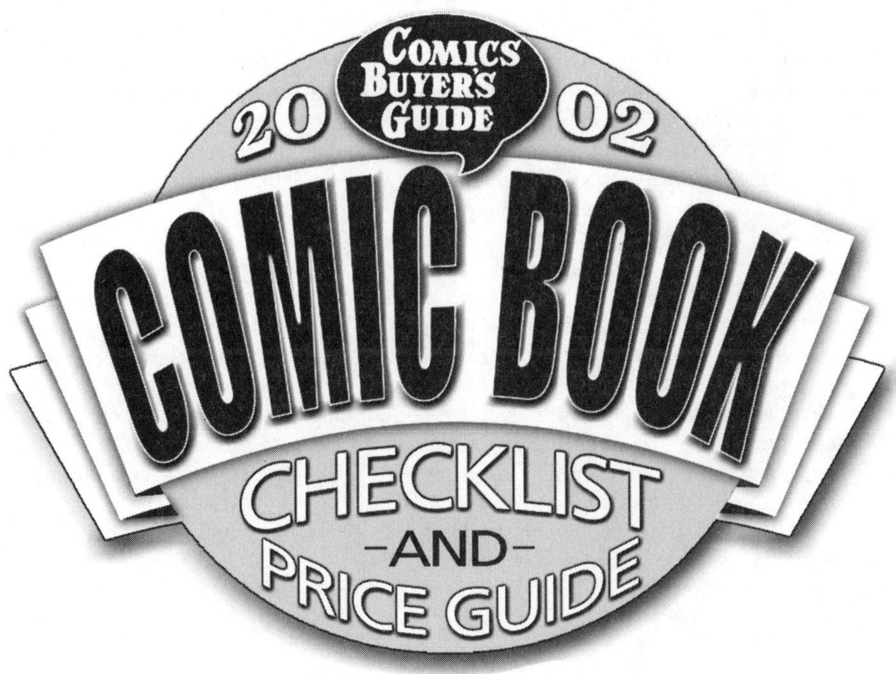

Brent Frankenhoff,
Peter Bickford,
& Maggie Thompson

Acknowledgments

As ever, there are so many people to thank that we're bound to miss a few. To anyone who should be thanked but isn't (you know who you are): We're sorry, and you know we couldn't have done this without you.

First and foremost, without the copious contributions of *ComicBase* developer Peter Bickford, this edition simply wouldn't exist. While his research has often paralleled our own, he has also obtained information that we didn't have access to. On the flip side, our information has added many titles to his computerized comics database program.

Moreover, we thank all the publishers who provided copies of their titles, so that we could maintain a database based on actually published material. Thanks also to the readers of our previous editions who have been providing additional data on their favorite titles. This year again, a special thanks goes out to Howard Michaels Jr., who provided an ongoing stream of information to make our compendium of information even more detailed and precise.

Thanks to our own behind-the-scenes people, including: Kevin Sauter for designing the cover; Bonnie Tetzlaff, database specialist; Tammy Kuhnle, computer services; Cheryl Hayburn and Wendy Wendt in our book production department; and the entire comics, toys, and games division at Krause Publications. An extra special thanks to Brent's wife, Kim, who understood when long weekends and evenings were required at the office to finish data entry and preparation. (If this last sentence seems familiar, it's because she's put up with this sort of thing for the last several years. This year's stresses including moving to a new home during the height of this book's production.)

Most of all, we acknowledge the work of Don Thompson, who nursed this project through the last 11 years of his life. We miss you, Don.

And we thank you all.

Maggie Thompson
Brent Frankenhoff
Iola, Wisconsin
October 26, 2001

Published by

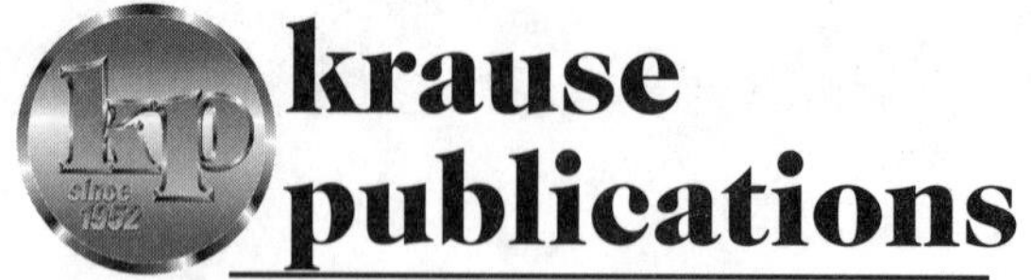

700 E. State St. • Iola, WI 54990-0001
Telephone: (715) 445-2214 • www.krause.com

Please call or write for our free catalog.
Our toll-free number to place an order or obtain a free catalog is (800) 258-0929
or please use our regular business telephone (715) 445-2214.

Library of Congress Catalog Number: 94-77503
ISBN: 0-87349-320-6

Printed in the United States of America

Contents

Introduction

By Maggie Thompson

This checklist and price guide is intended to function in a number of fashions.

There's more than one way to use it.

You can use it as a "have" list, in which you maintain an inventory of the comics you're collecting. (Make an "X" in the box for each one you have. If you prefer, you can circle the condition indicated. If you don't use the "X" system, you can use your own symbols indicating what you please, including condition, in the open box. You can then see at a glance what you're still looking for of a title you want to collect.)

You can use it as a guide to show prices you can expect to pay for items, if you look for them in comics shops throughout the country, online, or at conventions. The prices listed are arrived at by surveying comics shops, online sales, convention sales, and mail-order houses. With that information, our price guide reflects what a smart person with those choices would be willing to pay for a given issue.

You can use it as a guide for value, when you're buying or trading items. In that case, you'll want to keep in mind sales information you'll find on Page 9.

And you can carry it with you in your comics storage box, because it's sized to fit in a comics box.

Condition is vital.

Whether you're buying or selling comic books, one of the most important factors in setting the price is the condition of the material.

A scuffed, torn "reading copy" (that is, one that is suitable for reading but not for getting high prices at resale) will bring only a fraction of the price of a copy of the same issue which looks as though it has just come off the newsstand.

Picky collectors will even go through all the copies on a newsstand so as to buy the one in best condition. [Even a so-called "newsstand mint" copy of *Fantastic Four* #1 may have what is called "Marvel chipping" (a frayed right edge), since many of those early-'60s issues were badly cut by the printer.]

On the other hand, beat-up copies can provide bargains for collectors whose primary focus is *reading* the comic-book story. The same goes for reprints of comics which would otherwise be hard to find.

In fact, you may find prices on poor-condition copies even lower than the prices in this guide, depending on the attitude of the seller. It's a good time to get into collecting comics for the *fun* of it.

A major change in the comics-collecting world, CGC grading, has meant a huge jump in prices for certain hotly collected issues in almost-perfect condition. The third-party graders of Comics Guaranty LLC evaluate the condition of submitted copies and then encapsulate the graded issue in a labeled container. Because of the independent nature of the process and the reliability of the evaluating team, confidence in buying such items has meant a premium over the standard price in that condition. For example, at press time, a CGC 9.4 (Near Mint) is bringing at auction our Near Mint price ***plus*** *three times the Near Mint price*. More information on the company can be found on Page 6.

Our price guide is constantly evolving.

Each year, the most important changes in this guide from previous editions are, of course, the addition of countless chunks of data which we have compiled from consulting physical copies of the issues in question. (Thanks again to the many who helped.) Alone among checklists, this book contains original cover data and original pricing information for tens of thousands of comics.

We've also provided dozens and dozens of new cover photos with enough additional information, we hope, to whet a collector's appetite. We want to provide the most accurate picture of what you, as a customer, can expect to pay for comics when you walk into a shop or comics convention with your want list.

If You're New to Collecting ...

If you've just begun to collect comic books, you may find some aspects confusing. Here are some terms and some basics. (Don't forget to check other introductory material in this issue, as well.)

• **Cover variants:** These occur when publishers try to increase "collectibility" of and interest in a title by releasing an issue with an assortment of covers. This is in hopes that completists will want to buy multiple copies, instead of just one. (The practice has even spread to publications like *TV Guide*.) So how are these performing as "rare" back-issues? So far: poorly. Prices may rise at the time of release, but they usually fall again relatively quickly.

The same thing goes for other gimmicky extras. *Slingers* and *Fathom* were released with variant interiors — and readership dropped.

• **Issue identification:** If you've found a box of 1950s comics in the attic and wonder what to do next, the first thing to do is find out what you've got.

The same goes when you're looking for what you want to buy.

Here are some basics: Look at the copyright dates; if there are multiple dates, look at the *last* date. (If they're before 1950, chances are the comics are considered "Golden Age," and they're not covered in this price guide. Comics from the mid-1950s and later are Silver Age or more recent.)

Almost all comics are collected and identified by title and issue number. Look at the indicia, as outlined on page 7. That's what you'll use to find a specific issue in this or any other price guide. You'll want to check the issue title as given there — and the issue number.

• **Issue condition:** What does the comic book look like? Check pages 10 and 11 to get a feel for the shape your comics are in. If they're beaten-up, enjoy them for reading but don't expect to get a lot of money for them. For this reason, many beginning collectors focus on exactly such poor issues, getting the pleasure of reading without making a heavy investment.

• **Want to buy? To sell? To find out more about the field?** Check out page 9 for some indications.

• **Collecting with computer:** If you have a home computer, you'll find it increases your sources for buying and selling. (And *ComicBase* can help in your inventory.) Some sites of special interest include:

www.comicsbuyersguide.com
www.ebay.com
www.amazon.com

But they're not the only spots comics collectors will find fascinating. *Comics Buyer's Guide* has produced several guides for comics collecting on the Internet. Check it out!

Happy collecting!

What's Next?

The Internet has gained in its importance to collectors, e-mail is connecting collectors around the world, a third-party grading service has led to incredible price variations in some back issues, and computers are permitting collectors, as well as retailers, to monitor what they've got, what condition it's in, and what they want to buy.

One advance we continue to work on is the expansion of the information in our files on as many back issues as possible. To that end, the assistance of Human Computing's *ComicBase* program has been invaluable. Our combined informational base has grown rapidly, and we look forward to an even greater mutual compilation of data. Collectors who choose to do so will be able to access the information in both electronic and printed form. Both companies have for years been in an aggressive program to improve and increase the data for collectors, and collectors today are already experiencing services not available in the 1900s.

Maggie Thompson, October 26, 2001

CGC: Grading with confidence

Comics Buyer's Guide *broke the news on Comics Guaranty LLC, when the Certified Collectibles Group of companies announced it would serve the comic-book field. Today, CGC grading is widely used by online buyers and sellers to provide a standard on which both can agree.*

If you plan to have a comic book graded:

Information is available on the website, *www.CGCcomics.com*, and by calling (877) NM-COMIC.

There are several levels of service. At this point, the levels are:

- **Modern** (1975-today). Cost is $15 each, with a minimum of four graded.
- **Economy** (value of $0-$250). Cost is $25 each, with a minimum of three graded.
- **Standard** (value of $251-$1,000). Cost is $45 each.
- **Express** (value of $1,001-$5,000). Cost is $70 each.
- **Walkthru** (value of $5,001 or more). Cost is $110 each.

Graders do not determine a value; they identify defects and place a grade on the comic book. This lets online buyers purchase items evaluated by a common standard — and identifies for buyer and seller such matters as whether issues have been restored.

If you plan to buy a CGC-graded comic book:

First, yes: You *can* remove the comic book from the sealed container. If you retain the container and paperwork with the comic book, CGC even offers a discount on re-encapsulation.

A summary is as follows, but note the descriptions are ***CBG***'s guidelines, *not* officially CGC's:

10.0 Mint
9.9 Mint
9.8 Near Mint/Mint
9.6 Near Mint+
9.4 Near Mint (almost invisible stress marks, very tiny color flecks, ever so slight corner blunting)
9.2 Near Mint-
9.0 Very Fine/Near Mint
8.5 Very Fine+
8.0 Very Fine (relatively flat cover, slight staple discoloration, 2 slight stress lines, 1/4-inch crease not breaking color, slight yellowing)
7.5 Very Fine-
7.0 Fine/Very Fine
6.5 Fine+
6.0 Fine (slight surface wear, a few stress marks or 1/4-inch spine split, read a few times)
5.5 Fine-
5.0 Very Good/Fine
4.5 Very Good+
4.0 Very Good (average used comic book, wear, center crease, slightly rolled spine, minor soiling, 1/4-inch triangle from corner or edge, store stamps, name stamps, minor tears and folds, minor tape)
3.5 Very Good-
3.0 Good/Very Good
2.5 Good+
2.0 Good (all pages and covers, small pieces missing inside, cover piece as much as 1/2-inch triangle, 2-inch spine split, abraded — but retains structural integrity)
1.8 Good-
1.5 Fair/Good
1.0 Fair (soiled, ragged, unattractive, spine split to 2/3 its length, staples gone, coupon clipped)

Now filter eBay for "CGC." And remember to check ***CBG*** weekly for our latest market analyses.

— *Maggie Thompson*

Are There Any Questions?

Collectors looking for series beginning with a creator's name will find the titles under the series' name with the creator's name in parentheses at the end. For example, *Kurt Busiek's Astro City* can be found under *Astro City (Kurt Busiek's)*.
© 1995 Jukebox Productions.

Readers have been kind enough to ask many questions about our price guide. To help you make the best use of this volume, we're answering many of them here (and we're answering questions you **didn't** *ask, too, in an attempt to provide more information than you can possibly use).*

Why do we need a price guide at all?

We've spent 18 years developing a guide so that buyers and sellers of back issues will have help knowing what a consumer with various buying choices can expect to pay, if he's looking — for example — for that issue that will complete his run of the two DC series of *Shade the Changing Man*. The collector will find that even the highest-priced issue in the best condition probably won't cost more than about $3 — and that's the sort of information that can motivate a casual reader to become a collector.

Moreover, we try to provide helpful information to people who purchase it in order to have a (yes) guide to buying comics. Pricing information is just *part* of what we offer. In fact, we are increasingly intrigued by the more detailed information you'll find in this book — where we provide original cover date and price information wherever we can locate it, along with character appearances.

Why can't I find a title in your list?

We're working constantly to expand the listings themselves and increase the information on those we already provide. Check out what we have included, and — if you have something we're not listing — please let us know the details!

We need to know the information as given in the indicia of the issue (that's the tiny print, usually on the first few pages, that gives the publishing information): the full title, the number, and the issue month and year — and the U.S. price given on the cover. If you find work by a creator on our abbreviations list that we haven't noted in this guide, please include that information. If there's a significant event (especially as given in the abbreviations list), please include that, too. This is an *annual* volume designed to consolidate our information — but our weekly *Comics Buyer's Guide* runs updated information (with commentary on recent sales activity and previews of upcoming material), and we add to the data constantly — including updates to such market changes as the effects of CGC grading.

Check, too, on whether you're looking up the title as it appears in the indicia. For example, we list *The Vampire Lestat (Anne Rice's)*, not *Anne Rice's The Vampire Lestat*; we list *Mack Bolan: The Executioner (Don Pendleton's)*, not *Don Pendleton's Mack Bolan: The Executioner*. Many Marvel titles have adjectives. *Hulk*, for example, is listed as *Incredible Hulk*.

What's in this book?

This Silver Age and more recent price guide began as a quarterly update of activity in comics published since 1961, as reflected in prices comics shops were likely to charge. Moreover, the focus was pretty much limited to Silver Age super-hero titles — in fact, Silver Age super-hero titles *that were being published when the price guide began*. This meant that such titles as *OMAC*, a Silver Age title that starred a super-hero but was not still being published by 1983, didn't get listed in that earliest edition. It also meant that so-called "funny animal" titles, "war" titles, and the like were not included.

However, once the listings were begun (not by *Comics Buyer's Guide* staff, incidentally; the material was started for another publication), Don Thompson took over the compilation. From that point, every effort was made to include every issue of every comic book received in the office. However, since the entries were not on a database and had to be compressed to fit the space available, annotation, dates, and original prices were not usually part of the listing. On the other hand

(and because of Don's care, once he took over the project), material which was often overlooked by other reference publishers has been listed from the beginning in the *CBG* listings. *Concrete* and *Teenage Mutant Ninja Turtles*, for example, were first listed in *CBG*'s price listings. And we continue to fill in remaining information whenever we get it. Our cooperative agreement with *ComicBase* has led to the inclusion of hundreds of new titles and issues, as well as a wealth of variant editions.

What is the "Silver Age?"

Comic-book collectors divide the history of comics into the "Golden Age" and the "Silver Age." "Golden Age" indicates the first era of comic-book production — the '30s and '40s. It was a time of incredible creation in the field, when such characters as Superman and Batman first appeared. It's the era *before* material in this price guide was published.

"Silver Age" is used to indicate a period of comic-book production of slightly less (nostalgic?) luster than that of the Golden Age. It is usually considered to have begun with the publication of the first revival of a '40s super-hero: the appearance of The Flash in *Showcase* #4 (Sep-Oct 1956). However, that was a lone appearance at the time, so this price guide begins to catalog most titles from the time Marvel reentered the super-hero field with the publication of *Fantastic Four* #1 (1961).

This guide lists #8 and #10. Where's #9?

We haven't seen a copy. There was a time when comics collectors could safely assume that issue numbers would run in normal sequence, when no numbers were skipped and when there were no special numbers to confuse completists. That's not the case any more. What we need from those who want to help add to our information is confirmation that an item has *actually been published.*

This guide *does* include information on published material that was not widely distributed. Eternity's *Uncensored Mouse* #2, for example, was pulled from distribution after legal problems with The Walt Disney Company — but copies *do* exist. So few transactions involve it, however, that retailers have not yet established an standard price for the item.

So do you own all these comics?

No, many publishers and collectors have helped us over the years by sending photocopies of indicia, records of publication, annotations, and the like — all of which has permitted us to provide collectors with more information every year. What *ComicBase* and we cannot do — and *do* not do — is pull information from other price guides or from announcements of what is *scheduled* for publication. The former would not be proper; the latter leads to errors — the sort of errors that have been known to become imbedded in some price guides' information files.

This is also why information sometimes seems varied. Every effort has been made to make the notations consistent, but this list has more than 90,000 individual issues coordinated between *ComicBase* and Krause Publications, so this can be an arduous task. Nevertheless, we're whittling away at problems between weekly issues of *Comics Buyer's Guide* and the assorted other projects we take on.

This title switched publishers. Why wasn't that noted?

Chances are that the publishers involved didn't give us the information. Again, if you have the information, please provide it to us for inclusion in the next edition.

Why do some of your listings say (first series), (second series), etc., while others have (Vol. 1), (Vol. 2), and so on? Is there a difference?

Although publishers may begin a series again at #1, they often don't update the volume number in the indicia, which leads to the (first series) and (second series) notations. If the volume number changes (and it's a clear change, as in the case of Marvel's "Heroes Reborn" and "Heroes Return" title restarts), that is what differentiates the series.

On the other hand, when the volume number changes each year (as was the case with some early Silver Age material) but the series number is ongoing in sequence (Vol. 2, #21), then we don't note that change.

I've heard some of my squarebound comics referred to variously as "bookshelf

format," "prestige format," and "Dark Knight format." What's the difference?

Various formats — usually reserved for special projects (mini-series and one-shots) — have different names, depending on the publisher. We use the term "prestige format" generically to indicate a fancier package than the average comic book. Marvel refers to some titles in upscale formats as "bookshelf format," whereas DC initially solicited some of its titles in the format of *Batman: The Dark Knight* as "Dark Knight format." Details of fancy formats can be widely varied.

I tried to sell my comics to a retailer, but he wouldn't even offer me 10% of the prices you list. Is he trying to cheat me? Are your prices wrong?

Remember, our prices are based on what an informed collector with some choices is willing to pay for a comic book, not necessarily what a shop is charging or paying for that comic book. A shop has huge overhead and needs to tailor its stock to match the interest shown by its customers. If no one locally is buying comics starring Muggy-Doo, Boy Cat, it doesn't matter that *Muggy-Doo, Boy Cat* is bringing high prices elsewhere in the country.

Comics listed at their original prices may be showing no movement in most comics shops. In such cases, a retailer won't usually be interested in devoting store space to such titles, no matter *how* nice they are or *how* much you're discounting them.

I'm a publisher, and I'd be willing to buy a hundred copies of my first issue at the price you list. I get calls from all over America from would-be buyers who would pay 10 times the price you give here for out-of-print issues of my comics. What's going on?

A publisher like you hears from faithful fans across the nation. A comics shop deals with a market of one community or smaller. You're dealing with a narrow, focused market of aficionados of your product who are looking for the specific issues they're missing. And with more and more online offerings, those fans find it easier to seek you out. As a result, a publisher who has back issues for sale may get higher prices than readers will find in this checklist. It doesn't mean you're ripping off fans; it means fans looking to buy that material are competing within a nationwide pool; the Internet may eventually put everyone in the same pool.

While all copies destined for U.S. distribution were destroyed, approximately 700 copies of *Elseworlds 80-Page Giant* were released in England and many quickly made their way back to the States via online auctions.

***Can I just order the back-issue comics I want from* Comics Buyer's Guide?**

This price guide is just that: a guide to the average back-issue prices comics shops are likely to charge their customers. We maintain no back-issue stock for sale; we leave that to retailers who specialize in back issues. (Start with your local shops. You'll be able to check out the variety of material available and take a look in advance at what you're buying.)

Comics Buyer's Guide itself is the weekly newspaper of the comic-book field. As such, it carries ads from retailers across the country. You can check those advertisements for specific back issues that you're looking for. You can even take out a "wanted" ad to locate particular items, if that appeals to you. A free sample copy is available from *Comics Buyer's Guide* Sample Copy, 700 E. State St., Iola, WI 54990.

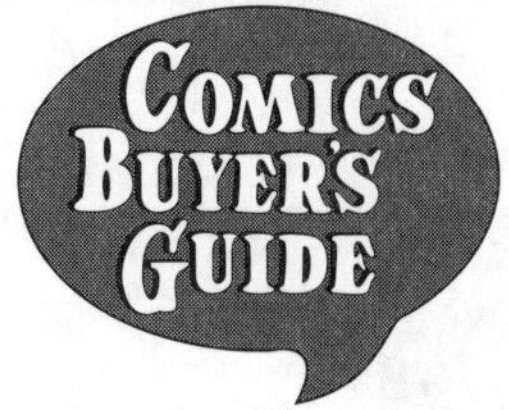

Finally —

We'd like to hear from you about this guide: additions, corrections, and comments. Write: Maggie Thompson, ***CBG 2002 Checklist and Price Guide***, 700 E. State St., Iola, WI 54990.

Maggie Thompson, October 26, 2001

Photo Grading Guide

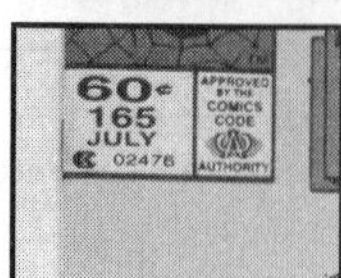

MINT: This is a perfect comic book. Its cover has full luster, with edges sharp and pages like new. There are no signs of wear or aging. It is not imperfectly printed or off-center. "Mint" means just what it says. **[roughly CGC 10.0]**

NEAR MINT: This is a nearly perfect comic book. Its cover shows barely perceptible signs of wear. Its spine is tight, and its cover has only minor loss of luster and only minor printing defects. Some discoloration is acceptable in older comics — as are signs of aging. **[roughly CGC 9.4]**

VERY FINE: This is a nice comic book with beginning signs of wear. There can be slight creases and wrinkles at the staples, but it is a flat, clean issue with definite signs of being read a few times. There is some loss of the original gloss, but it is in general an attractive comic book. **[roughly CGC 8.0]**

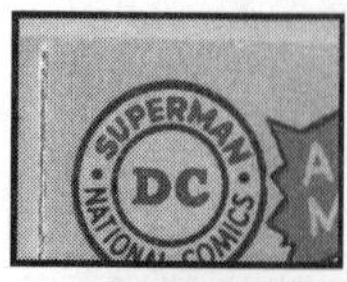

FINE: This comic book's cover is worn but flat and clean with no defacement. There is usually no cover writing or tape repair. Stress lines around the staples and more rounded corners are permitted. It is a good-looking issue at first glance. **[roughly CGC 6.0]**

VERY GOOD: Most of the original gloss is gone from this well-read issue. There are minor markings, discoloration, and/or heavier stress lines around the staples and spine. The cover may have minor tears and/or corner creases, and spine-rolling is permissible. These comics have problems but are nice. **[roughly CGC 4.0]**

GOOD: This is a very worn comic book with nothing missing. Creases, minor tears, rolled spine, and cover flaking are permissible. Older Golden Age comic books often come in this condition. **[roughly CGC 2.0]**

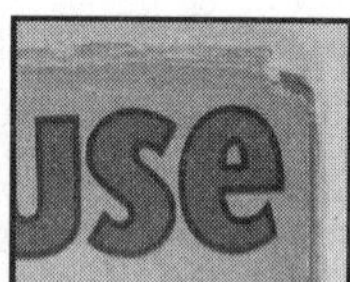

POOR: This issue is damaged and generally considered unsuitable for collecting. It may, however, still contain readable stories.

When comics are compared with the Photo Grading Guide, it's easy to see there are many comics which fall between categories in something of an infinite gradation. For example, a "Fair" condition comic book (which falls between "Good" and "Poor") may have a soiled, slightly damaged cover, a badly rolled spine, cover flaking, corners gone, tears, and the like. It is an issue with multiple problems but it is intact — and some collectors enjoy collecting in this grade for the fun of it. Tape may be present and is always considered a defect.

The condition of a comic book is a vital factor in determining its price.

Guide to Defects

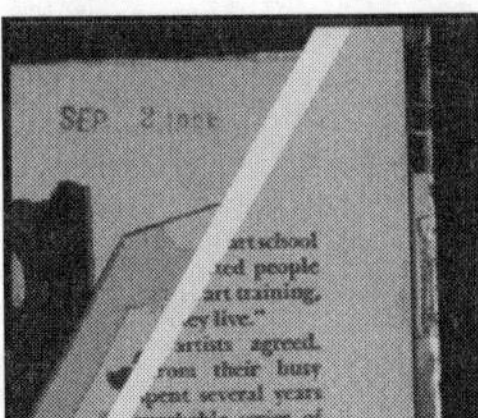

Stamped arrival date and **off-center cover** and **off-center stapling**. Minor defects. Some will not call it "Mint"; some will.

Writing defacing cover. Marking can include filling in light areas or childish scribbling. Usually no better than "Good."

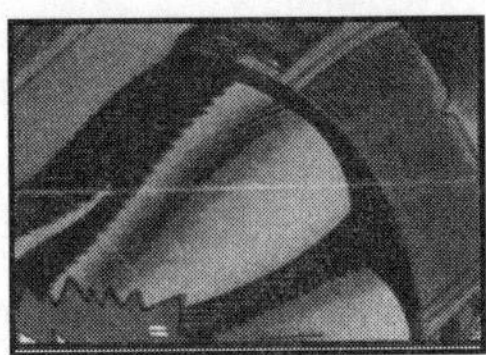

Subscription crease. Comic books sent by mail were often folded down the middle, leaving a permanent crease. Definitely no better than "Very Good"; probably no better than "Good."

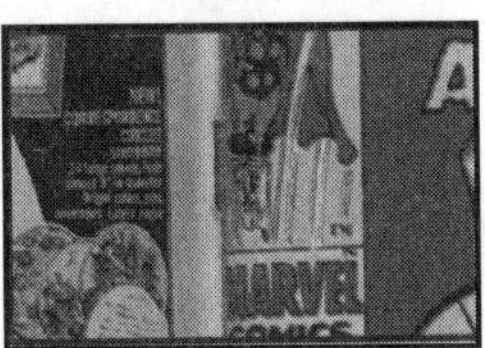

Rusty staple. Caused by dampness during storage, rust stains around staples may be minor — or more apparent. No better than "Very Good."

Chunk missing. Sizable piece missing. No better than "Fair."

Water damage. Varies from simple page-warping to staining shown here. Less damage than this could be "Very Good"; this is no better than "Good."

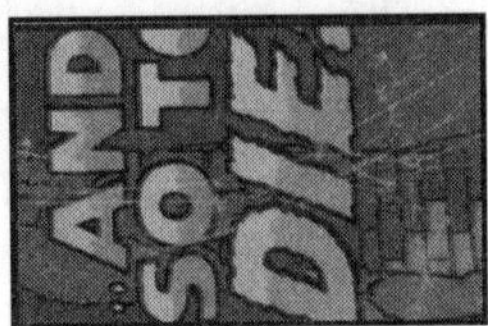

Multiple folds and wrinkles. No better than "Fair" condition.

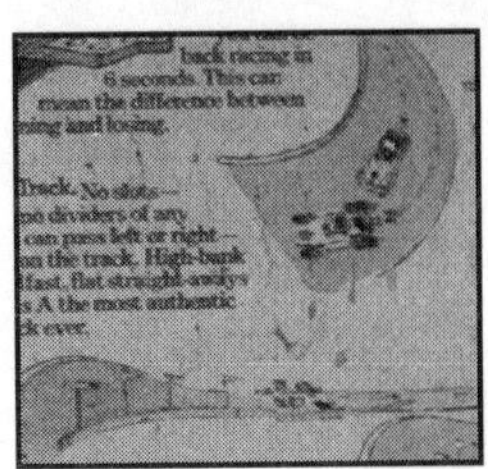

Stains. Can vary widely, depending on cause. These look like mud — but food, grease, and the like also stain. No better than "Good."

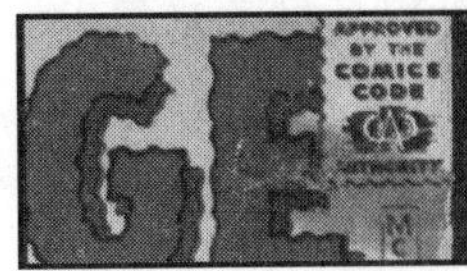

Tape. This extreme example of tape damage is used to show *why* tape shouldn't be used on a comic book — or *any* book — for repairs. *All* tape (even so-called "magic" tape) ages badly — as does rubber cement. Use of tape usually means "Fair," at best.

Rolled Spine. Caused by folding back each page while reading — rather than opening the issue flat. Repeated folding permanently bent the spine. *May* be corrected, but the issue is no better than "Very Good."

The problem of grading comics accurately is one which seems to have an easy solution. Theoretically, given a set of grading rules, determining the condition of a comic book should be simple. Unfortunately, flaws vary from item to item, and it can be difficult to pin one label on a particular issue — as with a sharp issue with a coupon removed. The examples shown here represent specific defects listed in each case. The condition of the individual issue as a whole is not necessarily that of the specific defect. (For example, the copy with stamped arrival date, off-center staple is *not* in mint condition aside from those defects.)

Abbreviations

AA — Alfredo Alcala
AAd — Art Adams
AF — Al Feldstein
AM — Al Milgrom
AMo — Alan Moore
AN — Alex Nino
AR — Alex Raymond
AT — Angelo Torres
ATh — Alex Toth
AW — Al Williamson
BA — Brent Anderson
BB — Brian Bolland
BE — Bill Elder
BEv — Bill Everett
BG — Butch Guice
BH — Bob Hall
BK — Bernie Krigstein
BL — Bob Layton
BMc — Bob McLeod
BO — Bob Oksner
BS — Barry Smith
BSz — Bill Sienkiewicz
BT — Bryan Talbot
BW — Basil Wolverton
BWa — Bill Ward
BWi — Bob Wiacek
BWr — Berni Wrightson
CB — Carl Barks
CCB — C.C. Beck
CI — Carmine Infantino
CR — P. Craig Russell
CS — Curt Swan
CV — Charles Vess
DA — Dan Adkins
DC — Dave Cockrum
DD — Dick Dillin
DaG — Dave Gibbons
DG — Dick Giordano
DGr — Dan Green
DH — Don Heck
DN — Don Newton
DP — Don Perlin
DR — Don Rosa
DS — Dan Spiegle
DSt — Dave Stevens
EC — Ernie Colon
EL — Erik Larsen
FB — Frank Brunner
FF — Frank Frazetta
FG — Floyd Gottfredson
FGu — Fred Guardineer
FH — Fred Hembeck
FM — Frank Miller
FMc — Frank McLaughlin
FR — Frank Robbins
FS — Frank Springer
FT — Frank Thorne
GC — Gene Colan
GD — Gene Day
GE — George Evans
GI — Graham Ingels
GK — Gil Kane
GM — Gray Morrow
GP — George Pérez
GT — George Tuska
HC — Howard Chaykin
HK — Harvey Kurtzman
HT — Herb Trimpe
IN — Irv Novick
JA — Jim Aparo
JAb — Jack Abel
JB — John Buscema
JBy — John Byrne
JCr — Johnny Craig
JD — Jayson Disbrow
JDu — Jan Duursema
JJ — Jeff Jones
JK — Jack Kirby
JKa — Jack Kamen
JKu — Joe Kubert
JL — Jose Luis Garcia Lopez
JLee — Jim Lee
JM — Jim Mooney
JO — Joe Orlando
JOy — Jerry Ordway
JR — John Romita
JR2 — John Romita Jr.
JS — John Stanley
JSa — Joe Staton
JSe — John Severin
JSh — Jim Sherman
JSn — Jim Starlin
JSo — Jim Steranko
JSt — Joe Sinnott
KB — Kurt Busiek
KG — Keith Giffen
KGa — Kerry Gammill
KJ — Klaus Janson
KN — Kevin Nowlan
KP — Keith Pollard
KS — Kurt Schaffenberger
LMc — Luke McDonnell
MA — Murphy Anderson
MB — Matt Baker
MD — Mort Drucker
ME — Mark Evanier
MG — Michael Golden
MGr — Mike Grell
MGu — Mike Gustovich
MK — Mike Kaluta
MM — Mort Meskin
MN — Mike Nasser
MP — Mike Ploog
MR — Marshall Rogers
MW — Matt Wagner
MZ — Mike Zeck
NA — Neal Adams
NC — Nick Cardy
NG — Neil Gaiman
NR — Nestor Redondo
PB — Pat Broderick
PD — Peter David
PG — Paul Gulacy
PM — Pete Morisi
PS — Paul Smith
RA — Ross Andru
RB — Rich Buckler
RBy — Reggie Byers
RCo — Rich Corben
RE — Ric Estrada
RH — Russ Heath
RHo — Richard Howell
RK — Roy Krenkel
RL — Rob Liefeld
RM — Russ Manning
RMo — Ruben Moreira
RT — Romeo Tanghal
SA — Sergio Aragonés
SB — Sal Buscema
SD — Steve Ditko
SR — Steve Rude
SRB — Steve Rude
TA — Tony DeZuniga
TMc — Todd McFarlane
TP — Tom Palmer
TS — Tom Sutton
TVE — Trevor Von Eeden
TY — Tom Yeates
VM — Val Mayerik
WE — Will Eisner
WH — Wayne Howard
WK — Walt Kelly
WP — Wendy Pini
WS — Walter Simonson
WW — Wally Wood

Issue information

A — Appearance of
Aut — Autographed edition
Bk — Book
C — Cameo of
D — Death of
DFE — Dynamic Forces Edition
GS — Giant Size
HOL — Hologram cover
HS — Holiday Special
I — Introduction of
J — Joining of
JSA — Justice Society of America
L — Leaving of
M or W — Wedding of
N — New costume
nn — no number
O — Origin of
R — Revival or return of
rep. — reprint
SE — Special Edition
Smr — Summer Special
SS — Swimsuit Special
tpb — trade paperback
V — versus
1 — first appearance of
2 — second appearance of
3 — third appearance of

# #

1, 001 NIGHTS OF BACCHUS, THE
DARK HORSE

	ORIG	GOOD	FINE	N-MINT
❑1, May 93, Up All Night With Sheherezade; Oh King, it has Come to my Ears That..., nn; b&w; One-Shot	3.95	0.90	2.25	4.50

100 BULLETS
DC

	ORIG	GOOD	FINE	N-MINT
❑1, Aug 99	2.50	0.90	2.25	4.50
❑2, Sep 99	2.50	0.70	1.75	3.50
❑3, Oct 99	2.50	0.70	1.75	3.50
❑4, Nov 99, Shot, Water Back, Part 1	2.50	0.60	1.50	3.00
❑5, Dec 99, Shot, Water Back, Part 2	2.50	0.60	1.50	3.00
❑6, Jan 00, Short Con, Long Odds, Part 1	2.50	0.50	1.25	2.50
❑7, Feb 00, Short Con, Long Odds, Part 2	2.50	0.50	1.25	2.50
❑8, Mar 00	2.50	0.50	1.25	2.50
❑9, Apr 00, The Right Ear, Left in the Cold, Part 1	2.50	0.50	1.25	2.50
❑10, May 00, The Right Ear, Left in the Cold, Part 2	2.50	0.50	1.25	2.50
❑11, Jun 00, Heartbreak, Sunnyside Up	2.50	0.50	1.25	2.50
❑12, Jul 00	2.50	0.50	1.25	2.50
❑13, Aug 00	2.50	0.50	1.25	2.50
❑14, Sep 00	2.50	0.50	1.25	2.50
❑15, Oct 00, Hang Up on the Hang Low, Part 1	2.50	0.50	1.25	2.50
❑16, Nov 00, Hang Up on the Hang Low, Part 2	2.50	0.50	1.25	2.50
❑17, Dec 00, Hang Up on the Hang Low, Part 3	2.50	0.50	1.25	2.50
❑18, Jan 01, Hang Up on the Hang Low, Part 4	2.50	0.50	1.25	2.50
❑19, Feb 01, Epilogue for a Road Dog	2.50	0.50	1.25	2.50
❑20, Mar 01, The Mimic	2.50	0.50	1.25	2.50
❑21, Apr 01, Selfish & Out to Sea, Part 1	2.50	0.50	1.25	2.50
❑22, May 01, Selfish & Out to Sea, Part 2	2.50	0.50	1.25	2.50
❑23, Jun 01, Red Prince Blues, Part 1	2.50	0.50	1.25	2.50
❑24	2.50	0.50	1.25	2.50
❑25	2.50	0.50	1.25	2.50
❑26	2.50	0.50	1.25	2.50

100 DEGREES IN THE SHADE
FANTAGRAPHICS

Value: Cover or less

- ❑1, b&w; adult ... 2.50
- ❑2, b&w; adult ... 2.50
- ❑3, b&w; adult ... 2.50
- ❑4, b&w; adult ... 2.50

100% TRUE?
DC

Value: Cover or less

- ❑1, Sum 96, b&w; magazine; excerpts from The Big Books of Death, Conspiracies, Weirdos, and Freaks ... 3.50
- ❑2, Win 97, b&w; magazine; excerpts from The Big Books of Death, Conspiracies, Weirdos, and Freaks; Winter, 1996 issue ... 3.50

101 WAYS TO END THE CLONE SAGA
MARVEL

Value: Cover or less

- ❑1, Jan 97, One-Shot ... 2.50

10TH MUSE
IMAGE

Value: Cover or less

- ❑1, Nov 00 ... 2.95
- ❑2/A, Jan 01, Character leaping from right on cover ... 2.95
- ❑2/B, Jan 01, Character leaping from left on cover ... 2.95
- ❑2/C, Jan 01, Photo cover ... 2.95
- ❑3/A, Mar 01, Drawn cover with woman summoning lightning 2.95
- ❑3/B, Mar 01, Photo cover with green border ... 2.95
- ❑3/C, Mar 01, Drawn cover with woman leaping forward ... 2.95
- ❑3/D, Mar 01, Wraparound Tower Records photo cover with red border ... 2.95

1111
CRUSADE

Value: Cover or less

- ❑1, Oct 96, BWr, nn; b&w; One-Shot; prose story with facing page illustrations; illustrated story ... 2.95

13: ASSASSIN COMICS MODULE
TSR

Value: Cover or less

- ❑1, The Wakening Storm ... 2.95
- ❑2 ... 2.95
- ❑3, How Dead is Dead?; Who are the Brotherhood? ... 2.95
- ❑4 ... 2.95
- ❑5, The Search for Maggie Darr, Part 1; Weapon ... 2.95
- ❑6, The Search for Maggie Darr, Part 2 ... 2.95
- ❑7, The Search for Maggie Darr, Part 3 ... 2.95
- ❑8, The Search for Maggie Darr, Part 4 ... 2.95

13 DAYS OF CHRISTMAS, THE: A TALE OF THE LOST LUNAR BESTIARY
SIRIUS

Value: Cover or less

- ❑1, b&w; wraparound cover ... 2.95

A gun and 100 untraceable bullets are given to certain individuals in order that they dispense "justice" in *100 Bullets*.

© 1999 DC Comics (Vertigo)

1963
IMAGE

	ORIG	GOOD	FINE	N-MINT
❑1, Apr 93, DaG, AMo (w), Mayhem on Mystery Mile, Mystery Incorporated	1.95	0.40	1.00	2.00
❑1/BR, Apr 93, DaG, AMo (w), Signed by Dave Gibbons; Bronze edition; Promotional limited edition	—	1.00	2.50	5.00
❑1/GO, Apr 93, DaG, AMo (w), Signed by Dave Gibbons; Gold edition; Profits donated to cancer research	—	1.00	2.50	5.00
❑1/SI, Apr 93, DaG, AMo (w), Signed by Dave Gibbons; silver edition; Profits donated to cancer research	—	1.00	2.50	5.00
❑2, May 93, AMo (w), When Wakes The War Beast!, No One Escapes...the Fury	1.95	0.40	1.00	2.00
❑3, Jun 93, AMo (w), Tales of the Uncanny; Double Deal in Dallas!, Tales of the Uncanny	1.95	0.40	1.00	2.00
❑4, Jul 93, Tales From Beyond; Showdown in the Shimmering Zone!, Tales From Beyond; Johnny Beyond	1.95	0.40	1.00	2.00
❑5, Aug 93, AMo (w), Horus, Lord of Light	1.95	0.40	1.00	2.00
❑6, Oct 93, AMo (w), The Tomorrow Syndicate	1.95	0.40	1.00	2.00

1984 MAGAZINE
WARREN

	ORIG	GOOD	FINE	N-MINT
❑1, Mar 84	—	1.20	3.00	6.00
❑2	—	0.80	2.00	4.00
❑3	—	0.80	2.00	4.00
❑4	—	0.80	2.00	4.00
❑5	—	0.80	2.00	4.00
❑6	—	0.80	2.00	4.00
❑7	—	0.80	2.00	4.00
❑8	—	0.80	2.00	4.00
❑9	—	0.80	2.00	4.00
❑10, Series continued in 1994 #11	—	0.80	2.00	4.00

1994 MAGAZINE
WARREN

	ORIG	GOOD	FINE	N-MINT
❑11, Series continued from 1984 #10	—	0.60	1.50	3.00
❑12	—	0.60	1.50	3.00
❑13	—	0.60	1.50	3.00
❑14	—	0.60	1.50	3.00
❑15	—	0.60	1.50	3.00
❑16, Dec 80, Telemetry; Sci-Fi Writer	1.95	0.60	1.50	3.00
❑17	—	0.60	1.50	3.00
❑18, Apr 81, FT, FT (w), Telemetry; Lost Love	2.00	0.60	1.50	3.00
❑19	2.00	0.60	1.50	3.00
❑20	2.00	0.60	1.50	3.00
❑21, Oct 81, FT, FT (w), Telemetry; Lord Machina	—	0.60	1.50	3.00
❑22	—	0.60	1.50	3.00
❑23	—	0.60	1.50	3.00
❑24	—	0.60	1.50	3.00
❑25	—	0.60	1.50	3.00
❑26	—	0.60	1.50	3.00
❑27	—	0.60	1.50	3.00
❑28	—	0.60	1.50	3.00
❑29, Final Issue	—	0.60	1.50	3.00

1ST FOLIO
PACIFIC

Value: Cover or less

- ❑1, Mar 84, Joe Kubert School 1.50

2000 A.D. MONTHLY (1ST SERIES)
EAGLE

	ORIG	GOOD	FINE	N-MINT
❑1, Apr 85, Judge Dredd: The Black Plague, Part 1; D.R. & Quinch: Go Straight	1.00	0.30	0.75	1.50
❑2, May 85, Judge Dredd: The Black Plague, Part 2; D.R. & Quinch Go Girl Crazy	1.00	0.30	0.75	1.50
❑3, Jun 85, Anderson, Psi Division; D.R. & Quinch go to Hollywood, Part 3	1.00	0.30	0.75	1.50
❑4, Jul 85, Judge Dredd: The Invisible Man; D.R. & Quinch Get Drafted, Part 2	1.00	0.30	0.75	1.50
❑5, Aug 85, Judge Dredd: Pirates of the Black Atlantic; D.R. & Quinch Get Drafted, Part 3	1.00	0.30	0.75	1.50
❑6, Sep 85, AMo (w)	1.00	0.30	0.75	1.50

2000 A.D. MONTHLY (2ND SERIES)
EAGLE

	ORIG	GOOD	FINE	N-MINT
❑1, Apr 86, Judge Anderson, D.R. & Quinch, Skizz	1.25	0.30	0.75	1.50
❑2, May 86	1.25	0.30	0.75	1.50
❑3, Jun 86	1.25	0.30	0.75	1.50
❑4	1.25	0.30	0.75	1.50

2000 A.D. PRESENTS
FLEETWAY

	ORIG	GOOD	FINE	N-MINT
❑4, Jul 86, Series continued from 2000 A.D. Monthly#3; Title changes to 2000 A.D. Presents; Quality begins publishing	1.25	0.30	0.75	1.50
❑5, Aug 86	1.25	0.30	0.75	1.50
❑6, Sep 86	1.25	0.30	0.75	1.50
❑7, Oct 86, DaG, AMo (w), Dan Dare: The Lost Worlds; Skizz	1.25	0.30	0.75	1.50
❑8, Nov 86	1.25	0.30	0.75	1.50
❑9, Dec 86, 52pgs.	1.25	0.30	0.75	1.50
❑10, Jan 87, 52pgs.	1.25	0.30	0.75	1.50
❑11, Feb 87, Dan Dare: Starship Commander; Harry Twenty on the High Rock, 52pgs.	1.25	0.30	0.75	1.50
❑12, Dec 87, AMo (w), Anderson, Psi Division; Dan Dare	1.50	0.30	0.75	1.50
❑13, Harry 20 on the High Rock; Dan Dare: Star Slayer	1.25	0.30	0.75	1.50
❑14	1.25	0.30	0.75	1.50
❑15, Dan Dare: Waterworld; Harry 20 on the High Rock	1.25	0.30	0.75	1.50
❑16	1.25	0.30	0.75	1.50
❑17	1.25	0.30	0.75	1.50
❑18	1.25	0.30	0.75	1.50
❑19	1.25	0.30	0.75	1.50
❑20, DaG, Dan Dare; The VCs	1.25	0.30	0.75	1.50
❑21	1.25	0.30	0.75	1.50
❑22	1.25	0.30	0.75	1.50
❑23	1.25	0.30	0.75	1.50
❑24, Series continues as 2000 A.D. Showcase	1.25	0.30	0.75	1.50
❑25, Series continues as 2000 A.D. Showcase (1st Series) #25	1.25	0.30	0.75	1.50

2000 A.D. SHOWCASE (1ST SERIES)
FLEETWAY
Value: Cover or less

- ❑25, Series continued from 2000 A.D. Presents #24 .... 1.25
- ❑26 .... 1.50
- ❑27, Inferno; Dan Dare, double issue #27/28 .... 1.50
- ❑28, Inferno; Dan Dare, double issue #27/28 .... 1.50
- ❑29, double issue #29/30 .... 1.50
- ❑30, double issue #29/30 .... 1.50
- ❑31, Zenith 1.50
- ❑32, Zenith 1.50
- ❑33, Zenith 1.50
- ❑34, Zenith 1.50
- ❑35, Zenith 1.50
- ❑36, Zenith 1.50
- ❑37, Zenith 1.50
- ❑38, Zenith 1.50
- ❑39, Zenith 1.50
- ❑40, Zenith 1.50
- ❑41, Zenith 1.50
- ❑42, Zenith 1.50
- ❑43, Zenith 1.50
- ❑44, Zenith 1.50
- ❑45, Zenith 1.75
- ❑46 .... 1.75
- ❑47 .... 1.75
- ❑48 .... 1.75
- ❑49 .... 1.75
- ❑50 .... 1.75
- ❑51 .... 1.75
- ❑52 .... 1.75
- ❑53 .... 1.75
- ❑54, Final Issue 1.75

2000 A.D. SHOWCASE (2ND SERIES)
FLEETWAY
Value: Cover or less

- ❑1, Below Zero; Luke Kirby: The Dark Path 2.95
- ❑2, Below Zero; Bix Barton 2.95
- ❑3 .... 2.95
- ❑4, Axa 2.95
- ❑5, Axa 2.95
- ❑6, Strontium Dogs 2.95
- ❑7, Strontium Dogs 2.95
- ❑8 .... 2.95
- ❑9 .... 2.95
- ❑10 .... 2.95
- ❑11 .... 2.95

2001 NIGHTS
VIZ

	ORIG	GOOD	FINE	N-MINT
❑1, Night 1, Earthglow; Night 2, Sea Of Fertility	3.75	0.80	2.00	4.00
❑2	3.95	0.80	2.00	4.00
❑3	3.95	0.80	2.00	4.00
❑4	3.75	0.80	2.00	4.00
❑5, Night 10, Medusa's Throne; Night 11, A Stranger's Footsteps	3.75	0.80	2.00	4.00
❑6	4.25	0.85	2.13	4.25
❑7	4.25	0.85	2.13	4.25
❑8	4.25	0.85	2.13	4.25
❑9	4.25	0.85	2.13	4.25
❑10, Children of the Earth, Final Issue	4.25	0.85	2.13	4.25

2001, A SPACE ODYSSEY
MARVEL

	ORIG	GOOD	FINE	N-MINT
❑1, Dec 76, JK, JK (w), Beast-Killer!	0.30	0.80	2.00	4.00
❑2, Jan 77, JK, JK (w), Vira The She-Demon!	0.30	0.50	1.25	2.50
❑3, Feb 77, JK, JK (w), Marak!	0.30	0.50	1.25	2.50
❑4, Mar 77, JK, JK (w), Wheels of Death!...	0.30	0.50	1.25	2.50
❑5, Apr 77, JK, JK (w), Norton Of New York 2040 A.D.	0.30	0.50	1.25	2.50
❑6, May 77, JK, JK (w), Inter-Galactica, The Ultimate Trip	0.30	0.50	1.25	2.50
❑7, Jun 77, JK, JK (w)	0.30	0.50	1.25	2.50
❑8, Jul 77, JK, JK (w), The Capture of X-51, 1: Machine Man (as "Mister Machine") ...	0.30	0.50	1.25	2.50
❑9, Aug 77, JK, JK (w)	0.30	0.50	1.25	2.50
❑10, Sep 77, JK, JK (w), Mister machine, O: Machine Man	0.30	0.50	1.25	2.50
❑GS 1, JK, treasury-sized adaptation of movie	1.50	2.00	5.00	10.00

2010
MARVEL

	ORIG	GOOD	FINE	N-MINT
❑1, Apr 84, movie Adaptation	0.75	0.30	0.75	1.50
❑2, May 84, movie Adaptation	0.75	0.30	0.75	1.50

2020 VISIONS
DC

	ORIG	GOOD	FINE	N-MINT
❑1, May 97, Lust for Life, Part 1	2.25	0.50	1.25	2.50
❑2, Jun 97, Lust for Life, Part 2	2.25	0.50	1.25	2.50
❑3, Jul 97, Lust for Life, Part 3	2.25	0.50	1.25	2.50
❑4, Aug 97, La Tormenta, Part 1	2.25	0.50	1.25	2.50
❑5, Sep 97, La Tormenta, Part 2	2.25	0.50	1.25	2.50
❑6, Oct 97, La Tormenta, Part 3	2.25	0.50	1.25	2.50
❑7, Nov 97, Renegade, Part 1	2.25	0.50	1.25	2.50
❑8, Dec 97, Renegade, Part 2	2.25	0.50	1.25	2.50
❑9, Jan 98, Renegade, Part 3	2.25	0.50	1.25	2.50
❑10, Feb 98, Repro-Man, Part 1	2.25	0.50	1.25	2.50
❑11, Mar 98, Repro-Man, Part 2	2.25	0.50	1.25	2.50
❑12, Apr 98, Repro-Man, Part 3	2.25	0.50	1.25	2.50

2099 A.D.
MARVEL
Value: Cover or less

- ❑1, May 95, enhanced cover... 3.95

2099 A.D. APOCALYPSE
MARVEL
Value: Cover or less

- ❑1, Dec 95, D: Punisher 2099; D: Hulk 2099, enhanced wraparound cover; continues in 2099 A.D. Genesis #1 .... 4.95

2099 A.D. GENESIS
MARVEL
Value: Cover or less

- ❑1, Jan 96, Midday Sun, A: Daredevil 2099; 1: X-Nation 2099 and Fantastic Four 2099, chromium cover 4.95

2099: MANIFEST DESTINY
MARVEL
Value: Cover or less

- ❑1, Mar 98, nn; One-Shot 5.99

2099 SPECIAL: THE WORLD OF DOOM
MARVEL
Value: Cover or less

- ❑1, May 95 .... 2.25

2099 UNLIMITED
MARVEL

	ORIG	GOOD	FINE	N-MINT
❑1, Jul 93, Nothing Ever Changes, A: Spider-Man 2099; 1: Hulk 2099	3.95	0.79	1.98	3.95
❑2, Oct 93, Thirty Mile Mall; Remote Control, 1: R Gang 2099, Return of Hulk 2099	3.95	0.79	1.98	3.95
❑3, Jan 94	3.95	0.79	1.98	3.95
❑4, Apr 94	3.95	0.79	1.98	3.95
❑5, Jul 94	3.95	0.79	1.98	3.95
❑6, Aug 94	3.95	0.79	1.98	3.95
❑7, Nov 94	3.95	0.79	1.98	3.95
❑8, Apr 95	3.95	0.79	1.98	3.95
❑9, Jul 95	3.95	0.79	1.98	3.95
❑10, Oct 95	3.95	0.79	1.98	3.95
❑Ash 1, foil cover; "2099 Limited" ashcan edition from Hero magazine	—	0.15	0.38	0.75

2099: WORLD OF TOMORROW
MARVEL
Value: Cover or less

- ❑1, Sep 96, The World of Tomorrow, wraparound cover; 2099 anthology 2.50
- ❑2, Oct 96, Revelations 2.50
- ❑3, Nov 96 .... 2.50
- ❑4, Dec 96, De-Evolution, A: Doom 2099 .... 2.50
- ❑5, Jan 97, Finders Keepers... 2.50
- ❑6, Feb 97, Final Decision 2.50
- ❑7, Mar 97, Blitzkrieg, A: Spider-Man 2099 .... 2.50
- ❑8, Apr 97, The Quiet Earth, Final Issue 2.50

21
IMAGE
Value: Cover or less

- ❑1, Feb 96 .... 2.50
- ❑1/A, Feb 96 .... 2.50
- ❑2, Mar 96 .... 2.50
- ❑3, Apr 96 .... 2.50

2112 (JOHN BYRNE'S...)
DARK HORSE
Value: Cover or less

- ❑1, Nov 91, JBy, JBy (w), 1: Sathanus, prestige format 9.95

	ORIG	GOOD	FINE	N-MINT

❑1-2, JBy, JBy (w), 1: Sathanus, 2nd Printing 9.95
❑, JBy, JBy (w), 1: Sathanus, 3rd Printing 9.95

22 BRIDES
EVENT

	ORIG	GOOD	FINE	N-MINT
❑1, Mar 96, Married to the Mob, Part 1	2.95	0.60	1.50	3.00
❑1/LE, Mar 96, Married to the Mob, Part 1	2.95	1.00	2.50	5.00
❑2, Jun 96, Married to the Mob, Part 2	2.95	0.59	1.48	2.95
❑3, Sep 96, Married to the Mob, Part 3	2.95	0.59	1.48	2.95
❑4, Jan 97, Married to the Mob, Part 4	2.95	0.59	1.48	2.95
❑4/A, Married to the Mob, Part 4, O: Painkiller Jane, Painkiller Jane on Dinosaur cover	2.95	0.80	2.00	4.00
❑CS 1, Married to the Mob, Collector's Set. Includes #1-4, poster	34.95	6.99	17.48	34.95

2-HEADED GIANT
A IS A

Value: Cover or less
❑1, Oct 95, b&w; Anthology 2.95

2 HOT GIRLS ON A HOT SUMMER NIGHT
FANTAGRAPHICS

	ORIG	GOOD	FINE	N-MINT
❑1, b&w; adult	2.25	0.60	1.50	3.00
❑2, b&w; adult	2.25	0.60	1.50	3.00
❑3, b&w; adult	2.25	0.60	1.50	3.00
❑4, b&w; adult	2.25	0.60	1.50	3.00

2 LIVE CREW COMICS
FANTAGRAPHICS

Value: Cover or less
❑1, b&w; adult 2.95

300
DARK HORSE

	ORIG	GOOD	FINE	N-MINT
❑1, May 98, FM, FM (w), Honor	2.95	0.70	1.75	3.50
❑2, Jun 98, FM, FM (w)	2.95	0.70	1.75	3.50
❑3, Jul 98, FM, FM (w), Glory	2.95	0.65	1.63	3.25
❑4, Aug 98, FM, FM (w), Combat	2.95	0.65	1.63	3.25
❑5, Sep 98, FM, FM (w), Victory	3.95	0.65	1.63	3.25

32 PAGES
SIRIUS

Value: Cover or less
❑1, Jan 01, To Be Continued...; Man Whole 2.95

.357!
MU

	ORIG	GOOD	FINE	N-MINT
❑1, b&w	2.25	0.50	1.25	2.50

39 SCREAMS, THE
THUNDER BAAS

Value: Cover or less
❑1 .... 2.00
❑2, Oh to be Desired for Just One Day; The Man Who Experimented on Animals 2.00
❑3 .... 2.00
❑4 .... 2.00
❑5 .... 2.00
❑6 .... 2.00

3-D ADVENTURE COMICS
STATS ETC.

	ORIG	GOOD	FINE	N-MINT
❑1, Aug 86, 1: Statman	1.50	0.40	1.00	2.00

3-D ALIEN TERROR
ECLIPSE

Value: Cover or less
❑1, Jun 86, GM, The Wishing World; Oral Hygienist 2.50

3-D EXOTIC BEAUTIES
3-D ZONE

Value: Cover or less
❑1, nn 3.50

3-D HEROES
BLACKTHORNE

	ORIG	GOOD	FINE	N-MINT
❑1, Rescue, In 3-D, glasses not included	2.00	0.50	1.25	2.50

3-D HOLLYWOOD
3-D ZONE

Value: Cover or less
❑1, paper dolls 2.95

3-D SPACE ZOMBIES
3-D ZONE

Value: Cover or less
❑1, nn 3.95

3-D SUBSTANCE
3-D ZONE

Value: Cover or less
❑1, SD, nn 2.95
❑2, SD 3.95

3-D THREE STOOGES
ECLIPSE

Value: Cover or less
❑1, Men In The Moon, Stuntgirl backup feature 2.50
❑2, The Bandit Moons 2.50
❑3, Uncivil Warriors; Dee-Fective Comics 2.50

3-D TRUE CRIME
3-D ZONE

Value: Cover or less
❑1 .... 3.95

3-D ZONE, THE
3-D ZONE

Value: Cover or less
❑1, WW 2.50
❑2, BW 2.50
❑3 .... 2.50
❑4, Electric Fear, Electric Fear 2.50
❑5, Krazy Kat 2.50
❑6, Rat Fink 2.50
❑7, JKu, Hollywood 2.50
❑8, JKu, High Seas 2.50
❑9, Red Mask 2.50
❑10, AW, Jet 2.50

John Byrne's Next Men villain Sathanus made his first appearance in *John Byrne's 2112*.

© 1991 John Byrne (Dark Horse).

❑11, Matt Fox 2.50
❑12, Presidents 2.50
❑13, Flash Gordon 2.50
❑14, Tyranostar 2.50
❑15, HK, humor 2.50
❑16, DS, space vixens 2.50
❑17, JKa; RA; WW; FF; AF, My Marriage was Doomed!; I Was a Stepmother at Twenty, Thrilling Love 2.50
❑18, BW 2.50
❑19, Cracked 2.50
❑20, Atomic Sub 2.50

3 GEEKS, THE
3 FINGER PRINTS

	ORIG	GOOD	FINE	N-MINT
❑1, Going to the Con, Part 1	2.50	0.70	1.75	3.50
❑1-2, Going to the Con, Part 1, 2nd Printing	2.50	0.50	1.25	2.50
❑2, Going to the Con, Part 2	2.50	0.55	1.38	2.75
❑3, Going to the Con, Part 3, Brain Boy back-up	2.50	0.55	1.38	2.75
❑4, Brain Boy back-up	2.50	0.70	1.75	3.50
❑5, The Collector City Club, Part 1	2.50	0.70	1.75	3.50
❑6, The Collector City Club, Part 2	2.50	0.70	1.75	3.50
❑7, Mission Jimpossible	2.50	0.70	1.75	3.50
❑8, Sep 98, Get A Job!, 48pgs.	3.50	0.70	1.75	3.50
❑9, Feb 99, Marvelous Movie Marathon; Close Call!, movie night	2.50	0.50	1.25	2.50
❑10, Apr 99, Happy Birthday Allen!, Part 1, Allen's birthday	2.50	0.50	1.25	2.50
❑11, Jun 99, Happy Birthday Allen!, Part 2, Allen's redemption	2.50	0.50	1.25	2.50

3 NINJAS KICK BACK
NOW

Value: Cover or less
❑1, Jun 94, Curveballs and Goofballs 1.95
❑2 .... 1.95
❑3 .... 1.95

3X3 EYES
INNOVATION

	ORIG	GOOD	FINE	N-MINT
❑1, b&w; Japanese	2.25	0.50	1.25	2.50
❑2, b&w; Japanese	2.25	0.45	1.13	2.25
❑3, b&w; Japanese	2.25	0.45	1.13	2.25
❑4, b&w; Japanese	2.25	0.45	1.13	2.25
❑5, b&w; Japanese	2.25	0.45	1.13	2.25

3X3 EYES: CURSE OF THE GESU
DARK HORSE

Value: Cover or less
❑1, Oct 95, b&w 2.95
❑2, Nov 95, b&w 2.95
❑3, Dec 95, b&w 2.95
❑4, Jan 96, b&w 2.95
❑5, Feb 96, b&w; Final Issue... 2.95

4
MARVEL

Value: Cover or less
❑1, Oct 00, BA; ARo, Universe X tie-in; Sue Richards restored to life 3.99

4-D MONKEY, THE
DR. LEUNG'S

	ORIG	GOOD	FINE	N-MINT
❑1	1.80	0.40	1.00	2.00
❑2	1.80	0.40	1.00	2.00
❑3	1.80	0.40	1.00	2.00
❑4	1.80	0.40	1.00	2.00
❑5	1.80	0.40	1.00	2.00
❑6	2.00	0.40	1.00	2.00
❑7	2.00	0.40	1.00	2.00
❑8	2.00	0.40	1.00	2.00
❑9	2.00	0.40	1.00	2.00
❑10	2.00	0.40	1.00	2.00
❑11	2.00	0.40	1.00	2.00
❑12	2.00	0.40	1.00	2.00

6, THE
VIRTUAL

Value: Cover or less
❑1, Lethal Origins, Part 1 .... 2.50
❑2, Lethal Origins, Part 2 .... 2.50
❑3, Lethal Origins, Part 3 .... 2.50

666: THE MARK OF THE BEAST
FLEETWAY

	ORIG	GOOD	FINE	N-MINT
❑1	1.95	0.50	1.25	2.50
❑2	1.95	0.40	1.00	2.00
❑3	1.95	0.40	1.00	2.00
❑4	1.95	0.40	1.00	2.00
❑5, The Dead	1.95	0.40	1.00	2.00

	ORIG	GOOD	FINE	N-MINT
❑6	1.95	0.40	1.00	2.00
❑7	1.95	0.40	1.00	2.00
❑8	1.95	0.40	1.00	2.00
❑9	1.95	0.40	1.00	2.00
❑10, The Drowning Pond	1.95	0.40	1.00	2.00
❑11	1.95	0.40	1.00	2.00
❑12, AMo (w), Alan Moore special	1.95	0.40	1.00	2.00
❑13	1.95	0.40	1.00	2.00
❑14	1.95	0.40	1.00	2.00
❑15	1.95	0.40	1.00	2.00
❑16	1.95	0.40	1.00	2.00
❑17	1.95	0.40	1.00	2.00
❑18, Final Issue	1.95	0.40	1.00	2.00

6, THE: LETHAL ORIGINS
VIRTUAL

Value: Cover or less

❑1, May 96, nn; digest 3.99

7TH MILLENNIUM
ALLIED

Value: Cover or less

❑1 .... 2.50
❑2 .... 2.50
❑3 .... 2.50
❑4 .... 2.50

7TH SYSTEM, THE
SIRIUS

Value: Cover or less

❑1, Jan 98, Kat & Mouse, b&w 2.95
❑2, Feb 98, b&w 2.95
❑3, Jul 98, b&w 2.95
❑4, Dec 98, b&w 2.95
❑6, b&w 2.95

80 PAGE GIANT MAGAZINE
DC

	ORIG	GOOD	FINE	N-MINT
❑1, Aug 64, Superman; Imaginary stories	0.25	52.00	130.00	260.00
❑2, Jimmy Olsen	0.25	16.00	40.00	80.00
❑3, Sep 64, Lois Lane	0.25	14.00	35.00	70.00
❑4, Oct 64, Flash	0.25	14.00	35.00	70.00
❑5, Nov 64, Batman	0.25	14.00	35.00	70.00
❑6, Jan 65, Superman	0.25	12.00	30.00	60.00
❑7, Feb 65, Sgt. Rock	0.25	12.00	30.00	60.00
❑8, Mar 65, Secret Origins	0.25	20.00	50.00	100.00
❑9, Apr 65, Flash; reprints "Flash of Two Worlds"	0.25	12.00	30.00	60.00
❑10, May 65, Superboy	0.25	10.00	25.00	50.00
❑11, Jun 65, Superman	0.25	10.00	25.00	50.00
❑12, Jul 65, Batman	0.25	10.00	25.00	50.00
❑13, Aug 65, Jimmy Olsen	0.25	10.00	25.00	50.00
❑14, Sep 65, Lois Lane	0.25	10.00	25.00	50.00
❑15, Oct 65, Batman/Superman	0.25	10.00	25.00	50.00

A

A1 (VOL. 1)
ATOMEKA

Value: Cover or less

❑1, 89, BSz; DaG, BB (c), The Big Button; Warpsmith: Ghostdance 9.95
❑2, 89, DaG; MW 9.95
❑3, 90, BB (c), The American; Deadface: The Book-Keeper from Atlantis 5.95
❑4, 90, BSz 5.95
❑5, 91, Cover Story; Bricktop: Sunglasses 7.95
❑6, 92, Tankgirl: She's F*cking Great!; Rescue 4.95
❑7 .... 7.95

A1 (VOL. 2)
MARVEL

Value: Cover or less

❑1, Along For The Ride; Cyrano De Bergerac's Voyage To The Moon 5.95
❑2, Max Zillion and Alto Ego: Pawn Shop; Deadline 5.95
❑3, Axel Pressbutton: The Movie; Pale Horses 5.95
❑4, Frankenstein Meets Shirley Temple, Part 4; King Leon, Part 3 5.95

A1 TRUE LIFE BIKINI CONFIDENTIAL, THE
ATOMEKA

	ORIG	GOOD	FINE	N-MINT
❑1, BB (c), Mr. Monster's Most Wanted!; Parcels of Events, b&w	1.00	1.39	3.47	6.95

ÄARDWOLF
AARDWOLF

Value: Cover or less

❑1, Dec 94, I, Gezheh; Stiffed 2.95
❑2, Feb 95 .... 2.95

AARON STRIPS
IMAGE

Value: Cover or less

❑1, Apr 97 .... 2.95
❑2, Jun 97 .... 2.95
❑3, Aug 97 .... 2.95
❑4, Oct 97, has "Aaron Warner's Year of the Monkey" back-up; goes to Amazing Aaron Productions 2.95
❑5, Jan 99, continued numbering from Image series 2.95
❑6, Mar 99 .... 2.95

ABBOTT & COSTELLO (CHARLTON)
CHARLTON

	ORIG	GOOD	FINE	N-MINT
❑1, Feb 68	—	5.00	12.50	25.00
❑2	—	3.60	9.00	18.00
❑3	—	3.60	9.00	18.00
❑4, There's No Business; Flowers of the Business World	0.12	2.40	6.00	12.00
❑5	—	2.40	6.00	12.00
❑6	—	2.40	6.00	12.00
❑7	—	2.40	6.00	12.00
❑8	—	2.40	6.00	12.00
❑9	—	2.40	6.00	12.00
❑10	—	2.40	6.00	12.00
❑11	—	2.00	5.00	10.00
❑12	—	2.00	5.00	10.00
❑13	—	2.00	5.00	10.00
❑14	—	2.00	5.00	10.00
❑15, Jun 70	0.15	2.00	5.00	10.00
❑16, Aug 70	0.15	2.00	5.00	10.00
❑17, Oct 70, daisy poster	0.15	2.00	5.00	10.00
❑18	—	2.00	5.00	10.00
❑19	—	2.00	5.00	10.00
❑20	—	2.00	5.00	10.00
❑21	—	2.00	5.00	10.00
❑22, Final Issue	—	2.00	5.00	10.00

A.B.C. WARRIORS
FLEETWAY

	ORIG	GOOD	FINE	N-MINT
❑1, ABC Warriors: The Tournament Of The Damned	1.95	0.40	1.00	2.00
❑2	1.95	0.40	1.00	2.00
❑3	1.95	0.40	1.00	2.00
❑4	1.95	0.40	1.00	2.00
❑5	1.95	0.40	1.00	2.00
❑6	1.95	0.40	1.00	2.00
❑7	1.95	0.40	1.00	2.00
❑8, Final Issue	1.95	0.40	1.00	2.00

ABC WARRIORS: KHRONICLES OF KHAOS
FLEETWAY

Value: Cover or less

❑1 .... 2.95
❑2 .... 2.95
❑3 .... 2.95
❑4 .... 2.95

ABE SAPIEN DRUMS OF THE DEAD
DARK HORSE

Value: Cover or less

❑1, Mar 98, Drums of the Dead; Heads, A: Hellboy, nn; One-Shot; Hellboy back-up 2.95

A. BIZARRO
DC

Value: Cover or less

❑1, Jul 99, Vivisimilitude........ 2.50
❑2, Aug 99, Silicon Dreamer... 2.50
❑3, Sep 99, Nine-Inch Sonic Pumpkins, A: Granny Goodness 2.50
❑4, Oct 99, Viva Bizarro!, A: Superman 2.50

A-BOMB
ANTARCTIC

Value: Cover or less

❑1, Dec 93 .... 2.95
❑2, Mar 94 .... 2.95
❑3, Jun 94, Barr Girls story 2.95
❑4, Sep 94, Barr Girls story 2.95
❑5, Dec 94 .... 2.95
❑6, Mar 95, Strip F*cker; Knight after Knight 2.95
❑7, Jun 95, Merry Maria Melon; Tavern Tales 2.95
❑8, Sep 95 .... 2.95
❑9, Nov 95 .... 2.95
❑10, Jan 96 .... 2.95
❑11, Mar 96 .... 2.95
❑12, May 96, Burma 1942, Part 2 .... 2.95
❑13, Jul 96 .... 2.95
❑14, Sep 96 .... 2.95
❑15, Nov 96, Passionate Immorality; Robin and Cindy: Kingdom Come 2.95
❑16, Jan 97, Not Ninja High School; Burma 1942, Part 2 2.95

ABOMINATIONS
MARVEL

Value: Cover or less

❑1, Dec 96, Blood Rush, follows events in Hulk: Future Imperfect 1.50
❑2, Jan 97, The Fading Dead.. 1.50
❑3, Feb 97, Blur of Time, Final Issue 1.50

ABRAHAM STONE (EPIC)
MARVEL

Value: Cover or less

❑1, Jul 95, JKu, JKu (w)......... 6.95
❑2, Aug 95, JKu, JKu (w) 6.95

ABSOLUTE VERTIGO
DC

	ORIG	GOOD	FINE	N-MINT
❑1, Win 95, previews of The Eaters, Jonah Hex: Riders of the Worm and Such, Preacher, Ghostdancing, Hellblazer	0.99	1.00	2.50	5.00

ORIG GOOD FINE N-MINT

ABSOLUTE ZERO
ANTARCTIC
Value: Cover or less
- ❑1, Feb 95, True Hero; Athena: Road Trip, 1: Athena 3.50
- ❑2, May 95, Mighty Tiny and the Mouse Marines; Like a Fisherman Needs a Bicycle 2.95
- ❑3, Aug 95 .... 2.95

ABSURD ART OF J.J. GRANDVILLE, THE
TOME PRESS
Value: Cover or less
- ❑1, b&w; no date of publication 2.50

ABYSS, THE
DARK HORSE

	ORIG	GOOD	FINE	N-MINT
❑1, Aug 89	2.25	0.50	1.25	2.50
❑2, Sep 89	2.25	0.50	1.25	2.50

AC ANNUAL
AC
Value: Cover or less
- ❑1 .... 3.95
- ❑2 .... 5.00
- ❑3, Rocketman Returns!; Iron Jaw's Identity Crisis! 3.50
- ❑4 .... 3.95

ACCELERATE
DC
Value: Cover or less
- ❑1, Aug 00 .... 2.95
- ❑2, Sep 00, I Love Living in the City 2.95
- ❑3, Oct 00, Message from the Underground 2.95
- ❑4, Nov 00, Year One 2.95

ACCIDENTAL DEATH, AN
FANTAGRAPHICS
Value: Cover or less
- ❑1, Dec 93, ES, nn; b&w.......... 3.50

ACCIDENT MAN
DARK HORSE
Value: Cover or less
- ❑1, 93 .... 2.50
- ❑2, 93 .... 2.50
- ❑3, 93 .... 2.50

ACCLAIM ADVENTURE ZONE
ACCLAIM
Value: Cover or less
- ❑1, 97, BL (w), The Boss; While the Cat's Away, nn; Ninjak on Cover 4.50
- ❑2, 97, BL (w), Extinction; Hero to the Fifth Power, nn; Turok on Cover 4.50
- ❑3, 97, BL (w), Dinosaur Rodeo; Reaction Time, nn; Turok and Dinosaur on Cover 4.50

ACE
HARRIER
Value: Cover or less
- ❑1, In The Days of The Ace Rock'n'Roll Club; If Monkeys Fly, b&w; no indicia.............. 1.95

ACE COMICS PRESENTS
ACE

	ORIG	GOOD	FINE	N-MINT
❑1, May 87, Daredevil (Golden Age) vs. The Claw; Silver Streak	1.75	0.40	1.00	2.00
❑2, Jul 87, Jack Bradbury	1.75	0.40	1.00	2.00
❑3, Sep 87, Bob and Swab; The Barker, The Golden Age of Klaus Nordling	1.75	0.40	1.00	2.00
❑4, Nov 87, Lou Fine	1.75	0.40	1.00	2.00

ACE MCCOY
AVALON
Value: Cover or less
- ❑1, FF, FF (c), From Comet to McCoy!; The Old Red Car, b&w 2.95
- ❑2, FF, FF (c), Circle of Fire; Moment of Truth, b&w 2.95
- ❑3, FF, FF (c), The Fastest Toy in Town, b&w 2.95

ACE OF SPADES
ZUZUPETAL
Value: Cover or less
- ❑1, The Ace Is Drawn 2.50

ACES
ECLIPSE

	ORIG	GOOD	FINE	N-MINT
❑1, Apr 88, Airmail; Flying Down to Ohio	2.95	0.60	1.50	3.00
❑2	2.95	0.60	1.50	3.00
❑3	2.95	0.60	1.50	3.00
❑4	2.95	0.60	1.50	3.00
❑5, Final Issue	2.95	0.60	1.50	3.00

ACES HIGH (RCP)
RCP
Value: Cover or less
- ❑1, Apr 99, BK; WW; GE, BK (w); WW (w); GE (w), The Way it was; The Stork with Talon (Text Story) 2.50
- ❑2, May 99, BK; WW; GE, BK (w); WW (w); GE (w), Chivalry!; The Ace of Aces (Text Story) 2.50
- ❑3, Jun 99, BK; WW; GE, BK (w); WW (w); GE (w), The Rules; The Spy 2.50
- ❑4, Jul 99, BK; WW; GE, BK (w); WW (w); GE (w), The Green Kids; The Good Luck Piece. 2.50
- ❑5, Aug 99, BK; WW; GE, BK (w); WW (w); GE (w), C'est la Guerre!; Airman Unknown (Text Story).................................. 2.50
- ❑Anl 1, BK; WW; GE, BK (w); WW (w); GE (w), Collects Aces High #1-5 .... 13.50

ACG CHRISTMAS SPECIAL
AVALON
Value: Cover or less
- ❑1, Only A Toy; Terrible Teddy, Cover reads "Christmas Horror" 2.95

ACG'S CIVIL WAR
ACG
Value: Cover or less
- ❑1, 95 .... 2.50

Many of DC's "triangle" numbers (showing what week the specific Superman-related title was to be read) have been added to individual issue notes this year.

ORIG GOOD FINE N-MINT

ACG'S HALLOWEEN SPECIAL
AVALON
Value: Cover or less
- ❑1, Bridal Night; The Flapping Head, Cover reads "Halloween Horror" 2.95

ACHILLES STORM: DARK SECRET
BRAINSTORM
Value: Cover or less
- ❑1 .... 2.95
- ❑2 .... 2.95

ACHILLES STORM/RAZMATAZ
AJA BLU
Value: Cover or less
- ❑1, Oct 90 .... 2.25
- ❑2, Jan 91 .... 2.25
- ❑3, May 91 .... 2.25

ACID BATH CASE, THE
KITCHEN SINK
Value: Cover or less
- ❑1 .... 4.95

ACK THE BARBARIAN
INNOVATION
Value: Cover or less
- ❑1, This Spell...This Monster!; Duck Soup, b&w.................. 2.25

ACME
FANDOM HOUSE
Value: Cover or less
- ❑1 .... 3.00
- ❑2 .... 3.00
- ❑3 .... 3.00
- ❑4 .... 3.00
- ❑5 .... 3.00
- ❑6 .... 3.00
- ❑7 .... 3.00
- ❑8, Fal 87 .... 2.00
- ❑9, Sum 89 .... 3.00

ACME NOVELTY LIBRARY, THE
FANTAGRAPHICS

	ORIG	GOOD	FINE	N-MINT
❑1, Win 93, Jimmy Corrigan: A Souvenir Book Of Views; Jimmy Corrigan: Jimmy Gets Out of the House, 1: Jimmy Corrigan	3.50	3.00	7.50	15.00
❑1-2, Dec 95, 2nd Printing; Jimmy Corrigan	3.50	0.80	2.00	4.00
❑2, Sum 94, Quimby the Mouse	4.95	1.80	4.50	9.00
❑2-2, Sum 95, 2nd Printing; Quimby the Mouse	4.95	1.00	2.50	5.00
❑3, Aut 94, digest-sized; Blind Man	3.95	1.40	3.50	7.00
❑4, Win 94, Sparky's Best Comics and Stories	4.95	1.20	3.00	6.00
❑4-2	4.95	0.99	2.47	4.95
❑5, Jimmy Corrigan, digest-sized; Jimmy Corrigan	3.95	1.00	2.50	5.00
❑6, Fal 95, digest-sized; Jimmy Corrigan	3.95	0.80	2.00	4.00
❑7, Oversized; Book of Jokes	6.95	1.39	3.47	6.95
❑8, Win 96, digest-sized; Jimmy Corrigan	4.75	0.79	1.98	3.95
❑9, Win 97, digest-sized; Jimmy Corrigan	4.50	0.90	2.25	4.50
❑10, Spr 98, digest-sized; Jimmy Corrigan	4.95	0.99	2.47	4.95
❑11, digest-sized; Jimmy Corrigan	4.50	0.90	2.25	4.50
❑12, Spr 99, digest-sized; Jimmy Corrigan	4.50	0.90	2.25	4.50

ACOLYTE, THE
MAD MONKEY
Value: Cover or less
- ❑1 .... 3.95

ACTION COMICS
DC

	ORIG	GOOD	FINE	N-MINT
❑0, Oct 94, Peer Pressure, Part 4, 1: Kenny Braverman, ▲1994-40	1.50	0.50	1.25	2.50
❑1-2, Superman; "Chuck" Dawson, 1: Lois Lane; 1: Tex Thomson; 1: Superman; 1: Zatara, 2nd printing (giveaway, 1976?)	0.50	3.60	9.00	18.00
❑, Superman; "Chuck" Dawson, 1: Lois Lane; 1: Tex Thomson; 1: Superman; 1: Zatara, 3rd printing (giveaway, 1983?)	0.50	2.80	7.00	14.00
❑1-4, Superman, O: Superman, 4th printing (Nestle Quik 16-page giveaway, 1988)	0.50	1.00	2.50	5.00
❑1-5, Superman; "Chuck" Dawson, 1: Lois Lane; 1: Tex Thomson; 1: Superman; 1: Zatara, 5th printing (1992)	1.00	0.80	2.00	4.00
❑1-6, Superman, 1: Superman, stamp; 6th printing (1998); U.S. Postal Service	—	0.40	1.00	2.00
❑252, May 59, 1: Supergirl; 1: Anti-Kryptonite	0.10	240.00	600.00	1200.00
❑253, Jun 59, 2: Supergirl, Supergirl	0.10	75.00	187.50	375.00
❑254, Jul 59, A: Bizarro	0.10	55.00	137.50	275.00
❑255, Aug 59, 1: Bizarro Lois Lane	0.10	45.00	112.50	225.00
❑256, Sep 59	0.10	20.00	50.00	100.00

	ORIG	GOOD	FINE	N-MINT
❑257, Oct 59	0.10	20.00	50.00	100.00
❑258, Nov 59	0.10	20.00	50.00	100.00
❑259, Dec 59	0.10	20.00	50.00	100.00
❑260, Jan 60	0.10	20.00	50.00	100.00
❑261, Feb 60, 1: Streaky the Supercat; 1: X-Kryptonite	0.10	20.00	50.00	100.00
❑262, Mar 60	0.10	18.00	45.00	90.00
❑263, Apr 60, O: Bizarro World	0.10	20.00	50.00	100.00
❑264, May 60	0.10	16.00	40.00	80.00
❑265, Jun 60, CS	0.10	16.00	40.00	80.00
❑266, Jul 60	0.10	16.00	40.00	80.00
❑267, Aug 60, 1: Chameleon Boy, Colossal Boy, Invisible Kid I (Lyle Norg)	0.10	48.00	120.00	240.00
❑268, Sep 60	0.10	16.00	40.00	80.00
❑269, Oct 60	0.10	16.00	40.00	80.00
❑270, Nov 60	0.10	16.00	40.00	80.00
❑271, Dec 60	0.10	13.00	32.50	65.00
❑272, Jan 61	0.10	13.00	32.50	65.00
❑273, Feb 61, V: Mxyzptlk	0.10	13.00	32.50	65.00
❑274, Mar 61	0.10	13.00	32.50	65.00
❑275, Apr 61	0.10	13.00	32.50	65.00
❑276, May 61, Triplicate Girl, Phantom Girl, Brainiac 5, Shrinking Violet, Bouncing Boy joins team	0.10	25.00	62.50	125.00
❑277, Jun 61	0.10	12.00	30.00	60.00
❑278, Jul 61	0.10	12.00	30.00	60.00
❑279, Aug 61	0.10	12.00	30.00	60.00
❑280, Sep 61	0.10	12.00	30.00	60.00
❑281, Oct 61	0.10	12.00	30.00	60.00
❑282, Nov 61	0.10	12.00	30.00	60.00
❑283, Dec 61, Legion of Super-Villains	0.12	12.00	30.00	60.00
❑284, Jan 62, Mon-El	0.12	12.00	30.00	60.00
❑285, Feb 62, NA, A: Legion of Super-Heroes, Supergirl goes public	0.12	20.00	50.00	100.00
❑286, Mar 62, Legion of Super-Villains	0.12	11.00	27.50	55.00
❑287, Apr 62, A: Legion of Super-Heroes	0.12	11.00	27.50	55.00
❑288, May 62, Mon-El	0.12	10.40	26.00	52.00
❑289, Jun 62, A: Legion of Super-Heroes	0.12	10.40	26.00	52.00
❑290, Jul 62, CS, A: Legion of Super-Heroes	0.12	10.40	26.00	52.00
❑291, Aug 62, NA	0.12	6.00	15.00	30.00
❑292, Sep 62, A: Superhorse (Comet)	0.12	6.00	15.00	30.00
❑293, Oct 62, O: Superhorse (Comet)	0.12	7.00	17.50	35.00
❑294, Nov 62, CS	0.12	6.00	15.00	30.00
❑295, Dec 62	0.12	6.00	15.00	30.00
❑296, Jan 63, CS	0.12	6.00	15.00	30.00
❑297, Feb 63	0.12	6.00	15.00	30.00
❑298, Mar 63, CS	0.12	6.00	15.00	30.00
❑299, Apr 63	0.12	6.00	15.00	30.00
❑300, May 63, 300th anniversary issue	0.12	9.60	24.00	48.00
❑301, Jun 63, The Trial of Superman	0.12	5.00	12.50	25.00
❑302, Jul 63, CS	0.12	5.00	12.50	25.00
❑303, Aug 63, CS	0.12	5.00	12.50	25.00
❑304, Sep 63, CS, 1: Black Flame	0.12	5.00	12.50	25.00
❑305, Oct 63	0.12	3.60	9.00	18.00
❑306, Nov 63	0.12	3.60	9.00	18.00
❑307, Dec 63	0.12	3.60	9.00	18.00
❑308, Jan 64	0.12	3.60	9.00	18.00
❑309, Feb 64, NA, A: Supergirl's parents, Legion	0.12	3.60	9.00	18.00
❑310, Mar 64, 1: Jewel Kryptonite	0.12	4.80	12.00	24.00
❑311, Apr 64	0.12	3.20	8.00	16.00
❑312, May 64	0.12	3.20	8.00	16.00
❑313, Jun 64, A: Batman	0.12	3.20	8.00	16.00
❑314, Jul 64, A: Batman	0.12	3.20	8.00	16.00
❑315, Aug 64	0.12	3.20	8.00	16.00
❑316, Sep 64	0.12	3.20	8.00	16.00
❑317, Oct 64	0.12	3.20	8.00	16.00
❑318, Nov 64	0.12	3.20	8.00	16.00
❑319, Dec 64	0.12	3.20	8.00	16.00
❑320, Jan 65	0.12	3.20	8.00	16.00
❑321, Feb 65, CS	0.12	3.20	8.00	16.00
❑322, Mar 65	0.12	3.20	8.00	16.00
❑323, Apr 65	0.12	3.20	8.00	16.00
❑324, May 65	0.12	3.20	8.00	16.00
❑325, Jun 65	0.12	3.20	8.00	16.00
❑326, Jul 65	0.12	3.20	8.00	16.00
❑327, Aug 65, Imaginary story: Three Generations of Superman	0.12	3.20	8.00	16.00
❑328, Sep 65	0.12	3.20	8.00	16.00
❑329, Oct 65	0.12	3.20	8.00	16.00
❑330, Nov 65	0.12	3.20	8.00	16.00
❑331, Dec 65	0.12	3.20	8.00	16.00
❑332, Jan 66, Imaginary Story: Superwoman vs. Superboy	0.12	3.20	8.00	16.00
❑333, Feb 66, Imaginary Story: Superwoman vs. Superboy	0.12	3.20	8.00	16.00
❑334, Mar 66, O: Supergirl, Giant-sized issue	0.25	7.20	18.00	36.00
❑335, Mar 66	0.12	2.80	7.00	14.00
❑336, Apr 66, O: Akvar	0.12	2.80	7.00	14.00
❑337, May 66	0.12	2.80	7.00	14.00
❑338, Jun 66, CS	0.12	2.80	7.00	14.00
❑339, Jul 66, CS	0.12	2.80	7.00	14.00
❑340, Aug 66, 1: Parasite	0.12	2.80	7.00	14.00
❑341, Sep 66, A: Batman	0.12	2.00	5.00	10.00
❑342, Oct 66	0.12	2.00	5.00	10.00
❑343, Nov 66	0.12	2.00	5.00	10.00
❑344, Dec 66, A: Batman	0.12	2.00	5.00	10.00
❑345, Jan 67, The Day Candid Camera Unmasked Clark Kent's Identity!; The Exile of Steel, A: Allen Funt	0.12	2.00	5.00	10.00
❑346, Feb 67	0.12	2.00	5.00	10.00
❑347, Apr 67, Giant-sized issue; Supergirl; reprints Superman #140 and Action #290 and #293	0.25	4.40	11.00	22.00
❑348, Mar 67	0.12	1.80	4.50	9.00
❑349, Apr 67	0.12	1.80	4.50	9.00
❑350, May 67	0.12	1.80	4.50	9.00
❑351, Jun 67	0.12	1.80	4.50	9.00
❑352, Jul 67	0.12	1.80	4.50	9.00
❑353, Aug 67	0.12	1.80	4.50	9.00
❑354, Sep 67	0.12	1.80	4.50	9.00
❑355, Oct 67	0.12	1.80	4.50	9.00
❑356, Nov 67	0.12	1.80	4.50	9.00
❑357, Dec 67, CS	0.12	1.80	4.50	9.00
❑358, Jan 68, CS	0.12	1.80	4.50	9.00
❑359, Feb 68, CS	0.12	1.80	4.50	9.00
❑360, Mar 68, Giant-sized issue; Supergirl.	0.25	3.60	9.00	18.00
❑361, Apr 68	0.12	1.60	4.00	8.00
❑362, May 68	0.12	1.60	4.00	8.00
❑363, Jun 68	0.12	1.60	4.00	8.00
❑364, Jul 68, D: Superman	—	1.60	4.00	8.00
❑365, Aug 68, D: Superman	0.12	1.60	4.00	8.00
❑366, Sep 68, D: Superman	0.12	1.60	4.00	8.00
❑367, Oct 68, CS	0.12	1.60	4.00	8.00
❑368, Nov 68	0.12	1.60	4.00	8.00
❑369, Dec 68	0.12	1.60	4.00	8.00
❑370, Jan 69	0.12	1.60	4.00	8.00
❑371, Feb 69	0.12	1.60	4.00	8.00
❑372, Mar 69	0.12	1.60	4.00	8.00
❑373, Apr 69, NA, A: Supergirl, Giant-sized issue	0.25	3.60	9.00	18.00
❑374, Mar 69	0.12	1.40	3.50	7.00
❑375, Apr 69	0.12	1.40	3.50	7.00
❑376, May 69	0.12	1.40	3.50	7.00
❑377, Jun 69, The Cage of Doom; The Face Behind the Lead Mask, Legion; Reprint from Adventure Comics #300	0.15	1.40	3.50	7.00
❑378, Jul 69, The Forbidden Fruit, Legion	0.15	1.40	3.50	7.00
❑379, Aug 69, One of us is an Imposter, Legion	0.15	1.40	3.50	7.00
❑380, Sep 69, Half a Legionaire?, Legion	0.15	1.40	3.50	7.00
❑381, Oct 69, The Hapless Hero, Legion	0.15	1.40	3.50	7.00
❑382, Nov 69, Kill a Friend to Save a World, Legion	0.15	1.40	3.50	7.00
❑383, Dec 69, Chameleon Boy's Secret Identity, Legion	0.15	1.40	3.50	7.00
❑384, Jan 70, Lament for a Legionnaire, Legion	0.15	1.40	3.50	7.00
❑385, Feb 70, The Fallen Star Boy, Legion	0.15	1.40	3.50	7.00
❑386, Mar 70, Zap Goes the Legion, Legion	0.15	1.40	3.50	7.00
❑387, Apr 70, One Hero Too Many, Legion.	0.15	1.40	3.50	7.00
❑388, May 70, Sun Boy's Lost Power, Legion; Reprints Legion story from Adventure Comics #302	0.15	1.40	3.50	7.00
❑389, Jun 70, The Mystery Legionnaire, Legion	0.15	1.40	3.50	7.00
❑390, Jul 70, The Tyrant and the Traitor, Legion	0.15	1.40	3.50	7.00
❑391, Aug 70, The Ordeal of Element Lad, Legion	0.15	1.40	3.50	7.00
❑392, Sep 70, Super-Sons; Last Legion of Super-Heroes	0.15	1.40	3.50	7.00
❑393, Oct 70	0.15	1.40	3.50	7.00
❑394, Nov 70	0.15	1.40	3.50	7.00
❑395, Dec 70	0.15	1.40	3.50	7.00
❑396, Jan 71, CS; MA, The Super-Panhandler of Metropolis	0.15	1.10	2.75	5.50
❑397, Feb 71	0.15	1.10	2.75	5.50
❑398, Mar 71	0.15	1.10	2.75	5.50
❑399, Apr 71	0.15	1.10	2.75	5.50
❑400, May 71	0.15	1.10	2.75	5.50
❑401, Jun 71	0.15	1.10	2.75	5.50
❑402, Jul 71, Supergirl back-up	0.15	1.10	2.75	5.50
❑403, Aug 71, Superboy back-ups; Vigilante	0.25	1.10	2.75	5.50
❑404, Sep 71	0.25	1.10	2.75	5.50

	ORIG	GOOD	FINE	N-MINT
❑405, Oct 71	0.25	1.10	2.75	5.50
❑406, Nov 71	0.25	1.10	2.75	5.50
❑407, Dec 71	0.25	1.10	2.75	5.50
❑408, Jan 72, GK, reprints The Atom #9	0.25	1.10	2.75	5.50
❑409, Feb 72	0.25	1.10	2.75	5.50
❑410, Feb 72	0.25	1.10	2.75	5.50
❑411, Apr 72, O: Eclipso	0.25	1.20	3.00	6.00
❑412, May 72	0.25	0.90	2.25	4.50
❑413, Jun 72	0.25	0.90	2.25	4.50
❑414, Jul 72	0.20	0.90	2.25	4.50
❑415, Aug 72	0.20	0.90	2.25	4.50
❑416, Sep 72	0.20	0.90	2.25	4.50
❑417, Oct 72	0.20	0.90	2.25	4.50
❑418, Nov 72	0.20	0.90	2.25	4.50
❑419, Dec 72, 1: Human Target	0.20	0.90	2.25	4.50
❑420, Jan 73	0.20	0.90	2.25	4.50
❑421, Feb 73, Green Arrow begins	0.20	0.90	2.25	4.50
❑422, Mar 73	0.20	0.90	2.25	4.50
❑423, Apr 73	0.20	0.90	2.25	4.50
❑424, Jun 73, CS; DG; MA, Green Arrow	0.20	0.90	2.25	4.50
❑425, Jul 73, CS; NA; DG; MA	0.20	1.60	4.00	8.00
❑426, Aug 73	0.20	0.80	2.00	4.00
❑427, Sep 73	0.20	0.80	2.00	4.00
❑428, Oct 73	0.20	0.80	2.00	4.00
❑429, Nov 73	0.20	0.80	2.00	4.00
❑430, Dec 73, Atom back-up	0.20	0.80	2.00	4.00
❑431, Jan 74, Green Arrow back-up	0.20	0.80	2.00	4.00
❑432, Feb 74	0.20	0.80	2.00	4.00
❑433, Mar 74	0.20	0.80	2.00	4.00
❑434, Apr 74	0.20	0.80	2.00	4.00
❑435, May 74	0.20	0.80	2.00	4.00
❑436, Jun 74	0.20	0.80	2.00	4.00
❑437, Jul 74, CI, Giant-sized issue (100 pages); Green Arrow	0.60	1.80	4.50	9.00
❑438, Aug 74, CS	0.20	0.80	2.00	4.00
❑439, Sep 74, CS, Atom back-up	0.20	0.80	2.00	4.00
❑440, Oct 74, CS; MGr, 1st Green Arrow by Mike Grell	0.20	1.80	4.50	9.00
❑441, Nov 74, CS; MGr, A: Flash, Green Arrow back-up	0.20	1.20	3.00	6.00
❑442, Dec 74, CS	0.20	0.80	2.00	4.00
❑443, Jan 75, Giant-sized issue (100 pages); JLA	0.60	1.80	4.50	9.00
❑444, Feb 75, A: Green Lantern, Green Arrow back-up	0.25	0.80	2.00	4.00
❑445, Mar 75	0.25	0.80	2.00	4.00
❑446, Apr 75	0.25	0.80	2.00	4.00
❑447, May 75	0.25	0.70	1.75	3.50
❑448, Jun 75	0.25	0.70	1.75	3.50
❑449, Jul 75, JK, Green Arrow giant	0.50	0.70	1.75	3.50
❑450, Aug 75	0.25	0.70	1.75	3.50
❑451, Sep 75, Green Arrow back-up	0.25	0.70	1.75	3.50
❑452, Oct 75	0.25	0.70	1.75	3.50
❑453, Nov 75, Atom back-up	0.25	0.70	1.75	3.50
❑454, Dec 75, last Atom back-up	0.25	0.70	1.75	3.50
❑455, Jan 76	0.25	0.70	1.75	3.50
❑456, Feb 76, Green Arrow back-up	0.25	0.70	1.75	3.50
❑457, Mar 76, Green Arrow back-up; Superman reveals ID to Pete Ross' son	0.30	0.70	1.75	3.50
❑458, Apr 76, CS; MGr, 1: Blackrock, Green Arrow	0.30	0.70	1.75	3.50
❑459, May 76	0.30	0.70	1.75	3.50
❑460, Jun 76, 1: Karb-Brak, Mxyzptlk back-up	0.30	0.70	1.75	3.50
❑461, Jul 76, V: Karb-Brak, Superman in colonial America; Bicentennial #30	0.30	0.70	1.75	3.50
❑462, Aug 76	0.30	0.70	1.75	3.50
❑463, Sep 76	0.30	0.70	1.75	3.50
❑464, Oct 76	0.30	0.70	1.75	3.50
❑465, Nov 76	0.30	0.70	1.75	3.50
❑466, Dec 76	0.30	0.70	1.75	3.50
❑467, Jan 77	0.30	0.70	1.75	3.50
❑468, Feb 77	0.30	0.70	1.75	3.50
❑469, Mar 77	0.30	0.70	1.75	3.50
❑470, Apr 77	0.30	0.70	1.75	3.50
❑471, May 77	0.30	0.70	1.75	3.50
❑472, Jun 77, CS, The Phantom Touch Of Death, V: Faora Hu-Ul	0.30	0.70	1.75	3.50
❑473, Jul 77	0.35	0.70	1.75	3.50
❑474, Aug 77	0.35	0.70	1.75	3.50
❑475, Sep 77	0.35	0.70	1.75	3.50
❑476, Oct 77	0.35	0.70	1.75	3.50
❑477, Nov 77	0.35	0.70	1.75	3.50
❑478, Dec 77	0.35	0.70	1.75	3.50
❑479, Jan 78	0.35	0.70	1.75	3.50
❑480, Feb 78	0.35	0.70	1.75	3.50
❑481, Mar 78, 1: Supermobile; V: Amazo	0.35	0.70	1.75	3.50

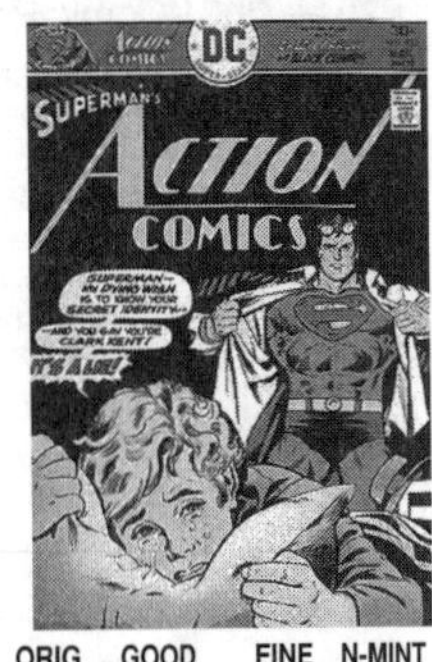

Unaware that Pete Ross had known his secret identity since their childhood days in Smallville, Superman revealed his secret to Ross' son in *Action Comics* #457.

	ORIG	GOOD	FINE	N-MINT
❑482, Apr 78	0.35	0.70	1.75	3.50
❑483, May 78, V: Amazo	0.35	0.70	1.75	3.50
❑484, Jun 78, 40th anniversary; Wedding of E-2 Superman and Lois Lane	0.35	0.70	1.75	3.50
❑485, Jul 78	0.35	0.70	1.75	3.50
❑486, Aug 78	0.35	0.70	1.75	3.50
❑487, Sep 78, O: Atom	0.50	0.70	1.75	3.50
❑488, Oct 78	0.50	0.70	1.75	3.50
❑489, Nov 78	0.50	0.70	1.75	3.50
❑490, Dec 78	0.40	0.70	1.75	3.50
❑491, Jan 79	0.40	0.70	1.75	3.50
❑492, Feb 79	0.40	0.70	1.75	3.50
❑493, Mar 79	0.40	0.70	1.75	3.50
❑494, Apr 79	0.40	0.70	1.75	3.50
❑495, May 79, 1: Silver Banshee	0.40	0.70	1.75	3.50
❑496, Jun 79	0.40	0.70	1.75	3.50
❑497, Jul 79	0.40	0.70	1.75	3.50
❑498, Aug 79	0.40	0.70	1.75	3.50
❑499, Sep 79	0.40	0.70	1.75	3.50
❑500, Oct 79, O: Superman, 500th anniversary issue; Giant-sized; Superman's life	1.00	0.80	2.00	4.00
❑501, Nov 79	0.40	0.60	1.50	3.00
❑502, Dec 79	0.40	0.60	1.50	3.00
❑503, Jan 80	0.40	0.60	1.50	3.00
❑504, Feb 80	0.40	0.60	1.50	3.00
❑505, Mar 80	0.40	0.60	1.50	3.00
❑506, Apr 80	0.40	0.60	1.50	3.00
❑507, May 80	0.40	0.60	1.50	3.00
❑508, Jun 80	0.40	0.60	1.50	3.00
❑509, Jul 80, JSt; JSn, Radio Shack promo insert	0.40	0.60	1.50	3.00
❑510, Aug 80	0.40	0.60	1.50	3.00
❑511, Sep 80	0.50	0.60	1.50	3.00
❑512, Oct 80	0.50	0.60	1.50	3.00
❑513, Nov 80	0.50	0.60	1.50	3.00
❑514, Dec 80	0.50	0.60	1.50	3.00
❑515, Jan 81, V: Vandal Savage	0.50	0.60	1.50	3.00
❑516, Feb 81, V: Vandal Savage	0.50	0.60	1.50	3.00
❑517, Mar 81	0.50	0.60	1.50	3.00
❑518, Apr 81, Aquaman back-up	0.50	0.60	1.50	3.00
❑519, May 81	0.50	0.60	1.50	3.00
❑520, Jun 81	0.50	0.60	1.50	3.00
❑521, Jul 81, 1: Vixen, Atom, Aquaman back-up	0.50	0.60	1.50	3.00
❑522, Aug 81, Atom back-up	0.50	0.60	1.50	3.00
❑523, Sep 81	0.50	0.60	1.50	3.00
❑524, Oct 81, Airwave and Atom back-up	0.60	0.60	1.50	3.00
❑525, Nov 81, 1: Neutron	0.60	0.60	1.50	3.00
❑526, Dec 81	0.60	0.60	1.50	3.00
❑527, Jan 82, 1: Lord Satanis, Airwave, Aquaman back-up	0.60	0.60	1.50	3.00
❑528, Feb 82, A: Brainiac, Aquaman back-up	0.60	0.60	1.50	3.00
❑529, Mar 82	0.60	0.60	1.50	3.00
❑530, Apr 82	0.60	0.60	1.50	3.00
❑531, May 82	0.60	0.60	1.50	3.00
❑532, Jun 82	0.60	0.60	1.50	3.00
❑533, Jul 82	0.60	0.60	1.50	3.00
❑534, Aug 82	0.60	0.60	1.50	3.00
❑535, Sep 82, Omega Man	0.60	0.60	1.50	3.00
❑536, Oct 82, Omega Man	0.60	0.60	1.50	3.00
❑537, Nov 82	0.60	0.60	1.50	3.00
❑538, Dec 82	0.60	0.60	1.50	3.00
❑539, Jan 83, GK, Flash, Atom	0.60	0.60	1.50	3.00
❑540, Feb 83, CS	0.60	0.60	1.50	3.00
❑541, Mar 83, CS	0.60	0.60	1.50	3.00
❑542, Apr 83, CS, V: Vandal Savage	0.60	0.60	1.50	3.00
❑543, May 83, CS, V: Neutron	0.60	0.60	1.50	3.00
❑544, Jun 83, CS; GK, GK (c); DG (c), Luthor Unleashed!; Rebirth!, 1: Lex Luthor (New); 1: Brainiac (New), 45th anniversary	1.50	0.60	1.50	3.00
❑545, Jul 83, V: New Brainiac	1.50	0.60	1.50	3.00
❑546, Aug 83, A: JLA, Titans	0.60	0.60	1.50	3.00

	ORIG	GOOD	FINE	N-MINT
❑547, Sep 83	1.50	0.60	1.50	3.00
❑548, Oct 83	1.50	0.60	1.50	3.00
❑549, Nov 83	1.50	0.60	1.50	3.00
❑550, Dec 83	0.75	0.60	1.50	3.00
❑551, Jan 84, 1: Red Star (Starfire)	0.75	0.60	1.50	3.00
❑552, Feb 84, 1: Legion of Forgotten Heroes; A: Animal Man	0.75	0.80	2.00	4.00
❑553, Mar 84, A: Legion of Forgotten Heroes; A: Animal Man	0.75	0.60	1.50	3.00
❑554, Apr 84	0.75	0.40	1.00	2.00
❑555, May 84, V: Parasite; A: Supergirl	0.75	0.40	1.00	2.00
❑556, Jun 84, V: Vandal Savage, Neutron	0.75	0.40	1.00	2.00
❑557, Jul 84	0.75	0.40	1.00	2.00
❑558, Aug 84	0.75	0.40	1.00	2.00
❑559, Sep 84	0.75	0.40	1.00	2.00
❑560, Oct 84, A: Ambush Bug	0.75	0.40	1.00	2.00
❑561, Nov 84	0.75	0.40	1.00	2.00
❑562, Dec 84	0.75	0.40	1.00	2.00
❑563, Jan 85, Ambush Bug vs. Mxyzptlk	0.75	0.40	1.00	2.00
❑564, Feb 85	0.75	0.40	1.00	2.00
❑565, Mar 85, A: Ambush Bug	0.75	0.40	1.00	2.00
❑566, Apr 85, V: Captain Strong	0.75	0.40	1.00	2.00
❑567, May 85	0.75	0.40	1.00	2.00
❑568, Jun 85	0.75	0.40	1.00	2.00
❑569, Jul 85	0.75	0.40	1.00	2.00
❑570, Aug 85	0.75	0.40	1.00	2.00
❑571, Sep 85	0.75	0.40	1.00	2.00
❑572, Oct 85	0.75	0.40	1.00	2.00
❑573, Nov 85	0.75	0.40	1.00	2.00
❑574, Dec 85	0.75	0.40	1.00	2.00
❑575, Jan 86	0.75	0.40	1.00	2.00
❑576, Feb 86	0.75	0.40	1.00	2.00
❑577, Mar 86	0.75	0.40	1.00	2.00
❑578, Apr 86	0.75	0.40	1.00	2.00
❑579, May 86	0.75	0.40	1.00	2.00
❑580, Jun 86	0.75	0.40	1.00	2.00
❑581, Jul 86	0.75	0.40	1.00	2.00
❑582, Aug 86	0.75	0.40	1.00	2.00
❑583, Sep 86, AMo (w), Whatever Happened to the Man of Tomorrow, Part 2, Last pre-Crisis on Infinite Earths Superman	0.75	1.00	2.50	5.00
❑584, Jan 87, DG; JBy, AMo (w), A: Titans, Post-Crisis Superman begins	0.75	0.50	1.25	2.50
❑585, Feb 87, DG; JBy, A: Phantom Stranger	0.75	0.40	1.00	2.00
❑586, Mar 87, DG; JBy, A: Orion, "Legends"	0.75	0.40	1.00	2.00
❑587, Apr 87, DG; JBy, A: Demon	0.75	0.40	1.00	2.00
❑588, May 87, DG; JBy, A: Hawkman	0.75	0.40	1.00	2.00
❑589, Jun 87, DG; JBy, A: Green Lantern Corps	0.75	0.40	1.00	2.00
❑590, Jul 87, DG; JBy, A: Metal Men	0.75	0.40	1.00	2.00
❑591, Aug 87, DG; JBy, A: Superboy	0.75	0.40	1.00	2.00
❑592, Sep 87, DG; JBy, A: Big Barda	0.75	0.40	1.00	2.00
❑593, Oct 87, DG; JBy, A: Mr. Miracle	0.75	0.40	1.00	2.00
❑594, Nov 87, JBy, A: Batman, Booster Gold	0.75	0.40	1.00	2.00
❑595, Dec 87, JBy, A: Batman, J'onn J'onzz	0.75	0.40	1.00	2.00
❑596, Jan 88, JBy, A: Spectre, "Millennium"	0.75	0.40	1.00	2.00
❑597, Feb 88, JBy, A: Lois Lane and Lana Lang	0.75	0.40	1.00	2.00
❑598, Mar 88, JBy, 1: Checkmate	0.75	0.50	1.25	2.50
❑599, Apr 88, RA; JBy, A: Metal Men, Bonus Book #1	0.75	0.40	1.00	2.00
❑600, May 88, JBy; GP, 600th anniversary issue; Giant-sized; "Genesis" prequel	2.50	1.00	2.50	5.00
❑601, Aug 88, 52pgs.; Superman, Blackhawk, Green Lantern, Deadman, Wild Dog, Secret Six; Action Comics begins weekly issues	1.50	0.40	1.00	2.00
❑602, Aug 88, 52pgs.; Superman, Blackhawk, Green Lantern, Deadman, Wild Dog, Secret Six	1.50	0.35	0.88	1.75
❑603, Aug 88, 52pgs.; Superman, Blackhawk, Green Lantern, Deadman, Wild Dog, Secret Six	1.50	0.35	0.88	1.75
❑604, Aug 88, 52pgs.; Superman, Blackhawk, Green Lantern, Deadman, Wild Dog, Secret Six	1.50	0.35	0.88	1.75
❑605, Aug 88, 52pgs.; Superman, Blackhawk, Green Lantern, Deadman, Wild Dog, Secret Six	1.50	0.35	0.88	1.75
❑606, Sep 88, 52pgs.; Superman, Blackhawk, Green Lantern, Deadman, Wild Dog, Secret Six	1.50	0.35	0.88	1.75
❑607, Sep 88, 52pgs.; Superman, Blackhawk, Green Lantern, Deadman, Wild Dog, Secret Six	1.50	0.35	0.88	1.75
❑608, Sep 88, 52pgs.	1.50	0.35	0.88	1.75
❑609, Sep 88, BB (c), 52pgs.; Black Canary	1.50	0.35	0.88	1.75

	ORIG	GOOD	FINE	N-MINT
❑610, Sep 88, Green Lantern: Risky Business; The Phantom Stranger: Kenny And The Demon!, 52pgs.	1.50	0.35	0.88	1.75
❑611, Oct 88, 52pgs.	1.50	0.35	0.88	1.75
❑612, Oct 88, 52pgs.	1.50	0.35	0.88	1.75
❑613, Oct 88, 52pgs.	1.50	0.35	0.88	1.75
❑614, Oct 88, 52pgs.	1.50	0.35	0.88	1.75
❑615, Oct 88, 52pgs.	1.50	0.35	0.88	1.75
❑616, Nov 88, 52pgs.	1.50	0.35	0.88	1.75
❑617, Nov 88, 52pgs.	1.50	0.35	0.88	1.75
❑618, Nov 88, 52pgs.	1.50	0.35	0.88	1.75
❑619, Nov 88, 52pgs.	1.50	0.35	0.88	1.75
❑620, Dec 88, 52pgs.	1.50	0.35	0.88	1.75
❑621, Dec 88, 52pgs.	1.50	0.35	0.88	1.75
❑622, Dec 88, 52pgs.	1.50	0.35	0.88	1.75
❑623, Dec 88, 52pgs.	1.50	0.35	0.88	1.75
❑624, Dec 88, 52pgs.	1.50	0.35	0.88	1.75
❑625, Dec 88, 52pgs.	1.50	0.35	0.88	1.75
❑626, Dec 88, 52pgs.	1.50	0.35	0.88	1.75
❑627, Dec 88, 52pgs.	1.50	0.35	0.88	1.75
❑628, Jan 89, 52pgs.	1.50	0.35	0.88	1.75
❑629, Jan 89, 52pgs.	1.50	0.35	0.88	1.75
❑630, Jan 89, 52pgs.	1.50	0.35	0.88	1.75
❑631, Jan 89, 52pgs.	1.50	0.35	0.88	1.75
❑632, Jan 89, 52pgs.	1.50	0.35	0.88	1.75
❑633, Jan 89, 52pgs.	1.50	0.35	0.88	1.75
❑634, Jan 89, 52pgs.	1.50	0.35	0.88	1.75
❑635, Jan 89, 52pgs.; crossover	1.50	0.35	0.88	1.75
❑636, Jan 89, 1: new Phantom Lady, 52pgs.	1.50	0.35	0.88	1.75
❑637, Jan 89, 1: Hero Hotline, 52pgs.	1.50	0.35	0.88	1.75
❑638, Feb 89, TD; JK, 2: Hero Hotline, 52pgs.	1.50	0.35	0.88	1.75
❑639, Feb 89, A: Hero Hotline, 52pgs.	1.50	0.35	0.88	1.75
❑640, Feb 89, A: Hero Hotline, 52pgs.	1.50	0.35	0.88	1.75
❑641, Feb 89, Blackhawk	1.50	0.35	0.88	1.75
❑642, Mar 89, 52pgs.; Last weekly issue	1.50	0.35	0.88	1.75
❑643, Jul 89, GP, Cover swipe from Superman #1; Title returns to Action Comics; Monthly issues begin again	0.75	0.35	0.88	1.75
❑644, Aug 89, GP	0.75	0.35	0.88	1.75
❑645, Sep 89, GP, V: Maxima	0.75	0.35	0.88	1.75
❑646, Oct 89, GP	0.75	0.35	0.88	1.75
❑647, Nov 89, GP, O: Brainiac	0.75	0.35	0.88	1.75
❑648, Dec 89, GP	0.75	0.35	0.88	1.75
❑649, Jan 90, GP	0.75	0.35	0.88	1.75
❑650, Feb 90, GP; JO, 52pgs.	1.50	0.35	0.88	1.75
❑651, Mar 90, V: Maxima, Krypton Man	0.75	0.35	0.88	1.75
❑652, Apr 90, Krypton Man	0.75	0.35	0.88	1.75
❑653, May 90	0.75	0.35	0.88	1.75
❑654, Jun 90, Batman	0.75	0.35	0.88	1.75
❑655, Jul 90	0.75	0.35	0.88	1.75
❑656, Aug 90	0.75	0.35	0.88	1.75
❑657, Sep 90, Toyman	0.75	0.35	0.88	1.75
❑658, Oct 90, CS, A: Sinbad	0.75	0.35	0.88	1.75
❑659, Nov 90	0.75	0.35	0.88	1.75
❑660, Dec 90, D: Lex Luthor (fake death)	0.75	0.50	1.25	2.50
❑661, Jan 91, Plastic Man	1.00	0.35	0.88	1.75
❑662, Feb 91, Clark tells Lois; Superman reveals identity to Lois Lane	1.00	0.50	1.25	2.50
❑662-2, Feb 91, 2nd Printing; Superman reveals identity to Lois Lane	1.00	0.30	0.75	1.50
❑663, Mar 91, Time and Time Again, Part 2, Superman in 1940s	1.00	0.35	0.88	1.75
❑664, Apr 91, Time and Time Again, Part 5, A: Chronos	1.00	0.35	0.88	1.75
❑665, May 91	1.00	0.35	0.88	1.75
❑666, Jun 91	1.00	0.35	0.88	1.75
❑667, Jul 91, 52pgs.	1.75	0.40	1.00	2.00
❑668, Aug 91	1.00	0.35	0.88	1.75
❑669, Sep 91, A: Thorn	1.00	0.35	0.88	1.75
❑670, Oct 91, 1: Lex Luthor II	1.00	0.35	0.88	1.75
❑671, Nov 91, Superman blackout	1.00	0.35	0.88	1.75
❑672, Dec 91	1.00	0.35	0.88	1.75
❑673, Jan 92, V: Hellgrammite	1.00	0.35	0.88	1.75
❑674, Apr 92, Supergirl	1.00	0.35	0.88	1.75
❑675, Mar 92, Panic in Sky	1.00	0.35	0.88	1.75
❑676, Apr 92	1.00	0.35	0.88	1.75
❑677, May 92	1.00	0.35	0.88	1.75
❑678, Jun 92, O: Luthor	1.00	0.40	1.00	2.00
❑679, Jul 92	1.00	0.35	0.88	1.75
❑680, Aug 92	1.25	0.35	0.88	1.75
❑681, Sep 92, V: Rampage	1.25	0.35	0.88	1.75
❑682, Oct 92, V: Hi-Tech	1.25	0.35	0.88	1.75
❑683, Nov 92, Doomsday	1.25	0.50	1.25	2.50
❑683-2, Nov 92, Doomsday, 2nd Printing	1.25	0.30	0.75	1.50
❑684, Dec 92, Doomsday, Doomsday	1.25	0.50	1.25	2.50
❑684-2, Dec 92, Doomsday, 2nd Printing	1.25	0.30	0.75	1.50
❑685, Jan 93, Funeral for a Friend, Part 2, ▲1993-4	1.25	0.40	1.00	2.00

	ORIG	GOOD	FINE	N-MINT
❑685-2, Jan 93, Funeral For a Friend, Part 2, ▲1993-4, 2nd Printing	1.25	0.25	0.63	1.25
❑685-3, Jan 93, Funeral For a Friend, Part 2, ▲1993-4, 3rd Printing	1.25	0.25	0.63	1.25
❑686, Feb 93, Funeral For a Friend, Part 6, Superman funeral; ▲1993-8	1.25	0.40	1.00	2.00
❑687, Jun 93, Reign of the Supermen; Born Again, A: ▲1993-12, 1st; 1: alien Superman, poster	1.50	0.30	0.75	1.50
❑687/CS, Jun 93, Reign of the Supermen; Born Again, 1: Last Son of Krypton; 1: alien Superman, die-cut cover, Die-cut cover; poster; ▲1993-12	1.95	0.50	1.25	2.50
❑688, Jul 93, Reign of the Supermen; Eye For An Eye, ▲1993-16	1.50	0.40	1.00	2.00
❑689, Jul 93, Reign of the Supermen; Who Is The Hero True, ▲1993-20	1.50	0.40	1.00	2.00
❑690, Aug 93, Reign of the Supermen	1.50	0.40	1.00	2.00
❑691, Sep 93, Reign of the Supermen, ▲1993-28	1.50	0.40	1.00	2.00
❑692, Oct 93, Clark Kent returns	1.50	0.40	1.00	2.00
❑693, Nov 93	1.50	0.40	1.00	2.00
❑694, Dec 93, V: Hi-Tech	1.50	0.35	0.88	1.75
❑695, Jan 94, Cauldron!, A: Lobo	1.50	0.35	0.88	1.75
❑695/SC, Jan 94, Cauldron!, A: Lobo, enhanced cover	2.50	0.50	1.25	2.50
❑696, Feb 94, Champion, Return of Doomsday; ▲1994-8	1.50	0.35	0.88	1.75
❑697, Mar 94, Bizarro's World, Part 3, Bizarro	1.50	0.35	0.88	1.75
❑698, Apr 94	1.50	0.35	0.88	1.75
❑699, May 94	1.50	0.35	0.88	1.75
❑700, Jun 94, The Fall Of Metropolis, Swan Song, Giant-size; Wedding of Pete Ross and Lana Lang; Destruction of the Daily Planet building; ▲1994-24	2.95	0.65	1.63	3.25
❑700/PL, Jun 94, no cover price; Platinum edition; Giant-size; ▲1994-24; Wedding of Pete Ross and Lana Lang; Destruction of the Daily Planet building	—	1.00	2.50	5.00
❑701, Jul 94, Fall of Metropolis	1.50	0.35	0.88	1.75
❑702, Aug 94, V: Bloodsport	1.50	0.35	0.88	1.75
❑703, Sep 94, "Zero Hour"	1.50	0.35	0.88	1.75
❑704, Nov 94, Dead Again, V: Eradictor and The Outsiders	1.50	0.35	0.88	1.75
❑705, Dec 94, Dead Again	1.50	0.35	0.88	1.75
❑706, Jan 95	1.50	0.35	0.88	1.75
❑707, Feb 95, V: Shadowdragon	1.50	0.35	0.88	1.75
❑708, Mar 95, A: Mister Miracle	1.50	0.35	0.88	1.75
❑709, Apr 95, V: Guy Gardner	1.50	0.35	0.88	1.75
❑710, Jun 95, Death of Clark Kent	1.95	0.39	0.98	1.95
❑711, Jul 95, Death of Clark Kent, D: Kenny Braverman (Conduit)	1.95	0.39	0.98	1.95
❑712, Aug 95	1.95	0.39	0.98	1.95
❑713, Sep 95	1.95	0.39	0.98	1.95
❑714, Oct 95, A: Joker	1.95	0.39	0.98	1.95
❑715, Nov 95, V: Parasite	1.95	0.39	0.98	1.95
❑716, Dec 95, Trial of Superman	1.95	0.39	0.98	1.95
❑717, Jan 96, Trial of Superman	1.95	0.39	0.98	1.95
❑718, Feb 96, By Darker Reason, 1: Demolitia, ▲1996-5	1.95	0.39	0.98	1.95
❑719, Mar 96, Hazard's Choice, A: Batman, ▲1996-9	1.95	0.39	0.98	1.95
❑720, Apr 96, Love Breaks, Lois Lane breaks off engagement to Clark Kent; ▲1996-14	1.95	0.40	1.00	2.00
❑720-2, Apr 96, 2nd Printing; ▲1996-14; Lois Lane breaks off engagement to Clark Kent	1.95	0.39	0.98	1.95
❑721, May 96, A: Mxyzptlk	1.95	0.39	0.98	1.95
❑722, Jun 96	1.95	0.39	0.98	1.95
❑723, Jul 96	1.95	0.39	0.98	1.95
❑724, Aug 96, O&D: Brawl	1.95	0.39	0.98	1.95
❑725, Sep 96, The Bottle City, Part 1, V: Tolos	1.95	0.39	0.98	1.95
❑726, Oct 96, Arms!, V: Barrage, ▲1996-40	1.95	0.39	0.98	1.95
❑727, Nov 96, Cold Comfort!, "Final Night"; ▲1996-44	1.95	0.39	0.98	1.95
❑728, Dec 96, Hawaiian Honeymoon; I Killed Superman, ▲1996-49	1.95	0.39	0.98	1.95
❑729, Jan 97, Generator X!, A: Mr. Miracle, Big Barda, ▲1997-3	1.95	0.39	0.98	1.95
❑730, Feb 97, The President of the United Hates, V: Superman Revenge Squad (Anomaly, Maxima, Misa, Barrage and Riot), ▲1997-8	1.95	0.39	0.98	1.95
❑731, Mar 97, ...Fire Burn and Cauldron Bubble!, V: Cauldron, ▲1997-12	1.95	0.39	0.98	1.95
❑732, Apr 97, The Saving Skull, V: Atomic Skull, more energy powers manifest; ▲1997-17	1.95	0.39	0.98	1.95
❑733, May 97, A: Ray, new uniform	1.95	0.39	0.98	1.95
❑734, Jun 97, Scorn vs. Rock	1.95	0.39	0.98	1.95
❑735, Jul 97, V: Saviour	1.95	0.39	0.98	1.95

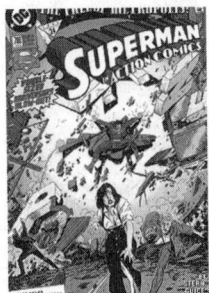

Pete Ross and Lana Lang tied the knot in *Action Comics* #700, more than two years before the wedding of Lois Lane and Clark Kent.

	ORIG	GOOD	FINE	N-MINT
❑736, Aug 97	1.95	0.39	0.98	1.95
❑737, Sep 97, Jimmy pursued by Intergang	1.95	0.39	0.98	1.95
❑738, Oct 97, 1: Inkling	1.95	0.39	0.98	1.95
❑739, Nov 97, Party Trappings, V: Locksmith; A: Sam Lane, Lois captured by Naga; ▲1997-46	1.95	0.39	0.98	1.95
❑740, Dec 97, A Bag, a Bone, & a Hank of Hair, V: Ripper, Face cover	1.95	0.39	0.98	1.95
❑741, Jan 98, A: Legion of Super-Heroes	1.95	0.39	0.98	1.95
❑742, Mar 98, forms diptych with Superman: Man of Steel #77	1.95	0.39	0.98	1.95
❑743, Apr 98, Operation: Ink!; A Persistence of You, Orgin of Inkling	1.95	0.39	0.98	1.95
❑744, May 98, "Millennium Giants"	1.95	0.39	0.98	1.95
❑745, Jun 98, Polyester Year, Part 1, V: Prankster	1.95	0.39	0.98	1.95
❑746, Jul 98, Polyester Year, Part 2, V: Prankster	1.95	0.39	0.98	1.95
❑747, Aug 98, A: Dominus	1.95	0.39	0.98	1.95
❑748, Sep 98, A: Waverider; V: Dominus	1.99	0.39	0.98	1.95
❑749, Dec 98, into Kandor	1.99	0.40	1.00	2.00
❑750, Jan 99, Confidence Job, 1: Crazytop, Giant-size; ▲1999-1	2.95	0.40	1.00	2.00
❑751, Feb 99, A: DEO agents; A: Geo-Force; A: Lex Luthor	1.99	0.40	1.00	1.99
❑752, Mar 99, A: Supermen of America	1.99	0.40	1.00	1.99
❑753, Apr 99, A: JLA; A: Justice League of America	1.99	0.40	1.00	1.99
❑754, May 99, The Aimless Blade of Science, V: Dominus	1.99	0.40	1.00	1.99
❑755, Jul 99, Necropolis, ▲1999-25	1.99	0.40	1.00	1.99
❑756, Aug 99, Comeback, V: Doomslayers	1.99	0.40	1.00	1.99
❑757, Sep 99, One-Man JLA; Secret Origins, Part 3, Superman as Hawkman; ▲1999-34	1.99	0.40	1.00	1.99
❑758, Oct 99, V: Intergang	1.99	0.40	1.00	1.99
❑759, Nov 99, SB, Who is Strange Visitor?, Part 3, A: Strange Visitor, ▲1999-42	1.99	0.40	1.00	1.99
❑760, Dec 99, ...Never-Ending Battle..., ▲1999-49	1.99	0.40	1.00	1.99
❑761, Jan 00, For a Thousand Years..., A: Wonder Woman, ▲2000-4	1.99	0.40	1.00	1.99
❑762, Feb 00	1.99	0.40	1.00	1.99
❑763, Mar 00	1.99	0.40	1.00	1.99
❑764, Apr 00, Quiet After the Storm, ▲2000-17	1.99	0.40	1.00	1.99
❑765, May 00, A Clown Comes to Metropolis, ▲2000-21	1.99	0.40	1.00	1.99
❑766, Jun 00	1.99	0.40	1.00	1.99
❑767, Jul 00	—	0.40	1.00	1.99
❑768, Aug 00, O, Captain, My Captain!, A: Mary Marvel; A: Captain Marvel; A: Captain Marvel Jr., ▲2000-33	2.25	0.40	1.00	1.99
❑769, Sep 00, Superman Arkham, Part 2; Supermanamrepus, ▲2000-37	2.25	0.45	1.13	2.25
❑770, Oct 00, The Reign of Emperor Joker, Part 5; He Who Laughs Last!, A: Joker, Giant-size; ▲2000-42	2.25	0.70	1.75	3.50
❑771, Nov 00, The Out of Towner, A: Nightwing, ▲2000-46; ▲2000-47	2.25	0.45	1.13	2.25
❑772, Dec 00, Kith & Kin, Part 1, A: Talia; A: Encantadora, ▲2000-50	2.25	0.45	1.13	2.25
❑773, Jan 01, Kith & Kin, Part 2, ▲2001-5	2.25	0.45	1.13	2.25
❑774, Feb 01, Fireside Chat, ▲2001-9	2.25	0.45	1.13	2.25
❑775, Mar 01, What's so Funny About Truth, Justice, & the American Way?, Giant-size; ▲2001-13	3.75	0.75	1.88	3.75
❑776, Apr 01, Escape from Krypton, ▲2001-17	2.25	0.45	1.13	2.25
❑777, May 01, Kancer, ▲2001-21	2.25	0.45	1.13	2.25
❑778, Jun 01	2.25	0.45	1.13	2.25
❑779, Jul 01	2.25	0.45	1.13	2.25
❑780, Aug 01	2.25	0.45	1.13	2.25
❑781, Sep 01	2.25	0.45	1.13	2.25
❑1000000, Nov 98, Brave New Hero	1.99	0.40	1.00	2.00
❑Anl 1	1.25	0.80	2.00	4.00

	ORIG	GOOD	FINE	N-MINT
❑Anl 2, CS; GP; JO, 1: The Eradicator	1.75	0.60	1.50	3.00
❑Anl 3, Armageddon 2001, Part 8, Armageddon 2001	2.00	0.50	1.25	2.50
❑Anl 4, Eclipso: The Darkness Within, Part 10, Living Daylights, Eclipso	2.50	0.50	1.25	2.50
❑Anl 5, JPH (w), Bloodlines, 1: Loose Cannon, Bloodlines; 1993 Annual	2.50	0.50	1.25	2.50
❑Anl 6, Elseworlds	2.95	0.59	1.48	2.95
❑Anl 7, Year One	3.95	0.79	1.98	3.95
❑Anl 8, Legends of the Dead Earth; A World of Hurt, A: Bizarro, 1996 annual; Legends of the Dead Earth	2.95	0.59	1.48	2.95
❑Anl 9, The Magnetic Medium, Pulp Heroes; 1997 Annual	3.95	0.79	1.98	3.95

A.C.T.I.O.N. FORCE (LIGHTNING)
LIGHTNING
Value: Cover or less

❑1, Jan 87 .... 1.75

ACTION GIRL COMICS
SLAVE LABOR

	ORIG	GOOD	FINE	N-MINT
❑1, Oct 94, Soundtrack; Action Girl: Cakes & Dresses	2.50	0.70	1.75	3.50
❑1-2, Feb 96, 2nd Printing	2.75	0.55	1.38	2.75
❑2, Jan 95	2.50	0.60	1.50	3.00
❑2-2, Oct 95, 2nd Printing	2.75	0.55	1.38	2.75
❑3, Apr 95	2.50	0.60	1.50	3.00
❑3-2, Feb 96, 2nd Printing	2.75	0.55	1.38	2.75
❑4, Jul 95	2.50	0.60	1.50	3.00
❑4-2, Jul 96, 2nd Printing	2.75	0.60	1.50	3.00
❑4-3, 3rd Printing	2.75	0.60	1.50	3.00
❑5, Oct 95	2.50	0.60	1.50	3.00
❑6, Jan 96	2.50	0.55	1.38	2.75
❑6-2, 2nd Printing	2.75	0.55	1.38	2.75
❑7, May 96	2.50	0.55	1.38	2.75
❑8, Jul 96	2.50	0.55	1.38	2.75
❑9	2.50	0.55	1.38	2.75
❑10, Jan 97	2.75	0.55	1.38	2.75
❑11, May 97, b&w	2.75	0.55	1.38	2.75
❑12, Jul 97	2.75	0.55	1.38	2.75
❑13, Oct 97	2.75	0.55	1.38	2.75
❑14, Jul 98	2.75	0.55	1.38	2.75

ACTION PLANET COMICS
ACTION PLANET
Value: Cover or less

- ❑1, Hero of the Beach; Nailz: the Fix, b&w; Anthology; Black and white 3.95
- ❑2, Sep 00, b&w; Anthology ... 3.95
- ❑3, Sep 97, b&w; Anthology ... 3.95
- ❑Ash 1, b&w; b&w preview of series; "Philly Ashcan Ed."; Black and white 2.00
- ❑GS 1, Oct 98, Menace Before Midnight!; A Brannigan's Ghost Escapade, A: Bitchula; A: Monsterman; A: Hem; A: Haw; A: Fire Dog; A: Wrathbone; A: Uncle Slam; A: Doc Thunder; A: Brannigan's Ghost; A: Wretch, Anthology; Giant-size; Giant size 5.95

ACTIONS SPEAK (SERGIO ARAGONÉS...)
DARK HORSE
Value: Cover or less

- ❑1, Jan 01, SA, SA (w) 2.99
- ❑2, Feb 01, SA, SA (w) 2.99
- ❑3, Mar 01, SA, SA (w) 2.99
- ❑4, Apr 01, SA, SA (w) 2.99
- ❑5, May 01, SA, SA (w) 2.99
- ❑6, Jun 01, SA, SA (w) 2.99

A.D.A.M.
THE TOY MAN

	ORIG	GOOD	FINE	N-MINT
❑1, In the Beginning	2.95	0.59	1.48	2.95
❑Ash 1, no cover price; preview	—	0.20	0.50	1.00

ADAM-12
GOLD KEY

	ORIG	GOOD	FINE	N-MINT
❑1, Dec 73	0.25	6.00	15.00	30.00
❑2	0.25	3.60	9.00	18.00
❑3	0.25	3.20	8.00	16.00
❑4	0.25	3.20	8.00	16.00
❑5	0.25	3.20	8.00	16.00
❑6	0.25	2.80	7.00	14.00
❑7, May 75, The Old Guard; Trouble in Tow, Photo cover	0.25	2.80	7.00	14.00
❑8	0.25	2.80	7.00	14.00
❑9	0.25	2.80	7.00	14.00
❑10, Feb 76, A Double Life; One Wild Night, Photo cover	0.25	2.80	7.00	14.00

ADAM AND EVE A.D.
BAM
Value: Cover or less

- ❑1, Sep 85 .... 1.50
- ❑2, Nov 85 .... 1.50
- ❑3, Jan 86 .... 1.50
- ❑4, Mar 86, Arcane 1.50
- ❑5, May 86 .... 1.50
- ❑6, Jul 86 .... 1.50
- ❑7, Oct 86, With Friends Like These 1.50
- ❑8, Nov 86 .... 1.50
- ❑9, Jan 87 .... 1.50
- ❑10, Mar 87 .... 1.50

ADAM BOMB COMICS
BLUE MONKEY
Value: Cover or less

❑1, Sum 99, b&w 2.00

ADAM STRANGE
DC
Value: Cover or less

- ❑1, Mar 90 .... 3.95
- ❑2, May 90 .... 3.95
- ❑3, Jul 90 .... 3.95

ADDAM OMEGA
ANTARCTIC
Value: Cover or less

- ❑1, Jan 97 .... 2.95
- ❑2, Apr 97 .... 2.95
- ❑3, Jun 97 .... 2.95
- ❑4, Aug 97 .... 2.95

ADDAMS FAMILY EPISODE GUIDE
COMIC CHRONICLES
Value: Cover or less

❑1, nn; b&w; illustrated episode guide to original TV series ... 5.95

ADELE & THE BEAST
NBM
Value: Cover or less

❑1, 90 .... 9.95

ADOLESCENT RADIOACTIVE BLACK BELT HAMSTERS, THE
ECLIPSE

	ORIG	GOOD	FINE	N-MINT
❑1, 1: The Adolescent Radioactive Black Belt Hamsters, b&w	1.50	0.40	1.00	2.00
❑1/GO, Gold edition; Published by Parody	2.95	0.59	1.48	2.95
❑1-2, 1: The Adolescent Radioactive Black Belt Hamsters, 2nd Printing	1.50	0.30	0.75	1.50
❑2, Spr 86	1.50	0.30	0.75	1.50
❑3, Jul 86	1.50	0.30	0.75	1.50
❑4, Nov 86	1.50	0.30	0.75	1.50
❑5, Feb 87	1.50	0.30	0.75	1.50
❑6, May 87	1.50	0.30	0.75	1.50
❑7, Aug 87, D: Bruce	1.50	0.30	0.75	1.50
❑8, Oct 87	2.00	0.40	1.00	2.00
❑9, Jan 88, Final Issue	2.00	0.40	1.00	2.00

ADOLESCENT RADIOACTIVE BLACK BELT HAMSTERS CLASSICS
PARODY
Value: Cover or less

- ❑1, Aug 92, b&w; Reprints ARBBH in 3-D #1 .... 2.50
- ❑2, b&w; Reprints ARBBH in 3-D #2 .... 2.50
- ❑3, Reprints ARBBH (Eclipse) #3 .... 2.50
- ❑4, Reprints ARBBH: Massacre the Japanese Invasion 2.50
- ❑5, holiday cover; Reprints ARBBH in 3-D #4 .... 2.50

ADOLESCENT RADIOACTIVE BLACK BELT HAMSTERS IN 3-D
ECLIPSE
Value: Cover or less

- ❑1, Jul 86 .... 2.50
- ❑2, Sep 86, Hamsters Go Hollywood 2.50
- ❑3, Nov 86, TS, The Night of the Living Dolls, aka Eclipse 3-D #13 .... 2.50
- ❑4, Dec 86, aka Eclipse 3-D #14 .... 2.50

ADOLESCENT RADIOACTIVE BLACK BELT HAMSTERS: LOST AND ALONE IN NEW YORK
PARODY PRESS
Value: Cover or less

❑1, Escape From New York 2.95

ADOLESCENT RADIOACTIVE BLACK BELT HAMSTERS MASSACRE THE JAPANESE INVASION
ECLIPSE
Value: Cover or less

❑1, Aug 89, b&w 2.50

ADOLESCENT RADIOACTIVE BLACK BELT HAMSTERS: THE LOST TREASURES
PARODY
Value: Cover or less

❑1, Big Name Artists Draw the Hamster!; Big Butt Hamhocks, b&w; cardstock cover; Reprints portions of ARBBH (Eclipse) #9 .... 2.95

AD POLICE
VIZ
Value: Cover or less

- ❑1, May 94, b&w 14.95
- ❑1-2, 2nd printing with fold-out cover 12.95

ADRENALYNN
IMAGE
Value: Cover or less

- ❑1, Aug 99 .... 2.50
- ❑2, Oct 99 .... 2.50
- ❑3, Dec 99 .... 2.50
- ❑4, Feb 00 .... 2.50

ADULT ACTION FANTASY FEATURING: TAWNY'S TALES
LOUISIANA LEISURE
Value: Cover or less

- ❑1, adult 2.50
- ❑2, adult 2.50

ADULTS ONLY! COMIC MAGAZINE
INKWELL

	ORIG	GOOD	FINE	N-MINT
❑1, Aug 79	2.00	0.50	1.25	2.50
❑2, Fal 85	2.50	0.50	1.25	2.50
❑3	2.50	0.50	1.25	2.50

ADVANCED DUNGEONS & DRAGONS
DC
Value: Cover or less

- ❑1, Dec 88 .... 1.25
- ❑2, Jan 89, JDu, The Bounty Seekers of Manshaka 1.25

	ORIG	GOOD	FINE	N-MINT
❑3, Feb 89				1.25
❑4, Mar 89				1.50
❑5, Apr 89				1.50
❑6, May 89				1.50
❑7, Jun 89				1.50
❑8, Jul 89, JDu, The Spirit Of Myrrth, Part 4				1.50
❑9, Aug 89				1.50
❑10, Sep 89				1.50
❑11, Oct 89				1.50
❑12, Nov 89				1.50
❑13, Dec 89				1.50
❑14, Jan 90				1.50
❑15, Feb 90				1.50
❑16, Mar 90				1.50
❑17, Apr 90				1.50
❑18, May 90				1.50
❑19, Jun 90				1.50
❑20, Jul 90				1.50
❑21, Aug 90				1.50
❑22, Sep 90				1.50
❑23, Nov 90				1.50
❑24, Dec 90				1.50
❑25, Jan 91				1.75
❑26, Feb 91				1.75
❑27, Mar 91				1.75
❑28, Apr 91				1.75
❑29, May 91				1.75
❑30, Jun 91				1.75
❑31, Jul 91				1.75
❑32, Aug 91				1.75
❑33, Sep 91				1.75
❑34, Oct 91				1.75
❑35, Nov 91				1.75
❑36, Dec 91, Final Issue				1.75
❑Anl 1				3.95

ADVENTURE COMICS
DC

	ORIG	GOOD	FINE	N-MINT
❑247, Apr 58, 1: Legion of Super-Heroes, Cosmic Boy, Saturn Girl, Lightning Lad, Superboy joins team	0.10	940.00	2350.00	4700.00
❑248, May 58, Green Arrow	0.10	28.00	70.00	140.00
❑249, Jun 58, Green Arrow	0.10	28.00	70.00	140.00
❑250, Jul 58, Green Arrow	0.10	28.00	70.00	140.00
❑251, Aug 58, Green Arrow	0.10	28.00	70.00	140.00
❑252, Sep 58, Green Arrow	0.10	28.00	70.00	140.00
❑253, Oct 58, Green Arrow; Robin meets Superboy	0.10	38.00	95.00	190.00
❑254, Nov 58, Green Arrow	0.10	28.00	70.00	140.00
❑255, Dec 58, 1: Red Kryptonite, Green Arrow	0.10	28.00	70.00	140.00
❑256, Jan 59, JK, O: Green Arrow	0.10	120.00	300.00	600.00
❑257, Feb 59	0.10	26.00	65.00	130.00
❑258, Mar 59	0.10	26.00	65.00	130.00
❑259, Apr 59	0.10	26.00	65.00	130.00
❑260, May 59, O: Aquaman	0.10	120.00	300.00	600.00
❑261, Jun 59, Lois Lane meets Superboy	0.10	16.00	40.00	80.00
❑262, Jul 59, O: Speedy	0.10	16.00	40.00	80.00
❑263, Aug 59	0.10	16.00	40.00	80.00
❑264, Sep 59	0.10	16.00	40.00	80.00
❑265, Oct 59, A: Superman	0.10	16.00	40.00	80.00
❑266, Nov 59, A: Superman	0.10	16.00	40.00	80.00
❑267, Dec 59, 2: Legion of Super-Heroes	0.10	157.00	392.50	785.00
❑268, Jan 60	0.10	16.00	40.00	80.00
❑269, Feb 60, 1: Aqualad	0.10	45.00	112.50	225.00
❑270, Mar 60, A: Congorilla	0.10	16.00	40.00	80.00
❑271, Apr 60, A: Congorilla; O: Lex Luthor	0.10	45.00	112.50	225.00
❑272, May 60, A: Congorilla	0.10	13.00	32.50	65.00
❑273, Jun 60, A: Congorilla	0.10	13.00	32.50	65.00
❑274, Jul 60, A: Congorilla	0.10	13.00	32.50	65.00
❑275, Aug 60, O: Superman/Batman Team-up; A: Congorilla	0.10	30.00	75.00	150.00
❑276, Sep 60, A: Congorilla; 1: Sun Boy	0.10	13.00	32.50	65.00
❑277, Oct 60, A: Congorilla	0.10	13.00	32.50	65.00
❑278, Nov 60, A: Congorilla; A: Supergirl	0.10	13.00	32.50	65.00
❑279, Dec 60, CS, 1: White Kryptonite; A: Congorilla	0.10	13.00	32.50	65.00
❑280, Jan 61, A: Congorilla; A: Lori Lemaris, Superboy meets Lori Lemaris	0.10	13.00	32.50	65.00
❑281, Feb 61, A: Congorilla	0.10	12.00	30.00	60.00
❑282, Mar 61, A: Congorilla; 1: Starboy	0.10	18.00	45.00	90.00
❑283, Apr 61, A: Congorilla; 1: Phantom Zone	0.10	20.00	50.00	100.00
❑284, May 61	0.10	12.00	30.00	60.00
❑285, Jun 61, 1: Bizarro World	0.10	23.00	57.50	115.00
❑286, Jul 61, 1: Bizarro Mxyzptlk	0.10	22.00	55.00	110.00
❑287, Aug 61, Tales of Bizarro World	0.10	12.00	30.00	60.00
❑288, Sep 61, Tales of Bizarro World, 1: Dev-Em	0.10	12.00	30.00	60.00
❑289, Oct 61, Tales of Bizarro World	0.10	12.00	30.00	60.00
❑290, Nov 61, Tales of Bizarro World, A: Legion of Super-Heroes; O: Sun Boy, Sun Boy joins Legion of Super-Heroes	0.10	22.00	55.00	110.00
❑291, Dec 61, Tales of Bizarro World, Superboy	0.12	9.00	22.50	45.00
❑292, Jan 62, Tales of Bizarro World, Superboy	0.12	9.00	22.50	45.00
❑293, Feb 62, CS, Tales of Bizarro World, 1: Legion of Super-Pets; 1: Mon-El in Legion; O: Mon-El	0.12	20.00	50.00	100.00
❑294, Mar 62, Tales of Bizarro World, 1: Bizarro Marilyn Monroe, Superboy	0.12	19.00	47.50	95.00
❑295, Apr 62, Tales of Bizarro World, Superboy	0.12	9.00	22.50	45.00
❑296, May 62, Tales of Bizarro World, Superboy	0.12	9.00	22.50	45.00
❑297, Jun 62, Tales of Bizarro World, Superboy	0.12	9.00	22.50	45.00

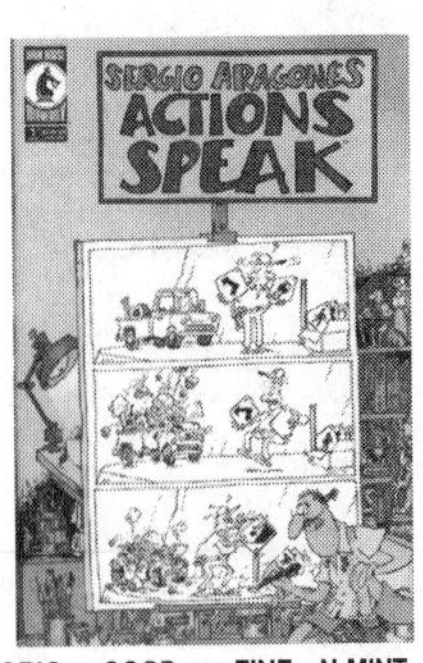

A new group of Sergio Aragonés' silent cartoons can be found in the six-issue *Sergio Aragonés' Actions Speak.*

© 2001 Sergio Aragonés (Dark Horse)

	ORIG	GOOD	FINE	N-MINT
❑298, Jul 62, Tales of Bizarro World, Superboy	0.12	9.00	22.50	45.00
❑299, Aug 62, 1: Gold Kryptonite, Superboy; Bizarro world story	0.10	11.00	27.50	55.00
❑300, Sep 62, The Face Behind the Lead Mask, 300th anniversary issue; Legion; Mon-El joins team; Legion of Super-Heroes begins as a regular back-up feature	0.12	65.00	162.50	325.00
❑301, Oct 62, O: Bouncing Boy	0.12	16.00	40.00	80.00
❑302, Nov 62, Legion	0.12	13.00	32.50	65.00
❑303, Dec 62, 1: Matter-Eater Lad, Matter-Eater Lad joins team; Legion	0.12	14.00	35.00	70.00
❑304, Jan 63, D: Lightning Lad, Legion	0.12	14.00	35.00	70.00
❑305, Feb 63, Legion	0.12	13.00	32.50	65.00
❑306, Mar 63, 1: Legion of Substitute Heroes	0.12	10.00	25.00	50.00
❑307, Apr 63, 1: Roxxas; 1: Element Lad, Element Lad joins team; Legion	0.12	11.00	27.50	55.00
❑308, May 63, 1: Proty; 1: Lightning Lass, Legion; Lightning Lass joins team	0.12	11.00	27.50	55.00
❑309, Jun 63, Legion	0.12	10.00	25.00	50.00
❑310, Jul 63, Legion	0.12	10.00	25.00	50.00
❑311, Aug 63, A: Legion of Substitute Heroes; 1: Legion of Super-Heroes Headquarters, Legion	0.12	9.00	22.50	45.00
❑312, Sep 63, D: Proty, Legion; Return of Lightning Lad	0.12	9.00	22.50	45.00
❑313, Oct 63, CS, Legion	0.12	7.00	17.50	35.00
❑314, Nov 63, Legion	0.12	7.00	17.50	35.00
❑315, Dec 63, Legion	0.12	7.00	17.50	35.00
❑316, Jan 64, profile pages; Legion	0.12	7.00	17.50	35.00
❑317, Feb 64, 1: Dream Girl, Dream Girl joins team; Legion	0.12	8.00	20.00	40.00
❑318, Mar 64, Legion	0.12	7.00	17.50	35.00
❑319, Apr 64, Legion	0.12	7.00	17.50	35.00
❑320, May 64, Legion	0.12	7.00	17.50	35.00
❑321, Jun 64, 1: Time Trapper, Legion	0.12	9.00	22.50	45.00
❑322, Jul 64, Legion	0.12	6.00	15.00	30.00
❑323, Aug 64, Legion	0.12	6.00	15.00	30.00
❑324, Sep 64, 1: Heroes of Lallor (later Wanderers); 1: Duplicate Boy, Legion	0.12	6.00	15.00	30.00
❑325, Oct 64, Legion	0.12	6.00	15.00	30.00
❑326, Nov 64, Legion	0.12	6.00	15.00	30.00
❑327, Dec 64, 1: Timber Wolf, Timber Wolf joins team	0.12	6.00	15.00	30.00
❑328, Jan 65, Legion	0.12	6.00	15.00	30.00
❑329, Feb 65, 1: Bizarro Legion of Super-Heroes, Legion	0.12	6.00	15.00	30.00
❑330, Mar 65, Dynamo Boy joins team; Legion	0.12	6.00	15.00	30.00
❑331, Apr 65, 1: Saturn Queen, Legion	0.12	6.00	15.00	30.00
❑332, May 65, Legion	0.12	6.00	15.00	30.00
❑333, Jun 65, Legion	0.12	6.00	15.00	30.00
❑334, Jul 65, Legion	0.12	6.00	15.00	30.00
❑335, Aug 65, 1: Starfinger; 1: Magnetic Kid, Legion	0.12	6.00	15.00	30.00
❑336, Sep 65, Legion	0.12	6.00	15.00	30.00
❑337, Oct 65, Legion; Wedding of Lightning Lad and Saturn Girl, Mon-El and Phantom Girl (fake weddings)	0.12	6.00	15.00	30.00
❑338, Nov 65, 1: Glorith; V: Time-Trapper, Glorith	0.12	6.00	15.00	30.00
❑339, Dec 65, Legion	0.12	6.00	15.00	30.00
❑340, Jan 66, CS, D: one of Triplicate Girl's bodies; 1: Computo, Legion	0.12	6.00	15.00	30.00
❑341, Feb 66, CS, Legion	0.12	3.60	9.00	18.00
❑342, Mar 66, CS, 1: Color Kid, Legion	0.12	3.20	8.00	16.00
❑343, Apr 66, CS, Legion	0.12	3.20	8.00	16.00
❑344, May 66, CS, Legion	0.12	3.20	8.00	16.00
❑345, Jun 66, CS, 1: Khunds; D: Blockade Boy, Weight Wizard, Legion	0.12	3.20	8.00	16.00
❑346, Jul 66, 1: Karate Kid, Princess Projectra, Ferro Lad, Karate Kid, Princess Projecta, Ferro Lad joins team; 1st a	0.12	3.60	9.00	18.00
❑347, Aug 66, Legion	0.12	3.20	8.00	16.00

	ORIG	GOOD	FINE	N-MINT
❑348, Sep 66, O: Sunboy; V: Doctor Regulus, Legion	0.12	3.60	9.00	18.00
❑349, Oct 66, 1: Rond Vidar	0.12	3.20	8.00	16.00
❑350, Nov 66, CS, 1: Prince Evillo; 1: Mysa Nal, Legion	0.12	3.20	8.00	16.00
❑351, Dec 66, CS, 1: White Witch	0.12	3.20	8.00	16.00
❑352, Jan 67, 1: The Fatal Five, Legion	0.12	2.60	6.50	13.00
❑353, Feb 67, D: Ferro Lad	0.12	3.60	9.00	18.00
❑354, Mar 67, Legion	0.12	2.40	6.00	12.00
❑355, Apr 67, CS, Adult Legion story	0.12	2.40	6.00	12.00
❑356, May 67, Legion	0.12	2.40	6.00	12.00
❑357, Jun 67, CS, 1: Controllers, Legion	0.12	2.40	6.00	12.00
❑358, Jul 67, Legion	0.12	2.40	6.00	12.00
❑359, Aug 67, Legion	0.12	2.40	6.00	12.00
❑360, Sep 67, Legion	0.12	2.40	6.00	12.00
❑361, Oct 67, A: Dominators; V: Unkillables, Legion	0.12	2.00	5.00	10.00
❑362, Nov 67, V: Mantis Morlo, Legion	0.12	2.00	5.00	10.00
❑363, Dec 67, V: Mantis Morlo, Legion	0.12	2.00	5.00	10.00
❑364, Jan 65, CS, Legion	0.12	2.00	5.00	10.00
❑365, Feb 68, NA, 1: Shadow Lass	0.12	2.00	5.00	10.00
❑366, Mar 68, NA, V: Validus, Legion; Shadow Lass joins Legion	0.12	2.00	5.00	10.00
❑367, Apr 68, 1: The Dark Circle, Legion	0.12	2.00	5.00	10.00
❑368, May 68, Legion	0.12	2.00	5.00	10.00
❑369, Jun 68, 1: Mordru, Legion	0.12	2.00	5.00	10.00
❑370, Jul 68, Legion	0.12	2.00	5.00	10.00
❑371, Aug 68, NA, 1: Legion Academy; 1: Chemical King, Legion; Colossal Boy leaves team	0.12	2.00	5.00	10.00
❑372, Sep 68, NA, Legion; Chemical King joins Legion; Timber Wolf joins Legion	0.12	2.00	5.00	10.00
❑373, Oct 68, Legion	0.12	1.80	4.50	9.00
❑374, Nov 68, Legion	0.12	1.80	4.50	9.00
❑375, Dec 68, NA, 1: Quantum Queen; 1: Wanderers	0.12	1.80	4.50	9.00
❑376, Jan 69, Legion	0.12	1.80	4.50	9.00
❑377, Feb 69, Heroes for Hire, Legion	0.12	1.80	4.50	9.00
❑378, Mar 69, Twelve Hours to Live, Legion	0.12	1.80	4.50	9.00
❑379, Apr 69, Burial in Space, Legion	0.12	1.80	4.50	9.00
❑380, Apr 69, The Legion's Space Odyssey, Legion; Legion of Super-Heroes stories end	0.12	1.80	4.50	9.00
❑381, Jun 69, Supergirl stories begin	0.15	2.00	5.00	10.00
❑382, Jul 69	0.15	1.60	4.00	8.00
❑383, Aug 69	0.15	1.60	4.00	8.00
❑384, Sep 69	0.15	1.60	4.00	8.00
❑385, Oct 69	0.15	1.60	4.00	8.00
❑386, Nov 69, A: Mxyzptlk, Supergirl	0.15	1.60	4.00	8.00
❑387, Dec 69, V: Lex Luthor, Supergirl	0.15	1.60	4.00	8.00
❑388, Jan 70, The Kindergarten Criminal!; The Romance Machine, V: Lex Luthor, Supergirl	0.15	1.60	4.00	8.00
❑389, Feb 70	0.15	1.60	4.00	8.00
❑390, Apr 70, Giant-size issue	0.25	1.60	4.00	8.00
❑391, Mar 70	0.15	1.60	4.00	8.00
❑392, Apr 70	0.15	1.60	4.00	8.00
❑393, May 70	0.15	1.60	4.00	8.00
❑394, Jun 70	0.15	1.60	4.00	8.00
❑395, Jul 70	0.15	1.60	4.00	8.00
❑396, Aug 70	0.15	1.60	4.00	8.00
❑397, Sep 70	0.15	1.60	4.00	8.00
❑398, Oct 70	0.15	1.60	4.00	8.00
❑399, Nov 70	0.15	1.60	4.00	8.00
❑400, Dec 70, 35th anniversary	0.15	2.40	6.00	12.00
❑401, Jan 71	0.15	1.20	3.00	6.00
❑402, Feb 71, Supergirl loses powers	0.15	1.20	3.00	6.00
❑403, Apr 71, Giant-size	0.25	3.00	7.50	15.00
❑404, Mar 71, Supergirl gets exo-skeleton	0.15	1.00	2.50	5.00
❑405, Apr 71	0.15	1.00	2.50	5.00
❑406, May 71	0.15	1.00	2.50	5.00
❑407, Jun 71	0.15	1.00	2.50	5.00
❑408, Jul 71	0.15	1.00	2.50	5.00
❑409, Aug 71, reprints Legion story from Adventure #313; Supergirl gets new costume	0.25	1.00	2.50	5.00
❑410, Sep 71	0.25	1.00	2.50	5.00
❑411, Oct 71	0.25	1.00	2.50	5.00
❑412, Nov 71, 1: Animal Man, Animal Man reprint; reprints Strange Adventures #180	0.25	0.90	2.25	4.50
❑413, Dec 71, 48pgs.	0.25	0.90	2.25	4.50
❑414, Jan 72, A: Animal Man	0.25	0.90	2.25	4.50
❑415, Feb 72, Animal Man reprint	0.25	0.90	2.25	4.50
❑416, Mar 72, wraparound cover; Giant-size issue; a.k.a. DC 100-Page Super Spectacular #DC-10; all-women issue	0.50	1.40	3.50	7.00
❑417, Mar 72, FF	0.25	0.90	2.25	4.50

	ORIG	GOOD	FINE	N-MINT
❑418, Apr 72, also contains previously unpublished Golden Age Doctor Mid-Nite story, Black Canary	0.25	0.90	2.25	4.50
❑419, May 72, Black Canary	0.25	0.90	2.25	4.50
❑420, Jun 72, Animal Man reprint	0.25	0.90	2.25	4.50
❑421, Jul 72, Animal Man reprint	0.20	0.90	2.25	4.50
❑422, Aug 72, GM; BO, Supergirl: Pawn of Peace; The Vigilante: Rodeo of Death	0.20	0.90	2.25	4.50
❑423, Sep 72	0.20	0.90	2.25	4.50
❑424, Oct 72	0.20	0.90	2.25	4.50
❑425, Jan 73, ATh, The Wings Of Jealous Gods; Sword Of The Dead, 1: Captain Fear	0.20	0.90	2.25	4.50
❑426, Mar 73	0.20	0.90	2.25	4.50
❑427, May 73	0.20	0.90	2.25	4.50
❑428, Aug 73, 1: Black Orchid	0.20	4.00	10.00	20.00
❑429, Oct 73, A: Black Orchid	0.20	2.00	5.00	10.00
❑430, Dec 73, A: Black Orchid	0.20	1.80	4.50	9.00
❑431, Feb 74, JA; ATh, The Wrath Of The Spectre; Is A Snerl Human?, A: Spectre.	0.20	1.80	4.50	9.00
❑432, Apr 74	0.20	1.00	2.50	5.00
❑433, Jun 74, JA, A: Spectre	0.20	1.00	2.50	5.00
❑434, Aug 74	0.20	1.00	2.50	5.00
❑435, Oct 74, JA, A: Spectre, Aquaman back-up	0.20	1.00	2.50	5.00
❑436, Dec 74, JA, A: Spectre, Aquaman back-up	0.20	1.00	2.50	5.00
❑437, Feb 75	0.25	1.00	2.50	5.00
❑438, Apr 75	0.25	1.00	2.50	5.00
❑439, Jun 75	0.25	1.00	2.50	5.00
❑440, Aug 75, O: Spectre-New	0.25	1.00	2.50	5.00
❑441, Oct 75	0.25	0.70	1.75	3.50
❑442, Dec 75	0.25	0.70	1.75	3.50
❑443, Feb 76, Seven Soldiers of Victory back-up; Aquaman	0.25	0.70	1.75	3.50
❑444, Apr 76, Aquaman	0.30	0.70	1.75	3.50
❑445, Jun 76	0.30	0.70	1.75	3.50
❑446, Aug 76, Bicentennial #31	0.30	0.70	1.75	3.50
❑447, Oct 76	0.30	0.70	1.75	3.50
❑448, Nov 76	0.30	0.70	1.75	3.50
❑449, Jan 77	0.30	0.70	1.75	3.50
❑450, Mar 77	0.30	0.70	1.75	3.50
❑451, May 77	0.30	0.70	1.75	3.50
❑452, Jul 77	0.35	0.70	1.75	3.50
❑453, Sep 77, A: Barbara Gordon, Superboy	0.35	0.70	1.75	3.50
❑454, Nov 77	0.35	0.70	1.75	3.50
❑455, Jan 78	0.35	0.70	1.75	3.50
❑456, Mar 78	0.35	0.70	1.75	3.50
❑457, May 78	0.35	0.70	1.75	3.50
❑458, Jul 78	0.35	0.70	1.75	3.50
❑459, Sep 78, JA; JSa; DN, no ads; expands contents and raises price to $1	1.00	0.70	1.75	3.50
❑460, Nov 78, JSa; SA; DN	1.00	0.70	1.75	3.50
❑461, Jan 79, JA; JSa; DN, Giant-size issue; incorporates JSA story from unpublished All-Star Comics #75	1.00	1.20	3.00	6.00
❑462, Mar 79, JSa; DG, D: E-2 Batman, Giant-size issue	1.00	1.20	3.00	6.00
❑463, May 79, JSa; DH; FMc	1.00	0.70	1.75	3.50
❑464, Jul 79, contains previously unpublished Deadman story from Showcase #105	1.00	0.70	1.75	3.50
❑465, Sep 79	1.00	0.70	1.75	3.50
❑466, Nov 79, final JSA case before group retired in the '50s	1.00	0.70	1.75	3.50
❑467, Jan 80	0.40	0.70	1.75	3.50
❑468, Feb 80	0.40	0.70	1.75	3.50
❑469, Mar 80, 1: Starman III (Prince Gavyn)	0.40	0.70	1.75	3.50
❑470, Apr 80, O: Starman III (Prince Gavyn)	0.40	0.70	1.75	3.50
❑471, May 80	0.40	0.70	1.75	3.50
❑472, Jun 80	0.40	0.70	1.75	3.50
❑473, Jul 80	0.40	0.70	1.75	3.50
❑474, Aug 80	0.40	0.70	1.75	3.50
❑475, Sep 80	0.50	0.70	1.75	3.50
❑476, Oct 80	0.50	0.70	1.75	3.50
❑477, Nov 80	0.50	0.70	1.75	3.50
❑478, Dec 80	0.50	0.70	1.75	3.50
❑479, Mar 81, Dial 'H' For Hero back-up, 1: Christopher King; 1: Victoria Grant	0.50	0.70	1.75	3.50
❑480, Apr 81, Dial 'H' For Hero back-up	0.50	0.60	1.50	3.00
❑481, May 81, Dial 'H' For Hero back-up	0.50	0.60	1.50	3.00
❑482, Jun 81, Dial 'H' For Hero back-up	0.50	0.60	1.50	3.00
❑483, Jul 81, Dial 'H' For Hero back-up, Dial H for Hero	0.50	0.60	1.50	3.00
❑484, Aug 81, Dial 'H' For Hero back-up	0.50	0.60	1.50	3.00
❑485, Sep 81, Dial 'H' For Hero back-up	0.50	0.60	1.50	3.00
❑486, Oct 81, Dial 'H' For Hero back-up	0.60	0.60	1.50	3.00
❑487, Nov 81, Dial 'H' For Hero back-up	0.60	0.60	1.50	3.00

	ORIG	GOOD	FINE	N-MINT
❑488, Dec 81, Dial 'H' For Hero back-up	0.60	0.60	1.50	3.00
❑489, Jan 82, Dial 'H' For Hero back-up	0.60	0.60	1.50	3.00
❑490, Feb 82, Dial 'H' For Hero back-up	0.60	0.60	1.50	3.00
❑491, Sep 82, digest size begins	0.95	0.60	1.50	3.00
❑492, Oct 82	1.25	0.60	1.50	3.00
❑493, Nov 82, A: Challengers of the Unknown	1.25	0.60	1.50	3.00
❑494, Dec 82, A: Challengers of the Unknown	1.25	0.60	1.50	3.00
❑495, Jan 83, A: Challengers of the Unknown	1.25	0.60	1.50	3.00
❑496, Feb 83, A: Challengers of the Unknown	1.25	0.60	1.50	3.00
❑497, Mar 83, A: Challengers of the Unknown	1.25	0.60	1.50	3.00
❑498, Apr 83	1.25	0.60	1.50	3.00
❑499, May 83	1.25	0.60	1.50	3.00
❑500, Jun 83	1.25	0.60	1.50	3.00
❑501, Jul 83	1.25	0.60	1.50	3.00
❑502, Aug 83	1.25	0.60	1.50	3.00
❑503, Sep 83, Final Issue	1.25	0.60	1.50	3.00

ADVENTURE COMICS (2ND SERIES)
DC

Value: Cover or less

- ❑1, May 99, JRo (w), Stars and Atoms, A: Starman; A: Atom 1.99
- ❑GS 1, Oct 98, JBy (w), Wonder Woman: Darkness Fallen; Green Arrow: Longshot, Giant size; Wonder Woman, Captain Marvel, Superboy, Green Arrow, Legion, Supergirl, Bizarro 4.95

ADVENTURERS, THE (AIRCEL)
AIRCEL

	ORIG	GOOD	FINE	N-MINT
❑1, The Gate of Chaos, regular cover	1.50	0.40	1.00	2.00
❑1/LE, The Gate of Chaos, skeleton cover; Limited ed	1.50	0.40	1.00	2.00
❑2, The Gate of Chaos	1.50	0.40	1.00	2.00

ADVENTURERS, THE (BOOK 1)
ADVENTURE

Value: Cover or less

- ❑0, 86, The Gate of Chaos 1.50
- ❑1, 86, The Gate of Chaos, 1: Argent (sorcerer); D: Tirian; 1: Bladehelm; 1: Shadolok; 1: Nightwind; 1: Dhakab; 1: Sultar; 1: Coron 1.50
- ❑1-2, The Gate of Chaos, 2nd Printing; published by Adventure 1.50
- ❑2, The Gate of Chaos 1.50
- ❑3, 86, The Gate of Chaos, no indicia 1.50
- ❑4, 86, The Gate of Chaos 1.50
- ❑5, 86, The Gate of Chaos 1.50
- ❑6, Jun 87, The Gate of Chaos 1.50
- ❑7, Jul 87, The Gate of Chaos 1.50
- ❑8, Sep 87, The Gate of Chaos 1.50
- ❑9, 86, The Gate of Chaos 1.75
- ❑10, 86, The Gate of Chaos 1.75

ADVENTURERS, THE (BOOK 2)
ADVENTURE

Value: Cover or less

- ❑0, Jul 88, b&w 1.95
- ❑1, Dec 87, The Grail Of Darkness, regular cover 1.95
- ❑1/LE, Dec 87, The Grail Of Darkness, Limited edition cover 1.95
- ❑2, Mar 88 .... 1.95
- ❑3, Apr 88 .... 1.95
- ❑4 .... 1.95
- ❑5 .... 1.95
- ❑6, Nov 88 .... 1.95
- ❑7, Mar 89, b&w 1.95
- ❑8 .... 1.95
- ❑9 .... 1.95
- ❑10 .... 1.95

ADVENTURERS, THE (BOOK 3)
ADVENTURE

Value: Cover or less

- ❑1, Oct 89, regular cover 2.25
- ❑1/LE, Oct 89, Limited edition cover 2.25
- ❑2, Nov 89 .... 2.25
- ❑3, Dec 89 .... 2.25
- ❑4, Jan 90 .... 2.25
- ❑5, Feb 90 .... 2.25
- ❑6, Mar 90 .... 2.25

ADVENTURES IN READING STARRING: THE AMAZING SPIDER-MAN
MARVEL

	ORIG	GOOD	FINE	N-MINT
❑1, Sep 90, Giveaway to promote literacy	—	0.20	0.50	1.00

ADVENTURES IN THE DC UNIVERSE
DC

	ORIG	GOOD	FINE	N-MINT
❑1, Apr 97, JLA	1.75	0.50	1.25	2.50
❑2, May 97, The Flash: Bombs Away!; Catwoman: Catch as Cat Can, O: The Flash III (Wally West)	1.75	0.40	1.00	2.00
❑3, Jun 97, Batman vs. Poison Ivy; Wonder Woman vs. Cheetah	1.75	0.40	1.00	2.00
❑4, Jul 97, Mr. Miracle; Green Lantern	1.75	0.40	1.00	2.00
❑5, Aug 97, A: Ultra the Multi-Alien, Martian Manhunter	1.75	0.40	1.00	2.00
❑6, Sep 97, Power Girl; Aquaman	1.75	0.40	1.00	2.00
❑7, Oct 97, Marvel Family: A: Lois Lane, Clark Kent	1.75	0.40	1.00	2.00
❑8, Nov 97, Question; Blue Beetle, Booster Gold	1.75	0.40	1.00	2.00
❑9, Dec 97, Flash vs. Gorilla Grodd	1.95	0.40	1.00	2.00
❑10, Jan 98, Legion of Super-Heroes	1.95	0.40	1.00	2.00
❑11, Feb 98, Wonder Woman, Green Lantern	1.95	0.40	1.00	2.00
❑12, Mar 98, Cipher Rules!, JLA vs. Cipher	1.95	0.40	1.00	2.00
❑13, Apr 98, Green Arrow; Impulse, Martian Manhunter	1.95	0.39	0.98	1.95

Judd Winick's *Adventures of Barry Ween, Boy Genius* got its start at Image before moving to Oni Press.

© 1999 Judd Winick (Image)

	ORIG	GOOD	FINE	N-MINT
❑14, May 98, Nightwing; Superboy, Flash	1.95	0.39	0.98	1.95
❑15, Jun 98, Aquaman; Captain Marvel	1.95	0.39	0.98	1.95
❑16, Jul 98, Green Arrow; Green Lantern	1.95	0.39	0.98	1.95
❑17, Aug 98, Creeper; Batman	1.95	0.39	0.98	1.95
❑18, Sep 98, JLA vs. Amazo	1.95	0.39	0.98	1.95
❑19, Oct 98, Final Issue; Wonder Woman, Catwoman	1.99	0.40	1.00	1.99
❑Anl 1, Something Wicked This Way Comes!, Doctor Fate, Impulse, Superboy, Thorn, Mr. Miracle; events crossover with Superman Adventures Annual #1 and Batman & Robin Adventures Annual #2	3.95	0.79	1.98	3.95

ADVENTURES IN THE MYSTWOOD
BLACKTHORNE

Value: Cover or less

- ❑1, Aug 86, Dreams...Sweet Dreams 2.00

ADVENTURES IN THE RIFLE BRIGADE
DC

Value: Cover or less

- ❑1, Oct 00, Once More into the Breach 2.50
- ❑2, Nov 00, Definitely Not Cricket 2.50
- ❑3, Dec 00, Up Yours, Fritz 2.50

ADVENTURES INTO THE UNKNOWN (A+)
A-PLUS

Value: Cover or less

- ❑1, FF; TS; AW, FF (w); TS (w); AW (w), Dog Day; The Timeless Tribe!, b&w; Reprint 2.50
- ❑2, FF; SD, Hell House; To My Pal Joey..., Reprint 2.50
- ❑3, AW, Skull of the Sorcerer; Hades Universe, Reprint 2.50
- ❑4, Roll Me Down; To Die A Witch's Death, Reprint 2.50

ADVENTURES MADE IN AMERICA
RIP OFF

Value: Cover or less

- ❑0, Preview 2.75
- ❑1 .... 2.75
- ❑2 .... 2.75
- ❑3 .... 2.75
- ❑4 .... 2.75
- ❑5 .... 2.75
- ❑6 .... 2.75

ADVENTURES OF AARON
CHIASMUS

Value: Cover or less

- ❑1 .... 2.50
- ❑2, Jul 95, Babysitter Gone Bad, Part 1 .... 2.50

ADVENTURES OF AARON (2ND SERIES)
IMAGE

Value: Cover or less

- ❑1, Mar 97, Babysitter Gone Bad, Part 1 .... 2.95
- ❑2, May 97, Babysitter Gone Bad, Part 2 .... 2.95
- ❑3, Sep 97, "Adventures of Dad" back-up 2.95
- ❑100, Jul 97, Anthology 2.95

ADVENTURES OF ADAM & BYRON
AMERICAN MULE

Value: Cover or less

- ❑1, May 98 .... 2.50

ADVENTURES OF BARON MUNCHAUSEN, THE
NOW

	ORIG	GOOD	FINE	N-MINT
❑1, Jul 89, Eighteenth Century Europe: The Age of Reason	1.75	0.40	1.00	2.00
❑2, Aug 89	1.75	0.40	1.00	2.00
❑3, Sep 89	1.75	0.40	1.00	2.00
❑4, Oct 89	1.75	0.40	1.00	2.00

ADVENTURES OF BARRY WEEN, BOY GENIUS, THE
IMAGE

Value: Cover or less

- ❑1, Mar 99, O: Barry Ween 2.95
- ❑2, Apr 99, Jeremy turned into dinosaur 2.95
- ❑3, May 99, at museum 2.95

ADVENTURES OF BARRY WEEN, BOY GENIUS 2.0, THE
ONI

Value: Cover or less

- ❑1, Feb 00, E.T. Go Home, b&w 2.95
- ❑2, Mar 00, b&w; in the old West 2.95
- ❑3, Apr 00, b&w 2.95

ADVENTURES OF BAYOU BILLY, THE
ARCHIE

Value: Cover or less

- ❑1, Sep 89, Swamp Fire, O: Bayou Billy, Archie, Jughead, Betty, and Veronica public service announcement inside back cover 1.00
- ❑2, Nov 89 .... 1.00
- ❑3, Jan 90 .... 1.00
- ❑4, Apr 90, Billy's Night Out 1.00
- ❑5, Jun 90 .... 1.00

ADVENTURES OF BOB HOPE, THE
DC

	ORIG	GOOD	FINE	N-MINT
❑67, Feb 61	0.10	8.00	20.00	40.00
❑68, Apr 61	0.10	8.00	20.00	40.00
❑69, Jun 61	0.10	8.00	20.00	40.00
❑70, Aug 61	0.10	8.00	20.00	40.00
❑71, Oct 61	0.10	6.40	16.00	32.00
❑72, Dec 61	0.10	6.40	16.00	32.00
❑73, Feb 62	0.12	6.40	16.00	32.00
❑74, Apr 62, MD	0.12	6.40	16.00	32.00
❑75, Jun 62, MD	0.12	6.40	16.00	32.00
❑76, Aug 62, MD	0.12	6.40	16.00	32.00
❑77, Oct 62	0.12	6.40	16.00	32.00
❑78, Dec 62	0.12	6.40	16.00	32.00
❑79, Feb 63	0.12	6.40	16.00	32.00
❑80, Apr 63	0.12	6.40	16.00	32.00
❑81, Jun 63	0.12	5.20	13.00	26.00
❑82, Aug 63, MD	0.12	5.20	13.00	26.00
❑83, Oct 63	0.12	5.20	13.00	26.00
❑84, Dec 63	0.12	5.20	13.00	26.00
❑85, Feb 64, MD	0.12	5.20	13.00	26.00
❑86, Apr 64	0.12	5.20	13.00	26.00
❑87, Jun 64, MD	0.12	5.20	13.00	26.00
❑88, Aug 64	0.12	5.20	13.00	26.00
❑89, Oct 64, MD	0.12	5.20	13.00	26.00
❑90, Dec 64, MD	0.12	5.20	13.00	26.00
❑91, Feb 65, MD	0.12	4.00	10.00	20.00
❑92, Apr 65	0.12	4.00	10.00	20.00
❑93, Jun 65	0.12	4.00	10.00	20.00
❑94, Aug 65, A: Aquaman	0.12	4.00	10.00	20.00
❑95, Oct 65, 1: Super-Hip and monster faculty	0.12	4.00	10.00	20.00
❑96, Dec 65	0.12	4.00	10.00	20.00
❑97, Feb 66	0.12	4.00	10.00	20.00
❑98, Apr 66	0.12	4.00	10.00	20.00
❑99, Jun 66	0.12	4.00	10.00	20.00
❑100, Aug 66, Super-Hip as President	0.12	4.00	10.00	20.00
❑101, Oct 66	0.12	4.00	10.00	20.00
❑102, Dec 66	0.12	4.00	10.00	20.00
❑103, Feb 67, A: Batman, Nancy, Ringo Starr, Frank Sinatra, Stanley and his Monster	0.12	4.00	10.00	20.00
❑104, May 67	0.12	4.00	10.00	20.00
❑105, Jun 67, A: David Janssen, Dan Blocker, Ed Sullivan, Don Adams	0.12	4.00	10.00	20.00
❑106, Aug 67, Badger's Baby Brother Beastley	0.12	8.00	20.00	40.00
❑107, Oct 67	0.12	8.00	20.00	40.00
❑108, Dec 67	0.12	8.00	20.00	40.00
❑109, Feb 68, NA, Final Issue	0.12	8.00	20.00	40.00

ADVENTURES OF B.O.C., THE
INVASION

Value: Cover or less

- ❑1, Nov 86, Escape From Darkness ... 1.50
- ❑2, Jan 87 ... 1.50
- ❑3, Mar 87 ... 1.50

ADVENTURES OF BROWSER & SEQUOIA, THE
SABERCAT

Value: Cover or less

- ❑1, Aug 99, Sequoia's First Hunt ... 2.95

ADVENTURES OF CAPTAIN AMERICA
MARVEL

Value: Cover or less

- ❑1, Sep 91 ... 4.95
- ❑2, Nov 91, Betrayed By Agent X, O: Bucky ... 4.95
- ❑3, Dec 91 ... 4.95
- ❑4, Jan 92 ... 4.95

ADVENTURES OF CAPTAIN JACK, THE
FANTAGRAPHICS

Value: Cover or less

- ❑1, Jun 86 ... 2.00
- ❑2, Sep 86 ... 2.00
- ❑3, Oct 86 ... 2.00
- ❑4, Nov 86 ... 2.00
- ❑5, Dec 86, Farmer Fred, I'm in Love with your Daughter!, no indicia ... 2.00
- ❑6, Jan 87 ... 2.00
- ❑7, Mar 87 ... 2.00
- ❑8, Jul 87 ... 2.00
- ❑9, Oct 87 ... 2.00
- ❑10, May 88 ... 2.00
- ❑11, Nov 88 ... 2.00
- ❑12, Jan 89 ... 2.00

ADVENTURES OF CAPTAIN NEMO, THE
RIP OFF

Value: Cover or less

- ❑1, b&w ... 2.50

ADVENTURES OF CHRISSIE CLAUS, THE
HERO

Value: Cover or less

- ❑1, Spr 91, Trouble in Toyland; You'd Better Watch Out ... 2.95
- ❑2, Jan 94, w/ trading card ... 2.95

ADVENTURES OF CHUK THE BARBARIC
WHITE WOLF

	ORIG	GOOD	FINE	N-MINT
❑1, Jul 87	1.25	0.30	0.75	1.50
❑2, Aug 87, becomes Chuk the Barbaric	1.25	0.30	0.75	1.50

ADVENTURES OF CYCLOPS AND PHOENIX, THE
MARVEL

Value: Cover or less

- ❑1, May 94, Wish You Were Here ... 2.95
- ❑2, Jun 94, Tenure ... 2.95
- ❑3, Jul 94 ... 2.95
- ❑4, Aug 94 ... 2.95

ADVENTURES OF DR. GRAVES
A-PLUS

Value: Cover or less

- ❑1, b&w; Reprint ... 2.50

ADVENTURES OF DOLO ROMY, THE
DÔLO BLUE

Value: Cover or less

- ❑1 ... 2.95

ADVENTURES OF DORIS NELSON, ATOMIC HOUSEWIFE
JAKE COMICS

Value: Cover or less

- ❑1, Aug 96, b&w; reprints Doris Nelson, Atomic Housewife ... 2.95

ADVENTURES OF EDGAR MUDD AND ELAINE, THE
WET EARTH

Value: Cover or less

- ❑1 ... 3.50

ADVENTURES OF EVIL & MALICE, THE
IMAGE

Value: Cover or less

- ❑1, Jun 99 ... 3.50
- ❑2, Aug 99 ... 3.50
- ❑3, Nov 99, cover says Oct, indicia says Nov ... 3.95

ADVENTURES OF FELIX THE CAT
HARVEY

	ORIG	GOOD	FINE	N-MINT
❑1	1.25	0.30	0.75	1.50

ADVENTURES OF FORD FAIRLANE, THE
DC

Value: Cover or less

- ❑1, May 90, Stayin' Alive ... 1.50
- ❑2, Jun 90, I Write The Songs ... 1.50
- ❑3, Jul 90 ... 1.50
- ❑4, Aug 90 ... 1.50

ADVENTURES OF JERRY LEWIS, THE
DC

	ORIG	GOOD	FINE	N-MINT
❑62, Jan 61	0.10	5.60	14.00	28.00
❑63, Mar 61	0.10	5.60	14.00	28.00
❑64, May 61	0.10	5.60	14.00	28.00
❑65, Jul 61	0.10	5.60	14.00	28.00
❑66, Sep 61	0.10	5.60	14.00	28.00
❑67, Nov 61	0.10	5.60	14.00	28.00
❑68, Jan 62	0.12	5.60	14.00	28.00
❑69, Mar 62	0.12	5.60	14.00	28.00
❑70, May 62	0.12	5.60	14.00	28.00
❑71, Jul 62	0.12	5.60	14.00	28.00
❑72, Sep 62, MD	0.12	5.60	14.00	28.00
❑73, Nov 62	0.12	5.60	14.00	28.00
❑74, Jan 63, Photo cover; adapts It's Only Money	0.12	5.60	14.00	28.00
❑75, Mar 63	0.12	5.60	14.00	28.00
❑76, May 63	0.12	5.60	14.00	28.00
❑77, Jul 63	0.12	5.60	14.00	28.00
❑78, Sep 63	0.12	5.60	14.00	28.00
❑79, Nov 63, 1: Mr. Yes	0.12	5.60	14.00	28.00
❑80, Jan 64	0.12	5.60	14.00	28.00
❑81, Mar 64	0.12	5.00	12.50	25.00
❑82, May 64	0.12	5.00	12.50	25.00
❑83, Jul 64	0.12	5.00	12.50	25.00
❑84, Sep 64, Jerry becomes The Fearless Tarantula	0.12	5.00	12.50	25.00
❑85, Nov 64, 1: Renfrew	0.12	5.00	12.50	25.00
❑86, Jan 65, BO, King Klonk The Killer Gorilla	0.12	5.00	12.50	25.00
❑87, Mar 65, A: Renfrew	0.12	5.00	12.50	25.00
❑88, May 65, 1: Witch Kraft	0.12	5.00	12.50	25.00
❑89, Jul 65	0.12	5.00	12.50	25.00
❑90, Sep 65	0.12	5.00	12.50	25.00
❑91, Nov 65	0.12	5.00	12.50	25.00
❑92, Jan 66, A: Superman	0.12	6.00	15.00	30.00
❑93, Mar 66	0.12	5.00	12.50	25.00
❑94, May 66	0.12	5.00	12.50	25.00
❑95, Jul 66	0.12	5.00	12.50	25.00
❑96, Sep 66	0.12	5.00	12.50	25.00
❑97, Nov 66, A: Batman, Robin, Penguin, Riddler, Joker	0.12	7.00	17.50	35.00
❑98, Jan 67, A: Ringo Starr, Ilya Kurakin (on stamps)	0.12	5.00	12.50	25.00
❑99, Mar 67	0.12	5.00	12.50	25.00
❑100, May 67, 1: Jerry Mess-terpiece pin-up	0.12	5.00	12.50	25.00
❑101, Jul 67	0.12	6.40	16.00	32.00
❑102, Sep 67, A: The Beatles	0.12	11.00	27.50	55.00
❑103, Nov 67	0.12	6.40	16.00	32.00
❑104, Jan 68, NA	0.12	6.40	16.00	32.00
❑105, Mar 68, A: Superman, Lex Luthor	0.12	6.40	16.00	32.00
❑106, May 68	0.12	2.80	7.00	14.00
❑107, Jul 68	0.12	2.80	7.00	14.00
❑108, Sep 68	0.12	2.80	7.00	14.00
❑109, Nov 68	0.12	2.80	7.00	14.00
❑110, Jan 69	0.12	2.80	7.00	14.00

	ORIG	GOOD	FINE	N-MINT
❑111, Mar 69	0.12	2.80	7.00	14.00
❑112, May 69, A: Flash	0.15	2.80	7.00	14.00
❑113, Jul 69	0.15	2.80	7.00	14.00
❑114, Sep 69	0.15	2.80	7.00	14.00
❑115, Nov 69	0.15	2.80	7.00	14.00
❑116, Jan 70	0.15	2.80	7.00	14.00
❑117, Mar 70, A: Wonder Woman	0.15	4.00	10.00	20.00
❑118, May 70	0.15	2.80	7.00	14.00
❑119, Jul 70	0.15	2.80	7.00	14.00
❑120, Sep 70	0.15	2.40	6.00	12.00
❑121, Nov 70	0.15	2.40	6.00	12.00
❑122, Jan 71	0.15	2.40	6.00	12.00
❑123, Mar 71	0.15	2.40	6.00	12.00
❑124, May 71, Final Issue	0.15	2.40	6.00	12.00

ADVENTURES OF KELLY BELLE: PERIL ON THE HIGH SEAS, THE
ATLANTIS

Value: Cover or less — ❑1, 96, b&w ... 2.95

ADVENTURES OF KOOL-AID MAN, THE
MARVEL

	ORIG	GOOD	FINE	N-MINT
❑1, nn; 60ó value on cover; giveaway	0.60	0.20	0.50	1.00
❑5	0.75	0.20	0.50	1.00

ADVENTURES OF LIBERAL MAN, THE
POLITICAL

Value: Cover or less

❑1, 1: Media Man; 1: Liberal Man ... 2.95

❑2, The Search for Equal Kick; Right Wing Radio Talk Show Hosts Must Die, Part 1, 1: 60's Man ... 2.95

❑3, Right Wing Radio Talk Show Hosts Must Die, Part 2; Contract With America: Terminate With Extreme Prejudice, Part 1 ... 2.95

❑4, Jul 96, Contract with America: Termiante with Extreme Predjudice, Part 2 ... 2.95

❑5, Sep 96, Contract with America: Termiante with Extreme Predjudice, Part 3; The 1996 Campaign: A Nation on the Precipice, Part 1 ... 2.95

❑6, Oct 96, The 1996 Campaign: A Nation on the Precipice, Part 2; A Clinton Carol ... 2.95

ADVENTURES OF LUTHER ARKWRIGHT, THE (DARK HORSE)
DARK HORSE

	ORIG	GOOD	FINE	N-MINT
❑1, 90, BT, BT (w), The Disruption Spiral, Reprints Adventures of Luther Arkwright (Valkyrie) #1	1.95	0.50	1.25	2.50
❑2, 90, BT, BT (w), Reprints Adventures of Luther Arkwright (Valkyrie) #2	1.95	0.40	1.00	2.00
❑3, May 90, BT, BT (w), Reprints Adventures of Luther Arkwright (Valkyrie) #3	1.95	0.40	1.00	2.00
❑4, 90, BT, BT (w), Reprints Adventures of Luther Arkwright (Valkyrie) #4	1.95	0.40	1.00	2.00
❑5, 90, BT, BT (w), Reprints Adventures of Luther Arkwright (Valkyrie) #5	1.95	0.40	1.00	2.00
❑6, 90, BT, BT (w), Reprints Adventures of Luther Arkwright (Valkyrie) #6	1.95	0.40	1.00	2.00
❑7, Nov 90, BT, BT (w), Destiny's Angel, Reprints Adventures of Luther Arkwright (Valkyrie) #7	1.95	0.40	1.00	2.00
❑8, Nov 90, BT, BT (w), Reprints Adventures of Luther Arkwright (Valkyrie) #8	1.95	0.40	1.00	2.00
❑9, 90, BT, BT (w), trading cards; Reprints Adventures of Luther Arkwright (Valkyrie) #9	1.95	0.40	1.00	2.00

ADVENTURES OF LUTHER ARKWRIGHT, THE (VALKYRIE)
VALKYRIE

	ORIG	GOOD	FINE	N-MINT
❑1, Oct 87, BT, BT (w), The Disruption Spiral	2.00	0.50	1.25	2.50
❑2, Dec 87, BT, BT (w)	2.00	0.50	1.25	2.50
❑3, Feb 88, BT, BT (w)	2.00	0.50	1.25	2.50
❑4, Apr 88, BT, BT (w)	2.00	0.50	1.25	2.50
❑5, Jun 88, BT, BT (w)	2.00	0.50	1.25	2.50
❑6, BT, BT (w)	2.00	0.50	1.25	2.50
❑7, Oct 88, BT, BT (w), Destiny's Angel	2.00	0.50	1.25	2.50
❑8, Dec 88, BT, BT (w)	2.00	0.50	1.25	2.50
❑9, Feb 89, BT, BT (w)	2.00	0.50	1.25	2.50
❑10, BT, BT (w), Essays	2.00	0.50	1.25	2.50

ADVENTURES OF MARK TYME, THE
JOHN SPENCER & CO.

	ORIG	GOOD	FINE	N-MINT
❑1	—	0.40	1.00	2.00
❑2, Fight for Life; Planet of Fear	—	0.40	1.00	2.00

ADVENTURES OF MR. PYRIDINE
FANTAGRAPHICS

Value: Cover or less — ❑1, b&w ... 2.50

ADVENTURES OF MISTY, THE
FORBIDDEN FRUIT

Value: Cover or less

❑1, Apr 91	2.95
❑2, May 91	2.95
❑3, Jun 91	2.95
❑4, Jul 91	2.95
❑5, Aug 91	2.95
❑6, Oct 91	2.95
❑7, Dec 91	2.95
❑8, Feb 92	2.95
❑9, Apr 92	2.95
❑10, Jun 92	2.95
❑11, Aug 92	3.50
❑12, Oct 92	3.50

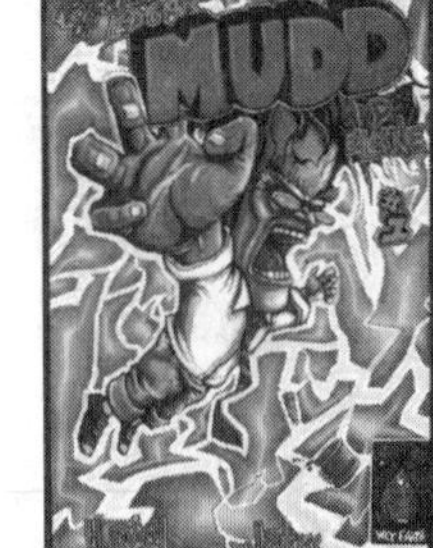

The Adventures of Edgar Mudd and Elaine began as a series of bedtime stories for the creators' children.

© 1998 Wet Earth

ADVENTURES OF MONKEY, THE
WOMP

	ORIG	GOOD	FINE	N-MINT
❑1, Jul 95	1.50	0.40	1.00	2.00
❑2, Jun 96	1.50	0.40	1.00	2.00
❑3, Jun 97	2.00	0.40	1.00	2.00
❑4, Jun 98, Freshmen back-up	2.00	0.40	1.00	2.00

ADVENTURES OF QUIK BUNNY
MARVEL

	ORIG	GOOD	FINE	N-MINT
❑1, nn; 60ó value on cover; giveaway	0.60	0.20	0.50	1.00

ADVENTURES OF RHEUMY PEEPERS & CHUNKY HIGHLIGHTS, THE
ONI PRESS

Value: Cover or less — ❑1, Feb 99, nn ... 2.95

ADVENTURES OF RICK RAYGUN, THE
STOP DRAGON

	ORIG	GOOD	FINE	N-MINT
❑1, Sep 86	1.75	0.40	1.00	2.00
❑2, Oct 86	1.75	0.40	1.00	2.00
❑3, Fal 86	1.75	0.40	1.00	2.00
❑4, Nov 86	1.75	0.40	1.00	2.00
❑5, Jan 87	1.75	0.40	1.00	2.00

ADVENTURES OF ROBIN HOOD, THE
GOLD KEY

	ORIG	GOOD	FINE	N-MINT
❑1, Mar 74	0.20	1.60	4.00	8.00
❑2, May 74	0.20	1.00	2.50	5.00
❑3, Jul 74	0.20	0.80	2.00	4.00
❑4, Aug 74	0.20	0.80	2.00	4.00
❑5, Sep 74	0.20	0.80	2.00	4.00
❑6, Nov 74	0.20	0.80	2.00	4.00
❑7	—	0.80	2.00	4.00

ADVENTURES OF ROMA
FORBIDDEN FRUIT

Value: Cover or less — ❑1, Jan 93, b&w; adult ... 3.50

ADVENTURES OF SNAKE PLISSKEN
MARVEL

Value: Cover or less — ❑1, Jan 97, Up and Running ... 2.50

ADVENTURES OF SPENCER SPOOK, THE
ACE

	ORIG	GOOD	FINE	N-MINT
❑1, Oct 86, The Comic Capercon; Spencer Spook, reprints stories from Giggle Comics #77 and Spencer Spook #102	1.95	0.40	1.00	2.00
❑2, Dec 86, Wrassle Hassle!; Hector the Specter, reprint from Giggle Comics #66	1.95	0.40	1.00	2.00
❑3, Jan 87	1.95	0.40	1.00	2.00
❑4, Mar 87	1.95	0.40	1.00	2.00
❑5	1.95	0.40	1.00	2.00
❑6	1.95	0.40	1.00	2.00

ADVENTURES OF SPIDER-MAN, THE
MARVEL

	ORIG	GOOD	FINE	N-MINT
❑1, Apr 96, Shot In The Dark, A: Punisher, animated series adaptations	0.99	0.30	0.75	1.50
❑2, May 96, V: Hammerhead	0.99	0.25	0.63	1.25
❑3, Jun 96, V: Mr. Sinister; A: X-Men	0.99	0.25	0.63	1.25
❑4, Jul 96	0.99	0.20	0.50	1.00
❑5, Aug 96, V: Rhino	0.99	0.20	0.50	1.00
❑6, Sep 96, A: Thing, Human Torch	0.99	0.20	0.50	1.00
❑7, Oct 96, V: Enforcers	0.99	0.20	0.50	1.00
❑8, Nov 96, Where Demons Ride!, V: Kingpin	0.99	0.20	0.50	1.00
❑9, Dec 96	0.99	0.20	0.50	1.00
❑10, Jan 97, To Catch a Spider, V: Beetle	0.99	0.20	0.50	1.00
❑11, Feb 97, Unions, Part 1, V: Doctor Octopus and Venom; A: Venom	0.99	0.20	0.50	1.00
❑12, Mar 97, Unions, Part 2, V: Doctor Octopus and Venom; A: Venom, Final Issue	0.99	0.20	0.50	1.00

ADVENTURES OF SUPERBOY, THE
DC

	ORIG	GOOD	FINE	N-MINT
❑19, Series continued from Superboy (2nd Series) #18	1.25	0.30	0.75	1.50
❑20, The Secret (Until Now) Origin of Knickknack, O: Knickknack	1.25	0.30	0.75	1.50
❑21	1.25	0.30	0.75	1.50
❑22, Final Issue	1.25	0.30	0.75	1.50

ADVENTURES OF SUPERMAN
DC

	ORIG	GOOD	FINE	N-MINT
❑0, Oct 94, Peer Pressure, Part 3, ▲1994-39	1.50	0.50	1.25	2.50
❑424, Jan 87, JOy, Man o' War!	0.75	0.50	1.25	2.50
❑425, Feb 87, JOy	0.75	0.40	1.00	2.00
❑426, Mar 87, JOy, 1: Bibbo, Legends	0.75	0.40	1.00	2.00
❑427, Apr 87, JOy	0.75	0.40	1.00	2.00
❑428, May 87, JOy	0.75	0.40	1.00	2.00
❑429, Jun 87, JOy	0.75	0.40	1.00	2.00
❑430, Jul 87, JOy	0.75	0.40	1.00	2.00
❑431, Aug 87, JOy	0.75	0.40	1.00	2.00
❑432, Sep 87, JOy, 1: Jose Delgado (Gangbuster)	0.75	0.40	1.00	2.00
❑433, Oct 87, JOy	0.75	0.40	1.00	2.00
❑434, Nov 87, JOy, 1: Gangbuster	0.75	0.40	1.00	2.00
❑435, Dec 87, JOy	0.75	0.40	1.00	2.00
❑436, Jan 88, JOy, Millennium, Millennium	0.75	0.40	1.00	2.00
❑437, Feb 88, JOy, Millennium, V: Gangbuster, Millennium	0.75	0.40	1.00	2.00
❑438, Mar 88, JOy, 1: Brainiac II (Milton Moses Fine)	0.75	0.40	1.00	2.00
❑439, Apr 88, JOy	0.75	0.40	1.00	2.00
❑440, May 88, JOy	0.75	0.40	1.00	2.00
❑441, Jun 88, JOy, V: Mxyzptlk	0.75	0.40	1.00	2.00
❑442, Jul 88, JBy; JOy	0.75	0.40	1.00	2.00
❑443, Aug 88, JOy	0.75	0.40	1.00	2.00
❑444, Sep 88, JOy, Supergirl	0.75	0.40	1.00	2.00
❑445, Oct 88, JOy	0.75	0.40	1.00	2.00
❑446, Nov 88, JOy, A: Gangbuster	0.75	0.40	1.00	2.00
❑447, Dec 88, JOy	0.75	0.40	1.00	2.00
❑448, Dec 88, JOy	0.75	0.40	1.00	2.00
❑449, Jan 89, Invasion!	0.75	0.40	1.00	2.00
❑450, Jan 89, Invasion!	0.75	0.40	1.00	2.00
❑451, Feb 89	0.75	0.40	1.00	2.00
❑452, Mar 89	0.75	0.40	1.00	2.00
❑453, Apr 89	0.75	0.40	1.00	2.00
❑454, May 89, 1: Draaga	0.75	0.40	1.00	2.00
❑455, Jun 89	0.75	0.40	1.00	2.00
❑456, Jul 89	0.75	0.40	1.00	2.00
❑457, Aug 89	0.75	0.40	1.00	2.00
❑458, Sep 89, Jimmy as Elastic Lad	0.75	0.40	1.00	2.00
❑459, Oct 89, Eradicator buried in Antarctic	0.75	0.40	1.00	2.00
❑460, Nov 89, 1: Fortress of Solitude	0.75	0.40	1.00	2.00
❑461, Dec 89	0.75	0.40	1.00	2.00
❑462, Jan 90	0.75	0.40	1.00	2.00
❑463, Feb 90, A: Flash, Superman/Flash race	0.75	0.60	1.50	3.00
❑464, Mar 90, V: Lobo, Krypton Man	0.75	0.60	1.50	3.00
❑465, Apr 90, Krypton Man	0.75	0.40	1.00	2.00
❑466, May 90, 1: Hank Henshaw (becomes cyborg Superman)	0.75	0.60	1.50	3.00
❑467, Jun 90, Batman	0.75	0.40	1.00	2.00
❑468, Jul 90	0.75	0.40	1.00	2.00
❑469, Aug 90, 1: Blaze	0.75	0.40	1.00	2.00
❑470, Sep 90	0.75	0.40	1.00	2.00
❑471, Oct 90, A: Sinbad	0.75	0.40	1.00	2.00
❑472, Nov 90	0.75	0.40	1.00	2.00
❑473, Dec 90, A: Green Lantern, Guy Gardner	0.75	0.40	1.00	2.00
❑474, Jan 91	1.00	0.40	1.00	2.00
❑475, Feb 91, Wonder Woman; Batman, Flash	1.00	0.40	1.00	2.00
❑476, Mar 91, Time and Time Again, Part 1, 1: The Linear Men; V: Linear Man	1.00	0.40	1.00	2.00
❑477, Apr 91, Time and Time Again, Part 4, A: Legion	1.00	0.40	1.00	2.00
❑478, May 91, Time and Time Again, Part 7, V: Dev-Em	1.00	0.40	1.00	2.00
❑479, Jun 91	1.00	0.40	1.00	2.00
❑480, Jul 91, Giant-size	1.75	0.45	1.13	2.25
❑481, Aug 91	1.00	0.35	0.88	1.75
❑482, Sep 91, V: Parasite	1.00	0.35	0.88	1.75
❑483, Oct 91, 1: Atomic Skull	1.00	0.35	0.88	1.75
❑484, Nov 91, Blackout	1.00	0.35	0.88	1.75
❑485, Dec 91, Blackout	1.00	0.35	0.88	1.75
❑486, Jan 92	1.00	0.35	0.88	1.75
❑487, Feb 92	1.00	0.35	0.88	1.75
❑488, Mar 92, Panic in Sky	1.00	0.35	0.88	1.75
❑489, Apr 92, Panic in Sky	1.00	0.35	0.88	1.75
❑490, May 92	1.00	0.35	0.88	1.75
❑491, Jun 92, V: Metallo	1.00	0.35	0.88	1.75
❑492, Jul 92, JOy (w), ...And Justice For All!, V: Agent Liberty, ▲1992-27	1.00	0.35	0.88	1.75
❑493, Aug 92, 1: Lord Satanus; V: Blaze	1.25	0.35	0.88	1.75
❑494, Sep 92, 1: Kismet	1.25	0.35	0.88	1.75
❑495, Oct 92, A: Forever People	1.25	0.35	0.88	1.75
❑496, Nov 92, Doomsday, Mxyzptlk	1.25	0.60	1.50	3.00
❑496-2, Doomsday, 2nd Printing	1.25	0.30	0.75	1.50
❑497, Dec 92, JOy (w), Doomsday, Under Fire, Doomsday; ▲1992-47	1.25	0.60	1.50	3.00
❑497-2, Dec 96, JOy (w), Doomsday, Under Fire, 2nd printing, ▲1992-47	1.25	0.40	1.00	2.00
❑498, Jan 93, JOy (w), Funeral for a Friend, Part 1, ▲1993-3	1.25	0.60	1.50	3.00
❑498-2, Jan 93, JOy (w), Funeral for a Friend, Part 1, 2nd Printing; ▲1993-3	1.25	0.40	1.00	2.00
❑499, Feb 93, JOy (w), Funeral for a Friend, Part 5, ▲1993-7	1.25	0.50	1.25	2.50
❑500, Jun 93, JOy (w), Life After Death, begins return from dead	2.50	0.60	1.50	3.00
❑500/CS, Jun 93, JOy (w), Life After Death, translucent cover; trading card; begins return from dead	2.95	0.70	1.75	3.50
❑500/SI, Jun 93, JOy (w), Life After Death, silver edition	—	2.00	5.00	10.00
❑501, Jun 93, Reign of the Supermen; ...When He Was a Boy, 1: Superboy (clone), ▲1993-15	1.50	0.40	1.00	2.00
❑501/SC, Jun 93, Reign of the Supermen; ...When He Was a Boy, 1: Superboy (clone), Die-cut cover; poster; ▲1993-15	1.95	0.40	1.00	2.00
❑502, Jul 93, Boy Meets Girl, A: Supergirl, ▲1993-19	1.50	0.35	0.88	1.75
❑503, Aug 93, Superboy vs. Cyborg	1.50	0.35	0.88	1.75
❑504, Sep 93	1.50	0.35	0.88	1.75
❑505, Oct 93, Reign Of The Superman, foil cover; ▲1993-31	2.50	0.35	0.88	1.75
❑505/SC, Oct 93, Reign Of The Superman, Postcard; ▲1993-31, Special (prism) cover edition	1.50	0.50	1.25	2.50
❑506, Nov 93	1.50	0.30	0.75	1.50
❑507, Dec 93, V: Bloodsport	1.50	0.30	0.75	1.50
❑508, Jan 94, Challengers	1.50	0.30	0.75	1.50
❑509, Feb 94, A: Auron	1.50	0.30	0.75	1.50
❑510, Mar 94, Bizarro's World, Part 2, Bizarro	1.50	0.30	0.75	1.50
❑511, Apr 94, A: Guardian	1.50	0.30	0.75	1.50
❑512, May 94, V: Parasite; A: Guardian	1.50	0.30	0.75	1.50
❑513, Jun 94, The Battle For Metropolis, ▲1994-23	1.50	0.30	0.75	1.50
❑514, Jul 94, Fall of Metropolis	1.50	0.30	0.75	1.50
❑515, Aug 94, Massacre in Metropolis, Part 2, V: Massacre	1.50	0.30	0.75	1.50
❑516, Sep 94, A: Alpha Centurion, "Zero Hour"	1.50	0.30	0.75	1.50
❑517, Nov 94, Dead Again	1.50	0.30	0.75	1.50
❑518, Dec 94, Dead Again, A: Darkseid	1.50	0.30	0.75	1.50
❑519, Jan 95, Dead Again, V: Brainiac, Dead Again; ▲1995-3	1.50	0.30	0.75	1.50
❑520, Feb 95, A: Thorn	1.50	0.30	0.75	1.50
❑521, Mar 95, A: Thorn	1.50	0.30	0.75	1.50
❑522, Apr 95, Return of Metropolis	1.50	0.30	0.75	1.50
❑523, May 95, Death of Clark Kent	1.50	0.30	0.75	1.50
❑524, Jun 95, Death of Clark Kent	1.95	0.40	1.00	2.00
❑525, Jul 95	1.95	0.40	1.00	2.00
❑526, Aug 95, Bloodsport vs. Bloodsport	1.95	0.40	1.00	2.00
❑527, Sep 95, Alpha-Centurion returns	1.95	0.40	1.00	2.00
❑528, Oct 95	1.95	0.40	1.00	2.00
❑529, Nov 95, Trial of Superman	1.95	0.40	1.00	2.00
❑530, Dec 95, SCU vs. Hellgrammite; "Trial of Superman/Underworld Unleashed"	1.95	0.40	1.00	2.00
❑531, Jan 96, Justice!, Cyborg Superman sentenced to a black hole; ▲1996-4	1.95	0.40	1.00	2.00
❑532, Feb 96, Troubled Waters, Return of Lori Lemaris; ▲1996-8	1.95	0.40	1.00	2.00
❑533, Mar 96, Scavenger Hunt, A: Impulse, ▲1996-12	1.95	0.40	1.00	2.00
❑534, May 96	1.95	0.40	1.00	2.00
❑535, Jun 96	1.95	0.40	1.00	2.00
❑536, Jul 96, Brainiac takes over Superman's body	1.95	0.40	1.00	2.00
❑537, Aug 96	1.95	0.40	1.00	2.00
❑538, Sep 96, Clark Kent named acting managing editor; Perry White has cancer	1.95	0.40	1.00	2.00
❑539, Oct 96, Doppelgangster, 1: Anomaly	1.95	0.40	1.00	2.00
❑540, Nov 96, Curtain Call, 1: Ferro, "Final Night"; ▲1996-43	1.95	0.40	1.00	2.00
❑541, Dec 96, Hawaiian Honeymoon; Happily Ever After, A: Superboy, Clark shot by terrorists	1.95	0.40	1.00	2.00
❑542, Jan 97, Power Struggle; Power Trip!	1.95	0.40	1.00	2.00
❑543, Feb 97, V: Superman Revenge Squad	1.95	0.40	1.00	2.00
❑544, Mar 97, Dead Men Walking, return of Intergang; ▲1997-11	1.95	0.40	1.00	2.00
❑545, Apr 97, V: Metallo, energy powers begin	1.95	0.40	1.00	2.00
❑546, May 97, V: Metallo, new uniform	1.95	0.40	1.00	2.00
❑547, Jun 97, In Kandor, A: Atom	1.95	0.40	1.00	2.00
❑548, Jul 97, A: Phantom Stranger	1.95	0.40	1.00	2.00
❑549, Aug 97, A: Newsboy Legion, Dingbats of Danger Street	1.95	0.40	1.00	2.00

	ORIG	GOOD	FINE	N-MINT
❑550, Sep 97, Jimmy's special airs	1.95	0.70	1.75	3.50
❑551, Oct 97, V: Cyborg Superman	1.95	0.39	0.98	1.95
❑552, Nov 97, Control of Power, V: Parasite, ▲1997-45	1.95	0.39	0.98	1.95
❑553, Dec 97, Energy Crisis, Face cover	1.95	0.39	0.98	1.95
❑554, Dec 97, V: Ripper	1.95	0.39	0.98	1.95
❑555, Feb 98, Superman Red vs. Superman Blue	1.95	0.39	0.98	1.95
❑556, Apr 98, Three to One!; I Was Alone Against Gargox, a Really Big Monster, V: Millennium Guard, ▲1998-13	1.95	0.39	0.98	1.95
❑557, May 98, Millennium Giants	1.95	0.39	0.98	1.95
❑558, Jun 98, set in Silver Age	1.95	0.39	0.98	1.95
❑559, Jul 98, set in Silver Age	1.95	0.39	0.98	1.95
❑560, Aug 98, A: Kismet, set in Silver Age	1.95	0.39	0.98	1.95
❑561, Sep 98, V: Dominus	1.99	0.40	1.00	2.00
❑562, Oct 98, D: "Machine" Gunn, Torcher, Daily Planet closed	1.99	0.40	1.00	2.00
❑563, Dec 98, V: Cyborg, in Kandor	1.99	0.40	1.00	2.00
❑564, Feb 99, A: Geo-Force	1.99	0.40	1.00	2.00
❑565, Mar 99, A: Captain Cold; A: Metropolis Special Crimes Unit; A: Captain Boomerang; A: Justice League of America; A: D.E.O. agents	1.99	0.40	1.00	2.00
❑566, Apr 99, A: Lex Luthor	1.99	0.40	1.00	2.00
❑567, May 99, The Pathway to Oblivion, Lois' robot guardian returns; ▲1999-19	1.99	0.40	1.00	2.00
❑568, Jun 99, Lookin' Good, ▲1999-24	1.99	0.40	1.00	2.00
❑569, Jul 99, Power, SCU forms meta-unit; ▲1999-28	1.99	0.40	1.00	2.00
❑570, Sep 99, One-Man JLA; The Invader from Earth, Superman as protector of Rann	1.99	0.40	1.00	2.00
❑571, Oct 99, Image is Everything, V: Atomic Skull	1.99	0.40	1.00	2.00
❑572, Nov 99, SB, Who is Strange Visitor, Part 2, A: Strange Visitor; V: War, ▲1999-41	1.99	0.40	1.00	2.00
❑573, Dec 99, Higher Ground, ▲1999-47	1.99	0.40	1.00	2.00
❑574, Jan 00, Something Borrowed, Something Blue, ▲2000-2	1.99	0.40	1.00	2.00
❑575, Feb 00, A Night at the Opera, ▲2000-6	1.99	0.40	1.00	2.00
❑576, Mar 00	1.99	0.40	1.00	2.00
❑577, Apr 00	1.99	0.40	1.00	2.00
❑578, May 00, Getting Away From it All, ▲2000-19	1.99	0.40	1.00	2.00
❑579, Jun 00, Pranked!, ▲2000-23	1.99	0.40	1.00	2.00
❑580, Jul 00, ▲2000-27	1.99	0.40	1.00	2.00
❑581, Aug 00, Adversaries!, V: Adversary, ▲2000-31; Lex Luthor announces candidacy for President	2.25	0.40	1.00	2.00
❑582, Sep 00, Superman: Arkham, Part 2; Crazy About You, ▲2000-35	2.25	0.40	1.00	2.00
❑583, Oct 00, The Reign of Emperor Joker, Part 2; Life is But a (Very Bad) Dream, ▲2000-40	2.25	0.45	1.13	2.25
❑584, Nov 00, Bachelor Party, 1: Devouris the Conqueror; A: Lord Satanus, ▲2000-44	2.25	0.45	1.13	2.25
❑585, Dec 00, Doubles, A: Prankster; A: Thorn; A: Adversary; A: Rampage, ▲2000-48	2.25	0.45	1.13	2.25
❑586, Jan 01, Soul of the City, ▲2000-52	2.25	0.45	1.13	2.25
❑587, Feb 01, Metropolis: Hell of a Town!, ▲2001-7	2.25	0.45	1.13	2.25
❑588, Mar 01, Pillar of Earth, ▲2001-11	2.25	0.45	1.13	2.25
❑589, Apr 01, Return to Krypton, Part 2, ▲2001-15	2.25	0.45	1.13	2.25
❑590, May 01, Don't Cry for me, Bialya, ▲2001-19	2.25	0.45	1.13	2.25
❑591, Jun 01, Infestation, Part 2, ▲2001-23	2.25	0.45	1.13	2.25
❑592	2.25	0.45	1.13	2.25
❑593	2.25	0.45	1.13	2.25
❑594	2.25	0.45	1.13	2.25
❑1000000, Nov 98, Keepers of Solitude, A: Resurrection Man	1.99	0.40	1.00	2.00
❑Anl 1, Sep 87	1.25	0.60	1.50	3.00
❑Anl 2, Aug 90, JBy, L.E.G.I.O.N. '90	2.00	0.60	1.50	3.00
❑Anl 3, Oct 91, Armageddon 2001, Part 11, Armageddon 2001	2.00	0.60	1.50	3.00
❑Anl 4, Eclipso: The Darkness Within, Part 19, Eclipso	2.50	0.60	1.50	3.00
❑Anl 5, Bloodlines, 1: Sparx, Bloodlines	2.50	0.60	1.50	3.00
❑Anl 6, The Super Seven, concludes in Superboy Annual #1 (1994); Elseworlds	2.95	0.59	1.48	2.95
❑Anl 7, V: Kalibak, Year One	3.95	0.79	1.98	3.95
❑Anl 8, Elseworlds; Legends of the Dead Earth	2.95	0.59	1.48	2.95
❑Anl 9, Terror of the Sierra Madre, Pulp Heroes	3.95	0.79	1.98	3.95

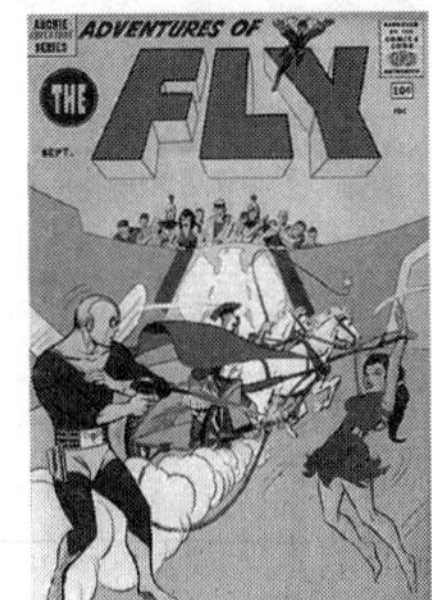

The Fly was just one of Archie's superheroes.

© 1960 Archie Comic Publications

ADVENTURES OF SUPERMAN, THE (MAGAZINE)
DC

	ORIG	GOOD	FINE	N-MINT
❑1	0.99	0.40	1.00	2.00
❑2, KGa; CS; JOy, JOy (w), Visions of Grandeur; The Racer's Edge, stickers	0.99	0.30	0.75	1.50
❑3, poster	0.99	0.30	0.75	1.50

ADVENTURES OF TAD MARTIN, THE
CALIBER

Value: Cover or less ❑1 .... 2.50

ADVENTURES OF THE FLY
ARCHIE

	ORIG	GOOD	FINE	N-MINT
❑1, Aug 59, O: Fly	0.10	70.00	175.00	350.00
❑2, Sep 59	0.10	45.00	112.50	225.00
❑3, Nov 59, JD	0.10	33.00	82.50	165.00
❑4, Jan 60	0.10	25.00	62.50	125.00
❑5, Mar 60	0.10	25.00	62.50	125.00
❑6, May 60	0.10	18.00	45.00	90.00
❑7, Jul 60	0.10	18.00	45.00	90.00
❑8, Sep 60, The Monster Gang; The Fly Versus Taxus the Tyrant	0.10	15.00	37.50	75.00
❑9, Nov 60	0.10	15.00	37.50	75.00
❑10, Jan 61	0.10	15.00	37.50	75.00
❑11, Mar 61	0.10	12.00	30.00	60.00
❑12, May 61	0.10	12.00	30.00	60.00
❑13, Jul 61	0.10	12.00	30.00	60.00
❑14, Sep 61	0.10	12.00	30.00	60.00
❑15, Nov 61	0.10	12.00	30.00	60.00
❑16, Jan 62	0.10	9.00	22.50	45.00
❑17	0.10	9.00	22.50	45.00
❑18	0.10	9.00	22.50	45.00
❑19, May 62	0.12	9.00	22.50	45.00
❑20, Jul 62	0.12	9.00	22.50	45.00
❑21	0.12	6.80	17.00	34.00
❑22, Oct 62	0.12	6.80	17.00	34.00
❑23, Nov 62	0.12	6.80	17.00	34.00
❑24, Feb 63	0.12	6.80	17.00	34.00
❑25	0.12	6.80	17.00	34.00
❑26	0.12	6.80	17.00	34.00
❑27	0.12	6.80	17.00	34.00
❑28	0.12	6.80	17.00	34.00
❑29	0.12	6.80	17.00	34.00
❑30, Oct 64	0.12	6.80	17.00	34.00
❑31, May 65, Final Issue; becomes Fly Man	0.12	6.80	17.00	34.00

ADVENTURES OF THE JAGUAR
ARCHIE

	ORIG	GOOD	FINE	N-MINT
❑1, Sep 61	0.10	18.00	45.00	90.00
❑2, Oct 61	0.10	11.00	27.50	55.00
❑3, Nov 61	0.10	9.00	22.50	45.00
❑4	0.12	7.00	17.50	35.00
❑5	0.12	7.00	17.50	35.00
❑6	0.12	5.00	12.50	25.00
❑7, Jul 62	0.12	5.00	12.50	25.00
❑8, Aug 62	0.12	5.00	12.50	25.00
❑9, Sep 62	0.12	5.00	12.50	25.00
❑10	0.12	5.00	12.50	25.00
❑11	0.12	3.60	9.00	18.00
❑12, May 63	0.12	3.60	9.00	18.00
❑13, Aug 63	0.12	3.60	9.00	18.00
❑14, Oct 63, "Kick" of the Month Club; The Jaguar's Sinister Safari	0.12	3.60	9.00	18.00
❑15, Nov 63, Final Issue	0.12	3.60	9.00	18.00

ADVENTURES OF THE LITTLE GREEN DINOSAUR, THE
LAST GASP

	ORIG	GOOD	FINE	N-MINT
❑1, b&w	0.50	1.00	2.50	5.00
❑2, Blackratt's Gold; Thrill to Bloodlust Comics, b&w	0.50	1.00	2.50	5.00

ADVENTURES OF THE MAD HUNDA DAY DAY, THE
THAUMATURGE

Value: Cover or less ❑1, Win 95, b&w 2.00

ADVENTURES OF THE MASK
DARK HORSE

	ORIG	GOOD	FINE	N-MINT
❑1, Jan 96, Who is that Masked Man?	2.50	0.50	1.25	2.50
❑2, Feb 96, V: Walter	2.50	0.50	1.25	2.50

	ORIG	GOOD	FINE	N-MINT
❑3, Mar 96	2.50	0.50	1.25	2.50
❑4, Apr 96, 1: Bombshell	2.50	0.50	1.25	2.50
❑5, May 96	2.50	0.50	1.25	2.50
❑6, Jun 96	2.50	0.50	1.25	2.50
❑7, Jul 96	2.50	0.50	1.25	2.50
❑8, Aug 96, Dog Days, Milo dons the mask	2.50	0.50	1.25	2.50
❑9, Sep 96, Shaken and Stirred, James Bond parody	2.50	0.50	1.25	2.50
❑10, Oct 96, V: Walter	2.50	0.50	1.25	2.50
❑11, Nov 96, Mask as Santa	2.50	0.50	1.25	2.50
❑12, Dec 96, Trial of the Mask, Final Issue	2.50	0.50	1.25	2.50
❑SE 1, Oct 96, nn; newsprint cover; Toys R Us Special Ed. Giveaway	—	0.20	0.50	1.00

ADVENTURES OF THE OUTSIDERS, THE
DC

	ORIG	GOOD	FINE	N-MINT
❑33, May 86, Continued from Batman and the Outsiders #32	0.75	0.20	0.50	1.00
❑34, Jun 86, V: Masters of Disaster	0.75	0.20	0.50	1.00
❑35, Jul 86	0.75	0.20	0.50	1.00
❑36, Aug 86	0.75	0.20	0.50	1.00
❑37, Sep 86	0.75	0.20	0.50	1.00
❑38, Oct 86	0.75	0.20	0.50	1.00
❑39, Nov 86, V: Nuclear Family	0.75	0.20	0.50	1.00
❑40, Dec 86, JA, Family Ties, V: Nuclear Family	0.75	0.20	0.50	1.00
❑41, Jan 87, JA, Breaking The Bank, V: Force of July	0.75	0.20	0.50	1.00
❑42, Feb 87	0.75	0.20	0.50	1.00
❑43, Mar 87	0.75	0.20	0.50	1.00
❑44, Apr 87, V: Duke of Oil	0.75	0.20	0.50	1.00
❑45, May 87, V: Duke of Oil	0.75	0.20	0.50	1.00
❑46, Jun 87, Final Issue	0.75	0.20	0.50	1.00

ADVENTURES OF THEOWN, THE
PYRAMID

	ORIG	GOOD	FINE	N-MINT
❑1, 86, Flight From Tomorrow	1.70	0.40	1.00	2.00
❑2, 86	1.70	0.40	1.00	2.00
❑3, 86	1.70	0.40	1.00	2.00

ADVENTURES OF THE SCREAMER BROTHERS
SUPERSTAR

Value: Cover or less

- ❑1, Dec 90 ... 1.50
- ❑2, Mar 91 ... 1.50
- ❑3, Jun 91 ... 1.50

ADVENTURES OF THE SCREAMER BROTHERS (VOL. 2)
SUPERSTAR

Value: Cover or less

- ❑1 ... 1.95
- ❑2 ... 1.95
- ❑3, Dec 91 ... 1.95

ADVENTURES OF THE SUPER MARIO BROS.
VALIANT

	ORIG	GOOD	FINE	N-MINT
❑1, Feb 91	1.50	0.50	1.25	2.50
❑2, Mar 91, swimsuit issue	1.50	0.50	1.25	2.50
❑3, Apr 91	1.50	0.50	1.25	2.50
❑4, May 91	1.50	0.50	1.25	2.50
❑5, Jun 91	1.50	0.50	1.25	2.50
❑6, Jul 91	1.50	0.50	1.25	2.50
❑7, Aug 91	1.50	0.50	1.25	2.50
❑8, Sep 91	1.50	0.50	1.25	2.50
❑9, Oct 91	1.50	0.50	1.25	2.50

ADVENTURES OF THE THING, THE
MARVEL

	ORIG	GOOD	FINE	N-MINT
❑1, Apr 92, JSt; JBy, JBy (w), Remembrance Of Things Past, Reprints Marvel Two-In-One #50; Thing vs. Thing	1.25	0.30	0.75	1.50
❑2, May 92	1.25	0.30	0.75	1.50
❑3, Jun 92	1.25	0.30	0.75	1.50
❑4, Jul 92, Only The Swamp Survives, A: Man-Thing, Reprints Marvel Two-In-One #77	1.25	0.30	0.75	1.50

ADVENTURES OF THE VITAL-MAN
BUDGIE

Value: Cover or less

- ❑1, Jun 91, b&w ... 2.00
- ❑2 ... 2.00
- ❑3 ... 2.00
- ❑4 ... 2.00

ADVENTURES OF THE X-MEN, THE
MARVEL

	ORIG	GOOD	FINE	N-MINT
❑1, Apr 96, The Green Revolution, Part 1, Wolverine vs. Hulk	0.99	0.30	0.75	1.50
❑2, May 96	0.99	0.25	0.63	1.25
❑3, Jun 96, A: Spider-Man; V: Mr. Sinister	0.99	0.25	0.63	1.25
❑4, Jul 96	0.99	0.25	0.63	1.25
❑5, Aug 96, V: Magneto	0.99	0.25	0.63	1.25
❑6, Sep 96, Magneto vs. Apocalypse	0.99	0.20	0.50	1.00
❑7, Oct 96	0.99	0.20	0.50	1.00
❑8, Nov 96, Vanished	0.99	0.20	0.50	1.00
❑9, Dec 96, V: Vanisher	0.99	0.20	0.50	1.00
❑10, Jan 97, Media Darlings, V: Mojo	0.99	0.20	0.50	1.00
❑11, Feb 97, Tower of Despair, A: Man-Thing	0.99	0.20	0.50	1.00
❑12, Mar 97, Better to Light A Small Candle..., Final Issue	0.99	0.20	0.50	1.00

ADVENTURES ON SPACE STATION FREEDOM
TADCORPS

	ORIG	GOOD	FINE	N-MINT
❑1, nn; educational giveaway on International Space Station	—	0.50	1.25	2.50

ADVENTURES ON THE FRINGE
FANTAGRAPHICS

Value: Cover or less

- ❑1, Mar 92 ... 2.25
- ❑2, May 92 ... 2.25
- ❑3, Jul 92 ... 2.25
- ❑4, Oct 92, Photo cover ... 2.25
- ❑5, Feb 93 ... 2.25

ADVENTURES ON THE PLANET OF THE APES
MARVEL

	ORIG	GOOD	FINE	N-MINT
❑1, Adapts movie	0.25	1.20	3.00	6.00
❑2, Nov 75, World of Captive Humans, Adapts movie	0.25	0.80	2.00	4.00
❑3, Adapts movie	0.25	0.80	2.00	4.00
❑4	0.25	0.80	2.00	4.00
❑5	0.25	0.80	2.00	4.00
❑6	0.25	0.80	2.00	4.00
❑7	0.25	0.70	1.75	3.50
❑8	0.25	0.70	1.75	3.50
❑9, Adapts Beneath the Planet of the Apes	0.25	0.70	1.75	3.50
❑10, Nov 76, AA, Children of the Bomb, Adapts Beneath the Planet of the Apes	0.25	0.70	1.75	3.50
❑11, Dec 76, AA, The Hell of Holocaust, Final Issue; Adapts Beneath the Planet of the Apes; Destruction of Earth	0.25	0.70	1.75	3.50

ADVENTURE STRIP DIGEST
WCG

	ORIG	GOOD	FINE	N-MINT
❑1, Aug 94	2.00	0.50	1.25	2.50
❑2, Apr 95, The EC Express	2.50	0.50	1.25	2.50
❑3	2.50	0.50	1.25	2.50
❑4, Jun 96, Hostile Takeover	2.50	0.50	1.25	2.50

ADVENTUROUS UNCLE SCROOGE MCDUCK, THE (WALT DISNEY'S...)
GLADSTONE

Value: Cover or less

- ❑1, Jan 98, CB, CB (w), The Twenty-Four Carat Moon; Time Bandits, Reprint; reprints Barks' "The Twenty-Four Carat Moon" ... 1.95
- ❑2, Mar 98, 50th anniversary of Uncle Scrooge ... 1.95

AEON FOCUS
AEON

	ORIG	GOOD	FINE	N-MINT
❑1, Mar 94, Justin Hampton's Twitch	2.75	0.59	1.48	2.95
❑2, Jun 94, Upton's Lives of the Saints: Saint Antony of Padua; I'm Not Angry, Anymore, Colin Upton's Other Other Even Bigger Than Slightly Smaller That Got Bigger Big Thing	2.75	0.59	1.48	2.95
❑3, Oct 94, El Sobrante, Filthy Habits	2.95	0.59	1.48	2.95
❑4, Nov 94, Ward Sutton's Ink Blot	2.95	0.59	1.48	2.95
❑5, Slip	2.50	0.59	1.48	2.95

AERTIMISAN: WAR OF SOULS
ALMAGEST

Value: Cover or less

- ❑1, Nov 97 ... 2.75
- ❑2, Jan 98 ... 2.75

AESOP'S DESECRATED MORALS
MAGNECOM

Value: Cover or less

- ❑1, b&w ... 2.95

AESOP'S FABLES
FANTAGRAPHICS

Value: Cover or less

- ❑1, Spr 91, FH, FH (w), The Wolf at the Cottage; The Ant and the Dove ... 2.50
- ❑2, Fal 91 ... 2.50
- ❑3, Win 91 ... 2.50

AETERNUS
BRICK

Value: Cover or less

- ❑1, Jun 97 ... 2.95

AETOS THE EAGLE
ORPHAN UNDERGROUND

Value: Cover or less

- ❑1, Sep 94, b&w ... 2.50

AETOS THE EAGLE (VOL. 2)
GROUND ZERO

Value: Cover or less

- ❑1, Aug 97, Aetos the Eagle ... 3.00
- ❑2, The Children of the Graves! ... 3.00
- ❑3 ... 3.00

AFFABLE TALES FOR YOUR IMAGINATON
LEE ROY BROWN

Value: Cover or less

- ❑1, Jan 87, b&w ... 3.00

AFTER APOCALYPSE
PARAGRAPHICS

Value: Cover or less

- ❑1, May 87 ... 1.95

AFTER DARK
MILLENNIUM

Value: Cover or less

- ❑1, Jack; Nico ... 2.95

ORIG GOOD FINE N-MINT

AFTERMATH
PINNACLE

Value: Cover or less
❑1, sequel to Messiah 1.50

AFTERMATH (CHAOS)
CHAOS

Value: Cover or less
❑1 .... 2.95

AFTER/SHOCK: BULLETINS FROM GROUND ZERO
LAST GASP

Value: Cover or less
❑1, b&w 2.00

AGAINST BLACKSHARD: 3-D-THE SAGA OF SKETCH, THE ROYAL ARTIST
SIRIUS

Value: Cover or less
❑1, The Saga of Sketch, the Royal Artist 2.25

AGENT, THE
MARVEL

Value: Cover or less
❑1 .... 9.95

AGENT "00" SOUL
TWIST RECORDS

	ORIG	GOOD	FINE	N-MINT
❑1, no price	—	0.40	1.00	2.00

AGENT 13: THE MIDNIGHT AVENGER
TSR

Value: Cover or less
❑1, DS, nn 7.95

AGENT LIBERTY SPECIAL
DC

Value: Cover or less
❑1, 91, Disgrace, O: Agent Liberty 2.00

AGENTS OF LAW
DARK HORSE

Value: Cover or less

❑1, Mar 95, KG (w), What Price Utopia? 2.50
❑2 .... 2.50
❑3 .... 2.50
❑4 .... 2.50
❑5 .... 2.50
❑6, Sep 95, V: Predators, Final Issue 2.50

AGENT THREE ZERO
GALAXINOVELS

Value: Cover or less
❑1, Mirror Image, Galaxinovels w/ Trading Card and Poster 3.95

AGENT THREE ZERO: THE BLUE SULTAN'S QUEST/BLUE SULTAN- GALAXI FACT FILES
GALAXINOVELS

Value: Cover or less

❑1, The Blue Sultan's Quest, Flip-book; poster; trading card ... 3.95
❑1/PL, Platinum edition 2.95
❑2 .... 2.95
❑3 .... 2.95
❑4 .... 2.95

AGENT UNKNOWN
RENEGADE

Value: Cover or less
❑1, Oct 87, Raw Deal; Upwardly Mobil 2.00
❑2, Jan 88 .... 2.00
❑3, Apr 88 .... 2.00

AGE OF APOCALYPSE: THE CHOSEN
MARVEL

Value: Cover or less
❑1 .... 2.50

AGE OF BRONZE
IMAGE

Value: Cover or less

❑1, Nov 98, ES, ES (w) 2.95
❑2, Jan 99, ES, ES (w) 2.95
❑3, Mar 99, ES, ES (w) 2.95
❑4, May 99, ES, ES (w) 2.95
❑5, Oct 99, ES, ES (w) 2.95
❑6, Jan 00, ES, ES (w), cover says Dec, indicia says Jan 3.50
❑7, Mar 00, ES, ES (w), cover says Apr, indicia says Mar 3.50
❑8, Aug 00, ES, ES (w), b&w.. 3.50
❑9, Dec 00, ES, ES (w), cover says Nov, indicia says Dec 3.50
❑10, Feb 01, ES, ES (w), Sacrifice, Part 1 .... 3.50
❑SE 1, Jul 99, ES, ES (w), House Of Horror, cover says Jun, indicia says Jul 2.95

AGE OF HEROES, THE
HALLOWEEN

Value: Cover or less

❑1, 96, Impressions, b&w 2.95
❑2, 96, b&w 2.95
❑3, Mar 97 .... 2.95
❑4, May 97 .... 2.95
❑5 .... 2.95
❑SE 1, reprints Age of Heroes #1 and 2 (Halloween) 4.95
❑SE 2, A Day's Wages, a Heroe's Burden 6.95

AGE OF HEROES, THE: WEX
IMAGE

Value: Cover or less
❑1, Nov 98, ES, Wex, b&w...... 2.95

AGE OF INNOCENCE: THE REBIRTH OF IRON MAN
MARVEL

Value: Cover or less
❑1, O: Happy Hogan; O: Pepper Potts; O: Iron Man 2.50

AGE OF REPTILES
DARK HORSE

Value: Cover or less

❑1, Nov 93 .... 2.50
❑2, Dec 93 .... 2.50
❑3, Jan 94 .... 2.50
❑4, Feb 94 .... 2.50

AGE OF REPTILES: THE HUNT
DARK HORSE

Value: Cover or less

❑1, May 96 .... 2.95
❑2, Jun 96 .... 2.95

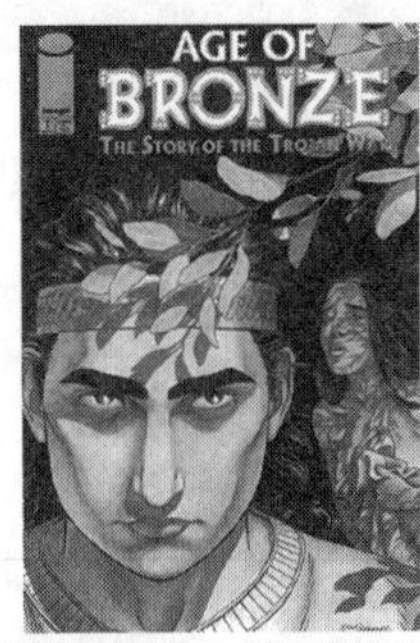

Eric Shanower received a 2001 Eisner Award for his work on *Age of Bronze.*

© 1998 Eric Shanower (Image)

ORIG GOOD FINE N-MINT

❑3, Jul 96 .... 2.95
❑4, Aug 96 .... 2.95
❑5, Sep 96, Final Issue 2.95

AGONY ACRES
AA² ENTERTAINMENT

	ORIG	GOOD	FINE	N-MINT
❑1, May 95	2.95	0.59	1.48	2.95
❑1/Ash	—	0.50	1.25	2.50
❑2, 96	2.95	0.59	1.48	2.95
❑3, b&w	2.95	0.59	1.48	2.95
❑4	2.95	0.59	1.48	2.95
❑5	2.95	0.59	1.48	2.95

AHLEA
RADIO

Value: Cover or less
❑1, Aug 97 .... 2.95
❑2, Oct 97 .... 2.95

AIDA-ZEE
NATE BUTLER

Value: Cover or less
❑1, KGa; NR; MA, Eterna-Teens; The Sons of Isaiah Glory..... 1.50

AIRBOY
ECLIPSE

	ORIG	GOOD	FINE	N-MINT
❑1, Jul 86, Chapter 1, On Wings Of Death; Part 2, Phoenix, D: Airboy I (Golden Age); 1: Airboy II (modern)	0.50	0.40	1.00	2.00
❑2, Jul 86, 1: Marisa; 1: Skywolf (Golden Age, in modern era)	0.50	0.30	0.75	1.50
❑3, Aug 86, A: The Heap	0.50	0.30	0.75	1.50
❑4, Aug 86, Misery	0.50	0.30	0.75	1.50
❑5, Sep 86, DSt, Return of Valkyrie; Revival of Valkyrie	0.50	0.30	0.75	1.50
❑6, Sep 86, 1: Iron Ace (in modern age)	0.50	0.30	0.75	1.50
❑7, Oct 86	0.50	0.30	0.75	1.50
❑8, Oct 86	0.50	0.30	0.75	1.50
❑9, Nov 86, 1: Flying Fool (in modern age); O: Airboy (Golden Age), Full-size issues begin	1.25	0.30	0.75	1.50
❑10, Nov 86, 1: Manic	1.25	0.25	0.63	1.25
❑11, Dec 86, O: Birdie; 1: Ito; O: Airboy (Golden Age), Skywolf back-up	1.25	0.25	0.63	1.25
❑12, Dec 86, 1: Kip Thorne, Iron Ace's identity revealed	1.25	0.25	0.63	1.25
❑13, Jan 87, 1: Bald Eagle (in modern age), Airfighters back-up	1.25	0.25	0.63	1.25
❑14, Jan 87	1.25	0.25	0.63	1.25
❑15, Feb 87	1.25	0.25	0.63	1.25
❑16, Feb 87, D: Manic	1.25	0.25	0.63	1.25
❑17, Mar 87, 1: Lacey Lyle; A: Harry Truman	1.25	0.25	0.63	1.25
❑18, Mar 87, 1: Black Angel (in modern age)	1.25	0.25	0.63	1.25
❑19, Apr 87, V: Rats	1.25	0.25	0.63	1.25
❑20, Apr 87, 1: The Rats (in modern age); V: Rats	1.25	0.25	0.63	1.25
❑21, May 87, GE, 1: Rat Mother	1.25	0.25	0.63	1.25
❑22, May 87, Arctic Deathzone, Part 1, 1: El Lobo Alado (Skywolf's father); 1: Lester Mansfield, Skywolf back-up story	1.25	0.25	0.63	1.25
❑23, Jun 87, Arctic Deathzone, Part 2	1.25	0.25	0.63	1.25
❑24, Jun 87, Arctic Deathzone, Part 3, A: Heap	1.25	0.25	0.63	1.25
❑25, Jul 87, A: Heap; 1: Manure Man	1.25	0.25	0.63	1.25
❑26, Jul 87, 1: Road Rats; 1: Flying Dutchman (in modern age)	1.25	0.25	0.63	1.25
❑27, Aug 87	1.25	0.25	0.63	1.25
❑28, Aug 87, 1: Black Axis	1.25	0.25	0.63	1.25
❑29, Sep 87	1.25	0.25	0.63	1.25
❑30, Sep 87	1.25	0.25	0.63	1.25
❑31, Oct 87	1.25	0.25	0.63	1.25
❑32, Oct 87	1.25	0.25	0.63	1.25
❑33, Nov 87	1.75	0.35	0.88	1.75
❑34, Dec 87, DS, Barbed Wire Noose; Skywolf: Hot Potato	1.75	0.35	0.88	1.75
❑35, Jan 88	1.75	0.35	0.88	1.75
❑36, Feb 88	1.75	0.35	0.88	1.75
❑37, Mar 88	1.75	0.35	0.88	1.75
❑38, Apr 88	1.75	0.35	0.88	1.75
❑39, May 88	1.75	0.35	0.88	1.75

	ORIG	GOOD	FINE	N-MINT
❑40, Jun 88	1.75	0.35	0.88	1.75
❑41, Jul 88	1.75	0.35	0.88	1.75
❑42, Aug 88	1.95	0.39	0.98	1.95
❑43, Sep 88	1.95	0.39	0.98	1.95
❑44, Oct 88	1.95	0.39	0.98	1.95
❑45, Nov 88	1.95	0.39	0.98	1.95
❑46, Jan 89, Airboy Diary	1.95	0.39	0.98	1.95
❑47, Mar 89, Airboy Diary	1.95	0.39	0.98	1.95
❑48, Apr 89, Airboy Diary	1.95	0.39	0.98	1.95
❑49, Jun 89, Airboy Diary	1.95	0.39	0.98	1.95
❑50, Oct 89, JKu, Final Issue; Giant-size	4.95	0.99	2.47	4.95

AIRBOY MEETS THE PROWLER
ECLIPSE

Value: Cover or less

- ❑1, Dec 87 ... 1.95

AIRBOY-MR. MONSTER SPECIAL
ECLIPSE

Value: Cover or less

- ❑1, Aug 87, The CafT at the Edge of the World ... 1.75

AIRBOY VERSUS THE AIRMAIDENS
ECLIPSE

Value: Cover or less

- ❑1, Jul 88 ... 1.95

AIR FIGHTERS CLASSICS
ECLIPSE

Value: Cover or less

- ❑1, Nov 87, cardstock cover; squarebound; Reprints Air Fighters Comics#1 ... 3.95
- ❑2, Jan 88, Airboy; Skywolf, O: Airboy, Reprints Air Fighters Comics#2 ... 3.95
- ❑3, Reprints Air Fighters Comics#3 ... 3.95
- ❑4, Reprints Air Fighters Comics#4 ... 3.95
- ❑5, Reprints Air Fighters Comics#5 ... 3.95
- ❑6, Reprints Air Fighters Comics#6 ... 3.95
- ❑7, Reprints Air Fighters Comics#7 ... 3.95

AIRFIGHTERS MEET SGT. STRIKE SPECIAL
ECLIPSE

Value: Cover or less

- ❑1, Jan 88, Tomorrow The Star ... 1.95

AIRLOCK
ECLECTUS

	ORIG	GOOD	FINE	N-MINT
❑1, Jun 90, Airlock; F-Mice: The Trouble with Flying, b&w	2.25	0.50	1.25	2.50
❑2	2.50	0.50	1.25	2.50
❑3	2.50	0.50	1.25	2.50

AIRMAIDENS SPECIAL
ECLIPSE

Value: Cover or less

- ❑1, Aug 87, Three Day Weekend, O: La Lupina ... 1.75

AIRMAN
MALIBU

Value: Cover or less

- ❑1, Shall The Sea Give Up Her Secrets?, 1: Thresher ... 1.95

AIRMEN, THE
MANSION

Value: Cover or less

- ❑1, Six Against Oblivion ... 2.50

AIR RAIDERS
MARVEL

Value: Cover or less

- ❑1, Sins Of The Father ... 1.00
- ❑2 ... 1.00
- ❑3 ... 1.00
- ❑4, May 86 ... 1.00
- ❑5 ... 1.00

AIRTIGHT GARAGE, THE
MARVEL

Value: Cover or less

- ❑1, Jul 93 ... 2.50
- ❑2, Aug 93 ... 2.50
- ❑3, Sep 93 ... 2.50
- ❑4, Oct 93 ... 2.50

AIR WAR STORIES
DELL

	ORIG	GOOD	FINE	N-MINT
❑1	0.12	4.40	11.00	22.00
❑2, Dec 65, The Hurricane that Wasn't; Admiral's Country	0.12	2.80	7.00	14.00
❑3	0.12	2.80	7.00	14.00
❑4	0.12	2.80	7.00	14.00
❑5	0.12	2.80	7.00	14.00
❑6	0.12	2.80	7.00	14.00
❑7	0.12	2.80	7.00	14.00
❑8, Final issue?	—	2.80	7.00	14.00

AIRWAVES
CALIBER

Value: Cover or less

- ❑1, Feb 91, Chapter 1; Taken Under ... 2.50
- ❑2 ... 2.50
- ❑3 ... 2.50
- ❑4 ... 2.50

A.K.A. GOLDFISH
CALIBER

Value: Cover or less

- ❑1, Joker ... 3.50
- ❑2, Ace ... 3.95
- ❑3, Jack ... 3.95
- ❑4, Queen ... 2.95
- ❑5, Mar 96, cardstock cover; King ... 3.95

AKIKO
SIRIUS

	ORIG	GOOD	FINE	N-MINT
❑1, Mar 96	2.50	1.20	3.00	6.00
❑2, Apr 96	2.50	0.90	2.25	4.50
❑3, May 96	2.50	0.80	2.00	4.00
❑4, Jun 96	2.50	0.80	2.00	4.00
❑5, 96, no indicia	2.50	0.80	2.00	4.00
❑6, Aug 96	2.50	0.70	1.75	3.50
❑7, Sep 96	2.50	0.70	1.75	3.50
❑8, Oct 96	2.50	0.70	1.75	3.50
❑9, Dec 96	2.50	0.70	1.75	3.50
❑10, Jan 97	2.50	0.70	1.75	3.50
❑11, Feb 97	2.50	0.50	1.25	2.50
❑12, Mar 97	2.50	0.50	1.25	2.50
❑13, Apr 97	2.50	0.50	1.25	2.50
❑14, May 97	2.50	0.50	1.25	2.50
❑15, Jul 97	2.50	0.50	1.25	2.50
❑16, Aug 97	2.50	0.50	1.25	2.50
❑17, Aug 97, indicia says "Aug"	2.50	0.50	1.25	2.50
❑18, Sep 97	2.50	0.50	1.25	2.50
❑19, Oct 97, The Story Tree, Beeba's story	2.50	0.50	1.25	2.50
❑20, Nov 97, The Story Tree, Beeba's story	2.50	0.50	1.25	2.50
❑21, Dec 97, Spuckler's Story, Part 1	2.50	0.50	1.25	2.50
❑22, Jan 98, Spuckler's Story, Part 2	2.50	0.50	1.25	2.50
❑23, Feb 98, Gax's Story, Part 1	2.50	0.50	1.25	2.50
❑24, Mar 98, Gax's Story, Part 2	2.50	0.50	1.25	2.50
❑25, May 98	2.95	0.50	1.25	2.50
❑26, Jul 98	2.50	0.50	1.25	2.50
❑27, Aug 98	2.50	0.50	1.25	2.50
❑28, Oct 98	2.50	0.50	1.25	2.50
❑29, Nov 98	2.50	0.50	1.25	2.50
❑30, Dec 98	2.50	0.50	1.25	2.50
❑31, Feb 98	2.50	0.50	1.25	2.50
❑32, Mar 98	2.50	0.50	1.25	2.50
❑33, May 98	2.50	0.50	1.25	2.50
❑34	2.50	0.50	1.25	2.50
❑35, Sep 99, Moonshopping, Part 1, b&w	2.50	0.50	1.25	2.50
❑36, Moonshopping, Part 2, b&w	2.50	0.50	1.25	2.50
❑37, Dec 99, Moonshopping, Part 3, b&w	2.50	0.50	1.25	2.50
❑38, Feb 00, Moonshopping, Part 4, b&w	2.50	0.50	1.25	2.50
❑39, May 00, Spucky and Gax in Illegal Aliens; Akiko in Dream Sequence, b&w	2.50	0.50	1.25	2.50
❑40, Aug 00, The Battle of Boach's Keep, b&w	2.95	0.59	1.48	2.95
❑41, Oct 00, The Battle of Boach's Keep, b&w	2.95	0.59	1.48	2.95

AKIKO ON THE PLANET SMOO
SIRIUS

	ORIG	GOOD	FINE	N-MINT
❑1, Dec 95, b&w; Fold-out cover	3.95	1.60	4.00	8.00
❑1/HC, b&w; Hardcover edition	9.95	3.99	9.98	19.95
❑1-2, May 98, b&w; 2nd Printing; cardstock cover	3.50	0.80	2.00	4.00
❑FAN 1, free promotional giveaway	—	0.60	1.50	3.00

AKIKO ON THE PLANET SMOO: THE COLOR EDITION
SIRIUS

Value: Cover or less

- ❑1, Feb 00, full color; cardstock cover ... 4.95

AKIRA
MARVEL

	ORIG	GOOD	FINE	N-MINT
❑1, Sep 88, 1st Printing	3.50	1.80	4.50	9.00
❑1-2, 2nd Printing	3.95	0.80	2.00	4.00
❑2, 1st Printing	3.50	1.00	2.50	5.00
❑2-2, 2nd Printing	3.95	0.80	2.00	4.00
❑3, 88	3.50	1.00	2.50	5.00
❑4	3.50	0.80	2.00	4.00
❑5, 88	3.50	0.80	2.00	4.00
❑6	3.50	0.80	2.00	4.00
❑7, 89	3.50	0.80	2.00	4.00
❑8	3.50	0.80	2.00	4.00
❑9	3.50	0.80	2.00	4.00
❑10	3.50	0.80	2.00	4.00
❑11	3.50	0.80	2.00	4.00
❑12	3.50	0.80	2.00	4.00
❑13	3.50	0.80	2.00	4.00
❑14	3.50	0.80	2.00	4.00
❑15	3.50	0.80	2.00	4.00
❑16, 89	3.50	0.80	2.00	4.00
❑17	3.95	0.80	2.00	4.00
❑18, 90	3.95	0.80	2.00	4.00
❑19	3.95	0.80	2.00	4.00
❑20	3.95	0.80	2.00	4.00
❑21	3.95	0.80	2.00	4.00
❑22	3.95	0.80	2.00	4.00
❑23	3.95	0.80	2.00	4.00
❑24	3.95	0.80	2.00	4.00
❑25	3.95	0.80	2.00	4.00
❑26	3.95	0.80	2.00	4.00
❑27	3.95	0.80	2.00	4.00
❑28	3.95	0.80	2.00	4.00
❑29	3.95	0.80	2.00	4.00
❑30	3.95	0.80	2.00	4.00

	ORIG	GOOD	FINE	N-MINT
❑31	3.95	0.79	1.98	3.95
❑32	3.95	0.79	1.98	3.95
❑33	3.95	0.79	1.98	3.95
❑34	3.95	0.79	1.98	3.95
❑35	3.95	0.79	1.98	3.95
❑36, A: Lady Miyako	3.95	0.79	1.98	3.95
❑37	3.95	0.79	1.98	3.95
❑38, Final Issue	3.95	0.79	1.98	3.95

A*K*Q*J
Fantagraphics

Value: Cover or less

❑1, b&w; Captain Jack	2.75

ALADDIN (DISNEY'S...)
Marvel

Value: Cover or less

❑1, Oct 94, Aladdin's Quest	1.50	❑6, Mar 95	1.50
❑2, Nov 94, The Pharaoh's Curse	1.50	❑7, Apr 95	1.50
❑3, Dec 94	1.50	❑8, May 95	1.50
❑4, Jan 95	1.50	❑9, Jun 95	1.50
❑5, Feb 95	1.50	❑10, Jul 95	1.50
		❑11, Aug 95	1.50

ALARMING ADVENTURES
Harvey

	ORIG	GOOD	FINE	N-MINT
❑1, Oct 62, The Lost Acre; The Night Visitor	0.12	12.00	30.00	60.00
❑2, Dec 62	0.12	8.00	20.00	40.00
❑3, Feb 63	0.12	7.00	17.50	35.00

ALBEDO (1ST SERIES)
Thoughts & Images

	ORIG	GOOD	FINE	N-MINT
❑0, Erma Felna; Bad Rubber, Blue cover; 500 printed	2.00	1.60	4.00	8.00
❑0/A, White cover (yellow table); Only 50 copies printed	2.00	6.00	15.00	30.00
❑0/B, White cover (no yellow); Less than 500 copies printed	2.00	3.00	7.50	15.00
❑0-2, 2nd Printing; Blue cover	2.00	1.00	2.50	5.00
❑0-3, 3rd Printing; Blue cover	0.50	0.60	1.50	3.00
❑0-4, Dec 86, 4th Printing; When and yellow cover from, blue cover back; additional material	1.00	0.50	1.25	2.50
❑1, 1: Usagi Yojimbo, Dark red cover	2.00	2.80	7.00	14.00
❑1/A, 1: Usagi Yojimbo, Bright red cover	2.00	2.00	5.00	10.00
❑1-2, 1: Usagi Yojimbo, 2nd Printing; Bright red cover	2.00	2.00	5.00	10.00
❑2, Nov 84, 2: Usagi Yojimbo	1.50	1.60	4.00	8.00
❑3, Apr 85, Usagi Yojimbo back-up	2.00	1.00	2.50	5.00
❑4, Jul 85, Usagi Yojimbo back-up	2.00	0.80	2.00	4.00
❑5, Oct 85	2.00	0.80	2.00	4.00
❑6, Jan 86	2.00	0.60	1.50	3.00
❑7, Mar 86	2.00	0.60	1.50	3.00
❑8, Jul 86	2.00	0.60	1.50	3.00
❑9, May 87	2.00	0.40	1.00	2.00
❑10, Sep 87, cardstock cover	2.00	0.40	1.00	2.00
❑11, Dec 87	2.00	0.40	1.00	2.00
❑12, Mar 88	2.00	0.40	1.00	2.00
❑13, Jun 88	2.00	0.40	1.00	2.00
❑14, Spr 89, Photo cover; Final Issue	2.00	0.40	1.00	2.00

ALBEDO (2ND SERIES)
Antarctic

	ORIG	GOOD	FINE	N-MINT
❑1, Jun 91	2.50	0.80	2.00	4.00
❑2, Sep 91	2.50	0.60	1.50	3.00
❑3, Dec 91	2.50	0.60	1.50	3.00
❑4, Mar 92	2.50	0.60	1.50	3.00
❑5, Jun 92	2.50	0.50	1.25	2.50
❑6, Sep 92	2.50	0.50	1.25	2.50
❑7, Dec 92	2.50	0.50	1.25	2.50
❑8, Mar 93	2.50	0.50	1.25	2.50
❑9, Jun 93	2.50	0.50	1.25	2.50
❑10, Oct 93	2.75	0.55	1.38	2.75
❑SE 1, Jul 93, full color; Color special	2.95	0.59	1.48	2.95

ALBEDO (3RD SERIES)
Antarctic

Value: Cover or less

❑1, Feb 94	2.95	❑3, Feb 95	2.95
❑2, Oct 94	2.95	❑4, Jan 96	2.95

ALBEDO (4TH SERIES)
Antarctic

	ORIG	GOOD	FINE	N-MINT
❑1, Dec 96	2.95	0.59	1.48	2.95
❑2, Jan 99, Erma Felna, EDF	2.95	0.60	1.50	2.99

ALBEDO (5TH SERIES)
Antarctic

Value: Cover or less

❑1	2.99

ALEC DEAR
Mediocre Concepts

	ORIG	GOOD	FINE	N-MINT
❑1, 96, The Hospital, b&w; no cover price; magazine-sized comic book with cardstock cover	—	0.40	1.00	2.00

ALEC: LOVE AND BEERGLASSES
Escape

	ORIG	GOOD	FINE	N-MINT
❑1	1.95	0.70	1.75	3.50

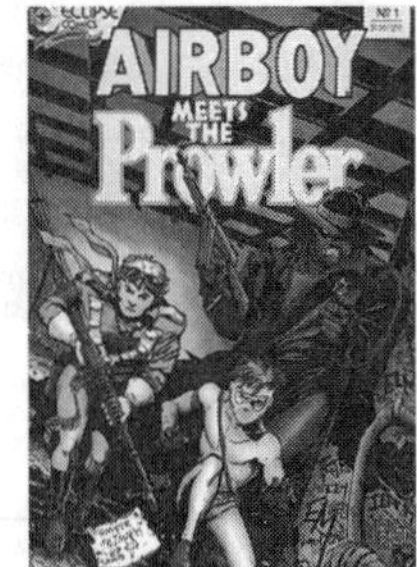

Golden Age hero Airboy met modern-day Eclipse vigilante The Prowler in a one-shot special.

© 1987 Eclipse

ALEX
Fantagraphics

Value: Cover or less

❑1	2.95	❑4, Oct 94	2.95
❑2, Apr 94	2.95	❑5, Nov 94	2.95
❑3, Jul 94	2.95		

ALEXIS (VOL. 2)
Eros

Value: Cover or less

❑1	2.95	❑4	2.95
❑2, Jul 95	2.95	❑5, Mar 96	2.95
❑3	2.95		

ALF
Marvel

Value: Cover or less

❑1, At Your Disposal; Snow Skin off My Nose, 1: Alf	1.00	❑32	1.00
❑2, All's Fair; Jungle Love, 2: Alf	1.00	❑33	1.00
❑3, Travels with Willie; One Tiny Mistake	1.00	❑34	1.00
❑4	1.00	❑35	1.00
❑5	1.00	❑36	1.00
❑6	1.00	❑37	1.00
❑7	1.00	❑38	1.00
❑8	1.00	❑39	1.00
❑9	1.00	❑40	1.00
❑10	1.00	❑41, May 81, T.V.F.X.N.F.S!	1.00
❑11	1.00	❑42, Jun 81, Send in the Clones!	1.00
❑12	1.00	❑43, Jul 81, Secure From General Quarter Pounders	1.00
❑13	1.00	❑44, Aug 81, X-Men parody	1.00
❑14	1.00	❑45, Sep 81	1.00
❑15	1.00	❑46, Oct 81	1.00
❑16	1.00	❑47, Nov 81	1.00
❑17	1.00	❑48, Dec 81, Th-Th-That's All, Folks!, Part 2	1.00
❑18	1.00	❑49	1.00
❑19	1.00	❑50, Final Issue; Giant-size	1.75
❑20, Babe in the Woods, Part 1	1.00	❑Anl 1, The Return Of Rhonda; Back To Human Nature, Dynamic Forces edition	1.75
❑21, Babe in the Woods, Part 2	1.00	❑Anl 2, BSz	2.00
❑22, X-Men parody	1.00	❑Anl 3, TMNT parody	2.00
❑23	1.00	❑HS 1, magazine-sized comic book with cardstock cover; Holiday Special #1	1.75
❑24	1.00	❑HS 2, Dynamic Forces edition; Holiday Special #2	2.00
❑25	1.00	❑SS 1, Spring Special	1.75
❑26	1.00		
❑27	1.00		
❑28	1.00		
❑29, "3-D" cover	1.00		
❑30	1.00		
❑31	1.00		

ALF COMICS MAGAZINE
Marvel

	ORIG	GOOD	FINE	N-MINT
❑1, digest	1.50	0.40	1.00	2.00
❑2, digest	1.50	0.40	1.00	2.00

ALIAS:
Now

Value: Cover or less

❑1, Jul 90	1.75	❑4, Oct 90	1.75
❑2, Aug 90	1.75	❑5, Nov 90	1.75
❑3, Sep 90	1.75		

ALIEN 3
Dark Horse

Value: Cover or less

❑1, 92	2.50	❑2, 92	2.50
		❑3, 92	2.50

ALIEN DUCKLINGS
Blackthorne

	ORIG	GOOD	FINE	N-MINT
❑1, Oct 86, Clone Home	1.75	0.40	1.00	2.00
❑2	1.75	0.40	1.00	2.00
❑3	1.75	0.40	1.00	2.00
❑4	1.75	0.40	1.00	2.00

ALIEN ENCOUNTERS (ECLIPSE)
Eclipse

	ORIG	GOOD	FINE	N-MINT
❑1, Pretending; Open Season	1.75	0.40	1.00	2.00
❑2	1.75	0.40	1.00	2.00
❑3, The Heroine; M.O.T.H.E.R. Knows Best	1.75	0.40	1.00	2.00

	ORIG	GOOD	FINE	N-MINT
❑4, Luv's Story; Now Jr. Behave Yourself	1.75	0.40	1.00	2.00
❑5	1.75	0.40	1.00	2.00
❑6, Standard Procedure; Freefall, Story "Nada" used as basis for movie "They Live"	1.75	0.40	1.00	2.00
❑7, Under Tartuka; So You Want to Be in Pictures?	1.75	0.40	1.00	2.00
❑8, Aug 86, Take One Capsule Every Million Years; Joyriding	1.75	0.40	1.00	2.00
❑9, The Conquered; Strangers on a Subway	1.75	0.40	1.00	2.00
❑10, GM; TS, The Exiles; Cracked Mirrors, "Exiles" Ray Bradbury adaptation	1.75	0.40	1.00	2.00
❑11, A World A'Hurtin'; Dave's Dilemma	2.00	0.40	1.00	2.00
❑12, What a Relief!; Eyes of the Sibyl	2.00	0.40	1.00	2.00
❑13, The Light at the End; Page One	2.00	0.40	1.00	2.00
❑14, The Buster Crabbe Collector; In Other News, Aliens Landed Today!, Final Issue	2.00	0.40	1.00	2.00

ALIEN ENCOUNTERS (FANTACO)
FANTACO

	ORIG	GOOD	FINE	N-MINT
❑1, 80	1.25	0.30	0.75	1.50

ALIEN FIRE
KITCHEN SINK

Value: Cover or less

❑1, Jan 87, Distant Light, Distant Country ... 2.00
❑2, May 87 ... 2.00
❑3, May 87 ... 2.00

ALIEN FIRE: PASS IN THUNDER
KITCHEN SINK

Value: Cover or less

❑1, May 95, nn; b&w; squarebound ... 6.95

ALIEN HERO
ZEN

Value: Cover or less

❑1, Feb 99, illustrated novella featuring Zen ... 8.95

ALIEN LEGION (VOL. 1)
MARVEL

Value: Cover or less

❑1, Apr 84, TD, Survival of the Fittest, Giant-size ... 2.00
❑2, Jun 84, Blind Trust ... 1.50
❑3, Aug 84, Last Gamble ... 1.50
❑4, Oct 84 ... 1.50
❑5, Dec 84 ... 1.50
❑6, Feb 85 ... 1.50
❑7, Apr 85 ... 1.50
❑8, Jun 85 ... 1.50
❑9, Aug 85 ... 1.50
❑10, Oct 85 ... 1.50
❑11, Dec 85 ... 1.50
❑12, Feb 86 ... 1.50
❑13, Apr 86 ... 1.50
❑14, Jun 86 ... 1.50
❑15, Aug 86 ... 1.50
❑16, Oct 86 ... 1.50
❑17, Dec 86 ... 1.50
❑18, Feb 87 ... 1.75
❑19, Apr 87 ... 1.75
❑20, Jun 87, Final Issue ... 1.75

ALIEN LEGION (VOL. 2)
MARVEL

	ORIG	GOOD	FINE	N-MINT
❑1, Oct 87, Dead And Buried	1.25	0.30	0.75	1.50
❑2, Dec 87	1.25	0.30	0.75	1.50
❑3, Feb 88	1.25	0.30	0.75	1.50
❑4, Apr 88	1.25	0.30	0.75	1.50
❑5, Jun 88	1.25	0.30	0.75	1.50
❑6, Aug 88	1.25	0.30	0.75	1.50
❑7, Oct 88	1.25	0.30	0.75	1.50
❑8, Dec 88	1.50	0.30	0.75	1.50
❑9, Feb 89	1.50	0.30	0.75	1.50
❑10, Apr 89	1.50	0.30	0.75	1.50
❑11, Jun 89	1.50	0.30	0.75	1.50
❑12, Aug 89	1.50	0.30	0.75	1.50
❑13, Oct 89	1.50	0.30	0.75	1.50
❑14, Dec 89	1.50	0.30	0.75	1.50
❑15, Feb 90	1.50	0.30	0.75	1.50
❑16, Apr 90	1.50	0.30	0.75	1.50
❑17, Jun 90	1.50	0.30	0.75	1.50
❑18, Aug 90, Final Issue	1.50	0.30	0.75	1.50

ALIEN LEGION: A GREY DAY TO DIE
MARVEL

Value: Cover or less

❑1 ... 5.95

ALIEN LEGION: BINARY DEEP
MARVEL

Value: Cover or less

❑1, Sep 93, nn ... 3.50

ALIEN LEGION: JUGGER GRIMROD
MARVEL

Value: Cover or less

❑1, Aug 92 ... 5.95

ALIEN LEGION: ONE PLANET AT A TIME
MARVEL

Value: Cover or less

❑1, One Planet At A Time ... 4.95
❑2, Heavy Hitters ... 4.95
❑3 ... 4.95

ALIEN LEGION: ON THE EDGE
MARVEL

Value: Cover or less

❑1 ... 4.50
❑2 ... 4.50
❑3 ... 4.50

ALIEN LEGION: TENANTS OF HELL
MARVEL

Value: Cover or less

❑1, 91, Hell Is A Planet, cardstock cover ... 4.50
❑2 ... 4.50

ALIEN NATION
DC

	ORIG	GOOD	FINE	N-MINT
❑1, Dec 88, movie Adaptation	2.50	0.60	1.50	3.00

ALIEN NATION: A BREED APART
ADVENTURE

Value: Cover or less

❑1, Nov 90 ... 2.50
❑2, Dec 90 ... 2.50
❑3, Jan 91 ... 2.50
❑4, Mar 91 ... 2.50

ALIEN NATION: THE FIRSTCOMERS
ADVENTURE

Value: Cover or less

❑1, May 91, The Firstcomers, Part 1 ... 2.50
❑2, Jun 91, The Firstcomers, Part 2 ... 2.50
❑3, Jul 91, The Firstcomers, Part 3 ... 2.50
❑4, Aug 91, The Firstcomers, Part 4 ... 2.50

ALIEN NATION: THE LOST EPISODE
MALIBU

Value: Cover or less

❑1, 92, nn; b&w; One-Shot; squarebound; adapts second season opener ... 4.95

ALIEN NATION: THE PUBLIC ENEMY
ADVENTURE

Value: Cover or less

❑1, Dec 91, Gefore The Fall ... 2.50
❑2, Jan 92, Fallen Angels! ... 2.50
❑3, Feb 92 ... 2.50
❑4, Mar 92 ... 2.50

ALIEN NATION: THE SKIN TRADE
ADVENTURE

Value: Cover or less

❑1, Mar 91, The Case of The Missing Milksop ... 2.50
❑2, Apr 91 ... 2.50
❑3, May 91 ... 2.50
❑4, Jun 91, The Big Goodbye ... 2.50

ALIEN NATION: THE SPARTANS
ADVENTURE

	ORIG	GOOD	FINE	N-MINT
❑1, Lost And Found, Yellow	2.50	0.50	1.25	2.50
❑1/A, 90, Lost And Found, Green	2.50	0.50	1.25	2.50
❑1/B, Lost And Found, Blue	2.50	0.50	1.25	2.50
❑1/C, Lost And Found, Red	2.50	0.50	1.25	2.50
❑1/LE, Lost And Found	2.50	0.80	2.00	4.00
❑2, 90, Stone Walled	2.50	0.50	1.25	2.50
❑3, 90, Take Back the Stars	2.50	0.50	1.25	2.50
❑4, 90	2.50	0.50	1.25	2.50

ALIEN RESURRECTION
DARK HORSE

Value: Cover or less

❑1, Oct 97 ... 2.50
❑2, Nov 97 ... 2.50

ALIENS, THE
GOLD KEY

	ORIG	GOOD	FINE	N-MINT
❑1, The Aliens; The Aliens: A Matter of Judgment, 1982 reprint of #1; Reprints The Aliens stories from Magnus, Robot Fighter	0.12	2.40	6.00	12.00

ALIENS (VOL. 1)
DARK HORSE

	ORIG	GOOD	FINE	N-MINT
❑1, May 88	1.95	1.00	2.50	5.00
❑1-2, 2nd Printing	1.95	0.50	1.25	2.50
❑, 3rd Printing	1.95	0.40	1.00	2.00
❑1-4, 4th Printing	1.95	0.40	1.00	2.00
❑1-5, 5th Printing	1.95	0.40	1.00	2.00
❑1-6, 6th Printing	1.95	0.40	1.00	2.00
❑2, Sep 88	1.95	0.70	1.75	3.50
❑2-2, 2nd Printing	1.95	0.50	1.25	2.50
❑2-3, 3rd Printing	1.95	0.40	1.00	2.00
❑2-4, 4th Printing	1.95	0.40	1.00	2.00
❑3, Jan 89	1.95	0.50	1.25	2.50
❑3-2, 2nd Printing	1.95	0.40	1.00	2.00
❑4, Mar 89	1.95	0.50	1.25	2.50
❑4-2, 2nd Printing	1.95	0.40	1.00	2.00
❑5, Jun 89	1.95	0.50	1.25	2.50
❑5-2, 2nd Printing	1.95	0.40	1.00	2.00
❑6, Jul 89	1.95	0.50	1.25	2.50
❑6-2, 2nd Printing	1.95	0.40	1.00	2.00

ALIENS (VOL. 2)
DARK HORSE

	ORIG	GOOD	FINE	N-MINT
❑1, Aug 89, full color	2.25	0.60	1.50	3.00
❑2, Dec 89	2.25	0.50	1.25	2.50
❑3, 90	2.25	0.50	1.25	2.50
❑4, May 90	2.25	0.50	1.25	2.50

ALIENS: ALCHEMY
DARK HORSE

Value: Cover or less

❑1, Oct 97 ... 2.95
❑2, Nov 97 ... 2.95
❑3, Nov 97 ... 2.95

ALIENS: APOCALYPSE-THE DESTROYING ANGELS
DARK HORSE

Value: Cover or less

❑1, Jan 99 ... 2.95
❑2, Feb 99 ... 2.95
❑3, Mar 99 ... 2.95
❑4, Apr 99 ... 2.95

ALIENS: BERSERKER
DARK HORSE

Value: Cover or less

❑1, Jan 95 ... 2.50
❑2, Feb 95 ... 2.50
❑3, Mar 95 ... 2.50
❑4, Apr 95 ... 2.50

ALIENS: COLONIAL MARINES
DARK HORSE
Value: Cover or less

- ❑1, Jan 93 ... 2.50
- ❑2, Feb 93 ... 2.50
- ❑3, Mar 93 ... 2.50
- ❑4, Apr 93 ... 2.50
- ❑5, May 93 ... 2.50
- ❑6, Jun 93 ... 2.50
- ❑7, Jul 93 ... 2.50
- ❑8, Aug 93 ... 2.50
- ❑9, Sep 93 ... 2.50
- ❑10, Oct 93, Final Issue ... 2.50

ALIENS: EARTH ANGEL
DARK HORSE
Value: Cover or less

- ❑1, Aug 94, JBy, JBy (w), nn; One-Shot ... 2.95

ALIENS: EARTH WAR
DARK HORSE

	ORIG	GOOD	FINE	N-MINT
❑1, Jun 90	2.50	0.60	1.50	3.00
❑1-2, 2nd Printing	2.50	0.50	1.25	2.50
❑2, Jul 90	2.50	0.50	1.25	2.50
❑3, Sep 90	2.50	0.50	1.25	2.50
❑4, Oct 90	2.50	0.50	1.25	2.50

ALIEN SEX/MONSTER LUST
FANTAGRAPHICS
Value: Cover or less

- ❑1, b&w; adult ... 2.50

ALIENS: GENOCIDE
DARK HORSE
Value: Cover or less

- ❑1 ... 2.50
- ❑2 ... 2.50
- ❑3 ... 2.50
- ❑4, Feb 92 ... 2.50

ALIENS: GLASS CORRIDOR
DARK HORSE
Value: Cover or less

- ❑1, Jun 98, nn; One-Shot ... 2.95

ALIENS: HAVOC
DARK HORSE

	ORIG	GOOD	FINE	N-MINT
❑1, Jun 97	2.95	0.59	1.48	2.95
❑2, Jul 97	2.95	0.79	1.98	3.95

ALIENS: HIVE
DARK HORSE
Value: Cover or less

- ❑1, Feb 92 ... 2.50
- ❑2, Mar 92 ... 2.50
- ❑3, Apr 92 ... 2.50
- ❑4, May 92 ... 2.50

ALIENS: KIDNAPPED
DARK HORSE
Value: Cover or less

- ❑1, Dec 97 ... 2.50
- ❑2, Jan 98 ... 2.50
- ❑3, Feb 98 ... 2.50

ALIENS: LABYRINTH
DARK HORSE
Value: Cover or less

- ❑1, Sep 93 ... 2.50
- ❑2, Oct 93 ... 2.50
- ❑3, Nov 93 ... 2.50
- ❑4, Dec 93 ... 2.50

ALIENS: LOVESICK
DARK HORSE
Value: Cover or less

- ❑1, Dec 96, One-Shot ... 2.95

ALIENS: MONDO HEAT
DARK HORSE
Value: Cover or less

- ❑1, Feb 96, nn; One-Shot ... 2.50

ALIENS: MONDO PEST
DARK HORSE
Value: Cover or less

- ❑1 ... 2.95

ALIENS: MUSIC OF THE SPEARS
DARK HORSE
Value: Cover or less

- ❑1, Jan 94 ... 2.50
- ❑2, Feb 94 ... 2.50
- ❑3, Mar 94 ... 2.50
- ❑4, Apr 94 ... 2.50

ALIENS: NEWT'S TALE
DARK HORSE
Value: Cover or less

- ❑1, Jun 92 ... 4.95
- ❑2, Aug 92 ... 4.95

ALIENS: PIG
DARK HORSE
Value: Cover or less

- ❑1, Mar 97 ... 2.95

ALIENS/PREDATOR: THE DEADLIEST OF THE SPECIES
DARK HORSE

	ORIG	GOOD	FINE	N-MINT
❑1, Jul 93	2.50	0.50	1.25	2.50
❑1/LE, Jul 93, no cover price	—	0.80	2.00	4.00
❑2, Sep 93, The Hunt	2.50	0.50	1.25	2.50
❑3, Nov 93	2.50	0.50	1.25	2.50
❑4, Jan 94	2.50	0.50	1.25	2.50
❑5, Mar 94	2.50	0.50	1.25	2.50
❑6, May 94	2.50	0.50	1.25	2.50
❑7, Aug 94	2.50	0.50	1.25	2.50
❑8, Oct 94	2.50	0.50	1.25	2.50
❑9, Dec 94	2.50	0.50	1.25	2.50
❑10, Feb 95, Queen's Gambit	2.50	0.50	1.25	2.50
❑11, May 95	2.50	0.50	1.25	2.50
❑12, Aug 95, Renegade, Final Issue	2.50	0.50	1.25	2.50

ALIENS: PURGE
DARK HORSE
Value: Cover or less

- ❑1, Aug 97, nn; One-Shot ... 2.95

DC published the adaptation of the 1988 film *Alien Nation* before Malibu's Adventure imprint began producing a series of mini-series based on the property.

© 1988 Twentieth Century Fox Film Corporation (DC)

ALIENS: ROGUE
DARK HORSE
Value: Cover or less

- ❑1, Apr 93 ... 2.50
- ❑2, May 93 ... 2.50
- ❑3, Jun 93 ... 2.50
- ❑4, Jul 93 ... 2.50

ALIENS: SACRIFICE
DARK HORSE
Value: Cover or less

- ❑1, nn ... 4.95

ALIENS: SALVATION
DARK HORSE
Value: Cover or less

- ❑1, DaG (w), nn ... 4.95

ALIENS: SALVATION AND SACRIFICE
DARK HORSE
Value: Cover or less

- ❑1, Mar 01, DaG (w) ... 12.95

ALIENS: SPECIAL
DARK HORSE
Value: Cover or less

- ❑1, Jun 97, 45 Seconds; Elder Gods, nn; One-Shot ... 2.50

ALIENS: STALKER
DARK HORSE
Value: Cover or less

- ❑1, Jun 98, nn; One-Shot ... 2.50

ALIENS: STRONGHOLD
DARK HORSE
Value: Cover or less

- ❑1, May 94 ... 2.50
- ❑2, Jun 94 ... 2.50
- ❑3, Jul 94 ... 2.50
- ❑4, Sep 94 ... 2.50

ALIENS: SURVIVAL
DARK HORSE
Value: Cover or less

- ❑1, Feb 98 ... 2.95
- ❑2, Mar 98 ... 2.95
- ❑3, Apr 98 ... 2.95

ALIENS VS. PREDATOR
DARK HORSE

	ORIG	GOOD	FINE	N-MINT
❑0, Jul 90, b&w; reprints story from Dark Horse Presents #34-36	1.95	0.80	2.00	4.00
❑1, Jun 90, full color	2.50	0.80	2.00	4.00
❑1-2, 2nd Printing	2.50	0.50	1.25	2.50
❑2, Aug 90	2.50	0.70	1.75	3.50
❑2-2, 2nd Printing	2.50	0.50	1.25	2.50
❑3, Oct 90	2.50	0.60	1.50	3.00
❑3-2, 2nd Printing	2.50	0.50	1.25	2.50
❑4, Dec 90	2.50	0.60	1.50	3.00
❑4-2, 2nd Printing	2.50	0.50	1.25	2.50
❑Anl 1, Jul 99, Hell-Bent; Lefty's Revenge, Anthology	4.95	0.99	2.47	4.95

ALIENS VS. PREDATOR: BOOTY
DARK HORSE
Value: Cover or less

- ❑1, Jan 96, nn; One-Shot ... 2.50

ALIENS VS. PREDATOR: DUEL
DARK HORSE
Value: Cover or less

- ❑1, Mar 95 ... 2.50
- ❑2 ... 2.50

ALIENS VS. PREDATOR: ETERNAL
DARK HORSE
Value: Cover or less

- ❑1, Jun 98 ... 2.50
- ❑2, Jul 98 ... 2.50
- ❑3, Aug 98 ... 2.50
- ❑4, Sep 98 ... 2.50

ALIENS VS. PREDATOR VS. THE TERMINATOR
DARK HORSE
Value: Cover or less

- ❑1, Apr 00, A: Ripley ... 2.95
- ❑2, May 00, A: Ripley ... 2.95
- ❑3, Jun 00, A: Ripley ... 2.95
- ❑4, Jul 00, A: Ripley ... 2.95

ALIENS VS. PREDATOR: WAR
DARK HORSE
Value: Cover or less

- ❑0 ... 2.50
- ❑1 ... 2.50
- ❑2, Jun 95 ... 2.50
- ❑3, Jul 95 ... 2.50
- ❑4, Aug 95 ... 2.50

ALIENS VS. PREDATOR: XENOGENESIS
DARK HORSE
Value: Cover or less

- ❑1, Dec 99 ... 2.95
- ❑2, Jan 00 ... 2.95
- ❑3, Feb 00 ... 2.95
- ❑4, Mar 00 ... 2.95

ALIENS: WRAITH
DARK HORSE

Value: Cover or less

- ❑1, Jul 98, nn; One-Shot 2.95

ALIENS: XENOGENESIS
DARK HORSE

Value: Cover or less

- ❑1, Aug 99 .... 2.95
- ❑2, Sep 99 .... 2.95
- ❑3 .... 2.95
- ❑4 .... 2.95

ALIEN: THE ILLUSTRATED STORY
HM COMMUNICATIONS

Issue	ORIG	GOOD	FINE	N-MINT
❑1	3.95	0.80	2.00	4.00

ALIEN WORLDS
PACIFIC

Issue	ORIG	GOOD	FINE	N-MINT
❑1, Dec 82, VM; NR; AW, The Few...The Far; Domain	1.50	0.50	1.25	2.50
❑2, May 83, Aurora; Vicious Circle	1.50	0.40	1.00	2.00
❑3, Jul 83, TY, The Inheritors; Pi in the Sky.	1.50	0.40	1.00	2.00
❑4, Sep 83, AW, Princess Pam; Girl of my Schemes	1.50	0.40	1.00	2.00
❑5, Lip Service; Game Wars	1.50	0.40	1.00	2.00
❑6, FB, Planet Perfict; The Test	1.50	0.40	1.00	2.00
❑7, The Small World of Lewis Stillman; Small Change	1.50	0.40	1.00	2.00
❑8, AW, ...And Miles To Go Before I Sleep; Soft Boiled, Eclipse Comics begins as publisher	1.50	0.40	1.00	2.00
❑9, FB, Final Issue	1.50	0.40	1.00	2.00
❑3D 1, Fair Play; Field Drill, Full-size issues begin	3.00	0.40	1.00	2.00

ALIEN WORLDS (BLACKTHORNE)
BLACKTHORNE

Value: Cover or less

- ❑1, b&w 5.95

ALISON DARE, LITTLE MISS ADVENTURES
ONI

Value: Cover or less

- ❑1, Sep 00, What I Did on My Summer Vacation or Tomb Raider, Too, b&w 4.50

ALISTER THE SLAYER
MIDNIGHT PRESS

Value: Cover or less

- ❑1, Oct 95 .... 2.50

ALIZARIN'S JOURNAL
AVATAR

Value: Cover or less

- ❑1, Mar 99, b&w 3.50

ALLAGASH INCIDENT, THE
TUNDRA

Value: Cover or less

- ❑1, Jul 93 .... 2.95

ALL-AMERICAN COMICS (2ND SERIES)
DC

Issue	ORIG	GOOD	FINE	N-MINT
❑1, May 99, Cold Heart, A: Green Lantern; A: Johnny Thunder	1.99	0.40	1.00	2.00

ALLEGRA
IMAGE

Issue	ORIG	GOOD	FINE	N-MINT
❑1, Aug 96, 1: Allegra	2.50	0.50	1.25	2.50
❑1/SC, Aug 96, foil cover	—	0.50	1.25	2.50
❑2, Sep 96	2.50	0.50	1.25	2.50
❑3, Nov 96	2.50	0.50	1.25	2.50
❑4, Dec 96	2.50	0.50	1.25	2.50

ALLEY CAT
IMAGE

Issue	ORIG	GOOD	FINE	N-MINT
❑1, Jul 99, Photo cover	2.50	0.50	1.25	2.50
❑1/A, school girl cover; Another Universe Edition	—	0.85	2.13	4.25
❑1/B, Wizard World Edition; reclining with claws extended	—	0.50	1.25	2.50
❑2, Aug 99	2.50	0.50	1.25	2.50
❑2/A, Aug 99, Monster Mart Edition; in red dress with stake in hand	3.00	0.60	1.50	3.00
❑3, Sep 99, in front of grave	2.50	0.50	1.25	2.50
❑3/A, Sep 99, Dorian cover	2.50	0.50	1.25	2.50
❑4, Oct 99, The Martyr, Part 1	2.50	0.50	1.25	2.50
❑5, Feb 00, The Martyr, Part 2, Photo cover	2.50	0.50	1.25	2.50
❑6, Feb 00, The Martyr, Part 3, Photo cover; with headdress	2.95	0.59	1.48	2.95
❑Ash 1, May 99, Photo cover; Limited Preview Edition on cover; holding arms over head	—	0.50	1.25	2.50
❑ASH 1/A, Photo cover; Dynamic Forces edition	—	1.00	2.50	5.00
❑ASH 1/B, Photo cover; Dynamic Forces edition; front shot; Wizard World logo at bottom right	—	0.60	1.50	3.00
❑ASH 1/C, sketch cover; Dynamic Forces edition	—	0.80	2.00	4.00
❑ASH 1/D, drawn color cover; Dynamic Forces edition; kneeling on rooftop	—	0.80	2.00	4.00

ALLEY CAT LINGERIE EDITION
IMAGE

Value: Cover or less

- ❑1, Oct 99, cardstock cover; photos and pin-ups 4.95

ALLEY OOP (DRAGON LADY)
DRAGON LADY

Value: Cover or less

- ❑1, O: Oop, Dinny 5.95
- ❑2, time machine 6.95
- ❑3, Hercules 7.95

ALLEY OOP ADVENTURES
ANTARCTIC

Value: Cover or less

- ❑1, Aug 98 .... 2.95
- ❑2, Oct 98 .... 2.95
- ❑3, Dec 98, Oop the Mighty!; Dinny and the Dinky Dino 2.95

ALLEY OOP QUARTERLY
ANTARCTIC

Value: Cover or less

- ❑1, Sep 99, Alley Oop's Survival Guide 2.50
- ❑2, Dec 99 .... 2.95
- ❑3, Mar 00 .... 2.95

ALL GIRLS SCHOOL MEETS ALL BOYS SCHOOL
ANGEL

Value: Cover or less

- ❑1, Dance of the Frustrated 3.00

ALL HALLOW'S EVE
INNOVATION

Value: Cover or less

- ❑1 .... 4.95

ALLIANCE, THE
IMAGE

Value: Cover or less

- ❑1, Aug 95, A Call to Arms 2.50
- ❑1/A, Aug 95, A Call to Arms, variant cover 2.50
- ❑2, Sep 95 .... 2.50
- ❑2/A, Sep 95, variant cover 2.50
- ❑3, Nov 95 .... 2.50
- ❑3/A, Nov 95, variant cover 2.50

ALL NEW ADVENTURES OF THE MIGHTY CRUSADERS
ARCHIE

Value: Cover or less

- ❑1, Mar 83, RB, RB (w), Atlantis Rising 1.00
- ❑2, May 83, RB, RB (w) 1.00
- ❑3, Jul 83, RB, RB (w), The Darkling Ingredient 1.00
- ❑4, RB, RB (w) 1.00

ALL NEW COLLECTORS' EDITION
DC

Issue	ORIG	GOOD	FINE	N-MINT
❑53, Dec 77, C-53	2.00	5.00	12.50	25.00
❑54, Jan 78, Superman vs. Wonder Woman, C-54	2.00	2.00	5.00	10.00
❑55, Feb 78, MGr, The Millennium Massacre, C-55; Legion; Wedding of Lightning Lad and Saturn Girl	2.00	3.00	7.50	15.00
❑56, Apr 78, NA, NA (w), Superman vs. Muhammad Ali, C-56	2.00	4.00	10.00	20.00
❑57, May 78, C-57	2.00	2.00	5.00	10.00
❑58, Jun 78, DG; RB, When Earths Collide, C-58; Superman vs. Shazam	2.00	2.00	5.00	10.00
❑60, Rudolph's Summer Fun, C-60	2.00	4.00	10.00	20.00
❑61, C-61	2.50	2.00	5.00	10.00
❑62, Mar 79, C-62	2.50	2.00	5.00	10.00

ALL NEW EXILES, THE
MALIBU

Value: Cover or less

- ❑0, Sep 95, "Black September"; Number infinity 1.50
- ❑0/SC, Sep 95, alternate cover; "Black September"; Number infinity 1.50
- ❑1, Oct 95 .... 1.50
- ❑2, Nov 95 .... 1.50
- ❑3, Dec 95 .... 1.50
- ❑4, Jan 96, V: UltraForce 1.50
- ❑5, Feb 96 .... 2.50
- ❑6, Mar 96 .... 1.50
- ❑7, Apr 96 .... 1.50
- ❑8, May 96 .... 1.50
- ❑10, Jul 96, V: Aladdin 1.50
- ❑11, Aug 96, V: Maxis, Final Issue; continues in UltraForce #12 .... 1.50

ALL NEW UNDERGROUND COMIX
LAST GASP

Issue	ORIG	GOOD	FINE	N-MINT
❑1	0.50	1.00	2.50	5.00
❑2	0.50	0.60	1.50	3.00
❑3	0.50	0.60	1.50	3.00

ALL-OUT WAR
DC

Issue	ORIG	GOOD	FINE	N-MINT
❑1, GE, The Viking Commando; Brother With Wings, O: Viking Commando	1.00	0.60	1.50	3.00
❑2	1.00	0.50	1.25	2.50
❑3	1.00	0.50	1.25	2.50
❑4, Apr 80, Execution on Demand; Death Comes in Threes	1.00	0.50	1.25	2.50
❑5, Jun 80	1.00	0.50	1.25	2.50
❑6, Aug 80, War Without a Name; Brothers on a Bulls-Eye	1.00	0.50	1.25	2.50

ALL SHOOK UP
RIP OFF

Value: Cover or less

- ❑1, Jun 90, nn; b&w; earthquake 3.50

ALL-STAR COMICS
DC

Issue	ORIG	GOOD	FINE	N-MINT
❑58, Feb 76, RE; WW, All Star Super Squad, 1: Power Girl, Power Girl joins team; regrouping of JSA; Series begins again after hiatus (1976)	0.25	0.80	2.00	4.00
❑59, Apr 76, V: Brainwave, Per Degaton	0.25	0.60	1.50	3.00
❑60, Jun 76, WW; KG, V: Vulcan	0.30	0.60	1.50	3.00

	ORIG	GOOD	FINE	N-MINT
❑61, Aug 76, WW; KG, V: Vulcan, Bicentennial #17	0.30	0.60	1.50	3.00
❑62, Oct 76, WW; KG, When Fall The Mighty, V: Zanadu; A: E-2 Superman	0.30	0.50	1.25	2.50
❑63, Dec 76, WW; KG, V: Injustice Gang, Solomon Grundy	0.30	0.50	1.25	2.50
❑64, Feb 77, WW, V: Vandal Savage; A: Shining Knight	0.30	0.50	1.25	2.50
❑65, Apr 77, WW, V: Vandal Savage	0.30	0.50	1.25	2.50
❑66, Jun 77, JSa; BL, V: Icicle, Wizard, Thinker	0.30	0.50	1.25	2.50
❑67, Aug 77, JSa; BL	0.35	0.50	1.25	2.50
❑68, Oct 77, JSa; BL, V: Psycho Pirate	0.35	0.50	1.25	2.50
❑69, Dec 77, JSa; BL, 1: The Huntress II (Helena Wayne), Original JSA vs. New JSA	0.35	0.70	1.75	3.50
❑70, Feb 78, JSa; BL, Huntress	0.35	0.50	1.25	2.50
❑71, Apr 78, JSa; BL	0.35	0.50	1.25	2.50
❑72, Jun 78, V: Thorn, Sportsmaster, original Huntress	0.35	0.50	1.25	2.50
❑73, Aug 78, JSa, V: Thorn, Sportsmaster, original Huntress	0.35	0.50	1.25	2.50
❑74, Oct 78, JSa, V: Master Summoner, Final Issue	0.50	0.50	1.25	2.50

ALL STAR COMICS (2ND SERIES)
DC

Value: Cover or less

❑1, May 99, JRo (w), Justice Society Returns; Time's Keeper. 2.95

❑2, May 99, JRo (w), Justice Society Returns; Time's Arrow... 2.95

❑GS 1, Sep 99, JRo (w), The Mighty Atom: Steam Engine; The Spectre & Starman:, 80pgs. 4.95

ALL-STAR INDEX, THE
ECLIPSE

Value: Cover or less

❑1, Feb 87, background on members of the JSA and first four issues of All-Star Comics (1st series) and DC Special #29 2.00

ALL-STAR SQUADRON
DC

	ORIG	GOOD	FINE	N-MINT
❑1, Sep 81, RB, The World on Fire!, 1: Danette Reilly (later Firebrand II)	0.50	0.50	1.25	2.50
❑2, Oct 81, JOy; RB	0.60	0.40	1.00	2.00
❑3, Nov 81, JOy; RB, The Dooms of Dark December!	0.60	0.40	1.00	2.00
❑4, Dec 81, JOy; RB, 1: Dragon King	0.60	0.30	0.75	1.50
❑5, Jan 82, JOy; RB, Never Step On A Feathered Serpent, 1: Firebrand II (Danette Reilly)	0.60	0.30	0.75	1.50
❑6, Feb 82	0.60	0.30	0.75	1.50
❑7, Mar 82, JKu	0.60	0.30	0.75	1.50
❑8, Apr 82, V: Kung; O: Steel	0.60	0.30	0.75	1.50
❑9, May 82, JKu, O: Baron Blitzkrieg	0.60	0.30	0.75	1.50
❑10, Jun 82, JKu	0.60	0.30	0.75	1.50
❑11, Jul 82, JKu	0.60	0.25	0.63	1.25
❑12, Aug 82, JKu, V: Hastor	0.60	0.25	0.63	1.25
❑13, Sep 82, JKu	0.60	0.25	0.63	1.25
❑14, Oct 82, JKu, Crisis on Earth-Prime, Part 2	0.60	0.25	0.63	1.25
❑15, Nov 82, JKu, Crisis on Earth-Prime, Part 4	0.60	0.25	0.63	1.25
❑16, Dec 82, JKu, V: Nuclear	0.60	0.25	0.63	1.25
❑17, Jan 83, JKu, Trial of Robotman	0.60	0.25	0.63	1.25
❑18, Feb 83, JKu, V: Villain from Valhalla	0.60	0.25	0.63	1.25
❑19, Mar 83, V: Brainwave	0.60	0.25	0.63	1.25
❑20, Apr 83, V: Brainwave	0.60	0.25	0.63	1.25
❑21, May 83, V: Cyclotron; 1: Deathbolt	0.60	0.25	0.63	1.25
❑22, Jun 83	0.60	0.25	0.63	1.25
❑23, Jul 83, 1: Amazing Man	0.60	0.25	0.63	1.25
❑24, Aug 83, 1: Brainwave Jr.; 1: Infinity Inc.	0.60	0.25	0.63	1.25
❑25, Sep 83, A: Infinity Inc.	0.60	0.25	0.63	1.25
❑26, Oct 83, A: Infinity Inc.	0.60	0.20	0.50	1.00
❑27, Nov 83, A: Spectre	0.60	0.20	0.50	1.00
❑28, Dec 83, A: Spectre	0.75	0.20	0.50	1.00
❑29, Jan 84, A: Seven Soldiers of Victory	0.75	0.20	0.50	1.00
❑30, Feb 84, V: Black Dragon Society	0.75	0.20	0.50	1.00
❑31, Mar 84, A: Uncle Sam	0.75	0.20	0.50	1.00
❑32, Apr 84	0.75	0.20	0.50	1.00
❑33, May 84, O: Freedom Fighters	0.75	0.20	0.50	1.00
❑34, Jun 84, V: Tsunami	0.75	0.20	0.50	1.00
❑35, Jul 84, D: Red Bee, Hourman vs. Baron Blitzkrieg	0.75	0.20	0.50	1.00
❑36, Aug 84, A: Captain Marvel	0.75	0.20	0.50	1.00
❑37, Sep 84, A: Marvel Family	0.75	0.20	0.50	1.00
❑38, Oct 84, A: Amazing Man	0.75	0.20	0.50	1.00
❑39, Nov 84, A: Amazing Man, Junior JSA kit repro	0.75	0.20	0.50	1.00
❑40, Dec 84, A: Monitor, Amazing Man vs. Real American	0.75	0.20	0.50	1.00
❑41, Jan 85, O: Starman	0.75	0.20	0.50	1.00

Dark Horse pitted three of its licensed properties against each other in the four-issue *Aliens vs. Predator vs. The Terminator.*

© 2000 Twentieth Century Fox Film Corporation (Dark Horse)

	ORIG	GOOD	FINE	N-MINT
❑42, Feb 85	0.75	0.20	0.50	1.00
❑43, Mar 85	0.75	0.20	0.50	1.00
❑44, Apr 85, V: Night and Fog	0.75	0.20	0.50	1.00
❑45, May 85, 1: Zyklon	0.75	0.20	0.50	1.00
❑46, Jun 85, Liberty Belle gets new powers	0.75	0.20	0.50	1.00
❑47, Jul 85, TMc, O: Doctor Fate	0.75	0.60	1.50	3.00
❑48, Aug 85, A: Shining Knight, Blackhawk	0.75	0.20	0.50	1.00
❑49, Sep 85, A: Doctor Occult	0.75	0.20	0.50	1.00
❑50, Oct 85, Crisis on Infinite Earths, A: Harbinger, Double-size issue; Mr. Mind to Earth-2; Crisis; Uncle Sam and others to Earth-X; Steel to Earth-1	0.75	0.25	0.63	1.25
❑51, Nov 85, Crisis on Infinite Earths, V: Monster Society of Evil (Oom, Mr. Who, Ramulus, Nyola, Mr. Mind)	0.75	0.20	0.50	1.00
❑52, Dec 85, A: Captain Marvel, Crisis	0.75	0.20	0.50	1.00
❑53, Jan 86, Superman vs. Monster Society; Crisis	0.75	0.20	0.50	1.00
❑54, Feb 86, V: Monster Society, Crisis	0.75	0.20	0.50	1.00
❑55, Mar 86, V: Ultra-Humanite in 1980s, Crisis	0.75	0.20	0.50	1.00
❑56, Apr 86, A: Seven Soldiers of Victory, Crisis	0.75	0.20	0.50	1.00
❑57, May 86, Crisis	0.75	0.20	0.50	1.00
❑58, Jun 86, A: Mekanique	0.75	0.20	0.50	1.00
❑59, Jul 86, 1: Aquaman in All-Star Squadron	0.75	0.20	0.50	1.00
❑60, Aug 86, The End of the Beginning, events of Crisis catch up with All-Star Squadron	0.75	0.20	0.50	1.00
❑61, Sep 86, O: Liberty Belle	0.75	0.20	0.50	1.00
❑62, Oct 86, O: Shining Knight	0.75	0.20	0.50	1.00
❑63, Nov 86, O: Robotman	0.75	0.20	0.50	1.00
❑64, Dec 86, retells Golden Age Superman story post-Crisis	0.75	0.20	0.50	1.00
❑65, Jan 87, O: Johnny Quick	0.75	0.20	0.50	1.00
❑66, Feb 87, O: Tarantula	0.75	0.20	0.50	1.00
❑67, Mar 87, Final Issue; final issue: JSA's first case	0.75	0.20	0.50	1.00
❑Anl 1, Nov 82, JOy, O: Atom, Wildcat, Guardian	1.00	0.25	0.63	1.25
❑Anl 2, Nov 83, JOy, The Ultra War; Divide For Conquest, A: Infinity Inc.; D: Cyclotron	1.00	0.25	0.63	1.25
❑Anl 3, Sep 84, GP; JOy; KG; DN, V: Ian Karkull	1.25	0.25	0.63	1.25

ALL-STAR WESTERN (2ND SERIES)
DC

	ORIG	GOOD	FINE	N-MINT
❑1, Sep 70, CI, Gun Duel at Copper Creek!; The Return of the Fadeaway Outlaw!, A: Pow-Wow Smith	0.15	5.00	12.50	25.00
❑2, Nov 70	0.15	2.00	5.00	10.00
❑3, Jan 71	0.15	2.00	5.00	10.00
❑4, Mar 71	0.15	1.60	4.00	8.00
❑5, May 71, JA; DG, Outlaw: Hangman Never Loses!; El Diablo: The Devil Rides for Vengeance!	0.15	1.60	4.00	8.00
❑6, Jul 71	0.15	1.20	3.00	6.00
❑7, Sep 71	0.25	1.20	3.00	6.00
❑8, Nov 71	0.25	1.20	3.00	6.00
❑9, Jan 72	0.25	1.20	3.00	6.00
❑10, Mar 72, NC; TD; GM, SA (w), Jonah Hex: Welcome to Paradise; El Diablo: The Devil's Secret, 1: Jonah Hex	0.25	27.00	67.50	135.00
❑11, May 72, NC; GM, Jonah Hex: The Hundred Dollar Deal!; El Diablo: Satan's Sanctuary, 2: Jonah Hex, Giant-size; Series continues as Weird Western Tales	0.25	18.00	45.00	90.00

ALL SUSPENSE
AVALON

Value: Cover or less

❑1, 98, The Ghost Who Loved a Girl!; Don't Let the Ghost Take Shape!, b&w; reprints Nemesis and Mark Midnight stories ... 2.95

ALL THE RULES HAVE CHANGED
RIP OFF

Value: Cover or less

❑1 9.95

ALL-THRILL COMICS
MANSION

Value: Cover or less

	ORIG	GOOD	FINE	N-MINT
❑845, Actually #1	2.95			

ALLY
ALLY-WINSOR

Value: Cover or less

	ORIG	GOOD	FINE	N-MINT
❑1, Fal 95, 1: Ally, b&w	2.95			
❑2	2.95			
❑3, Payback, Flip-book	2.95			

ALMURIC
DARK HORSE

Value: Cover or less

	ORIG	GOOD	FINE	N-MINT
❑1, Feb 91, nn	10.95			

ALONE IN THE SHADE SPECIAL
ALCHEMY

Value: Cover or less

	ORIG	GOOD	FINE	N-MINT
❑1, nn; b&w	2.00			

ALPHABET
DARK VISIONS

Value: Cover or less

	ORIG	GOOD	FINE	N-MINT
❑1, Dec 93, Eidolon: Unliving Hell, Part 1; The Enforcers	2.50			

ALPHA CENTURION SPECIAL
DC

Value: Cover or less

	ORIG	GOOD	FINE	N-MINT
❑1, Protector of Earth?, O: Alpha Centurion, One-Shot	2.95			

ALPHA FLIGHT
MARVEL

	ORIG	GOOD	FINE	N-MINT
❑1, Aug 83, JBy, JBy (w), Tundra!, 1: Puck, Marina; 1: Diamond Lil (not identified); 1: Wildheart (not identified)\, 2pgs.	1.00	0.50	1.25	2.50
❑2, Sep 83, JBy, JBy (w), Shadows Of The Past, 1: Guardian I (James Hudson); O: Alpha Flight; 1: The Master; O: Marina, Vindicator becomes Guardian I	0.60	0.35	0.88	1.75
❑3, Oct 83, JBy, JBy (w), Yesterday Man, O: Alpha Flight; O: The Master; O: Marina	0.60	0.35	0.88	1.75
❑4, Nov 83, JBy, JBy (w), O: Marina	0.60	0.35	0.88	1.75
❑5, Dec 83, JBy, JBy (w), What Fools These Mortals Be, 1: Elizabeth Twoyoungmen	0.60	0.35	0.88	1.75
❑6, Jan 84, JBy, JBy (w), Snowblind, O: Shaman, all-white issue	0.60	0.35	0.88	1.75
❑7, Feb 84, JBy, JBy (w), The Importance Of Being Deadly, O: Snowbird	0.60	0.35	0.88	1.75
❑8, Mar 84, JBy, JBy (w), Cold Hands Cold Heart	0.60	0.35	0.88	1.75
❑9, Apr 84, JBy, JBy (w), Things Aren't Always What They Seem, A: Thing; O: Aurora	0.60	0.35	0.88	1.75
❑10, May 84, JBy, JBy (w), Blood Battle, O: Sasquatch; O: Northstar	0.60	0.35	0.88	1.75
❑11, Jun 84, JBy, JBy (w), Set-Up, O: Sasquatch; 1: Diamond Lil (identified); 1: Wild Child	0.60	0.35	0.88	1.75
❑12, Jul 84, JBy, JBy (w), And One Shall Surely Die, D: Guardian, Double-size	0.60	0.35	0.88	1.75
❑13, Aug 84, JBy, JBy (w), Nightmare!, A: Wolverine	0.60	0.50	1.25	2.50
❑14, Sep 84, JBy, JBy (w), Biology Class	0.60	0.30	0.75	1.50
❑15, Oct 84, JBy, JBy (w), Blind Date, A: Sub-Mariner	0.60	0.30	0.75	1.50
❑16, Nov 84, JBy, JBy (w), ...And Forsaking All The Others, A: Sub-Mariner, Wolverine cameo	0.60	0.30	0.75	1.50
❑17, Dec 84, JBy, JBy (w), Dreams Die Hard..., X-Men crossover; Wolverine cameo	0.60	0.40	1.00	2.00
❑18, Jan 85, JBy, JBy (w), How Long Will A Man Lie In The Earth 'Ere He Rot?	0.60	0.30	0.75	1.50
❑19, Feb 85, JBy, JBy (w), Turn Again, Turn Again, Time In Thy Flight..., 1: Talisman II (Elizabeth Twoyoungmen)	0.60	0.30	0.75	1.50
❑20, Mar 85, JBy, JBy (w), Gold And Love Affairs, New headquarters	0.60	0.30	0.75	1.50
❑21, Apr 85, JBy, JBy (w), Love Wrought New Alchemy..., V: Diablo	0.65	0.30	0.75	1.50
❑22, May 85, JBy, JBy (w), Rub-Out	0.65	0.30	0.75	1.50
❑23, Jun 85, JBy, JBy (w), Night Of The Beast	0.65	0.30	0.75	1.50
❑24, Jul 85, JBy, JBy (w), Final Conflict, Double-size	1.25	0.30	0.75	1.50
❑25, Aug 85, JBy, JBy (w)	0.65	0.30	0.75	1.50
❑26, Sep 85, JBy, JBy (w), If At First You Don't Succeed...	0.65	0.30	0.75	1.50
❑27, Oct 85, JBy, JBy (w), Betrayal	0.65	0.30	0.75	1.50
❑28, Nov 85, JBy, JBy (w), Secret Wars II, Secret Wars II; Last Byrne issue	0.65	0.30	0.75	1.50
❑29, Dec 85, A: Hulk	0.65	0.30	0.75	1.50
❑30, Jan 86, Enter...Scramble!	0.65	0.30	0.75	1.50
❑31, Feb 86, The Grateful Dead!	0.75	0.30	0.75	1.50
❑32, Mar 86, Short Story	0.75	0.30	0.75	1.50
❑33, Apr 86, SB, A Friend In Need, A: X-Men, Wolverine	0.75	0.40	1.00	2.00
❑34, May 86, SB, Honor, O: Wolverine, Wolverine	0.75	0.50	1.25	2.50
❑35, Jun 86, SB, Wolverine	0.75	0.30	0.75	1.50
❑36, Jul 86, SB, Wolverine	0.75	0.30	0.75	1.50
❑37, Aug 86, Death Birth, Wolverine	0.75	0.30	0.75	1.50
❑38, Sep 86, Wolverine	0.75	0.30	0.75	1.50
❑39, Oct 86, The Invasion Of Atlantis!, Wolverine	0.75	0.30	0.75	1.50
❑40, Nov 86, Wolverine	0.75	0.30	0.75	1.50
❑41, Dec 86, Wolverine	0.75	0.30	0.75	1.50
❑42, Jan 87, Wolverine	0.75	0.30	0.75	1.50
❑43, Feb 87, Wolverine	0.75	0.30	0.75	1.50
❑44, Mar 87, D: Snowbird, Wolverine	0.75	0.30	0.75	1.50
❑45, Apr 87, Wolverine	0.75	0.30	0.75	1.50
❑46, May 87, Wolverine	0.75	0.30	0.75	1.50
❑47, Jun 87, Wolverine	0.75	0.30	0.75	1.50
❑48, Jul 87, Wolverine	0.75	0.30	0.75	1.50
❑49, Aug 87, Wolverine	0.75	0.30	0.75	1.50
❑50, Sep 87	1.25	0.30	0.75	1.50
❑51, Oct 87, JLee, A: Wolverine, 1st Jim Lee work at Marvel	0.75	0.50	1.25	2.50
❑52, Nov 87, A: Wolverine	1.00	0.40	1.00	2.00
❑53, Dec 87, A: Wolverine; 1: Laura Dean	1.00	0.40	1.00	2.00
❑54, Jan 88, O: Laura Dean	1.00	0.30	0.75	1.50
❑55, Feb 88, JLee	1.00	0.30	0.75	1.50
❑56, Mar 88, JLee, 1: The Dreamqueen	1.00	0.30	0.75	1.50
❑57, Apr 88, JLee	1.00	0.30	0.75	1.50
❑58, May 88, JLee	1.00	0.30	0.75	1.50
❑59, Jun 88, JLee	1.00	0.30	0.75	1.50
❑60, Jul 88, JLee	1.25	0.30	0.75	1.50
❑61, Aug 88, JLee	1.25	0.30	0.75	1.50
❑62, Sep 88, JLee	1.25	0.30	0.75	1.50
❑63, Oct 88	1.25	0.25	0.63	1.25
❑64, Nov 88	1.25	0.25	0.63	1.25
❑65, Dec 88	1.50	0.25	0.63	1.25
❑66, Jan 89	1.50	0.25	0.63	1.25
❑67, Feb 89, Wrath of the Dream Queen, Part 1, O: The Dream Queen	1.50	0.25	0.63	1.25
❑68, Mar 89, Wrath of the Dream Queen, Part 2	1.50	0.25	0.63	1.25
❑69, Apr 89, Wrath of the Dream Queen, Part 3	1.50	0.25	0.63	1.25
❑70, May 89, Wrath of the Dream Queen, Part 4	1.50	0.25	0.63	1.25
❑71, Jun 89, 1: Llan the Sorcerer	1.50	0.25	0.63	1.25
❑72, Jul 89	1.50	0.25	0.63	1.25
❑73, Aug 89	1.50	0.25	0.63	1.25
❑74, Sep 89	1.50	0.25	0.63	1.25
❑75, Oct 89, Double-size	1.95	0.45	1.13	2.25
❑76, Nov 89	1.50	0.30	0.75	1.50
❑77, Nov 89	1.95	0.30	0.75	1.50
❑78, Dec 89	1.50	0.30	0.75	1.50
❑79, Dec 89, Acts of Vengeance, Acts of Vengeance	1.50	0.30	0.75	1.50
❑80, Jan 90, Acts of Vengeance, Acts of Vengeance	1.50	0.30	0.75	1.50
❑81, Feb 90, Quest for Northstar, Part 1	1.50	0.30	0.75	1.50
❑82, Mar 90, Quest for Northstar, Part 2	1.50	0.30	0.75	1.50
❑83, Apr 90, O: Talisman II (Elizabeth Twoyoungmen)	1.50	0.30	0.75	1.50
❑84, May 90	1.50	0.30	0.75	1.50
❑85, Jun 90	1.50	0.30	0.75	1.50
❑86, Jul 90	1.50	0.30	0.75	1.50
❑87, Aug 90, 1: Windshear, Wolverine	1.50	0.40	1.00	2.00
❑88, Sep 90, Wolverine; Guardian I reappears as cyborg	1.50	0.40	1.00	2.00
❑89, Oct 90, Wolverine; Guardian returns	1.50	0.40	1.00	2.00
❑90, Nov 90	1.50	0.40	1.00	2.00
❑91, Dec 90, Doctor Doom	1.50	0.35	0.88	1.75
❑92, Jan 91, Compromising Positions	1.50	0.35	0.88	1.75
❑93, Feb 91	1.50	0.35	0.88	1.75
❑94, Mar 91, Fantastic 4	1.50	0.35	0.88	1.75
❑95, Apr 91	1.50	0.35	0.88	1.75
❑96, May 91	1.50	0.35	0.88	1.75
❑97, Jun 91, The Final Option, Part 1	1.50	0.35	0.88	1.75
❑98, Jul 91, The Final Option, Part 2	1.50	0.35	0.88	1.75
❑99, Aug 91, The Final Option, Part 3	1.50	0.35	0.88	1.75
❑100, Sep 91, The Final Option, Part 4, A: Avengers; A: Galactus, 52pgs.	2.00	0.35	0.88	1.75
❑101, Oct 91	1.50	0.35	0.88	1.75
❑102, Nov 91, 1: Weapon Omega	1.50	0.35	0.88	1.75
❑103, Dec 91	1.50	0.35	0.88	1.75
❑104, Jan 92	1.50	0.35	0.88	1.75
❑105, Feb 92, The Bachelor Party	1.75	0.35	0.88	1.75
❑106, Mar 92, The Walking Wounded, 1st Printing; Northstar admits he's gay	1.75	0.40	1.00	2.00
❑106-2, Mar 92, 2nd Printing; Northstar admits he's gay	1.75	0.35	0.88	1.75
❑107, Apr 92, A: X-Factor	1.75	0.35	0.88	1.75
❑108, May 92, The Global Village	1.75	0.35	0.88	1.75
❑109, Jun 92, By Right Of Memory	1.75	0.35	0.88	1.75
❑110, Jul 92	1.75	0.35	0.88	1.75

	ORIG	GOOD	FINE	N-MINT
❑111, Aug 92	1.75	0.35	0.88	1.75
❑112, Sep 92, Infinity War	1.75	0.35	0.88	1.75
❑113, Oct 92, Speaking Of Experience	1.75	0.35	0.88	1.75
❑114, Nov 92	1.75	0.35	0.88	1.75
❑115, Dec 92, Extreme Prejudice, Part 1, 1: Wyre	1.75	0.35	0.88	1.75
❑116, Jan 93, PB, Extreme Prejudice, Part 2	1.75	0.35	0.88	1.75
❑117, Feb 93, PB, Extreme Prejudice, Part 3	1.75	0.35	0.88	1.75
❑118, Mar 93, PB, The Clampdown, Part 1, 1: Wildheart	1.75	0.35	0.88	1.75
❑119, Apr 93, PB, The Clampdown, Part 2, V: Wrecking Crew	1.75	0.35	0.88	1.75
❑120, May 93, PB, The Clampdown, Part 3, Mutant Registration Act poster; with poster	2.25	0.45	1.13	2.25
❑121, Jun 93, A: Spider-Man	1.75	0.35	0.88	1.75
❑122, Jul 93, PB, The Holy Terror, Part 1; Puck: Brothers in Arms, Part 1	1.75	0.35	0.88	1.75
❑123, Aug 93, PB, The Holy Terror, Part 2; Puck: Brothers in Arms, Part 2	1.75	0.35	0.88	1.75
❑124, Sep 93, PB, The Holy Terror, Part 3, Infinity Crusade	1.75	0.35	0.88	1.75
❑125, Oct 93, PB, A: Box; A: Diamond Lil; A: Nemesis; A: Shaman; A: Wyre, Infinity Crusade crossover	1.75	0.35	0.88	1.75
❑126, Nov 93	1.75	0.35	0.88	1.75
❑127, Dec 93	1.75	0.35	0.88	1.75
❑128, Jan 94, No Future, Part 1	1.75	0.35	0.88	1.75
❑129, Feb 94, No Future, Part 2	1.75	0.35	0.88	1.75
❑130, Mar 94, No Future, Part 3, Final Issue	2.25	0.45	1.13	2.25
❑Anl 1, Sep 86	1.25	0.30	0.75	1.50
❑Anl 2, Dec 87	1.25	0.25	0.63	1.25
❑SE 1, Jun 92, Decisions Of Strength, A: Wolverine, No number on cover	2.50	0.59	1.48	2.95

ALPHA FLIGHT (VOL. 2)
MARVEL

Value: Cover or less

- ❑-1, Jul 97, Wedding of James Hudson and Heather McNeil; "Flashback" 1.99
- ❑1, Aug 97, Horoscope, wrap-around cover; gatefold summary 2.99
- ❑2, Sep 97, The Fighting Masters, "Presenting: The Master of Chaos" on cover; gatefold summary 1.99
- ❑2/A, Sep 97, The Fighting Masters, alternate cover; gatefold summary 1.99
- ❑3, Oct 97, gatefold summary 1.99
- ❑4, Nov 97, gatefold summary 1.99
- ❑5, Dec 97, gatefold summary 1.99
- ❑6, Jan 98, O: Sasquatch; A: Diamond Lil, Northstar, gatefold summary 1.99
- ❑7, Feb 98, gatefold summary 1.99
- ❑8, Mar 98, gatefold summary 1.99
- ❑9, Apr 98, V: Wolverine, gatefold summary 1.99
- ❑10, May 98, gatefold summary 1.99
- ❑11, Jun 98, gatefold summary 1.99
- ❑12, Jul 98, D: Sasquatch, gatefold summary 2.99
- ❑13, Aug 98, gatefold summary 1.99
- ❑14, Sep 98, gatefold summary 1.99
- ❑15, Oct 98, gatefold summary 1.99
- ❑16, Nov 98, gatefold summary 1.99
- ❑17, Dec 98, gatefold summary 1.99
- ❑18, Jan 99, Alpha: Omega, Part 1, gatefold summary 1.99
- ❑19, Alpha: Omega, Part 2, A: Old Alpha Flight team 1.99
- ❑20, Alpha: Omega, Part 3, A: Weapon X; A: Old Alpha Flight team, Final Issue 1.99
- ❑Anl 1998, wraparound cover; Alpha Flight/Inhumans '98 3.50

ALPHA FLIGHT SPECIAL
MARVEL

	ORIG	GOOD	FINE	N-MINT
❑1, Jul 91, The Final Option; Decisions of Faith, Reprints Alpha Flight #97	1.50	0.40	1.00	2.00
❑2, Aug 91, Reprints Alpha Flight #98	1.50	0.40	1.00	2.00
❑3, Sep 91, Reprints Alpha Flight #99	1.50	0.40	1.00	2.00
❑4, Oct 91, Reprints Alpha Flight #100	2.00	0.40	1.00	2.00

ALPHA ILLUSTRATED
ALPHA PRODUCTIONS

	ORIG	GOOD	FINE	N-MINT
❑0, Apr 94, b&w; free; Preview	—	0.20	0.50	1.00
❑1, Time Travel Means Never Having to Say You're Sorry, Black Icon, Work in Progress, Arena, Only friends The Lone Star Tapes, b&w	3.50	0.70	1.75	3.50

ALPHA KORPS
DIVERSITY

	ORIG	GOOD	FINE	N-MINT
❑1, Sep 96	2.50	0.50	1.25	2.50
❑Ash 1, The Price of Freedom Part 1, Preview issue	—	0.20	0.50	1.00

ALPHA TEAM OMEGA
FANTASY GRAPHICS

Value: Cover or less

- ❑1 1.25

ALPHA TRACK
FANTASY GENERAL

Value: Cover or less

- ❑1, Feb 85 1.75
- ❑2 1.75

ALPHA WAVE
DARKLINE

Value: Cover or less

- ❑1 1.75

ALTERED IMAGE
IMAGE

Value: Cover or less

- ❑1, Apr 98, The Day Reality Went Wild 2.50
- ❑2, Jun 98, Everybody Smoosh 2.50
- ❑3, Oct 98, Middle Age Crisis, cover says "Sep"; indicia says "Oct" 2.50

Northstar's sexual preference was revealed in *Alpha Flight* (Vol. 1) #106.

© 1992 Marvel

ALTER EGO
FIRST

	ORIG	GOOD	FINE	N-MINT
❑1, May 86, Alter Ego Lives!, 1: Alter Ego	1.25	0.30	0.75	1.50
❑2, Jul 86	1.25	0.30	0.75	1.50
❑3, Sep 86	1.25	0.30	0.75	1.50
❑4, Nov 86	1.25	0.30	0.75	1.50

ALTERNATE HEROES
PRELUDE

Value: Cover or less

- ❑1, Initiations, 1: The Crimehater; 1: The Solar Knight; 1: The Equalizer 1.95

ALTERNATING CRIMES
ALTERNATING CRIMES PUBLISHING

Value: Cover or less

- ❑1, Fal 96 2.95
- ❑2, Fal 97 3.25

ALTERNATIVE COMICS
REVOLUTIONARY

Value: Cover or less

- ❑1, Jan 94, Pearl Jam/Cure/REM 2.50

ALTERNITY
NAVIGATOR

	ORIG	GOOD	FINE	N-MINT
❑1, May 92	0.60	0.50	1.25	2.50

ALVAR MAYOR: DEATH AND SILVER
4WINDS

Value: Cover or less

- ❑1, b&w 8.98

ALVIN
DELL

	ORIG	GOOD	FINE	N-MINT
❑1, Oct 62, 12-021-212	0.12	7.00	17.50	35.00
❑2, Jan 63, 12-021-303	0.12	5.00	12.50	25.00
❑3, Apr 63, 12-021-306	0.12	3.60	9.00	18.00
❑4, Jul 63, 12-021-309	0.12	3.60	9.00	18.00
❑5, Oct 63, 12-021-312	0.12	3.60	9.00	18.00
❑6, Jan 64, 12-021-403	0.12	3.60	9.00	18.00
❑7, Apr 64, 12-021-406	0.12	3.60	9.00	18.00
❑8, Jul 64, 12-021-409	0.12	3.60	9.00	18.00
❑9, Oct 64, 12-021-412	0.12	3.60	9.00	18.00
❑10	0.12	3.60	9.00	18.00
❑11	0.12	2.80	7.00	14.00
❑12	0.12	2.80	7.00	14.00
❑13	0.12	2.80	7.00	14.00
❑14	0.12	2.80	7.00	14.00
❑15	0.12	2.80	7.00	14.00
❑16	0.12	2.80	7.00	14.00
❑17	0.12	2.80	7.00	14.00
❑18	0.12	2.80	7.00	14.00
❑19	0.12	2.80	7.00	14.00
❑20, Oct 69	0.15	2.80	7.00	14.00
❑21	0.15	2.00	5.00	10.00
❑22	0.15	2.00	5.00	10.00
❑23, Jan 72, 01-021-201	0.15	2.00	5.00	10.00
❑24, Apr 72, 01-021-204	0.15	2.00	5.00	10.00
❑25	—	2.00	5.00	10.00
❑26	—	2.00	5.00	10.00
❑27, Jul 73	0.20	2.00	5.00	10.00
❑28, Oct 73	0.20	2.00	5.00	10.00

ALVIN AND THE CHIPMUNKS
HARVEY

	ORIG	GOOD	FINE	N-MINT
❑1	1.25	0.30	0.75	1.50
❑2	1.50	0.30	0.75	1.50
❑3	1.50	0.30	0.75	1.50
❑4	1.50	0.30	0.75	1.50
❑5	1.50	0.30	0.75	1.50

AMANDA AND GUNN
IMAGE

Value: Cover or less

- ❑1, Apr 97, b&w 2.95
- ❑2, Jun 97, b&w 2.95
- ❑3, Aug 97, b&w 2.95
- ❑4, Oct 97, b&w 2.95

AMAZING ADULT FANTASY
MARVEL

	ORIG	GOOD	FINE	N-MINT
❑7, Dec 61, SD, SL (w), The Icy Fingers Of Fear, Series continued from Amazing Adventures #6	0.12	120.00	300.00	600.00
❑8, Jan 62, SD, SL (w)	0.12	95.00	237.50	475.00
❑9, Feb 62, SD, SL (w), The Terror of Tim Boo Ba	0.12	85.00	212.50	425.00

	ORIG	GOOD	FINE	N-MINT
❑10, Mar 62, SD, SL (w)	0.12	85.00	212.50	425.00
❑11, Apr 62, SD, SL (w), For The Rest Of Your Life; Secret Of The Universe	0.12	85.00	212.50	425.00
❑12, May 62, SD, SL (w)	0.12	85.00	212.50	425.00
❑13, Jun 62, SD, SL (w), The Unsuspected; Great Zeus	0.12	85.00	212.50	425.00
❑13-2, SD, SL (w), The Unsuspected; Great Zeus, 2nd Printing	0.12	0.40	1.00	2.00
❑14, Jul 62, SD, series continues as Amazing Fantasy; Professor X prototype; Series continued in Amazing Fantasy #15	0.12	105.00	262.50	525.00

AMAZING ADVENTURE
MARVEL

Value: Cover or less

❑1, Jul 88, Solo; Men of Peace, squarebound 4.95

AMAZING ADVENTURES (2ND SERIES)
MARVEL

	ORIG	GOOD	FINE	N-MINT
❑1, Jun 61, SD, SL (w), A: Doctor Droom	0.10	170.00	425.00	850.00
❑2, Jul 61, SD, SL (w), A: Doctor Droom	0.10	100.00	250.00	500.00
❑3, Aug 61, SD, SL (w), A: Doctor Droom	0.10	80.00	200.00	400.00
❑4, Sep 61, SD, SL (w), A: Doctor Droom	0.10	80.00	200.00	400.00
❑5, Oct 61, SD, SL (w), The Escape of...Monsteroso!; T.V. or...?, A: Doctor Droom	0.10	80.00	200.00	400.00
❑6, Nov 61, SD, SL (w), A: Doctor Droom, series continues as Amazing Adult Fantasy; Series continued in Amazing Adult Fantasy #7	0.10	80.00	200.00	400.00

AMAZING ADVENTURES (3RD SERIES)
MARVEL

	ORIG	GOOD	FINE	N-MINT
❑1, Aug 70, JK; JB, JK (w), The Inhumans; Then Came...The Black Widow, Inhumans	0.15	4.40	11.00	22.00
❑2, Sep 70	0.15	2.40	6.00	12.00
❑3, Nov 70, Black Widow; Inhumans	0.15	2.40	6.00	12.00
❑4, Jan 71, Black Widow; Inhumans	0.15	2.40	6.00	12.00
❑5, Mar 71, NA	0.15	2.40	6.00	12.00
❑6, May 71, NA; DH; SB, Hell on Earth!; Blood Will Tell!, Inhumans, Black Widow	0.15	1.80	4.50	9.00
❑7, Jul 71, NA, Inhumans, Black Widow	0.15	1.80	4.50	9.00
❑8, Sep 71, NA, Inhumans, Black Widow	0.15	1.80	4.50	9.00
❑9, Nov 71, A: Black Bolt	0.20	1.80	4.50	9.00
❑10, Jan 72	0.20	1.80	4.50	9.00
❑11, Mar 72, 1: Beast (in furry form)	0.20	7.00	17.50	35.00
❑12, May 72, A: Beast, Iron Man	0.20	2.00	5.00	10.00
❑13, Jul 72, 1: Robert "Buzz" Baxter	0.20	2.00	5.00	10.00
❑14, Sep 72	0.20	1.80	4.50	9.00
❑15, Nov 72, 1: Griffin	0.20	1.80	4.50	9.00
❑16, Jan 73	0.20	1.80	4.50	9.00
❑17, Mar 73	0.20	1.80	4.50	9.00
❑18, May 73, NA; HC, War of the Worlds, 1: Killraven	0.20	1.60	4.00	8.00
❑19, Jul 73, War of the Worlds, Killraven	0.20	0.60	1.50	3.00
❑20, Sep 73, HT, War of the Worlds; The Warlord Strikes!, Killraven	0.20	0.60	1.50	3.00
❑21, Nov 73, War of the Worlds, Killraven	0.20	0.60	1.50	3.00
❑22, Jan 74, War of the Worlds, Killraven	0.20	0.60	1.50	3.00
❑23, Mar 74, War of the Worlds, Killraven	0.20	0.60	1.50	3.00
❑24, May 74, HT, War of the Worlds; The Painting, V: High Overlord, Killraven; Marvel Value Stamp A/58 (The Mandarin)	0.25	0.60	1.50	3.00
❑25, Jul 74, War of the Worlds, V: Skar, Killraven	0.25	0.60	1.50	3.00
❑26, Sep 74, GC, War of the Worlds, Killraven	0.25	0.60	1.50	3.00
❑27, Nov 74, JSt; CR; JSn, War of the Worlds, O: Killraven, Killraven	0.25	0.60	1.50	3.00
❑28, Jan 75, CR, War of the Worlds, O: Volcana, Killraven	0.25	0.60	1.50	3.00
❑29, Mar 75, CR, War of the Worlds, Killraven	0.25	0.60	1.50	3.00
❑30, May 75, CR, War of the Worlds, Killraven	0.25	0.60	1.50	3.00
❑31, Jul 75, CR, War of the Worlds, Killraven	0.25	0.60	1.50	3.00
❑32, Sep 75, CR, Only The Computer Shows Me Respect!, Killraven	0.25	0.60	1.50	3.00
❑33, Nov 75, CR; HT, Sing Out Loudly...Death!, Killraven; Marvel Value Stamp A/52 (Quicksilver)	0.25	0.60	1.50	3.00
❑34, Jan 76, CR, A Death In The Family, D: Grok; D: Hawk, Killraven; Marvel Value Stamp B/10	0.25	0.60	1.50	3.00
❑35, Mar 76, JAb; CR; KG, The 24-Hour Man, Killraven	0.25	0.60	1.50	3.00
❑36, May 76, CR, Red Dust Legacy, Killraven	0.25	0.60	1.50	3.00
❑37, Jul 76, CR, Arena Kill!, O: Old Skull	0.25	0.60	1.50	3.00
❑38, Sep 76, CR; KG, Death's Dark Dreamer, Killraven	0.30	0.60	1.50	3.00
❑39, Nov 76, CR, Mourning Prey, Final Issue; Killraven	0.30	0.60	1.50	3.00

AMAZING ADVENTURES (4TH SERIES)
MARVEL

	ORIG	GOOD	FINE	N-MINT
❑1, Dec 79, JK, SL (w), X-Men, 1: the X-Men, Reprints first part of X-Men (1st Series) #1	0.40	0.50	1.25	2.50
❑2, Jan 80, JK, SL (w), When Mutants Clash, O: Cyclops, Reprints second half of X-Men (1st Series) #1; 2nd story reprinted from X-Men (1st Series) #39	0.40	0.35	0.88	1.75
❑3, Feb 80	0.40	0.35	0.88	1.75
❑4, Mar 80	0.40	0.35	0.88	1.75
❑5, Apr 80	0.40	0.35	0.88	1.75
❑6, May 80	0.40	0.35	0.88	1.75
❑7, Jun 80	0.40	0.35	0.88	1.75
❑8, Jul 80	0.40	0.35	0.88	1.75
❑9, Aug 80	0.40	0.35	0.88	1.75
❑10, Sep 80	—	0.35	0.88	1.75
❑11, Oct 80	0.50	0.35	0.88	1.75
❑12, Nov 80	0.50	0.35	0.88	1.75
❑13, Dec 80	0.50	0.35	0.88	1.75
❑14, Jan 81, Final Issue	0.50	0.35	0.88	1.75

AMAZING ADVENTURES OF ACE INTERNATIONAL, THE
STARHEAD

Value: Cover or less

❑1, Nov 93, b&w 2.95

AMAZING ADVENTURES OF FRANK AND JOLLY (ALAN GROENING'S...)
PRESS THIS

Value: Cover or less

❑1	1.75	❑6	1.75
❑2	1.75	❑7	1.75
❑3	1.75	❑8	1.75
❑4	1.75	❑9	1.75
❑5	1.75		

AMAZING ADVENTURES OF PROFESSOR JONES, THE
ANTARCTIC

Value: Cover or less

❑1, Nov 96	2.95	❑3	2.95
❑2, Dec 96	2.95	❑4	2.95

AMAZING COMICS PREMIERES
AMAZING

Value: Cover or less

❑1, Ninja Bots	1.95	❑4, Jul 87	1.95
❑2	1.95	❑5, Stargrazers	1.95
❑3, Shadowalker	1.95		

AMAZING CYNICALMAN, THE
ECLIPSE

	ORIG	GOOD	FINE	N-MINT
❑1, b&w	1.50	0.50	1.25	2.50

AMAZING FANTASY
MARVEL

	ORIG	GOOD	FINE	N-MINT
❑15, Aug 62, JK; SD, SL (w); SD (w), Spider-Man!, 1: Spider-Man	0.12	5600.00	14000.00	28000.00
❑16, Dec 95, KB (w), An Amazing World, cardstock cover; fills in gaps between Amazing Fantasy #15 and Amazing Spider-Man #1	3.95	0.90	2.25	4.50
❑17, Jan 96, KB (w), Amazing Adventures, cardstock cover	3.95	0.80	2.00	4.00
❑18, Mar 96, KB (w), The Amazing Spider-Man, cardstock cover; Final Issue	3.95	0.80	2.00	4.00

AMAZING HEROES SWIMSUIT SPECIAL
FANTAGRAPHICS

	ORIG	GOOD	FINE	N-MINT
❑4, Mar 93, published by Spoof Comics	3.95	0.79	1.98	3.95
❑5, Aug 93, published by Spoof Comics	4.95	0.99	2.47	4.95
❑Anl 1990, Jun 90	5.95	1.40	3.50	7.00
❑Anl 1991, Jun 91	6.95	2.00	5.00	10.00
❑Anl 1992, Jun 92	7.95	3.00	7.50	15.00

AMAZING HIGH ADVENTURE
MARVEL

Value: Cover or less

❑1, Aug 84, JSe, The Pike!; Gold	2.00	❑3, Oct 86	2.00
❑2, Sep 85, Too Long Last; The Conquest Of Kirurkan	2.00	❑4, Nov 86	2.00
		❑5, Dec 86	2.00

AMAZING SCARLET SPIDER, THE
MARVEL

	ORIG	GOOD	FINE	N-MINT
❑1, Nov 95, Virtual Mortality, Part 2	1.95	0.39	0.98	1.95
❑2, Dec 95, Cyberwar, Part 2, A: Green Goblin IV; A: Joystick	1.50	0.39	0.98	1.95
❑2/DM, Dec 95, Cyberwar, Part 2, Direct Edition	1.95	0.39	0.98	1.95

AMAZING SPIDER-MAN, THE
MARVEL

	ORIG	GOOD	FINE	N-MINT
❑-1, Jul 97, Flashback	1.99	0.50	1.25	2.50
❑1, Mar 63, JK; SD, SL (w); SD (w), Spider-Man; Spider-Man vs. the Chameleon, 1: Chameleon; 1: J. Jonah Jameson; O: Spider-Man; 1: John Jameson; A: Fantastic Four	0.12	4400.00	11000.00	22000.00
❑1/GR, SD, SL (w); SD (w), Spider-Man; Spider-Man vs. the Chameleon, 1: Chameleon; 1: J. Jonah Jameson; O: Spider-Man; A: Fantastic Four, record; Gold Records reprint	0.12	40.00	100.00	200.00
❑2, May 63, SD, SL (w); SD (w), Duel to the Death with the Vulture; The Uncanny Threat of the Terrible Tinkerer, 1: Vulture; 1: Tinkerer; 1: Mysterio (as "alien")	0.12	600.00	1500.00	3000.00

	ORIG	GOOD	FINE	N-MINT
❑3, Jul 63, SD, SL (w); SD (w), Spider-Man Versus Doctor Octopus, 1: Doctor Octopus	0.12	480.00	1200.00	2400.00
❑4, Sep 63, SD, SL (w); SD (w), Nothing Can Stop the Sandman, 1: Sandman (Marvel); 1: Betty Brant	0.12	350.00	875.00	1750.00
❑5, Oct 63, SD, SL (w); SD (w), Marked for Destruction by Dr. Doom, V: Doctor Doom	0.12	300.00	750.00	1500.00
❑6, Nov 63, SD, SL (w); SD (w), Face-to-Face with the Lizard, 1: The Lizard	0.12	250.00	625.00	1250.00
❑7, Dec 63, SD, SL (w); SD (w), Return of the Vulture, V: Vulture; 2: The Vulture	0.12	170.00	425.00	850.00
❑8, Jan 64, SD, SL (w); SD (w), The Terrible Threat of the Living Brain, V: Living Brain; A: Human Torch; V: Flash Thompson	0.12	170.00	425.00	850.00
❑9, Feb 64, SD, SL (w); SD (w), The Man Called Electro, 1: Electro; 1: Doctor Bromwell	0.12	190.00	475.00	950.00
❑10, Mar 64, JK; SD, SL (w); SD (w), The Enforcers, 1: Ox; 1: Enforcers; 1: Montana; 1: Big Man; 1: Fancy Dan	0.12	170.00	425.00	850.00
❑11, Apr 64, SD, SL (w); SD (w), Turning Point, V: Doctor Octopus	0.12	100.00	250.00	500.00
❑12, May 64, SD, SL (w); SD (w), Unmasked by Dr. Octopus, V: Doctor Octopus, Spider-Man unmasked	0.12	100.00	250.00	500.00
❑13, Jun 64, SD, SL (w); SD (w), The Menace of Mysterio, 1: Mysterio	0.12	126.00	315.00	630.00
❑14, Jul 64, SD, SL (w); SD (w), The Grotesque Adventure of the Green Goblin, 1: Green Goblin I (Norman Osborn); A: Enforcers; A: Hulk	0.12	330.00	825.00	1650.00
❑15, Aug 64, SD, SL (w); SD (w), Kraven the Hunter, 1: Mary Jane Watson (name mentioned); A: Chameleon; 1: Kraven the Hunter; 1: Anna May Watson	0.12	180.00	450.00	900.00
❑16, Sep 64, SD, SL (w); SD (w), Duel with Daredevil, 1: Princess Python; 1: The Great Gambonnos; V: Ringmaster and Circus of Crime; A: Daredevil	0.12	77.00	192.50	385.00
❑17, Oct 64, SD, SL (w); SD (w), The Return of the Green Goblin, V: Green Goblin I (Norman Osborn); A: Torch	0.12	120.00	300.00	600.00
❑18, Nov 64, SD, SL (w); SD (w), The End of Spider-Man, 1: Ned Leeds (later becomes Hobgoblin I); V: Sandman (Marvel)	0.12	77.00	192.50	385.00
❑19, Dec 64, SD, SL (w); SD (w), Spidey Strikes Back, V: Enforcers; V: Sandman (Marvel); 1: MacDonald "Mac" Gargan [later becomes the Scorpion]; 1: Rock Gimpy	0.12	65.00	162.50	325.00
❑20, Jan 65, SD, SL (w); SD (w), The Coming of the Scorpion, 1: The Scorpion	0.12	77.00	192.50	385.00
❑21, Feb 65, SD, SL (w); SD (w), Where Flies the Beetle, 2: The Beetle; V: Beetle; A: Torch	0.12	50.00	125.00	250.00
❑22, Mar 65, SD, SL (w); SD (w), The Clown, and His Masters of Menace, V: Ringmaster and Circus of Crime	0.12	50.00	125.00	250.00
❑23, Apr 65, SD, SL (w); SD (w), The Goblin and the Gangsters, V: Green Goblin I (Norman Osborn)	0.12	73.00	182.50	365.00
❑24, May 65, SD, SL (w); SD (w), Spider-Man Goes Mad, V: Mysterio	0.12	40.00	100.00	200.00
❑25, Jun 65, SD, SL (w); SD (w), Captured by J. Jonah Jameson, 1: Mary Jane Watson (cameo-face not shown); 1: Spider-Slayers; 1: Spencer Smythe	0.12	44.00	110.00	220.00
❑26, Jul 65, SD, SL (w); SD (w), The Man in the Crime-Master's Mask, A: Green Goblin I (Norman Osborn); 1: Patch; 1: Crime-Master	0.12	50.00	125.00	250.00
❑27, Aug 65, SD, SL (w); SD (w), Bring Back My Goblin to Me, A: Green Goblin I (Norman Osborn); D: Crime-Master	0.12	50.00	125.00	250.00
❑28, Sep 65, SD, SL (w); SD (w), The Molten Man, 1: Molten Man; 2: Spencer Smythe, Peter Parker graduates from high school	0.12	68.00	170.00	340.00
❑29, Oct 65, SD, SL (w); SD (w), Never Step on a Scorpion, V: The Scorpion	0.12	30.00	75.00	150.00
❑30, Nov 65, SD, V: Cat Burglar	0.12	30.00	75.00	150.00
❑31, Dec 65, SD, SL (w), If This Be My Destiny ..., 1: Harry Osborn; 1: Gwen Stacy; 1: Professor Warren	0.12	28.00	70.00	140.00
❑32, Jan 66, SD, Master Planner revealed as Doctor Octopus	0.12	28.00	70.00	140.00
❑33, Feb 66, SD, V: Doctor Octopus (as Master Planner)	0.12	28.00	70.00	140.00
❑34, Mar 66, SD, A: Green Goblin I (Norman Osborn); V: Kraven the Hunter	0.12	28.00	70.00	140.00
❑35, Apr 66, SD, V: Molten Man; 1: Spider Tracer	0.12	28.00	70.00	140.00
❑36, May 66, SD, 1: Looter (later Meteor Man in Marvel Team-Up #33)	0.12	28.00	70.00	140.00
❑37, Jun 66, SD, A: Patch; 1: Norman Osborn; V: Professor Mendel Stromm	0.12	26.00	65.00	130.00

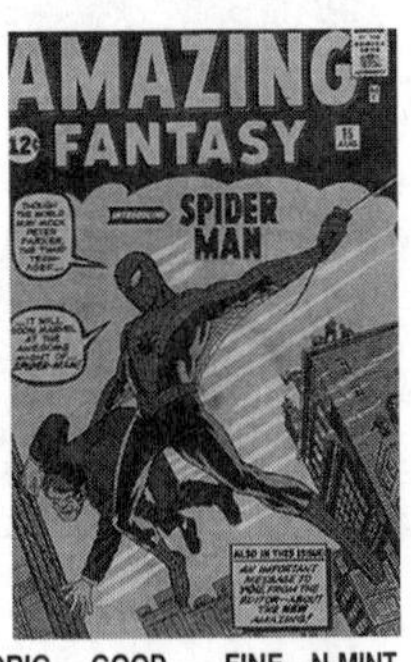

With the release of the movie scheduled for May 2002, early Spider-Man appearances, including his first, are climbing in value.

© 1962 Marvel

	ORIG	GOOD	FINE	N-MINT
❑38, Jul 66, SD, 2: Mary Jane Watson (cameo)	0.12	26.00	65.00	130.00
❑39, Aug 66, JR, V: Green Goblin I (Norman Osborn), Green Goblin revealed as Norman Osborn	0.12	40.00	100.00	200.00
❑40, Sep 66, JR, O: Green Goblin I (Norman Osborn)	0.12	55.00	137.50	275.00
❑41, Oct 66, JR, 1: Rhino	0.12	25.00	62.50	125.00
❑42, Nov 66, JR, 3: Mary Jane Watson (first time her face is shown); A: 3rd	0.12	27.00	67.50	135.00
❑43, Dec 66, JR, V: Rhino	0.12	18.00	45.00	90.00
❑44, Jan 67, JR, V: Lizard	0.12	18.00	45.00	90.00
❑45, Feb 67, JR, V: Lizard	0.12	18.00	45.00	90.00
❑46, Mar 67, JR, 1: Shocker	0.12	18.00	45.00	90.00
❑47, Apr 67, JR, V: Kraven the Hunter	0.12	18.00	45.00	90.00
❑48, May 67, JR, V: second Vulture	0.12	18.00	45.00	90.00
❑49, Jun 67, JR, V: Vulture; V: Kraven the Hunter	0.12	18.00	45.00	90.00
❑50, Jul 67, JR, 1: Kingpin	0.12	80.00	200.00	400.00
❑51, Aug 67, JR, 1: Robbie Robertson; O: Mysterio; V: Kingpin	0.12	28.00	70.00	140.00
❑52, Sep 67, JR, D: Big Man (Frederick Foswell); V: Kingpin; 1: Joe Robertson	0.12	12.00	30.00	60.00
❑53, Oct 67, JR, V: Doctor Octopus	0.12	12.00	30.00	60.00
❑54, Nov 67, JR, V: Doctor Octopus	0.12	12.00	30.00	60.00
❑55, Dec 67, JR, V: Doctor Octopus	0.12	12.00	30.00	60.00
❑56, Jan 68, JR, V: Doctor Octopus; 1: Captain Stacy	0.12	12.00	30.00	60.00
❑57, Feb 68, JR, A: Ka-Zar and Zabu	0.12	12.00	30.00	60.00
❑58, Mar 68, JR, V: J. Jonah Jameson; A: Ka-Zar and Zabu; V: Spencer Smythe	0.12	12.00	30.00	60.00
❑59, Apr 68, JR, SL (w); JR (w), The Brand of the Brainwasher, V: Kingpin (as Brainwasher); 1: Slade; 1: Doctor Winkler	0.12	12.00	30.00	60.00
❑60, May 68, JR, SL (w); JR (w), O, Bitter Victory, 2: Slade; 2: Doctor Winkler; V: Kingpin	0.12	12.00	30.00	60.00
❑61, Jun 68, JR, SL (w); JR (w), What a Tangled Web We Weave, V: Kingpin	0.12	10.00	25.00	50.00
❑62, Jul 68, JR, SL (w); JR (w), Make Way for Medusa, A: Medusa	0.12	10.00	25.00	50.00
❑63, Aug 68, JR, SL (w); JR (w), Wings in the Night, V: both Vultures	0.12	10.00	25.00	50.00
❑64, Sep 68, JR, SL (w); JR (w), The Vulture's Prey, V: Vulture	0.12	10.00	25.00	50.00
❑65, Oct 68, JR, SL (w); JR (w), The Impossible Escape	0.12	10.00	25.00	50.00
❑66, Nov 68, JR, SL (w); JR (w), The Madness of Mysterio, V: Mysterio	0.12	10.00	25.00	50.00
❑67, Dec 68, JR, SL (w); JR (w), To Squash a Spider, 1: Randy Robertson; V: Mysterio	0.12	10.00	25.00	50.00
❑68, Jan 69, JM; JR, SL (w); JR (w), Crisis on the Campus, 1: Louis Wilson; V: Kingpin	0.12	10.00	25.00	50.00
❑69, Feb 69, JM; JR, SL (w); JR (w), Mission: Crush the Kingpin, V: Kingpin	0.12	10.00	25.00	50.00
❑70, Mar 69, JM; JR, SL (w); JR (w), Spider-Man Wanted, 1: Vanessa Fisk (Kingpin's wife-face not shown); V: Kingpin	0.12	10.00	25.00	50.00
❑71, Apr 69, JM; JR, SL (w); JR (w), The Speedster and the Spider, A: Quicksilver	0.12	10.00	25.00	50.00
❑72, May 69, JR; JB, SL (w); JR (w), Rocked by the Shocker, V: Shocker	0.12	10.00	25.00	50.00
❑73, Jun 69, JR; JB, SL (w); JR (w), The Web Closes, 1: Silvermane; 1: Caesar Cicero; 1: Man-Mountain Marko	0.12	10.00	25.00	50.00
❑74, Jul 69, JM; JR, SL (w); JR (w), If This Be Bedlam, V: Silvermane; V: Caesar Cicero; V: Man-Mountain Marko	0.12	10.00	25.00	50.00
❑75, Aug 69, JM; JR, SL (w); JR (w), Death Without Warning, V: Silvermane; V: Caesar Cicero; V: Man-Mountain Marko	0.15	8.40	21.00	42.00
❑76, Sep 69, JM; JR; JB, SL (w), The Lizard Lives, A: Human Torch; V: Lizard	0.15	8.40	21.00	42.00
❑77, Oct 69, JM; JR; JB, SL (w); JR (w), In the Blaze of Battle, A: Human Torch; V: Lizard	0.15	8.40	21.00	42.00

	ORIG	GOOD	FINE	N-MINT
❑78, Nov 69, JM; JR; JB, SL (w); JR2 (w), The Night of the Prowler, 1: The Prowler.	0.15	9.60	24.00	48.00
❑79, Dec 69, JM; JR; JB, SL (w), To Prowl No More, V: Prowler; V: The Prowler.......	0.15	8.40	21.00	42.00
❑80, Jan 70, JR; JB, SL (w); JR (w), On the Trail of the Chameleon, V: Chameleon....	0.15	8.40	21.00	42.00
❑81, Feb 70, JR; JB, SL (w); JR (w), The Coming of the Kangaroo, 1: The Kangaroo	0.15	8.40	21.00	42.00
❑82, Mar 70, JR; JB, SL (w); JR (w), And Then Came Electro, V: Electro	0.15	8.40	21.00	42.00
❑83, Apr 70, JR, SL (w); JR (w), The Schemer, 1: Vanessa Fisk (Full-Kingpin's wife); 1: Richard Fisk ("The Schemer"); V: Schemer; V: Kingpin	0.15	8.40	21.00	42.00
❑84, May 70, JR; JB, SL (w); JR (w), The Kingpin Strikes Back, V: Schemer; V: Kingpin	0.15	8.40	21.00	42.00
❑85, Jun 70, JR; JB, SL (w); JR (w), The Secret of the Schemer, V: Schemer; V: Kingpin	0.15	8.40	21.00	42.00
❑86, Jul 70, JM; JR, SL (w); JR (w), Beware the Black Widow, O: Black Widow	0.15	8.40	21.00	42.00
❑87, Aug 70, JM; JR, SL (w); JR (w), Unmasked at Last, Peter reveals his secret identity	0.15	8.40	21.00	42.00
❑88, Sep 70, JR, SL (w), The Arms of Dr. Octopus, V: Doctor Octopus	0.15	8.40	21.00	42.00
❑89, Oct 70, JR; GK, SL (w), Doc Ock Lives, V: Doctor Octopus	0.15	8.40	21.00	42.00
❑90, Nov 70, GK, SL (w), And Death Shall Come, A: Doctor Octopus; D: Captain Stacy	0.15	10.00	25.00	50.00
❑91, Dec 70, JR; GK, SL (w), To Smash a Spider, 1: Sam Bullit	0.15	8.40	21.00	42.00
❑92, Jan 71, JR; GK, SL (w), When Iceman Attacks, A: Iceman; A: Sam Bullit	0.15	8.40	21.00	42.00
❑93, Feb 71, JR, SL (w); JR (w), The Lady and the Prowler, A: Prowler	0.15	8.40	21.00	42.00
❑94, Mar 71, JR; SB, SL (w); JR (w), On Wings of Death, O: Spider-Man; A: Beetle	0.15	12.00	30.00	60.00
❑95, Apr 71, JR; SB, SL (w); JR (w), Trap for a Terrorist, Spider-Man goes to London ..	0.15	7.60	19.00	38.00
❑96, May 71, GK, SL (w), And Now, the Goblin, A: Green Goblin I (Norman Osborn), Drug topics not approved by CCA	0.15	16.00	40.00	80.00
❑97, Jun 71, JR; GK, SL (w); JR (w), In the Grip of the Goblin, A: Green Goblin I (Norman Osborn), Drug topics not approved by CCA	0.15	16.00	40.00	80.00
❑98, Jul 71, GK, SL (w), The Goblin's Last Gasp, A: Green Goblin I (Norman Osborn), Drug topics not approved by CCA	0.15	16.00	40.00	80.00
❑99, Aug 71, GK, SL (w), A Day In The Life Of..., A: Johnny Carson	0.15	8.40	21.00	42.00
❑100, Sep 71, JR; GK, SL (w), The Spider or the Man?, A: Green Goblin I (Norman Osborn), 100th anniversary issue; Peter grows four extra arms	0.15	33.00	82.50	165.00
❑101, Oct 71, GK, GK (w), A Monster Called Morbius, 1: Morbius	0.15	20.00	50.00	100.00
❑101-2, GK, GK (w), A Monster Called Morbius, 1: Morbius, 2nd Printing; Metallic ink cover	1.75	0.45	1.13	2.25
❑102, Nov 71, GK, GK (w), Vampire at Large; The Way It Began, A: Morbius; A: Lizard, Giant-sized	0.25	15.00	37.50	75.00
❑103, Dec 71, GK, GK (w), Walk The Savage Land, 1: Gog; V: Kraven the Hunter	0.20	5.00	12.50	25.00
❑104, Jan 72, GK, GK (w), The Beauty and the Brute, 2: Gog; V: Kraven the Hunter..	0.20	5.00	12.50	25.00
❑105, Feb 72, GK, SL (w); GK (w), The Spider Slayer, V: Spencer Smythe; V: Spider Slayer	0.20	5.00	12.50	25.00
❑106, Mar 72, JR, SL (w); JR (w), Squash! Goes the Spider, V: Spencer Smythe; V: Spider Slayer	0.20	5.00	12.50	25.00
❑107, Apr 72, JR, SL (w); JR (w), Spidey Smashes Thru, V: Spencer Smythe; V: Spider Slayer	0.20	5.00	12.50	25.00
❑108, May 72, JR, SL (w); JR (w), Vengeance from Vietnam, 1: Sha Shan; A: Flash Thompson	0.20	5.00	12.50	25.00
❑109, Jun 72, JR, SL (w); JR (w), Enter: Dr. Strange, A: Doctor Strange	0.20	5.00	12.50	25.00
❑110, Jul 72, JR, SL (w); JR (w), The Birth of the Gibbon, 1: The Gibbon	0.20	5.00	12.50	25.00
❑111, Aug 72, JR, JR (w), To Stalk a Spider, V: The Gibbon, Kraven the Hunter	0.20	5.00	12.50	25.00
❑112, Sep 72, JR, JR (w), Spidey Cops Out, V: Doctor Octopus; A: The Gibbon	0.20	5.00	12.50	25.00
❑113, Oct 72, JSt; JR; JSn, JR (w), They Call the Doctor...Octopus, 1: Hammerhead; V: Doctor Octopus	0.20	6.00	15.00	30.00
❑114, Nov 72, JSt; JR; JSn, JR (w), Gang War, Shmang War! What I Want to Know is...Who the Heck is Hammerhead?, O: Hammerhead; 1: Doctor Jonas Harrow ...	0.20	5.00	12.50	25.00
❑115, Dec 72, JR, JR (w), The Last Battle, V: Hammerhead, Doctor Octopus	0.20	5.00	12.50	25.00
❑116, Jan 73, JR, SL (w); JR (w), Suddenly, the Smasher, V: Richard Raleigh; 1: Smasher (was Man Monster)	0.20	5.00	12.50	25.00
❑117, Feb 73, JR; HT, SL (w); JR (w), The Deadly Designs of the Disruptor, 1: Disruptor, reprints story from Spectacular Spider-Man (magazine) #1 with updates	0.20	5.00	12.50	25.00
❑118, Mar 73, JR, SL (w); JR (w), Countdown to Chaos, V: Disruptor, Smasher	0.20	5.00	12.50	25.00
❑119, Apr 73, JR, JR (w), The Gentleman's Name is Hulk, V: Hulk in Canada; A: Incredible Hulk	0.20	7.60	19.00	38.00
❑120, May 73, GK (w), The Fight and the Fury, V: Hulk; A: Incredible Hulk	0.20	7.60	19.00	38.00
❑121, Jun 73, JR; GK, GK (w), The Night Gwen Stacy Died, V: Green Goblin I (Norman Osborn); D: Gwen Stacy	0.20	22.00	55.00	110.00
❑122, Jul 73, JR; GK, GK (w), The Goblin's Last Gasp, D: Green Goblin I (Norman Osborn), Later revealed as false	0.20	24.00	60.00	120.00
❑123, Aug 73, JR; GK, GK (w), Just a Man Called Cage, A: Luke Cage	0.20	4.00	10.00	20.00
❑124, Sep 73, JR; GK, GK (w), The Mark of the Man-Wolf, 1: Man-Wolf	0.20	4.00	10.00	20.00
❑125, Oct 73, RA; JR, Wolfhunt, O: Man-Wolf	0.20	4.00	10.00	20.00
❑126, Nov 73, RA; JR, The Kangaroo Bounces Back, D: Kangaroo; A: Human Torch; A: Doctor Jonas Harrow	0.20	4.00	10.00	20.00
❑127, Dec 73, RA; JR, The Dark Wings of Death, V: third Vulture	0.20	4.00	10.00	20.00
❑128, Jan 74, RA; JR, The Vulture Hangs High, O: third Vulture	0.20	4.00	10.00	20.00
❑129, Feb 74, RA; GK, The Punisher Strikes Twice, 1: Jackal; 1: the Punisher	0.20	26.00	65.00	130.00
❑130, Mar 74, RA; JR, Betrayed!, V: Jackal; V: Hammerhead; V: Doctor Octopus; 1: Spider-Mobile	0.20	3.00	7.50	15.00
❑131, Apr 74, RA; GK, My Uncle...My Enemy?, V: Hammerhead; V: Doctor Octopus	0.20	3.00	7.50	15.00
❑132, May 74, JR; GK, The Master Plan Of The Molten Man, V: Molten Man	0.25	3.00	7.50	15.00
❑133, Jun 74, RA; JR, The Molten Man Breaks Out, V: Molten Man, Molten Man's relationship to Liz Allan revealed	0.25	3.00	7.50	15.00
❑134, Jul 74, RA; JR, Danger is a Man Name Tarantula, 1: Tarantula I (Anton Rodriguez); A: Punisher	0.25	5.20	13.00	26.00
❑135, Aug 74, RA; JR, Shoot-Out in Central Park, O: Tarantula I (Anton Rodriguez); A: Punisher	0.25	6.00	15.00	30.00
❑136, Sep 74, RA; JR, The Green Goblin Lives Again, 1: Green Goblin II (Harry Osborn)	0.25	7.00	17.50	35.00
❑137, Oct 74, RA; GK, The Green Goblin Strikes; Death-Trap Times Three, V: Green Goblin II (Harry Osborn)...............	0.25	7.00	17.50	35.00
❑138, Nov 74, RA; GK, Madness Means...The Mindworm!, 1: The Mindworm, Peter moves in with Flash Thompson	0.25	3.00	7.50	15.00
❑139, Dec 74, RA; GK, Day of the Grizzly, A: Jackal; 1: Grizzly	0.25	3.00	7.50	15.00
❑140, Jan 75, RA; GK, An One Will Fall, V: Jackal; 1: Gloria Grant; O: Grizzly	0.25	3.00	7.50	15.00
❑141, Feb 75, RA; JR, The Man's Name Appears to be Mysterio, V: second Mysterio, Spider-Mobile sinks in Hudson	0.25	3.00	7.50	15.00
❑142, Mar 75, RA; JR, Dead Man's Bluff, V: second Mysterio	0.25	3.00	7.50	15.00
❑143, Apr 75, RA; GK, And The Wind Cries: Cyclone!, 1: Cyclone	0.25	3.00	7.50	15.00
❑144, May 75, RA; GK, The Delusion Conspiracy, 1: Gwen Stacy clone; V: Cyclone	0.25	3.00	7.50	15.00
❑145, Jun 75, RA; GK, Gwen Stacy is Alive...and, Well...?!, V: Scorpion	0.25	3.00	7.50	15.00
❑146, Jul 75, RA; JR, Scorpion, Where is Thy Sting?, V: Jackal, Scorpion; A: Scorpion	0.25	3.00	7.50	15.00
❑147, Aug 75, RA; JR, The Tarantula is a Very Deadly Beast, V: Jackal, Tarantula	0.25	3.00	7.50	15.00
❑148, Sep 75, RA; GK, Jackal, Jackal, Who's Got the Jackal?, V: Jackal, Tarantula, Professor Warren revealed as Jackal...........	0.25	4.00	10.00	20.00
❑149, Oct 75, RA; GK, Even if I Live, I Die!, D: Spider-clone (faked death); D: Jackal; 1: Ben Reilly	0.25	5.00	12.50	25.00
❑150, Nov 75, GK, Spider-Man or Spider-Clone?, A: Ben Reilly, Spider-Man attempts to determine if he is the clone or the original	0.25	3.00	7.50	15.00
❑151, Dec 75, RA; JR, Skirmish Beneath the Streets, A: Ben Reilly; V: Shocker, Spider-Man disposes of clone's body (faked).....	0.25	2.00	5.00	10.00
❑152, Jan 76, RA; GK, Shattered by the Shocker, V: Shocker	0.25	2.00	5.00	10.00

	ORIG	GOOD	FINE	N-MINT
❑153, Feb 76, RA; GK, The Longest Hundred Yards	0.25	2.00	5.00	10.00
❑154, Mar 76, JR; SB, The Sandman Always Strikes Twice, V: Sandman (Marvel)	0.25	2.00	5.00	10.00
❑155, Apr 76, JR; SB, Whodunit!	0.25	2.00	5.00	10.00
❑156, May 76, RA; JR, On a Clear Day, You Can See the Mirage, 1: Mirage I (Desmond Charne), Wedding of Betty Brant and Ned Leeds	0.25	2.00	5.00	10.00
❑157, Jun 76, RA; JR, The Ghost That Haunted Octopus, return of Doctor Octopus	0.25	2.00	5.00	10.00
❑158, Jul 76, RA; GK, Hammerhead Is Out, V: Doctor Octopus, Hammerhead regains physical form	0.25	2.00	5.00	10.00
❑159, Aug 76, RA; GK, Arm-in-Arm-in-Arm-in-Arm-in-Arm-in-Arm with Doctor Octopus, 2: The Tinkerer; V: Doctor Octopus, Hammerhead	0.25	2.00	5.00	10.00
❑160, Sep 76, RA; GK, My Killer, the Car, V: Tinkerer, return of Spider-Mobile	0.30	2.00	5.00	10.00
❑161, Oct 76, RA; GK, And the Nightcrawler Came Prowling, Prowling, A: Nightcrawler; A: Punisher	0.30	2.00	5.00	10.00
❑162, Nov 76, RA, Let the Punisher Fit the Crime, A: Nightcrawler; A: Punisher	0.30	2.00	5.00	10.00
❑163, Dec 76, RA; DC, All the Kingpin's Men, V: Kingpin	0.30	1.20	3.00	6.00
❑164, Jan 77, RA; JR, Deadline!, V: Kingpin	0.30	1.20	3.00	6.00
❑165, Feb 77, RA; JR, Stegron Stalks the City, V: Stegron	0.30	1.20	3.00	6.00
❑166, Mar 77, RA; JR, War of the Reptile-Men, V: Stegron; V: Lizard	0.30	1.20	3.00	6.00
❑167, Apr 77, RA; JR, Stalked by the Spider-Slayer, 1: Will o' the Wisp	0.30	1.20	3.00	6.00
❑168, May 77, RA, Murder on the Wind, V: Will o' the Wisp	0.30	1.20	3.00	6.00
❑169, Jun 77, RA; AM, Confrontation, J. Jonah Jameson acquires photos showing Spider-Man disposing of clone's(?) body	0.30	1.20	3.00	6.00
❑170, Jul 77, RA, Madness Is All In The Mind, V: Doctor Faustus	0.30	1.20	3.00	6.00
❑171, Aug 77, RA, Photon Is Another Name For...?, A: Nova	0.30	1.20	3.00	6.00
❑172, Sep 77, RA, The Fiend from the Fire, 1: Rocket Racer	0.30	1.20	3.00	6.00
❑173, Oct 77, RA, If You Can't Stand the Heat, V: Molten Man	0.30	1.20	3.00	6.00
❑174, Nov 77, RA, The Hitman's Back in Town, V: Hitman; A: Punisher	0.35	1.20	3.00	6.00
❑175, Dec 77, RA, Big Apple Underground, V: Hitman; A: Punisher	0.35	1.20	3.00	6.00
❑176, Jan 78, RA, He Who Laughs Last, 1: Green Goblin III (Doctor Barton Hamilton)	0.35	1.20	3.00	6.00
❑177, Feb 78, RA, Goblin in the Middle, V: Silvermane; A: Green Goblin III (Doctor Barton Hamilton)	0.35	1.20	3.00	6.00
❑178, Mar 78, RA, Green Grows the Goblin, V: Silvermane; A: Green Goblin III (Doctor Barton Hamilton)	0.35	1.20	3.00	6.00
❑179, Apr 78, RA, The Goblin's Always Greener, V: Silvermane; A: Green Goblin III (Doctor Barton Hamilton)	0.35	1.20	3.00	6.00
❑180, May 78, RA, Who Was That Goblin I Saw You With?, V: Silvermane; A: Green Goblin III (Doctor Barton Hamilton)	0.35	1.20	3.00	6.00
❑181, Jun 78, GK; SB, Flashback!, O: Spider-Man	0.35	1.20	3.00	6.00
❑182, Jul 78, RA, The Rocket Racer's Back In Town!, V: Rocket Racer	0.35	1.20	3.00	6.00
❑183, Aug 78, RA, And Where the Big Wheel Stops, Nobody Knows, V: Rocket Racer; D: Big Wheel; V: Tinkerer	0.35	1.20	3.00	6.00
❑184, Sep 78, RA, White Dragon! Red Death!, 1: White Dragon II	0.35	1.20	3.00	6.00
❑185, Oct 78, RA, Spider, Spider, Burning Bright!; The Graduation of Peter Parker, V: White Dragon II; V: Dragon Gangs, Peter Parker graduates from college	0.35	1.20	3.00	6.00
❑186, Nov 78, KP, Chaos Is The Chameleon!, V: Chameleon	0.35	1.20	3.00	6.00
❑187, Dec 78, JSt; BMc; KP; JSn, JSn (w), The Power of Electro, V: Electro; A: Captain America; A: Shield	0.35	1.20	3.00	6.00
❑188, Jan 79, DC; KP, The Jigsaw Is Up!, V: Jigsaw	0.35	1.20	3.00	6.00
❑189, Feb 79, JBy, Mayhem by Moonlight, A: Man-Wolf	0.35	1.20	3.00	6.00
❑190, Mar 79, JM; KP; JBy, In Search of the Man-Wolf, A: Man-Wolf	0.35	1.20	3.00	6.00
❑191, Apr 79, KP; AM, Wanted for Murder: Spider-Man, V: Spencer Smythe; V: Spider Slayer	0.35	1.00	2.50	5.00
❑192, May 79, KP, 24 Hours Till Doomsday!, D: Spencer Smythe; V: The Fly	0.40	1.00	2.50	5.00
❑193, Jun 79, JM; KP, Wings Of The Fearsome Fly, V: The Fly	0.40	1.00	2.50	5.00

First introduced in *Amazing Spider-Man* #129, The Punisher has gone from a gun-toting mercenary to a vigilante during his nearly 30 years of existence.

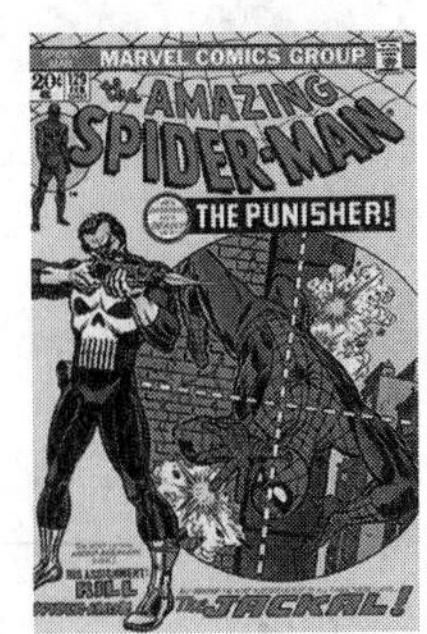

	ORIG	GOOD	FINE	N-MINT
❑194, Jul 79, KP; AM, Never Let the Black Cat Cross Your Path, 1: Black Cat	0.40	2.40	6.00	12.00
❑195, Aug 79, JM; KP; AM, Nine Lives Has the Black Cat, O: Black Cat, Peter Parker informed of Aunt May's death (faked death)	0.40	1.00	2.50	5.00
❑196, Sep 79, JM; KP; AM, Requiem!, D: Aunt May (faked death); V: Mysterio; V: Kingpin	0.40	1.00	2.50	5.00
❑197, Oct 79, JM; KP, The Kingpin's Midnight Massacre, V: Kingpin	0.40	1.00	2.50	5.00
❑198, Nov 79, JM; KP; SB, Mysterio Is Deadlier by the Dozen, V: Mysterio	0.40	1.00	2.50	5.00
❑199, Dec 79, JM; KP; SB, Now You See Me, Now You Die, V: Mysterio	0.40	1.00	2.50	5.00
❑200, Jan 80, JM; JR; KP, The Spider And The Burglar...a Sequel; Less Spider Than Man, D: unnamed burglar that shot Uncle Ben; O: Spider-Man, Giant sized; Aunt May revealed to be alive	0.75	2.80	7.00	14.00
❑201, Feb 80, JM; JR; KP, Man-Hunt!, A: Punisher	0.40	1.60	4.00	8.00
❑202, Mar 80, JM; JR; KP, One for Those Long Gone, A: Punisher	0.40	1.60	4.00	8.00
❑203, Apr 80, JR; KP, Bewitched, Bothered, And Be-Dazzled!, A: Dazzler	0.40	1.00	2.50	5.00
❑204, May 80, JR2; KP, The Black Cat Always Lands on Her Feet, A: Black Cat	0.40	1.00	2.50	5.00
❑205, Jun 80, KP; AM, ...In Love And War, A: Black Cat	0.40	1.00	2.50	5.00
❑206, Jul 80, JBy; AM, A Method In His Madness!	0.40	1.00	2.50	5.00
❑207, Aug 80, JM, Mesmero's Revenge, V: Mesmero	0.40	1.00	2.50	5.00
❑208, Sep 80, JR2; AM, Fusion!, 1: Fusion; 1: Lance Bannon	0.50	1.00	2.50	5.00
❑209, Oct 80, To Salvage My Honor!, V: Kraven the Hunter; 1: Calypso	0.50	1.20	3.00	6.00
❑210, Nov 80, JR2, The Prophecy Of Madame Web, 1: Madame Web	0.50	1.00	2.50	5.00
❑211, Dec 80, JM; JR2, The Spider And The Sea-Scourge, A: Sub-Mariner	0.50	0.80	2.00	4.00
❑212, Jan 81, JM; JR2, The Coming of Hydro-man, 1: Hydro-Man; O: Sandman (Marvel)	0.50	0.80	2.00	4.00
❑213, Feb 81, JM; JR2, All They Want To Do Is Kill You, Spider-Man, V: Wizard	0.50	0.80	2.00	4.00
❑214, Mar 81, JM; JR2, Then Shall We Both Be Betrayed, A: Sub-Mariner; V: Frightful Four	0.50	0.80	2.00	4.00
❑215, Apr 81, JM; JR2, By My Powers Shall I Be Vanquished!	0.50	0.80	2.00	4.00
❑216, May 81, JM; JR2, Marathon	0.50	0.80	2.00	4.00
❑217, Jun 81, JM; JR2, Here's Mud In Your Eye!	0.50	0.80	2.00	4.00
❑218, Jul 81, JR2, Eye Of The Beholder!	0.50	0.80	2.00	4.00
❑219, Aug 81, JM, Peter Parker -Criminal!	0.50	0.80	2.00	4.00
❑220, Sep 81, BMc, A Coffin For Spider-Man!, A: Moon Knight	0.50	0.80	2.00	4.00
❑221, Oct 81, Blues For Lonesome Pinky!	0.50	0.80	2.00	4.00
❑222, Nov 81, BH, Faster Than The Eye	0.50	0.80	2.00	4.00
❑223, Dec 81, JR2, Night Of The Ape	0.50	0.80	2.00	4.00
❑224, Jan 82, JR2, Let Fly These Aged Wings!	0.60	0.80	2.00	4.00
❑225, Feb 82, BWi; JR2, Fools...Like Us!, A: Foolkiller II (Greg Salinger)	0.60	0.80	2.00	4.00
❑226, Mar 82, JR2, A: Black Cat	0.60	0.80	2.00	4.00
❑227, Apr 82, JM; JR2, Goin' Straight, A: Black Cat	0.60	0.80	2.00	4.00
❑228, May 82, Murder By Spider	0.60	0.80	2.00	4.00
❑229, Jun 82, JR2, Nothing Can Stop the Juggernaut!	0.60	0.80	2.00	4.00
❑230, Jul 82, JR2, To Fight the Unbeatable Foe!	0.60	0.80	2.00	4.00
❑231, Aug 82, JM; JR2, Caught In The Act	0.60	0.80	2.00	4.00
❑232, Sep 82, JR2, Hyde...In Plain Sight	0.60	0.80	2.00	4.00
❑233, Oct 82, JM; JR2, Where The @ó%# Is Nose Norton?	0.60	0.80	2.00	4.00

	ORIG	GOOD	FINE	N-MINT
❑234, Nov 82, JR2; DGr, Now Shall Will-O'-The-Wisp Have His Revenge!, Free 16 page insert-Marvel Guide to Collecting Comics	0.60	0.80	2.00	4.00
❑235, Dec 82, JR2, Look Out, There's A Monster Coming!, O: Will o' the Wisp	0.60	0.80	2.00	4.00
❑236, Jan 83, JR2, Death Knell!, D: Tarantula I (Anton Rodriguez)	0.60	0.80	2.00	4.00
❑237, Feb 83, BH, High And Mighty!	0.60	0.80	2.00	4.00
❑238, Mar 83, 1: Hobgoblin (Ned Leeds), Came with "Tattooz" temporary tattoo decal	0.60	8.00	20.00	40.00
❑239, Apr 83, 2: Hobgoblin	0.60	4.00	10.00	20.00
❑240, May 83, JR2; BL, Wings Of Vengeance!	0.60	1.00	2.50	5.00
❑241, Jun 83, JR2, In The Beginning..., O: Vulture	0.60	1.00	2.50	5.00
❑242, Jul 83, JR2, Confrontations!	0.60	1.00	2.50	5.00
❑243, Aug 83	0.60	1.00	2.50	5.00
❑244, Sep 83, KJ; JR2, Ordeals!, A: 3rd; V: Hobgoblin	0.60	1.20	3.00	6.00
❑245, Oct 83, JR2, Sacrifice Play!, A: 4th, Lefty Donovan becomes Hobgoblin	0.60	1.60	4.00	8.00
❑246, Nov 83, JR2, The Daydreamers	0.60	1.00	2.50	5.00
❑247, Dec 83, JR2, Interruptions	0.60	1.00	2.50	5.00
❑248, Jan 84, And He Strikes Like A Thunderball!	0.60	1.00	2.50	5.00
❑249, Feb 84, V: Hobgoblin	0.60	1.20	3.00	6.00
❑250, Mar 84, KJ; JR2, Confessions!, A: Hobgoblin	0.60	1.40	3.50	7.00
❑251, Apr 84, Endings!, Last old costume	0.60	1.40	3.50	7.00
❑252, May 84, new costume	0.60	3.60	9.00	18.00
❑253, Jun 84, By Myself Betrayed!, 1: The Rose	0.60	1.00	2.50	5.00
❑254, Jul 84, With Great Power...	0.60	0.80	2.00	4.00
❑255, Aug 84, Even A Ghost Can Fear The Night!, V: Red Ghost	0.60	0.80	2.00	4.00
❑256, Sep 84, V: Puma	0.60	1.00	2.50	5.00
❑257, Oct 84, Beware The Claws Of Puma!, V: Puma; A: Hobgoblin	0.60	1.40	3.50	7.00
❑258, Nov 84, The Sinister Secret Of Spider-Man's New Costume!, A: Hobgoblin	0.60	1.60	4.00	8.00
❑259, Dec 84, O: Mary Jane Watson; A: Hobgoblin, Spider-Man back to old costume	0.60	1.60	4.00	8.00
❑260, Jan 85, The Challenge Of Hobgoblin!, V: Hobgoblin	0.60	1.40	3.50	7.00
❑261, Feb 85, The Sins Of My Father, V: Hobgoblin	0.60	1.40	3.50	7.00
❑262, Mar 85, BL, BL (w), Trade Secret, Photo cover; Spider-man unmasked	0.60	1.00	2.50	5.00
❑263, Apr 85, The Spectacular Spider-Kid, 1: Spider-Kid	0.65	0.80	2.00	4.00
❑264, May 85, Red 9 And Red Tape	0.65	0.80	2.00	4.00
❑265, Jun 85, 1: Silver Sable	0.65	1.20	3.00	6.00
❑265-2, 1: Silver Sable, 2nd Printing	1.25	0.40	1.00	2.00
❑266, Jul 85, SB, PD (w), Jump For My Love or Spring Is In The Air	0.65	0.60	1.50	3.00
❑267, Aug 85	0.65	0.60	1.50	3.00
❑268, Sep 85, A: Beyonder; A: Kingpin, Secret Wars II	0.65	0.60	1.50	3.00
❑269, Oct 85, Burn, Spider, Burn!, V: Firelord	0.65	0.60	1.50	3.00
❑270, Nov 85, The Hero And The Holocaust!, V: Firelord; A: Avengers; 1: Kate Cushing (Peter Parker's supervisor at the Bugle)	0.65	0.60	1.50	3.00
❑271, Dec 85, Whatever Happened To Crusher Hogan?	0.65	0.60	1.50	3.00
❑272, Jan 86, SB, Make Way For Slyde!, V: Slyde	0.65	0.60	1.50	3.00
❑273, Feb 86, Secret Wars II; To Challenge To Beyonder, A: Puma, Secret Wars II	0.75	0.60	1.50	3.00
❑274, Mar 86, Secret Wars II, A: Zarathos (the spirit of vengeance), Secret Wars II	0.75	0.60	1.50	3.00
❑275, Apr 86, The Choice And The Challenge, O: Spider-Man, double-sized; Hobgoblin story	1.25	1.40	3.50	7.00
❑276, May 86, Unmasked!, D: Fly; A: Hobgoblin	0.75	1.20	3.00	6.00
❑277, Jun 86, The Rules Of The Game	0.75	0.60	1.50	3.00
❑278, Jul 86, D: Wraith	0.75	0.60	1.50	3.00
❑279, Aug 86, Savage Is The Sable, Jack O' Lantern cover/story; Jack O' Lantern versus Silver Sable	0.75	0.80	2.00	4.00
❑280, Sep 86	0.75	0.60	1.50	3.00
❑281, Oct 86, V: Sinister Syndicate, Jack O' Lantern cover/story	0.75	1.60	4.00	8.00
❑282, Nov 86, The Fury Of X-Factor	0.75	0.60	1.50	3.00
❑283, Dec 86, With Foes Like These...	0.75	0.60	1.50	3.00
❑284, Jan 87, Gang War; Gang War, Part 1, A: Punisher	0.75	1.40	3.50	7.00
❑285, Feb 87, Gang War; Gang War, Part 2, A: Hobgoblin; A: Punisher	0.75	1.40	3.50	7.00
❑286, Mar 86, Gang War; Gang War, Part 3	0.75	1.00	2.50	5.00
❑287, Apr 87, EL, Gang War; Gang War, Part 4, A: Daredevil; A: Hobgoblin	0.75	1.00	2.50	5.00
❑288, May 87, Gang War; Gang War, Part 5, A: Hobgoblin	0.75	1.00	2.50	5.00
❑289, Jun 87, 1: Hobgoblin II (Jason Macendale), double-sized issue; Hobgoblin unmasked; Hobgoblin's identity revealed; Jack O' Lantern becomes Hobgoblin	1.25	2.00	5.00	10.00
❑290, Jul 87, JR2, The Big Question, Peter Parker proposes to Mary Jane	0.75	0.60	1.50	3.00
❑291, Aug 87, JR2, Dark Journey!, V: Spider-Slayer	0.75	0.60	1.50	3.00
❑292, Sep 87, Growing Pains!	0.75	0.60	1.50	3.00
❑293, Oct 87, MZ, Kraven's Last Hunt, Part 2; Crawling, V: Kraven the Hunter	0.75	1.20	3.00	6.00
❑294, Nov 87, BMc; MZ, Kraven's Last Hunt, Part 5; Thunder, V: Kraven the Hunter; D: Kraven	0.75	1.20	3.00	6.00
❑295, Dec 87, BSz, Mad Dogs	0.75	0.80	2.00	4.00
❑296, Jan 88, Force Of Arms, V: Doctor Octopus	0.75	0.80	2.00	4.00
❑297, Feb 88, I'll Take Manhattan!, V: Doctor Octopus	0.75	0.80	2.00	4.00
❑298, Mar 88, TMc, 1: Venom (cameo), w/o costume	0.75	3.00	7.50	15.00
❑299, Apr 88, TMc, 1: Venom (cameo)	0.75	2.00	5.00	10.00
❑300, May 88, TMc, O: Venom; 1: Venom (Full), 25th anniversary; Last black costume for Spider-Man	1.50	7.00	17.50	35.00
❑300/A, TMc, O: Venom; 1: Venom (Full), chromium cover; 25th anniversary; Last black costume for Spider-Man	—	2.80	7.00	14.00
❑300/B, TMc, O: Venom; 1: Venom (Full), chromium cover; Signed by David Micheline; 25th anniversary; Last black costume for Spider-Man	—	3.60	9.00	18.00
❑301, Jun 88, TMc	1.00	1.60	4.00	8.00
❑302, Jul 88, TMc	1.00	1.60	4.00	8.00
❑303, Aug 88, TMc	1.00	1.60	4.00	8.00
❑304, Sep 88, TMc	1.00	1.20	3.00	6.00
❑305, Sep 88, TMc	1.00	1.20	3.00	6.00
❑306, Oct 88, TMc	1.00	1.20	3.00	6.00
❑307, Oct 88, TMc, O: Chameleon	1.00	1.20	3.00	6.00
❑308, Nov 88, TMc, Dread	1.00	1.20	3.00	6.00
❑309, Nov 88, TMc, Styx And Stone	1.00	1.20	3.00	6.00
❑310, Dec 88, TMc, Shrike Force!	1.00	1.20	3.00	6.00
❑311, Jan 89, TMc, Inferno	1.00	1.20	3.00	6.00
❑312, Feb 89, TMc, Inferno; Hobgoblin vs. Green Goblin II (Harry Osborn)	1.00	1.80	4.50	9.00
❑313, Mar 89, TMc, Inferno	1.00	1.00	2.50	5.00
❑314, Apr 89, TMc, Down And Out In Forest Hills	1.00	1.00	2.50	5.00
❑315, May 89, TMc, A: Venom	1.00	1.60	4.00	8.00
❑316, Jun 89, TMc, A: Venom	1.00	1.60	4.00	8.00
❑317, Jul 89, TMc, A: Venom	1.00	1.60	4.00	8.00
❑318, Aug 89, TMc, Sting Your Partner!, A: Venom	1.00	1.20	3.00	6.00
❑319, Sep 89, TMc, The Scorpions Tale Of Woe!	1.00	1.20	3.00	6.00
❑320, Sep 89, TMc, Assassin Nation Plot, Part 1, A: Silver Sable	1.00	1.20	3.00	6.00
❑321, Oct 89, TMc, Assassin Nation Plot, Part 2, A: Silver Sable	1.00	0.80	2.00	4.00
❑322, Oct 89, TMc, Assassin Nation Plot, Part 3; Ceremony, A: Silver Sable	1.00	0.80	2.00	4.00
❑323, Nov 89, TMc, Assassin Nation Plot, Part 4, A: Silver Sable	1.00	0.80	2.00	4.00
❑324, Nov 89, TMc, A: Sabretooth	1.00	1.00	2.50	5.00
❑325, Nov 89, TMc	1.00	0.80	2.00	4.00
❑326, Dec 89, Acts of Vengeance, Acts of Vengeance	1.00	0.60	1.50	3.00
❑327, Dec 89, Acts of Vengeance, cosmic Spider-Man; Acts of Vengeance	1.00	0.60	1.50	3.00
❑328, Jan 90, TMc, Acts of Vengeance; Shaw's Gambit, Hulk; Acts of Vengeance; Last McFarlane Issue	1.00	0.90	2.25	4.50
❑329, Feb 90, Acts of Vengeance	1.00	0.60	1.50	3.00
❑330, Mar 90, A: Punisher	1.00	0.60	1.50	3.00
❑331, Apr 90, EL, A: Punisher	1.00	0.60	1.50	3.00
❑332, May 90, EL, A: Venom	1.00	0.60	1.50	3.00
❑333, Jun 90, A: Venom	1.00	0.60	1.50	3.00
❑334, Jul 90, EL, The Return Of The Sinister Six, Part 1, Sinister Six	1.00	0.50	1.25	2.50
❑335, Jul 90, EL, The Return Of The Sinister Six, Part 2; Shocks!, Sinister Six	1.00	0.50	1.25	2.50
❑336, Aug 90, EL, The Return Of The Sinister Six, Part 3; The Wagers Of Sin, Sinister Six	1.00	0.50	1.25	2.50
❑337, Aug 90, EL, The Return Of The Sinister Six, Part 4, Sinister Six	1.00	0.50	1.25	2.50
❑338, Sep 90, EL, The Return Of The Sinister Six, Part 5; Death From Above, Sinister Six	1.00	0.50	1.25	2.50

	ORIG	GOOD	FINE	N-MINT
❑339, Sep 90, EL, The Return Of The Sinister Six, Part 6; The Killing Cure, Sinister Six	1.00	0.50	1.25	2.50
❑340, Oct 90	1.00	0.50	1.25	2.50
❑341, Nov 90, Powerless; Spider-Man loses powers	1.00	0.50	1.25	2.50
❑342, Dec 90, Powerless	1.00	0.50	1.25	2.50
❑343, Jan 91, Spider-Man gets his powers back	1.00	0.50	1.25	2.50
❑344, Feb 91, 1: Cletus Kassidy (later becomes Carnage)-cameo; 1: Cardiac; 1: Cletus Kasady (later becomes Carnage)-cameo	1.00	1.00	2.50	5.00
❑345, Mar 91, A: Cletus Kassidy (later becomes Carnage)-full; O: Cletus Kasady	1.00	1.20	3.00	6.00
❑346, Apr 91, A: Venom	1.00	0.80	2.00	4.00
❑347, May 91, A: Venom	1.00	0.80	2.00	4.00
❑348, Jun 91, EL, Righteous Sand, A: Avengers	1.00	0.40	1.00	2.00
❑349, Jul 91, EL, Man Of Steal	1.00	0.40	1.00	2.00
❑350, Aug 91, EL, Doom Service!, V: Doctor Doom	1.50	0.40	1.00	2.00
❑351, Sep 91, The Three Faces Of Evil, V: Tri-Sentinel; A: Nova	1.00	0.40	1.00	2.00
❑352, Oct 91, Death Walk!, V: Tri-Sentinel; A: Nova	1.00	0.40	1.00	2.00
❑353, Nov 91, AM (w), Round Robin: The Sidekick's Revenge, Part 1; When Midnight Strikes!, A: Moon Knight; A: Punisher	1.00	0.40	1.00	2.00
❑354, Nov 91, AM (w), Round Robin: The Sidekick's Revenge, Part 2; Wilde At Heart!, A: Moon Knight; A: Punisher	1.00	0.40	1.00	2.00
❑355, Dec 91, AM (w), Round Robin: The Sidekick's Revenge, Part 3; Total Eclipse Of The Moon...Knight!, A: Moon Knight; A: Punisher	1.00	0.40	1.00	2.00
❑356, Dec 91, AM (w), Round Robin: The Sidekick's Revenge, Part 4; After Midnight!, A: Moon Knight; A: Punisher	1.00	0.40	1.00	2.00
❑357, Jan 92, AM (w), Round Robin: The Sidekick's Revenge, Part 5; A Bagel With Nova!, A: Moon Knight; A: Punisher	1.00	0.40	1.00	2.00
❑358, Jan 92, AM (w), Round Robin: The Sidekick's Revenge, Part 6, A: Moon Knight; A: Punisher	1.00	0.40	1.00	2.00
❑359, Feb 92, Toy Death!	1.25	0.40	1.00	2.00
❑360, Mar 92, Death Toy!, 1: Carnage (cameo); O: Cardiac	1.25	0.60	1.50	3.00
❑361, Apr 92, Carnage, Part 1, 1: Carnage (full appearance)	1.25	1.20	3.00	6.00
❑361-2, 2nd Printing; silver cover	1.25	0.30	0.75	1.50
❑362, May 92, Carnage, Part 2; Savage Alliance, A: Venom; A: Carnage	1.25	0.80	2.00	4.00
❑362-2, 2nd Printing	1.25	0.30	0.75	1.50
❑363, Jun 92, Carnage, Part 3, A: Venom; A: Carnage	1.25	0.60	1.50	3.00
❑364, Jul 92, The Pain Of Fast Air, V: Shocker, Peter Parker's parents (false parents) appear	1.25	0.40	1.00	2.00
❑365, Aug 92, Fathers And Sins; The Saga Of Spidey's Parents, 1: Spider-Man 2099, Hologram cover; Peter Parker meets his (false) parents; Gatefold poster with Venom and Carnage; Lizard back-up story	3.95	0.40	1.00	2.00
❑366, Sep 92, Skullwork!, V: Red Skull	1.25	0.40	1.00	2.00
❑367, Oct 92, Skullduggery	1.25	0.40	1.00	2.00
❑368, Nov 92, Invasion of the Spider-Slayers, Part 1; On Razored Wings, V: Spider-Slayers	1.25	0.40	1.00	2.00
❑369, Nov 92, Invasion of the Spider-Slayers, Part 2; Electric Doom, V: Spider-Slayers	1.25	0.40	1.00	2.00
❑370, Dec 92, Invasion of the Spider-Slayers, Part 3, V: Spider-Slayers	1.25	0.40	1.00	2.00
❑371, Dec 92, Invasion of the Spider-Slayers, Part 4; One Flew Over The Cuckoo's Nest, A: Black Cat; V: Spider-Slayers	1.25	0.40	1.00	2.00
❑372, Jan 93, Invasion of the Spider-Slayers, Part 5; Arachnophobia Too!, V: Spider-Slayers	1.25	0.40	1.00	2.00
❑373, Jan 93, Invasion of the Spider-Slayers, Part 6; The Bedlam Perspective, V: Spider-Slayers	1.25	0.40	1.00	2.00
❑374, Feb 93, V: Venom	1.25	0.40	1.00	2.00
❑375, Mar 93, The Bride Of Venom; True Friends, A: Venom, Metallic ink cover; 30th anniversary special; Sets stage for Venom #1	3.95	1.00	2.50	5.00
❑376, Apr 93, O: Cardiac; V: Cardiac, Styx and Stone	1.25	0.40	1.00	2.00
❑377, May 93, Dust to Dust, V: Cardiac	1.25	0.40	1.00	2.00
❑378, Jun 93, Maximum Carnage; Maximum Carnage, Part 3, A: Venom; A: Carnage	1.25	0.40	1.00	2.00
❑379, Jul 93, Maximum Carnage; Maximum Carnage, Part 7, A: Venom; A: Carnage	1.25	0.40	1.00	2.00
❑380, Aug 93, Maximum Carnage; Maximum Carnage, Part 10	1.25	0.40	1.00	2.00
❑381, Sep 93, Samson Unleashed, V: Hulk	1.25	0.40	1.00	2.00
❑382, Oct 93, Emerald Rage!, V: Hulk	1.25	0.40	1.00	2.00

Eric Larsen reintroduced The Sinister Six, a teaming of some of Spider-Man's fiercest enemies, in *Amazing Spider-Man* #334.

	ORIG	GOOD	FINE	N-MINT
❑383, Nov 93, Trial by Jury; Trial By Jury, Part 1	1.25	0.40	1.00	2.00
❑384, Dec 93, Trial by Jury; Trial By Jury, Part 2	1.25	0.40	1.00	2.00
❑385, Jan 94, Trial by Jury	1.25	0.40	1.00	2.00
❑386, Feb 94, Lifetheft; Lifetheft, Part 1, The Wings Of Age, V: Vulture	1.25	0.40	1.00	2.00
❑387, Mar 94, Lifetheft; Lifetheft, Part 2, V: Vulture	1.25	0.40	1.00	2.00
❑388, Apr 94, Lifetheft; Lifetheft, Part 3, V: Vulture; D: Peter Parker's parents (false parents), Double-size	2.25	0.65	1.63	3.25
❑388/SC, Apr 94, Lifetheft; Lifetheft, Part 3, V: Vulture; D: Peter Parker's parents (false parents), foil cover; Double-size	2.95	0.40	1.00	2.00
❑389, May 94, Pursuit	1.50	0.30	0.75	1.50
❑390, Jun 94, Shrieking, Part 1; Behind The Walls	1.50	0.30	0.75	1.50
❑390/CS, Jun 94, Shrieking, Part 1; Behind The Walls, animation cel; print; poster	2.95	0.60	1.50	3.00
❑391, Jul 94, Shrieking, Part 2; The Burning Fuse!, V: Shriek, Aunt May suffers stroke	1.50	0.30	0.75	1.50
❑392, Aug 94	1.50	0.30	0.75	1.50
❑393, Sep 94, V: Shriek, Carrion	1.50	0.30	0.75	1.50
❑394, Oct 94, Power & Responsibility, Part 2; Power and Responsibility, Part 2, A: Ben Reilly	1.50	0.40	1.00	2.00
❑394/SC, Oct 94, Power and Responsibility, Part 2; The Double, Part 2, A: Ben Reilly, enhanced cover; Flip-book; Giant-size	2.95	0.70	1.75	3.50
❑395, Nov 94, Back from the Edge, Part 1; Outcasts!, V: Puma	1.50	0.30	0.75	1.50
❑396, Dec 94, Back from the Edge, Part 3; Back From the Edge, Part 2, A: Daredevil	1.50	0.30	0.75	1.50
❑397, Jan 95, Back From the Edge, Part 3, V: Lizard, Double-size; flip book with illustrated story from The Ultimate Spider-Man back-up	2.25	0.45	1.13	2.25
❑398, Feb 95, Back From the Edge, Part 4, V: Doctor Octopus	1.50	0.30	0.75	1.50
❑399, Mar 95, Smoke & Mirrors, Part 2	1.50	0.30	0.75	1.50
❑400, Apr 95, SL (w), The Parker Legacy, Part 1; The Gift, D: Aunt May (fake death)	2.95	0.80	2.00	4.00
❑400/A, SL (w), The Parker Legacy, Part 1; The Gift, D: Aunt May (fake death), White cover; white cover edition (no ads, back-up story)	3.95	1.00	2.50	5.00
❑400/B, Apr 95, SL (w), The Parker Legacy, Part 1; The Gift, D: Aunt May (fake death), enhanced second cover	3.95	1.00	2.50	5.00
❑401, May 95, Mark of Kaine, Part 2; The Mark of Kaine, Part 2	1.50	0.30	0.75	1.50
❑402, Jun 95	1.50	0.30	0.75	1.50
❑403, Jul 95, Trial of Peter Parker, Part 2, A: Carnage	1.50	0.30	0.75	1.50
❑404, Aug 95, Maximum Clonage, Part 3	1.50	0.30	0.75	1.50
❑405, Sep 95, Exiled, Part 2	1.50	0.30	0.75	1.50
❑406, Oct 95, 1: Doctor Octopus II, OverPower cards inserted; (continues in Amazing Scarlet Spider); (continues in Amazing Scarlet Spider)	1.50	0.30	0.75	1.50
❑407, Jan 96, A: Sandman; A: Human Torch; A: Silver Sable	1.50	0.30	0.75	1.50
❑408, Feb 96, Media Blizzard, Part 2	1.50	0.30	0.75	1.50
❑409, Mar 96, Return of Kaine, Part 3; The Return of Kaine, Part 3	1.50	0.30	0.75	1.50
❑410, Apr 96, Web of Carnage, Part 2; And Now, Spider-Carnage	1.50	0.30	0.75	1.50
❑411, May 96, Blood Brothers, Part 2	1.50	0.30	0.75	1.50
❑412, Jun 96, Blood Brothers, Part 6	1.50	0.30	0.75	1.50
❑413, Jul 96	1.50	0.30	0.75	1.50
❑414, Aug 96, A: Delilah	1.50	0.30	0.75	1.50
❑415, Sep 96, Onslaught, V: Sentinel, "Onslaught: Impact 2"	1.50	0.30	0.75	1.50
❑416, Oct 96, Heroes' Farewell; Onslaught, post-Onslaught memories	1.50	0.30	0.75	1.50
❑417, Nov 96	1.50	0.30	0.75	1.50
❑418, Dec 96, Revelations, Part 3; Torment, birth of Peter and Mary Jane's baby; Return of Norman Osborn (face shown)	1.50	0.40	1.00	2.00
❑419, Jan 97, Beware Of The Black Tarantula!, V: Black Tarantula	1.50	0.30	0.75	1.50

	ORIG	GOOD	FINE	N-MINT
❑420, Feb 97, Twas the Night Before Christmas..., D: El Uno; A: X-Man	1.50	0.30	0.75	1.50
❑421, Mar 97, And Death Shall Fly Like a Dragon, 1: The Dragonfly	1.99	0.40	1.00	2.00
❑422, Apr 97, Exposed Wiring, O: Electro...	1.99	0.40	1.00	2.00
❑423, May 97, Choices, V: Electro	1.99	0.40	1.00	2.00
❑424, Jun 97, Then Came...Elektra, V: Elektra	1.99	0.40	1.00	2.00
❑425, Aug 97	1.99	0.40	1.00	2.00
❑426, Sep 97, gatefold summary	1.99	0.40	1.00	2.00
❑427, Oct 97, gatefold summary; return of Doctor Octopus	1.99	0.40	1.00	2.00
❑428, Nov 97, V: Doctor Octopus, gatefold summary	1.99	0.40	1.00	2.00
❑429, Dec 97, V: Absorbing Man, gatefold summary	1.99	0.40	1.00	2.00
❑430, Jan 98, A: Silver Surfer; V: Carnage, gatefold summary	1.99	0.40	1.00	2.00
❑431, Feb 98, Spider-Hunt, Part 2, A: Silver Surfer; V: Carnage, gatefold summary	1.99	0.40	1.00	2.00
❑432, Mar 98, gatefold summary	1.99	0.40	1.00	2.00
❑433, Apr 98, Identity Crisis, gatefold summary	1.99	0.40	1.00	2.00
❑434, May 98, Identity Crisis, gatefold summary	1.99	0.40	1.00	2.00
❑435, Jun 98, Identity Crisis, A: Ricochet, gatefold summary	1.99	0.40	1.00	2.00
❑436, Jul 98, gatefold summary	1.99	0.40	1.00	2.00
❑437, Aug 98, A: Synch, gatefold summary	1.99	0.40	1.00	2.00
❑438, Sep 98, A: Daredevil, gatefold summary	1.99	0.40	1.00	2.00
❑439, Sep 98, A: Zack and Lana, gatefold summary	1.99	0.40	1.00	2.00
❑440, Oct 98, The Gathering of Five, Part 2, V: Molten Man, gatefold summary	1.99	0.40	1.00	2.00
❑441, Nov 98, The Final Chapter, Part 1, A: Molten Man; D: Madame Web, Final Issue; gatefold summary	1.99	0.40	1.00	2.00
❑AIM 1, A: Doctor Octopus, nn; Giveaway from Aim Toothpaste; Spider-Man vs. Doctor Octopus	—	0.40	1.00	2.00
❑AIM 2, Crisis at Cape Canaveral, A: Green Goblin, nn; giveaway; Aim toothpaste giveaway	—	0.40	1.00	2.00
❑Anl 1, SD, SL (w); SD (w), The Sinister Six, 1: Sinister Six (Doctor Octopus, Vulture, Electro, Sandman, Mysterio, Kraven the Hunter)	0.25	115.00	287.50	575.00
❑Anl 2, SD, SL (w); SD (w), The Wondrous World of Dr. Strange; Smider-Man, A: Doctor Strange; 1: Xandu, 72pgs.; Cover reads "King-Size Special"; also reprints Amazing Spider-Man #1, 2, and 5	0.25	50.00	125.00	250.00
❑Anl 3, Nov 66, JR; DH, A: Avengers; A: Daredevil; V: Hulk, Cover reads "King-Size Special"	0.25	18.00	45.00	90.00
❑Anl 4, Nov 67, V: Wizard; V: Mysterio; A: Torch, Cover reads "King-Size Special"...	0.25	18.00	45.00	90.00
❑Anl 5, Nov 68, JR, SL (w); JR (w), The Parents of Peter Parker!; A Day at the Daily Bugle, A: Red Skull; 1: Peter Parker's parents, Cover reads "King-Size Special"; fate of Peter Parker's parents revealed...	0.25	18.00	45.00	90.00
❑Anl 5-2, JR, SL (w); JR (w), The Parents of Peter Parker!; A Day at the Daily Bugle, A: Red Skull; 1: Peter Parker's parents, 2nd Printing; Cover reads "King-Size Special"	0.25	0.30	0.75	1.50
❑Anl 6, Nov 69, SD, SL (w); SD (w), The Sinister Six; The Fabulous Fantastic Four Meet Spider-Man, Cover reads "King-Size Special"; reprints stories from Amazing Spider-Man #8, Annual #1 and Fantastic Four Annual #1	0.25	5.20	13.00	26.00
❑Anl 7, Dec 70, JR; SD, JR (c), SL (w); SD (w), Spider-Man vs. the Chameleon; Duel to the Death with the Vulture, Cover reads "King-Size Special"; reprints stories from Amazing Spider-Man #1, 2, and 38	0.25	5.20	13.00	26.00
❑Anl 8, Dec 71, SL (w), The Sinister Shocker; On the Trail of Spider-Man, Cover reads "King-Size Special"; reprints stories from Amazing Spider-Man #46 and 50 and Tales to Astonish #57	0.25	5.20	13.00	26.00
❑Anl 9, JM; JR, SL (w); JR (w), The Goblin Lives, A: Hobgoblin, Cover reads "King-Size Special"; reprints Spectacular Spider-Man (magazine) #2	0.35	5.20	13.00	26.00
❑Anl 10, Sep 76, GK, Step into My Parlor; Said the Spider to the Fly, 1: Human Fly.	0.50	2.00	5.00	10.00
❑Anl 11, DP; GK; JR2, Spawn of the Spider; Chaos at the Coffee Bean	0.50	2.00	5.00	10.00
❑Anl 12, JR (w); GK (w), The Gentleman's Name Is Hulk; The Fight and the Fury, Reprints Hulk story from Amazing Spider-Man #119-120	0.60	2.00	5.00	10.00
❑Anl 13, KP; JBy, The Arms of Doctor Octopus; Spider-Man! I Know Who You R, V: Doctor Octopus	0.75	2.00	5.00	10.00
❑Anl 14, FM, FM (w), Bend Sinister, V: Doctor Doom; A: Doctor Strange	0.75	2.00	5.00	10.00
❑Anl 15, FM, A: Punisher	0.75	1.20	3.00	6.00
❑Anl 16, 1: Captain Marvel II (Monica Rambeau)	1.00	1.40	3.50	7.00
❑Anl 17	1.00	1.20	3.00	6.00
❑Anl 18, Wedding of J. Jonah Jameson	1.00	1.20	3.00	6.00
❑Anl 19	1.25	1.20	3.00	6.00
❑Anl 20, D: Blizzard	1.25	1.20	3.00	6.00
❑Anl 21, The Wedding, newsstand edition; Wedding of Peter Parker and Mary Jane Watson	1.25	1.20	3.00	6.00
❑Anl 21/DM, The Wedding, Direct Market edition; Wedding of Peter Parker and Mary Jane Watson	1.25	1.20	3.00	6.00
❑Anl 22, Evolutionary War, Part 5, 1: Speedball; O: High Evolutionary; A: Daredevil..	1.75	0.80	2.00	4.00
❑Anl 23, Atlantis Attacks, Part 4; Abominations, O: Spider-Man, Atlantis Attacks	2.00	0.60	1.50	3.00
❑Anl 24, MZ; GK; SD, The Mercy Bomb; Quark Enterprises, or Honey, I Shrunk The Non-Mutant Super Hero, A: Ant-Man	2.00	0.60	1.50	3.00
❑Anl 25, The Vibranium Vendetta, Part 1; The Origin Of The Amazing Spider-Man, O: Spider-Man, Vibranium Vendetta; 1st solo Venom story	2.00	0.80	2.00	4.00
❑Anl 26, Hero Killers, Part 1, 1: Dreadnought 2000	2.25	0.60	1.50	3.00
❑Anl 27, 1: Annex, trading card; trading card	2.95	0.60	1.50	3.00
❑Anl 28, Carnage	2.95	0.60	1.50	3.00
❑Anl 1996	2.99	0.59	1.48	2.95
❑Anl 1997, V: Sundown, wraparound cover	2.99	0.60	1.50	2.99
❑Ash 1, O: Spider-Man, nn; b&w; ashcan edition; ashcan	0.75	0.15	0.38	0.75
❑GS 1, RA, Ship of Fiends; The Masque of the Black Death, A: Dracula	0.50	3.60	9.00	18.00
❑GS 2, RA, Masterstroke; Cross and Double-Cross	0.50	2.00	5.00	10.00
❑GS 3, RA, The Yesterday Connection; The Secret Out of Time	0.50	2.00	5.00	10.00
❑GS 4, RA, To Sow the Seeds of Death's Day; Attack of the War Machine, 1: Moses Magnum (Magnum Force); A: Punisher	0.50	4.00	10.00	20.00
❑GS 5, RA, Beware the Path of the Monster; The Lurker in the Swamp	0.50	1.40	3.50	7.00
❑GS 6, The Web and the Flame	0.50	1.40	3.50	7.00

AMAZING SPIDER-MAN, THE (PUBLIC SERVICE SERIES)

MARVEL

	ORIG	GOOD	FINE	N-MINT
❑1, TMc, Skating on Thin Ice!	1.25	0.50	1.25	2.50
❑1-2, TMc, US Edition; Skating on Thin Ice	1.50	0.40	1.00	2.00
❑2, TMc, Double Trouble!	1.50	0.50	1.25	2.50
❑2-2, TMc, US Edition; Double Trouble	1.50	0.40	1.00	2.00
❑3, TMc, Hit and Run!	1.50	0.50	1.25	2.50
❑3-2, TMc, A: Ghost Rider, US Edition; Hit and Run	1.50	0.40	1.00	2.00
❑4, Feb 93, TMc, 1: Turbine, Chaos in Calgary	1.50	0.50	1.25	2.50
❑4-2, US Edition; Chaos in Calgary	1.50	0.40	1.00	2.00

AMAZING SPIDER-MAN, THE (VOL. 2)

MARVEL

	ORIG	GOOD	FINE	N-MINT
❑1, Jan 99, JBy, wraparound cover	2.99	0.60	1.50	3.00
❑1/A, Jan 99, JBy	—	3.00	7.50	15.00
❑1/B, Jan 99, JBy	—	9.00	22.50	45.00
❑1/C, Jan 99, JBy, DFE alternate cover	—	1.00	2.50	5.00
❑1/D, Jan 99, JBy	—	3.00	7.50	15.00
❑1/E, JBy, Certificate of Authenticity; Marvel Authentix edition	—	2.00	5.00	10.00
❑2/A, Feb 99, JBy, V: Shadrac, Cover A; gatefold summary; new Spider-Man's identity revealed; Skeleton grabbing Spider-Man	1.99	0.40	1.00	1.99
❑2/B, Feb 99, JBy, V: Shadrac, Cover B; gatefold summary; new Spider-Man's identity revealed	1.99	0.40	1.00	1.99
❑3, Mar 99, JBy, O: Shadrac	1.99	0.40	1.00	1.99
❑4, Apr 99, JBy, Betrayals, V: Sandman; V: Trapster; A: Fantastic Four	1.99	0.40	1.00	1.99
❑5, May 99, A: new Spider-Woman	1.99	0.40	1.00	1.99
❑6, Jun 99, V: Spider-Woman	1.99	0.40	1.00	1.99
❑7, Jul 99, Flash Thompson's fantasy	1.99	0.40	1.00	1.99
❑8, Aug 99, V: Mysterio	1.99	0.40	1.00	1.99
❑9, Sep 99, A: Doctor Octopus	1.99	0.40	1.00	1.99
❑10, Oct 99, V: Captain Power; A: Doctor Octopus	1.99	0.40	1.00	1.99
❑11, Nov 99, V: Blob	1.99	0.40	1.00	1.99
❑12, Dec 99, Giant-size	2.99	0.60	1.50	2.99
❑13, Jan 00	1.99	0.40	1.00	1.99
❑14, Feb 00, DGr; JBy, JBy (w), A Surfeit of Spiders	1.99	0.40	1.00	1.99

	ORIG	GOOD	FINE	N-MINT
❑15, Mar 00, JBy, JBy (w), We're All Doomed...Again!	1.99	0.40	1.00	1.99
❑16, Apr 00	1.99	0.40	1.00	1.99
❑17, May 00	1.99	0.40	1.00	1.99
❑18, Jun 00	2.25	0.45	1.13	2.25
❑19, Jul 00, EL, Mirror Mirror, A: Venom	2.25	0.45	1.13	2.25
❑20, Aug 00, EL; JM; JR; KP; SD, EL (c), Setup!; Captured by J. Jonah Jameson, 100pgs.	2.99	0.80	2.00	3.99
❑21, Sep 00, EL, EL (c), Slayers to the Left of Me ..., V: Spider-Slayers	2.25	0.45	1.13	2.25
❑22, Oct 00	2.25	0.45	1.13	2.25
❑23, Nov 00, JR2, The Distinguished Gentleman from New York, Part 2	2.25	0.45	1.13	2.25
❑24, Dec 00, JR2, Maximum Security; The Distinguished Gentleman from New York, Part 3: Failure is Not an Option	2.25	0.45	1.13	2.25
❑25, Jan 01	2.25	0.45	1.13	2.25
❑26, Feb 01	2.25	0.45	1.13	2.25
❑27, Mar 01, JR2, The Stray, A: Mr. P; A: Mr. Q	2.25	0.45	1.13	2.25
❑28, Apr 01, Distractions	2.25	0.45	1.13	2.25
❑29, May 01, Mary Jane, Return of Mary Jane	2.25	0.45	1.13	2.25
❑30	2.25	0.45	1.13	2.25
❑31	2.25	0.45	1.13	2.25
❑32	2.25	0.45	1.13	2.25
❑33	2.25	0.45	1.13	2.25
❑Anl 1999, Jun 99, V: Wizard; V: Trapster, 1999 Annual	3.50	0.70	1.75	3.50
❑Anl 2001, Passages	2.99	0.60	1.50	2.99

AMAZING SPIDER-MAN 30TH ANNIVERSARY POSTER MAGAZINE
MARVEL

Value: Cover or less

❑1, nn ... 3.95

AMAZING SPIDER-MAN GIVEAWAYS
MARVEL

	ORIG	GOOD	FINE	N-MINT
❑1, (two different, both #1)	—	0.20	0.50	1.00
❑2, nn; Managing Materials	—	0.20	0.50	1.00
❑3, Feb 77, Planned Parenthood giveaway; miniature; ... vs. The Prodigy!	—	0.20	0.50	1.00
❑5, nn; child abuse; with New Mutants	—	0.20	0.50	1.00

AMAZING SPIDER-MAN, THE: SOUL OF THE HUNTER
MARVEL

Value: Cover or less

❑1, Aug 92, MZ, nn ... 5.95

AMAZING SPIDER-MAN SUPER SPECIAL, THE
MARVEL

Value: Cover or less

❑1, The Far Cry, Flip-book; two of the stories continue in Spider-Man Super Special #1; Amazing Scarlet Spider on other side ... 3.95

AMAZING STRIP
ANTARCTIC

Value: Cover or less

❑1, Feb 94 ... 2.95
❑2, Mar 94 ... 2.95
❑3, Apr 94 ... 2.95
❑4, May 94 ... 2.95
❑5, Jun 94 ... 2.95
❑6, Jul 94 ... 2.95
❑7, Aug 94 ... 2.95
❑8, Sep 94 ... 2.95
❑9, Nov 94 ... 2.95
❑10, Dec 94 ... 2.95

AMAZING WAHZOO
SOLSON

Value: Cover or less

❑1, 86, RB, Howard!; ...When Clouds Gather!, 1: Amazing Wahzoo; 1: Howard Wasnuski ... 1.75

AMAZING WORLD OF SUPERMAN
DC

	ORIG	GOOD	FINE	N-MINT
❑1, 73	2.00	0.60	1.50	3.00

AMAZING X-MEN
MARVEL

Value: Cover or less

❑1, Mar 95, The Crossing Guards ... 1.95
❑2, Apr 95 ... 1.95
❑3, May 95 ... 1.95
❑4, Jun 95 ... 1.95

AMAZON
DC

Value: Cover or less

❑1, Apr 96, JBy, JBy (w), Family History, O: Wonder Woman (Amalgam) ... 1.95

AMAZON, THE
COMICO

Value: Cover or less

❑1, Mar 89, Spirit Of The Amazon ... 1.95
❑2, Apr 89 ... 1.95
❑3, May 89 ... 1.95

AMAZON ATTACK 3-D
3-D ZONE

Value: Cover or less

❑1, nn ... 3.95

AMAZONS
FANTAGRAPHICS

Value: Cover or less

❑1, b&w ... 2.95

AMAZON TALES
FANTACO

Value: Cover or less

❑1, Texoma Red ... 2.95
❑2 ... 2.95
❑3 ... 2.95

Keith Giffen's Ambush Bug was one of the few comic-book characters to know he was a comic-book character.

AMAZON WARRIORS
AC

Value: Cover or less

❑1, 89, b&w Reprint ... 2.50

AMAZON WOMAN (1ST SERIES)
FANTACO

Value: Cover or less

❑1 ... 2.95
❑2 ... 2.95

AMAZON WOMAN (2ND SERIES)
FANTACO

Value: Cover or less

❑1, Curse Of The Amazon ... 2.95
❑2 ... 2.95
❑3 ... 2.95
❑4 ... 2.95

AMBER: NINE PRINCES IN AMBER (ROGER ZELAZNY'S...)
DC

Value: Cover or less

❑1, prestige format; adapts Zelazny story ... 6.95
❑2, prestige format; adapts Zelazny story ... 6.95
❑3, prestige format; adapts Zelazny story ... 6.95

AMBER: THE GUNS OF AVALON (ROGER ZELAZNY'S...)
DC

Value: Cover or less

❑1, prestige format ... 6.95
❑2, prestige format ... 6.95
❑3, Final Issue; prestige format ... 6.95

AMBUSH BUG
DC

	ORIG	GOOD	FINE	N-MINT
❑1, Jun 85, KG, KG (w), Wipe Out	0.75	0.20	0.50	1.00
❑2, Jul 85, KG, KG (w), Ambush Bug vs The koala Who Wlkas Like a Man!! (Awwwww, Cute)	0.75	0.20	0.50	1.00
❑3, Aug 85, KG, KG (w), The Ambush Bug History of the DC Universe	0.75	0.20	0.50	1.00
❑4, Sep 85, KG, KG (w), Coincidence; Professor Schwab's Mystery Picture	0.75	0.20	0.50	1.00

AMBUSH BUG NOTHING SPECIAL
DC

Value: Cover or less

❑1, Sep 92, KG, KG (w), The Book Of Jobs ... 2.50

AMBUSH BUG STOCKING STUFFER
DC

Value: Cover or less

❑1, Mar 86, KG, KG (w), I Knew I Should Have Taken That Left Toyn Back In Albakoyky ... 1.25

AMERICAN, THE
DARK HORSE

Value: Cover or less

❑1, Aug 87, Dead Wrong, 1: The American (modern), b&w ... 1.50
❑2, Oct 87 ... 1.75
❑3, Dec 87, America's Team ... 1.75
❑4, Apr 88 ... 1.75
❑5, Jul 88, Bearing Witness ... 1.75
❑6, Sep 88 ... 1.75
❑7, Oct 88, The Reality, Part 1 ... 1.75
❑8, Feb 89, The Reality, Part 2 ... 1.75
❑SE 1, b&w; Special edition ... 2.25

AMERICAN ARTISTS W.O.W. THE WORLD OF WARD
ALLIED

Value: Cover or less

❑1, BWa, Reprint ... 3.95

AMERICAN BOOK, THE
DARK HORSE

Value: Cover or less

❑1, Oct 88, O: American, b&w ... 5.95

AMERICAN CENTURY
VERTIGO

Value: Cover or less

❑1, May 01, HC (w), Borrowed Time: Interest Computed Daily ... 2.50
❑2, Jun 01, HC (w) ... 2.50
❑3, Jul 01, HC (w) ... 2.50
❑4, Aug 01, HC (w) ... 2.50
❑5, Aug 01, HC (w) ... 2.50

AMERICAN FLAGG
FIRST

	ORIG	GOOD	FINE	N-MINT
❑1, Oct 83, HC, 1: Reuben Flagg	1.00	0.50	1.25	2.50
❑2, Nov 83, HC	1.00	0.40	1.00	2.00
❑3, Dec 83, HC	1.00	0.40	1.00	2.00
❑4, Jan 84, HC	1.00	0.40	1.00	2.00
❑5, Feb 84, HC, HC (w), Southern Comfort, Part 2	1.00	0.40	1.00	2.00
❑6, Mar 84, HC	1.00	0.30	0.75	1.50
❑7, Apr 84, HC	1.00	0.30	0.75	1.50
❑8, May 84, HC	1.00	0.30	0.75	1.50
❑9, Jun 84, HC	1.00	0.30	0.75	1.50
❑10, Jul 84, HC	1.00	0.30	0.75	1.50

	ORIG	GOOD	FINE	N-MINT
❑11, Aug 84, HC	1.00	0.30	0.75	1.50
❑12, Sep 84, HC	1.00	0.30	0.75	1.50
❑13, Oct 84, HC	1.00	0.30	0.75	1.50
❑14, Nov 84, PB	1.25	0.25	0.63	1.25
❑15, Dec 84, HC	1.25	0.25	0.63	1.25
❑16, Jan 85, HC	1.25	0.25	0.63	1.25
❑17, Feb 85, HC	1.25	0.25	0.63	1.25
❑18, Mar 85, HC	1.25	0.25	0.63	1.25
❑19, Apr 85, HC	1.25	0.25	0.63	1.25
❑20, May 85, HC	1.25	0.25	0.63	1.25
❑21, Jun 85, AMo (w)	1.25	0.25	0.63	1.25
❑22, Jul 85, HC (c), AMo (w)	1.25	0.25	0.63	1.25
❑23, Aug 85, HC (c), AMo (w)	1.25	0.25	0.63	1.25
❑24, Sep 85, HC (c), AMo (w)	1.25	0.25	0.63	1.25
❑25, Oct 85, HC (c), AMo (w)	1.25	0.25	0.63	1.25
❑26, Nov 85, HC (c), AMo (w)	1.25	0.25	0.63	1.25
❑27, Dec 85, HC, AMo (w)	1.25	0.25	0.63	1.25
❑28, Apr 86, JSa; HC	1.25	0.25	0.63	1.25
❑29, May 86, JSa; HC	1.25	0.25	0.63	1.25
❑30, Jun 86, JSa; HC	1.25	0.25	0.63	1.25
❑31, Jul 86, HC, O: Bob Violence	1.25	0.25	0.63	1.25
❑32, Aug 86, HC	1.25	0.25	0.63	1.25
❑33, Sep 86	1.25	0.25	0.63	1.25
❑34	1.25	0.25	0.63	1.25
❑35, Dec 86	1.25	0.25	0.63	1.25
❑36, Jan 87	1.25	0.25	0.63	1.25
❑37, Feb 87	1.25	0.25	0.63	1.25
❑38, Mar 87, HC	1.25	0.25	0.63	1.25
❑39, Apr 87, HC	1.25	0.25	0.63	1.25
❑40, May 87, HC	1.25	0.25	0.63	1.25
❑41, Jun 87, HC	1.25	0.25	0.63	1.25
❑42, Jul 87, HC	1.25	0.25	0.63	1.25
❑43, Aug 87, HC	1.25	0.25	0.63	1.25
❑44, Sep 87, Reuben Redux?	1.25	0.25	0.63	1.25
❑45	1.25	0.25	0.63	1.25
❑46, HC (c), apology	1.25	0.35	0.88	1.75
❑47, HC	1.75	0.35	0.88	1.75
❑48, HC	1.75	0.35	0.88	1.75
❑49, HC	1.75	0.35	0.88	1.75
❑50, HC	1.75	0.35	0.88	1.75
❑SE 1, Nov 86, HC, HC (w), Back on the Track for '76, Special #1	1.75	0.35	0.88	1.75

AMERICAN FLAGG (HOWARD CHAYKIN'S...)
FIRST

	ORIG	GOOD	FINE	N-MINT
❑1, May 88	1.75	0.35	0.88	1.75
❑2, Jun 88	1.75	0.35	0.88	1.75
❑3, Jul 88	1.75	0.35	0.88	1.75
❑4, Aug 88	1.75	0.35	0.88	1.75
❑5, Sep 88	1.75	0.35	0.88	1.75
❑6, Oct 88	1.75	0.39	0.98	1.95
❑7, Nov 88	1.75	0.39	0.98	1.95
❑8, Dec 88	1.75	0.39	0.98	1.95
❑9, Jan 89	1.95	0.39	0.98	1.95
❑10, Feb 89	1.95	0.39	0.98	1.95
❑11, Mar 89	1.95	0.39	0.98	1.95
❑12, Apr 89	1.95	0.39	0.98	1.95

AMERICAN FLYER
LAST GASP

	ORIG	GOOD	FINE	N-MINT
❑1	0.50	0.60	1.50	3.00
❑2, The Wizard's Challenge; Star Wench on Mars	0.50	0.60	1.50	3.00

AMERICAN FREAK: A TALE OF THE UN-MEN
DC

	ORIG	GOOD	FINE	N-MINT
❑1, Feb 94, The Nature Of The Beast	1.95	0.40	1.00	2.00
❑2, Mar 94, The Covenant of Freaks	1.95	0.40	1.00	2.00
❑3, Apr 94, Blue Skies of Purgatory	1.95	0.40	1.00	2.00
❑4, May 94	1.95	0.40	1.00	2.00
❑5, Jun 94, The Dark Family	1.95	0.40	1.00	2.00

AMERICAN HEROES
PERSONALITY

Value: Cover or less

❑1, b&w 2.95

AMERICAN, THE: LOST IN AMERICA
DARK HORSE

Value: Cover or less

❑1, Jul 92 .... 2.50
❑2, Aug 92 .... 2.50
❑3, Sep 92 .... 2.50
❑4, Oct 92 .... 2.50

AMERICAN PRIMITIVE
3-D ZONE

Value: Cover or less

❑1, b&w; not 3-D 2.50

AMERICAN SPLENDOR
PEKAR

	ORIG	GOOD	FINE	N-MINT
❑1	—	2.00	5.00	10.00
❑2	—	1.20	3.00	6.00
❑3	—	1.00	2.50	5.00
❑4	—	1.00	2.50	5.00
❑5	—	1.00	2.50	5.00
❑6	—	0.80	2.00	4.00
❑7	—	0.80	2.00	4.00
❑8	—	0.80	2.00	4.00
❑9	—	0.80	2.00	4.00
❑10	—	0.80	2.00	4.00
❑11	—	0.60	1.50	3.00
❑12	—	0.60	1.50	3.00
❑13	—	0.60	1.50	3.00
❑14	—	0.60	1.50	3.00
❑15	—	0.60	1.50	3.00
❑17	4.95	0.99	2.47	4.95

AMERICAN SPLENDOR: BEDTIME STORIES
DARK HORSE

Value: Cover or less

❑1, Jun 00, Interviewing the Interviewer; "Pop's" Little Friend. 3.95

AMERICAN SPLENDOR: COMIC-CON COMICS
DARK HORSE

Value: Cover or less

❑1, Aug 96, An Invitation; Huckster, nn; b&w; Anthology 2.95

AMERICAN SPLENDOR: MUSIC COMICS
DARK HORSE

Value: Cover or less

❑1, Nov 97, nn; b&w; collects Pekar's stories about music. 2.95

AMERICAN SPLENDOR: ODDS & ENDS
DARK HORSE

Value: Cover or less

❑1, Dec 97, nn; b&w; collects short pieces 2.95

AMERICAN SPLENDOR: ON THE JOB
DARK HORSE

Value: Cover or less

❑1, May 97, nn; b&w; One-Shot 2.95

AMERICAN SPLENDOR: PORTRAIT OF THE AUTHOR IN HIS DECLINING YEARS
DARK HORSE

Value: Cover or less

❑1, Apr 01, Payback; Dennis McGee 3.99

AMERICAN SPLENDOR SPECIAL: A STEP OUT OF THE NEST
DARK HORSE

Value: Cover or less

❑1, Aug 94, b&w 2.95

AMERICAN SPLENDOR: TERMINAL
DARK HORSE

Value: Cover or less

❑1, Sep 99, The Terminal Years 2.95

AMERICAN SPLENDOR: TRANSATLANTIC COMICS
DARK HORSE

Value: Cover or less

❑1, Jul 98, nn 2.95

AMERICAN SPLENDOR: WINDFALL
DARK HORSE

Value: Cover or less

❑1, 95, Flight to Chicago; Ethnicity, b&w 3.95
❑2, Oct 95, b&w 3.95

AMERICAN TAIL, AN: FIEVEL GOES WEST
MARVEL

	ORIG	GOOD	FINE	N-MINT
❑1, Go West, Young Mousekewitz, movie Adaptation	1.00	0.25	0.63	1.25
❑2, movie Adaptation	1.00	0.25	0.63	1.25
❑3, movie Adaptation	1.00	0.25	0.63	1.25

AMERICAN WOMAN
ANTARCTIC

Value: Cover or less

❑1, Jun 98, 1: American Woman 2.95
❑2, Oct 98 .... 2.95

AMERICA'S BEST COMICS PREVIEW
AMERICA'S BEST

	ORIG	GOOD	FINE	N-MINT
❑1, AMo (w), Preview and Sketchbook, Included in Wizard #91	—	0.30	0.75	1.50

AMERICA'S BEST TV COMICS
ABC

	ORIG	GOOD	FINE	N-MINT
❑1, ca. 67, JR; JK, SL (w), Casper the Friendly Ghost: The Flying Horse; The Fantastic Four: Prisoners of the Pharaoh, nn; Giant-size; promotional comic published by Marvel for ABC to promote Saturday morning cartoons	0.25	11.00	27.50	55.00

AMERICA VS. THE JUSTICE SOCIETY
DC

Value: Cover or less

❑1, Jan 85, Chapter 1, I Accuse; Chapter 2, O: JSA, Giant-size 1.50
❑2, Feb 85, AA, O: All-Star Squadron 1.00
❑3, Mar 85, O: Freedom Fighters, Wizard 1.00
❑4, Apr 85, O: JSA revival, multiverse (Flash of Two Worlds) 1.00

AMERICOMICS
AC

Value: Cover or less

❑1, Apr 83, 1: the Shade (Americomics) 3.00
❑2, Jun 83 .... 2.00
❑3, Aug 83 .... 2.00
❑4, Oct 83, O: Dragonfly 2.00
❑5, Dec 83 .... 1.75
❑6, Mar 84 .... 1.75
❑SE 1, Jan 83, Sentinels of Justice, A: Captain Atom; A: Blue Beetle; A: Nightshade; A: The Question, Special 2.00

AMETHYST
DC

	ORIG	GOOD	FINE	N-MINT
❑1, Jan 85, The Long Way Home, 1: Fire Jade	0.75	0.20	0.50	1.00
❑2, Feb 85	0.75	0.20	0.50	1.00
❑3, Mar 85	0.75	0.20	0.50	1.00
❑4, Apr 85	0.75	0.20	0.50	1.00
❑5, May 85	0.75	0.20	0.50	1.00
❑6, Jun 85	0.75	0.20	0.50	1.00
❑7, Jul 85	0.75	0.20	0.50	1.00

	ORIG	GOOD	FINE	N-MINT
❑8, Aug 85	0.75	0.20	0.50	1.00
❑9, Sep 85	0.75	0.20	0.50	1.00
❑10, Oct 85	0.75	0.20	0.50	1.00
❑11, Nov 85	0.75	0.20	0.50	1.00
❑12, Dec 85	0.75	0.20	0.50	1.00
❑13, Feb 86, Crisis on Infinite Earths, A: Doctor Fate	0.75	0.20	0.50	1.00
❑14, Apr 86	0.75	0.20	0.50	1.00
❑15, Jun 86, 1: Flaw; 1: Child	0.75	0.20	0.50	1.00
❑16, Aug 86, Final Issue	0.75	0.20	0.50	1.00
❑SE 1, Oct 86, Special	1.25	0.20	0.50	1.00

AMETHYST (MINI-SERIES)
DC

Value: Cover or less

❑1, Nov 87, ...And Wait The Pointed Hour ... 1.25
❑2, Dec 87 ... 1.25
❑3, Jan 88 ... 1.25
❑4, Feb 88 ... 1.25

AMETHYST, PRINCESS OF GEMWORLD
DC

	ORIG	GOOD	FINE	N-MINT
❑1, May 83, The Birthright, O: Amethyst	0.60	0.20	0.50	1.00
❑2, Jun 83	0.60	0.20	0.50	1.00
❑3, Jul 83	0.60	0.20	0.50	1.00
❑4, Aug 83	0.60	0.20	0.50	1.00
❑5, Sep 83	0.60	0.20	0.50	1.00
❑6, Oct 83	0.60	0.20	0.50	1.00
❑7, Nov 83	0.60	0.20	0.50	1.00
❑8, Dec 83	0.60	0.20	0.50	1.00
❑9, Jan 84, Dreams of Glory, Dreams of Death!	0.75	0.20	0.50	1.00
❑10, Feb 84, Blackout	0.75	0.20	0.50	1.00
❑11, Mar 84	0.75	0.20	0.50	1.00
❑12, Apr 84	0.75	0.20	0.50	1.00
❑Anl 1	1.25	0.25	0.63	1.25

AMMO ARMAGEDDON
ATOMEKA

Value: Cover or less

❑1, Kicking The Monolithic Habit; Mechonismechs ... 4.95

AMORA (GRAY MORROW'S...)
FANTAGRAPHICS

Value: Cover or less

❑1, GM, GM (w), Blazing Stewardess; Panache Gordon: Sexual Lierator of the Universe, b&w; adult ... 2.95

AMUSING STORIES
RENEGADE

Value: Cover or less

❑1, Success Formula; It's Time to Meet...Urban Gorilla, A: Voyd; A: Blast; A: Thub; A: Prof Hackle; A: Ol' Doc Murphy; A: Gail Aardvark, b&w ... 2.00

AMY PAPUDA
NORTHSTAR

Value: Cover or less

❑1 ... 2.50
❑2, Hard Times Papuda ... 2.50

ANARCHY COMICS
LAST GASP

Value: Cover or less

❑1 ... 2.50
❑2 ... 2.50
❑3 ... 2.50
❑4, Armageddon Outtahere!; You rule the World! ... 2.50

ANARKY
DC

Value: Cover or less

❑1, May 99, Aberration, Part 1, A: JLA ... 2.50
❑2, Jun 99, Aberration, Part 2, A: Green Lantern ... 2.50
❑3, Jul 99, Aberration, Part 3, V: Green Lantern ... 2.50
❑4, Aug 99, War and Peace Part 1, A: Ra's Al Ghul ... 2.50
❑5, Sep 99, War and Peace Part 2, A: Ra's Al Ghul ... 2.50
❑6, Oct 99, War and Peace Part 3, A: Ra's Al Ghul ... 2.50
❑7, Nov 99, When Johnny Comes Marching Home, A: Haunted Tank, Day of Judgment ... 2.50
❑8, Dec 99, Final Issue ... 2.50

ANARKY (MINI-SERIES)
DC

Value: Cover or less

❑1, May 97, Metamorphosis, Part 1, A: Demon ... 2.50
❑2, Jun 97, Metamorphosis, Part 2, A: Darkseid ... 2.50
❑3, Jul 97, A: Batman ... 2.50
❑4, Aug 97 ... 2.50

ANDROMEDA (ANDROMEDA)
ANDROMEDA

Value: Cover or less

❑1, Mar 95 ... 2.50

ANDROMEDA (SILVER SNAIL)
SILVER SNAIL

Value: Cover or less

❑1 ... 2.00
❑2 ... 2.00
❑3 ... 2.00
❑4 ... 2.00
❑5 ... 2.00
❑6 ... 2.00

Andy Panda was created for Walter Lantz cartoons in 1939.

© 1976 Gold Key

ANDY PANDA (GOLD KEY)
GOLD KEY

	ORIG	GOOD	FINE	N-MINT
❑1	—	0.60	1.50	3.00
❑2	—	0.40	1.00	2.00
❑3	—	0.40	1.00	2.00
❑4	—	0.40	1.00	2.00
❑5	—	0.30	0.75	1.50
❑6	—	0.30	0.75	1.50
❑7, Feb 75	0.25	0.30	0.75	1.50
❑8	—	0.30	0.75	1.50
❑9	—	0.30	0.75	1.50
❑10	—	0.30	0.75	1.50
❑11	—	0.30	0.75	1.50
❑12	—	0.30	0.75	1.50
❑13	—	0.30	0.75	1.50
❑14, Jul 76	0.25	0.30	0.75	1.50
❑15	—	0.30	0.75	1.50
❑16	—	0.30	0.75	1.50
❑17, Jan 77	0.30	0.30	0.75	1.50
❑18	—	0.30	0.75	1.50
❑19	—	0.30	0.75	1.50
❑20	—	0.30	0.75	1.50
❑21	—	0.30	0.75	1.50
❑22	—	0.30	0.75	1.50
❑23	—	0.30	0.75	1.50

A-NEXT
MARVEL

Value: Cover or less

❑1, Oct 98, Second Coming, A: Jolt; A: Stinger; A: Juggernaut 2; A: Speedball; A: Jubilee; A: Thunderstryke; A: Mainframe; A: Tyrus, the Terrible, next generation of Avengers ... 1.99
❑2/A, Nov 98, Suddenly ... The Sentry!, 1: Earth Sentry ... 1.99
❑2/B, Nov 98, Suddenly ... The Sentry!, 1: Earth Sentry ... 1.99
❑3, Dec 98, V: Defenders; 1: Doc Magus ... 1.99
❑4, Jan 99, 1: American Dream, Freebooter, Bluestreak, Crimson Curse, Coal Tiger ... 1.99
❑5, Feb 99, Ghosts of the Past, A: Doctor Doom ... 1.99
❑6, Mar 99, Majority Rules!, A: Argos ... 1.99
❑7, Apr 99, The Last Days of the Avengers, 1: Iron Man (villain) 1.99
❑8, May 99 ... 1.99
❑9, Jun 99 ... 1.99
❑10, Jul 99, V: Thunder Guard 1.99
❑11, Aug 99, A: Captain America ... 1.99

ANGEL (DARK HORSE)
DARK HORSE

	ORIG	GOOD	FINE	N-MINT
❑1, Nov 99, Surrogates, Part 1; Surrogates, Part 2	2.95	0.59	1.48	2.95
❑1/A, Nov 99, Surrogates, Part 2; Surrogates, Part 1, Dynamic Forces gold logo variant	—	0.60	1.50	3.00
❑1/SC, Nov 99, Surrogates, Part 2; Surrogates, Part 1, Photo cover	2.95	0.59	1.48	2.95
❑2, Dec 99	2.95	0.59	1.48	2.95
❑2/SC, Dec 99, Photo cover	2.95	0.59	1.48	2.95
❑3, Jan 00	2.95	0.59	1.48	2.95
❑3/A, Jan 00, Dynamic Forces purple foil variant (white cover); Valentine's Day Edition	—	0.60	1.50	3.00
❑3/SC, Jan 00, Photo cover	2.95	0.59	1.48	2.95
❑4, Feb 00	2.95	0.59	1.48	2.95
❑4/SC, Feb 00, Photo cover	2.95	0.59	1.48	2.95
❑5, Mar 00	2.95	0.59	1.48	2.95
❑5/SC, Mar 00, Photo cover	2.95	0.59	1.48	2.95
❑6, Apr 00	2.95	0.59	1.48	2.95
❑6/SC, Apr 00, Photo cover	2.95	0.59	1.48	2.95
❑7, May 00	2.95	0.59	1.48	2.95
❑7/A, May 00, Dynamic Forces Lucky 7 foil variant (limited to 1500 copies)	—	0.60	1.50	3.00
❑7/SC, May 00, Photo cover	2.95	0.59	1.48	2.95
❑8, Jun 00, Beneath the Surface	2.95	0.59	1.48	2.95
❑8/SC, Jun 00, Beneath the Surface, Photo cover	2.95	0.59	1.48	2.95
❑9, Jul 00, Beneath the Surface	2.95	0.59	1.48	2.95
❑9/SC, Jul 00, Beneath the Surface, Photo cover	2.95	0.59	1.48	2.95
❑10, Aug 00, Strange Bedfellows; Strange Bedfellows, Part 1	2.95	0.59	1.48	2.95
❑10/SC, Aug 00, Strange Bedfellows; Strange Bedfellows, Part 1, Photo cover	2.95	0.59	1.48	2.95
❑11, Sep 00, Strange Bedfellows; Strange Bedfellows, Part 2	2.95	0.59	1.48	2.95
❑11/SC, Sep 00, Strange Bedfellows; Strange Bedfellows, Part 2, Photo cover	2.95	0.59	1.48	2.95

	ORIG	GOOD	FINE	N-MINT
❑12, Oct 00, Vermin; Vermin, Part 1	2.95	0.60	1.50	2.99
❑12/SC, Oct 00, Vermin; Vermin, Part 1, Photo cover	2.95	0.60	1.50	2.99
❑13, Nov 00, Vermin, Part 2	2.99	0.60	1.50	2.99
❑13/SC, Nov 00, Vermin, Part 2, Photo cover	2.99	0.60	1.50	2.99
❑14, Dec 00, Little Girl Lost	2.99	0.60	1.50	2.99
❑14/SC, Dec 00, Little Girl Lost, Photo cover	2.99	0.60	1.50	2.99
❑15, Feb 01, Past Lives, Part 1	2.99	0.60	1.50	2.99
❑15/SC, Feb 01, Photo cover	2.99	0.60	1.50	2.99
❑16, Mar 01, Past Lives, Part 3	2.99	0.60	1.50	2.99
❑16/SC, Mar 01, Photo cover	2.99	0.60	1.50	2.99
❑17, Apr 01, Cordelia	2.99	0.60	1.50	2.99
❑17/SC, Apr 01, Cordelia, Photo cover	2.99	0.60	1.50	2.99

ANGELA
IMAGE

	ORIG	GOOD	FINE	N-MINT
❑1, Dec 94, NG (w), A: Spawn	2.25	0.80	2.00	4.00
❑1/A, Dec 94, NG (w), A: Spawn, Pirate Spawn cover	—	0.80	2.00	4.00
❑2, Jan 95, NG (w), A: Spawn	2.25	0.60	1.50	3.00
❑3, Feb 95, NG (w)	2.25	0.60	1.50	3.00

ANGELA/GLORY: RAGE OF ANGELS
IMAGE

Value: Cover or less

- ❑1/A, Mar 96 2.50
- ❑1/B, Mar 96 2.50

ANGEL AND THE APE
DC

	ORIG	GOOD	FINE	N-MINT
❑1, Nov 68	—	6.00	15.00	30.00
❑2, Jan 69	—	4.40	11.00	22.00
❑3, Mar 69	—	3.60	9.00	18.00
❑4, May 69	—	3.60	9.00	18.00
❑5, Jul 69	—	3.60	9.00	18.00
❑6, Sep 69	—	3.60	9.00	18.00
❑7, Nov 69	—	3.60	9.00	18.00

ANGEL AND THE APE (MINI-SERIES)
DC

	ORIG	GOOD	FINE	N-MINT
❑1, Mar 91, PF, PF (w), Shaking The Family Tree	1.00	0.25	0.63	1.25
❑2, Apr 91, PF	1.00	0.25	0.63	1.25
❑3, May 91, PF	1.00	0.25	0.63	1.25
❑4, Jun 91, PF	1.00	0.25	0.63	1.25

ANGEL FIRE
CRUSADE

Value: Cover or less

- ❑1/A, Jun 97, wraparound photo cover 2.95
- ❑1/B, Jun 97, black background cover 2.95
- ❑1/C, Jun 97, white background cover 2.95
- ❑2, Aug 97, A: Shi 2.95
- ❑3, Oct 97, b&w 2.95

ANGEL GIRL
ANGEL

Value: Cover or less

- ❑0 2.95
- ❑0/Nude, Nude cover 5.00

ANGEL GIRL: BEFORE THE WINGS
ANGEL

Value: Cover or less

- ❑1, Aug 97 2.95

ANGEL GIRL VS. VAMPIRE GIRLS
ANGEL

Value: Cover or less

- ❑1 2.95
- ❑1/Nude, Nude edition 9.95

ANGEL LOVE
DC

	ORIG	GOOD	FINE	N-MINT
❑1, Aug 86	0.75	0.20	0.50	1.00
❑2, Sep 86	0.75	0.20	0.50	1.00
❑3, Oct 86	0.75	0.20	0.50	1.00
❑4, Nov 86	0.75	0.20	0.50	1.00
❑5, Dec 86, The Search for Mary Beth, Part 1	0.75	0.20	0.50	1.00
❑6, Jan 87, The Search for Mary Beth, Part 2	0.75	0.20	0.50	1.00
❑7, Feb 87, The Search for Mary Beth, Part 3	0.75	0.20	0.50	1.00
❑8, Mar 87, The Search for Mary Beth, Part 4	0.75	0.20	0.50	1.00
❑Anl 1	1.25	0.25	0.63	1.25
❑SE 1, Special	1.25	0.25	0.63	1.25

ANGEL OF DEATH
INNOVATION

Value: Cover or less

- ❑1, Do Dead Men Dream, Part 1 2.25
- ❑2, Do Dead Men Dream, Part 2 2.25
- ❑3, Do Dead Men Dream, Part 3 2.25
- ❑4 2.25

ANGELS OF DESTRUCTION
MALIBU

Value: Cover or less

- ❑1, Oct 96, BMB (w), One-Shot 2.50

ANGRYMAN
CALIBER

Value: Cover or less

- ❑1 2.50
- ❑2 2.50
- ❑3 2.50

ANGRYMAN (2ND SERIES)
ICONOGRAFIX

Value: Cover or less

- ❑1 2.50
- ❑2 2.50
- ❑3 2.50

ANGRY SHADOWS
INNOVATION

Value: Cover or less

- ❑1, b&w 4.95

ANIMA
DC

Value: Cover or less

- ❑0, Oct 94, Zero Summer, Series continued in Anima #8 1.75
- ❑1, Mar 94, Snap Shots 1.75
- ❑2, Apr 94, False Dawn 1.75
- ❑3, May 94, Running With The Wolf 1.75
- ❑4, Jun 94 1.75
- ❑5, Jul 94, Wheel of Fortune 1.75
- ❑6, Aug 94 1.95
- ❑7, Sep 94, BA (w), Zero Hour 1.95
- ❑8, Nov 94, Series continued from Anima #0 1.95
- ❑9, Dec 94, N.O. Future 1.95
- ❑10, Jan 95 1.95
- ❑11, Feb 95, A: Conan O'Brien 1.95
- ❑12, Mar 95 1.95
- ❑13, Apr 95 1.95
- ❑14, Jun 95 2.25
- ❑15, Jul 95, Final Issue 2.25

ANIMAL CONFIDENTIAL
DARK HORSE

Value: Cover or less

- ❑1, May 92, The Spy; Horseshoes Ain't Lucky, nn; b&w; One-Shot; Anthology 2.25

ANIMAL MAN
DC

	ORIG	GOOD	FINE	N-MINT
❑1, Sep 88, BB (c)	1.25	1.00	2.50	5.00
❑2, Oct 88, BB (c)	1.25	0.60	1.50	3.00
❑3, Nov 88, BB (c)	1.25	0.50	1.25	2.50
❑4, Dec 88, BB (c), A: B'wana Beast	1.25	0.50	1.25	2.50
❑5, Dec 88, BB (c), Road Runner-Coyote	1.25	0.50	1.25	2.50
❑6, Jan 89, BB (c), Invasion!	1.25	0.40	1.00	2.00
❑7, Jan 89, BB (c)	1.25	0.40	1.00	2.00
❑8, Feb 89, BB (c), V: Mirror Master	1.25	0.40	1.00	2.00
❑9, Mar 89, BB (c), A: JLA	1.25	0.40	1.00	2.00
❑10, Apr 89, BB (c), A: Vixen	1.25	0.40	1.00	2.00
❑11, May 89, BB (c), A: Vixen	1.50	0.40	1.00	2.00
❑12, Jun 89, BB (c), A: Vixen	1.50	0.40	1.00	2.00
❑13, Jul 89, BB (c)	1.50	0.40	1.00	2.00
❑14, Aug 89, BB (c)	1.50	0.40	1.00	2.00
❑15, Sep 89, BB (c)	1.50	0.40	1.00	2.00
❑16, Oct 89, BB (c)	1.50	0.40	1.00	2.00
❑17, Nov 89, BB (c)	1.50	0.40	1.00	2.00
❑18, Dec 89, BB (c)	1.50	0.40	1.00	2.00
❑19, Jan 90, BB (c)	1.50	0.40	1.00	2.00
❑20, Feb 90, BB (c)	1.50	0.40	1.00	2.00
❑21, Mar 90, BB (c)	1.50	0.40	1.00	2.00
❑22, Apr 90, BB (c)	1.50	0.40	1.00	2.00
❑23, May 90, BB (c), A: Phantom Stranger; A: Jason Blood, Arkham Asylum story	1.50	0.40	1.00	2.00
❑24, Jun 90, BB (c), A: Inferior Five	1.50	0.40	1.00	2.00
❑25, Jul 90, BB (c)	1.50	0.40	1.00	2.00
❑26, Aug 90, BB (c), Morrison puts himself in story	1.50	0.40	1.00	2.00
❑27, Sep 00, BB (c)	1.50	0.40	1.00	2.00
❑28, Oct 90, BB (c)	1.50	0.40	1.00	2.00
❑29, Nov 90, BB (c), D: The Notional Man	1.50	0.40	1.00	2.00
❑30, Dec 90, BB (c)	1.50	0.40	1.00	2.00
❑31, Jan 91, BB (c)	1.50	0.40	1.00	2.00
❑32, Feb 91, BB (c)	1.50	0.40	1.00	2.00
❑33, Mar 91, BB (c)	1.50	0.40	1.00	2.00
❑34, Apr 91, BB (c)	1.50	0.40	1.00	2.00
❑35, May 91, BB (c)	1.50	0.40	1.00	2.00
❑36, Jun 91, BB (c)	1.50	0.40	1.00	2.00
❑37, Jul 91, BB (c)	1.50	0.40	1.00	2.00
❑38, Aug 00, BB (c), Punisher parody	1.50	0.40	1.00	2.00
❑39, Sep 91	1.50	0.40	1.00	2.00
❑40, Oct 91, War of the Gods, Part 15	1.50	0.40	1.00	2.00
❑41, Nov 91	1.75	0.40	1.00	2.00
❑42, Dec 91	1.50	0.40	1.00	2.00
❑43, Jan 92	1.75	0.40	1.00	2.00
❑44, Feb 92	1.75	0.40	1.00	2.00
❑45, Mar 92	1.75	0.40	1.00	2.00
❑46, Apr 92	1.75	0.40	1.00	2.00
❑47, May 92	1.75	0.40	1.00	2.00
❑48, Jun 92	1.75	0.40	1.00	2.00
❑49, Jul 92	1.75	0.40	1.00	2.00
❑50, Aug 92, Giant-size	2.95	0.60	1.50	3.00
❑51, Sep 92, Flesh & Blood; Flesh and Blood, Part 1	1.75	0.40	1.00	2.00
❑52, Oct 92, Flesh & Blood; Flesh and Blood, Part 2	1.75	0.40	1.00	2.00
❑53, Nov 92, Flesh & Blood; Flesh and Blood, Part 3	1.75	0.40	1.00	2.00
❑54, Dec 92, Flesh & Blood; Flesh and Blood, Part 4	1.75	0.40	1.00	2.00
❑55, Jan 93, Flesh & Blood; Flesh and Blood, Part 5	1.75	0.40	1.00	2.00
❑56, Feb 93, Flesh & Blood; Flesh and Blood, Part 6, double-sized; Giant-size	3.50	0.70	1.75	3.50
❑57, Mar 93, Begin Vertigo line	1.75	0.40	1.00	2.00
❑58, Apr 93	1.75	0.40	1.00	2.00

Issue	ORIG	GOOD	FINE	N-MINT
❑59, May 93	1.75	0.40	1.00	2.00
❑60, Jun 93, BB (c)	1.95	0.40	1.00	2.00
❑61, Jul 93, Tooth and Claw, Part 1	1.95	0.40	1.00	2.00
❑62, Aug 93, Tooth and Claw, Part 2	1.95	0.40	1.00	2.00
❑63, Sep 93, Tooth and Claw, Part 3	1.95	0.40	1.00	2.00
❑64, Oct 93	1.95	0.40	1.00	2.00
❑65, Nov 93	1.95	0.40	1.00	2.00
❑66, Dec 93	1.95	0.40	1.00	2.00
❑67, Jan 94, Mysterious Ways, Part 1	1.95	0.40	1.00	2.00
❑68, Feb 94, Mysterious Ways, Part 2	1.95	0.40	1.00	2.00
❑69, Mar 94	1.95	0.40	1.00	2.00
❑70, Apr 94	1.95	0.40	1.00	2.00
❑71, May 94	1.95	0.39	0.98	1.95
❑72, Jun 94	1.95	0.39	0.98	1.95
❑73, Jul 94	1.95	0.39	0.98	1.95
❑74, Aug 94	1.95	0.39	0.98	1.95
❑75, Sep 94	1.95	0.39	0.98	1.95
❑76, Oct 94	1.95	0.39	0.98	1.95
❑77, Nov 94	1.95	0.39	0.98	1.95
❑78, Dec 94	1.95	0.39	0.98	1.95
❑79, Jan 95	1.95	0.39	0.98	1.95
❑80, Feb 95	1.95	0.39	0.98	1.95
❑81, Mar 95, Wild Type, Part 1	1.95	0.39	0.98	1.95
❑82, Apr 95, Wild Type, Part 2	1.95	0.39	0.98	1.95
❑83, May 95, Wild Type, Part 3	2.25	0.45	1.13	2.25
❑84, Jun 95	2.25	0.45	1.13	2.25
❑85, Jul 95	2.25	0.45	1.13	2.25
❑86, Aug 95	2.25	0.45	1.13	2.25
❑87, Sep 95	2.25	0.45	1.13	2.25
❑88, Oct 95	2.25	0.45	1.13	2.25
❑89, Nov 95, Final Issue	2.25	0.45	1.13	2.25
❑Anl 1, The Children's Crusade, Part 3, "Children's Crusade"	3.95	0.80	2.00	4.00

ANIMAL MYSTIC
CRY FOR DAWN

Issue	ORIG	GOOD	FINE	N-MINT
❑1	3.50	3.60	9.00	18.00
❑1/LE, limited edition with alternate cover and eight additional pages	3.50	5.00	12.50	25.00
❑1-2, 2nd Printing	3.50	0.80	2.00	4.00
❑2	3.50	2.40	6.00	12.00
❑2-2, 2nd Printing	3.50	0.80	2.00	4.00
❑3	3.50	1.60	4.00	8.00
❑3-2, 2nd Printing	3.50	0.80	2.00	4.00
❑4	3.50	1.00	2.50	5.00
❑4-2, 2nd Printing	3.50	0.80	2.00	4.00

ANIMAL MYSTIC WATER WARS
SIRIUS

Issue	ORIG	GOOD	FINE	N-MINT
❑1, 96	2.95	0.59	1.48	2.95
❑2	2.95	0.59	1.48	2.95
❑3	2.95	0.59	1.48	2.95
❑4, 97	2.95	0.59	1.48	2.95
❑5, May 98	2.95	0.59	1.48	2.95
❑6, Oct 98	2.95	0.59	1.48	2.95
❑Ash 1, Preview edition	—	0.50	1.25	2.50

ANIMAL RIGHTS COMICS
STABUR

Issue	ORIG	GOOD	FINE	N-MINT
❑1, The Silver Spring Monkeys, Part 1, Just Their Faces are Different, Benefit comic for PETA	—	0.50	1.25	2.50

ANIMANIACS
DC

Issue	ORIG	GOOD	FINE	N-MINT
❑1, May 95, Global Disorder; Ice Cream Of Genie, A: Pinky & The Brain	1.50	0.45	1.13	2.25
❑2, Jun 95	1.50	0.40	1.00	2.00
❑3, Jul 95	1.50	0.40	1.00	2.00
❑4, Aug 95	1.50	0.40	1.00	2.00
❑5, Sep 95	1.50	0.40	1.00	2.00
❑6, Oct 95	1.50	0.35	0.88	1.75
❑7, Nov 95	1.50	0.35	0.88	1.75
❑8, Dec 95	1.50	0.35	0.88	1.75
❑9, Jan 96, Pulp Fiction parody cover	1.50	0.35	0.88	1.75
❑10, Feb 96, A Comic Book is Born; The Ice Cream Man Cometh, gratuitous pin-up cover	1.50	0.35	0.88	1.75
❑11, Mar 96, Brain for Brain; Frankly Frankenstein, Brain duplicates himself	1.50	0.35	0.88	1.75
❑12, Apr 96, A Blast from Hipsville; The Mod Couple	1.50	0.35	0.88	1.75
❑13, May 96	1.75	0.35	0.88	1.75
❑14, Jun 96	1.75	0.35	0.88	1.75
❑15, Jul 96	1.75	0.35	0.88	1.75
❑16, Aug 96, Wrestling issue	1.75	0.35	0.88	1.75
❑17, Sep 96, Animaniacs judge a beauty contest	1.75	0.35	0.88	1.75
❑18, Oct 96, Dupe Du Jour; Good Idea/ French Idea, All France issue	1.75	0.35	0.88	1.75
❑19, Nov 96, The Y Files; Sheep!	1.75	0.35	0.88	1.75
❑20, Dec 96, Rebels Just Cause!; East of Burbank, James Dean tribute	1.75	0.35	0.88	1.75
❑21, Jan 97, Radio Dazed; ER: Emergency Roomies, Christmas issue	1.75	0.35	0.88	1.75
❑22, Feb 97	1.75	0.35	0.88	1.75
❑23, Mar 97, Hello Nurse, Agent of H.U.B.B.A.; Useless Facts	1.75	0.35	0.88	1.75
❑24, Apr 97	1.75	0.35	0.88	1.75
❑25, May 97, Anniversary issue	1.75	0.35	0.88	1.75
❑26, Jun 97, Pancake House of Horor!; Randy Beaman's Tales of Terror: Bubble Doom, Tales from the Crypt cover parody	1.75	0.35	0.88	1.75

Buffy the Vampire Slayer's beefy co-star graduated to his own series, both on TV and in the comics.

© 1999 Twentieth Century Fox Film Corporation (Dark Horse)

Issue	ORIG	GOOD	FINE	N-MINT
❑27, Jul 97, Slappy's plane is hijacked	1.75	0.35	0.88	1.75
❑28, Aug 97, Star Trek parody; Science issue	1.75	0.35	0.88	1.75
❑29, Sep 97, Hello Nurse	1.75	0.35	0.88	1.75
❑30, Oct 97, "Electra Woman and Dyna Girl" parody	1.75	0.35	0.88	1.75
❑31, Nov 97, 101 Darnations; The Usual Boo!, 101 Dalmations parody	1.75	0.35	0.88	1.75
❑32, Dec 97, Dot hosts a slumber party	1.95	0.39	0.98	1.95
❑33, Jan 98, 1: Sakko Warner, Lost World cover	1.95	0.39	0.98	1.95
❑34, Feb 98	1.95	0.39	0.98	1.95
❑35, Mar 98, A: Freakazoid	1.95	0.39	0.98	1.95
❑36, Apr 98	1.95	0.39	0.98	1.95
❑37, May 98	1.95	0.39	0.98	1.95
❑38, Jun 98, manga-style cover	1.95	0.39	0.98	1.95
❑39, Jul 98, A: Alfred Nobel	1.95	0.39	0.98	1.95
❑40, Sep 98, Spice Girls parody	1.99	0.39	0.98	1.95
❑41, Oct 98, Little Nemo and Little Mermaid parodies	1.99	0.39	0.98	1.95
❑42, Nov 98, Love Boat parody	1.99	0.40	1.00	1.99
❑43, Dec 98, Pinky & the Brain	1.99	0.40	1.00	1.99
❑44, Jan 99, Pinky & the Brain	1.99	0.40	1.00	1.99
❑45, Feb 99, Brain Loses His Mind; The Warner Twins, The Warner Twins; Featuring Pinky and the Brain	1.99	0.40	1.00	1.99
❑46, Mar 99, Dot the Vampire Slayer; Featuring Pinky and the Brain	1.99	0.40	1.00	1.99
❑47, Apr 99, Brainita, Evita parody; Featuring Pinky and the Brain	1.99	0.40	1.00	1.99
❑48, May 99	1.99	0.40	1.00	1.99
❑49, Jun 99, The Lit-Wit Issue; MacBoo, literature issue; Featuring Pinky and the Brain; It's the Animaniacal Guide to the Classics!!	1.99	0.40	1.00	1.99
❑50, Jul 99, Mime Time; Hello Nurse and the Animaniacs: Riki-Tiki Terror!, Hello Nurse as super-hero; Featuring Pinky and the Brain	1.99	0.40	1.00	1.99
❑51, Aug 99, Away With Wurds!; Crossed Signals, Featuring Pinky and the Brain...	1.99	0.40	1.00	1.99
❑52, Sep 99, Baby Bowl; Fear and Loathing on Mars!, football; Featuring Pinky and the Brain	1.99	0.40	1.00	1.99
❑53, Oct 99, Future Stock; The Contest, Featuring Pinky and the Brain	1.99	0.40	1.00	1.99
❑54, Nov 99	1.99	0.40	1.00	1.99
❑55, Dec 99, Theme Park Buttons; Waiting for Godot, Featuring Pinky and the Brain	1.99	0.40	1.00	1.99
❑56, Jan 00, Te Britches of Madison County; This Year's Model, Featuring Pinky and the Brain	1.99	0.40	1.00	1.99
❑57, Feb 00	1.99	0.40	1.00	1.99
❑58, Mar 00, From Bad to Nurse, Hello Nurse, Agent of H.U.B.B.A.	1.99	0.40	1.00	1.99
❑59, Apr 00, Far Lap, Featuring Pinky and the Brain	1.99	0.40	1.00	1.99
❑HS 1, Dec 94, 'Twas the Day Before Christmas; The Taming of the Screwy, double-sized	1.50	0.40	1.00	2.00

ANIMAX
MARVEL

Issue	ORIG	GOOD	FINE	N-MINT
❑1, Dec 86	0.75	0.20	0.50	1.00
❑2	0.75	0.20	0.50	1.00
❑3, The Retread Plot	0.75	0.20	0.50	1.00
❑4	0.75	0.20	0.50	1.00

ANIMERICA EXTRA
VIZ

Value: Cover or less

Issue	Price
❑1	4.95
❑2	4.95

ANIMERICA EXTRA (VOL. 2)
VIZ

Value: Cover or less

Issue	Price
❑1, 98	4.95
❑2, 99	4.95
❑3, 99	4.95
❑4, 99	4.95
❑5, 99	4.95
❑6, 99	4.95
❑7, 99	4.95

ANIMERICA EXTRA (VOL. 3)
VIZ

Value: Cover or less

Issue	Price
❑1	4.95
❑2	4.95

	ORIG	GOOD	FINE	N-MINT

❑3 .... 4.95
❑4 .... 4.95
❑5 .... 4.95
❑6, contains poster 4.95
❑7 .... 4.95
❑8 .... 4.95
❑9 .... 4.95
❑10 .... 4.95

ANIMISM
CENTURION

	ORIG	GOOD	FINE	N-MINT
❑1, Jan 87	—	0.30	0.75	1.50

ANIVERSE, THE
WEEBEE

	ORIG	GOOD	FINE	N-MINT
❑1	—	0.39	0.98	1.95
❑2	—	0.39	0.98	1.95

ANNEX
MARVEL

Value: Cover or less

❑1, Aug 94, Crucible Of Power, O: Annex 1.75
❑2, Sep 94 .... 1.75
❑3, Oct 94 .... 1.75
❑4, Nov 94 .... 1.75

ANNIE
MARVEL

	ORIG	GOOD	FINE	N-MINT
❑1, Oct 82, Official movie adaptation	0.60	0.20	0.50	1.00
❑1/SE, Treasury edition; Tabloid size	2.00	1.00	2.50	5.00
❑2, Nov 82, Official movie adaptation	0.60	0.20	0.50	1.00

ANNIE SPRINKLE IS MISS TIMED
RIP OFF

Value: Cover or less

❑1, Sep 91 .... 2.50
❑2, Oct 91 .... 2.50
❑3, Nov 91 .... 2.50
❑4, Dec 91 .... 2.50

ANOMALIES, THE
ABNORMAL FUN

Value: Cover or less

❑1, Oct 00 .... 2.95

ANOMALY
BUD PLANT

	ORIG	GOOD	FINE	N-MINT
❑1	0.50	1.60	4.00	8.00
❑2	0.50	1.00	2.50	5.00
❑3	0.50	1.00	2.50	5.00
❑4, Alice in Wonderlust; Leander and the Fat Queen	0.50	1.00	2.50	5.00

ANOMALY (BRASS RING)
BRASS RING

	ORIG	GOOD	FINE	N-MINT
❑1	—	0.79	1.98	3.95
❑2, Jun 00, Sting of the Scorpion; The Sincerest Form of Flattery	3.95	0.79	1.98	3.95

ANOTHER CHANCE TO GET IT RIGHT
DARK HORSE

Value: Cover or less

❑1 .... 9.95
❑1-2, Mar 95, 2nd Printing 9.95

ANOTHER DAY
RAISED BROW

Value: Cover or less

❑1, Oct 95, b&w 2.75

ANTARCTIC PRESS JAM 1996
ANTARCTIC

Value: Cover or less

❑1, Dec 96, Ninja High School; Twilight X, A: Ninja High School, Gold Digger, Twilight X, Tigers of Terra 2.95

ANTARES CIRCLE
ANTARCTIC

Value: Cover or less

❑1 .... 1.95
❑2 .... 1.95

ANT BOY
STEELDRAGON

Value: Cover or less

❑1 .... 1.75
❑2, Oct 88 .... 1.75

ANT FARM
GALLANT

Value: Cover or less

❑1, Jun 98, Legacy of Gray 2.50
❑2 .... 2.50

ANTHRO
DC

	ORIG	GOOD	FINE	N-MINT
❑1, Aug 68, It Could Be You	0.12	7.00	17.50	35.00
❑2, Oct 68	0.12	4.00	10.00	20.00
❑3, Dec 68	0.12	4.00	10.00	20.00
❑4, Feb 69	0.12	4.00	10.00	20.00
❑5, Apr 69	0.12	4.00	10.00	20.00
❑6, Aug 69, WW	0.12	4.00	10.00	20.00

ANTIETAM: THE FIERY TRAIL
HERITAGE COLLECTION

Value: Cover or less

❑1, 97, nn 3.50

ANTI-HITLER COMICS
NEW ENGLAND

Value: Cover or less

❑1 .... 2.75
❑2 .... 2.75

ANTI-SOCIAL
HELPLESS ANGER

Value: Cover or less

❑1, b&w 2.00
❑2 .... 2.50
❑3 .... 2.50
❑4 .... 2.75

ANTI SOCIAL FOR THE DISABLED
HELPLESS ANGER

Value: Cover or less

❑1, b&w 5.00

ANTI SOCIAL JR.
HELPLESS ANGER

Value: Cover or less

❑1, nn; b&w; 20pgs. 1.75

ANT-MAN'S BIG CHRISTMAS
MARVEL

Value: Cover or less

❑1, Feb 00, prestige format 5.95

ANTON'S DREKBOOK
FANTAGRAPHICS

Value: Cover or less

❑1, b&w; adult 2.50

ANUBIS
SUPER CREW

Value: Cover or less

❑1 .... 2.50

ANUBIS (2ND SERIES)
SUPER CREW

Value: Cover or less

❑1 .... 2.95

ANYTHING BUT MONDAY
ANYTHING BUT MONDAY PRODUCTIONS

	ORIG	GOOD	FINE	N-MINT
❑1, Dec 88	1.75	0.40	1.00	2.00
❑2, Reindeer Games; Sappy Days Are Here Again!	1.75	0.40	1.00	2.00

ANYTHING GOES!
FANTAGRAPHICS

Value: Cover or less

❑1, Oct 86, GK (c), Savage!; Who"s Stronger...?, full color 2.00
❑2, Dec 86, FM (c), In Pictopia; Those Wild and Mixed Up Locas, full color 2.00
❑3, Mar 87, NA (c), Cerebus in Breaking Up is Hard to Do (illustrated text piece); Last Blood, full color 2.00
❑4, May 87, Heartbreak Soup: Space Case; Dance Class, full color 2.00
❑5, Oct 87, TMNT 2.00
❑6, Oct 87, b&w 2.00

A-OK
ANTARCTIC

Value: Cover or less

❑1, Sep 92, The Mission 2.50
❑2, Nov 92 .... 2.50
❑3, Jan 93 .... 2.50
❑4, Feb 93, War! 2.50

APACHE DICK
ETERNITY

Value: Cover or less

❑1, The Dick And The Doll, Part 1 .... 2.25
❑2 .... 2.25
❑3 .... 2.25
❑4 .... 2.25

APACHE TRAIL
STEINWAY

	ORIG	GOOD	FINE	N-MINT
❑1, Apache Attack!; The Sheriff's Return!	0.10	11.00	27.50	55.00
❑2	0.10	8.00	20.00	40.00
❑3, Feb 58	0.10	8.00	20.00	40.00
❑4	0.10	8.00	20.00	40.00

APATHY KAT
EXPRESS

Value: Cover or less

❑1, 95, b&w 2.50
❑2, 96 .... 2.75
❑3, 96 .... 2.75
❑4, 96 .... 2.75

APE CITY
ADVENTURE

Value: Cover or less

❑1, Monkey Business, Planet of the Apes story 2.50
❑2, Planet of the Apes story 2.50
❑3, Planet of the Apes story 2.50
❑4, Planet of the Apes story 2.50

APE NATION
ADVENTURE

Value: Cover or less

❑1, Feb 91, Plans, full color; Alien Nation/Planet of Apes crossover; Alien Nation/Planet of the Apes crossover 2.50
❑1/LE, full color; limited edition; Alien Nation/Planet of the Apes crossover 5.95
❑2, Apr 91, Alien Nation/Planet of the Apes crossover 2.50
❑3, May 91, Alien Nation/Planet of the Apes crossover 2.50
❑4, Jun 91, Alien Nation/Planet of the Apes crossover 2.50

APEX
AZTEC

Value: Cover or less

❑1, Dimensions; Tale of Two Cities, b&w 2.00

APEX PROJECT, THE
STELLAR

Value: Cover or less

❑1 .... 1.00
❑2 .... 1.00

APHRODISIA
EROS

Value: Cover or less

❑1 .... 2.95
❑2, Mar 95 .... 2.95

APHRODITE IX
IMAGE

	ORIG	GOOD	FINE	N-MINT
❑0/A, Wizard Gold Foil Edition	—	2.00	5.00	10.00
❑0/B, Wizard Blue Foil Edition	—	2.00	5.00	10.00

	ORIG	GOOD	FINE	N-MINT
❑1/A, Sep 00, Aphrodite reclining against left edge of cover, gun up	2.50	0.50	1.25	2.50
❑1/B, Sep 00, Aphrodite walking on metallic planks	2.50	0.50	1.25	2.50
❑1/C, Sep 00, Red background, Aphrodite shooting on cover	2.50	0.50	1.25	2.50
❑1/D, Sep 00, Green background, standing with guns up	2.50	0.50	1.25	2.50
❑1/E, Sep 00, Tower records exclusive	—	1.00	2.50	5.00
❑1/F, Sep 00, Tower records exclusive w/foil	—	1.00	2.50	5.00
❑1/G, Sep 00, Wizard World exclusive	—	1.00	2.50	5.00
❑1/H, Sep 00, Wizard World exclusive w/foil	—	1.00	2.50	5.00
❑1/I, Sep 00, Dynamic Forces exclusive	—	1.00	2.50	5.00
❑2, Mar 01	2.50	0.50	1.25	2.50
❑Ash 1, Convention Preview	—	1.00	2.50	5.00

APOCALYPSE
Apocalypse
Value: Cover or less

❑1 3.95
❑2 3.95
❑3 3.95
❑4 3.95
❑5 3.95
❑6 3.95
❑7, Makabre 3.95

APOLLO SMILE
Mixx

	ORIG	GOOD	FINE	N-MINT
❑1	2.95	0.80	2.00	4.00
❑2	2.95	0.60	1.50	3.00

APPARITION, THE
Caliber
Value: Cover or less

❑1, 96, Whispered Promises, Part 1 2.95
❑2, 96 2.95
❑3, 96 2.95
❑4, 96 2.95
❑5, 96 2.95

APPARITION, THE: ABANDONED
Caliber
Value: Cover or less

❑1, 95, One-Shot; prestige format 3.95

APPARITION, THE: VISITATIONS
Caliber
Value: Cover or less

❑1, Aug 95, One-Shot 2.95

APPLE, P.I.
Parrot Communications
Value: Cover or less

❑1, Sep 96, pronounced "Apple Pie" 1.95

APPLESEED BOOK 1
Eclipse

	ORIG	GOOD	FINE	N-MINT
❑1, Sep 88	2.50	2.00	5.00	10.00
❑2, Oct 88	2.50	1.20	3.00	6.00
❑3, Nov 88, Even Bets; Hospitality, Squarebound	2.50	1.00	2.50	5.00
❑4, Jan 89	2.75	0.80	2.00	4.00
❑5, Feb 89	2.75	0.80	2.00	4.00

APPLESEED BOOK 2
Eclipse

	ORIG	GOOD	FINE	N-MINT
❑1, Feb 89	2.75	1.20	3.00	6.00
❑2, Mar 89	2.75	0.80	2.00	4.00
❑3, Apr 89	2.75	0.70	1.75	3.50
❑4, May 89	2.75	0.70	1.75	3.50
❑5, Jun 89	2.75	0.70	1.75	3.50

APPLESEED BOOK 3
Eclipse

	ORIG	GOOD	FINE	N-MINT
❑1, Aug 89, Squarebound	2.75	1.00	2.50	5.00
❑2	2.75	0.80	2.00	4.00
❑3	2.75	0.70	1.75	3.50
❑4	2.75	0.70	1.75	3.50
❑5	3.50	0.70	1.75	3.50

APPLESEED BOOK 4
Eclipse
Value: Cover or less

❑1, Jan 91 3.50
❑2 3.50
❑3 3.50
❑4 3.50
❑5 3.50

APPLESEED DATABOOK
Dark Horse
Value: Cover or less

❑1, Apr 94 3.50
❑2, May 94, Flip-book; Squarebound 3.50

APRIL HORRORS
Rip Off
Value: Cover or less

❑1, Sep 93, b&w 2.95

AQUABLUE
Dark Horse
Value: Cover or less

❑1, Nov 89 6.95

AQUABLUE: THE BLUE PLANET
Dark Horse
Value: Cover or less

❑1, Aug 90 8.95

AQUA KNIGHT PART 2
Viz
Value: Cover or less

❑1, Oct 00, The Bitter Trials of Desire 3.50
❑2 3.50
❑3 3.50
❑4 3.50
❑5 3.50

Anthro was one of DC's non-super-hero series of the late 1960s.

© 1968 National Periodical Publications (DC)

AQUAMAN (1ST SERIES)
DC

	ORIG	GOOD	FINE	N-MINT
❑1, Feb 62, 1: Quisp	0.12	120.00	300.00	600.00
❑2, Apr 62	0.12	55.00	137.50	275.00
❑3, Jun 62	0.12	30.00	75.00	150.00
❑4, Aug 62	0.12	30.00	75.00	150.00
❑5, Oct 62	0.12	30.00	75.00	150.00
❑6, Dec 62	0.12	18.00	45.00	90.00
❑7, Feb 63	0.12	18.00	45.00	90.00
❑8, Apr 63	0.12	18.00	45.00	90.00
❑9, Jun 63	0.12	18.00	45.00	90.00
❑10, Aug 63	0.12	18.00	45.00	90.00
❑11, Oct 63, 1: Mera	0.12	15.00	37.50	75.00
❑12, Dec 63	0.12	13.00	32.50	65.00
❑13, Feb 64	0.12	13.00	32.50	65.00
❑14, Apr 64	0.12	13.00	32.50	65.00
❑15, Jun 64	0.12	13.00	32.50	65.00
❑16, Aug 64	0.12	13.00	32.50	65.00
❑17, Oct 64	0.12	13.00	32.50	65.00
❑18, Dec 64, A: Justice League of America, Aquaman marries Mera	0.12	13.00	32.50	65.00
❑19, Feb 65	0.12	13.00	32.50	65.00
❑20, Apr 65	0.12	13.00	32.50	65.00
❑21, Jun 65, 1: Fisherman	0.12	9.00	22.50	45.00
❑22, Aug 65	0.12	9.00	22.50	45.00
❑23, Oct 65, Birth of Aquababy	0.12	9.00	22.50	45.00
❑24, Dec 65	0.12	9.00	22.50	45.00
❑25, Feb 66	0.12	9.00	22.50	45.00
❑26, Apr 66	0.12	9.00	22.50	45.00
❑27, Jun 66	0.12	9.00	22.50	45.00
❑28, Aug 66	0.12	9.00	22.50	45.00
❑29, Oct 66, 1: Ocean Master	0.12	9.00	22.50	45.00
❑30, Dec 66	0.12	9.00	22.50	45.00
❑31, Feb 67	0.12	7.00	17.50	35.00
❑32, Apr 67	0.12	7.00	17.50	35.00
❑33, Jun 67, 1: Aqua-Girl	0.12	12.00	30.00	60.00
❑34, Aug 67	0.12	6.00	15.00	30.00
❑35, Oct 67, 1: Black Manta	0.12	6.00	15.00	30.00
❑36, Dec 67	0.12	6.00	15.00	30.00
❑37, Feb 68	0.12	6.00	15.00	30.00
❑38, Apr 68	0.12	6.00	15.00	30.00
❑39, Jun 68	0.12	6.00	15.00	30.00
❑40, Aug 68	0.12	6.00	15.00	30.00
❑41, Oct 68	0.12	4.00	10.00	20.00
❑42, Dec 68	0.12	4.00	10.00	20.00
❑43, Feb 69	0.12	4.00	10.00	20.00
❑44, Apr 69	0.12	4.00	10.00	20.00
❑45, Jun 69	0.12	4.00	10.00	20.00
❑46, Aug 69	0.15	4.00	10.00	20.00
❑47, Oct 69	0.15	4.00	10.00	20.00
❑48, Dec 69, JA, O: Aquaman	0.15	5.00	12.50	25.00
❑49, Feb 70, JA	0.15	2.40	6.00	12.00
❑50, Apr 70, NA, A: Deadman	0.15	6.00	15.00	30.00
❑51, Jun 70, NA, A: Deadman	0.15	6.00	15.00	30.00
❑52, Aug 70, NA, A: Deadman	0.15	6.00	15.00	30.00
❑53, Oct 70, JA	0.15	1.40	3.50	7.00
❑54, Dec 70, JA	0.15	1.40	3.50	7.00
❑55, Feb 71, JA	0.15	1.40	3.50	7.00
❑56, Apr 71, JA, A Life For A Life, 1: Crusader	0.15	1.40	3.50	7.00
❑57, Aug 77, JA	0.35	1.00	2.50	5.00
❑58, Oct 77, JA, O: Aquaman	0.35	1.00	2.50	5.00
❑59, Dec 77	0.35	1.00	2.50	5.00
❑60, Feb 78	0.35	1.00	2.50	5.00
❑61, Apr 78	0.35	1.00	2.50	5.00
❑62, Jun 78	0.35	1.00	2.50	5.00
❑63, Sep 78, Final Issue	0.35	1.00	2.50	5.00

AQUAMAN (2ND SERIES)
DC

	ORIG	GOOD	FINE	N-MINT
❑1, Feb 86, New costume	0.75	0.80	2.00	4.00
❑2, Mar 86	0.75	0.60	1.50	3.00
❑3, Apr 86	0.75	0.60	1.50	3.00
❑4, May 86	0.75	0.60	1.50	3.00
❑SE 1, Jun 88	1.50	0.60	1.50	3.00

AQUAMAN (3RD SERIES)
DC

Value: Cover or less

- ❑1, Jun 89, CS; KG, Aquarium 1.00
- ❑2, Jul 89 1.00
- ❑3, Aug 89 1.00
- ❑4, Sep 89, CS, The Tide Of Battle 1.00
- ❑5, Oct 89 1.00
- ❑SE 1, Apr 89, CS, Legend of Aquaman 2.00

AQUAMAN (4TH SERIES)
DC

Value: Cover or less

- ❑1, Dec 91, A Small World Incident 1.00
- ❑2, Jan 92 1.00
- ❑3, Feb 92 1.00
- ❑4, Mar 92 1.00
- ❑5, Apr 92 1.00
- ❑6, May 92 1.25
- ❑7, Jun 92, What Matters Most 1.25
- ❑8, Jul 92, Demons in Thought & Deed, A: Batman; V: Nicodemus 1.25
- ❑9, Aug 92 1.25
- ❑10, Sep 92 1.25
- ❑11, Oct 92 1.25
- ❑12, Nov 92 1.25
- ❑13, Dec 92, A: Scavanger, Final Issue 1.25

AQUAMAN (5TH SERIES)
DC

	ORIG	GOOD	FINE	N-MINT
❑0, Oct 94, PD (w), Aquaman gets harpoon for arm	1.50	0.70	1.75	3.50
❑1, Aug 94, PD (w)	1.50	0.70	1.75	3.50
❑2, Sep 94, PD (w), Single Wet Female, V: Charybdis, Aquaman loses hand	1.50	0.70	1.75	3.50
❑3, Nov 94, PD (w), Arthur Goes Hawaiian, V: Superboy	1.50	0.40	1.00	2.00
❑4, Dec 94, PD (w), A Porpoise in Life, V: Lobo	1.50	0.40	1.00	2.00
❑5, Jan 95, PD (w)	1.50	0.40	1.00	2.00
❑6, Feb 95, PD (w)	1.50	0.40	1.00	2.00
❑7, Mar 95, PD (w)	1.50	0.40	1.00	2.00
❑8, Apr 95, PD (w)	1.50	0.40	1.00	2.00
❑9, Jun 95, PD (w)	1.75	0.35	0.88	1.75
❑10, Jul 95, PD (w)	1.75	0.35	0.88	1.75
❑11, Aug 95, PD (w)	1.75	0.35	0.88	1.75
❑12, Sep 95, PD (w), Mera returns	1.75	0.35	0.88	1.75
❑13, Oct 95, PD (w)	1.75	0.35	0.88	1.75
❑14, Nov 95, PD (w), Underworld Unleashed, "Underworld Unleashed"	1.75	0.35	0.88	1.75
❑15, Dec 95, PD (w)	1.75	0.35	0.88	1.75
❑16, Jan 96, PD (w), V: Justice League	1.75	0.35	0.88	1.75
❑17, Feb 96, PD (w), Numbers	1.75	0.35	0.88	1.75
❑18, Mar 96, PD (w), Biblical Sense, O: Dolphin	1.75	0.35	0.88	1.75
❑19, Apr 96, PD (w), Brother's Keeper, Aqualad returns	1.75	0.35	0.88	1.75
❑20, May 96, PD (w)	1.75	0.35	0.88	1.75
❑21, Jun 96, PD (w)	1.75	0.35	0.88	1.75
❑22, Jul 96, PD (w)	1.75	0.35	0.88	1.75
❑23, Aug 96, PD (w), A: Sea Devils, Power Girl, Tsunami, Arion	1.75	0.35	0.88	1.75
❑24, Sep 96, PD (w)	1.75	0.35	0.88	1.75
❑25, Oct 96, PD (w), Betwixt and Between	1.75	0.35	0.88	1.75
❑26, Nov 96, PD (w), Twilight, "Final Night"	1.75	0.35	0.88	1.75
❑27, Dec 96, PD (w), The Rising Sun, Aquaman declares war on Japan	1.75	0.35	0.88	1.75
❑28, Jan 97, PD (w), Setting Sun, A: Martian Manhunter	1.75	0.35	0.88	1.75
❑29, Feb 97, PD (w), V: Black Manta	1.75	0.35	0.88	1.75
❑30, Mar 97, PD (w), In Darkness He Waits	1.75	0.35	0.88	1.75
❑31, Apr 97, PD (w)	1.75	0.35	0.88	1.75
❑32, May 97, PD (w), A: Swamp Thing	1.75	0.35	0.88	1.75
❑33, Jun 97, PD (w)	1.75	0.35	0.88	1.75
❑34, Jul 97, PD (w), V: Triton	1.75	0.35	0.88	1.75
❑35, Aug 97, PD (w), V: Gamesman; A: Animal Man, Aquaman blind	1.75	0.35	0.88	1.75
❑36, Sep 97, PD (w)	1.75	0.35	0.88	1.75
❑37, Oct 97, PD (w), V: Parademons, "Genesis"	1.75	0.35	0.88	1.75
❑38, Nov 97, PD (w), Open for Business, Poseidonis becomes a tourist attraction	1.75	0.35	0.88	1.75
❑39, Dec 97, PD (w), Bad Relations, A: Neptune Perkins, Face cover	1.95	0.40	1.00	2.00
❑40, Jan 98, PD (w), V: Doctor Polaris	1.95	0.40	1.00	2.00
❑41, Feb 98, PD (w), A: Maxima	1.95	0.40	1.00	2.00
❑42, Mar 98, Necessary Poisons, V: Sea Wolf	1.95	0.40	1.00	2.00
❑43, Apr 98, "Millennium Giants"	1.95	0.40	1.00	2.00
❑44, May 98, A: Sentinel; A: Golden Age Flash	1.95	0.40	1.00	2.00
❑45, Jun 98, Destruction of Poseidonis	1.95	0.40	1.00	2.00
❑46, Jul 98	1.95	0.40	1.00	2.00
❑47, Aug 98	1.95	0.40	1.00	2.00
❑48, Sep 98	1.99	0.40	1.00	2.00
❑49, Oct 98	1.99	0.40	1.00	2.00
❑50, Dec 98, EL	1.99	0.40	1.00	2.00
❑51, Jan 99, EL (w), A: King Noble	1.99	0.40	1.00	2.00
❑52, Feb 99, EL (w), A: Noble; A: Lava Lord; A: Mera; A: Fire Trolls	1.99	0.40	1.00	2.00
❑53, Mar 99, EL (w), A: Shrapnel; A: Superman	1.99	0.40	1.00	2.00
❑54, Apr 99, EL (w), A: Lagoon Boy; A: Blubber; A: Landlovers; A: Shiva the Mermaid	1.99	0.40	1.00	2.00
❑55, May 99, Desperate Times	1.99	0.40	1.00	2.00
❑56, Jun 99, Madman Across the Water	1.99	0.40	1.00	2.00
❑57, Jul 99, Piranhaman Bites!	1.99	0.40	1.00	2.00
❑58, Aug 99, EL, EL (w), Watery Crave	1.99	0.40	1.00	2.00
❑59, Sep 99, EL (w), Drugs of Choice	1.99	0.40	1.00	2.00
❑60, Oct 99, EL (w), Marriage Vows, Wedding of Tempest and Dolphin	1.99	0.40	1.00	2.00
❑61, Nov 99	1.99	0.40	1.00	2.00
❑62, Dec 99, EL (w), Resolutions	1.99	0.40	1.00	2.00
❑63, Jan 00, King Arthur	1.99	0.40	1.00	2.00
❑64, Feb 00	1.99	0.40	1.00	2.00
❑65, Mar 00	1.99	0.40	1.00	2.00
❑66, Apr 00, Common Battleground	1.99	0.40	1.00	2.00
❑67, May 00, Clash of Kings	1.99	0.40	1.00	2.00
❑68, Jun 00	1.99	0.40	1.00	2.00
❑69, Jul 00	—	0.40	1.00	2.00
❑70, Aug 00, Unifaction by Division	—	0.40	1.00	2.00
❑71, Sep 00, To Enter the Lost World..., A: Warlord	2.50	0.50	1.25	2.50
❑72, Oct 00, World's Apart	2.50	0.50	1.25	2.50
❑73, Nov 00, Power Game	2.50	0.50	1.25	2.50
❑74, Dec 00, From the Core	2.50	0.50	1.25	2.50
❑75, Jan 01, No Future	2.50	0.50	1.25	2.50
❑1000000, Nov 98, The Banks and Shoals of Time	1.99	0.40	1.00	2.00
❑Anl 1, A: Wonder Woman, Superman,	3.50	0.70	1.75	3.50
❑Anl 2, Legends of the Dead Earth	2.95	0.59	1.48	2.95
❑Anl 3, Pulp Heroes	3.95	0.79	1.98	3.95
❑Anl 4, Ghosts	2.95	0.59	1.48	2.95
❑Anl 5, Sep 99, 20, 000 Apes under the Sea, JLApe	2.95	0.59	1.48	2.95

AQUAMAN SECRET FILES
DC

Value: Cover or less

- ❑1, Dec 98, EL, EL (w), Left for Dead; Aquacave Schematic, O: Aquaman; A: Charybdis 4.95

AQUAMAN: TIME AND TIDE
DC

	ORIG	GOOD	FINE	N-MINT
❑1, Dec 93, PD (w), Flash Back, O: Aquaman	1.50	0.50	1.25	2.50
❑2, Jan 94, PD (w)	1.50	0.50	1.25	2.50
❑3, Feb 94, PD (w), Snowball In Hell	1.50	0.50	1.25	2.50
❑4, Mar 94, PD (w), King Of The Sea, O: Ocean Master	1.50	0.50	1.25	2.50

AQUARIUM
CPM MANGA

Value: Cover or less

- ❑1/A, Apr 00, b&w; wraparound cover 2.95
- ❑1/B, Apr 00, b&w; alternate wraparound cover 2.95

ARABIAN NIGHTS ON THE WORLD OF MAGIC: THE GATHERING
ACCLAIM

Value: Cover or less

- ❑1, Dec 95, A Time to Gather. 2.50
- ❑2 2.50

ARAGONÉS 3-D
3-D ZONE

Value: Cover or less

- ❑1, SA, SA (w), paperback 4.95

ARAKNIS
MUSHROOM

Value: Cover or less

- ❑1, 95 2.50

ARAK SON OF THUNDER
DC

	ORIG	GOOD	FINE	N-MINT
❑1, Sep 81, The Sword And The Serpent, 1: Angelica; O: Arak	0.60	0.20	0.50	1.00
❑2, Oct 81, 1: Malagigi	0.60	0.20	0.50	1.00
❑3, Nov 81, 1: Valda	0.60	0.20	0.50	1.00
❑4, Dec 81	0.60	0.20	0.50	1.00
❑5, Jan 82	0.60	0.20	0.50	1.00
❑6, Feb 82	0.60	0.20	0.50	1.00
❑7, Mar 82	0.60	0.20	0.50	1.00
❑8, Apr 82	0.60	0.20	0.50	1.00
❑9, May 82	0.60	0.20	0.50	1.00
❑10, Jun 82	0.60	0.20	0.50	1.00
❑11, Jul 82	0.60	0.20	0.50	1.00
❑12, Aug 82	0.60	0.20	0.50	1.00
❑13, Sep 82	0.60	0.20	0.50	1.00
❑14, Oct 82	0.60	0.20	0.50	1.00
❑15, Nov 82	0.60	0.20	0.50	1.00
❑16, Dec 82	0.60	0.20	0.50	1.00
❑17, Jan 83	0.60	0.20	0.50	1.00
❑18, Feb 83	0.60	0.20	0.50	1.00
❑19, Mar 83	0.60	0.20	0.50	1.00

	ORIG	GOOD	FINE	N-MINT
❑20, Apr 83, O: Angelica	0.60	0.20	0.50	1.00
❑21, May 83	0.60	0.20	0.50	1.00
❑22, Jun 83	0.60	0.20	0.50	1.00
❑23, Jul 83	0.60	0.20	0.50	1.00
❑24, Aug 83	1.00	0.20	0.50	1.00
❑25, Sep 83	0.60	0.20	0.50	1.00
❑26, Oct 83	0.60	0.20	0.50	1.00
❑27, Nov 83	0.60	0.20	0.50	1.00
❑28, Dec 83	0.75	0.20	0.50	1.00
❑29, Jan 84	0.75	0.20	0.50	1.00
❑30, Feb 84	0.75	0.20	0.50	1.00
❑31, Mar 84	0.75	0.20	0.50	1.00
❑32, Apr 84	0.75	0.20	0.50	1.00
❑33, May 84	0.75	0.20	0.50	1.00
❑34, Jun 84	0.75	0.20	0.50	1.00
❑35, Jul 84	0.75	0.20	0.50	1.00
❑36, Aug 84	0.75	0.20	0.50	1.00
❑37, Sep 84	0.75	0.20	0.50	1.00
❑38, Nov 84	0.75	0.20	0.50	1.00
❑39, Dec 84	0.75	0.20	0.50	1.00
❑40, Jan 85	0.75	0.20	0.50	1.00
❑41, Feb 85	0.75	0.20	0.50	1.00
❑42, Mar 85	0.75	0.20	0.50	1.00
❑43, Apr 85	0.75	0.20	0.50	1.00
❑44, May 85	0.75	0.20	0.50	1.00
❑45, Jun 85	0.75	0.20	0.50	1.00
❑46, Jul 85	0.75	0.20	0.50	1.00
❑47, Aug 85	0.75	0.20	0.50	1.00
❑48, Sep 85	0.75	0.20	0.50	1.00
❑49, Oct 85	0.75	0.20	0.50	1.00
❑50, Nov 85, Giant-size	1.25	0.20	0.50	1.00
❑Anl 1	1.25	0.20	0.50	1.00

ARAMIS
COMICS INTERVIEW

Value: Cover or less

- ❑1 ... 1.95
- ❑2 ... 1.95
- ❑3 ... 1.95

ARCADE
PRINT MINT

	ORIG	GOOD	FINE	N-MINT
❑1, Mar 75, Cracking Jokes	1.25	2.00	5.00	10.00
❑2, Jun 75	1.25	1.60	4.00	8.00
❑3, Sep 75, That's Life; New York Journal...	1.25	1.60	4.00	8.00
❑4	—	1.60	4.00	8.00
❑5	—	1.40	3.50	7.00
❑6, Jun 76	1.50	1.20	3.00	6.00
❑7	1.50	1.00	2.50	5.00

ARCANA
DC

	ORIG	GOOD	FINE	N-MINT
❑Anl 1, The Children's Crusade, Part 6, "Children's Crusade"	3.95	0.80	2.00	4.00

ARCANA (WELLS & CLARK)
WELLS & CLARK

	ORIG	GOOD	FINE	N-MINT
❑1	3.00	0.60	1.50	3.00
❑2, Mar 95	2.25	0.60	1.50	3.00
❑3, May 95	2.25	0.60	1.50	3.00
❑4, Jul 95	2.25	0.45	1.13	2.25
❑5, Sep 95	2.25	0.45	1.13	2.25
❑6	2.25	0.45	1.13	2.25
❑7	2.25	0.45	1.13	2.25
❑8, Jul 96	2.25	0.45	1.13	2.25
❑9, Sep 96	2.25	0.45	1.13	2.25
❑10	2.25	0.45	1.13	2.25

ARCANE
ARCANE

Value: Cover or less

- ❑1 ... 2.00
- ❑2, Fly in My Eye ... 9.95

ARCANE (2ND SERIES)
GRAPHIK

Value: Cover or less

- ❑1, b&w ... 1.25

ARCANUM
IMAGE

	ORIG	GOOD	FINE	N-MINT
❑0.5, Dec 97, Certificate of Authenticity	—	1.00	2.50	5.00
❑0.5/GO, Dec 97, Signed by Brandon Peterson	—	1.20	3.00	6.00
❑1, Apr 97	2.50	0.50	1.25	2.50
❑1/A, Apr 97, variant cover	2.50	0.50	1.25	2.50
❑2, May 97	2.50	0.50	1.25	2.50
❑2/A, May 97, variant cover	2.50	0.50	1.25	2.50
❑3, Jun 97	2.50	0.50	1.25	2.50
❑3/A, Jun 97, variant cover	2.50	0.50	1.25	2.50
❑4, Jul 97	2.50	0.50	1.25	2.50
❑4/A, Jul 97, variant cover	2.50	0.50	1.25	2.50
❑5, Sep 97	2.50	0.59	1.48	2.95
❑6, Nov 97	2.50	0.59	1.48	2.95
❑7, Jan 98	2.50	0.59	1.48	2.95
❑8, Feb 98, Final Issue	2.50	0.59	1.48	2.95

After recounting Aquaman's conception and birth in *The Atlantis Chronicles*, writer Peter David provided adventures from The Sea King's early days as a hero in *Aquaman: Time and Tide.*

ARCHANGEL
MARVEL

Value: Cover or less

- ❑1, Feb 96, Phantom Wings, b&w; wraparound cover; One-Shot 2.50

ARCHANGELS: THE SAGA
ETERNAL

Value: Cover or less

- ❑1 ... 2.50
- ❑1-2, 2nd Printing ... 2.50
- ❑2 ... 2.50
- ❑3 ... 2.50
- ❑4 ... 2.50
- ❑5 ... 2.50
- ❑6 ... 2.50
- ❑7 ... 2.50
- ❑8 ... 2.50

ARCHER & ARMSTRONG
VALIANT

Value: Cover or less

- ❑0, Jul 92, O: Archer & Armstrong 2.50
- ❑0/GO, O: Archer & Armstrong, Gold edition ... 2.50
- ❑1, Aug 92, FM (c), Unity, Part 3, Unity ... 2.50
- ❑2, Sep 92, Unity, Part 11, Unity 2.50
- ❑3, Oct 92 ... 2.50
- ❑4, Nov 92 ... 2.50
- ❑5, Dec 92 ... 2.50
- ❑6, Jan 93 ... 2.50
- ❑7, Feb 93 ... 2.50
- ❑8, Mar 93, 1: Timewalker (Ivar), Double-sized: is also "Eternal Warrior #8"; Flip-book with Eternal Warrior #8 ... 4.50
- ❑9, Apr 93, BL (w), Darque Daze, 1: Mademoiselle Noir ... 2.50
- ❑10, May 93 ... 2.50
- ❑11, Jun 93, A Snatch in Time, A: Solar ... 2.50
- ❑12, Jul 93 ... 2.50
- ❑13, Jul 93 ... 2.50
- ❑14, Jul 93 ... 2.50
- ❑15, Jul 93 ... 2.50
- ❑16, Jul 93 ... 2.50
- ❑17, Jul 93 ... 2.50
- ❑18, Jul 93 ... 2.50
- ❑19, Jan 94 ... 2.50
- ❑20, Mar 94 ... 2.50
- ❑21, Apr 94, A: Shadowman ... 2.50
- ❑22, May 94, trading card ... 2.50
- ❑23, Jun 94 ... 2.50
- ❑24, Aug 94 ... 2.50
- ❑25, Sep 94, A: Eternal Warrior 2.50
- ❑26, Oct 94, The Chaos Effect: Gamma, Part 4, Final Issue; Flip-book with Eternal Warrior #26; indicia says August ... 2.75

ARCHIE
ARCHIE

	ORIG	GOOD	FINE	N-MINT
❑399, May 92	1.25	0.30	0.75	1.50
❑400, Jun 92	1.25	0.30	0.75	1.50
❑401, Jul 92	1.25	0.30	0.75	1.50
❑402, Aug 92	1.25	0.30	0.75	1.50
❑403, Sep 92	1.25	0.30	0.75	1.50
❑404, Oct 92	1.25	0.30	0.75	1.50
❑405, Nov 92	1.25	0.30	0.75	1.50
❑406, Dec 92	1.25	0.30	0.75	1.50
❑407, Jan 93	1.25	0.30	0.75	1.50
❑408, Feb 93	1.25	0.30	0.75	1.50
❑409, Mar 93	1.25	0.30	0.75	1.50
❑410, Apr 93	1.25	0.30	0.75	1.50
❑411, May 93	1.25	0.30	0.75	1.50
❑412, Jun 93	1.25	0.30	0.75	1.50
❑413, Jul 93, Archie: Food Choice; Archie: Quiz Biz!	1.25	0.30	0.75	1.50
❑414, Aug 93, prom poster	1.25	0.30	0.75	1.50
❑415, Sep 93	1.25	0.30	0.75	1.50
❑416, Oct 93	1.25	0.30	0.75	1.50
❑417, Nov 93	1.25	0.30	0.75	1.50
❑418, Dec 93	1.25	0.30	0.75	1.50
❑419, Jan 94	1.25	0.30	0.75	1.50
❑420, Feb 94	1.25	0.30	0.75	1.50
❑421, Mar 94	1.25	0.30	0.75	1.50
❑422, Apr 94	1.25	0.30	0.75	1.50
❑423, May 94	1.25	0.30	0.75	1.50
❑424, Jun 94	1.25	0.30	0.75	1.50
❑425, Jul 94	1.25	0.30	0.75	1.50
❑426, Aug 94	1.50	0.30	0.75	1.50
❑427, Sep 94	1.50	0.30	0.75	1.50
❑428, Oct 94	1.50	0.30	0.75	1.50
❑429, Nov 94, Love Showdown, Part 1	1.50	0.30	0.75	1.50
❑430, Dec 94	1.50	0.30	0.75	1.50
❑431, Jan 95	1.50	0.30	0.75	1.50
❑432, Feb 95, Technical Advisor; Snow Brawling, Treasure In The Attic	1.50	0.30	0.75	1.50

	ORIG	GOOD	FINE	N-MINT
❑433, Mar 95	1.50	0.30	0.75	1.50
❑434, Apr 95	1.50	0.30	0.75	1.50
❑435, May 95	1.50	0.30	0.75	1.50
❑436, Jun 95	1.50	0.30	0.75	1.50
❑437, Jul 95	1.50	0.30	0.75	1.50
❑438, Aug 95	1.50	0.30	0.75	1.50
❑439, Sep 95	1.50	0.30	0.75	1.50
❑440, Oct 95	1.50	0.30	0.75	1.50
❑441, Nov 95	1.50	0.30	0.75	1.50
❑442, Dec 95, House of Riverdale, Part 1, continues in Betty & Veronica #95	1.50	0.30	0.75	1.50
❑443, Jan 96, Photo cover	1.50	0.30	0.75	1.50
❑444, Feb 96	1.50	0.30	0.75	1.50
❑445, Mar 96	1.50	0.30	0.75	1.50
❑446, Apr 96	1.50	0.30	0.75	1.50
❑447, May 96	1.50	0.30	0.75	1.50
❑448, Jun 96	1.50	0.30	0.75	1.50
❑449, Jul 96	1.50	0.30	0.75	1.50
❑450, Aug 96	1.50	0.30	0.75	1.50
❑451, Sep 96	1.50	0.30	0.75	1.50
❑452, Oct 96	1.50	0.30	0.75	1.50
❑453, Nov 96	1.50	0.30	0.75	1.50
❑454, Dec 96	1.50	0.30	0.75	1.50
❑455, Jan 97	1.50	0.30	0.75	1.50
❑456, Feb 97	1.50	0.30	0.75	1.50
❑457, Mar 97	1.50	0.30	0.75	1.50
❑458, Apr 97	1.50	0.30	0.75	1.50
❑459, May 97	1.50	0.30	0.75	1.50
❑460, Jun 97	1.50	0.30	0.75	1.50
❑461, Jul 97	1.50	0.30	0.75	1.50
❑462, Aug 97	1.50	0.30	0.75	1.50
❑463, Sep 97	1.50	0.30	0.75	1.50
❑464, Oct 97	1.50	0.30	0.75	1.50
❑465, Nov 97	1.50	0.30	0.75	1.50
❑466, Dec 97	1.50	0.30	0.75	1.50
❑467, Jan 98	1.75	0.35	0.88	1.75
❑468, Feb 98	1.75	0.35	0.88	1.75
❑469, Mar 98	1.75	0.35	0.88	1.75
❑470, Apr 98	1.75	0.35	0.88	1.75
❑471, May 98	1.75	0.35	0.88	1.75
❑472, Jun 98	1.75	0.35	0.88	1.75
❑473, Jul 98	1.75	0.35	0.88	1.75
❑474, Aug 98	1.75	0.35	0.88	1.75
❑475, Sep 98, The Warning; Circus Atmosphere	1.75	0.35	0.88	1.75
❑476, Oct 98	1.75	0.35	0.88	1.75
❑477, Nov 98, Tuba or not Tuba; Hocus-Focus	1.75	0.35	0.88	1.75
❑478, Dec 98	1.75	0.35	0.88	1.75
❑479, Jan 99	1.75	0.35	0.88	1.75
❑480, Feb 99	1.75	0.35	0.88	1.75
❑481, Mar 99, Axe of Friendship	1.75	0.35	0.88	1.75
❑482, Apr 99, Losers Can Be Winners	1.79	0.36	0.89	1.79
❑483, May 99, Pup-ularity Contest	1.79	0.36	0.89	1.79
❑484, Jun 99	1.79	0.36	0.89	1.79
❑485, Jul 99	1.79	0.36	0.89	1.79
❑486, Aug 99	1.79	0.36	0.89	1.79
❑487, Sep 99	1.79	0.36	0.89	1.79
❑488, Oct 99	1.79	0.36	0.89	1.79
❑489, Nov 99	1.79	0.36	0.89	1.79
❑490, Dec 99	1.79	0.36	0.89	1.79
❑491, Jan 00	1.79	0.36	0.89	1.79
❑492, Feb 00	1.79	0.36	0.89	1.79
❑493, Mar 00	1.99	0.40	1.00	1.99
❑494, Apr 00	1.99	0.40	1.00	1.99
❑495, May 00	1.99	0.40	1.00	1.99
❑496, Jun 00	1.99	0.40	1.00	1.99
❑497, Jul 00	1.99	0.40	1.00	1.99
❑498, Aug 00	1.99	0.40	1.00	1.99
❑499, Sep 00	1.99	0.40	1.00	1.99
❑500, Oct 00	1.99	0.40	1.00	1.99
❑501, Nov 00	1.99	0.40	1.00	1.99
❑502, Dec 00	1.99	0.40	1.00	1.99
❑503, Jan 01	1.99	0.40	1.00	1.99
❑504, Feb 01	1.99	0.40	1.00	1.99
❑505, Mar 01	1.99	0.40	1.00	1.99
❑506, Apr 01	1.99	0.40	1.00	1.99
❑507, May 01	1.99	0.40	1.00	1.99
❑508, Jun 01	1.99	0.40	1.00	1.99
❑509, Jul 01	1.99	0.40	1.00	1.99
❑510, Aug 01	1.99	0.40	1.00	1.99
❑511, Sep 01	1.99	0.40	1.00	1.99
❑512, Oct 01	1.99	0.40	1.00	1.99
❑513, Nov 01	1.99	0.40	1.00	1.99
❑Anl 1, ca. 50	0.25	245.00	612.50	1225.00

	ORIG	GOOD	FINE	N-MINT
❑Anl 2, ca. 51	0.25	120.00	300.00	600.00
❑Anl 3, ca. 52	0.25	90.00	225.00	450.00
❑Anl 4, ca. 53	0.25	65.00	162.50	325.00
❑Anl 5, ca. 54	0.25	55.00	137.50	275.00
❑Anl 6, ca. 55	0.25	34.00	85.00	170.00
❑Anl 7, ca. 56	0.25	30.00	75.00	150.00
❑Anl 8, ca. 57	0.25	26.00	65.00	130.00
❑Anl 9, ca. 58	0.25	23.00	57.50	115.00
❑Anl 10, ca. 59	0.25	20.00	50.00	100.00
❑Anl 11, ca. 60	0.25	13.00	32.50	65.00
❑Anl 12, ca. 61	0.25	11.00	27.50	55.00
❑Anl 13, ca. 62	0.25	11.00	27.50	55.00
❑Anl 14, ca. 63	0.25	9.00	22.50	45.00
❑Anl 15, ca. 64	0.25	9.00	22.50	45.00
❑Anl 16, ca. 65	0.25	5.00	12.50	25.00
❑Anl 17, ca. 66	0.25	5.00	12.50	25.00
❑Anl 18, ca. 67	0.25	4.00	10.00	20.00
❑Anl 19, ca. 68	0.25	4.00	10.00	20.00
❑Anl 20, ca. 69	0.25	2.60	6.50	13.00
❑Anl 21, ca. 70	0.25	1.60	4.00	8.00
❑Anl 22, ca. 71	0.25	1.60	4.00	8.00
❑Anl 23, ca. 72	0.25	1.60	4.00	8.00
❑Anl 24, ca. 73	0.25	1.60	4.00	8.00
❑Anl 25, ca. 74	0.35	1.60	4.00	8.00
❑Anl 26, ca. 75	0.35	1.60	4.00	8.00

ARCHIE 3000
Archie

	ORIG	GOOD	FINE	N-MINT
❑1, May 89	0.75	0.60	1.50	3.00
❑2	0.75	0.40	1.00	2.00
❑3	0.75	0.40	1.00	2.00
❑4	0.75	0.40	1.00	2.00
❑5	0.75	0.40	1.00	2.00
❑6	0.75	0.15	0.38	0.75
❑7	0.75	0.15	0.38	0.75
❑8	0.75	0.15	0.38	0.75
❑9	0.75	0.15	0.38	0.75
❑10	0.75	0.15	0.38	0.75
❑11	0.75	0.15	0.38	0.75
❑12	0.75	0.15	0.38	0.75
❑13	0.75	0.15	0.38	0.75
❑14	0.75	0.15	0.38	0.75
❑15, May 91	0.75	0.15	0.38	0.75

ARCHIE ALL CANADIAN DIGEST
Archie

	ORIG	GOOD	FINE	N-MINT
❑1, Aug 96, digest; reprints Archie stories set in Canada	1.75	0.40	1.00	2.00

ARCHIE AND FRIENDS
Archie

	ORIG	GOOD	FINE	N-MINT
❑1, Dec 92, The Diary, Part 1; The Diary, Part 2, A: Hiram Lodge; A: Great Rondo	1.25	0.50	1.25	2.50
❑2, Feb 92	1.25	0.40	1.00	2.00
❑3, Apr 92	1.25	0.40	1.00	2.00
❑4, Jun 92	1.25	0.30	0.75	1.50
❑5, Aug 92	1.25	0.30	0.75	1.50
❑6, Oct 92, A: Sabrina	1.25	0.30	0.75	1.50
❑7, Mar 93	1.25	0.30	0.75	1.50
❑8	1.25	0.30	0.75	1.50
❑9, Jun 94	1.25	0.30	0.75	1.50
❑10, Aug 94	1.50	0.30	0.75	1.50
❑11, Oct 94	1.50	0.30	0.75	1.50
❑12, Dec 94	1.50	0.30	0.75	1.50
❑13, May 95	1.50	0.30	0.75	1.50
❑14, May 95	1.50	0.30	0.75	1.50
❑15, Aug 95	1.50	0.30	0.75	1.50
❑16, Nov 95	1.50	0.30	0.75	1.50
❑17, Feb 96	1.50	0.30	0.75	1.50
❑18, May 96	1.50	0.30	0.75	1.50
❑19, Aug 96, X-Men and E.R. parodies	1.50	0.30	0.75	1.50
❑20, Nov 96	1.50	0.30	0.75	1.50
❑21, Feb 97, The class puts on Romeo and Juliet	1.50	0.30	0.75	1.50
❑22, Apr 97, Friends parody	1.50	0.30	0.75	1.50
❑23, Jun 97	1.50	0.30	0.75	1.50
❑24, Aug 97	1.50	0.30	0.75	1.50
❑25, Oct 97	1.50	0.30	0.75	1.50
❑26, Dec 97	1.50	0.30	0.75	1.50
❑27, Feb 98	1.75	0.35	0.88	1.75
❑28, Apr 98	1.75	0.35	0.88	1.75
❑29, Jun 98, Pops opens a cyber-cafe	1.75	0.35	0.88	1.75
❑30, Aug 98	1.75	0.35	0.88	1.75
❑31, Oct 98	1.75	0.35	0.88	1.75
❑32, Dec 98	1.75	0.35	0.88	1.75
❑33, Feb 99	1.75	0.35	0.88	1.75
❑34, Apr 99, That's Snow Business	1.79	0.35	0.88	1.75
❑35, Jun 99	1.79	0.36	0.89	1.79

	ORIG	GOOD	FINE	N-MINT
❑36, Aug 99	1.79	0.36	0.89	1.79
❑37, Oct 99	1.79	0.36	0.89	1.79
❑38, Dec 99	1.79	0.36	0.89	1.79
❑39, Feb 00	1.99	0.36	0.89	1.79
❑40, Apr 00	1.99	0.36	0.89	1.79
❑41, Jun 00	1.99	0.36	0.89	1.79
❑42, Aug 00	1.99	0.40	1.00	1.99
❑43, Oct 00	1.99	0.40	1.00	1.99
❑44, Dec 00	1.99	0.40	1.00	1.99
❑45, Feb 01	1.99	0.40	1.00	1.99
❑46, Apr 01, Riverdale High Exposed!	1.99	0.40	1.00	1.99
❑47	1.99	0.40	1.00	1.99
❑48	1.99	0.40	1.00	1.99
❑49	1.99	0.40	1.00	1.99
❑50	1.99	0.40	1.00	1.99

ARCHIE ANNUAL DIGEST MAGAZINE
ARCHIE

Value: Cover or less

- ❑66, Jun 95 ... 1.75
- ❑67, Oct 95 ... 1.75
- ❑68, Apr 97 ... 1.79

ARCHIE...ARCHIE ANDREWS, WHERE ARE YOU? DIGEST MAGAZINE
ARCHIE

Value: Cover or less

- ❑97, Jan 95 ... 1.75
- ❑98, Feb 95 ... 1.75
- ❑99, Apr 95 ... 1.75
- ❑100, Jun 95 ... 1.75
- ❑101, Aug 95 ... 1.75
- ❑102, Oct 95 ... 1.75
- ❑103, Dec 95 ... 1.75
- ❑104, Jan 96 ... 1.75
- ❑105, Mar 96 ... 1.75
- ❑106, May 96 ... 1.75
- ❑107, Aug 96 ... 1.75
- ❑108, Nov 96 ... 1.79
- ❑109, Feb 97 ... 1.79
- ❑110, May 97 ... 1.79
- ❑111, Sep 97 ... 1.79
- ❑112, Nov 97 ... 1.79
- ❑113, Feb 98 ... 1.95

ARCHIE AS PUREHEART THE POWERFUL
ARCHIE

	ORIG	GOOD	FINE	N-MINT
❑1, Sep 66	0.15	10.00	25.00	50.00
❑2	0.15	7.00	17.50	35.00
❑3	0.15	5.00	12.50	25.00
❑4	0.15	5.00	12.50	25.00
❑5	0.15	5.00	12.50	25.00
❑6, Nov 67	0.15	5.00	12.50	25.00

ARCHIE DIGEST MAGAZINE
ARCHIE

	ORIG	GOOD	FINE	N-MINT
❑100	—	0.30	0.75	1.50
❑101	—	0.36	0.89	1.79
❑102	—	0.36	0.89	1.79
❑103	—	0.36	0.89	1.79
❑104	—	0.36	0.89	1.79
❑105	—	0.36	0.89	1.79
❑106	—	0.36	0.89	1.79
❑107	—	0.36	0.89	1.79
❑108	—	0.36	0.89	1.79
❑109	—	0.36	0.89	1.79
❑110	—	0.36	0.89	1.79
❑111	—	0.36	0.89	1.79
❑112	—	0.36	0.89	1.79
❑113	—	0.36	0.89	1.79
❑114	—	0.36	0.89	1.79
❑115	—	0.36	0.89	1.79
❑116	—	0.36	0.89	1.79
❑117	—	0.36	0.89	1.79
❑118	—	0.36	0.89	1.79
❑119	—	0.36	0.89	1.79
❑120	—	0.36	0.89	1.79
❑121	—	0.36	0.89	1.79
❑122	—	0.36	0.89	1.79
❑123	—	0.36	0.89	1.79
❑124	—	0.36	0.89	1.79
❑125	—	0.36	0.89	1.79
❑126	—	0.36	0.89	1.79
❑127	—	0.36	0.89	1.79
❑128	—	0.36	0.89	1.79
❑129	—	0.36	0.89	1.79
❑130	—	0.36	0.89	1.79
❑131, Dec 94	1.75	0.36	0.89	1.79
❑132	1.75	0.36	0.89	1.79
❑133, Apr 95	1.75	0.36	0.89	1.79
❑134, May 95	1.75	0.36	0.89	1.79
❑135, Jul 95	1.75	0.36	0.89	1.79
❑136, Sep 95	1.75	0.36	0.89	1.79
❑137, Nov 95	1.75	0.36	0.89	1.79
❑138, Jan 96	1.75	0.36	0.89	1.79
❑139, Mar 96	1.75	0.36	0.89	1.79
❑140, Apr 96	1.75	0.36	0.89	1.79
❑141	—	0.36	0.89	1.79
❑142	—	0.36	0.89	1.79

Archie's super-heroic adventures were recounted in *Archie as Pureheart the Powerful.*

	ORIG	GOOD	FINE	N-MINT
❑143	—	0.36	0.89	1.79
❑144, Dec 96, Archie: Name Exclaim!; L'il Jinx: Look of Knowledge	1.79	0.36	0.89	1.79
❑145, Jan 97	1.79	0.36	0.89	1.79
❑146, Mar 97	1.79	0.36	0.89	1.79
❑147, Apr 97	1.79	0.36	0.89	1.79
❑148, Jun 97	1.79	0.36	0.89	1.79
❑149, Aug 97	1.79	0.36	0.89	1.79
❑150, Sep 97	1.79	0.36	0.89	1.79
❑151, Nov 97	1.79	0.36	0.89	1.79
❑152, Jan 98	1.95	0.39	0.98	1.95
❑153, Mar 98	1.95	0.39	0.98	1.95
❑154, Apr 98	1.95	0.39	0.98	1.95
❑155, Jun 98	1.95	0.39	0.98	1.95
❑156, Jul 98	1.95	0.39	0.98	1.95
❑157, Sep 98	1.95	0.39	0.98	1.95
❑158, Oct 98	1.95	0.39	0.98	1.95
❑159, Dec 98	1.95	0.39	0.98	1.95
❑160, Jan 99	1.95	0.39	0.98	1.95
❑161, Mar 99	1.95	0.39	0.98	1.95
❑162, Apr 99	1.99	0.39	0.98	1.95
❑163, Jun 99	1.99	0.39	0.98	1.95
❑164, Jul 99	1.99	0.39	0.98	1.95
❑165, Sep 99	1.99	0.39	0.98	1.95
❑166, Oct 99	1.99	0.39	0.98	1.95
❑167, Nov 99	1.99	0.39	0.98	1.95
❑168, Jan 00	1.99	0.39	0.98	1.95
❑169, Feb 00	1.99	0.39	0.98	1.95
❑170, Apr 00	1.99	0.39	0.98	1.95
❑171, Jun 00	2.19	0.39	0.98	1.95
❑172, Jul 00	2.19	0.39	0.98	1.95
❑173, Aug 00	2.19	0.44	1.10	2.19
❑174, Oct 00	2.19	0.44	1.10	2.19
❑175, Nov 00	2.19	0.44	1.10	2.19
❑176, Jan 01	2.19	0.44	1.10	2.19
❑177, Feb 01	2.19	0.44	1.10	2.19
❑178, Mar 01	2.19	0.44	1.10	2.19
❑179	—	0.44	1.10	2.19
❑180	—	0.44	1.10	2.19
❑181	—	0.44	1.10	2.19
❑182	—	0.44	1.10	2.19
❑183	—	0.44	1.10	2.19

ARCHIE MEETS THE PUNISHER
MARVEL

	ORIG	GOOD	FINE	N-MINT
❑1, Aug 94, Archie cover	2.95	0.65	1.63	3.25

ARCHIE'S CHRISTMAS STOCKING (2ND SERIES)
ARCHIE

Value: Cover or less

- ❑1, Jan 94, DDC, A Jingle for Justice; Fresh Idea!, reprints from Archie's Christmas Stocking #4, 5, 20; calendar; For 1993 holiday season ... 2.00
- ❑2, For 1994 holiday season ... 2.00
- ❑3, For 1995 holiday season ... 2.00
- ❑4, For 1996 holiday season ... 2.00
- ❑5, For 1997 holiday season ... 2.25
- ❑6, For 1998 holiday season ... 2.25
- ❑7, For 1999 holiday season ... 2.29

ARCHIE'S DATE BOOK
SPIRE

	ORIG	GOOD	FINE	N-MINT
❑1, nn; religious	0.69	0.60	1.50	3.00

ARCHIE'S DOUBLE DIGEST MAGAZINE
ARCHIE

	ORIG	GOOD	FINE	N-MINT
❑75, Nov 94	2.75	0.60	1.50	3.00
❑76, Jan 95	2.75	0.60	1.50	3.00
❑77, Mar 95	2.75	0.60	1.50	3.00
❑78, May 95	2.75	0.60	1.50	3.00
❑79, Jul 95	2.75	0.60	1.50	3.00
❑80, Aug 95	2.75	0.55	1.38	2.75
❑81, Oct 95	2.75	0.55	1.38	2.75
❑82, Dec 95	2.75	0.55	1.38	2.75
❑83, Feb 96	2.75	0.55	1.38	2.75
❑84, Apr 96	2.75	0.55	1.38	2.75
❑85	2.75	0.55	1.38	2.75
❑86, Jul 96	2.75	0.55	1.38	2.75

	ORIG	GOOD	FINE	N-MINT
❑87, Sep 96	2.75	0.55	1.38	2.75
❑88, Oct 96	2.75	0.55	1.38	2.75
❑89, Leaf It To Reggie; Practice Makes Perfect	2.75	0.55	1.38	2.75
❑90, Feb 97	2.75	0.55	1.38	2.75
❑91, Mar 97	2.75	0.55	1.38	2.75
❑92, May 97	2.75	0.55	1.38	2.75
❑93, Jul 97	2.75	0.55	1.38	2.75
❑94, Aug 97	2.75	0.55	1.38	2.75
❑95, Oct 97	2.79	0.55	1.38	2.75
❑96, Dec 97	2.79	0.55	1.38	2.75
❑97, Feb 98	2.95	0.55	1.38	2.75
❑98, Mar 98	2.95	0.55	1.38	2.75
❑99, May 98	2.95	0.55	1.38	2.75
❑100, Jul 98	2.95	0.55	1.38	2.75
❑101, Aug 98	2.95	0.55	1.38	2.75
❑102, Sep 98	2.95	0.55	1.38	2.75
❑103, Nov 98, DDC (w)	2.95	0.59	1.48	2.95
❑104, Dec 98	2.95	0.59	1.48	2.95
❑105, Feb 99	2.95	0.59	1.48	2.95
❑106, Apr 99	2.95	0.59	1.48	2.95
❑107, May 99	2.99	0.60	1.50	2.99
❑108, Jun 99	2.99	0.60	1.50	2.99
❑109, Aug 99	2.99	0.60	1.50	2.99
❑110, Sep 99	2.99	0.60	1.50	2.99
❑111, Nov 99	2.99	0.59	1.48	2.95
❑112, Dec 99	2.99	0.60	1.50	2.99
❑113, Feb 00	2.99	0.59	1.48	2.95
❑114, Mar 00	2.99	0.60	1.50	2.99
❑115, May 00	2.99	0.59	1.48	2.95
❑116, Jul 00	3.19	0.59	1.48	2.95
❑117, Aug 00	3.19	0.64	1.60	3.19
❑118, Sep 00	3.19	0.64	1.60	3.19
❑119, Nov 00	3.19	0.64	1.60	3.19
❑120, Dec 00	3.19	0.64	1.60	3.19
❑121, Jan 01	3.19	0.64	1.60	3.19
❑122, Mar 01	3.19	0.64	1.60	3.19
❑123, Apr 01	3.29	0.66	1.64	3.29
❑124	—	0.66	1.64	3.29
❑125	—	0.66	1.64	3.29
❑126	—	0.66	1.64	3.29
❑127	—	0.66	1.64	3.29

ARCHIE'S FAMILY ALBUM
SPIRE

	ORIG	GOOD	FINE	N-MINT
❑1	0.49	0.50	1.25	2.50

ARCHIE'S HOLIDAY FUN DIGEST MAGAZINE
ARCHIE

	ORIG	GOOD	FINE	N-MINT
❑1, Feb 97	1.79	0.39	0.98	1.95
❑2, Feb 98	1.95	0.39	0.98	1.95
❑3, Feb 99	1.95	0.39	0.98	1.95
❑4, Feb 00	1.99	0.40	1.00	1.99
❑5, Jan 01	2.19	0.44	1.10	2.19

ARCHIE'S PAL JUGHEAD COMICS
ARCHIE

	ORIG	GOOD	FINE	N-MINT
❑46, Jun 93, Series continued from Jughead #45	1.25	0.30	0.75	1.50
❑47, Jul 93	1.25	0.30	0.75	1.50
❑48, Aug 93	1.25	0.30	0.75	1.50
❑49, Sep 93	1.25	0.30	0.75	1.50
❑50, Nov 93	1.25	0.30	0.75	1.50
❑51, Dec 93	1.25	0.30	0.75	1.50
❑52, Jan 94	1.25	0.30	0.75	1.50
❑53, Feb 94	1.25	0.30	0.75	1.50
❑54, Mar 94	1.25	0.30	0.75	1.50
❑55, Apr 94	1.25	0.30	0.75	1.50
❑56, May 94	1.25	0.30	0.75	1.50
❑57, Jun 94	1.25	0.30	0.75	1.50
❑58, Jul 94	1.25	0.30	0.75	1.50
❑59, Aug 94	1.50	0.30	0.75	1.50
❑60, Sep 94	1.50	0.30	0.75	1.50
❑61, Oct 94	1.50	0.30	0.75	1.50
❑62, Nov 94	1.50	0.30	0.75	1.50
❑63, Dec 94	1.50	0.30	0.75	1.50
❑64, Jan 95	1.50	0.30	0.75	1.50
❑65, Feb 95	1.50	0.30	0.75	1.50
❑66, Mar 95	1.50	0.30	0.75	1.50
❑67, Apr 95	1.50	0.30	0.75	1.50
❑68, May 95	1.50	0.30	0.75	1.50
❑69, Jun 95	1.50	0.30	0.75	1.50
❑70, Jul 95	1.50	0.30	0.75	1.50
❑71, Aug 95	1.50	0.30	0.75	1.50
❑72, Sep 95, Jellybean's real name revealed	1.50	0.30	0.75	1.50
❑73, Oct 95	1.50	0.30	0.75	1.50
❑74, Nov 95	1.50	0.30	0.75	1.50
❑75, Dec 95	1.50	0.30	0.75	1.50
❑76, Jan 96, House of Riverdale, Part 3	1.50	0.30	0.75	1.50
❑77, Feb 96	1.50	0.30	0.75	1.50
❑78, Mar 96	1.50	0.30	0.75	1.50
❑79, Apr 96	1.50	0.30	0.75	1.50
❑80, May 96	1.50	0.30	0.75	1.50
❑81, Jun 96	1.50	0.30	0.75	1.50
❑82, Jul 96	1.50	0.30	0.75	1.50
❑83, Aug 96	1.50	0.30	0.75	1.50
❑84, Sep 96	1.50	0.30	0.75	1.50
❑85, Oct 96	1.50	0.30	0.75	1.50
❑86, Nov 96	1.50	0.30	0.75	1.50
❑87, Dec 96, Fangs for the Memory; The Cash Flow Problem	1.50	0.30	0.75	1.50
❑88, Jan 97	1.50	0.30	0.75	1.50
❑89, Feb 97, 1: Trula Twist and J.U.S.T.	1.50	0.30	0.75	1.50
❑90, Mar 97, Jughead asks Trula out	1.50	0.30	0.75	1.50
❑91, Apr 97, Trula Twyst's true plan revealed	1.50	0.30	0.75	1.50
❑92, May 97	1.50	0.30	0.75	1.50
❑93, Jun 97, A: Trula Twyst	1.50	0.30	0.75	1.50
❑94, Jul 97, A: Trula Twyst	1.50	0.30	0.75	1.50
❑95, Aug 97	1.50	0.30	0.75	1.50
❑96, Sep 97	1.50	0.30	0.75	1.50
❑97, Oct 97, A: Trula Twyst	1.50	0.30	0.75	1.50
❑98, Nov 97	1.50	0.30	0.75	1.50
❑99, Dec 97, A: Trula Twyst	1.50	0.30	0.75	1.50
❑100, Jan 98, A Storm Over Uniforms, Part 1, continues in Archie #467	1.75	0.30	0.75	1.50
❑101, Feb 98, 1: Googie Gilmore	1.75	0.30	0.75	1.50
❑102, Mar 98	1.75	0.30	0.75	1.50
❑103, Apr 98	1.75	0.30	0.75	1.50
❑104, May 98	1.75	0.30	0.75	1.50
❑105, Jun 98	1.75	0.30	0.75	1.50
❑106, Jul 98, A: Googie Gilmore	1.75	0.30	0.75	1.50
❑107, Aug 98	1.75	0.30	0.75	1.50
❑108, Sep 98, Crown Town; Beach Bummed	1.75	0.35	0.88	1.75
❑109, Oct 98	1.75	0.35	0.88	1.75
❑110, Nov 98	1.75	0.35	0.88	1.75
❑111, Dec 98	1.75	0.35	0.88	1.75
❑112, Jan 99, A: Trula Twyst	1.75	0.35	0.88	1.75
❑113, Feb 99	1.75	0.35	0.88	1.75
❑114, Mar 99, A: Trula Twyst	1.75	0.35	0.88	1.75
❑115, Apr 99	1.79	0.35	0.88	1.75
❑116, May 99, Meals on Wheels	1.79	0.35	0.88	1.75
❑117, Jun 99, A: Trula Twyst	1.79	0.35	0.88	1.75
❑118, Jul 99, A: Trula Twyst	1.79	0.35	0.88	1.75
❑119, Aug 99, Ethel gets Jughead's baby pictures	1.79	0.35	0.88	1.75
❑120, Sep 99, A: Trula Twyst	1.79	0.35	0.88	1.75
❑121, Oct 99	1.79	0.35	0.88	1.75
❑122, Nov 99	1.79	0.35	0.88	1.75
❑123, Dec 99	1.79	0.35	0.88	1.75
❑124, Jan 00	1.79	0.35	0.88	1.75
❑125, Feb 00	1.79	0.35	0.88	1.75
❑126, Apr 00	1.79	0.35	0.88	1.75
❑127, May 00	1.79	0.35	0.88	1.75
❑128, Jul 00	1.99	0.40	1.00	1.99
❑129, Aug 00	1.99	0.40	1.00	1.99
❑130, Sep 00	1.99	0.40	1.00	1.99
❑131, Oct 00	1.99	0.40	1.00	1.99
❑132, Dec 00	1.99	0.40	1.00	1.99
❑133, Jan 01	1.99	0.40	1.00	1.99
❑134	1.99	0.40	1.00	1.99
❑135	1.99	0.40	1.00	1.99
❑136	1.99	0.40	1.00	1.99
❑137	1.99	0.40	1.00	1.99
❑138	1.99	0.40	1.00	1.99
❑139	1.99	0.40	1.00	1.99

ARCHIE'S PALS 'N' GALS DOUBLE DIGEST
ARCHIE

	ORIG	GOOD	FINE	N-MINT
❑1	2.50	0.80	2.00	4.00
❑2	2.50	0.60	1.50	3.00
❑3	2.50	0.60	1.50	3.00
❑4	2.75	0.60	1.50	3.00
❑5	2.75	0.60	1.50	3.00
❑6	2.75	0.55	1.38	2.75
❑7	2.75	0.55	1.38	2.75
❑8	2.75	0.55	1.38	2.75
❑9, Jan 95	2.75	0.55	1.38	2.75
❑10, Feb 95	2.75	0.55	1.38	2.75
❑11, Apr 95	2.75	0.55	1.38	2.75
❑12, Jun 95	2.75	0.55	1.38	2.75
❑13, Aug 95	2.75	0.55	1.38	2.75
❑14, Oct 95	2.75	0.55	1.38	2.75
❑15, Dec 95	2.75	0.55	1.38	2.75
❑16, Jan 96	2.75	0.55	1.38	2.75

	ORIG	GOOD	FINE	N-MINT
❑17, Mar 96	2.75	0.55	1.38	2.75
❑18, May 96	2.75	0.55	1.38	2.75
❑19, Jul 96	2.75	0.55	1.38	2.75
❑20, Aug 96	2.75	0.55	1.38	2.75
❑21	2.75	0.55	1.38	2.75
❑22, Dec 96, Now You Tell Me!; Leap Of Faith	2.75	0.55	1.38	2.75
❑23, Jan 97	2.75	0.55	1.38	2.75
❑24, Mar 97	2.75	0.55	1.38	2.75
❑25, May 97	2.75	0.55	1.38	2.75
❑26, Jul 97	2.75	0.55	1.38	2.75
❑27, Aug 97	2.79	0.55	1.38	2.75
❑28, Oct 97	2.79	0.55	1.38	2.75
❑29, Dec 97	2.79	0.55	1.38	2.75
❑30, Jan 98	2.95	0.59	1.48	2.95
❑31, Mar 98	2.95	0.59	1.48	2.95
❑32, May 98	2.95	0.59	1.48	2.95
❑33, Jun 98	2.95	0.59	1.48	2.95
❑34, Aug 98	2.95	0.59	1.48	2.95
❑35, Sep 98	2.95	0.59	1.48	2.95
❑36, Oct 98	2.95	0.59	1.48	2.95
❑37, Dec 98	2.95	0.59	1.48	2.95
❑38, Feb 99	2.95	0.59	1.48	2.95
❑39, Apr 99	2.95	0.59	1.48	2.95
❑40, May 99	2.99	0.60	1.50	2.99
❑41, Jun 99	2.99	0.60	1.50	2.99
❑42, Aug 99	2.99	0.60	1.50	2.99
❑43, Sep 99	2.99	0.60	1.50	2.99
❑44, Oct 99	2.99	0.60	1.50	2.99
❑45, Dec 99	2.99	0.60	1.50	2.99
❑46, Feb 00	2.99	0.60	1.50	2.99
❑47, Mar 00	2.99	0.60	1.50	2.99
❑48, May 00	2.99	0.60	1.50	2.99
❑49, Jun 00	3.19	0.64	1.60	3.19
❑50, Aug 00	3.19	0.64	1.60	3.19
❑51, Sep 00	3.19	0.64	1.60	3.19
❑52, Oct 00	3.19	0.64	1.60	3.19
❑53, Dec 00	3.19	0.64	1.60	3.19
❑54, Feb 01	3.19	0.64	1.60	3.19
❑55, Mar 01	3.19	0.64	1.60	3.19
❑56	—	0.66	1.64	3.29
❑57	—	0.66	1.64	3.29
❑58	—	0.66	1.64	3.29
❑59	—	0.66	1.64	3.29
❑60	—	0.66	1.64	3.29

ARCHIE'S R/C RACERS
ARCHIE

	ORIG	GOOD	FINE	N-MINT
❑1, On Your Mark; ...Get Ready..., Reggie appearanc	0.95	0.20	0.50	1.00
❑2	—	0.20	0.50	1.00
❑3	—	0.20	0.50	1.00
❑4	—	0.20	0.50	1.00
❑5	—	0.20	0.50	1.00
❑6	—	0.20	0.50	1.00
❑7	—	0.20	0.50	1.00
❑8	—	0.20	0.50	1.00
❑9	—	0.20	0.50	1.00
❑10	—	0.20	0.50	1.00

ARCHIE'S SPRING BREAK
ARCHIE

Value: Cover or less

- ❑1, 96 ... 2.00
- ❑2, 97 ... 2.00
- ❑3, 98 ... 2.25
- ❑4, 99 ... 2.29
- ❑5 ... 2.49

ARCHIE'S STORY & GAME DIGEST MAGAZINE
ARCHIE

Value: Cover or less

- ❑32, Jul 95 ... 1.75
- ❑33, Sep 95 ... 1.75
- ❑34, Mar 96 ... 1.75
- ❑35, May 96 ... 1.75
- ❑36 ... 1.75
- ❑37, Jan 97 ... 1.79
- ❑38, Aug 97 ... 1.79
- ❑39, Jan 98 ... 1.95

ARCHIE'S SUPER TEENS
ARCHIE

Value: Cover or less

- ❑1, 94, poster ... 2.00
- ❑2, 95 ... 2.00
- ❑3, 95 ... 2.00
- ❑4, 96 ... 2.00

ARCHIE'S VACATION SPECIAL
ARCHIE

Value: Cover or less

- ❑1, Sum 94, Have A Nice Trip, Part 1; Have A Nice Trip, Part 2, poster ... 2.00
- ❑2, Win 95 ... 2.00
- ❑3, Sum 95 ... 2.00
- ❑4, Sum 96 ... 2.00
- ❑5, Sum 97 ... 2.00
- ❑6, Sum 98 ... 2.25
- ❑7, Sum 99 ... 2.29
- ❑8, Sum 00 ... 2.49

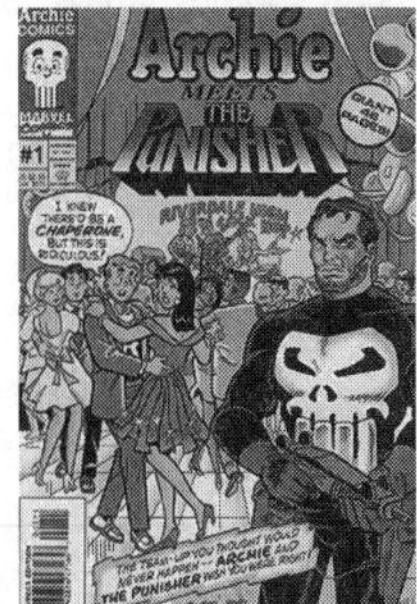

Frank Castle paid a visit to Riverdale in *Archie Meets The Punisher.*

ARCHIE'S WEIRD MYSTERIES
ARCHIE

	ORIG	GOOD	FINE	N-MINT
❑1, Feb 00	1.79	0.36	0.89	1.79
❑2, Mar 00	1.79	0.36	0.89	1.79
❑3, Apr 00	1.79	0.36	0.89	1.79
❑4, May 00	1.99	0.40	1.00	1.99
❑5, Jun 00	1.99	0.40	1.00	1.99
❑6, Jul 00	1.99	0.40	1.00	1.99
❑7, Aug 00	1.99	0.40	1.00	1.99
❑8, Sep 00	1.99	0.40	1.00	1.99
❑9, Oct 00	1.99	0.40	1.00	1.99
❑10, Dec 00	1.99	0.40	1.00	1.99
❑11, Feb 01	1.99	0.40	1.00	1.99
❑12, Apr 01	1.99	0.40	1.00	1.99
❑13	1.99	0.40	1.00	1.99
❑14	1.99	0.40	1.00	1.99
❑15	1.99	0.40	1.00	1.99
❑16	1.99	0.40	1.00	1.99
❑Ash 1, The Case of the Haunted Comic Shop, Giveaway from Diamond	—	0.20	0.50	1.00

ARCOMICS PREMIERE
ARCOMICS

Value: Cover or less

- ❑1, Jul 93, b&w; lenticular animation cover ... 2.95

ARCTIC COMICS
NICK BURNS

Value: Cover or less

- ❑1, Spring; Glossary, souvenir ... 1.00

AREA 52
IMAGE

Value: Cover or less

- ❑1, Jan 01, Here Nothing Can Go Wrong ... 2.95
- ❑2, Mar 01 ... 2.95
- ❑3, Apr 01 ... 2.95

AREA 88
ECLIPSE

	ORIG	GOOD	FINE	N-MINT
❑1, May 87, Mission 1, The Blue Skies Of Betrayal	1.50	0.70	1.75	3.50
❑1-2, Mission 1, The Blue Skies Of Betrayal, 2nd Printing	1.50	0.40	1.00	2.00
❑2	1.50	0.50	1.25	2.50
❑2-2, 2nd Printing	1.50	0.30	0.75	1.50
❑3	1.50	0.40	1.00	2.00
❑4	1.50	0.40	1.00	2.00
❑5	1.50	0.40	1.00	2.00
❑6	1.50	0.30	0.75	1.50
❑7	1.50	0.30	0.75	1.50
❑8	1.50	0.30	0.75	1.50
❑9	1.50	0.30	0.75	1.50
❑10	1.50	0.30	0.75	1.50
❑11	1.50	0.30	0.75	1.50
❑12	1.50	0.30	0.75	1.50
❑13	1.50	0.30	0.75	1.50
❑14	1.50	0.30	0.75	1.50
❑15	1.50	0.30	0.75	1.50
❑16, Jan 88	1.50	0.30	0.75	1.50
❑17, Jan 88	1.50	0.30	0.75	1.50
❑18, Feb 88	1.50	0.30	0.75	1.50
❑19, Feb 88	1.50	0.30	0.75	1.50
❑20, Mar 88	1.50	0.30	0.75	1.50
❑21, Mar 88	1.50	0.30	0.75	1.50
❑22, Apr 88	1.50	0.30	0.75	1.50
❑23, Apr 88	1.50	0.30	0.75	1.50
❑24, May 88	1.50	0.30	0.75	1.50
❑25, May 88	1.50	0.30	0.75	1.50
❑26, Jun 88	1.50	0.30	0.75	1.50
❑27, Jun 88	1.50	0.30	0.75	1.50
❑28, Jul 88	1.50	0.30	0.75	1.50
❑29, Jul 88	1.50	0.30	0.75	1.50
❑30, Aug 88	1.50	0.30	0.75	1.50
❑31, Aug 88	1.50	0.30	0.75	1.50
❑32, Sep 88	1.50	0.30	0.75	1.50
❑33, Sep 88	1.50	0.30	0.75	1.50

	ORIG	GOOD	FINE	N-MINT
❑34, Oct 88	1.50	0.30	0.75	1.50
❑35, Oct 88	1.50	0.30	0.75	1.50
❑36, Nov 88	1.50	0.30	0.75	1.50
❑37	1.75	0.35	0.88	1.75
❑38	1.75	0.35	0.88	1.75
❑39	1.75	0.35	0.88	1.75
❑40	1.75	0.35	0.88	1.75
❑41	1.75	0.35	0.88	1.75
❑42, Final Issue	2.00	0.35	0.88	1.75

AREALA: ANGEL OF WAR
ANTARCTIC

Value: Cover or less

❑1, Sep 98, O: Auria 2.95
❑2, Nov 98 .... 2.95
❑3, Feb 99 .... 2.95

ARENA
ALCHEMY

Value: Cover or less

❑1, b&w 1.50

ARGONAUTS, THE (ETERNITY)
ETERNITY

Value: Cover or less

❑1 .... 1.95
❑2, A Touch of Doomsday 1.95
❑3 .... 1.95
❑4 .... 1.95

ARGONAUTS, THE: SYSTEM CRASH
ALPHA PRODUCTIONS

Value: Cover or less

❑1, System Crash, Part 1 .... 2.50
❑2, System Crash, Part 2 .... 2.50

ARGON ZARK!
ARCLIGHT PUBLISHING

Value: Cover or less

❑1, 97, based on on-line comics series 6.95

ARGUS
DC

Value: Cover or less

❑1, Apr 95, Light In Dark, Part 1, God Of Vengeance 1.50
❑2, Jun 95 .... 1.75
❑3, Jul 95 .... 1.75
❑4, Aug 95 .... 1.75
❑5, Sep 95 .... 1.75
❑6, Oct 95, Final Issue 1.75

ARIA
IMAGE

	ORIG	GOOD	FINE	N-MINT
❑1, Jan 99, Fairy Tale Endings	2.50	0.60	1.50	3.00
❑1/A, Jan 99, Fairy Tale Endings, white background cover	2.50	0.80	2.00	4.00
❑1/B, Jan 99, Fairy Tale Endings, Woman looking from balcony on cover	2.50	0.80	2.00	4.00
❑2, Apr 99, The Shores of Sorrow	2.50	0.50	1.25	2.50
❑3, May 99	2.50	0.50	1.25	2.50
❑4/A, Nov 99, Among Ruins, Textured cover stock; Close-up shot of woman in green pointing at chest	2.50	0.50	1.25	2.50
❑4/B, Nov 99, Among Ruins, Variant cover with Angela	2.50	0.50	1.25	2.50
❑Ash 1, Nov 98, The World of Aria, b&w; preview issue	2.95	0.70	1.75	3.50

ARIA ANGELA
IMAGE

	ORIG	GOOD	FINE	N-MINT
❑1/A, Feb 00, Heavenly Creatures, Part 1, Aria and Angela in profile on cover	2.95	0.59	1.48	2.95
❑1/B, Feb 00, Heavenly Creatures, Part 1, Aria sitting on stairs on cover; Angela smiling, front	2.95	0.59	1.48	2.95
❑1/C, Feb 00, Heavenly Creatures, Part 1, Close-up on Aria (right half of 1/H cover in close-up)	2.95	0.59	1.48	2.95
❑1/D, Feb 00, Heavenly Creatures, Part 1, Woman walking through astral plane on cover	2.95	0.59	1.48	2.95
❑1/E, Feb 00, Heavenly Creatures, Part 1, Woman walking through astral plane on cover	2.95	0.59	1.48	2.95
❑1/F, Feb 00, Heavenly Creatures, Part 1, Two women, hawk on cover	2.95	0.59	1.48	2.95
❑1/G, Feb 00, Heavenly Creatures, Part 1, Woman with sword (between legs) on cover; Tower records variant	2.95	0.59	1.48	2.95
❑1/H, Feb 00, Heavenly Creatures, Part 1	2.95	0.59	1.48	2.95
❑1/I, Feb 00, Heavenly Creatures, Part 1, chromium cover	—	0.59	1.48	2.95
❑2, Oct 00, Heavenly Creatures, Part 2	2.95	0.59	1.48	2.95

ARIA ANGELA BLANC & NOIR
IMAGE

Value: Cover or less

❑1, Apr 00, Heavenly Creatures, Part 1, Reprints Aria Angela #1 in black & white 2.95

ARIA BLANC & NOIR
IMAGE

Value: Cover or less

❑1, Mar 99, wraparound cover; b&w reprint of Aria #1 .... 2.50
❑2, Mar 99, Fairy Tale Endings 2.50

ARIANE & BLUEBEARD
ECLIPSE

Value: Cover or less

❑1, CR, CR (w) 3.95

ARIANNE
SLAVE LABOR

	ORIG	GOOD	FINE	N-MINT
❑1, May 91	2.50	0.99	2.47	4.95
❑2, Oct 91	2.95	0.59	1.48	2.95

ARIANNE (MOONSTONE)
MOONSTONE

Value: Cover or less

❑1, Dec 95, b&w 4.95

ARIA: THE SOUL MARKET
IMAGE

Value: Cover or less

❑1 .... 2.95
❑2, Apr 01 .... 2.95

ARIK KHAN (A+)
A-PLUS

Value: Cover or less

❑1, Arik Kha: Crusade; Captain Crossbones, b&w, reprint 2.50
❑2 .... 2.50

ARIK KHAN (ANDROMEDA)
ANDROMEDA

Value: Cover or less

❑1 .... 1.95
❑2 .... 1.95
❑3 .... 1.95

ARION, LORD OF ATLANTIS
DC

	ORIG	GOOD	FINE	N-MINT
❑1, Nov 82, JDu, Star Spawn Sun Death, Story continued from Warlord #62	0.60	0.20	0.50	1.00
❑2, Dec 82, JDu, 1: Mara	0.60	0.20	0.50	1.00
❑3, Jan 83, JDu	0.60	0.20	0.50	1.00
❑4, Feb 83, JDu	0.60	0.20	0.50	1.00
❑5, Mar 83, JDu	0.60	0.20	0.50	1.00
❑6, Apr 83, JDu	0.60	0.20	0.50	1.00
❑7, May 83, JDu	0.60	0.20	0.50	1.00
❑8, Jun 83	0.60	0.20	0.50	1.00
❑9, Jul 83	0.60	0.20	0.50	1.00
❑10, Aug 83	0.60	0.20	0.50	1.00
❑11, Sep 83	0.60	0.20	0.50	1.00
❑12, Oct 83, JDu, Sanctuary Of Sorcery	0.60	0.20	0.50	1.00
❑13, Nov 83	0.60	0.20	0.50	1.00
❑14, Dec 83	0.75	0.20	0.50	1.00
❑15, Jan 84	0.75	0.20	0.50	1.00
❑16, Feb 84	0.75	0.20	0.50	1.00
❑17, Mar 84	0.75	0.20	0.50	1.00
❑18, Apr 84	0.75	0.20	0.50	1.00
❑19, May 84	0.75	0.20	0.50	1.00
❑20, Jun 84	0.75	0.20	0.50	1.00
❑21, Jul 84	0.75	0.20	0.50	1.00
❑22, Aug 84	0.75	0.20	0.50	1.00
❑23, Sep 84	0.75	0.20	0.50	1.00
❑24, Oct 84	0.75	0.20	0.50	1.00
❑25, Nov 84	0.75	0.20	0.50	1.00
❑26, Dec 84	0.75	0.20	0.50	1.00
❑27, Jan 85	0.75	0.20	0.50	1.00
❑28, Feb 85	0.75	0.20	0.50	1.00
❑29, Mar 85	0.75	0.20	0.50	1.00
❑30, Apr 85	0.75	0.20	0.50	1.00
❑31, May 85	0.75	0.20	0.50	1.00
❑32, Jun 85	0.75	0.20	0.50	1.00
❑33, Jul 85	0.75	0.20	0.50	1.00
❑34, Aug 85	0.75	0.20	0.50	1.00
❑35, Sep 85, Final Issue	0.75	0.20	0.50	1.00
❑SE 1, Special	1.25	0.20	0.50	1.00

ARION THE IMMORTAL
DC

Value: Cover or less

❑1, Jul 92, Excuse Me, Sir, How Do I Get To Carney Hall? 1.50
❑2, Aug 92, Shoot The Dog 1.50
❑3, Sep 92 .... 1.50
❑4, Oct 92 .... 1.50
❑5, Nov 92 .... 1.50
❑6, Dec 92, A: Power Girl, Final Issue 1.50

ARISTOCATS, THE
GOLD KEY

	ORIG	GOOD	FINE	N-MINT
❑1, Mar 71, movie Adaptation; 30045-103; poster	0.25	0.60	1.50	3.00

ARISTOCRATIC X-TRATERRESTRIAL TIME-TRAVELING THIEVES
COMICS INTERVIEW

	ORIG	GOOD	FINE	N-MINT
❑1, Feb 87	1.75	0.40	1.00	2.00
❑2, Apr 87	1.75	0.40	1.00	2.00
❑3, Jun 87	1.75	0.40	1.00	2.00
❑4, Aug 87	1.75	0.40	1.00	2.00
❑5, Oct 87	1.75	0.40	1.00	2.00
❑6, Dec 87	1.75	0.40	1.00	2.00
❑7, Feb 88	1.75	0.40	1.00	2.00
❑8, Apr 88	1.75	0.40	1.00	2.00
❑9, Jun 88	1.75	0.40	1.00	2.00
❑10, Aug 88	1.95	0.40	1.00	2.00
❑11, Oct 88	1.95	0.40	1.00	2.00
❑12, Dec 88	1.95	0.40	1.00	2.00

ARISTOCRATIC X-TRATERRESTRIAL TIME-TRAVELING THIEVES MICRO-SERIES
COMICS INTERVIEW

	ORIG	GOOD	FINE	N-MINT
❑1, Aug 86, One-Shot	1.75	0.40	1.00	2.00
❑1-2, 2nd Printing	1.75	0.40	1.00	2.00

ARISTOKITTENS, THE
GOLD KEY

	ORIG	GOOD	FINE	N-MINT
❑1	—	2.00	5.00	10.00
❑2	—	1.40	3.50	7.00
❑3	—	1.00	2.50	5.00
❑4	—	1.00	2.50	5.00
❑5	—	1.00	2.50	5.00
❑6	—	0.60	1.50	3.00
❑7	—	0.60	1.50	3.00
❑8	—	0.60	1.50	3.00
❑9	—	0.60	1.50	3.00

ARIZONA: A SIMPLE HORROR
LONDON NIGHT

Value: Cover or less

❑1 ..... 3.00

ARKAGA
IMAGE

Value: Cover or less

❑1, Sep 97 ..... 2.95
❑2 ..... 2.95

ARKEOLOGY
VALKYRIE

Value: Cover or less

❑1, Apr 89, nn; companion one-shot for The Adventures of Luther Arkwright 2.00

ARLINGTON HAMMER IN: "GET ME TO THE CHURCH ON TIME"
ONE SHOT

Value: Cover or less

❑1, nn; comic for sale at conventions only 2.50

A.R.M.
ADVENTURE

Value: Cover or less

❑1, Death by Ecstasy!, Introduction by Larry Niven 2.50
❑2 ..... 2.50
❑3 ..... 2.50

ARMADILLO COMICS
RIP OFF

	ORIG	GOOD	FINE	N-MINT
❑1	0.50	0.50	1.25	2.50
❑2	0.50	0.50	1.25	2.50

ARMAGEDDON
LAST GASP

	ORIG	GOOD	FINE	N-MINT
❑1	0.50	0.50	1.25	2.50
❑2	0.50	0.50	1.25	2.50

ARMAGEDDON (CHAOS)
CHAOS

Value: Cover or less

❑1, Oct 99, The Beginning of the End 2.95
❑2, Nov 99, Not of This Earth . 2.95
❑3, Dec 99, It Conquered the Earth 2.95
❑4, Jan 00 ..... 2.95

ARMAGEDDON 2001
DC

Value: Cover or less

❑1, May 91, Armageddon 2001, Part 1, 1: Waverider; 1: Monarch, 1st Printing 2.00
❑1-2, May 91, Armageddon 2001, Part 1, 1: Waverider; 1: Monarch, 2nd Printing 2.00
❑, May 91, Armageddon 2001, Part 1, 1: Waverider; 1: Monarch, 3rd printing (silver ink on cover) 2.00
❑2, Oct 91, Armageddon 2001, Part 14, Monarch's ID revealed 2.00

ARMAGEDDON FACTOR, THE
AC

Value: Cover or less

❑1, Jun 87 ..... 1.95
❑2, Aug 87 ..... 1.95
❑3 ..... 1.95

ARMAGEDDON FACTOR, THE: THE CONCLUSION
AC

Value: Cover or less

❑1, 90, The Last Days of Man on Earth, nn; b&w 3.95

ARMAGEDDON: INFERNO
DC

Value: Cover or less

❑1, Apr 92, Seeds Of Doom ... 1.00
❑2, May 92 ..... 1.00
❑3, Jun 92 ..... 1.00
❑4, Jul 92, JSA returns from limbo 1.00

ARMAGEDDONQUEST
STARHEAD

Value: Cover or less

❑1, 94, Tazio, adult 3.95
❑2, 94, adult 3.95

ARMAGEDDON RISING
MILLENNIUM

Value: Cover or less

❑1, 97, nn; b&w; Anthology; special foil edition; features characters from Song of the Sirens 4.95

ARMAGEDDON SQUAD, THE
HAZE STUDIOS

Value: Cover or less

❑1, b&w 1.50

ARMAGEDDON: THE ALIEN AGENDA
DC

Value: Cover or less

❑1, Nov 91, Days Of Thunder Lizards 1.00
❑2, Dec 91 ..... 1.00
❑3, Jan 92 ..... 1.00
❑4, Feb 92 ..... 1.00

ARComics introduced its line in *ARComics Premiere.* The one-shot had a lenticular animation card glued to its cover.

© 1993 ARComics

ARMATURE
OLYOPTICS

Value: Cover or less

❑1, Nov 96, Ghostarama 2.95
❑2 ..... 2.95

ARMED AND DANGEROUS (ACCLAIM)
ACCLAIM

Value: Cover or less

❑1, Apr 96, BH, BH (w), Picking Up The Pieces, b&w 2.95
❑2, May 96, BH, BH (w), Dire Street, b&w 2.95
❑3, Jun 96, BH, BH (w), b&w .. 2.95
❑4, Jul 96, BH, BH (w), b&w 2.95
❑SE 1, Aug 96, b&w; one-shot special; later indicias show this is really issue #5 of series 2.95

ARMED & DANGEROUS (KITCHEN SINK)
KITCHEN SINK

Value: Cover or less

❑1, Jul 95, magazine-sized graphic novel 9.95

ARMED & DANGEROUS: HELL'S SLAUGHTERHOUSE
ACCLAIM

Value: Cover or less

❑1, BH, BH (w), Terminal bar .. 2.95
❑2, BH, BH (w), Whiskey Dreams 2.95
❑3, BH, BH (w), The Brotherhood Of Cain 2.95
❑4, BH, BH (w) 2.95

ARMEN DEEP & BUG BOY
DILEMMA

Value: Cover or less

❑2, 95, b&w; cardstock cover 2.50

ARMITAGE
FLEETWAY

Value: Cover or less

❑1, cardstock cover 2.95
❑2, Armitage; Future Shock, cardstock cover 2.95

ARMOR
CONTINUITY

Value: Cover or less

❑1, NA (w) 2.00
❑2 ..... 2.00
❑3 ..... 2.00
❑4, Jul 88 ..... 2.00
❑5, Dec 88 ..... 2.00
❑6, Apr 89 ..... 2.00
❑7, Jan 90, NA (w), O: Armor . 2.00
❑8, Apr 90 ..... 2.00
❑9, Apr 91 ..... 2.00
❑10, Aug 91 ..... 2.00
❑11, Nov 91 ..... 2.00
❑12, Mar 92 ..... 2.00
❑13, Apr 92 ..... 2.00

ARMOR (2ND SERIES)
CONTINUITY

Value: Cover or less

❑1, Apr 93, Deathwatch 2000, Part 3, wraparound foil cardstock cover; 2 trading cards 2.50
❑2, May 93, Deathwatch 2000, Part 9, diecut outer cover; trading card 2.50
❑3, Aug 93, Deathwatch 2000, Part 15, trading card 2.50
❑4, Oct 93 ..... 2.50
❑5, Nov 93 ..... 2.50
❑6, Nov 93, Rise of Magic 2.50

ARMORED TROOPER VOTOMS
CPM

Value: Cover or less

❑1, Jul 96 ..... 2.95

ARMORINES
VALIANT

	ORIG	GOOD	FINE	N-MINT
❑0, Feb 93, no cover price; "Fall Fling Preview Edition"	—	0.40	1.00	2.00
❑1, Jun 94, Fathoms Below, Part 1, Fathoms Below	2.25	0.45	1.13	2.25
❑2, Aug 94, Fathoms Below, Part 2	2.25	0.45	1.13	2.25
❑3, Sep 94, Fathoms Below, Part 3	2.25	0.45	1.13	2.25
❑4, Oct 94, The Chaos Effect prelude	2.25	0.45	1.13	2.25
❑5, Nov 94, The Chaos Effect: Delta, Part 2, The Gathering, Continues from Harbinger #34	2.25	0.45	1.13	2.25
❑6, Dec 94, A: X-O	2.25	0.45	1.13	2.25
❑7, Jan 95, The Chaos Effect aftermath, wraparound cover	2.25	0.45	1.13	2.25
❑8, Feb 95	2.25	0.45	1.13	2.25
❑9, Mar 95	2.25	0.45	1.13	2.25
❑10, Apr 95	2.25	0.45	1.13	2.25
❑11, May 95	2.25	0.45	1.13	2.25
❑12, Jun 95, Final Issue	2.25	0.45	1.13	2.25

ARMORINES (VOL. 2)
ACCLAIM

	ORIG	GOOD	FINE	N-MINT
❑1, Oct 99, Return to Sender	3.95	0.79	1.98	3.95
❑2, Nov 99	3.95	0.79	1.98	3.95

	ORIG	GOOD	FINE	N-MINT
❑3, Dec 99, Return to Sender	2.50	0.79	1.98	3.95
❑4, Jan 00, Bugs Must Die, A: X-O Manowar	2.50	0.79	1.98	3.95

ARM'S LENGTH
THIRD WIND PRESS

Value: Cover or less
- ❑1, Jul 00, My Favorite Roadshow; The Artist at Sixty, b&w 3.95

ARMY ANTS (MICHAEL T. DESING'S...)
MICHAEL T. DESING

Value: Cover or less
- ❑8, b&w 2.50

ARMY OF DARKNESS
DARK HORSE

	ORIG	GOOD	FINE	N-MINT
❑1	2.50	1.20	3.00	6.00
❑2	2.50	1.00	2.50	5.00
❑3, Oct 93	2.50	1.00	2.50	5.00

ARMY SURPLUS KOMIKZ FEATURING: CUTEY BUNNY
QUAGMIRE

	ORIG	GOOD	FINE	N-MINT
❑1, Quagmire publishes	1.50	0.60	1.50	3.00
❑2	1.50	0.40	1.00	2.00
❑3	1.50	0.40	1.00	2.00
❑4	1.50	0.40	1.00	2.00
❑5, 85, b&w; Final Issue; X-Men parody; Eclipse publishes	1.50	0.40	1.00	2.00

ARRGH!
MARVEL

	ORIG	GOOD	FINE	N-MINT
❑1, Dec 74, TS, Fangs For The Memory!; Whacks' <Museum	0.25	1.00	2.50	5.00
❑2, Feb 75, TS	0.25	0.80	2.00	4.00
❑3, May 75, AA	0.25	0.60	1.50	3.00
❑4, Jul 75	0.25	0.60	1.50	3.00
❑5, Sep 75, RA, The Invisible Mr. Mann; Count Varicose	0.25	0.60	1.50	3.00

ARROW
MALIBU

Value: Cover or less
- ❑1, Shaft of Steel, Heart of Stone 1.95

ARROW ANTHOLOGY
ARROW

Value: Cover or less
- ❑1, Nov 97, The Fool, Jabberwocky, Great Scott, Night Streets, Battle Bot 3.95
- ❑2, Jan 98, Simone & Ajax, Battle Bot, Night Streets, Miss Chevious, Dark Oz 3.95
- ❑3, Mar 98, The Fool, Dragon Storm, Great Scott, Ninja Duck, Simone & Ajax, Samantha .. 3.95
- ❑4, Sep 98, August; Mr. Nightmare: Right Place, Wrong Time, August, Land of Oz, Corhawk, Mr. Nightmare, Simone & Ajax 3.95
- ❑5 .... 3.95

ARROWMAN
PARODY

Value: Cover or less
- ❑1, b&w 2.50

ARROW SPOTLIGHT
ARROW

Value: Cover or less
- ❑1, 98, A Christmas Calamity; What's Going On?, b&w; Simone & Ajax 2.95

ARSENAL
DC

Value: Cover or less
- ❑1, Oct 98, A: Black Canary ... 2.50
- ❑2, Nov 98, A: Green Arrow ... 2.50
- ❑3, Dec 98, V: Vandal Savage 2.50
- ❑4, Jan 99, DGry(w), V: Vandal Savage 2.50

ARSENAL SPECIAL
DC

Value: Cover or less
- ❑1, 96, The Readiness to Die, One-Shot 2.95

ARSENIC LULLABY
SILENT

Value: Cover or less
- ❑1, Dec 98, This Is the Enemy; Slow Boat to China, Part 1 .. 2.50

ART & BEAUTY MAGAZINE
KITCHEN SINK

Value: Cover or less
- ❑1, nn; b&w; adult; cardstock cover; over-sized 4.95

ARTBABE (VOL. 2)
FANTAGRAPHICS

Value: Cover or less
- ❑1, May 97 .... 2.95
- ❑2, Nov 97 .... 2.95
- ❑3, Aug 98 .... 2.95
- ❑4, Apr 99 .... 2.95

ART D'ECCO
FANTAGRAPHICS

Value: Cover or less
- ❑1, b&w 2.50
- ❑2, b&w 2.50
- ❑3 .... 2.75

ARTEMIS: REQUIEM
DC

Value: Cover or less
- ❑1, Jun 96, Into the Pit 1.75
- ❑2, Jul 96, Tribes 1.75
- ❑3, Aug 96 .... 1.75
- ❑4, Sep 96 .... 1.75
- ❑5, Oct 96 .... 1.75
- ❑6, Nov 96, Ev'ry Little Imp and Demon 1.75

ARTESIA
SIRIUS

Value: Cover or less
- ❑1, Jan 99 .... 2.95
- ❑2, Feb 99 .... 2.95
- ❑3, Mar 99 .... 2.95
- ❑4, Apr 99 .... 2.95
- ❑5, May 99 .... 2.95
- ❑6, Jun 99 .... 2.95

ARTESIA AFIELD
SIRIUS

Value: Cover or less
- ❑1, Jul 00, Who Kills a King, wraparound cover 2.95
- ❑2, Aug 00, Becomes a Worm, wraparound cover 2.95
- ❑3, Sep 00, Becomes a Raven, wraparound cover 2.95
- ❑4, Oct 00, Becomes a Ghost, wraparound cover 2.95

ARTHUR KING OF BRITAIN
TOME

Value: Cover or less
- ❑1 .... 2.95
- ❑2 .... 2.95
- ❑3 .... 2.95
- ❑4, The Monster of the Mont-Saint-Michel 2.95
- ❑5 .... 3.95

ARTHUR SEX
AIRCEL

Value: Cover or less
- ❑1, b&w; adult 2.50
- ❑2, b&w; adult 2.50
- ❑3, b&w; adult 2.50
- ❑4, b&w; adult 2.50
- ❑5, b&w; adult 2.50
- ❑6, b&w; adult 2.50
- ❑7, Nov 91, Castle of Ill Repute, Part 1, b&w; adult 2.50
- ❑8, b&w; adult 2.50

ARTILLERY ONE-SHOT
RED BULLET

Value: Cover or less
- ❑1, 95, b&w 2.50

ARTISTIC COMICS
KITCHEN SINK

Value: Cover or less
- ❑1, Aug 95, nn; b&w; adults only; new printing; squarebound .. 4.95
- ❑1-2, 2nd Printing 2.50

ARTISTIC LICENTIOUSNESS
STARHEAD

Value: Cover or less
- ❑1, b&w; adult 2.50
- ❑2, adult 2.95

ART OF ABRAMS, THE
LIGHTNING

Value: Cover or less
- ❑1, Dec 96, b&w pin-ups 3.50

ART OF AUBREY BEARDSLEY, THE
TOME PRESS

Value: Cover or less
- ❑1, b&w 2.95

ART OF HEATH ROBINSON
TOME PRESS

Value: Cover or less
- ❑1, b&w 2.95

ART OF HOMAGE STUDIOS, THE
IMAGE

	ORIG	GOOD	FINE	N-MINT
❑1, 93, 1: Gen13 (pin-ups, sketches)	4.95	1.10	2.75	5.50

ART OF MUCHA
TOME PRESS

Value: Cover or less
- ❑1, 92 .... 2.95

ART OF USAGI YOJIMBO, THE
RADIO

Value: Cover or less
- ❑1, Apr 97 .... 3.95
- ❑2, Jan 98 .... 3.95

ASCENSION
IMAGE

	ORIG	GOOD	FINE	N-MINT
❑0, Included with Wizard Top Cow Special	—	0.80	2.00	4.00
❑0/GO, Gold edition	—	1.00	2.50	5.00
❑0/LE, Gold cover; Signed by David Finch and Batt; Wizard "Certified Authentic"	—	1.80	4.50	9.00
❑0.5	—	1.00	2.50	5.00
❑1, Oct 97	2.50	0.60	1.50	3.00
❑1/A, Variant cover: Lucien holding head	—	0.80	2.00	4.00
❑1/B, Oct 97, Fan club edition; Top Cow Fan Club exclusive	—	1.00	2.50	5.00
❑1/C, Oct 97, American Entertainment exclusive	—	1.00	2.50	5.00
❑1/D, Oct 97, Sendaway edition; angels on pile of bodies	—	0.60	1.50	3.00
❑2, Nov 97	2.50	0.50	1.25	2.50
❑2/A, Nov 97, American Entertainment exclusive	—	1.00	2.50	5.00
❑2/GO, Gold edition	—	0.80	2.00	4.00
❑3, Dec 97	2.50	0.50	1.25	2.50
❑4, Feb 98	2.50	0.50	1.25	2.50
❑5, Mar 98	2.50	0.50	1.25	2.50
❑6, May 98	2.50	0.50	1.25	2.50
❑7, Jul 98	2.50	0.50	1.25	2.50
❑8, Aug 98	2.50	0.50	1.25	2.50
❑9, Oct 98	2.50	0.50	1.25	2.50
❑10, Nov 98	2.50	0.50	1.25	2.50
❑11, Feb 99	2.50	0.50	1.25	2.50
❑12, Apr 99	2.50	0.50	1.25	2.50

	ORIG	GOOD	FINE	N-MINT
❑13, May 99	2.50	0.50	1.25	2.50
❑14, Jun 99	2.50	0.50	1.25	2.50
❑15, Jul 99	2.50	0.50	1.25	2.50
❑16, Jul 99	2.50	0.50	1.25	2.50
❑17, Aug 99	2.50	0.50	1.25	2.50
❑18, Sep 99	2.50	0.50	1.25	2.50
❑19, Oct 99	—	0.50	1.25	2.50
❑20, Nov 99	2.50	0.50	1.25	2.50
❑21, Dec 99, cover says Nov, indicia says Dec	2.95	0.59	1.48	2.95
❑22, Mar 00	2.95	0.59	1.48	2.95
❑Ash 1, Jun 97, Convention Preview Edition; Preview edition	—	0.80	2.00	4.00

ASH
EVENT

	ORIG	GOOD	FINE	N-MINT
❑0, May 96, O: Ash, enhanced wraparound cover; "Present" edition	3.50	0.70	1.75	3.50
❑0/A, May 96, O: Ash, alternate enhanced wraparound cover; "Future" edition	3.50	0.70	1.75	3.50
❑0/B, Red foil logo-Present edition	—	0.80	2.00	4.00
❑0/C, Red foil logo-Future edition	—	0.80	2.00	4.00
❑0.5	—	0.50	1.25	2.50
❑0.5/LE, Wizard authentic edition	—	0.80	2.00	4.00
❑0.5/Pl, Platinum edition	—	0.80	2.00	4.00
❑1, Nov 94, Burn, Baby, Burn, 1: Ash	2.50	0.60	1.50	3.00
❑1/A, Nov 94, Burn, Baby, Burn, 1: Ash, Commemorative Omnichrome cover	—	0.80	2.00	4.00
❑1/B, Nov 94, Burn, Baby, Burn, 1: Ash, Dynamic Forces exclusive (DF on cover)	—	0.60	1.50	3.00
❑2	2.50	0.60	1.50	3.00
❑3, May 95	2.50	0.60	1.50	3.00
❑4, Jul 95	2.50	0.60	1.50	3.00
❑4/A, Red Edition	—	0.60	1.50	3.00
❑4/B, White edition	—	0.60	1.50	3.00
❑4/GO, Gold edition	—	0.60	1.50	3.00
❑5, Sep 95	2.50	0.60	1.50	3.00
❑6, Dec 95	2.50	0.50	1.25	2.50
❑6/A, Dec 95, alternate cover by Mark Texeira	2.50	0.50	1.25	2.50

ASH/22 BRIDES
EVENT

Value: Cover or less

- ❑1, Dec 96, Something Butt-Ugly This Way Comes! 2.95
- ❑2 .... 2.95

ASH: CINDER & SMOKE
EVENT

Value: Cover or less

- ❑1, May 97, House Afire 2.95
- ❑2 .... 2.95
- ❑2/A, variant cover 2.95
- ❑3 .... 2.95
- ❑3/A, variant cover 2.95
- ❑4 .... 2.95
- ❑4/A, variant cover 2.95
- ❑5 .... 2.95
- ❑5/A, variant cover 2.95
- ❑6 .... 2.95
- ❑6/A, variant cover 2.95

ASHEN VICTOR
VIZ

Value: Cover or less

- ❑1, 97 .... 2.95
- ❑2, 97 .... 3.25
- ❑3, 97, Pain and Anger 2.95
- ❑4, 97 .... 2.95

ASHES
CALIBER

Value: Cover or less

- ❑1 .... 2.50
- ❑2 .... 2.50
- ❑3 .... 2.50
- ❑4 .... 2.50
- ❑5 .... 2.50

ASH FILES, THE
EVENT

Value: Cover or less

- ❑1, Mar 97, background on series 2.95

ASH: FIRE AND CROSSFIRE
EVENT

	ORIG	GOOD	FINE	N-MINT
❑1, Jan 99, JRo (w), Fire and Crossfire, Part 1	2.95	0.59	1.48	2.95
❑1/A, Jan 99, JRo (w), Fire and Crossfire, Part 1	—	1.60	4.00	8.00
❑2, JRo (w)	2.95	0.59	1.48	2.95

ASHLEY DUST
KNIGHT PRESS

Value: Cover or less

- ❑1, Wurms 2.95
- ❑2, Dec 94 .... 2.95
- ❑3, Mar 95 .... 2.95

ASHPILE
SIDE SHOW

Value: Cover or less

- ❑1 .... 8.95

ASH: THE FIRE WITHIN
EVENT

Value: Cover or less

- ❑1, Sep 96, God's Never Been to Brooklyn 2.95
- ❑2 .... 2.95

Acclaim revived The Armorines in a second series to promote the videogame of the same name.

ASKANI'SON
MARVEL

Value: Cover or less

- ❑1, Jan 96, A Tiny Spark, cover says "Feb, " indicia says "Jan" 2.95
- ❑2, Apr 96, cover says "Mar", indicia says "Apr" 2.95
- ❑3, Apr 96, cardstock wraparound cover 2.95
- ❑4, May 96, cardstock wraparound cover; Final Issue 2.95

ASRIAL VS. CHEETAH
ANTARCTIC

Value: Cover or less

- ❑1, Mar 96 .... 2.95
- ❑2, Apr 96 .... 2.95

ASSASSINATION OF MALCOLM X, THE
ZONE

Value: Cover or less

- ❑1 .... 2.95

ASSASSINETTE
POCKET CHANGE

Value: Cover or less

- ❑1, silver foil cover 2.50
- ❑2 .... 2.50
- ❑3 .... 2.50
- ❑4 .... 2.50
- ❑5 .... 2.50
- ❑6 .... 2.50
- ❑7 .... 2.50

ASSASSINS
DC

Value: Cover or less

- ❑1, Apr 96, Political Suicide 1.95

ASSASSINS INC.
SILVERLINE

Value: Cover or less

- ❑1 .... 1.95
- ❑2 .... 1.95

ASTER
EXPRESS

Value: Cover or less

- ❑0, 95 .... 2.95
- ❑1, Oct 94, b&w 2.95
- ❑1/GO, b&w; Gold edition 10.00
- ❑2, Nov 94, enhanced cardstock cover 2.95
- ❑3 .... 2.95
- ❑3/A, Jan 95, alternate cover 2.95
- ❑3/B, Jan 95, enhanced cover 2.95
- ❑Ash 1, no cover price; b&w preview .... —

ASTER: THE LAST CELESTIAL KNIGHT
EXPRESS

Value: Cover or less

- ❑1, 95, Chronium Cover 3.75

ASTONISH!
WEHNER

Value: Cover or less

- ❑1, b&w 2.00

ASTONISHING EXCITEMENT
ALL-JONH

Value: Cover or less

- ❑503, Tricky & Nuby; Sanwich High 3.50

ASTONISHING TALES
MARVEL

	ORIG	GOOD	FINE	N-MINT
❑1, Aug 70, WW; JK, The Power of Ka-Zar!; Unto You is Born: The Doomsman!, A: Kraven the Hunter, Ka-Zar, Doctor Doom	0.15	5.00	12.50	25.00
❑2, Oct 70, WW; JK, A: Kraven the Hunter, Ka-Zar, Doctor Doom	0.15	2.40	6.00	12.00
❑3, Dec 70, WW, 1: Zaladane, Ka-Zar, Doctor Doom	0.15	3.00	7.50	15.00
❑4, Feb 71, WW, Ka-Zar, Doctor Doom	0.15	3.00	7.50	15.00
❑5, Apr 71, A: Red Skull, Ka-Zar, Doctor Doom	0.15	3.00	7.50	15.00
❑6, Jun 71, 1: Mockingbird (as Bobbi Morse), Ka-Zar, Doctor Doom	0.15	3.00	7.50	15.00
❑7, Aug 71, Ka-Zar, Doctor Doom	0.15	2.00	5.00	10.00
❑8, Oct 71, 52pgs.; Ka-Zar, Doctor Doom	0.25	2.00	5.00	10.00
❑9, Dec 71, Ka-Zar, Doctor Doom	0.20	0.80	2.00	4.00
❑10, Feb 72, SB, Ka-Zar, Doctor Doom	0.20	1.40	3.50	7.00
❑11, Apr 72, O: Ka-Zar	0.20	1.40	3.50	7.00
❑12, Jun 72, NA; JB, Terror Stalks the Everglades!, A: Man-Thing, Ka-Zar	0.20	1.60	4.00	8.00
❑13, Aug 72, DA; JB; RB, Man-Thing!, A: Man-Thing	0.20	0.60	1.50	3.00
❑14, Oct 72	0.20	0.60	1.50	3.00
❑15, Dec 72	0.20	0.60	1.50	3.00

	ORIG	GOOD	FINE	N-MINT
❑16, Feb 73	0.20	0.60	1.50	3.00
❑17, Apr 73	0.20	0.60	1.50	3.00
❑18, Jun 73	0.20	0.60	1.50	3.00
❑19, Aug 73	0.20	0.60	1.50	3.00
❑20, Oct 73	0.20	0.60	1.50	3.00
❑21, Dec 73	0.25	0.60	1.50	3.00
❑22, Feb 74	0.25	0.60	1.50	3.00
❑23, Apr 74	0.25	0.60	1.50	3.00
❑24, Jun 74	0.25	0.60	1.50	3.00
❑25, Aug 74, RB, 1: Deathlok I (Luther Manning), 1st PTrez work in comics	0.25	4.00	10.00	20.00
❑26, Oct 74, A: Deathlok	0.25	1.40	3.50	7.00
❑27, Dec 74, A: Deathlok	0.25	1.00	2.50	5.00
❑28, Feb 75, A: Deathlok	0.25	1.00	2.50	5.00
❑29, Apr 75, O: Guardians of the Galaxy; 1: Guardians of Galaxy	0.25	1.00	2.50	5.00
❑30, Jun 00, KP; RB, A: Deathlok	0.25	1.00	2.50	5.00
❑31, Aug 75, KP; GC; RB, SL (w), Twice Removed From Yesterday...; Tales of the Watcher: Why Won't They Believe Me?, A: Deathlok	0.25	1.00	2.50	5.00
❑32, A: Deathlok	0.25	1.00	2.50	5.00
❑33, Jan 76, A: Deathlok	0.25	1.00	2.50	5.00
❑34, A: Deathlok	0.25	1.00	2.50	5.00
❑35, A: Deathlok	0.25	1.00	2.50	5.00
❑36, Jul 76, A: Deathlok, Final Issue	0.25	1.00	2.50	5.00

ASTONISHING X-MEN
MARVEL

	ORIG	GOOD	FINE	N-MINT
❑1, Mar 95, Age of Apocalypse; Once More with Feeling	1.95	0.50	1.25	2.50
❑2, Apr 95	1.95	0.40	1.00	2.00
❑3, May 95	1.95	0.40	1.00	2.00
❑4, Jun 95	1.95	0.40	1.00	2.00

ASTONISHING X-MEN (2ND SERIES)
MARVEL

Value: Cover or less

❑1, Sep 99, Call to Arms! 2.50

ASTOUNDING SPACE THRILLS
DAY 1

Value: Cover or less

❑1, May 98, b&w 2.95
❑2, Jul 98, b&w 2.95
❑3, Jan 99, b&w 2.95

ASTOUNDING SPACE THRILLS: THE COMIC BOOK
DAY 1

Value: Cover or less

❑1, Apr 00, The Cydonian Contract; The Crater Kid: The Fear Chip 2.95
❑2, Jul 00, The Criminal Code; The Crater Kid: The Replacements 2.95
❑3, Sep 00, Gordo: Earthling Prime; The Crater Kid: The Holein Heaven 2.95
❑4, Dec 00, Hostile Takeover; The Crate Kid: The Blue Skull 2.95

ASTRIDER HUGO
RADIO COMIX

Value: Cover or less

❑1, Jul 00, b&w 3.95

ASTRO CITY (VOL. 1) (KURT BUSIEK'S...)
IMAGE

	ORIG	GOOD	FINE	N-MINT
❑1, Aug 95, BA, ARo (c), KB (w), In Dreams, 1: Samaritan; 1: The Samaritan; 1: Doctor Saturday; 1: The Menagerie Gang; 1: The Honor Guard	2.25	1.40	3.50	7.00
❑2, Sep 95, BA, ARo (c), KB (w), The Scoop, A: Honor Guard; A: Silver Agent	2.25	1.00	2.50	5.00
❑3, Oct 95, BA, ARo (c), KB (w), Dinner At Eight, A: Jack in the Box	2.25	0.80	2.00	4.00
❑4, Nov 95, BA, ARo (c), KB (w), A: Winged Victory; A: First Family; 1: The Hanged Man	2.25	0.80	2.00	4.00
❑5, Dec 95, BA, ARo (c), KB (w), A: Astro City Irregulars; A: Crackerjack	2.25	0.80	2.00	4.00
❑6, Jan 96, BA, ARo (c), KB (w), O: The Samaritan	2.25	0.80	2.00	4.00

ASTRO CITY (VOL. 2) (KURT BUSIEK'S...)
IMAGE

	ORIG	GOOD	FINE	N-MINT
❑0.5, Jan 00, BA, ARo (c), KB (w), The Nearness of You, Wizard promotional item	2.50	0.80	2.00	4.00
❑0.5/DM, Jan 98, BA, ARo (c), KB (w), The Nearness of You; Clash of Titans (A New York Romance), bonus story; Direct Market edition; reprints "The Nearness of You" and "Clash of Titans"	2.50	0.60	1.50	3.00
❑1, Sep 96, BA, ARo (c), KB (w), Welcome to Astro City	2.50	1.20	3.00	6.00
❑1/3D, BA, ARo (c), KB (w), Signed hardcover edition	4.95	1.00	2.50	5.00
❑2, Oct 96, BA, ARo (c), KB (w), Everyday Life, A: First Family	2.50	0.80	2.00	4.00
❑3, Nov 96, BA, ARo (c), KB (w), A: Astra, First Family	2.50	0.80	2.00	4.00
❑4, Dec 96, BA, ARo (c), KB (w), New Kid in Town, 1: Brian Kinney (The Altar Boy) (out of costume)	2.50	0.80	2.00	4.00
❑5, Jan 97, BA, ARo (c), KB (w), Learning the Game, O: The Altar Boy; 1: The Altar Boy (Brian Kinney in costume)	2.50	0.80	2.00	4.00
❑6, Feb 97, BA, ARo (c), KB (w), The Gathering Dark, 1: The Gunslinger, The Confessor revealed as vampire	2.50	0.80	2.00	4.00
❑7, Mar 97, BA, ARo (c), KB (w), Eye of the Storm, O: The Confessor I	2.50	0.70	1.75	3.50
❑8, Apr 97, BA, ARo (c), KB (w), Patterns, D: The Confessor I	2.50	0.70	1.75	3.50
❑9, May 97, BA, ARo (c), KB (w), My Father's Son, 1: The Confessor II	2.50	0.70	1.75	3.50
❑10, Oct 97, BA, ARo (c), KB (w), Shoe 'em All, O: The Junkman; O: Junkman	2.50	0.70	1.75	3.50
❑11, Nov 97, BA, ARo (c), KB (w), Serpent's Teeth, 1: The Jackson; 1: The Box, Jack-in-the-Box vs. alternate versions	2.50	0.50	1.25	2.50
❑12, Dec 97, BA, ARo (c), KB (w), Father's Day, 1: Jack-in-the-Box II (Roscoe James)	2.50	0.50	1.25	2.50
❑13, Feb 98, BA, ARo (c), KB (w), In the Spotlight, 1: Loony Leo	2.50	0.50	1.25	2.50
❑14, Apr 98, BA, ARo (c), KB (w), 1: Steeljack	2.50	0.50	1.25	2.50
❑15, Dec 98, BA, ARo (c), KB (w), The Long Treadmill, A: Steeljack; 1: new Golden-glove	2.50	0.50	1.25	2.50
❑16, Mar 99, BA, ARo (c), KB (w), The Tarnished Angel, O: El Hombre	2.50	0.50	1.25	2.50
❑17, May 99, BA, ARo (c), KB (w), The Voice of the Turtle, O: The Mock Turtle	2.50	0.50	1.25	2.50
❑18, Aug 99, BA, ARo (c), KB (w), The Empty Shell	2.50	0.50	1.25	2.50
❑19, Nov 99, BA, ARo (c), KB (w), The Only Chance	2.50	0.50	1.25	2.50
❑20, Jan 00, BA, ARo (c), KB (w), The Wow Finish	2.50	0.50	1.25	2.50
❑21, Mar 00, BA, ARo (c), KB (w), Where the Action Is	2.50	0.50	1.25	2.50
❑22, Aug 00, BA, ARo (c), KB (w), Great Expectations, 1: Crimson Cougar	2.50	0.50	1.25	2.50

ASTROCOMICS
HARVEY

	ORIG	GOOD	FINE	N-MINT
❑1, Flight Through the Ages; Richie Rich...Achooo!, Giveaway from American Airlines; Reprints Harvey Comics stories	—	0.40	1.00	2.00

ASTRONAUTS IN TROUBLE: SPACE 1959
AIT

	ORIG	GOOD	FINE	N-MINT
❑1	—	0.50	1.25	2.50

ASTROTHRILL
CHEEKY PRESS

Value: Cover or less

❑1, May 99, nn; cardstock cover; new material and reprints from Nemesister; CD 12.95

ASYLUM (MAXIMUM)
MAXIMUM

Value: Cover or less

❑1, Dec 95, RL (w), Beanworld, Part 1; Avengelyne, Warchild, Doubletap, Beanworld/Avengelyne flip covers; Flip-book 2.95
❑1/A, Dec 95, Warchild/Doubletake flip covers 2.95
❑2, Jan 96, Beanworld, Part 2; Cybrid: Chrysalis, Part 1, Flip-book 2.95
❑3, Apr 96, Beanworld, Part 3; Cybrid: Chrysalis, Part 2, A: Cybrid, Flip-book 2.95
❑4, Beanworld, Part 4; Christian: Heads I Win, Tails You Lose, Flip-book 2.95
❑5 2.95
❑6 2.95
❑7 2.95
❑8, Megaton Man, Part 2 2.95
❑9 2.95
❑10 2.95
❑11, Blindside: Look Up Look Down; Megaton Man, Part 3 2.99
❑12 2.99
❑13 2.99

ASYLUM (MILLENNIUM)
MILLENNIUM

Value: Cover or less

❑1, The Wishing Hour; The Latchkey Fiend 2.50
❑2, NG (w) 2.50
❑3, HC 4.95

ASYLUM (NCG)
NEW COMICS

Value: Cover or less

❑1, BWr, The Call; Spurs, b&w 1.95
❑2 2.25

ATARI FORCE
DC

	ORIG	GOOD	FINE	N-MINT
❑1, Jan 84, First Blood, 1: Blackjak; 1: Dart; 1: Atari Force (in standard comics); 1: Babe; 1: Dark Destroyer	0.75	0.20	0.50	1.00
❑2, Feb 84, 1: Martin Champion	0.75	0.20	0.50	1.00
❑3, Mar 84	0.75	0.20	0.50	1.00
❑4, Apr 84	0.75	0.20	0.50	1.00
❑5, May 84	0.75	0.20	0.50	1.00
❑6, Jun 84	0.75	0.20	0.50	1.00
❑7, Jul 84	0.75	0.20	0.50	1.00
❑8, Aug 84	0.75	0.20	0.50	1.00
❑9, Sep 84	0.75	0.20	0.50	1.00

	ORIG	GOOD	FINE	N-MINT
❑10, Oct 84	0.75	0.20	0.50	1.00
❑11, Nov 84	0.75	0.20	0.50	1.00
❑12, Dec 84	0.75	0.20	0.50	1.00
❑13, Jan 85	0.75	0.20	0.50	1.00
❑14, Feb 85	0.75	0.20	0.50	1.00
❑15, Mar 85	0.75	0.20	0.50	1.00
❑16, Apr 85	0.75	0.20	0.50	1.00
❑17, May 85	0.75	0.20	0.50	1.00
❑18, Jun 85	0.75	0.20	0.50	1.00
❑19, Jul 85	0.75	0.20	0.50	1.00
❑20, Aug 85, Final Issue	0.75	0.20	0.50	1.00
❑SE 1, 86, Codename: Dart: A Mercenary's Story; The Adventures of the Hukka!, Giant-size	2.00	0.40	1.00	2.00

A-TEAM, THE
MARVEL

	ORIG	GOOD	FINE	N-MINT
❑1, Mar 84, based on TV series	0.60	0.40	1.00	2.00
❑2, Apr 84, JM, Who Kidnapped Kuramoto?	0.60	0.40	1.00	2.00
❑3, May 84	0.60	0.40	1.00	2.00

ATHENA
ANTARCTIC

Value: Cover or less

- ❑0, Zero, Antarctic publishes.. 2.95
- ❑1, A.M. Press publishes 2.95
- ❑2 2.95
- ❑3 2.95
- ❑4 2.95
- ❑5 2.95
- ❑6 2.95

ATLANTIS CHRONICLES, THE
DC

	ORIG	GOOD	FINE	N-MINT
❑1, Mar 90, PD (w), The Deluge	2.95	0.60	1.50	3.00
❑2, Apr 90, PD (w)	2.95	0.60	1.50	3.00
❑3, May 90, PD (w)	2.95	0.60	1.50	3.00
❑4, Jun 90, PD (w)	2.95	0.60	1.50	3.00
❑5, Jul 90, PD (w)	2.95	0.60	1.50	3.00
❑6, Aug 90, PD (w)	2.95	0.60	1.50	3.00
❑7, Sep 90, PD (w), O: Aquaman, Final Issue	2.95	0.60	1.50	3.00

ATLAS
DARK HORSE

Value: Cover or less

- ❑1, Feb 94 2.50
- ❑2, Apr 94 2.50
- ❑3 2.50
- ❑4, Aug 94 2.50

ATOM, THE
DC

	ORIG	GOOD	FINE	N-MINT
❑1, Jul 62, GK; MA, 1: Plant Master	0.12	150.00	375.00	750.00
❑2, Sep 62, GK; MA	0.12	56.00	140.00	280.00
❑3, Nov 62, GK; MA, 1: Chronos	0.12	40.00	100.00	200.00
❑4, Jan 63, GK; MA	0.12	28.00	70.00	140.00
❑5, Mar 63, GK; MA	0.12	28.00	70.00	140.00
❑6, May 63, GK; MA	0.12	21.00	52.50	105.00
❑7, Jul 63, GK; MA, A: Hawkman	0.12	50.00	125.00	250.00
❑8, Sep 63, GK; MA, A: Justice League of America	0.12	21.00	52.50	105.00
❑9, Nov 63, GK; MA	0.12	21.00	52.50	105.00
❑10, Jan 64, GK; MA	0.12	21.00	52.50	105.00
❑11, Mar 64, GK; MA	0.12	16.00	40.00	80.00
❑12, May 64, GK; MA	0.12	16.00	40.00	80.00
❑13, Jul 64	0.12	16.00	40.00	80.00
❑14, Sep 64	0.12	16.00	40.00	80.00
❑15, Nov 64	0.12	16.00	40.00	80.00
❑16, Jan 65, GK; MA	0.12	10.00	25.00	50.00
❑17, Mar 65, GK; MA	0.12	10.00	25.00	50.00
❑18, May 65, GK; MA	0.12	10.00	25.00	50.00
❑19, Jul 65, GK; MA	0.12	10.00	25.00	50.00
❑20, Sep 65, GK; MA	0.12	10.00	25.00	50.00
❑21, Nov 65	0.12	7.60	19.00	38.00
❑22, Jan 66	0.12	7.60	19.00	38.00
❑23, Mar 66	0.12	7.60	19.00	38.00
❑24, May 66	0.12	7.60	19.00	38.00
❑25, Jul 66	0.12	7.60	19.00	38.00
❑26, Sep 66, 1: Bug-Eyed Bandit	0.12	7.60	19.00	38.00
❑27, Nov 66, V: Panther	0.12	7.60	19.00	38.00
❑28, Jan 67	0.12	7.60	19.00	38.00
❑29, Mar 67, A: Atom I (Al Pratt)	0.12	28.00	70.00	140.00
❑30, May 67	0.12	7.60	19.00	38.00
❑31, Jul 67, A: Hawkman	0.12	7.60	19.00	38.00
❑32, Sep 67	0.12	7.60	19.00	38.00
❑33, Nov 67	0.12	7.60	19.00	38.00
❑34, Jan 68	0.12	7.60	19.00	38.00
❑35, Mar 68, GK, Plight Of the Pin-Up Atom!	0.12	7.60	19.00	38.00
❑36, May 68, A: Atom I (Al Pratt)	0.12	10.00	25.00	50.00
❑37, Jul 68, A: Hawkman	0.12	7.60	19.00	38.00
❑38, Sep 68, Series continued in Atom and Hawkman #39	0.12	7.60	19.00	38.00
❑SE 1	2.50	0.50	1.25	2.50
❑SE 2, LMc, Critical Mass, 1995	2.50	0.50	1.25	2.50

Kurt Busiek's Astro City features Alex Ross covers and interior art by Brent Anderson.

ATOM AND HAWKMAN
DC

	ORIG	GOOD	FINE	N-MINT
❑39, Oct 68, JKu, Series continued from Atom #38	0.12	6.40	16.00	32.00
❑40, Dec 68, DD, The Explosive Exploit of the Split-Atom	0.12	6.40	16.00	32.00
❑41, Feb 69	0.12	6.40	16.00	32.00
❑42, Apr 69	0.12	6.40	16.00	32.00
❑43, Jun 69, JKu	0.12	6.40	16.00	32.00
❑44, Aug 69	—	6.40	16.00	32.00
❑45, Oct 69, Final Issue	—	6.40	16.00	32.00

ATOMIC AGE
EPIC

Value: Cover or less

- ❑1, Broken Silence 4.50
- ❑2 4.50
- ❑3 4.50
- ❑4, Everybody Mambo 4.50

ATOMIC AGE TRUCKSTOP WAITRESS
FANTAGRAPHICS

Value: Cover or less

- ❑1, b&w; adult 2.25

ATOMIC CITY TALES
KITCHEN SINK

Value: Cover or less

- ❑1, Night Of The Monkey, Part 1, Consumer Pangs; Night Of The Monkey, Part 2, Rat Race Blues 2.95
- ❑2 2.95
- ❑3 2.95
- ❑SE 1 2.95

ATOMIC MAN
BLACKTHORNE

Value: Cover or less

- ❑1 1.75
- ❑2 1.75
- ❑3 1.75

ATOMIC MOUSE (A+)
A+

Value: Cover or less

- ❑1 2.50
- ❑2 2.50
- ❑3 2.50

ATOMICOW
VISION

Value: Cover or less

- ❑1, Aug 90 2.50

ATOMIC RABBIT & FRIENDS
AVALON

Value: Cover or less

- ❑1, b&w; reprints Charlton stories 2.50

ATOMICS, THE
AAA POP

Value: Cover or less

- ❑1 2.95

ATOMIC TOYBOX
IMAGE

Value: Cover or less

- ❑1, Nov 99, Cruel Times, cover says Dec, indicia says Nov . 2.95
- ❑1/A, Nov 99 2.95
- ❑1/B, Nov 99 2.95

ATOMIK ANGELS (WILLIAM TUCCI'S...)
CRUSADE

	ORIG	GOOD	FINE	N-MINT
❑1, A: Freefall	2.95	0.59	1.48	2.95
❑1/SC, A: Freefall, variant cover	2.95	0.70	1.75	3.50
❑2	2.95	0.59	1.48	2.95
❑3	2.95	0.59	1.48	2.95
❑3/SC, Sep 96, alternate cover (orange background with Statue of Liberty)	2.95	0.70	1.75	3.50
❑4, Nov 96, flipbook with Manga Shi 2000 preview	2.95	0.59	1.48	2.95
❑SE 1, Feb 96, nn; b&w; "The Intrep-edition"; promotional comic for U.S.S. Intrepid	—	0.60	1.50	3.00

ATOM THE ATOMIC CAT
AVALON

Value: Cover or less

- ❑1, Two Little Prizes; House Moving, A: Li'l Lumberjack; A: Doctor Mole; A: Chappy; A: Aunt Tessie; A: Yin 2.95

ATTACK OF THE AMAZON GIRLS
FANTACO

Value: Cover or less

- ❑1, Amazon, Mara, Sirens, nn. 4.95

ATTACK OF THE MUTANT MONSTERS
A-PLUS

Value: Cover or less

- ❑1, SD, b&w; Reprint 2.50

AT THE SEAMS
ALTERNATIVE

Value: Cover or less
❑1, Jun 97, nn; b&w 2.95

ATTITUDE LAD
SLAVE LABOR

Value: Cover or less
❑1, Little Conversations 2.95

ATTU
4WINDS

Value: Cover or less
❑1, b&w 9.95
❑2, b&w 9.95

AUGUST
ARROW

Value: Cover or less
❑1 .... 2.95
❑2 .... 2.95
❑3 .... 2.95

AUTHORITY, THE
DC

	ORIG	GOOD	FINE	N-MINT
❑1, May 99, The Circle, Part 1, wraparound cover	2.50	1.00	2.50	5.00
❑2, Jun 99, The Circle, Part 2	2.50	0.80	2.00	4.00
❑3, Jul 99, The Circle, Part 3	2.50	0.80	2.00	4.00
❑4, Aug 99, The Circle, Part 4	2.50	0.60	1.50	3.00
❑5, Oct 99, Shiftships Part 1, cover says "Sep", indicia says "Oct"	2.50	0.60	1.50	3.00
❑6, Oct 99, Shiftships Part 2	2.50	0.60	1.50	3.00
❑7, Nov 99, Shiftships Part 3	2.50	0.60	1.50	3.00
❑8, Dec 99, Shiftships Part 4	2.50	0.60	1.50	3.00
❑9, Jan 00, Outer Dark, Part 1	2.50	0.60	1.50	3.00
❑10, Feb 00, Outer Dark, Part 2	2.50	0.60	1.50	3.00
❑11, Mar 00, Outer Dark, Part 3	2.50	0.50	1.25	2.50
❑12, Apr 00, Outer Dark, Part 4	2.50	0.50	1.25	2.50
❑13, May 00, The Nativity, Part 1	2.50	0.50	1.25	2.50
❑14, Jun 00, The Nativity, Part 2	2.50	0.50	1.25	2.50
❑15, Jul 00, The Nativity, Part 3	2.50	0.50	1.25	2.50
❑16, Aug 00, The Nativity, Part 4	2.50	0.50	1.25	2.50
❑17, Sep 00, Earth Inferno, Part 1	2.50	0.50	1.25	2.50
❑18, Sep 00, Earth Inferno, Part 2	2.50	0.50	1.25	2.50
❑19, Nov 00, Earth Inferno, Part 3	2.50	0.50	1.25	2.50
❑20, Jan 01, Earth Inferno, Part 4	2.50	0.50	1.25	2.50
❑21, Feb 01, Once Upon a Time...	2.50	0.50	1.25	2.50
❑22, Mar 01, Brave New World, Part 1	2.50	0.50	1.25	2.50
❑23, Apr 01, Brave New World, Part 2	2.50	0.50	1.25	2.50
❑24, May 01, Brave New World, Part 3	2.50	0.50	1.25	2.50
❑25, Jun 01, Brave New World, Part 4	2.50	0.50	1.25	2.50
❑Anl 2000, Dec 00, The Breaks	3.50	0.70	1.75	3.50

AUTOMATON
IMAGE

Value: Cover or less
❑1, The Measure of Life, Part 1 .... 2.95
❑2, To Never See Home Again, Part 2, no month of publication 2.95
❑3, Dawn's Last Light!, no month of publication 2.95

AUTUMN
CALIBER

Value: Cover or less
❑1, 95, Lammas 2.95
❑2, 95 .... 2.95
❑3 .... 2.95

AUTUMN ADVENTURES (WALT DISNEY'S)
DISNEY

Value: Cover or less
❑1 .... 2.95

AVALON
HARRIER

	ORIG	GOOD	FINE	N-MINT
❑1, Oct 86, Diana is...The Power; Mutant Love, O: Diana	1.95	0.39	0.98	1.95
❑2, Sparky's Dream; The Real Thing	1.95	0.39	0.98	1.95
❑3	1.95	0.39	0.98	1.95
❑4	1.95	0.39	0.98	1.95
❑5	1.95	0.39	0.98	1.95
❑6	1.95	0.39	0.98	1.95
❑7	1.95	0.39	0.98	1.95
❑8	1.95	0.39	0.98	1.95
❑9	1.95	0.39	0.98	1.95
❑10, Diana is...The Power: Self Analysis; For Better...	1.95	0.39	0.98	1.95
❑11	—	0.39	0.98	1.95
❑12	—	0.39	0.98	1.95
❑13	—	0.39	0.98	1.95
❑14	—	0.39	0.98	1.95

AVANT GUARD: HEROES AT THE FUTURE'S EDGE
DAY ONE

Value: Cover or less
❑1, Mar 94, b&w 2.50

AVATAARS: COVENANT OF THE SHIELD
MARVEL

Value: Cover or less
❑1 .... 2.99
❑2 .... 2.99
❑3, Nov 00, The Siege of Dread-keep 2.99

AVATAR
DC

Value: Cover or less
❑1, Forgotten Realms: Shadow-dale 5.95
❑2, Forgotten Realms: Tantras 5.95
❑3 .... 5.95

AVENGEBLADE
MAXIMUM

Value: Cover or less
❑1, RL (w) 2.95
❑2, RL (w) 2.95

AVENGELYNE (MINI-SERIES)
MAXIMUM

	ORIG	GOOD	FINE	N-MINT
❑1, May 95, RL, RL (w), 1: Avengelyne, Photo cover; one of 4 posters of Avengelyne	2.50	0.80	2.00	4.00
❑1/A, RL (w), 1: Avengelyne, Photo cover	2.50	0.80	2.00	4.00
❑1/GO, RL (w), 1: Avengelyne, Gold edition	—	1.60	4.00	8.00
❑1/SC, RL (w), 1: Avengelyne, chromium cover	3.50	0.80	2.00	4.00
❑2, Jun 95, RL (w), polybagged with card	2.50	0.60	1.50	3.00
❑3/A, RL (w), Avengelyne striking with sword on cover	2.50	0.60	1.50	3.00
❑3/B, RL (w), Avengelyne standing with demons prominent on cover	2.50	0.60	1.50	3.00
❑Ash 1, RL (w), Signed by creators	—	1.20	3.00	6.00

AVENGELYNE (VOL. 2)
MAXIMUM

	ORIG	GOOD	FINE	N-MINT
❑0	—	0.60	1.50	3.00
❑0.5, RL (w), Certificate of Authenticity; Wizard promotional mail-in edition	—	0.60	1.50	3.00
❑0.5/Pl, RL (w), Platinum edition with certificate of authenticity (Wizard promo)	—	1.20	3.00	6.00
❑1	2.50	0.60	1.50	3.00
❑1/SC, Apr 96, alternate cover (photo wraparound)	2.95	0.70	1.75	3.50
❑2, 1: Darkchylde	2.50	0.80	2.00	4.00
❑2/A, 1: Darkchylde, Photo cover	2.50	1.60	4.00	8.00
❑2/B, 1: Darkchylde, Nude cover	2.50	3.00	7.50	15.00
❑3	2.50	0.50	1.25	2.50
❑4, A: Cybrid	2.50	0.50	1.25	2.50
❑5, Aug 96, RL (w), A: Cybrid, flipbook with Blindside preview	2.99	0.60	1.50	2.99
❑6, RL (w)	2.99	0.60	1.50	2.99
❑7	2.99	0.60	1.50	2.99
❑8, RL (w)	2.99	0.60	1.50	2.99
❑9	2.99	0.60	1.50	2.99
❑10, Feb 97, RL (w), The Possession, Part 1	2.99	0.60	1.50	2.99
❑11, Mar 97, The Possession, Part 2	2.99	0.60	1.50	2.99
❑11/SC, Mar 97, The Possession, Part 2, alternate cover (multiple characters behind Avengelyne)	2.99	0.60	1.50	2.99
❑12	2.99	0.60	1.50	2.99
❑13	2.99	0.60	1.50	2.99
❑14	2.99	0.60	1.50	2.99
❑15, Final Issue	2.99	0.60	1.50	2.99

AVENGELYNE (VOL. 3)
AWESOME

Value: Cover or less
❑1, Mar 99, RL (w) 2.50

AVENGELYNE ARMAGEDDON
MAXIMUM

Value: Cover or less
❑1 .... 2.99
❑2 .... 2.99
❑3, Feb 97, RL (w) 2.99

AVENGELYNE BIBLE
MAXIMUM

Value: Cover or less
❑1, Oct 96 .... 3.50

AVENGELYNE: DEADLY SINS
MAXIMUM

	ORIG	GOOD	FINE	N-MINT
❑1	2.95	0.59	1.48	2.95
❑1/SC, Feb 95, alternate cover (photo)	2.95	0.70	1.75	3.50
❑2	2.95	0.59	1.48	2.95

AVENGELYNE/GLORY
MAXIMUM

Value: Cover or less
❑1, Sep 95, wraparound chromium cover 3.95
❑1/SC, variant cover 3.95

AVENGELYNE/GLORY: THE GODYSSEY
MAXIMUM

Value: Cover or less
❑1, RL (w) 2.99
❑1/SC, RL (w), Photo cover 2.99

AVENGELYNE: POWER
MAXIMUM

Value: Cover or less
❑1/A, Jan 96, RL (w), Red background on cover 2.50
❑1/B, Jan 96, RL (w), Blue background on cover 2.50
❑2 .... 2.50
❑3 .... 2.50

AVENGELYNE SWIMSUIT
MAXIMUM

	ORIG	GOOD	FINE	N-MINT
❑1, Aug 95, both drawn and photographed; pin-ups	2.95	0.59	1.48	2.95
❑1/SC, Aug 95, alternate cover; pin-ups, both drawn and photographed	2.95	0.70	1.75	3.50

AVENGELYNE/WARRIOR NUN AREALA

Maximum

Value: Cover or less

❑1/A, Nov 96, RL (w), Avengelynein front on cover 2.99

❑1/B, Nov 96, RL (w), Two women back-to-back on cover......... 2.99

AVENGERS, THE

Marvel

	ORIG	GOOD	FINE	N-MINT
❑-1, Flashback	1.99	0.40	1.00	2.00
❑0, Wizard promotional edition	—	0.60	1.50	3.00
❑1, Sep 63, JK, SL (w); JK (w), The Coming of the Avengers, O: Avengers, Team consists of Thor, Ant-Man, Wasp, Hulk, and Iron Man	0.12	460.00	1150.00	2300.00
❑1.5, Dec 99, The Death-Trap of Doctor Doom!, Issue #1-1/2	2.50	0.50	1.25	2.50
❑2, Nov 63, JK, SL (w); JK (w), The Avengers Battle the Space Phantom, 1: Space Phantom, Hulk leaves Avengers; Ant-Man becomes Giant-Man	0.12	120.00	300.00	600.00
❑3, Jan 64, JK, SL (w); JK (w), The Avengers Meet Sub-Mariner, Avengers vs. Sub-Mariner and Hulk	0.12	80.00	200.00	400.00
❑4, Mar 64, JK, SL (w); JK (w), Captain America Joins the Avengers, 1: Baron Zemo, Captain America returns; Capt. America returns	0.12	305.00	762.50	1525.00
❑5, May 64, JK, SL (w); JK (w), The Invasion of the Lava Man, Hulk leaves team	0.12	45.00	112.50	225.00
❑6, Jul 64, JK, SL (w); JK (w), Masters of Evil, 1: Masters of Evil	0.12	35.00	87.50	175.00
❑7, Aug 64, JK, SL (w); JK (w), Their Darkest Hour	0.12	35.00	87.50	175.00
❑8, Sep 64, JK, SL (w); JK (w), Kang, the Conqueror, 1: Kang	0.12	35.00	87.50	175.00
❑9, Oct 64, JK; DH, SL (w), The Coming of the Wonder Man, D: Wonder Man	0.12	37.00	92.50	185.00
❑10, Nov 64, JK; DH, SL (w), The Avengers Break Up, 1: Immortus; 1: Hercules	0.12	32.00	80.00	160.00
❑11, Dec 64, JK; DH, SL (w), The Mighty Avengers Meet Spider-Man, A: Spider-Man	0.12	28.00	70.00	140.00
❑12, Jan 65, JK; DH, SL (w), This Hostage Earth, V: Mole Man; 1: Monk Keefer (later becomes Ape-Man I)	0.12	18.00	45.00	90.00
❑13, Feb 65, JK; DH, SL (w), The Castle of Count Nefaria, 1: Count Nefaria	0.12	18.00	45.00	90.00
❑14, Mar 65, JK, SL (w); JK (w), Even Avengers Can Die, 1: Ogor and Kallusians	0.12	18.00	45.00	90.00
❑15, Apr 65, JK, SL (w); JK (w), Now, By My Hand, Shall Die a Villain, D: Baron Zemo I (Heinrich Zemo)	0.12	18.00	45.00	90.00
❑16, May 65, JK, SL (w); JK (w), The Old Order Changeth, Cap assembles new team of Hawkeye, Quicksilver, Scarlet Witch; New team begins: Captain America, Hawkeye, Quicksilver, and Scarlet Witch	0.12	18.00	45.00	90.00
❑17, Jun 65, JK, SL (w), Four Against the Minotaur	0.12	14.00	35.00	70.00
❑18, Jul 65, JK; DH, SL (w), When the Commissar Commands	0.12	14.00	35.00	70.00
❑19, Aug 65, JK; DH, SL (w), The Coming of the Swordsman, 1: Swordsman; O: Hawkeye	0.12	15.00	37.50	75.00
❑20, Sep 65, WW; DH, SL (w), Vengeance is Ours, V: Swordsman	0.12	8.00	20.00	40.00
❑21, Oct 65, JK; DH, SL (w), The Bitter Taste of Defeat, 1: Power Man I (Erik Josten)	0.12	8.00	20.00	40.00
❑22, Nov 65, JK; DH, SL (w), The Road Back	0.12	8.00	20.00	40.00
❑23, Dec 65, JK; DH, SL (w), Once an Avenger, 1: Ravonna	0.12	8.00	20.00	40.00
❑24, Jan 66, JK; DH, SL (w), From the Ashes of Defeat, A: Princess Ravonna; A: Doctor Doom; A: Kang	0.12	8.00	20.00	40.00
❑25, Feb 66, JK; DH, SL (w), Enter Dr. Doom, A: Doctor Doom; A: Human Torch; A: Thing; A: Invisible Girl; A: Mr. Fantastic	0.12	8.00	20.00	40.00
❑26, Mar 66, JK; DH, SL (w), The Voice of the Wasp, A: The Wasp; A: Sub-Mariner; A: Attuma; A: Tony Stark; A: Beetle; A: Puppet Master; A: Henry Pym	0.12	8.00	20.00	40.00
❑27, Apr 66, JK; DH, SL (w), Four Against the Floodtide, A: Attuma; A: Beetle; A: Henry Pym; A: Collector; A: Invisible Girl; A: Mr. Fantastic	0.12	8.00	20.00	40.00
❑28, May 66, JK; DH, SL (w), Among Us Walks a Goliath, 1: Goliath; 1: The Collector; A: Beetle, Giant-Man becomes Goliath; Goliath rejoins Avengers; Wasp rejoins Avengers	0.12	8.00	20.00	40.00
❑29, Jun 66, JK; DH, SL (w), This Power Unleashed, A: Swordsman; 1: Doctor Yen; 1: Hu Chen; A: S.H.I.E.L.D.; A: Black Widow, Power Man I	0.12	8.00	20.00	40.00
❑30, Jul 66, JK; DH, SL (w), Frenzy in a Far-Off Land, A: Swordsman; A: Hu Chen; A: Power Man I; 1: Prince Rey; 1: Keeper of the Flame; 1: Doctor Franz Anton; A: Black Widow, Quicksilver & Scarlet Witch leave Avengers	0.12	8.00	20.00	40.00

The Avengers faced Doctor Doom in a retro adventure in 1999's *Avengers* #15 .

	ORIG	GOOD	FINE	N-MINT
❑31, Aug 66, JK; DH, SL (w), Never Bug a Giant	0.12	5.20	13.00	26.00
❑32, Sep 66, DH, SL (w), The Sign of the Serpent, A: Tony Stark; A: Nick Fury; A: Quicksilver; A: Scarlet Witch; 1: Bill Foster (Giant-Man II); 1: Supreme Serpent I; 1: Sons of the Serpent; A: Black Widow	0.12	5.20	13.00	26.00
❑33, Oct 66, DH, SL (w), To Smash a Serpent, A: Black Widow	0.12	5.20	13.00	26.00
❑34, Nov 66, DH, SL (w), The Living Laser, 1: Lucy Barton; 1: Living Laser	0.12	5.20	13.00	26.00
❑35, Dec 66, DH, The Light that Failed, 2: Lucy Barton; A: Bill Foster; 2: Living Laser; 1: Ultrana (off page); A: Black Widow	0.12	5.20	13.00	26.00
❑36, Jan 67, DH, The Ultroids Attack, 1: Ixar; 1: Ultrana (full); 1: Ultroids; A: Black Widow, Quicksilver & Scarlet Witch rejoin Avengers	0.12	5.20	13.00	26.00
❑37, Feb 67, DH, To Conquer a Colossus, 2: Ixar; 2: Ultrana; 2: Ultroids; A: Black Widow, Ultroids consolidate into giant robot Ultroid	0.12	5.20	13.00	26.00
❑38, Mar 67, DH, In Our Midst, an Immortal, A: Black Widow; A: Hercules, Captain America leaves Avengers	0.12	5.20	13.00	26.00
❑39, Apr 67, DH, The Torment and the Triumph, A: Mad Thinker; A: Nick Fury; A: Dum Dum Dugan; A: Jasper Sitwell; A: S.H.I.E.L.D.; A: Black Widow; A: Hercules	0.12	5.20	13.00	26.00
❑40, May 67, DH, Suddenly, the Sub-Mariner, V: Sub-Mariner; A: Black Widow; A: Hercules	0.12	5.20	13.00	26.00
❑41, Jun 67, JB, Let Sleeping Dragons Lie, 1: Colonel Ling; 2: Doctor Yen; A: Diablo; A: Bill Foster; A: Dragon Man; A: Black Widow; A: Hercules, Mr. Fantastic cameo; Human Torch cameo	0.12	4.00	10.00	20.00
❑42, Jul 67, JB, The Plan and the Power, V: Diablo, Dragon Man	0.12	4.00	10.00	20.00
❑43, Aug 67, JB, Color Him the Red Guardian, A: Colonel Ling; 1: Red Guardian I (Alexi Shostakov); A: Edwin Jarvis; 1: General Yuri Brushov; A: Black Widow; A: Hercules	0.12	4.00	10.00	20.00
❑44, Sep 67, JB, The Valiant also Die, A: Colonel Ling; O: Black Widow (part); D: Red Guardian I (Alexi Shostakov); A: Black Widow; A: Hercules	0.12	4.00	10.00	20.00
❑45, Oct 67, DH, DH (w), Blitzkrieg in Central Park, A: Thor; A: Iron Man I; V: Super-Adaptoid, Hercules joins team; Hercules joins Avengers; Black Widow retires	0.12	4.00	10.00	20.00
❑46, Nov 67, 1: Whirlwind	0.12	4.00	10.00	20.00
❑47, Dec 67, D: Black Knight II (Nathan Garrett)	0.12	4.00	10.00	20.00
❑48, Jan 68, 1: Aragorn; 1: Black Knight III (Dane Whitman)	0.12	4.00	10.00	20.00
❑49, Feb 68, JB, Mine Is The Power!, A: Magneto, Quicksilver & Scarlet Witch leave Avengers	0.12	4.00	10.00	20.00
❑50, Mar 68, JB, To Tame A Titan!	0.12	4.00	10.00	20.00
❑51, Apr 68, JB, In The Clutches Of The Collector!	0.12	4.00	10.00	20.00
❑52, May 68, 1: Grim Reaper, Black Panther joins	0.12	4.80	12.00	24.00
❑53, Jun 68, JB, A: X-Men	0.12	7.00	17.50	35.00
❑54, Jul 68, JB, 1: Crimson Cowl	0.12	3.60	9.00	18.00
❑55, Aug 68, JB, 1: Ultron-5	0.12	3.60	9.00	18.00
❑56, Sep 68, JB	0.12	3.60	9.00	18.00
❑57, Oct 68, JB, 1: The Vision II (android)	0.12	13.00	32.50	65.00
❑58, Nov 68, JB, O: The Vision II (android)	0.12	9.00	22.50	45.00
❑59, Dec 68, JB, 1: Yellowjacket, Goliath becomes Yellowjacket	0.12	4.40	11.00	22.00
❑60, Jan 69, JB, Yellowjacket marries Wasp	0.12	4.40	11.00	22.00
❑61, Feb 69, JB, Some Say the World Will End in Fire, Some Say in Ice	0.12	3.60	9.00	18.00
❑62, Mar 69, JB, The Monarch and the Man-Ape, 1: The Man-Ape; 1: W'Kabi	0.12	3.60	9.00	18.00
❑63, Apr 69, GC, And in This Corner, Goliath, 1: Goliath-New (Hawkeye), Yellowjacket and Wasp rejoin Avengers	0.12	3.60	9.00	18.00

	ORIG	GOOD	FINE	N-MINT
❑64, May 69, GC, Like a Death Ray From the Sky	0.12	3.60	9.00	18.00
❑65, Jun 69, GC, Mightier Than the Sword?, O: Hawkeye	0.12	3.60	9.00	18.00
❑66, Jul 69, Betrayal!	0.15	3.60	9.00	18.00
❑67, Aug 69, We Stand at Armageddon	0.15	3.60	9.00	18.00
❑68, Sep 69, SB, And We Battle for the Earth	0.15	3.00	7.50	15.00
❑69, Oct 69, SB, Let he Game Begin, 1: Nighthawk II (Kyle Richmond)-Full; 1: Grandmaster	0.15	3.00	7.50	15.00
❑70, Nov 69, SB, When Strikes the Squadron Sinister	0.15	3.00	7.50	15.00
❑71, Dec 69, SB, Endgame, 1: Invaders (prototype)	0.15	4.00	10.00	20.00
❑72, Jan 70, SB, Did You Hear the One About Scorpio?, 1: Pisces I; 1: Taurus; 1: Zodiac I	0.15	2.40	6.00	12.00
❑73, Feb 70, HT, The Sting of the Serpent	0.15	2.40	6.00	12.00
❑74, Mar 70, JB, Pursue the Panther	0.15	2.40	6.00	12.00
❑75, Apr 70, JB, The Warlord and the Witch, 1: Arkon	0.15	2.80	7.00	14.00
❑76, May 70, JB, The Blaze of Battle, the Flames of Love	0.15	2.40	6.00	12.00
❑77, Jun 70, JB, Heroes for Hire, 1: the Split-Second Squad	0.15	2.40	6.00	12.00
❑78, Jul 70, JB, The Man-Ape Always Strikes Twice	0.15	2.40	6.00	12.00
❑79, Aug 70, JB, Lo, the Lethal Legion	0.15	2.40	6.00	12.00
❑80, Sep 70, JB, The Coming of Red Wolf, 1: Red Wolf	0.15	2.40	6.00	12.00
❑81, Oct 70, JB, When Dies a Legend	0.15	2.40	6.00	12.00
❑82, Nov 70, JB, Hostage	0.15	2.40	6.00	12.00
❑83, Dec 70, JB, Come On In, the Revolution's Fine, 1: Valkyrie	0.15	2.60	6.50	13.00
❑84, Jan 71, JB, The Sword and the Sorceress	0.15	2.40	6.00	12.00
❑85, Feb 71, JB, The World Is Not For Burning, 1: Doctor Spectrum I (Joe Ledger); 1: Tom Thumb; 1: American Eagle II (James Dore Jr.); 1: Hawkeye II (Wyatt McDonald); 1: Whizzer II (Stanley Stewart)	0.15	2.40	6.00	12.00
❑86, Mar 71, SB; JB, Brain-Child to the Dark Tower Came, 1: Brain-Child	0.15	2.40	6.00	12.00
❑87, Apr 71, Look Homeward, Avenger, O: Black Panther	0.15	5.00	12.50	25.00
❑88, May 71, SB, The Summons of Psyklop, 1: Psyklop, continues in Incredible Hulk #140	0.15	2.40	6.00	12.00
❑88-2, SB, The Summons of Psyklop, 1: Psyklop, 2nd Printing	0.15	0.30	0.75	1.50
❑89, Jun 71, SB, The Only Good Alien	0.15	2.40	6.00	12.00
❑90, Jul 71, SB, Judgment Day	0.15	2.40	6.00	12.00
❑91, Aug 71, SB, Take One Giant Step-Backward	0.15	2.40	6.00	12.00
❑92, Sep 71, NA; SB, All Things Must End	0.15	2.40	6.00	12.00
❑93, Nov 71, NA, This Beachhead Earth, Double-size	0.25	9.00	22.50	45.00
❑94, Dec 71, NA; JB, More Than Inhuman, 1: Mandroid armor, 52pgs	0.20	6.40	16.00	32.00
❑95, Jan 72, NA, Something Inhuman This Way Comes, O: Black Bolt	0.20	6.40	16.00	32.00
❑96, Feb 72, NA, The Andromeda Swarm	0.20	6.40	16.00	32.00
❑97, Mar 72, GK; SB; BEv; JB, NA (w), Godhood's End	0.20	3.60	9.00	18.00
❑98, Apr 72, Let Slip the Dogs of War, 1: The Warhawks, Goliath becomes Hawkeye again	0.20	4.80	12.00	24.00
❑99, May 72, They First Make Mad	0.20	4.80	12.00	24.00
❑100, Jun 72, Whatever Gods There Be, 100th anniversary issue	0.20	12.00	30.00	60.00
❑101, Jul 72, RB, Five Dooms to Save Tomorrow	0.20	2.00	5.00	10.00
❑102, Aug 72, RB, What to Do Till the Sentinels Come	0.20	2.00	5.00	10.00
❑103, Sep 72, RB, The Sentinels Are Alive and Well	0.20	2.00	5.00	10.00
❑104, Oct 72, RB, With a Bang and a Whimper	0.20	2.00	5.00	10.00
❑105, Nov 72, JB, In the Beginning Was the World Within	0.20	2.00	5.00	10.00
❑106, Dec 72, GT; RB, A Traitor Stalks Among Us	0.20	2.00	5.00	10.00
❑107, Jan 73, DC; GT; JSn, The Master Plan of the Space Phantom	0.20	2.00	5.00	10.00
❑108, Feb 73, DH, Check-and Mate	0.20	2.00	5.00	10.00
❑109, Mar 73, DH, The Measure of a Man, 1: Imus Champion, Hawkeye leaves Avengers	0.20	2.00	5.00	10.00
❑110, Apr 73, DH, And Now, Magneto, A: X-Men	0.20	3.60	9.00	18.00
❑111, May 73, DH, With Two Beside Them, A: X-Men	0.20	3.60	9.00	18.00
❑112, Jun 73, DH, The Lion God Lives, 1: Mantis	0.20	2.00	5.00	10.00
❑113, Jul 73, Your Young Men Shall Slay Visions, D: The Living Bombs, Silver Surfer	0.20	1.60	4.00	8.00

	ORIG	GOOD	FINE	N-MINT
❑114, Aug 73, Night of the Swordsman, Silver Surfer	0.20	1.60	4.00	8.00
❑115, Sep 73, Below Us the Battle, Silver Surfer	0.20	1.60	4.00	8.00
❑116, Oct 73, Betrayal, Silver Surfer	0.20	1.60	4.00	8.00
❑117, Nov 73, Holocaust, Silver Surfer	0.20	1.60	4.00	8.00
❑118, Dec 73, To the Death, Silver Surfer	0.20	1.60	4.00	8.00
❑119, Jan 74, Night of the Collector, Silver Surfer	0.20	1.60	4.00	8.00
❑120, Feb 74, JSt; DH; JSn, Death-Stars of the Zodiac	0.20	1.60	4.00	8.00
❑121, Mar 74, JB, Houses Divided Cannot Stand	0.20	1.60	4.00	8.00
❑122, Apr 74, Trapped in Outer Space	0.20	1.60	4.00	8.00
❑123, May 74, O: Mantis	0.25	1.60	4.00	8.00
❑124, Jun 74	0.25	1.60	4.00	8.00
❑125, Jul 74, A: Thanos	0.25	1.60	4.00	8.00
❑126, Aug 74	0.25	1.60	4.00	8.00
❑127, Sep 74, FF; SB, Bride and Doom, 1: Ultron-7; A: Inhumans; A: Fantastic Four	0.25	1.60	4.00	8.00
❑128, Oct 74, SB, Bewitched, Bothered, and Dead	0.25	1.60	4.00	8.00
❑129, Nov 74, SB, Bid Tomorrow Goodbye	0.25	1.60	4.00	8.00
❑130, Dec 74, SB, The Reality Problem, 1: The Slasher; V: Titanium Man, Radioactive Man, Crimson Dynamo, Slasher	0.25	1.60	4.00	8.00
❑131, Jan 75, SB, A Quiet Half-Hour in Saigon	0.25	1.30	3.25	6.50
❑132, Feb 75, SB, Kang War II	0.25	1.30	3.25	6.50
❑133, Mar 75, SB, Yesterday and Beyond	0.25	1.30	3.25	6.50
❑134, Apr 75, SB, The Times That Bind, O: Vision II (android)	0.25	1.30	3.25	6.50
❑135, May 75, GT, The Times That Bind, O: Vision II (android)-real origin; O: Moondragon	0.25	1.30	3.25	6.50
❑136, Jun 75, Iron Man: D.O.A.	0.25	1.30	3.25	6.50
❑137, Jul 75, GT, We Do Seek Out New Avengers	0.25	1.30	3.25	6.50
❑138, Aug 75, GT, Stranger in a Strange Man	0.25	1.30	3.25	6.50
❑139, Sep 75, GT, Prescription: Violence	0.25	1.30	3.25	6.50
❑140, Oct 75, GT, A Journey to the Center of the Ant	0.25	1.30	3.25	6.50
❑141, Nov 75, GP, The Phantom Empire, 1: Golden Archer II (Wyatt McDonald), Squadron Sinister	0.25	1.10	2.75	5.50
❑142, Dec 75, GP, Go West, Young Gods	0.25	1.10	2.75	5.50
❑143, Jan 76, GP, Right Between the Eons	0.25	1.10	2.75	5.50
❑144, Feb 76, GP, Claws, 1: Hellcat	0.25	1.10	2.75	5.50
❑145, Mar 76, DH, The Taking of the Avengers	0.25	1.10	2.75	5.50
❑146, Apr 76, DH; KP, The Assassin Never Fails!, 25¢ and 30¢ versions exist	0.25	1.10	2.75	5.50
❑147, May 76	0.25	1.10	2.75	5.50
❑148, Jun 76, 1: Cap'n Hawk	0.25	1.10	2.75	5.50
❑149, Jun 76	0.25	1.10	2.75	5.50
❑150, Aug 76, GP, New team: Captain America, Iron Man, Yellowjacket, Wasp, Beast, Vision II (android), and Scarlet Witch	0.25	1.10	2.75	5.50
❑151, Sep 76, GP, At Last: The Decision!, Wonder Man comes back from dead; New costume	0.30	1.10	2.75	5.50
❑152, Oct 76, 1: Black Talon II	0.30	1.10	2.75	5.50
❑153, Nov 76	0.30	1.10	2.75	5.50
❑154, Dec 76	0.30	1.10	2.75	5.50
❑155, Jan 77	0.30	1.10	2.75	5.50
❑156, Feb 77, 1: Tyrack	0.30	1.10	2.75	5.50
❑157, Mar 77	0.30	1.10	2.75	5.50
❑158, Apr 77	0.30	1.10	2.75	5.50
❑159, May 77, SB, Siege By Stealth And Storm	0.30	1.10	2.75	5.50
❑160, Jun 77	0.30	1.10	2.75	5.50
❑161, Jul 77, JBy; GP, ...The Trail	0.30	1.10	2.75	5.50
❑162, Aug 77, JBy; GP, The Bride Of Ultron!, 1: Jocasta	0.30	1.10	2.75	5.50
❑163, Sep 77, JBy; GP	0.30	1.10	2.75	5.50
❑164, Oct 77, JBy; GP	0.30	1.10	2.75	5.50
❑165, Nov 77, JBy, Hammer Of Vengeance	0.35	1.10	2.75	5.50
❑166, Dec 77, JBy	0.35	1.10	2.75	5.50
❑167, Jan 78, JBy	0.35	0.70	1.75	3.50
❑168, Feb 78, JBy	0.35	0.70	1.75	3.50
❑169, Mar 78, JBy	0.35	0.70	1.75	3.50
❑170, Apr 78, JBy	0.35	0.70	1.75	3.50
❑171, May 78, JBy	0.35	0.70	1.75	3.50
❑172, Jun 78	0.35	0.70	1.75	3.50
❑173, Jul 78	0.35	0.70	1.75	3.50
❑174, Aug 78	0.35	0.70	1.75	3.50
❑175, Sep 78	0.35	0.70	1.75	3.50
❑176, Oct 78	0.35	0.70	1.75	3.50
❑177, Nov 78, The Hope...and the Slaughter	0.35	0.70	1.75	3.50
❑178, Dec 78, JBy; CI, The Martyr Perplex	0.35	0.70	1.75	3.50

	ORIG	GOOD	FINE	N-MINT
❑179, Jan 79, JM, Slowly Slays the Stinger, 1: The Stinger II; 1: The Monolith	0.35	0.70	1.75	3.50
❑180, Feb 79, JM, Berserker's Holiday	0.35	0.70	1.75	3.50
❑181, Mar 79, TD; JBy; GP, On the Matter of Heroes, New team: Captain America, Falcon, Iron Man, Beast, Vision II (android), and Scarlet Witch	0.35	0.90	2.25	4.50
❑182, Apr 79, JBy, Honor Thy Father	0.35	0.80	2.00	4.00
❑183, May 79, JBy, The Redoubtable Return of Crusher Creel	0.40	0.80	2.00	4.00
❑184, Jun 79, JBy, Death on the Hudson	0.40	0.80	2.00	4.00
❑185, Jul 79, JBy, The Yesterday Quest!, O: Quicksilver; O: Scarlet Witch; 1: Chthon (in human body)	0.40	0.80	2.00	4.00
❑186, Aug 79, JBy, Nights Of Wundagore!	0.40	0.80	2.00	4.00
❑187, Sep 79, JBy, The Call Of Mountain Thing, 1: Chthon (in real human form)	0.40	0.80	2.00	4.00
❑188, Oct 79, FS; DGr; JBy, Elementary, Dear Avengers	0.40	0.80	2.00	4.00
❑189, Nov 79, JBy, Wings and Arrows	0.40	0.80	2.00	4.00
❑190, Dec 79, JBy, Heart of Stone, Daredevil	0.40	0.80	2.00	4.00
❑191, Jan 80, JBy; GP, Back to the Stone Age	0.40	0.80	2.00	4.00
❑192, Feb 80, Steel City Nightmare	0.40	0.50	1.25	2.50
❑193, Mar 80, DGr; SB, Battleground: Pittsburgh	0.40	0.50	1.25	2.50
❑194, Apr 80, GP, Interlude	0.40	0.50	1.25	2.50
❑195, May 80, GP, Assault on a Mind Cage, 1: Taskmaster	0.40	0.60	1.50	3.00
❑196, Jun 80, GP, The Terrible Toll of the Taskmaster, O: Taskmaster	0.40	0.60	1.50	3.00
❑197, Jul 80, CI, Prelude Of The War-Devil!	0.40	0.50	1.25	2.50
❑198, Aug 80, GP, Better Red than Ronin	0.40	0.50	1.25	2.50
❑199, Sep 80, GP, Last Stand on Long Island	0.50	0.50	1.25	2.50
❑200, Oct 80, GP, The Child Is Father To...?, double-sized; Ms. Marvel leaves team	0.75	0.50	1.25	2.50
❑201, Nov 80, GP, The Evil Reborn	0.50	0.50	1.25	2.50
❑202, Dec 80, GP, This Evil Undying, V: Ultron	0.50	0.50	1.25	2.50
❑203, Jan 81, CI, Night Of The Crawler	0.50	0.50	1.25	2.50
❑204, Feb 81, DN, Claws Across The Water, A: Yellow Claw	0.50	0.50	1.25	2.50
❑205, Mar 81, Shadow Of The Claw, A: Yellow Claw	0.50	0.50	1.25	2.50
❑206, Apr 81, GC, Fire In The Streets	0.50	0.50	1.25	2.50
❑207, May 81, GC, Beyond A Shadow	0.50	0.50	1.25	2.50
❑208, Jun 81, GC, Eve Of Destruction	0.50	0.50	1.25	2.50
❑209, Jul 81, The Resurrection Stone	0.50	0.50	1.25	2.50
❑210, Aug 81, DG; GC, You Don't Need The Weathermen To Know Which Way The Wind Blows!	0.50	0.50	1.25	2.50
❑211, Sep 81, DG; GC, By Force Of Mind!, Moon Knight, Dazzler; New team begins	0.50	0.50	1.25	2.50
❑212, Oct 81, Men Of Deadly Pride	0.50	0.50	1.25	2.50
❑213, Nov 81, BH, Court-Martial, Yellowjacket's court martial; Yellowjacket leaves	0.50	0.50	1.25	2.50
❑214, Dec 81, BH, Three Angels Have Fallen!, A: Ghost Rider	0.50	0.60	1.50	3.00
❑215, Jan 82, All the Ways of Power, A: Silver Surfer	0.60	0.50	1.25	2.50
❑216, Feb 82, To Avenge The Avengers!, A: Silver Surfer	0.60	0.50	1.25	2.50
❑217, Mar 82, BH, Double-Cross, Yellowjacket jailed; Yellowjacket & Wasp return	0.60	0.40	1.00	2.00
❑218, Apr 82, DP, Born Again(And Again And Again...)	0.60	0.40	1.00	2.00
❑219, May 82, BH, ...By Divine Right, A: Drax	0.60	0.40	1.00	2.00
❑220, Jun 82, BH, War Against The Gods!, A: Drax; D: Drax the Destroyer	0.60	0.40	1.00	2.00
❑221, Jul 82, BH, ...New Blood!, Wolverine on cover only; Hawkeye rejoins; She-Hulk joins	0.60	0.40	1.00	2.00
❑222, Aug 82, A Gathering Of Evil, V: Masters of Evil	0.60	0.40	1.00	2.00
❑223, Sep 82, Of Robin Hoods and Roustabouts, A: Ant-Man	0.60	0.40	1.00	2.00
❑224, Oct 82, Two from the Heart, Tony Stark/Wasp romance	0.60	0.40	1.00	2.00
❑225, Nov 82, The Fall Of Avalon, A: Black Knight; 1: Balor	0.60	0.40	1.00	2.00
❑226, Dec 82, An Eye For An Eye, 1: Valinor; A: Black Knight	0.60	0.40	1.00	2.00
❑227, Jan 83, SB, Testing...1...2...3!, O: Avengers; O: Giant-Man; O: Wasp; O: Goliath; O: Ant-Man; O: Yellowjacket, Captain Marvel II joins team; Captain Marvel II (female) joins team	0.60	0.40	1.00	2.00
❑228, Feb 83, AM, Trial of Yellowjacket; Trial And Error!	0.60	0.40	1.00	2.00
❑229, Mar 83, AM, Final Curtain!, V: Egghead	0.60	0.40	1.00	2.00
❑230, Apr 83, AM, The Last Farewell, D: Egghead, Yellowjacket leaves	0.60	0.40	1.00	2.00

The origins of several of Henry Pym's heroic alter egos, as well as The Wasp's origin, were retold in *Avengers* (Vol. 1) #227.

© 1983 Marvel

	ORIG	GOOD	FINE	N-MINT
❑231, May 83, AM, Up From The Depths!, Iron Man leaves	0.60	0.40	1.00	2.00
❑232, Jun 83, AM, Starfox!, A: Starfox, Starfox (Eros) joins	0.60	0.40	1.00	2.00
❑233, Jul 83, JSt; JBy, JBy (w), The Annihilation Gambit	0.60	0.40	1.00	2.00
❑234, Aug 83, AM, The Witch's Tale!, O: Quicksilver; O: Scarlet Witch	0.60	0.40	1.00	2.00
❑235, Sep 83, Havoc On The Home front, V: Wizard	0.60	0.40	1.00	2.00
❑236, Oct 83, AM, I Want To be An Avenger, Spider-Man; New logo	0.60	0.40	1.00	2.00
❑237, Nov 83, AM, Meltdowns And Mayhem, Spider-Man	0.60	0.40	1.00	2.00
❑238, Dec 83, AM, Unlimited Vision, O: Blackout I (Marcus Daniels)	0.60	0.40	1.00	2.00
❑239, Jan 84, AM, Late Night Of The Super-Stars!, A: David Letterman; D: Blackout I (Marcus Daniels)	0.60	0.40	1.00	2.00
❑240, Feb 84, AM, The Ghost Of Jessica Drew!, A: Spider-Woman, Spider-Woman revived	0.60	0.40	1.00	2.00
❑241, Mar 84, AM, Dark Angel!, A: Spider-Woman	0.60	0.40	1.00	2.00
❑242, Apr 84, AM, Easy Come...East Go!	0.60	0.40	1.00	2.00
❑243, May 84, AM, Chain Of Command!	0.60	0.40	1.00	2.00
❑244, Jun 84, AM, And The Rocket's Red Glare!, V: Dire Wraiths	0.60	0.40	1.00	2.00
❑245, Jul 84, AM, V: Dire Wraiths	0.60	0.40	1.00	2.00
❑246, Aug 84, AM, Gatherings, A: Sersi	0.60	0.40	1.00	2.00
❑247, Sep 84, AM, The Ties That Bind!, A: Uni-Mind	0.60	0.40	1.00	2.00
❑248, Oct 84, AM, To Save The Eternals!, A: Eternals	0.60	0.40	1.00	2.00
❑249, Nov 84, AM, The Snows Of Summer, A: Fantastic Four	0.60	0.40	1.00	2.00
❑250, Dec 84, AM, World Power, 52pgs.; Maelstrom	1.00	0.50	1.25	2.50
❑251, Jan 85, BH, Deceptions!	0.60	0.35	0.88	1.75
❑252, Feb 85, BH, Deciding Factor!	0.60	0.35	0.88	1.75
❑253, Mar 85	0.60	0.35	0.88	1.75
❑254, Apr 85	0.65	0.35	0.88	1.75
❑255, May 85, JB, The Legacy Of Thanos!	0.65	0.35	0.88	1.75
❑256, Jun 85, JB, This Power Unleashed!, Savage Land	0.65	0.35	0.88	1.75
❑257, Jul 85, JB, Pyrrhic Victory!, 1: Nebula	0.65	0.35	0.88	1.75
❑258, Aug 85, Spider-Man vs. Firelord	0.65	0.35	0.88	1.75
❑259, Sep 85, V: Skrulls	0.65	0.35	0.88	1.75
❑260, Oct 85, JB, Assault On Sanctuary II, A: Nebula, Secret Wars II	0.65	0.35	0.88	1.75
❑261, Nov 85, JB, Earth And Beyond, Secret Wars II	0.65	0.35	0.88	1.75
❑262, Dec 85, JB, Many Brave Hearts!, A: Sub-Mariner	0.65	0.35	0.88	1.75
❑263, Jan 86, 1: X-Factor; D: Melter	0.65	0.70	1.75	3.50
❑264, Feb 86	0.75	0.35	0.88	1.75
❑265, Mar 86, JB, Eve Of Destruction, Secret Wars II	0.75	0.35	0.88	1.75
❑266, Apr 86, JB, ...And The War's Desolation, Secret Wars II Epilogue	0.75	0.30	0.75	1.50
❑267, May 86, JB, Time-And Time Again, V: Kang	0.75	0.30	0.75	1.50
❑268, Jun 86, JB, V: Kang	0.75	0.30	0.75	1.50
❑269, Jul 86, JB, O: Rama-Tut; V: Kang	0.75	0.30	0.75	1.50
❑270, Aug 86, JB, Wild In The Streets, A: Namor	0.75	0.30	0.75	1.50
❑271, Sep 86, JB, Breakaway!	0.75	0.30	0.75	1.50
❑272, Oct 86, JB, A: Alpha Flight	0.75	0.30	0.75	1.50
❑273, Nov 86, JB, Rites Of Conquest!	0.75	0.30	0.75	1.50
❑274, Dec 86, JB, Divided...We Fall!	0.75	0.30	0.75	1.50
❑275, Jan 87, JB	0.75	0.30	0.75	1.50
❑276, Feb 87, JB, Revenge	0.75	0.30	0.75	1.50
❑277, Mar 87, JB, D: Blackout	0.75	0.30	0.75	1.50
❑278, Apr 87, JB, Pressure	0.75	0.30	0.75	1.50
❑279, May 87	0.75	0.30	0.75	1.50
❑280, Jun 87	0.75	0.30	0.75	1.50
❑281, Jul 87	0.75	0.30	0.75	1.50
❑282, Aug 87, V: Neptune	0.75	0.30	0.75	1.50
❑283, Sep 87	0.75	0.30	0.75	1.50

	ORIG	GOOD	FINE	N-MINT
❑284, Oct 87, on Olympus	0.75	0.30	0.75	1.50
❑285, Nov 87, V: Zeus	0.75	0.30	0.75	1.50
❑286, Dec 87, JB, The Fix Is On!, V: Super Adaptoid	0.75	0.30	0.75	1.50
❑287, Jan 88, JB, Invasion!, V: Fixer	0.75	0.30	0.75	1.50
❑288, Feb 88, JB, Heavy Metal, V: Sentry Sinister	0.75	0.30	0.75	1.50
❑289, Mar 88, JB, Attack!, V: Super Adaptoid, Sentry Sinister, Machine Man, Tess-One, Fixer	0.75	0.30	0.75	1.50
❑290, Apr 88, JB, The World According to the Adaptoid	0.75	0.30	0.75	1.50
❑291, May 88, JB, Shadows of the Future Past	1.00	0.30	0.75	1.50
❑292, Jun 88, JB, D: Leviathan III (Marina)	1.00	0.30	0.75	1.50
❑293, Jul 88, JB, And Flights Of Angels!, 1: Nebula; D: Marrina; D: Marina	1.00	0.30	0.75	1.50
❑294, Aug 88, JB, If Wishes Were Horses..., Captain Marvel leaves team; Capt. Marvel leaves team	1.00	0.30	0.75	1.50
❑295, Sep 88, JB, ...Beggars Would Ride!	1.00	0.30	0.75	1.50
❑296, Oct 88, JB, Hearts Of Oak...And Heads To Match!	1.00	0.30	0.75	1.50
❑297, Nov 88, JB, Futures Imperfect, D: Doctor Druid, Thor, Black Knight, She-Hulk leaves team; She-Hulk, Thor, and Black Knight leave	1.00	0.30	0.75	1.50
❑298, Dec 88, JB, Disaster!, Inferno	1.00	0.30	0.75	1.50
❑299, Jan 89, JB, I Love NY, Inferno	1.00	0.30	0.75	1.50
❑300, Feb 89, JB, Inferno, 68pgs.; 300th anniversary issue; Inferno; new team; Thor Joins	1.75	0.50	1.25	2.50
❑301, Mar 89, BH, Super-Nova Saga, Part 1; Super-Nova Unbound	1.00	0.30	0.75	1.50
❑302, Apr 89, RB, Super-Nova Saga, Part 2; Earth Rocks!	1.00	0.30	0.75	1.50
❑303, May 89, RB, Super-Nova Saga, Part 3; Reckoning	1.00	0.30	0.75	1.50
❑304, Jun 89, RB, ...Yearning To Breathe Free, V: U-Foes; 1: Portal; A: Puma	1.00	0.30	0.75	1.50
❑305, Jul 89, JBy, JBy (w), Attack Of The Lava Men!	1.00	0.30	0.75	1.50
❑306, Aug 89, JBy (w), There Is A Fire Down Below	1.00	0.30	0.75	1.50
❑307, Sep 89, JBy (w), To Crush An Eternal!	1.00	0.30	0.75	1.50
❑308, Oct 89, JBy (w), Journey	1.00	0.30	0.75	1.50
❑309, Nov 89, JBy (w), To Find Olympia!	1.00	0.30	0.75	1.50
❑310, Nov 89, JBy (w), Death in Olympia	1.00	0.30	0.75	1.50
❑311, Dec 89, JBy (w), Acts of Vengeance, Part 2, The Weakest Point, "Acts of Vengeance"	1.00	0.30	0.75	1.50
❑312, Dec 89, JBy (w), Acts of Vengeance, Part 11, Has The Whole World Gone Mad?!?, "Acts of Vengeance"	1.00	0.30	0.75	1.50
❑313, Jan 90, JBy (w), Acts of Vengeance, Part 20; Thieves' Honor, "Acts of Vengeance"	1.00	0.30	0.75	1.50
❑314, Feb 90, JBy (w), Along Came a Spider..., Spider-Man	1.00	0.30	0.75	1.50
❑315, Mar 90, JBy (w), Doomsday Plus One!, Spider-Man; Spider-Man x-over	1.00	0.30	0.75	1.50
❑316, Apr 90, JBy (w), Spiders and Stars, Spider-Man	1.00	0.30	0.75	1.50
❑317, May 90, JBy (w), Business as Usual, Spider-Man	1.00	0.30	0.75	1.50
❑318, Jun 90, A Vengeful God, Spider-Man	1.00	0.30	0.75	1.50
❑319, Jul 90, The Crossing Line!; The Crossing Line!, Part 1	1.00	0.30	0.75	1.50
❑320, Aug 90, The Crossing Line!; The Crossing Line!, Part 2, Underlying Currents, A: Alpha Flight	1.00	0.30	0.75	1.50
❑321, Aug 90, The Crossing Line!; The Crossing Line!, Part 3, Missing Links	1.00	0.30	0.75	1.50
❑322, Sep 90, The Crossing Line!; The Crossing Line!, Part 4, Bombs Away!, A: Alpha Flight	1.00	0.30	0.75	1.50
❑323, Sep 90, The Crossing Line!; The Crossing Line!, Part 5, One World's Not Enough For All Of Us, A: Alpha Flight	1.00	0.30	0.75	1.50
❑324, Oct 90, The Crossing Line!; The Crossing Line!, Part 6	1.00	0.30	0.75	1.50
❑325, Oct 90, Party Games	1.00	0.30	0.75	1.50
❑326, Nov 90, Wind From the East, 1: Rage	1.00	0.30	0.75	1.50
❑327, Dec 90, Into a Darkling Plain	1.00	0.30	0.75	1.50
❑328, Jan 91, Powers That Be, O: Turbo; O: Rage	1.00	0.30	0.75	1.50
❑329, Feb 91, Starting Line-Up	1.00	0.30	0.75	1.50
❑330, Mar 91, In A Strange Land	1.00	0.30	0.75	1.50
❑331, Apr 91, Pediments of Clay	1.00	0.30	0.75	1.50
❑332, May 91, The Many Faces Of Doom	1.00	0.30	0.75	1.50
❑333, Jun 91, HT, Life Of The Party!	1.00	0.30	0.75	1.50
❑334, Jul 91, The Collection Obsession, Part 1, First Encounter	1.00	0.30	0.75	1.50
❑335, Aug 91, The Collection Obsession, Part 2, Bloody Encounter	1.00	0.30	0.75	1.50
❑336, Aug 91, The Collection Obsession, Part 3, For Here We Make Your Stand	1.00	0.30	0.75	1.50
❑337, Sep 91, The Collection Obsession, Part 4, Mud And Glory?	1.00	0.30	0.75	1.50
❑338, Sep 91, Collection Obsession, Part 4; The Collection Obsession, Part 5, Infectious Compulses	1.00	0.30	0.75	1.50
❑339, Oct 91, The Collection Obsession, Part 6, Final Redemption	1.00	0.30	0.75	1.50
❑340, Oct 91, Clay Soldiers	1.00	0.30	0.75	1.50
❑341, Nov 91	1.00	0.30	0.75	1.50
❑342, Dec 91, By Reason Of Insanity?, A: New Warriors	1.00	0.30	0.75	1.50
❑343, Jan 92	1.00	0.30	0.75	1.50
❑344, Feb 92	1.25	0.30	0.75	1.50
❑345, Mar 92, Storm Gatherings, Operation: Galactic Storm, Part 5	1.25	0.30	0.75	1.50
❑346, Apr 92, Assassination, Operation: Galactic Storm, Part 12	1.25	0.30	0.75	1.50
❑347, May 92, Empire's End, D: Supreme Intelligence (apparent death), Operation: Galactic Storm, Part 19; Conclusion to Operation: Galactic Storm	1.75	0.40	1.00	2.00
❑348, Jun 92, Familiar Connections	1.25	0.30	0.75	1.50
❑349, Jul 92	1.25	0.30	0.75	1.50
❑350, Aug 92, Repercussions, Gatefold covers; reprint of Avengers #53; Dbl. Size	2.50	0.50	1.25	2.50
❑351, Aug 92, Retribution!	1.25	0.25	0.63	1.25
❑352, Sep 92, Fear the Reaper, Part 1, Son Of Darkness, V: Grim Reaper	1.25	0.25	0.63	1.25
❑353, Sep 92, Fear the Reaper, Part 2, To Wake The Dead, V: Grim Reaper	1.25	0.25	0.63	1.25
❑354, Oct 92, Fear the Reaper, Part 3, The Conqueror Worm, V: Grim Reaper	1.25	0.25	0.63	1.25
❑355, Oct 92, When Come The Gatherers!	1.25	0.25	0.63	1.25
❑356, Nov 92, Death In A Gathering Place	1.25	0.25	0.63	1.25
❑357, Dec 92	1.25	0.25	0.63	1.25
❑358, Jan 93, Arkon's Asylum	1.25	0.25	0.63	1.25
❑359, Feb 93, Gift Of The Gods	1.25	0.25	0.63	1.25
❑360, Mar 93, Alternate Visions, foil cover	2.95	0.59	1.48	2.95
❑361, Apr 93	1.25	0.25	0.63	1.25
❑362, May 93	1.25	0.25	0.63	1.25
❑363, Jun 93, A Gathering Of Hate, Silver embossed cover	2.95	0.59	1.48	2.95
❑364, Jul 93	1.25	0.25	0.63	1.25
❑365, Aug 93	1.25	0.25	0.63	1.25
❑366, Sep 93, sculpted foil cover	3.95	0.79	1.98	3.95
❑367, Oct 93, A: Black Knight; A: Sersi	1.25	0.25	0.63	1.25
❑368, Nov 93, Bloodties, Part 1	1.25	0.25	0.63	1.25
❑369, Dec 93, sculpted foil cover	2.95	0.59	1.48	2.95
❑370, Jan 94	1.25	0.25	0.63	1.25
❑371, Feb 94	1.25	0.25	0.63	1.25
❑372, Mar 94	1.25	0.25	0.63	1.25
❑373, Apr 94	1.25	0.25	0.63	1.25
❑374, May 94, cards	1.50	0.25	0.63	1.25
❑375, Jun 94, The Last Gathering, D: Proctor, Giant-size; poster; Dane Whitman and Sersi leave the Avengers	2.50	0.40	1.00	2.00
❑375/CS, Jun 94, The Last Gathering, D: Proctor, poster; Giant-size; Dane Whitman and Sersi leave the Avengers	2.50	0.50	1.25	2.50
❑376, Jul 94	1.50	0.30	0.75	1.50
❑377, Aug 94	1.50	0.30	0.75	1.50
❑378, Sep 94	1.50	0.30	0.75	1.50
❑379, Oct 94	1.50	0.30	0.75	1.50
❑379/A, Oct 94, Double-feature with Giant-Man	2.50	0.50	1.25	2.50
❑380, Nov 94, V: High Evolutionary	1.50	0.30	0.75	1.50
❑380/A, Nov 94, second indicia gives name as "Marvel Double Feature ... The Avengers/Giant Man"	2.50	0.50	1.25	2.50
❑381, Dec 94	1.50	0.30	0.75	1.50

	ORIG	GOOD	FINE	N-MINT
❑381/A, Dec 94, second indicia gives name as "Marvel Double Feature ... The Avengers/Giant Man"	2.50	0.50	1.25	2.50
❑382, Jan 95	1.50	0.30	0.75	1.50
❑382/A, Jan 95, second indicia gives name as "Marvel Double Feature ... The Avengers/Giant Man"	2.50	0.50	1.25	2.50
❑383, Feb 95	1.50	0.30	0.75	1.50
❑384, Mar 95	1.50	0.30	0.75	1.50
❑385, Apr 95	1.50	0.30	0.75	1.50
❑386, May 95	1.50	0.30	0.75	1.50
❑387, Jun 95, Taking A.I.M., Part 2	1.50	0.30	0.75	1.50
❑388, Jul 95, Taking A.I.M., Part 4	1.50	0.30	0.75	1.50
❑389, Aug 95	1.50	0.30	0.75	1.50
❑390, Sep 95	1.50	0.30	0.75	1.50
❑391, Oct 95	1.50	0.30	0.75	1.50
❑392, Nov 95, Mantis returns	1.50	0.30	0.75	1.50
❑393, Dec 95, A: Tony Stark, "The Crossing"; Wasp critically injured	1.50	0.30	0.75	1.50
❑394, Jan 96, 1: New Wasp, "The Crossing"	1.50	0.30	0.75	1.50
❑395, Feb 96, Avengers: Timeslide, D: Tony Stark	1.50	0.30	0.75	1.50
❑396, Mar 96, First Sign, Part 4, Balance Of Power	1.50	0.30	0.75	1.50
❑397, Apr 96, Crawling From the Wreckage	1.50	0.30	0.75	1.50
❑398, May 96	1.50	0.30	0.75	1.50
❑399, Jun 96	1.50	0.30	0.75	1.50
❑400, Jul 96, MWa (w), wraparound cover	2.50	0.80	2.00	4.00
❑401, Aug 96, MWa (w), A: Magneto, Rogue	1.50	0.50	1.25	2.50
❑402, Sep 96, MWa (w), Final Issue; "Onslaught: Impact 2"; story continues in X-Men #56 and Onslaught: Marvel	1.50	0.50	1.25	2.50
❑Anl 1, Sep 67, DH, The Monstrous Master Plan of the Mandarin; To Perish by the Sword, A: Thor; A: Living Laser; A: Power Man I; A: Edwin Jarvis; A: Black Widow; A: Mandarin; A: Iron Man I; A: Hercules, Cover reads "King-Size Special"	0.25	10.00	25.00	50.00
❑Anl 2, Sep 68, Cover reads "King-Size Special"	0.25	5.00	12.50	25.00
❑Anl 3, Sep 69, Cover reads "King-Size Special"	0.25	5.00	12.50	25.00
❑Anl 4, Jan 71, O: Moondragon, Reprint; Cover reads "King-Size Special"	0.25	1.80	4.50	9.00
❑Anl 5, Jan 72, Reprint; Cover reads "King-Size Special"	0.25	1.80	4.50	9.00
❑Anl 6, ca. 76, GP, V: Nuklo	0.50	1.20	3.00	6.00
❑Anl 7, ca. 77, JSt; JSn, D: Warlock; D: Gamora, Warlock	0.60	2.50	6.25	12.50
❑Anl 8, ca. 78, GP, Spectrums of Deceit, A: Ms. Marvel	0.60	1.00	2.50	5.00
❑Anl 9, ca. 79, DN, ...Today the Avengers Die!	0.60	0.80	2.00	4.00
❑Anl 10, ca. 81, MG, By Friends-Betrayed!, 1: Destiny; 1: Rogue, X-Men	0.75	4.00	10.00	20.00
❑Anl 11, ca. 82, AM, In Honor's Name	1.00	0.70	1.75	3.50
❑Anl 12, ca. 83, Moonrise, A: Inhumans	1.00	0.70	1.75	3.50
❑Anl 13, ca. 84, JBy; SD, In Memory Yet Green!, D: Nebulon	1.00	0.70	1.75	3.50
❑Anl 14, ca. 85, JBy	1.25	0.70	1.75	3.50
❑Anl 15, ca. 86, SD, Betrayal!	1.25	0.70	1.75	3.50
❑Anl 16, ca. 87	1.25	0.70	1.75	3.50
❑Anl 17, ca. 88, Evolutionary War, Part 11, Prometheus Mutants!	1.75	0.60	1.50	3.00
❑Anl 18, ca. 89, Atlantis Attacks, Part 8; Avengers Assembled, Atlantis Attacks	2.00	0.50	1.25	2.50
❑Anl 19, ca. 90, KB (w), The Terminus Factor, Part 5; Beat Me In St. Louis!, Terminus	2.00	0.50	1.25	2.50
❑Anl 20, ca. 91, Subterranean Odyssey, Part 1; Of Moles And Mutates, Subterranean Wars	2.00	0.50	1.25	2.50
❑Anl 21, ca. 92, Citizen Kang, Part 4, Kang's World; Chronopolis, 1: Terminatrix, Citizen Kang	2.25	0.50	1.25	2.50
❑Anl 22, ca. 93, 1: Bloodwraith, trading card; Polybagged with trading card	2.95	0.59	1.48	2.95
❑Anl 23, ca. 94	2.95	0.59	1.48	2.95
❑GS 1, 1: Whizzer I (Robert Frank); D: Miss America	0.50	2.40	6.00	12.00
❑GS 2, DC, A Blast From the Past, D: Swordsman; O: Rama-Tut	0.50	1.20	3.00	6.00
❑GS 3, DC, What Time Hath Put Asunder, O: Kang; O: Immortus	0.50	1.20	3.00	6.00

The adventures of British secret agents John Steed and Emma Peel were covered in Gold Key's *Avengers* one-shot.

© 1968 Gold Key

	ORIG	GOOD	FINE	N-MINT
❑GS 4, DH, Let All Men Bring Together, Vision and Scarlet Witch marry	0.50	1.20	3.00	6.00
❑GS 5, The Monstrous Master Plan of the Mandarin	0.50	1.00	2.50	5.00

AVENGERS (GOLD KEY)
GOLD KEY

	ORIG	GOOD	FINE	N-MINT
❑1, based on TV series	0.10	29.00	72.50	145.00

AVENGERS (VOL. 2)
MARVEL

	ORIG	GOOD	FINE	N-MINT
❑1, Nov 96, RL, Awaken The Thunder, Thor revived	2.95	0.60	1.50	3.00
❑1/A, Nov 96, RL, Awaken The Thunder, Alternate cover (Chap Yaep); Thor revived	2.95	0.60	1.50	3.00
❑2, Dec 96, JPH (w), First Blood, V: Kang; A: Mantis	1.95	0.40	1.00	2.00
❑3, Jan 97, JPH (w), In Love & War, A: Mantis, Nick Fury	1.95	0.40	1.00	2.00
❑4, Feb 97, RL (w); JPH (w), That Which Gods Have Joined Together..., V: Hulk	1.95	0.40	1.00	2.00
❑5, Mar 97, JPH (w), ...Let No Man Tear Asunder, Thor vs. Hulk	1.95	0.40	1.00	2.00
❑5/A, JPH (w), ...Let No Man Tear Asunder, White cover; Thor vs. Hulk	1.95	0.40	1.00	2.00
❑6, Apr 97, RL (w); JPH (w), Industrial Revolution, Part 1, continues in Iron Man #6	1.95	0.39	0.98	1.95
❑7, May 97, RL (w); JPH (w), Help!, V: Lethal Legion (Enchantress, Wonder Man, Ultron 5, Executioner, Scarlet Witch)	1.95	0.39	0.98	1.95
❑8, Shadowplay	1.95	0.39	0.98	1.95
❑9, Jul 97, V: Masters of Evil	1.95	0.39	0.98	1.95
❑10, Aug 97, V: dopplegangers, gatefold summary	1.99	0.39	0.98	1.95
❑11, Sep 97, V: Loki; D: Thor, gatefold summary	1.99	0.39	0.98	1.95
❑12, Oct 97, cover forms quadtych with Fantastic Four #12, Iron Man #12, and Captain America #12	1.99	0.60	1.50	2.99
❑13, Nov 97, cover forms quadtych with Fantastic Four #13, Iron Man #13, and Captain America #13; Final Issue	1.99	0.39	0.98	1.95

AVENGERS (VOL. 3)
MARVEL

	ORIG	GOOD	FINE	N-MINT
❑0, KB (w), Our Top Story Tonight, Promotional edition included with Wizard	—	0.20	0.50	1.00
❑1, Feb 98, GP, KB (w), Once an Avenger..., Part 1, gatefold summary	2.99	0.80	2.00	4.00
❑1/A, GP, KB (w), Once an Avenger..., Part 2, chromium cover; Signed by George PTrez	—	1.20	3.00	6.00
❑1/B, Jul 98, GP, KB (w), Once an Avenger..., Part 1, cardstock cover; Avengers Rough Cut	2.99	0.80	2.00	4.00
❑1/C, Feb 98, KB (w), alternate cover; gatefold summary	2.99	0.80	2.00	4.00
❑1/SC, GP, KB (w), Once an Avenger..., Part 1, variant cover	2.99	1.00	2.50	5.00
❑2, Mar 98, GP, KB (w), Once an Avenger..., Part 2; The Call, gatefold summary	1.99	0.60	1.50	3.00
❑2/SC, Mar 98, GP, KB (w), Once an Avenger..., Part 2; The Call, alternate cover; gatefold summary	1.99	0.60	1.50	3.00
❑3, Apr 98, KB (w), Once an Avenger..., Part 3; Fata Morgana, A: Wonder Man gatefold summary	1.99	0.40	1.00	2.00
❑4, May 98, KB (w), Too Many Avengers!, New team announced gatefold summary; New team begins	1.99	0.40	1.00	2.00
❑5, Jun 98, KB (w), Accusation Most Foul, V: Squadron Supreme, gatefold summary	1.99	0.40	1.00	2.00
❑6, Jul 98, GP, KB (w), Earth's Mightiest Frauds?, V: Squadron Supreme, gatefold summary	1.99	0.40	1.00	2.00
❑7, Aug 98, KB (w), Live Kree or Die, Part 4; The Court Martial of Carol Danvers, A: Supreme Intelligence, gatefold summary; Warbird leaves	1.99	0.40	1.00	1.99
❑8, Sep 98, KB (w), Turbulence!, 1: Triathlon; 1: Silverclaw, gatefold summary	1.99	0.40	1.00	1.99

	ORIG	GOOD	FINE	N-MINT
❑9, Oct 98, KB (w), The Villain Who Fell from Grace with the Earth, V: Moses Magnum, gatefold summary	1.99	0.40	1.00	1.99
❑10, Nov 98, KB (w), Pomp & Pageantry, V: Grim Reaper, gatefold summary; Anniversary issue	1.99	0.40	1.00	1.99
❑11, Dec 98, KB (w), ... Always an Avenger!, V: Grim Reaper; A: Swordsman; A: Hellcat; A: Captain Marvel; A: Doctor Druid; A: Mockingbird; A: Wonder Man, gatefold summary	1.99	0.40	1.00	1.99
❑12, Jan 99, GP, KB (w), Old Entanglements, V: Thunderbolts, wraparound cover; gatefold summary; double-sized; Continued from Thunderbolts #22	2.99	0.60	1.50	2.99
❑12/A, Jan 99, GP, KB (w), Old Entanglements, DFE alternate cover; Signed by George PTrez, Al Vey, and Tom Smith; Continued from Thunderbolts #22	29.95	4.00	10.00	20.00
❑12/SC, Jan 99, GP, KB (w), Old Entanglements, DFE alternate cover; Continued from Thunderbolts #22	6.95	1.39	3.47	6.95
❑13, Feb 99, GP, KB (w), Lords & Leaders, A: New Warriors	1.99	0.40	1.00	1.99
❑14, Mar 99, GP, KB (w), Hi Honey ... I'm Home!, A: Kurt Busiek; A: Beast; A: George P...rez; A: Lord Templar, Return of Beast to team	1.99	0.40	1.00	1.99
❑15, Apr 99, GP, KB (w), The Three Fold Path, A: Triathalon; A: Lord Templar	1.99	0.40	1.00	1.99
❑16, May 99, Mistaken Identity, V: Wrecking Crew	1.99	0.40	1.00	1.99
❑17, Jun 99, Cage of Freedom, V: Doomsday Man	1.99	0.40	1.00	1.99
❑18, Jul 99, The Battle for Imperion City, V: Wrecking Crew	1.99	0.40	1.00	1.99
❑19, Aug 99, This Evil Renewed, V: Ultron; A: Black Panther	1.99	0.40	1.00	1.99
❑20, Sep 99, This Evil Unfolding, V: Ultron	1.99	0.40	1.00	1.99
❑21, Oct 99, This Evil Unveiled, V: Ultron	1.99	0.40	1.00	1.99
❑22, Oct 99, This Evil Triumphant!, V: Ultron	1.99	0.40	1.00	1.99
❑23, Dec 99, Showdown, Wonder Man versus Vision	1.99	0.40	1.00	1.99
❑24, Jan 00, Harsh Judgments	1.99	0.40	1.00	1.99
❑25, Feb 00, The Ninth Day, A: Juggernaut, Giant-size	2.99	0.60	1.50	2.99
❑26, Mar 00	1.99	0.40	1.00	1.99
❑27, Apr 00	1.99	0.40	1.00	1.99
❑28, May 00	1.99	0.40	1.00	1.99
❑29, Jun 00, The Death-Song of Kulan Gath, Part 2; A Dream of Bitter Ash	2.25	0.45	1.13	2.25
❑30, Jul 00	2.25	0.45	1.13	2.25
❑31, Aug 00, And So It Begins ..., A: Grim Reaper; A: Madame Masque	2.25	0.45	1.13	2.25
❑32, Sep 00, Behind the Masque!, A: Madame Masque	2.25	0.45	1.13	2.25
❑33, Oct 00, Tainted Love, A: Thunderbolts; V: Count Nefaria; A: Madame Masque	2.25	0.45	1.13	2.25
❑34, Nov 00, The Nefaria Protocols, A: Thunderbolts; V: Count Nefaria; A: Madame Masque, double-sized issue	2.99	0.60	1.50	2.99
❑35, Dec 00, Maximum Security	2.25	0.45	1.13	2.25
❑36, Jan 01, KB (w), No Rest for the Weary, A: Ten-Thirtifor	2.25	0.45	1.13	2.25
❑37, Feb 01, KB (w), Scorched Earth, A: Bloodwraith	2.25	0.45	1.13	2.25
❑38, Mar 01, KB (w), Above and Beyond, Slashback issue; price reduced	1.99	0.40	1.00	1.99
❑39, Apr 01, KB (w), Condition: Green	2.25	0.45	1.13	2.25
❑40	2.25	0.45	1.13	2.25
❑41	2.25	0.45	1.13	2.25
❑42	2.25	0.45	1.13	2.25
❑43	2.25	0.45	1.13	2.25
❑44	2.25	0.45	1.13	2.25
❑Anl 1998, wraparound cover; gatefold summary; Avengers/Squadron Supreme '98	2.99	0.60	1.50	2.99
❑Anl 1999, Jul 99, Jarvis' story	3.50	0.70	1.75	3.50
❑Anl 2001, 2001 Annual	2.99	0.60	1.50	2.99

AVENGERS CASEBOOK
MARVEL

Value: Cover or less

❑1999 ... 2.99

AVENGERS: DEATH TRAP, THE VAULT
MARVEL

Value: Cover or less

❑1, Sep 91, also published as Venom: Deathtrap - The Vault ... 9.95

AVENGERS FOREVER
MARVEL

Value: Cover or less

❑1, Dec 98, KB (w), Destiny Made Manifest ... 2.99
❑1/WF, Dec 98, KB (w), Destiny Made Manifest, Westfield alternate cover ... 4.95
❑2, Jan 99, KB (w), Now is the Time for All Good Men ... 2.99
❑3, Feb 99, KB (w), City at the Heart of Forever ... 2.99
❑4/A, Mar 99, KB (w), Running Out of Time, A: 1950s Avengers, Avengers of Tomorrow cover 2.99
❑4/B, Mar 99, KB (w), Running Out of Time, Kang in the Old West cover ... 2.99
❑4/C, Mar 99, KB (w), Running Out of Time, Avengers throughout time cover ... 2.99
❑4/D, Mar 99, KB (w), Running Out of Time, Avengers of the '50s cover ... 2.99
❑5, Apr 99, KB (w), Past Imperfect...Future Tense!, A: Two-Gun Kid; A: Kid Colt; A: Avengers of Tomorrow; A: 1950s Avengers; A: Rawhide Kid ... 2.99
❑6, May 99, KB (w) ... 2.99
❑7, Jun 99, KB (w), Into a Limbo Large and Broad ... 2.99
❑8, Jul 99, KB (w), The Secret History of the Avengers, A: Human Torch ... 2.99
❑9, Aug 99, KB (w), Break: Reflections of the Conqueror ... 2.99
❑10, Oct 99, KB (w), Tomorrow and Tomorrow and Tomorrow ... 2.99
❑11, KB (w) ... 2.99
❑12, KB (w), Final Issue ... 2.99

AVENGERS INFINITY
MARVEL

Value: Cover or less

❑1 ... 2.99
❑2 ... 2.99
❑3, Nov 00, They Walk Among the Stars! ... 2.99
❑4, Dec 00, The Hand of the Infinites ... 2.99

AVENGERS LOG
MARVEL

Value: Cover or less

❑1, GP ... 1.95

AVENGERS SPOTLIGHT
MARVEL

	ORIG	GOOD	FINE	N-MINT
❑21, Aug 89, Starfox; Series continued from Solo Avengers #20	0.75	0.20	0.50	1.00
❑22, Sep 89, Swordsman	1.00	0.20	0.50	1.00
❑23, Oct 89, Vision	1.00	0.20	0.50	1.00
❑24, Nov 89, A Show of Hands, A: Trickshot	1.00	0.20	0.50	1.00
❑25, Nov 89, Forewarned is Disarmed, A: Trickshot; A: Mockingbird; A: Crossfire	1.00	0.20	0.50	1.00
❑26, Dec 89, Acts of Vengeance, Part 1, "Acts of Vengeance"	1.00	0.20	0.50	1.00
❑27, Dec 89, AM, Acts of Vengeance, Part 9, Hurting Inside, "Acts of Vengeance"	1.00	0.20	0.50	1.00
❑28, Jan 90, Acts of Vengeance, Part 18, "Acts of Vengeance"	1.00	0.20	0.50	1.00
❑29, Feb 90, Acts of Vengeance, Part 27, "Acts of Vengeance"	1.00	0.20	0.50	1.00
❑30, Mar 90, new Hawkeye costume	1.00	0.20	0.50	1.00
❑31, Apr 90	1.00	0.20	0.50	1.00
❑32, May 90	1.00	0.20	0.50	1.00
❑33, Jun 90	1.00	0.20	0.50	1.00
❑34, Jul 90	1.00	0.20	0.50	1.00
❑35, Aug 90, Call Me Whatshisname, A: Gilgamesh	1.00	0.20	0.50	1.00
❑36, Sep 90	1.00	0.20	0.50	1.00
❑37, Oct 90	1.00	0.20	0.50	1.00
❑38, Nov 90	1.00	0.20	0.50	1.00
❑39, Dec 90	1.00	0.20	0.50	1.00
❑40, Jan 91, Final Issue	1.00	0.20	0.50	1.00

AVENGERS STRIKE FILE
MARVEL

Value: Cover or less

❑1 ... 1.75

AVENGERS: THE CROSSING
MARVEL

Value: Cover or less

❑1, Sep 95, Chronium Cover ... 4.95

AVENGERS: THE TERMINATRIX OBJECTIVE
MARVEL

Value: Cover or less

❑1, Sep 93, MGu, Holo-grafix cover ... 2.50
❑2, MGu, A: Terminatrix, New Avengers vs. Old Avengers. 1.25
❑3, MGu ... 1.25
❑4, MGu ... 1.25

AVENGERS: TIMESLIDE
MARVEL

Value: Cover or less

❑1, Feb 96, The Crossing, A: early, nn; enhanced wraparound cardstock cover; One-Shot ... 4.95

AVENGERS TWO: WONDER MAN & BEAST
MARVEL

Value: Cover or less

❑1, May 00, Second Chances. 2.99
❑2, Jun 00 ... 2.99
❑3, Jul 00, It's Alive! ... 2.99

AVENGERS/ULTRAFORCE
MARVEL

Value: Cover or less

❑1, Oct 95, continues in UltraForce/Avengers #1; Foil logo ... 3.95

	ORIG	GOOD	FINE	N-MINT

AVENGERS: ULTRON UNLEASHED
MARVEL

Value: Cover or less

❑1, Aug 99, nn; collects Avengers (1st series) #57-58 and #170-171 .... 3.50

AVENGERS: UNITED THEY STAND
MARVEL

	ORIG	GOOD	FINE	N-MINT
❑1, Nov 99, The Ultimate Creation	1.99	0.60	1.50	2.99
❑2, Dec 99, Hail and Farewell	1.99	0.40	1.00	1.99

AVENGERS UNIVERSE
MARVEL

Value: Cover or less

❑1 .... —
❑2 .... —
❑3 .... —
❑4, Nov 00, reprints Iron Fist: Wolverine #1; indicia is for Iron Fist: Wolverine #1 .... 2.99
❑5, Dec 00, A Gathering of Forces, reprints Iron Fist: Wolverine #2; indicia is for Iron Fist: Wolverine #2 .... 2.99
❑6, Jan 01, Against the Wall, reprints Iron Fist: Wolverine #3; indicia is for Iron Fist: Wolverine #3 .... 2.99

AVENGERS UNPLUGGED
MARVEL

	ORIG	GOOD	FINE	N-MINT
❑1, Unchain my Heart	0.99	0.20	0.50	1.00
❑2, A: Gravitron	0.99	0.20	0.50	1.00
❑3, Jan 96, Ladies Nite, Luna; Black Widow	0.99	0.20	0.50	1.00
❑4, The Old Ball and Chain, Wedding of Thunderball and Titania; Peter David appears as reverend in story	0.99	0.20	0.50	1.00
❑5, Jun 96, A: Captain Marvel	0.99	0.20	0.50	1.00
❑6, Aug 96, Final Issue	0.99	0.20	0.50	1.00

AVENGERS WEST COAST
MARVEL

	ORIG	GOOD	FINE	N-MINT
❑47, Aug 89	0.75	0.30	0.75	1.50
❑48, Sep 89	1.00	0.30	0.75	1.50
❑49, Oct 89, Baptism of Fire, A: Great Lakes Avengers	1.00	0.30	0.75	1.50
❑50, Nov 89, A: 1st Silver Age, Golden Age Human Torch returns	1.00	0.30	0.75	1.50
❑51, Nov 89, I Sing of Arms and Heroes ..., A: Iron Man	1.00	0.30	0.75	1.50
❑52, Dec 89	1.00	0.30	0.75	1.50
❑53, Dec 89, Acts of Vengeance, Part 7; The Plan Proceeds, V: U-Foes, "Acts of Vengeance"	1.00	0.30	0.75	1.50
❑54, Jan 90, Acts of Vengeance, Part 16; The Troubled Earth, V: Mole Man, Fantastic Four #1 cover homage; "Acts of Vengeance"	1.00	0.30	0.75	1.50
❑55, Feb 90, Acts of Vengeance, Part 24; The Breaking Strain, V: Loki, "Acts of Vengeance"	1.00	0.30	0.75	1.50
❑56, Mar 90, JBy, Darker Than Scarlet	1.00	0.30	0.75	1.50
❑57, Apr 90, JBy, Family Reunion, A: Quicksilver; A: Magneto	1.00	0.30	0.75	1.50
❑58, May 90	1.00	0.30	0.75	1.50
❑59, Jun 90	1.00	0.30	0.75	1.50
❑60, Jul 90	1.00	0.30	0.75	1.50
❑61, Aug 90	1.00	0.25	0.63	1.25
❑62, Sep 90	1.00	0.25	0.63	1.25
❑63, Oct 90, 1: Living Lightning	1.00	0.25	0.63	1.25
❑64, Nov 90, A: Captain America	1.00	0.25	0.63	1.25
❑65, Dec 90	1.00	0.25	0.63	1.25
❑66, Jan 91, V: Ultron	1.00	0.25	0.63	1.25
❑67, Feb 91	1.00	0.25	0.63	1.25
❑68, Mar 91	1.00	0.25	0.63	1.25
❑69, Apr 91	1.00	0.25	0.63	1.25
❑70, May 91	1.00	0.25	0.63	1.25
❑71, Jun 91	1.00	0.25	0.63	1.25
❑72, Jul 91	1.00	0.25	0.63	1.25
❑73, Aug 91	1.00	0.25	0.63	1.25
❑74, Sep 91	1.00	0.25	0.63	1.25
❑75, Oct 91, A: Fantastic Four, Thundra, Double-size issue	1.50	0.30	0.75	1.50
❑76, Nov 91	1.00	0.25	0.63	1.25
❑77, Dec 91	1.00	0.25	0.63	1.25
❑78, Jan 92	1.00	0.25	0.63	1.25
❑79, Feb 92	1.25	0.25	0.63	1.25
❑80, Mar 92, Operation: Galactic Storm, Part 2; Turn of the Sentry, Galactic Storm	1.25	0.25	0.63	1.25
❑81, Apr 92, Operation: Galactic Storm, Part 9; They Also Serve ..., Galactic Storm	1.25	0.25	0.63	1.25
❑82, May 92, Operation: Galactic Storm, Part 16; Shi'ar Hatred, Galactic Storm	1.25	0.25	0.63	1.25

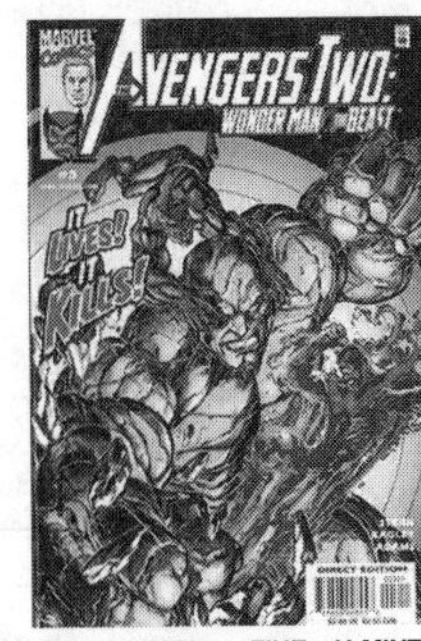

CBG columnist Tony Isabella's likeness can be found in the pages of *Avengers Two: Wonder Man & Beast.*

	ORIG	GOOD	FINE	N-MINT
❑83, Jun 92	1.25	0.25	0.63	1.25
❑84, Jul 92, O: Spider Woman	1.25	0.25	0.63	1.25
❑85, Aug 92	1.25	0.25	0.63	1.25
❑86, Sep 92	1.25	0.25	0.63	1.25
❑87, Oct 92	1.25	0.25	0.63	1.25
❑88, Nov 92	1.25	0.25	0.63	1.25
❑89, Dec 92	1.25	0.25	0.63	1.25
❑90, Jan 93	1.25	0.25	0.63	1.25
❑91, Feb 93	1.25	0.25	0.63	1.25
❑92, Mar 93	1.25	0.25	0.63	1.25
❑93, Apr 93	1.25	0.25	0.63	1.25
❑94, May 93	1.25	0.25	0.63	1.25
❑95, Jun 93	1.25	0.25	0.63	1.25
❑96, Jul 93, Infinity Crusade	1.25	0.25	0.63	1.25
❑97, Aug 93, Infinity Crusade	1.25	0.25	0.63	1.25
❑98, Sep 93	1.25	0.25	0.63	1.25
❑99, Oct 93, A: Hangman; A: Lethal Legion	1.25	0.25	0.63	1.25
❑100, Nov 93, sculpted foil cover	3.95	0.25	0.63	1.25
❑101, Dec 93, Bloodties, Part 3	1.25	0.25	0.63	1.25
❑102, Jan 94, Final Issue	1.25	0.25	0.63	1.25
❑Anl 4, ca. 89, Atlantis Attacks, Part 12, see West Coast Avengers for previous Annuals; "Atlantis Attacks"	2.00	0.50	1.25	2.50
❑Anl 5, ca. 90, The Terminus Factor, Part 4; When Titan Trash!, "Terminus Factor"	2.00	0.50	1.25	2.50
❑Anl 6, ca. 91, Subterranean Odyssey, Part 5, "Subterranean Wars"	2.00	0.50	1.25	2.50
❑Anl 7, ca. 92, Assault on Armor City, Part 2	2.25	0.45	1.13	2.25
❑Anl 8, ca. 93, 1: Raptor, trading card; Polybagged with trading card	2.95	0.59	1.48	2.95

AVENGERS/X-MEN: BLOODTIES
MARVEL

Value: Cover or less

❑1, Jan 95, Trade Paperback; collects Avengers #368 and 369, Avengers West Coast #101, Uncanny X-Men #307, and X-Men #26 .... 15.95

AVENUE D
FANTAGRAPHICS

Value: Cover or less

❑1, b&w; adult 3.50

A-V IN 3-D
AARDVARK-VANAHEIM

	ORIG	GOOD	FINE	N-MINT
❑1, Dec 84, Mist-Tree Tale In Tree-D, Requires 3-D glasses, Included; glasses	2.00	1.00	2.50	5.00

AWAKENING, THE
IMAGE

Value: Cover or less

❑1, 97, To Sleep Perchance to Dream! 2.95
❑2 .... 2.95
❑3 .... 2.95
❑4 .... 2.95

AWAKENING COMICS
AWAKENING COMICS

	ORIG	GOOD	FINE	N-MINT
❑1	3.50	0.70	1.75	3.50
❑2, Nov 97, Reminiscing; Karma Komix: Back to Bardo, A: Cerebus; A: Cerebus the Aardvark	3.50	0.70	1.75	3.50
❑3, Aug 98, wraparound cover; "The Everwinds Awakening War"	2.95	0.59	1.48	2.95
❑4, 1: Melvin G. Moose, Private Eye	—	0.59	1.48	2.95

AWAKENING COMICS 1999
AWAKENING COMICS

Value: Cover or less

❑1, 99, b&w; Anthology 3.50

AWESOME ADVENTURES
AWESOME

Value: Cover or less

❑1/A, Aug 99, AMo (w), Youngblood: Dandy in the Underworld, Woman standing (full length) on cover 2.50
❑1/B, Aug 99, AMo (w), Youngblood: Dandy in the Underworld, Woman standing (3/4 length) on cover 2.50

AWESOME HOLIDAY SPECIAL
Awesome

Value: Cover or less

❑1, Dec 97, AMo (w); JPH (w), Fighting America; Shaft, Flip cover; Youngblood side has gold foil logo ... 2.50

AWESOME PREVIEW
Awesome

	ORIG	GOOD	FINE	N-MINT
❑1, 97, nn; b&w and color previews of upcoming Awesome series given out at Comic-Con International: San Diego '97	—	0.20	0.50	1.00

AWKWARD
Slave Labor

Value: Cover or less

❑1 ... 4.95

AWKWARD UNIVERSE
Slave Labor

Value: Cover or less

❑1, Dec 95, nn; One-Shot ... 9.95

AXED FILES
Express

Value: Cover or less

❑1, 95, b&w ... 2.50

AXEL PRESSBUTTON
Eclipse

	ORIG	GOOD	FINE	N-MINT
❑1, Laser Eraser and Pressbutton; Zirk: Silver Sweater of the Spaceways	1.50	0.40	1.00	2.00
❑2	1.50	0.40	1.00	2.00
❑3	1.50	0.40	1.00	2.00
❑4	1.50	0.40	1.00	2.00
❑5, Continues as Pressbutton	1.75	0.40	1.00	2.00
❑6	1.75	0.40	1.00	2.00

AXIS ALPHA
Axis

Value: Cover or less

❑1, B.E.A.S.T.I.E.S.; Dethgrip ... 2.50

AXIS MUNDI
Amaze Ink

Value: Cover or less

❑2, b&w; wraparound cover; no indicia ... 2.95

AZ
Comico

Value: Cover or less

❑1, b&w ... 3.00

❑2, Comes Death, b&w ... 2.00

AZRAEL
DC

	ORIG	GOOD	FINE	N-MINT
❑1, Feb 95, A: Batman	1.95	0.60	1.50	3.00
❑2, Mar 95, Some Say In Ice, A: Batman	1.95	0.40	1.00	2.00
❑3, Apr 95	1.95	0.40	1.00	2.00
❑4, May 95	1.95	0.40	1.00	2.00
❑5, Jun 95	1.95	0.40	1.00	2.00
❑6, Jul 95	1.95	0.40	1.00	2.00
❑7, Aug 95	1.95	0.40	1.00	2.00
❑8, Sep 95	1.95	0.40	1.00	2.00
❑9, Oct 95	1.95	0.40	1.00	2.00
❑10, Nov 95, Underworld Unleashed, "Underworld Unleashed"	1.95	0.40	1.00	2.00
❑11, Dec 95	1.95	0.40	1.00	2.00
❑12, Jan 96	1.95	0.40	1.00	2.00
❑13, Feb 96, Demon Time, Part 1	1.95	0.40	1.00	2.00
❑14, Mar 96, Demon Time, Part 2	1.95	0.40	1.00	2.00
❑15, Mar 96, Contagion, Part 4; Contagion, Part 5, Marked as Contagion, Part 4 on cover	1.95	0.40	1.00	2.00
❑16, Apr 96, Contagion, Part 10	1.95	0.40	1.00	2.00
❑17	1.95	0.40	1.00	2.00
❑18	1.95	0.40	1.00	2.00
❑19	1.95	0.40	1.00	2.00
❑20	1.95	0.40	1.00	2.00
❑21, Sep 96, Angel in Waiting, Part 1	1.95	0.40	1.00	2.00
❑22, Oct 96, Angel in Hiding, Part 2	1.95	0.40	1.00	2.00
❑23, Oct 96, Angel in Hiding, Part 3	1.95	0.40	1.00	2.00
❑24, Dec 96, The Fall of Saint Dumas, Part 1	1.95	0.40	1.00	2.00
❑25, Jan 97, The Fall of Saint Dumas, Part 2	1.95	0.40	1.00	2.00
❑26, Feb 97, The Fall of Saint Dumas, Part 3	1.95	0.40	1.00	2.00
❑27, Mar 97, Angel Insane, Part 1	1.95	0.40	1.00	2.00
❑28, Apr 97, Angel Insane, Part 2	1.95	0.40	1.00	2.00
❑29, May 97	1.95	0.40	1.00	2.00
❑30, Jun 97, A: Ra's Al Ghul	1.95	0.40	1.00	2.00
❑31, Jul 97	1.95	0.40	1.00	2.00
❑32, Aug 97	1.95	0.40	1.00	2.00
❑33, Sep 97	1.99	0.40	1.00	2.00
❑34, Oct 97, V: Parademons, "Genesis"	1.95	0.40	1.00	2.00
❑35, Nov 97, The Angel and the Hitman, A: Hitman	1.95	0.40	1.00	2.00
❑36, Dec 97, Azrael and Bane, A: Batman; V: Bane, Face cover	1.95	0.40	1.00	2.00
❑37, Jan 98, V: Bane	1.95	0.40	1.00	2.00
❑38, Feb 98, V: Bane	1.95	0.40	1.00	2.00
❑39, Mar 98, V: Bane	1.95	0.40	1.00	2.00
❑40, Apr 98, Cataclysm, Part 4, V: Bane, continues in Detective Comics #720	1.95	0.40	1.00	2.00
❑41	1.99	0.40	1.00	2.00
❑42	1.99	0.40	1.00	2.00
❑43	1.99	0.40	1.00	2.00
❑44	1.99	0.40	1.00	2.00
❑45, Sep 98, V: Deathstroke	2.25	0.40	1.00	2.00
❑46	1.99	0.40	1.00	2.00
❑47, Dec 98, D: Senator Halivan; 1: Nicholas Scratch, Title changes to "Azrael: Agent of the Bat"; "Road to No Man's Land"; flip-book with Batman: Shadow of the Bat #80 (true title)	3.95	0.80	2.00	4.00
❑47/LE, Series name changes to "Azrael: Agent of the Bat"	15.95	3.19	7.97	15.95
❑48, Jan 99, Road to No Man's Land, V: Nicholas Scratch, "Road to No Man's Land"; Batman cameo	2.25	0.45	1.13	2.25
❑49, Feb 99, A: Nicholas Scratch; A: Batman, "Road to No Man's Land"	2.25	0.45	1.13	2.25
❑50, Mar 99, A: Batman, "No Man's Land"	2.25	0.45	1.13	2.25
❑51, Apr 99, A: Nicholas Scratch, "No Man's Land"; new costume	2.25	0.45	1.13	2.25
❑52, May 99, "No Man's Land"	2.25	0.45	1.13	2.25
❑53, Jun 99, Jellybean Deathtrap, V: Joker, "No Man's Land"	2.25	0.45	1.13	2.25
❑54, Jul 99, Step into the Light, A: Oracle, "No Man's Land"	2.25	0.45	1.13	2.25
❑55, Aug 99, Misery Dance, "No Man's Land"	2.25	0.45	1.13	2.25
❑56, Sep 99, The Night Foretold!, A: Batgirl, "No Man's Land"	2.25	0.45	1.13	2.25
❑57, Oct 99, Scratched Out!, A: Batgirl, "No Man's Land"	2.25	0.45	1.13	2.25
❑58, Nov 99, Ghosts, A: Saint Dumas, "No Man's Land"; Day of Judgment	2.25	0.45	1.13	2.25
❑59, Dec 99, Pilgrim's Return, No Man's Land	2.25	0.45	1.13	2.25
❑60, Jan 00, Evacuation, No Man's Land	2.25	0.45	1.13	2.25
❑61, Feb 00	2.25	0.45	1.13	2.25
❑62, Mar 00	2.25	0.45	1.13	2.25
❑63, Apr 00	2.25	0.45	1.13	2.25
❑64, May 00, Fugitive	2.25	0.45	1.13	2.25
❑65, Jun 00, The Witness	2.25	0.45	1.13	2.25
❑66, Jul 00, New Order	2.25	0.45	1.13	2.25
❑67, Aug 00, Maternal Instinct	2.25	0.45	1.13	2.25
❑68, Sep 00, Mirage	2.25	0.45	1.13	2.25
❑69, Oct 00, The Pursuit	2.50	0.50	1.25	2.50
❑70, Nov 00, Cry for Atonement	2.50	0.50	1.25	2.50
❑71, Dec 00, Brothers	2.50	0.50	1.25	2.50
❑72, Jan 01, Hell & Back	2.50	0.50	1.25	2.50
❑73, Feb 01, Losses, Part 1	2.50	0.50	1.25	2.50
❑74, Mar 01, Losses, Part 2	2.50	0.50	1.25	2.50
❑75, Apr 01, Losses, Part 3, Giant-size	3.95	0.79	1.98	3.95
❑76, May 01, There Shall Be a Beginning	2.50	0.50	1.25	2.50
❑77, Jun 01, Poison Road	2.50	0.50	1.25	2.50
❑78	2.50	0.50	1.25	2.50
❑79	2.50	0.50	1.25	2.50
❑80	2.50	0.50	1.25	2.50
❑1000000, Nov 98, Angel Wings, becomes Azrael: Agent of the Bat	2.25	0.45	1.13	2.25
❑Anl 1, 95, Year One; Requiem, Year One; 1995 Annual	3.95	0.79	1.98	3.95
❑Anl 2, 96, Legends of the Dead Earth	2.95	0.59	1.48	2.95
❑Anl 3, 97, Pulp Heroes	3.95	0.79	1.98	3.95

AZRAEL/ASH
DC

Value: Cover or less

❑1, 97 ... 4.95

AZRAEL PLUS
DC

Value: Cover or less

❑1, Dec 96, A: The Question ... 2.95

AZTEC ACE
Eclipse

	ORIG	GOOD	FINE	N-MINT
❑1, 1: Aztec Ace, Giant-size	2.25	0.50	1.25	2.50
❑2	1.50	0.40	1.00	2.00
❑3	1.50	0.40	1.00	2.00
❑4	—	0.40	1.00	2.00
❑5	—	0.40	1.00	2.00

	ORIG	GOOD	FINE	N-MINT
❑6	—	0.40	1.00	2.00
❑7	—	0.40	1.00	2.00
❑8	—	0.40	1.00	2.00
❑9	—	0.40	1.00	2.00
❑10	—	0.40	1.00	2.00
❑11	—	0.40	1.00	2.00
❑12	—	0.40	1.00	2.00
❑13	—	0.40	1.00	2.00
❑14	—	0.40	1.00	2.00
❑15	—	0.40	1.00	2.00

AZTEC ANTHROPOMORPHIC AMAZONS
ANTARCTIC

Value: Cover or less

❑1, Mar 94, b&w 2.75

AZTEC OF THE CITY
EL SALTO

Value: Cover or less

❑1, Nacimiento, 1: Aztec 2.25

AZTEC OF THE CITY (VOL. 2)
EL SALTO

Value: Cover or less

❑1 .... 2.50

❑2, May 96, Enter: La Llorna .. 2.50

While many collectors would consider *Azrael: Agent of the Bat* #47 to be the issue's correct title, it's really *Batman: Shadow of the Bat* #80, as determined by the UPC code.

AZTEK: THE ULTIMATE MAN
DC

Value: Cover or less

❑1, Aug 96, A town called Vanity 1.75
❑2, Sep 96, V: Major Force; A: Green Lantern 1.75
❑3, Oct 96, The Girl Who Was Death 1.75
❑4, Nov 96, The Lizard King ... 1.75
❑5, Dec 96, Deathtrap 1.75
❑6, Jan 97, A Child's Garden of Sinister Capers?, V: Joker ... 1.75
❑7, Feb 97, A: Batman 1.75
❑8, Mar 97, Invisible Hand 1.75
❑9, Apr 97, V: Parasite 1.75
❑10, May 97, A: JLA 1.75

B

BABE
DARK HORSE

Value: Cover or less

❑1, Jul 94, JBy, JBy (w), It Was a Dark and Stormy Night… 2.50
❑2, Aug 94, JBy, JBy (w) 2.50
❑3, Sep 94, JBy, JBy (w), Mr. Longshadow Regrets...; Prototykes: Into the Web, 1: The Prototykes 2.50
❑4, Oct 94, JBy, JBy (w), Meeting Adjourned 2.50

BABE 2
DARK HORSE

Value: Cover or less

❑1, Mar 95, JBy, JBy (w), Pipe Schemes 2.50
❑2, Apr 95, JBy, JBy (w) 2.50

BABES OF BROADWAY
BROADWAY

Value: Cover or less

❑1, May 96, pin-ups and previews of upcoming Broadway series 2.95

BABEWATCH
EXPRESS

Value: Cover or less

❑1, 95, b&w 2.50
❑1/A, 95 .... 2.95
❑1/SC, 95 .... 2.95

BABY ANGEL X
BRAINSTORM

Value: Cover or less

❑1, Nov, b&w; adult 2.95

BABY HUEY (VOL. 2)
HARVEY

Value: Cover or less

❑1 .... 1.25
❑2 .... 1.25
❑3 .... 1.25
❑4 .... 1.25
❑5, Nov 92, The Baby Sitter; Stumbo the Giant Baby 1.25
❑6 .... 1.25
❑7 .... 1.25
❑8 .... 1.50
❑9 .... 1.50

BABY HUEY DIGEST
HARVEY

Value: Cover or less

❑1 .... 1.75

BABY HUEY IN 3-D
BLACKTHORNE

Value: Cover or less

❑1 .... 2.50

BABYLON 5
DC

	ORIG	GOOD	FINE	N-MINT
❑1, Jan 95	1.95	2.00	5.00	10.00
❑2, Feb 95	1.95	1.60	4.00	8.00
❑3, Mar 95	1.95	1.20	3.00	6.00
❑4, Apr 95	1.95	1.20	3.00	6.00
❑5, Jun 95, Shadows Past and Present, Part 1	2.50	0.80	2.00	4.00
❑6, Jul 95, Shadows Past and Present, Part 2	2.50	0.80	2.00	4.00
❑7, Aug 95	2.50	0.80	2.00	4.00
❑8, Sep 95	2.50	0.70	1.75	3.50
❑9, Oct 95	2.50	0.70	1.75	3.50
❑10, Nov 95	2.50	0.70	1.75	3.50
❑11, Dec 95, Final Issue	2.50	0.70	1.75	3.50

BABYLON 5: IN VALEN'S NAME
DC

	ORIG	GOOD	FINE	N-MINT
❑1, Mar 98	2.50	0.80	2.00	4.00
❑2, Apr 98	2.50	0.60	1.50	3.00
❑3, May 98	2.50	0.60	1.50	3.00

BABYLON CRUSH
BONEYARD

Value: Cover or less

❑1, May 95, cardstock cover, b&w 2.95
❑2, Jul 95, Epitaphs, cardstock cover, b&w 2.95
❑3, Oct 95, b&w 2.95
❑4 .... 2.95
❑Xmas 1, Jan 98, A Present for Santa; Palm Leaf Christmas 2.95

BABY'S FIRST DEADPOOL BOOK
MARVEL

Value: Cover or less

❑1, Dec 98, Dresspool (activity); Make Way for Deadpool! (text), children's-book style stories 2.99

BABY, YOU'RE REALLY SOMETHING!
FANTAGRAPHICS

Value: Cover or less

❑1, FF, b&w; Reprint 2.50

BACCHUS (EDDIE CAMPBELL'S...)
EDDIE CAMPBELL

	ORIG	GOOD	FINE	N-MINT
❑1, May 99, The Face on the Bar-Room Floor	2.95	1.00	2.50	5.00
❑1-2	2.95	0.60	1.50	3.00
❑2	2.95	0.80	2.00	4.00
❑3	2.95	0.80	2.00	4.00
❑4	2.95	0.70	1.75	3.50
❑5	2.95	0.70	1.75	3.50
❑6	2.95	0.60	1.50	3.00
❑7	2.95	0.60	1.50	3.00
❑8	2.95	0.60	1.50	3.00
❑9, Jan 00, The Landscape of Sex	2.95	0.60	1.50	3.00
❑10	2.95	0.60	1.50	3.00
❑11	2.95	0.60	1.50	3.00
❑12	2.95	0.60	1.50	3.00
❑13	2.95	0.60	1.50	3.00
❑14	2.95	0.60	1.50	3.00
❑15	2.95	0.60	1.50	3.00
❑16	2.95	0.60	1.50	3.00
❑17	2.95	0.60	1.50	3.00
❑18, Oct 96, b&w	2.95	0.60	1.50	3.00
❑19	2.95	0.60	1.50	3.00
❑20	2.95	0.60	1.50	3.00
❑21	2.95	0.59	1.48	2.95
❑22	2.95	0.59	1.48	2.95
❑23	2.95	0.59	1.48	2.95
❑24	2.95	0.59	1.48	2.95
❑25	2.95	0.59	1.48	2.95
❑26	2.95	0.59	1.48	2.95
❑27	2.95	0.59	1.48	2.95
❑28	2.95	0.59	1.48	2.95
❑29	2.95	0.59	1.48	2.95
❑30	2.95	0.59	1.48	2.95
❑31	2.95	0.59	1.48	2.95
❑32	2.95	0.59	1.48	2.95
❑33	2.95	0.59	1.48	2.95
❑34	2.95	0.59	1.48	2.95
❑35	2.95	0.59	1.48	2.95
❑36	2.95	0.59	1.48	2.95
❑37	2.95	0.59	1.48	2.95
❑38	2.95	0.59	1.48	2.95
❑39	2.95	0.59	1.48	2.95
❑40	2.95	0.59	1.48	2.95
❑41	2.95	0.59	1.48	2.95
❑42	2.95	0.59	1.48	2.95

BACCHUS (HARRIER)
Harrier

	ORIG	GOOD	FINE	N-MINT
❑1, The Crazy Bastard	1.95	1.00	2.50	5.00
❑2	1.95	0.80	2.00	4.00

BACCHUS COLOR SPECIAL
Dark Horse

	ORIG	GOOD	FINE	N-MINT
❑1, Apr 95, nn; One-Shot	2.95	0.65	1.63	3.25

BACK DOWN THE LINE
Eclipse
Value: Cover or less

❑1, nn 8.95

BACKLASH
Image
Value: Cover or less

❑1, Nov 94, 1: Taboo, Double cover 1.95
❑2, Dec 94 1.95
❑3, Jan 95 2.50
❑4, Feb 95 2.50
❑5, Feb 95 2.50
❑6, Mar 95 2.50
❑7, Apr 95, 1: Crimson 2.50
❑8, May 95, WildStorm Rising, Part 8, bound-in trading cards 2.50
❑9, Jun 95 2.50
❑10, Jul 95, indicia says Jul, cover says Aug 2.50
❑11, Aug 95 2.50
❑12, Sep 95, 1: Mahkinot; 1: Serge, indicia says Sep, cover says Oct 2.95
❑13, Nov 95 2.50
❑14, Nov 95, indicia says Nov, cover says Dec 2.50
❑15, Dec 95, indicia says Dec, cover says Jan 2.50
❑16, Jan 96, indicia says Jan, cover says Feb 2.50
❑17, Feb 96 2.50
❑18, Mar 96 2.50
❑19, Apr 96, Fire from Heaven, Part 2 2.50
❑20, May 96, Fire from Heaven, Part 10 2.50
❑21, Jun 96 2.50
❑22, Jul 96 2.50
❑23, Aug 96 2.50
❑24, Sep 96, 1: Omni 2.50
❑25, Nov 96, 1: Gramalkin, Giant-size 3.95
❑26, Nov 96 2.50
❑27, Dec 96 2.50
❑28, Jan 97 2.50
❑29, Feb 97 2.50
❑30, Mar 97 2.50
❑31, Apr 97 2.50
❑32, May 97, Final Issue 2.50

BACKLASH & TABOO'S AFRICAN HOLIDAY
DC
Value: Cover or less

❑1, Sep 99 5.95

BACKLASH/SPIDER-MAN
Image
Value: Cover or less

❑1, Aug 96 2.50
❑1/A, Aug 96, crossover with Marvel, cover says Jul, indicia says Aug 2.50
❑1/B, Aug 96, alternate cover, crossover with Marvel, cover says Jul, indicia says Aug 2.50
❑2, Oct 96, crossover with Marvel 2.50

BACKPACK MARVELS: AVENGERS
Marvel
Value: Cover or less

❑1, Jan 01, GD; JBy, On the Matter of Heroes; Honor Thy Father... 6.95

BACKPACK MARVELS: X-MEN
Marvel
Value: Cover or less

❑1 6.95
❑2, Nov 00, PS, Romances; 'Til Death, Reprints Uncanny X-Men #167-173 6.95

BACK TO THE FUTURE
Harvey

	ORIG	GOOD	FINE	N-MINT
❑1, Sep 91, The Gang's All Here	1.25	0.30	0.75	1.50
❑2, Nov 91	1.25	0.30	0.75	1.50
❑3	1.25	0.30	0.75	1.50
❑4	1.25	0.30	0.75	1.50
❑SE 1, Universal Studios-Florida giveaway.	—	0.20	0.50	1.00

BACK TO THE FUTURE: FORWARD TO THE FUTURE
Harvey
Value: Cover or less

❑1, Oct 92 1.50
❑2, Nov 92 1.50
❑3, Jan 93 1.50

BAD APPLES
High Impact
Value: Cover or less

❑1 2.95

BAD ART COLLECTION, THE
Slave Labor
Value: Cover or less

❑1, Apr 96, nn; Oversized 1.95

BADAXE
Adventure
Value: Cover or less

❑1 2.25
❑2 2.25
❑3 2.25

BAD BOY
Oni Press
Value: Cover or less

❑1, Dec 97, nn; oversized one-shot 4.95

BAD COMICS
Cat-Head
Value: Cover or less

❑1, b&w 2.75

BAD COMPANY
Fleetway
Value: Cover or less

❑1, War Zombies, O: Bad Company 1.50
❑2 1.50
❑3 1.50
❑4 1.50
❑5 1.50
❑6 1.50
❑7 1.50
❑8 1.50
❑9 1.50
❑10 1.50
❑11 1.50
❑12 1.50
❑13 1.50
❑14 1.50
❑15 1.50
❑16 1.75
❑17 1.75
❑18 1.75
❑19, The Mean Area; Tharg's Future Shocks: The Perfect Wife?, Final Issue 1.75

BADE BIKER & ORSON
Mirage
Value: Cover or less

❑1, Nov 86 1.50
❑2, Jan 87 1.50
❑3, Mar 87 1.50
❑4, Jun 87 1.50

BAD EGGS, THE
Acclaim
Value: Cover or less

❑1, Jun 96, DP, BL (w), Sex, Lie and Vertebrates 2.95
❑2, Jul 96 2.95
❑3, Aug 96 2.95
❑4, Sep 96 2.95
❑5, Sep 96, That Dirty Yellow Mustard, Part 1, cover says Oct, indicia says Sep 2.95
❑6, Nov 96, That Dirty Yellow Mustard, Part 2, shoplifting instructions on cover 2.95
❑7, Dec 96, That Dirty Yellow Mustard, Part 3 2.95
❑8, Jan 97, DP, BL (w), That Dirty Yellow Mustard, Part 4; Much Do-Do About Nothing, A: Fabian Nicieza, Ivar, Turok 2.95

BADGE
Vanguard
Value: Cover or less

❑1, 81 2.95

BADGER
Capital

	ORIG	GOOD	FINE	N-MINT
❑1, Oct 83, SR, 1: Ham; 1: Badger	1.75	0.80	2.00	4.00
❑2, Feb 84	1.75	0.60	1.50	3.00
❑3, Mar 84	1.75	0.60	1.50	3.00
❑4, Apr 84	1.75	0.60	1.50	3.00
❑5, May 85, First Comics begins publishing	2.50	0.60	1.50	3.00
❑6, Jul 85	2.50	0.50	1.25	2.50
❑7, Sep 85	2.50	0.50	1.25	2.50
❑8, Nov 85	2.50	0.50	1.25	2.50
❑9, Jan 86	2.50	0.50	1.25	2.50
❑10, Mar 86	2.50	0.50	1.25	2.50
❑11, May 86	1.75	0.40	1.00	2.00
❑12, Jun 86	1.75	0.40	1.00	2.00
❑13, Jul 86	1.75	0.40	1.00	2.00
❑14, Aug 86	1.75	0.40	1.00	2.00
❑15, Sep 86	1.75	0.40	1.00	2.00
❑16, Oct 86	1.75	0.40	1.00	2.00
❑17, Nov 86	1.75	0.40	1.00	2.00
❑18, Dec 86	1.75	0.40	1.00	2.00
❑19, Jan 87	1.75	0.40	1.00	2.00
❑20, Feb 87	1.75	0.40	1.00	2.00
❑21, Mar 87	1.75	0.40	1.00	2.00
❑22, Apr 87	1.75	0.40	1.00	2.00
❑23, May 87	1.75	0.40	1.00	2.00
❑24, Jun 87	1.75	0.40	1.00	2.00
❑25, Jul 87	1.75	0.40	1.00	2.00
❑26, Aug 87, Roach Wrangler	1.75	0.40	1.00	2.00
❑27, Sep 87, Roach Wrangler	1.75	0.40	1.00	2.00
❑28, Oct 87	1.75	0.40	1.00	2.00
❑29, Nov 87	1.75	0.40	1.00	2.00
❑30, Dec 87	1.75	0.40	1.00	2.00
❑31, Jan 88	1.75	0.40	1.00	2.00
❑32, Feb 88	1.75	0.40	1.00	2.00
❑33, Mar 88	1.75	0.40	1.00	2.00
❑34, Apr 88	1.75	0.40	1.00	2.00
❑35, May 88	1.75	0.40	1.00	2.00
❑36, Jun 88	1.75	0.40	1.00	2.00
❑37, Jul 88	1.75	0.40	1.00	2.00
❑38, Aug 88	1.75	0.40	1.00	2.00
❑39, Sep 88	1.75	0.40	1.00	2.00
❑40, Oct 88	1.75	0.40	1.00	2.00
❑41, Nov 88	1.95	0.40	1.00	2.00
❑42, Dec 88	1.95	0.40	1.00	2.00
❑43, Jan 89	1.95	0.40	1.00	2.00
❑44, Feb 89, 1: Steve Marmel ("The Hilariator"-in comics)	1.95	0.40	1.00	2.00
❑45, Mar 89	1.95	0.40	1.00	2.00
❑46, Apr 89	1.95	0.40	1.00	2.00
❑47, May 89	1.95	0.40	1.00	2.00
❑48, Jun 89	1.95	0.40	1.00	2.00
❑49, Jul 89	1.95	0.40	1.00	2.00
❑50, Aug 89, Double-size	3.95	0.79	1.98	3.95
❑51, Sep 89	1.95	0.40	1.00	2.00
❑52, Oct 89	1.95	0.60	1.50	3.00
❑53, Nov 89	1.95	0.60	1.50	3.00
❑54, Dec 89	1.95	0.60	1.50	3.00
❑55, Jan 90	1.95	0.40	1.00	2.00

	ORIG	GOOD	FINE	N-MINT
❑56, Feb 90	1.95	0.40	1.00	2.00
❑57, Mar 90	1.95	0.40	1.00	2.00
❑58, Apr 90	1.95	0.40	1.00	2.00
❑59, May 90	1.95	0.40	1.00	2.00
❑60, Jun 90	1.95	0.40	1.00	2.00
❑61, Jul 90	1.95	0.40	1.00	2.00
❑62, Aug 90	1.95	0.40	1.00	2.00
❑63, Sep 90	1.95	0.40	1.00	2.00
❑64, Oct 90	2.25	0.45	1.13	2.25
❑65, Nov 90	2.25	0.45	1.13	2.25
❑66, Dec 90	2.25	0.45	1.13	2.25
❑67, Jan 91	2.25	0.45	1.13	2.25
❑68, Feb 91	2.25	0.45	1.13	2.25
❑69, Mar 91	2.25	0.45	1.13	2.25
❑70, Apr 91, Final Issue	2.25	0.45	1.13	2.25

BADGER (VOL. 2)
FIRST

Value: Cover or less

❑1, May 91, Badger Bedlam, O: Badger, Badger Bedlam 4.95

BADGER (VOL. 3)
IMAGE

Value: Cover or less

❑1, May 97, b&w; indicia says #78 in series 2.95
❑2, Jun 97, b&w; indicia says #79 in series 2.95
❑3, Jul 97, b&w; indicia says #80 in series 2.95
❑4, Aug 97, b&w; indicia says #81 in series 2.95
❑5, Sep 97, b&w; indicia says #82 in series 2.95
❑6, Oct 97, The Prime Minister of Klactoveedesteen, b&w; indicia says #83 in series 2.95
❑7, Nov 97, b&w; indicia says #84 in series 2.95
❑8, Dec 97, The Root of All Evil, b&w; indicia says #85 in series 2.95
❑9, Jan 98, Vapor Trail, b&w; indicia says #86 in series 2.95
❑10, Feb 98, Tuesday Ruby, b&w; indicia says #87 in series 2.95
❑11, Apr 98, The Crowded Skies, b&w; indicia says #88 in series 2.95

BADGER GOES BERSERK
FIRST

	ORIG	GOOD	FINE	N-MINT
❑1, Sep 89	1.95	0.40	1.00	2.00
❑2, Oct 89	1.95	0.40	1.00	2.00
❑3, Nov 89	1.95	0.40	1.00	2.00
❑4, Dec 89	1.95	0.40	1.00	2.00

BADGER: SHATTERED MIRROR
DARK HORSE

Value: Cover or less

❑1, Jul 94 ...... 2.50
❑2, Aug 94 ...... 2.50
❑3, Sep 94 ...... 2.50
❑4, Oct 94 ...... 2.50

BADGER: ZEN POP FUNNY-ANIMAL VERSION
DARK HORSE

Value: Cover or less

❑1, Jul 94 ...... 2.50
❑2, Aug 94 ...... 2.50

BAD GIRLS (BILL WARD'S...)
FORBIDDEN FRUIT

Value: Cover or less

❑1 ...... 1.50

BAD GIRLS OF BLACKOUT
BLACKOUT

Value: Cover or less

❑0, 95, Lady Vampire; Extremes Of Violet 3.50
❑1, 95 ...... 3.50
❑Anl 1 ...... 3.50

BAD HAIR DAY
SLAB-O-CONCRETE

	ORIG	GOOD	FINE	N-MINT
❑1, Postcard Comic	—	0.20	0.50	1.00

BAD KITTY
CHAOS

Value: Cover or less

❑1, Feb 01 ...... 2.99
❑2, Mar 01 ...... 2.99
❑3, Apr 01 ...... 2.99

BADLANDS
DARK HORSE

	ORIG	GOOD	FINE	N-MINT
❑1, Jul 91	2.25	0.50	1.25	2.50
❑2	2.25	0.50	1.25	2.50
❑3	2.25	0.50	1.25	2.50
❑4	2.25	0.50	1.25	2.50
❑5	2.25	0.50	1.25	2.50
❑6	2.25	0.50	1.25	2.50

BAD MEAT
FANTAGRAPHICS

Value: Cover or less

❑1, Jul 91, b&w; adult 2.25
❑2, adult 2.75

BAD NEWS
FANTAGRAPHICS

Value: Cover or less

❑3, b&w 3.50

BADROCK
IMAGE

Value: Cover or less

❑1/A, Mar 95, RL; BL, Todd McFarlane inks on cover 1.75
❑1/B, Mar 95, RL, Stephen Platt inks on cover 1.75
❑1/C, Mar 95, RL; BL, Dan Fraga inks on cover 1.75
❑2 ...... 1.75
❑3 ...... 1.75
❑Anl 1, Jul 95 ...... 2.95

The Image and Marvel universes crossed over in 1996 with *Backlash/Spider-Man.*

BADROCK & COMPANY
IMAGE

Value: Cover or less

❑1, Sep 94, KG (w) 2.50
❑2, Oct 94, KG (w) 2.50
❑3, Nov 94, KG (w) 2.50
❑4, Dec 94, KG (w) 2.50
❑5, Jan 95, KG (w) 2.50
❑6, Oct 95, KG (w), cover says Feb 95, indicia says Oct 94 ...... 2.50
❑SE 1, Sep 94, San Diego Comic-Con edition 2.50

BADROCK/WOLVERINE
IMAGE

Value: Cover or less

❑1/A, Jun 96, Savage 4.95
❑1/B, Jun 96, Savage 4.95
❑1/C, Jun 96, Savage 4.95
❑1/D, Jun 96, Savage 4.95

BAKER STREET
CALIBER

	ORIG	GOOD	FINE	N-MINT
❑1, Mar 89	1.95	0.50	1.25	2.50
❑2	1.95	0.50	1.25	2.50
❑3	1.95	0.50	1.25	2.50
❑4	1.95	0.50	1.25	2.50
❑5	2.50	0.50	1.25	2.50
❑6	2.50	0.50	1.25	2.50
❑7	2.50	0.50	1.25	2.50
❑8	2.50	0.50	1.25	2.50
❑9	2.50	0.50	1.25	2.50
❑10	2.50	0.50	1.25	2.50

BAKER STREET GRAFFITI
CALIBER

Value: Cover or less

❑1, b&w 2.50

BAKER STREET SKETCHBOOK
CALIBER

Value: Cover or less

❑1 ...... 3.95

BALANCE OF POWER
MU PRESS

	ORIG	GOOD	FINE	N-MINT
❑1, b&w	2.00	0.50	1.25	2.50
❑2	2.25	0.50	1.25	2.50
❑3, Mar 91	2.50	0.50	1.25	2.50
❑4, Jul 91	2.50	0.50	1.25	2.50

BALDER THE BRAVE
MARVEL

	ORIG	GOOD	FINE	N-MINT
❑1, Nov 85, SB, The Sword Of Prey	0.75	0.20	0.50	1.00
❑2, Jan 86	0.75	0.20	0.50	1.00
❑3, Mar 86	0.75	0.20	0.50	1.00
❑4, May 86	0.75	0.20	0.50	1.00

BALLAD OF HALO JONES, THE
FLEETWAY

	ORIG	GOOD	FINE	N-MINT
❑1, AMo (w), Tharg's Future Shocks: Sunburn, 1: Halo Jones, Reprints The Ballad of Halo Jones from 2000 A.D.	1.25	0.30	0.75	1.50
❑2, AMo (w), Fleurs Du Mall	1.25	0.30	0.75	1.50
❑3, AMo (w), A Postcard From Pluto	1.25	0.30	0.75	1.50
❑4, AMo (w)	1.25	0.30	0.75	1.50
❑5, AMo (w)	1.25	0.30	0.75	1.50
❑6, AMo (w)	1.25	0.30	0.75	1.50
❑7, AMo (w), The Last Dance; Anderson Division	1.25	0.30	0.75	1.50
❑8, AMo (w), Tarantula Rising; Halfway to Paradise	1.25	0.30	0.75	1.50
❑9, AMo (w)	1.25	0.30	0.75	1.50
❑10, AMo (w), Armies of the Night; Sooner or Later	1.25	0.30	0.75	1.50
❑11, AMo (w)	1.50	0.30	0.75	1.50
❑12, AMo (w), Final Issue	1.50	0.30	0.75	1.50

BALLAD OF UTOPIA, THE
BLACK DAZE

Value: Cover or less

❑1, Aug 98 ...... 2.95
❑2, Sep 99 ...... 2.95
❑3, Nov 99 ...... 2.95

BALL AND CHAIN
DC

Value: Cover or less

❑1, Nov 99 ...... 2.50
❑2, Dec 99, Marital Law 2.50
❑3, Jan 00, Love, Honore, and-Say What?! 2.50
❑4, Feb 00 ...... 2.50

	ORIG	GOOD	FINE	N-MINT

BALLISTIC
IMAGE

Value: Cover or less

❑1, Sep 95, A: Wetworks........ 2.50

❑2, Oct 95 .... 2.50

❑3, Nov 95 .... 2.50

BALLISTIC ACTION
IMAGE

Value: Cover or less

❑1, May 96, pin-ups 2.95

BALLISTIC IMAGERY
IMAGE

Value: Cover or less

❑1, Jan 96, Hellcop; True Stories of Cyberforce: Heatwave, Anthology.......................... 2.50

❑2... 2.50

BALLISTIC STUDIOS SWIMSUIT SPECIAL
IMAGE

Value: Cover or less

❑1, May 95, pin-ups 2.95

BALLISTIC/WOLVERINE
TOP COW

	ORIG	GOOD	FINE	N-MINT
❑1, Feb 97, Devil's Reign, Part 4, crossover with Marvel, continues in Wolverine/ Witchblade	2.95	0.70	1.75	3.50

BALLOONATIKS, THE
BEST

Value: Cover or less

❑1... 2.50

BAMBI AND HER FRIENDS
FRIENDLY

	ORIG	GOOD	FINE	N-MINT
❑1, Jan 91	2.50	0.50	1.25	2.50
❑2, Feb 91	2.50	0.50	1.25	2.50
❑3, Mar 91	2.50	0.59	1.48	2.95
❑4, Apr 91	2.50	0.59	1.48	2.95
❑5, May 91	2.50	0.59	1.48	2.95
❑6, Jun 91	2.95	0.59	1.48	2.95
❑7, Jul 91	2.95	0.59	1.48	2.95
❑8, Aug 91	2.95	0.59	1.48	2.95
❑9, Sep 91	2.95	0.59	1.48	2.95

BAMBI IN HEAT
FRIENDLY

Value: Cover or less

❑1... 2.95

❑2... 2.95

❑3, Bambi be Good!; When Larry Met Betty............................ 2.95

BAMBI THE HUNTER
FRIENDLY

Value: Cover or less

❑1... 2.95

❑2... 2.95

❑3... 2.95

❑4... 2.95

❑5... 2.95

BANANA SPLITS, THE (HANNA BARBERA...)
GOLD KEY

	ORIG	GOOD	FINE	N-MINT
❑1, Jun 69, The Loan Rangers; River Rock, 1: Bingo (in comics); 1: Drooper (in comics); 1: Fleegle (in comics); 1: Snorky (in comics)	0.15	6.00	15.00	30.00
❑2, Apr 70	0.15	3.00	7.50	15.00
❑3, Jul 70	0.15	2.40	6.00	12.00
❑4	0.15	2.40	6.00	12.00
❑5	0.15	2.40	6.00	12.00
❑6	0.15	2.00	5.00	10.00
❑7	0.15	2.00	5.00	10.00
❑8	0.15	2.00	5.00	10.00

BANDY MAN, THE
CALIBER

	ORIG	GOOD	FINE	N-MINT
❑1	2.95	0.70	1.75	3.50
❑2, Includes notes by Lee Schlessinger, preview of Level X; Origin of Bandy Man	2.95	0.65	1.63	3.25

BANG GANG
FANTAGRAPHICS

Value: Cover or less

❑1, b&w; adult......................... 2.50

BANGS AND THE GANG
SHHWINNG

Value: Cover or less

❑1, Feb 94, b&w; adult............ 2.95

BAOH
VIZ

	ORIG	GOOD	FINE	N-MINT
❑1, The Ultimate Weapons	2.95	0.80	2.00	4.00
❑2	2.95	0.70	1.75	3.50
❑3	2.95	0.70	1.75	3.50
❑4	2.95	0.65	1.63	3.25
❑5	2.95	0.65	1.63	3.25
❑6	2.95	0.65	1.63	3.25
❑7	2.95	0.65	1.63	3.25
❑8	2.95	0.65	1.63	3.25

BARABBAS
SLAVE LABOR

Value: Cover or less

❑1, Aug 86, Tempting Fate and Chasing Ghosts 1.50

❑2, Nov 85 .... 1.50

BARBARIAN COMICS
CALIFORNIA

	ORIG	GOOD	FINE	N-MINT
❑1	0.50	0.60	1.50	3.00
❑2, Hall of Kings; Hameka	0.50	0.50	1.25	2.50

BARBARIANS
ATLAS

	ORIG	GOOD	FINE	N-MINT
❑1, Jun 75, The Mountain Of Mutants, 1: Iron-jaw; O: Andrax	0.25	0.30	0.75	1.50

BARBARIANS (AVALON)
AVALON

Value: Cover or less

❑1, WH; JSa, The Guardian Spiders!; The Great Battles of History: Shiraz!......................... 2.95

❑2... 2.95

BARBARIANS AND BEAUTIES
AC

Value: Cover or less

❑1, 90...................................... 2.75

BARBARIC TALES
PYRAMID

	ORIG	GOOD	FINE	N-MINT
❑1, The Warriors Three; Damlog	1.50	0.34	0.85	1.70
❑2	1.50	0.34	0.85	1.70

BARBARIENNE (FANTAGRAPHICS)
FANTAGRAPHICS

Value: Cover or less

❑2, b&w; adult......................... 2.50

❑3, b&w; adult......................... 2.50

BARBARIENNE (HARRIER)
HARRIER

	ORIG	GOOD	FINE	N-MINT
❑1, Mar 87, Memree: The Girl in the Iron Gag	1.95	0.40	1.00	2.00
❑2	1.95	0.40	1.00	2.00
❑3	1.95	0.40	1.00	2.00
❑4	1.95	0.40	1.00	2.00
❑5	1.95	0.40	1.00	2.00
❑6, V: Cuirass	1.95	0.40	1.00	2.00
❑7, V: Cuirass	1.95	0.40	1.00	2.00
❑8, V: Cuirass	1.95	0.40	1.00	2.00

BARBIE
MARVEL

	ORIG	GOOD	FINE	N-MINT
❑1, Jan 91, The Fashion Show Must Go On; Dirty Dancing, "pink card"	1.00	1.00	2.50	5.00
❑1/A, Jan 91, door hanger	1.00	1.00	2.50	5.00
❑1/B, Jan 91, The Fashion Show Must Go On; Dirty Dancing, membership card	1.00	1.00	2.50	5.00
❑2, Feb 91, Surf 'n' Turf; The Co-Star	1.00	0.60	1.50	3.00
❑3, Mar 91, Ice Capades; Starry, Starry Night	1.00	0.50	1.25	2.50
❑4, Apr 91	1.00	0.50	1.25	2.50
❑5, May 91, Pleasure Cruise; Safety First	1.00	0.50	1.25	2.50
❑6, Jun 91, Horse Cents; Craft Shop	1.00	0.40	1.00	2.00
❑7, Jul 91, Oui, Oui, C'est Paris!; Bon Voyage	1.00	0.40	1.00	2.00
❑8, Aug 91	1.00	0.40	1.00	2.00
❑9, Sep 91	1.00	0.40	1.00	2.00
❑10, Oct 91	1.00	0.40	1.00	2.00
❑11, Nov 91	1.00	0.40	1.00	2.00
❑12, Dec 91	1.00	0.40	1.00	2.00
❑13, Jan 92	1.00	0.40	1.00	2.00
❑14, Feb 92	1.25	0.40	1.00	2.00
❑15, Mar 92	1.25	0.40	1.00	2.00
❑16, Apr 92	1.25	0.40	1.00	2.00
❑17, May 92	1.25	0.40	1.00	2.00
❑18, Jun 92	1.25	0.40	1.00	2.00
❑19, Jul 92	1.25	0.40	1.00	2.00
❑20, Aug 92	1.25	0.40	1.00	2.00
❑21, Sep 92	1.25	0.40	1.00	2.00
❑22, Oct 92	1.25	0.40	1.00	2.00
❑23, Nov 92	1.25	0.40	1.00	2.00
❑24, Dec 92	1.25	0.40	1.00	2.00
❑25, Jan 93	1.25	0.40	1.00	2.00
❑26, Feb 93	1.25	0.40	1.00	2.00
❑27, Mar 93	1.25	0.40	1.00	2.00
❑28, Apr 93	1.25	0.40	1.00	2.00
❑29, May 93	1.25	0.40	1.00	2.00
❑30, Jun 93	1.25	0.40	1.00	2.00
❑31, Jul 93	1.25	0.40	1.00	2.00
❑32, Aug 93	1.25	0.40	1.00	2.00
❑33, Sep 93	1.25	0.40	1.00	2.00
❑34, Oct 93, A: Teresa	1.25	0.40	1.00	2.00
❑35, Nov 93	1.25	0.40	1.00	2.00
❑36, Dec 93	1.25	0.40	1.00	2.00
❑37, Jan 94	1.25	0.40	1.00	2.00
❑38, Feb 94	1.25	0.40	1.00	2.00
❑39, Mar 94	1.25	0.40	1.00	2.00
❑40, Apr 94	1.25	0.40	1.00	2.00
❑41, May 94	1.25	0.40	1.00	2.00
❑42, Jun 94	1.50	0.40	1.00	2.00
❑43, Jul 94	1.50	0.40	1.00	2.00
❑44, Aug 94	1.50	0.40	1.00	2.00
❑45, Sep 94	1.50	0.40	1.00	2.00
❑46, Oct 94	1.50	0.40	1.00	2.00
❑47, Nov 94	1.50	0.40	1.00	2.00
❑48, Dec 94	1.50	0.40	1.00	2.00
❑49, Jan 95	1.50	0.40	1.00	2.00

	ORIG	GOOD	FINE	N-MINT
❑50, Feb 95	2.25	0.40	1.00	2.00
❑51, Mar 95	1.50	0.40	1.00	2.00
❑52, Apr 95	1.50	0.40	1.00	2.00
❑53, May 95	1.50	0.40	1.00	2.00
❑54, Jun 95	1.50	0.40	1.00	2.00
❑55, Jul 95	1.50	0.40	1.00	2.00
❑56, Aug 95	1.50	0.40	1.00	2.00
❑57, Sep 95	1.50	0.40	1.00	2.00
❑58, Oct 95	1.50	0.40	1.00	2.00
❑59, Nov 95	1.50	0.40	1.00	2.00
❑60, Dec 95, Halloween Hero	1.50	0.40	1.00	2.00
❑61, Jan 96	1.50	0.40	1.00	2.00
❑62, Feb 96, Nutcracker Suite references	1.50	0.40	1.00	2.00
❑63, Mar 96, Catch The Courage; Raging River, Final Issue	1.50	0.40	1.00	2.00

BARBIE FASHION
MARVEL

	ORIG	GOOD	FINE	N-MINT
❑1, Jan 91, Fall Fashion Issue; Be a Barbie Jewelry Designer, membership card	1.00	1.00	2.50	5.00
❑1/A, Jan 91, Fall Fashion Issue; Be a Barbie Jewelry Designer, doorknob hanger	1.00	1.00	2.50	5.00
❑2, Feb 91	1.00	0.60	1.50	3.00
❑3, Mar 91	1.00	0.50	1.25	2.50
❑4, Apr 91	1.00	0.50	1.25	2.50
❑5, May 91, Picture Perfect; Beauty Sleep	1.00	0.50	1.25	2.50
❑6, Jun 91, Ability; Be a Sport	1.00	0.40	1.00	2.00
❑7, Jul 91	1.00	0.40	1.00	2.00
❑8, Aug 91	1.00	0.40	1.00	2.00
❑9, Sep 91	1.00	0.40	1.00	2.00
❑10, Oct 91	1.00	0.40	1.00	2.00
❑11, Nov 91	1.00	0.40	1.00	2.00
❑12, Dec 91	1.00	0.40	1.00	2.00
❑13, Jan 92	1.00	0.40	1.00	2.00
❑14, Feb 92	1.00	0.40	1.00	2.00
❑15, Mar 92	1.00	0.40	1.00	2.00
❑16, Apr 92	1.00	0.40	1.00	2.00
❑17, May 92	1.00	0.40	1.00	2.00
❑18, Jun 92	1.00	0.40	1.00	2.00
❑19, Jul 92	1.00	0.40	1.00	2.00
❑20, Aug 92	1.00	0.40	1.00	2.00
❑21, Sep 92	1.00	0.40	1.00	2.00
❑22, Oct 92	1.00	0.40	1.00	2.00
❑23, Nov 92	1.00	0.40	1.00	2.00
❑24, Dec 92	1.00	0.40	1.00	2.00
❑25, Jan 93	1.00	0.40	1.00	2.00
❑26, Feb 93	1.00	0.40	1.00	2.00
❑27, Mar 93	1.00	0.40	1.00	2.00
❑28, Apr 93	1.00	0.40	1.00	2.00
❑29, May 93	1.00	0.40	1.00	2.00
❑30, Jun 93	1.00	0.40	1.00	2.00
❑31, Jul 93	1.25	0.40	1.00	2.00
❑32, Aug 93	1.25	0.40	1.00	2.00
❑33, Sep 93	1.25	0.40	1.00	2.00
❑34, Oct 93	1.25	0.40	1.00	2.00
❑35, Nov 93	1.25	0.40	1.00	2.00
❑36, Dec 93	1.25	0.40	1.00	2.00
❑37, Jan 94	1.25	0.40	1.00	2.00
❑38, Feb 94	1.25	0.40	1.00	2.00
❑39, Mar 94	1.25	0.40	1.00	2.00
❑40, Apr 94	1.25	0.40	1.00	2.00
❑41, May 94	1.25	0.40	1.00	2.00
❑42, Jun 94	1.50	0.40	1.00	2.00
❑43, Jul 94	1.50	0.40	1.00	2.00
❑44, Aug 94	1.50	0.40	1.00	2.00
❑45, Sep 94	1.50	0.40	1.00	2.00
❑46, Oct 94	1.50	0.40	1.00	2.00
❑47, Nov 94	1.50	0.40	1.00	2.00
❑48, Dec 94	1.50	0.40	1.00	2.00
❑49, Jan 95	1.50	0.40	1.00	2.00
❑50, Feb 95	2.25	0.40	1.00	2.00
❑51, Mar 95	1.50	0.40	1.00	2.00
❑52, Apr 95	1.50	0.40	1.00	2.00
❑53, May 95, Final Issue	1.50	0.40	1.00	2.00
❑54	1.50	0.40	1.00	2.00
❑55	1.50	0.40	1.00	2.00

BARBI TWINS ADVENTURES, THE
TOPPS

Value: Cover or less

❑1, Jul 95, Prelude to a Mission; Virtual Phony, Flip-book 2.50

BARB WIRE
DARK HORSE

	ORIG	GOOD	FINE	N-MINT
❑1, Apr 94, Devil in the Dark	2.00	0.50	1.25	2.50
❑2, May 94, The Wild, The Beautiful, & The Damned	2.00	0.50	1.25	2.50
❑3, Jun 94	2.00	0.50	1.25	2.50
❑4, Aug 94, Ghost in the Machine, Part 1	2.00	0.50	1.25	2.50
❑5, Sep 94, Ghost in the Machine, Part 2	2.50	0.50	1.25	2.50
❑6, Oct 94	2.50	0.50	1.25	2.50

The "actors" for a teen-age comedy comic book find themselves out of work and have to take on more "adult" roles in the Shhwinng!! Comics one-shot *Bangs and the Gang.*

© 1993 Anon Inc.

	ORIG	GOOD	FINE	N-MINT
❑7, Nov 94	2.50	0.50	1.25	2.50
❑8, Jan 95	2.50	0.50	1.25	2.50
❑9, Feb 95	2.50	0.50	1.25	2.50

BARB WIRE: ACE OF SPADES
DARK HORSE

Value: Cover or less

❑1, May 96 ...... 2.95
❑2, Jun 96 ...... 2.95
❑3, Jul 96 ...... 2.95
❑4, Sep 96 ...... 2.95

BARB WIRE COMICS MAGAZINE SPECIAL
DARK HORSE

Value: Cover or less

❑1, May 96, nn; magazine-sized adaptation of movie, b&w, poster 3.50

BARB WIRE MOVIE SPECIAL
DARK HORSE

Value: Cover or less

❑1, May 96, nn; adapts movie. 3.95

BAREFOOTZ FUNNIES
KITCHEN SINK

	ORIG	GOOD	FINE	N-MINT
❑1, The Eclipse; Hint & Run, b&w; adult	1.00	0.60	1.50	3.00
❑2, b&w; adult	0.75	0.40	1.00	2.00
❑3, Dec, b&w; adult	1.25	0.40	1.00	2.00

BAREFOOTZ THE COMIX BOOK STORIES (HOWARD CRUSE'S...)
RENEGADE

	ORIG	GOOD	FINE	N-MINT
❑1, The Boss Bug; Mamasoyboy Vumulukrishkrosh and a Pox on Your Panty Hose, A: Headrack; A: Barefootz; A: Dolly	1.70	0.50	1.25	2.50

BARF
REVOLUTIONARY

Value: Cover or less

❑1, Apr 90, b&w 1.95
❑2, Jun 90, b&w 2.50
❑3, Sep 90, b&w 2.50

BARNEY AND BETTY RUBBLE
CHARLTON

	ORIG	GOOD	FINE	N-MINT
❑1, Jan 73	—	2.80	7.00	14.00
❑2	—	1.80	4.50	9.00
❑3	—	1.20	3.00	6.00
❑4	—	1.20	3.00	6.00
❑5	—	1.20	3.00	6.00
❑6	—	1.00	2.50	5.00
❑7	—	1.00	2.50	5.00
❑8	—	1.00	2.50	5.00
❑9	—	1.00	2.50	5.00
❑10	—	1.00	2.50	5.00
❑11, Feb 75	—	1.00	2.50	5.00
❑12	—	0.80	2.00	4.00
❑13	—	0.80	2.00	4.00
❑14	—	0.80	2.00	4.00
❑15	—	0.80	2.00	4.00
❑16	—	0.80	2.00	4.00
❑17	—	0.80	2.00	4.00
❑18	—	0.80	2.00	4.00
❑19	—	0.80	2.00	4.00
❑20	—	0.80	2.00	4.00
❑21, Aug 76	0.30	0.80	2.00	4.00
❑22	—	0.80	2.00	4.00
❑23, Dec 76	—	0.80	2.00	4.00

BARNEY THE INVISIBLE TURTLE
AMAZING

Value: Cover or less

❑1, The Cold Clint of Death 1.95

BARR GIRLS, THE
ANTARCTIC

Value: Cover or less

❑1, Nov, b&w; adult 2.95

BARRON STOREY'S WATCH ANNUAL (VOL. 2)
VANGUARD

Value: Cover or less

❑1, b&w anthology, squarebound 5.95

BARRY WINDSOR-SMITH: STORYTELLER
DARK HORSE

Value: Cover or less

❑1, Oct 96 ...... 4.95
❑1/SC, Oct 96, alternate cover (logoless), cover with logos appears as back cover 4.95

	ORIG	GOOD	FINE	N-MINT
❑2, Nov 96	4.95			
❑3, Dec 96	4.95			
❑4, Jan 97	4.95			
❑5, Feb 97	4.95			
❑6, Mar 97	4.95			
❑7, May 97	4.95			
❑8, Jun 97	4.95			
❑9, Jul 97	4.95			

BAR SINISTER
WINDJAMMER

Value: Cover or less

- ❑1, Jun 95, MGr (w), 1: Bar Sinister 2.50
- ❑2, Jul 95, MGr (w) 2.50
- ❑3, Aug 95, MGr (w) 2.50
- ❑4, Sep 95, MGr 2.50

BARTMAN
BONGO

	ORIG	GOOD	FINE	N-MINT
❑1, The Comic Cover Caper, Silver ink cover; poster	2.95	0.80	2.00	4.00
❑2, 94, Where Stalks The Penalizer	1.95	0.50	1.25	2.50
❑3, 94, The Final Collision, trading card	2.25	0.50	1.25	2.50
❑4, 95	2.25	0.50	1.25	2.50
❑5, 95, 1: The Great Maggeena; 1: Lisa the Conjuror	2.25	0.50	1.25	2.50
❑6, 95, The Great Purple Hope, 1: Bart Dog	2.25	0.50	1.25	2.50

BASEBALL CLASSICS
PERSONALITY

Value: Cover or less

- ❑1 2.95
- ❑2 2.95

BASEBALL COMICS
KITCHEN SINK

Value: Cover or less

- ❑1, May 91, WE, trading cards 3.95
- ❑2, Slide, Sinner, Slide; The Spirit: The Good Old Days, cards on back cover 2.95

BASEBALL COMICS (PERSONALITY)
PERSONALITY

Value: Cover or less

- ❑1 2.95
- ❑2 2.95

BASEBALL GREATS
DARK HORSE

Value: Cover or less

- ❑1, Oct 92, The Jimmy Pierall Story, Jimmy Piersall, with cards 2.95
- ❑2, Bob Gibson 2.95
- ❑3, 2 trading cards 2.95

BASEBALL HALL OF SHAME IN 3-D
BLACKTHORNE

Value: Cover or less

- ❑1 2.50

BASEBALL LEGENDS
REVOLUTIONARY

Value: Cover or less

- ❑1, Mar 92, b&w; Babe Ruth 2.50
- ❑2, Apr 92, b&w; Ty Cobb 2.50
- ❑3, May 92, b&w; Ted Williams 2.50
- ❑4, Jun 92, b&w; Mickey Mantle 2.50
- ❑5, Jul 92, b&w; Joe Dimaggio 2.50
- ❑6, Aug 92, b&w; Jackie Robinson 2.50
- ❑7, Sep 92, b&w; Sandy Koufax 2.50
- ❑8, Oct 92, b&w; Willie Mays 2.50
- ❑9, Nov 92, b&w; Honus Wagner 2.50
- ❑10, Dec 92, full color; Roberto Clemente 2.75
- ❑11, Jan 93, full color; Yogi Berra 2.75
- ❑12, Feb 93, full color; Billy Martin 2.75
- ❑13, Mar 93, full color; Hank Aaron 2.95
- ❑14, Apr 93, b&w; Carl Yastrzemski 2.95
- ❑15, May 93, b&w; Satchel Paige 2.95
- ❑16, Jun 93, b&w; Johnny Bench 2.95
- ❑17, Jul 93, b&w; Shoeless Joe Jackson 2.95
- ❑18, Aug 93, b&w; Lou Gehrig 2.95
- ❑19, Sep 93, b&w; Casey Stengel 2.95

BASEBALL'S GREATEST HEROES
MAGNUM

	ORIG	GOOD	FINE	N-MINT
❑1, Mickey Mantle	—	0.50	1.25	2.50
❑2	—	0.50	1.25	2.50

BASEBALL SLUGGERS
PERSONALITY

Value: Cover or less

- ❑1 2.95
- ❑2 2.95
- ❑3 2.95
- ❑4 2.95

BASEBALL SUPERSTARS COMICS
REVOLUTIONARY

Value: Cover or less

- ❑1, Nov 91, Nolan Ryan 2.50
- ❑2, Feb 92, Bo Jackson 2.50
- ❑3, Mar 92, Ken Griffey Jr. 2.50
- ❑4, Apr 92, Pete Rose 2.50
- ❑5, May 92, Rickey Henderson 2.50
- ❑6, Jun 92, Jose Canseco 2.50
- ❑7, Jul 92, Cal Ripkin Jr. 2.50
- ❑8, Aug 92, Carlton Fisk 2.50
- ❑9, Sep 92, George Brett 2.50
- ❑10, Oct 92, Darryl Strawberry 2.50
- ❑11, Nov 92, Frank Thomas 2.50
- ❑12, Dec 92, full color; Ryne Sandberg 2.75
- ❑13, Jan 93, full color; Kirby Puckett 2.75
- ❑14, Feb 93, full color; Roberto and Sandi Alomar 2.75
- ❑15, Mar 93, full color; Roger Clemens 2.95
- ❑16, Apr 93, b&w; Mark McGuire 2.95
- ❑17, May 93, b&w; Avery/Glavine 2.95
- ❑18, Jun 93, b&w; Dennis Eckersley 2.95
- ❑19, Jul 93, b&w; Dave Winfield 2.95
- ❑20, Aug 93, b&w; Jim Abbott 2.95

BASEBALL THRILLS 3-D
3-D ZONE

Value: Cover or less

- ❑1, Wolrd Series; The Splendid Splinter, nn; glasses 2.95

BASICALLY STRANGE
JOHN C.

	ORIG	GOOD	FINE	N-MINT
❑1, Nov 82, WW (w), Bladerunner; To Kill Death	1.95	1.00	2.50	5.00

BAT, THE (APPLE)
APPLE

	ORIG	GOOD	FINE	N-MINT
❑1, Mar 94, The Bat, b&w	2.25	0.50	1.25	2.50

BAT, THE (MARY ROBERTS RINEHART'S)
ADVENTURE

Value: Cover or less

- ❑1, Aug 92, Another Angry Young Bastard Adventure; True-Life Stories that Make Me Laugh, b&w 2.50

BATBABE
SPOOF

Value: Cover or less

- ❑2 2.50

BATCH
CALIBER

Value: Cover or less

- ❑1, b&w 2.95

BATGIRL
DC

	ORIG	GOOD	FINE	N-MINT
❑1, Apr 00	2.50	0.60	1.50	3.00
❑2, May 00	2.50	0.50	1.25	2.50
❑3, Jun 00	2.50	0.50	1.25	2.50
❑4, Jul 00	2.50	0.50	1.25	2.50
❑5, Aug 00	2.50	0.50	1.25	2.50
❑6, Sep 00	2.50	0.50	1.25	2.50
❑7, Oct 00	2.50	0.50	1.25	2.50
❑8, Nov 00	2.50	0.50	1.25	2.50
❑9, Dec 00	2.50	0.50	1.25	2.50
❑10, Jan 01	2.50	0.50	1.25	2.50
❑11, Feb 01	2.50	0.50	1.25	2.50
❑12, Mar 01, Mute Witness, Officer Down	2.50	0.50	1.25	2.50
❑13, Apr 01	2.50	0.50	1.25	2.50
❑14, May 01	2.50	0.50	1.25	2.50
❑15, Jun 01	2.50	0.50	1.25	2.50
❑16	2.50	0.50	1.25	2.50
❑17	2.50	0.50	1.25	2.50
❑18	2.50	0.50	1.25	2.50

BATGIRL ADVENTURES, THE
DC

	ORIG	GOOD	FINE	N-MINT
❑1, Feb 98, V: Harley Quinn, Poison Ivy	2.95	0.65	1.63	3.25

BATGIRL SPECIAL
DC

	ORIG	GOOD	FINE	N-MINT
❑1, Jul 88	1.50	0.50	1.25	2.50

BATHING MACHINE
C&T

Value: Cover or less

- ❑1, b&w 2.50
- ❑2 1.50
- ❑3 1.50

BATHROOM GIRLS
MODERN

Value: Cover or less

- ❑1, 97, b&w 2.95
- ❑2, 98, b&w 2.95

BAT LASH
DC

	ORIG	GOOD	FINE	N-MINT
❑1, Nov 68	0.12	4.00	10.00	20.00
❑2, Jan 69	0.12	2.00	5.00	10.00
❑3, Mar 69	0.12	2.00	5.00	10.00
❑4, May 69	0.12	2.00	5.00	10.00
❑5, Jul 69	0.12	2.00	5.00	10.00
❑6, Sep 69	0.12	2.00	5.00	10.00
❑7, Nov 69, NC, SA (w), Final Issue	0.12	2.00	5.00	10.00

BATMAN
DC

	ORIG	GOOD	FINE	N-MINT
❑0, Oct 94, O: Batman	1.50	0.50	1.25	2.50
❑137, Feb 61, A: Mr. Marvel	0.10	27.00	67.50	135.00
❑138, Mar 61	0.10	27.00	67.50	135.00
❑139, Apr 61, 1: Batgirl (Golden Age)	0.10	27.00	67.50	135.00
❑140, Jun 61, A: Joker	0.10	27.00	67.50	135.00
❑141, Aug 61	0.10	27.00	67.50	135.00
❑142, Sep 61	0.10	27.00	67.50	135.00
❑143, Oct 61	0.10	27.00	67.50	135.00
❑144, Dec 61, A: Joker	0.12	27.00	67.50	135.00
❑145, Feb 62, A: Joker	0.12	27.00	67.50	135.00
❑146, Mar 62	0.12	21.00	52.50	105.00
❑147, May 62	0.12	21.00	52.50	105.00
❑148, Jul 62, A: Joker	0.12	27.00	67.50	135.00
❑149, Aug 62	0.12	21.00	52.50	105.00
❑150, Oct 62	0.12	21.00	52.50	105.00
❑151, Nov 62	0.12	16.00	40.00	80.00
❑152, Dec 62, A: Joker	0.12	18.00	45.00	90.00
❑153, Feb 63	0.12	14.00	35.00	70.00
❑154, Mar 63	0.12	14.00	35.00	70.00
❑155, Apr 63, 1: Penguin (in Silver Age)	0.12	65.00	162.50	325.00
❑156, Jun 63	0.12	14.00	35.00	70.00

	ORIG	GOOD	FINE	N-MINT
❑157, Aug 63	0.12	14.00	35.00	70.00
❑158, Sep 63	0.12	14.00	35.00	70.00
❑159, Nov 63, A: Joker	0.12	17.00	42.50	85.00
❑160, Dec 63	0.12	14.00	35.00	70.00
❑161, Feb 64	0.12	14.00	35.00	70.00
❑162, Mar 64	0.12	14.00	35.00	70.00
❑163, May 64, A: Joker	0.12	17.00	42.50	85.00
❑164, Jun 64	0.12	14.00	35.00	70.00
❑165, Aug 64	0.12	14.00	35.00	70.00
❑166, Sep 64	0.12	14.00	35.00	70.00
❑167, Nov 64	0.12	14.00	35.00	70.00
❑168, Dec 64	0.12	14.00	35.00	70.00
❑169, Feb 65, A: Penguin	0.12	16.00	40.00	80.00
❑170, Mar 65	0.12	14.00	35.00	70.00
❑171, May 65, Cl, A: 1s	0.12	85.00	212.50	425.00
❑172, Jun 65	0.12	9.60	24.00	48.00
❑173, Aug 65	0.12	9.60	24.00	48.00
❑174, Sep 65	0.12	9.60	24.00	48.00
❑175, Nov 65	0.12	9.60	24.00	48.00
❑176, Dec 65, A: Joker, 80pgs.	0.25	14.00	35.00	70.00
❑177, Dec 65	0.12	9.60	24.00	48.00
❑178, Feb 66	0.12	9.60	24.00	48.00
❑179, Mar 66, A: Riddler	0.12	21.00	52.50	105.00
❑180, May 66	0.12	9.60	24.00	48.00
❑181, Jun 66, 1: Poison Ivy	0.12	25.00	62.50	125.00
❑182, Aug 66, A: Joker, 80pgs.; Reprint	0.25	9.60	24.00	48.00
❑183, Aug 66, TV show reference	0.12	9.60	24.00	48.00
❑184, Sep 66, Mystery of the Missing Man-hunters; The Boy Wonder's Boo-boo Patrol!	0.12	9.60	24.00	48.00
❑185, Nov 66, 80pgs.	0.25	9.60	24.00	48.00
❑186, Nov 66, A: Joker	0.12	9.60	24.00	48.00
❑187, Dec 66, A: Joker, 80pgs.	0.25	12.00	30.00	60.00
❑188, Jan 67	0.12	5.60	14.00	28.00
❑189, Feb 67, 1: The Scarecrow (in Silver Age)	0.12	12.00	30.00	60.00
❑190, Mar 67, A: Penguin	0.12	7.00	17.50	35.00
❑191, May 67	0.12	5.60	14.00	28.00
❑192, Jun 67	0.12	5.60	14.00	28.00
❑193, Aug 67, 80pgs.	0.25	8.00	20.00	40.00
❑194, Aug 67	0.12	5.60	14.00	28.00
❑195, Sep 67	0.12	5.60	14.00	28.00
❑196, Nov 67	0.12	5.60	14.00	28.00
❑197, Dec 67, A: Catwoman	0.12	11.00	27.50	55.00
❑198, Jan 68, O: Batman; A: Joker, 80pgs.	0.25	14.00	35.00	70.00
❑199, Feb 68	0.12	5.60	14.00	28.00
❑200, Mar 68, NA, O: Batman; A: Joker; O: Robin I (Dick Grayson)	0.12	28.00	70.00	140.00
❑201, May 68, A: Joker	0.12	7.00	17.50	35.00
❑202, Jun 68	0.12	4.00	10.00	20.00
❑203, Aug 68, 80pgs.; Giant-size	0.25	4.00	10.00	20.00
❑204, Aug 68	0.12	3.60	9.00	18.00
❑205, Sep 68	0.12	3.60	9.00	18.00
❑206, Nov 68	0.12	3.60	9.00	18.00
❑207, Dec 68	0.12	3.60	9.00	18.00
❑208, Jan 69, O: Batman (new origin), 80pgs.	0.25	7.00	17.50	35.00
❑209, Jan 69	0.12	3.60	9.00	18.00
❑210, Mar 69	0.12	3.60	9.00	18.00
❑211, May 69	0.12	3.60	9.00	18.00
❑212, Jun 69	0.12	3.20	8.00	16.00
❑213, Aug 69, O: Robin I (Dick Grayson-new origin); A: Joker, Giant-size; Joker reprint	0.25	10.40	26.00	52.00
❑214, Aug 69	0.15	3.20	8.00	16.00
❑215, Sep 69	0.15	3.20	8.00	16.00
❑216, Nov 69	0.15	3.20	8.00	16.00
❑217, Dec 69	0.15	3.20	8.00	16.00
❑218, Feb 70, Giant-size	0.25	6.00	15.00	30.00
❑219, Feb 70, NA	0.15	6.00	15.00	30.00
❑220, Mar 70, NA	0.15	2.80	7.00	14.00
❑221, May 70, NA	0.15	2.80	7.00	14.00
❑222, Jun 70, NA, A: The Beatles	0.15	6.40	16.00	32.00
❑223, Aug 70, MA, Giant-size	0.25	6.00	15.00	30.00
❑224, Aug 70, NA	0.15	2.80	7.00	14.00
❑225, Sep 70, NA	0.15	2.80	7.00	14.00
❑226, Nov 70, NA	0.15	2.80	7.00	14.00
❑227, Dec 70, NA, Robin back-up	0.15	2.80	7.00	14.00
❑228, Feb 71, MA, Giant-size; giant	0.25	4.80	12.00	24.00
❑229, Feb 71	0.15	2.80	7.00	14.00
❑230, Mar 71	0.15	2.80	7.00	14.00
❑231, May 71	0.15	2.80	7.00	14.00
❑232, Jun 71, NA; DG, O: Batman; 1: Ra's Al Ghul	0.15	17.00	42.50	85.00
❑233, Aug 71, Giant-size; giant	0.25	4.80	12.00	24.00
❑234, Aug 71, NA; Cl, 1: Two-Face (in Silver Age)	0.25	23.00	57.50	115.00
❑235, Sep 71, Cl	0.25	2.60	6.50	13.00

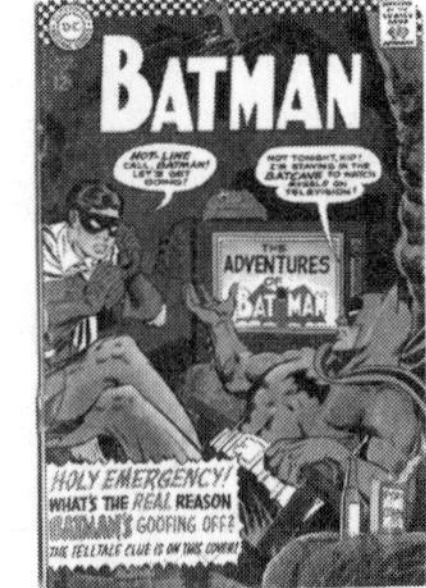

DC called attention to the *Batman* TV show in *Batman* #183.

© 1966 National Periodical Publications Inc. (DC)

	ORIG	GOOD	FINE	N-MINT
❑236, Nov 71, NA	0.25	2.60	6.50	13.00
❑237, Dec 71, NA, 1: The Reaper	0.25	8.00	20.00	40.00
❑238, Jan 72, NA; JKu, a.k.a. DC 100-Page Super Spectacular #DC-8, wraparound cover; Giant-size	0.50	4.80	12.00	24.00
❑239, Feb 72, NA; RB	0.25	2.60	6.50	13.00
❑240, Mar 72, NA; RB	0.25	2.60	6.50	13.00
❑241, May 72, NA; RB	0.25	2.60	6.50	13.00
❑242, Jun 72, RB	0.25	2.60	6.50	13.00
❑243, Aug 72, NA; DG, Ra's al Ghul	0.20	5.60	14.00	28.00
❑244, Sep 72, NA; DG, The Demon Lives Again!, Ra's al Ghul	0.20	5.60	14.00	28.00
❑245, Oct 72, IN; NA; DG, FM (c)	0.20	5.60	14.00	28.00
❑246, Dec 72	0.20	2.60	6.50	13.00
❑247, Feb 73	0.20	2.60	6.50	13.00
❑248, Apr 73	0.20	2.60	6.50	13.00
❑249, Jun 73	0.20	2.60	6.50	13.00
❑250, Jul 73	0.20	2.60	6.50	13.00
❑251, Sep 73, NA, A: Joker	0.20	9.00	22.50	45.00
❑252, Sep 73, 100pgs.	0.20	2.40	6.00	12.00
❑253, Nov 73, 100pgs.	0.20	2.40	6.00	12.00
❑254, Feb 74, GK; NA, 100pgs.	0.50	4.00	10.00	20.00
❑255, Apr 74, GK; NA; DG; Cl, 100pgs.	0.50	4.00	10.00	20.00
❑256, Jun 74, 100pgs.	0.60	4.00	10.00	20.00
❑257, Aug 74, 100pgs.	0.60	4.00	10.00	20.00
❑258, Oct 74, 100pgs.	0.60	4.00	10.00	20.00
❑259, Dec 74, 100pgs.	0.60	4.00	10.00	20.00
❑260, Feb 75, A: Joker, 100pgs.	0.60	5.60	14.00	28.00
❑261, Mar 75, 100pgs.	0.60	4.00	10.00	20.00
❑262, Apr 75, Giant-size	0.50	2.60	6.50	13.00
❑263, May 75	0.25	1.80	4.50	9.00
❑264, Jun 75, Death of a Daredevil, V: Devil Dayre	0.25	1.80	4.50	9.00
❑265, Jul 75	0.25	1.80	4.50	9.00
❑266, Aug 75, A: Catwoman, Catwoman goes back to old costume	0.25	1.80	4.50	9.00
❑267, Sep 75	0.25	1.80	4.50	9.00
❑268, Oct 75	0.25	1.80	4.50	9.00
❑269, Nov 75	0.25	1.80	4.50	9.00
❑270, Dec 75	0.25	1.80	4.50	9.00
❑271, Jan 76	0.25	1.80	4.50	9.00
❑272, Feb 76	0.25	1.80	4.50	9.00
❑273, Mar 76	0.25	1.80	4.50	9.00
❑274, Apr 76	0.30	1.80	4.50	9.00
❑275, May 76	0.30	1.80	4.50	9.00
❑276, Jun 76	0.30	1.80	4.50	9.00
❑277, Jul 76, Bicentennial #11	0.30	1.80	4.50	9.00
❑278, Aug 76	0.30	1.80	4.50	9.00
❑279, Sep 76	0.30	1.80	4.50	9.00
❑280, Oct 76	0.30	1.80	4.50	9.00
❑281, Nov 76	0.30	1.80	4.50	9.00
❑282, Dec 76	0.30	1.80	4.50	9.00
❑283, Jan 77, Omega Bomb Target: Gotham City, V: Omega	0.30	1.80	4.50	9.00
❑284, Feb 77	0.30	1.80	4.50	9.00
❑285, Mar 77	0.30	1.80	4.50	9.00
❑286, Apr 77, A: Joker	0.30	2.40	6.00	12.00
❑287, May 77	0.30	1.80	4.50	9.00
❑288, Jun 77	0.35	1.80	4.50	9.00
❑289, Jul 77	0.35	1.80	4.50	9.00
❑290, Aug 77	0.35	1.80	4.50	9.00
❑291, Sep 77, Underworld Olympics, Part 1, A: Joker	0.35	1.80	4.50	9.00
❑292, Oct 77, Underworld Olympics, Part 2	0.35	1.80	4.50	9.00
❑293, Nov 77, Underworld Olympics, Part 3, A: Superman; A: Lex Luthor	0.35	1.80	4.50	9.00
❑294, Dec 77, Underworld Olympics, Part 4, A: Joker	0.35	1.80	4.50	9.00
❑295, Jan 78	0.35	1.60	4.00	8.00
❑296, Feb 78, The Sinister Straws of the Scarecrow, V: Scarecrow	0.35	1.60	4.00	8.00
❑297, Mar 78	0.35	1.60	4.00	8.00
❑298, Apr 78	0.35	1.60	4.00	8.00

	ORIG	GOOD	FINE	N-MINT
❑299, May 78	0.35	1.60	4.00	8.00
❑300, Jun 78, 300th anniversary issue; Double-size	0.60	3.00	7.50	15.00
❑301, Jul 78	0.35	1.60	4.00	8.00
❑302, Aug 78	0.35	1.60	4.00	8.00
❑303, Sep 78	0.50	1.60	4.00	8.00
❑304, Oct 78	0.50	1.60	4.00	8.00
❑305, Nov 78	0.50	1.60	4.00	8.00
❑306, Dec 78	0.40	1.60	4.00	8.00
❑307, Jan 79	0.40	1.60	4.00	8.00
❑308, Feb 79	0.40	1.60	4.00	8.00
❑309, Mar 79	0.40	1.60	4.00	8.00
❑310, Apr 79	0.40	1.60	4.00	8.00
❑311, May 79	0.40	1.60	4.00	8.00
❑312, Jun 79	0.40	1.60	4.00	8.00
❑313, Jul 79	0.40	1.60	4.00	8.00
❑314, Aug 79	0.40	1.60	4.00	8.00
❑315, Sep 79	0.40	1.60	4.00	8.00
❑316, Oct 79	0.40	1.60	4.00	8.00
❑317, Nov 79	0.40	1.60	4.00	8.00
❑318, Dec 79, 1: Firebug	0.40	1.60	4.00	8.00
❑319, Jan 80	0.40	1.60	4.00	8.00
❑320, Feb 80	0.40	1.60	4.00	8.00
❑321, Mar 80, A: Joker; A: Catwoman	0.40	1.80	4.50	9.00
❑322, Apr 80	0.40	1.40	3.50	7.00
❑323, May 80	0.40	1.40	3.50	7.00
❑324, Jun 80	0.40	1.40	3.50	7.00
❑325, Jul 80	0.40	1.40	3.50	7.00
❑326, Aug 80, 1: Arkham Asylum	0.40	1.40	3.50	7.00
❑327, Sep 80	0.50	1.40	3.50	7.00
❑328, Oct 80	0.50	1.40	3.50	7.00
❑329, Nov 80	0.50	1.40	3.50	7.00
❑330, Dec 80	0.50	1.40	3.50	7.00
❑331, Jan 81, 1: Electrocutioner	0.50	1.40	3.50	7.00
❑332, Feb 81, 1st solo Catwoman story	0.50	1.60	4.00	8.00
❑333, Mar 81	0.50	1.40	3.50	7.00
❑334, Apr 81	0.50	1.40	3.50	7.00
❑335, May 81	0.50	1.40	3.50	7.00
❑336, Jun 81	0.50	1.40	3.50	7.00
❑337, Jul 81	0.50	1.40	3.50	7.00
❑338, Aug 81	0.50	1.40	3.50	7.00
❑339, Sep 81	0.50	1.40	3.50	7.00
❑340, Oct 81	0.60	1.40	3.50	7.00
❑341, Nov 81	0.60	1.40	3.50	7.00
❑342, Dec 81	0.60	1.40	3.50	7.00
❑343, Jan 82	0.60	1.40	3.50	7.00
❑344, Feb 82	0.60	1.40	3.50	7.00
❑345, Mar 82	0.60	1.40	3.50	7.00
❑346, Apr 82, V: Two-Face	0.60	1.40	3.50	7.00
❑347, May 82	0.60	1.40	3.50	7.00
❑348, Jun 82	0.60	1.40	3.50	7.00
❑349, Jul 82	0.60	1.40	3.50	7.00
❑350, Aug 82	0.60	1.40	3.50	7.00
❑351, Sep 82	0.60	1.40	3.50	7.00
❑352, Oct 82	0.60	1.40	3.50	7.00
❑353, Nov 82, A: Joker	0.60	1.90	4.75	9.50
❑354, Dec 82	0.60	1.40	3.50	7.00
❑355, Jan 83	0.60	1.40	3.50	7.00
❑356, Feb 83	0.60	1.40	3.50	7.00
❑357, Mar 83, 1: Jason Todd; 1: Killer Croc	0.60	1.80	4.50	9.00
❑358, Apr 83	0.60	1.40	3.50	7.00
❑359, May 83, A: Joker	0.60	1.80	4.50	9.00
❑360, Jun 83	0.60	1.40	3.50	7.00
❑361, Jul 83, 1: Harvey Bullock	0.60	1.40	3.50	7.00
❑362, Aug 83	0.60	1.40	3.50	7.00
❑363, Sep 83	0.60	1.40	3.50	7.00
❑364, Oct 83	0.60	1.40	3.50	7.00
❑365, Nov 83	0.60	1.40	3.50	7.00
❑366, Dec 83, 1: Jason Todd in Robin costume; A: Joker	0.75	2.00	5.00	10.00
❑367, Jan 84	0.75	1.40	3.50	7.00
❑368, Feb 84, AA; DN, 1: Robin II (Jason Todd)	0.75	1.60	4.00	8.00
❑369, Mar 84, V: Deadshot	0.75	1.20	3.00	6.00
❑370, Apr 84	0.75	1.20	3.00	6.00
❑371, May 84, V: Catman	0.75	1.00	2.50	5.00
❑372, Jun 84	0.75	1.00	2.50	5.00
❑373, Jul 84, V: Scarecrow	0.75	1.00	2.50	5.00
❑374, Aug 84, V: Penguin	0.75	1.00	2.50	5.00
❑375, Sep 84, V: Mr. Freeze	0.75	1.00	2.50	5.00
❑376, Oct 84	0.75	1.00	2.50	5.00
❑377, Nov 84	0.75	1.00	2.50	5.00
❑378, Dec 84, V: Mad Hatter	0.75	1.00	2.50	5.00
❑379, Jan 85, V: Mad Hatter	0.75	1.00	2.50	5.00
❑380, Feb 85	0.75	1.00	2.50	5.00

	ORIG	GOOD	FINE	N-MINT
❑381, Mar 85	0.75	1.00	2.50	5.00
❑382, Apr 85, GK (c), A: Catwoman	0.75	1.00	2.50	5.00
❑383, May 85	0.75	1.00	2.50	5.00
❑384, Jun 85, V: Calendar Man	0.75	1.00	2.50	5.00
❑385, Jul 85	0.75	1.00	2.50	5.00
❑386, Aug 85, 1: Black Mask	0.75	1.00	2.50	5.00
❑387, Sep 85, V: Black Mask	0.75	1.00	2.50	5.00
❑388, Oct 85, V: Captain Boomerang; V: Capt. Boomerang; V: Mirror Master	0.75	1.00	2.50	5.00
❑389, Nov 85, A: Catwoman	0.75	1.00	2.50	5.00
❑390, Dec 85, A: Catwoman	0.75	1.00	2.50	5.00
❑391, Jan 86, A: Catwoman	0.75	1.00	2.50	5.00
❑392, Feb 86	0.75	1.00	2.50	5.00
❑393, Mar 86	0.75	1.00	2.50	5.00
❑394, Apr 86	0.75	1.00	2.50	5.00
❑395, May 86	0.75	1.00	2.50	5.00
❑396, Jun 86	0.75	1.00	2.50	5.00
❑397, Jul 86, V: Two-Face	0.75	1.00	2.50	5.00
❑398, Aug 86, V: Two-Face, A: Catwoman; V: Two-Face; A: Catwoman	0.75	1.00	2.50	5.00
❑399, Sep 86	0.75	1.00	2.50	5.00
❑400, Oct 86, Double-size; Anniversary edition	1.50	2.80	7.00	14.00
❑401, Nov 86, Legends, Part 1, V: Magpie, Legends	0.75	0.80	2.00	4.00
❑402, Dec 86	0.75	0.80	2.00	4.00
❑403, Jan 87	0.75	0.80	2.00	4.00
❑404, Feb 87, FM (w), Year One; Batman: Year 1, Part 1, O: Batman; 1: Catwoman (new)	0.75	1.20	3.00	6.00
❑405, Mar 87, FM (w), Batman: Year 1, Part 2, Year One	0.75	1.00	2.50	5.00
❑406, Apr 87, FM (w), Batman: Year 1, Part 3, Year One	0.75	1.00	2.50	5.00
❑407, May 87, FM (w), Batman: Year 1, Part 4, Year One	0.75	1.00	2.50	5.00
❑408, Jun 87, O: Jason Todd (new origin)	0.75	0.80	2.00	4.00
❑409, Jul 87	0.75	0.60	1.50	3.00
❑410, Aug 87, V: Two-Face	0.75	0.60	1.50	3.00
❑411, Sep 87	0.75	0.60	1.50	3.00
❑412, Oct 87, 1: Mime	0.75	0.60	1.50	3.00
❑413, Nov 87	0.75	0.60	1.50	3.00
❑414, Dec 87, JA, JSn (w), Victims!, Millennium	0.75	0.60	1.50	3.00
❑415, Jan 88, Millennium, Millennium	0.75	0.60	1.50	3.00
❑416, Feb 88, JA, A: Nightwing	0.75	0.60	1.50	3.00
❑417, Mar 88, MZ (c), Ten Nights of the Beast, V: KGBeast	0.75	1.00	2.50	5.00
❑418, Apr 88, MZ (c), Ten Nights of the Beast, V: KGBeast	0.75	0.80	2.00	4.00
❑419, May 88, MZ (c), Ten Nights of the Beast, V: KGBeast	0.75	0.80	2.00	4.00
❑420, Jun 88, MZ (c), Ten Nights of the Beast, V: KGBeast	0.75	0.80	2.00	4.00
❑421, Jul 88	0.75	0.60	1.50	3.00
❑422, Aug 88	0.75	0.60	1.50	3.00
❑423, Sep 88, TMc (c)	0.75	0.60	1.50	3.00
❑424, Oct 88	0.75	0.60	1.50	3.00
❑425, Nov 88	0.75	0.60	1.50	3.00
❑426, Dec 88, Death in Family; A Death in the Family, Part 1	1.50	1.40	3.50	7.00
❑427, Dec 88, A Death in the Family, Part 2, D: Robin, newsstand	1.50	1.40	3.50	7.00
❑427/DM, Dec 88, D: Robin, direct sale	1.50	1.40	3.50	7.00
❑428, Jan 89, A Death in the Family, Part 3, D: Robin II (Jason Todd), Robin declared dead	0.75	1.40	3.50	7.00
❑429, Jan 89, JA, JSn (w), A Death in the Family, Part 4	0.75	1.00	2.50	5.00
❑430, Feb 89	0.75	1.00	2.50	5.00
❑431, Mar 89	0.75	0.40	1.00	2.00
❑432, Apr 89	0.75	0.40	1.00	2.00
❑433, May 89, JBy, JBy (w), Many Deaths of the Batman; The Many Deaths of Batman, Part 1	0.75	0.40	1.00	2.00
❑434, Jun 89, JBy, JBy (w), Many Deaths of the Batman; The Many Deaths of Batman, Part 2	0.75	0.40	1.00	2.00
❑435, Jul 89, JA; JBy, JBy (w), Many Deaths of the Batman; The Many Deaths of Batman, Part 3	0.75	0.40	1.00	2.00
❑436, Aug 89, Year 3; Batman: Year 3, Part 1	0.75	0.60	1.50	3.00
❑436-2, Batman: Year 3, Part 1, 2nd Printing	0.75	0.25	0.63	1.25
❑437, Aug 89, Year 3; Batman: Year 3, Part 2	0.75	0.40	1.00	2.00
❑438, Sep 89, Year 3; Batman: Year 3, Part 3	1.00	0.40	1.00	2.00
❑439, Sep 89, Year 3; Batman: Year 3, Part 4	1.00	0.40	1.00	2.00
❑440, Oct 89, JA, A Lonely Place of Dying; A Lonely Place of Dying, Part 1, 1: Timothy Drake	1.00	0.40	1.00	2.00

	ORIG	GOOD	FINE	N-MINT
❑441, Nov 89, A Lonely Place of Dying; A Lonely Place of Dying, Part 3	1.00	0.40	1.00	2.00
❑442, Dec 89, A Lonely Place of Dying, 1: Robin III (Timothy Drake)	1.00	0.60	1.50	3.00
❑443, Jan 90	1.00	0.30	0.75	1.50
❑444, Feb 90, JA, Crimesmith And Punishment, V: Crimesmith	1.00	0.30	0.75	1.50
❑445, Mar 90, JA, When the Earth Dies, Part 1, V: NKVDemon	1.00	0.30	0.75	1.50
❑446, Apr 90, V: NKVDemon	1.00	0.30	0.75	1.50
❑447, May 90, V: NKVDemon	1.00	0.30	0.75	1.50
❑448, Jun 90, V: Penguin	1.00	0.30	0.75	1.50
❑449, Jun 90, V: Penguin	1.00	0.30	0.75	1.50
❑450, Jul 90, V: Joker	1.00	0.30	0.75	1.50
❑451, Jul 90, V: Joker	1.00	0.30	0.75	1.50
❑452, Aug 90, Dark Knight, Dark City, Part 1, V: Riddler	1.00	0.30	0.75	1.50
❑453, Aug 90, Dark Knight, Dark City, Part 2, V: Riddler	1.00	0.30	0.75	1.50
❑454, Sep 90, Dark Knight, Dark City, Part 3, V: Riddler	1.00	0.30	0.75	1.50
❑455, Oct 90, Identity Crisis, Part 1	1.00	0.30	0.75	1.50
❑456, Nov 90, Identity Crisis, Part 2	1.00	0.30	0.75	1.50
❑457, Dec 90, A Master of Fear, 1: new Robin costume, Timothy Drake as Robin	1.00	0.60	1.50	3.00
❑457/DM, Dec 90, with #000 on indicia	1.00	0.60	1.50	3.00
❑457-2, Dec 90, A Master of Fear, 2nd Printing; Timothy Drake as Robin	1.00	0.40	1.00	2.00
❑458, Jan 91, 1: Harold	1.00	0.30	0.75	1.50
❑459, Feb 91	1.00	0.30	0.75	1.50
❑460, Mar 91, Sisters in Arms, Part 1, Catwoman	1.00	0.30	0.75	1.50
❑461, Apr 91, Sisters in Arms, Part 2, Catwoman	1.00	0.30	0.75	1.50
❑462, May 91, Spirit of the Beast, Part 1	1.00	0.30	0.75	1.50
❑463, Jun 91, Spirit of the Beast, Part 2	1.00	0.30	0.75	1.50
❑464, Jul 91, Spirit of the Beast, Part 3	1.00	0.30	0.75	1.50
❑465, Jul 91, Robin	1.00	0.30	0.75	1.50
❑466, Aug 91, Robin	1.00	0.30	0.75	1.50
❑467, Aug 91, Robin, covers form triptych	1.00	0.30	0.75	1.50
❑468, Sep 91, Robin, covers form triptych	1.00	0.30	0.75	1.50
❑469, Sep 91, Robin, covers form triptych	1.00	0.30	0.75	1.50
❑470, Oct 91, War of the Gods, Part 13, War of the Gods	1.00	0.30	0.75	1.50
❑471, Nov 91	1.00	0.30	0.75	1.50
❑472, Dec 91	1.00	0.30	0.75	1.50
❑473, Jan 92	1.00	0.30	0.75	1.50
❑474, Feb 92, Destroyer, Part 1, Anton Furst's Gotham City	1.00	0.30	0.75	1.50
❑475, Mar 92, V: Ventriloquist, Two-Face	1.00	0.30	0.75	1.50
❑476, Apr 92	1.00	0.30	0.75	1.50
❑477, May 92, A Gotham Tale, Photo cover	1.25	0.30	0.75	1.50
❑478, May 92, A Gotham Tale, Photo cover	1.25	0.30	0.75	1.50
❑479, Jun 92	1.25	0.30	0.75	1.50
❑480, Jun 92	1.25	0.30	0.75	1.50
❑481, Jul 92	1.25	0.30	0.75	1.50
❑482, Jul 92	1.25	0.30	0.75	1.50
❑483, Aug 92, JA, Crash & Burn: A Love Story	1.25	0.30	0.75	1.50
❑484, Sep 92	1.25	0.30	0.75	1.50
❑485, Oct 92	1.25	0.30	0.75	1.50
❑486, Nov 92, V: Metalhead	1.25	0.30	0.75	1.50
❑487, Dec 92	1.25	0.25	0.63	1.25
❑488, Jan 93, Robin trains Azrael	1.25	0.80	2.00	4.00
❑489, Feb 93, 1: Azrael (as Batman); A: Bane	1.25	0.80	2.00	4.00
❑490, Mar 93, Riddler on Venom	1.25	0.60	1.50	3.00
❑491, Apr 93, JA, Knightfall prequel	1.25	0.60	1.50	3.00
❑492, May 93, Knightfall, Part 1	1.25	0.60	1.50	3.00
❑492/SI, Knightfall, Part 1, Silver edition printing	—	1.20	3.00	6.00
❑492-2, Knightfall; Knightfall, Part 1, 2nd Printing	1.25	0.40	1.00	2.00
❑493, May 93, Knightfall, Part 3, V: Mr. Zsasz	1.25	0.40	1.00	2.00
❑494, Jun 93, JA, Knightfall, Part 5, V: Scarecrow	1.25	0.40	1.00	2.00
❑495, Jun 93, JA, Knightfall, Part 7, V: Poison Ivy	1.25	0.40	1.00	2.00
❑496, Jul 93, JA, Knightfall, Part 9, V: Joker	1.25	0.40	1.00	2.00
❑497, Jul 93, JA, Knightfall, Part 11, partial overlay outer cover; Bane cripples Batman	1.25	0.70	1.75	3.50
❑497-2, Jul 93, JA, Knightfall, Part 11, 2nd Printing, also has partial overlay; Bane cripples Batman	1.25	0.40	1.00	2.00
❑498, Aug 93, JA, Knightfall, Part 13; Knightfall, Part 15, Azrael takes on role of Batman	1.25	0.40	1.00	2.00
❑499, Sep 93, JA, Knightfall, Part 15; Knightfall, Part 17	1.25	0.40	1.00	2.00
❑500, Oct 93, JA, Knightfall, Part 19, Giant-size; Azrael vs. Bane, with poster	2.50	0.60	1.50	3.00

Batman faced Jason Todd's killer in *Batman* #429.

	ORIG	GOOD	FINE	N-MINT
❑500/CS, Oct 93, JA, Knightfall, Part 19, two-level cover; Postcards; Giant-size; diecut; Azrael vs. Bane; Collector's set	3.95	0.90	2.25	4.50
❑501, Nov 93, Knightquest: The Crusade; Knightquest: The Crusade, Code Name: Mekros	1.50	0.40	1.00	2.00
❑502, Dec 93, Knightquest: The Crusade; Knightquest: The Crusade, Phoenix In Chaos	1.50	0.40	1.00	2.00
❑503, Jan 94, Knightquest: The Crusade; Knightquest: The Crusade, Night Becomes Woman, A: Catwoman	1.50	0.40	1.00	2.00
❑504, Feb 94, Knightquest: The Crusade, A: Catwoman	1.50	0.40	1.00	2.00
❑505, Mar 94, Knightquest: The Crusade	1.50	0.40	1.00	2.00
❑506, Apr 94, Knightquest: The Crusade	1.50	0.40	1.00	2.00
❑507, May 94, Knightquest: The Crusade; Knightquest: The Crusade, Ballistic	1.50	0.40	1.00	2.00
❑508, Jun 94, Knightquest: The Crusade; Knightquest: The Crusade, Mortal Remains, D: Abattoir	1.50	0.40	1.00	2.00
❑509, Jul 94, KnightsEnd, Part 1	1.50	0.40	1.00	2.00
❑510, Aug 94, KnightsEnd, Part 7	1.50	0.40	1.00	2.00
❑511, Sep 94, Zero Hour, A: Batgirl	1.50	0.40	1.00	2.00
❑512, Nov 94, RT; MGu, Prodigal, Part 1; Prodigal, Part 1, Robin And Batman	1.50	0.40	1.00	2.00
❑513, Dec 94, Prodigal, Part 5	1.50	0.40	1.00	2.00
❑514, Jan 95, Prodigal, Part 9	1.50	0.40	1.00	2.00
❑515, Feb 95, Troika, Part 1, Return of Bruce Wayne as Batman	1.50	0.40	1.00	2.00
❑515/SC, Feb 95, Troika, Part 1, Embossed cover; Return of Bruce Wayne as Batman	2.50	0.50	1.25	2.50
❑516, Mar 95	1.50	0.40	1.00	2.00
❑517, Apr 95	1.50	0.40	1.00	2.00
❑518, May 95, V: Black Mask	1.50	0.40	1.00	2.00
❑519, Jun 95, Black Spider: Web of Scars	1.95	0.40	1.00	2.00
❑520, Jul 95	1.95	0.40	1.00	2.00
❑521, Aug 95, V: Killer Croc	1.95	0.40	1.00	2.00
❑522, Sep 95, V: Killer Croc, Swamp Thing	1.95	0.40	1.00	2.00
❑523, Oct 95, V: Scarecrow	1.95	0.40	1.00	2.00
❑524, Nov 95, V: Scarecrow	1.95	0.40	1.00	2.00
❑525, Dec 95, Underworld Unleashed, V: Mr. Freeze	1.95	0.40	1.00	2.00
❑526, Jan 96	1.95	0.40	1.00	2.00
❑527, Feb 96, The Face Schism, V: Two-Face	1.95	0.40	1.00	2.00
❑528, Mar 96, Rtwo-Face, Part 2	1.95	0.40	1.00	2.00
❑529, Apr 96, Contagion, Part 6	1.95	0.40	1.00	2.00
❑530, May 96, The Deadman Connection, Glow-in-the-dark cover	1.95	0.39	0.98	1.95
❑530/SC, May 96, The Deadman Connection, glow-in-the-darkcover	2.50	0.50	1.25	2.50
❑531, Jun 96, The Deadman Connection, Glow-in-the-dark cover	1.95	0.39	0.98	1.95
❑531/SC, Jun 96, The Deadman Connection, glow-in-the-darkcover	2.50	0.50	1.25	2.50
❑532, Jul 96, The Deadman Connection, Glow-in-the-dark cover	1.95	0.39	0.98	1.95
❑532/SC, Jul 96, The Deadman Connection, glow-in-the-dark cardstock cover	2.50	0.50	1.25	2.50
❑533, Aug 96, Legacy Prelude	1.95	0.40	1.00	2.00
❑534, Sep 96, Legacy, Part 5	1.95	0.40	1.00	2.00
❑535, Oct 96, The Ogre and the Ape, self-contained story, V: The Ogre and The Ape	2.95	0.40	1.00	2.00
❑535/SC, Oct 96, The Ogre and the Ape, V: The Ogre and The Ape, Die-cut cover; self-contained story	3.95	0.80	2.00	4.00
❑536, Nov 96, Darkest Night of the Man-Bat, Part 1, Final Night	1.95	0.40	1.00	2.00
❑537, Dec 96, Darkest Night of the Man-Bat, Part 2, V: Man-Bat	1.95	0.40	1.00	2.00
❑538, Jan 97, Darkest Night of the Man-Bat, Part 3, A: Man-Bat	1.95	0.40	1.00	2.00
❑539, Feb 97, Boneyard Blues	1.95	0.40	1.00	2.00
❑540, Mar 97, The Spectre of Vengeance, Part 1, A: Spectre	1.95	0.40	1.00	2.00

	ORIG	GOOD	FINE	N-MINT
❑541, Apr 97	1.95	0.40	1.00	2.00
❑542, May 97, Faceless, Part 1	1.95	0.40	1.00	2.00
❑543, Jun 97	1.95	0.40	1.00	2.00
❑544, Jul 97, A: Demon	1.95	0.40	1.00	2.00
❑545, Aug 97, A: Demon	1.95	0.40	1.00	2.00
❑546, Sep 97, A: Demon	1.95	0.40	1.00	2.00
❑547, Oct 97, Genesis	1.95	0.40	1.00	2.00
❑548, Nov 97, The Penguin Returns, Part 1, V: Penguin	1.95	0.40	1.00	2.00
❑549, Dec 97, The Penguin Returns, Part 2, V: Penguin, Face cover	1.95	0.40	1.00	2.00
❑550, Jan 98, 2: Chase	2.95	0.60	1.50	3.00
❑550/SC, Jan 98, 2: Chase, trading cards	3.50	0.70	1.75	3.50
❑551, Feb 98, A: Ragman	1.95	0.40	1.00	2.00
❑552, Mar 98, The Greatest Evil, A: Ragman	1.95	0.80	2.00	4.00
❑553, Apr 98, Cataclysm, Part 3, continues in Azrael #40	1.95	0.60	1.50	3.00
❑554, May 98, Cataclysm, Part 12; Cataclysm, V: Quakemaster, continues in Batman: HuntressSpoiler - Blunt Trauma #1	1.95	0.40	1.00	2.00
❑555, Jun 98, Aftershock, V: Ratcatcher	1.95	0.40	1.00	2.00
❑556, Jul 98, Aftershock	1.95	0.40	1.00	2.00
❑557, Aug 98, Aftershock, A: Ballistic	1.95	0.40	1.00	2.00
❑558, Sep 98, Aftershock	1.99	0.40	1.00	2.00
❑559, Oct 98, Aftershock	1.99	0.40	1.00	2.00
❑560, Dec 98, Road to No Man's Land, Bruce Wayne testifies	1.99	0.40	1.00	2.00
❑561, Jan 99, JA, Road to No Man's Land, Road to No Man's Land, Bruce Wayne testifies	1.99	0.40	1.00	2.00
❑562, Feb 99, JA, Mr. Wayne Goes to Washington, A: Mayor Grange, Road to No Man's Land, Gotham City is cut off	1.99	0.40	1.00	2.00
❑563, Mar 99, No Law and a New Order, Part 3; No Law & a New Order, A: Oracle, No Man's Land, V: Joker	1.99	0.60	1.50	3.00
❑564, Apr 99, Fear of Faith, Part 3, No Man's Land, A: Scarecrow/Huntress	1.99	0.50	1.25	2.50
❑565, May 99, Mosaic, Part 1, No Man's Land	1.99	0.40	1.00	2.00
❑566, Jun 99, The Visitor, No Man's Land, A: Superman; No Man's Land	1.99	0.40	1.00	2.00
❑567, Jul 99, Mark of Cain, Part 1, No Man's Land	1.99	0.40	1.00	2.00
❑568, Aug 99, BSz, Fruit of the Earth, Part 2, No Man's Land, A: Poison Ivy, V: Clayface; No Man's Land	1.99	0.40	1.00	2.00
❑569, Sep 99, I Cover the Waterfront, No Man's Land	1.99	0.40	1.00	1.99
❑570, Oct 99, The Code, Part 1, No Man's Land, V: Joker; No Man's Land	1.99	0.40	1.00	1.99
❑571, Nov 99, Goin' Downtown, Part 1, No Man's Land, V: Bane; No Man's Land	1.99	0.40	1.00	1.99
❑572, Dec 99, Jurisprudence, Part 1, No Man's Land	1.99	0.40	1.00	1.99
❑573, Jan 00, Shellgame, Part 1, No Man's Land	1.99	0.40	1.00	1.99
❑574, Feb 00, Endame, Part 2, No Man's Land	1.99	0.40	1.00	1.99
❑575, Mar 00	1.99	0.40	1.00	1.99
❑576, Apr 00, In the Dark Places	1.99	0.40	1.00	1.99
❑577, May 00	1.99	0.40	1.00	1.99
❑578, Jun 00, Mike and Allie	1.99	0.40	1.00	1.99
❑579, Jul 00, Orca, Part 1	—	0.40	1.00	1.99
❑580, Aug 00, Orca, Part 2; Going Under, V: Orca	2.25	0.40	1.00	1.99
❑581, Sep 00, Orca, Part 3; Diver Down, V: Orca	2.25	0.45	1.13	2.25
❑582, Oct 00, Fearless, Part 1	2.25	0.45	1.13	2.25
❑583, Nov 00, Fearless, Part 2	2.25	0.45	1.13	2.25
❑584, Dec 00, The Dark Knight Project	2.25	0.45	1.13	2.25
❑585, Jan 01, Measure for Measure	2.25	0.45	1.13	2.25
❑586, Feb 01, Penguin Dreams	2.25	0.45	1.13	2.25
❑587, Mar 01, Officer Down, Part 1	2.25	0.45	1.13	2.25
❑588, Apr 01, Close Before Striking, Part 1.	2.25	0.45	1.13	2.25
❑589, May 01, Close Before Striking, Part 2	2.25	0.45	1.13	2.25
❑590, Jun 01, Close Before Striking, Part 3	2.25	0.45	1.13	2.25
❑591	2.25	0.45	1.13	2.25
❑592	2.25	0.45	1.13	2.25
❑593	2.25	0.45	1.13	2.25
❑1000000, Nov 98, Peril Within the Prison Planet	1.99	0.40	1.00	1.99
❑Anl 1, ca. 61, How to be the Batman!; The Strange Costumes of Batman!, O: The Batcave	0.25	90.00	225.00	450.00
❑Anl 1-2, How to be the Batman!; The Strange Costumes of Batman!, O: The Batcave, Reprint (1999)	4.95	1.00	2.50	5.00
❑Anl 2, ca. 61	0.25	52.00	130.00	260.00
❑Anl 3, Sum 62, 80pgs.	0.25	40.00	100.00	200.00
❑Anl 4, Win 63, 80pgs.	0.25	20.00	50.00	100.00
❑Anl 5, Sum 63, 80pgs.	0.25	20.00	50.00	100.00
❑Anl 6, Win 64	0.25	15.00	37.50	75.00
❑Anl 7, Sum 64	—	15.00	37.50	75.00
❑Anl 8, 82, A: Ra's Al Ghul	1.00	1.40	3.50	7.00
❑Anl 9, 85, AN; PS; JOy	1.25	1.20	3.00	6.00
❑Anl 10, 86	1.25	1.20	3.00	6.00
❑Anl 11, 87, AMo (w)	1.25	1.20	3.00	6.00
❑Anl 12, 88	1.50	1.00	2.50	5.00
❑Anl 13, 89, Who's Who entries	1.75	1.00	2.50	5.00
❑Anl 14, 90, O: Two-Face	2.00	0.60	1.50	3.00
❑Anl 15, 91, Armageddon 2001, Part 3, A: Joker, 1st printing, Armageddon 2001	2.00	0.60	1.50	3.00
❑Anl 15-2, 2nd Printing	2.00	0.80	2.00	4.00
❑Anl 15-2, 2nd Printing	2.00	0.80	2.00	4.00
❑Anl 17, 93, Bloodlines, 1: Ballistic, Bloodlines	2.50	0.60	1.50	3.00
❑Anl 18, 94, Black Masterpiece, Elseworlds	2.95	0.60	1.50	3.00
❑Anl 19, 95, O: Scarecrow, Year One	3.95	0.79	1.98	3.95
❑Anl 20, 96, Legends of the Dead Earth	2.95	0.59	1.48	2.95
❑Anl 21, 97, Pulp Heroes	3.95	0.79	1.98	3.95
❑Anl 22, 98, Ghosts	2.95	0.59	1.48	2.95
❑Anl 23, Sep 99, Jungle Rules, JLApe	2.95	0.59	1.48	2.95
❑Anl 24, Oct 00, JA, Planet DC; Lost Boys, 1: The Boggart	3.50	0.70	1.75	3.50
❑GS 1, Aug 98, Batman: Maintaining Appearances; Penguin: Possessions, 80pgs.	4.95	0.99	2.47	4.95
❑GS 2, Oct 99, Gotham Roulette; Hunting for Answers, 80pgs.	4.95	0.99	2.47	4.95
❑GS 3, Jul 00, BSz, All the Deadly Days; A Month of Sundays, 80pgs.	5.95	1.19	2.97	5.95

BATMAN 3-D
DC

Value: Cover or less ❑1, JBy, nn 9.95

BATMAN ADVENTURES, THE
DC

	ORIG	GOOD	FINE	N-MINT
❑1, Oct 92, Penguin's Big Score, Act One: Charm School, A: Penguin, based on animated series, V: Penguin	1.25	0.80	2.00	4.00
❑1/SI, 92, Penguin's Big Score, Act One: Charm School, silver edition	1.95	0.39	0.98	1.95
❑2, Nov 92, V: Catwoman	1.25	0.50	1.25	2.50
❑3, Dec 92, V: Joker	1.25	0.50	1.25	2.50
❑4, Jan 93, Riot Act, Part 1, Robin	1.25	0.50	1.25	2.50
❑5, Feb 93, Riot Act, Part 2, V: Scarecrow.	1.25	0.50	1.25	2.50
❑6, Mar 93	1.25	0.40	1.00	2.00
❑7, Apr 93, V: Killer Croc, trading card	1.25	0.80	2.00	4.00
❑7/CS, Apr 93, trading card, V: Killer Croc.	1.25	0.80	2.00	4.00
❑8, May 93, Larceny, My Sweet	1.25	0.40	1.00	2.00
❑9, Jun 93	1.25	0.40	1.00	2.00
❑10, Jul 93, V: Riddler	1.25	0.40	1.00	2.00
❑11, Aug 93, V: Man-Bat	1.25	0.30	0.75	1.50
❑12, Sep 93, Batgirl: Day One, Batgirl	1.25	0.30	0.75	1.50
❑13, Oct 93	1.25	0.30	0.75	1.50
❑14, Nov 93, Robin	1.25	0.30	0.75	1.50
❑15, Dec 93	1.25	0.30	0.75	1.50
❑16, Jan 94, The Killing Book, V: Joker	1.50	0.30	0.75	1.50
❑17, Feb 94, The Tangled Web	1.50	0.30	0.75	1.50
❑18, Mar 94, Batgirl-Robin	1.50	0.30	0.75	1.50
❑19, Apr 94, V: Scarecrow	1.50	0.30	0.75	1.50
❑20, May 94	1.50	0.30	0.75	1.50
❑21, Jun 94, V: Man-Bat, A: Catwoman	1.50	0.30	0.75	1.50
❑22, Jul 94, V: Two-Face	1.50	0.30	0.75	1.50
❑23, Aug 94, V: Poison Ivy	1.50	0.30	0.75	1.50
❑24, Sep 94	1.50	0.30	0.75	1.50
❑25, Oct 94, A: Superman; A: Lex Luthor, Giant-size	2.50	0.50	1.25	2.50
❑26, Nov 94, A: Batgirl	1.50	0.30	0.75	1.50
❑27, Dec 94	1.50	0.30	0.75	1.50
❑28, Jan 95, A: Harley Quinn	1.50	0.30	0.75	1.50
❑29, Feb 95, V: Ra's Al Ghul	1.50	0.30	0.75	1.50
❑30, Mar 95, O: Mastermind (DC); O: Mister Nice; O: The Perfesser	1.50	0.30	0.75	1.50
❑31, Apr 95	1.50	0.30	0.75	1.50
❑32, Jun 95	1.50	0.30	0.75	1.50
❑33, Jul 95	1.75	0.35	0.88	1.75
❑34, Aug 95, V: Hugo Strange, A: Catwoman	1.75	0.35	0.88	1.75
❑35, Sep 95, V: Hugo Strange, A: Catwoman	1.75	0.35	0.88	1.75
❑36, Oct 95, V: Hugo Strange, A: Catwoman, Final Issue	1.75	0.35	0.88	1.75
❑Anl 1, 94	2.95	0.59	1.48	2.95
❑Anl 2, 95, A: The Demon	3.50	0.70	1.75	3.50
❑HS 1, Jan 95, V: Mr. Freeze, gatefold summary	2.95	0.59	1.48	2.95

BATMAN ADVENTURES, THE: MAD LOVE
DC

	ORIG	GOOD	FINE	N-MINT
❑1, Feb 94, O: Harley Quinn; A: Joker, nn.	3.95	3.00	7.50	15.00
❑1-2, 94, O: Harley Quinn; A: Joker, nn; prestige format	4.95	1.10	2.75	5.50

BATMAN ADVENTURES, THE: THE LOST YEARS
DC

Value: Cover or less

- ❑1, Jan, fills in time between first and second Batman animated series 1.95
- ❑2, Feb 98, A: Robin II........ 1.95
- ❑3, Mar 98, How You See 'em, V: Two-Face 1.95
- ❑4, Apr 98 .... 1.95
- ❑5, May 98, A: Nightwing........ 1.95

BATMAN/ALIENS
DARK HORSE

Value: Cover or less

- ❑1, Mar, BWr, prestige format; crossover with DC........ 4.95
- ❑2, Apr, BWr, prestige format; crossover with DC........ 4.95

BATMAN AND OTHER DC CLASSICS
DC

	ORIG	GOOD	FINE	N-MINT
❑1, FM; BB; GP, Reprints from Batman #47, Camelot 3000, Justice League (87), New Teen Titans, O: Batman	—	0.20	0.50	1.00

BATMAN AND ROBIN ADVENTURES, THE
DC

	ORIG	GOOD	FINE	N-MINT
❑1, Nov 95	1.75	0.60	1.50	3.00
❑2, Dec 95, V: Two-Face	1.75	0.40	1.00	2.00
❑3, Jan 96, Christmas Riddle, V: Riddler	1.75	0.40	1.00	2.00
❑4, Feb 96, Birdcage, V: Penguin	1.75	0.40	1.00	2.00
❑5, Mar 96, Second Banana, V: Joker	1.75	0.40	1.00	2.00
❑6, May 96	1.75	0.35	0.88	1.75
❑7, Jun 96, V: Scarface	1.75	0.35	0.88	1.75
❑8, Jul 96, Robin is enslaved by Poison Ivy	1.75	0.35	0.88	1.75
❑9, Aug 96, Batgirl versus Talia	1.75	0.35	0.88	1.75
❑10, Sep 96, V: Ra's Al Ghul	1.75	0.35	0.88	1.75
❑11, Oct 96, Windows to the Soul	1.75	0.35	0.88	1.75
❑12, Nov 96, To Live and Die in Gotham City!, V: Bane	1.75	0.35	0.88	1.75
❑13, Dec 96, Knightmare, V: Scarecrow	1.75	0.35	0.88	1.75
❑14, Jan 97, Dagger's Tale	1.75	0.35	0.88	1.75
❑15, Feb 97, A: Deadman	1.75	0.35	0.88	1.75
❑16, Mar 97, It Takes a Cat, A: Catwoman	1.75	0.35	0.88	1.75
❑17, Apr 97	1.75	0.35	0.88	1.75
❑18, May 97, V: Joker	1.75	0.35	0.88	1.75
❑19, Jun 97, Duty of the Huntress	1.75	0.35	0.88	1.75
❑20, Jul 97	1.75	0.35	0.88	1.75
❑21, Aug 97, Batgirl vs. Riddler	1.75	0.35	0.88	1.75
❑22, Sep 97, V: Two-Face	1.75	0.35	0.88	1.75
❑23, Oct 97, V: Killer Croc	1.75	0.35	0.88	1.75
❑24, Nov 97, Touch of Death, V: Poison Ivy	1.75	0.35	0.88	1.75
❑25, Dec 97, Demon in the Sky, V: Ra's Al Ghul, Face cover; Final Issue; Giant-size	2.95	0.59	1.48	2.95
❑Anl 1, Nov 96, Shadow of the Phantasm, sequel to Batman: Mask of the Phantasm	2.95	0.59	1.48	2.95
❑Anl 2, JSa, Token of Faith, A: Zatanna; A: Zatara, ties in with Adventures in the DC Universe Annual #1 and Superman Adventures Annual #1	3.95	0.79	1.98	3.95

BATMAN AND ROBIN ADVENTURES, THE: SUB-ZERO
DC

Value: Cover or less

- ❑1, 97, V: Mr. Freeze, nn; cover says 98; adapts direct-to-video movie; indicia says 97........ 3.95

BATMAN AND ROBIN: THE OFFICIAL ADAPTATION OF THE WARNER BROS. MOTION PICTURE
DC

Value: Cover or less

- ❑1, 97, nn; movie Adaptation; prestige format........ 5.95

BATMAN & SUPERMAN ADVENTURES: WORLD'S FINEST
DC

Value: Cover or less

- ❑1, 97, JSa, nn; prestige format; adapts 90-minute special........ 6.95

BATMAN AND SUPERMAN: WORLD'S FINEST
DC

	ORIG	GOOD	FINE	N-MINT
❑1, Apr 99, prestige format	4.95	0.50	1.25	2.50
❑1/Aut, Signed by Karl Kesel	—	3.79	9.48	18.95
❑2, May 99, A Tale of Two Cities	1.99	0.40	1.00	2.00
❑3, Jun 99, Light in the Darkness, V: Joker	1.99	0.40	1.00	2.00
❑4, Jul 99, Underworlds	1.99	0.40	1.00	1.99
❑5, Aug 99, A Woman's Work, A: Batgirl	1.99	0.40	1.00	1.99
❑6, Sep 99, The Imp-Possible Dream, A: Mr. Mxyzptlk; A: Bat-Mite	1.99	0.40	1.00	1.99
❑7, Oct 99, A Better World	1.99	0.40	1.00	1.99
❑8, Nov 99	1.99	0.40	1.00	1.99
❑9, Dec 99, When it Reigns...It Pours!	1.99	0.40	1.00	1.99
❑10, Jan 00, War of the Worlds!	4.95	0.40	1.00	1.99

BATMAN AND THE OUTSIDERS
DC

The three DC "Adventures" titles — *Batman and Robin Adventures, Adventures in the DC Universe,* and *Superman Adventures* — crossed over in their respective 1997 annuals.

	ORIG	GOOD	FINE	N-MINT
❑1, Aug 83, 1: Baron Bedlam; O: Geo-Force	0.60	0.60	1.50	3.00
❑2, Sep 83, JA, Markovia's Last Stand!, V: Baron Bedlam	0.60	0.40	1.00	2.00
❑3, Oct 83, JA, V: Agent Orange	0.60	0.40	1.00	2.00
❑4, Nov 83, JA	0.60	0.40	1.00	2.00
❑5, Dec 83, JA, A: New Teen Titans	0.75	0.40	1.00	2.00
❑6, Jan 84	0.75	0.30	0.75	1.50
❑7, Feb 84	0.75	0.30	0.75	1.50
❑8, Mar 84	0.75	0.30	0.75	1.50
❑9, Apr 84, 1: Masters of Disaster	0.75	0.30	0.75	1.50
❑10, May 84, V: Masters of Disaster	0.75	0.30	0.75	1.50
❑11, Jun 84, O: Katana	0.75	0.25	0.63	1.25
❑12, Jul 84, O: Katana	0.75	0.25	0.63	1.25
❑13, Aug 84	0.75	0.25	0.63	1.25
❑14, Oct 84, V: Maxie Zeus	0.75	0.25	0.63	1.25
❑15, Nov 84, V: Maxie Zeus	0.75	0.25	0.63	1.25
❑16, Dec 84, The Truth About Halo, Part 1.	0.75	0.25	0.63	1.25
❑17, Jan 85	0.75	0.25	0.63	1.25
❑18, Feb 85	0.75	0.25	0.63	1.25
❑19, Mar 85	0.75	0.25	0.63	1.25
❑20, Apr 85, The Truth About Halo, Part 2, 1: Syonide II	0.75	0.25	0.63	1.25
❑21, May 85	0.75	0.25	0.63	1.25
❑22, Jun 85, The Truth About Halo, Part 3	0.75	0.25	0.63	1.25
❑23, Jul 85, The Truth About Halo, Part 4	0.75	0.25	0.63	1.25
❑24, Aug 85	0.75	0.25	0.63	1.25
❑25, Sep 85	0.75	0.25	0.63	1.25
❑26, Oct 85, V: Kobra	0.75	0.25	0.63	1.25
❑27, Nov 85	0.75	0.25	0.63	1.25
❑28, Dec 85, The Truth About Looker, Part 1	0.75	0.25	0.63	1.25
❑29, Jan 86, The Truth About Looker, Part 2	0.75	0.25	0.63	1.25
❑30, Feb 86, The Truth About Looker, Part 3	0.75	0.25	0.63	1.25
❑31, Mar 86, The Truth About Looker, Part 4	0.75	0.25	0.63	1.25
❑32, Apr 86, Series continues as Adventures of the Outsiders; Batman leaves	0.75	0.25	0.63	1.25
❑Anl 1, FM (c), 1: Major Victory; 1: Force of July	1.25	0.30	0.75	1.50
❑Anl 2, JA, Wedding of Metamorpho and Sapphire Stag	1.25	0.25	0.63	1.25

BATMAN: ARKHAM ASYLUM - TALES OF MADNESS
DC

Value: Cover or less

- ❑1, May 98, Cataclysm, Part 16, One-Shot........ 2.95

BATMAN: A WORD TO THE WISE
DC

Value: Cover or less

- ❑1, nn; (DC giveaway); (DC give-away)........ 1.25

BATMAN: BANE
DC

Value: Cover or less

- ❑1, 97, nn; prestige format one-shot, cover is part of quadtych........ 4.95

BATMAN: BANE OF THE DEMON
DC

Value: Cover or less

- ❑1, Mar 98, O: Bane........ 1.95
- ❑2, Apr 98........ 1.95
- ❑3, May 98........ 1.95
- ❑4, Jun 98........ 1.95

BATMAN: BATGIRL
DC

Value: Cover or less

- ❑1, 97, nn; cover is part of quadtych; prestige format one-shot 4.95

BATMAN: BATGIRL (GIRLFRENZY)
DC

Value: Cover or less

- ❑1, Jun 98, Scars, V: Mr. Zsasz, One-Shot; Girlfrenzy; one-shot, V: Mr. Zsasz........ 1.95

BATMAN BEYOND
DC

	ORIG	GOOD	FINE	N-MINT
❑1, adapts first episode	1.99	0.50	1.25	2.50
❑2, Dec 99, Ebony Tears, adapts first episode	1.99	0.40	1.00	2.00
❑3, Jan 00, Zoologically Speaking, V: Blight	1.99	0.40	1.00	2.00
❑4, Feb 00, A: Demon	1.99	0.40	1.00	1.99
❑5, Mar 00	1.99	0.40	1.00	1.99
❑6, Apr 00, Most Dangerous Island	1.99	0.40	1.00	1.99
❑7, May 00, McGinnis' Secret	1.99	0.40	1.00	1.99
❑8, Jun 00	1.99	0.40	1.00	1.99
❑9, Jul 00, The Last of Her Kind	1.99	0.40	1.00	1.99
❑10, Aug 00, Toy Wonder, V: Golem	1.99	0.40	1.00	1.99

	ORIG	GOOD	FINE	N-MINT
❑11, Sep 00, The Perfect You	1.99	0.40	1.00	1.99
❑12, Oct 00, Terminal Velocity, V: Terminal	1.99	0.40	1.00	1.99
❑13, Nov 00, Commissioner of Fear, A: Batgirl; A: Scarecrow	1.99	0.40	1.00	1.99
❑14, Dec 00, May Flights of Demons Sing Thee to Thy Rest, A: Demon	1.99	0.40	1.00	1.99
❑15, Jan 01, Lightning and Rain	1.99	0.40	1.00	1.99
❑16, Feb 01, Snake Food	1.99	0.40	1.00	1.99
❑17, Mar 01, A Sinking Ship	1.99	0.40	1.00	1.99
❑18, Apr 01, Prey or Hunter, Hunter or Prey	1.99	0.40	1.00	1.99
❑19, May 01, Royal Mayhem	1.99	0.40	1.00	1.99
❑20	1.99	0.40	1.00	1.99
❑21	1.99	0.40	1.00	1.99
❑22	1.99	0.40	1.00	1.99
❑23	1.99	0.40	1.00	1.99

BATMAN BEYOND (MINI-SERIES)
DC

	ORIG	GOOD	FINE	N-MINT
❑1, Mar 99, Not On My Watch!, O: Batman II (Terry McGuiness), adapts first episode	1.99	0.50	1.25	2.50
❑2, Apr 99, Rebirth, part 2, O: Batman II (Terry McGuiness); A: Derek Powers, adapts first episode	1.99	0.40	1.00	2.00
❑3, May 99, Never Mix, Never Worry, V: Blight	1.99	0.40	1.00	2.00
❑4, Jun 99, JSa, Magic Is Everywhere!, A: Demon	1.99	0.40	1.00	2.00
❑5, Jul 99, Mummy, Oh! And Juliet	1.99	0.40	1.00	2.00
❑6, Aug 99, JSa, Permanent Inque Stains	1.99	0.40	1.00	2.00

BATMAN BEYOND: RETURN OF THE JOKER
DC

Value: Cover or less

❑1, Feb 01 .... 2.95

BATMAN BEYOND SPECIAL ORIGIN ISSUE
DC

	ORIG	GOOD	FINE	N-MINT
❑1, Jun 99, Rebirth, Free	—	0.10	0.25	0.50

BATMAN BLACK AND WHITE
DC

	ORIG	GOOD	FINE	N-MINT
❑1, Jun 96, JLee(c), b&w; Anthology	2.95	0.80	2.00	4.00
❑2, Jul 96, FM (c), b&w; Anthology	2.95	0.70	1.75	3.50
❑3, Aug 96, b&w; Anthology	2.95	0.70	1.75	3.50
❑4, Sep 96, ATh (c), b&w; Final Issue; Anthology	2.95	0.70	1.75	3.50

BATMAN: BLACKGATE
DC

Value: Cover or less

❑1, Jan 97, JSa, Hatred's Home, One-Shot 3.95

BATMAN: BLACKGATE-ISLE OF MEN
DC

Value: Cover or less

❑1, Apr 98, JA, Cataclysm, Part 8, one-shot, continues in Batman: Shadow of the Bat #74 .... 2.95

BATMAN: BOOK OF THE DEAD
DC

Value: Cover or less

❑1, Jun 99 .... 4.95

❑2, Jul 99 .... 4.95

BATMAN: BULLOCK'S LAW
DC

Value: Cover or less

❑1, Aug 99, Bullock's Law, One-Shot 4.95

BATMAN/CAPTAIN AMERICA
DC

Value: Cover or less

❑1, 96, JBy, JBy (w), prestige format crossover with Marvel, Elseworlds; prestige format crossover with Marvel; Elseworlds 5.95

BATMAN: CASTLE OF THE BAT
DC

Value: Cover or less

❑1, 94, prestige format; Elseworlds 5.95

BATMAN: CATWOMAN DEFIANT
DC

	ORIG	GOOD	FINE	N-MINT
❑1, nn; cover forms diptych with Batman: Penguin Triumphant; prestige format	4.95	1.00	2.50	5.00

BATMAN CHRONICLES, THE
DC

	ORIG	GOOD	FINE	N-MINT
❑1, Jun 95, Midnight Train; Anarky: Tomorrow Belongs to Us, Giant-size	2.95	0.80	2.00	4.00
❑2, Sep 95	2.95	0.70	1.75	3.50
❑3, Dec 95, BB (c), The Riddle of the Jinxed Sphinx; The First Cut is Deepest, O: Mr. Zsasz, A: Riddler, Killer Croc	2.95	0.70	1.75	3.50
❑4, Mar 96, Contagion; Hitman, A: Hitman	2.95	1.60	4.00	8.00
❑5, Jun 96, HC (c)	2.95	0.70	1.75	3.50
❑6, Sep 96, CS, Choices; Shadow Job	2.95	0.70	1.75	3.50
❑7, Dec 96, JO (c), A: Superman	2.95	0.70	1.75	3.50
❑8, Mar 97, SB, V: Ra's Al Ghul	2.95	0.70	1.75	3.50
❑9, Jun 97, Movie poster cover	2.95	0.70	1.75	3.50
❑10, Sep 97, BSz	2.95	0.70	1.75	3.50
❑11, Dec 97	2.95	0.70	1.75	3.50
❑12, Mar 98, Cataclysm, Part 10	2.95	0.70	1.75	3.50
❑13, Jun 98	2.95	0.59	1.48	2.95
❑14, Sep 98, Aftershock	2.95	0.59	1.48	2.95
❑15, Dec 98, Road to No Man's Land, A: Oracle; A: Question; A: Green Lantern; A: Man-Bat, team-up issue	2.95	0.59	1.48	2.95
❑16, Mar 99, Two Down, A: Two Face; A: Batgirl; A: Renee Montoya, No Man's Land	2.95	0.59	1.48	2.95
❑17, Jun 99, BSz, Little Bat Lost; Turn On, Tune In, Freak Out, No Man's Land; Man-Bat's child	2.95	0.59	1.48	2.95
❑18, Sep 99, DGry(w), Spiritual Currency, No Man's Land	2.95	0.59	1.48	2.95
❑19, Dec 99, Got a Date with an Angel; Rapscallions	2.95	0.59	1.48	2.95
❑20, Mar 00, Whippersnappers of Mass Destruction; Photo Finish	2.95	0.59	1.48	2.95
❑21	2.95	0.59	1.48	2.95
❑22, Sep 00, Pay the Ferryman; Cry, Uncle	2.95	0.59	1.48	2.95
❑23, Dec 00, The Bomb, the Bull, the Butler & the Bat; Automotive	2.95	0.59	1.48	2.95

BATMAN CHRONICLES GALLERY, THE
DC

Value: Cover or less

❑1, May 97, pin-ups 3.50

BATMAN CHRONICLES: THE GAUNTLET
DC

Value: Cover or less

❑1, 97, nn; prestige format; 1st Robin solo adventure 4.95

BATMAN/DAREDEVIL
DC

Value: Cover or less

❑1, King of New York 5.95

BATMAN: DARK ALLEGIANCES
DC

Value: Cover or less

❑1, 96, HC, HC (w) 5.95

BATMAN: DARK KNIGHT ADVENTURES
DC

Value: Cover or less

❑1 .... 7.95

BATMAN: DARK KNIGHT GALLERY
DC

Value: Cover or less

❑1, Jan 96, pin-ups 3.50

BATMAN: DARK KNIGHT OF THE ROUND TABLE
DC

Value: Cover or less

❑1, 99, prestige format; Elseworlds story 4.95

❑2, 99, DG, BL (w), prestige format; Elseworlds story 4.95

BATMAN: DARK VICTORY
DC

Value: Cover or less

❑0, JPH (w), Wizard giveaway .... —

❑1, Dec 99, JPH (w), War, prestige format 4.95

❑2, Jan 00, JPH (w), cardstock cover 2.95

❑3, Feb 00, JPH (w), cardstock cover 2.95

❑4, Mar 00, JPH (w), cardstock cover 2.95

❑5, Apr 00, JPH (w), Love, cardstock cover 2.95

❑6, May 00, JPH (w), Hate, cardstock cover 2.95

❑7, Jun 00, JPH (w), cardstock cover 2.95

❑8, Jul 00, JPH (w), Battle, cardstock cover 2.95

❑9, Aug 00, JPH (w), cardstock cover 2.95

❑10, Sep 00, JPH (w), Justice, cardstock cover 2.95

❑11, Oct 00, JPH (w), Passion, cardstock cover 2.95

❑12, Nov 00, JPH (w), Revenge, cardstock cover 2.95

❑13, Dec 00, JPH (w), Peace, prestige format 4.95

BATMAN: DAY OF JUDGMENT
DC

Value: Cover or less

❑1, Nov 99, Original Gangsters 3.95

BATMAN: DEATH OF INNOCENTS
DC

Value: Cover or less

❑1, Dec 96, JSa, one-shot about the dangers of landmines and unexploded ordnance 3.95

BATMAN/DEMON
DC

Value: Cover or less

❑1, 96, nn; prestige format one-shot 4.95

BATMAN/DEMON: A TRAGEDY
DC

Value: Cover or less

❑1 .... 5.95

BATMAN: DOA
DC

Value: Cover or less

❑1, BH, BH (w) 6.95

BATMAN FAMILY, THE
DC

	ORIG	GOOD	FINE	N-MINT
❑1, Oct 75	0.50	2.80	7.00	14.00
❑2, Dec 75	0.50	2.00	5.00	10.00
❑3, Feb 76	0.50	1.40	3.50	7.00
❑4, Apr 76, Batgirl: Cage Me or Kill Me!; Robin: Robin's Very White Christmas!, A: Fatman	0.50	1.40	3.50	7.00
❑5, Jun 76	0.50	1.40	3.50	7.00

	ORIG	GOOD	FINE	N-MINT
❑6, Aug 76	0.50	1.40	3.50	7.00
❑7, Sep 76	0.50	1.20	3.00	6.00
❑8, Nov 76	0.50	1.20	3.00	6.00
❑9, Jan 77, A: Duela Dent	0.50	1.40	3.50	7.00
❑10, Mar 77	0.50	1.40	3.50	7.00
❑11, May 77	0.50	1.00	2.50	5.00
❑12, Jul 77	0.60	1.00	2.50	5.00
❑13, Sep 77, V: Outsider, A: Man-Bat	0.60	1.00	2.50	5.00
❑14, Oct 77	0.60	1.00	2.50	5.00
❑15, Dec 77	0.60	1.00	2.50	5.00
❑16, Feb 78	0.60	1.00	2.50	5.00
❑17, Apr 78	1.00	1.20	3.00	6.00
❑18, Jun 78	1.00	1.20	3.00	6.00
❑19, Aug 78	1.00	1.20	3.00	6.00
❑20, Oct 78, Final Issue	1.00	1.20	3.00	6.00

BATMAN FOREVER: THE OFFICIAL COMIC ADAPTATION OF THE WARNER BROS. MOTION PICTURE
DC

Value: Cover or less

- ❑1, 95, nn; movie Adaptation.. 3.95
- ❑1/PR, nn; movie adaptation, prestige format ... 5.95

BATMAN: FULL CIRCLE
DC

	ORIG	GOOD	FINE	N-MINT
❑1, nn; prestige format	5.95	1.20	3.00	6.00

BATMAN GALLERY, THE
DC

Value: Cover or less

- ❑1, NA; FM; BB; JKu; DG; GP; TMc; MA ... 2.95

BATMAN: GCPD
DC

Value: Cover or less

- ❑1, Aug 96, JA, Model Citizens 2.25
- ❑2, Sep 96, JA ... 2.25
- ❑3, Oct 96, JA, This Year's Murder ... 2.25
- ❑4, Nov 96, JA, Mortl Remains 2.25

BATMAN: GHOSTS
DC

Value: Cover or less

- ❑1, 95, JPH (w), A Tale Of Halloween In Gotham City, nn; prestige format one-shot ... 4.95

BATMAN: GORDON OF GOTHAM
DC

Value: Cover or less

- ❑1, Jun 98, KJ; DG, Dumb as a Rock ... 1.95
- ❑2, Jul 98, KJ; DG ... 1.95
- ❑3, Aug 98, KJ; DG, To Al Capone... ... 1.95
- ❑4, Sep 98, KJ; DG ... 1.95

BATMAN: GORDON'S LAW
DC

Value: Cover or less

- ❑1, Dec 96, KJ, Dirty Deal ... 1.95
- ❑2, Jan 97, KJ, Suspicious Minds ... 1.95
- ❑3, Feb 97, KJ ... 1.95
- ❑4, Mar 97, KJ ... 1.95

BATMAN: GOTHAM ADVENTURES
DC

	ORIG	GOOD	FINE	N-MINT
❑1, Jun 98, based on animated series, Joker has a price on his head	2.95	0.60	1.50	3.00
❑2, Jul 98, V: Two-Face	1.95	0.50	1.25	2.50
❑3, Aug 98, Just Another Day, cover is toy package mock-up	1.95	0.50	1.25	2.50
❑4, Sep 98, V: Catwoman	1.99	0.50	1.25	2.50
❑5, Oct 98	1.99	0.50	1.25	2.50
❑6, Nov 98, A: Deadman	1.99	0.50	1.25	2.50
❑7, Dec 98, Dagger's Secret	1.99	0.50	1.25	2.50
❑8, Jan 99, 1: Hunchback; A: Batgirl	1.99	0.50	1.25	2.50
❑9, Feb 99, V: Sensei; A: Batgirl; A: League of Assassins	1.99	0.50	1.25	2.50
❑10, Mar 99, A: Robin III (Timothy Drake); A: Harley Quinn; A: Nightwing; A: Joker	1.99	0.50	1.25	2.50
❑11, Apr 99, V: Riddler	1.99	0.40	1.00	2.00
❑12, May 99, V: Two-Face	1.99	0.40	1.00	2.00
❑13, Jun 99, The End, A: final	1.99	0.40	1.00	2.00
❑14, Jul 99, Masks of Love, V: Harley Quinn	1.99	0.40	1.00	2.00
❑15, Aug 99, Cash 'n the Hood!, V: Venom; A: Bane	1.99	0.40	1.00	2.00
❑16, Sep 99, Captive Audience, Alfred is kidnapped	1.99	0.40	1.00	2.00
❑17, Oct 99, Daddy Dearest	1.99	0.40	1.00	2.00
❑18, Nov 99, Like a Bat Outta Gotham, A: Man-Bat	1.99	0.40	1.00	2.00
❑19, Dec 99	1.99	0.40	1.00	2.00
❑20, Jan 00, ...And Oh So Delicious!	1.99	0.40	1.00	2.00
❑21, Feb 00, How the World Goes!	1.99	0.40	1.00	2.00
❑22, Mar 00	1.99	0.40	1.00	2.00
❑23, Apr 00	1.99	0.40	1.00	2.00
❑24, May 00, Missed Connections	1.99	0.40	1.00	2.00
❑25, Jun 00, ...Recognized, in Flashes, and With Glory...	1.99	0.40	1.00	2.00
❑26, Jul 00	1.99	0.40	1.00	2.00
❑27, Aug 00	1.99	0.40	1.00	2.00

Robin's first solo adventure was recounted in the prestige format one-shot *Batman Chronicles: The Gauntlet.*

© 1997 DC Comics

	ORIG	GOOD	FINE	N-MINT
❑28, Sep 00	1.99	0.40	1.00	1.99
❑29, Oct 00, JSa, Six Hours to Kill	1.99	0.40	1.00	1.99
❑30, Nov 00, Deals	1.99	0.40	1.00	1.99
❑31, Dec 00, A: Joker	1.99	0.40	1.00	1.99
❑32, Jan 01, The Remote Controller	1.99	0.40	1.00	1.99
❑33, Feb 01, World Without Batman	1.99	0.40	1.00	1.99
❑34, Mar 01, When in Rome	1.99	0.40	1.00	1.99
❑35, Apr 01, Stepping Forward	1.99	0.40	1.00	1.99
❑36, May 01	1.99	0.40	1.00	1.99
❑37, Jun 01, Images, A: Joker	1.99	0.40	1.00	1.99
❑38	1.99	0.40	1.00	1.99
❑39	1.99	0.40	1.00	1.99
❑40	1.99	0.40	1.00	1.99

BATMAN: GOTHAM BY GASLIGHT
DC

	ORIG	GOOD	FINE	N-MINT
❑1, nn; 52pgs.; One-Shot; prestige format; first Elseworlds story; Victorian-era Batman; Prelude by Robert Bloch	3.95	0.80	2.00	4.00

BATMAN GOTHAM CITY SECRET FILES
DC

Value: Cover or less

- ❑1, Apr 00 ... 4.95

BATMAN: GOTHAM KNIGHTS
DC

Value: Cover or less

- ❑1, Mar 00 ... 2.50
- ❑2, Apr 00, DGry(w), Down with the Ship ... 2.50
- ❑3, May 00, Samsara, Part 1; Broken Nose ... 2.50
- ❑4, Jun 00 ... 2.50
- ❑5, Jul 00 ... 2.50
- ❑6, Aug 00 ... 2.50
- ❑7, Sep 00, DGry(w), Oblation 2.50
- ❑8, Oct 00, DGry(w), Transference, Part 1 ... 2.50
- ❑9, Nov 00, DGry(w), Transference, Part 2 ... 2.50
- ❑10, Dec 00, DGry(w), Transference, Part 3 ... 2.50
- ❑11, Jan 01, DGry(w), Transference, Part 4 ... 2.50
- ❑12, Feb 01, Damages ... 2.50
- ❑13, Mar 01, Officer Down, Part 7 ... 2.50
- ❑14, Apr 01, DGry(w), Sibling Rivalry ... 2.50
- ❑15, May 01, DGry(w), Far From the Tree ... 2.50
- ❑16 ... 2.50
- ❑17 ... 2.50
- ❑18 ... 2.50
- ❑19 ... 2.50

BATMAN/GREEN ARROW: THE POISON TOMORROW
DC

	ORIG	GOOD	FINE	N-MINT
❑1, nn; prestige format	5.95	1.20	3.00	6.00

BATMAN/GRENDEL (1ST SERIES)
DC

	ORIG	GOOD	FINE	N-MINT
❑1, MW, Devil's Riddle, prestige format	4.95	1.20	3.00	6.00
❑2, MW, Devil's Riddle, prestige format, cover indicates Grendel/Batman; Index title: Grendel/Batman: Devil's Masque	4.95	1.20	3.00	6.00

BATMAN/GRENDEL (2ND SERIES)
DC

	ORIG	GOOD	FINE	N-MINT
❑1, Jun 96, Batman/Grendel: Devil's Bones; prestige format crossover with Dark Horse; concludes in Grendel/Batman: Devil's Dance	4.95	1.00	2.50	5.00
❑2, Jul 96, MW, MW (w), prestige format; Grendel/Batman: Devil's Dance; continued from Batman/Grendel: Devil's Bones	4.95	1.00	2.50	5.00

BATMAN: HARLEY QUINN
DC

	ORIG	GOOD	FINE	N-MINT
❑1, ca. 99, nn; prestige format	5.95	1.30	3.25	6.50
❑1-2, 2nd Printing	5.95	1.19	2.97	5.95

BATMAN: HAUNTED GOTHAM
DC

Value: Cover or less

- ❑1, Hell's Hunting Ground, prestige format; Elseworlds ... 4.95
- ❑2, prestige format; Elseworlds 4.95
- ❑3, Shattered Serpent, prestige format; Elseworlds ... 4.95
- ❑4, prestige format; Elseworlds 4.95

BATMAN/HELLBOY/STARMAN
DC

Value: Cover or less

- ❑1, Jan 99, JRo (w), Gotham Gray Evil ... 2.50
- ❑1/Aut, JRo (w), Signed by James Robinson and Mike Mignola 24.99
- ❑2, Feb 99, JRo (w), A: Golden-Age Starman ... 2.50

BATMAN: HOLLYWOOD KNIGHT
DC

Value: Cover or less

- ❑1, Apr 01, DG, BL (w), Tinseltown Terror, Elseworlds 2.50
- ❑2, May 01, DG, BL (w), A Devil in the City of Angels, Elseworlds 2.50
- ❑3, Jun 01, DG, BL (w), Elseworlds 2.50

BATMAN: HOLY TERROR
DC

	ORIG	GOOD	FINE	N-MINT
❑1, Oct 91, nn; One-Shot; prestige format; Elseworlds	4.95	1.00	2.50	5.00

BATMAN/HOUDINI: THE DEVIL'S WORKSHOP
DC

	ORIG	GOOD	FINE	N-MINT
❑1, nn; prestige format; Elseworlds	3.95	0.90	2.25	4.50

BATMAN/HUNTRESS: CRY FOR BLOOD
DC

Value: Cover or less

- ❑1, Jun 00 .... 2.50
- ❑2, Jul 00 .... 2.50
- ❑3, Aug 00, A: Question 2.50
- ❑4, Sep 00, O: The Huntress .. 2.50
- ❑5, Oct 00 .... 2.50
- ❑6, Nov 00 .... 2.50

BATMAN: HUNTRESS/SPOILER - BLUNT TRAUMA
DC

Value: Cover or less

- ❑1, May 98, Cataclysm, Part 13, continues in Detective Comics #721 .... 2.95

BATMAN: I, JOKER
DC

Value: Cover or less

- ❑1, BH, BH (w), nn; One-Shot; prestige format; Elseworlds. 4.95

BATMAN: IN DARKEST KNIGHT
DC

Value: Cover or less

- ❑1, nn; One-Shot; prestige format; Elseworlds; Bruce Wayne as Green Lantern 4.95

BATMAN: JOKER'S APPRENTICE
DC

Value: Cover or less

- ❑1, May 99, TVE, Joker's Apprentice...................................... 3.95

BATMAN: JOKER TIME
DC

Value: Cover or less

- ❑1, BH, BH (w), prestige format................................ 4.95
- ❑2, BH, BH (w), prestige format 4.95
- ❑3, BH, BH (w), prestige format 4.95

BATMAN/JUDGE DREDD: DIE LAUGHING
DC

Value: Cover or less

- ❑1, prestige format; Joker in Mega-City One 4.95
- ❑2, prestige format; Joker in Mega-City One 4.95

BATMAN/JUDGE DREDD: JUDGMENT ON GOTHAM
DC

Value: Cover or less

- ❑1, nn.................................... 5.95

BATMAN/JUDGE DREDD: THE ULTIMATE RIDDLE
DC

	ORIG	GOOD	FINE	N-MINT
❑1, nn; prestige format	4.95	1.00	2.50	5.00

BATMAN/JUDGE DREDD: VENDETTA IN GOTHAM
DC

	ORIG	GOOD	FINE	N-MINT
❑1, nn	5.95	1.20	3.00	6.00

BATMAN: LEGEND OF THE DARK KNIGHT
DC

Value: Cover or less

- ❑1.. 4.95
- ❑2.. 4.95
- ❑3.. 4.95
- ❑4.. 4.95

BATMAN: LEGENDS OF THE DARK KNIGHT
DC

	ORIG	GOOD	FINE	N-MINT
❑0, Oct 94, Viewpoint	1.95	0.50	1.25	2.50
❑1, Nov 89, The Shaman of Gotham, Part 1, Outer cover comes in four different colors (yellow, blue, orange, pink); poster	1.50	0.80	2.00	4.00
❑2, Dec 89, The Shaman of Gotham, Part 2	1.50	0.60	1.50	3.00
❑3, Jan 90, The Shaman of Gotham, Part 3	1.00	0.60	1.50	3.00
❑4, Feb 90, The Shaman of Gotham, Part 4	1.50	0.60	1.50	3.00
❑5, Mar 90, The Shaman of Gotham, Part 5	1.50	0.60	1.50	3.00
❑6, Apr 90, KJ, Gothic, Part 1	1.50	0.50	1.25	2.50
❑7, May 90, KJ, Gothic, Part 2	1.50	0.50	1.25	2.50
❑8, Jun 90, KJ, Gothic, Part 3	1.50	0.50	1.25	2.50
❑9, Jul 90, KJ, Gothic, Part 4	1.50	0.50	1.25	2.50
❑10, Aug 90, KJ, Gothic, Part 5	1.50	0.50	1.25	2.50
❑11, Sep 90, TD; PG, Prey, Part 1	1.50	0.50	1.25	2.50
❑12, Oct 90, TD; PG, Prey, Part 2	1.50	0.50	1.25	2.50
❑13, Nov 90, TD; PG, Prey, Part 3	1.50	0.50	1.25	2.50
❑14, Dec 90, TD; PG, Prey, Part 4	1.50	0.50	1.25	2.50
❑15, Feb 91, TD; PG, Prey, Part 5	1.50	0.50	1.25	2.50
❑16, Mar 91, Venom, Part 1, Tie-in to Bane/KnightsEnd	1.50	0.70	1.75	3.50
❑17, Apr 91, Venom, Part 2, Tie-in to Bane/KnightsEnd	1.50	0.50	1.25	2.50
❑18, May 91, Venom, Part 3, Tie-in to Bane/KnightsEnd	1.50	0.50	1.25	2.50
❑19, Jun 91, Venom, Part 4, Tie-in to Bane/KnightsEnd	1.50	0.50	1.25	2.50
❑20, Jul 91, Venom, Part 5, Tie-in to Bane/KnightsEnd	1.75	0.50	1.25	2.50
❑21, Aug 91, Faith, Part 1	1.75	0.40	1.00	2.00
❑22, Sep 91, Faith, Part 2	1.75	0.40	1.00	2.00
❑23, Oct 91, Faith, Part 3	1.75	0.40	1.00	2.00
❑24, Nov 91, GK, Flyer, Part 1	1.75	0.40	1.00	2.00
❑25, Dec 91, GK, Flyer, Part 2	1.75	0.40	1.00	2.00
❑26, Jan 92, GK, Flyer, Part 3	1.75	0.40	1.00	2.00
❑27, Feb 92, Destroyer, Part 2, Gotham City Visions by Anton Furst feature	1.75	0.50	1.25	2.50
❑28, Mar 92, MW, Faces, Part 1, Two-Face	1.75	0.40	1.00	2.00
❑29, Apr 92, MW, Faces, Part 2, Two-Face	1.75	0.40	1.00	2.00
❑30, May 92, MW, Faces, Part 3, Two-Face	1.75	0.40	1.00	2.00
❑31, Jun 92, BA, Family	1.75	0.40	1.00	2.00
❑32, Jun 92, JRo (w), Blades; Blades, Part 1	1.75	0.40	1.00	2.00
❑33, Jul 92, JRo (w), Blades; Blades, Part 2	1.75	0.40	1.00	2.00
❑34, Jul 92, JRo (w), Blades; Blades, Part 3	1.75	0.40	1.00	2.00
❑35, Aug 92, Destiny, Part 1	1.75	0.40	1.00	2.00
❑36, Aug 92, Destiny, Part 2	1.75	0.40	1.00	2.00
❑37, Aug 92, Mercy, Series continues as Batman: Legends of the Dark Knight	1.75	0.40	1.00	2.00
❑38, Oct 92, Legends of the Dark Mite, A: Bat-Mite	1.75	0.40	1.00	2.00
❑39, Nov 92, BT, Mask, Part 1	1.75	0.40	1.00	2.00
❑40, Dec 92, BT, BT (w), Mask, Part 2	1.75	0.40	1.00	2.00
❑41, Jan 93, Sunset	1.75	0.40	1.00	2.00
❑42, Feb 93, CR, Hothouse; Hothouse, Part 1	1.75	0.40	1.00	2.00
❑43, Mar 93, CR, Hothouse; Hothouse, Part 2	1.75	0.40	1.00	2.00
❑44, Apr 93, Turf; Turf, Part 1	1.75	0.40	1.00	2.00
❑45, May 93, Turf; Turf, Part 2	1.75	0.40	1.00	2.00
❑46, Jun 93, RH, Heat; Heat, Part 1, V: Catman; A: Catwoman	1.75	0.40	1.00	2.00
❑47, Jul 93, RH, Heat; Heat, Part 2, V: Catman; A: Catwoman	1.75	0.40	1.00	2.00
❑48, Aug 93, Heat; Heat, Part 3, V: Catman; A: Catwoman	1.75	0.40	1.00	2.00
❑49, Aug 93, Heat; Heat, Part 4, V: Catman; A: Catwoman	1.75	0.40	1.00	2.00
❑50, Sep 93, A: Joker, foil cover; Giant-size	3.95	0.90	2.25	4.50
❑51, Sep 93, JKu (c), Snitch	1.75	0.40	1.00	2.00
❑52, Oct 93, Tao; Tao, Part 1	1.75	0.40	1.00	2.00
❑53, Oct 93, Tao; Tao, Part 2	1.75	0.40	1.00	2.00
❑54, Nov 93	1.75	0.40	1.00	2.00
❑55, Dec 93, Watchtower; Watchtower, Part 1	1.75	0.40	1.00	2.00
❑56, Jan 94, Watchtower; Watchtower, Part 2	1.75	0.40	1.00	2.00
❑57, Feb 94, Watchtower, Part 3	1.75	0.40	1.00	2.00
❑58, Mar 94, Storm	1.75	0.40	1.00	2.00
❑59, Apr 94, Knightquest: The Search; Quarry, Part 1	1.75	0.40	1.00	2.00
❑60, May 94, Knightquest: The Search; Quarry, Part 2	1.75	0.40	1.00	2.00
❑61, Jun 94, Knightquest: The Search; Quarry, Part 3	1.75	0.40	1.00	2.00
❑62, Jul 94, KnightsEnd, Part 4	1.75	0.40	1.00	2.00
❑63, Aug 94, KnightsEnd, Part 10	1.75	0.40	1.00	2.00
❑64, Sep 94	1.95	0.40	1.00	2.00
❑65, Nov 94, JSa, Going Sane; Going Sane, Part 1, V: Joker	1.95	0.40	1.00	2.00
❑66, Dec 94, JSa, Going Sane; Going Sane, Part 2, V: Joker	1.95	0.40	1.00	2.00
❑67, Jan 95, JSa, Going Sane; Going Sane, Part 3, V: Joker	1.95	0.40	1.00	2.00
❑68, Feb 95, Going Sane, V: Joker	1.95	0.40	1.00	2.00
❑69, Mar 95, Criminals; Criminals, Part 1	1.95	0.40	1.00	2.00
❑70, Apr 95, Criminals; Criminals, Part 2	1.95	0.40	1.00	2.00
❑71, May 95, Werewolf, Part 1 of 3	1.95	0.40	1.00	2.00
❑72, Jun 95, Werewolf, Part 2 of 3	1.95	0.40	1.00	2.00
❑73, Jul 95, Werewolf, Part 3 of 3	1.95	0.40	1.00	2.00
❑74, Aug 95, Engines, Part 1 of 2	1.95	0.40	1.00	2.00
❑75, Sep 95, Engines, Part 2 of 2	1.95	0.40	1.00	2.00
❑76, Oct 95, The Sleeping, Part 1 of 3	1.95	0.40	1.00	2.00
❑77, Nov 95, The Sleeping, Part 2 of 3	1.95	0.40	1.00	2.00
❑78, Dec 95, The Sleeping, Part 3 of 3	1.95	0.40	1.00	2.00
❑79, Jan, Favorite Things	1.95	0.40	1.00	2.00
❑80, Feb, Idols, Part 1	1.95	0.40	1.00	2.00
❑81, Mar, Idols, Part 2	1.95	0.40	1.00	2.00
❑82, May, Idols, Part 3	1.95	0.40	1.00	2.00
❑83, Jun, Infected, Part 1 of 2	1.95	0.40	1.00	2.00
❑84, Jul, Infected, Part 2 of 2	1.95	0.40	1.00	2.00
❑85, Aug, Citadel	1.95	0.40	1.00	2.00
❑86, Sep, Conspiracy, Part 1 of 3	1.95	0.40	1.00	2.00
❑87, Oct, Conspiracy, Part 2 of 3	1.95	0.40	1.00	2.00
❑88, Nov, Conspiracy, Part 3 of 3	1.95	0.40	1.00	2.00
❑89, Dec, Clay, Part 1 of 2, O: Clayface (Matt Hagen)	1.95	0.40	1.00	2.00

	ORIG	GOOD	FINE	N-MINT
❑90, Jan, Clay, Part 2 of 2	1.95	0.40	1.00	2.00
❑91, Feb, Freakout, Part 1 of 3	1.95	0.40	1.00	2.00
❑92, Mar, Freakout, Part 2 of 3	1.95	0.40	1.00	2.00
❑93, Apr, Freakout, Part 3 of 3	1.95	0.40	1.00	2.00
❑94, May 97, Stories, three eras of Batman	1.95	0.40	1.00	2.00
❑95, Jun, Dirty Tricks, Part 1 of 3	1.95	0.40	1.00	2.00
❑96, Jul, Dirty Tricks, Part 2 of 3	1.95	0.40	1.00	2.00
❑97, Aug, Dirty Tricks, Part 3 of 3	1.95	0.40	1.00	2.00
❑98, Sep 97, Steps, Part 1 of 2	1.95	0.40	1.00	2.00
❑99, Oct 97, Steps, Part 2 of 2	1.95	0.40	1.00	2.00
❑100, Nov 97, JRo (w), The Choice; A Great Day for Everyone, O: Robin I and Robin II; O: Robin I and Robin II, pin-up gallery; A: Joker, Double-size; pin-up gallery	3.95	0.90	2.25	4.50
❑101, Dec 97, The Incredible Adventures of Batman, Face cover; 100 years in the future	1.95	0.40	1.00	2.00
❑102, Jan 98, JRo (w), Spook, Part 1 of 3; Spook, Part 1	1.95	0.40	1.00	2.00
❑103, Feb 98, JRo (w), Spook, Part 2 of 3; Spook, Part 2	1.95	0.40	1.00	2.00
❑104, Mar 98, JRo (w), Spook, Part 3 of 3; Spook, Part 3	1.95	0.40	1.00	2.00
❑105, Apr, Duty, Part 1 of 2	1.95	0.40	1.00	2.00
❑106, May, Duty, Part 2 of 2, Gordon vs. Joker	1.95	0.40	1.00	2.00
❑107, Jun 98, Stalking, Part 1 of 2	1.95	0.40	1.00	2.00
❑108, Jul 98, Stalking, Part 2 of 2	1.95	0.40	1.00	2.00
❑109, Aug 98, The Primal Riddle, Part 1; Primal Riddle, Part 1, V: Riddler	1.95	0.40	1.00	2.00
❑110, Sep 98, The Primal Riddle, Part 2; Primal Riddle, Part 2, V: Riddler	1.99	0.40	1.00	2.00
❑111, Oct 98, The Primal Riddle, Part 3; Primal Riddle, Part 3, V: Riddler	1.99	0.40	1.00	2.00
❑112, Nov 98, Shipwreck, Part 1	1.99	0.40	1.00	2.00
❑113, Dec 98, Shipwreck, Part 2	1.99	0.40	1.00	2.00
❑114, Jan 99, Playground	1.99	0.40	1.00	2.00
❑115, Feb 99, LMc, The Darkness	1.99	0.40	1.00	2.00
❑116, Apr 99, Fear of Faith, Part 1, A: Huntress; A: Scarecrow, No Man's Land	1.99	0.40	1.00	2.00
❑117, May 99, Bread and Circuses, Part 1, V: Penguin, No Man's Land	1.99	0.40	1.00	2.00
❑118, Jun 99, Balance, No Man's Land	1.99	0.40	1.00	2.00
❑119, Jul 99, Claim Jumping, Part 1, A: Two-Face, No Man's Land	1.99	0.40	1.00	2.00
❑120, Aug 99, Assembly, A: Robin; 1: Batgirl III (in costume); A: Nightwing; A: Huntress, No Man's Land	1.99	0.60	1.50	3.00
❑121, Sep 99, Power Play, V: Mr. Freeze, No Man's Land	1.99	0.40	1.00	1.99
❑122, Oct 99, PG, Low Road to Golden Mountain, Part 1; ...Where the Lights are Burning Low, A: Lynx, No Man's Land	1.99	0.40	1.00	1.99
❑123, Nov 99, Underground Railroad, Part 1, No Man's Land	1.99	0.40	1.00	1.99
❑124, Dec 99, No Man's Land	1.99	0.40	1.00	1.99
❑125, Jan 00, Falling Back, No Man's Land; Batman attempts to reveal identity to Commissioner Gordon	1.99	0.40	1.00	1.99
❑126, Feb 00, DGry (w), Endgame, Part 1, No Man's Land	1.99	0.40	1.00	1.99
❑127, Mar 00, The Arrow and the Bat, Part 1	1.99	0.40	1.00	1.99
❑128, Apr 00, The Arrow and the Bat, Part 2	1.99	0.40	1.00	1.99
❑129, May 00, The Arrow and the Bat, Part 3	1.99	0.40	1.00	1.99
❑130, Jun 00, The Arrow and the Bat, Part 4	1.99	0.40	1.00	1.99
❑131, Jul 00	—	0.40	1.00	1.99
❑132, Aug 00, JRo, Siege, Part 1; Assembly, A: Silver St. Cloud	—	0.40	1.00	1.99
❑133, Sep 00, JRo, Siege, Part 2; Assault, A: Silver St. Cloud	—	0.40	1.00	1.99
❑134, Oct 00, JRo, Siege, Part 3; Breach, A: Silver St. Cloud	2.25	0.45	1.13	2.25
❑135, Nov 00, JRo, Siege, Part 4	2.25	0.45	1.13	2.25
❑136, Dec 00, JRo, Siege, Part 5	2.25	0.45	1.13	2.25
❑137, Jan 01, PG, Terror, Part 1	2.25	0.45	1.13	2.25
❑138, Feb 01, PG, Terror, Part 2	2.25	0.45	1.13	2.25
❑139, Mar 01, PG, Terror, Part 3	2.25	0.45	1.13	2.25
❑140, Apr 01, PG, Terror, Part 4	2.25	0.45	1.13	2.25
❑141, May 01, PG, Terror, Part 5	2.25	0.45	1.13	2.25
❑142, Jun 01, JA, The Demon Laughs, Part 1	2.25	0.45	1.13	2.25
❑143	2.25	0.45	1.13	2.25
❑144	2.25	0.45	1.13	2.25
❑145	2.25	0.45	1.13	2.25
❑Anl 1, Dec, Duel	3.95	0.90	2.25	4.50
❑Anl 2, Vows, Wedding of James Gordon	3.50	0.70	1.75	3.50
❑Anl 3, Bloodlines, 1: Cardinal Sin, Bloodlines	3.50	0.70	1.75	3.50
❑Anl 4, JSa, Elseworlds: Citizen Wayne, Elseworlds	3.50	0.70	1.75	3.50
❑Anl 5, Wings, O: Man-Bat, Year One	3.95	0.79	1.98	3.95
❑Anl 6, Legends of the Dead Earth	2.95	0.59	1.48	2.95

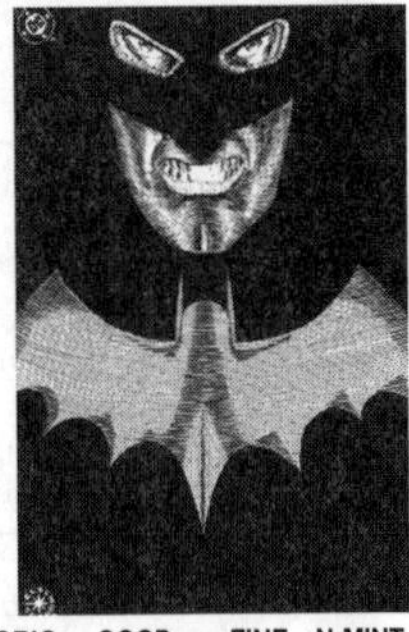

The world of Jules Verne and Batman met in the Elseworlds one-shot *Batman: Master of the Future.* The prestige-format issue followed the events of *Gotham by Gaslight.*

	ORIG	GOOD	FINE	N-MINT
❑Anl 7, A: Balloon Buster, Pulp Heroes	3.95	0.79	1.98	3.95
❑SE 1, prestige format	6.95	1.39	3.47	6.95

BATMAN: LEGENDS OF THE DARK KNIGHT: JAZZ
DC

Value: Cover or less

❑1, Apr 95 ... 2.50
❑2, May 95 ... 2.50
❑3, Jun 95 ... 2.50

BATMAN: MADNESS A LEGENDS OF THE DARK KNIGHT HALLOWEEN SPECIAL
DC

Value: Cover or less

❑1, JPH (w), One-Shot; prestige format ... 4.95

BATMAN: MANBAT
DC

	ORIG	GOOD	FINE	N-MINT
❑1, Oct, The Subterraneans, Part 1, prestige format; Elseworlds	4.95	1.00	2.50	5.00
❑2, Nov, The Subterraneans, Part 2, prestige format; Elseworlds	4.95	1.00	2.50	5.00
❑3, Dec, The Subterraneans, Part 3, prestige format; Elseworlds	4.95	1.00	2.50	5.00

BATMAN: MASK OF THE PHANTASM-THE ANIMATED MOVIE
DC

Value: Cover or less

❑1, Shady Lady, nn; newstand 2.95
❑1/PR, Shady Lady, nn; slick paper ... 4.95

BATMAN: MASQUE
DC

Value: Cover or less

❑1, MGr, MGr (w), nn; prestige format; Elseworlds; Phantom of the Opera theme; prestige format, Elseworlds, Phantom of the Opera theme ... 6.95

BATMAN: MASTER OF THE FUTURE
DC

Value: Cover or less

❑1, nn ... 5.95

BATMAN: MR. FREEZE
DC

Value: Cover or less

❑1, O: Mr. Freeze, nn; cover is part of quadtych; One-Shot; prestige format ... 4.95

BATMAN: MITEFALL
DC

Value: Cover or less

❑1, D: Bob Overdog, One-Shot; prestige format; prestige format one-shot ... 4.95

BATMAN: NO LAW AND A NEW ORDER
DC

Value: Cover or less

❑1, nn; collects Batman: No Man's Land #1, Batman #563, Batman: Shadow of the Bat #83, and Detective Comics #730 ... 5.95

BATMAN: NO MAN'S LAND
DC

	ORIG	GOOD	FINE	N-MINT
❑0, Dec 99, Ground Zero	4.95	0.99	2.47	4.95
❑1, Mar 99, No Law and a New Order, Part 1	2.95	0.59	1.48	2.95
❑1/Aut, No Law and a New Order, part 1, Signed by Alex Ross	—	3.59	8.98	17.95
❑1/SC, Mar, ARo (c), No Law and a New Order, part 1, lenticular animation cover	3.95	0.79	1.98	3.95
❑2, No Law and a New Order, part 2	2.95	0.59	1.48	2.95
❑3, No Law and a New Order, part 3	2.95	0.59	1.48	2.95
❑4, No Law and a New Order, part 4	2.95	0.59	1.48	2.95

BATMAN: NO MAN'S LAND GALLERY
DC

Value: Cover or less

❑1, Jul 99, pin-ups ... 3.95

BATMAN: NO MAN'S LAND SECRET FILES
DC

Value: Cover or less

❑1, Dec 99, The Message; Batcaves ... 4.95

BATMAN: NOSFERATU
DC

Value: Cover or less

❑1, nn; One-Shot; prestige format; Elseworlds ... 5.95

BATMAN: OUTLAWS
DC

Value: Cover or less

❑1, PG ... 4.95
❑2, PG ... 4.95
❑3, PG ... 4.95

BATMAN: PENGUIN TRIUMPHANT
DC

	ORIG	GOOD	FINE	N-MINT
❑1, JSa, nn; cover forms diptych with Batman: Catwoman Defiant; prestige format	4.95	1.00	2.50	5.00

BATMAN/PHANTOM STRANGER
DC

Value: Cover or less

❑1, nn; prestige format 4.95

BATMAN PLUS
DC

Value: Cover or less

❑1, Feb 97, DGry(w), Beauty and the Beast, A: Arsenal 2.95

BATMAN: POISON IVY
DC

Value: Cover or less

❑1, A: Poison Ivy; A: Batman; A: Croc, nn; cover is part of quadtych; One-Shot; prestige format 4.95

BATMAN/PREDATOR III
DC

Value: Cover or less

❑1, Nov 97 .... 1.95

❑2 .... 1.95

❑3 .... 1.95

❑4 .... 1.95

BATMAN/PUNISHER: LAKE OF FIRE
DC

	ORIG	GOOD	FINE	N-MINT
❑1, 94	4.95	1.00	2.50	5.00

BATMAN: REIGN OF TERROR
DC

Value: Cover or less

❑1, nn; prestige format; Elseworlds 4.95

BATMAN RETURNS: THE OFFICIAL COMIC ADAPTATION OF THE WARNER BROS. MOTION PICTURE
DC

	ORIG	GOOD	FINE	N-MINT
❑1, nn; movie Adaptation; Comic adaptation of Warner Bros. Movie	3.95	0.80	2.00	4.00
❑1/PR, nn; movie Adaptation; prestige format; Comic adaptation of Warner Bros. Movie	5.95	1.20	3.00	6.00

BATMAN: RIDDLER-THE RIDDLE FACTORY
DC

Value: Cover or less

❑1, MW (w), nn; cover forms diptych with Batman: Two-Face - Crime and Punishment; prestige format 4.95

BATMAN: RUN, RIDDLER, RUN
DC

	ORIG	GOOD	FINE	N-MINT
❑1, The Road To Hell, prestige format	4.95	1.00	2.50	5.00
❑2, prestige format	4.95	1.00	2.50	5.00
❑3, ...With Good Intentions, prestige format	4.95	1.00	2.50	5.00

BATMAN/SCARECROW 3-D
DC

Value: Cover or less

❑1, Dec 98, Concert of Fear, with glasses 3.95

❑1/SC, Dec 98, Concert of Fear 16.95

BATMAN/SCARFACE: A PSYCHODRAMA
DC

Value: Cover or less

❑1 .... 5.95

BATMAN: SCAR OF THE BAT
DC

Value: Cover or less

❑1, nn; prestige format; Elseworlds 4.95

BATMAN: SCOTTISH CONNECTION
DC

Value: Cover or less

❑1, Isle of Mists, nn; One-Shot; prestige format 5.95

BATMAN SECRET FILES
DC

Value: Cover or less

❑1, Oct, Gazing, background information 4.95

BATMAN: SEDUCTION OF THE GUN
DC

	ORIG	GOOD	FINE	N-MINT
❑1, Feb 93, Special edition on gun control; dedicated to John Reisenbach (Son of DC editor slain in gun killing)	2.50	0.70	1.75	3.50

BATMAN: SHADOW OF THE BAT
DC

	ORIG	GOOD	FINE	N-MINT
❑0, Oct, The Beginning Of Tomorrow, O: Batman, falls between issues #31 and 32	1.95	0.50	1.25	2.50
❑1, Jun, The Last Arkham, Part 1, Last Arkham	1.50	0.80	2.00	4.00
❑1/CS, Jun 92, The Last Arkham, Part 1, Arkham pop-up, posters, blueprint of Arkham Asylum, Bookmark; collector's set	2.00	1.10	2.75	5.50
❑2, Jul, The Last Arkham, Part 2, Last Arkham	1.50	0.60	1.50	3.00
❑3, Aug, The Last Arkham, Part 3, Last Arkham	1.50	0.60	1.50	3.00
❑4, Sep, The Last Arkham, Part 4, Last Arkham	1.50	0.60	1.50	3.00
❑5, Oct 92, The Black Spider	1.50	0.60	1.50	3.00
❑6, Nov 92, The Ugly American	1.50	0.50	1.25	2.50
❑7, Dec 92, The Misfits, Part 1	1.50	0.50	1.25	2.50
❑8, Jan 93, The Misfits, Part 2, Misfits	1.75	0.50	1.25	2.50
❑9, Feb 93, The Misfits, Part 3	1.75	0.50	1.25	2.50
❑10, Mar 93, The Thane of Gotham	1.75	0.50	1.25	2.50
❑11, Apr 93, The Human Flea, Part 1	1.75	0.50	1.25	2.50
❑12, May 93, The Human Flea, Part 2	1.75	0.50	1.25	2.50
❑13, Jun 93, The Nobody	1.75	0.50	1.25	2.50
❑14, Jul 93, JSa, Gotham Freaks, Part 1	1.75	0.50	1.25	2.50
❑15, Aug 93, JSa, Gotham Freaks, Part 2	1.75	0.50	1.25	2.50
❑16, Sep 93, The God of Fear, Part 1, V: Scarecrow	1.75	0.50	1.25	2.50
❑17, Sep 93, The God of Fear, Part 2, V: Scarecrow	1.75	0.50	1.25	2.50
❑18, Oct, Knightfall; The God of Fear, Part 3, V: Scarecrow	1.75	0.50	1.25	2.50
❑19, Oct, Knightquest: The Crusade; The Tally Man, Part 1, V: Tally Man	1.75	0.50	1.25	2.50
❑20, Nov, Knightquest: The Crusade; The Tally Man, Part 2, V: Tally Man	1.75	0.50	1.25	2.50
❑21, Nov, Knightquest: The Search; Bruce Wayne, Part 1	1.75	0.50	1.25	2.50
❑22, Dec, Knightquest: The Search; Bruce Wayne, Part 2	1.75	0.50	1.25	2.50
❑23, Jan, Knightquest: The Crusade; Bruce Wayne, Part 3	1.75	0.50	1.25	2.50
❑24, Feb, Knightquest: The Crusade; The Immigrant	1.75	0.50	1.25	2.50
❑25, Mar, Knightquest: The Crusade, A: Joe Public	1.75	0.50	1.25	2.50
❑26, Apr, Knightquest: The Crusade, V: Clayface	1.75	0.50	1.25	2.50
❑27, May, Knightquest: The Crusade	1.75	0.50	1.25	2.50
❑28, Jun, Knightquest: The Crusade	1.75	0.50	1.25	2.50
❑29, Jul, KnightsEnd, Part 2, Giant-size	2.95	0.50	1.25	2.50
❑30, Aug, KnightsEnd, Part 8	1.95	0.50	1.25	2.50
❑31, Sep 94, Zero Hour, R: Alfred as detective	1.95	0.50	1.25	2.50
❑32, Nov 94, Prodigal, Part 2	1.95	0.50	1.25	2.50
❑33, Dec 94, Prodigal, Part 6	1.95	0.50	1.25	2.50
❑34, Jan 95, Prodigal, Part 10	1.95	0.50	1.25	2.50
❑35, Feb 95	1.95	0.50	1.25	2.50
❑35/SC, Feb, enhanced cover	2.95	0.59	1.48	2.95
❑36, Mar 95, Black Canary: In the Name of the Father; Black Canary II (Dinah Lance) appearance, A: Black Canary	1.95	0.40	1.00	2.00
❑37, Apr 95	1.95	0.40	1.00	2.00
❑38, May 95	1.95	0.40	1.00	2.00
❑39, Jun 95, V: Anarky	1.95	0.40	1.00	2.00
❑40, Jul 95, V: Anarky	1.95	0.40	1.00	2.00
❑41, Aug 95	1.95	0.40	1.00	2.00
❑42, Sep, Feedback: The Day the Music Died	1.95	0.40	1.00	2.00
❑43, Oct 95, Ratcatcher: The Secret of the Universe, Part 1	1.95	0.40	1.00	2.00
❑44, Nov 95	1.95	0.40	1.00	2.00
❑45, Dec 95, Wayne Manor history	1.95	0.40	1.00	2.00
❑46, Jan, Cornelius Stirk, Part 1 of 2	1.95	0.40	1.00	2.00
❑47, Feb, Cornelius Stirk, Part 2 of 2	1.95	0.40	1.00	2.00
❑48, Mar, Contagion, Part 1, trading card bound in	1.95	0.40	1.00	2.00
❑49, Apr, Contagion, Part 7	1.95	0.40	1.00	2.00
❑50, May 96	1.95	0.40	1.00	2.00
❑51, Jun 96	1.95	0.39	0.98	1.95
❑52, Jul 96	1.95	0.39	0.98	1.95
❑53, Aug, Legacy Prelude, A: Huntress	1.95	0.39	0.98	1.95
❑54, Sep, Legacy, Part 4	1.95	0.39	0.98	1.95
❑55, Oct 96, Stamdard Operating Procedure	1.95	0.39	0.98	1.95
❑56, Nov 96, Leaves of Grass, Part 1, V: Poison Ivy	1.95	0.39	0.98	1.95
❑57, Dec 96, Leaves of Grass, Part 2, V: Poison Ivy	1.95	0.39	0.98	1.95
❑58, Jan 97, Leaves of Grass, Part 3, V: Floronic Man	1.95	0.39	0.98	1.95
❑59, Feb 97, Killer Killer, Part 1, V: Scarface	1.95	0.39	0.98	1.95
❑60, Mar 97, Killer Killer, Part 2, V: Scarface	1.95	0.39	0.98	1.95
❑61, Apr 97	1.95	0.39	0.98	1.95
❑62, May, Janus, Part 1, V: Two-Face	1.95	0.39	0.98	1.95
❑63, Jun, Janus, Part 2, V: Two-Face	1.95	0.39	0.98	1.95
❑64, Jul 97, The Wedding Present	1.95	0.39	0.98	1.95
❑65, Aug 97	1.95	0.39	0.98	1.95
❑66, Sep 97	1.95	0.39	0.98	1.95
❑67, Oct 97	1.95	0.39	0.98	1.95
❑68, Nov 97	1.95	0.39	0.98	1.95
❑69, Dec 97, The Spirit of 2000, Part 1, A: Fate	1.95	0.39	0.98	1.95
❑70, Jan 98, The Spirit of 2000, Part 2, A: Fate	1.95	0.39	0.98	1.95
❑71, Feb 98	1.95	0.39	0.98	1.95
❑72, Mar 98, 1: Drakken	1.95	0.39	0.98	1.95

	ORIG	GOOD	FINE	N-MINT
❑73, Apr, Cataclysm, Part 1, continues in Nightwing #19	1.95	0.39	0.98	1.95
❑74, May, Cataclysm, Part 9, continues in Batman Chronicles #12	1.95	0.39	0.98	1.95
❑75, Jun 98, V: Mr. Freeze; V: Clayface, Aftershock	2.95	0.39	0.98	1.95
❑76, Jul 98, Aftershock	1.95	0.39	0.98	1.95
❑77, Aug 98, Aftershock	1.95	0.39	0.98	1.95
❑78, Sep 98, Aftershock	1.99	0.39	0.98	1.95
❑79, Oct 98, Aftershock	1.99	0.40	1.00	1.99
❑80, Dec 98, Waxman and the Clown, Part 1, Road to No Man's Land; flipbook with Azrael: Agent of the Bat #47; Road to No Man's Land, flipbook with Azrael: Agent of the Bat #47	3.95	0.40	1.00	1.99
❑80/LE, Extra-sized flip-book	3.95	0.79	1.98	3.95
❑81, Jan 99, Waxman and the Clown, Part 2; Road to No Man's Land, A: Jeremiah Arkham, Road to No Man's Land	1.99	0.40	1.00	1.99
❑82, Feb 99, Waxman and the Clown, Part 3; Road to No Man's Land, Road to No Man's Land	1.99	0.40	1.00	1.99
❑83, Mar 99, No Law and a New Order, Part 2, 1: new Batgirl, No Man's Land	1.99	1.80	4.50	9.00
❑84, Apr 99, Fear of Faith, Part 2, A: Batgirl; A: Huntress; A: Scarecrow, No Man's Land	1.99	0.40	1.00	1.99
❑85, May 99, Bread and Circuses, Part 2, A: Batgirl; V: Penguin, No Man's Land	1.99	0.40	1.00	1.99
❑86, Jun 99, Home Sweet Home; No Man's Land: Home Sweet Home, No Man's Land	1.99	0.40	1.00	1.99
❑87, Jul 99, Claim Jumping, Part 2, A: Two-Face, No Man's Land	1.99	0.40	1.00	1.99
❑88, Aug 99, BSz, Fruit of the Earth, Part 1, A: Poison Ivy; V: Clayface, No Man's Land; continues in Batman #568	1.99	0.40	1.00	1.99
❑89, Sep 99, The King, V: Killer Croc, No Man's Land	1.99	0.40	1.00	1.99
❑90, Oct 99, PG, Low Road to Golden Mountain, Part 2; Positive Role Model, A: Lynx, No Man's Land	1.99	0.40	1.00	1.99
❑91, Nov 99	1.99	0.40	1.00	1.99
❑92, Dec 99, DGry(w), Stormy Weather, No Man's Land	1.99	0.40	1.00	1.99
❑93, Jan 00, BSz, Assembly Redux, No Man's Land	1.99	0.40	1.00	1.99
❑1000000, Nov 98, Aftershock	1.99	0.40	1.00	1.99
❑Anl 1, Bloodlines, 1: Joe Public, Bloodlines	3.50	0.80	2.00	4.00
❑Anl 2, Elseworlds	3.95	0.79	1.98	3.95
❑Anl 3, O: Poison Ivy, Year One	3.95	0.79	1.98	3.95
❑Anl 4, Nov 96, King Batman, Legends of the Dead Earth; 1996 Annual	2.95	0.59	1.48	2.95
❑Anl 5, V: Poison Ivy, 1997 Annual; Pulp Heroes	3.95	0.79	1.98	3.95

BATMAN-SPAWN: WAR DEVIL
DC

Value: Cover or less

❑1, KJ, nn; prestige format; crossover with Image 4.95

BATMAN SPECIAL
DC

	ORIG	GOOD	FINE	N-MINT
❑1, MG	1.25	0.40	1.00	2.00

BATMAN/SPIDER-MAN
DC

Value: Cover or less

❑1, V: Ra's Al Ghul; V: Kingpin, nn; prestige format; crossover with Marvel 4.95

BATMAN: SPOILER/HUNTRESS-BLUNT TRAUMA
DC

Value: Cover or less

❑1 .... 2.95
❑2 .... 2.95
❑3 .... 2.95
❑4 .... 2.95

BATMAN: SWORD OF AZRAEL
DC

	ORIG	GOOD	FINE	N-MINT
❑1, Oct 92, 1: Azrael, Wraparound, gatefold cover	1.75	1.20	3.00	6.00
❑1/SI, silver edition	1.95	0.39	0.98	1.95
❑2, Nov 92	1.75	0.80	2.00	4.00
❑2/SI, silver edition	1.95	0.39	0.98	1.95
❑3, Dec 92	1.75	0.60	1.50	3.00
❑3/SI, silver edition	1.95	0.39	0.98	1.95
❑4, Jan 93	1.75	0.60	1.50	3.00
❑4/SI, silver edition	1.95	0.39	0.98	1.95

BATMAN/TARZAN: CLAWS OF THE CAT-WOMAN
DARK HORSE

Value: Cover or less

❑1, Sep 99 .... 2.95
❑2, Oct 99 .... 2.95
❑3, Nov 99 .... 2.95
❑4, Dec 99 .... 2.95

BATMAN: THE ABDUCTION
DC

Value: Cover or less

❑1, 98, nn; One-Shot; prestige format; Batman kidnapped by aliens 5.95

A Civil War Batman made his appearance in *Batman: The Blue, The Grey, and The Bat.*

© 1992 DC Comics

BATMAN: THE BLUE, THE GREY, AND THE BAT
DC

Value: Cover or less

❑1, 92, nn; prestige format; Elseworlds 5.95

BATMAN: THE BOOK OF SHADOWS
DC

Value: Cover or less

❑1, nn; prestige format 5.95

BATMAN: THE CULT
DC

	ORIG	GOOD	FINE	N-MINT
❑1, Aug 88, BWr; JSn, JSn (w)	3.50	1.00	2.50	5.00
❑2, Sep 88, BWr; JSn, JSn (w)	3.50	0.80	2.00	4.00
❑3, Oct 88, BWr; JSn, JSn (w), Escape	3.50	0.80	2.00	4.00
❑4, Nov 88, BWr; JSn, JSn (w), Combat	3.50	0.80	2.00	4.00

BATMAN: THE DARK KNIGHT
DC

	ORIG	GOOD	FINE	N-MINT
❑1, Mar 01, FM, FM (w), The Dark Knight Returns, Squarebound	2.95	7.00	17.50	35.00
❑1-2, FM, FM (w), The Dark Knight Returns, 2nd Printing	2.95	1.80	4.50	9.00
❑, FM, FM (w), The Dark Knight Returns, 3rd Printing	2.95	1.50	3.75	7.50
❑2, Mar 01, FM, FM (w)	2.95	2.40	6.00	12.00
❑2-2, FM, FM (w), 2nd Printing	2.95	0.80	2.00	4.00
❑2-3, FM, FM (w), 3rd Printing	2.95	0.60	1.50	3.00
❑3, FM, FM (w), Hunt The Dark Knight, D: Joker (future)	2.95	1.60	4.00	8.00
❑3-2, FM, FM (w), Hunt The Dark Knight, D: Joker (future), 2nd Printing	2.95	0.60	1.50	3.00
❑4, FM, FM (w), The Dark Knight Falls, D: Alfred (future)	2.95	1.20	3.00	6.00

BATMAN: THE DOOM THAT CAME TO GOTHAM
DC

Value: Cover or less

❑1 .... 4.95
❑2 .... 4.95
❑3 .... 4.95

BATMAN: THE HILL
DC

Value: Cover or less

❑1, May 00, Heretic 2.95

BATMAN: THE KILLING JOKE
DC

	ORIG	GOOD	FINE	N-MINT
❑1, Jul 88, BB, AMo (w), V: Joker, prestige format; first printing	3.50	2.20	5.50	11.00
❑1-2, AMo (w), 2nd Printing	3.50	1.00	2.50	5.00
❑, AMo (w), 3rd Printing	4.95	1.00	2.50	5.00
❑1-4, AMo (w), 4th Printing	4.95	1.00	2.50	5.00
❑1-5, AMo (w), 5th Printing	4.95	1.00	2.50	5.00
❑1-6, AMo (w), 6th Printing	4.95	1.00	2.50	5.00
❑1-7, AMo (w), 7th Printing	4.95	1.00	2.50	5.00
❑1-8, AMo (w), 8th Printing	4.95	1.00	2.50	5.00

BATMAN: THE LONG HALLOWEEN
DC

	ORIG	GOOD	FINE	N-MINT
❑1, Dec 96, JPH (w), Crime, prestige format	4.95	2.40	6.00	12.00
❑2, Jan, JPH (w), Thanksgiving, V: Solomon Grundy, cardstock cover	2.95	1.80	4.50	9.00
❑3, Feb, JPH (w), V: Joker, cardstock cover	2.95	1.60	4.00	8.00
❑4, Mar, JPH (w), New Year's Eve, V: Joker, cardstock cover	2.95	1.40	3.50	7.00
❑5, Apr, JPH (w), A: Poison Ivy; A: Catwoman, cardstock cover	2.95	1.00	2.50	5.00
❑6, May, JPH (w), St. Patrick's Day, V: Poison Ivy, cardstock cover	2.95	1.00	2.50	5.00
❑7, Jun, JPH (w), V: Riddler, cardstock cover	2.95	0.80	2.00	4.00
❑8, Jul, JPH (w), V: Scarecrow, cardstock cover	2.95	0.80	2.00	4.00
❑9, Aug, JPH (w), cardstock cover	2.95	0.80	2.00	4.00
❑10, Sep, JPH (w), V: Mad Hatter; A: Catwoman; V: Scarecrow, cardstock cover	2.95	0.80	2.00	4.00
❑11, Oct, JPH (w), O: Two-Face, cardstock cover	2.95	0.70	1.75	3.50
❑12, Nov, JPH (w), Labor Day, D: Maroni, cardstock cover; identity of Holiday revealed	2.95	0.70	1.75	3.50
❑13, Dec 97, JPH (w), V: Arkham inmates; 1: Holiday, prestige format	4.95	1.20	3.00	6.00

ORIG GOOD FINE N-MINT

BATMAN: THE OFFICIAL COMIC ADAPTATION OF THE WARNER BROS. MOTION PICTURE
DC

	ORIG	GOOD	FINE	N-MINT
❑1, JOy, regular edition; newsstand format; Comic adaptation of Warner Bros. Movie	2.50	0.60	1.50	3.00
❑1/PR, prestige format; Comic adaptation of Warner Bros. Movie	4.95	1.00	2.50	5.00

BATMAN: THE ULTIMATE EVIL
DC

	ORIG	GOOD	FINE	N-MINT
❑1, prestige format; adapts Andrew Vachss novel	5.95	1.20	3.00	6.00
❑2, prestige format; adapts Andrew Vachss novel	5.95	1.20	3.00	6.00

BATMAN: THRILLKILLER
DC

Value: Cover or less

❑1, collects Thrillkiller #1-3 and Thrillkiller '62 .... 12.95

BATMAN: TOYMAN
DC

Value: Cover or less

❑1, Nov 98, Incident Report: The Cops' Story 2.25
❑2, Dec 98 .... 2.25
❑3, Jan 99, Wordless issue 2.25
❑4, Feb 99 .... 2.25

BATMAN: TURNING POINTS
DC

Value: Cover or less

❑1, Jan 01, 'Til Death Do Us Part 2.50
❑2, Jan 01, From Generation to Generation like Cancer 2.50
❑3, Jan 01, Haunted 2.50
❑4, Jan 01 .... 2.50
❑5, Jan 01, Old as the Stars ... 2.50

BATMAN: TWO-FACE-CRIME AND PUNISHMENT
DC

Value: Cover or less

❑1, nn; cover forms diptych with Batman: Riddler - The Riddle Factory; One-Shot; prestige format 4.95

BATMAN: TWO FACES
DC

Value: Cover or less

❑1, Nov 98, nn; Elseworlds..... 4.95
❑1/LE, Nov 98 .... 17.95

BATMAN: TWO-FACE STRIKES TWICE
DC

	ORIG	GOOD	FINE	N-MINT
❑1, JSa, The Two Faces Of Janus	4.95	1.00	2.50	5.00
❑2	4.95	1.00	2.50	5.00

BATMAN: VENGEANCE OF BANE II
DC

	ORIG	GOOD	FINE	N-MINT
❑1, nn; One-Shot	3.95	0.80	2.00	4.00

BATMAN: VENGEANCE OF BANE SPECIAL
DC

	ORIG	GOOD	FINE	N-MINT
❑1, Jan 93, 1: Bane	2.50	1.20	3.00	6.00

BATMAN VERSUS PREDATOR
DC

	ORIG	GOOD	FINE	N-MINT
❑1, DaG (w)	1.95	0.50	1.25	2.50
❑1/A, newsstand	1.95	0.50	1.25	2.50
❑1/B, Batman on front cover; prestige format; trading cards	4.95	1.00	2.50	5.00
❑1/C, Batman on back cover; prestige format; trading cards; Predator on front	4.95	1.00	2.50	5.00
❑1/PR, DaG (w)	4.95	1.00	2.50	5.00
❑2, DaG (w), newsstand	1.95	0.50	1.25	2.50
❑2/PR, DaG (w), prestige format; pin-ups	4.95	1.00	2.50	5.00
❑3, DaG (w), newsstand	1.95	0.50	1.25	2.50
❑3/PR, DaG (w), prestige format	4.95	1.00	2.50	5.00

BATMAN VERSUS PREDATOR II: BLOODMATCH
DC

Value: Cover or less

❑1, PG, Bloodmatch, Part 1, Crossover, no year in indicia 2.50
❑2, PG, Bloodmatch, Part 2, Crossover 2.50
❑3, PG, Bloodmatch, Part 3, Crossover 2.50
❑4, PG, Bloodmatch, Part 4, Crossover 2.50

BATMAN VS. THE INCREDIBLE HULK
DC

Value: Cover or less

❑1, Fal 81, oversized, (DC Special Series #27) 2.50
❑1-2, 2nd Printing, comics-sized 3.95

BATMAN VILLAINS SECRET FILES
DC

Value: Cover or less

❑1, Oct 98 .... 4.95

BATMAN: WAR ON CRIME
DC

Value: Cover or less

❑1, Nov 99, ARo 9.95

BATMAN/WILDCAT
DC

Value: Cover or less

❑1, Apr 97, Lights, Cameras, Death 2.25
❑2, May 97 .... 2.25
❑3, Jun 97 .... 2.25

BAT MEN
AVALON

Value: Cover or less

❑1, JSt, JSt (w), Babe Ruth: The Sultan of Swat; Hero Gallery 2.95

BATS, CATS & CADILLACS
NOW

	ORIG	GOOD	FINE	N-MINT
❑1, Oct 90	1.75	0.40	1.00	2.00
❑2, Nov 90	1.75	0.40	1.00	2.00

BAT-THING
DC

Value: Cover or less

❑1, Jun 97, Someone to Watch Over Me 1.95

BATTLE ANGEL ALITA PART 1
VIZ

	ORIG	GOOD	FINE	N-MINT
❑1, 1: Alita	2.75	0.80	2.00	4.00
❑2	2.75	0.70	1.75	3.50
❑3	2.75	0.70	1.75	3.50
❑4, Resurgence	2.75	0.60	1.50	3.00
❑5	2.75	0.60	1.50	3.00
❑6	2.75	0.60	1.50	3.00
❑7	2.75	0.60	1.50	3.00
❑8	2.75	0.60	1.50	3.00
❑9	2.75	0.60	1.50	3.00

BATTLE ANGEL ALITA PART 2
VIZ

	ORIG	GOOD	FINE	N-MINT
❑1	2.75	0.60	1.50	3.00
❑2	2.75	0.55	1.38	2.75
❑3	2.75	0.55	1.38	2.75
❑4	2.75	0.55	1.38	2.75
❑5	2.75	0.55	1.38	2.75
❑6	2.75	0.55	1.38	2.75
❑7	2.75	0.55	1.38	2.75

BATTLE ANGEL ALITA PART 3
VIZ

Value: Cover or less

❑1 .... 2.75
❑2 .... 2.75
❑3, The Skull Challenge 2.75
❑4 .... 2.75
❑5 .... 2.75
❑6 .... 2.75
❑7 .... 2.75
❑8 .... 2.75
❑9 .... 2.75
❑10 .... 2.75
❑11 .... 2.75
❑12 .... 2.75
❑13 .... 2.75

BATTLE ANGEL ALITA PART 4
VIZ

Value: Cover or less

❑1 .... 2.75
❑2, Dog Master Cycle 2: Melody of Redemption 2.75
❑3 .... 2.75
❑4 .... 2.75
❑5 .... 2.75
❑6 .... 2.75
❑7 .... 2.75

BATTLE ANGEL ALITA PART 5
VIZ

Value: Cover or less

❑1, Beyond the Yellow Door.... 2.75
❑2 .... 2.75
❑3 .... 2.75
❑4 .... 2.75
❑5 .... 2.75
❑6 .... 2.75
❑7 .... 2.95

BATTLE ANGEL ALITA PART 6
VIZ

Value: Cover or less

❑1 .... 2.95
❑2 .... 2.95
❑3 .... 2.95
❑4 .... 2.95
❑5 .... 2.95
❑6 .... 2.95
❑7 .... 2.95
❑8 .... 2.95

BATTLE ANGEL ALITA PART 7
VIZ

Value: Cover or less

❑1 .... 2.95
❑2 .... 2.95
❑3 .... 2.95
❑4 .... 2.95
❑5 .... 2.95
❑6 .... 2.95
❑7 .... 2.95
❑8 .... 2.95

BATTLE ANGEL ALITA PART 8
VIZ

Value: Cover or less

❑1 .... 2.95
❑2 .... 2.95
❑3 .... 2.95
❑4 .... 2.95
❑5 .... 2.95
❑6 .... 2.95
❑7 .... 2.95
❑8 .... 2.95
❑9 .... 2.95

BATTLE ARMOR
ETERNITY

Value: Cover or less

❑1, Oct 88 .... 1.95
❑2 .... 1.95
❑3 .... 1.95

BATTLE AXE
COMICS INTERVIEW

Value: Cover or less

❑1, b&w 2.50

BATTLEAXES
VERTIGO
Value: Cover or less

- ❑1, May 00, Medereus No More 2.50
- ❑2, Jun 00, How the Other Half Lives 2.50
- ❑3, Jul 00 2.50
- ❑4, Aug 00, The Fiery Finish!.. 2.50

BATTLE BEASTS
BLACKTHORNE

	ORIG	GOOD	FINE	N-MINT
❑1	1.50	0.35	0.88	1.75
❑2	1.50	0.30	0.75	1.50
❑3	1.50	0:30	0.75	1.50
❑4	1.75	0.35	0.88	1.75

BATTLE BINDER PLUS
ANTARCTIC
Value: Cover or less

- ❑1, Nov 94 3.50
- ❑2, Dec 94 2.95
- ❑3, Jan 95, Act 4 • Key Word.. 2.95
- ❑4, Feb 95 2.95
- ❑5, Mar 95 2.95
- ❑6, Apr 95, Final Issue 2.95

BATTLE CHASERS
IMAGE

	ORIG	GOOD	FINE	N-MINT
❑1, Apr 98	2.50	2.00	5.00	10.00
❑1/A, Apr 98, alternate cover, logo on back side of wraparound cover	2.50	2.40	6.00	12.00
❑1/B, Apr, Limited holochrome cover (limited to 5, 000 copies); Wrap-around	2.50	6.00	15.00	30.00
❑1/C, Gold "Come on...take a peek" cover (Monika)	—	5.00	12.50	25.00
❑1-2, Apr 98, 2nd Printing	2.50	0.80	2.00	4.00
❑2, May 98	2.50	1.00	2.50	5.00
❑2/A, Special "omnichrome" cover from Dynamic Forces	—	2.00	5.00	10.00
❑2/B, Battlechrome edition	—	3.00	7.50	15.00
❑3, Jul 98, Divine Intervention	2.50	0.80	2.00	4.00
❑4/A, Oct, four alternate back covers form quadtych	2.50	0.60	1.50	3.00
❑4/B, Oct, Old man on cover	2.50	0.60	1.50	3.00
❑4/C, Oct, four alternate back covers form quadtych	2.50	0.60	1.50	3.00
❑4/D, Oct, four alternate back covers form quadtych	2.50	0.60	1.50	3.00
❑5, May 99	2.50	0.50	1.25	2.50
❑6, Aug 99	2.50	0.50	1.25	2.50
❑7, Jan 01	2.50	0.50	1.25	2.50
❑8, May 01	2.50	0.50	1.25	2.50
❑Ash 1, 1: Battle Chasers, Preview edition	—	1.00	2.50	5.00
❑Ash 1/GO, 1: Battle Chasers, Preview edition; Gold logo	—	1.40	3.50	7.00
❑Dlx 1, Dec 99, hardcover; A Gathering of Heroes	24.95	4.99	12.48	24.95

BATTLE CLASSICS
DC

	ORIG	GOOD	FINE	N-MINT
❑1, Oct 78, Reprint	0.50	1.00	2.50	5.00

BATTLE FOR A THREE DIMENSIONAL WORLD
3-D COSMIC

	ORIG	GOOD	FINE	N-MINT
❑1, JK, no cover price	—	0.50	1.25	2.50

BATTLEFORCE
BLACKTHORNE
Value: Cover or less

- ❑1, full color 1.75
- ❑2, b&w 1.75

BATTLE GODS: WARRIORS OF THE CHAAK
DARK HORSE
Value: Cover or less

- ❑1, Apr 00 2.95
- ❑2, May 00 2.95
- ❑3, Jun 00 2.95

BATTLEGROUND EARTH
BEST
Value: Cover or less

- ❑1, b&w 2.50
- ❑2, b&w 2.50

BATTLE GROUP PEIPER
TOME PRESS
Value: Cover or less

- ❑1, b&w 2.95

BATTLE OF THE ULTRA-BROTHERS
VIZ
Value: Cover or less

- ❑1 4.95
- ❑2 4.95
- ❑3 4.95
- ❑4 4.95
- ❑5 4.95

BATTLESTAR GALACTICA (MARVEL)
MARVEL

	ORIG	GOOD	FINE	N-MINT
❑1, Mar 79	0.35	1.00	2.50	5.00
❑1-2, 20 Yahren reunion edition	4.99	1.00	2.49	4.99
❑2, Apr 79	0.35	0.60	1.50	3.00
❑3, May 79	0.40	0.60	1.50	3.00
❑4, Jun 79	0.40	0.60	1.50	3.00
❑5, Jul 79	0.40	0.60	1.50	3.00
❑6, Aug 79	0.40	0.60	1.50	3.00
❑7, Sep 79	0.40	0.60	1.50	3.00

Several comics publishers have licensed the rights to produce comics based on *Battlestar Galactica* since the TV series first aired, in 1978.

© 1996 Realm Press and Universal Studios

	ORIG	GOOD	FINE	N-MINT
❑8, Oct 79	0.40	0.60	1.50	3.00
❑9, Nov 79	0.40	0.60	1.50	3.00
❑10, Dec 79, PB, This Planet Hungers	0.40	0.60	1.50	3.00
❑11, Jan 80, Scavenge World	0.40	0.40	1.00	2.00
❑12, Feb 80, The Trap!	0.40	0.40	1.00	2.00
❑13, Mar 80	0.40	0.40	1.00	2.00
❑14, Apr 80	0.40	0.40	1.00	2.00
❑15, May 80, Derelict!	0.40	0.40	1.00	2.00
❑16, Jun 80	0.40	0.40	1.00	2.00
❑17, Jul 80	0.40	0.40	1.00	2.00
❑18, Aug 80	0.40	0.40	1.00	2.00
❑19, Sep 80	0.50	0.40	1.00	2.00
❑20, Oct 80	0.50	0.40	1.00	2.00
❑21, Nov 80, BA	0.50	0.40	1.00	2.00
❑22, Dec 80	0.50	0.40	1.00	2.00
❑23, Jan 81, Final Issue	0.50	0.40	1.00	2.00

BATTLESTAR GALACTICA (MAXIMUM)
MAXIMUM
Value: Cover or less

- ❑1, Jul 95, RL (w), War of Eden 2.50
- ❑2, Aug 95 2.50
- ❑3, Sep 95 2.50
- ❑4, Nov 95 2.50

BATTLESTAR GALACTICA (REALM)
REALM
Value: Cover or less

- ❑1/A, Dec 97, The Law of Volahd, Spaceships cover 2.99
- ❑1/B, Dec 97, The Law of Volahd, Cylons cover 2.99
- ❑2, Jan 98, The Law of Volahd 2.99
- ❑3, Mar 98, Prison of Souls..... 2.99
- ❑3/SC, Mar 98, Prison of Souls, alternate cover (eyes in background) 2.99

BATTLESTAR GALACTICA 1999 TOUR BOOK
REALM
Value: Cover or less

- ❑1/A, May 99 2.99
- ❑1/B, May, Dynamic Forces Edition, no cover price —
- ❑1/C, May 99, white background cover 6.99

BATTLESTAR GALACTICA: APOLLO'S JOURNEY
MAXIMUM
Value: Cover or less

- ❑1, Apr 95 2.95

BATTLESTAR GALACTICA EVE OF DESTRUCTION PRELUDE
REALM
Value: Cover or less

- ❑1 3.99

BATTLESTAR GALACTICA: JOURNEY'S END
MAXIMUM
Value: Cover or less

- ❑1, Aug 96 2.99
- ❑2 2.99
- ❑3 2.99
- ❑4 2.99

BATTLESTAR GALACTICA: SEARCH FOR SANCTUARY
REALM
Value: Cover or less

- ❑1 2.99

BATTLESTAR GALACTICA: SEASON III
REALM
Value: Cover or less

- ❑1, Jun 99, No Place Like Home 2.99
- ❑1/A, Jun 99, No Place Like Home, Special Convention Edition. 5.00
- ❑1/B, Jun 99, No Place Like Home 4.99
- ❑2, Jul 99 4.99

BATTLESTAR GALACTICA: STARBUCK
MAXIMUM
Value: Cover or less

- ❑1, RL (w) 2.95
- ❑2, RL (w) 2.95
- ❑3, Mar 96, RL (w) 2.95

BATTLESTAR GALACTICA: THE COMPENDIUM
MAXIMUM
Value: Cover or less

- ❑1 2.95

BATTLESTAR GALACTICA: THE ENEMY WITHIN
MAXIMUM
Value: Cover or less

- ❑1, Nov 95 2.50
- ❑2 2.50
- ❑3, Feb 96 2.95
- ❑3/SC, Feb 96, alternate cover 2.95

BATTLESTONE
IMAGE
Value: Cover or less

- ❑1, RL (w) 2.50
- ❑1/A, Nov 94 2.50
- ❑1/B, Nov 94, alternate cover.. 2.50
- ❑2, Dec 94, RL (w) 2.50

BATTLETECH
Malibu

Value: Cover or less

- ❑0, BattleTech: Overture 2.95

BATTLETECH (BLACKTHORNE)
Blackthorne

	ORIG	GOOD	FINE	N-MINT
❑1, Oct 97, full color	1.75	0.40	1.00	2.00
❑2, b&w	1.75	0.40	1.00	2.00
❑3, b&w	1.75	0.40	1.00	2.00
❑4, b&w	1.75	0.40	1.00	2.00
❑5, b&w	1.75	0.40	1.00	2.00
❑6, b&w	1.75	0.40	1.00	2.00

BATTLETECH: FALLOUT
Malibu

Value: Cover or less

- ❑1 .... 2.50
- ❑2 .... 2.50
- ❑3 .... 2.50
- ❑4 .... 2.50

BATTLETECH IN 3-D
Blackthorne

Value: Cover or less

- ❑1 .... 2.50

BATTLETIDE
Marvel

Value: Cover or less

- ❑1, Dec 92 .... 1.75
- ❑2, Jan 93 .... 1.75
- ❑3, Feb 93 .... 1.75
- ❑4, Mar 93 .... 1.75

BATTLETIDE II
Marvel

Value: Cover or less

- ❑1, Aug 93, Embossed cover . 2.95
- ❑2, Sep 93, A: Hulk 1.75
- ❑3, Oct 93, Pecs, Lies and Videoscapes 1.75
- ❑4, Nov 93 .... 1.75

BATTLEZONES: DREAM TEAM 2
Malibu

Value: Cover or less

- ❑1, Mar 96, pin-ups of battles between Malibu and Marvel characters 3.95

BATTRON
NEC

Value: Cover or less

- ❑1, b&w 2.75
- ❑2, b&w 2.75

BATTRON'S 4 QUEENS: GUNS, BABES & INTRIGUE
Commode

Value: Cover or less

- ❑1 .... 3.50

BAYWATCH COMIC STORIES
Acclaim

Value: Cover or less

- ❑1, May 4.95
- ❑2, Jun 4.95
- ❑3, Jul 4.95
- ❑4, Aug 4.95

B-BAR-B RIDERS
AC

	ORIG	GOOD	FINE	N-MINT
❑1, FF	—	0.40	1.00	2.00

BEACH HIGH
Big

Value: Cover or less

- ❑1, Feb, illustrated text story, one-shot 3.25

BEACH PARTY
Eternity

Value: Cover or less

- ❑1, b&w pin-ups 2.50

BEAGLE BOYS, THE
Gold Key

	ORIG	GOOD	FINE	N-MINT
❑1	—	4.00	10.00	20.00
❑2	—	3.00	7.50	15.00
❑3	—	3.00	7.50	15.00
❑4	—	3.00	7.50	15.00
❑5	—	2.40	6.00	12.00
❑6	—	2.40	6.00	12.00
❑7	—	2.40	6.00	12.00
❑8	—	2.40	6.00	12.00
❑9	—	2.40	6.00	12.00
❑10	—	2.40	6.00	12.00
❑11	—	1.60	4.00	8.00
❑12	—	1.60	4.00	8.00
❑13	—	1.60	4.00	8.00
❑14, Sep 72	0.15	1.60	4.00	8.00
❑15	—	1.60	4.00	8.00
❑16, A: Uncle Scrooge	—	1.60	4.00	8.00
❑17	—	1.60	4.00	8.00
❑18	—	1.60	4.00	8.00
❑19	—	1.60	4.00	8.00
❑20, Apr 74, Beagle Bloopers; Fakery in the Bakery	0.20	1.60	4.00	8.00
❑21	—	1.00	2.50	5.00
❑22	—	1.00	2.50	5.00
❑23	—	1.00	2.50	5.00
❑24	—	1.00	2.50	5.00
❑25	—	1.00	2.50	5.00
❑26	—	1.00	2.50	5.00
❑27	—	1.00	2.50	5.00
❑28	—	1.00	2.50	5.00
❑29	—	1.00	2.50	5.00
❑30	—	1.00	2.50	5.00
❑31	—	0.60	1.50	3.00
❑32	—	0.60	1.50	3.00
❑33, Jan 77	0.30	0.60	1.50	3.00
❑34, Apr 77	0.30	0.60	1.50	3.00
❑35, Jun 77	0.30	0.60	1.50	3.00
❑36, Aug 77	0.30	0.60	1.50	3.00
❑37, Sep 77	0.30	0.60	1.50	3.00
❑38, Oct 77	0.30	0.60	1.50	3.00
❑39	—	0.60	1.50	3.00
❑40	—	0.60	1.50	3.00
❑41	—	0.40	1.00	2.00
❑42	—	0.40	1.00	2.00
❑43	—	0.40	1.00	2.00
❑44	—	0.40	1.00	2.00
❑45	—	0.40	1.00	2.00
❑46	—	0.40	1.00	2.00
❑47	—	0.40	1.00	2.00

BEAGLE BOYS VERSUS UNCLE SCROOGE, THE
Whitman

	ORIG	GOOD	FINE	N-MINT
❑1	—	1.00	2.50	5.00
❑2	—	1.00	2.50	5.00
❑3	—	0.60	1.50	3.00
❑4	—	0.60	1.50	3.00
❑5	—	0.60	1.50	3.00
❑6	—	0.60	1.50	3.00
❑7, Sep 79	0.40	0.60	1.50	3.00
❑8	—	0.40	1.00	2.00
❑9	—	0.40	1.00	2.00
❑10	—	0.40	1.00	2.00
❑11	—	0.40	1.00	2.00
❑12	—	0.40	1.00	2.00

BEARFAX FUNNIES
Treasure

Value: Cover or less

- ❑1 .... 2.75

BEARSKIN: A GRIMM TALE
Thecomic.Com

	ORIG	GOOD	FINE	N-MINT
❑1, nn; b&w; no cover price; One-Shot	—	0.30	0.75	1.50

BEAST, THE
Marvel

Value: Cover or less

- ❑1, May 97, KG (w), Bad Karma, A: Gateway; A: Spiral; A: Viper; A: Cannonball; A: Karma..... 2.50
- ❑2, Jun 97 .... 2.50
- ❑3, Jul 97 .... 2.50

BEAST BOY
DC

Value: Cover or less

- ❑1, Jan 00 .... 2.95
- ❑2, Feb 00, Nobody's Hero 2.95
- ❑3, Mar 00 .... 2.95
- ❑4, Apr 00, Beast War! 2.95

B.E.A.S.T.I.E.S.
Axis

Value: Cover or less

- ❑1, Apr 94, Induction 1.95

BEAST WARRIORS OF SHAOLIN
Pied Piper

Value: Cover or less

- ❑1, Jul 87 .... 1.95
- ❑2 .... 1.95
- ❑3 .... 1.95

BEATLES, THE
Personality

	ORIG	GOOD	FINE	N-MINT
❑1, b&w	—	1.00	2.50	5.00
❑1/LE, limited edition, b&w	—	1.60	4.00	8.00
❑2, b&w	—	0.80	2.00	4.00

BEATLES EXPERIENCE, THE
Revolutionary

Value: Cover or less

- ❑1, Mar 91 .... 2.50
- ❑2, May 91 .... 2.50
- ❑3, Jul 91 .... 2.50
- ❑4, Sep 91 .... 2.50
- ❑5, Nov 91 .... 2.50
- ❑6, Jan 92 .... 2.50
- ❑7, Mar 92 .... 2.50
- ❑8, May 92 .... 2.50

BEATLES VS. THE ROLLING STONES, THE
Celebrity

Value: Cover or less

- ❑1, May 92 .... 2.95

BEATRIX
Vision

Value: Cover or less

- ❑1 .... 2.95
- ❑2, Mar 97 .... 2.95

BEAUTIES & BARBARIANS
AC

	ORIG	GOOD	FINE	N-MINT
❑1, WW	1.25	0.30	0.75	1.50

BEAUTIFUL PEOPLE
Slave Labor

Value: Cover or less

- ❑1, Apr 94, nn; Oversized 4.50

BEAUTIFUL STORIES FOR UGLY CHILDREN
DC

	ORIG	GOOD	FINE	N-MINT
❑1	2.00	0.50	1.25	2.50
❑2	2.00	0.50	1.25	2.50
❑3	2.00	0.50	1.25	2.50
❑4	2.00	0.50	1.25	2.50
❑5	2.00	0.50	1.25	2.50
❑6, Happy Birthday to Hell	2.50	0.50	1.25	2.50
❑7	2.00	0.50	1.25	2.50
❑8	2.00	0.50	1.25	2.50
❑9	2.00	0.50	1.25	2.50
❑10	2.00	0.50	1.25	2.50
❑11	2.00	0.50	1.25	2.50
❑12	2.50	0.50	1.25	2.50
❑13	2.50	0.50	1.25	2.50
❑14	2.50	0.50	1.25	2.50
❑15	2.50	0.50	1.25	2.50
❑16	2.50	0.50	1.25	2.50
❑17	2.50	0.50	1.25	2.50
❑18	2.50	0.50	1.25	2.50
❑19, Nice Girls Don't Massacre Ants	2.50	0.50	1.25	2.50
❑20	2.50	0.50	1.25	2.50
❑21	2.50	0.50	1.25	2.50
❑22	2.50	0.50	1.25	2.50
❑23	2.50	0.50	1.25	2.50
❑24	2.50	0.50	1.25	2.50
❑25	2.50	0.50	1.25	2.50
❑26	2.50	0.50	1.25	2.50
❑27	2.50	0.50	1.25	2.50
❑28, The Guilty Orphan	2.50	0.50	1.25	2.50
❑29, Gravity Sucks	2.50	0.50	1.25	2.50
❑30	2.50	0.50	1.25	2.50

BEAUTY AND THE BEAST
DISNEY

Value: Cover or less

- ❑1, nn; movie Adaptation 2.50
- ❑1/DM, nn; squarebound 4.95

BEAUTY AND THE BEAST (DISNEY'S...)
DISNEY

Value: Cover or less

- ❑1, Sep 94 1.50
- ❑2, Oct 94 1.50
- ❑3, Nov 94 1.50
- ❑4, Dec 94 1.50
- ❑5, Jan 95 1.50
- ❑6, Feb 95 1.50
- ❑7, Mar 95 1.50
- ❑8, Apr 95 1.50
- ❑9, May 95 1.50
- ❑10, Jun 95 1.50
- ❑11, Jul 95 1.50
- ❑12, Aug 95 1.50
- ❑13, Sep 95 1.50
- ❑HS 1, Extra-sized flip-book; digest; based on direct-to-video feature 4.50

BEAUTY AND THE BEAST (INNOVATION)
INNOVATION

Value: Cover or less

- ❑1, May 93 2.50
- ❑1/CS, poster 3.95
- ❑2, Jun 93 2.50
- ❑3, Jul 93 2.50
- ❑4, Aug 93 2.50
- ❑5, Sep 93 2.50
- ❑6, Oct 93, indicia says Jul, should be Oct 2.50

BEAUTY AND THE BEAST (MARVEL)
MARVEL

	ORIG	GOOD	FINE	N-MINT
❑1, Dec, DP	0.75	0.40	1.00	2.00
❑2, Feb, DP	0.75	0.40	1.00	2.00
❑3, Apr, DP	0.75	0.40	1.00	2.00
❑4, Jun, DP	0.75	0.40	1.00	2.00

BEAUTY AND THE BEAST (STAN SHAW'S...)
DARK HORSE

Value: Cover or less

- ❑1, nn 4.95

BEAUTY OF THE BEASTS
MU PRESS

Value: Cover or less

- ❑1, Nov 91, b&w 2.50
- ❑2, Jul 93, b&w 2.50

BEAVIS & BUTT-HEAD
MARVEL

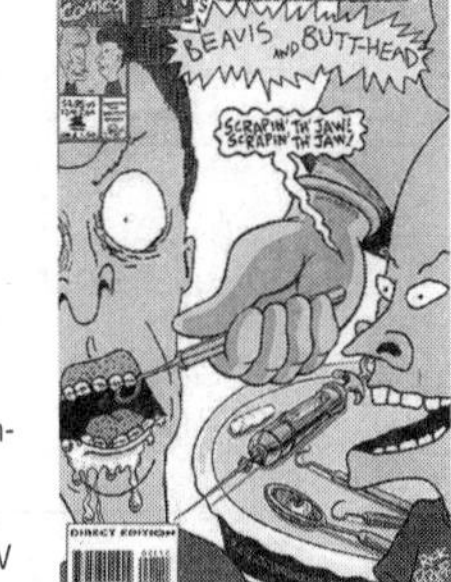

Mike Judge's irascible duo met The Punisher in the first issue of their Marvel comic book.

© 1994 Marvel Characters Inc. and MTV

	ORIG	GOOD	FINE	N-MINT
❑1, Mar 94, Dental Hygiene Dilemma; How to Sneak Home After School and Not Get Beat Up!, 1: Beavis & Butt-Head (in comics); A: Punisher	1.95	0.60	1.50	3.00
❑1-2, 2nd Printing	1.95	0.39	0.98	1.95
❑2, Apr 94	1.95	0.50	1.25	2.50
❑3, May 94	1.95	0.50	1.25	2.50
❑4, Jun 94	1.95	0.50	1.25	2.50
❑5, Jul 94	1.95	0.50	1.25	2.50
❑6, Aug 94	1.95	0.40	1.00	2.00
❑7, Sep 94	1.95	0.40	1.00	2.00
❑8, Oct 94	1.95	0.40	1.00	2.00
❑9, Nov 94	1.95	0.40	1.00	2.00
❑10, Dec 94	1.95	0.40	1.00	2.00
❑11, Jan 95	1.95	0.40	1.00	2.00
❑12, Feb 95	1.95	0.40	1.00	2.00
❑13, Mar 95	1.95	0.40	1.00	2.00
❑14, Apr 95	1.95	0.40	1.00	2.00
❑15, May 95	1.95	0.40	1.00	2.00
❑16, Jun 95	1.95	0.40	1.00	2.00
❑17, Jul 95	1.95	0.40	1.00	2.00
❑18, Aug 95	1.95	0.40	1.00	2.00
❑19, Sep 95	1.95	0.40	1.00	2.00
❑20, Oct 95, Printing for Dollar$	1.95	0.40	1.00	2.00
❑21, Nov 95	1.95	0.40	1.00	2.00
❑22, Dec 95	1.95	0.40	1.00	2.00
❑23, Jan 96	1.50	0.40	1.00	2.00
❑24, Feb 96	1.95	0.40	1.00	2.00
❑25, Mar 96	1.95	0.40	1.00	2.00
❑26, Apr 96	1.95	0.40	1.00	2.00
❑27, May 96	1.95	0.40	1.00	2.00
❑28, Jun, Final Issue	1.95	0.40	1.00	2.00

BECK & CAUL INVESTIGATIONS
CALIBER

Value: Cover or less

- ❑1, Jan 94, O: Caul (Mercedes Guillane) 2.95
- ❑2, Mar 94 2.95
- ❑3, May 94 2.95
- ❑4, Aug 94 2.95
- ❑5 2.95
- ❑Anl 1, May 95 3.50

BEDLAM!
ECLIPSE

Value: Cover or less

- ❑1, Aug 85, Lo; Sneaky Pete.. 1.75
- ❑2, Sep 85, Conquest of the Banana Planet; Scraps 1.75

BEDLAM (CHAOS)
CHAOS

Value: Cover or less

- ❑1, Sep 00 2.95
- ❑1/SC, Sep 00, Premium cover by David Michael Beck 2.95

BEELZELVIS
SLAVE LABOR

Value: Cover or less

- ❑1, Feb 94 2.95

BEER & ROAMING IN LAS VEGAS
SLAVE LABOR

	ORIG	GOOD	FINE	N-MINT
❑1, The Elvis Masters, b&w	12.95	2.59	6.47	12.95
❑Ash 1	—	0.20	0.50	1.00

BEER NUTZ
TUNDRA

Value: Cover or less

- ❑1 2.95
- ❑2 2.00
- ❑3, b&w 2.25

BEETHOVEN
HARVEY

Value: Cover or less

- ❑1, Mar 94, Beethoven's 2nd.. 1.50
- ❑2 1.50
- ❑3, Jul 94 1.50

BEETLE BAILEY (VOL. 2)
HARVEY

	ORIG	GOOD	FINE	N-MINT
❑1, Typing Orders!; The General's Shower.	1.25	0.40	1.00	2.00
❑2, The General's Bridge; Taxi Service	1.25	0.30	0.75	1.50
❑3	1.25	0.30	0.75	1.50
❑4	1.25	0.30	0.75	1.50
❑5	1.25	0.30	0.75	1.50
❑6	1.50	0.30	0.75	1.50
❑7	1.50	0.30	0.75	1.50
❑8	1.50	0.30	0.75	1.50
❑9, Final Issue	—	0.30	0.75	1.50
❑GS 1, Beetle Gets Shot!; Patch-Work Package, Giant-size	2.25	0.45	1.13	2.25
❑GS 2, Giant-size	2.25	0.45	1.13	2.25

BEETLE BAILEY BIG BOOK
HARVEY

Value: Cover or less

- ❑2 1.95

BEETLEJUICE
HARVEY

Value: Cover or less

- ❑1 1.50
- ❑2 1.50

BEETLEJUICE: CRIMEBUSTERS ON THE HAUNT
HARVEY

Value: Cover or less

- ❑1 1.50

BEETLEJUICE: ELLIOT MESS AND THE UNWASHABLES
HARVEY

Value: Cover or less

- ❑1 1.50
- ❑2, Oct 92, Oilcatraz Island 1.50
- ❑3, Nov 92, The Violence on the Lam 1.50

BEETLEJUICE HOLIDAY SPECIAL
HARVEY

	ORIG	GOOD	FINE	N-MINT
❑1, Feb 92	1.25	0.30	0.75	1.50

BEETLEJUICE IN THE NEITHERWORLD
HARVEY

Value: Cover or less

- ❑1, EC, The Neitherworld Beauty (You've Gotta be Kidding!) Pageant; Where the Ghouls Are 1.50
- ❑2 .... 1.50

BEFORE THE FANTASTIC FOUR: BEN GRIMM AND LOGAN
MARVEL

Value: Cover or less

- ❑1, Jul 00, Mission to Nowhere 2.99
- ❑2, Aug 00 .... 2.99
- ❑3, Sep 00 .... 2.99
- ❑4, Oct 00 .... 2.99

BEFORE THE FF: REED RICHARDS
MARVEL

Value: Cover or less

- ❑1, Sep 00, PD (w), Reed Richards & the Riddle of Bast, Part 1. 2.99
- ❑2, Oct 00, PD (w), Reed Richards & the Riddle of Bast, Part 2 .... 2.99
- ❑3, Dec 00, PD (w), Reed Richards & the Riddle of Bast, Part 3. 2.99
- ❑4, Dec 00, PD (w) 2.99

BEFORE THE FF: THE STORMS
MARVEL

Value: Cover or less

- ❑1, Dec 00, Burn Victims 2.99
- ❑2, Jan 01, Into the Fire 2.99
- ❑3, Feb 01, Firepower 2.99

BEHOLD 3-D
EDGE GROUP

Value: Cover or less

- ❑1, NR, Sunship G'hide-E1; Apollyon!, 3-D glasses inserted.. 3.95

BELIEVE IN YOURSELF PRODUCTIONS
BELIEVE IN YOURSELF PRODUCTIONS

Value: Cover or less

- ❑1/Ash, Ashcan Edition. Card-stock cover. Includes 6 page story only available in Ashcan format with 14 pin-u 3.50
- ❑1/B, Sapphire Edition. Only 25 made 25.00
- ❑1/LE 8.00

BELLA DONNA
PINNACLE

Value: Cover or less

- ❑1, b&w 1.75

BENEATH THE PLANET OF THE APES
GOLD KEY

	ORIG	GOOD	FINE	N-MINT
❑1, Dec 70, Beneath the Planet of the Apes, Photo cover; poster	0.25	7.00	17.50	35.00

BENZANGO OBSCURO
STARHEAD

Value: Cover or less

- ❑1 .... 2.75

BENZINE
ANTARCTIC

Value: Cover or less

- ❑1, Oct 00, Asrial Salusian Armored Corps; Tiger-X 4.95

BEOWULF
DC

	ORIG	GOOD	FINE	N-MINT
❑1, May 75, The Curse of Castle Hrothgar, 1: Beowulf; 1: Grendel (monster)	0.25	0.30	0.75	1.50
❑2, Jul 75	0.25	0.20	0.50	1.00
❑3, Sep 75	0.25	0.20	0.50	1.00
❑4, Nov 75	0.25	0.20	0.50	1.00
❑5, Jan 76	0.25	0.20	0.50	1.00
❑6, Mar 76, Final Issue	0.25	0.20	0.50	1.00

BEOWULF (COMIC.COM)
COMIC.COM

Value: Cover or less

- ❑1 .... 4.95
- ❑2 .... 4.95
- ❑3 .... 4.95

BERLIN
BLACK EYE

Value: Cover or less

- ❑1, Apr 96 .... 2.50
- ❑2, Jul 96 .... 2.50
- ❑3, Feb 97 .... 2.50
- ❑4, Feb 98 .... 2.50

BERLIN (DRAWN & QUARTERLY)
DRAWN & QUARTERLY

Value: Cover or less

- ❑7, Apr 00, b&w; smaller than normal comic book 2.95

BERNIE WRIGHTSON, MASTER OF THE MACABRE
PACIFIC

	ORIG	GOOD	FINE	N-MINT
❑1, BWr, BWr (w), The Muck Monster; The Pepper Lake Monster, Edgar Allen Poe adaptation ("The Black Cat")	1.50	0.50	1.25	2.50
❑2, BWr, BWr (w), Jennifer; Cool Air	1.50	0.40	1.00	2.00
❑3, BWr, BWr (w), King of the Mountain, Man; A Martian Saga	1.50	0.40	1.00	2.00
❑4, BWr, BWr (w), The Task; The Legend of Sleepy Hollow	1.50	0.40	1.00	2.00
❑5, Nov, BWr, BWr (w), Feed It!; Mother Load, Final Issue	1.50	0.40	1.00	2.00

BERZERKER
GAUNTLET

Value: Cover or less

- ❑1, Feb 93, EL; RL, Medina.... 2.95
- ❑2 .... 2.95
- ❑3 .... 2.95
- ❑4 .... 2.95
- ❑5 .... 2.95

BERZERKERS
IMAGE

Value: Cover or less

- ❑1, Aug 95, Berzerkers 2.50
- ❑1/SC, Aug 95, alternate cover 2.50
- ❑2, Sep 95, Into The Darklands 2.50
- ❑3, Oct 95 .... 2.50

BEST CELLARS
OUT OF THE CELLAR

Value: Cover or less

- ❑1, Monster Boy; Krystal Kalisto 2.50

BEST OF BARRON STOREY'S W.A.T.C.H. MAGAZINE
VANGUARD

Value: Cover or less

- ❑1, Dec 93 .... 2.95

BEST OF DARK HORSE PRESENTS, THE
DARK HORSE

Value: Cover or less

- ❑1, The Gray Embrace; Cortege, b&w; Reprint 5.95
- ❑2, b&w; Reprint 8.95

BEST OF DC, THE
DC

	ORIG	GOOD	FINE	N-MINT
❑1, Sep 79	0.95	0.60	1.50	3.00
❑2, Nov 79	0.95	0.60	1.50	3.00
❑3, Jan 80	0.95	0.60	1.50	3.00
❑4, Mar 80	0.95	0.60	1.50	3.00
❑5, May 80	0.95	0.60	1.50	3.00
❑6, Jul 80	0.95	0.60	1.50	3.00
❑7, Sep 80, Superboy	0.95	0.60	1.50	3.00
❑8, Nov 80, Superman, Other Identities	0.95	0.60	1.50	3.00
❑9, Jan 81	0.95	0.60	1.50	3.00
❑10, Mar 81	0.95	0.60	1.50	3.00
❑11, Apr 81	0.95	0.60	1.50	3.00
❑12, May 81	0.95	0.60	1.50	3.00
❑13, Jun 81	0.95	0.60	1.50	3.00
❑14, Jul 81	0.95	0.60	1.50	3.00
❑15, Aug 81, Superboy	0.95	0.60	1.50	3.00
❑16, Sep 81, Superman Anniversaries	0.95	0.60	1.50	3.00
❑17, Oct 81	0.95	0.60	1.50	3.00
❑18, Nov 81	0.95	0.60	1.50	3.00
❑19, Dec 81, Superman, Imaginary Stories	0.95	0.60	1.50	3.00
❑20, Jan 82	0.95	0.60	1.50	3.00
❑21, Feb, Justice Society	0.95	0.60	1.50	3.00
❑22, Mar 82	0.95	0.60	1.50	3.00
❑23, Apr 82	1.25	0.60	1.50	3.00
❑24, May, Legion	0.95	0.60	1.50	3.00
❑25, Jun 82	0.95	0.60	1.50	3.00
❑26, Jul, Brave and the Bold	0.95	0.60	1.50	3.00
❑27, Aug 82, Superman vs. Luthor	0.95	0.60	1.50	3.00
❑28, Sep 82	—	0.60	1.50	3.00
❑29, Oct 82	—	0.60	1.50	3.00
❑30, Nov, Batman	1.25	0.60	1.50	3.00
❑31, Dec, Justice League	1.25	0.60	1.50	3.00
❑32, Jan 83, Superman	1.25	0.60	1.50	3.00
❑33, Feb 83	—	0.60	1.50	3.00
❑34, Mar 83, Metal Men	1.25	0.60	1.50	3.00
❑35, Apr 83, Year's Best 82	1.75	0.60	1.50	3.00
❑36, May 83, Superman vs. Kryptonite	1.25	0.60	1.50	3.00
❑37, Jun 83	—	0.60	1.50	3.00
❑38, Jul 83	—	0.60	1.50	3.00
❑39, Aug 83	—	0.60	1.50	3.00
❑40, Sep 83, Superman, Krypton	1.25	0.60	1.50	3.00
❑41, Oct 83	—	0.60	1.50	3.00
❑42, Nov 83	—	0.60	1.50	3.00
❑43, Dec 83	—	0.60	1.50	3.00
❑44, Jan, Legion	1.25	0.60	1.50	3.00
❑45, Feb, Binky	1.25	0.60	1.50	3.00
❑46, Mar, Jimmy Olsen	1.25	0.60	1.50	3.00
❑47, Apr 84	—	0.60	1.50	3.00
❑48, May 84	—	0.60	1.50	3.00
❑49, Jun 84	—	0.60	1.50	3.00
❑50, Jul 84, Superman	1.25	0.60	1.50	3.00
❑51, Aug 84	—	0.60	1.50	3.00
❑52, Sep 84, Year's Best 83	1.75	0.60	1.50	3.00
❑53, Oct 84	—	0.60	1.50	3.00
❑54, Nov 84	—	0.60	1.50	3.00
❑55, Dec 84	—	0.60	1.50	3.00
❑56, Jan 85, Superman	1.50	0.60	1.50	3.00
❑57, Feb, Legion	1.50	0.60	1.50	3.00
❑58, Mar 85, Superman Jrs.	1.50	0.60	1.50	3.00
❑59, Apr 85, Superman	1.50	0.60	1.50	3.00
❑60, May 85	1.50	0.60	1.50	3.00

	ORIG	GOOD	FINE	N-MINT
❑61, Jun 85	1.50	0.60	1.50	3.00
❑62, Jul, Batman	1.50	0.60	1.50	3.00
❑63, Aug 85	1.50	0.60	1.50	3.00
❑64, Sep, Legion	1.50	0.60	1.50	3.00
❑65, Oct 85, Sugar & Spike	1.50	0.60	1.50	3.00
❑66, Nov 85, Superman	1.50	0.60	1.50	3.00
❑67, Dec 85	1.50	0.60	1.50	3.00
❑68, Jan 85, Sugar & Spike	1.50	0.60	1.50	3.00
❑69, Feb 85, Year's Best 85	1.50	0.60	1.50	3.00
❑70, Mar, Binky's Buddies	1.50	0.60	1.50	3.00

BEST OF DONALD DUCK AND UNCLE SCROOGE, THE
GOLD KEY

	ORIG	GOOD	FINE	N-MINT
❑1, Nov 64	0.25	10.00	25.00	50.00
❑2, Sep, CB, Luck of the North, Reprint	0.25	10.00	25.00	50.00

BEST OF FURRLOUGH
ANTARCTIC

Value: Cover or less

- ❑1, Jan 95, Romanics; Hairlift, b&w 3.95
- ❑2, Stosstrupp; Dog Star 3.95

BEST OF GOLD DIGGER
ANTARCTIC

Value: Cover or less

- ❑Anl 1, May 99, Proving Ground; Fish Tale, b&w 2.99

BEST OF NORTHSTAR, THE
NORTHSTAR

Value: Cover or less

- ❑1, b&w 1.95

BEST OF THE BRAVE AND THE BOLD, THE
DC

Value: Cover or less

- ❑1, Oct 88, NA; JKu, Batman, Green Arrow 2.50
- ❑2, Nov 88, NA; JKu, Batman, Flash 2.50
- ❑3, Dec 88, NA; JKu, Batman, Aquaman 2.50
- ❑4, Dec 88, NA; JKu, Batman, Creeper 2.50
- ❑5, Jan 89, NA; JKu, Batman, House of Mystery 2.50
- ❑6, Jan 89, NA; JKu, Batman, Teen Titans 2.50

BEST OF THE BRITISH INVASION
REVOLUTIONARY

Value: Cover or less

- ❑1, Sep 93, b&w 2.50
- ❑2, Jan 94, b&w 2.50

BEST OF TRIBUNE CO., THE
DRAGON LADY

Value: Cover or less

- ❑1 2.95
- ❑2 2.95
- ❑3 2.95
- ❑4, (becomes Thrilling Adventure Strips) 2.95

BETA SEXUS
FANTAGRAPHICS

Value: Cover or less

- ❑1, b&w; adult 2.75
- ❑2, Jul 94, b&w; adult 2.75

BETTA: TIME WARRIOR
IMMORTAL

Value: Cover or less

- ❑1, The Beginning's End, Part 1 2.95
- ❑2, The Beginning's End, Part 2 2.95
- ❑3, The Beginning's End, Part 3 2.95

BETTI COZMO
ANTARCTIC

Value: Cover or less

- ❑1, Apr 99 2.99
- ❑2, Jun 99 2.99

BETTIE PAGE COMICS
DARK HORSE

Value: Cover or less

- ❑1, Mar 96, Sandbar Skirmish; Mars Wants Bettie, one-shot, cardstock cover 3.95

BETTIE PAGE COMICS: SPICY ADVENTURE
DARK HORSE

Value: Cover or less

- ❑1, Jan 97, nn; One-Shot 2.95

BETTIE PAGE: QUEEN OF THE NILE
DARK HORSE

Value: Cover or less

- ❑1, Dec 99 2.95

BETTY
ARCHIE

	ORIG	GOOD	FINE	N-MINT
❑1, Sep 92	1.25	0.80	2.00	4.00
❑2	1.25	0.40	1.00	2.00
❑3	1.25	0.40	1.00	2.00
❑4, Feb 93	1.25	0.40	1.00	2.00
❑5, Apr 93	1.25	0.40	1.00	2.00
❑6, Jun 93, Gym Dandy; The Alternative Whirl	1.25	0.30	0.75	1.50
❑7, Aug 93	1.25	0.30	0.75	1.50
❑8, Sep 93	1.25	0.30	0.75	1.50
❑9, Oct 93	1.25	0.30	0.75	1.50
❑10, Nov 93	1.25	0.30	0.75	1.50
❑11, Dec 93	1.25	0.30	0.75	1.50
❑12, Feb 94	1.25	0.30	0.75	1.50
❑13, Apr 94	1.25	0.30	0.75	1.50
❑14, Jun 94	1.25	0.30	0.75	1.50

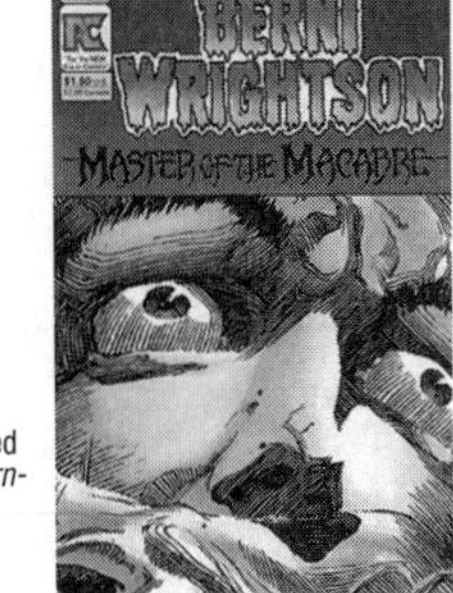

A number of horror stories were adapted by artist-writer Bernie Wrightson in *Bernie Wrightson, Master of the Macabre.*

	ORIG	GOOD	FINE	N-MINT
❑15, Jul 94	1.25	0.30	0.75	1.50
❑16, Aug 94	1.25	0.30	0.75	1.50
❑17, Sep 94	1.50	0.30	0.75	1.50
❑18, Oct 94	1.50	0.30	0.75	1.50
❑19, Nov, Love Showdown, Part 2	1.50	0.30	0.75	1.50
❑20, Dec 94	1.50	0.30	0.75	1.50
❑21, Jan 95	1.50	0.30	0.75	1.50
❑22, Feb 95	1.50	0.30	0.75	1.50
❑23, Mar 95	1.50	0.30	0.75	1.50
❑24, Apr 95	1.50	0.30	0.75	1.50
❑25, May 95	1.50	0.30	0.75	1.50
❑26, Jun 95	1.50	0.30	0.75	1.50
❑27, Jul 95	1.50	0.30	0.75	1.50
❑28, Aug 95	1.50	0.30	0.75	1.50
❑29, Sep 95	1.50	0.30	0.75	1.50
❑30, Oct 95	1.50	0.30	0.75	1.50
❑31, Nov 95	1.50	0.30	0.75	1.50
❑32, Dec 95	1.50	0.30	0.75	1.50
❑33, Jan 96	1.50	0.30	0.75	1.50
❑34, Feb 96	1.50	0.30	0.75	1.50
❑35, Mar 96	1.50	0.30	0.75	1.50
❑36, Apr 96	1.50	0.30	0.75	1.50
❑37, May 96	1.50	0.30	0.75	1.50
❑38, Jun 96	1.50	0.30	0.75	1.50
❑39, Jul 96	1.50	0.30	0.75	1.50
❑40, Aug 96	1.50	0.30	0.75	1.50
❑41, Sep 96	1.50	0.30	0.75	1.50
❑42, Oct, cover has reader sketches of Betty	1.50	0.30	0.75	1.50
❑43, Nov 96	1.50	0.30	0.75	1.50
❑44, Dec 96, The Nation's Most Wanted; Dream Catalog	1.50	0.30	0.75	1.50
❑45, Jan 97	1.50	0.30	0.75	1.50
❑46, Feb 97	1.50	0.30	0.75	1.50
❑47, Mar 97	1.50	0.30	0.75	1.50
❑48, Apr 97	1.50	0.30	0.75	1.50
❑49, May 97	1.50	0.30	0.75	1.50
❑50, Jun 97	1.50	0.30	0.75	1.50
❑51, Jul 97	1.50	0.30	0.75	1.50
❑52, Aug 97	1.50	0.30	0.75	1.50
❑53, Sep 97	1.50	0.30	0.75	1.50
❑54, Oct 97, The Zine Machine, Parts 3 and 4	1.50	0.30	0.75	1.50
❑55, Nov 97	1.50	0.30	0.75	1.50
❑56, Dec 97, return of Polly Cooper	1.50	0.30	0.75	1.50
❑57, Jan 98	1.75	0.35	0.88	1.75
❑58, Feb 98, Virtual Pets	1.75	0.35	0.88	1.75
❑59, Mar 98	1.75	0.35	0.88	1.75
❑60, Apr 98	1.75	0.35	0.88	1.75
❑61, May 98	1.75	0.35	0.88	1.75
❑62, Jun 98	1.75	0.35	0.88	1.75
❑63, Jul 98	1.75	0.35	0.88	1.75
❑64, Aug 98	1.75	0.35	0.88	1.75
❑65, Sep 98, A Day to Remember; Heel, Rover	1.75	0.35	0.88	1.75
❑66, Oct 98	1.75	0.35	0.88	1.75
❑67, Nov 98, The Good Sport!	1.75	0.35	0.88	1.75
❑68, Dec 98	1.75	0.35	0.88	1.75
❑69, Jan 99	1.75	0.35	0.88	1.75
❑70, Feb 99	1.75	0.35	0.88	1.75
❑71, Mar 99, A Day to Remember	1.75	0.35	0.88	1.75
❑72, Apr 99, Special Delivery	1.79	0.36	0.89	1.79
❑73, May 99, Pet Set Session	1.79	0.36	0.89	1.79
❑74, Jun 99	1.79	0.36	0.89	1.79
❑75, Jul 99	1.79	0.36	0.89	1.79
❑76, Aug 99	1.79	0.36	0.89	1.79
❑77, Sep 99	1.79	0.36	0.89	1.79
❑78, Oct 99	1.79	0.36	0.89	1.79
❑79, Nov 99	1.79	0.36	0.89	1.79
❑80, Dec 99	1.79	0.36	0.89	1.79
❑81, Jan 00	1.79	0.36	0.89	1.79
❑82, Feb 00	1.79	0.36	0.89	1.79
❑83, Mar 00	1.79	0.36	0.89	1.79

	ORIG	GOOD	FINE	N-MINT
❑84, Apr 00	1.79	0.36	0.89	1.79
❑85, May 00	1.79	0.36	0.89	1.79
❑86, Jun 00	1.79	0.36	0.89	1.79
❑87, Jul 00	1.99	0.40	1.00	1.99
❑88, Aug 00	1.99	0.40	1.00	1.99
❑89, Sep 00	1.99	0.40	1.00	1.99
❑90, Oct 00	1.99	0.40	1.00	1.99
❑91, Nov 00	1.99	0.40	1.00	1.99
❑92, Dec 00	1.99	0.40	1.00	1.99
❑93, Jan 01	1.99	0.40	1.00	1.99
❑94, Feb 01	1.99	0.40	1.00	1.99
❑95, Mar 01	1.99	0.40	1.00	1.99
❑96, Apr 01	1.99	0.40	1.00	1.99
❑97	1.99	0.40	1.00	1.99
❑98	1.99	0.40	1.00	1.99
❑99	1.99	0.40	1.00	1.99
❑100	1.99	0.40	1.00	1.99
❑101	1.99	0.40	1.00	1.99
❑102	1.99	0.40	1.00	1.99

BETTY AND VERONICA

ARCHIE

	ORIG	GOOD	FINE	N-MINT
❑1, Jun 87	0.75	1.00	2.50	5.00
❑2	0.75	0.60	1.50	3.00
❑3	0.75	0.60	1.50	3.00
❑4	0.75	0.50	1.25	2.50
❑5	0.75	0.50	1.25	2.50
❑6	0.75	0.40	1.00	2.00
❑7	0.75	0.40	1.00	2.00
❑8	0.75	0.40	1.00	2.00
❑9	0.75	0.40	1.00	2.00
❑10	0.75	0.40	1.00	2.00
❑11	0.75	0.40	1.00	2.00
❑12	0.75	0.40	1.00	2.00
❑13	0.75	0.40	1.00	2.00
❑14	0.75	0.40	1.00	2.00
❑15	0.75	0.40	1.00	2.00
❑16	0.75	0.40	1.00	2.00
❑17	0.75	0.40	1.00	2.00
❑18	0.75	0.40	1.00	2.00
❑19	0.75	0.40	1.00	2.00
❑20	0.75	0.40	1.00	2.00
❑21	1.00	0.35	0.88	1.75
❑22	1.00	0.35	0.88	1.75
❑23	1.00	0.35	0.88	1.75
❑24	1.00	0.35	0.88	1.75
❑25	1.00	0.35	0.88	1.75
❑26	1.00	0.35	0.88	1.75
❑27	1.00	0.35	0.88	1.75
❑28	1.00	0.35	0.88	1.75
❑29	1.00	0.35	0.88	1.75
❑30	1.00	0.35	0.88	1.75
❑31	1.00	0.35	0.88	1.75
❑32	1.00	0.35	0.88	1.75
❑33	1.00	0.35	0.88	1.75
❑34	1.00	0.35	0.88	1.75
❑35	1.00	0.35	0.88	1.75
❑36	1.00	0.35	0.88	1.75
❑37	1.00	0.35	0.88	1.75
❑38	1.00	0.35	0.88	1.75
❑39	1.00	0.35	0.88	1.75
❑40	1.00	0.35	0.88	1.75
❑41	1.00	0.35	0.88	1.75
❑42	1.00	0.35	0.88	1.75
❑43	1.00	0.35	0.88	1.75
❑44	1.00	0.35	0.88	1.75
❑45	1.00	0.35	0.88	1.75
❑46	1.00	0.35	0.88	1.75
❑47	1.00	0.35	0.88	1.75
❑48	1.00	0.35	0.88	1.75
❑49	1.00	0.35	0.88	1.75
❑50	1.00	0.35	0.88	1.75
❑51	1.00	0.30	0.75	1.50
❑52	1.00	0.30	0.75	1.50
❑53	1.00	0.30	0.75	1.50
❑54, Aug 92	1.25	0.30	0.75	1.50
❑55, Sep 92	1.25	0.30	0.75	1.50
❑56, Oct 92	1.25	0.30	0.75	1.50
❑57, Nov 92	1.25	0.30	0.75	1.50
❑58, Dec 92	1.25	0.30	0.75	1.50
❑59, Jan 93	1.25	0.30	0.75	1.50
❑60, Feb 93	1.25	0.30	0.75	1.50
❑61, Mar 93	1.25	0.30	0.75	1.50
❑62, Apr 93	1.25	0.30	0.75	1.50
❑63, May 93	1.25	0.30	0.75	1.50
❑64, Jun 93	1.25	0.30	0.75	1.50
❑65, Jul 93	1.25	0.30	0.75	1.50
❑66, Aug 93, DDC, Hold the Phone; Fab Job	1.25	0.30	0.75	1.50
❑67, Sep 93	1.25	0.30	0.75	1.50
❑68, Oct 93	1.25	0.30	0.75	1.50
❑69, Nov 93	1.25	0.30	0.75	1.50
❑70, Dec 93	1.25	0.30	0.75	1.50
❑71, Jan 94	1.25	0.30	0.75	1.50
❑72, Feb 94	1.25	0.30	0.75	1.50
❑73, Mar 94	1.25	0.30	0.75	1.50
❑74, Apr 94	1.25	0.30	0.75	1.50
❑75, May 94	1.25	0.30	0.75	1.50
❑76, Jun 94	1.25	0.30	0.75	1.50
❑77, Jul 94	1.25	0.30	0.75	1.50
❑78, Aug 94	1.50	0.30	0.75	1.50
❑79, Sep 94	1.50	0.30	0.75	1.50
❑80, Oct 94	1.50	0.30	0.75	1.50
❑81, Nov 94	1.50	0.30	0.75	1.50
❑82, Dec, Love Showdown, Part 3	1.50	0.30	0.75	1.50
❑83, Jan 95	1.50	0.30	0.75	1.50
❑84, Feb 95	1.50	0.30	0.75	1.50
❑85, Mar 95	1.50	0.30	0.75	1.50
❑86, Apr 95	1.50	0.30	0.75	1.50
❑87, May 95	1.50	0.30	0.75	1.50
❑88, Jun 95	1.50	0.30	0.75	1.50
❑89, Jul 95	1.50	0.30	0.75	1.50
❑90, Aug 95	1.50	0.30	0.75	1.50
❑91, Sep 95	1.50	0.30	0.75	1.50
❑92, Oct 95	1.50	0.30	0.75	1.50
❑93, Nov 95	1.50	0.30	0.75	1.50
❑94, Dec 95, Love Showdown, Part 3	1.50	0.30	0.75	1.50
❑95, Jan, House of Riverdale, Part 2, concludes in Archie's PalJughead #76	1.50	0.30	0.75	1.50
❑96, Feb 96	1.50	0.30	0.75	1.50
❑97, Mar 96	1.50	0.30	0.75	1.50
❑98, Apr 96	1.50	0.30	0.75	1.50
❑99, May 96	1.50	0.30	0.75	1.50
❑100, Jun 96	1.50	0.30	0.75	1.50
❑101	1.50	0.30	0.75	1.50
❑102, Aug 96	1.50	0.30	0.75	1.50
❑103, Sep 96	1.50	0.30	0.75	1.50
❑104, Oct 96	1.50	0.30	0.75	1.50
❑105, Nov 96	1.50	0.30	0.75	1.50
❑106, Dec 96, Hearing Aided; Style No-Show	1.50	0.30	0.75	1.50
❑107, Jan 97	1.50	0.30	0.75	1.50
❑108, Feb 97	1.50	0.30	0.75	1.50
❑109, Mar 97	1.50	0.30	0.75	1.50
❑110, Apr 97	1.50	0.30	0.75	1.50
❑111, May 97	1.50	0.30	0.75	1.50
❑112, Jun 97	1.50	0.30	0.75	1.50
❑113, Jul 97	1.50	0.30	0.75	1.50
❑114, Aug 97	1.50	0.30	0.75	1.50
❑115, Sep 97	1.50	0.30	0.75	1.50
❑116, Oct 97	1.50	0.30	0.75	1.50
❑117, Nov 97	1.50	0.30	0.75	1.50
❑118, Dec 97	1.50	0.30	0.75	1.50
❑119, Jan 98	1.75	0.35	0.88	1.75
❑120, Feb 98	1.75	0.35	0.88	1.75
❑121, Mar 98	1.75	0.35	0.88	1.75
❑122, Apr 98	1.75	0.35	0.88	1.75
❑123, May 98	1.75	0.35	0.88	1.75
❑124, Jun 98	1.75	0.35	0.88	1.75
❑125, Jul 98	1.75	0.35	0.88	1.75
❑126, Aug 98	1.75	0.35	0.88	1.75
❑127, Sep 98, DDC, Home Alone Comfort Zone; Faithfully Yours	1.75	0.35	0.88	1.75
❑128, Oct 98	1.75	0.35	0.88	1.75
❑129, Nov 98, DDC, Express Yourself; The Big Obsession	1.75	0.35	0.88	1.75
❑130, Dec 98	1.75	0.35	0.88	1.75
❑131, Jan 99	1.75	0.35	0.88	1.75
❑132, Feb 99	1.75	0.35	0.88	1.75
❑133, Mar 99, DDC, Fashion Fling	1.75	0.35	0.88	1.75
❑134, Apr 99	1.79	0.36	0.89	1.79
❑135, May 99, DDC, Media Manipulation	1.79	0.36	0.89	1.79
❑136, Jun 99	1.79	0.36	0.89	1.79
❑137, Jul 99	1.79	0.36	0.89	1.79
❑138, Aug 99	1.79	0.36	0.89	1.79
❑139, Sep 99	1.79	0.36	0.89	1.79
❑140, Oct 99	1.79	0.36	0.89	1.79
❑141, Nov 99	1.79	0.36	0.89	1.79
❑142, Dec 99	1.79	0.36	0.89	1.79
❑143, Jan 00	1.79	0.36	0.89	1.79
❑144, Feb 00	1.79	0.36	0.89	1.79
❑145, Mar 00	1.79	0.36	0.89	1.79
❑146, Apr 00	1.79	0.36	0.89	1.79

	ORIG	GOOD	FINE	N-MINT
❑147, May 00	1.79	0.36	0.89	1.79
❑148, Jun 00	1.79	0.36	0.89	1.79
❑149, Jul 00	1.99	0.40	1.00	1.99
❑150, Aug 00	1.99	0.40	1.00	1.99
❑151, Sep 00	1.99	0.40	1.00	1.99
❑152, Oct 00	1.99	0.40	1.00	1.99
❑153, Nov 00	1.99	0.40	1.00	1.99
❑154, Dec 00	1.99	0.40	1.00	1.99
❑155, Jan 01	1.99	0.40	1.00	1.99
❑156, Feb 01	1.99	0.40	1.00	1.99
❑157, Mar 01	1.99	0.40	1.00	1.99
❑158, Apr 01	1.99	0.40	1.00	1.99
❑159	1.99	0.40	1.00	1.99
❑160	1.99	0.40	1.00	1.99
❑161	1.99	0.40	1.00	1.99
❑162	1.99	0.40	1.00	1.99
❑163	1.99	0.40	1.00	1.99
❑164	1.99	0.40	1.00	1.99
❑165	1.99	0.40	1.00	1.99

BETTY & VERONICA ANNUAL DIGEST MAGAZINE
ARCHIE

Value: Cover or less

❑12, Jan 95	1.75	❑15, Jul 96	1.75
❑13, Sep 95	1.75	❑16, Aug 97	1.79
❑14, Feb 96	1.75		

BETTY AND VERONICA DIGEST MAGAZINE
ARCHIE

	ORIG	GOOD	FINE	N-MINT
❑72, Jan 95	1.75	0.35	0.88	1.75
❑73, Mar 95	1.75	0.35	0.88	1.75
❑74, Apr 95	1.75	0.35	0.88	1.75
❑75, Jun 95	1.75	0.35	0.88	1.75
❑76, Aug 95	1.75	0.35	0.88	1.75
❑77, Oct 95	1.75	0.35	0.88	1.75
❑78, Dec 95	1.75	0.35	0.88	1.75
❑79, Feb 96	1.75	0.35	0.88	1.75
❑80, Apr 96	1.75	0.35	0.88	1.75
❑81, Jun 96	1.75	0.35	0.88	1.75
❑82, Jul 96	1.75	0.35	0.88	1.75
❑83, Sep 96	1.75	0.35	0.88	1.75
❑84, Nov 96	1.79	0.36	0.89	1.79
❑85, Jan 97	1.79	0.36	0.89	1.79
❑86, Feb 97	1.79	0.36	0.89	1.79
❑87, Apr 97	1.79	0.36	0.89	1.79
❑88, Jun 97	1.79	0.36	0.89	1.79
❑89, Jul 97	1.79	0.36	0.89	1.79
❑90, Sep 97	1.79	0.36	0.89	1.79
❑91, Oct 97	1.79	0.36	0.89	1.79
❑92, Dec 97	1.79	0.36	0.89	1.79
❑93, Feb 98	1.95	0.39	0.98	1.95
❑94, Apr 98	1.95	0.39	0.98	1.95
❑95, May 98	1.95	0.39	0.98	1.95
❑96, Jul 98	1.95	0.39	0.98	1.95
❑97, Aug 98	1.95	0.39	0.98	1.95
❑98, Sep 98	1.95	0.39	0.98	1.95
❑99, Nov 98	1.95	0.39	0.98	1.95
❑100, Dec 98	1.95	0.39	0.98	1.95
❑101, Feb 99	1.95	0.39	0.98	1.95
❑102, Apr 99	1.99	0.40	1.00	1.99
❑103, May 99	1.99	0.40	1.00	1.99
❑104, Jul 99	1.99	0.40	1.00	1.99
❑105, Aug 99	1.99	0.40	1.00	1.99
❑106, Sep 99	1.99	0.40	1.00	1.99
❑107, Nov 99	1.99	0.40	1.00	1.99
❑108, Sep 99	1.99	0.40	1.00	1.99
❑109, Feb 00	1.99	0.40	1.00	1.99
❑110, Apr 00	1.99	0.40	1.00	1.99
❑111, May 00	1.99	0.40	1.00	1.99
❑112, Jul 00	2.19	0.40	1.00	1.99
❑113, Aug 00	2.19	0.40	1.00	1.99
❑114, Oct 00	2.19	0.40	1.00	1.99
❑115, Nov 00	2.19	0.40	1.00	1.99
❑116, Dec 00	2.19	0.40	1.00	1.99
❑117, Feb 01	2.19	0.44	1.10	2.19
❑118, Apr 01	2.19	0.44	1.10	2.19
❑119	—	0.44	1.10	2.19
❑120	—	0.44	1.10	2.19
❑121	—	0.44	1.10	2.19
❑122	—	0.44	1.10	2.19
❑123	—	0.44	1.10	2.19

BETTY AND VERONICA DOUBLE DIGEST
ARCHIE

	ORIG	GOOD	FINE	N-MINT
❑1	2.75	1.40	3.50	7.00
❑2	2.75	0.80	2.00	4.00
❑3	2.75	0.80	2.00	4.00
❑4	2.75	0.80	2.00	4.00

Archie Comics made it appear that the love triangle between Archie, Betty, and Veronica might finally be decided in the four-part "Love Showdown," when the girls learned that a new rival for Archie's affections was coming to town.

	ORIG	GOOD	FINE	N-MINT
❑5	2.75	0.80	2.00	4.00
❑6	2.75	0.80	2.00	4.00
❑7	2.75	0.80	2.00	4.00
❑8	2.75	0.80	2.00	4.00
❑9	2.75	0.80	2.00	4.00
❑10	2.75	0.80	2.00	4.00
❑11	2.75	0.60	1.50	3.00
❑12	2.75	0.60	1.50	3.00
❑13	2.75	0.60	1.50	3.00
❑14	2.75	0.60	1.50	3.00
❑15	2.75	0.60	1.50	3.00
❑16	2.75	0.60	1.50	3.00
❑17	2.75	0.60	1.50	3.00
❑18	2.75	0.60	1.50	3.00
❑19	2.75	0.60	1.50	3.00
❑20	2.75	0.60	1.50	3.00
❑21	2.75	0.60	1.50	3.00
❑22	2.75	0.60	1.50	3.00
❑23	2.75	0.60	1.50	3.00
❑24	2.75	0.60	1.50	3.00
❑25	2.75	0.60	1.50	3.00
❑26	2.75	0.60	1.50	3.00
❑27	2.75	0.60	1.50	3.00
❑28	2.75	0.60	1.50	3.00
❑29	2.75	0.60	1.50	3.00
❑30	2.75	0.60	1.50	3.00
❑31	2.75	0.60	1.50	3.00
❑32	2.75	0.60	1.50	3.00
❑33	2.75	0.60	1.50	3.00
❑34	2.75	0.60	1.50	3.00
❑35	2.75	0.60	1.50	3.00
❑36	2.75	0.60	1.50	3.00
❑37	2.75	0.60	1.50	3.00
❑38	2.75	0.60	1.50	3.00
❑39	2.75	0.60	1.50	3.00
❑40	2.75	0.60	1.50	3.00
❑41	2.75	0.60	1.50	3.00
❑42	2.75	0.60	1.50	3.00
❑43	2.75	0.60	1.50	3.00
❑44	2.75	0.60	1.50	3.00
❑45	2.75	0.60	1.50	3.00
❑46	2.75	0.60	1.50	3.00
❑47	2.75	0.60	1.50	3.00
❑48, Dec 94	2.75	0.60	1.50	3.00
❑49	2.75	0.60	1.50	3.00
❑50, Apr 95	2.75	0.60	1.50	3.00
❑51, Jun 95	2.75	0.60	1.50	3.00
❑52, Aug 95	2.75	0.60	1.50	3.00
❑53, Sep 95	2.75	0.60	1.50	3.00
❑54	2.75	0.60	1.50	3.00
❑55, Jan 96	2.75	0.60	1.50	3.00
❑56, Mar 96	2.75	0.60	1.50	3.00
❑57, Apr 96	2.75	0.60	1.50	3.00
❑58	2.75	0.60	1.50	3.00
❑59, Aug 96	2.75	0.60	1.50	3.00
❑60, Oct 96	2.75	0.60	1.50	3.00
❑61, Nov 96	2.75	0.60	1.50	3.00
❑62, Jan 97	2.75	0.60	1.50	3.00
❑63, Mar 97	2.75	0.60	1.50	3.00
❑64, Apr 97	2.75	0.60	1.50	3.00
❑65, Jun 97	2.75	0.60	1.50	3.00
❑66, Aug 97	2.79	0.60	1.50	3.00
❑67, Sep 97	2.79	0.60	1.50	3.00
❑68, Nov 97	2.79	0.60	1.50	3.00
❑69, Jan 98	2.95	0.60	1.50	3.00
❑70, Mar 98	2.95	0.60	1.50	3.00
❑71, Apr 98	2.95	0.60	1.50	3.00
❑72, Jun 98	2.95	0.60	1.50	3.00
❑73, Jul 98	2.95	0.60	1.50	3.00
❑74, Sep 98	2.95	0.60	1.50	3.00
❑75, Oct 98	2.95	0.60	1.50	3.00

	ORIG	GOOD	FINE	N-MINT
❑76, Dec 98	2.95	0.60	1.50	3.00
❑77, Jan 99	2.95	0.60	1.50	3.00
❑78, Mar 99	2.95	0.60	1.50	3.00
❑79, Apr 99	2.99	0.60	1.50	3.00
❑80, Jun 99	2.99	0.60	1.50	3.00
❑81, Jul 99	2.99	0.60	1.50	3.00
❑82, Sep 99	2.99	0.60	1.50	3.00
❑83, Oct 99	2.99	0.60	1.50	3.00
❑84, Dec 99	2.99	0.60	1.50	3.00
❑85, Jan 00	2.99	0.60	1.50	3.00
❑86, Mar 00	2.99	0.60	1.50	3.00
❑87, Apr 00	2.99	0.60	1.50	3.00
❑88, Jun 00	3.19	0.60	1.50	3.00
❑89, Jul 00	3.19	0.60	1.50	3.00
❑90, Sep 00	3.19	0.64	1.60	3.19
❑91, Oct 00	3.19	0.64	1.60	3.19
❑92, Nov 00	3.19	0.64	1.60	3.19
❑93, Jan 01	3.19	0.64	1.60	3.19
❑94, Feb 01	3.19	0.64	1.60	3.19
❑95, Apr 01	3.29	0.66	1.64	3.29

BETTY AND VERONICA SPECTACULAR
ARCHIE

	ORIG	GOOD	FINE	N-MINT
❑1, Oct 92	1.25	0.60	1.50	3.00
❑2	1.25	0.50	1.25	2.50
❑3, May 93	1.25	0.50	1.25	2.50
❑4	1.25	0.40	1.00	2.00
❑5, Oct 93	1.25	0.40	1.00	2.00
❑6, Feb 94	1.25	0.40	1.00	2.00
❑7, Apr 94	1.25	0.40	1.00	2.00
❑8, May 94	1.25	0.40	1.00	2.00
❑9, Jul 94	1.25	0.35	0.88	1.75
❑10, Sep 94	1.50	0.35	0.88	1.75
❑11, Nov 94	1.50	0.35	0.88	1.75
❑12, Jan 95	1.50	0.35	0.88	1.75
❑13, Feb 95	1.50	0.35	0.88	1.75
❑14, Apr 95	1.50	0.35	0.88	1.75
❑15, Jul 95	1.50	0.35	0.88	1.75
❑16, Oct 95	1.50	0.35	0.88	1.75
❑17, Jan 96	1.50	0.35	0.88	1.75
❑18, Apr 96	1.50	0.35	0.88	1.75
❑19, Jul 96	1.50	0.35	0.88	1.75
❑20, Oct 96	1.50	0.35	0.88	1.75
❑21, Jan, Betty becomes a fashion model	1.50	0.35	0.88	1.75
❑22, Mar 97	1.50	0.35	0.88	1.75
❑23, May 97	1.50	0.35	0.88	1.75
❑24, Jul, Betty and Veronica set up web pages	1.50	0.35	0.88	1.75
❑25, Sep 97	1.50	0.35	0.88	1.75
❑26, Nov 97	1.50	0.35	0.88	1.75
❑27, Feb 98	1.75	0.35	0.88	1.75
❑28, Mar 98	1.75	0.35	0.88	1.75
❑29, May 98	1.75	0.35	0.88	1.75
❑30, Jul 98	1.75	0.35	0.88	1.75
❑31, Sep 98, Lost At Sea; How Refreshing	1.75	0.35	0.88	1.75
❑32, Nov, Maid for Each Other, Betty and Veronica are maids for each other	1.75	0.35	0.88	1.75
❑33, Jan 99, talent competition	1.75	0.35	0.88	1.75
❑34, Mar 99, Give Me the Simple Life	1.75	0.35	0.88	1.75
❑35, May 99, Swing Time, Swing issue	1.79	0.36	0.89	1.79
❑36, Jul 99	1.79	0.36	0.89	1.79
❑37, Sep 99	1.79	0.36	0.89	1.79
❑38, Nov 99	1.79	0.36	0.89	1.79
❑39, Jan 00	1.79	0.36	0.89	1.79
❑40, Mar 00	1.79	0.36	0.89	1.79
❑41, May 00	1.79	0.36	0.89	1.79
❑42, Jul 00	1.99	0.40	1.00	1.99
❑43, Sep 00	1.99	0.40	1.00	1.99
❑44, Nov 00	1.99	0.40	1.00	1.99
❑45, Jan 01	1.99	0.40	1.00	1.99

BETTY & VERONICA SUMMER FUN
ARCHIE

	ORIG	GOOD	FINE	N-MINT
❑1, Sum 94	2.00	0.50	1.25	2.50
❑2, Sum 95	2.00	0.50	1.25	2.50
❑3, Sum 96	2.00	0.50	1.25	2.50
❑4, Sum 97	2.00	0.50	1.25	2.50
❑5, Sum 98, Surf on Turf; Dizzy Tizzy	2.25	0.45	1.13	2.25
❑6, Sum 99	2.29	0.46	1.14	2.29

BETTY BOOP 3-D
BLACKTHORNE

Value: Cover or less ❑1, Nov 86, The Contract........ 2.50

BETTY BOOP'S BIG BREAK
FIRST

Value: Cover or less ❑1, nn........ 5.95

BETTY IN BONDAGE (TEO JONELLI'S...)
SHUNGA

Value: Cover or less

❑1, b&w; adult	3.00
❑2, b&w; adult	3.00
❑3, b&w; adult	3.00
❑4, b&w; adult	3.00
❑5, adult	3.00
❑6, adult	3.00
❑7, adult	3.00
❑8, adult	3.00
❑Anl 1, adult; 1993 Annual	5.95
❑Anl 2, adult; 1994 Annual	5.95
❑Anl 3, adult; 1995 Annual	5.95

BETTY IN BONDAGE: BETTY MAE
SHUNGA

Value: Cover or less ❑1........ 6.95

BETTY PAGE 3-D COMICS
3-D ZONE

Value: Cover or less ❑1........ 3.95

BETTY PAGE 3-D PICTURE BOOK, THE
3-D ZONE

Value: Cover or less ❑1, photos, adult........ 3.95

BETTY PAGE CAPTURED JUNGLE GIRL 3-D
3-D ZONE

Value: Cover or less ❑1, photos........ 3.95

BETTY PAGES, THE
PURE IMAGINATION

	ORIG	GOOD	FINE	N-MINT
❑1, DSt, Ward, photos	5.00	1.20	3.00	6.00
❑1-2, 2nd Printing	5.00	1.00	2.50	5.00
❑2	5.00	1.00	2.50	5.00
❑2-2, 2nd Printing	5.00	1.00	2.50	5.00
❑3	5.00	1.00	2.50	5.00
❑4	5.00	1.00	2.50	5.00
❑5, Win 89	4.50	0.90	2.25	4.50
❑6	4.50	0.90	2.25	4.50
❑7	4.50	0.90	2.25	4.50
❑8	4.50	0.90	2.25	4.50
❑9	5.00	1.00	2.50	5.00

BETTY PAGE: THE 50'S RAGE
ILLUSTRATION

Value: Cover or less

❑1/A, Jan 93, tame cover	3.25
❑1/B, Jan 93, Adult cover	3.25
❑2/A, tame cover	3.25
❑2/B, Adult cover	3.25

BETTY'S DIARY
ARCHIE

	ORIG	GOOD	FINE	N-MINT
❑1, Apr 86	0.75	0.60	1.50	3.00
❑2	0.75	0.40	1.00	2.00
❑3	0.75	0.40	1.00	2.00
❑4	0.75	0.40	1.00	2.00
❑5	0.75	0.40	1.00	2.00
❑6	0.75	0.30	0.75	1.50
❑7	0.75	0.30	0.75	1.50
❑8	0.75	0.30	0.75	1.50
❑9	0.75	0.30	0.75	1.50
❑10	0.75	0.30	0.75	1.50
❑11	0.75	0.30	0.75	1.50
❑12	0.75	0.30	0.75	1.50
❑13	0.75	0.30	0.75	1.50
❑14	0.75	0.30	0.75	1.50
❑15	0.75	0.30	0.75	1.50
❑16	0.75	0.30	0.75	1.50
❑17	0.75	0.30	0.75	1.50
❑18	0.75	0.30	0.75	1.50
❑19	0.75	0.30	0.75	1.50
❑20	0.75	0.30	0.75	1.50
❑21	0.75	0.20	0.50	1.00
❑22	0.75	0.20	0.50	1.00
❑23	0.75	0.20	0.50	1.00
❑24	0.75	0.20	0.50	1.00
❑25	0.75	0.20	0.50	1.00
❑26	0.75	0.20	0.50	1.00
❑27	0.75	0.20	0.50	1.00
❑28	0.75	0.20	0.50	1.00
❑29	0.75	0.20	0.50	1.00
❑30	0.75	0.20	0.50	1.00
❑31	0.75	0.20	0.50	1.00
❑32	0.75	0.20	0.50	1.00
❑33	0.75	0.20	0.50	1.00
❑34	0.75	0.20	0.50	1.00
❑35	0.75	0.20	0.50	1.00
❑36	0.75	0.20	0.50	1.00
❑37	0.75	0.20	0.50	1.00
❑38	0.75	0.20	0.50	1.00
❑39	0.75	0.20	0.50	1.00
❑40	0.75	0.20	0.50	1.00

BETTY'S DIGEST MAGAZINE
ARCHIE

	ORIG	GOOD	FINE	N-MINT
❑1, Nov 96	1.79	0.40	1.00	2.00
❑2, Nov 97	1.79	0.40	1.00	2.00

BEVERLY HILLBILLIES, THE
DELL

	ORIG	GOOD	FINE	N-MINT
❑1, Apr 63, Photo cover	0.12	12.00	30.00	60.00
❑2, Jul 63	0.12	7.00	17.50	35.00
❑3, Oct 63	0.12	5.00	12.50	25.00
❑4, Jan 64	0.12	4.00	10.00	20.00
❑5, Apr 64	0.12	4.00	10.00	20.00
❑6, Jul 64	0.12	3.00	7.50	15.00
❑7, Oct 64	0.12	3.00	7.50	15.00
❑8, Jan 65	0.12	3.00	7.50	15.00
❑9, Apr 65	0.12	3.00	7.50	15.00
❑10, ca. 65	0.12	3.00	7.50	15.00
❑11, Dec 65	0.12	2.40	6.00	12.00
❑12, Mar 66	0.12	2.40	6.00	12.00
❑13, Jun 66	0.12	2.40	6.00	12.00
❑14, Sep 66	0.12	2.40	6.00	12.00
❑15	—	2.40	6.00	12.00
❑16	—	2.40	6.00	12.00
❑17	—	2.40	6.00	12.00
❑18	—	2.00	5.00	10.00
❑19, Oct 69, Same cover as #1	0.15	2.00	5.00	10.00
❑20, Oct 70	0.15	2.00	5.00	10.00
❑21	—	2.00	5.00	10.00

BEWARE (MARVEL)
MARVEL

	ORIG	GOOD	FINE	N-MINT
❑1, Mar 73, The Werewolf Was Afraid; On the Trail of the Witch	0.20	1.20	3.00	6.00
❑2, May 73	0.20	0.80	2.00	4.00
❑3, Jul 73	0.20	0.80	2.00	4.00
❑4, Sep 73	0.20	0.80	2.00	4.00
❑5, Nov 73	0.20	0.80	2.00	4.00
❑6, Jan 74	0.20	0.80	2.00	4.00
❑7, Mar 74	0.20	0.80	2.00	4.00
❑8, May 74, Series continued in Tomb of Darkness #9	0.25	0.80	2.00	4.00

BEWARE THE CREEPER
DC

	ORIG	GOOD	FINE	N-MINT
❑1, Jun 68, SD	0.12	8.00	20.00	40.00
❑2, Aug 68, SD	0.12	5.00	12.50	25.00
❑3, Oct 68, SD	0.12	5.00	12.50	25.00
❑4, Dec 68, SD	0.12	5.00	12.50	25.00
❑5, Feb 69, SD	0.12	4.00	10.00	20.00
❑6, Apr 69, SD, Final Issue	0.12	4.00	10.00	20.00

BEYOND
BLUE

Value: Cover or less ❑1, Jun 96 ... 2.95

BEYOND COMMUNION
CALIBER

Value: Cover or less ❑1 ... 2.95

BEYOND MARS
BLACKTHORNE

Value: Cover or less

❑0, book 1-3 ... 2.00

❑1 ... 6.95

❑2 ... 6.95

BEYOND THE GRAVE
CHARLTON

	ORIG	GOOD	FINE	N-MINT
❑1	0.25	1.20	3.00	6.00
❑2	0.25	0.80	2.00	4.00
❑3	0.25	0.80	2.00	4.00
❑4	0.25	0.60	1.50	3.00
❑5	0.25	0.60	1.50	3.00
❑6, Jun 76, The Stones of Brytagalon; Three Went Forth	0.25	0.50	1.25	2.50
❑7	0.25	0.50	1.25	2.50
❑8	0.25	0.50	1.25	2.50
❑9	0.25	0.50	1.25	2.50
❑10	0.25	0.50	1.25	2.50
❑11	0.25	0.50	1.25	2.50
❑12	0.25	0.50	1.25	2.50
❑13	0.25	0.50	1.25	2.50
❑14	0.25	0.50	1.25	2.50
❑15	0.25	0.50	1.25	2.50
❑16	0.25	0.50	1.25	2.50
❑17, Final Issue	0.25	0.50	1.25	2.50

BIG
DARK HORSE

	ORIG	GOOD	FINE	N-MINT
❑1, Mar 89, adaptation	2.00	0.50	1.25	2.50

BIG BAD BLOOD OF DRACULA
APPLE

Value: Cover or less

❑1, BWr, reprints, b&w ... 2.75

❑2 ... 2.95

The cover to the first issue of Dell's *The Beverly Hillbillies* was repeated on #19.

BIG BANG COMICS (VOL. 1)
CALIBER

	ORIG	GOOD	FINE	N-MINT
❑0, May 95, ARo (c), Knight Watchman: The Time Crimes of Grandfather Clock!; Thunder Girl: The Robber Robot, b&w and color	2.95	0.70	1.75	3.50
❑1, Spr 94, Knight Watchman: The Man Called Mr. Mask; The Badge: The Shrine of Crime, b&w	1.95	0.50	1.25	2.50
❑2, Sum 94, Ultiman vs. The Sub-oteurs; The Blitz: Night of 1000 Stars and Stripes, b&w	1.95	0.50	1.25	2.50
❑3, Oct 94, Round Table of America: The Criss Cross Crisis!, b&w	1.95	0.50	1.25	2.50
❑4, Feb 95, b&w	1.95	0.50	1.25	2.50

BIG BANG COMICS (VOL. 2)
IMAGE

	ORIG	GOOD	FINE	N-MINT
❑1, May 96, Mighty Man and the Critter Crime Wave; Knight Watchman, Mighty Man, Knight Watchman, Doctor Weird	1.95	0.60	1.50	3.00
❑2, Jun 96, Silver Age Shadowhawk, Knight Watchman, The Badge	2.50	0.55	1.38	2.75
❑3, Jul, Ultiman: The Crimes of Ultiman!; Thunder Girl Meets Her Evil Imitator, Knight Watchman, Ultiman, Thunder Girl	2.50	0.55	1.38	2.75
❑4, Sep, Knights of Justice	2.50	0.55	1.38	2.75
❑5, Oct 96, origins issue	2.95	0.59	1.48	2.95
❑6, Nov, Criss-Cross Crisis; Round Table of America: Criss Cross Crisis!	2.95	0.59	1.48	2.95
❑7, Dec 96, Mighty Man: Ominous Reprieve; Shanghai Breeze: Assassination Run, Mighty Man vs. Mighty Man	2.95	0.59	1.48	2.95
❑8, Jan 97, Mister U.S.: Birth of a Legend; A Hero Bestowed, 1: Mister U.S.	2.95	0.59	1.48	2.95
❑9, Mar 97, A: Blitz; A: Sphinx, Showplace	2.95	0.59	1.48	2.95
❑10, May 97	2.95	0.59	1.48	2.95
❑11, Jul, Knight Watchman vs. Faulty Towers	2.95	0.59	1.48	2.95
❑12, Sep 97, A: Savage Dragon	2.95	0.59	1.48	2.95
❑13, Aug 97, The Sphinx, cover says Jul, indicia says Aug	2.95	0.59	1.48	2.95
❑14, Oct 97, A: Savage Dragon	2.95	0.59	1.48	2.95
❑15, Oct, Dr. Weird: Terror in the Swamp; Blitz: Clickety Split, Doctor Weird vs. Bog Swamp Demon, cover says Dec, indicia says Oct/Nov	2.95	0.59	1.48	2.95
❑16, Jan 98, Thunder Girl: The Clock That Turned Back Time!; Shadow Lady, Thunder Girl	2.95	0.59	1.48	2.95
❑17, Feb 98, Murder by Microphone, Part 1; Shadow Lady: Murder by Microphone, Shadow Lady	2.95	0.59	1.48	2.95
❑18, Apr 98, End of Time!, A: Savage Dragon, Pantheon of Heroes	2.95	0.59	1.48	2.95
❑19, Jun 98, The Golden Age Beacon; The Hummingbird, O: The Beacon I (Scott Martin); O: The Hummingbird; O: The Beacon II (Doctor Julia Gardner), cover says Apr, indicia says Jun	2.95	0.59	1.48	2.95
❑20, Jul 98, D Is for Daughter, Deceit and Death!; Little Girl Lost..., A: The Sphinx; A: The Blitz; A: Knight Watchman; A: Dimensioneer, photo back cover	2.95	0.59	1.48	2.95
❑21, Aug 98, Murder by Microphone, Part 2; Shadow Lady: Murder by Microphone, Part 2, Shadow Lady	2.95	0.59	1.48	2.95
❑22, Sep 98, Knight Watchman: Crime From the Skies!; The Dimensioneer: Dr. Insect and his Ant Men!, Knight Watchman	2.95	0.59	1.48	2.95
❑23, Nov 98, The Sphinx; Who Do You Think You Are?, Tales of the Sphinx, Book 2	2.95	0.79	1.98	3.95
❑24, Apr 99, History of Big Bang Comics, Part 1, The Big Bang History of Comics	3.95	0.59	1.48	2.95
❑25, Jun 99, Father Flamingo and the Boys of Bad Town; The Shattering Showdown with The Super-Science Sprite!	3.95	0.59	1.48	2.95
❑26, Jul 99, Shadow Lady: Murder by Miicrophone, Part 3; Blue Bird: South of the Border	2.95	0.59	1.48	2.95
❑27, Oct 99, The Big Bang History of Comics, Part 2	3.95	0.79	1.98	3.95

	ORIG	GOOD	FINE	N-MINT
❑28, Dec 99, Knight Watchman: Knight of the Living Dead!; The Pink Flamingo's Bubble Trouble, Knight Watchman	3.95	0.79	1.98	3.95
❑29, Feb 00, Knight of the Living Dead; The Pink Feather Mystery	3.95	0.79	1.98	3.95
❑30, Mar 00	3.99	0.79	1.98	3.95
❑31, Apr 00	3.95	0.79	1.98	3.95
❑32, Jun 00, The Knight Watchman: The Pink Flamingo's Real Gone Rebop Roost; The Knight Watchman: Knight of the Living Dead, Part 3	3.95	0.79	1.98	3.95
❑33, Jul 00, The Round Table of America: Peril on Parallel Planets!; Gil Kane Tribute	3.95	0.79	1.98	3.95
❑34, Aug 00, Venus: Odyssey to Save the Gods; Renegade & Ladybug: Along Came the Ladybug	3.95	0.79	1.98	3.95
❑35, Jan 01, Big Bang vs. 1963; Mighty Man:Wicked Worm's Circus of Evil	3.95	0.79	1.98	3.95

BIG BLACK KISS
VORTEX

	ORIG	GOOD	FINE	N-MINT
❑1, Sep 89, HC, HC (w)	3.75	0.79	1.98	3.95
❑2, Oct 89, HC, HC (w)	3.75	0.79	1.98	3.95
❑3, Nov 89, HC, HC (w)	3.75	0.79	1.98	3.95

BIG BLACK THING (COLIN UPTON'S...)
UPTON

Value: Cover or less

❑1, b&w; adult 3.25

BIG BLOWN BABY
DARK HORSE

Value: Cover or less

❑1, Aug 96, Tales of Fetusdom; Procreation of the Gods 2.95
❑2, Sep 96 .... 2.95
❑3, Oct 96 .... 2.95
❑4, Nov 96 .... 2.95

BIG BOOB BONDAGE
ANTARCTIC

Value: Cover or less

❑1, Jan 97, b&w pin-ups, adult 2.95

BIG BRUISERS
IMAGE

Value: Cover or less

❑1, Jul 96 .... 3.50

BIG DOG FUNNIES
RIP OFF

Value: Cover or less

❑1, Jun 92, nn 2.50

BIGGER: WILL RISON & THE DEVIL'S CONCUBINE
FREE LUNCH

Value: Cover or less

❑1, Dec 98, Black and Blues... 2.95

BIG GUY AND RUSTY THE BOY ROBOT, THE
DARK HORSE

	ORIG	GOOD	FINE	N-MINT
❑1, Jul 95, FM (w)	4.95	1.20	3.00	6.00
❑2, Aug 95, FM (w)	4.95	1.20	3.00	6.00

BIG HAIR PRODUCTIONS
IMAGE

Value: Cover or less

❑1, Feb 00 .... 3.50

BIG LOU
SIDE SHOW

Value: Cover or less

❑1 .... 2.95

BIG MONSTER FIGHT
KIDGANG COMICS

Value: Cover or less

❑0 .... 2.50

BIG MOUTH
STARHEAD

Value: Cover or less

❑1, b&w 2.95
❑2, b&w 2.95
❑3 .... 2.95
❑4 .... 2.95
❑5, no indicia, b&w 2.95
❑6, Dec 96 .... 2.95
❑7, Jan 98 .... 2.95

BIG NUMBERS
MAD LOVE

Value: Cover or less

❑1, BSz, AMo (w) 5.50
❑2, BSz, AMo (w), Final published issue 5.50

BIG PRIZE, THE
ETERNITY

Value: Cover or less

❑1, May 88, The Time Drifter's Odyssey, b&w 1.95
❑2, Aug 85, b&w 1.95

BIG TIME
DELTA

Value: Cover or less

❑1, Mar 96 .... 1.95

BIG TOP BONDAGE
FANTAGRAPHICS

Value: Cover or less

❑1, b&w; adult 2.50

BIG TOWN (MARVEL)
MARVEL

	ORIG	GOOD	FINE	N-MINT
❑1, Jan 01, A: Avengers; A: X-Men, says Fantastic Four Big Town on cover; alternate Marvel history	3.50	0.70	1.75	3.50
❑2, Feb 01, A: Sub-Mariner; A: Avengers; A: Hulk	2.99	0.70	1.75	3.50
❑3, Mar 01, A: Sub-Mariner; A: Avengers; A: Hulk	2.99	0.70	1.75	3.50
❑4, Mar 01, A: Sub-Mariner; A: Avengers; A: Hulk	2.99	0.70	1.75	3.50

BIJOU FUNNIES
KITCHEN SINK

	ORIG	GOOD	FINE	N-MINT
❑1	—	35.00	87.50	175.00
❑1-2, 2nd Printing	—	8.00	20.00	40.00
❑2	—	10.00	25.00	50.00
❑3	—	7.00	17.50	35.00
❑3-2, 2nd Printing	—	3.00	7.50	15.00
❑3-3, 3rd Printing	—	2.00	5.00	10.00
❑4	—	5.00	12.50	25.00
❑5	—	5.00	12.50	25.00
❑6	—	4.00	10.00	20.00
❑7	—	4.00	10.00	20.00
❑8, Geek Brothers!; Snazzy Melvin Snoot!.	—	4.00	10.00	20.00
❑8-2, Geek Brothers!; Snazzy Melvin Snoot!, 2nd Printing	1.00	0.80	2.00	4.00

BIKER MICE FROM MARS
MARVEL

	ORIG	GOOD	FINE	N-MINT
❑1, Nov 93	1.50	0.40	1.00	2.00
❑2, Dec 93	1.50	0.40	1.00	2.00
❑3, Jan 94	1.50	0.40	1.00	2.00

BIKINI ASSASSIN TEAM, THE
CATFISH

Value: Cover or less

❑1 .... 2.50

BIKINI BATTLE 3-D
3-D ZONE

Value: Cover or less

❑1, nn; adult 3.95

BILL & TED'S BOGUS JOURNEY
MARVEL

Value: Cover or less

❑1, Sep 91 .... 2.95

BILL & TED'S EXCELLENT ADVENTURE MOVIE ADAPTATION
DC

	ORIG	GOOD	FINE	N-MINT
❑1, nn; adapts movie, wraparound cover, no cover price	—	0.30	0.75	1.50

BILL & TED'S EXCELLENT COMIC BOOK
MARVEL

	ORIG	GOOD	FINE	N-MINT
❑1, Dec 91	1.00	0.30	0.75	1.50
❑2, Jan 92	1.00	0.25	0.63	1.25
❑3, Feb 92	1.25	0.25	0.63	1.25
❑4, Mar 92	1.25	0.25	0.63	1.25
❑5, Apr 92	1.25	0.25	0.63	1.25
❑6, May 92	1.25	0.25	0.63	1.25
❑7, Jun 92	1.25	0.25	0.63	1.25
❑8, Jul 92	1.25	0.25	0.63	1.25
❑9, Aug 92	1.25	0.25	0.63	1.25
❑10, Sep 92, Don't Believe the Hype	1.25	0.25	0.63	1.25
❑11, Oct 92	1.25	0.25	0.63	1.25
❑12, Nov 92	1.25	0.25	0.63	1.25

BILL, THE GALACTIC HERO
TOPPS

Value: Cover or less

❑1, Jul 94, prestige format, based on Harry Harrison novel series 4.95
❑2 .... 4.95
❑3 .... 4.95

BILLI 99
DARK HORSE

Value: Cover or less

❑1 .... 3.50
❑2, Trespasses 3.50
❑3 .... 3.50
❑4 .... 3.95

BILL THE BULL: BURNT CAIN
BONEYARD

	ORIG	GOOD	FINE	N-MINT
❑1, Jul 92, eulogy for Michelle Davis (Hart Fisher's girlfriend)	2.50	0.99	2.47	4.95
❑2	2.50	0.99	2.47	4.95
❑3	4.95	0.99	2.47	4.95

BILL THE BULL: ONE SHOT, ONE BOURBON, ONE BEER
BONEYARD

Value: Cover or less

❑1, Dec 94, Whore 2.95
❑2, Mar, indicia says Mar 94, a misprint 2.95

BILL THE CLOWN
SLAVE LABOR

Value: Cover or less

❑1, Feb 92, b&w; 2nd Printing, b&w 2.50
❑1-2, Apr, 2nd Printing, b&w ... 2.95

BILL THE CLOWN: COMEDY ISN'T PRETTY
SLAVE LABOR

Value: Cover or less

❑1, Nov 92, b&w 2.50

BILL THE CLOWN: DEATH & CLOWN WHITE
SLAVE LABOR

Value: Cover or less

❑1, Sep 93, b&w 2.95

BILLY COLE
CULT

Value: Cover or less

❑1, Jun 94, b&w 2.75
❑2 .... 2.75
❑3 .... 2.75
❑4 .... 2.75

BILLY DOGMA
MODERN

Value: Cover or less

- ❑1, Apr 97 .... 2.95
- ❑2, Aug 97 .... 2.95
- ❑3, Dec 97 .... 2.95

BILLY JOE VAN HELSING: REDNECK VAMPIRE HUNTER
ALPHA

Value: Cover or less

- ❑1, Her Comes Billy Joe Van Helsing; The Devil and David Duke 2.50

BILLY NGUYEN
CALIBER

Value: Cover or less

- ❑1, b&w 2.95

BILLY NGUYEN, PRIVATE EYE
ATTITUDE

Value: Cover or less

- ❑1, Mar 88, Powers What Am. 2.00
- ❑2 .... 2.00
- ❑3 .... 2.00

BILLY RAY CYRUS
MARVEL MUSIC

Value: Cover or less

- ❑1, nn; prestige format 5.95

BINKY
DC

	ORIG	GOOD	FINE	N-MINT
❑72, Series continued from "Leave it to Binky #71"	0.25	1.20	3.00	6.00
❑73	0.25	1.20	3.00	6.00
❑74	0.25	1.20	3.00	6.00
❑75	0.25	1.20	3.00	6.00
❑76	0.25	1.00	2.50	5.00
❑77	0.25	1.00	2.50	5.00
❑78	0.25	1.00	2.50	5.00
❑79	0.25	1.00	2.50	5.00
❑80	0.25	1.00	2.50	5.00
❑81, Final issue of original series	0.25	1.00	2.50	5.00
❑82, 1977 one-shot revival	—	0.50	1.25	2.50

BINKY'S BUDDIES
DC

	ORIG	GOOD	FINE	N-MINT
❑1, Jan 69	0.12	5.00	12.50	25.00
❑2, Mar 69	0.12	3.00	7.50	15.00
❑3, May 69	0.12	2.40	6.00	12.00
❑4, Jul 69	0.12	2.00	5.00	10.00
❑5, Sep 69	0.12	2.00	5.00	10.00
❑6, Nov 69	0.12	2.00	5.00	10.00
❑7, Jan 70	0.12	2.00	5.00	10.00
❑8, Mar 70	0.12	2.00	5.00	10.00
❑9, May 70	0.12	2.00	5.00	10.00
❑10, Jul 70	0.12	2.00	5.00	10.00
❑11, Sep 70	0.12	2.00	5.00	10.00
❑12, Nov 70	0.12	2.00	5.00	10.00

BIO 90
BULLET

Value: Cover or less

- ❑1, b&w 2.50

BIO-BOOSTER ARMOR GUYVER
VIZ

	ORIG	GOOD	FINE	N-MINT
❑1, Awesome!	2.75	0.80	2.00	4.00
❑2	2.75	0.70	1.75	3.50
❑3	2.75	0.70	1.75	3.50
❑4	2.75	0.70	1.75	3.50
❑5	2.75	0.70	1.75	3.50
❑6	2.75	0.60	1.50	3.00
❑7	2.75	0.60	1.50	3.00
❑8, Explosive	2.75	0.60	1.50	3.00
❑9	2.75	0.60	1.50	3.00
❑10, Adversarial	2.75	0.60	1.50	3.00
❑11	2.75	0.60	1.50	3.00
❑12	2.75	0.60	1.50	3.00

BIO-BOOSTER ARMOR GUYVER PART 2
VIZ

	ORIG	GOOD	FINE	N-MINT
❑1, Betrayed!	2.75	0.60	1.50	3.00
❑2	2.75	0.60	1.50	3.00
❑3	2.75	0.60	1.50	3.00
❑4	2.75	0.60	1.50	3.00
❑5	2.75	0.60	1.50	3.00
❑6	2.75	0.60	1.50	3.00

BIO-BOOSTER ARMOR GUYVER PART 3
VIZ

Value: Cover or less

- ❑1 .... 2.75
- ❑2 .... 2.75
- ❑3 .... 2.75
- ❑4 .... 2.75
- ❑5 .... 2.75
- ❑6 .... 2.75
- ❑7 .... 2.75

BIO-BOOSTER ARMOR GUYVER PART 4
VIZ

Value: Cover or less

- ❑1 .... 2.75
- ❑2 .... 2.75
- ❑3 .... 2.95
- ❑4 .... 2.95
- ❑5 .... 2.95
- ❑6 .... 2.95

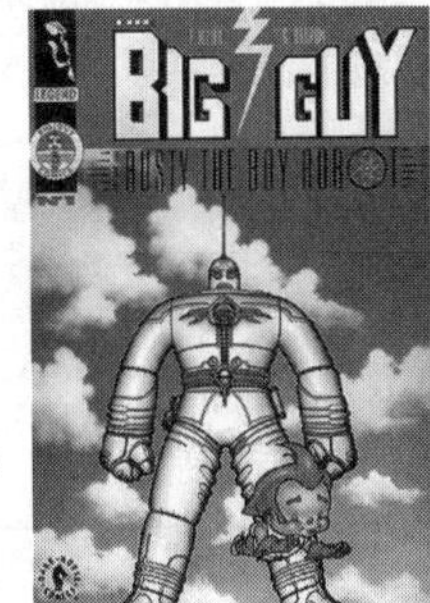

Frank Miller and Geof Darrow's *The Big Guy and Rusty the Boy Robot* inspired an animated series on Fox.

© 1995 Frank Miller and Geof Darrow (Dark Horse)

BIO-BOOSTER ARMOR GUYVER PART 5
VIZ

Value: Cover or less

- ❑1 .... 2.95
- ❑2 .... 2.95
- ❑3 .... 2.95
- ❑4 .... 2.95
- ❑5 .... 2.95
- ❑6 .... 2.95
- ❑7 .... 2.95

BIO-BOOSTER ARMOR GUYVER PART 6
VIZ

Value: Cover or less

- ❑1 .... 2.95
- ❑2 .... 2.95
- ❑3 .... 2.95
- ❑4 .... 2.95
- ❑5 .... 2.95
- ❑6 .... 2.95

BIOLOGIC SHOW, THE
FANTAGRAPHICS

Value: Cover or less

- ❑0, Oct 94, b&w; cardstock cover; magazine 2.95
- ❑1, Jan 95, b&w 2.75

BIONEERS
MIRAGE

Value: Cover or less

- ❑1, Aug 94, 1: Bioneers 2.75
- ❑2 .... 2.75
- ❑3 .... 2.75

BIONIC WOMAN, THE
CHARLTON

	ORIG	GOOD	FINE	N-MINT
❑1, Oct 77	0.35	1.20	3.00	6.00
❑2, Feb 78	0.35	0.80	2.00	4.00
❑3, Mar 78	0.35	0.80	2.00	4.00
❑4, May 78	0.35	0.80	2.00	4.00
❑5, Jun 78	0.35	0.80	2.00	4.00
❑25, Mar 81	—	0.40	1.00	2.00
❑26, May 81	—	0.40	1.00	2.00
❑27, Jul 81	—	0.40	1.00	2.00
❑28, Oct 81	—	0.40	1.00	2.00

BIRDLAND
FANTAGRAPHICS

Value: Cover or less

- ❑1, b&w; adult 1.95
- ❑2, adult 2.25
- ❑3, adult 2.25

BIRDLAND (VOL. 2)
FANTAGRAPHICS

Value: Cover or less

- ❑1, Jun 94, b&w 2.95

BIRDS OF PREY
DC

Value: Cover or less

- ❑1, Jan 99, Long Time Gone, A: Oracle; A: Hellhound 1.99
- ❑1/Aut, Jan 99, Long Time Gone, A: Oracle; A: Hellhound, Signed by Greg Land 14.99
- ❑2, Feb 99, A: Jackie Pajamas; A: Black Canary; A: Hellhound 1.99
- ❑3, Mar 99, A: Black Canary; A: Hellhound 1.99
- ❑4, Apr 99, A: Kobra; A: Ravens 1.99
- ❑5, May 99, A: Ravens 1.99
- ❑6, Jun 99, That's Rainbow 1.99
- ❑7, Jul 99, The Villain 1.99
- ❑8, Aug 99, On Wings, A: Nightwing 1.99
- ❑9, Sep 99, Girls Rules 1.99
- ❑10, Oct 99, The Wrong Guy .. 1.99
- ❑11, Nov 99, DG, State of War 1.99
- ❑12, Dec 99 .... 1.99
- ❑13, Jan 00, Apokolips Express, Part 1 .... 1.99
- ❑14, Feb 00, Apokolips Express, Part 2 .... 1.99
- ❑15, Mar 00 .... 1.99
- ❑16, Apr 00, BG, The Joker's Tale, A: Joker 1.99
- ❑17, May 00, BG, Nuclear Roulette 1.99
- ❑18, Jun 00, BG 1.99
- ❑19, Jul 00, BG .... —
- ❑20, Aug 00, BG, The Hunt for Oracle, Part 2 .... 2.50
- ❑21, Sep 00, BG, The Hunt for Oracle, Part 4 .... 2.50
- ❑22, Oct 00, BG; BSz, The Hostage Heart, Part 1 .... 2.50
- ❑23, Nov 00, BG, The Hostage Heart, Part 2 .... 2.50
- ❑24, Dec 00, BG, The Hostage Heart, Part 3 .... 2.50
- ❑25, Jan 01, BG, Old Habits ... 2.50
- ❑26, Feb 01, BG, The Suitor! .. 2.50
- ❑27, Mar 01, Officer Down, Part 3 .... 2.50
- ❑28, Apr 01, BG, History Lesson, Part 1 .... 2.50
- ❑29, May 01, BG, History Lesson, Part 2 .... 2.50
- ❑30 .... 2.50
- ❑31 .... 2.50
- ❑32 .... 2.50
- ❑33 .... 2.50

BIRDS OF PREY: BATGIRL
DC

Value: Cover or less

- ❑1, Feb 98 .... 2.95

BIRDS OF PREY: MANHUNT
DC

	ORIG	GOOD	FINE	N-MINT
❑1, Sep 96	1.95	0.45	1.13	2.25
❑2, Oct 96, Girl Crazy	1.95	0.40	1.00	2.00
❑3, Nov 96, The Man that got Away	1.95	0.40	1.00	2.00
❑4, Dec 96, Ladies' Choice, Final Issue	1.95	0.40	1.00	2.00

BIRDS OF PREY: REVOLUTION
DC

Value: Cover or less

❑1, One-Shot ... 2.95

BIRDS OF PREY: THE RAVENS
DC

Value: Cover or less

❑1, Jun 98, S.I.M.O.N. Says Armageddon, A: Cheshire; A: Pistolera; A: Termina; A: Vicious, One-Shot; Girlfrenzy ... 1.95

BIRDS OF PREY: WOLVES
DC

Value: Cover or less

❑1, Oct 97, One-Shot ... 2.95

BIRTHRIGHT
FANTAGRAPHICS

	ORIG	GOOD	FINE	N-MINT
❑1	2.00	0.50	1.25	2.50
❑2	2.00	0.50	1.25	2.50
❑3	2.00	0.50	1.25	2.50

BIRTHRIGHT (TSR)
TSR

	ORIG	GOOD	FINE	N-MINT
❑1, Serpent's Eye	—	0.30	0.75	1.50

BISHOP
MARVEL

Value: Cover or less

- ❑1, Dec 94, 1: Mountjoy, foil cover ... 2.95
- ❑2, Jan 95 ... 2.95
- ❑3, Feb 95 ... 2.95
- ❑4, Mar 95 ... 2.95

BISHOP THE LAST X-MAN
MARVEL

Value: Cover or less

- ❑1, Oct 99 ... 2.99
- ❑2, Nov 99 ... 2.99
- ❑3, Dec 99 ... 2.99
- ❑4 ... 2.99
- ❑5 ... 2.99
- ❑6 ... 2.99
- ❑7 ... 2.99
- ❑8 ... 2.99
- ❑9 ... 2.99
- ❑10 ... 2.99
- ❑11 ... 2.99
- ❑12, Sep 00, The Chronowar, Act 1: Helter Skelter, double-sized 2.99
- ❑13, Oct 00 ... 2.25
- ❑14, Nov 00, The Chronowar, Act 3: Remain in Light ... 2.25
- ❑15, Dec 00, Maximum Security; ... Been a Long Lonely, Lonely, Lonely, Lonely, Lonely Time! 2.25
- ❑16, Jan 01, Dream's End, Part 3, Final Issue ... 2.25

BISHOP: XSE
MARVEL

Value: Cover or less

- ❑1, Jan 98, Rook Takes Pawn, gatefold summary ... 2.50
- ❑2, Feb 98, gatefold summary 2.50
- ❑3 ... 2.50

BISLEY'S SCRAPBOOK
ATOMEKA

Value: Cover or less

❑1, Max Carnage; Kyrn, nn ... 2.50

BITCH IN HEAT
EROS

Value: Cover or less

- ❑1 ... 2.95
- ❑2 ... 2.95
- ❑3 ... 2.95
- ❑4 ... 2.95
- ❑5 ... 2.95
- ❑6 ... 2.95
- ❑7 ... 2.95
- ❑8, Apr 99 ... 2.95

BITTER CAKE
TIN CUP

Value: Cover or less

❑1, b&w ... 2.00

BIZARRE 3-D ZONE
BLACKTHORNE

Value: Cover or less

- ❑1, Jul 86 ... 2.25
- ❑2 ... 2.25
- ❑3 ... 2.25
- ❑4 ... 2.25
- ❑5, Jul 86, Dark Follower; July 4, 1976 ... 2.25

BIZARRE ADVENTURES
MARVEL

	ORIG	GOOD	FINE	N-MINT
❑25, Mar 81, A: Black Widow, Lethal Ladies; Was Marvel Preview	1.25	0.40	1.00	2.00
❑26, May 81, King Kull	1.25	0.40	1.00	2.00
❑27, Jul 81, X-Men	1.25	0.80	2.00	4.00
❑28, Oct 81, FM, FM (w), A: Elektra, Unlikely Heroes	1.50	0.60	1.50	3.00
❑29, Dec 81, Stephen King; Horror	1.50	0.40	1.00	2.00
❑30, Paradox; Tomorrow	1.50	0.40	1.00	2.00
❑31, FM, After the Violence Stops	1.50	0.40	1.00	2.00
❑32, Aug 82, Thor and other Gods	1.50	0.40	1.00	2.00
❑33, 1: Varnae, Photo cover; Dracula; Zombie; Horror	1.50	0.40	1.00	2.00
❑34, Feb 83, AM (w), Son of Santa!; Howard The Duck's Christmas, A: Howard the Duck, gatefold summary; Format changes to comic book	2.00	0.40	1.00	2.00

BIZARRE HEROES
KITCHEN SINK

Value: Cover or less

❑1, May 90, parody, b&w ... 2.50

BIZARRE HEROES (DON SIMPSON'S...)
FIASCO

	ORIG	GOOD	FINE	N-MINT
❑0, Dec 94	2.95	0.59	1.48	2.95
❑1, May 94, The Apocalypse Affiliation; Clone But Not Forgotten	2.95	0.65	1.63	3.25
❑2, Jun 94	2.95	0.59	1.48	2.95
❑3, Jul 94	2.95	0.59	1.48	2.95
❑4, Aug 94	2.95	0.59	1.48	2.95
❑5, Sep 94	2.95	0.59	1.48	2.95
❑6, Oct 94	2.95	0.59	1.48	2.95
❑7, Nov 94	2.95	0.59	1.48	2.95
❑8, Dec 94	2.95	0.59	1.48	2.95
❑9	2.95	0.59	1.48	2.95
❑10	2.95	0.59	1.48	2.95
❑11	2.95	0.59	1.48	2.95
❑12	2.95	0.59	1.48	2.95
❑13	2.95	0.59	1.48	2.95
❑14, Oct 95, Title changes to Bizarre Heroes	2.95	0.59	1.48	2.95
❑15, Jan 96, O: The Slick	2.95	0.59	1.48	2.95

BIZARRE SEX
KITCHEN SINK

	ORIG	GOOD	FINE	N-MINT
❑1, adult	—	3.60	9.00	18.00
❑2, adult	—	2.00	5.00	10.00
❑3, adult; White "remove this outer cover at your own risk" cover	—	1.60	4.00	8.00
❑4, adult; 2nd Printing; White "remove this outer cover at your own risk" cover	—	1.00	2.50	5.00
❑4-2, adult; 3rd Printing; White "remove this outer cover at your own risk" cover	—	0.80	2.00	4.00
❑4-3, adult	—	1.20	3.00	6.00
❑5, adult	—	1.20	3.00	6.00
❑6, adult	—	1.20	3.00	6.00
❑7, adult	—	1.20	3.00	6.00
❑8, adult	—	1.20	3.00	6.00
❑9, Aug 81, 1: Omaha, b&w; adult	2.00	4.00	10.00	20.00

B. KRIGSTEIN SAMPLER, A
INDEPENDENT

	ORIG	GOOD	FINE	N-MINT
❑1, The Man Who Shrunk; The Hypnotist...	—	0.50	1.25	2.50

BLAB!
KITCHEN SINK

Value: Cover or less

- ❑8, Sum 95, odd-sized anthology ... 16.95
- ❑9, Fal 97, odd-sized anthology ... 18.95
- ❑10, Fal 98, odd-sized anthology ... 19.95

BLACK & WHITE
IMAGE

	ORIG	GOOD	FINE	N-MINT
❑1, Feb 96, Beginnings	2.50	0.50	1.25	2.50
❑Ash 1, nn; no cover price; ashcan preview of series	—	0.20	0.50	1.00

BLACK & WHITE (MINI-SERIES)
IMAGE

Value: Cover or less

- ❑1, Oct 94, #1 Black ... 1.95
- ❑2, Nov 94 ... 1.95
- ❑3, Jan 95 ... 1.95

BLACK & WHITE (VIZ)
VIZ

Value: Cover or less

- ❑1 ... 3.25
- ❑2, The Color of Black ... 3.25
- ❑3 ... 3.25

BLACK AND WHITE COMICS
APEX NOVELTIES

	ORIG	GOOD	FINE	N-MINT
❑1, Squirrely the Squirrel; Namby Pamby and Her friends	0.75	0.80	2.00	4.00

BLACK AND WHITE THEATER
DOUBLE M

Value: Cover or less

- ❑1, Jun 96, b&w ... 2.95
- ❑2, b&w ... 2.95

BLACK ANGEL
VEROTIK

Value: Cover or less

❑1, Sep 96, nn; prestige format; reprints Golden Age stories. 9.95

BLACK AXE
MARVEL

Value: Cover or less

- ❑1, Apr 93, 1: Black Axe; A: Death's Head II ... 1.75
- ❑2, May 93, The Spirit of the Sword ... 1.75
- ❑3, Jun 93 ... 1.75
- ❑4, Jul 93 ... 1.75
- ❑5, Aug 93 ... 1.75
- ❑6, Sep 93 ... 1.75
- ❑7, Oct 93, A: She; A: Black Panther; A: Afrikka, Final Issue ... 1.75

BLACKBALL COMICS
BLACKBALL

Value: Cover or less

❑1, Mar 94, KG, KG (w), Folklaw; The Seuling Legacy ... 3.00

BLACK BOOK (BRIAN BOLLAND'S...)
Eclipse

	ORIG	GOOD	FINE	N-MINT
❑1, BB, Vampire Carnival; Plague of the Undead	1.75	0.40	1.00	2.00

BLACK CANARY
DC

	ORIG	GOOD	FINE	N-MINT
❑1, Jan 93, Hero Worship, Part 1	1.75	0.40	1.00	2.00
❑2, Feb 93, Hero Worship, Part 2	1.75	0.40	1.00	2.00
❑3, Mar 93, Hero Worship, Part 3	1.75	0.40	1.00	2.00
❑4, Apr 93	1.75	0.40	1.00	2.00
❑5, May 93	1.75	0.40	1.00	2.00
❑6, Jun 93	1.75	0.35	0.88	1.75
❑7, Jul 93	1.75	0.35	0.88	1.75
❑8, Aug 93, A: The Ray	1.75	0.35	0.88	1.75
❑9, Sep 93	1.75	0.35	0.88	1.75
❑10, Oct 93	1.75	0.35	0.88	1.75
❑11, Nov 93, TVE, Weaker Weasels	1.75	0.35	0.88	1.75
❑12, Dec 93, Final Issue	1.75	0.35	0.88	1.75

BLACK CANARY (MINI-SERIES)
DC

	ORIG	GOOD	FINE	N-MINT
❑1, Nov 91, New Wings, Part 1	1.75	0.50	1.25	2.50
❑2, Dec 91, New Wings, Part 2	1.75	0.40	1.00	2.00
❑3, Jan 92, New Wings, Part 3	1.75	0.40	1.00	2.00
❑4, Feb 92, New Wings, Part 4	1.75	0.40	1.00	2.00

BLACK CANARY/ORACLE: BIRDS OF PREY
DC

Value: Cover or less

❑1, One-Shot 3.95

BLACK CAT (THE ORIGINS)
Lorne-Harvey

Value: Cover or less

❑1, MA, ME (w), O: The Black Cat, color and b&w; reprints Black Cat and Sad Sack strips; text feature on Alfred Harvey 3.50

BLACK CAT THE WAR YEARS
Recollections

Value: Cover or less

❑1, Golden Age reprints, b&w. 1.00

BLACK CONDOR
DC

	ORIG	GOOD	FINE	N-MINT
❑1, Jun 92, A Dream of Flying, 1: Black Condor II; 1: The Black Condor II	1.25	0.30	0.75	1.50
❑2, Jul 92	1.25	0.25	0.63	1.25
❑3, Aug 92	1.25	0.25	0.63	1.25
❑4, Sep 92	1.25	0.25	0.63	1.25
❑5, Oct 92	1.25	0.25	0.63	1.25
❑6, Nov 92	1.25	0.25	0.63	1.25
❑7, Dec 92	1.25	0.25	0.63	1.25
❑8, Jan 93	1.25	0.25	0.63	1.25
❑9, Feb 93	1.25	0.25	0.63	1.25
❑10, Mar 93, A: The Ray	1.25	0.25	0.63	1.25
❑11, Apr 93	1.25	0.25	0.63	1.25
❑12, May, A: Batman, Final Issue	1.25	0.25	0.63	1.25

BLACK CROSS: DIRTY WORK
Dark Horse

Value: Cover or less

❑1, Apr 97, nn 2.95

BLACK CROSS SPECIAL
Dark Horse

	ORIG	GOOD	FINE	N-MINT
❑1, Jan 88, b&w	1.75	0.70	1.75	3.50
❑1-2, 2nd Printing	1.75	0.35	0.88	1.75

BLACK DIAMOND
AC

Value: Cover or less

❑1, May 83, 1: Black Diamond; 1: Darkfire; 1: Colt 2.00

❑2, Jul 83 2.00

❑3, Dec 83 2.00

❑4, Feb 84 2.00

❑5, May 84 2.00

BLACK DIAMOND EFFECT, THE
Black Diamond Effect

	ORIG	GOOD	FINE	N-MINT
❑1	3.10	0.60	1.50	3.00
❑2	3.10	0.62	1.55	3.10
❑3	3.10	0.62	1.55	3.10
❑4	3.10	0.62	1.55	3.10
❑5	3.10	0.62	1.55	3.10
❑6, Dec 92	2.75	0.60	1.50	3.00
❑7	3.10	0.62	1.55	3.10

BLACK DRAGON, THE
Marvel

	ORIG	GOOD	FINE	N-MINT
❑1, May 85	1.50	0.60	1.50	3.00
❑2, Jun 85	1.50	0.50	1.25	2.50
❑3, Jul 85	1.50	0.50	1.25	2.50
❑4, Aug 85	1.50	0.50	1.25	2.50
❑5, Sep 85	1.50	0.40	1.00	2.00
❑6, Oct 85	1.50	0.40	1.00	2.00

BLACK FLAG (IMAGE)
Image

Value: Cover or less

❑1, Jun 94, Once Upon A Time, 1: Sniper; 1: Geisha; 1: Black Rain, b&w; Fold-out cover 1.95

❑Ash 1, Guerrilla In The Midst!, 1: Sniper; 1: Geisha; 1: Black Rain, Preview edition 1.95

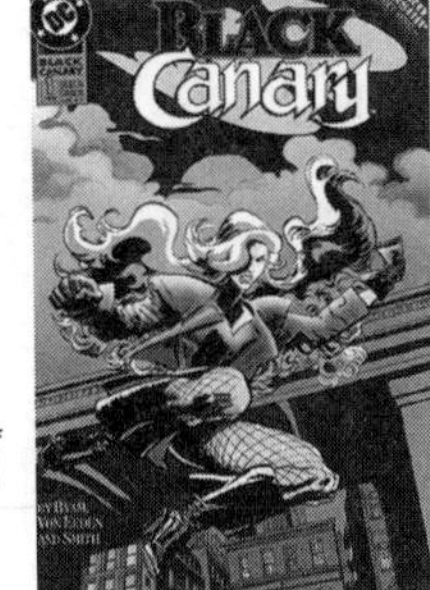

Before she teamed with Oracle in *Birds of Prey*, Black Canary had a mini-series and a short-lived ongoing series.

© 1993 DC Comics

BLACK FLAG (MAXIMUM)
Maximum Press

Value: Cover or less

❑0, Jul 95 2.50

❑1, Jan 95 2.50

❑2/A, Feb 95, Woman on cover 2.50

❑2/B, Variant cover with man.. 2.50

❑3, Mar 95 2.50

❑4/A, Apr, cover has black background 2.50

❑4/B, Apr, cover has white background 2.50

BLACK GOLIATH
Marvel

	ORIG	GOOD	FINE	N-MINT
❑1, Feb 76, GT, O: Black Goliath	0.25	1.00	2.50	5.00
❑2, Apr 76	0.25	0.70	1.75	3.50
❑3, Jun 76	0.25	0.60	1.50	3.00
❑4, Aug 76	0.25	0.60	1.50	3.00
❑5, Nov 76, Final Issue	0.30	0.60	1.50	3.00

BLACKHAWK (1ST SERIES)
DC

	ORIG	GOOD	FINE	N-MINT
❑150, Jul 60	0.10	9.60	24.00	48.00
❑151, Aug 60	0.10	9.60	24.00	48.00
❑152, Sep 60, four-color	0.10	9.60	24.00	48.00
❑153, Oct 60, four-color	0.10	9.60	24.00	48.00
❑154, Nov 60, four-color	0.10	9.60	24.00	48.00
❑155, Dec 60, four-color	0.10	9.60	24.00	48.00
❑156, Jan 61, four-color	0.10	9.60	24.00	48.00
❑157, Feb 61	0.10	9.60	24.00	48.00
❑158, Mar 61, four-color	0.10	9.60	24.00	48.00
❑159, Apr 61, four-color	0.10	9.60	24.00	48.00
❑160, May 61, four-color	0.10	9.60	24.00	48.00
❑161, Jun 61, four-color	0.10	9.60	24.00	48.00
❑162, Jul 61	0.10	9.60	24.00	48.00
❑163, Aug 61, four-color	0.10	9.60	24.00	48.00
❑164, Sep 61, O: Blackhawk; O: Blackhawks	0.10	12.00	30.00	60.00
❑165, Oct 61	0.10	9.60	24.00	48.00
❑166, Nov 61	0.10	9.60	24.00	48.00
❑167, Dec 61	0.12	4.40	11.00	22.00
❑168, Jan 62	0.12	4.40	11.00	22.00
❑169, Feb 62	0.12	4.40	11.00	22.00
❑170, Mar 62	0.12	4.40	11.00	22.00
❑171, Apr 62	0.12	4.40	11.00	22.00
❑172, May 62	0.12	4.40	11.00	22.00
❑173, Jun 62	0.12	4.40	11.00	22.00
❑174, Jul 62	0.12	4.40	11.00	22.00
❑175, Aug 62	0.12	4.40	11.00	22.00
❑176, Sep 62	0.12	4.40	11.00	22.00
❑177, Oct 62	0.12	4.40	11.00	22.00
❑178, Nov 62	0.12	4.40	11.00	22.00
❑179, Dec 62	0.12	4.40	11.00	22.00
❑180, Jan 63	0.12	4.40	11.00	22.00
❑181, Feb 63	0.12	2.40	6.00	12.00
❑182, Mar 63	0.12	2.40	6.00	12.00
❑183, Apr 63	0.12	2.40	6.00	12.00
❑184, May 63	0.12	2.40	6.00	12.00
❑185, Jun 63	0.12	2.40	6.00	12.00
❑186, Jul 63	0.12	2.40	6.00	12.00
❑187, Aug 63	0.12	2.40	6.00	12.00
❑188, Sep 63	0.12	2.40	6.00	12.00
❑189, Oct 63, O: Blackhawks	0.12	2.40	6.00	12.00
❑190, Nov 63	0.12	2.40	6.00	12.00
❑191, Dec 63	0.12	2.00	5.00	10.00
❑192, Jan 64	0.12	2.00	5.00	10.00
❑193, Feb 64	0.12	2.00	5.00	10.00
❑194, Mar 64	0.12	2.00	5.00	10.00
❑195, Apr 64	0.12	2.00	5.00	10.00
❑196, May 64	0.12	2.00	5.00	10.00
❑197, Jun 64, new look	0.12	2.00	5.00	10.00
❑198, Jul 64, O: Blackhawk; O: Blackhawks, four-color	0.12	2.40	6.00	12.00
❑199, Aug 64	0.12	2.00	5.00	10.00
❑200, Sep 64	0.12	2.00	5.00	10.00
❑201, Oct 64	0.12	1.60	4.00	8.00
❑202, Nov 64	0.12	1.60	4.00	8.00

	ORIG	GOOD	FINE	N-MINT
❑203, Dec 64, O: Chop-Chop	0.12	1.60	4.00	8.00
❑204, Jan 65	0.12	1.60	4.00	8.00
❑205, Feb 65	0.12	1.60	4.00	8.00
❑206, Mar 65	0.12	1.60	4.00	8.00
❑207, Apr 65	0.12	1.60	4.00	8.00
❑208, May 65	0.12	1.60	4.00	8.00
❑209, Jun 65	0.12	1.60	4.00	8.00
❑210, Jul 65	0.12	1.60	4.00	8.00
❑211, Aug 65	0.12	1.60	4.00	8.00
❑212, Sep 65	0.12	1.60	4.00	8.00
❑213, Oct 65	0.12	1.60	4.00	8.00
❑214, Nov 65	0.12	1.60	4.00	8.00
❑215, Dec 65	0.12	1.60	4.00	8.00
❑216, Jan 66	0.12	1.60	4.00	8.00
❑217, Feb 66	0.12	1.60	4.00	8.00
❑218, Mar 66	0.12	1.60	4.00	8.00
❑219, Apr 66	0.12	1.60	4.00	8.00
❑220, May 66	0.12	1.60	4.00	8.00
❑221, Jun 66	0.12	1.60	4.00	8.00
❑222, Jul 66	0.12	1.60	4.00	8.00
❑223, Aug 66	0.12	1.60	4.00	8.00
❑224, Sep 66	0.12	1.60	4.00	8.00
❑225, Oct 66	0.12	1.60	4.00	8.00
❑226, Nov 66	0.12	1.60	4.00	8.00
❑227, Dec 66	0.12	1.60	4.00	8.00
❑228, Jan 67	0.12	1.60	4.00	8.00
❑229, Feb 67	0.12	1.60	4.00	8.00
❑230, Mar 67, Blackhawks become super-heroes; New costumes	0.12	1.60	4.00	8.00
❑231, Apr 67, Blackhawks as super-heroes	0.12	1.60	4.00	8.00
❑232, May 67, Blackhawks as super-heroes	0.12	1.60	4.00	8.00
❑233, Jun 67, Blackhawks as super-heroes	0.12	1.60	4.00	8.00
❑234, Jul 67, Blackhawks as super-heroes	0.12	1.60	4.00	8.00
❑235, Aug 67, Blackhawks as super-heroes	0.12	1.60	4.00	8.00
❑236, Sep 67, Blackhawks as super-heroes	0.12	1.60	4.00	8.00
❑237, Nov 67, Blackhawks as super-heroes	0.12	1.60	4.00	8.00
❑238, Jan 68, Blackhawks as super-heroes	0.12	1.60	4.00	8.00
❑239, Mar 68, Blackhawks as super-heroes	0.12	1.60	4.00	8.00
❑240, May 68, Blackhawks as super-heroes	0.12	1.60	4.00	8.00
❑241, Jul 68, Blackhawks as super-heroes	0.12	1.60	4.00	8.00
❑242, Sep 68, Blackhawks back to old costumes	0.12	1.60	4.00	8.00
❑243, Nov 68, Last issue of 1960s run	0.12	1.60	4.00	8.00
❑244, Feb 76, GE, Death's Right Hand, New issues begin with old # sequence	0.25	0.80	2.00	4.00
❑245, Apr 76	0.30	0.80	2.00	4.00
❑246, Jun 76	0.30	0.80	2.00	4.00
❑247, Aug 76, Bicentennial #25	0.30	0.80	2.00	4.00
❑248, Sep 76	0.30	0.80	2.00	4.00
❑249, Nov 76	0.30	0.80	2.00	4.00
❑250, Jan 77, D: Chuck	0.30	0.80	2.00	4.00
❑251, Oct 82	0.60	0.80	2.00	4.00
❑252, Nov 82, V: War Wheel	0.60	0.80	2.00	4.00
❑253, Dec 82	0.60	0.80	2.00	4.00
❑254, Jan 83	0.60	0.80	2.00	4.00
❑255, Feb 83	0.60	0.80	2.00	4.00
❑256, Mar 83	0.60	0.80	2.00	4.00
❑257, Apr 83, HC (c)	0.60	0.80	2.00	4.00
❑258, May 83, HC (c)	0.60	0.80	2.00	4.00
❑259, Jun 83, HC (c)	0.60	0.80	2.00	4.00
❑260, Jul 83, HC, HC (c), ME (w), Detached Service Diary	0.60	0.80	2.00	4.00
❑261, Aug 83	0.60	0.50	1.25	2.50
❑262, Sep 83, DS, HC (c), ME (w), Der Fuehrer's Face!	0.60	0.50	1.25	2.50
❑263, Oct 83, GK (c), V: War Wheel	0.60	0.50	1.25	2.50
❑264, Nov 83	0.60	0.50	1.25	2.50
❑265, Dec 83	0.75	0.50	1.25	2.50
❑266, Jan 84	0.75	0.50	1.25	2.50
❑267, Feb 84	0.75	0.50	1.25	2.50
❑268, Mar 84	0.75	0.50	1.25	2.50
❑269, Apr 84, 1: Killer Shark I (General Haifisch)	0.75	0.50	1.25	2.50
❑270, May 84	0.75	0.50	1.25	2.50
❑271, Jul 84	0.75	0.50	1.25	2.50
❑272, Sep 84	0.75	0.50	1.25	2.50
❑273, Nov 84, HC (c), Final Issue	0.75	0.50	1.25	2.50

BLACKHAWK (2ND SERIES)
DC

	ORIG	GOOD	FINE	N-MINT
❑1, Mar 88, HC (w), Blood & Iron, no mature readers advisory	2.95	0.70	1.75	3.50
❑2, Apr 88, HC (w), Follow Blackjack's Example, Increase Your Quota For The Front Lines	2.95	0.70	1.75	3.50
❑3, May 88, HC (w), Blackout	2.95	0.70	1.75	3.50

BLACKHAWK (3RD SERIES)
DC

	ORIG	GOOD	FINE	N-MINT
❑1, Mar 89, All In Color For A Crime	1.50	0.40	1.00	2.00
❑2, Apr 89	1.50	0.35	0.88	1.75
❑3, May 89	1.50	0.35	0.88	1.75
❑4, Jun 89	1.50	0.35	0.88	1.75
❑5, Aug 89	1.50	0.35	0.88	1.75
❑6, Sep 89	1.50	0.30	0.75	1.50
❑7, Oct 89, WE, Reprint; Double-size	2.50	0.50	1.25	2.50
❑8, Nov 89	1.50	0.30	0.75	1.50
❑9, Dec 89	1.50	0.30	0.75	1.50
❑10, Jan 90	1.50	0.30	0.75	1.50
❑11	1.50	0.30	0.75	1.50
❑12	1.75	0.30	0.75	1.50
❑13	1.75	0.30	0.75	1.50
❑14	1.75	0.30	0.75	1.50
❑15	1.75	0.30	0.75	1.50
❑16	1.75	0.30	0.75	1.50
❑Anl 1	2.95	0.59	1.48	2.95
❑SE 1, Blackhawk Hardware, Special edition (1992); Special	3.50	0.70	1.75	3.50

BLACK HEART: ASSASSIN
IGUANA

Value: Cover or less

- ❑1, 1: Black Heart ... 2.95

BLACK HEART BILLY
SLAVE LABOR

Value: Cover or less

- ❑1, Mar 00, b&w ... 2.95

BLACK HOLE
KITCHEN SINK

Value: Cover or less

- ❑1, Biology 101; Planet Xeno . 3.50
- ❑2, Nov 95 ... 3.50
- ❑3, Jul 96 ... 3.50
- ❑4 ... 3.50
- ❑5, Mar 98 ... 3.95
- ❑6, Dec 98 ... 4.50

BLACK HOLE, THE (WALT DISNEY...)
WHITMAN

	ORIG	GOOD	FINE	N-MINT
❑1, movie Adaptation	0.40	0.40	1.00	2.00
❑2, movie Adaptation	0.40	0.30	0.75	1.50
❑3	0.40	0.30	0.75	1.50
❑4, Final Issue	0.40	0.30	0.75	1.50

BLACK HOOD
DC

Value: Cover or less

- ❑1, Dec 91, Justice. No Waiting!, 1: The Black Hood (Giles "Hit" Coffee); 1: The Black Hood (Nathan Cray); O: The Black Hood; 1: Pirate Blue ... 1.00
- ❑2, Jan 92 ... 1.00
- ❑3, Feb 92, 1: The Creeptures; 1: Tom Sickler ... 1.00
- ❑4, Mar 92, 1: Ozone ... 1.00
- ❑5, Apr 92, The Coming of the Crusaders, Part 4 ... 1.00
- ❑6, May 92 ... 1.00
- ❑7, Jun 92 ... 1.25
- ❑8, Aug 92 ... 1.25
- ❑9, Sep 92 ... 1.25
- ❑10, Oct 92 ... 1.25
- ❑11, Nov 92, 1: The Fox; 1: Fox 1.25
- ❑12, Dec 92, O: Black Hood, Final Issue ... 1.25
- ❑Anl 1, Earth Quest, Part 6, trading card ... 2.50

BLACK HOOD, THE (RED CIRCLE)
ARCHIE

	ORIG	GOOD	FINE	N-MINT
❑1, Jun 83, GM; ATh, The Mask...and the Man	1.00	0.60	1.50	3.00
❑2, Aug 83, GM; ATh, The Dark Destroyer	1.00	0.40	1.00	2.00
❑3, Oct 83, GM; ATh	1.00	0.40	1.00	2.00

BLACKJACK
DARK ANGEL

Value: Cover or less

- ❑1, Sep 96, Second Bite of the Cobra ... 2.95
- ❑2, Oct 96, Second Bite of the Cobra ... 2.95
- ❑3, Jan 97, Second Bite of the Cobra ... 2.95
- ❑4 ... 2.95
- ❑SE 1 ... 3.50

BLACK JACK (VIZ)
VIZ

Value: Cover or less

- ❑SE 1, Under the Knife ... 3.25

BLACKJACK (VOL. 2)
DARK ANGEL

Value: Cover or less

- ❑1, Apr 97 ... 2.95
- ❑2, Feb 98 ... 2.95

BLACK KISS
VORTEX

	ORIG	GOOD	FINE	N-MINT
❑1, Jun 88, HC, HC (w)	1.25	0.50	1.25	2.50
❑1-2, HC, HC (w), 2nd Printing	1.25	0.40	1.00	2.00
❑, HC, HC (w), 3rd Printing	1.25	0.40	1.00	2.00
❑2, Jul 88, HC, HC (w)	1.25	0.50	1.25	2.50
❑2-2, HC, HC (w), 2nd Printing	1.25	0.40	1.00	2.00
❑3, Aug 88, HC, HC (w)	1.25	0.40	1.00	2.00
❑4, Sep 88, HC, HC (w), polybagged with black insert card covering actual cover	1.25	0.40	1.00	2.00
❑5, Oct 88, HC, HC (w)	1.25	0.40	1.00	2.00
❑6, Nov 88, HC, HC (w)	1.25	0.40	1.00	2.00
❑7, Dec 88, HC, HC (w)	1.25	0.40	1.00	2.00

	ORIG	GOOD	FINE	N-MINT
❑8, Jan, HC, HC (w), indicia says 88 (misprint)	1.25	0.40	1.00	2.00
❑9, Mar, HC, HC (w), indicia says 88 (misprint)	1.25	0.40	1.00	2.00
❑10, Mar, HC, HC (w), indicia says 88 (misprint)	1.50	0.40	1.00	2.00
❑11, May 89, HC, HC (w)	1.50	0.40	1.00	2.00
❑12, Jul 89, HC, HC (w)	1.50	0.40	1.00	2.00

BLACK KNIGHT (LTD. SERIES)
MARVEL

	ORIG	GOOD	FINE	N-MINT
❑1, Jun 90, TD, The Rebirth Of The Black Knight, O: Black Knight II (Nathan Garrett); O: Black Knight I (Sir Percy); O: Black Knight III (Dane Whitman)	1.50	0.40	1.00	2.00
❑2, Jul 90, A: Captain Britain; A: Capt. Britain	1.50	0.30	0.75	1.50
❑3, Aug 90, RB, The Black Knight Has a Thousand Eyes..., 1: new Valkyrie; A: Doctor Strange	1.50	0.30	0.75	1.50
❑4, Sep 90, A: Valkyrie; A: Doctor Strange..	1.50	0.30	0.75	1.50

BLACK KNIGHT: EXODUS
MARVEL

Value: Cover or less

❑1, Dec 96, One-Shot 2.50

BLACK LAMB, THE
DC

Value: Cover or less

❑1, Nov 96, The Hated The Haunted The Hunted........... 2.50
❑2, Dec 96 .... 2.50
❑3, Jan 97, Steel Maiden........ 2.50
❑4, Feb 97 .... 2.50
❑5, Mar 97 .... 2.50
❑6, Apr 97 .... 2.50

BLACK LIGHTNING (1ST SERIES)
DC

	ORIG	GOOD	FINE	N-MINT
❑1, Apr 77, FS; TVE, 1: Black Lightning	0.30	1.00	2.50	5.00
❑2, May 77	0.30	0.60	1.50	3.00
❑3, Jul 77	0.35	0.60	1.50	3.00
❑4, Sep 77	0.35	0.60	1.50	3.00
❑5, Nov 77	0.35	0.60	1.50	3.00
❑6, Jan 78, 1: Syonide I	0.35	0.50	1.25	2.50
❑7, Mar 78	0.35	0.50	1.25	2.50
❑8, Apr 78	0.35	0.50	1.25	2.50
❑9, May 78	0.35	0.50	1.25	2.50
❑10, Jul 78	0.35	0.50	1.25	2.50
❑11, Sep 78, A: The Ray, Final Issue	0.50	0.50	1.25	2.50

BLACK LIGHTNING (2ND SERIES)
DC

	ORIG	GOOD	FINE	N-MINT
❑1, Feb 95, The Weekend Report	1.95	0.50	1.25	2.50
❑2, Mar 95, Teachers	1.95	0.40	1.00	2.00
❑3, Apr 95, Students	1.95	0.40	1.00	2.00
❑4, May 95	1.95	0.40	1.00	2.00
❑5, Jun 95	2.25	0.40	1.00	2.00
❑6, Jul 95, A: Gangbuster	2.25	0.55	1.38	2.75
❑7, Aug 95, A: Gangbuster	2.25	0.45	1.13	2.25
❑8, Sep 95	2.25	0.45	1.13	2.25
❑9, Oct 95	2.25	0.45	1.13	2.25
❑10, Nov 95	2.25	0.45	1.13	2.25
❑11, Dec 95	2.25	0.45	1.13	2.25
❑12, Jan 96	2.25	0.45	1.13	2.25
❑13, Feb, To Protect and Serve, Final Issue	2.25	0.45	1.13	2.25

BLACK MAGIC (DC)
DC

	ORIG	GOOD	FINE	N-MINT
❑1, Nov 73	0.20	1.40	3.50	7.00
❑2	0.20	0.80	2.00	4.00
❑3, Nasty Little Man	0.20	0.80	2.00	4.00
❑4, JK, The Girl the Earth Ate Up!; His Father's Footsteps!	0.20	0.80	2.00	4.00
❑5	0.20	0.80	2.00	4.00
❑6	0.20	0.80	2.00	4.00
❑7	0.20	0.80	2.00	4.00
❑8	0.20	0.80	2.00	4.00
❑9	0.20	0.80	2.00	4.00

BLACK MAGIC (ECLIPSE)
ECLIPSE

Value: Cover or less

❑1, Japanese, b&w 5.00
❑2 .... 3.50
❑3 .... 3.50
❑4 .... 3.50

BLACKMASK
DC

Value: Cover or less

❑1 .... 4.95
❑2 .... 4.95
❑3 .... 4.95

BLACK MIST
CALIBER

Value: Cover or less

❑1, Anguish of The Mist.......... 2.95
❑2 .... 2.95
❑3 .... 2.95
❑4 .... 2.95

BLACK MIST: BLOOD OF KALI
CALIBER

Value: Cover or less

❑1 .... 2.95
❑2 .... 2.95
❑3 .... 2.95

The origins of the first three Black Knights were recounted in the first issue of the four-issue mini-series.

© 1990 Marvel Comics

BLACK OPS
IMAGE

Value: Cover or less

❑1, Jan 96, 1: Redbird; 1: Geek & H.E.R.B.; 1: Shire 2.50
❑2, Feb 96, 1: Crane 2.50
❑3, Mar 96 .... 2.50
❑4, Apr 96 .... 2.50
❑5/A, Jun 96 .... 2.50
❑5/B, Jun 96, alternate cover .. 2.50

BLACK ORCHID
DC

	ORIG	GOOD	FINE	N-MINT
❑1, Sep 93, Sightings	1.95	0.50	1.25	2.50
❑1/PL, Sep 93, Sightings, Platinum edition.	—	1.00	2.50	5.00
❑2, Oct 93, Uprootings	1.95	0.45	1.13	2.25
❑3, Nov 93, The Tainted Zone	1.95	0.45	1.13	2.25
❑4, Dec 93	1.95	0.45	1.13	2.25
❑5, Jan 94, The Mind Fields, Part 1	1.95	0.45	1.13	2.25
❑6, Feb 94, The God In The Cage	1.95	0.40	1.00	2.00
❑7, Mar 94, Upon the Threshold	1.95	0.40	1.00	2.00
❑8, Apr 94	1.95	0.40	1.00	2.00
❑9, May 94, The Murmuring Of The Mists, The Whisper If Flowers	1.95	0.40	1.00	2.00
❑10, Jun 94, Florescence	1.95	0.40	1.00	2.00
❑11, Jul 94, Suzy And The Trade Of Fates.	1.95	0.40	1.00	2.00
❑12, Aug 94, Mr. Weems Takes a Wife	1.95	0.40	1.00	2.00
❑13, Sep 94	1.95	0.40	1.00	2.00
❑14, Oct 94	1.95	0.40	1.00	2.00
❑15, Nov 94	1.95	0.40	1.00	2.00
❑16, Dec 94	1.95	0.40	1.00	2.00
❑17, Jan 95, A Twisted Season, Part 1	1.95	0.39	0.98	1.95
❑18, Feb 95, Twisted Season, Part 2	1.95	0.39	0.98	1.95
❑19, Mar 95, Twisted Season, Part 3	1.95	0.39	0.98	1.95
❑20, Apr 95, Twisted Season, Part 4	1.95	0.39	0.98	1.95
❑21, May 95, Twisted Season, Part 5	2.25	0.45	1.13	2.25
❑22, Jun 95, Twisted Season, Part 6, Final Issue	2.25	0.45	1.13	2.25
❑Anl 1, The Children's Crusade, Part 2, Children's Crusade	3.95	0.80	2.00	4.00

BLACK ORCHID (MINI-SERIES)
DC

	ORIG	GOOD	FINE	N-MINT
❑1, Jan, NG (w)	1.95	1.00	2.50	5.00
❑1/PL, NG (w), Platinum edition	—	1.20	3.00	6.00
❑2, Jan, NG (w), A: Batman	1.95	1.00	2.50	5.00
❑3, Feb, NG (w)	1.95	1.00	2.50	5.00

BLACK PANTHER
MARVEL

	ORIG	GOOD	FINE	N-MINT
❑1, Jan 77, JK	0.30	2.40	6.00	12.00
❑2, Mar 77, JK, JK (w), The Six-Million Dollar Man	0.30	1.20	3.00	6.00
❑3, May 77, JK	0.30	1.00	2.50	5.00
❑4, Jul 77, JK	0.30	1.00	2.50	5.00
❑5, Sep 77, JK	0.30	1.00	2.50	5.00
❑6, Nov 77, JK, JK (c), JK (w), A Cup of Youth	0.35	1.00	2.50	5.00
❑7, Jan 78, JK	0.35	1.00	2.50	5.00
❑8, Mar 78, JK	0.35	1.00	2.50	5.00
❑9, May 78, JK	0.35	1.00	2.50	5.00
❑10, Jul 78, JK	0.35	1.00	2.50	5.00
❑11, Sep 78, JK	0.35	0.80	2.00	4.00
❑12, Nov 78, JK	0.35	0.80	2.00	4.00
❑13, Jan 79, JK	0.35	0.80	2.00	4.00
❑14, Mar 79	0.35	0.80	2.00	4.00
❑15, May 79, JK, A: Klaw, Final Issue	0.40	0.80	2.00	4.00

BLACK PANTHER (LTD. SERIES)
MARVEL

	ORIG	GOOD	FINE	N-MINT
❑1, Jul 88, Cry, The Accursed Country	1.25	0.40	1.00	2.00
❑2, Aug 88	1.25	0.40	1.00	2.00
❑3, Sep 88	1.25	0.40	1.00	2.00
❑4, Oct 88	1.25	0.40	1.00	2.00

BLACK PANTHER (VOL. 2)
MARVEL

	ORIG	GOOD	FINE	N-MINT
❑1, Nov, The Client, gatefold summary	2.50	1.00	2.50	5.00
❑1/SC, Nov 98, The Client, DFE alternate cover	6.95	1.40	3.50	7.00

	ORIG	GOOD	FINE	N-MINT
❑2/A, Dec, gatefold summary	2.50	0.80	2.00	4.00
❑2/B, Dec 98, gatefold summary	2.50	0.80	2.00	4.00
❑3, Jan, gatefold summary, A: Fantastic Four	2.50	0.60	1.50	3.00
❑4, Feb 99, A: Mephisto	2.50	0.60	1.50	3.00
❑5, Mar 99, A: Mephisto	2.50	0.60	1.50	3.00
❑6, Apr 99, V: Kraven the Hunter	2.50	0.50	1.25	2.50
❑7, May 99	2.50	0.50	1.25	2.50
❑8, Jun 99	2.50	0.50	1.25	2.50
❑9, Jul 99	2.50	0.50	1.25	2.50
❑10, Aug 99	2.50	0.50	1.25	2.50
❑11, Sep 99	2.50	0.50	1.25	2.50
❑12, Oct 99	2.50	0.50	1.25	2.50
❑13, Dec 99	2.50	0.50	1.25	2.50
❑14, Jan 00	2.50	0.50	1.25	2.50
❑15, Feb 00	2.50	0.50	1.25	2.50
❑16, Mar 00	2.50	0.50	1.25	2.50
❑17, Apr 00	2.50	0.50	1.25	2.50
❑18, May 00	2.50	0.50	1.25	2.50
❑19, Jun 00	2.50	0.50	1.25	2.50
❑20, Jul 00	2.50	0.50	1.25	2.50
❑21, Aug 00	2.50	0.50	1.25	2.50
❑22, Sep 00	2.50	0.50	1.25	2.50
❑23, Oct 00	2.50	0.50	1.25	2.50
❑24, Nov 00, Beloved	2.50	0.50	1.25	2.50
❑25, Dec 00, Maximum Security; Passage..	2.50	0.50	1.25	2.50
❑26, Jan 01, Sturm und Drang, A Story of Love and War, Part 1: Echoes, A: Storm.	2.50	0.50	1.25	2.50
❑27, Feb 01, Sturm und Drang, A Story of Love and War, Part 2: An Epidemic Insanity	2.50	0.50	1.25	2.50
❑28, Mar 01, Sturm und Drang, A Story of Love and War, Part 3: The Trade of Kings	2.50	0.50	1.25	2.50
❑29, Apr 01, Sturm und Drang, A Story of Love and War, Part 4: The Continuation of Politics by Other Means	2.50	0.50	1.25	2.50
❑30, May 01, The Story Thus Far, A: Captain America, World War II story	2.50	0.50	1.25	2.50
❑31	2.50	0.50	1.25	2.50
❑32	2.50	0.50	1.25	2.50
❑33	2.50	0.50	1.25	2.50
❑34	2.50	0.50	1.25	2.50

BLACK PANTHER: PANTHER'S PREY
MARVEL

Value: Cover or less

- ❑1, May 91 .... 4.95
- ❑2, Jun 91 .... 4.95
- ❑3, Aug 91 .... 4.95
- ❑4, Oct 91, Prey for the Night; Burie Alive 4.95

BLACK PEARL, THE
DARK HORSE

	ORIG	GOOD	FINE	N-MINT
❑1, Sep 96	2.95	0.70	1.75	3.50
❑2, Oct 96	2.95	0.60	1.50	3.00
❑3, Nov 96	2.95	0.60	1.50	3.00
❑4, Dec 96	2.95	0.60	1.50	3.00
❑5, Jan 97, Final Issue	2.95	0.60	1.50	3.00

BLACK PHANTOM
AC

Value: Cover or less

- ❑1, b&w 2.50
- ❑2 .... 2.50
- ❑3, b&w 2.75

BLACK SABBATH
ROCK-IT

Value: Cover or less

- ❑1, Feb 94 .... 3.95

BLACK SCORPION
SPECIAL STUDIO

Value: Cover or less

- ❑1, b&w 2.75
- ❑2, b&w 2.75
- ❑3, b&w 2.75

BLACK SEPTEMBER
MALIBU

	ORIG	GOOD	FINE	N-MINT
❑8, Sep, events affect the Infinity issues of the other Ultraverse titles	1.50	0.40	1.00	2.00

BLACKSTAR
IMPERIAL

	ORIG	GOOD	FINE	N-MINT
❑1	1.80	0.40	1.00	2.00
❑2	1.80	0.40	1.00	2.00

BLACK SUN: X-MEN
MARVEL

	ORIG	GOOD	FINE	N-MINT
❑1, Nov 00, Skin the Cat!	2.99	0.60	1.50	2.99
❑1/A, Nov 00, Dynamic Forces cover	2.99	1.00	2.50	5.00
❑2, Nov 00, X-Men Black Sun Second Spell: Spear the Angel!	2.99	0.60	1.50	2.99
❑3, Nov 00, X-Men Black Sun Third Spell: Bare the Claws!	2.99	0.60	1.50	2.99
❑4, Nov 00, X-Men Black Sun Fourth Spell: Light the Fire!	2.99	0.60	1.50	2.99
❑5, Nov 00, X-Men Black Sun Final Spell: Cast the Magik!	2.99	0.60	1.50	2.99

BLACK TERROR, THE (ECLIPSE)
ECLIPSE

Value: Cover or less

- ❑1, Oct 89 .... 4.95
- ❑1/Aut, Oct 89, Signed by Beau Smith 3.50
- ❑2, Mar 90 .... 4.95
- ❑2/Aut, Signed by Beau Smith 3.50
- ❑3, Jun 90, Seduction of Deceit 4.95
- ❑3/Aut, Jun 90, Signed by Beau Smith 3.50

BLACKTHORNE'S 3 IN 1
BLACKTHORNE

Value: Cover or less

- ❑1 .... 1.75
- ❑2, Feb 87 .... 1.75

BLACKTHORNE'S HARVEY FLIP BOOK
BLACKTHORNE

Value: Cover or less

- ❑1, A: Stumbo; A: Sad Sack, b&w 2.00

BLACK WIDOW
MARVEL

	ORIG	GOOD	FINE	N-MINT
❑1, Jun 99	2.99	0.70	1.75	3.50
❑2, Jul 99	2.99	0.60	1.50	3.00
❑3, Aug 99	2.99	0.60	1.50	3.00

BLACK WIDOW (VOL. 2)
MARVEL

Value: Cover or less

- ❑1, Jan 01, DGry(w), Breakdown, Part 1; Breakdown 2.99
- ❑2, Feb 01, DGry(w), Breakdown, Part 2 .... 2.99
- ❑3, May 01, DGry(w), Breakdown, Part 3 .... 2.99

BLACK WIDOW: WEB OF INTRIGUE
MARVEL

Value: Cover or less

- ❑1, Jun, collects Marvel Fanfare #10-13 .... 3.50

BLACKWULF
MARVEL

Value: Cover or less

- ❑1, Jun, Where Monsters Dwell, Embossed cover 2.50
- ❑2, Jul 94 .... 1.50
- ❑3, Aug 94 .... 1.50
- ❑4, Sep 94 .... 1.50
- ❑5, Oct 94 .... 1.50
- ❑6, Nov 94 .... 1.50
- ❑7, Dec 94 .... 1.50
- ❑8, Jan 95 .... 1.50
- ❑9, Feb 95 .... 1.50
- ❑10, Mar 95, Final Issue 1.50

BLACK ZEPPELIN (GENE DAY'S...)
RENEGADE

	ORIG	GOOD	FINE	N-MINT
❑1, Apr 85, GD, GD (w), The Strip	1.70	0.40	1.00	2.00
❑2	1.70	0.40	1.00	2.00
❑3	1.70	0.40	1.00	2.00
❑4	1.70	0.40	1.00	2.00
❑5	2.00	0.40	1.00	2.00

BLADE (1ST SERIES)
MARVEL

	ORIG	GOOD	FINE	N-MINT
❑1, May 97, TP; GC, The Final Glory of Deacon Frost, O: Blade, Reprint; giveaway ..	—	0.30	0.75	1.50

BLADE (2ND SERIES)
MARVEL

Value: Cover or less

- ❑1, Mar 98, GC, Crescent City Blues 3.50

BLADE (3RD SERIES)
MARVEL

Value: Cover or less

- ❑1, Oct 98, Blood Allies, Part 1, nn; One-Shot; movie Adaptation; gatefold summary 5.99
- ❑2/A, Dec 98, Blood Allies, Part 2, cover says Nov, indicia says Dec; gatefold summary 2.99
- ❑2/B, Dec 98, Blood Allies, Part 2 .... 2.99
- ❑3, Jan 99, cover says Dec, indicia says Jan; gatefold summary 2.99
- ❑4, A: Morbius 2.99

BLADE (BUCCANEER)
BUCCANEER

Value: Cover or less

- ❑1 .... 2.00
- ❑2 .... 2.00

BLADE OF SHURIKEN
ETERNITY

Value: Cover or less

- ❑1, May 87, RBy, RBy (w), The Blade of Shuriken 1.95
- ❑2, Jul 87, RBy, RBy (w) 1.95
- ❑3, Sep 87, RBy, RBy (w) 1.95
- ❑4, Nov 87, RBy, RBy (w) 1.95
- ❑5, Jan 88, RBy, RBy (w) 1.95

BLADE OF THE IMMORTAL
DARK HORSE

	ORIG	GOOD	FINE	N-MINT
❑1, Jun 96	2.95	0.70	1.75	3.50
❑2, Jul, Conquest, Part 1	2.95	0.60	1.50	3.00
❑3, Aug, Conquest, Part 2	2.95	0.60	1.50	3.00
❑4, Sep, Conquest, Part 3	2.95	0.60	1.50	3.00
❑5, Oct, Genius, Part 1	2.95	0.60	1.50	3.00
❑6, Nov, Genius, Part 2	2.95	0.59	1.48	2.95
❑7, Dec, Fanatic, Part 1	2.95	0.59	1.48	2.95
❑8, Jan, Fanatic, Part 2	2.95	0.59	1.48	2.95
❑9, Apr, Call of the Worm, Part 1, Giant-size	3.95	0.79	1.98	3.95
❑10, May, Call of the Worm, Part 2, Giant-size	3.95	0.79	1.98	3.95
❑11, Jun, Call of the Worm, Part 3, Giant-size	3.95	0.79	1.98	3.95

	ORIG	GOOD	FINE	N-MINT
❑12, Jul, Dreamsong, Part 1	2.95	0.59	1.48	2.95
❑13, Aug, Dreamsong, Part 2	2.95	0.59	1.48	2.95
❑14, Sep, Dreamsong, Part 3	2.95	0.59	1.48	2.95
❑15, Oct, Dreamsong, Part 4	2.95	0.59	1.48	2.95
❑16, Nov, Dreamsong, Part 5	2.95	0.59	1.48	2.95
❑17, Dec, Dreamsong, Part 6	2.95	0.59	1.48	2.95
❑18, Jan, Dreamsong, Part 7	2.95	0.59	1.48	2.95
❑19, Mar 98, Rin's Bane, Part 1	3.95	0.59	1.48	2.95
❑20, Apr 98, Rin's Bane, Part 2	3.95	0.59	1.48	2.95
❑21, May 98, On Silent Wings, Part 1	2.95	0.59	1.48	2.95
❑22, Jun 98, On Silent Wings, Part 2	2.95	0.59	1.48	2.95
❑23, Jul 98, On Silent Wings, Part 3	2.95	0.59	1.48	2.95
❑24, Aug 98, On Silent Wings, Part 4	2.95	0.59	1.48	2.95
❑25, Sep 98, On Silent Wings, Part 5	2.95	0.59	1.48	2.95
❑26, Oct 98, On Silent Wings, Part 6	3.95	0.59	1.48	2.95
❑27, Nov 98, On Silent Wings, Part 7	2.95	0.59	1.48	2.95
❑28, Dec 98, On Silent Wings, Part 8	2.95	0.59	1.48	2.95
❑29, Jan, Dark Shadows, Part 1	2.95	0.59	1.48	2.95
❑30, Feb, Dark Shadows, Part 2	2.95	0.59	1.48	2.95
❑31, Mar, Dark Shadows, Part 3	2.95	0.59	1.48	2.95
❑32, Apr, Dark Shadows, Part 4	2.95	0.59	1.48	2.95
❑33, May, Dark Shadows, Part 5	2.95	0.59	1.48	2.95
❑34, Jun, Food, 48pgs.	3.95	0.79	1.98	3.95
❑35, Jul, Heart of Darkness, Part 1	2.95	0.59	1.48	2.95
❑36, Aug, Heart of Darkness, Part 2	3.95	0.79	1.98	3.95
❑37, Sep, Heart of Darkness, Part 3	3.95	0.79	1.98	3.95
❑38, Oct, Heart of Darkness, Part 4	3.95	0.79	1.98	3.95
❑39, Nov 99	—	0.60	1.50	2.99
❑40, Dec 99	—	0.60	1.50	2.99
❑41, Jan 00	—	0.60	1.50	2.99
❑42, Feb 00	—	0.60	1.50	2.99
❑43, Mar 00, The Gathering, Part 1	—	0.60	1.50	2.99
❑44, Apr 00, The Gathering, Part 2	—	0.60	1.50	2.99
❑45, May 00, The Gathering, Part 3	—	0.60	1.50	2.99
❑46, Jun 00, The Gathering, Part 4	—	0.60	1.50	2.99
❑47, Jul 00, The Gathering, Part 5	—	0.60	1.50	2.99
❑48, Aug 00, The Gathering, Part 6	—	0.60	1.50	2.99
❑49, Sep 00, The Gathering, Part 7	—	0.60	1.50	2.99
❑50, Oct 00, The Gathering, Part 8	—	0.60	1.50	2.99
❑51, Nov 00, The Gathering, Part 9	—	0.60	1.50	2.99
❑52, Dec 00, The Gathering, Part 10	2.99	0.60	1.50	2.99
❑53, Jan 01, The Gathering, Part 11	2.99	0.60	1.50	2.99

BLADE RUNNER
MARVEL

	ORIG	GOOD	FINE	N-MINT
❑1, Oct 82, AW, movie Adaptation	0.60	0.20	0.50	1.00
❑2, Nov 82, AW, movie Adaptation	0.60	0.20	0.50	1.00

BLADESMEN, THE
BLUE COMET

Value: Cover or less

- ❑0, b&w 2.00
- ❑1, A Gathering of Hawks, b&w 2.00
- ❑2 2.25

BLADE: THE VAMPIRE-HUNTER
MARVEL

Value: Cover or less

- ❑1, Jul 94, Dark Visions, foil cover 2.95
- ❑2, Aug 94, Red Prophet 1.95
- ❑3, Sep 94 1.95
- ❑4, Oct 94 1.95
- ❑5, Nov 94 1.95
- ❑6, Dec 94 1.95
- ❑7, Jan 95 1.95
- ❑8, Feb 95 1.95
- ❑9, Mar 95 1.95
- ❑10, Apr, Final Issue 1.95

BLADE: VAMPIRE HUNTER
MARVEL

Value: Cover or less

- ❑1, Dec 99, Chaos, Part 1 3.50

BLAIR WHICH? (SERGIO ARAGONÉS'...)
DARK HORSE

Value: Cover or less

- ❑1, Dec 99, SA, ME (w) 2.95

BLAIR WITCH CHRONICLES, THE
ONI

Value: Cover or less

- ❑1, Mar 00, The Kearney Interview, b&w 2.95
- ❑2, Apr 00, The Offering 2.95
- ❑3, Jun 00 2.95
- ❑4, Jul 00, Fire 2.95

BLAIR WITCH: DARK TESTAMENTS
IMAGE

Value: Cover or less

- ❑1, Oct 00 2.95

BLAIR WITCH PROJECT, THE
ONI

	ORIG	GOOD	FINE	N-MINT
❑1, Aug 99, Curse; She Needs Me: Coffin Rock, 2nd Printing; prequel to movie	2.95	2.00	5.00	10.00
❑1-2, Curse; She Needs Me: Coffin Rock, 2nd Printing	2.95	0.59	1.48	2.95

BLANCHE GOES TO HOLLYWOOD
DARK HORSE

Value: Cover or less

- ❑1, nn; b&w 2.95

Oni's *Blair Witch Project* was so successful as to force multiple printings.

© 1999 Oni Press

BLANCHE GOES TO NEW YORK
DARK HORSE

Value: Cover or less

- ❑1, Nov 92, nn; b&w 2.95

BLARNEY
DISCOVERY

Value: Cover or less

- ❑1, cardstock cover, b&w 2.95

BLAST CORPS
DARK HORSE

Value: Cover or less

- ❑1, Oct, based on Nintendo 64 games 2.50

BLASTERS SPECIAL
DC

Value: Cover or less

- ❑1, May 89, PD (w) 2.00

BLAST-OFF
HARVEY

	ORIG	GOOD	FINE	N-MINT
❑1, Caution! Atoms!, A: The Three Rocketeers	—	5.20	13.00	26.00

BLAZE
MARVEL

Value: Cover or less

- ❑1, Aug 94, A Cold Blast From Ice Box Bob!, O: Johnny Blaze, silver enhanced cover 2.95
- ❑2, Sep 94 1.95
- ❑3, Oct 94 1.95
- ❑4, Nov 94 1.95
- ❑5, Dec 94 1.95
- ❑6, Jan 95 1.95
- ❑7, Feb 95 1.95
- ❑8, Mar 95 1.95
- ❑9, Apr 95 1.95
- ❑10, May 95 1.95
- ❑11, Jun 95 1.95
- ❑12, Jul, Final Issue 1.95

BLAZE: LEGACY OF BLOOD
MARVEL

Value: Cover or less

- ❑1, Dec 93, Legacy Of Blood, Part 1 1.75
- ❑2, Jan 94 1.75
- ❑3, Feb 94 1.75
- ❑4, Mar 94 1.75

BLAZE OF GLORY
MARVEL

Value: Cover or less

- ❑1, Feb 00, biweekly mini-series 2.99
- ❑2, Feb 00 2.99
- ❑3, Mar 00 2.99
- ❑4, Mar 00 2.99

BLAZING BATTLE TALES
SEABOARD

	ORIG	GOOD	FINE	N-MINT
❑1, Jul 75	0.25	0.50	1.25	2.50

BLAZING COMBAT
WARREN

	ORIG	GOOD	FINE	N-MINT
❑1, scarcer	—	20.00	50.00	100.00
❑2	—	7.00	17.50	35.00
❑3	—	7.00	17.50	35.00
❑4	—	7.00	17.50	35.00
❑Anl 1	—	10.00	25.00	50.00

BLAZING COMBAT (APPLE)
APPLE

Value: Cover or less

- ❑1 4.50
- ❑2, b&w; Reprint 4.50

BLAZING COMBAT: WORLD WAR I AND WORLD WAR II
APPLE

Value: Cover or less

- ❑1, Reprint 3.75
- ❑2, Jun 94, Reprint 3.75

BLAZING FOXHOLES
EROS

Value: Cover or less

- ❑1 2.95
- ❑2 2.95
- ❑3, Jan 95, The Percy Patrol 2.95

BLAZING WESTERN (AC)
AC

Value: Cover or less

- ❑1, b&w 2.50

BLAZING WESTERN (AVALON)
AVALON

Value: Cover or less

- ❑1, Cheyenne Kid: The Legend of the White Buffalo; You Ride With Crazy Horse 2.75

BLEAT
SLAVE LABOR

Value: Cover or less

- ❑1, Aug 95 2.95

BLEEDING HEART
FANTAGRAPHICS

Value: Cover or less

- ❑1 .... 2.50
- ❑2, Spr 92 .... 2.50
- ❑3 .... 2.50
- ❑4 .... 2.50
- ❑5, Aug 93 .... 2.50

BLINDSIDE
IMAGE

Value: Cover or less

- ❑1, Feb 98, Video Games of the Stars; Blip Tips I, 1: Donkey Kong; 1: Mario, video game magazine in comic-book format 1.00
- ❑1/A, Aug 96, wraparound cover 2.50
- ❑1/B, Aug 96, white background cover 2.50
- ❑2 .... 1.00
- ❑3 .... 1.00
- ❑4 .... 1.00
- ❑5 .... 1.00
- ❑6 .... 1.00
- ❑7 .... 1.00

BLINK
MARVEL

Value: Cover or less

- ❑1, Mar 01 .... 2.99
- ❑2, Apr 01, Through the Looking Glass … 2.99
- ❑3, May 01, On the Side of the Angels 2.99

BLIP
MARVEL

Value: Cover or less

- ❑1, Video Games of the Stars; Blip Tips I, 1: Donkey Kong; 1: Mario, video game magazine in comic-book format 1.00
- ❑2 .... 1.00
- ❑3 .... 1.00
- ❑4 .... 1.00
- ❑5 .... 1.00
- ❑6 .... 1.00
- ❑7 .... 1.00

BLIP (BARDIC)
BARDIC

Value: Cover or less

- ❑1, Feb 98, The Caretakers 1.25

BLIP AND THE C.C.A.D.S.
AMAZING

	ORIG	GOOD	FINE	N-MINT
❑1	1.95	0.40	1.00	2.00
❑2	1.95	0.40	1.00	2.00

BLISS ALLEY
IMAGE

Value: Cover or less

- ❑1, Jul 97 .... 2.95
- ❑2, Sep 97 .... 2.95

BLITE
FANTAGRAPHICS

Value: Cover or less

- ❑1, b&w 2.25

BLITZ
NIGHTWYND

Value: Cover or less

- ❑1 .... 2.50
- ❑2 .... 2.50
- ❑3 .... 2.50
- ❑4 .... 2.50

BLITZKRIEG
DC

	ORIG	GOOD	FINE	N-MINT
❑1, RE, Enemy	0.25	1.40	3.50	7.00
❑2	0.25	0.80	2.00	4.00
❑3, RE, The Execution; The Partisans!	0.25	0.80	2.00	4.00
❑4, Bicentennial #20	0.25	0.80	2.00	4.00
❑5, Final Issue	0.25	0.80	2.00	4.00

BLONDE, THE
FANTAGRAPHICS

Value: Cover or less

- ❑1 .... 2.50
- ❑2 .... 2.50
- ❑3 .... 2.50

BLONDE ADDICTION
BLITZWEASEL

Value: Cover or less

- ❑1 .... 2.95
- ❑2 .... 2.95
- ❑3 .... 2.95
- ❑4, flip-book with Blonde Avenger's Subplots 2.95

BLONDE AVENGER
BLITZ WEASEL

Value: Cover or less

- ❑27/A, Model Kombat 3.95
- ❑27/B, Model Kombat, Photo cover 3.95

BLONDE AVENGER, THE (MINI-SERIES)
EROS

Value: Cover or less

- ❑1 .... 2.75
- ❑2 .... 2.75
- ❑3 .... 2.75
- ❑4, Apr 94, Maneater 2.75

BLONDE AVENGER: CROSSOVER CRAZZEEE
BLITZWEASEL

Value: Cover or less

- ❑1, nn; One-Shot 3.95

BLONDE AVENGER MONTHLY
BLITZWEASEL

	ORIG	GOOD	FINE	N-MINT
❑1, Mar 96, Dangerous Island, Part 1, b&w.	2.95	0.80	2.00	4.00
❑2, Dangerous Island, Part 2	2.95	0.60	1.50	3.00
❑3, Dangerous Island, Part 3	2.95	0.59	1.48	2.95
❑4, Dangerous Island, Part 4	2.95	0.59	1.48	2.95
❑5, Dangerous Island, Part 5	2.95	0.59	1.48	2.95
❑6, Dangerous Island, Part 6	2.95	0.59	1.48	2.95

BLONDE AVENGER ONE-SHOT SPECIAL: THE SPYING GAME
BLITZWEASEL

Value: Cover or less

- ❑1, Mar 96, The Spying Game, b&w 2.95

BLONDE, THE: BONDAGE PALACE
FANTAGRAPHICS

Value: Cover or less

- ❑1 .... 2.95
- ❑2 .... 2.95
- ❑3 .... 2.95
- ❑5, May 94 .... 2.95

BLOOD
FANTACO

Value: Cover or less

- ❑1, b&w 3.95

BLOOD AND GLORY
MARVEL

Value: Cover or less

- ❑1, KJ, We The People…, A: Punisher, Embossed cover 5.95
- ❑2, KJ, Eternal Vigilance, A: Punisher 5.95
- ❑3, KJ, Establish the Blessings of Liberty, A: Terror, Inc.; A: Captain America; A: Punisher 5.95

BLOOD & ROSES ADVENTURES
KNIGHT PRESS

Value: Cover or less

- ❑1, May 95, b&w 2.95

BLOOD & ROSES: FUTURE PAST TENSE
SKY

	ORIG	GOOD	FINE	N-MINT
❑1, Dec 93, Silver logo regular edition	2.25	0.45	1.13	2.25
❑1/Ash, ashcan edition	—	0.60	1.50	3.00
❑1/GO, Gold logo promotional edition	—	0.60	1.50	3.00
❑2	2.25	0.45	1.13	2.25

BLOOD & ROSES: SEARCH FOR THE TIME-STONE
SKY

	ORIG	GOOD	FINE	N-MINT
❑1	2.50	0.50	1.25	2.50
❑1/Ash, ashcan edition	—	0.60	1.50	3.00
❑2	2.50	0.50	1.25	2.50

BLOOD AND SHADOWS
DC

Value: Cover or less

- ❑1 .... 5.95
- ❑2 .... 5.95
- ❑3 .... 5.95
- ❑4 .... 5.95

BLOOD AND THUNDER
CONQUEST

Value: Cover or less

- ❑1, b&w 2.95

BLOOD & WATER
SLAVE LABOR

Value: Cover or less

- ❑1, Oct 91, b&w 3.95

BLOOD: A TALE
MARVEL

Value: Cover or less

- ❑1, Uroborous 3.25
- ❑2, Communion 3.25
- ❑3, Theophany 3.25
- ❑4 .... 3.25

BLOOD: A TALE (VERTIGO)
DC

Value: Cover or less

- ❑1, Nov 96, Uroborous 2.95
- ❑2, Dec 96, Communion 2.95
- ❑3, Jan 97, Theophany 2.95
- ❑4, Feb 97, Ouroborous 2.95

BLOODBATH
DC

Value: Cover or less

- ❑1, Dec 93 .... 3.50
- ❑2, Dec 93 .... 3.50

BLOODBROTHERS
ETERNITY

Value: Cover or less

- ❑1 .... 1.95
- ❑2 .... 1.95
- ❑3 .... 1.95
- ❑4 .... 1.95

BLOODCHILDE
MILLENNIUM

Value: Cover or less

- ❑1, Dec 94, Portrait of a Surreal Killer 2.50
- ❑2, Feb 95 .... 2.50
- ❑3, May 95 .... 2.50
- ❑4, Jul 95, NG (w) 2.95

BLOOD CLUB
KITCHEN SINK

Value: Cover or less

- ❑1, nn; full color 5.95

BLOOD CLUB, FEATURING BIG BABY
KITCHEN SINK

Value: Cover or less

- ❑2, Series numbering continued from Curse of the Molemen 5.95

BLOODFANG
EPITATH STUDIOS

Value: Cover or less

- ❑1 .... 2.50

BLOOD FEAST
ETERNITY

Value: Cover or less

- ❑1, b&w; tame cover 2.50
- ❑1/SC, b&w; Explicit (photo) cover 2.50
- ❑2, b&w 2.50
- ❑2/SC, Explicit (photo) cover 2.50

BLOOD FEAST: THE SCREENPLAY
ETERNITY

Value: Cover or less

❑1, nn; b&w; not comics 4.95

BLOODFIRE
LIGHTNING

	ORIG	GOOD	FINE	N-MINT
❑0, O: Bloodfire, Giant-size	3.50	0.70	1.75	3.50
❑1, Mar 93, 1: Bloodfire, b&w; promotional copy	3.50	0.80	2.00	4.00
❑1/PL, Jun 93, platinum	3.50	0.70	1.75	3.50
❑1/SC, Jun 93, red foil	3.50	0.70	1.75	3.50
❑2, Jul 93	2.95	0.59	1.48	2.95
❑3, Aug 93	2.95	0.59	1.48	2.95
❑4, Sep 93	2.95	0.59	1.48	2.95
❑5, Oct 93, trading card	2.95	0.59	1.48	2.95
❑6, Nov 93, Paybacks Are Hell!	2.95	0.59	1.48	2.95
❑7, Dec 93	2.95	0.59	1.48	2.95
❑8, Jan 94, O: Prodigal	2.95	0.59	1.48	2.95
❑9, Feb 94	2.95	0.59	1.48	2.95
❑10, Mar 94	2.95	0.59	1.48	2.95
❑11	2.95	0.59	1.48	2.95
❑12	2.95	0.59	1.48	2.95

BLOODFIRE/HELLINA
LIGHTNING

	ORIG	GOOD	FINE	N-MINT
❑1, Aug 95, Common Enemy!, O: Hellina	3.00	0.60	1.50	3.00
❑1/Nude, Aug 95, Nude edition	9.95	1.00	2.50	5.00
❑1/PL, Common Enemy!, O: Hellina, Platinum edition	—	1.00	2.50	5.00

BLOOD GOTHIC
FANTACO

Value: Cover or less

❑1, The Thrice Cursed Calvin Brewster 4.95

❑2 4.95

BLOODHUNTER
BRAINSTORM

Value: Cover or less

❑1, Oct, b&w; cardstock cover 2.95

BLOOD IS THE HARVEST
ECLIPSE

Value: Cover or less

❑1, Jul 92 2.50

❑2 2.50

❑3 2.50

❑4 2.50

BLOOD JUNKIES
ETERNITY

Value: Cover or less

❑1 2.50

❑2 2.50

BLOOD LEGACY: THE STORY OF RYAN
IMAGE

Value: Cover or less

❑1, Jul 00 2.50

❑2, Aug 00 2.50

❑3, Sep 00 2.50

❑4, Nov 00 2.50

BLOODLETTING (1ST SERIES)
FANTACO

Value: Cover or less

❑1 2.95

BLOODLETTING (2ND SERIES)
FANTACO

Value: Cover or less

❑1 3.95

❑2 3.95

BLOODLINES
AIRCEL

	ORIG	GOOD	FINE	N-MINT
❑1, Overture, Part 1, Aircel publishes	1.70	0.60	1.50	3.00
❑2, Overture, Part 2	1.70	0.50	1.25	2.50
❑3, Overture, Part 3, Blackburn begins as publisher	1.70	0.50	1.25	2.50
❑4	1.70	0.50	1.25	2.50
❑5	1.75	0.50	1.25	2.50
❑6	1.75	0.50	1.25	2.50

BLOODLINES: A TALE FROM THE HEART OF AFRICA
MARVEL

Value: Cover or less

❑1 5.95

BLOODLUST
SLAVE LABOR

Value: Cover or less

❑1, Dec 90, Cross Of The Damned 2.25

BLOOD 'N' GUTS
AIRCEL

Value: Cover or less

❑1, Nov 90, 1: Blood & Guts, b&w 2.50

❑2 2.50

❑3 2.50

❑4 2.50

BLOOD OF DRACULA
APPLE

Geomancer Geoff Henry freed Bloodshot from the laboratory where he received his nanite-enhanced blood.

© 1993 Voyager Communications (Valiant)

	ORIG	GOOD	FINE	N-MINT
❑1	1.75	0.40	1.00	2.00
❑2	1.75	0.40	1.00	2.00
❑3, Enter Freely...And Of Your Own Will	1.75	0.40	1.00	2.00
❑4	1.75	0.40	1.00	2.00
❑5	1.75	0.40	1.00	2.00
❑6	1.95	0.40	1.00	2.00
❑7	1.95	0.40	1.00	2.00
❑8	1.95	0.40	1.00	2.00
❑9	1.95	0.40	1.00	2.00
❑10	1.95	0.40	1.00	2.00
❑11	1.95	0.40	1.00	2.00
❑12	1.95	0.40	1.00	2.00
❑13, BWr	2.25	0.40	1.00	2.00
❑14, BWr	2.25	0.45	1.13	2.25
❑15, record; flexidisc	3.75	0.75	1.88	3.75
❑16, BWr	2.25	0.45	1.13	2.25
❑17, BWr	2.25	0.45	1.13	2.25
❑18, BWr	2.25	0.45	1.13	2.25
❑19, BWr	2.25	0.45	1.13	2.25
❑20, Final issue?	2.25	0.45	1.13	2.25

BLOOD OF THE INNOCENT
WARP

Value: Cover or less

❑1 2.00

❑2, Light of the Sun, Dark of the Moon 2.00

❑3 2.00

❑4 2.00

BLOOD PACK
DC

Value: Cover or less

❑1, Mar 95, All Shook Up 1.50

❑2, Apr 95, A: Superboy 1.50

❑3, May 95 1.50

❑4, Jun 95 1.50

BLOODPOOL
IMAGE

Value: Cover or less

❑1, Aug 95, Discharged 2.50

❑1/SC, Aug 95, alternate cover 2.50

❑2, Sep 95 2.50

❑3, Oct 95 2.50

❑4, Nov 95 2.50

❑SE 1, Mar 96, Special 2.50

BLOOD REIGN
FATHOM

Value: Cover or less

❑1 2.95

❑2 2.95

❑3, Oct 91 2.95

BLOODSCENT
COMICO

Value: Cover or less

❑1, GC, Bloodscent; Acts of Darkness 2.00

BLOODSEED
MARVEL

Value: Cover or less

❑1, 1: Bloodseed 1.95

❑2, Gold cover; nudity; Final issue (series was rescheduled as 2-issue series) 1.95

BLOODSHED
DAMAGE!

	ORIG	GOOD	FINE	N-MINT
❑1	—	0.59	1.48	2.95
❑1/LE, no cover price, b&w	—	0.59	1.48	2.95
❑2	—	0.59	1.48	2.95
❑3, Lies, Ancuysm / You Know Who You Are!; Oh, The Guilt	—	0.59	1.48	2.95
❑Ash 1	—	0.40	1.00	2.00

BLOODSHOT
VALIANT

	ORIG	GOOD	FINE	N-MINT
❑0, Mar, O: Bloodshot, chromium cover, A: Eternal Warrior	3.50	0.70	1.75	3.50
❑0/GO, Mar, A: Eternal Warrior; O: Bloodshot, no cover price; Gold edition	—	0.80	2.00	4.00
❑1, Feb 93, DP, Blood of the Machine, Metallic embossed foil cover	3.50	0.70	1.75	3.50
❑2, Mar 93, V: X-O Manowar	2.50	0.50	1.25	2.50
❑3, Apr 93	2.25	0.45	1.13	2.25
❑4, May 93, A: Eternal Warrior	2.25	0.45	1.13	2.25
❑5, Jun 93, A: Eternal Warrior; A: Rai	2.25	0.45	1.13	2.25
❑6, Jul 93, 1: Ninjak	2.25	0.45	1.13	2.25
❑7, Aug 93, A: Ninjak	2.25	0.45	1.13	2.25
❑8, Sep 93	2.25	0.45	1.13	2.25
❑9, Oct 93	2.25	0.45	1.13	2.25
❑10, Nov 93	2.25	0.45	1.13	2.25
❑11, Dec 93	2.25	0.45	1.13	2.25
❑12, Jan 94, DP, Bloodshot's Day Off	2.25	0.45	1.13	2.25

	ORIG	GOOD	FINE	N-MINT
❑13, Feb 94	2.25	0.45	1.13	2.25
❑14, Mar 94	2.25	0.45	1.13	2.25
❑15, Apr 94	2.25	0.45	1.13	2.25
❑16, May 94, trading card	2.25	0.45	1.13	2.25
❑17, Jun 94, A: H.A.R.D.Corps	2.25	0.45	1.13	2.25
❑18, Aug 94	2.25	0.45	1.13	2.25
❑19, Sep 94	2.25	0.45	1.13	2.25
❑20, Oct, The Chaos Effect: Gamma, Part 1, Chaos Effect	2.25	0.45	1.13	2.25
❑21, Nov 94, V: Ax	2.25	0.45	1.13	2.25
❑22, Dec 94	2.25	0.45	1.13	2.25
❑23, Jan 95	2.25	0.45	1.13	2.25
❑24, Feb 95	2.25	0.45	1.13	2.25
❑25, Mar 95, Showdown in Clowntown, Part 1	2.25	0.45	1.13	2.25
❑26, Apr 95, Showdown in Clowntown, Part 2	2.25	0.45	1.13	2.25
❑27, May 95, Rampage, Part 1; Bloodshot Rampage, Part 1	2.25	0.45	1.13	2.25
❑28, May 95, Rampage, Part 3; Bloodshot Rampage, Part 3, V: Ninjak	2.25	0.45	1.13	2.25
❑29, Jun 95, Rampage, Part 5; Bloodshot Rampage, Part 5, Valiant becomes Acclaim imprint	2.25	0.45	1.13	2.25
❑30, Jul 95, Birthquake	2.25	0.45	1.13	2.25
❑31, Jul 95, Birthquake	2.25	0.45	1.13	2.25
❑32, Aug 95, Birthquake	2.25	0.45	1.13	2.25
❑33, Aug 95, Birthquake	2.25	0.45	1.13	2.25
❑34, Sep 95	2.50	0.50	1.25	2.50
❑35, Sep 95, V: Rampage	2.50	0.50	1.25	2.50
❑36, Oct 95, BA; MGr	2.50	0.50	1.25	2.50
❑37, Oct 95, BA	2.50	0.50	1.25	2.50
❑38, Nov 95	2.50	0.50	1.25	2.50
❑39, Nov 95	2.50	0.50	1.25	2.50
❑40, Dec 95	2.50	0.50	1.25	2.50
❑41, Dec 95	2.50	0.50	1.25	2.50
❑42, Jan 96	2.50	0.50	1.25	2.50
❑43, Jan 96	2.50	0.50	1.25	2.50
❑44	2.50	0.50	1.25	2.50
❑45, Mar 96	2.50	0.50	1.25	2.50
❑46, Apr 96	2.50	0.50	1.25	2.50
❑47, May 96	2.50	0.50	1.25	2.50
❑48, May 96	2.50	0.50	1.25	2.50
❑49, Jun 96	2.50	0.50	1.25	2.50
❑50, Jul 96	2.50	0.50	1.25	2.50
❑51, Aug 96, Final Issue	2.50	0.50	1.25	2.50
❑YB 1, Yearbook (annual) #1	3.95	0.79	1.98	3.95
❑YB 2, Yearbook (annual) #1	2.95	0.59	1.48	2.95

BLOODSHOT (VOL. 2)
ACCLAIM

	ORIG	GOOD	FINE	N-MINT
❑1, Jul 97, Behold, A Pale Horseman	2.50	0.50	1.25	2.50
❑1/SC, Jul 97, Behold, A Pale Horseman, alternate painted cover	2.50	0.50	1.25	2.50
❑2, Aug 97	2.50	0.50	1.25	2.50
❑3, Sep 97	2.50	0.50	1.25	2.50
❑4, Oct 97	2.50	0.50	1.25	2.50
❑5, Nov 97, Steranko tribute cover	2.50	0.50	1.25	2.50
❑6, Dec 97, The Society of The Mind	2.50	0.50	1.25	2.50
❑7, Jan 98, V: X-O Manowar	2.50	0.50	1.25	2.50
❑8, Feb 98, V: X-O Manowar	2.50	0.50	1.25	2.50
❑9, Mar 98	2.50	0.50	1.25	2.50
❑10, Apr, in Area 51	2.50	0.50	1.25	2.50
❑11	2.50	0.50	1.25	2.50
❑12, Feb 98, no cover date; indicia says Feb	2.50	0.50	1.25	2.50
❑13	2.50	0.50	1.25	2.50
❑14	2.50	0.50	1.25	2.50
❑15	2.50	0.50	1.25	2.50
❑16	2.50	0.50	1.25	2.50
❑Ash 1, Mar 97, no cover price, b&w preview of upcoming series; b&w preview of upcoming series	—	0.20	0.50	1.00

BLOODSTRIKE
IMAGE

	ORIG	GOOD	FINE	N-MINT
❑1, Apr 93, RL, Blood Brothers Prelude, 1: Fourplay; 1: Col. Cabbot; 1: Shogun; 1: Deadlock; 1: Tag, fading blood cover	2.95	0.60	1.50	3.00
❑2, Jun 93, 1: Lethal	1.95	0.40	1.00	2.00
❑3, Jul 93, Blood Brothers, Part 4	1.95	0.40	1.00	2.00
❑4, Oct 93, KG (w), Down Time	1.95	0.40	1.00	2.00
❑5, Nov 93, A: Supreme; 1: Noble	1.95	0.40	1.00	2.00
❑6, Dec 93, Chapel becomes team leader	1.95	0.40	1.00	2.00
❑7, Jan 94, A: Chapel	1.95	0.40	1.00	2.00
❑8, Feb 94	1.95	0.40	1.00	2.00
❑9, Mar 94, Extreme Prejudice, Part 3	1.95	0.40	1.00	2.00
❑10, Apr 94, Extreme Prejudice, Part 7	1.95	0.40	1.00	2.00
❑11, Jul 94	1.95	0.40	1.00	2.00
❑12, Aug 94	1.95	0.40	1.00	2.00
❑13, Aug 94	2.50	0.50	1.25	2.50
❑14, Sep 94	2.50	0.50	1.25	2.50
❑15, Oct 94, Extreme Sacrifice	1.95	0.50	1.25	2.50
❑16, Nov 94, Extreme Sacrifice	2.50	0.50	1.25	2.50
❑17, Dec 94, Extreme Sacrifice	1.95	0.50	1.25	2.50
❑18, Jan 95, Extreme Sacrifice; Extreme Sacrifice, Part 2, polybagged with trading card	2.50	0.50	1.25	2.50
❑19, Feb 95, Extreme Sacrifice Aftermath, polybagged	2.50	0.50	1.25	2.50
❑20, Mar 95	2.50	0.50	1.25	2.50
❑21, Apr 95	2.50	0.50	1.25	2.50
❑22, May 95	2.50	0.50	1.25	2.50
❑23	2.50	0.50	1.25	2.50
❑24	2.50	0.50	1.25	2.50
❑25, May 94, Images of Tomorrow; Published out of sequence as a preview of the future	1.95	0.39	0.98	1.95

BLOODSTRIKE ASSASSIN
IMAGE

Value: Cover or less

❑0, Oct 95	2.50	❑2, Jul 95	2.50
❑1	2.50	❑3, Aug 95	2.50
❑1/A, Jun 95	2.50	❑4	2.50
❑1/B, Jun 95, alternate cover	2.50		

BLOODSUCKER
FANTAGRAPHICS

Value: Cover or less

❑1, b&w; adult 2.50

BLOOD SWORD, THE
JADEMAN

Value: Cover or less

❑1	1.95	❑22	1.95
❑2	1.95	❑23	1.95
❑3	1.95	❑24	1.95
❑4	1.95	❑25	1.95
❑5	1.95	❑26	1.95
❑6	1.95	❑27	1.95
❑7	1.95	❑28	1.95
❑8	1.95	❑29	1.95
❑9	1.95	❑30	1.95
❑10	1.95	❑31	1.95
❑11	1.95	❑32	1.95
❑12	1.95	❑33	1.95
❑13	1.95	❑34	1.95
❑14	1.95	❑35	1.95
❑15	1.95	❑36	1.95
❑16	1.95	❑37	1.95
❑17	1.95	❑38	1.95
❑18	1.95	❑39	1.95
❑19	1.95	❑40	1.95
❑20	1.95	❑41	1.95
❑21	1.95	❑42	1.95

BLOOD SWORD DYNASTY
JADEMAN

Value: Cover or less

❑1	1.25	❑16	1.25
❑2	1.25	❑17	1.25
❑3	1.25	❑18	1.25
❑4	1.25	❑19	1.25
❑5	1.25	❑20	1.25
❑6	1.25	❑21	1.25
❑7	1.25	❑22	1.25
❑8	1.25	❑23	1.25
❑9	1.25	❑24	1.25
❑10	1.25	❑25	1.25
❑11	1.25	❑26	1.25
❑12	1.25	❑27	1.25
❑13	1.25	❑28	1.25
❑14	1.25	❑29	1.25
❑15	1.25		

BLOOD SYNDICATE
DC

Value: Cover or less

❑1, Apr 93, 1: Rob Chaplik; 1: Blood Syndicate	1.50	❑9, Dec 93, 1: Templo; O: Blood Syndicate	1.50
❑1/CS, Apr 93, 1: Rob Chaplik; 1: Blood Syndicate, trading card, part of mural, poster; poster, trading card	2.95	❑10, Jan 94, Shadow War; Shadow War, Part 4, 1: Bubba-saur, Metallic ink cover	2.50
❑2, May 93, 1: Boogieman; V: Holocaust	1.50	❑11, Feb 94, Aquamaria joins Blood Syndicate	1.50
❑3, Jun 93, 1: MOM; A: Boogieman	1.50	❑12, Mar 94, 1: The Rat Congress	1.50
❑4, Jul 93, D: Tech-9	1.50	❑13, Apr 94, Infestation, Part 1, 1: The White Roaches	1.50
❑5, Aug 93, 1: Kwai; 1: John Wing; 1: Demon Fox	1.50	❑14, May 94, Infestation, Part 2	1.50
❑6, Sep 93	1.50	❑15, Jun 94, Infestation, Part 3	1.50
❑7, Oct 93, 1: Cornelia; 1: Edmund	1.50	❑16, Jul 94, Worlds Collide, Part 6, A: Superman	1.50
❑8, Nov 93, 1: Kwai	1.50	❑17, Aug 94, Worlds Collide, Part 13	1.75
		❑18, Sep 94	1.75

ORIG GOOD FINE N-MINT

- ❑19, Oct 94 .... 1.75
- ❑20, Nov 94, A: Shadow Cabinet 1.75
- ❑21, Dec 94 .... 1.75
- ❑22, Jan 95, Some Dissembly Required 1.75
- ❑23, Feb 95 .... 1.75
- ❑24, Mar 95 .... 1.75
- ❑25, Apr 95, Giant-size; Tech-9 returns 2.95
- ❑26, May 95 .... 1.75
- ❑27, Jun 95 .... 1.75
- ❑28, Jul 95 .... 2.50
- ❑29, Aug 95, Long Hot Summer 0.99
- ❑30, Sep 95, The Long Hot Summer 2.50
- ❑31, Oct 95 .... 2.50
- ❑32, Nov 95 .... 2.50
- ❑33, Dec 95 .... 0.99
- ❑34, Jan 96 .... 2.50
- ❑35, Feb 96, The Beginning of the End, Final Issue 3.50

BLOODTHIRST: TERMINUS OPTION
ALPHA PRODUCTIONS

Value: Cover or less

- ❑1, Masquerade, b&w 3.50
- ❑2, Maelstrom 2.50

BLOODTHIRST: THE NIGHTFALL CONSPIRACY
ALPHA

Value: Cover or less

- ❑1 .... 2.50
- ❑2 .... 2.50

BLOODTHIRSTY PIRATE TALES
BLACK SWAN PRESS

Value: Cover or less

- ❑1 .... 2.50
- ❑2 .... 2.50
- ❑3 .... 2.50
- ❑4, Fal 96 .... 2.50
- ❑5, Spr 97, The Wrecking Annie; Pearl's Rekoning 2.50
- ❑6, Win 97 .... 2.50

BLOOD TIES
FULL MOON

Value: Cover or less

- ❑1, Genesis 2.25

BLOODWING
ETERNITY

Value: Cover or less

- ❑1, Jan 88 .... 1.95
- ❑2, Feb 88 .... 1.95
- ❑3, Mar 88 .... 1.95
- ❑4, Apr 88 .... 1.95
- ❑5, May 88 .... 1.95
- ❑6 .... 1.95

BLOODWULF
IMAGE

Value: Cover or less

- ❑1, Feb, DG, An Ill Wind Breaks, five different covers 2.50
- ❑2, Mar 95 .... 2.50
- ❑3, Apr 95 .... 2.50
- ❑4, May 95 .... 2.50
- ❑SS 1, Aug 95, A: Supreme, Giant-size 2.50

BLOODY BONES & BLACKEYED PEAS
GALAXY

Value: Cover or less

- ❑1 .... 1.00

BLOODYHOT
PARODY PRESS

	ORIG	GOOD	FINE	N-MINT
❑1	2.50	0.59	1.48	2.95

BLOODY MARY
DC

Value: Cover or less

- ❑1, Oct 96 .... 2.25
- ❑2, Nov 96 .... 2.25
- ❑3, Dec 96 .... 2.25
- ❑4, Jan, Final Issue 2.25

BLOODY MARY: LADY LIBERTY
DC

Value: Cover or less

- ❑1, Sep 97 .... 2.50
- ❑2, Oct 97 .... 2.50
- ❑3, Nov 97 .... 2.50
- ❑4, Dec 97 .... 2.50

BLUE
IMAGE

Value: Cover or less

- ❑1, Aug 99 .... 2.50
- ❑2, Apr 00 .... 2.50

BLUEBEARD
SLAVE LABOR

Value: Cover or less

- ❑1, Nov, JRo (w), b&w 2.95
- ❑2, Dec, JRo (w), b&w 2.95
- ❑3, Mar, JRo (w), b&w 2.95

BLUE BEETLE (DC)
DC

	ORIG	GOOD	FINE	N-MINT
❑1, Jun 86, Out from The Ashes, V: Firefist; O: Blue Beetle	0.75	0.30	0.75	1.50
❑2, Jul 86, This City's Not For Burning!, V: Firefist	0.75	0.20	0.50	1.00
❑3, Aug 86, V: Madmen	0.75	0.20	0.50	1.00
❑4, Sep 86, V: Doctor Alchemy	0.75	0.20	0.50	1.00
❑5, Oct 86, A: The Question	0.75	0.20	0.50	1.00
❑6, Nov 86, A: The Question	0.75	0.20	0.50	1.00
❑7, Dec 86, Gang War, D: Muse; A: The Question	0.75	0.20	0.50	1.00
❑8, Jan 87, V: Calculator	0.75	0.20	0.50	1.00
❑9, Feb, Legends	0.75	0.20	0.50	1.00
❑10, Mar, V: Chronos, Legends	0.75	0.20	0.50	1.00
❑11, Apr 87, A: Teen Titans	0.75	0.20	0.50	1.00
❑12, May 87, A: Teen Titans	0.75	0.20	0.50	1.00
❑13, Jun 87, A: Teen Titans	0.75	0.20	0.50	1.00
❑14, Jul 87	0.75	0.20	0.50	1.00
❑15, Aug 87	0.75	0.20	0.50	1.00
❑16, Sep 87	0.75	0.20	0.50	1.00
❑17, Oct 87	0.75	0.20	0.50	1.00
❑18, Nov 87	1.00	0.20	0.50	1.00
❑19, Dec 87	1.00	0.20	0.50	1.00
❑20, Jan 88, Millennium, Millennium	1.00	0.20	0.50	1.00
❑21, Feb 88, Millennium, Millennium	1.00	0.20	0.50	1.00
❑22, Mar 88	1.00	0.20	0.50	1.00
❑23, Apr 88	1.00	0.20	0.50	1.00
❑24, May 88, Final Issue	1.00	0.20	0.50	1.00

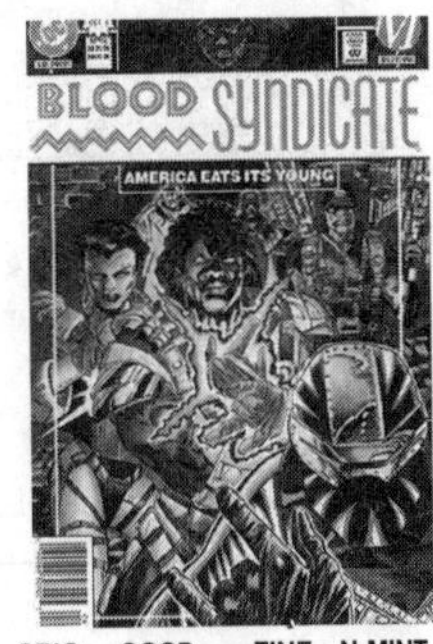

Members of The Blood Syndicate made an appearance in the four-issue *Static Shock: Rebirth of the Cool* mini-series.

© 1993 Milestone Media (DC)

BLUE BULLETEER, THE
AC

	ORIG	GOOD	FINE	N-MINT
❑1, Double Trouble For Lady Luger!, O: Blue Bulleteer, b&w	2.25	0.50	1.25	2.50

BLUE DEVIL
DC

	ORIG	GOOD	FINE	N-MINT
❑1, Jun 84, O: Blue Devil	0.75	0.30	0.75	1.50
❑2, Jul 84, V: Shockwave	0.75	0.20	0.50	1.00
❑3, Aug 84, V: Metallo	0.75	0.20	0.50	1.00
❑4, Sep 84, A: Zatanna	0.75	0.20	0.50	1.00
❑5, Oct 84, A: Zatanna	0.75	0.20	0.50	1.00
❑6, Nov 84, 1: Bolt	0.75	0.20	0.50	1.00
❑7, Dec 84, V: Trickster; V: Bolt	0.75	0.20	0.50	1.00
❑8, Jan 85, V: Trickster; V: Bolt	0.75	0.20	0.50	1.00
❑9, Feb 85, V: Trickster; V: Bolt	0.75	0.20	0.50	1.00
❑10, Mar 85	0.75	0.20	0.50	1.00
❑11, Apr 85	0.75	0.20	0.50	1.00
❑12, May 85, A: Demon	0.75	0.20	0.50	1.00
❑13, Jun 85, A: Zatanna; A: Green Lantern	0.75	0.20	0.50	1.00
❑14, Jul, 1: Kid Devil	0.75	0.20	0.50	1.00
❑15, Aug 85	0.75	0.20	0.50	1.00
❑16, Sep 85	0.75	0.20	0.50	1.00
❑17, Oct, Crisis on Infinite Earths, Crisis	0.75	0.20	0.50	1.00
❑18, Nov, Crisis on Infinite Earths, Crisis	0.75	0.20	0.50	1.00
❑19, Dec 85	0.75	0.20	0.50	1.00
❑20, Jan 86	0.75	0.20	0.50	1.00
❑21, Feb 86	0.75	0.20	0.50	1.00
❑22, Mar 86	0.75	0.20	0.50	1.00
❑23, Apr 86, A: Firestorm	0.75	0.20	0.50	1.00
❑24, May 86	0.75	0.20	0.50	1.00
❑25, Jun 86	0.75	0.20	0.50	1.00
❑26, Jul 86, V: Green Gargoyle	0.75	0.20	0.50	1.00
❑27, Aug 86	0.75	0.20	0.50	1.00
❑28, Sep 86	0.75	0.20	0.50	1.00
❑29, Oct 86	0.75	0.20	0.50	1.00
❑30, Nov 86, V: Flash's Rogues' Gallery, Double-size	1.25	0.25	0.63	1.25
❑31, Dec 86, Final Issue; Giant-size	1.25	0.25	0.63	1.25
❑Anl 1, Nov 85	1.25	0.25	0.63	1.25

BLUE HOLE
CHRISTINE SHIELDS

Value: Cover or less

- ❑1, Sworn to True; Adventures of the Kerosene Boy 2.95

BLUE LILY, THE
DARK HORSE

Value: Cover or less

- ❑1, Mar 93 .... 3.95
- ❑2 .... 3.95
- ❑3 .... 3.95
- ❑4 .... 3.95

BLUE LOCO
KITCHEN SINK

Value: Cover or less

- ❑1, cardstock cover 5.95

BLUE MOON
MU PRESS

Value: Cover or less

- ❑1, Sep 92 .... 2.50
- ❑2, Nov 92 .... 2.50
- ❑3, Feb 93 .... 2.50
- ❑4, May 93 .... 2.50
- ❑5, Dec 93 .... 2.50

BLUE MOON (VOL. 2)
AEON

Value: Cover or less

- ❑1, Aug 94, b&w 2.95

BLUE RIBBON COMICS (VOL. 2)
ARCHIE

	ORIG	GOOD	FINE	N-MINT
❑1, Nov 83, SD (c), The Strange New World of The Fly; The Fly Strikes, Red Circle publishes	1.50	0.50	1.25	2.50
❑2, Nov 83, AN, RB (c)	1.50	0.30	0.75	1.50
❑3, Dec 83	1.50	0.30	0.75	1.50

	ORIG	GOOD	FINE	N-MINT
❑4, Jan 84	1.00	0.30	0.75	1.50
❑5, Feb 84, A: Steel Sterling	0.75	0.30	0.75	1.50
❑6, Mar 84	0.75	0.30	0.75	1.50
❑7, Apr 84, RB (w), The Fox: Heads or Tales?; The Fox: Heads I Win, Tails You Lose!	0.75	0.30	0.75	1.50
❑8, May 84	0.75	0.30	0.75	1.50
❑9, Jun 84	0.75	0.30	0.75	1.50
❑10, Jul 84	0.75	0.30	0.75	1.50
❑11, Aug 84	0.75	0.30	0.75	1.50
❑12, Sep 84	0.75	0.30	0.75	1.50
❑13, Oct 84	0.75	0.30	0.75	1.50
❑14, Dec 84	0.75	0.30	0.75	1.50

B-MOVIE PRESENTS
B-Movie

	ORIG	GOOD	FINE	N-MINT
❑1, Captain Daring: Under a Black Venusian Sky; The World of X-Ray: Midnight Connection	1.50	0.34	0.85	1.70
❑2	1.50	0.34	0.85	1.70
❑3	1.50	0.34	0.85	1.70
❑4	1.50	0.34	0.85	1.70

BOARD OF SUPERHEROS
Not Available

Value: Cover or less

❑1, The Amazing Cynical Man Meets The Boss 0.50

BOBBY BENSON'S B-BAR-B RIDERS
AC

Value: Cover or less

❑1 .... 2.75

BOBBY RUCKERS
Art

Value: Cover or less

❑1, The Falling Woman 2.95

BOB, THE GALACTIC BUM
DC

	ORIG	GOOD	FINE	N-MINT
❑1, Feb 95, And the Maggot Cried "Death"	1.95	0.40	1.00	2.00
❑2, Mar 95, The Piker	1.95	0.40	1.00	2.00
❑3, Apr 95	1.95	0.40	1.00	2.00
❑4, Jun 95	1.95	0.40	1.00	2.00

BOB MARLEY, TALE OF THE TUFF GONG
Marvel

Value: Cover or less

❑1, GC, Iron; Dread-I-Story 5.95
❑2, GC 5.95
❑3, GC 5.95

"BOB'S" FAVORITE COMICS
Rip Off

Value: Cover or less

❑1-2, Car Dog Meets PeeBear; He might be a Subgenius, b&w; adult; 2nd Printing 2.50

BOB STEELE WESTERN
AC

Value: Cover or less

❑1, b&w; Reprint 2.75

BODY BAGS
Dark Horse

	ORIG	GOOD	FINE	N-MINT
❑1, Sep 96, Father's Day, Part 1	2.95	1.00	2.50	5.00
❑2, Oct 96, Father's Day, Part 2	2.95	1.20	3.00	6.00
❑3, Nov 96, Father's Day, Part 3	2.95	0.80	2.00	4.00
❑4, Jan 97, Father's Day, Part 4	2.95	0.70	1.75	3.50
❑Ash 1	—	0.60	1.50	3.00

BODY COUNT (AIRCEL)
Aircel

Value: Cover or less

❑1, Co-Ed Killers 2.25
❑2 .... 2.25
❑3 .... 2.25
❑4 .... 2.25

BODYCOUNT (IMAGE)
Image

Value: Cover or less

❑1, Mar 96 .... 2.50
❑2, Apr 96 .... 2.50
❑3, May 96 .... 2.50
❑4, Jul, Final Issue 2.50

BODY COUNT (MARVEL UK)
Marvel

	ORIG	GOOD	FINE	N-MINT
❑1, Oct 93, Free Previews of Marvel UK Creators	—	0.20	0.50	1.00

BODY DOUBLES
DC

Value: Cover or less

❑1, Oct 99, Girl Power!, A: Mystress 2.50
❑2, Nov 99 .... 2.50
❑3, Dec 99, Cold Snap 2.50
❑4, Jan 00 .... 2.50

BODY DOUBLES (VILLAINS)
DC

	ORIG	GOOD	FINE	N-MINT
❑1, Feb 98, New Year's Evil	1.95	0.40	1.00	2.00

BODYGUARD
Aircel

Value: Cover or less

❑1, Sep 90, PG (c), Boots 'n All; Stick Shift, b&w; adult; intro by Todd McFarlane 2.50
❑2, Oct 90, PG (c), Writer's Block; Clarry's Mum's Lamington Recipe, b&w; adult 2.50
❑3, Nov 90, b&w; adult 2.50

BODY PAINT
Eros

Value: Cover or less

❑1 .... 2.95
❑2, Jun 95 .... 2.95

BODY SWAP, THE
Roger Mason

	ORIG	GOOD	FINE	N-MINT
❑1	—	0.59	1.48	2.95

BOFFO IN HELL
Neatly Chiseled Features

Value: Cover or less

❑1, What Color is the Sky in Your World? 2.50

BOFFO LAFFS
Paragraphics

Value: Cover or less

❑1, first hologram cover 2.50
❑2 .... 1.95
❑3 .... 1.95
❑4 .... 1.95
❑5 .... 1.95

BOGIE MAN, THE
Fat Man

	ORIG	GOOD	FINE	N-MINT
❑1, Farewell, My Looney	1.95	0.50	1.25	2.50
❑2, The Treasure of The Ford Sierra	1.95	0.50	1.25	2.50
❑3, To Huv and Huvnae	1.95	0.50	1.25	2.50
❑4	1.95	0.50	1.25	2.50

BOGIE MAN, THE: CHINATOON
Atomeka

Value: Cover or less

❑1, Barefoot in the Pork 2.95
❑2 .... 2.95
❑3 .... 2.95
❑4 .... 2.95

BOGIE MAN: THE MANHATTAN PROJECT
Tundra

Value: Cover or less

❑1, nn 4.95

BOG SWAMP DEMON
Hall of Heroes

Value: Cover or less

❑1, Aug 96, Deliverance 2.50
❑2, Oct 96, no indicia 2.50
❑3, Dec 96 .... 2.50
❑4, Mar 97 .... 2.50

BOHOS
Image

Value: Cover or less

❑1, May, cover says Jun, indicia says May 2.95
❑2 .... 2.95
❑3, no month of publication 2.95

BO JACKSON VS. MICHAEL JORDAN
Celebrity

Value: Cover or less

❑1 .... 2.95
❑2 .... 2.95

BOLD ADVENTURE
Pacific

	ORIG	GOOD	FINE	N-MINT
❑1, Time Force	1.25	0.40	1.00	2.00
❑2	1.50	0.40	1.00	2.00
❑3, Final Issue	1.50	0.40	1.00	2.00

BOLT AND STARFORCE SIX
AC

Value: Cover or less

❑1, Jul 84 .... 1.75

BOLT SPECIAL
AC

	ORIG	GOOD	FINE	N-MINT
❑1	1.50	0.40	1.00	2.00

BOMARC
Nightwynd

Value: Cover or less

❑1 .... 2.50
❑2 .... 2.50
❑3 .... 2.50

BOMBA
DC

	ORIG	GOOD	FINE	N-MINT
❑1, Nightmare!, 1: Bomba	0.12	4.00	10.00	20.00
❑2	0.12	2.00	5.00	10.00
❑3	0.12	2.00	5.00	10.00
❑4	0.12	2.00	5.00	10.00
❑5	0.12	2.00	5.00	10.00
❑6	0.12	2.00	5.00	10.00
❑7, Final Issue	0.12	2.00	5.00	10.00

BOMBAST
Topps

Value: Cover or less

❑1, Apr 93, JSe, JK (c), Bombast Lives, trading card; Savage Dragon 2.95

BOMBASTIC
Screaming Dodo

Value: Cover or less

❑1, Nov 96, What's Up? 2.50
❑2, Feb 97 .... 2.50
❑3, May 97 .... 2.50
❑4, Aug 97 .... 2.50
❑5, Dec 97, cardstock cover 2.50

BONANZA
Gold Key

	ORIG	GOOD	FINE	N-MINT
❑1, A: Series continued from	0.12	22.00	55.00	110.00
❑2	0.12	15.00	37.50	75.00
❑3	0.12	10.00	25.00	50.00
❑4	0.12	10.00	25.00	50.00
❑5	0.12	10.00	25.00	50.00
❑6	0.12	6.00	15.00	30.00
❑7	0.12	6.00	15.00	30.00

	ORIG	GOOD	FINE	N-MINT
❑8	0.12	6.00	15.00	30.00
❑9	0.12	6.00	15.00	30.00
❑10	0.12	6.00	15.00	30.00
❑11	0.12	4.00	10.00	20.00
❑12	0.12	4.00	10.00	20.00
❑13	0.12	4.00	10.00	20.00
❑14	0.12	4.00	10.00	20.00
❑15	0.12	4.00	10.00	20.00
❑16	0.12	4.00	10.00	20.00
❑17	0.12	4.00	10.00	20.00
❑18, Feb 66, Strange Cargo; Dead Set on Winning	0.12	4.00	10.00	20.00
❑19	0.12	4.00	10.00	20.00
❑20	0.12	4.00	10.00	20.00
❑21	0.12	3.00	7.50	15.00
❑22	0.12	3.00	7.50	15.00
❑23	0.12	3.00	7.50	15.00
❑24	0.12	3.00	7.50	15.00
❑25, The Fugitive; Desert Salvage, reprints	0.12	3.00	7.50	15.00
❑26	—	3.00	7.50	15.00
❑27	—	3.00	7.50	15.00
❑28	—	3.00	7.50	15.00
❑29	—	3.00	7.50	15.00
❑30	—	3.00	7.50	15.00
❑31	—	2.00	5.00	10.00
❑32	—	2.00	5.00	10.00
❑33	—	2.00	5.00	10.00
❑34	—	2.00	5.00	10.00
❑35	—	2.00	5.00	10.00
❑36	—	2.00	5.00	10.00
❑37, Final Issue	—	2.00	5.00	10.00

BONDAGE CONFESSIONS
EROS

Value: Cover or less

❑1	2.95	❑3	2.95
❑2	2.95	❑4, Nov 98	2.95

BONDAGE FAIRIES
ANTARCTIC

	ORIG	GOOD	FINE	N-MINT
❑1, Mar 94	2.95	1.00	2.50	5.00
❑1-2, May 94, 2nd Printing	2.95	0.59	1.48	2.95
❑, Aug 94, 3rd Printing	2.95	0.59	1.48	2.95
❑1-4, Jan 95, 4th Printing	2.95	0.59	1.48	2.95
❑2, Apr 94	2.95	0.80	2.00	4.00
❑2-2, Jun 94, 2nd Printing	2.95	0.59	1.48	2.95
❑2-3, Oct 94, 3rd Printing	2.95	0.59	1.48	2.95
❑2-4, Apr 95, 4th Printing	2.95	0.59	1.48	2.95
❑3, May 94	2.95	0.65	1.63	3.25
❑3-2, Sep 94, 2nd Printing	2.95	0.59	1.48	2.95
❑3-3, Dec 94, 3rd Printing	2.95	0.59	1.48	2.95
❑4, Jun 94	2.95	0.65	1.63	3.25
❑4-2, Nov 94, 2nd Printing	2.95	0.59	1.48	2.95
❑4-3, Jan 95, 3rd Printing	2.95	0.59	1.48	2.95
❑5, Jul 94	2.95	0.65	1.63	3.25
❑5-2, Nov 94, 2nd Printing	2.95	0.59	1.48	2.95
❑5-3, Feb 95, 3rd Printing	2.95	0.59	1.48	2.95
❑6, Aug 94	2.95	0.59	1.48	2.95
❑6-2, Feb 95, 2nd Printing	2.95	0.59	1.48	2.95

BONDAGE FAIRIES EXTREME
EROS

Value: Cover or less	❑1, Oct 99	3.50

BONDAGE GIRLS AT WAR
EROS

Value: Cover or less

❑1	2.95	❑4	2.95
❑2	2.95	❑5, Feb 97	2.95
❑3	2.95		

BONE
CARTOON BOOKS

	ORIG	GOOD	FINE	N-MINT
❑1, Jul 91, 1: Fone Bone; 1: Smiley Bone; 1: Phoney Bone, 3000 printed	2.95	23.00	57.50	115.00
❑1-2, 1: Fone Bone; 1: Phoney Bone, 2nd Printing	2.95	2.00	5.00	10.00
❑, 1: Fone Bone; 1: Phoney Bone, 3rd Printing	2.95	0.60	1.50	3.00
❑1-4, 1: Fone Bone; 1: Phoney Bone, 4th Printing	2.95	0.60	1.50	3.00
❑1-5, 1: Fone Bone; 1: Phoney Bone, 5th Printing; fifth printing	2.95	0.60	1.50	3.00
❑1-6, 1: Fone Bone; 1: Phoney Bone, 6th Printing; sixth printing	2.95	0.60	1.50	3.00
❑1-7, 1: Fone Bone; 1: Phoney Bone, 7th Printing; seventh printing	2.95	0.60	1.50	3.00
❑1-8, 1: Fone Bone; 1: Phoney Bone, 8th Printing; eighth printing	2.95	0.60	1.50	3.00
❑1-9, Jan, 1: Fone Bone; 1: Phoney Bone, 9th Printing; Image reprint	2.95	0.60	1.50	3.00

Jeff Smith's *Bone* celebrated its 10th anniversary in 2001 with a reprint of the first issue accompanied by a PVC figure.

© 1991 Jeff Smith (Cartoon Books)

	ORIG	GOOD	FINE	N-MINT
❑2, Sep 91, 1: Thorn	2.95	12.00	30.00	60.00
❑2-2, 1: Thorn, 2nd Printing	2.95	1.60	4.00	8.00
❑2-3, 1: Thorn, 3rd Printing	2.95	0.60	1.50	3.00
❑2-4, 1: Thorn, 4th Printing	2.95	0.60	1.50	3.00
❑2-5, 1: Thorn, 5th Printing; fifth printing	2.95	0.60	1.50	3.00
❑2-6, 1: Thorn, 6th Printing; sixth printing	2.95	0.60	1.50	3.00
❑2-7, 1: Thorn, 7th Printing; seventh printing	2.95	0.60	1.50	3.00
❑2-8, Feb, Image reprint	2.95	0.60	1.50	3.00
❑3, Dec 91	2.95	7.00	17.50	35.00
❑3-2, 2nd Printing	2.95	1.00	2.50	5.00
❑3-3, 3rd Printing	2.95	0.60	1.50	3.00
❑3-4, 4th Printing	2.95	0.60	1.50	3.00
❑3-5, 5th Printing; fifth printing	2.95	0.60	1.50	3.00
❑3-6, 6th Printing; sixth printing	2.95	0.60	1.50	3.00
❑3-7, 7th Printing; seventh printing	2.95	0.60	1.50	3.00
❑3-8, Mar, Image reprint	2.95	0.60	1.50	3.00
❑4, Mar 92	2.95	5.00	12.50	25.00
❑4-2, 2nd Printing	2.95	0.80	2.00	4.00
❑4-3, Apr, 3rd Printing; Image reprint	2.95	0.60	1.50	3.00
❑4-4, 4th Printing	2.95	0.60	1.50	3.00
❑4-5, 5th Printing	2.95	0.60	1.50	3.00
❑4-6, 6th Printing	2.95	0.60	1.50	3.00
❑5, Jun 92	2.95	4.00	10.00	20.00
❑5-2, May, 2nd Printing; Image reprint	2.95	0.80	2.00	4.00
❑5-3, Jun, 3rd Printing; Image reprint	2.95	0.60	1.50	3.00
❑5-4, 4th Printing	2.95	0.60	1.50	3.00
❑5-5, 5th Printing	2.95	0.60	1.50	3.00
❑5-6, 6th Printing	2.95	0.60	1.50	3.00
❑5-7, 7th Printing	2.95	0.60	1.50	3.00
❑6, Nov 92	2.95	2.40	6.00	12.00
❑6-2, 2nd Printing	2.95	0.80	2.00	4.00
❑6-3, Jul, 3rd Printing; Image reprint	2.95	0.60	1.50	3.00
❑6-4, 4th Printing	2.95	0.60	1.50	3.00
❑6-5, 5th Printing	2.95	0.60	1.50	3.00
❑6-6, 6th Printing	2.95	0.60	1.50	3.00
❑7, Dec 92	2.95	2.40	6.00	12.00
❑7-2, 2nd Printing	2.95	0.60	1.50	3.00
❑7-3, Aug, 3rd Printing; Image reprint	2.95	0.60	1.50	3.00
❑7-4, 4th Printing	2.95	0.60	1.50	3.00
❑7-5, 5th Printing	2.95	0.60	1.50	3.00
❑8, Feb 93, The Great Cow Race, Part 1, Eisner award-winning story (1994)	2.95	2.00	5.00	10.00
❑8-2, The Great Cow Race, Part 1, 2nd Printing; Eisner award-winning story (1994)	2.95	0.60	1.50	3.00
❑8-3, The Great Cow Race, Part 1, 3rd Printing; Eisner award-winning story (1994)	2.95	0.60	1.50	3.00
❑8-4, The Great Cow Race, Part 1, 4th Printing; Eisner award-winning story (1994)	2.95	0.60	1.50	3.00
❑8-5, The Great Cow Race, Part 1, 5th Printing; fifth printing; Eisner award-winning story (1994)	2.95	0.60	1.50	3.00
❑8-6, The Great Cow Race, Part 1, 6th Printing; sixth printing; Eisner award-winning story (1994)	2.95	0.60	1.50	3.00
❑8-7, Sep, Image reprint	2.95	0.60	1.50	3.00
❑9, Jul 93, The Great Cow Race, Part 2, Eisner award-winning story (1994)	2.95	1.00	2.50	5.00
❑9-2, The Great Cow Race, Part 2, 2nd Printing; Eisner award-winning story (1994)	2.95	0.60	1.50	3.00
❑9-3, Oct, The Great Cow Race, Part 2, 3rd Printing; Image reprint; Eisner award-winning story (1994)	2.95	0.60	1.50	3.00
❑9-4, The Great Cow Race, Part 2, 4th Printing; Eisner award-winning story (1994)	2.95	0.60	1.50	3.00
❑10, Sep 93, The Great Cow Race, Part 3, Eisner award-winning story (1994)	2.95	0.80	2.00	4.00
❑10-2, The Great Cow Race, Part 3, 2nd Printing; Eisner award-winning story (1994)	2.95	0.60	1.50	3.00
❑10-3, Oct, The Great Cow Race, Part 3, 3rd Printing; Image reprint; Eisner award-winning story (1994)	2.95	0.60	1.50	3.00
❑11, Dec 93	2.95	0.80	2.00	4.00
❑11-2, Nov, 2nd Printing; Image reprint	2.95	0.60	1.50	3.00

	ORIG	GOOD	FINE	N-MINT
❑12, Feb 94	2.95	0.80	2.00	4.00
❑12-2, Dec, 2nd Printing; Image reprint	2.95	0.60	1.50	3.00
❑12-3, 3rd Printing	2.95	0.60	1.50	3.00
❑13, Mar 94	2.95	0.80	2.00	4.00
❑13-2, Jan, Image reprint	2.95	0.60	1.50	3.00
❑13.5, Wizard promotional edition	—	1.00	2.50	5.00
❑13.5/GO, Gold edition	—	1.00	2.50	5.00
❑14, May 94	2.95	0.60	1.50	3.00
❑14-2, Feb, Image reprint	2.95	0.60	1.50	3.00
❑15, Aug 94	2.95	0.60	1.50	3.00
❑15-2, Mar, Image reprint	2.95	0.60	1.50	3.00
❑16, Oct 94	2.95	0.60	1.50	3.00
❑16-2, Apr, Image reprint	2.95	0.59	1.48	2.95
❑17, Jan 95	2.95	0.59	1.48	2.95
❑17-2, May, Image reprint	2.95	0.59	1.48	2.95
❑18, Apr 95	2.95	0.59	1.48	2.95
❑18-2, Jun, Image reprint	2.95	0.59	1.48	2.95
❑19, Jun 95	2.95	0.59	1.48	2.95
❑19-2, Jul, Image reprint	2.95	0.59	1.48	2.95
❑20, Oct 95, moves to Image	2.95	0.59	1.48	2.95
❑20-2, Aug, Image reprint	2.95	0.59	1.48	2.95
❑21, Dec 95, Image begins as publisher	2.95	0.59	1.48	2.95
❑22, Feb 96	2.95	0.59	1.48	2.95
❑23, May 96, 1: Baby Rat Creature	2.95	0.59	1.48	2.95
❑24, Jun 96	2.95	0.59	1.48	2.95
❑25, Aug 96	2.95	0.59	1.48	2.95
❑26, Dec 96	2.95	0.59	1.48	2.95
❑27, Apr 97, Phoney captures Red Dragon; series returns to Cartoon Books	2.95	0.59	1.48	2.95
❑28, Aug 97, Cartoon Books begins as publisher	2.95	0.59	1.48	2.95
❑29, Nov 97	2.95	0.59	1.48	2.95
❑30, Jan 98	2.95	0.59	1.48	2.95
❑31, Apr 98	2.95	0.59	1.48	2.95
❑32, Jun 98	2.95	0.59	1.48	2.95
❑33, Aug 98	2.95	0.59	1.48	2.95
❑34, Dec 98	2.95	0.59	1.48	2.95
❑35, Mar 99	2.95	0.59	1.48	2.95
❑36, May 99	2.95	0.59	1.48	2.95
❑37, Aug 99, cover says Sep, indicia says Aug	2.95	0.59	1.48	2.95
❑38/A, Aug 00, Endgame	4.95	0.59	1.48	2.95
❑38/B, Aug 00, FM (c), Endgame, alternate cover	4.95	0.59	1.48	2.95
❑38/C, Aug 00, ARo (c), Endgame, alternate cover	4.95	0.59	1.48	2.95
❑39, Oct 00, Ghost Circles	2.95	0.59	1.48	2.95
❑40, Jan 01	2.95	0.59	1.48	2.95
❑41, Mar 01, The Dusty Trail to Atheia	2.95	0.59	1.48	2.95
❑42	2.95	0.59	1.48	2.95
❑43	2.95	0.59	1.48	2.95
❑44	2.95	0.59	1.48	2.95
❑SE 1, Special edition	2.00	0.40	1.00	2.00

BONES
MALIBU

Value: Cover or less

❑1 ... 1.95
❑2 ... 1.95
❑3 ... 1.95
❑4, Nov 87 ... 1.95

BONE SAW
TUNDRA

Value: Cover or less

❑1, b&w; adult ... 14.95

BONESHAKER
CALIBER

Value: Cover or less

❑1 ... 3.50

BONE SOURCEBOOK
IMAGE

Value: Cover or less

❑1/A, Nov 95, b&w; no cover price; promotional handout ... 2.00
❑1/B, Nov 95, San Diego Comic-Con edition ... 2.00

BONEYARD PRESS 1993 TOURBOOK
BONEYARD

Value: Cover or less

❑1, Distributor giveaway previewing Boneyard Press books .. 1.50

BONGO SPECIAL EDITION
BONGO

Value: Cover or less

❑1, hardcover collection of Simpsons #1, Bartman #1, Itchy&Scratchy #1, Radioactive Man #1 (1000 copies) ... 20.00

BOOF (ICONOGRAFIX)
ICONOGRAFIX

Value: Cover or less

❑1, b&w ... 2.50

BOOF (IMAGE)
IMAGE

Value: Cover or less

❑1, Jul 94, Boof's N' The Hood; The Buddy System, 1: Boof ... 1.95
❑1/A, Jul 94, Boof's N' The Hood; The Buddy System, 1: Boof, alternate cover ... 1.95
❑2, Aug 94 ... 1.95
❑2/A, Aug 94, alternate cover . 1.95
❑3, Sep 94, Drivin' This Crazy; Chained Heat ... 1.95
❑3/A, Sep 94, Drivin' This Crazy; Chained Heat, alternate cover 1.95
❑4, Oct 94 ... 1.95
❑5, Nov 94 ... 1.95
❑6, Dec 94 ... 1.95

BOOF AND THE BRUISE CREW
IMAGE

Value: Cover or less

❑1, Jul 94 ... 1.95
❑1/A, Jul 94, alternate cover ... 1.95
❑2, Aug 94 ... 1.95
❑2/A, Aug 94, alternate cover . 1.95
❑3, Sep 94, Shock Treatment; Model Me Beautiful ... 1.95
❑3/A, Sep 94, Shock Treatment; Model Me Beautiful, alternate cover ... 1.95
❑4, Oct 94 ... 1.95
❑5, Nov 94 ... 1.95
❑6, Dec 94 ... 1.95

BOOGEYMAN (SERGIO ARAGONÉS'...)
DARK HORSE

Value: Cover or less

❑1, Jun 98, SA, ME (w), The Dictator ... 2.95
❑2, Jul 98, SA, ME (w), The Great Prime Evil Forest; The Ship of Fear ... 2.95
❑3, Aug 98, SA, ME (w), The Unknown Man of Magic!; A Monster in the Barn! ... 2.95
❑4, Sep 98, SA, ME (w), The Great Conquistador; The Dare ... 2.95

BOOGIEMAN, THE
RION

Value: Cover or less

❑1, The Boogieman; Pumpkin Head, b&w ... 1.50

BOOK
DREAMSMITH STUDIOS

Value: Cover or less

❑1, May 98, b&w; Anthology ... 3.50

BOOK OF ANGELS
CALIBER

Value: Cover or less

❑1, nn; b&w; cardstock cover .. 3.95

BOOK OF ANTS
ARTISAN

Value: Cover or less

❑1 ... 2.95

BOOK OF BALLADS AND SAGAS, THE
GREEN MAN PRESS

	ORIG	GOOD	FINE	N-MINT
❑1, b&w	2.95	0.59	1.48	2.95
❑2, b&w	2.95	0.59	1.48	2.95
❑3, Jun 96, b&w	3.50	0.70	1.75	3.50
❑4, b&w	3.25	0.70	1.75	3.50

BOOK OF FATE, THE
DC

Value: Cover or less

❑1, Feb 97, KG (w), Lament, O: Jared Stevens; O: Fate ... 2.25
❑2, Mar 97, KG (w), Carnal Beckoning, A: Sentinel ... 2.25
❑3, Apr 97, KG (w), Caught in the Crossfire! ... 2.25
❑4, May 97, V: Two-Face ... 2.25
❑5, Jun 97 ... 2.25
❑6, Jul 97, Convergence, Part 1, continues in Night Force #8 2.25
❑7, Aug 97, V: Rats ... 2.25
❑8, Sep 97 ... 2.25
❑9, Oct 97 ... 2.25
❑10, Nov 97 ... 2.25
❑11, Dec 97, KG (w), The Perception of Doors, Face cover ... 2.25
❑12, Jan, KG, KG (w), One Man's Fate, A: Lobo, Final Issue; final issue, A: Lobo ... 2.50

BOOK OF NIGHT, THE
DARK HORSE

	ORIG	GOOD	FINE	N-MINT
❑1, Jul 87, CV, CV (w)	1.50	0.50	1.25	2.50
❑2, Aug 87, CV, CV (w)	1.50	0.40	1.00	2.00
❑3, Sep 87, CV, CV (w)	1.75	0.40	1.00	2.00

BOOK OF SPELLS
DOUBLE EDGE

Value: Cover or less

❑1 ... 2.00
❑2, Sep 94, The Crook ... 2.00
❑3 ... 2.00
❑4 ... 2.00

BOOK OF THE DAMNED: A HELLRAISER COMPANION (CLIVE BARKER'S...)
MARVEL

Value: Cover or less

❑1 ... 4.95
❑2 ... 4.95
❑3, Journale ... 4.95
❑4 ... 4.95

BOOK OF THE DEAD
MARVEL

	ORIG	GOOD	FINE	N-MINT
❑1, Dec 93, MP, Frankenstein!	1.75	0.40	1.00	2.00
❑2, Jan 94	1.75	0.40	1.00	2.00
❑3, Feb 94	1.75	0.40	1.00	2.00
❑4, Mar 94, MP, Dance To The Murder	1.75	0.40	1.00	2.00

BOOK OF THE TAROT
CALIBER

Value: Cover or less

❑1, nn; b&w ... 3.95

BOOK OF THOTH, THE
CIRCLE STUDIOS

Value: Cover or less

❑1, Jun 95 ... 2.50

BOOKS OF FAERIE, THE
DC

Value: Cover or less

❑1, Mar 97, The Foundling's Tale, A: Titania; A: Auberon; A: Timothy Hunter ... 2.50
❑2, Apr 97, The Widow's Tale . 2.50
❑3, May 97 ... 2.50

BOOKS OF FAERIE, THE: AUBERON'S TALE
DC

Value: Cover or less

- ❑1, Aug 98, The Regicide....... 2.50
- ❑2, Sep 98, The Pretender..... 2.50
- ❑3, Oct 98, The Usurper......... 2.50

BOOKS OF FAERIE, THE: MOLLY'S STORY
DC

Value: Cover or less

- ❑1, Sep 99, Twilight................ 2.50
- ❑2, Oct 99, Iron and Thorn..... 2.50
- ❑3, Nov 99............................. 2.50
- ❑4, Dec 99, The Importance of Being Evil........................... 2.50

BOOKS OF LORE: SPECIAL EDITION
PEREGRINE ENTERTAINMENT

Value: Cover or less

- ❑1, Sep, cardstock cover, b&w 2.95
- ❑1/LE, Jan, Collector's Edition, bagged with poster and limited and regular editions of #1.... 12.95
- ❑2, Nov 97............................. 2.95

BOOKS OF LORE: STORYTELLER
PEREGRINE ENTERTAINMENT

Value: Cover or less

- ❑1.. 2.95

BOOKS OF LORE: THE KAYNIN GAMBIT
PEREGRINE ENTERTAINMENT

Value: Cover or less

- ❑0, Dec 98............................. 2.95
- ❑1, Nov 98............................. 2.95
- ❑1/SC, Nov 98, alternate cover 2.95
- ❑2, Jan 99............................. 2.95
- ❑3, Mar 99............................. 2.95
- ❑Ash 1, Jul 98, b&w preview of Books Of Lore: The Kaynin Gambit................................ 5.00

The DC universe's magician Timothy Hunter was introduced in the four-issue *Books of Magic* mini-series.

© 1990 DC Comics

BOOKS OF MAGIC, THE
DC

	ORIG	GOOD	FINE	N-MINT
❑1, May 94, Bindings, Part 1	1.95	1.00	2.50	5.00
❑1/SI, May 94, Bindings, Part 1, no cover price; Silver (limited promotional) edition.	1.95	1.60	4.00	8.00
❑2, Jun 94, Bindings, Part 2	1.95	0.80	2.00	4.00
❑3, Jul 94, Bindings, Part 3	1.95	0.80	2.00	4.00
❑4, Aug 94, Bindings, Part 4	1.95	0.80	2.00	4.00
❑5, Sep 94, The Hidden School	1.95	0.60	1.50	3.00
❑6, Oct 94, Sacrifices, Part 1	1.95	0.60	1.50	3.00
❑7, Nov 94, Sacrifices, Part 2	1.95	0.60	1.50	3.00
❑8, Dec 94, Sacrifices, Part 3	1.95	0.60	1.50	3.00
❑9, Jan 95, The Artificial Heart, Part 1	1.95	0.60	1.50	3.00
❑10, Feb 95, The Artificial Heart, Part 2	1.95	0.60	1.50	3.00
❑11, Mar 95, The Artificial Heart, Part 3	1.95	0.50	1.25	2.50
❑12, Apr 95, Small Glass Worlds, Part 1	1.95	0.50	1.25	2.50
❑13, May 95, Small Glass Worlds, Part 2	1.95	0.50	1.25	2.50
❑14, Jul 95, What Fire Leaves Us	2.50	0.50	1.25	2.50
❑15, Aug 95, Playgrounds, Part 1	2.50	0.50	1.25	2.50
❑16, Sep 95, Playgrounds, Part 2	2.50	0.50	1.25	2.50
❑17, Oct 95	2.50	0.50	1.25	2.50
❑18, Nov 95	2.50	0.50	1.25	2.50
❑19, Dec 95	2.50	0.50	1.25	2.50
❑20, Jan 96	2.50	0.50	1.25	2.50
❑21, Feb 96, Heavy Petting	2.50	0.50	1.25	2.50
❑22, Mar 96, Needlepoint	2.50	0.50	1.25	2.50
❑23, Apr 96, Red Rover, Red Rover	2.50	0.50	1.25	2.50
❑24, May 96	2.50	0.50	1.25	2.50
❑25, Jun 96, A: appearance	2.50	0.50	1.25	2.50
❑26, Jul 96, Rites of Passage	2.50	0.50	1.25	2.50
❑27, Aug 96, Rites of Passage; Rites of Passage, Part 1	2.50	0.50	1.25	2.50
❑28, Sep 96, Rites of Passage; Rites of Passage, Part 2	2.50	0.50	1.25	2.50
❑29, Oct 96, Rites of Passage; Rites of Passage, Part 3	2.50	0.50	1.25	2.50
❑30, Nov 96, Rites of Passage; Rites of Passage, Part 4	2.50	0.50	1.25	2.50
❑31, Dec 96, Rites of Passage; Rites of Passage, Part 5	2.50	0.50	1.25	2.50
❑32, Jan 97, Rites of Passage; Rites of Passage, Part 6	2.50	0.50	1.25	2.50
❑33, Feb 97, Rites of Passage; Rites of Passage, Part 7	2.50	0.50	1.25	2.50
❑34, Mar 97, Rites of Passage; Rites of Passage, Part 8	2.50	0.50	1.25	2.50
❑35, Apr 97, Rites of Passage; Rites of Passage, Part 9	2.50	0.50	1.25	2.50
❑36, May 97, Rites of Passage; Rites of Passage, Part 10	2.50	0.50	1.25	2.50
❑37, Jun 97, Rites of Passage; Rites of Passage, Part 11	2.50	0.50	1.25	2.50
❑38, Jul 97, Rites of Passage	2.50	0.50	1.25	2.50
❑39, Aug 97	2.50	0.50	1.25	2.50
❑40, Sep 97	2.50	0.50	1.25	2.50
❑41, Oct 97	2.50	0.50	1.25	2.50
❑42, Nov 97, The Bridge	2.50	0.50	1.25	2.50
❑43, Dec 97, King of This	2.50	0.50	1.25	2.50
❑44, Jan 98	2.50	0.50	1.25	2.50
❑45, Feb 98, Slave of Heavens, Part 1	2.50	0.50	1.25	2.50
❑46, Mar 98, Slave of Heavens, Part 2	2.50	0.50	1.25	2.50
❑47, Apr 98, Slave of Heavens, Part 3	2.50	0.50	1.25	2.50
❑48, May 98, Slave of Heavens, Part 4	2.50	0.50	1.25	2.50
❑49, Jun 98, Slave of Heavens Conclusion	2.50	0.50	1.25	2.50
❑50, Jul 98, preview of issue #51	2.50	0.50	1.25	2.50
❑51, Aug 98, A Thousand Worlds of Tim	2.50	0.50	1.25	2.50
❑52, Sep 98	2.50	0.50	1.25	2.50
❑53, Oct 98	2.50	0.50	1.25	2.50
❑54, Nov 98	2.50	0.50	1.25	2.50
❑55, Dec 98	2.50	0.50	1.25	2.50
❑56, Jan 99, A: Cain	2.50	0.50	1.25	2.50
❑57, Feb 99, Books of Faerie back-up	2.50	0.50	1.25	2.50
❑58, Mar 99, Books of Faerie: Auberon Finds a Friend, Books of Faerie back-up	2.50	0.50	1.25	2.50
❑59, Apr 99, Books of Faerie: The Kelpie's Love, Books of Faerie back-up	2.50	0.50	1.25	2.50
❑60, May 99, In Defense of his Country	2.50	0.50	1.25	2.50
❑61, Jun 99, All Things Timothy	2.50	0.50	1.25	2.50
❑62, Jul 99, Wrong Side of the Tracks, Books of Faerie back-up	2.50	0.50	1.25	2.50
❑63, Aug 99, The Good Fella	2.50	0.50	1.25	2.50
❑64, Sep 99, Heart of the Storm	2.50	0.50	1.25	2.50
❑65, Oct 99, The Arrangement	2.50	0.50	1.25	2.50
❑66, Nov 99, A Day A Night A Dream; A Day, a Night & a Dream, Part 1	2.50	0.50	1.25	2.50
❑67, Dec 99, A Day, a Night & a Dream, Part 2	2.50	0.50	1.25	2.50
❑68, Jan 00, Pentimento	2.50	0.50	1.25	2.50
❑69, Feb 00, Cauldrons & Kettles	2.50	0.50	1.25	2.50
❑70, Mar 00	2.50	0.50	1.25	2.50
❑71, Apr 00	2.50	0.50	1.25	2.50
❑72, May 00, The Lord of the Hunt	2.50	0.50	1.25	2.50
❑73, The Closing, Part 1	2.50	0.50	1.25	2.50
❑Anl 1, Feb 97, 1997 Annual	3.95	0.79	1.98	3.95
❑Anl 2, Feb 98, Horn, 1998 Annual	3.95	0.79	1.98	3.95
❑Anl 3, Jun 99, The Thousand Deaths of Timothy Hunter, 1999 Annual	3.95	0.79	1.98	3.95

BOOKS OF MAGIC, THE (MINI-SERIES)
DC

	ORIG	GOOD	FINE	N-MINT
❑1, Dec 90, NG (w), The Invisible Labyrinth, 1: Timothy Hunter	3.95	1.20	3.00	6.00
❑2, Jan 91, NG (w)	3.95	1.00	2.50	5.00
❑3, Feb 91, NG (w)	3.95	1.00	2.50	5.00
❑4, Mar 91, NG (w), The Road to Nowhere, Paul Johnson	3.95	1.00	2.50	5.00

BOOM BOOM
AEON

Value: Cover or less

- ❑1, b&w................................. 2.50
- ❑2, Sep 94, b&w...................... 2.50

BOONDOGGLE
KNIGHT PRESS

Value: Cover or less

- ❑1, Mar 95............................. 2.95
- ❑2.. 2.95
- ❑3, Nov 95............................. 2.95
- ❑4.. 2.95
- ❑SE 1, Nov 96, Here Today Gone Tomorrow, b&w.................... 2.95

BOOSTER GOLD
DC

	ORIG	GOOD	FINE	N-MINT
❑1, Feb, V: Blackguard; 1: Booster Gold	0.75	0.25	0.63	1.25
❑2, Mar, 1: Mindancer	0.75	0.20	0.50	1.00
❑3, Apr	0.75	0.20	0.50	1.00
❑4, May	0.75	0.20	0.50	1.00
❑5, Jun	0.75	0.20	0.50	1.00
❑6, Jul, A: Superman	0.75	0.20	0.50	1.00
❑7, Aug, A: Superman	0.75	0.20	0.50	1.00
❑8, Sep, A: Legion	0.75	0.20	0.50	1.00
❑9, Oct, A: Legion	0.75	0.20	0.50	1.00
❑10, Nov	0.75	0.20	0.50	1.00
❑11, Dec	0.75	0.20	0.50	1.00
❑12, Jan	0.75	0.20	0.50	1.00
❑13, Feb	0.75	0.20	0.50	1.00
❑14, Mar, back to future	0.75	0.20	0.50	1.00
❑15, Apr	0.75	0.20	0.50	1.00
❑16, May, 1: Booster Gold International	0.75	0.20	0.50	1.00
❑17, Jun, A: CheshireHawk	0.75	0.20	0.50	1.00
❑18, Jul	0.75	0.20	0.50	1.00

	ORIG	GOOD	FINE	N-MINT
❑19, Aug, V: Rainbow Raider	0.75	0.20	0.50	1.00
❑20, Sep, blind	0.75	0.20	0.50	1.00
❑21, Oct	0.75	0.20	0.50	1.00
❑22, Nov, A: Justice League International	1.00	0.20	0.50	1.00
❑23, Dec, A: Superman	1.00	0.20	0.50	1.00
❑24, Jan, Millennium, Millennium	1.00	0.20	0.50	1.00
❑25, Feb, Final Issue; Millennium; Millennium, final issue	1.00	0.20	0.50	1.00

BOOTS OF THE OPPRESSOR
NORTHSTAR

Value: Cover or less ❑1 ... 2.95

BORDERGUARD
ETERNITY

Value: Cover or less
❑1, Nov 87, Borderguard, Part 1 1.95
❑2, Dec 87, Borderguard, Part 2 1.95

BORDER WORLDS (VOL. 1)
KITCHEN SINK

	ORIG	GOOD	FINE	N-MINT
❑1, Jul 86, Living In A Space Suit, Reprinted from Megaton Man	1.95	0.40	1.00	2.00
❑2, Sep 86, Empress Of China	1.95	0.40	1.00	2.00
❑3, Nov 86, View From the Edge	1.95	0.40	1.00	2.00
❑4, Jan 87	1.95	0.40	1.00	2.00
❑5, Apr 87, Differing World Views	1.95	0.40	1.00	2.00
❑6, Jun 87	1.95	0.40	1.00	2.00
❑7, Aug 87, Final Issue; pages 4-5 transposed	2.00	0.40	1.00	2.00
❑7/A, Final Issue; Corrected edition; corrected	2.00	0.40	1.00	2.00

BORDER WORLDS (VOL. 2)
KITCHEN SINK

Value: Cover or less ❑1, Marooned, b&w; adult ... 2.00

BORIS' ADVENTURE MAGAZINE
NICOTAT

Value: Cover or less ❑1, Aug 88, b&w ... 2.00

BORIS KARLOFF TALES OF MYSTERY
GOLD KEY

	ORIG	GOOD	FINE	N-MINT
❑3	—	4.80	12.00	24.00
❑4	—	4.00	10.00	20.00
❑5, The Sorcerer's Potion; Possessed	0.12	4.00	10.00	20.00
❑6	0.12	4.00	10.00	20.00
❑7	0.12	3.60	9.00	18.00
❑8	0.12	3.60	9.00	18.00
❑9, WW	0.12	6.00	15.00	30.00
❑10	0.12	3.00	7.50	15.00
❑11	0.12	4.40	11.00	22.00
❑12, Dec 65, The Convention; The Dunce, back cover pin-up	0.12	3.00	7.50	15.00
❑13, The Five Casks of Greed; The Door of Doom!	0.12	2.40	6.00	12.00
❑14	0.12	2.40	6.00	12.00
❑15, Captives of the Camera; The Phantom Rescue (text story)	0.12	3.00	7.50	15.00
❑16	0.12	2.40	6.00	12.00
❑17	0.12	2.40	6.00	12.00
❑18	0.12	2.40	6.00	12.00
❑19	0.12	2.40	6.00	12.00
❑20, The Medium; Death and Napoleon's Marshal (text story)	0.12	2.40	6.00	12.00
❑21, JJ, Screaming Skull	—	3.60	9.00	18.00
❑22	—	2.00	5.00	10.00
❑23, Sep 68, Past and Present Danger; Burn, Witch, Burn, 10053-809	0.15	2.00	5.00	10.00
❑24	0.15	2.00	5.00	10.00
❑25, Mar 69, The Thing Called Illona; The Strangling Pearls (text story)	0.15	2.00	5.00	10.00
❑26, Jun 69	0.15	2.00	5.00	10.00
❑27, Sep 69, Fantasties of the Fog; The Horror in the Velvet Mask (text story)	0.15	2.00	5.00	10.00
❑28, Creature of the Swamp; Son of Satan (text story)	0.15	2.00	5.00	10.00
❑29	0.15	2.00	5.00	10.00
❑30, The Grotesque One; The Living Skeleton (text story)	0.15	2.00	5.00	10.00
❑31	0.15	1.70	4.25	8.50
❑32, Nov 70, The Eyes of the Monster; The Cobra God (text story)	0.15	1.70	4.25	8.50
❑33	—	1.70	4.25	8.50
❑34	—	1.70	4.25	8.50
❑35	—	1.70	4.25	8.50
❑36	—	1.70	4.25	8.50
❑37	—	1.70	4.25	8.50
❑38	—	1.70	4.25	8.50
❑39	—	1.70	4.25	8.50
❑40	—	1.70	4.25	8.50
❑41	—	1.50	3.75	7.50
❑42	—	1.50	3.75	7.50
❑43	—	1.50	3.75	7.50
❑44	—	1.50	3.75	7.50
❑45	—	1.50	3.75	7.50
❑46	—	1.50	3.75	7.50
❑47	—	1.50	3.75	7.50
❑48	—	1.50	3.75	7.50
❑49, Aug 73, Blind to Danger; Royal Madness (text story), 90053-308	0.20	1.50	3.75	7.50
❑50	0.20	1.50	3.75	7.50
❑51	0.20	1.20	3.00	6.00
❑52	0.20	1.20	3.00	6.00
❑53, Molten Fury; Tender Feelings	0.20	1.20	3.00	6.00
❑54	—	1.20	3.00	6.00
❑55	—	1.20	3.00	6.00
❑56	—	1.20	3.00	6.00
❑57	—	1.20	3.00	6.00
❑58	—	1.20	3.00	6.00
❑59	—	1.20	3.00	6.00
❑60	—	1.00	2.50	5.00
❑61	—	1.00	2.50	5.00
❑62	—	1.00	2.50	5.00
❑63	—	1.00	2.50	5.00
❑64	—	1.00	2.50	5.00
❑65, The Pharaoh's Zoo; No Thing is My Enemy	0.25	1.00	2.50	5.00
❑66	—	1.00	2.50	5.00
❑67	—	1.00	2.50	5.00
❑68	—	1.00	2.50	5.00
❑69	—	1.00	2.50	5.00
❑70	—	1.00	2.50	5.00
❑71	—	1.00	2.50	5.00
❑72	—	1.00	2.50	5.00
❑73	—	1.00	2.50	5.00
❑74	—	1.00	2.50	5.00
❑75	—	0.60	1.50	3.00
❑76	—	0.60	1.50	3.00
❑77	—	0.60	1.50	3.00
❑78	—	0.60	1.50	3.00
❑79	—	0.60	1.50	3.00
❑80	—	0.60	1.50	3.00
❑81	—	0.60	1.50	3.00
❑82	—	0.60	1.50	3.00
❑83	—	0.60	1.50	3.00
❑84	—	0.60	1.50	3.00
❑85	—	0.60	1.50	3.00
❑86	—	0.60	1.50	3.00
❑87	—	0.60	1.50	3.00
❑88	—	0.60	1.50	3.00
❑89	—	0.60	1.50	3.00
❑90	—	0.60	1.50	3.00
❑91	—	0.60	1.50	3.00
❑92	—	0.60	1.50	3.00
❑93	—	0.60	1.50	3.00
❑94	—	0.60	1.50	3.00
❑95	—	0.60	1.50	3.00
❑96	—	0.60	1.50	3.00
❑97, Final Issue	—	0.60	1.50	3.00

BORIS THE BEAR
DARK HORSE

	ORIG	GOOD	FINE	N-MINT
❑1, Boris The Bear Slaughters The Teenage Radioactive Black Belt Mutant Ninja Critters, b&w	1.50	0.60	1.50	3.00
❑1-2, b&w; 2nd Printing	1.50	0.35	0.88	1.75
❑2, b&w	1.50	0.45	1.13	2.25
❑3, The Secret Hero Of The Super Wars, b&w	1.50	0.50	1.25	2.50
❑4, b&w; two different covers	1.50	0.50	1.25	2.50
❑5, b&w	1.50	0.50	1.25	2.50
❑6, b&w	1.50	0.50	1.25	2.50
❑7, b&w	1.50	0.45	1.13	2.25
❑8, The Return Of The Living Teenage Radioactive Mutant Ninja Critters, b&w	1.50	0.45	1.13	2.25
❑9, b&w	1.50	0.45	1.13	2.25
❑10, May 87, b&w	1.50	0.45	1.13	2.25
❑11, Jun 87, b&w	1.50	0.45	1.13	2.25
❑12, Jul 87, b&w	1.75	0.45	1.13	2.25
❑13, Nov 87, b&w	1.50	0.45	1.13	2.25
❑14, Dec 87, b&w	1.50	0.45	1.13	2.25
❑15, b&w	1.50	0.45	1.13	2.25
❑16, Mar 88, b&w	1.50	0.45	1.13	2.25
❑17, b&w	1.50	0.45	1.13	2.25
❑18, b&w	1.50	0.45	1.13	2.25
❑19, Sep 88, b&w	1.75	0.45	1.13	2.25
❑20, Nov 88, b&w	1.75	0.45	1.13	2.25
❑21, b&w	1.75	0.40	1.00	2.00
❑22, Apr 89, b&w	1.95	0.40	1.00	2.00
❑23, May 89, b&w	1.95	0.40	1.00	2.00
❑24, Jul 89, b&w	1.95	0.40	1.00	2.00

	ORIG	GOOD	FINE	N-MINT
❑25, b&w	1.95	0.40	1.00	2.00
❑26, Jul 90, b&w	1.95	0.40	1.00	2.00
❑27, Oct 90, b&w	1.95	0.40	1.00	2.00
❑28, b&w	1.95	0.40	1.00	2.00
❑29, Jan 91, b&w	1.95	0.40	1.00	2.00
❑30, Apr 91, b&w	2.50	0.50	1.25	2.50
❑31, Jun 91, b&w	2.25	0.50	1.25	2.50
❑32, Jul 91, b&w	2.25	0.50	1.25	2.50
❑33, Sep 91, b&w	2.25	0.50	1.25	2.50
❑34, Nov 91, b&w	2.25	0.50	1.25	2.50

BORIS THE BEAR INSTANT COLOR CLASSICS
DARK HORSE

	ORIG	GOOD	FINE	N-MINT
❑1, Jul 87, 1: Boris the Bear, Reprints Boris the Bear #1 in color	1.75	0.40	1.00	2.00
❑2, Aug 87	1.95	0.40	1.00	2.00
❑3, Dec 87	1.95	0.40	1.00	2.00

BORN AGAIN
SPIRE

	ORIG	GOOD	FINE	N-MINT
❑1, nn; Chuck Colson	0.39	0.60	1.50	3.00

BORN TO KILL
AIRCEL

Value: Cover or less
- ❑1, May 91, b&w 2.50
- ❑2 2.50
- ❑3 2.50

BOSTON BOMBERS, THE
CALIBER

Value: Cover or less
- ❑1, The Black Star Strikes 2.50
- ❑2 2.50
- ❑3 2.50
- ❑4 2.50
- ❑5 2.50
- ❑6 2.50

BOULEVARD OF BROKEN DREAMS
FANTAGRAPHICS

Value: Cover or less
- ❑1, nn 3.95

BOUND AND GAGGED
ICONOGRAFIX

Value: Cover or less
- ❑1, I, Debunker! 2.50

BOUND IN DARKNESS: INFINITY ISSUE
CFD

Value: Cover or less
- ❑1, b&w 2.50

BOUNTY
CALIBER

Value: Cover or less
- ❑1, Bounty; Navarro 2.50
- ❑2 2.50
- ❑3 2.50

BOUNTY OF ZONE-Z
SUNSET STRIPS

Value: Cover or less
- ❑1, nn 2.50

BOX
FANTAGRAPHICS

Value: Cover or less
- ❑1 2.25
- ❑2 2.25
- ❑3 2.25
- ❑4 2.25
- ❑5 2.25
- ❑6 2.25

BOXBOY
SLAVE LABOR

Value: Cover or less
- ❑1, Aug 93, Look! It's Boxboy!; The World of Boxboy 1.00
- ❑1-2, May 95, Look! It's Boxboy!; The World of Boxboy, 2nd Printing 1.25
- ❑2, Jul 95, No Restroom for the Weary; I Love Hockey 1.25

BOX OFFICE POISON
ANTARCTIC

	ORIG	GOOD	FINE	N-MINT
❑0, Collects stories from mini-comics	2.95	0.80	2.00	4.00
❑1, Oct 96, The Bohemian Girl	3.50	1.60	4.00	8.00
❑2, Dec 96, Boiling Frog	2.95	1.00	2.50	5.00
❑3, Feb 97, Ed-The Ink Stud	2.95	0.80	2.00	4.00
❑4, Mar 97, Ballad of Jane and Stephen	2.95	0.80	2.00	4.00
❑5	2.95	0.60	1.50	3.00
❑6	2.95	0.60	1.50	3.00
❑7, Nov 97	2.95	0.60	1.50	3.00
❑8, Feb, cover says Feb 97, indicia says Feb 98	2.95	0.59	1.48	2.95
❑9, Apr, Bumbles Bounce!, cover says May, indicia says Apr	2.95	0.59	1.48	2.95
❑10, Jul 98, When Titans Clash!	2.95	0.59	1.48	2.95
❑11, Oct 98	2.95	0.59	1.48	2.95
❑12, Dec 98, Which Celebrity Will You be Sleeping With?; A Rock in a Pond, wrap-around cover	2.95	0.59	1.48	2.95
❑13, Feb 99, Where will you be in ten years?; In the Company of Guys	2.95	0.60	1.50	2.99
❑14, Jun 99, Grudge!; The End	2.99	0.60	1.50	2.99
❑15, Aug 99, Another Satellite	2.95	0.60	1.50	2.99
❑16	2.99	0.60	1.50	2.99
❑17	2.99	0.60	1.50	2.99
❑18	2.99	0.60	1.50	2.99
❑20, Aug 00, Omen, b&w	2.99	0.60	1.50	2.99
❑SS 1, May 97, Super Special	4.95	0.99	2.47	4.95

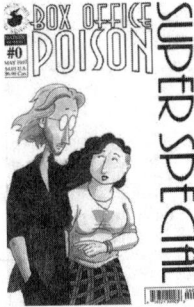

After a series of mini-comics, Alex Robinson's *Box Office Poison* ran 21 issues with Antarctic Press. The run was collected in a trade paperback by Top Shelf in 2001.

© 1996 Alex Robinson (Antarctic)

BOX OFFICE POISON: KOLOR KARNIVAL
ANTARCTIC

	ORIG	GOOD	FINE	N-MINT
❑1, May, Temptation, cover says Apr, indicia says May; Kolor Karnival	2.99	0.70	1.75	3.50

BOY AND HIS 'BOT, A
NOW

Value: Cover or less
- ❑1, Jan 87, digest-sized 1.95

BOY COMMANDOS (2ND SERIES)
DC

	ORIG	GOOD	FINE	N-MINT
❑1, Oct 73, JK	0.20	0.80	2.00	4.00
❑2, Dec 73, JK, Final Issue	0.20	0.60	1.50	3.00

BOZO: THE WORLD'S MOST FAMOUS CLOWN (LARRY HARMON'S...)
INNOVATION

Value: Cover or less
- ❑1, Bozo And The Manikin Circus; Seal Of Approval, some reprint; Reprints Four Color Comics #285 6.95

BOZZ CHRONICLES, THE
MARVEL

	ORIG	GOOD	FINE	N-MINT
❑1, Dec 85, 1: Bozz	1.50	0.40	1.00	2.00
❑2, Feb 86	1.50	0.40	1.00	2.00
❑3, Apr 86	1.50	0.40	1.00	2.00
❑4, Jun 86	1.50	0.40	1.00	2.00
❑5, Aug 86, The Cobblestone Jungle	1.50	0.40	1.00	2.00
❑6, Oct 86, Final Issue	1.50	0.40	1.00	2.00

BRADLEYS, THE
FANTAGRAPHICS

Value: Cover or less
- ❑1, Apr 99 2.95
- ❑2, May 99 2.95
- ❑3, Jul 99 2.95

BRAGADE
PARODY PRESS

Value: Cover or less
- ❑1, Mar 93 2.50

BRAINBANX
DC

Value: Cover or less
- ❑1, Mar 97, Down Upon the Darkness 2.50
- ❑2, Apr 97, The Word and the Light 2.50
- ❑3, May 97 2.50
- ❑4, Jun 97 2.50
- ❑5, Jul 97 2.50
- ❑6, Aug 97 2.50

BRAIN BAT 3-D
3-D ZONE

Value: Cover or less
- ❑1 3.95

BRAIN BOY
DELL

	ORIG	GOOD	FINE	N-MINT
❑2, A: Series numbering continued from	0.12	13.00	32.50	65.00
❑3	0.12	10.00	25.00	50.00
❑4	0.12	9.00	22.50	45.00
❑5	0.12	9.00	22.50	45.00
❑6, The Mindless Ones; The Devil Worshiper (text story), Final Issue	0.12	9.00	22.50	45.00

BRAIN CAPERS
FANTAGRAPHICS

Value: Cover or less
- ❑1 3.95

BRAIN FANTASY
LAST GASP

	ORIG	GOOD	FINE	N-MINT
❑1, Drooms Day; Flying Saucer Man	0.50	0.60	1.50	3.00

BRAND NEW YORK
MEAN

Value: Cover or less
- ❑1, Jul 97, b&w and red; cardstock cover 3.95
- ❑2 3.95

BRASS
IMAGE

Value: Cover or less
- ❑1, Aug 96, 1: Brass 2.50
- ❑1/Dlx, Oct, Folio edition 4.50
- ❑2, Sep 96 2.50
- ❑3, May 97 2.50

BRASS (WILDSTORM)
WILDSTORM

Value: Cover or less
- ❑1, Aug 00 2.50
- ❑2, Sep 00 2.50
- ❑3, Oct 00 2.50
- ❑4, Nov 00 2.50
- ❑5, Dec 00 2.50
- ❑6, Jan 01 2.50

BRATPACK
King Hell

	ORIG	GOOD	FINE	N-MINT
❑1, Aug 90, 1: Wild Boy; 1: Kid Vicious; 1: Luna; 1: Doctor Blasphemy, b&w	2.95	0.80	2.00	4.00
❑1-2, 1: Wild Boy; 1: Kid Vicious; 1: Luna; 1: Doctor Blasphemy, 2nd Printing	2.95	0.60	1.50	3.00
❑, 1: Wild Boy; 1: Kid Vicious; 1: Luna; 1: Doctor Blasphemy, 3rd Printing	2.95	0.60	1.50	3.00
❑2, Nov 90	2.95	0.59	1.48	2.95
❑3, Jan 91	2.95	0.59	1.48	2.95
❑4, Mar 91	2.95	0.59	1.48	2.95
❑5, May 91	2.95	0.59	1.48	2.95

BRAT PACK/MAXIMORTAL SUPER SPECIAL
King Hell

Value: Cover or less

❑1, Sep 96 ... 2.95

BRATS BIZARRE
Marvel

Value: Cover or less

❑1, May 94 ... 2.50

❑2, Jun 94, Bebe's Bogus Funeral ... 2.50

❑3, Jul 94, trading card ... 2.50

❑4, Aug 94 ... 2.50

BRAVE AND THE BOLD, THE
DC

	ORIG	GOOD	FINE	N-MINT
❑1, Aug 55, JKu, Viking Prince, Golden Gladiator, Silent Knight; Vi	0.10	500.00	1250.00	2500.00
❑2, Oct 55, Viking Prince, Golden Gladiator, Silent Knight	0.10	215.00	537.50	1075.00
❑3, Dec 55, Viking Prince, Golden Gladiator, Silent Knight	0.10	128.00	320.00	640.00
❑4, Feb 56, Viking Prince, Golden Gladiator, Silent Knight	0.10	120.00	300.00	600.00
❑5, Apr 56, Robin Hood, Silent Knight, Viking Prince	0.10	120.00	300.00	600.00
❑6, Jun 56, JKu, Robin Hood, Silent Knight, Golden Gladiator	0.10	80.00	200.00	400.00
❑7, Aug 56, JKu, Robin Hood, Silent Knight, Viking Prince	0.10	80.00	200.00	400.00
❑8, Oct 56, JKu, Robin Hood, Silent Knight, Golden Gladiator	0.10	80.00	200.00	400.00
❑9, Dec 56, JKu, Robin Hood, Silent Knight, Viking Prince	0.10	80.00	200.00	400.00
❑10, Feb 57, JKu, Robin Hood, Silent Knight, Viking Prince	0.10	80.00	200.00	400.00
❑11, Apr 57, JKu, Robin Hood, Silent Knight, Viking Prince	0.10	64.00	160.00	320.00
❑12, Jun 57, JKu, Robin Hood, Silent Knight, Viking Prince	0.10	64.00	160.00	320.00
❑13, Sep 57, JKu, Robin Hood, Silent Knight, Viking Prince	0.10	64.00	160.00	320.00
❑14, Nov 57, JKu, Robin Hood, Silent Knight, Viking Prince	0.10	64.00	160.00	320.00
❑15, Jan 58, JKu, Robin Hood, Silent Knight, Viking Prince	0.10	64.00	160.00	320.00
❑16, Mar 58, JKu, Silent Knight, Viking Prince	0.10	64.00	160.00	320.00
❑17, May 58, JKu, Silent Knight, Viking Prince	0.10	64.00	160.00	320.00
❑18, Jul 58, JKu, Silent Knight, Viking Prince	0.10	64.00	160.00	320.00
❑19, Sep 58, JKu, Silent Knight, Viking Prince	0.10	64.00	160.00	320.00
❑20, Nov 58, JKu, Silent Knight, Viking Prince	0.10	64.00	160.00	320.00
❑21, Jan 59, JKu, Silent Knight, Viking Prince	0.10	64.00	160.00	320.00
❑22, Mar 59, JKu, Silent Knight, Viking Prince	0.10	64.00	160.00	320.00
❑23, May 59, JKu, O: Viking Prince, Viking Prince	0.10	75.00	187.50	375.00
❑24, Jul 59, JKu, Viking Prince	0.10	64.00	160.00	320.00
❑25, Sep 59, 1: The Suicide Squad (Golden Age)	0.10	80.00	200.00	400.00
❑26, Nov 59, 2: Suicide Squad	0.10	60.00	150.00	300.00
❑27, Jan 60, 3: Suicide Squad	0.10	60.00	150.00	300.00
❑28, Mar 60, Starro the Conqueror!, 1: Snapper Carr; 1: Starro the Conqueror; 1: Justice League of America	0.10	1060.00	2650.00	5300.00
❑29, May 60, 2: Justice League of America	0.10	460.00	1150.00	2300.00
❑30, Jul 60, 1: Professor Ivo; 3: Justice League of America; 1: Amazo	0.10	400.00	1000.00	2000.00
❑31, Sep 60, 1: Cave Carson	0.10	68.00	170.00	340.00
❑32, Nov 60, Cave Carson	0.10	39.00	97.50	195.00
❑33, Jan 61, Cave Carson	0.10	39.00	97.50	195.00
❑34, Mar 61, JKu; JK, Creature of a Thousand Shapes, 1: Hawkman II (Katar Hol); 1: Hawkwoman II (Shayera Thal); 1: Byth; 1: Thanagar	0.10	390.00	975.00	1950.00
❑35, May 61, JKu; JK, Menace of the Matter Master; Valley of Vanishing Man, 1: Matter Master, Hawkman	0.10	105.00	262.50	525.00
❑36, Jul 61, JKu; JK, Strange Spells of the Sorcerer; Shadow Thief of Midway, 1: Shadow-Thief, Hawkman	0.10	80.00	200.00	400.00
❑37, Sep 61, Suicide Squad	0.10	50.00	125.00	250.00
❑38, Nov 61, Suicide Squad	0.10	45.00	112.50	225.00
❑39, Jan 62, Suicide Squad	0.10	45.00	112.50	225.00
❑40, Mar 62, Cave Carson	0.12	28.00	70.00	140.00
❑41, May 62, Cave Carson	0.12	28.00	70.00	140.00
❑42, Jul 62, JKu; JK, The Menace of the Dragonfly Raiders, A: Hawkman	0.12	60.00	150.00	300.00
❑43, Sep 62, JKu; JK, The Masked Marauders of Earth, O: Hawkman (Silver Age); 1: Manhawks	0.12	70.00	175.00	350.00
❑44, Nov 62, JKu; JK, Earth's Impossible Day; The Men Who Moved the World, A: Hawkman	0.12	52.00	130.00	260.00
❑45, Jan 63, CI, Strange Sports Stories	0.12	10.00	25.00	50.00
❑46, Mar 63, CI, Strange Sports Stories	0.12	10.00	25.00	50.00
❑47, May 63, CI, Strange Sports Stories	0.12	10.00	25.00	50.00
❑48, Jul 63, CI, Strange Sports Stories	0.12	10.00	25.00	50.00
❑49, Sep 63, CI, Strange Sports Stories	0.12	10.00	25.00	50.00
❑50, Nov 63, Green Arrow; Team-ups begin	0.12	35.00	87.50	175.00
❑51, Jan 64, Aquaman, Hawkman; Early Hawkman/Aquaman team-up	0.12	45.00	112.50	225.00
❑52, Mar 64, JK, Sgt. Rock	0.12	25.00	62.50	125.00
❑53, May 64, ATh, Atom & Flash	0.12	25.00	62.50	125.00
❑54, Jul 64, 1: Teen Titans	0.12	53.00	132.50	265.00
❑55, Sep 64, Metal Men, Atom	0.12	8.00	20.00	40.00
❑56, Nov 64, 1: Wynde, Flash	0.12	8.00	20.00	40.00
❑57, Jan 65, 1: Metamorpho	0.12	29.00	72.50	145.00
❑58, Mar 65, 2: Metamorpho	0.12	13.00	32.50	65.00
❑59, May 65, Batman; Batman/Green Lantern team-up	0.12	15.00	37.50	75.00
❑60, Jul 65, 1: Wonder Girl (Donna Troy), Teen Titans	0.12	16.00	40.00	80.00
❑61, Sep 65, MA, O: Black Canary; O: Starman I (Ted Knight), Starman	0.12	17.00	42.50	85.00
❑62, Nov 65, MA, Starman	0.12	17.00	42.50	85.00
❑63, Jan 66, Supergirl	0.12	6.00	15.00	30.00
❑64, Mar 66, A: Eclipso, Batman	0.12	11.00	27.50	55.00
❑65, May 66, Doom Patrol	0.12	4.00	10.00	20.00
❑66, Jul 66, Metamorpho, Metal Men	0.12	4.00	10.00	20.00
❑67, Sep 66, CI, Batman, Flash; Batman in all remaining issues	0.12	7.00	17.50	35.00
❑68, Nov 66, A: Joker, Metamorpho	0.12	12.00	30.00	60.00
❑69, Jan 67, Green Lantern	0.12	5.00	12.50	25.00
❑70, Mar 67, Hawkman	0.12	5.00	12.50	25.00
❑71, May 67, Green Arrow	0.12	5.00	12.50	25.00
❑72, Jul 67, CI, Spectre	0.12	4.40	11.00	22.00
❑73, Sep 67, Aquaman, Atom	0.12	4.00	10.00	20.00
❑74, Nov 67, Metal Men	0.12	4.00	10.00	20.00
❑75, Jan 68, Spectre	0.12	4.00	10.00	20.00
❑76, Mar 68, Plastic Man	0.12	4.00	10.00	20.00
❑77, May 68	0.12	4.00	10.00	20.00
❑78, Jul 68, 1: Copperhead, Wonder Woman	0.12	4.00	10.00	20.00
❑79, Sep 68, NA, A: Deadman, Deadman	0.12	8.00	20.00	40.00
❑80, Nov 68, NA, A: Creeper, Creeper	0.12	7.00	17.50	35.00
❑81, Jan 69, NA, A: Deadman, Flash	0.12	7.00	17.50	35.00
❑82, Mar 69, NA, A: Deadman; O: Ocean Master	0.12	7.00	17.50	35.00
❑83, May 69, NA, Titans	0.12	9.00	22.50	45.00
❑84, Jul 69, NA, Sgt. Rock	0.12	6.40	16.00	32.00
❑85, Sep 69, NA, Green Arrow; Green Arrow gets new costume	0.15	6.40	16.00	32.00
❑86, Nov 69, NA, Deadman	0.15	6.40	16.00	32.00
❑87, Jan 70, Wonder Woman	0.15	4.00	10.00	20.00
❑88, Mar 70, Wildcat	0.15	4.00	10.00	20.00
❑89, May 70, Phantom Stranger	0.15	4.00	10.00	20.00
❑90, Jul 70, Adam Strange	0.15	4.00	10.00	20.00
❑91, Sep 70, Black Canary	0.15	3.60	9.00	18.00
❑92, Nov 70, Bat Squad	0.15	3.60	9.00	18.00
❑93, Jan 71, NA, House of Mystery	0.15	6.00	15.00	30.00
❑94, Mar 71, Titans	0.15	3.60	9.00	18.00
❑95, May 71, Plastic Man	0.15	2.20	5.50	11.00
❑96, Jul 71, Sgt. Rock	0.15	2.20	5.50	11.00
❑97, 71, Wildcat	0.25	2.20	5.50	11.00
❑98, Nov 71, Phantom Stranger	0.25	2.20	5.50	11.00
❑99, Jan 72, NC, Flash	0.25	2.20	5.50	11.00
❑100, Mar 72, NA, 100th anniversary issue; Double-size; Green Arrow	0.25	6.00	15.00	30.00
❑101, May 72, Metamorpho	0.25	1.20	3.00	6.00
❑102, Jul 72, NA, Titans	0.25	1.80	4.50	9.00
❑103, Oct 72, Metal Men	0.20	1.20	3.00	6.00
❑104, Dec 72, JA, Deadman	0.20	1.20	3.00	6.00
❑105, Feb 73, JA, Wonder Woman	0.20	1.20	3.00	6.00
❑106, Apr 73, JA, Green Arrow	0.20	1.20	3.00	6.00
❑107, Jul 73, Black Canary	0.20	1.20	3.00	6.00
❑108, Sep 73, JA, Sgt. Rock	0.20	1.20	3.00	6.00
❑109, Nov 73, JA, Demon	0.20	1.20	3.00	6.00
❑110, Jan 74, JA, Wildcat	0.20	1.20	3.00	6.00
❑111, Mar 74, JA, Joker	0.20	2.40	6.00	12.00
❑112, May 74, 100pgs.; Mr. Miracle	0.60	2.40	6.00	12.00
❑113, Jul 74, JA, 100pgs.; Metal Men	0.60	2.40	6.00	12.00
❑114, Sep 74, JA, 100pgs.; Aquaman	0.60	2.40	6.00	12.00

	ORIG	GOOD	FINE	N-MINT
❑115, Nov 74, JA, O: Viking Prince, 100pgs.	0.60	2.40	6.00	12.00
❑116, Jan 75, JA, 100pgs.; Spectre	0.60	2.40	6.00	12.00
❑117, Mar 75, JA, 100pgs.; Sgt. Rock; reprints Secret Six #1	0.60	2.40	6.00	12.00
❑118, Apr 75, JA, Wildcat, Joker	0.25	2.40	6.00	12.00
❑119, Jun 75, JA, Man-Bat	0.25	0.80	2.00	4.00
❑120, Jul 75, JA, 68pgs.; Kamandi, 68 pgs., reprints Secret Six #2; Kamandi; reprints Secret Six #2	0.50	0.80	2.00	4.00
❑121, Sep 75, JA, Metal Men	0.25	0.80	2.00	4.00
❑122, Oct 75, Swamp Thing	0.25	0.80	2.00	4.00
❑123, Dec 75, JA, Plastic Man, Metamorpho	0.25	0.80	2.00	4.00
❑124, Jan 76, JA, Sgt. Rock	0.25	0.80	2.00	4.00
❑125, Mar 76, JA, Flash	0.25	0.80	2.00	4.00
❑126, Apr 76, JA, Aquaman	0.30	0.80	2.00	4.00
❑127, Jun 76, JA, Wildcat	0.30	0.80	2.00	4.00
❑128, Jul 76, JA, Mr. Miracle; Bicentennial #19	0.30	0.80	2.00	4.00
❑129, Sep 76, Green Arrow/Joker	0.30	2.20	5.50	11.00
❑130, Oct 76, Green Arrow/Joker	0.30	2.20	5.50	11.00
❑131, Dec 76, JA, A: Catwoman, Wonder Woman	0.30	1.20	3.00	6.00
❑132, Feb 77, JA, Kung Fu Fighter	0.30	0.70	1.75	3.50
❑133, Apr 77, JA, Deadman	0.30	0.70	1.75	3.50
❑134, May 77, JA, Green Lantern	0.30	0.70	1.75	3.50
❑135, Jul 77, JA, Metal Men	0.35	0.70	1.75	3.50
❑136, Sep 77, Green Arrow, Metal Men	0.35	0.70	1.75	3.50
❑137, Oct 77, Demon	0.35	0.70	1.75	3.50
❑138, Nov 77, JA, Mr. Miracle	0.35	0.70	1.75	3.50
❑139, Jan 78, JA, Hawkman	0.35	0.70	1.75	3.50
❑140, Mar 78, JA, Wonder Woman	0.35	0.70	1.75	3.50
❑141, May 78, Black Canary, Joker	0.35	2.20	5.50	11.00
❑142, Jul 78, JA, Aquaman	0.35	0.70	1.75	3.50
❑143, Sep 78, JA, O: Human Target	0.50	0.70	1.75	3.50
❑144, Nov 78, JA, Green Arrow	0.50	0.70	1.75	3.50
❑145, Dec 78, JA, Phantom Stranger	0.40	0.70	1.75	3.50
❑146, Jan 79, JA, E-2 Batman/Unknown Soldier	0.40	0.70	1.75	3.50
❑147, Feb 79, JA, A: Doctor Light	0.40	0.70	1.75	3.50
❑148, Mar 79, Plastic Man	0.40	0.70	1.75	3.50
❑149, Apr 79, JA, Teen Titans	0.40	0.70	1.75	3.50
❑150, May 79, JA, Superman	0.40	0.70	1.75	3.50
❑151, Jun 79, JA, Flash	0.40	0.70	1.75	3.50
❑152, Jul 79, JA, Atom	0.40	0.70	1.75	3.50
❑153, Aug 79, DN, Red Tornado	0.40	0.70	1.75	3.50
❑154, Sep 79, JA, Metamorpho	0.40	0.70	1.75	3.50
❑155, Oct 79, JA, Green Lantern	0.40	0.70	1.75	3.50
❑156, Nov 79, DN, Doctor Fate	0.40	0.70	1.75	3.50
❑157, Dec 79, JA, Kamandi, continues story from Kamandi #59; Kamandi; continues story from Kamandi #59	0.40	0.70	1.75	3.50
❑158, Jan 80, JA, Wonder Woman	0.40	0.70	1.75	3.50
❑159, Feb 80, JA, Ra's al Ghul	0.40	0.70	1.75	3.50
❑160, Mar 80, JA, Supergirl	0.40	0.70	1.75	3.50
❑161, Apr 80, JA, Adam Strange	0.40	0.70	1.75	3.50
❑162, May 80, JA, Sgt. Rock	0.40	0.70	1.75	3.50
❑163, Jun 80, DG, Black Lightning	0.40	0.70	1.75	3.50
❑164, Jul 80, The Mystery of the Mobile Museum!, A: Hawkman; A: Hawkgirl, Hawkman	0.40	0.70	1.75	3.50
❑165, Aug 80, DN, Man-Bat	0.40	0.70	1.75	3.50
❑166, Sep 80, 1: Nemesis, Black Canary	0.40	0.70	1.75	3.50
❑167, Oct 80, DA; DC, Blackhawk	0.50	0.70	1.75	3.50
❑168, Nov 80, JA, Green Arrow	0.50	0.70	1.75	3.50
❑169, Dec 80, JA, Zatanna	0.50	0.70	1.75	3.50
❑170, Jan 81, JA, Nemesis	0.50	0.70	1.75	3.50
❑171, Feb 81, GC, Scalphunter	0.50	0.70	1.75	3.50
❑172, Mar 81, CI, Firestorm	0.50	0.70	1.75	3.50
❑173, Apr 81, JA, Guardians	0.50	0.70	1.75	3.50
❑174, May 81, JA, Green Lantern	0.50	0.70	1.75	3.50
❑175, Jun 81, JA, Lois Lane	0.50	0.70	1.75	3.50
❑176, Jul 81, JA, Swamp Thing	0.50	0.70	1.75	3.50
❑177, Aug 81, JA, Elongated Man	0.50	0.70	1.75	3.50
❑178, Sep 81, JA, Creeper	0.50	0.70	1.75	3.50
❑179, Oct 81, EC, Legion	0.60	0.70	1.75	3.50
❑180, Nov 81, JA, Spectre, Nemesis	0.60	0.60	1.50	3.00
❑181, Dec 81, JA, Hawk & Dove, Nemesis	0.60	0.60	1.50	3.00
❑182, Jan 82, JA, E-2 Robin	0.60	0.60	1.50	3.00
❑183, Feb 82, CI, Riddler, Nemesis	0.60	0.60	1.50	3.00
❑184, Mar 82, JA, Huntress	0.60	0.60	1.50	3.00
❑185, Apr 82, Green Lantern	0.60	0.60	1.50	3.00
❑186, May 82, JA, Hawkman, Nemesis	0.60	0.60	1.50	3.00
❑187, Jun 82, JA, Metal Men, Nemesis	0.60	0.60	1.50	3.00
❑188, Jul 82, JA, A Grave As Wide As The World, Rose & Thorn	0.60	0.60	1.50	3.00
❑189, Aug 82, JA, Thorn, Nemesis	0.60	0.60	1.50	3.00
❑190, Sep 82, JA, Adam Strange, Nemesis	0.60	0.60	1.50	3.00

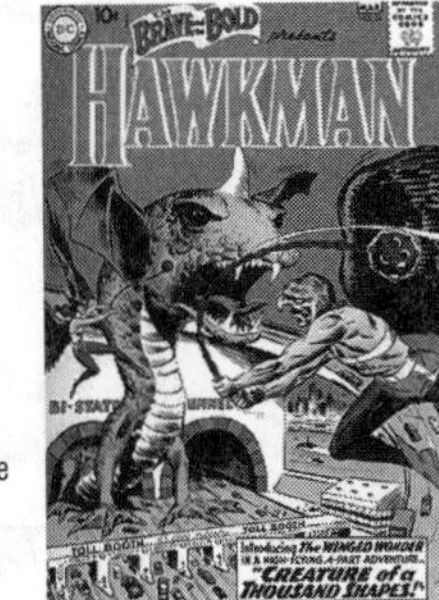

The Silver Age Hawkman and Hawkgirl were intergalactic police officers from the planet Thanagar.

© 1961 National Periodical Publications (DC)

	ORIG	GOOD	FINE	N-MINT
❑191, Oct 82, JA, A: Nemesis; A: Penguin, Joker	0.60	1.60	4.00	8.00
❑192, Nov 82, JA, V: Mr. IQ, Superboy	0.60	0.60	1.50	3.00
❑193, Dec 82, JA, D: Nemesis	0.60	0.60	1.50	3.00
❑194, Jan 84, CI, V: Rainbow Raider; V: Double-X, Flash; Flash, V: Rainbow Raider, Double-X	0.60	0.60	1.50	3.00
❑195, Feb 84, JA, I...Vampire	0.60	0.60	1.50	3.00
❑196, Mar 84, JA, Ragman	0.60	0.60	1.50	3.00
❑197, Apr 84, Catwoman; Wedding of Earth-2 Batman & Earth-2 Catwoman	0.60	0.80	2.00	4.00
❑198, May 84, Karate Kid	0.60	0.60	1.50	3.00
❑199, Jun 84, RA, Spectre	0.60	0.60	1.50	3.00
❑200, Jul 84, JA, 1: Outsiders; 1: Geo-Force; 1: Katana; 1: Halo, Final Issue; Giant-size; E-1 and E-2 Batman	1.50	1.40	3.50	7.00

BRAVE AND THE BOLD, THE (MINI-SERIES)
DC

	ORIG	GOOD	FINE	N-MINT
❑1, Dec 91, MGr (w)	1.75	0.50	1.25	2.50
❑2, Jan 92, MGr (w)	1.75	0.40	1.00	2.00
❑3, Feb 92, MGr (w)	1.75	0.40	1.00	2.00
❑4, Mar 92, MGr (w)	1.75	0.35	0.88	1.75
❑5, May 92, MGr (w)	1.75	0.35	0.88	1.75
❑6, Jun 92, MGr (w)	1.75	0.35	0.88	1.75

BRAVE OLD WORLD
DC

Value: Cover or less

- ❑1, Feb 00, The Century Turns, Abort, Retry, Reboot (Winter) 2.50
- ❑2, Mar 00, Melting Pot; Manual Override (Spring) 2.50
- ❑3, Apr 00, A Thousand Natural Shocks; Bugfix (Summer) 2.50
- ❑4, May 00, Weaker Vessels; Permanent Fatal Errors (Fall) 2.50

BRAVESTARR IN 3-D
BLACKTHORNE

Value: Cover or less

- ❑1 2.50
- ❑2 2.50

BRAVO FOR ADVENTURE
DRAGON LADY

Value: Cover or less

- ❑1, ATh 5.95

BRAVURA PREVIEW BOOK
MALIBU

	ORIG	GOOD	FINE	N-MINT
❑0, GK; HC; JSn, HC (w); JSn (w), 'Breed story; Power and Glory story, Coupon redemption promotion	—	0.60	1.50	3.00
❑1, Nov 93, no cover price; 1994 Preview book	1.50	0.30	0.75	1.50
❑2, Aug 94, (#1 on cover); 1995 Preview book	1.50	0.30	0.75	1.50

BREAKDOWNS
INFINITY

Value: Cover or less

- ❑1, Oct 86, Theater of the Absurd; Limaperg 1.70

BREAKFAST AFTER NOON
ONI

Value: Cover or less

- ❑1, May 00, b&w 2.95
- ❑2, Aug 00, b&w 2.95
- ❑3, Sep 00, b&w 2.95
- ❑4, b&w 2.95
- ❑5, b&w 2.95
- ❑6, b&w 2.95

BREAKNECK BLVD. (MOTION)
MOTION

Value: Cover or less

- ❑0, b&w 2.50
- ❑1, Jul, 1: Blu-J; 1: Blu-J, b&w, b&w 2.50
- ❑2, Sep 94, b&w 2.50

BREAKNECK BLVD. (SLAVE LABOR)
SLAVE LABOR

Value: Cover or less

- ❑1, Jul 95, Feel Every Beat 2.95
- ❑2, Oct 95, La Femme Incident 2.95
- ❑3, Jan 96 2.95
- ❑4, May 96, A Long Way From Home 2.95
- ❑5, Aug 96, Ten Percenter 2.95
- ❑6, Dec 96, More Fire than Flame 2.95

BREAK THE CHAIN
MARVEL MUSIC

Value: Cover or less

- ❑1, GP, polybagged with KRS-1 cassette tape 6.99

BREAK-THRU
MALIBU

	ORIG	GOOD	FINE	N-MINT
❑1, Dec, GP, Break-Thru, Part 1	2.50	0.50	1.25	2.50
❑1/LE, Ultra Limited; foil logo	2.50	0.80	2.00	4.00
❑2, Jan, GP, Break-Thru, Part 13	2.50	0.50	1.25	2.50

BREATHTAKER
DC

	ORIG	GOOD	FINE	N-MINT
❑1, Jul 90, 1: Breathtaker; 1: The Man	4.95	1.00	2.50	5.00
❑2, Aug 90	4.95	1.00	2.50	5.00
❑3, Sep 90, O: Breathtaker	4.95	1.00	2.50	5.00
❑4, Oct 90	4.95	1.00	2.50	5.00

'BREED
MALIBU

Value: Cover or less

- ❑1, Jan 94, JSn, JSn (w), coupon ... 2.50
- ❑2, Feb 94, JSn, JSn (w), coupon ... 2.50
- ❑3, Mar 94, JSn, JSn (w), coupon ... 2.50
- ❑4, Apr 94, JSn, JSn (w), coupon ... 2.50
- ❑5, May 94, JSn, JSn (w), coupon ... 2.50
- ❑6, Jun 94, JSn, JSn (w), coupon ... 2.50

'BREED II
MALIBU

Value: Cover or less

- ❑1, Nov 94, JSn, JSn (w) ... 2.95
- ❑2, Dec 94, JSn, JSn (w) ... 2.95
- ❑3, Jan 95, JSn, JSn (w) ... 2.95
- ❑4, Feb 95, JSn, JSn (w) ... 2.95
- ❑5, Mar 95, JSn, JSn (w) ... 2.95
- ❑6, Apr 95, JSn, JSn (w) ... 2.95

BRENDA STARR (AVALON)
AVALON

Value: Cover or less

- ❑1 ... 2.95
- ❑2 ... 2.95

BRENDA STARR CUT-OUTS AND COLORING BOOK
BLACKTHORNE

Value: Cover or less

- ❑1 ... 6.95

BRICKMAN
HARRIER

Value: Cover or less

- ❑1 ... 1.95

BRIDGMAN'S CONSTRUCTIVE ANATOMY
A-LIST

Value: Cover or less

- ❑1, Apr 98, b&w ... 2.95

BRIGADE
IMAGE

	ORIG	GOOD	FINE	N-MINT
❑0, Sep 93, RL (w), 1: Warcry, gatefold cover	1.95	0.45	1.13	2.25
❑1, May 93, RL (w), Blood Brothers, Part 1, 1: Hacker; 1: Boone	1.95	0.40	1.00	2.00
❑2, Jun, Blood Brothers, Part 3, foil cover	2.95	0.40	1.00	2.00
❑2/A, Jun 93, alternate cover	2.95	0.59	1.48	2.95
❑3, Sep 93, Blood Brothers, Part 5, 1: Roman	1.95	0.40	1.00	2.00
❑4, Oct 93	1.95	0.40	1.00	2.00
❑5, Nov 93	1.95	0.40	1.00	2.00
❑6, Dec 93, 1: Coral; 1: Worlok	1.95	0.39	0.98	1.95
❑7, Feb 94	1.95	0.39	0.98	1.95
❑8, Mar, Extreme Prejudice	1.95	0.39	0.98	1.95
❑9, Apr, Extreme Prejudice, Part 6	1.95	0.39	0.98	1.95
❑10, Jun 94	1.95	0.39	0.98	1.95
❑11, Aug 94, A: WildC.A.T.s	2.50	0.39	0.98	1.95
❑12, Sep 94, A: WildC.A.T.s	2.50	0.50	1.25	2.50
❑13, Oct 94	1.95	0.50	1.25	2.50
❑14, Nov 94	1.95	0.50	1.25	2.50
❑15, Dec 94	2.50	0.50	1.25	2.50
❑16, Jan 95, Extreme Sacrifice, Part 4; Extreme Sacrifice, Part 3, trading card	2.50	0.50	1.25	2.50
❑17, Feb, Extreme Sacrifice Aftermath	2.50	0.50	1.25	2.50
❑18, Mar 95	2.50	0.50	1.25	2.50
❑18/SC, Mar 95, alternate cover	2.50	0.50	1.25	2.50
❑19, Apr 95, A: Glory	2.50	0.50	1.25	2.50
❑20/A, May 95, A: Glory	2.50	0.50	1.25	2.50
❑20/B, May 95, A: Glory, alternate cover	2.50	0.50	1.25	2.50
❑21, Jun, Funeral of Shadowhawk	2.50	0.50	1.25	2.50
❑22, Jul 95	2.50	0.50	1.25	2.50
❑25, May 94, Images of Tomorrow; Published out of sequence as a preview of the future	1.95	0.39	0.98	1.95
❑26, Jun 94, Published out of sequence as a preview of the future	1.95	0.39	0.98	1.95
❑27, Final Issue	2.50	0.50	1.25	2.50

BRIGADE (MINI-SERIES)
IMAGE

Value: Cover or less

- ❑1, Aug 92, RL (c), 1: Brigade; 1: Genocide, trading cards ... 1.95
- ❑1/GO, Aug, 1: Brigade; 1: Genocide, Gold edition ... 5.00
- ❑2, Oct 92, RL (c), trading cards; coupon for Image Comics #0 ... 3.50
- ❑2/GO, Oct, Gold edition ... 3.50
- ❑3, Feb 93, RL (c), 1: the Birds of Prey ... 1.95
- ❑4, Jul, flip side of Youngblood #5 ... 2.50

BRIGADE SOURCEBOOK
IMAGE

Value: Cover or less

- ❑1, Aug 94 ... 2.95

BRIK HAUSS
BLACKTHORNE

Value: Cover or less

- ❑1, Jul 87, Brik Hauss and the Nuclear Cat-Astrophe ... 1.75

BRILLIANT BOY
CIRCUS

Value: Cover or less

- ❑1, Jan 97 ... 2.95
- ❑2, Mar 97 ... 2.50
- ❑3, May 97 ... 2.50
- ❑4 ... 2.50
- ❑5 ... 2.50

BRINKE OF DESTRUCTION
HIGH-TOP

Value: Cover or less

- ❑1, Dec 95 ... 2.95
- ❑1/CS, Dec 95, packaged with audio tape ... 6.99
- ❑2 ... 2.95
- ❑3 ... 2.95
- ❑SE 1, audio tape ... 6.95

BRINKE OF DISASTER
HIGH-TOP

Value: Cover or less

- ❑1 ... 2.25

BRINKE OF ETERNITY
CHAOS

Value: Cover or less

- ❑1, Apr 94 ... 2.75

BRIT-CIT BABES
FLEETWAY

Value: Cover or less

- ❑1, BB (c), nn ... 5.95

BROADWAY BABES
AVALON

Value: Cover or less

- ❑1, Moronica, Miss Nitwit of 1954; Moronica, Miss Nitwit of 1953, reprints Moronica stories, b&w ... 2.95

BROADWAY VIDEO SPECIAL COLLECTORS EDITION
BROADWAY

	ORIG	GOOD	FINE	N-MINT
❑1, Dec, cardstock cover; Promotional give-away; 1150 copies printed	—	0.20	0.50	1.00

BROID
ETERNITY

Value: Cover or less

- ❑1, b&w ... 2.75
- ❑2 ... 2.25
- ❑3 ... 2.25
- ❑4 ... 2.25

BROKEN AXIS
ANTARCTIC

Value: Cover or less

- ❑1, Oct, History of Silly Wars, b&w ... 2.95

BROKEN FENDER (VOL. 2)
TOP SHELF PRODUCTIONS

Value: Cover or less

- ❑2, b&w ... 2.95

BROKEN HEROES
SIRIUS

Value: Cover or less

- ❑1, Mar 98 ... 2.50
- ❑2, Apr 98 ... 2.50
- ❑3, May 98 ... 2.50
- ❑4, Jun 98 ... 2.50
- ❑5, Jul 98 ... 2.50
- ❑6, Aug 98 ... 2.50
- ❑7, Sep 98 ... 2.50
- ❑8, Oct 98 ... 2.50
- ❑9, Nov 98 ... 2.50
- ❑10, Dec 98 ... 2.50
- ❑11, Jan 99 ... 2.50
- ❑12, Feb 99 ... 2.50

BRONX
ETERNITY

Value: Cover or less

- ❑1 ... 2.50
- ❑2 ... 2.50
- ❑3 ... 2.50

BROOKLYN DREAMS
DC

Value: Cover or less

- ❑1 ... 4.95
- ❑2 ... 4.95
- ❑3 ... 4.95
- ❑4 ... 4.95

BROTHERMAN
BIG CITY

Value: Cover or less

- ❑1 ... 2.00
- ❑2 ... 2.00
- ❑3 ... 2.00
- ❑4 ... 2.00
- ❑5 ... 2.00
- ❑6 ... 2.00
- ❑7 ... 2.00
- ❑8 ... 2.00

BROTHER MAN: DICTATOR OF DISCIPLINE
BIG CITY

Value: Cover or less

- ❑11, Jul 96, magazine-sized ... 2.95

BROTHER POWER, THE GEEK
DC

	ORIG	GOOD	FINE	N-MINT
❑1, Oct 68, A Thing is Born, 1: Brother Power, the Geek	0.12	8.00	20.00	40.00
❑2	—	5.00	12.50	25.00

BROTHERS OF THE SPEAR
GOLD KEY

	ORIG	GOOD	FINE	N-MINT
❑1	0.15	4.00	10.00	20.00
❑2	0.20	2.00	5.00	10.00
❑3	0.20	1.20	3.00	6.00
❑4	0.20	1.20	3.00	6.00
❑5, Riders In The Sky	0.20	1.20	3.00	6.00
❑6	0.20	0.80	2.00	4.00
❑7	0.20	0.80	2.00	4.00
❑8	0.20	0.80	2.00	4.00

	ORIG	GOOD	FINE	N-MINT
❏9	0.20	0.80	2.00	4.00
❏10	0.20	0.80	2.00	4.00
❏11	0.20	0.80	2.00	4.00
❏12	0.20	0.80	2.00	4.00
❏13	0.20	0.80	2.00	4.00
❏14	0.20	0.80	2.00	4.00
❏15	0.20	0.80	2.00	4.00
❏16	0.20	0.80	2.00	4.00
❏17, Original series ends (1976)	0.20	0.80	2.00	4.00
❏18, One-shot continuation of series (1982)	—	0.50	1.25	2.50

BRUCE LEE
MALIBU
Value: Cover or less

Issue	Price
❏1, Jul 94, VM, One In Punch.	2.95
❏2, Aug 94, VM	2.95
❏3, Sep 94, VM, Tinsel Town Rebellion	2.95
❏4, Oct 94, VM	2.95
❏5, Nov 94, VM	2.95
❏6, Dec 94, VM	2.95

BRUCE WAYNE: AGENT OF S.H.I.E.L.D.
MARVEL
Value: Cover or less

Issue	Price
❏1, Apr 96, Mission: Destroy Hydra, O: Bruce Wayne, Agent of S.H.I.E.L.D., One-Shot	1.95

BRU-HED
SCHISM

	ORIG	GOOD	FINE	N-MINT
❏1, Mar 94, Don't Take the World Serious, 1: Grrim & Grritty; 1: Bru-Hed	2.50	0.70	1.75	3.50
❏1/Ash, 1: Grrim & Grritty; 1: Bru-Hed, Test-Market Ashcan edition	2.50	0.80	2.00	4.00
❏1/SC, Mar 94, metallic foil logo on cover	2.50	0.50	1.25	2.50
❏2, Jul 94, b&w	2.50	0.50	1.25	2.50
❏3, D: Grrim & Grritty, b&w; Pete Bickford thanked on letters page	2.50	0.50	1.25	2.50
❏4, Final Issue	2.50	0.50	1.25	2.50
❏Ash 1, 1: Grrim & Grritty; 1: Bru-Hed, Test-Market Ashcan edition; ashcan, b&w	2.50	0.80	2.00	4.00

BRU-HED'S BREATHTAKING BEAUTIES
SCHISM
Value: Cover or less

Issue	Price
❏1, b&w pin-ups, cardstock cover	2.50

BRU-HED'S BUNNIES, BADDIES & BUDDIES
SCHISM
Value: Cover or less

Issue	Price
❏1	2.50

BRU-HED'S GUIDE TO GETTIN' GIRLS NOW!
SCHISM
Value: Cover or less

Issue	Price
❏1	2.95
❏2	2.50

BRUISER
ANTHEM
Value: Cover or less

Issue	Price
❏1	2.45

BRUISER, THE
MYTHIC

	ORIG	GOOD	FINE	N-MINT
❏1, Win, no cover price, b&w	—	0.50	1.25	2.50

BRUNNER'S BEAUTIES
FANTAGRAPHICS
Value: Cover or less

Issue	Price
❏1, nn; pin-ups, adult, b&w	4.95

BRUTE, THE
ATLAS

	ORIG	GOOD	FINE	N-MINT
❏1, Feb 75, Night Of The Brute, 1: Brute	0.25	0.40	1.00	2.00
❏2, Apr 75	0.25	0.20	0.50	1.00
❏3, Jul 75	0.25	0.20	0.50	1.00

BRUTE FORCE
MARVEL
Value: Cover or less

Issue	Price
❏1, Aug 90, Fast Feud, 1: Brute Force	1.00
❏2, Sep 90	1.00
❏3, Oct 90	1.00
❏4, Nov 90	1.00

BUBBLEGUM CRISIS: GRAND MAL
DARK HORSE
Value: Cover or less

Issue	Price
❏1, Mar 94	2.50
❏2, Apr 94	2.50
❏3, May 94	2.50
❏4, Jun 94	2.50

BUCKAROO BANZAI
MARVEL

	ORIG	GOOD	FINE	N-MINT
❏1, Dec 84, movie Adaptation	0.75	0.20	0.50	1.00
❏2, Feb 85, movie Adaptation	0.75	0.20	0.50	1.00

BUCK GODOT, ZAP GUN FOR HIRE
PALLIARD PRESS

	ORIG	GOOD	FINE	N-MINT
❏1, Jul 93, PF, PF (w), The Gallimaufry, Part 1	2.95	0.70	1.75	3.50
❏2, Nov 93, PF, PF (w), The Gallimaufry, Part 2	2.95	0.60	1.50	3.00
❏3, Apr 94, PF, PF (w), The Gallimaufry, Part 3	2.95	0.59	1.48	2.95
❏4, Aug 94, PF, PF (w), The Gallimaufry, Part 4	2.95	0.59	1.48	2.95
❏5, Sep 95, PF, PF (w), The Gallimaufry, Part 5	2.95	0.59	1.48	2.95

Phil Foglio's *Buck Godot, Zap Gun for Hire* was a science-fiction series featuring an overweight bounty hunter.

	ORIG	GOOD	FINE	N-MINT
❏6, Oct 95, PF, PF (w), The Gallimaufry, Part 6	2.95	0.59	1.48	2.95
❏7, Aug 97, PF, PF (w), The Gallimaufry, Part 7	2.95	0.59	1.48	2.95
❏8, Mar 98, PF, PF (w), The Gallimaufry, Part 8, Final Issue	3.50	0.59	1.48	2.95

BUCK ROGERS (GOLD KEY/WHITMAN)
GOLD KEY

	ORIG	GOOD	FINE	N-MINT
❏1, Oct 64, The Space Slavers, 10/64; Gold Key publishes	0.15	7.00	17.50	35.00
❏2, Buck Rogers (movie adaptation), Part 1	0.40	0.80	2.00	4.00
❏3, Buck Rogers (movie adaptation), Part 2	0.40	0.80	2.00	4.00
❏4, Buck Rogers (movie adaptation), Part 3	—	0.80	2.00	4.00
❏5	—	0.60	1.50	3.00
❏6	—	0.60	1.50	3.00
❏7, Series begins under Whitman imprint	—	0.60	1.50	3.00
❏8	—	0.60	1.50	3.00
❏9	—	0.60	1.50	3.00
❏10	—	0.60	1.50	3.00
❏11	—	0.60	1.50	3.00
❏12	—	0.60	1.50	3.00
❏13	—	0.60	1.50	3.00
❏14	—	0.60	1.50	3.00
❏15	—	0.60	1.50	3.00
❏16, Final Issue	—	0.60	1.50	3.00

BUCK ROGERS COMICS MODULE
TSR
Value: Cover or less

Issue	Price
❏1, Rude Awakening; The Gauntlet (game), a board game for 2 players; Listed as 1 of 3	2.95
❏2	2.95
❏3	2.95
❏4	2.95
❏5	2.95
❏6	2.95
❏7	2.95
❏8	2.95
❏9	2.95

BUCKY O'HARE
CONTINUITY
Value: Cover or less

Issue	Price
❏1, Jan 91, MG	2.00
❏2, May 91, MG	2.00
❏3, Jul 91, MG	2.00
❏4, Dec 91, MG	2.00
❏5, Mar 92, MG	2.00

BUDDHA ON THE ROAD
AEON
Value: Cover or less

Issue	Price
❏1, Aug 96	2.95
❏2, Nov 96	2.95

BUFFALO WINGS
ANTARCTIC
Value: Cover or less

Issue	Price
❏1, Sep 93, b&w	2.50
❏2, Nov 93, b&w	2.75

BUFFY THE VAMPIRE SLAYER
DARK HORSE

	ORIG	GOOD	FINE	N-MINT
❏0.5, Wizard promotional edition	—	0.60	1.50	3.00
❏0.5/GO, Wizard promotional edition; Gold logo	—	1.60	4.00	8.00
❏0.5/Pl, Wizard promotional edition; Platinum logo	—	2.00	5.00	10.00
❏1, no month of publication	2.95	1.00	2.50	5.00
❏1/A, photo cover with foil logo; Another Universe	2.95	1.60	4.00	8.00
❏1/B, photo cover (Buffy holding gate) without foil logo; Another Universe	2.95	0.60	1.50	3.00
❏1/GO, art cover with gold foil logo; Gold logo; gold foil logo	2.95	1.40	3.50	7.00
❏1/SC, Photo cover	2.95	1.20	3.00	6.00
❏1-2, 2nd Printing	2.95	0.59	1.48	2.95
❏2, Oct 98, Halloween	2.95	0.80	2.00	4.00
❏2/SC, Oct 98, Halloween, Photo cover	2.95	1.00	2.50	5.00
❏3, Nov 98, Cold Turkey, no month of publication	2.95	0.80	2.00	4.00
❏3/SC, Nov 98, Cold Turkey, Photo cover	2.95	1.00	2.50	5.00
❏4, Dec 98, White Christmas	2.95	0.80	2.00	4.00
❏4/SC, Dec 98, White Christmas, Photo cover	2.95	0.80	2.00	4.00
❏5, Jan 99, Happy New Year	2.95	0.80	2.00	4.00

	ORIG	GOOD	FINE	N-MINT
❑5/SC, Jan 99, Happy New Year, Photo cover	2.95	0.80	2.00	4.00
❑6, Feb 99, New Kid on the Block, Part 1	2.95	0.60	1.50	3.00
❑6/SC, Feb 99, New Kid on the Block, Part 1, Photo cover	2.95	0.60	1.50	3.00
❑7, Mar 99, New Kid on the Block, Part 2	2.95	0.60	1.50	3.00
❑7/SC, Mar 99, New Kid on the Block, Part 2, Photo cover	2.95	0.60	1.50	3.00
❑8, Apr 99, The Final Cut	2.95	0.60	1.50	3.00
❑8/SC, Apr 99, The Final Cut, Photo cover	2.95	0.60	1.50	3.00
❑9, May 99, Hey, Good Lookin'	2.95	0.59	1.48	2.95
❑9/SC, May 99, Hey, Good Lookin', Photo cover	2.95	0.59	1.48	2.95
❑10, Jun 99, Hey, Good Lookin', part 2, teen magazine-style cover	2.95	0.59	1.48	2.95
❑10/SC, Jun 99, Hey, Good Lookin', part 2, Photo cover	2.95	0.59	1.48	2.95
❑11, Jul 99, A Boy Named Sue	2.95	0.59	1.48	2.95
❑11/SC, Jul 99, A Boy Named Sue, Photo cover	2.95	0.59	1.48	2.95
❑12, Aug 99, A Nice Girl Like You	2.95	0.59	1.48	2.95
❑12/SC, Aug 99, A Nice Girl Like You, Photo cover	2.95	0.59	1.48	2.95
❑13, Sep 99, Bad Blood, Part 4	2.95	0.59	1.48	2.95
❑13/SC, Sep 99, Bad Blood, Part 4, Photo cover	2.95	0.59	1.48	2.95
❑14, Oct 99, Bad Blood, Part 5	2.95	0.59	1.48	2.95
❑14/SC, Oct 99, Bad Blood, Part 5, Photo cover	2.95	0.59	1.48	2.95
❑15, Nov 99, Bad Blood, Part 6	2.95	0.59	1.48	2.95
❑15/SC, Nov 99, Bad Blood, Part 6, Photo cover	2.95	0.59	1.48	2.95
❑16, Dec 99, The Food Chain	2.95	0.59	1.48	2.95
❑16/SC, Dec 99, The Food Chain, Photo cover	2.95	0.59	1.48	2.95
❑17, Jan 00, Bad Blood, Part 7	2.95	0.59	1.48	2.95
❑17/SC, Jan 00, Bad Blood, Part 7, Photo cover	2.95	0.59	1.48	2.95
❑18, Feb 00	2.95	0.59	1.48	2.95
❑18/SC, Feb 00, Photo cover	2.95	0.59	1.48	2.95
❑19, Mar 00	2.95	0.59	1.48	2.95
❑19/SC, Mar 00, Photo cover	2.95	0.59	1.48	2.95
❑20, Apr 00	2.95	0.59	1.48	2.95
❑20/SC, Apr 00, Photo cover	2.95	0.59	1.48	2.95
❑21, May 00, The Blood of Carthage, Part 1	2.95	0.59	1.48	2.95
❑21/SC, May 00, The Blood of Carthage, Part 1, Photo cover	2.95	0.59	1.48	2.95
❑22, Jun 00, The Blood of Carthage, Part 2	2.95	0.59	1.48	2.95
❑22/SC, Jun 00, The Blood of Carthage, Part 2, Photo cover	2.95	0.59	1.48	2.95
❑23, Jul 00, The Blood of Carthage, Part 3	2.95	0.59	1.48	2.95
❑23/SC, Jul 00, The Blood of Carthage, Part 3, Photo cover	2.95	0.59	1.48	2.95
❑24, Aug 00, The Blood of Carthage, Part 4	2.95	0.59	1.48	2.95
❑24/SC, Aug 00, The Blood of Carthage, Part 4, Photo cover	2.95	0.59	1.48	2.95
❑25, Sep 00, The Blood of Carthage, Part 4	2.95	0.59	1.48	2.95
❑25/SC, Sep 00, The Blood of Carthage, Part 4, Photo cover	2.95	0.59	1.48	2.95
❑26, Oct 00, The Heart of a Slayer, Part 1	2.99	0.60	1.50	2.99
❑26/SC, Oct 00, The Heart of a Slayer, Part 1, Photo cover	2.99	0.60	1.50	2.99
❑27, Nov 00, The Heart of a Slayer, Part 2	2.99	0.60	1.50	2.99
❑27/SC, Nov 00, The Heart of a Slayer, Part 2, Photo cover	2.99	0.60	1.50	2.99
❑28, Dec 00, Cemetery of Lost Love	2.99	0.60	1.50	2.99
❑28/SC, Dec 00, Cemetery of Lost Love, Photo cover	2.99	0.60	1.50	2.99
❑29, Jan 01, Past Lives, Part 2	2.99	0.60	1.50	2.99
❑29/SC, Jan 01, Past Lives, Part 2, Photo cover	2.99	0.60	1.50	2.99
❑30, Feb 01, Past Lives, Part 4	2.99	0.60	1.50	2.99
❑30/SC, Feb 01, Past Lives, Part 4, Photo cover	2.99	0.60	1.50	2.99
❑31, Mar 01, Lost and Found	2.99	0.60	1.50	2.99
❑31/SC, Mar 01, Lost and Found, Photo cover	2.99	0.60	1.50	2.99
❑32, Apr 01, Invasion	2.99	0.60	1.50	2.99
❑32/SC, Apr 01, Invasion, Photo cover	2.99	0.60	1.50	2.99
❑33	2.99	0.60	1.50	2.99
❑33/SC, Photo cover	2.99	0.60	1.50	2.99
❑34	2.99	0.60	1.50	2.99
❑34/SC, Photo cover	2.99	0.60	1.50	2.99
❑35	2.99	0.60	1.50	2.99
❑35/SC, Photo cover	2.99	0.60	1.50	2.99
❑Anl 1999, Aug 99, The Latest Craze; Bad Dog, Photo cover; squarebound; 1999 Annual	4.95	0.99	2.47	4.95

BUFFY THE VAMPIRE SLAYER: ANGEL
DARK HORSE

	ORIG	GOOD	FINE	N-MINT
❑1, May 99	2.95	0.70	1.75	3.50
❑1/SC, May 99, Photo cover	2.95	0.70	1.75	3.50
❑2, Jun 99	2.95	0.60	1.50	3.00
❑2/SC, Jun 99, Photo cover	2.95	0.60	1.50	3.00
❑3, Jul 99	2.95	0.60	1.50	3.00
❑3/SC, Jul 99, Photo cover	2.95	0.60	1.50	3.00

BUFFY THE VAMPIRE SLAYER: GILES
DARK HORSE

Value: Cover or less

❑1, Oct 00, Beyond the Pale... 2.99
❑1/SC, Oct 00, Beyond the Pale, Photo cover... 2.99

BUFFY THE VAMPIRE SLAYER: JONATHAN
DARK HORSE

Value: Cover or less

❑1, Jan 01, Codename: Comrades... 2.99
❑1/SC, Jan 01, Codename: Comrades, Photo cover... 2.99

BUFFY THE VAMPIRE SLAYER: LOVER'S WALK
DARK HORSE

Value: Cover or less

❑1, Feb 01, One Small Promise; Punish Me With Kisses, Photo cover... 2.99

BUFFY THE VAMPIRE SLAYER: RING OF FIRE
DARK HORSE

Value: Cover or less

❑1, Aug 00, Photo cover... 9.95

BUFFY THE VAMPIRE SLAYER: SPIKE AND DRU
DARK HORSE

Value: Cover or less

❑1, Apr 99, Spike & Dru Paint the Town Red; The Queen of Hearts, Photo cover... 2.95
❑2... 2.95
❑3, All's Fair... 2.95
❑3/SC, Dec 00, All's Fair, Photo cover... 2.95

BUFFY THE VAMPIRE SLAYER: THE ORIGIN
DARK HORSE

Value: Cover or less

❑1, Jan 99... 2.95
❑1/LE, Jan 99, Limited edition foil cover... 19.95
❑1/SC, Jan 99, Photo cover... 2.95
❑2, Feb 99... 2.95
❑2/SC, Feb 99, Photo cover... 2.95
❑3, Mar 99... 2.95
❑3/SC, Mar 99, Photo cover... 2.95

BUFFY THE VAMPIRE SLAYER: WILLOW & TARA
DARK HORSE

Value: Cover or less

❑1, Apr 01... 2.99
❑1/SC, Apr 01... 2.99

BUG (MARVEL)
MARVEL

Value: Cover or less

❑1, Mar 97, Apples & Origins, V: Annihilus, One-Shot... 2.99

BUG (PLANET-X)
PLANET-X

Value: Cover or less

❑1... 1.50

BUG & STUMP
AAARGH!

Value: Cover or less

❑1, Aut 93, b&w; Australian; Australian, b&w... 2.95
❑2, Spr 94, b&w; Australian; Australian, b&w... 2.95

BUGBOY
IMAGE

Value: Cover or less

❑1, Jun 98, What I Did on My Vacation; Who Was That Masked Boy?, b&w... 3.95

BUGHOUSE
CAT-HEAD

	ORIG	GOOD	FINE	N-MINT
❑1, Mar 54, Opening Night, b&w	2.95	0.59	1.48	2.95
❑2, Nov 94, b&w	2.50	0.59	1.48	2.95
❑3, Jun 95, b&w	2.50	0.59	1.48	2.95
❑4, Sep 54, b&w; cardstock cover	2.75	0.59	1.48	2.95
❑5, Spr 97, b&w	2.95	0.59	1.48	2.95

BUG-HUNTERS
TRIDENT

Value: Cover or less

❑1, nn; b&w... 5.95

BUGS BUNNY
DC

	ORIG	GOOD	FINE	N-MINT
❑1, Jun 90	1.00	0.40	1.00	2.00
❑2, Jul 90	1.00	0.30	0.75	1.50
❑3, Aug 90	1.00	0.30	0.75	1.50

BUGS BUNNY MONTHLY, THE
DC

Value: Cover or less

❑1... 1.95
❑2... 1.95
❑3, Hoods in the Woods; The Great Bugsini... 1.95

BUG'S GIFT, A
DISCOVERY

Value: Cover or less

❑1, A Bug's Gift... 1.95

BULLET CROW, FOWL OF FORTUNE
ECLIPSE

Value: Cover or less

❑1... 2.00
❑2... 2.00

BULLETPROOF
KNOWN ASSOCIATES

Value: Cover or less

❑1, b&w... 3.95

BULLETPROOF COMICS
WET PAINT GRAPHICS

Value: Cover or less

❑1... 2.25
❑2, May 99... 2.25
❑3, Sep 99... 2.25

BULLETPROOF MONK
IMAGE

Value: Cover or less

- ❑1, Days of Thinking Why....... 2.95
- ❑2, Moments of Present Past . 2.95
- ❑3, Knowing you, Knowing me 2.95

BULLETS AND BRACELETS
MARVEL

Value: Cover or less

- ❑1, Apr 96, Final Trust 1.95

BULLWINKLE & ROCKY (BLACKTHORNE)
BLACKTHORNE

Value: Cover or less

- ❑1 .... 2.50
- ❑2 .... 2.50
- ❑3 .... 2.50
- ❑3D 1, Mar 87 .... 2.50

BULLWINKLE AND ROCKY (CHARLTON)
CHARLTON

	ORIG	GOOD	FINE	N-MINT
❑1, Jul 70, poster	0.15	6.00	15.00	30.00
❑2, Sep 70	0.15	3.60	9.00	18.00
❑3, Nov 70	0.15	3.00	7.50	15.00
❑4, Jan 71	0.15	2.40	6.00	12.00
❑5, Mar 71	0.15	2.40	6.00	12.00
❑6, May 71	0.15	2.40	6.00	12.00
❑7, Jul 71	0.15	2.40	6.00	12.00

BULLWINKLE AND ROCKY (GOLD KEY)
GOLD KEY

	ORIG	GOOD	FINE	N-MINT
❑1	0.12	28.00	70.00	140.00
❑2	0.12	20.00	50.00	100.00
❑3	0.12	8.00	20.00	40.00
❑4	0.12	8.00	20.00	40.00
❑5, Sep 72	0.15	8.00	20.00	40.00
❑6, Jan 73, Reprint	0.15	5.60	14.00	28.00
❑7, Reprint	0.12	5.60	14.00	28.00
❑8	0.12	5.60	14.00	28.00
❑9, Oct 73	0.20	5.60	14.00	28.00
❑10	0.20	5.60	14.00	28.00
❑11, Apr 74, Last issue of original run	0.20	5.60	14.00	28.00
❑12, Reprint; Series picks up after hiatus	—	2.80	7.00	14.00
❑13	—	4.00	10.00	20.00
❑14	—	3.20	8.00	16.00
❑15	—	1.80	4.50	9.00
❑16	—	1.80	4.50	9.00
❑17	—	1.80	4.50	9.00
❑18	—	1.80	4.50	9.00
❑19	—	1.80	4.50	9.00
❑20	0.40	1.80	4.50	9.00
❑21	0.40	1.40	3.50	7.00
❑22	0.40	1.40	3.50	7.00
❑23, Muscle Bound Moose	0.40	1.40	3.50	7.00
❑24	0.40	1.40	3.50	7.00
❑25, Final Issue	0.40	1.40	3.50	7.00

BULLWINKLE AND ROCKY (STAR)
MARVEL

	ORIG	GOOD	FINE	N-MINT
❑1, The "Invisible Ray" or "---!"	1.00	0.30	0.75	1.50
❑2	1.00	0.25	0.63	1.25
❑3	1.00	0.25	0.63	1.25
❑4	1.00	0.25	0.63	1.25
❑5	1.00	0.25	0.63	1.25
❑6	1.00	0.25	0.63	1.25
❑7	1.00	0.25	0.63	1.25
❑8, Bullwinkle and Rocky: The Moose Who Would be Mayor Or... Be-Caucus You're Mine!; Dudley Do-Right of the Mounties: A Nick in Time, Marvel publishes	1.00	0.25	0.63	1.25
❑9, Final Issue	1.00	0.25	0.63	1.25

BULLWINKLE FOR PRESIDENT IN 3-D
BLACKTHORNE

Value: Cover or less

- ❑1 .... 2.50

BUMBERCOMIX
STARHEAD

	ORIG	GOOD	FINE	N-MINT
❑1, Giveaway from arts festival	—	0.20	0.50	1.00

BURIAL OF THE RATS (BRAM STOKER'S...)
ROGER CORMAN'S COSMIC COMICS

Value: Cover or less

- ❑1 .... 2.50

BURIED TREASURE
PURE IMAGINATION

Value: Cover or less

- ❑1 .... 5.95
- ❑2 .... 5.95
- ❑3, moves to Caliber 5.95

BURIED TREASURE (2ND SERIES)
CALIBER

Value: Cover or less

- ❑1, FF; AW, reprints, b&w....... 2.50
- ❑2, Reprint............................. 2.50
- ❑3, WW; FF, reprints Frankenstein 2.50
- ❑4, FF 2.50

BURKE'S LAW
DELL

	ORIG	GOOD	FINE	N-MINT
❑1, Photo cover	0.12	4.80	12.00	24.00
❑2, Photo cover	0.12	4.00	10.00	20.00
❑3, Photo cover	0.12	4.00	10.00	20.00

When the DC and Marvel universes merged in *DC vs. Marvel/Marvel vs. DC*, a series of one-shots featuring the combined versions of the heroes and villains were published, including *Bullets and Bracelets.*

BURRITO
ACCENT!

	ORIG	GOOD	FINE	N-MINT
❑1, Jan 95	2.50	0.55	1.38	2.75
❑2, Apr 95	2.50	0.55	1.38	2.75
❑3, Jul 95	2.75	0.55	1.38	2.75
❑4, Nov 95	2.75	0.55	1.38	2.75
❑5, Jul 96, Discovered?! Is that You Finding Me or Me Finding You	2.75	0.55	1.38	2.75

BUSHIDO
ETERNITY

Value: Cover or less

- ❑1, Jul 88 .... 1.95
- ❑2 .... 1.95
- ❑3 .... 1.95
- ❑4 .... 1.95

BUSHIDO BLADE OF ZATOICHI WALRUS
SOLSON

Value: Cover or less

- ❑1 .... 2.00

BUSHWHACKED
EROS

Value: Cover or less

- ❑1 .... 2.95

BUSTER
CRISIS

Value: Cover or less

- ❑1 .... 2.50
- ❑2 .... 2.50

BUSTER THE AMAZING BEAR
URSUS STUDIOS

Value: Cover or less

- ❑1, Aug 92, Rude Awakening, says Aug 93 on cover, Aug 92 in indicia; Surprise Poster Insert... 2.50
- ❑2, Oct 93 .... 2.50
- ❑2-2, Oct 94, 2nd Printing....... 2.50
- ❑3, Jan 94 .... 2.50
- ❑4, May 94 .... 2.95
- ❑5, Nov 94 .... 2.50

BUSTLINE COMBAT
EROS

Value: Cover or less

- ❑1, May 99, Tanks for the Mammaries; The Island.................... 2.95

BUTCHER, THE
DC

Value: Cover or less

- ❑1, May 90, 1: John Butcher... 2.50
- ❑2, Jun 90 .... 2.50
- ❑3, Jul 90 .... 2.50
- ❑4, Aug 90 .... 2.50
- ❑5, Sep 90 .... 2.50

BUTCHER KNIGHT
IMAGE

Value: Cover or less

- ❑1/A, Dec 00, Demon's teeth cover 2.50
- ❑1/B, Dec 00, Woman standing next to demon on cover....... 2.50
- ❑1/C, Dec 00, Woman posing on demon on cover 2.50
- ❑1/D, Dec 00, White cover 2.50
- ❑2 .... 2.50
- ❑3, Apr 01 .... 2.50
- ❑4 .... 2.50

BUTT BISCUIT
FANTAGRAPHICS

Value: Cover or less

- ❑1 .... 2.25
- ❑2 .... 2.25
- ❑3 .... 2.25

BUTTERSCOTCH
FANTAGRAPHICS

Value: Cover or less

- ❑1 .... 2.50
- ❑2 .... 2.50
- ❑3 .... 2.50

BUTTON MAN: THE KILLING GAME
KITCHEN SINK

Value: Cover or less

- ❑1, Aug 95, oversized graphic novel.................................... 15.95

BUZ SAWYER QUARTERLY
DRAGON LADY

Value: Cover or less

- ❑1 .... 5.95
- ❑2 .... 5.95
- ❑3 .... 5.95

BUZZ
KITCHEN SINK

Value: Cover or less

- ❑1 .... 2.95
- ❑2 .... 2.95
- ❑3, Drink, Clown, Drink!; No Fran 2.95

BUZZ, THE
MARVEL

Value: Cover or less

- ❑1, Jul 00, SB, Comes a Hero! 2.99
- ❑2, Aug 00, SB....................... 2.99
- ❑3, Sep 00, SB, Moments of Truth 2.99

BUZZ AND COLONEL TOAD
BELMONT

Value: Cover or less

- ❑1 ... 2.50
- ❑2 ... 2.50
- ❑3, Jan 98 ... 2.50

BUZZARD
CAT-HEAD

	ORIG	GOOD	FINE	N-MINT
❑1	2.75	0.65	1.63	3.25
❑2, Oct 90	2.75	0.65	1.63	3.25
❑3	2.75	0.65	1.63	3.25
❑4	2.75	0.65	1.63	3.25
❑5	2.75	0.65	1.63	3.25
❑6, Aug 92	2.75	0.65	1.63	3.25
❑7, Feb 93	2.95	0.65	1.63	3.25
❑8	2.95	0.65	1.63	3.25
❑9	2.95	0.65	1.63	3.25
❑10	2.95	0.65	1.63	3.25
❑11	3.25	0.65	1.63	3.25
❑12	3.25	0.70	1.75	3.50
❑13	3.25	0.70	1.75	3.50
❑14	3.50	0.70	1.75	3.50
❑15	3.50	0.70	1.75	3.50
❑16	3.50	0.70	1.75	3.50
❑17	3.50	0.70	1.75	3.50
❑18	3.75	0.75	1.88	3.75
❑19, Old Grumpy; Caliente	3.75	0.75	1.88	3.75
❑20	3.75	0.75	1.88	3.75

BUZZBOY
SKYDOG PRESS

Value: Cover or less

- ❑1, May 98 ... 2.95
- ❑2, Aug 98 ... 2.95
- ❑3, Oct 98 ... 2.95
- ❑4, Win 98 ... 2.95

BY BIZARRE HANDS
DARK HORSE

Value: Cover or less

- ❑1, Apr 94, Tight Little Stitches In A Deadman's Back ... 2.50
- ❑2, May 94 ... 2.50
- ❑3 ... 2.50

BY THE TIME I GET TO WAGGA WAGGA
HARRIER

Value: Cover or less

- ❑1 ... 1.50

C

C•23
IMAGE

Value: Cover or less

- ❑1, Apr 98, 1: Protex; 1: Zenturion; 1: Primaid; 1: Tronix; 1: Armek; 1: The Hyperclan; 1: A-Mortal; 1: Zum; 1: Fluxus ... 2.50
- ❑2, May 98 ... 2.50
- ❑3, Jun 98, bound-in card ... 2.50
- ❑4, Jul 98 ... 2.50
- ❑5, Aug 98 ... 2.50
- ❑6, Sep 98, Planetary preview 2.50
- ❑7, Oct 98 ... 2.50
- ❑8, Nov 98 ... 2.50
- ❑8/SC, Nov 98, alternate cover (group) ... 2.50

CABBOT: BLOODHUNTER
MAXIMUM

Value: Cover or less

- ❑1 ... 2.50

CABINET OF DR. CALIGARI, THE
MONSTER

Value: Cover or less

- ❑1, Apr 92 ... 2.25
- ❑2, Jun 92 ... 2.25
- ❑3, Sep 92 ... 2.25

CABLE
MARVEL

	ORIG	GOOD	FINE	N-MINT
❑-1, Jul 97, Flashback	1.95	0.45	1.13	2.25
❑1, May 93, Embossed cover	3.50	0.80	2.00	4.00
❑2, Aug 93	2.00	0.50	1.25	2.50
❑3, Sep 93	2.00	0.50	1.25	2.50
❑4, Oct 93	2.00	0.50	1.25	2.50
❑5, Nov 93	2.00	0.50	1.25	2.50
❑6, Dec 93, A: Sinsear; A: Other	2.00	0.50	1.25	2.50
❑7, Jan 94	2.00	0.50	1.25	2.50
❑8, Feb 94	2.00	0.50	1.25	2.50
❑9, Mar 94	2.00	0.50	1.25	2.50
❑10, Apr 94	2.00	0.50	1.25	2.50
❑11, May 94	2.00	0.45	1.13	2.25
❑12, Jun 94	2.00	0.45	1.13	2.25
❑13, Jul 94	2.00	0.45	1.13	2.25
❑14, Aug 94	2.00	0.45	1.13	2.25
❑15, Sep 94, Ceremonies of Light	2.00	0.45	1.13	2.25
❑16, Oct 94, Final Sanction, Part 2	2.00	0.50	1.25	2.50
❑16/SC, Oct 94, Final Sanction, Part 2, enhanced cover	3.50	1.10	2.75	5.50
❑17, Nov 94	1.50	0.30	0.75	1.50
❑17/Dlx, Nov 94, Deluxe edition; deluxe	1.95	0.40	1.00	2.00
❑18, Dec 94	1.50	0.30	0.75	1.50
❑18/Dlx, Dec 94, Deluxe edition; deluxe	1.95	0.40	1.00	2.00
❑19, Jan 95	1.50	0.30	0.75	1.50
❑19/Dlx, Jan 95, Deluxe edition; deluxe	1.95	0.40	1.00	2.00
❑20, Feb 95	1.50	0.30	0.75	1.50
❑20/Dlx, Feb 95, JPH (w), An Hour of Last Things, A: X-Men, Deluxe edition; deluxe; A Legion Quest Addendum	1.95	0.40	1.00	2.00
❑21, Jul 95	1.95	0.40	1.00	2.00
❑22, Aug 95	1.95	0.40	1.00	2.00
❑23, Sep 95	1.95	0.40	1.00	2.00
❑24, Oct 95, no issue number on cover	1.95	0.40	1.00	2.00
❑25, Nov 95, JPH (w), What Was...What Is..., enhanced wraparound fold-out card-stock cover; Giant-size; 25th Issue Extravaganza	3.95	0.80	2.00	4.00
❑26, Dec 95, A: Weapon X	1.95	0.40	1.00	2.00
❑27, Jan 96, V: Sugar Man	1.95	0.40	1.00	2.00
❑28, Feb 96, V: Sugar Man	1.95	0.40	1.00	2.00
❑29, Mar 96, JPH (w), Man In The Mirror	1.95	0.40	1.00	2.00
❑30, Apr 96, JPH (w), For Every Action..., A: X-Man, Cable meets X-Man	1.95	0.40	1.00	2.00
❑31, May 96, V: X-Man	1.95	0.40	1.00	2.00
❑32, Jun 96	1.95	0.45	1.13	2.25
❑33, Jul 96	1.95	0.45	1.13	2.25
❑34, Aug 96, Onslaught: Phase 1; Onslaught, V: Hulk	1.95	0.45	1.13	2.25
❑35, Sep 96, Onslaught: Phase 2; Onslaught, V: Apocalypse	1.95	0.39	0.98	1.95
❑36, Oct 96	1.95	0.39	0.98	1.95
❑37, Nov 96, A: Weapon X	1.95	0.39	0.98	1.95
❑38, Dec 96, JPH (w), In Perspective, A: Micronauts	1.95	0.39	0.98	1.95
❑39, Jan 97, JPH (w), All Things Great And Small, A: Micronauts	1.95	0.39	0.98	1.95
❑40, Feb 97, Into The Dark	1.95	0.39	0.98	1.95
❑41, Mar 97, Depths of Time, A: Bishop	1.95	0.39	0.98	1.95
❑42, Apr 97, Tolerance	1.95	0.39	0.98	1.95
❑43, May 97, Legend of the Askani'Son; Broken Soldiers	1.95	0.39	0.98	1.95
❑44, Jun 97, JRo (w), Temptation in the Wilderness	1.95	0.39	0.98	1.95
❑45, Aug 97, gatefold summary; Operation Zero Tolerance	1.99	0.40	1.00	1.99
❑46, Sep 97, gatefold summary; Operation Zero Tolerance	1.99	0.40	1.00	1.99
❑47, Oct 97, gatefold summary; Operation Zero Tolerance	1.99	0.40	1.00	1.99
❑48, Nov 97, gatefold summary	1.99	0.40	1.00	1.99
❑49, Dec 97, gatefold summary	1.99	0.40	1.00	1.99
❑50, Jan 98, gatefold summary; Giant-size	1.99	0.59	1.48	2.95
❑51, Feb 98, gatefold summary	1.99	0.40	1.00	1.99
❑52, Mar 98, gatefold summary	1.99	0.40	1.00	1.99
❑53, Apr 98, gatefold summary	1.99	0.40	1.00	1.99
❑54, May 98, V: Klaw; A: Black Panther, gatefold summary	1.99	0.40	1.00	1.99
❑55, Jun 98, A: Domino, gatefold summary	1.99	0.40	1.00	1.99
❑56, Jul 98, gatefold summary	1.99	0.40	1.00	1.99
❑57, Aug 98, gatefold summary	1.99	0.40	1.00	1.99
❑58, Sep 98, gatefold summary	1.99	0.40	1.00	1.99
❑59, Oct 98, The Nemesis Contract, Part 1, V: Zzzax, gatefold summary	1.99	0.40	1.00	1.99
❑60, Nov 98, The Nemesis Contract, Part 2, 1: Agent 18, gatefold summary	1.99	0.40	1.00	1.99
❑61, Nov 98, The Nemesis Contract, Part 3, gatefold summary; captured by S.H.I.E.L.D.	1.99	0.40	1.00	1.99
❑62, Dec 98, The Nemesis Contract, Part 4; Blood Brothers, Part 1, A: Nick Fury, gatefold summary	1.99	0.40	1.00	1.99
❑63, Jan 99, Blood Brothers, Part 2, V: Stryfe, gatefold summary	1.99	0.40	1.00	1.99
❑64, Feb 99, O: Cable; A: Ozymandias, gatefold summary	1.99	0.40	1.00	1.99
❑65, Mar 99, 1: Acidroid; A: Rachel Summers	1.99	0.40	1.00	1.99
❑66, Apr 99, Sign of the End Times, part 1.	1.99	0.40	1.00	1.99
❑67, May 99, A: Avengers	1.99	0.40	1.00	1.99
❑68, Jun 99, A: Avengers	1.99	0.40	1.00	1.99
❑69, Jul 99	1.99	0.40	1.00	1.99
❑70, Aug 99	1.99	0.40	1.00	1.99
❑71, Sep 99, V: Hound Master	1.99	0.40	1.00	1.99
❑72, Oct 99	1.99	0.40	1.00	1.99
❑73, Nov 99	1.99	0.40	1.00	1.99
❑74, Dec 99	1.99	0.40	1.00	1.99
❑75, Jan 00	2.25	0.45	1.13	2.25
❑76, Feb 00	2.25	0.45	1.13	2.25
❑77, Mar 00	2.25	0.45	1.13	2.25
❑78, Apr 00	2.25	0.45	1.13	2.25

	ORIG	GOOD	FINE	N-MINT
❑79, May 00	2.25	0.45	1.13	2.25
❑80, Jun 00	2.25	0.45	1.13	2.25
❑81, Jul 00	2.25	0.45	1.13	2.25
❑82, Aug 00	2.25	0.45	1.13	2.25
❑83, Sep 00	2.25	0.45	1.13	2.25
❑84, Oct 00	2.25	0.45	1.13	2.25
❑85, Nov 00, Undertow	2.25	0.45	1.13	2.25
❑86, Dec 00, Last Man Standing	2.25	0.45	1.13	2.25
❑87, Jan 01, Dream's End, Part 2: Life Decisions	2.25	0.45	1.13	2.25
❑88, Feb 01, Earth Abides, A: Nightcrawler	2.25	0.45	1.13	2.25
❑89, Mar 01, Dark Tide Rising	2.25	0.45	1.13	2.25
❑90, Apr 01, Hearts of Darkness	2.25	0.45	1.13	2.25
❑91	2.25	0.45	1.13	2.25
❑92	2.25	0.45	1.13	2.25
❑93	2.25	0.45	1.13	2.25
❑94	2.25	0.45	1.13	2.25
❑95	2.25	0.45	1.13	2.25
❑96	2.25	0.45	1.13	2.25
❑Anl 1998, Engines of Destruction, Part 1, wraparound cover; Cable/Machine Man '98; continues in Machine Man/Bastion '98	2.99	0.60	1.50	2.99
❑Anl 1999, V: Sinister	3.50	0.70	1.75	3.50

CABLE: BLOOD AND METAL
MARVEL

	ORIG	GOOD	FINE	N-MINT
❑1, Oct 92, JR2	2.50	0.70	1.75	3.50
❑2, Nov 92, JR2	2.50	0.60	1.50	3.00

CABLE: SECOND GENESIS
MARVEL

Value: Cover or less

❑1, Sep 99, RL, RL (w), The Beginning of The End; The End of The Beginning, Reprint; collects New Mutants #1-2 and X-Force #1 ..... 3.99

CABLE TV
PARODY

Value: Cover or less

❑1, b&w 2.50

CADAVERA
MONSTER

Value: Cover or less

❑1, b&w 1.95
❑2, b&w 1.95

CADILLACS & DINOSAURS
MARVEL

Value: Cover or less

❑1, An Archipelago of Stone, Reprints Xenozoic Tales #1 in color 2.50
❑2, Reprints Xenozoic Tales #2 in color 2.50
❑3, Reprints Xenozoic Tales #3 in color 2.50
❑4, Reprints Xenozoic Tales #4 in color 2.50
❑5, Reprints Xenozoic Tales #5 in color 2.50
❑6, Reprints Xenozoic Tales #6 in color 2.50
❑3D 1, Jul 82, The Growing Pool, glasses; 100 Page giant 3.95

CADILLACS & DINOSAURS (VOL. 2)
TOPPS

	ORIG	GOOD	FINE	N-MINT
❑1, Feb 94, DG	2.50	0.50	1.25	2.50
❑1/SC, Feb 94, DG, foil cover	2.95	0.59	1.48	2.95
❑2, Mar 94, DG	2.50	0.50	1.25	2.50
❑2/Dlx, Mar 94, DG, poster by Moebius	2.50	0.50	1.25	2.50
❑3, Apr 94, DG	2.50	0.50	1.25	2.50
❑3/Dlx, Apr 94, poster	2.50	0.50	1.25	2.50
❑4, Jun 94, Man Eater, Part 1	2.50	0.50	1.25	2.50
❑4/SC, Jun 94	2.50	0.50	1.25	2.50
❑5, Man Eater, Part 2	—	0.50	1.25	2.50
❑6, Man Eater, Part 3	—	0.50	1.25	2.50
❑7, The Wild Ones!	2.50	0.50	1.25	2.50
❑8	2.50	0.50	1.25	2.50
❑9	2.50	0.50	1.25	2.50
❑10	2.50	0.50	1.25	2.50

CAFFEINE
SLAVE LABOR

Value: Cover or less

❑1, Jan 96 ..... 2.95
❑2, Apr 96 ..... 2.95
❑3, Jul 96 ..... 2.95
❑4, Nov 96 ..... 2.95
❑5, Jan 97 ..... 2.95
❑6, Apr 97 ..... 2.95
❑7, Jul 97 ..... 2.95
❑8, Nov 97 ..... 2.95
❑9 ..... 2.95
❑10, Final Issue 2.95

CAGE
MARVEL

Value: Cover or less

❑1, Apr 92 ..... 1.50
❑2, May 92 ..... 1.25
❑3, Jun 92, A: Punisher 1.25
❑4, Jul 92, A: Punisher 1.25
❑5, Aug 92, The Evil and the Cure, Part 1 ..... 1.25
❑6, Sep 92, The Evil and the Cure, Part 2 ..... 1.25
❑7, Oct 92 ..... 1.25
❑8, Nov 92 ..... 1.25
❑9, Dec 92 ..... 1.25
❑10, Jan 93 ..... 1.25
❑11, Feb 93 ..... 1.25
❑12, Mar 93, Iron Fist 1.75
❑13, Apr 93 ..... 1.25

Marvel's 1998 Annuals teamed two characters in the issue and its title — in this case, Cable and Machine Man.

© 1998 Marvel

❑14, May 93 ..... 1.25
❑15, Jun 93 ..... 1.25
❑16, Jul 93 ..... 1.25
❑17, Aug 93, Infinity Crusade 1.25
❑18, Sep 93, The Dark, Part 1 ..... 1.25
❑19, Oct 93, The Dark, Part 2 ..... 1.25
❑20, Nov 93, The Dark, Part 3, Final Issue 1.25

CAGED HEAT 3000
ROGER CORMAN'S COSMIC COMICS

Value: Cover or less

❑1, The Big Doll House 2.50
❑2 ..... 2.50

CAGES
TUNDRA

	ORIG	GOOD	FINE	N-MINT
❑1, b&w	3.50	1.40	3.50	7.00
❑2, b&w	3.50	1.00	2.50	5.00
❑3, b&w	3.50	0.90	2.25	4.50
❑4	3.95	0.90	2.25	4.50
❑5	3.95	0.90	2.25	4.50
❑6	3.95	0.90	2.25	4.50
❑7	3.95	0.80	2.00	4.00
❑8	3.95	0.80	2.00	4.00
❑9	3.95	0.99	2.47	4.95
❑10, Final Issue	4.95	0.99	2.47	4.95

CAIN
HARRIS

Value: Cover or less

❑1, trading card 2.95
❑2, Oct 93, two alternate covers 2.95

CALCULATED RISK
GENESIS

Value: Cover or less

❑1, b&w 3.00

CALIBER CHRISTMAS, A
CALIBER

	ORIG	GOOD	FINE	N-MINT
❑1, Dec 89, LifeQuest...A Time to Remember;, Crow; sampler	3.95	1.19	2.97	5.95

CALIBER CORE
CALIBER

	ORIG	GOOD	FINE	N-MINT
❑0, b&w; no cover price; intro to imprint	2.95	0.59	1.48	2.95
❑Ash 1, b&w; no cover price; intro to imprint	—	0.20	0.50	1.00

CALIBER PRESENTS
CALIBER

	ORIG	GOOD	FINE	N-MINT
❑1, b&w; Crow	1.95	1.20	3.00	6.00
❑2, b&w	1.95	0.40	1.00	2.00
❑3, b&w	1.95	0.40	1.00	2.00
❑4, b&w	1.95	0.40	1.00	2.00
❑5, b&w	1.95	0.40	1.00	2.00
❑6, Aug 89, Fugitive; This is only a Test	1.95	0.40	1.00	2.00
❑7	1.95	0.40	1.00	2.00
❑8	1.95	0.40	1.00	2.00
❑9	2.50	0.50	1.25	2.50
❑10	2.95	0.59	1.48	2.95
❑11	2.95	0.59	1.48	2.95
❑12	2.95	0.59	1.48	2.95
❑13	2.95	0.59	1.48	2.95
❑14	2.95	0.59	1.48	2.95
❑15, 64pgs.	3.50	0.70	1.75	3.50
❑16, 64pgs.	3.50	0.70	1.75	3.50
❑17, 64pgs.	3.50	0.70	1.75	3.50
❑18, 64pgs.	3.50	0.70	1.75	3.50
❑19, 64pgs.	3.50	0.70	1.75	3.50
❑20, 64pgs.	3.50	0.70	1.75	3.50
❑21, 64pgs.	3.50	0.70	1.75	3.50
❑22, 64pgs.	3.50	0.70	1.75	3.50
❑23, 64pgs.	3.50	0.70	1.75	3.50
❑24, Mack the Knife, A Night in Paradise, Sharks, Caliber Preview: The Zone Continuum, Puppy Love, Frames Edge, 64pgs.	3.50	0.70	1.75	3.50

CALIBER PRESENTS: CINDERELLA ON FIRE
CALIBER

Value: Cover or less

❑1, nn; b&w 2.95

CALIBER PRESENTS: GENERATOR COMICS
CALIBER

Value: Cover or less

❑1, nn; b&w 2.95

CALIBER PRESENTS: HYBRID STORIES
CALIBER

Value: Cover or less

- ❑1, The Dinner Guest; Baboon Boy, nn; b&w ... 2.95

CALIBER PRESENTS: PETIT MAL
CALIBER

Value: Cover or less

- ❑1, nn; b&w ... 2.95

CALIBER PRESENTS: ROMANTIC TALES
CALIBER

Value: Cover or less

- ❑1, Princess Leah, nn; b&w ... 2.95

CALIBER PRESENTS: SEPULCHER OPUS
CALIBER

Value: Cover or less

- ❑1, nn; b&w ... 2.95

CALIBER PRESENTS: SOMETHING INSIDE
CALIBER

Value: Cover or less

- ❑1, nn; b&w ... 3.50

CALIBER PRESENTS: SUB-ATOMIC SHOCK
CALIBER

Value: Cover or less

- ❑1, nn; b&w ... 2.95

CALIBER SPOTLIGHT
CALIBER

Value: Cover or less

- ❑1, May 95, A.K.A. Goldfish; Kabuki, b&w anthology with A.K.A. Goldfish, Kabuki, Kilroy is Here, Oz, and previews ... 2.95

CALIBRATIONS
CALIBER

Value: Cover or less

- ❑1, Stage Fright; Atmospherics, Part 1, b&w ... 2.95
- ❑2, Atmospherics, Part 2 ... 0.99
- ❑3, Atmospherics, Part 3 ... 0.99
- ❑4, Atmospherics, Part 4 ... 0.99
- ❑5, Atmospherics, Part 5 ... 0.99

CALIBRATIONS (VOL. 2)
CALIBER

	ORIG	GOOD	FINE	N-MINT
❑1, preview of The Lost and Atmospherics	0.99	0.20	0.50	1.00
❑2	0.99	0.20	0.50	1.00
❑3	0.99	0.20	0.50	1.00
❑4	0.99	0.20	0.50	1.00
❑5	0.99	0.20	0.50	1.00

CALIFORNIA COMICS
CALIFORNIA

	ORIG	GOOD	FINE	N-MINT
❑1	—	1.00	2.50	5.00
❑2	—	0.80	2.00	4.00

CALIFORNIA GIRLS
ECLIPSE

Value: Cover or less

- ❑1, Jun 87 ... 2.00
- ❑2, Jul 87 ... 2.00
- ❑3, Aug 87 ... 2.00
- ❑4, Sep 87 ... 2.00
- ❑5, Oct 87 ... 2.00
- ❑6, Nov 87 ... 2.00
- ❑7, Dec 87 ... 2.00
- ❑8, Jan 88, The Sound of Breaking Glass ... 2.00

CALIFORNIA RAISINS IN 3-D, THE
BLACKTHORNE

Value: Cover or less

- ❑1, Dec 87, a.k.a. Blackthorne in 3-D #31 ... 2.50
- ❑1-2 ... 2.50
- ❑ ... 2.50
- ❑2 ... 2.50
- ❑3 ... 2.50
- ❑4 ... 2.50
- ❑5 ... 2.50

CALIGARI 2050
MONSTER

Value: Cover or less

- ❑1 ... 2.25
- ❑2 ... 2.25
- ❑3 ... 2.25

CALLED FROM DARKNESS
ANARCHY

Value: Cover or less

- ❑1 ... 2.95

CALL ME PRINCESS
CPM

Value: Cover or less

- ❑1, May 99 ... 2.95
- ❑1/A, May 99 ... 2.95

CAMBION
SLAVE LABOR

Value: Cover or less

- ❑1, Dec 95 ... 2.95
- ❑2, Feb 96 ... 2.95
- ❑3, Feb 97, Rhythm's Gonna Get'cha, b&w; Published by Moonstone ... 2.95

CAMELOT 3000
DC

	ORIG	GOOD	FINE	N-MINT
❑1, Dec 82, BB, The Past And Future King!, O: Arthur; O: Merlin	1.00	0.50	1.25	2.50
❑2, Jan 83, BB	1.00	0.40	1.00	2.00
❑3, Feb 83, BB	1.00	0.40	1.00	2.00
❑4, Mar 83, BB	1.00	0.40	1.00	2.00
❑5, Apr 83, BB, The Tale Of Morgan LeFay	1.00	0.40	1.00	2.00
❑6, Jul 83, BB	1.00	0.40	1.00	2.00
❑7, Aug 83, BB	1.00	0.40	1.00	2.00
❑8, Sep 83, BB	1.00	0.40	1.00	2.00
❑9, Dec 83, BB	1.00	0.40	1.00	2.00
❑10, Mar 84, BB	1.00	0.40	1.00	2.00
❑11, Jul 84, BB	1.00	0.40	1.00	2.00
❑12, Apr 85, BB	1.00	0.40	1.00	2.00

CAMELOT ETERNAL
CALIBER

Value: Cover or less

- ❑1, Part 1, Avalon Denied, Prologue; After the Fall ... 2.50
- ❑2 ... 2.50
- ❑3 ... 2.50
- ❑4 ... 2.50
- ❑5 ... 2.50
- ❑6 ... 2.50
- ❑7 ... 2.50
- ❑8 ... 2.50

CAMP CANDY
MARVEL

Value: Cover or less

- ❑1, The Return of Headless Harry; The Owimpic Kid ... 1.00
- ❑2, The Counterfeit Campers; The Moose Who Loves Me ... 1.00
- ❑3 ... 1.00
- ❑4 ... 1.00
- ❑5 ... 1.00
- ❑6 ... 1.00
- ❑7 ... 1.00

CAMPING WITH BIGFOOT
SLAVE LABOR

Value: Cover or less

- ❑1, Sep 95 ... 2.95

CANADIAN ROCK SPECIAL
REVOLUTIONARY

Value: Cover or less

- ❑1, Apr 94, Ex-Poseurs, b&w; Rush ... 2.50

CANCER: THE CRAB BOY
SABRE'S EDGE

Value: Cover or less

- ❑1 ... 2.95
- ❑2 ... 2.95
- ❑3 ... 2.95
- ❑4 ... 2.95
- ❑5 ... 2.95

CANDIDE REVEALED
FANTAGRAPHICS

Value: Cover or less

- ❑1, b&w; adult ... 2.25

CANNIBALIS
RAGING RHINO

Value: Cover or less

- ❑1, b&w; adult ... 2.95

CANNON
FANTAGRAPHICS

	ORIG	GOOD	FINE	N-MINT
❑1, Feb 91, WW, WW (w), b&w	2.75	0.55	1.38	2.75
❑1-2, WW, 2nd Printing	2.95	0.59	1.48	2.95
❑2, Mar 91, WW, WW (w), b&w	2.75	0.59	1.48	2.95
❑2-2, WW, 2nd Printing	2.95	0.59	1.48	2.95
❑3, Apr 91, WW, WW (w), Love, Lust, and Larceny, O: Sue Stevens; O: Madame Toy	2.75	0.59	1.48	2.95
❑3-2, WW, O: Sue Stevens; O: Madame Toy, 2nd Printing	2.95	0.59	1.48	2.95
❑4, May 91, WW, WW (w)	2.75	0.59	1.48	2.95
❑5, Jun 91, WW, WW (w)	2.75	0.59	1.48	2.95
❑6, Jul 91, WW, WW (w)	2.75	0.59	1.48	2.95
❑7, Aug 91, WW, WW (w)	2.75	0.59	1.48	2.95
❑8, Sep 91, WW, WW (w)	2.95	0.59	1.48	2.95

CAPE CITY
DIMENSION X

Value: Cover or less

- ❑1, b&w ... 2.75
- ❑2, b&w ... 2.75

CAPITAL CAPERS PRESENTS
BLT STUDIOS

Value: Cover or less

- ❑1, Oct 94, Socialism Trek: The Search for Health Care, b&w 2.95

CAP'N OATMEAL
ALL AMERICAN

Value: Cover or less

- ❑1, b&w ... 2.25

CAP'N QUICK & A FOOZLE
ECLIPSE

Value: Cover or less

- ❑1, Jul 84, MR, Together Again...for the First Time, A: The Darklydale Dancers; A: The "Great Jones"; A: Granny; A: Mel; A: Cap'n Quick; A: Doberman; A: Foozle; A: Stat ... 1.50
- ❑2, Mar 85, MR ... 1.75
- ❑3, MR, Title changes to The Foozle ... 1.50

CAPTAIN ACTION
KARL ART

Value: Cover or less

- ❑0, 1: Captain Action (Karl Art); 1: Doctor Evil, preview of ongoing series; Insert in Space Bananas #1 ... 1.95

CAPTAIN ACTION (DC)
DC

	ORIG	GOOD	FINE	N-MINT
❑1, Nov 68, WW, O: Captain Action	0.12	8.00	20.00	40.00
❑2, Jan 69, WW; GK	0.12	5.00	12.50	25.00
❑3, Mar 69, WW; GK	0.12	5.00	12.50	25.00
❑4, May 69, GK	0.12	5.00	12.50	25.00
❑5, Jul 69, WW; GK	0.12	5.00	12.50	25.00

CAPTAIN AMERICA (VOL. 1)
MARVEL

	ORIG	GOOD	FINE	N-MINT
❑100, Apr 68, JK, A: Avengers, Series continued from Tales of Suspense #99	0.12	50.00	125.00	250.00
❑101, May 68, JK, 1: 4th Sleeper	0.12	10.00	25.00	50.00
❑102, Jun 68, JK	0.12	7.00	17.50	35.00
❑103, Jul 68, JK, The Weakest Link, A: Red Skull, Agent 13's identity revealed as Sharon Carter	0.12	7.00	17.50	35.00
❑104, Aug 68, JK, V: Red Skull	0.12	7.00	17.50	35.00
❑105, Sep 68, JK, V: Batroc	0.12	7.00	17.50	35.00
❑106, Oct 68, JK, SL (w), Cap Goes Wild!	0.12	7.00	17.50	35.00
❑107, Nov 68, JK, SL (w), If the Past Be Not Dead ..., A: Red Skull; 1: Doctor Faustus; 1: Dr. Faustus	0.12	7.00	17.50	35.00
❑108, Dec 68, JK	0.12	7.00	17.50	35.00
❑109, Jan 69, JK, SL (w), The Hero that Was!, O: Captain America	0.12	8.00	20.00	40.00
❑109-2, JK, The Hero that Was!, O: Captain America, 2nd Printing	0.12	0.40	1.00	2.00
❑110, Feb 69, JSo, 1: Viper; 1: Viper II (as Madame Hydra); A: Rick Jones; A: Hulk, Rick Jones dons Bucky costume	0.12	9.00	22.50	45.00
❑111, Mar 69, JSo	0.12	8.00	20.00	40.00
❑112, Apr 69, JK; GT, O: Captain America; O: Viper II (as Madame Hydra), album	0.12	6.00	15.00	30.00
❑113, May 69, JSo, Avengers	0.12	8.00	20.00	40.00
❑114, Jun 69, JR	0.12	3.20	8.00	16.00
❑115, Jul 69	0.12	3.20	8.00	16.00
❑116, Aug 69	0.15	3.20	8.00	16.00
❑117, Sep 69, JSt; GC, 1: Falcon	0.15	7.00	17.50	35.00
❑118, Oct 69, JSt; GC, SL (w), The Falcon Fights On, A: Falcon	0.15	2.80	7.00	14.00
❑119, Nov 69, JSt; GC, SL (w), Now Falls The Skull, A: Falcon	0.15	2.80	7.00	14.00
❑120, Dec 69, JSt; GC, SL (w), Crack Up On Campus, A: Falcon	0.15	2.80	7.00	14.00
❑121, Jan 70, GC, SL (w), The Coming Of The Man-Brute, O: Captain America	0.15	2.00	5.00	10.00
❑122, Feb 70, GC, SL (w), The Sting Of The Scorpion	0.15	1.80	4.50	9.00
❑123, Mar 70, GC, SL (w), Suprema, The Deadliest Of The Species, 1: Suprema (later becomes Mother Night)	0.15	1.80	4.50	9.00
❑124, Apr 70, GC, SL (w), Mission: Stop The Cyborg	0.15	1.80	4.50	9.00
❑125, May 70, GC, SL (w), Captured In Vietnam	0.15	1.80	4.50	9.00
❑126, Jun 70, GC, SL (w), The Fate of ... the Falcon!, A: Falcon; 1: Diamond Head	0.15	1.80	4.50	9.00
❑127, Jul 70, GC, SL (w), Who Calls Me Traitor?	0.15	1.80	4.50	9.00
❑128, Aug 70, GC, SL (w), Mission: Stamp Out Satan's Angels!	0.15	1.80	4.50	9.00
❑129, Sep 70, GC, SL (w), The Vengeance Of The Red Skull	0.15	1.80	4.50	9.00
❑130, Oct 70, GC, SL (w), Up Against The Wall!	0.15	1.80	4.50	9.00
❑131, Nov 70, GC, SL (w)	0.15	1.60	4.00	8.00
❑132, Dec 70, GC, SL (w)	0.15	1.60	4.00	8.00
❑133, Jan 71, GC, SL (w), Madness In The Slums!, O: Modok, Falcon becomes Captain America's partner	0.15	1.60	4.00	8.00
❑134, Feb 71, GC, SL (w)	0.15	1.60	4.00	8.00
❑135, Mar 71, GC, JR (c), SL (w), More Monster Than Man!	0.15	1.60	4.00	8.00
❑136, Apr 71, GC, SL (w), The World Below	0.15	1.60	4.00	8.00
❑137, May 71, BEv; GC, A: Spider-Man	0.15	1.60	4.00	8.00
❑138, Jun 71, JR, A: Spider-Man	0.15	1.60	4.00	8.00
❑139, Jul 71, JR; GC, SL (w), The Badge And The Betrayal!	0.15	1.60	4.00	8.00
❑140, Aug 71, JR, O: Grey Gargoyle	0.15	1.60	4.00	8.00
❑141, Sep 71, JR, SL (w), The Unholy Alliance!	0.15	1.20	3.00	6.00
❑142, Oct 71, JR, And In The End..., V: Grey Gargoyle	0.15	1.20	3.00	6.00
❑143, Nov 71, JR, Power To The People, Giant-size	0.25	1.20	3.00	6.00
❑144, Dec 71, JR	0.20	1.20	3.00	6.00
❑145, Jan 72, GK, Skyjacked!	0.20	1.20	3.00	6.00
❑146, Feb 72, SB, Mission: Destroy The Femme Force!	0.20	1.20	3.00	6.00
❑147, Mar 72	0.20	1.20	3.00	6.00
❑148, Apr 72	0.20	1.20	3.00	6.00
❑149, May 72, SB, All The Colors...Of Evil.	0.20	1.20	3.00	6.00
❑150, Jun 72	0.20	1.20	3.00	6.00
❑151, Jul 72	0.20	1.20	3.00	6.00
❑152, Aug 72, SB, Terror In The Night!	0.20	1.20	3.00	6.00
❑153, Sep 72, 1: Captain America IV; V: Red Skull; 1: Bucky III (Jack Monroe)	0.20	1.20	3.00	6.00
❑154, Oct 72	0.20	1.20	3.00	6.00

When aliens invaded Earth in the year 3000, King Arthur returned to aid England in its darkest hour in *Camelot 3000*, DC's first maxi-series.

	ORIG	GOOD	FINE	N-MINT
❑155, Nov 72, SB, The Incredible Origin Of The Other Captain America!, O: Captain America; O: Captain America II (Jack Monroe)	0.20	1.20	3.00	6.00
❑156, Dec 72	0.20	1.20	3.00	6.00
❑157, Jan 73	0.20	1.20	3.00	6.00
❑158, Feb 73	0.20	1.20	3.00	6.00
❑159, Mar 73	0.20	1.20	3.00	6.00
❑160, Apr 73, 1: Solarr	0.20	1.20	3.00	6.00
❑161, May 73, SB, ...If He Loseth His Soul!	0.20	1.00	2.50	5.00
❑162, Jun 73, SB, This Way Lies Madness!, O: Sharon Carter	0.20	1.00	2.50	5.00
❑163, Jul 73, SB, Beware Of Serpents!, 1: Dave Cox	0.20	1.00	2.50	5.00
❑164, Aug 73, Queen Of The Werewolves!, 1: Nightshade	0.20	1.00	2.50	5.00
❑165, Sep 73, SB, The Yellow Claw Strikes	0.20	1.00	2.50	5.00
❑166, Oct 73, SB, Night Of the Lurking Dead!	0.20	1.00	2.50	5.00
❑167, Nov 73, SB, Ashes To Ashes	0.20	1.00	2.50	5.00
❑168, Dec 73, SB, ...And A Phoenix Shall Arise, D: Phoenix I (Helmut Zemo); A: Baron Zemo (Helmut)	0.20	1.00	2.50	5.00
❑169, Jan 74, 1: Moonstone I (Lloyd Bloch)-cameo	0.20	1.00	2.50	5.00
❑170, Feb 74, SB, J'Accuse!, 1: Moonstone I (Lloyd Bloch)-full	0.20	1.00	2.50	5.00
❑171, Mar 74	0.20	1.00	2.50	5.00
❑172, Apr 74, SB, A: Banshee; A: X-Men	0.20	1.80	4.50	9.00
❑173, May 74, SB, The Sins Of The Secret Empire!, A: X-Men	0.25	1.80	4.50	9.00
❑174, Jun 74, SB, A: X-Men	0.25	1.80	4.50	9.00
❑175, Jul 74, SB, A: X-Men	0.25	1.80	4.50	9.00
❑176, Aug 74, SB	0.25	1.20	3.00	6.00
❑177, Sep 74, SB, recalls origin and quits	0.25	1.00	2.50	5.00
❑178, Oct 74, SB	0.25	1.00	2.50	5.00
❑179, Nov 74, SB, Slings And Arrows!	0.25	1.00	2.50	5.00
❑180, Dec 74, SB, 1: Viper II; O: Nomad; 1: Nomad (Steve Rogers)	0.25	1.40	3.50	7.00
❑181, Jan 75, SB, The Mark Of Madness!, 1: Captain America (new)	0.25	1.20	3.00	6.00
❑182, Feb 75	0.25	0.80	2.00	4.00
❑183, Mar 75, D: Captain America (new), Steve Rogers becomes Captain America again	0.25	1.00	2.50	5.00
❑184, Apr 75	0.25	0.80	2.00	4.00
❑185, May 75	0.25	0.80	2.00	4.00
❑186, Jun 75, O: Falcon (real origin)	0.25	1.00	2.50	5.00
❑187, Jul 75	0.25	0.80	2.00	4.00
❑188, Aug 75, SB, Druid-War	0.25	0.80	2.00	4.00
❑189, Sep 75, FR, Arena For A Fallen Hero	0.25	0.80	2.00	4.00
❑190, Oct 75, FR, Nightshade Is Deadlier The Second Time Around!	0.25	0.80	2.00	4.00
❑191, Nov 75, FR, The Trial Of The Falcon!	0.25	0.80	2.00	4.00
❑192, Dec 75, FR, Mad-Flight!, 1: Karla Sofen (becomes Moonstone)	0.25	0.80	2.00	4.00
❑193, Jan 76, JK, JK (w), Madbomb, Part 1; Screamer in the Brain!	0.25	0.80	2.00	4.00
❑194, Feb 76, JK, JK (w), Madbomb, Part 2; The Trojan Horde	0.25	0.80	2.00	4.00
❑195, Mar 76, JK, JK (w), Madbomb, Part 3; It's 1984!	0.25	0.80	2.00	4.00
❑196, Apr 76, JK, JK (w), Madbomb, Part 4; Kill-Derby	0.25	0.80	2.00	4.00
❑197, May 76, JK, JK (w), Madbomb, Part 5; The Rocks Are Burning!	0.25	0.80	2.00	4.00
❑198, Jun 76, JK, JK (w), Madbomb, Part 6; Captain America's Love Story	0.25	0.80	2.00	4.00
❑199, Jul 76, JK, JK (w), Madbomb, Part 7; The Man Who Sold the United States	0.25	0.80	2.00	4.00
❑200, Aug 76, JK, JK (w), Madbomb, Part 8, 200th anniversary issue	0.25	1.00	2.50	5.00
❑201, Sep 76, JK, JK (w), The Night People	0.30	0.60	1.50	3.00
❑202, Oct 76, JK	0.30	0.60	1.50	3.00
❑203, Nov 76, JK, JK (w), Alamo II	0.30	0.60	1.50	3.00
❑204, Dec 76, JK, JK (w), The Unburied One	0.30	0.60	1.50	3.00

	ORIG	GOOD	FINE	N-MINT
❑205, Jan 77, JK, JK (w), Agron Walks The Earth!	0.30	0.60	1.50	3.00
❑206, Feb 77, JK, JK (w), Face To Face With The Swine!, 1: Donna Maria Puentes	0.30	0.60	1.50	3.00
❑207, Mar 77, JK, JK (w), The Tiger And The Swine!	0.30	0.60	1.50	3.00
❑208, Apr 77, JK, JK (w), The River Of Death!, 1: Arnim Zola	0.30	0.60	1.50	3.00
❑209, May 77, JK, JK (w), Arnim Zola - The Bio-Fanatic!, 1: Doughboy; 1: Arnim Zola	0.30	0.60	1.50	3.00
❑210, Jun 77, JK, JK (w), Showdown Day!	0.30	0.60	1.50	3.00
❑211, Jul 77, JK, JK (w), Nazi "X"!	0.30	0.60	1.50	3.00
❑212, Aug 77, JK, JK (w), The Face Of A Hero	0.30	0.60	1.50	3.00
❑213, Sep 77, JK, JK (w), The Night Flyer!	0.30	0.60	1.50	3.00
❑214, Oct 77, JK, JK (w), Falcon	0.30	0.60	1.50	3.00
❑215, Nov 77, GK	0.35	0.60	1.50	3.00
❑216, Dec 77, GK	0.35	0.60	1.50	3.00
❑217, Jan 78, JB, 1: Blue Streak; 1: Quasar (Marvel Man)	0.35	0.60	1.50	3.00
❑218, Feb 78, SB	0.35	0.60	1.50	3.00
❑219, Mar 78, SB	0.35	0.60	1.50	3.00
❑220, Apr 78, GK; SB, The Ameridroid Lives!	0.35	0.60	1.50	3.00
❑221, May 78, GK; SB, Cul-De-Sac	0.35	0.60	1.50	3.00
❑222, Jun 78, SB, Monumental Menace	0.35	0.60	1.50	3.00
❑223, Jul 78, JBy; SB, Call Me Animus	0.35	0.60	1.50	3.00
❑224, Aug 78, MZ, Saturday Night Furor, 1: Señor Muerte II (Philip Garcia)	0.35	0.60	1.50	3.00
❑225, Sep 78, SB, Devastation	0.35	0.60	1.50	3.00
❑226, Oct 78, SB, Am I Still Captain America?	0.35	0.60	1.50	3.00
❑227, Nov 78, SB, This Deadly Gauntlet	0.35	0.60	1.50	3.00
❑228, Dec 78, SB, A Serpent Lurks Below	0.35	0.60	1.50	3.00
❑229, Jan 79, SB, Traitors All About Me!, A: Marvel Man (Quasar)	0.35	0.60	1.50	3.00
❑230, Feb 79, DP; SB, Assault on Alcatraz!, V: Hulk	0.35	0.60	1.50	3.00
❑231, Mar 79, DP; SB, Aftermath!, V: Grand Director	0.35	0.60	1.50	3.00
❑232, Apr 79, DP; SB, The Flame And The Fury	0.35	0.60	1.50	3.00
❑233, May 79, DP; SB, Crossfire, D: Sharon Carter	0.40	0.60	1.50	3.00
❑234, Jun 79, A: Daredevil	0.40	0.60	1.50	3.00
❑235, Jul 79, JAb; FM; SB, A: Daredevil	0.40	0.60	1.50	3.00
❑236, Aug 79, DP; SB, Death Dive!, D: Captain America IV	0.40	0.60	1.50	3.00
❑237, Sep 79, DP; SB, From The Ashes..., 1: Mike Farrel; 1: Copperhead; 1: Joshua Cooper; 1: Anna Kappelbaum, Steve moves to Brooklyn	0.40	0.60	1.50	3.00
❑238, Oct 79, JBy, Snowfall Fury	0.40	0.60	1.50	3.00
❑239, Nov 79, JBy, Mind-Stains On The Virgin Snow	0.40	0.60	1.50	3.00
❑240, Dec 79, Gang Wars!	0.40	0.60	1.50	3.00
❑241, Jan 80, FM, A: Punisher	0.40	1.30	3.25	6.50
❑242, Feb 80, JSt; DP, Facades!	0.40	0.50	1.25	2.50
❑243, Mar 80, DP; GP; RB, The Lazarus Conspiracy	0.40	0.50	1.25	2.50
❑244, Apr 80, DP; FM, The Way Of All Flesh!	0.40	0.50	1.25	2.50
❑245, May 80, FM, The Calypso Connection	0.40	0.50	1.25	2.50
❑246, Jun 80, GP, The Sins Of The Fathers	0.40	0.50	1.25	2.50
❑247, Jul 80, JBy, By The Dawn's Early Light!, 1: Machinesmith	0.40	0.50	1.25	2.50
❑248, Aug 80, JBy, 1: Bernie Rosenthal	0.40	0.50	1.25	2.50
❑249, Sep 80, JBy, Death, Where Is Thy Sting?, O: Machinesmith	0.50	0.50	1.25	2.50
❑250, Oct 80, JBy	0.50	0.50	1.25	2.50
❑251, Nov 80, JBy	0.50	0.50	1.25	2.50
❑252, Dec 80, JBy, Cold Fire	0.50	0.50	1.25	2.50
❑253, Jan 81, JBy, Should Old Acquaintance Be Forgot, D: Union Jack II (Brian Falsworth); 1: Joe Chapman (becomes Union Jack III)	0.50	0.50	1.25	2.50
❑254, Feb 81, JBy, Blood On The Moors, 1: Union Jack III (Joe Chapman); D: Union Jack I (Lord Falsworth); D: Baron Blood	0.50	0.50	1.25	2.50
❑255, Mar 81, FM; JBy, The Living Legend, 1: Sarah Rogers (Steve's mother); O: Captain America, 40th anniversary	0.50	0.50	1.25	2.50
❑256, Apr 81, GC, The Ghost Of Greymoor Castle!	0.50	0.40	1.00	2.00
❑257, May 81, Deadly Anniversary, A: Hulk	0.50	0.40	1.00	2.00
❑258, Jun 81, MZ, Blockbuster	0.50	0.40	1.00	2.00
❑259, Jul 81, MZ, Rite Of Passage!	0.50	0.40	1.00	2.00
❑260, Aug 81, AM (w), Prison Reform!	0.50	0.40	1.00	2.00
❑261, Sep 81, MZ, Celluloid Heroes!	0.50	0.40	1.00	2.00
❑262, Oct 81, MZ, Death of A Legend?	0.50	0.40	1.00	2.00
❑263, Nov 81, MZ, ...The Last Movie	0.50	0.40	1.00	2.00
❑264, Dec 81, MZ, The American Dreamers!, A: X-Men, X-Men cameo	0.50	0.40	1.00	2.00
❑265, Jan 82, MZ, Thunderhead, A: Nick Fury & Spider-Man	0.60	0.40	1.00	2.00
❑266, Feb 82, MZ, The Flight From Thunderhead!	0.60	0.40	1.00	2.00
❑267, Mar 82, MZ, The Man Who Made A Difference!, 1: Everyman	0.60	0.40	1.00	2.00

	ORIG	GOOD	FINE	N-MINT
❑268, Apr 82, MZ, Peace On Earth-Good Will To Man	0.60	0.40	1.00	2.00
❑269, May 82, MZ, A Mind Is A Terrible Thing To Waste, 1: Team America	0.60	0.40	1.00	2.00
❑270, Jun 82, MZ, Someone Who Cares	0.60	0.40	1.00	2.00
❑271, Jul 82, The Mystery Of Mr. X	0.60	0.40	1.00	2.00
❑272, Aug 82, MZ, Mean Streets, 1: Vermin	0.60	0.50	1.25	2.50
❑273, Sep 82, MZ, Cap And The Howlers...Together Again!	0.60	0.40	1.00	2.00
❑274, Oct 82, MZ, Death Of A Hero!, D: General Samuel "Happy Sam" Sawyer	0.60	0.40	1.00	2.00
❑275, Nov 82, MZ, Yesterday's Shadows, Bernie Rosenthal learns Cap's identity	0.60	0.40	1.00	2.00
❑276, Dec 82, MZ, Turning Point, 1: Baron Zemo II (Helmut Zemo), Later becomes Citizen V	0.60	0.70	1.75	3.50
❑277, Jan 83, MZ, In Thy Image	0.60	0.40	1.00	2.00
❑278, Feb 83, MZ	0.60	0.40	1.00	2.00
❑279, Mar 83, MZ, Of Monsters And Men	0.60	0.40	1.00	2.00
❑280, Apr 83, MZ, Sermon Of Straw	0.60	0.40	1.00	2.00
❑281, May 83, MZ, Before The Fall, A: Jack Monroe	0.60	0.40	1.00	2.00
❑282, Jun 83, MZ, 1: Nomad II (Jack Monroe); 1: Joseph Rogers (Steve's father)	0.60	0.80	2.00	4.00
❑282-2, MZ, 1: Nomad II (Jack Monroe), 2nd Printing; silver ink	1.75	0.40	1.00	2.00
❑283, Jul 83, MZ, America The Cursed, 2: Nomad (Jack Monroe)	0.60	0.60	1.50	3.00
❑284, Aug 83, MZ, A: Patriot (Jeffrey Mace)	0.60	0.40	1.00	2.00
❑285, Sep 83, MZ; SB, Letting Go, V: Porcupine; D: Patriot (Jeffrey Mace)	0.60	0.40	1.00	2.00
❑286, Oct 83, MZ, A: Deathlok	0.60	0.60	1.50	3.00
❑287, Nov 83, MZ, A: Deathlok	0.60	0.60	1.50	3.00
❑288, Dec 83, MZ, A: Deathlok	0.60	0.60	1.50	3.00
❑289, Jan 84, MZ, Tomorrow The World?, A: Bernie America, Assistant Editors' Month	0.60	0.40	1.00	2.00
❑290, Feb 84, JBy, Echoes, A: Mother Night; 1: Black Crow (in crow form), Zemo	0.60	0.40	1.00	2.00
❑291, Mar 84, HT, JBy (c), To Tame A Tumbler	0.60	0.40	1.00	2.00
❑292, Apr 84, An American Christmas!, O: Black Crow; 1: Black Crow (in human form)	0.60	0.40	1.00	2.00
❑293, May 84, Field Of Vision	0.60	0.40	1.00	2.00
❑294, Jun 84, The Measure Of A Man	0.60	0.40	1.00	2.00
❑295, Jul 84, The Centre Cannot hold!	0.60	0.40	1.00	2.00
❑296, Aug 84, Things Fall Apart!	0.60	0.40	1.00	2.00
❑297, Sep 84, All My Sins Remembered	0.60	0.40	1.00	2.00
❑298, Oct 84, Sturm Und Drang: The Life And Times Of The Red Skull, O: Red Skull	0.60	0.40	1.00	2.00
❑299, Nov 84, The Bunker, O: Red Skull	0.60	0.40	1.00	2.00
❑300, Dec 84, Das Ende!, V: Red Skull	0.60	0.40	1.00	2.00
❑301, Jan 85, All Good Things...	0.60	0.40	1.00	2.00
❑302, Feb 85, ...And Other Strangers!, 1: Machete	0.60	0.40	1.00	2.00
❑303, Mar 85, Double Dare, V: Batroc	0.60	0.40	1.00	2.00
❑304, Apr 85	0.65	0.40	1.00	2.00
❑305, May 85, Walk Upon England!, A: Captain Britain	0.65	0.40	1.00	2.00
❑306, Jun 85, Summoning!, A: Captain Britain	0.65	0.40	1.00	2.00
❑307, Jul 85, Stop Making Sense, 1: Madcap	0.65	0.40	1.00	2.00
❑308, Aug 85, JBy, Secret Wars II; The Body In Question, Secret Wars II	0.65	0.40	1.00	2.00
❑309, Sep 85, Nomad Madcap Cap..., V: Madcap, Nomad leaves team	0.65	0.40	1.00	2.00
❑310, Oct 85, 1: Asp II (Cleo); 1: Bushmaster; 1: Serpent Society; 1: Cottonmouth II; 1: Rattler; 1: Diamondback	0.65	0.40	1.00	2.00
❑311, Nov 85, Working..., V: Super-Adaptoid	0.65	0.40	1.00	2.00
❑312, Dec 85, Deface The Nation, 1: Flag-Smasher	0.65	0.40	1.00	2.00
❑313, Jan 86, JBy, Mission: Murder Modok!	0.65	0.40	1.00	2.00
❑314, Feb 86	0.75	0.40	1.00	2.00
❑315, Mar 86, D: Porcupine; V: Serpent Society	0.75	0.40	1.00	2.00
❑316, Apr 86	0.75	0.40	1.00	2.00
❑317, May 86	0.75	0.40	1.00	2.00
❑318, Jun 86, D: Death-Adder; D: The Blue Streak	0.75	0.40	1.00	2.00
❑319, Jul 86, Death Ringer I (Anthony Davis); Death Rapier, D: Bird-Man II (Achil	0.75	0.40	1.00	2.00
❑320, Aug 86, V: Scourge	0.75	0.40	1.00	2.00
❑321, Sep 86, MZ, 1: Ultimatum	0.75	0.40	1.00	2.00
❑322, Oct 86, 1: Super-Patriot	0.75	0.40	1.00	2.00
❑323, Nov 86, MZ, 1: Super-Patriot II (later becomes USAgent)	0.75	0.40	1.00	2.00
❑324, Dec 86, MZ	0.75	0.40	1.00	2.00
❑325, Jan 87, MZ, 1: Slug	0.75	0.40	1.00	2.00
❑326, Feb 87, MZ	0.75	0.40	1.00	2.00
❑327, Mar 87, MZ	0.75	0.40	1.00	2.00
❑328, Apr 87, The Hard Way!, 1: Demolition-Man	0.75	0.40	1.00	2.00
❑329, May 87, MZ	0.75	0.40	1.00	2.00

	ORIG	GOOD	FINE	N-MINT
❑330, Jun 87, MZ, A: Demolition-Man; A: D-Man	0.75	0.40	1.00	2.00
❑331, Jul 87, MZ	0.75	0.40	1.00	2.00
❑332, Aug 87, MZ, Steve Rogers quits as Captain America	0.75	0.80	2.00	4.00
❑333, Sep 87, MZ, 1: Captain America VI (John Walker), John Walker (Super-Patriot II) becomes Captain America	0.75	0.70	1.75	3.50
❑334, Oct 87, MZ, 1: Bucky IV (Lemar Hoskins)	0.75	0.60	1.50	3.00
❑335, Nov 87, 1: Watchdogs	0.75	0.50	1.25	2.50
❑336, Dec 87, MZ	0.75	0.50	1.25	2.50
❑337, Jan 88, MZ, 1: Puff Adder; 1: The Captain; 1: Fer-de-Lance	0.75	0.50	1.25	2.50
❑338, Feb 88, D: Professor Power	0.75	0.50	1.25	2.50
❑339, Mar 88, Fall of the Mutants, Fall of Mutants	0.75	0.50	1.25	2.50
❑340, Apr 88	0.75	0.50	1.25	2.50
❑341, May 88, 1: Battle Star; A: Iron Man; 1: Rock Python (cameo); 1: Left-Winger	0.75	0.40	1.00	2.00
❑342, Jun 88, 1: Rock Python (full appearance)	0.75	0.40	1.00	2.00
❑343, Jul 88, 1: Quill	0.75	0.40	1.00	2.00
❑344, Aug 88, Giant-size	1.50	0.40	1.00	2.00
❑345, Sep 88	0.75	0.40	1.00	2.00
❑346, Oct 88	0.75	0.40	1.00	2.00
❑347, Nov 88, Vengeance, D: Left-Winger	0.75	0.40	1.00	2.00
❑348, Dec 88, V: Flag Smasher	0.75	0.40	1.00	2.00
❑349, Jan 89	0.75	0.40	1.00	2.00
❑350, Feb 89, Giant-size; The Captain and Super-Patriot fight for title of Captain America	1.75	0.60	1.50	3.00
❑351, Mar 89, A: Nick Fury; D: Watchdog	0.75	0.40	1.00	2.00
❑352, Apr 89, 1: Machete; A: Soviet Super Soldiers	0.75	0.40	1.00	2.00
❑353, May 89, A: Soviet Super Soldiers	0.75	0.40	1.00	2.00
❑354, Jun 89, 1: U.S. Agent; A: Fabian Stankowitz, Super-Patriot becomes USAgent	0.75	0.40	1.00	2.00
❑355, Jul 89, RB, Missing Persons	0.75	0.30	0.75	1.50
❑356, Aug 89, AM, Camptown Rages!, 1: Mother Night	0.75	0.30	0.75	1.50
❑357, Sep 89, Bloodstone Hunt; The Bloodstone Hunt, Part 1, CBG Fan Awards parody ballot	1.00	0.30	0.75	1.50
❑358, Sep 89, The Bloodstone Hunt, Part 2, A: John Jameson	1.00	0.30	0.75	1.50
❑359, Oct 89, The Bloodstone Hunt, Part 3, 1: Crossbones (cameo)	1.00	0.30	0.75	1.50
❑360, Oct 89, Bloodstone Hunt, Part 4; The Bloodstone Hunt, Part 4, 1: Crossbones (full appearance)	1.00	0.30	0.75	1.50
❑361, Nov 89, The Bloodstone Hunt, Part 5	1.00	0.30	0.75	1.50
❑362, Nov 89, The Bloodstone Hunt, Part 6	1.00	0.30	0.75	1.50
❑363, Nov 89	1.00	0.30	0.75	1.50
❑364, Dec 89	1.00	0.30	0.75	1.50
❑365, Dec 89, Acts of Vengeance, Part 8, Acts of Vengeance	1.00	0.30	0.75	1.50
❑366, Jan 90, Acts of Vengeance, Part 17, Acts of Vengeance	1.00	0.30	0.75	1.50
❑367, Feb 90, Acts of Vengeance, Part 25, Acts of Vengeance; Red Skull vs. Magneto	1.00	0.30	0.75	1.50
❑368, Mar 90, O: Machinesmith	1.00	0.30	0.75	1.50
❑369, Apr 90, 1: Skeleton Crew	1.00	0.30	0.75	1.50
❑370, May 90	1.00	0.30	0.75	1.50
❑371, Jun 90, Cap's Night Out	1.00	0.30	0.75	1.50
❑372, Jul 90, Streets of Poison	1.00	0.30	0.75	1.50
❑373, Jul 90, Streets of Poison	1.00	0.30	0.75	1.50
❑374, Aug 90, Streets of Poison	1.00	0.30	0.75	1.50
❑375, Aug 90, Streets of Poison	1.00	0.30	0.75	1.50
❑376, Sep 90, Streets of Poison	1.00	0.30	0.75	1.50
❑377, Sep 90, Streets of Poison	1.00	0.30	0.75	1.50
❑378, Oct 90, Streets of Poison	1.00	0.30	0.75	1.50
❑379, Nov 90, A: Quasar; V: Nefarius	1.00	0.30	0.75	1.50
❑380, Dec 90	1.00	0.30	0.75	1.50
❑381, Jan 91, This Gun's For Hire	1.00	0.30	0.75	1.50
❑382, Feb 91	1.00	0.30	0.75	1.50
❑383, Mar 91, Double-size; 50th anniversary issue	2.00	0.60	1.50	3.00
❑384, Apr 91, Lair Of the Ice Worm, A: Jack Frost	1.00	0.30	0.75	1.50
❑385, May 91, Going To The Dogs	1.00	0.30	0.75	1.50
❑386, Jun 91, For Righteousness' Sake, A: U.S. Agent	1.00	0.30	0.75	1.50
❑387, Jul 91, Superia Stratagem; Superia Stratagem, Part 1, Red Skull back-up stories	1.00	0.30	0.75	1.50
❑388, Jul 91, Superia Stratagem; Superia Stratagem, Part 2, 1: Impala, Red Skull back-up stories	1.00	0.30	0.75	1.50

The Red Skull faced Magneto in the *Captain America* chapters of "Acts of Vengeance."

	ORIG	GOOD	FINE	N-MINT
❑389, Aug 91, Superia Stratagem; Superia Stratagem, Part 3, Red Skull back-up stories	1.00	0.30	0.75	1.50
❑390, Aug 91, Superia Stratagem; Superia Stratagem, Part 4	1.00	0.30	0.75	1.50
❑391, Sep 91, Superia Stratagem; Superia Stratagem, Part 5	1.00	0.30	0.75	1.50
❑392, Sep 91, Superia Stratagem; Superia Stratagem, Part 6	1.00	0.30	0.75	1.50
❑393, Oct 91, Skullbound	1.00	0.30	0.75	1.50
❑394, Nov 91, The Crimson Crusade	1.00	0.30	0.75	1.50
❑395, Dec 91, Rogues In The House	1.00	0.30	0.75	1.50
❑396, Jan 92, 1: Jack O'Lantern II	1.00	0.30	0.75	1.50
❑397, Feb 92	1.25	0.30	0.75	1.50
❑398, Mar 92, Operation: Galactic Storm, Part 1, Galactic Storm	1.25	0.30	0.75	1.50
❑399, Apr 92, Operation: Galactic Storm, Part 8, Galactic Storm	1.25	0.30	0.75	1.50
❑400, May 92, Operation: Galactic Storm, Part 15, O: Diamondback; O: Cutthroat, 80pgs.; Double-gatefold cover; Galactic Storm; reprints Avengers #4	2.25	0.50	1.25	2.50
❑401, Jun 92, Operation: Galactic Storm Aftermath	1.25	0.30	0.75	1.50
❑402, Jul 92, Man & Wolf, Part 1; Man and Wolf, Part 1, 1: Dredmund Druid; A: Wolverine	1.25	0.30	0.75	1.50
❑403, Jul 92, Man & Wolf, Part 2; Man and Wolf, Part 2, 2: Dredmund Druid; A: Wolverine	1.25	0.30	0.75	1.50
❑404, Aug 92, Man & Wolf, Part 3; Man and Wolf, Part 3, A: Wolverine	1.25	0.30	0.75	1.50
❑405, Aug 92, Man & Wolf, Part 4; Man and Wolf, Part 4, A: Wolverine	1.25	0.30	0.75	1.50
❑406, Sep 92, Man & Wolf, Part 5; Man and Wolf, Part 5, A: Wolverine	1.25	0.30	0.75	1.50
❑407, Sep 92, Man & Wolf, Part 6; Man and Wolf, Part 6, A: Cable; A: Wolverine	1.25	0.30	0.75	1.50
❑408, Oct 92, Infinity War, D: Cutthroat	1.25	0.30	0.75	1.50
❑409, Nov 92, Blood And Diamonds	1.25	0.30	0.75	1.50
❑410, Dec 92	1.25	0.30	0.75	1.50
❑411, Jan 93, Taking Aim, Part 1	1.25	0.30	0.75	1.50
❑412, Feb 93, Taking Aim, Part 2	1.25	0.30	0.75	1.50
❑413, Mar 93, Hostile Takeover, V: Modam	1.25	0.30	0.75	1.50
❑414, Apr 93, Savage Land	1.25	0.30	0.75	1.50
❑415, May 93	1.25	0.30	0.75	1.50
❑416, Jun 93	1.25	0.30	0.75	1.50
❑417, Jul 93	1.25	0.30	0.75	1.50
❑418, Aug 93	1.25	0.30	0.75	1.50
❑419, Sep 93, A: Silver Sable	1.25	0.30	0.75	1.50
❑420, Oct 93, The Faustus Affair, Part 2, A: Viper; A: Blazing Skull; A: Nomad	1.25	0.30	0.75	1.50
❑420/CS, Oct 93, The Faustus Affair, Part 2, A: Viper; A: Blazing Skull; A: Nomad, Includes copy of Dirt Magazine	2.95	0.59	1.48	2.95
❑421, Nov 93, The Faustus Affair, Part 4, A: Nomad	1.25	0.30	0.75	1.50
❑422, Dec 93	1.25	0.30	0.75	1.50
❑423, Jan 94, V: Namor	1.25	0.30	0.75	1.50
❑424, Feb 94	1.25	0.30	0.75	1.50
❑425, Mar 94, Fighting Chance; Fighting Chance, Part 1, Giant-size	1.75	0.50	1.25	2.50
❑425/SC, Mar 94, Fighting Chance; Fighting Chance, Part 1, Foil-embossed cover; Giant-size	2.95	0.65	1.63	3.25
❑426, Apr 94, Fighting Chance; Fighting Chance, Part 2	1.25	0.30	0.75	1.50
❑427, May 94, Fighting Chance; Fighting Chance, Part 3	1.50	0.30	0.75	1.50
❑428, Jun 94, Fighting Chance; Fighting Chance, Part 4	1.50	0.30	0.75	1.50
❑429, Jul 94, Fighting Chance; Fighting Chance, Part 5, 1: Kono the Sumo	1.50	0.30	0.75	1.50
❑430, Aug 94, Fighting Chance; Fighting Chance, Part 6	1.50	0.30	0.75	1.50
❑431, Sep 94, Fighting Chance; Fighting Chance, Part 7, 1: Free Spirit	1.50	0.30	0.75	1.50

	ORIG	GOOD	FINE	N-MINT
❑432, Oct 94, Fighting Chance; Fighting Chance, Part 8	1.50	0.30	0.75	1.50
❑433, Nov 94, Fighting Chance; Fighting Chance, Part 9	1.50	0.30	0.75	1.50
❑434, Dec 94, Fighting Chance; Fighting Chance, Part 10, 1: Jack Flag	1.50	0.30	0.75	1.50
❑435, Jan 95, Fighting Chance; Fighting Chance, Part 11, V: new Cobra	1.50	0.30	0.75	1.50
❑436, Feb 95, Fighting Chance; Fighting Chance, Part 12	1.50	0.30	0.75	1.50
❑437, Mar 95, Fighting Chance Epilogue	1.50	0.30	0.75	1.50
❑438, Apr 95, 1: Cap-Armor	1.50	0.30	0.75	1.50
❑439, May 95, V: Death-Stalker	1.50	0.30	0.75	1.50
❑440, Jun 95, Taking A.I.M., Part 1	1.50	0.30	0.75	1.50
❑441, Jul 95, Taking A.I.M., Part 3	1.50	0.30	0.75	1.50
❑442, Aug 95	1.50	0.30	0.75	1.50
❑443, Sep 95, D: Captain America	1.50	0.30	0.75	1.50
❑444, Oct 95, MWa (w), Title changes to Steve Rogers, Captain America; Red Skull brings Cap back to life; Return of Sharon Carter	1.50	0.80	2.00	4.00
❑445, Nov 95, MWa (w), Operation Rebirth, Part 1, Return of Sharon Carter; Cap revived	1.50	0.60	1.50	3.00
❑446, Dec 95, MWa (w), Operation Rebirth, Part 2, A: Red Skull	1.50	0.60	1.50	3.00
❑447, Jan 96, MWa (w), Operation Rebirth, Part 3	1.50	0.60	1.50	3.00
❑448, Feb 96, MWa (w), Operation Rebirth, Part 4, Giant-size	2.95	0.80	2.00	4.00
❑449, Mar 96, MWa (w)	1.50	0.40	1.00	2.00
❑450, Apr 96, MWa (w), Man Without a Country, Part 1, Title returns to Captain America; Cap's American citizenship is revoked	1.50	0.40	1.00	2.00
❑450/A, Apr 96, MWa (w), Man Without a Country, Part 1, alternate cover	1.50	0.50	1.25	2.50
❑451, May 96, MWa (w), Man Without a Country, Part 2	1.50	0.40	1.00	2.00
❑452, Jun 96, MWa (w)	1.50	0.40	1.00	2.00
❑453, Jul 96, MWa (w), Cap's citizenship restored	1.50	0.40	1.00	2.00
❑454, Aug 96, MWa (w), Sanctuary, Final Issue	1.50	0.40	1.00	2.00
❑Anl 1, Reprint; Cover reads "King-Size Special"	0.25	3.60	9.00	18.00
❑Anl 2, Reprint; Cover reads "King-Size Special"	0.25	2.40	6.00	12.00
❑Anl 3, JK	0.50	0.80	2.00	4.00
❑Anl 4, JK, 1: Crucible (Marvel); 1: Slither	0.50	0.80	2.00	4.00
❑Anl 5	0.75	0.60	1.50	3.00
❑Anl 6, The Invaders, Four Caps	1.00	0.60	1.50	3.00
❑Anl 7, The Last Enchantment, O: Kubik (Cosmic Cube), Cosmic Cube	1.00	0.60	1.50	3.00
❑Anl 8, A: Wolverine	1.25	3.20	8.00	16.00
❑Anl 9, Terminus Factor; The Terminus Factor, Part 1, A: Iron Man	2.00	0.60	1.50	3.00
❑Anl 10, DH, Von Strucker Gambit; The Von Strucker gambit, Part 3, O: Bushmaster; O: Captain America, 68pgs.	2.00	0.50	1.25	2.50
❑Anl 11, Citizen Kang, Part 1, Citizen Kang	2.25	0.50	1.25	2.50
❑Anl 12, 1: Battling Bantam, trading card; Polybagged with trading card	2.95	0.59	1.48	2.95
❑Anl 13, V: Red Skull	2.95	0.59	1.48	2.95
❑Ash 1, ashcan edition; no indicia; Mini "Ashcan" preview	0.75	0.20	0.50	1.00
❑GS 1	0.50	2.80	7.00	14.00
❑SE 1, JSo, JSo (c), Special Edition #1; reprint of Steranko issues	2.00	0.60	1.50	3.00
❑SE 2, JSo, JSo (c), Special Edition #2; reprint of Steranko issues	2.00	0.60	1.50	3.00

CAPTAIN AMERICA (VOL. 2)

MARVEL

	ORIG	GOOD	FINE	N-MINT
❑1, Nov 96, RL, RL (w); JPH (w), Courage, Captain America jumping forward on cover; Steve Rogers regains memories of WW II action	2.95	0.60	1.50	3.00
❑1/A, Nov 96, RL, RL (w); JPH (w), Courage, Variant cover (flag background)	2.95	0.60	1.50	3.00
❑1/B, Nov 96, RL, RL (w); JPH (w), Courage, variant cover; Signed by Rob Liefeld	2.95	1.00	2.50	5.00
❑2, Dec 96, RL, RL (w); JPH (w), Secrets, A: Nick Fury, Red Skull	1.95	0.40	1.00	2.00
❑3, Jan 97, RL, RL (w); JPH (w), Patriotism, V: Crossbones	1.95	0.40	1.00	2.00
❑4, Feb 97, RL, RL (w); JPH (w), Fire, V: Master Man	1.95	0.39	0.98	1.95
❑5, Mar 97, RL, RL (w); JPH (w), Victory	1.95	0.39	0.98	1.95
❑6, Apr 97, RL, RL (w); JPH (w), Industrial Revolution Epilogue; Soldier, A: Cable	1.95	0.39	0.98	1.95
❑7, May 97, JRo (w), Crossroads, O: Captain America (Heroes Reborn version)	1.95	0.39	0.98	1.95
❑8, Jun 97	1.95	0.39	0.98	1.95
❑9, Jul 97	1.95	0.39	0.98	1.95
❑10, Aug 97, A: Falcon, gatefold summary.	1.99	0.40	1.00	1.99
❑11, Sep 97, V: Nick Fury, gatefold summary	1.99	0.40	1.00	1.99
❑12, Oct 97, Heroes Reunited, Part 4, cover forms quadtych with Avengers #12; gatefold summary; Iron Man #12; and Fantastic Four #12	1.99	0.40	1.00	1.99
❑Ash 1, Mar 95, Collector's Preview	1.95	0.39	0.98	1.95
❑ASH 1/A, no cover price; Special Comicon Edition	—	0.20	0.50	1.00

CAPTAIN AMERICA (VOL. 3)

MARVEL

	ORIG	GOOD	FINE	N-MINT
❑1, Jan 98, MWa (w), V: Lady Deathstrike, wraparound cover; gatefold summary; follows events in Heroes Return; Cap in Japan	2.99	0.70	1.75	3.50
❑1/A, Jan 98, MWa (w), V: Lady Deathstrike, alternate cover; gatefold summary; follows events in Heroes Return; Cap in Japan	2.99	0.80	2.00	4.00
❑2, Feb 98, gatefold summary; Cap loses his shield	1.99	0.60	1.50	3.00
❑2/A, Feb 98, variant cover	1.99	0.60	1.50	3.00
❑3, Mar 98, BWi (w), Museum Piece, 1: New shield, gatefold summary	1.99	0.40	1.00	2.00
❑4, Apr 98, A: Hawkeye, gatefold summary; true identity of Sensational Hydra revealed	1.99	0.40	1.00	2.00
❑5, May 98, A: Thor, gatefold summary; Cap replaced by Skrull	1.99	0.40	1.00	2.00
❑6, Jun 98, gatefold summary; Skrulls revealed	1.99	0.40	1.00	2.00
❑7, Jul 98, V: Skrulls, gatefold summary	1.99	0.40	1.00	2.00
❑8, Aug 98, Live Kree or Die, Part 2, gatefold summary; Cap's shield destroyed; continues in Quicksilver #10	1.99	0.40	1.00	2.00
❑9, Sep 98, gatefold summary; Cap gets new virtual shield	1.99	0.40	1.00	2.00
❑10, Oct 98, V: USAgent, gatefold summary; Nightmare	1.99	0.40	1.00	2.00
❑11, Nov 98, V: Nightmare, gatefold summary	1.99	0.40	1.00	1.99
❑12, Dec 98, V: Nightmare, wraparound cover; gatefold summary; double-sized	2.99	0.60	1.50	2.99
❑12/LE, Dec 98	24.99	4.00	10.00	20.00
❑13, Jan 99, MWa (w), V: A.I.M., gatefold summary	1.99	0.40	1.00	1.99
❑14, Feb 99, MWa (w), A: Red Skull, gatefold summary	1.99	0.40	1.00	1.99
❑15, Mar 99, MWa (w), V: Red Skull	1.99	0.40	1.00	1.99
❑16, Apr 99, MWa (w), V: Red Skull	1.99	0.40	1.00	1.99
❑17, May 99, D: Red Skull; A: Korvac	1.99	0.40	1.00	1.99
❑18, Jun 99, V: Korvac	1.99	0.40	1.00	1.99
❑19, Jul 99, MWa (w), Triumph of the Will, A: Red Skull; A: Sharon Carter	1.99	0.40	1.00	1.99
❑20, Aug 99, A: USAgent, Sgt. Fury back-up (b&w)	1.99	0.40	1.00	1.99
❑21, Sep 99, A: Giant-Man, Wasp, Iron Man, Sgt. Fury back-up (b&w)	1.99	0.40	1.00	1.99
❑22, Oct 99, V: Klaw, Cap's shield restored	1.99	0.40	1.00	1.99
❑23, Nov 99	1.99	0.40	1.00	1.99
❑24, Dec 00	1.99	0.45	1.13	2.25
❑25, Jan 00	1.99	0.45	1.13	2.25
❑26, Feb 00, Twisted Tomorrows, Part 2, A: Falcon; V: Hatemonger	1.99	0.45	1.13	2.25
❑27, Mar 00	—	0.45	1.13	2.25
❑28, Apr 00	—	0.45	1.13	2.25
❑29, May 00	—	0.45	1.13	2.25
❑30, Jun 00, Waste of Dreams, A: Count Nefaria	2.25	0.45	1.13	2.25
❑31, Jul 00	2.25	0.45	1.13	2.25
❑32, Aug 00, JOy, Heart, World War II story	2.25	0.45	1.13	2.25
❑33, Sep 00	2.25	0.45	1.13	2.25
❑34, Oct 00	2.25	0.45	1.13	2.25
❑35, Nov 00, When Strikes Protocide!, V: Protocide	2.25	0.45	1.13	2.25
❑36, Dec 00, Maximum Security; Maelstrom Within, V: Mercurio	2.25	0.45	1.13	2.25
❑37, Jan 01, Brothers, V: Protocide	2.25	0.45	1.13	2.25
❑38, Feb 01, Across the Rubicon, A: Protocide	2.25	0.45	1.13	2.25
❑39, Mar 01, A Gulf So Wide	2.25	0.45	1.13	2.25
❑40, Apr 01, Fighting Back	2.25	0.45	1.13	2.25
❑41, May 01, Duel	2.25	0.45	1.13	2.25
❑42, Jun 01	2.25	0.45	1.13	2.25
❑43, Jul 01	2.25	0.45	1.13	2.25
❑44, Aug 01	2.25	0.45	1.13	2.25
❑45, Sep 01	2.25	0.45	1.13	2.25
❑Anl 1998, wraparound cover; Captain America/Citizen V '98	3.50	0.70	1.75	3.50
❑Anl 1999, V: Flag-Smasher	3.50	0.70	1.75	3.50
❑Anl 2000, Who is ... Protocide?!; The Test, O: Captain America; 1: Elite Agents of S.H.I.E.L.D.; O: Protocide, continued from Captain America #35	3.50	0.70	1.75	3.50

CAPTAIN AMERICA AND THE CAMPBELL KIDS
MARVEL

	ORIG	GOOD	FINE	N-MINT
❑1, nn; giveaway	—	0.20	0.50	1.00

CAPTAIN AMERICA: DEATHLOK LIVES!
MARVEL

Value: Cover or less

❑1, MZ, One Man in Search of Himself, Reprints from Captain America #286-288 ..... 4.95

CAPTAIN AMERICA: DRUG WAR
MARVEL

Value: Cover or less

❑1, Apr 93 ..... 2.00

CAPTAIN AMERICA GOES TO WAR AGAINST DRUGS
MARVEL

	ORIG	GOOD	FINE	N-MINT
❑1, PD (w), High Heat, nn; giveaway; Anti-drug giveaway	—	0.20	0.50	1.00

CAPTAIN AMERICA: MEDUSA EFFECT
MARVEL

Value: Cover or less

❑1, Mar 94, RB, The Medusa Effect 2.95

CAPTAIN AMERICA/NICK FURY: BLOOD TRUCE
MARVEL

Value: Cover or less

❑1, Feb 95, HC (w), prestige format one-shot 5.95

CAPTAIN AMERICA: SENTINEL OF LIBERTY
MARVEL

Value: Cover or less

❑1, Sep 98, Sentinel of Liberty, wraparound cover; gatefold summary 1.99
❑1/SC, Sentinel of Liberty, Rough-cut edition 2.99
❑2, Oct 98, gatefold summary; Invaders 1.99
❑3, Nov 98, gatefold summary; Invaders 1.99
❑4, Dec 98, gatefold summary; Invaders 1.99
❑5, Jan 99, MWa (w), Tales of Suspense, Part 1, A: Iron Man; A: S.H.I.E.L.D., gatefold summary; Tales of Suspense tribute 1.99
❑6, Feb 99, Tales of Suspense, Part 2, A: Iron Man, gatefold summary; double-sized; Tales of Suspense tribute 2.99
❑7, Mar 99, Bicentennial story 1.99
❑8, Apr 99, MWa (w), Flashpoint, A: Falcon; A: Sam Wilson ... 1.99
❑9, May 99, A: Falcon 1.99
❑10, Jun 99, V: Modok; A: Dino Manelli 1.99
❑11, Jul 99, V: Human Torch ... 1.99
❑12, Aug 99, A: Bucky, Final Issue 2.99

CAPTAIN AMERICA: THE LEGEND
MARVEL

Value: Cover or less

❑1, Sep 96, wraparound cover; background on Cap and his supporting cast 3.95

CAPTAIN AMERICA: THE MOVIE SPECIAL
MARVEL

Value: Cover or less

❑1, nn 3.50

CAPTAIN ATOM (CHARLTON)
CHARLTON

	ORIG	GOOD	FINE	N-MINT
❑78, Dec 65, O: Captain Atom, Series continued from Strange Suspense Stories #77	0.12	12.00	30.00	60.00
❑79, Mar 66	0.12	8.00	20.00	40.00
❑80, May 66, SD, Death Knell of the World	0.12	8.00	20.00	40.00
❑81, Jul 66	0.12	7.00	17.50	35.00
❑82, Sep 66	0.12	7.00	17.50	35.00
❑83, Nov 66, 1: Ted Kord (Blue Beetle)	0.12	7.00	17.50	35.00
❑84, Jan 67, 1: Captain Atom (new)	0.12	7.00	17.50	35.00
❑85, Mar 67	0.12	7.00	17.50	35.00
❑86, Jun 67	0.12	7.00	17.50	35.00
❑87, Aug 67, SD, The Menace: Of The Fiery Icer, Nightshade back-up story	0.12	7.00	17.50	35.00
❑88, Oct 67	0.12	7.00	17.50	35.00
❑89, Dec 67, Final Issue	0.12	7.00	17.50	35.00

CAPTAIN ATOM (DC)
DC

	ORIG	GOOD	FINE	N-MINT
❑1, Mar 87, PB, Point of Origin, O: Captain Atom, New costume	1.00	0.40	1.00	2.00
❑2, Apr 87	0.75	0.30	0.75	1.50
❑3, May 87, O: Captain Atom (fake origin)	0.75	0.30	0.75	1.50
❑4, Jun 87	0.75	0.30	0.75	1.50
❑5, Jul 87, A: Firestorm	0.75	0.30	0.75	1.50
❑6, Aug 87, V: Doctor Spectro	0.75	0.25	0.63	1.25
❑7, Sep 87	0.75	0.25	0.63	1.25
❑8, Oct 87, A: Plastique	0.75	0.25	0.63	1.25
❑9, Nov 87	0.75	0.25	0.63	1.25
❑10, Dec 87	0.75	0.25	0.63	1.25
❑11, Jan 88, A: Firestorm, Millennium	0.75	0.25	0.63	1.25
❑12, Feb 88, 1: Major Force	0.75	0.25	0.63	1.25
❑13, Mar 88	0.75	0.25	0.63	1.25
❑14, Apr 88	0.75	0.25	0.63	1.25
❑15, May 88, V: Major Force	0.75	0.25	0.63	1.25
❑16, Jun 88, A: JLI	0.75	0.25	0.63	1.25
❑17, Jul 88, A: Swamp Thing	1.00	0.25	0.63	1.25
❑18, Aug 88	1.00	0.25	0.63	1.25
❑19, Sep 88	1.00	0.25	0.63	1.25
❑20, Oct 88, A: Blue Beetle	1.00	0.25	0.63	1.25
❑21, Nov 88	1.00	0.25	0.63	1.25

When *Strange Suspense Stories* became *Captain Atom*, its title character's origin was retold.

© 1965 Charlton

	ORIG	GOOD	FINE	N-MINT
❑22, Dec 88, Plastique vs. Nightshade	1.00	0.25	0.63	1.25
❑23, V: Ghost, no month of publication	1.00	0.25	0.63	1.25
❑24, Invasion!; no month of publication	1.00	0.25	0.63	1.25
❑25, Jan 89, Invasion!; no month of publication	1.00	0.25	0.63	1.25
❑26, Feb 89, O: Captain Atom; A: JLA	1.00	0.25	0.63	1.25
❑27, Mar 89, PB, Truth and Consequences, O: Captain Atom	1.00	0.25	0.63	1.25
❑28, Apr 89, O: Captain Atom; V: Ghost	1.00	0.25	0.63	1.25
❑29, May 89, A Contrite Heart	1.00	0.25	0.63	1.25
❑30, Jun 89, Janus Directive	1.00	0.25	0.63	1.25
❑31, Jul 89, V: Rocket Red	1.00	0.25	0.63	1.25
❑32, Aug 89	1.00	0.25	0.63	1.25
❑33, Sep 89, Batman; new costume	1.00	0.25	0.63	1.25
❑34, Oct 89, V: Doctor Spectro	1.00	0.25	0.63	1.25
❑35, Nov 89, A: Major Force, back to old costume	1.00	0.25	0.63	1.25
❑36, Dec 89	1.00	0.25	0.63	1.25
❑37, Jan 90	1.00	0.25	0.63	1.25
❑38, Feb 90, V: Black Racer	1.00	0.25	0.63	1.25
❑39, Mar 90	1.00	0.25	0.63	1.25
❑40, Apr 90	1.00	0.25	0.63	1.25
❑41, May 90	1.00	0.25	0.63	1.25
❑42, Jun 90	1.00	0.25	0.63	1.25
❑43, Jul 90	1.00	0.25	0.63	1.25
❑44, Aug 90, A: Plastique	1.00	0.25	0.63	1.25
❑45, Sep 90	1.00	0.25	0.63	1.25
❑46, Oct 90, Superman	1.00	0.25	0.63	1.25
❑47, Nov 90	1.00	0.25	0.63	1.25
❑48, Dec 90	1.00	0.25	0.63	1.25
❑49, Jan 91, Trial of Plastique	1.00	0.25	0.63	1.25
❑50, Feb 91, D: Megala, Giant-size	2.00	0.40	1.00	2.00
❑51, Mar 91	1.00	0.25	0.63	1.25
❑52, Apr 91	1.00	0.25	0.63	1.25
❑53, May 91	1.00	0.25	0.63	1.25
❑54, Jun 91	1.00	0.25	0.63	1.25
❑55, Jul 91	1.00	0.25	0.63	1.25
❑56, Aug 91	1.00	0.25	0.63	1.25
❑57, Sep 91, War of the Gods, Part 7, Final Issue	1.00	0.25	0.63	1.25
❑Anl 1, V: Major Force, says 88 on cover, 87 in indicia	1.25	0.30	0.75	1.50
❑Anl 2, V: Queen Bee	1.50	0.30	0.75	1.50

CAPTAIN CANUCK
COMELY

	ORIG	GOOD	FINE	N-MINT
❑1, Jul 75	0.35	0.60	1.50	3.00
❑2, no month of publication	0.35	0.40	1.00	2.00
❑3, no month of publication	0.35	0.40	1.00	2.00
❑4, Aug 79, New publisher	0.50	0.30	0.75	1.50
❑5, Sep 79	0.50	0.30	0.75	1.50
❑6, Nov 79	0.50	0.30	0.75	1.50
❑7, Jan 80	0.50	0.30	0.75	1.50
❑8, Mar 80	0.50	0.30	0.75	1.50
❑9, May 80, says Jun on cover; May in indicia	0.50	0.30	0.75	1.50
❑10, Aug 80	0.50	0.30	0.75	1.50
❑11, Oct 80	0.50	0.30	0.75	1.50
❑12, Dec 80	0.50	0.30	0.75	1.50
❑13, Feb 81	0.50	0.30	0.75	1.50
❑14, Apr 81, Fire-Fight; Beyond, Final Issue	0.50	0.30	0.75	1.50

CAPTAIN CANUCK (2ND SERIES)
SEMPLE

	ORIG	GOOD	FINE	N-MINT
❑0/A, English	0.95	0.30	0.75	1.50
❑0/B, French	0.95	0.30	0.75	1.50
❑1	1.95	0.39	0.98	1.95
❑1/GO, gold; trading cards	2.95	0.59	1.48	2.95

CAPTAIN CANUCK FIRST SUMMER SPECIAL
COMELY

	ORIG	GOOD	FINE	N-MINT
❑1, Sep 80	0.95	0.30	0.75	1.50

CAPTAIN CANUCK REBORN
SEMPLE

	ORIG	GOOD	FINE	N-MINT
❑0, Sep 93	0.95	0.30	0.75	1.50
❑1, Jan 94	2.50	0.40	1.00	2.00
❑1/GO, Gold polybagged edition with trading cards	2.95	0.60	1.50	3.00

	ORIG	GOOD	FINE	N-MINT
❑2, Jul 94	2.50	0.50	1.25	2.50
❑3, b&w; cardstock cover; strip reprints	2.50	0.50	1.25	2.50

CAPTAIN CARROT AND HIS AMAZING ZOO CREW
DC

	ORIG	GOOD	FINE	N-MINT
❑1, Mar 82, The Pluto Syndrome, A: Starro; A: Superman	0.60	0.30	0.75	1.50
❑2, Apr 82, AA	0.60	0.20	0.50	1.00
❑3, May 82	0.60	0.20	0.50	1.00
❑4, Jun 82	0.60	0.20	0.50	1.00
❑5, Jul 82, A: Oklahoma Bones	0.60	0.20	0.50	1.00
❑6, Aug 82, V: Bunny from Beyond	0.60	0.20	0.50	1.00
❑7, Sep 82, A: Bow-zar the Barbarian	0.60	0.20	0.50	1.00
❑8, Oct 82, 1: Z-Building (Zoo Crew's Head-quarters)	0.60	0.20	0.50	1.00
❑9, Nov 82, A: Three Mouseketeers; A: Terrific Whatzie, Masters of the Universe preview	0.60	0.20	0.50	1.00
❑10, Dec 82	0.60	0.20	0.50	1.00
❑11, Jan 83	0.60	0.20	0.50	1.00
❑12, Feb 83, 1: Little Cheese, 1st Art Adams art; 1st Arthur Adams art	0.60	0.20	0.50	1.00
❑13, Mar 83	0.60	0.20	0.50	1.00
❑14, Apr 83, Crisis on Earth-C!, Part 1, Justa Lotta Animals	0.60	0.20	0.50	1.00
❑15, May 83, Justa Lotta Animals	0.60	0.20	0.50	1.00
❑16, Jun 83	0.60	0.20	0.50	1.00
❑17, Jul 83	0.60	0.20	0.50	1.00
❑18, Aug 83	0.60	0.20	0.50	1.00
❑19, Sep 83, V: Frogzilla	0.60	0.20	0.50	1.00
❑20, Nov 83, A: Changeling; V: Gorilla Grodd, Final Issue	0.60	0.20	0.50	1.00

CAPTAIN CONFEDERACY (EPIC)
MARVEL

	ORIG	GOOD	FINE	N-MINT
❑1, Nov 91, Crossroad	1.95	0.40	1.00	2.00
❑2, Dec 91	1.95	0.40	1.00	2.00
❑3, Jan 92, Hellhound on My Trail	1.95	0.40	1.00	2.00
❑4, Feb 92	1.95	0.40	1.00	2.00

CAPTAIN CONFEDERACY (STEELDRAGON)
STEELDRAGON

Value: Cover or less

- ❑1, The Making of a Hero 1.50
- ❑2 .... 1.50
- ❑3, Beer and Confidences; Ant Boy! 1.50
- ❑4 .... 1.50
- ❑5 .... 1.50
- ❑6, Sum 87 .... 1.50
- ❑7, Aut 87 .... 1.75
- ❑8, Win 87 .... 1.75
- ❑9, Spr 88 .... 1.75
- ❑10, Jun 88 .... 1.75
- ❑11, Jun 88 .... 1.75
- ❑12, Oct 88 .... 1.75
- ❑SE 1, Sum 87, O: Captain Confederacy 1.75
- ❑SE 2, Sum 87, O: Captain Confederacy 1.75

CAPTAIN COSMOS, THE LAST STARVEYOR
YBOR CITY

Value: Cover or less

- ❑1, JSa, The Beast from Hyper-space; Captain (text) 2.95

CAPTAIN CRAFTY
CONCEPTION

Value: Cover or less

- ❑1, Jun 94, b&w; wraparound cover 2.50
- ❑2, Win 94, b&w; wraparound cover 2.50
- ❑2.5, Apr 98 .... 1.00

CAPTAIN CRAFTY COLOR SPECTACULAR
CONCEPTION

Value: Cover or less

- ❑1, Aug 96, wraparound cover 2.50
- ❑2, Dec 96, wraparound cover 2.50

CAPTAIN DINGLEBERRY
SLAVE LABOR

Value: Cover or less

- ❑1 .... 2.95
- ❑2 .... 2.95
- ❑3 .... 2.95
- ❑4 .... 2.95
- ❑5, Jan 98, Bun Ca-Ca City and the Runsdance Kid 2.95
- ❑6, Feb 99, sticker 2.95

CAPTAIN EO 3-D
ECLIPSE

Value: Cover or less

- ❑1, Aug 87, nn; oversized (11x17) 3.50

CAPTAIN FORTUNE
RIP OFF

Value: Cover or less

- ❑1, Pressure 2.95
- ❑2, Treasure Moon, Part 1 .... 3.25
- ❑3, Treasure Moon, Part 2 .... 3.25
- ❑4, Treasure Moon, Part 3 .... 3.25

CAPTAIN GLORY
TOPPS

Value: Cover or less

- ❑0, Apr 93, JK; SD, trading card 2.95
- ❑1, SD, trading card 2.95

CAPTAIN GRAVITY
PENNY-FARTHING

	ORIG	GOOD	FINE	N-MINT
❑1, Dec 98, The Curse of Ah Puch	2.75	0.55	1.38	2.75
❑1/Aut, Dec 98, The Curse of Ah Puch	—	0.70	1.75	3.50
❑2, Jan 99	2.75	0.55	1.38	2.75
❑3, Feb 99	2.75	0.55	1.38	2.75
❑4, Mar 99	2.75	0.55	1.38	2.75

CAPTAIN GRAVITY: ONE TRUE HERO
PENNY-FARTHING

Value: Cover or less

- ❑1, Aug 99, One-Shot 2.95

CAPTAIN HARLOCK
ETERNITY

	ORIG	GOOD	FINE	N-MINT
❑1, An Exchange of Futures, b&w; Character created by Leiji Matsumoto	1.95	0.50	1.25	2.50
❑2	1.95	0.50	1.25	2.50
❑3	1.95	0.50	1.25	2.50
❑4	1.95	0.50	1.25	2.50
❑5	1.95	0.50	1.25	2.50
❑6	1.95	0.50	1.25	2.50
❑7	1.95	0.50	1.25	2.50
❑8	1.95	0.50	1.25	2.50
❑9	1.95	0.50	1.25	2.50
❑10	1.95	0.50	1.25	2.50
❑11	1.95	0.50	1.25	2.50
❑12	2.25	0.50	1.25	2.50
❑13	2.25	0.50	1.25	2.50
❑HS 1, b&w; prestige format	2.50	0.50	1.25	2.50

CAPTAIN HARLOCK: DEATHSHADOW RISING
ETERNITY

Value: Cover or less

- ❑1 .... 2.25
- ❑2 .... 2.25
- ❑3 .... 2.25
- ❑4 .... 2.25
- ❑5 .... 2.25
- ❑6 .... 2.25

CAPTAIN HARLOCK: THE FALL OF THE EMPIRE
ETERNITY

Value: Cover or less

- ❑1 .... 2.50
- ❑2, Aug 92 .... 2.50
- ❑3 .... 2.50
- ❑4 .... 2.50

CAPTAIN HARLOCK: THE MACHINE PEOPLE
ETERNITY

Value: Cover or less

- ❑1 .... 2.50
- ❑2 .... 2.50
- ❑3 .... 2.50
- ❑4, Flesh and Steel 2.50

CAPTAIN JOHNER & THE ALIENS
VALIANT

Value: Cover or less

- ❑1, May 95, RM, RM (w), The Aliens, cardstock cover; reprints back-ups from Magnus, Robot Fighter (Gold Key) #1-7 .... 2.95
- ❑2, May 95, RM, RM (w), An Alien Welcome, cardstock cover; reprints back-ups from Magnus, Robot Fighter (Gold Key) 2.95

CAPTAIN JUSTICE
MARVEL

Value: Cover or less

- ❑1, Once a Hero, Part 1, TV show 1.25
- ❑2, Once a Hero, Part 2, TV show 1.25

CAPTAIN MARVEL (1ST SERIES)
MARVEL

	ORIG	GOOD	FINE	N-MINT
❑1, May 68, GC, Out of the Holocaust-A Hero!, Indicia: Marvel's Space-Born Superhero: Captain Marvel	0.12	9.00	22.50	45.00
❑2, Jun 68, GC, From The Void Of Space Comes...The Super Skrull!, A: Sub-Mariner; V: Skrull	0.12	3.60	9.00	18.00
❑3, Jul 68, GC, From the Ashes of Defeat!, V: Skrull	0.12	3.00	7.50	15.00
❑4, Aug 68, GC, Alien And The Amphibian!, V: Sub-Mariner	0.12	3.00	7.50	15.00
❑5, Sep 68, DH, The Mark of The Metazoid	0.12	2.40	6.00	12.00
❑6, Oct 68, DH	0.12	1.80	4.50	9.00
❑7, Nov 68, DH, V: Quasimodo	0.12	1.80	4.50	9.00
❑8, Dec 68, DH, 1: Aakon (alien race)	0.12	1.80	4.50	9.00
❑9, Jan 69, DH	0.12	1.80	4.50	9.00
❑10, Feb 69, DH	0.12	1.80	4.50	9.00
❑11, Mar 69, Rebirth!, D: Una	0.12	1.80	4.50	9.00
❑12, Apr 69, The Man-Slayer	0.12	1.40	3.50	7.00
❑13, May 69	0.12	1.40	3.50	7.00
❑14, Jun 69, A: Iron Man	0.12	1.40	3.50	7.00
❑15, Aug 69	0.15	1.40	3.50	7.00
❑16, Sep 69	0.15	1.40	3.50	7.00
❑17, Oct 69, DA; GK, DA (c); GK (c), And a Child Shall Lead You!, O: Rick Jones retold, new costume	0.15	1.40	3.50	7.00
❑18, Nov 69	0.15	1.40	3.50	7.00
❑19, Dec 69, DA; GK	0.15	1.40	3.50	7.00
❑20, Jun 70, DA; GK, DA (c); GK (c), The Hunter and the Holocaust	0.15	1.40	3.50	7.00
❑21, Aug 70, A: Hulk, series goes on hiatus	0.15	1.40	3.50	7.00
❑22, Sep 72, V: Megaton, Title changes to Captain Marvel after hiatus	0.20	1.40	3.50	7.00
❑23, Nov 72, V: Megaton	0.20	1.40	3.50	7.00
❑24, Jan 73	0.20	1.40	3.50	7.00

	ORIG	GOOD	FINE	N-MINT
❑25, Mar 73, JSn	0.20	2.00	5.00	10.00
❑26, May 73, JSn, A: Thanos	0.20	2.00	5.00	10.00
❑27, Jul 73, JSn, A: Thanos; 1: Death (Marvel)	0.20	1.60	4.00	8.00
❑28, Sep 73, JSn; AM, A: Thanos	0.20	1.60	4.00	8.00
❑29, Nov 73, JSn; AM, O: Kronos; A: Thanos, Captain Marvel gets new powers	0.20	1.20	3.00	6.00
❑30, Jan 74, JSn; AM, V: Controller; A: Thanos	0.20	1.20	3.00	6.00
❑31, Mar 74, JSn, A: Thanos; 1: ISAAC	0.20	1.60	4.00	8.00
❑32, May 74, JSn, O: Drax; A: Thanos; O: Moondragon, Rick Jones vs. Thanos	0.25	1.60	4.00	8.00
❑33, Jul 74, JSn, O: Thanos	0.25	2.00	5.00	10.00
❑34, Sep 74, JAb; JSn, Blown Away!, 1: Nitro, Captain Marvel contracts cancer (will eventually die from it)	0.25	1.00	2.50	5.00
❑35, Nov 74, AA, V: Living Laser, Ant-Man	0.25	0.60	1.50	3.00
❑36, Jan 75, JSn, A: Thanos, Watcher	0.25	0.60	1.50	3.00
❑37, Mar 75	0.25	0.40	1.00	2.00
❑38, May 75, Trial of the Watcher	0.25	0.40	1.00	2.00
❑39, Jul 75, 1: Aron the Rogue Watcher	0.25	0.40	1.00	2.00
❑40, Sep 75	0.25	0.40	1.00	2.00
❑41, Nov 75, V: Ronan; A: Supreme Intelligence	0.25	0.40	1.00	2.00
❑42, Jan 76, V: Stranger	0.25	0.40	1.00	2.00
❑43, Mar 76, AM, Destroy! Destroy!, V: Drax	0.25	0.40	1.00	2.00
❑44, May 76, V: Drax	0.25	0.40	1.00	2.00
❑45, Jul 76	0.25	0.40	1.00	2.00
❑46, Sep 76, 1: Supremor	0.30	0.40	1.00	2.00
❑47, Nov 76, A: Human Torch; V: Sentry Sinister	0.30	0.40	1.00	2.00
❑48, Jan 77, V: Sentry Sinister; V: Cheetah; 1: Cheetah (Esteban Carracus)	0.30	0.40	1.00	2.00
❑49, Mar 77, V: Ronan	0.30	0.40	1.00	2.00
❑50, May 77, AM, To Begin Anew!, A: Adaptoid; A: Avengers; 1: Doctor Minerva	0.30	0.40	1.00	2.00
❑51, Jul 77, V: Mercurio	0.30	0.40	1.00	2.00
❑52, Sep 77	0.30	0.40	1.00	2.00
❑53, Nov 77	0.35	0.40	1.00	2.00
❑54, Jan 78	0.35	0.40	1.00	2.00
❑55, Mar 78, V: Death-Grip	0.35	0.40	1.00	2.00
❑56, May 78, PB, Survival Quest!, V: Death-Grip	0.35	0.40	1.00	2.00
❑57, Jul 78, BWi; PB, Star Burst, V: Thor; A: Thanos, (flashback); (flashback)	0.35	0.60	1.50	3.00
❑58, Sep 78, V: Drax	0.35	0.40	1.00	2.00
❑59, Nov 78, V: Drax; 1: Elysius	0.35	0.40	1.00	2.00
❑60, Jan 79	0.35	0.40	1.00	2.00
❑61, Mar 79, PB, Chaos And The Pit!	0.35	0.40	1.00	2.00
❑62, May 79, Final Issue	0.40	0.40	1.00	2.00
❑GS 1	0.50	2.00	5.00	10.00

CAPTAIN MARVEL (2ND SERIES)
MARVEL

Value: Cover or less

❑1, Nov 89, The Dream Is The Truth, One-Shot; New Captain Marvel (Monica Rambeau) gets her powers back 1.50

CAPTAIN MARVEL (3RD SERIES)
MARVEL

Value: Cover or less

❑2, Feb 94 .... 1.75

CAPTAIN MARVEL (4TH SERIES)
MARVEL

Value: Cover or less

❑1, Dec 95, Sins of the Fathers, Part 1, enhanced cardstock cover 2.95
❑2, Jan 96, Sins of the Fathers, Part 2, A: Rick and Marlo Jones 1.95
❑3, Feb 96, Sins of the Fathers, Part 3 .... 1.95
❑4, Mar 96, Sins of the Fathers, Part 4 .... 1.95
❑5, Apr 96, In the Name of God? 1.95
❑6, May 96 .... 1.95
❑7, Final Issue 1.95

CAPTAIN MARVEL (5TH SERIES)
MARVEL

	ORIG	GOOD	FINE	N-MINT
❑0, Wizard promotional edition	—	0.60	1.50	3.00
❑1, Jan 00, PD (w), First Contact, Regular cover (space background w/rocks)	2.95	0.60	1.50	3.00
❑1/A, Jan 00, PD (w), First Contact, 1: 10 ratio, Variant cover by Chris Cross (Marvel against white background)	2.95	0.80	2.00	4.00
❑2, Feb 00, PD (w), Does a Hulk Sit In the Woods?, A: Hulk; A: Moondragon; A: Wendigo	2.50	0.50	1.25	2.50
❑3, Mar 00, PD (w), One Down, Wendigo, D: Lorraine; A: Drax; A: Hulk; A: Moondragon; A: Wendigo	2.50	0.50	1.25	2.50
❑4, Apr 00, PD (w), Other Side of the Drax, A: Drax; A: Moondragon	2.50	0.50	1.25	2.50
❑5, May 00, PD (w), Visit to an Even Smaller Planet, A: Drax; A: Moondragon, in micro-verse	2.50	0.50	1.25	2.50
❑6, Jun 00, PD (w), It's a Small Universe After All	2.50	0.50	1.25	2.50
❑7, Jul 00	2.50	0.50	1.25	2.50

After a series of adventures with Mar-Vell, Rick Jones found himself similarly teamed with the Kree soldier's son in *Captain Marvel* (5th series).

© 2000 Marvel

	ORIG	GOOD	FINE	N-MINT
❑8, Aug 00	2.50	0.50	1.25	2.50
❑9, Sep 00, PD (w), Anything Can Happen Day, A: Silver Surfer; A: Super Skrull	2.50	0.50	1.25	2.50
❑10, Oct 00	2.50	0.50	1.25	2.50
❑11, Nov 00, JSn, PD (w), Together Again for the First Time!, A: Mar-Vell; A: Silver Surfer; A: Moondragon	2.50	0.50	1.25	2.50
❑12, Dec 00, PD (w), Maximum Security; Dead and In Person ...	2.50	0.50	1.25	2.50
❑13, Jan 01, PD (w), Am I Blue?	2.50	0.50	1.25	2.50
❑14, Feb 01, Truth or Dare	2.50	0.50	1.25	2.50
❑15, Mar 01, PD (w), Micro-Management...	2.50	0.50	1.25	2.50
❑16, Apr 01, PD (w), Marvel Mania	2.50	0.50	1.25	2.50
❑17, May 01, JSn, PD (w), Cheating Death, A: Thor	2.50	0.50	1.25	2.50
❑18	2.50	0.50	1.25	2.50
❑19	2.50	0.50	1.25	2.50
❑20	2.50	0.50	1.25	2.50
❑21	2.50	0.50	1.25	2.50

CAPTAIN NAUTICUS & THE OCEAN FORCE
EXPRESS

Value: Cover or less

❑1, May 94, More Trouble Than You Can Fathom!, 1: Captain Nauticus 2.95
❑1/LE, Oct 94, limited promotional edition 2.95
❑2, Dec 94, for The National Maritime Center Authority 2.95

CAPTAIN NICE
GOLD KEY

	ORIG	GOOD	FINE	N-MINT
❑1, Nov 67, One-Shot	0.12	7.00	17.50	35.00

CAPTAIN N: THE GAME MASTER
VALIANT

Value: Cover or less

❑1 .... 1.95
❑2, The Happy Zone; Villains' Do's and Don'ts 1.95
❑3 .... 1.95
❑4 .... 1.95
❑5 .... 1.95
❑6 .... 1.95

CAPTAIN OBLIVION
HARRIER

Value: Cover or less

❑1, Aug 87, Red Ant, White Ant, The Moon, The Moon, The Moon 1.95

CAPTAIN PARAGON
AC

Value: Cover or less

❑1, Dec 83, The Diamond Connection 1.50
❑2 .... 1.50
❑3 .... 1.50
❑4 .... 1.50

CAPTAIN PARAGON AND THE SENTINELS OF JUSTICE
AC

	ORIG	GOOD	FINE	N-MINT
❑1, The Shadows of Legends	1.75	0.35	0.88	1.75
❑2	1.75	0.35	0.88	1.75
❑3	1.75	0.35	0.88	1.75
❑4	1.75	0.35	0.88	1.75
❑5, O: Captain Paragon; O: Capt. Paragon, Title changes to Sentinels of Justice	1.50	0.35	0.88	1.75
❑6	1.50	0.35	0.88	1.75

CAPTAIN PHIL
STEELDRAGON

Value: Cover or less

❑1 .... 1.50

CAPTAIN PLANET AND THE PLANETEERS
MARVEL

Value: Cover or less

❑1, NA (c), A Hero for Earth!, O: the Planeteers, TV 1.00
❑2 .... 1.00
❑3 .... 1.00
❑4 .... 1.00
❑5 .... 1.25
❑6 .... 1.25
❑7 .... 1.25
❑8 .... 1.25
❑9 .... 1.25
❑10 .... 1.25
❑11 .... 1.25
❑12, Oct 92, Final Issue 1.25

CAPTAIN POWER AND THE SOLDIERS OF THE FUTURE
CONTINUITY

Value: Cover or less

❑1, NA, NA (w), newsstand cover; Captain Power standing 2.00
❑1/DM, NA, direct-sale cover; Captain Power kneeling 2.00
❑2, Jan 89, NA, NA (w) 2.00

CAPTAIN SALVATION
STREETLIGHT
Value: Cover or less

- ❑1 ... 1.95

CAPTAIN SATAN
MILLENNIUM
Value: Cover or less

- ❑1, Second Chances, Flip-book format ... 2.95
- ❑2, Flip-book format ... 2.95

CAPT. SAVAGE AND HIS LEATHERNECK RAIDERS
MARVEL

	ORIG	GOOD	FINE	N-MINT
❑1, Jan 68, O: Captain Savage and his Leatherneck Raiders; A: Sgt. Fury	0.12	2.80	7.00	14.00
❑2, Mar 68, V: Baron Strucker; O: Hydra	0.12	1.80	4.50	9.00
❑3, May 68, V: Baron Strucker, Hydra	0.12	1.60	4.00	8.00
❑4, Jul 68, V: Baron Strucker	0.12	1.60	4.00	8.00
❑5, Aug 68	0.12	1.60	4.00	8.00
❑6, Sep 68, Save a Howler, A: Izzy Cohen	0.12	1.40	3.50	7.00
❑7, Oct 68, Objective: Ben Grimm, A: Ben Grimm	0.12	1.40	3.50	7.00
❑8, Nov 68, Foul Ball, (becomes Captain Savage)	0.12	1.40	3.50	7.00
❑9, Dec 68, The Gun-Runner, Title changes to Captain Savage (and his Battlefield Raiders)	0.12	1.40	3.50	7.00
❑10, Jan 69, To the Last Man!	0.12	1.40	3.50	7.00
❑11, Feb 69, Death of a Leatherneck!, D: Baker; A: Sgt. Fury, Story continued in Sgt. Fury #64	0.12	1.20	3.00	6.00
❑12, Mar 69, Pray for Simon Savage!	0.12	1.20	3.00	6.00
❑13, Apr 69, DH, The Junk-Heap Juggernauts!	0.12	1.20	3.00	6.00
❑14, May 69, DH, Savage's First Mission!	0.12	1.20	3.00	6.00
❑15, Jul 69, Title changes to Capt. Savage	0.15	1.00	2.50	5.00
❑16, Sep 69	0.15	1.00	2.50	5.00
❑17, Nov 69, The Unsinkable Jay Little Bear	0.15	1.00	2.50	5.00
❑18, Jan 70, The High Cost of Fighting!	0.15	1.00	2.50	5.00
❑19, Mar 70, Final Issue	0.15	1.00	2.50	5.00

CAPTAIN'S JOLTING TALES
ONE SHOT
Value: Cover or less

- ❑1, Aug 91 ... 2.95
- ❑2, Oct 91 ... 3.50
- ❑3, trading card ... 3.50
- ❑3/Dlx, Dec 92 ... 3.50
- ❑4 ... 3.50

CAPTAIN STERNN: RUNNING OUT OF TIME
KITCHEN SINK

	ORIG	GOOD	FINE	N-MINT
❑1, Sep 93, BWr, BWr (w), b&w	4.95	1.10	2.75	5.50
❑2, Dec 93, BWr, BWr (w), b&w	4.95	1.00	2.50	5.00
❑3, Mar 94, BWr, BWr (w)	4.95	1.00	2.50	5.00
❑4, May 94, BWr, BWr (w)	4.95	1.00	2.50	5.00
❑5, Sep 94, BWr, BWr (w)	4.95	1.00	2.50	5.00

CAPT. STORM
DC

	ORIG	GOOD	FINE	N-MINT
❑1, Jun 64, Killer Hunt!, O: Captain Storm	0.12	5.00	12.50	25.00
❑2, Aug 64	0.12	3.20	8.00	16.00
❑3, Oct 64	0.12	3.20	8.00	16.00
❑4, Dec 64	0.12	3.20	8.00	16.00
❑5, Feb 65	0.12	3.20	8.00	16.00
❑6, Apr 65	0.12	2.40	6.00	12.00
❑7, Jun 65	0.12	2.00	5.00	10.00
❑8, Aug 65	0.12	2.00	5.00	10.00
❑9, Oct 65	0.12	2.00	5.00	10.00
❑10, Dec 65	0.12	2.00	5.00	10.00
❑11, Feb 66	0.12	2.00	5.00	10.00
❑12, Apr 66	0.12	2.00	5.00	10.00
❑13, Jun 66	0.12	2.00	5.00	10.00
❑14, Aug 66	0.12	2.00	5.00	10.00
❑15, Oct 66	0.12	2.00	5.00	10.00
❑16, Dec 66	0.12	1.60	4.00	8.00
❑17, Feb 67	0.12	1.60	4.00	8.00
❑18, Apr 67, Final Issue	0.12	1.60	4.00	8.00

CAPTAIN TAX TIME
PAUL HAYNES COMICS
Value: Cover or less

- ❑1 ... 3.50

CAPTAIN THUNDER AND BLUE BOLT
HERO
Value: Cover or less

- ❑1, Back to the Beginning, O: Blue Bolt; A: Captain Thunder ... 1.95
- ❑2 ... 1.95
- ❑3, O: Captain Thunder ... 1.95
- ❑4 ... 1.95
- ❑5 ... 1.95
- ❑6 ... 1.95
- ❑7 ... 1.95
- ❑8, 1: King's Gambit ... 1.95
- ❑9 ... 1.95
- ❑10 ... 1.95

CAPTAIN THUNDER AND BLUE BOLT (VOL. 2)
HERO
Value: Cover or less

- ❑1, Aug 92, Blow-Back ... 3.50
- ❑2 ... 3.50

CAPTAIN VICTORY AND THE GALACTIC RANGERS
PACIFIC

	ORIG	GOOD	FINE	N-MINT
❑1, Nov 81, JK, JK (w), 1: Mr. Mind	1.00	0.30	0.75	1.50
❑2, Jan 82, JK, JK (w)	1.00	0.25	0.63	1.25
❑3, Mar 82, NA; JK, JK (w), 1: Ms. Mystic	1.00	0.25	0.63	1.25
❑4, May 82, JK, JK (w)	1.00	0.25	0.63	1.25
❑5, Jul 82, JK, JK (w)	1.00	0.25	0.63	1.25
❑6, Sep 82, JK, JK (w)	1.00	0.25	0.63	1.25
❑7, Oct 82, JK, JK (w)	1.00	0.25	0.63	1.25
❑8, Dec 82, JK, JK (w)	1.00	0.25	0.63	1.25
❑9, Feb 83, JK, JK (w), Martius Klavus and The Unseen World, 1: Paranex the Fighting Fetus	1.00	0.25	0.63	1.25
❑10, Apr 83, JK, JK (w), The Voice; Rainmaker, A: Paranex the Fighting Fetus	1.00	0.25	0.63	1.25
❑11, Jun 83, JK, JK (w), O: Captain Victory	1.00	0.25	0.63	1.25
❑12, Oct 83, JK, JK (w)	1.00	0.25	0.63	1.25
❑13, Jan 84, JK, JK (w), indicia lists title as Captain Victory.	1.50	0.25	0.63	1.25
❑SE 1, Oct 83, JK, JK (w)	1.50	0.30	0.75	1.50

CAPTAIN VICTORY AND THE GALACTIC RANGERS (MINI-SERIES)
JACK KIRBY
Value: Cover or less

- ❑1, JK, no cover price ... 2.95
- ❑2, Sep 00, JK ... 2.95
- ❑3, JK ... 2.95

CAPTAIN WINGS COMPACT COMICS
AC
Value: Cover or less

- ❑1, Reprint ... 3.95
- ❑2, Reprint ... 3.95

CARAVAN KIDD
DARK HORSE
Value: Cover or less

- ❑1 ... 2.50
- ❑2 ... 2.50
- ❑3 ... 2.50
- ❑4 ... 2.50
- ❑5 ... 2.50
- ❑6 ... 2.50
- ❑7 ... 2.50
- ❑8 ... 2.50
- ❑9 ... 2.50
- ❑10 ... 2.50

CARAVAN KIDD PART 2
DARK HORSE
Value: Cover or less

- ❑1, May 93 ... 2.50
- ❑2, Jun 93 ... 2.50
- ❑3, Jul 93 ... 2.95
- ❑4, Aug 93 ... 2.50
- ❑5, Sep 93 ... 2.50
- ❑6, Oct 93 ... 2.50
- ❑7 ... 2.50
- ❑8 ... 2.50
- ❑9, Mar 94 ... 2.50
- ❑10, Apr 94 ... 2.50

CARAVAN KIDD PART 3
DARK HORSE
Value: Cover or less

- ❑1, May 94 ... 2.50
- ❑2, Jun 94 ... 2.50
- ❑3, Jul 94 ... 2.50
- ❑4, Aug 94 ... 2.50
- ❑5, Sep 94 ... 2.50
- ❑6, Oct 94 ... 2.50
- ❑7, Nov 94 ... 2.95
- ❑8, Dec 94 ... 2.95

CARBON KNIGHT
LUNAR STUDIOS
Value: Cover or less

- ❑1 ... 2.95
- ❑2 ... 2.95

CARE BEARS
MARVEL

	ORIG	GOOD	FINE	N-MINT
❑1, Nov 85, The Plot to Steal Summer	0.65	0.20	0.50	1.00
❑2	0.65	0.20	0.50	1.00
❑3	0.65	0.20	0.50	1.00
❑4	0.75	0.20	0.50	1.00
❑5	0.75	0.20	0.50	1.00
❑6	0.75	0.20	0.50	1.00
❑7	0.75	0.20	0.50	1.00
❑8	0.75	0.20	0.50	1.00
❑9	0.75	0.20	0.50	1.00
❑10	0.75	0.20	0.50	1.00
❑11	1.00	0.20	0.50	1.00
❑12	1.00	0.20	0.50	1.00
❑13, A: Madballs	1.00	0.20	0.50	1.00
❑14	1.00	0.20	0.50	1.00
❑15	1.00	0.20	0.50	1.00
❑16	1.00	0.20	0.50	1.00
❑17	1.00	0.20	0.50	1.00
❑18	1.00	0.20	0.50	1.00
❑19	1.00	0.20	0.50	1.00
❑20, Final Issue	1.00	0.20	0.50	1.00

CARL AND LARRY CHRISTMAS SPECIAL
COMICS INTERVIEW
Value: Cover or less

- ❑1, b&w ... 2.25

CARMILLA
AIRCEL
Value: Cover or less

- ❑1, Feb 91, b&w; adult; outer paper wrapper to cover nude cover ... 2.50
- ❑2, Mar 91, b&w; adult ... 2.50
- ❑3, Apr 91, b&w; adult ... 2.50
- ❑4, b&w; adult ... 2.50
- ❑5, b&w; adult ... 2.50
- ❑6, b&w; adult ... 2.50

CARNAGE
ETERNITY
Value: Cover or less

❑1, Wrath 1.95

CARNAGE: IT'S A WONDERFUL LIFE
MARVEL
Value: Cover or less

❑1, Oct 96 .... 1.95

CARNAGE: MINDBOMB
MARVEL
Value: Cover or less

❑1, Feb 96, foil cover; One-Shot 2.95

CARNAL COMICS PRESENTS DEMI'S WILD KINGDOM ADVENTURE
REVISIONARY

	ORIG	GOOD	FINE	N-MINT
❑1, Sep 99, b&w; adult; no cover price	—	0.70	1.75	3.50

CARNAL COMICS PRESENTS GINGER LYNN IS TORN
REVISIONARY
Value: Cover or less

❑1/A, Sep 99, b&w; adult; Photo cover 3.50

❑1/B, Sep 99, b&w; adult; alternate coveradult 3.50

CARNEYS, THE
ARCHIE
Value: Cover or less

❑1, Sum 94 .... 2.00

CARNOSAUR CARNAGE
ATOMEKA
Value: Cover or less

❑1, The Skin of Hadrosaurs; Battle at the Edge of Time 4.95

CARTOON CARTOONS
DC
Value: Cover or less

❑1, Mar 01, Ed, Edd n Eddy: Last Nail in the Edhouse; Johnny Bravo's Rules to Live By: Tip #12 Johnny on the Spot 1.99

❑2, Apr 01, Ed, Edd n Eddy: Half Bak-Ed; Cow and Chicken: Chicken and the Beanstalk 1.99

❑3, May 01, The Big Winner 1.99

❑4 .... 1.99

❑5 .... 1.99

❑6 .... 1.99

❑7 .... 1.99

CARTOON HISTORY OF THE UNIVERSE, THE
RIP OFF

	ORIG	GOOD	FINE	N-MINT
❑1, The Evolution of Everything, b&w; cardstock cover	2.50	0.90	2.25	4.50
❑2, b&w; cardstock cover	2.50	0.70	1.75	3.50
❑3, b&w; cardstock cover	2.50	0.70	1.75	3.50
❑4, b&w; cardstock cover	2.50	0.70	1.75	3.50
❑5, b&w; cardstock cover	2.50	0.70	1.75	3.50
❑6, b&w; cardstock cover	2.50	0.50	1.25	2.50
❑7, b&w; cardstock cover	2.50	0.50	1.25	2.50
❑8, b&w	2.95	0.59	1.48	2.95
❑9, b&w	2.95	0.59	1.48	2.95

CARTOONIST, THE
SIRIUS
Value: Cover or less

❑1, Nov, b&w; collects strips 2.95

CARTOON NETWORK
DC

	ORIG	GOOD	FINE	N-MINT
❑1, Cow and Chicken: Recycling Daze; Scooby Doo: Repeat Offender, nn; Give-away from DC Comics to promote comics; Reprints stories from Cartoon Networks Presents #6	—	0.20	0.50	1.00

CARTOON NETWORK CHRISTMAS SPECTACULAR
ARCHIE
Value: Cover or less

❑1, Too Much Christmas Spirit; It's A Gift, A: Scooby-Doo, The Flintstones, The Jetsons, Yogi Bear, Huckleberry Hound, Magilla Gorilla 2.00

CARTOON NETWORK PRESENTS
DC

	ORIG	GOOD	FINE	N-MINT
❑1, Aug 97, Dexter's Laboratory, Top Cat	1.75	0.40	1.00	2.00
❑2, Sep 97, Space Ghost, Yogi Bear	1.75	0.35	0.88	1.75
❑3, Oct 97, The Twiddle Method; Wally Gator: Fifteen Minutes of Fame, Hanna-Barbera crossover with Mr. Peebles, Ranger Smith, Officer Dibble, Mr. Twiddle, and Colonel Fusby; Wally Gator back-up; Cartoon All-Stars	1.75	0.35	0.88	1.75
❑4, Nov 97, Dial M for Monkey, Dial M for Monkey	1.75	0.35	0.88	1.75
❑5, Dec 97, A: Birdman, Herculoids, Toonami	1.95	0.39	0.98	1.95
❑6, Jan 98, Cow and Chicken: Recycling Daze; Scooby Doo: Repeat Offender, Cow and Chicken	1.95	0.39	0.98	1.95
❑7, Feb 98, Wacky Races	1.95	0.39	0.98	1.95
❑8, Mar 98, The Karate Chump!; Clothes Make the Man!, Fighting Monkies; Johnny Bravo	1.95	0.39	0.98	1.95
❑9, Apr 98, A: Herculoids, Birdman, Toonami	1.95	0.39	0.98	1.95
❑10, May 98, Cow & Chicken	1.95	0.39	0.98	1.95
❑11, Jun 98, Wacky Races	1.95	0.39	0.98	1.95
❑12, Aug 98, Cartoon All-Stars; Peter Potamus	1.95	0.39	0.98	1.95
❑13, Sep 98, Toonami, Birdman, Herculoids	1.99	0.39	0.98	1.95
❑14, Oct 98, Cow and Chicken	1.99	0.39	0.98	1.95
❑15, Nov 98, Wacky Races	1.99	0.40	1.00	1.99
❑16, Dec 98, Cartoon All-Stars; Top Cat	1.99	0.40	1.00	1.99
❑17, Jan 99, Winter Takes all, Toonami, Herculoids, Galaxy Trio; Toonami	1.99	0.40	1.00	1.99
❑18, Feb 99, Treasure Hunt, Cartoon All-Stars; Funtastic Treasure Hunt	1.99	0.40	1.00	1.99
❑19, Mar 99, Attack of the 50-Foot Chicken, Cow and Chicken	1.99	0.40	1.00	1.99
❑20, Apr 99, Cartoon All-Stars; Hong Kong Phooey, Atom Ant, Secret Squirrel	1.99	0.40	1.00	1.99
❑21, May 99, Cat on a Hot Tin Pooch; Galtar and the Golden Lance: Zorn to the Rescue!, Toonami, Blue Falcon and Dyno-Mutt, Galtar and the Golden Lance; Toonami	1.99	0.40	1.00	1.99
❑22, Jun 99, Night of the Iron Horse; Brain Food, A: Ranger Smith; A: Ranger Jones; A: El Kabonng; A: Boo Boo Bear; A: Magilla Gorilla; A: Quick Draw McGraw; A: Yogi Bear, Cartoon All-Stars; Baba Looey	1.99	0.40	1.00	1.99
❑23, Jul 99, Jabberjaw: Gammyjaws; Speed Buggy: Bah, Humbug!, Jabberjaw, Speed Buggy, Captain Caveman; Jabberjaw; Speed Buggy; Captain Caveman	1.99	0.40	1.00	1.99
❑24, Aug 99, Puppy Power; Goober and the Ghost Chasers: The Video Vanishes, Scrappy-Doo	1.99	0.40	1.00	1.99
❑SE 1/PL, no cover price; Platinum edition; Dexter's Laboratory	—	0.40	1.00	2.00

A platinum edition of *Cartoon Network Presents* #1 was produced in 1998.

CARTOON NETWORK PRESENTS SPACE GHOST
ARCHIE
Value: Cover or less

❑1, Mar 97 .... 1.50

CARTOON NETWORK STARRING
DC
Value: Cover or less

❑1, Sep 99, The Powerpuff Girls 1.99

❑2, Oct 99, Johnny in Paradise!, 1: Johnny Bravo (in comics) 1.99

❑3, Nov 99 .... 1.99

❑4, Dec 99, 45 Minutes 'til Show-time!, Space Ghost 1.99

❑5, Jan 00 .... 1.99

❑6, Feb 00 .... 1.99

❑7, Mar 00 .... 1.99

❑8, Apr 00 .... 1.99

❑9, May 00, Zorak: Wotta Felon!, Space Ghost 1.99

❑10, Jun 00 .... 1.99

❑11, Jul 00 .... 1.99

❑12, Aug 00 .... 1.99

❑13, Sep 00, Weak in the Sneeze; Flaming Desire 1.99

❑14, Oct 00, Under My Wheels, Johnny Bravo 1.99

❑15, Nov 00, Just Desserts, Space Ghost 1.99

❑16, Dec 00, Two Dips in the Ocean, Cow and Chicken 1.99

❑17, Jan 01, Giddy-Up Johnny!; Beach Blanket Bravo, preview of Sheep in the Big City; Johnny Bravo 1.99

❑18, Feb 01, Who Voo-Dooed It?; Lokar, Lothario, Space Ghost 1.99

CARTOON QUARTERLY
GLADSTONE

	ORIG	GOOD	FINE	N-MINT
❑1, Mickey Mouse	—	1.00	2.50	5.00

CARTOON TALES (DISNEY'S...)
DISNEY
Value: Cover or less

❑1, 101 Dalmatians; Lucky's Big Break 2.95

❑2, Just Us Justice Ducks, 21809; Darkwing Duck 2.95

❑3, F'Reeze a Jolly Good Fellow!; Contractual Desperation, 21810; Tale Spin: Surprise in the Skies; Reprints stories from Disney's Tale Spin #4, 6 .... 2.95

CARTUNE LAND
MAGIC CARPET
Value: Cover or less

❑1, In Other Worlds; the Changeling Earth, b&w 1.50

❑2, Jul 87, Fury of Desolation; Uncle Scourge, b&w 1.50

CARVERS
IMAGE
Value: Cover or less

❑1, Chilling Out 2.95

❑2, All Downhill 2.95

❑3, End Run 2.95

CAR WARRIORS
MARVEL
Value: Cover or less

❑1 .... 2.25

❑2 .... 2.25

❑3 .... 2.25

❑4 .... 2.25

CASANOVA
AIRCEL
Value: Cover or less

Issue	ORIG
❑1, b&w; adult	2.50
❑2, b&w; adult	2.50
❑3, b&w; adult	2.50
❑4, b&w; adult	2.50
❑5, b&w; adult	2.50
❑6, b&w; adult	2.50
❑7, b&w; adult	2.50
❑8, b&w; adult	2.50
❑9, Nov 91, b&w; adult	2.95
❑10, b&w; adult	2.95

CASE MORGAN, GUMSHOE PRIVATE EYE
FORBIDDEN FRUIT
Value: Cover or less

Issue	ORIG
❑1, b&w; adult	2.95
❑2, b&w; adult	2.95
❑3, b&w; adult	2.95
❑4, b&w; adult	2.95
❑5, b&w; adult	2.95
❑6, b&w; adult	2.95
❑7, b&w; adult	2.95
❑8, b&w; adult	2.95
❑9, b&w; adult	2.95
❑10, b&w; adult	2.95
❑11, b&w; adult	3.50

CASE OF BLIND FEAR, A
ETERNITY
Value: Cover or less

Issue	ORIG
❑1, Jan 89, The Madness, b&w; Sherlock Holmes, Invisible Man	1.95
❑2, Apr 89, The Woman, b&w; Sherlock Holmes, Invisible Man	1.95
❑3, b&w; Sherlock Holmes, Invisible Man	1.95
❑4, b&w; Sherlock Holmes, Invisible Man	1.95

CASES OF SHERLOCK HOLMES
RENEGADE

Issue	ORIG	GOOD	FINE	N-MINT
❑1, b&w; Renegade publishes	1.70	0.40	1.00	2.00
❑2, The Adventure of the Dancing Men, b&w	1.70	0.40	1.00	2.00
❑3, The Strange Adventure of The Vourdalak	2.00	0.40	1.00	2.00
❑4, The Adventure of the Six Napoleons	2.00	0.40	1.00	2.00
❑5, The Adventure of the Engineer's Thumb	2.00	0.40	1.00	2.00
❑6	2.00	0.40	1.00	2.00
❑7	2.00	0.40	1.00	2.00
❑8	2.00	0.40	1.00	2.00
❑9, The Adventure of the Copper Beeches	2.00	0.40	1.00	2.00
❑10, The Adventure of the Greek Interpreter	2.00	0.40	1.00	2.00
❑11, The Adventure of Black Peter	2.00	0.40	1.00	2.00
❑12	2.00	0.40	1.00	2.00
❑13, The Adventure of the Naval Treaty, Part 1	2.00	0.40	1.00	2.00
❑14, The Adventure of the Naval Treaty, Part 2	2.00	0.40	1.00	2.00
❑15, The Adventure of Charles Augustus Milverton	2.00	0.40	1.00	2.00
❑16, b&w; Northstar begins as publisher	2.25	0.45	1.13	2.25
❑17, The Adventure of the Abbey Grange, b&w	2.25	0.45	1.13	2.25
❑18, The Adventure of the Blue Carbuncle, b&w	2.25	0.45	1.13	2.25
❑19, The Man With the Twisted Lip	2.25	0.45	1.13	2.25
❑20, The Red-Headed League	2.25	0.45	1.13	2.25
❑21	2.25	0.45	1.13	2.25
❑22	2.25	0.45	1.13	2.25
❑23	2.25	0.45	1.13	2.25
❑24	2.25	0.45	1.13	2.25

CASEY JONES & RAPHAEL
MIRAGE
Value: Cover or less

Issue	ORIG
❑1, Oct 94	2.75
❑2, Exists?	2.75
❑3, Exists?	2.75
❑4, Exists?	2.75
❑5, Exists?	2.75

CASEY JONES: NORTH BY DOWNEAST
MIRAGE
Value: Cover or less

Issue	ORIG
❑1, May 94	2.75
❑2, Jul 94, Final Issue	2.75

CASPER ADVENTURE DIGEST
HARVEY

Issue	ORIG	GOOD	FINE	N-MINT
❑1, Oct 92	1.75	0.40	1.00	2.00
❑2, Dec 92	1.75	0.35	0.88	1.75
❑3, Jan 93	1.75	0.35	0.88	1.75
❑4, Apr 93	1.75	0.35	0.88	1.75
❑5, Jul 93	1.75	0.35	0.88	1.75
❑6, Oct 93	1.75	0.35	0.88	1.75
❑7	1.75	0.35	0.88	1.75
❑8	1.75	0.35	0.88	1.75

CASPER AND FRIENDS
HARVEY

Issue	ORIG	GOOD	FINE	N-MINT
❑1	1.25	0.30	0.75	1.50
❑2	1.25	0.30	0.75	1.50
❑3	1.25	0.30	0.75	1.50
❑4	1.25	0.30	0.75	1.50
❑5	1.25	0.30	0.75	1.50

CASPER AND FRIENDS MAGAZINE
MARVEL
Value: Cover or less

Issue	ORIG
❑1, Mar 97, A: Casper, Richie Rich, Baby Huey, magazine	3.99
❑2, May 97, A: Casper, Richie Rich, Baby Huey, magazine	3.99
❑3, Jul 97, A: Casper, Richie Rich, Baby Huey, magazine	3.99

CASPER & WENDY
HARVEY

Issue	ORIG	GOOD	FINE	N-MINT
❑1, Sep 72, Alice in Wonderland	0.25	1.60	4.00	8.00
❑2, Nov 72	0.25	0.80	2.00	4.00
❑3, Jan 73	0.25	0.80	2.00	4.00
❑4, Mar 73	0.25	0.80	2.00	4.00
❑5, May 73	0.25	0.80	2.00	4.00
❑6, Jul 73	0.25	0.60	1.50	3.00
❑7, Sep 73	0.25	0.60	1.50	3.00
❑8, Nov 73	0.25	0.60	1.50	3.00

CASPER DIGEST MAGAZINE
HARVEY

Issue	ORIG	GOOD	FINE	N-MINT
❑1	1.75	0.40	1.00	2.00
❑2	1.75	0.40	1.00	2.00
❑3	1.75	0.40	1.00	2.00
❑4	1.75	0.40	1.00	2.00
❑9, Sep 89	1.75	0.40	1.00	2.00
❑10, Feb 90, Thanskgiving Parade Special	1.75	0.40	1.00	2.00
❑11, May 90	1.75	0.40	1.00	2.00
❑12, Jul 90	1.75	0.40	1.00	2.00
❑13, Aug 90	1.75	0.40	1.00	2.00

CASPER DIGEST MAGAZINE (VOL. 2)
HARVEY
Value: Cover or less

Issue	ORIG
❑1	1.75
❑2	1.75
❑3	1.75
❑4, Jul 92, indicia says Casper Digest	1.75
❑5, Nov 92	1.75
❑6, Feb 93	1.75
❑7, May 93	1.75
❑8, Aug 93	1.75
❑9, Nov 93	1.75
❑10, Feb 94	1.75
❑11, May 94	1.75
❑12, Jul 94	1.75
❑13, Aug 94	1.75
❑14, Nov 94	1.75

CASPER ENCHANTED TALES DIGEST
HARVEY
Value: Cover or less

Issue	ORIG
❑1, May 92	1.75
❑2, Sep 92	1.75
❑3	1.75
❑4, Jun 93	1.75
❑5, Sep 93	1.75
❑6, Dec 93	1.75
❑7	1.75
❑8, Jun 94	1.75
❑9	1.75
❑10, Oct 94	1.75

CASPER GHOSTLAND
HARVEY
Value: Cover or less

Issue	ORIG
❑1, Win 58	1.25

CASPER GIANT SIZE
HARVEY
Value: Cover or less

Issue	ORIG
❑1	2.25
❑2	2.25
❑3	2.25
❑4	2.25

CASPER IN 3-D
BLACKTHORNE
Value: Cover or less

Issue	ORIG
❑1, Win 88, Roar Lion; Uncle Casper Vs. Uncle Trio	2.50

CASPER THE FRIENDLY GHOST (2ND SERIES)
HARVEY

Issue	ORIG	GOOD	FINE	N-MINT
❑1	1.25	0.40	1.00	2.00
❑2	1.25	0.30	0.75	1.50
❑3	1.25	0.30	0.75	1.50
❑4	1.25	0.30	0.75	1.50
❑5	1.25	0.30	0.75	1.50
❑6	1.25	0.30	0.75	1.50
❑7	1.25	0.30	0.75	1.50
❑8	1.25	0.30	0.75	1.50
❑9	1.25	0.30	0.75	1.50
❑10	1.25	0.30	0.75	1.50
❑11, Cloud Nine; The Poifect Boo	1.25	0.30	0.75	1.50
❑12	1.25	0.30	0.75	1.50
❑13	1.25	0.30	0.75	1.50
❑14	1.25	0.30	0.75	1.50
❑15	1.50	0.30	0.75	1.50
❑16	1.50	0.30	0.75	1.50
❑17	1.50	0.30	0.75	1.50
❑18	1.50	0.30	0.75	1.50
❑19	1.50	0.30	0.75	1.50
❑20	1.50	0.30	0.75	1.50
❑21	1.50	0.30	0.75	1.50
❑22	1.50	0.30	0.75	1.50
❑23	1.50	0.30	0.75	1.50
❑24, Jul 94	1.50	0.30	0.75	1.50
❑25, Aug 94	1.50	0.30	0.75	1.50

	ORIG	GOOD	FINE	N-MINT
❑26, Sep 94	1.50	0.30	0.75	1.50
❑27, Oct 94	1.50	0.30	0.75	1.50
❑28, Nov 94	1.50	0.30	0.75	1.50
❑GS 1, Helpless Hunt; I Am the Spirit of Helpfulness	2.25	0.45	1.13	2.25
❑GS 2	2.25	0.45	1.13	2.25
❑GS 3	2.25	0.45	1.13	2.25
❑GS 4	2.25	0.45	1.13	2.25

CASPER THE FRIENDLY GHOST BIG BOOK
HARVEY

Value: Cover or less

- ❑1 ... 1.95
- ❑2, The Mysterious Zooky; Tricks Not Treats ... 1.95
- ❑3 ... 1.95

CASTLE WAITING
OLIO

	ORIG	GOOD	FINE	N-MINT
❑1, Bahtalo Drom	2.95	1.80	4.50	9.00
❑1-2, Bahtalo Drom, 2nd Printing	2.95	0.59	1.48	2.95
❑, Bahtalo Drom, 3rd Printing	2.95	0.59	1.48	2.95
❑2	2.95	1.00	2.50	5.00
❑2-2, 2nd Printing	2.95	0.59	1.48	2.95
❑3, Akiko pin-up	2.95	0.80	2.00	4.00
❑3-2, 2nd Printing	2.95	0.59	1.48	2.95
❑4, Scott Roberts pin-up	2.95	0.70	1.75	3.50
❑4-2, 2nd Printing	2.95	0.59	1.48	2.95
❑5	2.95	0.70	1.75	3.50
❑5-2, 2nd Printing	2.95	0.59	1.48	2.95
❑6, profiles of 12 Witches begins	2.95	0.60	1.50	3.00
❑7	2.95	0.59	1.48	2.95
❑8, Hiatus issue	2.95	0.59	1.48	2.95
❑Ash 1, The Curse of Brambly Hedge, Limited ashcan edition given away (20 printed)	—	2.00	5.00	10.00

CASTLE WAITING (CARTOON)
CARTOON

Value: Cover or less

- ❑1, Jul 00, Solicitine, Part 1, b&w; follows events of Olio series ... 2.95
- ❑2, Oct 00, Solicitine, Part 2 ... 2.95
- ❑3, Dec 00, Solicitine, Part 3 ... 2.95
- ❑4, Mar 01, Solicitine, Part 4 ... 2.95

CASUAL HEROES
IMAGE

	ORIG	GOOD	FINE	N-MINT
❑1, Apr 96, I Love Myself Better Than You	2.25	0.50	1.25	2.50
❑2, Exists?	2.50	0.50	1.25	2.50
❑3, Exists?	2.50	0.50	1.25	2.50
❑4, Exists?	2.50	0.50	1.25	2.50
❑5, Exists?	2.50	0.50	1.25	2.50

CAT, THE
MARVEL

	ORIG	GOOD	FINE	N-MINT
❑1, Nov 72, WW, Beware The Claws Of The Cat!, 1: Cat, (Cat later becomes Tigra); (Cat later becomes Tigra)	0.20	4.00	10.00	20.00
❑2, Jan 73	0.20	2.80	7.00	14.00
❑3, Apr 73, A: Contains letter by Frank Miller (1st Miller	0.20	2.00	5.00	10.00
❑4, Jun 73	0.20	2.00	5.00	10.00

CAT, THE (AIRCEL)
AIRCEL

Value: Cover or less

- ❑1, b&w; adult ... 2.50
- ❑2, b&w; adult ... 2.50

CATALYST: AGENTS OF CHANGE
DARK HORSE

Value: Cover or less

- ❑1, Feb 94, Behind The Golden Curtain, cardstock cover with foil logo ... 2.00
- ❑2, Mar 94 ... 2.00
- ❑3, Apr 94, Golden Day ... 2.00
- ❑4, May 94, and so are Myths Made ... 2.00
- ❑5 ... 2.00
- ❑6, Aug 94 ... 2.00
- ❑7, Sep 94, We Lucky Few ... 2.00

CAT & MOUSE
EF GRAPHICS

	ORIG	GOOD	FINE	N-MINT
❑1, Jan 89, part color	2.00	0.40	1.00	2.00
❑1-2, 2nd Printing	1.75	0.40	1.00	2.00

CAT & MOUSE (AIRCEL)
AIRCEL

	ORIG	GOOD	FINE	N-MINT
❑1, Mar 90, A Game of Cat & Mouse, b&w	2.25	0.50	1.25	2.50
❑2, Apr 90	2.25	0.50	1.25	2.50
❑3, May 90	2.25	0.50	1.25	2.50
❑4, Jun 90	2.25	0.50	1.25	2.50
❑5, Jul 90, Working 11 to 7 Really Makes Life a Drag	2.25	0.50	1.25	2.50
❑6, Aug 90	2.25	0.50	1.25	2.50
❑7, Sep 90	2.25	0.50	1.25	2.50
❑8, Oct 90, Fight From the Inside	2.25	0.50	1.25	2.50
❑9, Nov 90	2.25	0.50	1.25	2.50
❑10, Dec 90	2.25	0.50	1.25	2.50
❑11, Jan 91, Into the Fire	2.25	0.50	1.25	2.50
❑12, Feb 91, Dead on Time!, D: Nail	2.25	0.50	1.25	2.50
❑13, Mar 91, Good Times Bad Times	2.25	0.50	1.25	2.50
❑14, Apr 91	2.25	0.50	1.25	2.50

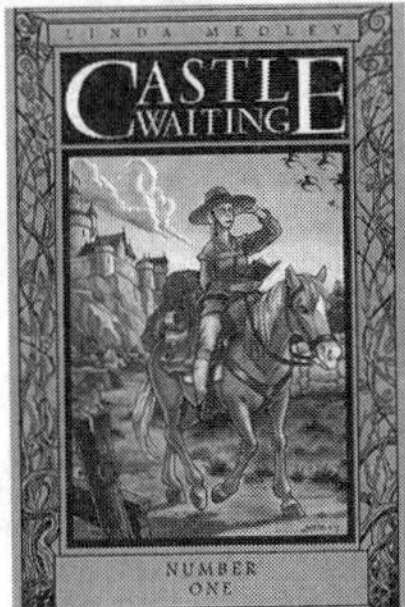

Linda Medley's *Castle Waiting* is an all-ages tale of medieval fantasy set in an alternate universe.

	ORIG	GOOD	FINE	N-MINT
❑15, May 91	2.25	0.50	1.25	2.50
❑16, Jun 91	2.25	0.50	1.25	2.50
❑17, Aug 91	2.25	0.50	1.25	2.50
❑18, Sep 91	2.25	0.50	1.25	2.50

CAT CLAW
ETERNITY

Value: Cover or less

- ❑1, Sep 90, O: Cat Claw, b&w ... 2.50
- ❑1-2, 2nd Printing ... 2.50
- ❑2, Nov 90 ... 2.50
- ❑3, Jan 91 ... 2.50
- ❑4, Feb 91 ... 2.50
- ❑5, Apr 91 ... 2.50
- ❑6, Jun 91 ... 2.50
- ❑7 ... 2.50
- ❑8 ... 2.50
- ❑9 ... 2.50

CATFIGHT
INSOMNIA

Value: Cover or less

- ❑1, Mar 95, The Lolli-pop Man Gets Licked!, 1: The Lolli-pop Man; 1: Catfight, b&w ... 2.75
- ❑1/GO, The Lolli-pop Man Gets Licked!, 1: The Lolli-pop Man; 1: Catfight, Gold edition ... 5.00

CATFIGHT: DREAM INTO ACTION
LIGHTNING

Value: Cover or less

- ❑1, Mar 96, A: CreeD, Hellina, Perg, Creed Guest Star ... 2.75

CATFIGHT: DREAM WARRIOR
LIGHTNING

Value: Cover or less

- ❑1 ... 2.75

CATFIGHT: ESCAPE FROM LIMBO
LIGHTNING

Value: Cover or less

- ❑1, Nov 96 ... 2.75

CATFIGHT: SWEET REVENGE
LIGHTNING

Value: Cover or less

- ❑1, Apr 97, b&w; alternate cover B ... 2.95

CATNIP
SIDE SHOW

Value: Cover or less

- ❑1 ... 2.95

CATSEYE
MANIC PRESS

	ORIG	GOOD	FINE	N-MINT
❑1, Dec 98	2.50	0.59	1.48	2.95
❑2	2.50	0.50	1.25	2.50
❑3	2.50	0.50	1.25	2.50
❑4	2.50	0.50	1.25	2.50
❑5	2.50	0.50	1.25	2.50
❑6	2.50	0.50	1.25	2.50
❑7	2.50	0.50	1.25	2.50
❑8	2.50	0.50	1.25	2.50

CATSEYE AGENCY
RIP OFF

Value: Cover or less

- ❑1, Sep 92, b&w ... 2.50
- ❑2, Oct 92, b&w ... 2.50

CAT, T.H.E. (DELL)
DELL

	ORIG	GOOD	FINE	N-MINT
❑1	0.12	3.60	9.00	18.00
❑2	0.12	2.40	6.00	12.00
❑3	0.12	2.40	6.00	12.00
❑4, Oct 67, The Czars Car Caper!; The 14th Year!, Photo cover	0.12	2.40	6.00	12.00

CATTLE BRAIN
ITCHY EYEBALL

Value: Cover or less

- ❑1, b&w ... 2.75
- ❑2, b&w ... 2.75
- ❑3, b&w ... 2.75

CATWOMAN
DC

	ORIG	GOOD	FINE	N-MINT
❑0, Oct 94, Cat Shadows, O: Catwoman	1.50	0.50	1.25	2.50
❑1, Aug 93, Life Lines, Part 1, O: Catwoman	1.95	1.00	2.50	5.00
❑2, Sep 93, Life Lines, Part 2	1.50	0.70	1.75	3.50
❑3, Oct 93, Life Lines, Part 3	1.50	0.60	1.50	3.00
❑4, Nov 93, Life Lines, Part 4	1.50	0.60	1.50	3.00
❑5, Dec 93	1.50	0.60	1.50	3.00
❑6, Jan 94, Knightquest: The Search	1.50	0.50	1.25	2.50
❑7, Feb 94, Knightquest: The Crusade	1.50	0.50	1.25	2.50
❑8, Mar 94, Zephyr	1.50	0.50	1.25	2.50
❑9, Apr 94	1.50	0.50	1.25	2.50

	ORIG	GOOD	FINE	N-MINT
❑10, May 94	1.50	0.50	1.25	2.50
❑11, Jun 94	1.50	0.50	1.25	2.50
❑12, Jul 94, KnightsEnd, Part 6	1.50	0.50	1.25	2.50
❑13, Aug 94, KnightsEnd Aftermath; KnightsEnd Aftermath, Part 2	1.50	0.50	1.25	2.50
❑14, Sep 94, Zero Hour, Zero Hour	1.50	0.50	1.25	2.50
❑15, Nov 94	1.50	0.50	1.25	2.50
❑16, Dec 94	1.50	0.50	1.25	2.50
❑17, Jan 95	1.50	0.50	1.25	2.50
❑18, Feb 95	1.50	0.50	1.25	2.50
❑19, Mar 95	1.50	0.50	1.25	2.50
❑20, Apr 95	1.50	0.50	1.25	2.50
❑21, May 95	1.95	0.50	1.25	2.50
❑22, Jul 95	1.95	0.50	1.25	2.50
❑23, Aug 95	1.95	0.50	1.25	2.50
❑24, Sep 95	1.95	0.50	1.25	2.50
❑25, Oct 95, A: Robin, Psyba-Rats, Giant-size	2.95	0.60	1.50	3.00
❑26, Nov 95	1.95	0.50	1.25	2.50
❑27, Dec 95	1.95	0.50	1.25	2.50
❑28, Jan 96	1.95	0.50	1.25	2.50
❑29, Feb 96, Thieves	1.95	0.50	1.25	2.50
❑30, Mar 96, The Great Plane Robbery	1.95	0.50	1.25	2.50
❑31, Mar 96, Contagion, Part 5	1.95	0.50	1.25	2.50
❑32, Apr 96, Contagion, Part 9	1.95	0.60	1.50	3.00
❑33, May 96, Contagion	1.95	0.60	1.50	3.00
❑34, Jun 96	1.95	0.50	1.25	2.50
❑35, Jul 96	1.95	0.50	1.25	2.50
❑36, Aug 96, Legacy, Part 2	1.95	0.50	1.25	2.50
❑37, Sep 96	1.95	0.50	1.25	2.50
❑38, Oct 96, Year Two, Part 1	1.95	0.50	1.25	2.50
❑39, Nov 96, Year Two, Part 2	1.95	0.50	1.25	2.50
❑40, Dec 96, Year Two, Part 3, V: Two-Face, Penguin	1.95	0.50	1.25	2.50
❑41, Jan 97, Stolen Yesterdays	1.95	0.40	1.00	2.00
❑42, Feb 97, She-Cats, Part 1, 1: Cybercat	1.95	0.40	1.00	2.00
❑43, Mar 97, She-Cats, Part 2, A: She-Cat	1.95	0.40	1.00	2.00
❑44, Apr 97	1.95	0.40	1.00	2.00
❑45, May 97, Nine Deaths of the Cat	1.95	0.40	1.00	2.00
❑46, Jun 97, V: Two-Face	1.95	0.40	1.00	2.00
❑47, Jul 97, V: Two-Face	1.95	0.40	1.00	2.00
❑48, Aug 97	1.95	0.40	1.00	2.00
❑49, Sep 97	1.95	0.40	1.00	2.00
❑50	—	0.40	1.00	2.00
❑50/A, Oct 97, yellow logo	2.95	0.59	1.48	2.95
❑50/B, Oct 97, purple logo	2.95	0.59	1.48	2.95
❑51, Nov 97, Big Game, V: Huntress	1.95	0.40	1.00	2.00
❑52, Dec 97, The Headhunter: Bigger Game, Face cover	1.95	0.40	1.00	2.00
❑53, Jan 98	1.95	0.40	1.00	2.00
❑54, Feb 98, self-contained story; 1st Devin Grayson script	1.95	0.40	1.00	2.00
❑55, Mar 98, DGry(w), Shared Mentality, self-contained story	1.95	0.40	1.00	2.00
❑56, Apr 98, Cataclysm, Part 6, continues in Robin #52	1.95	0.40	1.00	2.00
❑57, May 98, Cataclysm, Part 15, V: Poison Ivy, continues in Batman: Arkham Asylum - Tales of Madness #1	1.95	0.40	1.00	2.00
❑58, Jun 98, V: Scarecrow	1.95	0.40	1.00	2.00
❑59, Jul 98, V: Scarecrow	1.95	0.40	1.00	2.00
❑60, Aug 98, V: Scarecrow	1.95	0.40	1.00	2.00
❑61, Sep 98	1.99	0.40	1.00	2.00
❑62, Oct 98, A: Nemesis	1.99	0.40	1.00	2.00
❑63, Dec 98, V: Joker	1.99	0.40	1.00	2.00
❑64, Jan 99, DGry(w), A: Batman; V: Joker.	1.99	0.40	1.00	2.00
❑65, Feb 99, DGry(w), A: Batman; V: Joker; A: Scarecrow	1.99	0.40	1.00	2.00
❑66, Mar 99, DGry(w), I'll Take Manhattan, Part 1	1.99	0.40	1.00	2.00
❑67, Apr 99, DGry(w), I'll Take Manhattan, Part 2	1.99	0.40	1.00	2.00
❑68, May 99, DGry(w), I'll Take Manhattan, Part 3, V: Body Doubles, Lady Vic	1.99	0.40	1.00	2.00
❑69, Jun 99, DGry(w), I'll Take Manhattan, Part 4, A: Trickster	1.99	0.40	1.00	2.00
❑70, Jul 99, DGry(w), I'll Take Manhattan, Part 5	1.99	0.40	1.00	1.99
❑71, Aug 99, DGry(w), I'll Take Manhattan: Requiem for Selina Kyle	1.99	0.40	1.00	1.99
❑72, Sep 99, DGry(w), The Mission, No Man's Land	1.99	0.40	1.00	1.99
❑73, Oct 99, Ms. Direction, No Man's Land.	1.99	0.40	1.00	1.99
❑74, Nov 99, No Man's Land	1.99	0.40	1.00	1.99
❑75, Dec 99, The Rules, No Man's Land	1.99	0.40	1.00	1.99
❑76, Jan 00, Strange Bedfellows, No Man's Land	1.99	0.40	1.00	1.99
❑77, Feb 00	1.99	0.40	1.00	1.99
❑78, Mar 00	1.99	0.40	1.00	1.99
❑79, Apr 00, Meet Jane Doe	1.99	0.40	1.00	1.99
❑80, May 00, Kitten in a Cage	1.99	0.40	1.00	1.99
❑81, Jun 00	—	0.40	1.00	1.99
❑82, Jul 00	—	0.40	1.00	1.99
❑83, Aug 00	—	0.40	1.00	1.99
❑84, Sep 00, The Lesser of Two Evils	2.25	0.45	1.13	2.25
❑85, Oct 00, The Cat Came Back	2.25	0.45	1.13	2.25
❑86, Nov 00, Tears for Fluffy	2.25	0.45	1.13	2.25
❑87, Dec 00, Casa De Mujer-Gato	2.25	0.45	1.13	2.25
❑88, Jan 01, TK	2.25	0.45	1.13	2.25
❑89, Feb 01, Always Leave 'em Laughing	2.25	0.45	1.13	2.25
❑90, Mar 01, Office Down, Part 4	2.25	0.45	1.13	2.25
❑91, Apr 01, The Short Road	2.25	0.45	1.13	2.25
❑92, May 01, Tag	2.25	0.45	1.13	2.25
❑1000000, Nov 98	1.99	0.40	1.00	2.00
❑Anl 1, Elseworlds	2.95	0.70	1.75	3.50
❑Anl 2, Year One	3.95	0.79	1.98	3.95
❑Anl 3, Legends of the Dead Earth	2.95	0.59	1.48	2.95
❑Anl 4, Pulp Heroes	3.95	0.79	1.98	3.95

CATWOMAN (MINI-SERIES)
DC

	ORIG	GOOD	FINE	N-MINT
❑1, Feb 89, Metamorphosis, O: Catwoman (new origin)	1.50	1.00	2.50	5.00
❑2, Mar 89	1.50	0.80	2.00	4.00
❑3, Apr 89	1.50	0.60	1.50	3.00
❑4, May 89	1.50	0.60	1.50	3.00

CATWOMAN: GUARDIAN OF GOTHAM
DC

Value: Cover or less

❑1 ... 5.95

❑2 ... 5.95

CATWOMAN PLUS
DC

Value: Cover or less

❑1, Nov 97, Undead...And Loving It!; Wild Things, Part 3, A: Scream Queen, continues in Robin Plus #2 ... 2.95

CATWOMAN/VAMPIRELLA: THE FURIES
DC

Value: Cover or less

❑1, Feb 97, The Furies, A: Pantha, prestige format; crossover with Harris ... 5.95

CATWOMAN/WILDCAT
DC

Value: Cover or less

❑1, Aug 98, 2 Against the House ... 2.50

❑2, Sep 98 ... 2.50

❑3, Oct 98 ... 2.50

❑4, Nov 98 ... 2.50

CAVE BANG
EROS

Value: Cover or less

❑1, Oct 96 ... 2.95

❑2, Jul 00 ... 2.95

CAVE GIRL
AC

Value: Cover or less

❑1, O: Cave Girl, Reprint ... 2.95

CAVEMAN
CAVEMAN PUBLISHING

Value: Cover or less

❑1, Apr 98 ... 3.50

❑2, Jun 98 ... 3.50

❑3, Aug 98 ... 3.50

❑4, Oct 98 ... 3.50

❑GN 1, Evolution, Heck!, b&w; graphic novel ... 9.95

CAVEWOMAN
BASEMENT

	ORIG	GOOD	FINE	N-MINT
❑1, b&w	2.95	11.00	27.50	55.00
❑2, b&w	2.95	7.00	17.50	35.00
❑3, b&w	2.95	5.00	12.50	25.00
❑4, b&w	2.95	4.00	10.00	20.00
❑5, b&w	2.95	4.00	10.00	20.00
❑6, b&w	2.95	4.00	10.00	20.00

CAVEWOMAN: MISSING LINK
BASEMENT

Value: Cover or less

❑1, b&w ... 2.95

❑2, b&w ... 2.95

CAVEWOMAN: RAIN
BASEMENT

	ORIG	GOOD	FINE	N-MINT
❑1, trading card	2.95	0.80	2.00	4.00
❑1-2, 2nd Printing	2.95	0.59	1.48	2.95
❑, 3rd Printing	2.95	0.59	1.48	2.95
❑2	2.95	0.70	1.75	3.50
❑2-2, 2nd Printing	2.95	0.59	1.48	2.95
❑2-3, 3rd Printing	2.95	0.59	1.48	2.95
❑3	2.95	0.70	1.75	3.50
❑3-2, 2nd Printing	2.95	0.59	1.48	2.95
❑4	2.95	0.60	1.50	3.00
❑4-2, 2nd Printing	2.95	0.59	1.48	2.95
❑5	2.95	0.60	1.50	3.00
❑5-2, 2nd Printing	2.95	0.59	1.48	2.95

	ORIG	GOOD	FINE	N-MINT
❑6	2.95	0.60	1.50	3.00
❑7	2.95	0.60	1.50	3.00
❑8	2.95	0.60	1.50	3.00

CECIL KUNKLE (2ND SERIES)
DARKLINE

Value: Cover or less

❑1 .... 3.50
❑2 .... 3.50
❑3, b&w; Santa cover 2.00

CECIL KUNKLE (CHARLES A. WAGNER'S...)
RENEGADE

	ORIG	GOOD	FINE	N-MINT
❑1, May 86, Take Two...They're Good for You!, b&w	1.70	0.40	1.00	2.00

CELESTIAL MECHANICS: THE ADVENTURES OF WIDGET WILHELMINA JONES
INNOVATION

Value: Cover or less

❑1, Dec 90, What a Glorious Feeling, I'm Happy Again, b&w.. 2.75
❑2, Feb 91, We've Talked The Whole Night Through, b&w . 2.75
❑3, b&w 2.75

CELESTINE
IMAGE

Value: Cover or less

❑1, May 96 .... 2.50
❑1/SC, May 96, alternate cover 2.50
❑2, Jun 96 .... 2.50

CELL
ANTARCTIC

Value: Cover or less

❑1, Sep 96, b&w 2.95
❑2, Nov 96, b&w 2.95
❑3, Jan 97, b&w 2.95

CENOTAPH
NORTHSTAR

Value: Cover or less

❑1 .... 3.95

CENTRIFUGAL BUMBLE-PUPPY
FANTAGRAPHICS

	ORIG	GOOD	FINE	N-MINT
❑1, b&w	2.25	0.45	1.13	2.25
❑2, b&w	2.25	0.45	1.13	2.25
❑3, b&w	2.25	0.45	1.13	2.25
❑4, b&w	2.25	0.45	1.13	2.25
❑5, b&w	2.25	0.45	1.13	2.25
❑6, b&w	2.25	0.45	1.13	2.25
❑7	—	0.45	1.13	2.25
❑8	2.50	0.50	1.25	2.50

CENTURIONS
DC

	ORIG	GOOD	FINE	N-MINT
❑1, Jun 87, O: Centurions	0.75	0.20	0.50	1.00
❑2, Jul 87, DH, Seeing Is Not Believing!, O: Centurions	0.75	0.20	0.50	1.00
❑3, Aug 87	0.75	0.20	0.50	1.00
❑4, Sep 87	1.00	0.20	0.50	1.00

CENTURY: DISTANT SONS
MARVEL

Value: Cover or less

❑1, Feb 96, D: The Broker 2.95

CEREAL KILLINGS
FANTAGRAPHICS

	ORIG	GOOD	FINE	N-MINT
❑1, Mar 92, b&w	2.25	0.50	1.25	2.50
❑2, b&w	2.25	0.50	1.25	2.50
❑3, Lost Causes; Slump, b&w	2.25	0.50	1.25	2.50
❑4, b&w	2.50	0.50	1.25	2.50
❑5, b&w	2.50	0.50	1.25	2.50

CEREBUS BI-WEEKLY
AARDVARK-VANAHEIM

	ORIG	GOOD	FINE	N-MINT
❑1, Dec 88, A: Reprints Cerebus the Aardvark #1, 1st	1.25	0.40	1.00	2.00
❑2, Dec 88, Reprints Cerebus the Aardvark #2	1.25	0.30	0.75	1.50
❑3, Dec 88, Reprints Cerebus the Aardvark #3	1.25	0.30	0.75	1.50
❑4, Jan 89, Reprints Cerebus the Aardvark #4	1.25	0.30	0.75	1.50
❑5, Jan 89, Reprints Cerebus the Aardvark #5	1.25	0.30	0.75	1.50
❑6, Feb 89, Reprints Cerebus the Aardvark #6	1.25	0.30	0.75	1.50
❑7, Feb 89, Reprints Cerebus the Aardvark #7	1.25	0.30	0.75	1.50
❑8, Mar 89, Reprints Cerebus the Aardvark #8	1.25	0.30	0.75	1.50
❑9, Mar 89, Reprints Cerebus the Aardvark #9	1.25	0.30	0.75	1.50
❑10, Apr 89, Reprints Cerebus the Aardvark #10	1.25	0.30	0.75	1.50
❑11, Apr 89, Reprints Cerebus the Aardvark #11	1.25	0.30	0.75	1.50
❑12, May 89, Reprints Cerebus the Aardvark #12	1.25	0.30	0.75	1.50
❑13, May 89, Reprints Cerebus the Aardvark #13	1.25	0.30	0.75	1.50
❑14, May 89, Reprints Cerebus the Aardvark #14	1.25	0.30	0.75	1.50
❑15, Jun 89, A Day In The Pits, Reprints Cerebus the Aardvark #15	1.25	0.30	0.75	1.50

Catwoman was introduced in the 1940s, and her origin has been revised several times in the years since.

	ORIG	GOOD	FINE	N-MINT
❑16, Jun 89, Reprints Cerebus the Aardvark #16	1.25	0.30	0.75	1.50
❑17, Jul 89, 1: Hepcats, Reprints Cerebus the Aardvark #17 with new material	1.25	2.00	5.00	10.00
❑18, Jul 89, Reprints Cerebus the Aardvark #18	1.25	0.30	0.75	1.50
❑19, Aug 89, Reprints Cerebus the Aardvark #19	1.25	0.30	0.75	1.50
❑20, Aug 89, 1: Milk & Cheese, Reprints Cerebus the Aardvark #20 with new material	1.25	3.00	7.50	15.00
❑21, Sep 89, Reprints Cerebus the Aardvark #21	1.25	0.30	0.75	1.50
❑22, Sep 89, Reprints Cerebus the Aardvark #22	1.25	0.30	0.75	1.50
❑23, Oct 89, Reprints Cerebus the Aardvark #23	1.25	0.30	0.75	1.50
❑24, Oct 89, Reprints Cerebus the Aardvark #24	1.25	0.30	0.75	1.50
❑25, Nov 89, Reprints Cerebus the Aardvark #25	1.25	0.30	0.75	1.50
❑26, Nov 89, Reprints Cerebus the Aardvark #26	1.25	0.30	0.75	1.50

CEREBUS: CHURCH & STATE
AARDVARK-VANAHEIM

Value: Cover or less

❑1, Reprints Cerebus the Aardvark #51 .... 2.00
❑2, Reprints Cerebus the Aardvark #52 .... 2.00
❑3, Reprints Cerebus the Aardvark #53 .... 2.00
❑4, Reprints Cerebus the Aardvark #54 .... 2.00
❑5, Reprints Cerebus the Aardvark #55 .... 2.00
❑6, Reprints Cerebus the Aardvark #56 .... 2.00
❑7, Reprints Cerebus the Aardvark #57 .... 2.00
❑8, Reprints Cerebus the Aardvark #58 .... 2.00
❑9, Reprints Cerebus the Aardvark #59 .... 2.00
❑10, Reprints Cerebus the Aardvark #60 .... 2.00
❑11, Reprints Cerebus the Aardvark #61 .... 2.00
❑12, Reprints Cerebus the Aardvark #62 .... 2.00
❑13, Reprints Cerebus the Aardvark #63 .... 2.00
❑14, Reprints Cerebus the Aardvark #64 .... 2.00
❑15, Reprints Cerebus the Aardvark #65 .... 2.00
❑16, Reprints Cerebus the Aardvark #66 .... 2.00
❑17, Reprints Cerebus the Aardvark #67 .... 2.00
❑18, Reprints Cerebus the Aardvark #68 .... 2.00
❑19, Reprints Cerebus the Aardvark #69 .... 2.00
❑20, Sane As It Ever Was, Reprints Cerebus the Aardvark #70... 2.00
❑21, Reprints Cerebus the Aardvark #71 .... 2.00
❑22, Reprints Cerebus the Aardvark #72 .... 2.00
❑23, Reprints Cerebus the Aardvark #73 .... 2.00
❑24, Dec 92, Reprints Cerebus the Aardvark #74 .... 2.00
❑25, Jan 93, Reprints Cerebus the Aardvark #75 .... 2.00
❑26, Feb 93, Reprints Cerebus the Aardvark #76 .... 2.00
❑27, Mar 93, Reprints Cerebus the Aardvark #77 .... 2.00
❑28, Reprints Cerebus the Aardvark #78 .... 2.00
❑29, Spinning Straw Into Gold, Reprints Cerebus the Aardvark #79 .... 2.00
❑30, Reprints Cerebus the Aardvark #80 .... 2.00

CEREBUS COMPANION
WIN-MILL

Value: Cover or less

❑1, Dec 93 .... 3.95
❑2, Dec 94 .... 3.95

CEREBUS GUIDE TO SELF PUBLISHING
AARDVARK-VANAHEIM

Value: Cover or less

❑1, Nov 97, nn; collects Sim text pieces on the subject from Cerebus 3.95

CEREBUS: GUYS PARTY PACK
AARDVARK-VANAHEIM

Value: Cover or less

❑1, Guys, Reprints Cerebus the Aardvark #201-204 .... 3.95

CEREBUS HIGH SOCIETY
AARDVARK-VANAHEIM

	ORIG	GOOD	FINE	N-MINT
❑1	1.70	0.40	1.00	2.00
❑2	1.70	0.40	1.00	2.00
❑3	1.70	0.40	1.00	2.00
❑4	1.70	0.40	1.00	2.00
❑5, Apr 90	1.70	0.40	1.00	2.00

	ORIG	GOOD	FINE	N-MINT
❑6, Apr 90	1.70	0.40	1.00	2.00
❑7, May 90	1.70	0.40	1.00	2.00
❑8, May 90	1.70	0.40	1.00	2.00
❑9, Jun 90	1.70	0.40	1.00	2.00
❑10, Jun 90	1.70	0.40	1.00	2.00
❑11, Jul 90	2.00	0.40	1.00	2.00
❑12, Jul 90	2.00	0.40	1.00	2.00
❑13, Aug 90	2.00	0.40	1.00	2.00
❑14, Aug 90	2.00	0.40	1.00	2.00
❑15	2.00	0.40	1.00	2.00
❑16	2.00	0.40	1.00	2.00
❑17	2.00	0.40	1.00	2.00
❑18	2.00	0.40	1.00	2.00
❑19	2.00	0.40	1.00	2.00
❑20	2.00	0.40	1.00	2.00
❑21	2.00	0.40	1.00	2.00
❑22	2.00	0.40	1.00	2.00
❑23	2.00	0.40	1.00	2.00
❑24	2.00	0.40	1.00	2.00
❑25	2.00	0.40	1.00	2.00

CEREBUS JAM

AARDVARK-VANAHEIM

Value: Cover or less ❑1, Apr 85 .... 2.00

CEREBUS THE AARDVARK

AARDVARK-VANAHEIM

	ORIG	GOOD	FINE	N-MINT
❑0, Jun 93, b&w; Reprint; Reprints Cerebus the Aardvark #51, 112/113, 137/138	2.25	0.80	2.00	4.00
❑0/GO, Gold logo on cover; Reprints Cerebus the Aardvark #51, 112/113, 137/138	—	1.20	3.00	6.00
❑1, 1: Cerebus, genuine; Low circulation	1.00	55.00	137.50	275.00
❑1/CF, 1: Cerebus, Counterfeit edition (glossy cover stock on inside cover); Low circulation	1.00	7.00	17.50	35.00
❑2	1.00	14.00	35.00	70.00
❑3, 1: Red Sophia	1.00	13.00	32.50	65.00
❑4, 1: Elrod the Albino	1.00	8.00	20.00	40.00
❑5, Aug 78	1.00	7.00	17.50	35.00
❑6, Oct 78	1.00	7.00	17.50	35.00
❑7, Dec 78	1.00	4.80	12.00	24.00
❑8, Feb 79	1.00	4.80	12.00	24.00
❑9, Apr 79	1.00	4.80	12.00	24.00
❑10, Jun 79	1.00	4.80	12.00	24.00
❑11, Aug 79, 1: Captain Cockroach	1.00	4.00	10.00	20.00
❑12, Oct 79	1.00	4.00	10.00	20.00
❑13, Dec 79	1.00	4.00	10.00	20.00
❑14, Mar 80	1.00	4.00	10.00	20.00
❑15, Apr 80, A Day In The Pits	1.00	4.00	10.00	20.00
❑16, May 80	1.25	3.60	9.00	18.00
❑17, Jun 80	1.25	3.60	9.00	18.00
❑18, Jul 80	1.25	3.60	9.00	18.00
❑19, Aug 80	1.25	3.60	9.00	18.00
❑20, Sep 80	1.25	3.60	9.00	18.00
❑21, Oct 80, Low circulation	1.25	6.00	15.00	30.00
❑22, Nov 80, no cover price	—	3.20	8.00	16.00
❑23, Dec 80	1.50	1.40	3.50	7.00
❑24, Jan 81	1.50	1.40	3.50	7.00
❑25, Mar 81	1.50	1.40	3.50	7.00
❑26, May 81, High Society	1.50	1.40	3.50	7.00
❑27, Jun 81, High Society	1.50	1.40	3.50	7.00
❑28, Jul 81, High Society	1.50	1.40	3.50	7.00
❑29, Aug 81, High Society	1.50	1.40	3.50	7.00
❑30, Sep 81, High Society	1.50	1.40	3.50	7.00
❑31, Oct 81, High Society	1.50	1.40	3.50	7.00
❑32, Nov 81, High Society	1.50	1.20	3.00	6.00
❑33, Dec 81, High Society	1.50	1.20	3.00	6.00
❑34, Jan 82, High Society	1.50	1.20	3.00	6.00
❑35, Feb 82, High Society	1.50	1.20	3.00	6.00
❑36, Mar 82, High Society	1.50	1.20	3.00	6.00
❑37, Apr 82, High Society	1.50	1.20	3.00	6.00
❑38, May 82, High Society	1.50	1.20	3.00	6.00
❑39, Jun 82, High Society	1.50	1.20	3.00	6.00
❑40, Jul 82, High Society	1.50	1.20	3.00	6.00
❑41, Aug 82, High Society	1.50	1.00	2.50	5.00
❑42, Sep 82, High Society	1.50	1.00	2.50	5.00
❑43, Oct 82, High Society	1.50	1.00	2.50	5.00
❑44, Nov 82, High Society, sideways	1.50	1.00	2.50	5.00
❑45, Dec 82, High Society, sideways	1.50	1.00	2.50	5.00
❑46, Jan 83, High Society, sideways	1.40	1.00	2.50	5.00
❑47, Feb 83, High Society, sideways	1.40	1.00	2.50	5.00
❑48, Mar 83, High Society, sideways	1.40	1.00	2.50	5.00
❑49, Apr 83, High Society, rotating issue	1.40	1.00	2.50	5.00
❑50, May 83, High Society	1.40	1.00	2.50	5.00
❑51, Jun 83, Church & State, Low circulation	1.40	1.60	4.00	8.00
❑52, Jul 83, Church & State	1.40	1.00	2.50	5.00
❑53, Aug 83, Church & State, 1: Wolveroach (cameo)	1.40	1.00	2.50	5.00
❑54, Sep 83, Church & State, 1: Wolveroach (full story); A: Wolveroach	1.40	1.00	2.50	5.00
❑55, Oct 83, Church & State, A: Wolveroach	1.40	1.00	2.50	5.00
❑56, Nov 83, Church & State, 1: Normalman; A: Wolveroach	1.40	1.00	2.50	5.00
❑57, Dec 83, Church & State, 2: Normalman	1.40	0.80	2.00	4.00
❑58, Jan 84, Church & State	1.70	0.80	2.00	4.00
❑59, Feb 84, Church & State	1.70	0.80	2.00	4.00
❑60, Mar 84, Church & State	1.70	0.80	2.00	4.00
❑61, Apr 84, Church & State, A: Flaming Carrot, Flaming Carrot	1.70	1.00	2.50	5.00
❑62, May 84, Church & State, A: Flaming Carrot, Flaming Carrot	1.70	1.00	2.50	5.00
❑63, Jun 84, Church & State	1.70	0.60	1.50	3.00
❑64, Jul 84, Church & State	1.70	0.60	1.50	3.00
❑65, Aug 84, Church & State, Gerhard begins as background artist	1.70	0.60	1.50	3.00
❑66, Sep 84, Church & State	1.70	0.60	1.50	3.00
❑67, Oct 84, Church & State	1.70	0.60	1.50	3.00
❑68, Nov 84, Church & State	1.70	0.60	1.50	3.00
❑69, Dec 84, Church & State	1.70	0.60	1.50	3.00
❑70, Jan 85, Church & State	1.70	0.60	1.50	3.00
❑71, Feb 85, Church & State	1.70	0.60	1.50	3.00
❑72, Mar 85, Church & State	1.70	0.60	1.50	3.00
❑73, Apr 85, Church & State	1.70	0.60	1.50	3.00
❑74, May 85, Church & State	1.70	0.60	1.50	3.00
❑75, Jun 85, Church & State	1.70	0.60	1.50	3.00
❑76, Jul 85, Church & State	1.70	0.60	1.50	3.00
❑77, Aug 85, Church & State	1.70	0.60	1.50	3.00
❑78, Sep 85, Church & State	1.70	0.60	1.50	3.00
❑79, Oct 85, Church & State	1.70	0.60	1.50	3.00
❑80, Nov 85, Church & State	1.70	0.60	1.50	3.00
❑81, Dec 85, Church & State	1.70	0.60	1.50	3.00
❑82, Jan 86, Church & State	1.70	0.60	1.50	3.00
❑83, Feb 86, Church & State	1.70	0.60	1.50	3.00
❑84, Mar 86, Church & State	1.70	0.60	1.50	3.00
❑85, Apr 86, Church & State	1.70	0.60	1.50	3.00
❑86, May 86, Church & State	1.70	0.60	1.50	3.00
❑87, Jun 86, Church & State	1.70	0.60	1.50	3.00
❑88, Jul 86, Church & State	1.70	0.60	1.50	3.00
❑89, Aug 86, Church & State	1.70	0.60	1.50	3.00
❑90, Sep 86, Church & State	1.70	0.60	1.50	3.00
❑91, Oct 86, Church & State	1.70	0.60	1.50	3.00
❑92, Nov 86, Church & State	1.70	0.60	1.50	3.00
❑93, Dec 86, Church & State	1.70	0.60	1.50	3.00
❑94, Jan 87, Church & State	1.70	0.60	1.50	3.00
❑95, Feb 87, Church & State	1.70	0.60	1.50	3.00
❑96, Mar 87, Church & State	1.70	0.60	1.50	3.00
❑97, Apr 87, Church & State	1.70	0.60	1.50	3.00
❑98, May 87, Church & State	1.70	0.60	1.50	3.00
❑99, Jun 87, Church & State	1.70	0.60	1.50	3.00
❑100, Jul 87, Church & State	1.70	0.60	1.50	3.00
❑101, Aug 87, Church & State	1.70	0.50	1.25	2.50
❑102, Sep 87, Church & State	1.70	0.50	1.25	2.50
❑103, Oct 87, Church & State	1.70	0.50	1.25	2.50
❑104, Nov 87, Church & State, A: Flaming Carrot	1.70	0.50	1.25	2.50
❑105, Dec 87, Church & State; Ascension's End, Part 1	1.70	0.50	1.25	2.50
❑106, Jan 88, Church & State; Ascension's End, Part 2	2.00	0.50	1.25	2.50
❑107, Feb 88, Church & State	2.00	0.50	1.25	2.50
❑108, Mar 88, Church & State	2.00	0.50	1.25	2.50
❑109, Apr 88, Church & State	2.00	0.50	1.25	2.50
❑110, May 88, Church & State	2.00	0.50	1.25	2.50
❑111, Jun 88, Church & State	2.00	0.50	1.25	2.50
❑112, Jul 88, Double-issue #112 and #113	2.00	0.50	1.25	2.50
❑114, Sep 88, Jaka's Story; Jaka's Story, Part 1	2.00	0.50	1.25	2.50
❑115, Oct 88, Jaka's Story; Jaka's Story, Part 2	2.00	0.50	1.25	2.50
❑116, Nov 88, Jaka's Story; Jaka's Story, Part 3	2.00	0.50	1.25	2.50
❑117, Dec 88, Jaka's Story; Jaka's Story, Part 4	2.00	0.50	1.25	2.50
❑118, Jan 89, Jaka's Story; Jaka's Story, Part 5	2.00	0.50	1.25	2.50
❑119, Feb 89, Jaka's Story; Jaka's Story, Part 6	2.00	0.50	1.25	2.50
❑120, Mar 89, Jaka's Story; Jaka's Story, Part 7	2.00	0.50	1.25	2.50
❑121, Apr 89, Jaka's Story; Jaka's Story, Part 8	2.00	0.50	1.25	2.50
❑122, May 89, Jaka's Story; Jaka's Story, Part 9	2.00	0.50	1.25	2.50
❑123, Jun 89, Jaka's Story; Jaka's Story, Part 10	2.00	0.50	1.25	2.50

	ORIG	GOOD	FINE	N-MINT
❑124, Jul 89, Jaka's Story; Jaka's Story, Part 11	2.00	0.50	1.25	2.50
❑125, Aug 89, Jaka's Story; Jaka's Story, Part 12	2.00	0.50	1.25	2.50
❑126, Sep 89, Jaka's Story; Jaka's Story, Part 13	2.00	0.50	1.25	2.50
❑127, Oct 89, Jaka's Story; Jaka's Story, Part 14	2.00	0.50	1.25	2.50
❑128, Nov 89, Jaka's Story; Jaka's Story, Part 15	2.00	0.50	1.25	2.50
❑129, Dec 89, Jaka's Story; Jaka's Story, Part 16	2.00	0.50	1.25	2.50
❑130, Jan 90, Jaka's Story; Jaka's Story, Part 17	2.00	0.50	1.25	2.50
❑131, Feb 90, Jaka's Story; Jaka's Story, Part 18	2.00	0.50	1.25	2.50
❑132, Mar 90, Jaka's Story; Jaka's Story, Part 19	2.00	0.50	1.25	2.50
❑133, Apr 90, Jaka's Story; Jaka's Story, Part 19	2.00	0.50	1.25	2.50
❑134, May 90, Jaka's Story; Jaka's Story, Part 20	2.00	0.50	1.25	2.50
❑135, Jun 90, Jaka's Story; Jaka's Story, Part 21	2.00	0.50	1.25	2.50
❑136, Jul 90, Jaka's Story; Jaka's Story, Part 22	2.00	0.50	1.25	2.50
❑137, Aug 90, Jaka's Story	2.25	0.50	1.25	2.50
❑138, Sep 90, Jaka's Story, Photo cover	2.25	0.50	1.25	2.50
❑139, Oct 90, Melmoth; Melmoth, Part 0	2.25	0.50	1.25	2.50
❑140, Nov 90, Melmoth; Melmoth, Part 1	2.25	0.45	1.13	2.25
❑141, Dec 90, Melmoth; Melmoth, Part 2	2.25	0.45	1.13	2.25
❑142, Jan 91, Melmoth; Melmoth, Part 3	2.25	0.45	1.13	2.25
❑143, Feb 91, Melmoth; Melmoth, Part 4	2.25	0.45	1.13	2.25
❑144, Mar 91, Melmoth; Melmoth, Part 5	2.25	0.45	1.13	2.25
❑145, Apr 91, Melmoth; Melmoth, Part 6	2.25	0.45	1.13	2.25
❑146, May 91, Melmoth; Melmoth, Part 7	2.25	0.45	1.13	2.25
❑147, Jun 91, Melmoth; Melmoth, Part 8	2.25	0.45	1.13	2.25
❑148, Jul 91, Melmoth; Melmoth, Part 9	2.25	0.45	1.13	2.25
❑149, Aug 91, Melmoth; Melmoth, Part 10	2.25	0.45	1.13	2.25
❑150, Sep 91, Melmoth; Melmoth, Part 11	2.25	0.45	1.13	2.25
❑151, Oct 91, Mothers & Daughters; Mothers & Daughters, Part 1	2.25	0.45	1.13	2.25
❑152, Nov 91, Mothers & Daughters; Mothers & Daughters, Part 2	2.25	0.45	1.13	2.25
❑153, Dec 91, Mothers & Daughters; Mothers & Daughters, Part 3	2.25	0.45	1.13	2.25
❑154, Jan 92, Mothers & Daughters; Mothers & Daughters, Part 4	2.25	0.45	1.13	2.25
❑155, Feb 92, Mothers & Daughters; Mothers & Daughters, Part 5	2.25	0.45	1.13	2.25
❑156, Mar 92, Mothers & Daughters; Mothers & Daughters, Part 6	2.25	0.45	1.13	2.25
❑157, Apr 92, Mothers & Daughters; Mothers & Daughters, Part 7	2.25	0.45	1.13	2.25
❑158, May 92, Mothers & Daughters; Mothers & Daughters, Part 8	2.25	0.45	1.13	2.25
❑159, Jun 92, Mothers & Daughters; Mothers & Daughters, Part 9	2.25	0.45	1.13	2.25
❑160, Jul 92, Mothers & Daughters; Mothers & Daughters, Part 10	2.25	0.45	1.13	2.25
❑161, Aug 92, Mothers & Daughters; Mothers & Daughters, Part 11, Bone back-up	2.25	0.45	1.13	2.25
❑162, Sep 92, Mothers & Daughters; Mothers & Daughters, Part 12	2.25	0.45	1.13	2.25
❑163, Oct 92, Mothers & Daughters; Mothers & Daughters, Part 13	2.25	0.45	1.13	2.25
❑164, Nov 92, Mothers & Daughters; Mothers & Daughters, Part 14	2.25	0.45	1.13	2.25
❑165, Dec 92, Mothers & Daughters; Mothers & Daughters, Part 15	2.25	0.45	1.13	2.25
❑165-2, Dec 92, Mothers & Daughters, 2nd Printing	2.25	0.45	1.13	2.25
❑166, Jan 93, Mothers & Daughters; Mothers & Daughters, Part 16	2.25	0.45	1.13	2.25
❑167, Feb 93, Mothers & Daughters; Mothers & Daughters, Part 17	2.25	0.45	1.13	2.25
❑168, Mar 93, Mothers & Daughters; Mothers & Daughters, Part 18	2.25	0.45	1.13	2.25
❑169, Apr 93, Mothers & Daughters; Mothers & Daughters, Part 19	2.25	0.45	1.13	2.25
❑170, May 93, Mothers & Daughters; Mothers & Daughters, Part 20	2.25	0.45	1.13	2.25
❑171, Jun 93, Mothers & Daughters; Mothers & Daughters, Part 21	2.25	0.45	1.13	2.25
❑172, Jul 93, Mothers & Daughters; Mothers & Daughters, Part 22	2.25	0.45	1.13	2.25
❑173, Aug 93, Mothers & Daughters; Mothers & Daughters, Part 23	2.25	0.45	1.13	2.25
❑174, Sep 93, Mothers & Daughters; Mothers & Daughters, Part 24	2.25	0.45	1.13	2.25
❑175, Oct 93, Mothers & Daughters; Mothers & Daughters, Part 25	2.25	0.45	1.13	2.25

Jaka's early days in the court of Lord Julius were recounted in "Jaka's Story."

	ORIG	GOOD	FINE	N-MINT
❑176, Nov 93, Mothers & Daughters; Mothers & Daughters, Part 26	2.25	0.45	1.13	2.25
❑177, Dec 93, Mothers & Daughters; Mothers & Daughters, Part 27	2.25	0.45	1.13	2.25
❑178, Jan 94, Mothers & Daughters; Mothers & Daughters, Part 28	2.25	0.45	1.13	2.25
❑179, Feb 94, Mothers & Daughters; Mothers & Daughters, Part 29	2.25	0.45	1.13	2.25
❑180, Mar 94, Mothers & Daughters; Mothers & Daughters, Part 30	2.25	0.45	1.13	2.25
❑181, Apr 94, Mothers & Daughters; Mothers & Daughters, Part 31	2.25	0.45	1.13	2.25
❑182, May 94, Mothers & Daughters; Mothers & Daughters, Part 32	2.25	0.45	1.13	2.25
❑183, Jun 94, Mothers & Daughters; Mothers & Daughters, Part 33	2.25	0.45	1.13	2.25
❑184, Jul 94, Mothers & Daughters; Mothers & Daughters, Part 34	2.25	0.45	1.13	2.25
❑185, Aug 94, Mothers & Daughters; Mothers & Daughters, Part 35	2.25	0.45	1.13	2.25
❑186, Sep 94, Mothers & Daughters; Mothers & Daughters, Part 36	2.25	0.45	1.13	2.25
❑187, Oct 94, Mothers & Daughters; Mothers & Daughters, Part 37	2.25	0.45	1.13	2.25
❑188, Nov 94, Mothers & Daughters; Mothers & Daughters, Part 38	2.25	0.45	1.13	2.25
❑189, Dec 94, Mothers & Daughters; Mothers & Daughters, Part 39	2.25	0.45	1.13	2.25
❑190, Jan 94, Mothers & Daughters; Mothers & Daughters, Part 40	2.25	0.45	1.13	2.25
❑191, Feb 94, Mothers & Daughters	2.25	0.45	1.13	2.25
❑192, Mar 94, Mothers & Daughters	2.25	0.45	1.13	2.25
❑193, Apr 94, Mothers & Daughters	2.25	0.45	1.13	2.25
❑194, May 95, Mothers & Daughters	2.25	0.45	1.13	2.25
❑195, Jun 95, Mothers & Daughters	2.25	0.45	1.13	2.25
❑196, Jul 95, Mothers & Daughters	2.25	0.45	1.13	2.25
❑197, Aug 95, Mothers & Daughters	2.25	0.45	1.13	2.25
❑198, Sep 95, Mothers & Daughters	2.25	0.45	1.13	2.25
❑199, Oct 95, Mothers & Daughters	2.25	0.45	1.13	2.25
❑200, Nov 95, Mothers & Daughters, Patty Cake back-up	2.25	0.45	1.13	2.25
❑201, Dec 95, Guys, Part 1	2.25	0.45	1.13	2.25
❑202, Jan 96, Guys, Part 2	2.25	0.45	1.13	2.25
❑203, Feb 96, Guys, Part 3	2.25	0.45	1.13	2.25
❑204, Mar 96, Guys, Part 4	2.25	0.45	1.13	2.25
❑205, Apr 96, Guys, Part 5	2.25	0.45	1.13	2.25
❑206, May 96, Guys, Part 6	2.25	0.45	1.13	2.25
❑207, Jun 96, Guys, Part 7	2.25	0.45	1.13	2.25
❑208, Jul 96, Guys, Part 8	2.25	0.45	1.13	2.25
❑209, Aug 96, Guys, Part 9	2.25	0.45	1.13	2.25
❑210, Sep 96, Guys, Part 10	2.25	0.45	1.13	2.25
❑211, Oct 96, Guys, Part 11	2.25	0.45	1.13	2.25
❑212, Nov 96, Guys, Part 12	2.25	0.45	1.13	2.25
❑213, Dec 96, Guys, Part 13	2.25	0.45	1.13	2.25
❑214, Jan 97, Guys, Part 14	2.25	0.45	1.13	2.25
❑215, Feb 97, Guys, Part 15	2.25	0.45	1.13	2.25
❑216, Mar 97, Guys, Part 16	2.25	0.45	1.13	2.25
❑217, Apr 97, Guys, Part 17	2.25	0.45	1.13	2.25
❑218, May 97, Guys, Part 18	2.25	0.45	1.13	2.25
❑219, Jun 97, Guys, Part 19	2.25	0.45	1.13	2.25
❑220, Jul 97, Rick's Story, Part 1	2.25	0.45	1.13	2.25
❑221, Aug 97, Rick's Story, Part 2	2.25	0.45	1.13	2.25
❑222, Sep 97, Rick's Story, Part 3	2.25	0.45	1.13	2.25
❑223, Oct 97, Rick's Story, Part 4	2.25	0.45	1.13	2.25
❑224, Nov 97, Rick's Story, Part 5	2.25	0.45	1.13	2.25
❑225, Dec 97, Rick's Story, Part 6	2.25	0.45	1.13	2.25
❑226, Jan 98, Rick's Story, Part 7	2.25	0.45	1.13	2.25
❑227, Feb 98, Rick's Story, Part 8	2.25	0.45	1.13	2.25
❑228, Mar 98, Rick's Story, Part 9	2.25	0.45	1.13	2.25
❑229, Apr 98, Rick's Story, Part 10	2.25	0.45	1.13	2.25
❑230, May 98, Rick's Story, Part 11	2.25	0.45	1.13	2.25
❑231, Jun 98, Rick's Story, Part 12	2.25	0.45	1.13	2.25
❑232, Jul 98, Going Home, Part 1	2.25	0.45	1.13	2.25
❑233, Aug 98, Going Home, Part 2	2.25	0.45	1.13	2.25

	ORIG	GOOD	FINE	N-MINT
❑234, Sep 98, Going Home, Part 3	2.25	0.45	1.13	2.25
❑235, Oct 98, Going Home, Part 4	2.25	0.45	1.13	2.25
❑236, Nov 98, Going Home, Part 5	2.25	0.45	1.13	2.25
❑237, Dec 98, Going Home, Part 6	2.25	0.45	1.13	2.25
❑238, Jan 99, Going Home, Part 7	2.25	0.45	1.13	2.25
❑239, Feb 99, Going Home, Part 8	2.25	0.45	1.13	2.25
❑240, Mar 99, Going Home, Part 9	2.25	0.45	1.13	2.25
❑241, Apr 99, Going Home, Part 10	2.25	0.45	1.13	2.25
❑242, May 99, Going Home, Part 11	2.25	0.45	1.13	2.25
❑243, Jun 99, Going Home, Part 12	2.25	0.45	1.13	2.25
❑244, Jul 99, Going Home, Part 13	2.25	0.45	1.13	2.25
❑245, Aug 99, Going Home, Part 14	2.25	0.45	1.13	2.25
❑246, Sep 99, Going Home, Part 15	2.25	0.45	1.13	2.25
❑247, Oct 99, Going Home, Part 16	2.25	0.45	1.13	2.25
❑248, Nov 99, Going Home, Part 17	2.25	0.45	1.13	2.25
❑249, Dec 99, Going Home, Part 18	2.25	0.45	1.13	2.25
❑250, Jan 00, Going Home, Part 19	2.25	0.45	1.13	2.25
❑251, Feb 00, Going Home, Part 20	2.25	0.45	1.13	2.25
❑252, Mar 00, Going Home, Part 21	2.25	0.45	1.13	2.25
❑253, Apr 00, Going Home, Part 22	2.25	0.45	1.13	2.25
❑254, May 00, Going Home, Part 23	2.25	0.45	1.13	2.25
❑255, Jun 00, Going Home, Part 24	2.25	0.45	1.13	2.25
❑256, Jul 00, Going Home, Part 25	2.25	0.45	1.13	2.25
❑257, Aug 00, Going Home, Part 26	2.25	0.45	1.13	2.25
❑258, Sep 00, Going Home, Part 27	2.25	0.45	1.13	2.25
❑259, Oct 00, Going Home, Part 28	2.25	0.45	1.13	2.25
❑260, Nov 00, Going Home, Part 29	2.25	0.45	1.13	2.25
❑261, Dec 00, Going Home, Part 30	2.25	0.45	1.13	2.25
❑262	2.25	0.45	1.13	2.25
❑263	2.25	0.45	1.13	2.25
❑264	2.25	0.45	1.13	2.25
❑265	2.25	0.45	1.13	2.25
❑266	2.25	0.45	1.13	2.25
❑267	2.25	0.45	1.13	2.25
❑268	2.25	0.45	1.13	2.25

CEREBUS WORLD TOUR BOOK
AARDVARK-VANAHEIM

Value: Cover or less

❑1, nn; b&w 2.95

CHADZ FRENDZ
SMILING FACE

Value: Cover or less

❑1, Jan 98, Chad The Chicken; Don't Sleep in My Class 1.50

CHAINGANG
NORTHSTAR

Value: Cover or less

❑1, b&w 2.50

❑2 .... 2.50

CHAIN GANG WAR
DC

	ORIG	GOOD	FINE	N-MINT
❑1, Jul 93, Chain Reaction, Foil embossed cover	2.50	0.50	1.25	2.50
❑1/SI, Chain Reaction, Silver promotional edition	2.50	0.80	2.00	4.00
❑2, Aug 93	1.75	0.40	1.00	2.00
❑3, Sep 93, Weak Link	1.75	0.40	1.00	2.00
❑4, Oct 93	1.75	0.40	1.00	2.00
❑5, Nov 93, A: Batman; A: Azrael; A: Deathstroke, Embossed cover	2.50	0.40	1.00	2.00
❑6, Dec 93	1.75	0.35	0.88	1.75
❑7, Jan 94, Jail Break	1.75	0.35	0.88	1.75
❑8, Feb 94, The Crooked Man, Part 1	1.75	0.35	0.88	1.75
❑9, Mar 94, The Crooked Man, Part 2	1.75	0.35	0.88	1.75
❑10, Apr 94, The Crooked Man, Part 3	1.75	0.35	0.88	1.75
❑11, May 94, The Crooked Man, Part 4	1.75	0.35	0.88	1.75
❑12, Jun 94, Meltdown, D: Curtis Zecker, Final Issue; End of Chain Gang	1.75	0.40	1.00	2.00

CHAINSAW VIGILANTE
NEC

	ORIG	GOOD	FINE	N-MINT
❑1, Night Of Lumber Equipment And Minor Surgery, A: Tick	3.25	0.70	1.75	3.50
❑1/A, Orange cover	14.00	2.80	7.00	14.00
❑1/B, Gold foil cover	17.00	3.40	8.50	17.00
❑1/C, Pseudo-3D "platinum" foil cover	25.00	5.00	12.50	25.00
❑2	2.75	0.55	1.38	2.75
❑3	2.75	0.55	1.38	2.75

CHAINS OF CHAOS
HARRIS

Value: Cover or less

❑1, Nov 94, Link One 2.95

❑2, Dec 94 .... 2.95

❑3, Jan 95, Link III 2.95

CHAKAN
RAK

	ORIG	GOOD	FINE	N-MINT
❑1, b&w	—	0.80	2.00	4.00

CHALLENGERS OF THE FANTASTIC
MARVEL

	ORIG	GOOD	FINE	N-MINT
❑1, Jun 97	1.95	0.40	1.00	2.00

CHALLENGERS OF THE UNKNOWN
DC

	ORIG	GOOD	FINE	N-MINT
❑1, May 58, JK	0.10	400.00	1000.00	2000.00
❑2, Jul 58, JK	0.10	150.00	375.00	750.00
❑3, Sep 58, JK	0.10	125.00	312.50	625.00
❑4, Nov 58, WW; JK	0.10	102.00	255.00	510.00
❑5, Jan 59, WW; JK	0.10	102.00	255.00	510.00
❑6, Mar 59, WW; JK	0.10	102.00	255.00	510.00
❑7, May 59, WW; JK	0.10	102.00	255.00	510.00
❑8, Jul 59, WW; JK	0.10	102.00	255.00	510.00
❑9, Sep 59, JK	0.10	60.00	150.00	300.00
❑10, Nov 59, JK	0.10	60.00	150.00	300.00
❑11, Jan 60	0.10	40.00	100.00	200.00
❑12, Mar 60	0.10	40.00	100.00	200.00
❑13, May 60	0.10	40.00	100.00	200.00
❑14, Jul 60, 1: Multi-Man	0.10	40.00	100.00	200.00
❑15, Sep 60	0.10	40.00	100.00	200.00
❑16, Nov 60	0.10	24.00	60.00	120.00
❑17, Jan 61	0.10	24.00	60.00	120.00
❑18, Mar 61, 1: Cosmo (Challengers of the Unknown's Pet)	0.10	24.00	60.00	120.00
❑19, May 61	0.10	24.00	60.00	120.00
❑20, Jul 61	0.10	24.00	60.00	120.00
❑21, Sep 61	0.10	14.00	35.00	70.00
❑22, Nov 61	0.10	14.00	35.00	70.00
❑23, Jan 62	0.12	14.00	35.00	70.00
❑24, Mar 62	0.12	14.00	35.00	70.00
❑25, May 62	0.12	14.00	35.00	70.00
❑26, Jul 62	0.12	14.00	35.00	70.00
❑27, Sep 62	0.12	14.00	35.00	70.00
❑28, Nov 62	0.12	14.00	35.00	70.00
❑29, Jan 63	0.12	14.00	35.00	70.00
❑30, Mar 63	0.12	14.00	35.00	70.00
❑31, May 63, O: Challengers of the Unknown	0.12	16.00	40.00	80.00
❑32, Jul 63	0.12	8.40	21.00	42.00
❑33, Sep 63	0.12	8.40	21.00	42.00
❑34, Nov 63, 1: Multi-Woman	0.12	8.40	21.00	42.00
❑35, Jan 64	0.12	8.40	21.00	42.00
❑36, Mar 64	0.12	8.40	21.00	42.00
❑37, May 64	0.12	8.40	21.00	42.00
❑38, Jul 64	0.12	8.40	21.00	42.00
❑39, Sep 64	0.12	8.40	21.00	42.00
❑40, Nov 64, The Super Powers of the Challengers	0.12	8.40	21.00	42.00
❑41, Jan 65	0.12	4.80	12.00	24.00
❑42, Mar 65, The League Of Challenger Haters	0.12	4.80	12.00	24.00
❑43, May 65, Challengers of the Unknown get new uniforms	0.12	4.80	12.00	24.00
❑44, Jul 65	0.12	4.80	12.00	24.00
❑45, Sep 65	0.12	4.80	12.00	24.00
❑46, Nov 65	0.12	4.80	12.00	24.00
❑47, Jan 66	0.12	4.80	12.00	24.00
❑48, Mar 66, A: The Doom Patrol	0.12	4.80	12.00	24.00
❑49, May 66	0.12	4.80	12.00	24.00
❑50, Jul 66, Final Hour for the Challengers, 1: Villo	0.12	4.80	12.00	24.00
❑51, Sep 66, V: Sponge Man; A: Sea Devils	0.12	4.00	10.00	20.00
❑52, Nov 66	0.12	4.00	10.00	20.00
❑53, Jan 67	0.12	4.00	10.00	20.00
❑54, Mar 67	0.12	4.00	10.00	20.00
❑55, May 67, D: Red Ryan; 1: Tino Manarry	0.12	4.00	10.00	20.00
❑56, Jul 67	0.12	4.00	10.00	20.00
❑57, Sep 67	0.12	4.00	10.00	20.00
❑58, Nov 67, V: Neutro	0.12	4.00	10.00	20.00
❑59, Jan 68	0.12	4.00	10.00	20.00
❑60, Mar 68, Red Ryan returns	0.12	4.00	10.00	20.00
❑61, May 68	0.12	1.40	3.50	7.00
❑62, Jul 68	0.12	1.40	3.50	7.00
❑63, Sep 68	0.12	1.40	3.50	7.00
❑64, Nov 68, JK, O: Challengers of the Unknown, reprints Showcase #6	0.12	1.40	3.50	7.00
❑65, Jan 69, JK, O: Challengers of the Unknown, reprints Showcase #6	0.12	1.40	3.50	7.00
❑66, Mar 69	0.12	1.40	3.50	7.00
❑67, May 69	0.12	1.40	3.50	7.00
❑68, Jul 69, One Of Us Is A Madman	0.12	1.40	3.50	7.00
❑69, Sep 69, 1: Corinna	0.15	1.40	3.50	7.00
❑70, Nov 69	0.15	1.40	3.50	7.00
❑71, Jan 70	0.15	1.40	3.50	7.00
❑72, Mar 70	0.15	1.40	3.50	7.00
❑73, May 70	0.15	1.40	3.50	7.00
❑74, Jul 70, NA, A: Deadman	0.15	2.80	7.00	14.00
❑75, Sep 70, JK, V: Ultivac, reprints Showcase #7	0.15	1.40	3.50	7.00
❑76, Nov 70	0.15	1.40	3.50	7.00

	ORIG	GOOD	FINE	N-MINT
❑77, Jan 71	0.15	1.40	3.50	7.00
❑78, Feb 73	0.20	1.40	3.50	7.00
❑79, Apr 73, JKu (c), reprints stories from Challengers of the Unknown #1 and 2	0.20	1.40	3.50	7.00
❑80, Jul 73, series goes on hiatus for four years	0.20	1.40	3.50	7.00
❑81, Jul 77	0.20	1.20	3.00	6.00
❑82, Aug 77, A: Swamp Thing	0.20	1.00	2.50	5.00
❑83, Oct 77	0.20	1.00	2.50	5.00
❑84, Dec 77	0.20	1.00	2.50	5.00
❑85, Feb 78, A: Deadman, Swamp Thing	0.20	1.00	2.50	5.00
❑86, Apr 78, A: Deadman, Swamp Thing	0.20	1.00	2.50	5.00
❑87, Jul 78, KG, A: Deadman, Swamp Thing, Rip Hunter, Final Issue	0.35	1.00	2.50	5.00

CHALLENGERS OF THE UNKNOWN (2ND SERIES)
DC

	ORIG	GOOD	FINE	N-MINT
❑1, Feb 97, new team	2.25	0.50	1.25	2.50
❑2, Mar 97, Undead	2.25	0.50	1.25	2.50
❑3, Apr 97, Threshold	2.25	0.50	1.25	2.50
❑4, May 97, O: Challengers	2.25	0.50	1.25	2.50
❑5, Jun 97, Private Lives	2.25	0.50	1.25	2.50
❑6, Jul 97, Convergenge, Part 3, concludes in Scare Tactics #8	2.25	0.45	1.13	2.25
❑7, Aug 97, Last Days, Part 1, return of original Challengers	2.25	0.45	1.13	2.25
❑8, Sep 97, Last Days, Part 2, O: both Challenger teams	2.25	0.45	1.13	2.25
❑9, Oct 97, Last Days, Part 3	2.25	0.45	1.13	2.25
❑10, Nov 97, Broken Spirits	2.25	0.45	1.13	2.25
❑11, Dec 97, Times Fade Away, Face cover	2.25	0.45	1.13	2.25
❑12, Jan 98, A: Batman	2.25	0.45	1.13	2.25
❑13, Feb 98	2.25	0.45	1.13	2.25
❑14, Mar 98, Dark Waters	2.25	0.45	1.13	2.25
❑15, Apr 98, Millennium Giants; continues in Superman #134	2.25	0.60	1.50	3.00
❑16, May 98, tales of the original Challengers	2.25	0.45	1.13	2.25
❑17, Jun 98	2.25	0.45	1.13	2.25
❑18, Jul 98, Final Issue	2.50	0.50	1.25	2.50

CHALLENGERS OF THE UNKNOWN (MINI-SERIES)
DC

	ORIG	GOOD	FINE	N-MINT
❑1, Mar 91, JPH (w), The Challengers Must Die, O: Challengers of the Unknown (new origin)	1.75	0.50	1.25	2.50
❑2, Apr 91	1.75	0.40	1.00	2.00
❑3, May 91	1.75	0.40	1.00	2.00
❑4, Jun 91	1.75	0.40	1.00	2.00
❑5, Jul 91	1.75	0.40	1.00	2.00
❑6, Aug 91, GK (c)	1.75	0.40	1.00	2.00
❑7, Sep 91, JPH (w), Another World!	1.75	0.40	1.00	2.00
❑8, Oct 91	1.75	0.40	1.00	2.00

CHAMBER OF CHILLS
MARVEL

	ORIG	GOOD	FINE	N-MINT
❑1, Nov 72, A Dragon Stalks By Night	0.20	1.60	4.00	8.00
❑2, Jan 73	0.20	0.80	2.00	4.00
❑3, Mar 73	0.20	0.80	2.00	4.00
❑4, May 73	0.20	0.60	1.50	3.00
❑5, Jul 73	0.20	0.60	1.50	3.00
❑6, Sep 73	0.20	0.60	1.50	3.00
❑7, Nov 73	0.20	0.60	1.50	3.00
❑8, Jan 74	0.20	0.60	1.50	3.00
❑9, Mar 74	0.20	0.60	1.50	3.00
❑10, May 74	0.25	0.60	1.50	3.00
❑11, Jul 74	0.25	0.60	1.50	3.00
❑12, Sep 74	0.25	0.60	1.50	3.00
❑13, Nov 74	0.25	0.60	1.50	3.00
❑14, Jan 75	0.25	0.60	1.50	3.00
❑15, Mar 75	0.25	0.60	1.50	3.00
❑16, May 75	0.25	0.60	1.50	3.00
❑17, Jul 75	0.25	0.60	1.50	3.00
❑18, Sep 75	0.25	0.60	1.50	3.00
❑19, Nov 75	0.25	0.60	1.50	3.00
❑20, Jan 76	0.25	0.60	1.50	3.00
❑21, Mar 76	0.25	0.60	1.50	3.00
❑22, May 76	0.25	0.60	1.50	3.00
❑23, Jul 76	0.25	0.60	1.50	3.00
❑24, Sep 76	0.30	0.60	1.50	3.00
❑25, Nov 76	0.30	0.60	1.50	3.00

CHAMBER OF DARKNESS
MARVEL

	ORIG	GOOD	FINE	N-MINT
❑1, Oct 68, DH; JB, It's Only Magic!; Mr. Craven Buys His Scream House!	0.15	2.80	7.00	14.00
❑2, Dec 68	0.15	1.00	2.50	5.00
❑3, Feb 69	0.15	1.00	2.50	5.00
❑4, Apr 69, Conan try-out	0.15	4.00	10.00	20.00
❑5, Jun 69	0.15	0.80	2.00	4.00
❑6, Aug 69	0.15	0.80	2.00	4.00

A group of Marvel's super-powered adventurers, including Hercules, The Black Widow, Ghost Rider, Ice Man, and The Angel, joined forces as The Champions in 1975.

	ORIG	GOOD	FINE	N-MINT
❑7, Oct 69, BWr, 1st Bernie Wrightson work	0.15	1.60	4.00	8.00
❑8, Dec 69	0.15	0.80	2.00	4.00

CHAMBER OF EVIL
COMAX

Value: Cover or less

- ❑1, Demon Skull's Revenge.... 2.95

CHAMPION, THE
SPECIAL STUDIO

Value: Cover or less

- ❑1, b&w.... 2.50

CHAMPION OF KATARA
CRACK O'DAWN

Value: Cover or less

- ❑1.... 1.50

CHAMPION OF KATARA, THE
MU PRESS

Value: Cover or less

- ❑1, Jan 92, b&w.... 2.50
- ❑2, Apr 92.... 2.50

CHAMPION OF KATARA: DUM-DUMS & DRAGONS, THE
MU

Value: Cover or less

- ❑1, Jun 95, b&w.... 2.95
- ❑2, Jul 95, b&w.... 2.95
- ❑3, Aug 95, b&w.... 2.95

CHAMPIONS (ECLIPSE)
ECLIPSE

	ORIG	GOOD	FINE	N-MINT
❑1, Jun 86, The Curse of the Hellfire Crown, 1: Foxbat; 1: Icestar; 1: Flare; 1: Giant; 1: The Champions (game characters); 1: Marksman; 1: Rose	1.25	0.30	0.75	1.50
❑2, Sep 86	1.25	0.30	0.75	1.50
❑3, Oct 86	1.25	0.30	0.75	1.50
❑4, Nov 86	1.25	0.30	0.75	1.50
❑5, Feb 87, O: Flare	1.25	0.30	0.75	1.50
❑6, Feb 87	1.25	0.30	0.75	1.50

CHAMPIONS (HERO)
HERO

Value: Cover or less

- ❑1, Sep 87, Champions, 1: Madame Synn; 1: The Galloping Galooper.... 1.95
- ❑2, Oct 87, 1: The Fat Man; 1: Black Enchantress.... 1.95
- ❑3, Nov 87, O: Flare; 1: Sparkplug; 1: Icicle.... 1.95
- ❑4, Dec 87, 1: Exo-Skeleton Man; 1: Pulsar.... 1.95
- ❑5, Jan 88.... 1.95
- ❑6, Feb 88, 1: Mechanon.... 1.95
- ❑7, Mar 88.... 1.95
- ❑8, May 88, O: Foxbat.... 1.95
- ❑9, Jun 88, (also was Flare #0) 1.95
- ❑10, Jul 88.... 1.95
- ❑11, Sep 88.... 1.95
- ❑12, Oct 88.... 1.95
- ❑13.... 1.95
- ❑14.... 1.95
- ❑15, b&w.... 3.95
- ❑Anl 1, Dec 88, O: Dark Malice; O: Giant.... 2.75
- ❑Anl 2.... 4.50

CHAMPIONS, THE (MARVEL)
MARVEL

	ORIG	GOOD	FINE	N-MINT
❑1, Oct 75, DH, The World Still Needs...The Champions!, 1: The Champions; A: Venus	0.25	2.40	6.00	12.00
❑2, Jan 76	0.25	1.20	3.00	6.00
❑3, Feb 76	0.25	1.20	3.00	6.00
❑4, Mar 76	0.25	1.00	2.50	5.00
❑5, Apr 76, DH, 1: Rampage (Marvel); A: Ghost Rider	0.25	1.00	2.50	5.00
❑6, Jun 76	0.25	0.80	2.00	4.00
❑7, Aug 76	0.25	0.80	2.00	4.00
❑8, Oct 76, GK	0.30	0.80	2.00	4.00
❑9, Dec 76, BH; GK, The Battle Of Los Angeles, V: Darkstar, Titanium Man, Crimson Dynamo	0.30	0.80	2.00	4.00
❑10, Jan 77, DC	0.30	0.80	2.00	4.00
❑11, Feb 77, JBy	0.30	1.20	3.00	6.00
❑12, Mar 77, JBy, The Stranger?	0.30	1.20	3.00	6.00
❑13, May 77, JBy	0.30	1.20	3.00	6.00
❑14, Jul 77, JBy, 1: Swarm	0.30	1.20	3.00	6.00
❑15, Sep 77, JBy	0.30	1.20	3.00	6.00
❑16, Nov 77, BH; JBy, A: Doctor Doom	0.35	1.20	3.00	6.00
❑17, Jan 78, GT; JBy, V: Sentinels, Final Issue	0.35	1.20	3.00	6.00

CHAMPIONS CLASSICS
HERO

	ORIG	GOOD	FINE	N-MINT
❑1, Reprint	0.90	0.20	0.50	1.00
❑13, Oct 93, b&w reprint	3.95	0.79	1.98	3.95
❑14, Jan 94, b&w reprint	3.95	0.79	1.98	3.95

ORIG GOOD FINE N-MINT

CHAMPIONS CLASSICS/FLARE ADVENTURES
HERO
Value: Cover or less

- ❑2, flip-format 2.95
- ❑3, flip-format 2.95
- ❑4, flip-format 3.50
- ❑5, flip-format 3.50
- ❑6, flip-format 3.50
- ❑7, flip-format 3.50

CHAMPION SPORTS
DC

Issue	ORIG	GOOD	FINE	N-MINT
❑1, Nov 73, The Kid Who Beat the Oakland A's; The Little Racer	0.20	1.00	2.50	5.00
❑2, Jan 74, The Enchanted Bat; Street Fighter	0.20	0.70	1.75	3.50
❑3, Mar 74, Horse Story; The Saga of Wild Bill Hickok	0.20	0.70	1.75	3.50

CHANGE COMMANDER GOKU (1ST SERIES)
ANTARCTIC
Value: Cover or less

- ❑1, Oct 93, Battle Burn, Part 1, 1: Change Commander Goku. 2.95
- ❑2, Nov 93, Battle Burn, Part 2 2.95
- ❑3, Dec 93, Battle Burn, Part 3 2.95
- ❑4, Jan 94, Battle Burn, Part 4, 1: The True-Brewing Magnetic Man 2.95
- ❑5, Feb 94, Battle Burn, Part 5 2.95

CHANGE COMMANDER GOKU 2
ANTARCTIC
Value: Cover or less

- ❑1, Sep 96 2.95
- ❑2, Nov 96 2.95
- ❑3, Jan 97 2.95
- ❑4, Mar 97 2.95

CHANGES
TUNDRA
Value: Cover or less

- ❑1 7.95

CHANNEL ZERO
IMAGE
Value: Cover or less

- ❑1, Feb 98 2.95
- ❑2, Apr 98 2.95
- ❑3, Jun 98 2.95
- ❑4, Aug 98 2.95
- ❑5, Nov 98, Global Supermarket 2.95
- ❑6 2.95

CHANNEL ZERO: DUPE
IMAGE
Value: Cover or less

- ❑1, Jan 99, nn; b&w 2.95

CHAOS! BIBLE, THE
CHAOS
Value: Cover or less

- ❑1, Alien Evil; Root of All Evil.. 3.50

CHAOS! CHRONICLES
CHAOS
Value: Cover or less

- ❑1, Feb 00 3.50

CHAOS EFFECT, THE: ALPHA
VALIANT

Issue	ORIG	GOOD	FINE	N-MINT
❑1, BL (w), Chaos Rules, A: Timewalker, no cover price; trading card; giveaway	—	0.20	0.50	1.00
❑1/GO, BL (w), Chaos Rules, A: Timewalker, giveaway; Gold edition	—	0.30	0.75	1.50

CHAOS EFFECT, THE: EPILOGUE
VALIANT
Value: Cover or less

- ❑1, Dec 94, In Search of Faith Part 1, A: Timewalker; A: Faith, cardstock cover; Magnus in 20th century 2.95
- ❑2, Jan 95, In Search of Faith Part 2, cardstock cover; Magnus in 20th century 2.95

CHAOS EFFECT, THE: OMEGA
VALIANT

Issue	ORIG	GOOD	FINE	N-MINT
❑1, Nov 94, cardstock cover; Magnus to 20th century	2.25	0.45	1.13	2.25
❑1/GO, Nov 94, cardstock cover; Gold edition; Magnus to 20th century	—	0.60	1.50	3.00
❑2, Nov 94, BL (w), From Chaos Comes...Order, Omega	2.25	0.45	1.13	2.25
❑2/GO, Nov 94, BL (w), From Chaos Comes...Order, Gold edition	—	0.50	1.25	2.50

CHAOS! GALLERY
CHAOS!
Value: Cover or less

- ❑1, Aug 97, pin-ups 2.95

CHAOS! PRESENTS JADE
CHAOS
Value: Cover or less

- ❑1, May 01 2.99
- ❑2 2.99
- ❑3 2.99
- ❑4 2.99

CHAOS! QUARTERLY
CHAOS

Issue	ORIG	GOOD	FINE	N-MINT
❑1, Lady Death; Purgatori	4.95	1.00	2.50	5.00
❑2, Lady Demon; Robo-Evil	4.95	1.00	2.50	5.00
❑3	3.95	0.79	1.98	3.95

CHAPEL
IMAGE

Issue	ORIG	GOOD	FINE	N-MINT
❑1, Feb 95	2.50	0.60	1.50	2.99
❑2, Mar 95	2.50	0.50	1.25	2.50
❑2/SC, Mar 95, alternate cover; Chapel firing right, white lettering in logo	2.50	0.50	1.25	2.50

ORIG GOOD FINE N-MINT

CHAPEL (MINI-SERIES)
IMAGE

Issue	ORIG	GOOD	FINE	N-MINT
❑1	2.50	0.70	1.75	3.50
❑2	2.50	0.50	1.25	2.50

CHAPEL (VOL. 2)
IMAGE
Value: Cover or less

- ❑1, Aug 95 2.50
- ❑1/SC, Aug 95, alternate cover 2.50
- ❑2, Sep 95 2.50
- ❑3, Oct 95 2.50
- ❑4, Nov 95, Babewatch 2.50
- ❑5, Dec 95, V: Spawn 2.50
- ❑6, Feb 96, A: Spawn 2.50
- ❑7, Apr 96, Shadow Hunt, Part 2, V: Shadowhawk 2.50

CHARLEMAGNE
DEFIANT
Value: Cover or less

- ❑0, Feb 94, giveaway 10.00
- ❑1, Mar 94, Fire Will Come..., 1: Charlemagne 3.25
- ❑2, Apr 94, The Dance Of Eternity, A: War Dancer 2.50
- ❑3, May 94, Fear Itself, A: Doctor Michael Alexander 2.50
- ❑4, Jun 94 3.25
- ❑5 2.50
- ❑6 2.50
- ❑7 2.50
- ❑8, Final Issue 2.50

CHARLES BURNS' MODERN HORROR SKETCHBOOK
KITCHEN SINK
Value: Cover or less

- ❑1, nn 6.95

CHARLIE CHAN (ETERNITY)
ETERNITY
Value: Cover or less

- ❑1, Mar 89, b&w strip reprint... 1.95
- ❑2, Mar 89, b&w strip reprint... 1.95
- ❑3, Apr 89, b&w strip reprint ... 1.95
- ❑4, May 89, b&w strip reprint .. 1.95
- ❑5, Jul 89 2.25
- ❑6, Aug 89 2.25

CHARLIE THE CAVEMAN
FANTASY GENERAL

Issue	ORIG	GOOD	FINE	N-MINT
❑1, b&w	1.70	0.40	1.00	2.00

CHARLTON ACTION FEATURING STATIC
CHARLTON

Issue	ORIG	GOOD	FINE	N-MINT
❑11, Oct 85	0.75	0.30	0.75	1.50
❑12, Dec 85	0.75	0.30	0.75	1.50

CHARLTON BULLSEYE (VOL. 2)
CHARLTON

Issue	ORIG	GOOD	FINE	N-MINT
❑1, Jun 81, Blue Beetle & The Question: The Enigma!	0.50	0.60	1.50	3.00
❑2, Jul 81	0.60	0.40	1.00	2.00
❑3, Sep 81	0.60	0.40	1.00	2.00
❑4, Nov 81	0.60	0.40	1.00	2.00
❑5, Jan 82	0.60	0.40	1.00	2.00
❑6, Mar 82	0.60	0.40	1.00	2.00
❑7, May 82, The Games Of Ragnath, A: Captain Atom	0.60	0.40	1.00	2.00
❑8, Jul 82, Strange Encounter	0.60	0.40	1.00	2.00
❑9, Sep 82, GD, GD (w), Bludd The Ultimate Barbarian	0.60	0.40	1.00	2.00
❑10, Dec 82	—	0.20	0.50	1.00

CHARLTON CLASSICS
CHARLTON

Issue	ORIG	GOOD	FINE	N-MINT
❑1, Apr 80	—	0.40	1.00	2.00
❑2	—	0.40	1.00	2.00
❑3	—	0.40	1.00	2.00
❑4	—	0.40	1.00	2.00
❑5	—	0.40	1.00	2.00
❑6	—	0.40	1.00	2.00
❑7	—	0.40	1.00	2.00
❑8, Jun 81, Hercules	0.50	0.40	1.00	2.00
❑9, Aug 81	—	0.40	1.00	2.00

CHARLTON PREMIERE
CHARLTON

Issue	ORIG	GOOD	FINE	N-MINT
❑1, Sep 67, Its The Shape!; Introducing The Tyro Team	0.12	1.20	3.00	6.00
❑2, Nov 67	0.12	0.80	2.00	4.00
❑3, Jan 68	0.12	0.80	2.00	4.00
❑4, May 68	0.12	0.80	2.00	4.00

CHASE
DC

Issue	ORIG	GOOD	FINE	N-MINT
❑1, Feb 98, Baptized in Fire, trading cards; bound-in trading cards	2.50	0.60	1.50	3.00
❑2, Mar 98, Letdowns, A: Bolt, Sledge, Killer Frost, Copperhead	2.50	0.50	1.25	2.50
❑3, Apr 98	2.50	0.50	1.25	2.50
❑4, May 98, A: Clock King	2.50	0.50	1.25	2.50
❑5, Jun 98, A: Klarion	2.50	0.50	1.25	2.50
❑6, Jul 98	2.50	0.50	1.25	2.50
❑7, Aug 98	2.50	0.50	1.25	2.50
❑8, Sep 98	2.50	0.50	1.25	2.50
❑9, Oct 98, A: Green Lantern	2.50	0.50	1.25	2.50
❑1000000, Nov 98, Don't Believe It!, Final Issue	2.50	0.50	1.25	2.50

ORIG GOOD FINE N-MINT

CHASER PLATOON
AIRCEL
Value: Cover or less

- ❑1, Feb 91, Rhetoric, b&w 2.25
- ❑2, Mar 91, Reception, b&w ... 2.25
- ❑3, Apr 91, Strings, b&w 2.25
- ❑4, May 91, Last Day, b&w 2.25
- ❑5, b&w 2.25
- ❑6, b&w 2.25

CHASSIS (VOL. 1)
MILLENNIUM
Value: Cover or less

- ❑1, foil logo 2.95
- ❑1-2, May 97, 2nd Printing 2.95
- ❑2 ...... 2.95
- ❑3, Apr 98 ...... 2.95

CHASSIS (VOL. 2)
HURRICANE
Value: Cover or less

- ❑0 ...... 2.95
- ❑1, Jun 98, Old Ghosts and, New Blood, Part 1 ...... 2.95
- ❑2, Sep 98, Old Ghosts and, New Blood, Part 2 ...... 2.95
- ❑3, Jan 99 ...... 2.95

CHASSIS (VOL. 3)
IMAGE
Value: Cover or less

- ❑0, Apr 99, background information 2.95
- ❑1, Nov 99 ...... 2.95
- ❑1/A, Nov 99, Alternate cover with Chassis standing against blueprint background 2.95
- ❑2 ...... 2.95
- ❑3, Mar 00 ...... 2.95
- ❑4, Mar 00 ...... 2.95

CHASTITY
CHAOS!
Value: Cover or less

- ❑0.5, Jan 01 ...... 2.95

CHASTITY: LUST FOR LIFE
CHAOS!
Value: Cover or less

- ❑1, May 99 ...... 2.95
- ❑2, Jun 99 ...... 2.95

CHASTITY: REIGN OF TERROR
CHAOS!
Value: Cover or less

- ❑1, Oct 00 ...... 2.95

CHASTITY: ROCKED
CHAOS!
Value: Cover or less

- ❑1, Nov 98, Lust for Life 2.95
- ❑2, Dec 98, The Passenger 2.95
- ❑3, Jan 99 ...... 2.95
- ❑4, Feb 99 ...... 2.95

CHASTITY: THEATRE OF PAIN
CHAOS!

	ORIG	GOOD	FINE	N-MINT
❑1, Feb 97	2.95	0.59	1.48	2.95
❑1/SC, Feb 97, cardstock cover; Onyx Premium Edition	—	1.00	2.50	5.00
❑2, Apr 97	2.95	0.59	1.48	2.95
❑3, Jun 97, back cover pin-up	2.95	0.59	1.48	2.95
❑3/SC, Jun 97, no cover price; Final Curtain Edition; Limited Engagement	—	1.00	2.50	5.00

CHEAPSKIN
FANTAGRAPHICS
Value: Cover or less

- ❑1, b&w; adult 2.95

CHECKMATE
DC

	ORIG	GOOD	FINE	N-MINT
❑1, Apr 88, Opening Gambit, O: Checkmate	1.25	0.30	0.75	1.50
❑2, May 88, GK (c)	1.25	0.25	0.63	1.25
❑3, Jun 88, RL (c)	1.25	0.25	0.63	1.25
❑4, Jul 88, GK (c)	1.25	0.25	0.63	1.25
❑5, Aug 88	1.25	0.25	0.63	1.25
❑6, Sep 88	1.25	0.25	0.63	1.25
❑7, Oct 88, GK (c)	1.25	0.25	0.63	1.25
❑8, Nov 88, GK (c), A: Black Thorn	1.25	0.25	0.63	1.25
❑9, Dec 88	1.25	0.25	0.63	1.25
❑10, Win 88, GK (c)	1.25	0.25	0.63	1.25
❑11, Hol 88, GK (c), Invasion! First Strike	1.25	0.25	0.63	1.25
❑12, Feb 89, Invasion! Aftermath	1.25	0.25	0.63	1.25
❑13, Mar 89	1.50	0.30	0.75	1.50
❑14, Apr 89, A: Black Thorn	1.50	0.30	0.75	1.50
❑15, May 89, GK (c), Janus Directive, Part 1; The Janus Directive, Part 1, continues in Suicide Squad #27	1.50	0.30	0.75	1.50
❑16, May 89, GK (c), Janus Directive, Part 3, A: Major Force, continues in Suicide Squad #28	1.50	0.30	0.75	1.50
❑17, Jun 89, GK (c), Janus Directive, Part 5, continues in Manhunter #14	1.50	0.30	0.75	1.50
❑18, Jun 89, GK (c), Janus Directive, Part 9, continues in Suicide Squad #30	1.50	0.30	0.75	1.50
❑19, Jul 89, GK (c)	1.50	0.30	0.75	1.50
❑20, Aug 89	1.50	0.30	0.75	1.50
❑21, Oct 89	1.50	0.30	0.75	1.50
❑22, Nov 89	1.50	0.30	0.75	1.50
❑23, Dec 89	1.50	0.30	0.75	1.50
❑24, Jan 90	1.50	0.30	0.75	1.50
❑25, Feb 90	1.50	0.30	0.75	1.50
❑26	1.50	0.30	0.75	1.50

Checkmate applied chess terms to its agents, including Knights as soldiers, Rooks as planners, and the King and Queen as the agency heads.

© 1988 DC Comics

	ORIG	GOOD	FINE	N-MINT
❑27	1.50	0.30	0.75	1.50
❑28, Jun 90	1.50	0.30	0.75	1.50
❑29, Jul 90	1.50	0.30	0.75	1.50
❑30, Aug 90	1.50	0.30	0.75	1.50
❑31, Oct 90	1.50	0.30	0.75	1.50
❑32, Dec 90	1.50	0.30	0.75	1.50
❑33, Final Issue	1.50	0.30	0.75	1.50

CHECK-UP
FANTAGRAPHICS
Value: Cover or less

- ❑1, b&w 2.75

CHEECH WIZARD
LAST GASP
Value: Cover or less

- ❑1 ...... 0.75

CHEERLEADERS FROM HELL
CALIBER
Value: Cover or less

- ❑1, b&w 2.50

CHEESE HEADS, THE
TRAGEDY STRIKES
Value: Cover or less

- ❑1, b&w; second edition 2.50
- ❑1-2, b&w; second edition 2.95
- ❑2, b&w 2.50
- ❑3 ...... 2.95
- ❑4 ...... 2.95
- ❑5 ...... 2.95

CHEESE WEASEL
SIDE SHOW
Value: Cover or less

- ❑1, Color cover 2.95
- ❑2, Black & white covers begin 2.95
- ❑3 ...... 2.95
- ❑4 ...... 2.95
- ❑5 ...... 2.95
- ❑6 ...... 2.95
- ❑7 ...... 2.95

CHEESE WEASEL: INNOCENT UNTIL PROVEN GUILTY
SIDE SHOW
Value: Cover or less

- ❑1 ...... 9.95

CHEETA POP (VOL. 2)
EROS
Value: Cover or less

- ❑1 ...... 2.95
- ❑2 ...... 2.95
- ❑3, Jan 96, Morality and Monsters 2.95

CHEETA POP SCREAM QUEEN
ANTARCTIC
Value: Cover or less

- ❑1, May 94 ...... 2.95
- ❑2, Nov 94 ...... 2.95
- ❑3, Jan 95 ...... 2.95
- ❑4, Mar 95, Galaxy Marshall Gingaban vs. Claw King 2.95
- ❑5, May 95, Interview with a Pornstar 2.95

CHEMICAL WARFARE
CHECKER COMICS

	ORIG	GOOD	FINE	N-MINT
❑1, b&w	2.50	0.59	1.48	2.95
❑2, Sum 98, b&w	2.50	0.59	1.48	2.95
❑3	2.95	0.59	1.48	2.95

CHEQUE, MATE, THE
FANTAGRAPHICS
Value: Cover or less

- ❑1, nn; b&w 3.50

CHERRY
LAST GASP

	ORIG	GOOD	FINE	N-MINT
❑1, 1: Cherry Poptart, adult; 1977	2.50	1.50	3.75	7.50
❑1-2, 1: Cherry Poptart, adult; 2nd Printing; 1982	2.50	0.60	1.50	3.00
❑2, adult	2.50	0.80	2.00	4.00
❑3, adult; Title changes to Cherry; indicia says Cherry (nee Poptart)	2.50	0.80	2.00	4.00
❑4, adult	2.50	0.70	1.75	3.50
❑5, adult	2.50	0.70	1.75	3.50
❑6, adult	2.50	0.70	1.75	3.50
❑7, adult	2.50	0.70	1.75	3.50
❑8, Ellie Dee in the Land of Woz, adult; Oz parody Land of Woz	2.50	0.70	1.75	3.50
❑9, adult	2.50	0.70	1.75	3.50
❑10, The New Guy; Honor Farm Girls, adult	2.50	0.70	1.75	3.50
❑11, adult; 3-D issue; Cherry in 3D	3.50	0.79	1.98	3.95
❑11-2, adult; Kitchen Sink reprint	3.95	0.79	1.98	3.95
❑12, Sum 91, adult; Cherry goes to Iraq	2.95	0.60	1.50	3.00
❑13, adult; Last Cherry issue from Last Gasp	2.95	0.60	1.50	3.00

	ORIG	GOOD	FINE	N-MINT
❑14, Feb 93, Cherry Does The Time Warp, O: Cherry, adult; moves to Kitchen Sink; 1st issue at Kitchen Sink	2.95	0.59	1.48	2.95
❑15, Nov 93, adult	2.95	0.59	1.48	2.95
❑16, Nov 94, adult	2.95	0.59	1.48	2.95
❑17, Apr 95, adult; TMNT parody	2.95	0.59	1.48	2.95
❑18, Oct 95, adult	2.95	0.59	1.48	2.95
❑19, Sep 96, adult; moves to Cherry Comics	2.95	0.59	1.48	2.95
❑20, Mar 99, adult; was Kitchen Sink	2.95	0.59	1.48	2.95

CHERRY DELUXE
CHERRY

Value: Cover or less

- ❑1, Aug 98, NG (w), b&w; adult 4.00

CHERRY'S JUBILEE
TUNDRA

Value: Cover or less

- ❑1 .... 2.95
- ❑2 .... 2.95
- ❑3 .... 2.95
- ❑4 .... 2.95

CHERYL BLOSSOM (1ST SERIES)
ARCHIE

	ORIG	GOOD	FINE	N-MINT
❑1, Sep 95	1.50	0.50	1.25	2.50
❑2, Oct 95	1.50	0.40	1.00	2.00
❑3, Nov 95	1.50	0.40	1.00	2.00

CHERYL BLOSSOM (2ND SERIES)
ARCHIE

	ORIG	GOOD	FINE	N-MINT
❑1, Jul 96	1.50	0.40	1.00	2.00
❑2, Aug 96	1.50	0.30	0.75	1.50
❑3, Sep 96	1.50	0.30	0.75	1.50

CHERYL BLOSSOM (3RD SERIES)
ARCHIE

	ORIG	GOOD	FINE	N-MINT
❑1, Apr 97	1.50	0.40	1.00	2.00
❑2, May 97	1.50	0.30	0.75	1.50
❑3	1.50	0.30	0.75	1.50
❑4	1.50	0.30	0.75	1.50
❑5, Sep 97	1.50	0.30	0.75	1.50
❑6, Oct 97	1.50	0.30	0.75	1.50
❑7, Nov 97	1.50	0.30	0.75	1.50
❑8, Jan 98	1.75	0.35	0.88	1.75
❑9, Feb 98	1.75	0.35	0.88	1.75
❑10, Mar 98	1.75	0.35	0.88	1.75
❑11, Apr 98	1.75	0.35	0.88	1.75
❑12, May 98	1.75	0.35	0.88	1.75
❑13, Jun 98	1.75	0.35	0.88	1.75
❑14, Aug 98	1.75	0.35	0.88	1.75
❑15, Sep 98, Beach Bash; Party Hardly, cover forms triptych with issue #16 and #17	1.75	0.35	0.88	1.75
❑16, Oct 98	1.75	0.35	0.88	1.75
❑17, Nov 98, Cheryl-Mania; How Crafty	1.75	0.35	0.88	1.75
❑18, Jan 99, Cheryl as super-model with readers' fashions	1.75	0.35	0.88	1.75
❑19, Feb 99	1.75	0.35	0.88	1.75
❑20, Mar 99, Cinderblossom	1.75	0.35	0.88	1.75
❑21, Apr 99, Sugar World	1.79	0.36	0.89	1.79
❑22, May 99, Big in Japan	1.79	0.36	0.89	1.79
❑23, Jun 99	1.79	0.36	0.89	1.79
❑24, Aug 99	1.79	0.36	0.89	1.79
❑25, Sep 99	1.79	0.36	0.89	1.79
❑26, Oct 99	1.79	0.36	0.89	1.79
❑27, Nov 99	1.79	0.36	0.89	1.79

CHERYL BLOSSOM GOES HOLLYWOOD
ARCHIE

Value: Cover or less

- ❑1, Dec 96, She Ought to Be in Pictures, Part 1; She Ought to Be in Pictures, Part 2 .... 1.50
- ❑2, Jan 97 .... 1.50
- ❑3, Feb 97 .... 1.50

CHERYL BLOSSOM SPECIAL
ARCHIE

Value: Cover or less

- ❑1 .... 2.00
- ❑2 .... 2.00
- ❑3 .... 2.00
- ❑4 .... 2.00

CHESTY SANCHEZ
ANTARCTIC

Value: Cover or less

- ❑1, Nov 95, b&w 2.95
- ❑2, Mar 96, b&w 2.95
- ❑3 .... 2.95
- ❑SE 1, Feb 99, b&w; cardstock cover; Super Special Edition; Super Special; collects two-issue series 5.99

CHEVAL NOIR
DARK HORSE

	ORIG	GOOD	FINE	N-MINT
❑1, Aug 89, DSt (c), Lone Sloane; Fever In Urbicand, b&w	3.50	0.70	1.75	3.50
❑2, Oct 89, DSt (c), b&w	3.50	0.70	1.75	3.50
❑3	3.50	0.70	1.75	3.50
❑4	3.50	0.70	1.75	3.50
❑5, Mar 90, BB	3.50	0.70	1.75	3.50
❑6, Sunstroke; Fred and Bob	3.50	0.70	1.75	3.50
❑7, DSt (c)	3.50	0.70	1.75	3.50
❑8, Coutoo, Part 1	3.50	0.70	1.75	3.50
❑9, Coutoo, Part 2	3.50	0.70	1.75	3.50
❑10, Coutoo, Part 3	3.50	0.70	1.75	3.50
❑11, Coutoo, Part 4	3.50	0.70	1.75	3.50
❑12, Coutoo, Part 5	3.50	0.70	1.75	3.50
❑13	3.50	0.70	1.75	3.50
❑14	3.50	0.70	1.75	3.50
❑15	3.50	0.70	1.75	3.50
❑16, trading cards	3.50	0.75	1.88	3.75
❑17, trading cards	3.50	0.70	1.75	3.50
❑18, trading cards	3.50	0.70	1.75	3.50
❑19, trading cards	3.50	0.70	1.75	3.50
❑20	3.50	0.70	1.75	3.50
❑21	3.50	0.70	1.75	3.50
❑22	3.50	0.70	1.75	3.50
❑23	3.50	0.70	1.75	3.50
❑24	3.50	0.70	1.75	3.50
❑25	3.50	0.70	1.75	3.50
❑26, Jan 92	3.50	0.70	1.75	3.50
❑27, Feb 92	2.95	0.59	1.48	2.95
❑28, Mar 92	2.95	0.59	1.48	2.95
❑29, Apr 92	2.95	0.59	1.48	2.95
❑30, May 92	2.95	0.59	1.48	2.95
❑31, Jun 92	2.95	0.59	1.48	2.95
❑32, Jul 92	2.95	0.59	1.48	2.95
❑33, Aug 92, The Angriest Dog in the World; The Man From the Ciguri	2.95	0.59	1.48	2.95
❑34, Sep 92	2.95	0.59	1.48	2.95
❑35, Oct 92	2.95	0.59	1.48	2.95
❑36, Nov 92	2.95	0.59	1.48	2.95
❑37, Dec 92	2.95	0.59	1.48	2.95
❑38, Jan 93	2.95	0.59	1.48	2.95
❑39, Feb 93	2.95	0.59	1.48	2.95
❑40, Mar 93	2.95	0.59	1.48	2.95
❑41, Apr 93	2.95	0.59	1.48	2.95
❑42, May 93	2.95	0.59	1.48	2.95
❑43, Jun 93	2.95	0.59	1.48	2.95
❑44, Jul 93	2.95	0.59	1.48	2.95
❑45, Aug 93	2.95	0.59	1.48	2.95
❑46, Sep 93	2.95	0.59	1.48	2.95
❑47, Oct 93	2.95	0.59	1.48	2.95
❑48, Nov 93	2.95	0.59	1.48	2.95
❑49, Dec 93	2.95	0.59	1.48	2.95
❑50, Jan 94, Final Issue	2.95	0.59	1.48	2.95

CHIAROSCURO
DC

Value: Cover or less

- ❑1, Jul 95, Greater Than Light 2.50
- ❑2, Aug 95 .... 2.50
- ❑3, Sep 95, Clearly in Dreams 2.95
- ❑4, Oct 95, Dispero 2.95
- ❑5, Nov 95, Limb of Satan 2.95
- ❑6, Dec 95 .... 2.95
- ❑7, Jan 96 .... 2.95
- ❑8, Feb 96, The Giant 2.95
- ❑9, Mar 96, The Deluge 2.95
- ❑10, Apr 96, The Great Bird, Final Issue 2.95

CHI CHIAN
SIRIUS

Value: Cover or less

- ❑1 .... 2.95
- ❑2, 2nd Printing 2.95
- ❑2-2, 2nd Printing 2.95
- ❑2-3, 2nd Printing 2.95
- ❑3 .... 2.95
- ❑4 .... 2.95
- ❑5 .... 2.95
- ❑6 .... 2.95

CHICK MAGNET
VOLUPTUOUS

Value: Cover or less

- ❑1 .... 2.95

CHILDHOOD'S END
IMAGE

Value: Cover or less

- ❑1, Oct 97, b&w 2.95
- ❑2, <Never published?> 2.95
- ❑3, <Never published?> 2.95
- ❑4, <Never published?> 2.95
- ❑5, <Never published?> 2.95

CHILDREN OF FIRE
FANTAGOR

Value: Cover or less

- ❑1 .... 2.00
- ❑2 .... 2.00
- ❑3 .... 2.00

CHILDREN OF THE FALLEN ANGEL
ACE

Value: Cover or less

- ❑1, Feb 97, Gothic Moon 2.95

CHILDREN OF THE NIGHT
NIGHTWYND

Value: Cover or less

- ❑1, Dance Of Death, b&w 2.50
- ❑2, b&w 2.50
- ❑3, b&w 2.50
- ❑4, b&w 2.50

CHILDREN OF THE VOYAGER
MARVEL

Value: Cover or less

- ❑1, Sep 93, Shadows & Fog, Embossed cover; foil.......... 2.95
- ❑2, Oct 93, The Counterfeit Man 1.95
- ❑3, Nov 93, Candle Burning Brightly 1.95
- ❑4, Dec 93, State Of Grace 1.95

CHILDREN'S CRUSADE, THE
DC

	ORIG	GOOD	FINE	N-MINT
❑1, Dec 93, NG (w), The Children's Crusade, Part 1	3.95	0.90	2.25	4.50
❑2, Jan 94, NG (w), The Children's Crusade, Part 7	3.95	0.80	2.00	4.00

CHILD'S PLAY 2: THE OFFICIAL MOVIE ADAPTATION
INNOVATION

Value: Cover or less

- ❑1, movie Adaptation; Adapted from the screenplay by Don Mancini............................... 2.50
- ❑2, movie Adaptation 2.50
- ❑3, Andy and the Chucky Factory, movie Adaptation 2.50

CHILD'S PLAY 3
INNOVATION

Value: Cover or less

- ❑1, movie Adaptation............. 2.50
- ❑2, movie Adaptation............. 2.50
- ❑3, Good Guys Wear Blood, movie Adaptation 2.50
- ❑4, movie Adaptation 2.50

CHILD'S PLAY: THE SERIES
INNOVATION

Value: Cover or less

- ❑1, Night Of The Living Doll.... 2.50
- ❑2.. 2.50
- ❑3.. 2.50
- ❑4.. 2.50
- ❑5.. 2.50

CHILLER
MARVEL

Value: Cover or less

- ❑1.. 7.95
- ❑2.. 7.95

CHILLING TALES OF HORROR (2ND SERIES)
STANLEY

	ORIG	GOOD	FINE	N-MINT
❑1	0.50	1.80	4.50	9.00
❑2/A, Feb 71, Vampire's Prey; The Swami's Secret	0.50	1.60	4.00	8.00
❑2/B	0.50	1.60	4.00	8.00
❑3	0.50	1.20	3.00	6.00
❑4	0.50	1.20	3.00	6.00
❑5	0.50	1.20	3.00	6.00

CHILLY WILLY (WALTER LANTZ)
DELL

	ORIG	GOOD	FINE	N-MINT
❑1, 4C 967; 4C	0.10	6.00	15.00	30.00
❑2, Sep 61, 4C 1212	0.10	6.00	15.00	30.00

CHINAGO AND OTHER STORIES
TOME PRESS

Value: Cover or less

- ❑1, b&w.................................. 2.50

CHINA SEA
NIGHTWYND

Value: Cover or less

- ❑1, b&w.................................. 2.50
- ❑2, b&w.................................. 2.50
- ❑3, b&w.................................. 2.50
- ❑4, b&w.................................. 2.50

CHIPMUNKS & SQUIRRELS
ORIGINAL SYNDICATE

Value: Cover or less

- ❑1, Dec 94, The Game of the Name.................................. 5.95

CHIP 'N' DALE (2ND SERIES)
GOLD KEY

Characters from *Chi Chian* have appeared in animated bumpers on cable's Sci-Fi Channel.

	ORIG	GOOD	FINE	N-MINT
❑1	0.15	4.00	10.00	20.00
❑2	0.15	2.40	6.00	12.00
❑3, Apr 69	0.15	1.60	4.00	8.00
❑4	0.15	1.60	4.00	8.00
❑5, Dec 69	0.15	1.60	4.00	8.00
❑6, Mar 70	0.15	1.00	2.50	5.00
❑7	—	1.00	2.50	5.00
❑8, Sep 70	0.15	1.00	2.50	5.00
❑9	—	1.00	2.50	5.00
❑10	—	1.00	2.50	5.00
❑11, Jun 71	0.15	1.00	2.50	5.00
❑12	—	1.00	2.50	5.00
❑13	—	1.00	2.50	5.00
❑14, Mar 72	0.15	1.00	2.50	5.00
❑15, May 72	0.15	1.00	2.50	5.00
❑16, Jul 72	0.15	1.00	2.50	5.00
❑17	—	1.00	2.50	5.00
❑18	—	1.00	2.50	5.00
❑19	—	1.00	2.50	5.00
❑20	—	1.00	2.50	5.00
❑21	—	0.60	1.50	3.00
❑22, Jul 73	0.20	0.60	1.50	3.00
❑23	—	0.60	1.50	3.00
❑24	—	0.60	1.50	3.00
❑25	—	0.60	1.50	3.00
❑26	—	0.60	1.50	3.00
❑27	—	0.60	1.50	3.00
❑28	—	0.60	1.50	3.00
❑29	—	0.60	1.50	3.00
❑30	—	0.60	1.50	3.00
❑31	—	0.60	1.50	3.00
❑32	—	0.60	1.50	3.00
❑33	—	0.60	1.50	3.00
❑34	—	0.60	1.50	3.00
❑35	—	0.60	1.50	3.00
❑36	—	0.60	1.50	3.00
❑37	—	0.60	1.50	3.00
❑38	—	0.60	1.50	3.00
❑39	—	0.60	1.50	3.00
❑40	—	0.60	1.50	3.00
❑41	—	0.50	1.25	2.50
❑42	—	0.50	1.25	2.50
❑43	—	0.50	1.25	2.50
❑44	—	0.50	1.25	2.50
❑45	—	0.50	1.25	2.50
❑46	—	0.50	1.25	2.50
❑47	—	0.50	1.25	2.50
❑48	—	0.50	1.25	2.50
❑49	—	0.50	1.25	2.50
❑50	—	0.50	1.25	2.50
❑51	—	0.50	1.25	2.50
❑52	—	0.50	1.25	2.50
❑53	—	0.50	1.25	2.50
❑54	—	0.50	1.25	2.50
❑55	—	0.50	1.25	2.50
❑56	—	0.50	1.25	2.50
❑57	—	0.50	1.25	2.50
❑58, May 79	0.40	0.50	1.25	2.50
❑59	—	0.50	1.25	2.50
❑60	—	0.50	1.25	2.50
❑61	—	0.50	1.25	2.50
❑62, Oct 79	0.40	0.50	1.25	2.50
❑63	—	0.50	1.25	2.50
❑64	—	0.50	1.25	2.50
❑65	—	0.50	1.25	2.50
❑66	—	0.50	1.25	2.50
❑67	—	0.50	1.25	2.50
❑68	—	0.50	1.25	2.50
❑69	—	0.50	1.25	2.50
❑70	—	0.50	1.25	2.50
❑71	—	0.50	1.25	2.50
❑72	—	0.50	1.25	2.50
❑73	—	0.50	1.25	2.50
❑74	—	0.50	1.25	2.50
❑75	—	0.50	1.25	2.50
❑76	—	0.50	1.25	2.50
❑77	—	0.50	1.25	2.50
❑78	—	0.50	1.25	2.50
❑79	—	0.50	1.25	2.50
❑80	—	0.50	1.25	2.50
❑81	—	0.50	1.25	2.50
❑82	—	0.50	1.25	2.50
❑83	—	0.50	1.25	2.50

CHIP 'N' DALE (ONE-SHOT)
DISNEY

Value: Cover or less

- ❑1, Secret Casebook, nn......... 3.50

CHIP 'N' DALE RESCUE RANGERS (DISNEY'S...)
DISNEY

	ORIG	GOOD	FINE	N-MINT
❑1, Jun 90, Rescue Rangers to the Rescue, O: Rescue Rangers	1.50	0.40	1.00	2.00
❑2, O: Rescue Rangers	1.50	0.35	0.88	1.75
❑3	1.50	0.35	0.88	1.75
❑4, The King of Beasts Caper, Part 2	1.50	0.35	0.88	1.75
❑5	1.50	0.35	0.88	1.75
❑6	1.50	0.35	0.88	1.75
❑7	1.50	0.35	0.88	1.75

	ORIG	GOOD	FINE	N-MINT
❑8	1.50	0.35	0.88	1.75
❑9	1.50	0.35	0.88	1.75
❑10	1.50	0.35	0.88	1.75
❑11	1.50	0.35	0.88	1.75
❑12	1.50	0.35	0.88	1.75
❑13	1.50	0.35	0.88	1.75
❑14	1.50	0.35	0.88	1.75
❑15	1.50	0.35	0.88	1.75
❑16	1.50	0.35	0.88	1.75
❑17	1.50	0.35	0.88	1.75
❑18	1.50	0.35	0.88	1.75
❑19	1.50	0.35	0.88	1.75

CHIPS AND VANILLA
KITCHEN SINK

Value: Cover or less

❑1, Jun 88, b&w 1.75

CHIRALITY
CPM

Value: Cover or less

- ❑1, Mar 97, The Reunion, 1: Shiori; 1: Shizuma; 1: Vic; 1: Carol, adult 2.95
- ❑2, Apr 97, The Promise, 2: Shiori; 2: Vic; 2: Carol, adult; Carol reveals morph power 2.95
- ❑3, May 97, The Decision, 1: Patty, adult 2.95
- ❑4, Jun 97, The Memory, adult 2.95
- ❑5, Jul 97, The Flight, adult 2.95
- ❑6, Aug 97, The Mission, 1: Adam, adult 2.95
- ❑7, Sep 97, An Old Rival, adult 2.95
- ❑8, Oct 97, Cruelty, adult 2.95
- ❑9, Nov 97, Anguish, adult 2.95
- ❑10, Dec 97, Insanity, adult 2.95
- ❑11, Jan 98, Love, adult 2.95
- ❑12, Feb 98, adult 2.95
- ❑13, Mar 98, Selection, adult .. 2.95
- ❑14, Apr 98, Soul Desire, adult 2.95
- ❑15, May 98, Love and Loathing, adult 2.95
- ❑16, Jun 98, Infiltration, adult .. 2.95
- ❑17, Jul 98, Eye of the Storm, adult 2.95
- ❑18, Aug 98, adult; Final Issue 2.95

CHIRÖN
HAMMAC

	ORIG	GOOD	FINE	N-MINT
❑1, b&w; Hammac Publications	2.00	0.40	1.00	2.00
❑2, b&w; Hammac Publications	2.00	0.40	1.00	2.00
❑3, b&w; Alpha Productions takes over	1.95	0.40	1.00	2.00

C.H.I.X.
IMAGE

	ORIG	GOOD	FINE	N-MINT
❑1, Jan 98, Bad Girl parody comic book; Bad Girl paro	2.50	0.50	1.25	2.50
❑1/SC, Jan 98, X-Ray edition; Bad Girl parody comic book; Comic Cavalcade alternate	2.50	1.08	2.70	5.40

C.H.I.X. THAT TIME FORGOT
IMAGE

Value: Cover or less

❑1, Aug 98, That Time Forgot; Death How Cruel Ye Be, 2: Good Girl 2.95

CHOICES
ANGRY ISIS

Value: Cover or less

❑1, nn 4.00

CHOKE, THE
ANUBIS

Value: Cover or less

❑Anl 1, Jul 94, Chains 2.75

CHOPPER: EARTH, WIND & FIRE
FLEETWAY

Value: Cover or less

- ❑1, cardstock cover 2.95
- ❑2 .... 2.95

CHOPPER: SONG OF THE SURFER
FLEETWAY

Value: Cover or less

❑1 .... 9.95

CHOSEN, THE
MARTINEZ

Value: Cover or less

❑1, Jul 95, 1: Santo; 1: Rattler; 1: Rico Chico; 1: Santana (superhero); 1: Pache, nn; cover indicates Premiere Issue 2.50

CHRISTIAN COMICS & GAMES MAGAZINE
AIDA-ZEE

Value: Cover or less

- ❑0, b&w 3.50
- ❑1, b&w 3.50

CHRISTINA WINTERS: AGENT OF DEATH
EROS

Value: Cover or less

- ❑1 .... 2.95
- ❑2, Mar 95 .... 2.95

CHRISTMAS CLASSICS (WALT KELLY'S...)
ECLIPSE

Value: Cover or less

❑1, Dec 87, WK, WK (w), Christmas Comes to the Wood Land; The Adventures of Peter Wheat, Peter Wheat 1.75

CHRISTMAS PARADE (WALT DISNEY'S...)
GLADSTONE

Value: Cover or less

❑1, CB, You Can't Guess; Goofy 2.95

CHRISTMAS WITH SUPERSWINE
FANTAGRAPHICS

Value: Cover or less

❑1, b&w 2.00

CHRISTMAS WITH THE SUPER-HEROES
DC

	ORIG	GOOD	FINE	N-MINT
❑1, Jan 89, CS; FM; DG; MA, Wanted: Santa Claus - Dead Or Alive, Reprint	2.95	0.60	1.50	3.00
❑2, Dec 89, DG; JBy; GM	2.95	0.60	1.50	3.00

CHROMA-TICK, THE
NEW ENGLAND

	ORIG	GOOD	FINE	N-MINT
❑1, Feb 92, High Rise Hijinx, full color; trading cards; Reprints The Tick #1 in color	3.95	0.79	1.98	3.95
❑2, Jun 92, High Rise Hijinx, full color; trading cards; "Special Edition #2"; trading cards	3.95	0.79	1.98	3.95
❑3, full color; Reprint	3.50	0.70	1.75	3.50
❑4, Oct 92, full color; Bush cover	2.95	0.70	1.75	3.50
❑4/A, Perot cover	2.95	0.70	1.75	3.50
❑4/B, Clinton cover	2.95	0.70	1.75	3.50
❑5, full color	2.95	0.70	1.75	3.50
❑6, full color; trading card	3.50	0.90	2.25	4.50
❑7	3.50	0.70	1.75	3.50
❑8, A Matter of Cosmic Import	3.50	0.70	1.75	3.50
❑9	3.50	0.70	1.75	3.50

CHROME
HOT COMICS

Value: Cover or less

- ❑1, Oct 86, Shadow of the Torturer 1.50
- ❑2 .... 1.50
- ❑3 .... 1.50

CHROMIUM MAN, THE
TRIUMPHANT

Value: Cover or less

- ❑0, Apr 94 .... 2.50
- ❑1, Jan 94 .... 2.50
- ❑1/Ash, ashcan edition 2.50
- ❑2, indicia not updated through issue #7; says Jan 94; Violent Past 2.50
- ❑3 .... 2.50
- ❑4, Bonds And Choices, Unleashed! 2.50
- ❑5, Unleashed! 2.50
- ❑6, The Courier, Part 1 .... 2.50
- ❑7 .... 2.50
- ❑8, Mar 94 .... 2.50
- ❑9, Mar 94 .... 2.50
- ❑10, May 94 .... 2.50
- ❑11 .... 2.50
- ❑12 .... 2.50
- ❑13 .... 2.50
- ❑14 .... 2.50
- ❑15 .... 2.50

CHROMIUM MAN, THE: VIOLENT PAST
TRIUMPHANT

Value: Cover or less

- ❑1, Violent Past, Part 1 .... 2.50
- ❑2 .... 2.50

CHRONIC APATHY
ILLITERATURE PRESS

Value: Cover or less

- ❑1, Aug 95, b&w 2.95
- ❑2, Sep 95, b&w 2.95
- ❑3, Oct 95, b&w 2.95
- ❑4, Dec 95, b&w 2.95

CHRONIC IDIOCY
CALIBER

Value: Cover or less

- ❑1, b&w 2.50
- ❑2, b&w 2.50
- ❑3, b&w 2.50

CHRONICLES OF CORUM, THE
FIRST

	ORIG	GOOD	FINE	N-MINT
❑1	1.75	0.40	1.00	2.00
❑2	1.75	0.40	1.00	2.00
❑3	1.75	0.40	1.00	2.00
❑4	1.75	0.40	1.00	2.00
❑5	1.75	0.40	1.00	2.00
❑6	1.75	0.40	1.00	2.00
❑7	1.75	0.40	1.00	2.00
❑8	1.75	0.40	1.00	2.00
❑9	1.75	0.40	1.00	2.00
❑10	1.75	0.40	1.00	2.00
❑11	1.75	0.40	1.00	2.00
❑12	1.95	0.40	1.00	2.00

CHRONICLES OF CRIME AND MYSTERY: SHERLOCK HOLMES
NORTHSTAR

Value: Cover or less

❑1, b&w 2.25

CHRONICLES OF PANDA KHAN, THE
ABACUS

Value: Cover or less

- ❑1 .... 1.50
- ❑2 .... 2.00
- ❑3 .... 2.00
- ❑4 .... 2.00

CHRONOS
DC

Value: Cover or less

- ❑1, Mar 98, Time Out of Time . 2.50
- ❑2, Apr 98, Down on the Farm 2.50
- ❑3, May 98 .... 2.50
- ❑4, Jun 98, D: original Chronos 2.50
- ❑5, Jul 98 .... 2.50
- ❑6, Aug 98, A: Tattooed Man, funeral of original Chronos .. 2.50
- ❑7, Sep 98 .... 2.50
- ❑8, Oct 98 .... 2.50
- ❑9, Dec 98, A: Destiny 2.50
- ❑10, Jan 99, A: Azrael 2.50
- ❑11, Feb 99, Final Issue 2.50
- ❑1000000, Nov 98, A: Hourman 2.50

ORIG GOOD FINE N-MINT

CHRONOWAR
DARK HORSE

Value: Cover or less

- ❑1, Aug 96, b&w 2.95
- ❑2, Sep 96, b&w 2.95
- ❑3, Oct 96, b&w 2.95
- ❑4, Nov 96, b&w 2.95
- ❑5, Dec 96, b&w 2.95
- ❑6, Jan 97, b&w 2.95
- ❑7, Feb 97, b&w 2.95
- ❑8, Mar 97, b&w 2.95
- ❑9, Apr 97, b&w 2.95

CHUCK NORRIS
MARVEL

	ORIG	GOOD	FINE	N-MINT
❑1, Jan 87, SD, The Super Cruiser	0.75	0.30	0.75	1.50
❑2, Mar 87, SD	0.75	0.25	0.63	1.25
❑3, May 87, SD	0.75	0.25	0.63	1.25
❑4, Jul 87	0.75	0.25	0.63	1.25
❑5	0.75	0.25	0.63	1.25

CHUK THE BARBARIC
AVATAR

Value: Cover or less

- ❑3, no color cover 1.25

CHYNA
CHAOS!

Value: Cover or less

- ❑1, Sep 00, Guilt and Innocence 2.95

CINDER AND ASHE
DC

Value: Cover or less

- ❑1, May 88 .... 1.75
- ❑2, Jun 88 .... 1.75
- ❑3, Jul 88 .... 1.75
- ❑4, Aug 88 .... 1.75

CIRCLE UNLEASHED, THE
EPOCH

Value: Cover or less

- ❑1, May 95, Sacrifice 3.00

CIRCLE WEAVE, THE: APPRENTICE TO A GOD
ABALONE PRESS

Value: Cover or less

- ❑1, b&w 2.00
- ❑2, Into the Storm, b&w 2.00

CIRCUS WORLD
HAMMAC

Value: Cover or less

- ❑1, Tryouts, b&w 2.50
- ❑2 .... 2.50
- ❑3 .... 2.50

CITY OF SILENCE
IMAGE

Value: Cover or less

- ❑1, May 00 .... 2.50
- ❑2, Jun 00 .... 2.50
- ❑3, Jul 00 .... 2.50

CLAIR VOYANT
LIGHTNING

Value: Cover or less

- ❑1, Jun 96, b&w 3.50

CLAN APIS
ACTIVE SYNAPSE

	ORIG	GOOD	FINE	N-MINT
❑1, b&w; educational comic about bees	2.95	0.59	1.48	2.95
❑2	—	0.59	1.48	2.95
❑3	—	0.59	1.48	2.95
❑4	—	0.59	1.48	2.95
❑5, Apr 99, b&w	3.95	0.79	1.98	3.95

CLANDESTINE
MARVEL

	ORIG	GOOD	FINE	N-MINT
❑1, Oct 94, Family Reunion, Part 1, 1: The Crimson Crusader; 1: Imp, foil cover	2.95	0.60	1.50	3.00
❑2, Nov 94, Family Reunion, Part 2, wrap-around cover	2.50	0.50	1.25	2.50
❑3, Dec 94	2.50	0.50	1.25	2.50
❑4, Jan 95	2.50	0.50	1.25	2.50
❑5, Feb 95	2.50	0.50	1.25	2.50
❑6, Mar 95	2.50	0.50	1.25	2.50
❑7, Apr 95	2.50	0.50	1.25	2.50
❑8, May 95	2.50	0.50	1.25	2.50
❑9, Jun 95	2.50	0.50	1.25	2.50
❑10, Jul 95	2.50	0.50	1.25	2.50
❑11, Aug 95	2.50	0.50	1.25	2.50
❑12, Sep 95, Final Issue	2.50	0.50	1.25	2.50
❑Ash 1, Oct 94, Preview	1.50	0.30	0.75	1.50

CLASH
DC

Value: Cover or less

- ❑1 .... 4.95
- ❑2, The Power And The Glory 4.95
- ❑3 .... 4.95

CLASSIC ADVENTURE STRIPS
DRAGON LADY

	ORIG	GOOD	FINE	N-MINT
❑1, King of the Royal Mounted	2.95	0.80	2.00	4.00
❑2, Red Ryder	2.95	0.80	2.00	4.00
❑3, Dickie Dare, Flash Gordon	2.95	0.80	2.00	4.00
❑4, Nov 85, FR, FR (w), Buz Sawyer; Johnny Hazard; Steve Canyon	2.95	0.80	2.00	4.00
❑5, Jan 86, Wash Tubbs	2.95	0.80	2.00	4.00
❑6, Mandrake the Magician, Johnny Hazard, Rip Kirby	2.95	0.80	2.00	4.00
❑7, Buz Sawyer	2.95	0.80	2.00	4.00
❑8	2.95	0.80	2.00	4.00
❑9	2.95	0.80	2.00	4.00
❑10, Apr 87, MA, MA (w), Buck Rogers vs. Dr. Modor	2.95	0.80	2.00	4.00

Image poked fun at "Bad Girl" comics with its *C.H.I.X.* one-shots.

© 1998 Image

ORIG GOOD FINE N-MINT

CLASSIC ALEX TOTH ZORRO, THE
IMAGE

Value: Cover or less

- ❑1, Jul 98, ATh, ATh (w), Presenting Señor Zorro; Zorro's Secret Passage, Trade Paperback; reprints Eclipse collection.... 15.95
- ❑2, Aug 98, ATh, ATh (w), The Eagle's Brood; Gypsy Warning, Trade Paperback; reprints Eclipse collection 15.95

CLASSIC GIRLS
ETERNITY

Value: Cover or less

- ❑1, b&w; Reprint 2.50
- ❑2, b&w; Reprint 2.50
- ❑3, b&w; Reprint 2.50
- ❑4, b&w; Reprint 2.50

CLASSIC JONNY QUEST: SKULL & DOUBLE CROSSBONES
ILLUSTRATED PRODUCTIONS

	ORIG	GOOD	FINE	N-MINT
❑1, Mar 96, no cover price; smaller than normal size comic book; inserted with Jonny Quest videos	—	0.20	0.50	1.00

CLASSIC JONNY QUEST: THE QUETONG MISSILE MYSTERY
ILLUSTRATED PRODUCTIONS

	ORIG	GOOD	FINE	N-MINT
❑1, Mar 96, no cover price; smaller than normal size comic book; inserted with Jonny Quest videos	—	0.20	0.50	1.00

CLASSIC PUNISHER
MARVEL

Value: Cover or less

- ❑1, Dec 89, O: the Punisher, b&w; prestige format; Reprints Punisher stories from Marvel Preview #2, Marvel Super Action #1 .... 4.95

CLASSICS ILLUSTRATED (FIRST)
FIRST

	ORIG	GOOD	FINE	N-MINT
❑1, Feb 90, The Raven, Raven	3.75	0.80	2.00	4.00
❑2, Feb 90, Great Expectations, Great Expectations	3.75	0.80	2.00	4.00
❑3, Feb 90, Through the Looking Glass, Through the Looking Glass	3.75	0.80	2.00	4.00
❑4, Feb 90, BSz, Moby Dick, Moby Dick	3.75	0.80	2.00	4.00
❑5, Mar 90, Hamlet, Hamlet	3.75	0.80	2.00	4.00
❑6, Mar 90, CR, The Scarlet Letter, Scarlet Letter	3.75	0.80	2.00	4.00
❑7, Apr 90, The Count of Monte Cristo, Count of Monte Cristo	3.75	0.80	2.00	4.00
❑8, Apr 90, JK, Dr. Jekyll and Mr. Hyde, Doctor Jekyll & Mr. Hyde	3.75	0.80	2.00	4.00
❑9, May 90, MP, Tom Sawyer, Tom Sawyer	3.75	0.80	2.00	4.00
❑10, Jun 90, Call of the Wild, Call of the Wild	3.75	0.80	2.00	4.00
❑11, Jul 90, Rip Van Winkle, Rip Van Winkle	3.75	0.80	2.00	4.00
❑12, Aug 90, The Island of Dr. Moreau, Island of Doctor Moreau	3.75	0.80	2.00	4.00
❑13, Oct 90, Wuthering Heights, Wuthering Heights	3.75	0.80	2.00	4.00
❑14, Sep 90, CR, Fall of the House of Usher, Fall of the House of Usher	3.75	0.80	2.00	4.00
❑15, Nov 90, The Gift of the Magi, Gift of Magi	3.75	0.80	2.00	4.00
❑16, Dec 90, JSa, JSa (w), A Christmas Carol, Christmas Carol	3.75	0.80	2.00	4.00
❑17, Treasure Island, Treasure Island	3.75	0.80	2.00	4.00
❑18, The Devil's Dictionary, Jungle	3.95	0.80	2.00	4.00
❑19, Feb 91, Secret Agent, Secret Agent	3.95	0.80	2.00	4.00
❑20, Mar 91, The Invisible Man, Invisible Man	3.95	0.80	2.00	4.00
❑21, Cyrano de Bergerac, Cyrano de Bergerac	3.95	0.80	2.00	4.00
❑22, The Jungle Book, Jungle Books	3.95	0.80	2.00	4.00
❑23, Apr 91, Swiss Family Robinson, Robinson Crusoe	3.95	0.80	2.00	4.00
❑24, May 91, Rime of the Ancient Mariner, Rime of Ancient Mariner	3.95	0.80	2.00	4.00
❑25, May 91, Ivanhoe, Ivanhoe	3.95	0.80	2.00	4.00
❑26, Jun 91, Aesop's Fables, Aesop's Fables	3.95	0.80	2.00	4.00
❑27, The Jungle, Jungle	3.95	0.80	2.00	4.00

CLASSICS ILLUSTRATED STUDY GUIDE
ACCLAIM

Value: Cover or less

- ❑1, nn; All Quiet on the Western Front 4.99
- ❑2, nn; Around the World in 80 Days 4.99

❑3, Sep 97, nn; The Call of the Wild ... 4.99
❑4, nn; Captains Courageous. 4.99
❑5, nn; A Christmas Carol 4.99
❑6, nn; The Count of Monte Cristo ... 4.99
❑7, Aug 97, nn; David Copperfield ... 4.99
❑8, nn; Doctor Jekyll and Mr. Hyde ... 4.99
❑9, nn; Don Quixote ... 5.25
❑10, nn; Faust ... 4.99
❑11, nn; Frankenstein ... 4.99
❑12, nn; Great Expectations ... 4.99
❑13, Sep 97, nn; The Hunchback of Notre Dame ... 4.99
❑14, nn; The Iliad ... 4.99
❑15, nn; The Invisible Man 4.99
❑16, Aug 97, nn; Julius Caesar 4.99
❑17, Aug 97, nn; The Jungle Book ... 4.99
❑18, nn; Kidnapped ... 4.99
❑19, nn; Kim ... 4.99
❑20, nn; The Last of the Mohicans ... 4.99
❑21, Sep 97, nn; Lord Jim 4.99
❑22, Aug 97, nn; The Man in the Iron Mask ... 4.99
❑23, nn; The Master of Ballantrae ... 4.99
❑24, Apr 97, nn; A Midsummer Night's Dream ... 4.99
❑25, Apr 97, nn; Moby Dick 4.99
❑26, nn; new adaptation of Narrative of the Life of Frederick Douglass ... 4.99
❑27, nn; The Prince and the Pauper ... 4.99
❑28, Aug 97, Pudd'nhead Wilson, nn; Pudd'nhead Wilson 4.99
❑29, Sep 97, nn; Robinson Crusoe ... 4.99
❑30, nn; new adaptation of The Scarlet Pimpernel ... 4.99
❑31, nn; Silas Marner ... 4.99
❑32, nn; War of the Worlds 4.99
❑33, nn; Wuthering Heights 4.99
❑34, Feb 97, GE, Romeo and Juliet, nn ... 4.99
❑35 ... 4.99
❑36, Feb 97, Crime and Punishment, nn ... 4.99
❑37, Jul 97, Gulliver's Travels, nn ... 4.99
❑38, Feb 97, Tom Sawyer, nn ... 4.99

CLASSIC STAR WARS
DARK HORSE

	ORIG	GOOD	FINE	N-MINT
❑1, Aug 92	2.50	0.80	2.00	4.00
❑2, Sep 92	2.50	0.70	1.75	3.50
❑3, Oct 92	2.50	0.70	1.75	3.50
❑4, Nov 92	2.50	0.65	1.63	3.25
❑5, Dec 92, AW	2.50	0.65	1.63	3.25
❑6, Jan 93, AW	2.50	0.60	1.50	3.00
❑7, Feb 93, AW	2.50	0.60	1.50	3.00
❑8, Apr 93, AW, trading card	2.50	0.60	1.50	3.00
❑9, May 93, AW	2.50	0.60	1.50	3.00
❑10, Jun 93	2.50	0.60	1.50	3.00
❑11, Aug 93	2.50	0.60	1.50	3.00
❑12, Sep 93	2.50	0.60	1.50	3.00
❑13, Oct 93	2.50	0.60	1.50	3.00
❑14, Nov 93	2.50	0.60	1.50	3.00
❑15, Jan 94	2.50	0.60	1.50	3.00
❑16, Feb 94	2.50	0.60	1.50	3.00
❑17, Mar 94	2.50	0.60	1.50	3.00
❑18, Apr 94	2.50	0.60	1.50	3.00
❑19, May 94	2.50	0.60	1.50	3.00
❑20, Jun 94, Final Issue; trading card; Giant-size	3.50	0.70	1.75	3.50

CLASSIC STAR WARS: A LONG TIME AGO
DARK HORSE

Value: Cover or less

❑1, Mar 99 ... 12.95
❑2, Apr 99, GD; Cl; MG; AW... 12.95
❑3, May 99, no cover price 12.95
❑4, Jun 99, no cover price 12.95
❑5, Jul 99, Cl, no cover price .. 12.95
❑6, Aug 99 ... 12.95

CLASSIC STAR WARS: A NEW HOPE
DARK HORSE

Value: Cover or less

❑1, Jun 94, HC, movie Adaptation; prestige format; Collects Star Wars (Marvel) #1-3 ... 3.95
❑2, Jul 94, HC, movie Adaptation; prestige format; Collects Star Wars (Marvel) #4-6 ... 3.95

CLASSIC STAR WARS: DEVILWORLDS
DARK HORSE

Value: Cover or less

❑1, Aug 96, AMo (w) ... 2.50
❑2, Sep 96, AMo (w), Rust Never Sleeps ... 2.50

CLASSIC STAR WARS: HAN SOLO AT STARS' END
DARK HORSE

Value: Cover or less

❑1, Mar 97, AA, cardstock cover; adapts Brian Daley novel 2.95
❑2, Apr 97, AA, cardstock cover; adapts Brian Daley novel 2.95
❑3, May 97, AA, cardstock cover; adapts Brian Daley novel 2.95

CLASSIC STAR WARS: RETURN OF THE JEDI
DARK HORSE

Value: Cover or less

❑1, Oct 94, AW, polybagged with trading card ... 3.50
❑2, AW ... 3.95

CLASSIC STAR WARS: THE EARLY ADVENTURES
DARK HORSE

Value: Cover or less

❑1, Aug 94, RM, RM (w) ... 2.50
❑2, Sep 94, RM (w) ... 2.50
❑3, Oct 94, RM ... 2.50
❑4, Nov 94, RM ... 2.50
❑5, Dec 94, RM ... 2.50
❑6, Jan 95, RM ... 2.50
❑7, Feb 95, RM ... 2.50
❑8, Mar 95 ... 2.50
❑9, Apr 95 ... 2.50

CLASSIC STAR WARS: THE EMPIRE STRIKES BACK
DARK HORSE

Value: Cover or less

❑1, Aug 94, AW, prestige format 3.95
❑2, Sep 94, AW, prestige format 3.95

CLASSIC STAR WARS: THE VANDELHELM MISSION
DARK HORSE

Value: Cover or less

❑1, Mar 95, AW ... 2.50

CLASSIC X-MEN
MARVEL

	ORIG	GOOD	FINE	N-MINT
❑1, Sep 86	1.00	1.20	3.00	6.00
❑2, Oct 86, The Doomsmith Scenario!;, Reprints X-Men (1st Series) #94	1.00	0.70	1.75	3.50
❑3, Nov 86	1.00	0.60	1.50	3.00
❑4, Dec 86	1.00	0.60	1.50	3.00
❑5, Jan 87	1.00	0.60	1.50	3.00
❑6, Feb 87	1.00	0.50	1.25	2.50
❑7, Mar 87	1.00	0.50	1.25	2.50
❑8, Apr 87	1.00	0.50	1.25	2.50
❑9, May 87	1.00	0.50	1.25	2.50
❑10, Jun 87	1.00	0.50	1.25	2.50
❑11, Jul 87	1.00	0.50	1.25	2.50
❑12, Aug 87	1.00	0.50	1.25	2.50
❑13, Sep 87	1.00	0.50	1.25	2.50
❑14, Oct 87	1.00	0.50	1.25	2.50
❑15, Nov 87	1.00	0.50	1.25	2.50
❑16, Dec 87	1.00	0.50	1.25	2.50
❑17, Jan 88	1.00	0.50	1.25	2.50
❑18, Feb 88	1.00	0.50	1.25	2.50
❑19, Mar 88	1.00	0.50	1.25	2.50
❑20, Apr 88	1.00	0.50	1.25	2.50
❑21, May 88	1.00	0.50	1.25	2.50
❑22, Jun 88, FM	1.00	0.50	1.25	2.50
❑23, Jul 88	1.00	0.50	1.25	2.50
❑24, Aug 88	1.00	0.50	1.25	2.50
❑25, Sep 88	1.00	0.50	1.25	2.50
❑26, Oct 88	1.25	0.50	1.25	2.50
❑27, Nov 88	1.25	0.50	1.25	2.50
❑28, Dec 88	1.25	0.50	1.25	2.50
❑29, Jan 89	1.25	0.50	1.25	2.50
❑30, Feb 89	1.25	0.40	1.00	2.00
❑31, Mar 89, There's Something Awful on Muir Island; Spigot at the End of the Universe, Reprints X-Men (1st Series) #125	1.25	0.40	1.00	2.00
❑32, Apr 89	1.25	0.40	1.00	2.00
❑33, May 89	1.25	0.40	1.00	2.00
❑34, Jun 89	1.25	0.40	1.00	2.00
❑35, Jul 89	1.25	0.40	1.00	2.00
❑36, Aug 89	1.25	0.40	1.00	2.00
❑37, Sep 89	1.25	0.40	1.00	2.00
❑38, Oct 89	1.25	0.40	1.00	2.00
❑39, Nov 89	1.25	0.40	1.00	2.00
❑40, Nov 89	1.25	0.40	1.00	2.00
❑41, Dec 89	1.25	0.40	1.00	2.00
❑42, Dec 89	1.25	0.40	1.00	2.00
❑43, Jan 90	1.75	0.40	1.00	2.00
❑44, Feb 90	1.25	0.40	1.00	2.00
❑45, Mar 90, Series continues as X-Men Classic; Series continued in X-Men Classic #46	1.25	0.40	1.00	2.00

CLAUS
DRACO

Value: Cover or less

❑1, Dec 97 ... 2.95

CLAWS
CONQUEST

Value: Cover or less

❑1, b&w ... 2.95

CLAW THE UNCONQUERED
DC

	ORIG	GOOD	FINE	N-MINT
❑1, Jun 75, The Sword And The silent Scream, 1: Claw the Unconquered	0.25	0.40	1.00	2.00
❑2, Aug 75	0.25	0.30	0.75	1.50
❑3, Oct 75	0.25	0.25	0.63	1.25
❑4, Dec 75	0.25	0.20	0.50	1.00
❑5, Feb 76	0.25	0.20	0.50	1.00
❑6, Apr 76	0.25	0.20	0.50	1.00
❑7, Jun 76	0.30	0.20	0.50	1.00
❑8, Aug 76, Bicentennial #18	0.30	0.20	0.50	1.00
❑9, Oct 76, O: Claw the Unconquered	0.30	0.20	0.50	1.00
❑10, May 78	0.35	0.20	0.50	1.00
❑11, Jul 78	0.35	0.20	0.50	1.00
❑12, Sep 78, Final Issue	0.35	0.20	0.50	1.00

CLEM: MALL SECURITY
SPIT TAKE

Value: Cover or less

❑0, b&w ... 2.00

CLEOPATRA
RIP OFF

Value: Cover or less

❑1, Feb 92, nn; b&w; adult 2.50

CLERKS: THE COMIC BOOK
ONI

	ORIG	GOOD	FINE	N-MINT
❑1, Feb 98, KSm (w)	2.95	1.60	4.00	8.00
❑1-2, KSm (w), 2nd Printing	2.95	0.59	1.48	2.95

	ORIG	GOOD	FINE	N-MINT
❑, KSm (w), 3rd Printing	2.95	0.59	1.48	2.95
❑1-4, May 98, 4th Printing	2.95	0.59	1.48	2.95
❑2	2.95	0.59	1.48	2.95
❑HS 1, Dec 98, KSm (w), b&w; Double-size	2.95	0.70	1.75	3.50

CLIFFHANGER COMICS
AC
Value: Cover or less
- ❑1, b&w; Reprint 2.50
- ❑2, b&w; Reprint 2.50

CLIFFHANGER COMICS (2ND SERIES)
AC
Value: Cover or less
- ❑1, b&w; new and reprint 2.75
- ❑2, Aug 90, b&w; new and reprint 2.75

CLIMAXXX
AIRCEL
Value: Cover or less
- ❑1, Apr 91, full color; adult 3.50
- ❑2, May 91, full color; adult 3.50
- ❑3, Jun 91, full color; adult 3.50
- ❑4, Jul 91, full color; adult 3.50

CLINT
TRIGON
Value: Cover or less
- ❑1, Sep 86, Baby the Reign Must Fall 2.50
- ❑2, Jan 87, Magnun Force 2.50

CLINT: THE HAMSTER TRIUMPHANT
ECLIPSE
Value: Cover or less
- ❑1, b&w 1.50
- ❑2, b&w 1.50

CLOAK & DAGGER
MARVEL

	ORIG	GOOD	FINE	N-MINT
❑1, Jul 85, TD	0.65	0.40	1.00	2.00
❑2, Sep 85, Standing In The Shadows	0.65	0.30	0.75	1.50
❑3, Nov 85, TD, A: Spider-Man	0.65	0.30	0.75	1.50
❑4, Jan 86, Secret Wars II	0.65	0.30	0.75	1.50
❑5, Mar 85, TD, 1: Mayhem	0.75	0.25	0.63	1.25
❑6, May 85, TD	0.75	0.25	0.63	1.25
❑7, Jul 85, TD	0.75	0.25	0.63	1.25
❑8, Sep 85, TD	0.75	0.25	0.63	1.25
❑9, Nov 85	0.75	0.25	0.63	1.25
❑10, Jan 86, TD	0.75	0.25	0.63	1.25
❑11, Mar 86, TD, Final Issue; Giant-size	1.25	0.30	0.75	1.50

CLOAK & DAGGER (LTD. SERIES)
MARVEL

	ORIG	GOOD	FINE	N-MINT
❑1, Oct 83, The Priest, 1: Brigid O'Reilly	0.60	0.59	1.48	2.95
❑2, Nov 83, Bellyful of Blues!	0.60	0.59	1.48	2.95
❑3, Dec 83, Dark is My Love, and Deadly!	0.60	0.40	1.00	2.00
❑4, Jan 84, True Confessions, O: Cloak & Dagger	0.60	0.40	1.00	2.00

CLOAK AND DAGGER IN PREDATOR AND PREY
MARVEL
Value: Cover or less
- ❑1, nn; One-Shot; prestige format 5.95

CLOCK!
TOP SHELF
Value: Cover or less
- ❑3, b&w 2.95

CLONEZONE SPECIAL
DARK HORSE
Value: Cover or less
- ❑1, The Zone: Shakedown, b&w 2.00

CLOWN: NOBODY'S LAUGHING NOW, THE
FLEETWAY
Value: Cover or less
- ❑1, nn 4.95

CLOWNS
YAHOO PRO

	ORIG	GOOD	FINE	N-MINT
❑1, Simon the Pieman; Clowns	0.50	0.60	1.50	3.00

CLOWNS, THE
DARK HORSE
Value: Cover or less
- ❑1, Apr 98, CR, CR (w), Pagliacci, nn; b&w; adapts Leoncavallo opera 2.95

COBALT 60
TUNDRA
Value: Cover or less
- ❑1 4.95
- ❑2 4.95

COBALT BLUE
POWER

	ORIG	GOOD	FINE	N-MINT
❑1, Jan 78, MGu	0.50	0.40	1.00	2.00

COBALT BLUE (INNOVATION)
INNOVATION

	ORIG	GOOD	FINE	N-MINT
❑1, Sep 89, MGu	1.95	0.40	1.00	2.00
❑2, Oct 89, MGu	1.95	0.40	1.00	2.00
❑GN 1, KP, Graphic novel	5.95	1.19	2.97	5.95

COBRA
VIZ
Value: Cover or less
- ❑1 2.95
- ❑2 2.95
- ❑3 2.95
- ❑4 2.95
- ❑5 2.95
- ❑6 2.95
- ❑7 3.25
- ❑8 3.25

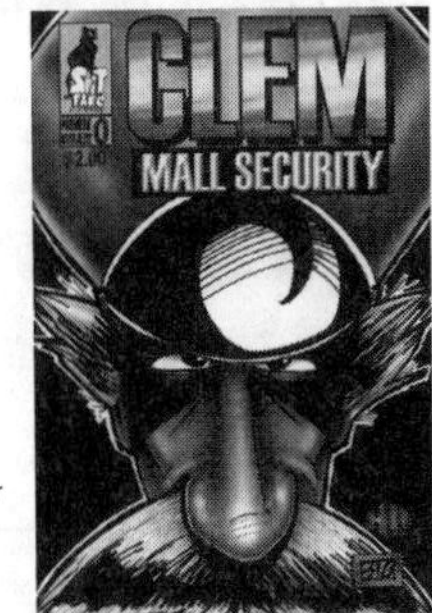

Spit Take followed in the footsteps of Sharkbait's *Pete, the P.O.'d Postal Worker* with its one-shot *Clem: Mall Security.*

© 1997 Spit Take Comics

- ❑9 3.25
- ❑10 3.25
- ❑11 3.25
- ❑12 3.25

CODA
CODA
Value: Cover or less
- ❑1 2.00
- ❑2 2.00
- ❑3 2.00
- ❑4 2.00

CODE BLUE
IMAGE
Value: Cover or less
- ❑1, Apr 98 2.95

CODENAME: DANGER
LODESTONE

	ORIG	GOOD	FINE	N-MINT
❑1, Aug 85, RB, Double Or Nothing	1.50	0.40	1.00	2.00
❑2, Oct 85	1.50	0.35	0.88	1.75
❑3, Jan 86, PS, I.O.U.	1.50	0.35	0.88	1.75
❑4, May 86	1.50	0.35	0.88	1.75

CODENAME: FIREARM
MALIBU
Value: Cover or less
- ❑0, JRo (w), Idle Thoughts, Part 1 2.95
- ❑1, JRo (w), The Adversary; Idle Thoughts, Part 2 2.95
- ❑2, JRo (w), Idle Thoughts, Part 3 2.95
- ❑3 2.95
- ❑4 2.95
- ❑5 2.95

CODENAME: GENETIX
MARVEL
Value: Cover or less
- ❑1, Feb 93, Nature Of The Beast, Part 1, 1: Genetix 1.75
- ❑2, Mar 93, Nature Of The Beast, Part 2, A: Wolverine 1.75
- ❑3, Apr 93, Nature Of The Beast, Part 3, A: Wolverine 1.75
- ❑4, May 93, Nature Of The Beast, Part 4 1.75

CODE NAME NINJA
SOLSON
Value: Cover or less
- ❑1, Silent Steps of the Ninja, b&w 2.00

CODENAME: SCORPIO
ANTARCTIC
Value: Cover or less
- ❑1, Oct 96, b&w 2.95
- ❑2, Apr 97, b&w 2.95
- ❑3, Jul 97, b&w 2.95
- ❑4, Sep 97, b&w 2.95

CODENAME: SPITFIRE
MARVEL

	ORIG	GOOD	FINE	N-MINT
❑10, Jul 87, Series continued from Spitfire and the Troubleshooters #9	0.75	0.20	0.50	1.00
❑11, Aug 87	0.75	0.20	0.50	1.00
❑12, Sep 87	0.75	0.20	0.50	1.00
❑13, Oct 87	0.75	0.20	0.50	1.00

CODENAME: STRIKEFORCE
SPECTRUM

	ORIG	GOOD	FINE	N-MINT
❑1, Jun 84, Strikeforce!	1.00	0.30	0.75	1.50

CODENAME: STRYKE FORCE
IMAGE

	ORIG	GOOD	FINE	N-MINT
❑0, Jun 95, indicia says Jun, cover says Jul	2.50	0.50	1.25	2.50
❑1, Jan 94	2.95	0.50	1.25	2.50
❑1/GO, Jan 94, Gold promotional edition	2.95	0.80	2.00	4.00
❑1/SC, Jan 94, blue embossed edition	2.95	0.80	2.00	4.00
❑2, Mar 94	1.95	0.39	0.98	1.95
❑3, Apr 94	1.95	0.39	0.98	1.95
❑4, Jun 94	1.95	0.39	0.98	1.95
❑5, Jul 94	1.95	0.39	0.98	1.95
❑6, Aug 94	1.95	0.39	0.98	1.95
❑7, Oct 94	1.95	0.39	0.98	1.95
❑8/A, Nov 94, same cover; Cyblade poster; different poster	1.95	0.39	0.98	1.95
❑8/B, Nov 94, same cover; Shi Poster; different poster	1.95	0.39	0.98	1.95
❑8/C, Nov 94, same cover; Tempest poster; different poster	1.95	0.39	0.98	1.95
❑9, Dec 94	1.95	0.39	0.98	1.95
❑10, Jan 95	1.95	0.39	0.98	1.95
❑11, Mar 95	1.95	0.39	0.98	1.95
❑12, Apr 95	1.95	0.39	0.98	1.95

	ORIG	GOOD	FINE	N-MINT
❑13, May 95	2.25	0.45	1.13	2.25
❑14, Aug 95	2.25	0.45	1.13	2.25

CODE OF HONOR
MARVEL

Value: Cover or less

❑1, Jan 97 ... 5.95
❑2, Mar 97, Verdicts ... 5.95
❑3, Apr 97, The Street ... 5.95
❑4, May 97, Sirens ... 5.95

CODY STARBUCK
STAR*REACH

Value: Cover or less

❑1, HC ... 2.00

COFFIN, THE
ONI

Value: Cover or less

❑1, Sep 00, b&w ... 2.95

COFFIN BLOOD
MONSTER

Value: Cover or less

❑1, b&w ... 3.95

COLD BLOODED
NORTHSTAR

Value: Cover or less

❑1, b&w ... 2.95

COLD-BLOODED CHAMELEON COMMANDOS
BLACKTHORNE

Value: Cover or less

❑1, 1: The Cold-Blooded Chameleon Commandos ... 1.75
❑2 ... 1.75
❑3 ... 1.75
❑4 ... 1.75
❑5 ... 1.75

COLD BLOODED: THE BURNING KISS
NORTHSTAR

Value: Cover or less

❑1, Nov 93, cardstock cover ... 4.95

COLD EDEN
LEGACY

Value: Cover or less

❑4, Nov 95, b&w; cover says Feb 96, indicia says Nov 95 ... 2.35

COLLECTION
ETERNITY

Value: Cover or less

❑1 ... 2.95

COLLECTOR'S DRACULA, THE
MILLENNIUM

Value: Cover or less

❑1, Nosferatu: Plague of Terror; Blood War ... 3.95
❑2 ... 3.95

COLLECTORS GUIDE TO THE ULTRAVERSE
MALIBU

	ORIG	GOOD	FINE	N-MINT
❑1, Aug 94	0.99	0.20	0.50	1.00

COLLIER'S
FANTAGRAPHICS

Value: Cover or less

❑1, b&w ... 2.75
❑2, b&w ... 3.25

COLONIA
COLONIA PRESS

Value: Cover or less

❑1, b&w ... 2.95
❑1-2, Landfall, b&w; 2nd Printing ... 2.95
❑2, b&w ... 2.95
❑3, b&w ... 2.95

COLORS IN BLACK
DARK HORSE

Value: Cover or less

❑1, Mar 95, The Life That Jack Built; The Red Hot Pizza Girl 2.95
❑2 ... 2.95
❑3 ... 2.95
❑4 ... 2.95

COLOSSUS
MARVEL

Value: Cover or less

❑1, Oct 97, A Most Dangerous Game, gatefold cover; gatefold summary ... 2.99

COLOSSUS: GOD'S COUNTRY
MARVEL

Value: Cover or less

❑1, One-Shot; prestige format 6.95

COLOUR OF MAGIC, THE (TERRY PRATCHETT'S...)
INNOVATION

Value: Cover or less

❑1 ... 2.50
❑2 ... 2.50
❑3 ... 2.50
❑4 ... 2.50

COLT SPECIAL
AC

Value: Cover or less

❑1, Aug 85 ... 1.50

COLUMBUS
DARK HORSE

Value: Cover or less

❑1, b&w ... 2.50

COLVILLE
KING INK

Value: Cover or less

❑1, Sep 97, nn; b&w ... 3.00

COMBAT (IMAGE)
IMAGE

Value: Cover or less

❑1, Jan 96 ... 2.50
❑2, Jan 96 ... 2.50

COMBAT KELLY (2ND SERIES)
MARVEL

	ORIG	GOOD	FINE	N-MINT
❑1, Jun 72, Stop the Luftwaffe...Win the War!, O: Combat Kelly, Combat Kelly becomes leader of Dum-Dum Dugan's Deadly Dozen (from Sgt. Fury #98)	0.20	1.60	4.00	8.00
❑2, Aug 72, Lonely Are The Brave;	0.20	1.00	2.50	5.00
❑3, Oct 72, O: Combat Kelly	0.20	1.00	2.50	5.00
❑4, Dec 72, A: Sgt. Fury and his Howling Commandos	0.20	0.60	1.50	3.00
❑5, Feb 73	0.20	0.60	1.50	3.00
❑6, Apr 73	0.20	0.60	1.50	3.00
❑7, Jun 73	0.20	0.60	1.50	3.00
❑8, Aug 73	0.20	0.60	1.50	3.00
❑9, Oct 73, D: Deadly Dozen, Final Issue; Combat Kelly leaves team	0.20	0.60	1.50	3.00

COMBAT ZONE
AVALON

Value: Cover or less

❑1, b&w; Reprint ... 2.95

COME AGAIN
EROS

Value: Cover or less

❑1, Feb 97 ... 2.95
❑2, May 97 ... 2.95

COMET, THE (IMPACT)
DC

Value: Cover or less

❑1, Jul 91, First Flight, O: Comet 1.00
❑2, Aug 91, 1: Applejack; 1: Lance Perry ... 1.00
❑3, Sep 91 ... 1.00
❑4, Oct 91, 1: Inferno; V: Black Hood ... 1.00
❑5, Nov 91, 1: The Hangman (as Roger Adams) ... 1.00
❑6, Dec 91, 1: Hangman; 1: The Hangman (in costume) ... 1.00
❑7, Jan 92, 1: Bob Phantom; 1: The Wolf ... 1.00
❑8, Feb 92, MWa (w), Shattered Secrets, V: Web; 1: The Black Witch ... 1.00
❑9, Mar 92 ... 1.00
❑10, Apr 92, The Coming Of The Crusaders, Part 2, trading card ... 1.00
❑11, May 92 ... 1.00
❑12, Jun 92 ... 1.00
❑13, Jul 92 ... 1.00
❑14, Aug 92 ... 1.25
❑15, Sep 92 ... 1.25
❑16, Oct 92 ... 1.25
❑17, Nov 92 ... 1.25
❑18, Dec 92, Final Issue ... 1.25
❑Anl 1, Earth Quest, Part 3, trading card ... 2.50

COMET, THE (RED CIRCLE)
ARCHIE

Value: Cover or less

❑1, Oct 83, CI, Comet, O: Comet ... 1.00
❑2, Dec 83, CI ... 1.00

COMET MAN
MARVEL

Value: Cover or less

❑1, Feb 87, The Coming Of The Comet Man, 1: Comet Man . 1.00
❑2, Mar 87 ... 1.00
❑3, Apr 87, When The Truth Is Found To Be Lies ... 1.00
❑4, May 87 ... 1.00
❑5, Jun 87 ... 1.00
❑6, Jul 87, Final Issue ... 1.00

COMET TALES
ROCKET

Value: Cover or less

❑1 ... 1.00
❑2 ... 1.00
❑3 ... 1.00

COMIC BOOK
MARVEL

Value: Cover or less

❑1, Jimmy the Turtle Food Collector, oversized anthology ... 6.95
❑2, oversized anthology ... 6.95

COMIC BOOK CONFIDENTIAL
SPHINX

	ORIG	GOOD	FINE	N-MINT
❑1, nn; giveaway promo for documentary film of same name	—	0.40	1.00	2.00

COMIC BOOK HEAVEN
SLAVE LABOR

	ORIG	GOOD	FINE	N-MINT
❑1	1.95	0.40	1.00	2.00
❑2	1.95	0.40	1.00	2.00

COMIC BOOK TALENT SEARCH, THE
SILVERWOLF

Value: Cover or less

❑1, Feb 87 ... 1.50

COMICO BLACK BOOK, THE
COMICO

	ORIG	GOOD	FINE	N-MINT
❑1	1.50	0.40	1.00	2.00

COMICO CHRISTMAS SPECIAL
COMICO

Value: Cover or less

❑1, Dec 88, SR, DSt (c) ... 2.50

COMICO COLLECTION
COMICO

Value: Cover or less

❑1, 10 comics & Grendel: Devil's Vagary ... 9.95

COMICS 101 PRESENTS
CHEAP THRILLS

	ORIG	GOOD	FINE	N-MINT
❑1, Aug 94, nn; b&w; two covers; Anthology; one inside the other	—	0.30	0.75	1.50

COMICS AND STORIES
DARK HORSE
Value: Cover or less

- ❑1, Apr 96, Wolf & Red 2.95
- ❑2, May 96 .... 2.95
- ❑3, Jun 96, Duck and Cover; Son of King Size Canar, Bad Luck Blackie 2.95
- ❑4, Jan 97, Kaboom!; Farm Harm, Screwball Squirrel 2.95

COMICS ARE DEAD
SLAP HAPPY
Value: Cover or less

- ❑1, 99, b&w; Anthology 4.95

COMICS ARTIST SHOWCASE, THE
SHOWCASE
Value: Cover or less

- ❑1, No Such Thing as Demond; A Tiger's Tale 1.00

COMICS' GREATEST WORLD
DARK HORSE
Value: Cover or less

- ❑1, Jun 93, preview copy of Comics' Greatest World: X; 1500 printed 1.00

COMICS' GREATEST WORLD-ARCADIA
DARK HORSE

	ORIG	GOOD	FINE	N-MINT
❑1, Jun 93, 1: X, X; Arcadia, Week 1	1.00	0.40	1.00	2.00
❑1/LE, Jun 93, enhanced cardstock cover; limited edition for Heroes World Distribution; X	1.00	0.50	1.25	2.50
❑2, Pit Bulls; Arcadia, Week 2	1.00	0.20	0.50	1.00
❑3, Jun 93, 1: Ghost, Ghost; Arcadia, Week 3	1.00	0.60	1.50	3.00
❑4, Monster; continues in Comics' Greatest World - Golden City; Arcadia, Week 4	1.00	0.20	0.50	1.00

COMICS' GREATEST WORLD-CINNABAR FLATS
DARK HORSE

	ORIG	GOOD	FINE	N-MINT
❑1, Jun 93, Division 13; Vortex, Week 1	1.00	0.20	0.50	1.00
❑1/A, Aug 93, cardstock cover; limited edition; limited edition for American Distribution; Division 13; Vortex, Week 1	—	0.50	1.25	2.50
❑1/LE, Aug 93, cardstock cover; limited edition; Division 13	—	0.50	1.25	2.50
❑2, Jun 93, Hero Zero; Vortex, Week 2	1.00	0.20	0.50	1.00
❑3, Jun 93, King Tiger; Vortex, Week 3	1.00	0.20	0.50	1.00
❑4, Jun 93, Out of the Vortex; continues in Out of the Vortex (Comics' Greatest World...); continues in Comics' Greatest World - Out of the Vortex; Vortex, Week 4	1.00	0.20	0.50	1.00

COMICS' GREATEST WORLD-GOLDEN CITY
DARK HORSE

	ORIG	GOOD	FINE	N-MINT
❑1, Jul 93, JO (c), Rebel; Golden City, Week 1	1.00	0.20	0.50	1.00
❑1/LE, JO (c), enhanced cardstock cover; limited edition for Heroes World Distribution; Rebel; Golden City, Week 1	1.00	0.50	1.25	2.50
❑2, Mecha; Golden City, Week 2	1.00	0.20	0.50	1.00
❑3, Jul 93, Titan; Golden City, Week 3	1.00	0.20	0.50	1.00
❑4, Aug 93, JDu, Catalyst, continues in Comics' Greatest World - Steel Harbor; Catalyst: Agents of Change; Golden City, Week 4	1.00	0.20	0.50	1.00

COMICS' GREATEST WORLD-STEEL HARBOR
DARK HORSE

	ORIG	GOOD	FINE	N-MINT
❑1, Aug 93, PG, 1: Barb Wire, Barb Wire; Steel Harbor, Week 1	1.00	0.50	1.25	2.50
❑2, The Machine; Steel Harbor, Week 2	1.00	0.20	0.50	1.00
❑3, Aug 93, Wolf Gang; Steel Harbor, Week 3	1.00	0.20	0.50	1.00
❑4, Aug 93, Motorhead; continues in Comics' Greatest World - Cinnabar Flats; Steel Harbor, Week 4	1.00	0.20	0.50	1.00

COMING OF APHRODITE
HERO
Value: Cover or less

- ❑1, b&w 3.95

COMIX BOOK
MARVEL

	ORIG	GOOD	FINE	N-MINT
❑1, The Bir, 1974	1.00	2.00	5.00	10.00
❑2	—	1.60	4.00	8.00
❑3	—	1.60	4.00	8.00
❑4	—	1.00	2.50	5.00
❑5	—	1.00	2.50	5.00

COMMAND REVIEW
THOUGHTS & IMAGES
Value: Cover or less

- ❑1, Jul 86, b&w; collects stories from Albedo #1-4 .... 4.00
- ❑2, Aug 87, b&w; collects stories from Albedo #5-8 .... 4.00
- ❑3, b&w 5.00
- ❑4, Jan 94, (former Thoughts & Imagess title) 4.95

COMMIES FROM MARS
LAST GASP

	ORIG	GOOD	FINE	N-MINT
❑1	1.50	0.40	1.00	2.00
❑2, Snak?; The Treaty	1.50	0.40	1.00	2.00
❑3	1.50	0.40	1.00	2.00
❑4	1.50	0.40	1.00	2.00

Jeff Nicholson followed his *Ultra-Klutz, Through the Habitrails*, and *Father & Son* series with the fantasy-based *Colonia*.

© 1999 Jeff Nicholson (Colonia Press)

	ORIG	GOOD	FINE	N-MINT
❑5	1.50	0.40	1.00	2.00
❑6, Life Drags on on the New Martian Earth; Counterpoint	2.50	0.50	1.25	2.50

COMMUNION
FANTAGRAPHICS
Value: Cover or less

- ❑1, b&w; adult 2.75

COMPLETE CHEECH WIZARD
RIP OFF
Value: Cover or less

- ❑1, Oct 86, b&w; Vaughn BodT 2.25
- ❑2, Jan 87, b&w; Vaughn BodT 2.25
- ❑3, May 87, b&w and color; Vaughn BodT 2.50
- ❑4, Nov 87, b&w and color; Vaughn BodT 2.50

COMPLETELY BAD BOYS
FANTAGRAPHICS
Value: Cover or less

- ❑1, b&w 2.50

CONAN
MARVEL
Value: Cover or less

- ❑1, Aug 95, Song Of The Death Pits, cardstock cover 2.95
- ❑2, Sep 95, The Treasure of Harach Gnar, cardstock cover 2.95
- ❑3, Oct 95, cardstock cover 2.95
- ❑4, Nov 95, A: Rune, cardstock cover 2.95
- ❑5, Dec 95, A: yeti, cardstock cover 2.95
- ❑6, Jan 96, cardstock cover 2.95
- ❑7, Feb 96, V: Man of Iron 2.95
- ❑8, Mar 96, cardstock cover 2.95
- ❑9, Apr 96, God Fall, cardstock cover 2.95
- ❑10, May 96, Queen of the Amazons, cardstock cover 2.95
- ❑11, Jun 96, cardstock cover 2.95
- ❑12, Final Issue 2.95

CONAN CLASSIC
MARVEL
Value: Cover or less

- ❑1, Jun 94, The Coming of Conan, 1: Conan, Reprints Conan the Barbarian #1 .... 1.50
- ❑2, Jul 94 .... 1.50
- ❑3, Aug 94 .... 1.50
- ❑4, Sep 94 .... 1.50
- ❑5, Oct 94 .... 1.50
- ❑6, Nov 94 .... 1.50
- ❑7, Dec 94 .... 1.50
- ❑8, Jan 95 .... 1.50
- ❑9, Feb 95 .... 1.50
- ❑10, Mar 95 .... 1.50
- ❑11, Apr 95, Final Issue 1.50

CONAN: DEATH COVERED IN GOLD
MARVEL
Value: Cover or less

- ❑1, Sep 99 .... 2.99
- ❑3, Nov 99 .... 2.99

CONAN: FLAME AND THE FIEND
MARVEL
Value: Cover or less

- ❑1, Aug 00 .... 2.99
- ❑2, Sep 00 .... 2.99
- ❑3, Oct 00 .... 2.99

CONAN: RETURN OF STYRM
MARVEL
Value: Cover or less

- ❑1, Sep 98, gatefold summary 2.99
- ❑2, Oct 98, gatefold summary 2.99
- ❑3, Nov 98, gatefold summary 2.99

CONAN: RIVER OF BLOOD
MARVEL
Value: Cover or less

- ❑1, Jun 98 .... 2.50
- ❑2, Jul 98 .... 2.50
- ❑3, Aug 98 .... 2.50

CONAN SAGA
MARVEL

	ORIG	GOOD	FINE	N-MINT
❑1, b&w; Reprint	2.00	0.60	1.50	3.00
❑2	2.00	0.50	1.25	2.50
❑3	2.00	0.50	1.25	2.50
❑4	2.00	0.50	1.25	2.50
❑5	2.00	0.50	1.25	2.50
❑6	2.00	0.50	1.25	2.50
❑7, Nov 87	2.00	0.50	1.25	2.50
❑8	2.00	0.50	1.25	2.50
❑9	2.00	0.50	1.25	2.50
❑10	2.00	0.50	1.25	2.50
❑11	2.00	0.50	1.25	2.50
❑12	2.00	0.50	1.25	2.50
❑13	2.00	0.50	1.25	2.50
❑14	2.00	0.50	1.25	2.50
❑15, The Curse of the Cat Goddess	2.00	0.50	1.25	2.50
❑16	2.00	0.50	1.25	2.50

	ORIG	GOOD	FINE	N-MINT
❑17	2.00	0.50	1.25	2.50
❑18	2.00	0.50	1.25	2.50
❑19	2.00	0.50	1.25	2.50
❑20	2.00	0.50	1.25	2.50
❑21	2.00	0.50	1.25	2.50
❑22	2.00	0.50	1.25	2.50
❑23	2.00	0.50	1.25	2.50
❑24	2.00	0.50	1.25	2.50
❑25	2.00	0.50	1.25	2.50
❑26	2.00	0.50	1.25	2.50
❑27	2.00	0.50	1.25	2.50
❑28, b&w; Reprint	2.25	0.50	1.25	2.50
❑29, b&w; Reprint	2.25	0.50	1.25	2.50
❑30, b&w; Reprint	2.25	0.50	1.25	2.50
❑31, b&w; Reprint	2.25	0.50	1.25	2.50
❑32, b&w; Reprint	2.25	0.50	1.25	2.50
❑33, b&w; Reprint	2.25	0.50	1.25	2.50
❑34, b&w; Reprint	2.25	0.50	1.25	2.50
❑35, b&w; Reprint	2.25	0.50	1.25	2.50
❑36, b&w; Reprint	2.25	0.50	1.25	2.50
❑37, b&w; Reprint	2.25	0.50	1.25	2.50
❑38, b&w; Reprint	2.25	0.50	1.25	2.50
❑39, b&w; Reprint	2.25	0.50	1.25	2.50
❑40, b&w; Reprint	2.25	0.50	1.25	2.50
❑41, b&w; Reprint	2.25	0.50	1.25	2.50
❑42, b&w; Reprint	2.25	0.50	1.25	2.50
❑43, b&w; Reprint	2.25	0.50	1.25	2.50
❑44, b&w; Reprint	2.25	0.50	1.25	2.50
❑45, b&w; Reprint	2.25	0.50	1.25	2.50
❑46, b&w; Reprint	2.25	0.50	1.25	2.50
❑47, b&w; Reprint	2.25	0.50	1.25	2.50
❑48, b&w; Reprint	2.25	0.50	1.25	2.50
❑49, b&w; Reprint	2.25	0.50	1.25	2.50
❑50, b&w; Reprint	2.25	0.50	1.25	2.50
❑51, b&w; Reprint	2.25	0.50	1.25	2.50
❑52, b&w; Reprint	2.25	0.50	1.25	2.50
❑53, Conan the Liberator, Part 1, b&w; Reprint	2.25	0.50	1.25	2.50
❑54, Sep 91, JB, Conan the Liberator, Part 2, b&w; Reprint	2.25	0.50	1.25	2.50
❑55, Oct 91, JB, Conan the Liberator, Part 3, b&w; Reprint	2.25	0.50	1.25	2.50
❑56, Nov 91, JB, Conan the Liberator, Part 4, b&w; Reprint	2.25	0.50	1.25	2.50
❑57, Dec 91, FB, The Scarlet Citadel, b&w; Reprint	2.25	0.50	1.25	2.50
❑58, Jan 92, b&w; Reprint	2.25	0.50	1.25	2.50
❑59, Feb 92, b&w; Reprint	2.25	0.50	1.25	2.50
❑60, Mar 92, JB, The Star of Khorala, b&w; Reprint	2.25	0.50	1.25	2.50
❑61, Apr 92, JB, The Sword of Skelos, b&w; Reprint	2.25	0.50	1.25	2.50
❑62, May 92, JB, The Eye of Erlik, b&w; Reprint	2.25	0.50	1.25	2.50
❑63, Jun 92, JB, For the Throne of Zamboula, b&w; Reprint	2.25	0.50	1.25	2.50
❑64, Jul 92, The City of Skulls, b&w; Reprint	2.25	0.50	1.25	2.50
❑65, Aug 92, JB, The Ivory Goddess, b&w; Reprint	2.25	0.50	1.25	2.50
❑66, Sep 92, The Phoenix on the Sword, b&w; Reprint	2.25	0.50	1.25	2.50
❑67, Oct 92, b&w; Reprint	2.25	0.50	1.25	2.50
❑68, Nov 92, JB, Bride of the Conqueror, b&w; Reprint	2.25	0.50	1.25	2.50
❑69, Dec 92, b&w; Reprint	2.25	0.50	1.25	2.50
❑70, Jan 93, b&w; Reprint	2.25	0.50	1.25	2.50
❑71, Feb 93, JB, Revenge of the Barbarian, b&w; Reprint	2.25	0.50	1.25	2.50
❑72, Mar 93, JB, b&w; Reprint	2.25	0.50	1.25	2.50
❑73, Apr 93, JB, b&w; Reprint	2.25	0.50	1.25	2.50
❑74, May 93, JB, b&w; Reprint	2.25	0.50	1.25	2.50
❑75, Jun 93, poster, handbook	3.95	0.80	2.00	4.00
❑76, Jul 93, b&w; Reprint	2.25	0.45	1.13	2.25
❑77, Aug 93, The Warrior and the Were-Woman, b&w; Reprint	2.25	0.45	1.13	2.25
❑78, Sep 93, b&w; Reprint	2.25	0.45	1.13	2.25
❑79, Oct 93, Red Sonja: Balek Lives!; The Tower of Blood, A: Red Sonja, b&w; Reprint; part 5 of chronology of Conan's Career; Reprints Conan the Barbarian #43-45	2.25	0.45	1.13	2.25
❑80, Nov 93, JB, The Trail of the Bloodstained God, b&w; Reprint	2.25	0.45	1.13	2.25
❑81, Dec 93, JB, The Curse of the Conjurer, b&w; Reprint	2.25	0.45	1.13	2.25
❑82, Jan 94, JB, The Oracle of Ophir, b&w; Reprint	2.25	0.45	1.13	2.25
❑83, Feb 94, b&w; Reprint	3.00	0.45	1.13	2.25
❑84, Mar 94, b&w; Reprint	2.25	0.45	1.13	2.25
❑85, Apr 94, b&w; Reprint	2.25	0.45	1.13	2.25
❑86, May 94, JB, Talons of the Man-Tiger, b&w; Reprint	2.25	0.45	1.13	2.25
❑87, Jun 94, JB, The City in the Storm, b&w; Reprint	2.25	0.45	1.13	2.25
❑88, Jul 94, JB, Vengeance in Asgalun, b&w; Reprint	2.25	0.45	1.13	2.25
❑89, Aug 94, JB, The Battle at the Black Walls, b&w; Reprint	2.25	0.45	1.13	2.25
❑90, Sep 94, b&w; Reprint	2.25	0.45	1.13	2.25
❑91, Oct 94, HC, The Sorceress of the Swamp, b&w; Reprint	2.25	0.45	1.13	2.25
❑92, Nov 94, JB, Two Against the Hawk City, b&w; Reprint; list of Conan adaptations	2.25	0.45	1.13	2.25
❑93, Dec 94, JB, The Queen and the Corsairs, b&w; Reprint	2.25	0.45	1.13	2.25
❑94, Jan 95, JB, Savage Doings in Shem!, b&w; Reprint	2.25	0.45	1.13	2.25
❑95, Feb 95, JB, Prelude to Death, b&w; Reprint	2.25	0.45	1.13	2.25
❑96, Mar 95, JB, The Devil has Many Legs!; The Men Who Drink Blood, b&w; Reprint; Red Sonja chronology; Reprints Conan the Barbarian #101-103 in black and white	2.25	0.45	1.13	2.25
❑97, Apr 95, JB, A War of Wizards!, b&w; Reprint; Final Issue	2.25	0.45	1.13	2.25

CONAN: SCARLET SWORD
MARVEL

Value: Cover or less

❑1, Dec 98, gatefold summary 2.99
❑2, Jan 99, gatefold summary. 2.99
❑3, Feb 99 2.99

CONAN THE ADVENTURER
MARVEL

Value: Cover or less

❑1, Jun 94, Barbarians at the Gate, Embossed foil cover; foil embossed 2.50
❑2, Jul 94 1.50
❑3, Aug 94 1.50
❑4, Sep 94, Between Twin Terrors 1.50
❑5, Oct 94 1.50
❑6, Nov 94 1.50
❑7, Dec 94 1.50
❑8, Jan 95 1.50
❑9, Feb 95 1.50
❑10, Mar 95 1.50
❑11, Apr 95 1.50
❑12, May 95 1.50
❑13, Jun 95 1.50
❑14, Jul 95, Final Issue 1.50

CONAN THE BARBARIAN
MARVEL

	ORIG	GOOD	FINE	N-MINT
❑1, Oct 70, The Coming of Conan!, A: Kull; 1: Conan	0.15	30.00	75.00	150.00
❑2, Dec 70, Howard story	0.15	9.00	22.50	45.00
❑3, Feb 71, TS, low dist.	0.15	11.00	27.50	55.00
❑4, Apr 71, SB; TS, The Tower of the Elephant	0.15	4.80	12.00	24.00
❑5, May 71, TS	0.15	4.00	10.00	20.00
❑6, Jun 71	0.15	4.00	10.00	20.00
❑7, Jul 71, 1: Thoth Amon	0.15	4.00	10.00	20.00
❑8, Aug 71	0.15	4.00	10.00	20.00
❑9, Aug 71	0.15	4.00	10.00	20.00
❑10, Oct 71, A: King Kull, Giant-size	0.25	3.20	8.00	16.00
❑11, Nov 71, Giant-size	0.25	3.20	8.00	16.00
❑12, Dec 71	0.20	3.00	7.50	15.00
❑13, Jan 72	0.20	3.00	7.50	15.00
❑14, Mar 72, 1: Elric	0.20	2.40	6.00	12.00
❑15, May 72, A: Elric	0.20	2.40	6.00	12.00
❑16, Jul 72, TS, The Frost Giant's Daughter, Reprint	0.20	2.00	5.00	10.00
❑17, Aug 72, GK	0.20	1.00	2.50	5.00
❑18, Aug 72, GK	0.20	1.00	2.50	5.00
❑19, Oct 72	0.20	1.60	4.00	8.00
❑20, Nov 72	0.20	1.60	4.00	8.00
❑21, Dec 72	0.20	1.60	4.00	8.00
❑22, Jan 73	0.20	1.60	4.00	8.00
❑23, Feb 73, TS, 1: Red Sonja	0.20	4.00	10.00	20.00
❑24, Mar 73, A: Red Sonja, Red Sonja; 1st full Red Sonja story	0.20	1.60	4.00	8.00
❑25, Apr 73, GK; JB; TS, mirrors	0.20	0.80	2.00	4.00
❑26, May 73, JB, The Hour Of The Griffin	0.20	0.60	1.50	3.00
❑27, Jun 73, JB, The Blood Of Bel-Hissar	0.20	0.60	1.50	3.00
❑28, Jul 73, GK; JB; TS, Moon Of Zimbabwe	0.20	0.60	1.50	3.00
❑29, Aug 73, GK; JB; TS	0.20	0.60	1.50	3.00
❑30, Sep 73, GK; JB; TS, The Hand Of Negral	0.20	0.60	1.50	3.00
❑31, Oct 73, JB, The Shadow In The tomb.	0.20	0.40	1.00	2.00
❑32, Nov 73, JB, Flame Winds Of Lost Khitai	0.20	0.40	1.00	2.00
❑33, Dec 73, JB, Death And Seven Wizards	0.20	0.40	1.00	2.00
❑34, Jan 74, JB, The Temptress In The Tower Of Flame	0.20	0.40	1.00	2.00
❑35, Feb 74, JB, The Hell Spawn Of Kara-Shehr	0.20	0.40	1.00	2.00
❑36, Mar 74, JB, Beware The Hyrkanians Bearing Gifts	0.20	0.40	1.00	2.00
❑37, Apr 74, NA; TS, Curse Of The Golden Skull	0.20	0.60	1.50	3.00

	ORIG	GOOD	FINE	N-MINT
❑38, May 74, Night-Lurker!	0.25	0.40	1.00	2.00
❑39, Jun 74, JB, Dragon From The Inland Sea!	0.25	0.40	1.00	2.00
❑40, Jul 74, RB, The Fiend From The Forgotten City	0.25	0.40	1.00	2.00
❑41, Aug 74, GK; JB, The Garden Of Death And Life	0.25	0.40	1.00	2.00
❑42, Sep 74, GK; JB, Night Of The Gargoyle	0.25	0.40	1.00	2.00
❑43, Oct 74, GK; JB, Tower Of Blood	0.25	0.40	1.00	2.00
❑44, Nov 74, JB, Of Flame And The Fiend	0.25	0.40	1.00	2.00
❑45, Dec 74, NA, The Last Ballad Of Laza-Lanti	0.25	0.40	1.00	2.00
❑46, Jan 75, JB, The Curse Of The Conjurer	0.25	0.40	1.00	2.00
❑47, Feb 75, JB, Goblins In The Moonlight	0.25	0.40	1.00	2.00
❑48, Mar 75, JB, The Rats Dance At Ravengard, O: Conan	0.25	0.40	1.00	2.00
❑49, Apr 75, JB, Wolf-Woman!	0.25	0.40	1.00	2.00
❑50, May 75, JB, The Dweller In The Pool	0.25	0.40	1.00	2.00
❑51, Jun 75, JB, Man Born Of Demon!, V: Unos	0.25	0.30	0.75	1.50
❑52, Jul 75, JB, The Altar And The Scorpion	0.25	0.30	0.75	1.50
❑53, Aug 75, JB, Brothers Of The Blade	0.25	0.30	0.75	1.50
❑54, Sep 75, JB, The Oracle Of Ophir	0.25	0.30	0.75	1.50
❑55, Oct 75, JB, Shadow On The Land!	0.25	0.30	0.75	1.50
❑56, Nov 75, JB, The Strange High Tower In The Mist!	0.25	0.30	0.75	1.50
❑57, Dec 75, MP, Incident in Argos	0.25	0.30	0.75	1.50
❑58, Jan 76, JB, Queen Of The Black Coast!, 2: BTlit	0.25	0.40	1.00	2.00
❑59, Feb 76, JB, The Ballad Of BTlit, O: BTlit	0.25	0.40	1.00	2.00
❑60, Mar 76, JB, Riders Of The River-Dragons	0.25	0.30	0.75	1.50
❑61, Apr 76, JB, On The Track Of The She-Pirate	0.25	0.30	0.75	1.50
❑62, May 76, JB, Lord Of The Lions	0.25	0.30	0.75	1.50
❑63, Jun 76, JB, Death Among The Ruins	0.25	0.30	0.75	1.50
❑64, Jul 76, JSn; AM, The Secret Of Skull River	0.25	0.30	0.75	1.50
❑65, Aug 76, GK; JB, Fiends Of The Feathered Serpent!	0.25	0.30	0.75	1.50
❑66, Sep 76, GK; JB, V: Dagon	0.30	0.30	0.75	1.50
❑67, Oct 76, GK; JB, Talons Of The Man Tiger!, A: Red Sonja, Red Sonja	0.30	0.30	0.75	1.50
❑68, Nov 76, GK; JB, A: Red Sonja, (continued from Marvel Feature #7); (continued from Marvel Feature #7)	0.30	0.30	0.75	1.50
❑69, Dec 76, The Demon Out Of The Deep!	0.30	0.30	0.75	1.50
❑70, Jan 77, JB	0.30	0.30	0.75	1.50
❑71, Feb 77, JB, The Secret Of Ashtoreth!	0.30	0.30	0.75	1.50
❑72, Mar 77, JB, Vengeance In Asgalun	0.30	0.30	0.75	1.50
❑73, Apr 77, JB, He Who Waits -In the Well Of Skelos	0.30	0.30	0.75	1.50
❑74, May 77, JB, The Battle At The Black Walls!	0.30	0.30	0.75	1.50
❑75, Jun 77, JB, Hawk Riders Of Harach!	0.30	0.30	0.75	1.50
❑76, Jul 77, JB, Swordless In Stygia	0.30	0.30	0.75	1.50
❑77, Aug 77, JB, When Giants Walk The Earth	0.30	0.30	0.75	1.50
❑78, Sep 77, JB, Curse Of The Undead Man	0.30	0.30	0.75	1.50
❑79, Oct 77, HC, The Lost Valley Of Iskander	0.30	0.30	0.75	1.50
❑80, Nov 77, HC, Trial By Combat!	0.35	0.30	0.75	1.50
❑81, Dec 77, HC, The Eye Of The Serpent	0.35	0.30	0.75	1.50
❑82, Jan 78, HC, The Sorceress Of The Swamp!	0.35	0.30	0.75	1.50
❑83, Feb 78, HC, The Dance Of The Skull	0.35	0.30	0.75	1.50
❑84, Mar 78, JB, Two Against The Hawk City!, 1: Zula	0.35	0.30	0.75	1.50
❑85, Apr 78, JB, Of Swordsmen And Sorcerers!, O: Zula	0.35	0.30	0.75	1.50
❑86, May 78, JB, The Devourer Of The Dead	0.35	0.30	0.75	1.50
❑87, Jun 78, JB, Demons At The Summit!, Reprints Savage Sword of Conan #3 in color	0.35	0.30	0.75	1.50
❑88, Jul 78, JB, The Queen And The Corsairs!, Return of Belit; Return of BTlit	0.35	0.30	0.75	1.50
❑89, Aug 78, JB, The Sword And the Serpent, V: Thoth-Amon	0.35	0.30	0.75	1.50
❑90, Sep 78, JB, The Diadem Of The Giant-Kings!	0.35	0.30	0.75	1.50
❑91, Oct 78, JB, Savage Doings In Shem!	0.35	0.30	0.75	1.50
❑92, Nov 78, JB, The Thing in the Crypt	0.35	0.30	0.75	1.50
❑93, Dec 78, JB, The Rage And Revenge, Belit regains throne; BTlit regains throne	0.35	0.30	0.75	1.50
❑94, Jan 79, JB, The Beast-King Of Abombi!	0.35	0.30	0.75	1.50
❑95, Feb 79, JB, The Return Of Amra!	0.35	0.30	0.75	1.50
❑96, Mar 79, JB, The Long Night Of Fang And Talon!, Part 1	0.35	0.30	0.75	1.50
❑97, Apr 79, JB, The Long Night Of Fang And Talon!, Part 2	0.35	0.30	0.75	1.50
❑98, May 79, JB, Sea-Woman	0.40	0.30	0.75	1.50

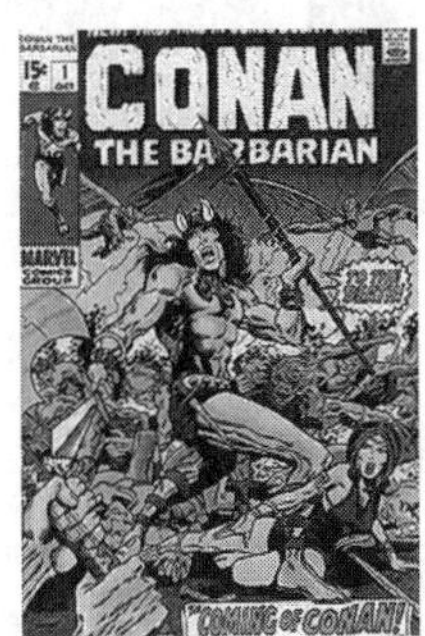

CONAN
THE BARBARIAN
15¢
1
MARVEL
COMING OF CONAN!

One of Robert E. Howard's other creations, Kull the Conqueror, made an appearance in the first issue of Marvel's *Conan the Barbarian.*

© 1970 Marvel

	ORIG	GOOD	FINE	N-MINT
❑99, Jun 79, JB, Devil Crabs Of the Dark Cliffs!	0.40	0.30	0.75	1.50
❑100, Jul 79, JB; TS, Death On The Black Coast, D: BTlit; D: Belit, Double-size issue	0.60	0.40	1.00	2.00
❑101, Aug 79, JB, The Devil Has Many Legs	0.40	0.20	0.50	1.00
❑102, Sep 79, JB, The Men Who Drink Blood	0.40	0.20	0.50	1.00
❑103, Oct 79, JB, Bride Of The Vampire!	0.40	0.20	0.50	1.00
❑104, Nov 79, JB, The Vale Of Lost Women	0.40	0.20	0.50	1.00
❑105, Dec 79, JB, Whispering Shadows	0.40	0.20	0.50	1.00
❑106, Jan 80, JB, Chaos In The Land Called Kush!0	0.40	0.20	0.50	1.00
❑107, Feb 80, JB, Demon Of The Night!	0.40	0.20	0.50	1.00
❑108, Mar 80, JB, The Moon-Eaters Of Darfar!	0.40	0.20	0.50	1.00
❑109, Apr 80, JB, Sons Of The Bear God!	0.40	0.20	0.50	1.00
❑110, May 80, JB, Beware The Bear Of Heaven	0.40	0.20	0.50	1.00
❑111, Jun 80, JB, Cimmerian Against A City	0.40	0.20	0.50	1.00
❑112, Jul 80, JB, Buryat Besieged!	0.40	0.20	0.50	1.00
❑113, Aug 80, JB, A Devil In The Family!	0.40	0.20	0.50	1.00
❑114, Sep 80, JB, The Shadow Of The Beast!	0.50	0.20	0.50	1.00
❑115, Oct 80, JB, A War Of Wizards, 10th anniversary; double-sized	0.75	0.30	0.75	1.50
❑116, Nov 80, NA; JB, A Crawler On The Midst!, Reprint	0.50	0.20	0.50	1.00
❑117, Dec 80, JB, The Corridor f Mullah Kajar	0.50	0.20	0.50	1.00
❑118, Jan 81, JB, Valley Of Forever Night	0.50	0.20	0.50	1.00
❑119, Feb 81, JB, The Voice Of One Long Gone	0.50	0.20	0.50	1.00
❑120, Mar 81, JB, Hand Of Erlik!	0.50	0.20	0.50	1.00
❑121, Apr 81, JB, The Price Of Perfection	0.50	0.20	0.50	1.00
❑122, May 81, JB, The City Where Time Stood Still	0.50	0.20	0.50	1.00
❑123, Jun 81, JB, The Horror Beneath The Hills	0.50	0.20	0.50	1.00
❑124, Jul 81, JB, The Eternity War!	0.50	0.20	0.50	1.00
❑125, Aug 81, JB, The Witches Of Nexxx	0.50	0.20	0.50	1.00
❑126, Sep 81, JB, The Blood Red Eye Of Truth	0.50	0.20	0.50	1.00
❑127, Oct 81, JB, The Snow Haired Woman Of The Wastes	0.50	0.20	0.50	1.00
❑128, Nov 81, GK, GK (c), And Life Sprang Forth From These	0.50	0.20	0.50	1.00
❑129, Dec 81	0.50	0.20	0.50	1.00
❑130, Jan 82, GK, The Quest Ends!	0.60	0.20	0.50	1.00
❑131, Feb 82, GK, The Ring Of Rhax	0.60	0.20	0.50	1.00
❑132, Mar 82, GK, Games Of Gharn	0.60	0.20	0.50	1.00
❑133, Apr 82, GK, The Witch Of Windsor	0.60	0.20	0.50	1.00
❑134, May 82, GK, A Hitch In Time	0.60	0.20	0.50	1.00
❑135, Jun 82, The Forest Of The Night	0.60	0.20	0.50	1.00
❑136, Jul 82, JB, The River Of Death	0.60	0.20	0.50	1.00
❑137, Aug 82, AA, Titan's Gambit	0.60	0.20	0.50	1.00
❑138, Sep 82, VM, The Isle Of The Dead	0.60	0.20	0.50	1.00
❑139, Oct 82, VM, In The Lair Of The Damned	0.60	0.20	0.50	1.00
❑140, Nov 82, JB, Spider Isle	0.60	0.20	0.50	1.00
❑141, Dec 82, JB, The Web Tightens	0.60	0.20	0.50	1.00
❑142, Jan 83, JB, The Maze, The Man, The Monster	0.60	0.20	0.50	1.00
❑143, Feb 83, JB, Life Among The Dead	0.60	0.20	0.50	1.00
❑144, Mar 83, JB, The Blade And The Beast	0.60	0.20	0.50	1.00
❑145, Apr 83, JB, Son Of Cimmeria	0.60	0.20	0.50	1.00
❑146, May 83, JB, Night Of The Three Sisters!	0.60	0.20	0.50	1.00
❑147, Jun 83, JB, Tower Of Mitra!	0.60	0.20	0.50	1.00
❑148, Jul 83, JB, The Plague Of Forlek	0.60	0.20	0.50	1.00
❑149, Aug 83, JB, Deathmark	0.60	0.20	0.50	1.00
❑150, Sep 83, JB, Tower Of Flame!	0.60	0.20	0.50	1.00
❑151, Oct 83, JB, Vale Of Death!	0.60	0.20	0.50	1.00
❑152, Nov 83, JB, The Dark Blade Of Jergal Zadh!	0.60	0.20	0.50	1.00
❑153, Dec 83, JB, The Bird Men Of Akah Ma'at!	0.60	0.20	0.50	1.00
❑154, Jan 84, The Man Bats Of Ur-Xanarrh!, Assistant Editors' Month	0.60	0.20	0.50	1.00

	ORIG	GOOD	FINE	N-MINT
❑155, Feb 84, JB, The Anger Of Conan	0.60	0.20	0.50	1.00
❑156, Mar 84, JB, The Curse!	0.60	0.20	0.50	1.00
❑157, Apr 84, JB, The Wizard	0.60	0.20	0.50	1.00
❑158, May 84, JB, Night Of The Wolf	0.60	0.20	0.50	1.00
❑159, Jun 84, JB, Cauldron Of The Doomed!	0.60	0.20	0.50	1.00
❑160, Jul 84, Veil of Darkness	0.60	0.20	0.50	1.00
❑161, Aug 84, JB, The House Of Skulls!	0.60	0.20	0.50	1.00
❑162, Sep 84, JB, Destroyer In The Flame	0.60	0.20	0.50	1.00
❑163, Oct 84, JB, Cavern Of The Vines Of Doom!	0.60	0.20	0.50	1.00
❑164, Nov 84, The Jeweled Sword Of Tem	0.60	0.20	0.50	1.00
❑165, Dec 84, JB, Temple Of The Dragon	0.60	0.20	0.50	1.00
❑166, Jan 85, JB, Blood Of The Titan	0.60	0.20	0.50	1.00
❑167, Feb 85, JB, The Creature From Time's Dawn!	0.60	0.20	0.50	1.00
❑168, Mar 85, JB, The Bird-Woman And The Beast!	0.60	0.20	0.50	1.00
❑169, Apr 85, JB	0.65	0.20	0.50	1.00
❑170, May 85, JB, Dominion Of The Dead!	0.65	0.20	0.50	1.00
❑171, Jun 85, JB, Barbarian Death Song	0.65	0.20	0.50	1.00
❑172, Jul 85, JB	0.65	0.20	0.50	1.00
❑173, Aug 85, JB, Honor Among Thieves	0.65	0.20	0.50	1.00
❑174, Sep 85, JB, Children Of The Night	0.65	0.20	0.50	1.00
❑175, Oct 85, JB, The Scarlet Personage!	0.65	0.20	0.50	1.00
❑176, Nov 85, JB, Argos Rain	0.65	0.20	0.50	1.00
❑177, Dec 85, JB, Well of Souls!	0.65	0.20	0.50	1.00
❑178, Jan 86, JB, Death Hunt	0.65	0.20	0.50	1.00
❑179, Feb 86, JB, The End Of All There Is	0.75	0.20	0.50	1.00
❑180, Mar 86, JB	0.75	0.20	0.50	1.00
❑181, Apr 86, JB, Maddoc's Reign	0.75	0.20	0.50	1.00
❑182, May 86, JB, Testament	0.75	0.20	0.50	1.00
❑183, Jun 86, JB, Blood Dawn	0.75	0.20	0.50	1.00
❑184, Jul 86	0.75	0.20	0.50	1.00
❑185, Aug 86	0.75	0.20	0.50	1.00
❑186, Sep 86, The Crimson Brotherhood	0.75	0.20	0.50	1.00
❑187, Oct 86, JB, Resurrection	0.75	0.20	0.50	1.00
❑188, Nov 86	0.75	0.20	0.50	1.00
❑189, Dec 86	0.75	0.20	0.50	1.00
❑190, Jan 87	0.75	0.20	0.50	1.00
❑191, Feb 87	0.75	0.20	0.50	1.00
❑192, Mar 87	0.75	0.20	0.50	1.00
❑193, Apr 87	0.75	0.20	0.50	1.00
❑194, May 87, Victory	1.00	0.20	0.50	1.00
❑195, Jun 87	1.00	0.20	0.50	1.00
❑196, Jul 87	1.00	0.20	0.50	1.00
❑197, Aug 87, Stand	1.00	0.20	0.50	1.00
❑198, Sep 87	1.00	0.20	0.50	1.00
❑199, Oct 87	1.00	0.20	0.50	1.00
❑200, Nov 87, The Fall Of Acheron, Double-size; 200th issue anniversary	1.50	0.30	0.75	1.50
❑201, Dec 87	1.00	0.20	0.50	1.00
❑202, Jan 88	1.00	0.20	0.50	1.00
❑203, Feb 88	1.00	0.20	0.50	1.00
❑204, Mar 88	1.00	0.20	0.50	1.00
❑205, Apr 88	1.00	0.20	0.50	1.00
❑206, May 88	1.00	0.20	0.50	1.00
❑207, Jun 88	1.00	0.20	0.50	1.00
❑208, Jul 88	1.00	0.20	0.50	1.00
❑209, Aug 88	1.00	0.20	0.50	1.00
❑210, Sep 88	1.00	0.20	0.50	1.00
❑211, Oct 88	1.00	0.20	0.50	1.00
❑212, Nov 88	1.00	0.20	0.50	1.00
❑213, Dec 88	1.00	0.20	0.50	1.00
❑214, Jan 89	1.00	0.20	0.50	1.00
❑215, Feb 89	1.00	0.20	0.50	1.00
❑216, Mar 89	1.00	0.20	0.50	1.00
❑217, Apr 89	1.00	0.20	0.50	1.00
❑218, May 89	1.00	0.20	0.50	1.00
❑219, Jun 89	1.00	0.20	0.50	1.00
❑220, Jul 89	1.00	0.20	0.50	1.00
❑221, Aug 89	1.00	0.20	0.50	1.00
❑222, Sep 89	1.00	0.20	0.50	1.00
❑223, Oct 89, The Wheel Of Life And Death	1.00	0.20	0.50	1.00
❑224, Nov 89	1.00	0.20	0.50	1.00
❑225, Nov 89	1.00	0.20	0.50	1.00
❑226, Dec 89	1.00	0.20	0.50	1.00
❑227, Dec 89	1.00	0.20	0.50	1.00
❑228, Jan 90	1.00	0.20	0.50	1.00
❑229, Feb 90	1.00	0.20	0.50	1.00
❑230, Mar 90	1.00	0.20	0.50	1.00
❑231, Apr 90	1.00	0.20	0.50	1.00
❑232, May 90, starts over	1.00	0.20	0.50	1.00
❑233, Jun 90	1.00	0.20	0.50	1.00
❑234, Jul 90	1.00	0.20	0.50	1.00
❑235, Aug 90	1.00	0.20	0.50	1.00
❑236, Sep 90	1.00	0.20	0.50	1.00
❑237, Oct 90	1.00	0.20	0.50	1.00
❑238, Nov 90	1.00	0.20	0.50	1.00
❑239, Dec 90	1.00	0.20	0.50	1.00
❑240, Jan 91, The End Must Come	1.00	0.20	0.50	1.00
❑241, Feb 91, TMc (c)	1.00	0.30	0.75	1.50
❑242, Mar 91, JLee(c)	1.00	0.30	0.75	1.50
❑243, Apr 91, Red Sonja	1.00	0.20	0.50	1.00
❑244, May 91, Red Sonja	1.00	0.20	0.50	1.00
❑245, Jun 91, Red Sonja	1.00	0.20	0.50	1.00
❑246, Jul 91, Red Sonja	1.00	0.20	0.50	1.00
❑247, Aug 91, Red Sonja	1.00	0.20	0.50	1.00
❑248, Sep 91, Red Sonja	1.00	0.20	0.50	1.00
❑249, Oct 91, Red Sonja	1.00	0.20	0.50	1.00
❑250, Nov 91, Double-size; 250th issue anniversary	1.50	0.30	0.75	1.50
❑251, Dec 91	1.00	0.20	0.50	1.00
❑252, Jan 92	1.00	0.20	0.50	1.00
❑253, Feb 92	1.25	0.25	0.63	1.25
❑254, Mar 92	1.25	0.25	0.63	1.25
❑255, Apr 92	1.25	0.25	0.63	1.25
❑256, May 92	1.25	0.25	0.63	1.25
❑257, Jun 92, V: Thoth-Amon	1.25	0.25	0.63	1.25
❑258, Jul 92, returns to Cimmeria	1.25	0.25	0.63	1.25
❑259, Aug 92	1.25	0.25	0.63	1.25
❑260, Sep 92	1.25	0.25	0.63	1.25
❑261, Oct 92	1.25	0.25	0.63	1.25
❑262, Nov 92	1.25	0.25	0.63	1.25
❑263, Dec 92	1.25	0.25	0.63	1.25
❑264, Jan 93	1.25	0.25	0.63	1.25
❑265, Feb 93	1.25	0.25	0.63	1.25
❑266, Mar 93	1.25	0.25	0.63	1.25
❑267, Apr 93	1.25	0.25	0.63	1.25
❑268, May 93	1.25	0.25	0.63	1.25
❑269, Jun 93	1.25	0.25	0.63	1.25
❑270, Jul 93	1.25	0.25	0.63	1.25
❑271, Aug 93	1.25	0.25	0.63	1.25
❑272, Sep 93	1.25	0.25	0.63	1.25
❑273, Oct 93, Conan the Punisher, A: Lord of the Purple Lotus	1.25	0.25	0.63	1.25
❑274, Nov 93	1.25	0.25	0.63	1.25
❑275, Dec 93, 64pgs.; Final Issue	2.50	0.50	1.25	2.50
❑Anl 1, ca. 73, Cover reads "King-Size Special"	0.35	1.20	3.00	6.00
❑Anl 2, Jan 76, JB, Conan The Cimmerian	0.50	0.80	2.00	4.00
❑Anl 3, ca. 77, NA; HC; JB, At The Mountain Of The Moon God, A: King Kull, Reprints Savage Sword of Conan #2	0.60	0.40	1.00	2.00
❑Anl 4, ca. 78, JB, The Return Of The Conqueror!, King Conan story	0.60	0.40	1.00	2.00
❑Anl 5, ca. 79, JB, Bride Of The Conqueror	0.75	0.40	1.00	2.00
❑Anl 6, ca. 81, JB, King Of The Forgotten People	0.75	0.40	1.00	2.00
❑Anl 7, ca. 82, JB, Conan of the Isles	1.00	0.30	0.75	1.50
❑Anl 8, ca. 83, VM, Dark Night Of The White Queen	1.00	0.30	0.75	1.50
❑Anl 9, ca. 84, Wrath Of The Shambling God!	1.00	0.30	0.75	1.50
❑Anl 10, ca. 85, Scorched Earth	1.25	0.25	0.63	1.25
❑Anl 11, ca. 86, Bride Of The Orulist	1.25	0.25	0.63	1.25
❑Anl 12, ca. 87, Legion of the Dead	1.25	0.25	0.63	1.25
❑GS 1, Sep 74, 1: BTlit	0.50	0.80	2.00	4.00
❑GS 2, Dec 74, GK, Conan Bound!	0.50	0.60	1.50	3.00
❑GS 3, Apr 75, GK, To Tarantia-And The Tower	0.50	0.60	1.50	3.00
❑GS 4, Jun 75, GK, Swords Of The South	0.50	0.60	1.50	3.00
❑GS 5, ca. 75, A Sword Called Stormbringer	0.50	0.60	1.50	3.00
❑SE 1, Red Nails, Reprint	2.50	0.50	1.25	2.50

CONAN THE BARBARIAN (VOL. 2)

MARVEL

Value: Cover or less

- ❑1, Jul 97 .... 2.50
- ❑2, Aug 97 .... 2.50
- ❑3, Oct 97 .... 2.50

CONAN THE BARBARIAN MOVIE SPECIAL

MARVEL

	ORIG	GOOD	FINE	N-MINT
❑1, Oct 82, JB, JB (w), movie Adaptation	0.60	0.20	0.50	1.00
❑2, Nov 82, JB, JB (w), movie Adaptation	0.60	0.20	0.50	1.00

CONAN THE BARBARIAN: THE USURPER

MARVEL

Value: Cover or less

- ❑1, Dec 97, gatefold cover; gatefold summary 2.50
- ❑2, Jan 98, gatefold summary 2.50
- ❑3 .... 2.50
- ❑4 .... 2.50

CONAN THE DESTROYER

MARVEL

	ORIG	GOOD	FINE	N-MINT
❑1, Jan 85, movie Adaptation	0.75	0.20	0.50	1.00
❑2, Mar 85, movie Adaptation	0.75	0.20	0.50	1.00

CONAN THE KING

MARVEL

	ORIG	GOOD	FINE	N-MINT
❑20, Continued from King Conan #19	1.00	0.30	0.75	1.50
❑21, Mar 84	1.00	0.30	0.75	1.50
❑22, May 84	1.00	0.30	0.75	1.50

	ORIG	GOOD	FINE	N-MINT
❑23, Jul 84	1.00	0.30	0.75	1.50
❑24, Sep 84	1.00	0.30	0.75	1.50
❑25, Nov 84	1.00	0.30	0.75	1.50
❑26, Jan 85	1.00	0.30	0.75	1.50
❑27, Mar 85	1.00	0.30	0.75	1.50
❑28, May 85	1.25	0.30	0.75	1.50
❑29, Jul 85	1.25	0.30	0.75	1.50
❑30, Sep 85	1.25	0.30	0.75	1.50
❑31, Nov 85	1.25	0.30	0.75	1.50
❑32, Jan 86	1.25	0.30	0.75	1.50
❑33, Mar 86	1.25	0.30	0.75	1.50
❑34, May 86	1.25	0.30	0.75	1.50
❑35, Jul 86	1.25	0.30	0.75	1.50
❑36, Sep 86	1.25	0.30	0.75	1.50
❑37, Nov 86	1.25	0.30	0.75	1.50
❑38, Jan 87	1.25	0.30	0.75	1.50
❑39, Mar 87	1.25	0.30	0.75	1.50
❑40, May 87	1.25	0.30	0.75	1.50
❑41, Jul 87	1.25	0.30	0.75	1.50
❑42, Sep 87	1.25	0.30	0.75	1.50
❑43, Nov 87	1.25	0.30	0.75	1.50
❑44, Jan 88	1.25	0.30	0.75	1.50
❑45, Mar 88	1.25	0.30	0.75	1.50
❑46, May 88	1.50	0.30	0.75	1.50
❑47, Jul 88	1.50	0.30	0.75	1.50
❑48, Sep 88	1.50	0.30	0.75	1.50
❑49, Nov 88	1.50	0.30	0.75	1.50
❑50, Jan 89	1.50	0.30	0.75	1.50
❑51, Mar 89	1.50	0.30	0.75	1.50
❑52, May 89	1.50	0.30	0.75	1.50
❑53, Jul 89	1.50	0.30	0.75	1.50
❑54, Sep 89	1.50	0.30	0.75	1.50
❑55, Nov 89, Final Issue	1.50	0.30	0.75	1.50

CONAN: THE LORD OF THE SPIDERS
MARVEL

Value: Cover or less

- ❑1, Mar 98, The Webs We Weave, gatefold cover; gatefold summary ... 2.50
- ❑2, Apr 98, gatefold summary. 2.50
- ❑3, May 98, gatefold summary 2.50

CONAN THE SAVAGE
MARVEL

Value: Cover or less

- ❑1, Aug 95, b&w magazine..... 2.95
- ❑2, Sep 95, Stalker in the Snows, Part 1, b&w magazine......... 2.95
- ❑3, Oct 95, Stalker in the Snows, Part 2, b&w magazine......... 2.95
- ❑4, Nov 95, Stalker in the Snows, Part 3, V: Rune, b&w magazine; indicia gives title as Conan . 2.95
- ❑5, Dec 95, VM, Stalkers of the Snows, Part 4, b&w magazine2.95
- ❑6, Jan 96, b&w magazine 2.95
- ❑7, Feb 96, b&w magazine 2.95
- ❑8, Mar 96, VM, Ivory; Fate, b&w magazine ... 2.95
- ❑9, Apr 96, b&w magazine...... 2.95
- ❑10, May 96, b&w magazine .. 2.95
- ❑11 ... 2.95
- ❑12 ... 2.95

CONAN VS. RUNE
MARVEL

Value: Cover or less

- ❑1, Nov 95, The Dark God, One-Shot ... 2.95

CONCRETE
DARK HORSE

	ORIG	GOOD	FINE	N-MINT
❑1, Mar 87, A Stone Among Stones	1.50	1.00	2.50	5.00
❑1-2, A Stone Among Stones, 2nd Printing.	1.50	0.40	1.00	2.00
❑2, Jun 87	1.50	0.60	1.50	3.00
❑3, Aug 87, O: Concrete	1.50	0.60	1.50	3.00
❑4, Oct 87, O: Concrete	1.75	0.50	1.25	2.50
❑5, Dec 87	1.75	0.50	1.25	2.50
❑6, Feb 88	1.75	0.50	1.25	2.50
❑7, Apr 88	1.75	0.50	1.25	2.50
❑8, Jun 88	1.75	0.50	1.25	2.50
❑9, Sep 88	1.75	0.50	1.25	2.50
❑10, Final Issue	1.75	0.40	1.00	2.00
❑Hero 1, Moving A Big Rock, Hero Special edition; Included with Hero Illustrated #23	—	0.20	0.50	1.00

CONCRETE: A NEW LIFE
DARK HORSE

Value: Cover or less

- ❑1, Oct 89, O: Concrete, b&w reprint ... 2.95

CONCRETE CELEBRATES EARTH DAY
DARK HORSE

Value: Cover or less

- ❑1, Apr 90, CV, CV (w), Like Disneyland, Only Toxic; Earth Streams, Moebius ... 3.50

CONCRETE COLOR SPECIAL
DARK HORSE

Value: Cover or less

- ❑1, Feb 89, The Damp Descent; Lifestyles of the Rich and Famous, reprint in color 2.95

CONCRETE: ECLECTICA
DARK HORSE

Value: Cover or less

- ❑1, Apr 93, wraparound cover from 1992 WonderCon program book ... 2.95
- ❑2, May 93, wraparound cover 2.95

Paul Chadwick's Concrete moved from his initial appearances in *Dark Horse Presents* to a 10-issue series and then a number of mini-series.

© 1987 Paul Chadwick (Dark Horse)

CONCRETE: FRAGILE CREATURE
DARK HORSE

Value: Cover or less

- ❑1, Jun 91, full color; wraparound cover ... 2.50
- ❑2, Jul 91, full color; wraparound cover ... 2.50
- ❑3, Aug 91, full color; wraparound cover ... 2.50
- ❑4, Feb 92, full color; wraparound cover ... 2.50

CONCRETE JUNGLE: THE LEGEND OF THE BLACK LION
ACCLAIM

Value: Cover or less

- ❑1, Speaking in Tongues......... 2.50

CONCRETE: KILLER SMILE
DARK HORSE

Value: Cover or less

- ❑1, Jul 94 ... 2.95
- ❑2, Aug 94 ... 2.95
- ❑3, Sep 94 ... 2.95
- ❑4, Oct 94 ... 2.95

CONCRETE: LAND & SEA
DARK HORSE

Value: Cover or less

- ❑1, Feb 89, b&w; wraparound cardstock cover; reprints first two Concrete stories with additional material ... 2.95

CONCRETE: ODD JOBS
DARK HORSE

Value: Cover or less

- ❑1, Jul 90, b&w reprint; Collects Concrete #5-6 ... 3.50

CONCRETE: STRANGE ARMOR
DARK HORSE

Value: Cover or less

- ❑1, Dec 97, O: Concrete 2.95
- ❑2, Jan 98, O: Concrete.......... 2.95
- ❑3, Mar 98, O: Concrete 2.95
- ❑4, Apr 98, O: Concrete 2.95
- ❑5, May 98, O: Concrete 2.95

CONCRETE: THINK LIKE A MOUNTAIN
DARK HORSE

	ORIG	GOOD	FINE	N-MINT
❑1, Mar 96, Green Fire, nn; b&w; promotional giveaway for mini-series	2.95	0.59	1.48	2.95
❑2, Apr 96, Hidden Graveyard	2.95	0.59	1.48	2.95
❑3, May 96, Arms and Boxes	2.95	0.59	1.48	2.95
❑4, Jun 96, Weight of the World	2.95	0.59	1.48	2.95
❑5, Jul 96, Nightwork	2.95	0.59	1.48	2.95
❑6, Aug 96, Charismatic Megafauna	2.95	0.59	1.48	2.95
❑Ash 1, nn; b&w; promotional giveaway for mini-series	—	0.20	0.50	1.00

CONDOM-MAN
AAAAHH!!

Value: Cover or less

- ❑1, Gold ink limited edition...... 3.95

CONDORMAN (WALT DISNEY)
WHITMAN

	ORIG	GOOD	FINE	N-MINT
❑1	0.50	0.20	0.50	1.00
❑2, Conclusion	0.50	0.20	0.50	1.00
❑3	0.50	0.20	0.50	1.00

CONEHEADS
MARVEL

Value: Cover or less

- ❑1, Jun 94, Homecoming........ 1.75
- ❑2, Jul 94 ... 1.75
- ❑3, Aug 94 ... 1.75
- ❑4, Sep 94 ... 1.75

CONFESSIONS OF A CEREAL EATER
NBM

Value: Cover or less

- ❑1, Daniel's Den; Movin' In, b&w2.95
- ❑2, A Quiet Evening at Home; Bailey Daze: Rat Tales, b&w 2.95
- ❑3, Yule Be Sorry; Junkers, b&w2.95

CONFESSIONS OF A TEENAGE VAMPIRE: THE TURNING
SCHOLASTIC

Value: Cover or less

- ❑1, Jul 97, nn; digest............... 4.99

CONFESSIONS OF A TEENAGE VAMPIRE: ZOMBIE SATURDAY NIGHT
SCHOLASTIC

Value: Cover or less

- ❑1, Jul 97, nn; digest............... 4.99

CONFESSOR, THE (DEMONICUS EX DEO)
DARK MATTER

Value: Cover or less

- ❑1, Purgation, b&w.................. 2.95

CONFRONTATION, THE
SACRED ORIGIN

	ORIG	GOOD	FINE	N-MINT
❑1, Jul 97, The Journey	2.95	0.59	1.48	2.95
❑2, Oct 97, Genesis	2.95	0.59	1.48	2.95

	ORIG	GOOD	FINE	N-MINT
❑3	2.95	0.59	1.48	2.95
❑4	2.95	0.59	1.48	2.95
❑SE 1, Convention exclusive edition	—	1.00	2.50	5.00

CONGO BILL
DC

Value: Cover or less

- ❑1, Oct 99, The Message 2.95
- ❑2, Nov 99 2.95
- ❑3, Dec 99, The Darkness 2.95
- ❑4, Jan 00, The Beast 2.95

CONGORILLA
DC

	ORIG	GOOD	FINE	N-MINT
❑1, Nov 92, Now I Lay Me Down to Sleep...	1.75	0.40	1.00	2.00
❑2, Dec 92	1.75	0.35	0.88	1.75
❑3, Jan 93	1.75	0.35	0.88	1.75
❑4, Feb 93	1.75	0.35	0.88	1.75

CONJURORS
DC

Value: Cover or less

- ❑1, Apr 99, The Birth of Magic, A: Phantom Stranger; A: Deadman; A: Challengers of the Unknown, Elseworlds story 2.95
- ❑2, May 99, The Death of Magic, Elseworlds story 2.95
- ❑3, Jun 99, Magic and Machine, Elseworlds story 2.95

CONQUEROR
HARRIER

Value: Cover or less

- ❑1 1.75
- ❑2, Ladies' Night; Local Problem 1.75
- ❑3 1.75
- ❑4 1.75
- ❑5 1.75
- ❑6 1.75
- ❑7, Aug 85 1.75
- ❑8, Oct 85 1.75
- ❑9, Dec 85 1.75
- ❑SE 1, Unicorn on Winchester; Mark of the Beast, Special edition (1987) 1.95

CONQUEROR OF THE BARREN EARTH
DC

	ORIG	GOOD	FINE	N-MINT
❑1, Feb 83, The Ravager	0.75	0.20	0.50	1.00
❑2, Mar 83	0.75	0.20	0.50	1.00
❑3, Apr 83	0.75	0.20	0.50	1.00
❑4, May 83	0.75	0.20	0.50	1.00

CONQUEROR UNIVERSE
HARRIER

Value: Cover or less

- ❑1, Castle in the Air; Sacrifice 2.75

CONSERVATION CORPS
ARCHIE

Value: Cover or less

- ❑1, Aug 93, Lost & Found 1.25
- ❑2, Sep 93 1.25
- ❑3, Nov 93 1.25

CONSPIRACY
MARVEL

Value: Cover or less

- ❑1, Feb 98, Show & Tell 2.99
- ❑2, Mar 98, Print the Legend 2.99

CONSPIRACY COMICS
REVOLUTIONARY

Value: Cover or less

- ❑1, Oct 91, Marilyn Monroe 2.50
- ❑2, Feb 92, b&w; John F. Kennedy 2.50
- ❑3, Jul 92, b&w; Robert F. Kennedy 2.50

CONSTELLATION GRAPHICS
STAGES

Value: Cover or less

- ❑1 1.50
- ❑2 1.50

CONSTRUCT
CALIBER

	ORIG	GOOD	FINE	N-MINT
❑1	—	0.59	1.48	2.95
❑2	—	0.59	1.48	2.95
❑3	—	0.59	1.48	2.95
❑4	—	0.59	1.48	2.95
❑5	—	0.59	1.48	2.95

CONTAMINATED ZONE, THE
BRAVE NEW WORDS

Value: Cover or less

- ❑1, Apr 91, The Status of Bio-Level 5, b&w 2.50
- ❑2, b&w 2.50
- ❑3, b&w 2.50

CONTEMPORARY BIO-GRAPHICS
REVOLUTIONARY

Value: Cover or less

- ❑1, Dec 91, Don't Start the Revolution Without Smilin' Stan Lee, b&w; Stan Lee 2.50
- ❑2, Apr 92, b&w; Boris Yeltsin 2.50
- ❑3, May 92, b&w; Gene Roddenberry 2.50
- ❑4, Jun 92, Pee Wee Herman 2.50
- ❑5, Sep 92, b&w; David Lynch 2.50
- ❑6, Oct 92, Ross Perot 2.50
- ❑7, Dec 92, b&w; Spike Lee 2.50
- ❑8, Jun 93, b&w; Image story 2.50

CONTENDER COMICS SPECIAL
CONTENDER

	ORIG	GOOD	FINE	N-MINT
❑1, b&w	—	0.20	0.50	1.00

CONTEST OF CHAMPIONS II
MARVEL

Value: Cover or less

- ❑1, Sep 99, The Gathering, Iron Man vs. Psylocke; Iron Man vs. X-Force 2.50
- ❑2, Sep 99, Human Torch vs. Spider-Girl, Storm, She-Hulk; Mr. Fantastic vs. Hulk 2.50
- ❑3, Oct 99, Thor vs. Storm; Cable vs. Scarlet Witch; New Warriors vs. Slingers 2.50
- ❑4, Nov 99, Black Panther vs Captain America 2.50
- ❑5, Nov 99, Rogue vs Warbird 2.50

CONTRACTORS
ECLIPSE

Value: Cover or less

- ❑1, b&w 2.00

CONVOCATIONS-A MAGIC: THE GATHERING GALLERY
ACCLAIM

Value: Cover or less

- ❑1, Jan 95, reproduces covers from several Magic mini-series; pin-ups 2.50

COOL WORLD
DC

Value: Cover or less

- ❑1, Apr 92 1.75
- ❑2, May 92 1.75
- ❑3, Jun 92 1.75
- ❑4, Sep 92 1.75

COOL WORLD MOVIE ADAPTATION
DC

Value: Cover or less

- ❑1, nn 3.50

COP CALLED TRACY, A
AVALON

Value: Cover or less

- ❑1, Dick Tracy 2.95
- ❑2, Dick Tracy 2.95
- ❑3, Dick Tracy 2.95
- ❑4, Dick Tracy 2.95
- ❑5, Dick Tracy 2.95
- ❑6, Dick Tracy 2.95
- ❑7, Dick Tracy 2.95
- ❑8, Dick Tracy 2.95
- ❑9, Dick Tracy 2.95
- ❑10, Dick Tracy 2.95
- ❑11, Dick Tracy 2.95
- ❑12, Dick Tracy 2.95
- ❑13, Dick Tracy 2.95
- ❑14, Dick Tracy 2.95
- ❑15, Dick Tracy 2.95
- ❑16, Dick Tracy 2.95

COPS
DC

Value: Cover or less

- ❑1, Aug 88, PB, Bad Vibes, 1: COPS, Giant-size 1.50
- ❑2, Sep 88 1.00
- ❑3, Oct 88 1.00
- ❑4, Nov 88 1.00
- ❑5, Dec 88 1.00
- ❑6, Win 88, PB, Ms. Demeanor's Capital Crime, Winter, 1988 1.00
- ❑7, Hol 88, Holdays, 1988 1.00
- ❑8, Jan 89 1.00
- ❑9, Feb 89 1.00
- ❑10, Mar 89 1.00
- ❑11, Apr 89 1.00
- ❑12, May 89 1.00
- ❑13, Jun 89 1.00
- ❑14, Jul 89 1.00
- ❑15, Aug 89, Final Issue 1.00

COPS: THE JOB
MARVEL

Value: Cover or less

- ❑1, Jun 92, First Day 1.25
- ❑2, Jul 92 1.25
- ❑3, Aug 92 1.25
- ❑4, Sep 92, Repercussions 1.25

COPYBOOK TALES, THE
SLAVE LABOR

Value: Cover or less

- ❑1, Jul 96, b&w 2.95
- ❑2, Oct 96, b&w 2.95
- ❑3, Jan 97, b&w 2.95
- ❑4, Apr 97, b&w 2.95
- ❑5, Jul 97, b&w 2.95
- ❑6, Aug 97, Cover swipe of X-Men (1st Series) #141 2.95

CORBEN SPECIAL, A
PACIFIC

Value: Cover or less

- ❑1, Adapted From Edgar Allan Poe 1.50

CORBO
SWORD IN STONE

Value: Cover or less

- ❑1 1.75

CORMAC MAC ART
DARK HORSE

Value: Cover or less

- ❑1, Jul 89, b&w 1.95
- ❑2, Aug 89, b&w 1.95
- ❑3, Mar 90, b&w 1.95
- ❑4, Apr 90, b&w 1.95

CORNY'S FETISH
DARK HORSE

Value: Cover or less

- ❑1, Apr 98, nn; b&w; One-Shot 4.95

CORPORATE CRIME COMICS
KITCHEN SINK

	ORIG	GOOD	FINE	N-MINT
❑1	—	0.50	1.25	2.50
❑2	—	0.50	1.25	2.50

CORTEZ AND THE FALL OF THE AZTECS
TOME

Value: Cover or less

- ❑1, b&w 2.95
- ❑2, b&w 2.95

CORUM: THE BULL AND THE SPEAR
FIRST

Value: Cover or less

- ❑1, The Past Through Tomorrow 1.95
- ❑2 1.95
- ❑3 1.95
- ❑4 1.95

CORVUS REX: A LEGACY OF SHADOWS
CROW

Value: Cover or less

- ❑1, Feb 96, nn; b&w; Prologue 1.95

COSMIC BOOK, THE
ACE

Value: Cover or less

❑1, Encounter; Tonango's Folly........ 1.95

COSMIC BOY
DC

	ORIG	GOOD	FINE	N-MINT
❑1, Dec 86, KG, Those Who Will Not Learn The Lessons Of History, Legends Spin-Off, Part 4	0.75	0.20	0.50	1.00
❑2, Jan 87, Legends Spin-Off, Part 8	0.75	0.20	0.50	1.00
❑3, Feb 87, Legends Spin-Off, Part 13	0.75	0.20	0.50	1.00
❑4, Mar 87, V: Time Trapper, Legends Spin-Off, Part 20	0.75	0.20	0.50	1.00

COSMIC HEROES
ETERNITY

Value: Cover or less

❑1, b&w; Buck Rogers........ 1.95
❑2, b&w; Buck Rogers........ 1.95
❑3, b&w; Buck Rogers........ 1.95
❑4, b&w; Buck Rogers........ 1.95
❑5, b&w; Buck Rogers........ 1.95
❑6, b&w; Buck Rogers........ 1.95
❑7........ 2.25
❑8........ 2.25
❑9........ 2.95
❑10........ 3.50
❑11........ 3.95

COSMIC KLITI
FANTAGRAPHICS

Value: Cover or less

❑1, GM, b&w; adult........ 2.25

COSMIC ODYSSEY
DC

Value: Cover or less

❑1, Nov 88, JSn (w), Discovery, V: Darkseid; A: Superman, Batman........ 3.50
❑2, Dec 88, JSn (w)........ 3.50
❑3, Dec 88, JSn (w), Decisions........ 3.50
❑4, Jan 89, JSn (w)........ 3.50

COSMIC POWERS
MARVEL

Value: Cover or less

❑1, Mar 94, Thanos........ 2.50
❑2, Apr 94, Terrax........ 2.50
❑3, May 94, Jack of Hearts & Ganymede........ 2.50
❑4, Jun 94, Legacy........ 2.50
❑5, Jul 94, Morg........ 2.50
❑6, Aug 94, Final Issue; Tyrant........ 2.50

COSMIC POWERS UNLIMITED
MARVEL

Value: Cover or less

❑1, May 95, A: Captain Marvel I (Mar-Vell)........ 3.95
❑2, Aug 95, cover says Sep; indicia says Aug........ 3.95
❑3, Dec 95........ 3.95
❑4, Feb 96........ 3.95
❑5, May 96........ 3.95

COSMIC RAY
IMAGE

Value: Cover or less

❑1/A, Jun 99, The Resurection of Cosmic Ray, green sunglasses cover........ 2.95
❑1/B, Jun 99, Murderer or Hero cover........ 2.95
❑2, Aug 99........ 2.95
❑3........ 2.95

COSMIC STELLER REBELLERS
HAMMAC

Value: Cover or less

❑1........ 1.50
❑2........ 1.50

COUGAR, THE
ATLAS

	ORIG	GOOD	FINE	N-MINT
❑1, Apr 75	0.25	0.40	1.00	2.00
❑2, Jul 75, O: Cougar	0.25	0.40	1.00	2.00

COUNTDOWN
WILDSTORM

Value: Cover or less

❑1, Jun 00........ 2.95
❑2, Jul 00........ 2.95
❑3, Aug 00........ 2.95
❑4, Sep 00........ 2.95
❑5, Oct 00........ 2.95
❑6, Nov 00........ 2.95
❑7, Dec 00........ 2.95
❑8, Jan 01........ 2.95

COUNT DUCKULA
MARVEL

	ORIG	GOOD	FINE	N-MINT
❑1, Jan 89, O: Count Duckula	1.00	0.30	0.75	1.50
❑2, Feb 89	1.00	0.20	0.50	1.00
❑3, Mar 89, Love at First Bite; Danger Mouse...A Twisted Tail, A: Penfold; 1: Danger Mouse	1.00	0.20	0.50	1.00
❑4, Apr 89, Danger Mouse	1.00	0.20	0.50	1.00
❑5, May 89, Danger Mouse	1.00	0.20	0.50	1.00
❑6, Jun 89, Danger Mouse	1.00	0.20	0.50	1.00
❑7, Jul 89, Danger Mouse	1.00	0.20	0.50	1.00
❑8, Aug 89, Geraldo Rivera	1.00	0.20	0.50	1.00
❑9, Sep 89	1.00	0.20	0.50	1.00
❑10, Oct 89	1.00	0.20	0.50	1.00
❑11, Nov 89	1.00	0.20	0.50	1.00
❑12, Dec 89	1.00	0.20	0.50	1.00
❑13, Jan 90	1.00	0.20	0.50	1.00
❑14, Feb 90	1.00	0.20	0.50	1.00
❑15, Mar 90	1.00	0.20	0.50	1.00

In the four-issue *Cosmic Boy* mini-series, Cosmic Boy attempted to reconcile several time anomalies caused by the 1986 revamp of Superman's origin.

COUNTERPARTS
TUNDRA

Value: Cover or less

❑1, Jan 93, The Sum of the Parts, b&w........ 2.95
❑2, Mar 93, b&w........ 2.95
❑3........ 2.95

COUPLE OF WINOS, A
FANTAGRAPHICS

Value: Cover or less

❑1, b&w........ 2.25

COURAGEOUS MAN ADVENTURES
MOORDAM

Value: Cover or less

❑1, b&w; Mr. Beat back-up........ 2.95
❑2, Spunky's Evil Twin!; The Security Secrets of the Silo of Sanctuary!, b&w........ 2.95
❑3........ 2.95

COUTOO
DARK HORSE

Value: Cover or less

❑1, nn; b&w; One-Shot........ 3.50

COVEN, THE
AWESOME

	ORIG	GOOD	FINE	N-MINT
❑1/A, JPH (w), Murder in the First, "Butt" cover	2.50	0.60	1.50	3.00
❑1/B, JPH (w), Murder in the First, Man with flaming hands on cover; Red border	2.50	0.80	2.00	4.00
❑1/C, JPH (w), Murder in the First, "Wizard Authentic" cover; Signed by Jeph Loeb	2.50	1.20	3.00	6.00
❑1/D, JPH (w), Murder in the First, Team on cover; White border	2.50	0.60	1.50	3.00
❑1/E, JPH (w), Murder in the First, Chromium cover otherwise same as 1/A; Dynamic Forces edition	2.50	1.00	2.50	5.00
❑1/F, JPH (w), Murder in the First, 1ø Edition; Flip book with Kaboom 1+	2.50	0.80	2.00	4.00
❑1/G, JPH (w), Murder in the First, "Flame Hands" cover	—	1.00	2.50	5.00
❑1-2, JPH (w), Murder in the First, "Fan Appreciation Edition"; Is really 2nd Printing	2.50	0.50	1.25	2.50
❑2, JPH (w)	2.50	0.80	2.00	4.00
❑2/GO, JPH (w), Gold edition limited to 5000 copies	—	1.00	2.50	5.00
❑3, JPH (w)	2.50	0.60	1.50	3.00
❑3/A, JPH (w), Red foil logo on cover; Signed by Loeb and Churchill	—	0.80	2.00	4.00
❑4, JPH (w)	2.50	0.60	1.50	3.00
❑5, JPH (w)	2.50	0.60	1.50	3.00
❑5/A, JPH (w), Variant cover, woman, ghouls standing in water	—	0.60	1.50	3.00
❑6, JPH (w)	2.50	0.50	1.25	2.50

COVEN, THE (VOL. 2)
AWESOME

	ORIG	GOOD	FINE	N-MINT
❑1, Aug 97, JPH (w), regular cover; Woman with glowing gloves facing forward	2.50	0.50	1.25	2.50
❑1/A, JPH (w), Two team-members flying on cover with white Coven logo; Chrome ("Covenchrome") edition with certificate of authenticity	—	1.00	2.50	5.00
❑1/B, JPH (w), Variant "scratch" cover by Ian Churchill	—	0.60	1.50	3.00
❑1/C, JPH (w), Gold edition	—	0.60	1.50	3.00
❑1/D, JPH (w), "Spellcaster" cover by Rob Liefeld	—	0.60	1.50	3.00
❑1/E, Aug 97, JPH (w), "Black Mass" cover by Ian Churchill	2.50	0.50	1.25	2.50
❑1/F, JPH (w), Dynamic Forces exclusive cover with two women surfing	—	0.80	2.00	4.00
❑2, JPH (w)	2.50	0.50	1.25	2.50
❑3, JPH (w)	2.50	0.50	1.25	2.50
❑4, JPH (w)	2.50	0.50	1.25	2.50

COVEN 13
NO MERCY

Value: Cover or less

❑1, Aug 97........ 2.50

COVEN: DARK ORIGINS
AWESOME

Value: Cover or less

❑1........ 2.50

COVEN, THE: FANTOM
AWESOME

	ORIG	GOOD	FINE	N-MINT
❑1, JPH (w)	—	0.60	1.50	3.00
❑1/GO, JPH (w), Gold logo	—	0.80	2.00	4.00

COVEN OF ANGELS
Jitterbug

	ORIG	GOOD	FINE	N-MINT
❑1, Nov 95	2.95	1.00	2.50	5.00
❑2, Buffalo Girls; Clown Story	2.95	1.20	3.00	6.00
❑Ash 1, Ashcan edition with Linsner cover	—	2.00	5.00	10.00

COVENTRY
Fantagraphics

Value: Cover or less

- ❑1, Nov 96, The Frogs of God, b&w; cardstock cover 3.95
- ❑2, Mar 97, Thirteen Dead Guys Named Bob, b&w; cardstock cover 3.95
- ❑3, Jul 97, Later That Same Day, b&w; cardstock cover 3.95

COW
MonsterPants

Value: Cover or less

- ❑1, Galactic Glamour; The Puppeteer 1.99
- ❑2 .... 1.99
- ❑3 .... 1.99

COW-BOY
Ogre Press

Value: Cover or less

- ❑1, O: Cow-Boy, b&w 4.00

COWBOY LOVE
Avalon

Value: Cover or less

- ❑1, b&w; Reprint 2.95

COYOTE
Marvel

	ORIG	GOOD	FINE	N-MINT
❑1, Apr 83, O: Coyote	1.50	0.50	1.25	2.50
❑2, Jun 83	1.50	0.40	1.00	2.00
❑3, Sep 83	1.50	0.40	1.00	2.00
❑4, Jan 84	1.50	0.30	0.75	1.50
❑5, Apr 84	1.50	0.30	0.75	1.50
❑6, Jun 84	1.50	0.30	0.75	1.50
❑7, Jul 84, SD	1.50	0.30	0.75	1.50
❑8, Oct 84, SD	1.50	0.30	0.75	1.50
❑9, Dec 84, SD	1.50	0.30	0.75	1.50
❑10, Jan 85	1.50	0.30	0.75	1.50
❑11, Mar 85, TMc, 1st Todd McFarlane art	1.50	0.50	1.25	2.50
❑12, May 85, TMc	1.50	0.40	1.00	2.00
❑13, Jul 85, TMc	1.50	0.40	1.00	2.00
❑14, Sep 85, TMc, A: Badger	1.50	0.30	0.75	1.50
❑15, Nov 85	1.50	0.30	0.75	1.50
❑16, Jan 86	1.50	0.30	0.75	1.50

CRABBS
Cat-Head

Value: Cover or less

- ❑1, b&w 3.75

CRACK BUSTERS
Showcase

Value: Cover or less

- ❑1 .... 1.95
- ❑2, Enter: The Mechanic! 1.95

CRAP
Fantagraphics

Value: Cover or less

- ❑1, Aug 93 .... 2.50
- ❑2, Nov 93 .... 2.50
- ❑3, Feb 94 .... 2.50
- ❑4, May 94 .... 2.50
- ❑5, Aug 94 .... 2.50

CRASH DUMMIES
Harvey

Value: Cover or less

- ❑1 .... 1.50
- ❑2 .... 1.50
- ❑3, Jun 94, The Space Dummies; My Daddy The Junkman 1.50

CRASH METRO & THE STAR SQUAD
Oni Press

Value: Cover or less

- ❑1, May 99, b&w 2.95

CRASH RYAN
Marvel

Value: Cover or less

- ❑1, Oct 84, Doomsday Eve 1.50
- ❑2, Nov 84, Doomsday 1.50
- ❑3, Dec 84, Fortress Japan! 1.50
- ❑4, Jan 85, The Final Battle! 1.50

CRAY BABY ADVENTURES SPECIAL, THE
Electric Milk

Value: Cover or less

- ❑1 .... 2.95

CRAY-BABY ADVENTURES, THE: WRATH OF THE PEDIDDLERS
Destination Entertainment

Value: Cover or less

- ❑1, b&w 2.95

CRAZY
Marvel

	ORIG	GOOD	FINE	N-MINT
❑1, Feb 73, reprints Not Brand Ecch	0.20	2.40	6.00	12.00
❑2, Apr 73, reprints Not Brand Ecch	0.20	1.40	3.50	7.00
❑3, Jun 73, Final Issue; reprints Not Brand Ecch	0.20	1.40	3.50	7.00

CRAZY (MAGAZINE)
Marvel

	ORIG	GOOD	FINE	N-MINT
❑1	0.40	2.00	5.00	10.00
❑2	0.40	1.20	3.00	6.00
❑3	0.40	1.00	2.50	5.00
❑4	0.40	1.00	2.50	5.00
❑5	0.40	1.00	2.50	5.00
❑6	0.40	0.60	1.50	3.00
❑7	0.40	0.60	1.50	3.00
❑8	0.50	0.60	1.50	3.00
❑9	0.50	0.60	1.50	3.00
❑10	0.50	0.60	1.50	3.00
❑11	0.50	0.60	1.50	3.00
❑12	0.50	0.60	1.50	3.00
❑13	0.50	0.60	1.50	3.00
❑14	0.50	0.60	1.50	3.00
❑15	0.50	0.60	1.50	3.00
❑16	0.50	0.40	1.00	2.00
❑17	0.50	0.40	1.00	2.00
❑18	0.50	0.40	1.00	2.00
❑19	0.50	0.40	1.00	2.00
❑20	—	0.40	1.00	2.00
❑21	—	0.30	0.75	1.50
❑22	—	0.30	0.75	1.50
❑23	—	0.30	0.75	1.50
❑24	—	0.30	0.75	1.50
❑25	—	0.30	0.75	1.50
❑26	—	0.30	0.75	1.50
❑27	—	0.30	0.75	1.50
❑28	—	0.30	0.75	1.50
❑29	—	0.30	0.75	1.50
❑30	—	0.30	0.75	1.50
❑31	—	0.30	0.75	1.50
❑32	—	0.30	0.75	1.50
❑33	—	0.30	0.75	1.50
❑34	—	0.30	0.75	1.50
❑35	—	0.30	0.75	1.50
❑36	—	0.30	0.75	1.50
❑37	—	0.30	0.75	1.50
❑38	—	0.30	0.75	1.50
❑39	—	0.30	0.75	1.50
❑40	—	0.30	0.75	1.50
❑41	—	0.30	0.75	1.50
❑42	—	0.30	0.75	1.50
❑43	—	0.30	0.75	1.50
❑44	—	0.30	0.75	1.50
❑45	—	0.30	0.75	1.50
❑46	—	0.30	0.75	1.50
❑47	—	0.30	0.75	1.50
❑48	—	0.30	0.75	1.50
❑49	—	0.30	0.75	1.50
❑50	—	0.30	0.75	1.50
❑51	—	0.30	0.75	1.50
❑52	—	0.30	0.75	1.50
❑53	—	0.30	0.75	1.50
❑54	—	0.30	0.75	1.50
❑55	—	0.30	0.75	1.50
❑56	—	0.30	0.75	1.50
❑57	—	0.30	0.75	1.50
❑58	—	0.30	0.75	1.50
❑59	—	0.30	0.75	1.50
❑60	—	0.30	0.75	1.50
❑61	—	0.30	0.75	1.50
❑62	—	0.30	0.75	1.50
❑63	—	0.30	0.75	1.50
❑64	—	0.30	0.75	1.50
❑65	—	0.30	0.75	1.50
❑66, Sep 80, Empire Strikes Back parody	—	0.30	0.75	1.50
❑67	—	0.30	0.75	1.50
❑68	—	0.30	0.75	1.50
❑69	—	0.30	0.75	1.50
❑70	—	0.30	0.75	1.50
❑71	—	0.30	0.75	1.50
❑72	—	0.30	0.75	1.50
❑73	—	0.30	0.75	1.50
❑74	—	0.30	0.75	1.50
❑75	—	0.30	0.75	1.50
❑76	—	0.30	0.75	1.50
❑77	—	0.30	0.75	1.50
❑78	—	0.30	0.75	1.50
❑79	—	0.30	0.75	1.50
❑80	0.90	0.30	0.75	1.50
❑81	0.90	0.30	0.75	1.50
❑82	1.25	0.30	0.75	1.50
❑83, Feb 81, Raiders of the Lost Ark parody	0.90	0.30	0.75	1.50
❑84	0.90	0.30	0.75	1.50
❑85	1.25	0.30	0.75	1.50
❑86	0.90	0.30	0.75	1.50
❑87	0.90	0.30	0.75	1.50
❑88	0.90	0.30	0.75	1.50
❑89	0.90	0.30	0.75	1.50

	ORIG	GOOD	FINE	N-MINT
❑90	0.90	0.30	0.75	1.50
❑91, Oct 82, Blade Runner parody	1.25	0.30	0.75	1.50
❑92, Dec 82, Star Trek II parody	1.25	0.30	0.75	1.50
❑93	1.25	0.30	0.75	1.50
❑94	1.25	0.30	0.75	1.50

CRAZY BOB
BLACKBIRD

Value: Cover or less
- ❑1, b&w ... 2.75
- ❑2, b&w ... 2.00

CRAZYFISH PREVIEW
CRAZYFISH

	ORIG	GOOD	FINE	N-MINT
❑1	—	0.10	0.25	0.50
❑2, Soulwind; Supermodels Don't Know Kung Fu	—	0.10	0.25	0.50

CRAZYMAN
CONTINUITY

Value: Cover or less
- ❑1, Apr 92, enhanced cover ... 3.95
- ❑2, May 92, BB, NA (c) ... 2.50
- ❑3, Jul 92 ... 2.50

CRAZYMAN (2ND SERIES)
CONTINUITY

Value: Cover or less
- ❑1, May 93, Die-cut comic book 3.95
- ❑2, Dec 93 ... 2.50
- ❑3, Dec 93 ... 2.50
- ❑4, Jan 94, indicia says #3 ... 2.50

CREATURE
ANTARCTIC

Value: Cover or less
- ❑1, Oct 97, A Deadly Silence, b&w ... 2.95
- ❑2, Dec 97, All Hell, b&w ... 2.95

CREATURE COMMANDOS
DC

Value: Cover or less
- ❑1, May 00, A Spear of Silence 2.50
- ❑2, Jun 00, From Here to Heaven is a Scar ... 2.50
- ❑3, Jul 00 ... 2.50
- ❑4, Aug 00 ... 2.50
- ❑5, Sep 00 ... 2.50
- ❑6, Oct 00, The Last Wall of the Castle ... 2.50
- ❑7, Nov 00, The Other Side of this Life ... 2.50
- ❑8, Dec 00, War Movie ... 2.50

CREATURE FEATURES
MOJO

Value: Cover or less
- ❑1, b&w; prestige format one-shot ... 4.95

CREATURE FEATURES (ART ADAMS'...)
DARK HORSE

Value: Cover or less
- ❑1, Aug 96, nn; Trade Paperback ... 13.95

CREATURES OF THE ID
CALIBER

	ORIG	GOOD	FINE	N-MINT
❑1, 1: Madman (Frank Einstein), b&w	2.95	3.00	7.50	15.00

CREATURES ON THE LOOSE
MARVEL

	ORIG	GOOD	FINE	N-MINT
❑10, Mar 71, JK; BWr, The Skull of Silence; Trull! The Inhuman!, Title changes to Creatures on the Loose; first King Kull story; Series continued from Tower of Shadows #9	0.15	3.00	7.50	15.00
❑11, May 71, Reprint	0.15	0.60	1.50	3.00
❑12, Jul 71, Reprint	0.15	0.60	1.50	3.00
❑13, Sep 71, Reprint	0.15	0.60	1.50	3.00
❑14, Nov 71, Reprint	0.20	0.60	1.50	3.00
❑15, Jan 72, Reprint	0.20	0.60	1.50	3.00
❑16, Mar 72, GK, Warrior of Mars, O: Gullivar Jones, Warrior of Mars	0.20	0.60	1.50	3.00
❑17, May 72, GK, River Of The Dead!, A: Gullivar Jones, Warrior of Mars	0.20	0.60	1.50	3.00
❑18, Jul 72, RA, Wasteland...On A Weirdling World!, A: Gullivar Jones, Warrior of Mars	0.20	0.60	1.50	3.00
❑19, Sep 72, JM, The Long Road to Nowhere!, A: Gullivar Jones, Warrior of Mars	0.20	0.60	1.50	3.00
❑20, Nov 72, GM, What Price Victory?, A: Gullivar Jones, Warrior of Mars	0.20	0.80	2.00	4.00
❑21, Jan 73, A: Gullivar Jones, Warrior of Mars	0.20	0.80	2.00	4.00
❑22, Mar 73, A: Thongor	0.20	0.60	1.50	3.00
❑23, May 73, VM, Where Broods the Demon!, A: Thongor	0.20	0.60	1.50	3.00
❑24, Jul 73, VM, Red Swords, Black Wings!, A: Thongor	0.20	0.60	1.50	3.00
❑25, Sep 73, VM, The Wizard of Lemuria!, A: Thongor	0.20	0.60	1.50	3.00
❑26, Nov 73, VM, Tower of the Serpent Women!, A: Thongor	0.20	0.60	1.50	3.00
❑27, Jan 74, VM, In the Crypts of Yamath!, A: Thongor	0.20	0.60	1.50	3.00
❑28, Mar 74, Mountain Thunder!, A: Thongor	0.20	0.60	1.50	3.00
❑29, May 74, Lord of Chaos!, A: Thongor	0.25	0.60	1.50	3.00
❑30, Jul 74, A: Man-Wolf	0.25	0.60	1.50	3.00
❑31, Sep 74, GT, The Beast Within!, A: Man-Wolf	0.25	0.60	1.50	3.00
❑32, Nov 74, A: Man-Wolf	0.25	0.60	1.50	3.00
❑33, Jan 75, A: Man-Wolf	0.25	0.60	1.50	3.00

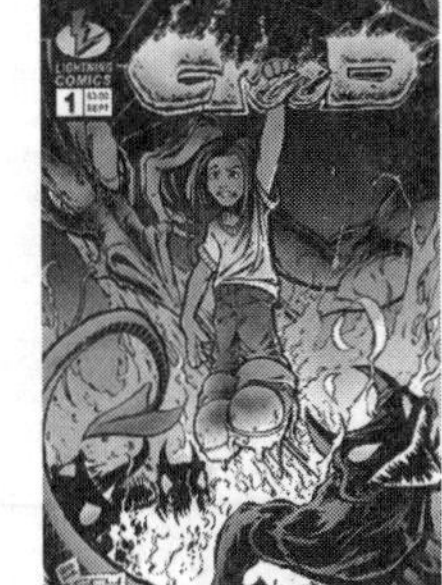

CreeD told the fantasy adventures of a boy and his frog.

© 1995 Trent Kaniuga (Lightning)

	ORIG	GOOD	FINE	N-MINT
❑34, Mar 75, A: Man-Wolf	0.25	0.60	1.50	3.00
❑35, May 75, A: Man-Wolf	0.25	0.60	1.50	3.00
❑36, Jul 75, A: Man-Wolf	0.25	0.60	1.50	3.00
❑37, Sep 75, A: Man-Wolf	0.25	0.60	1.50	3.00
❑KS 1, King-size special	—	1.00	2.50	5.00

CREECH, THE
IMAGE

Value: Cover or less
- ❑1, Oct 97, A Vision of Death, O: Creech ... 1.95
- ❑1/A, Oct 97, alternate cover .. 1.95
- ❑2, Nov 97, Awakening ... 2.50
- ❑3, Dec 97, The Resurrection . 2.50

CREED (1ST SERIES)
HALL OF HEROES

	ORIG	GOOD	FINE	N-MINT
❑1	—	1.00	2.50	5.00
❑2, Dec 94, Heaven Seed	—	0.80	2.00	4.00

CREED (2ND SERIES)
LIGHTNING

	ORIG	GOOD	FINE	N-MINT
❑1, Sep 95, b&w; reprints Hall of Heroes #1 and #2 with corrections; Black and white	3.00	0.55	1.38	2.75
❑1/A, full color	3.00	0.60	1.50	3.00
❑1/B, Purple edition	3.00	0.60	1.50	3.00
❑1/PL, Sep 95, enhanced cover; Platinum edition; Collector's edition	3.00	0.80	2.00	4.00
❑2, Jan 96	3.00	0.60	1.50	3.00
❑2/PL, Jan 96, alternate cover; Platinum edition	3.00	1.99	4.97	9.95
❑3, Jul 96, bagged with trading card	3.00	0.60	1.50	3.00
❑3/PL, Platinum edition	3.00	0.60	1.50	3.00

CREED: CRANIAL DISORDER
LIGHTNING

	ORIG	GOOD	FINE	N-MINT
❑1, Nov 96	—	0.60	1.50	3.00
❑2, Nov 96, alternate cover, cover says Dec, indicia says Nov	3.00	0.60	1.50	3.00
❑3, Apr 97, alternate cover	2.95	0.60	1.50	3.00

CREED: MECHANICAL EVOLUTION
GEARBOX

Value: Cover or less
- ❑1, Sep 00 ... 2.95

CREED/TEENAGE MUTANT NINJA TURTLES
LIGHTNING

Value: Cover or less
- ❑1, May 96, Dream Stone ... 3.00

CREED: THE GOOD SHIP AND THE NEW JOURNEY HOME
LIGHTNING

Value: Cover or less
- ❑1, Jul 97, b&w ... 2.95

CREED USE YOUR DELUSION
AVATAR

Value: Cover or less
- ❑1, Jan 98 ... 3.00
- ❑2 ... 3.00

CREEPER, THE
DC

Value: Cover or less
- ❑1, Dec 97, Screaming to Get Out ... 2.50
- ❑2, Jan 98 ... 2.50
- ❑3, Feb 98 ... 2.50
- ❑4, Mar 98 ... 2.50
- ❑5, Apr 98 ... 2.50
- ❑6, May 98 ... 2.50
- ❑7, Jun 98, V: Joker ... 2.50
- ❑8, Jul 98, A: Batman ... 2.50
- ❑9, Aug 98 ... 2.50
- ❑10, Sep 98 ... 2.50
- ❑11, Oct 98 ... 2.50
- ❑1000000, Nov 98, Insanitation, Final Issue ... 2.50

CREEPSVILLE
GO-GO

	ORIG	GOOD	FINE	N-MINT
❑1, Creepsville; Invasion of the Martianmen, b&w; trading cards	2.95	0.59	1.48	2.95
❑2, b&w; trading cards	2.95	0.59	1.48	2.95
❑3	2.25	0.59	1.48	2.95
❑4	2.25	0.59	1.48	2.95
❑5	2.25	0.59	1.48	2.95

CREEPY TALES
PINNACLE

Value: Cover or less
- ❑1, The Dinosaur Doctor; Hounded ... 1.75

CREEPY: THE LIMITED SERIES
DARK HORSE

	ORIG	GOOD	FINE	N-MINT
❑1, b&w; prestige format	3.95	0.80	2.00	4.00
❑2, KB (w), b&w; prestige format	3.95	0.80	2.00	4.00

	ORIG	GOOD	FINE	N-MINT
❑3, RHo (w), The Cast Without a Program; Fair Ground, b&w; prestige format	3.95	0.80	2.00	4.00
❑4, b&w; prestige format	3.95	0.80	2.00	4.00
❑FB 1993, KB (w), A: Vampirella, 1993 "Fear-book"; Relaunch of Vampirella for '90s	3.95	2.40	6.00	12.00

CREMATOR
CHAOS
Value: Cover or less

- ❑1, Dec 98, Welcome to Hell!. 2.95
- ❑2, Dec 99, wraparound cover 2.95
- ❑3, Jan 99 2.95
- ❑4, Feb 99 2.95
- ❑5, Apr 99 2.95

CRESCENT
B-LINE

	ORIG	GOOD	FINE	N-MINT
❑0, May 96	—	0.20	0.50	1.00

CRIME & JUSTICE
AVALON
Value: Cover or less

- ❑1, Mar 98, b&w; Reprint 2.95

CRIME AND PUNISHMENT MARSHAL LAW TAKES MANHATTAN
MARVEL
Value: Cover or less

- ❑1, nn; One-Shot; prestige format 4.95

CRIMEBUSTER
AC
Value: Cover or less

- ❑0, Back From The Dead-Again! 2.95

CRIMEBUSTER CLASSICS
AC
Value: Cover or less

- ❑1 3.50

CRIME CLASSICS
ETERNITY
Value: Cover or less

- ❑1, Jul 88, The Riddle of the Sealed Box, The Shadow ... 1.95
- ❑2, Jul 88, The Shadow 1.95
- ❑3, Aug 88, The Shadow 1.95
- ❑4, Sep 89, The Shadow 1.95
- ❑5, Jan 89, The Shadow 1.95
- ❑6, Feb 89, The Shadow 1.95
- ❑7, Mar 89, The Shadow 1.95
- ❑8, Apr 89, The Shadow 1.95
- ❑9, May 89, The Shadow 1.95
- ❑10, Jun 89, The Shadow 1.95
- ❑11, Aug 89, The Shadow 1.95
- ❑12, Sep 89, The Shadow 2.25
- ❑13, Oct 89, The Shadow 2.25

CRIME CLINIC
SLAVE LABOR
Value: Cover or less

- ❑1, Nov 95 2.95
- ❑2, May 95 2.95

CRIME PATROL (GEMSTONE)
GEMSTONE
Value: Cover or less

- ❑1, Apr 00, JCr, Captain Crime!; Death by Rocket Bomb!, Reprints Crime Patrol #1 (#7) 2.50
- ❑2, May 00, The Deadly Grease Monkey; The Alibi, Reprints Crime Patrol #2 (#8) 2.50
- ❑3, Jun 00, JCr; AF, JCr (w); AF (w), The Slaughter Syndicate; Madelon, Reprints Crime Patrol #3 (#9) 2.50
- ❑4, Jul 00, AF, AF (w), Dance-Hall Racket; The Ace of Spades, Reprints Crime Patrol #4 2.50
- ❑5, AF, AF (w), Kidnappers; The Werewolf's Curse!, Reprints Crime Patrol #5 2.50
- ❑Anl 1, Collects issues #1-5 13.50

CRIME PAYS
BONEYARD
Value: Cover or less

- ❑1, Oct 96, A: Bill the Bull, b&w; Anthology 3.95
- ❑2, Sep 97, Bar Slut; Crime Pays 2.95

CRIME-SMASHER (BLUE COMET)
BLUE COMET

	ORIG	GOOD	FINE	N-MINT
❑SE 1, Jul 87, Genesis 27	1.80	0.40	1.00	2.00

CRIME SUSPENSTORIES (RCP)
EC

	ORIG	GOOD	FINE	N-MINT
❑1, Nov 92, GI; WW; JCr; HK, GI (w); WW (w); JCr (w); HK (w), Murder May Boomerang; Reward (text story), Reprints Crime SuspenStories (EC) #1	1.50	0.40	1.00	2.00
❑2, Nov 93, Dead Ringer; A Moment of Madness, Reprints Crime SuspenStories (EC) #2	1.50	0.40	1.00	2.00
❑3, Feb 93, Poison; The Giggling Killer, Edgar Allen Poe adaptation: "Blood Red Wine" (adapts "The Cask of Amontillado"); Reprints Crime SuspenStories (EC) #3	1.50	0.40	1.00	2.00
❑4, May 93, JKa; JCr, JKa (w); JCr (w), Backlash; Premium Overdue, Reprints Crime SuspenStories (EC) #4	2.00	0.40	1.00	2.00
❑5, Aug 93, The Sewer; Mr. Biddy...Lady Killer, Reprints Crime SuspenStories (EC) #5	2.00	0.40	1.00	2.00
❑6, Nov 94, A Toast...To Death!; Out of my Mind!, Reprints Crime SuspenStories (EC) #6	2.00	0.40	1.00	2.00
❑7, Feb 94, Hatchet-Killer!; Revenge!, Reprints Crime SuspenStories (EC) #7	2.00	0.40	1.00	2.00
❑8, May 94, Out of the Frying Pan...; A Trace of Murder!, Reprints Crime SuspenStories (EC) #8	2.00	0.40	1.00	2.00
❑9, Aug 94, Understudy to a Corpse!; Medicine!, Reprints Crime SuspenStories (EC) #9	2.00	0.40	1.00	2.00
❑10, Nov 95, ...Rocks in His Head!; Lady Killer, Reprints Crime SuspenStories (EC) #10	2.00	0.40	1.00	2.00
❑11, Feb 95, Stiff Punishment!; One Man's Poison!, Reprints Crime SuspenStories (EC) #11	2.00	0.40	1.00	2.00
❑12, May 95, The Execution!; Murder the Lover!, Reprints Crime SuspenStories (EC) #12	2.00	0.40	1.00	2.00
❑13, Aug 95, Hear no Evil!; First Impulse!, Reprints Crime SuspenStories (EC) #13	2.00	0.40	1.00	2.00
❑14, Nov 96, Sweet Dreams!; The Perfect Place!, Reprints Crime SuspenStories (EC) #14	2.00	0.40	1.00	2.00
❑15, Feb 96, When the Cat's Away...; The Screaming Woman!, "The Screaming Woman" Ray Bradbury adaptation; Ray Bradbury story; Reprints Crime SuspenStories (EC) #15	2.00	0.40	1.00	2.00
❑16, May 96, JKa; JCr; JO; AW, JKa (w); JCr (w); JO (w); AW (w), Rendezvous!; Fission Bait!, Reprints Crime SuspenStories (EC) #16	2.50	0.50	1.25	2.50
❑17, Aug 96, JKa; BE; FF; JCr; AW, JKa (w); BE (w); FF (w); JCr (w); AW (w), Touch and Go!; One for the Money..., Ray Bradbury adaptation, "Touch and Go!"; Ray Bradbury story; Reprints Crime SuspenStories (EC) #17	2.50	0.50	1.25	2.50
❑18, Nov 97, BE; JCr, BE (w); JCr (w), Fall Guy for Murder; Juice for the Record!, Reprints Crime SuspenStories (EC) #18	2.50	0.50	1.25	2.50
❑19, Feb 97, JCr; GE, JCr (w); GE (w), The Killer; Wined-Up!, Reprints Crime SuspenStories (EC) #19	2.50	0.50	1.25	2.50
❑20, May 97, Reprints Crime SuspenStories (EC) #20	2.50	0.50	1.25	2.50
❑21, Aug 97, Reprints Crime SuspenStories (EC) #21	2.50	0.50	1.25	2.50
❑22, Nov 98, Reprints Crime SuspenStories (EC) #22	2.50	0.50	1.25	2.50
❑23, Feb 98, Reprints Crime SuspenStories (EC) #23	2.50	0.50	1.25	2.50
❑24, May 98, BK; JO, Double-Crossed; Crushed Ice, Reprints Crime SuspenStories (EC) #24	2.50	0.50	1.25	2.50
❑25, Aug 98, BK; GE, Three for the Money; Dog Food, Reprints Crime SuspenStories (EC) #25	2.50	0.50	1.25	2.50
❑26, Nov 99, JO, The Fixer; Dead Center, Reprints Crime SuspenStories (EC) #26	2.50	0.50	1.25	2.50
❑27, Feb 99, GI; JKa; BK; GE, Maniac at Large; Just Her Speed, Reprints Crime SuspenStories (EC) #27	2.50	0.50	1.25	2.50
❑Anl 1, Reprints Crime SuspenStories (EC) #1-5	8.95	1.79	4.47	8.95
❑Anl 2, Reprints Crime SuspenStories (EC) #6-10	9.95	1.99	4.97	9.95
❑Anl 3, Reprints Crime SuspenStories (EC) #11-15	9.95	1.99	4.97	9.95
❑Anl 4, Reprints Crime SuspenStories (EC) #15-19	10.50	2.10	5.25	10.50
❑Anl 5, Reprints Crime SuspenStories (EC) #20-23	10.95	2.19	5.47	10.95
❑Anl 6, Reprints Crime SuspenStories (EC) #24-27	10.95	2.19	5.47	10.95

CRIMSON
IMAGE

	ORIG	GOOD	FINE	N-MINT
❑1, Dawn to Dusk, Several figures on cover, one in cowboy hat smoking	2.50	0.70	1.75	3.50
❑1/A, May 98, Dawn to Dusk, Boy covered in blood/rain	2.50	0.70	1.75	3.50
❑1/B, May 98, chromium cover; Three figures on ledge	2.50	3.00	7.50	15.00
❑1/C, May 98, chromium cover; Dynamic Forces chromium edition with certificate of authenticity; Boy in graveyard	2.50	3.00	7.50	15.00
❑2, May 98, Unlife Story	2.50	0.60	1.50	3.00
❑2/A, Jun 98, Unlife Story, alternate cover (vampire)	2.50	3.00	7.50	15.00
❑2/B, Unlife Story, Crimson chrome edition	—	3.00	7.50	15.00
❑3, Jun 98, Payment in Blood	2.50	0.60	1.50	3.00
❑3/A, Jul 98, alternate cover (red background)	2.50	0.80	2.00	4.00
❑4, Jul 98, The Children of Judas, Part 1	2.50	0.50	1.25	2.50
❑5, Aug 98, The Children of Judas, Part 2	2.50	0.50	1.25	2.50
❑6, Sep 98, The Children of Judas, Part 3, Running Mates	2.50	0.50	1.25	2.50
❑7, Dec 98, Hark	2.50	0.50	1.25	2.50
❑7/A, Nov 98, DFE Hard-to-Get Foil covers pack	2.50	5.00	12.50	25.00

	ORIG	GOOD	FINE	N-MINT
❑7/B, Dec 98, alternate cover (angels)	2.50	0.60	1.50	3.00
❑7/C, Dec 98, alternate cover (archway)	2.50	0.60	1.50	3.00
❑8, Dec 99	2.50	0.50	1.25	2.50
❑9, Mar 99, Raptus	2.50	0.50	1.25	2.50
❑10, May 99, Lamentum	2.50	0.50	1.25	2.50
❑11, Jun 99, Memoria	2.50	0.50	1.25	2.50
❑12, Aug 99, Cantus Excio	2.50	0.50	1.25	2.50
❑13, Dec 99, Life Sentence	2.50	0.50	1.25	2.50
❑14, Jan 00, U-Turn	2.50	0.50	1.25	2.50
❑15, Feb 00	2.50	0.50	1.25	2.50
❑16, Mar 00	2.50	0.50	1.25	2.50
❑17, Apr 00, Twisted Paths	2.50	0.50	1.25	2.50
❑18	2.50	0.50	1.25	2.50
❑19	2.50	0.50	1.25	2.50
❑20, Oct 00, The Fire This Time	2.50	0.50	1.25	2.50
❑21, Nov 00, Blood and Tears	2.50	0.50	1.25	2.50
❑22, Dec 00, The Cleansing Fire	2.50	0.50	1.25	2.50
❑23, Jan 01, The Narrowing Gyre	2.50	0.50	1.25	2.50
❑24, Apr 01, Excelsus Dei	2.50	0.50	1.25	2.50
❑SE 1	6.95	1.39	3.47	6.95
❑SE 1/A, European cover	—	2.59	6.47	12.95
❑SE 1/Aut, DFE alternate cover; Signed by Humberto Ramos	—	3.99	9.98	19.95
❑SE 1/SC, DFE alternate cover	—	2.00	5.00	10.00

CRIMSON AVENGER
DC

	ORIG	GOOD	FINE	N-MINT
❑1, Jun 88, The Dark Cross Conspiracy, Part 1	1.00	0.30	0.75	1.50
❑2, Jul 88, The Dark Cross Conspiracy, Part 2	1.00	0.30	0.75	1.50
❑3, Aug 88, The Dark Cross Conspiracy, Part 3	1.00	0.30	0.75	1.50
❑4, Sep 88, The Dark Cross Conspiracy, Part 4	1.00	0.30	0.75	1.50

CRIMSON DREAMS
CRIMSON

Value: Cover or less

- ❑1 ... 2.00
- ❑2 ... 2.00
- ❑3 ... 2.00
- ❑4 ... 2.00
- ❑5 ... 2.00
- ❑6 ... 2.00
- ❑7 ... 2.00
- ❑8 ... 2.00
- ❑9 ... 2.00
- ❑10 ... 2.00
- ❑11 ... 2.00

CRIMSON LETTERS
ADVENTURE

Value: Cover or less

- ❑1, Adventurers b&w ... 2.25

CRIMSON NUN, THE
ANTARCTIC

Value: Cover or less

- ❑1, May 97, Old Enemies, New Friends ... 2.95
- ❑2, Jul 97, Into The Interior ... 2.95
- ❑3, Sep 97, The Mountains of Death ... 2.95
- ❑4, Nov 97, Stranger Than Fiction ... 2.95

CRIMSON PLAGUE
EVENT

Value: Cover or less

- ❑1, Jun 97, GP, GP (w) ... 2.95
- ❑1/LE, Jun 97, GP, GP (w), alternate limited edition only sold at 1997 Heroes Con ... 10.00

CRIMSON PLAGUE (GEORGE PÉREZ'S...)
IMAGE

Value: Cover or less

- ❑1, Jun 00, GP, GP (w) ... 2.95
- ❑2, Aug 00, GP, GP (w) ... 2.50

CRIMSON: SCARLET X BLOOD ON THE MOON
DC

Value: Cover or less

- ❑1, Oct 99, One-Shot ... 3.95

CRIMSON SOURCEBOOK
WILDSTORM

Value: Cover or less

- ❑1, Nov 99 ... 2.95

CRISIS ON INFINITE EARTHS
DC

	ORIG	GOOD	FINE	N-MINT
❑1, Apr 85, GP, The Summoning!, D: Alex Luthor; D: Crime Syndicate; 1: Blue Beetle in DC universe, wraparound cover	0.75	0.80	2.00	4.00
❑2, May 85, GP, 1: Anti-Monitor (as shadow, voice)	0.75	0.60	1.50	3.00
❑3, Jun 85, GP, D: Nighthawk; 1: Nighthawk (modern); D: Captain Storm; D: Sarge; D: Losers; D: Johnny Cloud; D: Kid Psycho; D: Gunner	0.75	0.50	1.25	2.50
❑4, Jul 85, GP, D: Liana; 1: Doctor Light II; 1: Lady Quark; D: Lord Volt; D: The Monitor	0.75	0.50	1.25	2.50
❑5, Aug 85, GP, 1: Anti-Monitor (fully shown)	0.75	0.50	1.25	2.50
❑6, Sep 85, GP, 1: New Wildcat	0.75	0.50	1.25	2.50
❑7, Oct 85, GP, O: the DC Multiverse; O: Anti-Monitor; O: DC Multiverse; D: Supergirl; O: Monitor, Double-size	1.25	0.80	2.00	4.00
❑8, Nov 85, GP, D: Flash II (Barry Allen)	0.75	1.20	3.00	6.00
❑9, Dec 85, GP, D: Lex Luthor (Earth-2); 1: Doctor Spectro in DC universe; D: five of six renegade Guardians	0.75	0.60	1.50	3.00

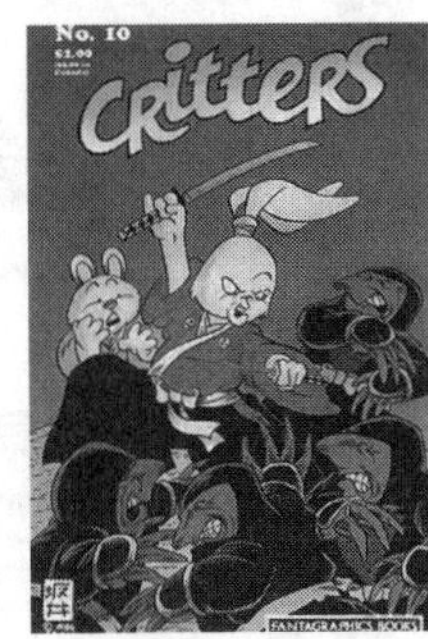

Stan Sakai's Usagi Yojimbo was a frequent feature in early issues of *Critters*.

© 1987 Stan Sakai (Fantagraphics)

	ORIG	GOOD	FINE	N-MINT
❑10, Jan 86, GP, D: Shaggy Man; D: Psimon; D: Chemo; D: Starman 3; D: Maaldor; D: Mirror Master; D: Immortal Man; D: Aqua-girl; D: Icicle	0.75	0.60	1.50	3.00
❑11, Feb 86, GP, 1: Ghost (at DC); D: Angle-Man	0.75	0.60	1.50	3.00
❑12, Mar 86, GP	1.25	0.80	2.00	4.00

CRISP
CRISP BISCUIT

	ORIG	GOOD	FINE	N-MINT
❑1, Apr 97, Littlefellas; Colin the Adorable Baby Rhino	1.95	0.60	1.50	3.00
❑2, Apr 98, A Perfect Weekend	1.95	0.60	1.50	3.00

CRISP BISCUIT
CRISP BISCUIT

	ORIG	GOOD	FINE	N-MINT
❑1, Jul 91, Murtle; She's Back	1.10	0.40	1.00	2.00

CRITICAL ERROR
DARK HORSE

Value: Cover or less

- ❑1, Jul 92, JBy, JBy (w), Critical Error, nn; color reprint of silent story from The Art of John Byrne ... 2.50

CRITICAL MASS
MARVEL

Value: Cover or less

- ❑1, Jan 89, GM; BSz, Extracting the Control Rods ... 4.95
- ❑2 ... 4.95
- ❑3 ... 4.95
- ❑4 ... 4.95
- ❑5 ... 4.95
- ❑6 ... 4.95
- ❑7 ... 5.95

CRITTERS
FANTAGRAPHICS

	ORIG	GOOD	FINE	N-MINT
❑1, Jun 86, A: Usagi Yojimbo, b&w	2.00	2.00	5.00	10.00
❑2, Jul 86, Captain Jack debut	2.00	0.60	1.50	3.00
❑3, Aug 86, A: Usagi Yojimbo	2.00	1.60	4.00	8.00
❑4, Sep 86	2.00	0.60	1.50	3.00
❑5, Oct 86	2.00	0.60	1.50	3.00
❑6, Nov 86, A: Usagi Yojimbo	2.00	1.00	2.50	5.00
❑7, Dec 86, A: Usagi Yojimbo	2.00	1.00	2.50	5.00
❑8, Jan 87	2.00	0.60	1.50	3.00
❑9, Feb 87	2.00	0.60	1.50	3.00
❑10, Mar 87, Usagi Yojimbo: Homecoming; Gnuff: The Ultimate ...rva, A: Usagi Yojimbo	2.00	0.80	2.00	4.00
❑11, Apr 87	2.00	0.60	1.50	3.00
❑12, May 87	2.00	0.60	1.50	3.00
❑13, Jun 87, The Great Race; Birthright II: Chapter II, Gnuff story; Birthright II story	2.00	0.60	1.50	3.00
❑14, Jul 87, A: Usagi Yojimbo	2.00	0.60	1.50	3.00
❑15, Aug 87	2.00	0.60	1.50	3.00
❑16, Sep 87	2.00	0.60	1.50	3.00
❑17, Oct 87	2.00	0.60	1.50	3.00
❑18, Nov 87, indicia says Sep 87	2.00	0.60	1.50	3.00
❑19, Dec 87	2.00	0.60	1.50	3.00
❑20, Jan 88	2.00	0.60	1.50	3.00
❑21, Feb 88	2.00	0.50	1.25	2.50
❑22, Mar 88, Watchmen parody cover; indicia repeated from issue #21	2.00	0.50	1.25	2.50
❑23, Apr 88, AMo (w), flexi-disc	3.95	0.79	1.98	3.95
❑24, May 88	2.00	0.50	1.25	2.50
❑25, Jun 88	2.00	0.50	1.25	2.50
❑26, Jul 88	2.00	0.50	1.25	2.50
❑27, Aug 88	2.00	0.50	1.25	2.50
❑28, Sep 88	2.00	0.50	1.25	2.50
❑29, Oct 88	2.00	0.50	1.25	2.50
❑30, Nov 88	2.00	0.50	1.25	2.50
❑31, Dec 88	2.00	0.50	1.25	2.50
❑32	2.00	0.50	1.25	2.50
❑33	2.00	0.50	1.25	2.50
❑34	2.00	0.50	1.25	2.50
❑35, Apr 89	2.00	0.50	1.25	2.50
❑36	2.00	0.50	1.25	2.50
❑37	2.00	0.50	1.25	2.50
❑38, Jul 89, 1: Stinz, Usagi Yojimbo	2.75	0.50	1.25	2.50
❑39, Fission Chicken	2.00	0.50	1.25	2.50
❑40, Gnuff	2.00	0.50	1.25	2.50
❑41, Sep 89, Platypus	2.00	0.40	1.00	2.00
❑42, Sep 89, Captain Jack	2.00	0.40	1.00	2.00
❑43	2.00	0.40	1.00	2.00
❑44	2.00	0.40	1.00	2.00

	ORIG	GOOD	FINE	N-MINT
❑45	2.00	0.40	1.00	2.00
❑46	2.00	0.40	1.00	2.00
❑47	2.00	0.40	1.00	2.00
❑48	2.00	0.40	1.00	2.00
❑49	2.00	0.40	1.00	2.00
❑50, Final Issue	4.95	0.99	2.47	4.95
❑SE 1, Jan 88, A: Usagi Yojimbo, Special #1	2.00	0.40	1.00	2.00

CRITTURS
MU PRESS

Value: Cover or less

❑0, Nov 92 ... 2.50

CROMWELL STONE
DARK HORSE

Value: Cover or less

❑1, nn; b&w ... 3.50

CROSS
DARK HORSE

Value: Cover or less

❑0, Oct 95 ... 2.95
❑1, Nov 95, Genesis ... 2.95
❑2, Dec 95, The Bet ... 2.95
❑3, Jan 96 ... 2.95
❑4, Feb 96 ... 2.95
❑5, Mar 96 ... 2.95
❑6, Apr 96 ... 2.95

CROSS AND THE SWITCHBLADE, THE
SPIRE

	ORIG	GOOD	FINE	N-MINT
❑1, Based on the book, The Cross and the Switchblade	0.35	0.60	1.50	3.00

CROSSED SWORDS
K-Z

	ORIG	GOOD	FINE	N-MINT
❑1, Dec 86	0.95	0.20	0.50	1.00

CROSSFIRE
ECLIPSE

	ORIG	GOOD	FINE	N-MINT
❑1, May 84, ME (w); DS (w), The Long, Hard Climb To Oblivion	1.50	0.50	1.25	2.50
❑2, Jun 84	1.50	0.35	0.88	1.75
❑3, Jul 84	1.50	0.35	0.88	1.75
❑4, Aug 84	1.50	0.35	0.88	1.75
❑5, Sep 84	1.50	0.35	0.88	1.75
❑6, Nov 84	1.50	0.35	0.88	1.75
❑7, Dec 84	1.50	0.35	0.88	1.75
❑8, Jan 85	1.50	0.35	0.88	1.75
❑9, Mar 85	1.50	0.35	0.88	1.75
❑10, Apr 85	1.50	0.35	0.88	1.75
❑11, May 85	1.50	0.35	0.88	1.75
❑12, Jun 85, DSt (c), Marilyn Monroe cover; Marilyn Monroe story	1.50	0.35	0.88	1.75
❑13, Jul 85	1.75	0.35	0.88	1.75
❑14, Aug 85	1.75	0.35	0.88	1.75
❑15, Oct 85	1.75	0.35	0.88	1.75
❑16, Jan 86	1.75	0.35	0.88	1.75
❑17, Mar 86	1.75	0.35	0.88	1.75
❑18, Jan 87, Black & white issues begin	2.00	0.35	0.88	1.75
❑19, Feb 87	2.00	0.35	0.88	1.75
❑20, Mar 87	2.00	0.35	0.88	1.75
❑21, Apr 87	2.00	0.35	0.88	1.75
❑22, Jun 87	2.00	0.35	0.88	1.75
❑23, Jul 87	2.00	0.35	0.88	1.75
❑24, Aug 87	2.00	0.35	0.88	1.75
❑25, Oct 87	2.00	0.35	0.88	1.75
❑26, Feb 88, Final Issue	2.00	0.35	0.88	1.75

CROSSFIRE AND RAINBOW
ECLIPSE

Value: Cover or less

❑1, Jun 86, DS, ME (w), Jay Endicott, This is Your Sex Life! .. 1.25
❑2, Jul 86, DS, ME (w) ... 1.25
❑3, Aug 86, DS, ME (w) ... 1.25
❑4, Sep 86, DS, DSt (c), ME (w) ... 1.25

CROSSGEN CHRONICLES
CROSSGEN

Value: Cover or less

❑1, Jun 00, lead-in to ongoing CrossGen series; background info on creators and series.. 3.95

CROSSGEN SAMPLER
CROSSGEN

	ORIG	GOOD	FINE	N-MINT
❑1, Feb 00, no cover price; previews of upcoming series	—	0.20	0.50	1.00

CROSSROADS
FIRST

	ORIG	GOOD	FINE	N-MINT
❑1, Jul 88, Sable, Whisper; Whisper, Sable	3.25	0.70	1.75	3.50
❑2, Aug 88, Payback, Sable, Badger	3.25	0.70	1.75	3.50
❑3, Sep 88, Badger, Luther Ironheart	3.25	0.70	1.75	3.50
❑4, Oct 88, Grimjack, Judah; Grimjack, Judah Maccabee	3.25	0.70	1.75	3.50
❑5, Nov 88, Grimjack, Nexus, Dreadstar	3.25	0.70	1.75	3.50

CROW, THE (CALIBER)
CALIBER

	ORIG	GOOD	FINE	N-MINT
❑1, Feb 89, O: The Crow, b&w (10, 000 print run)	1.95	7.00	17.50	35.00
❑1-2, O: The Crow, 2nd Printing (5, 000 print run)	1.95	1.00	2.50	5.00
❑, O: The Crow, 3rd printing (5, 000 print run)	1.95	0.80	2.00	4.00
❑2, Mar 89, (7000 print run)	1.95	5.00	12.50	25.00
❑2-2, Dec 89, 2nd Printing (5, 000 print run)	1.95	1.00	2.50	5.00
❑2-3, Jun 90, 3rd printing (5, 000 print run)	1.95	0.80	2.00	4.00
❑3, (5000 print run)	1.95	4.00	10.00	20.00
❑3-2, 2nd Printing (5, 000 print run)	1.95	1.00	2.50	5.00
❑4, only printing (12, 000 print run)	1.95	4.00	10.00	20.00

CROW, THE (IMAGE)
IMAGE

	ORIG	GOOD	FINE	N-MINT
❑1, Feb 99, Resurrection	2.50	0.60	1.50	3.00
❑1/A, Feb 99, Resurrection, gravestones	2.50	0.60	1.50	3.00
❑2, Mar 99, Shadows	2.50	0.50	1.25	2.50
❑3, Apr 99, Death	2.50	0.50	1.25	2.50
❑4, May 99, The Line Between the Devil's Teeth	2.50	0.50	1.25	2.50
❑5, Jun 99, In the Skin of An Angel Part 1	2.50	0.50	1.25	2.50
❑6, Jul 99, In the Skin of An Angel Part 2	2.50	0.50	1.25	2.50
❑7, Aug 99, Touch of Evil, Part 1	2.50	0.50	1.25	2.50
❑8, Sep 99, Touch of Evil, Part 2	2.50	0.50	1.25	2.50
❑9, Oct 99, Ashes to Ashes, Part 1	2.50	0.50	1.25	2.50
❑10, Nov 99, Ashes to Ashes, Part 2	2.50	0.50	1.25	2.50

CROW, THE (TUNDRA)
TUNDRA

Value: Cover or less

❑1, Jan 92, b&w; prestige format ... 4.95
❑2, Mar 92, b&w; prestige format ... 4.95
❑3, May 92, b&w; prestige format ... 4.95
❑4 ... 4.95

CROW, THE: CITY OF ANGELS
KITCHEN SINK

Value: Cover or less

❑1, Jul 96, adapts movie ... 2.95
❑1/SC, Jul 96, Photo cover; adapts movie ... 2.95
❑2, Aug 96, adapts movie ... 2.95
❑2/SC, Aug 96, Photo cover; adapts movie ... 2.95
❑3, Sep 96, Final Issue ... 2.95
❑3/SC, Sep 96, photo cover (head shot of Crow); Final Issue.... 2.95

CROW, THE: DEAD TIME
KITCHEN SINK

Value: Cover or less

❑1, Jan 96, b&w ... 2.95
❑2, Feb 96 ... 2.95
❑3, Mar 96 ... 2.95

CROW, THE: FLESH & BLOOD
KITCHEN SINK

Value: Cover or less

❑1, May 96, b&w ... 2.95
❑2, Jun 96, b&w ... 2.95
❑3, Jul 96, b&w ... 2.95

CROW OF THE BEARCLAN
BLACKTHORNE

Value: Cover or less

❑1, Oct 86 ... 1.50
❑2 ... 1.50
❑3 ... 1.50
❑4 ... 1.75
❑5 ... 1.75
❑6, Mar 88 ... 1.75

CROW, THE: WAKING NIGHTMARES
KITCHEN SINK

Value: Cover or less

❑1, Jan 97, b&w ... 2.95
❑2, Jan 98, b&w ... 2.95
❑3, Feb 98, b&w ... 2.95
❑4, May 98, b&w ... 2.95

CROW, THE: WILD JUSTICE
KITCHEN SINK

Value: Cover or less

❑1, Oct 96, b&w ... 2.95
❑2, Nov 96, b&w ... 2.95
❑3, Dec 96, b&w ... 2.95

CROZONIA
IMAGE

Value: Cover or less

❑1, The Tales From Crozonia.. 2.95

CRUCIAL FICTION
FANTAGRAPHICS

Value: Cover or less

❑1, b&w ... 2.50
❑2, b&w ... 2.25
❑3, b&w ... 2.25

CRUCIBLE
DC

	ORIG	GOOD	FINE	N-MINT
❑1, Feb 93, Hood Winked	0.99	0.30	0.75	1.50
❑2, Mar 93	1.25	0.25	0.63	1.25
❑3, Apr 93	1.25	0.25	0.63	1.25
❑4, May 93	1.25	0.25	0.63	1.25
❑5, Jun 93	1.25	0.25	0.63	1.25
❑6, Jul 93, Final Issue	1.25	0.25	0.63	1.25

CRUEL AND UNUSUAL
DC

Value: Cover or less

❑1, Jun 99 ... 2.95
❑2, Jul 99 ... 2.95
❑3, Aug 99 ... 2.95
❑4, Sep 99 ... 2.95

CRUEL & UNUSUAL PUNISHMENT
STARHEAD

Value: Cover or less

❑1, Nov 93, b&w; adult ... 2.75
❑2, Oct 94, b&w; adult ... 2.95

CRUEL WORLD
FANTAGRAPHICS

Value: Cover or less

❑1, b&w ... 3.50

CRUSADERS
GUILD

	ORIG	GOOD	FINE	N-MINT
❑1, Title continued in Southern Nights #2	—	0.20	0.50	1.00

CRUSADERS, THE
DC

Value: Cover or less

- ❑1, May 92, Blast From The Past, 1: The Crusaders (Impact); 1: The American Crusaders; 1: Captain Commando; 1: Kalathar, trading cards 1.00
- ❑2, Jun 92 .... 1.00
- ❑3, Jul 92, Slaves of New York 1.00
- ❑4, Aug 92 .... 1.00
- ❑5, Sep 92 .... 1.00
- ❑6, Oct 92 .... 1.00
- ❑7, Nov 92, Childhood's End, Part III 1.00
- ❑8, Dec 92, Final Issue 1.00

CRUSADES, THE
VERTIGO

Value: Cover or less

- ❑1, May 01, The First Crusade AD 2001 .... 2.50
- ❑2, Jun 01, The First Crusade AD 2001 .... 2.50
- ❑3 .... 2.50
- ❑4 .... 2.50
- ❑5 .... 2.50

CRUSADES, THE: URBAN DECREE
VERTIGO

Value: Cover or less

- ❑1 .... 3.95

CRUSH
AEON

Value: Cover or less

- ❑1, Nov 95, b&w; cardstock cover 2.95
- ❑2, Dec 95, b&w; cardstock cover 2.95
- ❑3, Jan 96, b&w; cardstock cover 2.95
- ❑4, Feb 96, b&w; cardstock cover 2.95

CRUSH, THE
IMAGE

Value: Cover or less

- ❑1, Jan 96, 1: The Crush, cover says Mar, indicia says Jan .. 2.25
- ❑2, Apr 96 .... 2.25
- ❑3, May 96 .... 2.25
- ❑4, Jun 96 .... 2.25
- ❑5, Jul 96 .... 2.25

CRUST
TOP SHELF

Value: Cover or less

- ❑1, b&w; no cover date 3.00

CRY FOR DAWN
CRY FOR DAWN

	ORIG	GOOD	FINE	N-MINT
❑1, Rainstorms & Maniacs; Tokens, 1: Dawn, b&w; adult	2.25	16.00	40.00	80.00
❑1/A, Rainstorms & Maniacs; Tokens, adult; Black light edition	—	3.00	7.50	15.00
❑1/CF, Rainstorms & Maniacs; Tokens, adult; Has blotchy tones on cover; Counterfeit version of #1	2.25	0.00	0.00	0.00
❑1-2, Rainstorms & Maniacs; Tokens, 1: Dawn, adult; 2nd Printing	2.25	10.00	25.00	50.00
❑, Rainstorms & Maniacs; Tokens, 1: Dawn, adult; 3rd Printing	2.25	8.00	20.00	40.00
❑2, adult	2.25	12.00	30.00	60.00
❑2-2, adult; 2nd Printing	2.25	5.00	12.50	25.00
❑3, adult	2.25	10.00	25.00	50.00
❑4, adult	2.25	6.00	15.00	30.00
❑4/AUT, adult	2.25	10.00	25.00	50.00
❑5, b&w; adult	2.25	5.00	12.50	25.00
❑5/AUT, adult	2.25	8.00	20.00	40.00
❑5-2, adult; 2nd Printing	2.25	2.40	6.00	12.00
❑6, b&w; adult	2.25	5.00	12.50	25.00
❑6/AUT, adult	2.25	6.00	15.00	30.00
❑7, b&w; adult	2.25	4.00	10.00	20.00
❑7/AUT, adult	2.25	5.00	12.50	25.00
❑8, b&w; adult	2.25	4.00	10.00	20.00
❑8/AUT, adult	2.25	5.00	12.50	25.00
❑9, b&w; adult	2.25	4.00	10.00	20.00
❑9/AUT, adult	2.25	5.00	12.50	25.00

CRYING FREEMAN PART 1
VIZ

	ORIG	GOOD	FINE	N-MINT
❑1, Mr. Yo,	3.50	1.20	3.00	6.00
❑2, Mr. Yo,	3.50	1.00	2.50	5.00
❑3, Mr. Yo,	3.50	1.00	2.50	5.00
❑4, Mr. Yo,	3.50	0.80	2.00	4.00
❑5, Mr. Yo, Crying Freeman gets tattooed;	3.50	0.80	2.00	4.00
❑6, Mr. Yo,	3.50	0.80	2.00	4.00
❑7, Mr. Yo; Fallen Flower,	3.50	0.80	2.00	4.00
❑8, Fallen Flower; Flowing Water,	3.50	0.80	2.00	4.00

CRYING FREEMAN PART 2
VIZ

	ORIG	GOOD	FINE	N-MINT
❑1, The Tiger Orchid,	3.50	0.80	2.00	4.00
❑2, The Tiger Orchid,	3.50	0.80	2.00	4.00
❑3, The Tiger Orchid; The Wind and the Crane,	3.50	0.80	2.00	4.00
❑4, The Wind and the Crane; The Marital Vows,	3.75	0.80	2.00	4.00
❑5, The Separation of Dragon and the Tiger; The Killing Ring,	3.95	0.80	2.00	4.00
❑6, The Killing Ring,	3.95	0.80	2.00	4.00
❑7, The Killing Ring,	3.95	0.80	2.00	4.00

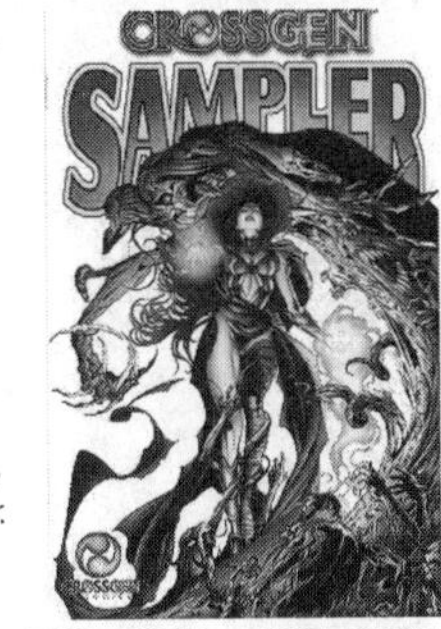

CrossGeneration Comics gave a preview of its first releases in *CrossGen Sampler.*

	ORIG	GOOD	FINE	N-MINT
❑8, Sister,	3.95	0.80	2.00	4.00
❑9, Sister,	3.95	0.80	2.00	4.00

CRYING FREEMAN PART 3
VIZ

	ORIG	GOOD	FINE	N-MINT
❑1, Tohgoku Oshu, 1st issue in color	4.95	1.10	2.75	5.50
❑2, Tohgoku Oshu, full color	4.95	1.00	2.50	5.00
❑3, Tohgoku Oshu, full color	4.95	1.00	2.50	5.00
❑4, Tohgoku Oshu, full color	4.95	1.00	2.50	5.00
❑5, Tohgoku Oshu, full color	4.95	1.00	2.50	5.00
❑6, Tohgoku Oshu, full color	4.95	1.00	2.50	5.00
❑7, Tohgoku Oshu, full color	4.95	1.00	2.50	5.00
❑8, Nothing Ventured, Nothing Gained, full color	4.95	1.00	2.50	5.00
❑9, Nothing Ventured, Nothing Gained, full color	4.95	1.00	2.50	5.00
❑10, Nothing Ventured, Nothing Gained, full color	4.95	1.00	2.50	5.00

CRYING FREEMAN PART 4
VIZ

	ORIG	GOOD	FINE	N-MINT
❑1, The Pomegranate	4.95	1.00	2.50	5.00
❑2, The Pomegranate	4.95	1.00	2.50	5.00
❑3, The Pomegranate	4.95	1.00	2.50	5.00
❑4, The Pomegranate	2.75	0.60	1.50	3.00
❑5, The Pomegranate	2.75	0.60	1.50	3.00
❑6, The Pomegranate	2.75	0.60	1.50	3.00
❑7, The Pomegranate	2.75	0.60	1.50	3.00
❑8, The Pomegranate	2.75	0.60	1.50	3.00

CRYING FREEMAN PART 5
VIZ

Value: Cover or less

- ❑1, Journey to Freedom, ... 2.75
- ❑2, Journey to Freedom, b&w 2.75
- ❑3, Journey to Freedom, b&w. 2.75
- ❑4, Journey to Freedom, b&w. 2.75
- ❑5, Journey to Freedom, b&w. 2.75
- ❑6, Journey to Freedom, b&w. 2.75
- ❑7, Journey to Freedom, b&w. 2.75
- ❑8, Journey to Freedom, b&w. 2.75
- ❑9, Journey to Freedom, b&w. 2.75
- ❑10, Journey to Freedom, b&w 2.75
- ❑11, b&w 2.75

CRYPT
IMAGE

Value: Cover or less

- ❑1, Aug 95 .... 2.50
- ❑2, Oct 95 .... 2.50

CRYPTIC TALES
SHOWCASE

Value: Cover or less

- ❑1 .... 1.95

CRYPTIC WRITINGS OF MEGADETH
CHAOS!

Value: Cover or less

- ❑1, Sep 97, Skull Beneath the Skin; Rattlehead, alternate cardstock cover; Necro Limited Premium Edition; comics adaptation of Megadeath songs 2.95
- ❑2, Dec 97, comics adaptation of Megadeath songs 2.95

CRYPT OF C*M
EROS

Value: Cover or less

- ❑1, Feb 99, The Cumback!; Mr. Keys 2.95

CRYPT OF DAWN
SIRIUS

	ORIG	GOOD	FINE	N-MINT
❑1, Oct 96, Enter the Crypt; Vicariosity	2.95	0.80	2.00	4.00
❑1/LE	—	2.80	7.00	14.00
❑2, Five Minutes of My Life; The Fool of the Web	2.95	0.60	1.50	3.00
❑3, Feb 98	2.95	0.60	1.50	3.00
❑4, Jun 98, color story	2.95	0.59	1.48	2.95
❑5, Nov 98	2.95	0.59	1.48	2.95
❑6, Mar 99	2.95	0.59	1.48	2.95

CRYPT OF SHADOWS
MARVEL

	ORIG	GOOD	FINE	N-MINT
❑1, Jan 73, BW, Midnight On Black Mountain, Reprints Adventures into Terror #7	0.20	1.20	3.00	6.00
❑2, Mar 73	0.20	0.80	2.00	4.00
❑3, May 73	0.20	0.80	2.00	4.00
❑4, Jul 73	0.20	0.70	1.75	3.50
❑5, Sep 73	0.20	0.70	1.75	3.50
❑6, Oct 73	0.20	0.60	1.50	3.00

	ORIG	GOOD	FINE	N-MINT
❑7, Nov 73	0.20	0.60	1.50	3.00
❑8, Jan 74	0.20	0.60	1.50	3.00
❑9, Mar 74	0.20	0.60	1.50	3.00
❑10, May 74	0.25	0.60	1.50	3.00
❑11, Jul 74	0.25	0.50	1.25	2.50
❑12, Sep 74	0.25	0.50	1.25	2.50
❑13	0.25	0.50	1.25	2.50
❑14	0.25	0.50	1.25	2.50
❑15	0.25	0.50	1.25	2.50
❑16	0.25	0.50	1.25	2.50
❑17	0.25	0.50	1.25	2.50
❑18	0.25	0.50	1.25	2.50
❑19	0.25	0.50	1.25	2.50
❑20	0.25	0.50	1.25	2.50
❑21	0.25	0.50	1.25	2.50

CRYSTAL BALLS
EROS

Value: Cover or less

❑1 .... 2.95
❑2, Sep 95, The Bridge 2.95

CRYSTAL BREEZE UNLEASHED
HIGH IMPACT

	ORIG	GOOD	FINE	N-MINT
❑1, b&w; adult; no cover price	—	0.60	1.50	3.00

CRYSTAL WAR, THE
ATLANTIS

Value: Cover or less

❑1 .... 3.50

CTHULHU (H.P. LOVECRAFT'S...)
MILLENNIUM

Value: Cover or less

❑1, BMB, The Festival, Part 1 .... 2.50
❑1/CS, BMB, The Festival, Part 1, trading cards 3.50
❑2, BMB, The Festival, Part 2, trading cards 2.50
❑3, BMB, The Festival, Part 3 .... 2.50

CUCKOO
GREEN DOOR

Value: Cover or less

❑1, b&w; cardstock cover 2.75
❑2, Win 96, b&w; cardstock cover 2.75
❑3, Spr 97, b&w; cardstock cover 2.75
❑4, Sum 97, b&w; cardstock cover 2.75
❑5, Fal 97, b&w; cardstock cover 2.75

CUD
FANTAGRAPHICS

	ORIG	GOOD	FINE	N-MINT
❑1, b&w; adult	2.25	0.50	1.25	2.50
❑2, b&w; adult	2.50	0.50	1.25	2.50
❑3, b&w; adult	2.50	0.50	1.25	2.50
❑4, b&w; adult	2.50	0.50	1.25	2.50
❑5, b&w; adult	2.50	0.50	1.25	2.50
❑6, b&w; adult	2.50	0.50	1.25	2.50
❑7, Aug 94, b&w; adult	2.50	0.50	1.25	2.50

CUDA B.C.
REBEL

Value: Cover or less

❑1 .... 2.00

CUD COMICS
DARK HORSE

	ORIG	GOOD	FINE	N-MINT
❑1, Nov 95, b&w	2.95	0.59	1.48	2.95
❑2, Jan 96, b&w	2.95	0.59	1.48	2.95
❑3, Mar 96, b&w	2.95	0.59	1.48	2.95
❑4, Jun 96	2.95	0.59	1.48	2.95
❑5, Sep 96, Eno and Plum: The Old Folks at Home; Most Girls Like Dick, b&w	2.95	0.59	1.48	2.95
❑6, Dec 96, b&w	2.95	0.59	1.48	2.95
❑7, Apr 97, b&w	2.95	0.59	1.48	2.95
❑8, Sep 97, b&w	2.95	0.59	1.48	2.95
❑Ash 1, A: Ashcan promotional giveaway from comic con	—	0.20	0.50	1.00

CUIRASS
HARRIER

Value: Cover or less

❑1, b&w 1.95

CULTURAL JET LAG
FANTAGRAPHICS

Value: Cover or less

❑1, b&w 2.50

CUPID'S REVENGE
EROS

Value: Cover or less

❑1 .... 2.95
❑2 .... 2.95

CURIO SHOPPE, THE
PHOENIX PRESS

Value: Cover or less

❑1, Mar 95, Serendipity; The Big Boner, b&w 2.50

CURSED WORLDS SOURCE BOOK
BLUE COMET

Value: Cover or less

❑1 .... 2.95

CURSE OF DRACULA, THE
DARK HORSE

Value: Cover or less

❑1, Jul 98, GC; MW, Go to Hell! 2.95
❑2, Aug 98, GC; MW 2.95
❑3, Sep 98, GC; MW 2.95

CURSE OF DREADWOLF
LIGHTNING

Value: Cover or less

❑1, Sep 94, Deadly Vision; Homecoming, b&w 2.75

CURSE OF RUNE
MALIBU

Value: Cover or less

❑1, May 95, Connections 2.50

CURSE OF THE MOLEMEN
KITCHEN SINK

	ORIG	GOOD	FINE	N-MINT
❑1, full color	2.95	0.99	2.47	4.95

CURSE OF THE SHE-CAT
AC

Value: Cover or less

❑1, Feb 89, b&w 2.50

CURSE OF THE SPAWN
IMAGE

	ORIG	GOOD	FINE	N-MINT
❑1, Sep 96, Dark Future, b&w promo	1.95	0.80	2.00	4.00
❑1/A, Sep 96	1.95	0.60	1.50	3.00
❑1/B, Sep 96, b&w	1.95	0.60	1.50	3.00
❑2, Oct 96	1.95	0.60	1.50	3.00
❑3, Nov 96	1.95	0.60	1.50	3.00
❑4, Dec 96, Damnation War	1.95	0.50	1.25	2.50
❑5, Dec 96, Suture	1.95	0.50	1.25	2.50
❑6, Feb 97	1.95	0.50	1.25	2.50
❑7, Mar 97	1.95	0.50	1.25	2.50
❑8, Apr 97, Carnival of Souls	1.95	0.50	1.25	2.50
❑9, May 97, A: Angela	1.95	0.50	1.25	2.50
❑10, Jun 97, A: Angela	1.95	0.50	1.25	2.50
❑11, Aug 97, A: Angela	1.95	0.50	1.25	2.50
❑12, Sep 97, Photo cover	1.95	0.50	1.25	2.50
❑13, Oct 97, Heart of Darkness	1.95	0.50	1.25	2.50
❑14, Nov 97, Apocalypse When	1.95	0.50	1.25	2.50
❑15, Dec 97, Sympathy for an Angel, Part 1	1.95	0.50	1.25	2.50
❑16, Jan 98, Sympathy for an Angel, Part 2	1.95	0.40	1.00	2.00
❑17, Feb 98, Twist of Fate	1.95	0.40	1.00	2.00
❑18, Mar 98, Gutshot	1.95	0.40	1.00	2.00
❑19, Apr 98, Curse the Curse	1.95	0.40	1.00	2.00
❑20, May 98, Dark Myth	1.95	0.40	1.00	2.00
❑21, Jun 98, Chaos Cometh	1.95	0.40	1.00	2.00
❑22, Jul 98, Deadland	1.95	0.40	1.00	2.00
❑23, Aug 98, Overt-Resurrection	1.95	0.40	1.00	2.00
❑24, Sep 98, Overt-Hell	1.95	0.39	0.98	1.95
❑25, Oct 98, Heart of Hell	1.95	0.39	0.98	1.95
❑26, Nov 98, Brother's Keeper	1.95	0.39	0.98	1.95
❑27, Dec 98, Return of the Suture, Part 1, Ghosts	1.95	0.39	0.98	1.95
❑28, Feb 99, Return of the Suture, Part 2, Bleed	1.95	0.39	0.98	1.95
❑29, Mar 99, Last Rites	1.95	0.39	0.98	1.95

CURSE OF THE WEIRD
MARVEL

	ORIG	GOOD	FINE	N-MINT
❑1, Dec 93, RH, Do Not Panic!; The Brain, Reprint; Reprints stories from Adventures in Terror #4, Astonishing Tales #10, others	1.25	0.30	0.75	1.50
❑2, Jan 94, The Ghost Of Grismore Castle!; Bat's Tale, Reprint	1.25	0.30	0.75	1.50
❑3, Feb 94, Reprint	1.25	0.30	0.75	1.50
❑4, Mar 94, Reprint; Final Issue	1.25	0.30	0.75	1.50

CURSE OF THE ZOMBIE
MARVEL

Value: Cover or less

❑4, Reprint 1.25

CUTEGIRL
NOT AVAILABLE

Value: Cover or less

❑1 .... 0.50
❑2, CuteGirl Finds A Pet; The Never Ending Struggle 0.50

CUTTING EDGE
MARVEL

Value: Cover or less

❑1, Dec 95, Ghosts of the Future, A: Omnibus; A: Hulk; A: Talbot, continued from The Incredible Hulk #436; continues in The Incredible Hulk #437 .... 2.95

CYBER 7
ECLIPSE

Value: Cover or less

❑1, b&w; Japanese 2.00
❑2, b&w; Japanese 2.00
❑3, b&w; Japanese 2.00
❑4, b&w; Japanese 2.00
❑5, b&w; Japanese 2.00
❑6, b&w; Japanese 2.00
❑7, b&w; Japanese 2.00

CYBER 7 BOOK TWO
ECLIPSE

Value: Cover or less

❑1, b&w; Japanese 2.00
❑2, b&w; Japanese 2.00
❑3, b&w; Japanese 2.00
❑4, b&w; Japanese 2.00
❑5, b&w; Japanese 2.00
❑6, b&w; Japanese 2.00
❑7, b&w; Japanese 2.00
❑8, b&w; Japanese 2.00
❑9, b&w; Japanese 2.00
❑10, b&w; Japanese 2.00

ORIG GOOD FINE N-MINT

CYBER CITY: PART 1
CPM

Value: Cover or less

- ❑1, Sep 95, adapts anime....... 2.95
- ❑2, Sep 95, adapts anime....... 2.95

CYBER CITY: PART 2
CPM

Value: Cover or less

- ❑1, Oct 95, adapts anime 2.95
- ❑2, Nov 95, adapts anime....... 2.95

CYBER CITY: PART 3
CPM

Value: Cover or less

- ❑1, Dec 95, adapts anime....... 2.95
- ❑2, Jan 96, adapts anime 2.95

CYBERCOM, HEART OF THE BLUE MESA
MATRIX

Value: Cover or less

- ❑1, Dec 87, First Impressions, b&w 2.00

CYBER CRUSH: ROBOTS IN REVOLT
FLEETWAY

Value: Cover or less

- ❑1, Death on the Orient Express; Robo-Hunter 1.95
- ❑2....... 1.95
- ❑3....... 1.95
- ❑4....... 1.95
- ❑5....... 1.95
- ❑6....... 1.95
- ❑7....... 1.95
- ❑8....... 1.95
- ❑9....... 1.95
- ❑10....... 1.95
- ❑11....... 1.95
- ❑12....... 1.95
- ❑13....... 1.95
- ❑14....... 1.95

CYBERELLA
DC

Value: Cover or less

- ❑1, Sep 96, HC (w), Silent Weapons, Quiet Wars, Part 1....... 2.25
- ❑2, Oct 96, HC (w), Silent Weapons, Quiet Wars, Part 2....... 2.25
- ❑3, Nov 96, HC (w), Silent Weapons, Quiet Wars, Part 3....... 2.25
- ❑4, Dec 96, HC (w), Silent Weapons, Quiet Wars, Part 4....... 2.25
- ❑5, Jan 97, HC (w), Silent Weapons, Quiet Wars, Part 5....... 2.25
- ❑6, Feb 97, HC (w), Silent Weapons, Quiet Wars, Part 6....... 2.25
- ❑7, Mar 97, HC (w), Silent Weapons, Quiet Wars, Part 7....... 2.50
- ❑8, Apr 97, HC (w)....... 2.50
- ❑9, May 97, Program Change, or My Mom, My Enemy....... 2.50
- ❑10, Jun 97....... 2.50
- ❑11, Jul 97....... 2.50
- ❑12, Aug 97, Final Issue....... 2.50

CYBERFARCE
PARODY

Value: Cover or less

- ❑1, b&w....... 2.50

CYBER FEMMES
SPOOF

Value: Cover or less

- ❑1....... 2.95

CYBERFORCE (VOL. 1)
IMAGE

	ORIG	GOOD	FINE	N-MINT
❑1, Oct 92, The Tin Men Of War, Part 1, 1: Cyberforce, coupon for Image Comics #0	1.95	0.80	2.00	4.00
❑2, Mar 93, The Tin Men Of War, Part 2	1.95	0.50	1.25	2.50
❑3, May 93, A: Pitt	1.95	0.40	1.00	2.00
❑4, Jul 93, foil cover	2.50	0.40	1.00	2.00

CYBERFORCE (VOL. 2)
IMAGE

	ORIG	GOOD	FINE	N-MINT
❑0, Sep 93, O: Cyberforce	1.95	0.50	1.25	2.50
❑1, Nov 93	1.95	0.50	1.25	2.50
❑1/GO, Nov, Gold edition	—	0.80	2.00	4.00
❑1-2, Nov 93, 2nd Printing	0.99	0.25	0.63	1.25
❑2, Feb 94, Killer Instinct, Part 2	1.95	0.50	1.25	2.50
❑2/PL, Feb 94, Platinum edition; foil-embossed outer wrap	—	0.60	1.50	3.00
❑3, Mar 94, Killer Instinct, Part 4	1.95	0.50	1.25	2.50
❑3/GO, Mar 94, Killer Instinct, Part 4, Gold edition	—	0.60	1.50	3.00
❑4, Apr 94	1.95	0.50	1.25	2.50
❑5, Jun 94	1.95	0.50	1.25	2.50
❑6, Jul 94	1.95	0.40	1.00	2.00
❑7, Sep 94	1.95	0.40	1.00	2.00
❑8, Oct 94, TMc, Image X-Month	2.50	0.55	1.38	2.75
❑9, Dec 94	1.95	0.50	1.25	2.50
❑10, Feb 95	1.95	0.50	1.25	2.50
❑10/GO, Feb 95, Gold edition	—	0.60	1.50	3.00
❑10/PL, Feb 95, Platinum edition	—	0.60	1.50	3.00
❑10/SC, Feb 95, alternate cover	1.95	0.60	1.50	3.00
❑11, Mar 95	1.95	0.50	1.25	2.50
❑12, Apr 95	1.95	0.50	1.25	2.50
❑13, Jun 95	2.25	0.50	1.25	2.50
❑14, Jul 95	2.25	0.50	1.25	2.50
❑15, Aug 95	2.25	0.50	1.25	2.50
❑16, Nov 95	2.25	0.50	1.25	2.50
❑17, Dec 95	2.25	0.45	1.13	2.25
❑18, Jan 96	2.25	0.50	1.25	2.50
❑18/A, Jan 96, alternate cover	2.25	0.50	1.25	2.50
❑19, Feb 96	2.50	0.50	1.25	2.50
❑20, Mar 96	2.50	0.50	1.25	2.50
❑21, May 96	2.50	0.50	1.25	2.50
❑22, May 96	2.50	0.50	1.25	2.50
❑23, Jun 96	2.50	0.50	1.25	2.50
❑24, Jun 96	2.50	0.50	1.25	2.50

Creatures from H.P. Lovecraft's Miskatonic mythos and other horror-based stories have popped up in comics from a number of publishers over the years.

	ORIG	GOOD	FINE	N-MINT
❑25, Aug 96, enhanced wraparound cardstock cover	3.95	0.79	1.98	3.95
❑26, Sep 96	2.50	0.50	1.25	2.50
❑27, Oct 96	2.50	0.50	1.25	2.50
❑27/SC, Oct 96, A: Ash, alternate cover	2.50	0.50	1.25	2.50
❑28, Nov 96, A: Gabriel (from Ash)	2.50	0.50	1.25	2.50
❑29, Dec 96	2.50	0.50	1.25	2.50
❑30, Feb 97, Devil's Reign Interlude; Devil's Reign	2.50	0.50	1.25	2.50
❑31, Mar 97	2.50	0.50	1.25	2.50
❑32, Apr 97	2.50	0.50	1.25	2.50
❑33, May 97	2.50	0.50	1.25	2.50
❑34, Jul 97	2.50	0.50	1.25	2.50
❑35, Sep 97	2.50	0.50	1.25	2.50
❑Anl 1, Mar 95	2.50	0.50	1.25	2.50
❑Anl 2, Aug 96	2.50	0.59	1.48	2.95

CYBERFORCE ORIGINS
IMAGE

	ORIG	GOOD	FINE	N-MINT
❑1, Jan 95, O: Cyblade	2.50	0.50	1.25	2.50
❑1/GO, O: Cyblade, Gold edition	—	0.80	2.00	4.00
❑1-2, O: Cyblade, 2nd Printing	0.99	0.25	0.63	1.25
❑2, Feb 95, O: Stryker	2.50	0.50	1.25	2.50
❑3, Nov 95, O: Impact	2.50	0.50	1.25	2.50

CYBERFORCE, STRYKE FORCE: OPPOSING FORCES
IMAGE

Value: Cover or less

- ❑1, Sep 95 .... 2.50
- ❑2, Oct 95....... 2.50

CYBERFORCE UNIVERSE SOURCEBOOK
IMAGE

Value: Cover or less

- ❑1, Aug 94 .... 2.50
- ❑2, Feb 95....... 2.50

CYBERFROG (HARRIS)
HARRIS

	ORIG	GOOD	FINE	N-MINT
❑0, Mar 97, Yo Mama is...An Alien	2.95	1.00	2.50	5.00
❑0/A, Mar 97, Yo Mama is...An Alien, Art Adams cover	2.95	1.60	4.00	8.00
❑1, Feb 96, Directing Traffik	2.95	1.00	2.50	5.00
❑2, Torn Together	2.95	0.80	2.00	4.00
❑3, Deathfly By Night	2.95	0.70	1.75	3.50
❑4, The Afterlife of Riley	2.95	0.70	1.75	3.50

CYBERFROG: 3RD ANNIVERSARY SPECIAL
HARRIS

Value: Cover or less

- ❑1, Jan 97 .... 2.50
- ❑2, Feb 97....... 2.50

CYBERFROG: RESERVOIR FROG
HARRIS

Value: Cover or less

- ❑1, Sep 96, Getting To Hate You, Eric Larsen/Ethan Van Sciver cover art 2.95
- ❑1/A, Getting To Hate You, Ethan Van Sciver Cover Art....... 2.95
- ❑2, Oct 96, Infestation, Ethan Van Sciver Cover Art 2.95
- ❑2/A, Infestation, Ethan Van Sciver Cover Art 2.95

CYBERFROG VS CREED
HARRIS

Value: Cover or less

- ❑1, Jul 97....... 2.95

CYBERHAWKS
PYRAMID

Value: Cover or less

- ❑1, b&w....... 1.80
- ❑2, b&w....... 1.80

CYBERLUST
AIRCEL

Value: Cover or less

- ❑1, b&w; adult....... 2.95
- ❑2, b&w; adult....... 2.95
- ❑3, b&w; adult....... 2.95

CYBERNARY
IMAGE

Value: Cover or less

- ❑1, Nov 95, Duet....... 2.50
- ❑2, Dec 95, Down Memory Lane 2.50
- ❑3, Jan 96 .... 2.50
- ❑4, Feb 96....... 2.50
- ❑5, Mar 96....... 2.50

CYBERPUNK (BOOK 1)
INNOVATION

Value: Cover or less

- ❑1....... 1.95
- ❑2....... 1.95

CYBERPUNK (BOOK 2)
INNOVATION

Value: Cover or less

❑1 .... 2.25

❑2 .... 2.25

CYBERPUNK GRAPHIC NOVEL
INNOVATION

Value: Cover or less

❑1 .... 6.95

CYBERPUNK: THE SERAPHIM FILES
INNOVATION

Value: Cover or less

❑1 .... 2.50

❑2 .... 2.50

CYBERPUNX
IMAGE

Value: Cover or less

❑1/A, Mar 96, RL (w), Woman with purple/white costume at bottom of cover 2.50

❑1/B, Mar 96, RL (w), Man with green hair at bottom of cover 2.50

❑1/C, Mar 96, RL (w), variant cover 2.50

❑1/D, Mar 96, RL (w), variant cover 2.50

CYBERRAD (1ST SERIES)
CONTINUITY

Value: Cover or less

❑1, Jan 91 .... 2.00

❑2, Apr 91 .... 2.00

❑3, May 91 .... 2.00

❑4, Jun 91 .... 2.00

❑5, glow cover 2.00

❑6, Nov 91, foldout poster 2.00

❑7, Mar 92 .... 2.00

CYBERRAD (2ND SERIES)
CONTINUITY

Value: Cover or less

❑1, Nov 92, Hologram cover ... 2.95

CYBERRAD DEATHWATCH 2000
CONTINUITY

Value: Cover or less

❑1, Apr 93, NA, NA (w), trading card 2.50

❑2, Jul 93, NA, NA (w), trading card; indicia drops Deathwatch 2000 .... 2.50

CYBER REALITY COMIX
WONDER COMIX

Value: Cover or less

❑1, Fal 94, Arena; Leah 3.95

❑2, Win 95 .... 3.95

CYBERSEXATION
ANTARCTIC

Value: Cover or less

❑1, Mar 97, Cyberfux, b&w; adult 2.95

CYBERSPACE 3000
MARVEL

Value: Cover or less

❑1, Jul 93, Judgment Day, Glow-in-the-dark cover 2.95

❑2, Aug 93 .... 1.75

❑3, Sep 93 .... 1.75

❑4, Oct 93, A: Silver Surfer; A: Dark Angel; A: Galactus 1.75

❑5, Nov 93, Bad Habits! 1.75

❑6, Dec 93 .... 1.75

❑7, Jan 94 .... 1.75

❑8, Feb 94, Final Issue 1.75

CYBERSUIT ARKADYNE
IANUS

Value: Cover or less

❑1, b&w 2.50

❑2, b&w 2.50

❑3, Jun 92, b&w 2.50

❑4 .... 2.50

❑5 .... 2.50

❑6 .... 2.50

CYBERTRASH AND THE DOG
SILVERLINE

Value: Cover or less

❑1, May 98 .... 2.95

CYBERZONE
JET-BLACK GRAFIKS

	ORIG	GOOD	FINE	N-MINT
❑1, Jul 94	2.50	0.60	1.50	3.00
❑2, Sep 94	2.50	0.50	1.25	2.50
❑3, Dec 94	2.50	0.50	1.25	2.50
❑4, Mar 95	2.50	0.50	1.25	2.50
❑5, May 95	2.50	0.50	1.25	2.50
❑6, Sep 95	2.50	0.50	1.25	2.50
❑7, Feb 96	2.50	0.50	1.25	2.50
❑8, Final Issue	2.50	0.50	1.25	2.50

CYBLADE/GHOST RIDER
MARVEL

Value: Cover or less

❑1, Jan 97, Devil's Reign, Part 2, crossover with Top Cow; continues in Ghost Rider/Ballistic 2.95

CYBORG GERBILS
TRIGON

Value: Cover or less

❑1 .... 2.50

❑2 .... 2.50

CYBRID
MAXIMUM

Value: Cover or less

❑1, Jul 95, RL (w), Chrysalis, Part 1 .... 2.95

CYCOPS
COMICS INTERVIEW

Value: Cover or less

❑1, Jun 88, Cyclops Blues, b&w 1.95

❑2, Sum 88, b&w 1.95

❑3, b&w 1.95

CY-GOR
IMAGE

Value: Cover or less

❑1, Jul 99, Fire in Mind 2.50

❑2, Aug 99, Fire in Mind, Part 2 .... 2.50

❑3, Sep 99, Needles and Pins 2.50

❑4, Oct 99, Exquisite Corpse .. 2.50

❑5, Nov 99, Then One Foggy Christmas Eve 2.50

CYLINDERHEAD
SLAVE LABOR

Value: Cover or less

❑1, Feb 89, b&w 1.95

CYNDER
IMMORTELLE

	ORIG	GOOD	FINE	N-MINT
❑1, 1: Cynder	2.50	0.60	1.50	3.00
❑2	2.50	0.60	1.50	3.00
❑3	2.50	0.50	1.25	2.50
❑Anl 1	2.95	0.60	1.50	3.00

CYNDER/HELLINA SPECIAL
IMMORTELLE

Value: Cover or less

❑1 .... 2.95

CYNTHERITA
SIDE SHOW

Value: Cover or less

❑1 .... 2.95

CZAR CHASM
C&T

Value: Cover or less

❑1, b&w 2.00

❑2, b&w 2.00

CYBLADE/SHI: THE BATTLE FOR INDEPENDENTS
IMAGE

	ORIG	GOOD	FINE	N-MINT
❑1, 1: Witchblade	2.95	1.00	2.50	5.00
❑1/A, 1: Witchblade, alternate cover; crossover; concludes in Shi/Cyblade: The Battle for Independents #2	2.95	1.20	3.00	6.00
❑1/B, crossover; concludes in Shi/Cyblade: The Battle for Independents #2; San Diego Preview	2.95	1.20	3.00	6.00
❑1/CS, boxed set; crossover with Crusade; also contains Shi/Cyblade: The Battle for Independents #2	—	6.00	15.00	30.00
❑Ash 1, preview of crossover with Crusade	—	0.40	1.00	2.00

D

DADAVILLE
CALIBER

Value: Cover or less

❑1, b&w 2.95

DAEMON MASK
AMAZING

Value: Cover or less

❑1, The Crimson Wings of Silence 1.95

DAEMONSTORM
CALIBER

	ORIG	GOOD	FINE	N-MINT
❑1, TMc (c), b&w	3.95	0.79	1.98	3.95
❑Ash 1, nn; b&w; preview of upcoming series	0.99	0.20	0.50	1.00

DAFFY QADDAFI
COMICS UNLIMITED

	ORIG	GOOD	FINE	N-MINT
❑1, A Dictator's Nightmare in Wonderland, A: Ronald Reagan; A: Daffy Duck; A: Moammar Qaddafi; A: Oliver North, b&w; Nancy Reagan cameo	1.75	0.40	1.00	2.00

DAGAR THE INVINCIBLE (TALES OF SWORD AND SORCERY...)
GOLD KEY

	ORIG	GOOD	FINE	N-MINT
❑1, Oct 72, The Sword Of Dagar, 1: Ostellon; 1: Scorpio; O: Dagar	0.15	1.60	4.00	8.00
❑2	0.15	0.80	2.00	4.00
❑3, The Wrath Of The Vampires, 1: Graylin	0.15	0.60	1.50	3.00
❑4	—	0.60	1.50	3.00
❑5	—	0.60	1.50	3.00
❑6, Dark Gods story	—	0.50	1.25	2.50
❑7	—	0.50	1.25	2.50
❑8	—	0.50	1.25	2.50
❑9	—	0.50	1.25	2.50
❑10	—	0.50	1.25	2.50
❑11	—	0.40	1.00	2.00
❑12	—	0.40	1.00	2.00
❑13	—	0.40	1.00	2.00
❑14	—	0.40	1.00	2.00
❑15	—	0.40	1.00	2.00
❑16	—	0.40	1.00	2.00
❑17	—	0.40	1.00	2.00
❑18, Final issue of original run (1976)	—	0.40	1.00	2.00
❑19, The Sword Of Dagar, O: Dagar, One-shot revival: 1982; Reprints Dagar #1	0.60	0.40	1.00	2.00

DAHMER'S ZOMBIE SQUAD
BONEYARD

Value: Cover or less

❑1, Feb 93 ... 3.95

DAI KAMIKAZE!
NOW

Value: Cover or less

❑1, Jun 87, Generations ... 3.00
❑1-2, Sep 87, Generations, 2nd Printing ... 1.75
❑2, Jul 87 ... 1.50
❑3, Aug 87 ... 1.50
❑4, Oct 87 ... 1.50
❑5, Nov 87 ... 1.75
❑6, Dec 87 ... 1.75
❑7, Jan 88 ... 1.75
❑8, Feb 88 ... 1.75
❑9, Apr 88 ... 1.75
❑10, Apr 88 ... 1.75
❑11, Jun 88 ... 1.75
❑12, Jul 88 ... 1.75

DAIKAZU
GROUND ZERO

Value: Cover or less

❑1, b&w ... 1.50
❑1-2, 2nd Printing ... 1.50
❑2, b&w ... 1.50
❑2-2, 2nd Printing ... 1.50
❑3, b&w ... 1.50
❑4, b&w ... 1.50
❑5, b&w ... 1.50
❑6, b&w ... 1.50
❑7, b&w ... 1.50
❑8 ... 1.75

DAILY BUGLE
MARVEL

Value: Cover or less

❑1, Dec 96, Front Page, b&w ... 2.50
❑2, Jan 97, Scoop, b&w ... 2.50
❑3, Feb 97, Deadline, b&w; Final Issue ... 2.50

DAISY AND DONALD
GOLD KEY

	ORIG	GOOD	FINE	N-MINT
❑1, May 73, CB, Dinner Date, The Beauty Business, The Shutterbug Duck, A: April; A: May; A: June	0.15	2.40	6.00	12.00
❑2	—	1.20	3.00	6.00
❑3	—	0.80	2.00	4.00
❑4, Feb 74, CB, Reprint	0.20	0.80	2.00	4.00
❑5	—	0.80	2.00	4.00
❑6	—	0.80	2.00	4.00
❑7	—	0.80	2.00	4.00
❑8	—	0.80	2.00	4.00
❑9	—	0.80	2.00	4.00
❑10	—	0.80	2.00	4.00
❑11, Jul 75	0.20	0.60	1.50	3.00
❑12	—	0.60	1.50	3.00
❑13	—	0.60	1.50	3.00
❑14	—	0.60	1.50	3.00
❑15	—	0.60	1.50	3.00
❑16	—	0.60	1.50	3.00
❑17	—	0.60	1.50	3.00
❑18	—	0.60	1.50	3.00
❑19	—	0.60	1.50	3.00
❑20	—	0.60	1.50	3.00
❑21	—	0.60	1.50	3.00
❑22	—	0.60	1.50	3.00
❑23	—	0.60	1.50	3.00
❑24	—	0.60	1.50	3.00
❑25	—	0.60	1.50	3.00
❑26	—	0.60	1.50	3.00
❑27	—	0.60	1.50	3.00
❑28	—	0.60	1.50	3.00
❑29	—	0.60	1.50	3.00
❑30	—	0.60	1.50	3.00
❑31	—	0.40	1.00	2.00
❑32	—	0.40	1.00	2.00
❑33	—	0.40	1.00	2.00
❑34	—	0.40	1.00	2.00
❑35	—	0.40	1.00	2.00
❑36	—	0.40	1.00	2.00
❑37	—	0.40	1.00	2.00
❑38	—	0.40	1.00	2.00
❑39	—	0.40	1.00	2.00
❑40, Sep 79	0.40	0.40	1.00	2.00
❑41	—	0.40	1.00	2.00
❑42	—	0.40	1.00	2.00
❑43	—	0.40	1.00	2.00
❑44	—	0.40	1.00	2.00
❑45	—	0.40	1.00	2.00
❑46	—	0.40	1.00	2.00
❑47	—	0.40	1.00	2.00
❑48	—	0.40	1.00	2.00
❑49	—	0.40	1.00	2.00
❑50	—	0.40	1.00	2.00
❑51	—	0.40	1.00	2.00
❑52	—	0.40	1.00	2.00
❑53	—	0.40	1.00	2.00
❑54	—	0.40	1.00	2.00
❑55	—	0.40	1.00	2.00
❑56	—	0.40	1.00	2.00

The cybernetically enhanced ape, Cy-Gor, spun off from Todd McFarlane's *Spawn* into his own five-issue mini-series. An action figure of the character was also created.

	ORIG	GOOD	FINE	N-MINT
❑57	—	0.40	1.00	2.00
❑58	—	0.40	1.00	2.00
❑59	—	0.40	1.00	2.00

DAKOTA NORTH
MARVEL

	ORIG	GOOD	FINE	N-MINT
❑1, Jun 86, Design for Dying	0.75	0.20	0.50	1.00
❑2, Aug 86	0.75	0.20	0.50	1.00
❑3, Oct 86	0.75	0.20	0.50	1.00
❑4, Dec 86	0.75	0.20	0.50	1.00
❑5, Feb 87	0.75	0.20	0.50	1.00

DALGODA
FANTAGRAPHICS

Value: Cover or less

❑1, Aug 84, Factions ... 2.25
❑2, Dec 84 ... 1.50
❑3, Feb 85 ... 1.50
❑4, Apr 85 ... 1.50
❑5, Jun 85 ... 2.00
❑6, Oct 85 ... 2.00
❑7, Jan 86 ... 2.00
❑8, Apr 86 ... 2.00

DALKIEL: THE PROPHECY
VEROTIK

Value: Cover or less

❑1, Aug 98, nn; adult; cardstock cover ... 3.95

DAMAGE
DC

	ORIG	GOOD	FINE	N-MINT
❑0, Oct 94, Back Again, Follows Damage #6	1.95	0.40	1.00	2.00
❑1, Apr 94, Damage	1.75	0.40	1.00	2.00
❑2, May 94	1.75	0.40	1.00	2.00
❑3, Jun 94	1.75	0.35	0.88	1.75
❑4, Jul 94	1.75	0.35	0.88	1.75
❑5, Aug 94, Iron Munro	1.95	0.39	0.98	1.95
❑6, Sep 94, A: New Titans, Zero Hour	1.95	0.39	0.98	1.95
❑7, Nov 94	1.95	0.39	0.98	1.95
❑8, Dec 94, Fragments, Part 1	1.95	0.39	0.98	1.95
❑9, Jan 95, Fragments, Part 2, A: Iron Munro	1.95	0.39	0.98	1.95
❑10, Feb 95, Fragments, Part 3, A: Iron Munro	1.95	0.39	0.98	1.95
❑11, Mar 95, Fragments, Part 4	1.95	0.39	0.98	1.95
❑12, Apr 95	1.95	0.39	0.98	1.95
❑13, Jun 95, Picking Up the Pieces, Part 1	1.95	0.45	1.13	2.25
❑14, Jul 95, Picking Up the Pieces, Part 2, A: Ray	2.25	0.45	1.13	2.25
❑15, Aug 95, Picking Up the Pieces, Part 3	2.25	0.45	1.13	2.25
❑16, Sep 95, The Siege of The Zi Charam, Part 4	2.25	0.45	1.13	2.25
❑17, Oct 95	2.25	0.45	1.13	2.25
❑18, Nov 95, Underworld Unleashed, Underworld Unleashed	2.25	0.45	1.13	2.25
❑19, Dec 95	2.25	0.45	1.13	2.25
❑20, Jan 96, Final Issue	2.25	0.45	1.13	2.25

DAMAGE CONTROL (VOL. 1)
MARVEL

	ORIG	GOOD	FINE	N-MINT
❑1, May 89, A Restoration Remedy, A: Thor; A: Spider-Man	1.00	0.30	0.75	1.50
❑2, Jun 89, A: Doctor Doom	1.00	0.20	0.50	1.00
❑3, Jul 89, A: Iron Man	1.00	0.20	0.50	1.00
❑4, Aug 89, A: Wolverine, Inferno	1.00	0.20	0.50	1.00

DAMAGE CONTROL (VOL. 2)
MARVEL

	ORIG	GOOD	FINE	N-MINT
❑1, Dec 89, No Vault Insurance, A: Thor; A: Captain America, Acts of Vengeance	1.00	0.30	0.75	1.50
❑2, Dec 89, Acts of Vengeance, Part 15, A: Punisher, Acts of Vengeance	1.00	0.20	0.50	1.00
❑3, Jan 90, Acts of Vengeance, Part 23, A: She-Hulk, Acts of Vengeance	1.00	0.20	0.50	1.00
❑4, Feb 90, A: Thor; A: Captain America; A: Shield; A: Punisher, Acts of Vengeance	1.00	0.20	0.50	1.00

DAMAGE CONTROL (VOL. 3)
MARVEL

Value: Cover or less

❑1, Jun 91, The Sure Thing, A: Spider-Man ... 1.25
❑2, Jul 91, A: Hulk ... 1.25
❑3, Aug 91, The Movie, A: Silver Surfer; A: Galactus ... 1.25
❑4, Sep 91, A: Silver Surfer ... 1.25

DAMNATION
FANTAGRAPHICS

Value: Cover or less

❑1, Sum 94, b&w; magazine ... 2.95

DAMNED
IMAGE

Value: Cover or less

Issue	ORIG
❑1, Jun 97, MZ	2.50
❑2, Jul 97, MZ	2.50
❑3, Aug 97, MZ	2.50
❑4, Sep 97, MZ, Final Issue	2.50

DANCE OF LIFEY DEATH
DARK HORSE

Value: Cover or less

Issue	ORIG
❑1, Jan 94, nn	3.95

DANCE PARTY DOA
SLAVE LABOR

Value: Cover or less

Issue	ORIG
❑1, Nov 93, Dance Party D.O.A.; Kake Gunther vs. the NFL, adult	3.95

DANGER GIRL
IMAGE

Issue	ORIG	GOOD	FINE	N-MINT
❑1, Mar 98, Dangerously Yours	2.95	0.80	2.00	4.00
❑1/A, Mar 98, Dangerously Yours, chromium cover; Signed by J. Scott Campbell	2.50	3.00	7.50	15.00
❑1/B, Mar 98, Dangerously Yours, deluxe oversized; magazine-sized	2.50	9.00	22.50	45.00
❑1/C, Mar 98, Dangerously Yours, Tour Edition; Woman holding rifle, white background	2.95	3.00	7.50	15.00
❑1/D, Dangerously Yours, Chromium a-go-go cover	—	16.00	40.00	80.00
❑2, May 98, Dangerous Liaisons	2.50	0.80	2.00	4.00
❑2/A, May 98, Dangerous Liaisons, Special holochrome cover	2.50	4.00	10.00	20.00
❑2/B, Dangerous Liaisons, Dynamic Forces cover, later recalled	—	7.00	17.50	35.00
❑2/GO, May 98, Dangerous Liaisons, Gold logo	2.50	1.60	4.00	8.00
❑3, Aug 98, Dangerous Curves, White background, 3 girls on cover	2.50	0.60	1.50	3.00
❑3/A, Aug 98, Dangerous Curves, Girls surrounding guy, knife cover	2.50	0.60	1.50	3.00
❑3/B, Aug 98, Dangerous Curves, "Filled to the Brim with Danger" cover	2.50	0.60	1.50	3.00
❑4, Dec 98, Maximum Danger	2.50	0.60	1.50	3.00
❑4/A, Dec 98, alternate cover (purple background)	2.50	0.60	1.50	3.00
❑5, Jul 99, Damgerous When Wet	2.50	0.50	1.25	2.50
❑5/A, Dynamic Forces variant; Woman in red bikini	—	2.00	5.00	10.00
❑5/B, Dynamic Forces variant; Woman in blue bikini	—	2.00	5.00	10.00
❑6, Dec 99, Dangerous Destinies	2.50	0.50	1.25	2.50
❑6/A, Dec 99, Dangerous Destinies, DFE gold foil edition	2.50	3.99	9.98	19.95
❑6/GO, Dec 99, Dangerous Destinies, DFE gold foil edition	2.50	2.00	5.00	10.00
❑7, Feb 01, Into the Danger Zone	5.95	1.19	2.97	5.95
❑Ash 1, Prelude to Danger, Preview edition	—	1.00	2.50	5.00
❑Ash 1/GO, Prelude to Danger, Preview edition; Gold logo	—	2.00	5.00	10.00

DANGEROUS TIMES
EVOLUTION

Value: Cover or less

Issue	ORIG
❑1, The Last Survivor of Mona	1.75
❑1-2, 2nd Printing	1.75
❑2	1.75
❑2-2, 2nd Printing	1.75
❑3, The Stone and the Icon	1.95
❑3-2, 2nd Printing	1.95
❑4, One Key Many Doors	1.95
❑4-2, 2nd Printing	1.95
❑5	1.95
❑5-2, 2nd Printing	1.95
❑6, Class Struggle	1.95
❑6-2, 2nd Printing	2.25

DANGER RANGER
CHECKER

Value: Cover or less

Issue	ORIG
❑1, Sum 98, Service of a Villain	1.95
❑2	1.95

DANGER TRAIL (MINI-SERIES)
DC

Value: Cover or less

Issue	ORIG
❑1, Apr 93, CI, The Serpent In The Garden File!	1.50
❑2, May 93, CI	1.50
❑3, Jun 93, CI	1.50
❑4, Jul 93, CI	1.50

DANGER UNLIMITED
DARK HORSE

Value: Cover or less

Issue	ORIG
❑1, Feb 94, JBy, JBy (w), The Phoenix Agenda, Part 1, 1: Danger Unlimited; 1: Doc Danger; 1: Thermal; 1: Hunk; 1: Torch of Liberty; 1: Miss Mirage	2.00
❑2, Mar 94, JBy, JBy (w), The Phoenix Agenda, Part 2	2.50
❑3, Apr 94, JBy, JBy (w), The Phoenix Agenda, Part 3, 1: Caucus	2.50
❑4, May 94, JBy, JBy (w), The Phoenix Agenda, Part 4	2.50

DAN TURNER: ACE IN THE HOLE
ETERNITY

Value: Cover or less

Issue	ORIG
❑1, b&w	2.50

DAN TURNER: DARK STAR OF DEATH
ETERNITY

Value: Cover or less

Issue	ORIG
❑1, b&w	2.50

DAN TURNER: HOMICIDE HUNCH
ETERNITY

Value: Cover or less

Issue	ORIG
❑1, Jul 91, b&w	2.50

DAN TURNER: STAR CHAMBER
ETERNITY

Value: Cover or less

Issue	ORIG
❑1, Sep 91, b&w	2.50

DARBY O'GILL AND THE LITTLE PEOPLE
GOLD KEY

Issue	ORIG	GOOD	FINE	N-MINT
❑1, Jan 70, nn; movie Adaptation; Four Color Comics #1024	0.15	20.00	50.00	100.00

D'ARC TANGENT
FFANTASY FFACTORY

Value: Cover or less

Issue	ORIG
❑1, Aug 82, PF, PF (w), Clues and Omens	2.00

DAREDEVIL
MARVEL

Issue	ORIG	GOOD	FINE	N-MINT
❑-1, Jul 97, Flashback	1.99	0.45	1.13	2.25
❑1, Apr 64, BEv, 1: Foggy Nelson; 1: Daredevil; D: Battling Jack Murdock; 1: Karen Page	0.12	360.00	900.00	1800.00
❑2, Jun 64, JO, V: Electro; A: Fantastic Four	0.12	100.00	250.00	500.00
❑3, Aug 64, JO, 1: Owl	0.12	65.00	162.50	325.00
❑4, Oct 64, JO, V: Killgrave; 1: The Purple Man	0.12	52.00	130.00	260.00
❑5, Dec 64, WW, V: Masked Matador	0.12	40.00	100.00	200.00
❑6, Feb 65, WW, V: Fellowship of Fear; 1: Mister Fear I (Zoltan Drago)	0.12	29.00	72.50	145.00
❑7, Apr 65, WW, A: Sub-Mariner; 1: red costume	0.12	40.00	100.00	200.00
❑8, Jun 65, WW, 1: Stilt Man	0.12	27.00	67.50	135.00
❑9, Aug 65, WW, That He May See!	0.12	26.00	65.00	130.00
❑10, Oct 65, WW, While the City Sleeps!, 1: Ape-Man I (Gordon "Monk" Keefer); 1: Bird-Man I (Henry Hawk); 1: Cat-Man I (Townshend Horgan); 1: Ani-Men; 1: Frog-Man I (Francois LeBlanc)	0.12	26.00	65.00	130.00
❑11, Dec 65, JR; JK	0.12	17.00	42.50	85.00
❑12, Jan 66, 2: Ka-Zar	0.12	17.00	42.50	85.00
❑13, Feb 66, O: Ka-Zar	0.12	17.00	42.50	85.00
❑14, Mar 66, A: Ka-Zar	0.12	17.00	42.50	85.00
❑15, Apr 66	0.12	17.00	42.50	85.00
❑16, May 66, A: Spider-Man; 1: Masked Marauder	0.12	18.00	45.00	90.00
❑17, Jun 66, A: Spider-Man	0.12	18.00	45.00	90.00
❑18, Jul 66, JR, 1: Gladiator I (Melvin Potter)	0.12	10.00	25.00	50.00
❑19, Aug 66, JR, A: Gladiator I (Melvin Potter)	0.12	10.00	25.00	50.00
❑20, Sep 66, GC, V: Owl	0.12	9.00	22.50	45.00
❑21, Oct 66, GC, V: Owl	0.12	6.80	17.00	34.00
❑22, Nov 66, GC, SL (w), The Tri-Man Lives!	0.12	6.80	17.00	34.00
❑23, Dec 66, GC	0.12	6.80	17.00	34.00
❑24, Jan 67, GC, A: Ka-Zar	0.12	6.80	17.00	34.00
❑25, Feb 67, GC	0.12	6.80	17.00	34.00
❑26, Mar 67, GC	0.12	6.80	17.00	34.00
❑27, Apr 67, GC, A: Spider-Man	0.12	7.60	19.00	38.00
❑28, May 67, GC	0.12	6.80	17.00	34.00
❑29, Jun 67, GC, SL (w), Unmasked!	0.12	6.80	17.00	34.00
❑30, Jul 67, GC, A: Thor	0.12	6.80	17.00	34.00
❑31, Aug 67, GC, Cobra	0.12	5.60	14.00	28.00
❑32, Sep 67, GC	0.12	5.60	14.00	28.00
❑33, Oct 67, GC, SL (w), Behold The Beetle	0.12	5.60	14.00	28.00
❑34, Nov 67, GC	0.12	5.60	14.00	28.00
❑35, Dec 67, GC, V: Trapster; A: Invisible Girl	0.12	5.60	14.00	28.00
❑36, Jan 68, GC, A: Doctor Doom; A: Fantastic Four	0.12	5.60	14.00	28.00
❑37, Feb 68, GC, V: Doctor Doom	0.12	5.60	14.00	28.00
❑38, Mar 68, GC, SL (w), The Living Prison!, A: Doctor Doom; A: Fantastic Four	0.12	5.60	14.00	28.00
❑39, Apr 68, GC, 1: Exterminator (later Death-Stalker)	0.12	5.60	14.00	28.00
❑40, May 68, GC, SL (w), The Fallen Hero.	0.12	5.60	14.00	28.00
❑41, Jun 68, GC, SL (w), The Death Of Mike Murdock!, D: Mike Murdock (Daredevil's "twin brother")	0.12	5.60	14.00	28.00
❑42, Jul 68, GC, 1: Jester	0.12	5.60	14.00	28.00
❑43, Aug 68, GC, V: Captain America; O: Daredevil	0.12	4.80	12.00	24.00
❑44, Sep 68, GC	0.12	4.00	10.00	20.00
❑45, Oct 68, GC, Photo cover	0.12	4.00	10.00	20.00
❑46, Nov 68, GC	0.12	4.00	10.00	20.00
❑47, Dec 68, GC	0.12	4.00	10.00	20.00
❑48, Jan 69, GC	0.12	4.00	10.00	20.00
❑49, Feb 69, GC, Daredevil Drops Out, 1: Samuel "Starr" Saxon	0.12	4.00	10.00	20.00
❑50, Mar 69	0.12	4.40	11.00	22.00
❑51, Apr 69, A: Captain America	0.12	4.40	11.00	22.00
❑52, May 69, A: Black Panther	0.12	4.40	11.00	22.00

	ORIG	GOOD	FINE	N-MINT
❑53, Jun 69, GC, O: Daredevil	0.12	5.00	12.50	25.00
❑54, Jul 69, GC, 1: Mister Fear II (Samuel "Starr" Saxon); A: Spider-Man	0.15	3.00	7.50	15.00
❑55, Aug 69, GC	0.15	3.00	7.50	15.00
❑56, Sep 69, GC	0.15	3.00	7.50	15.00
❑57, Oct 69, GC, Daredevil reveals identity to Karen Page	0.15	3.00	7.50	15.00
❑58, Nov 69, GC	0.15	3.00	7.50	15.00
❑59, Dec 69, GC	0.15	3.00	7.50	15.00
❑60, Jan 70, GC	0.15	2.40	6.00	12.00
❑61, Feb 70, GC	0.15	2.40	6.00	12.00
❑62, Mar 70, GC, O: Nighthawk II (Kyle Richmond)	0.15	2.40	6.00	12.00
❑63, Apr 70, GC	0.15	2.40	6.00	12.00
❑64, May 70, GC	0.15	2.40	6.00	12.00
❑65, Jun 70, GC	0.15	2.40	6.00	12.00
❑66, Jul 70, GC, And One Cried Murder	0.15	2.40	6.00	12.00
❑67, Aug 70, GC	0.15	2.40	6.00	12.00
❑68, Sep 70, GC	0.15	2.40	6.00	12.00
❑69, Oct 70, GC, 1: William Carver (Thunderbolt)	0.15	2.40	6.00	12.00
❑70, Nov 70, GC, The Tribune	0.15	2.40	6.00	12.00
❑71, Dec 70, GC	0.15	2.40	6.00	12.00
❑72, Jan 71, GC, 1: Tagak the Leopard Lord	0.15	1.80	4.50	9.00
❑73, Feb 71, GC	0.15	1.80	4.50	9.00
❑74, Mar 71, GC	0.15	1.80	4.50	9.00
❑75, Apr 71, GC	0.15	1.80	4.50	9.00
❑76, May 71, GC	0.15	1.80	4.50	9.00
❑77, Jun 71, GC	0.15	1.80	4.50	9.00
❑78, Jul 71, GC	0.15	1.80	4.50	9.00
❑79, Aug 71, GC	0.15	1.80	4.50	9.00
❑80, Sep 71, GC	0.15	1.80	4.50	9.00
❑81, Nov 71, GC, giant	0.25	1.80	4.50	9.00
❑82, Dec 71, GC	0.20	1.80	4.50	9.00
❑83, Jan 72, V: Mr. Hyde	0.20	1.80	4.50	9.00
❑84, Feb 72, GC, Night Of The Assassin	0.20	1.80	4.50	9.00
❑85, Mar 72	0.20	1.80	4.50	9.00
❑86, Apr 72	0.20	1.80	4.50	9.00
❑87, May 72	0.20	1.80	4.50	9.00
❑88, Jun 72, GC, Call Him Killgrave, O: Black Widow	0.20	1.80	4.50	9.00
❑89, Jul 72	0.20	1.80	4.50	9.00
❑90, Aug 72	0.20	1.80	4.50	9.00
❑91, Sep 72, 1: Mister Fear III (Larry Cranston)	0.20	1.80	4.50	9.00
❑92, Oct 72, GC, On The Eve Of The Talon	0.20	1.80	4.50	9.00
❑93, Nov 72	0.20	1.80	4.50	9.00
❑94, Dec 72	0.20	1.80	4.50	9.00
❑95, Jan 73	0.20	1.80	4.50	9.00
❑96, Feb 73	0.20	1.80	4.50	9.00
❑97, Mar 73, GC, He Who Saves, 1: Disciples of Doom; 1: Dark Messiah	0.20	1.80	4.50	9.00
❑98, Apr 73	0.20	1.80	4.50	9.00
❑99, May 73	0.20	1.80	4.50	9.00
❑100, Jun 73, GC, 1: Angar the Screamer, 100th anniversary issue	0.20	3.00	7.50	15.00
❑101, Jul 73	0.20	1.20	3.00	6.00
❑102, Aug 73, Stilt-Man Stalks The City	0.20	1.20	3.00	6.00
❑103, Sep 73, DH, ...Then Came Ramrod!, 1: Ramrod I	0.20	1.20	3.00	6.00
❑104, Oct 73	0.20	1.20	3.00	6.00
❑105, Nov 73, A: Thanos; 1: Moondragon	0.20	1.20	3.00	6.00
❑106, Dec 73, DH, Life Be Not Proud!, 1: Black Spectre (female group); A: Black Widow	0.20	1.20	3.00	6.00
❑107, Jan 74, SB, Blind Man's Bluff, A: Captain Marvel	0.20	1.20	3.00	6.00
❑108, Mar 74, Cry...Beetle!, Marvel Value Stamp A/22 (Man-Thing)	0.20	1.20	3.00	6.00
❑109, May 74	0.25	1.20	3.00	6.00
❑110, Jun 74, GC, Birthright!, Marvel Value Stamp	0.25	1.20	3.00	6.00
❑111, Jul 74, 1: Silver Samurai	0.25	1.20	3.00	6.00
❑112, Aug 74	0.25	1.20	3.00	6.00
❑113, Sep 74	0.25	1.20	3.00	6.00
❑114, Oct 74, A Quiet Night In The Swamp, 1: Death-Stalker, Marvel Value Stamp A/7 (Werewolf)	0.25	1.20	3.00	6.00
❑115, Nov 74, Death Stalks The City!, Marvel Value Stamp A/35 (Killraven)	0.25	1.20	3.00	6.00
❑116, Dec 74	0.25	1.20	3.00	6.00
❑117, Jan 75, Mind Tap!, Marvel Value Stamp A/88 (The Leader)	0.25	1.20	3.00	6.00
❑118, Feb 75, DH, Circus Spelled Sideways Is Death!, 1: Blackwing, Marvel Value Stamp A/28 (Hawkeye)	0.25	1.20	3.00	6.00
❑119, Mar 75	0.25	1.20	3.00	6.00
❑120, Apr 75, ...And A Hydra New Year!, Marvel Value Stamp A/99 (Sandman)	0.25	1.20	3.00	6.00

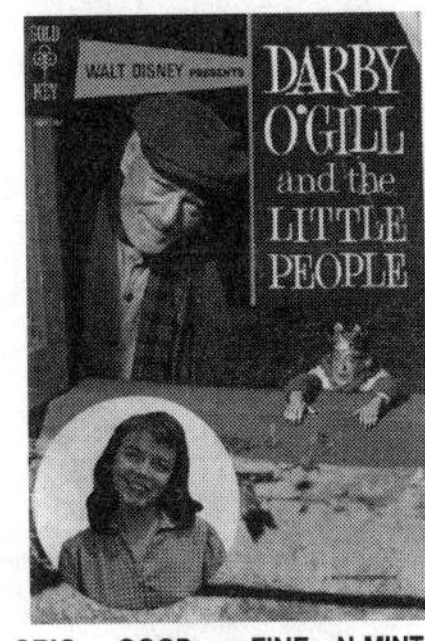

Before he was James Bond, a young Sean Connery was featured in Walt Disney's *Darby O'Gill and the Little People.* The copy listed here was reprinted by Gold Key for a 1970 re-release of the 1950s film.

© 1970 Walt Disney Productions (Gold Key)

	ORIG	GOOD	FINE	N-MINT
❑121, May 75, Foggy Nelson, Agent Of Shield	0.25	0.80	2.00	4.00
❑122, Jun 75, Hydra-And-Seek	0.25	0.80	2.00	4.00
❑123, Jul 75, Holocaust In The Halls Of Hydra!	0.25	0.80	2.00	4.00
❑124, Aug 75, KJ; GC, 1: Copperhead; 1: Blake Tower	0.25	0.80	2.00	4.00
❑125, Sep 75, KJ	0.25	0.80	2.00	4.00
❑126, Oct 75, KJ, 1: Torpedo	0.25	0.80	2.00	4.00
❑127, Nov 75, KJ	0.25	0.80	2.00	4.00
❑128, Dec 75, KJ, Death Stalks The Stairway To The Stars!	0.25	0.80	2.00	4.00
❑129, Jan 76, KJ	0.25	0.80	2.00	4.00
❑130, Feb 76, KJ	0.25	0.80	2.00	4.00
❑131, Mar 76, KJ, O: Bullseye	0.25	3.60	9.00	18.00
❑132, Apr 76	0.25	0.80	2.00	4.00
❑133, May 76, 1: Mind-Wave	0.25	0.60	1.50	3.00
❑134, Jun 76	0.25	0.60	1.50	3.00
❑135, Jul 76, What Is Happening?	0.25	0.60	1.50	3.00
❑136, Aug 76, JB, A Hanging For A Hero!	0.25	0.60	1.50	3.00
❑137, Sep 76, JB, The Murder Maze Strikes Twice!	0.30	0.60	1.50	3.00
❑138, Oct 76, JBy, Where Is Karen Page?, A: Death's Head (monster); A: Ghost Rider	0.30	0.60	1.50	3.00
❑139, Nov 76, SB	0.30	0.60	1.50	3.00
❑140, Dec 76, SB, Death Times Two	0.30	0.60	1.50	3.00
❑141, Jan 77, GK	0.30	0.60	1.50	3.00
❑142, Feb 77, JB, V: Cobra, Mr. Hyde	0.30	0.60	1.50	3.00
❑143, Mar 77, Hyde And Go Seek	0.30	0.60	1.50	3.00
❑144, Apr 77	0.30	0.60	1.50	3.00
❑145, May 77, JM; GT, Danger Rides The Bitter Wind	0.30	0.60	1.50	3.00
❑146, Jun 77, GK, V: Bullseye	0.30	0.60	1.50	3.00
❑147, Jul 77, KJ; GK, Breaking Point	0.30	0.60	1.50	3.00
❑148, Sep 77, KJ; GK	0.30	0.60	1.50	3.00
❑149, Nov 77, CI	0.35	0.60	1.50	3.00
❑150, Jan 78, KJ; CI, Catastrophe, 1: Paladin	0.35	0.60	1.50	3.00
❑151, Mar 78, KJ; GK, Crisis!, Daredevil reveals identity to Heather Glenn	0.35	0.60	1.50	3.00
❑152, May 78, KJ; CI, Prisoner, A: Paladin.	0.35	0.60	1.50	3.00
❑153, Jul 78, 1: Ben Urich	0.35	0.60	1.50	3.00
❑154, Sep 78, GC, Arena!	0.35	0.60	1.50	3.00
❑155, Nov 78, FR, The Man Without Fear?, Black Widow returns	0.35	0.60	1.50	3.00
❑156, Jan 79, GC, Ring Of Death!, A: 1960's Daredevil	0.35	0.60	1.50	3.00
❑157, Mar 79, KJ; GC, The Ungrateful Dead, 1: Ape-Man II (Roy McVey); 1: Cat-Man II (Sebastian Patane); 1: Bird-Man II (Achille DiBacco)	0.35	0.60	1.50	3.00
❑158, May 79, FM, D: Death-Stalker; D: Ape-Man II (Roy McVey); D: Cat-Man II (Sebastian Patane); V: Deathstalker	0.40	6.00	15.00	30.00
❑159, Jul 79, FM, V: Bullseye	0.40	3.20	8.00	16.00
❑160, Sep 79, FM, V: Bullseye	0.40	1.80	4.50	9.00
❑161, Nov 79, FM, V: Bullseye	0.40	1.80	4.50	9.00
❑162, Jan 80, SD	0.40	0.60	1.50	3.00
❑163, Mar 80, FM	0.40	1.20	3.00	6.00
❑164, May 80, FM	0.40	1.20	3.00	6.00
❑165, Jul 80, FM	0.40	1.20	3.00	6.00
❑166, Sep 80, FM	0.50	1.20	3.00	6.00
❑167, Nov 80, FM	0.50	1.20	3.00	6.00
❑168, Jan 81, FM, FM (w), 1: Elektra	0.50	4.80	12.00	24.00
❑169, Mar 81, FM, FM (w), V: Bullseye; A: Elektra	0.50	1.60	4.00	8.00
❑170, May 81, FM, FM (w), The Kingpin Must Die, V: Bullseye	0.50	1.60	4.00	8.00
❑171, Jun 81, FM, FM (w)	0.50	1.00	2.50	5.00
❑172, Jul 81, FM, FM (w)	0.50	1.00	2.50	5.00
❑173, Aug 81, FM, FM (w)	0.50	1.00	2.50	5.00
❑174, Sep 81, FM, FM (w)	0.50	1.00	2.50	5.00
❑175, Oct 81, FM, FM (w)	0.50	1.00	2.50	5.00
❑176, Nov 81, FM, FM (w), 1: Stick; A: Elektra	0.50	1.00	2.50	5.00
❑177, Dec 81, FM, FM (w), Where Angles Fear To Tread, A: Elektra	0.50	1.00	2.50	5.00

	ORIG	GOOD	FINE	N-MINT
❑178, Jan 82, FM, FM (w), Paper Chase, A: Elektra	0.60	1.00	2.50	5.00
❑179, Feb 82, FM, FM (w), Spiked, A: Elektra	0.60	1.00	2.50	5.00
❑180, Mar 82, FM, FM (w), A: Elektra	0.60	1.00	2.50	5.00
❑181, Apr 82, FM, FM (w), Last Hand, V: Bullseye; D: Elektra, double-sized; Punisher cameo out of costume	1.00	1.40	3.50	7.00
❑182, May 82, FM, FM (w), She's Alive, V: Punisher	0.60	0.80	2.00	4.00
❑183, Jun 82, FM, FM (w), Child's Play, V: Punisher	0.60	0.80	2.00	4.00
❑184, Jul 82, FM, FM (w), Good Guys Wear Red, V: Punisher	0.60	0.80	2.00	4.00
❑185, Aug 82, KJ; FM, FM (w), Guts	0.60	0.50	1.25	2.50
❑186, Sep 82, KJ; FM, FM (w), Stilts	0.60	0.50	1.25	2.50
❑187, Oct 82, KJ; FM, FM (w), Overkill, A: Black Widow	0.60	0.50	1.25	2.50
❑188, Nov 82, KJ; FM, FM (w), the Widow's Bite	0.60	0.50	1.25	2.50
❑189, Dec 82, KJ; FM, FM (w), Siege, D: Stick	0.60	0.60	1.50	3.00
❑190, Jan 83, KJ; FM, FM (w), Resurrection, A: Elektra, Double-size	1.00	0.60	1.50	3.00
❑191, Feb 83, FM, FM (w)	0.60	0.40	1.00	2.00
❑192, Mar 83, KJ, Promises	0.60	0.40	1.00	2.00
❑193, Apr 83, KJ, Bitsy's Revenge	0.60	0.40	1.00	2.00
❑194, May 83, Judgement	0.60	0.40	1.00	2.00
❑195, Jun 83, Betrayal	0.60	0.40	1.00	2.00
❑196, Jun 83, Enemies, A: Wolverine	0.60	1.20	3.00	6.00
❑197, Aug 83, Journey, V: Bullseye	0.60	0.40	1.00	2.00
❑198, Sep 83, Touch Of A Stranger	0.60	0.40	1.00	2.00
❑199, Oct 83, Daughter Of A Dark Wind	0.60	0.40	1.00	2.00
❑200, Nov 83, JBy (c), Redemption, V: Bullseye	0.60	0.40	1.00	2.00
❑201, Dec 83, The Day The Devil Didn't Dare!, A: Black Widow	0.60	0.40	1.00	2.00
❑202, Jan 84, Savages	0.60	0.40	1.00	2.00
❑203, Feb 84, Trumps!, 1: Trump	0.60	0.40	1.00	2.00
❑204, Mar 84, LMc, Vengeance Of The Victim!	0.60	0.40	1.00	2.00
❑205, Apr 84, The Gael!	0.60	0.40	1.00	2.00
❑206, May 84, Every Good And Perfect Gift...	0.60	0.40	1.00	2.00
❑207, Jun 84, Ultimatum!	0.60	0.40	1.00	2.00
❑208, Jul 84, The Deadliest Night Of My Life!	0.60	0.40	1.00	2.00
❑209, Aug 84, Blast From The Past!	0.60	0.40	1.00	2.00
❑210, Sep 84, Survivor!	0.60	0.40	1.00	2.00
❑211, Oct 84, This Hungry God	0.60	0.40	1.00	2.00
❑212, Nov 84, Lies	0.60	0.40	1.00	2.00
❑213, Dec 84, The Blindness Men Wish For	0.60	0.40	1.00	2.00
❑214, Jan 85, The Crumbling	0.60	0.40	1.00	2.00
❑215, Feb 85, Prophecy, A: Two-Gun Kid	0.60	0.40	1.00	2.00
❑216, Mar 85, The Second Secret	0.60	0.40	1.00	2.00
❑217, Apr 85, FM (c), The Sight Stealer	0.65	0.40	1.00	2.00
❑218, May 85, SB, All My Laurels You Have Riven Away!	0.65	0.40	1.00	2.00
❑219, Jun 85, FM; SB, FM (w), Badlands	0.65	0.40	1.00	2.00
❑220, Jul 85, Fog	0.65	0.40	1.00	2.00
❑221, Aug 85, Behold My Vengeance!	0.65	0.40	1.00	2.00
❑222, Sep 85, Fear In A Handful Of Dust, A: Black Widow	0.65	0.40	1.00	2.00
❑223, Oct 85, The Price, Secret Wars II	0.65	0.40	1.00	2.00
❑224, Nov 85, Abe, V: Sunturion	0.65	0.40	1.00	2.00
❑225, Dec 85, ...And Then you Die!, V: Vulture	0.65	0.40	1.00	2.00
❑226, Jan 86, FM, FM (w), Warriors	0.65	0.40	1.00	2.00
❑227, Feb 86, FM (w), A: Kingpin	0.75	0.40	1.00	2.00
❑228, Mar 86, FM (w)	0.75	0.40	1.00	2.00
❑229, Apr 86, FM (w), 1: Sister Maggie	0.75	0.40	1.00	2.00
❑230, May 86, FM (w)	0.75	0.40	1.00	2.00
❑231, Jun 86, FM (w)	0.75	0.40	1.00	2.00
❑232, Jul 86, FM (w), God And Country	0.75	0.40	1.00	2.00
❑233, Aug 86, FM (w), Armageddon	0.75	0.40	1.00	2.00
❑234, Sep 86, SD, Madcasting	0.75	0.40	1.00	2.00
❑235, Oct 86, SD, A Safe Place	0.75	0.40	1.00	2.00
❑236, Nov 86, American Dreamer	0.75	0.40	1.00	2.00
❑237, Dec 86, Context!	0.75	0.40	1.00	2.00
❑238, Jan 87, SB, Mutant Massacre; It Comes With The Claws, A: Sabretooth	0.75	0.60	1.50	3.00
❑239, Feb 87, Bad Plumbing!	0.75	0.40	1.00	2.00
❑240, Mar 87, The Face You Deserve	0.75	0.40	1.00	2.00
❑241, Apr 87, TMc, Black Christmas	0.75	0.40	1.00	2.00
❑242, May 87, KP, Caviar Killer	0.75	0.40	1.00	2.00
❑243, Jun 87, Don't Touch Me	0.75	0.40	1.00	2.00
❑244, Jul 87, Touch Me	0.75	0.40	1.00	2.00
❑245, Aug 87, Burn!, A: Black Panther	0.75	0.40	1.00	2.00
❑246, Sep 87, Bad Guy	0.75	0.40	1.00	2.00
❑247, Oct 87, KP, The Backwards Man	0.75	0.40	1.00	2.00
❑248, Nov 87, A: Wolverine	0.75	0.80	2.00	4.00
❑249, Dec 87, A: Wolverine	0.75	0.80	2.00	4.00
❑250, Jan 88, 1: Bullet	0.75	0.40	1.00	2.00
❑251, Feb 88, JR2, Save The Planet!	0.75	0.40	1.00	2.00
❑252, Mar 88, JR2, Ground Zero, double-sized; Fall of Mutants	1.25	0.60	1.50	3.00
❑253, Apr 88	0.75	0.40	1.00	2.00
❑254, May 88, JR2, Typhoid!, 1: Typhoid Mary, 1&0: Typhoid Mary	0.75	1.20	3.00	6.00
❑255, Jun 88, JR2, Temptation!, 2: Typhoid Mary	0.75	0.70	1.75	3.50
❑256, Jul 88, JR2, Blindspots, A: 3rd, 3: Typhoid Mary	0.75	0.50	1.25	2.50
❑257, Aug 88, JR2, The Bully, A: Punisher.	0.75	0.60	1.50	3.00
❑258, Sep 88, I Heard The Jungle Breathe, 1: Bengal	0.75	0.40	1.00	2.00
❑259, Oct 88, A: Typhoid Mary	0.75	0.40	1.00	2.00
❑260, Nov 88, double-sized	1.50	0.50	1.25	2.50
❑261, Dec 88, JR2, Meltdown!, A: Human Torch	0.75	0.40	1.00	2.00
❑262, Jan 89, JR2, I Found A Me In A Gloomy Hood, Astray..., Inferno	0.75	0.40	1.00	2.00
❑263, Feb 89, JR2, In Bitterness Not Far From Death..., Inferno	0.75	0.40	1.00	2.00
❑264, Mar 89, SD, Baby Boom!	0.75	0.40	1.00	2.00
❑265, Apr 89, JR2, We Again Beheld The Stars, Inferno	0.75	0.40	1.00	2.00
❑266, May 89, JR2, A Beer With The Devil	0.75	0.40	1.00	2.00
❑267, Jun 89, JR2, Cremains	0.75	0.40	1.00	2.00
❑268, Jul 89, JR2, Golden Rut	0.75	0.40	1.00	2.00
❑269, Aug 89, JR2, Lone Stranger	0.75	0.40	1.00	2.00
❑270, Sep 89, JR2, Blackheart!, 1: Blackheart; A: Spider-Man	1.00	0.40	1.00	2.00
❑271, Oct 89, JR2, Genetrix	1.00	0.30	0.75	1.50
❑272, Nov 89, 1: Shotgun II	1.00	0.30	0.75	1.50
❑273, Nov 89	1.00	0.30	0.75	1.50
❑274, Dec 89, JR2, Bombs And Lemonade	1.00	0.30	0.75	1.50
❑275, Dec 89, JR2, Acts of Vengeance, Acts of Vengeance	1.00	0.30	0.75	1.50
❑276, Jan 90, JR2, Acts of Vengeance, Acts of Vengeance	1.00	0.30	0.75	1.50
❑277, Feb 90, Of Crowns And Horns	1.00	0.30	0.75	1.50
❑278, Mar 90, JR2, The Deadly Seven	1.00	0.30	0.75	1.50
❑279, Apr 90, JR2, Before The Flame	1.00	0.30	0.75	1.50
❑280, May 90, JR2, Twilight Of The Idols	1.00	0.30	0.75	1.50
❑281, Jun 90, JR2, Heaven Is Knowing Who You Are, Silver Surfer cameo	1.00	0.30	0.75	1.50
❑282, Jul 90, A: Silver Surfer	1.00	0.30	0.75	1.50
❑283, Aug 90, The American Nightmare, A: Captain America	1.00	0.30	0.75	1.50
❑284, Sep 90, The Outsiders	1.00	0.30	0.75	1.50
❑285, Oct 90, The Shadowman	1.00	0.30	0.75	1.50
❑286, Nov 90, The Thief	1.00	0.30	0.75	1.50
❑287, Dec 90, The Fighter	1.00	0.30	0.75	1.50
❑288, Jan 91, The Student	1.00	0.30	0.75	1.50
❑289, Feb 91, The Hero	1.00	0.30	0.75	1.50
❑290, Mar 91, Bullseye!	1.00	0.30	0.75	1.50
❑291, Apr 91, All The News That Fits	1.00	0.30	0.75	1.50
❑292, May 91, Body Count, A: Punisher	1.00	0.30	0.75	1.50
❑293, Jun 91, Murder By Numbers, A: Punisher	1.00	0.30	0.75	1.50
❑294, Jul 91, The Infernal Mysteries	1.00	0.30	0.75	1.50
❑295, Aug 91, Through The Eyes Of The Enemy, A: Ghost Rider	1.00	0.30	0.75	1.50
❑296, Sep 91, Balancing Act	1.00	0.30	0.75	1.50
❑297, Oct 91, Last Rites, Part 1, V: Typhoid Mary	1.00	0.30	0.75	1.50
❑298, Nov 91, Last Rites, Part 2	1.00	0.30	0.75	1.50
❑299, Dec 91, Last Rites, Part 3	1.00	0.30	0.75	1.50
❑300, Jan 92, Last Rites, Part 4, double-sized; Kingpin deposed	2.00	0.60	1.50	3.00
❑301, Feb 92, V: Owl	1.25	0.30	0.75	1.50
❑302, Mar 92, Nocturnal Hunter, V: Owl	1.25	0.30	0.75	1.50
❑303, Apr 92, Dark And Deliverance, V: Owl	1.25	0.30	0.75	1.50
❑304, May 92, 34 Hours	1.25	0.30	0.75	1.50
❑305, Jun 92, Under The Knife, 1: Surgeon General	1.25	0.30	0.75	1.50
❑306, Jul 92, Emergency Procedure	1.25	0.30	0.75	1.50
❑307, Aug 92, Dead Man's Hand, Part 1	1.25	0.30	0.75	1.50
❑308, Sep 92, Dead Man's Hand, Part 4	1.25	0.30	0.75	1.50
❑309, Oct 92, Dead Man's Hand, Part 7; Cards on the Table	1.25	0.30	0.75	1.50
❑310, Nov 92, Devil De Rouge	1.25	0.30	0.75	1.50
❑311, Dec 92, Soul Search	1.25	0.30	0.75	1.50
❑312, Jan 93, Hot Flashes	1.25	0.30	0.75	1.50
❑313, Feb 93, So Cold It Burns	1.25	0.30	0.75	1.50
❑314, Mar 93, Shock Treatment	1.25	0.30	0.75	1.50
❑315, Apr 93, Shock Therapy, V: Mr. Fear..	1.25	0.30	0.75	1.50
❑316, May 93, Fare Play	1.25	0.30	0.75	1.50
❑317, Jun 93, Grease Is The Word, V: Stiltman	1.25	0.30	0.75	1.50

	ORIG	GOOD	FINE	N-MINT
❑318, Jul 93, Grease Monkeys, V: Devil-Man; V: Stiltman	1.25	0.30	0.75	1.50
❑319, Aug 93, first printing (white); Elektra returns	1.25	0.80	2.00	4.00
❑319-2, Aug 93, 2nd Printing; 2nd Printing (black); Elektra returns	1.25	0.25	0.63	1.25
❑320, Sep 93, Fall from Grace; Fall From Grace, Part 1, A: Silver Sable, red costume destroyed; New costume	1.25	0.70	1.75	3.50
❑321, Oct 93, Fall from Grace; Fall From Grace, Part 2	2.00	0.50	1.25	2.50
❑321/SC, Oct 93, Fall from Grace; Fall From Grace, Part 2, Special glow-in-the-dark cover	2.00	0.60	1.50	3.00
❑322, Nov 93, Fall from Grace; Fall From Grace, Part 3	1.25	0.40	1.00	2.00
❑323, Dec 93, Fall from Grace; Fall From Grace, Part 4, V: Venom	1.25	0.40	1.00	2.00
❑324, Jan 94, Fall From Grace, Part 5	1.25	0.40	1.00	2.00
❑325, Feb 94, Fall From Grace, Part 6, D: Hellspawn, Double-size; poster	2.50	0.60	1.50	3.00
❑326, Mar 94, Tree of Knowledge; Tree of Knowledge, Part 1	1.25	0.30	0.75	1.50
❑327, Apr 94, Tree of Knowledge, Part 2	1.25	0.30	0.75	1.50
❑328, May 94, Tree of Knowledge, Part 3	1.25	0.30	0.75	1.50
❑329, Jun 94, Tree of Knowledge, Part 4	1.50	0.30	0.75	1.50
❑330, Jul 94, Tree of Knowledge, Part 5, Gambit	1.50	0.30	0.75	1.50
❑331, Aug 94, Tree of Knowledge	1.50	0.30	0.75	1.50
❑332, Sep 94	1.50	0.30	0.75	1.50
❑333, Oct 94, Fathoms Of Humanity, Part 1	1.50	0.30	0.75	1.50
❑334, Nov 94, Fathoms Of Humanity, Part 2	1.50	0.30	0.75	1.50
❑335, Dec 94, Fathoms Of Humanity, Part 3	1.50	0.30	0.75	1.50
❑336, Jan 95, Fathoms Of Humanity, Part 4	1.50	0.30	0.75	1.50
❑337, Feb 95, Fathoms Of Humanity, Part 5	1.50	0.30	0.75	1.50
❑338, Mar 95, Wages of Sin, Part 1	1.50	0.30	0.75	1.50
❑339, Apr 95	1.50	0.30	0.75	1.50
❑340, May 95	1.50	0.30	0.75	1.50
❑341, Jun 95	1.50	0.30	0.75	1.50
❑342, Jul 95	1.50	0.30	0.75	1.50
❑343, Aug 95	1.50	0.30	0.75	1.50
❑344, Sep 95, Yellow and red-costumed Daredevil returns	1.95	0.40	1.00	2.00
❑345, Oct 95, Red-costumed Daredevil returns; OverPower card inserted	1.95	0.40	1.00	2.00
❑346, Nov 95	1.95	0.40	1.00	2.00
❑347, Dec 95, Identity of both Daredevils revealed	1.95	0.40	1.00	2.00
❑348, Jan 96, Purgatorio, A: Stick; A: Sister Maggie, cover says Dec, indicia says Jan	1.95	0.40	1.00	2.00
❑349, Feb 96, Paradiso, A: Stick; A: Sister Maggie	1.95	0.40	1.00	2.00
❑350, Mar 96, Paradiso, double-sized; Giant-size; Daredevil switches back to red costume	2.95	0.59	1.48	2.95
❑350/SC, Mar 96, Paradiso, gold ink on cover; double-sized; Giant-size; Daredevil switches back to red costume	3.50	0.70	1.75	3.50
❑351, Apr 96, Helping Hands, 1: The Vice Cop	1.95	0.40	1.00	2.00
❑352, May 96, Smoky Mirrors, V: Bullseye	1.95	0.40	1.00	2.00
❑353, Jun 96, V: Mr. Hyde	1.95	0.40	1.00	2.00
❑354, Jul 96, A: Spider-Man	1.50	0.30	0.75	1.50
❑355, Aug 96, V: Pyro	1.50	0.30	0.75	1.50
❑356, Sep 96, V: Enforcers	1.50	0.30	0.75	1.50
❑357, Oct 96, V: Enforcers	1.50	0.30	0.75	1.50
❑358, Nov 96, V: Mysterio	1.50	0.30	0.75	1.50
❑359, Dec 96, The Devil You Know!	1.50	0.30	0.75	1.50
❑360, Jan 97, Alone Against The Absorbing Man!, V: Absorbing Man	1.50	0.30	0.75	1.50
❑361, Feb 97, Unfinished Business, A: Black Widow	1.50	0.30	0.75	1.50
❑362, Mar 97, Never Look Back	1.99	0.40	1.00	1.99
❑363, Apr 97, GC, The City That Never Sleeps, V: Insomnia	1.99	0.39	0.98	1.95
❑364, May 97, No Rest for the Wicked!	1.99	0.39	0.98	1.95
❑365, Jun 97, A Question of Trust, V: Molten Man	1.99	0.40	1.00	1.99
❑366, Aug 97, gatefold summary	1.99	0.40	1.00	1.99
❑367, Sep 97, gatefold summary	1.99	0.40	1.00	1.99
❑368, Oct 97, V: Omega Red, gatefold summary	1.99	0.40	1.00	1.99
❑369, Nov 97, gatefold summary	1.99	0.40	1.00	1.99
❑370, Dec 97, A: Black Widow, gatefold summary	1.99	0.40	1.00	1.99
❑371, Jan 98, gatefold summary	1.99	0.40	1.00	1.99
❑372, Feb 98, A: Ghost Rider, gatefold summary	1.99	0.40	1.00	1.99
❑373, Mar 98, gatefold summary	1.99	0.40	1.00	1.99
❑374, Apr 98, gatefold summary	1.99	0.40	1.00	1.99
❑375, May 98, V: Mr. Fear, gatefold summary; Giant-size	2.99	0.59	1.48	2.95
❑376, Jun 98, Flying Blind, Part 1, Matt sent deep undercover, regains eyesight; gatefold summary	1.99	0.40	1.00	1.99

Daredevil's mentor, Stick, met his end in *Daredevil* #189.

© 1982 Marvel

	ORIG	GOOD	FINE	N-MINT
❑377, Jul 98, Flying Blind, Part 2, gatefold summary; Matt as Laurent Levasseur with new costume	1.99	0.40	1.00	1.99
❑378, Aug 98, Flying Blind, Part 3, gatefold summary	1.99	0.40	1.00	1.99
❑379, Sep 98, Flying Blind, Part 4, gatefold summary; Matt regains his identity and loses sight	1.99	0.40	1.00	1.99
❑380, Oct 98, A: Kingpin, Final Issue; gatefold summary; Giant-size	2.99	0.60	1.50	2.99
❑Anl 1, GC, Cover reads "King-Size Special"	0.25	5.00	12.50	25.00
❑Anl 2, Feb 71, Reprint; Cover reads "King-Size Special"	0.25	1.80	4.50	9.00
❑Anl 3, Reprint; Cover reads "King-Size Special"	0.25	1.80	4.50	9.00
❑Anl 4, Reprint	0.50	1.00	2.50	5.00
❑Anl 5, A Friend In Need; Role Reversal, Cover # of 4 seems to be a mistake; Atlantis Attacks; 1989 annual	2.00	0.80	2.00	4.00
❑Anl 6, Predator; Truth Or Dare, Lifeform	2.00	0.60	1.50	3.00
❑Anl 7, Crippling Death; Malicious Justice-Or Injustice, 1: Crippler, Von Strucker Gambit	2.00	0.50	1.25	2.50
❑Anl 8, System Bytes; The System Bytes, Part 2	2.25	0.50	1.25	2.50
❑Anl 9, Devouring Madness, On the Clock, Resurrections, 1: Devourer, trading card; trading card	2.95	0.59	1.48	2.95
❑Anl 10	2.95	0.59	1.48	2.95
❑Anl 1997, Sep 97, gatefold summary; Daredevil/Deadpool '97; combined annuals for Daredevil and Deadpool	2.99	0.60	1.50	2.99
❑GS 1	0.50	1.60	4.00	8.00

DAREDEVIL (VOL. 2)

MARVEL

Value: Cover or less

- ❑0.5, Nov 98, KSm (w), Guardian Devil, Part 1, gatefold summary —
- ❑1, Nov 98, KSm (c), KSm (w), Guardian Devil, Part 1, gatefold summary 2.50
- ❑1/LE, KSm (w), Guardian Devil, Part 1 29.95
- ❑1/SC, KSm (w), Guardian Devil, Part 1, DFE alternate cover. 6.95
- ❑2/A, Dec 98, KSm (c), KSm (w), Guardian Devil, Part 2, gatefold summary 2.50
- ❑2/B, KSm (w), Guardian Devil, Part 2 2.50
- ❑3, Jan 99, KSm (c), KSm (w), Guardian Devil, Part 3, Dystopia, A: Foggy Nelson; A: Karen Page, gatefold summary; Matt quits law firm 2.50
- ❑4, Feb 99, KSm (w), Guardian Devil, Part 4 2.50
- ❑5, Mar 99, KSm (w), Guardian Devil, Part 5, V: Bullseye; A: Doctor Strange; A: Mephisto; D: Karen Page 2.50
- ❑6, Apr 99, KSm (w), Guardian Devil, Part 6, V: Mysterio 2.50
- ❑7, May 99, KSm (w), D: Mysterio 2.50
- ❑8, Jun 99, KSm (w), A: Spider-Man, Karen's funeral 2.50
- ❑9, Dec 99 2.50
- ❑10 2.99
- ❑11 2.99
- ❑12 2.99
- ❑13, Oct 00, Trial and Error, Trial of Kingpin 2.99
- ❑14, Mar 01, An Object in Motion 2.99
- ❑15, Apr 01, Parts of a Hole, Conclusion 2.99
- ❑16 2.99
- ❑17 2.99
- ❑18 2.99
- ❑19 2.99
- ❑20 2.99
- ❑21 2.99

DAREDEVIL/BATMAN

MARVEL

Value: Cover or less

- ❑1, Eye For An Eye, nn; prestige format; crossover with DC 5.99

DAREDEVIL/BLACK WIDOW: ABATTOIR

MARVEL

Value: Cover or less

- ❑1, JSn (w) 14.95

DAREDEVIL: NINJA

MARVEL

Value: Cover or less

- ❑1, Dec 00, BMB (w) 2.99
- ❑2, Jan 01, BMB (w) 2.99
- ❑3, May 01, BMB (w) 2.99

DAREDEVIL/PUNISHER: CHILD'S PLAY

MARVEL

Value: Cover or less

- ❑1, FM, FM (w), Child's Play 4.95

DAREDEVIL/SHI

MARVEL

	ORIG	GOOD	FINE	N-MINT
❑1, Feb 97, None are so Blind; Blind Faith, crossover with Crusade	2.99	0.60	1.50	3.00

DAREDEVIL/SPIDER-MAN
MARVEL

Value: Cover or less

- ❑1, Jan 01, Unusual Suspects, Part 1; Unusual Suspects ... 2.99
- ❑2, Feb 01, Unusual Suspects, Part 2: The Sting ... 2.99
- ❑3, Mar 01, Unusual Suspects, Part 3: Bad Boys Don't Cry ... 2.99
- ❑4, Apr 01, Unusual Suspects, Part 4: Things Get Worse.... 2.99

DAREDEVIL THE MAN WITHOUT FEAR
MARVEL

	ORIG	GOOD	FINE	N-MINT
❑1, Oct 93, JR2; AW, FM (w), O: Daredevil, Partial foil cover	2.95	0.80	2.00	4.00
❑2, Nov 93, JR2; AW, FM (w), Partial foil cover	2.95	0.80	2.00	4.00
❑3, Dec 93, JR2; AW, FM (w), cardstock cover	2.95	0.80	2.00	4.00
❑4, Jan 94, JR2; AW, FM (w), Partial foil cover	2.95	0.70	1.75	3.50
❑5, Feb 94, JR2; AW, FM (w), cardstock cover	2.95	0.70	1.75	3.50

DAREDEVIL VS. VAPORA
MARVEL

Value: Cover or less

- ❑1, A Season for Tears, Fire-prevention comic ... 1.25

DARERAT/TADPOLE
MIGHTY PUMPKIN

Value: Cover or less

- ❑1, Feb 87, b&w; parody of Frank Miller's Daredevil work; flip book with Tadpole: Prankster back-up; color poster ... 1.95

DARIA JONTAK
JMJ

Value: Cover or less

- ❑1, Jan 01 ... 4.99

DARING ADVENTURES
B COMICS

	ORIG	GOOD	FINE	N-MINT
❑1	1.50	0.40	1.00	2.00
❑2, Jul 93	2.00	0.40	1.00	2.00
❑3	2.00	0.40	1.00	2.00

DARING ESCAPES
IMAGE

Value: Cover or less

- ❑1, Sep 98, Heart of the Matter ... 2.50
- ❑1/SC, Sep 98, alternate cover ... 2.50
- ❑2, Oct 98, Matters of Heart ... 2.50
- ❑3, Nov 98 ... 2.50
- ❑4 ... 2.50

DARING NEW ADVENTURES OF SUPERGIRL, THE
DC

	ORIG	GOOD	FINE	N-MINT
❑1, Nov 82, CI, A Very Strange And Special Girl, O: Supergirl; 1: Psi	0.60	0.50	1.25	2.50
❑2, Dec 82	0.60	0.40	1.00	2.00
❑3, Jan 83, 1: The Council	0.60	0.40	1.00	2.00
❑4, Feb 83, 1: The Gang	0.60	0.30	0.75	1.50
❑5, Mar 83	—	0.30	0.75	1.50
❑6, Apr 83, 1: Matrix-Prime	—	0.30	0.75	1.50
❑7, May 83	—	0.30	0.75	1.50
❑8, Jun 83, 1: Reactron; A: The Doom Patrol	—	0.30	0.75	1.50
❑9, Jul 83, A: The Doom Patrol	—	0.30	0.75	1.50
❑10, Aug 83	—	0.30	0.75	1.50
❑11, Sep 83	—	0.30	0.75	1.50
❑12, Oct 83	—	0.30	0.75	1.50
❑13, Nov 83, 1: Blackstarr, New costume; Series continues after this issue as "Supergirl"	—	0.30	0.75	1.50

DARK, THE
CONTINUM

Value: Cover or less

- ❑1 ... 2.00
- ❑1/A, Jan 95, enhanced cover ... 2.50
- ❑2 ... 2.25
- ❑3 ... 2.50
- ❑4, GP (c) ... 2.50

DARK, THE (AUGUST HOUSE)
AUGUST HOUSE

Value: Cover or less

- ❑1, Jan 95, enhanced cover ... 2.50

DARK, THE (VOL. 2)
CONTINUM

	ORIG	GOOD	FINE	N-MINT
❑1, May 93	1.95	0.40	1.00	2.00
❑1/SC, May 93, red foil cover	1.95	0.40	1.00	2.00
❑1-2, 2nd Printing; blue foil cover	1.95	0.40	1.00	2.00
❑2	1.95	0.40	1.00	2.00
❑3, foil cover	1.95	0.40	1.00	2.00
❑3/Aut, GP, foil cover; Signed by Joseph Naftali	1.95	0.40	1.00	2.00
❑4, Sep 93	1.95	0.40	1.00	2.00
❑5, Feb 94	1.95	0.40	1.00	2.00
❑6, Mar 94	1.95	0.40	1.00	2.00
❑7, Jul 94	1.95	0.40	1.00	2.00
❑7-2, 2nd Printing; blue foil cover	1.95	0.40	1.00	2.00

DARK ANGEL (1ST SERIES)
BONEYARD

Value: Cover or less

- ❑1, May 97, b&w ... 2.95
- ❑2, Sep 91, Jack the Green.... 2.25
- ❑3, Oct 91, The Marking ... 2.25

DARK ANGEL (3RD SERIES)
BONEYARD

Value: Cover or less

- ❑1, No Time for Tears; Lubricant ... 4.95
- ❑2, Aug 97, A Quiet Prequel ... 1.95
- ❑3, Sep 97 ... 1.95

DARK ANGEL: PHOENIX RESURRECTION
IMAGE

Value: Cover or less

- ❑1, May 00 ... 2.95
- ❑2, Aug 00 ... 2.95
- ❑3, Mar 01 ... 2.95

DARK ASSASSIN
SILVERWOLF

Value: Cover or less

- ❑1, Feb 87 ... 1.50

DARKCHYLDE
IMAGE

	ORIG	GOOD	FINE	N-MINT
❑0/A, Mar 98	2.50	0.50	1.25	2.50
❑0/B	2.50	0.50	1.25	2.50
❑0/C	2.50	0.50	1.25	2.50
❑0.5, Aug 97, Wizard 1/2 edition; purple background, girl sitting on skull	—	0.80	2.00	4.00
❑0.5/SC, Aug 97, Wizard 1/2 edition; Black background, demoness	—	0.80	2.00	4.00
❑1	2.50	1.00	2.50	5.00
❑1/AE, American Entertainment variant	—	1.00	2.50	5.00
❑1/B, Magazine-style variant	—	1.20	3.00	6.00
❑1/C, A Treasury of Sorrows, San Diego Comic-Con variant (Darkchylde with wings standing on front); Flip-book with Glory/Angela #1	2.50	1.00	2.50	5.00
❑2	2.50	0.70	1.75	3.50
❑2/A, Spider-Web/Moon variant cover	—	0.70	1.75	3.50
❑3	2.50	0.60	1.50	3.00
❑3/A, All-white variant	—	0.60	1.50	3.00
❑4/A, Mar 97, was Maximum Press title; Image begins as publisher	2.50	0.60	1.50	3.00
❑4/B, Mar 97, alternate cover; "Fear" Edition; Image begins as publisher	2.50	0.60	1.50	3.00
❑5/A, Sep 97, variant cover	2.50	0.50	1.25	2.50
❑5/B, Sep 97, alternate cover	2.50	0.50	1.25	2.50
❑5/C, Sep 97, alternate cover	2.50	0.50	1.25	2.50
❑Ash 1, Preview edition	—	0.60	1.50	3.00
❑Ash 1/GO, Preview edition; Gold logo	—	1.00	2.50	5.00
❑Ash 1/LE, Signed by Randy Queen	—	1.40	3.50	7.00

DARKCHYLDE REMASTERED
IMAGE

Value: Cover or less

- ❑0, Mar 98 ... 2.50
- ❑1/A, May 97, reprints Darkchylde #1 with corrections ... 2.50
- ❑1/B, May 97, alternate cover; reprints Darkchylde #1 with corrections ... 2.50
- ❑2, Sep 98, reprints Darkchylde #2 with corrections ... 2.50
- ❑3, Nov 98, reprints Darkchylde #3 with corrections ... 2.50

DARKCHYLDE SUMMER SWIMSUIT SPECTACULAR
DC

Value: Cover or less

- ❑1, Aug 99, pin-ups ... 3.95

DARKCHYLDE THE DIARY
IMAGE

Value: Cover or less

- ❑1/A, Jun 97, pin-ups with diary entries ... 2.50
- ❑1/B, Jun 97, alternate cover; pin-ups with diary entries ... 2.50
- ❑1/C, Jun 97, alternate cover; pin-ups with diary entries ... 2.50
- ❑1/D, Jun 97, alternate cover; pin-ups with diary entries ... 2.50

DARKCHYLDE: THE LEGACY
IMAGE

	ORIG	GOOD	FINE	N-MINT
❑1, Aug 98, cardstock cover	2.50	0.60	1.50	3.00
❑1/A, DFE alternate chrome cover; Signed by Randy Queen	—	3.00	7.50	15.00
❑1/SC, DFE alternate chrome cover	—	2.40	6.00	12.00
❑2, Dec 98	2.50	0.50	1.25	2.50
❑2/SC, Dec 98, alternate cover	2.50	0.60	1.50	3.00
❑3, Jun 99	2.50	0.50	1.25	2.50

DARK CLAW ADVENTURES
DC

Value: Cover or less

- ❑1, Jun 97, Face to Face ... 1.95

DARK CONVENTION BOOK, THE
CONTINUM

Value: Cover or less

- ❑1 ... 1.95

DARK CROSSINGS
IMAGE

Value: Cover or less

- ❑1, Jun 00, Dark Clouds Rising 5.95
- ❑2, Oct 00, Dark Clouds Overhead ... 5.95

DARK CROSSINGS: DARK CLOUDS OVERHEAD
IMAGE

Value: Cover or less

- ❑1, Jun 00, A: Darkness; A: Tomb Raider; A: Witchblade, cover says Dark Crossings: Dark Clouds Rising; prestige format ... 5.95

DARK CRYSTAL, THE
MARVEL

	ORIG	GOOD	FINE	N-MINT
❑1, Apr 83, movie Adaptation	0.60	0.25	0.63	1.25
❑2, May 83, movie Adaptation	0.60	0.25	0.63	1.25

DARK DESTINY
ALPHA

Value: Cover or less

❑1, Nov 94, Giant in the Earth 3.50

DARKDEVIL
MARVEL

Value: Cover or less

❑1, Nov 00, AM, From the Abyss ...!; The Cursed! 2.99
❑2, Dec 00, AM, The Cursed! 2.99
❑3, Jan 01, AM, Fathers of the Sin! 2.99

DARK DOMINION
DEFIANT

Value: Cover or less

❑1, Oct 93, Haunts of the Very Rich, Part 1; The Gathering Darkness, 1: Doctor Michael Alexander; 1: Chasm 2.50
❑2, Nov 93 .... 2.50
❑3, Dec 93, A Man's Home 2.50
❑4, Jan 94, Bad Moon Rising 2.50
❑5, Feb 94, Family Skeletons, Part 1 .... 2.50
❑6, Mar 94, Family Skeletons, Part 2 .... 2.50
❑7, Apr 94, Once a Hero, Part 1 .... 2.50
❑8, May 94, Once a Hero, Part 2 .... 2.50
❑9, Jun 94, Once a Hero, Part 3 .... 2.50
❑10 .... 2.50
❑11 .... 2.50
❑12 .... 2.50
❑13, Final Issue 2.50

DARKER IMAGE
IMAGE

	ORIG	GOOD	FINE	N-MINT
❑1, Mar 93, 1: Deathblow; 1: Maxx, trading card	2.50	0.50	1.25	2.50
❑1/GO, Mar 93, 1: Deathblow; 1: Maxx, trading card; Gold logo	2.50	0.80	2.00	4.00
❑1/LE, Mar 93, 1: Deathblow; 1: Maxx, trading card; White limited edition cover	—	0.80	2.00	4.00
❑Ash 1, b&w; ashcan edition	—	0.60	1.50	3.00

DARK FANTASY
APPLE

Value: Cover or less

❑1, Sep 92, Ph'tillph'tarr; Retro-spectacle, b&w 2.75

DARK FRINGE, THE
BRAINSTORM

Value: Cover or less

❑2, Dec 96, b&w 2.95

DARK GUARD
MARVEL

	ORIG	GOOD	FINE	N-MINT
❑1, Oct 93, Tour Of Duty, 1: The Time Guardian, Prism cover	2.25	0.59	1.48	2.95
❑2, Nov 93	1.75	0.35	0.88	1.75
❑3, Dec 93, Escalation!	1.75	0.35	0.88	1.75
❑4, Jan 94	1.75	0.35	0.88	1.75
❑5, Final Issue	1.75	0.35	0.88	1.75

DARKHAWK
MARVEL

	ORIG	GOOD	FINE	N-MINT
❑1, Mar 91, Dawn of the Darkhawk, 1: Darkhawk; A: Hobgoblin	1.00	0.40	1.00	2.00
❑2, Apr 91, A: Spider-Man; A: Hobgoblin	1.00	0.30	0.75	1.50
❑3, May 91, A: Spider-Man; A: Hobgoblin	1.00	0.30	0.75	1.50
❑4, Jun 91	1.00	0.30	0.75	1.50
❑5, Jul 91	1.00	0.30	0.75	1.50
❑6, Aug 91, A: Captain America; A: Daredevil	1.00	0.30	0.75	1.50
❑7, Sep 91	1.00	0.30	0.75	1.50
❑8, Oct 91	1.00	0.30	0.75	1.50
❑9, Nov 91, Honor Among Psychotics, A: Punisher	1.00	0.30	0.75	1.50
❑10, Dec 91	1.00	0.30	0.75	1.50
❑11, Jan 92	1.00	0.30	0.75	1.50
❑12, Feb 92, V: Tombstone	1.25	0.30	0.75	1.50
❑13, Mar 92, A: Venom	1.25	0.30	0.75	1.50
❑14, Apr 92, A: Venom	1.25	0.30	0.75	1.50
❑15, May 92	1.25	0.25	0.63	1.25
❑16, Jun 92, V: Peristrike Force	1.25	0.25	0.63	1.25
❑17, Jul 92, V: Peristrike Force	1.25	0.25	0.63	1.25
❑18, Aug 92	1.25	0.25	0.63	1.25
❑19, Sep 92	1.25	0.25	0.63	1.25
❑20, Oct 92	1.25	0.25	0.63	1.25
❑21, Nov 92, Return to Forever, Part 1, O: Darkhawk	1.25	0.25	0.63	1.25
❑22, Dec 92, Return to Forever, Part 2, A: Ghost Rider	1.25	0.25	0.63	1.25
❑23, Jan 93, Return to Forever, Part 3	1.25	0.25	0.63	1.25
❑24, Feb 93, Return to Forever, Part 4	1.25	0.25	0.63	1.25
❑25, Mar 93, Return to Forever, Part 5, O: Darkhawk armor, foil cover; Double-size	2.95	0.59	1.48	2.95
❑26, Apr 93	1.25	0.25	0.63	1.25
❑27, May 93	1.25	0.25	0.63	1.25
❑28, Jun 93, Time To Kill	1.25	0.25	0.63	1.25
❑29, Jul 93	1.25	0.25	0.63	1.25
❑30, Aug 93	1.25	0.25	0.63	1.25

Daredevil explained the dangers of gasoline vapors in the public service comic book *Daredevil vs. Vapora.*

© 1996 Marvel

	ORIG	GOOD	FINE	N-MINT
❑31, Sep 93	1.25	0.25	0.63	1.25
❑32, Oct 93	1.25	0.25	0.63	1.25
❑33, Nov 93	1.25	0.25	0.63	1.25
❑34, Dec 93	1.25	0.25	0.63	1.25
❑35, Jan 94, Operation Symbiote, Part 1, A: Venom	1.25	0.25	0.63	1.25
❑36, Feb 94, Operation Symbiote, Part 2, A: Venom	1.25	0.25	0.63	1.25
❑37, Mar 94, Operation Symbiote, Part 3, A: Venom	1.25	0.25	0.63	1.25
❑38, Apr 94, Amulet Quest, Part 1	1.25	0.25	0.63	1.25
❑39, May 94, Amulet Quest, Part 2	1.50	0.30	0.75	1.50
❑40, Jun 94, Amulet Quest, Part 3	1.50	0.30	0.75	1.50
❑41, Jul 94, Amulet Quest, Part 4	1.50	0.30	0.75	1.50
❑42, Aug 94	1.50	0.30	0.75	1.50
❑43, Sep 94	1.50	0.30	0.75	1.50
❑44, Oct 94	1.50	0.30	0.75	1.50
❑45, Nov 94	1.50	0.30	0.75	1.50
❑46, Dec 94	1.50	0.30	0.75	1.50
❑47, Jan 95	1.50	0.30	0.75	1.50
❑48, Feb 95	1.50	0.30	0.75	1.50
❑49, Mar 95	1.50	0.30	0.75	1.50
❑50, Apr 95, Final Issue; Giant-size	2.50	0.50	1.25	2.50
❑Anl 1	2.25	0.50	1.25	2.50
❑Anl 2, Dreamkiller; Force Of Evil, 1: Dreamkiller, trading card	2.95	0.59	1.48	2.95
❑Anl 3	2.95	0.59	1.48	2.95

DARKHOLD
MARVEL

Value: Cover or less

❑1/CS, Oct 92, Rise of the Midnight Sons, Part 4, 1: Darkhold Redeemers, poster; Midnight Sons 2.75
❑2, Nov 92, For God and Country 1.75
❑3, Dec 92 .... 1.75
❑4, Jan 93, Cry N' Garai!, A: Sabretooth 1.75
❑5, The Living Dead, A: Punisher 1.75
❑6, Duel 1.75
❑7, Day Of Infamy 1.75
❑8, Betrayal, Part 1 .... 1.75
❑9, Betrayal, Part 2 .... 1.75
❑10, Betrayal, Part 3 .... 1.75
❑11, Midnight Massacre, Part 3, Double-cover 1.75
❑12, For Want Of A Soul! 1.75
❑13, Stalker In The House, A: Missing Link, Missing CCA approval stamp 1.75
❑14 .... 1.75
❑15, Siege of Darkness, Part 4 .... 1.75
❑16, Siege of Darkness, Part 12, Final Issue 1.75

DARK HORSE CLASSICS: ALIENS VERSUS PREDATOR
DARK HORSE

Value: Cover or less

❑1, Feb 97, Reprints Aliens Vs. Predator #1 with new cover. 2.95
❑2, Mar 97, Reprints Aliens Vs. Predator #2 with new cover. 2.95
❑3, Apr 97, Reprints Aliens Vs. Predator #3 with new cover. 2.95
❑4, May 97, Reprints Aliens Vs. Predator #4 with new cover. 2.95
❑5, Jun 97, Reprints Aliens Vs. Predator #5 with new cover. 2.95
❑6, Jul 97, Reprints Aliens Vs. Predator #6 with new cover. 2.95

DARK HORSE CLASSICS: GODZILLA
DARK HORSE

Value: Cover or less

❑1, Apr 98 .... 2.95

DARK HORSE CLASSICS: GODZILLA: KING OF THE MONSTERS
DARK HORSE

Value: Cover or less

❑1, Jul 98 .... 2.95
❑2, Aug 98, Blast from the Past, Can G-Force Survive? In the Grip of Godzilla! 2.95
❑3, Sep 98, Dramatization, No Blast from the Past-Godzilla Rules! 2.95
❑4, Oct 98 .... 2.95
❑5, Nov 98 .... 2.95
❑6, Dec 98 .... 2.95

DARK HORSE CLASSICS: STAR WARS: DARK EMPIRE
DARK HORSE

Value: Cover or less

❑1, Mar 97, The Destiny of a Jedi 2.95
❑2, Apr 97, Devastator of Worlds 2.95
❑3, May 97, The Battle for Calamari 2.95
❑4, Jun 97, Confrontation on the Smugglers' Moon 2.95
❑5, Jul 97, Emperor Reborn 2.95
❑6, Aug 97, The Fate of a Galaxy 2.95

DARK HORSE CLASSICS: TERROR OF GODZILLA
DARK HORSE

Value: Cover or less

- ❑1, Aug 98, Translation by Mike Richardson and Randy Stradley of Viz Communications 2.95
- ❑2, Sep 98, Translation by Mike Richardson and Randy Stradley of Viz Communications 2.95
- ❑3, Oct 98, Translation by Mike Richardson and Randy Stradley of Viz Communications........ 2.95
- ❑4, Nov 98 .... 2.95
- ❑5, Dec 98 .... 2.95
- ❑6, Jan 99 .... 2.95

DARK HORSE COMICS
DARK HORSE

	ORIG	GOOD	FINE	N-MINT
❑1, Aug 92, Predator: Rite of Passage, Part 1; Time Cop: A Man Out of Time, Part 1, 1: Time Cop, wraparound gatefold cover; Predator, RoboCop, Time Cop, Renegade	2.50	0.70	1.75	3.50
❑2, Sep 92, Aliens: Horror Show, Part 1; Time Cop: A Man Out of Time, Part 3, RoboCop, Renegade, Time Cop, Predator..............	2.50	0.50	1.25	2.50
❑3, Oct 92, Time Cop: A Man Out of Time, Part 2; Renegade, Part 2, Aliens: Horror Show, RoboCop, Indiana Jones, Time Cop; RoboCop, Indiana Jones, Time Cop, Aliens: Horror Show................................	2.50	0.50	1.25	2.50
❑4, Nov 92, Predator: Blood Feud, Part 1; Mad Dogs, Part 1, Aliens, Predator, Indiana Jones, Mad Dogs.............................	2.50	0.50	1.25	2.50
❑5, Dec 92, Aliens: Horror Show, Part 3; Predator: Blood Feud, Part 2, Aliens, Predator, Indiana Jones, Mad Dogs................	2.50	0.50	1.25	2.50
❑6, Jan 93, Robocop: Invasions, Part 1; Mad Dogs, Part 3, RoboCop, Predator, Indiana Jones, Mad Dogs..................................	2.50	0.50	1.25	2.50
❑7, Feb 93, Star Wars: Tales of the Jedi, Part 1; Mad Dogs, Part 4, RoboCop, Star Wars, Mad Dogs, Predator	2.50	1.00	2.50	5.00
❑8, Mar 93, James Bond: Light of My Death, Part 1, 1: X, RoboCop, James Bond, Star Wars	2.50	1.00	2.50	5.00
❑9, Apr 93, James Bond: Light of My Death, Part 2, 2: X, James Bond, Star Wars, RoboCop...	2.50	0.80	2.00	4.00
❑10, May 93, Godzilla: Blast From the Past, Part 1; Predator: The Pride at Nghasa, Part 1, X, Predator, Godzilla, James Bond	2.50	0.60	1.50	3.00
❑11, Jul 93, Aliens: Taste; Godzilla: Blast From the Past, Part 2, Predator, Godzilla, James Bond, Aliens..............................	2.50	0.50	1.25	2.50
❑12, Aug 93, Predator: The Pride at Nghasa, Part 3, Aliens, Predator	2.50	0.50	1.25	2.50
❑13, Sep 93, The Mark: Taking Back the Streets, Part 1; Predator: Bad Blood, Part 2, Aliens, Predator, Thing from Another World	2.50	0.50	1.25	2.50
❑14, Oct 93, The Mark: Taking Back the Streets, Part 1; Predator: Bad Blood, Part 3, Predator, The Mark, Thing from Another World	2.50	0.50	1.25	2.50
❑15, Nov 93, The Thing From Another World: Questionable Research, Part 2	2.50	0.50	1.25	2.50
❑16, Dec 93, The Thing From Another World: Questionable Research, Part 4; Predator: The Hunted City, Part 1	2.50	0.50	1.25	2.50
❑17, Jan 94, Alien, Part 1; Star Wars: Droids, Part 1	2.50	0.50	1.25	2.50
❑18, Feb 94, Alien, Part 2; Star Wars: Droids, Part 2, Aliens, Star Wars: Droids, Predator	2.50	0.50	1.25	2.50
❑19, Mar 94, Alien, Part 3; Star Wars: Droids, Part 3, X, Aliens, Star Wars: Droids.........	2.50	0.50	1.25	2.50
❑20, Apr 94	2.50	0.50	1.25	2.50
❑21, May 94..	2.50	0.50	1.25	2.50
❑22..	2.50	0.50	1.25	2.50
❑23, Jul 94, Aliens, The Machine	2.50	0.50	1.25	2.50
❑24, Aug 94	2.50	0.50	1.25	2.50
❑25, Sep 94, James Bond: Minute of Midnight; Aliens Vs. Predator: Blood Time, Final Issue; Flip-book	2.50	0.50	1.25	2.50

DARK HORSE DOWN UNDER
DARK HORSE

Value: Cover or less

- ❑1, Jun 94, The Undertaker: Dead Reckoning, Part 1; Aquarine, b&w.................................... 2.50
- ❑2, Aug 94, The Undertaker: Dead Reckoning, Part 2, b&w....... 2.50
- ❑3, Oct 94, The Undertaker: Dead Reckoning, Part 3; Jace Riegel: The Scimitar Mutiny, b&w.... 2.50

DARK HORSE MAVERICK 2000
DARK HORSE

Value: Cover or less

- ❑0, Jul 00, Mercy!; Concrete: Family Night.............................. 3.95
- ❑1, Jul 00, FM (c), Mercy!; Concrete: Family Night, nn; b&w; Anthology 3.95

DARK HORSE MONSTERS
DARK HORSE

Value: Cover or less

- ❑1, Feb 97, Burn Out; Jungle of the Giants, Reprinted from Dark Horse Presents #33 & #47.. 2.95

DARK HORSE PRESENTS
DARK HORSE

	ORIG	GOOD	FINE	N-MINT
❑1, Black Cross; Lifestyles of the Rich and Famous, A: Black Cross; 1: Concrete.....	2.25	1.20	3.00	6.00
❑1-2, Black Cross; Lifestyles of the Rich and Famous, A: Black Cross; 1: Concrete, 2nd Printing...	2.25	0.45	1.13	2.25
❑, Black Cross; Lifestyles of the Rich and Famous, A: Black Cross; 1: Concrete, 3rd Printing; Commemorative edition; green border	2.25	0.45	1.13	2.25
❑1-4, 4th Printing; silver border..................	2.25	0.45	1.13	2.25
❑2, 2: Concrete	1.50	0.60	1.50	3.00
❑3, Nov 86, A: Concrete	1.50	0.50	1.25	2.50
❑4, Jan 87, A: Concrete	1.50	0.50	1.25	2.50
❑5, Feb 87, A: Concrete.............................	1.50	0.40	1.00	2.00
❑6, Apr 87, A: Concrete	1.50	0.40	1.00	2.00
❑7, May 87	1.50	0.40	1.00	2.00
❑8, Jun 87, A: Concrete	1.50	0.40	1.00	2.00
❑9, Jul 87	2.25	0.40	1.00	2.00
❑10, Sep 87, 1: The Mask; A: Concrete......	1.75	0.90	2.25	4.50
❑11, Oct 87, 2: The Mask...........................	2.25	0.70	1.75	3.50
❑12, Nov 87, A: The Mask; A: Concrete	1.75	0.50	1.25	2.50
❑13, Dec 87, A: The Mask	1.75	0.50	1.25	2.50
❑14, Jan 87, A: The Mask; A: Concrete......	1.75	0.60	1.50	3.00
❑15, Feb 88, A: The Mask	1.75	0.50	1.25	2.50
❑16, Mar 88, A: The Mask; A: Concrete	1.75	0.60	1.50	3.00
❑17, Apr 88, Spume, Muzzi & Woim, Roachmill	1.75	0.40	1.00	2.00
❑18, Jun 88, A: The Mask; A: Concrete......	1.75	0.70	1.75	3.50
❑19, Jul 88, A: The Mask...........................	1.75	0.50	1.25	2.50
❑20, Aug 88, A: The Mask; A: Concrete; A: Flaming Carrot, Double Size..................	2.95	0.60	1.50	3.00
❑21, Aug 88, A: The Mask	1.75	0.50	1.25	2.50
❑22, Sep 88, 1: Duckman	1.75	0.50	1.25	2.50
❑23, Oct 88	1.75	0.40	1.00	2.00
❑24, Nov 88, 1: Aliens, Aliens....................	1.75	1.20	3.00	6.00
❑25, Dec 88	1.75	0.40	1.00	2.00
❑26, Jan 89	1.75	0.40	1.00	2.00
❑27, Feb 89...	1.75	0.40	1.00	2.00
❑28, Mar 89, Double Size; Concrete, Mr. Monster..	2.95	0.60	1.50	3.00
❑29, Apr 89	1.75	0.40	1.00	2.00
❑30, May 89	1.75	0.40	1.00	2.00
❑31, Jul 89, Duckman	1.75	0.40	1.00	2.00
❑32, Jul 89, A: Concrete, Giant-size	3.50	0.70	1.75	3.50
❑33, Aug 89, Giant-size	2.25	0.50	1.25	2.50
❑34, Aug 89, Aliens; Zone, Aliens; Aliens story	1.75	0.60	1.50	3.00
❑35, Dec 89, Predator, Heartbreakers, A Tough Nut To Crack, Aliens	1.95	0.60	1.50	3.00
❑36, Oct 89, regular cover; Aliens vs. Predator..	1.95	0.60	1.50	3.00
❑36/A, Oct 89, Painted cover; Aliens vs. Predator	1.95	0.80	2.00	4.00
❑37, Nov 89	1.95	0.50	1.25	2.50
❑38, Apr 90, Concrete: Fire At Twilight; Mary: The Elephant, A: Concrete	1.95	0.40	1.00	2.00
❑39, May 90	1.95	0.40	1.00	2.00
❑40, Jun 90, MW, Giant-size.......................	2.95	0.60	1.50	3.00
❑41, Jul 90	2.95	0.40	1.00	2.00
❑42, Aug 90, Aliens; Kings In Disguise, Aliens	1.95	0.60	1.50	3.00
❑43, Sep 90, Aliens.....................................	1.95	0.60	1.50	3.00
❑44, Oct 90	1.95	0.40	1.00	2.00
❑45, Nov 90, MW...	1.95	0.40	1.00	2.00
❑46, Nov 90, Predator, Bacchus, Crash Ryan	1.95	0.40	1.00	2.00
❑47, Jan 91, monsters	1.95	0.40	1.00	2.00
❑48, Feb 91, Harlequin, 48pgs.; Dark Horse trading cards; Black Cross, Roachmill, Concrete, Mr. Monster	1.95	0.40	1.00	2.00
❑49, Mar 91, Restless Sleep, Dark Horse trading cards	1.95	0.40	1.00	2.00
❑50, Apr 91, Dark Horse trading cards	1.95	0.40	1.00	2.00
❑51, Jun 91, FM, FM (w), Sin City, Part 2; Harlequin, Part 4....................................	1.95	0.40	1.00	2.00
❑52, Jul 91, FM, FM (w), Sin City................	1.95	0.40	1.00	2.00
❑53, Aug 91, FM, FM (w), Sin City.............	1.95	0.40	1.00	2.00
❑54, Sep 91, FM; JBy; GM, JBy (w), Sin City, 1: Next Men	2.25	0.60	1.50	3.00
❑55, Oct 91, FM; JBy, FM (w); JBy (w), Sin City, Part 5; Sin City, Part 6, 2: Next Men	2.25	0.40	1.00	2.00
❑56, Nov 91, FM; JBy, FM (w), Aliens: Genocide (prelude); Sin City, Double-size; Aliens	3.95	0.60	1.50	3.00
❑57, Dec 91, FM; JBy, FM (w), Sin City, Giant-size	3.50	0.70	1.75	3.50
❑58, Jan 92, FM, FM (w), Sin City	1.95	0.40	1.00	2.00
❑59, Feb 92, Sin City; Alien Fire	2.25	0.50	1.25	2.50
❑60, Mar 92, FM, FM (w), Sin City	2.25	0.50	1.25	2.50

	ORIG	GOOD	FINE	N-MINT
❑61, Apr 92, FM, FM (w), Sin City	2.25	0.50	1.25	2.50
❑62, May 92, FM, FM (w), Sin City	2.25	0.50	1.25	2.50
❑63, Jun 92, FM (w), Marie Dakar, The Creep, Abandonment Games	2.25	0.50	1.25	2.50
❑64, Jul 92	2.25	0.50	1.25	2.50
❑65, Sep 92	2.25	0.50	1.25	2.50
❑66, Sep 92, Concrete; Dr. Giggles, Part 3, Concrete, Doctor Giggles, An Accidental Death; Concrete, Dr. Giggles, An Accidental Death	2.25	0.50	1.25	2.50
❑67, Nov 92, Zoo-Lou vs. Editor, Part 1; Zoo-Lou vs. Editor, Part 2, A: Zoo-Lou, Double-size issue	3.95	0.79	1.98	3.95
❑68, Dec 92, Predator: Race War (prelude), Predator: Race War	2.25	0.50	1.25	2.50
❑69, Feb 93, Predator: Race War, Part 1; Nestrobber: Survival Skills, Predator: Race War	2.25	0.50	1.25	2.50
❑70, Mar 93, The Madwoman of the Sacred Heart, Part 1	2.25	0.50	1.25	2.50
❑71, Apr 93, The Madwoman of the Sacred Heart, Part 2; Dominique: The Hardest Part, Part 1	2.25	0.50	1.25	2.50
❑72, Apr 93, The Madwoman of the Sacred Heart, Part 3; Eudaemon, Part 1	2.25	0.50	1.25	2.50
❑73, Jun 93, The Madwoman of the Sacred Heart, Part 4; Eudaemon, Part 2	2.25	0.50	1.25	2.50
❑74, Jun 93, The Madwoman of the Sacred Heart, Part 5; Eudaemon, Part 3	2.25	0.50	1.25	2.50
❑75, Jul 93, The Madwoman of the Sacred Heart, Part 6; The Chairman, Part 2	2.25	0.50	1.25	2.50
❑76, Aug 93, The Madwoman of the Sacred Heart, Part 7; The Chairman, Part 3	2.25	0.50	1.25	2.50
❑77, Sep 93	2.25	0.50	1.25	2.50
❑78, Oct 93	2.25	0.50	1.25	2.50
❑79, Nov 93	2.25	0.50	1.25	2.50
❑80, Dec 93	2.25	0.60	1.50	3.00
❑81, Jan 94	2.25	0.50	1.25	2.50
❑82, Feb 94	2.25	0.50	1.25	2.50
❑83, Mar 94	2.25	0.50	1.25	2.50
❑84, Apr 94	2.50	0.50	1.25	2.50
❑85, May 94, The Eighth Wonder, Part 1; Star Riders, Part 1	2.50	0.50	1.25	2.50
❑86, Jun 94, The Eighth Wonder, Part 2; Star Riders, Part 2	2.50	0.50	1.25	2.50
❑87, Jul 94, Hermes Versus The Eyeball Kid, Part 1; The Eighth Wonder, Part 3	2.50	0.50	1.25	2.50
❑88, Aug 94, Hellboy	2.50	0.50	1.25	2.50
❑89, Sep 94, Hellboy	2.50	0.50	1.25	2.50
❑90, Oct 94	2.50	0.50	1.25	2.50
❑91, Nov 94, Blackheart, Part 1	2.50	0.50	1.25	2.50
❑92, Dec 94, Blackheart, Part 2; Too Much Coffee Man, Part 1, A: Too Much Coffee Man	2.50	0.50	1.25	2.50
❑93, Jan 95, Blackheart, Part 3; Cud, Part 1, A: Too Much Coffee Man	2.50	0.50	1.25	2.50
❑94, Feb 95, Cud, Part 2; Too Much Coffee Man, Part 3	2.50	0.50	1.25	2.50
❑95, Mar 95, Cud, Part 3; Too Much Coffee Man, Part 4, A: Too Much Coffee Man	2.50	0.50	1.25	2.50
❑96, Apr 95	2.50	0.50	1.25	2.50
❑97, May 95	2.50	0.50	1.25	2.50
❑98, Jun 95	2.50	0.50	1.25	2.50
❑99, Jul 95	2.50	0.50	1.25	2.50
❑100.1, Aug 95, FM, FM (c), FM (w), Issue 100 #1	2.50	0.50	1.25	2.50
❑100.2, Aug 95, Hellboy cover and story; Issue 100 #2	2.50	0.50	1.25	2.50
❑100.3, Aug 95, Concrete cover and story; Issue 100 #3	2.50	0.50	1.25	2.50
❑100.4, Aug 95, DaG (c), FM (w), Martha Washington story; Issue 100 #4	2.50	0.50	1.25	2.50
❑100.5, Aug 95, Issue 100 #5	2.50	0.50	1.25	2.50
❑101, Sep 95, A: Aliens	2.50	0.50	1.25	2.50
❑102, Oct 95	2.50	0.50	1.25	2.50
❑103, Nov 95, Kirby centerfold; Mr. Painter, One-Trick Rip-Off, The Pink Tornado, Hairball	2.95	0.59	1.48	2.95
❑104, Dec 95	2.95	0.59	1.48	2.95
❑105, Jan 96	2.95	0.59	1.48	2.95
❑106, Feb 96	2.95	0.59	1.48	2.95
❑107, Mar 96	2.95	0.59	1.48	2.95
❑108, Apr 96	2.95	0.59	1.48	2.95
❑109, May 96	2.95	0.59	1.48	2.95
❑110, Jun 96	2.95	0.59	1.48	2.95
❑111, Jul 96	2.95	0.59	1.48	2.95
❑112, Aug 96	2.95	0.59	1.48	2.95
❑113, Sep 96, Lowlife, Part 1; Trypto the Acid Dog, Part 1	2.95	0.59	1.48	2.95
❑114, Oct 96, FM, FM (w), Star Slammers: Fever Dream; Lowlife, Part 2, Star Slammers, Lance Blastoff, Lowlife, Trypto the Acid Dog	2.95	0.59	1.48	2.95

Andrew Vachss' *Predator: Race War* mini-series got started in *Dark Horse Presents* #68 and 69.

© 1993 Dark Horse Comics

	ORIG	GOOD	FINE	N-MINT
❑115, Nov 96, FM (c), Lowlife, Part 3; Trypto the Acid Dog, Part 3, Doctor Spin, The Creep, Lowlife, Trypto the Acid Dog	2.95	0.59	1.48	2.95
❑116, Dec 96, Trypto the Acid Dog, Part 4; Dr. Spin, Part 2, Fat Dog Mendoza, Trypto the Acid Dog, Doctor Spin	2.95	0.59	1.48	2.95
❑117, Jan 97, Aliens: Headhunters; Dr. Spin, Part 3, Aliens, Trypto the Acid Dog, Doctor Spin	2.95	0.59	1.48	2.95
❑118, Feb 97, Hectic Planet; Dr. Spin, Monkeyman & O'Brien, Hectic Planet, Trypto the Acid Dog, Doctor Spin	2.95	0.59	1.48	2.95
❑119, Mar 97, Trout, Part 1; Hectic Planet, Part 2, Monkeyman & O'Brien, Hectic Planet, Trout, Predator	2.95	0.59	1.48	2.95
❑120, Apr 97, One Last Job, The Lords of Misrule, Trout, Hectic Planet	2.95	0.59	1.48	2.95
❑121, May 97, Jack Zero, Aliens, The Lords of Misrule, Trout	2.95	0.59	1.48	2.95
❑122, Jun 97, Jack Zero, Imago, Trout, The Lords of Misrule	2.95	0.59	1.48	2.95
❑123, Jul 97, Imago, Part 2; Trout, Imago, Jack Zero, Trout	2.95	0.59	1.48	2.95
❑124, Aug 97, Predator, Jack Zero, Outside, Inside	2.95	0.59	1.48	2.95
❑125, Sep 97, The Nocturnals, Part 1; Jack Zero	2.95	0.59	1.48	2.95
❑126, Oct 97, The Nocturnals, Part 2; Last Night I Dreamed	2.95	0.59	1.48	2.95
❑127, Nov 97, The Nocturnals, Part 3; Metalfer, Nocturnals, Metalfer, Stiltskin, Blue Monday	2.95	0.59	1.48	2.95
❑128, Jan 98, Dan & Larry: Don't Do That!, Part 1; Metalfer, Part 3, Dan & Larry, Metalfer, Stiltskin	2.95	0.59	1.48	2.95
❑129, Feb 98	2.95	0.59	1.48	2.95
❑130, Mar 98, Dan & Larry, Wanted Man, Mary Walker: The Woman	2.95	0.59	1.48	2.95
❑131, Apr 98, Girl Crazy, The Fall, Dan & Larry, Boogie Picker	2.95	0.59	1.48	2.95
❑132, Apr 98, The Fall, Dan & Larry, Dirty Pair	2.95	0.59	1.48	2.95
❑133, May 98, Carson of Venus, The Fall, Dirty Pair, Blue Monday	2.95	0.59	1.48	2.95
❑134, Jul 98	2.95	0.59	1.48	2.95
❑135, Sep 98, The Fall, Part 5; The Ark, Part 4, Carson of Venus, The Mark, The Fall, The Ark	2.95	0.70	1.75	3.50
❑136, Oct 98, The Ark, Part 3; Spirit of the Badlander, The Ark, Spirit of the Badlander	2.95	0.59	1.48	2.95
❑137, Nov 98, Predator, The Ark, My Vagabond Days	2.95	0.59	1.48	2.95
❑138, Dec 98, Terminator, The Moth, My Vagabond Days	2.95	0.59	1.48	2.95
❑139, Jan 99, Roachmill, Saint Slayer	2.95	0.59	1.48	2.95
❑140, Feb 99, Aliens, Usagi Yojimbo, Saint Slayer	2.95	0.59	1.48	2.95
❑141, Mar 99, Buffy the Vampire Slayer: Hello Moon; Buffy the Vampire Slayer: Cursed, Buffy the Vampire Slayer	2.95	0.59	1.48	2.95
❑142, Apr 99, The Book Room Horror; The Devil's Footprints: Worm Song, 1: Doctor Gosburo Coffin, Codex Arcana	2.95	0.59	1.48	2.95
❑143, May 99, TY (w), Tarzan: Tales of Pellucidar, Tarzan: Tales of Pellucidar	2.95	0.59	1.48	2.95
❑144, Jun 99, The Vortex, Burglar Girls, Galactic Jack	2.95	0.59	1.48	2.95
❑145, Jul 99, Burglar Girls	2.95	0.59	1.48	2.95
❑146, Sep 99, Aliens vs Predator	2.95	0.59	1.48	2.95
❑147, Oct 99, Ragnok	2.95	0.59	1.48	2.95
❑148, Oct 99	2.95	0.59	1.48	2.95
❑149, Dec 99	2.95	0.59	1.48	2.95
❑150, Jan 00, Buffy the Vampire Slayer: Killing Time; Concrete: Sympathy from a Devil, Giant-size	4.50	0.90	2.25	4.50
❑151	—	0.00	0.00	0.00
❑152	—	0.00	0.00	0.00
❑153	—	0.00	0.00	0.00
❑154	—	0.00	0.00	0.00

	ORIG	GOOD	FINE	N-MINT
❑155	—	0.00	0.00	0.00
❑156	—	0.00	0.00	0.00
❑157, Sep 00, Witch's Son, Part 2; The Goon, b&w	2.95	0.59	1.48	2.95
❑Anl 1997, Feb 98, Body Bags; The American: The Big Deal, b&w; cover says 1997, indicia says 1998	4.95	0.99	2.47	4.95
❑Anl 1998, Sep 98, Hellboy: The Right Hand of Doom; Phineas Page, b&w; Hellboy, Buffy, Skeleton Key, The Ark, My Vagabond Days, Infirmary	4.95	0.99	2.47	4.95
❑Anl 1999, Aug 99, Xena Warrior Princess: The Worm; Hellboy: Pancakes, Dark Horse Jr.	4.95	0.99	2.47	4.95
❑Anl 2000, Jun 00, Gabrielle: Atlas Shrugged; Silhouette: Haunted Past, Flipbook	4.95	0.99	2.47	4.95

DARK ISLAND
DAVDEZ

	ORIG	GOOD	FINE	N-MINT
❑1, May 98, b&w	2.95	0.59	1.48	2.95
❑2, Jun 98, b&w	2.50	0.59	1.48	2.95
❑3, Jul 98, b&w	2.50	0.50	1.25	2.50

DARKLIGHT: PRELUDE
SIRIUS

Value: Cover or less

- ❑1, b&w 2.95
- ❑2, b&w 2.95
- ❑3, b&w 2.95

DARKLON THE MYSTIC
PACIFIC

Value: Cover or less

- ❑1, Nov 83, JSn, JSn (w), The Price; Retribution 1.50

DARKMAN (MAGAZINE)
MARVEL

Value: Cover or less

- ❑1, Sep 90, b&w; Movie Adaptation, Magazine size; Magazine size 2.25

DARKMAN (VOL. 1)
MARVEL

	ORIG	GOOD	FINE	N-MINT
❑1, Oct 90	1.50	0.45	1.13	2.25
❑2, Nov 90, BH	1.50	0.30	0.75	1.50
❑3, Dec 90, BH	1.50	0.30	0.75	1.50

DARKMAN (VOL. 2)
MARVEL

Value: Cover or less

- ❑1, Apr 93, KB (w), Dark Obsession 3.95
- ❑2, May 93, KB (w) 2.95
- ❑3, Jun 93, KB (w), Dancin' In The Dark 2.95
- ❑4, Jul 93, KB (w) 2.95
- ❑5, Aug 93, KB (w) 2.95
- ❑6, Sep 93, KB (w), Final Issue 2.95

DARK MANSION OF FORBIDDEN LOVE, THE
DC

	ORIG	GOOD	FINE	N-MINT
❑1, TD, The Mystery Of The Missing Bride	0.25	7.00	17.50	35.00
❑2	0.25	4.00	10.00	20.00
❑3	0.25	4.00	10.00	20.00
❑4, Series continued in Forbidden Tales of Dark Mansion #5	0.25	4.00	10.00	20.00

DARKMINDS
IMAGE

	ORIG	GOOD	FINE	N-MINT
❑0.5, May 99, Electric Dream	2.50	0.50	1.25	2.50
❑1, Jul 98, A Deadly Paradox	2.50	0.80	2.00	4.00
❑1/GO, Aug 98, A Deadly Paradox, DFE gold foil edition	—	1.00	2.50	5.00
❑1/SC, Jul 98, alternate cover (solo figure)	2.50	1.00	2.50	5.00
❑1-2, 2nd Printing	2.50	0.50	1.25	2.50
❑2, Aug 98, The Neon Dragons	2.50	0.70	1.75	3.50
❑2/SC, Aug 98, alternate cover	2.50	0.70	1.75	3.50
❑3, Sep 98, Face of a Killer	2.50	0.60	1.50	3.00
❑3/SC, Sep 98, alternate cover	2.50	0.60	1.50	3.00
❑4, Oct 98, Deadly Intentions, cover says Dec, indicia says Oct	2.50	0.60	1.50	3.00
❑5, Nov 98, Unlikely Friends, Unlikely Enemies	2.50	0.60	1.50	3.00
❑6, Dec 98, Opposing Forces	2.50	0.60	1.50	3.00
❑7, Feb 99, The Darkest Mind	2.50	0.50	1.25	2.50
❑8, Apr 99	2.50	0.50	1.25	2.50

DARKMINDS (VOL. 2)
IMAGE

Value: Cover or less

- ❑0, Jul 00, The Bullet 2.50
- ❑1, Feb 00, The More Things Change 2.50
- ❑2, Mar 00 .... 2.50
- ❑3, Apr 00 .... 2.50
- ❑4, May 00 .... 2.50
- ❑5, Jun 00, The Prize 2.50
- ❑6, Sep 00, 9mm Answers 2.50
- ❑7, Oct 00, The Hunger 2.50
- ❑8, Nov 00, Born Again 2.50
- ❑9, Feb 01, A Million and One 2.50
- ❑10, Apr 01, Final Bow 2.50

DARKMINDS/WITCHBLADE
IMAGE

Value: Cover or less

- ❑1, Aug 00 .... 5.95

DARK MOON PROPHESY
DARK MOON PRODUCTIONS

	ORIG	GOOD	FINE	N-MINT
❑1, May 95, nn; free color and b&w preview of Dark Moon line	—	0.20	0.50	1.00

DARK NEMESIS (VILLAINS)
DC

Value: Cover or less

- ❑1, Feb 98, New Year's Evil 1.95

DARKNESS, THE
TOP COW

	ORIG	GOOD	FINE	N-MINT
❑0	2.50	0.60	1.50	3.00
❑0.5, Wizard mail-away promotion	—	0.60	1.50	3.00
❑0.5/SC, Christmas cover; Wizard mail-away promotion	—	1.00	2.50	5.00
❑0.5-2, Mar 01	2.95	0.59	1.48	2.95
❑1, Dec 96, Coming of Age	2.50	0.80	2.00	4.00
❑1/A, Dec 96, Marc Silvestri, Dark cover variant	2.50	0.80	2.00	4.00
❑1/B, Marc Silvestri, Wizard Ace edition	—	1.00	2.50	5.00
❑1/C, Marc Silvestri, Fan club edition	—	0.80	2.00	4.00
❑1/GO, Dec 96, Coming of Age, Gold edition	—	1.20	3.00	6.00
❑1/PL, Dec 96, Coming of Age, Platinum edition	—	2.00	5.00	10.00
❑2, Jan 97, Underworld	2.50	0.80	2.00	4.00
❑3, Mar 97, Almost an Angel	2.50	0.60	1.50	3.00
❑4, May 97, Brought to Light	2.50	0.60	1.50	3.00
❑5, Jun 97, Apocalypse Shortly	2.50	0.60	1.50	3.00
❑6, Jul 97, End of an Era	2.50	0.60	1.50	3.00
❑7, Aug 97, Coming of Age	2.50	0.50	1.25	2.50
❑7/A, Aug 97, Coming of Age, Variant cover with Michael Turner and babes	2.50	0.50	1.25	2.50
❑8, Oct 97, Coming of Age	2.50	0.50	1.25	2.50
❑8/A, Oct 97, Coming of Age, alternate cover	2.50	0.50	1.25	2.50
❑8/B, Oct 97, alternate cover	2.50	0.50	1.25	2.50
❑8/C, Oct 97, alternate cover	2.50	0.50	1.25	2.50
❑9, Nov 97, Family Ties, Part 2	2.50	0.50	1.25	2.50
❑9/A, Nov 97, Family Ties, Part 2, alternate cover	2.50	0.50	1.25	2.50
❑10, Dec 97, Family Ties, Part 3	2.50	0.50	1.25	2.50
❑10/A, Dec 97, Family Ties, Part 3, alternate cover (gold)	2.50	0.50	1.25	2.50
❑10/B, Dec 97, Family Ties, Part 3, alternate cover (gold)	2.50	0.50	1.25	2.50
❑11/A, Jan 98, Brought to Light, chromium cover	2.50	1.80	4.50	9.00
❑11/B, Brought to Light	2.50	0.50	1.25	2.50
❑11/C, Brought to Light	2.50	0.50	1.25	2.50
❑11/D, Brought to Light	2.50	0.50	1.25	2.50
❑11/E, Brought to Light	2.50	0.50	1.25	2.50
❑11/F, Brought to Light	2.50	0.50	1.25	2.50
❑11/G, Brought to Light	2.50	0.50	1.25	2.50
❑11/H, Brought to Light	2.50	0.50	1.25	2.50
❑11/I, Brought to Light	2.50	0.50	1.25	2.50
❑11/J, Brought to Light	2.50	0.50	1.25	2.50
❑12, Feb 98	2.50	0.50	1.25	2.50
❑13, Mar 98	2.50	0.50	1.25	2.50
❑14, Apr 98	2.50	0.50	1.25	2.50
❑15, Jun 98	2.50	0.50	1.25	2.50
❑16, Jul 98, Family Ties, Part 2	2.50	0.50	1.25	2.50
❑17, Sep 98, O: Magdalena	2.50	0.50	1.25	2.50
❑18, Nov 98	2.50	0.50	1.25	2.50
❑19, Jan 99	2.50	0.50	1.25	2.50
❑20/A, Apr 99, Regular Cover (with Darklings)	2.50	0.50	1.25	2.50
❑20/B, Apr 99, alternate cover	2.50	0.50	1.25	2.50
❑20/C, Apr 99, Alternate Cover (With Darklings)	2.50	0.50	1.25	2.50
❑21, May 99	2.50	0.50	1.25	2.50
❑22, Jun 99	2.50	0.50	1.25	2.50
❑23, Jul 99	2.50	0.50	1.25	2.50
❑24, Aug 99	2.50	0.50	1.25	2.50
❑25, Sep 99	2.50	0.50	1.25	2.50
❑25/A, Chrome variant	—	4.00	10.00	20.00
❑26, Oct 99	2.50	0.50	1.25	2.50
❑27, Oct 99	2.50	0.50	1.25	2.50
❑28, Jan 00	2.50	0.50	1.25	2.50
❑29	2.50	0.50	1.25	2.50
❑30, Apr 00	2.50	0.50	1.25	2.50
❑31	2.50	0.50	1.25	2.50
❑32, Jul 00	2.50	0.50	1.25	2.50
❑33, Aug 00	2.50	0.50	1.25	2.50
❑34, Oct 00	2.50	0.50	1.25	2.50
❑35, Nov 00	2.50	0.50	1.25	2.50
❑36, Dec 00	2.50	0.50	1.25	2.50
❑37, Feb 01	2.50	0.50	1.25	2.50
❑38, Apr 01	2.50	0.50	1.25	2.50
❑39, May 01	2.50	0.50	1.25	2.50
❑40	2.50	0.50	1.25	2.50
❑Ash 1, Jul 96, nn; no cover price; preview of upcoming series	—	0.80	2.00	4.00
❑ASH 1/A, Prelude; "Wizard Authentic" variant	—	0.60	1.50	3.00
❑Dlx 1, Darkness Preview; Collected Editions #1; Deluxe edition; Reprints The Darkness #1-6; Slipcased	14.95	2.99	7.47	14.95

	ORIG	GOOD	FINE	N-MINT

DARKNESS/BATMAN, THE
IMAGE

Value: Cover or less

- ❑1, Aug 99, JPH 5.95

DARKNESS INFINITY
IMAGE

Value: Cover or less

- ❑1, Aug 99 ..... 3.50

DARKNESS/PAINKILLER JANE
IMAGE

	ORIG	GOOD	FINE	N-MINT
❑Ash 1	—	0.60	1.50	3.00
❑ASH 1/A, variant cover	—	0.60	1.50	3.00

DARKNESS, THE: SPEAR OF DESTINY
IMAGE

Value: Cover or less

- ❑1, Apr 00, Collects The Darkness #15-18 ..... 12.95

DARKNESS/WITCHBLADE SPECIAL
IMAGE

Value: Cover or less

- ❑1, Dec 99 ..... 3.95

DARK OZ
ARROW

Value: Cover or less

- ❑1 ..... 2.75
- ❑2 ..... 2.75
- ❑3 ..... 2.75
- ❑4 ..... 2.75
- ❑5, indicia says 97, a misprint 2.75

DARK RAT
MAVERICK PULP COMIX

Value: Cover or less

- ❑1, Sep 97, b&w 2.50

DARK REALM
IMAGE

Value: Cover or less

- ❑1, Oct 00 ..... 2.95
- ❑2, Dec 00 ..... 2.95
- ❑3, Feb 01 ..... 2.95

DARK REGIONS
WHITE WOLF

Value: Cover or less

- ❑1, Feb 87, The Magic Stream; Ignor Ant 1.75
- ❑2 ..... 1.75
- ❑3, May 87 ..... 1.75

DARKSEID (VILLAINS)
DC

Value: Cover or less

- ❑1, Feb 98, SB, JBy (w), Shadows in a Greater Darkness, New Year's Evil 1.95

DARK SHADOWS (GOLD KEY)
GOLD KEY

	ORIG	GOOD	FINE	N-MINT
❑1, poster; based on TV series	—	25.00	62.50	125.00
❑1/A, based on TV series; with poster; Without poster	—	10.00	25.00	50.00
❑2	—	11.00	27.50	55.00
❑3, poster	—	10.00	25.00	50.00
❑4	—	8.00	20.00	40.00
❑5	—	8.00	20.00	40.00
❑6	—	6.40	16.00	32.00
❑7	—	6.40	16.00	32.00
❑8	—	6.40	16.00	32.00
❑9	—	6.40	16.00	32.00
❑10	—	6.40	16.00	32.00
❑11	—	6.00	15.00	30.00
❑12	—	6.00	15.00	30.00
❑13	—	6.00	15.00	30.00
❑14, Jun 72, The Mystic Painting, Part 1, A Tragedy Recalled; The Mystic Painting, Part 2, Stain of Guilt, Painted cover	0.15	6.00	15.00	30.00
❑15	—	6.00	15.00	30.00
❑16	—	4.80	12.00	24.00
❑17	—	4.80	12.00	24.00
❑18	—	4.80	12.00	24.00
❑19	—	4.80	12.00	24.00
❑20	—	4.80	12.00	24.00
❑21	—	3.60	9.00	18.00
❑22	—	3.60	9.00	18.00
❑23	—	3.60	9.00	18.00
❑24	—	3.60	9.00	18.00
❑25	—	3.60	9.00	18.00
❑26	—	3.60	9.00	18.00
❑27	—	3.60	9.00	18.00
❑28	—	3.60	9.00	18.00
❑29	—	3.60	9.00	18.00
❑30	—	3.60	9.00	18.00
❑31	—	3.00	7.50	15.00
❑32	—	3.00	7.50	15.00
❑33	—	3.00	7.50	15.00
❑34	—	3.00	7.50	15.00
❑35	—	3.00	7.50	15.00

DARK SHADOWS (INNOVATION)
INNOVATION

	ORIG	GOOD	FINE	N-MINT
❑1, Jun 92, A Time Of Innocence...And Confidences, TV series	2.50	0.60	1.50	3.00
❑2, Aug 92, TV series	2.50	0.50	1.25	2.50
❑3, Nov 92, TV series	2.50	0.50	1.25	2.50
❑4, Spr 93, TV series	2.50	0.50	1.25	2.50
❑5, Jun 93, Lost in Thought, Part 1, Book 2, #1	2.50	0.50	1.25	2.50
❑6, Lost in Thought, Part 2, Book 2, #2	2.50	0.50	1.25	2.50
❑7, Book 2, #3	2.50	0.50	1.25	2.50
❑8, Book 2, #4	2.50	0.50	1.25	2.50
❑9, A Motion and a Spirit, Book 3 #1	2.50	0.50	1.25	2.50

The connection between The Darkness and Witchblade was explored in the "Family Ties" crossover between the two characters' titles.

DARK SHRINE
ANTARCTIC PRESS

Value: Cover or less

- ❑1, May 99 ..... 2.99
- ❑2, Jun 99 ..... 2.50

DARKSTARS, THE
DC

Value: Cover or less

- ❑0, Oct 94, Wayward Son, O: Darkstars, Series continued in Darkstars #24 ..... 1.95
- ❑1, Oct 92, Mean Streets, 1: Darkstars 1.75
- ❑2, Nov 92 ..... 1.75
- ❑3, Dec 92 ..... 1.75
- ❑4, Jan 93 ..... 1.75
- ❑5, Feb 93, A: Hawkman; A: Hawkwoman 1.75
- ❑6, Mar 93, A: Hawkman 1.75
- ❑7, Apr 93 ..... 1.75
- ❑8, May 93 ..... 1.75
- ❑9, Jun 93 ..... 1.75
- ❑10, Jun 93 ..... 1.75
- ❑11, Aug 93, Trinity 1.75
- ❑12, Sep 93, Trinity 1.75
- ❑13, Oct 93 ..... 1.75
- ❑14, Nov 93 ..... 1.75
- ❑15, Dec 93 ..... 1.75
- ❑16, Jan 94 ..... 1.75
- ❑17, Feb 94 ..... 1.75
- ❑18, Mar 94, Eve of Destruction, Part 1 ..... 1.75
- ❑19, Apr 94, Flash 1.75
- ❑20, May 94, Flash 1.75
- ❑21, Jun 94 ..... 1.75
- ❑22, Jul 94, Tangled Webs 1.95
- ❑23, Aug 94, Series continued in Darkstars #0, Donna Troy joins Darkstars 1.95
- ❑24, Sep 94, Zero Hour 1.95
- ❑25, Nov 94 ..... 1.95
- ❑26, Dec 94 ..... 1.95
- ❑27, Jan 95 ..... 1.95
- ❑28, Feb 95 ..... 1.95
- ❑29, Mar 95 ..... 1.95
- ❑30, Apr 95 ..... 1.95
- ❑31, Jun 95 ..... 2.25
- ❑32, Jul 95 ..... 2.25
- ❑33, Aug 95 ..... 2.25
- ❑34, Sep 95, The Siege of The Zi Charam, Part 3 ..... 2.25
- ❑35, Oct 95 ..... 2.25
- ❑36, Nov 95, A: Flash 2.25
- ❑37, Dec 95, V: Guy Gardner 2.25
- ❑38, Jan 96, Final Issue 2.25

DARK TALES OF DAILY HORROR
ANTARCTIC

Value: Cover or less

- ❑1, Feb 94, b&w 2.95

DARK VISIONS
PYRAMID

	ORIG	GOOD	FINE	N-MINT
❑1, Nov 86, The Nightstalker; Dirty Needles	1.70	0.40	1.00	2.00
❑2	1.70	0.40	1.00	2.00

DARKWING DUCK
DISNEY

Value: Cover or less

- ❑1 ..... 1.50
- ❑2 ..... 1.50
- ❑3 ..... 1.50
- ❑4 ..... 1.50

DARKWING DUCK LIMITED SERIES (DISNEY'S...)
DISNEY

Value: Cover or less

- ❑1, Nov 91, Brawl in the Family, Part 1 ..... 1.50
- ❑2 ..... 1.50
- ❑3 ..... 1.50
- ❑4 ..... 1.50

DARK WOLF
ETERNITY

Value: Cover or less

- ❑1, b&w 1.95
- ❑2, b&w 1.95
- ❑3, b&w 1.95
- ❑4, b&w 1.95
- ❑5, Jun 88, Destruction, b&w 1.95
- ❑6, b&w 1.95
- ❑7, b&w 1.95
- ❑8, b&w 1.95
- ❑9, b&w 1.95
- ❑10, b&w 1.95
- ❑11, b&w 1.95
- ❑12, b&w 1.95
- ❑13, b&w 1.95
- ❑14, b&w 1.95
- ❑Anl 1, b&w 2.25

DARK WOLF (VOL. 2)
MALIBU

Value: Cover or less

- ❑1 ..... 1.95
- ❑2 ..... 1.95
- ❑3 ..... 1.95
- ❑4 ..... 1.95

DARQUE PASSAGES
VALIANT

Value: Cover or less

- ❑1, Jan 94 .... 2.00

DARQUE PASSAGES (VOL. 2)
ACCLAIM

Value: Cover or less

- ❑1, Apr 98 .... 2.50
- ❑2, Jan 98, no cover date; indicia says Jan 2.50
- ❑3, Feb 98, no cover date; indicia says Feb 2.50

DARQUE RAZOR
LONDON NIGHT

Value: Cover or less

- ❑1, Oct 97 .... 3.00

DART
IMAGE

Value: Cover or less

- ❑1, Feb 96 .... 2.50
- ❑1/A, Feb 96, alternate cover 2.50
- ❑2, Apr 96 .... 2.50
- ❑3, May 96 .... 2.50

DAWN
SIRIUS ENTERTAINMENT

	ORIG	GOOD	FINE	N-MINT
❑0.5, Wizard mail-away	—	1.00	2.50	5.00
❑0.5/SC, "Hey Kids" Variant cover; Wizard mail-away	—	4.40	11.00	22.00
❑1, Jul 95, Lucifer's Halo, Part 1	2.95	1.20	3.00	6.00
❑1/A, Lucifer's Halo, Part 1, "Black light" cover; blacklight edition	10.00	2.40	6.00	12.00
❑1/B, Lucifer's Halo, Part 1, "White Trash" edition	—	3.00	7.50	15.00
❑1/C, Lucifer's Halo, Part 1, "Look Sharp" edition	—	3.00	7.50	15.00
❑2, Sep 95, Lucifer's Halo, Part 1	2.95	1.00	2.50	5.00
❑2/A, Mystery Book	10.00	5.00	12.50	25.00
❑3	2.95	1.00	2.50	5.00
❑3/A	2.95	5.00	12.50	25.00
❑4	2.95	0.80	2.00	4.00
❑4/A	2.95	4.00	10.00	20.00
❑5	2.95	0.60	1.50	3.00
❑5/A	2.95	3.00	7.50	15.00
❑6	2.95	0.80	2.00	4.00
❑6/A	2.95	3.00	7.50	15.00

DAWN TENTH ANNIVERSARY SPECIAL
SIRIUS ENTERTAINMENT

Value: Cover or less

- ❑1, Sep 99 .... 2.95

DAWN: THE RETURN OF THE GODDESS
SIRIUS ENTERTAINMENT

Value: Cover or less

- ❑1, Apr 99 .... 2.95
- ❑1/LE 25.00
- ❑2, May 99, Access; Jaynis Goldbaum's Last Dance 2.95
- ❑3 .... 2.95
- ❑4, Jul 00, Atrocity; Ascension 2.95

DAYDREAMERS
MARVEL

Value: Cover or less

- ❑1, Aug 97, Once Upon a Time..., gatefold summary; teams Howard the Duck, Man-Thing, Franklin Richards, Leech, Artie, and Tana 2.50
- ❑2, Sep 97, Across the Universe, gatefold summary 2.50
- ❑3, Oct 97, Dark Eyes, gatefold summary 2.50

DAY OF JUDGMENT
DC

Value: Cover or less

- ❑1, Nov 99, The Summoning 2.95
- ❑2, Nov 99, Lost Souls 2.50
- ❑3, Nov 99 .... 2.50
- ❑4, Nov 99, D: Enchantress 2.50
- ❑5, Nov 99, Hal Jordan becomes Spectre 2.50

DAY OF JUDGMENT SECRET FILES
DC

Value: Cover or less

- ❑1, Nov 99, background on participants in event 4.95

DAY OF THE DEFENDERS
MARVEL

Value: Cover or less

- ❑1, Mar 01, RA; HT, The Monarch and the Mystic!; ... Where Stalks the Nightcrawler!, 1: The Defenders, nn; Reprint 3.50

DAYS OF WRATH
APPLE

Value: Cover or less

- ❑1, b&w 2.75
- ❑2, b&w 2.75
- ❑3, b&w 2.75
- ❑4, Jun 94, b&w 2.75

DAZZLER
MARVEL

	ORIG	GOOD	FINE	N-MINT
❑1, Mar 81, JR2, So Bright This Star, O: Dazzler; A: X-Men, direct; First Marvel direct market-only comic	0.50	0.40	1.00	2.00
❑2, Apr 81, AA; JR2, A: X-Men	0.50	0.30	0.75	1.50
❑3, May 81, The Jewels of Doom!, V: Doctor Doom	0.50	0.20	0.50	1.00
❑4, Jun 81, FS, Here Nightmares Abide!, V: Doctor Doom	0.50	0.20	0.50	1.00
❑5, Jul 81, 1: Blue Shield	0.50	0.20	0.50	1.00
❑6, Aug 81	0.50	0.20	0.50	1.00
❑7, Sep 81	0.50	0.20	0.50	1.00
❑8, Oct 81	0.50	0.20	0.50	1.00
❑9, Nov 81	0.50	0.20	0.50	1.00
❑10, Dec 81, A: Galactus	0.50	0.20	0.50	1.00
❑11, Jan 82, A: Galactus	0.60	0.20	0.50	1.00
❑12, Feb 82	0.60	0.20	0.50	1.00
❑13, Mar 82	0.60	0.20	0.50	1.00
❑14, Apr 82	0.60	0.20	0.50	1.00
❑15, May 82, FS; BSz	0.60	0.20	0.50	1.00
❑16, Jun 82, FS; BSz	0.60	0.20	0.50	1.00
❑17, Jul 82, FS, Angel	0.60	0.20	0.50	1.00
❑18, Aug 82, FS; FF; BSz	0.60	0.20	0.50	1.00
❑19, Sep 82	0.60	0.20	0.50	1.00
❑20, Oct 82	0.60	0.20	0.50	1.00
❑21, Nov 82, Photo cover; Double-size	1.00	0.20	0.50	1.00
❑22, Dec 82, V: Rogue	0.60	0.20	0.50	1.00
❑23, Jan 83	0.60	0.20	0.50	1.00
❑24, Feb 83	0.60	0.20	0.50	1.00
❑25, Mar 83	0.60	0.20	0.50	1.00
❑26, May 83	0.60	0.20	0.50	1.00
❑27, Jul 83, BSz (c)	0.60	0.20	0.50	1.00
❑28, Sep 83, BSz (c), A: Rogue	0.60	0.20	0.50	1.00
❑29, Nov 83, Photo cover	0.60	0.20	0.50	1.00
❑30, Jan 84, BSz (c)	0.60	0.20	0.50	1.00
❑31, Mar 84, BSz (c)	0.60	0.20	0.50	1.00
❑32, Jun 84, BSz (c), A: Inhumans	0.60	0.20	0.50	1.00
❑33, Aug 84, BSz (c)	0.60	0.20	0.50	1.00
❑34, Oct 84, BSz (c)	0.60	0.20	0.50	1.00
❑35, Jan 85, BSz (c)	0.60	0.20	0.50	1.00
❑36, Mar 85, JBy (c)	0.60	0.20	0.50	1.00
❑37, May 85	0.65	0.20	0.50	1.00
❑38, Jul 85, A: X-Men	0.65	0.20	0.50	1.00
❑39, Sep 85	0.65	0.20	0.50	1.00
❑40, Nov 85, Secret Wars II, Secret Wars II	0.65	0.20	0.50	1.00
❑41, Jan 86	0.65	0.20	0.50	1.00
❑42, Mar 86, Final Issue	0.75	0.20	0.50	1.00

DC 100 PAGE SUPER SPECTACULAR
DC

	ORIG	GOOD	FINE	N-MINT
❑4, back cover pin-up; Weird Mystery Tales	0.50	20.00	50.00	100.00
❑5, BO, Made For Love; How Do I Know When I'm Really in Love?, back cover pin-up; Love Stories	0.50	65.00	162.50	325.00
❑5-2, BO, Made For Love; How Do I Know When I'm Really in Love?, Replica edition; Love Stories	6.95	1.39	3.47	6.95
❑6, wraparound cover; World's Greatest Super-Heroes; reprints JLA #21-22	0.50	20.00	50.00	100.00
❑7, Dec 71, back cover pin-up; really DC-7; a.k.a. Superman #245	0.50	7.00	17.50	35.00
❑8, Jan 72, wraparound cover; really DC-8; a.k.a. Batman #238	0.50	10.00	25.00	50.00
❑9, Feb 72, Sgt. Rock, wraparound cover; really DC-9; a.k.a. Our Army at War #242	0.50	10.00	25.00	50.00
❑10, Mar 72, wraparound cover; really DC-10; a.k.a. Adventure Comics #416; Supergirl	0.50	7.00	17.50	35.00
❑11, Apr 72, wraparound cover; really DC-11; a.k.a. Flash #214	0.50	7.00	17.50	35.00
❑12, May 72, wraparound cover; really DC-12; a.k.a. Superboy #185	0.50	7.00	17.50	35.00
❑13, Jun 72, wraparound cover; really DC-13; a.k.a. Superman #252	0.50	7.00	17.50	35.00
❑14, Feb 73, wraparound cover; really DC-14; Batman	0.50	6.00	15.00	30.00
❑15, Mar 73, back cover pin-up; really DC-15; Superboy	0.50	6.00	15.00	30.00
❑16, back cover cover gallery; really DC-16; Sgt. Rock	0.50	5.00	12.50	25.00
❑17, Jun 73, back cover cover gallery; really DC-17; JLA	0.50	5.00	12.50	25.00
❑18, Jul 73, back cover cover gallery; Superman's 35th anniversary; really DC-18	0.50	5.00	12.50	25.00
❑19, Aug 73, RM, JKu (c), Tarzan and the Elephants' Guardian; Prisoners in Opar, back cover pin-up; really DC-19; Tarzan.	0.50	5.00	12.50	25.00
❑20, Sep 73, O: Two-Face, back cover cover gallery; really DC-20; Batman	0.50	5.00	12.50	25.00
❑21, Oct 73, back cover cover gallery; really DC-21; Superboy	0.50	5.00	12.50	25.00
❑22, Nov 73, really DC-22; Flash; Super Specs become part of individual series beginning with Shazam! #8	0.50	1.50	3.75	7.50

DC 2000
DC

Value: Cover or less

- ❑1 .... 6.95
- ❑2 .... 6.95

DC CHALLENGE
DC

	ORIG	GOOD	FINE	N-MINT
❑1, Nov 85, GC, ME (w), Outbreak!	1.25	0.30	0.75	1.50
❑2, Dec 85	1.25	0.30	0.75	1.50
❑3, Jan 86, CI, Viking Vengeance	1.25	0.30	0.75	1.50
❑4, Feb 86, KJ; GK	1.25	0.30	0.75	1.50
❑5, Mar 86, DaG	1.25	0.30	0.75	1.50
❑6, Apr 86	1.25	0.30	0.75	1.50
❑7, May 86, JSa	1.25	0.30	0.75	1.50
❑8, Jun 86	1.25	0.30	0.75	1.50
❑9, Jul 86	1.25	0.30	0.75	1.50
❑10, Aug 86, CS	1.25	0.30	0.75	1.50
❑11, Sep 86, RT; KG	1.25	0.30	0.75	1.50
❑12, Oct 86, GP	1.25	0.30	0.75	1.50

DC COMICS PRESENTS
DC

	ORIG	GOOD	FINE	N-MINT
❑1, Jul 78, Flash	0.35	0.60	1.50	3.00
❑2, Sep 78, Flash	0.50	0.60	1.50	3.00
❑3, Oct 78, Adam Strange	0.50	0.40	1.00	2.00
❑4, Dec 78, Metal Men	0.40	0.40	1.00	2.00
❑5, Jan 79, MA, Aquaman	0.40	0.40	1.00	2.00
❑6, Feb 79, CS, Green Lantern	0.40	0.40	1.00	2.00
❑7, Mar 79, DD, Red Tornado	0.40	0.40	1.00	2.00
❑8, Apr 79, MA, Swamp Thing	0.40	0.40	1.00	2.00
❑9, May 79, JSa, Wonder Woman	0.40	0.40	1.00	2.00
❑10, Jun 79, JSa, Sgt. Rock	0.40	0.40	1.00	2.00
❑11, Jul 79, JSa, Hawkman	0.40	0.40	1.00	2.00
❑12, Aug 79, DG; RB, Mr. Miracle	0.40	0.40	1.00	2.00
❑13, Sep 79, DD; DG, Legion; Legion of Super-Heroes	0.40	0.40	1.00	2.00
❑14, Oct 79, DD; DG, Superboy	0.40	0.30	0.75	1.50
❑15, Nov 79, JSa, Atom	0.40	0.30	0.75	1.50
❑16, Dec 79, Black Lightning	0.40	0.30	0.75	1.50
❑17, Jan 80, Firestorm	0.40	0.30	0.75	1.50
❑18, Feb 80, DD, Zatanna	0.40	0.30	0.75	1.50
❑19, Mar 80, JSa, Batgirl	0.40	0.30	0.75	1.50
❑20, Apr 80, Green Arrow	0.40	0.30	0.75	1.50
❑21, May 80, JSa, Elongated Man	0.40	0.30	0.75	1.50
❑22, Jun 80, Captain Comet	0.40	0.30	0.75	1.50
❑23, Jul 80, JSa, Doctor Fate	0.40	0.30	0.75	1.50
❑24, Aug 80, Deadman	0.40	0.30	0.75	1.50
❑25, Sep 80, Phantom Stranger	0.50	0.30	0.75	1.50
❑26, Oct 80, GP; JSn, JSn (w), Between Friend and Foe; Where Nightmares Begin, 1: Cyborg; 1: Starfire II (Koriand'r); 1: Raven; 1: New Teen Titans, Green Lantern	0.50	1.60	4.00	8.00
❑27, Nov 80, JSn, 1: Mongul, Martian Manhunter; Congorilla back-up	0.50	0.50	1.25	2.50
❑28, Dec 80, JSn, V: Mongul, Supergirl; Johnny Thunder Lawman back-up	0.50	0.30	0.75	1.50
❑29, Jan 81, RT; JSn, Spectre	0.50	0.30	0.75	1.50
❑30, Feb 81, CS, Black Canary	0.50	0.30	0.75	1.50
❑31, Mar 81, DG, Robin; Robotman back-up	0.50	0.30	0.75	1.50
❑32, Apr 81, Wonder Woman	0.50	0.30	0.75	1.50
❑33, May 81, Captain Marvel	0.50	0.30	0.75	1.50
❑34, Jun 81, Marvel Family	0.50	0.30	0.75	1.50
❑35, Jul 81, CS, Man-Bat	0.50	0.30	0.75	1.50
❑36, Aug 81, JSn, Starman	0.50	0.30	0.75	1.50
❑37, Sep 81, RT; JSn, Hawkgirl; Rip Hunter back-up	0.50	0.30	0.75	1.50
❑38, Oct 81, D: Crimson Avenger, Flash	0.60	0.30	0.75	1.50
❑39, Nov 81, JSn, A: Toyman	0.60	0.30	0.75	1.50
❑40, Dec 81, Metamorpho	0.60	0.30	0.75	1.50
❑41, Jan 82, 1: new Wonder Woman; A: Joker, Joker	0.60	0.45	1.13	2.25
❑42, Feb 82, Unknown Soldier; Golden Age Sandman back-up	0.60	0.25	0.63	1.25
❑43, Mar 82, CS, Legion	0.60	0.25	0.63	1.25
❑44, Apr 82, A: Joker, Dial 'H' for Hero	0.60	0.45	1.13	2.25
❑45, May 82, RB, Firestorm	0.60	0.25	0.63	1.25
❑46, Jun 82, 1: Global Guardians	0.60	0.25	0.63	1.25
❑47, Jul 82, 1: Masters of Universe	0.60	0.25	0.63	1.25
❑48, Aug 82, Aquaman; Black Pirate back-up; Aquaman, Black Pirate back-up	0.60	0.25	0.63	1.25
❑49, Sep 82, RB, Captain Marvel	0.60	0.25	0.63	1.25
❑50, Oct 82, CS, Clark Kent	0.60	0.25	0.63	1.25
❑51, Nov 82, FMc, Atom	0.60	0.25	0.63	1.25
❑52, Dec 82, KG, 1: Ambush Bug, Doom Patrol	0.60	0.50	1.25	2.50
❑53, Jan 83, 1: Atari Force, Atari Force preview; House of Mystery	0.60	0.20	0.50	1.00
❑54, Feb 83, DN, Green Arrow, Black Canary	0.60	0.20	0.50	1.00
❑55, Mar 83, V: Parasite; A: Superboy, Air Wave	0.60	0.20	0.50	1.00
❑56, Apr 83, CS, 1: Maaldor the Darklord, Power Girl	0.60	0.20	0.50	1.00

The groundwork was laid for the return of The Spectre in *Day of Judgment.*

	ORIG	GOOD	FINE	N-MINT
❑57, May 83, Atomic Knights	0.60	0.20	0.50	1.00
❑58, Jun 83, CS, GK (c), 1: The Untouchables (DC), Robin, Elongated Man	0.60	0.20	0.50	1.00
❑59, Jul 83, KG, Legion of Super-Heroes, Ambush Bug	0.60	0.20	0.50	1.00
❑60, Aug 83, Guardians of the Universe	0.60	0.20	0.50	1.00
❑61, Sep 83, OMAC	0.60	0.20	0.50	1.00
❑62, Oct 83, Freedom Fighters	0.60	0.20	0.50	1.00
❑63, Nov 83, Amethyst	0.60	0.20	0.50	1.00
❑64, Dec 83, Kamandi	0.75	0.20	0.50	1.00
❑65, Jan 84, Madame Xanadu	0.75	0.20	0.50	1.00
❑66, Feb 84, JK, 1: Blackbriar Thorn, Demon	0.75	0.20	0.50	1.00
❑67, Mar 84, V: Toyman, Santa Claus	0.75	0.20	0.50	1.00
❑68, Apr 84, CS; MA, Vixen	0.75	0.20	0.50	1.00
❑69, May 84, IN, Blackhawk	0.75	0.20	0.50	1.00
❑70, Jun 84, Metal Men	0.75	0.20	0.50	1.00
❑71, Jul 84, CS, Bizarro	0.75	0.20	0.50	1.00
❑72, Aug 84, Phantom Stranger, Joker	0.75	0.30	0.75	1.50
❑73, Sep 84, CI, Flash	0.75	0.20	0.50	1.00
❑74, Oct 84, Hawkman	0.75	0.20	0.50	1.00
❑75, Nov 84, Arion	0.75	0.20	0.50	1.00
❑76, Dec 84, A: Monitor, Wonder Woman	0.75	0.20	0.50	1.00
❑77, Jan 85, 1: The Forgotten Villains, Animal Man, Dolphin, Congorilla, Cave Carson, Immortal Man, Rip Hunter, Rick Flagg	0.75	0.60	1.50	3.00
❑78, Feb 85, Animal Man, Dolphin, Congorilla, Cave Carson, Immortal Man, Rip Hunter, Rick Flagg	0.75	0.60	1.50	3.00
❑79, Mar 85, Clark Kent	0.75	0.20	0.50	1.00
❑80, Apr 85, Legion	0.75	0.20	0.50	1.00
❑81, May 85, V: Kobra, Ambush Bug	0.75	0.20	0.50	1.00
❑82, Jun 85, Adam Strange	0.75	0.20	0.50	1.00
❑83, Jul 85, Outsiders	0.75	0.20	0.50	1.00
❑84, Aug 85, Challengers of the Unknown	0.75	0.20	0.50	1.00
❑85, Sep 85, AMo (w), Swamp Thing	0.75	1.60	4.00	8.00
❑86, Oct 85, V: Blackstarr, Crisis; Supergirl	0.75	0.20	0.50	1.00
❑87, Nov 85, 1: Superboy of Earth-Prime, Crisis	1.25	0.20	0.50	1.00
❑88, Dec 85, Crisis	0.75	0.20	0.50	1.00
❑89, Jan 86, Omega Men	0.75	0.20	0.50	1.00
❑90, Feb 86, O: Captain Atom, Firestorm	0.75	0.20	0.50	1.00
❑91, Mar 86, Captain Comet	0.75	0.20	0.50	1.00
❑92, Apr 86, Vigilante	0.75	0.20	0.50	1.00
❑93, May 86, Plastic Man, Elongated Man, Elastic Lad	0.75	0.20	0.50	1.00
❑94, Jun 86, Harbinger, Lady Quark, Pariah	0.75	0.20	0.50	1.00
❑95, Jul 86, Hawkman	0.75	0.20	0.50	1.00
❑96, Aug 86, Blue Devil	0.75	0.20	0.50	1.00
❑97, Sep 86, V: Phantom Zone Criminals; A: Mxyzptlk; A: Bizarro, Double-size	1.25	0.25	0.63	1.25
❑Anl 1, RB, Superman & E-2 Superman	1.00	0.60	1.50	3.00
❑Anl 2, 1: Superwoman	1.00	0.60	1.50	3.00
❑Anl 3, Doctor Sivana gains the Shazam! powers	1.25	0.60	1.50	3.00
❑Anl 4, A: Superwoman	1.25	0.60	1.50	3.00

DC GRAPHIC NOVEL
DC

Value: Cover or less

❑1, Star Raiders	5.95
❑2, Warlords	5.95
❑3, EC, Medusa Chain	5.95
❑4, JK, Hunger Dogs	5.95
❑5, Me and Joe Priest	5.95
❑6, Metalzoic	6.95
❑7, Space Clusters	5.95

DC/MARVEL: ALL ACCESS
DC

	ORIG	GOOD	FINE	N-MINT
❑1, Dec 96, The Crossing!, A: Superman, Spider-Man, Venom, crossover with Marvel	2.95	0.59	1.48	2.95
❑2, Jan 97, Two Sides of the Same Coin, A: Jubilee, Robin, Two-Face, Scorpion, crossover with Marvel	1.95	0.59	1.48	2.95
❑3, Jan 97, In The Doctor's House, A: Jubilee, Robin, Batman, Doctor Strange, Scorpion, JLA, X-Men, crossover with Marvel	1.95	0.59	1.48	2.95
❑4, Feb 97, A: JLA, X-Men, Doctor Strangefate, Amalgam universe, Final Issue; crossover with Marvel	2.95	0.59	1.48	2.95

DC ONE MILLION
DC
Value: Cover or less

- ❑1, Nov 98, Riders on the Storm ... 2.95
- ❑1/SC, Nov 98, Riders on the Storm ... 14.99
- ❑2, Nov 98 ... 2.95
- ❑3, Nov 98, Solaris Rising ... 2.95
- ❑4, Nov 98 ... 2.95
- ❑GS 1, Aug 99, System's Finest; Tales of the Legion of Executive Familiars, 80pgs. ... 4.95

DC SAMPLER
DC

	ORIG	GOOD	FINE	N-MINT
❑1, Sep 83	1.00	0.20	0.50	1.00
❑2, Sep 84, FH, no cover price; Promotional giveaway; Atari Force, etc.	—	0.20	0.50	1.00
❑3, FH, FH (c), AMo (w), no cover price; Promotional giveaway; The Saga of the Swamp Thing, etc.	—	0.20	0.50	1.00

DC SCIENCE FICTION GRAPHIC NOVEL
DC
Value: Cover or less

- ❑1, Hell on Earth ... 5.95
- ❑2, Nightwings ... 5.95
- ❑3, Frost and Fire ... 5.95
- ❑4, Merchants Venus ... 5.95
- ❑5, Demon with a Glass Hand 5.95
- ❑6, Magic Goes Away ... 5.95
- ❑7, Sand Kings ... 5.95

DC SILVER AGE CLASSICS ACTION COMICS
DC
Value: Cover or less

- ❑252, The Menace of Metallo!; Congo Bill Dies at Dawn, O: Supergirl, reprints Action Comics #252 ... 1.00

DC SILVER AGE CLASSICS ADVENTURE COMICS
DC
Value: Cover or less

- ❑247, The Legion of Super-Heroes; The 13 Superstition Arrows, O: Legion, reprints Adventure Comics #247 ... 1.00

DC SILVER AGE CLASSICS DETECTIVE COMICS
DC
Value: Cover or less

- ❑225, If I Were Batman; The Money That Came to Life!, 1: J'onn J'onzz, reprints Detective Comics #225 ... 1.00
- ❑327, CI, The Mystery of The Menacing Mask; Ten Miles to Nowhere, 1: new Batman, reprints Detective Comics #327 ... 1.00

DC SILVER AGE CLASSICS GREEN LANTERN
DC
Value: Cover or less

- ❑76, O: Green Lantern/Green Arrow team, reprints Green Lantern #76 ... 1.00

DC SILVER AGE CLASSICS HOUSE OF SECRETS
DC
Value: Cover or less

- ❑92, DD (w), Swamp Thing; After I Die, 1: Swamp Thing, reprints House of Secrets #92 ... 1.00

DC SILVER AGE CLASSICS SHOWCASE
DC
Value: Cover or less

- ❑4, JKu; CI, Mystery of the Human Thunderbolt!; The Man Who Broke the Time Barrier!, O: Flash, reprints Showcase #4 ... 1.00
- ❑22, GK, SOS Green LanternSecret of the Flaming Spear!; Menace of the Runaway Missile!, O: Green Lantern, reprints Showcase #22 ... 1.00

DC SILVER AGE CLASSICS SUGAR & SPIKE
DC

	ORIG	GOOD	FINE	N-MINT
❑99, not a reprint; first publication of Sugar and Spike #99	1.00	0.40	1.00	2.00

DC SILVER AGE CLASSICS THE BRAVE AND THE BOLD
DC

	ORIG	GOOD	FINE	N-MINT
❑28, Justice League Of America: Starro The Conqueror!, 1: The Justice League of America; 1: JLA, reprints The Braveand the Bold #28	1.00	0.25	0.63	1.25

DC SPECIAL
DC

	ORIG	GOOD	FINE	N-MINT
❑1, Dec 68, CI, 68pgs.; Flash, Batman, Adam Strange	0.25	2.80	7.00	14.00
❑2, Mar 69, 68pgs.; teen	0.25	1.60	4.00	8.00
❑3, Jun 69, 68pgs.; Green Arrow, Black Canary	0.25	1.60	4.00	8.00
❑4, Sep 69, 68pgs.	0.25	1.60	4.00	8.00
❑5, Dec 69, 68pgs.	0.25	1.60	4.00	8.00
❑6, Mar 70, 68pgs.	0.25	1.60	4.00	8.00
❑7, Jun 70, 68pgs.; Strange Sports	0.25	1.60	4.00	8.00
❑8, Sep 70, 68pgs.; Wanted	0.25	1.60	4.00	8.00
❑9, Dec 70, 68pgs.	0.25	1.60	4.00	8.00
❑10, Feb 71, 68pgs.	0.25	1.60	4.00	8.00
❑11, Apr 71, 68pgs.; Monsters	0.25	1.60	4.00	8.00
❑12, Jun 71, IN; RH; JKu, Battle For The Dragon Ship; The Ice Dragon, 68pgs.; Viking Prince	0.25	1.60	4.00	8.00
❑13, Aug 71, 68pgs.; Strange Sports	0.25	1.60	4.00	8.00
❑14, Oct 71, The Toyman's Castle; The Heat Is In For Captain Cold, Giant-size; Wanted: The World's Most Dangerous Villains	0.25	1.60	4.00	8.00
❑15, Dec 71, O: Plastic Man (Golden Age); O: Woozy Winks, Giant-size; Plastic Man reprints	0.25	2.00	5.00	10.00
❑16, Spr 75, RA; CI, Batman Battles the Living Beast-Bomb!; Wonder Woman - Gorilla!, Gorillas	0.50	1.20	3.00	6.00
❑17, Sum 75	0.50	1.20	3.00	6.00
❑18, Nov 75, Earth-Shaking Stories	0.50	1.20	3.00	6.00
❑19, Jan 76	0.50	1.20	3.00	6.00
❑20, Mar 76, Green Lantern	0.50	1.20	3.00	6.00
❑21, May 76, Monsters, War That Time Forgot	0.50	1.20	3.00	6.00
❑22, Jul 76, Three Musketeers, Robin Hood	0.50	1.20	3.00	6.00
❑23, Sep 76, Three Musketeers, Robin Hood	0.50	1.20	3.00	6.00
❑24, Oct 76, Robin Hood, Viking Prince	0.50	1.20	3.00	6.00
❑25, Dec 76, Robin Hood, Viking Prince	0.50	1.20	3.00	6.00
❑26, Feb 77, Enemy Ace	0.50	1.20	3.00	6.00
❑27, Apr 77, Captain Comet	0.50	1.20	3.00	6.00
❑28, Jun 77, Batman	0.60	1.20	3.00	6.00
❑29, Sep 77, JSa; BL, O: Justice Society of America (Secret Origin)	0.60	1.20	3.00	6.00

DC SPECIAL BLUE RIBBON DIGEST
DC

	ORIG	GOOD	FINE	N-MINT
❑1, Apr 80, Legion of Super Heroes	0.95	0.80	2.00	4.00
❑2, Jun 80, Flash	0.95	0.60	1.50	3.00
❑3, Aug 80, Justice Society	0.95	0.60	1.50	3.00
❑4, Oct 80, Green Lantern	0.95	0.60	1.50	3.00
❑5, Dec 80, Secret Origins	0.95	0.60	1.50	3.00
❑6, Jan 81, Death Held the Lantern High; The Phatom Hangman, House of Mystery	0.95	0.60	1.50	3.00
❑7, Mar 81, Flying Tigers, Haunted Tank, War That Time Forgot, Enemy Ace	0.95	0.60	1.50	3.00
❑8, Apr 81, Legion	0.95	0.60	1.50	3.00
❑9, May 81, The Atom	0.95	0.60	1.50	3.00
❑10, Jun 81, Warlord	0.95	0.60	1.50	3.00
❑11, Jul 81, Justice League, Justice Society, Seven Soldiers	0.95	0.60	1.50	3.00
❑12, Aug 81, Haunted Tank	0.95	0.60	1.50	3.00
❑13, Sep 81, Strange Sports	0.95	0.60	1.50	3.00
❑14, Oct 81, Science Fiction	0.95	0.60	1.50	3.00
❑15, Nov 81, Superboy, Green Lantern, Batman	0.95	0.60	1.50	3.00
❑16, Dec 81, Green Lantern/Green Arrow	0.95	0.60	1.50	3.00
❑17, Jan 82, Mystery	0.95	0.60	1.50	3.00
❑18, Feb 82, Sgt. Rock	0.95	0.60	1.50	3.00
❑19, Mar 82, Doom Patrol	0.95	0.60	1.50	3.00
❑20, Apr 82, Mystery	0.95	1.60	4.00	8.00
❑21, May 82, JK, War	0.95	0.60	1.50	3.00
❑22, Jun 82, Secret Origins	0.95	0.60	1.50	3.00
❑23, Jul 82, Green Arrow	0.95	0.60	1.50	3.00

DC SPECIAL SERIES
DC

	ORIG	GOOD	FINE	N-MINT
❑1, Sep 77, IN; JR; DD; MN; FMc, 5-Star Super-Hero Spectacular; Super-heroes	1.00	1.00	2.50	5.00
❑2, Sep 77, BWr, Dark Genesis!; The Man who Wanted Forever, Swamp Thing reprint; Swamp Thing	0.60	0.80	2.00	4.00
❑3, Oct 77, JK, Sgt. Rock	0.60	0.60	1.50	3.00
❑4, Oct 77, Unexpected Annual	—	0.60	1.50	3.00
❑5, Nov 77, The Second Coming of Superman, The First Coming of Superman, A: Brainiac; A: Luthor; A: Superman, a.k.a. Superman Spectacular; first DC Dollar Comic; Superman, Luthor	1.00	0.60	1.50	3.00
❑6, Nov 77, JLA	0.60	0.60	1.50	3.00
❑7, Dec 77, Ghosts	0.60	0.60	1.50	3.00
❑8, Feb 78, DG, Brave & Bold	0.60	0.60	1.50	3.00
❑9, Mar 78, SD, Wonder Woman vs. Hitler	1.00	2.40	6.00	12.00
❑10, Apr 78, MN, Super-Heroes	0.60	0.60	1.50	3.00
❑11, May 78, IN; KS; WW; MA, A: Johnny Quick, Flash; a.k.a. Flash Spectacular	1.00	0.60	1.50	3.00
❑12, Jun 78, Secrets of Haunted House	1.00	0.60	1.50	3.00
❑13, Jul 78, Sgt. Rock	1.00	0.60	1.50	3.00
❑14, Jul 78, Swamp Thing reprint	0.60	0.60	1.50	3.00
❑15, Aug 78, Batman, Ra's al Ghul	1.00	0.60	1.50	3.00
❑16, Sep 78, RH, D: Jonah Hex	1.00	2.80	7.00	14.00
❑17, Sep 79, Swamp Thing reprint	1.00	0.40	1.00	2.00
❑18, Oct 79, digest Sgt. Rock	0.95	0.40	1.00	2.00
❑19, Oct 79, O: Wonder Woman, digest; Secret Origins	0.95	0.50	1.25	2.50
❑20, Jan 80, BWr, The Lurker In Tunnel 13!; The Stalker From Beyond!, Swamp Thing reprint; a.k.a. Original Swamp Thing Saga	1.00	0.50	1.25	2.50
❑21, Mar 80, FM, Batman; Legion; 1st Frank Miller Batman	1.00	2.40	6.00	12.00
❑22, Sep 80, G.I. Combat	—	0.60	1.50	3.00
❑23, Feb 81, digest; Flash	0.75	0.60	1.50	3.00
❑24, Feb 81, Flash	0.75	0.60	1.50	3.00

	ORIG	GOOD	FINE	N-MINT
❑25, Sum 81, treasury-sized; Superman II movie adaptation	2.95	0.60	1.50	3.00
❑26, Sum 81, RT; RA, Fortress of Fear!, treasury-sized; Superman's Fortress	2.50	0.60	1.50	3.00
❑27, Dec 81, Final Issue; treasury-sized; Batman vs. The Incredible Hulk	2.50	2.00	5.00	10.00

DC SPOTLIGHT
DC

	ORIG	GOOD	FINE	N-MINT
❑1, Sep 85	—	0.20	0.50	1.00

DC SUPER-STARS
DC

	ORIG	GOOD	FINE	N-MINT
❑1, Mar 76, NC, Monster Bait; Introducing the Teen Titans, reprints; Double-size; Teen Titans reprint	0.50	1.20	3.00	6.00
❑2, Apr 76, Double-size; Space	0.50	0.60	1.50	3.00
❑3, May 76, CS, A: Legion of Super-Heroes, Superman; Reprints Legion of Super-Heroes story from Adventure Comics #354 and #355	0.50	0.80	2.00	4.00
❑4, Jun 76	0.50	0.40	1.00	2.00
❑5, Jul 76, Flash; Bicentennial #33	0.50	0.40	1.00	2.00
❑6, Aug 76	0.50	0.40	1.00	2.00
❑7, Sep 76	0.50	0.40	1.00	2.00
❑8, Oct 76, Reprints Showcase #15	0.50	0.80	2.00	4.00
❑9, Nov 76, Reprint; Man Behind the Gun	0.50	0.40	1.00	2.00
❑10, Dec 76, A: Joker, Sports stories and Batman story	0.50	1.00	2.50	5.00
❑11, Jan 77	0.50	0.40	1.00	2.00
❑12, Feb 77	0.50	0.40	1.00	2.00
❑13, Mar 77, SA	0.50	0.40	1.00	2.00
❑14, May 77, O: Shark; O: Grodd; O: Two-Face; O: Braniac; O: Doctor Light, 68pgs.	0.50	0.80	2.00	4.00
❑15, Jul 77, war stories	0.50	0.80	2.00	4.00
❑16, Sep 77, BL; DN, 1: The Star Hunters; 1: Star Hunters	0.60	0.60	1.50	3.00
❑17, Nov 77, JSa; MGr; BL, JSa (w); BL (w), Green Arrow; The Legion Of Super-Heroes, 1: The Huntress II (Helena Wayne); O: Green Arrow; 1: Huntress II (Helena Wayne), Secret Origins; Revealed that Earth-2 Batman had married Earth-2 Catwoman; Legion story	0.60	0.80	2.00	4.00
❑18, Jan 78, Deadman, Phantom Stranger	0.60	0.40	1.00	2.00

DCU HEROES SECRET FILES
DC

Value: Cover or less

- ❑1, Feb 99, Spies Like Us; A Guide to Resurrection Man's Powers ... 4.95

DC UNIVERSE CHRISTMAS, A
DC

Value: Cover or less

- ❑1, Batman: Wanted: Santa Claus-Dead or Alive!; The Flash: Present Tense ... 19.95

DC UNIVERSE HOLIDAY BASH
DC

	ORIG	GOOD	FINE	N-MINT
❑1, Superman: The Benefaction of Peace; Catwoman: Bearing Gifts We Traverse Afar, Preview edition; Holiday special for 1996 season	3.95	0.79	1.98	3.95
❑2, prestige format; Holiday special for 1997 season	3.95	0.99	2.47	4.95
❑3, Jan 99, Signed edition; Holiday special for 1998 season	4.95	0.99	2.47	4.95

DC UNIVERSE: TRINITY
DC

Value: Cover or less

- ❑1, Aug 93, A: Darkstars; A: L.E.G.I.O.N.; A: Green Lantern, foil cover ... 2.95
- ❑2, Sep 93, foil cover ... 2.95

DC UNIVERSE VILLAINS SECRET FILES
DC

Value: Cover or less

- ❑1, Apr 99, The Evil We Do ... 4.95

DEAD, THE
ARROW

Value: Cover or less

- ❑1 ... 2.95
- ❑1/A, alternate cover ... 2.95
- ❑2 ... 2.95
- ❑3 ... 2.95

DEAD, THE (2ND SERIES)
ARROW

Value: Cover or less

- ❑1, Gerald's Game, Part 1 ... 2.95

DEADBEATS
CLAYPOOL

	ORIG	GOOD	FINE	N-MINT
❑1, RHo, RHo (w)	2.50	0.80	2.00	4.00
❑2, RHo, RHo (w), They All Laughed!	2.50	0.60	1.50	3.00
❑3, RHo, RHo (w), Pawns	2.50	0.60	1.50	3.00
❑4, RHo, RHo (w)	2.50	0.60	1.50	3.00
❑5, RHo, RHo (w)	2.50	0.60	1.50	3.00
❑6, RHo, RHo (w)	2.50	0.50	1.25	2.50
❑7, RHo, RHo (w)	2.50	0.50	1.25	2.50
❑8, RHo, RHo (w), The Experiment	2.50	0.50	1.25	2.50
❑9, Nov 94	2.50	0.50	1.25	2.50

Issues in *DC Special Series* can only be determined by checking the indicia. The titles on the covers would make collectors think that each issue is its own separate series.

© 1977 DC Comics

	ORIG	GOOD	FINE	N-MINT
❑10, Jan 95	2.50	0.50	1.25	2.50
❑11, Mar 95	2.50	0.50	1.25	2.50
❑12, May 95	2.50	0.50	1.25	2.50
❑13, Jul 95	2.50	0.50	1.25	2.50
❑14, Sep 95	2.50	0.50	1.25	2.50
❑15, Nov 95	2.50	0.50	1.25	2.50
❑16, Jan 96	2.50	0.50	1.25	2.50
❑17, Mar 96	2.50	0.50	1.25	2.50
❑18, May 96	2.50	0.50	1.25	2.50
❑19, Jul 96	2.50	0.50	1.25	2.50
❑20, Sep 96	2.50	0.50	1.25	2.50
❑21, Nov 96	2.50	0.50	1.25	2.50
❑22, Jan 97	2.50	0.50	1.25	2.50
❑23, Mar 97	2.50	0.50	1.25	2.50
❑24, May 97	2.50	0.50	1.25	2.50
❑25, Jul 97	2.50	0.50	1.25	2.50
❑26, Sep 97, RHo (w), The Southland Family Saga!	2.50	0.50	1.25	2.50
❑27, Nov 97, RHo (w), Misery Loves Butchery!	2.50	0.50	1.25	2.50
❑28, Jan 98, RHo, RHo (w), Burying Dodger!	2.50	0.50	1.25	2.50
❑29, Mar 98	2.50	0.50	1.25	2.50
❑30, May 98	2.50	0.50	1.25	2.50
❑31, Jul 98	2.50	0.50	1.25	2.50
❑32, Oct 98	2.50	0.50	1.25	2.50
❑33, Dec 98	2.50	0.50	1.25	2.50
❑34, Feb 99	2.50	0.50	1.25	2.50
❑35, Apr 99	2.50	0.50	1.25	2.50
❑36, Jun 99	2.50	0.50	1.25	2.50
❑37, Aug 99	2.50	0.50	1.25	2.50
❑38, Oct 99	2.50	0.50	1.25	2.50
❑39, Dec 99	2.50	0.50	1.25	2.50
❑40, Feb 00	2.50	0.50	1.25	2.50
❑41, Apr 00, Guys' Night Out!	2.50	0.50	1.25	2.50
❑42, Jun 00, Dark Dealings!	2.50	0.50	1.25	2.50
❑43, Aug 00, RHo (w), Dodging the Bullet!	2.50	0.50	1.25	2.50

DEAD CLOWN
MALIBU

Value: Cover or less

- ❑1, Oct 96, Kill-Krazy Klown ... 2.50
- ❑2 ... 2.50
- ❑3, Feb 94 ... 2.50

DEAD CORPS(E)
DC

Value: Cover or less

- ❑1, Sep 98, Suckers of Mars ... 2.50
- ❑2, Oct 98, Out of the Coffin: The Death of C.J. Rataan ... 2.50
- ❑3, Nov 98 ... 2.50
- ❑4, Dec 98 ... 2.50

DEADENDERS
VERTIGO

Value: Cover or less

- ❑1, Mar 00, Stealing the Sun, Part 1 ... 2.50
- ❑2, Apr 00, Stealing the Sun, Part 2 ... 2.50
- ❑3, May 00, Stealing the Sun, Part 3 ... 2.50
- ❑4, Jun 00 ... 2.50
- ❑5, Jul 00, Suspended Between Now and Then, Part 1 ... 2.50
- ❑6, Aug 00, Suspended Between Now and Then, Part 2 ... 2.50
- ❑7, Sep 00, Suspended Between Now and Then, Part 3 ... 2.50
- ❑8, Oct 00, My Secret Affair ... 2.50
- ❑9, Nov 00, More Fun in the New World ... 2.50
- ❑10, Dec 00, On a Clear Day You Can See Forever ... 2.50
- ❑11, Jan 01, The Good News of the Cataclysm ... 2.50
- ❑12, Feb 01, At This Point in Time ... 2.50
- ❑13, Mar 01, Only for Seconds ... 2.50
- ❑14, Apr 01, Smashing Time, Part 1 ... 2.50
- ❑15, May 01, Smashing Time, Part 2 ... 2.50

DEADFACE
HARRIER

	ORIG	GOOD	FINE	N-MINT
❑1	—	1.00	2.50	5.00
❑2	—	0.80	2.00	4.00
❑3	—	0.60	1.50	3.00
❑4	—	0.60	1.50	3.00
❑5	—	0.60	1.50	3.00
❑6	—	0.50	1.25	2.50
❑7	—	0.50	1.25	2.50
❑8	—	0.50	1.25	2.50

DEADFACE: DOING THE ISLANDS WITH BACCHUS
DARK HORSE

Value: Cover or less

Issue	ORIG
❑1, Jul 91, b&w	2.95
❑2, Aug 91, b&w	2.95
❑3, Sep 91, b&w	2.95

DEADFACE: EARTH, WATER, AIR, AND FIRE
DARK HORSE

Value: Cover or less

Issue	ORIG
❑1, Dust in the Eyes, b&w	2.50
❑2, b&w	2.50
❑3, b&w	2.50
❑4, Staring At The Sun, b&w	2.50

DEADFORCE (ANTARCTIC)
ANTARCTIC PRESS

Issue	ORIG	GOOD	FINE	N-MINT
❑1, May 99, Death and Redemption, b&w	2.99	0.50	1.25	2.50
❑2, Jun 99	2.99	0.50	1.25	2.50
❑Ash 1	—	0.20	0.50	1.00

DEADFORCE (STUDIONOIR)
STUDIO NOIR

Value: Cover or less

Issue	ORIG
❑1, Jul 96, b&w	2.50

DEAD GRRRL: DEAD AT 21
BONEYARD

Value: Cover or less

Issue	ORIG
❑1, Apr 98	2.95

DEAD IN THE WEST
DARK HORSE

Value: Cover or less

Issue	ORIG
❑1, Oct 93, b&w; adult	3.95
❑2, Mar 94, b&w; adult	3.95

DEAD KID ADVENTURES
KNIGHT

Value: Cover or less

Issue	ORIG
❑1, Jul 98	2.95

DEAD KING: BURNT
CHAOS

Value: Cover or less

Issue	ORIG
❑1, May 98	2.95
❑2	2.95
❑3, Jul 98	2.95
❑4, Aug 98	2.95

DEADLINE USA
DARK HORSE

Value: Cover or less

Issue	ORIG
❑1, Sep 91, b&w; Reprint	9.95
❑2, b&w; Reprint	9.95
❑3, b&w; Reprint	9.95
❑4, Nail Boss; Timulo	3.95
❑5, Young Kafka; Wired World, A: Gwar	3.95
❑6	3.95
❑7	3.95
❑8, Final Issue	3.95

DEADLY DUO, THE
IMAGE

Value: Cover or less

Issue	ORIG
❑1, Nov 94	2.50
❑2, Dec 94	2.50
❑3, Jan 95	2.50

DEADLY DUO, THE (2ND SERIES)
IMAGE

Value: Cover or less

Issue	ORIG
❑1, Jul 95	2.50
❑2, Aug 95	2.50
❑3, Sep 95	2.50
❑4, Oct 95	2.50

DEADLY FOES OF SPIDER-MAN
MARVEL

Issue	ORIG	GOOD	FINE	N-MINT
❑1, May 91, KGa; AM, Punishment And Crime, Punisher, Rhino, Kingpin, others appear	1.00	0.30	0.75	1.50
❑2, Jun 91, KGa; AM, The Price Of Justice	1.00	0.30	0.75	1.50
❑3, Jul 91, AM, Shattered Dreams	1.00	0.30	0.75	1.50
❑4, Aug 91, AM, While The City Screams	1.00	0.30	0.75	1.50

DEADLY HANDS OF KUNG FU
MARVEL

Issue	ORIG	GOOD	FINE	N-MINT
❑1, Apr 74	0.75	3.00	7.50	15.00
❑2	0.75	1.40	3.50	7.00
❑3	0.75	1.00	2.50	5.00
❑4	0.75	1.00	2.50	5.00
❑5	0.75	1.00	2.50	5.00
❑6	0.75	0.80	2.00	4.00
❑7	0.75	0.80	2.00	4.00
❑8	0.75	0.80	2.00	4.00
❑9	0.75	0.80	2.00	4.00
❑10	0.75	0.80	2.00	4.00
❑11	0.75	0.80	2.00	4.00
❑12	0.75	0.80	2.00	4.00
❑13	0.75	0.80	2.00	4.00
❑14	0.75	0.80	2.00	4.00
❑15	1.25	0.80	2.00	4.00
❑16	1.00	0.80	2.00	4.00
❑17	1.00	0.80	2.00	4.00
❑18	1.00	0.80	2.00	4.00
❑19	1.00	0.80	2.00	4.00
❑20	1.00	0.80	2.00	4.00
❑21	1.00	0.60	1.50	3.00
❑22	1.00	0.60	1.50	3.00
❑23	1.00	0.60	1.50	3.00
❑24	1.00	0.60	1.50	3.00
❑25	1.00	0.60	1.50	3.00
❑26	1.00	0.60	1.50	3.00
❑27	1.00	0.60	1.50	3.00
❑28, Sep 76	1.00	0.60	1.50	3.00
❑29, Oct 76	1.00	0.60	1.50	3.00
❑30, Nov 76	1.00	0.60	1.50	3.00
❑31, Dec 76	1.00	0.60	1.50	3.00
❑32, Jan 77	1.00	0.60	1.50	3.00
❑33, Feb 77	1.00	0.60	1.50	3.00
❑SE 1	1.00	0.60	1.50	3.00

DEADMAN
DC

Issue	ORIG	GOOD	FINE	N-MINT
❑1, May 85, NA; CI, Who Has Been Lying In My Grave	1.75	0.50	1.25	2.50
❑2, Jun 85, NA	1.75	0.40	1.00	2.00
❑3, Jul 85, NA	1.75	0.40	1.00	2.00
❑4, Aug 85, NA	1.75	0.40	1.00	2.00
❑5, Sep 85, NA	1.75	0.40	1.00	2.00
❑6, Oct 85, NA	1.75	0.40	1.00	2.00
❑7, Nov 85, NA	1.75	0.40	1.00	2.00

DEADMAN (MINI-SERIES)
DC

Issue	ORIG	GOOD	FINE	N-MINT
❑1, Mar 86, Return...To Forever!	0.75	0.40	1.00	2.00
❑2, Apr 86	0.75	0.40	1.00	2.00
❑3, May 86	0.75	0.40	1.00	2.00
❑4, Jun 86	0.75	0.40	1.00	2.00

DEADMAN: EXORCISM
DC

Value: Cover or less

Issue	ORIG
❑1, prestige format	4.95
❑2, prestige format	4.95

DEADMAN: LOVE AFTER DEATH
DC

Value: Cover or less

Issue	ORIG
❑1, Dec 89, prestige format	3.95
❑2, Jan 90, prestige format	3.95

DEAD OF NIGHT
MARVEL

Issue	ORIG	GOOD	FINE	N-MINT
❑1, JSt, JSt (w), The Ghost Still Walks; House of Fear, Reprint	0.20	1.50	3.75	7.50
❑2, Reprint	0.20	1.00	2.50	5.00
❑3, Reprint	0.20	1.00	2.50	5.00
❑4, Reprint	0.20	0.80	2.00	4.00
❑5, Reprint	0.20	0.80	2.00	4.00
❑6, Reprint	0.20	0.80	2.00	4.00
❑7, Reprint	0.20	0.80	2.00	4.00
❑8, Reprint	0.20	0.80	2.00	4.00
❑9, Reprint	0.20	0.80	2.00	4.00
❑10, Reprint	0.20	0.80	2.00	4.00
❑11, Aug 75, 1: Scarecrow, Final Issue	0.25	0.80	2.00	4.00

DEAD OR ALIVE-A CYBERPUNK WESTERN
DARK HORSE

Value: Cover or less

Issue	ORIG
❑1, Apr 98	2.50
❑2, May 98	2.50
❑3, Jun 98	2.50
❑4, Jul 98	2.50

DEADPAN
ICHOR

Value: Cover or less

Issue	ORIG
❑1, Mar 95, If We Shadows Have Offended...	3.95

DEADPOOL
MARVEL

Issue	ORIG	GOOD	FINE	N-MINT
❑-1, Jul 97, O: Deadpool, Flashback	1.99	0.45	1.13	2.25
❑0, You Only Die Twice, Included as give-away with Wizard Magazine	—	0.30	0.75	1.50
❑1, Jan 97, wraparound cover	2.99	0.80	2.00	4.00
❑2, Feb 97, Operation: That Wacky Doctor's Game!	1.99	0.60	1.50	3.00
❑3, Mar 97, A: Siryn	1.99	0.50	1.25	2.50
❑4, Apr 97, V: Hulk	1.99	0.50	1.25	2.50
❑5, May 97	1.99	0.40	1.00	2.00
❑6, Jun 97	1.99	0.40	1.00	2.00
❑7, Aug 97, gatefold summary	1.99	0.40	1.00	2.00
❑8, Sep 97, Hey, It's Deadpool!, gatefold summary	1.99	0.40	1.00	2.00
❑9, Oct 97, gatefold summary	1.99	0.40	1.00	2.00
❑10, Nov 97, Stumped!, A: Great Lakes Avengers, gatefold summary; back-up feature on making of Deadpool #11	1.99	0.40	1.00	2.00
❑11, Dec 97, Why is it, to Save me, I Must Kill You?, A: Great Lakes Avengers, gatefold summary; Deadpool and Blind Al interact with Amazing Spider-Man #47	2.99	0.40	1.00	2.00
❑12, Jan 98, The Doctor is Skinned, gatefold summary; parody of Faces of the DC Universe month	1.99	0.40	1.00	2.00
❑13, Feb 98, gatefold summary	1.99	0.40	1.00	2.00
❑14, Mar 98, gatefold summary	1.99	0.40	1.00	2.00
❑15, Apr 98, gatefold summary	1.99	0.40	1.00	2.00
❑16, May 98, gatefold summary	1.99	0.40	1.00	2.00
❑17, Jun 98, gatefold summary	1.99	0.40	1.00	2.00
❑18, Jul 98, V: Ajax, gatefold summary	1.99	0.40	1.00	2.00
❑19, Aug 98, V: Ajax, gatefold summary	1.99	0.40	1.00	2.00

	ORIG	GOOD	FINE	N-MINT
❑20, Sep 98, gatefold summary	1.99	0.40	1.00	2.00
❑21, Oct 98, gatefold summary	1.99	0.40	1.00	2.00
❑22, Nov 98, A: Cable, gatefold summary	1.99	0.40	1.00	2.00
❑23, Dec 98, Dead Reckoning, Part 1, wrap-around cover; gatefold summary	2.99	0.60	1.50	2.99
❑24, Jan 99, Dead Reckoning, Part 2, A: Cosmic Messiah; A: Tiamat, gatefold summary	1.99	0.40	1.00	1.99
❑25, Feb 99, Dead Reckoning, Part 3, A: Captain America; A: Tiamat	1.99	0.60	1.50	2.99
❑26, Mar 99, Dead Reckoning Aftermath	1.99	0.40	1.00	1.99
❑27, Apr 99, A: Wolverine; V: Doc Bong	1.99	0.40	1.00	1.99
❑28, May 99	1.99	0.40	1.00	1.99
❑29, Jun 99	1.99	0.40	1.00	1.99
❑30, Jul 99	1.99	0.40	1.00	1.99
❑31, Aug 99	1.99	0.40	1.00	1.99
❑32, Sep 99	1.99	0.40	1.00	1.99
❑33, Oct 99	1.99	0.40	1.00	1.99
❑34, Nov 99	1.99	0.40	1.00	1.99
❑35, Dec 99	1.99	0.45	1.13	2.25
❑36	—	0.45	1.13	2.25
❑37	—	0.45	1.13	2.25
❑38	—	0.45	1.13	2.25
❑39	—	0.45	1.13	2.25
❑40	—	0.45	1.13	2.25
❑41	—	0.45	1.13	2.25
❑42	—	0.45	1.13	2.25
❑43	—	0.45	1.13	2.25
❑44	—	0.45	1.13	2.25
❑45	2.25	0.45	1.13	2.25
❑46, Nov 00, Cruel Summer, Part 1	2.25	0.45	1.13	2.25
❑47, Dec 00, Cruel Summer, Part 2	2.25	0.45	1.13	2.25
❑48, Jan 01, Cruel Summer, Part 3	2.25	0.45	1.13	2.25
❑49, Feb 01, Cat Magnet	2.25	0.45	1.13	2.25
❑50, Mar 01, The Promise, Part 1	2.25	0.45	1.13	2.25
❑51, Apr 01, The Promise, Part 2, A: Kid Deadpool, Detective Comics #39 cover homage	2.25	0.45	1.13	2.25
❑52, May 01, Talk of the Town	2.25	0.45	1.13	2.25
❑Anl 1998, wraparound cover; gatefold summary; Deadpool/Death '98	2.99	0.60	1.50	2.99

DEADPOOL (LTD. SERIES)
MARVEL

	ORIG	GOOD	FINE	N-MINT
❑1, Aug 94, MWa (w)	2.50	0.80	2.00	4.00
❑2, Sep 94, MWa (w)	2.50	0.60	1.50	3.00
❑3, Oct 94, A: Slayback; A: Executive Elite	2.50	0.60	1.50	3.00
❑4, Nov 94, MWa (w)	2.50	0.60	1.50	3.00

DEADPOOL TEAM-UP
MARVEL

Value: Cover or less

❑1, Dec 98, Turning Japanese...or Little Demon Inside, A: Widdle Wade, gatefold summary; Secret Wars II tie-in 2.99

DEADPOOL: THE CIRCLE CHASE
MARVEL

Value: Cover or less

- ❑1, Aug 93, The Circle Chase, Round 1, Embossed cover .. 2.50
- ❑2, Sep 93 ..... 2.00
- ❑3, Oct 93 ..... 2.00
- ❑4, Nov 93 ..... 2.00

DEADSHOT
DC

	ORIG	GOOD	FINE	N-MINT
❑1, Nov 88, Die But Once, O: Deadshot	1.00	0.30	0.75	1.50
❑2, Dec 88	1.00	0.25	0.63	1.25
❑3, Win 88	1.00	0.25	0.63	1.25
❑4, Hol 88	1.00	0.25	0.63	1.25

DEADTIME STORIES
NEW COMICS

Value: Cover or less

❑1, Oct 87, The Prospector Luckiest Strike!; A Toast to Mr. Dalrymple, b&w 1.75

DEADWALKERS
AIRCEL

Value: Cover or less

- ❑1/A, Jan 91, One of the Living, "gross" cover 2.50
- ❑1/B, Jan 91, "not-so-gross" cover 2.50
- ❑2, Feb 91 ..... 2.50
- ❑3, Mar 91 ..... 2.50
- ❑4, Apr 91 ..... 2.50

DEADWORLD (VOL. 1)
ARROW

	ORIG	GOOD	FINE	N-MINT
❑1, Eye Of The Zombie, b&w; Arrow publishes	1.50	0.60	1.50	3.00
❑2	—	0.50	1.25	2.50
❑3	—	0.50	1.25	2.50
❑4	—	0.50	1.25	2.50
❑5	—	0.50	1.25	2.50
❑6	—	0.50	1.25	2.50
❑7	—	0.50	1.25	2.50
❑8	—	0.50	1.25	2.50
❑9	—	0.50	1.25	2.50
❑10, b&w; Caliber begins as publisher	2.50	0.50	1.25	2.50
❑11, b&w	2.50	0.50	1.25	2.50
❑12, b&w	2.50	0.50	1.25	2.50
❑13, b&w	2.50	0.50	1.25	2.50

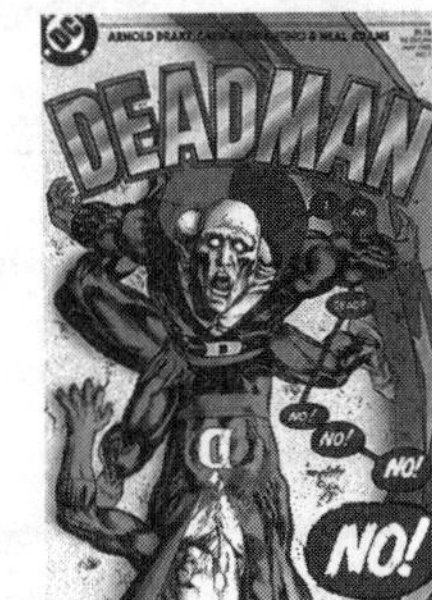

DC collected the Deadman stories that had previously appeared in *Strange Adventures* and other DC titles in 1985's seven-issue *Deadman* mini-series.

	ORIG	GOOD	FINE	N-MINT
❑14, b&w	2.50	0.50	1.25	2.50
❑15, b&w	2.50	0.50	1.25	2.50
❑16, b&w	2.50	0.50	1.25	2.50
❑17, b&w	2.50	0.50	1.25	2.50
❑18, b&w	2.50	0.50	1.25	2.50
❑19, b&w	2.50	0.50	1.25	2.50
❑20, b&w	2.50	0.50	1.25	2.50
❑21, b&w	2.50	0.50	1.25	2.50
❑22, b&w	2.50	0.50	1.25	2.50
❑23, b&w	2.50	0.50	1.25	2.50
❑24, b&w	2.50	0.50	1.25	2.50
❑25, b&w	2.50	0.50	1.25	2.50
❑26, b&w; Final Issue	3.50	0.50	1.25	2.50

DEADWORLD (VOL. 2)
CALIBER

Value: Cover or less

- ❑1, Dead Credits, b&w; Giant-size 5.95
- ❑2, b&w 2.95
- ❑3, b&w 2.95
- ❑4, b&w 2.95
- ❑5, b&w 2.95
- ❑6, b&w 2.95
- ❑7, b&w 2.95
- ❑8, b&w 2.95
- ❑9, b&w 2.95
- ❑10, b&w 2.95
- ❑11, b&w 2.95
- ❑12, b&w 2.95
- ❑13, b&w 2.95
- ❑14, b&w 2.95
- ❑15, b&w 2.95

DEADWORLD ARCHIVES
CALIBER

Value: Cover or less

- ❑1, b&w 2.50
- ❑2, b&w 2.50
- ❑3, b&w 2.50

DEADWORLD: BITS AND PIECES
CALIBER

Value: Cover or less

❑1, b&w; Reprint 2.95

DEADWORLD CHRONICLES: PLAGUE
CALIBER

Value: Cover or less

❑1 ..... 2.95

DEADWORLD: NECROPOLIS
CALIBER

Value: Cover or less

❑1 ..... 3.95

DEADWORLD: TO KILL A KING
CALIBER

Value: Cover or less

- ❑1, Sinergy as flip-book 2.95
- ❑1/LE, limited edition 5.95
- ❑2 ..... 2.95
- ❑3 ..... 2.95

DEAR JULIA
BLACK EYE

	ORIG	GOOD	FINE	N-MINT
❑1	—	0.59	1.48	2.95
❑2	—	0.59	1.48	2.95
❑3	—	0.59	1.48	2.95
❑4	—	0.59	1.48	2.95

DEATH3
MARVEL

Value: Cover or less

- ❑1, Sep 93, 1: Death Metal, Embossed cover 2.95
- ❑2, Oct 93, A: Charnel; A: Doctor Octopus; A: Ghost Rider; A: Iron Man; A: Thing; A: Kingpin ... 1.75
- ❑3, Nov 93 ..... 1.75
- ❑4, Dec 93 ..... 1.75

DEATH & CANDY
FANTAGRAPHICS

Value: Cover or less

❑1, Win 99, Car-Boy's Garden; The Excavation 3.95

DEATH & TAXES: THE REAL COSTS OF LIVING
PARODY

Value: Cover or less

❑1, b&w 2.50

DEATHANGEL
LIGHTNING

Value: Cover or less

- ❑1/A, Dec 97 ..... 2.95
- ❑1/B, Dec 97, alternate cover 2.95

DEATHBLOW
IMAGE

	ORIG	GOOD	FINE	N-MINT
❑0, Aug 96	2.95	0.50	1.25	2.50
❑1, Apr 93, JLee, JLee(w), Confessions, 1: Cybernary, Black varnish cover; Cybernary #1 as flip-book	2.50	0.60	1.50	3.00

	ORIG	GOOD	FINE	N-MINT
❑2, Aug 93, JLee, JLee(w), Cybernary #2 as flip-book	1.75	0.50	1.25	2.50
❑3, Feb 94, 1: Cisco, Cybernary #3 as flip-book	1.75	0.60	1.50	3.00
❑4, Apr 94	1.75	0.40	1.00	2.00
❑5, May 94	1.95	0.40	1.00	2.00
❑5/A, May 94, alternate cover; Variant cover edition	1.95	0.80	2.00	4.00
❑6, Jun 94	1.95	0.39	0.98	1.95
❑7, Jul 94	1.95	0.39	0.98	1.95
❑8, Aug 94	1.95	0.39	0.98	1.95
❑9, Oct 94, Dark Angel Saga, Part 9	1.95	0.39	0.98	1.95
❑10, Nov 94, wraparound cover	2.50	0.50	1.25	2.50
❑11, Dec 94	2.50	0.50	1.25	2.50
❑12, Jan 95	2.50	0.50	1.25	2.50
❑13, Feb 95	2.50	0.50	1.25	2.50
❑14, Mar 95	2.50	0.50	1.25	2.50
❑15, Apr 95	2.50	0.50	1.25	2.50
❑16, May 95, WildStorm Rising, Part 6, bound-in trading cards	2.50	0.39	0.98	1.95
❑16/SC	2.50	0.50	1.25	2.50
❑17, Jun 95	2.50	0.50	1.25	2.50
❑17/A, Jun 95, Chicago Comicon limited edition	2.50	0.60	1.50	3.00
❑18, Jul 95	2.50	0.50	1.25	2.50
❑19, Sep 95	2.50	0.50	1.25	2.50
❑20, Oct 95, Brothers-in-Arms, Part 1	2.50	0.50	1.25	2.50
❑21, Nov 95, Brothers-in-Arms, Part 2, A: Gen13	2.50	0.50	1.25	2.50
❑22, Dec 95, Brothers-in-Arms, Part 3	2.50	0.50	1.25	2.50
❑23, Jan 96, Brothers-in-Arms, Part 4	2.50	0.50	1.25	2.50
❑24, Feb 96, Brothers-in-Arms, Part 5, A: Grifter	2.50	0.50	1.25	2.50
❑25, Mar 96, Brothers-in-Arms, Part 6	2.50	0.50	1.25	2.50
❑26, Mar 96, Fire from Heaven Prelude 3	2.50	0.50	1.25	2.50
❑27, Apr 96, Fire from Heaven, Part 8	2.50	0.50	1.25	2.50
❑28, Jul 96, Fire from Heaven Finale 3	2.50	0.50	1.25	2.50
❑28/SC, Jul 96, Fire from Heaven Finale 3, alternate cover	2.50	0.50	1.25	2.50
❑29, Aug 96, Final Issue	2.50	0.50	1.25	2.50

DEATHBLOW: BYBLOWS
WILDSTORM

Value: Cover or less

❑1, Nov 99, AMo (w) ... 2.95
❑2, Dec 99, AMo (w) ... 2.95
❑3, Jan 00, AMo (w) ... 2.95

DEATHBLOW/WOLVERINE
IMAGE

Value: Cover or less

❑1, Sep 96, crossover with Marvel ... 2.50
❑2, Feb 97, Final Issue; crossover with Marvel ... 2.50

DEATH BY CHOCOLATE
SLEEPING GIANT

Value: Cover or less

❑1, Mar 96, nn; b&w ... 2.50

DEATH BY CHOCOLATE: SIR GEOFFREY AND THE CHOCOLATE CAR
SLEEPING GIANT

Value: Cover or less

❑1, nn; b&w ... 2.50

DEATH BY CHOCOLATE: THE METABOLATORS
SLEEPING GIANT

Value: Cover or less

❑1, nn; b&w ... 2.50

DEATH CRAZED TEENAGE SUPERHEROES
ARF! ARF!

Value: Cover or less

❑1 ... 1.50
❑2, D.O.A. ... 1.50

DEATH DEALER
VEROTIK

	ORIG	GOOD	FINE	N-MINT
❑1, Jul 95	5.95	1.20	3.00	6.00
❑2, May 96	6.95	1.39	3.47	6.95
❑3, Apr 97	6.95	1.39	3.47	6.95
❑4, Jul 97	6.95	1.39	3.47	6.95

DEATH DREAMS OF DRACULA
APPLE

Value: Cover or less

❑1, Have You Seen Me?; Slash!, b&w ... 2.50
❑2, b&w ... 2.50
❑3, b&w ... 2.50
❑4, b&w ... 2.50

DEATH GALLERY, A
DC

	ORIG	GOOD	FINE	N-MINT
❑1, portraits	2.95	0.60	1.50	3.00

DEATH HAWK
ADVENTURE

Value: Cover or less

❑1, Dreams Alone, b&w ... 1.95
❑2, To Enshrine the Past, b&w ... 1.95
❑3, b&w ... 1.95

DEATH HUNT
ETERNITY

Value: Cover or less

❑1, b&w ... 1.95

DEATHLOK (1ST SERIES)
MARVEL

Value: Cover or less

❑1, Jul 90, The Brains Of The Outfit, 1: Deathlok II (Mike Collins) ... 3.95
❑2, Aug 90 ... 3.95
❑3, Sep 90 ... 3.95
❑4, Oct 90 ... 3.95

DEATHLOK (2ND SERIES)
MARVEL

	ORIG	GOOD	FINE	N-MINT
❑1, Jul 91, The Wolf Is At The Door, Silver ink cover	1.75	0.50	1.25	2.50
❑2, Aug 91, The Souls Of Cyber-Folk, Part 1, A: Forge	1.75	0.40	1.00	2.00
❑3, Sep 91, The Souls Of Cyber-Folk, Part 2, V: Doctor Doom	1.75	0.40	1.00	2.00
❑4, Oct 91, The Souls Of Cyber-Folk, Part 3	1.75	0.40	1.00	2.00
❑5, Nov 91, The Souls Of Cyber-Folk, Part 4, X-Men & Fantastic Four X-over	1.75	0.40	1.00	2.00
❑6, Dec 91, Similar Machines, Part 1, Punisher x-over	1.75	0.40	1.00	2.00
❑7, Jan 92, Similar Machines, Part 2, Punisher x-over	1.75	0.40	1.00	2.00
❑8, Feb 92, The Ultimate War Machine, Punisher x-over	1.75	0.40	1.00	2.00
❑9, Mar 92, Nightmares of Vengeance, V: Ghost Rider	1.75	0.40	1.00	2.00
❑10, Apr 92, Wake Up! It's Time to Die!, V: Ghost Rider	1.75	0.40	1.00	2.00
❑11, May 92, Welcome to the Terrordome, 1: High-Tech	1.75	0.35	0.88	1.75
❑12, Jun 92, Biohazard Agenda, Part 1	1.75	0.35	0.88	1.75
❑13, Jul 92, Biohazard Agenda, Part 2	1.75	0.35	0.88	1.75
❑14, Aug 92, Biohazard Agenda, Part 3, O: Deathlok III (Luther Manning)	1.75	0.35	0.88	1.75
❑15, Sep 92, Biohazard Agenda, Part 4	1.75	0.35	0.88	1.75
❑16, Oct 92, Infinity War	1.75	0.35	0.88	1.75
❑17, Nov 92, CyberWar, Part 1	1.75	0.35	0.88	1.75
❑18, Dec 92, CyberWar, Part 2	1.75	0.35	0.88	1.75
❑19, Jan 93, CyberWar, Part 3, 1: Siege, foil cover	2.25	0.45	1.13	2.25
❑20, Feb 93, CyberWar, Part 4	1.75	0.35	0.88	1.75
❑21, Mar 93, CyberWar, Part 5	1.75	0.35	0.88	1.75
❑22, Apr 93	1.75	0.35	0.88	1.75
❑23, May 93, And We Are Not Saved!	1.75	0.35	0.88	1.75
❑24, Jun 93, And All Fashionable Vices Pass For Virtues	1.75	0.35	0.88	1.75
❑25, Jul 93, A: Black Panther, foil cover	2.95	0.35	0.88	1.75
❑26, Aug 93	1.75	0.35	0.88	1.75
❑27, Sep 93	1.75	0.35	0.88	1.75
❑28, Oct 93, A: Goddess; A: Timestream, Infinity Crusade crossover	1.75	0.35	0.88	1.75
❑29, Nov 93	1.75	0.35	0.88	1.75
❑30, Dec 93	1.75	0.35	0.88	1.75
❑31, Jan 94, Cyberstrike, Part 1	1.75	0.35	0.88	1.75
❑32, Feb 94, Cyberstrike, Part 2	1.75	0.35	0.88	1.75
❑33, Mar 94, Cyberstrike, Part 3	1.75	0.35	0.88	1.75
❑34, Apr 94, Cyberstrike, Part 4, Final Issue	1.75	0.35	0.88	1.75
❑Anl 1, Timestream	2.50	0.50	1.25	2.50
❑Anl 2, 1: Tracer, trading card; Polybagged	2.95	0.59	1.48	2.95
❑SE 1, May 91, Reprint	2.00	0.40	1.00	2.00
❑SE 2, Jun 91, Reprint	2.00	0.40	1.00	2.00
❑SE 3, Jun 91, Reprint	2.00	0.40	1.00	2.00
❑SE 4, Jun 91, Reprint	2.00	0.40	1.00	2.00

DEATHLOK (3RD SERIES)
MARVEL

	ORIG	GOOD	FINE	N-MINT
❑1, Sep 99, The Crawl From Small Things Part 1	1.99	0.40	1.00	2.00
❑2, Oct 99	1.99	0.40	1.00	1.99
❑3, Nov 99	1.99	0.40	1.00	1.99
❑4, Nov 99	1.99	0.40	1.00	1.99
❑5	1.99	0.40	1.00	1.99

DEATHMARK
LIGHTNING

Value: Cover or less

❑1, Dec 94, b&w ... 2.95

DEATHMATE
IMAGE

	ORIG	GOOD	FINE	N-MINT
❑1, Sep 93, BL (w), A Love To End All Time, silver cover; crossover; Prologue	2.95	0.59	1.48	2.95
❑1/GO, Sep 93, BL (w), A Love To End All Time, Gold cover (limited promotional edition); gold; Prologue	4.95	0.80	2.00	4.00
❑2, Sep 93, 1: Freefall; 1: Gen13 (full); 1: Burn-Out; 1: Fairchild, Black	4.95	0.60	1.50	3.00
❑2/GO, Sep 93, 1: Gen13 (full), Gold edition	2.95	1.20	3.00	6.00
❑3, Sep 93, Jerked Through Time, cover says Oct, indicia says Sep; Yellow	4.95	0.99	2.47	4.95
❑3/GO, Sep 93, Jerked Through Time, Gold edition; Yellow	2.95	1.20	3.00	6.00
❑4, Oct 93, Battlestone vs. Magnus Outlaw!, Blue	4.95	0.99	2.47	4.95
❑4/GO, Oct 93, Gold limited promotional edition; Gold edition; Blue	4.95	1.20	3.00	6.00

	ORIG	GOOD	FINE	N-MINT
❑5, Nov 93, Red	4.95	0.99	2.47	4.95
❑5/GO, Nov 93, Gold edition; Red	4.95	1.20	3.00	6.00
❑6, Feb 94, BL (w), Armageddon Interuptus, silver cover; Epilogue	2.95	0.59	1.48	2.95
❑6/GO, Feb 94, Gold edition	4.95	0.80	2.00	4.00

DEATH METAL
MARVEL
Value: Cover or less

- ❑1, Jan 94 ... 1.95
- ❑2, Feb 94 ... 1.95
- ❑3, Mar 94 ... 1.95
- ❑4, Apr 94 ... 1.95

DEATH METAL VS. GENETIX
MARVEL
Value: Cover or less

- ❑1, Dec 93, Offspring, Part 1, trading cards ... 2.95
- ❑2, Jan 94, Offspring, Part 2, trading cards ... 2.95

DEATH OF ANGEL GIRL, THE
ANGEL
Value: Cover or less

- ❑1, A war in Hell ... 2.95

DEATH OF ANTISOCIALMAN, THE
NOT AVAILABLE
Value: Cover or less

- ❑1 ... 0.50
- ❑2 ... 0.50
- ❑3 ... 0.50
- ❑4 ... 0.50
- ❑5 ... 0.50
- ❑6 ... 0.50
- ❑7 ... 0.50
- ❑8 ... 0.50
- ❑9 ... 0.50
- ❑10 ... 0.50

DEATH OF LADY VAMPRÉ
BLACKOUT
Value: Cover or less

- ❑1, O: Lady VamprT ... 2.95

DEATH OF STUPIDMAN, THE
PARODY PRESS
Value: Cover or less

- ❑1, Gloomsday ... 3.50

DEATH OF SUPERBABE
SPOOF
Value: Cover or less

- ❑1, b&w ... 3.95

DEATH OF VAMPIRELLA
HARRIS

	ORIG	GOOD	FINE	N-MINT
❑1, Feb 97, chromium cover; Memorial Edition; Green logo	—	3.00	7.50	15.00
❑1/SC, Feb 97, Holofoil chromium edition; 750 copies printed; Yellow logo	—	3.00	7.50	15.00

DEATH RACE 2020
COSMIC
Value: Cover or less

- ❑1, Apr 95, sequel to Corman film ... 2.50
- ❑2, May 95, Bride of Frankenstein ... 2.50
- ❑5, Aug 95 ... 2.50

DEATH RATTLE (VOL. 2)
KITCHEN SINK
Value: Cover or less

- ❑1, Killer Planet; Ill Bred, full color ... 2.00
- ❑2, God's Bosom; A Quagmire of Occult Stories, full color; Spirit story (previously unpublished) 2.00
- ❑3, A Dead Man's Chest; Bulto the Cosmic Slug, full color ... 2.00
- ❑4, The Power of Prayer; Bulto, full color ... 2.00
- ❑5, full color ... 2.00
- ❑6, Road Kill; Catcalls, b&w; Black and white; Listed as #5 in indicia ... 2.00
- ❑7, This Old House; The Blue Boot, b&w ... 2.00
- ❑8, 1: Xenozoic ... 2.00
- ❑9 ... 2.00
- ❑10, WW; FF; AW ... 2.00
- ❑11 ... 2.00
- ❑12 ... 2.00
- ❑13, Nov 87 ... 2.00
- ❑14, Jan 88 ... 2.00
- ❑15, The Big Day Off; The Priest Killer ... 2.00
- ❑16 ... 2.00
- ❑17, Jul 88, Slide, Sinner, Slide; Bulto: Screams of Delight.... 2.00
- ❑18, Oct 88, FM (c), Bulto: The Cow Camp; The Old Wisconsin That I Knew ... 2.00

DEATH RATTLE (VOL. 3)
KITCHEN SINK
Value: Cover or less

- ❑1, Oct 95, The Probability Chamber; The Day I Lost My Head, b&w ... 2.95
- ❑2, Dec 95, b&w ... 2.95
- ❑3, Feb 96 ... 2.95
- ❑4, Apr 96 ... 2.95
- ❑5, Jun 96, b&w ... 2.95
- ❑6 ... 2.95
- ❑36893, Nov 95, The Probability Chamber; The Day I Lost My Head, b&w; 2nd Printing ... 2.95

DEATHROW
HEROIC
Value: Cover or less

- ❑1, Sep 93, 1: X-187, b&w; trading card ... 3.50

DEATH'S HEAD
MARVEL
Value: Cover or less

- ❑1, Dec 88, Death's Head Revisited ... 1.75
- ❑2, Jan 89 ... 1.75
- ❑3, Feb 89 ... 1.75
- ❑4, Mar 89 ... 1.75
- ❑5, Apr 89 ... 1.75
- ❑6, May 89 ... 1.75
- ❑7, Jun 89 ... 1.75
- ❑8, Jul 89, Death's Head Revisited, A: Doctor Who ... 1.75
- ❑9, Aug 89, A: Fantastic 4 ... 1.75
- ❑10, Sep 89, A: Iron Man of 2020, Final Issue ... 1.75

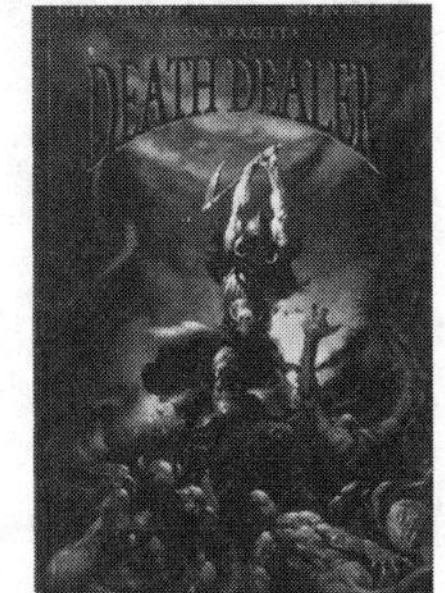

Frank Frazetta's Death Dealer paintings were the inspiration for Verotik's prestige-format series.

DEATH'S HEAD II (VOL. 1)
MARVEL

	ORIG	GOOD	FINE	N-MINT
❑1, Mar 92, The Wild Hunt, Part 1, D: Death's Head; 1: Death's Head II	1.75	0.50	1.25	2.50
❑1-2, Mar 92, The Wild Hunt, Part 1, D: Death's Head; 1: Death's Head II, 2nd Printing; Silver ink cover	1.75	0.35	0.88	1.75
❑2, Apr 92, Reed Richards Dies Tonight	1.75	0.40	1.00	2.00
❑2-2, Apr 92, 2nd Printing; Silver ink cover	1.75	0.35	0.88	1.75
❑3, May 92, 1: Tuck	1.75	0.40	1.00	2.00
❑4, Jun 92, A: Captain America; A: Wolverine	1.75	0.40	1.00	2.00

DEATH'S HEAD II (VOL. 2)
MARVEL

	ORIG	GOOD	FINE	N-MINT
❑1, Dec 92, The Lotus FX, Part 1, A: X-Men, gatefold cover	1.75	0.40	1.00	2.00
❑2, Jan 93, The Lotus FX, Part 2, A: X-Men	1.75	0.40	1.00	2.00
❑3, Feb 93, The Lotus FX, Part 3, A: X-Men	1.75	0.40	1.00	2.00
❑4, Mar 93, A: X-Men	1.75	0.40	1.00	2.00
❑5, Apr 93	1.75	0.35	0.88	1.75
❑6, May 93, Borgs 'n the Hood!	1.95	0.39	0.98	1.95
❑7, Jun 93	1.95	0.39	0.98	1.95
❑8, Jul 93	1.95	0.39	0.98	1.95
❑9, Aug 93	1.95	0.39	0.98	1.95
❑10, Sep 93	1.95	0.39	0.98	1.95
❑11, Oct 93, A: Charnel; 1: Death's Head III; A: Doctor Necker	1.95	0.39	0.98	1.95
❑12, Nov 93	1.95	0.39	0.98	1.95
❑13, Dec 93	1.95	0.39	0.98	1.95
❑14, Jan 94, foil cover; Prelude to Death's Head Gold #1	2.95	0.59	1.48	2.95
❑15, Feb 94	1.95	0.39	0.98	1.95
❑16, Mar 94, Final Issue	1.95	0.39	0.98	1.95

DEATH'S HEAD II & THE ORIGIN OF DIE-CUT
MARVEL
Value: Cover or less

- ❑1, Aug 93, The First Cut, O: Die Cut, foil cover ... 2.95
- ❑2, Sep 93, Death and Perfection, O: Die Cut ... 1.75

DEATH'S HEAD II GOLD
MARVEL
Value: Cover or less

- ❑1, foil cover ... 3.95

DEATH SHRIKE
BRAINSTORM
Value: Cover or less

- ❑1, Jul 93, Man of Sorrow, b&w ... 2.95

DEATHSNAKE, THE
EROS
Value: Cover or less

- ❑1 ... 2.95
- ❑2, Oct 94 ... 2.95

DEATHSTROKE THE TERMINATOR
DC

	ORIG	GOOD	FINE	N-MINT
❑0, Oct 94, Title changes to Deathstroke the Hunted	1.95	0.40	1.00	2.00
❑1, Aug 91, Full Cycle, Part 1, O: Deathstroke the Terminator	1.75	0.60	1.50	3.00
❑1-2, Full Cycle, Part 1, O: Deathstroke the Terminator, 2nd Printing	1.75	0.35	0.88	1.75
❑2, Sep 91, Full Cycle, Part 2	1.75	0.40	1.00	2.00
❑3, Oct 91, Full Cycle, Part 3	1.75	0.40	1.00	2.00
❑4, Nov 91, Full Cycle, Part 4, V: Ravager	1.75	0.40	1.00	2.00
❑5, Dec 91	1.75	0.40	1.00	2.00
❑6, Jan 92, City of Assassins, Part 1	1.75	0.40	1.00	2.00
❑7, Feb 92, City of Assassins, Part 2, Batman	1.75	0.40	1.00	2.00
❑8, Mar 92, City of Assassins, Part 3, Batman	1.75	0.40	1.00	2.00
❑9, Apr 92, City of Assassins, Part 4, 1: Vigilante III (Pat Trayce), Batman	1.75	0.40	1.00	2.00
❑10, Jun 92, Guns and Roses, Part 1, 1: new Vigilante	1.75	0.40	1.00	2.00
❑11, Jun 92, Guns and Roses, Part 2, Vigilante	1.75	0.40	1.00	2.00
❑12, Jul 92	1.75	0.40	1.00	2.00
❑13, Aug 92	1.75	0.40	1.00	2.00
❑14, Sep 92, Total Chaos, Part 1	1.75	0.40	1.00	2.00
❑15, Oct 92, Total Chaos, Part 4	1.75	0.40	1.00	2.00
❑16, Nov 92, Total Chaos, Part 7, D: Deathstroke the Terminator	1.75	0.40	1.00	2.00

	ORIG	GOOD	FINE	N-MINT
❑17, Dec 92, Titans Sell-Out, Part 2, Deathstroke the Terminator revived	1.75	0.40	1.00	2.00
❑18, Jan 93	1.75	0.40	1.00	2.00
❑19, Feb 93, Quarac destroyed	1.75	0.40	1.00	2.00
❑20, Mar 93	1.75	0.35	0.88	1.75
❑21, Apr 93	1.75	0.35	0.88	1.75
❑22, May 93	1.75	0.35	0.88	1.75
❑23, May 93	1.75	0.35	0.88	1.75
❑24, Jun 93	1.75	0.35	0.88	1.75
❑25, Jun 93	1.75	0.35	0.88	1.75
❑26, Jul 93	1.75	0.35	0.88	1.75
❑27, Aug 93, World Tour, Part 1	1.75	0.35	0.88	1.75
❑28, Sep 93, World Tour, Part 2	1.75	0.35	0.88	1.75
❑29, Oct 93, World Tour, Part 3	1.75	0.35	0.88	1.75
❑30, Nov 93, World Tour, Part 4	1.75	0.35	0.88	1.75
❑31, Dec 93, World Tour, Part 5	1.75	0.35	0.88	1.75
❑32, Jan 94, World Tour, Part 6	1.75	0.35	0.88	1.75
❑33, Feb 94, World Tour, Part 7	1.75	0.35	0.88	1.75
❑34, Mar 94, World Tour, Part 8	1.75	0.35	0.88	1.75
❑35, Apr 94	1.75	0.35	0.88	1.75
❑36, May 94	1.75	0.35	0.88	1.75
❑37, Jun 94, Sins of the Father!	1.75	0.35	0.88	1.75
❑38, Jul 94, A: Vigilante	1.95	0.39	0.98	1.95
❑39, Aug 94, Title becomes "Deathstroke the Hunted"	1.95	0.39	0.98	1.95
❑40, Sep 94, The Hunted, Part 1	1.95	0.39	0.98	1.95
❑41, Nov 94, The Hunted, Part 2	1.95	0.39	0.98	1.95
❑42, Dec 94, The Hunted, Part 3	1.95	0.39	0.98	1.95
❑43, Jan 95, The Hunted, Part 4	1.95	0.39	0.98	1.95
❑44, Feb 95, The Hunted, Part 5	1.95	0.39	0.98	1.95
❑45, Mar 95, The Hunted, Part 6	1.95	0.39	0.98	1.95
❑46, Apr 95	1.95	0.39	0.98	1.95
❑47, May 95	1.95	0.39	0.98	1.95
❑48, Jun 95	2.25	0.45	1.13	2.25
❑49, Jul 95	2.25	0.45	1.13	2.25
❑50, Aug 95, Giant-size; Title changes to Deathstroke	3.50	0.70	1.75	3.50
❑51, Sep 95	2.25	0.45	1.13	2.25
❑52, Oct 95, A: Hawkman	2.25	0.45	1.13	2.25
❑53, Nov 95	2.25	0.45	1.13	2.25
❑54, Dec 95	2.25	0.45	1.13	2.25
❑55, Jan 96, Night of the Karrion, Part 1	2.25	0.45	1.13	2.25
❑56, Feb 96, Night of the Karrion!, Part 2	2.25	0.45	1.13	2.25
❑57, Mar 96, Night of the Karrion, Part 3	2.25	0.45	1.13	2.25
❑58, Apr 96, Bad Blood, V: Joker	2.25	0.45	1.13	2.25
❑59, May 96	2.25	0.45	1.13	2.25
❑60, Jun 96, Final Issue	2.25	0.45	1.13	2.25
❑Anl 1, Eclipso: The Darkness Within, Part 13, A: Vigilante, Eclipso; 1992 Annual	3.50	0.70	1.75	3.50
❑Anl 2, Bloodlines, 1: Gunfire, Bloodlines	3.50	0.70	1.75	3.50
❑Anl 3, Elseworlds	3.95	0.79	1.98	3.95
❑Anl 4, Title changes to Deathstroke Annual, Year One; Title changes to Deathstroke Annual; Year One	3.95	0.79	1.98	3.95

DEATH TALKS ABOUT LIFE
DC

	ORIG	GOOD	FINE	N-MINT
❑1, NG (w), 16pgs.	—	0.40	1.00	2.00

DEATH: THE HIGH COST OF LIVING
DC

	ORIG	GOOD	FINE	N-MINT
❑1, Mar 93, NG (w)	1.95	0.80	2.00	4.00
❑1/PL, NG (w), Platinum edition	—	1.80	4.50	9.00
❑2, Apr 93, NG (w)	1.95	0.70	1.75	3.50
❑3, May 93, NG (w), Error editions with reversed pages exist-no difference in value; regular edition	1.95	0.60	1.50	3.00
❑3/A, May 93, with error	1.95	0.60	1.50	3.00

DEATH: THE TIME OF YOUR LIFE
DC

	ORIG	GOOD	FINE	N-MINT
❑1, Apr 96, NG (w), Things You Just Do When You're Bored	2.95	0.80	2.00	4.00
❑2, May 96, NG (w), Imaginary Solutions	2.95	0.70	1.75	3.50
❑3, Jun 96, NG (w), The Time Of Your Life	2.95	0.70	1.75	3.50

DEATHWATCH
HARRIER
Value: Cover or less

- ❑1, Jul 87, Deathbringer; A Dark Summer ... 1.95

DEATHWISH
MILESTONE
Value: Cover or less

- ❑1, Dec 94, This Ain't No Cryin' Game ... 2.50
- ❑2, Jan 95 ... 2.50
- ❑3, Feb 95 ... 2.50
- ❑4, Mar 95, Silence of the Rahm ... 2.50

DEATHWORLD
ADVENTURE
Value: Cover or less

- ❑1, Nov 90, b&w ... 2.50
- ❑2, Dec 90, b&w ... 2.50
- ❑3, Jan 91, b&w ... 2.50
- ❑4, Feb 91, b&w ... 2.50

DEATHWORLD BOOK II
ADVENTURE
Value: Cover or less

- ❑1, Apr 91, b&w ... 2.50
- ❑2, May 91, b&w ... 2.50
- ❑3, Jun 91, b&w ... 2.50
- ❑4, Jul 91, b&w ... 2.50

DEATHWORLD BOOK III
ADVENTURE
Value: Cover or less

- ❑1, Aug 91, b&w ... 2.50
- ❑2, Sep 91, b&w ... 2.50
- ❑3, Nov 91, b&w ... 2.50
- ❑4, Dec 91, b&w ... 2.50

DEATH WRECK
MARVEL
Value: Cover or less

- ❑1, Jan 94, 1: Death-Wreck ... 1.95
- ❑2, Feb 94 ... 1.95
- ❑3, Mar 94 ... 1.95
- ❑4, Apr 94 ... 1.95
- ❑5, May 94 ... 1.95
- ❑6, Jun 94 ... 1.95
- ❑7, Jul 94 ... 1.95

DEBBIE DOES COMICS
AIRCEL
Value: Cover or less

- ❑1, b&w; adult ... 2.95

DEBBIE DOES DALLAS
AIRCEL
Value: Cover or less

- ❑1, Mar 91, adult ... 2.50
- ❑1/3D, adult ... 3.95
- ❑1-2, adult; 2nd Printing ... 2.50
- ❑2, Apr 91, adult ... 2.50
- ❑3, May 91, adult ... 2.50
- ❑4, Jun 91, adult ... 2.50
- ❑5, Jul 91, adult ... 2.50
- ❑6, adult ... 2.50
- ❑7, Oct 91, adult ... 2.50
- ❑8, Nov 91, adult ... 2.50
- ❑9, Dec 91, adult ... 2.95
- ❑10, adult ... 2.95
- ❑11, adult ... 2.95
- ❑12, adult ... 2.95
- ❑13, adult ... 2.95
- ❑14, adult ... 2.95
- ❑15, adult ... 2.95
- ❑16, adult ... 2.95
- ❑17, adult ... 2.95
- ❑18, adult ... 2.95

DECADE OF DARK HORSE, A
DARK HORSE
Value: Cover or less

- ❑1, Jul 96, FM; MW, FM (w); MW (w), Sin City: Daddy's Little Girl; Predator: 1718, b&w and color; Sin City, Predator, Grendel stories ... 2.95
- ❑2, Aug 96, Star Wars: This Crumb For Hire; Ghost: Sweet Things, Star Wars, Ghost, Trekker stories ... 2.95
- ❑3, Sep 96, Aliens: Lucky; Nexus: All and Sundra, b&w and color; Aliens, Outlanders, Nexus, The Mask stories ... 2.95
- ❑4, Oct 96, Concrete: World Beneath the Skin; Black Cross, O: Godzilla, b&w and color, Concrete, Black Cross, Exon Depot, Godzilla stories, final issue ... 2.95

DECAPITATOR (RANDY BOWEN'S...)
DARK HORSE
Value: Cover or less

- ❑1, Jun 98 ... 2.95
- ❑2, Jul 98 ... 2.95
- ❑3, Aug 98 ... 2.95
- ❑4 ... 2.95

DECEPTION, THE
IMAGE
Value: Cover or less

- ❑1, Vanishing Act ... 2.95
- ❑2, Magic Words ... 2.95
- ❑3, Quicker than the Eye ... 2.95

DECORATOR, THE
FANTAGRAPHICS
Value: Cover or less

- ❑1, b&w; adult ... 2.50

DECOY
PENNY-FARTHING PRESS
Value: Cover or less

- ❑1, Mar 99 ... 2.75
- ❑1/Aut, Mar 99, Auographed edition ... 3.25
- ❑2, Apr 99 ... 2.75
- ❑3, May 99 ... 2.75
- ❑4, Jun 99 ... 2.75

DEE DEE
FANTAGRAPHICS
Value: Cover or less

- ❑1, Jul 96, b&w; adult ... 2.95

DEEP, THE
MARVEL

	ORIG	GOOD	FINE	N-MINT
❑1, Nov 77, CI, movie Adaptation	0.60	0.30	0.75	1.50

DEEP BLACK
CHAOS!

	ORIG	GOOD	FINE	N-MINT
❑1/A, Aug 97, no cover price; b&w pencilled pin-ups	—	0.40	1.00	2.00
❑1/B, Aug 97, all-white cardstock cover; b&w pencilled pin-ups	—	0.40	1.00	2.00

DEEPEST DIMENSION
REVOLUTIONARY
Value: Cover or less

- ❑1, Jun 93 ... 2.50
- ❑2, Aug 93, Sea Change ... 2.50

DEEP GIRL
ARIEL BORDEAUX
Value: Cover or less

- ❑1 ... 2.50
- ❑2 ... 2.50
- ❑3 ... 2.50
- ❑4 ... 2.50
- ❑5, Violet; I Am Ellsbette and... 2.50

DEEP TERROR
AVALON
Value: Cover or less

- ❑1, TS, The Legacy; Pay the Price...Twice!, b&w ... 2.95

DEE VEE
DEE VEE PRESS
Value: Cover or less

Issue	Price
❑1, Alec (a new work in progress); Vital Reality Six Ways to Tell a Loved One…	2.95
❑5, Feb 98, b&w; wraparound cover; Anthology	2.95
❑6, Apr 98, b&w; wraparound cover; Anthology	2.95
❑7, Jun 98, b&w; wraparound cover; Anthology	2.95

DEFCON 4
IMAGE
Value: Cover or less

Issue	Price
❑1/A, Feb 96, wraparound cover	2.50
❑1/B, Feb 96, alternate wraparound cover	2.50
❑2, Mar 96	2.50
❑3, Jun 96, cover says May, indicia says Jun	2.50
❑4, Sep 96	2.50
❑5	2.50

DEFENDERS, THE
MARVEL

Issue	ORIG	GOOD	FINE	N-MINT
❑1, Aug 72, SB, I Slay By the Stars!, Team consists of Doctor Strange, Hulk, and Sub-Mariner	0.20	10.00	25.00	50.00
❑2, Oct 72, SB, A: Silver Surfer	0.20	5.00	12.50	25.00
❑3, Dec 72, JM; SB, A: Silver Surfer	0.20	4.00	10.00	20.00
❑4, Feb 73, SB; FMc, Valkyrie joins Defenders	0.20	4.00	10.00	20.00
❑5, Apr 73, SB; FMc, D: Omegatron	0.20	4.00	10.00	20.00
❑6, Jun 73, SB; FMc	0.20	3.00	7.50	15.00
❑7, Aug 73, SB, A: Hawkeye	0.20	3.00	7.50	15.00
❑8, Sep 73, A: Avengers, Avengers appearace	0.20	3.00	7.50	15.00
❑9, Oct 73, A: Avengers, Avengers appearace	0.20	3.00	7.50	15.00
❑10, Nov 73, A: Avengers, Hulk vs. Thor	0.20	4.00	10.00	20.00
❑11, Dec 73, A: Avengers	0.20	1.40	3.50	7.00
❑12, Feb 74	0.20	1.40	3.50	7.00
❑13, May 74, 1: Nebulon	0.25	1.40	3.50	7.00
❑14, Jul 74	0.25	1.40	3.50	7.00
❑15, Sep 74, V: Magneto	0.25	2.00	5.00	10.00
❑16, Oct 74, SB, Alpha, The Ultimate Mutant, A: Magneto	0.25	1.60	4.00	8.00
❑17, Nov 74, 1: Bulldozer	0.25	1.00	2.50	5.00
❑18, Dec 74, V: Wrecking Crew; O: Bulldozer	0.25	1.00	2.50	5.00
❑19, Jan 75, KJ; SB, Doomball!	0.25	1.00	2.50	5.00
❑20, Feb 75, SB, A: Thing	0.25	1.00	2.50	5.00
❑21, Mar 75, SB	0.25	1.00	2.50	5.00
❑22, Apr 75, SB	0.25	1.00	2.50	5.00
❑23, May 75, SB, …The Snakes Shall Inherit The Earth	0.25	1.00	2.50	5.00
❑24, Jun 75, SB, -In The Jaws Of The Serpent, A: Son of Satan; A: Daredevil	0.25	1.00	2.50	5.00
❑25, Jul 75, A: Daredevil	0.25	1.00	2.50	5.00
❑26, Aug 75, A: Guardians of the Galaxy	0.25	1.20	3.00	6.00
❑27, Sep 75, 1: Starhawk II (Aleta)-cameo; A: Guardians of the Galaxy	0.25	1.20	3.00	6.00
❑28, Oct 75, A: Guardians of the Galaxy; 1: Starhawk II (Aleta)-full	0.25	1.20	3.00	6.00
❑29, Nov 75, A: Guardians of the Galaxy	0.25	1.20	3.00	6.00
❑30, Dec 75	0.25	0.80	2.00	4.00
❑31, Jan 76	0.25	0.80	2.00	4.00
❑32, Feb 76, O: Nighthawk II (Kyle Richmond)	0.25	0.80	2.00	4.00
❑33, Mar 76	0.25	0.80	2.00	4.00
❑34, Apr 76, JM; SB, I Think We're All Bozos In This Book!, V: Nebulon	0.25	0.80	2.00	4.00
❑35, May 76, 1: Red Guardian II (Doctor Tanja Belinskya)	0.25	0.80	2.00	4.00
❑36, Jun 76, KJ; SB, A Garden Of Earthly Demise!	0.25	0.80	2.00	4.00
❑37, Jul 76, KJ; SB	0.25	0.80	2.00	4.00
❑38, Aug 76, KJ; SB, Exile To Oblivion!	0.25	0.80	2.00	4.00
❑39, Sep 76, KJ; SB	0.30	0.80	2.00	4.00
❑40, Oct 76, KJ; SB, Love, Anarchy, And, Oh Yes… The Assassin!	0.30	0.80	2.00	4.00
❑41, Nov 76, KJ; SB	0.30	0.60	1.50	3.00
❑42, Dec 76, KJ; KG	0.30	0.60	1.50	3.00
❑43, Jan 77, KJ; KG	0.30	0.60	1.50	3.00
❑44, Feb 77, KJ; KG, Hellcat joins Defenders	0.30	0.60	1.50	3.00
❑45, Mar 77, KJ; KG	0.30	0.60	1.50	3.00
❑46, Apr 77, KJ; KG	0.30	0.60	1.50	3.00
❑47, May 77, KJ; KG, Moon Knight	0.30	0.60	1.50	3.00
❑48, Jun 77, DGr; KG, Sinister Savior!, O: Zodiac II	0.30	0.60	1.50	3.00
❑49, Jul 77, KG, O: Zodiac II	0.30	0.60	1.50	3.00
❑50, Aug 77, KG, O: Zodiac II	0.30	0.60	1.50	3.00
❑51, Sep 77, KG, A Round With The Ringer!, A: Moon Knight; 1: Ringer I (Anthony Davis), Moon Knight	0.30	0.50	1.25	2.50
❑52, Oct 77, KG, Defender Of The Realm!, V: Sub-Mariner; 1: Presence; A: Hulk	0.30	0.50	1.25	2.50

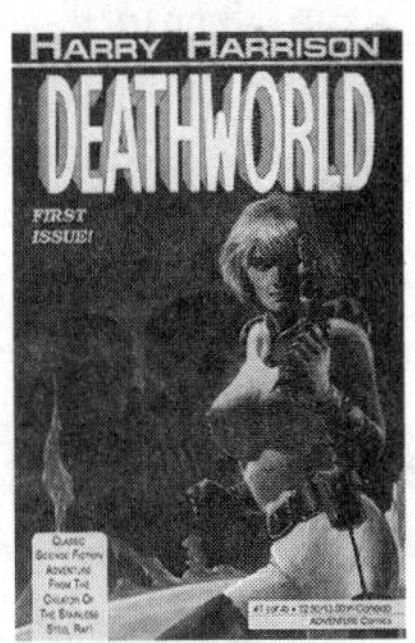

Harry Harrison's *Deathworld* books were adapted in a series of mini-series by Malibu's Adventure imprint.

Issue	ORIG	GOOD	FINE	N-MINT
❑53, Nov 77, MG, 1: Lunatik	0.35	0.50	1.25	2.50
❑54, Dec 77, KG; MG, A Study in Survival!	0.35	0.50	1.25	2.50
❑55, Jan 78, O: Red Guardian II (Doctor Tanja Belinskya)	0.35	0.50	1.25	2.50
❑56, Feb 78	0.35	0.50	1.25	2.50
❑57, Mar 78	0.35	0.50	1.25	2.50
❑58, Apr 78	0.35	0.50	1.25	2.50
❑59, May 78	0.35	0.50	1.25	2.50
❑60, Jun 78	0.35	0.50	1.25	2.50
❑61, Jul 78	0.35	0.50	1.25	2.50
❑62, Aug 78, JM; SB, Membership Madness!	0.35	0.50	1.25	2.50
❑63, Sep 78	0.35	0.50	1.25	2.50
❑64, Oct 78	0.35	0.50	1.25	2.50
❑65, Nov 78, DP, Of Ambitions And Giant Amoebas	0.35	0.50	1.25	2.50
❑66, Dec 78	0.35	0.50	1.25	2.50
❑67, Jan 79, We, The Unliving	0.35	0.50	1.25	2.50
❑68, Feb 79, HT, Valhalla Can Wait!	0.35	0.50	1.25	2.50
❑69, Mar 79, HT, The Anything Man!	0.35	0.50	1.25	2.50
❑70, Apr 79, HT, Catch A Falling Lunatik!, V: Lunatik	0.35	0.50	1.25	2.50
❑71, May 79, JAb; HT, Stranger And Stranger In A Strange Land, O: Lunatik	0.40	0.50	1.25	2.50
❑72, Jun 79, HT, Up From The Sky!, A: Lunatik	0.40	0.50	1.25	2.50
❑73, Jul 79, HT, Of Wizards, Shadows, And Kings, A: Foolkiller II (Greg Salinger)	0.40	0.50	1.25	2.50
❑74, Aug 79, HT, Fools Rush In!, A: Foolkiller II (Greg Salinger), Nighthawk II resigns from Defenders	0.40	0.50	1.25	2.50
❑75, Sep 79, HT, Poetic Justice, A: Foolkiller II (Greg Salinger)	0.40	0.50	1.25	2.50
❑76, Oct 79, HT, Little Triggers, O: Omega.	0.40	0.50	1.25	2.50
❑77, Nov 79, HT, Waiting For The End Of The World, D: James-Michael Starling (Omega the Unknown's counterpart)	0.40	0.50	1.25	2.50
❑78, Dec 79, HT, The Return Of The Original Defenders, Original Defenders return	0.40	0.40	1.00	2.00
❑79, Jan 80, HT, Chains Of Love	0.40	0.40	1.00	2.00
❑80, Feb 80, HT, Once A Defender	0.40	0.40	1.00	2.00
❑81, Mar 80, JAb; HT, War In Ogeon!	0.40	0.40	1.00	2.00
❑82, Apr 80, DP, Wizard Death!	0.40	0.40	1.00	2.00
❑83, May 80, DP, End Of The Tunnel	0.40	0.40	1.00	2.00
❑84, Jun 80, DP, Battle Royal	0.40	0.40	1.00	2.00
❑85, Jul 80	0.40	0.40	1.00	2.00
❑86, Aug 80	0.40	0.40	1.00	2.00
❑87, Sep 80, Inquest	0.50	0.40	1.00	2.00
❑88, Oct 80, Lord Of The Whales	0.50	0.40	1.00	2.00
❑89, Nov 80, A Death In The Family!	0.50	0.40	1.00	2.00
❑90, Dec 80, Mind Over Mandrill!, Daredevil	0.50	0.40	1.00	2.00
❑91, Jan 81, Defiance!, Daredevil	0.50	0.40	1.00	2.00
❑92, Feb 81, JSt; DP	0.50	0.40	1.00	2.00
❑93, Mar 81, JSt; DP, The Woman Behind The Man!	0.50	0.40	1.00	2.00
❑94, Apr 81, JSt; DP, Beware…The Six-Fingered Man!, 1: Gargoyle	0.50	0.40	1.00	2.00
❑95, May 81, JSt; DP, The Vampire Strikes Back!, O: Gargoyle; A: Dracula	0.50	0.40	1.00	2.00
❑96, Jun 81, JSt; DP, A: Ghost Rider	0.50	0.50	1.25	2.50
❑97, Jul 81, JSt; DP, Slouching Toward Bethlehem	0.50	0.40	1.00	2.00
❑98, Aug 81, JSt; DP, The Hand Closes!	0.50	0.40	1.00	2.00
❑99, Sep 81, JSt; DP, Final Conflict	0.50	0.40	1.00	2.00
❑100, Oct 81, JSt; DP, 100th anniversary issue; Giant-size; giant	0.75	0.40	1.00	2.00
❑101, Nov 81, JSt; DP, A: Silver Surfer	0.50	0.30	0.75	1.50
❑102, Dec 81, JAb; JSt; DP, Mind Games!	0.50	0.30	0.75	1.50
❑103, Jan 82, JSt; DP, 1: Null the Living Darkness	0.60	0.30	0.75	1.50
❑104, Feb 82, JSt; DP	0.60	0.30	0.75	1.50
❑105, Mar 82, JSt; DP	0.60	0.30	0.75	1.50
❑106, Apr 82, DP, D: Nighthawk II (Kyle Richmond); A: Daredevil	0.60	0.30	0.75	1.50
❑107, May 82, JSt; DP, On Death And Dying…, A: Enchantress	0.60	0.30	0.75	1.50

	ORIG	GOOD	FINE	N-MINT
❑108, Jun 82, DP, The Wasteland!	0.60	0.30	0.75	1.50
❑109, Jul 82	0.60	0.30	0.75	1.50
❑110, Aug 82, DP, ...Hunger...	0.60	0.30	0.75	1.50
❑111, Sep 82, DP, Fathers And Daughters	0.60	0.30	0.75	1.50
❑112, Oct 82, DP, Strange Visitor From Another Planet!, 1: Nuke I (Albert Gaines); 1: Power Princess	0.60	0.30	0.75	1.50
❑113, Nov 82	0.60	0.30	0.75	1.50
❑114, Dec 82, DP, Dance Of Darkness/Dance Of Light!	0.60	0.30	0.75	1.50
❑115, Jan 83, DP, A Very Wrong Turn!	0.60	0.30	0.75	1.50
❑116, Feb 83, DP, Two By Two	0.60	0.30	0.75	1.50
❑117, Mar 83, DP, The Gift	0.60	0.30	0.75	1.50
❑118, Apr 83, DP, The Double!	0.60	0.30	0.75	1.50
❑119, May 83, 1: Yandroth II	0.60	0.30	0.75	1.50
❑120, Jun 83	0.60	0.30	0.75	1.50
❑121, Jul 83	0.60	0.30	0.75	1.50
❑122, Aug 83, DP, Things To Come!	0.60	0.30	0.75	1.50
❑123, Sep 83, DP, of Elves And Androids!, 1: Cloud	0.60	0.30	0.75	1.50
❑124, Oct 83	0.60	0.30	0.75	1.50
❑125, Nov 83, DP, BSz (c), Hello, I Must Be Going. (Or...Mad Dogs And Elvishmen!), 1: Mad-Dog, double-sized; New Team begins: Valkyrie, Beast, Iceman, Angel, Gargoyle, and Moondragon	1.00	0.30	0.75	1.50
❑126, Dec 83, State Of The Union!, 1: Leviathan I (Edward Cobert)	0.60	0.30	0.75	1.50
❑127, Jan 84, SB, Cloud Hidden!	0.60	0.30	0.75	1.50
❑128, Feb 84, Assault On The Empire!	0.60	0.30	0.75	1.50
❑129, Mar 84, DP, Countdown!, V: New Mutants	0.60	0.30	0.75	1.50
❑130, Apr 84, MZ, And In The End!	0.60	0.30	0.75	1.50
❑131, May 84, If This Be Walrus...!	0.60	0.20	0.50	1.00
❑132, Jun 84, DP, The Phantom Of Gamma-Ray Flats!	0.60	0.20	0.50	1.00
❑133, Jul 84, 1: Manslaughter (cameo)	0.60	0.20	0.50	1.00
❑134, Aug 84, DP, Manslaughter!, 1: Manslaughter (full appearance)	0.60	0.20	0.50	1.00
❑135, Sep 84, DP, The Fire At Heaven's Gate!	0.60	0.20	0.50	1.00
❑136, Oct 84, DP, Bodies And Souls!	0.60	0.20	0.50	1.00
❑137, Nov 84, DP, Hearts And Minds!	0.60	0.20	0.50	1.00
❑138, Dec 84, DP, Three Women, O: Moondragon	0.60	0.20	0.50	1.00
❑139, Jan 85, DP, Hungry Like The Wolf!, Series continues as The New Defenders	0.60	0.20	0.50	1.00
❑140, Feb 85, DP, The Heartbreak Kid!	0.60	0.20	0.50	1.00
❑141, Mar 85	0.60	0.20	0.50	1.00
❑142, Apr 85, DP, M.O.N.S.T.E.R.!	0.65	0.20	0.50	1.00
❑143, May 85, DP, Another Runner..., 1: Andromeda; 1: Dragon of the Moon; 1: Runner; O: Moondragon	0.65	0.20	0.50	1.00
❑144, Jun 85, DP, Dragon Midnight	0.65	0.20	0.50	1.00
❑145, Jul 85, A: Johnny Blaze	0.65	0.20	0.50	1.00
❑146, Aug 85, LMc, Fun!	0.65	0.20	0.50	1.00
❑147, Sep 85, DP, ...And Games!, Sgt. Fury and His Howling Defenders on both cover and in indicia	0.65	0.20	0.50	1.00
❑148, Oct 85, SB, The Kickshaws Consignment	0.65	0.20	0.50	1.00
❑149, Nov 85, DP, Lonely An A Cloud-!, O: Andromeda	0.65	0.20	0.50	1.00
❑150, Dec 85, DP, The Stars In Their Courses!, O: Cloud, double-sized	1.25	0.20	0.50	1.00
❑151, Jan 86, DP, Second Degree Manslaughter	0.65	0.20	0.50	1.00
❑152, Feb 86, DP, Secret Wars II, O: Manslaughter, Final Issue; double-sized; Secret Wars II	1.25	0.20	0.50	1.00
❑Anl 1, Nov 76, JSn, O: Hulk	0.50	1.20	3.00	6.00
❑GS 1, JSn, The Way They Were!; Banished To Outer Space, A: Silver Surfer	0.50	1.20	3.00	6.00
❑GS 2	0.50	0.80	2.00	4.00
❑GS 3, DA; JM; JSn; DN, Games Godlings Play!;, 1: Korvac	0.50	0.80	2.00	4.00
❑GS 4, DH, Too Cold A Night For Dying!	0.50	0.80	2.00	4.00
❑GS 5, DH, Eelar Moves Mysterious Ways!	0.50	0.80	2.00	4.00

DEFENDERS (VOL. 2)
MARVEL

Value: Cover or less

❑1, Mar 01, EL, KB (w), Once More, The End of the World ..., A: Nighthawk; A: Sub-Mariner; A: Hellcat; A: Silver Surfer; A: Doctor Strange; A: Hulk	2.99
❑2, Apr 01, EL, KB (w), The Curse	2.25
❑3, May 01, EL, KB (w), The Armies of the Slain	2.25
❑4	2.25
❑5	2.25
❑6	2.25
❑7	2.25

DEFENDERS OF DYNATRON CITY
MARVEL

Value: Cover or less

❑1, Feb 92	1.25
❑2, Mar 92	1.25
❑3, Apr 92	1.25
❑4, May 92	1.25
❑5, Jun 92, This Island: Radium	1.25
❑6, Jul 92	1.25

DEFENDERS OF THE EARTH
MARVEL

	ORIG	GOOD	FINE	N-MINT
❑1, Jan 87, Flash Gordon, Mandrake, Phantom	0.75	0.20	0.50	1.00
❑2, Mar 87, Flash Gordon, Mandrake, Phantom	0.75	0.20	0.50	1.00
❑3, May 87, Flash Gordon, Mandrake, Phantom	0.75	0.20	0.50	1.00
❑4, Jul 87, Final Issue	1.00	0.20	0.50	1.00

DEFENSELESS DEAD, THE
ADVENTURE

Value: Cover or less

❑1, Feb 91, b&w; based on Larry Niven story	2.50
❑2, b&w; based on Larry Niven story	2.50
❑3, b&w; based on Larry Niven story	2.50

DEFIANT GENESIS
DEFIANT

	ORIG	GOOD	FINE	N-MINT
❑1, Oct 93, no cover price	—	0.20	0.50	1.00

DEFINITION
SLAVE LABOR

Value: Cover or less

❑1, Aug 97, nn; b&w; Oversized	12.95

DEITY (VOL. 1)
IMAGE

Value: Cover or less

❑0, May 98, Flip cover; exclusive New Dimension Comics edition	6.00
❑0/A, May 98	2.95
❑1, White background on cover	2.95
❑1/A, variant cover	2.95
❑2, Regular cover (power blasts)	2.95
❑2/A, variant cover; Brandishing gun, sword	2.95
❑3, Regular cover (brown background, bandages on face)	2.95
❑3/A, variant cover; Cyborg girl	2.95
❑4	2.95
❑4/A, variant cover	2.95
❑5, Feb 98	2.95
❑5/A, variant cover	2.95
❑6, Girl with backpack on cover	2.95
❑6/A, variant cover	2.95

DEITY (VOL. 2)
IMAGE

Value: Cover or less

❑1, Sep 98, Flipbook preview of Catseye	2.95
❑1/A, Sep 98, Variant cover with blue background, wielding sword	2.95
❑1/B, Sep 98, Variant cover with monster threatening	2.95
❑1/C, Sep 98, Variant cover with gratuitous bathing suit, cleavage	2.95
❑2, Nov 98	2.95
❑3, Jan 99	2.95
❑4, Jan 99	2.95
❑5, May 99	2.95
❑Ash 1, Jun 98, Special Preview edition	2.95

DEITY: REVELATIONS
IMAGE

Value: Cover or less

❑1, Jul 99, Woman on floating skateboard, figures in background	2.95
❑1/A, Jul 99, variant cover: woman holding her face on cover	2.95
❑1/B, Jul 99, variant cover	2.95
❑2, Sep 99, variant cover	2.95
❑3, Nov 99	2.95
❑4	2.95

DEJA VU
FANTACO

Value: Cover or less

❑1, BWr	2.95

DELIA CHARM
RED MENACE

Value: Cover or less

❑1	2.95
❑2	2.95

DELIRIUM
METRO

Value: Cover or less

❑1	2.00

DELTA SQUADRON
ANDERPOL

Value: Cover or less

❑1	2.00

DELTA TENN
ENTERTAINMENT

Value: Cover or less

❑1, Jul 87	1.50
❑2, Sep 87	1.50
❑3, Nov 87	1.50
❑4, Jan 88	1.50
❑5, Mar 88	1.50
❑6, May 88	1.50
❑7, Jul 88	1.50
❑8, Sep 88	1.50
❑9, b&w	1.50
❑10, b&w	1.50

DELTA, THE ULTIMATE DIFFERENCE
APEX ONE

	ORIG	GOOD	FINE	N-MINT
❑1, Oct 97, b&w; no cover price	—	0.40	1.00	2.00
❑2, Fal 98, b&w; cardstock cover	2.95	0.59	1.48	2.95

DEMENTED: SCORPION CHILD
DMF

Value: Cover or less

❑1, Nov 00, Boiling Water Clean	2.95
❑2	2.95
❑3	2.95
❑4	2.95
❑5	2.95

DEMI'S WILD KINGDOM ADVENTURE
OPUS

Value: Cover or less

❑1, Mar 00, b&w; adult; squarebound	9.95

DEMI THE DEMONESS
RIP OFF
Value: Cover or less

- ❑1, Mar 93 ... 2.95
- ❑2, Nov 93 ... 2.95
- ❑3, Mar 95, flip-book with Kit-Ra back-up ... 2.95
- ❑4, 1: Imed the Angelic ... 3.25
- ❑SE 1, "Choose your own adventure"-style special ... 5.95

DEMOLITION MAN
DC
Value: Cover or less

- ❑1, Nov 93, Send a Maniac to Catch One! ... 1.75
- ❑2, Dec 93 ... 1.75
- ❑3, Jan 94, The Man Who Remade The World! ... 1.75
- ❑4, Feb 94 ... 1.75

DEMON, THE (1ST SERIES)
DC

	ORIG	GOOD	FINE	N-MINT
❑1, Sep 72, JK, 1: Randu Singh; 1: Etrigan; 1: Jason Blood	0.20	2.00	5.00	10.00
❑2, Oct 72, JK	0.20	1.20	3.00	6.00
❑3, Nov 72, JK, JK (w), Batman	0.20	1.00	2.50	5.00
❑4, Dec 72, JK	0.20	1.00	2.50	5.00
❑5, Jan 73, JK	0.20	0.80	2.00	4.00
❑6, Feb 73, JK	0.20	0.80	2.00	4.00
❑7, Mar 73, JK, 1: Klarion the Witch Boy	0.20	0.80	2.00	4.00
❑8, Apr 73, JK	0.20	0.80	2.00	4.00
❑9, Jun 73, JK	0.20	0.80	2.00	4.00
❑10, Jul 73, JK	0.20	0.80	2.00	4.00
❑11, Aug 73, JK	0.20	0.80	2.00	4.00
❑12, Sep 73, JK	0.20	0.80	2.00	4.00
❑13, Oct 73, JK	0.20	0.80	2.00	4.00
❑14, Nov 73, JK	0.20	0.80	2.00	4.00
❑15, Dec 73, JK	0.20	0.80	2.00	4.00
❑16, Jan 74, JK	0.20	0.80	2.00	4.00

DEMON, THE (2ND SERIES)
DC

	ORIG	GOOD	FINE	N-MINT
❑1, Jan 87, MW, MW (w), Direction From The Darkness	0.75	0.30	0.75	1.50
❑2, Feb 87, MW	0.75	0.20	0.50	1.00
❑3, Mar 87, MW	0.75	0.20	0.50	1.00
❑4, Apr 87, MW, MW (w), Begins Our Tale of Woe	0.75	0.20	0.50	1.00

DEMON, THE (3RD SERIES)
DC

	ORIG	GOOD	FINE	N-MINT
❑0, Oct 94, O: Etrigan; O: Jason Blood	1.95	0.40	1.00	2.00
❑1, Jul 90, Lost Souls	1.50	0.80	2.00	4.00
❑2, Aug 90	1.50	0.50	1.25	2.50
❑3, Sep 90, Batman	1.50	0.50	1.25	2.50
❑4, Oct 90	1.50	0.45	1.13	2.25
❑5, Nov 90	1.50	0.45	1.13	2.25
❑6, Dec 90	1.50	0.45	1.13	2.25
❑7, Jan 91	1.50	0.45	1.13	2.25
❑8, Feb 91, Batman	1.50	0.45	1.13	2.25
❑9, Mar 91	1.50	0.45	1.13	2.25
❑10, Apr 91	1.50	0.45	1.13	2.25
❑11, May 91	1.50	0.60	1.50	3.00
❑12, Jun 91, A: Lobo	1.50	0.50	1.25	2.50
❑13, Jul 91, A: Lobo	1.50	0.50	1.25	2.50
❑14, Aug 91, A: Lobo	1.50	0.50	1.25	2.50
❑15, Sep 91, A: Lobo	1.50	0.50	1.25	2.50
❑16, Oct 91	1.50	0.40	1.00	2.00
❑17, Nov 91, War of the Gods, Part 19, War of the Gods	1.50	0.40	1.00	2.00
❑18, Dec 91	1.50	0.40	1.00	2.00
❑19, Jan 92, poster; Double-size; Lobo poster	2.50	0.50	1.25	2.50
❑20, Feb 92	1.50	0.40	1.00	2.00
❑21, Mar 92	1.50	0.40	1.00	2.00
❑22, Apr 92	1.50	0.40	1.00	2.00
❑23, May 92, Robin	1.50	0.40	1.00	2.00
❑24, Jun 92, Robin	1.50	0.40	1.00	2.00
❑25, Jul 92	1.50	0.30	0.75	1.50
❑26, Aug 92	1.50	0.30	0.75	1.50
❑27, Sep 92	1.50	0.30	0.75	1.50
❑28, Oct 92, Superman	1.75	0.30	0.75	1.50
❑29, Nov 92	1.75	0.35	0.88	1.75
❑30, Dec 92	1.75	0.35	0.88	1.75
❑31, Jan 93	1.75	0.35	0.88	1.75
❑32, Feb 93	1.75	0.35	0.88	1.75
❑33, Mar 93	1.75	0.35	0.88	1.75
❑34, Apr 93, Lobo	1.75	0.35	0.88	1.75
❑35, May 93, Lobo	1.75	0.35	0.88	1.75
❑36, Jun 93	1.75	0.35	0.88	1.75
❑37, Jul 93	1.75	0.35	0.88	1.75
❑38, Aug 93	1.75	0.35	0.88	1.75
❑39, Sep 93	1.75	0.35	0.88	1.75
❑40, Oct 93	1.75	0.35	0.88	1.75
❑41, Nov 93, Castle of the Damned	1.75	0.35	0.88	1.75
❑42, Dec 93	1.75	0.35	0.88	1.75

Moondragon's origins were revealed in *Defenders* (Vol. 1) #143.

	ORIG	GOOD	FINE	N-MINT
❑43, Jan 94, A: Hitman	1.75	1.60	4.00	8.00
❑44, Feb 94, A: Hitman	1.75	1.60	4.00	8.00
❑45, Mar 94, A: Hitman	1.75	1.60	4.00	8.00
❑46, Apr 94, A: Haunted Tank	1.75	0.35	0.88	1.75
❑47, May 94, A: Haunted Tank	1.75	0.35	0.88	1.75
❑48, Jun 94	1.75	0.39	0.98	1.95
❑49, Jul 94	1.95	0.39	0.98	1.95
❑50, Aug 94, 50th anniversary issue; Giant-size	2.95	0.59	1.48	2.95
❑51, Sep 94	1.95	0.39	0.98	1.95
❑52, Nov 94, Suffer the Children, Part 1, A: Hitman	1.95	0.39	0.98	1.95
❑53, Dec 94, Suffer the Children, Part 2, A: Hitman	1.95	0.39	0.98	1.95
❑54, Jan 95, Suffer the Children, Part 3, A: Hitman	1.95	0.39	0.98	1.95
❑55, Feb 95	1.95	0.39	0.98	1.95
❑56, Mar 95	1.95	0.39	0.98	1.95
❑57, Apr 95	1.95	0.39	0.98	1.95
❑58, May 95, Final Issue	1.95	0.39	0.98	1.95
❑Anl 1, Eclipso: The Darkness Within, Part 7, Eclipso	3.00	0.60	1.50	3.00
❑Anl 2, Bloodlines, 1: Hitman	3.50	2.40	6.00	12.00

DEMON BEAST INVASION
CPM
Value: Cover or less

- ❑1, Oct 96, b&w; adult; wrap-around cover ... 2.95

DEMON BEAST INVASION: THE FALLEN
CPM
Value: Cover or less

- ❑1, Sep 98, b&w; adult ... 2.95
- ❑2, Oct 98, b&w; adult ... 2.95

DEMONBLADE
NEW COMICS
Value: Cover or less

- ❑1, b&w ... 1.95

DEMON DREAMS
PACIFIC
Value: Cover or less

- ❑1, Feb 84, Bad Breath; Christmas Carol ... 1.50
- ❑2, May 84, The Toll Bridge; Mama's Place ... 1.50

DEMONGATE
SIRIUS
Value: Cover or less

- ❑1, May 96 ... 2.50
- ❑2, Jun 96 ... 2.50
- ❑3, Jul 96 ... 2.50
- ❑4 ... 2.50
- ❑5 ... 2.50
- ❑6 ... 2.50
- ❑7 ... 2.50
- ❑8, Jan 97 ... 2.50
- ❑9, Feb 97, b&w ... 2.50

DEMON GUN
CRUSADE
Value: Cover or less

- ❑1, Jun 96, To Whom Vengeance Belong, b&w ... 2.95
- ❑2, Sep 96, b&w ... 2.95
- ❑3, Jan 97, b&w ... 2.95

DEMON-HUNTER
ATLAS

	ORIG	GOOD	FINE	N-MINT
❑1, Sep 75, RB, RB (w), The Harvester of Eyes!, 1: Gideon Cross	0.25	0.40	1.00	2.00

DEMON HUNTER (AIRCEL)
AIRCEL
Value: Cover or less

- ❑1, Mar 89, b&w ... 1.95
- ❑2, Apr 89, b&w ... 1.95
- ❑3, May 89, b&w ... 1.95
- ❑4, Jun 89, b&w ... 1.95

DEMON HUNTER (DAVDEZ)
DAVDEZ
Value: Cover or less

- ❑1, Aug 98 ... 2.50

DEMONIC TOYS
ETERNITY
Value: Cover or less

- ❑1, Jan 92 ... 2.50
- ❑2 ... 2.50
- ❑3 ... 2.50
- ❑4 ... 2.50

DEMONIQUE
LONDON NIGHT
Value: Cover or less

- ❑1, Oct 94, b&w ... 3.00
- ❑2 ... 3.00
- ❑3 ... 3.00
- ❑4 ... 3.00

DEMON REALM
MEDEIA

Value: Cover or less

- ❑0 .... 2.50

DEMONS & DARK ELVES
WEIRDWORX

Value: Cover or less

- ❑1, b&w 2.95

DEMON'S BLOOD
ODYSSEY

	ORIG	GOOD	FINE	N-MINT
❑1	1.70	0.40	1.00	2.00

DEMONSLAYER
IMAGE

Value: Cover or less

- ❑1, Nov 99, Jaklyn's Tale, Part 1 .... 2.95
- ❑2, Dec 99, Jaklyn's Tale, Part 2 .... 2.95
- ❑3, Jan 00, Jaklyn's Tale, Part 3 .... 2.95

DEMONSLAYER (VOL. 2)
IMAGE

Value: Cover or less

- ❑1, Into Hell, Part 1 .... 2.95
- ❑2, Into Hell, Part 2 .... 2.95
- ❑3, Aug 00, Into Hell, Part 3 .... 2.95

DEMON'S TAILS
ADVENTURE

Value: Cover or less

- ❑1, b&w 2.50
- ❑2, b&w 2.50
- ❑3, b&w 2.50
- ❑4, b&w 2.50

DEMON WARRIOR, THE
EASTERN

Value: Cover or less

- ❑1, Aug 87, b&w 1.50
- ❑2, b&w 1.50
- ❑3, b&w 1.50
- ❑4, b&w 1.50

DEN
FANTAGOR

	ORIG	GOOD	FINE	N-MINT
❑1	2.00	0.60	1.50	3.00
❑2	2.00	0.60	1.50	3.00
❑3	2.00	0.60	1.50	3.00
❑4	2.00	0.60	1.50	3.00
❑5	2.00	0.60	1.50	3.00
❑6, Den, Giant Below; Hunter	2.00	0.50	1.25	2.50
❑7, Den, The Phoenix Fallen; Sea Serpents	2.00	0.50	1.25	2.50
❑8, Shuffled Seeds Scattered; The Cure	2.00	0.50	1.25	2.50
❑9, Strange Nativity; The Drinkers of Dust	2.00	0.50	1.25	2.50
❑10	2.00	0.50	1.25	2.50

DENIZENS OF DEEP CITY
KITCHEN SINK

Value: Cover or less

- ❑1, b&w 2.00
- ❑2, b&w 2.00
- ❑3, b&w 2.00
- ❑4, b&w 2.00
- ❑5, b&w 2.00
- ❑6, b&w 2.00
- ❑7, b&w 2.00
- ❑8, b&w 2.00
- ❑9 .... 2.00

DENNIS THE MENACE (FAWCETT)
STANDARD

	ORIG	GOOD	FINE	N-MINT
❑109, Jul 70	0.15	0.80	2.00	4.00
❑110, Sep 70	0.15	0.80	2.00	4.00
❑111, Nov 70	0.15	0.80	2.00	4.00
❑112, Jan 71	0.15	0.80	2.00	4.00
❑113, Mar 71	0.15	0.80	2.00	4.00
❑114, May 71	0.15	0.80	2.00	4.00
❑115, Jul 71	0.15	0.80	2.00	4.00
❑116, Sep 71, anti-pollution issue	0.15	0.80	2.00	4.00
❑117, Nov 71	0.15	0.80	2.00	4.00
❑118, Jan 72	—	0.80	2.00	4.00
❑119, Mar 72	—	0.80	2.00	4.00
❑120, May 72	0.25	0.80	2.00	4.00
❑121, Jul 72	0.25	0.60	1.50	3.00
❑122, Sep 72, Spirit of '72	0.25	0.60	1.50	3.00
❑123, Nov 72	0.25	0.60	1.50	3.00
❑124, Jan 73	—	0.60	1.50	3.00
❑125, Mar 73	—	0.60	1.50	3.00
❑126, May 73, A: Gina	0.25	0.60	1.50	3.00
❑127, Jul 73	—	0.60	1.50	3.00
❑128, Sep 73	—	0.60	1.50	3.00
❑129, Nov 73	0.25	0.60	1.50	3.00
❑130, Jan 74	0.25	0.60	1.50	3.00
❑131, Mar 74	0.25	0.60	1.50	3.00
❑132, May 74	—	0.60	1.50	3.00
❑133, Jul 74	0.25	0.60	1.50	3.00
❑134, Sep 74	—	0.60	1.50	3.00
❑135, Nov 74	—	0.60	1.50	3.00
❑136, Jan 75	—	0.60	1.50	3.00
❑137, Mar 75	—	0.60	1.50	3.00
❑138, May 75	—	0.60	1.50	3.00
❑139, Jul 75	—	0.60	1.50	3.00
❑140, Sep 75, at Winchester mansion	0.25	0.60	1.50	3.00
❑141, Nov 75	—	0.40	1.00	2.00
❑142, Jan 76	—	0.40	1.00	2.00
❑143, Mar 76	—	0.40	1.00	2.00
❑144, May 76	—	0.40	1.00	2.00
❑145, Jun 76	0.30	0.40	1.00	2.00
❑146, Jul 76	0.30	0.40	1.00	2.00
❑147, Sep 76	0.30	0.40	1.00	2.00
❑148, Nov 76	0.30	0.40	1.00	2.00
❑149, Jan 77	—	0.40	1.00	2.00
❑150, Mar 77	—	0.40	1.00	2.00
❑151, May 77	0.35	0.40	1.00	2.00
❑152, Jul 77	0.35	0.40	1.00	2.00
❑153, Sep 77	0.35	0.40	1.00	2.00
❑154, Nov 77	—	0.40	1.00	2.00
❑155, Jan 78	—	0.40	1.00	2.00
❑156, Mar 78	0.35	0.40	1.00	2.00
❑157, May 78	—	0.40	1.00	2.00
❑158, Jul 78	—	0.40	1.00	2.00
❑159, Sep 78, Welcome to the Pumpkin Festival; The Week Watcher	0.35	0.40	1.00	2.00
❑160, Nov 78	—	0.40	1.00	2.00
❑161, Jan 79	—	0.40	1.00	2.00
❑162, Mar 79	0.40	0.40	1.00	2.00
❑163, May 79	—	0.40	1.00	2.00
❑164, Jul 79	0.40	0.40	1.00	2.00
❑165	—	0.40	1.00	2.00
❑166, Final Issue	—	0.40	1.00	2.00

DENNIS THE MENACE (MARVEL)
MARVEL

	ORIG	GOOD	FINE	N-MINT
❑1, Nov 81	0.50	0.40	1.00	2.00
❑2, Dec 81	0.50	0.30	0.75	1.50
❑3, Jan 82	0.60	0.30	0.75	1.50
❑4, Feb 82	0.60	0.30	0.75	1.50
❑5, Mar 82	0.60	0.30	0.75	1.50
❑6, Apr 82	0.60	0.30	0.75	1.50
❑7, May 82	0.60	0.30	0.75	1.50
❑8, Jun 82	0.60	0.30	0.75	1.50
❑9, Jul 82	0.60	0.30	0.75	1.50
❑10, Aug 82	0.60	0.30	0.75	1.50
❑11, Sep 82	0.60	0.30	0.75	1.50
❑12, Oct 82	0.60	0.30	0.75	1.50
❑13, Nov 82	0.60	0.30	0.75	1.50

DENNIS THE MENACE AND HIS FRIENDS
FAWCETT

	ORIG	GOOD	FINE	N-MINT
❑1, ...and Joey (#2 on cover)	—	2.00	5.00	10.00
❑2, ...and Ruff (#2 on cover)	—	2.00	5.00	10.00
❑3, ...and Mr. Wilson (#1 on cover)	—	2.00	5.00	10.00
❑4, ...and Margaret (#1 on cover)	—	2.00	5.00	10.00
❑5, Jan 70, ...and Margaret (#5 on cover)	0.15	1.20	3.00	6.00
❑6, Jun 70, Joey	0.15	0.80	2.00	4.00
❑7, Aug 70	0.15	0.80	2.00	4.00
❑8, Oct 70	0.15	0.80	2.00	4.00
❑9, Jan 71	0.15	0.80	2.00	4.00
❑10, Jun 71	0.15	0.80	2.00	4.00
❑11, Aug 71	0.15	0.60	1.50	3.00
❑12, Oct 71, Mr. Wilson	0.15	0.60	1.50	3.00
❑13, Jan 72, Margaret	0.25	0.60	1.50	3.00
❑14, Jun 72	—	0.60	1.50	3.00
❑15, Aug 72, Ruff	0.25	0.60	1.50	3.00
❑16, Oct 72, Mr. Wilson	0.25	0.60	1.50	3.00
❑17, Jan 73	—	0.60	1.50	3.00
❑18, Jun 73, Joey	0.25	0.60	1.50	3.00
❑19, Aug 73, A Full House; Hairy Tale	0.25	0.60	1.50	3.00
❑20, Oct 73	—	0.60	1.50	3.00
❑21, Jan 74	—	0.60	1.50	3.00
❑22, Jun 74, Joey	0.25	0.60	1.50	3.00
❑23, Aug 74	—	0.60	1.50	3.00
❑24, Oct 74	—	0.60	1.50	3.00
❑25, Jan 75	—	0.60	1.50	3.00
❑26, Jun 75	—	0.60	1.50	3.00
❑27, Aug 75	—	0.60	1.50	3.00
❑28, Oct 75	—	0.60	1.50	3.00
❑29, Jan 76, Charge!; Up in the Air, ...and Margaret (#29)	0.30	0.60	1.50	3.00
❑30, Jun 76	—	0.60	1.50	3.00
❑31, Aug 76	0.30	0.50	1.25	2.50
❑32, Oct 76	—	0.50	1.25	2.50
❑33, Jan 77	—	0.50	1.25	2.50
❑34, Jun 77	—	0.50	1.25	2.50
❑35, Aug 77, Ruff	0.35	0.50	1.25	2.50
❑36, Oct 77	—	0.50	1.25	2.50
❑37	—	0.50	1.25	2.50
❑38, Apr 78, digest size begins	0.95	0.50	1.25	2.50
❑39	—	0.50	1.25	2.50
❑40	—	0.50	1.25	2.50
❑41	—	0.50	1.25	2.50
❑42	—	0.50	1.25	2.50

	ORIG	GOOD	FINE	N-MINT
❑43	—	0.50	1.25	2.50
❑44	—	0.50	1.25	2.50
❑45	—	0.50	1.25	2.50
❑46, Apr 80, Final Issue	—	0.50	1.25	2.50

DENNIS THE MENACE BIG BONUS SERIES
FAWCETT

	ORIG	GOOD	FINE	N-MINT
❑10, Feb 80	0.40	0.60	1.50	3.00
❑11, Apr 80	0.40	0.60	1.50	3.00

DENNIS THE MENACE BONUS MAGAZINE SERIES
FAWCETT

	ORIG	GOOD	FINE	N-MINT
❑76, Jan 70, Series continued from Dennis the Menace (Giants) #75	—	1.40	3.50	7.00
❑77, Feb 70	—	1.40	3.50	7.00
❑78, Mar 70	—	1.40	3.50	7.00
❑79, Apr 70	—	1.40	3.50	7.00
❑80, May 70	—	1.40	3.50	7.00
❑81, Jun 70	—	1.40	3.50	7.00
❑82, Jun 70	—	1.40	3.50	7.00
❑83, Jul 70	—	1.40	3.50	7.00
❑84, Jul 70, at the circus	0.25	1.40	3.50	7.00
❑85, Aug 70	0.25	1.40	3.50	7.00
❑86, Oct 70, Christmas	0.25	1.40	3.50	7.00
❑87, Oct 70	—	1.40	3.50	7.00
❑88, Jan 71	—	1.40	3.50	7.00
❑89, Feb 71	—	1.40	3.50	7.00
❑90, Mar 71	—	1.40	3.50	7.00
❑91, Apr 71	—	1.20	3.00	6.00
❑92, May 71	—	1.20	3.00	6.00
❑93, Jun 71	—	1.20	3.00	6.00
❑94, Jun 71	—	1.20	3.00	6.00
❑95, Jul 71, Pitter Patter Painter; Dennis Acts Up	0.35	1.20	3.00	6.00
❑96, Jul 71	0.35	1.20	3.00	6.00
❑97, Aug 71	0.35	1.20	3.00	6.00
❑98, Oct 71, Christmas	0.35	1.20	3.00	6.00
❑99, Oct 71	0.35	1.20	3.00	6.00
❑100, Jan 72	0.35	1.20	3.00	6.00
❑101, Feb 72	0.35	1.20	3.00	6.00
❑102, Mar 72, Wish I Was	0.35	1.20	3.00	6.00
❑103, Apr 72, Short Stuff Special	0.35	1.20	3.00	6.00
❑104, May 72	0.35	1.20	3.00	6.00
❑105, Jun 72	0.35	1.20	3.00	6.00
❑106, Jun 72	0.35	1.20	3.00	6.00
❑107, Jul 72	0.35	1.20	3.00	6.00
❑108, Jul 72	0.35	1.20	3.00	6.00
❑109, Aug 72	0.35	1.20	3.00	6.00
❑110, Oct 72, Christmas	0.35	1.20	3.00	6.00
❑111, Oct 72, Christmas	0.35	1.20	3.00	6.00
❑112, Jan 73, Go-Go Special	0.35	1.20	3.00	6.00
❑113, Feb 73, Tangled Tales	0.35	1.20	3.00	6.00
❑114, Mar 73, Hawaii	0.35	1.20	3.00	6.00
❑115, Apr 73	—	1.20	3.00	6.00
❑116, May 73	—	1.20	3.00	6.00
❑117, Jun 73	—	1.20	3.00	6.00
❑118, Jun 73	—	1.20	3.00	6.00
❑119, Jul 73, Summer Number and state flags	0.35	1.20	3.00	6.00
❑120, Jul 73	—	1.20	3.00	6.00
❑121, Aug 73, Way-Out Stories	0.35	1.00	2.50	5.00
❑122, Oct 73	—	1.00	2.50	5.00
❑123, Oct 73	—	1.00	2.50	5.00
❑124, Jan 74	—	1.00	2.50	5.00
❑125, Feb 74	—	1.00	2.50	5.00
❑126, Mar 74	—	1.00	2.50	5.00
❑127, Apr 74	—	1.00	2.50	5.00
❑128, May 74	—	1.00	2.50	5.00
❑129, Jun 74	—	1.00	2.50	5.00
❑130, Jun 74	—	1.00	2.50	5.00
❑131, Jul 74	—	1.00	2.50	5.00
❑132, Jul 74	—	1.00	2.50	5.00
❑133, Aug 74	—	1.00	2.50	5.00
❑134, Oct 74, Christmas	0.35	1.00	2.50	5.00
❑135, Oct 74	—	1.00	2.50	5.00
❑136, Jan 75, Crazy Daze	0.35	1.00	2.50	5.00
❑137, Feb 75	—	1.00	2.50	5.00
❑138, Mar 75	—	1.00	2.50	5.00
❑139, Apr 75	—	1.00	2.50	5.00
❑140, May 75, Big Deal	0.35	1.00	2.50	5.00
❑141, Jun 75	—	1.00	2.50	5.00
❑142, Jun 75	—	1.00	2.50	5.00
❑143, Jul 75	—	1.00	2.50	5.00
❑144, Jul 75, Welcome to Washington!; Down in Historic Virginia	0.35	1.00	2.50	5.00
❑145, Aug 75	—	1.00	2.50	5.00
❑146, Oct 75, Christmas	0.35	1.00	2.50	5.00
❑147, Oct 75	0.35	1.00	2.50	5.00
❑148, Jan 76	0.35	1.00	2.50	5.00

Dennis the Menace pointed out the evils of pollution in a special issue in 1971.

© 1971 Publisher-Hall Syndicate (Fawcett)

	ORIG	GOOD	FINE	N-MINT
❑149, Feb 76	0.35	1.00	2.50	5.00
❑150, Mar 76	0.35	1.00	2.50	5.00
❑151, Apr 76	0.35	0.80	2.00	4.00
❑152, May 76	0.35	0.80	2.00	4.00
❑153, Jun 76	0.35	0.80	2.00	4.00
❑154, Jun 76	0.35	0.80	2.00	4.00
❑155, Jul 76	0.35	0.80	2.00	4.00
❑156, Jul 76	0.35	0.80	2.00	4.00
❑157, Aug 76	0.35	0.80	2.00	4.00
❑158, Oct 76	0.35	0.80	2.00	4.00
❑159, Oct 76	0.35	0.80	2.00	4.00
❑160, Jan 77	0.35	0.80	2.00	4.00
❑161	0.35	0.80	2.00	4.00
❑162	0.35	0.80	2.00	4.00
❑163	0.35	0.80	2.00	4.00
❑164	0.35	0.80	2.00	4.00
❑165	0.35	0.80	2.00	4.00
❑166	0.35	0.80	2.00	4.00
❑167, Jun 77	0.35	0.80	2.00	4.00
❑168	—	0.80	2.00	4.00
❑169	—	0.80	2.00	4.00
❑170	—	0.80	2.00	4.00
❑171	—	0.60	1.50	3.00
❑172	—	0.60	1.50	3.00
❑173	—	0.60	1.50	3.00
❑174	—	0.60	1.50	3.00
❑175	—	0.60	1.50	3.00
❑176	—	0.60	1.50	3.00
❑177	—	0.60	1.50	3.00
❑178	—	0.60	1.50	3.00
❑179	—	0.60	1.50	3.00
❑180	—	0.60	1.50	3.00
❑181	—	0.60	1.50	3.00
❑182	—	0.60	1.50	3.00
❑183	—	0.60	1.50	3.00
❑184	—	0.60	1.50	3.00
❑185, Feb 79	0.40	0.60	1.50	3.00
❑186, Mar 79	0.40	0.60	1.50	3.00
❑187	0.40	0.60	1.50	3.00
❑188	0.40	0.60	1.50	3.00
❑189	0.40	0.60	1.50	3.00
❑190	0.40	0.60	1.50	3.00
❑191, Jul 79	0.40	0.60	1.50	3.00
❑192	0.40	0.60	1.50	3.00
❑193	0.40	0.60	1.50	3.00
❑194, Oct 79, Final Issue	0.40	0.60	1.50	3.00

DER VANDALE
INNERVISION

Value: Cover or less

❑1, b&w	2.50	❑2	2.50
❑1/SC, b&w; alternate cover	2.50	❑3	2.50

DESCENDANTS OF TOSHIN
ARROW

Value: Cover or less

❑1, Apr 99, nn; b&w	2.95

DESCENDING ANGELS
MILLENNIUM

Value: Cover or less

❑1, The Arrival; Nothing Good	2.95

DESERT PEACH, THE
THOUGHTS & IMAGES

	ORIG	GOOD	FINE	N-MINT
❑1, b&w; Thoughts & Images publishes	2.00	2.00	5.00	10.00
❑2, b&w	2.00	1.20	3.00	6.00
❑3, b&w	2.00	0.80	2.00	4.00
❑4, Mar 90, b&w	2.00	0.80	2.00	4.00
❑5, b&w; MU Press begins publishing	2.00	0.80	2.00	4.00
❑6, b&w	2.00	0.80	2.00	4.00
❑7	2.25	0.60	1.50	3.00
❑8	2.25	0.60	1.50	3.00
❑9	2.25	0.60	1.50	3.00
❑10	2.50	0.60	1.50	3.00
❑11	2.25	0.60	1.50	3.00
❑12	2.25	0.50	1.25	2.50
❑13	2.50	0.50	1.25	2.50
❑14	2.50	0.50	1.25	2.50

	ORIG	GOOD	FINE	N-MINT
❑15	2.50	0.50	1.25	2.50
❑16	2.50	0.50	1.25	2.50
❑17, b&w; Giant-size	3.95	0.79	1.98	3.95
❑18, b&w	2.50	0.50	1.25	2.50
❑19, b&w; aka Desert Peach: Self-Propelled Target; Aeon begins publishing	4.95	0.99	2.47	4.95
❑20, Sep 93, b&w; aka Desert Peach: Fever Dream	4.95	0.99	2.47	4.95
❑21, Jun 94, b&w	4.95	0.99	2.47	4.95
❑22, Nov 94, b&w	4.95	0.99	2.47	4.95
❑23, Jun 95, b&w; a.k.a. The Desert Peach: Visions	2.95	0.59	1.48	2.95
❑24, Sep 95, b&w; a.k.a. The Desert Peach: Ups and Downs	2.95	0.59	1.48	2.95
❑25	2.95	0.59	1.48	2.95
❑26, b&w; cardstock cover; a.k.a. The Desert Peach: Miki	2.95	0.59	1.48	2.95

DESERT STORM JOURNAL
APPLE

Value: Cover or less

- ❑1, Read My Lips: No More Viet-nams, Hussein on cover 2.75
- ❑1/A, Schwartzkopf on cover.. 2.75
- ❑2, b&w 2.75
- ❑3, b&w 2.75
- ❑4, b&w 2.75
- ❑5, b&w 2.75
- ❑6, b&w 2.75
- ❑7, b&w 2.75
- ❑8, b&w 2.75

DESERT STREAMS
DC

Value: Cover or less

- ❑1 ..... 5.95

DESPERADOES
IMAGE

Value: Cover or less

- ❑1, Sep 97, A Moment's Sunlight 2.50
- ❑1-2, Sep 97, 2nd Printing 2.50
- ❑2, Oct 97, The Gathering Gloom 2.95
- ❑3, Nov 97, Heroes and Villains 2.95
- ❑4, Dec 97, The Dance 2.95
- ❑5, Jun 98, Blankenship's Arm 2.95

DESPERADOES: EPIDEMIC!
DC

Value: Cover or less

- ❑1, Nov 99, nn; prestige format 5.95

DESPERATE TIMES
IMAGE

Value: Cover or less

- ❑1, Jun 98 ..... 2.95
- ❑2, Aug 98 ..... 2.95
- ❑3, Oct 98 ..... 2.95
- ❑4, Dec 98 ..... 2.95

DESTINY: A CHRONICLE OF DEATHS FORETOLD
DC

Value: Cover or less

- ❑1, prestige format 5.95
- ❑2, Black Death, prestige format 5.95
- ❑3, prestige format 5.95

DESTINY ANGEL
DARK FANTASY

Value: Cover or less

- ❑1, Magic Bullet, Part 1 ..... 3.95

DESTROY!!
ECLIPSE

	ORIG	GOOD	FINE	N-MINT
❑1, Nov 86, b&w; oversize	4.95	0.99	2.47	4.95
❑1/3D, 3-D	2.50	0.60	1.50	3.00

DESTROY ALL COMICS
SLAVE LABOR

Value: Cover or less

- ❑1, Nov 94, Oversized 3.50
- ❑2, Feb 95, Oversized 3.50
- ❑3, Aug 95, Oversized 3.50
- ❑4, Jan 96, Oversized 3.50
- ❑5, Apr 96, Oversized 3.50

DESTROYER, THE (MAGAZINE)
MARVEL

Value: Cover or less

- ❑1, Nov 89, His Name is Remo, O: Remo Williams 2.25
- ❑2, Dec 89, Golden Rule 2.25
- ❑3, Dec 89 ..... 2.25
- ❑4, Jan 90, SD, Mass Hysteria; How the Thieving Ninja Came to Be 2.25
- ❑5, Feb 90, The Fist of Gallah; How Remo Came to Sinanju 2.25
- ❑6, Mar 90 ..... 2.25
- ❑7, Apr 90, Stone Killer 2.25
- ❑8, May 90, America is Worth a Life 2.25

DESTROYER, THE (VALIANT)
VALIANT

Value: Cover or less

- ❑1, Apr 95, A Place of Our Own, cover says #0 ..... 2.95

DESTROYER, THE (VOL. 2)
MARVEL

Value: Cover or less

- ❑1, Mar 91, Drive-By Heaven 1.95

DESTROYER, THE (VOL. 3)
MARVEL

Value: Cover or less

- ❑1, Dec 91 ..... 1.95
- ❑2, Jan 92 ..... 1.95
- ❑3, Feb 92 ..... 1.95
- ❑4, Mar 92 ..... 1.95

DESTROYER DUCK
ECLIPSE

	ORIG	GOOD	FINE	N-MINT
❑1, Feb 82, JK; VM; SA, ME (w), It's Got the Whole World In Its Hand!, 1: Destroyer Duck; 1: Groo	1.50	1.00	2.50	5.00
❑2, Jan 83, JK; VM, The Starling, Part 1; Mommie Noises!	1.50	0.30	0.75	1.50
❑3, Jun 83, JK; VM, Pheromones!; The Starling, Part 2	1.50	0.30	0.75	1.50
❑4, Oct 83, JK; VM, The Starling, Part 3	1.50	0.30	0.75	1.50
❑5, Dec 83, JK; VM, Shatterer of Worlds!; The Starling, Part 4	1.50	0.30	0.75	1.50
❑6, Mar 84, VM, The Starling, Part 5	1.50	0.30	0.75	1.50
❑7, May 84, VM, The Vault of Virus!; The Starling, Part 6, Final Issue	1.50	0.30	0.75	1.50

DESTRUCTOR, THE
ATLAS

	ORIG	GOOD	FINE	N-MINT
❑1, Feb 75, WW; SD, ..The Birth Of A Hero, O: Destructor	0.25	0.40	1.00	2.00
❑2, Apr 75, SD	0.25	0.30	0.75	1.50
❑3, Jun 75, SD	0.25	0.30	0.75	1.50
❑4, Aug 75	0.25	0.30	0.75	1.50

DETECTIVE, THE: CHRONICLES OF MAX FACCIONI
CALIBER

Value: Cover or less

- ❑1, The Punch 2.95

DETECTIVE COMICS
DC

	ORIG	GOOD	FINE	N-MINT
❑0, Oct 94, Choice Of Weapons, O: Batman; O: Batmobile; O: Batarangs	1.50	0.50	1.25	2.50
❑287, Jan 61, O: Martian Manhunter	0.10	20.00	50.00	100.00
❑288, Feb 61	0.10	20.00	50.00	100.00
❑289, Mar 61	0.10	20.00	50.00	100.00
❑290, Apr 61	0.10	20.00	50.00	100.00
❑291, May 61	0.10	20.00	50.00	100.00
❑292, Jun 61, A: Batwoman	0.10	20.00	50.00	100.00
❑293, Jul 61	0.10	20.00	50.00	100.00
❑294, Aug 61	0.10	20.00	50.00	100.00
❑295, Sep 61	0.10	20.00	50.00	100.00
❑296, Oct 61	0.10	20.00	50.00	100.00
❑297, Nov 61	0.10	20.00	50.00	100.00
❑298, Dec 61, 1: Clayface II (Matt Hagen) .	0.12	45.00	112.50	225.00
❑299, Jan 62	0.12	14.00	35.00	70.00
❑300, Feb 62	0.12	14.00	35.00	70.00
❑301, Mar 62	0.12	13.00	32.50	65.00
❑302, Apr 62, A: Batwoman	0.12	10.80	27.00	54.00
❑303, May 62	0.12	10.80	27.00	54.00
❑304, Jun 62	0.12	10.80	27.00	54.00
❑305, Jul 62	0.12	10.80	27.00	54.00
❑306, Aug 62	0.12	10.80	27.00	54.00
❑307, Sep 62, A: Batwoman	0.12	10.80	27.00	54.00
❑308, Oct 62	0.12	10.80	27.00	54.00
❑309, Nov 62, A: Batwoman	0.12	10.80	27.00	54.00
❑310, Dec 62	0.12	10.80	27.00	54.00
❑311, Jan 63, A: Batwoman; 1: Cat-Man (DC)	0.12	10.80	27.00	54.00
❑312, Feb 63	0.12	10.80	27.00	54.00
❑313, Mar 63	0.12	10.80	27.00	54.00
❑314, Apr 63	0.12	10.80	27.00	54.00
❑315, May 63	0.12	10.80	27.00	54.00
❑316, Jun 63	0.12	10.80	27.00	54.00
❑317, Jul 63	0.12	10.80	27.00	54.00
❑318, Aug 63, A: Batwoman	0.12	10.80	27.00	54.00
❑319, Sep 63	0.12	10.80	27.00	54.00
❑320, Oct 63	0.12	10.80	27.00	54.00
❑321, Nov 63, A: Batwoman	0.12	10.80	27.00	54.00
❑322, Dec 63	0.12	10.80	27.00	54.00
❑323, Jan 64	0.12	10.80	27.00	54.00
❑324, Feb 64	0.12	10.80	27.00	54.00
❑325, Mar 64, A: Batwoman	0.12	10.80	27.00	54.00
❑326, Apr 64	0.12	10.80	27.00	54.00
❑327, May 64, CI, 25th anniversary; symbol change; 300th Batman in Detective Comics	0.12	15.00	37.50	75.00
❑328, Jun 64, D: Alfred	0.12	17.00	42.50	85.00
❑329, Jul 64	0.12	8.00	20.00	40.00
❑330, Aug 64	0.12	8.00	20.00	40.00
❑331, Sep 64	0.12	7.00	17.50	35.00
❑332, Oct 64, A: Joker	0.12	7.60	19.00	38.00
❑333, Nov 64	0.12	6.00	15.00	30.00
❑334, Dec 64, A: Joker	0.12	6.00	15.00	30.00
❑335, Jan 65	0.12	6.00	15.00	30.00
❑336, Feb 65	0.12	6.00	15.00	30.00
❑337, Mar 65	0.12	6.00	15.00	30.00
❑338, Apr 65	0.12	6.00	15.00	30.00
❑339, May 65	0.12	6.00	15.00	30.00
❑340, Jun 65	0.12	6.00	15.00	30.00
❑341, Jul 65, A: Joker	0.12	8.00	20.00	40.00

	ORIG	GOOD	FINE	N-MINT
❑342, Aug 65	0.12	6.00	15.00	30.00
❑343, Sep 65	0.12	5.60	14.00	28.00
❑344, Oct 65	0.12	5.60	14.00	28.00
❑345, Nov 65, 1: Blockbuster	0.12	5.60	14.00	28.00
❑346, Dec 65	0.12	5.60	14.00	28.00
❑347, Jan 66	0.12	5.60	14.00	28.00
❑348, Feb 66	0.12	5.60	14.00	28.00
❑349, Mar 66	0.12	5.60	14.00	28.00
❑350, Apr 66	0.12	5.60	14.00	28.00
❑351, May 66, 1: Cluemaster	0.12	5.60	14.00	28.00
❑352, Jun 66, Elongated Man back-up	0.12	5.60	14.00	28.00
❑353, Jul 66	0.12	5.60	14.00	28.00
❑354, Aug 66, 1: Doctor Tzin-Tzin	0.12	5.60	14.00	28.00
❑355, Sep 66	0.12	5.60	14.00	28.00
❑356, Oct 66, Alfred returns	0.12	5.60	14.00	28.00
❑357, Nov 66	0.12	5.60	14.00	28.00
❑358, Dec 66, 1: Spellbinder	0.12	5.60	14.00	28.00
❑359, Jan 67, 1: Batgirl (Barbara Gordon)	0.12	15.00	37.50	75.00
❑360, Feb 67	0.12	5.60	14.00	28.00
❑361, Mar 67	0.12	5.60	14.00	28.00
❑362, Apr 67, A: Riddler	0.12	5.60	14.00	28.00
❑363, May 67, A: Batgirl (Barbara Gordon)	0.12	5.60	14.00	28.00
❑364, Jun 67, A: Batgirl (Barbara Gordon)	0.12	5.60	14.00	28.00
❑365, Jul 67, A: Joker	0.12	8.00	20.00	40.00
❑366, Aug 67	0.12	5.60	14.00	28.00
❑367, Sep 67	0.12	5.60	14.00	28.00
❑368, Oct 67	0.12	5.60	14.00	28.00
❑369, Nov 67, NA, Robin teams with Batgirl; Elongated Man back-up	0.12	8.80	22.00	44.00
❑370, Dec 67, BK; GK, Elongated Man	0.12	5.60	14.00	28.00
❑371, Jan 68, A: Batgirl (Barbara Gordon)	0.12	5.60	14.00	28.00
❑372, Feb 68	0.12	4.40	11.00	22.00
❑373, Mar 68, A: Riddler	0.12	4.40	11.00	22.00
❑374, Apr 68	0.12	4.40	11.00	22.00
❑375, May 68	0.12	4.40	11.00	22.00
❑376, Jun 68, Elongated Man back-up	0.12	4.40	11.00	22.00
❑377, Jul 68	0.12	4.40	11.00	22.00
❑378, Aug 68	0.12	4.40	11.00	22.00
❑379, Sep 68	0.12	4.40	11.00	22.00
❑380, Oct 68	0.12	4.40	11.00	22.00
❑381, Nov 68	0.12	4.40	11.00	22.00
❑382, Dec 68	0.12	4.40	11.00	22.00
❑383, Jan 69	0.12	4.40	11.00	22.00
❑384, Feb 69	0.12	4.40	11.00	22.00
❑385, Mar 69	0.12	4.40	11.00	22.00
❑386, Apr 69	0.12	4.40	11.00	22.00
❑387, May 69, 1: Batman, Reprints Detective Comics #27	0.12	9.00	22.50	45.00
❑388, Jun 69, A: Joker	0.15	5.00	12.50	25.00
❑389, Jul 69	0.15	3.20	8.00	16.00
❑390, Aug 69	0.15	3.20	8.00	16.00
❑391, Sep 69	0.15	2.60	6.50	13.00
❑392, Oct 69, GK; MA, FR (w), The Gal Most Likely to Be...Batman's Widow!; Robin: Strike!, 1: Jason Bard	0.15	2.60	6.50	13.00
❑393, Nov 69	0.15	2.60	6.50	13.00
❑394, Dec 69	0.15	2.60	6.50	13.00
❑395, Jan 70, GK; NA; DG; MA	0.15	4.00	10.00	20.00
❑396, Feb 70, GK, NA (c), A: Batgirl	0.15	2.60	6.50	13.00
❑397, Mar 70, NA	0.15	4.00	10.00	20.00
❑398, Apr 70	0.15	2.60	6.50	13.00
❑399, May 70	0.15	2.60	6.50	13.00
❑400, Jun 70, NA; GC, 1: Man-Bat	0.15	9.00	22.50	45.00
❑401, Jul 70	0.15	2.00	5.00	10.00
❑402, Aug 70, NA	0.15	4.00	10.00	20.00
❑403, Sep 70, GK, NA (c), Robin	0.15	2.00	5.00	10.00
❑404, Oct 70, GK; NA; DG, Batgirl	0.15	3.60	9.00	18.00
❑405, Nov 70	0.15	2.00	5.00	10.00
❑406, Dec 70	0.15	2.00	5.00	10.00
❑407, Jan 71, NA, A: Man-Bat	0.15	4.00	10.00	20.00
❑408, Feb 71, NA	0.15	4.00	10.00	20.00
❑409, Mar 71, IN; DG, NA (c)	0.15	2.00	5.00	10.00
❑410, Apr 71, NA; DG; DH, Batgirl	0.15	4.00	10.00	20.00
❑411, May 71, 1: Talia	0.15	2.00	5.00	10.00
❑412, Jun 71	0.15	2.00	5.00	10.00
❑413, Jul 71	0.15	2.00	5.00	10.00
❑414, Aug 71, Giant-size	0.15	2.00	5.00	10.00
❑415, Sep 71, Giant-size	0.25	2.00	5.00	10.00
❑416, Oct 71, Giant-size	0.25	2.00	5.00	10.00
❑417, Nov 71, Giant-size	0.25	2.00	5.00	10.00
❑418, Dec 71, Giant-size	0.25	2.00	5.00	10.00
❑419, Jan 72, Giant-size	0.25	2.00	5.00	10.00
❑420, Feb 72, Giant-size	0.25	2.00	5.00	10.00
❑421, Mar 72, DH, Giant-size; Batgirl story	0.25	2.00	5.00	10.00
❑422, Apr 72, Giant-size	0.25	2.00	5.00	10.00

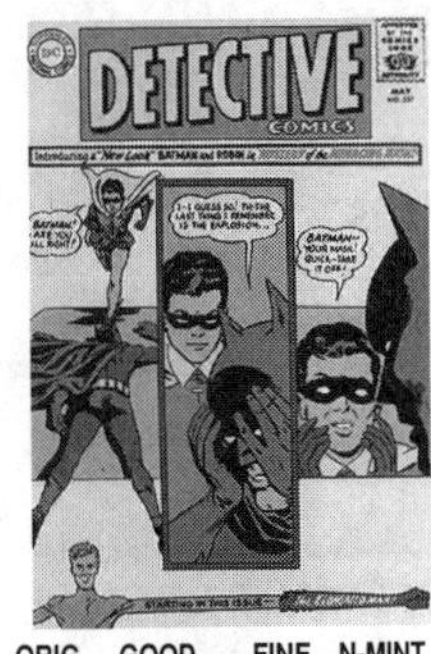

For the character's 25th anniversary, DC Editor Julius Schwartz added a yellow oval to the front of Batman's costume in *Detective Comics* #327.

	ORIG	GOOD	FINE	N-MINT
❑423, May 72, Giant-size	0.25	2.00	5.00	10.00
❑424, Jun 72, Giant-size	0.25	2.00	5.00	10.00
❑425, Jul 72	0.20	1.80	4.50	9.00
❑426, Aug 72	0.20	1.80	4.50	9.00
❑427, Sep 72	0.20	1.80	4.50	9.00
❑428, Oct 72, DD, The Invisible Thie of Bleakhill Manor	0.20	1.80	4.50	9.00
❑429, Nov 72	0.20	1.80	4.50	9.00
❑430, Dec 72	0.20	1.80	4.50	9.00
❑431, Jan 73	0.20	1.80	4.50	9.00
❑432, Feb 73	0.20	1.80	4.50	9.00
❑433, Mar 73	0.20	1.80	4.50	9.00
❑434, Apr 73, RB, Riddle of the Red-Handed Robber, 1: The Spook	0.20	1.80	4.50	9.00
❑435, Jul 73	0.20	1.80	4.50	9.00
❑436, Sep 73	0.20	1.80	4.50	9.00
❑437, Nov 73, 1: Manhunter	0.20	3.00	7.50	15.00
❑438, Jan 74, 100pgs.; Manhunter	0.50	2.80	7.00	14.00
❑439, Mar 74, O: Manhunter, 100pgs.; Manhunter	0.50	2.40	6.00	12.00
❑440, May 74, 100pgs.; Manhunter	0.60	2.40	6.00	12.00
❑441, Jul 74, 100pgs.; Manhunter	0.60	2.40	6.00	12.00
❑442, Sep 74, 100pgs.; Manhunter	0.60	2.40	6.00	12.00
❑443, Nov 74, D: Manhunter, 100pgs.	0.60	2.80	7.00	14.00
❑444, Jan 75, 100pgs.	0.60	2.40	6.00	12.00
❑445, Mar 75, 100pgs.	0.60	2.40	6.00	12.00
❑446, Apr 75, JA; RB, Slaughter in Silver; The Mystery of the Flyaway Car, 1: Sterling Silversmith, Hawkman back-up	0.25	1.60	4.00	8.00
❑447, May 75	0.25	1.60	4.00	8.00
❑448, Jun 75	0.25	1.60	4.00	8.00
❑449, Jul 75	0.25	1.60	4.00	8.00
❑450, Aug 75	0.25	1.60	4.00	8.00
❑451, Sep 75	0.25	1.60	4.00	8.00
❑452, Oct 75, The Case of the Ancient Weapons, Hawkman back-up	0.25	1.60	4.00	8.00
❑453, Nov 75	0.25	1.60	4.00	8.00
❑454, Dec 75, The Catch-Me-If-You-Can Crooks	0.25	1.60	4.00	8.00
❑455, Jan 76, Battle of the Backfiring Weapons	0.25	1.60	4.00	8.00
❑456, Feb 76	0.25	1.60	4.00	8.00
❑457, Mar 76, O: Batman, Elongated Man back-up	0.30	1.80	4.50	9.00
❑458, Apr 76	0.30	1.60	4.00	8.00
❑459, May 76	0.30	1.60	4.00	8.00
❑460, Jun 76	0.30	1.60	4.00	8.00
❑461, Jul 76, Bicentennial #29	0.30	1.60	4.00	8.00
❑462, Aug 76	0.30	1.60	4.00	8.00
❑463, Sep 76, 1: the Calculator; 1: Black Spider	0.30	1.60	4.00	8.00
❑464, Oct 76	0.30	1.60	4.00	8.00
❑465, Nov 76, TD, Elongated Man	0.30	1.60	4.00	8.00
❑466, Dec 76, MR; TD	0.30	2.60	6.50	13.00
❑467, Jan 77, MR; TD, The Man Who Skyjacked Hawkman	0.30	2.60	6.50	13.00
❑468, Mar 77, MR; TD	0.30	2.60	6.50	13.00
❑469, May 77, AM, ...By Death's Eerie Light!; The Origin of Dr. Phosphorus, 1: Doctor Phosphorous; 1: Doctor Phosphorus	0.30	1.60	4.00	8.00
❑470, Jun 77, AM, The Master Plan of Dr. Phosphorus!, A: Hugo Strange	0.35	1.60	4.00	8.00
❑471, Aug 77, The Dead Yet Live, A: Hugo Strange	0.35	2.60	6.50	13.00
❑472, Sep 77, MR, I Am the Batman	0.35	2.60	6.50	13.00
❑473, Oct 77, MR, The Malay Penguin	0.35	2.60	6.50	13.00
❑474, Dec 77, MR, The Deadshot Ricochet	0.35	2.80	7.00	14.00
❑475, Feb 78, MR, The Laughing Fish, A: Joker	0.35	4.80	12.00	24.00
❑476, Mar 78, MR, Sign of the Joker!, A: Joker	0.35	4.80	12.00	24.00
❑477, May 78, MR	0.35	2.60	6.50	13.00

	ORIG	GOOD	FINE	N-MINT
❑478, Jul 78, MR, The Coming of…Clayface III!, 1: Clayface III (Preston Payne)	0.35	2.60	6.50	13.00
❑479, Sep 78, MR; RB, True Heroes Never Die…; If a Man be Made of Clay…!, 1: The Fadeaway Man	0.50	2.60	6.50	13.00
❑480, Nov 78, MA; DN, The Case of the Off-Key Crimes	0.50	1.60	4.00	8.00
❑481, Dec 78, DA; MR; CR; JSn; DN, Double-size	1.00	2.40	6.00	12.00
❑482, Feb 79, CR; DG; HC; JSn, Double-size	1.00	1.80	4.50	9.00
❑483, Apr 79, DA; DG; MG; DN, 1: Maxie Zeus, Double-size	1.00	2.00	5.00	10.00
❑484, Jun 79, O: Robin I (Dick Grayson), Double-size	1.00	1.40	3.50	7.00
❑485, Aug 79, Double-size	1.00	1.20	3.00	6.00
❑486, Oct 79, Double-size	1.00	1.20	3.00	6.00
❑487, Dec 79, Double-size	1.00	1.20	3.00	6.00
❑488, Feb 80, Double-size	1.00	1.20	3.00	6.00
❑489, Apr 80, Double-size; Batgirl forgets Batman and Robin's secret identities	1.00	1.20	3.00	6.00
❑490, May 80, Double-size	1.00	1.20	3.00	6.00
❑491, Jun 80, Double-size	1.00	1.20	3.00	6.00
❑492, Jul 80, Double-size	1.00	1.20	3.00	6.00
❑493, Aug 80, Double-size	1.00	1.20	3.00	6.00
❑494, Sep 80, 1: Crime Doctor, Double-size	1.00	1.20	3.00	6.00
❑495, Oct 80, Double-size	1.00	1.20	3.00	6.00
❑496, Nov 80	0.50	1.20	3.00	6.00
❑497, Dec 80	0.50	1.20	3.00	6.00
❑498, Jan 81	0.50	1.20	3.00	6.00
❑499, Feb 81	0.50	1.20	3.00	6.00
❑500, Mar 81, JKu; TY; DG; Cl, The Strange Death of Dr. Erdel, A: Deadman, Slam Bradley, Hawkman, Robin, Double-size; 500th anniversary issue	1.50	2.00	5.00	10.00
❑501, Apr 81	0.50	1.00	2.50	5.00
❑502, May 81	0.50	1.00	2.50	5.00
❑503, Jun 81, JSn	0.50	1.00	2.50	5.00
❑504, Jul 81, JSn, A: Joker	0.50	1.60	4.00	8.00
❑505, Aug 81	0.50	1.00	2.50	5.00
❑506, Sep 81	0.50	1.00	2.50	5.00
❑507, Oct 81	0.60	1.00	2.50	5.00
❑508, Nov 81	0.60	1.00	2.50	5.00
❑509, Dec 81	0.60	1.00	2.50	5.00
❑510, Jan 82	0.60	1.00	2.50	5.00
❑511, Feb 82, 1: Mirage (DC)	0.60	1.00	2.50	5.00
❑512, Mar 82	0.60	1.00	2.50	5.00
❑513, Apr 82	0.60	1.00	2.50	5.00
❑514, May 82	0.60	1.00	2.50	5.00
❑515, Jun 82	0.60	1.00	2.50	5.00
❑516, Jul 82	0.60	1.00	2.50	5.00
❑517, Aug 82	0.60	1.00	2.50	5.00
❑518, Sep 82, 1: Velvet Tiger	0.60	1.00	2.50	5.00
❑519, Oct 82	0.60	1.00	2.50	5.00
❑520, Nov 82	0.60	1.00	2.50	5.00
❑521, Dec 82	0.60	1.00	2.50	5.00
❑522, Jan 83	0.60	1.00	2.50	5.00
❑523, Feb 83	0.60	1.00	2.50	5.00
❑524, Mar 83, 2: Jason Todd	0.60	1.20	3.00	6.00
❑525, Apr 83	0.60	1.00	2.50	5.00
❑526, May 83, AA; DN, A: Batman's 500th	1.50	2.80	7.00	14.00
❑527, Jun 83	0.60	0.70	1.75	3.50
❑528, Jul 83	0.60	0.70	1.75	3.50
❑529, Aug 83	0.60	0.70	1.75	3.50
❑530, Sep 83	0.60	0.70	1.75	3.50
❑531, Oct 83	0.60	0.60	1.50	3.00
❑532, Nov 83, A: Joker	0.60	1.40	3.50	7.00
❑533, Dec 83	0.75	0.60	1.50	3.00
❑534, Jan 84, V: Poison Ivy	0.75	0.60	1.50	3.00
❑535, Feb 84, V: Crazy Quilt; 2: Robin II (Jason Todd)	0.75	1.40	3.50	7.00
❑536, Mar 84, V: Deadshot	0.75	0.70	1.75	3.50
❑537, Apr 84	0.75	0.70	1.75	3.50
❑538, May 84, V: Catman	0.75	0.70	1.75	3.50
❑539, Jun 84, V: Catman	0.75	0.70	1.75	3.50
❑540, Jul 84, V: Scarecrow	0.75	0.70	1.75	3.50
❑541, Aug 84	0.75	0.70	1.75	3.50
❑542, Sep 84, V: Nocturna	0.75	0.70	1.75	3.50
❑543, Oct 84	0.75	0.70	1.75	3.50
❑544, Nov 84	0.75	0.70	1.75	3.50
❑545, Dec 84	0.75	0.70	1.75	3.50
❑546, Jan 85	0.75	0.70	1.75	3.50
❑547, Feb 85	0.75	0.70	1.75	3.50
❑548, Mar 85	0.75	0.70	1.75	3.50
❑549, Apr 85, AMo (w)	0.75	0.70	1.75	3.50
❑550, May 85, AMo (w), Green Arrow back-up	0.75	0.70	1.75	3.50
❑551, Jun 85, V: Calendar Man	0.75	0.70	1.75	3.50
❑552, Jul 85	0.75	0.70	1.75	3.50
❑553, Aug 85, V: Black Mask	0.75	0.70	1.75	3.50
❑554, Sep 85	0.75	0.70	1.75	3.50
❑555, Oct 85, V: Captain Boomerang; V: Mirror Master	0.75	0.70	1.75	3.50
❑556, Nov 85	0.75	0.70	1.75	3.50
❑557, Dec 85	0.75	0.70	1.75	3.50
❑558, Jan 86	0.75	0.70	1.75	3.50
❑559, Feb 86, A: Black Canary; A: Green Arrow; A: Catwoman	0.75	0.70	1.75	3.50
❑560, Mar 86, 1: Steelclaw	0.75	0.70	1.75	3.50
❑561, Apr 86	0.75	0.70	1.75	3.50
❑562, May 86	0.75	0.70	1.75	3.50
❑563, Jun 86, V: Two-Face	0.75	0.70	1.75	3.50
❑564, Jul 86, V: Two-Face; D: Steelclaw	0.75	0.70	1.75	3.50
❑565, Aug 86	0.75	0.70	1.75	3.50
❑566, Sep 86, A: Joker	0.75	0.70	1.75	3.50
❑567, Oct 86, JSn	0.75	0.70	1.75	3.50
❑568, Nov 86, Legends	0.75	0.70	1.75	3.50
❑569, Dec 86, V: Joker; A: Catwoman	0.75	1.20	3.00	6.00
❑570, Jan 87, A: Joker	0.75	1.20	3.00	6.00
❑571, Feb 87, V: Scarecrow	0.75	0.70	1.75	3.50
❑572, Mar 87, A: Slam Bradley, 50th anniversary issue; Giant-size	1.25	0.80	2.00	4.00
❑573, Apr 87, V: Mad Hatter	0.75	0.60	1.50	3.00
❑574, May 87, O: Batman	0.75	0.60	1.50	3.00
❑575, Jun 87, Year Two; Batman: Year 2, Part 1	0.75	1.20	3.00	6.00
❑576, Jul 87, TMc, Year Two; Batman: Year 2, Part 2	0.75	0.80	2.00	4.00
❑577, Aug 87, TMc, Year Two; Batman: Year 2, Part 3	0.75	0.80	2.00	4.00
❑578, Sep 87, TMc, Year Two; Batman: Year 2, Part 4	0.75	0.80	2.00	4.00
❑579, Oct 87, V: Two-Face	0.75	0.40	1.00	2.00
❑580, Nov 87, V: Two-Face	0.75	0.40	1.00	2.00
❑581, Dec 87, V: Two-Face	0.75	0.40	1.00	2.00
❑582, Jan 88, Millennium	0.75	0.40	1.00	2.00
❑583, Feb 88, 1: Ventriloquist	0.75	0.40	1.00	2.00
❑584, Mar 88	0.75	0.40	1.00	2.00
❑585, Apr 88	0.75	0.40	1.00	2.00
❑586, May 88, V: Rat-catcher	0.75	0.40	1.00	2.00
❑587, Jun 88	0.75	0.40	1.00	2.00
❑588, Jul 88	0.75	0.40	1.00	2.00
❑589, Aug 88, Bonus Book #5	0.75	0.40	1.00	2.00
❑590, Sep 88	0.75	0.40	1.00	2.00
❑591, Oct 88	0.75	0.40	1.00	2.00
❑592, Nov 88	0.75	0.40	1.00	2.00
❑593, Dec 88	0.75	0.40	1.00	2.00
❑594, Dec 88, 1: Joe Potato	0.75	0.40	1.00	2.00
❑595, Jan 89, 16 page extra feature; Bonus Book; Invasion!	0.75	0.40	1.00	2.00
❑596, Jan 89	0.75	0.40	1.00	2.00
❑597, Feb 89	0.75	0.40	1.00	2.00
❑598, Mar 89, Blind Justice; Blind Justice, Part 1, Double-size	2.95	0.60	1.50	3.00
❑599, Apr 89, Blind Justice; Blind Justice, Part 2	0.75	0.50	1.25	2.50
❑600, May 89, Blind Justice; Blind Justice, Part 3, Double-size	2.95	0.60	1.50	3.00
❑601, Jun 89, Tulpa, Part 1, A: Demon	0.75	0.40	1.00	2.00
❑602, Jul 89, Tulpa, Part 2, A: Demon	0.75	0.40	1.00	2.00
❑603, Aug 89, Tulpa, Part 3, A: Demon	0.75	0.40	1.00	2.00
❑604, Sep 89, Mud Pack; The Mud Pack, Part 1, poster	1.00	0.40	1.00	2.00
❑605, Sep 89, Mud Pack; The Mud Pack, Part 2	1.00	0.40	1.00	2.00
❑606, Oct 89, Mud Pack; The Mud Pack, Part 3	1.00	0.40	1.00	2.00
❑607, Oct 89, Mud Pack; The Mud Pack, Part 4	1.00	0.40	1.00	2.00
❑608, Nov 89, Letters To The Editor, 1: Anarky	1.00	0.40	1.00	2.00
❑609, Dec 89, Facts About Bats, 2: Anarky	1.00	0.40	1.00	2.00
❑610, Jan 90, Penguin	1.00	0.40	1.00	2.00
❑611, Feb 90, Penguin	1.00	0.30	0.75	1.50
❑612, Mar 90, Catman, Catwoman	1.00	0.30	0.75	1.50
❑613, Apr 90	1.00	0.30	0.75	1.50
❑614, May 90	1.00	0.30	0.75	1.50
❑615, Jun 90, Penguin	1.00	0.30	0.75	1.50
❑616, Jun 90	1.00	0.30	0.75	1.50
❑617, Jul 90, A: Joker	1.00	0.30	0.75	1.50
❑618, Jul 90, Rite of Passage, Part 1	1.00	0.30	0.75	1.50
❑619, Aug 90, Rite of Passage, Part 2	1.00	0.30	0.75	1.50
❑620, Aug 90, Rite of Passage, Part 3	1.00	0.30	0.75	1.50
❑621, Sep 90	1.00	0.30	0.75	1.50
❑622, Oct 90, The Demon Within, Part 1	1.00	0.30	0.75	1.50
❑623, Nov 90, The Demon Within, Part 2	1.00	0.30	0.75	1.50

	ORIG	GOOD	FINE	N-MINT
❑624, Dec 90, The Demon Within, Part 3	1.00	0.30	0.75	1.50
❑625, Jan 91	1.00	0.30	0.75	1.50
❑626, Feb 91	1.00	0.30	0.75	1.50
❑627, Mar 91, A: Batman's 600th, giant	2.95	0.60	1.50	3.00
❑628, Apr 91	1.00	0.30	0.75	1.50
❑629, May 91	1.00	0.30	0.75	1.50
❑630, Jun 91	1.00	0.30	0.75	1.50
❑631, Jul 91	1.00	0.30	0.75	1.50
❑632, Jul 91	1.00	0.30	0.75	1.50
❑633, Aug 91	1.00	0.30	0.75	1.50
❑634, Aug 91	1.00	0.30	0.75	1.50
❑635, Sep 91	1.00	0.30	0.75	1.50
❑636, Sep 91	1.00	0.30	0.75	1.50
❑637, Oct 91	1.00	0.30	0.75	1.50
❑638, Nov 91, JA, The Bomb	1.00	0.30	0.75	1.50
❑639, Dec 91	1.00	0.30	0.75	1.50
❑640, Jan 92	1.00	0.30	0.75	1.50
❑641, Feb 92, JA, Destroyer, Part 3, Anton Furst's Gotham City designs	1.00	0.30	0.75	1.50
❑642, Mar 92, V: Scarface	1.00	0.30	0.75	1.50
❑643, Apr 92	1.00	0.30	0.75	1.50
❑644, May 92, Electric City, Part 1	1.00	0.30	0.75	1.50
❑645, Jun 92, Electric City, Part 2	1.25	0.30	0.75	1.50
❑646, Jul 92, Electric City, Part 3	1.25	0.30	0.75	1.50
❑647, Aug 92	1.25	0.30	0.75	1.50
❑648, Aug 92	1.25	0.30	0.75	1.50
❑649, Sep 92	1.25	0.30	0.75	1.50
❑650, Sep 92	1.25	0.30	0.75	1.50
❑651, Oct 92	1.25	0.30	0.75	1.50
❑652, Oct 92, A: The Huntress III (Helena Bertinelli)	1.25	0.30	0.75	1.50
❑653, Nov 92, A: The Huntress III (Helena Bertinelli)	1.25	0.30	0.75	1.50
❑654, Dec 92, The General, Part 1	1.25	0.30	0.75	1.50
❑655, Jan 93, The General, Part 2, V: Ulysses	1.25	0.30	0.75	1.50
❑656, Feb 93, The General, Part 3, A: Bane	1.25	0.60	1.50	3.00
❑657, Mar 93	1.25	0.60	1.50	3.00
❑658, Apr 93, Deciphered	1.25	0.60	1.50	3.00
❑659, May 93, Knightfall, Part 2	1.25	0.50	1.25	2.50
❑659-2, May 93, Knightfall, Part 2, 2nd Printing	1.25	0.25	0.63	1.25
❑660, May 93, Knightfall, Part 4	1.25	0.40	1.00	2.00
❑661, Jun 93, Knightfall, Part 6	1.25	0.40	1.00	2.00
❑662, Jun 93, Knightfall, Part 8	1.25	0.40	1.00	2.00
❑663, Jul 93, Knightfall, Part 10	1.25	0.40	1.00	2.00
❑664, Aug 93, Knightfall, Part 12	1.25	0.40	1.00	2.00
❑665, Aug 93, Knightfall, Part 16	1.25	0.40	1.00	2.00
❑666, Sep 93, Knightfall, Part 18	1.25	0.40	1.00	2.00
❑667, Oct 93, Knightquest: The Crusade	1.25	0.30	0.75	1.50
❑668, Nov 93, Knightquest: The Crusade	1.25	0.30	0.75	1.50
❑669, Dec 93, Knightquest: The Crusade	1.25	0.30	0.75	1.50
❑670, Jan 94, Knightquest: The Crusade, V: Mr. Freeze	1.25	0.30	0.75	1.50
❑671, Feb 94, Knightquest: The Crusade	1.50	0.30	0.75	1.50
❑672, Mar 94, Knightquest: The Crusade	1.50	0.30	0.75	1.50
❑673, Apr 94, Knightquest: The Crusade; Knightquest, V: Joker	1.50	0.30	0.75	1.50
❑674, May 94, Knightquest: The Crusade; Knightquest	1.50	0.30	0.75	1.50
❑675, Jun 94, Knightquest: The Crusade; Knightquest	1.50	0.30	0.75	1.50
❑675/PL, Jun 94, no cover price; Platinum edition	—	0.60	1.50	3.00
❑675/SC, Jun 94, Knightquest: The Crusade; Knightquest, Special cover; premium edition	2.95	0.59	1.48	2.95
❑676, Jul 94, KnightsEnd, Part 3, Giant-size	2.50	0.50	1.25	2.50
❑677, Aug 94, KnightsEnd, Part 9, V: Nightwing	1.50	0.30	0.75	1.50
❑678, Sep 94, O: Batman, Zero Hour	1.50	0.30	0.75	1.50
❑679, Nov 94, Prodigal, Part 3, V: Ratcatcher	1.50	0.30	0.75	1.50
❑680, Dec 94, Prodigal, Part 7, V: Two-Face	1.50	0.30	0.75	1.50
❑681, Jan 95, Prodigal, Part 11	1.50	0.30	0.75	1.50
❑682, Feb 95	1.50	0.30	0.75	1.50
❑682/SC, Feb 95, enhanced cover	2.50	0.50	1.25	2.50
❑683, Mar 95, V: Penguin	1.50	0.30	0.75	1.50
❑684, Apr 95	1.50	0.30	0.75	1.50
❑685, May 95	1.50	0.30	0.75	1.50
❑686, Jun 95, War of the Dragons, Part 3, A: Nightwing; A: Huntress	1.95	0.40	1.00	2.00
❑687, Jul 95	1.95	0.40	1.00	2.00
❑688, Aug 95	1.95	0.40	1.00	2.00
❑689, Sep 95	1.95	0.40	1.00	2.00
❑690, Oct 95, V: Firefly	1.95	0.40	1.00	2.00
❑691, Nov 95, Underworld Unleashed, V: Spellbinder, Underworld Unleashed	1.95	0.40	1.00	2.00
❑692, Dec 95, Underworld Unleashed	1.95	0.40	1.00	2.00

The quartet of villains to use the Clayface name teamed up as The Mud Pack for a four-issue story beginning in *Detective Comics* #604.

	ORIG	GOOD	FINE	N-MINT
❑693, Jan 96, Systemic Shock, 1: Allergent; A: Poison Ivy	1.95	0.40	1.00	2.00
❑694, Feb 96, Violent Reactions, V: Allergent; A: Poison Ivy	1.95	0.40	1.00	2.00
❑695, Mar 96, Contagion, Part 2	1.95	0.40	1.00	2.00
❑696, Apr 96, Contagion, Part 8	1.95	0.40	1.00	2.00
❑697, Jun 96, V: Two-Face	1.95	0.40	1.00	2.00
❑698, Jul 96, V: Two-Face	1.95	0.40	1.00	2.00
❑699, Jul 96	1.95	0.40	1.00	2.00
❑700, Aug 96, Legacy, Part 1, Anniversary issue	2.95	0.70	1.75	3.50
❑700/SC, Aug 96, Legacy, Part 1, Anniversary issue; cardstock outer wrapper	4.95	1.00	2.50	5.00
❑701, Sep 96, Legacy, Part 6, V: Bane	1.95	0.40	1.00	2.00
❑702, Oct 96, Legacy Epilogue	1.95	0.40	1.00	2.00
❑703, Nov 96, Howling in the Dark, Final Night	1.95	0.40	1.00	2.00
❑704, Dec 96, Rocket Scientist, self-contained story	1.95	0.40	1.00	2.00
❑705, Jan 97, Badd Girls, V: Cluemaster; V: Riddler	1.95	0.40	1.00	2.00
❑706, Feb 97, Lethal Pursuits, V: Riddler	1.95	0.40	1.00	2.00
❑707, Mar 97, Riddled, V: Riddler	1.95	0.40	1.00	2.00
❑708, Apr 97, BSz, The Death Lottery, Part 1	1.95	0.40	1.00	2.00
❑709, May 97, BSz, The Death Lottery, Part 2	1.95	0.40	1.00	2.00
❑710, Jun 97	1.95	0.40	1.00	2.00
❑711, Jul 97	1.95	0.40	1.00	2.00
❑712, Aug 97	1.95	0.40	1.00	2.00
❑713, Sep 97	1.95	0.40	1.00	2.00
❑714, Oct 97, V: Firefly	1.95	0.40	1.00	2.00
❑715, Nov 97, Days of Fire, A: J'onn J'onzz	1.95	0.40	1.00	2.00
❑716, Dec 97, JA, Death Comes Home, Face cover	1.95	0.40	1.00	2.00
❑717, Jan 98	1.95	0.40	1.00	2.00
❑718, Feb 98, V: Finch	1.95	0.40	1.00	2.00
❑719, Mar 98, Cataclysm Prelude; Cataclysm	1.95	0.50	1.25	2.50
❑720, Apr 98, Cataclysm, Part 5, continues in Catwoman #56	1.95	0.70	1.75	3.50
❑721, May 98, Cataclysm, Part 14; Cataclysm, continues in Catwoman #57	1.95	0.60	1.50	3.00
❑722, Jun 98, Aftershock	1.95	0.50	1.25	2.50
❑723, Jul 98, Brotherhood of the Fist, Part 2, continues in Robin #55	1.95	0.40	1.00	2.00
❑724, Aug 98, Aftershock	1.95	0.40	1.00	2.00
❑725, Sep 98, Aftershock	1.99	0.40	1.00	2.00
❑726, Oct 98, A: Joker, Aftershock	1.99	0.39	0.98	1.95
❑727, Dec 98, Fight or Flight, Part 1, A: Robin; A: Nightwing, Road to No Man's Land	1.99	0.40	1.00	1.99
❑728, Jan 99, Fight or Flight, Part 2; Road to No Man's Land, A: Robin; A: Nightwing, Road to No Man's Land	1.99	0.40	1.00	1.99
❑729, Feb 99, Fight or Flight, Part 3; Road to No Man's Land, A: Commissioner Gordan; A: Robin; A: Nightwing, Road to No Man's Land	1.99	0.40	1.00	1.99
❑730, Mar 99, No Law and a New Order, Part 4; No Man's Land, Part 1, A: Scarface, No Man's Land	1.99	0.40	1.00	1.99
❑731, Apr 99, Fear of Faith, Part 4, A: Huntress; A: Scarecrow, No Man's Land	1.99	0.40	1.00	1.99
❑732, May 99, Mosaic, Part 2, A: Batgirl, No Man's Land	1.99	0.40	1.00	1.99
❑733, Jun 99, Crisis of Faith; Shades of Grey, No Man's Land	1.99	0.40	1.00	1.99
❑734, Jul 99, Mark of Cain, Part 2, A: Batgirl, No Man's Land	1.99	0.40	1.00	1.99
❑735, Aug 99, BSz, Fruit of the Earth, Part 3, A: Poison Ivy; V: Clayface, No Man's Land	1.99	0.40	1.00	1.99
❑736, Sep 99, Homecoming, No Man's Land	1.99	0.40	1.00	1.99
❑737, Oct 99, The Code, Part 2, V: Harley Quinn; V: Joker, No Man's Land	1.99	0.40	1.00	1.99
❑738, Nov 99, No Man's Land	1.99	0.40	1.00	1.99
❑739, Dec 99, Jurisprudence, Part 2, No Man's Land	1.99	0.40	1.00	1.99
❑740, Jan 00, Shellgame, Part 2, No Man's Land	1.99	0.40	1.00	1.99

	ORIG	GOOD	FINE	N-MINT
❑741, Feb 00	1.99	0.40	1.00	1.99
❑742, Mar 00	1.99	0.40	1.00	1.99
❑743, Apr 00, Evolution, Part 1	1.99	0.40	1.00	1.99
❑744, May 00, Evolution, Part 2	1.99	0.40	1.00	1.99
❑745, Jun 00, Evolution, Part 3	1.99	0.40	1.00	1.99
❑746, Jul 00	1.99	0.40	1.00	1.99
❑747, Aug 00	—	0.40	1.00	1.99
❑748, Sep 00, Urban Renewal, Part 1	—	0.40	1.00	1.99
❑749, Oct 00, Urban Renewal, Part 2	2.50	0.50	1.25	2.50
❑750, Nov 00, Dependence, Giant-size	4.95	0.99	2.47	4.95
❑751, Dec 00, A Walk in the Park, Part 1	2.50	0.50	1.25	2.50
❑752, Jan 01, A Walk in the Park, Part 2	2.50	0.50	1.25	2.50
❑753, Feb 01, The Adventures of Copernicus Dent: The Janus Double-Down!; Dead in the Water, Part 8	2.50	0.50	1.25	2.50
❑754, Mar 01, Officer Down, Part 6; The Jacobian, Part 9	2.50	0.50	1.25	2.50
❑755, Apr 01, Here's Your Hat, What's Your Hurry?	2.50	0.50	1.25	2.50
❑756, May 01, Lord of the Ring	2.50	0.50	1.25	2.50
❑757	2.50	0.50	1.25	2.50
❑758	2.50	0.50	1.25	2.50
❑759	2.50	0.50	1.25	2.50
❑760	2.50	0.50	1.25	2.50
❑1000000, Nov 98	1.99	0.40	1.00	1.99
❑1000000/SC	14.99	2.00	5.00	10.00
❑Anl 1, V: Penguin	1.50	1.00	2.50	5.00
❑Anl 2, Blood Secrets, Who's Who entries	2.00	0.80	2.00	4.00
❑Anl 3	2.00	0.50	1.25	2.50
❑Anl 4, Armageddon 2001, Part 12, Armageddon 2001	2.00	0.50	1.25	2.50
❑Anl 5, V: Joker, Eclipso	2.00	0.55	1.38	2.75
❑Anl 6, Bloodlines, 1: Geist, Bloodlines	2.50	0.50	1.25	2.50
❑Anl 7, Elseworlds	2.95	0.59	1.48	2.95
❑Anl 8, O: Riddler, Year One	3.95	0.79	1.98	3.95
❑Anl 9, War Bat, Legends of the Dead Earth; 1996 annual	2.95	0.59	1.48	2.95
❑Anl 10, Pulp Heroes	3.95	0.79	1.98	3.95

DETECTIVES, THE
ALPHA PRODUCTIONS

Value: Cover or less

❑1, Apr 93, b&w 4.95

DETECTIVES INC. (MICRO-SERIES)
ECLIPSE

	ORIG	GOOD	FINE	N-MINT
❑1, Apr 85, MR, A Terror of Dying Dreams; Cheerful Lies and Desperate Truths	1.75	0.40	1.00	2.00
❑2, Apr 85, MR, A Hostile Poolside Universe	1.75	0.40	1.00	2.00

DETECTIVES, INC.: A TERROR OF DYING DREAMS
ECLIPSE

Value: Cover or less

❑1, Jun 87, GC, sepia 1.75
❑2, Sep 87, GC, sepia 1.75
❑3, Dec 87, GC, sepia 1.75

DETENTION COMICS
DC

Value: Cover or less

❑1, Oct 96, Mama's Boy; The Lesson, One-Shot; Robin, Superboy, and Warrior stories 3.50

DETONATOR
CHAOS!

Value: Cover or less

❑1, Dec 94, Fear the Hero 2.75
❑2, Jan 94, Reunion, D: Mindbender; O: Detonator 2.75

DETOUR
ALTERNATIVE PRESS

Value: Cover or less

❑1, Oct 97, b&w 2.95

DETROIT! MURDER CITY COMIX
KENT MYERS

Value: Cover or less

❑1, b&w 2.50
❑2, b&w 2.50
❑3, b&w 2.50
❑4, Jun 94, b&w 2.95
❑5, Aug 94, b&w 2.95
❑6, Jan 95, German Secret Weapon!, A: Iggy Pop, b&w 2.95
❑7, May 95, b&w 2.95

DEVASTATOR
IMAGE

Value: Cover or less

❑1, b&w 2.95
❑2, b&w 2.95
❑3 ...... 2.95

DEVIANT
ANTARCTIC

Value: Cover or less

❑1, Mar 99, A Comic Book Journal of Strange Sexual Practices, b&w; adult 2.99

DEVIL CHEF
DARK HORSE

Value: Cover or less

❑1, Jul 94, b&w 2.50

DEVIL DINOSAUR
MARVEL

	ORIG	GOOD	FINE	N-MINT
❑1, Apr 78, JK, JK (w), 1: Moon Boy; 1: Devil Dinosaur	0.35	1.00	2.50	5.00
❑2, May 78, JK	0.35	0.60	1.50	3.00
❑3, Jun 78, JK	0.35	0.40	1.00	2.00
❑4, Jul 78, JK	0.35	0.40	1.00	2.00
❑5, Aug 78, JK	0.35	0.40	1.00	2.00
❑6, Sep 78, JK	0.35	0.40	1.00	2.00
❑7, Oct 78, JK	0.35	0.40	1.00	2.00
❑8, Nov 78, JK	0.35	0.40	1.00	2.00
❑9, Dec 78, JK, Final Issue	0.35	0.40	1.00	2.00

DEVIL DINOSAUR SPRING FLING
MARVEL

Value: Cover or less

❑1, Jun 97, A: Moon-Boy, One-Shot 2.99

DEVILINA
ATLAS

	ORIG	GOOD	FINE	N-MINT
❑1, Jan 75, b&w; magazine	0.75	1.80	4.50	9.00
❑2, May 75, b&w; magazine	0.75	2.40	6.00	12.00

DEVIL JACK
DOOM THEATER

Value: Cover or less

❑1 ...... 2.95

DEVILMAN
VEROTIK

	ORIG	GOOD	FINE	N-MINT
❑1, Jun 95, The Late Spring of Vienna	2.95	0.70	1.75	3.50
❑2	2.95	0.60	1.50	3.00
❑3	2.95	0.60	1.50	3.00
❑4	2.95	0.59	1.48	2.95
❑5	2.95	0.59	1.48	2.95
❑6	—	0.70	1.75	3.50

DEVIL'S ANGEL, THE
EROS

Value: Cover or less

❑1, FT, FT (w) 2.95

DEVIL'S BITE
BONEYARD

Value: Cover or less

❑1 ...... 2.95
❑2, The Duffel Bag, Indicia lists as #1 ...... 2.95

DEVIL'S REIGN
IMAGE

	ORIG	GOOD	FINE	N-MINT
❑0.5, Wizard mail-in	—	0.60	1.50	3.00
❑0.5/Aut	—	1.20	3.00	6.00
❑0.5/Pl, Platinum edition	—	1.00	2.50	5.00

DEVLIN
MAXIMUM

Value: Cover or less

❑1, Apr 96, A: Avengelyne 2.50

DEVLIN DEMON: NOT FOR NORMAL CHILDREN
DUBLIN

Value: Cover or less

❑1 ...... 2.95

DEWEY DESADE
ITEM

	ORIG	GOOD	FINE	N-MINT
❑1	3.50	0.70	1.75	3.50
❑2	3.50	0.70	1.75	3.50
❑Ash 1, Promotional, mini-ashcan (4 x 2)	—	0.05	0.13	0.25

DEXTER'S LABORATORY
DC

	ORIG	GOOD	FINE	N-MINT
❑1, Sep 99, Wow! Comic Relief	1.99	0.50	1.25	2.50
❑2, Oct 99, Let's Save thw World, You Jerk!, A: Mandark	1.99	0.40	1.00	2.00
❑3, Nov 99, Dexter's robot takes his place	1.99	0.40	1.00	2.00
❑4, Dec 99, Meanwhile…	1.99	0.40	1.00	2.00
❑5, Jan 00	1.99	0.40	1.00	2.00
❑6, Feb 00	1.99	0.40	1.00	2.00
❑7, Mar 00	1.99	0.40	1.00	2.00
❑8, Apr 00, Dee-Dee Fo-Fum	1.99	0.40	1.00	2.00
❑9, May 00, ...Perfect Chemistry!!	1.99	0.40	1.00	2.00
❑10, Jun 00	1.99	0.40	1.00	2.00
❑11, Jul 00	1.99	0.40	1.00	1.99
❑12, Aug 00	1.99	0.40	1.00	1.99
❑13, Sep 00, What: Funny?; Forget me Not	1.99	0.40	1.00	1.99
❑14, Oct 00, Teacher's Pet	1.99	0.40	1.00	1.99
❑15, Nov 00, Totally Tanked	1.99	0.40	1.00	1.99
❑16, Dec 00, Dee-Dee's Pony Tale	1.99	0.40	1.00	1.99
❑17, Jan 01, Dexter's New Clothes	1.99	0.40	1.00	1.99
❑18, Feb 01, Doot-Doot-Doot!	1.99	0.40	1.00	1.99
❑19, Mar 01, Spoon	1.99	0.40	1.00	1.99
❑20, Apr 01, Journey to the Center of Dee-Dee	1.99	0.40	1.00	1.99
❑21, May 01, The Big Move	1.99	0.40	1.00	1.99
❑22	1.99	0.40	1.00	1.99
❑23	1.99	0.40	1.00	1.99
❑24	1.99	0.40	1.00	1.99
❑25	1.99	0.40	1.00	1.99

DHAMPIRE: STILLBORN
DC

Value: Cover or less

❑1, prestige format 5.95

DIA DE LOS MUERTOS (SERGIO ARAGONÉS'...)
DARK HORSE

Value: Cover or less

❑1, Oct 98, SA, ME (w); SA (w), nn; One-Shot; Day of the Dead stories 2.95

ORIG GOOD FINE N-MINT

DIATOM
PHOTOGRAPHICS

Value: Cover or less

❑1, Apr 95, b&w; prestige format; fumetti 4.95
❑2 .... 4.95
❑3, Cap'n Ice 4.95

DICK DANGER
OLSEN

Value: Cover or less

❑1, Jan 98, The Star of Bengala; Dick Danger's Crime-Quiz .. 2.95
❑2 .... 2.95
❑3 .... 2.95
❑4 .... 2.95
❑5 .... 2.95

DICK TRACY (BLACKTHORNE)
BLACKTHORNE

Value: Cover or less

❑1, Jun 86 .... 6.95
❑2, Jun 86 .... 6.95
❑3, Jul 86 .... 6.95
❑4, Aug 86 .... 6.95
❑5, Oct 86 .... 6.95
❑6, Oct 86 .... 6.95
❑7, Dec 86 .... 6.95
❑8, Jan 87 .... 6.95
❑9, Jan 87 .... 6.95
❑10, Feb 87 .... 6.95
❑11, Mar 87 .... 6.95
❑12, Apr 87 .... 6.95
❑13, May 87 .... 6.95
❑14, Jun 87 .... 6.95
❑15, Jul 87 .... 6.95
❑16, Aug 87 .... 6.95
❑17, Sep 87 .... 6.95
❑18, Sep 87, V: Pruneface 6.95
❑19, Oct 87, V: Pruneface 6.95
❑20, Oct 87, V: Pruneface 6.95
❑21, Nov 87 .... 6.95
❑22, Nov 87 .... 6.95
❑23, Nov 87 .... 6.95
❑24, Dec 87, V: Flattop 6.95

DICK TRACY (DISNEY)
DISNEY

Value: Cover or less

❑1, Big City Blues, newsstand format 2.95
❑1/DM, Big City Blues, prestige format 4.95
❑2, vs. the Underworld, newsstand format 2.95
❑2/DM, vs. the Underworld, prestige format 4.95
❑3, Movie Adaptation, movie Adaptation; newsstand format 2.95
❑3/DM, movie Adaptation; prestige format 5.95

DICK TRACY 3-D
BLACKTHORNE

	ORIG	GOOD	FINE	N-MINT
❑1, Jul 86, Ocean Death Trap!, 3-D glasses	2.00	0.50	1.25	2.50

DICK TRACY ADVENTURES (GLADSTONE)
GLADSTONE

Value: Cover or less

❑1, Sep 91, JSt (c), V: B.B. Eyes 4.95

DICK TRACY ADVENTURES (HAMILTON)
HAMILTON

Value: Cover or less

❑1, b&w 3.95

DICK TRACY CRIMEBUSTER
AVALON

Value: Cover or less

❑1 .... 2.95
❑2 .... 2.95
❑3 .... 2.95
❑4 .... 2.95

DICK TRACY DETECTIVE
AVALON

Value: Cover or less

❑1 .... 2.95
❑2, Sleet Before the Storm 2.95
❑3, Is Ketchum Dead 2.95
❑4 .... 2.95

DICK TRACY MONTHLY
BLACKTHORNE

	ORIG	GOOD	FINE	N-MINT
❑1	2.00	0.50	1.25	2.50
❑2	2.00	0.40	1.00	2.00
❑3	2.00	0.40	1.00	2.00
❑4	2.00	0.40	1.00	2.00
❑5	2.00	0.40	1.00	2.00
❑6	2.00	0.40	1.00	2.00
❑7	2.00	0.40	1.00	2.00
❑8	2.00	0.40	1.00	2.00
❑9	2.00	0.40	1.00	2.00
❑10	2.00	0.40	1.00	2.00
❑11, Mar 87	2.00	0.40	1.00	2.00
❑12, no month in indicia	2.00	0.40	1.00	2.00
❑13	2.00	0.40	1.00	2.00
❑14	2.00	0.40	1.00	2.00
❑15	2.00	0.40	1.00	2.00
❑16	2.00	0.40	1.00	2.00
❑17	2.00	0.40	1.00	2.00
❑18	2.00	0.40	1.00	2.00
❑19	2.00	0.40	1.00	2.00
❑20	2.00	0.40	1.00	2.00
❑21	2.00	0.40	1.00	2.00
❑22	2.00	0.40	1.00	2.00
❑23	2.00	0.40	1.00	2.00
❑24	2.00	0.40	1.00	2.00
❑25, Series continues as Dick Tracy Weekly	2.00	0.40	1.00	2.00

DICK TRACY SPECIAL
BLACKTHORNE

Value: Cover or less

❑1, Jan 88, O: Tracy 2.95
❑2, Mar 88, O: Tracy 2.95
❑3, O: Tracy 2.95

Disney issued the three issues of its *Dick Tracy* movie adaptation in two editions: prestige format for the direct market and regular format for the newsstand.

ORIG GOOD FINE N-MINT

DICK TRACY: THE EARLY YEARS
BLACKTHORNE

Value: Cover or less

❑1, Aug 87 .... 6.95
❑2, Oct 87 .... 6.95
❑3, Apr 88 .... 6.95
❑4 .... 2.95

DICK TRACY "UNPRINTED STORIES"
BLACKTHORNE

Value: Cover or less

❑1, Sep 87 .... 2.95
❑2, Nov 87 .... 2.95
❑3, Jan 88 .... 2.95
❑4, Jun 88, D: Flattop Jr. 4.95

DICK TRACY WEEKLY
BLACKTHORNE

Value: Cover or less

❑26, Jan 88 .... 2.00
❑27, Jan 88 .... 2.00
❑28, Jan 88 .... 2.00
❑29, Jan 88 .... 2.00
❑30, Feb 88 .... 2.00
❑31, Feb 88 .... 2.00
❑32, Feb 88 .... 2.00
❑33, Feb 88 .... 2.00
❑34, Mar 88 .... 2.00
❑35, Mar 88 .... 2.00
❑36, Mar 88 .... 2.00
❑37, Mar 88 .... 2.00
❑38, Jun 88 .... 2.00
❑39, Jun 88 .... 2.00
❑40, Jun 88 .... 2.00
❑41, Jun 88 .... 2.00
❑42, Jul 88 .... 2.00
❑43, Jul 88 .... 2.00
❑44, Jul 88 .... 2.00
❑45, Jul 88 .... 2.00
❑46, Aug 88 .... 2.00
❑47, Aug 88 .... 2.00
❑48, Aug 88 .... 2.00
❑49, Aug 88 .... 2.00
❑50, Sep 88 .... 2.00
❑51, Sep 88 .... 2.00
❑52, Sep 88 .... 2.00
❑53, Sep 88 .... 2.00
❑54, Oct 88 .... 2.00
❑55, Oct 88 .... 2.00
❑56, Oct 88 .... 2.00
❑57, Oct 88 .... 2.00
❑58, Oct 88 .... 2.00
❑59, Oct 88 .... 2.00
❑60, Nov 88 .... 2.00
❑61, Nov 88 .... 2.00
❑62, Nov 88 .... 2.00
❑63, Nov 88 .... 2.00
❑64, Nov 88 .... 2.00
❑65, Nov 88 .... 2.00
❑66, Dec 88 .... 2.00
❑67, Dec 88 .... 2.00
❑68, Dec 88 .... 2.00
❑69, Dec 88 .... 2.00
❑70, Jan 89 .... 2.00
❑71, Jan 89 .... 2.00
❑72, Jan 89 .... 2.00
❑73, Jan 89 .... 2.00
❑74, Feb 89 .... 2.00
❑75, Feb 89 .... 2.00
❑76, Feb 89 .... 2.00
❑77, Feb 89 .... 2.00
❑78, Mar 89 .... 2.00
❑79, Mar 89 .... 2.00
❑80, Mar 89 .... 2.00
❑81, Mar 89 .... 2.00
❑82, Apr 89 .... 2.00
❑83, Apr 89 .... 2.00
❑84, Apr 89 .... 2.00
❑85, Apr 89 .... 2.00
❑86, May 89 .... 2.00
❑87, May 89 .... 2.00
❑88, May 89 .... 2.00
❑89, May 89 .... 2.00
❑90, Jun 89 .... 2.00
❑91, Jun 89 .... 2.00
❑92, Jun 89 .... 2.00
❑93, Jun 89 .... 2.00
❑94, Aug 89 .... 2.00
❑95, Aug 89 .... 2.00
❑96, Aug 89 .... 2.00
❑97, Aug 89, 1: Moon Maid 2.00
❑98, Sep 89 .... 2.00
❑99, Sep 89 .... 2.00

DICK WAD
SLAVE LABOR

Value: Cover or less

❑1, Sep 93, b&w; adult 2.50

DIEBOLD
SILENT PARTNERS

Value: Cover or less

❑1, b&w 2.95
❑2, b&w 2.95

DIE-CUT
MARVEL

Value: Cover or less

❑1, Nov 93, Beastswarm: The Howling, diecut cover 2.50
❑2, Dec 93 .... 1.75
❑3, Jan 94 .... 1.75
❑4, Feb 94 .... 1.75

DIE-CUT VS. G-FORCE
MARVEL

Value: Cover or less

❑1, Nov 93, Grave Incisions, Holo-Grafx cover 2.75
❑2, Dec 93, foil cover 2.75

DIESEL
ANTARCTIC

Value: Cover or less

❑1, Apr 97, Master of Dragon 2.95

DIGIMON DIGITAL MONSTERS
DARK HORSE

Value: Cover or less

- ❑1, May 00 ... 2.95
- ❑2, May 00 ... 2.95
- ❑3, May 00 ... 2.95
- ❑4, May 00 ... 2.95
- ❑5, Aug 00 ... 2.95
- ❑6, Sep 00 ... 2.95
- ❑7, Sep 00 ... 2.95
- ❑8, Sep 00 ... 2.95
- ❑9, Sep 00 ... 2.99
- ❑10, Oct 00 ... 2.99
- ❑11, Nov 00 ... 2.99
- ❑12, Nov 00 ... 2.99

DIGITAL DRAGON
PEREGRINE ENTERTAINMENT

Value: Cover or less

- ❑1, Jan 99, b&w ... 2.95
- ❑2, Apr 99, b&w ... 2.95

DIGITEK
MARVEL

Value: Cover or less

- ❑1, Dec 92, A Shock to the System, Part 1 ... 1.95
- ❑2, Jan 93, A Shock to the System, Part 2 ... 1.95
- ❑3, Feb 93, A Shock to the System, Part 3 ... 2.25
- ❑4, Mar 93, A Shock to the System, Part 4 ... 2.25

DIK SKYCAP
RIP OFF

Value: Cover or less

- ❑1, Dec 91, b&w ... 2.50
- ❑2, May 92, b&w ... 2.50

DILEMMA PRESENTS
DILEMMA

Value: Cover or less

- ❑1, Oct 94, b&w ... 2.50
- ❑2, b&w; Flip-book ... 2.50
- ❑3, Apr 95, b&w; Flip-book ... 2.50
- ❑4, b&w; Flip-book ... 2.50

DILTON'S STRANGE SCIENCE
ARCHIE

	ORIG	GOOD	FINE	N-MINT
❑1, May 89	0.75	0.40	1.00	2.00
❑2	0.75	0.30	0.75	1.50
❑3	0.75	0.30	0.75	1.50
❑4	0.75	0.30	0.75	1.50
❑5, May 90	0.75	0.30	0.75	1.50

DIMENSION 5
EDGE

Value: Cover or less

- ❑1, Oct 95, b&w; adult ... 3.95

DIMENSION X
KARL ART

Value: Cover or less

- ❑1, b&w ... 3.50

DIMENSION Z
PYRAMID

	ORIG	GOOD	FINE	N-MINT
❑1	1.70	0.40	1.00	2.00
❑2	1.70	0.40	1.00	2.00

DIMM COMICS PRESENTS
DIMM

	ORIG	GOOD	FINE	N-MINT
❑Ash 0, Jan 96, b&w; ashcan promotional comic	—	0.20	0.50	1.00
❑Ash 1, May 96, b&w; ashcan promotional comic	—	0.20	0.50	1.00

DIM-WITTED DARRYL
SLAVE LABOR

Value: Cover or less

- ❑1, Jun 98, Savory Meat; A Colorful World, b&w ... 2.95
- ❑2 ... 2.95
- ❑3 ... 2.95

DINGLEDORFS, THE
SKYLIGHT

Value: Cover or less

- ❑1, b&w ... 2.75

DINKY ON THE ROAD
BLIND BAT PRESS

Value: Cover or less

- ❑1, Jun 94, b&w ... 1.95

DINO ISLAND
MIRAGE

Value: Cover or less

- ❑1, Feb 93, covers form diptych ... 2.75
- ❑2, Mar 93, covers form diptych ... 2.75

DINO-RIDERS
MARVEL

	ORIG	GOOD	FINE	N-MINT
❑1, Mar 89	1.00	0.30	0.75	1.50
❑2, Apr 89	1.00	0.30	0.75	1.50
❑3, May 89	1.00	0.30	0.75	1.50

DINOSAUR BOP
MONSTER

Value: Cover or less

- ❑1, b&w ... 2.50
- ❑2, b&w ... 2.50

DINOSAUR ISLAND
MONSTER

	ORIG	GOOD	FINE	N-MINT
❑1, b&w	2.25	0.50	1.25	2.50

DINOSAUR MANSION
EDGE

Value: Cover or less

- ❑1, b&w; no indicia ... 2.95

DINOSAUR REX
UPSHOT

Value: Cover or less

- ❑1, full color ... 2.00
- ❑2, b&w ... 2.00
- ❑3, b&w ... 2.00

DINOSAURS
HOLLYWOOD

	ORIG	GOOD	FINE	N-MINT
❑1, TV based	2.95	0.60	1.50	3.00
❑2, TV based	2.95	0.60	1.50	3.00

DINOSAURS ATTACK!
ECLIPSE

Value: Cover or less

- ❑1, HT, The Timescan Disaster, trading cards ... 3.95
- ❑2 ... 3.95
- ❑3 ... 3.95

DINOSAURS, A CELEBRATION
MARVEL

Value: Cover or less

- ❑1, Horns and Heavy Armor ... 4.95
- ❑2, Bone heads and Duck-bills ... 4.95
- ❑3, Lizard-Hipped and Bird Hipped Dinosaurs; The Dinosaur Family Tree, Egg stealers and Earth shakers ... 4.95
- ❑4, Terrible Claws and Tyrants ... 4.95

DINOSAURS FOR HIRE (ETERNITY)
ETERNITY

	ORIG	GOOD	FINE	N-MINT
❑1, Mar 88, Rolling Thunder Lizards, b&w	1.95	0.40	1.00	2.00
❑1/3D, 3-D	2.95	0.59	1.48	2.95
❑1-2, Mar 88, Rolling Thunder Lizards, 2nd Printing	1.95	0.39	0.98	1.95
❑2, Jun 88	1.95	0.39	0.98	1.95
❑3	1.95	0.39	0.98	1.95
❑4	1.95	0.39	0.98	1.95
❑5	1.95	0.39	0.98	1.95
❑6	1.95	0.39	0.98	1.95
❑7	1.95	0.39	0.98	1.95
❑8	1.95	0.39	0.98	1.95
❑9	1.95	0.39	0.98	1.95

DINOSAURS FOR HIRE (MALIBU)
MALIBU

Value: Cover or less

- ❑1, Feb 93 ... 1.95
- ❑2, Mar 93 ... 1.95
- ❑3, Apr 93, A: Ex-Mutants ... 1.95
- ❑4, May 93 ... 1.95
- ❑5, Jun 93, V: Poacher ... 2.50
- ❑6, Jul 93, Jurassic Park parody cover ... 2.50
- ❑7, Aug 93, V: Turret, Hunter of Dinosaurs ... 2.50
- ❑8, Sep 93, Genesis, Part 2; The Extinction Agenda! ... 2.50
- ❑9, Oct 93, Genesis, Part 5 ... 2.50
- ❑10, Nov 93, Genesis, Comics' Greatest World parody cover ... 2.50
- ❑11, Dec 93, Genesis ... 2.50
- ❑12, Feb 94, Genesis, Ultraverse parody cover ... 2.50

DINOSAURS FOR HIRE: DINOSAURS RULE!
ETERNITY

Value: Cover or less

- ❑1, Dinosaurs Rule! ... 5.95

DINOSAURS FOR HIRE FALL CLASSIC
ETERNITY

Value: Cover or less

- ❑1, Nov 88, b&w; Fall Classic; Elvis ... 2.25

DINOSAURS FOR HIRE: GUNS 'N' LIZARDS
ETERNITY

Value: Cover or less

- ❑1, Guns 'n' Lizards ... 5.95

DIRECTORY TO A NONEXISTENT UNIVERSE
ECLIPSE

Value: Cover or less

- ❑1, Dec 87 ... 2.00

DIRE WOLVES: A CHRONICLE OF THE DEADWORLD
CALIBER

Value: Cover or less

- ❑1, b&w ... 3.95

DIRTBAG
TWIST N SHOUT

Value: Cover or less

- ❑1 ... 2.95
- ❑2 ... 2.95
- ❑3 ... 2.95
- ❑4 ... 2.95
- ❑5 ... 2.95
- ❑6, Crowd Control; Deeno in Tourist Trap ... 2.95
- ❑7, If It ain't Broke, Fix It; true Takes from the Periphery ... 2.95

DIRTY DOZEN, THE
DELL

	ORIG	GOOD	FINE	N-MINT
❑1, Oct 67, movie Adaptation; 12-180-710	0.12	5.00	12.50	25.00

DIRTY PAIR
ECLIPSE

	ORIG	GOOD	FINE	N-MINT
❑1, Dec 88, Cory! Emerson, b&w	2.00	1.20	3.00	6.00
❑2, Jan 89, b&w	2.00	0.80	2.00	4.00
❑3, Feb 89, b&w	2.00	0.80	2.00	4.00
❑4, Mar 89, b&w	2.00	0.80	2.00	4.00

DIRTY PAIR (4TH SERIES)
VIZ

Value: Cover or less

- ❑1, To Kill a Computer ... 4.95
- ❑2 ... 4.95
- ❑3 ... 4.95
- ❑4, Come Out, Come Out, Assassin ... 4.95
- ❑5, Address for Danger ... 4.95

DIRTY PAIR: DANGEROUS ACQUAINTANCES
DARK HORSE

	ORIG	GOOD	FINE	N-MINT
❑1, b&w	2.95	0.59	1.48	2.95
❑2, b&w	2.95	0.59	1.48	2.95
❑3, b&w	2.95	0.59	1.48	2.95
❑4, b&w	2.95	0.59	1.48	2.95
❑5, b&w	2.95	0.59	1.48	2.95

DIRTY PAIR, THE: FATAL BUT NOT SERIOUS
DARK HORSE

Value: Cover or less

- ❑1, Jul 95 ... 2.95
- ❑2, Aug 95 ... 2.95
- ❑3, Sep 95 ... 2.95
- ❑4, Oct 95 ... 2.95
- ❑5, Nov 95 ... 2.95

DIRTY PAIR II
ECLIPSE

	ORIG	GOOD	FINE	N-MINT
❑1, b&w	—	0.50	1.25	2.50
❑2, b&w	—	0.50	1.25	2.50
❑3	—	0.50	1.25	2.50
❑4	—	0.50	1.25	2.50
❑5	—	0.50	1.25	2.50

DIRTY PAIR III
ECLIPSE

	ORIG	GOOD	FINE	N-MINT
❑1, b&w	—	0.45	1.13	2.25
❑2, b&w	—	0.45	1.13	2.25
❑3	—	0.45	1.13	2.25
❑4	—	0.45	1.13	2.25
❑5	—	0.45	1.13	2.25

DIRTY PAIR, THE: RUN FROM THE FUTURE
DARK HORSE

Value: Cover or less

- ❑1, Jan 00, Smart Clothes, Foolish Criminals ... 2.95
- ❑1/A, Jan 00, Smart Clothes, Foolish Criminals, Alternate cover by Adam Warren ... 2.95
- ❑2 ... 2.95
- ❑3 ... 2.95
- ❑4 ... 2.95

DIRTY PAIR, THE: SIM HELL
DARK HORSE

	ORIG	GOOD	FINE	N-MINT
❑1, b&w	2.50	0.59	1.48	2.95
❑2, b&w	2.50	0.59	1.48	2.95
❑3, b&w	2.50	0.59	1.48	2.95
❑4, b&w	2.50	0.59	1.48	2.95
❑5	2.95	0.59	1.48	2.95

DIRTY PAIR, THE: SIM HELL REMASTERED
DARK HORSE

Value: Cover or less

- ❑1, May 01 ... 2.99

DIRTY PAIR, THE: START THE VIOLENCE
DARK HORSE

Value: Cover or less

- ❑1/A, Sep 99, Jason Pearson cover ... 2.95
- ❑1/B, Sep 99, variant cover ... 2.95

DIRTY PICTURES
AIRCEL

Value: Cover or less

- ❑1, Apr 91, b&w; adult ... 2.50
- ❑2, b&w; adult ... 2.50
- ❑3, b&w; adult ... 2.50

DIRTY PLOTTE
DRAWN AND QUARTERLY

Value: Cover or less

- ❑1 ... 2.50
- ❑2 ... 2.50
- ❑3 ... 2.50
- ❑4 ... 2.50
- ❑5 ... 2.50
- ❑6 ... 2.50
- ❑7 ... 2.95
- ❑8 ... 2.95
- ❑9 ... 2.95
- ❑10 ... 3.50

DISAVOWED
WILDSTORM

Value: Cover or less

- ❑1, Mar 00 ... 2.50
- ❑2, Apr 00, Point of View ... 2.50
- ❑3, May 00, Smoke and Mirrors ... 2.50

DISCIPLES, THE
IMAGE

Value: Cover or less

- ❑1, Apr 01 ... 2.95

DISHMAN
ECLIPSE

Value: Cover or less

- ❑1, Sep 88, Dishman Hands, 1: Dishman, b&w ... 2.50

DISNEY AFTERNOON, THE
MARVEL

Value: Cover or less

- ❑1, Nov 94, Kitchen Clean-up; The Paint Job, Darkwing Duck, Bonkers, Goof Troop, Tailspin ... 1.50
- ❑2, Dec 94 ... 1.50
- ❑3, Jan 95 ... 1.50
- ❑4, Feb 95 ... 1.50
- ❑5, Mar 95 ... 1.50
- ❑6, Apr 95 ... 1.50
- ❑7, May 95 ... 1.50
- ❑8, Jun 95 ... 1.50
- ❑9, Jul 95 ... 1.50
- ❑10, Aug 95, Final Issue ... 1.50

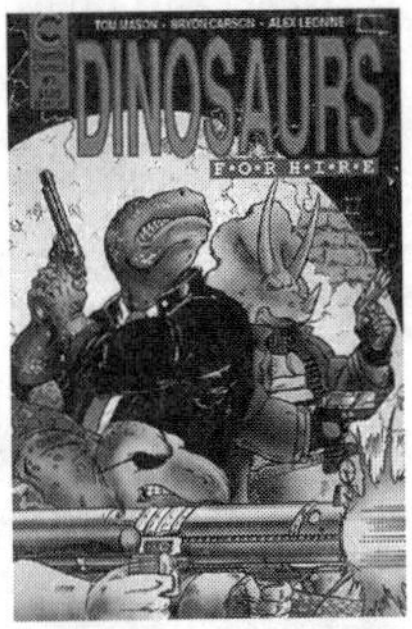

Disney issued the three issues of its *Dick Tracy* movie adaptation in two editions: prestige format for the direct market and regular format for the newsstand.

© 1988 Malibu Comics (Eternity)

DISNEY COMIC HITS
MARVEL

Value: Cover or less

- ❑1, Oct 95, Pocahontas ... 1.50
- ❑2, Nov 95, Timon and Pumbaa ... 1.50
- ❑3, Dec 95, Pocahontas, A: Captain John Smith; A: Pocahontas ... 1.50
- ❑4, Jan 96, Adapts Toy Story ... 2.50
- ❑5, Feb 96, Toy Story: Andy's Sleep Over; Beauty & The Beast: Magical Memories!, Winter Wonderland ... 1.50
- ❑6, Mar 96, Aladdin: Faking Thunderbirds ... 1.50
- ❑7, Apr 96, Pocahontas: Nature's Way ... 1.50
- ❑8, May 96 ... 1.50
- ❑9 ... 1.50
- ❑10, Jul 96, Hunchback of Notre Dame, adapts Hunchback of Notre Dame ... 2.50
- ❑11, Aug 96, Hunchback of Notre Dame ... 1.50
- ❑12, Sep 96, The Little Mermaid 1.50
- ❑13, Oct 96, Aladdin and the King of Thieves, adapts Aladdin and the King of Thieves ... 1.50
- ❑14, Nov 96, Timon & Pumbaa: Once Upon a Timon, Timon & Pumbaa ... 1.50
- ❑15, Dec 96, Toy Story adventures ... 1.50
- ❑16, Jan 97, adapts 101 Dalmations ... 1.50

DISNEYLAND BIRTHDAY PARTY (WALT DISNEY'S...)
GLADSTONE

	ORIG	GOOD	FINE	N-MINT
❑1, CB, Reprints Disneyland Birthday Party (Giant), Uncle Scrooge Goes to Disneyland	2.50	2.00	5.00	10.00
❑1/A, digest	—	2.00	5.00	10.00

DISNEY MOVIE BOOK
DISNEY

Value: Cover or less

- ❑1, Roger Rabbit in Tummy Trouble ... 7.95

DISNEY'S ACTION CLUB
ACCLAIM

Value: Cover or less

- ❑1, digest; Hercules, Hunchback, Lion King, Aladdin, Toy Story, Mighty Ducks ... 4.50
- ❑2, The Mighty Ducks: Puck Power; The Hunchback of Notre Dame: Misfortunes of War... 4.50
- ❑3, Aladdin: Monkey Business; Timon & Pumbaa: After Hours ... 4.50
- ❑4, Mighty Ducks: Rough Stuff; Find Aladdin, digest; Mighty Ducks, Toy Story, Aladdin, Hercules stories ... 4.50
- ❑5 ... 4.50
- ❑6 ... 4.50
- ❑7 ... 4.50

DISNEY'S COLOSSAL COMICS
DISNEY

Value: Cover or less

- ❑1 ... 2.00

DISNEY'S COLOSSAL COMICS COLLECTION
DISNEY

	ORIG	GOOD	FINE	N-MINT
❑1, digest	1.95	0.40	1.00	2.00
❑2, digest	1.95	0.40	1.00	2.00
❑3, digest	1.95	0.40	1.00	2.00
❑4, digest	1.95	0.40	1.00	2.00
❑5, digest	1.95	0.40	1.00	2.00
❑6, digest	1.95	0.40	1.00	2.00
❑7, digest	1.95	0.40	1.00	2.00
❑8, digest	1.95	0.40	1.00	2.00
❑9, digest	1.95	0.40	1.00	2.00
❑10, digest	1.95	0.40	1.00	2.00

DISNEY'S COMICS IN 3-D
DISNEY

Value: Cover or less

- ❑1, DR; FG; CB ... 2.95

DISNEY'S ENCHANTING STORIES
ACCLAIM

Value: Cover or less

- ❑1 ... 4.50
- ❑2, River of Youth; Service with a Smile, Pocahontas ... 4.50
- ❑3, DP, The Book Crook; Meg's Mismatched Monograms, Beauty & The Beast ... 4.50
- ❑4, Star Search; Clean-up Time, 101 Dalmations ... 4.50

DISOBEDIENT DAISY
FANTAGRAPHICS

Value: Cover or less

- ❑1, Aug 95, b&w; adult ... 2.95
- ❑2, Oct 95, b&w; adult ... 2.95

DISTANT SOIL, A (1ST SERIES)
Warp

Issue	ORIG	GOOD	FINE	N-MINT
❑1	1.50	2.00	5.00	10.00
❑2	1.50	1.20	3.00	6.00
❑3	1.50	1.00	2.50	5.00
❑4	1.50	1.00	2.50	5.00
❑5	1.50	1.00	2.50	5.00
❑6, Jun 85, The Chronicles of Panda Khan, 1: Panda Khan, Standard comic size	1.50	0.80	2.00	4.00
❑7	1.50	0.80	2.00	4.00
❑8, Dec 85	1.50	0.80	2.00	4.00
❑9, Mar 86	1.50	0.80	2.00	4.00

DISTANT SOIL, A (2ND SERIES)
Aria

Issue	ORIG	GOOD	FINE	N-MINT
❑1	1.75	1.20	3.00	6.00
❑1-2, 2nd Printing	1.75	0.60	1.50	3.00
❑, 3rd Printing	1.75	0.40	1.00	2.00
❑1-4, 4th Printing	1.75	0.35	0.88	1.75
❑2	1.75	0.80	2.00	4.00
❑2-2, 2nd Printing	1.75	0.50	1.25	2.50
❑3	1.75	0.80	2.00	4.00
❑3-2, 2nd Printing	1.75	0.50	1.25	2.50
❑4, Knights of the Angel	1.75	0.60	1.50	3.00
❑4-2, Knights of the Angel, 2nd Printing	1.75	0.40	1.00	2.00
❑5, Knights of the Angel	1.75	0.50	1.25	2.50
❑6, Knights of the Angel	1.75	0.40	1.00	2.00
❑7	1.75	0.40	1.00	2.00
❑8, Jun 94	1.75	0.40	1.00	2.00
❑9, Knights of the Angel, Part 4	2.50	0.40	1.00	2.00
❑10	2.50	0.50	1.25	2.50
❑11, Apr 95	2.50	0.50	1.25	2.50
❑12, Nov 95	2.50	0.50	1.25	2.50
❑13, Jun 96, Ascension, Part 1	2.50	0.59	1.48	2.95
❑14, Aug 96, Ascension, Part 2	2.50	0.59	1.48	2.95
❑15, Aug 96, Ascension, Part 3, Image begins as publisher	2.95	0.59	1.48	2.95
❑16, Oct 96, Ascension, Part 4	2.95	0.59	1.48	2.95
❑17, Dec 96, Ascension, Part 5	2.95	0.59	1.48	2.95
❑18, Feb 97	2.95	0.59	1.48	2.95
❑19, Apr 97	2.95	0.59	1.48	2.95
❑20, Jun 97	2.95	0.59	1.48	2.95
❑21, Sep 97, sketchbook pages	2.95	0.59	1.48	2.95
❑22, Dec 97	2.95	0.59	1.48	2.95
❑23, Feb 98, Ascension	2.95	0.59	1.48	2.95
❑24, Apr 98	2.95	0.59	1.48	2.95
❑25, Jun 98, Troll Bridge, 15th anniversary issue; double-sized	3.95	0.79	1.98	3.95
❑25/LE, Troll Bridge, Signed by Colleen Doran and Neil Gaiman; 15th anniversary issue	10.00	2.00	5.00	10.00
❑26, Nov 98, Christmas cover; not Christmas story	2.95	0.59	1.48	2.95
❑27, Apr 99	2.95	0.59	1.48	2.95
❑28, Jul 99	3.95	0.79	1.98	3.95
❑29	3.95	0.79	1.98	3.95
❑30, Aug 00	3.95	0.79	1.98	3.95
❑31, Jan 01, A World for Dreaming	3.95	0.79	1.98	3.95
❑32	3.95	0.79	1.98	3.95
❑33	3.95	0.79	1.98	3.95

DITKO PACKAGE
Ditko

Value: Cover or less

- ❑1, nn; squarebound ... 8.95

DIVA GRAFIX & STORIES
Starhead

Value: Cover or less

- ❑1, Nov 93, b&w; adult ... 3.95
- ❑2, b&w; adult ... 3.95

DIVAS
Caliber

Value: Cover or less

- ❑1, b&w ... 2.50
- ❑2, b&w ... 2.50
- ❑3, b&w ... 2.50
- ❑4, b&w ... 2.50

DIVINE INTERVENTION/GEN13
DC

Value: Cover or less

- ❑1, Nov 99 ... 2.50

DIVINE INTERVENTION/WILDCATS
DC

Value: Cover or less

- ❑1, Nov 99 ... 2.50

DIVINE RIGHT
Image

Issue	ORIG	GOOD	FINE	N-MINT
❑1, Sep 97, JLee, JLee(w), Blaze of Glory	2.50	0.80	2.00	4.00
❑1/A, Sep 97, JLee, JLee(w), Blaze of Glory, variant cover	2.50	0.80	2.00	4.00
❑1/B, Sep 97, JLee, JLee(w), Blaze of Glory, American Entertainment variant; Christy Blaze with flag in background	2.50	0.60	1.50	3.00
❑1/C, Sep 97, JLee, JLee(w), Blaze of Glory, Bagged edition	2.50	0.60	1.50	3.00
❑1/D, Sep 97, alternate cover; Spanish edition	2.50	0.50	1.25	2.50
❑1/E, Sep 97, Voyager pack with preview of Stormwatch	2.50	0.50	1.25	2.50
❑2, Oct 97, JLee, JLee(w), Disco Inferno, Sword battle scene on cover	2.50	0.60	1.50	3.00
❑2/SC, Oct 97, alternate cover; fight scene	2.50	0.50	1.25	2.50
❑3, Nov 97, JLee, JLee(w), Enemies of the State, A: Fairchild	2.50	0.50	1.25	2.50
❑3/SC, Nov 97, no cover price on outer cover	2.50	0.50	1.25	2.50
❑4, Dec 97, JLee, JLee(w), The Love Connection, White cover w/blue figure (no Fairchild)	2.50	0.50	1.25	2.50
❑4/SC, JLee, JLee(w), The Love Connection, Variant cover (Fairchild)	2.50	0.50	1.25	2.50
❑5, Feb 98, JLee, JLee(w), Party Crashers	2.50	0.50	1.25	2.50
❑5/SC, JLee, JLee(w), Party Crashers, Pacific Comicon variant cover edition	5.40	0.60	1.50	3.00
❑6, Aug 98, JLee, JLee(w), Truth or Consequences	2.50	0.50	1.25	2.50
❑7, Dec 98, JLee, JLee(w), Firewall Online	2.50	0.50	1.25	2.50
❑8, Jan 99, JLee, JLee(w), Into the Hollow Realm, Part 1	2.50	0.50	1.25	2.50
❑8/SC, Jan 99, alternate cover	2.50	0.50	1.25	2.50
❑9, Jul 99, JLee, JLee(w), The Fall of the Hollow Realm	2.50	0.50	1.25	2.50
❑10, Oct 99, JLee, JLee(w), Happily Ever After	2.50	0.50	1.25	2.50
❑11, Nov 99, JLee, JLee(w), Destiny Interruptus	2.50	0.50	1.25	2.50
❑Ash 1, Jul 97, JLee, JLee(w), 1: Divine Right, Team on cover	—	0.80	2.00	4.00
❑ASH 1/A, Jul 97, JLee, JLee(w), 1: Divine Right, variant cover; Faraday typing, woman's leg in foreground	—	0.80	2.00	4.00

DIVISION 13
Dark Horse

Value: Cover or less

- ❑1, Sep 94, KG (w) ... 2.50
- ❑2, Oct 94, KG (w) ... 2.50
- ❑3, Dec 94 ... 2.50

DJANGO AND ANGEL
Caliber

Value: Cover or less

- ❑1, b&w ... 2.50
- ❑2, b&w ... 2.50
- ❑3, b&w ... 2.50
- ❑4, b&w ... 2.50
- ❑5, b&w ... 2.50

DNAGENTS
Eclipse

Issue	ORIG	GOOD	FINE	N-MINT
❑1, Mar 83	1.50	0.50	1.25	2.50
❑2, Apr 83, ME (w), Stalked!	1.50	0.40	1.00	2.00
❑3, May 83, ME (w), Somewhat Alive!	1.50	0.40	1.00	2.00
❑4, Jul 83	1.50	0.40	1.00	2.00
❑5, Aug 83	1.50	0.40	1.00	2.00
❑6, Oct 83	1.50	0.35	0.88	1.75
❑7, Nov 83	1.50	0.35	0.88	1.75
❑8, Jan 84	1.50	0.35	0.88	1.75
❑9, Feb 84	1.50	0.35	0.88	1.75
❑10, Mar 84	1.50	0.35	0.88	1.75
❑11, May 84	1.50	0.35	0.88	1.75
❑12, May 84	1.50	0.35	0.88	1.75
❑13, Jun 84	1.25	0.35	0.88	1.75
❑14, Jul 84	1.50	0.35	0.88	1.75
❑15, Aug 84, EL	1.25	0.35	0.88	1.75
❑16, Sep 84	1.25	0.35	0.88	1.75
❑17, Dec 84	1.50	0.35	0.88	1.75
❑18, Jan 85	1.50	0.35	0.88	1.75
❑19, Feb 85	1.50	0.35	0.88	1.75
❑20, Mar 85	1.50	0.35	0.88	1.75
❑21, Apr 85	1.50	0.35	0.88	1.75
❑22, May 85	1.50	0.35	0.88	1.75
❑23, Jun 85	1.50	0.35	0.88	1.75
❑24, Jul 85, DSt (c)	1.50	0.35	0.88	1.75
❑3D 1, Jan 86, 3-Dminensional DNAgents	2.25	0.50	1.25	2.50

DNAGENTS SUPER SPECIAL
Antarctic

Value: Cover or less

- ❑1, Apr 94, b&w ... 3.50

DOC CHAOS: THE STRANGE ATTRACTOR
Vortex

Value: Cover or less

- ❑1, Apr 90, The Lust for Order Part 1 ... 3.00
- ❑2, The Lust for Order Part 2 ... 3.00
- ❑3, The Lust for Order Part 3 ... 3.00

DOC SAMSON
Marvel

Value: Cover or less

- ❑1, Jan 96, A: Hulk ... 1.95
- ❑2, Feb 96, Body Double, A: She-Hulk ... 1.95
- ❑3, Mar 96, Copycats, V: Punisher ... 1.95
- ❑4, Apr 96, The Final Analysis, A: Polaris ... 1.95

DOC SAVAGE (DC)
DC

	ORIG	GOOD	FINE	N-MINT
❑1, Nov 88, Fire In The Sky!; The Discord Makers, Part 1	1.75	0.40	1.00	2.00
❑2, Dec 88, The Discord Makers, Part 2	1.75	0.40	1.00	2.00
❑3, Dec 88	1.75	0.40	1.00	2.00
❑4, Jan 89	1.75	0.40	1.00	2.00
❑5, Jan 89	1.75	0.40	1.00	2.00
❑6, Mar 89	1.75	0.40	1.00	2.00
❑7, Apr 89	1.75	0.40	1.00	2.00
❑8, May 89	1.75	0.40	1.00	2.00
❑9, Jun 89	1.75	0.40	1.00	2.00
❑10, Jul 89	1.75	0.40	1.00	2.00
❑11, Aug 89, V: John Sunlight	1.75	0.40	1.00	2.00
❑12, Sep 89, V: John Sunlight	1.75	0.40	1.00	2.00
❑13, Oct 89, V: John Sunlight	2.00	0.40	1.00	2.00
❑14, Nov 89, V: John Sunlight	2.00	0.40	1.00	2.00
❑15, Dec 89	2.00	0.40	1.00	2.00
❑16, Jan 90	2.00	0.40	1.00	2.00
❑17, Feb 90, Shadow	2.00	0.40	1.00	2.00
❑18, Mar 90, Shadow	2.00	0.40	1.00	2.00
❑19, May 90, Air Lord	2.00	0.40	1.00	2.00
❑20, Jun 90, Air Lord	2.00	0.40	1.00	2.00
❑21, Jul 90, Air Lord	2.00	0.40	1.00	2.00
❑22, Aug 90	2.00	0.40	1.00	2.00
❑23, Sep 90	2.00	0.40	1.00	2.00
❑24, Oct 90, Final Issue	2.00	0.40	1.00	2.00
❑Anl 1	3.50	0.70	1.75	3.50

DOC SAVAGE (GOLD KEY)
GOLD KEY

	ORIG	GOOD	FINE	N-MINT
❑1, Nov 66, The Thousand-Headed Man, 10192-611	0.12	7.00	17.50	35.00

DOC SAVAGE (MARVEL)
MARVEL

	ORIG	GOOD	FINE	N-MINT
❑1, Oct 72, JM; RA, The Man Of Bronze!, adapts Man of Bronze	0.20	1.20	3.00	6.00
❑2, Dec 72, adapts Man of Bronze	0.20	0.70	1.75	3.50
❑3, Feb 73, adapts Death in Silver	0.20	0.60	1.50	3.00
❑4, Apr 73, adapts Death in Silver	0.20	0.60	1.50	3.00
❑5, Jun 73, adapts The Monsters	0.20	0.60	1.50	3.00
❑6, Aug 73, RA, GK (c), Where Giants Walk!, adapts The Monsters	0.20	0.60	1.50	3.00
❑7, Oct 73, adapts Brand of the Werewolf	0.20	0.60	1.50	3.00
❑8, Jan 74, adapts Brand of the Werewolf	0.20	0.60	1.50	3.00
❑GS 1, Reprints Doc Savage (Marvel) #1-2	0.50	1.20	3.00	6.00

DOC SAVAGE (MARVEL MAGAZINE)
MARVEL

	ORIG	GOOD	FINE	N-MINT
❑1, Aug 75	1.00	0.80	2.00	4.00
❑2, Oct 75	1.00	0.60	1.50	3.00
❑3, Jan 76	1.00	0.60	1.50	3.00
❑4, Apr 76	1.00	0.60	1.50	3.00
❑5, Jul 76	1.00	0.60	1.50	3.00
❑6, Oct 76	1.00	0.60	1.50	3.00
❑7, Jan 77	1.00	0.60	1.50	3.00
❑8, Spr 77	1.00	0.60	1.50	3.00

DOC SAVAGE (MINI-SERIES)
DC

	ORIG	GOOD	FINE	N-MINT
❑1, Nov 87, Into The Silver Pyramid	1.75	0.40	1.00	2.00
❑2, Dec 87	1.75	0.40	1.00	2.00
❑3, Jan 88	1.75	0.40	1.00	2.00
❑4, Feb 88	1.75	0.40	1.00	2.00

DOC SAVAGE: CURSE OF THE FIRE GOD
DARK HORSE

Value: Cover or less

- ❑1, Sep 95, PB ... 2.95
- ❑2, Oct 95, PB ... 2.95
- ❑3, Nov 95, PB ... 2.95
- ❑4, Dec 95, PB ... 2.95

DOC SAVAGE: DEVIL'S THOUGHTS
MILLENNIUM

Value: Cover or less

- ❑1 ... 2.50
- ❑2 ... 2.50
- ❑3 ... 2.50

DOC SAVAGE: DOOM DYNASTY
MILLENNIUM

Value: Cover or less

- ❑1, full color ... 2.50
- ❑2, full color ... 2.50

DOC SAVAGE: MANUAL OF BRONZE
MILLENNIUM

Value: Cover or less

- ❑1, Aug 92 ... 2.50

DOC SAVAGE: REPEL
MILLENNIUM

Value: Cover or less

- ❑1, only issue ever released ... 2.50

DOC SAVAGE: THE MAN OF BRONZE
MILLENNIUM

Value: Cover or less

- ❑1, The Monarch Of Armageddon, full color ... 2.50
- ❑2, The Monarch Of Armageddon ... 2.50
- ❑3 ... 2.50
- ❑4 ... 2.50

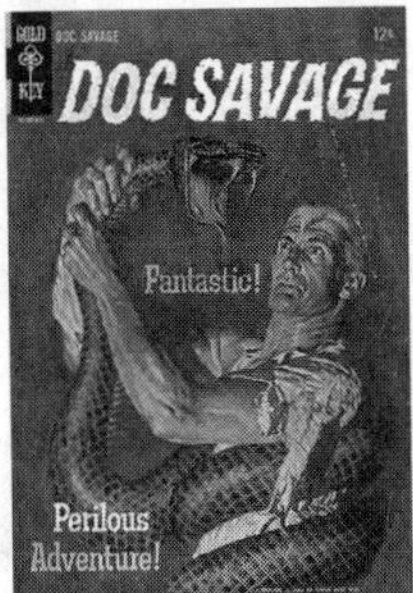

Gold Key was the first Silver Age publisher of the adventures of Lester Dent's pulp adventurer.

© 1966 Gold Key

DOC STEARN...MR. MONSTER
ECLIPSE

	ORIG	GOOD	FINE	N-MINT
❑1, Jan 85, Triumphant Unleashed, 1: Mr. Monster, Reprints Mr. Monster story from Vanguard Illustrated #7	1.75	0.50	1.25	2.50
❑2, Aug 85, DSt (c)	1.75	0.40	1.00	2.00
❑3, Oct 85	1.75	0.40	1.00	2.00
❑4, Dec 85	1.75	0.40	1.00	2.00
❑5, Feb 86	1.75	0.40	1.00	2.00
❑6, Jun 86	1.75	0.40	1.00	2.00
❑7, Dec 86	1.75	0.40	1.00	2.00
❑8, Mar 87, The Case of the Reluctant Werewolf	1.75	0.40	1.00	2.00
❑9, Apr 87, The Hemo Horror, A: Wolff & Byrd	1.75	0.40	1.00	2.00
❑10, Jun 87, BW (w), Swamp Monster; Rot, Final Issue; 6-D	1.75	0.40	1.00	2.00

DR. ANDY
ALLIANCE

Value: Cover or less

- ❑1, Aug 94, b&w ... 2.50

DR. ATOMIC
LAST GASP

	ORIG	GOOD	FINE	N-MINT
❑1, Dr. Atomic and His Spaceship; Dr. Atomic Invents the Iron Pig	0.50	1.00	2.50	5.00
❑2, The Giant Grass of Bangagong Valley;	0.50	0.80	2.00	4.00
❑3, Dr. Atomic Meets The Lochness Monster; Dr. Atomic and Mr. Hyde	0.50	0.80	2.00	4.00
❑4, The Pipe and the Dope Book	0.50	0.60	1.50	3.00
❑5, The Astral Flashlight; Kids Grow Giant Psychedelic Mushrooms 6 Feet Tall	0.50	0.60	1.50	3.00
❑6, The Chariots of The Sun;	0.50	0.60	1.50	3.00

DOCTOR BANG
RIP OFF

Value: Cover or less

- ❑1, Feb 92, b&w ... 2.50

DOCTOR BOOGIE
MEDIA ARTS

Value: Cover or less

- ❑1, Doctor Boogie vs. The Dirt Blobs ... 1.75

DOCTOR CHAOS
TRIUMPHANT

Value: Cover or less

- ❑1, The Demon of Destiny Drive; The Yellow Death, Unleashed! ... 2.50
- ❑2, KG, KG (w), Bubble Bath of the Damned!; Stretching Things, Unleashed! ... 2.50
- ❑3, Jan 94, Mr. Monster's Bedtime Story, The One Who Lurks! ... 2.50
- ❑4, Feb 94, Automatic Terror Machine; On the Job ... 2.50
- ❑5, Mar 94, Mr. Monster's Vacation; Mr. Monster's Nursery Digest: Up in the Air ... 2.50
- ❑6, Mar 94 ... 2.50
- ❑7 ... 2.50
- ❑8 ... 2.50
- ❑9 ... 2.50
- ❑10 ... 2.50
- ❑11 ... 2.50
- ❑12 ... 2.50

DOCTOR CYBORG
ATTENTION!

	ORIG	GOOD	FINE	N-MINT
❑1, 1: Doctor Cyborg, b&w	2.95	0.59	1.48	2.95
❑1/Ash, 1: Doctor Cyborg, nn; b&w; Preview edition of Doctor Cyborg #1; preview of series	0.99	0.20	0.50	1.00
❑2, b&w	2.95	0.59	1.48	2.95
❑3, b&w	2.95	0.59	1.48	2.95

DOCTOR DOOM'S REVENGE
MARVEL

	ORIG	GOOD	FINE	N-MINT
❑1, nn; giveaway comic included with computer game from Paragon Software	—	0.20	0.50	1.00

DOCTOR FATE
DC

Value: Cover or less

- ❑1, Dec 88, The Return Of Doctor Faith ... 1.25
- ❑2, Jan 89 ... 1.25
- ❑3, Jan 89 ... 1.25
- ❑4, Feb 89 ... 1.25
- ❑5, Apr 89 ... 1.25
- ❑6, May 89 ... 1.75
- ❑7, Jun 89 ... 1.75
- ❑8, Jul 89 ... 1.75
- ❑9, Aug 89 ... 1.75
- ❑10, Sep 89 ... 1.75
- ❑11, Nov 89 ... 1.75

	ORIG	GOOD	FINE	N-MINT

- ❑12, Dec 89 ... 1.75
- ❑13, Jan 90 ... 1.75
- ❑14, Feb 90 ... 1.75
- ❑15, Mar 90, A: JLI ... 1.50
- ❑16, Apr 90 ... 1.50
- ❑17, May 90 ... 1.50
- ❑18, Jun 90 ... 1.50
- ❑19, Jul 90 ... 1.50
- ❑20, Aug 90 ... 1.50
- ❑21, Oct 90 ... 1.50
- ❑22, Nov 90 ... 1.50
- ❑23, Dec 90 ... 1.50
- ❑24, Jan 91 ... 1.50
- ❑25, Feb 91, 1: Doctor Fate (New) ... 1.50
- ❑26, Mar 91 ... 1.50
- ❑27, Apr 91 ... 1.50
- ❑28, May 91 ... 1.50
- ❑29, Jun 91 ... 1.50
- ❑30, Jul 91 ... 1.50
- ❑31, Aug 91 ... 1.50
- ❑32, Sep 91, War of the Gods, Part 8, War of the Gods ... 1.75
- ❑33, Oct 91, War of the Gods, Part 14, War of the Gods ... 1.75
- ❑34, Nov 91 ... 1.75
- ❑35, Dec 91 ... 1.75
- ❑36, Jan 92 ... 1.75
- ❑37, Feb 92 ... 1.75
- ❑38, Mar 92 ... 1.75
- ❑39, Apr 92 ... 1.75
- ❑40, May 92 ... 1.75
- ❑41, Jun 92, Balances, Final Issue ... 1.75
- ❑Anl 1, Nov 89 ... 2.95

DOCTOR FATE (MINI-SERIES)
DC

	ORIG	GOOD	FINE	N-MINT
❑1, Jul 87, KG, Cycles	1.50	0.40	1.00	2.00
❑2, Aug 87, KG, Asylum	1.50	0.40	1.00	2.00
❑3, Sep 87, KG	1.50	0.40	1.00	2.00
❑4, Oct 87, KG, Incarnations, 1: Doctor Fate II (Eric Strauss & Linda Strauss); D: Doctor Fate I (Kent Nelson)	1.50	0.40	1.00	2.00

DOCTOR FAUSTUS
ANARCHY

	ORIG	GOOD	FINE	N-MINT
❑1, b&w	2.95	0.59	1.48	2.95
❑2, b&w	2.95	0.59	1.48	2.95
❑Ash 1, ashcan, b&w	—	0.40	1.00	2.00

DOCTOR FRANKENSTEIN'S HOUSE OF 3-D
3-D ZONE

Value: Cover or less

- ❑1, Oversized ... 3.95

DR. GIGGLES
DARK HORSE

Value: Cover or less

- ❑1, Discharge Granted, movie Adaptation ... 2.50
- ❑2, movie Adaptation ... 2.50

DOCTOR GORPON
ETERNITY

Value: Cover or less

- ❑1, Hands of Death, b&w ... 2.50
- ❑2, b&w ... 2.50
- ❑3, Aug 91, b&w ... 2.50

DR. GOYLE SPECIAL
ARROW

Value: Cover or less

- ❑1, b&w ... 2.95

DOCTOR MID-NITE
DC

Value: Cover or less

- ❑1, MW (w), D.O.A. ... 5.95
- ❑2, MW (w), A: Note-Lite; A: Black Shadow; A: Terrible Trio; A: Mouthpiece ... 5.95
- ❑3, MW (w) ... 5.95

DR. RADIUM AND THE GIZMOS OF BOOLA-BOOLA
SLAVE LABOR

Value: Cover or less

- ❑1, Jan 92, nn; b&w ... 4.95

DR. RADIUM, MAN OF SCIENCE
SLAVE LABOR

Value: Cover or less

- ❑1, Oct 92, b&w ... 2.50
- ❑2, Jan 93, b&w ... 2.50
- ❑3, Jul 93 ... 2.95
- ❑4, Jan 94 ... 2.95
- ❑5, Jan 95, b&w ... 2.95

DR. ROBOT SPECIAL
DARK HORSE

Value: Cover or less

- ❑1, Apr 00 ... 2.95

DOCTOR SOLAR, MAN OF THE ATOM
GOLD KEY

	ORIG	GOOD	FINE	N-MINT
❑1, 1: Doctor Solar (out of costume); O: Doctor Solar, 1st Gold Key comic	0.12	20.00	50.00	100.00
❑2, 1: Professor Harbinger	0.12	9.00	22.50	45.00
❑3	0.12	6.00	15.00	30.00
❑4	0.12	6.00	15.00	30.00
❑5, 1: Doctor Solar (in costume)	0.12	6.00	15.00	30.00
❑6	0.12	4.40	11.00	22.00
❑7, Mar 64, Keys of Kn, Painted cover	0.12	4.40	11.00	22.00
❑8	0.12	4.40	11.00	22.00
❑9	0.12	4.40	11.00	22.00
❑10	0.12	4.40	11.00	22.00
❑11	0.12	3.20	8.00	16.00
❑12, May 65, makes multiple versions of self	0.12	3.20	8.00	16.00
❑13	0.12	3.20	8.00	16.00
❑14, Sep 65, Solar's Midas Touch, Part 1; Solar's Science Forum, Painted cover	0.12	3.20	8.00	16.00
❑15, O: Doctor Solar	0.12	4.00	10.00	20.00
❑16, Jun 66, Secrets of Atom Valley; The War of the Suns, Part 1, Painted cover	0.12	3.20	8.00	16.00
❑17	0.12	3.20	8.00	16.00
❑18	0.12	3.20	8.00	16.00
❑19	0.12	3.20	8.00	16.00
❑20	0.12	3.20	8.00	16.00
❑21	0.12	2.40	6.00	12.00
❑22	0.12	2.40	6.00	12.00
❑23	0.12	2.40	6.00	12.00
❑24	0.12	2.40	6.00	12.00
❑25	0.12	2.40	6.00	12.00
❑26	0.12	2.40	6.00	12.00
❑27, End of original series	0.12	2.40	6.00	12.00
❑28, Series begins again (1981)	0.12	0.70	1.75	3.50
❑29	0.12	0.70	1.75	3.50
❑30, A: Magnus, Robot Fighter (Gold Key)	0.12	0.70	1.75	3.50
❑31, A: Magnus, Robot Fighter (Gold Key), Final Issue	0.12	0.70	1.75	3.50

DR. SPECK
BUG BOOKS

Value: Cover or less

- ❑1, b&w ... 2.95
- ❑2, b&w ... 2.95
- ❑3, b&w ... 2.95
- ❑4, b&w ... 2.95

DOCTOR STRANGE (1ST SERIES)
MARVEL

	ORIG	GOOD	FINE	N-MINT
❑169, Jun 68, DA, The Coming of ... Dr. Strange!, O: Doctor Strange, Series continued from Strange Tales #168	0.12	20.00	50.00	100.00
❑170, Jul 68, DA, V: Nightmare	0.12	7.00	17.50	35.00
❑171, Aug 68, DA	0.12	6.00	15.00	30.00
❑172, Sep 68, GC, V: Dormammu	0.12	6.00	15.00	30.00
❑173, Oct 68, GC, V: Dormammu	0.12	6.00	15.00	30.00
❑174, Nov 68, GC, The Power And The Pendulum, 1: Satannish	0.12	6.00	15.00	30.00
❑175, Dec 68, GC, Unto Us The Sons Of Satannish!	0.12	6.00	15.00	30.00
❑176, Jan 69, GC, O Grave Where is Thy Victory	0.12	6.00	15.00	30.00
❑177, Feb 69, GC, 1: new costume	0.12	5.00	12.50	25.00
❑178, Mar 69, GC, A: Black Knight	0.12	5.00	12.50	25.00
❑179, Apr 69, SD, A: Spider-Man, Reprint	0.12	5.00	12.50	25.00
❑180, May 69, GC, A: Eternity, Photo cover	0.12	5.00	12.50	25.00
❑181, Jun 69, GC	0.12	5.00	12.50	25.00
❑182, Sep 69, GC, V: Juggernaut	0.15	5.00	12.50	25.00
❑183, Nov 69, GC	0.15	5.00	12.50	25.00

DOCTOR STRANGE (2ND SERIES)
MARVEL

	ORIG	GOOD	FINE	N-MINT
❑1, Jun 74, DG; FB	0.25	5.00	12.50	25.00
❑2, Aug 74, DG; FB, A Separate Reality, 1: Silver Dagger; A: Defenders	0.25	2.40	6.00	12.00
❑3, Sep 74, DG; FB, V: Dormammu	0.25	1.20	3.00	6.00
❑4, Oct 74, DG; FB	0.25	1.20	3.00	6.00
❑5, Nov 74, DG; FB, O: Silver Dagger	0.25	1.20	3.00	6.00
❑6, Dec 74, GC	0.25	1.00	2.50	5.00
❑7, GC	0.25	1.00	2.50	5.00
❑8, GC, O: Clea	0.25	1.00	2.50	5.00
❑9, GC, O: Clea	0.25	1.00	2.50	5.00
❑10, Oct 75, GC	0.25	1.00	2.50	5.00
❑11, Dec 75, GC	0.25	0.60	1.50	3.00
❑12, Feb 76, GC	0.25	0.60	1.50	3.00
❑13, GC	0.25	0.60	1.50	3.00
❑14, GC	0.25	0.60	1.50	3.00
❑15, GC, Where There's Smoke...	0.25	0.60	1.50	3.00
❑16, GC	0.25	0.60	1.50	3.00
❑17, Aug 76, GC	0.25	0.60	1.50	3.00
❑18, Sep 76, GC	0.30	0.60	1.50	3.00
❑19, Oct 76, AA; GC, 1: Xander	0.30	0.60	1.50	3.00
❑20, Dec 76	0.30	0.60	1.50	3.00
❑21, Feb 77, O: Doctor Strange	0.30	0.50	1.25	2.50
❑22, Apr 77	0.30	0.50	1.25	2.50
❑23, Jun 77	0.30	0.50	1.25	2.50
❑24, Aug 77	0.30	0.50	1.25	2.50
❑25, Oct 77	0.30	0.50	1.25	2.50
❑26, Dec 77	0.35	0.40	1.00	2.00
❑27, Feb 78	0.35	0.40	1.00	2.00
❑28, Apr 78	0.35	0.40	1.00	2.00
❑29, Jun 78, TS, He Who Stalks!	0.35	0.40	1.00	2.00
❑30, Aug 78, TS, A Gathering Of Fear!	0.35	0.40	1.00	2.00
❑31, Oct 78, A Death For Immorality	0.35	0.40	1.00	2.00
❑32, Dec 78, The Dream Weaver	0.35	0.40	1.00	2.00
❑33, Feb 79, All My Dreams Against Me	0.35	0.40	1.00	2.00
❑34, Apr 79	0.35	0.40	1.00	2.00
❑35, Jun 79	0.40	0.40	1.00	2.00
❑36, Aug 79, DGr; GC, The Man Who Knew Stephen Sanders!	0.40	0.40	1.00	2.00
❑37, Oct 79	0.40	0.40	1.00	2.00
❑38, Dec 79, DGr; GC, Eye Of The Beholder	0.40	0.40	1.00	2.00
❑39, Feb 80	0.40	0.40	1.00	2.00
❑40, Apr 80	0.40	0.40	1.00	2.00
❑41, Jun 80	0.40	0.40	1.00	2.00

	ORIG	GOOD	FINE	N-MINT
❑42, Aug 80	0.40	0.40	1.00	2.00
❑43, Oct 80	0.50	0.40	1.00	2.00
❑44, Dec 80	0.50	0.40	1.00	2.00
❑45, Feb 81	0.50	0.40	1.00	2.00
❑46, Apr 81	0.50	0.40	1.00	2.00
❑47, Jun 81	0.50	0.40	1.00	2.00
❑48, Aug 81, A: Brother Voodoo	0.50	0.40	1.00	2.00
❑49, Oct 81, A: Baron Mordo	0.50	0.40	1.00	2.00
❑50, Dec 81, A: Baron Mordo	0.50	0.40	1.00	2.00
❑51, Feb 82, A Time For Love, A Time For Hate!	0.60	0.40	1.00	2.00
❑52, Apr 82	0.60	0.40	1.00	2.00
❑53, Jun 82	0.60	0.40	1.00	2.00
❑54, Aug 82, BA; PS	0.60	0.40	1.00	2.00
❑55, Oct 82, PS	0.60	0.40	1.00	2.00
❑56, Dec 82, PS	0.60	0.40	1.00	2.00
❑57, Feb 83, KN, Gather My Disciples Before Me!	0.60	0.40	1.00	2.00
❑58, Apr 83, DGr, ...At Loose Ends!	0.60	0.40	1.00	2.00
❑59, Jun 83, DGr, Children Of The Night!	0.60	0.40	1.00	2.00
❑60, Aug 83, DGr, A: Dracula	0.60	0.40	1.00	2.00
❑61, Oct 83, DGr, Power Be The Prize, A: Dracula	0.60	0.40	1.00	2.00
❑62, Dec 83, Deliver Us From Evil!, A: Dracula	0.60	0.40	1.00	2.00
❑63, Feb 84, Cry Of The Spirit	0.60	0.40	1.00	2.00
❑64, Apr 84, Art Rage	0.60	0.40	1.00	2.00
❑65, Jun 84, PS, Charlatan	0.60	0.40	1.00	2.00
❑66, Aug 84, PS, The Chosen One	0.60	0.40	1.00	2.00
❑67, Oct 84, Private Eyes	0.60	0.40	1.00	2.00
❑68, Dec 84, PS, Sword And Sorcery	0.60	0.40	1.00	2.00
❑69, Feb 85, PS, Sea Cruise	0.60	0.40	1.00	2.00
❑70, Apr 85, Deadly Exchange	0.65	0.40	1.00	2.00
❑71, Jun 85, PS, Into The Dark Dimension, O: Umar	0.65	0.40	1.00	2.00
❑72, Aug 85, PS, Secret Origin	0.65	0.40	1.00	2.00
❑73, Oct 85, PS, Final Triumph	0.65	0.40	1.00	2.00
❑74, Dec 85, And Now...The Beyonder, 1: Ecstasy, Secret Wars II	0.65	0.40	1.00	2.00
❑75, Feb 86, SB, Souls In Torment!, O: Wong (Doctor Strange's manservant)	0.75	0.40	1.00	2.00
❑76, Apr 86, What Song The Sirens Sang!	0.75	0.40	1.00	2.00
❑77, Jun 86, Khat?	0.75	0.40	1.00	2.00
❑78, Aug 86, New costume	0.75	0.40	1.00	2.00
❑79, Oct 86, Fata Morganna!	0.75	0.40	1.00	2.00
❑80, Dec 86, Don't Pay the Ferryman!	0.75	0.40	1.00	2.00
❑81, Feb 87, The Tongues Of Men And Angels...!, Final Issue	0.75	0.40	1.00	2.00
❑Anl 1	0.50	0.40	1.00	2.00
❑GS 1	0.50	1.00	2.50	5.00
❑SE 1, Mar 83, FB, Through An Orb Darkly; A Separate Reality	2.50	0.60	1.50	3.00

DOCTOR STRANGE (3RD SERIES)

MARVEL

Value: Cover or less

- ❑1, Feb 99, The Flight of Bones ... 2.99
- ❑2, Mar 99, The Flight of Bones ... 2.99
- ❑3, Apr 99, The Flight of Bones, A: Jonathan White ... 2.99
- ❑4, May 99, The Flight of Bones ... 2.99

DOCTOR STRANGE AND DOCTOR DOOM: TRIUMPH AND TORMENT

MARVEL

Value: Cover or less

- ❑1, Oct 89, hardcover ... 17.95

DOCTOR STRANGE CLASSICS

MARVEL

	ORIG	GOOD	FINE	N-MINT
❑1, Mar 84, SD, Reprint	1.50	0.40	1.00	2.00
❑2, Apr 84, SD, Reprint	1.50	0.40	1.00	2.00
❑3, May 84	1.50	0.40	1.00	2.00
❑4, Jun 84	1.50	0.40	1.00	2.00

DOCTOR STRANGEFATE

DC

Value: Cover or less

- ❑1, Apr 96, The Decrees Of Fate, A: Access ... 1.95

DOCTOR STRANGE/GHOST RIDER SPECIAL

MARVEL

Value: Cover or less

- ❑1, Apr 91, Strange Tales Part II, reprints Doctor Strange #28; Continued from Ghost Rider # 12 ... 1.50

DOCTOR STRANGE: SHAMBALLA

MARVEL

Value: Cover or less

- ❑1 ... 5.95

DOCTOR STRANGE: SORCERER SUPREME

MARVEL

	ORIG	GOOD	FINE	N-MINT
❑1, Nov 88, Love is the Spell...The Spell is Death!	1.25	0.60	1.50	3.00
❑2, Jan 89, Inferno	1.50	0.40	1.00	2.00
❑3, Mar 89	1.50	0.40	1.00	2.00
❑4, May 89	1.50	0.30	0.75	1.50

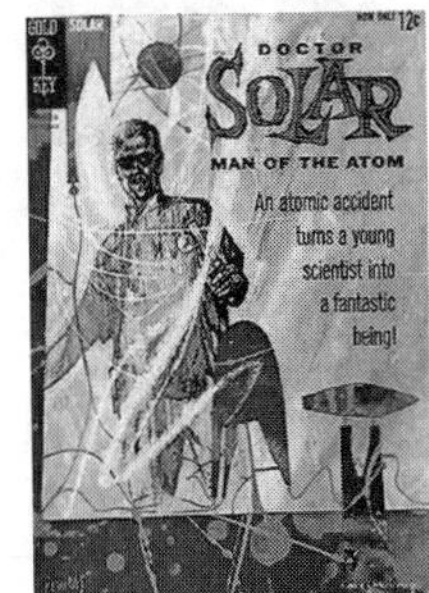

Gold Key's first comic book was *Doctor Solar, Man of the Atom.*

© 1963 Gold Key

	ORIG	GOOD	FINE	N-MINT
❑5, Jul 89	1.50	0.30	0.75	1.50
❑6, Aug 89	1.50	0.30	0.75	1.50
❑7, Sep 89	1.50	0.30	0.75	1.50
❑8, Oct 89, O: Mephisto; O: Satannish	1.50	0.30	0.75	1.50
❑9, Nov 89	1.50	0.30	0.75	1.50
❑10, Dec 89, A: Morbius	1.50	0.30	0.75	1.50
❑11, Dec 89, Acts of Vengeance, A: Hobgoblin, Acts of Vengeance	1.50	0.30	0.75	1.50
❑12, Dec 89, Acts of Vengeance, Acts of Vengeance	1.50	0.30	0.75	1.50
❑13, Jan 90, Acts of Vengeance, Acts of Vengeance	1.50	0.30	0.75	1.50
❑14, Feb 90, vampires	1.50	0.30	0.75	1.50
❑15, Mar 90, Amy Grant cover (unauthorized, caused Marvel to be sued); vampires	1.50	0.60	1.50	3.00
❑16, Apr 90, vampires	1.50	0.30	0.75	1.50
❑17, May 90, vampires	1.50	0.30	0.75	1.50
❑18, Jun 90, vampires	1.50	0.30	0.75	1.50
❑19, Jul 90, GC	1.50	0.30	0.75	1.50
❑20, Aug 90	1.50	0.30	0.75	1.50
❑21, Sep 90	1.50	0.30	0.75	1.50
❑22, Oct 90, O: Umar	1.50	0.30	0.75	1.50
❑23, Nov 90	1.50	0.30	0.75	1.50
❑24, Dec 90	1.50	0.30	0.75	1.50
❑25, Jan 91	1.50	0.30	0.75	1.50
❑26, Feb 91, werewolf	1.50	0.30	0.75	1.50
❑27, Mar 91, werewolf	1.50	0.30	0.75	1.50
❑28, Apr 91, Ghost Rider; Ghost Rider x-over	1.50	0.30	0.75	1.50
❑29, May 91	1.75	0.30	0.75	1.50
❑30, Jun 91	1.75	0.30	0.75	1.50
❑31, Jul 91, Infinity Gauntlet, Infinity Gauntlet	1.75	0.30	0.75	1.50
❑32, Aug 91, Infinity Gauntlet, Infinity Gauntlet	1.75	0.30	0.75	1.50
❑33, Sep 91, Infinity Gauntlet, Infinity Gauntlet	1.75	0.30	0.75	1.50
❑34, Oct 91, Infinity Gauntlet, Infinity Gauntlet	1.75	0.30	0.75	1.50
❑35, Nov 91, Infinity Gauntlet, Infinity Gauntlet	1.75	0.30	0.75	1.50
❑36, Dec 91, Infinity Gauntlet; Prelude to Warlock & the Infinity Watch #1	1.75	0.30	0.75	1.50
❑37, Jan 92	1.75	0.30	0.75	1.50
❑38, Feb 92	1.75	0.35	0.88	1.75
❑39, Mar 92	1.75	0.35	0.88	1.75
❑40, Apr 92	1.75	0.35	0.88	1.75
❑41, May 92, Wolverine	1.75	0.35	0.88	1.75
❑42, Jun 92, Infinity War, Galactus	1.75	0.35	0.88	1.75
❑43, Jul 92, Infinity War	1.75	0.35	0.88	1.75
❑44, Aug 92, Infinity War	1.75	0.35	0.88	1.75
❑45, Sep 92, Infinity War	1.75	0.35	0.88	1.75
❑46, Oct 92, Infinity War	1.75	0.35	0.88	1.75
❑47, Nov 92, Infinity War	1.75	0.35	0.88	1.75
❑48, Dec 92	1.75	0.35	0.88	1.75
❑49, Jan 93	1.75	0.35	0.88	1.75
❑50, Feb 93, The Heart Of Darkness, Prism cover; Prelude to Secret Defenders #1	2.95	0.59	1.48	2.95
❑51, Mar 93	1.75	0.35	0.88	1.75
❑52, Apr 93	1.75	0.35	0.88	1.75
❑53, May 93	1.75	0.35	0.88	1.75
❑54, Jun 93	1.75	0.35	0.88	1.75
❑55, Jul 93	1.75	0.35	0.88	1.75
❑56, Aug 93	1.75	0.35	0.88	1.75
❑57, Sep 93	1.75	0.35	0.88	1.75
❑58, Oct 93, A: Urthona	1.75	0.35	0.88	1.75
❑59, Nov 93	1.75	0.35	0.88	1.75
❑60, Dec 93, Siege of Darkness, Part 7, Spot varnish cover	1.75	0.35	0.88	1.75
❑61, Jan 94, Siege of Darkness, Part 15, Spot varnish cover	1.75	0.35	0.88	1.75
❑62, Feb 94	1.75	0.35	0.88	1.75
❑63, Mar 94	1.75	0.35	0.88	1.75
❑64, Apr 94	1.75	0.35	0.88	1.75
❑65, May 94	1.95	0.35	0.88	1.75
❑66, Jun 94	1.95	0.39	0.98	1.95
❑67, Jul 94	1.95	0.39	0.98	1.95
❑68, Aug 94	1.95	0.39	0.98	1.95

	ORIG	GOOD	FINE	N-MINT
❑69, Sep 94	1.95	0.39	0.98	1.95
❑70, Oct 94, A: Hulk	1.95	0.39	0.98	1.95
❑71, Nov 94, A: Hulk	1.95	0.39	0.98	1.95
❑72, Dec 94, Last Rites, Part 1	1.95	0.39	0.98	1.95
❑73, Jan 95, Last Rites, Part 2	1.95	0.39	0.98	1.95
❑74, Feb 95, Last Rites, Part 3	1.95	0.39	0.98	1.95
❑75, Mar 95, Last Rites, Part 4, Giant-size	2.50	0.50	1.25	2.50
❑75/SC, Mar 95, Last Rites, Part 4, foil cover; Giant-size	3.50	0.70	1.75	3.50
❑76, Apr 95	1.95	0.39	0.98	1.95
❑77, May 95	1.95	0.39	0.98	1.95
❑78, Jun 95	1.95	0.39	0.98	1.95
❑79, Jul 95	1.95	0.39	0.98	1.95
❑80, Aug 95, indicia changes to Doctor Strange, Sorcerer Supreme for remainder of run	1.95	0.39	0.98	1.95
❑81, Sep 95	1.95	0.39	0.98	1.95
❑82, Oct 95	1.95	0.39	0.98	1.95
❑83, Nov 95	1.95	0.39	0.98	1.95
❑84, Dec 95, The Homecoming, Part 1, A: Mordo	1.95	0.39	0.98	1.95
❑85, Jan 96, The Homecoming, Part 2, O: Mordo	1.95	0.39	0.98	1.95
❑86, Feb 96, The Homecoming, Part 3	1.95	0.39	0.98	1.95
❑87, Mar 96, The Homecoming, Part 4, D: Mordo	1.95	0.39	0.98	1.95
❑88, Apr 96, Fall of the Tempo, Part 1	1.95	0.39	0.98	1.95
❑89, May 96, Fall of the Tempo, Part 2	1.95	0.39	0.98	1.95
❑90, Jun 96, Final Issue	1.95	0.39	0.98	1.95
❑Anl 1	2.00	0.50	1.25	2.50
❑Anl 2, Return of Defenders; Return of the Defenders, Part 4	2.25	0.45	1.13	2.25
❑Anl 3, trading card	2.95	0.59	1.48	2.95
❑Anl 4, Strangers Among Us	2.95	0.59	1.48	2.95
❑Ash 1, b&w; no indicia	0.75	0.15	0.38	0.75

DR. STRANGE VS. DRACULA
MARVEL

Value: Cover or less

❑1, Mar 94, TP; GC, Reprint ... 1.75

DOCTOR STRANGE: WHAT IS IT THAT DISTURBS YOU STEPHEN?
MARVEL

Value: Cover or less

❑1, Oct 97, CR, squarebound . 5.99

DR. TOMORROW
ACCLAIM

Value: Cover or less

❑1, Sep 97, DP, BL (w), Age of Tomorrow ... 2.50
❑2, Oct 97, DP, BL (w), V: Teutonic Knight ... 2.50
❑3, Nov 97, DP, BL (w), V: Nazi X-O ... 2.50
❑4, Dec 97, BL (w), Tomorrow Ends Today ... 2.50
❑5, Jan 98, DP, BL (w), D: Cappy ... 2.50
❑6, Feb 98, DP, BL (w), 1: Mushroom Cloud ... 2.50
❑7, Mar 98, DP, BL (w), Tomorrow and Mushroom Cloud go to Vietnam ... 2.50
❑8, Apr 98, DP, GK (c), BL (w), V: Warmaster ... 2.50
❑9, Jan 98, DP, BL (w), no cover date; indicia says Jan 98 ... 2.50
❑10, Jan 98, DP, BL (w), no cover date; indicia says Jan 98 ... 2.50
❑11, DP, BL (w) ... 2.50
❑12, DP, BL (w) ... 2.50

DOCTOR WEIRD
CALIBER

Value: Cover or less

❑1, Oct 94, Where Monsters Dwell, b&w ... 2.95
❑2, May 95, b&w ... 2.95
❑SE 1, Feb 94, b&w ... 3.95

DR. WEIRD (VOL. 2)
OCTOBER

Value: Cover or less

❑1, Oct 97, Wasteland ... 2.95
❑2, Jul 98 ... 2.95

DOCTOR WHO
MARVEL

	ORIG	GOOD	FINE	N-MINT
❑1, Oct 97, DaG, BBC TV series; Reprint from Doctor Who Monthly (British)	1.50	0.50	1.25	2.50
❑2, Nov 84, DaG, Revenge Of Wrath, Reprint from Doctor Who Monthly (British)	1.50	0.40	1.00	2.00
❑3, Dec 84, DaG, Dogs Of Doom, Reprint from Doctor Who Monthly (British)	1.50	0.40	1.00	2.00
❑4, Jan 85, Reprint from Doctor Who Monthly (British)	1.50	0.40	1.00	2.00
❑5, Feb 85, Reprint from Doctor Who Monthly (British)	1.50	0.40	1.00	2.00
❑6, Mar 85, Reprint from Doctor Who Monthly (British)	1.50	0.40	1.00	2.00
❑7, Apr 85, Reprint from Doctor Who Monthly (British)	1.50	0.40	1.00	2.00
❑8, May 85, Reprint from Doctor Who Monthly (British)	1.50	0.40	1.00	2.00
❑9, Jun 85, Reprint from Doctor Who Monthly (British)	1.50	0.40	1.00	2.00
❑10, Jul 85, Reprint from Doctor Who Monthly (British)	1.50	0.40	1.00	2.00
❑11, Aug 85, Reprint from Doctor Who Monthly (British)	1.50	0.30	0.75	1.50
❑12, Sep 85, Reprint from Doctor Who Monthly (British)	1.50	0.30	0.75	1.50
❑13, Oct 85, Reprint from Doctor Who Monthly (British)	1.50	0.30	0.75	1.50
❑14, Nov 85, Reprint from Doctor Who Monthly (British)	1.50	0.30	0.75	1.50
❑15, Dec 85, Reprint from Doctor Who Monthly (British)	1.50	0.30	0.75	1.50
❑16, Jan 86, Reprint from Doctor Who Monthly (British)	1.50	0.30	0.75	1.50
❑17, Feb 86, Reprint from Doctor Who Monthly (British)	1.50	0.30	0.75	1.50
❑18, Mar 86, Reprint from Doctor Who Monthly (British)	1.50	0.30	0.75	1.50
❑19, Apr 86, Reprint from Doctor Who Monthly (British)	1.50	0.30	0.75	1.50
❑20, May 86, Reprint from Doctor Who Monthly (British)	1.50	0.30	0.75	1.50
❑21, Jun 86, Reprint from Doctor Who Monthly (British)	1.50	0.30	0.75	1.50
❑22, Jul 86, Reprint from Doctor Who Monthly (British)	1.50	0.30	0.75	1.50
❑23, Aug 86, Reprint from Doctor Who Monthly (British)	1.50	0.30	0.75	1.50

DR. WONDER
OLD TOWN

Value: Cover or less

❑1, Jun 96, Terror in the Town Square!; The Writer (text story), O: Doctor Wonder, b&w ... 2.95
❑2, Jul 96, b&w ... 2.95
❑3, Aug 96, b&w ... 2.95
❑4, Oct 96, b&w ... 2.95
❑5, Fal 97, Fan Page (t, b&w; magazine-sized ... 2.95

DOCTOR ZERO
MARVEL

	ORIG	GOOD	FINE	N-MINT
❑1, Apr 88, BSz (c), Shadows Of Troy	1.25	0.30	0.75	1.50
❑2, Jun 88, BSz (c)	1.25	0.30	0.75	1.50
❑3, Aug 88	1.25	0.30	0.75	1.50
❑4, Oct 88	1.50	0.30	0.75	1.50
❑5, Dec 88	1.50	0.30	0.75	1.50
❑6, Feb 89	1.50	0.30	0.75	1.50
❑7, Apr 89, DS, man Is But A Dream Of A Shadow	1.50	0.30	0.75	1.50
❑8, Jun 89, Final Issue	1.50	0.30	0.75	1.50

DOC WEIRD'S THRILL BOOK
PURE IMAGINATION

	ORIG	GOOD	FINE	N-MINT
❑1, FF; ATh; AW	1.75	0.40	1.00	2.00
❑2, WW, Jack Cole	1.75	0.40	1.00	2.00
❑3, WW	2.00	0.40	1.00	2.00

DODEKAIN
ANTARCTIC

Value: Cover or less

❑1, Nov 94, b&w ... 2.95
❑2, Dec 94, b&w ... 2.95
❑3, Jan 95, b&w ... 2.95
❑4, Feb 95, b&w ... 2.95
❑5, Mar 95, b&w ... 2.95
❑6, Apr 95, b&w ... 2.95
❑7, May 95, b&w ... 2.95
❑8, Jun 95, b&w; Final Issue ... 2.95

DOG BOY
FANTAGRAPHICS

	ORIG	GOOD	FINE	N-MINT
❑1	1.75	0.40	1.00	2.00
❑2	1.75	0.35	0.88	1.75
❑3, May 87, The Brainstorm	1.75	0.35	0.88	1.75
❑4	1.75	0.35	0.88	1.75
❑5	1.75	0.35	0.88	1.75
❑6	1.75	0.35	0.88	1.75
❑7, Sep 87	1.75	0.35	0.88	1.75
❑8	1.75	0.35	0.88	1.75
❑9	1.75	0.35	0.88	1.75

DOG MOON
DC

Value: Cover or less

❑1, nn; One-Shot ... 6.95

DOGS OF WAR
DEFIANT

Value: Cover or less

❑1, Apr 94, Reassignment ... 2.50
❑2, May 94, What Makes Brothers... ... 2.50
❑3, Jun 94, I've Got A Little List... ... 2.50
❑4 ... 2.50
❑5 ... 2.50
❑6 ... 2.50
❑7 ... 2.50
❑8, Final Issue ... 2.50

DOG SOUP
DOG SOUP

Value: Cover or less

❑1, b&w ... 2.50

DOGS-O-WAR
CRUSADE

Value: Cover or less

❑1, b&w ... 2.95
❑2, Jul 96, b&w ... 2.95
❑3, Jan 97, b&w; Final Issue ... 2.95

DOG T.A.G.S.: TRAINED ANIMAL GUN SQUADRON
BUGGED OUT

Value: Cover or less

- ❑1, Jun 93, b&w ... 1.95

DOIN' TIME WITH OJ
BONEYARD

	ORIG	GOOD	FINE	N-MINT
❑1, Dec 94, b&w	2.95	0.70	1.75	3.50

DOJINSHI
ANTARCTIC

Value: Cover or less

- ❑1, Oct 92, b&w ... 2.95
- ❑2, Dec 92, b&w ... 2.95
- ❑3, Feb 93, b&w ... 2.95
- ❑4, Apr 93, b&w ... 2.95

DOLL
RIP OFF

	ORIG	GOOD	FINE	N-MINT
❑1, Feb 89, b&w; adult	2.50	0.60	1.50	3.00
❑2, Mar 89, b&w; adult	2.50	0.50	1.25	2.50
❑3, May 89, b&w; adult	2.50	0.50	1.25	2.50
❑4, Feb 90, b&w; adult	2.50	0.50	1.25	2.50
❑5, Mar 91, b&w; adult	2.50	0.50	1.25	2.50
❑6, May 91, b&w; adult	2.50	0.50	1.25	2.50
❑7, Jun 91, b&w; adult	2.50	0.50	1.25	2.50
❑8, Sep 92, b&w; adult	2.95	0.59	1.48	2.95

DOLLMAN (MINI-SERIES)
ETERNITY

Value: Cover or less

- ❑1, Nov 91, The Brain From Beyond, 1: Dollman (Brick Bardo), full color; movie tie-in ... 2.50
- ❑2, full color; movie tie-in ... 2.50
- ❑3, full color; movie tie-in ... 2.50
- ❑4, Blaze Of Glory, full color; movie tie-in ... 2.50

DOLL PARTS
SIRIUS

Value: Cover or less

- ❑1, Oct 00, b&w ... 2.95

DOLLS
SIRIUS

Value: Cover or less

- ❑1, Jun 96 ... 2.95

DOLLZ, THE
IMAGE

Value: Cover or less

- ❑1, Apr 01 ... 2.95

DOME: GROUND ZERO, THE
DC

Value: Cover or less

- ❑1, nn; prestige format; computer-generated ... 7.95

DOMINATION FACTOR: AVENGERS
MARVEL

Value: Cover or less

- ❑1, Nov 99, says 1.2 on cover, 1 in indicia ... 2.50
- ❑2, Nov 99, JOy (w), Strange Tales, says 2.4 on cover, 2 in indicia ... 2.50

DOMINATION FACTOR: FANTASTIC FOUR
MARVEL

Value: Cover or less

- ❑1, Dec 99, BMc, Arrival, cover forms diptych with Domination Factor: Avengers #1 ... 2.50
- ❑2, Dec 99, BMc, Flashback Times Four, says 2.3 on cover, 2 in indicia ... 2.50

DOMINION
ECLIPSE

	ORIG	GOOD	FINE	N-MINT
❑1, b&w; Japanese	2.00	0.60	1.50	3.00
❑2, b&w; Japanese	2.00	0.50	1.25	2.50
❑3, b&w; Japanese	2.00	0.50	1.25	2.50
❑4, b&w; Japanese	2.00	0.40	1.00	2.00
❑5, b&w; Japanese	2.00	0.40	1.00	2.00
❑6, b&w; Japanese	2.00	0.40	1.00	2.00

DOMINION: CONFLICT 1
DARK HORSE

	ORIG	GOOD	FINE	N-MINT
❑1, Mar 96, b&w	2.95	0.59	1.48	2.95
❑2, Apr 96, b&w	2.95	0.59	1.48	2.95
❑3, May 96, b&w	2.95	0.59	1.48	2.95
❑4, Jun 96, b&w	2.95	0.59	1.48	2.95
❑5, Jul 96, b&w	2.95	0.59	1.48	2.95
❑6, Aug 96, b&w; Final Issue	2.95	0.59	1.48	2.95

DOMINION: PHANTOM OF THE AUDIENCE
DARK HORSE

Value: Cover or less

- ❑1, nn ... 2.50

DOMINIQUE: FAMILY MATTERS
CALIBER

Value: Cover or less

- ❑1, b&w ... 2.95

DOMINIQUE: KILLZONE
CALIBER

Value: Cover or less

- ❑1, b&w; One-Shot ... 2.95

DOMINIQUE: PROTECT AND SERVE
CALIBER

Value: Cover or less

- ❑1, b&w; One-Shot ... 2.95

DOMINIQUE: WHITE KNUCKLE DRIVE
CALIBER

Value: Cover or less

- ❑1, b&w; One-Shot ... 2.95

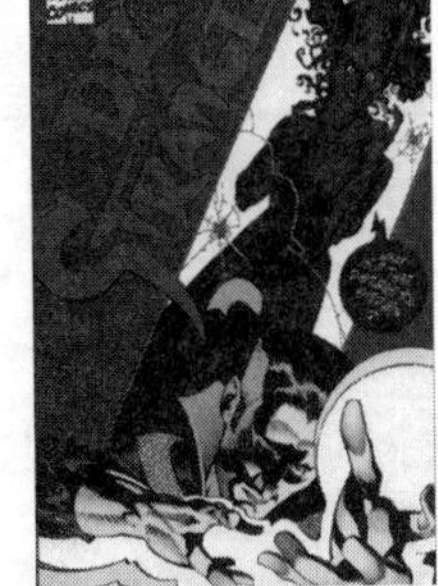

P. Craig Russell's Doctor Strange story was released as a prestige-format one-shot in 1997.

DOMINO
MARVEL

	ORIG	GOOD	FINE	N-MINT
❑1, Jan 97, Rise and Fall	1.95	0.40	1.00	2.00
❑2, Feb 97, V: Deathstrike	1.95	0.40	1.00	2.00
❑3, Mar 97, Hard Luck	1.95	0.40	1.00	2.00

DOMINO CHANCE
CHANCE

	ORIG	GOOD	FINE	N-MINT
❑1, b&w	1.50	0.50	1.25	2.50
❑1-2, b&w; 2nd Printing	1.50	0.30	0.75	1.50
❑2, Jul 82, b&w	1.50	0.40	1.00	2.00
❑3, Sep 82, b&w	1.50	0.40	1.00	2.00
❑4, b&w	1.50	0.40	1.00	2.00
❑5, Jul 83, b&w	1.50	0.40	1.00	2.00
❑6, b&w	1.50	0.40	1.00	2.00
❑7, 1: Gizmo, b&w	1.50	0.40	1.00	2.00
❑8, 2: Gizmo, b&w	1.50	0.40	1.00	2.00
❑9, b&w	1.50	0.40	1.00	2.00

DOMINO CHANCE: ROACH EXTRAORDINAIRE
AMAZING

Value: Cover or less

- ❑1 ... 1.95

DOMINO LADY
FANTAGRAPHICS

Value: Cover or less

- ❑1, Dec 90, b&w; adult ... 1.95
- ❑2, Jan 91, b&w; adult ... 1.95
- ❑3, Mar 91, b&w; adult ... 1.95

DOMINO LADY'S JUNGLE ADVENTURE
FANTAGRAPHICS

	ORIG	GOOD	FINE	N-MINT
❑1, b&w; adult	2.50	0.55	1.38	2.75
❑2, b&w; adult	2.75	0.55	1.38	2.75
❑3, Nov 92, b&w; adult	2.75	0.55	1.38	2.75

DOMU: A CHILD'S DREAM
DARK HORSE

Value: Cover or less

- ❑1 ... 5.95
- ❑2 ... 5.95
- ❑3, May 95 ... 5.95

DONALD AND MICKEY
GLADSTONE

Value: Cover or less

- ❑19, Sep 93, CB, Reprint ... 1.50
- ❑20, Nov 93, CB, 64pgs. ... 2.95
- ❑21, Jan 94, CB, Reprint ... 1.50
- ❑22, Mar 94, CB, Reprint ... 1.50
- ❑23, May 94, CB, Reprint ... 1.50
- ❑24, Jul 94, CB, Reprint ... 1.50
- ❑25, Sep 94, 64pgs. ... 2.95
- ❑26, Nov 94, newsstand distribution by Marvel ... 1.50
- ❑27, Jan 95 ... 1.50
- ❑28, Mar 95 ... 1.50
- ❑29, May 95 ... 1.50
- ❑30, Jul 95 ... 1.50

DONALD AND SCROOGE
DISNEY

Value: Cover or less

- ❑1 ... 1.75
- ❑2 ... 1.75
- ❑3 ... 1.75

DONALD DUCK (WALT DISNEY'S...)
DELL

	ORIG	GOOD	FINE	N-MINT
❑246, CB, Series begins again (1986); Gladstone publishes	0.75	1.60	4.00	8.00
❑247, Nov 86, CB	0.75	1.00	2.50	5.00
❑248, Dec 86, CB	0.75	1.00	2.50	5.00
❑249, Jan 87, CB	0.75	1.00	2.50	5.00
❑250, Feb 87, CB, reprints 1st Barks comic	0.75	1.60	4.00	8.00
❑251, Mar 87, CB	0.75	0.80	2.00	4.00
❑252, Apr 87, CB	0.75	0.80	2.00	4.00
❑253, May 87, CB	0.75	0.80	2.00	4.00
❑254, Jun 87	0.75	0.80	2.00	4.00
❑255, Jul 87	0.95	0.80	2.00	4.00
❑256, Aug 87	0.95	0.80	2.00	4.00
❑257, Sep 87, CB, forest fire	0.95	0.80	2.00	4.00
❑258, Oct 87, CB	0.95	0.80	2.00	4.00
❑259, Nov 87, CB	0.95	0.80	2.00	4.00
❑260, Dec 87, CB	0.95	0.80	2.00	4.00
❑261, Jan 88, CB	0.95	0.60	1.50	3.00
❑262, Mar 88, CB	0.95	0.60	1.50	3.00
❑263, Jun 88, CB	0.95	0.60	1.50	3.00
❑264, Jul 88, CB	0.95	0.60	1.50	3.00
❑265, Aug 88	0.95	0.60	1.50	3.00
❑266, Sep 88	0.95	0.60	1.50	3.00

	ORIG	GOOD	FINE	N-MINT
❑267, Oct 88	0.95	0.60	1.50	3.00
❑268, Nov 88	0.95	0.60	1.50	3.00
❑269, Jan 89	0.95	0.60	1.50	3.00
❑270, Mar 89	0.95	0.60	1.50	3.00
❑271, Apr 89, says Jun on cover, Apr in indicia	0.95	0.50	1.25	2.50
❑272, Jul 89	0.95	0.50	1.25	2.50
❑273, Aug 89	0.95	0.50	1.25	2.50
❑274, Sep 89	0.95	0.50	1.25	2.50
❑275, Oct 89, WK; CB, Donocchio	0.95	0.50	1.25	2.50
❑276, Nov 89, CB	0.95	0.50	1.25	2.50
❑277, Jan 90, CB	0.95	0.50	1.25	2.50
❑278, Mar 90, DR; CB	0.95	0.50	1.25	2.50
❑279, May 90, CB, Series ends again (1990)	0.95	0.50	1.25	2.50
❑280, Sep 93, Series begins again (1993)	1.50	0.30	0.75	1.50
❑281, Nov 93	1.50	0.30	0.75	1.50
❑282, Jan 94, CB, Reprint	1.50	0.30	0.75	1.50
❑283, Mar 94, DR	1.50	0.30	0.75	1.50
❑284, May 94, CB, Reprint	1.50	0.30	0.75	1.50
❑285, Jul 94, CB, Reprint	1.50	0.30	0.75	1.50
❑286, Sep 94, Giant-size; Donald Duck's 60th	2.95	0.60	1.50	3.00
❑287, Nov 94	1.50	0.30	0.75	1.50
❑288, Jan 95	1.50	0.30	0.75	1.50
❑289, Mar 95	1.50	0.30	0.75	1.50
❑290, May 95	1.50	0.30	0.75	1.50
❑291, Jul 95	1.50	0.30	0.75	1.50
❑292, Sep 95	1.95	0.30	0.75	1.50
❑293, Nov 95	1.95	0.30	0.75	1.50
❑294, Jan 96, CB, The Persistent Postman, Reprint	1.95	0.30	0.75	1.50
❑295, Mar 96, newsprint covers begin	1.50	0.30	0.75	1.50
❑296, May 96	1.50	0.30	0.75	1.50
❑297, Jul 96	1.50	0.30	0.75	1.50
❑298, Sep 96	1.50	0.30	0.75	1.50
❑299, Nov 96	1.50	0.30	0.75	1.50
❑300, Jan 97	2.25	0.30	0.75	1.50
❑301, Mar 97, newsprint covers end	1.95	0.30	0.75	1.50
❑302, May 97, CB, CB (c), The Gold Finder, Reprint	1.95	0.39	0.98	1.95
❑303, Jul 97	1.95	0.39	0.98	1.95
❑304, Sep 97, CB, Bubbleweight Champ, Reprint	1.95	0.39	0.98	1.95
❑305, Nov 97, CB, CB (w), Mocking Bird Ridge; The Autograph, Reprint	1.95	0.39	0.98	1.95
❑306, Jan 98	1.95	0.39	0.98	1.95
❑307, Mar 98, Final Issue	1.95	0.39	0.98	1.95

DONALD DUCK ADVENTURES (DISNEY)

DISNEY

	ORIG	GOOD	FINE	N-MINT
❑1, Jun 90, DR, DR (w), The Money Pit	1.50	0.50	1.25	2.50
❑2, Jul 90, CB	1.50	0.40	1.00	2.00
❑3, Aug 90	1.50	0.40	1.00	2.00
❑4, Sep 90, CB	1.50	0.40	1.00	2.00
❑5, Oct 90	1.50	0.40	1.00	2.00
❑6, Nov 90	1.50	0.40	1.00	2.00
❑7, Dec 90	1.50	0.40	1.00	2.00
❑8, Jan 91	1.50	0.40	1.00	2.00
❑9, Feb 91, CB, reprint of 1: Uncle Scrooge	1.50	0.40	1.00	2.00
❑10, Mar 91	1.50	0.40	1.00	2.00
❑11, Apr 91, Mad #1 cover parody	1.50	0.40	1.00	2.00
❑12, May 91	1.50	0.40	1.00	2.00
❑13, Jun 91	1.50	0.40	1.00	2.00
❑14, Jul 91, CB	1.50	0.40	1.00	2.00
❑15, Aug 91	1.50	0.40	1.00	2.00
❑16, Sep 91	1.50	0.40	1.00	2.00
❑17, Oct 91, Time Tetrad, Part 1	1.50	0.40	1.00	2.00
❑18, Nov 91, That Ol' Soft Soap	1.50	0.40	1.00	2.00
❑19, Dec 91	1.50	0.40	1.00	2.00
❑20, Jan 92	1.50	0.40	1.00	2.00
❑21, Feb 92, CB, golden Christmas tree	1.50	0.30	0.75	1.50
❑22, Mar 92, DR	1.50	0.30	0.75	1.50
❑23, Apr 92, CB	1.50	0.30	0.75	1.50
❑24, May 92, DR	1.50	0.30	0.75	1.50
❑25, Jun 92, map piece	1.50	0.30	0.75	1.50
❑26, Jul 92, CB, map piece	1.50	0.30	0.75	1.50
❑27, Aug 92, CB, map piece	1.50	0.30	0.75	1.50
❑28, Sep 92, Olympics	1.50	0.30	0.75	1.50
❑29, Oct 92	1.50	0.30	0.75	1.50
❑30, Nov 92	1.50	0.30	0.75	1.50
❑31, Dec 92	1.50	0.30	0.75	1.50
❑32, Jan 93	1.50	0.30	0.75	1.50
❑33, Feb 93	1.50	0.30	0.75	1.50
❑34, Mar 93, DR, Return of Super-Duck	1.50	0.30	0.75	1.50
❑35, Apr 93, CB, Reprint	1.50	0.30	0.75	1.50
❑36, May 93, CB, Reprint	1.50	0.30	0.75	1.50
❑37, Jun 93, DR; CB, Reprint	1.50	0.30	0.75	1.50
❑38, Jul 93	1.50	0.30	0.75	1.50
❑39, Aug 93	1.50	0.30	0.75	1.50
❑40, Sep 93	1.50	0.30	0.75	1.50
❑41, Oct 93	1.50	0.30	0.75	1.50
❑42, Nov 93, CB (c)	1.50	0.30	0.75	1.50
❑43	—	0.30	0.75	1.50
❑44, Dec 93, Gladstone resumes publishing its series	1.50	0.30	0.75	1.50

DONALD DUCK ADVENTURES (GLADSTONE)

GLADSTONE

	ORIG	GOOD	FINE	N-MINT
❑1, Nov 87, CB	0.95	0.50	1.25	2.50
❑2, Jan 88, CB	0.95	0.40	1.00	2.00
❑3, Mar 88, CB, Lost in the Andes	0.95	0.40	1.00	2.00
❑4, May 88, CB	0.95	0.40	1.00	2.00
❑5, Jul 88, DR; CB	0.95	0.40	1.00	2.00
❑6, Aug 88, CB	0.95	0.30	0.75	1.50
❑7, Sep 88, CB	0.95	0.30	0.75	1.50
❑8, Oct 88, DR; CB	0.95	0.30	0.75	1.50
❑9, Nov 88, CB	0.95	0.30	0.75	1.50
❑10, Dec 88, CB	0.95	0.30	0.75	1.50
❑11, Feb 89, CB	0.95	0.30	0.75	1.50
❑12, May 89, DR; CB, Return to Plain Awful	1.50	0.30	0.75	1.50
❑13, Jul 89, CB, DR (c)	1.50	0.30	0.75	1.50
❑14, Aug 89, CB	1.50	0.30	0.75	1.50
❑15, Sep 89, CB	1.50	0.30	0.75	1.50
❑16, Oct 89, CB	1.50	0.30	0.75	1.50
❑17, Nov 89, CB	1.50	0.30	0.75	1.50
❑18, Dec 89, CB, No Such Varmint	1.50	0.30	0.75	1.50
❑19, Feb 90, CB	1.50	0.30	0.75	1.50
❑20, Apr 90, CB, Old Castle's Secret, series goes on hiatus during Disney run	1.50	0.30	0.75	1.50
❑21, Aug 93, CB, DR (c), Reprint	1.50	0.30	0.75	1.50
❑22, Oct 93, CB, The Pixilated Parrot, Reprint	1.50	0.30	0.75	1.50
❑23, Dec 93, DR (c)	1.50	0.30	0.75	1.50
❑24, Feb 94, The Black Moon	1.50	0.30	0.75	1.50
❑25, Apr 94	1.50	0.30	0.75	1.50
❑26, Jun 94, CB, 64pgs.	2.95	0.59	1.48	2.95
❑27, Aug 94	1.50	0.30	0.75	1.50
❑28, Oct 94, CB, Sheriff of Bullet Valley, cover uses portion of Barks painting; Reprint	1.50	0.30	0.75	1.50
❑29, Dec 94, newsstand distribution by Marvel	1.50	0.30	0.75	1.50
❑30, Feb 95, CB, Christmas for Shacktown, 64pgs.; Reprint	2.95	0.59	1.48	2.95
❑31, Apr 95	1.50	0.30	0.75	1.50
❑32, Jun 95	1.50	0.30	0.75	1.50
❑33, Aug 95, CB, The Golden Helmet, Reprint	1.95	0.39	0.98	1.95
❑34, Oct 95, newsprint covers begin	1.50	0.30	0.75	1.50
❑35, Dec 95	1.50	0.30	0.75	1.50
❑36, Feb 96	1.50	0.30	0.75	1.50
❑37, Apr 96	1.50	0.30	0.75	1.50
❑38, Jun 96	1.50	0.30	0.75	1.50
❑39, Aug 96	1.50	0.30	0.75	1.50
❑40, Oct 96	1.50	0.30	0.75	1.50
❑41, Dec 96	1.50	0.30	0.75	1.50
❑42, Feb 97	1.50	0.30	0.75	1.50
❑43, Apr 97, newsprint covers end	1.50	0.30	0.75	1.50
❑44, Jun 97	1.95	0.39	0.98	1.95
❑45, Aug 97	1.95	0.39	0.98	1.95
❑46, Oct 97	1.95	0.39	0.98	1.95
❑47, Dec 97, CB, Trick or Treat, Reprint	1.95	0.39	0.98	1.95
❑48, Feb 98, Final Issue	1.95	0.39	0.98	1.95

DONALD DUCK ALBUM (WALT DISNEY'S)

DELL

	ORIG	GOOD	FINE	N-MINT
❑1, May 61, FC 1182	0.10	9.00	22.50	45.00

DONALD DUCK & MICKEY MOUSE

GLADSTONE

Value: Cover or less

	Value
❑1, Sep 95	1.50
❑2, Nov 95	1.50
❑3, Jan 96	1.50
❑4, Mar 96	1.50
❑5, May 96	1.50
❑6, Jul 96	1.50
❑7, Sep 96	1.50

DONALD DUCK BEACH PARTY (WALT DISNEY'S...)

DELL

	ORIG	GOOD	FINE	N-MINT
❑1	0.25	20.00	50.00	100.00
❑2	0.25	13.00	32.50	65.00
❑3	0.25	11.00	27.50	55.00
❑4	0.25	11.00	27.50	55.00
❑5, The Gem Jam	0.25	11.00	27.50	55.00
❑6	0.25	11.00	27.50	55.00

DONATELLO TEENAGE MUTANT NINJA TURTLE

MIRAGE

	ORIG	GOOD	FINE	N-MINT
❑1, b&w	1.50	0.40	1.00	2.00

DONIELLE: ENSLAVED AT SEA
RAGING RHINO

Value: Cover or less

- ❑1, b&w; adult 2.95
- ❑2, b&w; adult 2.95
- ❑3, b&w; adult 2.95
- ❑4, b&w; adult 2.95

DONNA MATRIX
REACTOR

	ORIG	GOOD	FINE	N-MINT
❑1, Aug 93, 1: Donna Matrix, computer-generated	2.95	0.70	1.75	3.50

DONNA MIA
AVATAR

Value: Cover or less

- ❑1 .... 3.00
- ❑2 .... 3.00
- ❑3 .... 3.00

DONNA'S DAY
SLAB-O-CONCRETE

	ORIG	GOOD	FINE	N-MINT
❑1, Postcard comic book	—	0.20	0.50	1.00

DOOFER
FANTAGRAPHICS

Value: Cover or less

- ❑1, b&w 2.75

DOOFUS
FANTAGRAPHICS

Value: Cover or less

- ❑1, Dec 94, What Color is Your Parachute?; Team America, b&w 2.75
- ❑2, Spr 97, b&w 2.75

DOOM
MARVEL

Value: Cover or less

- ❑1, Oct 00 .... 2.99
- ❑2, Nov 00, Slaves 2.99
- ❑3, Dec 00, Fight Back to Baxter 2.99

DOOM 2099
MARVEL

	ORIG	GOOD	FINE	N-MINT
❑1, Jan 93, PB, Muses of Fire!, 1: Doom 2099, Metallic ink cover	1.75	0.50	1.25	2.50
❑2, Feb 93, PB	1.25	0.35	0.88	1.75
❑3, Mar 93, PB	1.25	0.35	0.88	1.75
❑4, Apr 93	1.25	0.35	0.88	1.75
❑5, May 93, 1: Fever	1.25	0.35	0.88	1.75
❑6, Jun 93	1.25	0.30	0.75	1.50
❑7, Jul 93	1.25	0.30	0.75	1.50
❑8, Aug 93	1.25	0.30	0.75	1.50
❑9, Sep 93	1.25	0.30	0.75	1.50
❑10, Oct 93, PB, A: Xandra, Covers of Doom 2099 10-12 combine to form triptych	1.25	0.30	0.75	1.50
❑11, Nov 93, Covers of Doom 2099 10-12 combine to form triptych	1.25	0.25	0.63	1.25
❑12, Dec 93, Covers of Doom 2099 10-12 combine to form triptych	1.25	0.25	0.63	1.25
❑13, Jan 94	1.25	0.25	0.63	1.25
❑14, Feb 94, Fall of the Hammer, Part 4	1.25	0.25	0.63	1.25
❑15, Mar 94	1.25	0.25	0.63	1.25
❑16, Apr 94	1.25	0.25	0.63	1.25
❑17, May 94	1.50	0.25	0.63	1.25
❑18, May 94, poster	1.50	0.30	0.75	1.50
❑19, Jul 94	1.50	0.30	0.75	1.50
❑20, Aug 94, X Nation, A: X-Men 2099	1.50	0.30	0.75	1.50
❑21, Sep 94	1.50	0.30	0.75	1.50
❑22, Oct 94	1.50	0.30	0.75	1.50
❑23, Nov 94	1.50	0.30	0.75	1.50
❑24, Dec 94	1.50	0.30	0.75	1.50
❑25, Jan 95, Special cover	2.25	0.45	1.13	2.25
❑25/SC, Jan 95, enhanced cover; Giant-size	2.95	0.59	1.48	2.95
❑26, Feb 95	1.50	0.30	0.75	1.50
❑27, Mar 95	1.50	0.30	0.75	1.50
❑28, Apr 95	1.50	0.39	0.98	1.95
❑29, May 95	1.95	0.39	0.98	1.95
❑29/SC, May 95, enhanced acetate overlay cover	3.50	0.70	1.75	3.50
❑30, Jun 95	1.95	0.39	0.98	1.95
❑31, Jul 95	1.95	0.39	0.98	1.95
❑32, Aug 95	1.95	0.39	0.98	1.95
❑33, Sep 95	1.95	0.39	0.98	1.95
❑34, Oct 95	1.95	0.39	0.98	1.95
❑35, Nov 95	1.95	0.39	0.98	1.95
❑36, Dec 95	1.95	0.39	0.98	1.95
❑37, Jan 96	1.95	0.39	0.98	1.95
❑38, Feb 96, X-Nation	1.95	0.39	0.98	1.95
❑39, Mar 96, JB, May the Circle by Unbroken	1.95	0.39	0.98	1.95
❑39/SC, Special cover	3.50	0.70	1.75	3.50
❑40, Apr 96, JB, The Rage Against Time, Part 1, Doom 2099 comes to present	1.95	0.39	0.98	1.95
❑41, May 96, V: Daredevil; V: Namor	1.95	0.39	0.98	1.95
❑42, Jun 96, V: Fantastic Four	1.95	0.39	0.98	1.95
❑43, Jul 96, story continues in Fantastic Four 2099 #7	1.95	0.39	0.98	1.95
❑44, Aug 96, Final Issue; continues in 2099: World of Tomorrow	1.95	0.39	0.98	1.95

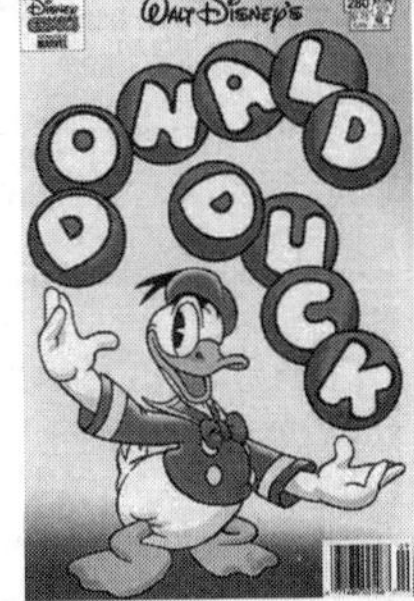

When Disney Comics took over publication of its comic books from Gladstone, it put the long-running *Donald Duck* on hiatus for more than three years.

© 1993 Walt Disney Corporation (Gladstone)

DOOM FORCE SPECIAL
DC

Value: Cover or less

- ❑1, Judgment Day, 1: Doom Force, X-Force parody 2.95

DOOM PATROL, THE (1ST SERIES)
DC

	ORIG	GOOD	FINE	N-MINT
❑86, 1: Madame Rouge; 1: The Brain; 1: Monsieur Mallah, Series continued from My Greatest Adventure #85	0.12	15.00	37.50	75.00
❑87	0.12	10.00	25.00	50.00
❑88, O: The Chief	0.12	8.00	20.00	40.00
❑89	0.12	8.00	20.00	40.00
❑90	0.12	8.00	20.00	40.00
❑91, 1: Mento	0.12	7.60	19.00	38.00
❑92	0.12	7.60	19.00	38.00
❑93, Feb 65	0.12	7.60	19.00	38.00
❑94, Mar 65	0.12	7.60	19.00	38.00
❑95, May 65	0.12	7.60	19.00	38.00
❑96, Jun 65	0.12	7.60	19.00	38.00
❑97, Aug 65, 1: Garguax	0.12	7.60	19.00	38.00
❑98, Sep 65	0.12	7.60	19.00	38.00
❑99, Nov 65, 1: Changeling	0.12	9.00	22.50	45.00
❑100, Dec 65, O: Changeling	0.12	10.00	25.00	50.00
❑101, Feb 66	0.12	5.00	12.50	25.00
❑102, Mar 66, A: Challengers of the Unknown	0.12	5.00	12.50	25.00
❑103, May 66	0.12	5.00	12.50	25.00
❑104, Jun 66	0.12	5.00	12.50	25.00
❑105, Aug 66	0.12	5.00	12.50	25.00
❑106, Sep 66, O: Negative Man	0.12	5.00	12.50	25.00
❑107, Nov 66	0.12	5.00	12.50	25.00
❑108, Dec 66	0.12	5.00	12.50	25.00
❑109, Feb 67	0.12	5.00	12.50	25.00
❑110, Mar 67	0.12	5.00	12.50	25.00
❑111, May 67	0.12	5.00	12.50	25.00
❑112, Jun 67	0.12	5.00	12.50	25.00
❑113, Aug 67	0.12	5.00	12.50	25.00
❑114, Sep 67	0.12	5.00	12.50	25.00
❑115, Nov 67	0.12	5.00	12.50	25.00
❑116, Dec 67	0.12	5.00	12.50	25.00
❑117, Feb 68	0.12	5.00	12.50	25.00
❑118, Mar 68	0.12	5.00	12.50	25.00
❑119, May 68	0.12	5.00	12.50	25.00
❑120, Jun 68	0.12	5.00	12.50	25.00
❑121, Aug 68, JO, D: The Doom Patrol	0.12	10.00	25.00	50.00
❑122, Feb 73, Reprints begin (1973)	0.12	0.40	1.00	2.00
❑123, Apr 73	0.12	0.40	1.00	2.00
❑124, Jun 73	0.12	0.40	1.00	2.00

DOOM PATROL (2ND SERIES)
DC

	ORIG	GOOD	FINE	N-MINT
❑1, Oct 87, The Doom Patrol, The Doom Patrol returns from their supposed deaths	0.75	0.40	1.00	2.00
❑2, Nov 87, Satellite Of Doom	0.75	0.20	0.50	1.00
❑3, Dec 87, 1: Lodestone; 1: Rhea Jones	0.75	0.20	0.50	1.00
❑4, Jan 88, Trouble In Kansas City, O: Lodestone	0.75	0.20	0.50	1.00
❑5, Feb 88	0.75	0.20	0.50	1.00
❑6, Mar 88, EL, Heroes And Villains	0.75	0.20	0.50	1.00
❑7, Apr 88, 1: Shrapnel	0.75	0.20	0.50	1.00
❑8, May 88, EL, The Morning After	0.75	0.20	0.50	1.00
❑9, Jun 88, Bonus Book	0.75	0.20	0.50	1.00
❑10, Jul 88, A: Superman	0.75	0.20	0.50	1.00
❑11, Aug 88	1.00	0.20	0.50	1.00
❑12, Sep 88	1.00	0.20	0.50	1.00
❑13, Oct 88	1.00	0.20	0.50	1.00
❑14, Nov 88, 1: Dorothy Spinner; A: Power Girl	1.00	0.20	0.50	1.00
❑15, Dec 88, V: Animal-Vegetable-Mineral Man	1.00	0.20	0.50	1.00
❑16, Dec 88	1.00	0.20	0.50	1.00
❑17, Jan 89, D: Celsius, Invasion!	1.00	0.20	0.50	1.00
❑18, Jan 89, Invasion, Invasion!	1.00	0.20	0.50	1.00

	ORIG	GOOD	FINE	N-MINT
❑19, Feb 89, Crawling From the Wreckage, Part 1, 1: Crazy Jane, 1st Grant Morrison; New, very strange direction for The Doom Patrol	1.50	0.60	1.50	3.00
❑20, Mar 89, 1: The Scissormen	1.50	0.40	1.00	2.00
❑21, Apr 89	1.50	0.40	1.00	2.00
❑22, May 89	1.50	0.40	1.00	2.00
❑23, Jun 89	1.50	0.40	1.00	2.00
❑24, Jul 89	1.50	0.40	1.00	2.00
❑25, Aug 89	1.50	0.40	1.00	2.00
❑26, Sep 89, 1: The Brotherhood of Dada	1.50	0.40	1.00	2.00
❑27, Nov 89	1.50	0.40	1.00	2.00
❑28, Dec 89	1.50	0.40	1.00	2.00
❑29, Jan 90, Superman cover	1.50	0.40	1.00	2.00
❑30, Feb 90	1.50	0.40	1.00	2.00
❑31, Apr 90	1.50	0.40	1.00	2.00
❑32, May 90	1.50	0.40	1.00	2.00
❑33, Jun 90	1.50	0.40	1.00	2.00
❑34, Jul 90, The Soul Of A New Machine	1.50	0.40	1.00	2.00
❑35, Aug 90, 1: Flex Mentallo; 1: Danny the Street	1.50	0.40	1.00	2.00
❑36, Sep 90	1.50	0.40	1.00	2.00
❑37, Oct 90, Persephone	1.50	0.40	1.00	2.00
❑38, Nov 90	1.50	0.40	1.00	2.00
❑39, Dec 90	1.50	0.40	1.00	2.00
❑40, Jan 91, Battlefield Of Dreams	1.50	0.40	1.00	2.00
❑41, Feb 91, Fallen Angel	1.50	0.40	1.00	2.00
❑42, Mar 91, 1: The Fact; O: Flex Mentallo	1.50	0.40	1.00	2.00
❑43, Apr 91	1.50	0.40	1.00	2.00
❑44, May 91, 1: The Candlemaker	1.50	0.40	1.00	2.00
❑45, Jul 91	1.50	0.40	1.00	2.00
❑46, Aug 91	1.50	0.40	1.00	2.00
❑47, Sep 91	1.50	0.40	1.00	2.00
❑48, Oct 91	1.50	0.40	1.00	2.00
❑49, Nov 91	1.50	0.40	1.00	2.00
❑50, Dec 91, Tales Of Hoffman, Giant-size	2.50	0.50	1.25	2.50
❑51, Jan 92, 1: Yankee Doodle Dandy	1.50	0.40	1.00	2.00
❑52, Feb 92, After The Cabaret	1.50	0.35	0.88	1.75
❑53, Mar 92, And Men Shall Call Him Hero!, Fantastic Four parody	1.50	0.35	0.88	1.75
❑54, Apr 92, Aenigma Regis, Photo cover	1.50	0.35	0.88	1.75
❑55, May 92, The Blood Of The Lamb	1.50	0.35	0.88	1.75
❑56, Jun 92	1.50	0.35	0.88	1.75
❑57, Jul 92, The Nature Of The Catastrophe, Giant-size	1.50	0.50	1.25	2.50
❑58, Aug 92	1.50	0.35	0.88	1.75
❑59, Sep 92, Dying Inside	1.50	0.35	0.88	1.75
❑60, Oct 92, Brief Candles	1.50	0.35	0.88	1.75
❑61, Nov 92	1.75	0.35	0.88	1.75
❑62, Dec 92, Planet Love	1.75	0.35	0.88	1.75
❑63, Jan 93, The Empire of Chairs	1.75	0.35	0.88	1.75
❑64, Mar 93, Sliding in the Wreckage, Part 1, Begins Vertigo line	1.75	0.35	0.88	1.75
❑65, Apr 93, Sliding in the Wreckage, Part 2	1.75	0.35	0.88	1.75
❑66, May 93, Sliding in the Wreckage, Part 3	1.75	0.39	0.98	1.95
❑67, Jun 93, E Rose In The Autos	1.95	0.39	0.98	1.95
❑68, Jul 93	1.95	0.39	0.98	1.95
❑69, Aug 93, Down Among The Underpinnings	1.95	0.39	0.98	1.95
❑70, Sep 93	1.95	0.39	0.98	1.95
❑71, Oct 93, The Fox And The Crow	1.95	0.39	0.98	1.95
❑72, Nov 93	1.95	0.39	0.98	1.95
❑73, Dec 93, The Dream Patrol: Return Of The Widowmen	1.95	0.39	0.98	1.95
❑74, Jan 94	1.95	0.39	0.98	1.95
❑75, Feb 94, The Teireseias Wars, Part 1	1.95	0.39	0.98	1.95
❑76, Mar 94, The Teireseias Wars, Part 2	1.95	0.39	0.98	1.95
❑77, Apr 94, The Teireseias Wars, Part 3	1.95	0.39	0.98	1.95
❑78, May 94, The Teireseias Wars, Part 4	1.95	0.39	0.98	1.95
❑79, Jun 94, The Teireseias Wars, Part 5	1.95	0.39	0.98	1.95
❑80, Jul 94, The Dogs of Soul	1.95	0.39	0.98	1.95
❑81, Aug 94, Masquerade, Part 1	1.95	0.39	0.98	1.95
❑82, Sep 94, Masquerade, Part 2	1.95	0.39	0.98	1.95
❑83, Oct 94	1.95	0.39	0.98	1.95
❑84, Nov 94, Imagine Ari's Friends, Part 1	1.95	0.39	0.98	1.95
❑85, Dec 94, Imagine Ari's Friends, Part 2	1.95	0.39	0.98	1.95
❑86, Jan 95, Imagine Ari's Friends, Part 3	1.95	0.39	0.98	1.95
❑87, Feb 95, Imagine Ari's Friends, Part 4, Final Issue	1.95	0.39	0.98	1.95
❑Anl 1	1.50	0.30	0.75	1.50
❑Anl 2, The Children's Crusade, Part 5, Children's Crusade	3.95	0.79	1.98	3.95

DOOM PATROL AND SUICIDE SQUAD SPECIAL
DC

	ORIG	GOOD	FINE	N-MINT
❑1, Feb 88, EL, Red Pawn	1.50	0.40	1.00	2.00

DOOMSDAY + 1 (AVALON)
AVALON

Value: Cover or less

❑1, JBy 2.95

❑2, JBy 2.95

DOOMSDAY + 1 (CHARLTON)
CHARLTON

	ORIG	GOOD	FINE	N-MINT
❑1, Jul 75, JBy	0.25	1.60	4.00	8.00
❑2, Sep 75, JBy	0.25	1.00	2.50	5.00
❑3, Nov 75, JBy, Peace Keepers	0.25	0.80	2.00	4.00
❑4, Jan 76, JBy	0.25	0.80	2.00	4.00
❑5, Mar 76, JBy	0.25	0.80	2.00	4.00
❑6, May 76, JBy	0.25	0.80	2.00	4.00
❑7, Jun 78, JBy, Reprints Doomsday + 1 #1	0.35	0.60	1.50	3.00
❑8, JBy, Reprints Doomsday + 1 #2	0.35	0.60	1.50	3.00
❑9, JBy, Peace Keepers, Reprints Doomsday + 1 #3	0.35	0.60	1.50	3.00
❑10, JBy, Reprints Doomsday + 1 #4	—	0.60	1.50	3.00
❑11, JBy, Reprints Doomsday + 1 #5	—	0.60	1.50	3.00
❑12, JBy, Reprints Doomsday + 1 #6	—	0.60	1.50	3.00

DOOMSDAY ANNUAL
DC

Value: Cover or less

❑1, JOy (w), Communion 3.95

DOOMSDAY SQUAD, THE
FANTAGRAPHICS

	ORIG	GOOD	FINE	N-MINT
❑1, Aug 86, JBy, Doomsday: Minus Two	2.00	0.40	1.00	2.00
❑2, JBy	2.00	0.40	1.00	2.00
❑3, JBy, The Peace Keepers; Village of Fear, A: Usagi Yojimbo	2.00	0.60	1.50	3.00
❑4, JBy	2.00	0.40	1.00	2.00
❑5, JBy	2.00	0.40	1.00	2.00
❑6, JBy	2.00	0.40	1.00	2.00
❑7, JBy	2.00	0.40	1.00	2.00

DOOM'S IV
IMAGE

	ORIG	GOOD	FINE	N-MINT
❑0.5, Dec 94, Preview promotional edition	—	0.50	1.25	2.50
❑1, Jul 94, RL (w)	2.50	0.50	1.25	2.50
❑1/A, Jul 94, RL (w), Alternate cover with left half of yellow two-part picture	2.50	0.50	1.25	2.50
❑1/B, Jul 94, RL (w), Alternate cover with right half of yellow two-part picture	2.50	0.50	1.25	2.50
❑2, Aug 94	2.50	0.50	1.25	2.50
❑2/A, Aug 94	2.50	0.50	1.25	2.50
❑3, Sep 94	2.50	0.50	1.25	2.50
❑4, Oct 94	2.50	0.50	1.25	2.50

DOORMAN (CALIBER)
CALIBER

Value: Cover or less

❑1 .... 2.95

DOORMAN (CULT)
CULT PRESS

	ORIG	GOOD	FINE	N-MINT
❑1, My Brother's Keeper, b&w; Double-cover	2.95	0.59	1.48	2.95
❑2, Identical..., Part 1, b&w	2.95	0.50	1.25	2.50
❑3, Identical..., Part 2, b&w	2.95	0.50	1.25	2.50
❑4, b&w	2.95	0.59	1.48	2.95
❑Ash 1, ashcan	—	0.20	0.50	1.00

DOORMAN: FAMILY SECRETS
CALIBER

Value: Cover or less

❑1, Brothers and Sisters 2.95

DOORWAY TO NIGHTMARE
DC

	ORIG	GOOD	FINE	N-MINT
❑1, Feb 78, VM	0.35	0.50	1.25	2.50
❑2, Apr 78	0.35	0.40	1.00	2.00
❑3, Jun 78	0.35	0.40	1.00	2.00
❑4, Aug 78	0.35	0.40	1.00	2.00
❑5, Oct 78, Final Issue	0.50	0.40	1.00	2.00

DOPE COMIX
KITCHEN SINK

	ORIG	GOOD	FINE	N-MINT
❑1	1.50	0.80	2.00	4.00
❑2, Wam Bong Hai; Li'l Nirvana Sees God	1.50	0.60	1.50	3.00
❑3, The Guide; The Old Son of a Bitch	1.50	0.60	1.50	3.00
❑4, Mark Was There!; Tea For Two	1.50	0.60	1.50	3.00
❑5, My First Marijuana Experience!; Dancing Water Voles	1.50	0.60	1.50	3.00

DOPIN' DAN
LAST GASP

	ORIG	GOOD	FINE	N-MINT
❑1	0.75	1.00	2.50	5.00
❑2, Heads or Tails; The Four Thousand Three Hundred and Twenty Four Hour	0.75	0.60	1.50	3.00
❑3, Pay Day; I Ride the Vomit Comet	0.75	0.60	1.50	3.00

DORIS NELSON: ATOMIC HOUSEWIFE
JAKE COMICS

Value: Cover or less

❑1, Dec 95, b&w 2.75

DORK
SLAVE LABOR

	ORIG	GOOD	FINE	N-MINT
❑1, Jun 93, Murrrr-derrr Fa-mi-leeee!!!; Comic Industry Trading Cards, b&w	2.50	0.60	1.50	3.00
❑1-2, Aug 95, Murrrr-derrr Fa-mi-leeee!!!; Comic Industry Trading Cards, b&w; 2nd Printing	2.75	0.55	1.38	2.75
❑, Mar 97, b&w; 3rd Printing	2.75	0.55	1.38	2.75

	ORIG	GOOD	FINE	N-MINT
❑2, May 94, The Murder Family: A Date With Death; Kyle and Evan: Critics at Large, b&w	2.50	0.50	1.25	2.50
❑2-2, Jan 96, The Murder Family: A Date With Death; Kyle and Evan: Critics at Large, b&w; 2nd Printing	2.75	0.55	1.38	2.75
❑3, Aug 95, Generation Ecch!; Fun!, b&w	2.75	0.55	1.38	2.75
❑3-2, Sep 96, Generation Ecch!; Fun!, b&w; 2nd Printing	2.75	0.55	1.38	2.75
❑4, Mar 97, The Murder Family: Death and Taxidermists; They Make Me Sick, b&w	2.75	0.55	1.38	2.75
❑5, Jan 98, Let the Fun Begin; It Came From the Pit, b&w	2.95	0.59	1.48	2.95
❑6, May 98, b&w	2.95	0.59	1.48	2.95
❑7, Aug 99, What Does it Look Like I'm Doing!; Cluttered, Like My Head, b&w	2.95	0.59	1.48	2.95
❑8, Sep 00, b&w	3.50	0.70	1.75	3.50
❑9	2.95	0.59	1.48	2.95

DORK HOUSE COMICS
PARODY PRESS

Value: Cover or less

- ❑1 ... 2.50

DORKIER IMAGES
PARODY PRESS

	ORIG	GOOD	FINE	N-MINT
❑1, Mar 93, Bloodwoof; The Faxx, Standard edition	2.50	0.50	1.25	2.50
❑1/SC, gold, silver, blue edition	2.95	0.60	1.50	3.00

DORK TOWER
CORSAIR PUBLISHING

	ORIG	GOOD	FINE	N-MINT
❑1, Jul 98	2.95	0.80	2.00	4.00
❑2, Oct 98, Night in the City	2.95	0.60	1.50	3.00
❑3, Jan 99, Global Village Idiot	2.95	0.60	1.50	3.00
❑4, May 99, The Fandom Menace, Star Wars	2.95	0.60	1.50	3.00
❑5, Jul 99, Babylon 5	2.95	0.59	1.48	2.95
❑6	2.95	0.59	1.48	2.95
❑7	2.95	0.59	1.48	2.95
❑8, Mar 00, High Sobriety	2.95	0.59	1.48	2.95
❑9, Aug 00, b&w; switches to Dork Storm	2.95	0.59	1.48	2.95
❑10, Aug 00, Road Rules	2.95	0.59	1.48	2.95
❑11, Sep 00, World of Dorkness	2.95	0.59	1.48	2.95
❑12, Nov 00, Warhamster	2.95	0.59	1.48	2.95
❑13	2.95	0.59	1.48	2.95
❑14	2.95	0.59	1.48	2.95
❑15	2.95	0.59	1.48	2.95
❑16	2.95	0.59	1.48	2.95

DOUBLE DRAGON
MARVEL

Value: Cover or less

- ❑1, Jul 91, 1: Double Dragon (Billy & Jimmy Lee) ... 1.00
- ❑2 ... 1.00
- ❑3 ... 1.00
- ❑4 ... 1.00
- ❑5, Nov 91 ... 1.00
- ❑6, Final Issue ... 1.00

DOUBLE EDGE: ALPHA
MARVEL

Value: Cover or less

- ❑1, Aug 95, Reset, chromium cover; Punisher ... 4.95

DOUBLE EDGE: OMEGA
MARVEL

Value: Cover or less

- ❑1, Oct 95, Glory Days, D: Nick Fury, enhanced wraparound cover; Punisher ... 4.95

DOUBLE IMAGE
IMAGE

Value: Cover or less

- ❑1, Feb 01, Codeflesh; The Bod, Flip-book ... 2.95
- ❑2, Feb 01, Codeflesh; The Bod, Flip-book ... 2.95
- ❑3, Apr 01, The Bod; Codeflesh, Flip-book ... 2.95

DOUBLE IMPACT
HIGH IMPACT

	ORIG	GOOD	FINE	N-MINT
❑1, Mar 95, nn; no cover price; no indicia; gray polybag; preview of Double Impact #3 and 4; San Diego Comic-Con ed.	3.95	0.79	1.98	3.95
❑1/LE, nn; no cover price; no indicia; black polybag; letters pages and pin-ups; limited to 5000	3.95	0.79	1.98	3.95
❑2	—	0.60	1.50	3.00
❑3	—	0.60	1.50	3.00
❑4, Sep 95, no information on cover whatsoever	—	0.60	1.50	3.00

DOUBLE IMPACT (VOL. 2)
HIGH IMPACT

Value: Cover or less

- ❑0 ... 2.95
- ❑1, Chronium Cover ... 4.00
- ❑2 ... 3.00
- ❑3 ... 3.00
- ❑4 ... 3.00
- ❑5 ... 3.00
- ❑6 ... 3.00
- ❑7, May 96 ... 3.00

The Doom Patrol faced a number of strange villains including The Animal, Vegetable, Mineral Man.

DOUBLE IMPACT: ART ATTACK
ABC STUDIOS

Value: Cover or less

- ❑1 ... 3.00
- ❑1/A, China & Jazz Nude Edition ... 6.00
- ❑1/B, Nude Jazz Edition ... 6.00

DOUBLE IMPACT: ASSASSINS FOR HIRE
HIGH IMPACT

	ORIG	GOOD	FINE	N-MINT
❑1, b&w; adult; cardstock cover; Hard Core! Edition	—	0.59	1.48	2.95

DOUBLE IMPACT BIKINI SPECIAL
HIGH IMPACT

Value: Cover or less

- ❑1, Sep 98, b&w; pin-ups ... 3.00

DOUBLE IMPACT: FROM THE ASHES
HIGH IMPACT

Value: Cover or less

- ❑1, b&w; adult ... 3.00
- ❑2, b&w; adult ... 5.95

DOUBLE IMPACT/HELLINA
ABC STUDIOS

	ORIG	GOOD	FINE	N-MINT
❑1, Jan 98, b&w; crossover with Lightning	3.00	0.60	1.50	3.00
❑1/Aut, Mar 96	—	1.00	2.50	5.00
❑1/GO, Mar 96, Gold nude cover	—	1.00	2.50	5.00
❑1/Nude, Jan 98, Nude cover	3.00	0.80	2.00	4.00
❑1/SC, Mar 96, Nude cover	—	0.80	2.00	4.00

DOUBLE IMPACT: ONE STEP BEYOND
HIGH IMPACT

Value: Cover or less

- ❑1 ... 3.00
- ❑1/SC, Leather cover ... 20.00

DOUBLE IMPACT: RAISING HELL
ABC STUDIOS

	ORIG	GOOD	FINE	N-MINT
❑1, Sep 97, b&w; adult	2.95	0.59	1.48	2.95
❑1/Nude, Sep 97, b&w; adult; nude photo cover	2.95	0.80	2.00	4.00

DOUBLE IMPACT: RAW
ABC STUDIOS

	ORIG	GOOD	FINE	N-MINT
❑1, Nov 97, cardstock cover	2.95	0.59	1.48	2.95
❑1/A, Nov 97, no cover price; Eurotika Edition	—	0.80	2.00	4.00
❑1/Nude, Nov 97, nude photo cover; Eurotika Edition	—	0.80	2.00	4.00
❑1-2, 2nd Printing	3.50	0.70	1.75	3.50
❑2	2.95	0.59	1.48	2.95
❑2/Nude, nude photo cover	2.95	0.80	2.00	4.00
❑3	2.95	0.59	1.48	2.95

DOUBLE IMPACT: RAW (VOL. 2)
ABC STUDIOS

	ORIG	GOOD	FINE	N-MINT
❑1/Nude, Sep 98, Nude cover	3.00	0.80	2.00	4.00

DOUBLE IMPACT: SUICIDE RUN
HIGH IMPACT

Value: Cover or less

- ❑1 ... 3.00
- ❑1/A ... 8.00
- ❑1/Leather, no cover price ... —
- ❑1/Nude ... 6.00

DOUBLE IMPACT: TRIGGER HAPPY
HIGH IMPACT

	ORIG	GOOD	FINE	N-MINT
❑1	3.00	0.60	1.50	3.00
❑1/B, Jazz Edition	3.00	0.60	1.50	3.00
❑1/LE, no cover price; Gold edition; limited to 300 copies	—	0.80	2.00	4.00

D.P.7
MARVEL

Value: Cover or less

- ❑1, Nov 86, The Clinic, O: D.P.7 ... 0.75
- ❑2, Dec 86 ... 0.75
- ❑3, Jan 87 ... 0.75
- ❑4, Feb 87 ... 0.75
- ❑5, Mar 87, Exorcism ... 0.75
- ❑6, Apr 87 ... 0.75
- ❑7, May 87 ... 0.75
- ❑8, Jun 87 ... 0.75
- ❑9, Jul 87 ... 0.75
- ❑10, Aug 87 ... 0.75
- ❑11, Sep 87 ... 0.75
- ❑12, Oct 87 ... 0.75
- ❑13, Nov 87 ... 0.75
- ❑14, Dec 87 ... 0.75
- ❑15, Jan 88 ... 0.75
- ❑16, Feb 88 ... 0.75
- ❑17, Mar 88 ... 0.75
- ❑18, Apr 88 ... 0.75
- ❑19, May 88 ... 1.25
- ❑20, Jun 88 ... 1.25

❑21, Jul 88 ..... 1.25
❑22, Aug 88 ..... 1.25
❑23, Sep 88, A: Psi-Force 1.25
❑24, Oct 88 ..... 1.25
❑25, Nov 88, A: Nightmask 1.25
❑26, Dec 88 ..... 1.50
❑27, Jan 89 ..... 1.50
❑28, Feb 89 ..... 1.50
❑29, Mar 89 ..... 1.50
❑30, Apr 89, 1: Captain Manhattan 1.50
❑31, May 89 ..... 1.50
❑32, Jun 89, Final Issue 1.50
❑Anl 1, Nov 87, 1: the Witness; O: D.P.7 ..... 1.25

DRACULA (BRAM STOKER'S...)
TOPPS

	ORIG	GOOD	FINE	N-MINT
❑1, Oct 92, trading cards	2.95	0.59	1.48	2.95
❑1/SC, Oct 92, no cover price	—	0.70	1.75	3.50
❑2, Nov 92, trading cards	2.95	0.59	1.48	2.95
❑3, Dec 92, trading cards	2.95	0.59	1.48	2.95
❑4, Jan 93, trading cards	2.95	0.59	1.48	2.95

DRACULA (ETERNITY)
ETERNITY

Value: Cover or less

❑1 ..... 3.50
❑1-2, 2nd Printing 2.50
❑2, b&w 2.50
❑3, b&w 2.50
❑4, b&w 2.50

DRACULA 3-D
3-D ZONE

Value: Cover or less

❑1, nn 3.95

DRACULA CHRONICLES, THE
TOPPS

Value: Cover or less

❑1, I Am Dracula 2.50
❑2 ..... 2.50
❑3 ..... 2.50

DRACULA IN HELL
APPLE

Value: Cover or less

❑1, b&w; adult 2.50
❑2, b&w; adult 2.50

DRACULA LIVES
MARVEL

	ORIG	GOOD	FINE	N-MINT
❑1, Jun 73	0.75	0.80	2.00	4.00
❑2, Aug 73, O: Dracula	0.75	0.60	1.50	3.00
❑3, Oct 73, A: Soloman Kane	0.75	0.60	1.50	3.00
❑4, Jan 74, title changes to Dracula Lives!	0.75	0.60	1.50	3.00
❑5, Mar 74, adapts Bram Stoker novel	0.75	0.60	1.50	3.00
❑6, May 74	0.75	0.60	1.50	3.00
❑7, Jul 74, Master Of The Sky	0.75	0.60	1.50	3.00
❑8, Sep 74	0.75	0.60	1.50	3.00
❑9, Nov 74	0.75	0.60	1.50	3.00
❑10, Jan 75	0.75	0.60	1.50	3.00
❑11, Mar 75	0.75	0.50	1.25	2.50
❑12, May 75	0.75	0.50	1.25	2.50
❑13, Jul 75, Final Issue	0.75	0.50	1.25	2.50
❑14	—	0.50	1.25	2.50
❑15	—	0.50	1.25	2.50
❑16	—	0.50	1.25	2.50
❑17	—	0.50	1.25	2.50
❑18	—	0.50	1.25	2.50
❑19	—	0.50	1.25	2.50
❑20	—	0.50	1.25	2.50
❑21	—	0.40	1.00	2.00
❑22	—	0.40	1.00	2.00
❑23	—	0.40	1.00	2.00
❑24	—	0.40	1.00	2.00
❑25	—	0.40	1.00	2.00
❑26	—	0.40	1.00	2.00
❑27	—	0.40	1.00	2.00
❑28	—	0.40	1.00	2.00
❑29	—	0.40	1.00	2.00
❑30	—	0.40	1.00	2.00
❑31	—	0.40	1.00	2.00
❑32	—	0.40	1.00	2.00
❑33	—	0.40	1.00	2.00
❑34	—	0.40	1.00	2.00
❑35	—	0.40	1.00	2.00
❑36, MP; VM; GC, Death Rides the Rails; Lo, the Monster Strikes, A: Blade the Vampire Slayer	0.08	0.40	1.00	2.00
❑37	—	0.40	1.00	2.00
❑38	—	0.40	1.00	2.00
❑39	—	0.40	1.00	2.00
❑40	—	0.40	1.00	2.00
❑41	—	0.40	1.00	2.00
❑42	—	0.40	1.00	2.00
❑43	—	0.40	1.00	2.00
❑44	—	0.40	1.00	2.00
❑45	—	0.40	1.00	2.00
❑46	—	0.40	1.00	2.00
❑47	—	0.40	1.00	2.00
❑48	—	0.40	1.00	2.00
❑49	—	0.40	1.00	2.00
❑50	—	0.40	1.00	2.00
❑51	—	0.30	0.75	1.50
❑52	—	0.30	0.75	1.50
❑53	—	0.30	0.75	1.50
❑54	—	0.30	0.75	1.50
❑55	—	0.30	0.75	1.50
❑56	—	0.30	0.75	1.50
❑57	—	0.30	0.75	1.50
❑58	—	0.30	0.75	1.50
❑59	—	0.30	0.75	1.50
❑60	—	0.30	0.75	1.50
❑61	—	0.30	0.75	1.50
❑62	—	0.30	0.75	1.50
❑63	—	0.30	0.75	1.50
❑64	—	0.30	0.75	1.50
❑65	—	0.30	0.75	1.50
❑66	—	0.30	0.75	1.50
❑67	—	0.30	0.75	1.50
❑68	—	0.30	0.75	1.50
❑69	—	0.30	0.75	1.50
❑70	—	0.30	0.75	1.50
❑71	—	0.30	0.75	1.50
❑72	—	0.30	0.75	1.50
❑73	—	0.30	0.75	1.50
❑74	—	0.30	0.75	1.50
❑75	—	0.30	0.75	1.50
❑76	—	0.30	0.75	1.50
❑77	—	0.30	0.75	1.50
❑78	—	0.30	0.75	1.50
❑79	—	0.30	0.75	1.50
❑80	—	0.30	0.75	1.50
❑81	—	0.30	0.75	1.50
❑82	—	0.30	0.75	1.50
❑83	—	0.30	0.75	1.50
❑84	—	0.30	0.75	1.50
❑85	—	0.30	0.75	1.50
❑86	—	0.30	0.75	1.50
❑87	—	0.30	0.75	1.50
❑Anl 1, b&w; magazine	1.25	0.25	0.63	1.25

DRACULA: LORD OF THE UNDEAD
MARVEL

Value: Cover or less

❑1, Dec 98, When Darkness Returns, gatefold summary 2.99
❑2, Dec 98, gatefold summary 2.99
❑3, Dec 98, gatefold summary 2.99

DRACULA: RETURN OF THE IMPALER
SLAVE LABOR

Value: Cover or less

❑1, Jul 93 ..... 2.95
❑2, Jan 94 ..... 2.95
❑3, Mar 94 ..... 2.95
❑4, Oct 94 ..... 2.95

DRACULA'S DAUGHTER
FANTAGRAPHICS

Value: Cover or less

❑1, b&w; adult 2.50

DRACULA: THE LADY IN THE TOMB
ETERNITY

Value: Cover or less

❑1, b&w 2.50

DRACULA: THE SUICIDE CLUB
ADVENTURE

Value: Cover or less

❑1, Aug 92 ..... 2.50
❑2, Sep 92 ..... 2.50
❑3, Oct 92 ..... 2.50
❑4, Nov 92 ..... 2.50

DRACULA VERSUS ZORRO
TOPPS

	ORIG	GOOD	FINE	N-MINT
❑1, Oct 93, TY	2.95	0.80	2.00	4.00
❑2, Nov 93, TY	2.95	0.70	1.75	3.50

DRACULA VERSUS ZORRO (VOL. 2)
TOPPS

Value: Cover or less

❑1, Apr 94 ..... 5.95

DRACULA VERSUS ZORRO (VOL. 3)
IMAGE

Value: Cover or less

❑1, Sep 98, TY 2.95
❑2, Oct 98, TY 2.95

DRACULA: VLAD THE IMPALER
TOPPS

Value: Cover or less

❑1, I Am Dracula!, trading cards; trading cards 2.95
❑2, Dark Legend A-Borning, trading cards; trading cards 2.95
❑3, To Rise Again!, trading cards; trading cards 2.95

DRACULINA (2ND SERIES)
DRACULINA

Value: Cover or less

❑1, Blood Of The Bride, O: Draculina 2.50

DRACULINA'S COZY COFFIN
DRACULINA

Value: Cover or less

❑1, b&w; no indicia 2.50
❑2, b&w; no indicia 2.50

ORIG GOOD FINE N-MINT

DRAFT, THE
MARVEL

Value: Cover or less

- ❑1, Jul 88, HT, D.P.7, Nightmask 3.50

DRAGON
COMICS INTERVIEW

Value: Cover or less

- ❑1, Aug 87, weekly 1.75
- ❑2, Aug 87, weekly 1.75
- ❑3, Aug 87, weekly 1.75
- ❑4, Aug 87, weekly 1.75

DRAGON (2ND SERIES)
IMAGE

Issue	ORIG	GOOD	FINE	N-MINT
❑1, Mar 96	0.99	0.40	1.00	2.00
❑2, Apr 96	0.99	0.40	1.00	2.00
❑3, May 96	0.99	0.40	1.00	2.00
❑4, Jun 96	0.99	0.40	1.00	2.00
❑5, Jul 96, A: Badrock, Final Issue	0.99	0.40	1.00	2.00

DRAGONBALL
VIZ

Issue	ORIG	GOOD	FINE	N-MINT
❑1, Bloomers and the Monkey King, 'Manga Style ' Edition	2.95	1.20	3.00	6.00
❑2, 'Manga Style ' Edition	2.95	0.80	2.00	4.00
❑3, 'Manga Style ' Edition	2.95	0.80	2.00	4.00
❑4, 'Manga Style ' Edition	2.95	0.80	2.00	4.00
❑5, 'Manga Style ' Edition	2.95	0.80	2.00	4.00
❑6, 'Manga Style ' Edition	2.95	0.80	2.00	4.00
❑7, 'Manga Style ' Edition	2.95	0.80	2.00	4.00
❑8	2.95	0.60	1.50	3.00
❑9	2.95	0.60	1.50	3.00
❑10	2.95	0.60	1.50	3.00
❑11	2.95	0.60	1.50	3.00
❑12	2.95	0.60	1.50	3.00

DRAGONBALL PART TWO
VIZ

Issue	ORIG	GOOD	FINE	N-MINT
❑1	2.95	0.80	2.00	4.00
❑2	2.95	0.60	1.50	3.00
❑3	2.95	0.60	1.50	3.00
❑4	2.95	0.60	1.50	3.00
❑5	2.95	0.60	1.50	3.00
❑6	2.95	0.60	1.50	3.00
❑7	2.95	0.60	1.50	3.00
❑8	2.95	0.60	1.50	3.00

DRAGONBALL Z
VIZ

Issue	ORIG	GOOD	FINE	N-MINT
❑1	2.95	1.20	3.00	6.00
❑2	2.95	0.80	2.00	4.00
❑3	2.95	0.80	2.00	4.00
❑4	2.95	0.80	2.00	4.00
❑5	2.95	0.80	2.00	4.00
❑6	2.95	0.59	1.48	2.95
❑7	2.95	0.59	1.48	2.95
❑8	2.95	0.59	1.48	2.95
❑9	2.95	0.59	1.48	2.95
❑10	2.95	0.59	1.48	2.95

DRAGONBALL Z PART 2
VIZ

Issue	ORIG	GOOD	FINE	N-MINT
❑1, Here They Come...in Time to Kill!; Let the Games Begin!, 'Manga Style ' Edition	2.95	0.70	1.75	3.50
❑2, 'Manga Style ' Edition	2.95	0.60	1.50	3.00
❑3, 'Manga Style ' Edition	2.95	0.60	1.50	3.00
❑4, 'Manga Style ' Edition	2.95	0.60	1.50	3.00
❑5, 'Manga Style ' Edition	2.95	0.60	1.50	3.00
❑6, 'Manga Style ' Edition	2.95	0.59	1.48	2.95
❑7, 'Manga Style ' Edition	2.95	0.59	1.48	2.95
❑8	2.95	0.59	1.48	2.95
❑9	2.95	0.59	1.48	2.95
❑10	2.95	0.59	1.48	2.95
❑11	2.95	0.59	1.48	2.95

DRAGON, THE: BLOOD & GUTS
IMAGE

Value: Cover or less

- ❑1, Mar 95 .... 2.50
- ❑2, Apr 95 .... 2.50
- ❑3, May 95 .... 2.50

DRAGON CHIANG
ECLIPSE

Value: Cover or less

- ❑1, nn, b&w 3.95

DRAGONFIRE (VOL. 1)
NIGHTWYND

Value: Cover or less

- ❑1, b&w 2.50
- ❑2, b&w 2.50
- ❑3, b&w 2.50
- ❑4, b&w 2.50

DRAGONFIRE (VOL. 2)
NIGHTWYND

Value: Cover or less

- ❑1, b&w 2.50
- ❑2, b&w 2.50
- ❑3, b&w 2.50
- ❑4, b&w 2.50

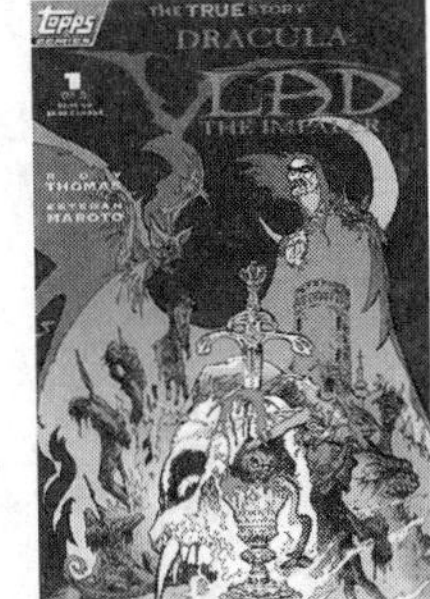

Topps delved into the legends behind Dracula, including his real-life inspiration, Vlad the Impaler, for a three-issue mini-series.

ORIG GOOD FINE N-MINT

DRAGONFIRE: THE CLASSIFIED FILES
NIGHTWYND

Value: Cover or less

- ❑1, b&w 2.50
- ❑2, b&w 2.50
- ❑3, b&w 2.50
- ❑4, b&w 2.50

DRAGONFIRE: THE EARLY YEARS
NIGHT WYND

Value: Cover or less

- ❑1, b&w 2.50
- ❑2, b&w 2.50
- ❑3, b&w 2.50
- ❑4, b&w 2.50
- ❑5, b&w 2.50
- ❑6, b&w 2.50
- ❑7, b&w 2.50
- ❑8, b&w 2.50

DRAGONFIRE: UFO WARS
NIGHTWYND

Value: Cover or less

- ❑1, b&w 2.50
- ❑2, b&w 2.50
- ❑3, b&w 2.50

DRAGONFLIGHT
ECLIPSE

Value: Cover or less

- ❑1, Feb 91, Anne McCaffrey... 4.95
- ❑2, Anne McCaffrey 4.95
- ❑3, Anne McCaffrey 4.95

DRAGON FLUX
ANTARCTIC

Value: Cover or less

- ❑2, Jun 96, b&w 2.95
- ❑3, Nov 96, b&w 2.95

DRAGONFLY
AC

Value: Cover or less

- ❑1, Aug 85 .... 1.75
- ❑2 .... 1.75
- ❑3 .... 1.75
- ❑4 .... 1.75
- ❑5 .... 1.75
- ❑6, Feb 87 .... 1.75
- ❑7, Jul 87 .... 1.75
- ❑8 .... 1.95

DRAGONFORCE
AIRCEL

Issue	ORIG	GOOD	FINE	N-MINT
❑1, 1: Sental; 1: Kamikaze; 1: Alloy; 1: Dragonforce; 1: Maire; 1: Kohl, b&w	1.95	0.40	1.00	2.00
❑2, b&w	1.95	0.40	1.00	2.00
❑3, b&w	1.95	0.40	1.00	2.00
❑4, b&w	1.95	0.40	1.00	2.00
❑5, b&w	1.95	0.40	1.00	2.00
❑6, b&w	1.95	0.40	1.00	2.00
❑7, b&w	1.95	0.40	1.00	2.00
❑8, b&w	1.95	0.40	1.00	2.00
❑9, b&w	1.95	0.40	1.00	2.00
❑10, b&w	1.95	0.40	1.00	2.00
❑11, b&w	1.95	0.40	1.00	2.00
❑12, b&w	1.95	0.40	1.00	2.00
❑13, b&w	1.95	0.40	1.00	2.00

DRAGONFORCE CHRONICLES
AIRCEL

Value: Cover or less

- ❑1, Change, b&w; Reprint 2.95
- ❑2, b&w; Reprint 2.95
- ❑3, b&w; Reprint 2.95
- ❑4, b&w; Reprint 2.95
- ❑5, b&w; Reprint 2.95

DRAGONHEART
TOPPS

Value: Cover or less

- ❑1, May 96, movie Adaptation 2.95
- ❑2, Jun 96, 64pgs.; movie Adaptation 4.95

DRAGON KNIGHTS
SLAVE LABOR

Value: Cover or less

- ❑1, Aug 98, b&w 1.75
- ❑2 .... 1.75
- ❑3 .... 1.75

DRAGON LADY
DRAGON LADY PRESS

Value: Cover or less

- ❑1, King of Mounted 6.95
- ❑2, Red Ryder 6.95
- ❑3, Captain Easy 5.95
- ❑4, AW, Secret Agent X-9 .... 5.95
- ❑5, Brick Bradford 5.95
- ❑6, ATh (c), Secret Agent X-9 . 5.95
- ❑7, Captain Easy 5.95
- ❑8, ATh (c), Terry 5.95

DRAGONLANCE
DC

	ORIG	GOOD	FINE	N-MINT
❑1, Dec 88, Fire & Light	1.25	0.40	1.00	2.00
❑2, Win 88	1.25	0.30	0.75	1.50
❑3, Hol 88	1.25	0.25	0.63	1.25
❑4, Jan 89	1.25	0.25	0.63	1.25
❑5, Feb 89	1.25	0.25	0.63	1.25
❑6, Mar 89	1.50	0.30	0.75	1.50
❑7, Apr 89	1.50	0.30	0.75	1.50
❑8, Jun 89	1.50	0.30	0.75	1.50
❑9, Jul 89	1.50	0.30	0.75	1.50
❑10	1.50	0.30	0.75	1.50
❑11	1.50	0.30	0.75	1.50
❑12	1.50	0.30	0.75	1.50
❑13	1.50	0.30	0.75	1.50
❑14	1.50	0.30	0.75	1.50
❑15	1.50	0.30	0.75	1.50
❑16	1.50	0.30	0.75	1.50
❑17	1.50	0.30	0.75	1.50
❑18	1.50	0.30	0.75	1.50
❑19	1.50	0.30	0.75	1.50
❑20	1.50	0.30	0.75	1.50
❑21	1.50	0.30	0.75	1.50
❑22	1.50	0.30	0.75	1.50
❑23	1.50	0.30	0.75	1.50
❑24	1.50	0.35	0.88	1.75
❑25	1.75	0.35	0.88	1.75
❑26	1.75	0.35	0.88	1.75
❑27	1.75	0.35	0.88	1.75
❑28	1.75	0.35	0.88	1.75
❑29	1.75	0.35	0.88	1.75
❑30	1.75	0.35	0.88	1.75
❑31	1.75	0.35	0.88	1.75
❑32	1.75	0.35	0.88	1.75
❑33	1.75	0.35	0.88	1.75
❑34, Final Issue	1.75	0.35	0.88	1.75
❑Anl 1	2.95	0.59	1.48	2.95

DRAGONLANCE COMIC BOOK
TSR

	ORIG	GOOD	FINE	N-MINT
❑1	—	0.20	0.50	1.00

DRAGONLANCE SAGA
TSR

Value: Cover or less

	ORIG
❑1, TY	9.95
❑2, TY	9.95
❑3, TY	9.95
❑4	9.95
❑5	9.95

DRAGON LINES
MARVEL

Value: Cover or less

	ORIG
❑1, The Year Of The Monkey, Embossed cover	2.50
❑2, Snapping The Dragon's Spine	1.95
❑3	1.95
❑4	1.95

DRAGON LINES: WAY OF THE WARRIOR
MARVEL

Value: Cover or less

	ORIG
❑1	2.25
❑2	2.25

DRAGON OF THE VALKYR
RAK

Value: Cover or less

	ORIG
❑1, b&w	1.75
❑2	1.75
❑3	1.75

DRAGON QUEST
SILVERWOLF

	ORIG	GOOD	FINE	N-MINT
❑1, b&w	—	0.40	1.00	2.00
❑2	—	0.40	1.00	2.00

DRAGONRING
AIRCEL

Value: Cover or less

	ORIG
❑1, Demon Hunter, b&w	2.00
❑2, b&w	2.00
❑3, b&w	2.00
❑4, The King of Rock and Roll, b&w	2.00
❑5, b&w	2.00
❑6, In the Box, b&w	2.00

DRAGONRING (VOL. 2)
AIRCEL

Value: Cover or less

	ORIG
❑1	2.00
❑2	2.00
❑3, Homecoming	2.00
❑4, Culmination	2.00
❑5, Tiger's Teeth	2.00
❑6	2.00
❑7	2.00
❑8	2.00
❑9, Edge of the Pit	2.00
❑10	2.00
❑11	2.00
❑12	2.00
❑13, The Gathering Storm	2.00
❑14, Tiger's Tale	2.00
❑15	2.00

DRAGONROK SAGA, THE
HANTHERCRAFT

Value: Cover or less

	ORIG
❑1	2.50
❑2	2.50
❑3	2.50
❑4	2.50
❑5	2.50
❑6	2.50
❑7	2.50
❑8	2.50
❑9	2.50
❑10	2.50

DRAGON'S BANE
HALL OF HEROES

Value: Cover or less

	ORIG
❑1, Rebirth	2.50
❑Ash 1, Chicago Comic Con Ashcan limited to 100 copies	4.95

DRAGON'S CLAWS
MARVEL

	ORIG	GOOD	FINE	N-MINT
❑1, Jul 88, The Game!, 1: Dragon's Claws	1.25	0.30	0.75	1.50
❑2, Aug 88	1.50	0.30	0.75	1.50
❑3, Sep 88, Heroes' Welcome	1.50	0.30	0.75	1.50
❑4, Oct 88	1.50	0.30	0.75	1.50
❑5, Nov 88, 1: Death's Head I	1.75	0.40	1.00	2.00
❑6, Dec 88	1.75	0.35	0.88	1.75
❑7, Jan 89	1.75	0.35	0.88	1.75
❑8, Feb 89	1.75	0.35	0.88	1.75
❑9, Mar 89	1.75	0.35	0.88	1.75
❑10, Apr 89	1.75	0.35	0.88	1.75
❑11	1.75	0.35	0.88	1.75
❑12	1.75	0.35	0.88	1.75

DRAGONS IN THE MOON
AIRCEL

Value: Cover or less

	ORIG
❑1, Oct 90, b&w	2.50
❑2, Oct 90, b&w	2.50
❑3, Oct 90, b&w	2.50
❑4, Oct 90, b&w	2.50

DRAGONSLAYER
MARVEL

	ORIG	GOOD	FINE	N-MINT
❑1, Oct 81, movie Adaptation	0.50	0.30	0.75	1.50
❑2, Nov 81, movie Adaptation	0.50	0.30	0.75	1.50

DRAGON'S STAR
MATRIX

	ORIG	GOOD	FINE	N-MINT
❑1, Dec 87, Beginnings	1.75	0.40	1.00	2.00
❑2	1.75	0.40	1.00	2.00
❑3	1.75	0.40	1.00	2.00

DRAGON'S STAR 2
CALIBER

Value: Cover or less

	ORIG
❑1, Entanglements	2.95
❑2	2.95
❑3	2.95

DRAGON'S TEETH
DRAGON'S TEETH

Value: Cover or less

	ORIG
❑1, b&w	2.95

DRAGON STRIKE
MARVEL

	ORIG	GOOD	FINE	N-MINT
❑1, Before The Strike!	1.25	0.30	0.75	1.50

DRAGONSTRIKE PRIME
ILLUSION STUDIOS

Value: Cover or less

	ORIG
❑2, Dec 96, b&w	1.95

DRAGON WARS, THE
IRONCAT

Value: Cover or less

	ORIG
❑1	2.95
❑2	2.95
❑3	2.95
❑4	2.95
❑5	2.95
❑6	2.95

DRAKKON WARS, THE
REALM

Value: Cover or less

	ORIG
❑0, Jul 97, Battlestar Galactica story written by Richard Hatch	2.99

DRAKUUN
DARK HORSE

Value: Cover or less

	ORIG
❑1, Feb 97, Rise of the Dragon Princess, Part 1	2.95
❑2, Mar 97, Rise of the Dragon Princess, Part 2	2.95
❑3, Apr 97, Rise of the Dragon Princess, Part 3	2.95
❑4, May 97, Rise of the Dragon Princess, Part 4	2.95
❑5, Jun 97, Rise of the Dragon Princess, Part 5	2.95
❑6, Jul 97, Rise of the Dragon Princess, Part 6	2.95
❑7, Aug 97, The Revenge of Gustav, Part 1	2.95
❑8, Sep 97, The Revenge of Gustav, Part 2	2.95
❑9, Oct 97, The Revenge of Gustav, Part 3	2.95
❑10, Nov 97, The Revenge of Gustav, Part 4	2.95
❑11, Dec 97, The Revenge of Gustav, Part 5	2.95
❑12, Jan 98, The Revenge of Gustav, Part 6	2.95
❑13, Feb 98, Shadow of the Warlock, Part 1	2.95
❑14, Mar 98, Shadow of the Warlock, Part 2	2.95
❑15, Apr 98, Shadow of the Warlock, Part 3	2.95
❑16, May 98, Shadow of the Warlock, Part 4	2.95
❑17, Jun 98, Shadow of the Warlock, Part 5	2.95
❑18, Jul 98, Shadow of the Warlock, Part 6	2.95
❑19, Oct 98, The Hidden War, Part 1	2.95
❑20, Nov 98, The Hidden War, Part 2	2.95

	ORIG	GOOD	FINE	N-MINT

❑21, Dec 98, The Hidden War, Part 3 .... 2.95
❑22, Jan 99, The Hidden War, Part 4 .... 2.95
❑23, Feb 99, The Hidden War, Part 5 .... 2.95
❑24, Mar 99, The Hidden War, Part 6 .... 2.95

DRAMA
SIRIUS ENTERTAINMENT

	ORIG	GOOD	FINE	N-MINT
❑1, Jun 95, The Fall of the Goddess; Psychobabble, nn; One-Shot	2.95	1.60	4.00	8.00
❑1/LE, limited to 1400 copies	15.00	4.00	10.00	20.00

DRAWN & QUARTERLY
DRAWN & QUARTERLY

	ORIG	GOOD	FINE	N-MINT
❑1, b&w	—	0.60	1.50	3.00
❑2	—	0.60	1.50	3.00
❑3	—	0.60	1.50	3.00
❑4	—	0.60	1.50	3.00
❑5	—	0.60	1.50	3.00
❑6	—	0.60	1.50	3.00
❑7	—	0.60	1.50	3.00
❑8, Apr 92, b&w	3.75	0.75	1.88	3.75

DREADLANDS
MARVEL

Value: Cover or less

❑1 .... 3.95
❑2 .... 3.95
❑3 .... 3.95
❑4, Winter and Spring 3.95

DREAD OF NIGHT
HAMILTON

Value: Cover or less

❑1, b&w 3.95
❑2, b&w 3.95

DREADSTAR
MARVEL

	ORIG	GOOD	FINE	N-MINT
❑1, Nov 82, JSn, JSn (w), The Quest, Story continued from Epic Illustrated #15	1.50	0.50	1.25	2.50
❑2, Jan 83, O: Willow, Willow	1.50	0.40	1.00	2.00
❑3, Mar 83, Lord Papal	1.50	0.40	1.00	2.00
❑4, May 83	1.50	0.40	1.00	2.00
❑5, Jul 83	1.50	0.40	1.00	2.00
❑6, Sep 83	1.50	0.35	0.88	1.75
❑7, Nov 83	1.50	0.35	0.88	1.75
❑8, Jan 84	1.50	0.35	0.88	1.75
❑9, Mar 84	1.50	0.35	0.88	1.75
❑10, Apr 84	1.50	0.35	0.88	1.75
❑11, Jun 84	1.50	0.35	0.88	1.75
❑12, Jul 84, New costume	1.50	0.35	0.88	1.75
❑13, Aug 84	1.50	0.35	0.88	1.75
❑14, Oct 84, Fights Lord Papal	1.50	0.35	0.88	1.75
❑15, Nov 84	1.50	0.35	0.88	1.75
❑16, Dec 84	1.50	0.30	0.75	1.50
❑17, Feb 85	1.50	0.30	0.75	1.50
❑18, Apr 85	1.50	0.30	0.75	1.50
❑19, Jun 85	1.50	0.30	0.75	1.50
❑20, Aug 85	1.50	0.30	0.75	1.50
❑21, Oct 85	1.50	0.30	0.75	1.50
❑22, Dec 85	1.50	0.30	0.75	1.50
❑23, Feb 86	1.50	0.30	0.75	1.50
❑24, Apr 86	1.50	0.30	0.75	1.50
❑25, Jun 86	1.50	0.30	0.75	1.50
❑26, Aug 86	1.50	0.30	0.75	1.50
❑27, Nov 86, First Comics begins publishing	1.75	0.35	0.88	1.75
❑28, Jan 87	1.75	0.35	0.88	1.75
❑29, Mar 87	1.75	0.35	0.88	1.75
❑30, May 87	1.75	0.35	0.88	1.75
❑31, Jul 87	1.75	0.35	0.88	1.75
❑32, Sep 87	1.75	0.35	0.88	1.75
❑33, Nov 87	1.75	0.35	0.88	1.75
❑34, Jan 88	1.75	0.35	0.88	1.75
❑35, Mar 88	1.75	0.35	0.88	1.75
❑36, May 88	1.75	0.35	0.88	1.75
❑37, Jul 88	1.75	0.35	0.88	1.75
❑38, Sep 88	1.75	0.35	0.88	1.75
❑39, Nov 88, Crossroads	1.95	0.39	0.98	1.95
❑40, Jan 89	1.95	0.39	0.98	1.95
❑41, Mar 89, PD (w), Peter David writing starts	1.95	0.39	0.98	1.95
❑42, May 89	1.95	0.39	0.98	1.95
❑43, Jun 89	1.95	0.39	0.98	1.95
❑44, Jul 89	1.95	0.39	0.98	1.95
❑45, Aug 89	1.95	0.39	0.98	1.95
❑46, Sep 89	1.95	0.39	0.98	1.95
❑47, Oct 89	1.95	0.39	0.98	1.95
❑48, Nov 89	1.95	0.39	0.98	1.95
❑49, Dec 89	1.95	0.39	0.98	1.95
❑50, Jan 90, Embossed cover; Double-size	3.95	0.55	1.38	2.75
❑51, Feb 90	1.95	0.39	0.98	1.95
❑52, Mar 90	1.95	0.39	0.98	1.95
❑53, Apr 90	1.95	0.39	0.98	1.95
❑54, May 90	1.95	0.39	0.98	1.95
❑55, Jun 90	1.95	0.45	1.13	2.25
❑56, Jul 90	1.95	0.45	1.13	2.25
❑57, Aug 90	1.95	0.45	1.13	2.25
❑58, Sep 90	1.95	0.45	1.13	2.25
❑59, Oct 90	2.25	0.45	1.13	2.25
❑60, Nov 90	2.25	0.45	1.13	2.25
❑61, Dec 90	2.25	0.45	1.13	2.25
❑62, Jan 91	2.25	0.45	1.13	2.25
❑63, Feb 91	2.25	0.45	1.13	2.25
❑64, Mar 91, Final Issue	2.25	0.45	1.13	2.25
❑Anl 1, Apr 91, JSn, The Price	2.00	0.40	1.00	2.00

In the early 1980s, Marvel produced dozens of movie adaptations, including the two-issue *Dragonslayer* adaptation.

© 1981 Marvel

DREADSTAR (MALIBU)
MALIBU

	ORIG	GOOD	FINE	N-MINT
❑0.5, Mar 94, Promotional edition included in Hero Illustrated	—	0.40	1.00	2.00
❑1, Apr 94, PD (w), coupon	2.50	0.50	1.25	2.50
❑2, May 94, PD (w), Contradiction, coupon	2.50	0.50	1.25	2.50
❑3, Jun 94, PD (w), Backstory, coupon	2.50	0.50	1.25	2.50
❑4, Sep 94, PD (w), coupon	2.50	0.50	1.25	2.50
❑5, Oct 94, PD (w), Convergence, D: Dreadstar (Vanth), coupon	2.50	0.50	1.25	2.50
❑6, Jan 95, PD (w), Final Issue; coupon	2.50	0.50	1.25	2.50

DREADSTAR & CO.
MARVEL

	ORIG	GOOD	FINE	N-MINT
❑1, Jul 85, JSn, JSn (w), The Hand Of Darkness, Reprint	0.75	0.20	0.50	1.00
❑2, Aug 85, JSn, JSn (w), Willow's Story, Reprint	0.75	0.25	0.63	1.25
❑3, Sep 85, JSn, JSn (w), Holocaust, Reprint	0.75	0.25	0.63	1.25
❑4, Reprint	0.75	0.25	0.63	1.25
❑5, Reprint	0.75	0.25	0.63	1.25
❑6, Reprint	0.75	0.25	0.63	1.25

DREAM ANGEL
ANGEL ENTERTAINMENT

Value: Cover or less

❑0, Fal 96, b&w 2.95

DREAM ANGEL AND ANGEL GIRL
ANGEL

Value: Cover or less

❑1 .... 3.00

DREAM ANGEL: THE QUANTUM DREAMER
ANGEL

Value: Cover or less

❑0, I Saw It in a Dream...! 2.95
❑1 .... 2.95
❑2 .... 2.95

DREAM CORRIDOR (HARLAN ELLISON'S...)
DARK HORSE

	ORIG	GOOD	FINE	N-MINT
❑1, Mar 95, JBy, I Have No Mouth and I Must Scream, Part 1; Midnight in the Sunken Cathedral (text story)	2.95	0.70	1.75	3.50
❑2, Apr 95, JBy, I Have No Mouth and I Must Scream, Part 2; S.R.O.	2.95	0.65	1.63	3.25
❑3, May 95, JBy, I Have No Mouth and I Must Scream, Part 3	2.95	0.60	1.50	3.00
❑4, Jun 95, JBy, I Have No Mouth and I Must Scream, Part 4; Catman, Part 1	2.95	0.60	1.50	3.00
❑5, Aug 95, Catman, Part 2; How's the Night Life on Cissalda?	2.95	0.60	1.50	3.00
❑6, Sep 95, Opposites Attract; One Life, Furnished in Early Poverty	2.95	0.60	1.50	3.00
❑SE 1, Jan 95, On The Slab; Quicktime, prestige format	4.95	1.00	2.50	5.00
❑SE 1-2, Sep 95, 2nd Printing; prestige format	4.95	0.99	2.47	4.95

DREAM CORRIDOR QUARTERLY (HARLAN ELLISON'S...)
DARK HORSE

Value: Cover or less

❑1, Aug 96, Opposites Attract; Rock God, prestige format... 5.95

DREAMERY, THE
ECLIPSE

Value: Cover or less

❑1, Dec 86, Andri's Christmas Shoes; Jabberwocky, A: Chicken; A: Andri Lowhard; A: Veit Wassergarn; A: Berdach Feuerbach; A: Stinz Lowhard; A: Frau Wassergarn; A: Bruna Lowhard, b&w; Councilman Stinz story 2.00
❑2, Feb 87, Alice, Part I, 1: White Rabbit; 1: Alice, b&w; Lela Dowling bio 2.00

❑3, The Carp of Easter; Alice, Part II, A: Andri Lowhard; A: Ede; A: Odo; A: Stinz Lowhard; 2: Alice; A: Bruna Lowhard, b&w; Councilman Stinz story; Donna Barr bio 2.00
❑4, Alice, Part III; The Dreamery Gallery, 1: Cheshire Cat; A: Alice, b&w 2.00
❑5, Alice, Part IV; Nothing Like Gone, A: Andri Lowhard; A: Doctor Foon; A: Loch Ness Monster; A: Stinz Lowhard; A: Alice; A: Quidam, b&w; Councilman Stinz story; Time Release entirely done on a Macintosh computer 2.00
❑6, Alice, Part V; Chicken, A: Chicken; O: Feuerbach family; 2: Cheshire Cat; 2: White Rabbit; A: Berdach Feuerbach; A: Stinz Lowhard; A: The Devil; A: Alice, b&w; Councilman Stinz story 2.00
❑7, Alice, Part VI; The Last Horselaugh, A: Uwe Wassergarn; A: Margl Dammling; A: White Rabbit; A: Albert Dammling; A: Stinz Lowhard; A: Alice; A: Hans Bruchteil, b&w; Last installment Alice; Young Stinz story 2.00
❑8, The Adventures of Prince Ivan: On the Birth of Prince Ivan; A Breathing Spill, 1: Prince Iv, b&w 2.00
❑9, Animal Attraction; The Tale of Prince Ivan the Not-So-Experienced, Part the Second, b&w; Young Stinz story 2.00
❑10, The Proving Ground; The Raccoon Platoon Tune (song), A: Stinz Lowhard; A: Paul Lowhard, b&w; Young Stinz story; Sti 2.00
❑11, Smoked Out; Prince Ivan, Part IV, A: Rauchl Schorsche, b&w; Young Stinz story; Wolf Pack 2.00
❑12, Sprunghack Hans; Next: How Prince Ivan Meets Various Insects and Critters, and What They Do for His Credit Rating, Part Five, A: Andri Lowhard; O: Sprunghack Han; A: Stinz Lowhard, b&w; Councilman Stinz story 2.00
❑13, Not My Problem; The Tale of Prince Ivan the Slightly Experienced, Part VI, A: Baron von Geisel; A: Rolf; 1: Little Humpback Horse (full); A: Stinz Lowhard; A: Prince Ivan; A: Bruna Lowhard; A: Raoul, b&w; Councilman Stinz story 2.00
❑14, Hooves of Death; The Philosophy of Raccoons, b&w; Cover reads "The Ninjery"; Final Issue; Ninja themed stories 2.00

DREAMING, THE
DC

	ORIG	GOOD	FINE	N-MINT
❑1, Jun 96, The Goldie Factor, Part 1	2.50	0.80	2.00	4.00
❑2, Jul 96, The Goldie Factor, Part 2	2.50	0.60	1.50	3.00
❑3, Aug 96, The Goldie Factor, Part 3	2.50	0.60	1.50	3.00
❑4, Sep 96, The Lost Boy, Part 1	2.50	0.60	1.50	3.00
❑5, Oct 96, The Lost Boy, Part 2, Photo cover	2.50	0.60	1.50	3.00
❑6, Nov 96, The Lost Boy, Part 3	2.50	0.60	1.50	3.00
❑7, Dec 96, The Lost Boy, Part 4	2.50	0.60	1.50	3.00
❑8, Jan 97, His Brother's Keeper, cover says Nov 96, indicia says Jan 97; self-contained story	2.50	0.60	1.50	3.00
❑9, Feb 97, BT (w), Weird Romance, Part 1	2.50	0.60	1.50	3.00
❑10, Mar 97, BT (w), Weird Romance, Part 2	2.50	0.60	1.50	3.00
❑11, Apr 97, BT (w), Weird Romance, Part 3	2.50	0.50	1.25	2.50
❑12, May 97, BT (w), Weird Romance, Part 4	2.50	0.50	1.25	2.50
❑13, Jun 97, Coyote's Kiss, Part 1	2.50	0.50	1.25	2.50
❑14, Jul 97, Coyote's Kiss, Part 2	2.50	0.50	1.25	2.50
❑15, Aug 97, Day's Work Night's Rest	2.50	0.50	1.25	2.50
❑16, Sep 97, Ice	2.50	0.50	1.25	2.50
❑17, Oct 97, Souvenirs, Part 1	2.50	0.50	1.25	2.50
❑18, Nov 97, Souvenirs, Part 2	2.50	0.50	1.25	2.50
❑19, Dec 97, Souvenirs, Part 3, A: The Corinthian	2.50	0.50	1.25	2.50
❑20, Jan 98, The Dark Rose, Part 1	2.50	0.50	1.25	2.50
❑21, Feb 98, The Dark Rose, Part 2	2.50	0.50	1.25	2.50
❑22, Mar 98, The Unkindness of One, Part 1; Unkindness of One, Part 1	2.50	0.50	1.25	2.50
❑23, Apr 98, The Unkindness of One, Part 2; Unkindness of One, Part 2	2.50	0.50	1.25	2.50
❑24, May 98, The Unkindness of One, Part 3; Unkindness of One, Part 1	2.50	0.50	1.25	2.50
❑25, Jun 98, My Year As A Man	2.50	0.50	1.25	2.50
❑26, Jul 98, Restitution	2.50	0.50	1.25	2.50
❑27, Aug 98, Many Mansions: Stormy Weather	2.50	0.50	1.25	2.50
❑28, Sep 98, Many Mansions: Dreams the Burning Dream, House of Mystery burns down	2.50	0.50	1.25	2.50
❑29, Oct 98, Many Mansions: Ashes	2.50	0.50	1.25	2.50
❑30, Nov 98, Many Mansions: Temporary Overflow, A: Lucien	2.50	0.50	1.25	2.50
❑31, Dec 98, Many Mansions: November Eve, Anthology	3.95	0.50	1.25	2.50
❑32, Jan 99, London Pride, A: Peggy Gadling; A: Mad Hettie; A: Hob Gadling	2.50	0.50	1.25	2.50
❑33, Feb 99, The Little Mermaid	2.50	0.50	1.25	2.50
❑34, Mar 99, Many Mansions: Ruin, A: Eve; A: Cain; A: Abel	2.50	0.50	1.25	2.50
❑35, Apr 99, Kaleidoscope	2.50	0.50	1.25	2.50
❑36, May 99, Slow Dying; The Gyres, Part 1	2.50	0.50	1.25	2.50
❑37, Jun 99, Pariah; The Gyres, Part 2	2.50	0.50	1.25	2.50
❑38, Jul 99, Apostate; The Gyres, Part 3	2.50	0.50	1.25	2.50
❑39, Aug 99, The Lost Language of Flowers	2.50	0.50	1.25	2.50
❑40, Sep 99, Fox and Hounds, Part 1	2.50	0.50	1.25	2.50
❑41, Oct 99, Fox and Hounds, Part 2	2.50	0.50	1.25	2.50
❑42, Nov 99, Fox and Hounds, Part 3	2.50	0.50	1.25	2.50
❑43, Dec 99, Fox and Hounds, Part 4	2.50	0.50	1.25	2.50
❑44, Jan 00, Homesick	2.50	0.50	1.25	2.50
❑45, Feb 00	2.50	0.50	1.25	2.50
❑46, Mar 00	2.50	0.50	1.25	2.50
❑47, Apr 00, Ttrinket	2.50	0.50	1.25	2.50
❑48, May 00, Scary Monsters	2.50	0.50	1.25	2.50
❑49, Jun 00	2.50	0.50	1.25	2.50
❑50, Jul 00	2.50	0.50	1.25	2.50
❑51, Aug 00	2.50	0.50	1.25	2.50
❑52, Sep 00, Exiles, Part 1	2.50	0.50	1.25	2.50
❑53, Oct 00, Exiles, Part 2	2.50	0.50	1.25	2.50
❑54, Nov 00, Exiles, Part 3	2.50	0.50	1.25	2.50
❑55, Dec 00, The Further Adventures of Danny Nod, Heroic Library Assistant	2.50	0.50	1.25	2.50
❑56, Jan 01, The First Adventure of Miss Catterina Poe	2.50	0.50	1.25	2.50
❑57, Feb 01, Rise, Part 1	2.50	0.50	1.25	2.50
❑58, Mar 01, Rise, Part 2	2.50	0.50	1.25	2.50
❑59, Apr 01, Rise, Part 3	2.50	0.50	1.25	2.50
❑60, May 01, Rise, Part 4	2.50	0.50	1.25	2.50
❑SE 1, Jul 98, Trial and Error, wraparound cover	5.95	1.19	2.97	5.95

DREAM-QUEST OF UNKNOWN KADATH, THE (H.P. LOVECRAFT'S...)
MOCK MAN
Value: Cover or less

❑1 .... 2.95
❑1-2, Mar 98 .... 2.95
❑2 .... 2.95
❑3 .... 2.95
❑4 .... 2.95
❑5, Final Issue 2.95

DREAMS CANNOT DIE!
MARK'S GIANT ECONOMY SIZE
Value: Cover or less

❑1, Jun 96, Trade Paperback .. 17.95

DREAMS 'N' SCHEMES OF COL. KILGORE
SPECIAL STUDIO
Value: Cover or less

❑1, Mar 91, b&w 2.50
❑2, May 91, b&w 2.50

DREAMS OF A DOG
RIP OFF
Value: Cover or less

❑1, May 90, b&w 2.00
❑2, Jun 92, b&w 2.50

DREAMS OF EVERYMAN
RIP OFF
Value: Cover or less

❑1, Jun 92, nn 2.50

DREAMS OF THE DARKCHYLDE
DARKCHYLDE
Value: Cover or less

❑1, Oct 00, No Possible Harm 2.95

DREAM TEAM
MALIBU
Value: Cover or less

❑1, Jul 95, Malibu/Marvel Pin-ups 4.95

DREAMTIME
BLIND BAT PRESS
Value: Cover or less

❑1, May 95, b&w 2.50
❑2, b&w; no indicia 2.50

DREAMWALKER (AVATAR)
AVATAR
Value: Cover or less

❑0, Nov 98, b&w; One-Shot 3.00

DREAMWALKER (CALIBER)
CALIBER
Value: Cover or less

❑1, b&w 2.95
❑2, b&w 2.95
❑3, b&w 2.95
❑4, Jul 97, b&w 2.95
❑5, Sep 97, b&w 2.95
❑6, Jul 98, b&w 2.95

DREAMWALKER (DREAMWALKER)
DREAMWALKER
Value: Cover or less

❑1, b&w 2.95
❑2, b&w 2.95
❑3, b&w 2.95
❑4, b&w 2.95
❑5, b&w 2.95

DREAMWALKER (MARVEL)
MARVEL
Value: Cover or less

❑1 .... 6.95

DREAMWALKER: AUTUMN LEAVES
AVATAR
Value: Cover or less

❑1, Sep 99, b&w 3.00
❑2, Oct 99, b&w 3.00

DREAMWALKER: CAROUSEL
AVATAR
Value: Cover or less

❑1, Mar 99, b&w 3.00
❑2, Apr 99, b&w 3.00

DREAMWALKER: SUMMER RAIN
AVATAR
Value: Cover or less

❑1, Jul 99, b&w; One-Shot 3.00

	ORIG	GOOD	FINE	N-MINT

DREAM WEAVER
Robert Lankford
Value: Cover or less

❑1, Aug 87 .... 1.95

DREAM WEAVERS
Golden Realm Unlimited
Value: Cover or less

❑1 .... 2.50
❑2 .... 1.50

DREAM WOLVES
Dramenon Studios
Value: Cover or less

❑1, b&w 3.00
❑2, Dec 94, b&w; cardstock cover 3.00
❑3, Jan 95, b&w; cardstock cover 3.00
❑4, Feb 95, b&w 3.00

DREAM WOLVES SWIMSUIT BIZARRE
Gothic
Value: Cover or less

❑0, Dec 95 .... 3.00

DREDD BY BISLEY
Fleetway
Value: Cover or less

❑1, Judge Dredd: A Mega-City Primer; Heavy Metal Dredd: The Legend of Johnny Biker, nn 5.95

DREDD RULES!
Fleetway

	ORIG	GOOD	FINE	N-MINT
❑1	2.95	0.70	1.75	3.50
❑2	2.95	0.60	1.50	3.00
❑3, That Sweet Stuff; Alzheimer's Block	2.95	0.60	1.50	3.00
❑4	2.95	0.60	1.50	3.00
❑5	2.95	0.60	1.50	3.00
❑6, Breakdown on 9th St.; On Meeting Your Enemy	2.95	0.59	1.48	2.95
❑7	2.95	0.59	1.48	2.95
❑8	2.95	0.59	1.48	2.95
❑9	2.95	0.59	1.48	2.95
❑10, Judge Dredd: A Mega-City Primer; Judge Dredd: Bill Bailey, Won't You Please Come Home	2.95	0.59	1.48	2.95
❑11	2.95	0.59	1.48	2.95
❑12	2.95	0.59	1.48	2.95
❑13	2.95	0.59	1.48	2.95
❑14, V: Santa	2.95	0.59	1.48	2.95
❑15	2.95	0.59	1.48	2.95
❑16	2.95	0.59	1.48	2.95
❑17	2.95	0.59	1.48	2.95
❑18	2.95	0.59	1.48	2.95
❑19	2.95	0.59	1.48	2.95
❑20	2.95	0.59	1.48	2.95

DRIFTER
Brainstorm
Value: Cover or less

❑1, b&w 2.95

DRIFTERS
Infinity

	ORIG	GOOD	FINE	N-MINT
❑1	1.70	0.40	1.00	2.00

DRIFTERS, THE
Cornerstone
Value: Cover or less

❑1, b&w 2.00

DROIDS
Marvel

	ORIG	GOOD	FINE	N-MINT
❑1, Apr 86	0.75	0.80	2.00	4.00
❑2, Jun 86, JR, The Ultimate Weapon	0.75	0.50	1.25	2.50
❑3, Aug 86	0.75	0.50	1.25	2.50
❑4, Oct 86	0.75	0.50	1.25	2.50
❑5, Dec 86	0.75	0.50	1.25	2.50
❑6, Feb 87, A New Hope told from droids' p.o.v.	0.75	0.50	1.25	2.50
❑7, Apr 87, A New Hope told from droids' p.o.v.	0.75	0.50	1.25	2.50
❑8, Jun 87, Final Issue; A New Hope told from droids' p.o.v.	1.00	0.50	1.25	2.50

DROOL MAGAZINE
Co. & Sons

	ORIG	GOOD	FINE	N-MINT
❑1, Survival of the Fittest; Shockwork Lemon	0.50	0.60	1.50	3.00

DROOPY
Dark Horse
Value: Cover or less

❑1, Oct 95, Droopy: Dr. Droopenstein; Screwball Squirrel: The Violent Zone, Screwball Squirrel back-up 2.50
❑2, Nov 95, Wolf and Red back-up 2.50
❑3, Dec 95, Droopy: Satan's Little Helpers, Final Issue; Screwball Squirrel back-up 2.50

DROPSIE AVENUE: THE NEIGHBORHOOD
Kitchen Sink Press
Value: Cover or less

❑1, Jun 95, WE, b&w 15.95

John Byrne adapted Harlan Ellison's *I Have No Mouth and I Must Scream* for the first four issues of Dark Horse's *Harlan Ellison's Dream Corridor.*

© 1995 Kilimanjaro Corporation (Dark Horse)

	ORIG	GOOD	FINE	N-MINT

DRUID
Marvel
Value: Cover or less

❑1, May 95, Sick Of This, O: Doctor Druid 2.50
❑2, Jun 95 .... 1.95
❑3, Jul 95 .... 1.95
❑4, Aug 95, Final Issue 1.95

DRUNKEN FIST
Jademan
Value: Cover or less

❑1 .... 1.95
❑2 .... 1.95
❑3 .... 1.95
❑4 .... 1.95
❑5 .... 1.95
❑6 .... 1.95
❑7 .... 1.95
❑8 .... 1.95
❑9 .... 1.95
❑10 .... 1.95
❑11 .... 1.95
❑12 .... 1.95
❑13 .... 1.95
❑14 .... 1.95
❑15 .... 1.95
❑16 .... 1.95
❑17 .... 1.95
❑18 .... 1.95
❑19 .... 1.95
❑20 .... 1.95
❑21 .... 1.95
❑22 .... 1.95
❑23 .... 1.95
❑24 .... 1.95
❑25 .... 1.95
❑26 .... 1.95
❑27 .... 1.95
❑28 .... 1.95
❑29 .... 1.95
❑30 .... 1.95
❑31 .... 1.95
❑32 .... 1.95
❑33 .... 1.95
❑34 .... 1.95
❑35 .... 1.95
❑36 .... 1.95
❑37 .... 1.95
❑38 .... 1.95
❑39 .... 1.95
❑40 .... 1.95
❑41 .... 1.95
❑42 .... 1.95

DRY ROT
Zolton
Value: Cover or less

❑1, b&w 2.95

DUCK AND COVER
Cat-Head
Value: Cover or less

❑1, b&w 2.00
❑2, b&w 2.00

DUCKBOTS
Blackthorne

	ORIG	GOOD	FINE	N-MINT
❑1	1.75	0.40	1.00	2.00
❑2	1.75	0.40	1.00	2.00

DUCKMAN
Dark Horse

	ORIG	GOOD	FINE	N-MINT
❑1, Sep 90, 1: Duckman, b&w	1.95	0.40	1.00	2.00
❑2, b&w	1.95	0.40	1.00	2.00
❑SE 1, Apr 90, nn; b&w; One-Shot	1.95	0.40	1.00	2.00

DUCKMAN (TOPPS)
Topps
Value: Cover or less

❑1, Nov 94, Naked Duck; The Sewer People, coupon for trading card 2.50
❑2, Dec 94, Where's Grandma-ma?, V: King Chicken 2.50
❑3, Mar 95, Night of the Living Duck 2.50
❑4, Mar 95 .... 2.50
❑5, May 95 .... 2.50
❑6, Star Trek: Abduckshuns 2.50

DUCKMAN: THE MOB FROG SAGA
Topps
Value: Cover or less

❑1, Nov 94 .... 2.50
❑2, Dec 94 .... 2.50
❑3, Feb 95 .... 2.50

DUCKTALES (DISNEY)
Disney

	ORIG	GOOD	FINE	N-MINT
❑1, Dime After Dime, nn	—	0.60	1.50	3.00

DUCKTALES (DISNEY'S...)
Disney

	ORIG	GOOD	FINE	N-MINT
❑1, Jun 90, The Ice Demon	1.50	0.40	1.00	2.00
❑2, Jul 90	1.50	0.30	0.75	1.50
❑3, Aug 90, The Fall of New Atlantis!, V: Magica de Spell	1.50	0.30	0.75	1.50
❑4, Sep 90	1.50	0.30	0.75	1.50
❑5, Oct 90	1.50	0.30	0.75	1.50

	ORIG	GOOD	FINE	N-MINT
❑6, Nov 90	1.50	0.30	0.75	1.50
❑7, Dec 90	1.50	0.30	0.75	1.50
❑8, Jan 91, Of Badges 'n' Beagles!	1.50	0.30	0.75	1.50
❑9, Feb 91, The Gold Odyssey, Part 1; Terror at the Top of the World	1.50	0.30	0.75	1.50
❑10, Mar 91, The Gold Odyssey, Part 2; Moon of Gold	1.50	0.30	0.75	1.50
❑11, Apr 91, The Gold Odyssey, Part 3; The Once and Future Warlock	1.50	0.30	0.75	1.50
❑12, May 91, The Gold Odyssey, Part 4; Lost Beyond the Milky Way	1.50	0.30	0.75	1.50
❑13, Jun 91, The Gold Odyssey, Part 5	1.50	0.30	0.75	1.50
❑14, Jul 91, The Gold Odyssey, Part 6; Planet Blue	1.50	0.30	0.75	1.50
❑15, Aug 91, The Gold Odyssey, Part 7; Gold Odyssey, Part 7	1.50	0.30	0.75	1.50
❑16, Sep 91, The Great Chase	1.50	0.30	0.75	1.50
❑17, Oct 91, Time Tetrad, Part 4	1.50	0.30	0.75	1.50
❑18, Nov 91, Dime in Time, Part 2	1.50	0.30	0.75	1.50

DUCKTALES (GLADSTONE)
GLADSTONE

	ORIG	GOOD	FINE	N-MINT
❑1, Oct, CB	1.50	0.40	1.00	2.00
❑2	1.50	0.30	0.75	1.50
❑3	1.50	0.30	0.75	1.50
❑4	1.50	0.30	0.75	1.50
❑5	1.50	0.30	0.75	1.50
❑6	1.50	0.30	0.75	1.50
❑7	1.50	0.30	0.75	1.50
❑8	1.50	0.30	0.75	1.50
❑9, CB	1.50	0.30	0.75	1.50
❑10, CB	1.50	0.30	0.75	1.50
❑11, CB	1.50	0.30	0.75	1.50
❑12, CB, The City Under The Ice; Mythtic Mystery	1.50	0.30	0.75	1.50
❑13, CB	1.50	0.30	0.75	1.50

DUCKTALES: THE MOVIE
DISNEY

Value: Cover or less

❑1, Treasure of the Lost Lamp, adaptation 5.95

DUDLEY DO-RIGHT
CHARLTON

	ORIG	GOOD	FINE	N-MINT
❑1, Aug 70	0.15	4.00	10.00	20.00
❑2, Oct 70	0.15	2.40	6.00	12.00
❑3, Dec 70	0.15	2.00	5.00	10.00
❑4, Feb 71	0.15	1.60	4.00	8.00
❑5, Apr 71	0.15	1.60	4.00	8.00
❑6, Jun 71	0.15	1.60	4.00	8.00
❑7, Aug 71	0.15	1.60	4.00	8.00

DUMB-ASS EXPRESS
MCMANN & TATE

Value: Cover or less

❑1, Assie: Yo Assie's Mine!; Interior Decorator Man, A: Carneys, slightly oversized 2.95

DUMM $2099
PARODY PRESS

Value: Cover or less

❑1, Cover forms triptych with Rummage $2099, Pummeler $2099 .... 2.95

DUNCAN'S KINGDOM
IMAGE

Value: Cover or less

❑1 .... 2.95

❑2 .... 2.95

DUNE
MARVEL

	ORIG	GOOD	FINE	N-MINT
❑1, Apr 85, BSz, movie Adaptation	0.75	0.30	0.75	1.50
❑2, May 85, BSz, movie Adaptation	0.75	0.30	0.75	1.50
❑3, Jun 85, BSz, movie Adaptation	0.75	0.30	0.75	1.50

DUNG BOYS, THE
KITCHEN SINK

Value: Cover or less

❑1, Apr 96, b&w 2.95

❑2, May 96, nude cover with black bars 2.95

❑3, Jun 96, Final Issue 2.95

DUNGEONEERS, THE
SILVERWOLF

Value: Cover or less

❑1 .... 1.50

❑2, Oct 86, Into the Ogres' Lair 1.50

❑3 .... 1.50

❑4 .... 1.50

DUPLEX PLANET ILLUSTRATED
FANTAGRAPHICS

	ORIG	GOOD	FINE	N-MINT
❑1, Jan 93, My First Funeral; What's the Wildest Party You Were At?, b&w; record	2.95	0.59	1.48	2.95
❑2	2.50	0.50	1.25	2.50
❑3	2.50	0.50	1.25	2.50
❑4	2.50	0.50	1.25	2.50
❑5	2.95	0.59	1.48	2.95
❑6	—	0.59	1.48	2.95
❑7, b&w	2.50	0.50	1.25	2.50
❑8, May 94, b&w	2.50	0.50	1.25	2.50
❑9, Jul 94, b&w	2.50	0.50	1.25	2.50
❑10, Sep 94, b&w	2.50	0.50	1.25	2.50
❑11, Dec 94, Bern & Edwina; The King of Love	2.75	0.50	1.25	2.50
❑12	—	0.50	1.25	2.50
❑13	—	0.50	1.25	2.50
❑14	—	0.50	1.25	2.50
❑15, Apr 96, b&w	4.95	0.99	2.47	4.95

DURANGO KID, THE
AC

Value: Cover or less

❑1, Reprint; some color 2.50

❑2, FF, b&w 2.75

❑3 .... 4.95

DUSK
DEADWOOD PRESS

Value: Cover or less

❑1, b&w; cardstock cover 3.00

DUSTY STAR
IMAGE

Value: Cover or less

❑0, Apr 97, b&w; collects stories from Negative Burn #28 and #37 .... 2.95

❑1, Jun 97, Aeroplane, b&w 2.95

DV8
DC

	ORIG	GOOD	FINE	N-MINT
❑0, Dec 98	2.50	0.60	1.50	3.00
❑0.5, Jan 97, Wizard 1/2 Promotional edition	5.00	1.00	2.50	5.00
❑0.5/A, variant cover; Signed by Warren Ellis; Wizard 1/2 Promotional edition	—	1.00	2.50	5.00
❑0.5/GO, Signed by Warren Ellis; Wizard 1/2 "Authentic Gold" promotional edition	10.00	1.20	3.00	6.00
❑0.5/Pl, Jan 97, Wizard 1/2 Platinum promotional edition; Wizard promotional item; platinum version	5.00	1.00	2.50	5.00
❑1/A, Aug 96, Lust for Life, cover says Sep, indicia says Aug	2.50	0.60	1.50	3.00
❑1/B, Aug 96, Lust for Life, cover says Sep, indicia says Aug	2.50	0.60	1.50	3.00
❑1/C, Aug 96, Lust for Life, cover says Sep, indicia says Aug	2.50	0.80	2.00	4.00
❑1/D, Aug 96, Lust for Life, cover says Sep, indicia says Aug	2.50	0.60	1.50	3.00
❑1/E, Aug 96, JLee(c), Lust for Life, cover says Sep, indicia says Aug	2.50	0.60	1.50	3.00
❑1/F, Aug 96, Lust for Life, cover says Sep, indicia says Aug	2.50	0.60	1.50	3.00
❑1/G, Aug 96, Lust for Life, cover says Sep, indicia says Aug	2.50	0.60	1.50	3.00
❑1/H, Aug 96, Lust for Life, cover says Sep, indicia says Aug	2.50	0.60	1.50	3.00
❑2, Nov 96, Some Weird Sin	2.50	0.50	1.25	2.50
❑3, Dec 96, Neighborhood Threat	2.50	0.50	1.25	2.50
❑4, Jan 97, Miss Drugstore	2.50	0.50	1.25	2.50
❑5, Feb 97	2.50	0.50	1.25	2.50
❑6, Mar 97	2.50	0.50	1.25	2.50
❑7, Apr 97, cover says May, indicia says Apr	2.50	0.50	1.25	2.50
❑8, May 97, cover says Jun, indicia says May	2.50	0.50	1.25	2.50
❑9, Jun 97	2.50	0.50	1.25	2.50
❑10, Jul 97	2.50	0.50	1.25	2.50
❑11, Sep 97, Facets	2.50	0.50	1.25	2.50
❑12, Oct 97, Marriage Of Convenience	2.50	0.50	1.25	2.50
❑13, Nov 97, The Sad Tale of Senator Killory	2.50	0.50	1.25	2.50
❑14/A, Dec 97, Barely Legal, Has woman on cover	2.50	0.50	1.25	2.50
❑14/B, Dec 97, Barely Legal, Whole group on cover; white background	2.50	0.50	1.25	2.50
❑14/C, Dec 97, Voyager pack with preview of Danger Girl	2.50	1.20	3.00	6.00
❑15, Jan 98, Settling Accounts	2.50	0.50	1.25	2.50
❑16, Feb 98, Intersection	2.50	0.50	1.25	2.50
❑17, Apr 98, Gen-Passive	2.50	0.50	1.25	2.50
❑18, May 98, Same as it Ever Was, A: Grifter	2.50	0.50	1.25	2.50
❑19, Jun 98, Larger Concerns	2.50	0.50	1.25	2.50
❑20, Jul 98, Lounging in the Ammo Dump	2.50	0.50	1.25	2.50
❑21, Aug 98, Anthrax!	2.50	0.50	1.25	2.50
❑22, Choices	2.50	0.50	1.25	2.50
❑22/A, Sep 98, alternate cover (white background)	2.50	0.50	1.25	2.50

	ORIG	GOOD	FINE	N-MINT
❑23, Oct 98, Gone to Ground	2.50	0.50	1.25	2.50
❑24, Nov 98, Slipstream Prologue; Slipstream	2.50	0.50	1.25	2.50
❑25, Dec 98, Slipstream	2.50	0.50	1.25	2.50
❑26, May 99, Lost and Found	2.50	0.50	1.25	2.50
❑27, Jun 99, Family	2.50	0.50	1.25	2.50
❑28, Jul 99	2.50	0.50	1.25	2.50
❑29, Aug 99, An Affront of Liberty	2.50	0.50	1.25	2.50
❑30, Sep 99, Things Fall Apart, Part 1	2.50	0.50	1.25	2.50
❑31, Oct 99, Things Fall Apart, Part 2	2.50	0.50	1.25	2.50
❑32, Nov 99	2.50	0.50	1.25	2.50
❑Anl 1, Jan 98, Head Trips	2.95	0.59	1.48	2.95
❑Anl 1999, Mar 99, nn; wraparound cover; continued from Gen13 Annual 1999	3.50	0.70	1.75	3.50

DV8 RAVE
IMAGE

	ORIG	GOOD	FINE	N-MINT
❑1, Jul 96	1.75	0.40	1.00	2.00

DV8 VS. BLACK OPS
IMAGE

Value: Cover or less

Issue	Value
❑1, Oct 97, The Techtromis Design, Part 1	2.50
❑2, Nov 97, The Techtromis Design, Part 2	2.50
❑3, Dec 97, The Techtromis Design, Part 3	2.50

DYKE'S DELIGHT
FANNY

	ORIG	GOOD	FINE	N-MINT
❑1, Auntie Studs: The Early Years	—	0.59	1.48	2.95
❑2, Auntie Studs: Rebel Without A Cat!	—	0.59	1.48	2.95

DYLAN DOG
DARK HORSE

Value: Cover or less

Issue	Value
❑1, Mar 99	4.95
❑2, Apr 99	4.95
❑3, May 99	4.95
❑4, Jun 99	4.95
❑5, Jul 99	4.95
❑6, Aug 99	4.95

DYNAMIC CLASSICS
DC

	ORIG	GOOD	FINE	N-MINT
❑1, Sep 78, Batman:The Secret of the Waiting Graves; Manhunter: The Himalaya Incident	0.50	0.50	1.25	2.50

DYNAMO
TOWER

	ORIG	GOOD	FINE	N-MINT
❑1, Aug 66, WW	0.25	8.00	20.00	40.00
❑2, Oct 66, WW	0.25	6.00	15.00	30.00
❑3, Mar 67, WW	0.25	6.00	15.00	30.00
❑4, Jun 67, WW	0.25	6.00	15.00	30.00

The misadventures of the world's most inept Canadian Mountie received their own series in 1970.

© 1970 Jay Ward Productions (Charlton)

DYNAMO JOE
FIRST

	ORIG	GOOD	FINE	N-MINT
❑1, May 86	1.25	0.30	0.75	1.50
❑2, Jun 86, Boldshot Brimfire!	1.25	0.25	0.63	1.25
❑3, Jul 86	1.25	0.25	0.63	1.25
❑4, Feb 87	1.25	0.25	0.63	1.25
❑5, Mar 87	1.25	0.25	0.63	1.25
❑6, Apr 87	1.25	0.25	0.63	1.25
❑7, May 87	1.25	0.25	0.63	1.25
❑8, Jun 87	1.25	0.25	0.63	1.25
❑9, Jul 87	1.25	0.25	0.63	1.25
❑10, Aug 87	1.25	0.25	0.63	1.25
❑11, Sep 87	1.25	0.25	0.63	1.25
❑12, Oct 87	1.75	0.35	0.88	1.75
❑13, Nov 87	1.75	0.35	0.88	1.75
❑14, Dec 87	1.75	0.35	0.88	1.75
❑15, Jan 88	1.75	0.35	0.88	1.75
❑SE 1, Jan 87	1.25	0.25	0.63	1.25

DYNOMUTT
MARVEL

	ORIG	GOOD	FINE	N-MINT
❑1, Nov 77, Scooby Doo	—	1.20	3.00	6.00
❑2, Jan 78, Scooby Doo	—	0.80	2.00	4.00
❑3, Mar 78, Scooby Doo	—	0.60	1.50	3.00
❑4, May 78, Scooby Doo	—	0.60	1.50	3.00
❑5, Jul 78, Scooby Doo	—	0.60	1.50	3.00
❑6, Sep 78, Scooby Doo	—	0.60	1.50	3.00

DYSTOPIK SNOMEN
SLAVE LABOR

Value: Cover or less

Issue	Value
❑1, Oct 94, was college newspaper strip	4.95

DYSTOPIK SNOMEN (VOL. 2)
SLAVE LABOR

Value: Cover or less

Issue	Value
❑1, Sep 95, Purple Angst Kafe	1.50
❑2, Dec 95, The Anxiety Engine	1.75

E

EAGLE (COMIC ZONE)
COMIC ZONE

Value: Cover or less

Issue	Value
❑1, b&w	2.75
❑2, b&w	2.75
❑3, b&w	2.75

EAGLE (CRYSTAL)
CRYSTAL

Value: Cover or less

Issue	Value
❑1, Sep 86, Night of 1000 Ninjas	1.50
❑1/LE, limited edition	—
❑2	1.50
❑3	1.50
❑4	1.50
❑5	1.50
❑6	1.50
❑7	1.75
❑8	1.75
❑9	1.75
❑10	1.75
❑11	1.75
❑12	2.50
❑13, Jan 88	1.95
❑14	1.95
❑15	1.95
❑16	1.95
❑17, b&w	1.95
❑18, Sep 88, b&w	1.95
❑19, Oct 88, b&w	1.95
❑20, b&w	1.95
❑21, b&w	1.95
❑22, b&w	1.95
❑23	2.25

EAGLES DARE
AAGER

Value: Cover or less

Issue	Value
❑1	1.95
❑2, Sep 94	1.95

EAGLE: THE DARK MIRROR SAGA
COMIC ZONE

Value: Cover or less

Issue	Value
❑1, Jan 92, Reflections in a Dark Mirror	2.75
❑2	2.75
❑3	2.75

EARLY DAYS OF THE SOUTHERN KNIGHTS
COMICS INTERVIEW

Value: Cover or less

Issue	Value
❑1	4.95
❑1-2, 2nd Printing	4.95
❑2, Feb 87	4.95
❑3, Jul 87	4.95
❑4	4.95
❑5	5.95
❑6, Nov 88	6.50
❑7, Jan 89	6.95
❑8, Mar 89	6.95

EARTH 4
CONTINUITY

Value: Cover or less

Issue	Value
❑1	2.50
❑2, Dec 93	2.50
❑3	2.50
❑4, Jan 94	2.50

EARTH 4 (VOL. 2)
CONTINUITY

Value: Cover or less

Issue	Value
❑1, Dec 93	2.50
❑2, Dec 93	2.50
❑3, Dec 93	2.50
❑4, Jan 94	2.50

EARTH 4 DEATHWATCH 2000
CONTINUITY

Value: Cover or less

Issue	Value
❑0, Apr 93, Trading Cards	2.50
❑1, Apr 93, trading cards; indicia says #0, a misprint	2.50
❑2, May 93, trading card	2.50
❑3, Aug 93, trading card; Deathwatch 2000 dropped from indicia	2.50

EARTH C.O.R.E.
INDEPENDENT

Value: Cover or less

Issue	Value
❑1	1.95

EARTHLORE
ETERNITY

	ORIG	GOOD	FINE	N-MINT
❑1	1.80	0.40	1.00	2.00
❑2	1.80	0.40	1.00	2.00

EARTHWORM JIM
MARVEL

Value: Cover or less

Issue	Value
❑1, Dec 95, based on video game	2.25
❑2, Jan 96	2.25
❑3, Feb 96	2.25
❑4	2.25

EARTH X
Marvel

Issue	ORIG	GOOD	FINE	N-MINT
❑0, Mar 99, ARo (w)	3.99	0.80	2.00	4.00
❑0/A, Mar 99, ARo (w), A: Watcher; A: X-51, Covers of series form giant picture; Signed by Jim Krueger, John Paul Leon, Bill Rheinhold, and Alex Ross	—	1.20	3.00	6.00
❑0/B, Mar 99, ARo (w), A: Watcher; A: X-51, Covers of series form giant picture	—	0.80	2.00	4.00
❑0/C, Mar 99, ARo (w), A: Watcher; A: X-51, DFE alternate cover by Alex Ross; Signed by Jim Krueger, John Paul Leon, Bill Rheinhold, and Alex Ross	—	1.20	3.00	6.00
❑1, Apr 99, ARo (w), A: Hydra; A: Inhumans, Covers of series form giant picture	2.99	0.60	1.50	3.00
❑1/A, Apr 99, ARo (w), A: Hydra; A: Inhumans, Covers of series form giant picture; Signed by Jim Krueger, John Paul Leon, Bill Rheinhold, and Alex Ross	—	1.20	3.00	6.00
❑1/B, Apr 99, ARo (w), A: Hydra; A: Inhumans, DFE alternate cover	—	0.70	1.75	3.50
❑1/C, Apr 99, ARo (w), A: Hydra; A: Inhumans, DFE alternate cover; Signed by Jim Krueger, John Paul Leon, Bill Rheinhold, and Alex Ross	—	1.20	3.00	6.00
❑2, May 99, ARo (w)	2.99	0.60	1.50	2.99
❑3, Jun 99, ARo (w)	2.99	0.60	1.50	2.99
❑4, Jul 99, ARo (w)	2.99	0.60	1.50	2.99
❑5, Aug 99, ARo (w)	2.99	0.60	1.50	2.99
❑6, Sep 99, ARo (w)	2.99	0.60	1.50	2.99
❑7, Oct 99, ARo (w)	2.99	0.60	1.50	2.99
❑8, Nov 99, ARo (w)	2.99	0.60	1.50	2.99
❑9, Dec 99, ARo (w)	2.99	0.60	1.50	2.99
❑10, ARo (w)	2.99	0.60	1.50	2.99
❑11, ARo (w)	2.99	0.60	1.50	2.99
❑12, Apr 00, ARo (w)	2.99	0.60	1.50	2.99
❑13, Jun 00, ARo (w), "X" issue	3.99	0.80	2.00	3.99

EARTH X SKETCHBOOK
Marvel

Issue	ORIG	GOOD	FINE	N-MINT
❑1, Mar 99	—	1.20	3.00	6.00

EAST MEETS WEST
Innovation

Value: Cover or less

Issue	Price
❑1, Apr 90, DSt	2.50

EAT-MAN
Viz

Value: Cover or less

Issue	Price	Issue	Price
❑1, Aperitif, b&w	2.95	❑4, b&w	2.95
❑2, b&w	2.95	❑5, b&w	2.95
❑3, b&w	2.95	❑6, b&w	2.95

EAT-MAN SECOND COURSE
Viz

Value: Cover or less

Issue	Price	Issue	Price
❑1, b&w	2.95	❑4, b&w	3.25
❑2, b&w	3.50	❑5, b&w	2.95
❑3, b&w	3.50		

EB'NN
Now

Value: Cover or less

Issue	Price	Issue	Price
❑3, Jun 86	1.50	❑5, Nov 86, MW (c)	1.50
❑4, Aug 86	1.50	❑6, Jan 87	1.50

EB'NN THE RAVEN
Crowquill

Issue	ORIG	GOOD	FINE	N-MINT
❑1	—	0.80	2.00	4.00
❑2	—	0.60	1.50	3.00

EBONY WARRIOR
Africa Rising

Value: Cover or less

Issue	Price
❑1, Apr 93	1.95

E.C. CLASSIC REPRINTS
East Coast Comix

Issue	ORIG	GOOD	FINE	N-MINT
❑1, JO; GE, AF (w), Upon Reflection; Blind Alleys, Reprint; Reprints Crypt of Terror #1 (a series meant to have been launched when EC ceased publishing horror)	1.00	0.60	1.50	3.00
❑2, JKa; WW; JO; AW, AF (w), The Martians!; Captivity, Reprint; Reprints Weird Science #15	1.00	0.60	1.50	3.00
❑3, Reprint; Reprints Shock SuspenStories #12	1.00	0.50	1.25	2.50
❑4, Reprint; Reprints Haunt of Fear #12	1.00	0.50	1.25	2.50
❑5, The End!; The Trip!, Reprint; Reprints Weird Fantasy #13	1.00	0.50	1.25	2.50
❑6, BK; GE, Three for the Money; Dog Food, Reprint; Reprints Crime SuspenStories #25	1.00	0.50	1.25	2.50
❑7, Two of a Kind!; Graft in Concrete!, Reprint; Reprints Vault of Horror #26	1.00	0.50	1.25	2.50
❑8, Under Cover!; Sugar 'n Spice 'n ..., Reprint; Reprints Shock SuspenStories #6	1.00	0.50	1.25	2.50
❑9, Betsy!; Trial by Arms!, Reprint; Reprints Two-Fisted Tales #34	1.00	0.50	1.25	2.50
❑10, Creep Course; No Silver Atoll, Reprint; Reprints Haunt of Fear #23	1.25	0.50	1.25	2.50
❑11, Lost in the Microcosm; Dream of Doom, Reprint; Reprints Weird Science #12	1.25	0.50	1.25	2.50
❑12, Kickback; Ge, Dad, It's a Daisy, Reprint; Reprints Shock SuspenStories #2	1.25	0.50	1.25	2.50

EC CLASSICS
Cochran

Issue	ORIG	GOOD	FINE	N-MINT
❑1	4.95	1.00	2.50	5.00
❑2	4.95	1.00	2.50	5.00
❑3	4.95	1.00	2.50	5.00
❑4	4.95	1.00	2.50	5.00
❑5, AW, The Exile!; Mad Journey!, Reprints from Weird Fantasy #14, 15, 16, 17	4.95	1.00	2.50	5.00
❑6	4.95	1.00	2.50	5.00

ECHO
Image

Value: Cover or less

Issue	Price	Issue	Price
❑0, Jul 00, Thick as Thieves	2.50	❑3	2.50
❑1	2.95	❑4, Jun 00, Desperate Times	2.50
❑2	2.50	❑5, Sep 00, Welcoming Party	2.50

ECHO OF FUTUREPAST
Continuity

Value: Cover or less

Issue	Price	Issue	Price
❑1, NA; MG, Bucky O'Hare; Tippie Toe Jones	2.95	❑6, Jul 85, NA; MG; ATh, Tiipie Toe Jones; Virus	2.95
❑2, NA; MG, Frankenstein; Virus	2.95	❑7, Aug 85	2.95
❑3, Nov 84	2.95	❑8, Dec 85, NA, AE-35; Star rat	2.95
❑4, Feb 85	2.95	❑9, Jan 86, NA, The Damned City; Tippie Toe Jones	2.95
❑5, Apr 85	2.95		

ECLIPSE GRAPHIC ALBUM SERIES
Eclipse

Issue	ORIG	GOOD	FINE	N-MINT
❑1, PG, Sabre	—	1.60	4.00	8.00
❑1-2, PG, 2nd Printing; Sabre	—	1.20	3.00	6.00
❑, PG, 3rd Printing; Sabre: 10th anniversary; Sabre	5.95	1.19	2.97	5.95
❑2, CR, CR (w), Night Music	—	1.00	2.50	5.00
❑3, May 80, MR, Detectives, Inc.	6.95	1.40	3.50	7.00
❑4, GC, Stewart the Rat	5.95	1.20	3.00	6.00
❑5, JSn, JSn (w), The Price	—	2.40	6.00	12.00
❑6, MR, I am Coyote	—	1.20	3.00	6.00
❑7, DSt, DSt (w), The Rocketeer	—	1.60	4.00	8.00
❑7/HC, DSt, DSt (w), Hardcover edition; The Rocketeer	19.95	3.99	9.98	19.95
❑7-2, DSt, DSt (w), 2nd Printing; The Rocketeer	7.95	1.60	4.00	8.00
❑7-3, DSt, DSt (w), 3rd Printing; The Rocketeer	8.95	1.80	4.50	9.00
❑8, Zorro	—	1.20	3.00	6.00
❑9, Somerset Holmes; The Sacred and the Profane	—	2.80	7.00	14.00
❑10, BA, Sacred & Profane; Somerset Holmes	—	2.80	7.00	14.00
❑10/HC, BA, Hardcover edition; Somerset Holmes	24.95	4.99	12.48	24.95
❑11, Floyd Farland	3.95	0.80	2.00	4.00
❑12, Jul 87, Silverheels	7.95	1.80	4.50	9.00
❑12/HC, Jul 87, Hardcover edition; Silverheels	14.95	2.99	7.47	14.95
❑12/LE, Jul 87, Silverheels	24.95	4.99	12.48	24.95
❑13, The Sisterhood of Steel	8.95	2.00	5.00	10.00
❑14, Samurai, Son of Death	—	1.00	2.50	5.00
❑15, Termites From Mars; Fraternity, Twisted Tales	3.95	0.79	1.98	3.95
❑16, Air Fighters Classics #1	—	0.90	2.25	4.50
❑17, PG, Valkyrie: Prisoner of the Past, Valkyrie: Prisoner of the Past	6.95	1.39	3.47	6.95
❑18, Air Fighters Classics #2	—	0.90	2.25	4.50
❑19, Scout: The Four Monsters, Scout: Four Monsters; Collects Scout #1-7	14.95	2.99	7.47	14.95
❑20, Air Fighters Classics #3	—	0.90	2.25	4.50
❑21, XYR "choose your own adventure" game	3.95	0.79	1.98	3.95
❑22, Alien Worlds	—	1.00	2.50	5.00
❑23, Air Fighters Classics #4	—	0.90	2.25	4.50
❑24, Heartbreak Comics; Heartbreak	—	1.00	2.50	5.00
❑25, ATh, ATh (w), Alex Toth's Zorro #1	—	1.80	4.50	9.00
❑26, ATh, ATh (w), Alex Toth's Zorro #2	—	1.80	4.50	9.00
❑27, She; Fast Fiction	—	1.20	3.00	6.00
❑28, TY; BSz; DaG, AMo (w), A Dream of Flying, Brought to Light	—	1.80	4.50	9.00
❑29, Miracleman Book One	—	2.60	6.50	13.00
❑30, AMo (w), Brought to Light, Real Love: The Best of Simon & Kirby Romance Comics	—	1.80	4.50	9.00
❑30/HC, BSz, AMo (w), Brought to Light, Hardcover edition	—	6.00	15.00	30.00
❑31, Pigeons From Hell, Pigeons from Hell	—	1.40	3.50	7.00
❑31/LE, Pigeons From Hell, Limited hardcover edition	—	6.00	15.00	30.00

	ORIG	GOOD	FINE	N-MINT
❑32, Reform School Girl; Trapped!, Teen-aged Dope Slaves & Reform School Girls	9.95	1.99	4.97	9.95
❑33, Bogie	9.95	1.99	4.97	9.95
❑34, Air Fighters Classics #5	3.95	0.79	1.98	3.95
❑35, Into the Shadow of the Sun, Rael; Rael	7.95	1.59	3.97	7.95
❑36, CR, Ariane & Bluebeard	4.95	0.99	2.47	4.95
❑37, Air Fighters Classics #6	3.95	0.79	1.98	3.95
❑38, Doctor Watchstop; Dr. Watchstop	8.95	1.79	4.47	8.95
❑39, MGr, James Bond 007: Permission to Die 1	4.95	0.99	2.47	4.95
❑40, MGr, James Bond 007: Permission to Die 2	4.95	0.99	2.47	4.95
❑41, MGr, James Bond 007: Permission to Die 3	4.95	0.99	2.47	4.95
❑42, MGr, James Bond 007: Licence to Kill	8.95	1.79	4.47	8.95
❑43, Tapping the Vein #1	7.95	1.59	3.97	7.95
❑44, Hobbit #1	5.95	1.19	2.97	5.95
❑45, Toadswart	10.95	2.19	5.47	10.95
❑46, Tapping the Vein #2	7.95	1.59	3.97	7.95
❑47, Scout: Mount Fire	14.95	2.99	7.47	14.95
❑48, Moderne Man Comics	9.95	1.99	4.97	9.95
❑49, Tapping the Vein #3	6.95	1.39	3.47	6.95
❑50, Miracleman Book Two	12.95	2.59	6.47	12.95
❑51, Tapping the Vein 4	7.95	1.59	3.97	7.95
❑52, James Bond 007: Permission to Die #3	4.95	0.99	2.47	4.95

ECLIPSE MAGAZINE
ECLIPSE
Value: Cover or less

- ❑1, May 81, MR, 1: Ms. Tree, Foozle, b&w ... 2.95
- ❑2, Jul 81, MG (c), 1: Coyote.. 2.95
- ❑3, Nov 81, VM; GC, Coyote, Part 2; Vamp Dance, 1: Ragamuffins ... 2.95
- ❑4, Jan 82 ... 2.95
- ❑5, Mar 82 ... 2.95
- ❑6, Jul 82 ... 2.95
- ❑7, Nov 82, 1: Masked Man.... 2.95
- ❑8, Jan 83, MR (c) ... 2.95

ECLIPSE MONTHLY
ECLIPSE
Value: Cover or less

- ❑1, Aug 83, SD, SD (w), Cap'n Quick and a Foozie; The Bank Robbery ... 2.00
- ❑2, Sep 83, KJ; GC ... 2.00
- ❑3, Oct 83 ... 2.00
- ❑4, Jan 84 ... 1.50
- ❑5, Feb 84 ... 1.50
- ❑6, Mar 84 ... 1.50
- ❑7, Apr 84 ... 1.50
- ❑8, May 84 ... 1.50
- ❑9, Jun 84 ... 1.75
- ❑10, Jul 84, Flying Too High With Some Guy In The Sky; Robber's Roost ... 1.75

ECLIPSO
DC

	ORIG	GOOD	FINE	N-MINT
❑1, Nov 92	1.25	0.40	1.00	2.00
❑2, Dec 92	1.25	0.35	0.88	1.75
❑3, Jan 93	1.25	0.35	0.88	1.75
❑4, Feb 93	1.25	0.30	0.75	1.50
❑5, Mar 93	1.25	0.30	0.75	1.50
❑6, Apr 93	1.25	0.25	0.63	1.25
❑7, May 93	1.25	0.25	0.63	1.25
❑8, Jun 93, Good Night Mr. Holmes	1.25	0.25	0.63	1.25
❑9, Jul 93	1.25	0.25	0.63	1.25
❑10, Aug 93	1.75	0.25	0.63	1.25
❑11, Sep 93	1.25	0.25	0.63	1.25
❑12, Oct 93	1.25	0.25	0.63	1.25
❑13, Nov 93, Hour of Darkness	1.25	0.25	0.63	1.25
❑14, Dec 93	1.25	0.25	0.63	1.25
❑15, Jan 94	1.25	0.30	0.75	1.50
❑16, Feb 94, Fallout	1.50	0.30	0.75	1.50
❑17, Mar 94	1.50	0.30	0.75	1.50
❑18, Apr 94, Final Issue	1.50	0.30	0.75	1.50
❑Anl 1, Bloodlines, 1: Prism, Bloodlines	2.50	0.50	1.25	2.50

ECLIPSO: THE DARKNESS WITHIN
DC

	ORIG	GOOD	FINE	N-MINT
❑1, Jul 92, KG, KG (w), Eclipso: The Darkness Within, Part 1, Without plastic gem (newsstand version)	2.50	0.50	1.25	2.50
❑1/DM, Jul 92, KG, KG (w), Eclipso: The Darkness Within, Part 1, plastic diamond glued to cover; Direct Market edition	2.50	0.60	1.50	3.00
❑2, Jul 92, Eclipso: The Darkness Within, Part 20	2.50	0.50	1.25	2.50

ECTOKID
MARVEL
Value: Cover or less

- ❑1, Sep 93, Foil embossed cover ... 2.50
- ❑2, Oct 93, JRo (w), O: Ectokid 1.75
- ❑3, Nov 93 ... 1.75
- ❑4, Dec 93, JRo (w), An Innocent Abroad ... 1.75
- ❑5, Jan 94 ... 1.75
- ❑6, Feb 94 ... 1.75
- ❑7, Mar 94 ... 1.75
- ❑8, Apr 94 ... 1.75
- ❑9, May 94 ... 1.75

ECTOKID UNLEASHED!
MARVEL
Value: Cover or less

- ❑1, Oct 94, Unnatural Causes! 2.95

ED
3CG COMICS
Value: Cover or less

- ❑1, Mar 97, b&w ... 2.95

Videogame character Earthworm Jim became a comic-book character in 1996.

© 1996 Marvel

EDDY CURRENT
MAD DOG
Value: Cover or less

- ❑1, Jul 87 ... 2.00
- ❑2, Sep 87 ... 2.00
- ❑3, Oct 87 ... 2.00
- ❑4, Nov 87 ... 2.00
- ❑5, Jan 88 ... 2.00
- ❑6, Feb 88 ... 2.00
- ❑7, Apr 88, A: Amazing Broccoli ... 2.00
- ❑8, Jun 88 ... 2.00
- ❑9, Jul 88 ... 2.00
- ❑10, Sep 88 ... 2.00
- ❑11, Nov 88 ... 2.00
- ❑12, Dec 88 ... 2.00

EDEN DESCENDANTS, THE
QUESTER ENTERTAINMENT
Value: Cover or less

- ❑1, b&w; cardstock cover ... 3.95

EDEN MATRIX, THE
ADHESIVE
Value: Cover or less

- ❑1/A ... 2.95
- ❑1/B ... 2.95

EDGAR ALLAN POE
ETERNITY
Value: Cover or less

- ❑1, b&w; Black Cat ... 1.95
- ❑2, b&w; Pit & Pendulum ... 1.95
- ❑3, Dec 88, b&w; Red Death .. 1.95
- ❑4, b&w; Rue Morgue ... 1.95
- ❑5, b&w; Tell-Tale Heart ... 1.95

EDGE
BRAVURA
Value: Cover or less

- ❑1, Jul 94, GK, 1: Phaseshifter; 1: Winged Victory; 1: Free Agent; 1: Barricade; 1: Will Power; 1: Edge; 1: Intruder; 1: The Ultimates, coupon ... 2.50
- ❑2, Aug 94, GK, coupon ... 2.50
- ❑3, Apr 95, GK, coupon ... 2.95
- ❑4, GK, coupon ... 2.95

EDGE OF CHAOS
PACIFIC

	ORIG	GOOD	FINE	N-MINT
❑1, Jul, GM	1.00	0.20	0.50	1.00
❑2, GM	—	0.20	0.50	1.00
❑3, GM	—	0.20	0.50	1.00

EEK! THE CAT
HAMILTON
Value: Cover or less

- ❑1, Feb 94, TV show ... 1.95
- ❑2, Mar 94, TV show ... 1.95
- ❑3, Apr 94, TV show ... 1.95

EERIE (I.W.)
I.W.

	ORIG	GOOD	FINE	N-MINT
❑1, Mister Lucifer: Up Pops the Devil!; Gregory the Ghost	0.10	4.00	10.00	20.00
❑2	0.10	3.00	7.50	15.00

EERIE TALES
SUPER

	ORIG	GOOD	FINE	N-MINT
❑12, The Werewolf of Warsham Manor!; King of the Living Dead, Reprints(?)	0.12	3.00	7.50	15.00

EGON
DARK HORSE
Value: Cover or less

- ❑1, Jan 98 ... 2.95

EGYPT
DC
Value: Cover or less

- ❑1, Aug 95, The Book of the Remains ... 2.50
- ❑2, Sep 95, The Book of the Shadows ... 2.50
- ❑3, Oct 95, The Book of the Double ... 2.50
- ❑4, Nov 95, The Book of the Heart ... 2.50
- ❑5, Dec 95, The Book of the Angel ... 2.50
- ❑6, Jan 96, The Book of the Power ... 2.50
- ❑7, Feb 96, The Book of the Name, Final Issue ... 2.50

EHLISSA
HIGHLAND GRAPHICS
Value: Cover or less

- ❑1, Strange New World, Color on cover ... 2.00
- ❑1-2, Strange New World, 2nd Printing; Black & white cover 2.00
- ❑, Strange New World, 3rd Printing; Black & white cover ... 2.00
- ❑2, 1: Kalendes, Color on cover 2.00
- ❑2-2, 2nd Printing; Black & white cover ... 2.00
- ❑3, Color on cover ... 2.00
- ❑3-2, 2nd Printing; Black & white cover ... 2.00
- ❑4, Mar 94, Color on cover ... 2.00
- ❑4-2, 2nd Printing; Black & white cover ... 2.00
- ❑5, Color on cover ... 2.00

- ❑5-2, 2nd Printing; Black & white cover 2.00
- ❑6, Color on cover 2.00
- ❑6-2, 2nd Printing; Black & white cover 2.00
- ❑7, Color on cover 2.00
- ❑7-2, 2nd Printing; Black & white cover 2.00
- ❑8, Color on cover 2.00
- ❑8-2, 2nd Printing; Black & white cover 2.00
- ❑9, Color on cover 2.00
- ❑9-2, 2nd Printing; Black & white cover 2.00
- ❑10, Color on cover 2.00
- ❑10-2, 2nd Printing; Black & white cover 2.00
- ❑11, Yesterme, Yesteryou, Color on cover 2.00
- ❑11-2, Yesterme, Yesteryou, 2nd Printing; Black & white cover 2.00
- ❑12, Color on cover 2.00
- ❑12-2, 2nd Printing; Black & white cover 2.00
- ❑13, Color on cover 2.00
- ❑13-2, 2nd Printing; Black & white cover 2.00
- ❑14, Color on cover 2.00
- ❑14-2, 2nd Printing; Black & white cover 2.00
- ❑15, One Step Ahead of the Sheet, 1: Ransard Maclin, Color cover 2.00
- ❑15-2, One Step Ahead of the Sheet, 1: Ransard Maclin, Black & white cover 2.00
- ❑16, Color on cover 2.00
- ❑16-2, 2nd Printing; Black & white cover 2.00
- ❑17, Color on cover 2.00
- ❑17-2, 2nd Printing; Black & white cover 2.00
- ❑18, Color on cover 2.00
- ❑18-2, 2nd Printing; Black & white cover 2.00
- ❑19, Color on cover 2.00
- ❑19-2, 2nd Printing; Black & white cover 2.00
- ❑20, Color on cover 2.00
- ❑20-2, 2nd Printing; Black & white cover 2.00
- ❑21 2.00
- ❑22, Welcome to Zhuruk 2.00
- ❑23 2.00
- ❑24 2.00
- ❑25 2.00
- ❑26 2.00
- ❑27, Feb 95 2.00
- ❑28, Mar 95 2.00
- ❑29, Apr 95 2.00
- ❑30, May 95, Stanzas From the Edge, 1: Nathan 2.00
- ❑31, Jun 95, has #27's indicia. 2.00
- ❑32, Interlude in Pre-Historia, 1: Lanith 2.00
- ❑33 2.00

EIGHTBALL
FANTAGRAPHICS

	ORIG	GOOD	FINE	N-MINT
❑1	—	2.40	6.00	12.00
❑1-2, 2nd Printing	—	1.00	2.50	5.00
❑, 3rd Printing	—	0.70	1.75	3.50
❑1-4, 4th Printing	2.95	0.60	1.50	3.00
❑2	2.00	1.40	3.50	7.00
❑3	2.00	1.20	3.00	6.00
❑4	2.75	1.20	3.00	6.00
❑5, Like a Velvet Glove Cast in Iron; Just Another Day…	2.75	1.00	2.50	5.00
❑6	2.75	1.00	2.50	5.00
❑7	2.75	0.80	2.00	4.00
❑8	2.95	0.80	2.00	4.00
❑9	2.75	0.60	1.50	3.00
❑10	2.75	0.60	1.50	3.00
❑11	2.95	0.60	1.50	3.00
❑12, Nov 93	2.75	0.60	1.50	3.00
❑13	2.95	0.60	1.50	3.00
❑14	2.95	0.60	1.50	3.00
❑15	2.95	0.60	1.50	3.00
❑16, Nov 95, 36pgs.; cardstock cover	3.95	0.80	2.00	4.00
❑17	3.95	0.59	1.48	2.95
❑18, Mar 97	3.95	0.59	1.48	2.95
❑19, May 98	3.95	0.59	1.48	2.95
❑20, Feb 99, cardstock cover	4.50	0.59	1.48	2.95
❑21, Feb 00	4.95	0.59	1.48	2.95
❑22	2.95	0.59	1.48	2.95
❑23	2.95	0.59	1.48	2.95

EIGHTH WONDER, THE
DARK HORSE

Value: Cover or less

- ❑1, Nov 97, nn; b&w; cover says The 8th Wonder, indicia says The Eighth Wonder; One-Shot 2.95

ELDER DRAGONS
ACCLAIM

Value: Cover or less

- ❑1, Apr 95 2.50
- ❑2, May 95 2.50

EL DIABLO
DC

Value: Cover or less

- ❑1, Aug 89, 1: El Diablo, Double-size 2.50
- ❑2, Sep 89 1.50
- ❑3, Oct 89 1.50
- ❑4, Dec 89 1.50
- ❑5, Jan 90 1.50
- ❑6, Feb 90 1.50
- ❑7, Mar 90 1.75
- ❑8, Apr 90 1.75
- ❑9, May 90 1.75
- ❑10, Jun 90 1.75
- ❑11, Jul 90 1.75
- ❑12, Aug 90, Golden Age Vigilante 2.00
- ❑13, Sep 90 2.00
- ❑14, Oct 90 2.00
- ❑15, Dec 90 2.00
- ❑16, Jan 91, Final Issue 2.00

EL DIABLO (MINI-SERIES)
VERTIGO

Value: Cover or less

- ❑1, Mar 01 2.50
- ❑2, Apr 01 2.50
- ❑3, May 01 2.50
- ❑4, Jun 01 2.50

ELECTRIC FEAR
SPARKS

	ORIG	GOOD	FINE	N-MINT
❑1, Win 84	1.25	0.30	0.75	1.50
❑2, Spr 86	1.25	0.30	0.75	1.50

ELECTRIC GIRL
MIGHTY GREMLIN

Value: Cover or less

- ❑1, May 98 3.50
- ❑2, Spr 99 2.95
- ❑3, Sum 99 2.95

ELECTRIC WARRIOR
DC

Value: Cover or less

- ❑1, May 86, The Whole Nasty Night 2.00
- ❑2, Jun 86, Gene Tricks Berserk! 1.50
- ❑3, Jul 86 1.50
- ❑4, Aug 86 1.50
- ❑5, Sep 86 1.50
- ❑6, Oct 86 1.50
- ❑7, Nov 86 1.50
- ❑8, Dec 86 1.50
- ❑9, Jan 87 1.50
- ❑10, Feb 87 1.50
- ❑11, Mar 87 1.50
- ❑12, Apr 87 1.50
- ❑13, May 87 1.50
- ❑14, Jun 87 1.50
- ❑15, Jul 87 1.50
- ❑16, Aug 87 1.50
- ❑17, Sep 87 1.50
- ❑18, Oct 87 1.50

ELEKTRA
MARVEL

	ORIG	GOOD	FINE	N-MINT
❑-1, Jul 97, A: Daredevil, Flashback	1.95	0.40	1.00	2.00
❑1, Nov 96, Afraid of the Dark	1.99	0.50	1.25	2.50
❑1/A, Afraid of the Dark, variant cover	1.95	0.50	1.25	2.50
❑2, Dec 96, Fathers Day, V: Bullseye	1.95	0.50	1.25	2.50
❑3, Jan 97, I Know How You Feel	1.95	0.50	1.25	2.50
❑4, Feb 97, A Little Piece of Paradise	1.95	0.40	1.00	2.00
❑5, Mar 97, Fourteen Days	1.95	0.40	1.00	2.00
❑6, Apr 97, Fury, V: Razorfist	1.95	0.40	1.00	2.00
❑7, May 97, Out of the Night	1.95	0.40	1.00	2.00
❑8, Jun 97	1.95	0.40	1.00	2.00
❑9, Aug 97, gatefold summary	1.99	0.40	1.00	2.00
❑10, Sep 97, gatefold summary	1.99	0.40	1.00	2.00
❑11, Oct 97, American Samurai, Part 1, A: Daredevil, gatefold summary	1.99	0.40	1.00	2.00
❑12, Nov 97, American Samurai, Part 2, A: Daredevil, gatefold summary	1.99	0.40	1.00	2.00
❑13, Dec 97, American Samurai, Part 3, A: Daredevil, gatefold summary	1.99	0.40	1.00	2.00
❑14, Jan 98, gatefold summary	1.99	0.40	1.00	2.00
❑15, Feb 98, gatefold summary	1.99	0.40	1.00	2.00
❑16, Mar 98, gatefold summary	1.99	0.40	1.00	2.00
❑17, Apr 98, gatefold summary	1.99	0.40	1.00	2.00
❑18, May 98, gatefold summary	1.99	0.40	1.00	2.00
❑19, Jun 98, Final Issue; gatefold summary	1.99	0.40	1.00	2.00

ELEKTRA (MINI-SERIES)
MARVEL

	ORIG	GOOD	FINE	N-MINT
❑1, Mar 95, The Force of The Killer, enhanced cover	2.95	0.60	1.50	3.00
❑2, Apr 95, enhanced cover	2.95	0.60	1.50	3.00
❑3, May 95, enhanced cover	2.95	0.60	1.50	3.00
❑4, Jun 95, enhanced cover	2.95	0.60	1.50	3.00

ELEKTRA: ASSASSIN
MARVEL

	ORIG	GOOD	FINE	N-MINT
❑1, Aug 86, FM; BSz, FM (w)	1.50	1.00	2.50	5.00
❑2, Sep 86, FM; BSz, FM (w)	1.50	0.80	2.00	4.00
❑3, Oct 86, FM; BSz, FM (w)	1.50	0.60	1.50	3.00
❑4, Nov 86, FM; BSz, FM (w), Young Love.	1.50	0.60	1.50	3.00
❑5, Dec 86, FM; BSz, FM (w)	1.50	0.60	1.50	3.00
❑6, Jan 87, FM; BSz, FM (w)	1.50	0.50	1.25	2.50
❑7, Feb 87, FM; BSz, FM (w)	1.75	0.50	1.25	2.50
❑8, Mar 87, FM; BSz, FM (w), Relatively scarce	1.75	0.60	1.50	3.00

ELEKTRA/CYBLADE
IMAGE

	ORIG	GOOD	FINE	N-MINT
❑1, Mar 97, Devil's Reign, Part 7, crossover with Marvel; concludes in Silver Surfer/ Weapon Zero	2.95	0.70	1.75	3.50
❑1/A, Mar 97, Devil's Reign, Part 7, alternate cover; crossover with Marvel; concludes in Silver Surfer/Weapon Zero	2.95	0.59	1.48	2.95

ELEKTRA LIVES AGAIN
MARVEL

Value: Cover or less

- ❑1, Mar 91, NG (w), hardcover 24.95

ELEKTRA MEGAZINE
MARVEL

Value: Cover or less

- ❑1, Nov 96, FM, FM (w), Reprints Elektra stories from Daredevil 3.95
- ❑2, Nov 96, FM, FM (w), D: Elektra; A: Punisher, Reprints Elektra stories from Daredevil 3.95

ELEKTRA SAGA, THE
MARVEL

	ORIG	GOOD	FINE	N-MINT
❑1, Feb 84, FM, FM (w), Daredevil reprint	2.00	0.80	2.00	4.00
❑2, Mar 84, FM, FM (w), Daredevil reprint	2.00	0.70	1.75	3.50
❑3, Apr 84, FM, FM (w), Daredevil reprint	2.00	0.70	1.75	3.50
❑4, May 84, FM, FM (w), Daredevil reprint	2.00	0.70	1.75	3.50

ELEMENTALS (VOL. 1)
COMICO

	ORIG	GOOD	FINE	N-MINT
❑1	1.50	0.50	1.25	2.50
❑2, The Natural Order, Part 1	1.50	0.40	1.00	2.00
❑3	1.50	0.40	1.00	2.00

	ORIG	GOOD	FINE	N-MINT
❑4, Jun 85	1.50	0.40	1.00	2.00
❑5, Dec 85	1.50	0.40	1.00	2.00
❑6, Feb 86	1.50	0.30	0.75	1.50
❑7, Apr 86	1.50	0.30	0.75	1.50
❑8, Jun 86	1.50	0.30	0.75	1.50
❑9, Aug 86	1.50	0.30	0.75	1.50
❑10, Oct 86	1.50	0.30	0.75	1.50
❑11, Dec 86	1.50	0.30	0.75	1.50
❑12, Feb 87	1.50	0.30	0.75	1.50
❑13, Apr 87	1.50	0.30	0.75	1.50
❑14, Jun 87	1.50	0.30	0.75	1.50
❑15, Jul 87	1.50	0.30	0.75	1.50
❑16, Aug 87	1.50	0.30	0.75	1.50
❑17, Sep 87	1.50	0.30	0.75	1.50
❑18, Oct 87	1.50	0.30	0.75	1.50
❑19, Nov 87	1.50	0.30	0.75	1.50
❑20, Dec 87	1.50	0.30	0.75	1.50
❑21, Jan 88	1.50	0.30	0.75	1.50
❑22, Feb 88	1.50	0.30	0.75	1.50
❑23, Mar 88	1.75	0.35	0.88	1.75
❑24, Apr 88	1.75	0.35	0.88	1.75
❑25, May 88	1.75	0.35	0.88	1.75
❑26, Jun 88	1.75	0.35	0.88	1.75
❑27, Jul 88	1.75	0.35	0.88	1.75
❑28, Aug 88	1.75	0.35	0.88	1.75
❑29, Sep 88, Final Issue	1.75	0.35	0.88	1.75
❑SE 1, Mar 86, Episodes, Child abuse special	1.75	0.40	1.00	2.00
❑SE 2, Jan 89	1.95	0.39	0.98	1.95

ELEMENTALS (VOL. 2)
COMICO

	ORIG	GOOD	FINE	N-MINT
❑1, Mar 89	1.95	0.50	1.25	2.50
❑2, Apr 89	1.95	0.40	1.00	2.00
❑3, May 89	1.95	0.40	1.00	2.00
❑4, Jun 89	2.50	0.50	1.25	2.50
❑5, Jul 89	2.50	0.50	1.25	2.50
❑6, Aug 89	2.50	0.50	1.25	2.50
❑7, Sep 89	2.50	0.50	1.25	2.50
❑8, Oct 89	2.50	0.50	1.25	2.50
❑9, Nov 89	2.50	0.50	1.25	2.50
❑10, Dec 89, Oblivion War	2.50	0.50	1.25	2.50
❑11, Jan 90, Oblivion War	2.50	0.50	1.25	2.50
❑12, Feb 90, Oblivion War	2.50	0.50	1.25	2.50
❑13, Mar 90, Oblivion War	2.50	0.50	1.25	2.50
❑14, May 90	2.50	0.50	1.25	2.50
❑15, Jul 90	2.50	0.50	1.25	2.50
❑16, May 91	2.50	0.50	1.25	2.50
❑17, May 91	2.50	0.50	1.25	2.50
❑18, Jun 91	2.50	0.50	1.25	2.50
❑19, Aug 91	2.50	0.50	1.25	2.50
❑20, Oct 91	2.50	0.50	1.25	2.50
❑21, Nov 91, Demon Massacre	2.50	0.50	1.25	2.50
❑22, Mar 92, Forever in this Halflife	2.50	0.50	1.25	2.50
❑23, May 92, 1: New Monolith	2.50	0.50	1.25	2.50
❑24	2.50	0.50	1.25	2.50
❑25, Nov 92	2.50	0.50	1.25	2.50
❑26, Apr 93	2.50	0.50	1.25	2.50
❑27	2.50	0.50	1.25	2.50
❑28	2.50	0.50	1.25	2.50
❑29	2.50	0.50	1.25	2.50
❑30	2.50	0.50	1.25	2.50
❑31	2.50	0.50	1.25	2.50
❑32, Birth of a Nation, Part 1	2.50	0.50	1.25	2.50
❑33, Birth of a Nation, Part 2	2.50	0.50	1.25	2.50
❑34	2.50	0.50	1.25	2.50
❑35, Never published?	2.50	0.50	1.25	2.50
❑36, Never published?	2.50	0.50	1.25	2.50
❑37, Never published?	2.50	0.50	1.25	2.50
❑38, Never published?	2.50	0.50	1.25	2.50
❑39, Never published?	2.50	0.50	1.25	2.50
❑40, Never published?	2.50	0.50	1.25	2.50
❑41, Never published?	2.50	0.50	1.25	2.50
❑SE 1, Special Edition #1	1.75	0.35	0.88	1.75
❑SE 2, Special Edition #2	1.95	0.39	0.98	1.95

ELEMENTALS (VOL. 3)
COMICO

Value: Cover or less

❑1	2.95	❑2	2.95
		❑3, May 96	2.95

ELEMENTALS: HOW THE WAR WAS WON
COMICO

Value: Cover or less

❑1, Jun 96 .... 2.95

ELEMENTALS LINGERIE
COMICO

Value: Cover or less

❑1, May 96, pin-ups 2.95

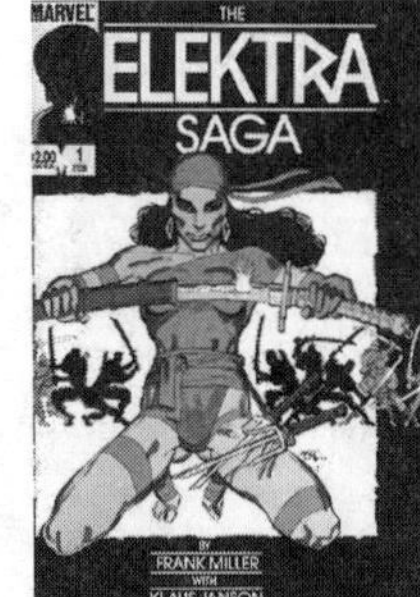

Frank Miller's Elektra stories that originally appeared in *Daredevil* were collected in the four-issue *Elektra Saga*.

© 1984 Marvel

ELEMENTALS SEX SPECIAL
COMICO

Value: Cover or less

❑1, Oct 91	2.95	❑3, Sep 92	2.95
❑2, Jun 92	2.95	❑4, Feb 93	2.95

ELEMENTAL'S SEXY LINGERIE SPECIAL
COMICO

Value: Cover or less

❑1/A, Jan 93, without poster	2.95	❑1/B, Jan 93, poster	5.95

ELEMENTALS SWIMSUIT SPECTACULAR 1996
COMICO

Value: Cover or less

❑1, Jun 96, pin-ups 2.95

ELEMENTALS: THE VAMPIRES' REVENGE
COMICO

Value: Cover or less

❑1, Jun 96 .... 2.95

ELEVEN OR ONE
SIRIUS ENTERTAINMENT

	ORIG	GOOD	FINE	N-MINT
❑1, Apr 95, nn; reprints new story from Angry Christ Comics tpb	2.95	0.80	2.00	4.00
❑1-2, 2nd Printing	2.95	0.60	1.50	3.00

ELFHEIM
NIGHTWYND

Value: Cover or less

❑1, b&w	2.50	❑3, b&w	2.50
❑2, b&w	2.50	❑4, b&w	2.50

ELFHEIM (VOL. 2)
NIGHTWYND

Value: Cover or less

❑1, b&w	2.50	❑3, b&w	2.50
❑2, b&w	2.50	❑4, b&w	2.50

ELFHEIM (VOL. 3)
NIGHTWYND

Value: Cover or less

❑1, b&w	2.50	❑3, b&w	2.50
❑2, b&w	2.50	❑4, b&w	2.50

ELFHEIM (VOL. 4)
NIGHTWYND

Value: Cover or less

❑1, b&w	2.50	❑2, b&w	2.50

ELFHEIM: DRAGON DREAM (VOL. 5)
NIGHT WYND

Value: Cover or less

❑1	2.50	❑3	2.50
❑2	2.50	❑4	2.50

ELFIN ROMANCE
MT. WILSON

	ORIG	GOOD	FINE	N-MINT
❑1, Feb 94, b&w	1.25	0.30	0.75	1.50
❑2, Apr 94, b&w	1.25	0.30	0.75	1.50
❑3, Apr 94, b&w	1.25	0.30	0.75	1.50
❑4, Jun 94, b&w	2.00	0.40	1.00	2.00
❑5, b&w	—	0.40	1.00	2.00
❑6, Oct 94, b&w	1.75	0.35	0.88	1.75
❑7, Dec 96, b&w	3.25	0.65	1.63	3.25

ELFLORD
AIRCEL

Value: Cover or less

❑1, b&w	2.00	❑4	2.00
❑1-2, 2nd Printing	2.00	❑5	2.00
❑2	2.00	❑6	2.00
❑2-2, 2nd Printing	2.00	❑7, Never published?	2.00
❑3	2.00	❑8, Never published?	2.00

ELFLORD (2ND SERIES)
AIRCEL

Value: Cover or less

❑1	2.00	❑9	2.00
❑2	2.00	❑10	2.00
❑3	2.00	❑11	2.00
❑4	2.00	❑12	2.00
❑5	2.00	❑13	2.00
❑6	2.00	❑14	2.00
❑7	2.00	❑15	2.00
❑8	2.00	❑15.5	2.00

- ❑16 .... 2.00
- ❑17 .... 2.00
- ❑18 .... 2.00
- ❑19 .... 2.00
- ❑20 .... 2.00
- ❑21, Finale and DTnoument, double-sized 4.95
- ❑22, Red Sails in the Sunset .. 2.00
- ❑23 .... 1.95
- ❑24 .... 1.95
- ❑25 .... 1.95
- ❑26 .... 1.95
- ❑27 .... 1.95
- ❑28 .... 1.95
- ❑29 .... 1.95
- ❑30 .... 1.95
- ❑31 .... 1.95

ELFLORD (3RD SERIES)

NIGHT WYND

Value: Cover or less

- ❑1, b&w 2.50
- ❑2, b&w 2.50
- ❑3, b&w 2.50
- ❑4, b&w 2.50

ELFLORD (4TH SERIES)

WARP

Value: Cover or less

- ❑1, Jan 97, b&w 2.95
- ❑2, Feb 97, b&w 2.95
- ❑3, Mar 97, b&w 2.95
- ❑4, Apr 97, b&w 2.95

ELFLORD (5TH SERIES)

WARP

Value: Cover or less

- ❑1, Cuts Loose, b&w 2.95
- ❑2, Only Human, b&w 2.95
- ❑3, See No See, b&w 2.95
- ❑4, Dec 97, Armageddon Outta Here, b&w 2.95
- ❑5, Got Those Old Need to Get Outta Here Right Now Blues 2.95
- ❑6, The long March 2.95
- ❑7, The Best Ate Plans 2.95

ELFLORD CHRONICLES, THE

AIRCEL

Value: Cover or less

- ❑1, Oct 90, b&w; Reprint 2.50
- ❑2, Oct 90, b&w; Reprint 2.50
- ❑3, War of Shadows, b&w; Reprint 2.50
- ❑4, Dreams in the Mist, b&w; Reprint 2.50
- ❑5, Jan 91, Light of Darkness, b&w; Reprint 2.50
- ❑6, Feb 91, b&w; Reprint 2.50
- ❑7, Mar 91, b&w; Reprint 2.75
- ❑8, Apr 91 .... 2.75
- ❑9 .... 2.75
- ❑10 .... 2.75
- ❑11 .... 2.75
- ❑12 .... 2.75

ELFLORD: DRAGON'S EYE

NIGHT WYND

Value: Cover or less

- ❑1 .... 2.50
- ❑2 .... 2.50
- ❑3 .... 2.50

ELFLORD THE RETURN

MAD MONKEY

Value: Cover or less

- ❑1 .... 6.96

ELFLORD: THE RETURN OF THE KING

NIGHT WYND

Value: Cover or less

- ❑1 .... 2.50
- ❑2 .... 2.50
- ❑3 .... 2.50
- ❑4 .... 2.50

ELFLORE

NIGHTWYND

	ORIG	GOOD	FINE	N-MINT
❑1, b&w	—	0.50	1.25	2.50
❑2, b&w	—	0.50	1.25	2.50
❑3, b&w	—	0.50	1.25	2.50
❑4, b&w	—	0.50	1.25	2.50

ELFLORE (VOL. 2)

NIGHTWYND

	ORIG	GOOD	FINE	N-MINT
❑1, Foxfire, b&w	—	0.50	1.25	2.50
❑2, Foxfire, b&w	—	0.50	1.25	2.50
❑3, Foxfire, b&w	—	0.50	1.25	2.50
❑4, Foxfire, b&w	—	0.50	1.25	2.50

ELFLORE (VOL. 3)

NIGHTWYND

Value: Cover or less

- ❑1, b&w 2.50
- ❑2, b&w 2.50
- ❑3, b&w 2.50
- ❑4, b&w 2.50

ELFLORE: HIGH SEAS

NIGHT WYND

Value: Cover or less

- ❑1 .... 2.50
- ❑2 .... 2.50
- ❑3 .... 2.50

ELFQUEST

WARP

	ORIG	GOOD	FINE	N-MINT
❑1, Apr 79, WP, WP (w)	1.00	5.60	14.00	28.00
❑1-2, WP, WP (w), 2nd Printing	1.25	2.00	5.00	10.00
❑, WP, WP (w), 3rd Printing	1.50	1.20	3.00	6.00
❑1-4, WP, WP (w), 4th Printing	1.50	0.80	2.00	4.00
❑2, Aug 78, WP, WP (w), Raid at Sorrow's End	1.00	3.20	8.00	16.00
❑2-2, WP, WP (w), Raid at Sorrow's End, 2nd Printing	1.25	1.00	2.50	5.00
❑2-3, WP, WP (w), Raid at Sorrow's End, 3rd Printing	1.50	0.60	1.50	3.00
❑2-4, WP, WP (w), Raid at Sorrow's End, 4th Printing	1.50	0.40	1.00	2.00
❑3, Dec 78, WP, WP (w), The Challenge	1.00	3.20	8.00	16.00
❑3-2, WP, WP (w), The Challenge, 2nd Printing	1.25	0.40	1.00	2.00
❑3-3, WP, WP (w), The Challenge, 3rd Printing	1.50	0.60	1.50	3.00
❑3-4, WP, WP (w), The Challenge, 4th Printing	1.50	0.40	1.00	2.00
❑4, Apr 79, WP, WP (w), Wolfsong	1.00	3.20	8.00	16.00
❑4-2, WP, WP (w), Wolfsong, 2nd Printing	1.25	1.00	2.50	5.00
❑4-3, WP, WP (w), Wolfsong, 3rd Printing	1.50	0.60	1.50	3.00
❑4-4, WP, WP (w), Wolfsong, 4th Printing	1.50	0.30	0.75	1.50
❑5, Aug 79, WP, WP (w), Voice of the Sun	1.00	3.20	8.00	16.00
❑5-2, WP, WP (w), Voice of the Sun, 2nd Printing	1.25	0.40	1.00	2.00
❑5-3, WP, WP (w), Voice of the Sun, 3rd Printing	1.50	0.60	1.50	3.00
❑6, Jan 80, WP, WP (w), The Quest Begins	1.25	2.40	6.00	12.00
❑6-2, WP, WP (w), The Quest Begins, 2nd Printing	1.50	0.80	2.00	4.00
❑6-3, WP, WP (w), The Quest Begins, 3rd Printing	1.50	0.40	1.00	2.00
❑7, May 80, WP, WP (w), The Dreamberry Tales	1.25	2.00	5.00	10.00
❑7-2, WP, WP (w), The Dreamberry Tales, 2nd Printing	1.50	0.80	2.00	4.00
❑7-3, WP, WP (w), The Dreamberry Tales, 3rd Printing	1.50	0.40	1.00	2.00
❑8, Sep 80, WP, WP (w), Hands of the Symbol Maker	1.25	2.00	5.00	10.00
❑8-2, WP, WP (w), Hands of the Symbol Maker, 2nd Printing	1.50	0.80	2.00	4.00
❑8-3, WP, WP (w), Hands of the Symbol Maker, 3rd Printing	1.50	0.40	1.00	2.00
❑9, Feb 81, WP, WP (w), The Lodestone	1.25	2.00	5.00	10.00
❑9-2, WP, WP (w), The Lodestone, 2nd Printing	1.50	0.80	2.00	4.00
❑9-3, WP, WP (w), The Lodestone, 3rd Printing	1.50	0.40	1.00	2.00
❑10, Jun 81, WP, WP (w), The Forbidden Grove	1.50	1.50	3.75	7.50
❑11, Oct 81, WP, WP (w), Lair of the Bird Spirits	1.50	1.50	3.75	7.50
❑12, Feb 82, WP, WP (w), What is the Way?	1.50	1.50	3.75	7.50
❑13, Jun 82, WP, WP (w), The Secret of the Wolfriders	1.50	1.50	3.75	7.50
❑14, Oct 82, WP, WP (w), The Fall	1.50	1.50	3.75	7.50
❑15, Feb 83, WP, WP (w), The Quest Usurped	1.50	1.50	3.75	7.50
❑16, Jun 83, WP, WP (w), The Go-Backs; A Distant Soil, preview of "A Distant Soil"	1.50	2.00	5.00	10.00
❑17, Oct 83, WP, WP (w), The First War, Elf orgy	1.50	1.40	3.50	7.00
❑18, Feb 84, WP, WP (w), The Treasure	1.50	1.40	3.50	7.00
❑19, Jun 84, WP, WP (w), Quest's End, Part 1	1.50	1.40	3.50	7.00
❑20, Oct 84, WP, WP (w), Quest's End, Part 2	1.50	1.40	3.50	7.00
❑21, Feb 85, WP, WP (w), Final Issue; all letters issue	1.50	1.40	3.50	7.00

ELFQUEST (EPIC)

EPIC

	ORIG	GOOD	FINE	N-MINT
❑1, Aug 85, WP, WP (w)	0.75	0.65	1.63	3.25
❑2, Sep 85, WP, WP (w)	0.75	0.50	1.25	2.50
❑3, Oct 85, WP, WP (w)	0.75	0.50	1.25	2.50
❑4, Nov 85, WP, WP (w)	0.75	0.50	1.25	2.50
❑5, Dec 85, WP, WP (w)	0.75	0.50	1.25	2.50
❑6, Jan 86, WP, WP (w)	0.75	0.45	1.13	2.25
❑7, Feb 86, WP, WP (w)	0.75	0.45	1.13	2.25
❑8, Mar 86, WP, WP (w)	0.75	0.45	1.13	2.25
❑9, Apr 86, WP, WP (w)	0.75	0.45	1.13	2.25
❑10, May 86, WP, WP (w)	0.75	0.45	1.13	2.25
❑11, Jun 86, WP, WP (w)	0.75	0.40	1.00	2.00
❑12, Jul 86, WP, WP (w)	0.75	0.40	1.00	2.00
❑13, Aug 86, WP, WP (w)	0.75	0.40	1.00	2.00
❑14, Sep 86, WP, WP (w)	0.75	0.40	1.00	2.00
❑15, Oct 86, WP, WP (w)	0.75	0.40	1.00	2.00
❑16, Nov 86, WP, WP (w)	0.75	0.40	1.00	2.00
❑17, Dec 86, WP, WP (w)	0.75	0.40	1.00	2.00
❑18, Jan 87, WP, WP (w)	0.75	0.40	1.00	2.00
❑19, Feb 87, WP, WP (w)	0.75	0.40	1.00	2.00
❑20, Mar 87, WP, WP (w)	0.75	0.40	1.00	2.00
❑21, Apr 87, WP, WP (w)	0.75	0.30	0.75	1.50
❑22, May 87, WP, WP (w)	1.00	0.30	0.75	1.50
❑23, Jun 87, WP, WP (w)	1.00	0.30	0.75	1.50
❑24, Jul 87, WP, WP (w)	1.00	0.30	0.75	1.50
❑25, Aug 87, WP, WP (w)	1.00	0.30	0.75	1.50
❑26, Sep 87, WP, WP (w)	1.00	0.30	0.75	1.50
❑27, Oct 87, WP, WP (w)	1.00	0.30	0.75	1.50
❑28, Nov 87, WP, WP (w)	1.00	0.30	0.75	1.50
❑29, Dec 87, WP, WP (w)	1.00	0.30	0.75	1.50
❑30, Jan 88, WP, WP (w)	1.00	0.30	0.75	1.50
❑31, Feb 88, WP, WP (w)	1.00	0.30	0.75	1.50
❑32, Mar 88, WP, WP (w), Final Issue	1.00	0.30	0.75	1.50

ELFQUEST (VOL. 2)
WARP

	ORIG	GOOD	FINE	N-MINT
❑1, May 96	4.95	1.20	3.00	6.00
❑2, Jun 96	4.95	1.00	2.50	5.00
❑3, Jul 96	4.95	1.00	2.50	5.00
❑4, Aug 96	4.95	1.00	2.50	5.00
❑5, Sep 96	4.95	1.00	2.50	5.00
❑6, Nov 96	4.95	1.00	2.50	5.00
❑7, Dec 96	4.95	1.00	2.50	5.00
❑8, Jan 97	4.95	1.00	2.50	5.00
❑9, Feb 97	4.95	1.00	2.50	5.00
❑10, Mar 97	4.95	1.00	2.50	5.00
❑11, Apr 97	4.95	0.99	2.47	4.95
❑12, May 97	4.95	0.99	2.47	4.95
❑13, Jun 97	4.95	0.99	2.47	4.95
❑14, Jul 97	4.95	0.99	2.47	4.95
❑15, Aug 97	4.95	0.99	2.47	4.95
❑16, Sep 97	4.95	0.99	2.47	4.95
❑17, Oct 97	4.95	0.99	2.47	4.95
❑18, Nov 97	4.95	0.99	2.47	4.95
❑19, Dec 97	4.95	0.99	2.47	4.95
❑20, Jan 98	4.95	0.99	2.47	4.95
❑21, Feb 98	4.95	0.99	2.47	4.95
❑22, Mar 98	4.95	0.99	2.47	4.95
❑23, Apr 98	4.95	0.99	2.47	4.95
❑24, May 98	4.95	0.99	2.47	4.95
❑25, Jun 98, needlepoint style cover	4.95	0.99	2.47	4.95
❑26, Jul 98	4.95	0.99	2.47	4.95
❑27, Aug 98	4.95	0.99	2.47	4.95
❑28, Sep 98	4.95	0.99	2.47	4.95
❑29, Oct 98	4.95	0.99	2.47	4.95
❑30, Nov 98	4.95	0.99	2.47	4.95
❑31, Dec 98, Christmas cover	4.95	0.99	2.47	4.95
❑32, Jan 99	2.95	0.59	1.48	2.95
❑33, Feb 99, Final Issue	2.95	0.59	1.48	2.95

ELFQUEST (WARP REPRINTS)
WARP

Value: Cover or less

❑1, May 89	1.50	❑3, Jul 89	1.50
❑2, Jun 89	1.50	❑4, Aug 89	1.50

ELFQUEST: BLOOD OF TEN CHIEFS
WARP

	ORIG	GOOD	FINE	N-MINT
❑1, Aug 93	2.00	0.50	1.25	2.50
❑2, Sep 93	2.00	0.50	1.25	2.50
❑3, Nov 93	2.00	0.50	1.25	2.50
❑4, Jan 94	2.00	0.50	1.25	2.50
❑5, Mar 94	2.25	0.50	1.25	2.50
❑6, May 94	2.25	0.50	1.25	2.50
❑7, Jun 94	2.25	0.50	1.25	2.50
❑8, Jul 94	2.25	0.50	1.25	2.50
❑9, Aug 94	2.25	0.50	1.25	2.50
❑10, Sep 94	2.25	0.50	1.25	2.50
❑11, Oct 94	2.25	0.50	1.25	2.50
❑12, Nov 94	2.25	0.50	1.25	2.50
❑13, Dec 94	2.25	0.50	1.25	2.50
❑14, Jan 95	2.25	0.50	1.25	2.50
❑15, Feb 95	2.25	0.50	1.25	2.50
❑16, Apr 95	2.25	0.50	1.25	2.50
❑17, May 95	2.50	0.50	1.25	2.50
❑18, Jun 95	2.50	0.50	1.25	2.50
❑19, Aug 95, contains Elfquest timeline	2.50	0.50	1.25	2.50
❑20, Sep 95, Final Issue	2.50	0.50	1.25	2.50

ELFQUEST: HIDDEN YEARS
WARP

	ORIG	GOOD	FINE	N-MINT
❑1, May 92	2.00	0.60	1.50	3.00
❑2, Jul 92	2.00	0.50	1.25	2.50
❑3, Sep 92, This story was previewed in Harbinger #11 (character reads it as in a comic book)	2.00	0.50	1.25	2.50
❑4, Nov 92	2.00	0.50	1.25	2.50
❑5, Jan 93	2.00	0.50	1.25	2.50
❑6, Mar 93	2.00	0.50	1.25	2.50
❑7, May 93	2.00	0.50	1.25	2.50
❑8, Jul 93	2.00	0.50	1.25	2.50
❑9, Sep 93	2.00	0.50	1.25	2.50
❑9.5, Nov 93, double-sized	2.95	0.59	1.48	2.95
❑10, Jan 94	2.00	0.50	1.25	2.50
❑11, Mar 94	2.25	0.50	1.25	2.50
❑12, Apr 94	2.25	0.50	1.25	2.50
❑13, May 94	2.25	0.50	1.25	2.50
❑14, Jun 94, WP (w), Shards, Part 5	2.25	0.50	1.25	2.50
❑15, Jul 94	3.50	0.50	1.25	2.50
❑16, Aug 94	2.25	0.50	1.25	2.50
❑17, Oct 94	2.25	0.50	1.25	2.50
❑18, Dec 94	2.25	0.50	1.25	2.50
❑19, Jan 95	2.25	0.50	1.25	2.50

Wendy and Richard Pini's *Elfquest* led to a publishing house for the couple and has spun off animation and action figures.

© 1979 Wendy and Richard Pini (Warp)

	ORIG	GOOD	FINE	N-MINT
❑20, Apr 95	2.50	0.50	1.25	2.50
❑21, May 95	2.50	0.50	1.25	2.50
❑22, Jul 95	2.50	0.50	1.25	2.50
❑23, Aug 95, contains Elfquest timeline	2.50	0.50	1.25	2.50
❑24, Sep 95	2.50	0.50	1.25	2.50
❑25, Oct 95, b&w	2.25	0.50	1.25	2.50
❑26, Dec 95, b&w	2.25	0.50	1.25	2.50
❑27, b&w	2.25	0.50	1.25	2.50
❑28, b&w	2.25	0.50	1.25	2.50
❑29, b&w	2.25	0.50	1.25	2.50

ELFQUEST: JINK
WARP

	ORIG	GOOD	FINE	N-MINT
❑1, Nov 94	2.25	0.50	1.25	2.50
❑2, Dec 94	2.25	0.50	1.25	2.50
❑3, Jan 95, WP (w), Neverending Story	2.25	0.50	1.25	2.50
❑4, Apr 95	2.50	0.50	1.25	2.50
❑5, May 95	2.50	0.50	1.25	2.50
❑6, Jul 95, contains Elfquest world map	2.50	0.50	1.25	2.50
❑7, Aug 95, contains Elfquest timeline	2.50	0.50	1.25	2.50
❑8, Oct 95, b&w for remainder of series	2.25	0.50	1.25	2.50
❑9, Nov 95	2.25	0.50	1.25	2.50
❑10, Dec 95	2.25	0.50	1.25	2.50
❑11, Jan 96	2.25	0.50	1.25	2.50
❑12, Feb 96	2.25	0.50	1.25	2.50

ELFQUEST: KAHVI
WARP

Value: Cover or less

❑1, Oct 95	2.25	❑4, Jan 96	2.25
❑2, Nov 95	2.25	❑5, Feb 96	2.25
❑3, Dec 95	2.25	❑6, Mar 96	2.25

ELFQUEST: KINGS CROSS
WARP

Value: Cover or less

❑1, Nov 97, b&w	2.95
❑2, Dec 97, b&w	2.95

ELFQUEST: KINGS OF THE BROKEN WHEEL
WARP

	ORIG	GOOD	FINE	N-MINT
❑1, Jun 90, WP	2.00	0.50	1.25	2.50
❑2, Aug 90, WP	2.00	0.40	1.00	2.00
❑3, Sep 90, WP	2.00	0.40	1.00	2.00
❑4, Dec 90, WP	2.00	0.40	1.00	2.00
❑5, Feb 91, WP	2.00	0.40	1.00	2.00
❑6, May 91, WP	2.00	0.40	1.00	2.00
❑7, Aug 91, WP	2.00	0.40	1.00	2.00
❑8, Nov 91, WP	2.00	0.40	1.00	2.00
❑9, Feb 92, WP	2.00	0.40	1.00	2.00

ELFQUEST: METAMORPHOSIS
WARP

Value: Cover or less

❑1, Apr 96, WP, The Wild Hunt; Rogue's Curse	2.95

ELFQUEST: NEW BLOOD
WARP

	ORIG	GOOD	FINE	N-MINT
❑1, Aug 92, JBy, full color; gatefold summary; "Elfquest Summer Special"	2.00	1.00	2.50	5.00
❑2, Oct 92	2.00	0.50	1.25	2.50
❑3, Dec 92	2.00	0.50	1.25	2.50
❑4, Feb 93	2.00	0.50	1.25	2.50
❑5, Apr 93, Windkin	2.00	0.50	1.25	2.50
❑6, Jun 93	2.00	0.50	1.25	2.50
❑7, Jul 93	2.00	0.50	1.25	2.50
❑8, Aug 93	2.00	0.50	1.25	2.50
❑9, Sep 93	2.00	0.50	1.25	2.50
❑10, Oct 93	2.00	0.50	1.25	2.50
❑11, Nov 93	2.00	0.45	1.13	2.25
❑12, Dec 93	2.00	0.45	1.13	2.25
❑13, Jan 94	2.00	0.45	1.13	2.25
❑14, Feb 94	2.25	0.45	1.13	2.25
❑15, Mar 94	2.25	0.45	1.13	2.25
❑16, Apr 94	2.25	0.45	1.13	2.25
❑17, May 94	2.25	0.45	1.13	2.25
❑18, Jun 94, Forevergreen, Part 6	2.25	0.45	1.13	2.25
❑19, Jul 94	2.25	0.45	1.13	2.25
❑20, Aug 94	2.25	0.45	1.13	2.25
❑21, Sep 94	2.25	0.45	1.13	2.25
❑22, Oct 94	2.25	0.45	1.13	2.25
❑23, Nov 94	2.25	0.45	1.13	2.25

	ORIG	GOOD	FINE	N-MINT
❑24, Dec 94	2.25	0.45	1.13	2.25
❑25, Jan 95	2.25	0.45	1.13	2.25
❑26, Feb 95	2.25	0.45	1.13	2.25
❑27, Apr 95	2.50	0.50	1.25	2.50
❑28, May 95	2.50	0.50	1.25	2.50
❑29, Jul 95	2.50	0.50	1.25	2.50
❑30, Aug 95, contains Elfquest timeline	2.50	0.50	1.25	2.50
❑31, Sep 95	2.50	0.50	1.25	2.50
❑32, Oct 95	2.25	0.50	1.25	2.50
❑33, Nov 95	2.25	0.50	1.25	2.50
❑34, Dec 95	2.25	0.45	1.13	2.25
❑35, Jan 96	2.25	0.45	1.13	2.25
❑SE 1, Jul 93, JBy	3.95	0.79	1.98	3.95

ELFQUEST: SHARDS
WARP

	ORIG	GOOD	FINE	N-MINT
❑1, Aug 94, WP (w)	2.25	0.50	1.25	2.50
❑2, Sep 94, WP (w)	2.25	0.50	1.25	2.50
❑3, Oct 94, WP (w)	2.25	0.50	1.25	2.50
❑4, Nov 94, WP (w)	2.25	0.50	1.25	2.50
❑5, Dec 94, WP (w)	2.25	0.50	1.25	2.50
❑6, Jan 95, WP (w)	2.25	0.45	1.13	2.25
❑7, Mar 95, WP (w)	2.50	0.45	1.13	2.25
❑8, May 95, WP (w)	2.50	0.45	1.13	2.25
❑9, Jun 95, WP (w)	2.50	0.50	1.25	2.50
❑10, Aug 95, WP (w), contains Elfquest timeline	2.50	0.50	1.25	2.50
❑11, Sep 95, WP (w)	2.50	0.50	1.25	2.50
❑12, Oct 95, WP (w)	2.25	0.50	1.25	2.50
❑13, Dec 95	2.25	0.45	1.13	2.25
❑14, Feb 96	2.25	0.45	1.13	2.25
❑15, Apr 96	2.25	0.45	1.13	2.25
❑16, Jun 96	2.25	0.45	1.13	2.25
❑Ash 1, ashcan preview/ San Diego Comic-Con premium	0.50	0.20	0.50	1.00

ELFQUEST: SIEGE AT BLUE MOUNTAIN
WARP

	ORIG	GOOD	FINE	N-MINT
❑1, Mar 87, JSa; WP, WP (w), b&w	1.75	0.80	2.00	4.00
❑1-2, WP, WP (w)	1.75	0.50	1.25	2.50
❑2, May 87, JSa; WP, WP (w)	1.75	0.60	1.50	3.00
❑2-2, WP, WP (w), 2nd Printing	1.75	0.45	1.13	2.25
❑2-3, 2nd Printing	—	0.60	1.50	3.00
❑3, Jul 87, JSa; WP, WP (w)	1.75	0.50	1.25	2.50
❑3-2, WP, WP (w), 2nd Printing	1.75	0.40	1.00	2.00
❑4, Sep 87, JSa; WP, WP (w)	1.75	0.50	1.25	2.50
❑5, Nov 87, JSa; WP, WP (w)	1.75	0.50	1.25	2.50
❑6, Aug 88, JSa; WP, WP (w)	1.95	0.50	1.25	2.50
❑7, Oct 88, JSa; WP, WP (w)	1.95	0.50	1.25	2.50
❑8, Dec 88, JSa; WP, WP (w)	1.95	0.50	1.25	2.50

ELFQUEST: THE REBELS
WARP

Value: Cover or less

- ❑1, Nov 94, To Colder Seas.... 2.25
- ❑2, Dec 94 .... 2.25
- ❑3, Jan 95 .... 2.25
- ❑4, Mar 95 .... 2.50
- ❑5, Apr 95 .... 2.50
- ❑6, Jun 95 .... 2.50
- ❑7, Jul 95, contains Elfquest world map 2.50
- ❑8, Sep 95 .... 2.50
- ❑9, Oct 95 .... 2.25
- ❑10, Nov 95 .... 2.25
- ❑11, Jan 96 .... 2.25
- ❑12, Feb 96 .... 2.25

ELFQUEST: TWO-SPEAR
WARP

Value: Cover or less

- ❑1, Oct 95, Discoveries 2.25
- ❑2, Nov 95 .... 2.25
- ❑3, Dec 95 .... 2.25
- ❑4, Jan 96 .... 2.25
- ❑5, Feb 96 .... 2.25

ELFQUEST: WAVEDANCERS
WARP

Value: Cover or less

- ❑1, Dec 93, Search for the True Crown, Part 1, O: The Wavedancers 2.00
- ❑2, Feb 94, Search for the True Crown, Part 2 .... 2.25
- ❑3, Apr 94, Search for the True Crown, Part 3 .... 2.25
- ❑4, Jun 94, Search for the True Crown, Part 4 .... 2.25
- ❑5, Aug 94, Search for the True Crown, Part 5 .... 2.25
- ❑6, Oct 94 .... 2.25
- ❑SE 1 .... 2.25

ELFQUEST: WORLDPOOL
WARP

Value: Cover or less

- ❑1, Jul 97, The Perception of Doors, b&w 2.95

ELF-THING
ECLIPSE

Value: Cover or less

- ❑1, Mar 87, This Elf... This Monster, b&w 1.50

ELFTREK
DIMENSION

Value: Cover or less

- ❑1, Jul 86, parody of Star Trek, Elfquest 1.75
- ❑2, Oct 86, The Hassle with Troublets, parody of Star Trek, Elfquest 1.75

ELF WARRIOR
ADVENTURE

Value: Cover or less

- ❑1 .... 1.95
- ❑2 .... 1.95
- ❑3 .... 1.95
- ❑4 .... 1.95

EL GATO NEGRO
AZTECA

Value: Cover or less

- ❑1, Oct 93, The Burning, Part 1; Unknown Passing, Unforgettable Return, b&w 2.00
- ❑2, Sum 94, The Burning, Part 2, b&w 2.00
- ❑3, Fal 95, b&w 2.00
- ❑4 .... 2.50

EL-HAZARD
VIZ

Value: Cover or less

- ❑1 .... 2.95

ELIMINATOR, THE
MALIBU

Value: Cover or less

- ❑0, MZ, 1: Manic; 1: Zothros; 1: Eliminator; A: Collects Eliminator 2.95
- ❑1, May 95, MZ, 1: Mannequin; 1: Siren, 7th Infinity Gem revealed 2.50
- ❑1/SC, MZ, 1: Mannequin; 1: Siren, Black cover edition; 7th Infinity Gem revealed 3.95
- ❑2 .... 2.50
- ❑3 .... 2.50

ELIMINATOR (ETERNITY)
ETERNITY

Value: Cover or less

- ❑1, b&w 2.50
- ❑2, b&w 2.50

ELIMINATOR FULL COLOR SPECIAL
ETERNITY

Value: Cover or less

- ❑1, Lowell Cunningham 2.95

ELONGATED MAN
DC

	ORIG	GOOD	FINE	N-MINT
❑1, Jan 92	1.00	0.25	0.63	1.25
❑2, Feb 92	1.00	0.20	0.50	1.00
❑3, Mar 92	1.00	0.20	0.50	1.00
❑4, Apr 92	1.00	0.20	0.50	1.00

ELRIC
PACIFIC

	ORIG	GOOD	FINE	N-MINT
❑1, Apr 83, CR	1.50	0.40	1.00	2.00
❑2, Aug 83, CR	1.50	0.35	0.88	1.75
❑3, Oct 83, CR	2.50	0.35	0.88	1.75
❑4, Dec 83, CR	1.50	0.35	0.88	1.75
❑5, Feb 84, CR	1.50	0.35	0.88	1.75
❑6, Apr 84, CR	1.50	0.35	0.88	1.75

ELRIC (TOPPS)
TOPPS

	ORIG	GOOD	FINE	N-MINT
❑0, CR, NG (w), One Life	2.95	0.70	1.75	3.50
❑1	2.95	0.59	1.48	2.95
❑2	2.95	0.59	1.48	2.95
❑3	2.95	0.59	1.48	2.95
❑4, CR, CR (w), Chaos Wars	2.95	0.59	1.48	2.95

ELRIC: SAILOR ON THE SEAS OF FATE
FIRST

	ORIG	GOOD	FINE	N-MINT
❑1, Jun 85	1.75	0.40	1.00	2.00
❑2, Aug 85	1.75	0.35	0.88	1.75
❑3, Oct 85	1.75	0.35	0.88	1.75
❑4, Dec 85	1.75	0.35	0.88	1.75
❑5, Feb 86	1.75	0.35	0.88	1.75
❑6, Apr 86	1.75	0.35	0.88	1.75
❑7, Jun 86	1.75	0.35	0.88	1.75

ELRIC: STORMBRINGER
DARK HORSE

Value: Cover or less

- ❑1, CR 2.95
- ❑2, CR 2.95
- ❑3, CR 2.95
- ❑4, CR 2.95
- ❑5, CR 2.95
- ❑6, CR 2.95
- ❑7, CR 2.95

ELRIC: THE BANE OF THE BLACK SWORD
FIRST

	ORIG	GOOD	FINE	N-MINT
❑1, Aug 88	1.75	0.40	1.00	2.00
❑2, Oct 88	1.95	0.40	1.00	2.00
❑3, Dec 88	1.95	0.40	1.00	2.00
❑4, Feb 89	1.95	0.40	1.00	2.00
❑5, Apr 89	1.95	0.40	1.00	2.00
❑6, Jun 89	1.95	0.40	1.00	2.00

ELRIC: THE VANISHING TOWER
FIRST

Value: Cover or less

- ❑1, Aug 87, JDu 1.75
- ❑2, Oct 87, JDu 1.75
- ❑3, Dec 87, JDu 1.75
- ❑4, Feb 88, JDu 1.75
- ❑5, Apr 88, JDu 1.75
- ❑6, Jun 88, JDu, Tall Tower Vanishing 1.75

ELRIC: WEIRD OF THE WHITE WOLF
FIRST

Value: Cover or less

- ❑1, Oct 86, CR 1.75
- ❑2, Dec 86, CR 1.75
- ❑3, Feb 87, CR 1.75
- ❑4, Apr 87, CR 1.75
- ❑5, Jun 87, CR 1.75

ELSEWHERE PRINCE, THE
MARVEL

Value: Cover or less

- ❑1, May 90, ES 1.95
- ❑2, Jun 90, ES 1.95
- ❑3, Jul 90, ES 1.95
- ❑4, Aug 90, ES 1.95
- ❑5, Sep 90, ES 1.95
- ❑6, Oct 90, ES 1.95

ELSEWORLDS 80-PAGE GIANT
DC

	ORIG	GOOD	FINE	N-MINT
❑1, U.S. copies destroyed, only released in England; less than 700 copies estimated to exist	4.95	48.00	120.00	240.00

ELSEWORLD'S FINEST
DC

Value: Cover or less

	ORIG
❑1, A: Lana Lang; A: Clark Kent; A: Captain Marvel; A: Lex Luthor; A: Bruce Wayne; A: Jimmy Olsen, prestige format; Superman and Batman in the 1920s; Elseworlds story	4.95
❑2, prestige format; Superman and Batman in the 1920s	4.95

ELSEWORLD'S FINEST: SUPERGIRL & BATGIRL
DC

Value: Cover or less

	ORIG
❑1, nn; One-Shot; prestige format	5.95
❑1/LE	18.95

ELVEN
MALIBU

	ORIG	GOOD	FINE	N-MINT
❑0, Oct 94, Gimme Shelter; Prime-Itive Attraction, 1: Elven	2.95	0.59	1.48	2.95
❑1, Feb 95, Eye for an Eye...Pain for Pain, A: Prime	2.50	0.45	1.13	2.25
❑1/LE, Eye for an Eye...Pain for Pain, A: Prime, Limited foil edition	—	0.50	1.25	2.50
❑2, Mar 95	2.50	0.45	1.13	2.25
❑3, Apr 95	2.50	0.45	1.13	2.25
❑4, May 95	2.50	0.45	1.13	2.25

ELVIRA, MISTRESS OF THE DARK
CLAYPOOL

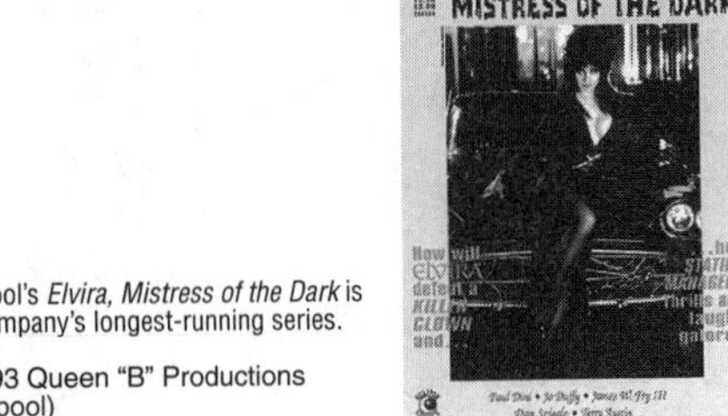

Claypool's *Elvira, Mistress of the Dark* is the company's longest-running series.

© 1993 Queen "B" Productions (Claypool)

	ORIG	GOOD	FINE	N-MINT
❑1, May 93	2.50	0.80	2.00	4.00
❑2, Jun 93, Kurt Busiek	2.50	0.60	1.50	3.00
❑3, Jul 93, Kurt Busiek	2.50	0.60	1.50	3.00
❑4, Aug 93	2.50	0.60	1.50	3.00
❑5, Sep 93, Kurt Busiek	1.50	0.60	1.50	3.00
❑6, Oct 93	1.50	0.60	1.50	3.00
❑7, Nov 93, Kurt Busiek	1.50	0.60	1.50	3.00
❑8, Dec 93	2.50	0.60	1.50	3.00
❑9, Jan 94, Kurt Busiek	2.50	0.60	1.50	3.00
❑10, Feb 94, Kurt Busiek	2.50	0.60	1.50	3.00
❑11, Mar 94, Kurt Busiek	2.50	0.55	1.38	2.75
❑12, Apr 94	2.50	0.55	1.38	2.75
❑13, May 94	2.50	0.55	1.38	2.75
❑14, Jun 94	2.50	0.55	1.38	2.75
❑15, Jul 94	2.50	0.55	1.38	2.75
❑16, Aug 94	2.50	0.55	1.38	2.75
❑17, Sep 94	2.50	0.55	1.38	2.75
❑18, Oct 94	2.50	0.55	1.38	2.75
❑19, Nov 94	2.50	0.55	1.38	2.75
❑20, Dec 94	2.50	0.55	1.38	2.75
❑21, Jan 95	2.50	0.50	1.25	2.50
❑22, Feb 95	2.50	0.50	1.25	2.50
❑23, Mar 95	2.50	0.50	1.25	2.50
❑24, Apr 95	2.50	0.50	1.25	2.50
❑25, May 95, Kurt Busiek	2.50	0.50	1.25	2.50
❑26, Jun 95	2.50	0.50	1.25	2.50
❑27, Jul 95	2.50	0.50	1.25	2.50
❑28, Aug 95	2.50	0.50	1.25	2.50
❑29, Sep 95	2.50	0.50	1.25	2.50
❑30, Oct 95	2.50	0.50	1.25	2.50
❑31, Nov 95	2.50	0.50	1.25	2.50
❑32, Dec 95	2.50	0.50	1.25	2.50
❑33, Jan 96	2.50	0.50	1.25	2.50
❑34, Feb 96	2.50	0.50	1.25	2.50
❑35, Mar 96	2.50	0.50	1.25	2.50
❑36, Apr 96	2.50	0.50	1.25	2.50
❑37, May 96	2.50	0.50	1.25	2.50
❑38, Jun 96	2.50	0.50	1.25	2.50
❑39, Jul 96, A: Portia Prinz	2.50	0.50	1.25	2.50
❑40, Aug 96	2.50	0.50	1.25	2.50
❑41, Sep 96	2.50	0.50	1.25	2.50
❑42, Oct 96	2.50	0.50	1.25	2.50
❑43, Nov 96	2.50	0.50	1.25	2.50
❑44, Dec 96	2.50	0.50	1.25	2.50
❑45, Jan 97	2.50	0.50	1.25	2.50
❑46, Feb 97	2.50	0.50	1.25	2.50
❑47, Mar 97	2.50	0.50	1.25	2.50
❑48, Apr 97	2.50	0.50	1.25	2.50
❑49, May 97	2.50	0.50	1.25	2.50
❑50, Jun 97	2.50	0.50	1.25	2.50
❑51, Jul 97	2.50	0.50	1.25	2.50
❑52, Aug 97	2.50	0.50	1.25	2.50
❑53, Sep 97	2.50	0.50	1.25	2.50
❑54, Oct 97	2.50	0.50	1.25	2.50
❑55, Nov 97	2.50	0.50	1.25	2.50
❑56, Dec 97	2.50	0.50	1.25	2.50
❑57, Jan 98	2.50	0.50	1.25	2.50
❑58, Feb 98	2.50	0.50	1.25	2.50
❑59, Mar 98	2.50	0.50	1.25	2.50
❑60, Apr 98	2.50	0.50	1.25	2.50
❑61, May 98	2.50	0.50	1.25	2.50
❑62, Jun 98	2.50	0.50	1.25	2.50
❑63, Jul 98	2.50	0.50	1.25	2.50
❑64, Aug 98	2.50	0.50	1.25	2.50
❑65, Sep 98	2.50	0.50	1.25	2.50
❑66, Oct 98	2.50	0.50	1.25	2.50
❑67, Nov 98, The Search for Schlock	2.50	0.50	1.25	2.50
❑68, Dec 98	2.50	0.50	1.25	2.50
❑69, Jan 99	2.50	0.50	1.25	2.50
❑70, Feb 99	2.50	0.50	1.25	2.50
❑71, Mar 99	2.50	0.50	1.25	2.50
❑72, Apr 99	2.50	0.50	1.25	2.50
❑73, May 99	2.50	0.50	1.25	2.50
❑74, Jun 99	2.50	0.50	1.25	2.50
❑75, Jul 99	2.50	0.50	1.25	2.50
❑76, Aug 99	2.50	0.50	1.25	2.50
❑77, Sep 99	2.50	0.50	1.25	2.50
❑78, Oct 99	2.50	0.50	1.25	2.50
❑79, Nov 99	2.50	0.50	1.25	2.50
❑80, Dec 99, Christmas on the Prowl	2.50	0.50	1.25	2.50
❑81, Jan 00	2.50	0.50	1.25	2.50
❑82, Feb 00	2.50	0.50	1.25	2.50
❑83, Mar 00	2.50	0.50	1.25	2.50
❑84, Apr 00	2.50	0.50	1.25	2.50
❑85, May 00, Telechubby Alien Autopsy	2.50	0.50	1.25	2.50
❑86, Jun 00, Snoop Troop	2.50	0.50	1.25	2.50
❑87, Jul 00, Picture Perfect, Part 1: Portrait of the Artist as a B-Movie Bimbo!	2.50	0.50	1.25	2.50
❑88, Aug 00, Picture Perfect, Part 2: A Brush with Disaster!; ... That Old Get-up and Glow!	2.50	0.50	1.25	2.50
❑89, Sep 00, Picture Perfect, Part 3: S'Mource of My Discontent!; Web-Mistress of the Dark!	2.50	0.50	1.25	2.50
❑90, Oct 00, Creepy Hollow; Boys on the Slide!	2.50	0.50	1.25	2.50
❑91	2.50	0.50	1.25	2.50
❑92	2.50	0.50	1.25	2.50
❑93	2.50	0.50	1.25	2.50
❑94	2.50	0.50	1.25	2.50
❑95	2.50	0.50	1.25	2.50
❑96	2.50	0.50	1.25	2.50
❑97	2.50	0.50	1.25	2.50
❑98	2.50	0.50	1.25	2.50
❑99	2.50	0.50	1.25	2.50

ELVIRA'S HOUSE OF MYSTERY
DC

	ORIG	GOOD	FINE	N-MINT
❑1, Jan 86, Play or Pay!, Photo cover; Double-size	1.50	0.60	1.50	3.00
❑2, Apr 86	0.75	0.40	1.00	2.00
❑3, May 86	0.75	0.40	1.00	2.00
❑4, Jun 86	0.75	0.30	0.75	1.50
❑5, Jul 86	0.75	0.30	0.75	1.50
❑6, Aug 86, sideways issue	0.75	0.30	0.75	1.50
❑7, Sep 86, science-fiction issue	0.75	0.30	0.75	1.50
❑8, Oct 86	0.75	0.30	0.75	1.50
❑9, Nov 86	0.75	0.30	0.75	1.50
❑10, Dec 86, A: Cain	0.75	0.30	0.75	1.50
❑11, Jan 87, DSt (c), Final Issue; Double-size	1.25	0.30	0.75	1.50
❑SE 1, Christmas stories	1.25	0.40	1.00	2.00

ELVIS MANDIBLE, THE
DC

Value: Cover or less

	ORIG
❑1, nn; b&w; One-Shot	3.50

ELVIS PRESLEY EXPERIENCE, THE
REVOLUTIONARY

Value: Cover or less

	ORIG
❑1, Aug 92, b&w	2.50
❑2, Oct 92, b&w	2.50
❑3, Jan 93, b&w	2.50
❑4, Feb 93, b&w	2.50
❑5, Jul 93, b&w	2.50
❑6, Aug 93, b&w	2.50
❑7, Apr 94, b&w	2.50

ELVIS SHRUGGED
REVOLUTIONARY

Value: Cover or less

	ORIG
❑1, Feb 92, b&w	2.50
❑2, Aug 92, b&w	2.50
❑3, Apr 92, b&w	3.95

E-MAN (1ST SERIES)
CHARLTON

	ORIG	GOOD	FINE	N-MINT
❑1, Oct 73, O: E-Man	0.20	1.60	4.00	8.00
❑2, Dec 73, X-Men parody	0.20	1.00	2.50	5.00
❑3, Jun 74, X-Men parody	0.25	1.00	2.50	5.00
❑4, Aug 74	0.25	1.00	2.50	5.00
❑5, Nov 74	0.25	0.70	1.75	3.50
❑6, Jan 75, JBy	0.25	0.70	1.75	3.50

	ORIG	GOOD	FINE	N-MINT
❑7, Mar 75, JBy	0.25	0.70	1.75	3.50
❑8, May 75, JBy, Nova becomes E-Man's partner	0.25	0.70	1.75	3.50
❑9, Jul 75, JBy	0.25	0.70	1.75	3.50
❑10, Sep 75, JBy	0.25	0.70	1.75	3.50

E-MAN (2ND SERIES)
FIRST

	ORIG	GOOD	FINE	N-MINT
❑1, Apr 83, JSa, O: E-Man	1.00	0.30	0.75	1.50
❑2, Jun 83, JSa, A: F-Men, (X-Men parody); (X-Men parody)	1.00	0.25	0.63	1.25
❑3, Jun 83, JSa	1.00	0.25	0.63	1.25
❑4, Jul 83, JSa	1.00	0.25	0.63	1.25
❑5, Aug 83, JSa	1.00	0.25	0.63	1.25
❑6, Sep 83, JSa, O: E-Man	1.00	0.25	0.63	1.25
❑7, Oct 83, JSa	1.00	0.25	0.63	1.25
❑8, Nov 83, JSa	1.00	0.25	0.63	1.25
❑9, Dec 83, JSa	1.00	0.25	0.63	1.25
❑10, Jan 84, JSa, O: Nova Kane	1.00	0.25	0.63	1.25
❑11, Feb 84, JSa	1.00	0.25	0.63	1.25
❑12, Mar 84, JSa	1.00	0.25	0.63	1.25
❑13, Apr 84, JSa	1.00	0.25	0.63	1.25
❑14, May 84, JSa	1.00	0.25	0.63	1.25
❑15, Jun 84, JSa	1.00	0.25	0.63	1.25
❑16, Jul 84, JSa	1.00	0.25	0.63	1.25
❑17, Aug 84, JSa	1.00	0.25	0.63	1.25
❑18, Sep 84, JSa	1.00	0.25	0.63	1.25
❑19, Oct 84, JSa	1.00	0.25	0.63	1.25
❑20, Nov 84, JSa	1.25	0.25	0.63	1.25
❑21, Dec 84, JSa	1.25	0.25	0.63	1.25
❑22, Feb 85, JSa	1.25	0.25	0.63	1.25
❑23, Apr 85, JSa	1.25	0.25	0.63	1.25
❑24, Jun 85, JSa, O: Michael Mauser	1.25	0.25	0.63	1.25
❑25, Aug 85, JSa, Final Issue	1.25	0.25	0.63	1.25

E-MAN (3RD SERIES)
COMICO
Value: Cover or less

❑1, Sep 89, JSa, E-Man: Quark and the Real World; Michael Mauser, Private Eye: Into Thin Air, O: Vamfire; O: E-Man; O: Nova Kane 2.75

E-MAN (4TH SERIES)
COMICO
Value: Cover or less

❑1, Jan 90, JSa 2.50
❑2, Feb 90, JSa, The Price of Paradise 2.50
❑3, Mar 90, JSa 2.50

E-MAN (5TH SERIES)
ALPHA
Value: Cover or less

❑1, Oct 93, JSa, E-Man Meets 'e'-Man; Mr. Jigsaw: A Day in the Park, 1: Eco-Man, full color 3.25

E-MAN RETURNS
ALPHA PRODUCTIONS
Value: Cover or less

❑1, Mar 94, b&w 2.75

EMBLEM
ANTARCTIC
Value: Cover or less

❑1, May 94, b&w; adult 3.50
❑2, Jun 94, b&w; adult 2.95
❑3, Jul 94, b&w; adult 2.95
❑5, Oct 94, b&w; adult 2.95
❑6, Nov 94, b&w; adult 2.95
❑7, Dec 94, b&w; adult 2.95
❑8, Feb 95, b&w; adult 2.95

EMBRACE
LONDON NIGHT

	ORIG	GOOD	FINE	N-MINT
❑1, Carmen Electra cover	—	0.60	1.50	3.00
❑1/LE	—	1.99	4.97	9.95

EMERALDAS
ETERNITY
Value: Cover or less

❑1, b&w 2.25
❑2, The Children of Eden, Part 2, b&w 2.25
❑3, b&w 2.25
❑4, b&w 2.25

EMERGENCY!
CHARLTON

	ORIG	GOOD	FINE	N-MINT
❑1, JBy	0.30	4.40	11.00	22.00
❑2	0.30	3.60	9.00	18.00
❑3	0.30	3.00	7.50	15.00
❑4, Final Issue; Scarce	0.30	3.00	7.50	15.00

EMERGENCY! (MAGAZINE)
CHARLTON

	ORIG	GOOD	FINE	N-MINT
❑1	1.00	6.40	16.00	32.00
❑2	1.00	5.60	14.00	28.00
❑3, Oct 76	1.00	4.80	12.00	24.00
❑4, Dec 76	1.00	5.20	13.00	26.00

EMISSARY
STRATEIA STUDIOS
Value: Cover or less

❑1, Jul 98 2.95

EMMA DAVENPORT
LOHMAN HILLS

	ORIG	GOOD	FINE	N-MINT
❑1, Apr 95, b&w	2.75	0.60	1.50	3.00
❑2, Jun 95, b&w	2.75	0.55	1.38	2.75
❑3, Aug 95, b&w	2.75	0.55	1.38	2.75
❑4, Oct 95, b&w	2.75	0.55	1.38	2.75
❑5, Dec 95, b&w	2.75	0.55	1.38	2.75
❑6, Feb 96, b&w	2.75	0.55	1.38	2.75
❑7, Apr 96, b&w	2.75	0.55	1.38	2.75
❑8, Feb 96, b&w; crossover with Femforce.	2.75	0.55	1.38	2.75

EMPIRE
ETERNITY
Value: Cover or less

❑1, Mar 88, The Uncrowned Lion 1.95
❑2 1.95
❑3 1.95
❑4 1.95

EMPIRE (IMAGE)
IMAGE
Value: Cover or less

❑1, May 00, MWa (w) 2.50
❑2, Sep 00, MWa (w) 2.50

EMPIRE LANES (KEYLINE)
KEYLINE
Value: Cover or less

❑1 1.75

EMPIRE LANES (NORTHERN LIGHTS)
NORTHERN LIGHTS
Value: Cover or less

❑1 1.75
❑2 1.75
❑3 1.75
❑4 1.75

EMPIRE LANES (VOL. 2)
KEYLINE
Value: Cover or less

❑1, The Innocent 2.95

EMPIRES OF NIGHT
REBEL STUDIOS
Value: Cover or less

❑1, Dec 93, b&w 2.25
❑2 2.25
❑3 2.25
❑4 2.25

EMPTY LOVE STORIES
SLAVE LABOR
Value: Cover or less

❑1, Nov 94, ARo (c), White Trash Romance!; One of the Walking Dead, b&w 2.95
❑2, Aug 96, b&w 2.95

EMPTY LOVE STORIES (2ND SERIES)
FUNNY VALENTINE
Value: Cover or less

❑1, Jul 98, ARo (c), b&w; reprints Slave Labor issue 2.95
❑SE 1, Jan 98, nn; b&w; Anthology 2.95

EMPTY SKULL COMICS
FANTAGRAPHICS
Value: Cover or less

❑1, Apr 96, nn; b&w; cardstock cover; Oversized 4.95

EMPTY ZONE
SIRIUS
Value: Cover or less

❑1 2.50
❑2 2.50
❑3 2.50
❑4 2.50

EMPTY ZONE (2ND SERIES)
SIRIUS
Value: Cover or less

❑1 2.95
❑2 2.95
❑3 2.95
❑4 2.95
❑5 2.95
❑6 2.95
❑7 2.95
❑8 2.95

EMPTY ZONE: TRANCEMISSIONS
SIRIUS
Value: Cover or less

❑1 2.95

ENCHANTED
SIRIUS

	ORIG	GOOD	FINE	N-MINT
❑1	2.50	0.59	1.48	2.95
❑2	2.50	0.59	1.48	2.95
❑3	2.50	0.59	1.48	2.95

ENCHANTED VALLEY
BLACKTHORNE
Value: Cover or less

❑1 1.75
❑2 1.75

ENCHANTED WORLDS
BLACKMORE
Value: Cover or less

❑1, b&w 2.75

ENCHANTER
ECLIPSE
Value: Cover or less

❑1 2.00
❑2 2.00
❑3 2.00
❑4 2.00
❑5 2.00
❑6 2.00
❑7 2.00
❑8, May 86 2.00

ENCHANTER: APOCALYPSE MOON
EXPRESS
Value: Cover or less

❑1, b&w; illustrated novella 2.95

ENCHANTER: PRELUDE TO APOCALYPSE
Express

Value: Cover or less

- ❑1, b&w 2.50
- ❑2, b&w 2.50
- ❑3, b&w 2.50

ENCHANTERS, THE
Hidden Poet

Value: Cover or less

- ❑1, Jun 96, School Daze 2.50

ENCYCLOPÆDIA DEADPOOLICA, THE
Marvel

Value: Cover or less

- ❑1, Dec 98, Deadpool reference 2.99

END, THE: IN THE BEGINNING
AFC Studio

Value: Cover or less

- ❑1, Jun 00, b&w 2.95

ENDLESS GALLERY, THE
DC

Value: Cover or less

- ❑1, pin-ups; Introduction by Neil Gaiman 3.50

ENEMY
Dark Horse

Value: Cover or less

- ❑1, May 94 .... 2.50
- ❑2, Jun 94 .... 2.50
- ❑3, Jul 94 .... 2.50
- ❑4, Aug 94, O: The Enemy 2.50
- ❑5, Sep 94 .... 2.50

ENEMY ACE SPECIAL
DC

	ORIG	GOOD	FINE	N-MINT
❑1, Oct 90, JK, reprints Showcase and Our Army at War	1.00	0.60	1.50	3.00

ENEMY ACE: WAR IDYLL
DC

Value: Cover or less

- ❑1, nn; prestige format 4.95

ENEMY ACE: WAR IN HEAVEN
DC

Value: Cover or less

- ❑1 .... 5.95
- ❑2 .... 5.95

ENFORCE
Reoccurring Images

Value: Cover or less

- ❑1, 1: EnForce 2.95

ENIGMA
DC

Value: Cover or less

- ❑1, Mar 93 .... 2.50
- ❑2, Apr 93 .... 2.50
- ❑3, May 93 .... 2.50
- ❑4, Jun 93 .... 2.50
- ❑5, Jul 93 .... 2.50
- ❑6, Aug 93 .... 2.50
- ❑7, Sep 93, Sex in Arizona 2.50
- ❑8, Oct 93 .... 2.50

ENO & PLUM
Oni Press

Value: Cover or less

- ❑1, Mar 98, b&w 2.95

ENTROPY TALES
Entropy

Value: Cover or less

- ❑1, Star Fox: Sweet Sixteen; Night Wolf: IntroductionMighty Slug 1.50
- ❑2 .... 1.50
- ❑3 .... 1.50
- ❑4 .... 1.50

ENTS
Manic Press

Value: Cover or less

- ❑1, b&w 2.50
- ❑2, b&w 2.50
- ❑3, b&w 2.50

EO
Rebel

	ORIG	GOOD	FINE	N-MINT
❑1	3.00	0.60	1.50	3.00
❑1/LE, Limited "Premier" edition	—	1.00	2.50	5.00
❑2	3.00	0.60	1.50	3.00
❑2/LE, limited edition	—	0.60	1.50	3.00
❑3	3.00	0.60	1.50	3.00
❑4	3.00	0.60	1.50	3.00

EPIC ILLUSTRATED
Marvel

	ORIG	GOOD	FINE	N-MINT
❑1, Spr 80, The Answer; Home Spun, A: Silver Surfer; 1: Dreadstar	2.00	1.00	2.50	5.00
❑2, Sum 80	2.00	0.70	1.75	3.50
❑3, Aut 80	2.00	0.70	1.75	3.50
❑4, Win 80	2.00	0.60	1.50	3.00
❑5, Apr 81	2.00	0.60	1.50	3.00
❑6, Jun 81	2.00	0.50	1.25	2.50
❑7, Aug 81	2.00	0.50	1.25	2.50
❑8, Oct 81	2.00	0.50	1.25	2.50
❑9, Dec 81	2.00	0.50	1.25	2.50
❑10, Feb 82	2.00	0.50	1.25	2.50
❑11, Apr 82	2.50	0.50	1.25	2.50
❑12, Jun 82	2.50	0.50	1.25	2.50
❑13, Aug 82	2.50	0.50	1.25	2.50
❑14, Oct 82	2.50	0.50	1.25	2.50
❑15, Dec 82	2.50	0.50	1.25	2.50
❑16, Feb 83	2.50	0.50	1.25	2.50
❑17, Apr 83	2.50	0.50	1.25	2.50
❑18, Jun 83	2.50	0.50	1.25	2.50
❑19, Aug 83	2.50	0.50	1.25	2.50
❑20, Oct 83	2.50	0.50	1.25	2.50
❑21, Dec 83	2.50	0.50	1.25	2.50
❑22, Feb 84	2.50	0.50	1.25	2.50
❑23, Apr 84	2.50	0.50	1.25	2.50

When the subject merited it, Revolutionary devoted a mini-series to a rock artist's career. In addition to Elvis Presley, mini-series featuring The Beatles and Pink Floyd appeared.

	ORIG	GOOD	FINE	N-MINT
❑24, Jun 84	2.50	0.50	1.25	2.50
❑25, Aug 84	2.50	0.50	1.25	2.50
❑26, Oct 84, The Last Galactus Story	2.50	0.50	1.25	2.50
❑27, Dec 84, The Last Galactus Story	2.50	0.50	1.25	2.50
❑28, Feb 85, The Last Galactus Story	2.50	0.50	1.25	2.50
❑29, Apr 85, The Last Galactus Story	2.50	0.50	1.25	2.50
❑30, Jun 85, The Last Galactus Story	2.50	0.50	1.25	2.50
❑31, Aug 85, The Last Galactus Story	2.50	0.50	1.25	2.50
❑32, Oct 85, The Last Galactus Story	2.50	0.50	1.25	2.50
❑33, Dec 85, The Last Galactus Story	2.50	0.50	1.25	2.50
❑34, Feb 86, The Last Galactus Story, Final Issue	2.50	0.50	1.25	2.50

EPIC LITE
Marvel

	ORIG	GOOD	FINE	N-MINT
❑1	3.95	0.80	2.00	4.00

EPSILON WAVE, THE
Independent

Value: Cover or less

- ❑1, Oct 85, 1: Nightmare (super-hero), Independent Comics publishes 1.50
- ❑2, Dec 85 .... 1.50
- ❑3, Feb 86 .... 1.50
- ❑4, Apr 86 .... 1.50
- ❑5, May 86, Elite begins as publisher 1.75
- ❑6, Jun 86 .... 1.75
- ❑7, Aug 86 .... 1.75
- ❑8 .... 1.75

EQUINE THE UNCIVILIZED
Graphxpress

Value: Cover or less

- ❑1, b&w 2.00
- ❑2 .... 2.00
- ❑3 .... 2.00
- ❑4 .... 2.00
- ❑5 .... 2.00
- ❑6 .... 2.00

EQUINOX CHRONICLES
Innovation

Value: Cover or less

- ❑1, b&w 2.25
- ❑2, The Road to Apocalypse, b&w 2.25

ERADICATOR
DC

Value: Cover or less

- ❑1, Aug 96, Pinocchio: Prince of Lies 1.75
- ❑2, Sep 96 .... 1.75
- ❑3, Oct 96, Matters of Conscience 1.75

ERADICATORS, THE
Silverwolf

Value: Cover or less

- ❑1, Jun 86 .... 1.50
- ❑2, Jul 86 .... 1.50
- ❑3, Aug 86 .... 1.50
- ❑4, Sep 86 .... 1.50

ERIC PRESTON IS THE FLAME
B-Movie

	ORIG	GOOD	FINE	N-MINT
❑1	0.95	0.20	0.50	1.00

ERNIE
Kitchen Sink

Value: Cover or less

- ❑1, comics 2.00

EROS FORUM
Fantagraphics

Value: Cover or less

- ❑1, b&w; adult 2.50
- ❑3, b&w; adult 2.95

EROS GRAPHIC ALBUM
Eros

Value: Cover or less

- ❑1, Birdland 9.95
- ❑2, The Young Witches 12.95
- ❑3, Anton's Collected Drek 10.95
- ❑4, 2 Hot Girls on a Hot Summer Night 10.95
- ❑5, Ironwood Volume 1 .... 14.95
- ❑6, Ironwood Book Two 16.95
- ❑7, Karate Girl 12.95
- ❑8, Liz & Beth Volume 1 .... 12.95
- ❑9, The Blonde Vol. 1, Double Cross 9.95
- ❑10, Talk Dirty 12.95
- ❑11, FT, FT (w), Lann 11.95
- ❑12, Liz & Beth Volume 2 .... 12.95
- ❑13, Time Wankers 12.95
- ❑14, XXX-Women 14.95
- ❑15, Ramba 14.95
- ❑16, Coley Running Wild 14.95
- ❑17, FT; VM, Mara of the Celts 15.95
- ❑18, The Blonde Vol. 2, Bondage Palace 12.95
- ❑19, Domino Lady 14.95
- ❑20, Liz & Beth Vol. 3 .... 12.95
- ❑21, FT, FT (w), The Iron Devil 14.95
- ❑22, Ramba Vol. 2 .... 14.95
- ❑23, City of Dreams 12.95
- ❑24, The Blonde: Phoebus III.. 12.95
- ❑25, I Want to be your Dog 16.95
- ❑26, Beta Sexus 13.95
- ❑27, Hot Nights in Rangoon 11.95
- ❑28, Sheedeva 16.95
- ❑29, Ramba Vol. 3 .... 16.95
- ❑30, Karate Girl: Tengu Wars .. 13.95

❑31, The Young Witches II: London Babylon ... 19.95
❑32, Finger Filth ... 16.95
❑33, Caged Heat ... 16.95
❑34, Buffy Collection ... 14.95
❑35, Diary of a Dominatrix ... 14.95
❑36, Mara: Celtic Shamaness. 19.95

EROS HAWK
EROS

Value: Cover or less

❑1 ... 2.75
❑2 ... 2.75
❑3 ... 2.75
❑4 ... 2.75

EROS HAWK III
FANTAGRAPHICS

Value: Cover or less

❑1, Jul 94, b&w ... 2.75

EROTIC FABLES & FAERIE TALES
FANTAGRAPHICS

Value: Cover or less

❑1, b&w; adult ... 2.50
❑2, b&w; adult ... 2.50

EROTICOM
CALIBER

Value: Cover or less

❑1 ... 2.50

EROTICOM II
CALIBER

Value: Cover or less

❑1, b&w; pin-ups ... 2.95

EROTIC ORBITS
COMAX

Value: Cover or less

❑1, b&w; adult ... 2.95

EROTIC TALES
AIRCEL

Value: Cover or less

❑1, b&w; adult ... 2.95
❑2, b&w; adult ... 2.95
❑3, b&w; adult ... 2.95

EROTIC WORLDS OF FRANK THORNE, THE
FANTAGRAPHICS

	ORIG	GOOD	FINE	N-MINT
❑1, Oct 90, FT, FT (w), The Deathman's Head; The Wizard and The Woman, adult; sexy cover	2.95	0.59	1.48	2.95
❑1/A, Oct 90, FT, FT (w), The Deathman's Head; The Wizard and The Woman, adult; Violent cover	2.95	0.59	1.48	2.95
❑2, FT, FT (w), adult	2.50	0.59	1.48	2.95
❑3, FT, FT (w), adult	2.50	0.59	1.48	2.95
❑4, FT, FT (w), adult	2.50	0.59	1.48	2.95
❑5, FT, FT (w), adult	2.50	0.59	1.48	2.95
❑6, FT, FT (w), adult	2.50	0.59	1.48	2.95

EROTIQUE
AIRCEL

Value: Cover or less

❑1, b&w; adult ... 2.50

ERSATZ PEACH, THE
AEON

Value: Cover or less

❑1, Jul 95, nn; see also The Desert Peach; Charity fund-raiser; Desert Peach stories by various artists and writers ... 7.95

ESC
COMICO

Value: Cover or less

❑1, Zaminidar, Part 1 ... 2.95
❑2, Sep 96, Zaminidar, Part 2. 2.95
❑3, Zaminidar, Part 3 ... 2.95
❑4, Zaminidar, Part 4 ... 2.95

ESCAPE TO THE STARS
SOLSON

Value: Cover or less

❑1, RB, Cul-de-Sac ... 1.75

ESPERS
ECLIPSE

	ORIG	GOOD	FINE	N-MINT
❑1, Jul 86	1.25	0.50	1.25	2.50
❑2, Sep 86	1.25	0.40	1.00	2.00
❑3, Nov 86, Thunderhead	1.25	0.40	1.00	2.00
❑4, Feb 87	1.25	0.40	1.00	2.00
❑5, Apr 87, The Liquidators, Story continued in Interface #1	1.75	0.40	1.00	2.00

ESPERS (VOL. 2)
HALLOWEEN

	ORIG	GOOD	FINE	N-MINT
❑1, b&w	2.95	0.60	1.50	3.00
❑2, Undertow, b&w	2.95	0.60	1.50	3.00
❑3, b&w	2.95	0.60	1.50	3.00
❑4, b&w	2.95	0.60	1.50	3.00
❑5, b&w	2.95	0.60	1.50	3.00
❑6, Revelations	2.95	0.60	1.50	3.00

ESPERS (VOL. 3)
IMAGE

	ORIG	GOOD	FINE	N-MINT
❑1, Black Magic, Part 1, b&w	2.95	0.70	1.75	3.50
❑2, Black Magic, Part 2, b&w	2.95	0.60	1.50	3.00
❑3, Aug 97, Black Magic, Part 3, b&w	2.95	0.60	1.50	3.00
❑4, Black Magic, Part 4, b&w	2.95	0.60	1.50	3.00
❑5, The Bad Joe, b&w	2.95	0.60	1.50	3.00
❑6, Cold Comforts, b&w	2.95	0.60	1.50	3.00
❑7, Down Rio Way, b&w	2.95	0.60	1.50	3.00
❑8	2.95	0.60	1.50	3.00
❑9	2.95	0.60	1.50	3.00

ESPIONAGE
DELL

	ORIG	GOOD	FINE	N-MINT
❑1, The Chameleon; Small Spy-Big Explosion	0.12	3.30	8.25	16.50
❑2	0.12	2.80	7.00	14.00

ESSENTIAL ELFQUEST, THE
WARP

	ORIG	GOOD	FINE	N-MINT
❑1, Apr 95, WP (w), Blood of Ten Chiefs; Shard, nn; giveaway; Free Preview	—	0.30	0.75	1.50

ESSENTIAL VERTIGO: SWAMP THING
DC

	ORIG	GOOD	FINE	N-MINT
❑1, Nov 96, AMo (w), Reprints Saga of the Swamp Thing #21	1.95	0.50	1.25	2.50
❑2, Dec 96, AMo (w), Swamped, Reprints Saga of the Swamp Thing #22	1.95	0.40	1.00	2.00
❑3, Jan 97, AMo (w), Reprints Saga of the Swamp Thing #23	1.95	0.40	1.00	2.00
❑4, Feb 97, AMo (w), Reprints Saga of the Swamp Thing #24	1.95	0.40	1.00	2.00
❑5, Mar 97, AMo (w), The Sleep of Reason..., Reprints Saga of the Swamp Thing #25	1.95	0.40	1.00	2.00
❑6, Apr 97, Reprints Saga of the Swamp Thing #26	1.95	0.40	1.00	2.00
❑7, May 97, Reprints Saga of the Swamp Thing #27	1.95	0.40	1.00	2.00
❑8, Jun 97, Reprints Saga of the Swamp Thing #28	1.95	0.40	1.00	2.00
❑9, Jul 97, Reprints Saga of the Swamp Thing #29	1.95	0.40	1.00	2.00
❑10, Aug 97, Reprints Saga of the Swamp Thing #30	1.95	0.40	1.00	2.00
❑11, Sep 97, Reprints Saga of the Swamp Thing #31	1.95	0.40	1.00	2.00
❑12, Oct 97, Reprints Saga of the Swamp Thing #32	1.95	0.40	1.00	2.00
❑13, Nov 97, AMo (w), Pog, Reprints Saga of the Swamp Thing #32	1.95	0.40	1.00	2.00
❑14, Dec 97, AMo (w), Abandoned Houses, Reprints Saga of the Swamp Thing #34	1.95	0.40	1.00	2.00
❑15, Jan 98, Reprints Saga of the Swamp Thing #34	1.95	0.40	1.00	2.00
❑16, Feb 98, Reprints Saga of the Swamp Thing #35	1.95	0.40	1.00	2.00
❑17, Mar 98, Reprints Saga of the Swamp Thing #36	1.95	0.40	1.00	2.00
❑18, Apr 98, Reprints Saga of the Swamp Thing #37	1.95	0.40	1.00	2.00
❑19, May 98, Reprints Saga of the Swamp Thing #38	1.95	0.40	1.00	2.00
❑20, Jun 98, Reprints Saga of the Swamp Thing #39	1.95	0.40	1.00	2.00
❑21, Jul 98, Reprints Saga of the Swamp Thing #40	1.95	0.40	1.00	2.00
❑22, Aug 98, Reprints Saga of the Swamp Thing #41	1.95	0.40	1.00	2.00
❑23, Sep 98, Reprints Saga of the Swamp Thing #42	2.25	0.45	1.13	2.25
❑24, Oct 98, Final Issue	2.25	0.45	1.13	2.25

ESSENTIAL VERTIGO: THE SANDMAN
DC

	ORIG	GOOD	FINE	N-MINT
❑1, Aug 96, NG (w), Preludes & Nocturnes, Reprints Sandman #1	1.95	0.60	1.50	3.00
❑2, Sep 96, NG (w), Preludes & Nocturnes, Reprints Sandman #2	1.95	0.50	1.25	2.50
❑3, Oct 96, NG (w), Preludes & Nocturnes, Reprints Sandman #3	1.95	0.50	1.25	2.50
❑4, Oct 96, NG (w), Preludes & Nocturnes, Reprints Sandman #4	1.95	0.50	1.25	2.50
❑5, Dec 96, NG (w), Preludes & Nocturnes, Reprints Sandman #5	1.95	0.50	1.25	2.50
❑6, Jan 97, NG (w), Preludes & Nocturnes, Reprints Sandman #6	1.95	0.40	1.00	2.00
❑7, Feb 97, NG (w), Reprints Sandman #7	1.95	0.40	1.00	2.00
❑8, Mar 97, NG (w), The Sound of her Wings, 1: Death (Sandman), Reprints Sandman #8	1.95	0.40	1.00	2.00
❑9, Apr 97, NG (w), Reprints Sandman #9.	1.95	0.40	1.00	2.00
❑10, May 97, NG (w), A Doll's House, Part 1, Reprints Sandman #10	1.95	0.40	1.00	2.00
❑11, Jun 97, NG (w), A Doll's House, Part 2, Reprints Sandman #11	1.95	0.40	1.00	2.00
❑12, Jul 97, NG (w), A Doll's House, Part 3, Reprints Sandman #12	1.95	0.40	1.00	2.00
❑13, Aug 97, NG (w), A Doll's House, Part 4, Reprints Sandman #13	1.95	0.40	1.00	2.00
❑14, Sep 97, NG (w), A Doll's House, Part 5, Reprints Sandman #14	1.95	0.40	1.00	2.00
❑15, Oct 97, NG (w), A Doll's House, Part 6, Reprints Sandman #15	1.95	0.40	1.00	2.00
❑16, Nov 97, NG (w), A Doll's House, Part 7, Reprints Sandman #16	1.95	0.40	1.00	2.00
❑17, Dec 97, NG (w), Calliope, Reprints Sandman #17	1.95	0.40	1.00	2.00
❑18, Jan 98, NG (w), A Dream of a Thousand Cats, Reprints Sandman #18	1.95	0.40	1.00	2.00
❑19, Feb 98, NG (w), Reprints Sandman #19	1.95	0.40	1.00	2.00
❑20, Mar 98, NG (w), Reprints Sandman #20	1.95	0.40	1.00	2.00

	ORIG	GOOD	FINE	N-MINT
❑21, Apr 98, NG (w), Season of Mists, Part 0, Reprints Sandman #21	1.95	0.39	0.98	1.95
❑22, May 98, NG (w), Reprints Sandman #22	1.95	0.39	0.98	1.95
❑23, Jun 98, NG (w), Reprints Sandman #23	1.95	0.39	0.98	1.95
❑24, Jul 98, NG (w), Reprints Sandman #24	1.95	0.39	0.98	1.95
❑25, Aug 98, NG (w), Reprints Sandman #25	1.95	0.39	0.98	1.95
❑26, Sep 98, NG (w), Reprints Sandman #26	2.25	0.45	1.13	2.25
❑27, Oct 98, NG (w), Reprints Sandman #27	2.25	0.45	1.13	2.25
❑28, Nov 98, NG (w), Reprints Sandman #28	2.25	0.45	1.13	2.25
❑29, Dec 98, NG (w), Reprints Sandman #29	2.25	0.45	1.13	2.25
❑30, Jan 99, NG (w), Reprints Sandman #30	2.25	0.45	1.13	2.25
❑31, Feb 99, NG (w), Three Septembers and a January, Reprints Sandman #31	2.25	0.45	1.13	2.25
❑32, Mar 99, BT, NG (w), Song of Orpheus, Final Issue; Reprints Sandman Special #1	4.50	0.90	2.25	4.50

ESSENTIAL X-MEN
MARVEL

	ORIG	GOOD	FINE	N-MINT
❑1, Reprints from Various X-Men Titles	—	1.00	2.50	5.00
❑2, Reprints from Various X-Men Titles	—	0.80	2.00	4.00
❑3, Reprints from Various X-Men Titles	—	0.80	2.00	4.00
❑4, Reprints from Various X-Men Titles	—	0.80	2.00	4.00
❑5, Reprints from Various X-Men Titles	—	0.80	2.00	4.00
❑6, Reprints from Various X-Men Titles	—	0.60	1.50	3.00
❑7, Reprints from Various X-Men Titles	—	0.60	1.50	3.00
❑8, Reprints from Various X-Men Titles	—	0.60	1.50	3.00
❑9, Reprints from Various X-Men Titles	—	0.60	1.50	3.00
❑10, Reprints from Various X-Men Titles	—	0.60	1.50	3.00
❑11, Reprints from Various X-Men Titles	—	0.60	1.50	3.00
❑12, Reprints from Various X-Men Titles	—	0.60	1.50	3.00
❑13, Reprints from Various X-Men Titles	—	0.60	1.50	3.00
❑14, Reprints from Various X-Men Titles	—	0.60	1.50	3.00
❑15, Reprints from Various X-Men Titles	—	0.60	1.50	3.00
❑16, Reprints from Various X-Men Titles	—	0.60	1.50	3.00
❑17, Reprints from Various X-Men Titles	—	0.60	1.50	3.00
❑18, Reprints from Various X-Men Titles	—	0.60	1.50	3.00
❑19, Reprints from Various X-Men Titles	—	0.60	1.50	3.00
❑20, Reprints from Various X-Men Titles	—	0.60	1.50	3.00
❑21, Reprints from Various X-Men Titles	—	0.60	1.50	3.00
❑22, Reprints from Various X-Men Titles	—	0.60	1.50	3.00
❑23, Reprints from Various X-Men Titles	—	0.60	1.50	3.00
❑24, Reprints from Various X-Men Titles	—	0.60	1.50	3.00
❑25, Reprints from Various X-Men Titles	—	0.60	1.50	3.00
❑26, Reprints from Various X-Men Titles	—	0.60	1.50	3.00
❑27, Reprints from Various X-Men Titles	—	0.60	1.50	3.00
❑28, Reprints from Various X-Men Titles	—	0.60	1.50	3.00
❑29, Reprints from Various X-Men Titles	—	0.60	1.50	3.00
❑30, Reprints from Various X-Men Titles	—	0.60	1.50	3.00
❑31, Reprints from Various X-Men Titles	—	0.60	1.50	3.00
❑32, On Consecrated Ground; Omega, Reprints from Various X-Men Titles	—	0.60	1.50	3.00

ETC
DC

Value: Cover or less

❑1, full color 2.50
❑2, full color 2.50
❑3, full color 2.50
❑4, full color 2.50
❑5, full color 2.50

ETERNAL ROMANCE
BEST DESTINY

	ORIG	GOOD	FINE	N-MINT
❑1, Feb 97, Till Death Do Us Part; The Night Student, b&w	2.50	0.60	1.50	3.00
❑2, May 97, My Phantom Lover!; Once Bitten, Twice Shy!, b&w	2.50	0.50	1.25	2.50
❑3, Dec 97, Kiss of Death!; Angel or Alien ..	2.50	0.50	1.25	2.50
❑4, Jul 98, Destine's Scream Date; The Green Eyed Monster!	2.50	0.50	1.25	2.50

ETERNAL ROMANCE LABOR OF LOVE SKETCHBOOK
BEST DESTINY

Value: Cover or less

❑1, Labor of Love sketchbook. 250 printed 2.50

ETERNALS, THE
MARVEL

	ORIG	GOOD	FINE	N-MINT
❑1, Jul 76, JK, JK (w), The Day of the Gods, O: Eternals; 1: Ikaris; 1: Brother Tode; 1: Margo Damian; 1: Kro, 1st appearan	0.25	0.50	1.25	2.50
❑2, Aug 76, JK, 1: Arishem the Judge; 1: Ajak	0.25	0.40	1.00	2.00
❑3, Sep 76, JK, 1: Sersi	0.30	0.40	1.00	2.00
❑4, Oct 76, JK, 1: Gammenon the Gatherer	0.30	0.40	1.00	2.00
❑5, Nov 76, JK, 1: Zuras (Thena); 1: Makkari	0.30	0.40	1.00	2.00
❑6, Dec 76, JK	0.30	0.30	0.75	1.50
❑7, Jan 77, JK, 1: Nezarr	0.30	0.30	0.75	1.50
❑8, Feb 77, JK, 1: Karkas	0.30	0.30	0.75	1.50
❑9, Mar 77, JK, 1: Sprite I	0.30	0.30	0.75	1.50
❑10, Apr 77, JK	0.30	0.30	0.75	1.50
❑11, May 77, JK, 1: Aginar	0.30	0.30	0.75	1.50
❑12, Jun 77, JK, 1: Uni-Mind	0.30	0.30	0.75	1.50
❑13, Jul 77, JK, 1: One Above All; 1: Gilgamesh	0.30	0.30	0.75	1.50
❑14, Aug 77, JK, A: Hulk	0.30	0.30	0.75	1.50
❑15, Sep 77, JK, A: Hulk	0.30	0.30	0.75	1.50

DC reprinted a portion of Alan Moore's run on *Swamp Thing* in black and white in its *Essential Vertigo: Swamp Thing* series.

	ORIG	GOOD	FINE	N-MINT
❑16, Oct 77, JK	0.30	0.30	0.75	1.50
❑17, Nov 77, JK	0.35	0.30	0.75	1.50
❑18, Dec 77, JK	0.35	0.30	0.75	1.50
❑19, Jan 78, JK, 1: Ziran	0.35	0.30	0.75	1.50
❑Anl 1, Oct 77, JK	0.50	0.30	0.75	1.50

ETERNALS, THE (LTD. SERIES)
MARVEL

	ORIG	GOOD	FINE	N-MINT
❑1, Oct 85, 1: Khoryphos, Giant-size	1.25	0.25	0.63	1.25
❑2, Nov 85, 1: Ghaur	0.75	0.20	0.50	1.00
❑3, Dec 85	0.75	0.20	0.50	1.00
❑4, Jan 86	0.75	0.20	0.50	1.00
❑5, Feb 86	0.75	0.20	0.50	1.00
❑6, Mar 86	0.75	0.20	0.50	1.00
❑7, Apr 86	0.75	0.20	0.50	1.00
❑8, May 86	0.75	0.20	0.50	1.00
❑9, Jun 86	0.75	0.20	0.50	1.00
❑10, Jul 86, O: Ghaur; D: Margo Damian ...	0.75	0.20	0.50	1.00
❑11, Aug 86	0.75	0.20	0.50	1.00
❑12, Sep 86, Giant-size	1.25	0.25	0.63	1.25

ETERNALS: THE HEROD FACTOR
MARVEL

Value: Cover or less

❑1, Nov 91, D: Doctor Damian; D: Ajak 2.50

ETERNAL THIRST
ALPHA PRODUCTIONS

Value: Cover or less

❑3, Treachery, b&w 1.95
❑4, b&w 1.95
❑5, b&w 1.95

ETERNAL WARRIOR
VALIANT

	ORIG	GOOD	FINE	N-MINT
❑1, Aug 92, FM (c), Unity, Part 2, Unity	2.25	0.60	1.50	3.00
❑1/GF, Aug 92, Unity, Part 2, Gold foil logo (dealer promotion)	2.25	1.00	2.50	5.00
❑1/GO, Aug 92, Unity, Part 2, Gold logo (dealer promotion)	2.25	0.80	2.00	4.00
❑2, Sep 92, Unity, Part 10, Unity	2.25	0.50	1.25	2.50
❑3, Oct 92, A: Armstrong	2.25	0.50	1.25	2.50
❑4, Nov 92, 1: Bloodshot (cameo)	2.25	0.50	1.25	2.50
❑5, Dec 92, A: Bloodshot	2.25	0.50	1.25	2.50
❑6, Jan 93, V: Master Darque	2.25	0.45	1.13	2.25
❑7, Feb 93	2.25	0.45	1.13	2.25
❑8, Mar 93, Double-size; combined with Archer & Armstrong #8	4.50	0.90	2.25	4.50
❑9, Apr 93, Book of the Geomancer, Part 1	2.25	0.45	1.13	2.25
❑10, May 93, Book of the Geomancer, Part 2	2.25	0.45	1.13	2.25
❑11, Jun 93, A Gift Before Dying	2.25	0.45	1.13	2.25
❑12, Jul 93, Return of the Immortal Enemy, Part 1	2.25	0.45	1.13	2.25
❑13, Aug 93, Return of the Immortal Enemy, Part 2, V: Eternal Enemy	2.25	0.45	1.13	2.25
❑14, Sep 93, A: Bloodshot	2.25	0.45	1.13	2.25
❑15, Oct 93, A: Bloodshot	2.25	0.45	1.13	2.25
❑16, Nov 93	2.25	0.45	1.13	2.25
❑17, Dec 93	2.25	0.45	1.13	2.25
❑18, Jan 94	2.25	0.45	1.13	2.25
❑19, Feb 94, A: Doctor Mirage	2.25	0.45	1.13	2.25
❑20, Mar 94	2.25	0.45	1.13	2.25
❑21, Apr 94	2.25	0.45	1.13	2.25
❑22, May 94, trading card	2.25	0.45	1.13	2.25
❑23, Jun 94	2.25	0.45	1.13	2.25
❑24, Aug 94, V: Archer & Armstrong	2.25	0.45	1.13	2.25
❑25, Sep 94, A: Archer & Armstrong	2.25	0.45	1.13	2.25
❑26, Oct 94, The Chaos Effect: Gamma, Part 4, indicia says August; Flip-book with Archer & Armstrong #26	2.75	0.55	1.38	2.75
❑27, Nov 94	2.25	0.45	1.13	2.25
❑28, Dec 94	2.25	0.45	1.13	2.25
❑29, Jan 95	2.25	0.45	1.13	2.25
❑30, Feb 95	2.25	0.45	1.13	2.25
❑31, Mar 95	2.25	0.45	1.13	2.25
❑32, Apr 95	2.25	0.45	1.13	2.25
❑33, May 95, Mortal Kin, Part 1	1.95	0.45	1.13	2.25

	ORIG	GOOD	FINE	N-MINT
❑34, Jun 95	2.25	0.45	1.13	2.25
❑35, Jul 95, outer white cover with warning; Birthquake	2.50	0.50	1.25	2.50
❑36, Jul 95, Birthquake	2.50	0.50	1.25	2.50
❑37, Aug 95	2.50	0.50	1.25	2.50
❑38, Aug 95, V: Spider Queen	2.50	0.50	1.25	2.50
❑39, Sep 95	2.50	0.50	1.25	2.50
❑40, Sep 95	2.50	0.50	1.25	2.50
❑41, Oct 95	2.50	0.50	1.25	2.50
❑42, Oct 95	2.50	0.50	1.25	2.50
❑43, Nov 95	2.50	0.50	1.25	2.50
❑44, Nov 95	2.50	0.50	1.25	2.50
❑45, Dec 95	2.50	0.50	1.25	2.50
❑46, Dec 95	2.50	0.50	1.25	2.50
❑47, Jan 96	2.50	0.50	1.25	2.50
❑48, Jan 96	2.50	0.50	1.25	2.50
❑49, Feb 96	2.50	0.50	1.25	2.50
❑50, Mar 96, A: Geomancer, Final Issue	2.50	0.50	1.25	2.50
❑SE 1, Feb 96, The Wings of Justice	2.50	0.50	1.25	2.50
❑YB 1, cardstock cover; Yearbook 1	3.95	0.79	1.98	3.95
❑YB 2, cardstock cover; Yearbook 2	3.95	0.79	1.98	3.95

ETERNAL WARRIOR: FIST AND STEEL
ACCLAIM

Value: Cover or less

❑1, May 96, A: Geomancer..... 2.50
❑2, Jun 96, A: Geomancer...... 2.50

ETERNAL WARRIORS
ACCLAIM

	ORIG	GOOD	FINE	N-MINT
❑1, Jun 97, Time and Treachery, One-Shot	3.95	0.79	1.98	3.95
❑1/SC, Jun 97, alternate painted cover	3.95	0.79	1.98	3.95
❑Ash 1, Feb 97, b&w; no cover price; preview of Time and Treachery one-shot	—	0.20	0.50	1.00

ETERNAL WARRIORS: ARCHER & ARMSTRONG
ACCLAIM

Value: Cover or less

❑1, Dec 97, price stickered on cover 3.95

ETERNAL WARRIORS BLACKWORKS
ACCLAIM

Value: Cover or less

❑1, Mar 98, A: Goat 3.95

ETERNAL WARRIORS: DIGITAL ALCHEMY
ACCLAIM

Value: Cover or less

❑1, Sep 97, One-Shot 3.95

ETERNAL WARRIORS: MOG
ACCLAIM

Value: Cover or less

❑1, Mar 98, One-Shot 3.95

ETERNAL WARRIOR SPECIAL
ACCLAIM

Value: Cover or less

❑1, Feb 96, Eternal Warrior in WW II 2.50

ETERNAL WARRIORS: THE IMMORTAL ENEMY
ACCLAIM

Value: Cover or less

❑1, Final issue of VH-2 universe 3.95

ETERNAL WARRIORS: TIME AND TREACHERY
ACCLAIM

Value: Cover or less

❑1 ..... 3.95

ETERNITY SMITH (VOL. 1)
RENEGADE

	ORIG	GOOD	FINE	N-MINT
❑1, Sep 86, full color	1.25	0.30	0.75	1.50
❑2, Nov 86	1.50	0.30	0.75	1.50
❑3, Jan 87	1.50	0.30	0.75	1.50
❑4, Mar 87, And Death Comes Softly Knocking	1.50	0.30	0.75	1.50
❑5, May 87	1.50	0.30	0.75	1.50

ETERNITY SMITH (VOL. 2)
HERO

Value: Cover or less

❑1, Sep 87, Final Ashowdown 1.95
❑2, Oct 87 ..... 1.95
❑3, Nov 87 ..... 1.95
❑4, Dec 87 ..... 1.95
❑5, Jan 88 ..... 1.95
❑6, Feb 88 ..... 1.95
❑7, Apr 88 ..... 1.95
❑8, Jun 88 ..... 1.95
❑9, Aug 88, A: Walter Koenig, Final Issue 1.95

ETERNITY TRIPLE ACTION
ETERNITY

Value: Cover or less

❑1, Amazon Gazonga, Part 1; Gigantor, Part 1, b&w..... 2.50
❑2, Amazon Gazonga, Part 2; Gigantor, Part 2, b&w..... 2.50
❑3, Amazon Gazonga, Part 3; Gigantor, Part 3, b&w..... 2.50

EUDAEMON, THE
DARK HORSE

Value: Cover or less

❑1, Aug 93 ..... 2.50
❑2 ..... 2.50
❑3 ..... 2.50

EUGENUS
EUGENUS

Value: Cover or less

❑1, b&w 3.50
❑2, b&w 3.50
❑3 ..... 2.50

EUREKA
RADIO COMIX

Value: Cover or less

❑1, Apr 00, b&w 2.95
❑2, Jul 00, b&w 2.95
❑3, Sep 00, b&w 2.95

EUROPA AND THE PIRATE TWINS
POWDER MONKEY PRODUCTIONS

	ORIG	GOOD	FINE	N-MINT
❑1, Oct 96, b&w	2.95	0.59	1.48	2.95
❑1/A, Oct 96, b&w; no cover price	2.95	0.59	1.48	2.95
❑Ash 1, Mar 96, nn; b&w; no cover price; smaller than normal comic	—	0.20	0.50	1.00

EVANGELINE (VOL. 1)
COMICO

	ORIG	GOOD	FINE	N-MINT
❑1, 1: Evangeline	1.50	0.50	1.25	2.50
❑2	1.50	0.40	1.00	2.00

EVANGELINE (VOL. 2)
FIRST

	ORIG	GOOD	FINE	N-MINT
❑1	1.75	0.50	1.25	2.50
❑2	1.75	0.40	1.00	2.00
❑3	1.75	0.40	1.00	2.00
❑4	1.75	0.40	1.00	2.00
❑5	1.75	0.40	1.00	2.00
❑6	1.75	0.40	1.00	2.00
❑7	1.75	0.40	1.00	2.00
❑8	1.75	0.40	1.00	2.00
❑9	1.75	0.40	1.00	2.00
❑10	1.95	0.40	1.00	2.00
❑11	1.95	0.40	1.00	2.00
❑12	1.95	0.40	1.00	2.00

EVANGELINE SPECIAL
LODESTONE

Value: Cover or less

❑1 ..... 2.00

EVEL KNIEVEL
MARVEL

	ORIG	GOOD	FINE	N-MINT
❑1, giveaway	—	0.70	1.75	3.50

E.V.E. PROTOMECHA
IMAGE

Value: Cover or less

❑1 ..... 2.50
❑2 ..... 2.50
❑3 ..... 2.50
❑4, Nov 00 ..... 2.50
❑5 ..... 2.50
❑6, Sep 00 ..... 2.50

EVERWINDS
SLAVE LABOR

Value: Cover or less

❑1, Aug 97, Everwinds, A: Lethargic Lad, b&w 2.95
❑2, Oct 97, 'Shrooms, b&w 2.95
❑3, Dec 97, b&w 2.95
❑4, Mar 98, A Woman's Touch; Genesis 2.95

EVERYMAN, THE
MARVEL

Value: Cover or less

❑1, Nov 91, nn 4.50

EVIL ERNIE (CHAOS!)
CHAOS!

	ORIG	GOOD	FINE	N-MINT
❑0	—	0.60	1.50	3.00
❑0/PL, Platinum edition	—	1.00	2.50	5.00
❑1, Jul 98, Vampire Vengeance, Part 1	2.95	0.60	1.50	3.00
❑2, Aug 98, Vampire Vengeance, Part 2	2.95	0.60	1.50	3.00
❑3, Sep 98, Vampire Vengeance, Part 3	2.95	0.60	1.50	3.00
❑4, Oct 98, Fear Itself	2.95	0.60	1.50	3.00
❑5, Nov 98, Fear Itself	2.95	0.59	1.48	2.95
❑6, Dec 98, Fear Itself	2.95	0.59	1.48	2.95
❑7, Jan 99, Christmas Evil	2.95	0.59	1.48	2.95
❑8, Feb 99, Trauma	2.95	0.59	1.48	2.95
❑9, Mar 99, Trauma	2.95	0.59	1.48	2.95
❑10, Apr 99, Trauma	2.95	0.59	1.48	2.95

EVIL ERNIE (ETERNITY)
ETERNITY

	ORIG	GOOD	FINE	N-MINT
❑1, 1: Lady Death; 1: Evil Ernie, b&w	2.50	5.60	14.00	28.00
❑1/LE, 1: Lady Death; 1: Evil Ernie, new material; Limited edition reprint (1992)	—	3.00	7.50	15.00
❑2, b&w	2.50	4.00	10.00	20.00
❑3, b&w	2.50	3.20	8.00	16.00
❑4, b&w	2.50	3.00	7.50	15.00
❑5, b&w	2.50	3.00	7.50	15.00

EVIL ERNIE: BADDEST BATTLES
CHAOS

	ORIG	GOOD	FINE	N-MINT
❑1	1.50	0.30	0.75	1.50
❑1/SC, Splatterfest Premium Edition cover.	—	0.30	0.75	1.50

	ORIG	GOOD	FINE	N-MINT

EVIL ERNIE: DEPRAVED
CHAOS!

Value: Cover or less

❑1, Jul 99	2.95
❑2, Aug 99	2.95
❑3, Sep 99	2.95

EVIL ERNIE: DESTROYER
CHAOS!

Value: Cover or less

❑1, Oct 97	2.95
❑2, Nov 97	2.95
❑3, Dec 97	2.95
❑4, Jan 98	2.95
❑5, Feb 98	2.95
❑6	2.95
❑7	2.95
❑8	2.95
❑9	2.95
❑Ash 1, Sep 97	2.50

EVIL ERNIE: NEW YEAR'S EVIL
CHAOS!

	ORIG	GOOD	FINE	N-MINT
❑1, nn	—	1.00	2.50	5.00

EVIL ERNIE: PIECES OF ME
CHAOS!

Value: Cover or less

❑1, Nov 00, b&w	2.95

EVIL ERNIE: REVENGE
CHAOS!

	ORIG	GOOD	FINE	N-MINT
❑0	—	0.50	1.25	2.50
❑1	2.50	0.60	1.50	3.00
❑1/Dlx, Master of Annihilation premium edition	—	0.90	2.25	4.50
❑1/LE, Glow-in-the-dark limited edition	—	0.90	2.25	4.50
❑2	2.50	0.60	1.50	3.00
❑3, Jan 95	2.50	0.50	1.25	2.50
❑4, Feb 95	2.50	0.50	1.25	2.50

EVIL ERNIE: STRAIGHT TO HELL
CHAOS!

	ORIG	GOOD	FINE	N-MINT
❑1, Beyond the Black, Coffin fold-out cover	2.95	0.60	1.50	3.00
❑1/A, Beyond the Black, chromium cover	—	1.00	2.50	5.00
❑2, Dec 95	2.95	0.60	1.50	3.00
❑3	2.95	0.60	1.50	3.00
❑4	2.95	0.60	1.50	3.00
❑5, May 96, Final Issue	2.95	0.60	1.50	3.00

EVIL ERNIE: THE RESURRECTION
CHAOS!

	ORIG	GOOD	FINE	N-MINT
❑1, O: Evil Ernie	2.95	0.80	2.00	4.00
❑1/GO, O: Evil Ernie, Gold promotional edition	—	2.00	5.00	10.00
❑2	2.95	0.70	1.75	3.50
❑3	2.95	0.70	1.75	3.50
❑4, A: Lady Death	2.95	0.60	1.50	3.00
❑Ash 1	—	1.00	2.50	5.00

EVIL ERNIE VS. THE MOVIE MONSTERS
CHAOS!

	ORIG	GOOD	FINE	N-MINT
❑1, One-Shot	—	0.60	1.50	3.00

EVIL ERNIE VS. THE SUPER HEROES
CHAOS!

	ORIG	GOOD	FINE	N-MINT
❑1, Aug 95, O: Evil Ernie	2.95	0.60	1.50	3.00
❑1/SC, Aug 95, O: Evil Ernie, no cover price; Limited edition enhanced cover; premium edition (10, 000 copies)	—	0.80	2.00	4.00
❑2, Sep 98	2.95	0.59	1.48	2.95

EVIL ERNIE: WAR OF THE DEAD
CHAOS!

Value: Cover or less

❑1, Nov 99	2.95
❑2, Dec 99	2.95
❑3, Jan 00	2.95

EVIL ERNIE: YOUTH GONE WILD
CHAOS!

Value: Cover or less

❑1, Nov 96, b&w; reprints Eternity's Evil Ernie	1.95
❑2, Dec 96, b&w; reprints Eternity's Evil Ernie	1.95
❑3, Jan 97, b&w; reprints Eternity's Evil Ernie	1.95
❑4, Feb 97, b&w; reprints Eternity's Evil Ernie	1.95
❑5, Mar 97, b&w; reprints Eternity's Evil Ernie	1.95
❑SE 1, script to Evil Ernie #1; "Director's Cut" #1	4.95

EVIL EYE
FANTAGRAPHICS

Value: Cover or less

❑1, Jun 98	2.95
❑2, Oct 98	2.95
❑3, Apr 99	2.95

EVILMAN SAVES THE WORLD
MOONSTONE

Value: Cover or less

❑1, Jul 96, nn; b&w	2.95

EWOKS
MARVEL

	ORIG	GOOD	FINE	N-MINT
❑1, May 85, The Rainbow Bridge	0.65	0.40	1.00	2.00
❑2, Jul 85	0.65	0.30	0.75	1.50
❑3, Sep 85, Flight to Danger	0.65	0.30	0.75	1.50

The Eternal Warrior made his first appearance in his own series during Valiant's first inter-company crossover, "Unity."

© 1992 Voyager Communications (Valiant)

	ORIG	GOOD	FINE	N-MINT
❑4, Nov 85	0.65	0.25	0.63	1.25
❑5, Jan 86	0.65	0.25	0.63	1.25
❑6, Mar 86	0.75	0.25	0.63	1.25
❑7, May 86	0.75	0.25	0.63	1.25
❑8, Jul 86	0.75	0.25	0.63	1.25
❑9, Sep 86	0.75	0.25	0.63	1.25
❑10, Nov 86	0.75	0.25	0.63	1.25
❑11, Jan 87	0.75	0.25	0.63	1.25
❑12, Mar 87	0.75	0.25	0.63	1.25
❑13, May 87	0.75	0.25	0.63	1.25
❑14, Jul 87	1.00	0.25	0.63	1.25

EXCALIBUR
MARVEL

	ORIG	GOOD	FINE	N-MINT
❑-1, Jul 97, Flashback	1.99	0.40	1.00	2.00
❑1, Oct 88, Warwolves of London!	1.50	0.50	1.25	2.50
❑2, Nov 88, 1: Kylun; 1: Tweedledope (in America)	1.50	0.40	1.00	2.00
❑3, Dec 88	1.50	0.40	1.00	2.00
❑4, Jan 89, 1: Knave (in America); 1: Executioner (in America); 1: The Crazy Gang (in America); 1: Red Queen (in America); 1: Jester (in America), 1st appearan	1.50	0.40	1.00	2.00
❑5, Feb 89	1.50	0.40	1.00	2.00
❑6, Mar 89, Inferno, Inferno	1.50	0.35	0.88	1.75
❑7, Apr 89, Inferno, Inferno	1.50	0.35	0.88	1.75
❑8, May 89	1.50	0.35	0.88	1.75
❑9, Jun 89	1.50	0.35	0.88	1.75
❑10, Jul 89	1.50	0.35	0.88	1.75
❑11, Aug 89	1.50	0.35	0.88	1.75
❑12, Sep 89	1.50	0.35	0.88	1.75
❑13, Oct 89, Cross-Time Caper	1.50	0.35	0.88	1.75
❑14, Nov 89, Cross-Time Caper	1.50	0.35	0.88	1.75
❑15, Nov 89, Cross-Time Caper	1.50	0.35	0.88	1.75
❑16, Dec 89, Cross-Time Caper	1.50	0.35	0.88	1.75
❑17, Dec 89, Cross-Time Caper	1.50	0.35	0.88	1.75
❑18, Jan 90, Cross-Time Caper	1.50	0.35	0.88	1.75
❑19, Feb 90	1.50	0.35	0.88	1.75
❑20, Mar 90	1.50	0.35	0.88	1.75
❑21, Apr 90, Cross-Time Caper	1.50	0.35	0.88	1.75
❑22, May 90, Cross-Time Caper	1.50	0.35	0.88	1.75
❑23, Jun 90, Cross-Time Caper	1.50	0.35	0.88	1.75
❑24, Jul 90, Cross-Time Caper	1.75	0.35	0.88	1.75
❑25, Aug 90	1.75	0.35	0.88	1.75
❑26, Aug 90	1.75	0.35	0.88	1.75
❑27, Aug 90, A: Nth Man	1.75	0.35	0.88	1.75
❑28, Sep 90	1.75	0.35	0.88	1.75
❑29, Sep 90	1.75	0.35	0.88	1.75
❑30, Oct 90	1.75	0.35	0.88	1.75
❑31, Nov 90	1.75	0.35	0.88	1.75
❑32, Girl's School Heck, Part 1, with $1.75 price	1.75	0.35	0.88	1.75
❑32/A, Dec 90, Girl's School Heck, Part 1, with $1.50 price	1.50	0.35	0.88	1.75
❑32/B, with $1.75 price	1.75	0.35	0.88	1.75
❑33, Jan 91, Girl's School Heck, Part 2	1.75	0.35	0.88	1.75
❑34, Feb 91, Girl's School Heck, Part 3	1.75	0.35	0.88	1.75
❑35, Mar 91	1.75	0.35	0.88	1.75
❑36, Apr 91, Outlaws	1.75	0.35	0.88	1.75
❑37, May 91, The Promethean Exchange, Part 1	1.75	0.35	0.88	1.75
❑38, Jun 91, The Promethean Exchange, Part 2	1.75	0.35	0.88	1.75
❑39, Jul 91, The Promethean Exchange, Part 3	1.75	0.35	0.88	1.75
❑40, Aug 91	1.75	0.35	0.88	1.75

	ORIG	GOOD	FINE	N-MINT
❑41, Sep 91	1.75	0.35	0.88	1.75
❑42, Oct 91	1.75	0.35	0.88	1.75
❑43, Nov 91	1.75	0.35	0.88	1.75
❑44, Nov 91, 1: Micromax	1.75	0.35	0.88	1.75
❑45, Dec 91, 1: Necrom	1.75	0.35	0.88	1.75
❑46, Jan 92	1.75	0.35	0.88	1.75
❑47, Feb 92, 1: Cerise	1.75	0.35	0.88	1.75
❑48, Mar 92, 1: Feron	1.75	0.35	0.88	1.75
❑49, Apr 92	1.75	0.35	0.88	1.75
❑50, May 92, O: Feron, glow in the dark cover; Double-size	2.75	0.55	1.38	2.75
❑51, Jun 92	1.75	0.35	0.88	1.75
❑52, Jul 92, O: Phoenix III (Rachel Summers); A: X-Men	1.75	0.35	0.88	1.75
❑53, Aug 92, A: Spider-Man	1.75	0.35	0.88	1.75
❑54, Sep 92	1.75	0.35	0.88	1.75
❑55, Oct 92	1.75	0.35	0.88	1.75
❑56, Nov 92, A: X-Men	1.75	0.35	0.88	1.75
❑57, Nov 92	1.75	0.35	0.88	1.75
❑58, Dec 92	1.75	0.35	0.88	1.75
❑59, Dec 92	1.75	0.35	0.88	1.75
❑60, Jan 93	1.75	0.35	0.88	1.75
❑61, Jan 93	1.75	0.35	0.88	1.75
❑62, Feb 93	1.75	0.35	0.88	1.75
❑63, Mar 93	1.75	0.35	0.88	1.75
❑64, Apr 93	1.75	0.35	0.88	1.75
❑65, May 93	1.75	0.35	0.88	1.75
❑66, Jun 93	1.75	0.35	0.88	1.75
❑67, Jul 93	1.75	0.35	0.88	1.75
❑68, Aug 93	1.75	0.35	0.88	1.75
❑69, Sep 93	1.75	0.35	0.88	1.75
❑70, Oct 93, O: Cerise; A: Shi'Ar; A: Starjammers	1.75	0.35	0.88	1.75
❑71, Nov 93, Hologram cover	3.95	0.80	2.00	4.00
❑72, Dec 93	1.75	0.35	0.88	1.75
❑73, Jan 94	1.75	0.35	0.88	1.75
❑74, Feb 94	1.75	0.35	0.88	1.75
❑75, Mar 94, 1: Britannic, Giant-size	2.25	0.45	1.13	2.25
❑75/SC, Mar 94, 1: Britannic, Holo-grafix cover; Giant-size	3.50	0.70	1.75	3.50
❑76, Apr 94	2.25	0.35	0.88	1.75
❑77, May 94	1.95	0.39	0.98	1.95
❑78, Jun 94, The Douglock Chronicles, Part 1	1.95	0.39	0.98	1.95
❑79, Jul 94, The Douglock Chronicles, Part 2	1.95	0.39	0.98	1.95
❑80, Aug 94	1.95	0.39	0.98	1.95
❑81, Sep 94	1.95	0.39	0.98	1.95
❑82, Oct 94, Life Signs, Part 3, Giant-size	2.50	0.50	1.25	2.50
❑82/SC, Oct 94, Life Signs, Part 3, foil cover; Giant-size	3.50	0.70	1.75	3.50
❑83, Nov 94, Soul Sword Trilogy, Part 1	1.50	0.30	0.75	1.50
❑83/Dlx, Nov 94, Soul Sword Trilogy, Part 1, Deluxe edition	1.95	0.39	0.98	1.95
❑84, Dec 94, Soul Sword Trilogy, Part 2	1.50	0.30	0.75	1.50
❑84/Dlx, Dec 94, Soul Sword Trilogy, Part 2, Deluxe edition	1.95	0.39	0.98	1.95
❑85, Jan 95, Soul Sword Trilogy, Part 3	1.50	0.30	0.75	1.50
❑85/Dlx, Jan 95, Soul Sword Trilogy, Part 3, Deluxe edition	1.95	0.39	0.98	1.95
❑86, Feb 95	1.50	0.39	0.98	1.95
❑86/Dlx, Feb 95, Deluxe edition	1.95	0.39	0.98	1.95
❑87, Jul 95	1.95	0.39	0.98	1.95
❑88, Aug 95	1.95	0.39	0.98	1.95
❑89, Sep 95	1.95	0.39	0.98	1.95
❑90, Oct 95, OverPower cards inserted	1.95	0.39	0.98	1.95
❑91, Nov 95	1.95	0.39	0.98	1.95
❑92, Dec 95, Colossus Is Here!, A: Pete Wisdom; A: Colossus	1.95	0.39	0.98	1.95
❑93, Jan 96, Rahne's past	1.95	0.39	0.98	1.95
❑94, Feb 96, Days of Future Tense	1.95	0.39	0.98	1.95
❑95, Mar 96, A: X-Man	1.95	0.39	0.98	1.95
❑96, Apr 96	1.95	0.39	0.98	1.95
❑97, May 96	1.95	0.39	0.98	1.95
❑98, Jun 96	1.95	0.39	0.98	1.95
❑99, Jul 96	1.95	0.39	0.98	1.95
❑100, Aug 96, Onslaught: Impact 1, wrap-around cover; Giant-size	2.95	0.59	1.48	2.95
❑101, Sep 96	1.95	0.39	0.98	1.95
❑102, Oct 96, bound-in trading cards	1.95	0.39	0.98	1.95
❑103, Nov 96	1.95	0.39	0.98	1.95
❑104, Dec 96	1.95	0.39	0.98	1.95
❑105, Jan 97, KG (w), Hard Truths	1.95	0.39	0.98	1.95
❑106, Feb 97, A Portrait of the Artist	1.95	0.39	0.98	1.95
❑107, Mar 97, Focus	1.95	0.39	0.98	1.95
❑108, Apr 97, The Old Ways	1.95	0.39	0.98	1.95
❑109, May 97, Dragon Moon Rising, V: Spiral	1.95	0.39	0.98	1.95
❑110, Jun 97, Hearts Bled Crimson	1.95	0.40	1.00	1.99
❑111, Aug 97, gatefold summary	1.99	0.40	1.00	1.99
❑112, Sep 97, gatefold summary	1.99	0.40	1.00	1.99
❑113, Oct 97, A: High Evolutionary, gatefold summary	1.99	0.40	1.00	1.99
❑114, Nov 97, gatefold summary	1.99	0.40	1.00	1.99
❑115, Dec 97, gatefold summary	1.99	0.40	1.00	1.99
❑116, Jan 98, gatefold summary	1.99	0.40	1.00	1.99
❑117, Feb 98, gatefold summary	1.99	0.40	1.00	1.99
❑118, Mar 98, gatefold summary	1.99	0.40	1.00	1.99
❑119, Apr 98, V: Nightmare, gatefold summary	1.99	0.40	1.00	1.99
❑120, May 98, gatefold summary	1.99	0.40	1.00	1.99
❑121, Jun 98, gatefold summary	1.99	0.40	1.00	1.99
❑122, Jul 98, V: Prime Sentinels, gatefold summary	1.99	0.40	1.00	1.99
❑123, Aug 98, V: Mimic, gatefold summary	1.99	0.40	1.00	1.99
❑124, Sep 98, gatefold summary; Captain Britain's bachelor party	1.99	0.40	1.00	1.99
❑125, Oct 98, Final Issue; gatefold summary; Giant-size; Wedding of Captain Britain, Meggan	2.99	0.60	1.50	3.00
❑Anl 1, Soul Sword Trilogy, Part 3, 1: Ghath, trading card; trading card	2.95	0.59	1.48	2.95
❑Anl 2	2.95	0.59	1.48	2.95

EXCALIBUR (MINI-SERIES)
MARVEL

Value: Cover or less

- ❑1, Feb 01, Camelot Lost 2.99
- ❑2, Mar 01, The Ruined Land 2.99
- ❑3, Apr 01, Destiny's Children 2.99

EXCALIBUR: AIR APPARENT
MARVEL

	ORIG	GOOD	FINE	N-MINT
❑1, Dec 91, nn; Air Apparent Special Edition	4.95	1.00	2.50	5.00

EXCALIBUR: MOJO MAYHEM
MARVEL

Value: Cover or less

- ❑1, Dec 89, nn 4.50

EXCALIBUR: THE POSSESSION
MARVEL

Value: Cover or less

- ❑1, Jul 91 .... 2.95

EXCALIBUR: THE SWORD IS DRAWN
MARVEL

	ORIG	GOOD	FINE	N-MINT
❑1, Sword is Drawn, 1: Excalibur, prestige format	3.25	1.00	2.50	5.00
❑1-2, 1: Excalibur, 2nd Printing	3.50	0.70	1.75	3.50
❑, 1: Excalibur, 3rd Printing	3.50	0.70	1.75	3.50

EXCALIBUR: WEIRD WAR III
MARVEL

Value: Cover or less

- ❑1, Dec 90 .... 9.95

EXCALIBUR: XX CROSSING
MARVEL

Value: Cover or less

- ❑1, May 92, A: X-Men, indicia says May, cover says Jul 2.50

EXCITING X-PATROL
MARVEL

Value: Cover or less

- ❑1, Jun 97, The Curse of Brother Brood! 1.95

EXHIBITIONIST, THE
EROS

Value: Cover or less

- ❑1 .... 2.75
- ❑2, Aug 94 .... 2.75

EXILE
EYEBALL SOUP DESIGNS

Value: Cover or less

- ❑1, May 96, b&w; cardstock cover 2.95
- ❑2, Jul 96, b&w; cardstock cover 2.95

During the "Cross-Time Caper," the members of Excalibur visited a number of alternate dimensions, including one where the characters from Edgar Rice Burroughs' Martian novels lived.

© 1989 Marvel

EXILED, THE
Exiled Studios

Value: Cover or less

- ❑1, Jan 98, Cry Baby 2.75
- ❑2, Apr 98 .... 2.75
- ❑3, Jun, cover says 98, indicia says 97 .... 2.75

EXILE EARTH
River City

Value: Cover or less

- ❑1 .... 1.95
- ❑2 .... 1.95

EXILES
Malibu

	ORIG	GOOD	FINE	N-MINT
❑1, 1: The Exiles, b&w	1.95	0.40	1.00	2.00
❑1/SC, 1: The Exiles, Hologram cover; hologram	—	1.00	2.50	5.00
❑2, Sep 93	1.95	0.40	1.00	2.00
❑3, Oct 93, Rune, Part E, 40pgs.; Rune	2.50	0.50	1.25	2.50
❑4, Nov 93, D: Exiles, Final Issue	1.95	0.40	1.00	2.00

EXILES (ALPHA)
Alpha Productions

Value: Cover or less

- ❑1, b&w 1.95

EXIT (VOL. 2)
Caliber

Value: Cover or less

- ❑1, Traitors, Part 1 .... 2.95
- ❑2, Traitors, Part 2 .... 2.95
- ❑3, Traitors, Part 3 .... 2.95
- ❑4, Traitors, Part 4 .... 2.95
- ❑5, Traitors, Part 5 .... 2.95

EXIT 6
Plastic Spoon Press

Value: Cover or less

- ❑1, Aug 98, b&w 2.95
- ❑2/Ash, Aug 98, preview of upcoming issue 2.95
- ❑3, Jan 99 .... 2.95
- ❑3/Ash, Aug 98, preview of upcoming issue 2.95

EXIT FROM SHADOW
Bronze Man

Value: Cover or less

- ❑4, indicia has name change, cover doesn't; was Secret Killers 2.95

EX-MUTANTS (AMAZING)
Pied Piper

	ORIG	GOOD	FINE	N-MINT
❑1	1.80	0.40	1.00	2.00
❑2	1.80	0.40	1.00	2.00
❑3	1.80	0.40	1.00	2.00
❑4	1.95	0.40	1.00	2.00
❑5, Enter the New Humans, A: New Humans	1.95	0.40	1.00	2.00
❑6, Jul 87	1.95	0.40	1.00	2.00
❑7	1.95	0.40	1.00	2.00
❑8	1.95	0.40	1.00	2.00
❑SE 1, Spr 87, b&w	1.80	0.40	1.00	2.00

EX-MUTANTS (ETERNITY)
Eternity

	ORIG	GOOD	FINE	N-MINT
❑1, A Breed Apart	1.80	0.40	1.00	2.00
❑2	1.95	0.40	1.00	2.00
❑3	1.95	0.40	1.00	2.00
❑4, Oct 88, RL (c)	1.95	0.40	1.00	2.00
❑5	1.95	0.40	1.00	2.00
❑6	1.95	0.40	1.00	2.00
❑7	1.95	0.40	1.00	2.00
❑8	1.95	0.40	1.00	2.00
❑9	1.95	0.40	1.00	2.00
❑10	1.95	0.40	1.00	2.00
❑11	1.95	0.40	1.00	2.00
❑12	1.95	0.40	1.00	2.00
❑13	1.95	0.40	1.00	2.00
❑14	1.95	0.40	1.00	2.00
❑15	1.95	0.39	0.98	1.95
❑Anl 1	1.95	0.39	0.98	1.95

EX-MUTANTS (MALIBU)
Malibu

	ORIG	GOOD	FINE	N-MINT
❑1, Nov 92, O: Ex-Mutants	1.95	0.40	1.00	2.00
❑1/SC, O: Ex-Mutants, shiny cover	—	0.50	1.25	2.50
❑2, Dec 92	1.95	0.39	0.98	1.95
❑3, Jan 93	1.95	0.39	0.98	1.95
❑4, Feb 93	1.95	0.39	0.98	1.95
❑5, Mar 93	1.95	0.39	0.98	1.95
❑6, Apr 93	1.95	0.39	0.98	1.95
❑7, May 93	1.95	0.39	0.98	1.95
❑8	1.95	0.39	0.98	1.95
❑9	1.95	0.39	0.98	1.95
❑10	1.95	0.39	0.98	1.95
❑11	2.25	0.39	0.98	1.95
❑12	2.25	0.45	1.13	2.25
❑13, Genesis begins publishing	2.25	0.45	1.13	2.25
❑14, Genesis	2.25	0.45	1.13	2.25
❑15, Genesis	2.50	0.45	1.13	2.25
❑16, Feb 94, Genesis	2.50	0.45	1.13	2.25
❑17, Mar 94, Genesis	2.50	0.50	1.25	2.50
❑18, Apr 94, Final Issue; Genesis	2.50	0.50	1.25	2.50

EX-MUTANTS MICROSERIES: ERIN (LAWRENCE & LIM'S...)
Pied Piper

Value: Cover or less

- ❑1, b&w 1.95

EX-MUTANTS PIN-UP BOOK
Eternity

Value: Cover or less

- ❑1 .... 1.95

EXODUS REVELATION
Exodus

	ORIG	GOOD	FINE	N-MINT
❑1, Nov 94, b&w; no cover price	—	0.20	0.50	1.00

EXOSQUAD
Topps

Value: Cover or less

- ❑0, Jan 94, JSa, 1: Exosquad, cardstock cover 1.00

EXOTICA
Cry for Dawn

	ORIG	GOOD	FINE	N-MINT
❑1, b&w; adult	—	0.80	2.00	4.00

EXOTIC FANTASY
Fantagraphics

Value: Cover or less

- ❑1, b&w; adult; sketches 4.95
- ❑2, b&w; adult; sketches 4.95
- ❑3, b&w; adult; sketches 4.95

EXPERIENCE, THE
Aircel

	ORIG	GOOD	FINE	N-MINT
❑1, b&w; adult	—	0.65	1.63	3.25

EXPLORERS
Explorer

Value: Cover or less

- ❑1, b&w 2.95
- ❑2, b&w 2.95
- ❑3, b&w 2.95

EXPLORERS (VOL. 2)
Caliber

Value: Cover or less

- ❑1, b&w 2.95
- ❑2, b&w 2.95

EXPLORERS OF THE UNKNOWN
Archie

Value: Cover or less

- ❑1, Jun 90 .... 1.00
- ❑2 .... 1.00
- ❑3 .... 1.00
- ❑4 .... 1.00
- ❑5 .... 1.00
- ❑6 .... 1.00

EXPOSE
Cracked Pepper

Value: Cover or less

- ❑1, Dec 93, b&w 2.50

EXPOSURE
Image

Value: Cover or less

- ❑1, Black Sabbath 2.50
- ❑2, The Strange Case of Mrs. Christenson!, Part 1 .... 2.50
- ❑2/A, The Strange Case of Mrs. Christenson!, Part 1, Photo cover 2.50
- ❑3, Jan 00, The Strange Case of Mrs. Christenson!, Part 2 .... 2.50
- ❑4 .... 2.50
- ❑5, Second Coming 3.50
- ❑6, Second Coming 3.50

EXQUISITE CORPSE
Dark Horse

Value: Cover or less

- ❑1, Yellow issue 2.50
- ❑2, Red Issue 2.50
- ❑3, Green Issue 2.50

EXTINCT!
New England

Value: Cover or less

- ❑1, b&w; Reprint 3.50
- ❑2, b&w; Reprint 3.50

EXTINCTIONERS
Shanda Fantasy Arts

Value: Cover or less

- ❑1, Apr 99, b&w — 2.95
- ❑2 — 2.95

EXTRA! (GEMSTONE)
Gemstone

Value: Cover or less

- ❑1, Jan 00, JSe; JCr, JSe (w); JCr (w), Dateline: Cayo Romano, Cuba!; Camera! — 2.50
- ❑2, JSe; JCr, JSe (w); JCr (w), Dateline: Oslo; Stromboli — 2.50
- ❑3, JSe; JCr, JSe (w); JCr (w), Dateline: Algiers; Steve Rampart — 2.50
- ❑4, JSe; JCr, JSe (w); JCr (w), Dateline: New York City; Steve Rampart — 2.50
- ❑5, JSe; JCr, JSe (w); JCr (w), Dateline: Long Island Sound; Steve Rampart — 2.50
- ❑Anl 1 — 13.50

EXTRA TERRESTRIAL TRIO, THE
Smiling Face

Value: Cover or less

- ❑1 — 2.95

EXTREME
Image

	ORIG	GOOD	FINE	N-MINT
❑0, Aug 93, RL, RL (w), Cybrid; Law & Order	2.50	0.50	1.25	2.50
❑0/A, Aug 93, RL, RL (w), Cybrid; Law & Order	2.50	0.50	1.25	2.50
❑0/B, Aug 93, RL, RL (w), Cybrid; Law & Order, San Diego Con edition	2.50	0.50	1.25	2.50
❑0/GO, Aug 93, RL, RL (w), Cybrid; Law & Order, Gold edition	—	0.60	1.50	3.00
❑HS 1, RL, RL (w), Cybrid; Law & Order, nn; no cover price; "Extreme Hero" promotional edition from Hero Magazine	—	0.20	0.50	1.00

EXTREME DESTROYER EPILOGUE
Image

Value: Cover or less

- ❑1, Jan 96, RL (w) — 2.50

EXTREME DESTROYER PROLOGUE
Image

Value: Cover or less

- ❑1, Jan 96, RL (w), bagged with card — 2.50

EXTREME JUSTICE
DC

	ORIG	GOOD	FINE	N-MINT
❑0, Jan 95	1.50	0.40	1.00	2.00
❑1, Feb 95, Mad Dogs and Super-Heroes	1.50	0.35	0.88	1.75
❑2, Mar 95	1.50	0.35	0.88	1.75
❑3, Apr 95	1.50	0.35	0.88	1.75
❑4, May 95	1.50	0.35	0.88	1.75
❑5, Jun 95	1.75	0.35	0.88	1.75
❑6, Jul 95	1.75	0.35	0.88	1.75
❑7, Aug 95	1.75	0.35	0.88	1.75
❑8, Sep 95	1.75	0.35	0.88	1.75
❑9, Oct 95, 1: Zan and Jayna	1.75	0.35	0.88	1.75
❑10, Nov 95	1.75	0.35	0.88	1.75
❑11, Dec 95	1.75	0.35	0.88	1.75
❑12, Jan 96	1.75	0.35	0.88	1.75
❑13, Feb 96, King's Heeling, V: Monarch	1.75	0.35	0.88	1.75
❑14, Mar 96, Kings Revealed and Kings Revealing	1.75	0.35	0.88	1.75
❑15, Apr 96, Duel of Duals	1.75	0.35	0.88	1.75
❑16, May 96	1.75	0.35	0.88	1.75
❑17, Jun 96	1.75	0.35	0.88	1.75
❑18, Jul 96, Final Issue	1.75	0.35	0.88	1.75

EXTREME SACRIFICE
Image

Value: Cover or less

- ❑1, Jan 95, RL, RL (w), Prelude, polybagged with trading card — 2.50
- ❑2, Jan 95, RL, RL (w), Epilogue — 2.50

EXTREMES OF VIOLET
Blackout

Value: Cover or less

- ❑0 — 2.95
- ❑1 — 2.95
- ❑2 — 2.95

EXTREME SUPER CHRISTMAS SPECIAL
Image

Value: Cover or less

- ❑1, Dec 94 — 2.95

EXTREME SUPER TOUR BOOK
Image

	ORIG	GOOD	FINE	N-MINT
❑1	—	0.20	0.50	1.00
❑1/GO, Gold edition	—	0.40	1.00	2.00

EXTREME TOUR BOOK
Image

	ORIG	GOOD	FINE	N-MINT
❑1, no cover price	—	0.50	1.25	2.50
❑1/GO, Gold edition	—	0.50	1.25	2.50

EXTREMIST, THE
DC

	ORIG	GOOD	FINE	N-MINT
❑1, Sep 93, 1: The Extremist	1.95	0.50	1.25	2.50
❑1/PL, Sep 93, 1: The Extremist, Platinum edition	—	0.80	2.00	4.00
❑2, Oct 93	1.95	0.50	1.25	2.50
❑3, Nov 93	1.95	0.50	1.25	2.50
❑4, Dec 93	1.95	0.50	1.25	2.50

EYE, THE
Hamster

Value: Cover or less

- ❑SE 1, Jun 99, Face to Face with Myopia!, Special edition — 2.95

EYEBALL KID, THE
Dark Horse

	ORIG	GOOD	FINE	N-MINT
❑1, 1: Eyeball Kid (in comic books), b&w	2.25	0.50	1.25	2.50
❑2, b&w	2.25	0.50	1.25	2.50
❑3, b&w; Final Issue	2.25	0.50	1.25	2.50

EYEBEAM
Adhesive

Value: Cover or less

- ❑1, b&w; strip reprints — 2.50
- ❑2, b&w; strip reprints — 2.50
- ❑3, b&w; strip reprints — 2.50
- ❑4, b&w; strip reprints — 2.50
- ❑5, b&w; strip reprints — 2.50

EYE OF MONGOMBO
Fantagraphics

Value: Cover or less

- ❑1, b&w — 2.00
- ❑2, b&w — 2.00
- ❑3, b&w — 2.00
- ❑4, b&w — 2.00
- ❑5, b&w — 2.00
- ❑6, b&w — 2.00
- ❑7, Dec 91, b&w — 2.25

EYE OF THE STORM
Rival

Value: Cover or less

- ❑1, Dec 94 — 2.95

EXTREMELY SILLY
Antarctic

	ORIG	GOOD	FINE	N-MINT
❑1	—	0.60	1.50	3.00

EXTREMELY SILLY (VOL. 2)
Antarctic

Value: Cover or less

- ❑1, Nov 96, b&w; Star Trek parody — 1.25

EXTREMELY YOUNGBLOOD
Image

Value: Cover or less

- ❑1, Sep 96, One-Shot — 3.50

EXTREME PREJUDICE
Image

Value: Cover or less

- ❑0, Nov 94 — 2.50

EXTREME PREVIEWS
Image

	ORIG	GOOD	FINE	N-MINT
❑1, Mar 96	—	0.20	0.50	1.00

EXTREME PREVIEWS 1997
Image

	ORIG	GOOD	FINE	N-MINT
❑1, nn; no cover price; pin-ups	—	0.20	0.50	1.00

F

F-3 BANDIT
Antarctic

Value: Cover or less

- ❑1, Jan 95, mini-poster — 2.95
- ❑2, Mar 95, American Were-woman, trading card — 2.95
- ❑3, May 95, Alto Through the Look-ing-glass, trading card — 2.95
- ❑4, Jul 95, trading card — 2.95
- ❑5, Sep 95, trading card — 2.95
- ❑6, Nov 95 — 2.95
- ❑7, Jan 96 — 2.95
- ❑8, Mar 96 — 2.95
- ❑9, May 96, b&w — 2.95
- ❑10, Jul 96, b&w; Final Issue; trading card — 2.95

F5
Image

	ORIG	GOOD	FINE	N-MINT
❑1	—	0.59	1.48	2.95
❑2, Jun 00	2.50	0.50	1.25	2.50
❑3, Aug 00	2.50	0.50	1.25	2.50
❑4, Oct 00	2.50	0.50	1.25	2.50
❑Ash 1, Jan 00, Preview issue	2.50	0.50	1.25	2.50

FAANS
Six Handed Press

Value: Cover or less

- ❑1, b&w — 2.95

FABLES BY THE BROTHERS DIMM
Dimm

Value: Cover or less

- ❑1, Apr 95, The Electric Forest; Ragnarok!, b&w — 1.50

FABULOUS FURRY FREAK BROTHERS, THE
Rip Off

	ORIG	GOOD	FINE	N-MINT
❑0, 1985 Compilation	2.95	0.59	1.48	2.95
❑1, The Freaks Pull A Heist; Freak Brothers Go To College!, b&w; Collected Adventures of the...; 1971	0.70	11.00	27.50	55.00
❑1-2, The Freaks Pull A Heist; Freak Brothers Go To College!, Collected Adventures of the...; 1980	2.95	0.59	1.48	2.95
❑2, Shootout at the County Slammer; Buster Foyt Esq., b&w; Further Adventures of the...	0.50	7.00	17.50	35.00
❑2-2, Shootout at the County Slammer; Buster Foyt Esq., Further Adventures of the...; 1989	2.95	0.59	1.48	2.95
❑3, The Adventures of Freewheelin' Franklin; Government Spies, b&w; A Year Passes Like Nothing With...	0.50	3.00	7.50	15.00

	ORIG	GOOD	FINE	N-MINT
❑4, The 7th Voyage of the Fabulous Furry Freak Brothers: A Mexican Odyssey, b&w; Brother Can You Spare 75¢ For...	0.75	2.60	6.50	13.00
❑5, b&w; Fabulous Furry Freak Brothers	—	2.00	5.00	10.00
❑6, b&w; Six Snappy Sockeroos From the Archives Of...	—	0.80	2.00	4.00
❑7, b&w	2.50	0.40	1.00	2.00
❑8, full color	2.95	0.40	1.00	2.00
❑9, full color	2.95	0.40	1.00	2.00
❑10, full color	2.95	0.40	1.00	2.00
❑11, full color	2.50	0.59	1.48	2.95
❑12, b&w	2.95	0.59	1.48	2.95
❑13, b&w; reprints stories from High Times.	2.95	0.59	1.48	2.95

FACE
DC

Value: Cover or less

- ❑1, Jan 95 ... 4.95

FACTOR-X
MARVEL

	ORIG	GOOD	FINE	N-MINT
❑1, Mar 95, Sinister Neglect	1.95	0.40	1.00	2.00
❑2, Apr 95	1.95	0.40	1.00	2.00
❑3, May 95	1.95	0.40	1.00	2.00
❑4, Jun 95	1.95	0.40	1.00	2.00

FACULTY FUNNIES
ARCHIE

	ORIG	GOOD	FINE	N-MINT
❑1, Jun 89	0.75	0.60	1.50	3.00
❑2	0.75	0.40	1.00	2.00
❑3	0.75	0.40	1.00	2.00
❑4	0.75	0.40	1.00	2.00
❑5	0.75	0.40	1.00	2.00

FAERIE CODEX
RAVEN

Value: Cover or less

- ❑1, b&w ... 2.95
- ❑2, b&w ... 2.95
- ❑3, Dec 97, b&w ... 2.95

FAFHRD AND THE GRAY MOUSER
MARVEL

Value: Cover or less

- ❑1, Oct 90, AW; MM, HC (w), Ill Met in Lankhmar ... 4.50
- ❑2, AW; MM, HC (w), The Circle Curse; The Howling Tower.. 4.50
- ❑3, AW; MM, HC (w), The Price of Pain Ease; Bazaar of the Bizarre ... 4.50
- ❑4, AW; MM, HC (w), Lean Times in Lankhmar; When The Sea King's Away ... 4.50

FAILED UNIVERSE
BLACKTHORNE

Value: Cover or less

- ❑1, Dec 86, Make Mine Mediocre ... 1.75

FAITH
DC

Value: Cover or less

- ❑1, Nov 99, An Act of Confession ... 2.50
- ❑2, Dec 99, The Coverage of Sound ... 2.50
- ❑3, Jan 00, Satanico Pandemonium ... 2.50
- ❑4, Feb 00 ... 2.50
- ❑5, Mar 00, Coma Monkeys.... 2.50

FAITH (LIGHTNING)
LIGHTNING

Value: Cover or less

- ❑1/A, Jul 97, b&w ... 2.95

FAITH: A FABLE
CARBON-BASED BOOKS

Value: Cover or less

- ❑1, Jan 00, nn; b&w; Trade Paperback; smaller than normal comic book ... 8.95

FALCON
MARVEL

	ORIG	GOOD	FINE	N-MINT
❑1, Nov 83, PS	0.60	0.30	0.75	1.50
❑2, Dec 83	0.60	0.30	0.75	1.50
❑3, Jan 84	0.60	0.30	0.75	1.50
❑4, Feb 84	0.60	0.30	0.75	1.50

FALL, THE (BIG BAD WORLD)
BIG BAD WORLD

Value: Cover or less

- ❑1, b&w ... 3.00

FALL, THE (CALIBER)
CALIBER

Value: Cover or less

- ❑1, b&w ... 2.95

FALLEN ANGEL ON THE WORLD OF MAGIC: THE GATHERING
ACCLAIM

Value: Cover or less

- ❑1, May 96, One-Shot; prestige format; polybagged with Fallen Angel card ... 5.95

FALLEN ANGELS
MARVEL

Howard Chaykin took a second swing at adapting Fritz Leiber's Lankhmar stories in Marvel's *Fafhrd and the Gray Mouser* mini-series.

© 1990 Marvel

	ORIG	GOOD	FINE	N-MINT
❑1, Apr 87	0.75	0.30	0.75	1.50
❑2, May 87	0.75	0.25	0.63	1.25
❑3, Jun 87, 1: Chance II	0.75	0.25	0.63	1.25
❑4, Jul 87	0.75	0.25	0.63	1.25
❑5, Aug 87, D: Don	0.75	0.25	0.63	1.25
❑6, Sep 87	0.75	0.25	0.63	1.25
❑7, Oct 87	0.75	0.25	0.63	1.25
❑8, Nov 87	0.75	0.25	0.63	1.25

FALLEN EMPIRES ON THE WORLD OF MAGIC: THE GATHERING
ACCLAIM

Value: Cover or less

- ❑1, Sep 95, Rumors of War, Magic cards; polybagged with pack of Fallen Empires cards ... 2.75
- ❑2, Oct 95, polybagged with sheet of creature tokens ... 2.75

FALLING MAN, THE
IMAGE

Value: Cover or less

- ❑1, Feb 98, b&w ... 2.95

FALLOUT 3000 (MIKE DEODATO'S...)
CALIBER

Value: Cover or less

- ❑1 ... 2.95

FALLS THE GOTHAM RAIN
COMICO

Value: Cover or less

- ❑1 ... 4.95

FAMILY AFFAIR
GOLD KEY

	ORIG	GOOD	FINE	N-MINT
❑1, Feb 70, poster	0.15	4.40	11.00	22.00
❑2	0.15	3.60	9.00	18.00
❑3, Jul 70	0.15	2.40	6.00	12.00
❑4, Oct 70, Final Issue	0.15	2.40	6.00	12.00

FAMILY MAN
DC

Value: Cover or less

- ❑1, JSa, To Protect and Serve, b&w; digest ... 4.95
- ❑2, b&w; digest ... 4.95
- ❑3, b&w; digest ... 4.95

FAMOUS FEATURES (JERRY IGER'S ...)
PACIFIC

	ORIG	GOOD	FINE	N-MINT
❑1, Jul 84, Flamingo	1.50	0.40	1.00	2.00

FAMOUS FIRST EDITION
DC

	ORIG	GOOD	FINE	N-MINT
❑4, Nov 74, really F-4; reprints Whiz Comics #2	1.00	2.00	5.00	10.00
❑5, Jan 75, really F-5; reprints Batman #1..	1.00	1.60	4.00	8.00
❑6, May 75, really F-6; reprints Wonder Woman #1	1.00	1.60	4.00	8.00
❑7, Jul 75, really F-7; reprints All-Star #3....	1.00	2.00	5.00	10.00
❑8, Sep 75, really F-8; reprints Flash Comics #1	1.00	1.60	4.00	8.00
❑26, Superman, 1: Superman, really C-26; reprints Action Comics #1	1.00	1.60	4.00	8.00
❑28, really C-28; reprints Detective Comics #1; reprints Detective Comics #27	1.00	1.60	4.00	8.00
❑30, 1: Wonder Woman, really C-30; reprints Sensation Comics #1	1.00	1.60	4.00	8.00
❑61, Mar 79, really C-61; reprints Superman #1	1.00	1.20	3.00	6.00

FANA
COMAX

Value: Cover or less

- ❑1, b&w; adult ... 2.95

FANA THE JUNGLE GIRL
COMAX

Value: Cover or less

- ❑1, b&w ... 2.95

FANBOY
DC

Value: Cover or less

- ❑1, Mar 99, SA, ME (w), A: Superman ... 2.50
- ❑2, Apr 99, KN; GK; DaG; SA; WP, ME (w), A: Green Lantern ... 2.50
- ❑3, May 99, BA; BSz; SA, ME (w), A: JLA ... 2.50
- ❑4, Jun 99, SA, ME (w), Our Fanboy at War, A: Sgt. Rock, Our Army at War take-off ... 2.50
- ❑5, Jul 99, ME (w), A: Batman ... 2.50
- ❑6, Aug 99, SA, ME (w), A: Wonder Woman ... 2.50

FANG (CONQUEST)
CONQUEST

Value: Cover or less

- ❑1, b&w ... 2.95

FANG (SIRIUS)
SIRIUS ENTERTAINMENT

Value: Cover or less

- ❑1, Feb 95 ... 2.95
- ❑2, Apr 95 ... 2.95
- ❑3, Jun 95 ... 2.95

FANG (TANGRAM)
TANGRAM

Value: Cover or less

❑1, nn; b&w ... 2.95

FANGRAPHIX
FANGRAPHIX

Value: Cover or less

❑1 ... 1.95
❑2 ... 1.95
❑3 ... 1.95

FANGS OF THE COBRA
MYTHIC

Value: Cover or less

❑1, Win 96, color and b&w ... 2.95

FANG: TESTAMENT
SIRIUS ENTERTAINMENT

Value: Cover or less

❑1 ... 2.50
❑2 ... 2.50
❑3 ... 2.50
❑4 ... 2.50

FANNY
FANNY

	ORIG	GOOD	FINE	N-MINT
❑1	—	0.60	1.50	3.00
❑2	—	0.60	1.50	3.00
❑3, b&w	3.95	0.79	1.98	3.95

FANNY HILL
SHUNGA

Value: Cover or less

❑1, b&w; adult ... 2.50

FANTAESCAPE
ZINZINNATI

Value: Cover or less

❑1, Jun 88 ... 1.75

FANTAGOR
LAST GASP

	ORIG	GOOD	FINE	N-MINT
❑1, Twilight of The Dogs; Razar The Unhero	0.50	0.60	1.50	3.00
❑2	0.50	0.60	1.50	3.00
❑3, The Temple; Fugue	0.50	0.60	1.50	3.00

FANTASCI
APPLE

	ORIG	GOOD	FINE	N-MINT
❑1, Dull to Dynamic in One Difficult Lesson; A Hero Named Harold, b&w	1.50	0.40	1.00	2.00
❑2, Hunter XX: Storm Patterns; The Elves of Awe San Tan, b&w	1.50	0.40	1.00	2.00
❑3, Feelings, Wo-Wo-Wo Feelings; A Hero Named Harold, b&w; Apple Comics publisher Begins	1.50	0.40	1.00	2.00
❑4, The Fatman Boogie; Swamp thingies, Questions Without Answers!	1.75	0.40	1.00	2.00
❑5	1.75	0.35	0.88	1.75
❑6	1.75	0.35	0.88	1.75
❑7	1.75	0.35	0.88	1.75
❑8, Jul 88	1.75	0.35	0.88	1.75
❑9	1.95	0.39	0.98	1.95

FANTASTIC ADVENTURES (ACE)
ACE

Value: Cover or less

❑1, Mar 87, GT, GT (w), Skool Yardley: ...Our man on the Corner; The Ace Killer From Outer Space ... 1.75
❑2, Jun 87 ... 1.75
❑3, Oct 87 ... 1.75

FANTASTIC FABLES (BASIL WOLVERTON'S...)
DARK HORSE

Value: Cover or less

❑1, Oct 93, BW, BW (w), Meteor Morgan; Spacehawk, b&w; Reprint ... 2.50
❑2 ... 2.50

FANTASTIC FANZINE
ARROW

Value: Cover or less

❑1 ... 1.50
❑2 ... 1.50
❑3 ... 1.50

FANTASTIC FIVE
MARVEL

Value: Cover or less

❑1, Oct 99 ... 1.99
❑2, Nov 99 ... 1.99
❑2/A, Nov 99, variant cover ... 1.99
❑3, Dec 99, Side by Side with Spider-Girl! ... 1.99

FANTASTIC FORCE
MARVEL

	ORIG	GOOD	FINE	N-MINT
❑1, Nov 94, Legacy, 1: Fantastic Force, foil cover	2.50	0.50	1.25	2.50
❑2, Dec 94	1.75	0.40	1.00	2.00
❑3, Jan 95	1.75	0.40	1.00	2.00
❑4, Feb 95	1.75	0.35	0.88	1.75
❑5, Mar 95	1.75	0.35	0.88	1.75
❑6, Apr 95	1.75	0.35	0.88	1.75
❑7, May 95	1.75	0.35	0.88	1.75
❑8, Jun 95	1.75	0.35	0.88	1.75
❑9, Jul 95	1.75	0.35	0.88	1.75
❑10, Aug 95	1.75	0.35	0.88	1.75
❑11, Sep 95	1.75	0.35	0.88	1.75
❑12, Oct 95, Moments of Truth	1.75	0.35	0.88	1.75
❑13, Nov 95, She-Hulk joins team	1.75	0.35	0.88	1.75
❑14, Dec 95, A: Wakanda; A: Human Torch; A: Black Panther; A: She-Hulk	1.75	0.35	0.88	1.75
❑15, Jan 96, cover says Jan 95, indicia says Jan 96; Team disbands	1.75	0.35	0.88	1.75
❑16, Feb 96	1.75	0.35	0.88	1.75
❑17, Mar 96, Agendas Diabolik!	1.75	0.35	0.88	1.75
❑18, Apr 96, A Force of One, Final Issue	1.75	0.35	0.88	1.75

FANTASTIC FOUR (VOL. 1)
MARVEL

	ORIG	GOOD	FINE	N-MINT
❑1, Nov 61, JK, SL (w); JK (w), The Fantastic Four, 1: FF, Mole Man; 1: Fantastic Four, Mole Man	0.10	3300.00	8250.00	16500.00
❑1/GR, JK, SL (w); JK (w), The Fantastic Four, Golden Record reprint	—	36.00	90.00	180.00
❑2, Jan 62, JK, SL (w); JK (w), The Fantastic Four Meet the Skrulls from Outer Space; Prisoner of the Skrulls, O: The Fantastic Four; 1: The Skrulls	0.10	640.00	1600.00	3200.00
❑3, Mar 62, JK, SL (w); JK (w), The Menace of the Miracle Man; The Monster Lives, 1: Baxter Building; 1: Pogo Plane; 1: Fantasti-Car; 1: The Miracle Man (Marvel); 1: Fantasti-Copter, Fantastic Four wear uniforms for first time	0.12	440.00	1100.00	2200.00
❑4, May 62, JK, SL (w); JK (w), The Coming of the Sub-Mariner; On the Trail of the Torch, D: Giganto; 1: Sub-Mariner (in Silver Age)	0.12	480.00	1200.00	2400.00
❑5, Jul 62, JK, SL (w); JK (w), Prisoners of Doctor Doom; Back to the Past, 1: Doctor Doom	0.12	540.00	1350.00	2700.00
❑6, Sep 62, JK, SL (w); JK (w), Captives of the Deadly Duo; When Super-Menaces Unite, A: Doctor Doom; 1: The Yancy Street Gang (name only), Doctor Doom & Sub-Mariner vs. Fantastic Four	0.12	240.00	600.00	1200.00
❑7, Oct 62, JK, SL (w); JK (w), Prisoners of Kurrgo, Master of Planet X; It Came from the Skies, 1: The Xantha; 1: Kurrgo	0.12	145.00	362.50	725.00
❑8, Nov 62, JK, SL (w); JK (w), Prisoners of the Puppet Master; The Hands of the Puppet Maker, 1: Alicia Masters; 1: Puppet Master	0.12	140.00	350.00	700.00
❑9, Dec 62, JK, SL (w); JK (w), The End of the Fantastic Four; Sub-Mariner Gives the Orders, A: Sub-Mariner	0.12	140.00	350.00	700.00
❑10, Jan 63, JK, SL (w); JK (w), The Return of Doctor Doom; Back from the Dread, 1: Stan Lee (as character in story); 1: Jack Kirby (as character in story); V: Doctor Doom; 1: The Ovoids	0.12	140.00	350.00	700.00
❑11, Feb 63, JK, SL (w); JK (w), A Visit with the Fantastic Four; The Impossible Man, 1: The Popuppians; 1: Impossible Man; 1: Willie Lumpkin (Fantastic Four's mailman)-Silver Age; O: Fantastic Four	0.12	110.00	275.00	550.00
❑12, Mar 63, JK, SL (w); JK (w), The Incredible Hulk; Mission: Stop the Hulk, 1: The Wrecker I (Dr. Karl Kort); V: Hulk, Thing fights Hulk for 1st time	0.12	220.00	550.00	1100.00
❑13, Apr 63, JK, SL (w); JK (w), The Fantastic Four, Versus the Red Ghost and His Indescribable Super-Apes; Menace on the Moon, 1: The Watcher; 1: Red Ghost	0.12	90.00	225.00	450.00
❑14, May 63, JK, SL (w); JK (w), The Merciless Puppet Master, V: Sub-Mariner; V: Puppet Master	0.12	60.00	150.00	300.00
❑15, Jun 63, JK, SL (w); JK (w), The Fantastic Four Battle the Mad Thinker and His Awesome Android, 1: Mad Thinker; 1: Awesome Android	0.12	60.00	150.00	300.00
❑16, Jul 63, JK, A: The Wasp; V: Doctor Doom; A: Ant Man; V: Dr. Doom	0.12	60.00	150.00	300.00
❑17, Aug 63, JK, V: Doctor Doom; A: Ant Man; V: Dr. Doom	0.12	60.00	150.00	300.00
❑18, Sep 63, JK, 1: Super-Skrull	0.12	60.00	150.00	300.00
❑19, Oct 63, JK, 1: Rama-Tut	0.12	60.00	150.00	300.00
❑20, Nov 63, JK, A: Watcher; 1: Molecule Man	0.12	65.00	162.50	325.00
❑21, Dec 63, JK, 1: Hate-Monger; A: Nick Fury	0.12	40.00	100.00	200.00
❑22, Jan 64, JK, V: Mole Man	0.12	28.00	70.00	140.00
❑23, Feb 64, JK, V: Doctor Doom	0.12	28.00	70.00	140.00
❑24, Mar 64, JK, 1: Moloids	0.12	28.00	70.00	140.00
❑25, Apr 64, JK, A: Avengers; A: Avengers, Rick Jones; A: Rick Jones; V: Hulk, first mention of Thing's Aunt Petunia; Hulk Battles Thing	0.12	77.00	192.50	385.00
❑26, May 64, JK, A: Avengers; A: Rick Jones; V: Hulk	0.12	77.00	192.50	385.00
❑27, Jun 64, JK, V: Sub-Mariner; A: Doctor Strange	0.12	28.00	70.00	140.00
❑28, Jul 64, JK, V: Mad Thinker; V: Puppet Master; A: X-Men	0.12	42.00	105.00	210.00
❑29, Aug 64, JK, A: Watcher; V: Red Ghost	0.12	22.00	55.00	110.00
❑30, Sep 64, JK, 1: Diablo	0.12	22.00	55.00	110.00
❑31, Oct 64, JK, V: Mole Man; A: Avengers	0.12	17.00	42.50	85.00
❑32, Nov 64, JK, 1: Sue and Johnny's parents (Franklin and Mary); V: Super-Skrull	0.12	17.00	42.50	85.00

	ORIG	GOOD	FINE	N-MINT
❑33, Dec 64, JK, A: Sub-Mariner; 1: Attuma	0.12	17.00	42.50	85.00
❑34, Jan 65, JK, 1: Thomas Gideon (later becomes Glorian)	0.12	17.00	42.50	85.00
❑35, Feb 65, JK, V: Diablo; 1: Dragon Man	0.12	17.00	42.50	85.00
❑36, Mar 65, JK, 1: Medusa; 1: Frightful Four	0.12	17.00	42.50	85.00
❑37, Apr 65, JK	0.12	17.00	42.50	85.00
❑38, May 65, JK, 1: Trapster I (Peter Petruski); A: Frightful Four, Paste-Pot Pete becomes Trapster I	0.12	17.00	42.50	85.00
❑39, Jun 65, JK, V: Doctor Doom; A: Daredevil	0.12	17.00	42.50	85.00
❑40, Jul 65, JK, V: Doctor Doom; A: Daredevil	0.12	17.00	42.50	85.00
❑41, Aug 65, JK, V: Frightful Four	0.12	9.00	22.50	45.00
❑42, Sep 65, JK, V: Frightful Four	0.12	9.00	22.50	45.00
❑43, Oct 65, JK, V: Doctor Doom; V: Dr. Doom; V: Frightful Four	0.12	9.00	22.50	45.00
❑44, Nov 65, JK, SL (w), The Gentleman's Name is Gorgon!, 1: Gorgon; A: Medusa; A: Dragon Man	0.12	9.00	22.50	45.00
❑45, Dec 65, JK, A: Sandman; 1: Black Bolt; 1: Lockjaw; A: Trapster I; 1: Triton; 1: Crystal; V: Dragon Man; V: Maximus; 1: Inhumans; 1: Karnak	0.12	11.00	27.50	55.00
❑46, Jan 66, JK, SL (w); JK (w), Those Who Would Destroy Us, A: Inhumans	0.12	10.00	25.00	50.00
❑47, Feb 66, JK, SL (w); JK (w), Beware the Hidden Land, V: Maximus; A: Inhumans	0.12	9.00	22.50	45.00
❑48, Mar 66, JK, SL (w); JK (w), The Coming of Galactus, 1: Silver Surfer; A: Inhumans; 1: Galactus	0.12	180.00	450.00	900.00
❑49, Apr 66, JK, SL (w); JK (w), If This Be Doomsday, A: Watcher; A: Silver Surfer; V: Galactus	0.12	49.00	122.50	245.00
❑50, May 66, JK, SL (w); JK (w), The Starting Saga of the Silver Surfer, A: Watcher; A: Silver Surfer; 1: Wyatt Wingfoot; V: Galactus	0.12	53.00	132.50	265.00
❑51, Jun 66, JK, SL (w); JK (w), This Man, This Monster, 1: Negative Zone	0.12	8.40	21.00	42.00
❑52, Jul 66, JK, SL (w); JK (w), The Black Panther, 1: Black Panther, (had costume with cape); (had costume with cape)	0.12	15.00	37.50	75.00
❑53, Aug 66, JK, SL (w); JK (w), The Way It Began, 1: Klaw; 2: Black Panther	0.12	10.00	25.00	50.00
❑54, Sep 66, JK, SL (w); JK (w), Whosoever Finds the Evil Eye, 1: Prester John; A: Black Panther; A: Inhumans	0.12	8.00	20.00	40.00
❑55, Oct 66, JK, SL (w); JK (w), When Strikes the Silver Surfer, A: Silver Surfer, Thing vs. Silver Surfer	0.12	13.00	32.50	65.00
❑56, Nov 66, JK, SL (w); JK (w), Klaw, the Murderous Master of Sound, V: Klaw	0.12	9.00	22.50	45.00
❑57, Dec 66, JK, SL (w); JK (w), Enter Doctor Doom, V: Sandman; V: Wizard; V: Doctor Doom; A: Inhumans	0.12	9.00	22.50	45.00
❑58, Jan 67, JK, SL (w); JK (w), The Dismal Dregs of Defeat, A: Silver Surfer; A: Lockjaw; V: Doctor Doom	0.12	9.00	22.50	45.00
❑59, Feb 67, JK, SL (w); JK (w), Doomsday, A: Silver Surfer; V: Doctor Doom; A: Inhumans	0.12	9.00	22.50	45.00
❑60, Mar 67, JK, SL (w); JK (w), The Peril and the Power, A: Watcher; A: Silver Surfer; V: Doctor Doom; A: Black Panther; A: Inhumans	0.12	9.00	22.50	45.00
❑61, Apr 67, JK, SL (w); JK (w), Where Stalks the Sandman?, V: Sandman; A: Silver Surfer; A: Inhumans	0.12	7.60	19.00	38.00
❑62, May 67, JK, SL (w); JK (w), And One Shall Save Him, A: Sandman; 1: Blastaar	0.12	7.60	19.00	38.00
❑63, Jun 67, JK, SL (w); JK (w), Blastaar, The Living Bomb-Burst, V: Sandman; V: Blastaar	0.12	7.60	19.00	38.00
❑64, Jul 67, JK, SL (w); JK (w), The Sentry Sinister, 1: Supreme Intelligence	0.12	7.60	19.00	38.00
❑65, Aug 67, JK, SL (w); JK (w), From Beyond This Planet Earth, 1: Ronan the Accuser; 1: Kree Supreme Intelligence; 1: Kree	0.12	7.60	19.00	38.00
❑66, Sep 67, JK, SL (w); JK (w), What Lurks Behind the Beehive, 1: The Enclave (unnamed); 1: Him (later Warlock); O: The Enclave; A: Crystal	0.12	7.00	17.50	35.00
❑67, Oct 67, JK, SL (w); JK (w), When Opens the Cocoon, A: Him (later Warlock)	0.12	8.00	20.00	40.00
❑68, Nov 67, JK, SL (w); JK (w), His Mission: Destroy the Fantastic Four, V: Mad Thinker	0.12	6.00	15.00	30.00
❑69, Dec 67, JK, SL (w); JK (w), By Ben Betrayed!, V: Mad Thinker	0.12	6.00	15.00	30.00
❑70, Jan 68, JK, SL (w); JK (w), When Fall The Mighty, V: Mad Thinker	0.12	6.00	15.00	30.00
❑71, Feb 68, JK, SL (w); JK (w), And So It Ends, V: Mad Thinker	0.12	5.20	13.00	26.00
❑72, Mar 68, JK, SL (w); JK (w), Where Soars the Silver Surfer, A: Silver Surfer	0.12	7.00	17.50	35.00
❑73, Apr 68, JK, SL (w); JK (w), The Flames of Battle, V: Doctor Doom; A: Thor; A: Spider-Man; A: Daredevil	0.12	5.60	14.00	28.00

Published in late 1961, *Fantastic Four* (Vol. 1) #1 initiated what came to be known as "The Marvel Age of Comics."

© 1961 Marvel

	ORIG	GOOD	FINE	N-MINT
❑74, May 68, JK, SL (w); JK (w), When Calls Galactus, A: Silver Surfer; V: Galactus	0.12	6.00	15.00	30.00
❑75, Jun 68, JK, SL (w); JK (w), Worlds Within Worlds, A: Silver Surfer; V: Galactus	0.12	6.00	15.00	30.00
❑76, Jul 68, JK, SL (w); JK (w), Stranded in Sub-Atomica, A: Silver Surfer; V: Psycho-Man; V: Galactus	0.12	5.60	14.00	28.00
❑77, Aug 68, JK, SL (w); JK (w), Shall Earth Endure?, A: Silver Surfer; V: Psycho-Man; V: Galactus	0.12	5.60	14.00	28.00
❑78, Sep 68, JK, SL (w); JK (w), The Thing No More!, V: Wizard	0.12	5.60	14.00	28.00
❑79, Oct 68, JK, SL (w); JK (w), A Monster Forever?, V: Mad Thinker	0.12	5.60	14.00	28.00
❑80, Nov 68, JK, SL (w); JK (w), Where Treads the Living Totem	0.12	5.60	14.00	28.00
❑81, Dec 68, JK, SL (w); JK (w), Enter-The Exquisite Elemental, V: Wizard, Crystal joins Fantastic Four	0.12	4.40	11.00	22.00
❑82, Jan 69, JK, SL (w); JK (w), The Mark of the Madman, V: Maximus; A: Inhumans	0.12	4.40	11.00	22.00
❑83, Feb 69, JK, SL (w); JK (w), Shall Man Survive?, V: Maximus; A: Inhumans	0.12	4.40	11.00	22.00
❑84, Mar 69, JK, SL (w); JK (w), The Name Is Doom, V: Doctor Doom	0.12	4.40	11.00	22.00
❑85, Apr 69, JK, SL (w); JK (w), Within This Tortured Land, V: Doctor Doom	0.12	4.40	11.00	22.00
❑86, May 69, JK, SL (w); JK (w), The Victims, V: Doctor Doom	0.12	4.40	11.00	22.00
❑87, Jun 69, JK, SL (w); JK (w), The Power And The Pride!, V: Doctor Doom	0.12	4.40	11.00	22.00
❑88, Jul 69, JK, SL (w); JK (w), A House There Was!, V: Mole Man	0.12	4.40	11.00	22.00
❑89, Aug 69, JK, SL (w); JK (w), The Madness of the Mole Man, V: Mole Man	0.15	3.60	9.00	18.00
❑90, Sep 69, JK, SL (w); JK (w), The Skrull Takes a Slave, V: Mole Man	0.15	3.60	9.00	18.00
❑91, Oct 69, JK, SL (w); JK (w), The Thing Enslaved, 1: Torgo	0.15	3.60	9.00	18.00
❑92, Nov 69, JK, SL (w); JK (w), Ben Grimm, Killer!, V: Torgo	0.15	3.60	9.00	18.00
❑93, Dec 69, JK, SL (w); JK (w), At the Mercy of Torgo, V: Torgo	0.15	3.60	9.00	18.00
❑94, Jan 70, JK, SL (w); JK (w), The Return of the Frightful Four, V: Sandman; V: Wizard; V: Trapster; 1: Agatha Harkness	0.15	3.60	9.00	18.00
❑95, Feb 70, JK, SL (w); JK (w), Tomorrow, World War Three, 1: The Monocle	0.15	3.60	9.00	18.00
❑96, Mar 70, JK, SL (w); JK (w), The Mad Thinker and His Androids of Death, V: Mad Thinker	0.15	3.60	9.00	18.00
❑97, Apr 70, JK, SL (w); JK (w), The Monster from the Lost Lagoon	0.15	3.60	9.00	18.00
❑98, May 70, JK, SL (w); JK (w), Mystery on the Moon, A: Neil Armstrong	0.15	3.60	9.00	18.00
❑99, Jun 70, JK, SL (w); JK (w), The Torch Goes Wild, A: Inhumans	0.15	3.60	9.00	18.00
❑100, Jul 70, JK, SL (w); JK (w), The Long Journey Home, V: Lots of villains, 100th anniversary issue; anniversary; Doctor Doom, Sandman, Sub-Mariner, others appear	0.15	12.00	30.00	60.00
❑101, Aug 70, JK, SL (w); JK (w), Bedlam In The Baxter Building!, 1: Top Man; 1: Gimlet	0.15	3.20	8.00	16.00
❑102, Sep 70, JK, JR (c), SL (w); JK (w), The Strength Of The Sub-Mariner, A: Sub-Mariner; V: Magneto	0.15	3.20	8.00	16.00
❑103, Oct 70, JR, SL (w); JR (w), At War With Atlantis!, A: Sub-Mariner; V: Magneto; 2: Agatha Harkness; A: Richard M. Nixon	0.15	2.60	6.50	13.00
❑104, Nov 70, JR, SL (w), Our World Enslaved!, A: Sub-Mariner; V: Magneto; A: Richard M. Nixon	0.15	2.60	6.50	13.00
❑105, Dec 70, JR, SL (w), The Monster In The Streets!, 1: Dr. Phillip Zolten Rambow; 1: The "monster" (Larry Rambow)	0.15	2.60	6.50	13.00
❑106, Jan 71, JR, SL (w); JR (w), The Monster's Secret, 2: Dr. Phillip Zolten Rambow; 2: The "monster" (Larry Rambow)	0.15	2.60	6.50	13.00

	ORIG	GOOD	FINE	N-MINT
❑107, Feb 71, JB, SL (w), And Now The Thing!, 1: Janus (the scientist)	0.15	2.60	6.50	13.00
❑108, Mar 71, JK; JB, SL (w); JR (w); JK (w), The Monstrous Mystery of the Nega-Man, 2: Janus (the scientist)	0.15	2.60	6.50	13.00
❑109, Apr 71, JB, SL (w), Death In The Negative Zone!, V: Annihilus; A: Captain Marvel; D: Janus (the scientist)	0.15	2.60	6.50	13.00
❑110, May 71, JB, SL (w), One From Four Leaves Three!, V: Annihilus; A: J. Jonah Jameson; A: Joe Robertson	0.15	2.60	6.50	13.00
❑111, Jun 71, JB, SL (w), The Thing Amok, A: J. Jonah Jameson; A: Hulk; 1: Collins (landlord of Baxter building); A: Peter Parker; A: Joe Robertson	0.15	2.60	6.50	13.00
❑112, Jul 71, JB, SL (w), Battle of the Behemoths, A: J. Jonah Jameson; A: Hulk; A: Bruce Banner; 2: Collins, Thing vs. Hulk	0.15	8.40	21.00	42.00
❑113, Aug 71, JB, SL (w), The Power of the Overmind, 1: Overmind; A: The Watcher; A: Bruce Banner	0.15	2.20	5.50	11.00
❑114, Sep 71, JB, SL (w), But Who Shall Stop The Over-Mind?, V: Overmind; A: The Watcher	0.15	2.20	5.50	11.00
❑115, Oct 71, JB, SL (w), The Secret of the Eternals, 1: Eternals; 1: The Eternals (a.k.a. Eternians); O: Overmind; A: The Watcher	0.15	2.20	5.50	11.00
❑116, Nov 71, JB, The Alien, the Ally, and Armageddon; Now Falls the Final Hour, O: Stranger; A: Doctor Doom; A: Edwin Jarvis; A: The Watcher; A: The Stranger, Giant-size	0.25	1.80	4.50	9.00
❑117, Dec 71, JB, The Flame and the Quest, A: Kaliban; V: Diablo; 1: Asmodeus; A: Crystal; 1: Chiron	0.20	1.80	4.50	9.00
❑118, Jan 72, JB, Thunder in the Ruins; What Mad World, 1: Sue Storm Grimm of Earth-A; A: Lockjaw; 1: Ben Grimm of Earth-A; V: Diablo; A: Crystal; 1: Reed Richards of Earth-A	0.20	1.80	4.50	9.00
❑119, Feb 72, JB, Three Stood Together, V: Klaw; A: Black Panther	0.20	1.80	4.50	9.00
❑120, Mar 72, JB, SL (w); JB (w), The Horror That Walks on Air, A: General T. E. "Thunderbolt" Ross; 1: Air-Walker (robot form); V: Air-Walker Automaton	0.20	1.80	4.50	9.00
❑121, Apr 72, JB, SL (w); JB (w), The Mysterious Mind-Blowing Secret of Gabriel, A: Silver Surfer; 2: Air-Walker (robot form); V: Air-Walker Automaton; A: Galactus	0.20	3.00	7.50	15.00
❑122, May 72, JB, SL (w), Galactus Unleashed, A: Silver Surfer; V: Galactus	0.20	3.00	7.50	15.00
❑123, Jun 72, JB, SL (w), This World Enslaved, A: Silver Surfer; A: General T. E. "Thunderbold" Ross; A: Richard M. Nixon; V: Galactus	0.20	3.00	7.50	15.00
❑124, Jul 72, JB, SL (w), The Return of the Monster	0.20	1.60	4.00	8.00
❑125, Aug 72, JB, SL (w), The Monster's Secret	0.20	1.60	4.00	8.00
❑126, Sep 72, JB, The Way It Began, O: Fantastic Four	0.20	1.60	4.00	8.00
❑127, Oct 72, JB, Where the Sun Dares Not Shine, V: Mole Man	0.20	1.60	4.00	8.00
❑128, Nov 72, JB, Death in a Dark and Lonely Place, V: Mole Man; V: Tyrannus	0.20	1.80	4.50	9.00
❑129, Dec 72, JB, The Frightful Four-Plus One, 1: Thundra; A: Medusa	0.20	1.60	4.00	8.00
❑130, Jan 73, JB, Battleground: The Baxter Building, V: Sandman; V: Wizard; V: Thundra; V: Trapster; A: Inhumans	0.20	1.40	3.50	7.00
❑131, Feb 73, RA, JB (c), Revolt in Paradise, V: Maximus; A: Inhumans; 1: Omega (the ultimate Alpha Primitive)	0.20	1.40	3.50	7.00
❑132, Mar 73, JB, Omega! The Ultimate Enemy!, V: Maximus, Medusa Joins	0.20	1.40	3.50	7.00
❑133, Apr 73, JB (c), Thundra at Dawn, V: Sandman; V: Wizard; V: Thundra; V: Trapster	0.20	1.40	3.50	7.00
❑134, May 73, JB, A Dragon Stalks the Skies, V: Dragon Man	0.20	1.40	3.50	7.00
❑135, Jun 73, JB, The Eternity Machine, V: Dragon Man	0.20	1.40	3.50	7.00
❑136, Jul 73, JB, Rock Around the Cosmos, V: Shaper of Worlds	0.20	1.40	3.50	7.00
❑137, Aug 73, JB, Rumble on Planet 3, V: Shaper of Worlds	0.20	1.40	3.50	7.00
❑138, Sep 73, JB, Madness Is the Miracle Man, V: Miracle Man	0.20	1.40	3.50	7.00
❑139, Oct 73, JB, Target: Tomorrow!, V: Miracle Man	0.20	1.40	3.50	7.00
❑140, Nov 73, JB, RB (c), Annihilus Revealed, V: Annihilus	0.20	1.40	3.50	7.00
❑141, Dec 73, JB, JR (c), The End of the Fantastic Four, V: Annihilus	0.20	1.40	3.50	7.00
❑142, Jan 74, RB, 1: Darkoth the Death-Demon; V: Doctor Doom	0.20	1.40	3.50	7.00
❑143, Feb 74, RB, GK (c), V: Doctor Doom	0.20	1.40	3.50	7.00
❑144, Mar 74, RB, V: Doctor Doom	0.20	1.40	3.50	7.00
❑145, Apr 74, RA, GK (c), A: Doctor Doom	0.20	1.40	3.50	7.00
❑146, May 74, RA, GK (c)	0.25	1.40	3.50	7.00
❑147, Jun 74, RB, A: Sub-Mariner	0.25	1.40	3.50	7.00
❑148, Jul 74, RB, V: Frightful Four	0.25	1.40	3.50	7.00
❑149, Aug 74, RB	0.25	1.40	3.50	7.00
❑150, Sep 74, RB, GK (c), A: Avengers; A: Inhumans, Wedding of Crystal and Quicksilver	0.25	1.40	3.50	7.00
❑151, Oct 74, RB, 1: Mahkizmo; O: Thundra	0.25	1.20	3.00	6.00
❑152, Nov 74, RB	0.25	1.20	3.00	6.00
❑153, Dec 74, RB, GK (c), V: Mahkizmo	0.25	1.20	3.00	6.00
❑154, Jan 75, GK (c)	0.25	1.20	3.00	6.00
❑155, Feb 75, RB, A: Silver Surfer; V: Doctor Doom	0.25	1.40	3.50	7.00
❑156, Mar 75, RB, A: Silver Surfer; V: Doctor Doom; V: Dr. Doom	0.25	1.40	3.50	7.00
❑157, Apr 75, RB, A: Silver Surfer; V: Doctor Doom; V: Dr. Doom	0.25	1.40	3.50	7.00
❑158, May 75, RB, V: Xemu	0.25	1.20	3.00	6.00
❑159, Jun 75, RB, A: Inhumans; V: Xemu	0.25	1.20	3.00	6.00
❑160, Jul 75, JB, GK (c), V: Arkon	0.25	1.20	3.00	6.00
❑161, Aug 75, RB, All the World Wars at Once, A: Phineas; A: Lockjaw; A: Ben Grimm of Earth-A; A: Sue Grimm of Earth-A; A: Reed Richards of Earth-A; A: Valeria	0.25	0.80	2.00	4.00
❑162, Sep 75, RB, The Shape of Things to Come, A: Phineas; A: Ben Grimm of Earth-A; A: Arkon; A: Gaard (Johnny Storm of Earth-A, reconstructed); A: Reed Richards of Earth-A; A: Valeria; A: The "Old One"; A: Albert E. DeVoor	0.25	0.80	2.00	4.00
❑163, Oct 75, RB, Finale; Arkon at Bay, A: Arkon; A: Gaard (Johnny Storm of Earth-A, reconstructed); A: Reed Richards of Earth-A; A: Albert E. DeVoor	0.25	0.80	2.00	4.00
❑164, Nov 75, GP, JK (c), The Crusader Syndrome, 1: Frankie Raye; 1: Crusader (Marvel Boy); 1: Crusader (a.k.a. Marvel Boy)	0.25	0.80	2.00	4.00
❑165, Dec 75, GP, The Light of Other Worlds, D: Crusader; O: Crusader (a.k.a. Marvel Boy)	0.25	0.80	2.00	4.00
❑166, Jan 76, GP, RB (c), If It's Tuesday, This Must Be the Hulk, A: Puppet Master; V: Hulk	0.25	0.80	2.00	4.00
❑167, Feb 76, GP, JK (c), Titans Two, A: Puppet Master; V: Hulk	0.25	0.80	2.00	4.00
❑168, Mar 76, RB, Where Have All The Powers Gone?, A: Wreaker, Thing replaced by Luke Cage (Power Man)	0.25	0.80	2.00	4.00
❑169, Apr 76, RB, Five Characters in Search of a Madman, A: Luke Cage	0.25	0.80	2.00	4.00
❑170, May 76, GP, A Sky-Full Of Fear!, A: Luke Cage	0.25	0.80	2.00	4.00
❑171, Jun 76, GP; RB, JK (c), Death is a Golden Gorilla, 1: Gorr; V: Galactus	0.25	0.60	1.50	3.00
❑172, Jul 76, GP, JK (c), Cry, the Bedeviled Planet, A: The Destroyer; A: The High Evolutionary; 2: Gorr; V: Galactus	0.25	0.60	1.50	3.00
❑173, Aug 76, JB, JK (c), Counter-Earth Must Die-At the Hand of Galactus, A: Torgo; A: The High Evolutionary; A: Gorr; V: Galactus	0.25	0.60	1.50	3.00
❑174, Sep 76, JB, JK (c), Starquest, A: Torgo; A: The High Evolutionary; A: Gorr; V: Galactus	0.30	0.60	1.50	3.00
❑175, Oct 76, JB, JK (c), When Giants Walk The Sky!, A: The High Evolutionary; A: Gorr; A: The Impossible Man; V: Galactus	0.30	0.60	1.50	3.00
❑176, Nov 76, GP, JK (c), Improbable As It May Seem, The Impossible Man Is Back In Town, V: Sandman; A: Jack Kirby; V: Wizard; A: Stan Lee; A: Roy Thomas; V: Trapster; A: The Impossible Man	0.30	0.60	1.50	3.00
❑177, Dec 76, GP, JK (c), Look Out for the Frightful Four, V: Sandman; V: Wizard; V: Brute; A: Impossible Man; V: Trapster; 1: Captain Ultra; A: Tigra; 1: Texas Twister.	0.30	0.60	1.50	3.00
❑178, Jan 77, GP, JR (c), Call My Killer the Brute, V: Sandman; V: Wizard; V: Brute; V: Trapster; A: The Impossible Man	0.30	0.60	1.50	3.00
❑179, Feb 77, AM (c), A Robinson Crusoe in the Negative Zone, V: Mad Thinker; V: Annihilus; A: Impossible Man; A: Reed Richards of Counter-Earth; 1: Metalloid; A: Thundra; A: Tigra	0.30	0.60	1.50	3.00
❑180, Mar 77, JK, JK (c), SL (w); JK (w), Bedlam in the Baxter Building, reprints FF #101	0.30	0.60	1.50	3.00

	ORIG	GOOD	FINE	N-MINT
❑181, Apr 77, JK (c), Side by Side With - Annihilus?, V: Mad Thinker; V: Annihilus; V: Reed Richards of Counter-Earth	0.30	0.50	1.25	2.50
❑182, May 77, SB, Enter: The Mad Thinker, V: Mad Thinker; V: Annihilus; V: Reed Richards of Counter-Earth	0.30	0.50	1.25	2.50
❑183, Jun 77, SB, GP (c), Battleground: The Baxter Building!, V: Mad Thinker; V: Annihilus; V: Brute; A: Impossible Man; A: Thundra; A: Tigra	0.30	0.50	1.25	2.50
❑184, Jul 77, GP, Aftermath: The Eliminator, A: Impossible Man; A: Thundra; A: Tigra.	0.30	0.50	1.25	2.50
❑185, Aug 77, GP, Here There Be Witches, A: Impossible Man; 2: New Salem's Witches; 1: Nicholas Scratch	0.30	0.50	1.25	2.50
❑186, Sep 77, GP, Enter: Salem's Seven, A: Impossible Man; O: New Salem's Witches; 2: Nicholas Scratch	0.30	0.50	1.25	2.50
❑187, Oct 77, GP, Trouble Times Two, A: Impossible Man; V: Klaw; V: Molecule Man	0.30	0.50	1.25	2.50
❑188, Nov 77, GP, The Rampage of Reed Richards, A: Impossible Man; V: Klaw; V: Molecule Man; A: The Watcher	0.35	0.50	1.25	2.50
❑189, Dec 77, JK, KP (c), SL (w); JK (w), The Torch That Was, reprints FF Annual #4	0.35	0.50	1.25	2.50
❑190, Jan 78, SB, JK (c), The Way It Was, Thing recounts FF's career	0.35	0.50	1.25	2.50
❑191, Feb 78, GP, Four No More, A: Thundra; V: Plunderer, Fantastic Four resign	0.35	0.50	1.25	2.50
❑192, Mar 78, GP, He Who Soweth the Wind, A: Texas Twister	0.35	0.50	1.25	2.50
❑193, Apr 78, KP, KP (w), Day Of The Death-Demon, A: Impossible Man; V: Diablo; 1: Victor Von Doom II (not face); O: Darketh the Death-Demon	0.35	0.50	1.25	2.50
❑194, May 78, KP, GP (c), KP (w), Vengeance is Mine, A: Sub-Mariner; A: Impossible Man; V: Diablo; A: Darketh	0.35	0.50	1.25	2.50
❑195, Jun 78, KP, GP (c), Beware the Ravaging Retrievers, A: Sub-Mariner; A: Impossible Man; A: Lord Vashti; 2: Victor Von Doom II (not face)	0.35	0.50	1.25	2.50
❑196, Jul 78, KP, GP (c), Who in the World Is the Invincible Man?, A: Doctor Doom; A: Victor Von Doom II	0.35	0.50	1.25	2.50
❑197, Aug 78, KP, GP (c), The Riotous Return of the Red Ghost, V: Doctor Doom; A: Nick Fury; A: Dr. Doom; A: Victor Von Doom II; V: Red Ghost, Reed Richards gets powers back	0.35	0.50	1.25	2.50
❑198, Sep 78, KP, JB (c), Invasion!, V: Doctor Doom; A: Victor Von Doom II; A: Prince Zorba, Team gets together to fight Doctor Doom	0.35	0.50	1.25	2.50
❑199, Oct 78, KP, The Son of Doctor Doom, A: Doctor Doom; D: Victor Von Doom II; A: Prince Zorba	0.35	0.50	1.25	2.50
❑200, Nov 78, KP, When Titans Clash; Beginning of the End, V: Doctor Doom, Prince Zorba	0.60	0.60	1.50	3.00
❑201, Dec 78, KP, Home Deadly Home, A: Quasimodo; A: Prince Zorba	0.35	0.40	1.00	2.00
❑202, Jan 79, KP; JB, There's One Iron Man Too Many, A: Tony Stark; A: Quasimodo; A: Iron Man	0.35	0.40	1.00	2.00
❑203, Feb 79, KP, And a Child Shall Slay Them	0.35	0.40	1.00	2.00
❑204, Mar 79, KP, The Andromeda Attack, A: Spider-Man; 1: Skrull X; A: Edwin Jarvis; A: Monocle; A: The Watcher; A: Man-Wolf; 1: Queen Adora (of Xandar)	0.35	0.40	1.00	2.00
❑205, Apr 79, KP, When Worlds Die, A: Emperor Dorrek; 1: Thoran Rul (Protector); A: Monocle; A: The Watcher; 2: Queen Adora (of Xandar)	0.35	0.40	1.00	2.00
❑206, May 79, KP, The Death of the Fantastic Four	0.40	0.40	1.00	2.00
❑207, Jun 79, SB, Might of the Monocle, A: Spider-Man; 1: The Enclave (identified); A: Monocle; A: Medusa; A: Barney Bushkin	0.40	0.40	1.00	2.00
❑208, Jul 79, SB, The Power of the Sphinx, O: Protector; A: Powerhouse; A: Doctor Sun; A: Crimebuster; A: Thoran Rul (Protector); A: Diamondhead; A: Comet; A: Queen Adora; A: Sphinx; A: Nova	0.40	0.40	1.00	2.00
❑209, Aug 79, JBy, Trapped in the Sargasso of Space, 1: Herbie	0.40	0.40	1.00	2.00
❑210, Sep 79, JBy, In Search of Galactus, 2: Herbie; A: Galactus	0.40	0.40	1.00	2.00
❑211, Oct 79, JBy, If This Be Terrax, 1: Terrax the Tamer; A: The Watcher; A: Galactus.	0.40	0.40	1.00	2.00
❑212, Nov 79, JBy, The Battle of the Titans, A: Skrull X; A: Sayge; A: The Watcher; A: Sphinx; A: Galactus	0.40	0.40	1.00	2.00

Jack Kirby ended his run on *Fantastic Four* (Vol. 1) with #102.

© 1970 Marvel

	ORIG	GOOD	FINE	N-MINT
❑213, Dec 79, JBy, In Final Battle, A: Sayge; A: The Watcher; A: Sphinx; A: Galactus.	0.40	0.40	1.00	2.00
❑214, Jan 80, JBy, And Then There Was One, A: Dum Dum Dugan; D: Skrull X; A: Queen Adora	0.40	0.40	1.00	2.00
❑215, Feb 80, JBy	0.40	0.40	1.00	2.00
❑216, Mar 80, JBy	0.40	0.40	1.00	2.00
❑217, Apr 80, JBy, A: Dazzler	0.40	0.40	1.00	2.00
❑218, May 80, JSt; JBy, When A Spider-Man Comes Calling!	0.40	0.40	1.00	2.00
❑219, Jun 80	0.40	0.40	1.00	2.00
❑220, Jul 80, JBy, JBy (w), ...And The Lights Went Out All Ever The World, O: Fantastic Four	0.40	0.40	1.00	2.00
❑221, Aug 80, JBy	0.40	0.40	1.00	2.00
❑222, Sep 80, The Possession Of Franklin Richards!	0.50	0.40	1.00	2.00
❑223, Oct 80	0.50	0.40	1.00	2.00
❑224, Nov 80	0.50	0.40	1.00	2.00
❑225, Dec 80, BSz, The Blind God's Tears, A: Thor	0.50	0.40	1.00	2.00
❑226, Jan 81	0.50	0.40	1.00	2.00
❑227, Feb 81, BSz, The Brain Parasites!	0.50	0.40	1.00	2.00
❑228, Mar 81, BSz, Ego-Spawn	0.50	0.40	1.00	2.00
❑229, Apr 81, BSz, The Thing From The Black Hole	0.50	0.40	1.00	2.00
❑230, May 81, BSz, Firefrost And The Ebon Seeker	0.50	0.40	1.00	2.00
❑231, Jun 81, BSz, In All The Gathered Gloom!	0.50	0.40	1.00	2.00
❑232, Jul 81, JBy, JBy (w), Back To The Basics!	0.50	0.50	1.25	2.50
❑233, Aug 81, JBy, JBy (w), Mission For A Dead Man!	0.50	0.50	1.25	2.50
❑234, Sep 81, JBy, JBy (w), The Man With The Power!	0.50	0.50	1.25	2.50
❑235, Oct 81, JBy, JBy (w), Four Against Ego!, V: Ego	0.50	0.50	1.25	2.50
❑236, Nov 81, JBy, JBy (w), Terror In A Tiny Town, V: Doctor Doom; O: Fantastic Four, 20th Anniversary Issue	1.00	0.50	1.25	2.50
❑237, Dec 81, JBy, JBy (w), The Eyes Have It!, 1: Julie Angel	0.50	0.50	1.25	2.50
❑238, Jan 82, JBy, JBy (w), The Lady Is For Burning!, O: Frankie Raye; A: Aunt Petunia	0.60	0.50	1.25	2.50
❑239, Feb 82, JBy, JBy (w), Wendy's Friends	0.60	0.50	1.25	2.50
❑240, Mar 82, JBy, JBy (w), 1: Luna	0.60	0.50	1.25	2.50
❑241, Apr 82, JBy, JBy (w), Render Unto Caesar, A: Black Panther	0.60	0.50	1.25	2.50
❑242, May 82, JBy, JBy (w), Terrax The Untamed, A: Daredevil	0.60	0.50	1.25	2.50
❑243, Jun 82, JBy, JBy (w)	0.60	0.50	1.25	2.50
❑244, Jul 82, JBy, JBy (w), Beginnings And Endings, 1: Nova II (Frankie Raye), Frankie Raye becomes herald of Galactus	0.60	0.50	1.25	2.50
❑245, Aug 82, JBy, JBy (w), Childhood's End	0.60	0.50	1.25	2.50
❑246, Sep 82, JBy, JBy (w), Too Many Dooms!	0.60	0.50	1.25	2.50
❑247, Oct 82, JBy, JBy (w), This Land Is Mine!, 1: Kristoff Vernard	0.60	0.50	1.25	2.50
❑248, Nov 82, JBy, JBy (w), Nightmare!	0.60	0.50	1.25	2.50
❑249, Dec 82, JBy, JBy (w), Man And Super-Man!, V: Gladiator	0.60	0.50	1.25	2.50
❑250, Jan 83, JBy, JBy (w), X-Factor, A: Spider-Man; A: Captain America; A: X-Men, Double-size	1.00	0.60	1.50	3.00
❑251, Feb 83, JBy, JBy (w), Into The Negative Zone!, Negative Zone	0.60	0.50	1.25	2.50
❑252, Mar 83, JBy, JBy (w), Cityscape, "Tattooz" temporary tattoo decals; sideways format	0.60	0.50	1.25	2.50
❑253, Apr 83, JBy, JBy (w), Quest	0.60	0.50	1.25	2.50
❑254, May 83, JBy, JBy (w), The Minds Of Mantracora, A: She-Hulk	0.60	0.50	1.25	2.50
❑255, Jun 83, JBy, JBy (w), Trapped!	0.60	0.50	1.25	2.50
❑256, Jul 83, JBy, JBy (w), The Annihilation Gambit	0.60	0.50	1.25	2.50

	ORIG	GOOD	FINE	N-MINT
❑257, Aug 83, JBy, JBy (w), Fragments	0.60	0.50	1.25	2.50
❑258, Sep 83, JBy, JBy (w)	0.60	0.50	1.25	2.50
❑259, Oct 83, JBy, JBy (w), Choices	0.60	0.50	1.25	2.50
❑260, Nov 83, JBy, JBy (w), When Titans Clash!, A: Silver Surfer; A: Doctor Doom; D: Terrax, Silver Surfer, Doctor Doom	0.60	0.60	1.50	3.00
❑261, Dec 83, JBy, A: Watcher; A: Silver Surfer	0.60	0.50	1.25	2.50
❑262, Jan 84, JBy, JBy (w), The Trial Of Reed Richards, O: Galactus, Trial of Reed Richards; John Byrne appears in story	0.60	0.50	1.25	2.50
❑263, Feb 84, JBy	0.60	0.50	1.25	2.50
❑264, Mar 84, JBy, JBy (w), Inferno, V: Karisma, Cover swipe of Fantastic Four #1	0.60	0.50	1.25	2.50
❑265, Apr 84, JBy, 1: Roberta the Receptionist; 1: Lyja (as Alicia Masters), She-Hulk joins Fantastic Four (replaces Thing, who left in Secret Wars)	0.60	0.50	1.25	2.50
❑266, May 84, KGa; JBy, JBy (w), Call Her Karisma!	0.60	0.50	1.25	2.50
❑267, Jun 84, JBy, Sue has a miscarriage	0.60	0.50	1.25	2.50
❑268, Jul 84, JBy, A: Doctor Octopus; A: Hulk	0.60	0.50	1.25	2.50
❑269, Aug 84, JBy, JBy (w), Skyfall, 1: Terminus	0.60	0.50	1.25	2.50
❑270, Sep 84, JBy, JBy (w), Planet-Fall, V: Terminus	0.60	0.50	1.25	2.50
❑271, Oct 84, JBy, JBy (w), Happy Birthday Darling!	0.60	0.50	1.25	2.50
❑272, Nov 84, JBy, JBy (w), Cowboys And Idioms!, 1: Nathaniel Richards (Reed's father)	0.60	0.50	1.25	2.50
❑273, Dec 84, JBy, JBy (w), Fathers And Others, O: Kang	0.60	0.50	1.25	2.50
❑274, Jan 85, JBy, JBy (w), Monster Mash, Thing solo story; alien costume freed	0.60	0.50	1.25	2.50
❑275, Feb 85, JBy, JBy (w), The Naked Truth	0.60	0.50	1.25	2.50
❑276, Mar 85, JBy, JBy (w)	0.60	0.50	1.25	2.50
❑277, Apr 85, JBy, JBy (w), Back From Beyond	0.65	0.50	1.25	2.50
❑278, May 85, JBy, JBy (w), True Lies, O: Doctor Doom, Kristoff becomes second Doctor Doom	0.65	0.50	1.25	2.50
❑279, Jun 85, JBy, JBy (w), Crack Of Doom!	0.65	0.50	1.25	2.50
❑280, Jul 85, JBy, JBy (w), 1: Hate-Monger III ("H.M. Unger"), Sue becomes Malice	0.65	0.50	1.25	2.50
❑281, Aug 85, JBy, JBy (w), With Malice Towards All!	0.65	0.50	1.25	2.50
❑282, Sep 85, JBy, JBy (w), Inwards To Infinity!, Secret Wars II	0.65	0.50	1.25	2.50
❑283, Oct 85, JBy, JBy (w), Torment	0.65	0.50	1.25	2.50
❑284, Nov 85, JBy, JBy (w), Revolution!, Invisible Girl becomes Invisible Woman	0.65	0.50	1.25	2.50
❑285, Dec 85, JBy, JBy (w), Secret Wars II, Secret Wars II	0.65	0.50	1.25	2.50
❑286, Jan 86, JBy, JBy (w), Like A Phoenix!, 2: X-Factor; A: X-Men, return of Jean Grey	0.65	0.60	1.50	3.00
❑287, Feb 86, JBy, JBy (w), Prisoner Of The Flesh, A: Doctor Doom	0.75	0.40	1.00	2.00
❑288, Mar 86, JBy, Secret Wars II, A: Doctor Doom, Secret Wars II; Doom vs. Beyonder; Doctor Doom vs. Beyonder	0.75	0.40	1.00	2.00
❑289, Apr 86, JBy, D: Basilisk I (Basil Elks)	0.75	0.40	1.00	2.00
❑290, May 86, JBy, JBy (w), Risk	0.75	0.40	1.00	2.00
❑291, Jun 86, JBy, JBy (w), The Times They Are A' Changing!	0.75	0.40	1.00	2.00
❑292, Jul 86, JBy, JBy (w), The Man Who Dreamed The World!, A: Nick Fury	0.75	0.40	1.00	2.00
❑293, Aug 86, JBy, Central City Does Not Answer!	0.75	0.40	1.00	2.00
❑294, Sep 86, JOy, Hero Worship	0.75	0.40	1.00	2.00
❑295, Nov 86, JOy, Welcome To The Future!	0.75	0.40	1.00	2.00
❑296, Nov 86, 25th anniversary issue of Fantastic Four; Double-size; Thing comes back	1.50	0.50	1.25	2.50
❑297, Dec 86, SB; JB, Heart Of The Sun!	0.75	0.40	1.00	2.00
❑298, Jan 87, SB; JB, Closer Than Brothers!	0.75	0.40	1.00	2.00
❑299, Feb 87	0.75	0.40	1.00	2.00
❑300, Mar 87, SB; JB, Dearly Beloved..., Wedding of Johnny Storm and Alicia; "Alicia" later revealed to be Lyja (a Skrull)	0.75	0.50	1.25	2.50
❑301, Apr 87, JB, Dark Dreams	0.75	0.40	1.00	2.00
❑302, May 87, SB; JB, And Who Shall Survive?!	0.75	0.40	1.00	2.00
❑303, Jun 87, JB, Alternatives	0.75	0.40	1.00	2.00
❑304, Jul 87, JSt; JB, Pressure Drop, Reed and Sue take leave of absence	0.75	0.40	1.00	2.00
❑305, Aug 87, JSt; JB, All In The Family!	0.75	0.40	1.00	2.00
❑306, Sep 87, A: Ms. Marvel (Sharon Ventura)	0.75	0.40	1.00	2.00
❑307, Oct 87, Crystal and new Ms. Marvel joins team	0.75	0.40	1.00	2.00
❑308, Nov 87, JSt; JB, Fasaud!, 1: Fasaud	0.75	0.40	1.00	2.00
❑309, Dec 87, JSt; JB, Danger On The Air!	0.75	0.40	1.00	2.00
❑310, Jan 88, Ms. Marvel becomes She-Thing	0.75	0.40	1.00	2.00
❑311, Feb 88	0.75	0.40	1.00	2.00
❑312, Mar 88, Fall of the Mutants, A: Doctor Doom, Fall of Mutants	0.75	0.40	1.00	2.00
❑313, Apr 88	0.75	0.40	1.00	2.00
❑314, May 88, JSt; KP, The Scenic Route!, V: Belasco	0.75	0.40	1.00	2.00
❑315, Jun 88, JSt; KP, No Way Out!	0.75	0.40	1.00	2.00
❑316, Jul 88, JSt; KP, Cold Storage!	0.75	0.40	1.00	2.00
❑317, Aug 88	0.75	0.40	1.00	2.00
❑318, Sep 88, Doctor Doom	0.75	0.40	1.00	2.00
❑319, Oct 88, Giant-size; Doctor Doom v. Beyonder; Doctor Doom vs. Beyonder; Beyonder returns, merges with Molecule Man	1.50	0.50	1.25	2.50
❑320, Nov 88, Thing vs. Hulk	0.75	0.40	1.00	2.00
❑321, Dec 88, 1: Aron the Rogue Watcher, Ms. Marvel vs. She-Hulk	0.75	0.30	0.75	1.50
❑322, Jan 89, Inferno	0.75	0.30	0.75	1.50
❑323, Feb 89, Inferno	0.75	0.30	0.75	1.50
❑324, Mar 89, KP, I Die Like The Stars!, Inferno	0.75	0.30	0.75	1.50
❑325, Apr 89, RB, A Christmas Tale	0.75	0.30	0.75	1.50
❑326, May 89, Reed and Sue return to team	0.75	0.30	0.75	1.50
❑327, Jun 89, Thing reverts to human form	0.75	0.30	0.75	1.50
❑328, Jul 89, KP, Bad Dream!	0.75	0.30	0.75	1.50
❑329, Aug 89, RB, ...And You Can't Wake Up!	0.75	0.30	0.75	1.50
❑330, Sep 89, RB, Good Dreams!, V: Doom	1.00	0.30	0.75	1.50
❑331, Oct 89, RB, Metal Man!, V: Ultron	1.00	0.30	0.75	1.50
❑332, Nov 89, RB, Love's Labour Lost!	1.00	0.30	0.75	1.50
❑333, Nov 89, RB, The Dream Is Death, Part 2	1.00	0.30	0.75	1.50
❑334, Dec 89, Acts of Vengeance, Part 5, Acts of Vengeance	1.00	0.30	0.75	1.50
❑335, Dec 89, Acts of Vengeance, Part 14, Acts of Vengeance	1.00	0.30	0.75	1.50
❑336, Jan 90, Acts of Vengeance, Part 22, Acts of Vengeance	1.00	0.30	0.75	1.50
❑337, Feb 90	1.00	0.40	1.00	2.00
❑338, Mar 90, Kangs For The Memories!	1.00	0.40	1.00	2.00
❑339, Apr 90	1.00	0.40	1.00	2.00
❑340, May 90	1.00	0.40	1.00	2.00
❑341, Jun 90, The Ultimate Solution	1.00	0.40	1.00	2.00
❑342, Jul 90, Burnout!, A: Spider-Man	1.00	0.40	1.00	2.00
❑343, Aug 90, Nukebusters!	1.00	0.40	1.00	2.00
❑344, Sep 90, Nukebusters II	1.00	0.40	1.00	2.00
❑345, Oct 90, The Mesozoic Mambo!	1.00	0.40	1.00	2.00
❑346, Nov 90, 70 Million Years BC...And Then Some!	1.00	0.40	1.00	2.00
❑347, Dec 90, Big Trouble On Little Earth!, A: Spider-Man; A: Wolverine; A: Ghost Rider; A: Hulk	1.00	0.50	1.25	2.50
❑347-2, Dec 90, Big Trouble On Little Earth!, A: Wolverine; A: Ghost Rider; A: Hulk, 2nd Printing	1.00	0.30	0.75	1.50
❑348, Jan 91, Where Monsters Dwell!, A: Spider-Man; A: Wolverine; A: Ghost Rider; A: Hulk	1.00	0.50	1.25	2.50
❑348-2, Jan 91, 2nd Printing	1.00	0.30	0.75	1.50
❑349, Feb 91, Eggs Got Legs!, A: Spider-Man; A: Wolverine; A: Ghost Rider; A: Hulk; A: Punisher	1.00	0.50	1.25	2.50
❑350, Mar 91, The More Things Change...!, A: Doctor Doom, Giant-size; Return of Thing	1.50	0.50	1.25	2.50
❑351, Apr 91, Strange Interlude	1.00	0.40	1.00	2.00
❑352, May 91, No Time Like The Present!, Reed and Doctor Doom battle through time	1.00	0.40	1.00	2.00
❑353, Jun 91, So Little Time, So Much To Do	1.00	0.40	1.00	2.00
❑354, Jul 91, The Cross Time Express!	1.00	0.40	1.00	2.00
❑355, Aug 91, AM, Rage	1.00	0.40	1.00	2.00
❑356, Sep 91, War With The New Warriors!, Alicia is Skrull; Fantastic Four vs. New Warriors	1.00	0.40	1.00	2.00
❑357, Oct 91, The Monster Among Us!, 1: Lyja (in true form), Skrull's identity revealed as Lyja	1.00	0.40	1.00	2.00
❑358, Nov 91, Whatever Happened To Alicia?!, 1: Paibok the Power Skrull, Die-cut cover; Double-size; 30th Anniversary Issue	2.50	0.50	1.25	2.50
❑359, Dec 91, Devos The Devastator!, 1: Devos the Devastator, The real Alicia returns	1.00	0.30	0.75	1.50
❑360, Jan 92, At The Mercy Of Dreadface!	1.00	0.30	0.75	1.50
❑361, Feb 92, Miracle On Yancy Street, Doctor Doom	1.25	0.30	0.75	1.50
❑362, Mar 92, Here Comes The Wild Blood!	1.25	0.30	0.75	1.50
❑363, Apr 92, Innerverse, 1: Occulus	1.25	0.30	0.75	1.50
❑364, May 92, Omnipotent Is Occulus!	1.25	0.30	0.75	1.50
❑365, Jun 92, With Defeat Comes Death!	1.25	0.30	0.75	1.50
❑366, Jul 92, Infinity War	1.25	0.30	0.75	1.50
❑367, Aug 92, Infinity War	1.25	0.30	0.75	1.50
❑368, Sep 92, Infinity War	1.25	0.30	0.75	1.50
❑369, Oct 92, Infinity War	1.25	0.30	0.75	1.50

	ORIG	GOOD	FINE	N-MINT
❑370, Nov 92, Infinity War, 1: Lyja the Lazerfist	1.25	0.30	0.75	1.50
❑371, Dec 92, This Flame, This Fury, All-white embossed cover	2.00	0.70	1.75	3.50
❑371-2, Dec 92, This Flame, This Fury, 2nd Printing; red embossed cover	2.00	0.50	1.25	2.50
❑372, Jan 93	1.25	0.25	0.63	1.25
❑373, Feb 93, A: Silver Sable	1.25	0.25	0.63	1.25
❑374, Mar 93, Spider-Man, Hulk, Ghost Rider, Wolverine team up again; Secret Defenders x-over	1.25	0.25	0.63	1.25
❑375, Apr 93, It Is Always Darkest Before The...Doom!, Prism cover	2.95	0.60	1.50	3.00
❑376, May 93, To A Future Darkly!, Franklin returns from future as a young man	1.25	0.25	0.63	1.25
❑377, Jun 93, If This Be War!, 1: Huntara, Secret Defenders x-over	1.25	0.25	0.63	1.25
❑378, Jul 93	1.25	0.25	0.63	1.25
❑379, Aug 93	1.25	0.30	0.75	1.50
❑380, Sep 93	1.25	0.30	0.75	1.50
❑381, Oct 93, D: Doctor Doom; A: Hunger; D: Mister Fantastic (apparent death)	1.25	0.60	1.50	3.00
❑382, Nov 93	1.25	0.40	1.00	2.00
❑383, Dec 93	1.25	0.25	0.63	1.25
❑384, Jan 94, A: Ant-Man (Scott Lang)	1.25	0.25	0.63	1.25
❑385, Feb 94, Starblast, Part 7	1.25	0.25	0.63	1.25
❑386, Mar 94, Starblast, Part 11, 1: Egg (Lyja's baby), Birth of Lyja's baby	1.25	0.25	0.63	1.25
❑387, Apr 94, Nobody Gets Out Alive!	1.25	0.25	0.63	1.25
❑387/SC, Apr 94, diecut cover	2.95	0.60	1.50	3.00
❑388, May 94, A: Avengers, cards	1.50	0.30	0.75	1.50
❑389, Jun 94	1.50	0.30	0.75	1.50
❑390, Jun 94, A: Galactus	1.50	0.30	0.75	1.50
❑391, Aug 94, A: Galactus	1.50	0.30	0.75	1.50
❑392, Sep 94	1.50	0.30	0.75	1.50
❑393, Oct 94, A: Puppet Master, Nathaniel Richards takes over Latveria	1.50	0.30	0.75	1.50
❑394, Nov 94	1.50	0.30	0.75	1.50
❑394/CS, Nov 94, polybagged with 16-page Marvel Action Hour preview, acetate print, and other items	2.95	0.59	1.48	2.95
❑395, Dec 94, A: Wolverine	1.50	0.30	0.75	1.50
❑396, Jan 95	1.50	0.30	0.75	1.50
❑397, Feb 95, V: Aron	1.50	0.30	0.75	1.50
❑398, Mar 95, Watcher's Lie, Part 1	1.50	0.30	0.75	1.50
❑398/SC, Mar 95, Watcher's Lie, Part 1, foil cover	2.50	0.50	1.25	2.50
❑399, Apr 95, Watcher's Lie, Part 2	1.50	0.30	0.75	1.50
❑399/SC, Apr 95, Watcher's Lie, Part 2, enhanced cardstock cover	2.50	0.50	1.25	2.50
❑400, May 95, Watcher's Lie, Part 3, foil cover; 400th anniversary issue; Giant-size	3.95	0.79	1.98	3.95
❑401, Jun 95, Atlantis Rising, Part 4	1.50	0.30	0.75	1.50
❑402, Jul 95, A: Thor, Atlantis Rising	1.50	0.30	0.75	1.50
❑403, Aug 95	1.50	0.30	0.75	1.50
❑404, Sep 95	1.50	0.30	0.75	1.50
❑405, Oct 95, A: Green Goblin; A: Zarko; A: Young Allies; A: Red Raven; A: Conan; A: Iron Man 2020, The Thing becomes human	1.50	0.30	0.75	1.50
❑406, Nov 95, 1: Hyperstorm, Return of Doctor Doom	1.50	0.30	0.75	1.50
❑407, Dec 95, Return of Reed Richards, Return of Reed Richards	1.50	0.30	0.75	1.50
❑408, Jan 96, Strange Days, V: Hyperstorm	1.50	0.30	0.75	1.50
❑409, Feb 96, The Thing's face is healed	1.50	0.30	0.75	1.50
❑410, Mar 96, The Ties That Bind!, O: Kristoff	1.50	0.30	0.75	1.50
❑411, Apr 96, Black Bolt...Berserk!, V: Black Bolt; A: Inhumans	1.50	0.30	0.75	1.50
❑412, May 96	1.50	0.30	0.75	1.50
❑413, Jun 96, Franklin Richards becomes a child again	1.50	0.30	0.75	1.50
❑414, Jul 96, O: Hyperstorm	1.50	0.30	0.75	1.50
❑415, Aug 96, Onslaught: Phase 1; Onslaught, Franklin captured by Onslaught	1.50	0.40	1.00	2.00
❑416, Sep 96, Onslaught: Phase 2; Onslaught, wraparound cover; Final Issue; Giant-size	2.50	0.70	1.75	3.50
❑Anl 1, JK, V: Sub-Mariner; A: Doctor Doom; A: Spider-Man; O: Fantastic Four; 1: Krang	0.25	100.00	250.00	500.00
❑Anl 2, O: Doctor Doom; 1: Boris	0.25	55.00	137.50	275.00
❑Anl 3, Wedding of Reed Richards and Susan Storm; Virtually all Marvel super-heroes appear	0.25	22.00	55.00	110.00
❑Anl 4, Nov 66, JK, SL (w); JK (w), The Torch That Was, 1: Quasimodo, Return of Golden Age Human Torch; reprints FF #25 and 26	0.25	11.00	27.50	55.00
❑Anl 5, Nov 67, JK, SL (w); JK (w), Divide and Conquer; This Is a Plot?, A: Inhumans, Black Panther; 1: Psycho-Man; A: Black Panther; A: Inhumans	0.25	14.00	35.00	70.00

When the original team was unavailable, a new team of four heroes — Spider-Man, Ghost Rider, Wolverine, and The Hulk — banded together as an ersatz Fantastic Four.

© 1991 Marvel

	ORIG	GOOD	FINE	N-MINT
❑Anl 6, Nov 68, JK, SL (w); JK (w), Let There Be Life, 1: Annihilus; 1: Franklin Richards	0.25	9.00	22.50	45.00
❑Anl 7, Nov 69, JK, SL (w); JK (w), The Fantastic Four Meet the Mole Man; Origin of Doctor Doom, reprints FF #1, FF Annual #2	0.25	3.60	9.00	18.00
❑Anl 8, Dec 70, JK, Sub-Mariner Versus the Human Race; Inside the Baxter Bldg., reprints FF Annual #1	0.25	2.40	6.00	12.00
❑Anl 9, Dec 71, JK, SL (w); JK (w), Lo, There Shall Be an Ending; The Bouncing Ball of Doom, reprints stories from FF #43, Annual #3, and Strange Tales #131	0.25	2.00	5.00	10.00
❑Anl 10, JK, SL (w); JK (w), Bedlam at the Baxter Building; The Torch That Was, reprints stories from FF Annual #3 and 4; Reprints wedding of Reed and Sue Richards	0.35	1.60	4.00	8.00
❑Anl 11, JB, JK (c), And Then the Invaders; Nine Against Destiny, V: Invaders; A: The Watcher	0.50	1.20	3.00	6.00
❑Anl 12, BH; KP, The End of the Inhumans and the Fantastic Four; Hither Comes Crystal, A: Black Bolt; A: Gorgon; A: Lockjaw; A: Quicksilver; A: Triton; A: Crystal; A: Medusa; A: Sphinx; A: Karnak	0.60	1.00	2.50	5.00
❑Anl 13, SB, Nightlife; Encounter, A: Mole Man; A: Daredevil	0.60	1.00	2.50	5.00
❑Anl 14, GP, Cat's Paw	0.75	1.00	2.50	5.00
❑Anl 15, GP, Time For The Prime Ten, Skrulls	0.75	0.60	1.50	3.00
❑Anl 16, JBy; SD, The Coming Of Dragon Lord!	0.75	0.60	1.50	3.00
❑Anl 17, JBy, JBy (w), Legacy	1.00	0.60	1.50	3.00
❑Anl 18, JBy (w), Something Old, Something New!, Kree-Skrull War	1.00	0.60	1.50	3.00
❑Anl 19, JBy, A: Avengers	1.25	0.60	1.50	3.00
❑Anl 20	1.25	0.60	1.50	3.00
❑Anl 21, Evolutionary War, Part 6	1.75	0.60	1.50	3.00
❑Anl 22, RB, Atlantis Attacks, Part 14, Atlantis Attacks	2.00	0.60	1.50	3.00
❑Anl 23, Future Present; Days of Future Present, Part 1, 1: Kosmos	2.00	0.60	1.50	3.00
❑Anl 24, Korvac Quest, Part 1, A: Guardians of Galaxy; O: Fantastic Four, Korvac Quest	2.00	0.50	1.25	2.50
❑Anl 25, Citizen Kang, Part 3, 1: Temptress, Citizen Kang	2.25	0.50	1.25	2.50
❑Anl 26, 1: Wildstreak, Polybagged with trading card	2.95	0.60	1.50	3.00
❑Anl 27	2.95	0.60	1.50	3.00
❑Ash 1, O: Fantastic Four, ashcan edition	0.75	0.15	0.38	0.75
❑GS 1, JK; RB, The Mind of the Monster; Someone's Been Sleeping in My Head, Thing battles Hulk	0.35	3.00	7.50	15.00
❑GS 2	0.50	1.60	4.00	8.00
❑GS 3	0.50	1.40	3.50	7.00
❑GS 4, JK; JB, JK (w), Madrox the Multiple Man; We Have to Fight the X-Men, 1: Madrox the Multiple Man; A: Medusa; A: Professor X	0.50	1.60	4.00	8.00
❑GS 5	0.50	1.20	3.00	6.00
❑GS 6	0.50	1.20	3.00	6.00
❑SE 1, JBy, Reprints Sub-Mariner vs. Fantastic Four from Annual #1	2.00	0.50	1.25	2.50

FANTASTIC FOUR (VOL. 2)

MARVEL

	ORIG	GOOD	FINE	N-MINT
❑1, Nov 96, JLee, JLee(w), Renaissance, O: Fantastic Four (new origin)	2.95	0.60	1.50	3.00
❑1/A, Nov 96, JLee, JLee(w), Renaissance, O: Fantastic Four (new origin), alternate cover	2.95	0.80	2.00	4.00
❑1/B, JLee, JLee(w), Renaissance, Signed by Jim Lee; Certificate of Authenticity	—	1.00	2.50	5.00
❑2, Dec 96, JLee, JLee(w), Repercussions, V: Namor	1.95	0.40	1.00	2.00
❑3, Jan 97, JLee, JLee(w), Revelations, A: Avengers; V: Namor	1.95	0.40	1.00	2.00
❑4, Feb 97, JLee, JLee(w), The Heart Of Darkness, V: Doctor Doom; A: Black Panther	1.95	0.40	1.00	2.00

	ORIG	GOOD	FINE	N-MINT
❑4/A, JLee, JLee(w), The Heart Of Darkness	1.95	0.40	1.00	2.00
❑5, Mar 97, JLee, JLee(w), Auld Acquaintance, V: Doctor Doom	1.95	0.40	1.00	2.00
❑6, Apr 97, JLee, JLee(w), Industrial Revolution Prologue; Retribution, A: Silver Surfer; V: Super Skrull, continues in Avengers #6	1.95	0.40	1.00	2.00
❑7, May 97, JLee(w), Into the Negative Zone, A: Blastaar; A: Wolverine; A: Galactus	1.95	0.40	1.00	2.00
❑8, Jun 97, JLee(w), The Ties that Bind, A: Inhumans	1.95	0.40	1.00	2.00
❑9, Jul 97, A: Firelord; A: Inhumans	1.99	0.40	1.00	2.00
❑10, Aug 97, A: Inhumans, gatefold summary	1.99	0.40	1.00	2.00
❑11, Sep 97, V: Terrax, gatefold summary	1.99	0.40	1.00	2.00
❑12, Oct 97, Heroes Reunited, Part 1, covers forms quadtych with Avengers #12, Iron Man #12, and Captain America #12; gatefold summary	1.99	0.60	1.50	2.99
❑13, Nov 97, World War 3, Part 1, A: WildC.A.T.s; A: Wetworks; A: StormWatch, covers forms quadtych with Avengers #13, Iron Man #13, and Captain America #13; Final Issue; gatefold summary	1.99	0.40	1.00	2.00

FANTASTIC FOUR (VOL. 3)
MARVEL

	ORIG	GOOD	FINE	N-MINT
❑1, Jan 98, Vive la Fantastique!, Cover has green background with team facing forward; gatefold summary; Giant-size	2.99	0.70	1.75	3.50
❑1/A, Jan 98, Vive la Fantastique!, alternate cover; gatefold summary	2.99	0.80	2.00	4.00
❑2, Feb 98, gatefold summary	1.99	0.50	1.25	2.50
❑2/A, Feb 98, alternate cover; gatefold summary	1.99	0.50	1.25	2.50
❑3, Mar 98, Happy New Year, Reed Richards...Now Die!, 1: Crucible, gatefold summary	1.99	0.50	1.25	2.50
❑4, Apr 98, A: Silver Surfer; 1: Billie the Postman; V: Terminus, gatefold summary	2.99	0.40	1.00	2.00
❑5, May 98, V: Crucible, gatefold summary	1.99	0.40	1.00	2.00
❑6, Jun 98, A: Iron Fist, gatefold summary; Thing vs. Technet	1.99	0.40	1.00	2.00
❑7, Jul 98, V: Warwolves, gatefold summary	1.99	0.40	1.00	2.00
❑8, Aug 98, gatefold summary	1.99	0.40	1.00	2.00
❑9, Sep 98, A: Spider-Man, gatefold summary	1.99	0.40	1.00	2.00
❑10, Oct 98, V: Trapster, gatefold summary	1.99	0.40	1.00	2.00
❑11, Nov 98, A: Her, gatefold summary	1.99	0.40	1.00	2.00
❑12, Dec 98, V: Crucible; V: Her, wraparound cover; gatefold summary	2.99	0.60	1.50	3.00
❑13, Jan 99, V: Ronan, gatefold summary	1.99	0.60	1.50	3.00
❑14, Feb 99, A: Ronan the Accuser; V: Ronan, gatefold summary	1.99	0.40	1.00	2.00
❑15, Mar 99, A: Watcher; A: Ronan the Accuser; V: Ronan; A: Iron Man; A: Shi'Ar; A: S.H.I.E.L.D.; A: Kree, Iron Man crossover, Part 1	1.99	0.40	1.00	2.00
❑16, Apr 99, Unnatural Selection, V: Kree	1.99	0.40	1.00	2.00
❑17, May 99	1.99	0.40	1.00	1.99
❑18, Jun 99	1.99	0.40	1.00	1.99
❑19, Jul 99, V: Annihilus	1.99	0.40	1.00	1.99
❑20, Aug 99	1.99	0.40	1.00	1.99
❑21, Sep 99	1.99	0.40	1.00	1.99
❑22, Oct 99	1.99	0.40	1.00	1.99
❑23, Nov 99	1.99	0.40	1.00	1.99
❑24, Dec 99	1.99	0.40	1.00	1.99
❑25, Jan 00	1.99	0.45	1.13	2.25
❑26, Feb 00	—	0.45	1.13	2.25
❑27, Mar 00	—	0.45	1.13	2.25
❑28, Apr 00	—	0.45	1.13	2.25
❑29, May 00	—	0.45	1.13	2.25
❑30, Jun 00	—	0.45	1.13	2.25
❑31, Jul 00	—	0.45	1.13	2.25
❑32, Aug 00	—	0.45	1.13	2.25
❑33, Sep 00	—	0.45	1.13	2.25
❑34, Oct 00	2.25	0.45	1.13	2.25
❑35, Nov 00	2.25	0.45	1.13	2.25
❑36, Dec 00, Day of the Dark Sun, A: Diablo; A: Spider-Man; A: Daredevil	2.25	0.45	1.13	2.25
❑37, Jan 01	2.25	0.45	1.13	2.25
❑38, Feb 01, Flesh and Stone	2.25	0.45	1.13	2.25
❑39, Mar 01, Things Change, A: Avengers; A: Grey Gargoyle, Thing can switch from rock form to human and back	2.25	0.45	1.13	2.25
❑40, Apr 01, Into the Breach, Baxter Building reopens	2.25	0.45	1.13	2.25
❑41, May 01, JPH (w), Marooned, A: First	2.25	0.45	1.13	2.25
❑42	2.25	0.45	1.13	2.25
❑43	2.25	0.45	1.13	2.25
❑44	2.25	0.45	1.13	2.25
❑45	2.25	0.45	1.13	2.25
❑Anl 1998, Fantastic Four/Fantastic 4 '98; alternate universe FF	3.50	0.70	1.75	3.50
❑Anl 1999, Fantastic Four/Fantastic 4 '99	3.50	0.70	1.75	3.50

FANTASTIC FOUR 2099
MARVEL

	ORIG	GOOD	FINE	N-MINT
❑1, Jan 96, enhanced wraparound cover	3.95	0.79	1.98	3.95
❑2, Feb 96, JB, Frightful 4	1.95	0.40	1.00	2.00
❑3, Mar 96, Difficult to Recall	1.95	0.40	1.00	2.00
❑4, Apr 96, Negative Results, A: Spider-Man 2099	1.95	0.40	1.00	2.00
❑5, May 96, A: Doctor Strange	1.95	0.40	1.00	2.00
❑6, Jun 96, A: Doctor Strange; A: Spider-Man 2099	1.95	0.40	1.00	2.00
❑7, Jul 96, V: Attuma; A: Doom 2099	1.95	0.40	1.00	2.00
❑8, Aug 96, A: Doom 2099	1.95	0.40	1.00	2.00

FANTASTIC FOUR: ATLANTIS RISING
MARVEL

Value: Cover or less

- ❑1, Jun 95, Atlantis Rising, Part 1, acetate outer cover; Atlantis rises from sea 3.95
- ❑2, Jul 95, Atlantis Rising, acetate outer cover 3.95
- ❑Ash 1, May 95, O: The Inhumans, Collector's Preview 2.25

FANTASTIC FOUR: FIREWORKS
MARVEL

Value: Cover or less

- ❑1, Jan 99, A: Inhumans, Marvel Remix 2.99
- ❑2, Feb 99, A: Inhumans, Marvel Remix 2.99
- ❑3, Mar 99, A: Inhumans, Marvel Remix 2.99

FANTASTIC FOUR ROAST
MARVEL

	ORIG	GOOD	FINE	N-MINT
❑1, May 82, TD; FM; JB; MG; FH; MA, When Titans Chuckle!, Celebrates 20th Anniversary of Fantastic Four	1.00	0.40	1.00	2.00

FANTASTIC FOUR SPECIAL
MARVEL

	ORIG	GOOD	FINE	N-MINT
❑1, May 84, JBy (c), reprints FF Annual #1	2.00	0.60	1.50	3.00

FANTASTIC FOUR: THE LEGEND
MARVEL

Value: Cover or less

- ❑1, Oct 96, O: Fantastic Four and supporting cast, highlights of group's history 3.95

FANTASTIC FOUR: THE WORLD'S GREATEST COMICS MAGAZINE
MARVEL

Value: Cover or less

- ❑1, Feb 01, EL; KG, EL (c), EL (w), The Baxter Building Besieged! 2.99
- ❑2, Mar 01, KG, MG (c), EL (w), The Sinister Secret of the Sentry! 2.99
- ❑3, Apr 01, KG, EL (w), When Strike These Sentinels! 2.99
- ❑4 ..... 2.99
- ❑5 ..... 2.99
- ❑6 ..... 2.99
- ❑7 ..... 2.99
- ❑8 ..... 2.99
- ❑9 ..... 2.99
- ❑10 ..... 2.99
- ❑11 ..... 2.99
- ❑12 ..... 2.99

FANTASTIC FOUR UNLIMITED
MARVEL

	ORIG	GOOD	FINE	N-MINT
❑1, Mar 93, HT, Echoes!	3.95	0.90	2.25	4.50
❑2, Jun 93	3.95	0.80	2.00	4.00
❑3, Sep 93	3.95	0.80	2.00	4.00
❑4, Dec 93, Thing vs. Hulk	3.95	0.79	1.98	3.95
❑5, Mar 94	3.95	0.79	1.98	3.95
❑6, Jun 94, V: Namor	3.95	0.79	1.98	3.95
❑7, Sep 94, V: early Marvel monsters, wraparound cover	3.95	0.79	1.98	3.95
❑8, Dec 94, V: Doom	3.95	0.79	1.98	3.95
❑9, Mar 95	3.95	0.79	1.98	3.95
❑10, Jul 95	3.95	0.79	1.98	3.95
❑11, Sep 95, A: Inhumans	3.95	0.79	1.98	3.95
❑12, Dec 95, HT, A: Doctor Doom; A: Hyperstorm, wraparound cover; Final Issue; how Reed and Doom vanished	3.95	0.79	1.98	3.95

FANTASTIC FOUR UNPLUGGED
MARVEL

	ORIG	GOOD	FINE	N-MINT
❑1, Sep 95, Adapt This!	0.99	0.25	0.63	1.25
❑2, Nov 95, reading of Reed Richards' will	0.99	0.20	0.50	1.00
❑3, Jan 96	0.99	0.20	0.50	1.00
❑4, Mar 96	0.99	0.20	0.50	1.00
❑5, May 96, Bomb Scared!, V: Blastaar	0.99	0.20	0.50	1.00
❑6, Jul 96	0.99	0.20	0.50	1.00

FANTASTIC FOUR VS. X-MEN
MARVEL

	ORIG	GOOD	FINE	N-MINT
❑1, Feb 87, Are You Sure?!	1.50	0.50	1.25	2.50
❑2, Mar 87	1.50	0.50	1.25	2.50
❑3, Apr 87	1.50	0.50	1.25	2.50
❑4, May 87	1.50	0.50	1.25	2.50

	ORIG	GOOD	FINE	N-MINT

FANTASTIC PANIC
ANTARCTIC
Value: Cover or less

- ❑1, Aug 93 ... 2.75
- ❑2, Oct 93 ... 2.75
- ❑3, Dec 93 ... 2.75
- ❑4, Feb 94 ... 2.75
- ❑5, Apr 94 ... 2.75
- ❑6, Jun 94 ... 2.75
- ❑7, Aug 94 ... 2.75
- ❑8, Oct 94 ... 2.75

FANTASTIC PANIC (VOL. 2)
ANTARCTIC
Value: Cover or less

- ❑1, Nov 95 ... 2.95
- ❑2, Jan 96 ... 2.95
- ❑3, Mar 96 ... 2.95
- ❑4, May 96 ... 2.95
- ❑5, Jul 96 ... 2.95
- ❑6, Sep 96 ... 2.95
- ❑7, Nov 96 ... 2.95
- ❑8, Dec 96, You Can't Do it ... 2.95

FANTASTIC VOYAGES OF SINDBAD
GOLD KEY

	ORIG	GOOD	FINE	N-MINT
❑1, Oct 65, pin-up on back cover	0.12	3.20	8.00	16.00
❑2	0.12	2.00	5.00	10.00

FANTASTIC WORLDS
FLASHBACK COMICS
Value: Cover or less

- ❑1, Sep 95, b&w ... 2.95

FANTASY FEATURES
AC
Value: Cover or less

- ❑1, Eric the Dragon Slayer: Death Hunt; Back to Syros ... 1.75
- ❑2 ... 1.95

FANTASY GIRLS
COMAX
Value: Cover or less

- ❑1, b&w; adult ... 2.50

FANTASY MASTERPIECES (VOL. 1)
MARVEL

	ORIG	GOOD	FINE	N-MINT
❑1, Feb 66, JK; DH; SD, Golden Age reprints	0.12	3.60	9.00	18.00
❑2, Apr 66, JK; DH; SD, Golden Age reprints; Fin Fang Foom	0.12	3.00	7.50	15.00
❑3, Jun 66, The Hunchback Of Hollywood And The Movie Murder, Golden Age reprints; Captain America, other Golden Age super-heroes appear	0.25	2.80	7.00	14.00
❑4, Aug 66, The Menace Of Dr. Grimm!; The Case Of The Fake Monkey Fiends, Golden Age reprints; Captain America, other Golden Age super-heroes appear	0.25	2.40	6.00	12.00
❑5, Oct 66, Captain America And The Ringmaster Of Death; The Gruesome Secret Of The Dragon Of Doom, Golden Age reprints; Captain America, other Golden Age super-heroes appear	0.25	2.40	6.00	12.00
❑6, Dec 66, Golden Age reprints; Captain America, other Golden Age super-heroes appear	0.25	2.40	6.00	12.00
❑7, Feb 67, Golden Age reprints; Captain America, other Golden Age super-heroes appear	0.25	2.40	6.00	12.00
❑8, Apr 67, Golden Age reprints; Sub-Mariner vs. Human Torch (original)	0.25	2.60	6.50	13.00
❑9, Jun 67, O: Human Torch (original), Golden Age reprints; Reprinted from Marvel Comics #1	0.25	2.40	6.00	12.00
❑10, Aug 67, The All Winners Squad!; The Whizzer, 1: All Winners Squad, Golden Age reprints; Reprinted from All Winners #19	0.25	2.00	5.00	10.00
❑11, Oct 67, The Human Torch, O: Toro, Series continues as Marvel Super-Heroes; Reprinted from Human Torch #1	0.25	2.00	5.00	10.00

FANTASY MASTERPIECES (VOL. 2)
MARVEL

	ORIG	GOOD	FINE	N-MINT
❑1, Dec 79, SL (w), Silver Surfer reprint	0.75	0.80	2.00	4.00
❑2, Jan 80, SL (w)	0.75	0.50	1.25	2.50
❑3, Feb 80, SL (w)	0.75	0.50	1.25	2.50
❑4, Mar 80, SL (w)	0.75	0.50	1.25	2.50
❑5, Apr 80, SL (w)	0.75	0.50	1.25	2.50
❑6, May 80, JB, SL (w), Worlds Without End!	0.75	0.40	1.00	2.00
❑7, Jun 80, SL (w)	0.75	0.40	1.00	2.00
❑8, Jul 80, SL (w)	0.75	0.40	1.00	2.00
❑9, Aug 80, SL (w)	0.75	0.40	1.00	2.00
❑10, Sep 80, JB, SL (w), A World he Never Made	0.75	0.40	1.00	2.00
❑11, Oct 80	0.75	0.40	1.00	2.00
❑12, Nov 80	0.75	0.40	1.00	2.00
❑13, Dec 80	0.75	0.40	1.00	2.00
❑14, Jan 81	0.50	0.40	1.00	2.00

FANTASY QUARTERLY
INDEPENDENT PUB. SYND.

	ORIG	GOOD	FINE	N-MINT
❑1, Spr 78, 1: Elfquest, b&w; back-up story with art by Sim	1.00	8.00	20.00	40.00

FAREWELL, MOONSHADOW
DC
Value: Cover or less

- ❑1, Jan 97, nn; One-Shot; prestige format ... 7.95

A sampling of Marvel's Golden Age output (when the company was known as Timely) can be found reprinted relatively inexpensively in *Fantasy Masterpieces*.

	ORIG	GOOD	FINE	N-MINT

FAREWELL TO WEAPONS
MARVEL
Value: Cover or less

- ❑1, nn ... 2.25

FAR WEST
ANTARCTIC
Value: Cover or less

- ❑1, Nov 98, 1: Meg ... 2.95
- ❑2, Jan 99 ... 2.95
- ❑3, Mar 99 ... 2.95
- ❑4, May 99 ... 2.95

FASHION IN ACTION
ECLIPSE

	ORIG	GOOD	FINE	N-MINT
❑Smr 1, Aug 86, A Force of HabitThe RevenantThe Men in Black!; Luftmann's Move, gatefold summary	1.75	0.40	1.00	2.00
❑WS 1, anniversary	2.00	0.40	1.00	2.00

FASHION POLICE, THE
BRYCE ALAN

	ORIG	GOOD	FINE	N-MINT
❑1	—	0.50	1.25	2.50

FAST FORWARD
DC
Value: Cover or less

- ❑1, phobias ... 4.95
- ❑2, Lester Fenton & The Walking Dead; Brothers & Sisters, family ... 4.95
- ❑3, Riding The Sun; Toybox, Storytellers ... 4.95

FASTLANE ILLUSTRATED
FASTLANE

	ORIG	GOOD	FINE	N-MINT
❑0.5, Fastlane Illustrated, Chapter 1; Sidewinder, Giveaway at 1994 San Diego Comicon	—	0.30	0.75	1.50
❑1, Sep 94, b&w	2.50	0.50	1.25	2.50
❑2, Jun 95, b&w	2.50	0.50	1.25	2.50
❑3, Jul 96, b&w; wraparound cover	2.50	0.50	1.25	2.50

FATAL BEAUTY
ILLUSTRATION
Value: Cover or less

- ❑ASH 1/A, Jun 96, Adult cover ... 3.95

FAT ALBERT
GOLD KEY

	ORIG	GOOD	FINE	N-MINT
❑1	—	1.60	4.00	8.00
❑2	—	1.20	3.00	6.00
❑3	—	1.00	2.50	5.00
❑4	—	1.00	2.50	5.00
❑5	—	1.00	2.50	5.00
❑6	—	1.00	2.50	5.00
❑7	—	0.80	2.00	4.00
❑8	—	0.80	2.00	4.00
❑9	—	0.80	2.00	4.00
❑10	—	0.80	2.00	4.00
❑11	—	0.80	2.00	4.00
❑12	—	0.80	2.00	4.00
❑13	—	0.80	2.00	4.00
❑14	—	0.80	2.00	4.00
❑15	—	0.80	2.00	4.00
❑16	—	0.80	2.00	4.00
❑17	—	0.80	2.00	4.00
❑18, Apr 77	0.30	0.80	2.00	4.00
❑19	—	0.80	2.00	4.00
❑20	—	0.80	2.00	4.00
❑21	—	0.80	2.00	4.00
❑22	—	0.80	2.00	4.00
❑23	—	0.80	2.00	4.00
❑24	—	0.80	2.00	4.00
❑25	—	0.80	2.00	4.00
❑26	—	0.80	2.00	4.00
❑27	—	0.80	2.00	4.00
❑28	—	0.80	2.00	4.00
❑29	—	0.80	2.00	4.00

FATALE
BROADWAY

	ORIG	GOOD	FINE	N-MINT
❑1, Jan 96, Inherit the Earth, Embossed cover	2.50	0.50	1.25	2.50
❑2, Feb 96	2.50	0.50	1.25	2.50

	ORIG	GOOD	FINE	N-MINT
❑3, Mar 96	2.50	0.50	1.25	2.50
❑4, May 96	2.50	0.50	1.25	2.50
❑5, Jul 96, The Word	2.95	0.59	1.48	2.95
❑6, Oct 96, Final Issue	2.95	0.59	1.48	2.95
❑Ash 1, Sep 95, b&w; giveaway preview edition	—	0.20	0.50	1.00

FAT DOG MENDOZA
DARK HORSE

Value: Cover or less

❑1, Dec 92, b&w 2.50

FATE
DC

	ORIG	GOOD	FINE	N-MINT
❑0, Oct 94, Twisted Fate, D: Doctor Fate III (Kent & Inza Nelson); 1: Doctor Fate IV (Jared Stevens)	1.95	0.50	1.25	2.50
❑1, Nov 94, Kings And Desperate Men, O: Doctor Fate IV (Jared Stevens)	1.95	0.50	1.25	2.50
❑2, Dec 94	1.95	0.40	1.00	2.00
❑3, Jan 95, The Horde	1.95	0.40	1.00	2.00
❑4, Feb 95	1.95	0.40	1.00	2.00
❑5, Mar 95	1.95	0.40	1.00	2.00
❑6, Apr 95	1.95	0.40	1.00	2.00
❑7, May 95	1.95	0.40	1.00	2.00
❑8, Jun 95	2.25	0.45	1.13	2.25
❑9, Jul 95	2.25	0.45	1.13	2.25
❑10, Aug 95	2.25	0.45	1.13	2.25
❑11, Sep 95	2.25	0.45	1.13	2.25
❑12, Oct 95, A: Sentinel	2.25	0.45	1.13	2.25
❑13, Nov 95, Underworld Unleashed, Underworld Unleashed	2.25	0.45	1.13	2.25
❑14, Dec 95	2.25	0.45	1.13	2.25
❑15, Jan 96, Chasers	2.25	0.45	1.13	2.25
❑16, Feb 96, Gone South	2.25	0.45	1.13	2.25
❑17, Mar 96, Bad Blood	2.25	0.45	1.13	2.25
❑18, May 96	2.25	0.45	1.13	2.25
❑19, Jun 96	2.25	0.45	1.13	2.25
❑20, Jul 96, The Hand of Fate, Part 1	2.25	0.45	1.13	2.25
❑21, Aug 96, The Hand of Fate, Part 2	2.25	0.45	1.13	2.25
❑22, Sep 96, The Hand of Fate, Part 3, Final Issue; Kent and Inza Nelson go to heaven	2.25	0.45	1.13	2.25

FATE'S FIVE
INNERVISION

Value: Cover or less

❑1, b&w 2.50
❑2 ..... 2.50
❑3 ..... 2.50
❑4 ..... 2.50

FAT FREDDY'S CAT
RIP OFF

	ORIG	GOOD	FINE	N-MINT
❑1, I Led Nine Lives!, b&w	2.50	3.60	9.00	18.00
❑1-2, I Led Nine Lives!, b&w; 2nd Printing; 1988 printing	2.95	0.80	2.00	4.00
❑, I Led Nine Lives!, 1988 printing	2.95	0.70	1.75	3.50
❑2, b&w	2.50	1.80	4.50	9.00
❑3, b&w	2.50	1.60	4.00	8.00
❑4, b&w	2.50	0.80	2.00	4.00
❑5, b&w	2.50	0.80	2.00	4.00
❑6, b&w	2.50	0.60	1.50	3.00
❑7, b&w	2.95	0.60	1.50	3.00

FAT FREDDY'S COMICS & STORIES
RIP OFF

Value: Cover or less

❑1, Dec 83 ..... 2.50
❑2, Dec 85 ..... 2.50

FAT FURY SPECIAL
AVALON

Value: Cover or less

❑1, b&w; reprints Herbie stories 2.95

FATHER & SON
KITCHEN SINK

	ORIG	GOOD	FINE	N-MINT
❑1, Jul 95, The Seventies; Great Jobs, b&w	2.75	0.55	1.38	2.75
❑2, Sep 95, b&w	2.75	0.55	1.38	2.75
❑3, Dec 95, b&w	2.75	0.55	1.38	2.75
❑4, Jan 96, b&w	2.75	0.55	1.38	2.75
❑Ash 1, Jul 95, ashcan edition limited to 200, b&w	—	0.40	1.00	2.00
❑SE 1, Reality Soldiers; Road Trip, b&w; "Like, Special #1"	3.95	0.79	1.98	3.95

FATHOM (1ST SERIES)
COMICO

Value: Cover or less

❑1, May 87, Auld Lang Syne .. 1.50
❑2, Jun 87 ..... 1.50
❑3, Jul 87, wraparound cover . 1.50

FATHOM (2ND SERIES)
COMICO

Value: Cover or less

❑1 ..... 2.50
❑2 ..... 2.50
❑3, Genie In A Bottle, Chapter 3 ..... 2.50

FATHOM (3RD SERIES)
IMAGE

	ORIG	GOOD	FINE	N-MINT
❑0, Wizard Promotional Edition: Given away with subsrciption to Wizard	—	0.60	1.50	3.00
❑0/A, Green holografix cover	—	1.20	3.00	6.00
❑0/B, Signed by Michael Turner; Wizard authentic edition	—	1.60	4.00	8.00
❑1/A, Aug 98, Variant covers, some pages	2.50	0.80	2.00	4.00
❑1/B, Aug 98, Variant covers, some pages; Fathom standing underwater	2.50	0.80	2.00	4.00
❑1/C, Aug 98, Fathom, dolphins on cover w/ inset close-up	2.50	0.80	2.00	4.00
❑1/D, Museum edition; Limited to 50 copies	—	30.00	75.00	150.00
❑2, Sep 98	2.50	0.60	1.50	3.00
❑3, Oct 98	2.50	0.60	1.50	3.00
❑3/SC, Monster Edition: No cover price	—	1.00	2.50	5.00
❑4, Mar 99	2.50	0.50	1.25	2.50
❑5, May 99	2.50	0.50	1.25	2.50
❑6, Jun 99	2.50	0.50	1.25	2.50
❑7, Aug 99	2.50	0.50	1.25	2.50
❑8, Sep 99	2.50	0.50	1.25	2.50
❑9, Oct 99	2.50	0.50	1.25	2.50
❑9/A, Holofoil edition	—	2.40	6.00	12.00
❑9/B, Platinum Holofoil edition	—	1.60	4.00	8.00
❑9/C, Aspen on outcropping	—	2.00	5.00	10.00
❑9/D, Green logo variant w/Aspen on rock outcropping	—	3.00	7.50	15.00
❑10, Jan 00	2.50	0.50	1.25	2.50
❑10/A, Perfect 10 DFE Alternate cover	—	1.00	2.50	5.00
❑10/B, Perfect 10 DFE Alternate cover with Gold Stamp and certificate of authenticity	—	2.00	5.00	10.00
❑11, Apr 00	2.50	0.50	1.25	2.50
❑12, Jul 00, Witchblade in background, Fathom crawling on cover	2.50	0.50	1.25	2.50
❑12/A	—	1.60	4.00	8.00
❑12/B, Holofoil edition	—	1.50	3.75	7.50
❑12/C, DF Alternate edition	—	1.60	4.00	8.00
❑12/D, DF Alternate edition with certificate of authenticity; Gold logo	—	2.00	5.00	10.00

FATHOM SWIMSUIT SPECIAL
IMAGE

Value: Cover or less

❑1 ..... 2.95
❑2000, Dec 00 ..... 2.95

FAT NINJA, THE
SILVERWOLF

Value: Cover or less

❑1, b&w 1.50
❑2, b&w 1.50
❑3, b&w 1.50
❑4, b&w 1.50
❑5, b&w 1.50

FATT FAMILY, THE
SIDE SHOW

Value: Cover or less

❑1, 1: The Fatt Family, b&w 2.95

FAULTLINES
DC

Value: Cover or less

❑1, May 97, Fresh Meat, Old Lies 2.50
❑2, Jun 97 ..... 2.50
❑3, Jul 97 ..... 2.50
❑4, Aug 97 ..... 2.50
❑5, Sep 97 ..... 2.50
❑6, Oct 97 ..... 2.50

FAUNA REBELLION, THE
FANTAGRAPHICS

Value: Cover or less

❑1, Mar 90, Where There's Smoke, b&w 2.00
❑2, b&w 2.00
❑3, b&w 2.00

FAUST
NORTHSTAR

	ORIG	GOOD	FINE	N-MINT
❑1	2.00	3.60	9.00	18.00
❑1-2, 2nd Printing	2.00	1.00	2.50	5.00
❑, 3rd Printing	2.25	0.60	1.50	3.00
❑2	2.00	2.40	6.00	12.00
❑2-2, 2nd Printing	2.00	0.80	2.00	4.00
❑2-3, 3rd Printing	2.25	0.60	1.50	3.00
❑3	2.25	1.60	4.00	8.00
❑3-2, 2nd Printing	2.25	0.60	1.50	3.00
❑4, Blues Wif' the Moon; Fritzwhitstle	2.25	1.00	2.50	5.00
❑4-2, Blues Wif' the Moon; Fritzwhitstle, 2nd Printing	2.25	0.60	1.50	3.00
❑5	2.25	1.00	2.50	5.00
❑5-2, 2nd Printing	2.25	0.60	1.50	3.00
❑6, becomes Rebel title	2.25	0.80	2.00	4.00
❑6-2, 2nd Printing	2.25	0.60	1.50	3.00
❑7, Delicate Tone	2.25	0.80	2.00	4.00
❑7-2, Delicate Tone, 2nd Printing; gatefold cover	2.25	0.50	1.25	2.50
❑8, Jaded Love	2.25	0.80	2.00	4.00
❑8-2, Jaded Love, 2nd Printing	2.25	0.50	1.25	2.50
❑9	2.25	0.70	1.75	3.50
❑9-2, 2nd Printing	2.25	0.50	1.25	2.50
❑10	2.25	0.70	1.75	3.50
❑10-2, 2nd Printing	2.25	0.50	1.25	2.50
❑11, The Tantric Manifold	2.25	0.50	1.25	2.50

FAUST 777: THE WRATH
AVATAR

Value: Cover or less

- ❑0, Dec 98, Darkness in Collision, Part 1 ... 3.00

FAUST: THE BOOK OF M
AVATAR

	ORIG	GOOD	FINE	N-MINT
❑1	—	0.60	1.50	3.00

FEAR
MARVEL

	ORIG	GOOD	FINE	N-MINT
❑1, Nov 70	0.25	2.00	5.00	10.00
❑2, Jan 71	0.25	1.20	3.00	6.00
❑3, Mar 71	0.25	0.80	2.00	4.00
❑4, Jul 71, JK; SD, Lo-Karr, Bringer of Doom!; Mister Gregory and the Ghost!	0.25	0.80	2.00	4.00
❑5, SD, I Am the Gorilla-Man; One Look Means Doom!	0.25	0.80	2.00	4.00
❑6, Feb 72, DH; SD, SL (w), Midnight Monster; There is a Brain Behind the Fangs!	0.25	0.80	2.00	4.00
❑7, May 72	0.20	0.80	2.00	4.00
❑8, Jun 72	0.20	0.80	2.00	4.00
❑9, Aug 72	0.20	0.80	2.00	4.00
❑10, Oct 72, HC, Man-Thing stories begin ("Adventures into Fear")	0.20	2.40	6.00	12.00
❑11, Dec 72, Man-Thing	0.20	1.20	3.00	6.00
❑12, Feb 73, Man-Thing	0.20	0.80	2.00	4.00
❑13, Apr 73, Man-Thing	0.20	0.80	2.00	4.00
❑14, Jun 73, Man-Thing	0.20	0.80	2.00	4.00
❑15, Aug 73, Man-Thing	0.20	0.80	2.00	4.00
❑16, Sep 73, Man-Thing	0.20	0.80	2.00	4.00
❑17, Oct 73, V: Wundarr, Man-Thing	0.20	0.80	2.00	4.00
❑18, Nov 73, Man-Thing	0.20	0.80	2.00	4.00
❑19, Dec 73, 1: Howard the Duck, Man-Thing	0.20	2.80	7.00	14.00
❑20, Feb 74, PG, Morbius the Living Vampire!; Midnight in the Wax Museum!, Morbius stories begin	0.20	2.00	5.00	10.00
❑21, Apr 74, Morbius	0.20	0.80	2.00	4.00
❑22, Jun 74, Morbius	0.25	0.80	2.00	4.00
❑23, Aug 74, CR, A: Morbius, 1st Russell art	0.25	0.80	2.00	4.00
❑24, Oct 74, A: Blade the Vampire Slayer; V: Blade, Morbius	0.25	1.20	3.00	6.00
❑25, Dec 74, Morbius	0.25	0.60	1.50	3.00
❑26, Feb 75, Morbius	0.25	0.60	1.50	3.00
❑27, Apr 75, V: Simon Stroud, Morbius	0.25	0.60	1.50	3.00
❑28, Jun 75, FR, The Doorway Screaming Into Hell!, Morbius	0.25	0.60	1.50	3.00
❑29, Aug 75, DH, Through A Helleyes Darkly!, A: Morbius; A: Simon Stroud; A: Helleyes	0.25	0.60	1.50	3.00
❑30, Oct 75, Morbius	0.25	0.60	1.50	3.00
❑31, Dec 75, Final Issue; Morbius	0.25	0.60	1.50	3.00

FEAR EFFECT SPECIAL
IMAGE

Value: Cover or less

- ❑1, May 00 ... 2.95

FEDS 'N' HEADS
PRINT MINT

	ORIG	GOOD	FINE	N-MINT
❑1, Wonder Wart-Hog Meets The Elusive, Chimerical Chameleon!; O	0.50	0.80	2.00	4.00

FEEDERS
DARK HORSE

Value: Cover or less

- ❑1, Oct 99, After Prohibition; The Case of Doctor Feelgood: The TV Freak ... 2.95

FEELGOOD FUNNIES
RIP OFF

	ORIG	GOOD	FINE	N-MINT
❑1, After Prohibition; The Case of Doctor Feelgood: The TV Freak	0.50	0.60	1.50	3.00

FELICIA HARDY: THE BLACK CAT
MARVEL

Value: Cover or less

- ❑1, Jul 94, Chimera Lost, Part 1 ... 1.50
- ❑2, Aug 94, Chimera Lost, Part 2 ... 1.50
- ❑3, Sep 94, Chimera Lost, Part 3 ... 1.50
- ❑4, Oct 94, Chimera Lost, Part 4, Final Issue ... 1.50

FELIX THE CAT
HARVEY

Value: Cover or less

- ❑1, Feb 48 ... 1.25
- ❑2, Apr 48 ... 1.25
- ❑3 ... 1.25
- ❑4 ... 1.25
- ❑5 ... 1.25
- ❑6 ... 1.25
- ❑7 ... 1.25

FELIX THE CAT AND FRIENDS
FELIX

Value: Cover or less

- ❑1 ... 1.95
- ❑2 ... 1.95
- ❑3 ... 1.95
- ❑4 ... 1.95
- ❑5 ... 1.95

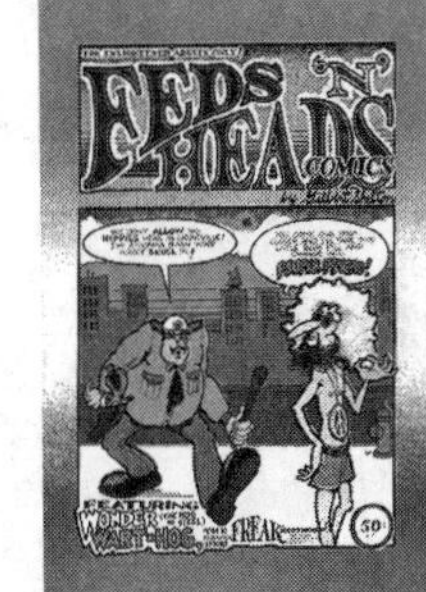

A Wonder Wart-Hog adventure appears in Print Mint's *Feds 'n' Heads.*

FELIX THE CAT BIG BOOK (VOL. 2)
HARVEY

Value: Cover or less

- ❑1, Sep 92, The Rainmaker; Bolts in the Blue ... 1.95

FELIX THE CAT BLACK & WHITE
FELIX

Value: Cover or less

- ❑1, The Felix CafT; Magic Bag Mishap ... 1.95
- ❑2 ... 1.95
- ❑3 ... 1.95
- ❑4 ... 1.95
- ❑5 ... 1.95
- ❑6 ... 1.95
- ❑7 ... 2.25
- ❑8 ... 2.25

FELIX THE CAT DIGEST MAGAZINE
HARVEY

Value: Cover or less

- ❑1 ... 1.75

FEM 5
EXPRESS

Value: Cover or less

- ❑1, four cover variants ... 2.95
- ❑1/A, Breakthrough, variant cover ... 2.95
- ❑1/B, Breakthrough, variant cover ... 2.95
- ❑1/C, Breakthrough, variant cover ... 2.95
- ❑1/D, Breakthrough, variant cover ... 2.95
- ❑2 ... 2.95

FEMALE SEX PIRATES
FRIENDLY

Value: Cover or less

- ❑1, Scourge of the Seas ... 2.95

FEM FANTASTIQUE
AC

Value: Cover or less

- ❑1, Jul 88, Rad; Dragonfly, b&w ... 1.95

FEMFORCE
AC

	ORIG	GOOD	FINE	N-MINT
❑1, Trek for the Time Twister!, O: Femforce, full color	1.75	1.00	2.50	5.00
❑2, full color	1.75	0.70	1.75	3.50
❑3, full color	1.75	0.60	1.50	3.00
❑4, full color	1.75	0.60	1.50	3.00
❑5, full color	1.75	0.60	1.50	3.00
❑6, Feb 87, full color	1.75	0.50	1.25	2.50
❑7, May 87, full color	1.75	0.50	1.25	2.50
❑8, Jul 87, full color	1.75	0.50	1.25	2.50
❑9, Aug 87, full color	1.95	0.50	1.25	2.50
❑10, full color	1.95	0.50	1.25	2.50
❑11, Mar 88, full color	1.95	0.50	1.25	2.50
❑12, May 88, full color	1.95	0.50	1.25	2.50
❑13, May 88, full color	1.95	0.50	1.25	2.50
❑14, full color	1.95	0.50	1.25	2.50
❑15, Aug 88, full color	1.95	0.50	1.25	2.50
❑16	2.25	0.50	1.25	2.50
❑17, Jan 89	2.25	0.50	1.25	2.50
❑18	2.25	0.50	1.25	2.50
❑19, Apr 89	2.25	0.50	1.25	2.50
❑20, b&w	2.50	0.50	1.25	2.50
❑21, b&w	2.50	0.50	1.25	2.50
❑22, b&w	2.50	0.50	1.25	2.50
❑23, b&w	2.50	0.50	1.25	2.50
❑24, Apr 90, b&w	2.50	0.50	1.25	2.50
❑25, May 90, b&w	2.50	0.50	1.25	2.50
❑26, Jun 90, b&w	2.50	0.50	1.25	2.50
❑27, Jul 90, b&w	2.50	0.50	1.25	2.50
❑28, Aug 90, b&w	2.50	0.50	1.25	2.50
❑29, Sep 90, b&w	2.50	0.50	1.25	2.50
❑30, Nov 90, b&w	2.50	0.50	1.25	2.50
❑31, Dec 90	2.75	0.55	1.38	2.75
❑32, Jan 91	2.75	0.55	1.38	2.75
❑33, Feb 91	2.75	0.55	1.38	2.75
❑34, Mar 91	2.75	0.55	1.38	2.75
❑35, Apr 91	2.75	0.55	1.38	2.75
❑36, May 91	2.75	0.55	1.38	2.75
❑37, Jun 91	2.75	0.55	1.38	2.75
❑38, Jul 91	2.75	0.55	1.38	2.75
❑39, Aug 91	2.75	0.55	1.38	2.75
❑40, Sep 91	2.75	0.55	1.38	2.75

	ORIG	GOOD	FINE	N-MINT
❑41, Oct 91	2.75	0.55	1.38	2.75
❑42, Nov 91	2.75	0.55	1.38	2.75
❑43, Dec 91	2.75	0.55	1.38	2.75
❑44	2.75	0.55	1.38	2.75
❑45	2.75	0.55	1.38	2.75
❑46	2.75	0.55	1.38	2.75
❑47	2.75	0.55	1.38	2.75
❑48	2.75	0.55	1.38	2.75
❑49	2.75	0.55	1.38	2.75
❑50, flexi-disc; contains flexidisccolor	2.95	0.59	1.48	2.95
❑51, Photo cover	2.75	0.55	1.38	2.75
❑52, In the Clutches of the Claw!, Part 3	2.75	0.55	1.38	2.75
❑53	2.75	0.55	1.38	2.75
❑54	2.75	0.55	1.38	2.75
❑55	2.75	0.55	1.38	2.75
❑56	2.75	0.55	1.38	2.75
❑57, The Capricorn Chronicles, Part 3, full color	2.75	0.55	1.38	2.75
❑58, O: Microman	2.75	0.55	1.38	2.75
❑59	2.75	0.55	1.38	2.75
❑60	2.75	0.55	1.38	2.75
❑61	2.75	0.55	1.38	2.75
❑62	2.75	0.55	1.38	2.75
❑63, Assault of the 60 Foot Woman, Chapter 1	2.95	0.59	1.48	2.95
❑64	2.95	0.59	1.48	2.95
❑65	2.95	0.59	1.48	2.95
❑66	2.95	0.59	1.48	2.95
❑67	2.95	0.59	1.48	2.95
❑68	2.95	0.59	1.48	2.95
❑69	2.95	0.59	1.48	2.95
❑70	2.95	0.59	1.48	2.95
❑71	2.95	0.59	1.48	2.95
❑72	2.95	0.59	1.48	2.95
❑73	2.95	0.59	1.48	2.95
❑74	2.95	0.59	1.48	2.95
❑75	2.95	0.59	1.48	2.95
❑76	2.95	0.59	1.48	2.95
❑77	2.95	0.59	1.48	2.95
❑78	2.95	0.59	1.48	2.95
❑79	2.95	0.59	1.48	2.95
❑80, V: Iron Jaw	2.95	0.59	1.48	2.95
❑81	2.95	0.59	1.48	2.95
❑82, Twilight's Last Gleaming, Part 1	2.95	0.59	1.48	2.95
❑83	2.95	0.59	1.48	2.95
❑84, The Death of Joan Wayne	2.95	0.59	1.48	2.95
❑85	2.95	0.59	1.48	2.95
❑86	2.95	0.59	1.48	2.95
❑87, A: AC staff, 10th anniversary issue	3.50	0.59	1.48	2.95
❑88	2.95	0.59	1.48	2.95
❑89	2.95	0.59	1.48	2.95
❑90	2.95	0.59	1.48	2.95
❑91	2.95	0.59	1.48	2.95
❑92	2.95	0.59	1.48	2.95
❑93	2.95	0.59	1.48	2.95
❑94	2.95	0.59	1.48	2.95
❑95	2.95	0.59	1.48	2.95
❑96	2.95	0.59	1.48	2.95
❑97, b&w	2.95	0.59	1.48	2.95
❑98, b&w; subtitled in Spanish	2.95	0.59	1.48	2.95
❑99, b&w	2.95	0.59	1.48	2.95
❑100, b&w; photo back cover	3.95	0.79	1.98	3.95
❑100/CS, poster	6.90	1.38	3.45	6.90
❑101, The Yesterday Syndrome, Part 1, b&w	4.95	0.99	2.47	4.95
❑102, The Yesterday Syndrome, Part 2, b&w	4.95	0.99	2.47	4.95
❑103, b&w	4.95	0.99	2.47	4.95
❑104, Return from the Ashes, Part 1; Prelude to Darkness, b&w	4.95	0.99	2.47	4.95
❑105, Return from the Ashes, Part 2, b&w	4.95	0.99	2.47	4.95
❑106, Return from the Ashes, Part 3, b&w	4.95	0.99	2.47	4.95
❑107, Rampage; Old Flames	4.95	0.99	2.47	4.95
❑108	4.95	0.99	2.47	4.95
❑109	4.95	0.99	2.47	4.95
❑110/A, Rayda on cover	2.95	0.59	1.48	2.95
❑110/B, Femforce on cover	2.95	0.59	1.48	2.95
❑111	2.95	0.59	1.48	2.95
❑112	2.95	0.59	1.48	2.95
❑113	2.95	0.59	1.48	2.95
❑114	2.95	0.59	1.48	2.95
❑SE 1, Nov 84	1.50	0.30	0.75	1.50

FEMFORCE FRIGHTBOOK
AC

Value: Cover or less

❑1, b&w 2.95

FEMFORCE IN THE HOUSE OF HORROR
AC

Value: Cover or less

❑1, b&w 2.50

FEMFORCE: NIGHT OF THE DEMON
AC

Value: Cover or less

❑1, nn; b&w 2.75

FEMFORCE: OUT OF THE ASYLUM SPECIAL
AC

Value: Cover or less

❑1, Aug 87, b&w 2.50

FEMFORCE PIN UP PORTFOLIO
AC

Value: Cover or less

❑1 .... 2.50
❑2 .... 2.50
❑3 .... 2.50
❑4, Dec 91 .... 2.50
❑5 .... 5.00

FEMFORCE UP CLOSE
AC

	ORIG	GOOD	FINE	N-MINT
❑1, full color; Nightveil	2.75	0.60	1.50	3.00
❑2, Stardust	2.75	0.60	1.50	3.00
❑3, Dragonfly	2.75	0.60	1.50	3.00
❑4, O: She Cat	2.95	0.59	1.48	2.95
❑5, Blue Bulleteer	2.95	0.59	1.48	2.95
❑6, Ms. Victory	2.95	0.59	1.48	2.95
❑7, Ms. Victory	2.95	0.59	1.48	2.95
❑8, Tara, Garganta	2.95	0.59	1.48	2.95
❑9, Synn	2.95	0.59	1.48	2.95
❑10, b&w; Yankee Girl	2.95	0.59	1.48	2.95
❑11, b&w; Nightveil	2.95	0.59	1.48	2.95

FEMME MACABRE
LONDON NIGHT

Value: Cover or less

❑1 .... 2.95

FEMME NOIRE
CAT-HEAD

Value: Cover or less

❑1, The Shamness; Wimp Rock Babylon 1.75
❑2, Love Triangle; Yarhooty! ... 1.75

FENRY
RAVEN

Value: Cover or less

❑1, Yesterday's Spirit 6.95

FERRET (1ST SERIES)
MALIBU

Value: Cover or less

❑1, Flesh and Steel 1.95

FERRET, THE (2ND SERIES)
MALIBU

Value: Cover or less

❑1, In The Midnight Hour 1.95
❑1/SC, In The Midnight Hour, die-cut 2.50
❑2, Deadline Medix, poster 2.50
❑3, Countdown To Oblivion 2.50
❑4, poster 2.25
❑5, Thicker Than Water 2.25
❑6 .... 2.25
❑7 .... 2.25
❑8 .... 2.25
❑9, Jan 94 .... 2.50
❑10, Feb 94 .... 2.50

FEUD
MARVEL

Value: Cover or less

❑1, Jul 93, embossed cardstock cover 2.50
❑2, Aug 93 .... 1.95
❑3, Sep 93 .... 1.95
❑4, Oct 93, A: Mammals; A: Skids; A: Throckmorton; A: Dust Devils; A: Stoker 1.95

FEVER
WONDER COMIX

Value: Cover or less

❑1, Fear (Text Story); I Suspect the Sea (Poem), b&w; Anthology 1.95

FEVER DREAMS
KITCHEN SINK

	ORIG	GOOD	FINE	N-MINT
❑1, The Unicorn Quest; To Meet the Faces You Meet	0.50	0.60	1.50	3.00

FIFTH FORCE FEATURING HAWK AND ANIMAL, THE
ANTARCTIC

Value: Cover or less

❑1, Apr 99, 1: Hawk and Animal (in comics) 1.99
❑2, Jul 99 .... 2.50

FIFTIES TERROR
ETERNITY

Value: Cover or less

❑1, b&w; Reprint 1.95
❑2, b&w; Reprint 1.95
❑3, b&w; Reprint 1.95
❑4, b&w; Reprint 1.95
❑5, b&w; Reprint 1.95
❑6, b&w; Reprint 1.95

FIFTY WHO MADE DC GREAT
DC

Value: Cover or less

❑1, Oct 85, Tribute Issue 2.95

FIGHTING AMERICAN (AWESOME)
AWESOME

Value: Cover or less

❑1/A, RL, RL (w); JPH (w), Back in the Ring, Diving at guns, bayonets on cover 2.50
❑1/B, RL, RL (w); JPH (w), Back in the Ring, Holding flag on cover 2.50
❑1/C, RL, RL (w); JPH (w), Back in the Ring, Comics Cavalcade regular edition (two heroes diving toward a gun at lower left corner) 2.50
❑1/D, RL, RL (w); JPH (w), Back in the Ring, Comics Cavalcade Liberty Gold Foil Edition 15.95
❑2, RL, RL (w); JPH (w) 2.50
❑3, RL, RL (w); JPH (w) 2.50

FIGHTING AMERICAN (MINI-SERIES)
DC
Value: Cover or less

- ❑1, Feb 94, Brothers' Keepers Losers Weepers, O: Fighting American 1.50
- ❑2, Mar 94, Here Comes the Media Circus 1.50
- ❑3, Apr 94 .... 1.50
- ❑4, May 94 .... 1.50
- ❑5, Jun 94 .... 1.50
- ❑6, Jul 94, The Fighting Ugly American 1.50

FIGHTING AMERICAN: DOGS OF WAR
AWESOME

	ORIG	GOOD	FINE	N-MINT
❑1, Sep 98, JSn (w), Dogs of War!	2.50	0.50	1.25	2.50
❑1/A, Sep 98, JSn (w), Dogs of War!, 98 Tour Edition cover	—	0.60	1.50	3.00

FIGHTING AMERICAN: RULES OF THE GAME
AWESOME
Value: Cover or less

- ❑1, Nov 97 .... 2.50
- ❑1/A, Nov 97, JPH (w), Do Not Pass "Go", Fighting American standing on cover 2.50
- ❑1/B, Nov 97, JPH (w), Do Not Pass "Go", Woman pointing gun on cover 2.50

FIGHTING AMERICAN SPECIAL COMICON EDITION
AWESOME

	ORIG	GOOD	FINE	N-MINT
❑1, nn; no cover price; b&w preview of upcoming series given out at Comic-Con International: San Diego 1997	—	0.20	0.50	1.00

FIGHTING FEM CLASSICS
FORBIDDEN FRUIT
Value: Cover or less

- ❑1, b&w; adult 3.50

FIGHTING FEMS
FORBIDDEN FRUIT
Value: Cover or less

- ❑1, b&w; adult 3.50
- ❑2, b&w; adult 3.50

FIGHT MAN
MARVEL
Value: Cover or less

- ❑1, Jun 93, The Big Fight! 2.00

FIGHT THE ENEMY
TOWER

	ORIG	GOOD	FINE	N-MINT
❑1	0.25	4.20	10.50	21.00
❑2, Saga of the Lucky 7, Michel's Revenge; K.P. McGoof	0.25	3.20	8.00	16.00
❑3	0.25	3.20	8.00	16.00

FIGMENTS
BLACKTHORNE
Value: Cover or less

- ❑1 .... 1.75
- ❑2 .... 1.75

FIGMENTS UNLIMITED
GRAPHIK
Value: Cover or less

- ❑1 .... 1.25
- ❑2 .... 1.25
- ❑3, Vengeance is Mine 1.25

FILES OF MS. TREE, THE
RENEGADE

	ORIG	GOOD	FINE	N-MINT
❑1, Jun 84, b&w	—	0.60	1.50	3.00
❑2, Sep 85, b&w	—	0.60	1.50	3.00
❑3, b&w	—	0.60	1.50	3.00

FILIBUSTING COMICS
FANTAGRAPHICS
Value: Cover or less

- ❑1, Jan 95, b&w 2.75

FILTHY ANIMALS
RADIO
Value: Cover or less

- ❑1, Aug 97, Of Toons & Poons 2.95
- ❑2 .... 2.95
- ❑3, Aug 98 .... 2.95
- ❑4 .... 2.95

FILTHY HABITS
AEON
Value: Cover or less

- ❑1, Jul 96, b&w 2.95
- ❑2, Nov 96, Lobsters Away!; Man Was She Fine, b&w 2.95
- ❑3, Feb 97, An Incidental Death; Really Small Hitler, b&w 2.95

FINAL CYCLE, THE
DRAGON'S TEETH
Value: Cover or less

- ❑1, b&w 1.75
- ❑2, b&w 1.75
- ❑3, b&w 1.75
- ❑4, b&w 1.75

FINAL MAN, THE
C&T
Value: Cover or less

- ❑1, b&w 1.50

FINAL NIGHT, THE
DC

	ORIG	GOOD	FINE	N-MINT
❑1, Nov 96, Dusk	1.95	0.50	1.25	2.50
❑2, Nov 96, Darker Grows the Night	1.95	0.40	1.00	2.00
❑3, Nov 96, Keeping Hope Alive	1.95	0.40	1.00	2.00
❑4, Nov, The Final Knight, D: Hal Jordan	1.95	0.40	1.00	2.00

FINALS
DC
Value: Cover or less

- ❑1, Sep 99, Back to School 2.95
- ❑2, Oct 99, All-Nighters 2.95
- ❑3, Nov 99, Hell Week 2.95
- ❑4, Dec 99, Pomp & Circumstance Beyond Our Control 2.95

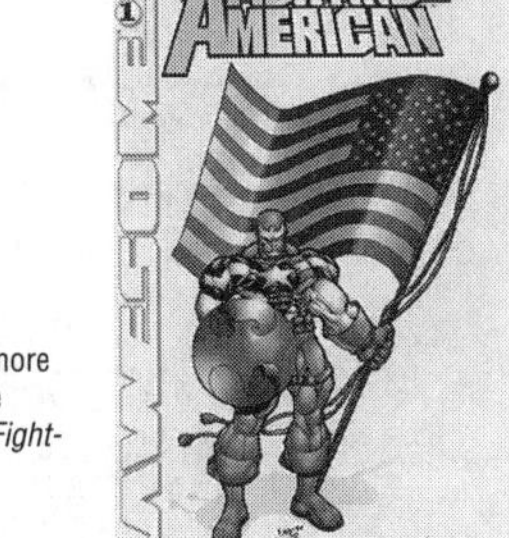

In 1997, Rob Liefeld attempted a more serious take on Jack Kirby and Joe Simon's Captain America parody, *Fighting American.*

© 1997 Joe Simon (Awesome)

FINAL TABOO
AIRCEL
Value: Cover or less

- ❑1, b&w; adult 2.50
- ❑2, b&w; adult 2.50

FINDER
LIGHTSPEED PRESS

	ORIG	GOOD	FINE	N-MINT
❑1, Nov 96, Salutation, b&w; wraparound cover	2.95	0.70	1.75	3.50
❑2, Jan 97, b&w	2.95	0.70	1.75	3.50
❑3, Mar 97, b&w	2.95	0.70	1.75	3.50
❑4	3.50	0.70	1.75	3.50
❑5	3.50	0.70	1.75	3.50
❑6	3.50	0.70	1.75	3.50
❑7	3.50	0.70	1.75	3.50
❑8	3.50	0.70	1.75	3.50
❑9	3.50	0.70	1.75	3.50
❑10	3.50	0.70	1.75	3.50
❑11	—	0.70	1.75	3.50
❑12	—	0.70	1.75	3.50
❑13	—	0.70	1.75	3.50
❑14	—	0.70	1.75	3.50
❑15, Dec 99, The King of the Cats, Part 1	2.95	0.59	1.48	2.95
❑16, Feb 00, The King of the Cats, Part 2	2.95	0.59	1.48	2.95
❑17, May 00, The King of the Cats, Part 3	2.95	0.59	1.48	2.95
❑18	2.95	0.59	1.48	2.95
❑19	2.95	0.59	1.48	2.95
❑20	2.95	0.59	1.48	2.95
❑21	2.95	0.59	1.48	2.95
❑22	2.95	0.59	1.48	2.95
❑23	2.95	0.59	1.48	2.95
❑Ash 1	—	0.20	0.50	1.00

FINDER FOOTNOTES
LIGHTSPEED
Value: Cover or less

- ❑1 .... 6.00

FINIEOUS TREASURY, THE
TSR
Value: Cover or less

- ❑1, nn; collects Finieous Fingers strips from Dragon magazine; magazine-sized 3.00

FINK, INC.
FINK, INC.
Value: Cover or less

- ❑1 .... 3.50

FIRE
CALIBER
Value: Cover or less

- ❑1, BMB, BMB (w), b&w 2.95
- ❑2, BMB, BMB (w), b&w 2.95

FIREARM
MALIBU
Value: Cover or less

- ❑0, Aug 93, with videotape 14.95
- ❑1, Sep 93, JRo (w), American Pastimes, Part 1, 1: Firearm 1.95
- ❑1/LE, JRo (w), American Pastimes, Part 1, 1: Firearm, foil cover; limited promotional edition 25.00
- ❑2, Oct 93, JRo (w), Rune, Part I; American Pastimes, Part 2, 1: Mosely, Rune 2.50
- ❑3, Nov 93, JRo (w), American Pastimes, Part 3, 1: The Sportsmen 1.95
- ❑4, Dec 93, JRo (w), American Pastimes, Part 4; Break-Thru, Break-Thru 1.95
- ❑5, Jan 94, JRo (w), Said T.E. Lawrence, Picking Up His Fork... .... 1.95
- ❑6, Feb 94, JRo (w), Missing Child, A: Prime 1.95
- ❑7, Mar 94, JRo (w), Mystery Tour 1.95
- ❑8, May 94, JRo (w), Kirby 1.95
- ❑9, Jun 94, JRo (w), Idle Thoughts, 1: Willy Manila; 1: Ms. Rule 1.95
- ❑10, Jul 94, JRo (w), South of Watford, then Way, Way North, Part 1; Hang Time, 1: Faulkner; 1: Iron Clad; 1: Aeon, Flip book with Ultraverse Premiere #5 .... 3.50
- ❑11, Jul 94, JRo (w), South of Watford, then Way, Way North, Part 2, 1: Right Man; 1: Doctor Z, flip-book with Ultraverse Premiere #5 .... 1.95
- ❑12, Aug 94, JRo (w), Rafferty Saga Prologue; The Rafferty Saga, 1: Rafferty; D: Last; D: Doctor Z; D: Lukasz 1.95
- ❑13, Sep 94, JRo (w), Rafferty Saga, Part 1; The Rafferty Saga, Part 1 .... 1.95
- ❑14, Oct 94, JRo (w), Rafferty Saga, Part 2; The Rafferty Saga, Part 2, D: Vinaigrette; D: Organism 0.9B 1.95
- ❑15, Nov 94, JRo (w), Rafferty Saga, Part 3; The Rafferty Saga, Part 3 .... 1.95

❑16, Dec 94, JRo (w), Rafferty Saga, Part 4; The Rafferty Saga, Part 4, D: Sigma ... 1.95
❑17, Jan 95, JRo (w), Rafferty Saga, Part 5; The Rafferty Saga, Part 5, D: The Silence; A: Elvis Presley (impersonator) ... 1.95
❑18, Feb 95, JRo (w), Rafferty Saga Finale; The Rafferty Saga, D: Rafferty ... 2.50
❑19, JRo (w) ... 1.95

FIREBRAND
DC

	ORIG	GOOD	FINE	N-MINT
❑1, Feb 96, Ashes To Ashes, 1: Firebrand III (Alex Sanchez)	1.75	0.40	1.00	2.00
❑2, Mar 96, Burning Bright	1.75	0.35	0.88	1.75
❑3, Apr 96, The Best of Families	1.75	0.35	0.88	1.75
❑4, May 96	1.75	0.35	0.88	1.75
❑5, Jun 96	1.75	0.35	0.88	1.75
❑6, Jul 96	1.75	0.35	0.88	1.75
❑7, Aug 96	1.75	0.35	0.88	1.75
❑8, Sep 96	1.75	0.35	0.88	1.75
❑9, Oct 96, Final Notice, Final Issue	1.75	0.35	0.88	1.75

FIRE FROM HEAVEN
IMAGE

	ORIG	GOOD	FINE	N-MINT
❑0.5	—	0.40	1.00	2.00
❑1, Mar 96, wraparound cover	2.50	0.50	1.25	2.50
❑2, Jul 96, Finale 2	2.50	0.50	1.25	2.50

FIRE SALE
RIP OFF

Value: Cover or less

❑1, Dec 89, b&w; benefit ... 2.50

FIRESTAR
MARVEL

	ORIG	GOOD	FINE	N-MINT
❑1, Mar 86, O: Firestar; A: New Mutants; A: X-Men	0.75	0.30	0.75	1.50
❑2, Apr 86, A: Wolverine	0.75	0.30	0.75	1.50
❑3, May 86	0.75	0.20	0.50	1.00
❑4, Jun 86	0.75	0.20	0.50	1.00

FIRESTORM
DC

	ORIG	GOOD	FINE	N-MINT
❑1, Mar 78, JR; AM, Make Way for Firestorm!, 1: Firestorm	0.35	0.60	1.50	3.00
❑2, Apr 78, AM	0.35	0.35	0.88	1.75
❑3, Jun 78, AM, 1: Killer Frost	0.35	0.35	0.88	1.75
❑4, Aug 78, AM	0.35	0.35	0.88	1.75
❑5, Oct 78, AM	0.35	0.35	0.88	1.75

FIRESTORM, THE NUCLEAR MAN
DC

	ORIG	GOOD	FINE	N-MINT
❑65, Nov 87, A: new Firestorm; A: Green Lantern, Series continued from Fury of Firestorm #64	0.75	0.20	0.50	1.00
❑66, Dec 87, A: Green Lantern	0.75	0.20	0.50	1.00
❑67, Jan 88, Millennium, Millennium	0.75	0.20	0.50	1.00
❑68, Feb 88, Millennium, Millennium	0.75	0.20	0.50	1.00
❑69, Mar 88	0.75	0.20	0.50	1.00
❑70, Apr 88	0.75	0.20	0.50	1.00
❑71, May 88, Hammer and Tong	0.75	0.20	0.50	1.00
❑72, Jun 88	0.75	0.20	0.50	1.00
❑73, Jul 88, A: Soyuz	0.75	0.20	0.50	1.00
❑74, Aug 88	0.75	0.20	0.50	1.00
❑75, Sep 88	1.00	0.20	0.50	1.00
❑76, Oct 88, A: Firehawk; V: Brimstone	1.00	0.20	0.50	1.00
❑77, Nov 88	1.00	0.20	0.50	1.00
❑78, Dec 88	1.00	0.20	0.50	1.00
❑79, no cover date	1.00	0.20	0.50	1.00
❑80, Invasion!, A: Firehawk, Power Girl, no cover date; Invasion!	1.00	0.20	0.50	1.00
❑81, Jan 89, Invasion!, A: Soyuz, Invasion! Aftermath	1.00	0.20	0.50	1.00
❑82, Feb 89	1.00	0.20	0.50	1.00
❑83, Mar 89	1.00	0.20	0.50	1.00
❑84, Apr 89	1.00	0.20	0.50	1.00
❑85, May 89, new Firestorm	1.00	0.20	0.50	1.00
❑86, Jun 89, Janus Directive	1.00	0.20	0.50	1.00
❑87, Jul 89	1.00	0.20	0.50	1.00
❑88, Aug 89	1.00	0.20	0.50	1.00
❑89, Sep 89	1.00	0.20	0.50	1.00
❑90, Oct 89, The Elemental War, Part 1, 1: Naiad	1.00	0.20	0.50	1.00
❑91, Nov 89	1.00	0.20	0.50	1.00
❑92, Dec 89	1.00	0.20	0.50	1.00
❑93, Jan 90	1.00	0.20	0.50	1.00
❑94, Feb 90	1.00	0.20	0.50	1.00
❑95, Mar 90	1.00	0.20	0.50	1.00
❑96, Apr 90	1.00	0.20	0.50	1.00
❑97, May 90	1.00	0.20	0.50	1.00
❑98, Jun 90	1.00	0.20	0.50	1.00
❑99, Jul 90	1.00	0.20	0.50	1.00
❑100, Aug 90, Final Issue; Giant-size	2.95	0.59	1.48	2.95
❑Anl 5	—	0.25	0.63	1.25

FIRE TEAM
AIRCEL

Value: Cover or less

❑1, b&w ... 2.50
❑2, Jan 91, Retribution, b&w ... 2.50
❑3, Feb 91, Showdown, b&w ... 2.50
❑4, b&w ... 2.50
❑5, River of Shame, b&w ... 2.50
❑6, b&w ... 2.50

FIRKIN
KNOCKABOUT

	ORIG	GOOD	FINE	N-MINT
❑1, adult	2.50	0.50	1.25	2.50
❑2, gentlemen; Ladies, adult	2.50	0.50	1.25	2.50
❑6, b&w; adult	—	0.50	1.25	2.50

FIRST ADVENTURES
FIRST

Value: Cover or less

❑1, Dec 85, Whisper: The Terminal Zone, Part 1; Blaze Barlow: Guns and Butter ... 1.25
❑2, Jan 86, Whisper: The Terminal Zone, Part 2; Blaze Barlow: When Titans Party ... 1.25
❑3, Feb 86, Whisper: The Terminal Zone, Part 3 ... 1.25
❑4, Mar 86, Whisper: The Terminal Zone, Part 4 ... 1.25
❑5, Apr 86, Dynamo Joe: Call of Duty; Whisper: The Terminal Zone, Part 5 ... 1.25

FIRST ISSUE SPECIAL
DC

	ORIG	GOOD	FINE	N-MINT
❑1, Apr 75, JK, JK (w), Atlas The Great!, 1: Atlas, Atlas	0.25	0.40	1.00	2.00
❑2, May 75, Green Team	0.25	0.40	1.00	2.00
❑3, Jun 75, Metamorpho	0.25	0.40	1.00	2.00
❑4, Jul 75, Lady Cop, Lady Cop	0.25	0.40	1.00	2.00
❑5, Aug 75, JK, JK (w), Manhunter, 1: Manhunter II (Mark Shaw); 1: Manhunters	0.25	0.40	1.00	2.00
❑6, Sep 75, JK, JK (w), Dingbat Of Danger Street, Dingbats of Danger St.; Dingbats	0.25	0.40	1.00	2.00
❑7, Oct 75, SD, A: Creeper	0.25	0.40	1.00	2.00
❑8, Nov 75, MGr, MGr (w), Land of Fear!, 1: Warlord; 1: Skartaris; 1: Deimos	0.25	0.80	2.00	4.00
❑9, Dec 75, A: Doctor Fate	0.25	0.40	1.00	2.00
❑10, Jan 76, Outsiders	0.25	0.40	1.00	2.00
❑11, Feb 76, Codename: Assassin, Code Name: Assassin	0.25	0.40	1.00	2.00
❑12, Mar 76, Starman, 1: Starman II (Mikaal Tomas)	0.30	0.40	1.00	2.00
❑13, Apr 76, Lest Night Fall Forever!, Return of the New Gods	0.30	0.60	1.50	3.00

FIRST KINGDOM, THE
BUD PLANT

	ORIG	GOOD	FINE	N-MINT
❑1	0.75	0.60	1.50	3.00
❑2	1.00	0.50	1.25	2.50
❑3	1.00	0.50	1.25	2.50
❑4	1.00	0.50	1.25	2.50
❑5	1.00	0.50	1.25	2.50
❑6	—	0.40	1.00	2.00
❑7	1.00	0.40	1.00	2.00
❑8	1.00	0.40	1.00	2.00
❑9	—	0.40	1.00	2.00
❑10	—	0.40	1.00	2.00
❑11	—	0.40	1.00	2.00
❑12	—	0.40	1.00	2.00
❑13	—	0.40	1.00	2.00
❑14	—	0.40	1.00	2.00
❑15	—	0.40	1.00	2.00
❑16	—	0.40	1.00	2.00
❑17	—	0.40	1.00	2.00
❑18	—	0.40	1.00	2.00
❑19	1.75	0.40	1.00	2.00
❑20	—	0.40	1.00	2.00
❑21	—	0.40	1.00	2.00
❑22	—	0.40	1.00	2.00
❑23	—	0.40	1.00	2.00
❑24, Final Issue	—	0.40	1.00	2.00

FIRST MAN
IMAGE

Value: Cover or less

❑1, Jun 97, cover says 1st Man, indicia says First Man ... 2.50

FIRST SIX PACK
FIRST

	ORIG	GOOD	FINE	N-MINT
❑1, Jul 87, Nexus, Badger, Jon, etc.	0.50	0.20	0.50	1.00
❑2, MGr (w); HC (w); JSn (w), Psychoblast, Shatter, American Flagg, Jon Sable, Dreadstar, Whisper	0.50	0.20	0.50	1.00

FIRST TRIP TO THE MOON
AVALON

Value: Cover or less

❑1, b&w; reprints Charlton story ... 2.50

FIRST WAVE
ANDROMEDA

Value: Cover or less

❑1, Dec 00, Photo cover ... 2.99

FISHMASTERS
SLAVE LABOR

Value: Cover or less

❑1, May 94, 1: The Fishmasters, adapts TV show ... 2.95

ORIG GOOD FINE N-MINT

FISH POLICE (MARVEL)
MARVEL
Value: Cover or less

- ❑1, Oct 92, Hairballs, Part 1 ... 1.25
- ❑2, Nov 92, Hairballs, Part 2... 1.25
- ❑3, Dec 92, Hairballs, Part 3... 1.25
- ❑4, Jan 93, Hairballs, Part 4 ... 1.25
- ❑5, Feb 93 ... 1.25
- ❑6, Mar 93, S.H.A.R.K. Bait 1.25

FISH POLICE (VOL. 1)
FISHWRAP
Value: Cover or less

- ❑1, Hairballs, Indicia title: Inspector Gill of the Fish Police..... 1.25
- ❑1-2, Hairballs, 2nd Printing; Indicia changed to "Fish Police" 1.25
- ❑2 ... 1.25
- ❑3 ... 1.25
- ❑4 ... 1.50
- ❑5, Aug 86 ... 1.50
- ❑6 ... 1.50
- ❑7, Feb 86, indicia says Feb 86 ... 1.50
- ❑8 ... 1.50
- ❑9 ... 1.50
- ❑10 ... 1.50
- ❑11 ... 1.50

FISH POLICE, THE (VOL. 2)
COMICO
Value: Cover or less

- ❑5 ... 1.75
- ❑6 ... 1.75
- ❑7 ... 1.75
- ❑8 ... 1.75
- ❑9 ... 1.75
- ❑10 ... 1.75
- ❑11 ... 1.75
- ❑12 ... 1.75
- ❑13 ... 1.75
- ❑14, Dec 88 ... 1.75
- ❑15 ... 1.75
- ❑16 ... 1.75
- ❑17, Jun 89 ... 2.50
- ❑18, Aug 89, b&w; Black & white format begins, Apple Comics 2.25
- ❑19, Oct 89, b&w ... 2.25
- ❑20, Mar 90, b&w ... 2.25
- ❑21, b&w ... 2.25
- ❑22, b&w ... 2.25
- ❑23, b&w ... 2.25
- ❑24, b&w ... 2.25
- ❑25, Nov 90, b&w ... 2.25
- ❑26, b&w ... 2.25
- ❑SE 1 ... 2.50

FISH SHTICKS
APPLE
Value: Cover or less

- ❑1, Nov 91, b&w ... 2.75
- ❑2, b&w ... 2.75
- ❑3, May 92, b&w ... 2.75
- ❑4, b&w ... 2.75
- ❑5, b&w ... 2.75
- ❑6, b&w ... 2.75

FISSION CHICKEN
FANTAGRAPHICS

	ORIG	GOOD	FINE	N-MINT
❑1, b&w	—	0.40	1.00	2.00
❑2, b&w	—	0.40	1.00	2.00
❑3, b&w	—	0.40	1.00	2.00
❑4, b&w	—	0.40	1.00	2.00

FISSION CHICKEN: PLAN NINE FROM VORTOX
MU PRESS
Value: Cover or less

- ❑1, Jul 94 ... 3.95

FIST OF GOD, THE
ETERNITY

	ORIG	GOOD	FINE	N-MINT
❑1, May 88	1.95	0.45	1.13	2.25
❑2, Jul 88	1.95	0.39	0.98	1.95
❑3, Sep 88	1.95	0.39	0.98	1.95
❑4, Nov 88	1.95	0.39	0.98	1.95

FIST OF THE NORTH STAR
VIZ
Value: Cover or less

- ❑1, A Cry From the Heart, Part 1 2.95
- ❑2 ... 2.95
- ❑3 ... 2.95
- ❑4 ... 2.95
- ❑5, O: Fist ... 2.95
- ❑6 ... 2.95
- ❑7 ... 2.95
- ❑8 ... 2.95

FIST OF THE NORTH STAR PART 2
VIZ
Value: Cover or less

- ❑1 ... 2.75
- ❑2 ... 2.75
- ❑3 ... 2.95
- ❑4 ... 2.95
- ❑5 ... 2.95
- ❑6 ... 2.95
- ❑7 ... 2.95
- ❑8 ... 2.95

FIST OF THE NORTH STAR PART 3
VIZ
Value: Cover or less

- ❑1, The Wolf Pack of Death.... 2.95
- ❑2 ... 2.95
- ❑3 ... 2.95
- ❑4 ... 2.95
- ❑5 ... 2.95

FIST OF THE NORTH STAR PART 4
VIZ
Value: Cover or less

- ❑1 ... 2.95
- ❑2 ... 2.95
- ❑3 ... 2.95
- ❑4 ... 2.95
- ❑5 ... 2.95
- ❑6 ... 2.95
- ❑7 ... 2.95

FIVE LITTLE COMICS
SCOTT MCCLOUD
Value: Cover or less

- ❑1, Another Little Epic; Some Words Albert Likes ... 4.00

FIVE YEARS OF PAIN
BONEYARD
Value: Cover or less

- ❑1, Jan 97 ... 3.95

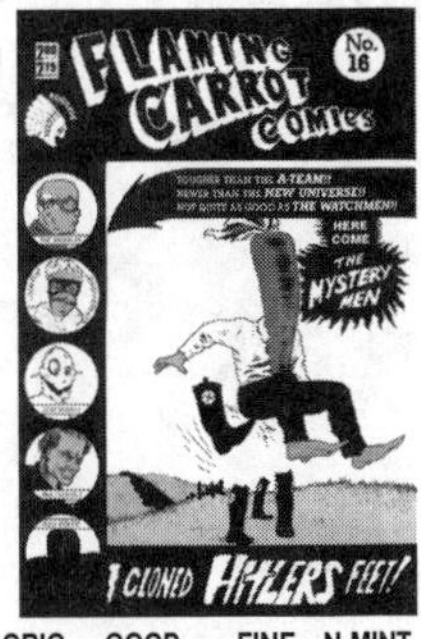

While Bob Burden's Flaming Carrot has yet to appear in a movie, a group of super-heroes from the series, The Mystery Men, did make it to the silver screen in 1999.

© 1987 Bob Burden (Renegade)

ORIG GOOD FINE N-MINT

FLAG FIGHTERS
IRONCAT
Value: Cover or less

- ❑1, Sep 97, Flag Fight, b&w ... 2.95
- ❑2, b&w ... 2.95
- ❑3, Nov 97, b&w ... 2.95
- ❑4 ... 2.95
- ❑5 ... 2.95

FLAME TWISTERS
BROWN STUDY
Value: Cover or less

- ❑1, Oct 94, Oppressions of the Bleak, b&w ... 2.50
- ❑2, Mar 95, b&w ... 2.50

FLAMING CARROT (KILLIAN)
KILIAN

	ORIG	GOOD	FINE	N-MINT
❑1, Sum 81, One-Shot; magazine	1.95	8.00	20.00	40.00

FLAMING CARROT COMICS
AARDVARK-VANAHEIM

	ORIG	GOOD	FINE	N-MINT
❑1, May 84, 1: Flaming Carrot, Aardvark-Vanaheim publishes	2.00	6.00	15.00	30.00
❑2, Jul 84	2.00	3.00	7.50	15.00
❑3, Sep 84	2.00	2.40	6.00	12.00
❑4, Nov 84	2.00	2.00	5.00	10.00
❑5, Jan 85	2.00	1.60	4.00	8.00
❑6, Mar 85, becomes Flaming Carrot Comics	1.70	1.60	4.00	8.00
❑7, May 85, Renegade begins publishing	2.00	1.40	3.50	7.00
❑8, Aug 85	2.00	1.00	2.50	5.00
❑9, Oct 85	2.00	1.00	2.50	5.00
❑10, Dec 85	2.00	0.80	2.00	4.00
❑11, Mar 86	1.70	0.80	2.00	4.00
❑12, May 86	1.70	0.80	2.00	4.00
❑13, Jul 86	1.70	0.60	1.50	3.00
❑14, Oct 86	2.00	0.60	1.50	3.00
❑15, Jan 87, Monster Fighter	2.00	0.60	1.50	3.00
❑15/A, Jan 87, Monster Fighter, no cover price	—	0.80	2.00	4.00
❑16, Jun 87, 1: Mystery Men	2.00	0.80	2.00	4.00
❑17, Jul 87, A: Mystery Men	2.00	0.60	1.50	3.00
❑18, Jun 01, Dark Horse begins publishing	2.00	0.60	1.50	3.00
❑19, Jun 01, Hills Like Pink Elephants	2.00	0.60	1.50	3.00
❑20, Nov 88	2.00	0.60	1.50	3.00
❑21, Spr 89	2.00	0.60	1.50	3.00
❑22, Jun 89	2.00	0.60	1.50	3.00
❑23, Nov 89	2.00	0.60	1.50	3.00
❑24, Apr 90, A Beautiful Day in the Neighborhood, 48pgs.	2.95	0.60	1.50	3.00
❑25, Apr 91, Dark City..., A: Teenage Mutant Ninja Turtles, trading cards	2.00	0.70	1.75	3.50
❑26, Jun 91, A: Teenage Mutant Ninja Turtles	2.25	0.50	1.25	2.50
❑27, TMc (c), A: Teenage Mutant Ninja Turtles; A: Mystery Men, no indicia	2.25	0.50	1.25	2.50
❑28, Aug 92	2.25	0.50	1.25	2.50
❑29, Oct 92, Night Of The Hunted	2.50	0.50	1.25	2.50
❑30, Dec 92, brown background	2.50	0.50	1.25	2.50
❑30/A, Dec 92, blue background	2.50	0.50	1.25	2.50
❑31, Oct 94, Alas Poor Carrot!, A: Herbie, Final Issue; Story originally scheduled for Herbie (Dark Horse) #3	2.50	0.50	1.25	2.50
❑Anl 1, Jan 97, A: Mystery Men, b&w; cardstock cover; 1997 Annual	5.00	1.00	2.50	5.00

FLAMING CARROT STORIES
DARK HORSE
Value: Cover or less

- ❑1, Green Bones Dancing, "Version A" ... 5.00

FLARE
HERO

	ORIG	GOOD	FINE	N-MINT
❑1, 52pgs.	—	0.55	1.38	2.75
❑2, 52pgs.	2.75	0.55	1.38	2.75
❑3, Jan 89, 52pgs.	2.75	0.55	1.38	2.75

FLARE (VOL. 2)
HERO
Value: Cover or less

- ❑1 ... 2.75
- ❑2 ... 2.75
- ❑3, Jan 89, The Adventures of Sky Marshal; Freedom's Just another Word, 1: Britannia... 2.75

Issue	Price
❑4	2.75
❑5, Eternity Smith	2.75
❑6, 1: Tigress	2.75
❑7	2.75
❑8, b&w	3.50
❑9, b&w	3.50
❑10, b&w	3.50
❑11, Apr 93, b&w	2.95
❑12, Jun 93, b&w	3.95
❑13, Aug 93, b&w	3.95
❑14, Oct 93, b&w	3.95
❑15, Jan 94	3.95
❑16	2.95
❑Anl 1, b&w	—

FLARE ADVENTURES
HERO

	ORIG	GOOD	FINE	N-MINT
❑1, Reprint	0.90	0.20	0.50	1.00
❑2, Flip-book format with Champions Classics #2	2.95	0.59	1.48	2.95
❑3, Betrayal By Design; Dolf and the Formal Dance, Flip-book format with Champions Classics #3	2.95	0.59	1.48	2.95
❑4, b&w; Flip-book format with Champions Classics #4	—	0.79	1.98	3.95
❑5, b&w; Flip-book format with Champions Classics #5	—	0.79	1.98	3.95
❑6, b&w; Flip-book format with Champions Classics #6	—	0.79	1.98	3.95
❑7, b&w; Flip-book format with Champions Classics #7	—	0.79	1.98	3.95
❑8, Turnabout, b&w; Flip-book format with Champions Classics #8	3.95	0.79	1.98	3.95
❑9, b&w; Flip-book format	3.95	0.79	1.98	3.95
❑10, b&w; Flip-book format	3.95	0.79	1.98	3.95
❑11, b&w; Flip-book format	3.95	0.79	1.98	3.95
❑12, b&w; Flip-book format	3.95	0.79	1.98	3.95
❑13, b&w; Flip-book format	3.95	0.79	1.98	3.95

FLARE FIRST EDITION
HERO

	ORIG	GOOD	FINE	N-MINT
❑1, contents will vary	—	0.70	1.75	3.50
❑2, contents will vary	—	0.70	1.75	3.50
❑3, b&w	—	0.70	1.75	3.50
❑4, b&w	—	0.90	2.25	4.50
❑5, b&w	—	0.90	2.25	4.50
❑6, b&w	3.95	0.79	1.98	3.95
❑7, b&w	3.95	0.79	1.98	3.95
❑8, b&w	3.95	0.79	1.98	3.95
❑9, Sparkplug	3.95	0.79	1.98	3.95
❑10	3.95	0.79	1.98	3.95
❑11, Oct 93, b&w	3.95	0.79	1.98	3.95

FLASH, THE (1ST SERIES)
DC

	ORIG	GOOD	FINE	N-MINT
❑105, Feb 59, CI, O: Flash II (Barry Allen); 1: Mirror Master, numbering continued from Flash Comics	0.10	960.00	2400.00	4800.00
❑106, May 59, CI, 1: The Pied Piper; 1: Gorilla Grodd; 1: Gorilla City; O: Pied Piper	0.10	270.00	675.00	1350.00
❑107, Jul 59, CI, 2: Gorilla Grodd	0.10	137.00	342.50	685.00
❑108, Sep 59, CI, A: Gorilla Grodd	0.10	130.00	325.00	650.00
❑109, Nov 59, CI, Return of the Mirror Master!; Secret of the Sunken Satellite!	0.10	100.00	250.00	500.00
❑110, Jan 60, CI; MA, The Challenge of the Weathe Wizard!; Meet Kid Flash!, 1: Kid Flash; 1: Weather Wizard	0.10	250.00	625.00	1250.00
❑111, Mar 60, CI, The Invasion of the Cloud Creatures!; Kid Flash: The Challenge of the Crimson Crows!, 2: Kid Flash	0.10	65.00	162.50	325.00
❑112, May 60, CI, The Mystery of the Elongated Man!; Kid Flash: Danger on Wheels!, 1: Elongated Man	0.10	73.00	182.50	365.00
❑113, Jul 60, CI, Danger in the Air!; The Man Who Claimed the Earth!, 1: Trickster	0.10	65.00	162.50	325.00
❑114, Aug 60, CI, The Big Freeze!; Kid Flash: King of the Beatniks!, O: Captain Cold	0.10	48.00	120.00	240.00
❑115, Sep 60, CI; MA, The Day Flash Weighed 1000 Pounds!; The Elongated Man's Secret Weapon!	0.10	40.00	100.00	200.00
❑116, Nov 60, CI, The Man Who Stole Central City!; Kid Flash: The Race to Thunder Hill!	0.10	40.00	100.00	200.00
❑117, Dec 60, CI, 1: Captain Boomerang	0.10	48.00	120.00	240.00
❑118, Feb 61, CI	0.10	40.00	100.00	200.00
❑119, Mar 61, CI, Wedding of Elongated Man and Sue Dearborn	0.10	40.00	100.00	200.00
❑120, May 61, CI	0.10	40.00	100.00	200.00
❑121, Jun 61, CI	0.10	30.00	75.00	150.00
❑122, Aug 61, CI, 1: Top, The	0.10	30.00	75.00	150.00
❑123, Sep 61, Flash of Two Worlds, 1: Earth-2 (as an alternate Earth); O: Flash II (Barry Allen); A: Flash I (Jay Garrick), 1st	0.10	190.00	475.00	950.00
❑124, Nov 61, CI	0.10	22.00	55.00	110.00
❑125, Dec 61, CI, 1: cosmic treadmill	0.12	18.00	45.00	90.00
❑126, Feb 62, CI	0.12	18.00	45.00	90.00
❑127, Mar 62, CI	0.12	18.00	45.00	90.00
❑128, May 62, CI, 1: Abra Kadabra	0.12	18.00	45.00	90.00
❑129, Jun 62, CI, A: Flash I (Jay Garrick)	0.12	50.00	125.00	250.00
❑130, Aug 62, CI	0.12	18.00	45.00	90.00
❑131, Sep 62, CI, A: Green Lantern	0.12	18.00	45.00	90.00
❑132, Nov 62, CI	0.12	18.00	45.00	90.00
❑133, Dec 62, CI	0.12	18.00	45.00	90.00
❑134, Feb 63, CI	0.12	18.00	45.00	90.00
❑135, Mar 63, CI	0.12	18.00	45.00	90.00
❑136, May 63, CI	0.12	18.00	45.00	90.00
❑137, Jun 63, CI, A: Flash I (Jay Garrick), Vandal Savage	0.12	50.00	125.00	250.00
❑138, Sep 63, CI	0.12	16.00	40.00	80.00
❑139, Sep 63, CI, 1: Professor Zoom	0.12	23.00	57.50	115.00
❑140, Nov 63, CI, 1: Heat Wave	0.12	16.00	40.00	80.00
❑141, Dec 63, CI	0.12	12.00	30.00	60.00
❑142, Feb 64, CI	0.12	12.00	30.00	60.00
❑143, Mar 64, CI	0.12	12.00	30.00	60.00
❑144, May 64, CI	0.12	12.00	30.00	60.00
❑145, Jun 64, CI	0.12	12.00	30.00	60.00
❑146, Aug 64, CI	0.12	12.00	30.00	60.00
❑147, Sep 64, CI	0.12	12.00	30.00	60.00
❑148, Nov 64, CI	0.12	12.00	30.00	60.00
❑149, Dec 64, CI	0.12	12.00	30.00	60.00
❑150, Feb 65, CI	0.12	12.00	30.00	60.00
❑151, Mar 65, CI, A: Flash I (Jay Garrick)	0.12	15.00	37.50	75.00
❑152, May 65, CI	0.12	9.00	22.50	45.00
❑153, Jun 65, CI	0.12	9.00	22.50	45.00
❑154, Aug 65, CI	0.12	9.00	22.50	45.00
❑155, Sep 65, CI	0.12	9.00	22.50	45.00
❑156, Nov 65, CI	0.12	9.00	22.50	45.00
❑157, Dec 65, CI	0.12	9.00	22.50	45.00
❑158, Feb 66, CI	0.12	9.00	22.50	45.00
❑159, Mar 66, CI	0.12	9.00	22.50	45.00
❑160, Apr 66, CI, Giant-size	0.25	12.00	30.00	60.00
❑161, May 66, CI	0.12	7.00	17.50	35.00
❑162, Jun 66, CI	0.12	7.00	17.50	35.00
❑163, Aug 66, CI	0.12	7.00	17.50	35.00
❑164, Sep 66, CI	0.12	7.00	17.50	35.00
❑165, Nov 66, CI, Wedding of Flash II (Barry Allen) and Iris West	0.12	8.00	20.00	40.00
❑166, Dec 66, CI	0.12	7.00	17.50	35.00
❑167, Feb 67, CI, O: Flash II (Barry Allen); 1: Mopee	0.12	7.00	17.50	35.00
❑168, Mar 67	0.12	7.00	17.50	35.00
❑169, May 67, O: Flash II (Barry Allen), 80pgs.; Giant-size	0.25	11.00	27.50	55.00
❑170, Jun 67	0.12	7.00	17.50	35.00
❑171, Jun 67, V: Dr. Light; V: Doctor Light	0.12	6.40	16.00	32.00
❑172, Aug 67	0.12	6.40	16.00	32.00
❑173, Sep 67	0.12	6.40	16.00	32.00
❑174, Nov 67, V: Rogue's Gallery, Flash II reveals identity to wife	0.12	6.40	16.00	32.00
❑175, Dec 67, Flash II races Superman	0.12	20.00	50.00	100.00
❑176, Feb 68	0.12	6.40	16.00	32.00
❑177, Mar 68	0.12	6.40	16.00	32.00
❑178, May 68, Giant-size	0.25	8.00	20.00	40.00
❑179, May 68, Flash visits DC Comics	0.12	6.40	16.00	32.00
❑180, Jun 68	0.12	6.40	16.00	32.00
❑181, Aug 68	0.12	4.00	10.00	20.00
❑182, Sep 68	0.12	4.00	10.00	20.00
❑183, Nov 68	0.12	4.00	10.00	20.00
❑184, Dec 68	0.12	4.00	10.00	20.00
❑185, Feb 69	0.12	4.00	10.00	20.00
❑186, Mar 69	0.12	4.00	10.00	20.00
❑187, May 69, Giant-size	0.25	6.00	15.00	30.00
❑188, May 69	0.12	3.60	9.00	18.00
❑189, Jun 69, JKu (c)	0.12	3.60	9.00	18.00
❑190, Aug 69	0.15	3.60	9.00	18.00
❑191, Sep 69	0.15	3.00	7.50	15.00
❑192, Nov 69	0.15	3.00	7.50	15.00
❑193, Dec 69	0.15	3.00	7.50	15.00
❑194, Feb 70	0.15	3.00	7.50	15.00
❑195, Mar 70	0.15	3.00	7.50	15.00
❑196, May 70, Giant-size	0.25	6.00	15.00	30.00
❑197, May 70	0.15	3.00	7.50	15.00
❑198, Jun 70	0.15	3.00	7.50	15.00
❑199, Aug 70	0.15	3.00	7.50	15.00
❑200, Sep 70	0.15	3.00	7.50	15.00
❑201, Nov 70	0.15	2.00	5.00	10.00
❑202, Dec 70	0.15	2.00	5.00	10.00
❑203, Feb 71	0.15	2.00	5.00	10.00
❑204, Mar 71	0.15	2.00	5.00	10.00
❑205, May 71, Giant-size	0.25	2.00	5.00	10.00
❑206, May 71	0.15	2.00	5.00	10.00
❑207, Jun 71	0.15	2.00	5.00	10.00
❑208, Aug 71, Giant-size; Elongated Man back-up	0.25	2.00	5.00	10.00
❑209, Sep 71, V: Trickster; V: Captain Boomerang, Giant-size	0.25	2.00	5.00	10.00

	ORIG	GOOD	FINE	N-MINT
❑210, Dec 71, Giant-size; in future	0.25	2.00	5.00	10.00
❑211, Dec 71, Giant-size; Golden Age Flash back-up	0.25	2.00	5.00	10.00
❑212, Feb 72	0.25	2.00	5.00	10.00
❑213, Mar 72	0.25	2.00	5.00	10.00
❑214, Apr 72, CI, O: Metal Men, wraparound cover; a.k.a. DC 100-Page Super Spectacular #DC-11; reprints O: Metal Men; Reprints Showcase #37	0.50	3.20	8.00	16.00
❑215, May 72, V: Vandal Savage; A: Golden Age Flash, giant	0.25	3.00	7.50	15.00
❑216, Jun 72	0.25	2.00	5.00	10.00
❑217, Sep 72, IN; NA; DG; FMc, The Flash Times Five is Fatal; The Killing of an Archer!, Part 1, Green Lantern/Green Arrow back-up; Green Arrow back-up	0.20	2.00	5.00	10.00
❑218, Nov 72, NA	0.20	2.00	5.00	10.00
❑219, Jan 73, NA, last Green Arrow back-up	0.20	2.00	5.00	10.00
❑220, Mar 73	0.20	1.40	3.50	7.00
❑221, May 73	0.20	1.40	3.50	7.00
❑222, Aug 73	0.20	1.40	3.50	7.00
❑223, Oct 73, NA, Green Lantern back-up	0.20	1.40	3.50	7.00
❑224, Dec 73	0.20	1.40	3.50	7.00
❑225, Feb 74	0.20	1.40	3.50	7.00
❑226, Apr 74, NA, A: Captain Cold; A: Capt. Cold	0.20	2.00	5.00	10.00
❑227, Jun 74	0.20	1.40	3.50	7.00
❑228, Aug 74	0.20	1.40	3.50	7.00
❑229, Oct 74, V: Rag Doll, 100pgs.	0.60	2.40	6.00	12.00
❑230, Dec 74, V: Dr. Alchemy; V: Doctor Alchemy	0.20	1.40	3.50	7.00
❑231, Feb 75	0.25	1.40	3.50	7.00
❑232, Apr 75, 100pgs.	0.60	2.40	6.00	12.00
❑233, May 75, 100pgs.	0.25	0.80	2.00	4.00
❑234, Jun 75	0.25	0.80	2.00	4.00
❑235, Aug 75, V: Vandal Savage; A: Golden Age Flash; A: Green Lantern	0.25	0.80	2.00	4.00
❑236, Sep 75, A: Golden Age Flash; A: Doctor Fate; A: Dr. Fate	0.25	0.80	2.00	4.00
❑237, Nov 75	0.25	0.80	2.00	4.00
❑238, Dec 75	0.25	0.80	2.00	4.00
❑239, Feb 76	0.25	0.80	2.00	4.00
❑240, Mar 76	0.30	0.80	2.00	4.00
❑241, May 76	0.30	0.80	2.00	4.00
❑242, Jun 76	0.30	0.80	2.00	4.00
❑243, Aug 76	0.30	0.80	2.00	4.00
❑244, Sep 76	0.30	0.80	2.00	4.00
❑245, Nov 76	0.30	0.80	2.00	4.00
❑246, Jan 77	0.30	0.80	2.00	4.00
❑247, Mar 77	0.30	0.80	2.00	4.00
❑248, Apr 77	0.30	0.80	2.00	4.00
❑249, May 77	0.30	0.80	2.00	4.00
❑250, Jun 77, V: Golden Glider	0.35	0.80	2.00	4.00
❑251, Aug 77	0.35	0.80	2.00	4.00
❑252, Sep 77	0.35	0.80	2.00	4.00
❑253, Sep 77	0.35	0.80	2.00	4.00
❑254, Oct 77, V: Rogue's Gallery	0.35	0.80	2.00	4.00
❑255, Nov 77	0.35	0.80	2.00	4.00
❑256, Dec 77, V: Rogue's Gallery	0.35	0.80	2.00	4.00
❑257, Jan 78	0.35	0.80	2.00	4.00
❑258, Feb 78	0.35	0.80	2.00	4.00
❑259, Mar 78	0.35	0.80	2.00	4.00
❑260, Apr 78	0.35	0.80	2.00	4.00
❑261, May 78	0.35	0.80	2.00	4.00
❑262, Jun 78, V: Golden Glider	0.35	0.80	2.00	4.00
❑263, Jul 78, V: Golden Glider	0.35	0.80	2.00	4.00
❑264, Aug 78	0.35	0.80	2.00	4.00
❑265, Sep 78	0.50	0.80	2.00	4.00
❑266, Oct 78	0.50	0.80	2.00	4.00
❑267, Nov 78	0.50	0.80	2.00	4.00
❑268, Dec 78	0.40	0.80	2.00	4.00
❑269, Jan 79	0.40	0.80	2.00	4.00
❑270, Mar 79	0.40	0.80	2.00	4.00
❑271, Mar 79, RB	0.40	0.70	1.75	3.50
❑272, Apr 79, RB	0.40	0.70	1.75	3.50
❑273, May 79, RB	0.40	0.70	1.75	3.50
❑274, Jun 79, RB	0.40	0.70	1.75	3.50
❑275, Jul 79, D: Iris West Allen (Flash II's wife)	0.40	0.70	1.75	3.50
❑276, Aug 79, A: JLA	0.40	0.70	1.75	3.50
❑277, Sep 79, A: JLA	0.40	0.70	1.75	3.50
❑278, Oct 79	0.40	0.70	1.75	3.50
❑279, Nov 79	0.40	0.70	1.75	3.50
❑280, Dec 79	0.40	0.70	1.75	3.50
❑281, Jan 80	0.40	0.70	1.75	3.50
❑282, Feb 80	0.40	0.70	1.75	3.50
❑283, Mar 80	0.40	0.70	1.75	3.50

Wally West was doused by chemicals and acquired super-speed, becoming Kid Flash, in *The Flash* (1st series) #110.

	ORIG	GOOD	FINE	N-MINT
❑284, Apr 80	0.40	0.70	1.75	3.50
❑285, May 80	0.40	0.70	1.75	3.50
❑286, Jun 80, 1: Rainbow Raider	0.40	0.70	1.75	3.50
❑287, Jul 80	0.40	0.70	1.75	3.50
❑288, Aug 80	0.40	0.70	1.75	3.50
❑289, Sep 80, DH; GP, George PTrez's first work at DC	0.50	1.00	2.50	5.00
❑290, Oct 80, GP, A: Firestorm	0.50	0.60	1.50	3.00
❑291, Nov 80	0.50	0.60	1.50	3.00
❑292, Dec 80	0.50	0.60	1.50	3.00
❑293, Jan 81	0.50	0.60	1.50	3.00
❑294, Feb 81	0.50	0.60	1.50	3.00
❑295, Mar 81, V: Grodd	0.50	0.60	1.50	3.00
❑296, Apr 81	0.50	0.60	1.50	3.00
❑297, May 81	0.50	0.60	1.50	3.00
❑298, Jun 81	0.50	0.60	1.50	3.00
❑299, Jul 81	0.50	0.60	1.50	3.00
❑300, Aug 81, CI, O: Flash; A: New Teen Titans, wraparound cover; Giant-size	1.00	1.00	2.50	5.00
❑301, Sep 81	0.50	0.60	1.50	3.00
❑302, Oct 81	0.60	0.60	1.50	3.00
❑303, Nov 81	0.60	0.60	1.50	3.00
❑304, Dec 81, 1: Colonel Computron	0.60	0.60	1.50	3.00
❑305, Jan 82	0.60	0.70	1.75	3.50
❑306, Feb 82, KG; CI	0.60	0.70	1.75	3.50
❑307, Mar 82, KG; CI, Doctor Fate back-up; Dr. Fate back-up	0.60	0.50	1.25	2.50
❑308, Apr 82, KG; CI	0.60	0.50	1.25	2.50
❑309, May 82, KG; CI	0.60	0.50	1.25	2.50
❑310, Jun 82, KG; CI	0.60	0.50	1.25	2.50
❑311, Jul 82, KG; CI	0.60	0.50	1.25	2.50
❑312, Aug 82, KG; CI, 1: Creed Phillips	0.60	0.50	1.25	2.50
❑313, Sep 82, KG; CI	0.60	0.50	1.25	2.50
❑314, Oct 82, 1: The Eradicator	0.60	0.50	1.25	2.50
❑315, Nov 82	0.60	0.50	1.25	2.50
❑316, Dec 82	0.60	0.50	1.25	2.50
❑317, Jan 83	0.60	0.50	1.25	2.50
❑318, Feb 83, 1: Big Sir	0.60	0.50	1.25	2.50
❑319, Mar 83	0.60	0.50	1.25	2.50
❑320, Apr 83	0.60	0.50	1.25	2.50
❑321, May 83	0.60	0.50	1.25	2.50
❑322, Jun 83, Flash Vs. Reverse Flash	0.60	0.50	1.25	2.50
❑323, Jul 83, Flash Vs. Reverse Flash	0.60	0.50	1.25	2.50
❑324, Aug 83	0.60	0.50	1.25	2.50
❑325, Sep 83	0.60	0.50	1.25	2.50
❑326, Oct 83	0.60	0.50	1.25	2.50
❑327, Nov 83	0.60	0.50	1.25	2.50
❑328, Dec 83	0.75	0.50	1.25	2.50
❑329, Jan 84, V: Grodd	0.75	0.50	1.25	2.50
❑330, Feb 84	0.75	0.50	1.25	2.50
❑331, Mar 84	0.75	0.50	1.25	2.50
❑332, Apr 84, A: Green Lantern	0.75	0.50	1.25	2.50
❑333, May 84	0.75	0.50	1.25	2.50
❑334, Jun 84	0.75	0.50	1.25	2.50
❑335, Jul 84	0.75	0.50	1.25	2.50
❑336, Aug 84	0.75	0.50	1.25	2.50
❑337, Sep 84, V: Pied Piper	0.75	0.50	1.25	2.50
❑338, Oct 84, V: Big Sir	0.75	0.50	1.25	2.50
❑339, Nov 84, V: Big Sir	0.75	0.50	1.25	2.50
❑340, Dec 84, Trial begins	0.75	0.50	1.25	2.50
❑341, Jan 85	0.75	0.50	1.25	2.50
❑342, Feb 85	0.75	0.50	1.25	2.50
❑343, Mar 85	0.75	0.50	1.25	2.50
❑344, Apr 85, O: Kid Flash	0.75	0.50	1.25	2.50
❑345, May 85	0.75	0.50	1.25	2.50
❑346, Jun 85	0.75	0.50	1.25	2.50
❑347, Jul 85	0.75	0.50	1.25	2.50
❑348, Aug 85	0.75	0.50	1.25	2.50
❑349, Sep 85	0.75	0.50	1.25	2.50
❑350, Oct 85, Final Issue; Double-size	1.25	1.30	3.25	6.50
❑Anl 1, Dec 63, O: Elongated Man, Kid Flash, Golden-Age Flash story; O: Elongated Man, 80pgs.	0.25	70.00	175.00	350.00

FLASH (2ND SERIES)
DC

	ORIG	GOOD	FINE	N-MINT
❑0, Oct 94, O: Flash III (Wally West)	1.50	0.50	1.25	2.50
❑1, Jun 87, Wally West as Flash	0.75	0.80	2.00	4.00
❑2, Jul 87, Stone!, V: Vandal Savage	0.75	0.60	1.50	3.00
❑3, Aug 87, V: Kilg%re; V: Kilgore; 1: Tina McGee	0.75	0.50	1.25	2.50
❑4, Sep 87, V: Kilg%re; V: Kilgore	0.75	0.50	1.25	2.50
❑5, Oct 87	0.75	0.50	1.25	2.50
❑6, Nov 87	0.75	0.50	1.25	2.50
❑7, Dec 87, 1: Red Trinity	0.75	0.50	1.25	2.50
❑8, Jan 88, Millennium	0.75	0.50	1.25	2.50
❑9, Feb 88, 1: Chunk, Millennium	0.75	0.50	1.25	2.50
❑10, Mar 88	0.75	0.50	1.25	2.50
❑11, Apr 88	0.75	0.50	1.25	2.50
❑12, May 88, Bonus Book #2	0.75	0.50	1.25	2.50
❑13, Jun 88, V: Vandal Savage	0.75	0.50	1.25	2.50
❑14, Jul 88, V: Vandal Savage	0.75	0.50	1.25	2.50
❑15, Aug 88, GP (c)	0.75	0.50	1.25	2.50
❑16, Sep 88, GP (c)	0.75	0.50	1.25	2.50
❑17, Oct 88, GP (c)	1.00	0.50	1.25	2.50
❑18, Nov 88	1.00	0.50	1.25	2.50
❑19, Dec 88, bonus story; Bonus Book #9	1.00	0.50	1.25	2.50
❑20	1.00	0.50	1.25	2.50
❑21, Invasion!	1.00	0.40	1.00	2.00
❑22, Jan 89, A: Manhunter, Invasion!	1.00	0.40	1.00	2.00
❑23, Feb 89	1.00	0.40	1.00	2.00
❑24, Mar 89	1.00	0.40	1.00	2.00
❑25, Apr 89	1.00	0.40	1.00	2.00
❑26, May 89	1.00	0.40	1.00	2.00
❑27, Jun 89	1.00	0.40	1.00	2.00
❑28, Jul 89	1.00	0.40	1.00	2.00
❑29, Aug 89, A: Phantom Lady	1.00	0.40	1.00	2.00
❑30, Sep 89	1.00	0.40	1.00	2.00
❑31, Oct 89	1.00	0.30	0.75	1.50
❑32, Nov 89	1.00	0.30	0.75	1.50
❑33, Dec 89	1.00	0.30	0.75	1.50
❑34, Jan 90	1.00	0.30	0.75	1.50
❑35, Feb 90	1.00	0.30	0.75	1.50
❑36, Mar 90	1.00	0.30	0.75	1.50
❑37, Apr 90	1.00	0.30	0.75	1.50
❑38, May 90	1.00	0.30	0.75	1.50
❑39, Jun 90	1.00	0.30	0.75	1.50
❑40, Jul 90	1.00	0.30	0.75	1.50
❑41, Aug 90	1.00	0.30	0.75	1.50
❑42, Sep 90	1.00	0.30	0.75	1.50
❑43, Oct 90	1.00	0.30	0.75	1.50
❑44, Nov 90	1.00	0.30	0.75	1.50
❑45, Dec 90, V: Grodd	1.00	0.30	0.75	1.50
❑46, Jan 91, A: Vixen; V: Grodd	1.00	0.30	0.75	1.50
❑47, Feb 91, A: Vixen; V: Grodd	1.00	0.30	0.75	1.50
❑48, Mar 91	1.00	0.30	0.75	1.50
❑49, Apr 91	1.00	0.30	0.75	1.50
❑50, May 91, Giant size	1.75	0.50	1.25	2.50
❑51, Jun 91	1.00	0.30	0.75	1.50
❑52, Jul 91	1.00	0.30	0.75	1.50
❑53, Aug 91, Superman	1.00	0.30	0.75	1.50
❑54, Sep 91	1.00	0.30	0.75	1.50
❑55, Oct 91, War of the Gods, Part 10, War of the Gods	1.00	0.30	0.75	1.50
❑56, Nov 91, Icicle	1.00	0.30	0.75	1.50
❑57, Dec 91, Icicle	1.00	0.30	0.75	1.50
❑58, Jan 92	1.00	0.30	0.75	1.50
❑59, Feb 92, A: Power Girl	1.00	0.30	0.75	1.50
❑60, Mar 92	1.00	0.30	0.75	1.50
❑61, Apr 92	1.00	0.30	0.75	1.50
❑62, May 92, MWa (w), Year One; Flash: Year 1, Part 1, O: Flash	1.00	0.40	1.00	2.00
❑63, May 92, Year One; Flash: Year 1, Part 2, O: Flash	1.00	0.40	1.00	2.00
❑64, Jun 92, Year One; Flash: Year 1, Part 3, O: Flash	1.00	0.30	0.75	1.50
❑65, Jun 92, Year One; Flash: Year 1, Part 4, O: Flash	1.00	0.30	0.75	1.50
❑66, Jul 92, Aquaman	1.25	0.30	0.75	1.50
❑67, Aug 92, V: Abra Kadabra	1.25	0.30	0.75	1.50
❑68, Sep 92, V: Abra Kadabra	1.25	0.30	0.75	1.50
❑69, Oct 92, V: Grodd; A: Green Lantern; V: Grodd, Hector Hammond; V: Hector Hammond	1.25	0.30	0.75	1.50
❑70, Nov 92, Gorilla Warfare (conclusion), V: Grodd; A: Green Lantern; V: Grodd, Hector Hammond; V: Hector Hammond	1.25	0.30	0.75	1.50
❑71, Dec 92, V: Dr. Alchemy; V: Doctor Alchemy	1.25	0.30	0.75	1.50
❑72, Jan 93	1.25	0.30	0.75	1.50
❑73, Feb 93, A: Jay Garrick	1.25	0.30	0.75	1.50
❑74, Mar 93	1.25	0.30	0.75	1.50
❑75, Apr 93	1.25	0.30	0.75	1.50
❑76, May 93	1.25	0.30	0.75	1.50
❑77, Jun 93	1.25	0.30	0.75	1.50
❑78, Jul 93	1.25	0.30	0.75	1.50
❑79, Jul 93	2.50	0.30	0.75	1.50
❑80, Aug 93, regular cover	1.25	0.30	0.75	1.50
❑80/SC, Aug 93, foil cover	2.50	0.50	1.25	2.50
❑81, Sep 93, A: Starfire; A: Nightwing	1.25	0.30	0.75	1.50
❑82, Oct 93, A: Starfire; A: Nightwing	1.25	0.30	0.75	1.50
❑83, Oct 93	1.25	0.30	0.75	1.50
❑84, Nov 93, V: Razer	1.25	0.30	0.75	1.50
❑85, Dec 93, V: Razer	1.50	0.30	0.75	1.50
❑86, Jan 94	1.50	0.30	0.75	1.50
❑87, Feb 94	1.50	0.30	0.75	1.50
❑88, Mar 94, MWa (w)	1.50	0.40	1.00	2.00
❑89, Apr 94, MWa (w)	1.50	0.40	1.00	2.00
❑90, May 94, MWa (w)	1.50	0.40	1.00	2.00
❑91, Jun 94, MWa (w)	1.50	0.80	2.00	4.00
❑92, Jul 94, MWa (w), Reckless Youth, Part 1, 1: Impulse	1.50	1.80	4.50	9.00
❑93, Aug 94, MWa (w), Reckless Youth, Part 2, 2: Impulse	1.50	0.90	2.25	4.50
❑94, Sep 94, MWa (w), Reckless Youth, Part 3, Zero Hour	1.50	0.80	2.00	4.00
❑95, Nov 94, Terminal Velocity, Part 1	1.50	0.60	1.50	3.00
❑96, Dec 94, Terminal Velocity, Part 2	1.50	0.40	1.00	2.00
❑97, Jan 95, MWa (w), Terminal Velocity, Part 3	1.50	0.40	1.00	2.00
❑98, Feb 95, Terminal Velocity, Part 4	1.50	0.40	1.00	2.00
❑99, Mar 95, Terminal Velocity, Part 5	1.50	0.40	1.00	2.00
❑100, Apr 95, Terminal Velocity, Part 6, Giant-size	2.50	0.60	1.50	3.00
❑100/SC, Apr 95, Terminal Velocity, Part 6, Holo-grafix cover; Giant-size	3.50	0.80	2.00	4.00
❑101, May 95	1.75	0.35	0.88	1.75
❑102, Jun 95, V: Mongul	1.75	0.35	0.88	1.75
❑103, Jul 95	1.75	0.35	0.88	1.75
❑104, Aug 95	1.75	0.35	0.88	1.75
❑105, Sep 95, V: Mirror Master	1.75	0.35	0.88	1.75
❑106, Oct 95, return of Frances Kane	1.75	0.35	0.88	1.75
❑107, Nov 95, Underworld Unleashed, A: Captain Marvel, Underworld Unleashed	1.75	0.35	0.88	1.75
❑108, Dec 95, Dead Heat, Part 1	1.75	0.35	0.88	1.75
❑109, Jan 96, Dead Heat, Part 2, continues in Impulse #10	1.75	0.35	0.88	1.75
❑110, Feb 96, MWa (w), Dead Heat, Part 4, continues in Impulse #11	1.75	0.35	0.88	1.75
❑111, Mar 96, MWa (w), Dead Heat Finale	1.75	0.35	0.88	1.75
❑112, Apr 96, MWa (w), Future Perfect, A: John Fox	1.75	0.35	0.88	1.75
❑113, May 96, Race Against Time, Part 1	1.75	0.35	0.88	1.75
❑114, Jun 96, Race Against Time, Part 2, A: Don and Dawn Allen	1.75	0.35	0.88	1.75
❑115, Jul 96, Race Against Time, Part 3	1.75	0.35	0.88	1.75
❑116, Aug 96, Race Against Time, Part 4	1.75	0.35	0.88	1.75
❑117, Sep 96, Race Against Time, Part 5, Flash returns to present	1.75	0.35	0.88	1.75
❑118, Oct 96, Race Against Time	1.75	0.35	0.88	1.75
❑119, Nov 96, Pray for the Dawn, Final Night	1.75	0.35	0.88	1.75
❑120, Dec 96, Presidential Race, Part 1, A: Trickster, Wally West asked to leave Keystone	1.75	0.35	0.88	1.75
❑121, Jan 97, Presidential Race, Part 2, V: Top	1.75	0.35	0.88	1.75
❑122, Feb 97, Running Away From Home, Flash becomes a commuting super-hero	1.75	0.35	0.88	1.75
❑123, Mar 97, The Flash of Two Cities	1.75	0.35	0.88	1.75
❑124, Apr 97, Quicker than the Eye, V: Major Disaster	1.75	0.35	0.88	1.75
❑125, May 97, V: Major Disaster	1.75	0.35	0.88	1.75
❑126, Jun 97, V: Major Disaster, return of Rogues Gallery	1.75	0.35	0.88	1.75
❑127, Jul 97, A: Jay Garrick; A: Neron; V: Soulless Rogues Gallery	1.75	0.35	0.88	1.75
❑128, Aug 97, A: Green Lantern; A: Martian Manhunter; A: Superman; V: Soulless Rogues Gallery; A: Wonder Woman	1.75	0.35	0.88	1.75
❑129, Sep 97, V: Neron	1.75	0.35	0.88	1.75
❑130, Oct 97, Emergency Stop, Part 1, Wally has his legs broken	1.75	0.35	0.88	1.75
❑131, Nov 97, Emergency Stop, Part 2, Wally gets new costume	1.75	0.35	0.88	1.75
❑132, Dec 97, Emergency Stop, Part 3, A: Mirror Master, Face cover	1.95	0.39	0.98	1.95
❑133, Jan 98, V: Mirror Master	1.95	0.39	0.98	1.95
❑134, Feb 98, A: Jay Garrick; A: Sentinel; A: Ted Knight; A: Johnny Thunder; A: Wildcat; A: Thinker	1.95	0.39	0.98	1.95

	ORIG	GOOD	FINE	N-MINT
❑135, Mar 98, Three of a Kind, Part 3, cover forms triptych with Green Arrow #130 and Green Lantern #96	1.95	0.39	0.98	1.95
❑136, Apr 98, The Human Race, Part 1, A: Krakkl	1.95	0.39	0.98	1.95
❑137, May 98, The Human Race, Part 2	1.95	0.39	0.98	1.95
❑138, Jun 98, The Human Race, Part 3	1.95	0.39	0.98	1.95
❑139, Jul 98, The Black Flash, Part 1, D: Linda Park	1.95	0.39	0.98	1.95
❑140, Aug 98, The Black Flash, Part 2, Linda's funeral	1.99	0.39	0.98	1.95
❑141, Sep 98, The Black Flash, Part 3, V: Black Flash	1.99	0.39	0.98	1.95
❑142, Oct 98, Wedding of Wally and Linda	1.99	0.39	0.98	1.95
❑143, Dec 98, V: Cobalt Blue	1.99	0.40	1.00	1.99
❑144, Jan 99, O: Cobalt Blue	1.99	0.40	1.00	1.99
❑145, Feb 99, Chain Lightning, Part 1, A: Cobalt Blue	1.99	0.40	1.00	1.99
❑146, Mar 99, Chain Lightning, Part 2, A: Cobalt Blue	1.99	0.40	1.00	1.99
❑147, Apr 99, Chain Lightning, Part 3, A: Cobalt Blue; A: Reverse Flash	1.99	0.40	1.00	1.99
❑148, May 99, Chain Lightning, Part 4, A: Barry Allen	1.99	0.40	1.00	1.99
❑149, Jun 99, Chain Lightning, Part 5, Crisis ending changed	1.99	0.40	1.00	1.99
❑150, Jul 99, Chain Lightning, Part 6, Wally vs. Anti-Monitor	2.95	0.59	1.48	2.95
❑151, Aug 99, Territorealis, Teen Titans adventure	1.99	0.40	1.00	1.99
❑152, Sep 99, New Kid in Town	1.99	0.40	1.00	1.99
❑153, Oct 99, The Folded Man, V: Folded Man	1.99	0.40	1.00	1.99
❑154, Nov 99, new Flash reveals identity	1.99	0.40	1.00	1.99
❑155, Dec 99, Payback Unlimited	1.99	0.40	1.00	1.99
❑156, Jan 00	1.99	0.40	1.00	1.99
❑157, Feb 00	1.99	0.40	1.00	1.99
❑158, Mar 00	1.99	0.40	1.00	1.99
❑159, Apr 00, Whirlwind Ceremony	1.99	0.40	1.00	1.99
❑160, May 00, Honeymoon on the Run	1.99	0.40	1.00	1.99
❑161, Jun 00	—	0.40	1.00	1.99
❑162, Jul 00	—	0.40	1.00	1.99
❑163, Aug 00	—	0.40	1.00	1.99
❑164, Sep 00, Lightning in a Bottle; Joining the Tea Party, Part 1	2.25	0.45	1.13	2.25
❑165, Oct 00, Joining the Tea Party, Part 2	2.25	0.45	1.13	2.25
❑166, Nov 00, Joining the Tea Party, Part 3	2.25	0.45	1.13	2.25
❑167, Dec 00, Joining the Tea Party, Part 4	2.25	0.45	1.13	2.25
❑168, Jan 01, Joining the Tea Party, Part 5	2.25	0.45	1.13	2.25
❑169, Feb 01, Joining the Tea Party, Part 6	2.25	0.45	1.13	2.25
❑170, Mar 01, Blood Will Run, Part 1	2.25	0.45	1.13	2.25
❑171, Apr 01, Blood Will Run, Part 2	2.25	0.45	1.13	2.25
❑172, May 01, Blood Will Run, Part 3	2.25	0.45	1.13	2.25
❑173	2.25	0.45	1.13	2.25
❑174	2.25	0.45	1.13	2.25
❑175	2.25	0.45	1.13	2.25
❑176	2.25	0.45	1.13	2.25
❑1000000, Nov 98, MWa (w), Fast Forward	1.99	0.40	1.00	1.99
❑Anl 1, Death Touch	1.25	0.60	1.50	3.00
❑Anl 2, Private Lives	1.50	0.40	1.00	2.00
❑Anl 3, Who's Who entries	1.75	0.45	1.13	2.25
❑Anl 4, Armageddon 2001, Part 7, Armageddon 2001	2.00	0.45	1.13	2.25
❑Anl 5, Eclipso: The Darkness Within, Part 9, Eclipso	2.50	0.55	1.38	2.75
❑Anl 6, Bloodlines, 1: Argus, Bloodlines	2.50	0.50	1.25	2.50
❑Anl 7, Elseworlds	2.95	0.59	1.48	2.95
❑Anl 8, Year One	3.50	0.70	1.75	3.50
❑Anl 9, Legends of the Dead Earth	2.95	0.59	1.48	2.95
❑Anl 10, Pulp Heroes; 1997 Annual	3.95	0.79	1.98	3.95
❑Anl 11, A: Johnny Quick, Ghosts; 1998 Annual	2.95	0.79	1.98	3.95
❑Anl 12, Oct 99, The Apes of Wrath, JLApe; 1999 Annual	2.95	0.59	1.48	2.95
❑GS 1, Aug 98, A Celebration of the Heroic Legacy; The Speed of Life, A: Flash IV (John Fox); A: Captain Boomerang; A: Flash I (Jay Garrick); A: Impulse; A: Jesse Quick; A: Flash III (Wally West); A: Lightning, 80pgs.	4.95	0.99	2.47	4.95
❑GS 2, Apr 99, 80pgs.	4.95	0.99	2.47	4.95
❑SE 1, Cl, JKu (c), 1: John Fox, 50th anniversary issue; 3 Flashes	2.95	0.70	1.75	3.50
❑TV 1, A: Kid Flash, Photo cover; TV Special; Stories about TV show Flash	3.95	0.79	1.98	3.95

FLASH & GREEN LANTERN: THE BRAVE AND THE BOLD
DC

Value: Cover or less

❑1, Oct 99, MWa (w), Those Who Worship Evil's Might 2.50
❑2, Nov 99, A: Kid Flash; V: Major Disaster; V: Mirror Master ... 2.50
❑3, Dec 99, MWa (w), A World of Hurt 2.50
❑4, Jan 00, MWa (w), How Many Times Can a Man Turn His Head? 2.50
❑5, Feb 00, MWa (w), The Man Without Fearlessness! 2.50
❑6, Mar 00, MWa (w), Running on Empty 2.50

Following the death of his mentor in *Crisis on Infinite Earths*, Wally West assumed the mantle of The Flash.

© 1987 DC Comics

FLASHBACK
SPECIAL

Value: Cover or less

❑1	3.00
❑2	3.00
❑3	3.00
❑4	3.00
❑5	3.00
❑6	3.00
❑7	3.00
❑8	3.00
❑9	3.00
❑10	3.00
❑11	3.00
❑12	3.00
❑13	3.00
❑14	3.00
❑15	3.00
❑16	3.00
❑17	3.00
❑18	3.00
❑19	3.00
❑20	3.00
❑21	3.00
❑22	3.00
❑23	3.00
❑24	3.00
❑25	3.00
❑26	3.00
❑27, Silver Streak; The Sky Wolf	3.00

FLASH GORDON (DC)
DC

	ORIG	GOOD	FINE	N-MINT
❑1, Jun 88, Into The Maelstrom	1.25	0.40	1.00	2.00
❑2, Jul 88	1.25	0.30	0.75	1.50
❑3, Aug 88	1.25	0.30	0.75	1.50
❑4, Sep 88	1.25	0.30	0.75	1.50
❑5, Oct 88	1.25	0.30	0.75	1.50
❑6, Nov 88	1.25	0.30	0.75	1.50
❑7, Dec 88	1.25	0.30	0.75	1.50
❑8, Win 88	1.25	0.30	0.75	1.50
❑9, Hol 88	1.25	0.30	0.75	1.50

FLASH GORDON (MARVEL)
MARVEL

Value: Cover or less

❑1, Jun 95, AW, Treachery in Torneo, cardstock wraparound cover 2.95
❑2, Jul 95, wraparound cardstock cover; Final Issue 2.95

FLASH GORDON: THE MOVIE
GOLDEN PRESS

	ORIG	GOOD	FINE	N-MINT
❑1, AW	1.95	0.50	1.25	2.50

FLASH/GREEN LANTERN: FASTER FRIENDS
DC

Value: Cover or less

❑1, prestige format; continued from Green Lantern/Flash: Faster Friends 4.95

FLASHMARKS
FANTAGRAPHICS

Value: Cover or less

❑1, b&w 2.95

FLASH PLUS
DC

Value: Cover or less

❑1, Jan 97, Doorway to Nightmare, A: Nightwing 2.95

FLASHPOINT
DC

Value: Cover or less

❑1, Dec 99, Elseworlds 2.95
❑2, Jan 00 .... 2.95
❑3, Feb 00 .... 2.95

FLASH SECRET FILES, THE
DC

Value: Cover or less

❑1, Nov 97, Secret Origin; Interview: Max Mercury, O: Flash II (Barry Allen); O: Flash I (Jay Garrick); O: Flash III (Wally West), bios on major cast members and villains; timeline 4.95
❑2, Nov 99, updates on cast ... 4.95

FLAXEN
DARK HORSE

Value: Cover or less

❑1, RHo, ME (w), photo back cover; centerfold 2.95

FLAXEN: ALTER EGO
CALIBER

Value: Cover or less

❑1, Mar 95, BMB, Shakedown 2.95

FLEENER
ZONGO

Value: Cover or less

- ❑1, b&w 2.95
- ❑2, b&w 2.95
- ❑3, b&w 2.95

FLESH
FLEETWAY

Value: Cover or less

- ❑1, Flesh: The Legend Of Shamana 2.95
- ❑2, Flesh: The Legend Of Shamana 2.95
- ❑3, Flesh: The Legend Of Shamana 2.95
- ❑4, Flesh: The Legend Of Shamana 2.95

FLESH & BLOOD
BRAINSTORM

	ORIG	GOOD	FINE	N-MINT
❑1, The Storm Is Rising, Partial foil cover	2.95	0.59	1.48	2.95
❑1/Ash, Ashcan preview from 1995 Philadelphia Comic Con	—	0.20	0.50	1.00

FLESH & BLOOD: PRE-EXISTING CONDITIONS
BLINDWOLF

Value: Cover or less

- ❑1, Flesh & Blood: Pre-Existing Conditions; The Angel 2.95

FLESH AND BONES
UPSHOT

Value: Cover or less

- ❑1, The Bojeffries Saga, full color 2.00
- ❑2, full color 2.00
- ❑3, full color 2.00
- ❑4, full color 2.00

FLESH CRAWLERS
KITCHEN SINK

Value: Cover or less

- ❑1 2.50
- ❑2 2.50
- ❑3 2.50

FLESH GORDON
AIRCEL

Value: Cover or less

- ❑1, Mar 92 2.95
- ❑2, Apr 92 2.95
- ❑3, May 92 2.95
- ❑4, Jun 92 2.95

FLESHPOT
EROS

Value: Cover or less

- ❑1, Oct 97 2.95

FLEX MENTALLO
DC

	ORIG	GOOD	FINE	N-MINT
❑1, Jun 96, After the Fact, Part 1	2.50	1.70	4.25	8.50
❑2, Jul 96, After the Fact, Part 2, EC parody cover	2.50	1.10	2.75	5.50
❑3, Aug 96, After the Fact, Part 3, Dark Knight parody cover	2.50	1.10	2.75	5.50
❑4, Sep 96, After the Fact, Part 4	2.50	1.10	2.75	5.50

FLICKERING FLESH
BONEYARD

Value: Cover or less

- ❑1, Mar 93 2.50

FLICKER'S FLEAS
FIFTH WHEEL

Value: Cover or less

- ❑1 3.00

FLINCH
DC

Value: Cover or less

- ❑1, Jun 99, Rocket-Man; Nice Neighborhood 2.50
- ❑2, Jul 99, Maggie and Her Microscope; Found Object 2.50
- ❑3, Aug 99, Night Terrors; A Walk in The Park 2.50
- ❑4, Sep 99, PG, A Gift of Friendship; Fair Trade 2.50
- ❑5, Oct 99, Betrothed; Peeping Bob 2.50
- ❑6, Nov 99 2.50
- ❑7, Dec 99, Parade; It Takes a Village 2.50
- ❑8, Jan 00, Guts; You've Got Hate Mail 2.50
- ❑9 2.50
- ❑10 2.50
- ❑11, Apr 00, Red Romance; Emergent 2.50
- ❑12, May 00, Waching You; Mondays 2.50
- ❑13 2.50
- ❑14, Sep 00, Resolve; Grave Wisdom, If Wishes Had Wings 2.50
- ❑15, Nov 00, A Night to Forget; Watchful 2.50
- ❑16, Jan 01, The Wedding Breakfast; A Temporary Life 2.50

FLINT ARMBUSTER JR. SPECIAL
ALCHEMY

Value: Cover or less

- ❑1, nn; b&w 2.95

FLINTSTONE KIDS, THE
MARVEL

Value: Cover or less

- ❑1 1.00
- ❑2 1.00
- ❑3 1.00
- ❑4 1.00
- ❑5 1.00
- ❑6 1.00
- ❑7, Get Lost, Freddy!; 3 Cheers 4 Betty! 1.00
- ❑8 1.00
- ❑9 1.00
- ❑10 1.00
- ❑11 1.00

FLINTSTONES, THE (ARCHIE)
ARCHIE

Value: Cover or less

- ❑1, Sep 95 1.50
- ❑2, Oct 95 1.50
- ❑3, Nov 95 1.50
- ❑4, Dec 95 1.50
- ❑5, Jan 96 1.50
- ❑6, Feb 96 1.50
- ❑7, Mar 96 1.50
- ❑8, Apr 96 1.50
- ❑9, May 96 1.50
- ❑10, Jun 96 1.50
- ❑12, Aug 96 1.50
- ❑13, Sep 96 1.50
- ❑14, Oct 96 1.50
- ❑15, Nov 96 1.50
- ❑16, Dec 96 1.50
- ❑17, Jan 97 1.50
- ❑18, Feb 97, Fred becomes a cartoonist 1.50
- ❑19, Mar 97, A: Great Gazoo 1.50
- ❑20, Apr 97 1.50
- ❑21, May 97 1.50
- ❑22, Jun 97, A: Gruesomes 1.50

FLINTSTONES, THE (HARVEY)
HARVEY

	ORIG	GOOD	FINE	N-MINT
❑1	1.25	0.50	1.25	2.50
❑2	1.25	0.40	1.00	2.00
❑3	1.25	0.40	1.00	2.00
❑4	1.25	0.40	1.00	2.00
❑5	1.25	0.40	1.00	2.00
❑6	1.50	0.40	1.00	2.00
❑7	1.50	0.40	1.00	2.00
❑8	1.50	0.40	1.00	2.00
❑9	1.50	0.40	1.00	2.00
❑10	1.50	0.40	1.00	2.00
❑11	1.50	0.40	1.00	2.00
❑12	1.50	0.40	1.00	2.00
❑13	1.50	0.40	1.00	2.00

FLINTSTONES, THE (MARVEL)
MARVEL

	ORIG	GOOD	FINE	N-MINT
❑1, Oct 77	0.30	1.00	2.50	5.00
❑2, Dec 77	0.35	0.60	1.50	3.00
❑3, Feb 78	0.35	0.60	1.50	3.00
❑4, Apr 78	0.35	0.60	1.50	3.00
❑5, Jun 78	0.35	0.60	1.50	3.00
❑6, Aug 78	0.35	0.60	1.50	3.00
❑7, Oct 78	0.35	0.60	1.50	3.00
❑8, Dec 78	0.35	0.60	1.50	3.00
❑9, Feb 79	0.35	0.60	1.50	3.00

FLINTSTONES 3-D
BLACKTHORNE

Value: Cover or less

- ❑1, Apr 87, A-Weigh We Go!, a.k.a. Blackthorne 3-D #19 2.50
- ❑2, Fal 87, Sheriff for a Day, a.k.a. Blackthorne 3-D #22 2.50
- ❑3 2.50
- ❑4 2.50

FLINTSTONES AND THE JETSONS, THE
DC

	ORIG	GOOD	FINE	N-MINT
❑1, Aug 97, The Flintstones: Fired!; The Jetsons: Fired!	1.75	0.40	1.00	2.00
❑2, Sep 97, The Flintstones: The First Purple Dinosaur on TV; The Jetsons: Garbage in, Garbage Out	1.75	0.40	1.00	2.00
❑3, Oct 97, Spacely turned into baby	1.75	0.40	1.00	2.00
❑4, Nov 97, Gazoo turns Fred and Barney into women	1.75	0.40	1.00	2.00
❑5, Dec 97, Wild Weekend; The Groovy Gruesomes, Judy and Elroy throw a party	1.75	0.40	1.00	2.00
❑6, Jan 98, Dodo a-Go-Go; The Jetsons: Morphin' Than a Barrel of Monkeys	1.95	0.40	1.00	2.00
❑7, Feb 98, Spies issue	1.95	0.40	1.00	2.00
❑8, Mar 98, Kung Fu issue	1.95	0.40	1.00	2.00
❑9, Apr 98, I, Rosey!	1.95	0.40	1.00	2.00
❑10, May 98	1.95	0.40	1.00	2.00
❑11, Jun 98, Time travel	1.95	0.40	1.00	2.00
❑12, Jul 98	1.95	0.40	1.00	2.00
❑13, Aug 98	1.95	0.40	1.00	2.00
❑14, Oct 98	1.99	0.40	1.00	2.00
❑15, Nov 98, The Return of Superstone; Cybersox, Super-Fred	1.99	0.40	1.00	2.00
❑16, Dec 98	1.99	0.40	1.00	2.00
❑17, Jan 99	1.99	0.40	1.00	2.00
❑18, Feb 99, It's a Wonderful Prehistoric Life, A: Great Gazoo, It's A Wonderful Life homage	1.99	0.40	1.00	2.00
❑19, Mar 99, Jetsons Bizarro story	1.99	0.40	1.00	2.00
❑20, Apr 99	1.99	0.40	1.00	2.00
❑21, May 99, It's About Time!, Fred and George switch places	1.99	0.40	1.00	1.99

FLINTSTONES BIG BOOK, THE
HARVEY

Value: Cover or less

- ❑1 1.95
- ❑2 1.95

FLINTSTONES DOUBLEVISION, THE
HARVEY

Value: Cover or less

- ❑1, Sep 94, polybagged with double vision glasses, adaptation of movie 2.95

FLINTSTONES GIANT SIZE
HARVEY

	ORIG	GOOD	FINE	N-MINT
❑2	2.25	0.50	1.25	2.50
❑3	2.25	0.50	1.25	2.50

FLINTSTONES WITH PEBBLES AND BAMM-BAMM, THE
GOLD KEY

	ORIG	GOOD	FINE	N-MINT
❑1, Regular paper (non-glossy) cover	0.25	10.00	25.00	50.00

FLOATERS
DARK HORSE

Value: Cover or less

- ❑1, b&w 2.50
- ❑2, b&w 2.50
- ❑3, b&w 2.50
- ❑4, b&w 2.50
- ❑5 2.50

FLOCK OF DREAMERS
KITCHEN SINK PRESS

Value: Cover or less

- ❑1, Nov 97, nn; b&w; Anthology 12.95

FLOOD RELIEF
MALIBU

	ORIG	GOOD	FINE	N-MINT
❑1, Ultraverse Red Cross giveaway	—	1.00	2.50	5.00

FLOWERS
DRAWN AND QUARTERLY

Value: Cover or less

- ❑1 2.95

FLOWERS ON THE RAZORWIRE
BONEYARD

Value: Cover or less

- ❑1, Crows; Silent Treatment, b&w 2.95
- ❑2, Blood Notes, Part 2; Tears: The Crucifixion, b&w 2.95
- ❑3, Red Coats; Biffo's Blues, b&w 2.95
- ❑4, Nov 94, Poem #81 (text); I Wish I Were the Candyman, b&w 2.95
- ❑5, May 95, Dark Angel: The Quiet Demon; It Was Only a Dream, b&w 2.95
- ❑6, May 95, b&w 2.95
- ❑7, Oct 95, b&w 2.95
- ❑8, b&w 2.95
- ❑9, b&w 2.95
- ❑10, Apr 97, b&w 2.95

FLY, THE (ARCHIE)
ARCHIE

	ORIG	GOOD	FINE	N-MINT
❑1, May 83, The Return Of The Sinister Spider	1.00	0.60	1.50	3.00
❑2, Jul 83	1.00	0.30	0.75	1.50
❑3, Oct 83	1.00	0.30	0.75	1.50
❑4, Dec 83, SD	1.00	0.30	0.75	1.50
❑5, Feb 84	0.75	0.30	0.75	1.50
❑6, Apr 84	0.75	0.30	0.75	1.50
❑7, Jun 84	0.75	0.30	0.75	1.50
❑8, Aug 84	0.75	0.30	0.75	1.50
❑9, Oct 84	0.75	0.30	0.75	1.50

FLY, THE (IMPACT)
DC

Value: Cover or less

- ❑1, Aug 91, Forged In Fire, O: The Fly 1.00
- ❑2, Sep 91 1.00
- ❑3, Oct 91, 1: Lt. Walker Odell 1.00
- ❑4, Nov 91, V: Black Hood 1.00
- ❑5, Dec 91, V: Arachnus 1.00
- ❑6, Jan 92, 1: Dolphus; 1: General Mechanix; 1: Blackjack 1.00
- ❑7, Feb 92, 1: Jason Troy Sr. 1.00
- ❑8, Mar 92 1.00
- ❑9, Apr 92, The Coming of The Crusaders, Part 3, 1: Fireball, trading cards 1.00
- ❑10, May 92 1.00
- ❑11, Jun 92 1.25
- ❑12, Jul 92, 1: Domino (Impact) 1.25
- ❑13, Aug 92, 1: Tremor 1.25
- ❑14, Sep 92 1.25
- ❑15, Oct 92 1.25
- ❑16, Nov 92, Curfew Violation 1.25
- ❑17, Dec 92, Final Issue 1.25
- ❑Anl 1, trading card 2.50

FLYING COLORS 10TH ANNIVERSARY SPECIAL
FLYING COLORS

Value: Cover or less

- ❑1, Sep 98, Funboys: Raiders of the 1951 Chevy Fleetline (delux); Burrito: Godzilla Madness 2.95

FLYING SAUCERS (DELL)
DELL

	ORIG	GOOD	FINE	N-MINT
❑1	0.12	4.40	11.00	22.00
❑2	0.12	2.50	6.25	12.50
❑3	0.12	2.50	6.25	12.50
❑4, Race With a...?	0.12	2.50	6.25	12.50
❑5, Final Issue	0.12	2.50	6.25	12.50

FLY MAN
ARCHIE

	ORIG	GOOD	FINE	N-MINT
❑32, Series continued from Adventures of the Fly #31	0.12	3.60	9.00	18.00
❑33	0.12	3.20	8.00	16.00
❑34	0.12	3.20	8.00	16.00
❑35	0.12	3.20	8.00	16.00
❑36, Mar 66, Fly Man's Strangest Dilemma; The Shield: Sufer, Shield, Suffer!, O: The Web	0.12	3.20	8.00	16.00
❑37	0.12	3.20	8.00	16.00
❑38	0.12	3.20	8.00	16.00
❑39, Series continued in Mighty Comics #40	0.12	3.20	8.00	16.00

To celebrate his store's 10th anniversary, Flying Colors Owner Joe Field commissioned a comic book with contributions from such creators as Dan Brereton.

© 1998 Joe Field

FOCUS
DC

	ORIG	GOOD	FINE	N-MINT
❑1, Sum 87, GP; BSz, no cover price	—	0.20	0.50	1.00

FOES
RAM

Value: Cover or less

- ❑1 1.95

FOODANG
CONTINUM

	ORIG	GOOD	FINE	N-MINT
❑1, Jul 94, b&w; foil cover	1.95	0.39	0.98	1.95
❑Ash 1, 1: Foodang, Ashcan promotional edition; Previews Foodang #1; Flip Book with The Dark Ashcan #1	—	0.20	0.50	1.00

FOODANG (2ND SERIES)
AUGUST HOUSE

Value: Cover or less

- ❑1, Jan 95, enhanced cover; oversized trading card 2.50

FOOFUR
MARVEL

Value: Cover or less

- ❑1 1.00
- ❑2 1.00
- ❑3 1.00
- ❑4, Fernando's Hideaway 1.00
- ❑5 1.00
- ❑6 1.00

FOOLKILLER
MARVEL

	ORIG	GOOD	FINE	N-MINT
❑1, Oct 90, O: FoolKiller III; A: Greg Salinger (FoolKiller II); 1: FoolKiller III (Kurt Gerhardt)	1.75	0.40	1.00	2.00
❑2, Nov 90	1.75	0.40	1.00	2.00
❑3, Dec 90, cover says Nov, indicia says Dec	1.75	0.40	1.00	2.00
❑4, Jan 91	1.75	0.40	1.00	2.00
❑5, Feb 91, Body Count	1.75	0.40	1.00	2.00
❑6, Apr 91, Fool's Paradise	1.75	0.40	1.00	2.00
❑7	1.75	0.40	1.00	2.00
❑8, Jul 91, A: Spider-Man, Spider-Man	1.75	0.40	1.00	2.00
❑9	1.75	0.40	1.00	2.00
❑10	1.75	0.40	1.00	2.00

FOOT SOLDIERS, THE
DARK HORSE

Value: Cover or less

- ❑1, Jan 96 2.95
- ❑2, Feb 96 2.95
- ❑3, Mar 96 2.95
- ❑4, Apr 96 2.95

FOOT SOLDIERS (VOL. 2)
IMAGE

Value: Cover or less

- ❑1, Sep 97, Walls; Arch Enemies, Part 1, b&w 2.95
- ❑2, Nov 97, Arch Enemies, Part 2, b&w 2.95
- ❑3, Jan 98, Arch Enemies, Part 3, b&w 2.95
- ❑4, Mar 98, Arch Enemies, Part 4, b&w 2.95
- ❑5, May 98, Arch Enemies, Part 5; The Battle of Old, b&w 2.95

FORBIDDEN FRANKENSTEIN
FANTAGRAPHICS

Value: Cover or less

- ❑1, b&w; adult 2.25
- ❑2, b&w; adult 2.50

FORBIDDEN KINGDOM, THE
EASTERN

Value: Cover or less

- ❑1, Nov 87 1.95

FORBIDDEN KNOWLEDGE
LAST GASP

	ORIG	GOOD	FINE	N-MINT
❑1, The Notorious Hell-Fire-Club; Alcibiades The Phalos Smasher	0.75	0.80	2.00	4.00

FORBIDDEN KNOWLEDGE: ADVENTURE BEYOND THE DOORWAY TO SOULS WITH RADICAL DREAMER
MARK'S GIANT ECONOMY SIZE

Value: Cover or less

- ❑1, nn; b&w; infinity cover; One-Shot 3.50

FORBIDDEN PLANET
INNOVATION

	ORIG	GOOD	FINE	N-MINT
❑1, Relief Ship, movie Adaptation	2.50	0.50	1.25	2.50
❑2, movie Adaptation	2.50	0.50	1.25	2.50
❑3, Sep 92, movie Adaptation	2.50	0.50	1.25	2.50
❑4, movie Adaptation	2.50	0.50	1.25	2.50

FORBIDDEN SUBJECTS
ANGEL

Value: Cover or less

❑0 .... 2.95
❑0/A, Nude edition A 3.95
❑0/B, Nude edition B 3.95

FORBIDDEN SUBJECTS: CANDY KISSES
ANGEL

Value: Cover or less

❑1, Censored cover 3.00
❑1/B, Adult cover 3.00

FORBIDDEN TALES OF DARK MANSION
DC

	ORIG	GOOD	FINE	N-MINT
❑5, Series continued from The Dark Mansion of Forbidden Love #4	—	1.60	4.00	8.00
❑6, Jul 72, The Psychic Blood-Hound; Mind-Bending Tales	0.20	1.60	4.00	8.00
❑7, HC, JO (w), Eye of the Beholder; Realm of the Mystic	0.20	1.60	4.00	8.00
❑8	0.20	1.60	4.00	8.00
❑9	0.20	1.60	4.00	8.00
❑10	0.20	1.60	4.00	8.00
❑11	0.20	1.60	4.00	8.00
❑12, A Change Of Bodies; Death Laughed Last	0.20	1.60	4.00	8.00
❑13	—	1.60	4.00	8.00
❑14	—	1.60	4.00	8.00
❑15, Final Issue	—	1.60	4.00	8.00

FORBIDDEN VAMPIRE
ANGEL

Value: Cover or less

❑0 .... 2.95

FORBIDDEN WORLDS
ACG

	ORIG	GOOD	FINE	N-MINT
❑73, 1: Herbie	—	55.00	137.50	275.00
❑74	—	7.00	17.50	35.00
❑75	—	7.00	17.50	35.00
❑76	—	7.00	17.50	35.00
❑77	—	7.00	17.50	35.00
❑78	—	7.00	17.50	35.00
❑79	—	7.00	17.50	35.00
❑80	—	7.00	17.50	35.00
❑81	—	4.80	12.00	24.00
❑82	—	4.80	12.00	24.00
❑83	—	4.80	12.00	24.00
❑84	—	4.80	12.00	24.00
❑85	—	4.80	12.00	24.00
❑86, Flying saucer cover	—	6.00	15.00	30.00
❑87	—	4.80	12.00	24.00
❑88	—	4.80	12.00	24.00
❑89	—	4.80	12.00	24.00
❑90	—	4.80	12.00	24.00
❑91	—	4.00	10.00	20.00
❑92	—	4.00	10.00	20.00
❑93	—	4.00	10.00	20.00
❑94, A: Herbie	—	11.00	27.50	55.00
❑95	—	4.00	10.00	20.00
❑96	—	4.00	10.00	20.00
❑97	—	4.00	10.00	20.00
❑98	—	4.00	10.00	20.00
❑99	—	4.00	10.00	20.00
❑100	—	4.00	10.00	20.00
❑101	—	3.20	8.00	16.00
❑102	—	3.20	8.00	16.00
❑103	—	3.20	8.00	16.00
❑104	—	3.20	8.00	16.00
❑105	—	3.20	8.00	16.00
❑106	—	3.20	8.00	16.00
❑107, The Endless Rooms!; Mysterious Island	0.12	3.20	8.00	16.00
❑108	0.12	3.20	8.00	16.00
❑109	0.12	3.20	8.00	16.00
❑110, A: Herbie	0.12	7.00	17.50	35.00
❑111	0.12	3.20	8.00	16.00
❑112, This Man is Dangerous!; The Case for E.S.P.	0.12	3.20	8.00	16.00
❑113	0.12	3.20	8.00	16.00
❑114, A: Herbie	0.12	7.00	17.50	35.00
❑115	0.12	3.20	8.00	16.00
❑116, A: Herbie	0.12	6.00	15.00	30.00
❑117	0.12	3.20	8.00	16.00
❑118, Mar 64	0.12	3.20	8.00	16.00
❑119	0.12	3.20	8.00	16.00
❑120	0.12	3.20	8.00	16.00
❑121, The Man Without a Mind; Back to Yesterday!	0.12	2.40	6.00	12.00
❑122	0.12	2.40	6.00	12.00
❑123	0.12	2.40	6.00	12.00
❑124	0.12	2.40	6.00	12.00
❑125, 1: Magicman	0.12	5.00	12.50	25.00
❑126	0.12	2.40	6.00	12.00
❑127	0.12	2.40	6.00	12.00
❑128, Magicman Meets Merlin!; Only Tough Guys Get Places!, A: Magicman	0.12	2.80	7.00	14.00
❑129	0.12	2.40	6.00	12.00
❑130, Magicman vs. The Wizard of Science!; Stone Age Man, A: Magicman	0.12	2.80	7.00	14.00
❑131	—	2.40	6.00	12.00
❑132	—	2.40	6.00	12.00
❑133	—	2.40	6.00	12.00
❑134	—	2.40	6.00	12.00
❑135	—	2.40	6.00	12.00
❑136	—	2.40	6.00	12.00
❑137	—	2.40	6.00	12.00
❑138	—	2.40	6.00	12.00
❑139	—	2.40	6.00	12.00
❑140	—	2.40	6.00	12.00
❑141	—	2.00	5.00	10.00
❑142	—	2.00	5.00	10.00
❑143	—	2.00	5.00	10.00
❑144	—	2.00	5.00	10.00
❑145, Final Issue	—	2.00	5.00	10.00

FORBIDDEN WORLDS (A+)
A-PLUS

Value: Cover or less

❑1, SD, An Old Man; Traveler, b&w; Reprint 2.50

FORBIDDEN WORLDS (AVALON)
AVALON

Value: Cover or less

❑1, His Own Little World; Lash Thunder Space Explorer 2.95

FORBIDDEN X ANGEL
ANGEL

Value: Cover or less

❑1 .... 2.95

FORBIDDEN ZONE
GALAXY ENTERTAINMENT

Value: Cover or less

❑1, Motion: Tales of the Millennium; M80 .... 5.95

FORCE 10
CROW

	ORIG	GOOD	FINE	N-MINT
❑1, Children Of The Revolution, Part 1, 1: Impel	2.50	0.50	1.25	2.50
❑1/Ash, Children Of The Revolution, Part 1, 1: Force 10; 1: Leprechaun; 1: Teknik; 1: Lodestar; 1: Rukh; 1: Spook; 1: Armadillos; 1: Flux, Ashcan preview edition	—	0.60	1.50	3.00

FORCE OF BUDDHA'S PALM, THE
JADEMAN

Value: Cover or less

❑1 .... 1.95
❑2 .... 1.95
❑3 .... 1.95
❑4 .... 1.95
❑5 .... 1.95
❑6 .... 1.95
❑7 .... 1.95
❑8 .... 1.95
❑9 .... 1.95
❑10 .... 1.95
❑11 .... 1.95
❑12 .... 1.95
❑13 .... 1.95
❑14 .... 1.95
❑15 .... 1.95
❑16 .... 1.95
❑17 .... 1.95
❑18 .... 1.95
❑19 .... 1.95
❑20 .... 1.95
❑21 .... 1.95
❑22 .... 1.95
❑23 .... 1.95
❑24 .... 1.95
❑25 .... 1.95
❑26 .... 1.95
❑27 .... 1.95
❑28 .... 1.95
❑29 .... 1.95
❑30 .... 1.95
❑31 .... 1.95
❑32 .... 1.95
❑33 .... 1.95
❑34 .... 1.95
❑35 .... 1.95
❑36 .... 1.95
❑37 .... 1.95
❑38 .... 1.95
❑39 .... 1.95
❑40 .... 1.95
❑41 .... 1.95
❑42 .... 1.95

FORCE SEVEN
LONE STAR

Value: Cover or less

❑1, Aug 99, S.O.S. 2.95
❑2, Sep 99, Fire in the Sky 2.95
❑3, Mar 00, Extinction 2.95

FORCE WORKS
MARVEL

	ORIG	GOOD	FINE	N-MINT
❑1, Jul 94, Daybreak, Pop-up cover; Giant-size	3.95	0.79	1.98	3.95
❑2, Aug 94	1.50	0.40	1.00	2.00
❑3, Sep 94	1.50	0.40	1.00	2.00
❑4, Oct 94	1.50	0.30	0.75	1.50
❑5, Nov 94	1.50	0.30	0.75	1.50
❑5/CS, Nov 94, with sericel	2.95	0.59	1.48	2.95
❑6, Dec 94	1.50	0.30	0.75	1.50
❑7, Jan 95	1.50	0.30	0.75	1.50
❑8, Feb 95	1.50	0.30	0.75	1.50
❑9, Mar 95	1.50	0.30	0.75	1.50
❑10, Apr 95	1.50	0.30	0.75	1.50
❑11, May 95	1.50	0.30	0.75	1.50

	ORIG	GOOD	FINE	N-MINT
❑12, Jun 95	2.50	0.50	1.25	2.50
❑13, Jul 95	1.50	0.30	0.75	1.50
❑14, Aug 95	1.50	0.30	0.75	1.50
❑15, Sep 95	1.50	0.30	0.75	1.50
❑16, Oct 95	1.50	0.30	0.75	1.50
❑17, Nov 95	1.50	0.30	0.75	1.50
❑18, Dec 95, The Crossing, A: Hawkeye; A: Avengers; A: War Machine	1.50	0.30	0.75	1.50
❑19, Jan 96, A: Mantis, Kang	1.50	0.30	0.75	1.50
❑20, Feb 96	1.50	0.30	0.75	1.50
❑21, Mar 96, Afterimage	1.50	0.30	0.75	1.50
❑22, Apr 96, Pain Threshold, Final Issue	1.50	0.30	0.75	1.50
❑Ash 1, ashcan edition; ashcan	0.75	0.15	0.38	0.75

FORE/PUNK
PARODY PRESS

Value: Cover or less

- ❑1/A, punk cover ... 2.50
- ❑1/B, fore cover ... 2.50

FORETERNITY
ANTARCTIC

Value: Cover or less

- ❑1, Jul 97, b&w ... 2.95
- ❑2, Sep 97, b&w ... 2.95
- ❑3, Nov 97, b&w ... 2.95
- ❑4, Jan 98, b&w ... 2.95

FOREVER AMBER
IMAGE

Value: Cover or less

- ❑1/A, Jul 99 ... 2.95
- ❑1/B, Jul 99, Welcome to My World, alternate cover has white background ... 2.95
- ❑2, Aug 99, The Center of Attention ... 2.95
- ❑3, Sep 99, Let the Lawyers Sort it Out ... 2.95
- ❑4, Oct 99 ... 2.95

FOREVER NOW
ENTERTAINMENT

Value: Cover or less

- ❑1 ... 1.50
- ❑2 ... 1.50

FOREVER PEOPLE, THE
DC

	ORIG	GOOD	FINE	N-MINT
❑1, Mar 71, JK, JK (w), In Search Of A Dream!, O: Forever People	0.15	5.20	13.00	26.00
❑2, May 71, JK, JK (w), Super War!, 1: Mantis (DC); 1: Desaad	0.15	3.60	9.00	18.00
❑3, Jul 71, JK, JK (w), 1: Glorious Godfrey	0.15	3.00	7.50	15.00
❑4, Sep 71, JK, JK (w)	0.25	3.00	7.50	15.00
❑5, Nov 71, JK, JK (w), Giant-size	0.25	3.00	7.50	15.00
❑6, Jan 72, JK, JK (w), The Omega Effect, A: Sandman; A: Sandy, Giant-size	0.25	1.80	4.50	9.00
❑7, Mar 72, JK, JK (w)	0.25	1.80	4.50	9.00
❑8, May 72, JK, JK (w)	0.25	1.80	4.50	9.00
❑9, Jul 72, JK, JK (w)	0.25	1.80	4.50	9.00
❑10, Jul 72, JK, JK (w)	0.20	1.80	4.50	9.00
❑11, Nov 72, JK, JK (w), 1: The Pursuer	0.20	1.80	4.50	9.00

FOREVER PEOPLE (MINI-SERIES)
DC

	ORIG	GOOD	FINE	N-MINT
❑1, Feb 88, The Day After Forever	1.25	0.40	1.00	2.00
❑2, Mar 88, From Earth to Forever	1.25	0.30	0.75	1.50
❑3, Apr 88, Forever's End?	1.25	0.30	0.75	1.50
❑4, May 88	1.25	0.30	0.75	1.50
❑5, Jun 88	1.25	0.30	0.75	1.50
❑6, Jul 88	1.25	0.30	0.75	1.50

FOREVER WARRIORS
CFD

Value: Cover or less

- ❑1, May 97, RB, RB (w), The Wizard of Odd!; Trial by Holocaust! ... 2.95

FORGOTTEN REALMS (DC)
DC

Value: Cover or less

- ❑1, The Hand of Vaprak, Part 1 ... 1.50
- ❑2, The Hand of Vaprak, Part 2 ... 1.50
- ❑3, The Hand of Vaprak, Part 3 ... 1.50
- ❑4, The Hand of Vaprak, Part 4 ... 1.50
- ❑5 ... 1.50
- ❑6 ... 1.50
- ❑7 ... 1.50
- ❑8 ... 1.50
- ❑9 ... 1.50
- ❑10 ... 1.50
- ❑11 ... 1.50
- ❑12 ... 1.50
- ❑13 ... 1.50
- ❑14 ... 1.50
- ❑15 ... 1.50
- ❑16 ... 1.75
- ❑17 ... 1.75
- ❑18 ... 1.75
- ❑19 ... 1.75
- ❑20 ... 1.75
- ❑21 ... 1.75
- ❑22 ... 1.75
- ❑23 ... 1.75
- ❑24 ... 1.75
- ❑25, Wake OF The Realms Master, Final Issue ... 1.75
- ❑Anl 1, GK (c) ... 2.95

FORGOTTEN REALMS: THE GRAND TOUR
TSR

	ORIG	GOOD	FINE	N-MINT
❑1, Grand Tour, nn; no cover price	—	0.20	0.50	1.00

FORTUNE AND GLORY
ONI

Value: Cover or less

- ❑1, Dec 99, BMB (w), b&w ... 4.95
- ❑2, Feb 00, BMB (w), b&w ... 4.95
- ❑3, Apr 00, BMB (w), b&w ... 4.95

Magicman was one of ACG's few super-heroes.

FORTUNE'S FOOL, THE STORY OF JINXER
CRANIUM

Value: Cover or less

- ❑0, Jul 99 ... 2.95

FORTUNE'S FRIENDS: HELL WEEK
ARIA

Value: Cover or less

- ❑1, graphic novel ... 6.95

FORTY WINKS
ODD JOBS LIMITED

Value: Cover or less

- ❑1, Nov 97 ... 2.95
- ❑2, Dec 97 ... 2.95
- ❑3, Mar 98 ... 2.95
- ❑4, Jun 98 ... 2.95

FORTY WINKS CHRISTMAS SPECIAL
PEREGRINE ENTERTAINMENT

Value: Cover or less

- ❑1, Aug 98, b&w ... 2.95

FORTY WINKS SUPER SPECIAL EDITION: TV PARTY TONITE!
PEREGRINE ENTERTAINMENT

Value: Cover or less

- ❑1, Apr 99, b&w ... 2.95

FOTON EFFECT, THE
ACED

Value: Cover or less

- ❑1, Oct 86 ... 1.50
- ❑2 ... 1.50
- ❑3 ... 1.50

FOUL!
TRAITORS GAIT

	ORIG	GOOD	FINE	N-MINT
❑1, Scottish Manager; Freaky Formations	2.00	0.60	1.50	3.00

FOUR HORSEMEN
VERTIGO

Value: Cover or less

- ❑1, Feb 00, Famine ... 2.50
- ❑2, Mar 00 ... 2.50
- ❑3, Apr 00, Pestilence ... 2.50
- ❑4, May 00, Death ... 2.50

FOUR KUNOICHI, THE: BLOODLUST
LIGHTNING

Value: Cover or less

- ❑1, Dec 96, b&w; Standard edition ... 2.75
- ❑1/Nude, Nude cover ... 9.95
- ❑1/PL, Platinum edition ... 9.95
- ❑1/PLND, Platinum Nude edition ... 29.95

FOUR KUNOICHI: ENTER THE SINJA
LIGHTNING

Value: Cover or less

- ❑1, Feb 97, b&w ... 2.95

FOUR-STAR BATTLE TALES
DC

	ORIG	GOOD	FINE	N-MINT
❑1, Feb 73, The Last Target; Indians Don't Fight By The Book!	0.20	1.30	3.25	6.50
❑2	0.20	0.80	2.00	4.00
❑3	0.20	0.80	2.00	4.00
❑4	0.20	0.80	2.00	4.00
❑5, Nov 73, Final Issue	0.20	0.80	2.00	4.00

FOUR STAR SPECTACULAR
DC

	ORIG	GOOD	FINE	N-MINT
❑1, Apr 76, Giant-size	0.50	1.00	2.50	5.00
❑2, Jun 76, Giant-size	0.50	0.80	2.00	4.00
❑3, Aug 76, Giant-size; Bicentennial #15	0.50	0.80	2.00	4.00
❑4, Oct 76, Giant-size	0.50	0.80	2.00	4.00
❑5, Dec 76, Superboy: The Man Who Hunted Superboy; Vigilante: The Unlucky Horseshoe, Giant-size	0.50	0.80	2.00	4.00
❑6, Feb 77, Final Issue; Giant-size	0.50	0.80	2.00	4.00

FOURTH WORLD (JACK KIRBY'S...)
DC

	ORIG	GOOD	FINE	N-MINT
❑1, Mar 97, JBy, JBy (w), Born of Thunder, Born of Flame	1.95	0.50	1.25	2.50
❑2, Apr 97, JBy, JBy (w)	1.95	0.40	1.00	2.00
❑3, May 97, JBy, JBy (w)	1.95	0.40	1.00	2.00
❑4, Jun 97, JBy, JBy (w), Back from the Source	1.95	0.40	1.00	2.00
❑5, Jul 97, JBy, JBy (w)	1.95	0.40	1.00	2.00
❑6, Aug 97, JBy, JBy (w)	1.95	0.40	1.00	2.00
❑7, Sep 97, JBy, JBy (w)	1.95	0.40	1.00	2.00
❑8, Oct 97, JBy, JBy (w), Genesis	1.95	0.40	1.00	2.00
❑9, Nov 97, JBy, JBy (w), Sons of the Father	1.95	0.40	1.00	2.00
❑10, Dec 97, JBy, JBy (w), Aftermath, Face cover	1.95	0.40	1.00	2.00
❑11, Jan 98, JBy, JBy (w)	1.95	0.40	1.00	2.00

	ORIG	GOOD	FINE	N-MINT
❑12, Feb 98, JBy, JBy (w)	1.95	0.40	1.00	2.00
❑13, Mar 98, JBy, JBy (w)	1.95	0.40	1.00	2.00
❑14, Apr 98, JBy, JBy (w), Darkseid and Ares escape Source Wall	1.95	0.40	1.00	2.00
❑15, May 98, JBy, JBy (w)	1.95	0.40	1.00	2.00
❑16, Jun 98, JBy, JBy (w)	1.95	0.40	1.00	2.00
❑17, Jul 98, JBy, JBy (w)	1.95	0.40	1.00	2.00
❑18, Aug 98, JBy, JBy (w)	1.95	0.40	1.00	2.00
❑19, Sep 98, JBy, JBy (w), Return of Supertown	2.25	0.45	1.13	2.25
❑20, Oct 98, JBy, A: Superman	2.25	0.45	1.13	2.25

FOURTH WORLD GALLERY, THE
DC

Value: Cover or less

- ❑1, nn; pin-ups based on Jack Kirby creations ... 3.50

FOX AND THE CROW
DC

	ORIG	GOOD	FINE	N-MINT
❑73, May 62	0.10	8.00	20.00	40.00
❑74	—	8.00	20.00	40.00
❑75	—	8.00	20.00	40.00
❑76	—	8.00	20.00	40.00
❑77	—	8.00	20.00	40.00
❑78	—	8.00	20.00	40.00
❑79	—	8.00	20.00	40.00
❑80	—	8.00	20.00	40.00
❑81	—	5.00	12.50	25.00
❑82	—	5.00	12.50	25.00
❑83	—	5.00	12.50	25.00
❑84	—	5.00	12.50	25.00
❑85	—	5.00	12.50	25.00
❑86	—	5.00	12.50	25.00
❑87	—	5.00	12.50	25.00
❑88	—	5.00	12.50	25.00
❑89	—	5.00	12.50	25.00
❑90	—	5.00	12.50	25.00
❑91	—	5.00	12.50	25.00
❑92	—	5.00	12.50	25.00
❑93	—	5.00	12.50	25.00
❑94	—	5.00	12.50	25.00
❑95, 1: Stanley and His Monster	—	9.00	22.50	45.00
❑96	—	4.00	10.00	20.00
❑97	—	4.00	10.00	20.00
❑98	—	4.00	10.00	20.00
❑99	—	4.00	10.00	20.00
❑100	—	4.40	11.00	22.00
❑101	—	3.20	8.00	16.00
❑102	—	3.20	8.00	16.00
❑103	—	3.20	8.00	16.00
❑104	—	3.20	8.00	16.00
❑105, Nov 67, A: Stanley and His Monster	—	3.20	8.00	16.00
❑106	—	3.20	8.00	16.00
❑107	—	3.20	8.00	16.00
❑108, Final Issue; Series continued in Stanley and His Monster	—	3.20	8.00	16.00

FOX COMICS
FANTAGRAPHICS

Value: Cover or less

- ❑24, b&w ... 2.95
- ❑25, b&w ... 2.95
- ❑26, b&w ... 2.95
- ❑SE 1, b&w; Australian; Special ... 2.95

FOX COMICS LEGENDS SERIES
FANTAGRAPHICS

	ORIG	GOOD	FINE	N-MINT
❑1, Jul 92, b&w; Three Stooges	2.25	0.50	1.25	2.50
❑2, The Unauthorized Biography of Elvis, b&w; Elvis	2.50	0.50	1.25	2.50

FOXFIRE (MALIBU)
MALIBU

Value: Cover or less

- ❑1, Feb 96, Interview with an Ultra ... 1.50
- ❑2, Mar 96, Tunnel Vision, V: UltraForce ... 1.50

FOXFIRE (NIGHT WYND)
NIGHTWYND

Value: Cover or less

- ❑1, b&w ... 2.50
- ❑2, b&w ... 2.50
- ❑3, b&w ... 2.50

FOX KIDS FUNHOUSE
ACCLAIM

Value: Cover or less

- ❑1, digest; The Tick, Life with Louie, Bobby's World ... 4.50
- ❑2, Raw, Uncooked Justice!; Bobby's World: Nasty Neighbor ... 4.50

FRAGGLE ROCK (MARVEL)
MARVEL

Value: Cover or less

- ❑1, Reprint ... 1.00
- ❑2, Reprint ... 1.00
- ❑3, Reprint ... 1.00
- ❑4, Reprint ... 1.00
- ❑5, Reprint ... 1.00

FRAGGLE ROCK (STAR)
MARVEL

	ORIG	GOOD	FINE	N-MINT
❑1, Apr 85, The Magic Time Machine	0.65	0.20	0.50	1.00
❑2, Jun 85, #1!	0.65	0.20	0.50	1.00
❑3, Aug 85	0.65	0.20	0.50	1.00
❑4, Oct 85	0.65	0.20	0.50	1.00
❑5, Dec 85	0.65	0.20	0.50	1.00
❑6, Feb 86	0.65	0.20	0.50	1.00
❑7, Apr 86	0.75	0.20	0.50	1.00
❑8, Jun 86	0.75	0.20	0.50	1.00

FRAGMENTS
SCREAMING CAT

Value: Cover or less

- ❑1 ... 2.50

FRANCIS, BROTHER OF THE UNIVERSE
MARVEL

	ORIG	GOOD	FINE	N-MINT
❑1	0.75	0.30	0.75	1.50

FRANK (FANTAGRAPHICS)
FANTAGRAPHICS

Value: Cover or less

- ❑1, Sep 96, b&w ... 2.95
- ❑2, Dec 97, b&w ... 3.95

FRANK (NEMESIS)
NEMESIS

Value: Cover or less

- ❑1, Apr 94, Tail-Bone Connects to the Elbow, newsstand ... 1.75
- ❑1/DM, Apr 94, Tail-Bone Connects to the Elbow, variant cover; direct sale ... 2.50
- ❑2, May 94, newsstand ... 1.75
- ❑2/DM, May 94, direct sale ... 2.50
- ❑3, Jun 94, newsstand ... 1.75
- ❑3/DM, Jun 94, direct sale ... 2.50
- ❑4, Jul 94, newsstand ... 2.50
- ❑4/DM, Jul 94, direct sale ... 2.50

FRANKENSTEIN (ETERNITY)
ETERNITY

Value: Cover or less

- ❑1, b&w ... 1.95
- ❑2, b&w ... 1.95
- ❑3, b&w ... 1.95

FRANKENSTEIN (MARY SHELLEY'S...)
TOPPS

Value: Cover or less

- ❑1, Oct 94 ... 2.95
- ❑2 ... 2.95
- ❑3, trading cards ... 2.95
- ❑4 ... 2.95

FRANKENSTEIN (THE MONSTER OF...)
MARVEL

	ORIG	GOOD	FINE	N-MINT
❑1, Jan 73, O: Frankenstein's Monster	0.20	4.80	12.00	24.00
❑2, Mar 73, MP, MP (w), Bride Of The Monster!, O: Bride of Frankenstein	0.20	2.40	6.00	12.00
❑3, May 73	0.20	1.80	4.50	9.00
❑4, Jul 73	0.20	1.80	4.50	9.00
❑5, Sep 73	0.20	1.80	4.50	9.00
❑6, Oct 73, Cover changes titles to "The Frankenstein Monster"	0.20	1.40	3.50	7.00
❑7, Nov 73	0.20	1.40	3.50	7.00
❑8, Jan 74, A: Dracula	0.20	2.00	5.00	10.00
❑9, Mar 74, A: Dracula	0.20	2.00	5.00	10.00
❑10, May 74	0.25	1.20	3.00	6.00
❑11, Jul 74, V: Ivan	0.25	1.00	2.50	5.00
❑12, Sep 74, The monster comes to the modern day	0.25	1.00	2.50	5.00
❑13, Nov 74	0.25	1.00	2.50	5.00
❑14, Jan 75	0.25	1.00	2.50	5.00
❑15, Mar 75, Tactics of Death!; The Shadow, Back-up story reprinted from Tales of Suspense #10	0.25	1.00	2.50	5.00
❑16, May 75, 1: Berserker; 1: Veronica Frankenstein	0.25	1.00	2.50	5.00
❑17, Jul 75, V: Berserker, Monster regains speech	0.25	1.00	2.50	5.00
❑18, Sep 75, Final Issue	0.25	1.00	2.50	5.00

FRANKENSTEIN/DRACULA WAR, THE
TOPPS

Value: Cover or less

- ❑1, Feb 95, The Gathering Storm ... 2.50
- ❑2 ... 2.50
- ❑3 ... 2.50

FRANKENSTEIN: OR THE MODERN PROMETHEUS
CALIBER

Value: Cover or less

- ❑1 ... 2.95

FRANK FRAZETTA FANTASY ILLUSTRATED
FRANK FRAZETTA FANTASY ILLUSTRATED

	ORIG	GOOD	FINE	N-MINT
❑1, Spr 98	5.99	1.40	3.50	7.00
❑1/SC, Spr 98, alternate cover	5.99	1.60	4.00	8.00
❑2, Sum 98, Battle Chasers story	5.99	2.00	5.00	10.00
❑2/SC, Sum 98, alternate cover	5.99	1.20	3.00	6.00
❑3, Fal 98	5.99	1.20	3.00	6.00
❑3/SC, Fal 98, alternate cover	5.99	1.20	3.00	6.00
❑4, Win 98	5.99	1.20	2.99	5.99
❑4/SC, Win 98, alternate cover	5.99	1.20	3.00	6.00
❑5, Mar 99	5.99	1.20	2.99	5.99
❑5/SC, Mar 99, alternate cover	5.99	1.50	3.75	7.50
❑6, May 99	5.99	1.20	3.00	6.00
❑6/SC, May 99, alternate cover	5.99	1.40	3.50	7.00

	ORIG	GOOD	FINE	N-MINT
❑7, Jul 99	5.99	1.20	2.99	5.99
❑7/SC, Jul 99, alternate cover	5.99	1.20	2.99	5.99

FRANK IN THE RIVER
TUNDRA
Value: Cover or less
❑1 ... 2.95

FRANK THE UNICORN
FRAGMENTS WEST
Value: Cover or less
❑1, Sep 86 ... 2.00
❑2, Nov 86 ... 2.00
❑3, Jan 87 ... 2.00
❑4 ... 2.00
❑5 ... 2.00
❑6 ... 2.00
❑7 ... 2.00
❑8 ... 2.00
❑9 ... 2.00

FRANK ZAPPA: VIVA LA BIZARRE
REVOLUTIONARY
Value: Cover or less
❑1, Feb 94, b&w ... 2.50

FREAK FORCE
IMAGE
Value: Cover or less
❑1, Dec 93, EL (w); KG (w), 1: Freak Force ... 1.95
❑2, Jan 94 ... 1.95
❑3, Feb 94 ... 1.95
❑4, Mar 94, A: Vanguard ... 1.95
❑5, Apr 94 ... 1.95
❑6, Jun 94, Identity of Mighty Man revealed ... 1.95
❑7, Jul 94 ... 1.95
❑8, Aug 94 ... 2.50
❑9, Sep 94, A: Cyber Force ... 2.50
❑10, Oct 94 ... 2.50
❑11, Nov 94 ... 2.50
❑12, Dec 94 ... 2.50
❑13, Jan 95, Jerry Ordway pin-up ... 2.50
❑13/A, Jan 95, alternate cover ... 2.50
❑14, Feb 95 ... 2.50
❑15, Mar 95, A: Maxx ... 2.50
❑16, Apr 95 ... 2.50
❑17, Jun 95 ... 2.50
❑18, Jul 95, Final Issue ... 2.50

FREAK FORCE (MINI-SERIES)
IMAGE
Value: Cover or less
❑1, Apr 97 ... 2.95
❑2, May 97 ... 2.95
❑3, Jul 97 ... 2.95

FREAK OUT ON INFANT EARTHS
BLACKTHORNE
Value: Cover or less
❑1, Jan 87 ... 2.00
❑2 ... 2.00

FREAKS
FANTAGRAPHICS
Value: Cover or less
❑1, movie Adaptation ... 2.25
❑2, movie Adaptation ... 2.25
❑3, movie Adaptation ... 2.25

FREAKS' AMOUR
DARK HORSE
Value: Cover or less
❑1, The Grinning Man ... 3.95
❑2 ... 3.95
❑3 ... 3.95

FRED & BIANCA CENSORSHIP SUCKS SPECIAL
COMICS INTERVIEW
Value: Cover or less
❑1, b&w; Reprint ... 2.25

FRED & BIANCA MOTHER'S DAY MASSACRE
COMICS INTERVIEW
Value: Cover or less
❑1, b&w; Reprint ... 2.25

FRED & BIANCA VALENTINE'S DAY MASSACRE
COMICS INTERVIEW
Value: Cover or less
❑1, b&w; Reprint ... 2.25

FREDDY KRUEGER'S NIGHTMARE ON ELM STREET
MARVEL
Value: Cover or less
❑1, Oct 89, TD; AA; RB, Dreamstalkers, Part 1, O: Freddy Krueger, b&w; magazine ... 2.25
❑2, Nov 89, TD; AA, Dreamstalkers, Part 2, b&w; magazine ... 2.25

FREDDY'S DEAD: THE FINAL NIGHTMARE
INNOVATION

	ORIG	GOOD	FINE	N-MINT
❑1, Little John In Slumberland, movie Adaptation	2.50	0.50	1.25	2.50
❑1/3D, part 3-D	—	0.50	1.25	2.50
❑2, movie Adaptation	2.50	0.50	1.25	2.50
❑3, Memories...Like The Killings In My Mind, movie Adaptation	2.50	0.50	1.25	2.50
❑3/3D, 3-D version of #3; Requires glasses provided at movie showings	2.50	0.50	1.25	2.50

FREDERIC REMINGTON: THE MAN WHO PAINTED THE WEST
TOME PRESS
Value: Cover or less
❑1, b&w ... 2.95

FRED HEMBECK DESTROYS THE MARVEL UNIVERSE
MARVEL
Value: Cover or less
❑1, Jul 89, FH, FH (w), When Titans Croak!, D: Everyone ... 1.50

FRED HEMBECK SELLS THE MARVEL UNIVERSE
MARVEL

	ORIG	GOOD	FINE	N-MINT
❑1, Oct 90, FH, FH (w), The New Adventures Of Brother Voodoo!	1.25	0.30	0.75	1.50

FRED THE POSSESSED FLOWER
HAPPY PREDATOR
Value: Cover or less
❑1, The Plant Behind the Scenes ... 2.95
❑2 ... 2.95
❑3 ... 2.95

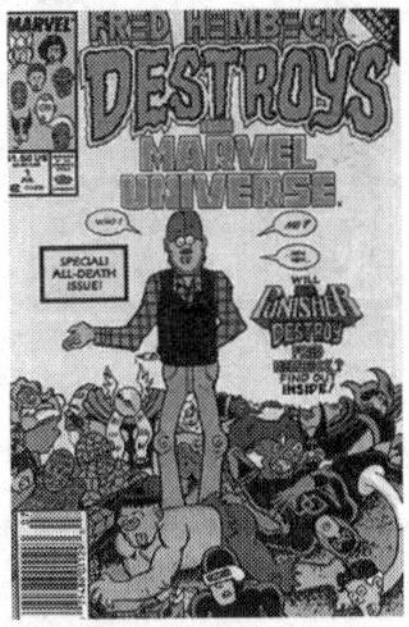

With the help of Crackers, Crown Prince of Death, Fred Hembeck killed every Marvel hero in the appropriately named *Fred Hembeck Destroys the Marvel Universe.*

	ORIG	GOOD	FINE	N-MINT

❑4 ... 2.95
❑5 ... 2.95
❑6 ... 2.95

FREEBOOTERS/YOUNG GODS/PARADOXMAN PREVIEW
DARK HORSE
Value: Cover or less
❑1 ... 1.00

FREE CEREBUS
AARDVARK-VANAHEIM

	ORIG	GOOD	FINE	N-MINT
❑1, nn; giveaway	—	0.20	0.50	1.00

FREEDOM FIGHTERS
DC

	ORIG	GOOD	FINE	N-MINT
❑1, Apr 76, RE, V: Silver Ghost, Freedom Fighters arrive on Earth-1	0.25	0.80	2.00	4.00
❑2, Jun 76, V: Silver Ghost	0.30	0.60	1.50	3.00
❑3, Aug 76, A: Wonder Woman, Bicentennial #8	0.30	0.60	1.50	3.00
❑4, Oct 76, A: Wonder Woman	0.30	0.50	1.25	2.50
❑5, Dec 76	0.30	0.50	1.25	2.50
❑6, Feb 77	0.30	0.40	1.00	2.00
❑7, Apr 77	0.30	0.40	1.00	2.00
❑8, Jun 77, V: Crusaders	0.30	0.40	1.00	2.00
❑9, Aug 77, V: Crusaders	0.35	0.40	1.00	2.00
❑10, Oct 77, Murder In Miniature, O: Doll Man; V: Cat-Man	0.35	0.40	1.00	2.00
❑11, Dec 77, O: Ray	0.35	0.40	1.00	2.00
❑12, Feb 78, O: Firebrand I (Rod Reilly)	0.35	0.40	1.00	2.00
❑13, Apr 78, O: Black Condor	0.35	0.40	1.00	2.00
❑14, Jun 78, A: Batgirl; A: Batwoman	0.35	0.40	1.00	2.00
❑15, Aug 78, O: Phantom Lady, Final Issue; events continue in Secret Society of Super Villains #16	0.35	0.40	1.00	2.00

FREEFLIGHT
THINKBLOTS
Value: Cover or less
❑1, Apr 94, Void, Part 1; How Much Longer? ... 2.95

FREEJACK
NOW
Value: Cover or less
❑1, Apr 92, newsstand ... 1.95
❑1/DM, Apr 92, movie Adaptation; direct-sale edition ... 2.50
❑2, May 92, newsstand ... 1.95
❑2/DM, May 92, direct-sale ... 2.50
❑3, Jun 92, newsstand ... 1.95
❑3/DM, Jun 92, direct-sale ... 2.50

FREE LAUGHS
DESCHAINE
Value: Cover or less
❑1, b&w ... 1.00

FREE SPEECHES
ONI
Value: Cover or less
❑1, Aug 98, The Comic Book Legal Defense Fun, nn; collects Nadine Strossen, Dave Sim, Neil Gaiman, and Frank Miller speeches; collects Nadine Strossen, Dave Sims, Neil Gaiman, and Frank Miller speeches; Fundraiser for Comic Book Legal Defense Fund ... 2.95

FREE-VIEW
ACCLAIM

	ORIG	GOOD	FINE	N-MINT
❑1, Mar 93	—	0.20	0.50	1.00

FREEWAY NINJA HANZO
SLEEPYHOUSE
Value: Cover or less
❑1, Lured from the Depths, Heavyweight premiere issue ... 3.50

FREEX
MALIBU

	ORIG	GOOD	FINE	N-MINT
❑1, Jul 93, Freaked, 1: Pressure; 1: Freex, coupon for Ultraverse #0	1.95	0.40	1.00	2.00
❑1/Hol, Jul 93, Freaked, 1: Pressure; 1: Freex, Hologram cover; coupon for Ultraverse #0; Ultra Limited	—	1.00	2.50	5.00
❑2, Aug 93, Blown Apart, 1: Rush	1.95	0.40	1.00	2.00
❑3, Sep 93, 1: Bloodhounds	1.95	0.40	1.00	2.00
❑4, Oct 93, Rune, Part E, 40pgs.; Rune	2.50	0.50	1.25	2.50
❑5, Nov 93	1.95	0.39	0.98	1.95
❑6, Dec 93, Break-Thru, Break-Thru	1.95	0.39	0.98	1.95

	ORIG	GOOD	FINE	N-MINT
❑7, Jan 94, Too Much Pressure, O: Hardcase; O: Pressure	1.95	0.39	0.98	1.95
❑8, Feb 94	1.95	0.39	0.98	1.95
❑9, Mar 94, O: Sweetface; 1: Contrary	1.95	0.39	0.98	1.95
❑10, Apr 94, O: Boomboy	1.95	0.39	0.98	1.95
❑11, May 94, The Destiny Trail, Part 1, O: Plug	1.95	0.39	0.98	1.95
❑12, Aug 94, The Destiny Trail, Part 2, 1: The Guardian	1.95	0.39	0.98	1.95
❑13, Sep 94, The Destiny Trail, Part 3, 1: Prometheus	1.95	0.39	0.98	1.95
❑14, Oct 94, The Destiny Trail, Part 4, 1: The Savior	1.95	0.39	0.98	1.95
❑15, Jan 95, Death's Axis; Neverland Blues, Part 3, 1: Oyabun; 1: Manic; 1: Eliminator, Flip-book with Ultraverse Premiere #9	3.50	0.70	1.75	3.50
❑16, Jan 95, Saying Goodbye	1.95	0.39	0.98	1.95
❑17, Feb 95, Call Him Mr. Thebes, A: Rune	2.50	0.50	1.25	2.50
❑18, Feb 95, Forever in Dreams, 1: Tulath; 1: A.J. Analla, Final Issue	2.50	0.50	1.25	2.50
❑GS 1, 1: Pixx, Giant-Size Freex #1	2.50	0.50	1.25	2.50

FRENCH ICE
Renegade
Value: Cover or less

- ❑1, The Sanitation Department; The Visit, b&w — 2.00
- ❑2, Apr 87, b&w — 2.00
- ❑3, May 87, b&w — 2.00
- ❑4, Jun 87, b&w — 2.00
- ❑5, Jul 87, b&w — 2.00
- ❑6, Sep 87, b&w — 2.00
- ❑7, Oct 87, b&w — 2.00
- ❑8, Nov 87, b&w — 2.00
- ❑9, Dec 87, b&w — 2.00
- ❑10, Jan 88, b&w — 2.00
- ❑11, Feb 88, b&w — 2.00
- ❑12, Mar 88, b&w — 2.00
- ❑13, Apr 88, b&w — 2.00

FRENCH TICKLERS
Kitchen Sink
Value: Cover or less

- ❑1, Oct 89, b&w — 2.00
- ❑2, Oct 89, b&w — 2.00
- ❑3, Oct 89, b&w — 2.00

FRENZY
Independent
Value: Cover or less

- ❑1 — 1.00
- ❑1/A — 1.00

FRIENDS
Renegade
Value: Cover or less

- ❑1, May 87, b&w — 2.00
- ❑2, b&w — 2.00
- ❑3, b&w — 2.00

FRIENDS OF MAXX
Image
Value: Cover or less

- ❑1, Apr 96, Dude Japan — 2.95
- ❑2, Nov 96, Broadminded, Broadminded — 2.95
- ❑3, Mar 97 — 2.95

FRIGHT
Atlas

	ORIG	GOOD	FINE	N-MINT
❑1, Jun 75, And Unto Dracula Was Born A Son, O: Son of Dracula	0.25	0.40	1.00	2.00

FRIGHT (ETERNITY)
Eternity

	ORIG	GOOD	FINE	N-MINT
❑1	1.95	0.40	1.00	2.00
❑2	1.95	0.40	1.00	2.00
❑3, The Claws of Death!; The Man With No Face	1.95	0.40	1.00	2.00
❑4, Hickory Dickory Dock; The Day that Satan Died	1.95	0.40	1.00	2.00
❑5, The 13 Dead Things; Gothic Fairy Tales: I Never Heard of a Ghost Actually Killing Anyone!!	1.95	0.40	1.00	2.00
❑6	1.95	0.40	1.00	2.00
❑7	1.95	0.40	1.00	2.00
❑8, The Night in the Horror Hotel; The Lunatic Mummy	1.95	0.40	1.00	2.00
❑9, The Butchered at Earth's Core!!!; Messrs. Crypts and Graves: Undertakers	1.95	0.40	1.00	2.00
❑10, Them, Part 1; A Tale of Horror	1.95	0.40	1.00	2.00
❑11, Tomorrow the Snowman Will Kill You!; The Mummy Khafre	1.95	0.40	1.00	2.00
❑12, The Fetid Belle of the Mississippi; Get Up and Die Again	1.95	0.40	1.00	2.00

FRIGHT NIGHT
Now

	ORIG	GOOD	FINE	N-MINT
❑1, Oct 88, Adapts movie	1.75	0.40	1.00	2.00
❑2, Nov 88, Adapts movie	1.75	0.40	1.00	2.00
❑3, Dec 88, The Dead Remember	1.75	0.40	1.00	2.00
❑4, Feb 89, Eight Arms to Hold You	1.75	0.40	1.00	2.00
❑5, Mar 89, The Spider Boy	1.75	0.40	1.00	2.00
❑6, Apr 89, The Legion of Endless Night, Part 1	1.75	0.40	1.00	2.00
❑7, May 89, The Legion of Endless Night, Part 2	1.75	0.40	1.00	2.00
❑8, Jun 89, The Revenge of Evil Ed, Part 1	1.75	0.40	1.00	2.00
❑9, Jul 89, The Revenge of Evil Ed, Part 2	1.75	0.40	1.00	2.00
❑10, Aug 89, Psychedelic Death, Part 1	1.75	0.40	1.00	2.00
❑11, Sep 89, Psychedelic Death, Part 2	1.75	0.40	1.00	2.00
❑12, Oct 89, Bull Whipped	1.75	0.40	1.00	2.00
❑13, Nov 89, Pup Pet	1.75	0.40	1.00	2.00
❑14, Dec 89, The Resurrection of Dracula, Part 1	1.75	0.40	1.00	2.00
❑15, Jan 90, The Resurrection of Dracula, Part 2	1.75	0.40	1.00	2.00
❑16, Feb 90, Potion Motion	1.75	0.40	1.00	2.00
❑17, Mar 90, Blood Ball	1.75	0.40	1.00	2.00
❑18, Apr 90	1.75	0.40	1.00	2.00
❑19, May 90, Daddy's Girl	1.75	0.40	1.00	2.00
❑20, Jun 90, The Charge of the Dead Brigade	1.75	0.40	1.00	2.00
❑21, Jul 90	1.75	0.40	1.00	2.00
❑22, Aug 90	1.75	0.40	1.00	2.00

FRIGHT NIGHT 1993 HALLOWEEN ANNUAL
Now
Value: Cover or less

- ❑1, nn; 3-D — 2.95

FRIGHT NIGHT 3-D
Now
Value: Cover or less

- ❑1, Jun 92, with glasses — 2.95
- ❑2, Fal 92, Dracula — 2.95

FRIGHT NIGHT 3-D WINTER SPECIAL
Now
Value: Cover or less

- ❑1, Win 93, nn; Brainbats — 2.95

FRIGHT NIGHT II GRAPHIC NOVEL
Now
Value: Cover or less

- ❑1, movie Adaptation — 3.95

FRINGE
Caliber
Value: Cover or less

- ❑1, b&w — 2.50
- ❑2, b&w — 2.50
- ❑3, b&w — 2.50
- ❑4, b&w — 2.50
- ❑5, b&w — 2.50
- ❑6, b&w — 2.50
- ❑7, b&w — 2.50
- ❑8, b&w — 2.50

FROGMEN, THE
Dell

	ORIG	GOOD	FINE	N-MINT
❑2, Continued from Four Color Comics #1258	0.12	6.00	15.00	30.00
❑3	0.12	5.00	12.50	25.00
❑4	0.12	3.60	9.00	18.00
❑5, ATh	0.12	4.00	10.00	20.00
❑6	0.12	3.60	9.00	18.00
❑7	0.12	3.20	8.00	16.00
❑8	0.12	3.20	8.00	16.00
❑9	0.12	3.20	8.00	16.00
❑10, Strange Disappearance	0.12	3.20	8.00	16.00
❑11, Final Issue	0.12	3.20	8.00	16.00

FROM BEYONDE
Studio Insidio
Value: Cover or less

- ❑1, b&w — 2.25

FROM BEYOND THE UNKNOWN
DC

	ORIG	GOOD	FINE	N-MINT
❑1, Nov 69	0.15	6.00	15.00	30.00
❑2, Jan 70	0.15	3.20	8.00	16.00
❑3, Mar 70	0.15	2.40	6.00	12.00
❑4, May 70	0.15	2.40	6.00	12.00
❑5, Jul 70	0.15	2.40	6.00	12.00
❑6, Sep 70	0.15	2.00	5.00	10.00
❑7, Nov 70, JKu (c), 64pgs.	0.25	2.00	5.00	10.00
❑8, Jan 71, 64pgs.	0.25	2.00	5.00	10.00
❑9, Mar 71, 64pgs.	0.25	2.00	5.00	10.00
❑10, May 71, CS (c), 64pgs.	0.25	2.00	5.00	10.00
❑11, Jul 71, 64pgs.	0.25	1.80	4.50	9.00
❑12, Sep 71, JKu (c), 64pgs.	0.25	1.80	4.50	9.00
❑13, Nov 71, 64pgs.	0.25	1.80	4.50	9.00
❑14, Jan 72, JKu (c), 64pgs.	0.25	1.80	4.50	9.00
❑15, Mar 72, 64pgs.	0.25	1.80	4.50	9.00
❑16, May 72, CI; MA, The World Wrecker; Doom From Station X, 64pgs.	0.25	1.80	4.50	9.00
❑17, Jul 72, 64pgs.	0.25	1.80	4.50	9.00
❑18, Sep 72	0.20	1.60	4.00	8.00
❑19, Nov 72	0.20	1.60	4.00	8.00
❑20, Jan 73	0.20	1.60	4.00	8.00
❑21, Mar 73	0.20	1.60	4.00	8.00
❑22, May 73	0.20	1.60	4.00	8.00
❑23, Aug 73	0.20	1.60	4.00	8.00
❑24, Oct 73	0.20	1.60	4.00	8.00
❑25, Dec 73, Final Issue	0.20	1.60	4.00	8.00

FROM HELL
Tundra

	ORIG	GOOD	FINE	N-MINT
❑1, AMo (w)	4.95	1.60	4.00	8.00
❑1-2, Feb 92, AMo (w), 2nd Printing	4.95	1.00	2.50	5.00
❑, AMo (w), 3rd printing (Kitchen Sink)	4.95	1.00	2.50	5.00
❑1-4, 4th printing (Kitchen Sink)	4.95	0.99	2.47	4.95
❑2, AMo (w)	4.95	1.20	3.00	6.00
❑2-2, AMo (w), 2nd printing (Kitchen Sink)	4.95	1.00	2.50	5.00

	ORIG	GOOD	FINE	N-MINT
❑2-3, AMo (w), 3rd Printing	4.95	1.00	2.50	5.00
❑3, Dec 93, AMo (w)	4.95	1.20	3.00	6.00
❑3-2, AMo (w), 2nd Printing	4.95	1.00	2.50	5.00
❑3-3, AMo (w), 3rd Printing	4.95	1.00	2.50	5.00
❑4, Mar 94, AMo (w)	4.95	1.00	2.50	5.00
❑4-2, AMo (w), 2nd Printing	4.95	1.00	2.50	5.00
❑4-3, AMo (w), 3rd Printing	4.95	1.00	2.50	5.00
❑5, Jun 94, AMo (w)	4.95	0.99	2.47	4.95
❑6, Nov 94, AMo (w)	4.95	0.99	2.47	4.95
❑7, Apr 95, AMo (w)	4.95	0.99	2.47	4.95
❑8, Jul 95, AMo (w)	4.95	0.99	2.47	4.95
❑9, Apr 96, AMo (w)	4.95	0.99	2.47	4.95
❑10, Aug 96, AMo (w), Final Issue	4.95	0.99	2.47	4.95
❑11, Sep 98, AMo (w)	4.95	0.99	2.47	4.95

FROM HELL: DANCE OF THE GULL CATCHERS
KITCHEN SINK

Value: Cover or less

❑1, nn; sequel to From Hell..... 4.95

FROM THE DARKNESS
ADVENTURE

	ORIG	GOOD	FINE	N-MINT
❑1	—	1.20	3.00	6.00
❑2	—	1.00	2.50	5.00
❑3, b&w	—	0.80	2.00	4.00
❑4, b&w	—	0.80	2.00	4.00

FROM THE DARKNESS BOOK II: BLOOD VOWS
CRY FOR DAWN

Value: Cover or less

❑1..... 2.50
❑2..... 2.50
❑3..... 2.50

FRONTIER
SLAVE LABOR

Value: Cover or less

❑1, Jul 94..... 2.95

FRONTIERS '86 PRESENTS
FRONTIERS

Value: Cover or less

❑1, Crusaders..... 1.50
❑2, Crusaders..... 1.50

FRONTLINE COMBAT (RCP)
EC

Value: Cover or less

❑1, Aug 95, RH; WW; HK, Unterseeboot 113; The Fatal Step (text story), Reprints Frontline Combat (EC) #1..... 2.00
❑2, Nov 95, WW; BE; HK, WW (w); BE (w); JSe (w); HK (w), Bouncing Bertha; Zero Hour!, Reprints Frontline Combat (EC) #2..... 2.00
❑3, Feb 96, Tin Can, Reprints Frontline Combat (EC) #3..... 2.00
❑4, May 96, Air Burst!, Reprints Frontline Combat (EC) #4..... 2.00
❑5, Aug 96, Reprints Frontline Combat (EC) #5..... 2.50
❑6, Nov 96, BE; JSe, BE (w); JSe (w), A Platoon!; Bellyrobber!, Reprints Frontline Combat (EC) #6..... 2.50
❑7, Feb 97, WW; BE; JSe, WW (w); BE (w); JSe (w), Iwo Jima!; The Landing!, Reprints Frontline Combat (EC) #7..... 2.50
❑8, May 97, WW; BE; JSe; ATh, WW (w); BE (w); JSe (w); ATh (w), Thunderjet!; Caesar!, Reprints Frontline Combat (EC) #8..... 2.50
❑9, Aug 97, WW; BE; JSe, WW (w); BE (w); JSe (w), Abe Lincoln!; First Shot!, Reprints Frontline Combat (EC) #9..... 2.50
❑10, Nov 97, WW; BE; JSe, WW (w); BE (w); JSe (w); GE (w), A Baby!; Geronimo! Napoleon!, Reprints Frontline Combat (EC) #10..... 2.50
❑11, Feb 98, Reprints Frontline Combat (EC) #11..... 2.50
❑12, May 98, Reprints Frontline Combat (EC) #12..... 2.50
❑13, Aug 98, Reprints Frontline Combat (EC) #13..... 2.50
❑14, Nov 98, Reprints Frontline Combat (EC) #14..... 2.50
❑15, Feb 99, Reprints Frontline Combat (EC) #15..... 2.50
❑Anl 1, WW; BE; HK, WW (w); BE (w); JSe (w); HK (w), Collects Frontline Combat #1-5..... 10.95
❑Anl 2, WW; BE; JSe; ATh, WW (w); BE (w); JSe (w); ATh (w); GE (w), Collects Frontline Combat #6-10..... 12.95

FROST
CALIBER

Value: Cover or less

❑1, b&w..... 1.95

FROSTBITER: WRATH OF THE WENDIGO
CALIBER

Value: Cover or less

❑1..... 2.95
❑2..... 2.95
❑3..... 2.95

FROST: THE DYING BREED
CALIBER

Value: Cover or less

❑1, Memorial, b&w..... 2.95
❑2, b&w..... 2.95
❑3, b&w..... 2.95

FROZEN EMBRYO
SLAVE LABOR

Value: Cover or less

❑1, Dec 92..... 2.95

F-TROOP
GOLD KEY

	ORIG	GOOD	FINE	N-MINT
❑1, Aug 66, Don't Cross Your Bridges; The Buffalo Hunter, Photo cover	0.12	10.00	25.00	50.00
❑2	0.12	8.00	20.00	40.00
❑3	0.12	7.20	18.00	36.00
❑4	0.12	7.20	18.00	36.00
❑5	0.12	7.20	18.00	36.00
❑6	0.12	6.40	16.00	32.00
❑7, Final Issue	0.12	6.40	16.00	32.00

Renegade adapted the adventures of eccentric old crank Carmen Cru from their original French in *French Ice*.

© 1987 Renegade

FUGITIVE
CALIBER

Value: Cover or less

❑1, Delaney's Heroes; Where No Madmad Has Gone Before..... 2.50

FUGITOID
MIRAGE

	ORIG	GOOD	FINE	N-MINT
❑1, Teenage Mutant Ninja Turtles tie-in; Continued from TMNT #4; continued in TMNT #5	1.50	0.60	1.50	3.00

FULL METAL FICTION
LONDON NIGHT

Value: Cover or less

❑1, Mar 97, Razor: Year one; Arizona: The Wild..... 3.95

FULL THROTTLE
AIRCEL

Value: Cover or less

❑1, Escape from Eden, b&w..... 2.95
❑2, b&w..... 2.95

FUN BOYS SPRING SPECIAL
TUNDRA

Value: Cover or less

❑1, nn; b&w..... 1.95

FUN COMICS
STAR PUBLICATIONS

	ORIG	GOOD	FINE	N-MINT
❑9, Jan 53, Giant-size; Series continued from Holiday Comics #8	0.25	22.00	55.00	110.00
❑10, Apr 53	0.10	17.00	42.50	85.00
❑11, Jul 53, 1: Mighty Bear	0.10	17.00	42.50	85.00
❑12, Oct 53, Series continued in Mighty Bear #13	0.10	17.00	42.50	85.00

FUN COMICS (BILL BLACK'S...)
AC

Value: Cover or less

❑1..... 2.00
❑2..... 2.00
❑3..... 2.00
❑4, Stardust Descending; The Mystic Origin of Nightfall, Captain Paragon, Nightfall..... 2.00

FUN HOUSE
MN DESIGN

Value: Cover or less

❑1, nn; full color; photos..... 6.50

FUN HOUSE (J.R. WILLIAMS'...)
STARHEAD

Value: Cover or less

❑1, Nov 93, b&w; adult; Collections of Comics, Strips..... 3.95

FUN-IN
GOLD KEY

	ORIG	GOOD	FINE	N-MINT
❑1, Feb 70	0.15	3.20	8.00	16.00
❑2	0.15	2.00	5.00	10.00
❑3	0.15	1.80	4.50	9.00
❑4	0.15	1.80	4.50	9.00
❑5, Jan 71, Motormouse and Autocat, Dastardly and Muttley	0.15	1.60	4.00	8.00
❑6, Mar 71, Dastardly and Muttley, It's the Wolf	0.15	1.60	4.00	8.00
❑7, May 71, Motormouse and Autocat, Dastardly and Muttley, It's the Wolf	0.15	1.20	3.00	6.00
❑8	—	1.20	3.00	6.00
❑9	—	1.20	3.00	6.00
❑10	—	1.20	3.00	6.00
❑11	—	0.80	2.00	4.00
❑12	—	0.80	2.00	4.00
❑13	—	0.80	2.00	4.00
❑14	—	0.80	2.00	4.00
❑15	—	0.80	2.00	4.00

FUNKY PHANTOM
GOLD KEY

	ORIG	GOOD	FINE	N-MINT
❑1	0.20	5.20	13.00	26.00
❑2	0.20	3.00	7.50	15.00
❑3	0.20	2.00	5.00	10.00
❑4	0.20	2.00	5.00	10.00
❑5	0.20	2.00	5.00	10.00
❑6	0.20	1.60	4.00	8.00
❑7	0.20	1.60	4.00	8.00
❑8, The Ben Franklin Bridge Plot; Ghost of the Lost City of Cibola, A: Prissy Atwater; A: Elmo; A: Augie; A: Skip; A: April	0.20	1.60	4.00	8.00
❑9	—	1.60	4.00	8.00

	ORIG	GOOD	FINE	N-MINT
❑10	—	1.60	4.00	8.00
❑11	—	1.20	3.00	6.00
❑12	—	1.20	3.00	6.00
❑13	—	1.20	3.00	6.00

FUNNY STUFF STOCKING STUFFER
DC

Value: Cover or less

❑1, Mar 85, Christmas Comes but Once...Next Year!; See Ya Later Aviator! ... 1.25

FUNNYTIME FEATURES
EENIEWEENIE

Value: Cover or less

❑1, Jul 94, Arachnid Kid: Our Country At War, b&w ... 2.50
❑1-2, b&w; 2nd Printing ... 2.50
❑2, b&w ... 2.50
❑3, b&w ... 2.50
❑4, b&w ... 2.50
❑5, b&w ... 2.50
❑6, b&w ... 2.50
❑7, A: Shi, b&w ... 2.50

FUNTASTIC WORLD OF HANNA-BARBERA
MARVEL

	ORIG	GOOD	FINE	N-MINT
❑1, Dec 77, Flintstone's Christmas Party	1.25	2.60	6.50	13.00
❑2	1.25	1.80	4.50	9.00
❑3	1.25	1.20	3.00	6.00

FUN WITH MILK & CHEESE
SLAVE LABOR

Value: Cover or less

❑1, Apr 94, nn; b&w; collects stories; has pages 59 and 62 switched ... 9.95

FURIES (AVATAR)
AVATAR

Value: Cover or less

❑0, Nude cover ... 5.00

FURIES, THE (CARBON-BASED)
CARBON-BASED

Value: Cover or less

❑1, May 96, b&w ... 2.75
❑2, Jul 96, b&w ... 2.75
❑3, Sep 96, b&w ... 2.75
❑4, Nov 96, b&w ... 2.75
❑5, Jan 97, b&w ... 2.75
❑6, Mar 97, b&w ... 2.75

FURKINDRED, THE
MU PRESS

Value: Cover or less

❑1, Jan 92, Otter Madness, b&w ... 6.95
❑2, Nov 92, Renewal of Porpoise, b&w ... 7.95

FURRLOUGH
ANTARCTIC

	ORIG	GOOD	FINE	N-MINT
❑1, Nov 91, Panzercorps: The Prototype; Empires: Thunderhead	2.50	0.70	1.75	3.50
❑2, Feb 92, Romanics: Res Futura; Why Desert Winds Howl	2.50	0.60	1.50	3.00
❑3, May 92, Stosstrupp, Part 3; Panzercorps: Rainy Season	2.50	0.60	1.50	3.00
❑4, Jul 92, Stosstrupp; Romanics: Gravia Avspicia	2.50	0.55	1.38	2.75
❑5, Nov 92, Final Cliche; Stosstrupp	2.50	0.55	1.38	2.75
❑6, Jan 93, Romanics: Viri Magni Momenti; Hairlift	2.50	0.55	1.38	2.75
❑7, Mar 93, Stosstrupp, Part 6; Dog Starr, Part 1	2.50	0.55	1.38	2.75
❑8, May 93, Germany, 1945; Dog Starr, Part 2	2.50	0.55	1.38	2.75
❑9, Jul 93, Risuko, Part 1; Under Realm	2.50	0.55	1.38	2.75
❑10, Sep 93, Walter Kitty, Part 1; Ice Cream Parlor	2.50	0.55	1.38	2.75
❑11, Nov 93, Stosstrupp, Part 8; Under Realm	2.75	0.55	1.38	2.75
❑12, Dec 93, Walter Kitty, Part 2; Scud	2.75	0.55	1.38	2.75
❑13, Jan 94, Watering Hole, Part 1; Bat Lancers	2.75	0.55	1.38	2.75
❑14, Feb 94, Watering Hole, Part 2; Walter Kitty, Part 3	2.75	0.55	1.38	2.75
❑15, Mar 94, Stosstrupp, Part 9; Collars & Cuffs	2.75	0.55	1.38	2.75
❑16, Apr 94, Live by the Bulley, Die by the Blade; Watering Hole, Part 3	2.75	0.55	1.38	2.75
❑17, May 94, Here Comes a Candle, Part 1; The Sound & The Furry, Part 3	2.75	0.55	1.38	2.75
❑18, Jun 94, Stosstrupp, Part 10; Here Comes a Candle, Part 2	2.75	0.55	1.38	2.75
❑19, Jul 94, The Adventure; Here Comes a Candle, Part 4	2.75	0.55	1.38	2.75
❑20, Aug 94, Jack, Part 1; Here Comes a Candle, Part 3	2.75	0.55	1.38	2.75
❑21, Sep 94, Zaibatsu Tears, Part 1; Here Comes a Candle Part 5	2.75	0.55	1.38	2.75
❑22, Oct 94, Here Comes a Candle, Part 6; Guardian Knights: The Renegar Affair, Part 1	2.75	0.55	1.38	2.75
❑23, Nov 94, Here Comes a Candle, Part 7; Under Realm, Part 4, Giant-size	3.50	0.70	1.75	3.50
❑24, Dec 94, Zaibatsu Tears; Here Comes a Candle, Part 8	2.75	0.55	1.38	2.75
❑25, Jan 95, Here Comes a Candle, Part 9; Bronze Fur	2.75	0.55	1.38	2.75
❑26, Feb 95, Here Comes a Candle, Part 10; Watering Hole, Part 4	2.75	0.55	1.38	2.75
❑27, Mar 95, Here Comes a Candle, Part 11; Bronze Fur, Part 2	2.75	0.55	1.38	2.75
❑28, Apr 95, Here Comes a Candle, Part 12; Stellar Babe	2.75	0.55	1.38	2.75
❑29, May 95, Here Comes a Candle, Part 13; Bronze Fur, Part 3	2.75	0.55	1.38	2.75
❑30, Jun 95, Here Comes a Candle, Part 14; Scavengers	2.75	0.55	1.38	2.75
❑31, Jul 95, Here Comes a Candle, Part 15; Bronze Fur, Part 4	2.75	0.55	1.38	2.75
❑32, Aug 95, Here Comes a Candle, Part 16; Stinz: Bad Memories	2.75	0.55	1.38	2.75
❑33, Sep 95, Bronze Fur, Part 5; Massacre on Main Street	2.75	0.55	1.38	2.75
❑34, Oct 95, Here Comes a Candle, Part 18; Weekend Wehrmacht	2.75	0.55	1.38	2.75
❑35, Nov 95, Here Comes a Candle; Bronze Fur, Giant-size; fourth anniversary special	3.50	0.70	1.75	3.50
❑36, Dec 95, Escape to New York, Part 1; Ultimate Weapon	3.50	0.59	1.48	2.95
❑37, Jan 96, Zaibatsu Tears: Puppet Warriors, Part 2; Stellar Babe	3.50	0.59	1.48	2.95
❑38, Feb 96, Escape to New York, Part 2; Luna	3.50	0.59	1.48	2.95
❑39, Mar 96, The Adventures of Swimmer, Part 1; Stellar Babe	3.50	0.59	1.48	2.95
❑40, Apr 96, Escape to New York, Part 3; The Adventures of Swimmer, Part 2	3.50	0.59	1.48	2.95
❑41, May 96, Star Run, Part 1; Occupational Hazard	2.95	0.59	1.48	2.95
❑42, Jun 96, Escape to New York, Part 4; Star Run, Part 2	2.95	0.59	1.48	2.95
❑43, Jul 96, Fort Ord Follies; Star Run	2.95	0.59	1.48	2.95
❑44, Aug 96, Escape to New York, Part 5; Freedom, Part 1	2.95	0.59	1.48	2.95
❑45, Sep 96, Star Run, Part 4; Freedom, Part 2	2.95	0.59	1.48	2.95
❑46, Oct 96, Freedom, Part 3; Escape to New York	2.95	0.59	1.48	2.95
❑47, Nov 96, Ninjara, Part 1; The Adventures of Swimmer, 48pgs.	3.95	0.59	1.48	2.95
❑48, Dec 96, Ninjara, Part 2; Heebas, Part 1	2.95	0.59	1.48	2.95
❑49, Jan 97, Star Run, Part 6; Tiger Orange, Part 1	2.95	0.59	1.48	2.95
❑50, Feb 97, Tobias Wah: Vampyre Hunter, Part 1; Distractions, Furrlough index; Giant-size	3.95	0.79	1.98	3.95
❑51, Mar 97, Star Run, Part 7; The Pranksters	2.95	0.59	1.48	2.95
❑52, Apr 97	2.95	0.59	1.48	2.95
❑53, May 97	2.95	0.59	1.48	2.95
❑54, Jun 97	2.95	0.59	1.48	2.95
❑55, Jul 97	2.95	0.59	1.48	2.95
❑56, Aug 97	2.95	0.59	1.48	2.95
❑57, Sep 97	2.95	0.59	1.48	2.95
❑58, Oct 97	2.95	0.59	1.48	2.95
❑59, Nov 97	2.95	0.59	1.48	2.95
❑60, Dec 97	2.95	0.59	1.48	2.95
❑61, Jan 98	2.95	0.59	1.48	2.95
❑62, Feb 98	2.95	0.59	1.48	2.95
❑63, Mar 98	2.95	0.59	1.48	2.95
❑64, Apr 98	2.95	0.59	1.48	2.95
❑65, May 98	2.95	0.59	1.48	2.95
❑66, Jun 98	2.95	0.59	1.48	2.95
❑67, Jul 98	2.95	0.59	1.48	2.95
❑68, Aug 98	2.95	0.59	1.48	2.95
❑69, Sep 98	2.95	0.59	1.48	2.95
❑70, Oct 98	2.95	0.59	1.48	2.95
❑71, Nov 98	2.95	0.59	1.48	2.95
❑72, Dec 98	2.95	0.59	1.48	2.95
❑73, Jan 99	2.95	0.59	1.48	2.95
❑79, Jul 99	2.95	0.59	1.48	2.95
❑80, Aug 99	2.95	0.59	1.48	2.95
❑81, Sep 99	2.95	0.59	1.48	2.95
❑82, Oct 99	2.95	0.59	1.48	2.95
❑83, Nov 99	2.95	0.59	1.48	2.95
❑84, Dec 99	2.95	0.59	1.48	2.95
❑85, Jan 00	2.95	0.59	1.48	2.95
❑86, Feb 00	2.95	0.59	1.48	2.95
❑87, Mar 00	2.95	0.59	1.48	2.95
❑88, Apr 00	2.95	0.59	1.48	2.95
❑89, May 00	2.95	0.59	1.48	2.95
❑90, Jun 00	2.95	0.59	1.48	2.95
❑91, Jul 00	2.95	0.59	1.48	2.95
❑92, Aug 00	2.95	0.59	1.48	2.95
❑93, Sep 00	2.95	0.59	1.48	2.95
❑94, Oct 00	2.95	0.59	1.48	2.95
❑95	—	0.59	1.48	2.95

	ORIG	GOOD	FINE	N-MINT
❑96	—	0.59	1.48	2.95
❑97	—	0.59	1.48	2.95
❑98	—	0.59	1.48	2.95
❑99	—	0.59	1.48	2.95
❑100	—	0.59	1.48	2.95
❑101	—	0.59	1.48	2.95
❑102	—	0.59	1.48	2.95
❑103	2.99	0.60	1.50	2.99

FURTHER ADVENTURES OF CYCLOPS AND PHOENIX, THE
MARVEL
Value: Cover or less

- ❑1, Jun 96, Digging Up the Past, O: Mr. Sinister 1.95
- ❑2, Jul 96 ..... 1.95
- ❑3, Aug 96 ..... 1.95
- ❑4, Sep 96 ..... 1.95

FURTHER ADVENTURES OF INDIANA JONES, THE
MARVEL

	ORIG	GOOD	FINE	N-MINT
❑1, Jan 83, TD; JBy	0.60	0.40	1.00	2.00
❑2, Feb 83, TD; JBy	0.60	0.30	0.75	1.50
❑3, Mar 83	0.60	0.30	0.75	1.50
❑4, Apr 83	0.60	0.30	0.75	1.50
❑5, May 83	0.60	0.30	0.75	1.50
❑6, Jun 83	0.60	0.30	0.75	1.50
❑7, Jul 83	0.60	0.30	0.75	1.50
❑8, Aug 83	0.60	0.30	0.75	1.50
❑9, Sep 83	0.60	0.30	0.75	1.50
❑10, Oct 83	0.60	0.30	0.75	1.50
❑11, Nov 83	0.60	0.30	0.75	1.50
❑12, Dec 83	0.60	0.30	0.75	1.50
❑13, Jan 84	0.60	0.30	0.75	1.50
❑14, Feb 84	0.60	0.30	0.75	1.50
❑15, Mar 84	0.60	0.30	0.75	1.50
❑16, Apr 84	0.60	0.30	0.75	1.50
❑17, May 84	0.60	0.30	0.75	1.50
❑18, Jun 84	0.60	0.30	0.75	1.50
❑19, Jul 84	0.60	0.30	0.75	1.50
❑20, Aug 84	0.60	0.30	0.75	1.50
❑21, Sep 84	0.60	0.30	0.75	1.50
❑22, Oct 84	0.60	0.30	0.75	1.50
❑23, Nov 84	0.60	0.30	0.75	1.50
❑24, Dec 84	0.60	0.30	0.75	1.50
❑25, Jan 85, SD	0.60	0.30	0.75	1.50
❑26, Feb 85, SD	0.60	0.30	0.75	1.50
❑27, Mar 85, SD	0.60	0.30	0.75	1.50
❑28, Apr 85, SD	0.65	0.30	0.75	1.50
❑29, May 85, SD	0.65	0.30	0.75	1.50
❑30, Jul 85, SD	0.65	0.30	0.75	1.50
❑31, Sep 85, SD	0.65	0.30	0.75	1.50
❑32, Nov 85, SD	0.65	0.30	0.75	1.50
❑33, Jan 86	0.65	0.30	0.75	1.50
❑34, Mar 86, Final Issue	0.75	0.30	0.75	1.50

FURTHER ADVENTURES OF NYOKA THE JUNGLE GIRL, THE
AC

	ORIG	GOOD	FINE	N-MINT
❑1, The Many Perils of Nyoka; The Serpent Strikes!	1.95	0.45	1.13	2.25
❑2, Photo cover	1.95	0.45	1.13	2.25
❑3, The Skull Squad!; Jungle Jousts of Death, b&w; Photo cover	2.25	0.45	1.13	2.25
❑4, b&w	2.25	0.45	1.13	2.25
❑5	2.50	0.50	1.25	2.50

FURTHER ADVENTURES OF YOUNG JEFFY DAHMER, THE
BONEYARD

	ORIG	GOOD	FINE	N-MINT
❑1, b&w; adult	2.75	0.80	2.00	4.00

FURTHER FATTENING ADVENTURES OF PUDGE, GIRL BLIMP, THE
STAR*REACH

	ORIG	GOOD	FINE	N-MINT
❑1, Comic size	—	0.60	1.50	3.00
❑1/A, large size	—	0.60	1.50	3.00
❑2, Comic size	3.00	0.60	1.50	3.00
❑3, Comic size	3.00	0.60	1.50	3.00

FURY
MARVEL

	ORIG	GOOD	FINE	N-MINT
❑1, May 94, O: Nick Fury; O: Hydra; O: S.H.I.E.L.D.	2.95	0.60	1.50	3.00

FURY/AGENT 13
MARVEL
Value: Cover or less

- ❑1, Jun 98, ...And Destroy!, A: Howling Commandos, gatefold summary 2.99
- ❑2, Jul 98, gatefold summary; Fury returns to Marvel universe... 2.99

FURY/BLACK WIDOW: DEATH DUTY
MARVEL
Value: Cover or less

- ❑1, Feb 95, prestige format..... 5.95

FURY OF FIRESTORM, THE
DC

	ORIG	GOOD	FINE	N-MINT
❑1, Jun 82, PB, Day of the Bison, 1: Black Bison; 1: Lorraine Reilly; O: Firestorm	0.60	0.50	1.25	2.50
❑2, Jul 82, PB	0.60	0.35	0.88	1.75

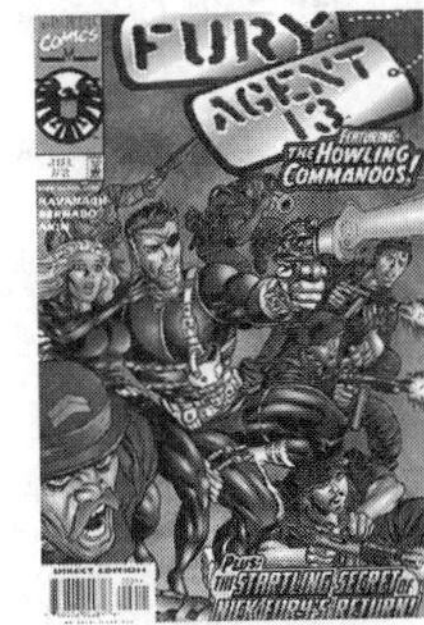

Nick Fury returned to active duty in the two-issue *Fury/Agent 13* mini-series.

© 1998 Marvel

	ORIG	GOOD	FINE	N-MINT
❑3, Aug 82, PB, A Cold Time in the Old Town Tonight ..., A: Killer Frost	0.60	0.35	0.88	1.75
❑4, Sep 82, PB, The Icy Heart of Killer Frost!, A: Killer Frost; A: Justice League of America	0.60	0.35	0.88	1.75
❑5, Oct 82, PB, The Pied Piper's Pipes of Peril, A: Pied Piper	0.60	0.35	0.88	1.75
❑6, Nov 82, PB, The Pandrakos Plot, Master of the Universe preview insert	0.60	0.30	0.75	1.50
❑7, Dec 82, PB, Plastique is Another Word for Fear!, 1: Plastique	0.60	0.30	0.75	1.50
❑8, Jan 83, Typhoon Warning, A: Typhoon	0.60	0.30	0.75	1.50
❑9, Feb 83, Baby, the Rain Must Fall!, A: Typhoon	0.60	0.30	0.75	1.50
❑10, Mar 83, PB, Prowl, A: Hyena	0.60	0.30	0.75	1.50
❑11, Apr 83, PB, Waking Darkness	0.60	0.25	0.63	1.25
❑12, May 83, PB, Howl	0.60	0.25	0.63	1.25
❑13, Jun 83, PB, Split!	0.60	0.25	0.63	1.25
❑14, Jul 83, PB, Enforcer, 1: Enforcer I (Leroy Merkyn); 1: Mica (Enforcer II)	0.60	0.25	0.63	1.25
❑15, Aug 83, PB, Breakout, A: Multiplex	0.60	0.25	0.63	1.25
❑16, Sep 83, PB, Blackout!	0.60	0.25	0.63	1.25
❑17, Oct 83, GT; PB, On Wings of Fire, 1: Firehawk	0.60	0.25	0.63	1.25
❑18, Nov 83, GT, Squeeze Play, 1: Enforcer II (Mica)	0.60	0.25	0.63	1.25
❑19, Jan 84, GC, Golden Boy!, V: Goldenrod	0.75	0.25	0.63	1.25
❑20, Feb 84, Frostbite!, 1: Louise Lincoln; V: Killer Frost; A: Firehawk	0.75	0.25	0.63	1.25
❑21, Mar 84, V: Killer Frost; D: Killer Frost I (Crystal Frost)	0.75	0.20	0.50	1.00
❑22, Apr 84, PB, The Secret Origin of Firestorm, O: Firestorm	0.75	0.20	0.50	1.00
❑23, May 84, V: Byte	0.75	0.20	0.50	1.00
❑24, Jun 84, 1: Byte; 1: Blue Devil; 1: Bug	0.75	0.20	0.50	1.00
❑25, Jul 84, V: Black Bison; 1: Silver Deer	0.75	0.20	0.50	1.00
❑26, Aug 84, V: Black Bison	0.75	0.20	0.50	1.00
❑27, Sep 84	0.75	0.20	0.50	1.00
❑28, Oct 84, V: Slipknot	0.75	0.20	0.50	1.00
❑29, Nov 84, 1: Breathtaker (villain); V: Stratos; 1: Mindboggler	0.75	0.20	0.50	1.00
❑30, Dec 84, GK (c), V: Mindboggler	0.75	0.20	0.50	1.00
❑31, Jan 85, V: Mindboggler	0.75	0.20	0.50	1.00
❑32, Feb 85, A: Phantom Stranger	0.75	0.20	0.50	1.00
❑33, Mar 85	0.75	0.20	0.50	1.00
❑34, Apr 85, V: Killer Frost; 1: Killer Frost II (Louise Lincoln)	0.75	0.20	0.50	1.00
❑35, May 85, V: Plastique; V: Killer Frost	0.75	0.20	0.50	1.00
❑36, Jun 85, V: Plastique; V: Killer Frost	0.75	0.20	0.50	1.00
❑37, Jul 85	0.75	0.20	0.50	1.00
❑38, Aug 85	0.75	0.20	0.50	1.00
❑39, Sep 85	0.75	0.20	0.50	1.00
❑40, Oct 85	0.75	0.20	0.50	1.00
❑41, Nov 85, Crisis On Infinite Earths, Crisis	0.75	0.20	0.50	1.00
❑42, Dec 85, Crisis On Infinite Earths, Crisis	0.75	0.20	0.50	1.00
❑43, Jan 86	0.75	0.20	0.50	1.00
❑44, Feb 86, V: Typhoon	0.75	0.20	0.50	1.00
❑45, Mar 86	0.75	0.20	0.50	1.00
❑46, Apr 86, A: Blue Devil	0.75	0.20	0.50	1.00
❑47, May 86, A: Blue Devil; V: Multiplex	0.75	0.20	0.50	1.00
❑48, Jun 86, 1: Moonbow	0.75	0.20	0.50	1.00
❑49, Jul 86	0.75	0.20	0.50	1.00
❑50, Aug 86	1.25	0.20	0.50	1.00
❑51, Sep 86	0.75	0.20	0.50	1.00
❑52, Oct 86	0.75	0.20	0.50	1.00
❑53, Nov 86	0.75	0.20	0.50	1.00
❑54, Dec 86	0.75	0.20	0.50	1.00
❑55, Jan 87, A: Cosmic Boy; V: Brimstone, Legends	0.75	0.20	0.50	1.00
❑56, Feb 87, A: Hawk, Legends	0.75	0.20	0.50	1.00
❑57, Mar 87	0.75	0.20	0.50	1.00
❑58, Apr 87, V: Parasite; 1: Parasite II	0.75	0.20	0.50	1.00
❑59, May 87, V: Parasite; A: Firehawk	0.75	0.20	0.50	1.00
❑60, Jun 87	0.75	0.20	0.50	1.00
❑61, Jul 87, V: Typhoon, regular cover	0.75	0.20	0.50	1.00
❑61/A, Jul 87, V: Typhoon, Alternate cover (test cover)	0.75	0.80	2.00	4.00

	ORIG	GOOD	FINE	N-MINT
❑62, Aug 87	0.75	0.20	0.50	1.00
❑63, Sep 87, A: Captain Atom	0.75	0.20	0.50	1.00
❑64, Oct 87, A: Suicide Squad, Final Issue; series continues as Firestorm, the Nuclear Man	0.75	0.20	0.50	1.00
❑Anl 1, All the Answers ...	1.25	0.40	1.00	2.00
❑Anl 2, text story	1.25	0.30	0.75	1.50
❑Anl 3	1.25	0.30	0.75	1.50
❑Anl 4	1.25	0.30	0.75	1.50
❑Anl 5, A: Suicide Squad; 1: Firestorm (new), Title changes to Firestorm Annual	1.25	0.30	0.75	1.50

FURY OF HELLINA
LIGHTNING

Value: Cover or less

❑1, Jan 95, b&w 2.75

FURY OF S.H.I.E.L.D.
MARVEL

	ORIG	GOOD	FINE	N-MINT
❑1, Apr 95, HC (w), Hell Hath No Fury, Part 1, chromium cover	2.50	0.60	1.50	3.00
❑2, May 95, HC (w), Hell Hath No Fury, Part 2, A: Iron Man	1.95	0.40	1.00	2.00
❑3, Jun 95, HC (w), Hell Hath No Fury, Part 3, A: Iron Man	1.95	0.40	1.00	2.00
❑4, Jul 95, HC (w), Hell Hath No Fury, Part 4, polybagged with decoder	2.50	0.50	1.25	2.50

FUSION
ECLIPSE

Value: Cover or less

❑1, Jan 87, b&w 2.00
❑2, Mar 87, b&w 2.00
❑3, May 87, The Soulstar Commission Part 3, b&w 2.00
❑4, Jul 87, b&w 2.00
❑5, Sep 87, b&w 2.00
❑6, Nov 87, b&w 2.00
❑7, Jan 88, b&w 2.00
❑8, Mar 88, b&w 2.00
❑9, May 88, b&w 2.00
❑10, Jul 88, b&w 2.00
❑11, Sep 88, b&w 2.00
❑12, Nov 88, b&w 2.00
❑13, Jan 89, b&w 2.00
❑14, Mar 89, b&w 2.00
❑15, May 89, The Nestling Part 2, b&w 2.00
❑16, Jul 89, Trouble with Babies, b&w 2.00
❑17, Sep 89, b&w 2.00

FUTABA-KUN CHANGE
IRONCAT

Value: Cover or less

❑1 .... 2.95
❑2 .... 2.95
❑3 .... 2.95

FUTABA-KUN CHANGE (VOL. 3)
IRONCAT

Value: Cover or less

❑1, Jul 99, Futaba-Kun Fights to Win 2.95
❑2 .... 2.95
❑3 .... 2.95
❑4 .... 2.95

FUTURAMA
SLAVE LABOR

	ORIG	GOOD	FINE	N-MINT
❑1, Apr 89, b&w	1.75	0.40	1.00	2.00
❑2, Jun 89, b&w	1.75	0.40	1.00	2.00
❑3, Aug 89, b&w	1.75	0.40	1.00	2.00

FUTURAMA (BONGO)
BONGO

Value: Cover or less

❑1, Monkey Sea, Monkey Doom! 2.50
❑2, ... But Deliver Us To Evil! .. 2.50

FUTURE BEAT
OASIS

Value: Cover or less

❑1, Jul 86, ...It's Better This Way; The Exodus 1.50
❑2 .... 1.50

FUTURE COP: L.A.P.D.
DC

	ORIG	GOOD	FINE	N-MINT
❑1, Jan 99, magazine-sized	4.95	0.99	2.47	4.95
❑Ash 1, Situation Critical	—	0.20	0.50	1.00

FUTURE COURSE
REOCCURRING IMAGES

Value: Cover or less

❑1 .... 2.95

FUTURETECH
MUSHROOM

Value: Cover or less

❑1, Feb 95, b&w; 2nd Printing (first printing published by BlackLine Studios, Oct 94) 3.50

FUTURIANS (VOL. 2)
AARDWOLF

Value: Cover or less

❑1, Aug 95 .... 2.95

FUTURIANS BY DAVE COCKRUM, THE
LODESTONE

	ORIG	GOOD	FINE	N-MINT
❑1, Oct 85, DC, DC (w), Aftermath!, 2: The Futurians; 1: Hammerhand; 1: Doctor Zeus, Story continued from Marvel Graphic Novel #9	1.50	0.40	1.00	2.00
❑2, Dec 85, DC, DC (w)	1.50	0.40	1.00	2.00
❑3, Apr 86, DC, DC (w), Final Issue	1.50	0.40	1.00	2.00

FUZZY BUZZARD AND FRIENDS
HALL OF HEROES

Value: Cover or less

❑1, Apr 95, The Upside Down Cake; Tricky Answers 2.50

G

G-8 AND HIS BATTLE ACES
BLAZING

Value: Cover or less

❑1, Grun--The Green Terror!, full color; Spider's Web #1 .... 1.50

GABRIEL
CALIBER

Value: Cover or less

❑1, b&w; One-Shot; prestige format 3.95

GAG REFLEX (SKIP WILLIAMSON'S...)
WILLIAMSON

Value: Cover or less

❑1, Jan 94, b&w 2.95

GAIJIN (CALIBER)
CALIBER

Value: Cover or less

❑1, The Dark Edge of Beauty, b&w 3.50

GAIJIN (MATRIX)
MATRIX

Value: Cover or less

❑1, Feb 87, First Assault 1.75

GAJIT GANG, THE
AMAZING

Value: Cover or less

❑1 .... 1.95

GALACTICA: THE NEW MILLENNIUM
REALM

Value: Cover or less

❑1, Sep 99, Fear of Flying 2.99

GALACTIC GUARDIANS
MARVEL

Value: Cover or less

❑1, Jul 94, Amid The Encircling Gloom 1.50
❑2, Aug 94, I Have Loved the Stars Too Fondly to be Fearful of the Night 1.50
❑3, Sep 94 .... 1.50
❑4, Oct 94 .... 1.50

GALACTIC PATROL
ETERNITY

Value: Cover or less

❑1, Jul 90, A Lensman Side Story; Decoy, b&w 2.25
❑2, b&w 2.25
❑3, b&w 2.25
❑4, b&w 2.25
❑5, b&w 2.25

GALACTUS THE DEVOURER
MARVEL

	ORIG	GOOD	FINE	N-MINT
❑1, Sep 99, Hunger!	3.50	0.70	1.75	3.50
❑2, Oct 99	2.50	0.70	1.75	3.50
❑3, Nov 99	2.50	0.70	1.75	3.50
❑4, Dec 99, JB, Truth or Consequences	2.50	0.70	1.75	3.50
❑5	3.50	0.70	1.75	3.50
❑6	3.50	0.70	1.75	3.50

GALAXINA
AIRCEL

Value: Cover or less

❑1, b&w; adult 2.95
❑2, b&w; adult 2.95
❑3, b&w; adult 2.95
❑4, adult 2.95

GALAXION
HELIKON

	ORIG	GOOD	FINE	N-MINT
❑1, May 97, A Monent in Time, b&w	2.75	0.55	1.38	2.75
❑2, Jul 97, b&w	2.75	0.55	1.38	2.75
❑3, Sep 97, b&w	2.75	0.55	1.38	2.75
❑4, Nov 97, b&w	2.75	0.55	1.38	2.75
❑5, Jan 98, b&w	2.75	0.55	1.38	2.75
❑6, Mar 98, b&w	2.75	0.55	1.38	2.75
❑7	2.75	0.55	1.38	2.75
❑8	2.75	0.55	1.38	2.75
❑9	2.75	0.55	1.38	2.75
❑10	2.75	0.55	1.38	2.75
❑11, Nov 99, Confined and Released	2.75	0.55	1.38	2.75
❑SE 1, May 98, b&w	0.99	0.20	0.50	1.00

GALAXY GIRL
DYNAMIC

Value: Cover or less

❑1, b&w 2.50

GALL FORCE: ETERNAL STORY
CPM

Value: Cover or less

❑1, Mar 95 .... 2.95
❑2, May 95 .... 2.95
❑3, Jul 95 .... 2.95
❑4, Sep 95 .... 2.95

GAMBIT (1ST SERIES)
ETERNITY

Value: Cover or less

❑1, Sep 88, Trust Me, b&w 1.95

GAMBIT (2ND SERIES)
ORACLE
Value: Cover or less

- ❑1, Sep 86 ... 1.50
- ❑2, Nov 86 ... 1.50

GAMBIT (3RD SERIES)
MARVEL

	ORIG	GOOD	FINE	N-MINT
❑1, Dec 93, Tithing, foil cover	2.50	0.60	1.50	3.00
❑1/GO, Dec 93, Gold promotion edition	—	0.80	2.00	4.00
❑2, Jan 94	2.00	0.50	1.25	2.50
❑3, Feb 94	2.00	0.50	1.25	2.50
❑4, Mar 94	2.00	0.50	1.25	2.50

GAMBIT (4TH SERIES)
MARVEL
Value: Cover or less

- ❑1, Sep 97, gatefold summary 2.50
- ❑2, Oct 97, gatefold summary 2.50
- ❑3 ... 2.50
- ❑4 ... 2.50

GAMBIT (5TH SERIES)
MARVEL

	ORIG	GOOD	FINE	N-MINT
❑1, Feb 99, The Man of Steal, A: X-Cutioner; A: X-Men	1.99	0.60	1.50	3.00
❑1/A, Feb 99, The Man of Steal, A: X-Cutioner; A: X-Men, DFE alternate cover	—	1.00	2.50	5.00
❑1/B, Feb 99, The Man of Steal, A: X-Cutioner; A: X-Men, DFE alternate cover; Signed by Fabian Nicieza and Steve Skroce	—	2.00	5.00	10.00
❑1/C, Feb 99, The Man of Steal, A: X-Cutioner; A: X-Men, Marvel Authentix printed sketch cover; "Certificate of Authenticity"; 600 printed	—	2.00	5.00	10.00
❑2, Mar 99, A: Storm	1.99	0.50	1.25	2.50
❑3, Apr 99, A: Mengo Brothers; A: Courier	1.99	0.50	1.25	2.50
❑4, May 99, Old Wounds, Fresh Blood!	1.99	0.50	1.25	2.50
❑5, Jun 99	1.99	0.40	1.00	1.99
❑6, Jul 99, early adventure	1.99	0.40	1.00	1.99
❑7, Aug 99	1.99	0.40	1.00	1.99
❑8, Sep 99	1.99	0.40	1.00	1.99
❑9, Oct 99	1.99	0.40	1.00	1.99
❑10, Nov 99	1.99	0.40	1.00	1.99
❑11, Dec 99	1.99	0.40	1.00	1.99
❑12, Jan 00	—	0.45	1.13	2.25
❑13, Feb 00	—	0.45	1.13	2.25
❑14, Mar 00	—	0.45	1.13	2.25
❑15, Apr 00	—	0.45	1.13	2.25
❑16, May 00	—	0.45	1.13	2.25
❑17, Jun 00	—	0.45	1.13	2.25
❑18, Jul 00	—	0.45	1.13	2.25
❑19, Aug 00	—	0.45	1.13	2.25
❑20, Sep 00	2.25	0.45	1.13	2.25
❑21, Oct 00	2.25	0.45	1.13	2.25
❑22, Nov 00, Follow the Leader	2.25	0.45	1.13	2.25
❑23, Dec 00, Maximum Security; Shell Game	2.25	0.45	1.13	2.25
❑24, Jan 01, Sunrise Sunset	2.25	0.45	1.13	2.25
❑25, Feb 01, Stop Draggin' My Heart Around, double-sized	2.99	0.60	1.50	2.99
❑Anl 1999, Sep 99	3.50	0.70	1.75	3.50
❑GS 1, Feb 98, The Hearts of Thieves; Dreams Die, Giant sized	3.99	0.80	2.00	3.99

GAMBIT AND BISHOP
MARVEL
Value: Cover or less

- ❑1, Mar 01 ... 2.25
- ❑2, Apr 01, Enter ... The Witness! ... 2.25
- ❑3, May 01, That's Stryfe That's What People Say! ... 2.25
- ❑4, Jun 01, My Brother, My Enemy! ... 2.25
- ❑5, May 01, Are We Ourselves ... 2.25

GAMBIT AND BISHOP ALPHA
MARVEL
Value: Cover or less

- ❑1, Feb 01, May Tomorrow Never Die! ... 2.25

GAMBIT AND BISHOP GENESIS
MARVEL
Value: Cover or less

- ❑1, Mar 01, Gambit: Out of the Frying Pan; Bishop's Crossing, reprints Uncanny X-Men #266, Uncanny X-Men #283, and X-Men (2nd series) #8 ... 3.50

GAMBIT & THE X-TERNALS
MARVEL
Value: Cover or less

- ❑1, Mar 95, Some of us Looking to the Stars ... 1.95
- ❑2, Apr 95 ... 1.95
- ❑3, May 95 ... 1.95
- ❑4, Jun 95 ... 1.95

GAME BOY
VALIANT
Value: Cover or less

- ❑1, GM, GM (w), In the Palm of Your Hand... ... 1.95
- ❑2 ... 1.95
- ❑3 ... 1.95
- ❑4, GM, GM (w), Pipes is Pipes ... 1.95

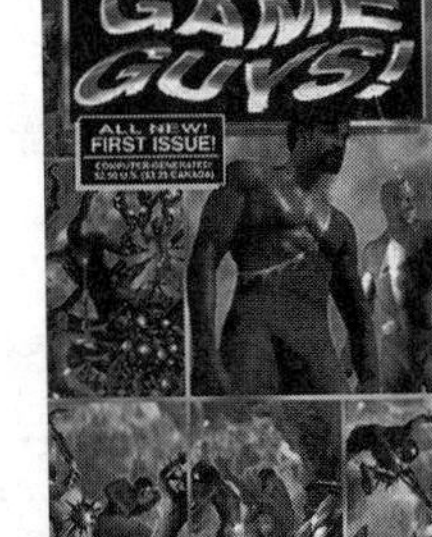

Wonder Comics used a combination of photography and computer effects to produce its comics, including the one-shot *Game Guys.*

© 1996 Wonder Comics

GAME GUYS!
WONDER
Value: Cover or less

- ❑1, A Thousand Ways To Die ... 2.50

GAMERA
DARK HORSE
Value: Cover or less

- ❑1, Aug 96, The Shadow of Evil-Gyaos!, V: Gyaos ... 2.95
- ❑2, Sep 96, Wreckoning ... 2.95
- ❑3, Oct 96, V: Zigra and Viras ... 2.95
- ❑4, Nov 96, The Last Hope, Final Issue ... 2.95

GAMMARAUDERS
DC
Value: Cover or less

- ❑1, Jan 89, Shut Down on the Big Nada! ... 1.25
- ❑2, Mar 89 ... 1.25
- ❑3, Apr 89 ... 1.25
- ❑4, May 89 ... 1.25
- ❑5, Jul 89 ... 1.25
- ❑6 ... 1.25
- ❑7 ... 2.00
- ❑8 ... 2.00
- ❑9 ... 2.00
- ❑10, Final Issue ... 2.00

GAMORRA SWIMSUIT SPECIAL
IMAGE
Value: Cover or less

- ❑1, Jun 96, pin-ups ... 2.50

GANGBANG GIRLS: ALL WET
ANGEL
Value: Cover or less

- ❑1 ... 3.00

GANGLAND
DC
Value: Cover or less

- ❑1, Jun 98, DaG, DaG (w), Clean House; Chains, cover overlay ... 2.95
- ❑2, Jul 98 ... 2.95
- ❑3, Aug 98, Gang Buff; Original Gangster ... 2.95
- ❑4, Sep 98 ... 2.95

GANTAR-THE LAST NABU
TARGET
Value: Cover or less

- ❑1, Dec 86, Cometh The Agonistes ... 1.75
- ❑2, Feb 87 ... 1.75
- ❑3 ... 1.75
- ❑4 ... 1.75
- ❑5 ... 1.75
- ❑6 ... 1.75
- ❑7 ... 1.75

GARGOYLE
MARVEL

	ORIG	GOOD	FINE	N-MINT
❑1, Jun 85	0.75	0.30	0.75	1.50
❑2, Jul 85	0.75	0.30	0.75	1.50
❑3, Aug 85	0.75	0.30	0.75	1.50
❑4, Sep 85	0.75	0.30	0.75	1.50

GARGOYLES
MARVEL
Value: Cover or less

- ❑1, Feb 95, enhanced cover ... 2.50
- ❑2, Mar 95, Always Darkest Before the Dawn ... 1.50
- ❑3, Apr 95 ... 1.50
- ❑4, May 95 ... 1.50
- ❑5, Jun 95 ... 1.50
- ❑6, Jul 95 ... 1.50
- ❑7, Aug 95 ... 1.50
- ❑8, Sep 95 ... 1.50
- ❑9, Oct 95, The Egg and I ... 1.50
- ❑10, Nov 95 ... 1.50
- ❑11, Dec 95, A: Elisa; A: Xanatos, Final Issue ... 1.50

GAROU: THE LONE WOLF
BARE BONES
Value: Cover or less

- ❑1, Jul 99, Fear No Evil ... 2.00

GARRISON'S GORILLAS
DELL

	ORIG	GOOD	FINE	N-MINT
❑1, Jan 68, Break Out; The Gremlins, Photo cover	0.12	4.00	10.00	20.00
❑2, Apr 68, There's a Rat in the Underground; Big Bertha, Photo cover	0.12	2.40	6.00	12.00
❑3	0.12	2.40	6.00	12.00
❑4	0.12	2.40	6.00	12.00
❑5, Break Out; The Gremlins, Reprints #1	0.12	2.00	5.00	10.00

GASP!
QUEBECOR

	ORIG	GOOD	FINE	N-MINT
❑1, Buckie Godot; Die, Previews Tyrant, Rare Bit Fiends, Wandering Star, and more. Contains new Buck Godot, Zap Gun for Hire story.	—	0.20	0.50	1.00

ORIG GOOD FINE N-MINT

GATECRASHER: RING OF FIRE
BLACK BULL
Value: Cover or less

❑1, MWa (w), Yellow cover with five figures ... 2.50
❑1/A, MWa (w), Green cover with two figures ... 2.50
❑2, MWa (w) ... 2.50
❑3, MWa (w) ... 2.50
❑3/A, MWa (w), variant cover.. 2.50
❑4, MWa (w) ... 2.50
❑4/A, MWa (w), Variant (woman in lingerie, shipped 1:4) ... 2.50

GATEKEEPER
GATEKEEPER
Value: Cover or less
❑1, b&w ... 2.50

GATES OF EDEN
FANTACO
Value: Cover or less
❑1, JBy; FH ... 3.50

GATES OF PANDRAGON
IANUS
Value: Cover or less
❑1, b&w ... 2.25

GATEWAY TO HORROR (BASIL WOLVERTON'S...)
DARK HORSE
Value: Cover or less
❑1, Aug 87, BW, b&w ... 1.75

GATHERING OF TRIBES
KC ARTS

	ORIG	GOOD	FINE	N-MINT
❑1, nn; no cover price; giveaway	—	0.20	0.50	1.00

GAUNTLET, THE
AIRCEL
Value: Cover or less

❑1, Jul 92 ... 2.95
❑2, Aug 92 ... 2.95
❑3, Sep 92 ... 2.95
❑4, Oct 92 ... 2.95
❑5, Nov 92 ... 2.95
❑6, Dec 92 ... 2.95
❑7, Jan 93 ... 2.95
❑8, Feb 93 ... 2.95

GAY COMICS (BOB ROSS)
BOB ROSS

	ORIG	GOOD	FINE	N-MINT
❑1	—	2.50	6.25	12.50
❑2	—	1.60	4.00	8.00
❑3	—	1.20	3.00	6.00
❑4	—	1.20	3.00	6.00
❑5	—	1.20	3.00	6.00
❑6	—	0.90	2.25	4.50
❑7	—	0.90	2.25	4.50
❑8	—	0.90	2.25	4.50
❑9, Win 86	2.00	0.90	2.25	4.50
❑10	2.00	0.70	1.75	3.50
❑11, Wee-Wee's Gayhouse	2.00	0.70	1.75	3.50
❑12, Spr 88	2.50	0.70	1.75	3.50
❑13, Sum 91	2.50	0.70	1.75	3.50
❑14	2.00	0.70	1.75	3.50
❑15, Queer Fish	2.00	0.70	1.75	3.50
❑16, Pigeonholed, Desert Peach story	2.95	0.70	1.75	3.50
❑17	2.95	0.60	1.50	3.00
❑18	2.95	0.60	1.50	3.00
❑19, Alison Bechdel Special	2.95	0.60	1.50	3.00
❑20, super-heroes	2.95	0.60	1.50	3.00
❑21	2.95	0.60	1.50	3.00
❑22, Sum 94, Funny Animals Special with Omaha the Cat Dancer story	2.95	1.00	2.50	5.00
❑23, Funny Animals Special	3.50	1.00	2.50	5.00
❑24, A: The Maxx	3.50	1.00	2.50	5.00

GAZILLION
IMAGE
Value: Cover or less

❑1, Nov 98 ... 2.50
❑1/SC, Nov 98, alternate cover; framed ... 2.50

GD MINUS 18
ANTARCTIC
Value: Cover or less
❑1, Feb 98, b&w; Gold Digger Special ... 2.95

GEAR
FIREMAN
Value: Cover or less

❑1, Nov 98 ... 2.95
❑2 ... 2.95
❑3 ... 2.95
❑4 ... 2.95
❑5 ... 2.95
❑6 ... 2.95

GEAR STATION, THE
IMAGE
Value: Cover or less

❑1, Mar 00, This Hero's Journey ... 2.50
❑2 ... 2.50
❑3, Jun 00, Crossing the Threshold ... 2.50
❑4, Jul 00, Final Destination ... 2.50
❑5, Nov 00 ... 2.50

GEEKSVILLE
3 FINGER PRINTS

	ORIG	GOOD	FINE	N-MINT
❑1, Aug 99, The 3 Geeks: Factor M; Innocent Bystander, b&w	2.75	0.60	1.50	3.00
❑2, Oct 99, True Tales From the Comic Shop; Innocent Bystander, b&w	2.75	0.60	1.50	3.00
❑3, Dec 99, b&w	2.75	0.55	1.38	2.75

GEEKSVILLE (VOL. 2)
IMAGE

	ORIG	GOOD	FINE	N-MINT
❑0, Mar 00, b&w	2.75	0.60	1.50	3.00
❑1, May 00, b&w	2.75	0.60	1.50	3.00
❑2, Jul 00, The 3 Geeks: Breaking into the Biz, Part Two: How Much?!?; Innocent Bystander: Drive West on Sunset, b&w	2.95	0.59	1.48	2.95
❑3, Sep 00, The 3 Geeks: Breaking into the Biz, Part 3; Babes and Blades, b&w	2.95	0.59	1.48	2.95
❑4, Nov 00, The 3 Geeks: Breaking into the Biz, Part 4; Dark Sky, Part 2, b&w	2.95	0.59	1.48	2.95
❑5, Jan 01, The 3 Geeks: Divide and Conquer, Part 1; Innocent Bystander: Nighthawks	2.95	0.59	1.48	2.95
❑6, Mar 01, All Good Things..., Final Issue	2.95	0.59	1.48	2.95

GEISHA
ONI PRESS
Value: Cover or less

❑1, Sep 98 ... 2.95
❑2, Oct 98 ... 2.95
❑3, Nov 98 ... 2.95
❑4, Dec 98 ... 2.95

GEMINAR
IMAGE
Value: Cover or less
❑SE 1, Jul 00 ... 4.95

GEMINI BLOOD
DC
Value: Cover or less

❑1, Sep 96, Species: Paratwa, Part 1 ... 2.25
❑2, Oct 96, Species: Paratwa, Part 2 ... 2.25
❑3, Nov 96, Species: Paratwa, Part 3 ... 2.25
❑4, Dec 96, Species: Paratwa, Part 4 ... 2.25
❑5, Jan 97, Species: Paratwa, Part 5 ... 2.25
❑6, Feb 97, Species: Paratwa, Part 6 ... 2.25
❑7, Mar 97, Infrangibility ... 2.25
❑8, Apr 97, Loothka Bl-Modal, Part 1 ... 2.25
❑9, May 97, Loothka Bl-Modal, Part 2 ... 2.25

GEN12
IMAGE
Value: Cover or less

❑1, Feb 98, The Legacy ... 2.50
❑2, Mar 98 ... 2.50
❑3, Apr 98 ... 2.50
❑4, May 98 ... 2.50
❑5, Jun 98 ... 2.50

GEN[13]
IMAGE

	ORIG	GOOD	FINE	N-MINT
❑-1, American Entertainment exclusive	—	0.80	2.00	4.00
❑0, Coming Home; Desert Bloom	2.50	0.60	1.50	3.00
❑1/3D, Feb 98, Among Friends and Enemies, 1: Alex Fairchild; 1: The Bounty Hunters; 1: Trance, 3D Edition; with glasses	4.95	0.80	2.00	4.00
❑1/A, Mar 95, Among Friends and Enemies, 1: Alex Fairchild; 1: The Bounty Hunters; 1: Trance, Cover 1 of 13: Charge!; Common	2.95	0.80	2.00	4.00
❑1/B, Mar 95, Among Friends and Enemies, 1: Alex Fairchild; 1: The Bounty Hunters; 1: Trance, Cover 2 of 13: Thumbs Up; Common	2.95	0.80	2.00	4.00
❑1/C, Mar 95, Among Friends and Enemies, 1: Alex Fairchild; 1: The Bounty Hunters; 1: Trance, Cover 3 of 13: Li'l GEN13	2.95	1.00	2.50	5.00
❑1/D, Mar 95, Among Friends and Enemies, 1: Alex Fairchild; 1: The Bounty Hunters; 1: Trance, Cover 4 of 13: Barbari-GEN	2.95	1.00	2.50	5.00
❑1/E, Mar 95, Among Friends and Enemies, 1: Alex Fairchild; 1: The Bounty Hunters; 1: Trance, Cover 5 of 13: Your Friendly Neighborhood Grunge	2.95	1.00	2.50	5.00
❑1/F, Mar 95, Among Friends and Enemies, 1: Alex Fairchild; 1: The Bounty Hunters; 1: Trance, Cover 6 of 13: Gen13 Goes Madison Avenue	2.95	1.00	2.50	5.00
❑1/G, Mar 95, Among Friends and Enemies, 1: Alex Fairchild; 1: The Bounty Hunters; 1: Trance, Cover 7 of 13: Lin-GEN-re	2.95	2.00	5.00	10.00
❑1/H, Mar 95, Among Friends and Enemies, 1: Alex Fairchild; 1: The Bounty Hunters; 1: Trance, Cover 8 of 13: GEN-et Jackson	2.95	2.00	5.00	10.00
❑1/I, Mar 95, Among Friends and Enemies, 1: Alex Fairchild; 1: The Bounty Hunters; 1: Trance, Cover 9 of 13: That's the Way We Became the GEN13	2.95	1.00	2.50	5.00
❑1/J, Mar 95, Among Friends and Enemies, 1: Alex Fairchild; 1: The Bounty Hunters; 1: Trance, Cover 10 of 13: All Dolled Up	2.95	1.00	2.50	5.00
❑1/K, Mar 95, Among Friends and Enemies, 1: Alex Fairchild; 1: The Bounty Hunters; 1: Trance, Cover 11 of 13: Verti-GEN	2.95	1.00	2.50	5.00
❑1/L, Mar 95, Among Friends and Enemies, 1: Alex Fairchild; 1: The Bounty Hunters; 1: Trance, Cover 12 of 13: Picto-Fiction	2.95	1.00	2.50	5.00
❑1/M, Mar 95, Among Friends and Enemies, 1: Alex Fairchild; 1: The Bounty Hunters; 1: Trance, Cover 13 of 13: Do-It-Yourself-Cover	2.95	1.00	2.50	5.00

	ORIG	GOOD	FINE	N-MINT
❑1/N, Among Friends and Enemies, 1: Alex Fairchild; 1: The Bounty Hunters; 1: Trance, Included all variant covers, plus new puzzle cover	39.95	12.00	30.00	60.00
❑1-2, Fairchild in French maid outfit on cover; "Encore edition"	2.50	0.50	1.25	2.50
❑2, May 95, Wildstorm Rising, Part 4, 1: Helmut, Flip cover; trading cards	2.50	0.50	1.25	2.50
❑3, Jul 95	2.50	0.50	1.25	2.50
❑4, Jul 95, 1: Lucius, indicia says Jul, cover says Aug	2.50	0.50	1.25	2.50
❑5, Oct 95	2.50	0.50	1.25	2.50
❑6, Nov 95, 1: The Order of the Cross; 1: Frostbite	2.50	0.50	1.25	2.50
❑7, Jan 96, 1: Evo; 1: Copycat, indicia says Jan, cover says Dec	2.50	0.50	1.25	2.50
❑8, Feb 96, 1: Sublime; 1: Powerhaus	2.50	0.50	1.25	2.50
❑9, Mar 96, 1: Absolom	2.50	0.50	1.25	2.50
❑10, Apr 96, Fire from Heaven, Part 3, 1: Sigma	2.50	0.50	1.25	2.50
❑11, May 96, Fire from Heaven, Part 9	2.50	0.50	1.25	2.50
❑11/A, May 96, Fire from Heaven, Part 9, European Tour Edition	2.50	0.60	1.50	3.00
❑12, Aug 96	2.50	0.50	1.25	2.50
❑13/A, Aug 96, A: Archie, Jughead, Betty, Veronica, Reggie	1.30	0.30	0.75	1.50
❑13/B, Sep 96, A: TMNTs, Bone, Beanworld, Spawn, Madman, cover says Oct, indicia says Sep	1.30	0.30	0.75	1.50
❑13/C, Nov 96, A: Madman, Maxx, Shi, Francine, Katchoo, Monkeyman, O'Brien, Hellboy	1.30	0.30	0.75	1.50
❑13/CS, A: Spawn; A: Teenage Mutant Ninja Turtles; A: Shi; A: Bone; A: Hellboy; A: Madman; A: Maxx, Collected Edition of #13A, B, and C	6.95	1.39	3.47	6.95
❑13/D, A: Spawn; A: Teenage Mutant Ninja Turtles; A: Shi; A: Bone; A: Hellboy; A: Madman; A: Maxx, Variant cover collected edition; Collected Edition of #13A, B, and C	6.95	1.39	3.47	6.95
❑14, Nov 96	2.50	0.50	1.25	2.50
❑15, Dec 96	2.50	0.50	1.25	2.50
❑16, Jan 97, Babes in Toyland	2.50	0.50	1.25	2.50
❑17, Feb 97	2.50	0.50	1.25	2.50
❑18, Apr 97	2.50	0.50	1.25	2.50
❑19, May 97	2.50	0.50	1.25	2.50
❑20, Jun 97	2.50	0.50	1.25	2.50
❑21, Aug 97, in space	2.50	0.50	1.25	2.50
❑22, Sep 97, Homecoming	2.50	0.50	1.25	2.50
❑23, Oct 97, Life in the Big City	2.50	0.50	1.25	2.50
❑24, Nov 97, Judgment Day	2.50	0.50	1.25	2.50
❑25, Dec 97, ...Where Angels Fear to Tread...	3.50	0.70	1.75	3.50
❑25/A, Dec 97, ...Where Angels Fear to Tread..., alternate cover; white background	3.50	0.70	1.75	3.50
❑25/B, Dec 97, ...Where Angels Fear to Tread..., chromium cover	3.50	0.70	1.75	3.50
❑25/CS, Dec 97, ...Where Angels Fear to Tread..., preview of Danger Girl; Voyager pack	3.50	0.80	2.00	4.00
❑26, Feb 98, When Worlds Collide	2.50	0.50	1.25	2.50
❑26/A, Feb 98, alternate cover; fight scene	2.50	0.50	1.25	2.50
❑27, Mar 98, Search and Seizure	2.50	0.50	1.25	2.50
❑28, Apr 98, Remote Control	2.50	0.50	1.25	2.50
❑29, May 98, A Firm Grip on Reality!	2.50	0.50	1.25	2.50
❑30, Jun 98, Stranger Than Fiction	2.50	0.50	1.25	2.50
❑30/A, Jun 98, alternate swimsuit cover	2.50	0.50	1.25	2.50
❑31, Jul 98, Paradigm Shift	2.50	0.50	1.25	2.50
❑32, Aug 98, Red Skies at Morning	2.50	0.50	1.25	2.50
❑33, Sep 98, Burning the Candle at Both Ends, Planetary preview	2.50	0.50	1.25	2.50
❑34, Oct 98, Overture	2.50	0.50	1.25	2.50
❑34/A, Oct 98, Variant cover by Arthur Adams (Fairchild posing); black background	2.50	0.50	1.25	2.50
❑35, Nov 98, But You Can't Hide	2.50	0.50	1.25	2.50
❑36, Dec 98, That Was Then	2.50	0.50	1.25	2.50
❑36/A, Dec 98, KN (c), That Was Then, Variant cover by Kevin Nowlan (corn dogs)	2.50	0.50	1.25	2.50
❑37, Mar 99	2.50	0.50	1.25	2.50
❑38, Apr 99	2.50	0.50	1.25	2.50
❑38/SC, Variant cover by Doug Mahnke (Grunge w/popcorn)	2.50	0.50	1.25	2.50
❑39, May 99, Death and the Broken Promise, Part 1	2.50	0.50	1.25	2.50
❑40, Jun 99, Death and the Broken Promise, Part 2	2.50	0.50	1.25	2.50
❑40/SC, Jun 99, Death and the Broken Promise, Part 2, Variant cover by Kyle Baker (Roxy in shower)	2.50	0.50	1.25	2.50
❑41, Jul 99, Death and the Broken Promise, Part 3	2.50	0.50	1.25	2.50

Gatecrasher: Ring of Fire was the first release from Wizard's Black Bull imprint.

	ORIG	GOOD	FINE	N-MINT
❑42, Aug 99	2.50	0.50	1.25	2.50
❑43, Sep 99, A Savage Breast, Part 1	2.50	0.50	1.25	2.50
❑44, Oct 99, A Savage Breast, Part 2, A: Mr. Majestic	2.50	0.50	1.25	2.50
❑45, Nov 99	2.50	0.50	1.25	2.50
❑46, Dec 00, The Grunge that ate Manhattan	2.50	0.50	1.25	2.50
❑47, Jan 00	2.50	0.50	1.25	2.50
❑48, Feb 00	2.50	0.50	1.25	2.50
❑49, Mar 00	2.50	0.50	1.25	2.50
❑50, Apr 00, Over my Dead Body, Giant-size	3.95	0.79	1.98	3.95
❑51, May 00	2.50	0.50	1.25	2.50
❑52, Jun 00	2.50	0.50	1.25	2.50
❑53, Jul 00	2.50	0.50	1.25	2.50
❑54, Aug 00, The Fairchild Trilogy, Part 1	2.50	0.50	1.25	2.50
❑55, Sep 00, The Fairchild Trilogy, Part 2	2.50	0.50	1.25	2.50
❑56, Oct 00, The Fairchild Trilogy, Part 3	2.50	0.50	1.25	2.50
❑57, Nov 00, Priscilla, Queen of the Monsters	2.50	0.50	1.25	2.50
❑58, Dec 00, Gotta Kill 'Em All!	2.50	0.50	1.25	2.50
❑59, Jan 01, Ghost, No Shell, Over Easy	2.50	0.50	1.25	2.50
❑60, Feb 01, Behind the Powers	2.50	0.50	1.25	2.50
❑61, Mar 01, Goin' Back to Cali to Cali, to Cali	2.50	0.50	1.25	2.50
❑62, Apr 01, Please Pull Ahead, or Would You Like Misogyny With That?	2.50	0.50	1.25	2.50
❑63, May 01, Fire on High	2.50	0.50	1.25	2.50
❑64	2.50	0.50	1.25	2.50
❑65	2.50	0.50	1.25	2.50
❑66	2.50	0.50	1.25	2.50
❑67	2.50	0.50	1.25	2.50
❑3D 1, Mauling!, European Tour Edition	4.95	1.00	2.50	5.00
❑3D 1/A, Mauling!, Fairchild holding open dinosaur mouth on cover; double-sized	4.95	1.00	2.50	5.00
❑Anl 1, May 97, 1997 Annual	2.95	0.59	1.48	2.95
❑Anl 1999, Mar 99, nn; wraparound cover; continues in DV8 Annual 1999	3.50	0.70	1.75	3.50
❑Anl 2000, Dec 00, Return of the Demon	3.50	0.70	1.75	3.50

GEN^{13} (MINI-SERIES)
IMAGE

	ORIG	GOOD	FINE	N-MINT
❑0, Sep 94	2.50	0.70	1.75	3.50
❑0.5, Mar 94, Wizard promotional edition	—	0.40	1.00	2.00
❑0.5/A, Signed by Jim Lee	—	2.00	5.00	10.00
❑1, Feb 94, 1: Freefall (full appearance); 1: Burnout (full appearance); 1: Grunge (full appearance), coupon for Gen 13 Ashcan; first printing	2.50	1.20	3.00	6.00
❑1/A, Oct 97, 1: Freefall (full appearance); 1: Burnout (full appearance); 1: Grunge (full appearance), alternate cover; 3-D; with glasses	4.95	0.99	2.47	4.95
❑1/B, Oct 97, 1: Freefall (full appearance); 1: Burnout (full appearance); 1: Grunge (full appearance), 3-D; with glasses	4.95	1.00	2.50	5.00
❑1/C, 1: Freefall (full appearance); 1: Burnout (full appearance); 1: Grunge (full appearance), Fairchild flexing on cover	2.50	1.20	3.00	6.00
❑1-2, Jun 94, 1: Burnout (full appearance); 1: Grunge (full appearance), 2nd Printing; coupon for Gen 13 Ashcan	2.50	0.60	1.50	3.00
❑2, Mar 94, Species: Paratwa, Part 2, coupon for Gen 13 Ashcan	2.50	0.60	1.50	3.00
❑3, Apr 94, A: Pitt, coupon for Gen 13 Ashcan	1.95	0.60	1.50	3.00
❑4, May 94, A: Pitt, wraparound cover, coupon for Gen 13 Ashcan	1.95	0.50	1.25	2.50
❑5, Jul 94	1.95	0.50	1.25	2.50
❑5/A, Jul 94, alternate cover	1.95	0.50	1.25	2.50
❑Ash 1, ashcan edition	—	1.20	3.00	6.00

GEN^{13}: A CHRISTMAS CAPER
WILDSTORM

Value: Cover or less

❑1, Jan 00 .... 5.95

GEN^{13}: BACKLIST
IMAGE

Value: Cover or less

❑1, Nov 96, collects Gen<V>13<V> #1/2, Gen<V>13<V> #0, Gen<V>13<V> #1, Gen<V>13<V>: The Unreal World, and Wildstorm! #1; collects Gen13 #1/2, Gen13 #0, Gen13 #1, Gen13: The Unreal World, and Wildstorm! #1; col 2.50

GEN^{13} BIKINI PIN-UP SPECIAL
IMAGE

	ORIG	GOOD	FINE	N-MINT
❑1, American Entertainment Exclusive	—	1.00	2.50	5.00

GEN^{13} BOOTLEG
IMAGE

	ORIG	GOOD	FINE	N-MINT
❑1/A, Nov 96, Team standing, Fairchild front on cover	2.50	0.60	1.50	3.00
❑1/B, Team falling	2.50	0.60	1.50	3.00
❑2, Dec 96, Lindquist's Fault	2.50	0.50	1.25	2.50
❑3, Jan 97, A Gen13 Fairy Tale	2.50	0.50	1.25	2.50
❑4, Feb 97, Little Girl Lost	2.50	0.50	1.25	2.50
❑5, Mar 97	2.50	0.50	1.25	2.50
❑6, Apr 97	2.50	0.50	1.25	2.50
❑7, May 97, JRo (w)	2.50	0.50	1.25	2.50
❑8, Jun 97, manga-style story	2.50	0.50	1.25	2.50
❑9, Jul 97, manga-style story; action movie references	2.50	0.50	1.25	2.50
❑10, Aug 97, manga-style story; video game references	2.50	0.50	1.25	2.50
❑11, Sep 97, The Castle of Doctor Monstro, Part 1	2.50	0.50	1.25	2.50
❑12, Oct 97, The Castle of Doctor Monstro, Part 2	2.50	0.50	1.25	2.50
❑13, Nov 97, The Trickster	2.50	0.50	1.25	2.50
❑14, Dec 97	2.50	0.50	1.25	2.50
❑15, Jan 98, Hangin', Part 1	2.50	0.50	1.25	2.50
❑16, Feb 98, Hangin', Part 2	2.50	0.50	1.25	2.50
❑17/A, Mar 98, Virgil Chu's Reality, alternate cover; videogame	2.50	0.50	1.25	2.50
❑17/B, Mar 98, Virgil Chu's Reality, alternate cover; videogame	2.50	0.50	1.25	2.50
❑18/A, May 98, Surfing cover; surfin'	2.50	0.50	1.25	2.50
❑18/B, May 98, Beach cover; surfin'	2.50	0.50	1.25	2.50
❑19, Jun 98	2.50	0.50	1.25	2.50
❑20, Jul 98, The Numbskulls, Final Issue	2.50	0.50	1.25	2.50
❑Anl 1, Feb 98, New York Confidential	2.95	0.59	1.48	2.95

GEN^{13}: CARNY FOLK
WILDSTORM

Value: Cover or less

- ❑1, Jan 00, Scenes at an Exhibition; I Want my Mommaaaaa!! ... 3.50

GEN^{13}/FANTASTIC FOUR
WILDSTORM

Value: Cover or less

- ❑1, Qeelock's Really Big New York Adventure ... 5.95

GEN^{13}/GENERATION X
IMAGE

	ORIG	GOOD	FINE	N-MINT
❑1/A, Jul 97, Generation Gap, crossover with Marvel	2.95	0.59	1.48	2.95
❑1/B, Jul 97, Generation Gap, alternate cover; crossover with Marvel	2.95	0.59	1.48	2.95
❑1/C, Aug 97, Generation Gap, Limited cover; 3D Edition	4.95	1.00	2.50	5.00
❑1/D, Jul 97, Generation Gap, alternate cover; 3D Edition; crossover with Marvel; with glasses	4.95	1.00	2.50	5.00
❑1/E, Generation Gap, San Diego Comic-Con edition	2.95	0.80	2.00	4.00

GEN^{13}: GOING WEST
DC

Value: Cover or less

- ❑1, Jun 99, Where the B uffalo Roam, nn; One-Shot ... 2.50

GEN^{13}: GRUNGE SAVES THE WORLD
DC

Value: Cover or less

- ❑1, May 99, prestige format ... 5.95

GEN^{13} INTERACTIVE
IMAGE

	ORIG	GOOD	FINE	N-MINT
❑1, Oct 97, Any Color You Like	2.50	0.50	1.25	2.50
❑2, Nov 97, Up For Grabs	2.50	0.50	1.25	2.50
❑3, Jan 98, How to Start a Panic, cover says Dec, indicia says Jan	2.50	0.50	1.25	2.50

GEN^{13}: MAGICAL DRAMA QUEEN ROXY
IMAGE

	ORIG	GOOD	FINE	N-MINT
❑1, Oct 98	3.50	0.70	1.75	3.50
❑1/A, Oct 98, alternate cover	3.50	1.20	3.00	6.00
❑1/B, Oct 98, DFE alternate cover; Signed by Adam Warren	3.50	1.60	4.00	8.00
❑2, Nov 98	3.50	0.70	1.75	3.50
❑2/A, Nov 98, alternate cover	3.50	0.70	1.75	3.50
❑3, Dec 98	3.50	0.70	1.75	3.50
❑3/A, Dec 98, alternate cover	3.50	0.70	1.75	3.50

GEN^{13}/MAXX
IMAGE

Value: Cover or less

- ❑1, Dec 95 ... 3.50

GEN^{13}: MEDICINE SONG
WILDSTORM

Value: Cover or less

- ❑1, BA ... 5.95

GEN^{13}/MONKEYMAN & O'BRIEN
IMAGE

	ORIG	GOOD	FINE	N-MINT
❑1, Jun 98	2.50	0.50	1.25	2.50
❑1/A, Jun 98, alternate cover	2.50	0.80	2.00	4.00
❑1/B, Jun 98, Variant chromium cover	—	1.20	3.00	6.00
❑1/C, Monkeyman holding team on cover, blue/gold background	—	1.20	3.00	6.00
❑2, Aug 98	2.50	0.50	1.25	2.50
❑2/A, Aug 98, alternate cover	2.50	0.50	1.25	2.50

GEN^{13}: ORDINARY HEROES
IMAGE

Value: Cover or less

- ❑1, Feb 96, Desolation Row ... 2.50
- ❑2, Jul 96 ... 2.50

GEN^{13} RAVE
IMAGE

	ORIG	GOOD	FINE	N-MINT
❑1, Mar 95, wraparound cover	1.50	0.60	1.50	3.00

GEN^{13}: SCIENCE FRICTION
WILDSTORM

Value: Cover or less

- ❑1 ... 5.95

GEN^{13}: THE UNREAL WORLD
IMAGE

Value: Cover or less

- ❑1, Jul 96, 1: Cull, One-Shot ... 2.95

GEN^{13}: WIRED
DC

Value: Cover or less

- ❑1, Apr 99 ... 2.50

GEN^{13} YEARBOOK '97
IMAGE

Value: Cover or less

- ❑1, Jun 97, Yearbook-style info on team ... 2.50

GEN^{13} 'ZINE
IMAGE

	ORIG	GOOD	FINE	N-MINT
❑1, Dec 96, b&w; digest	1.95	0.40	1.00	2.00

GEN-ACTIVE
WILDSTORM

Value: Cover or less

- ❑1, May 00, Nature vs. Nurture, Superchick Smackdown cover ... 3.95
- ❑1/A, May 00, Nature vs. Nurture, Woman with knife on cover ... 3.95
- ❑2, Group cover ... 3.95
- ❑2/A, Woman kicking on cover ... 3.95
- ❑3, Nov 00, Devil May Care ... 3.95
- ❑4, Feb 01, Abandon All Hope ... 3.95
- ❑5, May 01, Father's Day ... 3.95

GENE DOGS
MARVEL

Value: Cover or less

- ❑1, Oct 93, Storm Warning, A: MyS-TECH, trading cards; four trading cards; Polybagged .. 2.75
- ❑2, Nov 93 ... 1.75
- ❑3, Dec 93, Showdown in Siberia! ... 1.75
- ❑4, Jan 94 ... 1.75

GENERATION HEX
DC

Value: Cover or less

- ❑1, Jun 97, Humanity's Last Stand ... 1.95

GENERATION NEXT
MARVEL

Value: Cover or less

- ❑1, Mar 95, From the Top ... 1.95
- ❑2, Apr 95 ... 1.95
- ❑3, May 95 ... 1.95
- ❑4, Jun 95 ... 1.95

GENERATION X
MARVEL

	ORIG	GOOD	FINE	N-MINT
❑-1, Jul 97, JRo (w), The Beginning of a Beautiful Friendship, A: Stan Lee, Flashback	1.99	0.40	1.00	2.00
❑0.5	—	0.50	1.25	2.50
❑0.5/LE, Signed by Larry Hama; holofoil sticker; Certificate of Authenticity	—	1.20	3.00	6.00
❑1, Nov 94, Third Genesis, enhanced cover	3.95	0.80	2.00	4.00
❑2, Dec 94	1.50	0.35	0.88	1.75
❑2/Dlx, Dec 94, Deluxe edition	1.95	0.40	1.00	2.00
❑3, Jan 95	1.50	0.35	0.88	1.75
❑3/Dlx, Jan 95, Deluxe edition	1.95	0.40	1.00	2.00
❑4, Feb 95	1.50	0.35	0.88	1.75
❑4/Dlx, Feb 95, Deluxe edition	1.95	0.40	1.00	2.00
❑5, Jul 95	1.95	0.40	1.00	2.00
❑6, Aug 95	1.95	0.40	1.00	2.00
❑7, Sep 95	1.95	0.40	1.00	2.00
❑8, Oct 95	1.95	0.40	1.00	2.00
❑9, Nov 95	1.95	0.40	1.00	2.00
❑10, Dec 95, Banshee vs. Omega Red!, A: Banshee; V: Omega Red; A: Wolverine	1.95	0.40	1.00	2.00
❑11, Jan 96	1.95	0.40	1.00	2.00
❑12, Feb 96, V: Emplate	1.95	0.40	1.00	2.00
❑13, Mar 96, V: Emplate	1.95	0.40	1.00	2.00
❑14, Apr 96	1.95	0.40	1.00	2.00
❑15, May 96	1.95	0.40	1.00	2.00
❑16, Jun 96	1.95	0.40	1.00	2.00
❑17, Jul 96	1.95	0.40	1.00	2.00
❑18, Aug 96, Onslaught: Impact 1	1.95	0.40	1.00	2.00

	ORIG	GOOD	FINE	N-MINT
❑19, Sep 96, Onslaught: Impact 2	1.95	0.40	1.00	2.00
❑20, Oct 96, A: Howard the Duck	1.95	0.40	1.00	2.00
❑21, Nov 96, A: Howard the Duck	1.95	0.40	1.00	2.00
❑22, Dec 96, All Hallows Eve, A: Nightmare	1.95	0.40	1.00	2.00
❑23, Jan 97, We Give Thanks	1.95	0.40	1.00	2.00
❑24, Feb 97, Home for the Holidays	1.95	0.40	1.00	2.00
❑25, Mar 97, wraparound cover; Giant-size	2.99	0.60	1.50	3.00
❑26, Apr 97, Adrift	1.95	0.40	1.00	2.00
❑27, May 97, The Last X Man	1.95	0.40	1.00	2.00
❑28, Jun 97, Oh, Now I Get It...	1.95	0.40	1.00	2.00
❑29, Aug 97, gatefold summary; Operation Zero Tolerance	1.99	0.40	1.00	2.00
❑30, Sep 97, gatefold summary; Operation Zero Tolerance	1.99	0.40	1.00	2.00
❑31, Oct 97, gatefold summary; Operation Zero Tolerance	1.99	0.40	1.00	2.00
❑32, Nov 97, V: Circus of Crime, gatefold summary	1.99	0.40	1.00	2.00
❑33, Dec 97, gatefold summary	1.99	0.40	1.00	2.00
❑34, Jan 98, V: White Queen, gatefold summary	1.99	0.40	1.00	2.00
❑35, Feb 98, gatefold summary	1.99	0.40	1.00	2.00
❑36, Mar 98, gatefold summary	1.99	0.40	1.00	2.00
❑37, Apr 98, gatefold summary	1.99	0.40	1.00	2.00
❑38, May 98, Mystery Train, gatefold summary	1.99	0.40	1.00	2.00
❑39, Jun 98, Return From Forever, gatefold summary	1.99	0.40	1.00	2.00
❑40, Jul 98, gatefold summary	1.99	0.40	1.00	2.00
❑41, Aug 98, gatefold summary	1.99	0.40	1.00	2.00
❑42, Sep 98, gatefold summary	1.99	0.40	1.00	2.00
❑43, Oct 98, gatefold summary; White Queen powerless	1.99	0.40	1.00	2.00
❑44, Nov 98, gatefold summary	1.99	0.40	1.00	2.00
❑45, Dec 98, gatefold summary; White Queen regains powers	1.99	0.40	1.00	2.00
❑46, Dec 98, gatefold summary	1.99	0.40	1.00	2.00
❑47, Jan 99, A: Forge, gatefold summary	1.99	0.40	1.00	2.00
❑48, Feb 99, A: Jubilee	1.99	0.40	1.00	2.00
❑49, Mar 99, A: Maggott	1.99	0.40	1.00	2.00
❑50, Apr 99, War of the Mutants, part 1, A: Dark Beast	2.99	0.60	1.50	3.00
❑50/Aut, War of the Mutants, part 1, A: Dark Beast, Signed by Terry Dodson	—	1.60	4.00	8.00
❑51, May 99	1.99	0.40	1.00	2.00
❑52, Jun 99	1.99	0.40	1.00	2.00
❑53, Jul 99	1.99	0.40	1.00	2.00
❑54, Aug 99	1.99	0.40	1.00	2.00
❑55, Sep 99	1.99	0.40	1.00	2.00
❑56, Oct 99	1.99	0.40	1.00	2.00
❑57, Nov 99	2.99	0.60	1.50	2.99
❑58, Dec 99	2.99	0.60	1.50	2.99
❑59, Jan 00	1.99	0.40	1.00	1.99
❑60, Feb 00	—	0.45	1.13	2.25
❑61, Mar 00	—	0.45	1.13	2.25
❑62, Apr 00	—	0.45	1.13	2.25
❑63, May 00	—	0.45	1.13	2.25
❑64, Jun 00	—	0.45	1.13	2.25
❑65, Jul 00	—	0.45	1.13	2.25
❑66, Aug 00	—	0.45	1.13	2.25
❑67, Sep 00	—	0.45	1.13	2.25
❑68, Oct 00	2.25	0.45	1.13	2.25
❑69, Nov 00, Come On Die Young, Part 3	2.25	0.45	1.13	2.25
❑70, Dec 00	2.25	0.45	1.13	2.25
❑71, Jan 01, Four Days, Part 1	2.25	0.45	1.13	2.25
❑72, Feb 01, Four Days, Part 2	2.25	0.45	1.13	2.25
❑73, Mar 01, Four Days, Part 3	2.25	0.45	1.13	2.25
❑74, Apr 01, Four Days, Part 4	2.25	0.45	1.13	2.25
❑Anl 1995, wraparound cover	3.95	0.79	1.98	3.95
❑Anl 1996, MG (w), Everyday People, wraparound cover; Generation X '96	2.99	0.60	1.50	2.99
❑Anl 1997, wraparound cover; gatefold summary; Generation X '97	2.99	0.60	1.50	2.99
❑Anl 1998, wraparound cover; gatefold summary; Generation X/Dracula '98	3.50	0.70	1.75	3.50
❑Anl 1999	3.50	0.70	1.75	3.50
❑Ash 1, ashcan edition	0.75	0.15	0.38	0.75
❑HS 1, Feb 98, Yes, Jubilee-there is a Santa Clause, Giant-size; Holiday Special	3.50	0.70	1.75	3.50
❑SE 1, Feb 98, Yes, Jubilee-there is a Santa Clause, A: Orphan-Maker; A: Nanny	3.50	0.70	1.75	3.50

GENERATION X/GEN^{13}
MARVEL

	ORIG	GOOD	FINE	N-MINT
❑1, nn; wraparound cover; One-Shot; crossover with Image	3.99	0.80	2.00	4.00
❑1/A, variant cover	2.95	0.80	2.00	4.00

Marvel's *The Generic Comic* contained one super-hero, a story, and other basic elements.

© 1983 Marvel

GENERATION X UNDERGROUND
MARVEL

Value: Cover or less

- ❑1, May 98, The Big Game; Jubilee's Scrapbook, b&w; cardstock cover ... 2.50

GENERIC COMIC, THE
MARVEL

	ORIG	GOOD	FINE	N-MINT
❑1, Apr 83	0.60	0.50	1.25	2.50

GENESIS (DC)
DC

Value: Cover or less

- ❑1, Oct 97, JBy (w), Resonance ... 1.95
- ❑2, Oct 97, JBy (w) ... 1.95
- ❑3, Oct 97, JBy (w) ... 1.95
- ❑4, Oct 97, JBy (w) ... 1.95

GENESIS (MALIBU)
MALIBU

Value: Cover or less

- ❑0, Oct 93, CS; RB, Rock in a Hard Place; Revelations, foil cover 3.50

GENESIS: THE #1 COLLECTION
IMAGE

Value: Cover or less

- ❑1, Reprints Backlash #1, DV8 #1, Deathblow #1, Gen13 #1, Grifter #1, StormWatch #1, Union #1, Wetworks #1, WildC.A.T.s #1, Urban Storm ... 9.99

GENETIX
MARVEL

Value: Cover or less

- ❑1, Oct 93, Deadly Harvest, Part 1, A: Genetix, wraparound cover; trading cards ... 2.75
- ❑2, Nov 93, Deadly Harvest, Part 2 ... 1.75
- ❑3, Dec 93, Deadly Harvest, Part 3 ... 1.75
- ❑4, Jan 94, Deadly Harvest, Part 4 ... 1.75
- ❑5, Feb 94, Deadly Harvest, Part 5 ... 1.75
- ❑6, Mar 94, Deadly Harvest, Part 6 ... 1.75

GENOCIDE
RENEGADE TRIBE

Value: Cover or less

- ❑1, Aug 94 ... 2.95
- ❑1-2, Aug 94, 2nd Printing ... 2.95

GENOCYBER
VIZ

Value: Cover or less

- ❑1, b&w; Japanese ... 2.75
- ❑2, b&w; Japanese ... 2.75
- ❑3, The Birth of Genocyber, Part 2, b&w; Japanese ... 2.75
- ❑4, b&w; Japanese ... 2.75
- ❑5, b&w; Japanese ... 2.75

GEN OF HIROSHIMA
EDUCOMICS

	ORIG	GOOD	FINE	N-MINT
❑1, Jan 80	1.50	0.40	1.00	2.00
❑2	2.00	0.40	1.00	2.00

GENSAGA
EXPRESS

Value: Cover or less

- ❑1 ... 2.50

GENUS
ANTARCTIC

Value: Cover or less

- ❑1, May 93, Antarctic publishes 2.95
- ❑2, Sep 93 ... 2.95
- ❑3, Nov 93 ... 2.95
- ❑4, Jan 94 ... 2.95
- ❑5, Mar 94 ... 2.95
- ❑6, May 94 ... 2.95
- ❑7, Jul 94 ... 2.95
- ❑8, Sep 94 ... 2.95
- ❑9, Nov 94 ... 2.95
- ❑10, Jan 95 ... 3.50
- ❑11, Mar 95 ... 2.95
- ❑12, May 95, Terry Times Three; Rat & Ruin ... 2.95
- ❑13, Jul 95, Mink: Hometown Blues; Gainful Enjoyment ... 2.95
- ❑14, Sep 95 ... 2.95
- ❑15, Nov 95 ... 2.95
- ❑16, Jan 96 ... 2.95
- ❑17, Mar 96 ... 2.95
- ❑18, May 96 ... 2.95
- ❑19, Jul 96 ... 2.95
- ❑20, Sep 96 ... 3.95
- ❑21, Nov 96 ... 2.95
- ❑22, Jan 97, The Right Size; Savage Squirrels Dating Tips ... 2.95
- ❑23, Apr 97, all-skunk issue; Radio Comix publishes ... 2.95
- ❑24, Jun 97 ... 2.95
- ❑25, Aug 97 ... 2.95
- ❑26, Oct 97 ... 2.95
- ❑27, Dec 97 ... 2.95
- ❑28, Feb 98 ... 2.95
- ❑29, Apr 98 ... 2.95
- ❑30, Jun 98 ... 2.95
- ❑31, Aug 98 ... 2.95
- ❑32, Oct 98 ... 2.95
- ❑33, Dec 98 ... 2.95
- ❑34 ... 2.95

ORIG GOOD FINE N-MINT

❑35 2.95
❑36 2.95
❑37 2.95
❑38 2.95
❑39 2.95
❑40 2.95
❑41, Apr 00, Rat Maze; Crammin' 2.95
❑42, Jun 00, Anthony; Big Little Brother 2.95
❑43, Aug 00, Anthony; Collars & Cuffs 2.95

GENUS GREATEST HITS
ANTARCTIC
Value: Cover or less
❑1, Apr 96 4.50
❑2, May 97 4.95

GENUS SPOTLIGHT
RADIO
Value: Cover or less
❑1, Jul 98, Skunkworks 2.95
❑2, Nov 98, Skunkworks 2.95

GEOBREEDERS
CPM MANGA
Value: Cover or less
❑1 2.95
❑2 2.95
❑3 2.95
❑4 2.95
❑5 2.95
❑6 2.95
❑7 2.95
❑8 2.95
❑9 2.95
❑10 2.95
❑11 2.95
❑12 2.95
❑13 2.95
❑14 2.95
❑15 2.95
❑16 2.95
❑17 2.95
❑18 2.95
❑19 2.95
❑20 2.95
❑21 2.95
❑22 2.95
❑23 2.95
❑24 2.95
❑25 2.95
❑26 2.95
❑27 2.95
❑28 2.95
❑29 2.95

GEOMANCER
VALIANT
Value: Cover or less
❑1, Nov 94, Awakenings, 1: Clay McHenry; A: Eternal Warrior, Chromium wraparound cover 3.75
❑2, Dec 94, A: Eternal Warrior 2.25
❑3, Jan 95, Challenge 2.25
❑4, Feb 95 2.25
❑5, Mar 95, Riot Gear, Part 1, A: Turok 2.25
❑6, Apr 95, Riot Gear, Part 2, A: Turok 2.25
❑7, May 95 2.25
❑8, Jun 95, Final Issue 2.25

GEORGE OF THE JUNGLE
GOLD KEY

	ORIG	GOOD	FINE	N-MINT
❑1, Feb 69, George, Tom Slick, and Super Chicken stories	0.15	8.00	20.00	40.00
❑2, Oct 69, George, Tom Slick, and Super Chicken stories	0.15	5.00	12.50	25.00

GEPETTO FILES, THE
QUICK TO FLY
Value: Cover or less
❑1, Sep 98, Santa; Cold Timmy 3.00

GERIATRIC GANGRENE JUJITSU GERBILS
PLANET-X
Value: Cover or less
❑1, b&w 1.50
❑2 1.50

GERIATRICMAN
C&T
Value: Cover or less
❑1, b&w 1.75

GE ROUGE
VEROTIK
Value: Cover or less
❑0.5, Oct 98, adult 2.95
❑1, Glenn Danzig, adult 2.95
❑2, Glenn Danzig, adult 2.95
❑3, Glenn Danzig, adult 2.95

GERTIE THE DINOSAUR COMICS
GERTIE THE DINOSAUR
Value: Cover or less
❑1, Jul 00 2.95

GESTALT (CALIBER)
CALIBER
Value: Cover or less
❑0, From the Pages of Seeker 2.95

GESTALT (NEC)
NEW ENGLAND
Value: Cover or less
❑1, Apr 93, The Voices of Delirium, b&w 1.95
❑2 1.95

GET ALONG GANG
MARVEL

	ORIG	GOOD	FINE	N-MINT
❑1, May 85, The Ice Cold Mystery; Getting Ready	0.65	0.20	0.50	1.00
❑2	0.65	0.20	0.50	1.00
❑3	0.65	0.20	0.50	1.00
❑4	0.65	0.20	0.50	1.00
❑5	0.65	0.20	0.50	1.00
❑6	0.65	0.20	0.50	1.00

GET LOST (VOL. 2)
NEW COMICS
Value: Cover or less
❑1, b&w; Reprint 1.95
❑2, RA, RA (w), The Invincible Mr. Mann; I Killed Cock Robin, b&w; Reprint 1.95
❑3, BB (c), They Called Him Sam; Der Spider Und Der Fly, b&w; Reprint 1.95

GET REAL COMICS
TIDES CENTER
Value: Cover or less
❑1 1.95

GET SMART
DELL

	ORIG	GOOD	FINE	N-MINT
❑1, Jun 66	0.12	8.00	20.00	40.00
❑2, Sep 66	0.12	5.60	14.00	28.00
❑3, Nov 66	0.12	4.00	10.00	20.00
❑4, Jan 67	0.12	4.00	10.00	20.00
❑5, Mar 67	0.12	4.00	10.00	20.00
❑6, Apr 67	0.12	3.60	9.00	18.00
❑7, Jun 67, four-color	0.12	3.60	9.00	18.00
❑8, Sep 67	0.12	3.60	9.00	18.00

GHETTO BITCH
EROS
Value: Cover or less
❑1, b&w; adult 2.75

GHETTO BLASTERS, THE
WHIPLASH
Value: Cover or less
❑1, Sep 97, b&w 2.50

GHOST
DARK HORSE
Value: Cover or less
❑1, Apr 95, Arcadia Nocturne, Part 1 2.50
❑2, May 95, Arcadia Nocturne, Part 2 2.50
❑3, Jun 95, Arcadia Nocturne, Part 3 2.50
❑4, Jul 95, A: Barb Wire 2.50
❑5, Aug 95, V: Predator 2.50
❑6, Sep 95 2.50
❑7, Oct 95 2.50
❑8, Nov 95 2.50
❑9, Dec 95, A: X 2.50
❑10, Jan 96 2.50
❑11, Feb 96, Crack in the Wall 2.50
❑12, Mar 96, preview of Ghost/Hellboy crossover 2.50
❑13, Apr 96 2.50
❑14, May 96 2.50
❑15, Jun 96, A: X 2.50
❑16, Jul 96, Hell and Back 2.50
❑17, Aug 96, Dead City 2.50
❑18, Sep 96, Black Heart, Part 1, A: Barb Wire 2.50
❑19, Nov 96, Black Heart, Part 2, A: Barb Wire 2.50
❑20, Dec 96, Exhuming Elisa, Part 1 2.50
❑21, Jan 97, Exhuming Elisa, Part 2, A: X 2.50
❑22, Feb 97, Exhuming Elisa, Part 3 2.50
❑23, Mar 97, Exhuming Elisa, Part 4 2.50
❑24, Apr 97, Exhuming Elisa, Part 5 2.50
❑25, May 97, Elisa Exhumed, A: X; D: Crux; A: King Tiger; O: Ghost, 48pgs.; photo front and back covers; Giant-size 3.50
❑26, Jun 97, October Knight 2.95
❑27, Jul 97, October Day 2.95
❑28, Aug 97, Painful Music, Part 1 2.95
❑29, Sep 97, Painful Music, Part 2, flip-book with Timecop story 2.95
❑30, Oct 97, Painful Music, Part 3 2.95
❑31, Nov 97, Painful Music, Part 4 2.95
❑32, Dec 97, A Pathless Land. 2.95
❑33, Jan 98, Jade Cathedral, Part 1 2.95
❑34, Feb 98, Jade Cathedral, Part 2 2.95
❑35, Mar 98, Jade Cathedral, Part 3 2.95
❑36, Apr 98, Jade Cathedral, Part 4 2.95
❑SE 1, Jul 94, Ghost Special 3.95
❑SE 2, Jun 98, Photo cover; Immortal Coil 3.95
❑SE 3, Dec 98, Scary Monsters 3.95

GHOST (VOL. 2)
DARK HORSE

	ORIG	GOOD	FINE	N-MINT
❑1, Sep 98, No World So Dark	2.95	0.70	1.75	3.50
❑2, Oct 98	2.95	0.60	1.50	3.00
❑3, Nov 98	2.95	0.60	1.50	3.00
❑4, Dec 98, Stare at the Sun, Part 1	2.95	0.60	1.50	3.00
❑5, Jan 99, Stare at the Sun, Part 2	2.95	0.60	1.50	3.00
❑6, Feb 99, Stare at the Sun, Part 3	2.95	0.59	1.48	2.95
❑7, Mar 99, Shifter, Part 1	2.95	0.59	1.48	2.95
❑8, Apr 99, Shifter, Part 2	2.95	0.59	1.48	2.95
❑9, May 99, Shifter, Part 3	2.95	0.59	1.48	2.95
❑10, Jun 99, Shifter, Part 4, A: Vortex	2.95	0.59	1.48	2.95
❑11, Jul 99, Blood & Roses	2.95	0.59	1.48	2.95
❑12, Sep 99, Red Shadows, Part 1	2.95	0.59	1.48	2.95
❑13, Oct 99, Red Shadows, Part 2	2.95	0.59	1.48	2.95
❑14, Nov 99, Red Shadows, Part 3	2.95	0.59	1.48	2.95
❑15, Dec 99, Red Shadows, Part 4	2.95	0.59	1.48	2.95
❑16, Jan 00, When the Devil Daydreams, Part 1	2.95	0.59	1.48	2.95
❑17, Feb 00	2.95	0.59	1.48	2.95
❑18, Mar 00	2.95	0.59	1.48	2.95
❑19, Apr 00, Wish in One Hand...	2.95	0.59	1.48	2.95
❑20, Jun 00	2.95	0.59	1.48	2.95
❑21, Jul 00, A: X	2.95	0.59	1.48	2.95
❑22, Aug 00, Caesura	2.95	0.59	1.48	2.95

GHOST AND THE SHADOW
DARK HORSE
Value: Cover or less
❑1, Dec 95, nn; One-Shot 2.95

GHOST/BATGIRL
DARK HORSE
Value: Cover or less
❑1, The Resurrection Engine, Part 1 2.95
❑2, Oct 00, The Resurrection Engine, Part 2 2.95
❑3, Nov 00, The Resurrection Engine, Part 3 2.99
❑4, Dec 00, The Resurrection Engine, Part 4 2.99

GHOSTBUSTERS
First

	ORIG	GOOD	FINE	N-MINT
❑1, A Halloween Haunting	1.25	0.30	0.75	1.50
❑2	1.25	0.30	0.75	1.50
❑3	1.25	0.30	0.75	1.50
❑4	1.25	0.30	0.75	1.50
❑5	1.25	0.30	0.75	1.50
❑6	1.25	0.30	0.75	1.50

GHOSTBUSTERS II
Now

	ORIG	GOOD	FINE	N-MINT
❑1, Oct 89, Together Again For The First Time, Part 2, movie Adaptation	1.95	0.40	1.00	2.00
❑2, Nov 89, The Slime of their Lives, movie Adaptation	1.95	0.40	1.00	2.00
❑3, Dec 89, movie Adaptation	1.95	0.40	1.00	2.00

GHOSTDANCING
DC

Value: Cover or less

- ❑1, Mar 95, First Tremor 1.95
- ❑2, Apr 95, Second Tremor 1.95
- ❑3, Jun 95, Third Tremor 2.50
- ❑4, Jul 95 .... 2.50
- ❑5, Aug 95, Fifth Tremor 2.50
- ❑6, Sep 95, The Big One 2.50

GHOST HANDBOOK
Dark Horse

Value: Cover or less

- ❑1, Aug 99, nn; background on characters 2.95

GHOST/HELLBOY SPECIAL
Dark Horse

Value: Cover or less

- ❑1, May 96 .... 2.50
- ❑2, Jun 96, Final Issue 2.50

GHOST IN THE SHELL
Dark Horse

	ORIG	GOOD	FINE	N-MINT
❑1, Mar 95	3.95	3.00	7.50	15.00
❑2, Apr 95	3.95	2.00	5.00	10.00
❑3, Apr 95	3.95	1.60	4.00	8.00
❑4, Jun 95	3.95	1.60	4.00	8.00
❑5, Jul 95	3.95	1.20	3.00	6.00
❑6, Aug 95	3.95	1.20	3.00	6.00
❑7, Sep 95	3.95	1.00	2.50	5.00
❑8, Oct 95, Final Issue	3.95	1.00	2.50	5.00

GHOST RIDER, THE
Marvel

	ORIG	GOOD	FINE	N-MINT
❑1, Feb 67, The Origin of The Ghost Rider; Kid Colt Outlaw: The Menace of the Mask Maker, 1: Ghost Rider, Western; back-up reprints story from Kid Colt Outlaw #105	0.12	4.80	12.00	24.00
❑2, Apr 67, V: Tarantula, Western; back-up reprints story from Kid Colt Outlaw #99	0.12	3.00	7.50	15.00
❑3, Jun 67, Western; back-up reprints story from Kid Colt Outlaw #116	0.12	3.00	7.50	15.00
❑4, Aug 67, A: Tarantula; V: Sting-Ray a.k.a. Scorpion, Western; back-up reprints story from Two-Gun Kid #69	0.12	2.00	5.00	10.00
❑5, Sep 67, V: Tarantula, Western	0.12	2.00	5.00	10.00
❑6, Oct 67, V: Towering Oak, Western	0.12	2.00	5.00	10.00
❑7, Nov 67, Final Issue; Western	0.12	2.00	5.00	10.00

GHOST RIDER (VOL. 1)
Marvel

	ORIG	GOOD	FINE	N-MINT
❑1, Aug 73, GK, 1: Son of Satan (partially shown)	0.20	6.00	15.00	30.00
❑2, Oct 73	0.20	2.80	7.00	14.00
❑3, Dec 73, JM, Wheels On Fire	0.20	1.80	4.50	9.00
❑4, Feb 74, JM, Death Stalks Demolition Derby	0.20	1.80	4.50	9.00
❑5, Apr 74	0.20	1.80	4.50	9.00
❑6, Jun 74	0.25	1.40	3.50	7.00
❑7, Aug 74	0.20	1.40	3.50	7.00
❑8, Oct 74, JM, Satan Himself!, 1: Inferno; A: Roxanne	0.20	1.20	3.00	6.00
❑9, Dec 74	0.20	1.20	3.00	6.00
❑10, Feb 75, A: Hulk	0.20	1.20	3.00	6.00
❑11, Apr 75, KJ; GK; SB, A: Hulk	0.25	0.90	2.25	4.50
❑12, Jun 75, D: Phantom Eagle	0.25	0.90	2.25	4.50
❑13, Aug 75	0.25	0.90	2.25	4.50
❑14, Oct 75	0.25	0.90	2.25	4.50
❑15, Dec 75	0.25	0.90	2.25	4.50
❑16, Feb 76	0.25	0.90	2.25	4.50
❑17, Apr 76	0.25	0.90	2.25	4.50
❑18, Jun 76, A: Spider-Man	0.25	0.90	2.25	4.50
❑19, Aug 76	0.25	0.90	2.25	4.50
❑20, Oct 76, KJ; GK; JBy, A: Daredevil	0.30	1.20	3.00	6.00
❑21, Dec 76, D: Eel I (Leopold Stryke)	0.30	0.70	1.75	3.50
❑22, Feb 77, 1: Enforcer (Marvel)	0.30	0.70	1.75	3.50
❑23, Apr 77, 1: Water Wizard	0.30	0.70	1.75	3.50
❑24, Jun 77	0.30	0.70	1.75	3.50
❑25, Aug 77	0.30	0.70	1.75	3.50
❑26, Oct 77	0.30	0.70	1.75	3.50
❑27, Dec 77	0.35	0.70	1.75	3.50

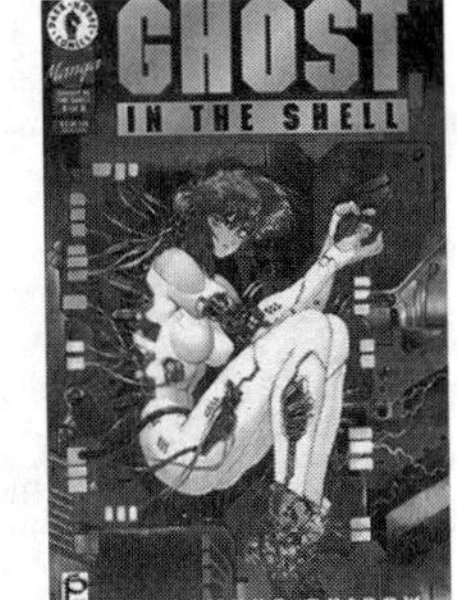

Ghost in the Shell is the story of a computer intelligence that gains sentience.

	ORIG	GOOD	FINE	N-MINT
❑28, Feb 78	0.35	0.70	1.75	3.50
❑29, Apr 78	0.35	0.70	1.75	3.50
❑30, Jun 78	0.35	0.70	1.75	3.50
❑31, Aug 78	0.35	0.50	1.25	2.50
❑32, Oct 78	0.35	0.50	1.25	2.50
❑33, Dec 78	0.35	0.50	1.25	2.50
❑34, Feb 79	0.35	0.50	1.25	2.50
❑35, Apr 79	0.35	0.50	1.25	2.50
❑36, Jun 79	0.40	0.50	1.25	2.50
❑37, Aug 79	0.40	0.50	1.25	2.50
❑38, Oct 79	0.40	0.50	1.25	2.50
❑39, Dec 79	0.40	0.50	1.25	2.50
❑40, Jan 80	0.40	0.50	1.25	2.50
❑41, Feb 80	0.40	0.50	1.25	2.50
❑42, Mar 80	0.40	0.50	1.25	2.50
❑43, Apr 80	0.40	0.50	1.25	2.50
❑44, May 80	0.40	0.50	1.25	2.50
❑45, Jun 80	0.40	0.50	1.25	2.50
❑46, Jul 80	0.40	0.50	1.25	2.50
❑47, Aug 80	0.40	0.50	1.25	2.50
❑48, Sep 80	0.50	0.50	1.25	2.50
❑49, Oct 80	0.50	0.50	1.25	2.50
❑50, Nov 80, DP, A: Night Rider, Giant-size	0.75	0.80	2.00	4.00
❑51, Dec 80	0.50	0.50	1.25	2.50
❑52, Jan 81	0.50	0.50	1.25	2.50
❑53, Feb 81	0.50	0.50	1.25	2.50
❑54, Mar 81	0.50	0.50	1.25	2.50
❑55, Apr 81	0.50	0.50	1.25	2.50
❑56, May 81, 1: Night Rider II (Hamilton Slade)	0.50	0.50	1.25	2.50
❑57, Jun 81	0.50	0.50	1.25	2.50
❑58, Jul 81	0.50	0.50	1.25	2.50
❑59, Aug 81	0.50	0.50	1.25	2.50
❑60, Sep 81	0.50	0.50	1.25	2.50
❑61, Oct 81	0.50	0.50	1.25	2.50
❑62, Nov 81	0.50	0.50	1.25	2.50
❑63, Dec 81	0.50	0.50	1.25	2.50
❑64, Jan 82	0.60	0.50	1.25	2.50
❑65, Feb 82	0.60	0.50	1.25	2.50
❑66, Mar 82	0.60	0.50	1.25	2.50
❑67, Apr 82	0.60	0.50	1.25	2.50
❑68, May 82, O: Ghost Rider (Johnny Blaze)	0.60	0.60	1.50	3.00
❑69, Jun 82	0.60	0.50	1.25	2.50
❑70, Jul 82	0.60	0.50	1.25	2.50
❑71, Aug 82	0.60	0.50	1.25	2.50
❑72, Sep 82, 1: Fire-Eater	0.60	0.50	1.25	2.50
❑73, Oct 82	0.60	0.50	1.25	2.50
❑74, Nov 82, 1: Centurius	0.60	0.50	1.25	2.50
❑75, Dec 82	0.60	0.50	1.25	2.50
❑76, Jan 83	0.60	0.50	1.25	2.50
❑77, Feb 83, O: Centurius; O: Zarathos	0.60	0.50	1.25	2.50
❑78, Mar 83	0.60	0.50	1.25	2.50
❑79, Apr 83	0.60	0.50	1.25	2.50
❑80, May 83, O: Centurius	0.60	0.50	1.25	2.50
❑81, Jun 83, D: Ghost Rider, Zarathos leaves Johnny Blaze-end of Ghost Rider I	0.60	0.70	1.75	3.50

GHOST RIDER (VOL. 2)
Marvel

	ORIG	GOOD	FINE	N-MINT
❑-1, Jul 97, Flashback	1.95	0.39	0.98	1.95
❑1, May 90, Life's Blood, 1: Deathwatch; 1: Ghost Rider II (Dan Ketch)	1.95	0.60	1.50	3.00
❑1-2, Sep 90, 1: Deathwatch; 1: Ghost Rider II (Dan Ketch), 2nd Printing (gold)	1.95	0.39	0.98	1.95
❑2, Jun 90, Do Be Afraid Of The Dark!, 1: Blackout II	1.50	0.40	1.00	2.00
❑3, Jul 90, Death Watch, V: Deathwatch; V: Kingpin; V: Blackout	1.50	0.40	1.00	2.00
❑4, Aug 90, V: Mr. Hyde, Scarcer	1.50	0.40	1.00	2.00
❑5, Sep 90, Getting Paid!, A: Punisher	1.50	0.40	1.00	2.00
❑5/SC, Jun 94, Getting Paid!, A: Punisher, Die-cut cover	2.95	0.59	1.48	2.95
❑5-2, Sep 90, Getting Paid!, A: Punisher, 2nd printing (gold)	1.50	0.30	0.75	1.50

	ORIG	GOOD	FINE	N-MINT
❑6, Oct 90, A: Punisher	1.50	0.40	1.00	2.00
❑7, Nov 90, V: Scarecrow	1.50	0.40	1.00	2.00
❑8, Dec 90	1.50	0.40	1.00	2.00
❑9, Jan 91, A: X-Factor	1.50	0.40	1.00	2.00
❑10, Feb 91, Stars Of Blood	1.50	0.40	1.00	2.00
❑11, Mar 91	1.50	0.30	0.75	1.50
❑12, Apr 91, A: Doctor Strange	1.50	0.30	0.75	1.50
❑13, May 91, 1: Snowblind; A: Doctor Strange	1.50	0.30	0.75	1.50
❑14, Jun 91, Johnny Blaze; Ghost Rider vs. Johnny Blaze	1.50	0.30	0.75	1.50
❑15, Jul 91, Last Hope, glow in the dark cover	1.75	0.40	1.00	2.00
❑15-2, Last Hope, glow in the dark cover; 2nd Printing (gold)	1.75	0.40	1.00	2.00
❑16, Aug 91, A: Johnny Blaze; A: Spider-Man; A: Hobgoblin	1.75	0.35	0.88	1.75
❑17, Sep 91, You've Got to Have Faith, A: Spider-Man; A: Hobgoblin	1.75	0.35	0.88	1.75
❑18, Oct 91, Lost Souls!, Painted cover	1.75	0.35	0.88	1.75
❑19, Nov 91, The Deal	1.75	0.35	0.88	1.75
❑20, Dec 91, Sign Of Death	1.75	0.35	0.88	1.75
❑21, Jan 92, Bad To The Bone!	1.75	0.35	0.88	1.75
❑22, Feb 92, Death's Eyes	1.75	0.35	0.88	1.75
❑23, Mar 92, Death Drive, V: Deathwatch	1.75	0.35	0.88	1.75
❑24, Apr 92, Death Duel, D: Snowblind; V: Deathwatch	1.75	0.35	0.88	1.75
❑25, May 92, You Can't Go Home Again, Pop-up centerfold, double-sized	2.75	0.40	1.00	2.00
❑26, Jun 92, ...Blood Feud!, A: X-Men	1.75	0.35	0.88	1.75
❑27, Jul 92, Vengeance. Pure And Simple., A: X-Men	1.75	0.35	0.88	1.75
❑28, Aug 92, Rise of the Midnight Sons, Part 1, 1: Lilith II, poster	2.50	0.50	1.25	2.50
❑29, Sep 92, Biting the Hand that Feeds You!, A: Beast; A: Wolverine	1.75	0.35	0.88	1.75
❑30, Oct 92, Nightmares of Truth, V: Nightmare	1.75	0.35	0.88	1.75
❑31, Nov 92, Rise of the Midnight Sons, Part 6, poster	2.50	0.50	1.25	2.50
❑32, Dec 92, Fight For Life	1.75	0.35	0.88	1.75
❑33, Jan 93, What Does it Matter?	1.75	0.35	0.88	1.75
❑34, Feb 93, Victims Of Our Past	1.75	0.35	0.88	1.75
❑35, Mar 93, You Can't Always Get What You Want	1.75	0.35	0.88	1.75
❑36, Apr 93, Transformations In Pain	1.75	0.35	0.88	1.75
❑37, May 93, Forward to the Shadows	1.75	0.35	0.88	1.75
❑38, Jun 93, Blood Obligations	1.75	0.35	0.88	1.75
❑39, Jul 93	1.75	0.35	0.88	1.75
❑40, Aug 93, black cover	2.25	0.45	1.13	2.25
❑41, Sep 93	1.75	0.35	0.88	1.75
❑42, Oct 93, Road to Vengeance: The Missing Link, Part 3, A: John Blaze; A: Ghostie; A: Centurius; A: Deathwatch, Neon cover	1.75	0.35	0.88	1.75
❑43, Nov 93, Road to Vengeance: The Missing Link	1.75	0.35	0.88	1.75
❑44, Dec 93, Siege of Darkness, Part 2, Neon cover	1.75	0.35	0.88	1.75
❑45, Jan 94, Siege of Darkness, Part 10, Spot-varnished cover	1.75	0.35	0.88	1.75
❑46, Feb 94, If a Skull Could Weep...	1.75	0.35	0.88	1.75
❑47, Mar 94, Under Fire, Part 1	1.75	0.35	0.88	1.75
❑48, Apr 94, Under Fire, Part 2, A: Spider-Man	1.75	0.35	0.88	1.75
❑49, May 94, Under Fire, Part 3	1.75	0.35	0.88	1.75
❑50, Jun 94, Reborn Again, foil cover; Giant-size	2.50	0.50	1.25	2.50
❑50/SC, Reborn Again; A Lover's Eyes, Die-cut cover; Giant-size	2.95	0.59	1.48	2.95
❑51, Jul 94	1.95	0.39	0.98	1.95
❑52, Aug 94, A Trail of Flames	1.95	0.39	0.98	1.95
❑53, Sep 94, Reunions	1.95	0.39	0.98	1.95
❑54, Oct 94, A Thirst for Celebrity	1.95	0.39	0.98	1.95
❑55, Nov 94	1.95	0.39	0.98	1.95
❑56, Dec 94	1.95	0.39	0.98	1.95
❑57, Jan 95, Where to Life?, A: Wolverine	1.95	0.39	0.98	1.95
❑58, Feb 95, Betrayals, Part 1	1.95	0.39	0.98	1.95
❑59, Mar 95, Betrayals, Part 1; Betrayals, Part 2	1.95	0.39	0.98	1.95
❑60, Apr 95, Betrayals, Part 2; Betrayals, Part 3	1.95	0.39	0.98	1.95
❑61, May 95, Betrayals, Part 3; Betrayals, Part 4, Giant-size	2.50	0.50	1.25	2.50
❑62, Jun 95, In Chains, Part 1	1.95	0.39	0.98	1.95
❑63, Jul 95, In Chains, Part 2	1.95	0.39	0.98	1.95
❑64, Aug 95, In Chains, Part 3	1.95	0.39	0.98	1.95
❑65, Sep 95, In Chains, Part 4 Over the Edge; In Chains, Part 4	1.95	0.39	0.98	1.95
❑66, Oct 95, D: Blackout	1.95	0.39	0.98	1.95
❑67, Nov 95, A: Gambit	1.95	0.39	0.98	1.95
❑68, Dec 95, A: Wolverine; A: Gambit	1.95	0.39	0.98	1.95
❑69, Jan 96	1.95	0.39	0.98	1.95
❑70, Feb 96	1.95	0.39	0.98	1.95
❑71, Mar 96, Blue Shadows	1.95	0.39	0.98	1.95
❑72, Apr 96	1.95	0.39	0.98	1.95
❑73, May 96, V: Snowblind	1.95	0.39	0.98	1.95
❑74, Jun 96	1.95	0.39	0.98	1.95
❑75, Jul 96	1.50	0.30	0.75	1.50
❑76, Aug 96	1.50	0.30	0.75	1.50
❑77, Sep 96, A: Doctor Strange	1.50	0.30	0.75	1.50
❑78, Oct 96	1.50	0.30	0.75	1.50
❑79, Nov 96	1.50	0.30	0.75	1.50
❑80, Dec 96, Storm Of Blood	1.50	0.30	0.75	1.50
❑81, Jan 97, Caught Between A Duck And A Hard Place, A: Howard the Duck	1.50	0.30	0.75	1.50
❑82, Feb 97, The Duck and the Amok, A: Moonboy; A: Howard the Duck; A: Devil Dinosaur	1.50	0.30	0.75	1.50
❑83, Mar 97, House of Burning Souls	1.95	0.39	0.98	1.95
❑84, Apr 97, Loss of Blood	1.95	0.39	0.98	1.95
❑85, May 97, Ashes of my Soul, A: Scarecrow	1.95	0.39	0.98	1.95
❑86, Jun 97, Faultlines	1.95	0.39	0.98	1.95
❑87, Aug 97, Wallow, gatefold summary	1.99	0.39	0.98	1.95
❑88, Sep 97, A Kind Face, gatefold summary	1.99	0.39	0.98	1.95
❑89, Oct 97, Doghead & Spiked Tails, gatefold summary	1.99	0.39	0.98	1.95
❑90, Nov 97, The Last Temptation, Part 1, gatefold summary	1.99	0.39	0.98	1.95
❑91, Dec 97, Down Among the Dead Men..., gatefold summary	1.99	0.39	0.98	1.95
❑92, Jan 98, gatefold summary	1.99	0.39	0.98	1.95
❑93, Feb 98, Final Issue; gatefold summary; Giant-size	2.99	0.60	1.50	2.99
❑Anl 1, trading card	2.95	0.59	1.48	2.95
❑Anl 2, Wish for Pain; Raising Cain, V: Scarecrow	2.95	0.59	1.48	2.95

GHOST RIDER 2099

MARVEL

	ORIG	GOOD	FINE	N-MINT
❑1, May 94, Burning Chrome, 1: Ghost Rider 2099	1.50	0.40	1.00	2.00
❑1/CS, May 94, Burning Chrome, Poly-bagged with trading card	2.25	0.50	1.25	2.50
❑2, Jun 94, Detonation Boulevard, Poly-bagged with poster	1.50	0.30	0.75	1.50
❑3, Jul 94	1.50	0.30	0.75	1.50
❑4, Aug 94	1.50	0.30	0.75	1.50
❑5, Sep 94	1.50	0.30	0.75	1.50
❑6, Oct 94	1.50	0.30	0.75	1.50
❑7, Nov 94	1.50	0.30	0.75	1.50
❑8, Dec 94	1.50	0.30	0.75	1.50
❑9, Jan 95	1.50	0.30	0.75	1.50
❑10, Feb 95	1.50	0.30	0.75	1.50
❑11, Mar 95	1.50	0.30	0.75	1.50
❑12, Apr 95	1.50	0.30	0.75	1.50
❑13, May 95	1.95	0.39	0.98	1.95
❑14, Jun 95	1.95	0.39	0.98	1.95
❑15, Jul 95, 1: Heartbreaker	1.95	0.39	0.98	1.95
❑16, Aug 95	1.95	0.39	0.98	1.95
❑17, Sep 95	1.95	0.39	0.98	1.95
❑18, Oct 95	1.95	0.39	0.98	1.95
❑19, Nov 95	1.95	0.39	0.98	1.95
❑20, Dec 95, A: Zero Cochrane; A: Arch-fiends; A: Heartbreaker; A: L-Cypher	1.95	0.39	0.98	1.95
❑21, Jan 96	1.95	0.39	0.98	1.95
❑22, Feb 96	1.95	0.39	0.98	1.95
❑23, Mar 96, Bad Craziness	1.95	0.39	0.98	1.95
❑24, Apr 96, Road To Ruin	1.95	0.39	0.98	1.95
❑25, May 96, wraparound cover; Final Issue; double-sized	2.95	0.50	1.25	2.50

GHOST RIDER & CABLE: SERVANTS OF THE DEAD

MARVEL

Value: Cover or less

❑1, Sep 91, cardstock cover; no indicia; Reprints Ghost Rider/Cable series from Marvel Comics Presents 3.95

GHOST RIDER AND THE MIDNIGHT SONS MAGAZINE

MARVEL

Value: Cover or less

❑1 .... 3.95

GHOST RIDER/BALLISTIC

MARVEL

Value: Cover or less

❑1, Feb 97, Devil's Reign, Part 3; Devil's Reign, crossover with Top Cow; continues in Ballistic/Wolverine 2.95

GHOST RIDER/BLAZE: SPIRITS OF VENGEANCE

MARVEL

Value: Cover or less

❑1, Aug 92, Rise of the Midnight Sons, Part 2, without poster 2.75
❑1/CS, Rise of the Midnight Sons, Part 2, poster 2.75
❑2, Sep 92, Steel Vengeance 1.75
❑3, Oct 92, Fathers 1.75
❑4, Nov 92 .... 1.75
❑5, Dec 92, Spirits of Venom, Part 2, Venom 1.75
❑6, Jan 93, Spirits of Venom, Part 4 .... 1.75
❑7, Feb 93 .... 1.75
❑8, Mar 93, Devil Dance 1.75
❑9, Apr 93, Carnival of Death, Part 1 .... 1.75

ORIG GOOD FINE N-MINT

- ❑10, May 93, Carnival of Death, Part 2 .... 1.75
- ❑11, Jun 93 .... 1.75
- ❑12, Jul 93, Obligations, Glow-in-the-dark cover 2.75
- ❑13, Aug 93, Midnight Massacre, Part 5, black cover 2.50
- ❑14, Sep 93, Truth is Only Skin Deep 1.75
- ❑15, Oct 93, Road to Vengeance, Part 4, A: Vengeance; A: Centurious; A: Lilith, Neon ink cover; Blaze's new costume and powers 1.75
- ❑16, Nov 93 .... 1.75
- ❑17, Dec 93, Siege of Darkness, Part 8, Neon inks on cover.. 1.75
- ❑18, Jan 94, Siege of Darkness, Part 16, Spot-varnished cover 1.75
- ❑19, Feb 94, Alone! 1.75
- ❑20, Mar 94 .... 1.75
- ❑21, Apr 94 .... 1.75
- ❑22, May 94 .... 1.95
- ❑23, Jun 94, An Ending, Final Issue 1.95

GHOST RIDER/CAPTAIN AMERICA: FEAR
MARVEL

Value: Cover or less

- ❑1, Oct 92, nn; Fold-out cover 5.95

GHOST RIDER: CROSSROADS
MARVEL

Value: Cover or less

- ❑1, Dec 95, A: Ghost Rider I (Johnny Blaze); A: Ghost Rider II (Dan Ketch), enhanced wrap-around cardstock cover; One-Shot 3.95

GHOST RIDER POSTER MAGAZINE
MARVEL

Value: Cover or less

- ❑1 .... 4.95

GHOST RIDER; WOLVERINE; PUNISHER: THE DARK DESIGN
MARVEL

Value: Cover or less

- ❑1, Dec 91, D: Mephisto, Double fold-out cover; squarebound 5.95

GHOST SHIP
SLAVE LABOR

Value: Cover or less

- ❑1, Mar 96, Scurvy; Nikolas Leads to Harder Things, b&w; cardstock cover 3.50
- ❑2, Jun 96, Crucial Beast; I Just Want One Real Friend in This World, b&w; cardstock cover 2.95
- ❑3, Oct 96, Father's Day; How Eynops Fell in Love, b&w; cardstock cover 2.95

GHOSTS OF DRACULA
ETERNITY

Value: Cover or less

- ❑1, b&w 2.50
- ❑2, b&w 2.50
- ❑3, b&w 2.50
- ❑4, b&w 2.50
- ❑5, b&w 2.50

GHOST STORIES
DELL

	ORIG	GOOD	FINE	N-MINT
❑1	—	6.00	15.00	30.00
❑2	—	3.20	8.00	16.00
❑3	—	2.00	5.00	10.00
❑4	—	2.00	5.00	10.00
❑5	—	2.00	5.00	10.00
❑6	—	1.60	4.00	8.00
❑7	—	1.60	4.00	8.00
❑8	—	1.60	4.00	8.00
❑9	—	1.60	4.00	8.00
❑10	—	1.60	4.00	8.00
❑11	—	1.20	3.00	6.00
❑12	—	1.20	3.00	6.00
❑13, Mar 66, Final Encounter; Dead Heat	0.12	1.20	3.00	6.00
❑14	—	1.20	3.00	6.00
❑15	—	1.20	3.00	6.00
❑16	—	1.20	3.00	6.00
❑17	—	1.20	3.00	6.00
❑18	—	1.20	3.00	6.00
❑19	—	1.20	3.00	6.00
❑20	—	1.20	3.00	6.00
❑21	—	1.00	2.50	5.00
❑22	—	1.00	2.50	5.00
❑23, Jan 70	0.15	1.00	2.50	5.00
❑24, To My Killer with Affection; Have I Been Here Before?	0.15	1.00	2.50	5.00
❑25	0.15	1.00	2.50	5.00
❑26	0.15	1.00	2.50	5.00
❑27, Jan 71, Larger than Life; Blood Will Tell	0.15	1.00	2.50	5.00
❑28, Piece of the Past!; Needed: One Miracle!	0.15	1.00	2.50	5.00
❑29	—	1.00	2.50	5.00
❑30	—	1.00	2.50	5.00
❑31	—	1.00	2.50	5.00
❑32	—	1.00	2.50	5.00
❑33	—	1.00	2.50	5.00
❑34	—	1.00	2.50	5.00
❑35	—	1.00	2.50	5.00
❑36	—	1.00	2.50	5.00
❑37, Final Issue	—	1.00	2.50	5.00

GHOULS
ETERNITY

Value: Cover or less

- ❑1, b&w; Reprint 2.25

The origins of various aspects of Kang the Conqueror were revealed in *Giant-Size Avengers* #2 and #3.

© 1974 Marvel

GIANT BATMAN ANNUAL REPLICA EDITION
DC

	ORIG	GOOD	FINE	N-MINT
❑1, cardstock cover; reprints Batman Annual #1	4.95	1.00	2.50	5.00

GIANTKILLER
DC

Value: Cover or less

- ❑1, Aug 99 .... 2.50
- ❑2, Sep 99 .... 2.50
- ❑3, Oct 99 .... 2.50
- ❑4, Nov 99 .... 2.50
- ❑5, Dec 99 .... 2.50
- ❑6, Jan 00 .... 2.50

GIANTKILLER A TO Z
DC

Value: Cover or less

- ❑1, Aug 99, nn; no indicia; biographical monster information 2.50

GIANT-SIZE AMAZING SPIDER-MAN
MARVEL

Value: Cover or less

- ❑1, Aug 99, 80pgs.; cardstock cover; reprints stories from Spider-Man Adventures #6, #11, #12, and Marvel Tales #205 .... 4.50

GIANT-SIZE AVENGERS
MARVEL

	ORIG	GOOD	FINE	N-MINT
❑1, Aug 74, RB, 1: Whizzer I (Robert Frank); D: Miss America, Reprint	0.50	2.40	6.00	12.00
❑2, Nov 74, DC, A Blast From the Past, D: Swordsman; O: Rama-Tut, reprints Fantastic Four #19 (Rama-Tut)	0.50	1.20	3.00	6.00
❑3, Feb 75, DC, What Time Hath Put Asunder, O: Kang; A: Frankenstein's Monster; A: Human Torch; O: Immortus; A: Zemo; A: Wonder Man, continued from Avengers #132; reprints Avengers #2	0.50	1.20	3.00	6.00
❑4, DH, Let All Men Bring Together, Wedding of Vision and Scarlet Witch; Wedding of Vision & Scarlet Witch	0.50	1.20	3.00	6.00
❑5, Dec 75, The Monstrous Master Plan of the Mandarin, Reprint	0.50	1.00	2.50	5.00

GIANT-SIZE CAPTAIN AMERICA
MARVEL

	ORIG	GOOD	FINE	N-MINT
❑1, O: Captain America	0.50	2.80	7.00	14.00

GIANT-SIZE CAPTAIN MARVEL
MARVEL

	ORIG	GOOD	FINE	N-MINT
❑1, A: Captain America; A: Hulk, Reprint	0.50	2.00	5.00	10.00

GIANT-SIZE CHILLERS (1ST SERIES)
MARVEL

	ORIG	GOOD	FINE	N-MINT
❑1, Jun 74, GC, 1: Lilith, Dracula	0.35	2.60	6.50	13.00

GIANT-SIZE CHILLERS (2ND SERIES)
MARVEL

	ORIG	GOOD	FINE	N-MINT
❑1	0.50	1.80	4.50	9.00
❑2	0.50	1.20	3.00	6.00
❑3	0.50	1.20	3.00	6.00

GIANT-SIZE CONAN
MARVEL

	ORIG	GOOD	FINE	N-MINT
❑1, Sep 74, GK; BB; TS, 1: BTlit	0.50	1.00	2.50	5.00
❑2, Dec 74, TS, Conan Bound!	0.50	0.80	2.00	4.00
❑3, Apr 75, GK, To Tarantia-And The Tower	0.50	0.80	2.00	4.00
❑4, Jun 75, GK, Swords Of The South	0.50	0.80	2.00	4.00
❑5, Jun 75, A Sword Called Stormbringer	0.50	0.80	2.00	4.00

GIANT-SIZE CREATURES
MARVEL

	ORIG	GOOD	FINE	N-MINT
❑1, Jul 74, DP, Tigra the Were-Woman!; Where Walks the Werewolf!, 1: Tigra, reprint from Creatures on the Loose #13; Marvel Value Stamp A-34 (Mr. Fantastic)	0.35	2.00	5.00	10.00

GIANT-SIZE DAREDEVIL
MARVEL

	ORIG	GOOD	FINE	N-MINT
❑1	0.50	1.60	4.00	8.00

GIANT-SIZE DEFENDERS
MARVEL

	ORIG	GOOD	FINE	N-MINT
❑1, Jul 74, JSn, The Way They Were!; Banished To Outer Space, A: Silver Surfer, Silver Surfer	0.50	1.20	3.00	6.00
❑2, Oct 74, KJ; GK, Son of Satan	0.50	0.80	2.00	4.00

	ORIG	GOOD	FINE	N-MINT
❑3, Jan 75, DA; JM; JSn; DN, Games Godlings Play!;, 1: Korvac	0.50	0.80	2.00	4.00
❑4, Apr 75, DH, Too Cold A Night For Dying!	0.50	0.80	2.00	4.00
❑5, Jul 75, DH, Eelar Moves Mysterious Ways!, A: Guardians of the Galaxy	0.50	0.80	2.00	4.00

GIANT-SIZE DOC SAVAGE
MARVEL

	ORIG	GOOD	FINE	N-MINT
❑1, Jan 75, RA, The Man of Bronze!, reprints Doc Savage (Marvel) #1 and 2; adapts Man of Bronze	0.50	1.20	3.00	6.00

GIANT-SIZE DOCTOR STRANGE
MARVEL

	ORIG	GOOD	FINE	N-MINT
❑1, DA; GT, Nightmare!; The Mystic and the Machine!, Reprints stories from Strange Tales #164, 165, 166, 167, 168	0.50	1.00	2.50	5.00

GIANT-SIZE DRACULA
MARVEL

	ORIG	GOOD	FINE	N-MINT
❑2, Sep 74, DH, Call them Triad...Call them Death!; The Girl in the Black Hood!, reprinted stories from Tales to Astonish #32, Menace #2, Astonishing Tales #18; Series continued from Giant-Size Chillers (1st Series) #1	0.50	1.20	3.00	6.00
❑3, Dec 74, DH	0.50	1.00	2.50	5.00
❑4, Mar 75, DH	0.50	1.00	2.50	5.00
❑5, Jun 75, JBy	0.50	1.00	2.50	5.00

GIANT-SIZE FANTASTIC FOUR
MARVEL

	ORIG	GOOD	FINE	N-MINT
❑1, May 74, JK; RB, The Mind of the Monster; Someone's Been Sleeping in My Head, A: Hulk; A: Fantastic Four, published as Giant-Size Super-Stars; Thing battles Hulk	0.35	3.00	7.50	15.00
❑2, Aug 74, JB, GK (c), A: Willie Lumpkin; V: Tempus, Title changes to Giant-Size Fantastic Four; also reprints Fantastic Four #13	0.50	1.60	4.00	8.00
❑3, Nov 74, RB, also reprints Fantastic Four #21	0.50	1.40	3.50	7.00
❑4, Feb 75, JK; JB, RB (c), JK (w), Madrox the Multiple Man; We Have to Fight the X-Men, 1: Madrox the Multiple Man; A: Medusa; A: Professor X	0.50	1.60	4.00	8.00
❑5, May 75, reprints Fantastic Four Annual #5 and Fantastic Four #15	0.50	1.20	3.00	6.00
❑6, Oct 75, Final Issue; reprints Fantastic Four Annual #6	0.50	1.20	3.00	6.00

GIANT-SIZE HULK
MARVEL

	ORIG	GOOD	FINE	N-MINT
❑1, reprints Hulk Annual #1	0.50	1.60	4.00	8.00

GIANT-SIZE INVADERS
MARVEL

	ORIG	GOOD	FINE	N-MINT
❑1, Jun 75, The Coming of the Invaders, 1: Invaders, reprints O: Sub-Mariner	0.50	1.00	2.50	5.00

GIANT-SIZE IRON MAN
MARVEL

	ORIG	GOOD	FINE	N-MINT
❑1, Reprint	0.50	1.00	2.50	5.00

GIANT-SIZE KID COLT
MARVEL

	ORIG	GOOD	FINE	N-MINT
❑1	0.50	4.00	10.00	20.00
❑2	0.50	3.00	7.50	15.00
❑3	0.50	3.00	7.50	15.00

GIANT-SIZE MAN-THING
MARVEL

	ORIG	GOOD	FINE	N-MINT
❑1, Aug 74, JK; SD, V: Glob	0.50	1.60	4.00	8.00
❑2	0.50	1.20	3.00	6.00
❑3, Feb 75	0.50	1.20	3.00	6.00
❑4, FB, Howard the Duck	0.50	2.00	5.00	10.00
❑5, Aug 75, FB, Howard the Duck	0.50	1.60	4.00	8.00

GIANT-SIZE MARVEL TRIPLE ACTION
MARVEL

	ORIG	GOOD	FINE	N-MINT
❑1, Reprint	0.50	0.80	2.00	4.00
❑2, Jul 75, Reprint	0.50	0.80	2.00	4.00

GIANT-SIZE MASTER OF KUNG FU
MARVEL

	ORIG	GOOD	FINE	N-MINT
❑1, Sep 74, CR	0.50	1.60	4.00	8.00
❑2, Dec 74	0.50	0.80	2.00	4.00
❑3, Mar 75	0.50	0.80	2.00	4.00
❑4, Jun 75, JK, Yellow Claw	0.50	0.80	2.00	4.00

GIANT-SIZE MINI COMICS
ECLIPSE

Value: Cover or less

- ❑1, Aug 86, b&w 1.50
- ❑2, Oct 86, Mightyguy: The Big Break!; Danger is Fun!, b&w 1.50
- ❑3, Dec 86, b&w 1.50
- ❑4, Feb 87, b&w 1.50

GIANT SIZE OFFICIAL PRINCE VALIANT
PIONEER

Value: Cover or less

- ❑1, b&w; Hal Foster 3.95

GIANT-SIZE POWER MAN
MARVEL

	ORIG	GOOD	FINE	N-MINT
❑1	0.50	0.80	2.00	4.00

GIANT-SIZE SPIDER-MAN
MARVEL

	ORIG	GOOD	FINE	N-MINT
❑1, Jul 74, RA, JR (c), Ship of Fiends; The Masque of the Black Death, A: Dracula, reprints story from Strange Tales Annual #2	0.50	3.60	9.00	18.00
❑2, Oct 74, RA; GK, JR (c), Masterstroke; Cross and Double-Cross, A: Shang-Chi, reprints story from Amazing Spider-Man Annual #3	0.50	2.00	5.00	10.00
❑3, Jan 75, RA, GK (c), The Yesterday Connection; The Secret Out of Time, A: Doc Savage, also reprints story from Amazing Spider-Man #16	0.50	2.00	5.00	10.00
❑4, Apr 75, RA, GK (c), To Sow the Seeds of Death's Day; Attack of the War Machine, 1: Moses Magnum (Magnum Force); A: Punisher	0.50	4.00	10.00	20.00
❑5, Jul 75, RA, GK (c), Beware the Path of the Monster; The Lurker in the Swamp, V: Lizard; A: Man-Thing	0.50	1.40	3.50	7.00
❑6, The Web and the Flame, reprints Amazing Spider-Man Annual #4	0.50	1.40	3.50	7.00

GIANT SIZE SPIDER-MAN (2ND SERIES)
MARVEL

Value: Cover or less

- ❑1, Dec 98, reprints stories from Marvel Team-Up 3.99

GIANT-SIZE SUPER-HEROES
MARVEL

	ORIG	GOOD	FINE	N-MINT
❑1, Jun 74, GK, Man-Wolf at Midnight; Duel of the Deadly Duo, A: Morbius; A: Spider-Man; A: Man-Wolf	0.35	3.00	7.50	15.00

GIANT-SIZE SUPER-VILLAIN TEAM-UP
MARVEL

	ORIG	GOOD	FINE	N-MINT
❑1, Mar 75	0.50	0.80	2.00	4.00
❑2, Jun 75, Doctor Doom, Sub-Mariner	0.50	0.80	2.00	4.00

GIANT-SIZE THOR
MARVEL

	ORIG	GOOD	FINE	N-MINT
❑1, GK, Reprint	0.50	0.80	2.00	4.00

GIANT-SIZE WEREWOLF BY NIGHT
MARVEL

	ORIG	GOOD	FINE	N-MINT
❑2, SD, Title changes to Giant Size Werewolf by Night; Frankenstein reprint	0.50	0.60	1.50	3.00
❑3, Jan 75, GK, Castle Curse!	0.50	0.60	1.50	3.00
❑4, GK	0.50	0.60	1.50	3.00
❑5, GK	0.50	0.60	1.50	3.00

GIANT-SIZE X-MEN
MARVEL

	ORIG	GOOD	FINE	N-MINT
❑1, Sum 75, DC; GK, Second Geesis!, 1: Illyana Rasputin; 1: Nightcrawler; 1: Storm; 1: Colossus; 1: Thunderbird; 1: X-Men (new)	0.50	120.00	300.00	600.00
❑2, KJ; GK, reprints X-Men #57-59	0.50	12.00	30.00	60.00

GIANT SUPERMAN ANNUAL REPLICA EDITION
DC

	ORIG	GOOD	FINE	N-MINT
❑1, cardstock cover; reproduction of Giant Superman Annual #1	4.95	1.00	2.50	5.00

GIANT THB PARADE
HORSE

	ORIG	GOOD	FINE	N-MINT
❑1, b&w; over-sized	4.95	1.00	2.50	5.00

G.I. COMBAT
DC

	ORIG	GOOD	FINE	N-MINT
❑87, 1: Haunted Tank	0.10	48.00	120.00	240.00
❑88	0.10	10.00	25.00	50.00
❑89	0.10	10.00	25.00	50.00
❑90	0.10	10.00	25.00	50.00
❑91	0.12	10.00	25.00	50.00
❑92	0.12	10.00	25.00	50.00
❑93	0.12	10.00	25.00	50.00
❑94	0.12	10.00	25.00	50.00
❑95	0.12	10.00	25.00	50.00
❑96	0.12	10.00	25.00	50.00
❑97	0.12	10.00	25.00	50.00
❑98, Mar 63	0.12	10.00	25.00	50.00
❑99, May 63	0.12	10.00	25.00	50.00
❑100, Jul 63	0.12	10.00	25.00	50.00
❑101, Sep 63	0.12	8.00	20.00	40.00
❑102, Nov 63	0.12	8.00	20.00	40.00
❑103, Jan 64, Painted cover	0.12	8.00	20.00	40.00
❑104, Mar 64, Sgt. Mule back-up	0.12	8.00	20.00	40.00
❑105, May 64	0.12	8.00	20.00	40.00
❑106, Jul 64	0.12	8.00	20.00	40.00
❑107, Sep 64	0.12	8.00	20.00	40.00
❑108, Nov 64	0.12	8.00	20.00	40.00
❑109, Jan 65	0.12	8.00	20.00	40.00

	ORIG	GOOD	FINE	N-MINT
❑110, Mar 65, Choose Your War; Battle Exterminator!	0.12	8.00	20.00	40.00
❑111, May 65	0.12	7.00	17.50	35.00
❑112, Jul 65	0.12	7.00	17.50	35.00
❑113, Sep 65	0.12	7.00	17.50	35.00
❑114, Nov 65, O: Haunted Tank	0.12	15.00	37.50	75.00
❑115, Jan 66	0.12	5.00	12.50	25.00
❑116, Mar 66, A: Johnny Cloud	0.12	5.00	12.50	25.00
❑117, May 66	0.12	5.00	12.50	25.00
❑118, Jul 66	0.12	5.00	12.50	25.00
❑119, Sep 66	0.12	5.00	12.50	25.00
❑120, Nov 66, A: Sgt. Rock; A: Johnny Cloud	0.12	5.00	12.50	25.00
❑121, Jan 67	0.12	4.00	10.00	20.00
❑122, Mar 67	0.12	4.00	10.00	20.00
❑123, May 67	0.12	4.00	10.00	20.00
❑124, Jul 67	0.12	4.00	10.00	20.00
❑125, Sep 67	0.12	4.00	10.00	20.00
❑126, Nov 67	0.12	4.00	10.00	20.00
❑127, Jan 68	0.12	4.00	10.00	20.00
❑128, Mar 68	0.12	4.00	10.00	20.00
❑129, May 68, Hold That Town for a Dead Man!; Combat Nightmare	0.12	4.00	10.00	20.00
❑130, Jul 68, RH (c), A: Attila the Hun's ghost	0.12	4.00	10.00	20.00
❑131, Sep 68	0.12	4.00	10.00	20.00
❑132, Nov 68	0.12	4.00	10.00	20.00
❑133, Jan 69	0.12	4.00	10.00	20.00
❑134, Mar 69	0.12	4.00	10.00	20.00
❑135, May 69, JKu (c)	0.12	4.00	10.00	20.00
❑136, Jul 69	0.15	4.00	10.00	20.00
❑137, Sep 69, JKu (c)	0.15	4.00	10.00	20.00
❑138, Nov 69, 1: Losers	0.15	7.60	19.00	38.00
❑139, Jan 70	0.15	4.00	10.00	20.00
❑140, Mar 70	—	4.00	10.00	20.00
❑141, May 70	—	1.50	3.75	7.50
❑142, Jul 70	—	1.50	3.75	7.50
❑143, Sep 70	—	1.50	3.75	7.50
❑144, Nov 70	—	1.50	3.75	7.50
❑145, Jan 71	—	1.50	3.75	7.50
❑146, Mar 71, Giant-size	0.25	1.50	3.75	7.50
❑147, May 71, Giant-size	0.25	1.50	3.75	7.50
❑148, Jul 71, Giant-size	0.25	1.50	3.75	7.50
❑149, Sep 71, JKu (c), Sgt. Rock back-up	0.25	1.50	3.75	7.50
❑150, Nov 71, JKu (c), 1: New Haunted Tank, reprints 1: Ice Cream Soldier	0.25	1.50	3.75	7.50
❑151, Jan 72	—	1.50	3.75	7.50
❑152, Mar 72	0.25	1.50	3.75	7.50
❑153, May 72	0.25	1.50	3.75	7.50
❑154, Jul 72, JKu (c)	0.25	1.50	3.75	7.50
❑155, Sep 72	—	1.50	3.75	7.50
❑156, Nov 72	—	1.50	3.75	7.50
❑157, Jan 73	—	1.50	3.75	7.50
❑158, Feb 73	—	1.50	3.75	7.50
❑159, Mar 73	—	1.50	3.75	7.50
❑160, May 73	—	1.50	3.75	7.50
❑161, Jun 73	0.20	1.20	3.00	6.00
❑162, Jul 73	0.20	1.20	3.00	6.00
❑163, Aug 73	0.20	1.20	3.00	6.00
❑164, Sep 73	0.20	1.20	3.00	6.00
❑165, Oct 73	0.20	1.20	3.00	6.00
❑166, Nov 73	0.20	1.20	3.00	6.00
❑167, Dec 73	0.20	1.20	3.00	6.00
❑168, Jan 74	0.20	1.20	3.00	6.00
❑169, Feb 74, Reprint	0.20	1.20	3.00	6.00
❑170, Mar 74	0.20	1.20	3.00	6.00
❑171, Jun 74	0.20	1.20	3.00	6.00
❑172, Aug 74	0.20	1.20	3.00	6.00
❑173, Oct 74, JKu (c)	0.20	1.20	3.00	6.00
❑174, Dec 74, JKu (c)	0.20	1.20	3.00	6.00
❑175	—	1.20	3.00	6.00
❑176	—	1.20	3.00	6.00
❑177	—	1.20	3.00	6.00
❑178	—	1.20	3.00	6.00
❑179	—	1.20	3.00	6.00
❑180	—	1.20	3.00	6.00
❑181	—	0.90	2.25	4.50
❑182	—	0.90	2.25	4.50
❑183	—	0.90	2.25	4.50
❑184	—	0.90	2.25	4.50
❑185	—	0.90	2.25	4.50
❑186	—	0.90	2.25	4.50
❑187	—	0.90	2.25	4.50
❑188	—	0.90	2.25	4.50
❑189, Apr 76	0.30	0.90	2.25	4.50
❑190, May 76	—	0.90	2.25	4.50
❑191, Jun 76	—	0.90	2.25	4.50

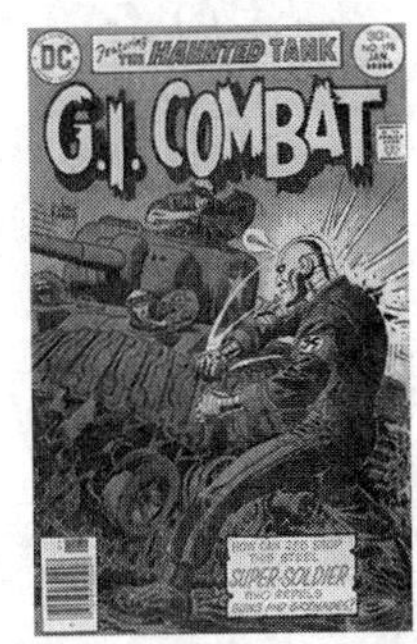

The spirit of Confederate General Jeb Stuart watched over the crew of a World War II tank in "The Haunted Tank" stories in *G.I. Combat.*

	ORIG	GOOD	FINE	N-MINT
❑192, Jul 76, Bicentennial #27	—	0.90	2.25	4.50
❑193, Aug 76	—	0.90	2.25	4.50
❑194, Sep 76	—	0.90	2.25	4.50
❑195, Oct 76	—	0.90	2.25	4.50
❑196, Nov 76	—	0.90	2.25	4.50
❑197, Dec 76	—	0.90	2.25	4.50
❑198, Jan 77, The Haunted Tank: The Devil Rides a Panzer; The Ship that Wouldn't Die	—	0.90	2.25	4.50
❑199, Feb 77	—	0.90	2.25	4.50
❑200, Mar 77	—	0.90	2.25	4.50
❑201, Apr 77	1.00	0.50	1.25	2.50
❑202, Jun 77	1.00	0.50	1.25	2.50
❑203, Aug 77, JKu (c)	1.00	0.50	1.25	2.50
❑204, Oct 77, JKu (c)	1.00	0.50	1.25	2.50
❑205, Dec 77, JKu (c)	1.00	0.50	1.25	2.50
❑206, Feb 78	1.00	0.50	1.25	2.50
❑207, Apr 78	1.00	0.50	1.25	2.50
❑208, Jun 78	1.00	0.50	1.25	2.50
❑209, Aug 78, JKu (c)	1.00	0.50	1.25	2.50
❑210, Oct 78	1.00	0.50	1.25	2.50
❑211, Dec 78, JKu (c)	1.00	0.50	1.25	2.50
❑212, Feb 79, JKu (c)	1.00	0.50	1.25	2.50
❑213, Apr 79	1.00	0.50	1.25	2.50
❑214, Jun 79	1.00	0.50	1.25	2.50
❑215, Aug 79	1.00	0.50	1.25	2.50
❑216, Oct 79	1.00	0.50	1.25	2.50
❑217, Dec 79	1.00	0.50	1.25	2.50
❑218, Feb 80	1.00	0.50	1.25	2.50
❑219, Apr 80, JKu (c)	1.00	0.50	1.25	2.50
❑220, Jun 80	1.00	0.50	1.25	2.50
❑221, Aug 80	1.00	0.50	1.25	2.50
❑222, Oct 80	1.00	0.50	1.25	2.50
❑223, Nov 80	1.00	0.50	1.25	2.50
❑224, Dec 80	1.00	0.50	1.25	2.50
❑225, Jan 81	1.00	0.50	1.25	2.50
❑226, Feb 81	1.00	0.50	1.25	2.50
❑227, Mar 81, The Haunted Tank: I, Tank; The Spy Who Died Twice!	1.00	0.50	1.25	2.50
❑228, Apr 81	1.00	0.50	1.25	2.50
❑229, May 81, JKu (c)	1.00	0.50	1.25	2.50
❑230, Jun 81	1.00	0.50	1.25	2.50
❑231, Jul 81	1.00	0.50	1.25	2.50
❑232, Aug 81, 1: Kana	1.00	0.50	1.25	2.50
❑233, Sep 81	1.00	0.50	1.25	2.50
❑234, Oct 81	1.00	0.50	1.25	2.50
❑235, Nov 81, JKu (c)	1.00	0.50	1.25	2.50
❑236, Dec 81	1.00	0.50	1.25	2.50
❑237, Jan 82, JKu (c)	1.00	0.50	1.25	2.50
❑238, Feb 82, JKu (c)	1.00	0.50	1.25	2.50
❑239, Mar 82, JKu (c)	1.00	0.50	1.25	2.50
❑240, Apr 82, JKu (c)	1.00	0.50	1.25	2.50
❑241, May 82, JKu (c)	1.00	0.50	1.25	2.50
❑242, Jun 82, JKu (c), 1: The Mercenaries	1.00	0.50	1.25	2.50
❑243, Jul 82	1.00	0.50	1.25	2.50
❑244, Aug 82, A: Mercenaries	1.00	0.50	1.25	2.50
❑245, Sep 82	1.00	0.50	1.25	2.50
❑246, Oct 82, A: Haunted Tank; A: Falcon; A: Captain Storm; A: Sgt. Rock; A: Gunner & Sarge; A: Johnny Cloud; A: Ninja, Double-size; 30th anniversary	1.50	0.50	1.25	2.50
❑247, Nov 82	1.00	0.50	1.25	2.50
❑248, Dec 82	1.00	0.50	1.25	2.50
❑249, Jan 83	1.00	0.50	1.25	2.50
❑250, Feb 83	1.00	0.50	1.25	2.50
❑251, Mar 83, JKu (c)	1.00	0.40	1.00	2.00
❑252, Apr 83	1.00	0.40	1.00	2.00
❑253, May 83	1.00	0.40	1.00	2.00
❑254, Jun 83	1.00	0.40	1.00	2.00
❑255, Jul 83	1.00	0.40	1.00	2.00
❑256, Aug 83	1.00	0.40	1.00	2.00
❑257, Sep 83	1.00	0.40	1.00	2.00
❑258, Oct 83, JKu (c)	1.00	0.40	1.00	2.00

	ORIG	GOOD	FINE	N-MINT
❑259, Nov 83, One Last Shot; Sweet Taste Of Death	—	0.40	1.00	2.00
❑260, Dec 83	1.25	0.40	1.00	2.00
❑261, Jan 84	1.25	0.40	1.00	2.00
❑262, Feb 84	1.25	0.40	1.00	2.00
❑263, Mar 84	1.25	0.40	1.00	2.00
❑264, Apr 84	1.25	0.40	1.00	2.00
❑265, May 84	1.25	0.40	1.00	2.00
❑266, Jun 84	1.25	0.40	1.00	2.00
❑267, Jul 84, KG, JKu (c)	1.25	0.40	1.00	2.00
❑268, Aug 84	1.25	0.40	1.00	2.00
❑269, Sep 84, JKu (c)	1.25	0.40	1.00	2.00
❑270, Oct 84	1.25	0.40	1.00	2.00
❑271, Nov 84	1.25	0.40	1.00	2.00
❑272, Dec 84	1.25	0.40	1.00	2.00
❑273, Jan 85	1.25	0.40	1.00	2.00
❑274, Feb 85, JKu (c), A: Attila; A: Monitor	1.25	0.40	1.00	2.00
❑275, Mar 85	1.25	0.40	1.00	2.00
❑276, Apr 85	1.25	0.40	1.00	2.00
❑277, May 85, JKu (c)	1.25	0.40	1.00	2.00
❑278, Jul 85, JKu (c)	1.25	0.40	1.00	2.00
❑279, Sep 85, JKu (c)	1.25	0.40	1.00	2.00
❑280, Nov 85, JKu (c)	1.25	0.40	1.00	2.00
❑281, Jan 86, JKu (c)	1.25	0.40	1.00	2.00
❑282, Mar 86, JKu (c), Mercenaries	0.75	0.40	1.00	2.00
❑283, May 86, Mercenaries	0.75	0.40	1.00	2.00
❑284, Jul 86, JKu (c), Mercenaries	0.75	0.40	1.00	2.00
❑285, Sep 86, JKu (c), Mercenaries	0.75	0.40	1.00	2.00
❑286, Nov 86, JKu (c), Mercenaries	0.75	0.40	1.00	2.00
❑287, Jan 87, JKu (c), Haunted Tank	0.75	0.40	1.00	2.00
❑288, Mar 87, JKu (c), Final Issue; Haunted Tank	0.75	0.40	1.00	2.00

GIDEON HAWK
BIG SHOT

Value: Cover or less

- ❑1, Jan 95, The Jewel of Shambali ... 2.00
- ❑2, Mar 95, b&w ... 2.00
- ❑3, Jun 95, b&w ... 2.00

GIFT, THE: A FIRST PUBLISHING HOLIDAY SPECIAL
FIRST

Value: Cover or less

- ❑1, Nov 90, A: Dreadstar, Nexus, Badger, nn ... 5.95

GIFTS OF THE NIGHT
DC

Value: Cover or less

- ❑1, Feb 99 ... 2.95
- ❑2, Mar 99 ... 2.95
- ❑3, Apr 99 ... 2.95
- ❑4, May 99 ... 2.95

GIGANTOR
ANTARCTIC

Value: Cover or less

- ❑1 ... 2.50

GIGOLO
EROS

Value: Cover or less

- ❑1 ... 2.95
- ❑2, Nov 95, W is for Wimmens Record ... 2.95

G.I. GOVERNMENT ISSUED
PARANOID

Value: Cover or less

- ❑1 ... 2.00
- ❑2, Aug 94 ... 2.00

G.I. JACKRABBITS
EXCALIBUR

Value: Cover or less

- ❑1, Dec 86 ... 1.50

GI JOE (VOL. 1)
DARK HORSE

	ORIG	GOOD	FINE	N-MINT
❑1, Dec 95, From the Ashes, Part 1, 1: Short Fuse; 1: Tall Sally	1.95	0.40	1.00	2.00
❑2, Jan 96	1.95	0.40	1.00	2.00
❑3, Mar 96, Island Assault	1.95	0.40	1.00	2.00
❑4, Apr 96, All This and World War II; The Last, Wild Heart, Part 1, Final Issue	1.95	0.40	1.00	2.00

GI JOE (VOL. 2)
DARK HORSE

Value: Cover or less

- ❑1, Jun 96, Red Scream, Part 1 ... 2.50
- ❑2, Jul 96, Red Scream, Part 2 ... 2.50
- ❑3, Aug 96 ... 2.50
- ❑4, Sep 96, Final Issue ... 2.50

G.I. JOE AND THE TRANSFORMERS
MARVEL

	ORIG	GOOD	FINE	N-MINT
❑1, Jan 87, HT, Blood On The Tracks	0.75	0.20	0.50	1.00
❑2, Feb 87	0.75	0.20	0.50	1.00
❑3, Mar 87	0.75	0.20	0.50	1.00
❑4, Apr 87	0.75	0.20	0.50	1.00

G.I. JOE COMICS MAGAZINE
MARVEL

Value: Cover or less

- ❑1, Dec 86, digest ... 1.50
- ❑2, Feb 87, digest ... 1.50
- ❑3, Apr 87, digest ... 1.50
- ❑4, Jun 87, digest ... 1.50
- ❑5, Aug 87, digest ... 1.50
- ❑6, Oct 87, digest ... 1.50
- ❑7, Dec 87, digest ... 1.50
- ❑8, Feb 88, digest ... 1.50
- ❑9, Apr 88, digest ... 1.50
- ❑10, Jun 88, digest ... 1.50
- ❑11, Aug 88, digest ... 1.50
- ❑12, Oct 88, digest ... 1.50
- ❑13, Dec 88, digest ... 1.50

G.I. JOE EUROPEAN MISSIONS
MARVEL

Value: Cover or less

- ❑1, Jun 88 ... 1.50
- ❑2, Jul 88 ... 1.50
- ❑3, Aug 88 ... 1.50
- ❑4, Sep 88 ... 1.50
- ❑5, Oct 88 ... 1.50
- ❑6, Nov 88 ... 1.50
- ❑7, Dec 88 ... 1.50
- ❑8, Jan 89 ... 1.50
- ❑9, Feb 89 ... 1.50
- ❑10, Mar 89 ... 1.50
- ❑11, Apr 89 ... 1.50
- ❑12, May 89 ... 1.75
- ❑13, Jun 89 ... 1.75
- ❑14, Jul 89 ... 1.75
- ❑15, Aug 89 ... 1.75

G.I. JOE IN 3-D
BLACKTHORNE

	ORIG	GOOD	FINE	N-MINT
❑1, Jul 87, of Birds and Men	2.50	0.50	1.25	2.50
❑2, Oct 87	2.50	0.50	1.25	2.50
❑3, Jan 88, The Quiet War	2.50	0.50	1.25	2.50
❑4, Apr 88	2.50	0.50	1.25	2.50
❑5, Jul 88	2.50	0.50	1.25	2.50
❑6	2.00	0.50	1.25	2.50

G.I. JOE ORDER OF BATTLE
MARVEL

Value: Cover or less

- ❑1, Dec 86, HT, The Official G.I. Joe Handbook ... 1.25
- ❑2, Jan 87, Rocky Balboa ... 1.25
- ❑3, Feb 87 ... 1.25
- ❑4, Mar 87 ... 1.25

G.I. JOE, A REAL AMERICAN HERO
MARVEL

	ORIG	GOOD	FINE	N-MINT
❑1, Jun 82, HT, Operation: Lady Doomsday, Giant-size	1.50	0.60	1.50	3.00
❑2, Aug 82	0.60	0.50	1.25	2.50
❑2-2, 2nd Printing	0.60	0.20	0.50	1.00
❑3, Sep 82, JAb; HT	0.60	0.40	1.00	2.00
❑3-2, 2nd Printing	0.60	0.20	0.50	1.00
❑4, Oct 82, JAb; HT	0.60	0.40	1.00	2.00
❑4-2, 2nd Printing	0.60	0.20	0.50	1.00
❑5, Nov 82, JAb; HT	0.60	0.40	1.00	2.00
❑5-2, 2nd Printing	0.60	0.20	0.50	1.00
❑6, Dec 82, HT	0.60	0.40	1.00	2.00
❑6-2, 2nd Printing	0.60	0.20	0.50	1.00
❑7, Jan 83, HT	0.60	0.40	1.00	2.00
❑7-2, 2nd Printing	0.60	0.20	0.50	1.00
❑8, Feb 83, HT	0.60	0.40	1.00	2.00
❑8-2, 2nd Printing	0.60	0.20	0.50	1.00
❑9, Mar 83	0.60	0.40	1.00	2.00
❑9-2, 2nd Printing	0.60	0.20	0.50	1.00
❑10, Apr 83	0.60	0.40	1.00	2.00
❑10-2, 2nd Printing	0.60	0.20	0.50	1.00
❑11, May 83	0.60	0.40	1.00	2.00
❑11-2, 2nd Printing	0.60	0.20	0.50	1.00
❑12, Jun 83	0.60	0.40	1.00	2.00
❑12-2, 2nd Printing	0.60	0.20	0.50	1.00
❑13, Jul 83	0.60	0.40	1.00	2.00
❑13-2, 2nd Printing	0.60	0.20	0.50	1.00
❑14, Aug 83	0.60	0.40	1.00	2.00
❑14-2, 2nd Printing	0.60	0.20	0.50	1.00
❑15, Sep 83	0.60	0.40	1.00	2.00
❑15-2, 2nd Printing	0.60	0.20	0.50	1.00
❑16, Oct 83	0.60	0.40	1.00	2.00
❑16-2, 2nd Printing	0.60	0.20	0.50	1.00
❑17, Nov 83	0.60	0.40	1.00	2.00
❑17-2, 2nd Printing	0.60	0.20	0.50	1.00
❑18, Dec 83	0.60	0.40	1.00	2.00
❑18-2, 2nd Printing	0.60	0.20	0.50	1.00
❑19, Jan 84	0.60	0.40	1.00	2.00
❑19-2, 2nd Printing	0.60	0.20	0.50	1.00
❑20, Feb 84	0.60	0.40	1.00	2.00
❑20-2, 2nd Printing	0.60	0.20	0.50	1.00
❑21, Mar 84, "silent" issue	0.60	0.40	1.00	2.00
❑21-2, 2nd Printing	0.60	0.20	0.50	1.00
❑22, Apr 84	0.60	0.40	1.00	2.00
❑22-2, 2nd Printing	0.60	0.20	0.50	1.00
❑23, May 84	0.60	0.40	1.00	2.00
❑23-2, 2nd Printing	0.60	0.20	0.50	1.00
❑24, Jun 84	0.60	0.40	1.00	2.00
❑24-2, 2nd Printing	0.60	0.20	0.50	1.00
❑25, Jul 84	0.60	0.40	1.00	2.00
❑25-2, 2nd Printing	0.60	0.20	0.50	1.00
❑26, Aug 84, O: Snake Eyes	0.60	0.40	1.00	2.00
❑26-2, O: Snake Eyes, 2nd Printing	0.60	0.20	0.50	1.00
❑27, Sep 84, O: Snake Eyes	0.60	0.40	1.00	2.00
❑27-2, O: Snake Eyes, 2nd Printing	0.60	0.20	0.50	1.00
❑28, Oct 84	0.60	0.40	1.00	2.00
❑28-2, 2nd Printing	0.60	0.20	0.50	1.00
❑29, Nov 84	0.60	0.40	1.00	2.00
❑29-2, 2nd Printing	0.60	0.20	0.50	1.00

	ORIG	GOOD	FINE	N-MINT
❑30, Dec 84	0.60	0.40	1.00	2.00
❑30-2, 2nd Printing	0.60	0.20	0.50	1.00
❑31, Jan 85	0.60	0.30	0.75	1.50
❑31-2, 2nd Printing	0.60	0.20	0.50	1.00
❑32, Feb 85	0.60	0.30	0.75	1.50
❑32-2, 2nd Printing	0.60	0.20	0.50	1.00
❑33, Mar 85	0.60	0.30	0.75	1.50
❑33-2, 2nd Printing	0.60	0.20	0.50	1.00
❑34, Apr 85	0.75	0.30	0.75	1.50
❑34-2, 2nd Printing	0.75	0.20	0.50	1.00
❑35, May 85	0.75	0.30	0.75	1.50
❑35-2, 2nd Printing	0.75	0.20	0.50	1.00
❑36, Jun 85	0.75	0.30	0.75	1.50
❑36-2, 2nd Printing	0.75	0.20	0.50	1.00
❑37, Jul 85	0.75	0.30	0.75	1.50
❑38, Aug 85	0.75	0.30	0.75	1.50
❑39, Sep 85	0.75	0.30	0.75	1.50
❑40, Oct 85	0.75	0.30	0.75	1.50
❑41, Nov 85	0.75	0.30	0.75	1.50
❑42, Dec 85	0.75	0.30	0.75	1.50
❑43, Jan 86	0.75	0.30	0.75	1.50
❑44, Feb 86	0.75	0.30	0.75	1.50
❑45, Mar 86	0.75	0.30	0.75	1.50
❑46, Apr 86	0.75	0.30	0.75	1.50
❑47, May 86	0.75	0.30	0.75	1.50
❑48, Jun 86	0.75	0.30	0.75	1.50
❑49, Jul 86	0.75	0.30	0.75	1.50
❑50, Aug 86, The Battle Of Springfield, double-sized; Double-size	1.25	0.35	0.88	1.75
❑51, Sep 86	0.75	0.25	0.63	1.25
❑52, Oct 86	0.75	0.25	0.63	1.25
❑53, Nov 86	0.75	0.25	0.63	1.25
❑54, Dec 86	0.75	0.25	0.63	1.25
❑55, Jan 87	0.75	0.25	0.63	1.25
❑56, Feb 87	0.75	0.25	0.63	1.25
❑57, Mar 87	0.75	0.25	0.63	1.25
❑58, Apr 87	0.75	0.25	0.63	1.25
❑59, May 87	1.00	0.25	0.63	1.25
❑60, Jun 87, TMc	1.00	0.30	0.75	1.50
❑61, Jul 87	1.00	0.25	0.63	1.25
❑62, Aug 87	1.00	0.25	0.63	1.25
❑63, Sep 87	1.00	0.25	0.63	1.25
❑64, Oct 87	1.00	0.25	0.63	1.25
❑65, Nov 87	1.00	0.25	0.63	1.25
❑66, Dec 87	1.00	0.25	0.63	1.25
❑67, Jan 88	1.00	0.25	0.63	1.25
❑68, Feb 88	1.00	0.25	0.63	1.25
❑69, Mar 88	1.00	0.25	0.63	1.25
❑70, Apr 88	1.00	0.25	0.63	1.25
❑71, May 88	1.00	0.25	0.63	1.25
❑72, Jun 88	1.00	0.25	0.63	1.25
❑73, Jul 88	1.00	0.25	0.63	1.25
❑74, Aug 88	1.00	0.25	0.63	1.25
❑75, Sep 88	1.00	0.25	0.63	1.25
❑76, Sep 88	1.00	0.25	0.63	1.25
❑77, Oct 88	1.00	0.25	0.63	1.25
❑78, Oct 88	1.00	0.25	0.63	1.25
❑79, Nov 88	1.00	0.25	0.63	1.25
❑80, Nov 88	1.00	0.25	0.63	1.25
❑81, Dec 88	1.00	0.20	0.50	1.00
❑82, Jan 89	1.00	0.20	0.50	1.00
❑83, Feb 89	1.00	0.20	0.50	1.00
❑84, Mar 89	1.00	0.20	0.50	1.00
❑85, Apr 89	1.00	0.20	0.50	1.00
❑86, May 89	1.00	0.20	0.50	1.00
❑87, Jun 89	1.00	0.20	0.50	1.00
❑88, Jul 89	1.00	0.20	0.50	1.00
❑89, Aug 89	1.00	0.20	0.50	1.00
❑90, Sep 89	1.00	0.20	0.50	1.00
❑91, Oct 89	1.00	0.20	0.50	1.00
❑92, Nov 89	1.00	0.20	0.50	1.00
❑93, Nov 89	1.00	0.20	0.50	1.00
❑94, Dec 89	1.00	0.20	0.50	1.00
❑95, Dec 89	1.00	0.20	0.50	1.00
❑96, Jan 90	1.00	0.20	0.50	1.00
❑97, Feb 90	1.00	0.20	0.50	1.00
❑98, Mar 90	1.00	0.20	0.50	1.00
❑99, Apr 90	1.00	0.20	0.50	1.00
❑100, May 90, Giant size	1.50	0.20	0.50	1.00
❑101, Jun 90	1.00	0.20	0.50	1.00
❑102, Jul 90	1.00	0.20	0.50	1.00
❑103, Aug 90	1.00	0.20	0.50	1.00
❑104, Sep 90	1.00	0.20	0.50	1.00
❑105, Oct 90	1.00	0.20	0.50	1.00
❑106, Nov 90	1.00	0.20	0.50	1.00

Marvel's comic-book and animated adventures of *G.I. Joe* tied in with Hasbro's toy line.

© 1982 Marvel

	ORIG	GOOD	FINE	N-MINT
❑107, Dec 90	1.00	0.20	0.50	1.00
❑108, Jan 91, Dossiers begin	1.00	0.20	0.50	1.00
❑109, Feb 91	1.00	0.20	0.50	1.00
❑110, Mar 91	1.00	0.20	0.50	1.00
❑111, Apr 91	1.00	0.20	0.50	1.00
❑112, May 91	1.00	0.20	0.50	1.00
❑113, Jun 91	1.00	0.20	0.50	1.00
❑114, Jul 91, 1: Metal-Head	1.00	0.20	0.50	1.00
❑115, Aug 91	1.00	0.20	0.50	1.00
❑116, Sep 91	1.00	0.20	0.50	1.00
❑117, Oct 91	1.00	0.20	0.50	1.00
❑118, Nov 91	1.00	0.20	0.50	1.00
❑119, Dec 91	1.00	0.20	0.50	1.00
❑120, Jan 92	1.00	0.20	0.50	1.00
❑121, Feb 92	1.25	0.25	0.63	1.25
❑122, Mar 92	1.25	0.25	0.63	1.25
❑123, Apr 92	1.25	0.25	0.63	1.25
❑124, May 92	1.25	0.25	0.63	1.25
❑125, Jun 92	1.25	0.25	0.63	1.25
❑126, Jul 92	1.25	0.25	0.63	1.25
❑127, Sep 92	1.25	0.25	0.63	1.25
❑128, Sep 92	1.25	0.25	0.63	1.25
❑129, Oct 92	1.25	0.25	0.63	1.25
❑130, Nov 92	1.25	0.25	0.63	1.25
❑131, Dec 92	1.25	0.25	0.63	1.25
❑132, Jan 93	1.25	0.25	0.63	1.25
❑133, Feb 93	1.25	0.25	0.63	1.25
❑134, Mar 93, A: Snake Eyes	1.25	0.25	0.63	1.25
❑135, Apr 93, Polybagged with trading card; Team members are regrouped into three strike teams	1.75	0.35	0.88	1.75
❑136, May 93, trading card	1.75	0.25	0.63	1.25
❑137, Jun 93, trading card	1.75	0.25	0.63	1.25
❑138, Jul 93, trading card	1.75	0.25	0.63	1.25
❑139, Aug 93, Transformers	1.25	0.25	0.63	1.25
❑140, Sep 93, Transformers	1.25	0.25	0.63	1.25
❑141, Oct 93, A: Cobra Commander; A: Megatron; A: Transformers: Generation 2	1.25	0.25	0.63	1.25
❑142, Nov 93, Transformers	1.25	0.25	0.63	1.25
❑143, Dec 93	1.25	0.25	0.63	1.25
❑144, Jan 94	1.25	0.25	0.63	1.25
❑145, Feb 94	1.25	0.25	0.63	1.25
❑146, Mar 94	1.25	0.25	0.63	1.25
❑147, Apr 94	1.25	0.25	0.63	1.25
❑148, May 94	1.25	0.25	0.63	1.25
❑149, Jun 94	1.25	0.25	0.63	1.25
❑150, Jul 94, Giant-size	2.00	0.40	1.00	2.00
❑151, Aug 94	1.25	0.25	0.63	1.25
❑152, Sep 94	1.25	0.25	0.63	1.25
❑153, Oct 94	1.50	0.30	0.75	1.50
❑154, Nov 94	1.50	0.30	0.75	1.50
❑155, Dec 94, Final Issue	1.50	0.30	0.75	1.50
❑YB 1, Mar 85, Yearbook (annual) #1	1.50	0.50	1.25	2.50
❑YB 2, Mar 86, Yearbook (annual) #2	1.50	0.40	1.00	2.00
❑YB 3, Mar 87, Yearbook (annual) #3	1.50	0.40	1.00	2.00
❑YB 4, Feb 88, Yearbook (annual) #4	1.50	0.30	0.75	1.50

G.I. JOE SPECIAL MISSIONS

Marvel

	ORIG	GOOD	FINE	N-MINT
❑1, Oct 86	0.75	0.20	0.50	1.00
❑2, Dec 86	0.75	0.20	0.50	1.00
❑3, Feb 87	0.75	0.20	0.50	1.00
❑4, Apr 87	0.75	0.20	0.50	1.00
❑5, Jun 87	1.00	0.20	0.50	1.00
❑6, Aug 87	1.00	0.20	0.50	1.00
❑7, Oct 87	1.00	0.20	0.50	1.00
❑8, Dec 87	1.00	0.20	0.50	1.00
❑9, Feb 88	1.00	0.20	0.50	1.00
❑10, Apr 88	1.00	0.20	0.50	1.00
❑11, Jun 88	1.00	0.20	0.50	1.00
❑12, Aug 88	1.00	0.20	0.50	1.00
❑13, Sep 88	1.00	0.20	0.50	1.00
❑14, Oct 88	1.00	0.20	0.50	1.00

	ORIG	GOOD	FINE	N-MINT
❑15, Nov 88	1.00	0.20	0.50	1.00
❑16, Dec 88	1.00	0.20	0.50	1.00
❑17, Jan 89	1.00	0.20	0.50	1.00
❑18, Feb 89	1.00	0.20	0.50	1.00
❑19, Mar 89	1.00	0.20	0.50	1.00
❑20, Apr 89	1.00	0.20	0.50	1.00
❑21, May 89	1.00	0.20	0.50	1.00
❑22, Jun 89	1.00	0.20	0.50	1.00
❑23, Jul 89	1.00	0.20	0.50	1.00
❑24, Aug 89	1.00	0.20	0.50	1.00
❑25, Sep 89	1.00	0.20	0.50	1.00
❑26, Oct 89	1.00	0.20	0.50	1.00
❑27, Nov 89	1.00	0.20	0.50	1.00
❑28, Nov 89	1.00	0.20	0.50	1.00

GILGAMESH II
DC

Value: Cover or less

- ❑1, JSn, JSn (w), A Mad New World, O: Gilgamesh, prestige format ... 3.95
- ❑2, JSn, prestige format ... 3.95
- ❑3, JSn, prestige format ... 3.95
- ❑4, JSn, prestige format ... 3.95

GIMME
HEAD IMPORTS

	ORIG	GOOD	FINE	N-MINT
❑1, Swine hog; Sh*\tty Jokes	0.50	0.60	1.50	3.00

G.I. MUTANTS
ETERNITY

Value: Cover or less

- ❑1, Ruin and Robots ... 1.95
- ❑2 ... 1.95
- ❑3 ... 1.95
- ❑4 ... 1.95

GINGER FOX
COMICO

Value: Cover or less

- ❑1, Sep 88, Yellow ... 1.75
- ❑2, Oct 88 ... 1.75
- ❑3, Nov 88 ... 1.75
- ❑4, Dec 88 ... 1.75

GIN-RYU
BELIEVE IN YOURSELF

	ORIG	GOOD	FINE	N-MINT
❑1, Mar 95	2.75	0.55	1.38	2.75
❑2, May 95	2.75	0.55	1.38	2.75
❑3	2.75	0.55	1.38	2.75
❑3/Ash	—	0.20	0.50	1.00

G.I. R.A.M.B.O.T.
WONDER COLOR

Value: Cover or less

- ❑1, Apr 87, Coming of Age ... 1.95

GIRL
DC

Value: Cover or less

- ❑1, Jul 96, Terminal City ... 2.50
- ❑2, Aug 96 ... 2.50
- ❑3, Sep 96 ... 2.50

GIRL, THE
RIP OFF

Value: Cover or less

- ❑1, Feb 91, b&w; adult ... 2.50
- ❑1-2, Oct 92, b&w; adult; 2nd Printing ... 2.50
- ❑2, May 91, b&w; adult ... 2.50
- ❑3, Aug 91, b&w; adult ... 2.50
- ❑4, Dec 91, b&w; adult ... 2.50

GIRL CALLED...WILLOW!, A
ANGEL

Value: Cover or less

- ❑1, Fal 96, b&w ... 2.95

GIRL CALLED...WILLOW! SKETCHBOOK, A
ANGEL

Value: Cover or less

- ❑1, b&w; wraparound cover; pin-ups and rough pencil sketches ... 2.95

GIRL CRAZY
DARK HORSE

Value: Cover or less

- ❑1, May 96, What's Knittin' Kitten?, b&w ... 2.95
- ❑2, Jul 96, b&w ... 2.95
- ❑3, Jul 96, b&w ... 2.95

GIRL FROM U.N.C.L.E., THE
GOLD KEY

	ORIG	GOOD	FINE	N-MINT
❑1, Oct 66, The Fatal Accidents Affair, pin-up on back cover; 10197-701	0.12	7.00	17.50	35.00
❑2, Photo cover	0.12	4.40	11.00	22.00
❑3, Photo cover	0.12	3.60	9.00	18.00
❑4, Photo cover	0.12	2.80	7.00	14.00
❑5, The Harem-Scarem Affair; Leopold Swift-Courier: Bubble Trouble, Photo cover; Final Issue	0.12	2.80	7.00	14.00

GIRL GENIUS
STUDIO FOGLIO

	ORIG	GOOD	FINE	N-MINT
❑1, Feb 01, PF, PF (w), b&w; cardstock cover	2.95	0.59	1.48	2.95
❑Ash 1, Oct 00, b&w; no cover price; preview of upcoming series; smaller than normal comic book	—	0.20	0.50	1.00

GIRLHERO
HIGH DRIVE

	ORIG	GOOD	FINE	N-MINT
❑1, Aug 93, b&w	3.00	0.60	1.50	3.00

	ORIG	GOOD	FINE	N-MINT
❑2, Feb 94, b&w	2.95	0.60	1.50	3.00
❑3, Jul 94, b&w	2.95	0.60	1.50	3.00

GIRL ON GIRL COLLEGE KINK: NEW YEAR'S BABES
ANGEL

Value: Cover or less

- ❑1, New Year's Babes ... 3.00

GIRL ON GIRL: FEEDIN' TIME
ANGEL

Value: Cover or less

- ❑1 ... 3.00

GIRL ON GIRL: TICKLISH
ANGEL

Value: Cover or less

- ❑1, Tickle Football ... 3.00

GIRLS OF '95: GOOD, BAD & DEADLY
LOST CAUSE

Value: Cover or less

- ❑1, Feb 96, Bad to the Bone!; ... 3.95

GIRLS OF NINJA HIGH SCHOOL
ANTARCTIC

	ORIG	GOOD	FINE	N-MINT
❑1, b&w	3.75	0.75	1.88	3.75
❑2, b&w	3.75	0.75	1.88	3.75
❑3, b&w	3.95	0.75	1.88	3.75
❑4, Apr 94, b&w; 1994 Annual	3.95	0.79	1.98	3.95
❑5, Apr 95, The Test of Endurance; The N Files, 1995 Annual	4.50	0.90	2.25	4.50
❑6, Welcome Home, 1996 Annual	3.95	0.79	1.98	3.95
❑7, May 97, 1997 Annual	3.95	0.79	1.98	3.95
❑8/A, May 98, Flights of Fantasy; Sprockets and Rockets, 1998 Annual	2.95	0.79	1.98	3.95
❑8/B, May 98, Ninja Tricks 3-1/2; Treasure Hunt, alternate cover (manga-style); 1998 Annual	2.95	0.79	1.98	3.95
❑9, Apr 99, Women of Ninja High School Unite!, Derek Cheung, Kyle A. Carrozza, back cover pin-up; Nylon Menaces: Dandelion; Minerva: Blind Spot	2.99	0.60	1.50	2.99

GIRL SQUAD X
FANTACO

Value: Cover or less

- ❑1, b&w ... 2.95

GIRL TALK
FANTAGRAPHICS

Value: Cover or less

- ❑4, Sum 96, b&w; Anthology ... 3.50

GIRL: THE RULE OF DARKNESS
CRY FOR DAWN

Value: Cover or less

- ❑1, b&w; adult ... 2.50

GIRL WHO WOULD BE DEATH, THE
DC

Value: Cover or less

- ❑1, Dec 98 ... 2.50
- ❑2, Jan 99, Warning: Impersonating Death May Be Hazardous to Your Health ... 2.50
- ❑3, Feb 99 ... 2.50
- ❑4, Mar 99 ... 2.50

GIVE IT UP! AND OTHER SHORT STORIES
NBM

Value: Cover or less

- ❑1, Jul 95, b&w; hardcover; Peter Kuper adaptations of Kafka stories ... 14.95

GIVE ME LIBERTY
DARK HORSE

Value: Cover or less

- ❑1, Jun 90, DG; DaG, FM (w), Homes & Gardens, 1: Martha Washington, prestige format ... 4.95
- ❑2, Sep 90, DG; DaG, FM (w), prestige format ... 4.95
- ❑3, Dec 90, DG; DaG, FM (w), Health & Welfare, prestige format ... 4.95
- ❑4, Apr 91, DG; DaG, FM (w), prestige format ... 4.95

GIVE ME LIBERTY! (RIP OFF)
RIP OFF

	ORIG	GOOD	FINE	N-MINT
❑1, Jan 76	0.75	0.80	2.00	4.00

G.I. WAR TALES
DC

	ORIG	GOOD	FINE	N-MINT
❑1	0.20	1.60	4.00	8.00
❑2, Jul 73, The Killing Ground!; Warrior (text story), Suicide Volunteer, Reprints stories from Star Spangled War Stories #134, G.I. Combat #133	0.20	1.00	2.50	5.00
❑3, Aug 73, RH; JKu, Split-Second Target; The G.I. Who Replaced Himself!, Reprints stories from All American Men of War #55, 38	0.20	0.80	2.00	4.00
❑4	0.20	0.80	2.00	4.00

GIZMO (CHANCE)
CHANCE

	ORIG	GOOD	FINE	N-MINT
❑1, That Was No Teddy Bear That Was My...	1.50	0.60	1.50	3.00

GIZMO (MIRAGE)
MIRAGE

Value: Cover or less

- ❑1, b&w ... 1.50
- ❑2, b&w ... 1.50
- ❑3, b&w ... 1.50
- ❑4, b&w ... 1.50
- ❑5, b&w ... 1.50
- ❑6, Jul 87, b&w ... 1.50

GIZMO AND THE FUGITOID
MIRAGE

	ORIG	GOOD	FINE	N-MINT
❑1, Jun 89, b&w	1.75	0.40	1.00	2.00
❑2, Jun 89, b&w	1.75	0.40	1.00	2.00

GLADIATOR/SUPREME
MARVEL

Value: Cover or less

❑1, Mar 97, KG (w) 4.99

GLAMOROUS GRAPHIX PRESENTS
GLAMOROUS GRAPHIX

Value: Cover or less

❑1, Jan 96, b&w; Becky Sunshine; pin-ups 3.95

GLASS JAW
CLAY HEELED PRESS

Value: Cover or less

❑1, no date 2.95

GLOBAL FORCE
SILVERLINE

Value: Cover or less

❑1, full color 1.95

GLORIANNA
PRESS THIS

Value: Cover or less

❑1, The Conscience of King, nn; b&w; One-Shot 3.95

GLORY
IMAGE

Value: Cover or less

❑0, Feb 96 .... 2.50
❑1, Mar 95, Who Wrote the Book of Love?, Part 1 .... 2.50
❑1/A, Mar 95, Who Wrote the Book of Love?, Part 1, alternate cover; Image publishes 2.50
❑2, Apr 95, Who Wrote the Book of Love?, Part 2 .... 2.50
❑3, May 95, Who Wrote the Book of Love?, Part 3 .... 2.50
❑4, Jun 95, Who Wrote the Book of Love?, Part 4 .... 2.50
❑4/A, Jun 95, Who Wrote the Book of Love?, Part 4, Quesada/Palmiotti variant cover 2.50
❑5, Aug 95, polybagged with trading card 2.50
❑6, Sep 95 .... 2.50
❑7, Oct 95 .... 2.50
❑8, Nov 95, Babewatch 2.50
❑9, Dec 95, Extreme Destroyer, Part 5, polybagged with Glory card 2.50
❑10, Mar 96, A: Angela 2.50
❑11, Apr 96 .... 2.50
❑12, May 96, Giant-size; double-sized anniversary issue 3.50
❑12/A, May 96, alternate cover (photo); double-sized anniversary issue 3.50
❑13, Jun 96 .... 2.50
❑14, Jul 96 .... 2.50
❑15, Sep 96 .... 2.50
❑16, Maximum begins as publisher 2.50
❑17 .... 2.50
❑18 .... 2.50
❑19 .... 2.50
❑20, Feb 97 .... 2.50
❑21 .... 2.50
❑22 .... 2.50
❑23, Final Issue 2.50

GLORY & FRIENDS BIKINI FEST
IMAGE

Value: Cover or less

❑1, Sep 95, pin-ups 2.50
❑1/SC, Sep 95, alternate cover (photo); pin-ups 2.50

GLORY & FRIENDS CHRISTMAS SPECIAL
IMAGE

Value: Cover or less

❑1, Dec 95, Home For The Holidays?; Bloodpool 2.50

GLORY & FRIENDS LINGERIE SPECIAL
IMAGE

Value: Cover or less

❑1, Sep 95, pin-ups 2.95
❑1/SC, Sep 95, alternate cover (photo); pin-ups 2.95

GLORY/ANGELA: ANGELS IN HELL
IMAGE

Value: Cover or less

❑1, Apr 96, One-Shot; flipbook with Darkchylde preview 2.50

GLORY/AVENGELYNE
IMAGE

Value: Cover or less

❑1/A, Oct 95, no title information on cover 3.95
❑1/B, Oct 95, no title information on cover 3.95

GLORY/CELESTINE: DARK ANGEL
IMAGE

Value: Cover or less

❑1, Sep 96, The Doomsday Talisman 2.50
❑2 .... 2.50

GLYPH
LABOR OF LOVE

Value: Cover or less

❑1, nn; b&w; Anthology; magazine 4.95
❑2, b&w; Anthology; magazine 4.95
❑3, b&w; Anthology; magazine 4.95

G-MEN
CALIBER

Value: Cover or less

❑1, b&w 2.50

GNATRAT: THE DARK GNAT RETURNS
PRELUDE

Value: Cover or less

❑1, b&w; Batman parody; continues in Darerat/Tadpole 1.95

GNATRAT: THE MOVIE
INNOVATION

Value: Cover or less

❑1, b&w; Batman parody 2.25

Phil Foglio's *Girl Genius* is set in a world of steampunk technology.

G'N'R'S GREATEST HITS
REVOLUTIONARY

Value: Cover or less

❑1, Oct 93, b&w 2.50

GOBBLEDYGOOK (1ST SERIES)
MIRAGE

	ORIG	GOOD	FINE	N-MINT
❑1, 1: The Teenage Mutant Ninja Turtles	—	25.00	62.50	125.00
❑2	—	16.00	40.00	80.00

GOBBLEDYGOOK (2ND SERIES)
MIRAGE

Value: Cover or less

❑1, Dec 86, Don't Sleep on Main Street; Technofear! 6.00

GOBLIN LORD
GOBLIN STUDIOS

Value: Cover or less

❑1, Oct 96 .... 2.50
❑2 .... 2.50
❑3, Feb 97 .... 2.50

GOBLIN MAGAZINE, THE
WARREN

	ORIG	GOOD	FINE	N-MINT
❑1	2.25	1.60	4.00	8.00
❑2	2.25	1.00	2.50	5.00
❑3, Nov 82, The Goblin; The Tin Man	2.25	1.00	2.50	5.00
❑4	2.25	1.00	2.50	5.00

GOBLIN MARKET
TOME PRESS

Value: Cover or less

❑1, b&w; poem 2.50

GOBLIN STUDIOS
GOBLIN STUDIOS

Value: Cover or less

❑1 .... 2.25
❑2 .... 2.25
❑3 .... 2.25
❑4 .... 2.25
❑5, Aug 95 .... 2.25

GODDESS
DC

Value: Cover or less

❑1, Jun 95, Dangerous To Man 2.95
❑2, Jul 95 .... 2.95
❑3, Aug 95 .... 2.95
❑4, Sep 95 .... 2.95
❑5, Oct 95 .... 2.95
❑6, Nov 95 .... 2.95
❑7, Dec 95 .... 2.95
❑8, Jan 96, Mine Eyes Have Seen the Glory, Final Issue 2.95

GODDESS (TWILIGHT TWINS)
TWILIGHT TWINS

Value: Cover or less

❑1, b&w; Zolastraya 2.00

GODHEAD
ANUBIS

	ORIG	GOOD	FINE	N-MINT
❑1, Distortion	2.75	3.00	7.50	15.00
❑1/LE, Distortion, 1: Jhatori, limited edition	2.75	5.00	12.50	25.00
❑2	2.75	1.20	3.00	6.00
❑2/LE	2.75	0.60	1.50	3.00
❑3	2.75	0.80	2.00	4.00

GODS & TULIPS
WESTHAMPTON

Value: Cover or less

❑1, NG (w), Good Comics and Why you should Sell Them; On Signings 3.00

GODS FOR HIRE
HOT

	ORIG	GOOD	FINE	N-MINT
❑1, Dec 86	1.50	0.40	1.00	2.00
❑2, Jan 87	1.75	0.40	1.00	2.00

GOD'S HAMMER
CALIBER

Value: Cover or less

❑1, b&w 2.50
❑2, b&w 2.50
❑3, b&w 2.50

GOD'S SMUGGLER
SPIRE

	ORIG	GOOD	FINE	N-MINT
❑1, God's Smuggler, Based on the book "God's Smuggler" by Brother Andrew	0.39	1.00	2.50	5.00

GODWHEEL
MALIBU

Value: Cover or less

❑0, Jan 95, The Crucible; Destiny, 1: Primevil, Flip cover 2.50
❑1, Jan 95, The Decision; The Quest, A: Thor; 1: Primevil, Flip cover 2.50
❑2, Feb 95, The Wheel; Pumpkin Trouble, Flip cover 2.50
❑3, Feb 95, GP, Reinventing the Wheel; Thunder in Vahdala, A: Thor, Flip cover; Marvel, Malibu universes cross 2.50

GODZILLA
Marvel

	ORIG	GOOD	FINE	N-MINT
❑1, Aug 77, JM; HT, The Coming!	0.30	1.20	3.00	6.00
❑2, Sep 77	0.30	0.70	1.75	3.50
❑3, Oct 77, A: Champions	0.30	0.60	1.50	3.00
❑4, Nov 77, 1: Doctor Demonicus; V: Batragon	0.35	0.60	1.50	3.00
❑5, Dec 77, O: Doctor Demonicus	0.35	0.60	1.50	3.00
❑6, Jan 78	0.35	0.60	1.50	3.00
❑7, Feb 78, V: Red Ronin	0.35	0.60	1.50	3.00
❑8, Mar 78, V: Red Ronin	0.35	0.60	1.50	3.00
❑9, Apr 78	0.35	0.60	1.50	3.00
❑10, May 78	0.35	0.60	1.50	3.00
❑11, Jun 78, V: Red Ronin, Yetrigar	0.35	0.50	1.25	2.50
❑12, Jul 78	0.35	0.50	1.25	2.50
❑13, Aug 78	0.35	0.50	1.25	2.50
❑14, Sep 78	0.35	0.50	1.25	2.50
❑15, Oct 78	0.35	0.50	1.25	2.50
❑16, Nov 78	0.35	0.50	1.25	2.50
❑17, Dec 78, Godzilla shrunk by Henry Pym's gas	0.35	0.50	1.25	2.50
❑18, Jan 79	0.35	0.50	1.25	2.50
❑19, Feb 79, HT, With Dugan On The Docks!	0.35	0.50	1.25	2.50
❑20, Mar 79, A: Fantastic Four	0.35	0.50	1.25	2.50
❑21, Apr 79, A: Devil Dinosaur	0.35	0.50	1.25	2.50
❑22, May 79, A: Devil Dinosaur	0.40	0.50	1.25	2.50
❑23, Jun 79, A: Avengers	0.40	0.50	1.25	2.50
❑24, Jul 79, V: Avengers; A: Spider-Man; V: Fantastic Four, Final Issue	0.40	0.50	1.25	2.50

GODZILLA (DARK HORSE)
Dark Horse

	ORIG	GOOD	FINE	N-MINT
❑0, May 95, Blast From the Past, reprints and expands story from Dark Horse Comics #10 and 11	2.50	0.80	2.00	4.00
❑1, Jun 95	2.50	0.60	1.50	3.00
❑2, Jul 95	2.50	0.60	1.50	3.00
❑3, Aug 95, V: Bagorah, the Bat Monster	2.50	0.60	1.50	3.00
❑4, Sep 95, V: Bagorah, the Bat Monster	2.50	0.60	1.50	3.00
❑5, Oct 95, Target: Godzilla, Part 1	2.50	0.60	1.50	3.00
❑6, Nov 95, Target: Godzilla, Part 2	2.50	0.59	1.48	2.95
❑7, Dec 95, Target: Godzilla, Part 3	2.50	0.59	1.48	2.95
❑8, Jan 96, Target: Godzilla, Part 4	2.50	0.59	1.48	2.95
❑9, Mar 96, Lost in Time, Part 1	2.50	0.59	1.48	2.95
❑10, Apr 96, Lost in Time, Part 2, Godzilla vs. Spanish Armada	2.50	0.59	1.48	2.95
❑11, May 96, Godzilla travels through time to sink the Titanic	2.50	0.59	1.48	2.95
❑12, Jun 96	2.95	0.59	1.48	2.95
❑13, Jun 96, V: Burtannus	2.95	0.59	1.48	2.95
❑14, Jul 96, To Climb the Highest Monster!	2.95	0.59	1.48	2.95
❑15, Aug 96, The Yamazaki Endowment, V: Lord Howe Monster	2.95	0.59	1.48	2.95
❑16, Final Issue	2.95	0.59	1.48	2.95

GODZILLA (MINI-SERIES)
Dark Horse

	ORIG	GOOD	FINE	N-MINT
❑1, Jul 87, b&w; movie Adaptation; manga	1.95	0.80	2.00	4.00
❑2, b&w; movie Adaptation; manga	1.95	0.60	1.50	3.00
❑3, b&w; movie Adaptation; manga	1.95	0.60	1.50	3.00
❑4, b&w; movie Adaptation; manga	1.95	0.60	1.50	3.00
❑5, b&w; movie Adaptation; manga	1.95	0.60	1.50	3.00
❑6, b&w; movie Adaptation; manga	1.95	0.60	1.50	3.00

GODZILLA COLOR SPECIAL
Dark Horse

	ORIG	GOOD	FINE	N-MINT
❑1, Aug 92	—	0.80	2.00	4.00

GODZILLA, KING OF THE MONSTERS SPECIAL
Dark Horse

	ORIG	GOOD	FINE	N-MINT
❑1/A, Aug 87	1.50	0.60	1.50	3.00
❑1/B, misprinted cover; fewer than 100	—	0.60	1.50	3.00

GODZILLA VS. BARKLEY
Dark Horse

	ORIG	GOOD	FINE	N-MINT
❑1, nn	2.95	0.60	1.50	3.00

GODZILLA VERSUS HERO ZERO
Dark Horse

Value: Cover or less

	ORIG
❑1, Jul 95, A: San Diego Comic-Con	2.50

GOG (VILLAINS)
DC

Value: Cover or less

	ORIG
❑1, Feb 98, JOy, MWa (w), The Road to Hell, New Year's Evil	1.95

GO GIRL!
Image

Value: Cover or less

	ORIG
❑1, Aug 00	3.50
❑2, Nov 00, A Day in the Wonderful Life	3.50
❑3, Nov 01, The Teacher From Hell!	3.50

GOING HOME
Aardvark-Vanaheim

	ORIG	GOOD	FINE	N-MINT
❑1, no date	—	0.40	1.00	2.00

GOJIN
Antarctic

Value: Cover or less

	ORIG
❑1, Apr 95	3.50
❑2, Jun 95	2.95
❑3, Aug 95	2.95
❑3/A, Aug 95, alternate cover	2.95
❑4, b&w	2.95
❑5, b&w	2.95
❑6, b&w	2.95
❑7, b&w	2.95
❑8, Jun 96, b&w	2.95

GOLD DIGGER
Antarctic

	ORIG	GOOD	FINE	N-MINT
❑1, Sep 92	2.50	11.00	27.50	55.00
❑2, Nov 92	2.50	7.00	17.50	35.00
❑3, Jan 93	2.50	5.00	12.50	25.00
❑4, Mar 93	2.50	4.00	10.00	20.00

GOLD DIGGER (2ND SERIES)
Antarctic

	ORIG	GOOD	FINE	N-MINT
❑1, Jul 93	2.50	3.00	7.50	15.00
❑2, Aug 93	2.50	2.00	5.00	10.00
❑3, Sep 93	2.50	1.60	4.00	8.00
❑4, Oct 93	2.75	1.60	4.00	8.00
❑5, Nov 93, has issue #0 on cover; production mistake	2.75	1.60	4.00	8.00
❑6, Dec 93	2.75	1.20	3.00	6.00
❑7, Jan 94	2.75	1.20	3.00	6.00
❑8, Feb 94	2.75	1.20	3.00	6.00
❑9, Mar 94	2.75	1.20	3.00	6.00
❑10, Apr 94	2.75	1.20	3.00	6.00
❑11, May 94	2.75	0.80	2.00	4.00
❑12, Jun 94	2.75	0.80	2.00	4.00
❑13, Jul 94	2.75	0.80	2.00	4.00
❑14, Aug 94	2.75	0.80	2.00	4.00
❑15, Sep 94	2.75	0.80	2.00	4.00
❑16, Oct 94	2.75	0.80	2.00	4.00
❑17, Nov 94	2.75	0.80	2.00	4.00
❑18, Dec 94	2.75	0.80	2.00	4.00
❑19, Feb 95	2.75	0.80	2.00	4.00
❑20, Apr 95	2.75	0.80	2.00	4.00
❑21, May 95	2.75	0.70	1.75	3.50
❑22, Jun 95	2.75	0.70	1.75	3.50
❑23, Jul 95	2.75	0.70	1.75	3.50
❑24, Aug 95	2.75	0.70	1.75	3.50
❑25, Oct 95	2.75	0.70	1.75	3.50
❑26, Nov 95	2.75	0.70	1.75	3.50
❑27, Dec 95	2.75	0.70	1.75	3.50
❑28, Feb 96	2.75	0.70	1.75	3.50
❑29, Apr 96	2.95	0.70	1.75	3.50
❑30, Jul 96	2.95	0.70	1.75	3.50
❑31, Aug 96	2.95	0.70	1.75	3.50
❑32, Oct 96, Time Warp, Part 1	2.95	0.70	1.75	3.50
❑33, Dec 96, Time Warp, Part 3	2.95	0.70	1.75	3.50
❑34, Feb 97, Time Warp, Part 5	2.95	0.70	1.75	3.50
❑35, Apr 97, Time Warp, Part 7	2.95	0.70	1.75	3.50
❑36, Jul 97	2.95	0.70	1.75	3.50
❑37, Aug 97	2.95	0.70	1.75	3.50
❑38, Jan 98, cover says Nov 97, indicia says Jan 98	2.95	0.70	1.75	3.50
❑39, Mar 98	2.95	0.70	1.75	3.50
❑40, May 98	2.95	0.70	1.75	3.50
❑41, Jun 98	2.95	0.70	1.75	3.50
❑42, Jul 98	2.95	0.70	1.75	3.50
❑43, Aug 98	2.95	0.70	1.75	3.50
❑44, Sep 98	2.95	0.70	1.75	3.50
❑45, Oct 98	2.95	0.70	1.75	3.50
❑46, Dec 98	2.95	0.70	1.75	3.50
❑47, Jan 99	2.95	0.70	1.75	3.50
❑48, Feb 99	2.99	0.70	1.75	3.50
❑49, Apr 99	2.99	0.70	1.75	3.50
❑50, Jun 99	2.99	0.70	1.75	3.50
❑50/CS, Jun 99, poster; poster edition	2.99	1.20	2.99	5.99
❑Anl 1, Sep 95	3.95	0.79	1.98	3.95
❑Anl 2, Sep 96, b&w	3.95	0.79	1.98	3.95
❑Anl 3, Sep 97, Proving Ground; A Fishy Revenge, b&w; 1997 Annual	3.95	0.79	1.98	3.95
❑Anl 4, Sep 98, Fatal Fury; Return of the Lich King, b&w; 1998 Annual	3.95	0.79	1.98	3.95
❑GN 1, Graphic Novel	10.95	2.19	5.47	10.95
❑SE 1, Special edition	2.75	0.55	1.38	2.75

GOLD DIGGER (3RD SERIES)
Antarctic

	ORIG	GOOD	FINE	N-MINT
❑1, Jul 99, new color series	2.50	1.20	3.00	6.00
❑2, Aug 99, new color series	2.50	0.80	2.00	4.00
❑3	—	0.60	1.50	3.00
❑4	—	0.60	1.50	3.00
❑5	—	0.60	1.50	3.00
❑6	—	0.60	1.50	3.00
❑7	—	0.60	1.50	3.00

	ORIG	GOOD	FINE	N-MINT
❑8	—	0.60	1.50	3.00
❑9	—	0.60	1.50	3.00
❑10	—	0.60	1.50	3.00
❑11	—	0.60	1.50	3.00
❑12	—	0.60	1.50	3.00
❑13	—	0.60	1.50	3.00
❑14	—	0.60	1.50	3.00
❑15	—	0.60	1.50	3.00
❑16	—	0.60	1.50	3.00
❑17	—	0.60	1.50	3.00
❑18	—	0.60	1.50	3.00
❑19	—	0.60	1.50	3.00
❑20	—	0.60	1.50	3.00
❑21	—	0.59	1.48	2.95
❑22	—	0.59	1.48	2.95
❑23	—	0.59	1.48	2.95
❑24	2.95	0.59	1.48	2.95

GOLD DIGGER: BETA
ANTARCTIC

Value: Cover or less

❑1, Feb 98 .... 2.95

GOLD DIGGER: EDGE GUARD
RADIO COMIX

Value: Cover or less

❑1, Aug 00 .... 2.95

GOLD DIGGER MANGAZINE
ANTARCTIC

	ORIG	GOOD	FINE	N-MINT
❑1, Mar 94	2.75	0.60	1.50	2.99
❑1-2, Apr 99, 2nd Printing	2.99	0.60	1.50	2.99

GOLD DIGGER PERFECT MEMORY
ANTARCTIC

Value: Cover or less

❑1, Jul 96, b&w; story synopses, character profiles, and other material 4.50

GOLDEN AGE, THE
DC

	ORIG	GOOD	FINE	N-MINT
❑1, PS, JRo (w), The World Was at Peace, Elseworlds	4.95	1.10	2.75	5.50
❑2, PS, JRo (w), We Had the Bomb, O: Dynaman, Elseworlds	4.95	1.10	2.75	5.50
❑3, PS, JRo (w), We Had Prosperity, Elseworlds	4.95	1.10	2.75	5.50
❑4, Apr 01, PS, JRo (w), We Had it All, D: Miss America; D: Doll Man; D: Hawkman; D: Ultra-Humanite; D: Dynaman, Elseworlds	4.95	1.10	2.75	5.50

GOLDEN AGE OF TRIPLE-X, THE
REVISIONARY

Value: Cover or less

❑1, b&w; adult 3.50

GOLDEN AGE OF TRIPLE-X: JOHN HOLMES SPECIAL
RE-VISIONARY

Value: Cover or less

❑1 .... 2.95

GOLDEN AGE SECRET FILES
DC

Value: Cover or less

❑1, Feb 01, The Dawn of the Golden Age; The Crimson Avenger Speaks! 4.95

GOLDEN DRAGON
SYNCHRONICITY

Value: Cover or less

❑1, Anything That Doesn't Kill You Makes You Stronger 1.50

GOLDEN FEATURES (JERRY IGER'S...)
BLACKTHORNE

Value: Cover or less

❑1 .... 2.00
❑2 .... 2.00
❑3, Jun 86 .... 2.00
❑4, Aug 86 .... 2.00
❑5, Oct 86 .... 2.00
❑6 .... 2.00

GOLDEN WARRIOR
INDUSTRIAL DESIGN

Value: Cover or less

❑1, Mar 97, b&w 2.95

GOLDEN WARRIOR ICZER ONE
ANTARCTIC

Value: Cover or less

❑1, Apr 94, b&w 2.95
❑2, May 94, b&w 2.95
❑3, Jun 94, b&w 2.95
❑4, Jul 94, b&w 2.95
❑5, Aug 94, b&w; Final Issue .. 2.95

GOLDYN 3-D
BLACKTHORNE

Value: Cover or less

❑1 .... 2.00

GOLGO 13
LEAD PUBLISHING CO.

Value: Cover or less

❑1, The Impossible Hit, b&w... 1.00
❑2, full color 1.50

NBA star Charles Barkley played one-on-one with the king of the Japanese monsters, Godzilla, in this Dark Horse one-shot.

© 1998 Dark Horse

ORIG GOOD FINE N-MINT

GOLGO 13 (2ND SERIES)
VIZ

Value: Cover or less

❑1, b&w 4.95
❑2, b&w 4.95
❑3, b&w 4.95

GOLGOTHIKA
CALIBER

Value: Cover or less

❑1, Leviathan 2.95

GO-MAN!
CALIBER

Value: Cover or less

❑1, b&w 2.50
❑2, b&w 2.50
❑3, b&w 2.50
❑4, b&w 2.50

GON
DC

Value: Cover or less

❑1, Gon Eats and Sleeps, b&w; digest 5.95
❑2, Gon Again!, b&w; digest ... 5.95
❑3, Here Today Gon Tomorrow!, b&w; digest 5.95
❑4, Going, Going...Gon, b&w; digest 5.95
❑5, Gon Swimmin', b&w; digest 6.95

GONAD THE BARBARIAN
ETERNITY

	ORIG	GOOD	FINE	N-MINT
❑1	1.95	0.45	1.13	2.25

GON COLOR SPECTACULAR
DC

Value: Cover or less

❑1, nn; comic-book-sized one-shot; prestige format 5.95

GON UNDERGROUND
PARADOX

Value: Cover or less

❑1 .... 7.95

GOOD-BYE, CHUNKY RICE
TOP SHELF

Value: Cover or less

❑1, Oct 99, nn; b&w; graphic novel 14.95

GOOD GIRL ART QUARTERLY
AC

	ORIG	GOOD	FINE	N-MINT
❑1, Jul 90, new & reprints	3.50	0.79	1.98	3.95
❑2, Fal 90	3.95	0.79	1.98	3.95
❑3, Win 91	3.95	0.79	1.98	3.95
❑4, Spr 91	3.95	0.79	1.98	3.95
❑5, Sum 91	3.95	0.79	1.98	3.95
❑6, Fal 91, Fall 1991	3.95	0.79	1.98	3.95
❑7, Win 92	3.95	0.79	1.98	3.95
❑8, Spr 92	3.95	0.79	1.98	3.95
❑9, Sum 92	3.95	0.79	1.98	3.95
❑10, Fal 92	3.95	0.79	1.98	3.95
❑11, Win 93	3.95	0.79	1.98	3.95
❑12, Spr 93	3.95	0.79	1.98	3.95
❑13, Sum 93	3.95	0.79	1.98	3.95
❑14, Fal 93	3.95	0.79	1.98	3.95
❑15, Win 94	3.95	0.79	1.98	3.95
❑16	3.95	0.79	1.98	3.95
❑17	3.95	0.79	1.98	3.95
❑18	3.95	0.79	1.98	3.95
❑19	6.95	1.39	3.47	6.95

GOOD GIRLS
FANTAGRAPHICS

Value: Cover or less

❑1, Apr 87, Ms. Lonelyhearts, b&w 2.00
❑2, Oct 87, Number 23 .... 2.00
❑3 .... 2.00
❑4, Feb 89, Dreamland 2.00
❑6, Jun 91, b&w 2.00

GOOD GUYS, THE
DEFIANT

Value: Cover or less

❑1, Nov 93, JM (w), To Wish A Mile High, 1: Master Ridgely Gatesman; 1: The Good Guys, Giant-size 3.50
❑2, Dec 93, Steppin' Out! 2.50
❑3, Jan 94, And From The Darkness...Chasm 2.50
❑4, Feb 94 .... 3.25
❑5, Mar 94, Monster Truck...... 2.50
❑6, Apr 94, Assault On Scourge Island 2.50
❑7, May 94, Master Of The World, A: Charlemagne 2.50
❑8, Jun 94 .... 2.50
❑9, Jul 94 .... 2.50
❑10 .... 2.50
❑11 .... 2.50
❑12 .... 2.50

GOODY GOOD COMICS
FANTAGRAPHICS

Value: Cover or less

❑1, Jun 00, Extend the Hand of Love to All Who Can Use It, Doofus, Greaseball, Mike Hayes 2.95

GOOFY ADVENTURES
DISNEY

	ORIG	GOOD	FINE	N-MINT
❑1, Jun 90, Balboa de Goofy; Goofy Frankenstein, Part 1	1.50	0.50	1.25	2.50
❑2, Jul 90, Goofy Frankenstein, Part 2; Goofy Peary & the North Pole	1.50	0.30	0.75	1.50
❑3, Aug 90, Covered Wagons, Ho!; Alexander the Goof	1.50	0.30	0.75	1.50
❑4, Sep 90, The Great Goofdini; The Goofy Goalie	1.50	0.30	0.75	1.50
❑5, Oct 90	1.50	0.30	0.75	1.50
❑6, Nov 90	1.50	0.30	0.75	1.50
❑7, Dec 90, Three Musketeers	1.50	0.30	0.75	1.50
❑8, Jan 91, Goofy Washington; A Goofy Look at Movies	1.50	0.30	0.75	1.50
❑9, Feb 91, James Goof - Master Spy; Goofy Caruso, James Bond parody	1.50	0.30	0.75	1.50
❑10, Mar 91, Samurai Goofy; A Goofy Look at Doors	1.50	0.30	0.75	1.50
❑11, Apr 91, Goofis Kahn; A Goofy Look at Weather	1.50	0.30	0.75	1.50
❑12, May 91, Arizona Goof and the Lost Temple, Part 1	1.50	0.30	0.75	1.50
❑13, Jun 91, Arizona Goof and the Lost Temple, Part 2	1.50	0.30	0.75	1.50
❑14, Jul 91, Alexander the Goof: The Early Years; Goofylution	1.50	0.30	0.75	1.50
❑15, Aug 91, Super Goof vs. the Cold Ray; A Goofy Look at Sleep, Super-Goof	1.50	0.30	0.75	1.50
❑16, Sep 91, Sheerluck Goof and the Giggling Ghost of Nottenny Moor, Sherlock Holmes parody	1.50	0.30	0.75	1.50
❑17, Oct 91, GC, Back in Time; Goofy Thuh Kid, Final Issue	1.50	0.30	0.75	1.50

GOON PATROL
PINNACLE

Value: Cover or less

❑1, A Transylvanian Affair; The Origin of the Beanman 1.75

GORDON YAMAMOTO AND THE KING OF THE GEEKS
HUMBLE

Value: Cover or less

❑1, Oct 97, b&w 2.95

GORE SHRIEK
FANTACO

	ORIG	GOOD	FINE	N-MINT
❑1, b&w; 1st Greg Capullo story	1.50	0.60	1.50	3.00
❑2, b&w	1.50	0.60	1.50	3.00
❑3, b&w	2.95	0.60	1.50	3.00
❑4, b&w	2.95	0.60	1.50	3.00
❑5, Fallen Leaves; Mal Occhio	3.50	0.70	1.75	3.50
❑6	3.50	0.70	1.75	3.50
❑Anl 1, b&w	4.95	0.99	2.47	4.95

GORE SHRIEK (VOL. 2)
FANTACO

Value: Cover or less

❑1, b&w 2.50

❑2, b&w 2.50

❑3, b&w 2.50

GORE SHRIEK DELECTUS
FANTACO

Value: Cover or less

❑1, nn 8.95

GORGANA'S GHOUL GALLERY
AC

Value: Cover or less

❑1, b&w; Reprint 2.95

❑2, I Released the Muck Man!; Deadtime Story, Reprint 2.95

GORGON
VENUS

Value: Cover or less

❑1, Jun 96, Dark Bandit 2.95

❑2, Jun 96 2.95

❑3, Jun 96 2.95

❑4, Jun 96 2.95

❑5, Aug 96 2.95

GORILLA GUNSLINGER
MOJO

	ORIG	GOOD	FINE	N-MINT
❑0, The Good, The Bad...and The Gorilla, Sampler	0.50	0.20	0.50	1.00

GOTCHA!
RIP OFF

Value: Cover or less

❑1, Sep 91, b&w; adult 2.50

G.O.T.H.
VEROTIK

	ORIG	GOOD	FINE	N-MINT
❑1	—	0.60	1.50	3.00
❑2	—	0.60	1.50	3.00
❑3	—	0.60	1.50	3.00

GOTHAM NIGHTS
DC

	ORIG	GOOD	FINE	N-MINT
❑1, Mar 92, Giants	1.25	0.30	0.75	1.50
❑2, Apr 92, The Lessons Of Life	1.25	0.30	0.75	1.50
❑3, May 92, Organisms	1.25	0.30	0.75	1.50
❑4, Jun 92	1.25	0.30	0.75	1.50

GOTHAM NIGHTS II
DC

	ORIG	GOOD	FINE	N-MINT
❑1, Mar 95	1.95	0.40	1.00	2.00
❑2, Apr 95	1.95	0.40	1.00	2.00
❑3, May 95, Final Blows	1.95	0.40	1.00	2.00
❑4, Jun 95, Ashes to Ashes	1.95	0.40	1.00	2.00

GOTHIC
5TH PANEL

	ORIG	GOOD	FINE	N-MINT
❑1, Apr 97, Foundation, b&w	1.95	0.50	1.25	2.50
❑2	2.50	0.50	1.25	2.50

GOTHIC MOON
ANARCHY BRIDGEWORKS

Value: Cover or less

❑1 5.95

GOTHIC NIGHTS
REBEL

Value: Cover or less

❑1, b&w 2.00

❑2 2.00

GOTHIC RED
BONEYARD

Value: Cover or less

❑1 2.95

❑3, Mar 97, b&w 2.95

GOTHIC SCROLLS, THE: DRAYVEN
DAVDEZ

Value: Cover or less

❑1, Dec 97, The Beginning 2.95

❑2, Feb 98 2.50

❑3, Mar 98 2.50

❑Ash 1, Aug 97, cover says Sep, indicia says Aug; Preview edition 1.50

GRACKLE, THE
ACCLAIM

Value: Cover or less

❑1, Jan 97, PG, Doublecross, Part 1, b&w 2.95

❑2, Feb 97, PG, Doublecross, Part 2, b&w 2.95

❑3, Mar 97, PG, Doublecross, Part 3, b&w 2.95

❑4, Apr 97, PG, Doublecross, Part 4, b&w 2.95

GRAFFITI KITCHEN
TUNDRA

Value: Cover or less

❑1, nn 2.95

GRAFIK MUZIK
CALIBER

	ORIG	GOOD	FINE	N-MINT
❑1, A: Madman, b&w	3.50	4.00	10.00	20.00
❑2	2.50	2.40	6.00	12.00
❑3	2.50	1.60	4.00	8.00
❑4	2.50	1.60	4.00	8.00

GRAMMAR PATROL, THE
CASTEL PUBLICATIONS

Value: Cover or less

❑1 2.00

GRAPHIC
FANTACO

Value: Cover or less

❑1 3.95

GRAPHIC HEROES IN HOUSE OF CARDS
GRAPHIC STAFFING

	ORIG	GOOD	FINE	N-MINT
❑1, nn; personalized promotional piece for temporary graphics employees	—	0.10	0.25	0.50

GRAPHIC STORY MONTHLY
FANTAGRAPHICS

	ORIG	GOOD	FINE	N-MINT
❑1, b&w	2.95	0.80	2.00	4.00
❑2, b&w	2.95	0.70	1.75	3.50
❑3, b&w	2.95	0.70	1.75	3.50
❑4, b&w	2.95	0.70	1.75	3.50
❑5, b&w	2.95	0.70	1.75	3.50
❑6, b&w	2.95	0.70	1.75	3.50
❑7	3.50	0.70	1.75	3.50

GRAPHIQUE MUSIQUE
SLAVE LABOR

	ORIG	GOOD	FINE	N-MINT
❑1, Dec 89, b&w	2.95	1.60	4.00	8.00
❑2, Mar 90, b&w	2.95	1.60	4.00	8.00
❑3, May 90, b&w	2.95	1.60	4.00	8.00

GRATEFUL DEAD COMIX
KITCHEN SINK

	ORIG	GOOD	FINE	N-MINT
❑1, full color	4.95	1.20	3.00	6.00
❑2, full color	4.95	1.00	2.50	5.00
❑3, full color	4.95	1.00	2.50	5.00
❑4, full color	4.95	1.00	2.50	5.00
❑5, full color	4.95	1.00	2.50	5.00
❑6, full color	4.95	1.00	2.50	5.00
❑7, full color	4.95	1.00	2.50	5.00

GRATEFUL DEAD COMIX (VOL. 2)
KITCHEN SINK

Value: Cover or less

❑1, comic-book size 3.95

❑2, Apr 94 3.95

GRAVEDIGGERS
ACCLAIM
Value: Cover or less

- ❑1, Nov 96, Magic Bullet, b&w ... 2.95
- ❑2, Dec 96, The Wrong Man, b&w ... 2.95
- ❑3, Jan 97, Losses Unknown, b&w ... 2.95
- ❑4, Feb 97, b&w; Final Issue .. 2.95

GRAVEDIGGER TALES
AVALON
Value: Cover or less

- ❑1, b&w ... 2.95

GRAVESTONE
MALIBU
Value: Cover or less

- ❑1, Orpheus Descending ... 2.25
- ❑2 ... 2.25
- ❑3, Sep 93, Near Death Experience, Genesis ... 2.25
- ❑4 ... 2.25
- ❑5, Genesis ... 2.25
- ❑6, Genesis ... 2.25
- ❑7, Feb 94, Genesis; last issue 2.25

GRAVESTOWN
ARIEL
Value: Cover or less

- ❑1, Oct 97 ... 2.95

GRAVE TALES
HAMILTON
Value: Cover or less

- ❑1, Oct 91, b&w ... 3.95
- ❑2, b&w ... 3.95
- ❑3, b&w ... 3.95

GREASE MONKEY
KITCHEN SINK
Value: Cover or less

- ❑1, Oct 95, Art Lovers ... 3.50
- ❑2, Oct 95, The Gift ... 3.50

GREASE MONKEY (IMAGE)
IMAGE
Value: Cover or less

- ❑1, Jan 98 ... 2.95
- ❑2, Mar 98, Gorilla Tactics ... 2.95

GREAT AMERICAN WESTERN
AC

	ORIG	GOOD	FINE	N-MINT
❑1, Dark Rider; Santee	1.75	0.40	1.00	2.00
❑2	2.95	0.59	1.48	2.95
❑3	2.95	0.59	1.48	2.95
❑4	3.50	0.70	1.75	3.50
❑5	5.00	1.00	2.50	5.00

GREAT BIG BEEF
ERR

	ORIG	GOOD	FINE	N-MINT
❑97, Jun 96, b&w	1.97	0.40	1.00	2.00
❑98, Jan 97, b&w; cover says Apr, indicia says Jan	1.98	0.40	1.00	2.00
❑99, Sep 97, b&w	1.99	0.40	1.00	2.00

GREATEST AMERICAN COMIC BOOK
OCEAN
Value: Cover or less

- ❑1, Spider-Man parody; Batman ... 2.55

GREATEST DIGGS OF ALL TIME!
RIP OFF
Value: Cover or less

- ❑1, Feb 91, nn; b&w ... 2.00

GREAT EXPLOITS
DECKER

	ORIG	GOOD	FINE	N-MINT
❑1, Oct 57, Frog Men Against Belzar; Explorer Joe: Murder in the Himilayas	0.10	4.80	12.00	24.00

GREAT GALAXIES
ZUB

	ORIG	GOOD	FINE	N-MINT
❑0, The Glory; Nal Ralone, Interstellar Archeologist, 1: The Warp Patrol, b&w	2.95	0.59	1.48	2.95
❑1, News Maker; Antique Death, O: Captain Dean, b&w	2.50	0.50	1.25	2.50
❑2, Final Objective; Death Stealer, b&w	2.50	0.50	1.25	2.50
❑3, A Real Thrill; Stolen Kisses, b&w	2.50	0.50	1.25	2.50
❑4, Funeral; Hacker!, b&w	2.50	0.50	1.25	2.50
❑5, The Warp Wars Saga, b&w	2.50	0.50	1.25	2.50
❑6/Ash, Glass Coffin, Flip book with Telluria Ashcan #6	—	0.10	0.25	0.50

GREAT MORONS IN HISTORY
REVOLUTIONARY
Value: Cover or less

- ❑1, Oct 93, b&w; Dan Quayle . 2.50

GREAT SOCIETY COMIC BOOK, THE
PARALLAX

	ORIG	GOOD	FINE	N-MINT
❑1, Super LBJ is Missing	1.00	2.80	7.00	14.00
❑2	1.00	2.00	5.00	10.00

GREEENLOCK
AIRCEL
Value: Cover or less

- ❑1, b&w ... 2.50

GREEN ARROW
DC

Whenever he ate an irradiated peanut, Goofy acquired super-powers and fought crime as Super Goof.

© 1991 Walt Disney Productions

	ORIG	GOOD	FINE	N-MINT
❑0, Oct 94, 1: Connor Hawke (as adult)	1.95	0.50	1.25	2.50
❑1, Feb 88, DG, MGr (c), MGr (w), Hunters Moon, Part 1, Painted cover	1.00	0.60	1.50	3.00
❑2, Mar 88, DG, MGr (c), MGr (w), Hunters Moon, Part 2, Painted cover	1.00	0.50	1.25	2.50
❑3, Apr 88, DG; FMc, MGr (c), MGr (w), The Champions, Part 1, Painted cover	1.00	0.40	1.00	2.00
❑4, May 88, MGr (c), MGr (w), The Champions, Part 2	1.00	0.40	1.00	2.00
❑5, Jun 88, Gauntlet, Part 1	1.00	0.40	1.00	2.00
❑6, Jul 88, Gauntlet, Part 2	1.00	0.40	1.00	2.00
❑7, Aug 88	1.00	0.40	1.00	2.00
❑8, Sep 88	1.00	0.40	1.00	2.00
❑9, Oct 88, Here There Be Dragons, Part 1	1.00	0.40	1.00	2.00
❑10, Nov 88, MGr (c), Here There Be Dragons, Part 2	1.00	0.40	1.00	2.00
❑11, Dec 88, MGr (c), Here There Be Dragons, Part 3	1.00	0.30	0.75	1.50
❑12, Dec 88, MGr (c), Here There Be Dragons, Part 4	1.00	0.30	0.75	1.50
❑13, Jan 89, Moving Target, Part 1	1.25	0.30	0.75	1.50
❑14, Jan 89, Moving Target, Part 2	1.25	0.30	0.75	1.50
❑15, Feb 89, Seattle & Die, Part 1	1.25	0.30	0.75	1.50
❑16, Mar 89, Seattle & Die, Part 2	1.25	0.30	0.75	1.50
❑17, Apr 89, The Horseman, Part 1	1.25	0.30	0.75	1.50
❑18, May 89, The Horseman, Part 2	1.25	0.30	0.75	1.50
❑19, Jun 89, The Trial of Oliver Queen, Part 1	1.25	0.30	0.75	1.50
❑20, Jul 89, The Trial of Oliver Queen, Part 2	1.25	0.30	0.75	1.50
❑21, Aug 89, Blood of the Dragon, Part 1, 1: Connor Hawke (baby)	1.25	0.50	1.25	2.50
❑22, Aug 89, Blood of the Dragon, Part 2	1.25	0.30	0.75	1.50
❑23, Sep 89, Blood of the Dragon, Part 3	1.25	0.30	0.75	1.50
❑24, Sep 89, Blood of the Dragon, Part 4	1.25	0.30	0.75	1.50
❑25, Oct 89, Witch Hunt, Part 1	1.25	0.30	0.75	1.50
❑26, Nov 89, Witch Hunt, Part 2	1.25	0.30	0.75	1.50
❑27, Dec 89, A: Warlord	1.25	0.30	0.75	1.50
❑28, Jan 90, A: Warlord	1.25	0.30	0.75	1.50
❑29, Feb 90, Coyote Tears, Part 1	1.25	0.30	0.75	1.50
❑30, Mar 90, Coyote Tears, Part 2	1.20	0.30	0.75	1.50
❑31, Apr 90, The Canary is a Bird of Prey, Part 1	1.20	0.30	0.75	1.50
❑32, May 90, The Canary is a Bird of Prey, Part 2	1.20	0.30	0.75	1.50
❑33, Jun 90	1.20	0.30	0.75	1.50
❑34, Jul 90	1.20	0.30	0.75	1.50
❑35, Aug 90, The Black Arrow Saga, Part 1, Black Arrow	1.25	0.30	0.75	1.50
❑36, Sep 90, The Black Arrow Saga, Part 2, Black Arrow	1.25	0.30	0.75	1.50
❑37, Sep 90, The Black Arrow Saga, Part 3, Black Arrow	1.25	0.30	0.75	1.50
❑38, Oct 90, The Black Arrow Saga, Part 4, Black Arrow	1.25	0.30	0.75	1.50
❑39, Nov 90	1.25	0.30	0.75	1.50
❑40, Dec 90	1.25	0.30	0.75	1.50
❑41, Dec 90	1.25	0.30	0.75	1.50
❑42, Jan 91	1.25	0.30	0.75	1.50
❑43, Feb 91	1.25	0.30	0.75	1.50
❑44, Mar 91, Rock and Runes, Part 1	1.25	0.30	0.75	1.50
❑45, Apr 91, Rock and Runes, Part 2	1.25	0.30	0.75	1.50
❑46, May 91, Round the Horn, Part 1	1.25	0.30	0.75	1.50
❑47, Jun 91, Round the Horn, Part 2	1.50	0.30	0.75	1.50
❑48, Jun 91, Round the Horn, Part 3	1.50	0.30	0.75	1.50
❑49, Jul 91	1.50	0.30	0.75	1.50
❑50, Aug 91, Giant-size	2.50	0.50	1.25	2.50
❑51, Aug 91	1.50	0.30	0.75	1.50
❑52, Sep 91	1.50	0.30	0.75	1.50
❑53, Oct 91	1.50	0.30	0.75	1.50
❑54, Nov 91	1.50	0.30	0.75	1.50
❑55, Dec 91, MGr (w), Justice is Mine, Part 1	1.50	0.30	0.75	1.50
❑56, Jan 92, Justice is Mine, Part 2	1.50	0.30	0.75	1.50
❑57, Feb 92, ...And Not a Drop to Drink, Part 1	1.25	0.30	0.75	1.50
❑58, Mar 92, ...And Not a Drop to Drink, Part 2	1.25	0.30	0.75	1.50
❑59, Apr 92, Predator, Part 1	1.25	0.30	0.75	1.50
❑60, May 92, Predator, Part 2	1.25	0.30	0.75	1.50
❑61, May 92	1.50	0.30	0.75	1.50

	ORIG	GOOD	FINE	N-MINT
❑62, Jun 92	1.50	0.30	0.75	1.50
❑63, Jun 92, The Hunt for the Red Dragon, Part 1	1.50	0.30	0.75	1.50
❑64, Jul 92, The Hunt for the Red Dragon, Part 2	1.50	0.30	0.75	1.50
❑65, Aug 92, The Hunt for the Red Dragon, Part 3	1.50	0.30	0.75	1.50
❑66, Sep 92, The Hunt for the Red Dragon, Part 4	1.50	0.30	0.75	1.50
❑67, Oct 92, Bum Rap, Part 1	1.50	0.30	0.75	1.50
❑68, Nov 92, Bum Rap, Part 2	1.50	0.30	0.75	1.50
❑69, Dec 92, MGr (w), Reunion Tour, Part 1	1.75	0.35	0.88	1.75
❑70, Jan 93, Reunion Tour, Part 2	1.75	0.35	0.88	1.75
❑71, Feb 93, Wild in the Streets, Part 1	1.75	0.35	0.88	1.75
❑72, Mar 93, Wild in the Streets, Part 2	1.75	0.35	0.88	1.75
❑73, Apr 93, Trigger, Part 1	1.75	0.35	0.88	1.75
❑74, May 93, Trigger, Part 2	1.75	0.35	0.88	1.75
❑75, Jun 93, Giant-size	2.50	0.50	1.25	2.50
❑76, Jul 93, Killing Camp, Part 1, O: Green Lantern and Green Arrow	1.75	0.35	0.88	1.75
❑77, Aug 93, Killing Camp, Part 2	1.75	0.35	0.88	1.75
❑78, Sep 93, Killing Camp, Part 3	1.75	0.35	0.88	1.75
❑79, Oct 93, New Dogs, Old Tricks, Part 1	1.75	0.35	0.88	1.75
❑80, Nov 93, MGr (w), New Dogs, Old Tricks, Part 2	1.75	0.35	0.88	1.75
❑81, Dec 93	1.75	0.35	0.88	1.75
❑82, Jan 94, JA, Night of the Bow	1.75	0.35	0.88	1.75
❑83, Feb 94	1.75	0.35	0.88	1.75
❑84, Mar 94	1.75	0.35	0.88	1.75
❑85, Apr 94, A: Deathstroke	1.75	0.35	0.88	1.75
❑86, May 94, Catwoman	1.75	0.35	0.88	1.75
❑87, Jun 94	1.75	0.39	0.98	1.95
❑88, Jul 94, JA, The Hero Descending, A: JLA	1.95	0.39	0.98	1.95
❑89, Aug 94	1.95	0.39	0.98	1.95
❑90, Sep 94, Crossroads Conclusion; Zero Hour, Zero Hour	1.95	0.45	1.13	2.25
❑91, Nov 94	1.95	0.39	0.98	1.95
❑92, Dec 94	1.95	0.39	0.98	1.95
❑93, Jan 95	1.95	0.39	0.98	1.95
❑94, Feb 95	1.95	0.39	0.98	1.95
❑95, Mar 95	1.95	0.39	0.98	1.95
❑96, Apr 95, Where Angels Fear to Tread, Part 1	1.95	0.60	1.50	3.00
❑97, Jun 95, Where Angels Fear to Tread, Part 2	2.25	0.60	1.50	3.00
❑98, Jul 95, Where Angels Fear to Tread, Part 3	2.25	0.60	1.50	3.00
❑99, Aug 95, Where Angels Fear to Tread, Part 4	2.25	0.60	1.50	3.00
❑100, Sep 95, Where Angels Fear to Tread, Part 5, enhanced cover; Giant-size	3.95	1.40	3.50	7.00
❑101, Oct 95, Where Angels Fear to Tread, Part 6, D: Oliver Queen; D: Green Arrow I (Oliver Queen)	2.25	5.20	13.00	26.00
❑102, Nov 95, Underworld Unleashed, Underworld Unleashed	2.25	0.45	1.13	2.25
❑103, Dec 95, A: Green Lantern	2.25	0.45	1.13	2.25
❑104, Jan 96	2.25	0.45	1.13	2.25
❑105, Feb 96, Open Season, A: Robin	2.25	0.45	1.13	2.25
❑106, Mar 96, Enter the Roustabout	2.25	0.45	1.13	2.25
❑107, Apr 96, Viva Los Dragons!	2.25	0.45	1.13	2.25
❑108, May 96, A: Thorn	2.25	0.45	1.13	2.25
❑109, Jun 96	2.25	0.45	1.13	2.25
❑110, Jul 96, Hard-Traveling Heroes: The Next Generation, Part 2	2.25	0.45	1.13	2.25
❑111, Aug 96, Hard-Traveling Heroes: The Next Generation, Part 4	2.25	0.45	1.13	2.25
❑112, Sep 96, The Lotus Seed, Part 1	2.25	0.45	1.13	2.25
❑113, Oct 96, The Lotus Seed, Part 2	2.25	0.45	1.13	2.25
❑114, Nov 96, The Thousand Year Night, Final Night	2.25	0.45	1.13	2.25
❑115, Dec 96, The Iron Death, Part 1, A: Shado, Black Canary	2.25	0.45	1.13	2.25
❑116, Jan 97, The Iron Death, Part 2, A: Black Canary, Oracle, Shado	2.25	0.45	1.13	2.25
❑117, Feb 97, The Iron Death, Part 3; The Death that Walks, A: Black Canary	2.25	0.45	1.13	2.25
❑118, Mar 97, Endangered Species, Part 1	2.25	0.45	1.13	2.25
❑119, Apr 97, Endangered Species, Part 2, A: Warlord	2.25	0.45	1.13	2.25
❑120, May 97, A: Warlord	2.25	0.45	1.13	2.25
❑121, Jun 97	2.25	0.45	1.13	2.25
❑122, Jul 97, Stormbringers, Part 1	2.25	0.45	1.13	2.25
❑123, Aug 97, Stormbringers, Part 2	2.25	0.45	1.13	2.25
❑124, Sep 97	2.25	0.45	1.13	2.25
❑125, Oct 97, Hate Crimes, Part 1, Giant-size; continues in Green Lantern #92	3.50	0.70	1.75	3.50
❑126, Nov 97, Hate Crimes, Part 3	2.50	0.50	1.25	2.50
❑127, Dec 97, Doubleback, Face cover	2.50	0.50	1.25	2.50
❑128, Jan 98, Deadly Comrades, Part 1	2.50	0.50	1.25	2.50
❑129, Feb 98, Deadly Comrades, Part 2	2.50	0.50	1.25	2.50
❑130, Mar 98, Three of a Kind, Part 2, cover forms triptych with Flash #135 and Green Lantern #96	2.50	0.50	1.25	2.50
❑131, Apr 98	2.50	0.50	1.25	2.50
❑132, May 98, Like A God, Part 1	2.50	0.50	1.25	2.50
❑133, Jun 98, Like A God, Part 2, A: JLA	2.50	0.50	1.25	2.50
❑134, Jul 98, Brotherhood of the Fist, Part 1, A: Batman, continues in Detective Comics #723	2.50	0.50	1.25	2.50
❑135, Aug 98, Brotherhood of the Fist, Part 5, V: Lady Shiva	2.50	0.50	1.25	2.50
❑136, Sep 98, Greener Pastures, Part 1, A: Hal Jordan	2.50	0.50	1.25	2.50
❑137, Oct 98, Full Circle, A: Superman, Final Issue	2.50	0.50	1.25	2.50
❑1000000, Nov 98, All Down the Years, Final Issue	2.50	0.50	1.25	2.50
❑Anl 1, Sep 88, A: Batman	2.00	0.70	1.75	3.50
❑Anl 2, Aug 89, A: Question	2.50	0.60	1.50	3.00
❑Anl 3, Dec 90, A: Question	2.50	0.60	1.50	3.00
❑Anl 4, Jun 91, 50th Anniversary; Robin Hood	2.95	0.60	1.50	3.00
❑Anl 5, Eclipso: The Darkness Within, Part 8, Eclipso, Batman	3.00	0.60	1.50	3.00
❑Anl 6, Bloodlines, 1: Hook, Bloodlines	3.50	0.70	1.75	3.50
❑Anl 7, Year One, Year One	3.95	0.79	1.98	3.95

GREEN ARROW (2ND SERIES)
DC

	ORIG	GOOD	FINE	N-MINT
❑1, Apr 01, KSm (w), Quiver, Part 1, Return of Oliver Queen	2.50	1.20	3.00	6.00
❑2, May 01, KSm (w), Quiver, Part 2	2.50	0.50	1.25	2.50
❑3	2.50	0.50	1.25	2.50
❑4	2.50	0.50	1.25	2.50
❑5	2.50	0.50	1.25	2.50
❑6	2.50	0.50	1.25	2.50

GREEN ARROW (MINI-SERIES)
DC

	ORIG	GOOD	FINE	N-MINT
❑1, May 83, DG, O: Green Arrow	0.60	0.60	1.50	3.00
❑2, Jun 83, TVE; DG, A Slight Case Of Vertigo..!	0.60	0.50	1.25	2.50
❑3, Jul 83, DG	0.60	0.40	1.00	2.00
❑4, Aug 83, DG	0.60	0.40	1.00	2.00

GREEN ARROW: THE LONGBOW HUNTERS
DC

	ORIG	GOOD	FINE	N-MINT
❑1, Aug 87, MGr, MGr (w), The Hunters, 1: Shado	2.95	0.80	2.00	4.00
❑1-2, MGr, MGr (w), The Hunters, 1: Shado, 2nd Printing	2.95	0.60	1.50	3.00
❑, MGr, MGr (w), The Hunters, 1: Shado, 3rd Printing	2.95	0.60	1.50	3.00
❑2, Sep 87, MGr, MGr (w), Dragon Hunt	2.95	0.60	1.50	3.00
❑3, Oct 87, MGr, MGr (w), Tracking Snow	2.95	0.60	1.50	3.00

GREEN ARROW: THE WONDER YEAR
DC

	ORIG	GOOD	FINE	N-MINT
❑1, Feb 93, MGr; GM, MGr (w)	1.75	0.40	1.00	2.00
❑2, Mar 93, MGr; GM, MGr (w)	1.75	0.40	1.00	2.00
❑3, Apr 93, MGr; GM, MGr (w)	1.75	0.40	1.00	2.00
❑4, May 93, MGr; GM, MGr (w)	1.75	0.40	1.00	2.00

GREEN CANDLES
DC

Value: Cover or less

❑1, b&w; digest	5.95
❑2, b&w; digest	5.95
❑3, b&w; digest	5.95

GREENER PASTURES
KRONOS

Value: Cover or less

❑1	2.50
❑1-2, Jan 97, 2nd Printing	2.50
❑2, Oct 94	2.50
❑3, Feb 95	2.50
❑4, Dec 95	2.50
❑4.5, Feb 96	1.95
❑5, Aug 96	2.95
❑6, Nov 96	2.95
❑7, Feb 97	2.95

GREEN GOBLIN
MARVEL

Value: Cover or less

❑1, Oct 95, Enter the Green Goblin, 1: Green Goblin IV (Phil Urich), enhanced cardstock cover; trading cards	2.95
❑2, Nov 95, V: Rhino	1.95
❑3, Dec 95, CyberWar, A: Joystick; V: Scarlet Spider, Story continued from Amazing Scarlet Spider #2	1.95
❑4, Jan 96, V: Hobgoblin	1.95
❑5, Feb 96	1.95
❑6, Mar 96, A: Daredevil	1.95
❑7, Apr 96, Slammed-!	1.95
❑8, May 96	1.95
❑9, Jun 96	1.95
❑10, Jul 96	1.95
❑11, Aug 96	1.95
❑12, Sep 96, Onslaught: Impact 2	1.95
❑13, Oct 96, Final Issue	1.95

	ORIG	GOOD	FINE	N-MINT

GREEN-GREY SPONGE-SUIT SUSHI TURTLES
MIRAGE

	ORIG	GOOD	FINE	N-MINT
❑1, full color; cardstock cover; parody	3.33	0.70	1.75	3.50

GREENHAVEN
AIRCEL

Value: Cover or less

Issue	Value
❑1, full color	2.00
❑2, full color	2.00
❑3, full color; Continued in Elflord #21	2.00

GREEN HORNET, THE (VOL. 1)
NOW

	ORIG	GOOD	FINE	N-MINT
❑1, Nov 89, JSo (c), My Last Case, O: 1940s Green Hornet; O: Green Hornet I	2.95	0.70	1.75	3.50
❑1-2, Apr 90, My Last Case, O: The Green Hornet, 2nd Printing; expanded family history of Green Hornet; prestige format; perfect bound	3.95	0.79	1.98	3.95
❑2, Dec 89	1.75	0.50	1.25	2.50
❑3, Jan 90	1.75	0.40	1.00	2.00
❑4, Feb 90, SR (c)	1.75	0.40	1.00	2.00
❑5, Mar 90	1.75	0.40	1.00	2.00
❑6, Apr 90	1.75	0.40	1.00	2.00
❑7, May 90, BSz (c), Bloodlines, 1: new Kato, Mishi becomes new Kato	1.75	0.40	1.00	2.00
❑8, Jun 90	1.75	0.40	1.00	2.00
❑9, Jul 90	1.75	0.40	1.00	2.00
❑10, Aug 90	1.75	0.40	1.00	2.00
❑11, Sep 90	1.75	0.40	1.00	2.00
❑12, Oct 90	1.75	0.40	1.00	2.00
❑13, Nov 90	1.75	0.40	1.00	2.00
❑14, Feb 91, Final Issue	1.75	0.40	1.00	2.00

GREEN HORNET, THE (VOL. 2)
NOW

Value: Cover or less

Issue	Value
❑1, Sep 91, Money Talks	1.95
❑2, Oct 91	1.95
❑3, Nov 91	1.95
❑4, Dec 91	1.95
❑5, Jan 92	1.95
❑6, Feb 92	1.95
❑7, Mar 92	1.95
❑8, Apr 92	1.95
❑9, May 92	1.95
❑10, Jun 92	1.95
❑11, Jul 92, V: Crimson Wasp.	1.95
❑12, Aug 92, The Odyssey of the Crimson Wasp, Part 1, V: Crimson Wasp, button; bagged; with button	2.50
❑13, Sep 92, The Odyssey of the Crimson Wasp, Part 2	1.95
❑14, Oct 92, The Odyssey of the Crimson Wasp, Part 3	1.95
❑15, Nov 92	1.95
❑16, Dec 92	1.95
❑17, Jan 93	1.95
❑18, Feb 93	1.95
❑19, Mar 93	1.95
❑20, Apr 93	1.95
❑21, May 93, V: Mr. Death	1.95
❑22, Jun 93, trading card; newsstand, trading card; newsstand; Has UPC, Comics Code seal	2.95
❑22/DM, Jun 93, alternate cover; direct sale; trading card; No Comics Code seal	2.95
❑23, Jul 93, hologram trading card	2.95
❑24, Aug 93, Pin-up	1.95
❑25, Sep 93	1.95
❑26, Oct 93	2.95
❑27, Nov 93, trading card	2.95
❑28, Dec 93	1.95
❑29, Jan 94	1.95
❑30, Feb 94	1.95
❑31, Mar 94	2.50
❑32, Apr 94	1.95
❑33, May 94	1.95
❑34, Jun 94	1.95
❑35, Jul 94	1.95
❑36, Aug 94	1.95
❑37, Sep 94	1.95
❑38, Nov 94	2.50
❑39, Dec 94	1.95
❑40, Jan 95	2.50
❑Anl 1, Dec 92	2.50
❑Anl 1994, Oct 94	2.95

GREEN HORNET ANNIVERSARY SPECIAL
NOW

Value: Cover or less

Issue	Value
❑1, Aug 92, bagged; with button	2.50
❑2	1.95
❑3	1.95

GREEN HORNET, THE: DARK TOMORROW
NOW

Value: Cover or less

Issue	Value
❑1, Jun 93, A Blacker Shade of Green	2.50
❑2, Jul 93	2.50
❑3, Aug 93	2.50

GREEN HORNET, THE: SOLITARY SENTINEL
NOW

Value: Cover or less

Issue	Value
❑1, Dec 92, Strike Force	2.50
❑2, Jan 93, Black Marauders	2.50
❑3, Feb 93, Crime Vs. Crime	2.50

GREENHOUSE WARRIORS
TUNDRA UK

Value: Cover or less

Issue	Value
❑1	2.95
❑2	3.95
❑3	3.95
❑4	3.95

GREEN LANTERN (2ND SERIES)
DC

	ORIG	GOOD	FINE	N-MINT
❑1, Aug 60, GK, 1: the Guardians; O: Green Lantern II (Hal Jordan)	0.10	560.00	1400.00	2800.00
❑2, Oct 60, GK, 1: Pieface; 1: Qward	0.10	150.00	375.00	750.00
❑3, Dec 60, GK	0.10	90.00	225.00	450.00
❑4, Feb 61, GK	0.10	68.00	170.00	340.00
❑5, Apr 61, GK, 1: Hector Hammond	0.10	68.00	170.00	340.00
❑6, Jun 61, GK, 1: Tomar	0.10	55.00	137.50	275.00
❑7, Aug 61, GK, 1: Sinestro	0.10	50.00	125.00	250.00

An adventure from the early days of his career was recounted in *Green Arrow: The Wonder Year.*

	ORIG	GOOD	FINE	N-MINT
❑8, Oct 61, GK	0.10	50.00	125.00	250.00
❑9, Dec 61, GK	0.10	50.00	125.00	250.00
❑10, Jan 62, GK	0.12	50.00	125.00	250.00
❑11, Mar 62, GK, 1: The Green Lantern Corps	0.12	35.00	87.50	175.00
❑12, Apr 62, GK, 1: Doctor Polaris	0.12	35.00	87.50	175.00
❑13, Jun 62, GK, A: Flash II (Barry Allen)	0.12	40.00	100.00	200.00
❑14, Jul 62, GK, 1: Sonar	0.12	30.00	75.00	150.00
❑15, Sep 62, GK	0.12	29.00	72.50	145.00
❑16, Oct 62, GK, 1: Zamarons; 1: Star Sapphire	0.12	29.00	72.50	145.00
❑17, Dec 62, GK	0.12	27.00	67.50	135.00
❑18, Jan 63, GK	0.12	27.00	67.50	135.00
❑19, Mar 63, GK	0.12	27.00	67.50	135.00
❑20, Apr 63, GK, Parasite Planet Peril!, A: Flash II (Barry Allen)	0.12	27.00	67.50	135.00
❑21, Jun 63, GK, O: Doctor Polaris; O: Dr. Polaris	0.12	24.00	60.00	120.00
❑22, Jul 63, GK	0.12	24.00	60.00	120.00
❑23, Sep 63, GK, 1: Tattooed Man	0.12	24.00	60.00	120.00
❑24, Oct 63, GK, 1: The Shark	0.12	24.00	60.00	120.00
❑25, Dec 63, GK	0.12	24.00	60.00	120.00
❑26, Jan 64, GK	0.12	24.00	60.00	120.00
❑27, Mar 64, GK	0.12	24.00	60.00	120.00
❑28, Apr 64, GK, 1: Goldface	0.12	24.00	60.00	120.00
❑29, Jun 64, GK, 1: Black Hand; A: Justice League of America	0.12	26.00	65.00	130.00
❑30, Jul 64, GK	0.12	24.00	60.00	120.00
❑31, Sep 64, GK	0.12	20.00	50.00	100.00
❑32, Oct 64, GK	0.12	20.00	50.00	100.00
❑33, Dec 64, GK	0.12	20.00	50.00	100.00
❑34, Jan 65, GK	0.12	20.00	50.00	100.00
❑35, Mar 65, GK	0.12	20.00	50.00	100.00
❑36, Apr 65, GK	0.12	20.00	50.00	100.00
❑37, Jun 65, GK, 1: Evil Star	0.12	20.00	50.00	100.00
❑38, Jul 65, GK	0.12	20.00	50.00	100.00
❑39, Sep 65, GK	0.12	20.00	50.00	100.00
❑40, Oct 65, A: Green Lantern I (Alan Scott); 1: Krona; O: the Guardians	0.12	93.00	232.50	465.00
❑41, Dec 65, GK, A: Star Sapphire	0.12	12.00	30.00	60.00
❑42, Jan 66, GK	0.12	12.00	30.00	60.00
❑43, Mar 66, GK, A: Flash II (Barry Allen); 1: Major Disaster	0.12	12.00	30.00	60.00
❑44, Apr 66, GK	0.12	12.00	30.00	60.00
❑45, Jun 66, GK, A: Green Lantern I (Alan Scott); 1: Prince Peril	0.12	18.00	45.00	90.00
❑46, Jul 66, GK	0.12	12.00	30.00	60.00
❑47, Sep 66, GK	0.12	12.00	30.00	60.00
❑48, Oct 66, GK	0.12	12.00	30.00	60.00
❑49, Dec 66, GK	0.12	12.00	30.00	60.00
❑50, Jan 67, GK	0.12	12.00	30.00	60.00
❑51, Mar 67	0.12	8.00	20.00	40.00
❑52, Apr 67, A: Green Lantern I (Alan Scott)	0.12	9.00	22.50	45.00
❑53, Jun 67	0.12	8.00	20.00	40.00
❑54, Jul 67	0.12	8.00	20.00	40.00
❑55, Sep 67	0.12	8.00	20.00	40.00
❑56, Oct 67	0.12	8.00	20.00	40.00
❑57, Dec 67	0.12	8.00	20.00	40.00
❑58, Jan 68	0.12	8.00	20.00	40.00
❑59, Mar 68, 1: Guy Gardner	0.12	40.00	100.00	200.00
❑60, Apr 68	0.12	5.20	13.00	26.00
❑61, Jun 68, A: Green Lantern I (Alan Scott)	0.12	8.00	20.00	40.00
❑62, Jul 68	0.12	5.20	13.00	26.00
❑63, Sep 68	0.12	5.20	13.00	26.00
❑64, Oct 68	0.12	5.20	13.00	26.00
❑65, Dec 68	0.12	5.20	13.00	26.00
❑66, Jan 69	0.12	5.20	13.00	26.00
❑67, Mar 69	0.12	5.20	13.00	26.00
❑68, Apr 69	0.12	5.20	13.00	26.00
❑69, Jun 69	0.12	5.20	13.00	26.00
❑70, Jul 69, GK	0.15	5.20	13.00	26.00
❑71, Sep 69, GK	0.15	4.00	10.00	20.00
❑72, Oct 69, GK	0.15	4.00	10.00	20.00

	ORIG	GOOD	FINE	N-MINT
❑73, Dec 69, GK	0.15	4.00	10.00	20.00
❑74, Jan 70, GK	0.15	4.00	10.00	20.00
❑75, Mar 70, GK	0.15	4.00	10.00	20.00
❑76, Apr 70, NA, A: Green Arrow, Green Lantern/Green Arrow series	0.15	27.00	67.50	135.00
❑77, Jun 70, NA, A: Green Arrow, Green Lantern/Green Arrow series	0.15	13.00	32.50	65.00
❑78, Jul 70, NA, A: Green Arrow, Green Lantern/Green Arrow series	0.15	13.00	32.50	65.00
❑79, Sep 70, NA, A: Green Arrow, Green Lantern/Green Arrow series	0.15	10.00	25.00	50.00
❑80, Oct 70, NA, A: Green Arrow, Green Lantern/Green Arrow series	0.15	10.00	25.00	50.00
❑81, Dec 70, NA, A: Green Arrow, Green Lantern/Green Arrow series	0.15	7.00	17.50	35.00
❑82, Mar 71, NA, A: Green Arrow, Green Lantern/Green Arrow series	0.15	7.00	17.50	35.00
❑83, May 71, NA, A: Green Arrow, Green Lantern/Green Arrow series	0.15	7.00	17.50	35.00
❑84, Jul 71, NA; BWr, Green Arrow; Green Lantern/Green Arrow series	0.15	7.00	17.50	35.00
❑85, Sep 71, NA, Green Arrow; Anti-drug issue; Green Lantern/Green Arrow series	0.25	10.00	25.00	50.00
❑86, Nov 71, NA, Green Lantern/Green Arrow series; Green Arrow; Anti-drug issue	0.25	10.00	25.00	50.00
❑87, Jan 72, GK; NA, 1: John Stewart; A: Green Arrow, Guy Gardner cameo; Green Lantern/Green Arrow series	0.25	8.00	20.00	40.00
❑88, Mar 72, GK, A: Green Arrow	0.25	1.80	4.50	9.00
❑89, May 72, NA, A: Green Arrow, Green Lantern/Green Arrow series	0.25	3.00	7.50	15.00
❑90, Sep 76, MGr, MGr (w), A: Green Arrow, Green Lantern/Green Arrow series	0.30	1.00	2.50	5.00
❑91, Nov 76, MGr	0.30	1.00	2.50	5.00
❑92, Dec 76, MGr	0.30	1.00	2.50	5.00
❑93, Feb 77, MGr	0.30	0.80	2.00	4.00
❑94, Apr 77, MGr	0.30	0.80	2.00	4.00
❑95, Jun 77, MGr	0.35	0.80	2.00	4.00
❑96, Aug 77, MGr	0.35	0.80	2.00	4.00
❑97, Oct 77, MGr	0.35	0.80	2.00	4.00
❑98, Nov 77, MGr	0.35	0.80	2.00	4.00
❑99, Dec 77, MGr	0.35	0.80	2.00	4.00
❑100, Jan 78, MGr, 1: Air Wave; 1: Air Wave II (Harry "Hal" Jordan), 100th anniversary issue	0.35	1.20	3.00	6.00
❑101, Feb 78, McGinty	0.35	0.80	2.00	4.00
❑102, Mar 78, MGr, A: Green Arrow	0.35	0.80	2.00	4.00
❑103, Apr 78, MGr, A: Green Arrow	0.35	0.80	2.00	4.00
❑104, May 78, MGr, A: Green Arrow	0.35	0.80	2.00	4.00
❑105, Jun 78, MGr, A: Green Arrow	0.35	0.80	2.00	4.00
❑106, Jul 78, MGr, A: Green Arrow	0.35	0.80	2.00	4.00
❑107, Aug 78, MGr, A: Green Arrow	0.35	0.80	2.00	4.00
❑108, Sep 78, MGr, A: Green Arrow, Golden Age Green Lantern back-up	0.50	0.80	2.00	4.00
❑109, Oct 78, MGr, A: Green Arrow, Golden Age Green Lantern back-up	0.50	0.80	2.00	4.00
❑110, Nov 78, MGr, A: Green Arrow	0.50	0.80	2.00	4.00
❑111, Dec 78, MGr, A: Green Arrow	0.40	0.80	2.00	4.00
❑112, Jan 79, O: Green Lantern I (Alan Scott)	0.40	1.60	4.00	8.00
❑113, Feb 79	0.40	0.60	1.50	3.00
❑114, Mar 79	0.40	0.60	1.50	3.00
❑115, Apr 79	0.40	0.60	1.50	3.00
❑116, May 79, Guy Gardner becomes a Green Lantern	0.40	2.40	6.00	12.00
❑117, Jun 79	0.40	0.60	1.50	3.00
❑118, Jul 79	0.40	0.60	1.50	3.00
❑119, Aug 79	0.40	0.50	1.25	2.50
❑120, Sep 79	0.40	0.50	1.25	2.50
❑121, Oct 79	0.40	0.50	1.25	2.50
❑122, Nov 79, A: Guy Gardner	0.40	0.70	1.75	3.50
❑123, Dec 79, Guy Gardner as Green Lantern	0.40	1.20	3.00	6.00
❑124, Jan 80	0.40	0.50	1.25	2.50
❑125, Feb 80	0.40	0.50	1.25	2.50
❑126, Mar 80	0.40	0.50	1.25	2.50
❑127, Apr 80, JSa	0.40	0.50	1.25	2.50
❑128, May 80, JSa	0.40	0.50	1.25	2.50
❑129, Jun 80, JSa	0.40	0.50	1.25	2.50
❑130, Jun 80, JSa	0.40	0.50	1.25	2.50
❑131, Aug 80, JSa	0.40	0.45	1.13	2.25
❑132, Sep 80, JSa	0.50	0.45	1.13	2.25
❑133, Oct 80, JSa, A: Doctor Polaris; A: Dr. Polaris	0.50	0.45	1.13	2.25
❑134, Nov 80, JSa, A: Doctor Polaris; A: Dr. Polaris	0.50	0.45	1.13	2.25
❑135, Dec 80, JSa, A: Doctor Polaris; A: Dr. Polaris	0.50	0.45	1.13	2.25
❑136, Jan 81, JSa	0.50	0.50	1.25	2.50
❑137, Feb 81, JSa, 1: Citadel	0.50	0.50	1.25	2.50
❑138, Mar 81, JSa	0.50	0.50	1.25	2.50
❑139, Apr 81, JSa	0.50	0.50	1.25	2.50
❑140, May 81, JSa	0.50	0.40	1.00	2.00
❑141, Jun 81, JSa, 1: Primus; 1: Demonia; 1: Kalista; 1: Auron; 1: Omega Men; 1: Harpis; 1: Broot	0.50	0.60	1.50	3.00
❑142, Jul 81, JSa, A: Omega Men; 1: The Gordanians	0.50	0.50	1.25	2.50
❑143, Aug 81, JSa, A: Omega Men	0.50	0.50	1.25	2.50
❑144, Sep 81, JSa, A: Omega Men	0.50	0.50	1.25	2.50
❑145, Oct 81, JSa	0.60	0.40	1.00	2.00
❑146, Nov 81, JSa	0.60	0.40	1.00	2.00
❑147, Dec 81, JSa	0.60	0.40	1.00	2.00
❑148, Jan 82, JSa	0.60	0.40	1.00	2.00
❑149, Feb 82, JSa	0.60	0.40	1.00	2.00
❑150, Mar 82, JSa, 150th anniversary issue	1.00	0.60	1.50	3.00
❑151, Apr 82	0.60	0.40	1.00	2.00
❑152, May 82	0.60	0.40	1.00	2.00
❑153, Jun 82	0.60	0.40	1.00	2.00
❑154, Jul 82	0.60	0.40	1.00	2.00
❑155, Aug 82	0.60	0.40	1.00	2.00
❑156, Sep 82	0.60	0.40	1.00	2.00
❑157, Oct 82	0.60	0.40	1.00	2.00
❑158, Nov 82	0.60	0.40	1.00	2.00
❑159, Dec 82	0.60	0.40	1.00	2.00
❑160, Jan 83, Omega Men	0.60	0.40	1.00	2.00
❑161, Feb 83, Omega Men	0.60	0.30	0.75	1.50
❑162, Mar 83, KP	0.60	0.30	0.75	1.50
❑163, Apr 83, KP	0.60	0.30	0.75	1.50
❑164, May 83, KP, 1: The Green Man	0.60	0.30	0.75	1.50
❑165, Jun 83, KP	0.60	0.30	0.75	1.50
❑166, Jul 83	0.60	0.30	0.75	1.50
❑167, Aug 83, 1: Spider Guild	0.60	0.30	0.75	1.50
❑168, Sep 83	0.60	0.30	0.75	1.50
❑169, Oct 83	0.60	0.30	0.75	1.50
❑170, Nov 83, GK (c)	0.60	0.30	0.75	1.50
❑171, Dec 83	0.75	0.30	0.75	1.50
❑172, Jan 84	0.75	0.30	0.75	1.50
❑173, Feb 84, DG, V: Javelin; A: Monitor	0.75	0.30	0.75	1.50
❑174, Mar 84, DG	0.75	0.30	0.75	1.50
❑175, Apr 84, DG, V: Shark; A: Flash	0.75	0.30	0.75	1.50
❑176, May 84, DG, V: Shark; 1: Demolition Team	0.75	0.30	0.75	1.50
❑177, Jun 84, GK (c), V: Hector Hammond	0.75	0.30	0.75	1.50
❑178, Jul 84, DG, V: Demolition Team; A: Monitor; 1: The Predator (Carol Ferris)	0.75	0.30	0.75	1.50
❑179, Aug 84, DG, A: Predator; V: Demolition Team	0.75	0.30	0.75	1.50
❑180, Sep 84, DG, A: Flash; A: Green Arrow; A: Superman	0.75	0.30	0.75	1.50
❑181, Oct 84, DG, Hal Jordan quits as Green Lantern; Hal Jordan resigns as Green Lantern	0.75	0.30	0.75	1.50
❑182, Nov 84, DG, John Stewart becomes new Green Lantern; retells origin	0.75	0.30	0.75	1.50
❑183, Dec 84	0.75	0.30	0.75	1.50
❑184, Jan 85, GK, reprints origin of Guy Gardner	0.75	0.30	0.75	1.50
❑185, Feb 85, DG	0.75	0.30	0.75	1.50
❑186, Mar 85, DG, V: Eclipso	0.75	0.30	0.75	1.50
❑187, Apr 85	0.75	0.30	0.75	1.50
❑188, May 85, John Stewart reveals ID to public	0.75	0.30	0.75	1.50
❑189, Jun 85, V: Sonar	0.75	0.30	0.75	1.50
❑190, Jul 85, V: Predator	0.75	0.30	0.75	1.50
❑191, Aug 85	0.75	0.30	0.75	1.50
❑192, Sep 85	0.75	0.30	0.75	1.50
❑193, Oct 85	0.75	0.30	0.75	1.50
❑194, Nov 85, Crisis; Guy Gardner returns; Guy Gardner vs. Hal Jordan	0.75	0.50	1.25	2.50
❑195, Dec 85, Crisis; Guy Gardner becomes new Green Lantern of Earth	0.75	0.60	1.50	3.00
❑196, Jan 86, Crisis	0.75	0.30	0.75	1.50
❑197, Feb 86, Crisis; Guy Gardner vs. John Stewart	0.75	0.30	0.75	1.50
❑198, Mar 86, Crisis; giant; Hal Jordan returns as Green Lantern	1.25	0.30	0.75	1.50
❑199, Apr 86, Crisis; Hal Jordan returns as GL	0.75	0.30	0.75	1.50
❑200, May 86, Crisis; Guardians join Zamarons	1.25	0.40	1.00	2.00
❑201, Jun 86, Crisis aftermath	0.75	0.30	0.75	1.50
❑202, Jul 86	0.75	0.30	0.75	1.50
❑203, Aug 86, O: Ch'p	0.75	0.30	0.75	1.50
❑204, Sep 86	0.75	0.30	0.75	1.50

	ORIG	GOOD	FINE	N-MINT
❑205, Oct 86, Series continues as Green Lantern Corps	0.75	0.30	0.75	1.50
❑SE 1, Dec 88, With This Ring...!	1.50	0.50	1.25	2.50
❑SE 2	1.50	0.50	1.25	2.50

GREEN LANTERN (3RD SERIES)
DC

	ORIG	GOOD	FINE	N-MINT
❑0, Oct 94, Second Chances, V: Hal Jordan; O: Green Lantern (Kyle Rayner), Oa destroyed	1.50	0.60	1.50	3.00
❑1, Jun 90, PB, Down to Earth	1.00	0.60	1.50	3.00
❑2, Jul 90, PB, Pursuit Of Happiness!	1.00	0.50	1.25	2.50
❑3, Aug 90, Hal vs. Guy	1.00	0.40	1.00	2.00
❑4, Sep 90	1.00	0.40	1.00	2.00
❑5, Oct 90	1.00	0.40	1.00	2.00
❑6, Nov 90	1.00	0.30	0.75	1.50
❑7, Dec 90	1.00	0.30	0.75	1.50
❑8, Jan 91	1.00	0.30	0.75	1.50
❑9, Feb 91, A: G'Nort	1.00	0.30	0.75	1.50
❑10, Mar 91, A: G'Nort	1.00	0.30	0.75	1.50
❑11, Apr 91, A: G'Nort	1.00	0.30	0.75	1.50
❑12, May 91, A: G'Nort	1.00	0.30	0.75	1.50
❑13, Jun 91, Giant-size	1.75	0.45	1.13	2.25
❑14, Jul 91	1.00	0.30	0.75	1.50
❑15, Aug 91	1.00	0.30	0.75	1.50
❑16, Sep 91	1.00	0.30	0.75	1.50
❑17, Oct 91	1.00	0.30	0.75	1.50
❑18, Nov 91	1.00	0.30	0.75	1.50
❑19, Dec 91, GK (c), 50th anniversary issue; 50th Anniversary; Giant-size	1.75	0.40	1.00	2.00
❑20, Jan 92	1.00	0.30	0.75	1.50
❑21, Feb 92	1.00	0.30	0.75	1.50
❑22, Mar 92	1.00	0.30	0.75	1.50
❑23, Apr 92	1.00	0.30	0.75	1.50
❑24, May 92	1.00	0.30	0.75	1.50
❑25, Jun 92, Giant size; Hal Jordan vs. Guy Gardner	1.75	0.45	1.13	2.25
❑26, Jul 92, Evil Star Rising, Part 1	1.00	0.30	0.75	1.50
❑27, Aug 92, Evil Star Rising, Part 2	1.25	0.25	0.63	1.25
❑28, Sep 92, Evil Star Rising, Part 3	1.25	0.25	0.63	1.25
❑29, Sep 92	1.25	0.25	0.63	1.25
❑30, Oct 92, V: Gorilla Grodd; A: Flash	1.25	0.25	0.63	1.25
❑31, Oct 92, V: Grodd; A: Flash; V: Hector Hammond	1.25	0.25	0.63	1.25
❑32, Nov 92	1.25	0.25	0.63	1.25
❑33, Nov 92	1.25	0.25	0.63	1.25
❑34, Dec 92	1.25	0.25	0.63	1.25
❑35, Jan 93	1.25	0.25	0.63	1.25
❑36, Feb 93	1.25	0.25	0.63	1.25
❑37, Mar 93	1.25	0.25	0.63	1.25
❑38, Apr 93, Adam Strange	1.25	0.25	0.63	1.25
❑39, May 93	1.25	0.25	0.63	1.25
❑40, May 93, A: Darkstar	1.25	0.25	0.63	1.25
❑41, Jun 93	1.25	0.25	0.63	1.25
❑42, Jun 93	1.25	0.25	0.63	1.25
❑43, Jul 93	1.25	0.25	0.63	1.25
❑44, Aug 93	1.25	0.25	0.63	1.25
❑45, Sep 93	1.25	0.25	0.63	1.25
❑46, Oct 93, Reign of The Supermen, A: Superman; V: Mongul	1.25	0.80	2.00	4.00
❑47, Nov 93, A: Green Arrow	1.25	0.40	1.00	2.00
❑48, Jan 94, Emerald Twilight; Emerald Twilight, Part 1	1.50	1.20	3.00	6.00
❑49, Feb 94, Emerald Twilight; Emerald Twilight, Part 2	1.50	1.20	3.00	6.00
❑50, Mar 94, Emerald Twilight; Emerald Twilight, Part 3, D: Kilowog; D: Sinestro; 1: Green Lantern IV (Kyle Rayner), Glow-in-the-dark cover; Double-size	2.95	1.20	3.00	6.00
❑51, May 94, Changing The Guard, New costume	1.50	0.60	1.50	3.00
❑52, Jun 94, V: Mongul	1.50	0.40	1.00	2.00
❑53, Jul 94, A: Superman	1.50	0.40	1.00	2.00
❑54, Aug 94, V: Major Force	1.50	0.40	1.00	2.00
❑55, Sep 94, Zero Hour, A: Alan Scott; A: Green Lantern I, Zero Hour	1.50	0.40	1.00	2.00
❑56, Nov 94	1.50	0.40	1.00	2.00
❑57, Dec 94, A: New Titans, continues in New Titans #116	1.50	0.40	1.00	2.00
❑58, Jan 95, Conjuring	1.50	0.40	1.00	2.00
❑59, Feb 95, V: Doctor Polaris; V: Dr. Polaris	1.50	0.40	1.00	2.00
❑60, Mar 95, Capital Punishment, Part 3, V: Major Force; A: Guy Gardner	1.50	0.40	1.00	2.00
❑61, Apr 95, V: Kalibak; A: Darkstar	1.50	0.40	1.00	2.00
❑62, May 95	1.50	0.40	1.00	2.00
❑63, Jun 95, Parallax View, Part 1	1.75	0.40	1.00	2.00
❑64, Jul 95, Parallax View, Part 2	1.75	0.40	1.00	2.00
❑65, Aug 95, The Siege of The Zi Charam, Part 2, continues in Darkstars #34	1.75	0.40	1.00	2.00

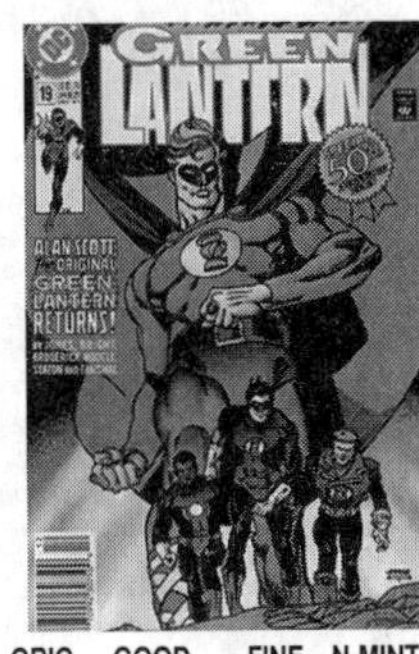

Golden Age Green Lantern creator Martin Nodell contributed several story pages to *Green Lantern* (3rd series) #19, which honored his creation's 50th anniversary.

© 1991 DC Comics

	ORIG	GOOD	FINE	N-MINT
❑66, Sep 95, teams with Flash	1.75	0.40	1.00	2.00
❑67, Oct 95	1.75	0.40	1.00	2.00
❑68, Nov 95, A: Donna Troy, Underworld Unleashed	1.75	0.40	1.00	2.00
❑69, Dec 95, Underworld Unleashed, Underworld Unleashed	1.75	0.40	1.00	2.00
❑70, Jan 96, A: John Stewart	1.75	0.40	1.00	2.00
❑71, Feb 96, Hero Quest, Part 1, A: Batman; A: Sentinel; A: Robin	1.75	0.40	1.00	2.00
❑72, Mar 96, Hero Quest, Part 2, A: Captain Marvel	1.75	0.40	1.00	2.00
❑73, Apr 96, Hero Quest, Part 3, A: Wonder Woman	1.75	0.40	1.00	2.00
❑74, Jun 96	1.75	0.40	1.00	2.00
❑75, Jul 96	1.75	0.40	1.00	2.00
❑76, Jul 96, Hard-Traveling Heroes: The Next Generation, Part 1	1.75	0.40	1.00	2.00
❑77, Aug 96, Hard-Traveling Heroes: The Next Generation, Part 3	1.75	0.40	1.00	2.00
❑78, Sep 96	1.75	0.40	1.00	2.00
❑79, Oct 96, Hard Time, V: Sonar	1.75	0.40	1.00	2.00
❑80, Nov 96, Light in Darkness, V: Dr. Light; V: Doctor Light, Final Night	1.75	0.40	1.00	2.00
❑81, Dec 96, Funeral for a Hero, Funeral of Hal Jordan; Memorial for Hal Jordan	1.75	0.60	1.50	3.00
❑81/SC, Dec 96, Funeral for a Hero, Embossed cover; Funeral of Hal Jordan; Kane back-up story; reprints origin; Memorial for Hal Jordan	3.95	0.80	2.00	4.00
❑82, Jan 97, Adventures in Babysitting	1.75	0.35	0.88	1.75
❑83, Feb 97, Retribution, Part 1	1.75	0.35	0.88	1.75
❑84, Mar 97, Retribution, Part 2	1.75	0.35	0.88	1.75
❑85, Apr 97, Retribution, Part 3	1.75	0.35	0.88	1.75
❑86, May 97, A: Obsidian; A: Jade	1.75	0.35	0.88	1.75
❑87, Jun 97, A: Access; A: Martian Manhunter	1.75	0.35	0.88	1.75
❑88, Jul 97	1.75	0.35	0.88	1.75
❑89, Aug 97	1.75	0.35	0.88	1.75
❑90, Sep 97	1.75	0.35	0.88	1.75
❑91, Oct 97, Torture, V: Desaad, Genesis	1.75	0.35	0.88	1.75
❑92, Nov 97, Hate Crimes, Part 2, concludes in Green Arrow #126	1.75	0.35	0.88	1.75
❑93, Dec 97, All Hallow's Eve, A: Deadman, Face cover	1.75	0.39	0.98	1.95
❑94, Jan 98, Idol Worship, Part 1, A: Superboy	1.95	0.39	0.98	1.95
❑95, Feb 98	1.95	0.39	0.98	1.95
❑96, Mar 98, Three of a Kind, Part 1, cover forms triptych with Flash #135 and Green Arrow #130	1.95	0.39	0.98	1.95
❑97, Apr 98, Loose Ends, V: Grayven	1.95	0.39	0.98	1.95
❑98, May 98, Future Shock, Part 1, 1: Cary Wren as Green Lantern; A: Legion of Super-Heroes	1.95	0.39	0.98	1.95
❑99, Jun 98, Future Shock, Part 2	1.95	0.39	0.98	1.95
❑100/A, Jul 98, Hal Jordan cover (Kyle Rayner cover inside)	2.95	0.59	1.48	2.95
❑100/Aut, Jul 98, Emerald Knights, Signed by Ron Marz	—	1.60	4.00	8.00
❑100/B, Jul 98, Kyle Rayner cover (Hal Jordan cover inside)	2.95	0.59	1.48	2.95
❑101, Aug 98, Emerald Knights, Part 1; Emerald Knights	1.95	0.39	0.98	1.95
❑102, Aug 98, Emerald Knights, Part 2; Emerald Knights, V: Kalibak	1.95	0.39	0.98	1.95
❑103, Sep 98, Emerald Knights, Part 3; Emerald Knights, A: JLA	1.99	0.39	0.98	1.95
❑104, Sep 98, Emerald Knights, Part 4; Emerald Knights, A: Green Arrow	1.99	0.39	0.98	1.95
❑105, Oct 98, Emerald Knights, Part 5; Emerald Knights, V: Parallax	1.99	0.39	0.98	1.95
❑106, Oct 98, Emerald Knights, Part 6; Emerald Knights, Hal returned to past	1.99	0.39	0.98	1.95
❑107, Dec 98, Kyle gives a ring to Jade	1.99	0.40	1.00	1.99
❑108, Jan 99, Wonder Woman	1.99	0.40	1.00	1.99
❑109, Feb 99, Green Lantern IV (Jade)	1.99	0.40	1.00	1.99

	ORIG	GOOD	FINE	N-MINT
❑110, Mar 99, A: Conner Hawke; A: Green Arrow; A: Green Lantern (Alan Scott)	1.99	0.40	1.00	1.99
❑111, Apr 99, A: John Stewart; V: Fatality	1.99	0.40	1.00	1.99
❑112, May 99, Kyle returns	1.99	0.40	1.00	1.99
❑113, Jun 99, Burning in Effigy, Part 1	1.99	0.40	1.00	1.99
❑114, Jul 99, Burning in Effigy, Part 2	1.99	0.40	1.00	1.99
❑115, Aug 99, The Package, A: Booster Gold; A: Plastic Man	1.99	0.40	1.00	1.99
❑116, Sep 99, Machinations, Misconceptions and, Revelations!, A: Booster Gold; A: Plastic Man	1.99	0.40	1.00	1.99
❑117, Oct 99, Found Art, V: Manhunter	1.99	0.40	1.00	1.99
❑118, Nov 99, Women, A: Enchantress, Day of Judgment	1.99	0.40	1.00	1.99
❑119, Dec 99, A: new Spectre	1.99	0.40	1.00	1.99
❑120, Jan 00, Target	1.99	0.40	1.00	1.99
❑121, Feb 00, New World	1.99	0.40	1.00	1.99
❑122, Mar 00	1.99	0.40	1.00	1.99
❑123, Apr 00	1.99	0.40	1.00	1.99
❑124, May 00, Control Freak	1.99	0.40	1.00	1.99
❑125, Jun 00, Tomb Raider	1.99	0.40	1.00	1.99
❑126, Jul 00	—	0.40	1.00	1.99
❑127, Aug 00	—	0.40	1.00	1.99
❑128, Sep 00	—	0.40	1.00	1.99
❑129, Oct 00, Something Old, Something New	2.25	0.45	1.13	2.25
❑130, Nov 00, Prodigal Son	2.25	0.45	1.13	2.25
❑131, Dec 00	2.25	0.45	1.13	2.25
❑132, Jan 01, While Rome Burned, Part 1	2.25	0.45	1.13	2.25
❑133, Feb 01, While Rome Burned, Part 2	2.25	0.45	1.13	2.25
❑134, Mar 01, While Rome Burned, Part 3	2.25	0.45	1.13	2.25
❑135, Apr 01, While Rome Burned, Part 4	2.25	0.45	1.13	2.25
❑136, May 01, While Rome Burned, Part 5	2.25	0.45	1.13	2.25
❑137, Jun 01, The Bonds of Friends and Lovers	2.25	0.45	1.13	2.25
❑138	2.25	0.45	1.13	2.25
❑139	2.25	0.45	1.13	2.25
❑140	2.25	0.45	1.13	2.25
❑1000000, Nov 98, One Million	1.99	0.40	1.00	1.99
❑3D 1, Dec 98, V: Dr. Light; V: Doctor Light	3.95	0.79	1.98	3.95
❑3D 1/LE	16.95	3.39	8.48	16.95
❑Anl 1, Eclipso: the Darkness Within, Part 3, Eclipso: The Darkness Within	2.50	0.60	1.50	3.00
❑Anl 2, Bloodlines, 1: Nightblade, Bloodlines: Outbreak	2.50	0.50	1.25	2.50
❑Anl 3, Elseworlds	2.95	0.60	1.50	3.00
❑Anl 4, Year One; Kyle and Hal switch places	3.50	0.70	1.75	3.50
❑Anl 5, Legends of the Dead Earth	2.95	0.59	1.48	2.95
❑Anl 6, Pulp Heroes; John Carter of Mars theme	3.95	0.79	1.98	3.95
❑Anl 7, Ghosts	2.95	0.59	1.48	2.95
❑Anl 8, Oct 99, KG (w), Grunts, JLApe	2.95	0.59	1.48	2.95
❑Anl 9, Oct 00, Mother of Heaven, 1: Sala, Planet DC	3.50	0.70	1.75	3.50
❑Anl 1963, 80pgs.; cardstock cover; published in 1998 in style of 1963 annuals	4.95	0.99	2.47	4.95
❑GS 1, Dec 98, A: G'Nort, 80pgs.	4.95	0.99	2.47	4.95
❑GS 2, Jun 99, Team-Ups from A to Z; Phases, A: Aquaman; A: Big Barda; A: Zatanna; A: Impulse; A: Deadman; A: Guy Gardner; A: Plastic Man, 80pgs.	4.95	0.99	2.47	4.95

GREEN LANTERN: 1001 EMERALD NIGHTS
DC

Value: Cover or less

❑1, Elseworlds 6.95

GREEN LANTERN/ADAM STRANGE
DC

Value: Cover or less

❑1, Oct 00, We Rann All Night 2.50

GREEN LANTERN/ATOM
DC

Value: Cover or less

❑1, Oct 00, Unusual Suspects 2.50

GREEN LANTERN: CIRCLE OF FIRE
DC

Value: Cover or less

❑1, Oct 00, Darkness Visible .. 4.95

❑2, Oct 00, Full Circle 4.95

GREEN LANTERN CORPS, THE
DC

	ORIG	GOOD	FINE	N-MINT
❑205, Series continued from Green Lantern (2nd Series) #204	—	0.30	0.75	1.50
❑206, Nov 86	0.75	0.30	0.75	1.50
❑207, Dec 86, Legends	0.75	0.30	0.75	1.50
❑208, Jan 87	0.75	0.30	0.75	1.50
❑209, Feb 87	0.75	0.30	0.75	1.50
❑210, Mar 87	0.75	0.30	0.75	1.50
❑211, Apr 87	0.75	0.30	0.75	1.50
❑212, May 87	0.75	0.30	0.75	1.50
❑213, Jun 87	0.75	0.30	0.75	1.50
❑214, Jul 87	0.75	0.30	0.75	1.50
❑215, Aug 87	0.75	0.30	0.75	1.50
❑216, Sep 87	0.75	0.30	0.75	1.50
❑217, Oct 87	0.75	0.30	0.75	1.50
❑218, Nov 87	0.75	0.30	0.75	1.50
❑219, Dec 87	0.75	0.30	0.75	1.50
❑220, Jan 88, Millennium	0.75	0.30	0.75	1.50
❑221, Feb 88, Millennium	0.75	0.30	0.75	1.50
❑222, Mar 88	0.75	0.30	0.75	1.50
❑223, Apr 88	0.75	0.30	0.75	1.50
❑224, May 88, GK, Final Issue; Giant-size	1.50	0.30	0.75	1.50
❑Anl 1	—	0.50	1.25	2.50
❑Anl 2	—	0.45	1.13	2.25
❑Anl 3, KB (w)	—	0.40	1.00	2.00

GREEN LANTERN CORPS QUARTERLY
DC

Value: Cover or less

- ❑1, Sum 92, The Book of Every-thing 2.50
- ❑2, Aut 92, Hector Hammond vs. Alan Scott 2.50
- ❑3, Win 92, The Book of Stories, D: Black Canary I 2.50
- ❑4, Spr 93, Alan Scott vs. Solomon Grundy 2.50
- ❑5, Sum 93, 1: Adam 2.50
- ❑6, Aut 93, Alan Scott vs. New Harlequin 2.95
- ❑7, Win 93, Horrors 2.95
- ❑8, Spr 94, The Book of Endings, Jack Chance vs. Lobo 2.95

GREEN LANTERN: EMERALD DAWN
DC

	ORIG	GOOD	FINE	N-MINT
❑1, Dec 89, The Sign, O: Green Lantern; O: Green Lantern II (Hal Jordan)	1.00	0.40	1.00	2.00
❑2, Jan 90	1.00	0.30	0.75	1.50
❑3, Feb 90	1.00	0.30	0.75	1.50
❑4, Mar 90, KG (w), The Corps	1.00	0.30	0.75	1.50
❑5, Apr 90	1.00	0.30	0.75	1.50
❑6, May 90	1.00	0.30	0.75	1.50

GREEN LANTERN: EMERALD DAWN II
DC

	ORIG	GOOD	FINE	N-MINT
❑1, Apr 91, KG (w), The Powers That Be	1.00	0.30	0.75	1.50
❑2, May 91, KG (w)	1.00	0.20	0.50	1.00
❑3, Jun 91, KG (w)	1.00	0.20	0.50	1.00
❑4, Jul 91, KG (w)	1.00	0.20	0.50	1.00
❑5, Aug 91, KG (w)	1.00	0.20	0.50	1.00
❑6, Sep 91, KG (w)	1.00	0.20	0.50	1.00

GREEN LANTERN/FIRESTORM
DC

Value: Cover or less

❑1, Oct 00, Missing Pieces...... 2.50

GREEN LANTERN/FLASH: FASTER FRIENDS
DC

Value: Cover or less

❑1, nn; prestige format; concludes in Flash/Green Lantern: Faster Friends 4.95

GREEN LANTERN GALLERY
DC

Value: Cover or less

❑1, Dec 96, GK (c), pin-ups..... 3.50

GREEN LANTERN: GANTHET'S TALE
DC

Value: Cover or less

❑1, JBy, nn; enhanced cover; One-Shot; prestige format; Larry Niven 5.95

GREEN LANTERN/GREEN ARROW
DC

	ORIG	GOOD	FINE	N-MINT
❑1, Oct 83, NA; DG, No Evil Shall Escape My Sight!, Reprint	2.00	0.70	1.75	3.50
❑2, Nov 83, NA; DG, Journey to Desolation, Reprint	2.00	0.60	1.50	3.00
❑3, Dec 83, NA; DG, A Kind of Loving, A Way of Death, Reprint	2.00	0.60	1.50	3.00
❑4, Jan 84, NA; DG, Ulysses Star is Still Alive!, Reprint	2.00	0.60	1.50	3.00
❑5, Feb 84, NA; DG; BWr, Peril In Plastic; Even an Immortal can Die!, Reprint	2.00	0.60	1.50	3.00
❑6, Mar 84, NA; DG, Death be My Destiny!, Reprint	2.00	0.60	1.50	3.00
❑7, Apr 84, NA; DG, ...And a Child Shall Destroy Them!, Reprint	2.50	0.60	1.50	3.00

GREEN LANTERN/GREEN LANTERN
DC

Value: Cover or less

❑1, Oct 00, Against the Dying of the Light 2.50

GREEN LANTERN: MOSAIC
DC

Value: Cover or less

- ❑1, Jun 92, Do You Want To See? 1.25
- ❑2, Jul 92, Nuts, D: Ch'p (Green Lantern squirrel) 1.25
- ❑3, Aug 92, Something Red.... 1.25
- ❑4, Sep 92, Not Yet 1.25
- ❑5, Oct 92, The Child-Man And The Great White Hero 1.25
- ❑6, Nov 92 .... 1.25
- ❑7, Dec 92 .... 1.25
- ❑8, Jan 93 .... 1.25
- ❑9, Feb 93 .... 1.25
- ❑10, Mar 93 .... 1.25
- ❑11, Apr 93, I Am Myself Mosaic 1.25
- ❑12, May 93, Any Means Necessary 1.25

	ORIG	GOOD	FINE	N-MINT

- ❑13, Jun 93, What Xenophobia Means To Me 1.25
- ❑14, Jul 93, LMc, The Sleep of Monsters Produces Reason 1.25
- ❑15, Aug 93, What Dis Be 1.25
- ❑16, Sep 93, LMc, Great Speckled Bird 1.25
- ❑17, Oct 93 ...... 1.25
- ❑18, Nov 93, Final Issue 1.25

GREEN LANTERN PLUS
DC

Value: Cover or less

- ❑1, Dec 96, A: Ray 2.95

GREEN LANTERN/POWER GIRL
DC

Value: Cover or less

- ❑1, Oct 00, Deep Down Below the Surface 2.50

GREEN LANTERN SECRET FILES
DC

Value: Cover or less

- ❑1, Jul 98, background on all Green Lanterns 4.95
- ❑2, Sep 99, JSa; GK, Keeping Secrets; Jade in Hidden Thorns, background on all Green Lanterns 4.95

GREEN LANTERN/SENTINEL: HEART OF DARKNESS
DC

Value: Cover or less

- ❑1, Mar 98, Fathers & Sons, covers form triptych 1.95
- ❑2, Apr 98, covers form triptych 1.95
- ❑3, May 98, covers form triptych 1.95

GREEN LANTERN/SILVER SURFER: UNHOLY ALLIANCES
DC

Value: Cover or less

- ❑1, A: Cyborg Superman; A: Thanos; A: Terrax; A: Parallax, nn; One-Shot; prestige format; crossover with Marvel 4.95

GREEN LANTERN/SUPERMAN: LEGEND OF THE GREEN FLAME
DC

Value: Cover or less

- ❑1, NG (w) 5.95

GREEN LANTERN: THE NEW CORPS
DC

	ORIG	GOOD	FINE	N-MINT
❑1, prestige format	4.95	0.99	2.47	4.95
❑1/Aut, Signed by Scott Eaton	—	1.60	4.00	8.00
❑2, prestige format	4.95	0.99	2.47	4.95

GREEN LANTERN VS. ALIENS
DC

Value: Cover or less

- ❑1, Sep 00 ...... 2.95
- ❑2, Oct 00 ...... 2.95
- ❑3, Nov 00 ...... 2.95
- ❑4, Dec 00 ...... 2.95

GREENLEAF IN EXILE
CAT'S PAW

Value: Cover or less

- ❑1 ...... 2.95
- ❑2 ...... 2.95
- ❑3 ...... 2.95
- ❑4 ...... 2.95
- ❑5 ...... 2.95
- ❑6 ...... 2.95

GREENLOCK
AIRCEL

Value: Cover or less

- ❑1, Mar 91, b&w; One-Shot 2.50

GREEN SKULL, THE
KNOWN ASSOCIATES

Value: Cover or less

- ❑1, nn; One-Shot 2.50

GREGORY
DC

	ORIG	GOOD	FINE	N-MINT
❑1, The Thing From Outside!; The Incredibly Odd And Mystifying Spectacle Of Herman Vermin, b&w	7.95	1.59	3.97	7.95
❑1-2, 2nd Printing	7.95	1.59	3.97	7.95
❑2, Herman Vermin's Very Own Best-selling & Critically Acclaimed Book with Gregory	4.95	0.99	2.47	4.95
❑3, It's The Terwilliger Show; I Gregory	4.95	1.59	3.97	7.95
❑3/GO, It's The Terwilliger Show; I Gregory, Gold logo edition (limited printing)	7.95	2.00	5.00	10.00
❑4, b&w; Fat Boy	4.95	0.99	2.47	4.95

GREMLIN TROUBLE
ANTI-BALLISTIC

	ORIG	GOOD	FINE	N-MINT
❑1, Unfortunate Encounters, 1: Cypher; 1: Xynophylyen, The Chief Imp; 1: Remi-el	2.95	0.70	1.75	3.50
❑2, Working within the System, 2: High Commi; 2: Cypher	2.95	0.60	1.50	3.00
❑3, Rude Awakenings	2.95	0.60	1.50	3.00
❑4, Fun with Electricity, Part 1, 2: Grommet; 1: Prince Frothbar of the Mountain Fairies; A: Murt; A: Cam; 2: Dr. Candy Tsai; A: High Commissioner Del Delage	2.95	0.60	1.50	3.00
❑5, Fun with Electricity, Part 2, 2: Prince	2.95	0.60	1.50	3.00
❑6, Fun with Electricity, Part 3, A: Prince Hex; A: Xynophylyen, The Chief Imp; A: Cam; A: Dr. Candy Tsai; A: Sorcerer General; A: High Commissioner Del Delage	2.95	0.59	1.48	2.95
❑7, Cypher in Fairyland, 2: King of the Mountain Fai	2.95	0.59	1.48	2.95

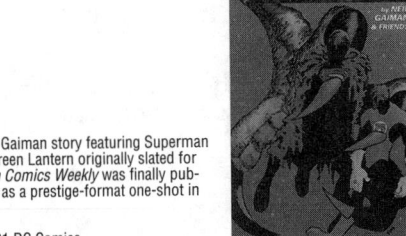

A Neil Gaiman story featuring Superman and Green Lantern originally slated for *Action Comics Weekly* was finally published as a prestige-format one-shot in 2001.

	ORIG	GOOD	FINE	N-MINT
❑8, Candy's Picnic Adventure, A: Grommet; A: Prince Hex; 1: Tuberian Nebulian Cruiser ship; A: Cam; A: Dr. Candy Tsai; 1: Goblin General Grafsnout; A: Prince Frothbar, Instigation of the Gremlin-Goblin War	2.95	0.59	1.48	2.95
❑9, The Technolution Is Not a Tea Party, A: High Commissioner Ragweed; 1: Dr. Pi Yukawa; 1: Candy Tsai and the Moist Towelettes; A: Dr. Candy Tsai; 1: Dr. Brandy Schwarzchild	2.95	0.59	1.48	2.95
❑10, The Tuberians Are Coming	2.95	0.59	1.48	2.95
❑11, Cypher Gets a Job, A: Dr. Candy Tsai; 2: X the Unmentionable; A: Sorcerer General; A: Annette, Xynophylyen; Grommet cameo; Mr. Wingnut cameo	2.95	0.59	1.48	2.95
❑12, The Battle at Site Z, 1: Ballpoint P. Greml	2.95	0.59	1.48	2.95
❑13, The Battle at Forest Meadows, Part 1, 2: Ballpoint P. Gremlin; A: Grommet; 2: General Grafsnout; A: Cam; A: Dr. Candy Tsai; A: Annette, Dr. Brandy Schwarzchild	2.95	0.59	1.48	2.95
❑14, The Battle at Forest Meadows, Part 2, 2: Tuberians; A: Princess Pentangle; A: General Grafsnout; 2: The Moist Towel; A: Annette	2.95	0.59	1.48	2.95
❑15	2.95	0.59	1.48	2.95
❑16	2.95	0.59	1.48	2.95
❑19	2.95	0.59	1.48	2.95

GRENDEL (1ST SERIES)
COMICO

	ORIG	GOOD	FINE	N-MINT
❑1, MW, b&w	1.50	13.00	32.50	65.00
❑2, MW, b&w	1.50	9.00	22.50	45.00
❑3, MW, b&w	1.50	8.00	20.00	40.00

GRENDEL (2ND SERIES)
COMICO

	ORIG	GOOD	FINE	N-MINT
❑1, Oct 86, MW, MW (w)	1.50	1.40	3.50	7.00
❑1-2, MW, MW (w), 2nd Printing	1.50	0.50	1.25	2.50
❑2, Nov 86, MW, MW (w)	1.50	1.00	2.50	5.00
❑3, Dec 86, MW, MW (w)	1.50	0.80	2.00	4.00
❑4, Jan 87, DSt (c), MW (w), Touch Not the Devil	1.50	0.80	2.00	4.00
❑5, Feb 87, MW, MW (w)	1.50	0.80	2.00	4.00
❑6, Mar 87, MW, MW (w)	1.50	0.60	1.50	3.00
❑7, Apr 87, MW, MW (w)	1.50	0.60	1.50	3.00
❑8, May 87, MW, MW (w)	1.50	0.60	1.50	3.00
❑9, Jun 87, MW, MW (w)	1.50	0.60	1.50	3.00
❑10, Jul 87, MW, MW (w)	1.50	0.60	1.50	3.00
❑11, Aug 87, MW, MW (w)	1.50	0.60	1.50	3.00
❑12, Sep 87, MW, MW (w), D: Grendel	1.50	0.60	1.50	3.00
❑13, Oct 87, MW, MW (w), new Grendel	1.50	0.60	1.50	3.00
❑14, Nov 87, MW, MW (w), new Grendel	1.50	0.60	1.50	3.00
❑15, Dec 87, MW, MW (w), new Grendel	1.50	0.60	1.50	3.00
❑16, Jan 88, MW, MW (w), Mage begins	1.50	0.80	2.00	4.00
❑17, Feb 88, MW, MW (w)	1.50	0.50	1.25	2.50
❑18, Apr 88, MW, MW (w)	1.75	0.60	1.50	3.00
❑19, May 88, MW, MW (w)	1.75	0.50	1.25	2.50
❑20, Jun 88, MW, MW (w)	1.75	0.50	1.25	2.50
❑21, Jul 88, MW, MW (w)	1.75	0.50	1.25	2.50
❑22, Aug 88, MW, MW (w)	1.75	0.50	1.25	2.50
❑23, Sep 88, MW, MW (w)	1.75	0.50	1.25	2.50
❑24, Oct 88, MW, MW (w)	1.75	0.50	1.25	2.50
❑25, Nov 88, MW, MW (w)	1.75	0.50	1.25	2.50
❑26, Dec 88, MW, MW (w)	1.75	0.50	1.25	2.50
❑27, Jan 89, MW, MW (w)	1.95	0.50	1.25	2.50
❑28, Feb 89, MW, MW (w)	1.95	0.50	1.25	2.50
❑29, Mar 89, MW, MW (w)	1.95	0.50	1.25	2.50
❑30, Apr 89, MW, MW (w)	1.95	0.50	1.25	2.50
❑31, May 89, MW, MW (w)	1.95	0.50	1.25	2.50
❑32, Jun 89, MW, MW (w)	1.95	0.50	1.25	2.50
❑33, Jul 89, MW, MW (w), Giant-size	2.75	0.75	1.88	3.75
❑34, Aug 89, MW, MW (w)	2.50	0.50	1.25	2.50
❑35, Sep 89, MW, MW (w)	2.50	0.50	1.25	2.50
❑36, Oct 89, MW, MW (w)	2.50	0.50	1.25	2.50
❑37, Nov 89, MW, MW (w)	2.50	0.50	1.25	2.50

	ORIG	GOOD	FINE	N-MINT
❑38, Dec 89, MW, MW (w)	2.50	0.50	1.25	2.50
❑39, Jan 90, MW, MW (w)	2.50	0.50	1.25	2.50
❑40, Feb 90, MW, MW (w), Final Issue; flip book with Grendel Tales Special Preview	3.50	0.70	1.75	3.50

GRENDEL: BLACK, WHITE, & RED
DARK HORSE

	ORIG	GOOD	FINE	N-MINT
❑1, Nov 98, MW (w)	3.95	0.80	2.00	4.00
❑2, Dec 98, MW (w), Devil's Cue; Devil's Requiem	3.95	0.80	2.00	4.00
❑3, Jan 99, MW (w), Devil's Apogee; Devil's Curse	3.95	0.80	2.00	4.00
❑4, Feb 99, MW (w), Devil's Cage; Devil's Witness	3.95	0.80	2.00	4.00

GRENDEL CLASSICS
DARK HORSE

Value: Cover or less

❑1, Jul 95, MW, Devil Tracks, cardstock cover.......... 3.95

❑2, Aug 95, MW, Devil Eyes, cardstock cover; Final Issue....... 3.95

GRENDEL CYCLE
DARK HORSE

Value: Cover or less

❑1, Oct 95, nn; prestige format; background information on the various series including a timeline....... 5.95

GRENDEL: DEVIL BY THE DEED
COMICO

	ORIG	GOOD	FINE	N-MINT
❑1, MW, nn; cardstock cover; graphic novel; reprints Comico one-shot	10.00	0.80	2.00	4.00
❑1/LE, MW, Limited to 2000	—	3.50	8.75	17.50
❑1-2, Jul 93, MW, nn; cardstock cover; reprints Comico one-shot	3.95	0.79	1.98	3.95

GRENDEL: DEVIL CHILD
DARK HORSE

Value: Cover or less

❑1, Jun 99, cardstock cover.... 2.95

❑2, Aug 99, cardstock cover ... 2.95

GRENDEL: DEVIL QUEST
DARK HORSE

Value: Cover or less

❑1, Nov 95, MW, MW (w), nn; One-Shot; prestige format........... 4.95

GRENDEL: DEVIL'S LEGACY
COMICO

Value: Cover or less

❑1, MW (w)........ 2.95

❑2, MW (w)........ 2.95

❑3, Apr 00, MW (w)........ 2.95

❑4, MW (w), Touch not the Devil 2.95

❑5, Jul 00, MW (w), Devil in Despair........ 2.95

❑6, Aug 00, MW (w), Challenge the Devil........ 2.95

❑7, Sep 00, MW (w), Devil's Dance........ 2.95

❑8, Oct 00, MW (w), After the Devil........ 2.95

❑9, Nov 00, MW (w), Devil's Revenge........ 2.95

❑10, Dec 00, MW (w), Devil on Edge........ 2.95

❑11, Jan 01, MW (w), Devil"s Rampage........ 2.95

❑12, Feb 01, MW (w), Devil's Ends........ 2.95

GRENDEL: DEVIL'S VAGARY
COMICO

	ORIG	GOOD	FINE	N-MINT
❑1, b&w and red; 16pgs	5.00	1.60	4.00	8.00

GRENDEL TALES
DARK HORSE

Value: Cover or less

❑1........ 2.95

❑2........ 2.95

❑3........ 2.95

❑4........ 2.95

❑5........ 2.95

❑6........ 2.95

GRENDEL TALES: DEVILS AND DEATHS
DARK HORSE

Value: Cover or less

❑1, Oct 94, MW, MW (w), Devil's Lot; Meat Machine, Part 1... 2.95

❑2, Nov 94, MW, MW (w), Meat Machine, Part 2........ 2.95

GRENDEL TALES: DEVIL'S CHOICES
DARK HORSE

Value: Cover or less

❑1, Mar 95........ 2.95

❑2, Apr 95........ 2.95

❑3, May 95........ 2.95

❑4, Jun 95........ 2.95

GRENDEL TALES: DEVIL'S HAMMER
DARK HORSE

Value: Cover or less

❑1, Feb 94, MW, MW (w), Black Blood; Devil Quest, Part 1... 2.95

❑2, Mar 94........ 2.95

❑3, Apr 94........ 2.95

GRENDEL TALES: FOUR DEVILS, ONE HELL
DARK HORSE

	ORIG	GOOD	FINE	N-MINT
❑1, Aug 93, JRo (w), Four Beginnings, One Case, cardstock cover	2.95	0.60	1.50	3.00
❑2, Sep 93, JRo (w), Three searchers, One Lucky Streak, cardstock cover	2.95	0.60	1.50	3.00
❑3, Oct 93, JRo (w), cardstock cover	2.95	0.60	1.50	3.00
❑4, Oct 93, JRo (w), One Rite, Three Wrongs, cardstock cover	2.95	0.60	1.50	3.00
❑5, Dec 93, JRo (w), One Carnival, Three Captives, cardstock cover	2.95	0.60	1.50	3.00
❑6, Jan 94, JRo (w), Four Fates, One Finale, cardstock cover; Grendel-Prime returns	2.95	0.60	1.50	3.00

GRENDEL TALES: HOMECOMING
DARK HORSE

Value: Cover or less

❑1, Dec 94, MW, MW (w), Part 1; Babylon Crash, Part 1, cardstock cover........ 2.95

❑2, Jan 95, MW, MW (w), Part 2; Babylon Crash, Part 2, cardstock cover........ 2.95

❑3, Feb 95, MW (w), Part 3; Devil Quest, cardstock cover........ 2.95

GRENDEL TALES: THE DEVIL IN OUR MIDST
DARK HORSE

Value: Cover or less

❑1, May 94, Devil Quest, Part 2........ 2.95

❑2, Jun 94, Devil Quest, Part 3........ 2.95

❑3, Jul 94........ 2.95

❑4, Aug 94........ 2.95

❑5, Sep 94........ 2.95

GRENDEL TALES: THE DEVIL MAY CARE
DARK HORSE

Value: Cover or less

❑1, Dec 95, cardstock cover ... 2.95

❑2, Jan 96, cardstock cover.... 2.95

❑3, Feb 96, cardstock cover ... 2.95

❑4, Mar 96, cardstock cover ... 2.95

❑5, Apr 96, cardstock cover 2.95

❑6, May 96, cardstock cover; Final Issue........ 2.95

GRENDEL TALES: THE DEVIL'S APPRENTICE
DARK HORSE

Value: Cover or less

❑1, Sep 97........ 2.95

❑2, Oct 97........ 2.95

❑3, Nov 97........ 2.95

GRENDEL: THE DEVIL INSIDE
COMICO

Value: Cover or less

❑1, MW (w)........ 11.95

GRENDEL: WAR CHILD
DARK HORSE

	ORIG	GOOD	FINE	N-MINT
❑1, Aug 92, MW, MW (w), Part 41 of Grendel total series	2.50	0.70	1.75	3.50
❑2, Sep 92, MW (w), Part 42 of Grendel total series	2.50	0.60	1.50	3.00
❑3, Oct 92, MW (w), Part 43 of Grendel total series	2.50	0.60	1.50	3.00
❑4, Nov 92, MW (w), Part 44 of Grendel total series	2.50	0.60	1.50	3.00
❑5, Dec 92, MW (w), Part 45 of Grendel total series	2.50	0.60	1.50	3.00
❑6, Jan 93, MW (w), Part 46 of Grendel total series	2.50	0.50	1.25	2.50
❑7, Jan 93, MW (w), Part 47 of Grendel total series	2.50	0.50	1.25	2.50
❑8, Mar 93, MW (w), Part 48 of Grendel total series	2.50	0.50	1.25	2.50
❑9, Apr 93, MW (w), Part 49 of Grendel total series	2.50	0.50	1.25	2.50
❑10, Jun 93, MW (w), Final Issue; Double-size; Part 50 of Grendel total series	3.50	0.75	1.88	3.75

GREY
VIZ

	ORIG	GOOD	FINE	N-MINT
❑1	2.95	1.00	2.50	5.00
❑2	2.95	0.80	2.00	4.00
❑3	2.95	0.70	1.75	3.50
❑4	2.95	0.70	1.75	3.50
❑5	2.95	0.70	1.75	3.50
❑6	2.95	0.65	1.63	3.25
❑7	3.25	0.65	1.63	3.25
❑8	3.25	0.65	1.63	3.25
❑9	3.25	0.65	1.63	3.25

GREY LEGACY
FRAGILE ELITE

Value: Cover or less

❑1, b&w........ 2.75

GREYLORE
SIRIUS COMICS

Value: Cover or less

❑1, Dec 85, A Pox Upon Him.. 1.50

❑2, Jan 86........ 1.50

❑3, Jan 86........ 1.50

❑4, Jan 86........ 1.50

❑5, Jan 86........ 1.50

GREYMATTER
ALAFFINITY

Value: Cover or less

❑1, Oct 93........ 2.95

❑2, Nov 93, Show & Tell........ 2.95

❑3, Dec 93, Revolution Less Revelation........ 2.95

❑4, Jan 94, No Time To Say Hello Goodbye........ 2.95

❑5, Apr 94........ 2.95

❑6, Sep 94, cover forms diptych with #7........ 2.95

❑7, Oct 94, cover forms diptych with #6........ 2.95

❑8, Mar 95........ 2.95

❑9, Dec 95........ 2.95

❑10, Mar 96........ 2.95

❑11, Jun 96........ 2.95

GRIFFIN, THE (AMAZE INK)
SLAVE LABOR

Value: Cover or less

❑1, May 97........ 2.95

GRIFFIN, THE (DC)
DC
Value: Cover or less

- ❑1, Nov 91, The Griffin Returns; Friendly Fire, O: The Griffin 4.95
- ❑2, Dec 91 4.95
- ❑3 4.95
- ❑4 4.95
- ❑5, Run Like Hell; Against The Wall 4.95
- ❑6 4.95

GRIFFIN, THE (SLAVE LABOR)
SLAVE LABOR
Value: Cover or less

- ❑1, Jul 88, b&w 1.75
- ❑1-2, Apr 89, b&w; 2nd Printing 1.75
- ❑2, Dec 88 1.75
- ❑3, Apr 89 1.75

GRIFFITH OBSERVATORY
FANTAGRAPHICS
Value: Cover or less

- ❑1, nn 4.95

GRIFTER (VOL. 1)
IMAGE

	ORIG	GOOD	FINE	N-MINT
❑1, May 95, WildStorm Rising, Part 5, bound-in trading cards	1.95	0.50	1.25	2.50
❑1/DM, Wildstorm Rising, Part 5, trading card; Direct Market edition	2.50	0.60	1.50	3.00
❑2, Jun 95	1.95	0.40	1.00	2.00
❑3, Jul 95, indicia says Jul, cover says Aug	1.95	0.40	1.00	2.00
❑4	1.95	0.40	1.00	2.00
❑5, Oct 95, indicia says Oct, cover says Jun	1.95	0.40	1.00	2.00
❑6, Nov 95	1.95	0.40	1.00	2.00
❑7, Dec 95	1.95	0.40	1.00	2.00
❑8, Jan 96	1.95	0.40	1.00	2.00
❑9, Feb 96, City of Angels, Part 3	1.95	0.40	1.00	2.00
❑10, Mar 96, City of Angels, Part 4, Final Issue	1.95	0.40	1.00	2.00

GRIFTER (VOL. 2)
IMAGE
Value: Cover or less

- ❑1, Jul 96 2.50
- ❑2, Aug 96 2.50
- ❑3, Sep 96 2.50
- ❑4, Oct 96 2.50
- ❑5, Nov 96 2.50
- ❑6, Dec 96, cover says Nov, indicia says Dec 2.50
- ❑7, Jan 97 2.50
- ❑8, Feb 97 2.50
- ❑9, Mar 97 2.50
- ❑10, Apr 97 2.50
- ❑11, May 97 2.50
- ❑12, Jun 97 2.50
- ❑13, Jul 97 2.50
- ❑14, Aug 97, Final Issue 2.50

GRIFTER AND THE MASK
DARK HORSE
Value: Cover or less

- ❑1, Sep 96, Cleaving Las Vegas, Part 1, crossover with Image 2.50
- ❑2, Oct 96, Cleaving Las Vegas, Part 2, crossover with Image 2.50

GRIFTER/BADROCK
IMAGE
Value: Cover or less

- ❑1/A, Oct 95 2.50
- ❑1/B, Oct 95, alternate cover 2.50
- ❑2/A, Nov 95, flipbook with Badrock #2A 2.50
- ❑2/B, Nov 95, flipbook with Badrock #2A 2.50

GRIFTER: ONE SHOT
IMAGE
Value: Cover or less

- ❑1, Jan 95 4.95

GRIFTER/SHI
IMAGE
Value: Cover or less

- ❑1, Apr 96, cover says Mar, indicia says Apr; crossover with Crusade 2.95
- ❑2, May 96, crossover with Crusade 2.95

GRIM GHOST, THE
ATLAS

	ORIG	GOOD	FINE	N-MINT
❑1, Jan 75, Enter The Grim Ghost, 1: Grim Ghost	0.25	0.40	1.00	2.00
❑2, Mar 75	0.25	0.40	1.00	2.00
❑3, Jul 75	0.25	0.40	1.00	2.00

GRIMJACK
FIRST

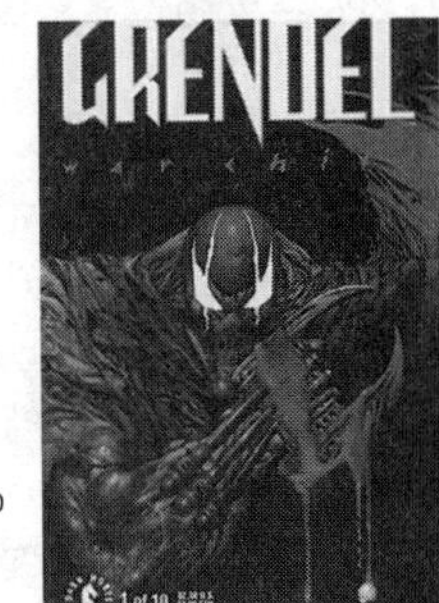

Grendel: War Child was the first series to follow Comico's original *Grendel* series.

© 1992 Matt Wagner (Dark Horse)

	ORIG	GOOD	FINE	N-MINT
❑1, Aug 84, A Shade Of Truth	1.25	0.40	1.00	2.00
❑2, Sep 84	1.25	0.35	0.88	1.75
❑3, Oct 84	1.25	0.35	0.88	1.75
❑4, Nov 84	1.25	0.35	0.88	1.75
❑5, Dec 84	1.25	0.35	0.88	1.75
❑6, Jan 85	1.25	0.35	0.88	1.75
❑7, Feb 85	1.25	0.35	0.88	1.75
❑8, Mar 85	1.25	0.35	0.88	1.75
❑9, Apr 85	1.25	0.35	0.88	1.75
❑10, May 85	1.25	0.35	0.88	1.75
❑11, Jun 85	1.25	0.35	0.88	1.75
❑12, Jul 85	1.25	0.35	0.88	1.75
❑13, Aug 85	1.25	0.35	0.88	1.75
❑14, Sep 85	1.25	0.35	0.88	1.75
❑15, Oct 85	1.25	0.35	0.88	1.75
❑16, Nov 85	1.25	0.35	0.88	1.75
❑17, Dec 85	1.25	0.35	0.88	1.75
❑18, Jan 86	1.25	0.35	0.88	1.75
❑19, Feb 86	1.25	0.35	0.88	1.75
❑20, Mar 86	1.25	0.35	0.88	1.75
❑21, Apr 86	1.25	0.30	0.75	1.50
❑22, May 86	1.25	0.30	0.75	1.50
❑23, Jun 86	1.25	0.30	0.75	1.50
❑24, Jul 86	1.25	0.30	0.75	1.50
❑25, Aug 86	1.25	0.30	0.75	1.50
❑26, Sep 86, TS, Twisted Metal, A: Teenage Mutant Ninja Turtles	1.25	0.60	1.50	3.00
❑27, Oct 86	1.25	0.30	0.75	1.50
❑28, Nov 86	1.25	0.30	0.75	1.50
❑29, Dec 86	1.25	0.30	0.75	1.50
❑30, Jan 87, Dynamo Joe	1.25	0.30	0.75	1.50
❑31, Feb 87	1.25	0.30	0.75	1.50
❑32, Mar 87	1.25	0.30	0.75	1.50
❑33, Apr 87	1.25	0.30	0.75	1.50
❑34, May 87	1.25	0.30	0.75	1.50
❑35, Jun 87	1.25	0.30	0.75	1.50
❑36, Jul 87, D: Grimjack	1.25	0.30	0.75	1.50
❑37, Aug 87	1.25	0.30	0.75	1.50
❑38, Sep 87	1.25	0.30	0.75	1.50
❑39, Oct 87	1.75	0.30	0.75	1.50
❑40, Nov 87	1.75	0.39	0.98	1.95
❑41, Dec 87	1.75	0.39	0.98	1.95
❑42, Jan 88	1.75	0.39	0.98	1.95
❑43, Feb 88	1.75	0.39	0.98	1.95
❑44, Mar 88	1.75	0.39	0.98	1.95
❑45, Apr 88	1.75	0.39	0.98	1.95
❑46, May 88	1.75	0.39	0.98	1.95
❑47, Jun 88	1.75	0.39	0.98	1.95
❑48, Jul 88	1.75	0.39	0.98	1.95
❑49, Aug 88, Hellbent	1.75	0.39	0.98	1.95
❑50, Sep 88, Blood Bath	1.75	0.39	0.98	1.95
❑51, Oct 88	1.75	0.39	0.98	1.95
❑52, Nov 88, Crossroads	1.95	0.39	0.98	1.95
❑53, Dec 88	1.95	0.39	0.98	1.95
❑54, Jan 89	1.95	0.39	0.98	1.95
❑55, Feb 89, new Grimjack	1.95	0.39	0.98	1.95
❑56, Mar 89	1.95	0.39	0.98	1.95
❑57, Apr 89	1.95	0.39	0.98	1.95
❑58, May 89	1.95	0.39	0.98	1.95
❑59, Jun 89	1.95	0.39	0.98	1.95
❑60, Jul 89	1.95	0.39	0.98	1.95
❑61, Aug 89	1.95	0.39	0.98	1.95
❑62, Sep 89, Reunion, Bloody Lies	1.95	0.39	0.98	1.95
❑63, Oct 89	1.95	0.39	0.98	1.95
❑64, Nov 89	1.95	0.39	0.98	1.95
❑65, Dec 89	1.95	0.39	0.98	1.95
❑66, Jan 90, Demon Wars	1.95	0.39	0.98	1.95
❑67, Feb 90, Demon Wars	1.95	0.39	0.98	1.95
❑68, Mar 90, Demon Wars	1.95	0.39	0.98	1.95
❑69, Apr 90, Demon Wars	1.95	0.39	0.98	1.95
❑70, May 90	1.95	0.39	0.98	1.95
❑71, Jun 90	1.95	0.40	1.00	2.00
❑72, Jul 90	1.95	0.40	1.00	2.00
❑73, Aug 90	1.95	0.40	1.00	2.00
❑74, Sep 90	1.95	0.40	1.00	2.00
❑75, Oct 90, Giant 75th issue	5.95	0.70	1.75	3.50
❑76	2.25	0.40	1.00	2.00
❑77	2.25	0.40	1.00	2.00
❑78	2.25	0.40	1.00	2.00
❑79	2.25	0.40	1.00	2.00
❑80	2.25	0.40	1.00	2.00
❑81, Final Issue	2.25	0.40	1.00	2.00

GRIMJACK CASEFILES
FIRST
Value: Cover or less

- ❑1, Reprint; Truman 1.95
- ❑2, Reprint; Truman 1.95
- ❑3, Reprint; Truman 1.95
- ❑4, Reprint; Truman 1.95
- ❑5, Reprint; Truman 1.95

GRIMLOCK
EMPYRE
Value: Cover or less

- ❑1, Jan 96, b&w 2.95
- ❑2, b&w; no cover date 2.95

GRIMMAX
DEFIANT

	ORIG	GOOD	FINE	N-MINT
❑0, Aug 94, no cover price	—	0.20	0.50	1.00

GRINGO
CALIBER

Value: Cover or less ❑1, b&w ... 1.95

GRIPS
SILVERWOLF

	ORIG	GOOD	FINE	N-MINT
❑1	—	0.80	2.00	4.00
❑1/LE	9.95	10.00	25.00	50.00
❑2	—	0.60	1.50	3.00
❑3	—	0.60	1.50	3.00
❑4	—	0.60	1.50	3.00

GRIPS (VOL. 2)
GREATER MERCURY

	ORIG	GOOD	FINE	N-MINT
❑1	—	0.80	2.00	4.00

GRIT BATH
FANTAGRAPHICS

	ORIG	GOOD	FINE	N-MINT
❑1, b&w	2.50	0.50	1.25	2.50
❑2, no cover price	—	0.50	1.25	2.50
❑3, Aug 94, no cover price	—	0.50	1.25	2.50

GROO (DARK HORSE)
DARK HORSE

Value: Cover or less

- ❑1, Jan 98, SA, ME (w) ... 2.95
- ❑2, Feb 98, SA, ME (w) ... 2.95
- ❑3, Mar 98, SA, ME (w) ... 2.95
- ❑4, Apr 98, SA, ME (w) ... 2.95

GROO (IMAGE)
IMAGE

	ORIG	GOOD	FINE	N-MINT
❑1, Dec 94, SA, ME (w), The Promised Land	1.95	0.50	1.25	2.50
❑2, Jan 95, SA, ME (w), The Aqualarre, indicia says issue #1	1.95	0.50	1.25	2.50
❑3, Feb 95, SA, ME (w)	1.95	0.50	1.25	2.50
❑4, Mar 95, SA, ME (w), A Drink of Water	1.95	0.40	1.00	2.00
❑5, Apr 95, SA, ME (w)	1.95	0.40	1.00	2.00
❑6, May 95, SA, ME (w)	1.95	0.40	1.00	2.00
❑7, Jun 95, SA, ME (w)	1.95	0.40	1.00	2.00
❑8, Jul 95, SA, ME (w)	1.95	0.40	1.00	2.00
❑9, Aug 95, SA, ME (w)	2.25	0.45	1.13	2.25
❑10, Sep 95, SA, ME (w)	2.25	0.45	1.13	2.25
❑11, Oct 95, SA, ME (w), The Gamblers	2.25	0.45	1.13	2.25
❑12, Nov 95, SA, ME (w), Final Issue	2.25	0.45	1.13	2.25

GROO AND RUFFERTO (SERGIO ARAGONÉS'...)
DARK HORSE

Value: Cover or less

- ❑1, Dec 98, SA, ME (w); SA (w), Rufferto sent through time ... 2.95
- ❑2, Jan 99, SA, ME (w); SA (w) 2.95
- ❑3, Feb 99, SA, ME (w); SA (w) 2.95
- ❑4, Mar 99, SA, ME (w); SA (w) 2.95

GROO CHRONICLES, THE
MARVEL

Value: Cover or less

- ❑1, SA, ME (w), Friends and Enemies; The Missive!, Reprint; squarebound ... 3.50
- ❑2, SA, ME (w), The Caravan, Reprint; squarebound ... 3.50
- ❑3, SA, ME (w), The Turn of the Wheel!; Shanghaied!, Reprint; squarebound ... 3.50
- ❑4, SA, ME (w), The Wizard War; The Music of Murkos!, Reprint; squarebound ... 3.50
- ❑5, SA, ME (w), Chakaal; Groo and the Poachers, Reprint; squarebound ... 3.50
- ❑6, SA, ME (w), Warriors Two; The Swords of Groo, Reprint; squarebound ... 3.50

GROO: MIGHTIER THAN THE SWORD (SERGIO ARAGONÉS...)
DARK HORSE

Value: Cover or less

- ❑1, Jan 00, SA, ME (w) ... 2.95
- ❑2, Feb 00, SA, ME (w) ... 2.95
- ❑3, Mar 00, SA, ME (w) ... 2.95
- ❑4, Apr 00, SA, ME (w) ... 2.95

GROO THE WANDERER
MARVEL

	ORIG	GOOD	FINE	N-MINT
❑1, Mar 85, SA, ME (w), The Song of Groo, 1: Minstrel	0.75	1.40	3.50	7.00
❑2, Apr 85, SA, ME (w), Dragon Killer!	0.75	1.00	2.50	5.00
❑3, May 85, SA, ME (w), The Medallion	0.75	0.80	2.00	4.00
❑4, Jun 85, SA, ME (w), World Without Women	0.75	0.80	2.00	4.00
❑5, Jul 85, SA, ME (w), Slavers	0.75	0.70	1.75	3.50
❑6, Aug 85, SA, ME (w), Eye of the Kabula.	0.75	0.70	1.75	3.50
❑7, Sep 85, SA, ME (w), The Ivory Graveyard	0.75	0.70	1.75	3.50
❑8, Oct 85, SA, ME (w), The Treasure Of Kantor	0.75	0.70	1.75	3.50
❑9, Nov 85, SA, ME (w), Pigs And Apples	0.75	0.70	1.75	3.50
❑10, Dec 85, SA, ME (w), Groo Meets The Hero	0.75	0.70	1.75	3.50
❑11, Jan 86, SA, ME (w), A Hero's Task	0.75	0.60	1.50	3.00
❑12, Feb 86, SA, ME (w), Groo Meets The Thespians	0.75	0.60	1.50	3.00
❑13, Mar 86, SA, ME (w), Groo And The Tale Of King Sage	0.75	0.60	1.50	3.00
❑14, Apr 86, SA, ME (w), The Quarry	0.75	0.60	1.50	3.00
❑15, May 86, SA, ME (w), Groo And The Monks	0.75	0.60	1.50	3.00
❑16, Jun 86, SA, ME (w), Groo and the Shipyard	0.75	0.60	1.50	3.00
❑17, Jul 86, SA, ME (w), Pescatel (The Hatchery)	0.75	0.60	1.50	3.00
❑18, Aug 86, SA, ME (w), Groo Sister's City!	0.75	0.60	1.50	3.00
❑19, Sep 86, SA, ME (w), Groo And The Siege!	0.75	0.60	1.50	3.00
❑20, Oct 86, SA, ME (w), Groo And The Siege (Second Try)	0.75	0.60	1.50	3.00
❑21, Nov 86, SA, ME (w), Groo And The Witches Of Brujas	0.75	0.50	1.25	2.50
❑22, Dec 86, SA, ME (w), Groo and the Ambassador	0.75	0.50	1.25	2.50
❑23, Jan 87, SA, ME (w), Groo Meets Pal n Drumm	0.75	0.50	1.25	2.50
❑24, Feb 87, SA, ME (w), Arcadio's Quest.	0.75	0.50	1.25	2.50
❑25, Mar 87, SA, ME (w), Divide and Conquer!	0.75	0.50	1.25	2.50
❑26, Apr 87, SA, ME (w), Arba Dakarba	0.75	0.50	1.25	2.50
❑27, May 87, SA, ME (w), Spies!	1.00	0.50	1.25	2.50
❑28, Jun 87, SA, ME (w), Gourmet Kings	1.00	0.50	1.25	2.50
❑29, Jul 87, SA, ME (w), Rufferto	1.00	0.50	1.25	2.50
❑30, Aug 87, SA, ME (w), Rufferto II	1.00	0.50	1.25	2.50
❑31, Sep 87, SA, ME (w), The Arms Deal	1.00	0.40	1.00	2.00
❑32, Oct 87, SA, ME (w), The Bankers of Avara	1.00	0.40	1.00	2.00
❑33, Nov 87, SA, ME (w), The Pirates of Salgari	1.00	0.40	1.00	2.00
❑34, Dec 87, SA, ME (w), The Amulet	1.00	0.40	1.00	2.00
❑35, Jan 88, SA, ME (w), Wishes	1.00	0.40	1.00	2.00
❑36, Feb 88, SA, ME (w), Rhyme Nor Reason	1.00	0.40	1.00	2.00
❑37, Mar 88, SA, ME (w), The Village of Miggledy	1.00	0.40	1.00	2.00
❑38, Apr 88, SA, ME (w), Mealtime	1.00	0.40	1.00	2.00
❑39, May 88, SA, ME (w), A Groo's Best Friend	1.00	0.40	1.00	2.00
❑40, Jun 88, SA, ME (w), The Glass Carafe	1.00	0.40	1.00	2.00
❑41, Jul 88, SA, ME (w), Granny Groo	1.00	0.40	1.00	2.00
❑42, Aug 88, SA, ME (w), The Weddings of Groo	1.00	0.40	1.00	2.00
❑43, Sep 88, SA, ME (w), Slave!	1.00	0.40	1.00	2.00
❑44, Oct 88, SA, ME (w), Ruffeto Reverie	1.00	0.40	1.00	2.00
❑45, Nov 88, SA, ME (w), Rufferto Reality!.	1.00	0.40	1.00	2.00
❑46, Dec 88, SA, ME (w), Groo's Clothes	1.00	0.40	1.00	2.00
❑47, Jan 89, SA, ME (w), The 300% Solution	1.00	0.40	1.00	2.00
❑48, Feb 89, SA, ME (w), The Wanderer!	1.00	0.40	1.00	2.00
❑49, Mar 89, SA, ME (w), The Protector, A: Chakaal	1.00	0.40	1.00	2.00
❑50, Apr 89, SA, ME (w), Chakaal Again!, A: Chakaal, Giant-size	1.50	0.60	1.50	3.00
❑51, May 89, SA, ME (w), The Valley of Mas and Menos, A: Chakaal	1.00	0.40	1.00	2.00
❑52, Jun 89, SA, ME (w), The Arana, A: Chakaal	1.00	0.40	1.00	2.00
❑53, Jul 89, SA, ME (w), Dragons for Sale, A: Chakaal	1.00	0.40	1.00	2.00
❑54, Aug 89, SA, ME (w), The Armadas	1.00	0.40	1.00	2.00
❑55, Sep 89, SA, ME (w), The Island of Felicidad	1.00	0.40	1.00	2.00
❑56, Oct 89, SA, ME (w), A Minstrel's Tale.	1.00	0.40	1.00	2.00
❑57, Nov 89, SA, ME (w), The Captain of Chinampa	1.00	0.40	1.00	2.00
❑58, Nov 89, SA, ME (w), The Idol	1.00	0.40	1.00	2.00
❑59, Dec 89, SA, ME (w), One Fine Day	1.00	0.40	1.00	2.00
❑60, Dec 89, SA, ME (w), The Mendicants.	1.00	0.40	1.00	2.00
❑61, Jan 90, SA, ME (w), The Horses of Caballo!	1.00	0.40	1.00	2.00
❑62, Feb 90, SA, ME (w), Horse Sense	1.00	0.40	1.00	2.00
❑63, Mar 90, SA, ME (w), Real Estate	1.00	0.40	1.00	2.00
❑64, Apr 90, SA, ME (w), The Painter	1.00	0.40	1.00	2.00
❑65, May 90, SA, ME (w), The Garbage Issue	1.00	0.40	1.00	2.00
❑66, Jun 90, SA, ME (w), The Gurus	1.00	0.40	1.00	2.00
❑67, Jul 90, SA, ME (w), Dragon Quest	1.00	0.40	1.00	2.00
❑68, Aug 90, SA, ME (w), The Hero of Lerolero	1.00	0.40	1.00	2.00
❑69, Sep 90, SA, ME (w), One if By Land, Two if By Sea!	1.00	0.40	1.00	2.00
❑70, Oct 90, SA, ME (w), The Greatest Hero	1.00	0.40	1.00	2.00
❑71, Nov 90, SA, ME (w), Laughingstock	1.00	0.30	0.75	1.50
❑72, Dec 90, SA, ME (w), Shaman	1.00	0.30	0.75	1.50
❑73, Jan 91, SA, ME (w), The Scepter of King Cetro, Part 1	1.00	0.30	0.75	1.50
❑74, Feb 91, SA, ME (w), The Scepter of King Cetro, Part 2	1.00	0.30	0.75	1.50
❑75, Mar 91, SA, ME (w), The Scepter of King Cetro, Part 3	1.00	0.30	0.75	1.50
❑76, Apr 91, SA, ME (w), The Mines of Minas	1.00	0.30	0.75	1.50
❑77, May 91, SA, ME (w), Rufferto's Magic Wish	1.00	0.30	0.75	1.50
❑78, Jun 91, SA, ME (w), The Book Burners, bookburners	1.00	0.30	0.75	1.50
❑79, Jul 91, SA, ME (w), The Monks of Monjes	1.00	0.30	0.75	1.50
❑80, Aug 91, SA, ME (w), Legend of Thaais, Part 1; The Legend of Thaais, Part 1	1.00	0.30	0.75	1.50

	ORIG	GOOD	FINE	N-MINT
❑81, Sep 91, SA, ME (w), Legend of Thaais, Part 2; The Legend of Thaais, Part 2	1.00	0.30	0.75	1.50
❑82, Oct 91, SA, ME (w), Legend of Thaais, Part 3; The Legend of Thaais, Part 3	1.00	0.30	0.75	1.50
❑83, Nov 91, SA, ME (w), Legend of Thaais, Part 4; The Legend of Thaais, Part 4	1.00	0.30	0.75	1.50
❑84, Dec 91, SA, ME (w)	1.00	0.30	0.75	1.50
❑85, Jan 92, SA, ME (w)	1.00	0.30	0.75	1.50
❑86, Feb 92, SA, ME (w), The Two Doors	1.00	0.30	0.75	1.50
❑87, Mar 92, SA, ME (w), The Supreme General	2.25	0.45	1.13	2.25
❑88, Apr 92, SA, ME (w), Prairie War	2.25	0.45	1.13	2.25
❑89, May 92, SA, ME (w)	2.25	0.45	1.13	2.25
❑90, Jun 92, SA, ME (w)	2.25	0.45	1.13	2.25
❑91, Jul 92, SA, ME (w)	2.25	0.45	1.13	2.25
❑92, Aug 92, SA, ME (w), Groo finds fountain of youth	2.25	0.45	1.13	2.25
❑93, Sep 92, SA, ME (w), Groo finds fountain of youth	2.25	0.45	1.13	2.25
❑94, Oct 92, SA, ME (w), Water	2.25	0.45	1.13	2.25
❑95, Nov 92, SA, ME (w), The Menagerie	2.25	0.45	1.13	2.25
❑96, Dec 92, SA, ME (w), Wager of the Gods, Part 1; The Wager of the Gods, Part 1	2.25	0.45	1.13	2.25
❑97, Jan 93, SA, ME (w), Wager of the Gods, Part 2; The Wager of the Gods, Part 2	2.25	0.45	1.13	2.25
❑98, Feb 93, SA, ME (w), Wager of the Gods, Part 3; The Wager of the Gods, Part 3	2.25	0.45	1.13	2.25
❑99, Mar 93, SA, ME (w), Wager of the Gods, Part 4	2.25	0.45	1.13	2.25
❑100, Apr 93, SA, ME (w), 100th anniversary issue; Groo learns to read	2.95	0.59	1.48	2.95
❑101, May 93, SA, ME (w)	2.25	0.45	1.13	2.25
❑102, Jun 93, SA, ME (w)	2.25	0.45	1.13	2.25
❑103, Aug 93, SA, ME (w)	2.25	0.45	1.13	2.25
❑104, Sep 93, SA, ME (w), A Home for Oso, O: Rufferto (Groo's Dog)	2.25	0.45	1.13	2.25
❑105, Oct 93, SA, ME (w), The Curse of Criaturas	2.25	0.45	1.13	2.25
❑106, Nov 93, SA, ME (w), Man of the People, Part 1	2.25	0.45	1.13	2.25
❑107, Dec 93, SA, ME (w), Man of the People, Part 2	2.25	0.45	1.13	2.25
❑108, Jan 94, SA, ME (w), Man of the People, Part 3	2.25	0.45	1.13	2.25
❑109, Feb 94, SA, ME (w), Man of the People, Part 4	2.25	0.45	1.13	2.25
❑110, Mar 94, SA, ME (w)	2.25	0.45	1.13	2.25
❑111, Apr 94, SA, ME (w)	2.25	0.45	1.13	2.25
❑112, May 94, SA, ME (w)	2.25	0.45	1.13	2.25
❑113, Jun 94, SA, ME (w)	2.25	0.45	1.13	2.25
❑114, Jul 94, SA, ME (w)	2.25	0.45	1.13	2.25
❑115, Aug 94, SA, ME (w)	2.25	0.45	1.13	2.25
❑116, Sep 94, SA, ME (w)	2.25	0.45	1.13	2.25
❑117, Oct 94, SA, ME (w)	2.25	0.45	1.13	2.25
❑118, Nov 94, SA, ME (w)	2.25	0.45	1.13	2.25
❑119, Dec 94, SA, ME (w)	2.25	0.45	1.13	2.25
❑120, Jan 95, SA, ME (w), Final Issue	2.25	0.45	1.13	2.25
❑SE 1, Oct 84, SA, ME (w), The Swords of Groo; The Music of Murkos, 1: Groo, reprints; Eclipse publishes	2.00	0.60	1.50	3.00

GROO THE WANDERER (SERGIO ARAGONÉS'...)

PACIFIC

	ORIG	GOOD	FINE	N-MINT
❑1, Dec 82, SA, ME (w), Friends and Enemies, 1: Sage	1.00	2.20	5.50	11.00
❑2, Feb 83, SA, ME (w), The Missive!	1.00	1.40	3.50	7.00
❑3, Apr 83, SA, ME (w), The Caravan	1.00	1.20	3.00	6.00
❑4, Sep 83, SA, ME (w), The Turn of the Wheel	1.00	1.20	3.00	6.00
❑5, Oct 83, SA, ME (w), Shanghaied!	1.00	1.20	3.00	6.00
❑6, Dec 83, SA, ME (w), The Wizard War	1.00	1.00	2.50	5.00
❑7, Feb 84, SA, ME (w), Chakaal	1.00	1.00	2.50	5.00
❑8, Apr 84, SA, ME (w), Groo The Wanderer Warriors Two	1.00	1.00	2.50	5.00

GROOTLORE

FANTAGRAPHICS

Value: Cover or less

- ❑1, b&w ... 2.00
- ❑2, b&w ... 2.00

GROOTLORE (VOL. 2)

FANTAGRAPHICS

Value: Cover or less

- ❑1, b&w ... 2.00
- ❑2, b&w ... 2.00
- ❑3 ... 2.25

GROOVY

MARVEL

	ORIG	GOOD	FINE	N-MINT
❑1, A: Monkees	0.12	7.00	17.50	35.00
❑2, May 68, Misery Loves Company	0.12	4.40	11.00	22.00
❑3, Marvel Comics Group Publisher	0.12	4.40	11.00	22.00

GROSS POINT

DC

	ORIG	GOOD	FINE	N-MINT
❑1, Aug 97, MWa (w), Welcome to Gross Point	2.50	0.60	1.50	3.00
❑2, Sep 97	2.50	0.50	1.25	2.50
❑3, Oct 97	2.50	0.50	1.25	2.50
❑4, Nov 97, Mourning Becomes Elective	2.50	0.50	1.25	2.50
❑5, Dec 97, The Duck of Mystery	2.50	0.50	1.25	2.50
❑6, Dec 97, You Can't Get There From Here	2.50	0.50	1.25	2.50
❑7, Jan 98	2.50	0.50	1.25	2.50
❑8, Feb 98	2.50	0.50	1.25	2.50
❑9, Mar 98, Possession is Nine-Tenths of the Flaw	2.50	0.50	1.25	2.50
❑10, Apr 98	2.50	0.50	1.25	2.50
❑11, May 98	2.50	0.50	1.25	2.50
❑12, Jun 98	2.50	0.50	1.25	2.50
❑13, Jul 98	2.50	0.50	1.25	2.50
❑14, Aug 98, Final Issue	2.50	0.50	1.25	2.50

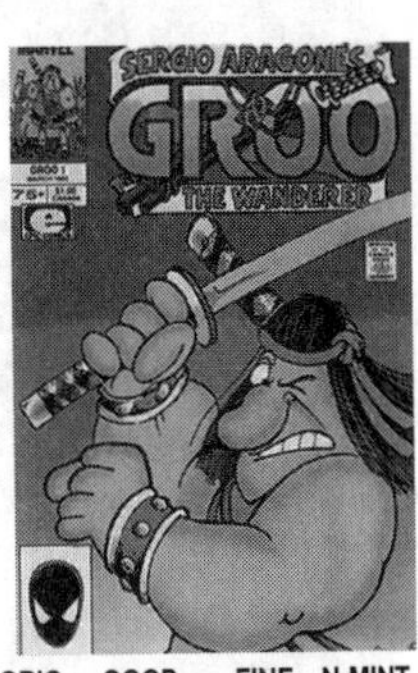

The Minstrel, who often commented on Groo's misadventures in rhyme, was introduced in the first issue of Marvel's *Groo the Wanderer.*

© 1985 Sergio Aragonés and Mark Evanier (Marvel/Epic)

GROUND POUND! COMIX

BLACKTHORNE

Value: Cover or less

- ❑1, Jan 87, Ronald's Surprise Birthday; Ronald The Barbarian ... 2.00

GROUND ZERO

ETERNITY

Value: Cover or less

- ❑1, b&w ... 2.50
- ❑2, b&w ... 2.50

GROUP LARUE, THE (MIKE BARON'S...)

INNOVATION

Value: Cover or less

- ❑1, Aug 89, Enter The Group LaRue! ... 1.95
- ❑2 ... 1.95
- ❑3 ... 1.95
- ❑4 ... 1.95

GRRL SCOUTS (JIM MAHFOOD'S...)

ONI PRESS

Value: Cover or less

- ❑1, Mar 99, b&w ... 2.95
- ❑2, Jun 99, b&w ... 2.95
- ❑3, Sep 99, b&w ... 2.95

GRRRL SQUAD

AMAZING AARON

Value: Cover or less

- ❑1, Mar 99, b&w; One-Shot ... 2.95

GRUN

HARRIER

Value: Cover or less

- ❑1, Jun 87 ... 1.95
- ❑2, Aug 87 ... 1.95
- ❑3, Oct 87 ... 1.95
- ❑4 ... 1.95

GRUNTS

MIRAGE

Value: Cover or less

- ❑1, Nov 87, b&w ... 2.00

GUARDIAN, THE

SPECTRUM

Value: Cover or less

- ❑1, Mar 84 ... 1.00
- ❑2, Jun 84 ... 1.00

GUARDIAN KNIGHTS: DEMON'S KNIGHT

LIMELIGHT

Value: Cover or less

- ❑1, b&w; no indicia ... 2.95
- ❑2, b&w; no indicia ... 2.95

GUARDIANS OF METROPOLIS, THE

DC

Value: Cover or less

- ❑1, Nov 94, No One Can Stop... Trevorr! ... 1.50
- ❑2, Dec 94, Donovan's Circus! ... 1.50
- ❑3, Jan 95, All this and World War II ... 1.50
- ❑4, Feb 95, Race the Devil!, V: Female Furies ... 1.50

GUARDIANS OF THE GALAXY

MARVEL

	ORIG	GOOD	FINE	N-MINT
❑1, Jun 90, Taserface!	1.00	0.40	1.00	2.00
❑2, Jul 90, V: The Stark	1.00	0.35	0.88	1.75
❑3, Aug 90	1.00	0.35	0.88	1.75
❑4, Sep 90, A: Firelord	1.00	0.35	0.88	1.75
❑5, Oct 90, V: Force	1.00	0.35	0.88	1.75
❑6, Nov 90, A: Captain America's shield	1.00	0.30	0.75	1.50
❑7, Dec 90, V: Malevolence	1.00	0.30	0.75	1.50
❑8, Jan 91, 1: Rancor	1.00	0.30	0.75	1.50
❑9, Feb 91, V: Rancor; 1: Replica	1.00	0.30	0.75	1.50
❑10, Mar 91	1.00	0.30	0.75	1.50
❑11, Apr 91, 1: Phoenix	1.00	0.30	0.75	1.50
❑12, May 91, V: Overkill	1.00	0.30	0.75	1.50

	ORIG	GOOD	FINE	N-MINT
❑13, Jun 91, 1: Spirit of Vengeance	1.00	0.40	1.00	2.00
❑14, Jul 91, A: Spirit of Vengeance	1.00	0.40	1.00	2.00
❑15, Aug 91, 1: Protege	1.00	0.30	0.75	1.50
❑16, Sep 91, Giant-size	1.50	0.35	0.88	1.75
❑17, Oct 91	1.00	0.30	0.75	1.50
❑18, Nov 91, 1: Talon	1.00	0.30	0.75	1.50
❑19, Dec 91, 1: Talon	1.00	0.30	0.75	1.50
❑20, Jan 92, A: Captain America's shield, Vance Astro becomes Major Victory	1.00	0.30	0.75	1.50
❑21, Feb 92, V: Rancor	1.25	0.30	0.75	1.50
❑22, Mar 92	1.25	0.30	0.75	1.50
❑23, Apr 92	1.25	0.30	0.75	1.50
❑24, May 92, A: Silver Surfer	1.25	0.30	0.75	1.50
❑25, Jun 92, V: Galactus, regular cover	2.50	0.50	1.25	2.50
❑25/SC, Jun 92, V: Galactus, foil cover	2.50	0.50	1.25	2.50
❑26, Jul 92, O: Guardians of the Galaxy	1.25	0.30	0.75	1.50
❑27, Aug 92, Infinity War, O: Talon	1.25	0.30	0.75	1.50
❑28, Sep 92, Infinity War, V: Doctor Octopus, Infinity War	1.25	0.30	0.75	1.50
❑29, Oct 92, Infinity War, Infinity War	1.25	0.30	0.75	1.50
❑30, Nov 92	1.25	0.25	0.63	1.25
❑31, Dec 92	1.25	0.25	0.63	1.25
❑32, Jan 93, A: Doctor Strange; A: Dr. Strange	1.25	0.25	0.63	1.25
❑33, Feb 93	1.25	0.25	0.63	1.25
❑34, Mar 93, Yellowjacket joins team	1.25	0.25	0.63	1.25
❑35, Apr 93, 1: Galactic Guardians, regular cover	1.25	0.25	0.63	1.25
❑35/SC, Apr 93, 1: Galactic Guardians, sculpted cover	2.95	0.59	1.48	2.95
❑36, May 93, V: Dormammu	1.25	0.25	0.63	1.25
❑37, Jun 93, D: Doctor Strange; D: Dr. Strange	1.25	0.25	0.63	1.25
❑38, Jul 93, A: Beyonder	1.25	0.25	0.63	1.25
❑39, Aug 93, Holo-grafix cover; Rancor vs. Doom	2.95	0.59	1.48	2.95
❑40, Sep 93, V: Composite	1.25	0.25	0.63	1.25
❑41, Oct 93, V: Loki; A: Composite; A: Starhawk; A: Inhumans	1.25	0.25	0.63	1.25
❑42, Nov 93	1.25	0.25	0.63	1.25
❑43, Dec 93, 1: Woden	1.25	0.25	0.63	1.25
❑44, Jan 94	1.25	0.25	0.63	1.25
❑45, Feb 94	1.25	0.25	0.63	1.25
❑46, Mar 94	1.25	0.25	0.63	1.25
❑47, Apr 94, Protege vs. Beyonder	1.25	0.25	0.63	1.25
❑48, May 94, V: Overkill	1.50	0.30	0.75	1.50
❑49, Jun 94, A: Celestial	1.50	0.30	0.75	1.50
❑50, Jul 94, Future History, Part 1, Giant-size	2.00	0.40	1.00	2.00
❑50/SC, Jul 94, Future History, Part 1, foil cover; Giant-size	2.95	0.59	1.48	2.95
❑51, Aug 94	1.50	0.30	0.75	1.50
❑52, Sep 94	1.50	0.30	0.75	1.50
❑53, Oct 94, Drax vs. Wolfhound	1.50	0.30	0.75	1.50
❑54, Nov 94, final fate of Spider-Man	1.50	0.30	0.75	1.50
❑55, Dec 94, V: Ripjak	1.50	0.30	0.75	1.50
❑56, Jan 95, V: Ripjak	1.50	0.30	0.75	1.50
❑57, Feb 95, A: Bubonicus	1.50	0.30	0.75	1.50
❑58, Mar 95	1.50	0.30	0.75	1.50
❑59, Apr 95, A: Silver Surfer	1.50	0.30	0.75	1.50
❑60, May 95, A: Silver Surfer	1.50	0.30	0.75	1.50
❑61, Jun 95	1.50	0.30	0.75	1.50
❑62, Jul 95, Final Issue; Giant-size	2.50	0.50	1.25	2.50
❑Anl 1, Jul 91, Korvac Quest, Part 4, Korvac Quest	2.00	0.60	1.50	3.00
❑Anl 2, The System Bytes, Part 4	2.25	0.50	1.25	2.50
❑Anl 3, trading card	2.95	0.59	1.48	2.95
❑Anl 4, Future History, Part 3	2.95	0.59	1.48	2.95

GUERRILLA GROUNDHOG
ECLIPSE

Value: Cover or less

- ❑1, Jan 87 ... 1.50
- ❑2, Mar 87, Guerrilla Groundhog Goes to Washington ... 1.50

GUERRILLA WAR
DELL

	ORIG	GOOD	FINE	N-MINT
❑12, Series continued from Jungle War Stories #11	0.12	1.60	4.00	8.00
❑13	0.12	1.60	4.00	8.00
❑14, Death From Below!; End of the Rope!, Final Issue	0.12	1.60	4.00	8.00

GUFF!
DARK HORSE

Value: Cover or less

- ❑1, Apr 98, Timoteo; Zombie Girl, nn; b&w; One-Shot; bound-in Meanie Babies card ... 1.95

GUMBY 3-D
BLACKTHORNE

Value: Cover or less

- ❑1 ... 2.50
- ❑2, The Eggs And Trixie ... 2.50
- ❑3 ... 2.50
- ❑4 ... 2.50
- ❑5 ... 2.50
- ❑6 ... 2.50
- ❑7 ... 2.50

GUMBY'S SUMMER FUN SPECIAL
COMICO

Value: Cover or less

- ❑1, Jul 87, Gumby's Summer Fun Adventure ... 4.00

GUMBY'S WINTER FUN SPECIAL
COMICO

Value: Cover or less

- ❑1, Gumby's Winter Fun Adventure ... 2.50

GUN FIGHTERS IN HELL
REBEL

Value: Cover or less

- ❑1 ... 2.25
- ❑2 ... 2.25
- ❑3, b&w ... 2.25
- ❑4 ... 2.25
- ❑5 ... 2.25

GUNFIRE
DC

	ORIG	GOOD	FINE	N-MINT
❑0, Oct 94, Forward Thrust!, Continued in Gunfire #6	1.95	0.40	1.00	2.00
❑1, May 94, Deadly Homecoming	1.75	0.40	1.00	2.00
❑2, Jun 94, On The Rebound	1.75	0.40	1.00	2.00
❑3, Jul 94, Enter: Purge	1.75	0.40	1.00	2.00
❑4, Aug 94, Squeeze Play	1.75	0.40	1.00	2.00
❑5, Sep 94, The Day of the Exomorphic Man, Continued in Gunfire #0	1.75	0.40	1.00	2.00
❑6, Nov 94, It's All Done With Mirrors!	1.95	0.40	1.00	2.00
❑7, Dec 94, The Big Blow-Out!	1.95	0.40	1.00	2.00
❑8, Jan 95, The Trail of the Dragon!	1.95	0.40	1.00	2.00
❑9, Feb 95, Hard News	1.95	0.40	1.00	2.00
❑10, Mar 95, The Hong Kong Shuffle	1.95	0.40	1.00	2.00
❑11, Apr 95	1.95	0.40	1.00	2.00
❑12, May 95	1.95	0.40	1.00	2.00
❑13, Jun 95, Final Issue	2.25	0.45	1.13	2.25

GUN FURY
AIRCEL

Value: Cover or less

- ❑1, b&w ... 1.95
- ❑2, b&w ... 1.95
- ❑3, b&w ... 1.95
- ❑4, b&w ... 1.95
- ❑5, b&w ... 1.95
- ❑6, b&w ... 1.95
- ❑7, May 89, Patrol, b&w ... 1.95
- ❑8, Jun 89, In God We Trust, b&w ... 1.95
- ❑9, b&w ... 1.95
- ❑10, b&w ... 1.95

GUN FURY RETURNS
AIRCEL

Value: Cover or less

- ❑1, Jul 90, b&w ... 2.25
- ❑2, Aug 90, Enter the Yesmen, b&w ... 2.25
- ❑3, Sep 90, b&w ... 2.25
- ❑4, Oct 90, b&w ... 2.25

GUNG HO
AVALON

Value: Cover or less

- ❑1, b&w; Reprint ... 2.95

GUNHAWKS
MARVEL

	ORIG	GOOD	FINE	N-MINT
❑1, Oct 72, 1: Reno Jones and Kid Cassidy	0.20	1.40	3.50	7.00
❑2, Dec 72	0.20	1.00	2.50	5.00
❑3, Feb 73	0.20	1.00	2.50	5.00
❑4, Apr 73, Trial By Ordeal	0.20	0.80	2.00	4.00
❑5, Jun 73, V: Reverend Mr. Graves	0.20	0.80	2.00	4.00
❑6, Aug 73, D: Kid Cassidy	0.20	0.80	2.00	4.00
❑7, Oct 73, Final Issue; Title changes to Gunhawk	0.20	0.80	2.00	4.00

GUNHED
VIZ

	ORIG	GOOD	FINE	N-MINT
❑1, full color; Japanese	—	1.40	3.50	7.00
❑2, full color; Japanese	—	1.40	3.50	7.00
❑3, full color; Japanese	—	1.40	3.50	7.00

GUNNER
GUN DOG

Value: Cover or less

- ❑1, Mar 99 ... 2.95

GUN RUNNER
MARVEL

Value: Cover or less

- ❑1, Oct 93, wraparound cover; 4 trading cards; four cards; Polybagged ... 2.75
- ❑2, Nov 93, Desert Storm ... 1.75
- ❑3, Dec 93, Heaven Can't Wait! 1.75
- ❑4, Jan 94, Thicker than Water! 1.75
- ❑5, Feb 94, You Can't Go Home Again! ... 1.75
- ❑6, Mar 94, Showdown on a Dying World ... 1.75

GUNSMITH CATS
DARK HORSE

Value: Cover or less

- ❑1, Sep 95 ... 2.95
- ❑2, Sep 95 ... 2.95
- ❑3, Sep 95, Bonnie and Clyde 2.95
- ❑4, Sep 95 ... 2.95
- ❑5, Sep 95 ... 2.95
- ❑6, Oct 95 ... 2.95
- ❑7, Nov 95 ... 2.95
- ❑8, Dec 95 ... 2.95
- ❑9, Jan 96 ... 2.95
- ❑10, Feb 96 ... 2.95

ORIG GOOD FINE N-MINT

GUNSMITH CATS: BAD TRIP
DARK HORSE
Value: Cover or less

- ❑1, Jun 98, Psychedelic.......... 2.95
- ❑2, Jun 98.............................. 2.95
- ❑3, Aug 98, Hammer Release 2.95
- ❑4, Sep 98, Poison of the Scorpion 2.95
- ❑5, Oct 98, Lost Game........... 2.95
- ❑6, Nov 98, Cool Down........... 2.95

GUNSMITH CATS: BEAN BANDIT
DARK HORSE
Value: Cover or less

- ❑1, Jan 99, Rolling Bean 2.95
- ❑2, Feb 99, Sleeper................ 2.95
- ❑3, Mar 99, V26...................... 2.95
- ❑4, Apr 99, Hot Motor 2.95
- ❑5, May 99............................ 2.95
- ❑6, Jun 99.............................. 2.95
- ❑7, Jul 99............................... 2.95
- ❑8, Aug 99, Crossfire.............. 2.95
- ❑9, Sep 99, Game, Set........... 2.95

GUNSMITH CATS: GOLDIE VS. MISTY
DARK HORSE
Value: Cover or less

- ❑1, Nov 97, Misty Brown........ 2.95
- ❑2, Dec 97, ...Decoy 2.95
- ❑3, Jan 98, ...Handicap.......... 2.95
- ❑4, Feb 98, ...Fast Burning 2.95
- ❑5, Mar 98, ...Minnie May....... 2.95
- ❑6, Apr 98, ...Injection............ 2.95
- ❑7, May 98, ...Bad Trip........... 2.95

GUNSMITH CATS: KIDNAPPED
DARK HORSE
Value: Cover or less

- ❑1, Nov 99.............................. 2.95
- ❑2, Dec 99.............................. 2.95
- ❑3, Jan 00, Long Night 2.95
- ❑4, Feb 00.............................. 2.95
- ❑5, Mar 00.............................. 2.95
- ❑6, Apr 00.............................. 2.95
- ❑7, May 00, Bloody Rally........ 2.95
- ❑8, Jun 00, 9mm vs. 40mm..... 2.95
- ❑9, Jul 00, Family.................... 2.95
- ❑10, Aug 00, Home Sweet Home 2.95

GUNSMITH CATS: MISTER V
DARK HORSE
Value: Cover or less

- ❑1, Oct 00, Goldie...Again...... 3.50
- ❑2, Nov 00, Breakthrough....... 3.50
- ❑3, Dec 00, Father.................. 3.50
- ❑4, Jan 01, Last Night............ 3.50
- ❑5, Feb 01, Daddy's 12-Gauge 3.50
- ❑6, Mar 01, Smokin' High....... 3.50
- ❑7, Apr 01, Guns n' Doses...... 3.50
- ❑8... 3.50
- ❑9... 3.50
- ❑10... 3.50
- ❑11... 3.50

GUNSMITH CATS: SHADES OF GRAY
DARK HORSE
Value: Cover or less

- ❑1, May 97, Hammerless........ 2.95
- ❑2, Jun 97, Big Game............. 2.95
- ❑3, Jul 97, SIG-SG550 .... 2.95
- ❑4, Aug 97, Lost...................... 2.95
- ❑5, Sep 97, Slide Stop............ 2.95

GUNSMITH CATS: THE RETURN OF GRAY
DARK HORSE
Value: Cover or less

- ❑1, Aug 96, Magnum Primer... 2.95
- ❑2, Sep 96, Sight-In, Part 1 .... 2.95
- ❑3, Oct 96, Sight-In, Part 2..... 2.95
- ❑4, Nov 96, Hard Touch.......... 2.95
- ❑5, Dec 96, Wood Bullet......... 2.95
- ❑6, Jan 97.............................. 2.95
- ❑7, Feb 97, Bean Bandit......... 2.95

GUNS OF SHAR-PEI
CALIBER
Value: Cover or less

- ❑1, b&w.................................. 2.95
- ❑2, b&w.................................. 2.95
- ❑3, b&w.................................. 2.95

GUNS OF THE DRAGON
DC
Value: Cover or less

- ❑1, Oct 98, Dragon Island....... 2.50
- ❑2, Nov 98.............................. 2.50
- ❑3, Dec 98.............................. 2.50
- ❑4, Jan 99.............................. 2.50

GUN THAT WON THE WEST, THE
WINCHESTER

	ORIG	GOOD	FINE	N-MINT
❑1, giveaway	—	4.40	11.00	22.00

GUTWALLOW
NUMBSKULL
Value: Cover or less

- ❑1, Feb 98, b&w..................... 2.95

GUY GARDNER
DC

	ORIG	GOOD	FINE	N-MINT
❑1, Oct 92, JSa, A New Guy In Town	1.25	0.40	1.00	2.00
❑2, Nov 92	1.25	0.35	0.88	1.75
❑3, Dec 92	1.25	0.30	0.75	1.50
❑4, Jan 93	1.25	0.30	0.75	1.50
❑5, Feb 93	1.25	0.30	0.75	1.50
❑6, Mar 93, JSa, Two for the Seesaw	1.25	0.25	0.63	1.25
❑7, Apr 93, JSa, Mexicali Gold	1.25	0.25	0.63	1.25
❑8, May 93, JSa, The Lord of the Ring	1.25	0.25	0.63	1.25
❑9, Jun 93, JSa, The Medusa Plague	1.25	0.25	0.63	1.25
❑10, Jul 93, JSa, Manifest Destiny	1.25	0.25	0.63	1.25
❑11, Aug 93, JSa, Yesterday's Sins, Part 1	1.25	0.25	0.63	1.25
❑12, Sep 93, JSa, Dream a Deadly Dream	1.25	0.25	0.63	1.25
❑13, Oct 93	1.25	0.25	0.63	1.25
❑14, Nov 93	1.25	0.25	0.63	1.25
❑15, Dec 93, Collateral Damage	1.50	0.30	0.75	1.50
❑16, Jan 94, Total Warfare, Series continued in Guy Gardner: Warrior #17	1.50	0.30	0.75	1.50

Gunhawk Reno Jones was a major character in the *Blaze of Glory* mini-series.

© 1972 Marvel Comics

ORIG GOOD FINE N-MINT

GUY GARDNER REBORN
DC
Value: Cover or less

- ❑1, JSt; JSa 4.95
- ❑2, JSa.................................... 4.95
- ❑3, JSa.................................... 4.95

GUY GARDNER: WARRIOR
DC

	ORIG	GOOD	FINE	N-MINT
❑0, Oct 94, O: Guy Gardner's Warrior persona	1.50	0.35	0.88	1.75
❑17, Feb 94, Warrior Road, Title changes to Guy Gardner: Warrior; Series continued from Guy Gardner #16	1.50	0.30	0.75	1.50
❑18, Mar 94	1.50	0.30	0.75	1.50
❑19, Apr 94	1.50	0.30	0.75	1.50
❑20, May 94	1.50	0.30	0.75	1.50
❑21, Jun 94, Emerald Fallout, Part 4, V: Parallax	1.50	0.30	0.75	1.50
❑22, Jul 94	1.50	0.30	0.75	1.50
❑23, Aug 94	1.50	0.30	0.75	1.50
❑24, Sep 94, Zero Hour	1.50	0.30	0.75	1.50
❑25, Nov 94, 25th anniversary issue; Giant-size	2.50	0.50	1.25	2.50
❑26, Dec 94	1.50	0.30	0.75	1.50
❑27, Jan 95	1.50	0.30	0.75	1.50
❑28, Feb 95, Capital Punishment, Part 2	1.50	0.30	0.75	1.50
❑29, Mar 95, Giant-size	1.50	0.30	0.75	1.50
❑29/SC, May 95, enhanced foldout cover; Giant-size	2.95	0.59	1.48	2.95
❑30, Apr 95	1.50	0.30	0.75	1.50
❑31, Jun 95	1.75	0.35	0.88	1.75
❑32, Jul 95	1.75	0.35	0.88	1.75
❑33, Aug 95	1.75	0.35	0.88	1.75
❑34, Sep 95, The Way of The Warrior, Part 7	1.75	0.35	0.88	1.75
❑35, Oct 95	1.75	0.35	0.88	1.75
❑36, Nov 95, Underworld Unleashed, Underworld Unleashed	1.75	0.35	0.88	1.75
❑37, Dec 95, Underworld Unleashed	1.75	0.35	0.88	1.75
❑38, Jan 96	1.75	0.35	0.88	1.75
❑39, Feb 96, Merriment, Mistletoe, and Mayhem!, Christmas party at Warriors	1.75	0.35	0.88	1.75
❑40, Mar 96, Good Things Ain't Been Comin' in The Packages I've Been Getting'	1.75	0.35	0.88	1.75
❑41, Apr 96, Guys & Babes in Toyland	1.75	0.35	0.88	1.75
❑42, May 96, Guy becomes a woman	1.75	0.35	0.88	1.75
❑43, Jun 96	1.75	0.35	0.88	1.75
❑44, Jul 96, A Warrior's Passing, Part 2, V: Major Force, Final Issue	1.75	0.35	0.88	1.75
❑Anl 1, Year One; 1995 Annual	3.50	0.70	1.75	3.50
❑Anl 2, Legends of the Dead Earth; 1996 Annual	2.95	0.59	1.48	2.95

GUY PUMPKINHEAD
SAINT GRAY
Value: Cover or less

- ❑1... 2.50

GUZZI LEMANS
ANTARCTIC
Value: Cover or less

- ❑1, Aug 96, b&w 2.95
- ❑2, Oct 96, b&w; Final Issue ... 2.95

GYRE
ABACULUS

	ORIG	GOOD	FINE	N-MINT
❑1, Dec 97, Soul Keeper, Part 1, b&w	2.95	0.70	1.75	3.50
❑2, Feb 98, Soul Keeper, Part 2; Six Degrees: The Five Giants, Part 6, b&w	2.95	0.59	1.48	2.95
❑3, Soul Keeper, Part 3; Six Degrees: The Five Giants, Part 7	2.95	0.59	1.48	2.95
❑Ash 1, Preview of Gyre #1	—	0.10	0.25	0.50
❑SE 1, Head Count; Dead Babies	4.50	0.90	2.25	4.50

GYRE: TRADITIONS & INTERRUPTIONS
ABACULUS

	ORIG	GOOD	FINE	N-MINT
❑1, nn; b&w; Promotional book for series	0.99	0.20	0.50	1.00

GYRO COMICS
RIP OFF
Value: Cover or less

- ❑1, b&w.................................. 2.00
- ❑2, b&w.................................. 2.00
- ❑3, b&w.................................. 2.00

H

HACKER FILES, THE
DC

	ORIG	GOOD	FINE	N-MINT
❑1, Aug 92, TS, Soft War, Part 1, 1: Jack Marshall	1.95	0.45	1.13	2.25
❑2, Sep 92, Soft War, Part 2	1.95	0.39	0.98	1.95
❑3, Oct 92, Soft War, Part 3	1.95	0.39	0.98	1.95
❑4, Nov 92, Soft War, Part 4	1.95	0.39	0.98	1.95
❑5, Dec 92, Operation: Moonwitch, Part 1	1.95	0.39	0.98	1.95
❑6, Jan 93, Operation: Moonwitch, Part 2	1.95	0.39	0.98	1.95
❑7, Feb 93, TS, Working Class Hero, Part 1	1.95	0.39	0.98	1.95
❑8, Mar 93, TS, Working Class Hero, Part 2	1.95	0.39	0.98	1.95
❑9, Apr 93, Working Class Hero, Part 3	1.95	0.39	0.98	1.95
❑10, May 93, TS, Working Class Hero, Part 4	1.95	0.39	0.98	1.95
❑11, Jun 93	1.95	0.39	0.98	1.95
❑12, Jul 93	1.95	0.39	0.98	1.95

HACKMASTERS OF EVERKNIGHT
KENZER AND COMPANY

Value: Cover or less

❑1, May 00 2.95
❑2, Jul 00 2.95
❑3 2.95
❑4 2.95
❑5 2.95
❑6 2.95
❑7 2.95
❑8 2.95

HAIRBAT
SCREAMING RICE

Value: Cover or less

❑1, b&w 2.50
❑2, b&w 2.50
❑3, b&w 2.50

HAIRBAT (VOL. 2)
SLAVE LABOR

Value: Cover or less

❑1, Jul 95 2.95

HAIR BEAR BUNCH, THE
GOLD KEY

	ORIG	GOOD	FINE	N-MINT
❑1, Feb 72	0.15	2.40	6.00	12.00
❑2, May 72	0.15	1.40	3.50	7.00
❑3, Aug 72	0.15	1.40	3.50	7.00
❑4, Nov 72	0.15	1.40	3.50	7.00
❑5, Feb 73	0.15	1.40	3.50	7.00
❑6, May 73	0.15	1.00	2.50	5.00
❑7, Aug 73	0.15	1.00	2.50	5.00
❑8, Nov 73	0.15	1.00	2.50	5.00
❑9, Feb 74	0.15	1.00	2.50	5.00

HAIRBUTT THE HIPPO
RATRACE

Value: Cover or less

❑1, Spr 97, b&w; no indicia 2.95
❑2, Sum 97, b&w; no indicia 2.95

HAIRBUTT THE HIPPO CRIME FILES
RAT RACE

Value: Cover or less

❑1, Dec 95, Sadly Ever Thus; Sins of My Father 3.50
❑2, Exists? 3.50
❑3, Exists? 3.50
❑4, Exists? 3.50
❑5, Exists? 3.50
❑6, Exists? 3.50

HALIFAX EXPLOSION
HALIFAX

Value: Cover or less

❑1, Apr 97, b&w 2.50

HALL OF FAME
J.C.

	ORIG	GOOD	FINE	N-MINT
❑1	1.00	0.30	0.75	1.50
❑2	1.00	0.30	0.75	1.50
❑3	1.00	0.30	0.75	1.50

HALL OF HEROES
HALL OF HEROES

Value: Cover or less

❑1, May 97, b&w 2.50

HALL OF HEROES HALLOWEEN SPECIAL
HALL OF HEROES

Value: Cover or less

❑1, Oct 97, nn; b&w; One-Shot 2.50

HALL OF HEROES PRESENTS (1ST SERIES)
HALL OF HEROES

Value: Cover or less

❑1, Aug 93, Wrath of Fire 2.50
❑2, Sep 93, The World of Nadir 2.50
❑3, Nov 93, Silent Wind 2.50

HALL OF HEROES PRESENTS (2ND SERIES)
HALL OF HEROES

Value: Cover or less

❑0/A, Mar 97, b&w; Slingers cover 2.50
❑0/B, Mar 97, b&w; Salamandroid cover 2.50
❑0/C, Mar 97, b&w; The Fuzz cover 2.50
❑1, Jul 96, Sinister, b&w 2.50
❑2, Sep 96, Elijah's Fury in the Last Days; Elijah's Fury in Last Day, b&w 2.50
❑3/A, Power of the Golem, b&w; no indicia 2.50
❑3/B, alternate b cover with Nazi swastika in background 2.50
❑4, May 97, Turaxx 2.50
❑5, Sep 97, The Becoming; extra-wide 2.50

HALLOWED KNIGHT
SHEA

Value: Cover or less

❑1, Apr 97, b&w 2.95
❑2, Sep 97, b&w 2.95

HALLOWEEN
CHAOS

Value: Cover or less

❑1, Nov 00, Photo cover; based on movie 2.95

HALLOWEEN HORROR
ECLIPSE

	ORIG	GOOD	FINE	N-MINT
❑1, Oct 87, Mother Hubbard; The Secret of Thurman Renauld, a.k.a. Seduction of the Innocent #7	1.75	0.40	1.00	2.00

HALLOWEEN MEGAZINE
MARVEL

Value: Cover or less

❑1, Dec 96, GC, Night of the Screaming House; To Kill a Vampire!, O: Blade, the Vampire Hunter, reprints stories from Tomb of Dracula 3.95

HALLOWEEN TERROR
ETERNITY

Value: Cover or less

❑1, The Long Way Home; Kin, b&w 2.50

HALLS OF HORROR (JOHN BOLTON'S...)
ECLIPSE

Value: Cover or less

❑1, Jun 85, The Monster Cabaret; The Werewolf 1.75
❑2, Jun 85, Where Monsters Roamed; Father Shandor 1.75
❑3 1.75

HALO, AN ANGEL'S STORY
SIRIUS

Value: Cover or less

❑1, Apr 96 2.95
❑2, May 96 2.95

HAMMER, THE
DARK HORSE

Value: Cover or less

❑1, Oct 97 2.95
❑2, Nov 97 2.95
❑3, Dec 97 2.95
❑4, Jan 98 2.95

HAMMERLOCKE
DC

Value: Cover or less

❑1, Sep 92, Now These Her Princes, 1: Hammerlocke 2.50
❑2, Oct 92 1.75
❑3, Nov 92 1.75
❑4, Dec 92 1.75
❑5, Jan 93 1.75
❑6, Feb 93 1.75
❑7, Mar 93 1.75
❑8, Apr 93 1.75
❑9, May 93, Final Issue 1.75

HAMMER OF GOD
FIRST

Value: Cover or less

❑1, SR, SR (w), Red Carnation 1.95
❑2 1.95
❑3 1.95
❑4 1.95

HAMMER OF GOD: BUTCH
DARK HORSE

Value: Cover or less

❑1, May 94, Butch 2.50
❑2, Jul 94 2.50
❑3, Aug 94, Final Issue 2.50

HAMMER OF GOD: PENTATHLON
DARK HORSE

Value: Cover or less

❑1, nn 2.50

HAMMER OF GOD: SWORD OF JUSTICE
FIRST

Value: Cover or less

❑1 4.95
❑2 4.95

HAMMER, THE: THE OUTSIDER
DARK HORSE

Value: Cover or less

❑1, Feb 99 2.95
❑2, Mar 99 2.95
❑3, Apr 99 2.95

HAMMER, THE: UNCLE ALEX
DARK HORSE

Value: Cover or less

❑1, Aug 98 2.95

HAMSTER VICE (BLACKTHORNE)
BLACKTHORNE

Value: Cover or less

❑1, Rumble Roach 2.00
❑2 2.00
❑3 2.00
❑4 2.00
❑5 2.00
❑6 2.00
❑7 2.00
❑8, Jul 87 2.00
❑9 1.50
❑3D 1, Nov 86, Zombie Quest 3D 2.50
❑3D 2, Feb 87, a.k.a. Blackthorne 3-D #15 2.50

HAMSTER VICE (ETERNITY)
ETERNITY

Value: Cover or less

❑1, Apr 89, b&w 1.95
❑2, b&w 1.95

HAND OF FATE
ECLIPSE

Value: Cover or less

❑1, Feb 88, Night of the Siren, full color 1.75
❑2, Mar 88, Night of the Widow, full color 1.75
❑3, Apr 88, b&w 2.00

HAND SHADOWS
Doyan

Value: Cover or less

- ❑1 ... 1.50
- ❑2, Nov 86, Gone Fission; Christopher Q. Cosmos, Space Janitor ... 1.50

HANDS OFF!
Ward Sutton

Value: Cover or less

- ❑1, b&w; One-Shot ... 2.95

HANDS OF THE DRAGON
Atlas

	ORIG	GOOD	FINE	N-MINT
❑1, Jun 75	0.25	0.60	1.50	3.00

HANNA-BARBERA ALL-STARS
Archie

Value: Cover or less

- ❑1, Oct 95, Anthology ... 1.50
- ❑2, Dec 95, Anthology ... 1.50
- ❑3, Feb 96, Anthology ... 1.50
- ❑4, Apr 96, Anthology ... 1.50

HANNA-BARBERA BIG BOOK
Harvey

Value: Cover or less

- ❑1, Jun 93, The Old Gray Bear; Bargain Day at Stonehill! ... 1.95
- ❑3 ... 2.50

HANNA-BARBERA GIANT SIZE
Harvey

Value: Cover or less

- ❑2, Nov 92, Rememger ... 2.25

HANNA-BARBERA PARADE
Charlton

	ORIG	GOOD	FINE	N-MINT
❑1, Sep 71, A: Lippy the Lion; A: Flintstones; A: TouchT Turtle,; A: Peter Potamus; A: Wally Gator; A: Hardy Har Har; A: Yakky & Fibber	0.15	6.00	15.00	30.00
❑2	0.15	4.00	10.00	20.00
❑3	0.15	3.20	8.00	16.00
❑4	0.15	2.80	7.00	14.00
❑5	0.15	2.80	7.00	14.00
❑6, The Flintstones: One Breakfast Comi, A: Pebbles Flintstone; A: Fred Flintstone; A: Wilma Flintstone, Dixie cameo; Pixie cameo	0.15	2.40	6.00	12.00
❑7	0.15	2.40	6.00	12.00
❑8	0.15	2.40	6.00	12.00
❑9	0.15	2.40	6.00	12.00
❑10	0.15	2.40	6.00	12.00

HANNA-BARBERA PRESENTS
Archie

Value: Cover or less

- ❑1, Nov 95, Atom Ant and Secret Squirrel ... 1.50
- ❑2, Jan 96, Wacky Races ... 1.50
- ❑3, Mar 96, Yogi Bear ... 1.50
- ❑4, May 96, Quick Draw McGraw and Magilla Gorilla ... 1.50
- ❑5, Jul 96, A Pup Named Scooby-Doo ... 1.50
- ❑6, Aug 96, Superstar Olympics 1.50
- ❑8, Oct 96, Frankenstein Jr. and the Impossibles ... 1.50

HANNA-BARBERA PRESENTS ALL-NEW COMICS
Harvey

	ORIG	GOOD	FINE	N-MINT
❑1, giveaway promo	—	0.20	0.50	1.00

HANNA-BARBERA SUPER TV HEROES
Gold Key

	ORIG	GOOD	FINE	N-MINT
❑1, Herculoids	0.15	12.00	30.00	60.00
❑2, Birdman	0.15	7.60	19.00	38.00
❑3, Space Ghost	0.15	7.00	17.50	35.00
❑4, Jan 69, Herculoids, Birdman, Shazzan, Moby Dick, Mighty Mightor	0.15	6.00	15.00	30.00
❑5	0.15	6.00	15.00	30.00
❑6, Space Ghost	0.15	7.20	18.00	36.00
❑7, Space Ghost	0.15	7.20	18.00	36.00

HANSI, THE GIRL WHO LOVED THE SWASTIKA
Spire

	ORIG	GOOD	FINE	N-MINT
❑1	0.39	1.00	2.50	5.00

HAP HAZARD
Fandom House

Value: Cover or less

- ❑1, b&w ... 2.00

HAPPENSTANCE JACK, III
-Ism

	ORIG	GOOD	FINE	N-MINT
❑1, May 98, What the Hell Were We Thinking?	2.98	0.60	1.50	3.00

HAPPY
Wonder Comics

Value: Cover or less

- ❑1, b&w ... 2.00

HAPPY BIRTHDAY GNATRAT!
Dimension

Value: Cover or less

- ❑1 ... 1.95

HAPPY BIRTHDAY MARTHA WASHINGTON
Dark Horse

	ORIG	GOOD	FINE	N-MINT
❑1, Mar 95, DaG, FM (w), Collateral Damage, cardstock cover	2.95	0.60	1.50	3.00

HAPPYDALE: DEVILS IN THE DESERT
DC

Value: Cover or less

- ❑1, prestige format ... 6.95
- ❑2, prestige format ... 6.95

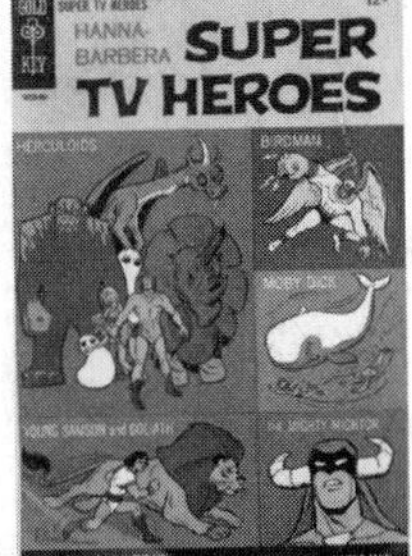

Many of Hanna-Barbera's action heroes, including The Herculoids, Space Ghost, and Birdman, made appearances in Gold Key's *Hanna-Barbera Super TV Heroes.*

© 1969 Gold Key and Hanna-Barbera

HARBINGER
Valiant

	ORIG	GOOD	FINE	N-MINT
❑0, Feb 93, O: Sting, sendaway; Special issue given as a premium from coupons in Harbinger #1-6	—	0.50	1.25	2.50
❑0-2, O: Sting, 2nd Printing; Included with Harbinger trade paperback	—	0.50	1.25	2.50
❑1, Jan 92, Childred of the Eighth Day, 1: Harbinger kids; O: Harbinger; 1: Torque; 1: Kris; 1: Sting; 1: Zeppelin; 1: Flamingo, coupon for Harbinger #0	1.95	0.80	2.00	4.00
❑2, Feb 92, coupon for Harbinger #0	1.95	0.50	1.25	2.50
❑3, Mar 92, V: Ax, coupon for Harbinger #0	1.95	0.50	1.25	2.50
❑4, Apr 92, coupon for Harbinger #0; Scarce	1.95	0.50	1.25	2.50
❑5, May 92, A: Solar, coupon for Harbinger #0	2.50	0.50	1.25	2.50
❑6, Jun 92, D: Torque, coupon for Harbinger #0	2.50	0.50	1.25	2.50
❑7, Jul 92	2.25	0.50	1.25	2.50
❑8, Aug 92, FM (c), Unity, Part 8, Unity	2.50	0.50	1.25	2.50
❑9, Sep 92, Unity, Part 16, Unity; Birth of Magnus	2.50	0.50	1.25	2.50
❑10, Oct 92, 1: H.A.R.D Corps	2.50	0.50	1.25	2.50
❑11, Nov 92, A: H.A.R.D Corps	2.50	0.50	1.25	2.50
❑12, Dec 92, Twilight of the Eighth Day, Part 1	2.50	0.50	1.25	2.50
❑13, Jan 93, Twilight of the Eighth Day, Part 2, Dark Knight cover	2.50	0.50	1.25	2.50
❑14, Feb 93, Twilight of the Eighth Day, Part 3	2.50	0.50	1.25	2.50
❑15, Mar 93	2.50	0.50	1.25	2.50
❑16, Apr 93	2.50	0.50	1.25	2.50
❑17, May 93	2.50	0.50	1.25	2.50
❑18, Jun 93, 1: Screen	2.50	0.50	1.25	2.50
❑19, Jul 93, Enter Kaliph	2.50	0.50	1.25	2.50
❑20, Aug 93, serial number coupon for contest	2.50	0.50	1.25	2.50
❑21, Sep 93	2.50	0.50	1.25	2.50
❑22, Oct 93, A: Archer & Armstrong	2.50	0.50	1.25	2.50
❑23, Nov 93	2.50	0.50	1.25	2.50
❑24, Dec 93	2.50	0.50	1.25	2.50
❑25, Jan 94, Armageddon, D: Rock; V: Harada, Giant-size; Sting vs. Harada; Harada put into coma; Sting loses powers	3.50	0.70	1.75	3.50
❑26, Feb 94, 1: Jolt; 1: Microwave; 1: Amazon; 1: Anvil; 1: Sonix, new team; Zephyr rejoins Harbinger foundation	2.50	0.50	1.25	2.50
❑27, Mar 94	2.50	0.50	1.25	2.50
❑28, Apr 94	2.50	0.50	1.25	2.50
❑29, May 94, trading card	2.50	0.50	1.25	2.50
❑30, Jun 94, Bad Omen, Part 1, A: H.A.R.D.Corps	2.50	0.50	1.25	2.50
❑31, Aug 94, A: H.A.R.D.Corps	2.50	0.50	1.25	2.50
❑32, Sep 94, A: Eternal Warrior	2.50	0.50	1.25	2.50
❑33, Oct 94, A: Dr. Eclipse; A: Doctor Eclipse	2.50	0.50	1.25	2.50
❑34, Nov 94, The Chaos Effect: Delta, Part 1, Chaos Effect	2.50	0.50	1.25	2.50
❑35, Dec 94	2.50	0.50	1.25	2.50
❑36, Jan 95, A: Magnus	2.50	0.50	1.25	2.50
❑37, Feb 95, Painted cover	2.50	0.50	1.25	2.50
❑38, Mar 95	2.50	0.50	1.25	2.50
❑39, Apr 95	2.50	0.50	1.25	2.50
❑40, May 95	2.50	0.50	1.25	2.50
❑41, Jun 95, Final Issue	2.50	0.50	1.25	2.50

HARBINGER: ACTS OF GOD
Acclaim

Value: Cover or less

- ❑1 ... 3.95

HARBINGER FILES
Valiant

Value: Cover or less

- ❑1, Aug 94, O: Toyo Harada ... 2.50
- ❑2, Feb 95, 1: The Harbinger .. 2.50

HARDBALL
Aircel

Value: Cover or less

- ❑1 ... 2.95
- ❑2 ... 2.95
- ❑3, Aug 91 ... 2.95
- ❑4 ... 2.95

HARD BOILED
DARK HORSE

Value: Cover or less

- ❑1, Sep 90, FM (w) 4.95
- ❑2, Dec 90, FM (w) 5.95
- ❑3, Mar 92, FM (w) 5.95

HARDCASE
MALIBU

	ORIG	GOOD	FINE	N-MINT
❑1, Jun 93, Winners Never Quit, 1: Hardcase; 1: Nicholas Lone (Solitaire); 1: NM-E	1.95	0.50	1.25	2.50
❑1/Hol, Jun 93, Holographic cover	—	1.00	2.50	5.00
❑1/LE, Jun 93, Ultrafoil limited edition	1.95	0.60	1.50	3.00
❑2, Jul 93, Hard Choices, 1: Choice, trading card, coupon; trading card	1.95	0.40	1.00	2.00
❑3, Aug 93, Hard Decisions, 1: Trouble; 1: Gun Nut; 1: The Needler	1.95	0.40	1.00	2.00
❑4, Sep 93, Strangers In The Night, O: Hardcase, Fold-out cover	1.95	0.40	1.00	2.00
❑5, Oct 93, Friends and Enemies, Part 1; Rune, Part D, Rune	2.50	0.40	1.00	2.00
❑6, Nov 93, Friends and Enemies, Part 2	1.95	0.39	0.98	1.95
❑7, Dec 93, Break-Thru: Sudden Surprises, Break-Thru	1.95	0.39	0.98	1.95
❑8, Jan 94, A: Solution	1.95	0.39	0.98	1.95
❑9, Feb 94, BA	1.95	0.39	0.98	1.95
❑10, Mar 94	1.95	0.39	0.98	1.95
❑11, Apr 94	1.95	0.39	0.98	1.95
❑12, May 94	1.95	0.39	0.98	1.95
❑13, Jun 94, The Turning Point, 1: Wynn; 1: Karr	1.95	0.39	0.98	1.95
❑14, Jul 94, Transition	1.95	0.39	0.98	1.95
❑15, Aug 94, Slash and Burn	1.95	0.39	0.98	1.95
❑16, Oct 94, KB (w), Battle Royale, Part 1; Fall, Flip book with Ultraverse Premiere #7	3.50	0.70	1.75	3.50
❑17, Nov 94, Battle Royale, Part 2, 1: The Genius	1.95	0.39	0.98	1.95
❑18, Dec 94, Battle Royale, Part 3	1.95	0.39	0.98	1.95
❑19, Jan 95, Here Today..., 1: Bismark; 1: Trauma	1.95	0.39	0.98	1.95
❑20, Feb 95, Reversals	2.50	0.50	1.25	2.50
❑21, Mar 95, Hard Road	2.50	0.50	1.25	2.50
❑22, Apr 95, Mundi Quest, Part 1, D: Trouble	2.50	0.50	1.25	2.50
❑23, May 95, Mundi Quest, Part 2	2.50	0.50	1.25	2.50
❑24, Jun 95	2.50	0.50	1.25	2.50
❑25, Jul 95	2.50	0.50	1.25	2.50
❑26, Aug 95, Final Issue	2.95	0.59	1.48	2.95

HARDCORE STATION
DC

Value: Cover or less

- ❑1, Jul 98, JSn, JSn (w), Genesis 2.50
- ❑2, Aug 98, JSn, JSn (w) 2.50
- ❑3, Sep 98, JSn, JSn (w), A: Green Lantern 2.50
- ❑4, Oct 98, JSn, JSn (w) 2.50
- ❑5, Nov 98, JSn, JSn (w), A: JLA 2.50
- ❑6, Dec 98, JSn, JSn (w), A: JLA 2.50

H.A.R.D. CORPS, THE
VALIANT

Value: Cover or less

- ❑1, Dec 92, Fold-out cover 2.50
- ❑1/GO, Fold-out cover; Gold (promotional) edition 2.50
- ❑2, Jan 93 .... 2.25
- ❑3, Feb 93, BL (w), Slaughter Street 2.25
- ❑4, Apr 93 .... 2.25
- ❑5, Apr 93, A: Bloodshot 2.25
- ❑6, May 93 .... 2.25
- ❑7, Jun 93, V: Spider-Aliens 2.25
- ❑8, Jul 93, The B-Team, or Some Like it Hot(Shot) 2.25
- ❑9, Aug 93 .... 2.25
- ❑10, Sep 93, A: Turok 2.25
- ❑11, Oct 93 .... 2.25
- ❑12, Nov 93 .... 2.25
- ❑13, Dec 93, D: Superstar 2.25
- ❑14, Jan 94, The Trouble With Midnight 2.25
- ❑15, Feb 94 .... 2.25
- ❑16, Mar 94 .... 2.25
- ❑17, Apr 94, V: Armorines 2.25
- ❑18, May 94, trading card 2.25
- ❑19, Jun 94, Bad Omen, Part 2, Harada awakes from coma 2.25
- ❑20, Jul 94, A: Harbinger 2.25
- ❑21, Sep 94, The Return of the Midnight Earl, Part 1 .... 2.25
- ❑22, Oct 94, The Return of the Midnight Earl, Part 2 .... 2.25
- ❑23, Nov 94, The Chaos Effect: Delta, Part 4, Chaos Effect 2.25
- ❑24, Dec 94 .... 2.50
- ❑25, Jan 95 .... 2.50
- ❑26, Feb 95 .... 2.50
- ❑27, Mar 95 .... 2.50
- ❑28, Apr 95 .... 2.50
- ❑29, May 95 .... 2.25
- ❑30, Jun 95, Final Issue 2.25

HARDKORR
AIRCEL

Value: Cover or less

- ❑1, Jun 91, b&w; adult 2.50
- ❑2, Jul 91, b&w; adult 2.50
- ❑3, Aug 91, b&w; adult 2.50
- ❑4, Sep 91, b&w; adult 2.50

HARD LOOKS
DARK HORSE

Value: Cover or less

- ❑1, DaG, Dumping Ground; Statute of Limitations, b&w 2.50
- ❑2, b&w 2.50
- ❑3, Crippler; Step on a Crack, b&w 2.50
- ❑4, b&w 2.50
- ❑5, Treatment; Crime Partner (text story), b&w 2.50
- ❑6, Dead Game; Bandit, b&w 2.95
- ❑7, b&w 2.95
- ❑8, b&w 2.95
- ❑9, KJ, Cain; Working Roots, b&w 2.95
- ❑10, KJ, Cain; Working Roots (text story), b&w 3.50

HARD ROCK COMICS
REVOLUTIONARY

	ORIG	GOOD	FINE	N-MINT
❑1, Mar 92, b&w; Metallica; early	2.50	0.80	2.00	4.00
❑2, Apr 92, b&w; Motley Crue	2.50	0.60	1.50	3.00
❑3, May 92, b&w; Jane's Addiction	2.50	0.50	1.25	2.50
❑4, Jun 92, b&w; Nirvana	2.50	0.50	1.25	2.50
❑5, Jul 92, b&w; Kiss: Tales From the Tours	2.50	1.60	4.00	8.00
❑5-2, 2nd Printing; Kiss: Tales From the Tours	2.50	1.20	3.00	6.00
❑6, Sep 92, b&w; Def Leppard II	2.50	0.50	1.25	2.50
❑7, Oct 92, b&w; Red Hot Chili Peppers	2.50	0.50	1.25	2.50
❑8, Nov 92, b&w; Soundgarden, Pearl Jam	2.50	0.50	1.25	2.50
❑9, Dec 92, b&w; Queen II	2.50	0.50	1.25	2.50
❑10, Jan 93, b&w; Birth of Punk	2.50	0.50	1.25	2.50
❑11, Feb 93, b&w; Pantera	2.50	0.50	1.25	2.50
❑12, Mar 93, b&w; Hendrix	2.50	0.50	1.25	2.50
❑13, Apr 93, b&w; Dead Kennedys	2.50	0.50	1.25	2.50
❑14, May 93, b&w; Van Halen II	2.50	0.50	1.25	2.50
❑15, Jun 93, Megadeath, Motorhead, b&w	2.50	0.50	1.25	2.50
❑16, Jul 93, b&w; Joan Jett, Lita Ford	2.50	0.50	1.25	2.50
❑17, never published; British Metal	2.50	0.50	1.25	2.50
❑18, Sep 93, b&w; Queensryche II	2.50	0.50	1.25	2.50
❑19, Oct 93, b&w; Tesla, Spirit, UKJ	2.50	0.50	1.25	2.50
❑20, Nov 93, The Sweet; Ratt, b&w; Ratt, P-Funk, Sweet	2.50	0.50	1.25	2.50

HARDWARE
DC

	ORIG	GOOD	FINE	N-MINT
❑1, Apr 93, The Man In The Machine, Chapter 1, 1: Hardware; 1: Edwin Alva; 1: Reprise, newsstand	1.50	0.30	0.75	1.50
❑1/CS, Apr 93, The Man In The Machine, Chapter 1, 1: Hardware; 1: Edwin Alva; 1: Reprise, trading card, poster, Part of mural; bagged	2.95	0.60	1.50	3.00
❑1/PL, Apr 93, The Man In The Machine, Chapter 1, 1: Hardware; 1: Edwin Alva; 1: Reprise, no cover price; Platinum (promotional) edition; platinum	2.95	0.70	1.75	3.50
❑2, May 93, The Man In The Machine, Chapter 2, 1: Barraki Young	1.50	0.30	0.75	1.50
❑3, May 93, Confrontations, 1: Systematic	1.50	0.30	0.75	1.50
❑4, Jun 93, Resolution	1.50	0.30	0.75	1.50
❑5, Jul 93, 1: Deathwish; 1: Deacon Stuart	1.50	0.30	0.75	1.50
❑6, Aug 93	1.50	0.30	0.75	1.50
❑7, Sep 93, O: Deathwish	1.50	0.30	0.75	1.50
❑8, Oct 93	1.50	0.30	0.75	1.50
❑9, Nov 93, 1: Technique	1.50	0.30	0.75	1.50
❑10, Dec 93, 1: Transit; 1: Harm	1.50	0.30	0.75	1.50
❑11, Jan 94, Shadow War; Shadow War, Part 1, 1: The Star Chamber; 1: Dharma; 1: Shadowspire	1.50	0.30	0.75	1.50
❑12, Feb 94, RB, No Harm Done	1.50	0.30	0.75	1.50
❑13, Mar 94, Weekend Getaway	1.50	0.30	0.75	1.50
❑14, Apr 94	1.50	0.30	0.75	1.50
❑15, May 94	1.50	0.30	0.75	1.50
❑16, Jun 94, 1: Hardware Version 2.0	2.50	0.50	1.25	2.50
❑16/SC, Jun 94, 1: Hardware Version 2.0, Fold-out cover	3.95	0.79	1.98	3.95
❑17, Jul 94, Worlds Collide; Worlds Collide, Part 2	1.50	0.30	0.75	1.50
❑18, Aug 94, Worlds Collide, Part 9	1.75	0.35	0.88	1.75
❑19, Sep 94	1.75	0.35	0.88	1.75
❑20, Oct 94	1.75	0.35	0.88	1.75
❑21, Nov 94	1.75	0.35	0.88	1.75
❑22, Dec 94	1.75	0.35	0.88	1.75
❑23, Jan 95, My Brother's Keeper?	1.75	0.35	0.88	1.75
❑24, Feb 95	1.75	0.35	0.88	1.75
❑25, Mar 95, Giant-size	2.95	0.59	1.48	2.95
❑26, Apr 95	1.75	0.35	0.88	1.75
❑27, May 95	1.75	0.35	0.88	1.75
❑28, Jun 95	1.75	0.35	0.88	1.75
❑29, Jul 95, cover has both .99 and 2.50 cover price	2.50	0.50	1.25	2.50
❑30, Aug 95, Long Hot Summer	2.50	0.50	1.25	2.50
❑31, Sep 95, The Long Hot Summer, D: Edwin Alva	2.50	0.50	1.25	2.50
❑32, Oct 95	2.50	0.50	1.25	2.50
❑33, Nov 95, HC (c)	2.50	0.50	1.25	2.50
❑34, Dec 95	2.50	0.50	1.25	2.50
❑35, Jan 96	2.50	0.50	1.25	2.50
❑36, Feb 96, T-Minus	2.50	0.50	1.25	2.50
❑37, Mar 96, Pressure Suit	2.50	0.50	1.25	2.50
❑38, Apr 96, Unsuited	2.50	0.50	1.25	2.50
❑39, May 96	2.50	0.50	1.25	2.50
❑40, Jun 96	2.50	0.50	1.25	2.50
❑41, Jul 96	2.50	0.50	1.25	2.50
❑42, Aug 96	2.50	0.50	1.25	2.50

	ORIG	GOOD	FINE	N-MINT
❑43, Sep 96, Doorway to Nightmares	2.50	0.50	1.25	2.50
❑44, Oct 96, Closure	2.50	0.50	1.25	2.50
❑45, Nov 96, Sweating it Out, return of Edwin Alva	2.50	0.50	1.25	2.50
❑46, Dec 96, Give them the Works	2.50	0.50	1.25	2.50
❑47, Jan 97	2.50	0.50	1.25	2.50
❑48, Feb 97	2.50	0.50	1.25	2.50
❑49, Mar 97	2.50	0.50	1.25	2.50
❑50, Apr 97, Final Issue; Giant-size	3.95	0.79	1.98	3.95
❑51, Final Issue	2.50	0.50	1.25	2.50

HARDWIRED
BANGTRO

Value: Cover or less

❑1, May 94 ... 2.25

HARI KARI
BLACK OUT

Value: Cover or less

❑0, Her Art is Death, indicia says "#0 #1" ... 2.95
❑1 ... 2.95

HARI KARI: LIVE & UNTAMED
BLACKOUT

Value: Cover or less

❑0, Moons Over My Hammy, photo feature ... 2.95
❑0/SC, Moons Over My Hammy, variant cover; photo feature ... 9.95
❑1 ... 2.95

HARI KARI PRIVATE GALLERY
BLACKOUT

Value: Cover or less

❑0, Pin-Ups ... 2.95

HARI KARI: REBIRTH
BLACK OUT

Value: Cover or less

❑1, Picking Up The Pieces ... 2.95

HARI KARI RESURRECTION
BLACKOUT

Value: Cover or less

❑1 ... 2.95

HARI KARI: THE BEGINNING
BLACK OUT

Value: Cover or less

❑1 ... 2.95

HARI KARI: THE DIARY OF KARI SUN
BLACKOUT

Value: Cover or less

❑1-2, prose accompanied with pin-ups ... 2.95

HARI KARI: THE SILENCE OF EVIL
BLACK OUT

Value: Cover or less

❑0 ... 2.95

HARLEM GLOBETROTTERS
GOLD KEY

	ORIG	GOOD	FINE	N-MINT
❑1, Apr 72	0.15	2.40	6.00	12.00
❑2, Jul 72	0.15	1.60	4.00	8.00
❑3, Oct 72, Granny's Royal Ruckus, A: Meadowlark; A: B.J.; A: Dribbles; A: Granny; A: Geese; A: Pabs; A: Gip; A: Curly	0.15	1.40	3.50	7.00
❑4, Jan 73	—	1.40	3.50	7.00
❑5, Apr 73, four-color; 32pgs.	—	1.40	3.50	7.00
❑6, Jul 73	0.20	1.00	2.50	5.00
❑7, Oct 73	0.20	1.00	2.50	5.00
❑8, Jan 74	0.20	1.00	2.50	5.00
❑9, Apr 74	0.20	1.00	2.50	5.00
❑10, Jul 74	0.20	1.00	2.50	5.00
❑11, Oct 74	0.20	1.00	2.50	5.00
❑12, Jan 75	0.20	1.00	2.50	5.00

HARLEM HEROES
FLEETWAY

Value: Cover or less

❑1, The Harlem Heroes, Part 1, b&w ... 1.95
❑2, b&w ... 1.95
❑3, b&w ... 1.95
❑4, b&w ... 1.95
❑5, b&w ... 1.95
❑6, b&w ... 1.95

HARLEQUIN
CALIBER

Value: Cover or less

❑1, nn; b&w ... 2.95

HARLEY QUINN
DC

Value: Cover or less

❑1, Dec 00, Harley Quinn Romance ... 2.95
❑2, Jan 01, A Heart Broken in Two! ... 2.25
❑3, Feb 01, A: Catwoman ... 2.25
❑4, Mar 01, The Wilde Life ... 2.25
❑5, Apr 01, Larger than Life ... 2.25
❑6, May 01, Who Wants to Rob a Millionaire? ... 2.25
❑7, Jun 01, Gods and Monsters 2.25
❑8 ... 2.25
❑9 ... 2.25
❑10 ... 2.25

HARLEY RIDER
HUNGNESS

Value: Cover or less

❑1, FS; GM, History of the Harley Davidson; A Harley Davidson Legend in San Francisco ... 2.00

HAROLD HEDD (LAST GASP)
LAST GASP ECO-FUNNIES

	ORIG	GOOD	FINE	N-MINT
❑1	0.50	1.60	4.00	8.00
❑2, Police Should Be Obscene and Not Absurd; Wings over Tijuana	1.50	0.80	2.00	4.00

In addition to their animated antics on the basketball court, The Harlem Globetrotters inspired an animated series and a comic-book series.

© 1972 Gold Key

HAROLD HEDD IN "HITLER'S COCAINE"
KITCHEN SINK

	ORIG	GOOD	FINE	N-MINT
❑1, Hitler's Cocaine	2.00	0.60	1.50	3.00
❑2	2.00	0.60	1.50	3.00

HARPY PIN-UP SPECIAL
PEREGRINE ENTERTAINMENT

Value: Cover or less

❑1, May 98, b&w ... 3.00

HARPY PREVIEW
GROUND ZERO

Value: Cover or less

❑1, Oct 96, b&w ... 3.00

HARPY: PRIZE OF THE OVERLORD
GROUND ZERO

Value: Cover or less

❑1, Dec 96, b&w ... 3.00
❑2, Feb 97, b&w ... 3.00
❑3, Apr 97, b&w; cover says Blood of the Demon ... 3.00

HARRIER PREVIEW
HARRIER

Value: Cover or less

❑1, Cuirass: The Fallen Star; Nightbird: Bird in Flight, 1: Cuirass, Night Bird ... 1.95

HARRIERS
EXPRESS

	ORIG	GOOD	FINE	N-MINT
❑1, Foil stamped cover	2.95	0.59	1.48	2.95
❑2	2.50	0.59	1.48	2.95
❑3	2.50	0.59	1.48	2.95

HARROWERS, THE (CLIVE BARKER'S...)
MARVEL

Value: Cover or less

❑1, Dec 93, GC, First Strike!, glow in the dark cover ... 2.95
❑2, Jan 94 ... 2.50
❑3, Feb 94 ... 2.50
❑4, Mar 94 ... 2.50
❑5, Apr 94 ... 2.50
❑6, May 94 ... 2.50

HARRY THE COP
SLAVE LABOR

Value: Cover or less

❑1, Apr 92, b&w ... 2.95
❑1-2, Oct 92, b&w; 2nd Printing 2.95

HARSH REALM
HARRIS

Value: Cover or less

❑1, The Case, full color ... 2.95
❑2, The City, full color ... 2.95
❑3, The Hazards, full color ... 2.95
❑4, full color ... 2.95
❑5, Jun 94, The Crucible, full color ... 2.95
❑6, Jul 94, The End ... 2.95

HARTE OF DARKNESS
ETERNITY

Value: Cover or less

❑1, b&w ... 2.50
❑2, b&w ... 2.50
❑3, b&w ... 2.50
❑4, b&w ... 2.50

HARVEY
MARVEL

	ORIG	GOOD	FINE	N-MINT
❑1, Oct 70, humor	0.20	3.60	9.00	18.00
❑2, Dec 70, humor	0.20	2.00	5.00	10.00
❑3, Jun 72, humor	0.20	1.60	4.00	8.00
❑4, Aug 72, humor	0.20	1.20	3.00	6.00
❑5, Oct 72, humor	0.20	1.20	3.00	6.00
❑6, Dec 72, humor	0.20	1.20	3.00	6.00

HATE
FANTAGRAPHICS

	ORIG	GOOD	FINE	N-MINT
❑1, Spr 90, b&w	2.00	2.40	6.00	12.00
❑1-2, 2nd Printing	2.00	0.70	1.75	3.50
❑, 3rd Printing	2.00	0.40	1.00	2.00
❑2, Sum 90	2.00	1.40	3.50	7.00
❑2-2, 2nd Printing	2.00	0.60	1.50	3.00
❑2-3, 3rd Printing	2.00	0.40	1.00	2.00
❑3, Fal 90	2.00	1.20	3.00	6.00
❑3-2, 2nd Printing	2.00	0.50	1.25	2.50
❑3-3, 3rd Printing	2.50	0.50	1.25	2.50
❑4, Spr 91	2.00	1.00	2.50	5.00
❑4-2, 2nd Printing	2.00	0.40	1.00	2.00
❑5, Sum 91	2.00	0.80	2.00	4.00
❑5-2, 2nd Printing	2.00	0.40	1.00	2.00

	ORIG	GOOD	FINE	N-MINT
❑6, Fal 91	2.25	0.80	2.00	4.00
❑7, Win 91	2.25	0.60	1.50	3.00
❑8, Spr 92	2.25	0.60	1.50	3.00
❑9, Sum 92	2.25	0.60	1.50	3.00
❑10, Fal 92	2.25	0.60	1.50	3.00
❑11, Win 93	2.50	0.50	1.25	2.50
❑12, Spr 93	2.50	0.50	1.25	2.50
❑13, Sum 93	2.50	0.50	1.25	2.50
❑14, Fal 93	2.50	0.50	1.25	2.50
❑15, Spr 94	2.50	0.50	1.25	2.50
❑16, Fal 94, color story	2.95	0.59	1.48	2.95
❑17, Win 95, Let's Get Serious, full color	2.95	0.59	1.48	2.95
❑18, Apr 95, full color	2.95	0.59	1.48	2.95
❑19, Jun 95, full color	2.95	0.59	1.48	2.95
❑20, Sep 95, color and b&w	2.95	0.59	1.48	2.95
❑21, Dec 95	2.95	0.59	1.48	2.95
❑22, Apr 96	2.95	0.59	1.48	2.95
❑23, Jun 96, full color	2.95	0.59	1.48	2.95
❑24, Sep 96, full color	2.95	0.59	1.48	2.95
❑25, Dec 96, full color	2.95	0.59	1.48	2.95
❑26, Mar 97	2.95	0.59	1.48	2.95
❑27, May 97	2.95	0.59	1.48	2.95
❑28, Jul 97	2.95	0.59	1.48	2.95
❑29, Jan 98	2.95	0.59	1.48	2.95
❑30, Jun 98, Final Issue; color and b&w	3.95	0.59	1.48	2.95

HATEBALL
FANTAGRAPHICS

	ORIG	GOOD	FINE	N-MINT
❑1, nn; giveaway	—	0.20	0.50	1.00

HATE JAMBOREE!
FANTAGRAPHICS

Value: Cover or less

❑1, Oct 98, b&w and color; newsprint cover ... 4.50

HAUNTED MAN, THE
DARK HORSE

Value: Cover or less

❑1, Mar 00, A Present of the Past ... 2.95
❑2 ... 2.95
❑3 ... 2.95

HAUNT OF FEAR, THE (GLADSTONE)
GLADSTONE

Value: Cover or less

❑1, May 91 ... 2.00
❑2, Jul 91 ... 2.00

HAUNT OF FEAR (RCP)
COCHRAN

Value: Cover or less

❑1, Sep 91, A Little Stranger!; Take Your Pick!, O: Old Witch, Giant-size; Reprints Haunt of Fear #14, Weird Fantasy #13 ... 2.00
❑2, Nov 91, Giant-size ... 2.00
❑3, Jan 92, Giant-size ... 2.00
❑4, Mar 92, Giant-size ... 2.00
❑5, May 92, Giant-size ... 2.00

HAUNT OF FEAR, THE (RCP)
EC

	ORIG	GOOD	FINE	N-MINT
❑1, Nov 92, Reprints The Haunt of Fear (EC) #1	1.50	0.40	1.00	2.00
❑2, Feb 93, Reprints The Haunt of Fear (EC) #2	1.50	0.40	1.00	2.00
❑3, May 93, Reprints The Haunt of Fear (EC) #3	1.50	0.40	1.00	2.00
❑4, Aug 93, Reprints The Haunt of Fear (EC) #4	2.00	0.40	1.00	2.00
❑5, Nov 93, Reprints The Haunt of Fear (EC) #5	2.00	0.40	1.00	2.00
❑6, Feb 94, A Strange Undertaking...; So They Finally Pinned You Down, Reprints The Haunt of Fear (EC) #6	2.00	0.40	1.00	2.00
❑7, May 94, Room For One More; The Basket, Reprints The Haunt of Fear (EC) #7	2.00	0.40	1.00	2.00
❑8, Aug 94, Hounded to Death; The Very Strange Mummy, Reprints The Haunt of Fear (EC) #8	2.00	0.40	1.00	2.00
❑9, Nov 94, Warts so Horrible?; Forbidden Fruit, Reprints The Haunt of Fear (EC) #9	2.00	0.40	1.00	2.00
❑10, Feb 95, Grave Business; The Vamp, Reprints The Haunt of Fear (EC) #10	2.00	0.40	1.00	2.00
❑11, May 95, Ooze in the Cellar?; The Acid Test!, Reprints The Haunt of Fear (EC) #11	2.00	0.40	1.00	2.00
❑12, Aug 95, Poetic Justice!; ...On a Dead Man's Chest!, Reprints The Haunt of Fear (EC) #12	2.00	0.40	1.00	2.00
❑13, Nov 95, For the Love of Death!; Fed Up!, Reprints The Haunt of Fear (EC) #13	2.00	0.40	1.00	2.00
❑14, Feb 96, A Little Stranger!; Take Your Pick!, O: The Old Witch, Reprints The Haunt of Fear (EC) #14	2.00	0.40	1.00	2.00
❑15, May 96, Chatter-Boxed!; All Washed Up!, Reprints The Haunt of Fear (EC) #15	2.00	0.40	1.00	2.00
❑16, Aug 96, JKa; GE, JKa (w); GE (w), Nobody There!; A Creep in the Deep!, Ray Bradbury story; Reprints The Haunt of Fear (EC) #16; Ray Bradbury adaptation	2.50	0.50	1.25	2.50
❑17, Nov 96, JKa; GE, JKa (w); GE (w), Horror We? How's Bayou?; Gorilla My Dreams!, Reprints The Haunt of Fear (EC) #17	2.50	0.50	1.25	2.50
❑18, Feb 97, JKa; GE, JKa (w); GE (w), Pipe Down; Bedtime Gory!, Ray Bradbury story; Reprints The Haunt of Fear (EC) #18	2.50	0.50	1.25	2.50
❑19, May 97, JKa; GE, JKa (w); GE (w), Sucker Bait!; Lover, Come Hack to Me!, Reprints The Haunt of Fear (EC) #19; Mentioned in Seduction of the Innocent "A comic book baseball game"	2.50	0.50	1.25	2.50
❑20, Aug 97, Reprints The Haunt of Fear (EC) #20	2.50	0.50	1.25	2.50
❑21, Nov 97, Reprints The Haunt of Fear (EC) #21	2.50	0.50	1.25	2.50
❑22, Feb 98, Reprints The Haunt of Fear (EC) #22	2.50	0.50	1.25	2.50
❑23, May 98, Reprints The Haunt of Fear (EC) #23	2.50	0.50	1.25	2.50
❑24, Aug 98, Reprints The Haunt of Fear (EC) #24	2.50	0.50	1.25	2.50
❑25, Nov 98, Reprints The Haunt of Fear (EC) #25	2.50	0.50	1.25	2.50
❑26, Feb 99, Marriage Vows; The Shadow Knows, Reprints The Haunt of Fear (EC) #26	2.50	0.50	1.25	2.50
❑27, May 99, JKa (w); GE (w), About Face; Game Washed Out, Reprints The Haunt of Fear (EC) #27	2.50	0.50	1.25	2.50
❑28, Aug 99, JKa; BK, JKa (w); BK (w), Purge; Numbskull, Reprints The Haunt of Fear (EC) #28	2.50	0.50	1.25	2.50
❑Anl 1, Reprints The Haunt of Fear #1-5	8.95	1.79	4.47	8.95
❑Anl 2, A Strange Undertaking; So They Finally Pinned You Down!, Reprints The Haunt of Fear #6-10	9.95	1.99	4.97	9.95
❑Anl 3, Ooze In The Cellar?; The Acid Test!, Reprints The Haunt of Fear #11-15	10.95	2.19	5.47	10.95
❑Anl 4, Reprints The Haunt of Fear #16-20	10.50	2.10	5.25	10.50
❑Anl 5, Reprints The Haunt of Fear #21-25	—	2.39	5.97	11.95
❑Anl 6, Marriage Vows; The Shadow Knows, Reprints The Haunt of Fear #26-28	8.95	1.79	4.47	8.95

HAUNT OF HORROR
MARVEL

	ORIG	GOOD	FINE	N-MINT
❑1, Aug 73	0.75	1.00	2.50	5.00
❑2	0.75	0.80	2.00	4.00
❑3	0.75	0.80	2.00	4.00
❑4	0.75	0.80	2.00	4.00
❑5, May 74	0.75	0.80	2.00	4.00

HAVOC, INC.
RADIO COMIX

Value: Cover or less

❑1, Mar 98 ... 2.95
❑2, Jun 98 ... 2.95
❑3, Sep 98 ... 2.95
❑4, Dec 98 ... 2.95
❑5 ... 2.95
❑6 ... 2.95
❑7 ... 2.95
❑8, Jul 00 ... 2.95

HAVOK & WOLVERINE: MELTDOWN
MARVEL

	ORIG	GOOD	FINE	N-MINT
❑1, Jan 88	3.50	0.80	2.00	4.00
❑2, Feb 88, Tender Loving Lies!	3.50	0.80	2.00	4.00
❑3, Mar 88, Duel	3.50	0.80	2.00	4.00
❑4, Apr 88	3.50	0.80	2.00	4.00

HAWK AND DOVE (2ND SERIES)
DC

	ORIG	GOOD	FINE	N-MINT
❑1, Oct 88, RL, Ghosts And Demons, 1: Dove II	1.00	0.60	1.50	3.00
❑2, Nov 88, RL	1.00	0.50	1.25	2.50
❑3, Dec 88, RL	1.00	0.40	1.00	2.00
❑4, Win 88, RL	1.00	0.40	1.00	2.00
❑5, Hol 89, RL, O: Dove	1.00	0.40	1.00	2.00

HAWK AND DOVE (3RD SERIES)
DC

	ORIG	GOOD	FINE	N-MINT
❑1, Jun 89, Gauntlet!	1.00	0.30	0.75	1.50
❑2, Jul 89	1.00	0.20	0.50	1.00
❑3, Aug 89	1.00	0.20	0.50	1.00
❑4, Sep 89	1.00	0.20	0.50	1.00
❑5, Oct 89	1.00	0.20	0.50	1.00
❑6, Nov 89	1.00	0.20	0.50	1.00
❑7, Dec 89	1.00	0.20	0.50	1.00
❑8, Jan 90	1.00	0.20	0.50	1.00
❑9, Feb 90	1.00	0.20	0.50	1.00
❑10, Mar 90	1.00	0.20	0.50	1.00
❑11, Apr 90	1.00	0.20	0.50	1.00
❑12, May 90, A: New Titans	1.00	0.20	0.50	1.00
❑13, Jun 90	1.00	0.20	0.50	1.00
❑14, Jul 90	1.00	0.20	0.50	1.00
❑15, Aug 90	1.00	0.20	0.50	1.00
❑16, Sep 90	1.00	0.20	0.50	1.00

	ORIG	GOOD	FINE	N-MINT
❑17, Oct 90	1.00	0.20	0.50	1.00
❑18, Nov 90	1.00	0.20	0.50	1.00
❑19, Dec 90	1.00	0.20	0.50	1.00
❑20, Jan 91	1.00	0.20	0.50	1.00
❑21, Feb 91	1.00	0.20	0.50	1.00
❑22, Mar 91	1.00	0.20	0.50	1.00
❑23, Apr 91	1.00	0.20	0.50	1.00
❑24, May 91	1.00	0.20	0.50	1.00
❑25, Jun 91, Giant-size	2.00	0.40	1.00	2.00
❑26, Aug 92, O: Hawk and Dove	1.25	0.25	0.63	1.25
❑27, Sep 91	1.25	0.25	0.63	1.25
❑28, Oct 91, War of the Gods, Giant-size; War of the Gods	2.00	0.40	1.00	2.00
❑Anl 1, Oct 90, Titans West	2.00	0.40	1.00	2.00
❑Anl 2, Sep 91, Armageddon 2001, Part 5, Armageddon 2001	2.00	0.40	1.00	2.00

HAWK AND DOVE (4TH SERIES)
DC

Value: Cover or less

- ❑1, Nov 97, Feathers, O: new team 2.50
- ❑2, Dec 97, Flight Into Madness, A: Vixen 2.50
- ❑3, Jan 98, Hellhound on my Trail! 2.50
- ❑4, Feb 98, Road Rules!, A: Vixen; V: Count Vertigo 2.50
- ❑5, Mar 98, Final Issue 2.50

HAWK & THE DOVE, THE (1ST SERIES)
DC

	ORIG	GOOD	FINE	N-MINT
❑1, Aug 68, SD, The Dove is a Very Gentle Bird	0.12	7.00	17.50	35.00
❑2, Oct 68, SD, DG (w), Jailbreak!	0.12	4.00	10.00	20.00
❑3, Dec 68, GK, DG (w), After the Cat; Twice Burned!	0.12	4.00	10.00	20.00
❑4, Feb 69, GK, DG (w), The Sell-Out!	0.12	4.00	10.00	20.00
❑5, Mar 69, GK, DG (w), Walk With Me, O' Brother...Death Has Taken My Hand!, A: Teen Titans	0.12	4.00	10.00	20.00
❑6, Jun 69, GK, GK (w); DG (w), Judgment in a Small, Dark Place, Final Issue	0.12	4.00	10.00	20.00

HAWK & WINDBLADE
WARP

Value: Cover or less

- ❑1, Aug 97, All the Lonely Places 2.95
- ❑2 2.95

HAWKEYE (VOL. 1)
MARVEL

	ORIG	GOOD	FINE	N-MINT
❑1, Sep 83, Listen to the Mockingbird, O: Hawkeye	0.60	0.50	1.25	2.50
❑2, Oct 83	0.60	0.40	1.00	2.00
❑3, Nov 83, 1: Oddball	0.60	0.40	1.00	2.00
❑4, Dec 83	0.60	0.40	1.00	2.00

HAWKEYE (VOL. 2)
MARVEL

Value: Cover or less

- ❑1, Jan 94, Shafted 1.75
- ❑2, Feb 94 1.75
- ❑3, Mar 94 1.75
- ❑4, Apr 94 1.75

HAWKEYE: EARTH'S MIGHTIEST MARKSMAN
MARVEL

Value: Cover or less

- ❑1, Oct 98, Battered by Batroc!; Assaulted by Oddball!, A: Firestar, Justice; V: Taskmaster, Oddball, One-Shot 2.99

HAWKMAN (1ST SERIES)
DC

	ORIG	GOOD	FINE	N-MINT
❑1, May 64, MA, Rivalry of the Winged Wonders; Master of the Sky Weapons	0.12	100.00	250.00	500.00
❑2, Jul 64, MA, Secret of the Sizzling Sparklers; Wings Across Time	0.12	38.00	95.00	190.00
❑3, Sep 64, MA, The Fear That Haunted Hawkman; Birds in the Gilded Cage	0.12	23.00	57.50	115.00
❑4, Nov 64, MA, The Girl Who Split in Two; The Machine That Magnetized Men, 1: Zatanna	0.12	30.00	75.00	150.00
❑5, Jan 65, MA, Steal, Shadow-Steal	0.12	23.00	57.50	115.00
❑6, Mar 65, MA, World Where Evolution Ran Wild	0.12	17.00	42.50	85.00
❑7, May 65, MA, Amazing Return of the I.Q. Gang; Attack of the Crocodile Man	0.12	17.00	42.50	85.00
❑8, Jul 65, MA, Giant in the Golden Mask; Battle of the Bird-Man Bandits	0.12	17.00	42.50	85.00
❑9, Sep 65, MA, Master Trap of the Matter Master	0.12	17.00	42.50	85.00
❑10, Nov 65, MA, Hawkman Clips the Claws of C.A.W.; The Magic Mirror Mystery	0.12	17.00	42.50	85.00
❑11, Jan 66, MA, The Shrike Strikes at Night	0.12	11.20	28.00	56.00
❑12, Mar 66, MA, The Million-Year-Long War	0.12	11.20	28.00	56.00
❑13, May 66, MA, Quest of the Immortal Queen	0.12	11.20	28.00	56.00
❑14, Jul 66, MA, The Treasure of the Talking Head	0.12	11.20	28.00	56.00

The various aspects of Hawkman were merged into one being during "Zero Hour" and given a new origin.

© 1994 DC Comics

	ORIG	GOOD	FINE	N-MINT
❑15, Sep 66, MA, Scourge of the Human Race	0.12	11.20	28.00	56.00
❑16, Nov 66, MA, Lord of the Flying Gorillas	0.12	8.40	21.00	42.00
❑17, Jan 67, MA, Ruse of the Robbing Raven; Enigma of the Escape-Happy Jewel Thieves	0.12	8.40	21.00	42.00
❑18, Mar 67, MA, World That Vanished, V: Manhawks; A: Adam Strange	0.12	8.40	21.00	42.00
❑19, May 67, MA, Parasite Planet Peril	0.12	8.40	21.00	42.00
❑20, Jul 67, MA, Death of the Living Flame; Lion-Mane-The Tabu Menace	0.12	7.60	19.00	38.00
❑21, Sep 67, MA, Attack of the Jungle Juggernaut	0.12	7.60	19.00	38.00
❑22, Nov 67, DD, Quoth the Falcon, "Hawkman Die"	0.12	7.60	19.00	38.00
❑23, Jan 68, DD, The Hawkman From 1, 000, 000 B.C.	0.12	7.60	19.00	38.00
❑24, Mar 68, DD, The Robot Raiders From Planet Midnight; The Man Who Grew Wings	0.12	7.60	19.00	38.00
❑25, May 68, DD, Return of the Death Goddess	0.12	7.60	19.00	38.00
❑26, Jul 68, DD, Last Stand on Thanagar	0.12	7.60	19.00	38.00
❑27, Sep 68, DD, ... When the Snow-Fiend Strikes, Final Issue	0.12	7.60	19.00	38.00

HAWKMAN (2ND SERIES)
DC

	ORIG	GOOD	FINE	N-MINT
❑1, Aug 86, RHo, Shadow War; Secrets....	0.75	0.40	1.00	2.00
❑2, Sep 86, RHo, Shadows..., V: Shadow Thief	0.75	0.30	0.75	1.50
❑3, Oct 86, RHo, Secrets, Shadows and Sinners, V: Shadow Thief	0.75	0.30	0.75	1.50
❑4, Nov 86, RHo, For the Benefit of Mr. Kite, A: Zatanna	0.75	0.25	0.63	1.25
❑5, Dec 86, RHo, The Lionmane Diversion, V: Lionmane	0.75	0.25	0.63	1.25
❑6, Jan 87, RHo, A Lion in the Streets, V: Lionmane	0.75	0.25	0.63	1.25
❑7, Feb 87, V: Darkwing	0.75	0.25	0.63	1.25
❑8, Mar 87, V: Darkwing	0.75	0.25	0.63	1.25
❑9, Apr 87	0.75	0.25	0.63	1.25
❑10, May 87, A: Superman	0.75	0.25	0.63	1.25
❑11, Jun 87	0.75	0.25	0.63	1.25
❑12, Jul 87	0.75	0.25	0.63	1.25
❑13, Aug 87	0.75	0.25	0.63	1.25
❑14, Sep 87	0.75	0.25	0.63	1.25
❑15, Oct 87	0.75	0.25	0.63	1.25
❑16, Nov 87	1.00	0.25	0.63	1.25
❑17, Dec 87	1.00	0.25	0.63	1.25
❑SE 1, Mar 86, RHo, RHo (w), Last Rights.	1.25	0.30	0.75	1.50

HAWKMAN (3RD SERIES)
DC

	ORIG	GOOD	FINE	N-MINT
❑0, Oct 94, Old Scores, O: Hawkman (new)	1.95	0.40	1.00	2.00
❑1, Sep 93, JDu, Winged Fury, foil cover....	2.50	0.50	1.25	2.50
❑2, Oct 93, JDu, Dead End	1.75	0.35	0.88	1.75
❑3, Nov 93	1.75	0.35	0.88	1.75
❑4, Dec 93	1.75	0.35	0.88	1.75
❑5, Jan 94, A Rage of Hawks	1.75	0.35	0.88	1.75
❑6, Feb 94	1.75	0.35	0.88	1.75
❑7, Mar 94, Mongrel; King of the Netherworld, Part 1	1.75	0.35	0.88	1.75
❑8, Apr 94, Mongrel	1.75	0.35	0.88	1.75
❑9, May 94	1.75	0.35	0.88	1.75
❑10, Jun 94	1.75	0.35	0.88	1.75
❑11, Jul 94, A: Carter Hall	1.75	0.35	0.88	1.75
❑12, Aug 94	1.95	0.39	0.98	1.95
❑13, Sep 94, Zero Hour; Godspawn, Conclusion	1.95	0.39	0.98	1.95
❑14, Nov 94, Eyes of the Hawk, Part 1; Old Ephraim's Folly	1.95	0.39	0.98	1.95
❑15, Dec 94, Eyes of the Hawk, Part 2; Among the Minnows, A: Aquaman	1.95	0.39	0.98	1.95
❑16, Jan 95, Eyes of the Hawk, Part 3; The Roar of the Bull, A: Wonder Woman	1.95	0.39	0.98	1.95

	ORIG	GOOD	FINE	N-MINT
❑17, Feb 95, Eyes of the Hawk, Part 4; Sting of the Viper	1.95	0.39	0.98	1.95
❑18, Mar 95, Identity	1.95	0.39	0.98	1.95
❑19, Apr 95, Mayhem in Motion	1.95	0.39	0.98	1.95
❑20, May 95, Clash of Wings	1.95	0.39	0.98	1.95
❑21, Jun 95, Party Lines, V: Gentleman Ghost; V: Shadow Thief	2.25	0.45	1.13	2.25
❑22, Jul 95, The Way of The Warrior, Part 3; Storm Over Thanagar	2.25	0.45	1.13	2.25
❑23, Aug 95, The Way of The Warrior, Part 6; Essential Warfare	2.25	0.45	1.13	2.25
❑24, Sep 95, Lion Hunt, Part 1; Hunting the Lion, Part 1	2.25	0.45	1.13	2.25
❑25, Oct 95, Lion Hunt, Part 2; Hunting the Lion, Part 2	2.25	0.45	1.13	2.25
❑26, Nov 95, Underworld Unleashed; Fear Visits, A: Scarecrow, Underworld Unleashed	2.25	0.45	1.13	2.25
❑27, Dec 95, Underworld Unleashed; Hawkmad, A: Neuron, Silent Knight; A: Neuron, Underworld Unleashed	2.25	0.45	1.13	2.25
❑28, Jan 96, Free Fall, V: Doctor Polaris; V: Dr. Polaris	2.25	0.45	1.13	2.25
❑29, Feb 96, Voices of Descent, Part 1, A: Vandal Savage	2.25	0.45	1.13	2.25
❑30, Mar 96, Voices of Descent, Part 2	2.25	0.45	1.13	2.25
❑31, Apr 96, Hunter, Hunted, Prey!, Part 1	2.25	0.45	1.13	2.25
❑32, Jun 96, Hunter, Hunted, Prey!, Part 2	2.25	0.45	1.13	2.25
❑33, Jul 96, Hunter, Hunted, Prey!, Part 3, D: Hawkman; A: Arion, Final Issue	2.25	0.45	1.13	2.25
❑Anl 1, Bloodlines, 1: Mongrel, Bloodlines	3.50	0.70	1.75	3.50
❑Anl 2, Year One	3.95	0.79	1.98	3.95

HAWKMOON: THE JEWEL IN THE SKULL
FIRST

Value: Cover or less

- ❑1, May 86 ... 1.75
- ❑2, Jul 86 ... 1.75
- ❑3, Sep 86 ... 1.75
- ❑4, Nov 86 ... 1.75

HAWKMOON: THE MAD GOD'S AMULET
FIRST

Value: Cover or less

- ❑1, Jan 87 ... 1.75
- ❑2, Feb 87 ... 1.75
- ❑3, Mar 87 ... 1.75
- ❑4, Apr 87 ... 1.75

HAWKMOON: THE RUNESTAFF
FIRST

	ORIG	GOOD	FINE	N-MINT
❑1	1.75	0.40	1.00	2.00
❑2	1.75	0.40	1.00	2.00
❑3	1.95	0.40	1.00	2.00
❑4	1.95	0.40	1.00	2.00

HAWKMOON: THE SWORD OF THE DAWN
FIRST

Value: Cover or less

- ❑1, Sep 87 ... 1.75
- ❑2, Nov 87 ... 1.75
- ❑3, Jan 88 ... 1.75
- ❑4, Mar 88 ... 1.75

HAWKSHAWS
IMAGE

Value: Cover or less

- ❑1, Mar 00, b&w ... 2.95

HAWK, STREET AVENGER
TAURUS PUBLISHING

Value: Cover or less

- ❑1, Jun 96, b&w ... 2.50

HAWKWORLD
DC

	ORIG	GOOD	FINE	N-MINT
❑1, Jun 90	1.50	0.50	1.25	2.50
❑2, Jul 90	1.50	0.35	0.88	1.75
❑3, Aug 90	1.50	0.35	0.88	1.75
❑4, Sep 90	1.50	0.35	0.88	1.75
❑5, Oct 90	1.50	0.35	0.88	1.75
❑6, Dec 90	1.50	0.35	0.88	1.75
❑7, Jan 91	1.50	0.35	0.88	1.75
❑8, Feb 91	1.50	0.35	0.88	1.75
❑9, Mar 91	1.50	0.35	0.88	1.75
❑10, Apr 91	1.50	0.35	0.88	1.75
❑11, May 91	1.50	0.30	0.75	1.50
❑12, Jun 91	1.50	0.30	0.75	1.50
❑13, Jul 91	1.50	0.30	0.75	1.50
❑14, Aug 91	1.50	0.30	0.75	1.50
❑15, Sep 91, War of the Gods, Part 4, War of the Gods	1.50	0.30	0.75	1.50
❑16, Oct 91, War of the Gods, Part 12, War of the Gods	1.50	0.30	0.75	1.50
❑17, Nov 91	1.50	0.30	0.75	1.50
❑18, Dec 91	1.50	0.30	0.75	1.50
❑19, Jan 92	1.50	0.30	0.75	1.50
❑20, Feb 92	1.50	0.30	0.75	1.50
❑21, Mar 92	1.25	0.30	0.75	1.50
❑22, Apr 92	1.50	0.30	0.75	1.50
❑23, May 92	1.50	0.30	0.75	1.50
❑24, Jul 92	1.50	0.30	0.75	1.50
❑25, Aug 92	1.50	0.30	0.75	1.50
❑26, Sep 92	1.50	0.30	0.75	1.50
❑27, Oct 92, Flight's End, Part 1, 1: The White Dragon	1.75	0.35	0.88	1.75
❑28, Nov 92, Flight's End, Part 2	1.75	0.35	0.88	1.75
❑29, Dec 92, Flight's End, Part 3	1.75	0.35	0.88	1.75
❑30, Jan 93, Flight's End, Part 4, 1: The Netherworld; 1: Count Viper	1.75	0.35	0.88	1.75
❑31, Feb 93, Flight's End, Part 5	1.75	0.35	0.88	1.75
❑32, Mar 93, Flight's End, Part 6, Final Issue	1.75	0.35	0.88	1.75
❑Anl 1, Dec 90, A: Flash	2.95	0.60	1.50	3.00
❑Anl 2, Aug 91, Armageddon Factor; Armageddon 2001, Part 6	2.95	0.59	1.48	2.95
❑Anl 2-2, Aug 91, 2nd Printing; silver	2.95	0.59	1.48	2.95
❑Anl 3, Eclipso: The Darkness Within, Part 11, Eclipso	2.95	0.59	1.48	2.95

HAWKWORLD (MINI-SERIES)
DC

	ORIG	GOOD	FINE	N-MINT
❑1, Aug 89, Flashzone, O: Hawkman, New costume	3.95	0.80	2.00	4.00
❑2, Sep 89, Truman	3.95	0.80	2.00	4.00
❑3, Oct 89, Truman	3.95	0.80	2.00	4.00

HAYWIRE
DC

Value: Cover or less

- ❑1, Oct 88, Kaleidoscope, 1: Haywire ... 1.25
- ❑2, Nov 88, Black Dragon ... 1.25
- ❑3, Dec 88 ... 1.25
- ❑4, Dec 88, Recognitions ... 1.25
- ❑5, Jan 89 ... 1.25
- ❑6, Jan 89 ... 1.25
- ❑7, Mar 89, V: White Lotus ... 1.50
- ❑8, Apr 89 ... 1.50
- ❑9, May 89 ... 1.50
- ❑10, Jun 89 ... 1.50
- ❑11, Jul 89 ... 1.50
- ❑12, Aug 89 ... 1.50
- ❑13, Sep 89, Final Issue ... 1.50

HAZARD
IMAGE

	ORIG	GOOD	FINE	N-MINT
❑1, Jun 96	1.75	0.35	0.88	1.75
❑2, Jul 96, cover says Jun, indicia says Jul	1.75	0.35	0.88	1.75
❑3, Jul 96	1.75	0.35	0.88	1.75
❑4, Aug 96	1.75	0.35	0.88	1.75
❑5, Sep 96	1.75	0.35	0.88	1.75
❑6, Oct 96, cover says Sep, indicia says Oct	1.75	0.45	1.13	2.25
❑7, Nov 96, Final Issue	2.25	0.45	1.13	2.25

HAZARD! (MOTION)
MOTION

Value: Cover or less

- ❑1, b&w; Breakneck Blvd. ... 2.50

HAZARD! (RECKLESS VISION)
RECKLESS VISION

Value: Cover or less

- ❑1, b&w; first Breakneck Blvd. Story ... 2.50

H-BOMB
ANTARCTIC

Value: Cover or less

- ❑1, Apr 93, b&w; adult ... 2.95

HEADBANGER
PARODY PRESS

Value: Cover or less

- ❑1, A Different Drummer ... 2.50

HEADBUSTER
ANTARCTIC

Value: Cover or less

- ❑1, Sep 98, b&w ... 2.95

HEADHUNTERS
IMAGE

Value: Cover or less

- ❑1, Apr 97, b&w; cover says Mar, indicia says Apr ... 2.95
- ❑2, May 97, b&w ... 2.95
- ❑3, Jun 97, b&w ... 2.95

HEADLESS HORSEMAN
ETERNITY

Value: Cover or less

- ❑1, b&w ... 2.25
- ❑2, b&w ... 2.25

HEADMAN
INNOVATION

Value: Cover or less

- ❑1, Head Games ... 2.50

HEAP
SKYWALD

	ORIG	GOOD	FINE	N-MINT
❑1, Sep 71, JAb; TS, Shadows of Satan; When The Sea Goes Dry!	0.25	2.80	7.00	14.00

HEARTBREAK COMICS
ECLIPSE

Value: Cover or less

- ❑1, b&w; magazine ... 3.95

HEARTBREAKERS
DARK HORSE

Value: Cover or less

- ❑1, Apr 96 ... 2.95
- ❑2, May 96 ... 2.95
- ❑3, Jun 96 ... 2.95
- ❑4, Jul 96, Final Issue ... 2.95

HEARTBREAKERS SUPERDIGEST: YEAR TEN
IMAGE

Value: Cover or less

- ❑1, Dec 99, The Last Strand; Sailing Vessels of the Southwest Sands ... 13.95

ORIG GOOD FINE N-MINT

HEARTLAND
DC

Value: Cover or less
- ❑1, Mar 97, One-Shot 4.95

HEART OF DARKNESS
HARDLINE

Value: Cover or less
- ❑1 .... 2.95

HEART OF EMPIRE
DARK HORSE

Value: Cover or less
- ❑1, Apr 99, BT, BT (w) 2.95
- ❑2, May 99, BT, BT (w) 2.95
- ❑3, Jun 99, BT, BT (w) 2.95
- ❑4, Jul 99, BT, BT (w) 2.95
- ❑5, Aug 99, BT, BT (w) 2.95
- ❑6, Sep 99, BT, BT (w) 2.95
- ❑7, Oct 99, BT, BT (w) 2.95
- ❑8, Nov 99, BT, BT (w) 2.95
- ❑9, Dec 99, BT, BT (w) 2.95

HEARTS OF DARKNESS
MARVEL

Value: Cover or less
- ❑1, Dec 91, JR2, Ghost Rider, Wolverine, and Punisher vs. Blackheart 4.95

HEARTTHROBS (VERTIGO)
DC

Value: Cover or less
- ❑1, Jan 99, BB (w), The Princess and the Frog; The Prince and the Witch 2.95
- ❑2, Feb 99, The Other Side of Town; Romancing the Stone 2.95
- ❑3, Mar 99, Apposites Attract; Mister Right 2.95
- ❑4, Apr 99, Heartache 1.0; Love... with a Twist 2.95

HEATHCLIFF
MARVEL

Issue	ORIG	GOOD	FINE	N-MINT
❑1, Apr 85	0.65	0.30	0.75	1.50
❑2	0.65	0.20	0.50	1.00
❑3	0.65	0.20	0.50	1.00
❑4	0.65	0.20	0.50	1.00
❑5, Computer Cat; Tale of Two Kitties	0.65	0.20	0.50	1.00
❑6	0.65	0.20	0.50	1.00
❑7	0.75	0.20	0.50	1.00
❑8	0.75	0.20	0.50	1.00
❑9	0.75	0.20	0.50	1.00
❑10	0.75	0.20	0.50	1.00
❑11	0.75	0.20	0.50	1.00
❑12, Spaced-Out Cat; The Kitnap Kaper	0.75	0.20	0.50	1.00
❑13	0.75	0.20	0.50	1.00
❑14	0.75	0.20	0.50	1.00
❑15	0.75	0.20	0.50	1.00
❑16	1.00	0.20	0.50	1.00
❑17	1.00	0.20	0.50	1.00
❑18	1.00	0.20	0.50	1.00
❑19	1.00	0.20	0.50	1.00
❑20	1.00	0.20	0.50	1.00
❑21	1.00	0.20	0.50	1.00
❑22	1.00	0.20	0.50	1.00
❑23	1.00	0.20	0.50	1.00
❑24	1.00	0.20	0.50	1.00
❑25	1.00	0.20	0.50	1.00
❑26	1.00	0.20	0.50	1.00
❑27	1.00	0.20	0.50	1.00
❑28	1.00	0.20	0.50	1.00
❑29	1.00	0.20	0.50	1.00
❑30	1.00	0.20	0.50	1.00
❑31	1.00	0.20	0.50	1.00
❑32	1.00	0.20	0.50	1.00
❑33	1.00	0.20	0.50	1.00
❑34	1.00	0.20	0.50	1.00
❑35	1.00	0.20	0.50	1.00
❑36	1.00	0.20	0.50	1.00
❑37	1.00	0.20	0.50	1.00
❑38	1.00	0.20	0.50	1.00
❑39	1.00	0.20	0.50	1.00
❑40	1.00	0.20	0.50	1.00
❑41	1.00	0.20	0.50	1.00
❑42	1.00	0.20	0.50	1.00
❑43	1.00	0.20	0.50	1.00
❑44	1.00	0.20	0.50	1.00
❑45	1.00	0.20	0.50	1.00
❑46	1.00	0.20	0.50	1.00
❑47, Batman parody	1.00	0.20	0.50	1.00
❑48	1.00	0.20	0.50	1.00
❑49	1.00	0.20	0.50	1.00
❑50, Giant-size; giant	1.50	0.30	0.75	1.50
❑51	1.00	0.20	0.50	1.00
❑52	1.00	0.20	0.50	1.00
❑53	1.00	0.20	0.50	1.00
❑54	1.00	0.20	0.50	1.00
❑55	1.00	0.20	0.50	1.00
❑56, Final Issue	1.00	0.20	0.50	1.00
❑Anl 1	1.25	0.25	0.63	1.25

THB creator Paul Pope brought his stylistic art to DC's *Heavy Liquid.*

ORIG GOOD FINE N-MINT

HEATHCLIFF'S FUNHOUSE
MARVEL

Issue	ORIG	GOOD	FINE	N-MINT
❑1, May 87, Karate Kitty; Undercover Cat	1.00	0.25	0.63	1.25
❑2, Jun 87	1.00	0.20	0.50	1.00
❑3, Jul 87	1.00	0.20	0.50	1.00
❑4, Aug 87	1.00	0.20	0.50	1.00
❑5, Sep 87	1.00	0.20	0.50	1.00
❑6, Oct 87	1.00	0.20	0.50	1.00
❑7, Nov 87	1.00	0.20	0.50	1.00
❑8, Dec 87	1.00	0.20	0.50	1.00
❑9, Jan 88	1.00	0.20	0.50	1.00
❑10, Feb 88	1.00	0.20	0.50	1.00

HEATSEEKER
FANTACO

Value: Cover or less
- ❑1, nn 5.95

HEAVY ARMOR
FANTASY GENERAL

Value: Cover or less
- ❑1 .... 1.70
- ❑2 .... 1.70
- ❑3 .... 1.70

HEAVY HITTERS
MARVEL

Value: Cover or less
- ❑Anl 1, Lawdog: Unrealed; Feud: A Movable Beast 3.75

HEAVY LIQUID
DC

Value: Cover or less
- ❑1, Oct 99 .... 5.95
- ❑2, Nov 99 .... 5.95
- ❑3, Dec 99 .... 5.95
- ❑4, Jan 00 .... 5.95
- ❑5, Feb 00 .... 5.95

HEAVY METAL MONSTERS
REVOLUTIONARY

Issue	ORIG	GOOD	FINE	N-MINT
❑1, Jan 92, b&w	2.50	0.60	1.50	3.00
❑2, 3-D	3.95	0.79	1.98	3.95

HECK!
RIP OFF

Value: Cover or less
- ❑1, b&w; Trade Paperback 7.95

HECKLER, THE
DC

Value: Cover or less
- ❑1, Sep 92, KG (w) 1.25
- ❑2, Oct 92, KG (w) 1.25
- ❑3, Nov 92, KG (w) 1.25
- ❑4, Dec 92, KG (w) 1.25
- ❑5, Jan 93, KG (w) 1.25
- ❑6, Feb 93, KG (w) 1.25
- ❑7, KG (w) 1.25

HECTIC PLANET
SLAVE LABOR

Value: Cover or less
- ❑6, Nov 93, previously titled Pirate Corp$! 2.50
- ❑6-2, Jan 96, 2nd Printing 2.75

HEE HAW
CHARLTON

Issue	ORIG	GOOD	FINE	N-MINT
❑1, Aug 70	0.15	2.40	6.00	12.00
❑2, Oct 70	0.15	1.60	4.00	8.00
❑3, Dec 70	0.15	1.20	3.00	6.00
❑4, Feb 71	0.15	1.20	3.00	6.00
❑5, Apr 71	0.15	1.20	3.00	6.00
❑6, Jun 71	0.15	1.20	3.00	6.00
❑7, Aug 71	0.15	1.20	3.00	6.00

HE IS JUST A RAT
EXCLAIM! BRAND COMICS

Value: Cover or less
- ❑1, Spr 95 .... 2.75
- ❑2, Fal 95 .... 2.75
- ❑3, Spr 96 .... 2.75
- ❑4, Fal 96 .... 2.75
- ❑5, Spr 97 .... 2.75

HELLBENDER
ETERNITY

Value: Cover or less
- ❑1, b&w; Shuriken 2.25

HELLBLAZER
DC

Issue	ORIG	GOOD	FINE	N-MINT
❑1, Jan 88, Hunger, 40pgs	1.25	1.20	3.00	6.00
❑2, Feb 88, A Feast For Friends	1.25	0.80	2.00	4.00
❑3, Mar 88, Going For It	1.25	0.80	2.00	4.00

	ORIG	GOOD	FINE	N-MINT
❑4, Apr 88, Waiting For The Man	1.25	0.80	2.00	4.00
❑5, May 88, When Johhny Comes Marching Home	1.25	0.80	2.00	4.00
❑6, Jun 88	1.25	0.70	1.75	3.50
❑7, Jul 88, Ghosts in the Machine	1.25	0.70	1.75	3.50
❑8, Aug 88	1.25	0.70	1.75	3.50
❑9, Sep 88, Shot to Hell	1.25	0.70	1.75	3.50
❑10, Oct 88, Sex and Death	1.25	0.70	1.75	3.50
❑11, Nov 88, Newcastle: A Taste of Things to Come	1.25	0.60	1.50	3.00
❑12, Dec 88, The Devil You Know	1.25	0.60	1.50	3.00
❑13, Dec 88, On the Beach	1.25	0.60	1.50	3.00
❑14, Jan 89, The Fear Machine, Part 1	1.25	0.60	1.50	3.00
❑15, Jan 89, The Fear Machine, Part 2	1.25	0.60	1.50	3.00
❑16, Feb 89, The Fear Machine, Part 3	1.25	0.60	1.50	3.00
❑17, Apr 89, The Fear Machine, Part 4	1.25	0.60	1.50	3.00
❑18, May 89, The Fear Machine, Part 5	1.50	0.60	1.50	3.00
❑19, Jun 89, The Fear Machine, Part 6	1.50	0.60	1.50	3.00
❑20, Jul 89, The Fear Machine, Part 7	1.50	0.60	1.50	3.00
❑21, Aug 89, The Fear Machine, Part 8	1.50	0.50	1.25	2.50
❑22, Sep 89, The Fear Machine, Part 9	1.50	0.50	1.25	2.50
❑23, Oct 89, Larger than Life	1.50	0.50	1.25	2.50
❑24, Nov 89, The Family Man	1.50	0.50	1.25	2.50
❑25, Jan 90, Early Warning	1.50	0.50	1.25	2.50
❑26, Feb 90, How I Learned to Love The Bomb	1.50	0.50	1.25	2.50
❑27, Mar 90, NG (w), Hold Me	1.50	2.00	5.00	10.00
❑28, Apr 90, Thicker than Water, D: Thomas Constantine	1.50	0.60	1.50	3.00
❑29, May 90	1.50	0.60	1.50	3.00
❑30, Jun 90, Fatality	1.50	0.60	1.50	3.00
❑31, Jul 90, Mourning of the Magician	1.50	0.60	1.50	3.00
❑32, Aug 90, New Tricks	1.50	0.60	1.50	3.00
❑33, Sep 90, Sundays are Different	1.50	0.60	1.50	3.00
❑34, Oct 90, The Bogeyman	1.50	0.60	1.50	3.00
❑35, Nov 90, Dead-Boy's Heart	1.50	0.60	1.50	3.00
❑36, Dec 90	1.50	0.60	1.50	3.00
❑37, Jan 91, Man's Work	1.50	0.60	1.50	3.00
❑38, Feb 91, Boy's Games	1.50	0.60	1.50	3.00
❑39, Mar 91	1.50	0.60	1.50	3.00
❑40, Apr 91, Magus	2.25	0.70	1.75	3.50
❑41, 91, Dangerous Habits, Part 1, 1st Garth Ennis story	1.50	1.20	3.00	6.00
❑42, Jun 91, Dangerous Habits, Part 2	1.50	0.80	2.00	4.00
❑43, Jul 91, Dangerous Habits, Part 3	1.50	0.80	2.00	4.00
❑44, Aug 91, Dangerous Habits, Part 4	1.75	0.80	2.00	4.00
❑45, Sep 91, Dangerous Habits, Part 5	1.75	0.80	2.00	4.00
❑46, Oct 91, Dangerous Habits, Part 6	1.75	0.80	2.00	4.00
❑47, Nov 91, The Pub Where I Was Born	1.75	0.60	1.50	3.00
❑48, Dec 91, Love Kills	1.75	0.60	1.50	3.00
❑49, Jan 92, Lord Of The Dance	1.75	0.60	1.50	3.00
❑50, Feb 92, Remarkable Lives, Giant-size	3.00	0.80	2.00	4.00
❑51, Mar 92, Counting to Ten	1.75	0.50	1.25	2.50
❑52, Apr 92, Royal Blood, Part 1	1.75	0.50	1.25	2.50
❑53, May 92, Royal Blood, Part 2	1.75	0.50	1.25	2.50
❑54, Jun 92, Royal Blood, Part 3	1.75	0.50	1.25	2.50
❑55, Jul 92, Royal Blood, Part 4	1.75	0.50	1.25	2.50
❑56, Aug 92, This is the Diary of Danny Drake	1.75	0.50	1.25	2.50
❑57, Sep 92, Mortal Clay	1.75	0.50	1.25	2.50
❑58, Oct 92, Body and Soul	1.75	0.50	1.25	2.50
❑59, Nov 92, Guys and Dolls, Part 1	1.75	0.50	1.25	2.50
❑60, Dec 92, Guys and Dolls, Part 2	1.75	0.50	1.25	2.50
❑61, Jan 93, She's Buying a Stairway to Heaven	1.75	0.50	1.25	2.50
❑62, Feb 93, End of the Line, "Death Talks About Life" AIDS-awareness insert	1.75	0.50	1.25	2.50
❑63, Mar 93, Forty	1.75	0.50	1.25	2.50
❑64, Apr 93, Fear and Loathing, Part 1	1.75	0.50	1.25	2.50
❑65, May 93, Fear and Loathing, Part 2	1.75	0.50	1.25	2.50
❑66, Jun 93, Fear and Loathing, Part 3	1.95	0.50	1.25	2.50
❑67, Jul 93, End Of The Line	1.95	0.50	1.25	2.50
❑68, Aug 93, Down all the Days	1.95	0.50	1.25	2.50
❑69, Sep 93, Rough Trade	1.95	0.50	1.25	2.50
❑70, Oct 93, Heartland	1.95	0.50	1.25	2.50
❑71, Nov 93, Finest Hour	1.95	0.50	1.25	2.50
❑72, Dec 93, Damnation's Flame, Part 1	1.95	0.50	1.25	2.50
❑73, Jan 94, Damnation's Flame, Part 2	1.95	0.50	1.25	2.50
❑74, Feb 94, Damnation's Flame, Part 3	1.95	0.50	1.25	2.50
❑75, Mar 94, Damnation's Flame, Part 4, Double-size	2.95	0.50	1.25	2.50
❑76, Apr 94, Confessions Of An Irish Rebel	1.95	0.50	1.25	2.50
❑77, May 94, And The Crowd Goes Wild	1.95	0.50	1.25	2.50
❑78, Jun 94, Rake at the Gates of Hell, Part 1	1.95	0.50	1.25	2.50
❑79, Jul 94, Rake at the Gates of Hell, Part 2	1.95	0.50	1.25	2.50
❑80, Aug 94, Rake at the Gates of Hell, Part 3	1.95	0.50	1.25	2.50
❑81, Sep 94, Rake at the Gates of Hell, Part 4	1.95	0.50	1.25	2.50

	ORIG	GOOD	FINE	N-MINT
❑82, Oct 94, Rake at the Gates of Hell, Part 5	1.95	0.50	1.25	2.50
❑83, Nov 94, Rake at the Gates of Hell, Part 6	1.95	0.50	1.25	2.50
❑84, Dec 94, In Another Part Of Hell	1.95	0.50	1.25	2.50
❑85, Jan 95, Warped Notions, Part 1	1.95	0.50	1.25	2.50
❑86, Feb 95, Warped Notions, Part 2	1.95	0.50	1.25	2.50
❑87, Mar 95, Warped Notions, Part 3	1.95	0.50	1.25	2.50
❑88, Apr 95, Warped Notions, Part 4	1.95	0.50	1.25	2.50
❑89, May 95, Dreamtime	2.25	0.50	1.25	2.50
❑90, Jun 95, Dangerous Ground	2.25	0.50	1.25	2.50
❑91, Jul 95, Riding the Green Lanes	2.25	0.50	1.25	2.50
❑92, Aug 95, Critical Mass, Part 1	2.25	0.50	1.25	2.50
❑93, Sep 95, Critical Mass, Part 2	2.25	0.50	1.25	2.50
❑94, Oct 95, Critical Mass, Part 3	2.25	0.50	1.25	2.50
❑95, Nov 95, Critical Mass, Part 4	2.25	0.50	1.25	2.50
❑96, Dec 95, Critical Mass, Part 5	2.25	0.50	1.25	2.50
❑97, Jan 96, The Nature Of The Beast	2.25	0.50	1.25	2.50
❑98, Feb 96, Walking the Dog	2.25	0.50	1.25	2.50
❑99, Mar 96, Punkin' up the Great Outdoors	2.25	0.50	1.25	2.50
❑100, Apr 96, Sins of the Father	3.50	0.50	1.25	2.50
❑101, May 96, Football: It's a Funny Old Game	2.25	0.50	1.25	2.50
❑102, Jun 96, Difficult Beginnings, Part 1	2.25	0.50	1.25	2.50
❑103, Jul 96, Difficult Beginnings, Part 2	2.25	0.50	1.25	2.50
❑104, Aug 96, Difficult Beginnings, Part 3	2.25	0.50	1.25	2.50
❑105, Sep 96, A Taste of Heaven	2.25	0.50	1.25	2.50
❑106, Oct 96, In the Line of Fire, Part 1	2.25	0.50	1.25	2.50
❑107, Nov 96, In the Line of Fire, Part 2	2.25	0.50	1.25	2.50
❑108, Dec 96, In the Line of Fire, Part 2; Days of Wine and Roses	2.25	0.50	1.25	2.50
❑109, Jan 97, The Wild Hunt	2.25	0.50	1.25	2.50
❑110, Feb 97, Last Man Standing, Part 1	2.25	0.50	1.25	2.50
❑111, Mar 97, Last Man Standing, Part 2	2.25	0.50	1.25	2.50
❑112, Apr 97, Last Man Standing, Part 3	2.25	0.50	1.25	2.50
❑113, May 97, Last Man Standing, Part 4	2.25	0.50	1.25	2.50
❑114, Jun 97, Last Man Standing, Part 5	2.25	0.50	1.25	2.50
❑115, Jul 97, In the Red Corner	2.25	0.50	1.25	2.50
❑116, Aug 97, Widdershins, Part 1	2.25	0.50	1.25	2.50
❑117, Sep 97, Widdershins, Part 2	2.25	0.50	1.25	2.50
❑118, Oct 97, Life and Death and Taxis	2.25	0.50	1.25	2.50
❑119, Nov 97, Undertow	2.25	0.50	1.25	2.50
❑120, Dec 97, Desperately Seeking Something, A: Alan Moore, 10th anniversary; Giant-size	3.50	0.70	1.75	3.50
❑121, Jan 98, Up the Down Staircase, Part 1	2.25	0.45	1.13	2.25
❑122, Feb 98, Up the Down Staircase, Part 2	2.25	0.45	1.13	2.25
❑123, Mar 98, Up the Down Staircase, Part 3	2.25	0.45	1.13	2.25
❑124, Apr 98, Up the Down Staircase, Part 4	2.25	0.45	1.13	2.25
❑125, May 98, How to Play With Fire, Part 1	2.25	0.45	1.13	2.25
❑126, Jun 98, How to Play With Fire, Part 2	2.25	0.45	1.13	2.25
❑127, Jul 98, How to Play With Fire, Part 3	2.25	0.45	1.13	2.25
❑128, Aug 98, How to Play With Fire, Part 4	2.25	0.45	1.13	2.25
❑129, Sep 98, Son of Man, Part 1	2.50	0.45	1.13	2.25
❑130, Oct 98, Son of Man, Part 2	2.50	0.45	1.13	2.25
❑131, Nov 98, Son of Man, Part 3	2.50	0.45	1.13	2.25
❑132, Dec 98, Son of Man, Part 4	2.50	0.45	1.13	2.25
❑133, Jan 99, Son of Man, Part 5	2.50	0.45	1.13	2.25
❑134, Feb 99, Haunted, Part 1	2.50	0.50	1.25	2.50
❑135, Mar 99, Haunted, Part 2	2.50	0.50	1.25	2.50
❑136, Apr 99, Haunted, Part 3	2.50	0.50	1.25	2.50
❑137, May 99, Haunted, Part 4	2.50	0.50	1.25	2.50
❑138, Jun 99, Haunted, Part 5	2.50	0.50	1.25	2.50
❑139, Jul 99, Haunted, Part 6	2.50	0.50	1.25	2.50
❑140, Aug 99, Locked	2.50	0.50	1.25	2.50
❑141, Oct 99, The Crib	2.50	0.50	1.25	2.50
❑142, Nov 99, Setting Sun, One Last Love Song	2.50	0.50	1.25	2.50
❑143, Dec 99, Telling Tales	2.50	0.50	1.25	2.50
❑144, Jan 00, Ashes & Honey, Part 1	2.50	0.50	1.25	2.50
❑145, Feb 00	2.50	0.50	1.25	2.50
❑146, Mar 00, Hard Time, Part 1	2.50	0.50	1.25	2.50
❑147, Apr 00, Hard Time, Part 2	2.50	0.50	1.25	2.50
❑148, May 00, Hard Time, Part 3	2.50	0.50	1.25	2.50
❑149, Jun 00, Hard Time, Part 4	2.50	0.50	1.25	2.50
❑150	2.50	0.50	1.25	2.50
❑151	2.50	0.50	1.25	2.50
❑152, Sep 00, Good Intentions, Part 2	2.50	0.50	1.25	2.50
❑153, Oct 00, Good Intentions, Part 3	2.50	0.50	1.25	2.50
❑154, Nov 00, Good Intentions, Part 4	2.50	0.50	1.25	2.50
❑155, Dec 00, Good Intentions, Part 5	2.50	0.50	1.25	2.50
❑156, Jan 01, Good Intentions, Part 6	2.50	0.50	1.25	2.50
❑157, Feb 01, ...And Buried	2.50	0.50	1.25	2.50
❑158, Mar 01, Freezes Over, Part 1	2.50	0.50	1.25	2.50
❑159, Apr 01, Freezes Over, Part 2	2.50	0.50	1.25	2.50
❑160, May 01, Freezes Over, Part 3	2.50	0.50	1.25	2.50
❑161, Jun 01, Freezes Over, Part 4	2.50	0.50	1.25	2.50
❑162	2.50	0.50	1.25	2.50

	ORIG	GOOD	FINE	N-MINT
❑163	2.50	0.50	1.25	2.50
❑164	2.50	0.50	1.25	2.50
❑Anl 1, Oct 89, BT, The Bloody Saint	2.95	1.20	3.00	6.00
❑SE 1, Jan 93, Confessional	3.95	1.00	2.50	5.00

HELLBLAZER SPECIAL: BAD BLOOD
VERTIGO
Value: Cover or less

❑1, Sep 00 .... 2.95
❑2, Oct 00 .... 2.95
❑3, Nov 00 .... 2.95
❑4, Dec 00 .... 2.95

HELLBLAZER/THE BOOKS OF MAGIC
DC

❑1, Dec 97, Ascent	2.50	0.60	1.50	3.00
❑2, Jan 98	2.50	0.60	1.50	3.00

HELLBOY: ALMOST COLOSSUS
DARK HORSE
Value: Cover or less

❑1, Jun 97, Almost Colossus; Autopsy in B-Flat 2.95
❑2, Jul 97, Almost Colossus; Autopsy in B-Flat 2.95

HELLBOY: BOX FULL OF EVIL
DARK HORSE
Value: Cover or less

❑1, Aug 99, Box Full of Evil, Part 1 .... 2.95
❑2, Sep 99, Box Full of Evil, Part 2; Abe Sapien vs. Science .. 2.95

HELLBOY CHRISTMAS SPECIAL
DARK HORSE
Value: Cover or less

❑1, Dec 97, A Christmas Underground; Ernie's Holiday Ditty, nn; One-Shot 3.95

HELLBOY: CONQUEROR WORM
DARK HORSE
Value: Cover or less

❑1, May 01 .... 2.99
❑2 .... 2.99
❑3 .... 2.99
❑4 .... 2.99

HELLBOY, THE CORPSE AND THE IRON SHOES
DARK HORSE

❑1, The Corpse; The Iron Shoes, nn; collects the story serialized in the distributor catalog Advance Comics #75-82	2.95	0.70	1.75	3.50

HELLBOY JR.
DARK HORSE
Value: Cover or less

❑1, Oct 99, Hellbooy Jr.'s Magical Mushroom Trip; The Wolvertons 2.95
❑2, Nov 99, The House of Candy Pain; Sparky Bear 2.95

HELLBOY JR. HALLOWEEN SPECIAL
DARK HORSE
Value: Cover or less

❑1, Oct 97, Maggots, Maggots, Everywhere; Wheezy the Sick Little Witch, nn; wraparound cover; One-Shot; Hellboy Jr. pinup 3.95

HELLBOY: SEED OF DESTRUCTION
DARK HORSE

❑1, Mar 94, O: Hellboy; 1: Monkeyman & O'Brien (in back-up story)	2.50	0.80	2.00	4.00
❑2, Apr 94	2.50	0.70	1.75	3.50
❑3, May 94	2.50	0.70	1.75	3.50
❑4, Jun 94	2.50	0.70	1.75	3.50

HELLBOY: THE WOLVES OF SAINT AUGUST
DARK HORSE
Value: Cover or less

❑1, nn; One-Shot; prestige format; collects the story from Dark Horse Presents #88-91 .... 4.95

HELLBOY: WAKE THE DEVIL
DARK HORSE
Value: Cover or less

❑1, Jun 96, Silent as the Grave back-up 2.95
❑2, Jul 96, The MonsterMen: Silent as the Grave, Silent as the Grave back-up 2.95
❑3, Aug 96, The MonsterMen: Silent as the Grave, Silent as the Grave back-up 2.95
❑4, Sep 96, The MonsterMen: Silent as the Grave, Silent as the Grave back-up 2.95
❑5, Oct 96, The MonsterMen: Silent as the Grave, Silent as the Grave back-up 2.95

HELL CAR COMIX
ALTERNATING CRIMES PUBLISHING
Value: Cover or less

❑1, Fal 98 .... 2.95

HELLCAT
MARVEL
Value: Cover or less

❑1, Sep 00, One Life to Live ... 2.99

HELL CITY, HELL
DIABLO MUSICA
Value: Cover or less

❑1, shrinkwrapped with CD-ROM 2.25

HELLCOP
IMAGE
Value: Cover or less

❑1, Aug 98, ...Like of Woman Scorned, cover says Oct, indicia says Aug 2.50
❑1/A, Aug 98, ...Like of Woman Scorned, alternate cover; Man kneeling with gun, woman, faces in background 2.50

A younger version of Mike Mignola's Hellboy has had two separate adventures from Dark Horse.

© 1999 Mike Mignola (Dark Horse)

ORIG GOOD FINE N-MINT

❑2, Nov 98, The Fates Roared 2.50
❑2/A, Nov 98, alternate cover . 2.50
❑3, Jan 99, Into the Abyss of an Empty Heart 2.50
❑4, Mar 99, Pandemonium Reigned 2.50

HELL ETERNAL
DC
Value: Cover or less

❑1, nn; One-Shot; prestige format 6.95

HELLGIRL: DEMONSEED
KNIGHT
Value: Cover or less

❑1, Mar 95 .... 2.95

HELLHOLE
IMAGE
Value: Cover or less

❑1, Jul 99 .... 2.50
❑2, Oct 99 .... 2.50

HELLHOUNDS
DARK HORSE
Value: Cover or less

❑1, b&w; Japanese 2.50
❑2 .... 2.95

HELLHOUNDS: PANZER CORPS
DARK HORSE
Value: Cover or less

❑1, b&w 2.50
❑2, b&w 2.50
❑3, Apr 94, Stray Dog, b&w 2.50
❑4, May 94, b&w 2.50
❑5, Jun 94, b&w 2.95
❑6, Jul 94, b&w 2.95

HELLHOUND: THE REDEMPTION QUEST
MARVEL
Value: Cover or less

❑1, Hellhound On My Trail 2.25
❑2, Jan 94 .... 2.25
❑3, Feb 94 .... 2.25
❑4, Mar 94 .... 2.25

HELLINA
LIGHTNING
Value: Cover or less

❑1, Sep 94, b&w 2.75

HELLINA 1997 PIN-UP SPECIAL
LIGHTNING
Value: Cover or less

❑1, Feb 97, cover version A; b&w pin-ups 3.50

HELLINA/CATFIGHT
LIGHTNING

❑1, Oct 95, b&w	2.75	0.60	1.50	3.00
❑1/A, Olive metallic edition	—	0.60	1.50	3.00
❑1-2, Aug 97, b&w; reprints Hellina, Catfight	2.95	0.59	1.48	2.95

HELLINA: CHRISTMAS IN HELL
LIGHTNING
Value: Cover or less

❑1, Dec 96, b&w 2.95
❑1/A, Dec 96, nude cover A 9.95
❑1/B, Dec 96, nude cover B 9.95

HELLINA/CYNDER
LIGHTNING
Value: Cover or less

❑1, Sep 97 .... 2.95

HELLINA/DOUBLE IMPACT
LIGHTNING
Value: Cover or less

❑1 .... 2.75
❑1/A, Feb 96, crossover with High Impact 3.00
❑1/B, Feb 96, alternate cover . 3.00
❑1/Nude, Feb 96, polybagged nude cover; Nude edition with certificate of authenticity 9.95
❑1/PL, Platinum edition .... —

HELLINA: GENESIS
LIGHTNING
Value: Cover or less

❑1, Apr 96, b&w; bagged with Hellina poster 3.50

HELLINA: HEART OF THORNS
LIGHTNING
Value: Cover or less

❑2, Sep 96, A: Perg 2.75
❑2/Nude, Sep 96, nude cover edition 9.95

HELLINA: HELLBORN
LIGHTNING
Value: Cover or less

❑1, Dec 97, b&w 2.95

HELLINA: HELL'S ANGEL
LIGHTNING
Value: Cover or less

❑1, Nov 96, b&w 2.75
❑2, Dec 96, b&w 2.75

ORIG GOOD FINE N-MINT

HELLINA: IN THE FLESH
LIGHTNING

Value: Cover or less

- ❑1, Aug 97, b&w 2.95

HELLINA: KISS OF DEATH
LIGHTNING

Value: Cover or less

- ❑1, Jul 95, b&w 2.75
- ❑1/GO, Gold edition 2.75
- ❑1/Nude, Jul 95, b&w; Nude edition 9.95
- ❑1-2, Mar 97, alternate cover; Encore edition 2.95

HELLINA: NAKED DESIRE
LIGHTNING

Value: Cover or less

- ❑1, May 97 .... 2.95

HELLINA/NIRA X
LIGHTNING

Value: Cover or less

- ❑1, Aug 96, crossover with Entity 3.00

HELLINA: SKYBOLT TOYZ LIMITED EDITION
LIGHTNING

Value: Cover or less

- ❑1/A, Aug 97, b&w; reprints Hellina #1 .... 1.50
- ❑1/B, Aug 97, alternate cover . 1.50

HELLINA: TAKING BACK THE NIGHT
LIGHTNING

Value: Cover or less

- ❑1 .... 4.50

HELLINA: WICKED WAYS
LIGHTNING

	ORIG	GOOD	FINE	N-MINT
❑1/A, Nov 95, b&w; alternate cover; polybagged	2.75	0.55	1.38	2.75
❑1/B, Nov 95, polybagged	3.00	0.60	1.50	3.00
❑1/Nude, Nov 95, cover C; polybagged	9.95	1.99	4.97	9.95
❑1/SI, silver edition	—	0.55	1.38	2.75

HELLRAISER (CLIVE BARKER'S...)
MARVEL

	ORIG	GOOD	FINE	N-MINT
❑HS 1, Nude edition with certificate of authenticity; Dark Holiday Special	4.95	0.99	2.47	4.95
❑Smr 1, Giant-size	5.95	1.19	2.97	5.95
❑Spr 1, Spring Special	6.95	1.39	3.47	6.95

HELLRAISER III: HELL ON EARTH
MARVEL

	ORIG	GOOD	FINE	N-MINT
❑1, Cruising The Ruins; Dark Star Rising, movie Adaptation	4.95	1.00	2.50	5.00

HELLRAISER POSTERBOOK (CLIVE BARKER'S...)
MARVEL

Value: Cover or less

- ❑1, BSz 4.95

HELLRAISER: SPRING SLAUGHTER
MARVEL

Value: Cover or less

- ❑1 .... 6.95

HELLSAINT
BLACK DIAMOND

Value: Cover or less

- ❑1, Mar 98, Retribution 2.50

HELL'S ANGEL
MARVEL

Value: Cover or less

- ❑1, O: Hell's Angel 1.75
- ❑2 .... 1.75
- ❑3 .... 1.75
- ❑4, A: X-Men 1.75
- ❑5, A: X-Men, Series continued as Dark Angel #6 .... 1.75

HELLSHOCK
IMAGE

Value: Cover or less

- ❑1, Jan 97, A Kairos Moment . 2.95
- ❑1/A, Jan 97, A Kairos Moment 2.95
- ❑2, Feb 97, The Milk of Paradise 2.95
- ❑3, Jan 98, The Science of Faith 2.95
- ❑4, Never published? 2.95
- ❑5, Never published? 2.95
- ❑6, Never published? 2.95
- ❑7, Never published? 3.95

HELLSHOCK (MINI-SERIES)
IMAGE

	ORIG	GOOD	FINE	N-MINT
❑1, Jul 94, The Sign Of The Cross, Part 1	1.95	0.40	1.00	2.00
❑2, Aug 94	1.95	0.40	1.00	2.00
❑3, Oct 94, Falling Angel, O: Hellshock	1.95	0.40	1.00	2.00
❑4	1.95	0.40	1.00	2.00
❑4/A, Nov 94, variant cover	1.95	0.40	1.00	2.00
❑4/B, Nov 94	1.95	0.39	0.98	1.95
❑Ash 1, ashcan	—	0.20	0.50	1.00

HELLSPAWN
IMAGE

Value: Cover or less

- ❑1, Aug 00, BMB (w), The Clown, Part 1 .... 2.50
- ❑2, Sep 00, BMB (w), The Clown, Part 2 .... 2.50
- ❑3, Oct 00, BMB (w), Hate Me 2.50
- ❑4, Nov 00, BMB (w), Hate You 2.50
- ❑5, Jan 01, BMB (w), Selling Fear 2.50
- ❑6, Feb 01, BMB (w), The Big Leagues 2.50
- ❑7, Apr 01, Shed 2.50
- ❑8 .... 2.50
- ❑9 .... 2.50
- ❑10 .... 2.50
- ❑11 .... 2.50
- ❑12 .... 2.50

ORIG GOOD FINE N-MINT

HELLSPOCK
EXPRESS

Value: Cover or less

- ❑1, b&w; One-Shot 2.95

HELLSTALKER
REBEL CREATIONS

Value: Cover or less

- ❑1 .... 2.25
- ❑2, Jul 89, Tricks of The Trade 2.25

HELLSTORM: PRINCE OF LIES
MARVEL

Value: Cover or less

- ❑1, Apr 93, Storm Clouds, parchment cover 2.95
- ❑2, May 93 .... 2.00
- ❑3, Jun 93, Paradise Lost 2.00
- ❑4, Jul 93 .... 2.00
- ❑5, Aug 93 .... 2.00
- ❑6, Sep 93, Lisa 2.00
- ❑7, Oct 93 .... 2.00
- ❑8, Nov 93 .... 2.00
- ❑9, Dec 93 .... 2.00
- ❑10, Jan 94 .... 2.00
- ❑11, Feb 94 .... 2.00
- ❑12, Mar 94 .... 2.00
- ❑13, Apr 94 .... 2.00
- ❑14, May 94 .... 2.00
- ❑15, Jun 94 .... 2.00
- ❑16, Jul 94 .... 2.00
- ❑17, Aug 94 .... 2.00
- ❑18, Sep 94 .... 2.00
- ❑19, Oct 94 .... 2.00
- ❑20, Nov 94 .... 2.00
- ❑21, Dec 94, Final Issue 2.00

HELM PREMIERE
HELM

Value: Cover or less

- ❑1, Mar 95, b&w; Preview edition 2.95

HELSING
CALIBER

Value: Cover or less

- ❑1, b&w 2.95
- ❑1/A, Cover has woman in black standing 2.95
- ❑2, b&w 2.95

HELTER SKELTER
ANTARCTIC

Value: Cover or less

- ❑0, May 97, b&w 2.95
- ❑1, Jun 97, b&w 2.95
- ❑2, Sep 97, b&w 2.95
- ❑3, Nov 97, b&w 2.95
- ❑4, Dec 97, b&w 2.95
- ❑5, Jan 98, b&w 2.95

HELYUN: BONES OF THE BACKWOODS
SLAVE LABOR

Value: Cover or less

- ❑1, Nov 91, b&w 2.95

HELYUN BOOK 1
SLAVE LABOR

Value: Cover or less

- ❑1, Aug 90, nn; b&w 6.95

HEMBECK
FANTACO

	ORIG	GOOD	FINE	N-MINT
❑1, Best of Dateline: @!!?#	2.50	0.50	1.25	2.50
❑2, Feb 80, FH, Hembeck 1980 or The Son of the Best of Dateline: @!!?#	2.50	0.50	1.25	2.50
❑3, Jun 80, Abbott & Costello Meet Bride of Hembeck	1.25	0.30	0.75	1.50
❑4, Nov 80, Bah Hembeck!	1.25	0.30	0.75	1.50
❑5, Feb 81, FH, Hembeck File	2.50	0.50	1.25	2.50
❑6, Sep 81, cardstock cover; Jimmy Olsen's Pal	2.25	0.45	1.13	2.25
❑7, Jan 83, Dial H for Hembeck	1.95	0.39	0.98	1.95

HEMP FOR VICTORY
STARHEAD

Value: Cover or less

- ❑1, Sep 93, b&w; based on 1943 USDA film 2.50

HENRY V
CALIBER

Value: Cover or less

- ❑1, b&w 2.95

HEPCATS
DOUBLE DIAMOND

	ORIG	GOOD	FINE	N-MINT
❑1, May 89, Joey Gunther	2.00	2.00	5.00	10.00
❑1/LE, Special edition with new material	2.00	1.20	3.00	6.00
❑2, Jul 89	2.00	1.20	3.00	6.00
❑2/LE, Special edition with new material	2.00	0.80	2.00	4.00
❑3, Aug 89, Snowblind, Part 1	2.00	1.00	2.50	5.00
❑4, Nov 89, Snowblind, Part 2	2.00	0.80	2.00	4.00
❑5, Feb 89, Snowblind, Part 3	2.00	0.80	2.00	4.00
❑6, Snowblind, Part 4	2.25	0.80	2.00	4.00
❑7, Snowblind, Part 5	2.25	0.80	2.00	4.00
❑8, Snowblind, Part 6	2.25	0.80	2.00	4.00
❑9, Snowblind, Part 7	2.25	0.60	1.50	3.00
❑10, Snowblind, Part 8	2.50	0.60	1.50	3.00
❑11, Jan 94, Snowblind, Part 9	2.50	0.60	1.50	3.00
❑12, Jul 94, Snowblind, Part 10	2.50	0.60	1.50	3.00
❑13	2.50	0.60	1.50	3.00
❑14	2.50	0.50	1.25	2.50
❑SE 1, Reprint	2.00	0.80	2.00	4.00
❑SE 2, Reprint	2.00	0.80	2.00	4.00

HEPCATS (ANTARCTIC)
ANTARCTIC

	ORIG	GOOD	FINE	N-MINT
❑0, Nov 96, Friday	2.95	0.80	2.00	4.00
❑0/A, Saturday, Comics Cavalcade Commemorative Edition	5.95	1.19	2.97	5.95
❑0/Dlx, Nov 96, Radio Hepcats edition; polybagged with compact disc	9.95	1.99	4.97	9.95

	ORIG	GOOD	FINE	N-MINT
❑1, Dec 96	2.95	0.70	1.75	3.50
❑2, Jan 97, Trial by Intimacy	2.95	0.70	1.75	3.50
❑3, Feb 97, Snowblind, Part 1	2.95	0.60	1.50	3.00
❑4, Mar 97, Snowblind, Part 2	2.95	0.60	1.50	3.00
❑5, Apr 97, Snowblind, Part 3	2.95	0.60	1.50	3.00
❑6, Jan 98, Snowblind, Part 4	2.95	0.59	1.48	2.95
❑7, Mar 98, Snowblind, Part 5	2.95	0.59	1.48	2.95
❑8, Snowblind, Part 6	2.95	0.59	1.48	2.95
❑9, Apr 98, Snowblind, Part 7	2.95	0.59	1.48	2.95
❑10, May 98, Snowblind, Part 8	2.95	0.59	1.48	2.95
❑11, May 98, Snowblind, Part 9	2.95	0.59	1.48	2.95
❑12, Jun 98, Snowblind, Part 10	2.95	0.59	1.48	2.95

HERBIE (A+)
A-PLUS

Value: Cover or less

- ❑1, Herbie And the Spirits!; Make Way For That Fat Fury, O: The Fat Fury, Reprints (including part of Herbie #8) 2.50
- ❑2, Reprint 2.50
- ❑3, Pirate Gold!; Herbie Claus is Coming to Town!, Reprint 2.50
- ❑4, Reprint 2.50
- ❑5, Reprint 2.50
- ❑6, Reprint 2.50

HERBIE (ACG)
AMERICAN COMICS GROUP

	ORIG	GOOD	FINE	N-MINT
❑1, Apr 64, A: Khrushchev; A: Sonny Liston; A: Lyndon Johnson; A: Castro	0.12	20.00	50.00	100.00
❑2, Jun 64, A: Marie Antoinette	0.12	13.00	32.50	65.00
❑3, Aug 64, A: Churchill	0.12	10.00	25.00	50.00
❑4, Sep 64, A: Clantons; A: Doc Holliday	0.12	10.00	25.00	50.00
❑5, Oct 64, A: Dean Martin; A: Beatles; A: Frank Sinatra	0.12	10.00	25.00	50.00
❑6, Dec 64, A: Ava Gardner; A: Gregory Peck	0.12	7.60	19.00	38.00
❑7, Feb 65, A: Khruschcev; A: Mao; A: Harry Truman	0.12	7.60	19.00	38.00
❑8, Mar 65, A: Lyndon Johnson; O: Fat Fury; A: Barry Goldwater; A: George Washington	0.12	10.00	25.00	50.00
❑9, Apr 65	0.12	7.60	19.00	38.00
❑10, Jun 65	0.12	7.60	19.00	38.00
❑11, Aug 65, A: Lyndon Johnson; A: Columbus; A: Queen Isabella; A: Adlai Stevenson	0.12	6.00	15.00	30.00
❑12, Sep 65, Fat Fury story	0.12	6.00	15.00	30.00
❑13, Oct 65, Pirate Gold!; Mom's New Coat!	0.12	6.00	15.00	30.00
❑14, Dec 65, A: Nemesis; A: Fat Fury; A: Magicman	0.12	6.00	15.00	30.00
❑15, Feb 66, A: Napoleon; A: Josephine	0.12	6.00	15.00	30.00
❑16, Mar 66, A: Fat Fury; A: Mao Tse Tung	0.12	6.00	15.00	30.00
❑17, Apr 66	0.12	6.00	15.00	30.00
❑18, Jun 66	0.12	6.00	15.00	30.00
❑19, Aug 66, A: Cleopatra	0.12	6.00	15.00	30.00
❑20, Sep 66, Fat Fury vs. Dracula	0.12	6.00	15.00	30.00
❑21, Oct 66	0.12	6.00	15.00	30.00
❑22, Dec 66, A: Ben Franklin; A: Queen Elizabeth; A: Charles de Gaulle, Fat Fury learns magic	0.12	6.00	15.00	30.00
❑23, Feb 67, Final Issue	0.12	6.00	15.00	30.00

HERBIE (DARK HORSE)
DARK HORSE

Value: Cover or less

- ❑1, Oct 92, JBy (w), The Most Beautiful Mom In The World; Make Way For That Fat Fury!, Reprint 2.50
- ❑2, Nov 92, Reprint; Final Issue; Series cancelled 2.50

HERCULES (CHARLTON)
CHARLTON

	ORIG	GOOD	FINE	N-MINT
❑1, Oct 67	0.12	2.40	6.00	12.00
❑2, Dec 67, When Man Meets Monster!	0.12	1.40	3.50	7.00
❑3, Feb 68	0.12	1.00	2.50	5.00
❑4, Jun 68	0.12	1.00	2.50	5.00
❑5, Jul 68	0.12	1.00	2.50	5.00
❑6, Sep 68	0.12	0.80	2.00	4.00
❑7, Nov 68	0.12	0.80	2.00	4.00
❑8, Dec 68, The Boar; The Legend of Hercules	0.12	0.80	2.00	4.00
❑8/A, Magazine-sized issue; Low distribution	0.35	1.80	4.50	9.00
❑9, Feb 69	0.12	0.80	2.00	4.00
❑10, Apr 67	0.12	0.80	2.00	4.00
❑11	0.12	0.80	2.00	4.00
❑12, Jul 67	0.12	0.80	2.00	4.00
❑13, Oct 67, Final Issue	0.12	0.80	2.00	4.00

HERCULES (VOL. 1)
MARVEL

	ORIG	GOOD	FINE	N-MINT
❑1, Sep 82, BL, BL (w), What Fools These Immortals Be!	0.60	0.30	0.75	1.50
❑2, Oct 82, LMc; BL, BL (w), For The Love Of Gods	0.60	0.30	0.75	1.50
❑3, Nov 82, BL	0.60	0.30	0.75	1.50
❑4, Dec 82, BL (w), -Not Just Another Galactus Story!	0.60	0.30	0.75	1.50

The Fat Fury faced off against The Prince of Darkness in *Herbie* #20.

© 1966 American Comics Group

HERCULES (VOL. 2)
MARVEL

	ORIG	GOOD	FINE	N-MINT
❑1, Mar 84, BL, BL (w), My Love Is...Green?	0.60	0.30	0.75	1.50
❑2, Apr 84, BL, BL (w), Red Wolf Stalks The Stars!	0.60	0.25	0.63	1.25
❑3, May 84, BL, BL (w), Deadly Legacy	0.60	0.25	0.63	1.25
❑4, Jun 84, BL, BL (w), A Pearl Of Great Price!	0.60	0.25	0.63	1.25

HERCULES: HEART OF CHAOS
MARVEL

Value: Cover or less

- ❑1, Aug 97, Even an Immortal Can Die!, gatefold summary 2.50
- ❑2, Sep 97, gatefold summary 2.50
- ❑3, Oct 97, gatefold summary 2.50

HERCULES: OFFICIAL COMICS MOVIE ADAPTATION
ACCLAIM

Value: Cover or less

- ❑1, nn; digest; adapts movie 4.50

HERCULES PROJECT, THE
MONSTER

Value: Cover or less

- ❑1, b&w 1.95
- ❑2, War, b&w 1.95

HERCULES: THE LEGENDARY JOURNEYS
TOPPS

	ORIG	GOOD	FINE	N-MINT
❑1, Jun 96, The Trial of Hercules, Part 1, wraparound cover	2.95	0.60	1.50	3.00
❑2, Jul 96, The Trial of Hercules, Part 2	2.95	0.60	1.50	3.00
❑3/A, Aug 96, A: Xena, art cover	2.95	0.80	2.00	4.00
❑3/B, Aug 96, A: Xena, Photo cover	2.95	1.00	2.50	5.00
❑3/GO, 1: Xena, Photo cover; Gold logo variant	—	1.00	2.50	5.00
❑4, Sep 96, A: Xena	2.95	0.70	1.75	3.50
❑5, Oct 96, A: Xena	2.95	0.70	1.75	3.50

HERCULES UNBOUND
DC

	ORIG	GOOD	FINE	N-MINT
❑1, Nov 75, WW, Hercules Unbound!	0.25	0.80	2.00	4.00
❑2, Jan 76	0.25	0.50	1.25	2.50
❑3, Mar 76	0.25	0.50	1.25	2.50
❑4, May 76	0.30	0.50	1.25	2.50
❑5, Jul 76	0.30	0.50	1.25	2.50
❑6, Sep 76	0.30	0.50	1.25	2.50
❑7, Nov 76	0.30	0.50	1.25	2.50
❑8, Jan 77	0.30	0.50	1.25	2.50
❑9, Mar 77	0.30	0.50	1.25	2.50
❑10, May 77	0.30	0.50	1.25	2.50
❑11, Jul 77	0.35	0.50	1.25	2.50
❑12, Sep 77, Final Issue	0.35	0.50	1.25	2.50

HERE COME THE BIG PEOPLE
EVENT

Value: Cover or less

- ❑1, Sep 97 2.95
- ❑1/A, Sep 97, Alternate cover (large woman burping man) 2.95

HERETIC, THE
DARK HORSE

Value: Cover or less

- ❑1, Nov 96, Of Little Faith, Part 1, Maximum Velocity back-up 2.95
- ❑2, Jan 97, Of Little Faith, Part 2; Maximum Velocity: Pursuit, Maximum Velocity back-up 2.95
- ❑3, Feb 97, Of Little Faith, Part 3; Maximum Velocity: Capture, Maximum Velocity back-up 2.95
- ❑4, Mar 97, Of Little Faith, Part 4, Maximum Velocity back-up 2.95

HERETICS
IGUANA

Value: Cover or less

- ❑1, Nov 93, Foil-embossed logo 2.95

HERMES VS. THE EYEBALL KID
DARK HORSE

Value: Cover or less

- ❑1, Dec 94, b&w 2.95
- ❑2, Jan 95, b&w 2.95
- ❑3, Feb 95, b&w 2.95

HERO
MARVEL

Value: Cover or less

- ❑1, May 90, A Hero Is Born! 1.50
- ❑2, Jun 90 1.50
- ❑3, Jul 90, Essential Evil 1.50
- ❑4, Aug 90 1.50
- ❑5, Sep 90 1.50
- ❑6, Oct 90 1.50

HERO ALLIANCE (INNOVATION)
INNOVATION

Value: Cover or less

- ❑1, Sep 89, Easy Target 1.75
- ❑2, Oct 89, Easy Target 1.75
- ❑3, Dec 89, Feast of Shadows 1.95
- ❑4, Feb 90 1.95

	ORIG	GOOD	FINE	N-MINT

- ❑5, Mar 90 ... 1.95
- ❑6, Apr 90 ... 1.95
- ❑7, May 90 ... 1.95
- ❑8, Jul 90 ... 1.95
- ❑9, Sep 90 ... 1.95
- ❑10, Oct 90 ... 1.95
- ❑11, Nov 90 ... 1.95
- ❑12, Dec 90 ... 1.95
- ❑13, Mar 91 ... 1.95
- ❑14, Apr 91 ... 1.95
- ❑15, May 91 ... 1.95
- ❑16, Jun 91 ... 1.95
- ❑17, Jul 91 ... 2.50
- ❑Anl 1, Sep 90 ... 2.75
- ❑SE 1 ... 2.50

HERO ALLIANCE (WONDER COLOR)
Wonder Color

Value: Cover or less

- ❑1, May 87, But What Have You Done For Us Lately? ... 1.95

HERO ALLIANCE & JUSTICE MACHINE: IDENTITY CRISIS
Innovation

Value: Cover or less

- ❑1, Oct 90 ... 2.75

HERO ALLIANCE: END OF THE GOLDEN AGE
Innovation

Value: Cover or less

- ❑1, Jul 89 ... 1.75
- ❑2, Jul 89 ... 1.75
- ❑3, Aug 89 ... 1.75

HERO ALLIANCE QUARTERLY
Innovation

Value: Cover or less

- ❑1, Sep 91 ... 2.75
- ❑2, Dec 91 ... 2.75
- ❑3, Mar 92, Child Endangerment ... 2.75
- ❑4 ... 2.75

HERO BEAR AND THE KID
Astonish

Value: Cover or less

- ❑1, Small Beginnings, b&w and red ... 2.95
- ❑2, Dreams, b&w and red ... 2.95

HEROES (BLACKBIRD)
Blackbird

	ORIG	GOOD	FINE	N-MINT
❑1	—	1.00	2.50	5.00
❑2	1.75	0.35	0.88	1.75
❑3	1.75	0.35	0.88	1.75
❑4, Nov 87	2.00	0.40	1.00	2.00
❑5	2.00	0.40	1.00	2.00
❑6	2.00	0.40	1.00	2.00

HEROES (LONDON EDITIONS)
London Editions

	ORIG	GOOD	FINE	N-MINT
❑1, Mar 91, The Soul-Thief From The Stars; How to Trap a Devil!, postcard reprint of Adventure Comcis #300	0.50	0.60	1.50	3.00
❑2, Mar 91, Postcards	0.50	0.50	1.25	2.50

HEROES (MILESTONE)
DC

Value: Cover or less

- ❑1, May 96 ... 2.50
- ❑2, Jun 96, Home of the Heroes, V: Shadow Cabinet ... 2.50
- ❑3, Jul 96 ... 2.50
- ❑4, Aug 96 ... 2.50
- ❑5, Sep 96 ... 2.50
- ❑6, Nov 96, KP, All for Love or The World Well Lost ... 2.50

HEROES AGAINST HUNGER
DC

	ORIG	GOOD	FINE	N-MINT
❑1, Aug 86, CI; DaG, JSn (w), A Song Of Pain And Sorrow!, Charity benefit comic for Ethiopian famine victims	1.50	0.60	1.50	3.00

HEROES FOR HIRE
Marvel

Value: Cover or less

- ❑1, Jul 97, Heroes and Villains, wraparound cover; Hulk, Hercules, Iron Fist, Luke Cage, Black Knight, White Tiger ... 2.99
- ❑2/A, Aug 97, gatefold summary; Jim Hammond (original Human Torch) joins team ... 1.99
- ❑2/B, Aug 97, alternate cover; gatefold summary; Jim Hammond (original Human Torch) joins team ... 1.99
- ❑3, Sep 97, gatefold summary 1.99
- ❑4, Oct 97, Controlled!, V: Controller, gatefold summary ... 1.99
- ❑5, Nov 97, A: Sersi; A: Jane Foster, gatefold summary ... 1.99
- ❑6, Dec 97, gatefold summary 1.99
- ❑7, Jan 98, gatefold summary 1.99
- ❑8, Feb 98, gatefold summary 1.99
- ❑9, Mar 98, A: Punisher, gatefold summary ... 1.99
- ❑10, Apr 98, gatefold summary 1.99
- ❑11, May 98, V: Wild Pack, gatefold summary ... 1.99
- ❑12, Jun 98, gatefold summary 2.99
- ❑13, Jul 98, A: Brother Voodoo, gatefold summary; Ant-Man inside Hammond's body ... 1.99
- ❑14, Aug 98, gatefold summary; Black Knight vs. dragons ... 1.99
- ❑15, Sep 98, gatefold summary 1.99
- ❑16, Oct 98, The Siege of Wundagore, Part 3, gatefold summary ... 1.99
- ❑17, Nov 98, A: She-Hulk, gatefold summary ... 1.99
- ❑18, Dec 98, A: Shang-Chi; A: Wolverine, Shang-Chi; A: Wolverine, gatefold summary ... 1.99
- ❑19, Jan 99, A: Shang-Chi; A: Wolverine, Shang-Chi; A: Wolverine, Final Issue; gatefold summary ... 1.99
- ❑Anl 1998, The Siege of Wundagore, Part 5, wraparound cover; gatefold summary; Heroes for Hire/Quicksilver '98 ... 2.99

HEROES FOR HOPE
Marvel

	ORIG	GOOD	FINE	N-MINT
❑1, Dec 85, famine relief	1.50	1.00	2.50	5.00

HEROES FROM WORDSMITH
Special Studio

Value: Cover or less

- ❑1, b&w ... 2.50

HEROES, INC. PRESENTS CANNON
Armed Services

	ORIG	GOOD	FINE	N-MINT
❑1, WW, WW (w), Cannon; The Misfits, nn.	0.15	2.40	6.00	12.00

HEROES OF FAITH
Coretoons

Value: Cover or less

- ❑1, Jun 92 ... 2.50

HEROES OF ROCK 'N FIRE
Wonder Comix

Value: Cover or less

- ❑1, Apr 87 ... 1.95

HEROES REBORN
Marvel

	ORIG	GOOD	FINE	N-MINT
❑0.5, RL, JPH (w), Faith, With certificate of authenticity	—	0.60	1.50	3.00

HEROES REBORN: ASHEMA
Marvel

Value: Cover or less

- ❑1, Jan 00 ... 1.99

HEROES REBORN: DOOM
Marvel

Value: Cover or less

- ❑1, Jan 00 ... 1.99

HEROES REBORN: DOOMSDAY
Marvel

Value: Cover or less

- ❑1, Jan 00 ... 1.99

HEROES REBORN: MASTERS OF EVIL
Marvel

Value: Cover or less

- ❑1, Feb 99, Battleship Downs. 1.99

HEROES REBORN MINI COMIC
Marvel

	ORIG	GOOD	FINE	N-MINT
❑1	—	0.10	0.25	0.50

HEROES REBORN: REBEL
Marvel

Value: Cover or less

- ❑1, Jan 00, Wild Blue ... 1.99

HEROES REBORN: REMNANTS
Marvel

Value: Cover or less

- ❑1, Jan 00, The Day the Earth Got III! ... 1.99

HEROES REBORN: THE RETURN
Marvel

	ORIG	GOOD	FINE	N-MINT
❑1, Dec 97, PD (w)	2.50	0.50	1.25	2.50
❑1/SC, Dec 97, PD (w), Franklin Richards on cover	2.50	0.80	2.00	4.00
❑2, Dec 97, PD (w)	2.50	0.50	1.25	2.50
❑2/SC, Dec 97, PD (w), Spider-Man/Hulk variant cover	2.50	0.60	1.50	3.00
❑3, Dec 97, PD (w)	2.50	0.50	1.25	2.50
❑3/SC, Dec 97, PD (w), Iron Man variant cover	2.50	0.60	1.50	3.00
❑4, Dec 97, PD (w), Fourth & Goal	2.50	0.50	1.25	2.50
❑4/SC, Dec 97, PD (w), Fourth & Goal, Reed Richards variant cover	2.50	0.60	1.50	3.00
❑Ash 1, JLee; RL, Onslaught Update	—	0.20	0.50	1.00

HEROES REBORN: YOUNG ALLIES
Marvel

Value: Cover or less

- ❑1, Jan 00 ... 1.99

HERO FOR HIRE
Marvel

	ORIG	GOOD	FINE	N-MINT
❑1, Jun 72, JR; GT, Out of Hell...A Hero!, 1: Power Man II (Luke Cage); 1: Diamondback	0.20	4.80	12.00	24.00
❑2, Aug 72, V: Diamondback	0.20	2.40	6.00	12.00
❑3, Oct 72, V: Mace	0.20	1.60	4.00	8.00
❑4, Dec 72	0.20	1.20	3.00	6.00
❑5, Jan 73	0.20	1.20	3.00	6.00
❑6, Feb 73	0.20	1.00	2.50	5.00
❑7, Mar 73	0.20	1.00	2.50	5.00
❑8, Apr 73, A: Doctor Doom	0.20	1.00	2.50	5.00
❑9, May 73	0.20	1.00	2.50	5.00
❑10, Jun 73, 1: Señor Muerte I (Ramon Garcia)	0.20	1.00	2.50	5.00
❑11, Jul 73, D: Señor Muerte I (Ramon Garcia)	0.20	0.80	2.00	4.00
❑12, Aug 73, 1: Chemistro I (Curtis Carr)	0.20	0.80	2.00	4.00
❑13, Sep 73, V: Lionfang	0.20	0.80	2.00	4.00
❑14, Oct 73, Retribution!, O: Luke Cage; V: Big Ben	0.20	0.80	2.00	4.00
❑15, Nov 73, Sub-Mariner back-up	0.20	0.80	2.00	4.00
❑16, Dec 73, V: Stiletto; D: Rackham, series continues as Power Man	0.20	0.80	2.00	4.00

HERO HOTLINE
DC

	ORIG	GOOD	FINE	N-MINT
❑1, Apr 89	1.75	0.40	1.00	2.00
❑2, May 89	1.75	0.40	1.00	2.00
❑3, Jun 89, 1: Snafu	1.75	0.40	1.00	2.00
❑4, Jul 89	1.75	0.40	1.00	2.00
❑5, Aug 89	1.75	0.40	1.00	2.00
❑6, Sep 89	1.75	0.40	1.00	2.00

ORIG GOOD FINE N-MINT

HEROIC
LIGHTNING

Value: Cover or less

- ❑1 ... 1.75

HEROIC 17
PENNACLE

Value: Cover or less

- ❑1, Sep 93, The Future Shock! 2.95

HEROIC TALES
LONE STAR

Value: Cover or less

- ❑1, Jun 97, Amazon: Steel of a Soldier's Heart, Part 1, Amazon 2.50
- ❑2, Aug 97, Amazon: Steel of a Soldier's Heart, Part 2; The Universal Monster's Guide to Men, Amazon ... 2.50
- ❑3, Oct 97, Amazon: Steel of a Soldier's Heart, Part 3; Ace of Diamonds ... 2.50
- ❑4, Dec 97, Amazon: Not Without Dust and Heart, Part 1; The B-Movie Grimoire of Lesser Monsters ... 2.50
- ❑5, Feb 98, Amazon: Not Without Dust and Heart, Part 2; Ace of Diamonds Preview II ... 2.50
- ❑6, May 98, Blackheart: A Victim of Fate; Amazon Meets Mr. Muscles, Amazon and Blackheart 2.50
- ❑7, Jul 98, The Children of Atlas, Part 1; Single Combat, Amazon and Gunslinger ... 2.50
- ❑8, Aug 98, Atlas: The Judgment of Atlas; The Children of Atlas, Part 2, Atlas ... 2.50
- ❑9, Apr 00, Gunslinger: Claws & Effect ... 2.50
- ❑10, May 00, Blackheart: A Matter of the Heart; Ape Company. 2.50

HEROINES INC.
AVATAR

Value: Cover or less

- ❑1, b&w ... 1.75

HEROMAN
DIMENSION

Value: Cover or less

- ❑1, Oct 86, The Origin of Heroman ... 1.75

HERO ON A STICK
BIG-BABY

Value: Cover or less

- ❑1 ... 2.95

HERO SANDWICH
SLAVE LABOR

	ORIG	GOOD	FINE	N-MINT
❑1, Feb 87, They Say Nobody Lives Forever...	1.50	0.40	1.00	2.00
❑2, May 87	1.50	0.30	0.75	1.50
❑3, Aug 87	1.50	0.30	0.75	1.50
❑4, Jan 88	1.75	0.35	0.88	1.75
❑5, Oct 88	1.75	0.35	0.88	1.75
❑6, Feb 89	1.75	0.35	0.88	1.75
❑7, Mar 90	2.25	0.45	1.13	2.25
❑8, Jun 91	2.50	0.50	1.25	2.50
❑9, May 92	2.50	0.50	1.25	2.50

HERO ZERO
DARK HORSE

Value: Cover or less

- ❑0, Sep 94 ... 2.50

HERU, SON OF AUSAR
ANIA

Value: Cover or less

- ❑1, Apr 93, The Coming Of Heru, 1: Heru, trading cards ... 1.95

HE SAID/SHE SAID COMICS
FIRST AMENDMENT

Value: Cover or less

- ❑1, Amy Fisher/Joey Buttafuoco ... 3.00
- ❑2, Woody Allen/Mia Farrow .. 3.00
- ❑3, Bill Clinton/Gennifer Flowers 3.00
- ❑4, Tonya Harding/Jeff Gillooly 3.00
- ❑5, O.J. Simpson/Nicole Brown 3.00

HEX
DC

	ORIG	GOOD	FINE	N-MINT
❑1, Sep 85, Once Upon A Time...In The West?!?, 1: Stiletta; 1: Hex (future Jonah Hex), continued from Jonah Hex #92	0.75	0.40	1.00	2.00
❑2, Oct 85, Can She Bake a Cherry Pie?	0.75	0.25	0.63	1.25
❑3, Nov 85, The Lotus Eaters!	0.75	0.25	0.63	1.25
❑4, Dec 85, Worms	0.75	0.25	0.63	1.25
❑5, Jan 86, The Seattle Chain Saw Massacre	0.75	0.25	0.63	1.25
❑6, Feb 86	0.75	0.25	0.63	1.25
❑7, Mar 86	0.75	0.25	0.63	1.25
❑8, Apr 86, Day of the Cyborg!	0.75	0.25	0.63	1.25
❑9, May 86	0.75	0.25	0.63	1.25
❑10, Jun 86, A: Legion	0.75	0.25	0.63	1.25
❑11, Jul 86, Night of the Bat, A: Batman of future	0.75	0.25	0.63	1.25
❑12, Aug 86, A: Batman of future	0.75	0.25	0.63	1.25
❑13, Sep 86, The Dogs of War, 1: Dogs of War	0.75	0.25	0.63	1.25
❑14, Oct 86	0.75	0.25	0.63	1.25
❑15, Nov 86, Chain of Doom	0.75	0.25	0.63	1.25
❑16, Dec 86, KG, The Slayer and the Slave!	0.75	0.25	0.63	1.25
❑17, Jan 87, KG	0.75	0.25	0.63	1.25
❑18, Feb 87, KG, Final Issue	1.00	0.25	0.63	1.25

HEXBREAKER: A BADGER GRAPHIC NOVEL
FIRST

Value: Cover or less

- ❑1, Mar 88 ... 8.95

Western bounty hunter Jonah Hex found himself in a post-apocalyptic future in the short-lived *Hex*.

ORIG GOOD FINE N-MINT

HEX OF THE WICKED WITCH
ASYLUM

Value: Cover or less

- ❑0/A, Aug 99 ... 1.95
- ❑0/B, Aug 99, Deluxe edition... 3.95

HEY, BOSS!
VISIONARY

	ORIG	GOOD	FINE	N-MINT
❑1	1.50	0.40	1.00	2.00

HEY, MISTER
INSOMNIA

Value: Cover or less

- ❑1, May 97, b&w ... 2.50
- ❑2, Nov 97, b&w ... 2.50
- ❑3, Aug 98, b&w ... 2.95
- ❑4, Dec 98, b&w ... 2.95

HEY MISTER: AFTERSCHOOL SPECIAL
TOP SHELF

Value: Cover or less

- ❑1, nn; b&w; digest; collects five-issue mini-comics series...... 4.95

HIDEO LI FILES, THE
RAGING RHINO

Value: Cover or less

- ❑1, b&w; adult ... 2.95

HIDING PLACE, THE
DC

Value: Cover or less

- ❑1 ... 12.95

HIEROGLYPH
DARK HORSE

Value: Cover or less

- ❑1, Nov 99 ... 2.95
- ❑2, Dec 99 ... 2.95
- ❑3, Jan 00 ... 2.95
- ❑4, Feb 00 ... 2.95

HIGH CALIBER
CALIBER

Value: Cover or less

- ❑1, b&w; Trade Paperback...... 9.95

HIGH OCTANE THEATRE
INFINITI

Value: Cover or less

- ❑1, Codename: Jezebel: Dead Little Lady; Jeremy Sifter: For Hire, sticker ... 2.50

HIGH SCHOOL AGENT
SUN

Value: Cover or less

- ❑1 ... 2.50

HIGH SHINING BRASS
APPLE

Value: Cover or less

- ❑1, Point, b&w ... 2.75
- ❑2, b&w ... 2.75
- ❑3, b&w ... 2.75
- ❑4 ... 2.95

HIGH STAKES ADVENTURES
ANTARCTIC

Value: Cover or less

- ❑1, Dec 98, The Big Game; Giant Fighter ... 2.95
- ❑1/Dlx, Dec 98, The Big Game; Giant Fighter, Deluxe edition 5.95

HIGHTOP NINJA
AUTHORITY

Value: Cover or less

- ❑1 ... 2.95
- ❑2 ... 2.95
- ❑3 ... 2.95

HIGH VOLTAGE
BLACK OUT

Value: Cover or less

- ❑0 ... 2.95

HILLY ROSE
ASTRO

	ORIG	GOOD	FINE	N-MINT
❑1, May 95	2.95	1.00	2.50	5.00
❑1/A	2.95	0.80	2.00	4.00
❑2, Jul 95, Heartbreak News, Chapter 2	2.95	0.80	2.00	4.00
❑3, Oct 95	2.95	0.60	1.50	3.00
❑4, Dec 95	2.95	0.60	1.50	3.00
❑5, Feb 96	2.95	0.60	1.50	3.00
❑6, Apr 96	2.95	0.60	1.50	3.00
❑7, Aug 96	2.95	0.60	1.50	3.00
❑8, Dec 96	2.95	0.60	1.50	3.00
❑9, Apr 97	2.95	0.60	1.50	3.00

HIP FLASK
COMICRAFT

Value: Cover or less

- ❑0.5, Aug 98, JPH (w), San Dego Comic-Con preview ... 2.95

HIS NAME IS...SAVAGE
Adventure House Press

	ORIG	GOOD	FINE	N-MINT
❑1, GK, nn; magazine	0.35	5.00	12.50	25.00

HISTORY OF MARVELS COMICS, THE
Marvel

	ORIG	GOOD	FINE	N-MINT
❑1, Jul 00	—	0.20	0.50	1.00

HISTORY OF THE DC UNIVERSE
DC

	ORIG	GOOD	FINE	N-MINT
❑1, Sep 86, GP	2.95	0.65	1.63	3.25
❑2, Nov 86, GP	2.95	0.65	1.63	3.25

HISTORY OF VIOLENCE
DC

Value: Cover or less

❑1, b&w ... 9.95

HITCHHIKER'S GUIDE TO THE GALAXY, THE
DC

Value: Cover or less

❑1 ... 4.95
❑2 ... 4.95
❑3 ... 4.95

HITMAN
DC

	ORIG	GOOD	FINE	N-MINT
❑1, Apr 96, A Rage in Arkham, Part 1, A: Batman	2.25	1.00	2.50	5.00
❑2, Jun 96, A Rage in Arkham, Part 2, V: Joker	2.25	0.60	1.50	3.00
❑3, Jul 96	2.25	0.60	1.50	3.00
❑4, Aug 96, Ten Thousand Bullets, Part 1	2.25	0.60	1.50	3.00
❑5, Sep 96, Ten Thousand Bullets, Part 2	2.25	0.60	1.50	3.00
❑6, Oct 96, Ten Thousand Bullets, Part 3, cover says Part 4 of 4	2.25	0.60	1.50	3.00
❑7, Nov 96, Ten Thousand Bullets, Part 4, D: Johnny Navarone; D: Nightfist	2.25	0.50	1.25	2.50
❑8, Dec 96, Final Night, O: Hitman, Final Night	2.25	0.50	1.25	2.50
❑9, Dec 96, Local Hero, Part 1; Local Heroes, Part 1	2.25	0.50	1.25	2.50
❑10, Jan 97, Local Hero, Part 2; Local Heroes, Part 2	2.25	0.50	1.25	2.50
❑11, Feb 97, Local Hero, Part 3; Local Heroes, Part 3	2.25	0.45	1.13	2.25
❑12, Mar 97, Local Hero, Part 4; Local Heroes, Part 4, A: Green Lantern	2.25	0.45	1.13	2.25
❑13, Apr 97, Zombie Night at the Gotham Aquarium, Part 1	2.25	0.45	1.13	2.25
❑14, May 97, Zombie Night at the Gotham Aquarium, Part 2; Zombie Night at the Aquarium	2.25	0.45	1.13	2.25
❑15, Jun 97, Ace of Killers; Ace of Killers, Part 1	2.25	0.45	1.13	2.25
❑16, Jul 97, Ace of Killers; Ace of Killers, Part 2, A: Catwoman	2.25	0.45	1.13	2.25
❑17, Aug 97, Ace of Killers; Ace of Killers, Part 3	2.25	0.45	1.13	2.25
❑18, Sep 97, Ace of Killers; Ace of Killers, Part 4	2.25	0.45	1.13	2.25
❑19, Oct 97, Ace of Killers; Ace of Killers, Part 5	2.25	0.45	1.13	2.25
❑20, Nov 97, Ace of Killers; Ace of Killers, Part 6	2.25	0.45	1.13	2.25
❑21, Dec 97, Kiss Me, Face cover	2.25	0.45	1.13	2.25
❑22, Jan 98	2.25	0.45	1.13	2.25
❑23, Feb 98, Who Dares Wins, Part 1	2.25	0.45	1.13	2.25
❑24, Mar 98, Who Dares Wins, Part 2	2.25	0.45	1.13	2.25
❑25, Apr 98	2.25	0.45	1.13	2.25
❑26, May 98	2.25	0.45	1.13	2.25
❑27, Jun 98	2.25	0.45	1.13	2.25
❑28, Jul 98	2.25	0.45	1.13	2.25
❑29, Aug 98, Tommy's Heroes, Part 1	2.25	0.45	1.13	2.25
❑30, Sep 98, Tommy's Heroes, Part 2	2.50	0.50	1.25	2.50
❑31, Oct 98, Tommy's Heroes, Part 3	2.50	0.50	1.25	2.50
❑32, Dec 98, Tommy's Heroes, Part 4	2.50	0.50	1.25	2.50
❑33, Jan 99, Tommy's Heroes, Part 5	2.50	0.50	1.25	2.50
❑34, Feb 99, Superfriends?, A: Superman	2.50	0.50	1.25	2.50
❑35, Mar 99, Katie, Part 1, 1: Frances Monaghan	2.50	0.50	1.25	2.50
❑36, Apr 99, Katie, Part 2, 2: Frances Monaghan; D: Tommy's mother	2.50	0.50	1.25	2.50
❑37, May 99, Dead Man's Land; Dead Man's Land, Part 1	2.50	0.50	1.25	2.50
❑38, Jun 99, Dead Man's Land; Dead Man's Land, Part 2	2.50	0.50	1.25	2.50
❑39, Jul 99, For Tomorrow, Part 1	2.50	0.50	1.25	2.50
❑40, Aug 99, For Tomorrow, Part 2	2.50	0.50	1.25	2.50
❑41, Sep 99, For Tomorrow, Part 3	2.50	0.50	1.25	2.50
❑42, Oct 99, For Tomorrow, Part 4	2.50	0.50	1.25	2.50
❑43, Nov 99	2.50	0.50	1.25	2.50
❑44, Dec 99, Fresh Meat, Part 1	2.50	0.50	1.25	2.50
❑45, Jan 00, Fresh Meat, Part 2	2.50	0.50	1.25	2.50
❑46, Feb 00, The Old Dog, Part 1	2.50	0.50	1.25	2.50
❑47, Mar 00, The Old Dog, Part 2	2.50	0.50	1.25	2.50
❑48, Apr 00	2.50	0.50	1.25	2.50
❑49, May 00, The Old Dog, Part 3	2.50	0.50	1.25	2.50
❑50, Jun 00	—	0.50	1.25	2.50
❑51, Jul 00	2.50	0.50	1.25	2.50
❑52, Aug 00	2.50	0.50	1.25	2.50
❑53, Sep 00, Closing Time, Part 1	2.50	0.50	1.25	2.50
❑54, Oct 00, Closing Time, Part 2	2.50	0.50	1.25	2.50
❑55, Nov 00, Closing Time, Part 3	2.50	0.50	1.25	2.50
❑56, Dec 00, Closing Time, Part 4	2.50	0.50	1.25	2.50
❑57, Jan 01, Closing Time, Part 5	2.50	0.50	1.25	2.50
❑58, Feb 01, Closing Time, Part 6	2.50	0.50	1.25	2.50
❑59, Mar 01, Closing Time, Part 7	2.50	0.50	1.25	2.50
❑60, Jun 01, Closing Time, Part 8, D: Hitman, Final Issue	2.50	0.50	1.25	2.50
❑1000000, Nov 98	2.50	0.50	1.25	2.50
❑Anl 1, Pulp Heroes; 1997 Annual	3.95	0.79	1.98	3.95

HITMAN/LOBO: THAT STUPID BASTICH
DC

Value: Cover or less

❑1, Sep 00 ... 3.95

HITOMI 2
Antarctic

Value: Cover or less

❑1, Aug 93, b&w ... 2.50
❑2, Oct 93, b&w ... 2.75
❑3, Dec 93, b&w ... 2.75
❑4, Feb 94, b&w ... 2.75
❑5, Apr 94, b&w ... 2.75
❑6, Jul 94, b&w ... 2.75
❑7, Nov 94, b&w ... 2.75
❑8, Mar 95, b&w ... 2.75
❑9, May 95, Shadow Hunter, b&w ... 2.75
❑10, May 97, b&w ... 3.95

HITOMI AND HER GIRL COMMANDOS
Antarctic

Value: Cover or less

❑1, Apr 92, b&w ... 2.50
❑2, Jun 92, b&w ... 2.50
❑3, Aug 92, b&w ... 2.50
❑4, Oct 92, b&w ... 2.50

HIT THE BEACH
Antarctic

Value: Cover or less

❑1, Jul 93, b&w ... 2.95
❑1/GO, Jul 93, Deluxe edition; gold foil ... 4.95
❑2, Jul 94, b&w ... 2.95
❑3, Jul 95, b&w ... 2.95
❑4, Jul 97, b&w ... 2.95
❑5, Jul 98, b&w; regular edition 2.95
❑5/CS, Jul 98, b&w; Special edition; polybagged with postcard ... 4.95
❑6, Jul 99 ... 3.95

HOBBIT, THE (J.R.R. TOLKIEN'S...)
Eclipse

Value: Cover or less

❑1 ... 4.95
❑2 ... 4.95
❑3 ... 4.95

HOCKEY MASTERS
Revolutionary

Value: Cover or less

❑1, Dec 93, b&w ... 2.95

HOE, THE
Thunderball

Value: Cover or less

❑1 ... 2.50

HOKUM & HEX
Marvel

Value: Cover or less

❑1, Sep 93, Strange Angels, O: Trip Munroe, Embossed cover 2.50
❑2, Oct 93, A Convocation Of Clowns, A: Trip Monroe; A: Analyzer; A: Felon Bale ... 1.75
❑3, Nov 93 ... 1.75
❑4, Dec 93, Fire And Rust, D: Z-Man ... 1.75
❑5, Jan 94 ... 1.75
❑6, Feb 94, Bloodshed, Part 1 1.75
❑7, Mar 94, Bloodshed, Part 2 1.75
❑8, Apr 94 ... 1.75
❑9, May 94, Final Issue ... 1.75

HOLIDAY FOR SCREAMS
Malibu

Value: Cover or less

❑1, nn; b&w ... 4.95

HOLIDAY OUT
Renegade

Value: Cover or less

❑1, b&w ... 2.00
❑2, b&w ... 2.00
❑3, b&w ... 2.00

HOLLOW EARTH, THE
Vision

Value: Cover or less

❑1 ... 2.50
❑2 ... 2.50
❑3, Jan 97, Follow the Leader. 2.50

HOLLYWOOD SUPERSTARS
Marvel

Value: Cover or less

❑1, Nov 90, ME (w), Stuntwork 2.95
❑2, Jan 91, ME (w) ... 2.25
❑3, Feb 91, ME (w) ... 2.25
❑4, Mar 91, ME (w) ... 2.25
❑5, Apr 91, ME (w) ... 2.25

HOLO BROTHERS, THE
Monster

	ORIG	GOOD	FINE	N-MINT
❑1, b&w	1.95	0.40	1.00	2.00
❑2, b&w	1.95	0.40	1.00	2.00
❑3	2.25	0.45	1.13	2.25
❑4	2.25	0.45	1.13	2.25
❑5	2.25	0.45	1.13	2.25

	ORIG	GOOD	FINE	N-MINT
❑6	2.25	0.45	1.13	2.25
❑7	2.25	0.45	1.13	2.25
❑8	2.25	0.45	1.13	2.25
❑9	2.25	0.45	1.13	2.25
❑10	2.25	0.45	1.13	2.25
❑SE 1, O: Holo. Brothers	2.25	0.45	1.13	2.25

HOLY AVENGER
SLAVE LABOR

Value: Cover or less
❑1, Apr 96 .... 4.95

HOLY CROSS
FANTAGRAPHICS

Value: Cover or less
❑0, b&w 4.95
❑1 .... 2.95
❑2, Oct 94, b&w 2.95

HOMAGE STUDIOS SWIMSUIT SPECIAL
IMAGE

	ORIG	GOOD	FINE	N-MINT
❑1, Apr 93, pin-ups	1.95	0.40	1.00	2.00

HOMELANDS ON THE WORLD OF MAGIC: THE GATHERING
ACCLAIM

Value: Cover or less
❑1, nn; One-Shot; prestige format; polybagged with Homelands card 5.95

HOMICIDE
DARK HORSE

Value: Cover or less
❑1, Apr 90, b&w 1.95

HOMICIDE: TEARS OF THE DEAD
CHAOS

Value: Cover or less
❑1 .... 2.95

HOMO PATROL
HELPLESS ANGER

Value: Cover or less
❑1, nn; b&w; adult 3.50

HONEYMOONERS, THE (LODESTONE)
LODESTONE

Value: Cover or less
❑1, Oct 86, The Home Game, Photo cover 1.50

HONEYMOONERS, THE (TRIAD)
TRIAD

Value: Cover or less
❑1, Sep 87, Photo cover 2.00
❑2, Sep 87, photo back cover; reprints #1's indicia 2.00
❑3, She's a Wonderful Wife, wraparound cover; Deluxe edition; squarebound 3.50
❑4, Jan 88, In the Pink, photo back cover 2.00
❑5, Feb 88, wraparound cover 2.00
❑6, Mar 88, photo back cover. 2.00
❑7, Apr 88, A: Captain Lou Albano, wraparound cover 2.00
❑8, May 88, wraparound cover 2.00
❑9, Jul 88, wraparound cover; squarebound 3.95
❑10, Apr 89, Minneapolis Here We Come, Photo cover 2.00
❑11, Jun 89, Take Me Out to the Ballgame!, Photo cover 2.00
❑12, Aug 89, My Fare Lady, Photo cover 2.00
❑13 .... 2.00

HONG ON THE RANGE
IMAGE

Value: Cover or less
❑1, Dec 97, I Woke Up Wicked 2.50
❑2, Jan 98 .... 2.50
❑3, Feb 98, The Good, The Bad, and The Control-Natural 2.50

HONK!
FANTAGRAPHICS

Value: Cover or less
❑1, Nov 86, b&w 2.75
❑2, Jan 87, b&w 2.75
❑3, Mar 87, b&w 2.75
❑4, May 87, b&w 2.75
❑5, Jul 87, b&w 2.75

HONKO THE CLOWN
C&T

Value: Cover or less
❑1, b&w 2.00

HONOR AMONG THIEVES
GATEWAY

Value: Cover or less
❑1 .... 1.50

HOOD, THE
SOUTH CENTRAL

Value: Cover or less
❑1, b&w 2.75

HOOD MAGAZINE
OAKLAND

Value: Cover or less
❑1 .... 3.00
❑2 .... 3.00

HOODOO
3-D ZONE

Value: Cover or less
❑1, Nov 88, Old Dave; The Black Cat Bone, b&w 2.50

HOOK
MARVEL

	ORIG	GOOD	FINE	N-MINT
❑1, Feb 92, CV (w)	1.00	0.25	0.63	1.25
❑2, Feb 92, CV (w)	1.00	0.25	0.63	1.25
❑3, Mar 92, CV (w)	1.00	0.25	0.63	1.25
❑4, Mar 92, CV (w)	1.00	0.25	0.63	1.25

HOOK (MAGAZINE)
MARVEL

Value: Cover or less
❑1, nn; magazine 2.95

Charles Vess was the writer for Marvel's adaptation of *Hook*.

HOON, THE
EENIEWEENIE

Value: Cover or less
❑1, Jun 95, b&w 2.50
❑2 .... 2.50
❑3 .... 2.50
❑4 .... 2.50
❑5 .... 2.50
❑6 .... 2.50

HOON, THE (VOL. 2)
CALIBER

Value: Cover or less
❑1 .... 2.95
❑2 .... 2.95

HOPSTER'S TRACKS
BONGO

Value: Cover or less
❑1, b&w 2.95
❑2, b&w 2.95

HORDE
SWING SHIFT

Value: Cover or less
❑1, b&w 2.00

HORNY BIKER SLUTS
LAST GASP

Value: Cover or less
❑5, b&w; adult 2.95

HORNY COMIX & STORIES
RIP OFF

Value: Cover or less
❑1, Apr 91, b&w; adult 2.50
❑2, Jul 91, b&w; adult 2.50
❑3, Dec 91, b&w; adult 2.50
❑4, May 92, b&w; adult 2.50

HORNY TOADS (WALLACE WOOD'S...)
FANTAGRAPHICS

Value: Cover or less
❑1, b&w; adult 2.95

HOROBI PART 1
VIZ

Value: Cover or less
❑1, Omen 1, b&w; Japanese .. 3.75
❑2, b&w; Japanese 3.75
❑3, b&w; Japanese 3.75
❑4, b&w; Japanese 3.75
❑5, b&w; Japanese 3.75
❑6, b&w; Japanese 3.75
❑7, b&w; Japanese 3.75
❑8, b&w; Japanese 3.75

HOROBI PART 2
VIZ

Value: Cover or less
❑1, Genocide 56, b&w; Japanese 4.25
❑2, b&w; Japanese 4.25
❑3, b&w; Japanese 4.25
❑4, b&w; Japanese 4.25
❑5, b&w; Japanese 4.25
❑6, b&w; Japanese 4.25
❑7, b&w; Japanese 4.25

HORRIBLE TRUTH ABOUT COMICS, THE
ALTERNATIVE

Value: Cover or less
❑1, Jan 99, nn; b&w 2.95

HORROR HOUSE
AC

Value: Cover or less
❑1, JKa; WW, JKa (w); WW (w), The Painted Beast! 2.95

HORROR, THE ILLUSTRATED BOOK OF FEARS
NORTHSTAR

	ORIG	GOOD	FINE	N-MINT
❑1, Timed Exposure; Bug House	3.95	0.80	2.00	4.00
❑2, Feb 90, Hurry Monster; Black Dot	3.95	0.80	2.00	4.00

HORROR IN THE DARK
FANTAGOR

Value: Cover or less
❑1, RCo, RCo (w), Tales of the Black Diamond, Blood Birth; Lame lem Love, b&w; adult. 2.00
❑2, RCo, RCo (w), Tales of the Black Diamond, Bath of Blood; Gogy, b&w; adult 2.00
❑3, b&w; adult 2.00
❑4, b&w; adult 2.00

HORRORIST, THE
DC

Value: Cover or less
❑1, Dec 95, Antarctica, Part 1, A: John Constantine 5.95
❑2, Jan 96, Antarctica, Part 2, A: John Constantine 5.95

HORROR OF COLLIER COUNTY, THE
DARK HORSE

Value: Cover or less
❑1, Oct 99, Them 2.95
❑2 .... 2.95
❑3 .... 2.95
❑4 .... 2.95
❑5 .... 2.95

HORRORS OF THE HAUNTER
AC

Value: Cover or less

❑1, b&w; Reprint 2.95

HORSE
SLAVE LABOR

Value: Cover or less

❑1, Sep 89, b&w 2.95
❑2 .... 2.95
❑3 .... 2.95

HORSEMAN
KEVLAR

Value: Cover or less

❑0, May, b&w; no cover price; Commemorative edition; published after Crusade issue #1 2.95
❑0/GO, May 96, gold foil-embossed cardstock cover; published after Crusade issue #1 .... 2.95
❑0/SI, no cover price or indicia; published after Crusade issue #1 .... 2.95
❑1, Mar 96, A: Shi 2.95
❑1/A, Nov 96, Kevlar edition ... 2.95
❑2, Jan 97 .... 2.95

HOSIE'S HEROINES
SLAVE LABOR

Value: Cover or less

❑1, Apr 93, The Asteroidisiac; Vic Blister...The Case of the Atomic Tongue, adult 2.95

HOSTILE TAKEOVER
MALIBU

Value: Cover or less

❑Ash 1, Sep 94, nn; ashcan; Ultraverse Preview 0.75

HOTEL HARBOUR VIEW
VIZ

Value: Cover or less

❑1, b&w; Japanese 9.95

HOTHEAD PAISAN: HOMICIDAL LESBIAN TERRORIST
GIANT ASS

Value: Cover or less

❑13 .... 3.50

HOT LINE
EROS

Value: Cover or less

❑1, Nov 92, Nymphos, Nazis, & Necrophiles 2.50

HOT MEXICAN LOVE COMICS
HOT MEXICAN LOVE COMICS

Value: Cover or less

❑1 .... 3.95
❑2 .... 3.95

HOT N' COLD HEROES
A-PLUS

Value: Cover or less

❑1, MZ; JBy, The Last Monster Hunter!; Yellow Jacket, 1: Hellsing, b&w 2.50
❑2, Mar 91, reprints O: Nemesis, Magicman 2.50

HOT NIGHTS IN RANGOON
EROS

Value: Cover or less

❑1 .... 2.95
❑2 .... 2.95
❑3, Nov 94 .... 2.95

HOT SHOTS
HOT

Value: Cover or less

❑1, full color 1.95

HOT SHOTS: AVENGERS
MARVEL

Value: Cover or less

❑1, Oct 95, BSz; ARo, One-Shot; pin-ups 2.95

HOT SHOTS: SPIDER-MAN
MARVEL

Value: Cover or less

❑1, Jan 96, nn; pin-ups 2.95

HOT SHOTS: X-MEN
MARVEL

Value: Cover or less

❑1, Jan 96, BSz; ARo, nn; pin-ups; Introduction by Scott Lobdell 2.95

HOTSPUR
ECLIPSE

Value: Cover or less

❑1, Jun 87, We're Not in Cincinnati Anymore 1.75
❑2 .... 1.75
❑3 .... 1.75

HOT STUF'
SAL QUARTUCCIO

	ORIG	GOOD	FINE	N-MINT
❑1	1.50	0.80	2.00	4.00
❑2	1.50	0.60	1.50	3.00
❑3, Dec 76, RCo, RCo (w), Prologue; The Pawn	1.50	0.60	1.50	3.00
❑4, Mar 77, GM; ATh, GM (w); ATh (w), Soace Station Dora; The Vanguard	1.50	0.60	1.50	3.00
❑5	1.50	0.60	1.50	3.00
❑6, Dec 77, EC; MN, EC (w); MN (w), 12 Parts; The Apprentice	2.00	0.60	1.50	3.00
❑7	—	0.60	1.50	3.00
❑8	—	0.60	1.50	3.00

HOT STUFF (VOL. 2)
HARVEY

	ORIG	GOOD	FINE	N-MINT
❑1	1.25	0.30	0.75	1.50
❑2	1.25	0.25	0.63	1.25
❑3	1.25	0.25	0.63	1.25
❑4	1.25	0.25	0.63	1.25
❑5, Story Book Land; Smile-durn You, Smile	1.25	0.25	0.63	1.25
❑6	1.25	0.25	0.63	1.25
❑7	1.25	0.25	0.63	1.25
❑8	1.25	0.25	0.63	1.25
❑9	1.50	0.30	0.75	1.50
❑10	1.50	0.30	0.75	1.50
❑11	1.50	0.30	0.75	1.50
❑12	1.50	0.30	0.75	1.50

HOT STUFF BIG BOOK
HARVEY

Value: Cover or less

❑1 .... 1.95
❑2 .... 1.95

HOT STUFF DIGEST
HARVEY

Value: Cover or less

❑1 .... 2.25
❑2 .... 2.25
❑3 .... 1.75
❑4 .... 1.75
❑5 .... 1.75

HOT STUFF GIANT SIZE
HARVEY

Value: Cover or less

❑1 .... 2.25
❑2 .... 2.25
❑3 .... 2.25

HOT STUFF SIZZLERS
HARVEY

Value: Cover or less

❑1, Jul 60 .... 1.25

HOT TAILS
EROS

	ORIG	GOOD	FINE	N-MINT
❑1	—	0.70	1.75	3.50

HOT WHEELS
DC

	ORIG	GOOD	FINE	N-MINT
❑1, Apr 70	0.15	6.00	15.00	30.00
❑2, Jun 70	0.15	4.00	10.00	20.00
❑3, Aug 70	0.15	3.20	8.00	16.00
❑4, Oct 70	0.15	3.20	8.00	16.00
❑5, Dec 70	0.15	3.20	8.00	16.00
❑6, Feb 71	0.15	3.20	8.00	16.00

HOURMAN
DC

	ORIG	GOOD	FINE	N-MINT
❑1, Apr 99, Through the Hourglass, A: Snapper Carr; A: Justice League of America; V: Amazo	2.50	0.50	1.25	2.50
❑1/Aut, A: Snapper Carr; A: Justice League of America; A: Amazo, Signed by David Meikis	—	3.19	7.97	15.95
❑2, May 99, A: Tomorrow Woman	2.50	0.50	1.25	2.50
❑3, Jun 99, Timepoint	2.50	0.50	1.25	2.50
❑4, Jul 99, V: Lord of Time	2.50	0.50	1.25	2.50
❑5, Aug 99, The Death of Hourman, A: Golden Age Hourman	2.50	0.50	1.25	2.50
❑6, Sep 99, The JLAndroids, V: Amazo	2.50	0.50	1.25	2.50
❑7, Oct 99, The Human League, V: Amazo	2.50	0.50	1.25	2.50
❑8, Nov 99, A Week With No Hourman, Day of Judgment	2.50	0.50	1.25	2.50
❑9, Dec 99, Where Does the Time Go?	2.50	0.50	1.25	2.50
❑10, Jan 00, Bride of the Gombezi	2.50	0.50	1.25	2.50
❑11, Feb 00, Hourman One Million, Part 1	2.50	0.50	1.25	2.50
❑12, Mar 00, Hourman One Million, Part 2	2.50	0.50	1.25	2.50
❑13, Apr 00, Hourman One Million, Part 3	2.50	0.50	1.25	2.50
❑14, May 00, Secrets and Lies	2.50	0.50	1.25	2.50
❑15, Jun 00, Friend of the Devil	2.50	0.50	1.25	2.50
❑16, Jul 00	2.50	0.50	1.25	2.50
❑17, Aug 00	2.50	0.50	1.25	2.50
❑18, Sep 00	2.50	0.50	1.25	2.50
❑19, Oct 00, The Thief of Time	2.50	0.50	1.25	2.50
❑20, Nov 00, My So-Called Afterlife	2.50	0.50	1.25	2.50
❑21, Dec 00, Maybe I'm Amazo	2.50	0.50	1.25	2.50
❑22, Jan 01, The Chrono-Bums	2.50	0.50	1.25	2.50
❑23, Feb 01, The Unbelievable Truth	2.50	0.50	1.25	2.50
❑24, Mar 01, Minutes to Go	2.50	0.50	1.25	2.50
❑25, Apr 01, ...But You'll Never See the End of the Road if You're Travelling With Me.	2.50	0.50	1.25	2.50

HOUSE II THE SECOND STORY
MARVEL

Value: Cover or less

❑1, Oct 87, movie Adaptation.. 2.00

HOUSE OF FRIGHTENSTEIN
AC

Value: Cover or less

❑1, b&w; Reprint 2.95

HOUSE OF MYSTERY
DC

	ORIG	GOOD	FINE	N-MINT
❑143, J'onn J'onzz; Martian Manhunter begins	0.12	22.00	55.00	110.00
❑144	0.12	11.00	27.50	55.00
❑145	0.12	9.00	22.50	45.00
❑146	0.12	9.00	22.50	45.00
❑147	0.12	9.00	22.50	45.00
❑148, Jan 65	0.12	9.00	22.50	45.00

	ORIG	GOOD	FINE	N-MINT
❑149, Mar 65, ATh	0.12	9.00	22.50	45.00
❑150, Apr 65	0.12	9.00	22.50	45.00
❑151, Jun 65	0.12	9.00	22.50	45.00
❑152, Jul 65	0.12	9.00	22.50	45.00
❑153, Sep 65, J'onn J'onzz	0.12	9.00	22.50	45.00
❑154, Oct 65	0.12	9.00	22.50	45.00
❑155, Dec 65	0.12	9.00	22.50	45.00
❑156, Jan 66, 1: Robby Reed; 1: Dial "H" For Hero	0.12	16.00	40.00	80.00
❑157, Mar 66	0.12	8.00	20.00	40.00
❑158, Apr 66	0.12	8.00	20.00	40.00
❑159, Jun 66	0.12	8.00	20.00	40.00
❑160, Jul 66, Dial "H" for Hero; Robby Reed becomes Plastic Man	0.12	15.00	37.50	75.00
❑161, Sep 66, Dial "H" for Hero	0.12	7.00	17.50	35.00
❑162, Oct 66	0.12	7.00	17.50	35.00
❑163, Dec 66	0.12	7.00	17.50	35.00
❑164, Jan 67	0.12	7.00	17.50	35.00
❑165, Mar 67	0.12	7.00	17.50	35.00
❑166, Apr 67	0.12	7.00	17.50	35.00
❑167, Jun 67	0.12	7.00	17.50	35.00
❑168, Jul 67	0.12	7.00	17.50	35.00
❑169, Sep 67, 1: Gem Girl	0.12	7.00	17.50	35.00
❑170, Oct 67	0.12	7.00	17.50	35.00
❑171, Dec 67, The Micro-Monsters!; Manhunter From Mars, Dial "H" for Hero	0.12	7.00	17.50	35.00
❑172, Feb 68	0.12	7.00	17.50	35.00
❑173, Apr 68, Revolt of the H-Dial; So You're Faceless!	0.12	7.00	17.50	35.00
❑174, Jun 68, NA, Mystery format begins	0.12	2.40	6.00	12.00
❑175, Aug 68, NA, 1: Cain	0.12	2.40	6.00	12.00
❑176, Oct 68, NA	0.12	2.40	6.00	12.00
❑177, Dec 68, NA	0.12	2.40	6.00	12.00
❑178, Feb 69, NA	0.12	2.80	7.00	14.00
❑179, Apr 69, NA; JO; BWr, Sour Note!; The Man Who Murdered Himself, Bernie Wrightson's first professional work	0.12	5.00	12.50	25.00
❑180, Jun 69, GK; NA; BWr; SA	0.12	1.80	4.50	9.00
❑181, Aug 69, NA; BWr	0.15	1.80	4.50	9.00
❑182, Oct 69, WH; AT; NA, The Devil's Doorway; Grave Results!	0.15	1.80	4.50	9.00
❑183, Dec 69, WW; NA; BWr	0.15	1.80	4.50	9.00
❑184, Feb 70, AT; WW; GK; NA; BWr	0.15	1.80	4.50	9.00
❑185, Apr 70, WW; NA; BWr; AW, Voice From The Dead...; The Beautiful Beast	0.15	1.80	4.50	9.00
❑186, Jun 70, NA; BWr	0.15	2.00	5.00	10.00
❑187, Aug 70, WH; AT; NA	0.15	1.20	3.00	6.00
❑188, Oct 70, NA; BWr	0.15	1.80	4.50	9.00
❑189, AT; NA	0.15	0.80	2.00	4.00
❑190, Feb 71, AT; NA	0.15	0.80	2.00	4.00
❑191, Apr 71, NA, No Strings Attached!; Cain's Game Room	0.15	0.80	2.00	4.00
❑192, Jun 71, NA; GM, Fright!; A Witch Must Die!	0.15	0.80	2.00	4.00
❑193, BWr	0.15	0.80	2.00	4.00
❑194, Sep 71, BWr	0.25	0.80	2.00	4.00
❑195, Oct 71, BWr, Swamp Thing prototype?	0.25	2.00	5.00	10.00
❑196, Nov 71, NA	0.25	0.80	2.00	4.00
❑197, Dec 71, NA	0.25	0.80	2.00	4.00
❑198, Jan 72	0.25	0.80	2.00	4.00
❑199, Feb 72, WW; NA; JK	0.25	0.80	2.00	4.00
❑200, Mar 72	0.25	0.80	2.00	4.00
❑201, Apr 72, BWr; SA	0.25	0.80	2.00	4.00
❑202, May 72, SA	0.25	0.80	2.00	4.00
❑203, Jun 72	0.25	0.80	2.00	4.00
❑204, Jul 72, AN; BWr	0.20	1.40	3.50	7.00
❑205, Aug 72	0.20	0.80	2.00	4.00
❑206, Sep 72	0.20	0.80	2.00	4.00
❑207, Oct 72, JSt; BWr; JSn	0.20	0.80	2.00	4.00
❑208, Nov 72	0.20	0.80	2.00	4.00
❑209, Dec 72, AA; BWr	0.20	0.80	2.00	4.00
❑210, Jan 73	0.20	0.80	2.00	4.00
❑211, Feb 73, AA; NR; BWr	0.20	0.80	2.00	4.00
❑212, Mar 73, AN	0.20	0.80	2.00	4.00
❑213, Apr 73, BWr	0.20	0.80	2.00	4.00
❑214, May 73, BWr	0.20	0.80	2.00	4.00
❑215, Jun 73	0.20	0.80	2.00	4.00
❑216, Jul 73	0.20	0.80	2.00	4.00
❑217, Sep 73, BWr (c)	0.20	0.80	2.00	4.00
❑218, Oct 73	0.20	0.80	2.00	4.00
❑219, Nov 73, BWr	0.20	0.80	2.00	4.00
❑220, Dec 73	0.20	0.80	2.00	4.00
❑221, Jan 74, BWr	0.20	0.80	2.00	4.00
❑222, Feb 74	0.20	0.80	2.00	4.00
❑223, Mar 74	0.20	0.80	2.00	4.00
❑224, Apr 74, AN; NA; BWr, A: Phantom Stranger, 100pgs.; Phantom Stranger	0.60	3.00	7.50	15.00

DC tested the waters for a Plastic Man revival in its "Dial 'H' for Hero" series in *House of Mystery* #160 by having Robby Reed turn into the ductile detective when he used his H-dial.

	ORIG	GOOD	FINE	N-MINT
❑225, Jun 74, AN, 100pgs.	0.60	1.80	4.50	9.00
❑226, Aug 74, AA; NR; BWr, Garden, A: Phantom Stranger, 100pgs.	0.60	1.80	4.50	9.00
❑227, Oct 74, NR, 100pgs.	0.60	1.80	4.50	9.00
❑228, Dec 74, AT; NA; NR, 100pgs.	0.60	1.80	4.50	9.00
❑229, Feb 75, 100pgs.	0.60	1.80	4.50	9.00
❑230, Apr 75	0.25	0.60	1.50	3.00
❑231, May 75	0.25	0.60	1.50	3.00
❑232, Jun 75	0.25	0.60	1.50	3.00
❑233, Jul 75	0.25	0.60	1.50	3.00
❑234, Aug 75	0.25	0.60	1.50	3.00
❑235, Sep 75	0.25	0.60	1.50	3.00
❑236, Oct 75, NA; BWr; SD	0.25	0.60	1.50	3.00
❑237, Nov 75	0.25	0.60	1.50	3.00
❑238, Dec 75	0.25	0.60	1.50	3.00
❑239, Feb 76	0.25	0.60	1.50	3.00
❑240, Apr 76	0.30	0.60	1.50	3.00
❑241, May 76	0.30	0.60	1.50	3.00
❑242, Jun 76, The Balloon Vendor!; Blood Money	0.30	0.60	1.50	3.00
❑243, Jul 76, Bicentennial #10	0.30	0.60	1.50	3.00
❑244, Aug 76	0.30	0.60	1.50	3.00
❑245, Sep 76	0.30	0.60	1.50	3.00
❑246, Oct 76	0.30	0.60	1.50	3.00
❑247, Nov 76	0.30	0.60	1.50	3.00
❑248, Dec 76	0.30	0.60	1.50	3.00
❑249, Jan 77	0.30	0.60	1.50	3.00
❑250, Feb 77	0.30	0.60	1.50	3.00
❑251, Mar 77, WW; NA, giant	1.00	0.60	1.50	3.00
❑252, May 77, AN; NA, giant	1.00	0.60	1.50	3.00
❑253, Jul 77, AN; NA, giant	1.00	0.60	1.50	3.00
❑254, Sep 77, WH; AN; SD, giant	1.00	0.60	1.50	3.00
❑255, Nov 77, BWr, giant	1.00	0.60	1.50	3.00
❑256, Jan 78, BWr, giant	1.00	0.60	1.50	3.00
❑257, Mar 78, MG, giant	1.00	0.60	1.50	3.00
❑258, May 78, SD, giant	1.00	0.60	1.50	3.00
❑259, Jul 78, MG; DN, giant	1.00	0.60	1.50	3.00
❑260, Sep 78	1.00	0.60	1.50	3.00
❑261, Oct 78	—	0.60	1.50	3.00
❑262, Nov 78	—	0.60	1.50	3.00
❑263, Dec 78	—	0.60	1.50	3.00
❑264, Jan 79	—	0.60	1.50	3.00
❑265, Feb 79	—	0.60	1.50	3.00
❑266, Mar 79	—	0.60	1.50	3.00
❑267, Apr 79, The Mouse of History	0.40	0.60	1.50	3.00
❑268, May 79	0.40	0.60	1.50	3.00
❑269, Jun 79	0.40	0.60	1.50	3.00
❑270, Jul 79	0.40	0.60	1.50	3.00
❑271, Aug 79	0.40	0.60	1.50	3.00
❑272, Sep 79	0.40	0.60	1.50	3.00
❑273, Oct 79	0.40	0.60	1.50	3.00
❑274, Nov 79, JO	0.40	0.60	1.50	3.00
❑275, Dec 79	0.40	0.60	1.50	3.00
❑276, Jan 80	0.40	0.60	1.50	3.00
❑277, Feb 80	0.40	0.60	1.50	3.00
❑278, Mar 80	0.40	0.60	1.50	3.00
❑279, Apr 80	0.40	0.60	1.50	3.00
❑280, May 80	0.40	0.60	1.50	3.00
❑281, Jun 80	0.40	0.60	1.50	3.00
❑282, Jul 80, JSn	—	0.60	1.50	3.00
❑283, Aug 80	—	0.60	1.50	3.00
❑284, Sep 80	—	0.60	1.50	3.00
❑285, Oct 80	—	0.60	1.50	3.00
❑286, Nov 80	—	0.60	1.50	3.00
❑287, Dec 80	—	0.60	1.50	3.00
❑288, Jan 81	—	0.60	1.50	3.00
❑289, Feb 81, 1: I, Vampire	0.50	0.60	1.50	3.00
❑290, Mar 81, I, Vampire	0.50	0.60	1.50	3.00
❑291, Apr 81, I, Vampire	0.50	0.60	1.50	3.00
❑292, May 81	0.50	0.60	1.50	3.00
❑293, Jun 81, I, Vampire	0.50	0.60	1.50	3.00

	ORIG	GOOD	FINE	N-MINT
❑294, Jul 81	0.50	0.60	1.50	3.00
❑295, Aug 81	0.50	0.60	1.50	3.00
❑296, Sep 81	0.50	0.60	1.50	3.00
❑297, Oct 81	0.50	0.60	1.50	3.00
❑298, Nov 81	0.60	0.60	1.50	3.00
❑299, Dec 81, I, Vampire	0.60	0.60	1.50	3.00
❑300, Jan 82	0.60	0.60	1.50	3.00
❑301, Feb 82	0.60	0.60	1.50	3.00
❑302, Mar 82, I, Vampire	0.60	0.60	1.50	3.00
❑303, Apr 82, I, Vampire	0.60	0.60	1.50	3.00
❑304, May 82, I, Vampire	0.60	0.60	1.50	3.00
❑305, Jun 82, I, Vampire	0.60	0.60	1.50	3.00
❑306, Jul 82, I, Vampire	0.60	0.60	1.50	3.00
❑307, Aug 82, I, Vampire	0.60	0.60	1.50	3.00
❑308, Sep 82, I, Vampire	0.60	0.60	1.50	3.00
❑309, Oct 82, I, Vampire	0.60	0.60	1.50	3.00
❑310, Nov 82, I, Vampire	0.60	0.60	1.50	3.00
❑311, Dec 82, I, Vampire	0.60	0.60	1.50	3.00
❑312, Jan 83, I, Vampire	0.60	0.60	1.50	3.00
❑313, Feb 83	0.60	0.60	1.50	3.00
❑314, Mar 83, I, Vampire	0.60	0.60	1.50	3.00
❑315, Apr 83, I, Vampire	0.60	0.60	1.50	3.00
❑316, May 83	0.60	0.60	1.50	3.00
❑317, Jun 83	0.60	0.60	1.50	3.00
❑318, Jul 83, I, Vampire	0.60	0.60	1.50	3.00
❑319, Aug 83, D: I, Vampire	0.60	0.60	1.50	3.00
❑320, Sep 83	0.60	0.60	1.50	3.00
❑321, Oct 83, Final Issue	0.60	0.60	1.50	3.00

HOUSE OF SECRETS
DC

	ORIG	GOOD	FINE	N-MINT
❑61, 1: Eclipso	0.12	24.00	60.00	120.00
❑62, Sep 63	0.12	15.00	37.50	75.00
❑63, Nov 63	0.12	12.00	30.00	60.00
❑64, Jan 64	0.12	12.00	30.00	60.00
❑65, Mar 64	0.12	12.00	30.00	60.00
❑66, May 64, Eclipso cover	0.12	15.00	37.50	75.00
❑67, Jul 64	0.12	10.00	25.00	50.00
❑68, Sep 64	0.12	9.60	24.00	48.00
❑69, Nov 64	0.12	9.60	24.00	48.00
❑70, Jan 65	0.12	9.60	24.00	48.00
❑71, Mar 65	0.12	9.60	24.00	48.00
❑72, May 65, Eclipso	0.12	9.60	24.00	48.00
❑73, Jul 65, 1: Prince Ra-Man	0.12	9.60	24.00	48.00
❑74, Sep 65, Eclipso	0.12	9.60	24.00	48.00
❑75, Nov 65	0.12	9.60	24.00	48.00
❑76, Jan 66, Eclipso	0.12	9.60	24.00	48.00
❑77, Mar 66	0.12	9.60	24.00	48.00
❑78, May 66	0.12	9.60	24.00	48.00
❑79, Jul 66	0.12	9.60	24.00	48.00
❑80, Sep 66	0.12	11.00	27.50	55.00
❑81, Sep 69, 1: Abel, Mystery format begins	0.15	2.40	6.00	12.00
❑82, Nov 69, NA	0.15	1.80	4.50	9.00
❑83, Jan 70, ATh	0.15	1.80	4.50	9.00
❑84, Mar 70, NA (c)	0.15	1.80	4.50	9.00
❑85, May 70, GK; NA	0.15	1.80	4.50	9.00
❑86, Jul 70, GM, NA (c), Strain; The Ballard Of Little Joe	0.15	1.80	4.50	9.00
❑87, Sep 70, BWr, NA (c)	0.15	1.80	4.50	9.00
❑88, Nov 70	0.15	1.80	4.50	9.00
❑89, Jan 71, GM	0.15	1.80	4.50	9.00
❑90, Mar 71, NA; GM; RB, 1st Buckler DC art	0.15	1.80	4.50	9.00
❑91, May 71, WW; NA; MA	0.15	1.80	4.50	9.00
❑92, Jul 71, DD (w), Swamp Thing; After I Die, 1: Swamp Thing	0.15	80.00	200.00	400.00
❑93, Sep 71, JA; BWr	—	1.00	2.50	5.00
❑94, Nov 71, BWr; ATh	—	1.00	2.50	5.00
❑95, Jan 72	—	1.00	2.50	5.00
❑96, Mar 72	—	1.00	2.50	5.00
❑97, May 72	—	1.00	2.50	5.00
❑98, Jul 72	—	1.00	2.50	5.00
❑99, Sep 72	—	1.00	2.50	5.00
❑100, Oct 72	—	1.00	2.50	5.00
❑101, Nov 72	—	0.80	2.00	4.00
❑102, Dec 72	—	0.80	2.00	4.00
❑103, Jan 73	—	0.80	2.00	4.00
❑104, Feb 73	0.20	0.80	2.00	4.00
❑105, Mar 73	0.20	0.80	2.00	4.00
❑106, Apr 73	0.20	0.80	2.00	4.00
❑107, May 73	0.20	0.80	2.00	4.00
❑108, Jun 73	0.20	0.80	2.00	4.00
❑109, Jul 73	0.20	0.80	2.00	4.00
❑110, Aug 73	0.20	0.80	2.00	4.00
❑111, Sep 73	0.20	0.60	1.50	3.00
❑112, Oct 73	0.20	0.60	1.50	3.00
❑113, Nov 73	0.20	0.60	1.50	3.00
❑114, Dec 73	0.20	0.60	1.50	3.00
❑115, Jan 74	0.20	0.60	1.50	3.00
❑116, Feb 74	0.20	0.60	1.50	3.00
❑117, Mar 74, AN; AA	0.20	0.60	1.50	3.00
❑118, Apr 74	0.20	0.60	1.50	3.00
❑119, May 74	0.20	0.60	1.50	3.00
❑120, Jun 74	0.20	0.60	1.50	3.00
❑121, Jul 74	0.20	0.60	1.50	3.00
❑122, Aug 74	0.20	0.60	1.50	3.00
❑123, Sep 74, ATh	0.20	0.60	1.50	3.00
❑124, Oct 74	—	0.60	1.50	3.00
❑125, Nov 74	—	0.60	1.50	3.00
❑126, Dec 74	—	0.60	1.50	3.00
❑127, Jan 75	0.25	0.60	1.50	3.00
❑128, Feb 75	0.25	0.60	1.50	3.00
❑129, Mar 75	0.25	0.60	1.50	3.00
❑130, Apr 75	0.25	0.60	1.50	3.00
❑131, May 75	0.25	0.60	1.50	3.00
❑132, Jun 75	0.25	0.60	1.50	3.00
❑133, Jul 75	0.25	0.60	1.50	3.00
❑134, Aug 75	0.25	0.60	1.50	3.00
❑135, Sep 75	0.25	0.60	1.50	3.00
❑136, Nov 75	0.25	0.60	1.50	3.00
❑137, Jan 76	0.25	0.60	1.50	3.00
❑138, Mar 76	0.25	0.60	1.50	3.00
❑139, May 76	0.25	0.60	1.50	3.00
❑140, Jul 76, O: Patchwork Man	0.25	0.60	1.50	3.00
❑141, Sep 76, O: Patchwork Man	0.25	0.60	1.50	3.00
❑142, Nov 76	—	0.60	1.50	3.00
❑143, Jan 77	—	0.60	1.50	3.00
❑144, Mar 77	—	0.60	1.50	3.00
❑145, May 77	—	0.60	1.50	3.00
❑146, Jul 77	—	0.60	1.50	3.00
❑147, Sep 77	—	0.60	1.50	3.00
❑148, Nov 77	—	0.60	1.50	3.00
❑149, Jan 78	—	0.60	1.50	3.00
❑150, Mar 78	0.35	0.60	1.50	3.00
❑151, May 78, MG	—	0.60	1.50	3.00
❑152, Jul 78	—	0.60	1.50	3.00
❑153, Sep 78	—	0.60	1.50	3.00
❑154, Nov 78, Series continued in The Unexpected	0.50	0.60	1.50	3.00

HOUSE OF SECRETS (2ND SERIES)
DC

	ORIG	GOOD	FINE	N-MINT
❑1, Oct 96, Foundation, Part 1	2.50	0.80	2.00	4.00
❑2, Nov 96, Foundation, Part 2	2.50	0.60	1.50	3.00
❑3, Dec 96, Foundation, Part 3	2.50	0.60	1.50	3.00
❑4, Jan 97, Foundation, Part 4	2.50	0.60	1.50	3.00
❑5, Feb 97, Foundation Epilogue	2.50	0.60	1.50	3.00
❑6, Mar 97, Other Rooms	2.50	0.60	1.50	3.00
❑7, Apr 97, Blueprint: Foundation A	2.50	0.60	1.50	3.00
❑8, May 97, The Road To You - Getting There, Part 1	2.50	0.60	1.50	3.00
❑9, Jun 97, The Road To You - Getting There, Part 2	2.50	0.60	1.50	3.00
❑10, Jul 97, The Road To You - Getting There, Part 3	2.50	0.60	1.50	3.00
❑11, Aug 97, The Book of Law, Part 1	2.50	0.60	1.50	3.00
❑12, Sep 97, The Book of Law, Part 2	2.50	0.60	1.50	3.00
❑13, Oct 97, The Book of Law, Part 3	2.50	0.60	1.50	3.00
❑14, Nov 97, The Book of Law, Part 4	2.50	0.60	1.50	3.00
❑15, Dec 97, The Book of Law, Part 5	2.50	0.60	1.50	3.00
❑16, Feb 98, The Book of Law Epilogue	2.50	0.60	1.50	3.00
❑17, Mar 98, The Road To You: Leaving There, Part 1, covers form triptych	2.50	0.60	1.50	3.00
❑18, Apr 98, The Road To You: Leaving There, Part 2, covers form triptych	2.50	0.60	1.50	3.00
❑19, May 98, The Road To You: Leaving There, Part 3, covers form triptych	2.50	0.60	1.50	3.00
❑20, Jun 98, Other Rooms	2.50	0.60	1.50	3.00
❑21, Jul 98, Basement, Part 1	2.50	0.50	1.25	2.50
❑22, Aug 98, Basement, Part 2	2.50	0.50	1.25	2.50
❑23, Sep 98, Basement, Part 3	2.50	0.50	1.25	2.50
❑24, Nov 98, Attic	2.50	0.50	1.25	2.50
❑25, Dec 98, Blueprint: Elevation B	2.50	0.50	1.25	2.50

HOUSEWIVES AT PLAY
EROS

Value: Cover or less

❑1	2.95
❑2	2.95
❑3	2.95

HOWARD THE DUCK
MARVEL

	ORIG	GOOD	FINE	N-MINT
❑1, Jan 76, FB, Howard The Barbarian, A: Spider-Man; 1: Beverly	0.25	1.60	4.00	8.00
❑2, Mar 76, FB, Cry Turnip!	0.25	0.40	1.00	2.00
❑3, May 76, JB, Four Feathers of Death!	0.25	0.40	1.00	2.00

	ORIG	GOOD	FINE	N-MINT
❑4, Jul 76, GC, The Sleep of the Just	0.25	0.40	1.00	2.00
❑5, Sep 76, GC, I Want Mo-o-oney!	0.30	0.40	1.00	2.00
❑6, Nov 76, GC, The Secret House of Forbidden Cookies!	0.30	0.40	1.00	2.00
❑7, Dec 76, GC, The Way The Cookie Crumbles!	0.30	0.40	1.00	2.00
❑8, Jan 77, GC, Open Season!	0.30	0.40	1.00	2.00
❑9, Feb 77, GC, Scandal Plucks Duck	0.30	0.40	1.00	2.00
❑10, Mar 77, GC	0.30	0.40	1.00	2.00
❑11, Apr 77, GC, Quack-Up	0.30	0.40	1.00	2.00
❑12, May 77, GC, 1: Kiss (rock group)	0.30	0.80	2.00	4.00
❑13, Jun 77, GC, Rock, Roll Over, and Writhe; A Duck Possessed, A: Kiss (rock group)	0.30	0.60	1.50	3.00
❑14, Jul 77, GC, A Duck Possessed!	0.30	0.30	0.75	1.50
❑15, Aug 77, GC, The Island of Dr. Bong, 1: Doctor Bong	0.30	0.30	0.75	1.50
❑16, Sep 77, Zen and the Art of Comic Book Writing, O: Doctor Bong, all-text issue	0.30	0.30	0.75	1.50
❑17, Oct 77, GC, Doctor Bong!, O: Doctor Bong	0.30	0.30	0.75	1.50
❑18, Nov 77, GC, Metamorphosis	0.35	0.30	0.75	1.50
❑19, Dec 77, GC, Howard The Human	0.35	0.30	0.75	1.50
❑20, Jan 78, GC, Scrubba-Dub Death!, V: Sudol	0.35	0.30	0.75	1.50
❑21, Feb 78, CI, If You Knew Soofi...!, V: Soofi	0.35	0.30	0.75	1.50
❑22, Mar 78, VM, May The Farce Be With You!	0.35	0.30	0.75	1.50
❑23, Apr 78, VM, Star Waaugh	0.35	0.30	0.75	1.50
❑24, May 78, GC, The Night After You Save The Universe?	0.35	0.30	0.75	1.50
❑25, Jun 78, GC, Getting Smooth!, A: Ringmaster	0.35	0.30	0.75	1.50
❑26, Jul 78, GC, Repercussions...!, A: Ringmaster	0.35	0.30	0.75	1.50
❑27, Sep 78, GC, Circus Maximus, A: Ringmaster	0.35	0.30	0.75	1.50
❑28, Nov 78, CI, Cooking With Gas	0.35	0.30	0.75	1.50
❑29, Jan 79, ME (w), Help Stamp Out Ducks!	0.35	0.30	0.75	1.50
❑30, Mar 79, GC, If This Be Bongsday!, V: Doctor Bong	0.35	0.30	0.75	1.50
❑31, May 79, GC; AM, The Final Bong!, V: Doctor Bong	0.40	0.30	0.75	1.50
❑32, Jan 86, PS, Going Underground, O: Howard the Duck	0.65	0.30	0.75	1.50
❑33, Sep 86, VM, Material Duck, Final Issue	1.50	0.30	0.75	1.50
❑Anl 1, Oct 77, VM, Thief Of Bagmom!	0.50	0.30	0.75	1.50

HOWARD THE DUCK (MAGAZINE)
MARVEL

	ORIG	GOOD	FINE	N-MINT
❑1, Oct 79, VM, Thief of Bagmom!; Calling All Carpets!, contains nudity	1.00	0.60	1.50	3.00
❑2, Dec 79, KJ; GC, Animal Indecency; The Crash of '79	1.25	0.40	1.00	2.00
❑3, Feb 80, GC, A Christmas for Carol; Duck Soup	1.25	0.40	1.00	2.00
❑4, Mar 80, KJ; JB; GC, The Maltese Cockroach; The Playduck Interview, A: Beatles; A: Kiss	1.25	0.80	2.00	4.00
❑5, May 80	1.25	0.40	1.00	2.00
❑6, Jul 80	1.25	0.40	1.00	2.00
❑7, Sep 80, GC, Of Dice & Ducks!; Street People, A: Man-Thing	1.25	0.40	1.00	2.00
❑8, Nov 80, MR; GC, The Grey Panther; How the Duck Got his Pants, Batman parody	1.25	0.40	1.00	2.00
❑9, Mar 81	1.25	0.40	1.00	2.00

HOWARD THE DUCK HOLIDAY SPECIAL
MARVEL

Value: Cover or less ❑1, Feb 97, Wreck the Malls with Hydra's Folly! ... 2.50

HOWARD THE DUCK: THE MOVIE
MARVEL

	ORIG	GOOD	FINE	N-MINT
❑1, Dec 86, O: Howard the Duck	0.75	0.20	0.50	1.00
❑2, Jan 87	0.75	0.20	0.50	1.00
❑3, Feb 87, Duck Day Afternoon	0.75	0.20	0.50	1.00

HOWL
ETERNITY

Value: Cover or less ❑2, b&w; Reprint ... 2.25

❑1, b&w; Reprint ... 2.25

HOW THE WEST WAS WON
GOLD KEY

	ORIG	GOOD	FINE	N-MINT
❑1, Jul 63, nn; movie Adaptation	0.12	3.60	9.00	18.00

HOW TO DRAW COMICS COMIC, THE
SOLSON

Value: Cover or less ❑1, JR2; JBy ... 1.95

HOW TO DRAW FELIX THE CAT AND HIS FRIENDS
FELIX

Value: Cover or less ❑1, b&w ... 2.25

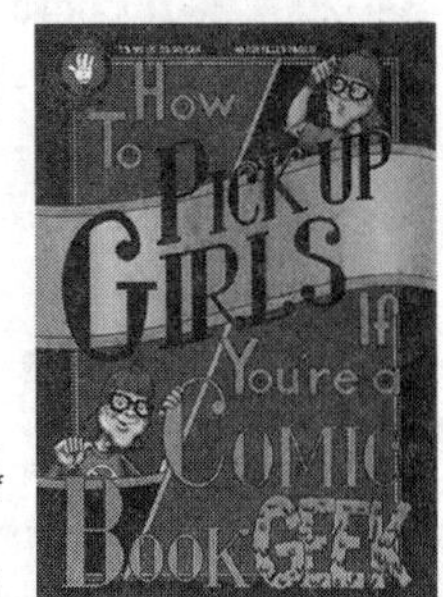

Rich Koslowski introduced his 3 Geeks in the color one-shot *How to Pick Up Girls If You're a Comic Book Geek.*

© 1996 Rich Koslowski (3 Finger Prints)

HOW TO DRAW TEENAGE MUTANT NINJA TURTLES
SOLSON

Value: Cover or less ❑1 ... 2.25

HOW TO PICK UP GIRLS IF YOU'RE A COMIC BOOK GEEK
3 FINGER PRINTS

Value: Cover or less ❑1, nn; cardstock cover ... 3.95

HOW TO PUBLISH COMICS
SOLSON

Value: Cover or less ❑1 ... 2.00

HUCKLEBERRY HOUND & QUICK DRAW MCGRAW GIANT-SIZE FLIP BOOK
HARVEY

Value: Cover or less ❑1 ... 2.25

HUEY, DEWEY, AND LOUIE JUNIOR WOODCHUCKS
GOLD KEY

	ORIG	GOOD	FINE	N-MINT
❑1	0.15	7.00	17.50	35.00
❑2	0.15	3.60	9.00	18.00
❑3	0.15	3.00	7.50	15.00
❑4	0.15	2.40	6.00	12.00
❑5	0.15	2.40	6.00	12.00
❑6	0.15	2.40	6.00	12.00
❑7	0.15	2.40	6.00	12.00
❑8	0.15	2.40	6.00	12.00
❑9	0.15	2.40	6.00	12.00
❑10	0.15	2.40	6.00	12.00
❑11	0.15	2.00	5.00	10.00
❑12, Jan 72, CB (w), Hound of the Moaning Hills; Storm Dancers	0.15	2.00	5.00	10.00
❑13, Mar 72	0.15	2.00	5.00	10.00
❑14, May 72	0.15	2.00	5.00	10.00
❑15, Jul 72	0.15	2.00	5.00	10.00
❑16, Sep 72	0.15	2.00	5.00	10.00
❑17, Nov 72	—	2.00	5.00	10.00
❑18	—	2.00	5.00	10.00
❑19	—	2.00	5.00	10.00
❑20	—	2.00	5.00	10.00
❑21	—	1.60	4.00	8.00
❑22	—	1.60	4.00	8.00
❑23	—	1.60	4.00	8.00
❑24	—	1.60	4.00	8.00
❑25	—	1.60	4.00	8.00
❑26	—	1.60	4.00	8.00
❑27	—	1.60	4.00	8.00
❑28	—	1.60	4.00	8.00
❑29	—	1.60	4.00	8.00
❑30	—	1.60	4.00	8.00
❑31	—	1.60	4.00	8.00
❑32	—	1.60	4.00	8.00
❑33	—	1.60	4.00	8.00
❑34	—	1.60	4.00	8.00
❑35	—	1.60	4.00	8.00
❑36	—	1.60	4.00	8.00
❑37	—	1.60	4.00	8.00
❑38	—	1.60	4.00	8.00
❑39	—	1.60	4.00	8.00
❑40	—	1.60	4.00	8.00
❑41	—	1.20	3.00	6.00
❑42	—	1.20	3.00	6.00
❑43	—	1.20	3.00	6.00
❑44	—	1.20	3.00	6.00
❑45	—	1.20	3.00	6.00
❑46	—	1.20	3.00	6.00
❑47	—	1.20	3.00	6.00
❑48, Feb 78	0.35	1.20	3.00	6.00
❑49, Apr 78	0.35	1.20	3.00	6.00
❑50, Jun 78	—	1.20	3.00	6.00
❑51, Aug 78	—	1.20	3.00	6.00
❑52, Sep 78	—	1.20	3.00	6.00
❑53, Dec 78	—	1.20	3.00	6.00
❑54	—	1.20	3.00	6.00
❑55	—	1.20	3.00	6.00

	ORIG	GOOD	FINE	N-MINT
❑56	—	1.20	3.00	6.00
❑57	—	1.20	3.00	6.00
❑58	—	1.20	3.00	6.00
❑59	—	1.20	3.00	6.00
❑60	—	1.20	3.00	6.00
❑61	—	0.80	2.00	4.00
❑62	—	0.80	2.00	4.00
❑63	—	0.80	2.00	4.00
❑64	—	0.80	2.00	4.00
❑65	—	0.80	2.00	4.00
❑66	—	0.80	2.00	4.00
❑67	—	0.80	2.00	4.00
❑68	—	0.80	2.00	4.00
❑69	—	0.80	2.00	4.00
❑70	—	0.80	2.00	4.00
❑71	—	0.80	2.00	4.00
❑72	—	0.80	2.00	4.00
❑73	—	0.80	2.00	4.00
❑74	—	0.80	2.00	4.00
❑75	—	0.80	2.00	4.00
❑76	—	0.80	2.00	4.00
❑77	—	0.80	2.00	4.00
❑78	—	0.80	2.00	4.00
❑79	—	0.80	2.00	4.00
❑80	—	0.80	2.00	4.00
❑81	—	0.80	2.00	4.00

HUGGA BUNCH
MARVEL

	ORIG	GOOD	FINE	N-MINT
❑1	0.75	0.20	0.50	1.00
❑2	0.75	0.20	0.50	1.00
❑3	0.75	0.20	0.50	1.00
❑4, Storm Watch	0.75	0.20	0.50	1.00
❑5	1.00	0.20	0.50	1.00
❑6	1.00	0.20	0.50	1.00

HUGO
FANTAGRAPHICS

Value: Cover or less

	ORIG
❑1	1.95
❑2	1.95
❑3, Jul 85, My Bonnie Lies Under the Ocean	1.95

HULK
MARVEL

	ORIG	GOOD	FINE	N-MINT
❑1, Apr 99, JBy (w), The Gathering Storm, wraparound cover	2.99	0.60	1.50	3.00
❑1/A, Apr 99, JBy (w), The Gathering Storm, DFE gold foil cover; Signed by Ron Garney	—	1.60	4.00	8.00
❑1/Aut, Apr 99, JBy (w), The Gathering Storm, Signed by Ron Garney	—	1.60	4.00	8.00
❑1/GO, Apr 99, JBy (w), The Gathering Storm, DFE gold foil cover	—	1.00	2.50	5.00
❑2, May 99, JBy (w)	1.99	0.40	1.00	2.00
❑3, Jun 99, JBy (w)	1.99	0.40	1.00	2.00
❑4, Jul 99, JBy (w)	1.99	0.40	1.00	2.00
❑5, Aug 99, JBy (w), A: Avengers	1.99	0.40	1.00	2.00
❑6, Sep 99, JBy (w), A: Man-Thing	1.99	0.40	1.00	2.00
❑7, Oct 99, JBy (w), A: Avengers; A: Man-Thing	1.99	0.40	1.00	2.00
❑8, Nov 99, V: Wolverine	1.99	0.40	1.00	2.00
❑9, Dec 99	1.99	0.40	1.00	2.00
❑10, Jan 00	—	0.45	1.13	2.25
❑11, Feb 00	—	0.45	1.13	2.25
❑12, Mar 00	—	0.45	1.13	2.25
❑13, Apr 00	—	0.45	1.13	2.25
❑14, May 00	—	0.45	1.13	2.25
❑15, Jun 00	—	0.45	1.13	2.25
❑16, Jul 00	—	0.45	1.13	2.25
❑17, Aug 00	—	0.45	1.13	2.25
❑18, Sep 00, The Dogs of War, Part 5	2.25	0.45	1.13	2.25
❑19, Oct 00, The Dogs of War, Part 6	2.25	0.45	1.13	2.25
❑20, Nov 00, The Dogs of War, Part 7	2.25	0.45	1.13	2.25
❑21, Dec 00, Maximum Security; The Truth is Really Out There	2.25	0.45	1.13	2.25
❑22, Jan 01, Disorganized Crime, Part 1	2.25	0.45	1.13	2.25
❑23, Feb 01, Disorganized Crime, Part 2: Chicago Dope	2.25	0.45	1.13	2.25
❑24, Mar 01, JR2, Dear Betty ..., A: Thunderbolt Ross; A: Abomination, lower cover price; part of Marvel's Slashback program	1.99	0.40	1.00	1.99
❑25, Apr 01, JR2, Always on My Mind, A: Abomination, double-sized	2.99	0.60	1.50	2.99
❑26, May 01, Do You Know Where You're Going?	2.25	0.45	1.13	2.25
❑27	2.25	0.45	1.13	2.25
❑28	2.25	0.45	1.13	2.25
❑29	2.25	0.45	1.13	2.25
❑30	2.25	0.45	1.13	2.25
❑Anl 1999	3.50	0.70	1.75	3.50
❑Anl 2000, Basic Instinct, A: Avengers; A: She-Hulk	3.50	0.70	1.75	3.50

HULK, THE
MARVEL

	ORIG	GOOD	FINE	N-MINT
❑10, Aug 78, format changes to color magazine; Title changes to The Hulk	1.50	0.80	2.00	4.00
❑11, Oct 78, GC, The Boy Who Cried Hulk; Graven Image of Death	1.50	1.00	2.50	5.00
❑12, Dec 78	1.50	0.60	1.50	3.00
❑13, Feb 79	1.50	0.60	1.50	3.00
❑14, Apr 79, A Cure for Chaos; Countdown to Dark	1.50	0.60	1.50	3.00
❑15, Jun 79, The Top Secret!; An Eclipse Waning	1.50	0.60	1.50	3.00
❑16, Aug 79	1.50	0.60	1.50	3.00
❑17, Oct 79	1.50	0.60	1.50	3.00
❑18, Dec 79, Cast Away; Shadows in the Heart of the City	1.50	0.60	1.50	3.00
❑19, Feb 80, Master Mind; It's a Monster ...	1.50	0.60	1.50	3.00
❑20, Apr 80	1.50	0.60	1.50	3.00
❑21, Jun 80, BMc; HC, Into the Myth Realm; Dominic Fortune: All in Color for a Crime	1.50	0.60	1.50	3.00
❑22, Aug 80, The Failure of Hydropolis; Ghoul of my Dreams	1.50	0.60	1.50	3.00
❑23, Oct 80, A Very Personal Hell; Clothes Call	1.50	0.60	1.50	3.00
❑24, Dec 80, HC; GC, The Man Who Would be President; It's Not Easy Being Green	1.50	0.60	1.50	3.00
❑25, Feb 81, AA; GC, Dreans of Iron...Dreams of Steel!; Carnival of Fools	1.50	0.60	1.50	3.00
❑26, Apr 81, GC, Namaste; Where Troops Have Encamped	1.50	0.60	1.50	3.00
❑27, Jun 81, GC, Feudin'; Happy Accidents, Final Issue	1.50	0.60	1.50	3.00

HULK 2099
MARVEL

Value: Cover or less

	ORIG
❑1, Dec 94, No Exit	2.50
❑2, Jan 95	1.50
❑3, Feb 95	1.50
❑4, Mar 95	1.50
❑5, Apr 95	1.50
❑6, May 95	1.50
❑7, Jun 95	1.95
❑8, Jul 95, V: Doom 2099	1.95
❑9, Aug 95	1.95
❑10, Sep 95, Final Issue; continued in 2099 A.D. Apocalypse #1	1.95

HULK/PITT
MARVEL

Value: Cover or less

	ORIG
❑1, Dec 96, nn	5.99

HULK: PROJECT H.I.D.E.
MARVEL

	ORIG	GOOD	FINE	N-MINT
❑1, Aug 98, nn; no cover price; prototype for children's comic	—	0.20	0.50	1.00

HULK SMASH
MARVEL

Value: Cover or less

	ORIG
❑1, Mar 01	2.99
❑2, Apr 01	2.99

HULK VERSUS THING
MARVEL

Value: Cover or less

	ORIG
❑1, Dec 99, JK; JB; JSn, The Hulk vs. The Thing; The Avengers Take Over, Reprints Fantastic Four #24, 26, 112, Marvel Features #11	3.99

HUMAN FLY, THE
MARVEL

	ORIG	GOOD	FINE	N-MINT
❑1, Sep 77, Death-Walk!; The Making of a Hero! (text), A: Spider-Man; 1: Human Fly	0.30	0.50	1.25	2.50
❑2, Oct 77, CI, Race to Destruction!, A: Ghost Rider	0.30	0.40	1.00	2.00
❑3, Nov 77	0.35	0.30	0.75	1.50
❑4, Dec 77	0.35	0.30	0.75	1.50
❑5, Jan 78	0.35	0.30	0.75	1.50
❑6, Feb 78	0.35	0.30	0.75	1.50
❑7, Mar 78	0.35	0.30	0.75	1.50
❑8, Apr 78	0.35	0.30	0.75	1.50
❑9, May 78, A: Daredevil	0.35	0.30	0.75	1.50
❑10, Jun 78	0.35	0.30	0.75	1.50
❑11, Jul 78	0.35	0.30	0.75	1.50
❑12, Aug 78	0.35	0.30	0.75	1.50
❑13, Sep 78	0.35	0.30	0.75	1.50
❑14, Oct 78	0.35	0.30	0.75	1.50
❑15, Nov 78	0.35	0.30	0.75	1.50
❑16, Dec 78	0.35	0.30	0.75	1.50
❑17, Jan 79	0.35	0.30	0.75	1.50
❑18, Feb 79	0.35	0.30	0.75	1.50
❑19, Mar 79, Final Issue	0.35	0.30	0.75	1.50

HUMAN GARGOYLES, THE
ETERNITY

Value: Cover or less

	ORIG
❑1, Jun 88, b&w	1.95
❑2, Aug 88, b&w	1.95
❑3, b&w	1.95
❑4, b&w	1.95

HUMAN HEAD COMIX
ICONOGRAFIX

Value: Cover or less

	ORIG
❑1, b&w	2.50

HUMAN POWERHOUSE, THE
PURE IMAGINATION

Value: Cover or less

	ORIG
❑1, End of A Legend, b&w	2.00

HUMAN TARGET
DC

Value: Cover or less

	ORIG
❑1, Apr 99	2.95
❑2, May 99	2.95
❑3, Jun 99	2.95
❑4, Jul 99	2.95

HUMAN TARGET SPECIAL
DC

Value: Cover or less

❑1, Nov 91, DG, The Mack Attack Contract, One-Shot 2.00

HUMAN TORCH, THE (2ND SERIES)
MARVEL

	ORIG	GOOD	FINE	N-MINT
❑1, Sep 74, JK, Johnny Storm, The Human Torch, Torch vs. Torch (reprinted from Strange Tales)	0.25	1.00	2.50	5.00
❑2, Nov 74, JK, Prisoner Of The Wizard	0.25	0.60	1.50	3.00
❑3, Jan 75, JK, Prisoner of the 5th Dimension!; Reptile's Revenge!, Reprints Torch story from Strange Tales #103, Sub-Mariner #23	0.25	0.60	1.50	3.00
❑4, Mar 75	0.25	0.60	1.50	3.00
❑5, May 75	0.25	0.60	1.50	3.00
❑6, Jul 75	0.25	0.60	1.50	3.00
❑7, Sep 75	0.25	0.60	1.50	3.00
❑8, Nov 75, JK, The Painter Of A Thousand Perils!, Final Issue	0.25	0.60	1.50	3.00

HUMAN TORCH COMICS
MARVEL

Value: Cover or less

❑1, BEv (w), A: Rathia; A: Namor 3.99

HUMMINGBIRD
SLAVE LABOR

Value: Cover or less

❑1, Jun 96, Trouble; Jack Shit 4.95

HUMONGOUS MAN
ALTERNATIVE

Value: Cover or less

❑1, Sep 97, Deceiving Appearances, b&w 2.25

❑2, Nov 97, b&w 2.25

HUMOR ON THE CUTTING...EDGE
EDGE

Value: Cover or less

❑1, b&w 2.95

❑2, b&w 2.95

❑3, b&w 2.95

❑4, b&w 2.95

HUNCHBACK OF NOTRE DAME, THE (DISNEY'S...)
MARVEL

Value: Cover or less

❑1, Jul 96, cardstock cover; adapts movie; square binding 4.95

HUNTER'S HEART
DC

Value: Cover or less

❑1, b&w; digest 5.95

❑2, b&w; digest 5.95

❑3, b&w; digest 5.95

HUNT FOR BLACK WIDOW, THE
FLEETWAY

Value: Cover or less

❑1, Judge Dredd 2.95

HUNTING, THE
NORTHSTAR

Value: Cover or less

❑1, Nov 93 .... 3.95

HUNTRESS, THE
DC

	ORIG	GOOD	FINE	N-MINT
❑1, Apr 89, Darker Still, 1: The Huntress III (Helena Bertinelli)	1.00	0.40	1.00	2.00
❑2, May 89, JSa, Uneasy Lies The Head...	1.00	0.35	0.88	1.75
❑3, Jun 89	1.00	0.30	0.75	1.50
❑4, Jul 89	1.00	0.30	0.75	1.50
❑5, Aug 89	1.00	0.30	0.75	1.50
❑6, Sep 89	1.00	0.25	0.63	1.25
❑7, Oct 89	1.00	0.25	0.63	1.25
❑8, Nov 89	1.00	0.25	0.63	1.25
❑9, Dec 89	1.00	0.25	0.63	1.25
❑10, Jan 90	1.00	0.25	0.63	1.25
❑11, Feb 90	1.00	0.25	0.63	1.25
❑12, Mar 90	1.00	0.25	0.63	1.25
❑13, Apr 90	1.00	0.25	0.63	1.25
❑14, May 90, JSa, Networking	1.00	0.25	0.63	1.25
❑15, Jun 90	1.25	0.25	0.63	1.25
❑16, Jul 90	1.25	0.25	0.63	1.25
❑17, Aug 90, A: Batman	1.25	0.25	0.63	1.25
❑18, Sep 90, A: Batman	1.25	0.25	0.63	1.25
❑19, Oct 90, A: Batman, Final Issue	1.25	0.25	0.63	1.25

HUNTRESS, THE (MINI-SERIES)
DC

Value: Cover or less

❑1, Jun 94, Darker Still 1.50

❑2, Jul 94 .... 1.50

❑3, Aug 94 .... 1.50

❑4, Sep 94 .... 1.50

HUP
LAST GASP

Value: Cover or less

❑1, b&w 2.50

❑2, The Mighty Power Fems Versus The Horrible Homunculi; If I Were a King 2.50

❑3 .... 2.50

❑4, Can You Stand Alone And Face The Universe?; Academy Awards 2.95

HURRICANE GIRLS
ANTARCTIC

	ORIG	GOOD	FINE	N-MINT
❑1, Jul 95	2.95	0.70	1.75	3.50
❑2, Sep 95	2.95	0.70	1.75	3.50
❑3, Nov 95	2.95	0.70	1.75	3.50
❑4	2.95	0.70	1.75	3.50
❑5	2.95	0.70	1.75	3.50
❑6	2.95	0.70	1.75	3.50
❑7, Aug 96, Final Issue	2.95	0.70	1.75	3.50

A new Hulk for the late 21st century joined other heroes of that era as part of Marvel's 2099 line.

© 1994 Marvel Comics

HURRICANE LEROUX
INFERNO

Value: Cover or less

❑1, Bayou Tapestry, 1: Hurricane LeRoux 2.50

HUSTLER COMIX
L.F.P.

Value: Cover or less

❑1, Spr 97, adult; magazine 4.99

❑2, Sum 97, adult; magazine .. 4.99

❑3, Fal 97, adult; magazine 4.99

❑4, Win 97, adult; magazine 4.99

HUSTLER COMIX (VOL. 2)
L.F.P.

Value: Cover or less

❑1, Spr 98, Venusian Assault; Dead Girl, adult; magazine .. 4.99

❑2, May 98, adult; magazine ... 4.99

❑3, Jul 98, adult; magazine 4.99

❑4, Sep 98, adult; magazine ... 4.99

❑5, Nov 98, adult; Final Issue; magazine 4.99

HUSTLER COMIX XXX
L.F.P.

Value: Cover or less

❑1, Jan 99, adult; magazine 5.99

HUTCH OWEN'S WORKING HARD
NEW HAT

Value: Cover or less

❑1, b&w 3.95

HY-BREED, THE
DIVISION

	ORIG	GOOD	FINE	N-MINT
❑3, b&w	2.25	0.45	1.13	2.25
❑4, b&w	2.90	0.60	1.50	3.00
❑5, b&w	2.50	0.50	1.25	2.50
❑6, b&w	2.50	0.50	1.25	2.50
❑7, b&w	2.50	0.50	1.25	2.50

HYBRID: ETHERWORLDS
DIMENSION 5

Value: Cover or less

❑1 .... 2.50

❑2 .... 2.50

❑3 .... 2.50

HYBRIDS (1ST SERIES)
CONTINUITY

Value: Cover or less

❑0, Apr 93, NA (w), Deathwatch 2000, Part 2, silver and red foil covers 1.00

❑1, Apr 93, Deathwatch 2000, Part 4, diecut cardstock cover; trading cards 2.50

❑2, Jun 93, Deathwatch 2000, Part 13, thermal cover; trading card 2.50

❑3, Aug 93, Deathwatch 2000, Part 18, trading card; Deathwatch 2000 dropped from indicia; Published out of sequence after #5 .... 2.50

❑4, Published out of sequence after #5, #3 .... 2.50

❑5, Deathwatch 2000, trading card 2.50

HYBRIDS (2ND SERIES)
CONTINUITY

Value: Cover or less

❑1, Jan 94, Rise of Magic, Embossed cover 2.50

HYBRIDS: THE ORIGIN
CONTINUITY

Value: Cover or less

❑1, really Revengers: Hybrids Special #1 .... 2.50

❑2, Jul 93, NA (w), Who's Really Buried in Grant's Tomb, "Revengers Special" on cover 2.50

❑3, Sep 93, "Revengers Special" on cover 2.50

❑4, Dec 93 .... 2.50

❑5, Jan 94 .... 2.50

HYDE-25
HARRIS

Value: Cover or less

❑0, Apr 95, Storm Before The Calm, 1: Vampirella, coupon for poster offer; Reprints Vampirella (Magazine) #1 in color 2.95

HYDROGEN BOMB FUNNIES
RIP OFF

	ORIG	GOOD	FINE	N-MINT
❑1, Mr. Sketchum; Wonder Warthog and the Inva	0.50	1.00	2.50	5.00

HYENA
TUNDRA

Value: Cover or less

❑1, b&w 3.95

❑2, b&w 3.95

❑3, b&w 3.95

❑4 .... 3.95

ORIG GOOD FINE N-MINT

HYPER DOLLS
IRONCAT

Value: Cover or less

- ❑1 ... 2.95
- ❑2 ... 2.95

HYPER DOLLS (VOL. 2)
IRONCAT

Value: Cover or less

- ❑1 ... 2.95
- ❑2 ... 2.95
- ❑3 ... 2.95
- ❑4 ... 2.95
- ❑5 ... 2.95
- ❑6, Jul 99 ... 2.95

HYPERKIND
MARVEL

Value: Cover or less

- ❑1, Sep 93, Paxis Reborn, O: Hyperkind, Foil-embossed cover ... 2.50
- ❑2, Oct 93 ... 1.75
- ❑3, Nov 93 ... 1.75
- ❑4, Dec 93 ... 1.75
- ❑5, Jan 94 ... 1.75
- ❑6, Feb 94 ... 1.75
- ❑7, Mar 94 ... 1.75
- ❑8, Apr 94 ... 1.75
- ❑9, May 94, Final Issue ... 1.75

HYPERKIND UNLEASHED!
MARVEL

Value: Cover or less

- ❑1, Aug 94, Hyperkind No More ... 2.95

HYPERSONIC
DARK HORSE

Value: Cover or less

- ❑1, Nov 97 ... 2.95
- ❑2, Dec 97 ... 2.95
- ❑3, Jan 98 ... 2.95
- ❑4, Jan 98 ... 2.95

HYPER VIOLENTS
CFD

Value: Cover or less

- ❑1, Jul 96, b&w ... 2.95

I

I AM LEGEND
ECLIPSE

Value: Cover or less

- ❑1, b&w ... 5.95
- ❑2 ... 5.95
- ❑3 ... 5.95
- ❑4 ... 5.95

I BEFORE E
FANTAGRAPHICS

Value: Cover or less

- ❑1, b&w ... 3.95
- ❑1-2, May 94, 2nd Printing ... 3.95
- ❑2, b&w ... 3.95

I•BOTS (ISAAC ASIMOV'S...) (1ST SERIES)
TEKNO

	ORIG	GOOD	FINE	N-MINT
❑1, Dec 95, GP, HC (w), Out of the Blue, 1: the I•Bots	1.95	0.40	1.00	2.00
❑2, Dec 95, GP, HC (w)	1.95	0.40	1.00	2.00
❑3, Jan 96, GP, HC (w)	2.25	0.45	1.13	2.25
❑4, Feb 96, GP, HC (w)	2.25	0.45	1.13	2.25
❑5, Mar 96, GP, HC (w)	2.25	0.45	1.13	2.25
❑6, Apr 96, GP, HC (w)	2.25	0.45	1.13	2.25
❑7, May 96, GP, HC (w), A: Lady Justice	2.25	0.45	1.13	2.25

I•BOTS (ISAAC ASIMOV'S...) (2ND SERIES)
BIG

Value: Cover or less

- ❑1, Jun 96, PB, The Big Crossover, Part 12, A: Lady Justice ... 2.25
- ❑2, Jul 96, GK (c) ... 2.25
- ❑3, Aug 96, GK (c) ... 2.25
- ❑4, Sep 96, GK (c) ... 2.25
- ❑5, Oct 96 ... 2.25
- ❑6, Nov 96, E.C. tribute cover. 2.25
- ❑7, Dec 96, Rebirth, Part 1, forms triptych ... 2.25
- ❑8, Jan 97, PB, Rebirth, Part 2, forms triptych ... 2.25
- ❑9, Feb 97, forms triptych ... 2.25

ICARUS (AIRCEL)
AIRCEL

Value: Cover or less

- ❑1 ... 2.00
- ❑2 ... 2.00
- ❑3 ... 2.00
- ❑4 ... 2.00
- ❑5 ... 2.00

ICARUS (KARDIA)
KARDIA

Value: Cover or less

- ❑1, Jun 92 ... 2.25

ICE AGE ON THE WORLD OF MAGIC: THE GATHERING
ACCLAIM

Value: Cover or less

- ❑1, Jul 95, The Twilight Kingdom, bound-in Magic card (Chub Toad) ... 2.50
- ❑2, Aug 95, bound-in Chub Toad card from Ice Age ... 2.50
- ❑3, Sep 95, polybagged with sheet of creature tokens ... 2.50
- ❑4, Oct 95, polybagged with sheet of creature tokens ... 2.50

ICEMAN
MARVEL

	ORIG	GOOD	FINE	N-MINT
❑1, Dec 84, The Fuse!, O: Iceman	0.75	0.50	1.25	2.50
❑2, Feb 85	0.75	0.40	1.00	2.00
❑3, Apr 85	0.75	0.40	1.00	2.00
❑4, Jun 85, The Price You Pay!	0.75	0.40	1.00	2.00

ICICLE
HERO

Value: Cover or less

- ❑1 ... 4.95
- ❑2, b&w ... 3.50
- ❑3, b&w ... 3.50
- ❑4, A: Chrissie Claus, b&w ... 3.50
- ❑5, b&w ... 3.95

I COME IN PEACE
GREATER MERCURY

Value: Cover or less

- ❑1, "I" Am The Peace Keeper. 2.50

ICON
DC

	ORIG	GOOD	FINE	N-MINT
❑1, May 93, By Their Own Bootstraps, 1: Icon; 1: Rocket; 1: S.H.R.E.D.	1.50	0.40	1.00	2.00
❑1/CS, May 93, O: Icon; O: Rocket, poster; trading card	2.95	0.59	1.48	2.95
❑2, Jun 93, 1: Payback	1.50	0.30	0.75	1.50
❑3, Jul 93	1.50	0.30	0.75	1.50
❑4, Aug 93, A: Blood Syndicate, Rocket's pregnant	1.50	0.30	0.75	1.50
❑5, Sep 93, V: Blood Syndicate	1.50	0.30	0.75	1.50
❑6, Oct 93, V: Blood Syndicate	1.50	0.30	0.75	1.50
❑7, Nov 93, The Moment of Truth	1.50	0.30	0.75	1.50
❑8, Dec 93, O: Icon	1.50	0.30	0.75	1.50
❑9, Jan 94, Shadow War; Shadow War, Part 2	1.50	0.30	0.75	1.50
❑10, Feb 94, V: Holocaust	1.50	0.30	0.75	1.50
❑11, Mar 94, KB (w), What I Did on my Vacation, 1: Todd Loomis	1.50	0.30	0.75	1.50
❑12, Apr 94, 1: Gideon's Cord	1.50	0.30	0.75	1.50
❑13, May 94, 1: Buck Wild	1.50	0.30	0.75	1.50
❑14, Jun 94	1.50	0.30	0.75	1.50
❑15, Jul 94, Worlds Collide; Worlds Collide, Part 4, A: Superboy	1.75	0.35	0.88	1.75
❑16, Aug 94, Worlds Collide; Worlds Collide, Part 11, A: Superman	1.75	0.35	0.88	1.75
❑17, Sep 94, Mothership Connection, Part 1; The Mothership Connection, Part 1	1.75	0.35	0.88	1.75
❑18, Oct 94, Mothership Connection Interlude; The Mothership Connection, Part 2	1.75	0.35	0.88	1.75
❑19, Nov 94, Mothership Connection, Part 2	1.75	0.35	0.88	1.75
❑20, Dec 94, Mothership Connection, Part 3, A: Hardware; A: Dharma; A: Wise Son; A: Static	1.75	0.35	0.88	1.75
❑21, Jan 95, Mothership Connection Conclusion	1.75	0.35	0.88	1.75
❑21, Jan 95, Mothership Connection Conclusion	1.75	0.35	0.88	1.75
❑22, Feb 95, A: DMZ; A: Hardware; 1: New Rocket; A: Static	1.75	0.35	0.88	1.75
❑23, Mar 95	1.75	0.35	0.88	1.75
❑24, Apr 95, Rocket's baby born	1.75	0.35	0.88	1.75
❑25, May 95, Giant-size	2.95	0.59	1.48	2.95
❑26, Jun 95, V: Oblivion	1.75	0.35	0.88	1.75
❑27, Jul 95, Icon returns from space	2.50	0.50	1.25	2.50
❑28, Aug 95, Long Hot Summer	2.50	0.50	1.25	2.50
❑29, Sep 95, Long Hot Summer; The Long Hot Summer	2.50	0.50	1.25	2.50
❑30, Oct 95, Funeral of Buck Wild	2.50	0.50	1.25	2.50
❑31, Nov 95	0.99	0.20	0.50	1.00
❑32, Dec 95	2.50	0.50	1.25	2.50
❑33, Jan 96, Inertia	2.50	0.50	1.25	2.50
❑34, Feb 96, Rocket's Tale	2.50	0.50	1.25	2.50
❑35, Mar 96, Arena?	2.50	0.50	1.25	2.50
❑36, Apr 96	2.50	0.50	1.25	2.50
❑37, Sep 96, Icon in the 1920s	2.50	0.50	1.25	2.50
❑38, Oct 96, Blood Reign, Part 1, V: Holocaust	2.50	0.50	1.25	2.50
❑39, Nov 96, Blood Reign, Part 2, V: Holocaust	2.50	0.50	1.25	2.50
❑40, Dec 96, Blood Reign, Part 3, V: Blood Syndicate	2.50	0.50	1.25	2.50
❑41, Jan 97, Blood Reign, Part 4	2.50	0.50	1.25	2.50
❑42, Feb 97, Final Issue	2.50	0.50	1.25	2.50

ICON DEVIL
SPIDER

Value: Cover or less

- ❑1 ... 1.60
- ❑2 ... 1.60

ICON DEVIL (VOL. 2)
SPIDER

Value: Cover or less

- ❑2, b&w ... 2.25

ICONOGRAFIX SPECIAL
ICONOGRAFIX

Value: Cover or less

- ❑1, b&w ... 2.50

ICZER 3
CPM

Value: Cover or less

- ❑1, Sep 96, b&w ... 2.95
- ❑2, Oct 96, b&w ... 2.95

ORIG GOOD FINE N-MINT

ICONOGRAFIX SPECIAL
ICONOGRAFIX
Value: Cover or less
- ❑1, b&w 2.50

ICZER 3
CPM
Value: Cover or less
- ❑1, Sep 96, b&w 2.95
- ❑2, Oct 96, b&w 2.95

ID
FANTAGRAPHICS
Value: Cover or less
- ❑1, b&w; adult 2.50
- ❑2, b&w; adult 2.50
- ❑3, b&w; adult 2.50
- ❑3-2, Jun 95, b&w; adult; 2nd Printing 2.95

ID4: INDEPENDENCE DAY
MARVEL

	ORIG	GOOD	FINE	N-MINT
❑0, Jun 96, prequel to movie	1.95	0.50	1.25	2.50
❑1, Jul 96, adapts movie	1.95	0.39	0.98	1.95
❑2, Aug 96, adapts movie	1.95	0.39	0.98	1.95

I DIE AT MIDNIGHT
VERTIGO
Value: Cover or less
- ❑1 .... 2.95

IDIOTLAND
FANTAGRAPHICS
Value: Cover or less
- ❑1, b&w 2.95
- ❑2, b&w 2.50
- ❑3, b&w 2.50
- ❑4, b&w 2.50
- ❑5, b&w 2.50
- ❑6, Aug 94, b&w 2.50

IDLE WORSHIP
VISCERAL
Value: Cover or less
- ❑1, Breeder; Haze 2.95

IDOL
MARVEL
Value: Cover or less
- ❑1 .... 2.95
- ❑2 .... 2.95
- ❑3, The Deep Six 2.95

I FEEL SICK
SLAVE LABOR
Value: Cover or less
- ❑1, Aug 99 .... 3.95

IGRAT ILLUSTRATIONS, THE
VEROTIK
Value: Cover or less
- ❑1, Apr 97, nn; adult; embossed cardstock cover; pin-ups 3.95

I HAD A DREAM
KING INK EMPIRE
Value: Cover or less
- ❑1, Jun 95, The Abyss 2.95

ILIAD
SLAVE LABOR
Value: Cover or less
- ❑1, Dec 97, Ikarus: The Plight; Toad, b&w; Anthology 2.95
- ❑2, Jan 98, Ikarus: The Seed; Toad, b&w; Anthology 2.95

ILIAD II
MICMAC

	ORIG	GOOD	FINE	N-MINT
❑1, b&w	1.70	0.40	1.00	2.00
❑2, b&w	1.70	0.40	1.00	2.00
❑3, b&w	1.70	0.40	1.00	2.00

ILLEGAL ALIENS
ECLIPSE
Value: Cover or less
- ❑1, nn; b&w 2.50

ILLUMINATIONS (VOL. 2)
MONOLITH
Value: Cover or less
- ❑1, Return To The Eve 2.50
- ❑2 .... 2.50
- ❑3 .... 2.50

ILLUMINATOR
MARVEL
Value: Cover or less
- ❑1, Genesis, 1: Illuminator 4.99
- ❑2 .... 4.99
- ❑3 .... 2.95

ILLUMINATUS (EYE-N-APPLE)
EYE-N-APPLE
Value: Cover or less
- ❑1 .... 2.00

ILLUMINATUS! (RIP OFF)
RIP OFF
Value: Cover or less
- ❑1, Oct 90, b&w 2.50
- ❑2, Dec 90, b&w 2.50
- ❑3, Apr 91, b&w 2.50

ILLUSTRATED CLASSEX
COMIC ZONE
Value: Cover or less
- ❑1, b&w; adult 2.75

ILLUSTRATED DORE: BOOK OF GENESIS
TOME PRESS
Value: Cover or less
- ❑1, b&w 2.50

ILLUSTRATED DORE: BOOK OF THE APOCRYPHA
TOME PRESS
Value: Cover or less
- ❑1, b&w 2.50

ILLUSTRATED EDITIONS
THWACK! POW!
Value: Cover or less
- ❑1, Feb 95, The Horned Toad 1.95

ILLUSTRATED TALES (JAXON'S...)
FTR
Value: Cover or less
- ❑1, God's Bosom; Bulto...A mountain of Silver 1.95

Concepts from famous science-fiction authors and personalities, including Leonard Nimoy, Isaac Asimov, and Gene Roddenberry, inspired many of Tekno's releases.

© 1995 Tekno

ORIG GOOD FINE N-MINT

I LOVE LUCY
ETERNITY
Value: Cover or less
- ❑1, May 90, b&w; strip reprint 2.95
- ❑2, Jun 90, b&w; strip reprint 2.95
- ❑3, Jul 90, b&w; strip reprint 2.95
- ❑4, Aug 90, b&w; strip reprint 2.95
- ❑5, Sep 90, b&w; strip reprint 2.95
- ❑6, Oct 90, b&w; strip reprint 2.95

I LOVE LUCY BOOK TWO
ETERNITY
Value: Cover or less
- ❑1, Nov 90, b&w; strip reprints 2.95
- ❑2, Dec 90, b&w; strip reprints 2.95
- ❑3, Jan 91, b&w; strip reprints 2.95
- ❑4, Feb 91, b&w; strip reprints 2.95
- ❑5, Mar 91, b&w; strip reprints 2.95
- ❑6, Apr 91, b&w; strip reprints 2.95

I LOVE LUCY IN 3-D
ETERNITY
Value: Cover or less
- ❑1 .... 3.95

I LOVE LUCY IN FULL COLOR
ETERNITY
Value: Cover or less
- ❑1, comic book reprint; Collects I Love Lucy # 4, 5, 8, 16 .... 5.95

I LOVE YOU (AVALON)
AVALON
Value: Cover or less
- ❑1, Devil-May-Care!; My Errant Heart 2.95

I LOVE YOU SPECIAL
AVALON
Value: Cover or less
- ❑1, b&w 2.95

I, LUSIPHUR
MULEHIDE

	ORIG	GOOD	FINE	N-MINT
❑1	—	5.00	12.50	25.00
❑2	—	3.00	7.50	15.00
❑3	—	4.00	10.00	20.00
❑4	—	3.00	7.50	15.00
❑5	—	2.50	6.25	12.50
❑6	—	2.00	5.00	10.00
❑7, series continues as Poison Elves	—	2.00	5.00	10.00

IMAGE
IMAGE

	ORIG	GOOD	FINE	N-MINT
❑0, Troll; StormWatch, Mail-away coupon-redemption promo from coupons in early Image comics	—	0.80	2.00	4.00

IMAGE OF THE BEAST, THE
LAST GASP

	ORIG	GOOD	FINE	N-MINT
❑1	0.75	0.60	1.50	3.00

IMAGE PLUS
IMAGE
Value: Cover or less
- ❑1, May 93 .... 2.25

IMAGES OF A DISTANT SOIL
IMAGE
Value: Cover or less
- ❑1, Feb 97, b&w; pin-ups by various artists 2.95

IMAGES OF OMAHA
KITCHEN SINK
Value: Cover or less
- ❑1, b&w; adult; cardstock cover; benefit comic; intro by Harlan Ellison; afterword by Neil Gaiman 3.95
- ❑2, b&w; adult; cardstock cover; benefit comic 3.95

IMAGES OF SHADOWHAWK
IMAGE
Value: Cover or less
- ❑1, Sep 93, KG, KG (w) 1.95
- ❑2, Oct 93, KG, KG (w), A: Trencher 1.95
- ❑3, Jan 94, KG, KG (w), A: Trencher 1.95

IMAGI-MATION
IMAGI-MATION
Value: Cover or less
- ❑1, Gnatman 1.75

IMMORTAL COMBAT
EXPRESS
Value: Cover or less
- ❑1, Feb 95, cardstock cover; Entity Illustrated Novella #5 .... 2.95

IMMORTAL DOCTOR FATE, THE
DC

	ORIG	GOOD	FINE	N-MINT
❑1, Jan 85, JSa; KG; MN, This Immortal Destiny, O: Doctor Fate	1.25	0.30	0.75	1.50
❑2, Feb 85, KG	1.25	0.30	0.75	1.50
❑3, Mar 85, KG	1.25	0.30	0.75	1.50

IMMORTAL II
IMAGE

Value: Cover or less

- ❑1, Apr 97, b&w; cover also says May, indicia says Apr 2.50
- ❑1/A, Apr 97, b&w; cover says Immortal Two, indicia says Immortal II 2.50
- ❑2, Jun 97, b&w; cover says Immortal Two, indicia says Immortal II 2.50
- ❑3, Aug 97, b&w; cover says Immortal Two, indicia says Immortal II 2.50
- ❑4, Sep 97, b&w; cover says Immortal Two, indicia says Immortal II 2.50
- ❑5, Feb 98, b&w; cover says Immortal Two, indicia says Immortal II 2.50

IMMORTALS, THE
COMICS BY DAY

Value: Cover or less

- ❑1 .... 1.00

IMP
SLAVE LABOR

Value: Cover or less

- ❑1, Jun 94 .... 2.95

IMPACT (RCP)
RCP

Value: Cover or less

- ❑1, Apr 99, BK; GE, BK (w); GE (w), Tough Cop; Thirty Dollars (Text Story) 2.50
- ❑2, May 99, JO, JO (w), Mother Knows Best; The Suit 2.50
- ❑3, Jun 99, Life Sentence; The Debt 2.50
- ❑4, Jul 99, GE, GE (w), The Lonely One; Fall in Winter 2.50
- ❑5, Aug 99, GI; BK; JO; GE, GI (w); BK (w); JO (w); GE (w), The Art Interest; One Armed Wonder (Text Story) 2.50
- ❑Anl 1, BK; JO; GE, BK (w); JO (w); GE (w), Collects Impact (RCP) #1-5 .... 13.50

IMPACT CHRISTMAS SPECIAL
DC

Value: Cover or less

- ❑1, CI, The Gift of Magi; American Crusader, A: Jaguar; A: Comet; A: Fly; A: Web; A: Shield 2.50

IMPACT COMICS WHO'S WHO
DC

Value: Cover or less

- ❑1 .... 4.95
- ❑2 .... 4.95
- ❑3, trading cards 4.95

IMPERIAL GUARD
MARVEL

Value: Cover or less

- ❑1, Jan 97 .... 1.99
- ❑2, Feb 97, Up From The Depths, wraparound cover 1.99
- ❑3, Mar 97, A Mad God Awakens!, A: Supreme Intelligence, Final Issue 1.99

IMPOSSIBLE MAN SUMMER VACATION SPECTACULAR
MARVEL

Value: Cover or less

- ❑1, Aug 90, Impquest 2.00
- ❑2, Aug 91 .... 2.00

IMPULSE
DC

	ORIG	GOOD	FINE	N-MINT
❑1, Apr 95, MWa (w), The Single Synapse Theory, O: Impulse	1.50	0.80	2.00	4.00
❑2, May 95, MWa (w), Crossfire	1.50	0.70	1.75	3.50
❑3, Jun 95, MWa (w), How to Win Friends and Influence People	1.75	0.50	1.25	2.50
❑4, Jul 95, MWa (w), Bad Influence, 1: White Lightning	1.75	0.50	1.25	2.50
❑5, Aug 95, MWa (w), Lightning Strikes	1.75	0.50	1.25	2.50
❑6, Sep 95, MWa (w), Secret Identity, Child abuse	1.75	0.45	1.13	2.25
❑7, Oct 95, MWa (w)	1.75	0.45	1.13	2.25
❑8, Nov 95, MWa (w), V: Blockbuster, Underworld Unleashed	1.75	0.45	1.13	2.25
❑9, Dec 95, MWa (w), Underworld Unleashed, A: Xs	1.75	0.45	1.13	2.25
❑10, Jan 96, MWa (w), Dead Heat, Part 3, continues in Flash #110	1.75	0.40	1.00	2.00
❑11, Feb 96, MWa (w), Dead Heat, Part 5, D: Johnny Quick	1.75	0.40	1.00	2.00
❑12, Mar 96, MWa (w), Sonic Youth	1.75	0.40	1.00	2.00
❑13, May 96, MWa (w)	1.75	0.40	1.00	2.00
❑14, Jun 96, MWa (w), V: Trickster; V: White Lightning	1.75	0.40	1.00	2.00
❑15, Jul 96, MWa (w), V: Trickster; V: White Lightning	1.75	0.40	1.00	2.00
❑16, Aug 96, MWa (w), more of Max Mercury's past revealed	1.75	0.40	1.00	2.00
❑17, Sep 96, MWa (w), A: Zatanna	1.75	0.40	1.00	2.00
❑18, Oct 96, Virtually Wasted	1.75	0.40	1.00	2.00
❑19, Nov 96, MWa (w), A Game of Spew	1.75	0.40	1.00	2.00
❑20, Dec 96, MWa (w), First Base, Bart plays baseball	1.75	0.35	0.88	1.75
❑21, Jan 97, MWa (w), A Little Knowledge, A: Legion	1.75	0.35	0.88	1.75
❑22, Feb 97, MWa (w), A: Jesse Quick	1.75	0.35	0.88	1.75
❑23, Mar 97, MWa (w), Lessons Learned, Impulse's mother returns	1.75	0.35	0.88	1.75
❑24, Apr 97, MWa (w), Impulse goes to 30th century	1.75	0.35	0.88	1.75
❑25, May 97, MWa (w), You and Me Against the World, Impulse in 30th century	1.75	0.35	0.88	1.75
❑26, Jun 97, MWa (w), Impulse returns to 20th century	1.75	0.35	0.88	1.75
❑27, Jul 97, MWa (w)	1.75	0.35	0.88	1.75
❑28, Aug 97, 1: Arrowette	1.75	0.35	0.88	1.75
❑29, Sep 97	1.75	0.35	0.88	1.75
❑30, Oct 97, Genesis; Impulse gains new powers	1.75	0.35	0.88	1.75
❑31, Nov 97, Solving the Puzzle	1.75	0.35	0.88	1.75
❑32, Dec 97, Unhealed Wounds, Face cover	1.95	0.39	0.98	1.95
❑33, Jan 98, V: White Lightning; 1: Jasper Pierson	1.95	0.39	0.98	1.95
❑34, Feb 98, Max and Impulse travel in time	1.95	0.39	0.98	1.95
❑35, Mar 98, Max and Impulse turned into apes	1.95	0.39	0.98	1.95
❑36, Apr 98	1.95	0.39	0.98	1.95
❑37, May 98, 1: Glory Shredder	1.95	0.39	0.98	1.95
❑38, Jun 98, Manchester floods	1.95	0.39	0.98	1.95
❑39, Jul 98, A: Trickster	1.95	0.39	0.98	1.95
❑40, Aug 98	1.95	0.39	0.98	1.95
❑41, Sep 98, A: Arrowette	2.25	0.45	1.13	2.25
❑42, Oct 98, Virtual pets	2.25	0.45	1.13	2.25
❑43, Dec 98	2.25	0.45	1.13	2.25
❑44, Jan 99, Halloween	2.25	0.45	1.13	2.25
❑45, Feb 99, A: Bart's mother, Christmas	2.25	0.45	1.13	2.25
❑46, Mar 99, Chain Lightning tie-in; Chain Lightning, A: Flash II (Barry Allen)	2.25	0.45	1.13	2.25
❑47, Apr 99, A: Superman, Superboy cameo	2.25	0.45	1.13	2.25
❑48, May 99, V: Riddler	2.25	0.45	1.13	2.25
❑49, Jun 99, The Old Reform School Dodge	2.25	0.45	1.13	2.25
❑50, Jul 99, First Fool's, A: Batman; V: Joker	2.25	0.45	1.13	2.25
❑51, Aug 99, It's All Relative	2.25	0.45	1.13	2.25
❑52, Sep 99, Tumbling Down	2.25	0.45	1.13	2.25
❑53, Oct 99, Threats, V: Kalibak; V: Inertia	2.25	0.45	1.13	2.25
❑54, Nov 99, Night of Camping, Day of Judgment	2.25	0.45	1.13	2.25
❑55, Dec 99, It Ain't Easy Being Greenery	2.25	0.45	1.13	2.25
❑56, Jan 00, The Best of Both, A: Young Justice	2.25	0.45	1.13	2.25
❑57, Feb 00, A Plastic Christmas, A: Plastic Man	2.25	0.45	1.13	2.25
❑58, Mar 00	2.25	0.45	1.13	2.25
❑59, Apr 00	2.25	0.45	1.13	2.25
❑60, May 00, What Would Flash Do?	2.25	0.45	1.13	2.25
❑61, Jun 00, The Sidekick Swap	2.25	0.45	1.13	2.25
❑62, Jul 00	2.25	0.45	1.13	2.25
❑63, Aug 00	2.25	0.45	1.13	2.25
❑64, Sep 00	2.25	0.45	1.13	2.25
❑65, Oct 00, Bart Allen's Evil Twin	2.50	0.50	1.25	2.50
❑66, Nov 00, Mercury Falling	2.50	0.50	1.25	2.50
❑67, Dec 00, Friends Like These...	2.50	0.50	1.25	2.50
❑68, Jan 01, I Rann and I Rann and I Rann...	2.50	0.50	1.25	2.50
❑69, Feb 01, Strange Impulses	2.50	0.50	1.25	2.50
❑70, Mar 01, Impulse, the Movie	2.50	0.50	1.25	2.50
❑71, Apr 01, The Return of Lucius Keller, Part 1	2.50	0.50	1.25	2.50
❑72, May 01, The Return of Lucius Keller, Part 2	2.50	0.50	1.25	2.50
❑73, Jun 01, Dark Tomorrow	2.50	0.50	1.25	2.50
❑74	2.50	0.50	1.25	2.50
❑75	2.50	0.50	1.25	2.50
❑76	2.50	0.50	1.25	2.50
❑1000000, Nov 98, A: John Fox	2.25	0.45	1.13	2.25
❑Anl 1, MWa (w), Legends of the Dead Earth	2.95	0.59	1.48	2.95
❑Anl 2, Showdown, A: Vigilante, Pulp Heroes	3.95	0.79	1.98	3.95

IMPULSE/ATOM DOUBLE-SHOT
DC

Value: Cover or less

- ❑1, Feb 98, Roll Back 1.95

IMPULSE: BART SAVES THE UNIVERSE
DC

Value: Cover or less

- ❑1, A: Linear Men; V: Extant, nn; prestige format; Batman cameo; Flash I (Jay Garrick) cameo; Flash II (Barry Allen) cameo; Flash III (Wally West) cameo 5.95

IMPULSE PLUS
DC

Value: Cover or less

- ❑1, Sep 97, Speed Freak, A: Grossout, continues in Superboy Plus #2 .... 2.95

IMP-UNITY
SPOOF

Value: Cover or less

- ❑1, b&w; parody 2.95

INCOMPLETE DEATH'S HEAD, THE
MARVEL
Value: Cover or less

Issue	Price
❏1, Jan 93, Connections; The Crossroads of Time, 1: Death's Head, Die-cut cover; Reprint; Giant-size	2.95
❏2, Feb 93	1.75
❏3, Mar 93, Contractual Obligations	1.75
❏4, Apr 93	1.75
❏5, May 93	1.75
❏6, Jun 93, Do Not Forsake Me Oh My Darling!	1.75
❏7, Jul 93	1.75
❏8, Aug 93	1.75
❏9, Sep 93	1.75
❏10, Oct 93, A: Tuck; A: Hob-Monster; A: Fantastic Four	1.75
❏11, Nov 93	1.75
❏12, Dec 93, Final Issue; double-sized	2.50

INCREDIBLE HULK, THE
MARVEL

	ORIG	GOOD	FINE	N-MINT
❏-1, Jul 97, PD (w), Grave Matters, O: Hulk, Flashback	1.99	0.40	1.00	2.00
❏1, JK, 1: Betty Ross; 1: Rick Jones; 1: Hulk; 1: General "Thunderbolt" Ross, Hulk's skin is gray (printing mistake)	0.12	2200.00	5500.00	11000.00
❏2, JK; SD, O: Hulk, Hulk's skin is printed in green	0.12	540.00	1350.00	2700.00
❏3, JK, 1: Bruto the Strongman; 1: Teena the Fat Lady; 1: The Clown; O: Hulk; 1: Cannonball (villain); 1: Ringmaster	0.12	330.00	825.00	1650.00
❏4, JK, O: Hulk	0.12	265.00	662.50	1325.00
❏5, 1: Tyrannus	0.12	265.00	662.50	1325.00
❏6, SD, 1: Teen Brigade; 1: Metal Master, Moves to "Tales To Astonish" following this issue	0.12	360.00	900.00	1800.00
❏102, Apr 68, O: Hulk, Numbering continued from "Tales To Astonish"	0.12	30.00	75.00	150.00
❏103, May 68, 1: Space Parasite	0.12	12.00	30.00	60.00
❏104, Jun 68, V: Rhino	0.12	11.00	27.50	55.00
❏105, Jul 68, 1: Missing Link; V: Gargoyle	0.12	9.00	22.50	45.00
❏106, Aug 68, HT	0.12	9.00	22.50	45.00
❏107, Sep 68, HT, V: Mandarin	0.12	9.00	22.50	45.00
❏108, Oct 68, HT, A: Nick Fury	0.12	9.00	22.50	45.00
❏109, Nov 68, HT, SL (w), The Monster and the Man-Beast!	0.12	6.00	15.00	30.00
❏110, Dec 68, HT	0.12	6.00	15.00	30.00
❏111, Jan 69, DA; HT	0.12	5.00	12.50	25.00
❏112, Feb 69, DA; HT	0.12	5.00	12.50	25.00
❏113, Mar 69, DA; HT, V: Sandman	0.12	5.00	12.50	25.00
❏114, Apr 69, DA; HT	0.12	5.00	12.50	25.00
❏115, May 69	0.12	5.00	12.50	25.00
❏116, Jun 69	0.12	5.00	12.50	25.00
❏117, Jul 69	0.12	5.00	12.50	25.00
❏118, Aug 69, A: Sub-Mariner	0.15	3.60	9.00	18.00
❏119, Sep 69	0.15	3.60	9.00	18.00
❏120, Oct 69	0.15	3.00	7.50	15.00
❏121, Nov 69	0.15	3.00	7.50	15.00
❏122, Dec 69, HT, A: Thing, Hulk vs. Thing	0.15	5.00	12.50	25.00
❏123, Jan 70	0.15	3.00	7.50	15.00
❏124, Feb 70, HT, The Rhino Says No!, V: Rhino	0.15	3.00	7.50	15.00
❏125, Mar 70, HT, ... And Now, The Absorbing Man!, V: Absorbing Man	0.15	3.00	7.50	15.00
❏126, Apr 70	0.15	1.80	4.50	9.00
❏127, May 70, V: Mogol	0.15	1.80	4.50	9.00
❏128, Jun 70	0.15	1.80	4.50	9.00
❏129, Jul 70	0.15	1.80	4.50	9.00
❏130, Aug 70	0.15	1.80	4.50	9.00
❏131, Sep 70, HT, Iron Man	0.15	1.80	4.50	9.00
❏132, Oct 70, JSe; HT, V: Hydra	0.15	1.80	4.50	9.00
❏133, Nov 70	0.15	1.80	4.50	9.00
❏134, Dec 70	0.15	1.80	4.50	9.00
❏135, Jan 71, V: Kang	0.15	1.80	4.50	9.00
❏136, Feb 71, 1: Xeron	0.15	1.80	4.50	9.00
❏137, Mar 71	0.15	1.80	4.50	9.00
❏138, Apr 71	0.15	1.80	4.50	9.00
❏139, May 71	0.15	1.80	4.50	9.00
❏140, Jun 71, HT, The Brute that Shouted Love at the Heart of the Atom!, 1: Jarella	0.15	1.80	4.50	9.00
❏140-2, HT, The Brute that Shouted Love at the Heart of the Atom!, 1: Jarella, 2nd Printing	0.15	0.30	0.75	1.50
❏141, Jul 71, 1: Doc Samson	0.15	4.00	10.00	20.00
❏142, Aug 71	0.15	1.60	4.00	8.00
❏143, Sep 71, V: Doctor Doom	0.15	1.60	4.00	8.00
❏144, Oct 71, V: Doctor Doom	0.15	1.60	4.00	8.00
❏145, Nov 71, JSe; HT, O: Hulk, Giant-size	0.25	1.80	4.50	9.00
❏146, Dec 71, JSe; HT	0.20	1.20	3.00	6.00
❏147, Jan 72, JSe; HT	0.20	1.20	3.00	6.00
❏148, Feb 72, JSe; HT	0.20	1.20	3.00	6.00
❏149, Mar 72, JSe; HT, 1: Inheritor	0.20	1.20	3.00	6.00
❏150, Apr 72, JSe; HT, 1: Viking; A: Havoc; A: Lorna Dane	0.20	1.20	3.00	6.00
❏151, May 72	0.20	1.20	3.00	6.00

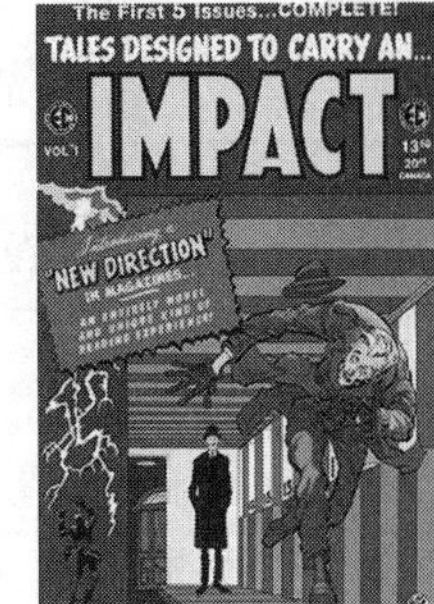

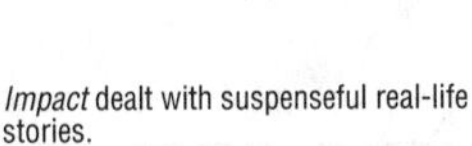

Impact dealt with suspenseful real-life stories.

	ORIG	GOOD	FINE	N-MINT
❏152, Jun 72	0.20	1.20	3.00	6.00
❏153, Jul 72, A: Matt Murdock; A: Peter Parker; A: Fantastic Four	0.20	1.20	3.00	6.00
❏154, Aug 72, V: Chameleon; A: Ant-Man	0.20	1.20	3.00	6.00
❏155, Sep 72, 1: Shaper of Worlds; V: Captain Axis	0.20	1.20	3.00	6.00
❏156, Oct 72	0.20	1.20	3.00	6.00
❏157, Nov 72	0.20	1.20	3.00	6.00
❏158, Dec 72, A: Warlock; V: Rhino on Counter-Earth	0.20	1.20	3.00	6.00
❏159, Jan 73, V: Abomination	0.20	1.20	3.00	6.00
❏160, Feb 73	0.20	1.20	3.00	6.00
❏161, Mar 73, HT, V: Beast; D: Mimic	0.20	1.20	3.00	6.00
❏162, Apr 73, HT, V: Wendigo	0.20	1.40	3.50	7.00
❏163, May 73, HT, 1: Gremlin	0.20	1.20	3.00	6.00
❏164, Jun 73, HT, 1: Captain Omen	0.20	1.20	3.00	6.00
❏165, Jul 73, HT, V: Aquon	0.20	1.20	3.00	6.00
❏166, Aug 73, HT, 1: Zzzax	0.20	1.20	3.00	6.00
❏167, Sep 73, HT, V: Modok	0.20	1.20	3.00	6.00
❏168, Oct 73, HT, 1: Harpy	0.20	1.20	3.00	6.00
❏169, Nov 73, HT, Calamity In The Clouds!, V: Bi-Beast I	0.20	1.20	3.00	6.00
❏170, Dec 73, HT, D: Bi-Beast I	0.20	1.20	3.00	6.00
❏171, Jan 74, HT, V: Rhino; V: Abomination	0.20	1.20	3.00	6.00
❏172, Feb 74, HT, A: X-Men	0.20	1.70	4.25	8.50
❏173, Mar 74, HT, V: Cobalt Man	0.20	1.20	3.00	6.00
❏174, Apr 74, HT, V: Cobalt Man	0.20	1.20	3.00	6.00
❏175, May 74, HT, V: Inhumans	0.25	1.20	3.00	6.00
❏176, Jun 74, HT, A: Warlock, on Counter-Earth	0.25	1.40	3.50	7.00
❏177, Jul 74, HT, D: Warlock	0.25	2.00	5.00	10.00
❏178, Aug 74, HT, D: Warlock, Warlock returns	0.25	2.00	5.00	10.00
❏179, Sep 74, HT, Missing Link	0.25	1.00	2.50	5.00
❏180, Oct 74, HT, A: Wendigo; 1: Wolverine (cameo)	0.25	22.00	55.00	110.00
❏181, Nov 74, HT, And Now...The Wolverine!, 1: Wolverine (full appearance); A: Wendigo, Marvel Value Stamp A/54: Shanna the She-Devil	0.25	120.00	300.00	600.00
❏182, Dec 74, 1: Crackajack; V: Anvil; A: Wolverine; V: Hammer	0.25	12.00	30.00	60.00
❏183, Jan 75, V: Zzzax	0.25	0.80	2.00	4.00
❏184, Feb 75	0.25	0.80	2.00	4.00
❏185, Mar 75	0.25	0.80	2.00	4.00
❏186, Apr 75, D: Devastator I (Kirov Petrovna)	0.25	0.80	2.00	4.00
❏187, May 75, V: Gremlin	0.25	0.80	2.00	4.00
❏188, Jun 75, V: Gremlin	0.25	0.80	2.00	4.00
❏189, Jul 75, V: Mole Man	0.25	0.80	2.00	4.00
❏190, Aug 75, 1: Glorian; V: Toad Men	0.25	0.80	2.00	4.00
❏191, Sep 75, V: Shaper of Worlds	0.25	0.75	1.88	3.75
❏192, Oct 75	0.25	0.75	1.88	3.75
❏193, Nov 75, V: Doc Samson	0.25	0.75	1.88	3.75
❏194, Dec 75	0.25	0.75	1.88	3.75
❏195, Jan 76, V: Abomination	0.25	0.75	1.88	3.75
❏196, Feb 76, V: Abomination	0.25	0.75	1.88	3.75
❏197, Mar 76, V: Gardner; V: Man-Thing	0.25	0.75	1.88	3.75
❏198, Apr 76, A: Man-Thing	0.25	0.75	1.88	3.75
❏199, May 76, JSa; SB, ..And Shield Shall Follow!, V: Doc Samson	0.25	0.75	1.88	3.75
❏200, Jun 76, JSt; SB, A: Surfer and others, 200th anniversary issue	0.25	2.40	6.00	12.00
❏200/A, Jun 76, JSt; SB, A: Surfer and others, 30¢ variant edition; 200th anniversary issue	0.30	4.40	11.00	22.00
❏201, Jul 76, JSt; SB	0.25	0.60	1.50	3.00
❏202, Aug 76, JSt; SB, A: Jarella	0.25	0.60	1.50	3.00
❏203, Sep 76, JSt; SB, V: Psyklop	0.25	0.60	1.50	3.00
❏204, Oct 76, JSe; HT, 1: Kronus; O: Hulk	0.30	0.60	1.50	3.00
❏205, Nov 76, JSa; SB, Do Not Forsake Me!	0.30	0.60	1.50	3.00
❏206, Dec 76	0.30	0.60	1.50	3.00
❏207, Jan 77, A: Defenders	0.30	0.60	1.50	3.00
❏208, Feb 77	0.30	0.60	1.50	3.00

	ORIG	GOOD	FINE	N-MINT
❑209, Mar 77, V: Absorbing Man	0.30	0.60	1.50	3.00
❑210, Apr 77, A: Doctor Druid	0.30	0.60	1.50	3.00
❑211, May 77, A: Doctor Druid	0.30	0.60	1.50	3.00
❑212, Jun 77, V: Constrictor	0.30	0.60	1.50	3.00
❑213, Jul 77, V: Quintronic Man	0.30	0.60	1.50	3.00
❑214, Aug 77, SB, Jack of Hearts	0.30	0.60	1.50	3.00
❑215, Sep 77, Home Is Where The Hurt Is, 1: Bi-Beast II	0.30	0.60	1.50	3.00
❑216, Oct 77, V: Bi-Beast II	0.30	0.60	1.50	3.00
❑217, Nov 77, V: Circus of Crime	0.35	0.60	1.50	3.00
❑218, Dec 77, Doc Samson vs. Rhino	0.35	0.60	1.50	3.00
❑219, Jan 78	0.35	0.60	1.50	3.00
❑220, Feb 78	0.35	0.60	1.50	3.00
❑221, Mar 78, AA; SB, Show Me The Way To Go Home, A: Stingray	0.35	0.60	1.50	3.00
❑222, Apr 78, AA; JSn	0.35	0.60	1.50	3.00
❑223, May 78	0.35	0.60	1.50	3.00
❑224, Jun 78	0.35	0.60	1.50	3.00
❑225, Jul 78	0.35	0.60	1.50	3.00
❑226, Aug 78	0.35	0.60	1.50	3.00
❑227, Sep 78, Doc Samson	0.35	0.60	1.50	3.00
❑228, Oct 78, 1: Moonstone	0.35	0.70	1.75	3.50
❑229, Nov 78, A: Doc Samson; A: Moonstone	0.35	0.60	1.50	3.00
❑230, Dec 78	0.35	0.60	1.50	3.00
❑231, Jan 79	0.35	0.60	1.50	3.00
❑232, Feb 79, SB, A: Captain America	0.35	0.60	1.50	3.00
❑233, Mar 79, SB, A: Marvel Man (Quasar)	0.35	0.60	1.50	3.00
❑234, Apr 79, SB, 1: Quasar, (Marvel Man changed name to Quasar); (Marvel Man changed name to Quasar)	0.35	0.60	1.50	3.00
❑235, May 79, SB, A: Machine Man	0.40	0.60	1.50	3.00
❑236, Jun 79, SB, Kill Or Be Killed, A: Machine Man	0.40	0.60	1.50	3.00
❑237, Jul 79, SB	0.40	0.60	1.50	3.00
❑238, Aug 79, SB	0.40	0.60	1.50	3.00
❑239, Sep 79, SB	0.40	0.60	1.50	3.00
❑240, Oct 79, SB	0.40	0.60	1.50	3.00
❑241, Nov 79, SB	0.40	0.50	1.25	2.50
❑242, Dec 79, SB, V: Tyranus	0.40	0.50	1.25	2.50
❑243, Jan 80, SB, A: Power Man and Iron Fist	0.40	0.50	1.25	2.50
❑244, Feb 80, SB, D: It, the Living Colossus	0.40	0.50	1.25	2.50
❑245, Mar 80, SB	0.40	0.50	1.25	2.50
❑246, Apr 80, SB, A: Captain Marvel	0.40	0.50	1.25	2.50
❑247, May 80, SB, A: Jarella	0.40	0.50	1.25	2.50
❑248, Jun 80, SB, V: Gardener	0.40	0.50	1.25	2.50
❑249, Jul 80, SB, A: Jack Frost	0.40	0.50	1.25	2.50
❑250, Aug 80, SB, Monster!, A: Silver Surfer; 1: Sabra (cameo), Giant-sized	0.75	1.20	3.00	6.00
❑251, Sep 80, SB, Whatever Happened To The 3D Man?, A: 3-D Man	0.50	0.50	1.25	2.50
❑252, Oct 80, SB, The Changelings, Part 1, A: Changelings	0.50	0.50	1.25	2.50
❑253, Nov 80, SB, The Changelings, Part 2, A: Changelings; A: Doc Samson	0.50	0.50	1.25	2.50
❑254, Dec 80, SB, Waiting For The U-Foes!, 1: Ironclad; 1: U-Foes; 1: Vector; 1: X-Ray	0.50	0.50	1.25	2.50
❑255, Jan 81, SB, Thunder Under The East River!, V: Thor	0.50	0.50	1.25	2.50
❑256, Feb 81, SB, Power In The Promised Land!, O: Sabra; 1: Sabra (full)	0.50	0.50	1.25	2.50
❑257, Mar 81, SB, Crypt Of Chaos, 1: Arabian Knight	0.50	0.50	1.25	2.50
❑258, Apr 81, SB, ...To Hunt The Hulk!, 1: Ursa Major; V: Soviet Super-Soldiers	0.50	0.50	1.25	2.50
❑259, May 81, SB, The Family That Dies Together, O: Vanguard; A: Soviet Super-Soldiers; O: Presence	0.50	0.50	1.25	2.50
❑260, Jun 81, SB, Sunset Of A Samurai!	0.50	0.50	1.25	2.50
❑261, Jul 81, SB, Encounter On Easter Island, V: Absorbing Man	0.50	0.50	1.25	2.50
❑262, Aug 81, SB, People In Glass Houses Shouldn't Hurt hulks!	0.50	0.50	1.25	2.50
❑263, Sep 81, SB, I Feel The Earth Move Under My Feet, And The Sky Come Tumbling Down, V: Landslide, Avalanche	0.50	0.50	1.25	2.50
❑264, Oct 81, SB, He Flies By Night	0.50	0.50	1.25	2.50
❑265, Nov 81, SB, You Can't Always Get What You Want, But If You Try Sometime You Might Just Find You Get What You Need!, 1: Firebird; 1: Shooting Star; V: Rangers	0.50	0.50	1.25	2.50
❑266, Dec 81, SB, Devolution!, V: High Evolutionary	0.50	0.50	1.25	2.50
❑267, Jan 82, SB, The Goliath, The Gargoyle, And The Galaxy Master!, V: Glorian	0.60	0.50	1.25	2.50
❑268, Feb 82, SB, And They Called The Wind Pariah!, O: Rick Jones	0.60	0.50	1.25	2.50
❑269, Mar 82, SB, Enter: The Hulk Hunters!	0.60	0.50	1.25	2.50
❑270, Apr 82, SB	0.60	0.50	1.25	2.50
❑271, May 82, SB, Rocket Raccoon!, 1: Rocket Raccoon, 20th Anniversary Issue	0.60	0.50	1.25	2.50

	ORIG	GOOD	FINE	N-MINT
❑272, Jun 82, SB, Weidsong Of The Wen-di-go!, A: Alpha Flight	0.60	0.50	1.25	2.50
❑273, Jul 82, SB, Once A Hulk, Always A Hulk!, A: Alpha Flight	0.60	0.50	1.25	2.50
❑274, Aug 82, SB, Home The Hard Way!	0.60	0.50	1.25	2.50
❑275, Sep 82, JSt; SB, Megalith!, V: Megalith	0.60	0.50	1.25	2.50
❑276, Oct 82, JSt; SB, The Return Of The U-Foes!, V: U-Foes	0.60	0.50	1.25	2.50
❑277, Nov 82, SB, What Friends Are For!, V: U-Foes	0.60	0.50	1.25	2.50
❑278, Dec 82, JSt; SB, Amnesty, Hulk granted amnesty	0.60	0.50	1.25	2.50
❑279, Jan 83, SB, Everybody Loves A Parade, Right?	0.60	0.50	1.25	2.50
❑280, Feb 83, SB, Alone In A Crowd!	0.60	0.50	1.25	2.50
❑281, Mar 83, JSt; SB, Audition!	0.60	0.50	1.25	2.50
❑282, Apr 83, JSt; SB, Again Arsenal!, A: She-Hulk	0.60	0.50	1.25	2.50
❑283, May 83, SB, A: Avengers	0.60	0.50	1.25	2.50
❑284, Jun 83, JSt; SB, Time-Lost!, A: Avengers; V: Leader	0.60	0.50	1.25	2.50
❑285, Jul 83, SB, Today Is The First Day Of the Rest Of My Life!	0.60	0.50	1.25	2.50
❑286, Aug 83, SB, Hero	0.60	0.50	1.25	2.50
❑287, Sep 83, SB, Loose Ends!	0.60	0.50	1.25	2.50
❑288, Oct 83, JM; SB, Yellow Fever?!, V: Modok	0.60	0.50	1.25	2.50
❑289, Nov 83, JSt; SB, A.I.M. For The Top!, V: A.I.M.	0.60	0.50	1.25	2.50
❑290, Dec 83, SB, V: Modame; V: Modok	0.60	0.50	1.25	2.50
❑291, Jan 84, SB, O: Thunderbolt Ross, Assistant Editor Month	0.60	0.50	1.25	2.50
❑292, Feb 84, SB	0.60	0.50	1.25	2.50
❑293, Mar 84, SB, V: Fantastic Four	0.60	0.50	1.25	2.50
❑294, Apr 84, SB	0.60	0.50	1.25	2.50
❑295, May 84, SB, V: Boomerang, Secret Wars aftermath	0.60	0.50	1.25	2.50
❑296, Jun 84, SB, V: ROM	0.60	0.50	1.25	2.50
❑297, Jul 84, SB	0.60	0.50	1.25	2.50
❑298, Aug 84, SB, A: Nightmare	0.60	0.50	1.25	2.50
❑299, Sep 84, SB, A: Doctor Strange	0.60	0.50	1.25	2.50
❑300, Oct 84, SB, V: Everybody, Giant-size; 300th anniversary edition; Hulk banished to Crossroads	1.00	0.80	2.00	4.00
❑301, Nov 84, SB, BSz (c)	0.60	0.50	1.25	2.50
❑302, Dec 84, SB	0.60	0.50	1.25	2.50
❑303, Jan 85, SB	0.60	0.50	1.25	2.50
❑304, Feb 85, SB	0.60	0.50	1.25	2.50
❑305, Mar 85, SB, V: U-Foes	0.60	0.50	1.25	2.50
❑306, Apr 85, SB	0.65	0.50	1.25	2.50
❑307, May 85, SB	0.65	0.50	1.25	2.50
❑308, Jun 85, SB	0.65	0.50	1.25	2.50
❑309, Jul 85, SB	0.65	0.50	1.25	2.50
❑310, Aug 85, SB	0.65	0.50	1.25	2.50
❑311, Sep 85, AW (c)	0.65	0.50	1.25	2.50
❑312, Oct 85, BSz (c), Secret Wars II	0.65	0.50	1.25	2.50
❑313, Nov 85, A: Alpha Flight	0.65	0.50	1.25	2.50
❑314, Dec 85, JBy, A: Doc Samson	0.65	0.50	1.25	2.50
❑315, Jan 86, JBy, Hulk and Banner separated	0.65	0.60	1.50	3.00
❑316, Feb 86, JBy, A: Avengers	0.75	0.60	1.50	3.00
❑317, Mar 86, JBy	0.75	0.60	1.50	3.00
❑318, Apr 86, JBy	0.75	0.60	1.50	3.00
❑319, May 86, JBy, Member of the Wedding, Wedding of Bruce Banner and Betty Ross	0.75	0.60	1.50	3.00
❑320, Jun 86, AM, AM (w), Honeymoon's Over!!, V: Doc Samson	0.75	0.40	1.00	2.00
❑321, Jul 86, AM, AM (w), ...And The Walls Come Tumbling Down!, V: Avengers	0.75	0.40	1.00	2.00
❑322, Aug 86, AM, AM (w), Must The Hulk Die?	0.75	0.40	1.00	2.00
❑323, Sep 86, AM, AM (w), Certain Intangibles	0.75	0.40	1.00	2.00
❑324, Oct 86, O: Hulk; 1: Grey Hulk (new)	0.75	1.20	3.00	6.00
❑325, Nov 86, 1: Rick Jones as green Hulk	0.75	0.60	1.50	3.00
❑326, Dec 86, Green Hulk vs. Grey Hulk	0.75	0.70	1.75	3.50
❑327, Jan 87, V: Zzzax	0.75	0.50	1.25	2.50
❑328, Feb 87, PD (w), 1st Peter David writing	0.75	0.50	1.25	2.50
❑329, Mar 87	0.75	0.40	1.00	2.00
❑330, Apr 87, TMc, D: Thunderbolt Ross	0.75	0.80	2.00	4.00
❑331, May 87, TMc, PD (w), 2nd Peter David issue; gray Hulk revealed	0.75	0.80	2.00	4.00
❑332, Jun 87, TMc	0.75	0.80	2.00	4.00
❑333, Jul 87, TMc	0.75	0.80	2.00	4.00
❑334, Aug 87, TMc	0.75	0.80	2.00	4.00
❑335, Sep 87, TMc	0.75	0.40	1.00	2.00
❑336, Oct 87, TMc, A: X-Factor	0.75	0.60	1.50	3.00
❑337, Nov 87, TMc, A: X-Factor	0.75	0.60	1.50	3.00
❑338, Dec 87, TMc, 1: Mercy	0.75	0.60	1.50	3.00

	ORIG	GOOD	FINE	N-MINT
❑339, Jan 88, TMc, A: Ashcan, Leader	0.75	0.60	1.50	3.00
❑340, Feb 88, TMc, V: Wolverine	0.75	2.40	6.00	12.00
❑341, Mar 88, TMc, V: Man-Bull	0.75	0.40	1.00	2.00
❑342, Apr 88, TMc, A: Leader	0.75	0.40	1.00	2.00
❑343, May 88, TMc	0.75	0.40	1.00	2.00
❑344, Jun 88, TMc	0.75	0.40	1.00	2.00
❑345, Jul 88, TMc, Double-size	1.50	0.40	1.00	2.00
❑346, Aug 88, TMc, PD (w)	0.75	0.40	1.00	2.00
❑347, Sep 88, PD (w), in Vegas	0.75	0.40	1.00	2.00
❑348, Oct 88, PD (w), V: Absorbing Man	0.75	0.40	1.00	2.00
❑349, Nov 88, PD (w), A: Spider-Man	0.75	0.40	1.00	2.00
❑350, Dec 88, PD (w), Hulk vs. Thing	0.75	0.60	1.50	3.00
❑351, Jan 89, PD (w)	0.75	0.40	1.00	2.00
❑352, Feb 89, PD (w)	0.75	0.40	1.00	2.00
❑353, Mar 89, PD (w)	0.75	0.40	1.00	2.00
❑354, Apr 89, PD (w)	0.75	0.40	1.00	2.00
❑355, May 89, PD (w), A: Glorian	0.75	0.40	1.00	2.00
❑356, Jun 89, PD (w)	0.75	0.40	1.00	2.00
❑357, Jul 89, PD (w), Possibilities	0.75	0.40	1.00	2.00
❑358, Aug 89, PD (w), Inferno-2 Hulk - - - 0	0.75	0.40	1.00	2.00
❑359, Sep 89, PD (w)	1.00	0.40	1.00	2.00
❑360, Oct 89, Nightmoves, V: Nightmare	1.00	0.40	1.00	2.00
❑361, Nov 89, PD (w), Iron Man	1.00	0.40	1.00	2.00
❑362, Nov 89, PD (w), A: Werewolf by Night	1.00	0.40	1.00	2.00
❑363, Dec 89, PD (w), Acts of Vengeance, V: Grey Gargoyle, Acts of Vengeance	1.00	0.40	1.00	2.00
❑364, Dec 89, PD (w), Countdown, Part 1, V: Abomination	1.00	0.40	1.00	2.00
❑365, Jan 90, PD (w), Countdown, Part 2, V: Thing	1.00	0.40	1.00	2.00
❑366, Feb 90, PD (w), Countdown, Part 3, V: Leader	1.00	0.40	1.00	2.00
❑367, Mar 90, PD (w), Countdown, Part 4, V: Madman, 1st Dale Keown art	1.00	0.80	2.00	4.00
❑368, Apr 90, PD (w), V: Mr. Hyde; 1: Pantheon	1.00	0.80	2.00	4.00
❑369, May 90, PD (w), V: Freedom Force	1.00	0.80	2.00	4.00
❑370, Jun 90, PD (w), A: Sub-Mariner; A: Doctor Strange	1.00	0.80	2.00	4.00
❑371, Jul 90, PD (w), A: Sub-Mariner; A: Doctor Strange	1.00	0.80	2.00	4.00
❑372, Aug 90, PD (w), Green Hulk returns	1.00	1.00	2.50	5.00
❑373, Sep 90, PD (w)	1.00	0.50	1.25	2.50
❑374, Oct 90, PD (w), V: Super Skrull	1.00	0.50	1.25	2.50
❑375, Nov 90, PD (w), V: Super Skrull	1.00	0.50	1.25	2.50
❑376, Dec 90, PD (w), 1: Agamemnon (as hologram), Green Hulk vs. Grey Hulk	1.00	0.50	1.25	2.50
❑377, Jan 91, PD (w), Honey, I Shrunk the Hulk!, 1: Hulk (new, smart), Fluorescent inks on cover	1.00	0.80	2.00	4.00
❑377-2, Jan 91, PD (w), 1: Hulk (new, smart), Fluorescent inks on cover; 2nd printing (gold)	1.00	0.40	1.00	2.00
❑377-3, Jan 91, 3rd Printing	1.75	0.35	0.88	1.75
❑378, Feb 91, PD (w), Rhino as Santa	1.00	0.30	0.75	1.50
❑379, Mar 91, PD (w), A: Pantheon	1.00	0.40	1.00	2.00
❑380, Apr 91, PD (w), Doc Samson solo story	1.00	0.40	1.00	2.00
❑381, May 91, PD (w), Exposition, Hulk joins Pantheon	1.00	0.40	1.00	2.00
❑382, Jun 91, PD (w), Moving On	1.00	0.40	1.00	2.00
❑383, Jul 91, PD (w), Green Canard, V: Abomination	1.00	0.40	1.00	2.00
❑384, Aug 91, PD (w), V: Abomination, Infinity Gauntlet; tiny Hulk	1.00	0.40	1.00	2.00
❑385, Sep 91, PD (w), Infinity Gauntlet, Infinity Gauntlet	1.00	0.40	1.00	2.00
❑386, Oct 91, PD (w), Little Hitler, A: Sabra	1.00	0.40	1.00	2.00
❑387, Nov 91, PD (w), Hiding Behind Mosques, A: Sabra	1.00	0.40	1.00	2.00
❑388, Dec 91, PD (w), Thicker Than Water, 1: Speedfreek	1.00	0.40	1.00	2.00
❑389, Jan 92, PD (w), A: Man-Thing	1.00	0.40	1.00	2.00
❑390, Feb 92, PD (w), War & Pieces, Part 1; This Means War	1.25	0.40	1.00	2.00
❑391, Mar 92, PD (w), War & Pieces, Part 2; X-Calation, A: X-Factor	1.25	0.40	1.00	2.00
❑392, Apr 92, PD (w), War & Pieces, Part 3; War And Pieces: Conclusion Fortunes Of War, A: X-Factor	1.25	0.40	1.00	2.00
❑393, May 92, PD (w), The Closing Circles; Classic Battles Of The Hulk, 30th Anniversary of the Hulk, Green Foil Cover	2.50	0.60	1.50	3.00
❑393-2, May 92, PD (w), The Closing Circles; Classic Battles Of The Hulk, 2nd Printing; non-foil cover; 30th Anniversary of the Hulk	2.50	0.50	1.25	2.50
❑394, Jun 92, PD (w), Cold Storage, 1: Trauma	1.25	0.30	0.75	1.50

The Hulk and Wolverine faced off in *Incredible Hulk* #340.

	ORIG	GOOD	FINE	N-MINT
❑395, Jul 92, PD (w), Return To Vegas, A: Punisher	1.25	0.30	0.75	1.50
❑396, Aug 92, PD (w), V: Doctor Octopus; V: Mr. Frost; A: Punisher	1.25	0.30	0.75	1.50
❑397, Sep 92, PD (w), Ghost of the Past, Part 1; Ghosts of the Past, Part 1, V: U-Foes.	1.25	0.30	0.75	1.50
❑398, Oct 92, PD (w), Ghost of the Past, Part 2; Ghosts of the Past, Part 2, V: Leader.	1.25	0.30	0.75	1.50
❑399, Nov 92, JDu, PD (w), Ghost of the Past, Part 3; Ghosts of the Past, Part 3, D: Marlo	1.25	0.30	0.75	1.50
❑400, Dec 92, JDu, PD (w), Ghost of the Past, Part 4; Ghosts of the Past, Part 4, D: Leader, Prism cover; Marlo revived	2.50	0.60	1.50	3.00
❑400-2, Dec 92, 2nd Printing	2.50	0.50	1.25	2.50
❑401, Jan 93, JDu, PD (w), Filling Slots, V: U-Foes; 1: Agamemnon (physical)	1.25	0.30	0.75	1.50
❑402, Feb 93, JDu, PD (w), The Forest For The Trees, V: Juggernaut; A: Doc Samson	1.25	0.30	0.75	1.50
❑403, Mar 93, PD (w), In Memory Not Yet Green, V: Juggernaut	1.25	0.30	0.75	1.50
❑404, Apr 93, PD (w), V: Juggernaut; A: Avengers	1.25	0.30	0.75	1.50
❑405, May 93, PD (w), Downtime	1.25	0.30	0.75	1.50
❑406, Jun 93, PD (w), American Pie, A: Captain America; A: Doc Samson	1.25	0.30	0.75	1.50
❑407, Jul 93, PD (w), More Or Ness, 1: Piecemeal	1.25	0.30	0.75	1.50
❑408, Aug 93, PD (w), A Sinking Feeling, V: Madman; D: Perseus	1.25	0.30	0.75	1.50
❑409, Sep 93, PD (w), Royal Pain, A: Motormouth; A: Killpower	1.25	0.30	0.75	1.50
❑410, Oct 93, PD (w), Jailhouse Rock, A: Nick Fury; A: S.H.I.E.L.D.; A: Doctor Samson	1.25	0.30	0.75	1.50
❑411, Nov 93, PD (w), A: Nick Fury	1.25	0.30	0.75	1.50
❑412, Dec 93, PD (w), Blame That, V: Bi-Beast; A: She-Hulk	1.25	0.30	0.75	1.50
❑413, Jan 94, PD (w), Troyjan War, Part 1; The Troyjan War, Part 1	1.25	0.30	0.75	1.50
❑414, Feb 94, PD (w), Troyjan War, Part 2; The Troyjan War, Part 2, A: Silver Surfer	1.25	0.30	0.75	1.50
❑415, Mar 94, PD (w), Troyjan War, Part 3; The Troyjan War, Part 3, A: Starjammers	1.25	0.30	0.75	1.50
❑416, Apr 94, PD (w), Troyjan War, Part 4; The Troyjan War, Part 4	1.25	0.30	0.75	1.50
❑417, May 94, PD (w), Rick's bachelor party	1.50	0.30	0.75	1.50
❑418, Jun 94, PD (w), We Are Gathered Here, A: (of Sandman) appearance, Wedding of Rick Jones and Marlo; Peter David (writer) puts himself in script	1.50	0.40	1.00	2.00
❑418/SC, Jun 94, PD (w), We Are Gathered Here, A: (of Sandman) appearance, Die-cut cover; Wedding of Rick Jones and Marlo; Peter David (writer) puts himself in script	2.50	0.60	1.50	3.00
❑419, Jul 94, PD (w), The Last Waltz, V: Talos the Tamed	1.50	0.30	0.75	1.50
❑420, Aug 94, PD (w), D: Jim Wilson	1.50	0.30	0.75	1.50
❑421, Sep 94, PD (w), Myth Conceptions, Part 1, V: Thor	1.50	0.30	0.75	1.50
❑422, Oct 94, PD (w), Myth Conceptions, Part 2	1.50	0.30	0.75	1.50
❑423, Nov 94, PD (w), Myth Conceptions, Part 3, A: Hel	1.50	0.30	0.75	1.50
❑424, Dec 94, PD (w), Fall of the Pantheon, Part 1	1.50	0.30	0.75	1.50
❑425, Jan 95, PD (w), Fall of the Pantheon, Part 2, Giant-size	2.25	0.45	1.13	2.25
❑425/SC, Jan 95, PD (w), Hologram cover; Giant-size	3.50	0.70	1.75	3.50
❑426, Feb 95, PD (w), One Fell Off, Hulk reverts to Banner	1.50	0.30	0.75	1.50
❑426/Dlx, Feb 95, PD (w), One Fell Off, Deluxe edition	1.95	0.39	0.98	1.95
❑427, Mar 95, PD (w), A: Man-Thing	1.95	0.30	0.75	1.50
❑427/Dlx, PD (w)	1.95	0.39	0.98	1.95
❑428, Apr 95, PD (w), A: Man-Thing	1.95	0.30	0.75	1.50
❑428/Dlx, PD (w)	1.95	0.39	0.98	1.95

	ORIG	GOOD	FINE	N-MINT
❑429, May 95, PD (w)	1.95	0.30	0.75	1.50
❑429/Dlx, PD (w)	1.95	0.39	0.98	1.95
❑430, Jun 95, PD (w), V: Speedfreek	1.95	0.39	0.98	1.95
❑431, Jul 95, PD (w), V: Abomination	1.95	0.39	0.98	1.95
❑432, Aug 95, PD (w), V: Abomination	1.95	0.39	0.98	1.95
❑433, Sep 95, PD (w), Over the Edge, A: Nick Fury; A: Punisher	1.95	0.39	0.98	1.95
❑434, Oct 95, PD (w), A: Howling Commandoes, Funeral of Nick Fury; OverPower cards inserted	1.95	0.39	0.98	1.95
❑435, Nov 95, PD (w), V: Rhino, Casey at the Bat tribute	1.95	0.39	0.98	1.95
❑436, Dec 95, PD (w), Ghosts of the Future, Part 1, A: Maestro, continued in Cutting Edge #1	1.95	0.39	0.98	1.95
❑437, Jan 96, PD (w), Ghosts of the Future, Part 2	1.95	0.39	0.98	1.95
❑438, Feb 96, PD (w), Ghosts of the Future, Part 3	1.95	0.39	0.98	1.95
❑439, Mar 96, PD (w), Ghosts of the Future, Part 4	1.95	0.39	0.98	1.95
❑440, Apr 96, PD (w), Ghosts of the Future, Part 5, V: Thor	1.95	0.39	0.98	1.95
❑441, May 96, PD (w), A: She-Hulk, Pulp Fiction tribute cover	1.95	0.39	0.98	1.95
❑442, Jun 96, PD (w), A: Molecule Man; A: Doc Samson; A: She-Hulk, no Hulk	1.95	0.39	0.98	1.95
❑443, Jul 96, PD (w), A: Janis	1.95	0.30	0.75	1.50
❑444, Aug 96, PD (w), Onslaught: Impact 1; Onslaught, V: Cable	1.50	0.30	0.75	1.50
❑445, Sep 96, PD (w), Onslaught: Impact 2; Onslaught, A: Avengers	1.50	0.30	0.75	1.50
❑446, Oct 96, PD (w), post-Onslaught; Hulk turns savage and highly radioactive	1.50	0.30	0.75	1.50
❑447, Nov 96, PD (w)	1.50	0.30	0.75	1.50
❑448, Dec 96, PD (w), Line In The Sand, A: Pantheon	1.50	0.30	0.75	1.50
❑449, Jan 97, PD (w), 1: The Thunderbolts.	1.50	1.80	4.50	9.00
❑450, Feb 97, PD (w), Hurray for Hulk; A Little Leeway, A: Doctor Strange, Giant-size; connection to Heroes Reborn universe revealed	2.95	1.00	2.50	5.00
❑451, Mar 97, PD (w), Island Getaway, Hulk takes over Duck Key	1.99	0.40	1.00	2.00
❑452, Apr 97, PD (w), Take Charge Guy, Hulk vs. Hurricane Betty	1.99	0.40	1.00	2.00
❑453, May 97, PD (w), Lock and Key, Hulk vs. Hulk	1.99	0.40	1.00	2.00
❑454, Jun 97, PD (w), Best Intentions	1.99	0.40	1.00	2.00
❑455, Aug 97, A: Apocalypse; V: X-Men, gatefold summary; Thunderbolt Ross returns	1.99	0.40	1.00	2.00
❑456, Sep 97, gatefold summary; Apocalypse transforms Hulk into War	1.99	0.40	1.00	2.00
❑457, Oct 97, V: Juggernaut, gatefold summary	1.99	0.40	1.00	2.00
❑458, Nov 97, A: Mercy; V: Mr. Hyde, gatefold summary	1.99	0.40	1.00	2.00
❑459, Dec 97, A: Mercy; V: Abomination, gatefold summary	1.99	0.40	1.00	2.00
❑460, Jan 98, gatefold summary; The Hulk and Bruce Banner are reunited; return of Maestro	1.99	0.40	1.00	2.00
❑461, Feb 98, V: Destroyer, gatefold summary	1.99	0.40	1.00	2.00
❑462, Mar 98, gatefold summary	1.99	0.40	1.00	2.00
❑463, Apr 98, gatefold summary	1.99	0.40	1.00	2.00
❑464, May 98, JK, A: Silver Surfer, gatefold summary	1.99	0.40	1.00	2.00
❑465, Jun 98, A: Tony Stark; A: Reed Richards, gatefold summary	1.99	0.40	1.00	2.00
❑466, Jul 98, D: Betty Banner, gatefold summary	1.99	0.40	1.00	2.00
❑467, Aug 98, gatefold summary; final Peter David-written issue	1.99	0.40	1.00	2.00
❑468, Sep 98, gatefold summary; 1st Joe Casey issue	1.99	0.40	1.00	2.00
❑469, Oct 98, V: Super-Adaptoid, gatefold summary	1.99	0.40	1.00	2.00
❑470, Nov 98, V: Circus of Crime, gatefold summary	1.99	0.40	1.00	2.00
❑471, Dec 98, V: Circus of Crime, gatefold summary	1.99	0.40	1.00	2.00
❑472, Jan 99, The Great Astonishment, Part 1, A: Xantarean, gatefold summary	1.99	0.40	1.00	2.00
❑473, Feb 99, The Great Astonishment, Part 2, A: Xantarean; A: Abomination; A: Watchers; A: Xanterean, gatefold summary	1.99	0.40	1.00	1.99
❑474, Mar 99, The Great Astonishment, Part 3, A: Xantarean; A: Thunderbolt Ross; A: Abomination; A: Watchers; A: Xanterean, Final Issue	2.99	0.40	1.00	1.99
❑Anl 1, JSo (c)	0.25	10.00	25.00	50.00
❑Anl 2, Oct 67, Reprint	0.25	7.20	18.00	36.00
❑Anl 3, Jan 71, Reprint; Cover reads "King-Size Special"	0.25	1.80	4.50	9.00
❑Anl 4, Jan 72, JR; JK, SL (w), Not All my Power Can Save Me!; I, Against a World!, Cover reads "Special"; Reprint	0.50	1.40	3.50	7.00
❑Anl 5, V: Goom; V: Taboo; V: Blip; V: Diablo, Blip; V: Diablo; V: Groot; V: Xemnu	0.50	1.40	3.50	7.00
❑Anl 6, HT, 1: Paragon; A: Doctor Strange; A: Warlock, Doctor Strange	0.60	0.60	1.50	3.00
❑Anl 7, BL; JBy, A: Angel; A: Iceman	0.60	0.60	1.50	3.00
❑Anl 8, Alpha Flight	0.75	0.60	1.50	3.00
❑Anl 9, SD; AM, A Game Of Monsters And Kings	0.75	0.50	1.25	2.50
❑Anl 10, Nothing Stops The Hulk!, Captain Universe	0.75	0.50	1.25	2.50
❑Anl 11, FM, 1st Frank Miller Marvel pencils	1.00	0.40	1.00	2.00
❑Anl 12, HT, Amazing Grace!	1.00	0.40	1.00	2.00
❑Anl 13	1.00	0.40	1.00	2.00
❑Anl 14	1.25	0.40	1.00	2.00
❑Anl 15, Subterranean Odyssey, Part 2, V: Abomination	1.25	0.45	1.13	2.25
❑Anl 16, Lifeform, Part 3; The Quality Of Mercy, Lifeform	2.00	0.50	1.25	2.50
❑Anl 17, Subterranean Wars	2.00	0.40	1.00	2.00
❑Anl 18, PD (w), Return Of The Defenders, Part 1, Return of Defenders	2.25	0.55	1.38	2.75
❑Anl 19, 1: Lazarus, Polybagged with trading card	2.95	0.59	1.48	2.95
❑Anl 20	2.95	0.59	1.48	2.95
❑Anl 1997, Sins of the Father; Where the Wild Things Are, Hulk vs. Gladiator; Incredible Hulk '97	2.99	0.60	1.50	2.99
❑Anl 1998, Lifesblood, wraparound cover; gatefold summary; Hulk/Sub-Mariner '98	2.99	0.60	1.50	2.99
❑Ash 1, ashcan edition	0.75	0.15	0.38	0.75
❑GS 1	0.50	1.60	4.00	8.00

INCREDIBLE HULK AND WOLVERINE

MARVEL

	ORIG	GOOD	FINE	N-MINT
❑1, Oct 86, Reprints The Incredible Hulk #181-182, other story	2.00	1.40	3.50	7.00
❑1-2, 2nd Printing; Reprints The Incredible Hulk #181-182, other story	—	0.80	2.00	4.00

INCREDIBLE HULK, THE: FUTURE IMPERFECT

MARVEL

	ORIG	GOOD	FINE	N-MINT
❑1, Jan 93, GP, PD (w), 1: The Maestro, Embossed cover; prestige format; indicia lists date as Jan 93	5.95	1.20	3.00	6.00
❑2, Dec 92, GP, PD (w), Embossed cover; prestige format; indicia lists date as Dec 92	5.95	1.20	3.00	6.00

INCREDIBLE HULK: HERCULES UNLEASHED

MARVEL

Value: Cover or less

❑1, Oct 96, One-Shot; follows events of Onslaught 2.50

INCREDIBLE HULK MEGAZINE, THE

MARVEL

Value: Cover or less

❑1, Dec 96, Quality of Life; Heaven is a Very Small Place, 1: The Abomination; O: Hulk, Reprint 3.95

INCREDIBLE HULK POSTER MAGAZINE

MARVEL

Value: Cover or less

❑1/A, comics 3.95

❑1/B, TV show 1.50

INCREDIBLE HULK VERSUS QUASIMODO, THE

MARVEL

	ORIG	GOOD	FINE	N-MINT
❑1, Mar 83, SB, The Hulk Meets The Hunchback Of Notre Dame!, Based on Saturday morning cartoon	0.60	0.30	0.75	1.50

INCREDIBLE HULK VS. SUPERMAN

MARVEL

Value: Cover or less

❑1, Jul 99, prestige format 5.99

INCREDIBLE HULK VS. VENOM

MARVEL

Value: Cover or less

❑1, Apr 94, nn 2.50

INCUBUS

PALLIARD PRESS

Value: Cover or less

❑1, b&w; adult 2.95

❑2, b&w; adult 2.95

INDEPENDENT PUBLISHER'S GROUP SPOTLIGHT

HERO

Value: Cover or less

❑0, Jul 93, Deathrow vs. X-187!: Turf-Wars; Flare: Joyride 3.50

INDEPENDENT VOICES

PEREGRINE ENTERTAINMENT

Value: Cover or less

❑1, Sep 98, b&w; SPX '98 anthology 1.95

❑2, b&w; CBLDF benefit comic book 2.95

❑36924, May 00, b&w; 2nd Printing; CBLDF benefit comic book 2.95

ORIG GOOD FINE N-MINT

INDIANA JONES AND THE ARMS OF GOLD
DARK HORSE
Value: Cover or less

❑1, Feb 94 .... 2.50
❑2, Mar 94 .... 2.50
❑3, Apr 94 .... 2.50
❑4, May 94 .... 2.50
❑5 .... 2.50
❑6, Apr 94 .... 2.50

INDIANA JONES AND THE FATE OF ATLANTIS
DARK HORSE
Value: Cover or less

❑1, Mar 91, trading cards; trading cards 2.50
❑1-2, 2nd Printing 2.50
❑2, May 91, trading cards 2.50
❑3, Jul 91 .... 2.50
❑4, Sep 91 .... 2.50

INDIANA JONES AND THE GOLDEN FLEECE
DARK HORSE
Value: Cover or less

❑1, Jun 94 .... 2.50
❑2, Jul 94 .... 2.50

INDIANA JONES AND THE IRON PHOENIX
DARK HORSE
Value: Cover or less

❑1, Dec 94 .... 2.50
❑2, Jan 95 .... 2.50
❑3, Feb 95 .... 2.50
❑4, Mar 95 .... 2.50

INDIANA JONES AND THE LAST CRUSADE
MARVEL
Value: Cover or less

❑1, Oct 89, movie Adaptation; comic book 1.00
❑2, Oct 89, comic book 1.00
❑3, Nov 89, comic book 1.00
❑4, Nov 89, comic book 1.00

INDIANA JONES AND THE LAST CRUSADE (MAGAZINE)
MARVEL
Value: Cover or less

❑1, Aug 89, b&w; magazine 2.95

INDIANA JONES AND THE SARGASSO PIRATES
DARK HORSE
Value: Cover or less

❑1, Dec 95, A Watery Grave ... 2.50
❑2, Jan 96 .... 2.50
❑3, Feb 96 .... 2.50
❑4, Mar 96, Final Issue 2.50

INDIANA JONES AND THE SHRINE OF THE SEA DEVIL
DARK HORSE
Value: Cover or less

❑1, Sep 94, One-Shot 2.50

INDIANA JONES AND THE SPEAR OF DESTINY
DARK HORSE
Value: Cover or less

❑1, Apr 95, The Land Below ... 2.50
❑2, May 95 .... 2.50
❑3, Jun 95 .... 2.50
❑4, Jul 95 .... 2.50

INDIANA JONES AND THE TEMPLE OF DOOM
MARVEL

Issue	ORIG	GOOD	FINE	N-MINT
❑1, Sep 84, movie Adaptation	0.75	0.30	0.75	1.50
❑2, Oct 84, movie Adaptation	0.75	0.30	0.75	1.50
❑3, Nov 84, movie Adaptation	0.75	0.30	0.75	1.50

INDIANA JONES: THUNDER IN THE ORIENT
DARK HORSE
Value: Cover or less

❑1, Sep 93 .... 2.50
❑2, Oct 93 .... 2.50
❑3, Nov 93 .... 2.50
❑4, Dec 93 .... 2.50
❑5, Mar 94 .... 2.50
❑6, Apr 94 .... 2.50

INDUSTRIAL GOTHIC
DC
Value: Cover or less

❑1, Dec 95, Anywhere but Here 2.50
❑2, Jan 96, Damn Your Hands 2.50
❑3, Feb 96, Traces of Lilac 2.50
❑4, Mar 96, The Truncheon's Waltz 2.50
❑5, Apr 96, The Aluminum Tower, Final Issue 2.50

INDUSTRIAL STRENGTH PREVIEW
SILVER SKULL
Value: Cover or less

❑1, b&w 1.50

INEDIBLE ADVENTURES OF CLINT THE CARROT
HOT LEG
Value: Cover or less

❑1, Mar 94, b&w 2.50

INFECTIOUS
FANTACO
Value: Cover or less

❑1, One-Shot 3.95

INFERIOR FIVE, THE
DC

Issue	ORIG	GOOD	FINE	N-MINT
❑1, Apr 67, Five Characters In Search Of A Plot, Poliwko cover	0.12	4.40	11.00	22.00
❑2, Jun 67	0.12	3.20	8.00	16.00
❑3, Aug 67	0.12	2.80	7.00	14.00
❑4, Oct 67	0.12	2.80	7.00	14.00
❑5, Dec 67	0.12	2.80	7.00	14.00
❑6, Feb 68, A: DC heroes	0.12	2.80	7.00	14.00
❑7, Apr 68	0.12	2.80	7.00	14.00
❑8, Jun 68	0.12	2.80	7.00	14.00
❑9, Aug 68	0.12	2.80	7.00	14.00
❑10, Oct 68, A: other heroes, Final issue of original run (1968)	0.12	2.80	7.00	14.00

Dark Horse's first Indiana Jones comic book shared its title with the *Fate of Atlantis* computer game.

© 1991 Lucasfilm Ltd. and Dark Horse

Issue	ORIG	GOOD	FINE	N-MINT
❑11, Sep 72, reprints Showcase #62; Series begins again (1972)	0.20	2.00	5.00	10.00
❑12, Nov 72, Final Issue; reprints Showcase #63	0.20	2.00	5.00	10.00

INFERNO (AIRCEL)
AIRCEL
Value: Cover or less

❑1, Oct 90, The White Wolf; Genesis the Magician, b&w; adult 2.50
❑2, Nov 90, The Hound of Hell; The Axe, b&w; adult 2.50
❑3, Dec 90, b&w; adult 2.50
❑4, Jan 91, Metalady; The Avenging Navajo, b&w; adult 2.50

INFERNO (CALIBER)
CALIBER
Value: Cover or less

❑1, Aug 95, b&w 2.95

INFERNO (DC)
DC
Value: Cover or less

❑1, Oct 97, Run Come See the Sun, spin-off from Legion of Super-Heroes 2.50
❑2, Nov 97 .... 2.50
❑3, Jan 98, Girls Interrupted 2.50
❑4, Feb 98 .... 2.50

INFINITY CHARADE, THE
PARODY PRESS

Issue	ORIG	GOOD	FINE	N-MINT
❑1/A	2.50	0.50	1.25	2.50
❑1/B	2.50	0.50	1.25	2.50
❑1/GO, Gold limited edition (1500 printed)	3.95	0.80	2.00	4.00

INFINITY CRUSADE, THE
MARVEL
Value: Cover or less

❑1, Jun 93, 1: Goddess, Gold foil cover 3.50
❑2, Jul 93 .... 2.50
❑3, Aug 93 .... 2.50
❑4, Sep 93 .... 2.50
❑5, Oct 93, JSn (w), A: Goddess; A: Thanos; A: Hulk 2.50
❑6, Nov 93 .... 2.50

INFINITY GAUNTLET
MARVEL

Issue	ORIG	GOOD	FINE	N-MINT
❑1, Jul 91, GP, JSn (w), God, A: Silver Surfer; A: Avengers; A: Spider-Man; A: Thanos	2.50	0.60	1.50	3.00
❑2, Aug 91, GP, JSn (w), A: Silver Surfer; A: Avengers; A: Spider-Man; A: Thanos	2.50	0.50	1.25	2.50
❑3, Sep 91, GP, JSn (w), A: Silver Surfer; A: Avengers; A: Spider-Man; A: Thanos	2.50	0.50	1.25	2.50
❑4, Oct 91, GP, JSn (w), A: Silver Surfer; A: Avengers; A: Spider-Man; A: Thanos	2.50	0.50	1.25	2.50
❑5, Nov 91, GP (c), JSn (w)	2.50	0.50	1.25	2.50
❑6, Dec 91, GP (c), JSn (w)	2.50	0.50	1.25	2.50

INFINITY, INC.
DC

Issue	ORIG	GOOD	FINE	N-MINT
❑1, Mar 84, JOy, Generations, O: Infinity Inc	1.25	0.40	1.00	2.00
❑2, May 84, JOy, O: ends; V: Ultra-Humanite	1.25	0.30	0.75	1.50
❑3, Jun 84, JOy, V: Solomon Grundy	1.25	0.30	0.75	1.50
❑4, Jul 84, JOy	1.25	0.30	0.75	1.50
❑5, Aug 84, JOy	1.25	0.30	0.75	1.50
❑6, Sep 84, JOy	1.25	0.30	0.75	1.50
❑7, Oct 84, JOy, A: E-2 Superman	1.25	0.30	0.75	1.50
❑8, Nov 84, JOy	1.25	0.30	0.75	1.50
❑9, Dec 84, JOy	1.25	0.30	0.75	1.50
❑10, Jan 85, JOy	1.25	0.30	0.75	1.50
❑11, Feb 85, more on Infinity's origin	1.25	0.25	0.63	1.25
❑12, Mar 85, 1: Yolanda Montez, Brainwave Junior's new powers	1.25	0.25	0.63	1.25
❑13, Apr 85, V: Thorn	1.25	0.25	0.63	1.25
❑14, May 85, TMc, 1: Marcie Cooper; 1: Chroma	1.25	0.70	1.75	3.50
❑15, Jun 85, TMc, A: Chroma	1.25	0.50	1.25	2.50
❑16, Jul 85, TMc, 1: Mr. Bones	1.25	0.50	1.25	2.50
❑17, Aug 85, TMc, 1: Helix	1.25	0.50	1.25	2.50
❑18, Sep 85, TMc, Crisis on Infinite Earths, V: Helix, Crisis	1.25	0.50	1.25	2.50
❑19, Oct 85, TMc, Crisis on Infinite Earths, A: JLA; A: Steel; 1: Mekanique, Crisis	1.25	0.50	1.25	2.50
❑20, Nov 85, TMc, Crisis on Infinite Earths, 1: Rick Tyler, Crisis	1.25	0.50	1.25	2.50
❑21, Dec 85, TMc, Crisis on Infinite Earths, 1: Hourman II (Rick Tyler); 1: Doctor Midnight (new), Crisis	1.50	0.50	1.25	2.50

	ORIG	GOOD	FINE	N-MINT
❑22, Jan 86, TMc, Crisis on Infinite Earths, Crisis	1.50	0.50	1.25	2.50
❑23, Feb 86, TMc, Crisis on Infinite Earths, V: Solomon Grundy, Crisis	1.50	0.50	1.25	2.50
❑24, Mar 86, TMc, Crisis on Infinite Earths, Star Spangled Kid, Jonni Thunder vs. Last Criminal; Crisis	1.50	0.50	1.25	2.50
❑25, Apr 86, TMc, Crisis aftermath; Hourman II joins team; Doctor Midnight joins team; Wildcat II joins team	1.50	0.50	1.25	2.50
❑26, May 86, TMc, A: Helix	1.50	0.50	1.25	2.50
❑27, Jun 86, TMc, Lyta's memories erased	1.50	0.50	1.25	2.50
❑28, Jul 86, TMc, V: Mr. Bones	1.50	0.50	1.25	2.50
❑29, Jul 86, TMc, V: Helix	1.50	0.50	1.25	2.50
❑30, Sep 86, TMc, What Private Griefs ..., JSA mourned	1.50	0.50	1.25	2.50
❑31, Oct 86, TMc, 1: Skyman; A: Jonni Thunder	1.50	0.50	1.25	2.50
❑32, Nov 86, TMc, V: Psycho Pirate	1.50	0.50	1.25	2.50
❑33, Dec 86, TMc, O: Obsidian	1.50	0.50	1.25	2.50
❑34, Jan 87, TMc, V: Global Guardians	1.50	0.50	1.25	2.50
❑35, Feb 87, TMc, V: Injustice Unlimited	1.50	0.50	1.25	2.50
❑36, Mar 87, TMc, V: Solomon Grundy	1.50	0.50	1.25	2.50
❑37, Apr 87, TMc, O: Northwing	1.50	0.50	1.25	2.50
❑38, May 87	1.50	0.25	0.63	1.25
❑39, Jun 87, The Saga of Solomon Grundy, O: Solomon Grundy	1.50	0.25	0.63	1.25
❑40, Jul 87	1.50	0.25	0.63	1.25
❑41, Aug 87	1.50	0.25	0.63	1.25
❑42, Sep 87, Farewell To Fury!, Fury leaves team	1.50	0.25	0.63	1.25
❑43, Oct 87	1.50	0.25	0.63	1.25
❑44, Nov 87	1.50	0.25	0.63	1.25
❑45, Dec 87, A: Titans	1.50	0.25	0.63	1.25
❑46, Jan 88, V: Floronic Man, Millennium	1.75	0.30	0.75	1.50
❑47, Feb 88, V: Harlequin, Millennium	1.75	0.25	0.63	1.25
❑48, Mar 88, O: Nuklon	1.75	0.25	0.63	1.25
❑49, Apr 88, A: Sandman	1.75	0.25	0.63	1.25
❑50, May 88, Giant-size	2.50	0.50	1.25	2.50
❑51, Jun 88, D: Skyman	1.75	0.25	0.63	1.25
❑52, Jul 88, V: Helix	1.75	0.25	0.63	1.25
❑53, Aug 88, V: Injustice Unlimited, Final Issue	1.75	0.35	0.88	1.75
❑Anl 1, Nov 85, TMc, O: Jade and Obsidian, Crisis	2.00	0.50	1.25	2.50
❑Anl 2, Jul 88, crossover with Young All-Stars Annual #1	2.00	0.50	1.25	2.50
❑SE 1, cover forms diptych with Outsiders Special #1	1.50	0.30	0.75	1.50

INFINITY OF WARRIORS, THE
OMINOUS

Value: Cover or less

❑1, Oct 94, The Infinity of Warriors, Revelation of The Molochs.. 1.95

INFINITY WAR, THE
MARVEL

Value: Cover or less

❑1, Jun 92, JSn (w), gatefold cover 2.50
❑2, Jul 92, JSn (w), Ethereal Revisionism, O: Magus, gatefold cover 2.50
❑3, Aug 92, JSn (w), gatefold cover 2.50
❑4, Sep 92, JSn (w), Mortiferous Artifice, gatefold cover 2.50
❑5, Oct 92, JSn (w), Psychomachia, gatefold cover 2.50
❑6, Nov 92, JSn (w), The Animus Engagement, gatefold cover 2.50

INFOCHAMELEON: COMPANY CULT
MEDIAWARP

Value: Cover or less

❑1, Feb 97, b&w; One-Shot 4.50

INFORMER, THE
FEATURE

	ORIG	GOOD	FINE	N-MINT
❑1, Apr 54, The Blood Stained Mink; The End of Hector Spectre	0.10	8.00	20.00	40.00
❑2	0.10	5.60	14.00	28.00
❑3	0.10	4.80	12.00	24.00
❑4	0.10	4.80	12.00	24.00
❑5	0.10	4.80	12.00	24.00

INHUMANOIDS, THE
MARVEL

	ORIG	GOOD	FINE	N-MINT
❑1, Jan 87, The Coming Of The Inhumanoids!, 1: Earth Corps	0.75	0.20	0.50	1.00
❑2, Mar 87	0.75	0.20	0.50	1.00
❑3, May 87	0.75	0.20	0.50	1.00
❑4, Jul 87	1.00	0.20	0.50	1.00

INHUMANS, THE
MARVEL

	ORIG	GOOD	FINE	N-MINT
❑1, Oct 75, GP, V: Blastaar	0.25	1.60	4.00	8.00
❑2	0.25	1.00	2.50	5.00
❑3	0.25	1.00	2.50	5.00
❑4	0.25	0.80	2.00	4.00
❑5	0.30	0.80	2.00	4.00
❑6, Oct 76	0.25	0.70	1.75	3.50
❑7, Nov 76	0.30	0.70	1.75	3.50
❑8, Dec 76	0.30	0.70	1.75	3.50
❑9, Feb 77	0.30	0.70	1.75	3.50
❑10, Apr 77	0.30	0.60	1.50	3.00
❑11, Jun 77	0.30	0.60	1.50	3.00
❑12, Aug 77, V: Hulk, Final Issue	0.30	0.60	1.50	3.00
❑SE 1, Apr 90, RHo, The Remembrances Of Revolutions Past, O: Medusa; A: Fantastic Four	1.50	0.50	1.25	2.50

INHUMANS (VOL. 2)
MARVEL

Value: Cover or less

❑1, Nov 98, trading card; gatefold summary 2.99
❑1/LE, Nov 98 19.95
❑1/SC, Nov 98, DFE alternate cover 6.95
❑2/A, Dec 98, Genotypical, Woman in circle on cover; gatefold summary 2.99
❑2/B, Dec 98, Genotypical, gatefold summary 2.99
❑3, Jan 99 2.99
❑4, Feb 99 2.99
❑5, Mar 99, Earth vs. Attilan war 2.99
❑6, Apr 99 2.99
❑7, May 99 2.99
❑8, Jun 99, Woof 2.99
❑9, Jul 99 2.99
❑10, Aug 99 2.99
❑11, Sep 99 2.99
❑12, Oct 99 2.99

INHUMANS (VOL. 3)
MARVEL

Value: Cover or less

❑1, Jun 00, Stars Our Destiny. 2.99
❑2 2.99
❑3 2.99
❑4 2.99

INHUMANS, THE: THE GREAT REFUGE
MARVEL

Value: Cover or less

❑1, May 95 2.95

INMATES PRISONERS OF SOCIETY
DELTA

Value: Cover or less

❑1, Aug 97 2.95
❑2, Mar 98 2.95
❑3, Jul 98 2.95
❑4, Nov 98 2.95

INNERCIRCLE
MUSHROOM

Value: Cover or less

❑0.1, Feb 95, Assimilation Begins... 2.50

INNER-CITY PRODUCTS
HYPE

Value: Cover or less

❑1, b&w 2.00

INNOCENT BYSTANDER
OLLIE OLLIE! OXEN FREE PRESS

	ORIG	GOOD	FINE	N-MINT
❑1, 1: Balac-Soon; 1: Lao Shan	2.50	0.59	1.48	2.95
❑2	2.75	0.59	1.48	2.95
❑3	2.75	0.59	1.48	2.95
❑4, Sum 97	2.75	0.59	1.48	2.95
❑5, Win 98	2.95	0.59	1.48	2.95
❑6, Fal 98	2.95	0.59	1.48	2.95

INNOVATION PREVIEW SPECIAL
INNOVATION

Value: Cover or less

❑1, Jun 89, sampler 1.00

INNOVATION SPECTACULAR
INNOVATION

Value: Cover or less

❑1, Dec 90 2.95
❑2, Jan 91 2.95

INNOVATION SUMMER FUN SPECIAL
INNOVATION

Value: Cover or less

❑1 3.50

INOVATORS
DARK MOON

Value: Cover or less

❑1, Apr 95, Second Chances, cardstock cover 2.50

IN RAGE
CFD

Value: Cover or less

❑1, Cherokee; Censorshit 2.50

INSANE
DARK HORSE

Value: Cover or less

❑1, Dec 87, Dim Jack; Mundane's Bar 1.75
❑2 1.75

INSANE CLOWN POSSE
CHAOS!

	ORIG	GOOD	FINE	N-MINT
❑1, Jun 99, The Upz & Downz of the Wicked Clownz	2.95	0.59	1.48	2.95
❑1/A, Tower Reocrds variant	—	1.60	4.00	8.00
❑2, The Amazing Jeckel Brothers	2.95	0.59	1.48	2.95
❑2/CS, CD	—	1.40	3.50	7.00
❑3, Oct 99, Raze the Desertz of Glass	2.95	0.59	1.48	2.95
❑3/A, Tower Reocrds variant	—	2.00	5.00	10.00
❑4, Jan 00, The Pendulum, Part 1, Says #1 on cover with Pendulum below issue number; polybagged with first of 12 Pendulum CDs	5.95	0.59	1.48	2.95

	ORIG	GOOD	FINE	N-MINT
❑4/CS, CD	—	1.60	4.00	8.00
❑5	2.95	0.59	1.48	2.95
❑5/CS, CD	—	1.60	4.00	8.00
❑6	2.95	0.59	1.48	2.95
❑7	2.95	0.59	1.48	2.95
❑7/CS, CD	—	1.60	4.00	8.00

INSIDE OUT KING, THE
FREE FALL

Value: Cover or less

❑1 .... 2.95
❑1-2, 2nd Printing 2.95

INSOMNIA
FANTAGRAPHICS

Value: Cover or less

❑1, nn 2.95

INSTANT PIANO
DARK HORSE

Value: Cover or less

❑1, Aug 94, The Eltingville Comic-Book Science-Fiction Fantasy-Horror and Role-Playing Clu, b&w 3.95
❑2, Dec 94, b&w 3.95
❑3, Feb 95, b&w 3.95
❑4, Jun 95, b&w 3.95

INTENSE!
PURE IMAGINATION

Value: Cover or less

❑2, BW, b&w; Reprint 3.00

INTERACTIVE COMICS
ADVENTURE

Value: Cover or less

❑1, Saves World, nn 4.95
❑2, nn; b&w 4.95

INTERFACE
MARVEL

Value: Cover or less

❑1, Dec 89, Espers 1.95
❑2, Feb 90, Assassins 1.95
❑3, Apr 90, Awareness 1.95
❑4, Jun 90, Information 1.95
❑5, Aug 90, Destruction 1.95
❑6, Oct 90, Wet Work 2.25
❑7, Nov 90, Fallout 2.25
❑8, Dec 90, Closure, Final Issue 2.25

INTERNATIONAL COWGIRL MAGAZINE
ICONOGRAFIX

Value: Cover or less

❑1, b&w 2.95
❑2, b&w 2.95

INTERPLANETARY LIZARDS OF THE TEXAS PLAINS
LEADBELLY

Value: Cover or less

❑0 .... 2.50
❑1, b&w 2.00
❑2, b&w 2.00
❑3, The Dark Ages 2.00
❑8, b&w 2.50

INTERVIEW WITH THE VAMPIRE (ANNE RICE'S...)
INNOVATION

	ORIG	GOOD	FINE	N-MINT
❑1, 91, The Last Sunrise	2.50	0.80	2.00	4.00
❑2, 91	2.50	0.60	1.50	3.00
❑3, 91	2.50	0.50	1.25	2.50
❑4, 91, And a Little Child...	2.50	0.50	1.25	2.50
❑5, 92	2.50	0.50	1.25	2.50
❑6, 92	2.50	0.50	1.25	2.50
❑7, 92, In Despair	2.50	0.50	1.25	2.50
❑8, 93	2.50	0.50	1.25	2.50
❑9	2.50	0.50	1.25	2.50
❑10, Phantoms	2.50	0.50	1.25	2.50
❑11	2.50	0.50	1.25	2.50
❑12	2.50	0.50	1.25	2.50

IN THE DAYS OF THE ACE ROCK 'N' ROLL CLUB
FANTAGRAPHICS

Value: Cover or less

❑1, nn; b&w 4.95

IN THE DAYS OF THE MOB
DC

	ORIG	GOOD	FINE	N-MINT
❑1, Fal 71	0.50	0.40	1.00	2.00

IN THE PRESENCE OF MINE ENEMIES
SPIRE

	ORIG	GOOD	FINE	N-MINT
❑1	0.39	1.00	2.50	5.00

IN THIN AIR
TOME PRESS

Value: Cover or less

❑1/A, b&w; With alternate ending #1 .... 2.95
❑1/B, b&w; With alternate ending #2 .... 2.95

INTRAZONE
BRAINSTORM

Value: Cover or less

❑1, Mar 93, Field Report, b&w 2.95
❑1/LE, Field Report, trading card; limited edition 5.95
❑2, Apr 93, b&w 2.95
❑2/LE, trading card; limited edition 5.95

INTRIGUE
IMAGE

Value: Cover or less

❑1/A, Aug 99 .... 2.50
❑1/B, Aug 99, alternate cover with woman firing directly at reader; Woman's face in background 2.50
❑2/A, Sep 99, Woman posting next to target on cover 2.50
❑2/B, Sep 99, alternate cover . 2.50
❑3, Feb 00 .... 2.95

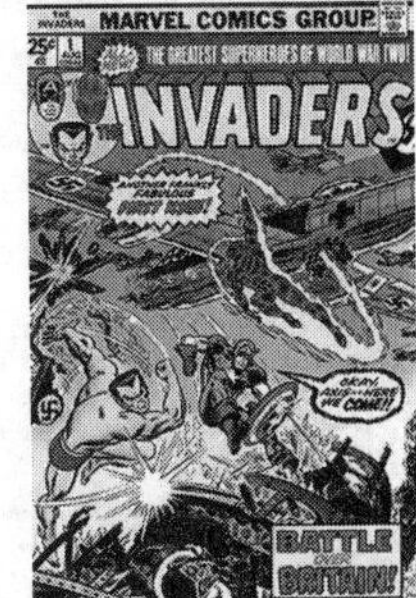

In a bit of retroactive continuity, Marvel's Golden Age heroes banded together as The Invaders to fight The Axis during World War II.

INTRUDER COMICS MODULE
TSR

Value: Cover or less

❑1, Breakthrough! 2.95
❑2 .... 2.95
❑3 .... 2.95
❑4 .... 2.95
❑5, Alexandria; The Intuder Archives, "Intruder II" on cover 2.95
❑6, Second Hand Twilight Part 1, "Intruder II" on cover 2.95
❑7, Intruder II 2.95
❑8, Intruder II 2.95
❑9, Intruder II 2.95

INU-YASHA
VIZ

Value: Cover or less

❑1 .... 2.95
❑2 .... 2.95
❑3 .... 2.95
❑4 .... 2.95
❑5 .... 2.95
❑6 .... 3.25
❑7 .... 3.25
❑8 .... 3.25
❑9 .... 3.25
❑10 .... 3.25
❑11 .... 3.25
❑12 .... 3.25
❑13 .... 3.25
❑14 .... 3.25
❑15 .... 3.25

INU-YASHA PART 2
VIZ

Value: Cover or less

❑1 .... 2.95
❑2 .... 2.95
❑3 .... 3.25
❑4 .... 3.25
❑5 .... 3.25
❑6 .... 3.25
❑7 .... 3.25
❑8 .... 3.25
❑9 .... 3.25

INU-YASHA PART 3
VIZ

Value: Cover or less

❑1 .... 3.25
❑2 .... 3.25
❑3 .... 3.25
❑4 .... 3.25
❑5 .... 3.25
❑6 .... 3.25
❑7 .... 3.25

INVADERS, THE
MARVEL

	ORIG	GOOD	FINE	N-MINT
❑1, Aug 75, FR, The Ring of the Nebulas, continued from Giant-Size Invaders #1; Marvel Value Stamp #A/37: The Watcher	0.25	2.00	5.00	10.00
❑2, Oct 75, 1: Brain Drain; 1: Mailbag; V: Donar	0.25	1.40	3.50	7.00
❑3, Nov 75, 1: U-Man, Captain America vs. Namor vs. Torch	0.25	1.00	2.50	5.00
❑4, Jan 76, V: U-Man	0.25	1.00	2.50	5.00
❑5, Mar 76, V: Red Skull; 1: Fin	0.25	1.00	2.50	5.00
❑6, May 76, A: Liberty Legion	0.25	0.80	2.00	4.00
❑7, Jul 76, V: Baron Blood	0.25	0.80	2.00	4.00
❑8, Sep 76, A: Union Jack	0.30	0.80	2.00	4.00
❑9, Oct 76, V: Baron Blood	0.30	0.80	2.00	4.00
❑10, Nov 76, V: Reaper, reprints Captain America #22	0.30	0.70	1.75	3.50
❑11, Dec 76, 1: Spitfire; V: Blue Bullet	0.30	0.70	1.75	3.50
❑12, Jan 77, 1: Spitfire	0.30	0.70	1.75	3.50
❑13, Feb 77, A: Golem	0.30	0.70	1.75	3.50
❑14, Mar 77, 1: Crusaders; 1: Dyna-Mite; 1: Spirit of '76	0.30	0.70	1.75	3.50
❑15, Apr 77, FS; FR, God Save The King!, V: Crusaders	0.30	0.70	1.75	3.50
❑16, May 77, V: Master Man	0.30	0.70	1.75	3.50
❑17, Jun 77, V: Warrior Woman	0.30	0.70	1.75	3.50
❑18, Jul 77, A: Destroyer; 1: Mighty Destroyer	0.30	0.70	1.75	3.50
❑19, Aug 77, 1: Union Jack II (Brian Falsworth); A: Hitler; 1: the Sub-Mariner, Mighty Destroyer becomes Union Jack II; Reprints Motion Picture Funnies Weekly	0.30	0.70	1.75	3.50
❑20, Sep 77, 1: Sub-Mariner; A: Union Jack; A: Spitfire, Reprints Sub-Mariner story from Motion Picture Funnies Weekly	0.30	1.00	2.50	5.00
❑21, Oct 77, FS; FR, The Battle Of Berlin, Part 2	0.30	0.60	1.50	3.00
❑22, Nov 77, O: Toro (new origin); V: Asbestos Lady	0.35	0.60	1.50	3.00
❑23, Dec 77, V: Scarlet Scarab	0.35	0.60	1.50	3.00
❑24, Jan 78, reprints Marvel Mystery #17	0.35	0.60	1.50	3.00

	ORIG	GOOD	FINE	N-MINT
❑25, Feb 78, V: Scarlet Scarab	0.35	0.50	1.25	2.50
❑26, Mar 78, V: Agent Axis; 1: Destroyer II (Roger Aubrey)	0.35	0.50	1.25	2.50
❑27, Apr 78	0.35	0.50	1.25	2.50
❑28, May 78, 1: Human Top (David Mitchell); 1: Kid Commandos; 1: Golden Girl	0.35	0.50	1.25	2.50
❑29, Jun 78, Attack Of The Teutonic Knight, V: Teutonic Knight; O: Invaders	0.35	0.50	1.25	2.50
❑30, Jul 78	0.35	0.50	1.25	2.50
❑31, Aug 78, V: Frankenstein	0.35	0.50	1.25	2.50
❑32, Sep 78, V: Thor	0.35	0.50	1.25	2.50
❑33, Oct 78, V: Thor	0.35	0.50	1.25	2.50
❑34, Nov 78, V: Destroyer	0.35	0.50	1.25	2.50
❑35, Dec 78, A: Whizzer	0.35	0.50	1.25	2.50
❑36, Jan 79, V: Iron Cross	0.35	0.50	1.25	2.50
❑37, Feb 79, A: Liberty Legion; V: Iron Cross	0.35	0.50	1.25	2.50
❑38, Mar 79, 1: Lady Lotus; A: U-Man	0.35	0.50	1.25	2.50
❑39, Apr 79	0.35	0.50	1.25	2.50
❑40, May 79, V: Baron Blood	0.40	0.50	1.25	2.50
❑41, Sep 79, V: Super Axis (Baron Blood, U-Man, Warrior Woman, Master Man), Final Issue; Double-size	0.60	0.70	1.75	3.50
❑Anl 1	0.50	1.00	2.50	5.00
❑GS 1	0.50	1.00	2.50	5.00

INVADERS, THE (LTD. SERIES)
MARVEL

Value: Cover or less

- ❑1, May 93, The Invaders Return ... 1.75
- ❑2, Jun 93, Havoc In Hollywood, V: Battle Axis ... 1.75
- ❑3, Jul 93, A: Vision ... 1.75
- ❑4, Aug 93 ... 1.75

INVADERS FROM HOME
DC

Value: Cover or less

- ❑1 ... 2.50
- ❑2 ... 2.50
- ❑3 ... 2.50
- ❑4, The Faceless Horror ... 2.50
- ❑5 ... 2.50
- ❑6 ... 2.50

INVADERS FROM MARS
ETERNITY

Value: Cover or less

- ❑1, b&w; movie Adaptation ... 2.50
- ❑2, b&w; movie Adaptation ... 2.50
- ❑3, Apr 90, The Son of Man, b&w; movie Adaptation ... 2.50

INVADERS FROM MARS (BOOK II)
ETERNITY

Value: Cover or less

- ❑1, b&w; sequel ... 2.50
- ❑2, b&w; sequel ... 2.50
- ❑3, b&w; sequel ... 2.50

INVASION!
DC

	ORIG	GOOD	FINE	N-MINT
❑1, Jan 89, TMc, KG (w), The Alien Alliance, 1: Vril Dox II; 1: Dominators; 1: Blasters; 1: Garryn Bek, 84pgs.	2.95	0.60	1.50	3.00
❑2, Feb 89, TMc, 1: Lyrissa Mallor; 1: L.E.G.I.O.N.; 1: Strata, 84pgs.	2.95	0.60	1.50	3.00
❑3, Mar 89, 84pgs.	2.95	0.60	1.50	3.00

INVASION '55
APPLE

Value: Cover or less

- ❑1, Oct 90, b&w ... 2.25
- ❑2, b&w ... 2.25
- ❑3, b&w ... 2.25

INVASION OF THE MIND SAPPERS
FANTAGRAPHICS

Value: Cover or less

- ❑1, Jan 96, nn; b&w; cardstock cover ... 8.95

INVASION OF THE SPACE AMAZONS FROM THE PURPLE PLANET
GRIZMART PRODUCTIONS

Value: Cover or less

- ❑1, May 97, b&w ... 2.25
- ❑2, Fal 97, b&w ... 2.25
- ❑3, Win 97, b&w ... 2.25

INVERT
CALIBER

Value: Cover or less

- ❑1, nn; b&w ... 2.95

INVINCIBLE FOUR OF KUNG FU & NINJA
DR. LEUNG'S

	ORIG	GOOD	FINE	N-MINT
❑1	1.80	0.40	1.00	2.00
❑2	1.80	0.40	1.00	2.00
❑3	1.80	0.40	1.00	2.00
❑4	1.80	0.40	1.00	2.00
❑5	1.80	0.40	1.00	2.00

INVINCIBLE MAN
JUNKO

Value: Cover or less

- ❑1, Sum 98, b&w; Glossy cover; 1500 printed ... 100.00
- ❑1/LE, b&w; has $100 cover price; 500 printed ... 100.00

INVISIBLE 9
FLYPAPER

Value: Cover or less

- ❑1, May 98 ... 2.95

INVISIBLE DIRTY OLD MAN, THE
RED GIANT

	ORIG	GOOD	FINE	N-MINT
❑1	—	0.70	1.75	3.50

INVISIBLE PEOPLE
KITCHEN SINK

Value: Cover or less

- ❑1, WE, WE (w), Sanctum ... 2.95
- ❑2, WE, WE (w), The Power ... 3.95
- ❑3, WE, WE (w), Mortal Combat ... 3.95

INVISIBLES, THE
DC

	ORIG	GOOD	FINE	N-MINT
❑1, Sep 94, Dead Beatles, 1: King Mob, Giant-size	2.95	0.70	1.75	3.50
❑2, Oct 94, Down and Out in Heaven and Hell, Part 1	1.95	0.50	1.25	2.50
❑3, Nov 94, Down and Out in Heaven and Hell, Part 2	1.95	0.50	1.25	2.50
❑4, Dec 94, Down and Out in Heaven and Hell, Part 3	1.95	0.40	1.00	2.00
❑5, Jan 95, Arcadia, Part 1, There are at least four cover variants, denoted A through D.	1.95	0.40	1.00	2.00
❑6, Feb 95, Arcadia, Part 2	1.95	0.40	1.00	2.00
❑7, Mar 95, Arcadia, Part 3	1.95	0.40	1.00	2.00
❑8, Apr 95, Arcadia, Part 4	1.95	0.40	1.00	2.00
❑9, Jun 95	2.50	0.50	1.25	2.50
❑10, Jul 95	2.50	0.50	1.25	2.50
❑11, Aug 95	2.50	0.50	1.25	2.50
❑12, Sep 95	2.50	0.50	1.25	2.50
❑13, Oct 95	2.50	0.50	1.25	2.50
❑14, Nov 95	2.50	0.50	1.25	2.50
❑15, Dec 95	2.50	0.50	1.25	2.50
❑16, Jan 96	2.50	0.50	1.25	2.50
❑17, Feb 96, Entropy in the U.K., Part 1	2.50	0.50	1.25	2.50
❑18, Mar 96, Entropy in the U.K., Part 2	2.50	0.60	1.50	3.00
❑19, Apr 96, Entropy in the U.K., Part 3	2.50	0.60	1.50	3.00
❑20, May 96	2.50	0.60	1.50	3.00
❑21, Jun 96	2.50	0.60	1.50	3.00
❑22, Jul 96	2.50	0.60	1.50	3.00
❑23, Aug 96	2.50	0.60	1.50	3.00
❑24, Sep 96	2.50	0.60	1.50	3.00
❑25, Oct 96, And a Half Dozen of the Other, Final Issue	2.50	0.80	2.00	4.00

INVISIBLES, THE (VOL. 2)
DC

	ORIG	GOOD	FINE	N-MINT
❑1, Feb 97, Black Science, Part 1	2.50	0.60	1.50	3.00
❑2, Mar 97, Black Science, Part 2	2.50	0.50	1.25	2.50
❑3, Apr 97, Black Science, Part 3	2.50	0.50	1.25	2.50
❑4, May 97	2.50	0.50	1.25	2.50
❑5, Jun 97, Time Machine Go	2.50	0.50	1.25	2.50
❑6, Jul 97, The Girl Most LikelyTo	2.50	0.50	1.25	2.50
❑7, Aug 97	2.50	0.50	1.25	2.50
❑8, Sep 97, Sensitive Criminals, Part 1	2.50	0.50	1.25	2.50
❑9, Oct 97, Sensitive Criminals, Part 2	2.50	0.50	1.25	2.50
❑10, Nov 97, Sensitive Criminals, Part 3	2.50	0.50	1.25	2.50
❑11, Dec 97, American Death Camp, Part 1	2.50	0.50	1.25	2.50
❑12, Jan 98, American Death Camp, Part 2	2.50	0.50	1.25	2.50
❑13, Feb 98, American Death Camp, Part 3	2.50	0.50	1.25	2.50
❑14, Mar 98	2.50	0.50	1.25	2.50
❑15, Apr 98	2.50	0.50	1.25	2.50
❑16, May 98	2.50	0.50	1.25	2.50
❑17, Aug 98	2.50	0.50	1.25	2.50
❑18, Sep 98	2.50	0.50	1.25	2.50
❑19, Oct 98	2.50	0.50	1.25	2.50
❑20, Nov 98	2.50	0.50	1.25	2.50
❑21, Jan 99	2.50	0.50	1.25	2.50
❑22, Feb 99, The Tower	2.50	0.50	1.25	2.50

INVISIBLES, THE (VOL. 3)
DC

Value: Cover or less

- ❑1, Final Issue; Issues count from 12 to 1 ... 2.95
- ❑2, May 00, The Invisible Kingdom, Part 3, Issues count from 12 to 1 ... 2.95
- ❑3, The Invisible Kingdom, Part 2, Issues count from 12 to 1 ... 2.95
- ❑4, The Invisible Kingdom, Part 1, Issues count from 12 to 1 ... 2.95
- ❑5, Jan 00, Karmageddon, Part 4, Issues count from 12 to 1 ... 2.95
- ❑6, Dec 99, Karmageddon, Part 3, Issues count from 12 to 1 ... 2.95
- ❑7, Oct 99, Karmageddon, Part 2, Issues count from 12 to 1 ... 2.95
- ❑8, Aug 99, Karmageddon, Part 1, Issues count from 12 to 1 ... 2.95
- ❑9, Jul 99, Satanstorm, Part 4, Issues count from 12 to 1 ... 2.95
- ❑10, Jun 99, Satanstorm, Part 3, Issues count from 12 to 1 ... 2.95
- ❑11, May 99, Satanstorm, Part 2, Issues count from 12 to 1 ... 2.95
- ❑12, Apr 99, Satanstorm, Part 1, Issues count from 12 to 1 ... 2.95

INVISOWORLD
ETERNITY

Value: Cover or less

- ❑1 ... 1.95

IO
INVICTUS

Value: Cover or less

- ❑1, Oct 94 ... 2.25
- ❑3, Win 95, b&w; ashcan ... 2.25

IRONCAT
IRONCAT

Value: Cover or less

- ❑1 ... 2.95
- ❑2, The Virgin of Steel ... 2.95

IRON CORPORAL (AVALON)
AVALON

Value: Cover or less

- ❑1, Here Lies John Williams; Alias Death, b&w ... 2.95

IRON CORPORAL, THE (CHARLTON)
CHARLTON

	ORIG	GOOD	FINE	N-MINT
❑23, Continues From Army War Heroes	0.75	0.30	0.75	1.50
❑24, Dec 85, Alias Death	0.75	0.30	0.75	1.50
❑25	0.75	0.30	0.75	1.50

IRON DEVIL, THE
FANTAGRAPHICS

Value: Cover or less

- ❑1, FT, FT (w), b&w; adult 2.95
- ❑2, FT, FT (w), b&w; adult 2.95
- ❑3, Mar 94, FT, FT (w), b&w; adult 2.95

IRON FIST
MARVEL

	ORIG	GOOD	FINE	N-MINT
❑1, Nov 75, JBy, A Duel of Iron!, A: Iron Man	0.25	4.00	10.00	20.00
❑2, Dec 75, JBy	0.25	2.40	6.00	12.00
❑3, Feb 76, JBy	0.25	1.60	4.00	8.00
❑4, JBy	0.25	1.60	4.00	8.00
❑5, JBy	0.25	1.60	4.00	8.00
❑6, JBy, Death Match!	0.25	1.20	3.00	6.00
❑7, Sep 76, JBy	0.30	1.20	3.00	6.00
❑8, Oct 76, JBy	0.30	1.20	3.00	6.00
❑9, Nov 76, JBy	0.30	1.20	3.00	6.00
❑10, Dec 76, JBy	0.30	1.20	3.00	6.00
❑11, Feb 77, JBy	0.30	1.00	2.50	5.00
❑12, Apr 77, JBy	0.30	1.00	2.50	5.00
❑13, Jun 77, JBy, V: Boomerang	0.30	1.00	2.50	5.00
❑14, Aug 77, JBy, Snowfire, 1: Sabretooth	0.30	16.00	40.00	80.00
❑15, Sep 77, JBy, Enter, the X-Men, A: Wolverine; A: X-Men, Final Issue	0.30	7.00	17.50	35.00
❑15/A, JBy, A: X-Men, 35¢ cover price; Final Issue; Limited distribution	0.35	9.00	22.50	45.00

IRON FIST (2ND SERIES)
MARVEL

Value: Cover or less

- ❑1, Sep 96, The Descent 1.50
- ❑2, Oct 96 .... 1.50

IRON FIST (3RD SERIES)
MARVEL

Value: Cover or less

- ❑1, Jul 98, gatefold summary . 2.50
- ❑2, Aug 98, gatefold summary 2.50
- ❑3, Sep 98, gatefold summary 2.50

IRON FIST: WOLVERINE
MARVEL

Value: Cover or less

- ❑1, Nov 00, Dark Horizon 2.99
- ❑2, Dec 00, A Gathering of Heroes 2.99
- ❑3, Jan 01 .... 2.99
- ❑4, Feb 01, Endgame, A: Luke Cage 2.99

IRONHAND OF ALMURIC
DARK HORSE

Value: Cover or less

- ❑1, Crownless In Koth, b&w ... 2.00
- ❑2, b&w 2.00
- ❑3, b&w 2.00
- ❑4, b&w 2.00

IRONJAW
ATLAS

	ORIG	GOOD	FINE	N-MINT
❑1, Jan 75, NA (c), The Saga of Iron Jaw	0.25	0.30	0.75	1.50
❑2, Mar 75, NA (c), Ironjaw the King!	0.25	0.20	0.50	1.00
❑3, May 75	0.25	0.20	0.50	1.00
❑4, Jul 75, And Who Will Forge the Jaw of Iron?, O: Ironjaw	0.25	0.20	0.50	1.00

IRON LANTERN
MARVEL

Value: Cover or less

- ❑1, Jun 97, PS, KB (w), Showdown at Stark Aircraft! 1.95

IRON MAN (VOL. 1)
MARVEL

	ORIG	GOOD	FINE	N-MINT
❑1, May 68, JCr; GC, O: Iron Man	0.12	55.00	137.50	275.00
❑2, Jun 68, JCr, 1: Demolisher	0.12	16.00	40.00	80.00
❑3, Jul 68, JCr	0.12	10.00	25.00	50.00
❑4, Aug 68, JCr	0.12	9.60	24.00	48.00
❑5, Sep 68, JCr	0.12	9.60	24.00	48.00
❑6, Oct 68, GT; JCr	0.12	8.00	20.00	40.00
❑7, Nov 68, GT; JCr, The Maggia Strikes	0.12	8.00	20.00	40.00
❑8, Dec 68, GT; JCr	0.12	7.00	17.50	35.00
❑9, Jan 69, GT; JCr, ... There Lives a Green Goliath!, V: Hulk (robot)	0.12	7.00	17.50	35.00
❑10, Feb 69, GT; JCr	0.12	7.00	17.50	35.00
❑11, Mar 69, V: Mandarin	0.12	5.60	14.00	28.00
❑12, Apr 69, 1: Controller; 1: Janice Cord; 1: The Controller	0.12	5.60	14.00	28.00
❑13, May 69, V: Controller	0.12	5.60	14.00	28.00
❑14, Jun 69, V: Night Phantom	0.12	5.60	14.00	28.00
❑15, Jul 69, V: Unicorn	0.12	5.60	14.00	28.00
❑16, Aug 69, V: Unicorn	0.15	3.60	9.00	18.00
❑17, Sep 69, 1: Madame Masque I (Whitney Frost)	0.15	3.60	9.00	18.00
❑18, Oct 69, O: Madame Masque I	0.15	3.60	9.00	18.00
❑19, Nov 69, O: Madame Masque I, Tony Stark's heart repaired	0.15	3.60	9.00	18.00

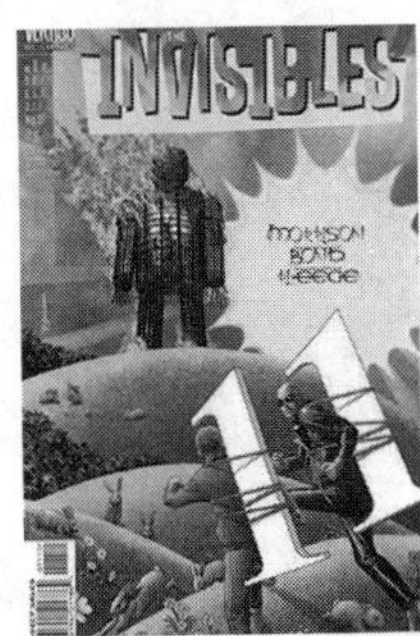

The third and final *Invisibles* series numbered its issues in reverse order, beginning with #12 and counting down to #1.

	ORIG	GOOD	FINE	N-MINT
❑20, Dec 69, V: Lucifer	0.15	3.60	9.00	18.00
❑21, Jan 70, 1: Crimson Dynamo III, Tony Stark quits as Iron Man	0.15	3.00	7.50	15.00
❑22, Feb 70, V: Crimson Dynamo; D: Janice Cord	0.15	3.00	7.50	15.00
❑23, Mar 70	0.15	3.00	7.50	15.00
❑24, Apr 70, V: Minotaur	0.15	3.00	7.50	15.00
❑25, May 70, V: Sub-Mariner	0.15	3.00	7.50	15.00
❑26, Jun 70, A: Val-Larr	0.15	3.00	7.50	15.00
❑27, Jul 70, 1: Firebrand (Marvel); V: Firebrand	0.15	3.00	7.50	15.00
❑28, Aug 70, V: Controller	0.15	3.00	7.50	15.00
❑29, Sep 70	0.15	3.00	7.50	15.00
❑30, Oct 70	0.15	3.00	7.50	15.00
❑31, Nov 70, V: Smashers; 1: Kevin O'Brien (later Guardsman)	0.15	2.40	6.00	12.00
❑32, Dec 70, V: Mechanoid	0.15	2.40	6.00	12.00
❑33, Jan 71, V: Spymaster	0.15	2.40	6.00	12.00
❑34, Feb 71, V: Spymaster	0.15	2.40	6.00	12.00
❑35, Mar 71, A: Daredevil	0.15	2.40	6.00	12.00
❑36, Apr 71, DH, ...Among Men Stalks The Ramrod!, V: Ramrod	0.15	2.40	6.00	12.00
❑37, May 71	0.15	2.40	6.00	12.00
❑38, Jun 71, V: Jonah	0.15	2.40	6.00	12.00
❑39, Jul 71, V: White Dragon	0.15	2.40	6.00	12.00
❑40, Aug 71, D: White Dragon I	0.15	2.40	6.00	12.00
❑41, Sep 71, V: Slasher	0.15	2.00	5.00	10.00
❑42, Oct 71	0.15	2.00	5.00	10.00
❑43, Nov 71, JM; GT, 1: Guardsman; V: Mikas, Giant-size	0.25	2.00	5.00	10.00
❑44, Jan 72, GT, V: Night Phantom	0.20	2.00	5.00	10.00
❑45, Mar 72, GT	0.20	2.00	5.00	10.00
❑46, May 72, GT, 1: Marianne Rodgers; D: Guardsman	0.20	2.00	5.00	10.00
❑47, Jun 72, O: Iron Man	0.20	2.40	6.00	12.00
❑48, Jul 72, V: Firebrand	0.20	1.60	4.00	8.00
❑49, Aug 72, V: Adaptoid	0.20	1.60	4.00	8.00
❑50, Sep 72, V: Princess Python	0.20	1.60	4.00	8.00
❑51, Oct 72	0.20	1.20	3.00	6.00
❑52, Nov 72, V: Raga	0.20	1.20	3.00	6.00
❑53, Dec 72, JSn, V: Black Lama	0.20	1.20	3.00	6.00
❑54, Jan 73, V: Sub-Mariner; 1: Moondragon (as "Madame MacEvil")	0.20	2.40	6.00	12.00
❑55, Feb 73, JSn, 1: Starfox; 1: Blood Brothers; 1: Kronos; 1: Thanos; 1: Drax the Destroyer; 1: Mentor	0.20	12.00	30.00	60.00
❑56, Mar 73, JSn, 1: Fangor	0.20	2.40	6.00	12.00
❑57, Apr 73	0.20	1.20	3.00	6.00
❑58, May 73, V: Mandarin	0.20	1.20	3.00	6.00
❑59, Jun 73	0.20	1.20	3.00	6.00
❑60, Jul 73	0.20	1.20	3.00	6.00
❑61, Aug 73	0.20	1.20	3.00	6.00
❑62, Sep 73	0.20	1.20	3.00	6.00
❑63, Oct 73	0.20	1.20	3.00	6.00
❑64, Nov 73, survey	0.20	1.20	3.00	6.00
❑65, Dec 73, O: Doctor Spectrum	0.20	1.20	3.00	6.00
❑66, Feb 74, A: Thor, Marvel Value Stamp A80	0.20	1.20	3.00	6.00
❑67, Apr 74, A: Sunfire	0.20	1.20	3.00	6.00
❑68, Jun 74, GT, O: Iron Man; A: Sunfire	0.25	1.20	3.00	6.00
❑69, Aug 74, GT, Confrontation, V: Yellow Claw; V: Unicorn; V: Mandarin; V: Sunfire	0.25	1.20	3.00	6.00
❑70, Sep 74, GT, Who Shall Stop...Ultimo?	0.25	1.20	3.00	6.00
❑71, Nov 74, GT	0.25	1.00	2.50	5.00
❑72, Jan 75, NA; GT, comic con	0.25	1.00	2.50	5.00
❑73, Mar 75	0.25	1.00	2.50	5.00
❑74, May 75, V: Modok	0.25	1.00	2.50	5.00
❑75, Jun 75	0.25	1.00	2.50	5.00
❑76, Jul 75, GT, ...There Lives A Green Goliath	0.25	1.00	2.50	5.00
❑77, Aug 75	0.25	1.00	2.50	5.00
❑78, Sep 75, in Vietnam	0.25	1.00	2.50	5.00

	ORIG	GOOD	FINE	N-MINT
❑79, Oct 75	0.25	1.00	2.50	5.00
❑80, Nov 75, JKu (c)	0.25	1.00	2.50	5.00
❑81, Dec 75, Marvel Value Stamp	0.25	1.00	2.50	5.00
❑82, Jan 76, repeats letter column from #81; Marvel Value Stamp B2	0.25	1.00	2.50	5.00
❑83, Feb 76, HT, The Rage of the Red Ghost, V: Red Ghost, Marvel Value Stamp B16	0.25	1.00	2.50	5.00
❑84, Mar 76, HT, Night Of The Walking Bomb, Marvel Value Stamp B56	0.25	1.00	2.50	5.00
❑85, Apr 76	0.25	1.00	2.50	5.00
❑86, May 76, V: Blizzard, Marvel Value Stamp B84	0.25	1.00	2.50	5.00
❑87, Jun 76, Marvel Value Stamp	0.25	1.00	2.50	5.00
❑88, Jul 76, GT, Fear Wears Two Faces!, Marvel Value Stamp 66	0.25	1.00	2.50	5.00
❑89, Aug 76, GT, Brute Fury!, A: Daredevil	0.25	1.00	2.50	5.00
❑90, Sep 76	0.30	1.00	2.50	5.00
❑91, Oct 76, GT, Breakout!	0.30	1.00	2.50	5.00
❑92, Nov 76, GT, Burn, Hero…Burn, V: Melter	0.30	1.00	2.50	5.00
❑93, Dec 76	0.30	1.00	2.50	5.00
❑94, Jan 77, HT, Frenzy At Fifty Fathoms	0.30	1.00	2.50	5.00
❑95, Feb 77	0.30	1.00	2.50	5.00
❑96, Mar 77, GT, Only A Friend Can Save Him, 1: New Guardsman, Michael O'Brien becomes New Guardsman	0.30	1.00	2.50	5.00
❑97, Apr 77	0.30	1.00	2.50	5.00
❑98, May 77	0.30	1.00	2.50	5.00
❑99, Jun 77, GT, At The Mercy Of The Mandarin!, V: Mandarin	0.30	1.00	2.50	5.00
❑100, Jul 77, GT, JSn (c), 100th anniversary issue; Mandarin	0.30	1.20	3.00	6.00
❑101, Aug 77, GT, Then Came The Monster!, 1: Dreadknight	0.30	0.80	2.00	4.00
❑102, Sep 77, 1: Dreadknight	0.30	0.80	2.00	4.00
❑103, Oct 77, A: Jack of Hearts	0.30	0.80	2.00	4.00
❑104, Nov 77	0.35	0.80	2.00	4.00
❑105, Dec 77, GT, Every Hand Against Him!, A: Jack of Hearts	0.35	0.80	2.00	4.00
❑106, Jan 78	0.35	0.80	2.00	4.00
❑107, Feb 78, KP, And, In the End …, V: Midas	0.35	0.80	2.00	4.00
❑108, Mar 78, CI, Growing Pains!	0.35	0.80	2.00	4.00
❑109, Apr 78, V: Vanguard; V: Darkstar, Vanguard; V: Darkstar	0.35	0.80	2.00	4.00
❑110, May 78, KP, Sojourners Through Space!, A: Jack of Hearts	0.35	0.80	2.00	4.00
❑111, Jun 78, The Man, the Metal, And The Mayhem, Wundagore	0.35	0.80	2.00	4.00
❑112, Jul 78, AA; KP, Moon Wars!	0.35	0.80	2.00	4.00
❑113, Aug 78, HT, The Horn Of The Unicorn!	0.35	0.80	2.00	4.00
❑114, Sep 78	0.35	0.80	2.00	4.00
❑115, Oct 78, DGr, Betrayal!	0.35	0.80	2.00	4.00
❑116, Nov 78, JR2; BL, Anguish, Once Removed, D: Ape-Man I (Gordon "Monk" Keefer); D: Bird-Man I (Henry Hawk); D: Cat-Man I (Townshend Patane); D: Count Nefaria; D: Frog-Man I (Francois LeBlanc), 1st David Michelinie written issue	0.35	0.80	2.00	4.00
❑117, Dec 78, JR2; BL, 1: Beth Cabe	0.35	0.80	2.00	4.00
❑118, Jan 79, BL; JBy, 1: Mrs. Arbogast; 1: James Rhodes (Rhodey)	0.35	1.20	3.00	6.00
❑119, Feb 79, JR2; BL, No S.H.I.E.L.D. To Protect Me!, Stark battles with alcohol	0.35	1.00	2.50	5.00
❑120, Mar 79, A: Sub-Mariner; 1: Justin Hammer, Stark battles with alcohol	0.35	0.80	2.00	4.00
❑121, Apr 79, A: Sub-Mariner, Stark battles with alcohol	0.35	0.80	2.00	4.00
❑122, May 79, A: Sub-Mariner; O: Iron Man, Stark battles with alcohol	0.40	0.80	2.00	4.00
❑123, Jun 79, Stark battles with alcohol	0.40	0.80	2.00	4.00
❑124, Jul 79, JR2, Pieces Of Hate!, Stark battles with alcohol	0.40	0.80	2.00	4.00
❑125, Aug 79, JR2, The Monaco Prelude, A: Scott Lang (Ant-Man), Stark battles with alcohol	0.40	0.80	2.00	4.00
❑126, Sep 79, V: Justin Hammer, Stark battles with alcohol	0.40	0.80	2.00	4.00
❑127, Oct 79, Stark battles with alcohol	0.40	0.80	2.00	4.00
❑128, Nov 79, JR2; BL, Demon In A Bottle, Stark begins recovery from alcohol	0.40	0.80	2.00	4.00
❑129, Dec 79, SB, Dread Night Of the Dreadnought!, V: Dreadnought	0.40	0.60	1.50	3.00
❑130, Jan 80	0.40	0.60	1.50	3.00
❑131, Feb 80, A: Hulk	0.40	0.60	1.50	3.00
❑132, Mar 80, A: Hulk	0.40	0.60	1.50	3.00
❑133, Apr 80, BL, The Hero Within!, A: Ant-Man; A: Hulk	0.40	0.60	1.50	3.00
❑134, May 80, BL, The Challenge	0.40	0.60	1.50	3.00
❑135, Jun 80, BL, Return Of The Hero, V: Titanium Man	0.40	0.60	1.50	3.00
❑136, Jul 80, The Beginning Of The Endotherm!	0.40	0.60	1.50	3.00
❑137, Aug 80, BL, Fatades!	0.40	0.60	1.50	3.00
❑138, Sep 80, TP; BL, Fatades And Ruses, 1: Dreadnought (silver)	0.50	0.60	1.50	3.00
❑139, Oct 80, BL, Fatades, Ruses, & Masques, Bethany Cabe knows Tony is Iron Man	0.50	0.60	1.50	3.00
❑140, Nov 80, BL, The Use Of Deadly Force!	0.50	0.60	1.50	3.00
❑141, Dec 80, JR2; BL, The Caribbean Connection	0.50	0.60	1.50	3.00
❑142, Jan 81, JR2; BL, Sky Die!, 1: Space Armor	0.50	0.60	1.50	3.00
❑143, Feb 81, JR2; BL, Meter On The Sun!, 1: Sunturion	0.50	0.60	1.50	3.00
❑144, Mar 81, JR2; BL, Sunfall, O: James Rhodes (Rhodey)	0.50	0.60	1.50	3.00
❑145, Apr 81, JR2; BL, Raiders' Rampage!	0.50	0.60	1.50	3.00
❑146, May 81, JR2; BL, Blacklash…And The Burning!, V: Blacklash	0.50	0.60	1.50	3.00
❑147, Jun 81, JR2; BL, Holocaust At High Noon	0.50	0.60	1.50	3.00
❑148, Jul 81, JR2; BL, Siege!	0.50	0.60	1.50	3.00
❑149, Aug 81, JR2; BL, Doomquest, V: Doctor Doom; V: Dr. Doom	0.50	0.60	1.50	3.00
❑150, Sep 81, JR2; BL, Knightmare, V: Doctor Doom; V: Dr. Doom, double-sized; In Camelot	0.75	0.70	1.75	3.50
❑151, Oct 81, LMc; BL, G.A.R.D.'s Gauntlet, A: Ant-Man	0.50	0.50	1.25	2.50
❑152, Nov 81, JR2; BL, Escape From Heaven's Hand!, 1: Stealth Armor	0.50	0.50	1.25	2.50
❑153, Dec 81, JR2; BL, Light Makes Might!	0.50	0.50	1.25	2.50
❑154, Jan 82, JR2; BL, The Other Side Of Madness, D: Unicorn I (Milos Masaryk)	0.60	0.50	1.25	2.50
❑155, Feb 82, JR2; BL, The Back Getters!	0.60	0.50	1.25	2.50
❑156, Mar 82, JR2, The Mauler Mandate!	0.60	0.50	1.25	2.50
❑157, Apr 82, Spores!	0.60	0.50	1.25	2.50
❑158, May 82, CI, Moms	0.60	0.50	1.25	2.50
❑159, Jun 82, PS, When Strikes Diablo, Diablo	0.60	0.50	1.25	2.50
❑160, Jul 82, SD, A Cry Of Beasts, Serpent Squad	0.60	0.50	1.25	2.50
❑161, Aug 82, LMc, If The Moonman Should Fial!, Moon Knight	0.60	0.50	1.25	2.50
❑162, Sep 82, The Menace Within!	0.60	0.50	1.25	2.50
❑163, Oct 82, LMc, Knight's Errand!, 1: Iron Monger (voice only); 1: Indries Moomji; 1: Chessmen; 1: Obadiah Stane (voice only)	0.60	0.50	1.25	2.50
❑164, Nov 82, LMc, Deadly Blessing	0.60	0.50	1.25	2.50
❑165, Dec 82, LMc, Endgame	0.60	0.50	1.25	2.50
❑166, Jan 83, LMc, One Of Those Days…, 1: Iron Monger (full appearance); 1: Obadiah Stane (full appearance)	0.60	0.50	1.25	2.50
❑167, Feb 83, LMc, The Empty Shell, Alcohol problem returns	0.60	0.50	1.25	2.50
❑168, Mar 83, LMc, The Iron Scream, Machine Man; Stark battles with alcohol.	0.60	0.50	1.25	2.50
❑169, Apr 83, LMc, Blackout!, Jim Rhodes takes over Stark's job as Iron Man; Stark battles with alcohol	0.60	0.80	2.00	4.00
❑170, May 83, LMc, And Who Shall Clothe Himself In Iron, 1: James Rhodes as Iron Man; 1: Morley Erwin, Stark battles with alcohol	0.60	0.80	2.00	4.00
❑171, Jun 83, LMc, Ball And Chain, V: Thunderball; 1: Clytemnestra Erwin, Stark battles with alcohol	0.60	0.50	1.25	2.50
❑172, Jul 83, LMc, Firebrand's Revenge!, A: Captain America, Stark battles with alcohol	0.60	0.50	1.25	2.50
❑173, Aug 83, LMc, Judas Is A Woman, Stark International becomes Stane International; Stark battles with alcohol	0.60	0.50	1.25	2.50
❑174, Sep 83, LMc, Armor Chase, V: Chessmen, S.H.I.E.L.D. acquires armor; Stark battles with alcohol	0.60	0.50	1.25	2.50
❑175, Oct 83, LMc, This Treasure Of Red And Gold, Stark battles with alcohol	0.60	0.50	1.25	2.50
❑176, Nov 83, LMc, Turf, Stark battles with alcohol	0.60	0.50	1.25	2.50
❑177, Dec 83, LMc, Have Armor, Will Travel, V: Flying Tiger, Stark battles with alcohol (alcohol storyline continues through next several issues)	0.60	0.50	1.25	2.50
❑178, Jan 84, LMc, Once An Avenger, Always An Avenger	0.60	0.50	1.25	2.50
❑179, Feb 84, LMc, Mission Into Darkness, V: Mandarin	0.60	0.50	1.25	2.50
❑180, Mar 84, LMc, This Ancient Enemy, V: Mandarin	0.60	0.50	1.25	2.50

	ORIG	GOOD	FINE	N-MINT
❑181, Apr 84, LMc, Though My Life Be Forfeit..., V: Mandarin	0.60	0.50	1.25	2.50
❑182, May 84, LMc, Deliverance, alcoholism cured again	0.60	0.50	1.25	2.50
❑183, Jun 84, LMc, All The Kinds Of Fear, V: Taurus	0.60	0.50	1.25	2.50
❑184, Jul 84, LMc, On The Road..., Tony Stark founds new company in California	0.60	0.50	1.25	2.50
❑185, Aug 84, LMc, Terror In Tulaluma!	0.60	0.50	1.25	2.50
❑186, Sep 84, LMc, Though This Fault Be Mine, V: Vibro	0.60	0.50	1.25	2.50
❑187, Oct 84, LMc, The Vengeance Of Vibro!, V: Vibro	0.60	0.50	1.25	2.50
❑188, Nov 84, DP, And Grimm Shall Be Their Name!, V: Brothers Grimm; 1: Circuits Maximus	0.60	0.50	1.25	2.50
❑189, Dec 84, LMc, A Thing That Bores From Within..., V: Termite	0.60	0.50	1.25	2.50
❑190, Jan 85, LMc, Losing Touch!, V: Termite; A: Scarlet Witch	0.60	0.50	1.25	2.50
❑191, Feb 85, LMc, The Iron Destiny, Tony Stark returns as Iron Man in original armor	0.60	0.50	1.25	2.50
❑192, Mar 85, Iron Man (Stark) vs. Iron Man (Rhodey)	0.60	0.50	1.25	2.50
❑193, Apr 85, LMc, The Choice And The Challenge, West Coast Avengers learn Tony is Iron Man	0.65	0.50	1.25	2.50
❑194, May 85, LMc, Otherwhere!, A: West Coast Avengers; D: Enforcer (Marvel); 1: Scourge	0.65	0.50	1.25	2.50
❑195, Jun 85, A: Shaman	0.65	0.50	1.25	2.50
❑196, Jul 85	0.65	0.50	1.25	2.50
❑197, Aug 85, Secret Wars II	0.65	0.50	1.25	2.50
❑198, Sep 85, SB, Revelations!, O: Iron Monger; O: Obadiah Stane	0.65	0.50	1.25	2.50
❑199, Oct 85, HT, And One Of Them Must Die!, D: Morley Erwin, James Rhodes crippled	0.65	0.50	1.25	2.50
❑200, Nov 85, D: Iron Monger; D: Obadiah Stane; 1: Red and white battlesuit; A: Iron Monger (full, double-sized; Tony Stark returns as Iron Man; New armor (red & white)	1.25	0.60	1.50	3.00
❑201, Dec 85, Sky Duel!	0.60	0.40	1.00	2.00
❑202, Jan 86, V: Fixer; A: Ka-Zar	0.60	0.40	1.00	2.00
❑203, Feb 86, The Maze	0.75	0.40	1.00	2.00
❑204, Mar 86	0.75	0.40	1.00	2.00
❑205, Apr 86, V: Modok	0.75	0.40	1.00	2.00
❑206, May 86, Prisons	0.75	0.40	1.00	2.00
❑207, Jun 86, Heat	0.75	0.40	1.00	2.00
❑208, Jul 86, Firefang!	0.75	0.40	1.00	2.00
❑209, Aug 86, A Renaissance Of Magic!	0.75	0.40	1.00	2.00
❑210, Sep 86, Happy's Story, A: Happy Hogan	0.75	0.40	1.00	2.00
❑211, Oct 86	0.75	0.40	1.00	2.00
❑212, Nov 86, Precious Legacy	0.75	0.40	1.00	2.00
❑213, Dec 86, A: Dominic Fortune	0.75	0.40	1.00	2.00
❑214, Jan 87, Bring Me Spider-Woman!, Construction of Stark Enterprises begins	0.75	0.40	1.00	2.00
❑215, Feb 87, The Shattered Sky	0.75	0.40	1.00	2.00
❑216, Mar 87, Requiescat...And Revenge!, D: Clytemnestra Erwin	0.75	0.40	1.00	2.00
❑217, Apr 87, Metamorphosis Oddity, 1: undersea armor	0.75	0.40	1.00	2.00
❑218, May 87, BL, Deep Trouble!, 1: Deep Sea armor	0.75	0.40	1.00	2.00
❑219, Jun 87, BL, Ghost Story, V: Ghost	0.75	0.40	1.00	2.00
❑220, Jul 87, Ghost Of A Chance, D: Spymaster	0.75	0.40	1.00	2.00
❑221, Aug 87	0.75	0.40	1.00	2.00
❑222, Sep 87, The Party	0.75	0.40	1.00	2.00
❑223, Oct 87, Counter Force, 1: Rae LaCoste	0.75	0.40	1.00	2.00
❑224, Nov 87, BL, Low Noon	0.75	0.40	1.00	2.00
❑225, Dec 87, Armor Wars; Armor Wars, Part 1, Giant-size	1.25	0.60	1.50	3.00
❑226, Jan 88, Armor Wars; Armor Wars, Part 2	0.75	0.50	1.25	2.50
❑227, Feb 88, Armor Wars; Armor Wars, Part 3	0.75	0.50	1.25	2.50
❑228, Mar 88, Armor Wars, Part 4	0.75	0.50	1.25	2.50
❑229, Apr 88, Armor Wars; Armor Wars, Part 5, D: Gremlin a.k.a Titanium Man II	0.75	0.60	1.50	3.00
❑230, May 88, Armor Wars; Armor Wars, Part 6, V: Firepower, apparent death of Iron Man	0.75	0.50	1.25	2.50
❑231, Jun 88, Armor Wars; Armor Wars, Part 7, V: Firepower, new armor	0.75	0.50	1.25	2.50
❑232, Jul 88, Armor Wars, Part 8, offset	0.75	0.50	1.25	2.50
❑232/A, Jul 88, Flexographic	0.75	0.50	1.25	2.50
❑233, Aug 88, Slaughterday!, 1: Kathy Dare; A: Ant-Man	0.75	0.40	1.00	2.00
❑234, Sep 88, Fallout!, A: Spider-Man	0.75	0.40	1.00	2.00

The second Titanium Man met his end during "Armor Wars."

	ORIG	GOOD	FINE	N-MINT
❑235, Oct 88, Epitaph In Grey	0.75	0.30	0.75	1.50
❑236, Nov 88, Stone Cold!	0.75	0.30	0.75	1.50
❑237, Dec 88, Star Hunter!	0.75	0.30	0.75	1.50
❑238, Jan 89, Two Live Or Die In L.A.!, 1: Madame Masque II	0.75	0.30	0.75	1.50
❑239, Feb 89, Unholy Ghost!	0.75	0.30	0.75	1.50
❑240, Mar 89, Ghost Righter!	0.75	0.30	0.75	1.50
❑241, Apr 89, China See!	0.75	0.30	0.75	1.50
❑242, May 89, Master Blaster, Stark shot by Kathy Dare	0.75	0.30	0.75	1.50
❑243, Jun 89, BL, Heartbeaten, Stark crippled	0.75	0.40	1.00	2.00
❑244, Jul 89, Giant-size; Carl Walker a.k.a. Force becomes Iron Man; New armor to allow Stark to walk again	1.50	0.60	1.50	3.00
❑245, Aug 89, PS, Inside Angry	0.75	0.30	0.75	1.50
❑246, Sep 89, BL, Heavy Mettle!	1.00	0.30	0.75	1.50
❑247, Oct 89, BL, Malled!	1.00	0.30	0.75	1.50
❑248, Nov 89, BL, Footsteps, Stark cured by implanted bio-chip	1.00	0.30	0.75	1.50
❑249, Nov 89, BL, The Doctor's Passion, Doctor Doom	1.00	0.30	0.75	1.50
❑250, Dec 89, BL, Acts of Vengeance, Part 3, V: Doctor Doom, double-sized; Acts of Vengeance	1.50	0.35	0.88	1.75
❑251, Dec 89, HT, Acts of Vengeance, Part 12, V: Wrecker, Acts of Vengeance	1.00	0.25	0.63	1.25
❑252, Jan 90, HT, Acts of Vengeance, Part 21, V: Chemistro, Acts of Vengeance	1.00	0.25	0.63	1.25
❑253, Feb 90, GC, JBy (c), Laughing All The Way To The Graveyard	1.00	0.25	0.63	1.25
❑254, Mar 90, BL, BL (w), Graduation Day.	1.00	0.25	0.63	1.25
❑255, Apr 90, HT, Switching Channels	1.00	0.25	0.63	1.25
❑256, May 90, JR2, BL (w), Soliloquy in Silence	1.00	0.25	0.63	1.25
❑257, Jun 90, Retribution	1.00	0.25	0.63	1.25
❑258, Jul 90, JR2, JBy (w), Armor Wars II; Armor Wars II, Part 1	1.00	0.30	0.75	1.50
❑259, Aug 90, JR2, JBy (w), Armor Wars II; Armor Wars II, Part 2	1.00	0.30	0.75	1.50
❑260, Sep 90, JR2, JBy (w), Armor Wars II; Armor Wars II, Part 3	1.00	0.30	0.75	1.50
❑261, Oct 90, JR2, JBy (w), Armor Wars II; Armor Wars II, Part 4	1.00	0.30	0.75	1.50
❑262, Nov 90, JR2, JBy (w), Armor Wars II; Armor Wars II, Part 5	1.00	0.30	0.75	1.50
❑263, Dec 90, JR2, JBy (w), Armor Wars II; Armor Wars II, Part 6	1.00	0.30	0.75	1.50
❑264, Jan 91, JR2, JBy (w), Armor Wars II; Armor Wars II, Part 7	1.00	0.30	0.75	1.50
❑265, Feb 91, JR2, JBy (w), Armor Wars II; Armor Wars II, Part 8	1.00	0.30	0.75	1.50
❑266, Mar 91, Armor Wars II	1.00	0.30	0.75	1.50
❑267, Apr 91, JBy (w), The Persistence Of Memory	1.00	0.30	0.75	1.50
❑268, May 91, JBy (w), First Blood, O: Iron Man	1.00	0.30	0.75	1.50
❑269, Jun 91, JBy (w), The Hallow Man	1.00	0.30	0.75	1.50
❑270, Jul 91, JBy (w), The Price	1.00	0.30	0.75	1.50
❑271, Aug 91, JBy (w), The Dragon Seed, Part 1	1.00	0.30	0.75	1.50
❑272, Sep 91, JBy (w), The Dragon Seed, Part 2	1.00	0.30	0.75	1.50
❑273, Oct 91, JBy (w), The Dragon Seed, Part 3	1.00	0.30	0.75	1.50
❑274, Nov 91, JBy (w), The Dragon Seed, Part 4, V: Fin Fang Foom	1.00	0.30	0.75	1.50
❑275, Dec 91, JBy (w), The Dragon Seed, Part 5, V: Dragon Lords; V: Mandarin; V: Fin Fang Foom, Giant-size	1.50	0.30	0.75	1.50
❑276, Jan 92, JBy (w), With Friends Like These...	1.00	0.30	0.75	1.50
❑277, Feb 92, JBy (w), War Games	1.25	0.30	0.75	1.50
❑278, Mar 92, Operation: Galactic Storm, Part 6, 1: new Space Armor, Galactic Storm	1.25	0.30	0.75	1.50

	ORIG	GOOD	FINE	N-MINT
❑279, Apr 92, Operation: Galactic Storm, Part 13, V: Ronan the Accuser, Galactic Storm	1.25	0.30	0.75	1.50
❑280, May 92, Technical Difficulties, A: The Stark	1.25	0.30	0.75	1.50
❑281, Jun 92, 1: War Machine armor	1.25	0.60	1.50	3.00
❑282, Jul 92, 2: War Machine armor	1.25	0.60	1.50	3.00
❑283, Aug 92	1.25	0.30	0.75	1.50
❑284, Sep 92, Legacy Of Iron, D: Tony Stark; 1: War Machine	1.25	0.40	1.00	2.00
❑285, Oct 92, Ashes To Ashes	1.25	0.25	0.63	1.25
❑286, Nov 92, Dust To Dust	1.25	0.25	0.63	1.25
❑287, Dec 92, Meltdown!	1.25	0.25	0.63	1.25
❑288, Jan 93, Ground Zero, 48pgs.; Embossed cover; 30th anniversary special; Tony Stark revived	2.50	0.50	1.25	2.50
❑289, Feb 93	1.25	0.25	0.63	1.25
❑290, Mar 93, This Years Model, 48pgs.; Metallic ink cover; New Armor	2.95	0.70	1.75	3.50
❑291, Apr 93, Judgement Day, James Rhodes leaves to become War Machine	1.25	0.25	0.63	1.25
❑292, May 93, Mixed Reactions	1.25	0.25	0.63	1.25
❑293, Jun 93, Controlling Interests	1.25	0.25	0.63	1.25
❑294, Jul 93, Orbital Resonances	1.25	0.25	0.63	1.25
❑295, Aug 93, Infinity Crusade	1.25	0.25	0.63	1.25
❑296, Sep 93, Trade War	1.25	0.25	0.63	1.25
❑297, Oct 93, Whipsaw!, A: Omega Red; A: M.O.D.A.M	1.25	0.25	0.63	1.25
❑298, Nov 93	1.25	0.25	0.63	1.25
❑299, Dec 93, V: Ultimo	1.25	0.25	0.63	1.25
❑300, Jan 94, V: Ultimo; A: Iron Legion (all substitute Iron Men), Giant size; Stark dons new (modular) armor	2.50	0.50	1.25	2.50
❑300/SC, Jan 94, Special (embossed foil) cover edition; Giant size; Stark dons new (modular) armor	3.95	0.79	1.98	3.95
❑301, Feb 94, Crash & Burn, Part 1	1.25	0.25	0.63	1.25
❑302, Mar 94, Crash & Burn, Part 2	1.25	0.25	0.63	1.25
❑303, Apr 94, Crash & Burn, Part 3	1.25	0.25	0.63	1.25
❑304, May 94, Crash & Burn, Part 4, 1: Hulkbuster Armor	1.50	0.25	0.63	1.25
❑305, Jun 94, Crash & Burn, Part 5, A: Hulk	1.50	0.30	0.75	1.50
❑306, Jul 94, Crash & Burn, Part 6, Stark restructures company	1.50	0.30	0.75	1.50
❑307, Aug 94	1.50	0.30	0.75	1.50
❑308, Sep 94	1.50	0.30	0.75	1.50
❑309, Oct 94	1.50	0.30	0.75	1.50
❑310, Nov 94, Friends...And Other Enemies	1.50	0.30	0.75	1.50
❑310/CS, Nov 94, polybagged with 16-page preview, acetate print, and other items	2.95	0.59	1.48	2.95
❑311, Dec 94	1.50	0.30	0.75	1.50
❑312, Jan 95	2.25	0.30	0.75	1.50
❑313, Feb 95	1.50	0.30	0.75	1.50
❑314, Mar 95	1.50	0.30	0.75	1.50
❑315, Apr 95, V: Titanium Man	1.50	0.30	0.75	1.50
❑316, May 95	1.50	0.30	0.75	1.50
❑317, Jun 95, D: Titanium Man I, flip book with War Machine: Brothers in Arms part 3 back-up	2.50	0.50	1.25	2.50
❑318, Jul 95	1.50	0.30	0.75	1.50
❑319, Aug 95, O: Iron Man	1.50	0.30	0.75	1.50
❑320, Sep 95	1.50	0.30	0.75	1.50
❑321, Oct 95, OverPower cards inserted	1.50	0.30	0.75	1.50
❑322, Nov 95, The Darkest Page to Turn	1.50	0.30	0.75	1.50
❑323, Dec 95, Iron Man vs. the Avengers, A: Hawkeye; A: Avengers	1.50	0.30	0.75	1.50
❑324, Jan 96	1.50	0.30	0.75	1.50
❑325, Feb 96, Avengers: Timeslide, wraparound cover; Giant-size; Tony Stark vs. young Tony Stark	2.95	0.60	1.50	3.00
❑326, Mar 96, First Sign, Part 3	1.95	0.30	0.75	1.50
❑327, Apr 96, Frostbite!, V: Frostbite, reading of Tony Stark's will	1.95	0.30	0.75	1.50
❑328, May 96	1.50	0.30	0.75	1.50
❑329, Jun 96, Fujikawa International takes over Stark Enterprises	1.50	0.30	0.75	1.50
❑330, Jul 96	1.50	0.30	0.75	1.50
❑331, Aug 96	1.50	0.30	0.75	1.50
❑332, Sep 96, Onslaught: Impact 2, Final Issue	1.50	0.30	0.75	1.50
❑Anl 1, Aug 70, War And Remembrance, Reprint	0.25	4.00	10.00	20.00
❑Anl 2, Nov 71, Reprint	0.25	1.80	4.50	9.00
❑Anl 3	0.50	1.20	3.00	6.00
❑Anl 4, Cover reads "King-Size Special"	0.50	0.80	2.00	4.00
❑Anl 5	1.00	0.60	1.50	3.00
❑Anl 6, LMc, In Dreams What Death May Come!, A: Eternals; D: Zuras (spirit leaves body), New Iron Man appears	1.00	0.60	1.50	3.00
❑Anl 7, LMc, When Giants Walk The Earth!, 1: Goliath III (Erik Josten), West Coast Avengers; Was formerly known as Power Man I	1.00	0.60	1.50	3.00
❑Anl 8, When Innocence Dies!, A: X-Factor	1.25	0.60	1.50	3.00
❑Anl 9	1.25	0.60	1.50	3.00
❑Anl 10, Atlantis Attacks, Part 1, Atlantis Attacks	2.00	0.50	1.25	2.50
❑Anl 11, The Terminus Factor, Part 2; Terminus Factor, A: Machine Man	2.00	0.40	1.00	2.00
❑Anl 12, Subterranean Wars; Subterranean Odyssey, Part 4, 1: Trapster II	2.00	0.40	1.00	2.00
❑Anl 13, GC, Assault on Armor City, Part 3; Assault On Armor City, A: Darkhawk, Avengers West Coast	2.25	0.40	1.00	2.00
❑Anl 14, trading card	2.95	0.59	1.48	2.95
❑Anl 15, V: Controller	2.95	0.59	1.48	2.95
❑Ash 1, Nov 94, "Iron Man & Force Works" on cover; Collectors' Preview	1.95	0.39	0.98	1.95
❑GS 1	0.50	1.00	2.50	5.00

IRON MAN (VOL. 2)

MARVEL

	ORIG	GOOD	FINE	N-MINT
❑1, Nov 96, JLee(w), Heart Of The Matter, O: Iron Man (new); O: Hulk (new), Giant-size	2.95	0.70	1.75	3.50
❑1/A, Nov 96, JLee(w), Heart Of The Matter, O: Iron Man (new), variant cover; Giant-size	2.95	0.70	1.75	3.50
❑2, Dec 96, JLee(w), Hulk Smash!, V: Hulk	1.95	0.40	1.00	2.00
❑3, Jan 97, JLee(w), Misperceptions, 1: Whirlwind; A: Fantastic Four	1.95	0.40	1.00	2.00
❑4, Feb 97, JLee(w), Bring me the Head of the Hulk!, V: Living Laser	1.95	0.40	1.00	2.00
❑4/A, JLee(w), Bring me the Head of the Hulk!, variant cover	1.95	0.40	1.00	2.00
❑5, Mar 97, JLee(w), Inherit the Whirlwind, V: Whirlwind	1.95	0.39	0.98	1.95
❑6, Apr 97, Industrial Revolution, Part 2, A: Onslaught, concludes in Captain America #6	1.95	0.39	0.98	1.95
❑7, May 97, JLee(w), Look Back in Anger	1.95	0.39	0.98	1.95
❑8, Jun 97	1.95	0.39	0.98	1.95
❑9, Jul 97	1.95	0.39	0.98	1.95
❑10, Aug 97, gatefold summary	1.99	0.39	0.98	1.95
❑11, Sep 97, A: Doctor Doom, gatefold summary	1.99	0.39	0.98	1.95
❑12, Oct 97, Heroes Reunited, cover forms quadtych with Fantastic Four #12, Avengers #12, and Captain America #12; gatefold summary	1.99	0.70	1.75	3.50
❑13, Nov 97, World War 3, cover forms quadtych with Fantastic Four #13, Avengers #13, and Captain America #13; gatefold summary	1.99	0.50	1.25	2.50

IRON MAN (VOL. 3)

MARVEL

	ORIG	GOOD	FINE	N-MINT
❑1, Feb 98, KB (w), Looking Forward, 1: Stark Solutions, wraparound cover; gatefold summary; Giant-size	2.99	0.70	1.75	3.50
❑1/A, Feb 98, KB (w), Looking Forward, 1: Stark Solutions, wraparound cover; gatefold summary	2.99	0.80	2.00	4.00
❑2, Mar 98, KB (w), Hidden Assets, gatefold summary	1.99	0.40	1.00	2.00
❑2/SC, KB (w), Hidden Assets, variant cover	1.99	0.60	1.50	3.00
❑3, Apr 98, KB (w), gatefold summary	1.99	0.40	1.00	2.00
❑4, May 98, KB (w), V: Firebrand, gatefold summary	1.99	0.40	1.00	2.00
❑5, Jun 98, KB (w), V: Firebrand, gatefold summary	1.99	0.40	1.00	2.00
❑6, Jul 98, KB (w), A: Black Widow, gatefold summary	1.99	0.40	1.00	2.00
❑7, Aug 98, KB (w), Live Kree or Die!, Part 1, A: Warbird, gatefold summary	1.99	0.40	1.00	2.00
❑8, Sep 98, KB (w), gatefold summary; Tony beaten	1.99	0.40	1.00	2.00
❑9, Oct 98, KB (w), Revenge of the Mandarin, Part 1, A: Winter Guard, gatefold summary	1.99	0.40	1.00	2.00
❑10, Nov 98, KB (w), Revenge of the Mandarin, Part 2, gatefold summary	1.99	0.40	1.00	2.00
❑11, Dec 98, KB (w), A: Warbird; V: War Machine armor, gatefold summary; new home	1.99	0.40	1.00	2.00
❑12, Jan 99, KB (w), Spoils of War!, A: Warbird; V: War Machine armor, gatefold summary	1.99	0.40	1.00	2.00

	ORIG	GOOD	FINE	N-MINT
❑13, Feb 99, KB (w), A Question of Control, V: Controller, gatefold summary; double-sized	2.99	0.60	1.50	3.00
❑13/Aut, KB (w), A: Controller, Signed by Sean Chen	—	1.20	3.00	6.00
❑14, Mar 99, KB (w), To Challenge the Fantastic, A: Watcher; A: Ronan the Accuser; V: Ronan; A: S.H.I.E.L.D.; A: Fantastic Four, Fantastic Four crossover, part 2	1.99	0.40	1.00	1.99
❑15, Apr 99, KB (w), Exploded View, V: Nitro	1.99	0.40	1.00	1.99
❑16, May 99, KB (w), Scale Model	1.99	0.40	1.00	1.99
❑17, Jun 99, KB (w), Your Young Men Shall Slay Dragons!, A: Fin Fang Foom	1.99	0.40	1.00	1.99
❑18, Jul 99, KB (w), Machinery of War, Part 1; Sunset Intrigues, A: Warbird	1.99	0.40	1.00	1.99
❑19, Aug 99, KB (w), Machinery of War, Part 2; Smart Weapons, Foolish Choices, V: War Machine	1.99	0.40	1.00	1.99
❑20, Sep 99, KB (w), Machinery of War, Part 3; Cheating Death, V: War Machine	1.99	0.40	1.00	1.99
❑21, Oct 99, KB (w), Eighth Day Prelude; Burning Need, 1: Inferno, continues in Thor #17	1.99	0.40	1.00	1.99
❑22, Nov 99, KB (w), Eighth Day, Part 2; The Thrill of the Chase, A: Thor; 1: Carnivore, continues in Peter Parker, Spider-Man #11	1.99	0.40	1.00	1.99
❑23, Dec 99, KB (w), Ultimate Danger, A: Ultimo	1.99	0.40	1.00	1.99
❑24, Jan 00	1.99	0.40	1.00	1.99
❑25, Feb 00, KB (w), Ultimate Devastation, A: Ultimo; A: Warbird, double-sized	2.99	0.45	1.13	2.25
❑26, Mar 00, The Mask in the Iron Man, Part 1; A Boy and His Toys	1.99	0.45	1.13	2.25
❑27, Apr 00	—	0.45	1.13	2.25
❑28, May 00	—	0.45	1.13	2.25
❑29, Jun 00	—	0.45	1.13	2.25
❑30, Jul 00	—	0.45	1.13	2.25
❑31, Aug 00	—	0.45	1.13	2.25
❑32, Sep 00, The Sons of Yinsen, Part 2; Gods & Monsters, A: Wong-Chu, concludes in Iron Man Annual 2000	2.25	0.45	1.13	2.25
❑33, Oct 00, Power, Part 1; Heroes	2.25	0.45	1.13	2.25
❑34, Nov 00, Power, Part 2; Villain$	2.25	0.45	1.13	2.25
❑35, Dec 00, Maximum Security; Power, Part 3	2.25	0.45	1.13	2.25
❑36, Jan 01, Danger Deep	2.25	0.45	1.13	2.25
❑37, Feb 01, Remote Control, Part 1	2.25	0.45	1.13	2.25
❑38, Mar 01, Remote Control, Part 2	2.25	0.45	1.13	2.25
❑39, Apr 01, Remote Control, Part 3	2.25	0.45	1.13	2.25
❑40, May 01, Remote Control, Part 4	2.25	0.45	1.13	2.25
❑Anl 1998, MWa (w), Life & Liberty, V: Modok, wraparound cover; Iron Man/Captain America '98	3.50	0.70	1.75	3.50
❑Anl 1999, Aug 99	3.50	0.70	1.75	3.50
❑Anl 2000, The Sons of Yinsen, Part 3; The Invisible Iron Man, D: Wong-Chu	3.50	0.70	1.75	3.50

IRON MAN 2020
MARVEL

Value: Cover or less

❑1, One-Shot 5.95

IRON MAN & SUB-MARINER
MARVEL

	ORIG	GOOD	FINE	N-MINT
❑1, Apr 68, JCr; GC, Iron Man: The Torrent Without...The Tumult Within!; Sub-Mariner: Call Him Destiny...Or Call Him Death!, O: Destiny	0.12	22.00	55.00	110.00

IRON MAN: BAD BLOOD
MARVEL

Value: Cover or less

❑1, Sep 00, BL, BL (w), A Gathering Dark 2.99	❑3, Nov 00, BL, BL (w), Enemy Mind 2.99
❑2, Oct 00, BL, BL (w), Smashing Seattle 2.99	❑4, Dec 00, BL, BL (w), Terminal Space 2.99

IRON MAN: CRASH
MARVEL

Value: Cover or less

❑1, Computer-generated art ... 12.95

IRON MAN: THE IRON AGE
MARVEL

Value: Cover or less

❑1, Aug 98, KB (w), Challenges, prestige format; retells early Iron Man adventures 5.99

❑2, Sep 98, KB (w), prestige format; retells early Iron Man adventures 5.99

IRON MAN: THE LEGEND
MARVEL

Value: Cover or less

❑1, Sep 96, O: Iron Man, wraparound cover; One-Shot; summation of history of character 3.95

IRON MANUAL
MARVEL

	ORIG	GOOD	FINE	N-MINT
❑1, no cover date; background info on Iron Man's armor	1.75	0.40	1.00	2.00

Bill Cosby and Robert Culp were secret agents masquerading as a Rhodes Scholar and a tennis player, respectively, in TV's *I Spy*.

© 1966 CBS and Gold Key

IRON MAN/X-O MANOWAR: HEAVY METAL
MARVEL

Value: Cover or less

❑1, Sep 96, crossover with Acclaim 2.50

IRON MARSHAL
JADEMAN

Value: Cover or less

❑1	1.75	❑17	1.75
❑2	1.75	❑18	1.75
❑3	1.75	❑19	1.75
❑4	1.75	❑20	1.75
❑5	1.75	❑21	1.75
❑6	1.75	❑22	1.75
❑7	1.75	❑23	1.75
❑8	1.75	❑24	1.75
❑9	1.75	❑25	1.75
❑10	1.75	❑26, A Humiliating Plot	1.75
❑11	1.75	❑27	1.75
❑12	1.75	❑28, The Exterminator	1.75
❑13	1.75	❑29	1.75
❑14	1.75	❑30	1.75
❑15	1.75	❑31	1.75
❑16	1.75	❑32	1.75

IRON SAGA'S ANTHOLOGY
IRON SAGA

Value: Cover or less

❑1 .... 1.75

IRON WINGS
ACTION PRESS

Value: Cover or less

❑1, May 99 .... 2.50

IRON WINGS (VOL. 2)
IMAGE

Value: Cover or less

❑1, Apr 00, The Legends Begin Here... .... 2.50

IRONWOLF
DC

Value: Cover or less

❑1, HC, HC (w), 1: IronWolf, Reprints IronWolf adventures from Weird Worlds #8-10 .... 2.00

IRONWOOD
FANTAGRAPHICS

Value: Cover or less

❑1, b&w; adult	1.95	❑6, b&w; adult	2.25
❑2, b&w; adult	2.25	❑7, Mar 92, b&w; adult	2.50
❑3, b&w; adult	2.25	❑8, b&w; adult	2.50
❑4, b&w; adult	2.25	❑9, b&w; adult	2.50
❑5, b&w; adult	2.25	❑10, Sep 94, b&w; adult	2.75

I SAW IT
EDUCOMICS

Value: Cover or less

❑1, b&w; Hiroshima 2.00

ISIS
DC

	ORIG	GOOD	FINE	N-MINT
❑1, Oct 76	—	1.60	4.00	8.00
❑2	—	1.00	2.50	5.00
❑3, The Wrath Of Set!	0.30	0.80	2.00	4.00
❑4	—	0.80	2.00	4.00
❑5	—	0.80	2.00	4.00
❑6	—	0.80	2.00	4.00
❑7, O: Isis	—	0.80	2.00	4.00
❑8, Dec 77, Final Issue	—	0.80	2.00	4.00

ISLAND OF DR. MOREAU, THE
MARVEL

	ORIG	GOOD	FINE	N-MINT
❑1, Oct 77, movie Adaptation	0.50	0.60	1.50	3.00

ISMET
CANIS

Value: Cover or less

❑1	1.25	❑4	1.25
❑2	1.25	❑5	1.25
❑3	1.25		

I SPY
GOLD KEY

	ORIG	GOOD	FINE	N-MINT
❑1, Aug 66, photo cover and pin-up back cover; based on TV series	0.12	12.00	30.00	60.00
❑2, Apr 67, photo cover and pin-up back cover; based on TV series	0.12	8.00	20.00	40.00

	ORIG	GOOD	FINE	N-MINT
❑3, Nov 67, photo cover and pin-up back cover; based on TV series	0.12	8.00	20.00	40.00
❑4, Feb 68, photo cover and pin-up back cover; based on TV series	0.12	7.00	17.50	35.00
❑5, Jun 68, Photo cover; based on TV series	0.12	7.00	17.50	35.00
❑6, Sep 68, Photo cover; based on TV series	0.15	7.00	17.50	35.00

ITCHY & SCRATCHY COMICS
BONGO

	ORIG	GOOD	FINE	N-MINT
❑1, Around The World In 80 Pieces, poster.	2.25	0.50	1.25	2.50
❑2, The Itchy & Scratchy Movie II	1.95	0.40	1.00	2.00
❑3, When Bongos Collide; When Bongos Collide, Part 1, A: Bart Simpson, decoder screen	2.25	0.45	1.13	2.25
❑HS 1, Itchy & Scratchy Holiday Hi-Jinx Special	1.95	0.40	1.00	2.00

ITCHY PLANET
FANTAGRAPHICS

Value: Cover or less

❑1, Spr 88 .... 2.25
❑2, Sum 88 .... 2.25
❑3 .... 2.25

IT'S ONLY A MATTER OF LIFE AND DEATH
FANTAGRAPHICS

Value: Cover or less

❑1, b&w 3.95

IT'S SCIENCE WITH DR. RADIUM
SLAVE LABOR

	ORIG	GOOD	FINE	N-MINT
❑1, Sep 86, Dr. Radium in the King of the KingsLast Chance	1.50	0.40	1.00	2.00
❑2, Jan 87	1.50	0.40	1.00	2.00
❑3, Mar 87	1.50	0.40	1.00	2.00
❑4, May 87, Alien Terror (Oh, My!); A Deal with God	1.50	0.40	1.00	2.00
❑5, Jul 87	1.50	0.40	1.00	2.00
❑6, Oct 87	1.50	0.40	1.00	2.00
❑7, Feb 88	1.75	0.40	1.00	2.00
❑SE 1, Jan 89, b&w	2.95	0.59	1.48	2.95

IT! THE TERROR FROM BEYOND SPACE
MILLENNIUM

Value: Cover or less

❑1, Murmur of the Heart, Die-cut cover 2.50
❑2 .... 2.50
❑3 .... 2.50
❑4 .... 2.50

I WANT TO BE YOUR DOG
FANTAGRAPHICS

Value: Cover or less

❑1, b&w; adult 1.95
❑2, b&w; adult 1.95
❑3, b&w; adult 1.95
❑4, b&w; adult 1.95
❑5, adult 2.25

J

J2
MARVEL

Value: Cover or less

❑1, Oct 98, gatefold summary; son of Juggernaut 1.99
❑1/A 1.99
❑2, Nov 98, V: X-People, gatefold summary 1.99
❑3, Dec 98, A: Sub-Mariner; A: Doctor Strange; A: Dr. Strange; A: Hulk 1.99
❑4, Jan 99, A: Doc Magus; 1: Nemesus 1.99
❑5, Feb 99, Here Comes Wild Thing, A: Elektra; A: Wolverine; 1: Wild Thing 1.99
❑6, Mar 99, Majority Rules!, A: Magneta, Wild Thing story .. 1.99
❑7, Apr 99, The Last Days of the Original Juggernaut; The Day J2 Lost 1, 000 Pounds, A: Parody; A: Uncanny X-People; A: Cyclops, Wild Thing story.... 1.99
❑8, May 99 .... 1.99
❑9, Jun 99, 1: Big Julie 1.99
❑10, Jul 99, A: Wolverine 1.99
❑11, Aug 99, A: Iron Fist; A: Sons of the Tiger, Iron Fist; A: Sons of the Tiger 1.99
❑12, Oct 99 .... 1.99

JAB
ADHESIVE

Value: Cover or less

❑1 .... 2.50
❑2 .... 2.50
❑3, Spr 93, bullet hole 2.50
❑4 .... 2.50
❑5, Dead End Cruiser; Untitled 2.50

JAB (CUMMINGS DESIGN)
CUMMINGS DESIGN GROUP

Value: Cover or less

❑3, Aut 94, b&w 2.95

JAB (FUNNY PAPERS)
FUNNY PAPERS

Value: Cover or less

❑1, b&w 2.50
❑2, b&w 2.50

JACKAROO, THE
ETERNITY

Value: Cover or less

❑1, Feb 90, Australia Nights, b&w; Australian 2.25
❑2, Mar 90, b&w; Australian.... 2.25
❑3, Apr 90, b&w; Australian 2.25

JACK FROST
AMAZING

Value: Cover or less

❑1, Behold Tomorrow, b&w..... 1.95
❑2, b&w 1.95

JACK HUNTER
BLACKTHORNE

Value: Cover or less

❑1, Mar 88, JKu (c) 1.25

JACK OF HEARTS
MARVEL

	ORIG	GOOD	FINE	N-MINT
❑1, Jan 84	0.60	0.25	0.63	1.25
❑2, Feb 84, Heart To Heart	0.60	0.25	0.63	1.25
❑3, Mar 84	0.60	0.25	0.63	1.25
❑4, Apr 84, Heart Attack	0.60	0.25	0.63	1.25

JACK'S LUCK RUNS OUT
BEEKEEPER CARTOON AMUSEMENTS

Value: Cover or less

❑1, nn 3.50

JACK THE RIPPER
ETERNITY

Value: Cover or less

❑1, b&w 2.25
❑2, b&w 2.25
❑3, b&w 2.25

JACK THE RIPPER (CALIBER)
CALIBER

Value: Cover or less

❑1, b&w; One-Shot 2.95

JACQUELYN THE RIPPER
FANTAGRAPHICS

Value: Cover or less

❑1, Oct 94, b&w 2.95
❑2, Oct 94, b&w 2.95

JACQUE'S VOICE OF DOOM
DOOMED COMICS

Value: Cover or less

❑1, b&w; strip reprints 1.50

JADEMAN COLLECTION
JADEMAN

Value: Cover or less

❑1 .... 2.50
❑2 .... 2.50

JADEMAN KUNG FU SPECIAL
JADEMAN

Value: Cover or less

❑1, Oriental Heroes; The Blood Sword, Perviews of Jademan's Titles 1.50

JADE WARRIORS
IMAGE

Value: Cover or less

❑1, To Die For, Part 1 .... 2.50
❑1/A, To Die For, Part 1, alternate cover; Painted 2.50
❑2, Jan 00, To Die For, Part 2 .... 2.50

JAGUAR, THE
DC

Value: Cover or less

❑1, Aug 91, Savage Birthright, O: Jaguar; 1: Luiza Timmerman; 1: Maxx-13; 1: Maxim Ruiz; 1: Tracy Dickerson; 1: Timon de Guzman; 1: The Jaguar (Maria de Guzman) 1.00
❑2, Sep 91 .... 1.00
❑3, Oct 91, V: Maxx-13 .... 1.00
❑4, Nov 91, A: Black Hood; 1: Victor Drago 1.00
❑5, Dec 91, 1: Void 1.00
❑6, Jan 92 .... 1.00
❑7, Mar 92 .... 1.00
❑8, Apr 92 .... 1.00
❑9, May 92, The Coming of The Crusaders, Part 6, 1: Moonlighter, trading card 1.00
❑10, Jun 92 .... 1.00
❑11, Jul 92 .... 1.00
❑12, Aug 92 .... 1.25
❑13, Sep 92 .... 1.25
❑14, Oct 92, Frightmare in Rio!, Final Issue 1.25
❑Anl 1, trading card. 2.50

JAGUAR GOD
VEROTIK

	ORIG	GOOD	FINE	N-MINT
❑0, Feb 96	2.95	1.00	2.50	5.00
❑1, Mar 95	2.95	1.00	2.50	5.00
❑2, Aug 95	2.95	0.80	2.00	4.00
❑3, Mar 96	2.95	0.70	1.75	3.50
❑4	2.95	0.70	1.75	3.50
❑5, Sep 96	2.95	0.70	1.75	3.50
❑6, Apr 97	2.95	0.59	1.48	2.95
❑7, Jun 97	2.95	0.59	1.48	2.95
❑8	2.95	0.59	1.48	2.95

JAILBAIT
EROS

Value: Cover or less

❑1, Dec 98 .... 2.95

JAKE THRASH
AIRCEL

Value: Cover or less

❑1, full color 2.00
❑2, full color 2.00

JAM, THE
SLAVE LABOR

	ORIG	GOOD	FINE	N-MINT
❑1, Nov 89, b&w	1.95	0.50	1.25	2.50
❑2, Jan 90, b&w	1.95	0.40	1.00	2.00
❑3, Mar 90, b&w	1.95	0.40	1.00	2.00
❑4, May 90	2.25	0.59	1.48	2.95
❑5, Mar 91	2.25	0.59	1.48	2.95
❑6	2.50	0.50	1.25	2.50
❑7, Mar 94, b&w	2.50	0.50	1.25	2.50
❑8, Feb 95, b&w	2.50	0.59	1.48	2.95
❑9, Aug 95, b&w	2.95	0.59	1.48	2.95
❑10, b&w	2.95	0.59	1.48	2.95
❑11, b&w	2.95	0.59	1.48	2.95
❑12	2.95	0.59	1.48	2.95
❑13	2.95	0.59	1.48	2.95

ORIG GOOD FINE N-MINT

JAMAR CHRONICLES, THE
SWEAT SHOP PRESS
Value: Cover or less
- ❑1, b&w 2.00

JAMES BOND 007: A SILENT ARMAGEDDON
DARK HORSE
Value: Cover or less
- ❑1, Mar 93, cardstock cover ... 2.95
- ❑2, May 93, cardstock cover ... 2.95

JAMES BOND 007/GOLDENEYE
TOPPS
Value: Cover or less
- ❑1, Jan 96, movie Adaptation . 2.95
- ❑2 .... 2.95
- ❑3 .... 2.95

JAMES BOND 007: SERPENT'S TOOTH
DARK HORSE
Value: Cover or less
- ❑1, Jul 92, PG, prestige format 4.95
- ❑2, Aug 92, PG, prestige format 4.95
- ❑3, Feb 93, PG, prestige format 4.95

JAMES BOND 007: SHATTERED HELIX
DARK HORSE
Value: Cover or less
- ❑1, Jun 94, The Greenhouse Effect 2.50
- ❑2, Jul 94 .... 2.50

JAMES BOND 007: THE QUASIMODO GAMBIT
DARK HORSE
Value: Cover or less
- ❑1, Jan 95, cardstock cover.... 3.95
- ❑2, Feb 95, cardstock cover ... 3.95
- ❑3, May 95, cardstock cover ... 3.95

JAMES BOND FOR YOUR EYES ONLY
MARVEL

	ORIG	GOOD	FINE	N-MINT
❑1, Oct 81, HC, movie Adaptation	0.50	0.30	0.75	1.50
❑2, Nov 81, HC, movie Adaptation	0.50	0.30	0.75	1.50

JAMES BOND JR.
MARVEL
Value: Cover or less
- ❑1, Jan 92, The Beginning, TV cartoon 1.00
- ❑2, Feb 92, TV cartoon 1.25
- ❑3, Mar 92, TV cartoon 1.25
- ❑4, Apr 92, TV cartoon 1.25
- ❑5, May 92, TV cartoon 1.25
- ❑6, Jun 92, TV cartoon 1.25
- ❑7, Jul 92, TV cartoon 1.25
- ❑8, Aug 92, TV cartoon 1.25
- ❑9, Sep 92, TV cartoon 1.25
- ❑10, Oct 92, TV cartoon 1.25
- ❑11, Nov 92, TV cartoon 1.25
- ❑12, Dec 92, Final Issue; TV cartoon 1.25

JAMES BOND: PERMISSION TO DIE
ECLIPSE

	ORIG	GOOD	FINE	N-MINT
❑1, Jul 91, MGr, MGr (w)	3.95	1.00	2.50	5.00
❑2, Aug 91, MGr, MGr (w)	3.95	1.00	2.50	5.00
❑3, Sep 91, MGr, MGr (w)	4.95	1.00	2.50	5.00

JAM QUACKY
JQ PRODUCTIONS
Value: Cover or less
- ❑1, b&w 2.00

JAM SPECIAL, THE
MATRIX
Value: Cover or less
- ❑1 .... 2.50

JAM SUPER COOL COLOR-INJECTED TURBO ADVENTURE FROM HELL
COMICO
Value: Cover or less
- ❑1 .... 2.50

JAM URBAN ADVENTURE, THE
TUNDRA
Value: Cover or less
- ❑1, full color 2.95
- ❑2, full color 2.95
- ❑3, full color 2.95

JANE BONDAGE
EROS
Value: Cover or less
- ❑1 .... 2.95
- ❑2, Sep 95 .... 2.95

JANE BOND: THUNDERBALLS
FANTAGRAPHICS
Value: Cover or less
- ❑1, b&w; adult 2.50

JANE DOE
RAGING RHINO
Value: Cover or less
- ❑1, Androgyne Anger Extreme, b&w; adult 2.95
- ❑2, Slice bySlice, b&w; adult... 2.95
- ❑3, b&w; adult 2.95

JANX
ES GRAPHICS
Value: Cover or less
- ❑1 .... 1.00
- ❑2 .... 1.00

J.A.P.A.N.
OUTEREALM
Value: Cover or less
- ❑1, As The Sun Rises 1.80

JAR OF FOOLS PART ONE
PENNY DREADFUL
Value: Cover or less
- ❑1, Jun 94, nn; b&w 5.95

JASON AND THE ARGONAUTS
TOME PRESS
Value: Cover or less
- ❑1, b&w 2.50
- ❑2, b&w 2.50
- ❑3, b&w 2.50
- ❑4, b&w 2.50
- ❑5, b&w 2.50

Mike Grell took a stab at the adventures of James Bond with the three-issue *James Bond: Permission to Die.*

© 1991 Eclipse and EON Productions

ORIG GOOD FINE N-MINT

JASON GOES TO HELL: THE FINAL FRIDAY
TOPPS
Value: Cover or less
- ❑1, glowing cover; trading cards 2.95
- ❑2, trading cards 2.95
- ❑3, trading cards 2.95

JASON MONARCH
ORACLE
Value: Cover or less
- ❑1, Jason Monarch, Star Menagerie, b&w 2.00

JASON VS. LEATHERFACE
TOPPS
Value: Cover or less
- ❑1, Oct 95, Goin' South 2.95
- ❑2, Nov 95 .... 2.95
- ❑3 .... 2.95

JAVA TOWN
SLAVE LABOR
Value: Cover or less
- ❑1, May 92, b&w 2.95
- ❑2, Nov 93, Java Town; We Want to Own a Coffee Shop B Cuz, b&w 2.95
- ❑3, Jul 94, b&w 2.95
- ❑4, Jul 95, b&w 2.95
- ❑5, Nov 95, b&w 2.95
- ❑6, Jun 96, b&w 2.95

JAVERTS
FIRSTLIGHT
Value: Cover or less
- ❑1 .... 2.95

JAX AND THE HELL HOUND
BLACKTHORNE
Value: Cover or less
- ❑1, Nov 86, Escape 1.75
- ❑2, Feb 87, Death Cance........ 1.75
- ❑3 .... 1.75
- ❑4 .... 1.75

JAY ANACLETO SKETCHBOOK
IMAGE
Value: Cover or less
- ❑1, Apr 99, no cover price....... —
- ❑1/A, Apr 99, Has cover price . 5.95

JAY & SILENT BOB
ONI PRESS

	ORIG	GOOD	FINE	N-MINT
❑1, Jul 98, KSm (w)	2.95	0.80	2.00	4.00
❑1/SC, KSm (w), Photo cover	2.95	1.00	2.50	5.00
❑1-2, Oct 98, KSm (w), 2nd Printing	2.95	0.59	1.48	2.95
❑2, Oct 98, KSm (w)	2.95	0.60	1.50	3.00
❑3, Dec 98, KSm (w), Photo cover	2.95	0.60	1.50	3.00
❑4, Oct 99, KSm (w)	2.95	0.60	1.50	3.00

JAZZ
HIGH IMPACT

	ORIG	GOOD	FINE	N-MINT
❑1	—	0.59	1.48	2.95
❑2, May 96	—	0.59	1.48	2.95

JAZZ AGE CHRONICLES (CALIBER)
CALIBER
Value: Cover or less
- ❑1, Vote Early and Often Part 1, b&w 2.50
- ❑2, May 90, Vote Early and Often Part 2, b&w 2.50
- ❑3, b&w 2.50
- ❑4, b&w 2.50
- ❑5, b&w 2.50

JAZZ AGE CHRONICLES (EF)
EF GRAPHICS
Value: Cover or less
- ❑1, Jan 89, The Case of the Beguiling Baroness Part 1 .... 1.50
- ❑2, Mar 89, The Case of the Beguiling Baroness Part 2 .... 1.50
- ❑3, May 89, The Case of the Beguiling Baroness Part 3... 1.50

JAZZBO COMICS THAT SWING
SLAVE LABOR
Value: Cover or less
- ❑1, Nov 94, Get Rhythm with Jazzbo! Comics; Yum Cha to Drink Tea and Eat Dim Sum 2.95
- ❑2, Apr 95, Year of the Egg, Chapter One; Year of the Egg, Chapter Two, Replacement God preview 2.95

JAZZ: SOLITAIRE
HIGH IMPACT

	ORIG	GOOD	FINE	N-MINT
❑1, May 98	2.95	0.59	1.48	2.95
❑1/A, May 98, wraparound photo cover	—	0.70	1.75	3.50
❑1/GO, May 98, no cover price; gold foil logo	—	0.70	1.75	3.50
❑2, May 98	3.00	0.60	1.50	3.00
❑2/A, no cover price	5.95	1.00	2.50	5.00
❑2/B, nude cover (blue background)	5.95	1.00	2.50	5.00
❑3	3.00	0.60	1.50	3.00

	ORIG	GOOD	FINE	N-MINT
❑3/A, Nude cover	5.95	1.00	2.50	5.00
❑3/B, wraparound nude cover	5.95	1.00	2.50	5.00

JCP FEATURES
J.C.

	ORIG	GOOD	FINE	N-MINT
❑1, Feb 81, NA; DG, THUNDER Agents	2.00	0.60	1.50	3.00

JEFFREY DAHMER: AN UNAUTHORIZED BIOGRAPHY OF A SERIAL KILLER
BONEYARD PRESS

	ORIG	GOOD	FINE	N-MINT
❑1	2.50	0.80	2.00	4.00
❑1-2	2.75	0.55	1.38	2.75

JEFFREY DAHMER VS. JESUS CHRIST
BONEYARD PRESS

	ORIG	GOOD	FINE	N-MINT
❑1, Feb 93, wraparound cover	2.75	0.80	2.00	4.00
❑1/Aut	3.95	1.00	2.50	5.00

JEMM, SON OF SATURN
DC

	ORIG	GOOD	FINE	N-MINT
❑1, Sep 84, KJ; GC, The Arrival, 1: Jemm, Son of Saturn	0.75	0.30	0.75	1.50
❑2, Oct 84	0.75	0.20	0.50	1.00
❑3, Nov 84, O: Jemm	0.75	0.20	0.50	1.00
❑4, Dec 84	0.75	0.20	0.50	1.00
❑5, Jan 85	0.75	0.20	0.50	1.00
❑6, Feb 85	0.75	0.20	0.50	1.00
❑7, Mar 85, KJ; GC, Firefight	0.75	0.20	0.50	1.00
❑8, Apr 85	0.75	0.20	0.50	1.00
❑9, May 85	0.75	0.20	0.50	1.00
❑10, Jun 85	0.75	0.20	0.50	1.00
❑11, Jul 85	0.75	0.20	0.50	1.00
❑12, Aug 85	0.75	0.20	0.50	1.00

JENNY FINN
ONI PRESS

Value: Cover or less

❑1, Jun 99 .... 2.95
❑2, Sep 99 .... 2.95
❑3 .... 2.95
❑4 .... 2.95

JENNY SPARKS: THE SECRET HISTORY OF THE AUTHORITY
WILDSTORM

Value: Cover or less

❑1, Aug 00 .... 2.50
❑2, Sep 00, Rough Trade 2.50
❑3, Oct 00, A Tale of Two Cities 2.50
❑4, Nov 00, Many Happy Returns 2.50
❑5, Dec 00, There's Nothing I Haven't Sung About 2.50

JEREMIAH: A FISTFUL OF SAND
ADVENTURE

Value: Cover or less

❑1, b&w 2.50
❑2, b&w 2.50

JEREMIAH: BIRDS OF PREY
ADVENTURE

Value: Cover or less

❑1, b&w 2.50
❑2, Apr 91, b&w 2.50

JEREMIAH: THE HEIRS
ADVENTURE

Value: Cover or less

❑1, b&w 2.50
❑2, b&w 2.50

JERSEY DEVIL
SOUTH JERSEY REBELLION

Value: Cover or less

❑1, no indicia 2.25
❑2, 48pgs. 2.95
❑3 .... 2.25
❑4 .... 2.25
❑5 .... 2.25
❑6 .... 2.25
❑7, no indicia 2.25

JESSE JAMES
AC

Value: Cover or less

❑1, JK, b&w; Reprint 3.95

JESTER'S MOON, THE
ONE SHOT PRESS

	ORIG	GOOD	FINE	N-MINT
❑1, Aug 96, nn; b&w	0.99	0.20	0.50	1.00

JESUS COMICS (FOOLBERT STURGEON'S...)
RIP OFF

	ORIG	GOOD	FINE	N-MINT
❑1	0.50	1.00	2.50	5.00
❑2	0.50	0.80	2.00	4.00
❑3, Jesus Joins the Academic Community; Craddock's Crusade, A Will Hatcher Adventure	0.50	0.80	2.00	4.00

JET
AUTHORITY

Value: Cover or less

❑1, Dec 96 .... 2.95

JET (WILDSTORM)
WILDSTORM

Value: Cover or less

❑1, Nov 00, Midnight 2 Midnight, Part 1 .... 2.50
❑2, Dec 00, Midnight 2 Midnight, Part 2 .... 2.50
❑3, Jan 01, Midnight 2 Midnight, Part 3 .... 2.50
❑4, Feb 01, Crimes and Mr. Meaner 2.50

JET BLACK
MONOLITH

Value: Cover or less

❑1, Sep 97, O: Jet Black 2.50

JET COMICS
SLAVE LABOR

Value: Cover or less

❑1, Oct 97, From Out of the Blue, 1: Alex Chambers; 1: Spectrum, b&w 2.95
❑2, Feb 98, Whole Lot of Shakin' Goin' On!, b&w 2.95
❑3, Mar 98, The Wet and the Wild!, Final Issue 2.95

JET DREAM
GOLD KEY

	ORIG	GOOD	FINE	N-MINT
❑1, Jun 68, Painted cover	0.12	3.00	7.50	15.00

JETSONS, THE (ARCHIE)
ARCHIE

Value: Cover or less

❑1, Sep 95, Journey Back Park; Johnny Space Cadet, A: The Flintstones 1.50
❑2, Oct 95 .... 1.50
❑3, Nov 95 .... 1.50
❑4, Dec 95 .... 1.50
❑5, Jan 96 .... 1.50
❑6, Feb 96 .... 1.50
❑7, Mar 96 .... 1.50
❑8, Apr 96 .... 1.50
❑9 .... 1.50
❑10 .... 1.50
❑11 .... 1.50
❑12 .... 1.50

JETSONS, THE (CHARLTON)
CHARLTON

	ORIG	GOOD	FINE	N-MINT
❑1, Nov 70	0.15	7.00	17.50	35.00
❑2, Jan 71	0.15	4.40	11.00	22.00
❑3, Mar 71	0.15	2.80	7.00	14.00
❑4, May 71	0.15	2.80	7.00	14.00
❑5, Jul 71	0.15	2.80	7.00	14.00
❑6, Sep 71	0.15	2.00	5.00	10.00
❑7, Nov 71	0.20	2.00	5.00	10.00
❑8, Jan 72	0.20	2.00	5.00	10.00
❑9, Mar 72	0.20	2.00	5.00	10.00
❑10, May 72	0.20	2.00	5.00	10.00
❑11, Jul 72	0.20	1.40	3.50	7.00
❑12, Sep 72	0.20	1.40	3.50	7.00
❑13, Nov 72	0.20	1.40	3.50	7.00
❑14	0.20	1.40	3.50	7.00
❑15, Feb 73	0.20	1.40	3.50	7.00
❑16, Apr 73	0.20	1.40	3.50	7.00
❑17, Jun 73	0.20	1.40	3.50	7.00
❑18, Aug 73	0.20	1.40	3.50	7.00
❑19, Oct 73	0.20	1.40	3.50	7.00
❑20, Dec 73	0.20	1.40	3.50	7.00

JETSONS, THE (GOLD KEY)
GOLD KEY

	ORIG	GOOD	FINE	N-MINT
❑1	—	22.00	55.00	110.00
❑2	—	16.00	40.00	80.00
❑3	—	12.00	30.00	60.00
❑4	—	12.00	30.00	60.00
❑5	—	12.00	30.00	60.00
❑6	—	9.00	22.50	45.00
❑7	—	9.00	22.50	45.00
❑8	—	9.00	22.50	45.00
❑9	—	9.00	22.50	45.00
❑10	—	9.00	22.50	45.00
❑11	—	6.00	15.00	30.00
❑12	—	6.00	15.00	30.00
❑13	—	6.00	15.00	30.00
❑14	—	6.00	15.00	30.00
❑15	—	6.00	15.00	30.00
❑16	—	6.00	15.00	30.00
❑17	—	6.00	15.00	30.00
❑18	—	6.00	15.00	30.00
❑19	—	6.00	15.00	30.00
❑20	—	6.00	15.00	30.00
❑21	—	3.60	9.00	18.00
❑22	—	3.60	9.00	18.00
❑23	—	3.60	9.00	18.00
❑24	—	3.60	9.00	18.00
❑25	—	3.60	9.00	18.00
❑26	—	3.60	9.00	18.00
❑27	—	3.60	9.00	18.00
❑28	—	3.60	9.00	18.00
❑29	—	3.60	9.00	18.00
❑30	—	3.60	9.00	18.00
❑31	—	3.00	7.50	15.00
❑32	—	3.00	7.50	15.00
❑33	—	3.00	7.50	15.00
❑34	—	3.00	7.50	15.00
❑35, Jul 70	0.15	3.00	7.50	15.00
❑36, Oct 70	0.15	3.00	7.50	15.00

JETSONS, THE (HARVEY)
HARVEY

	ORIG	GOOD	FINE	N-MINT
❑1	1.25	0.30	0.75	1.50
❑2, Two Worlds Collide; Stuffed Skunk	1.25	0.30	0.75	1.50
❑3	1.25	0.30	0.75	1.50
❑4	1.25	0.30	0.75	1.50
❑5	1.50	0.30	0.75	1.50

JETSONS BIG BOOK, THE
HARVEY

Value: Cover or less

- ❑1, A Visit to Bedrock; Hijacked 1.95
- ❑2 .... 1.95
- ❑3 .... 1.95

JETSONS GIANT SIZE
HARVEY

	ORIG	GOOD	FINE	N-MINT
❑1	2.25	0.60	1.50	3.00
❑2	2.25	0.50	1.25	2.50
❑3	2.25	0.50	1.25	2.50

JEW IN COMMUNIST PRAGUE, A
NBM

Value: Cover or less

- ❑1, oversized graphic novel 11.95
- ❑2, oversized graphic novel 11.95

JEZEBEL JADE
COMICO

Value: Cover or less

- ❑1, Oct 88, The Bones of Galahad, wraparound cover 2.00
- ❑2, Nov 88, wraparound cover 2.00
- ❑3, Dec 88, wraparound cover 2.00

JEZEBELLE
WILDSTORM

Value: Cover or less

- ❑1/A, Mar 01, Woman leaping backward on cover, two hands with energy glow 2.50
- ❑1/B, Mar 01, Woman standing on cover, one hand in energy ball 2.50
- ❑2, Apr 01 .... 2.50
- ❑3, May 01 .... 2.50
- ❑4 .... 2.50
- ❑5 .... 2.50
- ❑6 .... 2.50

JFK ASSASSINATION
ZONE

Value: Cover or less

- ❑1, Frame 313 .... 2.95

JHEREG
MARVEL

Value: Cover or less

- ❑1 .... 8.95

JIGABOO DEVIL
MILLENNIUM

Value: Cover or less

- ❑0, b&w 2.95

JIGSAW
HARVEY

	ORIG	GOOD	FINE	N-MINT
❑1, A Nightmare In Space!, 1: Jigsaw (Harvey)	0.12	2.40	6.00	12.00
❑2	0.12	1.40	3.50	7.00

JIM (VOL. 1)
FANTAGRAPHICS

	ORIG	GOOD	FINE	N-MINT
❑1	2.95	2.00	5.00	10.00
❑2	2.95	1.40	3.50	7.00
❑3	2.95	1.00	2.50	5.00
❑4	2.95	1.00	2.50	5.00

JIM (VOL. 2)
FANTAGRAPHICS

	ORIG	GOOD	FINE	N-MINT
❑1, Dec 93, Manhog Beyond The Face, b&w	2.95	1.20	3.00	6.00
❑2, b&w	2.95	0.80	2.00	4.00
❑3, b&w	2.95	0.80	2.00	4.00
❑4, b&w	2.95	0.60	1.50	3.00
❑5, b&w	3.50	0.60	1.50	3.00
❑6, May 96, b&w	3.50	0.70	1.75	3.50
❑SE 1, Frank's Real Pa Special Edition	3.95	0.80	2.00	4.00

JIMBO
BONGO

Value: Cover or less

- ❑1, b&w; adult 2.95
- ❑2, b&w; adult 2.95
- ❑3, adult; indicia says #2 .... 2.95
- ❑4, b&w; adult; no indicia 2.95
- ❑5, adult 2.95
- ❑6, adult 2.95
- ❑7, adult 2.95

JINGLE BELLE
ONI

Value: Cover or less

- ❑1, b&w 2.95
- ❑2, b&w 2.95

JINGLE BELLE'S ALL-STAR HOLIDAY HULLABALOO
ONI

Value: Cover or less

- ❑1, Nov 00, SA, SA (w), A Carol's Christmas, That Olde Christmas Spirit, Visions of Sugar Plums, Blue Belles, Belles' Belles, Coal Comfort, b&w 4.95

JINN
IMAGE

Value: Cover or less

- ❑1, Mar 00 .... 2.95
- ❑2 .... 2.95
- ❑3, Oct 00 .... 2.95

JINX
CALIBER

	ORIG	GOOD	FINE	N-MINT
❑1, BMB, BMB (w), b&w; Caliber publishes	2.95	0.70	1.75	3.50
❑2, BMB, BMB (w), Jinx Meets Goldfish, b&w	2.95	0.60	1.50	3.00
❑3, BMB, BMB (w), Goldfish and Jinx Go on a Date, b&w	2.95	0.60	1.50	3.00
❑4, BMB, BMB (w), The Treasure, b&w	2.95	0.60	1.50	3.00
❑5, Nov 96, BMB, BMB (w), The Confession, b&w	2.95	0.60	1.50	3.00
❑6, BMB, BMB (w), Jinx and Goldfish Team Up, b&w; series moves to Image	2.95	0.60	1.50	3.00
❑7, BMB, BMB (w), Jinx to the Rescue	2.95	0.60	1.50	3.00
❑8, BMB, BMB (w), Charity Special	4.95	0.99	2.47	4.95
❑9, BMB, BMB (w), Homeless Edition	4.95	0.99	2.47	4.95
❑10, BMB, BMB (w), b&w; was Caliber series; Image publishes	2.95	0.59	1.48	2.95
❑11, BMB, BMB (w), b&w	2.95	0.59	1.48	2.95
❑12, BMB, BMB (w), Stoplights; David Hasselhoff	3.95	0.79	1.98	3.95
❑13, BMB, BMB (w), Follically Challenged; Low Blood Sugar, b&w	2.95	0.79	1.98	3.95
❑14, BMB, BMB (w), Pitch the Bagel, b&w	3.95	0.79	1.98	3.95
❑15, BMB, BMB (w), Borderland; The Kiss Off	3.95	0.79	1.98	3.95
❑16, BMB, BMB (w), Torso	3.95	0.79	1.98	3.95
❑17, BMB, BMB (w), Torso	3.95	0.79	1.98	3.95
❑18, BMB, BMB (w), Fire	2.95	0.59	1.48	2.95
❑19, BMB, BMB (w), Defining Moments in Bendis History; A Day in the Life of...a Howard Stern Fan, Buried Treasures	2.95	0.59	1.48	2.95
❑20, BMB, BMB (w), Superman is Dead; Mike, b&w; True Crime Confessions	3.95	0.79	1.98	3.95
❑21, BMB, BMB (w), Torso	3.95	0.79	1.98	3.95

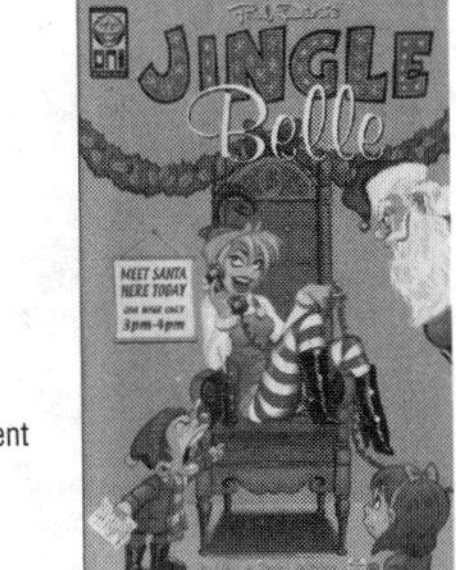

The misadventures of Santa's delinquent daughter are chronicled in Paul Dini's stories of Jingle Belle.

JINX POP CULTURE HOO-HAH, THE
IMAGE

Value: Cover or less

- ❑1, BMB, BMB (w), I Married A Sci-Fi-Geek; A Day in the Life of A Film Geek, nn; b&w; One-Shot 3.95

JIZZ
FANTAGRAPHICS

Value: Cover or less

- ❑1, b&w; adult 2.00
- ❑2, b&w; adult 2.00
- ❑3, b&w; adult 2.00
- ❑4, b&w; adult 2.00
- ❑5, adult 2.25
- ❑6, adult 2.25
- ❑7, adult 2.25
- ❑8, adult 2.50
- ❑9, adult 2.95
- ❑10, b&w; adult 2.50

JLA
DC

	ORIG	GOOD	FINE	N-MINT
❑1, Jan 97, Them!, Superman, Batman, Flash, Wonder Woman, Green Lantern, Martian Manhunter, Aquaman team	1.95	2.40	6.00	12.00
❑2, Feb 97	1.95	2.00	5.00	10.00
❑3, Mar 97	1.95	1.60	4.00	8.00
❑4, Apr 97	1.95	1.20	3.00	6.00
❑5, May 97, V: T.O. Morrow; V: Prof. Ivo, Membership drive	1.95	1.00	2.50	5.00
❑6, Jun 97, Fire in the Sky, A: Abnegazar; 1: Zauriel; A: Ghast; A: Neron	1.95	0.80	2.00	4.00
❑7, Jul 97	1.95	0.60	1.50	3.00
❑8, Aug 97, V: Key	1.95	0.60	1.50	3.00
❑9, Sep 97, V: Key	1.95	0.60	1.50	3.00
❑10, Oct 97, Rock of Ages, Part 1, V: New Injustice Gang	1.95	0.60	1.50	3.00
❑11, Nov 97, Rock of Ages, Part 2	1.95	0.50	1.25	2.50
❑12, Dec 97, Rock of Ages, Part 3	1.95	0.50	1.25	2.50
❑13, Dec 97, Rock of Ages, Part 4, Face cover; Aquaman, Green Lantern, and Flash in future	1.95	0.50	1.25	2.50
❑14, Jan 98, Rock of Ages, Part 5	1.95	0.50	1.25	2.50
❑15, Feb 98, Rock of Ages, Part 6	1.95	0.50	1.25	2.50
❑16, Mar 98, Camelot, V: Prometheus, Watchtower blueprints	1.95	0.40	1.00	2.00
❑17, Apr 98, V: Prometheus	1.95	0.40	1.00	2.00
❑18, May 98, 1: Julian September	1.95	0.40	1.00	2.00
❑19, Jun 98, A: Atom	1.95	0.40	1.00	2.00
❑20, Jul 98, V: Adam Strange	1.95	0.40	1.00	2.00
❑21, Aug 98, A: Aleaa; V: Adam Strange	1.95	0.40	1.00	2.00
❑22, Sep 98, A: Daniel (Sandman)	1.99	0.40	1.00	2.00
❑23, Oct 98, V: Star Conqueror; A: Daniel	1.99	0.40	1.00	2.00
❑24, Dec 98, Ultra-Marines Saga, Part 1, 1: Ultramarine Corps	1.99	0.40	1.00	2.00
❑25, Jan 99, Ultra-Marines Saga, Part 2, V: Ultramarine Corps	1.99	0.40	1.00	2.00
❑26, Feb 99, Ultra-Marines Saga, Part 3, V: Shaggy Man; A: Ultra-Marines	1.99	0.40	1.00	2.00
❑27, Mar 99, A: Justice Society of America; V: Amazo	1.99	0.40	1.00	2.00

	ORIG	GOOD	FINE	N-MINT
❑28, Apr 99, Crisis Times Five, Part 1, A: Triumph; A: Justice Society of America	1.99	0.40	1.00	2.00
❑29, May 99, JSa (w), Crisis Times Five, Part 2, A: Captain Marvel; A: Justice Society of America	1.99	0.40	1.00	2.00
❑30, Jun 99, Crisis Times Five, Part 3, A: Justice Society of America	1.99	0.40	1.00	2.00
❑31, Jul 99, Crisis Times Five, Part 4	1.99	0.40	1.00	2.00
❑32, Aug 99, MWa (w); DGry(w), Inside Job, JLA in No Man's Land	1.99	0.40	1.00	2.00
❑33, Sep 99, MWa (w), Altered Egos	1.99	0.40	1.00	2.00
❑34, Oct 99, The Ant and the Avalanche	1.99	0.40	1.00	2.00
❑35, Nov 99, A: new Spectre, Day of Judgment	1.99	0.40	1.00	2.00
❑36, Dec 99, World War III, Part 1	1.99	0.40	1.00	2.00
❑37, Jan 00, World War III, Part 2	1.99	0.40	1.00	2.00
❑38, Feb 00, World War III, Part 3	1.99	0.40	1.00	2.00
❑39, Mar 00, World War III, Part 4	1.99	0.40	1.00	2.00
❑40, Apr 00, World War III, Part 5	1.99	0.40	1.00	2.00
❑41, May 00, World War III, Part 6, Giant-size	2.99	0.60	1.50	2.99
❑42, Jun 00	1.99	0.40	1.00	1.99
❑43, Jul 00, MWa (w), Tower of Babel, Part 1	1.99	0.40	1.00	1.99
❑44, Aug 00, MWa (w), Tower of Babel, Part 2	1.99	0.40	1.00	1.99
❑45, Sep 00, MWa (w), Tower of Babel, Part 3	2.25	0.45	1.13	2.25
❑46, Oct 00, MWa (w), Tower of Babel, Part 4	2.25	0.45	1.13	2.25
❑47, Nov 00, MWa (w), The Queen of Fables, Part 1	2.25	0.45	1.13	2.25
❑48, Dec 00, MWa (w), The Queen of Fables, Part 2	2.25	0.45	1.13	2.25
❑49, Jan 01, MWa (w), The Queen of Fables, Part 3	2.25	0.45	1.13	2.25
❑50, Feb 01, MWa (w), Dream Team, Giant-size	3.75	0.75	1.88	3.75
❑51, Apr 01, MWa (w), Man and Superman	2.25	0.45	1.13	2.25
❑52, May 01, MWa (w), Element of Surprise	2.25	0.45	1.13	2.25
❑53	2.25	0.45	1.13	2.25
❑54	2.25	0.45	1.13	2.25
❑55	2.25	0.45	1.13	2.25
❑56	2.25	0.45	1.13	2.25
❑1000000, Nov 98, Prisoners of the Twentieth Century, One Million	1.99	0.40	1.00	1.99
❑Anl 1, Hardboiled Hangover, Pulp Heroes	3.95	0.79	1.98	3.95
❑Anl 2, Ghosts	2.95	0.79	1.98	3.95
❑Anl 3, Sep 99, Gorilla Warfare, JLApe	2.95	0.59	1.48	2.95
❑GS 1, Jul 98, 80pgs.	4.95	0.99	2.47	4.95
❑GS 2, Nov 99, The Game; With Friends Like These...!, 80pgs.	4.95	0.99	2.47	4.95
❑GS 3, Oct 00, The Century War II, 80pgs.	4.95	0.99	2.47	4.95

JLA: ACT OF GOD
DC

Value: Cover or less

❑1 .... 4.95
❑2 .... 4.95
❑3 .... 4.95

JLA: BLACK BAPTISM
DC

Value: Cover or less

❑1, May 01, Magicide 2.50
❑2, Jun 01, Trials in Darkness 2.50
❑3, Jul 01 .... 2.50
❑4, Aug 01 .... 2.50

JLA: CREATED EQUAL
DC

Value: Cover or less

❑1 .... 5.95
❑2, The Children of the Spring 5.95

JLA: FOREIGN BODIES
DC

Value: Cover or less

❑1, One-Shot; prestige format 5.95

JLA GALLERY
DC

Value: Cover or less

❑1, nn; wraparound cover; pin-ups 2.95

JLA: HEAVEN'S LADDER
DC

Value: Cover or less

❑1, MWa (w) 9.95

JLA IN CRISIS SECRET FILES
DC

Value: Cover or less

❑1, Nov 98, summaries of events from Crisis through One Million 4.95

JLA: PARADISE LOST
DC

	ORIG	GOOD	FINE	N-MINT
❑1, Jan 98, Someone to Watch Over Me	1.95	0.40	1.00	2.00
❑2, Feb 98	1.95	0.40	1.00	2.00
❑3, Mar 98, Revelations	1.95	0.40	1.00	2.00

JLA: PRIMEVAL
DC

Value: Cover or less

❑1 .... 5.95

JLA SECRET FILES
DC

Value: Cover or less

❑1, Sep 97, Secret Origin; The New Superman Meets the JLA: Day in the Life: Martian Manhunter, O: New JLA, bios of team members and key villains; timeline 4.95
❑2, Aug 98, O: new League line-up, bios of team members and key villains 3.95
❑3, Dec 00, Blame; Lost Pages 4.95

JLA: SECRET SOCIETY OF SUPER-HEROES
DC

Value: Cover or less

❑1, HC (w) 5.95
❑2, HC (w) 5.95

JLA: SEVEN CASKETS
DC

Value: Cover or less

❑1 .... 5.95

JLA SHOWCASE
DC

Value: Cover or less

❑GS 1, Feb 00, 80pgs. 4.95

JLA: SUPERPOWER
DC

Value: Cover or less

❑1, Nov 99, One-Shot; prestige format 5.95

JLA: THE NAIL
DC

	ORIG	GOOD	FINE	N-MINT
❑1, Aug 98, Elseworlds	4.95	1.10	2.75	5.50
❑2, Sep 98, Elseworlds	4.95	1.00	2.50	5.00
❑3, Oct 98, Elseworlds	4.95	1.00	2.50	5.00

JLA/TITANS
DC

Value: Cover or less

❑1, Dec 98 .... 2.95
❑1/LE, Dec 98 .... 23.95
❑2, Jan 99 .... 2.95
❑3, Feb 99, preview for new series 2.95

JLA: TOMORROW WOMAN
DC

Value: Cover or less

❑1, Jun 98, Tomorrow Never Knows, One-Shot; Girlfrenzy; set during events of JLA #5 .... 1.95

JLA VERSUS PREDATOR
DC

Value: Cover or less

❑1 .... 5.95

JLA/WILDC.A.T.S
DC

Value: Cover or less

❑1, nn; prestige format; crossover with Image; Crime Machine 5.95

JLA/WITCHBLADE
DC

Value: Cover or less

❑1 .... 5.95

JLA: WORLD WITHOUT GROWN-UPS
DC

	ORIG	GOOD	FINE	N-MINT
❑1, Aug 98, wraparound cover; prestige format	4.95	1.10	2.75	5.50
❑2, Sep 98	4.95	1.00	2.50	5.00

JLA: YEAR ONE
DC

	ORIG	GOOD	FINE	N-MINT
❑1, Jan 98	2.95	0.70	1.75	3.50
❑2, Feb 98, Group Dynamic	1.95	0.60	1.50	3.00
❑3, Mar 98	1.95	0.60	1.50	3.00
❑4, Apr 98, While You Were Out...	1.95	0.60	1.50	3.00
❑5, May 98, A League Divided, A: Doom Patrol	1.95	0.60	1.50	3.00
❑6, Jun 98, Sum of Their Parts	1.95	0.39	0.98	1.95
❑7, Jul 98, The American Way, A: Superman	1.95	0.39	0.98	1.95
❑8, Aug 98, Loose Ends	1.95	0.39	0.98	1.95
❑9, Sep 98, Change the World	1.99	0.39	0.98	1.95
❑10, Oct 98, Heaven and Earth	1.99	0.40	1.00	1.99
❑11, Nov 98, Stalag Earth, A: Challengers; A: Freedom Fighters; A: Blackhawks; A: Metal Men	1.99	0.40	1.00	1.99
❑12, Dec 98, Justice For All, Final Issue	2.95	0.59	1.48	2.95

JLX
DC

Value: Cover or less

❑1, Apr 96, A League Of Their Own 1.95

JLX UNLEASHED
DC

Value: Cover or less

❑1, Jun 97, The Unextinguishable Flame! 1.95

JOE DIMAGGIO
CELEBRITY

Value: Cover or less

❑1, trading cards 6.95

JOE PSYCHO & MOO FROG
GOBLIN STUDIOS

	ORIG	GOOD	FINE	N-MINT
❑1	2.50	0.50	1.25	2.50
❑2	2.50	0.50	1.25	2.50
❑3	2.50	0.50	1.25	2.50
❑4	2.50	0.50	1.25	2.50
❑5	2.50	0.50	1.25	2.50
❑Ash 1, b&w; no cover price; Kinko's Ashcan Edition	—	0.20	0.50	1.00

JOE PSYCHO FULL COLOR EXTRAVAGARBONZO
GOBLIN STUDIOS

Value: Cover or less

❑1, nn 2.95

JOE SINN
CALIBER

Value: Cover or less

- ❑1, Made In Taiwo, b&w ... 2.95
- ❑1/LE, limited edition ... 5.95
- ❑2, An Open Refrigerator To The Soul, b&w; Final issue (others never released) ... 2.95

JOHN CARTER OF MARS (EDGAR RICE BURROUGHS'...)
GOLD KEY

	ORIG	GOOD	FINE	N-MINT
❑1, Apr 64	0.12	5.60	14.00	28.00
❑2, Jul 64	0.12	3.20	8.00	16.00
❑3, Oct 64	0.12	3.20	8.00	16.00

JOHN CARTER, WARLORD OF MARS
MARVEL

	ORIG	GOOD	FINE	N-MINT
❑1, Jun 77, DC; GK, O: John Carter, Warlord of Mars	0.30	1.20	3.00	6.00
❑2, Jul 77, GK, V: White Apes	0.30	0.80	2.00	4.00
❑3, Aug 77, Amazons Of Mars!, V: White Apes	0.30	0.60	1.50	3.00
❑4, Sep 77, GK	0.30	0.60	1.50	3.00
❑5, Oct 77, GK, V: Stara Kan	0.30	0.60	1.50	3.00
❑6, Nov 77	0.35	0.50	1.25	2.50
❑7, Dec 77	0.35	0.50	1.25	2.50
❑8, Jan 78	0.35	0.50	1.25	2.50
❑9, Feb 78	0.35	0.50	1.25	2.50
❑10, Mar 78	0.35	0.50	1.25	2.50
❑11, Apr 78, O: Dejah Thoris	0.35	0.50	1.25	2.50
❑12, May 78	0.35	0.50	1.25	2.50
❑13, Jun 78	0.35	0.50	1.25	2.50
❑14, Jul 78	0.35	0.50	1.25	2.50
❑15, Aug 78	0.35	0.50	1.25	2.50
❑16, Sep 78	0.35	0.50	1.25	2.50
❑17, Oct 78	0.35	0.50	1.25	2.50
❑18, Nov 78, FM	0.35	0.50	1.25	2.50
❑19, Dec 78	0.35	0.50	1.25	2.50
❑20, Jan 79	0.35	0.50	1.25	2.50
❑21, Feb 79	0.35	0.50	1.25	2.50
❑22, Mar 79	0.35	0.50	1.25	2.50
❑23, Apr 79	0.35	0.50	1.25	2.50
❑24, May 79	0.40	0.50	1.25	2.50
❑25, Jul 79	0.40	0.50	1.25	2.50
❑26, Aug 79	0.40	0.50	1.25	2.50
❑27, Sep 79	0.40	0.50	1.25	2.50
❑28, Oct 79	0.40	0.50	1.25	2.50
❑Anl 1	0.50	0.20	0.50	1.00
❑Anl 2	0.60	0.20	0.50	1.00
❑Anl 3	0.60	0.20	0.50	1.00

JOHN F. KENNEDY
DELL

	ORIG	GOOD	FINE	N-MINT
❑1, Aug 64, DG, 12-378-410; memorial comic book; Biography	0.12	8.40	21.00	42.00
❑1-2, DG, 2nd Printing; Biography	0.12	5.60	14.00	28.00
❑, DG, 3rd Printing; Biography	0.12	4.00	10.00	20.00

JOHN LAW DETECTIVE
ECLIPSE

	ORIG	GOOD	FINE	N-MINT
❑1, Apr 83, WE, WE (w), Sand Saref...; Nubbin the Shoeshine Boy and the Strange, Ghastly Affair of the Half Dead Mr. Lox	1.50	0.40	1.00	2.00

JOHNNY ATOMIC
ETERNITY

Value: Cover or less

- ❑1, b&w ... 2.50
- ❑2, b&w ... 2.50
- ❑3, b&w ... 2.50

JOHNNY COMET
AVALON COMMUNICATIONS

Value: Cover or less

- ❑1, FF ... 2.95
- ❑2, FF ... 2.95
- ❑3, FF ... 2.95
- ❑4, FF, Slow Joe, The Thinker ... 2.95
- ❑5, FF ... 2.95

JOHNNY COSMIC
THORBY

Value: Cover or less

- ❑1, The Relativity of Reality, Flip-book with Spacegal Comics #2 ... 2.95

JOHNNY DYNAMITE
DARK HORSE

Value: Cover or less

- ❑1, Sep 94, Revenge for a Black-Eyed Blonde, b&w and red ... 2.95
- ❑2, Oct 94, b&w and red ... 2.95
- ❑3, Nov 94, b&w and red ... 2.95
- ❑4, Dec 94, b&w and red ... 2.95

JOHNNY GAMBIT
HOT

Value: Cover or less

- ❑1 ... 1.75

JOHNNY HAZARD
PIONEER

Value: Cover or less

- ❑1, Dec 88, HC (c), b&w ... 2.00

JOHNNY HAZARD QUARTERLY
DRAGON LADY

Value: Cover or less

- ❑1, ATh (c) ... 5.95
- ❑2, ATh (c) ... 5.95
- ❑3, ATh (c) ... 5.95
- ❑4, ATh (c) ... 5.95

With two of its members, Superman and Batman, facing Predators, it was only a matter of time before the entire Justice League would battle the intergalactic hunters.

© 2000 20th Century Fox Film Entertainment, Dark Horse, and DC Comics

JOHNNY NEMO MAGAZINE, THE
ECLIPSE

Value: Cover or less

- ❑1, Sep 95, The Spice of Death; Sindi Shade ... 2.75
- ❑2 ... 2.75
- ❑3 ... 2.75
- ❑4, Exists? ... 2.75
- ❑5, Exists? ... 2.75
- ❑6, Exists? ... 2.75

JOHNNY THE HOMICIDAL MANIAC
SLAVE LABOR

	ORIG	GOOD	FINE	N-MINT
❑1, Aug 95, Traumatize Thy Neighbor, A: Squee, b&w	2.95	5.20	13.00	26.00
❑1-2, Dec 95, Traumatize Thy Neighbor, b&w; 2nd Printing	2.95	0.90	2.25	4.50
❑, Aug 96, b&w; 3rd Printing	2.95	0.60	1.50	3.00
❑1-4, May 97, b&w; 4th Printing	2.95	0.60	1.50	3.00
❑2, Nov 95, b&w	2.95	3.20	8.00	16.00
❑2-2, Jul 96, b&w; 2nd Printing	2.95	0.60	1.50	3.00
❑3, Feb 96, A Transient Smile, b&w	2.95	2.40	6.00	12.00
❑3-2, Jul 96, b&w; 2nd Printing	2.95	0.59	1.48	2.95
❑4, May 96, b&w	2.95	1.80	4.50	9.00
❑4-2, Apr 97, b&w; 2nd Printing	2.95	0.59	1.48	2.95
❑5, Aug 96, b&w	2.95	1.20	3.00	6.00
❑5-2, Apr 97, b&w; 2nd Printing	2.95	0.60	1.50	3.00
❑6, Aug 96, b&w	2.95	0.80	2.00	4.00
❑7, Aug 96, Wobbly Headed Bob; Meanwhile... Before The Sun Rises, b&w	2.95	0.80	2.00	4.00
❑SE 1, Reprints Johnny the Homicidal Maniac #1 with cardstock outer cover; Limited to 2000	20.00	4.00	10.00	20.00

JOHNNY THUNDER
DC

	ORIG	GOOD	FINE	N-MINT
❑1, Mar 73	0.20	2.40	6.00	12.00
❑2, May 73	0.20	1.60	4.00	8.00
❑3, Aug 73	0.20	1.60	4.00	8.00

JOKER, THE
DC

	ORIG	GOOD	FINE	N-MINT
❑1, May 75, IN; DG, The Joker's Double Jeopardy, A: Two-Face	0.25	2.40	6.00	12.00
❑2, Jul 75	0.25	1.60	4.00	8.00
❑3, Oct 75	0.25	1.20	3.00	6.00
❑4, Dec 75, V: Green Arrow	0.25	1.20	3.00	6.00
❑5, Feb 76	0.25	1.20	3.00	6.00
❑6, Apr 76	0.25	1.00	2.50	5.00
❑7, Jun 76	0.30	1.00	2.50	5.00
❑8, Aug 76, Bicentennial #7	0.30	1.00	2.50	5.00
❑9, Sep 76, A: Catwoman, Final Issue	0.30	1.00	2.50	5.00

JOKER/MASK
DARK HORSE

Value: Cover or less

- ❑1, May 00 ... 2.95
- ❑2, Jun 00 ... 2.95
- ❑3, Jul 00 ... 2.95
- ❑4, Aug 00 ... 2.95

JOLLY JACK STARJUMPER SUMMER OF '92 ONE-SHOT, THE
CONQUEST

Value: Cover or less

- ❑1, nn; b&w ... 2.95

JONAH HEX
DC

	ORIG	GOOD	FINE	N-MINT
❑1, Apr 77	0.30	5.60	14.00	28.00
❑2, Jun 77, V: El Papagayo	0.30	2.00	5.00	10.00
❑3, Aug 77	0.35	1.40	3.50	7.00
❑4, Sep 77	0.35	1.40	3.50	7.00
❑5, Oct 77	0.35	1.40	3.50	7.00
❑6, Nov 77	0.35	1.20	3.00	6.00
❑7, Dec 77, O: Jonah Hex	0.35	1.20	3.00	6.00
❑8, Jan 78, O: Jonah's facial scars	0.35	1.00	2.50	5.00
❑9, Feb 78	0.35	1.00	2.50	5.00
❑10, Mar 78	0.35	1.00	2.50	5.00
❑11, Apr 78	0.35	0.80	2.00	4.00
❑12, May 78	0.35	0.80	2.00	4.00
❑13, Jun 78	0.35	0.80	2.00	4.00
❑14, Jul 78	0.35	0.80	2.00	4.00
❑15, Aug 78	0.35	0.80	2.00	4.00

	ORIG	GOOD	FINE	N-MINT
❑16, Sep 78	0.35	0.80	2.00	4.00
❑17, Oct 78	0.35	0.80	2.00	4.00
❑18, Nov 78	0.35	0.80	2.00	4.00
❑19, Dec 78	0.35	0.80	2.00	4.00
❑20, Jan 79	0.35	0.80	2.00	4.00
❑21, Feb 79	0.35	0.60	1.50	3.00
❑22, Mar 79	0.35	0.60	1.50	3.00
❑23, Apr 79	0.35	0.60	1.50	3.00
❑24, May 79	0.35	0.60	1.50	3.00
❑25, Jun 79	0.35	0.60	1.50	3.00
❑26, Jul 79	0.35	0.60	1.50	3.00
❑27, Aug 79	0.35	0.60	1.50	3.00
❑28, Sep 79	0.35	0.60	1.50	3.00
❑29, Oct 79	0.35	0.60	1.50	3.00
❑30, Nov 79	0.35	0.60	1.50	3.00
❑31, Dec 79	0.35	0.60	1.50	3.00
❑32, Jan 80	0.40	0.60	1.50	3.00
❑33, Feb 80	0.40	0.60	1.50	3.00
❑34, Mar 80	0.40	0.60	1.50	3.00
❑35, Apr 80	0.40	0.60	1.50	3.00
❑36, May 80	0.40	0.60	1.50	3.00
❑37, Jun 80, A: Stonewall Jackson	0.40	0.60	1.50	3.00
❑38, Jul 80	0.40	0.60	1.50	3.00
❑39, Aug 80	0.40	0.60	1.50	3.00
❑40, Sep 80	0.50	0.60	1.50	3.00
❑41, Oct 80	0.50	0.60	1.50	3.00
❑42, Nov 80	0.50	0.60	1.50	3.00
❑43, Dec 80	0.50	0.60	1.50	3.00
❑44, Jan 81	0.50	0.60	1.50	3.00
❑45, Feb 81	0.50	0.60	1.50	3.00
❑46, Mar 81	0.50	0.60	1.50	3.00
❑47, Apr 81	0.50	0.60	1.50	3.00
❑48, May 81	0.50	0.60	1.50	3.00
❑49, Jun 81	0.50	0.60	1.50	3.00
❑50, Jul 81	0.50	0.60	1.50	3.00
❑51, Aug 81	0.50	0.50	1.25	2.50
❑52, Sep 81	0.50	0.50	1.25	2.50
❑53, Oct 81	0.60	0.50	1.25	2.50
❑54, Nov 81	0.60	0.50	1.25	2.50
❑55, Dec 81	0.60	0.50	1.25	2.50
❑56, Jan 82	0.60	0.50	1.25	2.50
❑57, Feb 82, El Diablo back-up	0.60	0.50	1.25	2.50
❑58, Mar 82, El Diablo back-up	0.60	0.50	1.25	2.50
❑59, Apr 82, El Diablo back-up	0.60	0.50	1.25	2.50
❑60, May 82, El Diablo back-up	0.60	0.50	1.25	2.50
❑61, Jun 82, in China	0.60	0.50	1.25	2.50
❑62, Jul 82, in China	0.60	0.50	1.25	2.50
❑63, Aug 82	0.60	0.50	1.25	2.50
❑64, Sep 82	0.60	0.50	1.25	2.50
❑65, Oct 82	0.60	0.50	1.25	2.50
❑66, Nov 82	0.60	0.50	1.25	2.50
❑67, Dec 82	0.60	0.50	1.25	2.50
❑68, Jan 83	0.60	0.50	1.25	2.50
❑69, Feb 83	0.60	0.50	1.25	2.50
❑70, Mar 83	0.60	0.50	1.25	2.50
❑71, Apr 83	0.60	0.50	1.25	2.50
❑72, May 83	0.60	0.50	1.25	2.50
❑73, Jun 83	0.60	0.50	1.25	2.50
❑74, Jul 83	0.60	0.50	1.25	2.50
❑75, Aug 83	0.60	0.50	1.25	2.50
❑76, Sep 83, Caged!	0.60	0.50	1.25	2.50
❑77, Oct 83	0.60	0.50	1.25	2.50
❑78, Nov 83	0.60	0.50	1.25	2.50
❑79, Dec 83	0.75	0.50	1.25	2.50
❑80, Jan 84	0.75	0.50	1.25	2.50
❑81, Feb 84	0.75	0.50	1.25	2.50
❑82, Mar 84	0.75	0.50	1.25	2.50
❑83, Apr 84	0.75	0.50	1.25	2.50
❑84, May 84	0.75	0.50	1.25	2.50
❑85, Jun 84, V: Gray Ghost	0.75	0.50	1.25	2.50
❑86, Aug 84	0.75	0.50	1.25	2.50
❑87, Oct 84	0.75	0.50	1.25	2.50
❑88, Dec 84	0.75	0.50	1.25	2.50
❑89, Feb 85, V: Gray Ghost	0.75	0.50	1.25	2.50
❑90, Apr 85	0.75	0.50	1.25	2.50
❑91, Jun 85	0.75	0.50	1.25	2.50
❑92, Aug 85, Final Issue; events continue in Hex	0.75	0.50	1.25	2.50

JONAH HEX AND OTHER WESTERN TALES
DC

	ORIG	GOOD	FINE	N-MINT
❑1, Oct 79	0.95	1.20	3.00	6.00
❑2, Dec 79	0.95	1.20	3.00	6.00
❑3, Feb 80	0.95	1.20	3.00	6.00

JONAH HEX: RIDERS OF THE WORM AND SUCH
DC

	ORIG	GOOD	FINE	N-MINT
❑1, Mar 95, No Rest For The Wicked And The Good Don't Need Any	2.95	0.60	1.50	3.00
❑2, Apr 95, Wilde's West	2.95	0.60	1.50	3.00
❑3, May 95, Big Worm	2.95	0.60	1.50	3.00
❑4, Jun 95, Autumns Of Our Discontent	2.95	0.60	1.50	3.00
❑5, Jul 95	2.95	0.60	1.50	3.00

JONAH HEX: SHADOWS WEST
DC

Value: Cover or less

- ❑1, Feb 99, Long Tom, Part 1 .... 2.95
- ❑2, Mar 99 .... 2.95
- ❑3, Apr 99 .... 2.95

JONAH HEX: TWO-GUN MOJO
DC

	ORIG	GOOD	FINE	N-MINT
❑1, Aug 93, Slow Go Smith	2.95	0.80	2.00	4.00
❑1/SI, Aug 93, Silver (limited promotional) edition; platinum	—	1.20	3.00	6.00
❑2, Sep 93	2.95	0.60	1.50	3.00
❑3, Oct 93	2.95	0.60	1.50	3.00
❑4, Nov 93	2.95	0.60	1.50	3.00
❑5, Dec 93	2.95	0.60	1.50	3.00

JONAS! (MIKE DEODATO'S...)
CALIBER

Value: Cover or less

- ❑1, Jonas; Land of Fire 2.95

JONATHAN FOX
MARIAH GRAPHICS

Value: Cover or less

- ❑1 .... 2.00

JONES TOUCH
FANTAGRAPHICS

Value: Cover or less

- ❑1, adult 2.75

JONNI THUNDER
DC

	ORIG	GOOD	FINE	N-MINT
❑1, Feb 85, DG, ...Not In The Stars, But In Ourselves...!, 1: Jonni Thunder, origin	0.75	0.25	0.63	1.25
❑2, Apr 85, DG	0.75	0.25	0.63	1.25
❑3, Jun 85, DG	0.75	0.25	0.63	1.25
❑4, Aug 85, DG	0.75	0.25	0.63	1.25

JONNY DEMON
DARK HORSE

Value: Cover or less

- ❑1, May 94, KB (w), Living Though It! 2.50
- ❑2, Jun 94, KB (w) 2.50
- ❑3, Jul 94, KB (w) 2.50

JONNY DOUBLE
DC

Value: Cover or less

- ❑1, Sep 98, Two-Finger Discount 2.95
- ❑2, Oct 98 .... 2.95
- ❑3, Nov 98 .... 2.95
- ❑4, Dec 98 .... 2.95

JONNY QUEST (COMICO)
COMICO

	ORIG	GOOD	FINE	N-MINT
❑1, Jun 86, The Sands Of Khasa Tahid	1.50	0.60	1.50	3.00
❑2, Jul 86	1.50	0.50	1.25	2.50
❑3, Aug 86, DSt (c)	1.50	0.50	1.25	2.50
❑4, Sep 86, TY, Marley Frost is Here to Stay	1.50	0.50	1.25	2.50
❑5, Oct 86, DSt (c)	1.50	0.50	1.25	2.50
❑6, Nov 86, Philosopher's Stone	1.50	0.40	1.00	2.00
❑7, Dec 86	1.50	0.40	1.00	2.00
❑8, Jan 87	1.50	0.40	1.00	2.00
❑9, Feb 87, MA, Fire in Green Meadows	1.50	0.40	1.00	2.00
❑10, Mar 87, Winters of Discontent	1.50	0.40	1.00	2.00
❑11, Apr 87, BA, BSz (c)	1.50	0.30	0.75	1.50
❑12, May 87	1.50	0.30	0.75	1.50
❑13, Jun 87, CI	1.50	0.30	0.75	1.50
❑14, Jul 87	1.50	0.30	0.75	1.50
❑15, Aug 87	1.75	0.35	0.88	1.75
❑16, Sep 87	1.75	0.35	0.88	1.75
❑17, Oct 87, SR, ME (w), Space Ghost	1.75	0.35	0.88	1.75
❑18, Nov 87	1.75	0.35	0.88	1.75
❑19, Dec 87	1.75	0.35	0.88	1.75
❑20, Jan 88	1.75	0.35	0.88	1.75
❑21, Feb 88	1.75	0.35	0.88	1.75
❑22, Mar 88	1.75	0.35	0.88	1.75
❑23, Apr 88	1.75	0.35	0.88	1.75
❑24, May 88	1.75	0.35	0.88	1.75
❑25, Jun 88	1.75	0.35	0.88	1.75
❑26, Jul 88	1.75	0.35	0.88	1.75
❑27, Aug 88	1.75	0.35	0.88	1.75
❑28, Sep 88	1.75	0.35	0.88	1.75
❑29, Oct 88	1.75	0.35	0.88	1.75
❑30, Nov 88	1.75	0.35	0.88	1.75
❑31, Dec 88	1.75	0.35	0.88	1.75
❑SE 1, Sep 88, Special #1	1.95	0.35	0.88	1.75
❑SE 2, Oct 88, Special #2	1.95	0.35	0.88	1.75

JONNY QUEST CLASSICS
COMICO

Value: Cover or less

- ❑1, May 87 .... 2.00
- ❑2, Jun 87 .... 2.00
- ❑3, Jul 87 .... 2.00

JON SABLE, FREELANCE
FIRST

	ORIG	GOOD	FINE	N-MINT
❑1, Jun 83, MGr, MGr (w), The Iron Monster!, 1: Sable	1.00	0.60	1.50	3.00
❑2, Jul 83, MGr, MGr (w)	1.00	0.40	1.00	2.00
❑3, Aug 83, MGr, MGr (w), O: Sable	1.00	0.40	1.00	2.00

	ORIG	GOOD	FINE	N-MINT
❑4, Sep 83, MGr, MGr (w), O: Sable	1.00	0.40	1.00	2.00
❑5, Oct 83, MGr, MGr (w), O: Sable	1.00	0.40	1.00	2.00
❑6, Nov 83, MGr, MGr (w), O: Sable	1.00	0.40	1.00	2.00
❑7, Dec 83, MGr, MGr (w)	1.00	0.40	1.00	2.00
❑8, Jan 84, MGr, MGr (w)	1.00	0.40	1.00	2.00
❑9, Feb 84, MGr, MGr (w)	1.00	0.40	1.00	2.00
❑10, Mar 84, MGr, MGr (w)	1.00	0.40	1.00	2.00
❑11, Apr 84, MGr, MGr (w)	1.00	0.40	1.00	2.00
❑12, May 84, MGr, MGr (w)	1.00	0.40	1.00	2.00
❑13, Jun 84, MGr, MGr (w)	1.00	0.40	1.00	2.00
❑14, Jul 84, MGr, MGr (w)	1.00	0.40	1.00	2.00
❑15, Aug 84, MGr, MGr (w)	1.00	0.40	1.00	2.00
❑16, Sep 84, MGr, MGr (w)	1.00	0.40	1.00	2.00
❑17, Oct 84, MGr, MGr (w)	1.00	0.40	1.00	2.00
❑18, Oct 84, MGr, MGr (w)	1.25	0.40	1.00	2.00
❑19, Dec 84, MGr, MGr (w)	1.25	0.40	1.00	2.00
❑20, Jan 85, MGr, MGr (w)	1.25	0.40	1.00	2.00
❑21, Feb 85, MGr, MGr (w)	1.25	0.35	0.88	1.75
❑22, Mar 85, MGr, MGr (w)	1.25	0.35	0.88	1.75
❑23, Apr 85, MGr, MGr (w)	1.25	0.35	0.88	1.75
❑24, May 85, MGr, MGr (w)	1.25	0.35	0.88	1.75
❑25, Jun 85, MGr (w), Shatter back-up story	1.25	0.35	0.88	1.75
❑26, Jul 85, MGr (w), Shatter back-up story	1.25	0.35	0.88	1.75
❑27, Aug 85, MGr (w), Shatter back-up story	1.25	0.35	0.88	1.75
❑28, Sep 85, MGr (w), Shatter back-up story	1.25	0.35	0.88	1.75
❑29, Oct 85, MGr (w), Shatter back-up story	1.25	0.35	0.88	1.75
❑30, Nov 85, MGr (w), Shatter back-up story	1.25	0.35	0.88	1.75
❑31, Dec 85, MGr, MGr (w)	1.25	0.35	0.88	1.75
❑32, Jan 86, MGr, MGr (w)	1.25	0.35	0.88	1.75
❑33, Feb 86, MGr, MGr (w)	1.25	0.35	0.88	1.75
❑34, Mar 86, MGr, MGr (w)	1.75	0.35	0.88	1.75
❑35, Apr 86, MGr, MGr (w)	1.75	0.35	0.88	1.75
❑36, May 86, MGr, MGr (w)	1.75	0.35	0.88	1.75
❑37, Jun 86, MGr, MGr (w)	1.75	0.35	0.88	1.75
❑38, Jul 86, MGr, MGr (w)	1.75	0.35	0.88	1.75
❑39, Aug 86, MGr, MGr (w)	1.75	0.35	0.88	1.75
❑40, Sep 86, MGr, MGr (w)	1.75	0.35	0.88	1.75
❑41, Oct 86, MGr, MGr (w)	1.75	0.35	0.88	1.75
❑42, Nov 86, MGr, MGr (w)	1.75	0.35	0.88	1.75
❑43, Dec 86, MGr, MGr (w)	1.75	0.35	0.88	1.75
❑44, Jan 87, MGr, MGr (c), MGr (w)	1.75	0.35	0.88	1.75
❑45, Mar 87, MGr, MGr (c), MGr (w)	1.75	0.35	0.88	1.75
❑46, Apr 87, MGr, MGr (c), MGr (w)	1.75	0.35	0.88	1.75
❑47, May 87, MGr, MGr (c), MGr (w)	1.75	0.35	0.88	1.75
❑48, Jun 87, MGr, MGr (c), MGr (w)	1.75	0.35	0.88	1.75
❑49, Jul 87, MGr, MGr (c), MGr (w)	1.75	0.35	0.88	1.75
❑50, Aug 87, MGr, MGr (c), MGr (w)	1.75	0.35	0.88	1.75
❑51, Sep 87, MGr, MGr (c), MGr (w)	1.75	0.35	0.88	1.75
❑52, Oct 87, MGr, MGr (c), MGr (w)	1.75	0.35	0.88	1.75
❑53, Nov 87, MGr, MGr (c), MGr (w)	1.75	0.35	0.88	1.75
❑54, Dec 87, MGr, MGr (c), MGr (w)	1.75	0.35	0.88	1.75
❑55, Jan 88, MGr, MGr (c), MGr (w)	1.75	0.35	0.88	1.75
❑56, Feb 88, MGr, MGr (c), MGr (w), Final Issue	1.75	0.35	0.88	1.75

JONTAR RETURNS
MILLER

Value: Cover or less

❑1, b&w	2.00	❑3, b&w	2.00
❑2, b&w	2.00	❑4, b&w	2.00

JOURNEY
AARDVARK-VANAHEIM

	ORIG	GOOD	FINE	N-MINT
❑1, Mar 83	1.60	0.80	2.00	4.00
❑2	1.70	0.60	1.50	3.00
❑3	1.70	0.50	1.25	2.50
❑4	1.70	0.50	1.25	2.50
❑5	1.70	0.50	1.25	2.50
❑6	1.70	0.50	1.25	2.50
❑7	1.70	0.50	1.25	2.50
❑8, Mar 84, Part 9 Partners; Part 10 Up-Country Shelter	1.70	0.50	1.25	2.50
❑9	1.70	0.50	1.25	2.50
❑10	1.70	0.50	1.25	2.50
❑11	1.70	0.40	1.00	2.00
❑12	1.70	0.40	1.00	2.00
❑13	1.70	0.40	1.00	2.00
❑14, Sep 84	1.70	0.40	1.00	2.00
❑15	—	0.40	1.00	2.00
❑16	—	0.40	1.00	2.00
❑17	—	0.40	1.00	2.00
❑18	—	0.40	1.00	2.00
❑19	—	0.40	1.00	2.00
❑20	—	0.40	1.00	2.00
❑21	—	0.40	1.00	2.00
❑22	—	0.40	1.00	2.00
❑23	—	0.40	1.00	2.00

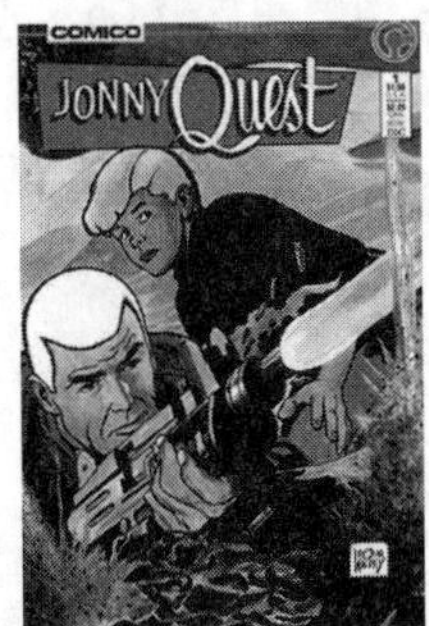

Comico published the further adventures of Jonny, Hadji, Race, and Professor Benton Quest in its *Jonny Quest* comics series.

© 1986 Hanna-Barbera (Comico)

	ORIG	GOOD	FINE	N-MINT
❑24	—	0.40	1.00	2.00
❑25	—	0.40	1.00	2.00
❑26	—	0.40	1.00	2.00
❑27	—	0.40	1.00	2.00

JOURNEY INTO MYSTERY (1ST SERIES)
MARVEL

	ORIG	GOOD	FINE	N-MINT
❑-1, Jul 97, Flashback	1.99	0.40	1.00	2.00
❑83, Aug 62, JK; SD, 1: Thor	0.12	820.00	2050.00	4100.00
❑83/GR, 1: Thor, Golden Records reprint (with record)	—	22.00	55.00	110.00
❑84, Sep 62, JK; DH; SD, 1: Jane Foster; 1: Loki; 2: Thor; 1: Executioner	0.12	180.00	450.00	900.00
❑85, Oct 62, JK; SD, 1: Heimdall; 1: Tyr; 1: Odin; 1: Loki; 1: Balder	0.12	110.00	275.00	550.00
❑86, Nov 62, JK; DH; SD, 1: Odin; 1: Tomorrow Man	0.12	65.00	162.50	325.00
❑87, Dec 62, JK; SD	0.12	48.00	120.00	240.00
❑88, Jan 63, JK; SD	0.12	48.00	120.00	240.00
❑89, Feb 63, JK; SD, O: Thor	0.12	52.00	130.00	260.00
❑90, Mar 63, SD, 1: Carbon-Copy	0.12	28.00	70.00	140.00
❑91, Apr 63, JSt; SD, 1: Sandu	0.12	24.00	60.00	120.00
❑92, May 63, JSt; SD, 1: Frigga; A: Loki	0.12	24.00	60.00	120.00
❑93, Jun 63, JK; SD, 1: Radioactive Man (Dr. Chen Lu)-Marvel	0.12	28.00	70.00	140.00
❑94, Jul 63, JSt; SD, Loki	0.12	24.00	60.00	120.00
❑95, Aug 63, JSt; SD	0.12	24.00	60.00	120.00
❑96, Sep 63, JSt; SD, Merlin	0.12	24.00	60.00	120.00
❑97, Oct 63, JK, 1: Lava Men; V: Molto; 1: Tales of Asgard; 1: Surtur; V: Ymir	0.12	28.00	70.00	140.00
❑98, Nov 63, JK	0.12	20.00	50.00	100.00
❑99, Dec 63, JK, 1: Mr. Hyde	0.12	20.00	50.00	100.00
❑100, Jan 64, JK	0.12	20.00	50.00	100.00
❑101, Feb 64, JK, A: Giant Man; A: Iron Man	0.12	14.00	35.00	70.00
❑102, Mar 64, JK, 1: The Norns; 1: Sif; 1: Hela	0.12	15.00	37.50	75.00
❑103, Apr 64, JK, 1: Enchantress; V: Executioner	0.12	15.00	37.50	75.00
❑104, May 64, JK, giants	0.12	15.00	37.50	75.00
❑105, Jun 64, JK, V: Hyde; V: Cobra	0.12	15.00	37.50	75.00
❑106, Jul 64, JK, O: Balder	0.12	15.00	37.50	75.00
❑107, Aug 64, JK, 1: Grey Gargoyle	0.12	15.00	37.50	75.00
❑108, Sep 64, JK, A: Doctor Strange	0.12	15.00	37.50	75.00
❑109, Oct 64, JK, A: Magneto	0.12	17.00	42.50	85.00
❑110, Nov 64, JK, V: Hyde; V: Cobra; V: Loki	0.12	15.00	37.50	75.00
❑111, Dec 64, JK, V: Hyde; V: Cobra; V: Loki	0.12	15.00	37.50	75.00
❑112, Jan 65, JK, V: Hulk	0.12	28.00	70.00	140.00
❑113, Feb 65, JK, V: Grey Gargoyle	0.12	15.00	37.50	75.00
❑114, Mar 65, JK, 1: Absorbing Man	0.12	15.00	37.50	75.00
❑115, Apr 65, JK, O: Loki	0.12	16.00	40.00	80.00
❑116, May 65, JK, A: Loki; A: Daredevil	0.12	15.00	37.50	75.00
❑117, Jun 65, JK, A: Loki	0.12	13.00	32.50	65.00
❑118, Jul 65, JK, 1: The Destroyer	0.12	13.00	32.50	65.00
❑119, Aug 65, JK, 1: Volstagg; 1: Fandrall; 1: Hogun; 1: Warriors Three	0.12	14.00	35.00	70.00
❑120, Sep 65, JK	0.12	13.00	32.50	65.00
❑121, Oct 65, JK	0.12	13.00	32.50	65.00
❑122, Nov 65, JK	0.12	13.00	32.50	65.00
❑123, Dec 65, JK, SL (w), While A Universe Trembles!, Tales of Asgard storyline (back-up story)	0.12	13.00	32.50	65.00
❑124, Jan 66, JK	0.12	13.00	32.50	65.00
❑125, Feb 66, JK, Series continues in Thor #126	0.12	13.00	32.50	65.00
❑503, Nov 96, D: Red Norvell; A: Lost Gods, Series continued from Thor #502	1.50	0.30	0.75	1.50
❑504, Dec 96, The Lost Gods: If This Be My Quest...!, A: Ulik	1.50	0.30	0.75	1.50
❑505, Jan 97, The Lost Gods: What Power is This?, V: Wrecking Crew; A: Spider-Man	1.50	0.30	0.75	1.50
❑506, Feb 97, The Lost Gods: And Death Be Thy Foe!	1.50	0.30	0.75	1.50
❑507, Mar 97, The Lost Gods: First Blood..	1.99	0.30	0.75	1.50
❑508, Apr 97, The Lost Gods: Deadly Reunion!, V: Red Norvell	1.99	0.30	0.75	1.50
❑509, May 97, The Lost Gods: Howie's Tale, return of Loki	1.99	0.30	0.75	1.50
❑510, Jun 97, The Lost Gods: Lest Despair Doth Claim Thee!, V: Red Norvell	1.99	0.30	0.75	1.50
❑511, Aug 97, gatefold summary; Loki vs. Seth	1.99	0.40	1.00	1.99
❑512, Sep 97, gatefold summary	1.99	0.40	1.00	1.99

	ORIG	GOOD	FINE	N-MINT
❑513, Oct 97, gatefold summary; Asgardian storyline concludes	1.99	0.40	1.00	1.99
❑514, Nov 97, gatefold summary; Shang-Chi	1.99	0.40	1.00	1.99
❑515, Dec 97, gatefold summary; Shang-Chi	1.99	0.40	1.00	1.99
❑516, Jan 98, gatefold summary; Shang-Chi	1.99	0.40	1.00	1.99
❑517, Feb 98, gatefold summary; Black Widow	1.99	0.40	1.00	1.99
❑518, Mar 98, gatefold summary; Black Widow	1.99	0.40	1.00	1.99
❑519, Apr 98, gatefold summary; Black Widow	1.99	0.40	1.00	1.99
❑520, May 98, gatefold summary; Hannibal King	1.99	0.40	1.00	1.99
❑521, Jun 98, Final Issue; gatefold summary; Hannibal King	1.99	0.40	1.00	1.99
❑Anl 1, JK, A: Zeus; 1: Hercules, King-Size Annual; continues as Thor Annual	0.25	25.00	62.50	125.00

JOURNEY INTO MYSTERY (2ND SERIES)
MARVEL

	ORIG	GOOD	FINE	N-MINT
❑1, Oct 72, TP; GK, Dig Me No Grave!, Robert Howard adaptation: "Dig Me No Grave"	0.20	1.40	3.50	7.00
❑2, Dec 72	0.20	0.80	2.00	4.00
❑3, Feb 73	0.20	0.80	2.00	4.00
❑4, Apr 73, H.P. Lovecraft adaptation: "Haunter of the Dark"	0.20	0.60	1.50	3.00
❑5, Jun 73, Robert Bloch adaptation: "Shadow From the Steeple"	0.20	0.60	1.50	3.00
❑6, Aug 73	0.20	0.50	1.25	2.50
❑7, Oct 73	0.20	0.50	1.25	2.50
❑8, Dec 73	0.20	0.50	1.25	2.50
❑9, Feb 74	0.20	0.50	1.25	2.50
❑10, Apr 74	0.20	0.50	1.25	2.50
❑11, Jun 74	0.25	0.50	1.25	2.50
❑12, Aug 74	0.25	0.50	1.25	2.50
❑13, Oct 74	0.25	0.50	1.25	2.50
❑14, Dec 74	0.25	0.50	1.25	2.50
❑15, Feb 75	0.25	0.50	1.25	2.50
❑16, Apr 75	0.25	0.50	1.25	2.50
❑17, Jun 75	0.25	0.50	1.25	2.50
❑18, Aug 75	0.25	0.50	1.25	2.50
❑19, Oct 75, Final Issue	0.25	0.50	1.25	2.50

JOURNEYMAN
IMAGE

Value: Cover or less

- ❑1, Aug 99 .... 2.95
- ❑2, Sep 99 .... 2.95
- ❑3, Oct 99 .... 2.95

JOURNEYMAN/DARK AGES, THE
LUCID

Value: Cover or less

- ❑1, Sum 97, nn; b&w; San Diego edition 3.00

JOURNEY: WARDRUMS
FANTAGRAPHICS

Value: Cover or less

- ❑1 .... 2.00
- ❑2 .... 2.00

JR. CARROT PATROL
DARK HORSE

Value: Cover or less

- ❑1, b&w 2.00
- ❑2, The Backwards Machine, b&w 2.00

JSA
DC

Value: Cover or less

- ❑1, Aug 99, JRo (w), Justice Be Done 2.50
- ❑2, Sep 99, JRo (w), The Wheel of Life, V: Mordru 2.50
- ❑3, Oct 99, JRo (w), Old Souls, V: Mordru 2.50
- ❑4, Nov 99, V: Mordru, identity of new Doctor Fate revealed 2.50
- ❑5, Dec 99, JRo (w), Grounded 2.50
- ❑6, Jan 00, Justice, Like Lightning 2.50
- ❑7, Feb 00 .... 2.50
- ❑8, Mar 00 .... 2.50
- ❑9, Apr 00, Black Planet 2.50
- ❑10, May 00, Wild Hunt 2.50
- ❑11 .... 2.50
- ❑12 .... 2.50
- ❑13 .... 2.50
- ❑14, Sep 00, Chaos Theory 2.50
- ❑15, Oct 00, Crime and Punishment 2.50
- ❑16, Nov 00, Injustice Be Done, Part 1 .... 2.50
- ❑17, Dec 00, Injustice Be Done, Part 2 .... 2.50
- ❑18, Jan 01, Injustice Be Done, Part 3 .... 2.50
- ❑19, Feb 01, Injustice Be Done, Part 4 .... 2.50
- ❑20, Mar 01, Injustice Be Done, Part 5 .... 2.50
- ❑21, Apr 01, Guardian Angels 2.50
- ❑22, May 01, Lost Friends 2.50
- ❑23 .... 2.50
- ❑24 .... 2.50
- ❑25 .... 2.50
- ❑26 .... 2.50
- ❑Anl 1, Oct 00, Genesis, 1: Nemesis, Planet DC 3.50

JSA SECRET FILES
DC

Value: Cover or less

- ❑1, Aug 99, JRo (w), Gathering of Storm; Dead EndsHistory 101, background information on team's formation and members 4.95
- ❑2 .... 4.95

JSA: THE LIBERTY FILE
DC

Value: Cover or less

- ❑1, Feb 00 .... 6.95
- ❑2, Mar 00 .... 6.95

JUDGE CHILD
EAGLE

	ORIG	GOOD	FINE	N-MINT
❑1, BB, Judge Dredd: The Judge Child Quest	1.50	0.40	1.00	2.00
❑2, Judge Dredd: The Judge Child Quest	1.50	0.40	1.00	2.00
❑3, Judge Dredd: The Judge Child Quest	1.50	0.40	1.00	2.00
❑4, Judge Dredd: The Judge Child Quest	1.50	0.40	1.00	2.00
❑5, Judge Dredd: The Judge Child Quest	1.50	0.40	1.00	2.00

JUDGE DREDD (DC)
DC

	ORIG	GOOD	FINE	N-MINT
❑1, Aug 94	1.95	0.50	1.25	2.50
❑2, Sep 94	1.95	0.45	1.13	2.25
❑3, Oct 94	1.95	0.45	1.13	2.25
❑4, Nov 94, 48 Hours: A Two-Day Story-Day One: Aftershock	1.95	0.40	1.00	2.00
❑5, Dec 94	1.95	0.40	1.00	2.00
❑6, Jan 95, Malice in Wonderland	1.95	0.40	1.00	2.00
❑7, Feb 95	1.95	0.40	1.00	2.00
❑8, Mar 95	1.95	0.40	1.00	2.00
❑9, Apr 95, homage to Judge Dredd #1 (first series)	1.95	0.40	1.00	2.00
❑10, May 95	1.95	0.40	1.00	2.00
❑11, Jun 95, Dredd Again	2.25	0.45	1.13	2.25
❑12, Jul 95	2.25	0.45	1.13	2.25
❑13, Aug 95, Block Wars, Part 1	2.25	0.45	1.13	2.25
❑14, Sep 95, Block Wars, Part 2	2.25	0.45	1.13	2.25
❑15, Oct 95, Block Wars, Part 3	2.25	0.45	1.13	2.25
❑16, Nov 95	2.25	0.45	1.13	2.25
❑17, Dec 95	2.25	0.45	1.13	2.25
❑18, Jan 96, Final Issue	2.25	0.45	1.13	2.25

JUDGE DREDD (VOL. 1)
EAGLE

	ORIG	GOOD	FINE	N-MINT
❑1, Nov 83, BB, A: Judge Death; 1: Judge Dredd (in U.S.)	1.00	1.00	2.50	5.00
❑2, Dec 83, BB	1.00	0.70	1.75	3.50
❑3, Jan 84, BB, V: Judge Death; A: Judge Anderson	1.00	0.60	1.50	3.00
❑4, Feb 84, BB	1.00	0.60	1.50	3.00
❑5, Mar 84	1.00	0.60	1.50	3.00
❑6, Apr 84	1.00	0.50	1.25	2.50
❑7, May 84	1.00	0.50	1.25	2.50
❑8, Jun 84	1.00	0.50	1.25	2.50
❑9, Jul 84	1.00	0.50	1.25	2.50
❑10, Aug 84	1.00	0.50	1.25	2.50
❑11, Sep 84	1.00	0.40	1.00	2.00
❑12, Oct 84	1.00	0.40	1.00	2.00
❑13, Nov 84	1.00	0.40	1.00	2.00
❑14, Dec 84	1.00	0.40	1.00	2.00
❑15, Jan 85, Judge Dredd: Block War; Judge Dredd: Umpty Candy, Umpty Candy	1.00	0.40	1.00	2.00
❑16, Feb 85, V: Fink Angel	1.00	0.40	1.00	2.00
❑17, Mar 85	1.00	0.40	1.00	2.00
❑18, Apr 85, Block Mania	1.00	0.40	1.00	2.00
❑19, May 85	1.00	0.40	1.00	2.00
❑20, Jun 85	1.00	0.40	1.00	2.00
❑21, Jul 85	1.00	0.40	1.00	2.00
❑22, Aug 85	1.00	0.40	1.00	2.00
❑23, Sep 85	1.00	0.40	1.00	2.00
❑24, Oct 85	1.25	0.40	1.00	2.00
❑25, Nov 85	1.25	0.40	1.00	2.00
❑26, Dec 85	1.25	0.40	1.00	2.00
❑27, Jan 86	1.25	0.40	1.00	2.00
❑28, Feb 86	1.25	0.40	1.00	2.00
❑29, Mar 86	1.25	0.40	1.00	2.00
❑30, Apr 86	1.25	0.40	1.00	2.00
❑31, May 86, V: Mean Machine; V: Judge Child	1.25	0.40	1.00	2.00
❑32, Jun 86, V: Mean Machine	1.25	0.40	1.00	2.00
❑33, Jul 86, League of Fatties	1.25	0.40	1.00	2.00
❑34, Aug 86	1.25	0.40	1.00	2.00
❑35, Sep 86, Final Issue	1.25	0.40	1.00	2.00

JUDGE DREDD (VOL. 2)
FLEETWAY

	ORIG	GOOD	FINE	N-MINT
❑1	0.75	0.60	1.50	3.00
❑2, Cry of the Werewolf	—	0.50	1.25	2.50
❑3	—	0.40	1.00	2.00
❑4	—	0.40	1.00	2.00
❑5, Feb 87, poster	0.75	0.40	1.00	2.00
❑6, Mar 87, Christmas issue	1.25	0.40	1.00	2.00
❑7	0.95	0.40	1.00	2.00
❑8, Jul 87, wraparound cover	1.25	0.40	1.00	2.00
❑9, Aug 87	1.25	0.40	1.00	2.00
❑10, Sep 87	1.25	0.40	1.00	2.00
❑11, Oct 87	1.25	0.40	1.00	2.00
❑12, Starborn Thing, Part 1, dropped publication date from cover and indicia for rest of series	1.25	0.40	1.00	2.00

	ORIG	GOOD	FINE	N-MINT
❑13, Starborn Thing, Part 2	1.25	0.40	1.00	2.00
❑14, BB, Attack Of The 50 Foot Woman; The Switch	1.25	0.40	1.00	2.00
❑15, City Of The Damned	1.25	0.40	1.00	2.00
❑16, Dredd Angel	1.25	0.40	1.00	2.00
❑17, Dredd Angel; Bob's Law	1.25	0.40	1.00	2.00
❑18	1.25	0.40	1.00	2.00
❑19, Judge Dredd: Condo; Judge Dredd: The Prankster	1.25	0.40	1.00	2.00
❑20, Channel Illegal	1.50	0.40	1.00	2.00
❑21, double issue #21, 22	1.50	0.40	1.00	2.00
❑22	—	0.40	1.00	2.00
❑23, double issue #23, 24	1.50	0.40	1.00	2.00
❑24	—	0.40	1.00	2.00
❑25, Riders on the Storm!; The Long Sleep	1.50	0.40	1.00	2.00
❑26, The Urge	1.50	0.40	1.00	2.00
❑27	1.50	0.40	1.00	2.00
❑28, The Hunters Club	1.50	0.40	1.00	2.00
❑29, Requiem for a Heavy-Weight	1.50	0.40	1.00	2.00
❑30	1.50	0.40	1.00	2.00
❑31	1.50	0.40	1.00	2.00
❑32	1.50	0.40	1.00	2.00
❑33, Judge Dredd: The Gun, The Badge, The Man; Judge Dredd: Bride Of Death	1.50	0.40	1.00	2.00
❑34, The Seven Samurai; Bride of Death	1.50	0.40	1.00	2.00
❑35	1.50	0.40	1.00	2.00
❑36, Judge Dredd: Tomb Of The Judges!; Judge Dredd In Atlantis	1.50	0.40	1.00	2.00
❑37, Judge Dredd In Atlantis; Rumble In The Jungle, Part 1	1.50	0.40	1.00	2.00
❑38, Rumble In The Jungle, Part 2	1.50	0.40	1.00	2.00
❑39, Judge Dredd: The Big Sleep; Judge Dredd: Phantom of the Shoppera	1.75	0.40	1.00	2.00
❑40	1.75	0.40	1.00	2.00
❑41, Judge Dredd: The Lurker; Judge Dredd: The Ugly Mug Ball, Reprinted from 2000 A.D. #449; Reprinted from 2000 A.D. #447; Reprinted from 2000 A.D. #445	1.75	0.40	1.00	2.00
❑42, Judge Dredd: West Side Rumble; Judge Dredd: Thirteenth Assessment, Reprints story from 2000 A.D. #434; Reprints story from 2000 A.D. #421; Reprints story from 2000 A.D. #422	1.75	0.40	1.00	2.00
❑43, Judge Dredd: The DNA Man; Judge Dredd: Monsteroso, Reprints story from 2000 A.D. #113-115; Reprints story from 2000 A.D. #412	1.75	0.40	1.00	2.00
❑44, Judge Dredd: Firebug; Judge Dredd: The Genie, Reprint from 2000 A.D. #60; Reprint from 2000 A.D. #514; Reprint from 2000 A.D. #304	1.75	0.40	1.00	2.00
❑45, BT, Judge Dredd: The Secret Diary of Adrian Cockroach; Judge Dredd: Last Voyage of the Flying Dutchman, Reprint from 2000 A.D. #457; Reprint from 2000 A.D. #458; Reprint from 2000 A.D. #459; Reprint from 2000 A.D. #119	1.75	0.40	1.00	2.00
❑46	1.75	0.40	1.00	2.00
❑47	1.75	0.40	1.00	2.00
❑48, Judge Dredd: An Elm Street Nightmare; Judge Dredd: The Confeshuns Of P.I. Maybe	1.75	0.40	1.00	2.00
❑49, Judge Dredd: Dead Ringer; Judge Dredd: Block War, Stories 2000 A.D. #493; From 2000 A.D. #182; From 2000 A.D. #490; From 2000 A.D. #491	1.75	0.40	1.00	2.00
❑50, Judge Dredd: On The Superslab	1.75	0.40	1.00	2.00
❑51	1.75	0.40	1.00	2.00
❑52, Judge Dredd: On The Air; Judge Dredd: The Witness	1.95	0.40	1.00	2.00
❑53, Judge Dredd: The Blood Donor; Judge Dredd: Russell's Inflatable Muscles, Reprinted from 2000 A.D. #519; From 2000 A.D. #25	1.95	0.40	1.00	2.00
❑54, Judge Dredd: Cardboard City; Judge Dredd: Carry on Judging, Reprinted from 2000 A.D. #643-645; Reprinted from 2000 1990 Mega-Special	1.95	0.40	1.00	2.00
❑55, Judge Dredd: What Would Be Horrible?; Reasons To Be Fearful	1.95	0.40	1.00	2.00
❑56, Judge Dredd: Cry of the Werewolf	1.95	0.40	1.00	2.00
❑57	1.95	0.40	1.00	2.00
❑58	1.95	0.40	1.00	2.00
❑59, Judge Dredd: The Wreckers!; Judge Dredd: The Last Invader	1.95	0.39	0.98	1.95
❑60	1.95	0.39	0.98	1.95
❑61, Series continued in Judge Dredd Classics #62	1.95	0.39	0.98	1.95
❑SE 1	—	0.50	1.25	2.50

JUDGE DREDD: AMERICA
FLEETWAY

Value: Cover or less

- ❑1, America 2.95
- ❑2 2.95

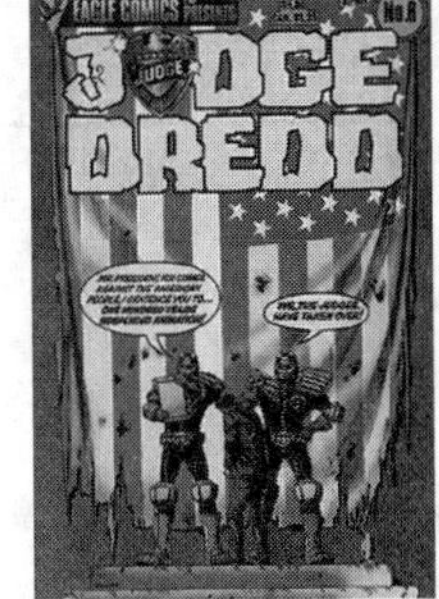

A popular character in England in the pages of *2000 A.D.*, Judge Dredd's adventures have been reprinted in the United States for many years.

JUDGE DREDD CLASSICS
FLEETWAY

Value: Cover or less

- ❑62 1.95
- ❑63 1.95
- ❑64, Judge Dredd: Loonies' Moon; Judge Dredd: The Mega-Rackets 1.95
- ❑65, BB, Judge Dredd: The Exo-men, Part 2 1.95
- ❑66, Judge Dredd: Monkey Business At The Charles Darwin Block 1.95
- ❑67, The Fink; Date With Destiny 1.95
- ❑68 1.95
- ❑69, DaG, Judge Dredd: Battle of the Black Atlantic; Judge Dredd: Dredd and the Mob Blitzers. 1.95
- ❑70 1.95
- ❑71, Judge Dredd: Bright Eyes...Burning Like Fire!; Judge Dredd: The Weather Man 1.95
- ❑72 1.95
- ❑73, Judge Dredd: The Big Sleep; Judge Dredd: The Art of Kenny Who? 1.95
- ❑74, AMo (w), Judge Dredd: High Society; Judge Dredd: The House on Runner's Walk 1.95
- ❑75, Judge Dredd: Death of a Judge; Judge Dredd: Rumble in the Jungle 1.95
- ❑76, Judge Dredd: Diary of a Mad Citizen; Judge Dredd: The Mega Rackets 1.95
- ❑77, Judge Dredd: The Falucci Tape, Final Issue 1.95

JUDGE DREDD: EMERALD ISLE
FLEETWAY

Value: Cover or less

- ❑1, nn 4.95

JUDGE DREDD: LEGENDS OF THE LAW
DC

	ORIG	GOOD	FINE	N-MINT
❑1, Dec 94, BA, The Organ Donors, Part 1	1.95	0.50	1.25	2.50
❑2, Jan 95, BA, The Organ Donors, Part 2	1.95	0.40	1.00	2.00
❑3, Feb 95, BA, The Organ Donors, Part 3	1.95	0.40	1.00	2.00
❑4, Mar 95, BA, The Organ Donors, Part 4	1.95	0.40	1.00	2.00
❑5, Apr 95, Trial by Gunfire, Part 1	1.95	0.40	1.00	2.00
❑6, May 95, Trial by Gunfire, Part 2	1.95	0.40	1.00	2.00
❑7, Jun 95, Trial by Gunfire, Part 3	2.25	0.45	1.13	2.25
❑8, Jul 95, JBy, Fall from Grace, Part 1	2.25	0.45	1.13	2.25
❑9, Aug 95, JBy, Fall from Grace, Part 2	2.25	0.45	1.13	2.25
❑10, Sep 95, JBy, Fall from Grace, Part 3	2.25	0.45	1.13	2.25
❑11, Oct 95, JBy (c), Dredd of Knight, Part 1	2.25	0.45	1.13	2.25
❑12, Nov 95, Dredd of Knight, Part 2	2.25	0.45	1.13	2.25
❑13, Dec 95, Dredd of Knight, Part 3, Final Issue	2.25	0.45	1.13	2.25

JUDGE DREDD: RAPTAUR
FLEETWAY

Value: Cover or less

- ❑1, Judge Dredd: Raptaur, Judge Dredd 2.95
- ❑2, Judge Dredd: Raptaur, Judge Dredd 2.95

JUDGE DREDD'S CRIME FILE (EAGLE)
EAGLE

	ORIG	GOOD	FINE	N-MINT
❑1	1.50	0.60	1.50	3.00
❑2	1.50	0.60	1.50	3.00
❑3	1.50	0.60	1.50	3.00
❑4, Nov 85, Umpty Baggers	1.50	0.60	1.50	3.00
❑5, Palais De Boing; The Psychos!	1.50	0.60	1.50	3.00
❑6	1.50	0.60	1.50	3.00

JUDGE DREDD'S CRIME FILE (FLEETWAY)
FLEETWAY

Value: Cover or less

- ❑1, BB (c) 5.95
- ❑2, BB (c), Judge Dredd: Anatomy Of A Crime; Judge Dredd: Vampire Effect 5.95
- ❑3, BB (c), The Problem With Sonny Bono; The Body Sharks 5.95
- ❑4, BB (c) 5.95

JUDGE DREDD'S HARDCASE PAPERS
FLEETWAY

Value: Cover or less

- ❑1, Tarantula; Law of the Jungle 5.95
- ❑2 5.95
- ❑3 5.95
- ❑4 5.95

JUDGE DREDD THE MEGAZINE
FLEETWAY QUALITY

Value: Cover or less

- ❑1 4.95
- ❑2 4.95
- ❑3 4.95

JUDGE DREDD: THE OFFICIAL MOVIE ADAPTATION
DC

Value: Cover or less

- ❑1, nn; movie Adaptation; prestige format 5.95

J.U.D.G.E.: SECRET RAGE
IMAGE

Value: Cover or less

❑1, Mar 00 ... 2.95

JUDGMENT DAY
AWESOME

Value: Cover or less

❑1, Jun 97, RL, AMo (w), Alpha ... 2.50
❑1/A, RL, AMo (w), variant cover; Alpha ... 2.50
❑1-2, RL, AMo (w), 2nd Printing; Alpha ... 2.50
❑2, Jul 97, RL (c), AMo (w), The Trial, Omega ... 2.50
❑2/A, Jul 97, RL, AMo (w), The Trial, variant cover; Omega ... 2.50
❑3, RL, AMo (w), Final Judgment ... 2.50
❑3/A, RL, AMo (w), Final Judgment ... 2.50

JUDGMENT DAY (LIGHTNING)
LIGHTNING

Value: Cover or less

❑1/A, Sep 93, red foil cover; Red prism border ... 3.50
❑1/B, Sep 93, purple foil cover ... 3.50
❑1/C, Sep 93, misprint ... 3.50
❑1/D, Aug 93, promotional copy; metallic ink ... 3.50
❑1/GO, Sep 93, Gold foil cover; Gold prism border ... 3.50
❑1/PL, Aug 93, promotional copy; platinum ... 3.50
❑2, Oct 93, trading card ... 2.95
❑3, Nov 93, O: X-Treme ... 2.95
❑4, Dec 93 ... 2.95
❑5, Jan 94 ... 2.95
❑6, Feb 94, O: Salubrio ... 2.95
❑7, Mar 94, O: Safeguard ... 2.95
❑8, Apr 94 ... 2.95

JUDGMENT DAY: AFTERMATH
AWESOME

Value: Cover or less

❑1, GK, AMo (w), Trial by Tempest ... 3.50
❑1/A, GK, AMo (w), Trial by Tempest, Purple cover by Evans ... 3.50

JUDGMENT DAY SOURCEBOOK
AWESOME

	ORIG	GOOD	FINE	N-MINT
❑1, no cover price; American Entertainment exclusive preview of series	—	0.20	0.50	1.00

JUDGMENT PAWNS
ANTARCTIC

Value: Cover or less

❑1, Feb 97, Life is a Game We Play Part 1, b&w ... 2.95
❑2, Apr 97, Life is a Game We Play Part 2, b&w ... 2.95
❑3, Jul 97, Life is a Game We Play Part 3, b&w ... 2.95

JUDOMASTER
CHARLTON

	ORIG	GOOD	FINE	N-MINT
❑89, Jun 66, Series continued from Gun Master #89	0.12	2.40	6.00	12.00
❑90, Aug 66	0.12	1.80	4.50	9.00
❑91, Oct 66, A: Sarge Steel	0.12	1.80	4.50	9.00
❑92, Dec 66	0.12	1.80	4.50	9.00
❑93, Feb 67	0.12	1.80	4.50	9.00
❑94, Apr 67	0.12	1.80	4.50	9.00
❑95, Jun 67, DG; FMc, FMc (w), The Plot to Destroy Judomaster; The Art of Stealth	0.12	1.80	4.50	9.00
❑96, Aug 67	0.12	1.80	4.50	9.00
❑97, Oct 67	0.12	1.80	4.50	9.00
❑98, Dec 67, Final Issue	0.12	1.80	4.50	9.00

JUGGERNAUT, THE
MARVEL

Value: Cover or less

❑1, Apr 97, A Night in Spite, One-Shot ... 2.99

JUGGERNAUT, THE (2ND SERIES)
MARVEL

Value: Cover or less

❑1, Nov 99, The Eighth Day, Part 4 ... 2.99

JUGHEAD (VOL. 2)
ARCHIE

	ORIG	GOOD	FINE	N-MINT
❑1	0.75	0.60	1.50	3.00
❑2	—	0.40	1.00	2.00
❑3	—	0.40	1.00	2.00
❑4	—	0.30	0.75	1.50
❑5	—	0.30	0.75	1.50
❑6	—	0.30	0.75	1.50
❑7	—	0.30	0.75	1.50
❑8	—	0.30	0.75	1.50
❑9	—	0.30	0.75	1.50
❑10	—	0.30	0.75	1.50
❑11	—	0.30	0.75	1.50
❑12	—	0.30	0.75	1.50
❑13	—	0.30	0.75	1.50
❑14	—	0.30	0.75	1.50
❑15	—	0.30	0.75	1.50
❑16	—	0.30	0.75	1.50
❑17	—	0.30	0.75	1.50
❑18	—	0.30	0.75	1.50
❑19	—	0.30	0.75	1.50
❑20	—	0.30	0.75	1.50
❑21	—	0.30	0.75	1.50
❑22	—	0.30	0.75	1.50
❑23	—	0.30	0.75	1.50
❑24	—	0.30	0.75	1.50
❑25	—	0.30	0.75	1.50
❑26	—	0.30	0.75	1.50
❑27	—	0.30	0.75	1.50
❑28	—	0.30	0.75	1.50
❑29	—	0.30	0.75	1.50
❑30	—	0.30	0.75	1.50
❑31	—	0.30	0.75	1.50
❑32	—	0.30	0.75	1.50
❑33	—	0.30	0.75	1.50
❑34	—	0.30	0.75	1.50
❑35, A Portrait of the Artist as a Young Jughead; Breaking Up is Hard To Do	1.25	0.30	0.75	1.50
❑36	—	0.30	0.75	1.50
❑37	—	0.30	0.75	1.50
❑38	—	0.30	0.75	1.50
❑39	—	0.30	0.75	1.50
❑40	—	0.30	0.75	1.50
❑41	—	0.30	0.75	1.50
❑42	—	0.30	0.75	1.50
❑43	—	0.30	0.75	1.50
❑44	—	0.30	0.75	1.50
❑45, Series continued in Archie's Pal Jughead #46	—	0.30	0.75	1.50

JUGHEAD AS CAPTAIN HERO
ARCHIE

	ORIG	GOOD	FINE	N-MINT
❑1	—	5.00	12.50	25.00
❑2	—	2.80	7.00	14.00
❑3	—	1.80	4.50	9.00
❑4, Apr 67	0.12	1.20	3.00	6.00
❑5	0.12	1.20	3.00	6.00
❑6	0.12	1.20	3.00	6.00
❑7, Nov 67	0.12	1.20	3.00	6.00

JUGHEAD'S BABY TALES
ARCHIE

Value: Cover or less

❑1, Spr 94 ... 2.00
❑2, Win 94, Monkey Business, Part 1; Monkey Business, Part 2, A: Archie; A: Big Ethel, Continued from Baby Tales #1 ... 2.00

JUGHEAD'S DINER
ARCHIE

	ORIG	GOOD	FINE	N-MINT
❑1, Apr 90	1.00	0.40	1.00	2.00
❑2	1.00	0.30	0.75	1.50
❑3	1.00	0.30	0.75	1.50
❑4	1.00	0.30	0.75	1.50
❑5	1.00	0.30	0.75	1.50
❑6	1.00	0.30	0.75	1.50
❑7	1.00	0.30	0.75	1.50

JUGHEAD'S DOUBLE DIGEST
ARCHIE

	ORIG	GOOD	FINE	N-MINT
❑1	2.25	1.20	3.00	6.00
❑2	—	0.80	2.00	4.00
❑3	—	0.80	2.00	4.00
❑4	—	0.80	2.00	4.00
❑5	—	0.80	2.00	4.00
❑6	—	0.60	1.50	3.00
❑7	—	0.60	1.50	3.00
❑8	—	0.60	1.50	3.00
❑9	—	0.60	1.50	3.00
❑10	—	0.60	1.50	3.00
❑11	—	0.60	1.50	3.00
❑12	—	0.60	1.50	3.00
❑13	—	0.60	1.50	3.00
❑14	—	0.60	1.50	3.00
❑15	—	0.60	1.50	3.00
❑16	—	0.60	1.50	3.00
❑17	—	0.60	1.50	3.00
❑18	—	0.60	1.50	3.00
❑19	—	0.60	1.50	3.00
❑20	—	0.60	1.50	3.00
❑21	—	0.60	1.50	3.00
❑22	—	0.60	1.50	3.00
❑23	—	0.60	1.50	3.00
❑24	—	0.60	1.50	3.00
❑25	—	0.60	1.50	3.00
❑26	—	0.60	1.50	3.00
❑27, Dec 93	2.75	0.60	1.50	3.00
❑28	2.75	0.60	1.50	3.00
❑29, Mar 95	2.75	0.60	1.50	3.00
❑30, May 95	2.75	0.60	1.50	3.00
❑31, Jul 95	2.75	0.55	1.38	2.75
❑32, Sep 95	2.75	0.55	1.38	2.75
❑33, Nov 95	2.75	0.55	1.38	2.75
❑34, Jan 96	2.75	0.55	1.38	2.75
❑35, Feb 96	2.75	0.55	1.38	2.75
❑36, Apr 96	2.75	0.55	1.38	2.75

	ORIG	GOOD	FINE	N-MINT
❑37, Jun 96	2.75	0.55	1.38	2.75
❑38, Aug 96	2.75	0.55	1.38	2.75
❑39, Sep 96	2.75	0.55	1.38	2.75
❑40, Nov 96, duplicate pages at front	2.75	0.55	1.38	2.75
❑41, Jan 97	2.75	0.55	1.38	2.75
❑42, Feb 97	2.75	0.55	1.38	2.75
❑43, Apr 97	2.75	0.55	1.38	2.75
❑44, Jun 97	2.75	0.55	1.38	2.75
❑45, Jul 97	2.75	0.55	1.38	2.75
❑46, Sep 97	2.79	0.56	1.39	2.79
❑47, Nov 97	2.79	0.56	1.39	2.79
❑48, Dec 97	2.79	0.56	1.39	2.79
❑49, Feb 98	2.95	0.56	1.39	2.79
❑50, Apr 98	2.95	0.56	1.39	2.79
❑51, Jun 98	2.95	0.56	1.39	2.79
❑52, Jul 98	2.95	0.56	1.39	2.79
❑53, Aug 98	2.95	0.56	1.39	2.79
❑54, Oct 98	2.95	0.56	1.39	2.79
❑55, Nov 98, DDC	2.95	0.59	1.48	2.95
❑56, Jan 99	2.95	0.59	1.48	2.95
❑57, Feb 99	2.95	0.59	1.48	2.95
❑58, Apr 99	2.99	0.59	1.48	2.95
❑59, Jun 99	2.99	0.60	1.50	2.99
❑60, Jul 99	2.99	0.60	1.50	2.99
❑61, Aug 99	2.99	0.60	1.50	2.99
❑62, Oct 99	2.99	0.60	1.50	2.99
❑63, Nov 99	2.99	0.60	1.50	2.99
❑64, Jan 00	2.99	0.60	1.50	2.99
❑65, Feb 00	2.99	0.60	1.50	2.99
❑66, Apr 00	2.99	0.60	1.50	2.99
❑67, May 00	2.99	0.60	1.50	2.99
❑68, Jul 00	3.19	0.64	1.60	3.19
❑69, Aug 00	3.19	0.64	1.60	3.19
❑70, Oct 00	3.19	0.64	1.60	3.19
❑71, Nov 00	3.19	0.64	1.60	3.19
❑72, Jan 01	3.19	0.64	1.60	3.19
❑73, Feb 01	3.19	0.64	1.60	3.19
❑74, Mar 01	3.19	0.64	1.60	3.19
❑75	—	0.66	1.64	3.29
❑76	—	0.66	1.64	3.29
❑77	—	0.66	1.64	3.29
❑78	—	0.66	1.64	3.29
❑79	—	0.66	1.64	3.29

JUGHEAD'S PAL HOT DOG
ARCHIE

Value: Cover or less

❑1, Jan 90 .... 1.00
❑2 .... 1.00
❑3 .... 1.00
❑4 .... 1.00
❑5 .... 1.00

JUGHEAD'S TIME POLICE
ARCHIE

	ORIG	GOOD	FINE	N-MINT
❑1, Jul 90	1.00	0.25	0.63	1.25
❑2, Sep 90	1.00	0.20	0.50	1.00
❑3, Nov 90	1.00	0.20	0.50	1.00
❑4, Jan 91	1.00	0.20	0.50	1.00
❑5, Mar 91, A: Abe Lincoln	1.00	0.20	0.50	1.00
❑6, May 91, O: Time Beanie	1.00	0.20	0.50	1.00

JUGHEAD WITH ARCHIE DIGEST MAGAZINE
ARCHIE

	ORIG	GOOD	FINE	N-MINT
❑122, Jan 95	1.75	0.35	0.88	1.75
❑123, May 95	1.75	0.35	0.88	1.75
❑124, Aug 95	1.75	0.35	0.88	1.75
❑125, Oct 95	1.75	0.35	0.88	1.75
❑126, Jan 96	1.75	0.35	0.88	1.75
❑127	1.75	0.35	0.88	1.75
❑128, Sep 96	1.79	0.36	0.89	1.79
❑129	1.79	0.36	0.89	1.79
❑130, Glutton For Hire; Double Takes	1.79	0.36	0.89	1.79
❑131, Feb 97	1.79	0.36	0.89	1.79
❑132, Mar 97	1.79	0.36	0.89	1.79
❑133, May 97	1.79	0.36	0.89	1.79
❑134, Jul 97	1.79	0.36	0.89	1.79
❑135, Aug 97	1.79	0.36	0.89	1.79
❑136, Oct 97	1.79	0.36	0.89	1.79
❑137, Dec 97	1.79	0.36	0.89	1.79
❑138, Jan 98	1.95	0.39	0.98	1.95
❑139, Mar 98	1.95	0.39	0.98	1.95
❑140, May 98	1.95	0.39	0.98	1.95
❑141, Jun 98	1.95	0.39	0.98	1.95
❑142, Aug 98	1.95	0.39	0.98	1.95
❑143, Oct 98, DDC	1.95	0.39	0.98	1.95
❑144, Nov 98	1.95	0.39	0.98	1.95
❑145, Dec 98	1.95	0.39	0.98	1.95
❑146, Feb 99	1.95	0.39	0.98	1.95
❑147, Apr 99	1.95	0.39	0.98	1.95
❑148, May 99	1.99	0.39	0.98	1.95
❑149, Jun 99	1.99	0.40	1.00	1.99
❑150, Aug 99	1.99	0.40	1.00	1.99

Charlton hero Judomaster was introduced to the DC universe in *Crisis on Infinite Earths*. He later made an appearance in *L.A.W. (Living Assault Weapons)*.

© 1966 Charlton

	ORIG	GOOD	FINE	N-MINT
❑151, Sep 99	1.99	0.40	1.00	1.99
❑152, Nov 99	1.99	0.40	1.00	1.99
❑153, Dec 99	1.99	0.40	1.00	1.99
❑154, Feb 00	1.99	0.40	1.00	1.99
❑155, Mar 00	1.99	0.40	1.00	1.99
❑156, May 00	1.99	0.40	1.00	1.99
❑157, Jul 00	2.19	0.44	1.10	2.19
❑158, Aug 00	2.19	0.44	1.10	2.19
❑159, Sep 00	2.19	0.44	1.10	2.19
❑160, Nov 00	2.19	0.44	1.10	2.19
❑161, Dec 00	2.19	0.44	1.10	2.19
❑162, Jan 01	2.19	0.44	1.10	2.19
❑163, Mar 01	2.19	0.44	1.10	2.19

JUGULAR
BLACK OUT

Value: Cover or less

❑0, The Immigrants 2.95

JUMPER
ZAV

Value: Cover or less

❑1, Into the Void, b&w 3.00
❑2, b&w 3.00

JUN
DISNEY

Value: Cover or less

❑1 .... 1.50

JUNGLE ACTION
MARVEL

	ORIG	GOOD	FINE	N-MINT
❑1, Reprint	0.20	1.20	3.00	6.00
❑2, Reprint	0.20	0.80	2.00	4.00
❑3, Reprint	0.20	0.80	2.00	4.00
❑4, Apr 73, Tharn the Magnificent: Menace From the Past!; Lorna the Jungle Girl: Wildfire!, Reprint	0.20	0.80	2.00	4.00
❑5, Jul 73, Black Panther; Black Panther begins	0.20	0.80	2.00	4.00
❑6, Sep 73, Black Panther	0.20	0.60	1.50	3.00
❑7, Nov 73, Black Panther	0.20	0.60	1.50	3.00
❑8, Jan 74, KJ; RB, Malice By Crimson Moonlight!, O: Black Panther, Black Panther	0.20	0.60	1.50	3.00
❑9, May 74, Black Panther	0.25	0.60	1.50	3.00
❑10, Jul 74, Black Panther	0.25	0.50	1.25	2.50
❑11, Sep 74, Black Panther	0.25	0.50	1.25	2.50
❑12, Nov 74, Black Panther	0.25	0.50	1.25	2.50
❑13, Jan 75, Black Panther	0.25	0.50	1.25	2.50
❑14, Mar 75, Black Panther	0.25	0.50	1.25	2.50
❑15, May 75, Black Panther	0.25	0.50	1.25	2.50
❑16, Jul 75, Black Panther	0.25	0.50	1.25	2.50
❑17, Sep 75, Black Panther	0.25	0.50	1.25	2.50
❑18, Nov 75, Black Panther	0.25	0.50	1.25	2.50
❑19, Jan 76, 1: Baron Macabre, Black Panther	0.25	0.50	1.25	2.50
❑20, Mar 76, Black Panther	0.25	0.50	1.25	2.50
❑21, May 76, Black Panther	0.25	0.50	1.25	2.50
❑22, Jul 76, Black Panther	0.25	0.50	1.25	2.50
❑23, Sep 76, Black Panther	0.30	0.50	1.25	2.50
❑24, Nov 76, 1: Wind Eagle, Black Panther	0.30	0.50	1.25	2.50

JUNGLE BOOK, THE
DISNEY

Value: Cover or less

❑1/A, movie Adaptation; saddle-stitched 2.95
❑1/B, movie Adaptation; squarebound 5.95

JUNGLE COMICS (A-LIST)
A-LIST

Value: Cover or less

❑1, Spr 97, Sheena: Queen of the Jungle, gatefold summary; Sheena; Reprints Sheena 3-D special #1 in color 2.95
❑2, Fal 97, Wambi 2.95
❑3, Win 97, Congo King; Death Stalks the Congo 2.95
❑4, Mar 98 .... 2.95
❑5, Oct 98, Sheena 2.95

JUNGLE GIRLS
AC

	ORIG	GOOD	FINE	N-MINT
❑1, Aug 88, b&w	1.95	0.40	1.00	2.00
❑2	2.25	0.45	1.13	2.25
❑3	2.75	0.55	1.38	2.75

	ORIG	GOOD	FINE	N-MINT
❑4	2.75	0.55	1.38	2.75
❑5	2.75	0.55	1.38	2.75
❑6, MB, Reprint	2.95	0.59	1.48	2.95
❑7, MB, Reprint	2.95	0.59	1.48	2.95
❑8, Sheena Queen of the Jungle; Camila Wild Girl of the Congo, b&w	2.95	0.59	1.48	2.95
❑9, b&w	2.95	0.59	1.48	2.95
❑10, b&w	2.95	0.59	1.48	2.95
❑11, b&w	2.95	0.59	1.48	2.95
❑12, b&w	2.95	0.59	1.48	2.95
❑13, b&w	2.95	0.59	1.48	2.95
❑14, b&w	2.95	0.59	1.48	2.95
❑15, b&w	2.95	0.59	1.48	2.95
❑16, b&w	2.95	0.59	1.48	2.95

JUNGLE GIRLS! (ETERNITY)
ETERNITY

Value: Cover or less

- ❑8 ... 2.95

JUNGLE JIM (AVALON)
AVALON

Value: Cover or less

- ❑1, WW, SD (w), The Witch Doctor of Borges Island; The One They Fear, published in 1998 ... 2.95

JUNGLE JIM (CHARLTON)
CHARLTON

	ORIG	GOOD	FINE	N-MINT
❑22, Feb 69, Series continued from Jungle Jim (Dell) #21	0.12	4.80	12.00	24.00
❑23, Apr 69	0.12	3.60	9.00	18.00
❑24, Jun 69	0.12	3.60	9.00	18.00
❑25, Aug 69, The Best of Everything; The Hunters And The Hunted!	0.12	3.20	8.00	16.00
❑26, Oct 69	0.12	3.20	8.00	16.00
❑27, Dec 69	0.12	3.20	8.00	16.00
❑28, Feb 70, Final Issue	0.15	3.20	8.00	16.00

JUNGLE JIM (KING)
KING

	ORIG	GOOD	FINE	N-MINT
❑5, Dec 67	0.15	1.80	4.50	9.00

JUNGLE LOVE
AIRCEL

Value: Cover or less

- ❑1, b&w; adult ... 2.95
- ❑2, b&w; adult ... 2.95
- ❑3, b&w; adult ... 2.95

JUNGLE TALES OF TARZAN
CHARLTON

	ORIG	GOOD	FINE	N-MINT
❑1, Jan 65	0.12	9.00	22.50	45.00
❑2, Mar 65	0.12	7.00	17.50	35.00
❑3, May 65	0.12	7.00	17.50	35.00
❑4, Jul 65	0.12	7.00	17.50	35.00

JUNIOR JACKALOPE
NEVADA CITY PUBLISHING

Value: Cover or less

- ❑1, b&w ... 1.50
- ❑2, b&w ... 1.50

JUNIOR WOODCHUCKS (WALT DISNEY'S...)
DISNEY

Value: Cover or less

- ❑1, Jul 91, CB, Bubbleweight Champ, Reprint ... 1.50
- ❑2, Aug 91 ... 1.50
- ❑3, Sep 91 ... 1.50
- ❑4, Oct 91, The Cave Caper!; Sleepy Valley ... 1.50

JUNK CULTURE
DC

Value: Cover or less

- ❑1, Jul 97 ... 2.50
- ❑2, Aug 97 ... 2.50

JUNKER
FLEETWAY

Value: Cover or less

- ❑1 ... 2.95
- ❑2 ... 2.95
- ❑3 ... 2.95
- ❑4 ... 2.95

JUNKFOOD NOIR
OKTOBER BLACK PRESS

Value: Cover or less

- ❑1, Jun 96, Murder, b&w ... 1.95

JUNKYARD ENFORCER
BOXCAR PRODUCTIONS

Value: Cover or less

- ❑1, Aug 98, b&w ... 2.95

JUPITER
SANDBERG

Value: Cover or less

- ❑1 ... 2.95
- ❑2 ... 2.95
- ❑3 ... 2.95

JURASSIC LARK DELUXE EDITION
PARODY PRESS

Value: Cover or less

- ❑1, b&w ... 2.95

JURASSIC PARK
TOPPS

	ORIG	GOOD	FINE	N-MINT
❑0, Nov 93, GK, Genesis; Betrayal, Polybagged with trade paperback; Flip book with two prequels to the movie	—	0.40	1.00	2.00
❑0/DM, Nov 93, GK, GP (c), movie Adaptation; trading cards (came packed with trade paperback)	2.95	0.60	1.50	3.00
❑1, Jun 93, GK, DC (c)	2.50	0.60	1.50	3.00
❑1/DM, Jun 93, GK, DC (c), trading cards	2.50	0.60	1.50	3.00
❑2, Jul 93, GK	2.50	0.60	1.50	3.00
❑2/DM, Jul 93, GK, trading cards	2.95	0.60	1.50	3.00
❑3, Jul 93, GK	2.50	0.60	1.50	3.00
❑3/DM, Jul 93, GK, trading cards	2.95	0.60	1.50	3.00
❑4, Aug 93, GK	2.50	0.60	1.50	3.00
❑4/DM, Aug 93, GK, hologram card	2.95	0.60	1.50	3.00

JURASSIC PARK ADVENTURES
TOPPS

Value: Cover or less

- ❑1, Jun 94 ... 1.95
- ❑2 ... 1.95
- ❑3 ... 1.95
- ❑4, Animals/Men ... 1.95
- ❑5 ... 1.95
- ❑6 ... 1.95
- ❑7 ... 1.95
- ❑8 ... 1.95
- ❑9 ... 1.95
- ❑10 ... 1.95

JURASSIC PARK: RAPTOR
TOPPS

Value: Cover or less

- ❑1, Nov 93, trading cards; Zorro #0 ... 2.95
- ❑2, Dec 93, Dark Cargo!, trading cards; cards ... 2.95

JURASSIC PARK: RAPTORS ATTACK
TOPPS

Value: Cover or less

- ❑1, Mar 94, Rush! ... 2.50
- ❑2, Apr 94 ... 2.50
- ❑3, May 94, Animals/Gods ... 2.50
- ❑4, Jun 94 ... 2.50

JURASSIC PARK: RAPTORS HIJACK
TOPPS

Value: Cover or less

- ❑1, The Wild! ... 2.50
- ❑2 ... 2.50
- ❑3 ... 2.50
- ❑4 ... 2.50

JUST A PILGRIM
BLACK BULL

Value: Cover or less

- ❑1, May 01 ... 2.99
- ❑2 ... 2.99
- ❑3 ... 2.99
- ❑4 ... 2.99
- ❑5 ... 2.99

JUSTICE (ANTARCTIC)
ANTARCTIC

Value: Cover or less

- ❑1, May 94, b&w ... 3.50

JUSTICE (MARVEL)
MARVEL

	ORIG	GOOD	FINE	N-MINT
❑1, Nov 86, Brave New World, 1: Justice	0.75	0.25	0.63	1.25
❑2, Dec 86	0.75	0.20	0.50	1.00
❑3, Jan 87	0.75	0.20	0.50	1.00
❑4, Feb 87	0.75	0.20	0.50	1.00
❑5, Mar 87	0.75	0.20	0.50	1.00
❑6, Apr 87, Sara	0.75	0.20	0.50	1.00
❑7, May 87	0.75	0.20	0.50	1.00
❑8, Jun 87	0.75	0.20	0.50	1.00
❑9, Jul 87	0.75	0.20	0.50	1.00
❑10, Aug 87	0.75	0.20	0.50	1.00
❑11, Sep 87	0.75	0.20	0.50	1.00
❑12, Oct 87	0.75	0.20	0.50	1.00
❑13, Nov 87	0.75	0.20	0.50	1.00
❑14, Dec 87	0.75	0.20	0.50	1.00
❑15, Jan 88	0.75	0.20	0.50	1.00
❑16, Feb 88	0.75	0.20	0.50	1.00
❑17, Mar 88	0.75	0.20	0.50	1.00
❑18, Apr 88	0.75	0.25	0.63	1.25
❑19, May 88	1.25	0.25	0.63	1.25
❑20, Jun 88	1.25	0.25	0.63	1.25
❑21, Jul 88	1.25	0.25	0.63	1.25
❑22, Aug 88	1.25	0.25	0.63	1.25
❑23, Sep 88	1.25	0.25	0.63	1.25
❑24, Oct 88	1.25	0.25	0.63	1.25
❑25, Nov 88	1.25	0.25	0.63	1.25
❑26, Dec 88	1.50	0.30	0.75	1.50
❑27, Jan 89	1.50	0.30	0.75	1.50
❑28, Feb 89	1.50	0.30	0.75	1.50
❑29, Mar 89	1.50	0.30	0.75	1.50
❑30, Apr 89, Psi Unseen; Psycho Killer, A: Psi-Force	1.50	0.30	0.75	1.50
❑31, May 89	1.50	0.30	0.75	1.50
❑32, Jun 89, Final Issue	1.50	0.30	0.75	1.50

JUSTICE BRIGADE
TCB COMICS

Value: Cover or less

- ❑1, b&w ... 1.50
- ❑2, b&w ... 1.50
- ❑3, b&w ... 1.50
- ❑4, b&w ... 1.50
- ❑5, b&w ... 1.50
- ❑6, b&w ... 1.50
- ❑7, b&w ... 1.50
- ❑8, b&w ... 1.50

JUSTICE: FOUR BALANCE
MARVEL

Value: Cover or less

- ❑1, Sep 94, Rock Crushes Scissors ... 1.75
- ❑2, Oct 94 ... 1.75
- ❑3, Nov 94, Marco-" "-Polo ... 1.75
- ❑4, Dec 94 ... 1.75

JUSTICE, INC.
DC

	ORIG	GOOD	FINE	N-MINT
❑1, Jun 75, This Night, An Avenger Is Born!, O: The Avenger, adapts Justice Inc. novel	0.25	0.60	1.50	3.00
❑2, Aug 75, JK, adapts The Skywalker	0.25	0.40	1.00	2.00
❑3, Oct 75, JK, The Monster Bug!, 1: Fergus MacMurdie	0.25	0.40	1.00	2.00
❑4, Dec 75, JK, JKu (c)	0.25	0.40	1.00	2.00

JUSTICE, INC. (MINI-SERIES)
DC

	ORIG	GOOD	FINE	N-MINT
❑1, Trust, O: The Avenger, prestige format	3.95	0.80	2.00	4.00
❑2, Betrayal, prestige format	3.95	0.80	2.00	4.00

JUSTICE LEAGUE
DC

	ORIG	GOOD	FINE	N-MINT
❑1, May 87, 1: Maxwell Lord	0.75	0.70	1.75	3.50
❑2, Jun 87, 1: Wandjina; 1: Bluejay; 1: Silver Sorceress	0.75	0.50	1.25	2.50
❑3, Jul 87, V: Rocket Reds	0.75	0.50	1.25	2.50
❑3/LE, Jul 87, alternate cover; Superman logo on cover (limited edition)	0.75	3.00	7.50	15.00
❑4, Aug 87, V: Royal Flush Gang, Booster Gold joins team	0.75	0.50	1.25	2.50
❑5, Sep 87, Batman vs. Guy Gardner	0.75	0.40	1.00	2.00
❑6, Oct 87, KG, KG (w), Massacre In Gray, Series continues in Justice League International #7	0.75	0.40	1.00	2.00

JUSTICE LEAGUE AMERICA
DC

	ORIG	GOOD	FINE	N-MINT
❑0, Oct 94, Home Again, New team begins: Wonder Woman, Flash III (Wally West), Fire, Metamorpho, Crimson Fox, Hawkman, Obsidian, Nuklon	1.50	0.40	1.00	2.00
❑26, May 89, A: Huntress, Continued from "Justice League International"	0.75	0.35	0.88	1.75
❑27, Jun 89, Exorcist homage cover	0.75	0.35	0.88	1.75
❑28, Jul 89	0.75	0.35	0.88	1.75
❑29, Aug 89	1.00	0.35	0.88	1.75
❑30, Sep 89	1.00	0.35	0.88	1.75
❑31, Oct 89, Teasdale Imperative, Part 1, A: Justice League Europe	1.00	0.35	0.88	1.75
❑32, Nov 89, Teasdale Imperative, Part 3, A: Justice League Europe	1.00	0.35	0.88	1.75
❑33, Dec 89, A: Kilowog	1.00	0.35	0.88	1.75
❑34, Jan 90	1.00	0.35	0.88	1.75
❑35, Feb 90	1.00	0.35	0.88	1.75
❑36, Mar 90, A: G'Nort; 1: Scarlet Skier; 1: Mr. Nebula	1.00	0.35	0.88	1.75
❑37, Apr 90	1.00	0.35	0.88	1.75
❑38, May 90, V: Despero	1.00	0.35	0.88	1.75
❑39, Jun 90, V: Despero	1.00	0.35	0.88	1.75
❑40, Jul 90, V: Despero	1.00	0.35	0.88	1.75
❑41, Aug 90	1.00	0.35	0.88	1.75
❑42, Sep 90, membership drive; Return of Mr. Miracle; Orion joins team; Lightray joins team	1.00	0.35	0.88	1.75
❑43, Oct 90	1.00	0.35	0.88	1.75
❑44, Nov 90	1.00	0.35	0.88	1.75
❑45, Jan 91	1.00	0.35	0.88	1.75
❑46, Jan 91, Glory Bound, Part 1, 1: General Glory, Medley art begins	1.00	0.35	0.88	1.75
❑47, Feb 91, Glory Bound, Part 2	1.00	0.35	0.88	1.75
❑48, Mar 91, Glory Bound, Part 3	1.00	0.35	0.88	1.75
❑49, Apr 91, Glory Bound, Part 4	1.00	0.35	0.88	1.75
❑50, May 91, Glory Bound, Part 5, Double-size	1.75	0.35	0.88	1.75
❑51, Jun 91	1.00	0.25	0.63	1.25
❑52, Jul 91, Guy Gardner vs. Blue Beetle	1.00	0.25	0.63	1.25
❑53, Aug 91, Breakdowns; Breakdowns, Part 1	1.00	0.25	0.63	1.25
❑54, Sep 91, Breakdowns; Breakdowns, Part 3	1.00	0.25	0.63	1.25
❑55, Oct 91, Breakdowns; Breakdowns, Part 5, V: Global Guardians	1.00	0.25	0.63	1.25
❑56, Nov 91, Breakdowns; Breakdowns, Part 7, back to Happy Harbor	1.00	0.25	0.63	1.25
❑57, Dec 91, Breakdowns; Breakdowns, Part 9, V: Extremists	1.00	0.25	0.63	1.25
❑58, Jan 92, Breakdowns; Breakdowns, Part 11, V: Despero; V: Lobo	1.00	0.25	0.63	1.25
❑59, Feb 92, Breakdowns; Breakdowns, Part 13	1.00	0.25	0.63	1.25
❑60, Mar 92, Breakdowns; Breakdowns, Part 15	1.00	0.25	0.63	1.25
❑61, Apr 92, 1: Bloodwynd; V: Weapons Master, new JLA	1.00	0.25	0.63	1.25
❑62, May 92, V: Weapons Master	1.00	0.25	0.63	1.25
❑63, Jun 92, Bloodwynd joins team; Guy Gardner leaves team	1.25	0.25	0.63	1.25
❑64, Jul 92, The Revenge Of Starbreaker, V: Starbreaker	1.25	0.25	0.63	1.25
❑65, Aug 92, V: Starbreaker	1.25	0.25	0.63	1.25

Following the events of the "Legends" crossover, DC revived *Justice League of America* as simply *Justice League.*

	ORIG	GOOD	FINE	N-MINT
❑66, Sep 92, Guy returns	1.25	0.25	0.63	1.25
❑67, Oct 92, Transitions, Transmissions, And Transactions	1.25	0.25	0.63	1.25
❑68, Nov 92	1.25	0.25	0.63	1.25
❑69, Dec 92, Doomsday, Doomsday	1.25	0.70	1.75	3.50
❑69-2, Doomsday, 2nd Printing	1.25	0.35	0.88	1.75
❑70, Jan 93, Funeral For a Friend, Part 1, cover wrapper; Funeral for a Friend	1.25	0.50	1.25	2.50
❑70-2, Jan 93, Funeral For a Friend, Part 1, 2nd Printing; cover wrapper; Funeral for a Friend	1.25	0.35	0.88	1.75
❑71, Feb 93, A New Look, black cover wrapper; Wonder Woman joins team; Ray joins team; Agent Liberty joins team; Black Condor joins team	1.25	0.40	1.00	2.00
❑71/SC, A New Look, Split cover; New team begins	1.25	0.50	1.25	2.50
❑72, Mar 93, V: Doctor Destiny	1.25	0.30	0.75	1.50
❑73, Apr 93, Destiny's Hand 2, V: Doctor Destiny	1.25	0.30	0.75	1.50
❑74, May 93, V: Doctor Destiny	1.25	0.30	0.75	1.50
❑75, Jun 93, V: Doctor Destiny	1.25	0.30	0.75	1.50
❑76, Jul 93	1.25	0.30	0.75	1.50
❑77, Jul 93	1.25	0.30	0.75	1.50
❑78, Aug 93, A: Jay Garrick	1.25	0.30	0.75	1.50
❑79, Aug 93, V: new Extremists	1.25	0.30	0.75	1.50
❑80, Sep 93, Booster gets new armor	1.25	0.30	0.75	1.50
❑81, Oct 93, Ray vs. Captain Atom	1.25	0.30	0.75	1.50
❑82, Nov 93	1.25	0.30	0.75	1.50
❑83, Dec 93	1.50	0.30	0.75	1.50
❑84, Jan 94	1.50	0.30	0.75	1.50
❑85, Feb 94	1.50	0.30	0.75	1.50
❑86, Mar 94, Cults of the Machine	1.50	0.30	0.75	1.50
❑87, Apr 94	1.50	0.30	0.75	1.50
❑88, May 94	1.50	0.30	0.75	1.50
❑89, Jun 94, Judgment Day	1.50	0.30	0.75	1.50
❑90, Jul 94, Judgment Day	1.50	0.30	0.75	1.50
❑91, Aug 94, Heroes Passage, Funeral of Ice	1.50	0.30	0.75	1.50
❑92, Sep 94, The Program, A: Triumph, Zero Hour	1.50	0.30	0.75	1.50
❑93, Nov 94	1.50	0.30	0.75	1.50
❑94, Dec 94	1.50	0.30	0.75	1.50
❑95, Jan 95, Where the Wild Things Are	1.50	0.30	0.75	1.50
❑96, Feb 95	1.50	0.30	0.75	1.50
❑97, Mar 95	1.50	0.30	0.75	1.50
❑98, Apr 95	1.50	0.30	0.75	1.50
❑99, May 95	1.50	0.30	0.75	1.50
❑100, Jun 95, Giant-size anniversary edition	2.95	0.59	1.48	2.95
❑100/SC, Holo-grafix cover; Giant-size anniversary edition	3.95	0.79	1.98	3.95
❑101, Jul 95, Way of the Warrior, Part 2	1.75	0.35	0.88	1.75
❑102, Aug 95, Way of the Warrior, Part 5	1.75	0.35	0.88	1.75
❑103, Sep 95	1.75	0.35	0.88	1.75
❑104, Oct 95	1.75	0.35	0.88	1.75
❑105, Nov 95, Underworld Unleashed, Underworld Unleashed	1.75	0.35	0.88	1.75
❑106, Dec 95, Underworld Unleashed	1.75	0.35	0.88	1.75
❑107, Jan 96	1.75	0.35	0.88	1.75
❑108, Feb 96, One Hand in Darkness, 1: Equinox	1.75	0.35	0.88	1.75
❑109, Mar 96, All that Yazz, A: Equinox	1.75	0.35	0.88	1.75
❑110, Apr 96, New Devils for Old, A: El Diablo	1.75	0.35	0.88	1.75
❑111, Jun 96, The Purge, Part 1	1.75	0.35	0.88	1.75
❑112, Jul 96, The Purge, Part 2	1.75	0.35	0.88	1.75
❑113, Aug 96, The Purge, Part 3, Final Issue	1.75	0.35	0.88	1.75
❑Anl 4, Justice League Antarctica	2.00	0.60	1.50	3.00
❑Anl 5, Armageddon 2001	2.00	0.60	1.50	3.00
❑Anl 5-2, Armageddon 2001, Part 4, 2nd Printing; Silver ink cover; silver	2.00	0.50	1.25	2.50
❑Anl 6, DC, Eclipso: The Darkness Within, Part 6, Eclipso	2.50	0.50	1.25	2.50
❑Anl 7, Only the Lucky Ones Die!, 1: Terror-smith, Bloodlines	2.50	0.50	1.25	2.50
❑Anl 8, Elseworlds	2.95	0.59	1.48	2.95

	ORIG	GOOD	FINE	N-MINT
❑Anl 9, Year One	3.50	0.70	1.75	3.50
❑Anl 10, Te Alliance, Legends of the Dead Earth; events continue in Ray #26; 1996.	2.95	0.59	1.48	2.95
❑SE 1	1.50	0.30	0.75	1.50
❑SE 2	2.95	0.59	1.48	2.95
❑SP 1/A, Team Work, Green Lantern on cover; Double-size; Justice League Spectacular	1.50	0.40	1.00	2.00
❑SP 1/B, Superman on cover; Double-size; Justice League Spectacular	1.50	0.40	1.00	2.00

JUSTICE LEAGUE: A MIDSUMMER'S NIGHTMARE
DC

Value: Cover or less

❑1, Sep 96, True Lies, forms triptych with other two issues... 2.95

❑2, Oct 96, forms triptych with other two issues 2.95

❑3, Nov 96, forms triptych with other two issues 2.95

JUSTICE LEAGUE EUROPE
DC

	ORIG	GOOD	FINE	N-MINT
❑1, Apr 89, KG, KG (w), How Ya Gonna Keep 'Em Down Of The Farm After They've Seen Paree?, 1: Catherine Cobert	0.75	0.50	1.25	2.50
❑2, May 89	0.75	0.30	0.75	1.50
❑3, Jun 89	0.75	0.30	0.75	1.50
❑4, Jul 89, V: Queen Bee	0.75	0.30	0.75	1.50
❑5, Aug 89, A: Sapphire, Java	0.75	0.30	0.75	1.50
❑6, Sep 89, 1: Crimson Fox	0.75	0.30	0.75	1.50
❑7, Oct 89, Teasdale Imperative, A: Justice League America; A: Justice League of America	1.00	0.30	0.75	1.50
❑8, Nov 89, Teasdale Imperative, A: Justice League America; A: Justice League of America	1.00	0.30	0.75	1.50
❑9, Dec 89, A: Superman	1.00	0.30	0.75	1.50
❑10, Jan 90	1.00	0.30	0.75	1.50
❑11, Feb 90, Guy Gardner vs. Metamorpho	1.00	0.30	0.75	1.50
❑12, Mar 90	1.00	0.30	0.75	1.50
❑13, Apr 90	1.00	0.30	0.75	1.50
❑14, May 90	1.00	0.30	0.75	1.50
❑15, Jun 90, 1: Extremists	1.00	0.30	0.75	1.50
❑16, Jun 90, V: Extremists	1.00	0.30	0.75	1.50
❑17, Aug 90, V: Extremists	1.00	0.30	0.75	1.50
❑18, Sep 90, V: Extremists	1.00	0.30	0.75	1.50
❑19, Oct 90, V: Extremists	1.00	0.30	0.75	1.50
❑20, Nov 90	1.00	0.30	0.75	1.50
❑21, Dec 90	1.00	0.25	0.63	1.25
❑22, Jan 91	1.00	0.25	0.63	1.25
❑23, Feb 91	1.00	0.25	0.63	1.25
❑24, Mar 91	1.00	0.25	0.63	1.25
❑25, Apr 91	1.00	0.25	0.63	1.25
❑26, May 91	1.00	0.25	0.63	1.25
❑27, Jun 91	1.00	0.25	0.63	1.25
❑28, Jul 91	1.00	0.25	0.63	1.25
❑29, Aug 91, Breakdowns; Breakdowns, Part 2	1.00	0.25	0.63	1.25
❑30, Sep 91, Breakdowns; Breakdowns, Part 4, V: Jack O'Lantern	1.00	0.25	0.63	1.25
❑31, Oct 91, Breakdowns; Breakdowns, Part 6, evicted from JLI Embassy	1.00	0.25	0.63	1.25
❑32, Nov 91, Breakdowns; Breakdowns, Part 8	1.00	0.25	0.63	1.25
❑33, Dec 91, Breakdowns; Breakdowns, Part 10, V: Despero; V: Lobo	1.00	0.25	0.63	1.25
❑34, Jan 92, Breakdowns; Breakdowns, Part 12, V: Despero; V: Lobo	1.00	0.25	0.63	1.25
❑35, Feb 92, Breakdowns; Breakdowns, Part 14, V: Extremists	1.00	0.25	0.63	1.25
❑36, Mar 92, Breakdowns	1.00	0.25	0.63	1.25
❑37, Apr 92, new team	1.00	0.25	0.63	1.25
❑38, May 92	1.00	0.25	0.63	1.25
❑39, Jun 92	1.25	0.25	0.63	1.25
❑40, Jul 92	1.25	0.25	0.63	1.25
❑41, Aug 92	1.25	0.25	0.63	1.25
❑42, Sep 92, Wonder Woman joins team	1.25	0.25	0.63	1.25
❑43, Oct 92	1.25	0.25	0.63	1.25
❑44, Oct 92	1.25	0.25	0.63	1.25
❑45, Dec 92, Red Winter, Part 1	1.25	0.25	0.63	1.25
❑46, Jan 93, Red Winter, Part 2	1.25	0.25	0.63	1.25
❑47, Feb 93, Red Winter, Part 3	1.25	0.25	0.63	1.25
❑48, Mar 93, Red Winter, Part 4, A: Justice Society of America	1.25	0.25	0.63	1.25
❑49, Apr 93, Red Winter, Part 5	1.25	0.25	0.63	1.25
❑50, May 93, Red Winter, Part 6, A: Justice Society of America; V: Sonar, Series continues as Justice League International	2.50	0.25	0.63	1.25
❑Anl 1, Global Guardians	2.00	0.40	1.00	2.00
❑Anl 2, Armageddon 2001, Part 13, A: Legion; A: General Glory; A: Hex; A: Bat Lash; A: Anthro; A: Elongated Man; A: Demon, Armageddon 2001	2.00	0.40	1.00	2.00
❑Anl 3, Eclipso: The Darkness Within, Part 16, Eclipso; series continues as Justice League International Annual	2.50	0.50	1.25	2.50

JUSTICE LEAGUE INTERNATIONAL
DC

	ORIG	GOOD	FINE	N-MINT
❑7, Nov 87, Title changes to Justice League International; Captain Marvel leaves team; Captain Atom joins team; Rocket Red joins team	1.25	0.50	1.25	2.50
❑8, Dec 87	0.75	0.30	0.75	1.50
❑9, Jan 88, Millennium	0.75	0.30	0.75	1.50
❑10, Feb 88, 1: G'Nort, Millennium	0.75	0.30	0.75	1.50
❑11, Mar 88	0.75	0.25	0.63	1.25
❑12, Apr 88	0.75	0.25	0.63	1.25
❑13, May 88, A: Suicide Squad	0.75	0.25	0.63	1.25
❑14, Jun 88	0.75	0.25	0.63	1.25
❑15, Jul 88, 1: L-Ron; 1: Manga Khan	0.75	0.25	0.63	1.25
❑16, Aug 88	0.75	0.25	0.63	1.25
❑17, Sep 88	0.75	0.25	0.63	1.25
❑18, Oct 88, A: Lobo, Bonus Book	0.75	0.25	0.63	1.25
❑19, Nov 88, A: Lobo	0.75	0.25	0.63	1.25
❑20, Dec 88, A: Lobo	0.75	0.25	0.63	1.25
❑21, A: Lobo, no month of publication	0.75	0.25	0.63	1.25
❑22, Invasion!; no month of publication; Oberon solo story	0.75	0.25	0.63	1.25
❑23, Jan 89, V: Injustice League, Invasion!	0.75	0.25	0.63	1.25
❑24, Feb 89, 1: JL Europe, Giant-size; Bonus Book	1.50	0.40	1.00	2.00
❑25, Apr 89, becomes Justice League America	0.75	0.25	0.63	1.25
❑51, Jun 93, was Justice League Europe	1.25	0.25	0.63	1.25
❑52, Jul 93	1.25	0.25	0.63	1.25
❑53, Aug 93	1.25	0.25	0.63	1.25
❑54, Sep 93	1.25	0.25	0.63	1.25
❑55, Sep 93	1.25	0.25	0.63	1.25
❑56, Oct 93	1.25	0.25	0.63	1.25
❑57, Oct 93	1.25	0.25	0.63	1.25
❑58, Nov 93	1.25	0.25	0.63	1.25
❑59, Dec 93, Ordinary People	1.50	0.30	0.75	1.50
❑60, Jan 94	1.50	0.30	0.75	1.50
❑61, Feb 94, Born of Man and Woman	1.50	0.30	0.75	1.50
❑62, Mar 94	1.50	0.30	0.75	1.50
❑63, Apr 94	1.50	0.30	0.75	1.50
❑64, May 94	1.50	0.30	0.75	1.50
❑65, Jun 94, Judgment Day; Judgment Day, Part 3	1.50	0.30	0.75	1.50
❑66, Jul 94, Judgment Day	1.50	0.30	0.75	1.50
❑67, Aug 94, Aftershocks, Part 3	1.50	0.30	0.75	1.50
❑68, Sep 94, Return of the Hero, Part 3, A: Triumph, Final Issue; Zero Hour	1.50	0.30	0.75	1.50
❑Anl 1	1.25	0.40	1.00	2.00
❑Anl 2, V: Joker	1.50	0.40	1.00	2.00
❑Anl 3	1.75	0.40	1.00	2.00
❑Anl 4, Bloodlines, 1: Lionheart, Bloodlines	2.50	0.50	1.25	2.50
❑Anl 5, Jun 94, No Rules to Follow, Elseworlds	2.95	0.59	1.48	2.95
❑SE 1, KG (w), The Show Must Go On…And On…And On…And On…, Mr. Miracle	1.50	0.30	0.75	1.50
❑SE 2, Huntress	2.95	0.59	1.48	2.95

JUSTICE LEAGUE OF AMERICA
DC

	ORIG	GOOD	FINE	N-MINT
❑1, Nov 60, 1: Despero	0.10	690.00	1725.00	3450.00
❑2, Jan 61, A: Merlin	0.10	162.00	405.00	810.00
❑3, Mar 61, 1: Hyathis; 1: Kanjar Ro	0.10	122.00	305.00	610.00
❑4, May 61, Green Arrow joins team	0.10	90.00	225.00	450.00
❑5, Jul 61, 1: Doctor Destiny	0.10	73.00	182.50	365.00
❑6, Sep 61, 1: Professor Amos Fortune	0.10	57.00	142.50	285.00
❑7, Nov 61	0.10	57.00	142.50	285.00
❑8, Jan 62	0.12	57.00	142.50	285.00
❑9, Feb 62, O: Justice League of America	0.12	88.00	220.00	440.00
❑10, Mar 62, 1: Felix Faust; 1: Lord of Time	0.12	52.00	130.00	260.00
❑11, May 62	0.12	40.00	100.00	200.00
❑12, Jun 62, 1: Doctor Light I (Dr. Arthur Light)	0.12	40.00	100.00	200.00
❑13, Aug 62	0.12	40.00	100.00	200.00
❑14, Sep 62, Atom joins Justice League of America	0.12	40.00	100.00	200.00
❑15, Nov 62	0.12	40.00	100.00	200.00
❑16, Dec 62	0.12	33.00	82.50	165.00
❑17, Feb 63, 1: Tornado Champion (Red Tornado)	0.12	33.00	82.50	165.00
❑18, Mar 63	0.12	33.00	82.50	165.00
❑19, May 63	0.12	33.00	82.50	165.00
❑20, Jun 63	0.12	33.00	82.50	165.00
❑21, Aug 63, 1: Earth-2 (named), Return of Justice Society of America; Justice League of America teams up with Justice Society of America	0.12	68.00	170.00	340.00
❑22, Sep 63, Return of Justice Society of America; Justice League of America teams up with Justice Society of America	0.12	57.00	142.50	285.00
❑23, Nov 63, 1: Queen Bee	0.12	18.00	45.00	90.00
❑24, Dec 63	0.12	18.00	45.00	90.00

	ORIG	GOOD	FINE	N-MINT
❑25, Feb 64	0.12	18.00	45.00	90.00
❑26, Mar 64	0.12	18.00	45.00	90.00
❑27, May 64	0.12	18.00	45.00	90.00
❑28, Jun 64	0.12	18.00	45.00	90.00
❑29, Aug 64, Crisis on Earth-Three, Part 1, 1: Crime Syndicate; 1: Earth-3; A: Justice Society; A: Justice Society of America	0.12	23.00	57.50	115.00
❑30, Sep 64, Justice League of America teams up with Justice Society of America	0.12	23.00	57.50	115.00
❑31, Nov 64, Riddle of the Runaway Room, Hawkman joins team	0.12	16.00	40.00	80.00
❑32, Dec 64, Attack of the Star-Bolt Warrior, V: Brain Storm; 1: Brainstorm	0.12	10.40	26.00	52.00
❑33, Feb 65, Enemy From the Timeless World	0.12	8.40	21.00	42.00
❑34, Mar 65, The Deadly Dreams of Doctor Destiny, V: Dr. Destiny; V: Doctor Destiny; A: Joker	0.12	11.60	29.00	58.00
❑35, May 65, Battle Against the Bodiless Uniforms	0.12	8.40	21.00	42.00
❑36, Jun 65, The Case of the Disabled Justice League	0.12	8.40	21.00	42.00
❑37, Aug 65, Earth Without a Justice League, A: Justice Society of America; 1: Earth-A	0.12	17.00	42.50	85.00
❑38, Sep 65, Crisis on Earth-A, A: Justice Society of America	0.12	17.00	42.50	85.00
❑39, Nov 65, Starro the Conqueror; Case of the Stolen Super-Powers, 80pgs.; reprints Brave and the Bold #28, 30, and Justice League of America #5	0.25	18.00	45.00	90.00
❑40, Nov 65, Indestructible Creatures of Nightmare Island, social issue	0.12	8.40	21.00	42.00
❑41, Dec 65, The Keymaster of the World!, 1: The Key; V: Key	0.12	8.40	21.00	42.00
❑42, Feb 66, Metamorpho Says No!, A: Metamorpho	0.12	6.40	16.00	32.00
❑43, Mar 66, The Card Crimes of the Royal Flush Gang!, 1: Royal Flush Gang	0.12	6.40	16.00	32.00
❑44, May 66, The Plague that Struck the Justice League!	0.12	6.40	16.00	32.00
❑45, Jun 66, The Super-Struggle Against Shaggy Man!, V: Shaggy Man	0.12	6.40	16.00	32.00
❑46, Aug 66, Crisis Between Earth-One and Earth-Two!, V: Solomon Grundy, Blockbuster; 1: Sandman I (in Silver Age); A: Justice Society of America	0.12	21.00	52.50	105.00
❑47, Sep 66, The Bridge Between Earths!, V: Anti-Matter Man; A: Justice Society of America	0.12	9.60	24.00	48.00
❑48, Dec 66, Challenge of the Weapons Master; Secret of the Sinister Sorcerers, 80pgs.; Reprint	0.25	9.00	22.50	45.00
❑49, Nov 66, Threat of the True-or-False Sorcerer!	0.12	4.00	10.00	20.00
❑50, Dec 66, The Lord of Time Attacks the 20th Century!	0.12	4.00	10.00	20.00
❑51, Feb 67, Z-As in Zatanna-And Zero Hour!, A: Elongated Man	0.12	4.00	10.00	20.00
❑52, Mar 67, Missing in Action-5 Justice Leaguers!	0.12	4.00	10.00	20.00
❑53, May 67, Secret Behind the Stolen Super-Weapons!	0.12	4.00	10.00	20.00
❑54, Jun 67, History-Making Crimes of the Royal-Flush Gang	0.12	4.00	10.00	20.00
❑55, Aug 67, The Super-Crisis that Struck Earth-Two, Justice League of America teams up with Justice Society of America	0.12	10.80	27.00	54.00
❑56, Sep 67, The Negative-Crisis on Earths One-Two, Justice League of America teams up with Justice Society of America	0.12	7.60	19.00	38.00
❑57, Nov 67, Man, They Name Is-Brother!	0.12	3.60	9.00	18.00
❑58, Dec 67, The Wheel of Misfortune!; For Sale-The Justice League!, Reprint; Giant-size; G-41	0.25	4.40	11.00	22.00
❑59, Dec 67, The Justice Leaguers' Impossible Adventure!	0.12	3.60	9.00	18.00
❑60, Feb 68, Winged Warriors of The Immortal Queen!	0.12	3.60	9.00	18.00
❑61, Mar 68	0.12	3.00	7.50	15.00
❑62, May 68	0.12	3.00	7.50	15.00
❑63, Jun 68	0.12	3.00	7.50	15.00
❑64, Aug 68, DP, A: Justice Society of America, Return of Red Tornado	0.12	3.00	7.50	15.00
❑65, Sep 68, DP, V: T.O.Morrow, Justice League of America teams up with Justice Society of America	0.12	3.00	7.50	15.00
❑66, Nov 68, DP	0.12	3.00	7.50	15.00
❑67, Dec 68, Reprint	0.25	3.00	7.50	15.00

The first team-up of the Justice League of America and the Justice Society of America occurred in *Justice League of America #21*.

	ORIG	GOOD	FINE	N-MINT
❑68, Jan 69, DD	0.12	3.00	7.50	15.00
❑69, Feb 69, DD, Wonder Woman leaves Justice League of America	0.12	3.00	7.50	15.00
❑70, Mar 69, DD, A: Creeper	0.12	3.00	7.50	15.00
❑71, May 69, DD, 1: Blue Jay, Martian Manhunter leaves Justice League of America	0.12	3.00	7.50	15.00
❑72, Jun 69, DD	0.12	3.00	7.50	15.00
❑73, Aug 69, DD, A: Justice Society of America	0.15	3.00	7.50	15.00
❑74, Sep 69, DD, Where Death Fears to Tread!, A: Justice Society; D: Larry Lance, Black Canary goes to Earth-1	0.15	2.60	6.50	13.00
❑75, Nov 69, DD, 1: Black Canary II (Dinah Lance)	0.15	2.60	6.50	13.00
❑76, Dec 69, DD; MA, giant; reprints #7 and #12; pin-ups of Justice Society of America and Seven Soldiers	0.25	3.00	7.50	15.00
❑77, Dec 69, DD	0.15	1.80	4.50	9.00
❑78, Feb 70, DD	0.15	1.80	4.50	9.00
❑79, Mar 70, DD	0.15	1.80	4.50	9.00
❑80, May 70, DD	0.15	1.80	4.50	9.00
❑81, Jun 70, DD	0.15	1.60	4.00	8.00
❑82, Aug 70, DD	0.15	1.60	4.00	8.00
❑83, Sep 70, DD, A: Spectre	0.15	1.60	4.00	8.00
❑84, Nov 70, DD	0.15	1.60	4.00	8.00
❑85, Dec 70, Reprint; Giant-size	0.25	2.40	6.00	12.00
❑86, Dec 70, DD	0.15	1.40	3.50	7.00
❑87, Feb 71, DD, 1: Silver Sorceress	0.15	1.40	3.50	7.00
❑88, Mar 71, DD	0.15	1.40	3.50	7.00
❑89, May 71, DD	0.15	1.40	3.50	7.00
❑90, Jun 71, DD	0.15	1.40	3.50	7.00
❑91, Aug 71, DD, Aftershocks, Part 1	0.25	1.40	3.50	7.00
❑92, Sep 71, DD, 1: Starbreaker	0.25	1.40	3.50	7.00
❑93, Nov 71, Reprint; Giant-size	0.35	2.40	6.00	12.00
❑94, Nov 71, DD; NA, O: Sandman I (Wesley Dodds); A: Deadman; 1: Merlyn, Reprints Adventure Comics #40	0.25	8.00	20.00	40.00
❑95, Dec 71, DD, O: Doctor Fate; O: Doctor Midnight, Reprints More Fun Comics #67 and All-American Comics #25	0.25	2.40	6.00	12.00
❑96, Feb 72, DD, V: Cosmic Vampire	0.25	2.40	6.00	12.00
❑97, Mar 72, DD, O: Justice League of America	0.25	2.40	6.00	12.00
❑98, May 72, DD, A: Sargon	0.25	1.40	3.50	7.00
❑99, Jun 72, DD, A: Sargon	0.25	2.40	6.00	12.00
❑100, Aug 72, DD, Return of Seven Soldiers of Victory	0.20	2.40	6.00	12.00
❑101, Sep 72, DD, Justice League of America teams up with Justice Society of America	0.20	2.00	5.00	10.00
❑102, Oct 72, DD, D: Red Tornado, Justice League of America teams up with Justice Society of America	0.20	2.00	5.00	10.00
❑103, Dec 72, DD; DG, A: Phantom Stranger	0.20	1.20	3.00	6.00
❑104, Feb 73, DD; DG, The Shaggy Man Will Get You if You Don't Watch Out!, V: Shaggy Man; V: Hector Hammond	0.20	1.20	3.00	6.00
❑105, May 73, DD; DG, Elongated Man joins the Justice League of America	0.20	1.20	3.00	6.00
❑106, Aug 73, DD; DG, Red Tornado (new) joins the Justice League of America	0.20	1.20	3.00	6.00
❑107, Oct 73, DD; DG, 1: Earth-X; 1: Freedom Fighters; A: Justice Society of America	0.20	2.40	6.00	12.00
❑108, Dec 73, DD; DG, A: Freedom Fighters; A: Justice Society of America	0.20	1.80	4.50	9.00
❑109, Feb 74, DD; DG, Hawkman resigns from Justice League of America	0.20	1.20	3.00	6.00

	ORIG	GOOD	FINE	N-MINT
❑110, Apr 74, DD; DG, The Man Who Murdered Santa Claus; The Plight of a Nation, 100pgs.; Justice Society of America pin-up	0.50	1.20	3.00	6.00
❑111, Jun 74, DD; DG, V: Libra, 100pgs.	0.60	1.20	3.00	6.00
❑112, Aug 74, DD; DG, V: Amazo, 100pgs.	0.60	1.20	3.00	6.00
❑113, Oct 74, DD; DG, 100pgs.	0.60	1.20	3.00	6.00
❑114, Dec 74, DD; DG, The Return of Anakronus!; Crisis on Earth-Three!, V: Anakronus, 100pgs.; Return of Snapper Carr	0.60	1.20	3.00	6.00
❑115, Feb 75, DD; DG, 100pgs.	0.60	1.20	3.00	6.00
❑116, Mar 75, DD; DG, V: Matter Master, 100pgs.; Return of Hawkman	0.60	1.20	3.00	6.00
❑117, Apr 75, DD; FMc, Hawkman rejoins JLA	0.25	0.80	2.00	4.00
❑118, May 75, DD; FMc	0.25	0.80	2.00	4.00
❑119, Jun 75, DD; FMc	0.25	0.80	2.00	4.00
❑120, Jul 75, DD; FMc, V: Kanjar Ro; A: Adam Strange	0.25	0.80	2.00	4.00
❑121, Aug 75, DD; FMc	0.25	0.80	2.00	4.00
❑122, Sep 75, DD; FMc, V: Dr. Light; V: Doctor Light	0.25	0.80	2.00	4.00
❑123, Oct 75, DD; FMc, 1: Earth-Prime (named); A: Justice Society of America	0.25	0.80	2.00	4.00
❑124, Nov 75, DD; FMc, A: Justice Society of America	0.25	0.80	2.00	4.00
❑125, Dec 75, DD; FMc	0.25	0.80	2.00	4.00
❑126, Jan 76, DD; FMc, Joker	0.26	0.80	2.00	4.00
❑127, Feb 76, DD; FMc	0.25	0.80	2.00	4.00
❑128, Mar 76, DD; FMc, Wonder Woman rejoins	0.25	0.80	2.00	4.00
❑129, Apr 76, DD; FMc, D: Red Tornado (new)	0.30	0.80	2.00	4.00
❑130, May 76, DD; FMc	0.30	0.80	2.00	4.00
❑131, Jun 76, DD; FMc	0.30	0.70	1.75	3.50
❑132, Jul 76, DD; FMc, Bicentennial #6	0.30	0.70	1.75	3.50
❑133, Aug 76, DD; FMc	0.30	0.70	1.75	3.50
❑134, Sep 76, DD; FMc	0.30	0.70	1.75	3.50
❑135, Oct 76, DD; FMc, Crisis on Earth-S, 1: Earth-S (named)	0.30	0.70	1.75	3.50
❑136, Nov 76, DD; FMc, Crisis on Earth-S	0.30	0.70	1.75	3.50
❑137, Dec 76, DD; FMc, Crisis on Earth-S, A: Marvel Family, Superman vs. Captain Marvel (Golden Age)	0.30	0.70	1.75	3.50
❑138, Jan 77, DD; FMc, double-sized	0.30	0.70	1.75	3.50
❑139, Feb 77, DD; FMc, double-sized	0.50	0.70	1.75	3.50
❑140, Mar 77, DD; FMc, A: Manhunters, double-sized	0.50	0.70	1.75	3.50
❑141, Apr 77, DD; FMc, A: Manhunters, double-sized	0.50	0.70	1.75	3.50
❑142, May 77, DD; FMc, 1: The Construct, double-sized	0.50	0.70	1.75	3.50
❑143, Jun 77, DD; FMc, 1: Privateer, double-sized	0.60	0.70	1.75	3.50
❑144, Jul 77, DD; FMc, O: Justice League of America, double-sized	0.60	0.70	1.75	3.50
❑145, Aug 77, DD; FMc	0.60	0.70	1.75	3.50
❑146, Sep 77, DD; FMc	0.60	0.70	1.75	3.50
❑147, Oct 77, DD; FMc, A: Legion; V: Mordru	0.60	0.70	1.75	3.50
❑148, Nov 77, DD; FMc, A: Legion; V: Mordru	0.60	0.70	1.75	3.50
❑149, Dec 77, DD; FMc, 1: Star-Tsar	0.60	0.70	1.75	3.50
❑150, Jan 78, DD; FMc, V: Key	0.60	0.70	1.75	3.50
❑151, Feb 78, DD; FMc	0.60	0.60	1.50	3.00
❑152, Mar 78, DD; FMc	0.60	0.60	1.50	3.00
❑153, Apr 78, DD; FMc, 1: Ultraa	0.60	0.60	1.50	3.00
❑154, May 78, DD; FMc, V: Dr. Destiny; V: Doctor Destiny	0.60	0.60	1.50	3.00
❑155, Jun 78, DD; FMc	0.60	0.60	1.50	3.00
❑156, Jul 78, DD; FMc, A: Phantom Stranger	0.60	0.60	1.50	3.00
❑157, Aug 78, DD; FMc	0.60	0.60	1.50	3.00
❑158, Sep 78, DD; FMc	0.50	0.60	1.50	3.00
❑159, Oct 78, DD; FMc, JSa (w), A: Jonah Hex; A: Miss Liberty; A: Viking Prince; A: Black Pirate; A: Justice Society of America; A: Enemy Ace	0.60	0.60	1.50	3.00
❑160, Nov 78, DD; FMc, JSa (w), A: Jonah Hex; A: Miss Liberty; A: Viking Prince; A: Black Pirate; A: Justice Society of America; A: Enemy Ace	0.60	0.60	1.50	3.00
❑161, Dec 78, DD; FMc, Zatanna joins the Justice League of America	0.40	0.60	1.50	3.00
❑162, Jan 79, DD; FMc	0.40	0.60	1.50	3.00
❑163, Feb 79, DD; FMc	0.40	0.60	1.50	3.00
❑164, Mar 79, DD; FMc	0.40	0.60	1.50	3.00
❑165, Apr 79, DD; FMc	0.40	0.60	1.50	3.00
❑166, May 79, DD; FMc, V: Secret Society of Super-Villains	0.40	0.60	1.50	3.00
❑167, Jun 79, DD; FMc	0.40	0.60	1.50	3.00
❑168, Jul 79, DD; FMc, V: Secret Society of Super-Villains	0.40	0.60	1.50	3.00
❑169, Aug 79, DD; FMc	0.40	0.60	1.50	3.00
❑170, Sep 79, DD; FMc, A: Supergirl	0.40	0.60	1.50	3.00
❑171, Oct 79, DD; FMc, D: Mr. Terrific; A: Justice Society of America	0.40	0.60	1.50	3.00
❑172, Nov 79, DD; FMc, A: Justice Society of America	0.40	0.50	1.25	2.50
❑173, Dec 79, DD; FMc, A: Black Lightning	0.40	0.50	1.25	2.50
❑174, Jan 80, DD; FMc, A: Black Lightning	0.40	0.50	1.25	2.50
❑175, Feb 80, DD; FMc, V: Dr. Destiny; V: Doctor Destiny	0.40	0.50	1.25	2.50
❑176, Mar 80, DD; FMc, V: Dr. Destiny; V: Doctor Destiny	0.40	0.50	1.25	2.50
❑177, Apr 80, DD; FMc, V: Despero; A: J'onn J'onzz	0.40	0.50	1.25	2.50
❑178, May 80, DD; FMc, JSn (c), V: Despero	0.40	0.50	1.25	2.50
❑179, Jun 80, DD; FMc, JSn (c), Firestorm joins the Justice League of America	0.40	0.50	1.25	2.50
❑180, Jul 80, DD; FMc, JSn (c)	0.40	0.50	1.25	2.50
❑181, Aug 80, DD; FMc, A: Snapper Carr, Green Arrow leaves team	0.40	0.50	1.25	2.50
❑182, Sep 80, DD; FMc, DC (c), A: Felix Faust, Elongated Man back-up	0.50	0.50	1.25	2.50
❑183, Oct 80, DD; FMc, JSn (c), JSa (w), A: Mr. Miracle; A: Metron; V: Darkseid; A: Justice Society of America; V: Fiddler; V: Shade; V: Icicle; A: Orion	0.50	0.50	1.25	2.50
❑184, Nov 80, DD; FMc, GP (c), JSa (w), A: New Gods; V: Injustice Society; V: Darkseid; A: Justice Society of America	0.50	0.50	1.25	2.50
❑185, Dec 80, DD; FMc, JSn (c), JSa (w), A: New Gods; V: Injustice Society; V: Darkseid; A: Justice Society of America	0.50	0.50	1.25	2.50
❑186, Jan 81, GP; FMc, V: Shaggy Man	0.50	0.50	1.25	2.50
❑187, Feb 81, RA; DH; FMc, DG (c)	0.50	0.50	1.25	2.50
❑188, Mar 81, RA; DH; FMc, DG (c)	0.50	0.50	1.25	2.50
❑189, Apr 81, RB; FMc, BB (c), V: Starro	0.50	0.50	1.25	2.50
❑190, May 81, RB, BB (c), V: Starro	0.50	0.50	1.25	2.50
❑191, Jun 81, RB, DG (c), V: The Key; V: Amazo	0.50	0.50	1.25	2.50
❑192, Jul 81, GP, O: Red Tornado; A: T.O. Morrow	0.50	0.50	1.25	2.50
❑193, Aug 81, GP, 1: All-Star Squadron; 1: Danette Reilly	0.50	0.50	1.25	2.50
❑194, Sep 81, GP	0.50	0.50	1.25	2.50
❑195, Oct 81, GP, V: Secret Society of Super-Villains; A: Justice Society of America	0.60	0.50	1.25	2.50
❑196, Nov 81, GP, V: Secret Society of Super-Villains; A: Justice Society of America	0.60	0.50	1.25	2.50
❑197, Dec 81, GP, V: Secret Society of Super-Villains; A: Justice Society of America	0.60	0.50	1.25	2.50
❑198, Jan 82, RA; DH, DG (c), A: Jonah Hex; A: Cinnamon; A: Bat Lash; V: Lord of Time; A: Scalphunter	0.60	0.50	1.25	2.50
❑199, Feb 82, DH, GP (c), A: Jonah Hex; A: Cinnamon; A: Bat Lash; V: Lord of Time; A: Scalphunter	0.60	0.50	1.25	2.50
❑200, Mar 82, A: Snapper Carr; O: JLA, Anniversary issue; Green Arrow rejoins	1.50	0.80	2.00	4.00
❑201, Apr 82, DH, GP (c), V: Ultraa	0.60	0.40	1.00	2.00
❑202, May 82, DH, GP (c)	0.60	0.40	1.00	2.00
❑203, Jun 82, DH, GP (c), V: New Royal Flush Gang; V: Hector Hammond	0.60	0.40	1.00	2.00
❑204, Jul 82, DH, GP (c), V: New Royal Flush Gang; V: Hector Hammond	0.60	0.40	1.00	2.00
❑205, Aug 82, DH, GP (c), V: New Royal Flush Gang; V: Hector Hammond	0.60	0.40	1.00	2.00
❑206, Sep 82, RT; DH, DC (c), V: Abnegazar; V: Ghast; V: Rath	0.60	0.40	1.00	2.00
❑207, Oct 82, RT; DH, GP (c), JSa (w), V: Crime Syndicate; A: All-Star Squadron; V: Per Degaton; A: Justice Society of America, Justice Society of America, Justice League of America, and All-Star Squadron team up	0.60	0.40	1.00	2.00
❑208, Nov 82, DH, GP (c), JSa (w), The Bomb-Blast Heard 'Round the World!, V: Crime Syndicate; A: All-Star Squadron; V: Per Degaton; A: Justice Society of America, Justice Society of America, Justice League of America, and All-Star Squadron team up	0.60	0.40	1.00	2.00
❑209, Dec 82, DH, GP (c), JSa (w), Let Old Acquaintances Be Forgot, V: Crime Syndicate; A: All-Star Squadron; V: Per Degaton; A: Justice Society of America, Justice Society of America, Justice League of America, and All-Star Squadron team up	0.60	0.35	0.88	1.75
❑210, Jan 83, RB, first publication of story slated for 1977 DC tabloid	0.60	0.35	0.88	1.75
❑211, Feb 83, RB, first publication of story slated for 1977 DC tabloid	0.60	0.35	0.88	1.75

	ORIG	GOOD	FINE	N-MINT
❑212, Mar 83, RB, GP (c), concludes story slated for 1977 DC tabloid	0.60	0.35	0.88	1.75
❑213, Apr 83, RT; DH, GP (c)	0.60	0.35	0.88	1.75
❑214, May 83, RT; DH, GP (c)	0.60	0.35	0.88	1.75
❑215, Jun 83, RT; DH, GP (c)	0.60	0.35	0.88	1.75
❑216, Jul 83, DH	0.60	0.35	0.88	1.75
❑217, Aug 83, GP (c), D: Garn Daanuth	0.60	0.35	0.88	1.75
❑218, Sep 83, A: Amazo; V: Prof. Ivo	0.60	0.35	0.88	1.75
❑219, Oct 83, JSa, GP (c), JSa (w), A: Thunderbolt; A: Justice Society of America	0.60	0.35	0.88	1.75
❑220, Nov 83, JSa, GP (c), JSa (w), The Doppelganger Gambit, O: Black Canary; A: Sargon; A: Justice Society of America	0.60	0.35	0.88	1.75
❑221, Dec 83, Beasts	0.75	0.30	0.75	1.50
❑222, Jan 84	0.75	0.30	0.75	1.50
❑223, Feb 84	0.75	0.30	0.75	1.50
❑224, Mar 84, KB (w), V: Paragon	0.75	0.30	0.75	1.50
❑225, Apr 84	0.75	0.30	0.75	1.50
❑226, May 84, RA (c)	0.75	0.30	0.75	1.50
❑227, Jun 84	0.75	0.30	0.75	1.50
❑228, Jul 84, J'onn J'onzz returns	0.75	0.30	0.75	1.50
❑229, Aug 84	0.75	0.30	0.75	1.50
❑230, Sep 84	0.75	0.30	0.75	1.50
❑231, Oct 84, JSa, KB (w); JSa (w), A: Phantom Stranger; A: Supergirl; A: Justice Society of America	0.75	0.30	0.75	1.50
❑232, Nov 84, JSa, KB (w); JSa (w), V: Crime Syndicate; A: Supergirl; A: Justice Society of America	0.75	0.30	0.75	1.50
❑233, Dec 84, Rebirth, Part 1, A: Vibe, cover forms four-part poster with issues #234-236; New team begins	0.75	0.30	0.75	1.50
❑234, Jan 85, Rebirth, Part 2, A: Vixen; A: Monitor	0.75	0.30	0.75	1.50
❑235, Feb 85, Rebirth, Part 3, V: The Cadre; V: Overmaster; O: Steel	0.75	0.30	0.75	1.50
❑236, Mar 85, Rebirth, Part 4, A: Gypsy; V: The Cadre; V: Overmaster	0.75	0.30	0.75	1.50
❑237, Apr 85, V: Mad Maestro; A: The Flash; A: Superman; A: Wonder Woman	0.75	0.30	0.75	1.50
❑238, May 85, Savage Symphony, D: Anton Allegro	0.75	0.30	0.75	1.50
❑239, Jun 85, In the Shadow of the Ox, D: General Mustapha Maksai, Wonder Woman leaves Justice League	0.75	0.30	0.75	1.50
❑240, Jul 85, KB (w), The Future Ain't What it Used to Be, 1: Doctor Anomaly	0.75	0.30	0.75	1.50
❑241, Aug 85, GT, Sea Change, V: Amazo	0.75	0.30	0.75	1.50
❑242, Sep 85, GT, Battle Cry; Assault on Mount Mayhem, V: Amazo	0.75	0.30	0.75	1.50
❑243, Oct 85, GT, Storm Cloud, V: Amazo, Aquaman leaves the Justice League of America	0.75	0.30	0.75	1.50
❑244, Nov 85, JSa, JSa (w), Crisis on Infinite Earths, A: Infinity, Inc.; A: Justice Society of America, Crisis; Steel vs. Steel	0.75	0.30	0.75	1.50
❑245, Dec 85, LMc, Crisis on Infinite Earths, A: Lord of Time, Crisis; Steel in future	0.75	0.30	0.75	1.50
❑246, Jan 86, LMc, Be It Ever So Humble..., evicted from HQ	0.75	0.30	0.75	1.50
❑247, Feb 86, LMc, ...There's No Place Like Home, back to Happy Harbor	0.75	0.30	0.75	1.50
❑248, Mar 86, LMc, Interweavings, J'onn J'onzz solo story	0.75	0.30	0.75	1.50
❑249, Apr 86, LMc, All Fall Down	0.75	0.30	0.75	1.50
❑250, May 86, LMc, The Return of the Justice League of America, A: original JLA, Giant-size; Batman rejoins Justice League of America	1.25	0.30	0.75	1.50
❑251, Jun 86, LMc, Hunters and Prey, V: Despero	0.75	0.30	0.75	1.50
❑252, Jul 86, LMc, Arrival, V: Despero	0.75	0.30	0.75	1.50
❑253, Aug 86, LMc, Pyre, O: Despero	0.75	0.30	0.75	1.50
❑254, Sep 86, LMc, JO (w), Desperate Climax; Secret of the Temple, V: Despero, Mask preview	0.75	0.30	0.75	1.50
❑255, Oct 86, LMc, Rising, O: Gypsy	0.75	0.30	0.75	1.50
❑256, Nov 86, LMc, Back to Godhead	0.75	0.30	0.75	1.50
❑257, Dec 86, LMc, Coming Down, Zatanna leaves Justice League	0.75	0.30	0.75	1.50
❑258, Jan 87, LMc, Legends, Part 5; The End of the Justice League of America, Part 1, D: Vibe, Legends	0.75	0.30	0.75	1.50
❑259, Feb 87, LMc, Legends, Part 9; The End of the Justice League of America, Part 2, Legends; Gypsy leaves team	0.75	0.30	0.75	1.50
❑260, Mar 87, LMc, Legends, Part 14; The End of the Justice League of America, Part 3, D: Steel, Legends	0.75	0.30	0.75	1.50
❑261, Apr 87, LMc, Legends, Part 21; The End of the Justice League of America, Part 4, Final Issue; group disbands	0.75	0.80	2.00	4.00

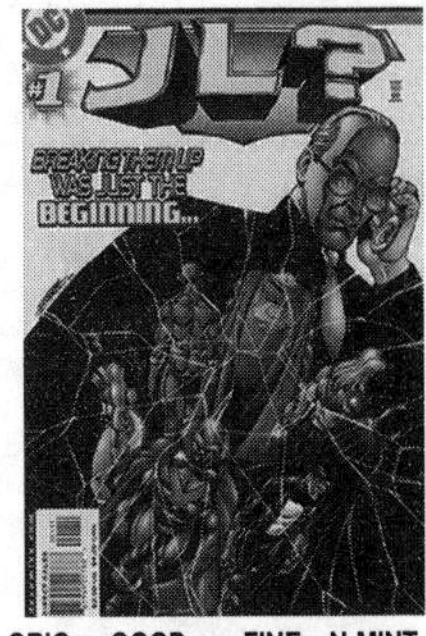

As preparation for an impending alien invasion, the JLA's members were stripped of their knowledge of their team and individually formed other Justice League of ... teams as part of DC's "Justice Leagues" event.

	ORIG	GOOD	FINE	N-MINT
❑Anl 1, Oct 83, A: Sandman; A: John Stewart; V: Dr. Destiny; V: Doctor Destiny; A: John Stewart, Sandman	1.00	0.90	2.25	4.50
❑Anl 2, Oct 84, 1: New JLA (Vixen, Vibe, Gypsy, Steel); 1: Gypsy	1.25	0.70	1.75	3.50
❑Anl 3, Nov 85, Crisis on Infinite Earths, 1: Red Tornado (in current form), Crisis	1.25	0.70	1.75	3.50

JUSTICE LEAGUE OF AMERICA INDEX
Eclipse

Value: Cover or less

❑1, Apr 86 ... 1.50
❑2, Apr 86 ... 1.50
❑3, May 86 ... 1.50
❑4, May 86 ... 1.50
❑5, Oct 86 ... 2.00
❑6, Nov 86 ... 2.00
❑7, Jan 87 ... 2.00
❑8, Title changes to Justice League of America Index ... 2.00

JUSTICE LEAGUE OF AMERICA SUPER SPECTACULAR
DC

Value: Cover or less

❑1, 100pgs.; Reprint ... 5.95

JUSTICE LEAGUE QUARTERLY
DC

Value: Cover or less

❑1, Win 90, KG (w), Corporate Maneuvers, 1: The Conglomerate ... 2.95
❑2, Spr 91, V: Mr. Nebula ... 2.95
❑3, Jun 91, cover says Sum, indicia says Jun ... 2.95
❑4, Fal 91, cover says Aut, indicia says Fal ... 2.95
❑5, Win 91, A: Global Guardians ... 2.95
❑6, Spr 92, A: Global Guardians ... 2.95
❑7, Sum 92, A: Global Guardians ... 3.50
❑8, Sum 92, cover says Aut, indicia says Sum; new Conglomerate ... 3.50
❑9, Win 92 ... 3.50
❑10, Spr 93 ... 3.50
❑11, Sum 93 ... 3.50
❑12, Sum 93, covers says Aut, indicia says Sum; Conglomerate 3.50
❑13, Aut 93, cover says Win, indicia says Aut ... 3.50
❑14, Spr 94, A: Captain Atom; A: Blue Beetle; A: Thunderbolt; A: Nightshade ... 3.50
❑15, Jun 94, A: Praxis, cover says Sum, indicia says Jun ... 3.50
❑16, Sep 94, A: General Glory 3.50
❑17, Win 94, Final Issue ... 3.50

JUSTICE LEAGUES: JL?
DC

Value: Cover or less

❑1, Mar 01, Justice Leagues, Part 1 ... 2.50

JUSTICE LEAGUES: JLA
DC

Value: Cover or less

❑1, Mar 01, Justice Leagues, Part 6 ... 2.50

JUSTICE LEAGUES: JUSTICE LEAGUE OF ALIENS
DC

Value: Cover or less

❑1, Mar 01, Justice Leagues, Part 5 ... 2.50

JUSTICE LEAGUES: JUSTICE LEAGUE OF AMAZONS
DC

Value: Cover or less

❑1, Mar 01, Justice Leagues, Part 2 ... 2.50

JUSTICE LEAGUES:JUSTICE LEAGUE OF ARKHAM
DC

Value: Cover or less

❑1, Mar 01, Justice Leagues, Part 4 ... 2.50

JUSTICE LEAGUES: JUSTICE LEAGUE OF ATLANTIS
DC

Value: Cover or less

❑1, Mar 01, Justice Leagues, Part 3 ... 2.50

JUSTICE LEAGUE TASK FORCE
DC

	ORIG	GOOD	FINE	N-MINT
❑0, Oct 94, MWa (w), The Gathering, A: Triumph	1.50	0.35	0.88	1.75
❑1, Jun 93, The Tyranny Gun!, membership card; membership card	1.25	0.40	1.00	2.00
❑2, Jul 93	1.25	0.30	0.75	1.50
❑3, Aug 93	1.25	0.30	0.75	1.50
❑4, Sep 93	1.25	0.30	0.75	1.50
❑5, Oct 93, KnightQuest: The Search	1.25	0.30	0.75	1.50
❑6, Nov 93, KnightQuest: The Search	1.25	0.25	0.63	1.25
❑7, Dec 93, transsexual J'onn J'onzz	1.25	0.30	0.75	1.50

	ORIG	GOOD	FINE	N-MINT
❑8, Jan 94, PD (w), How Green was my Daalie, transsexual J'onn J'onzz	1.50	0.30	0.75	1.50
❑9, Feb 94, JPH (w), Saturday Night's All Right for Fightin'!, A: New Bloods	1.50	0.30	0.75	1.50
❑10, Mar 94, Purification Plague, Part 1, V: Aryan Brigade	1.50	0.30	0.75	1.50
❑11, Apr 94, V: Aryan Brigade	1.50	0.30	0.75	1.50
❑12, May 94	1.50	0.30	0.75	1.50
❑13, Jun 94, MWa (w), Judgment Day; Judgment Day, Part 2	1.50	0.30	0.75	1.50
❑14, Jul 94, Judgment Day	1.50	0.30	0.75	1.50
❑15, Aug 94, Aftershocks, Part 2	1.50	0.30	0.75	1.50
❑16, Sep 94, A: Triumph, Zero Hour	1.50	0.30	0.75	1.50
❑17, Nov 94, Savage Legacy, Part 1	1.50	0.30	0.75	1.50
❑18, Dec 94, Savage Legacy, Part 2	1.50	0.30	0.75	1.50
❑19, Jan 95, Savage Legacy, Part 3, V: Vandal Savage	1.50	0.30	0.75	1.50
❑20, Feb 95	1.50	0.30	0.75	1.50
❑21, Mar 95	1.50	0.30	0.75	1.50
❑22, Apr 95	1.50	0.30	0.75	1.50
❑23, May 95	1.50	0.30	0.75	1.50
❑24, Jun 95	1.75	0.35	0.88	1.75
❑25, Jul 95	1.75	0.35	0.88	1.75
❑26, Aug 95	1.75	0.35	0.88	1.75
❑27, Sep 95	1.75	0.35	0.88	1.75
❑28, Oct 95	1.75	0.35	0.88	1.75
❑29, Nov 95	1.75	0.35	0.88	1.75
❑30, Dec 95, Underworld Unleashed	1.75	0.35	0.88	1.75
❑31, Jan 96, The Accused	1.75	0.35	0.88	1.75
❑32, Feb 96, The Ninth Hour	1.75	0.35	0.88	1.75
❑33, Mar 96, The Stand	1.75	0.35	0.88	1.75
❑34, May 96	1.75	0.35	0.88	1.75
❑35, Jun 96, A: Warlord	1.75	0.35	0.88	1.75
❑36, Jul 96	1.75	0.35	0.88	1.75
❑37, Aug 96, Final Issue	1.75	0.35	0.88	1.75

JUSTICE MACHINE (COMICO)
COMICO

	ORIG	GOOD	FINE	N-MINT
❑1, Jan 87, MGu, Heroes And Villains	1.50	0.50	1.25	2.50
❑2, Feb 87, MGu	1.50	0.40	1.00	2.00
❑3, Mar 87, MGu	1.50	0.35	0.88	1.75
❑4, Apr 87, MGu	1.50	0.35	0.88	1.75
❑5, May 87, MGu	1.50	0.35	0.88	1.75
❑6, Jun 87, MGu	1.50	0.35	0.88	1.75
❑7, Jul 87, MGu	1.50	0.35	0.88	1.75
❑8, Aug 87, MGu, D: Demon	1.50	0.35	0.88	1.75
❑9, Sep 87, MGu	1.50	0.35	0.88	1.75
❑10, Oct 87, MGu	1.50	0.35	0.88	1.75
❑11, Nov 87, MGu	1.50	0.35	0.88	1.75
❑12, Dec 87, MGu	1.50	0.35	0.88	1.75
❑13, Jan 88, MGu	1.50	0.35	0.88	1.75
❑14, Feb 88, MGu	1.50	0.35	0.88	1.75
❑15, Mar 88	1.75	0.35	0.88	1.75
❑16, Apr 88	1.75	0.35	0.88	1.75
❑17, May 88	1.75	0.35	0.88	1.75
❑18, Jun 88	1.75	0.35	0.88	1.75
❑19, Jul 88	1.75	0.35	0.88	1.75
❑20, Aug 88	1.75	0.35	0.88	1.75
❑21, Sep 88	1.75	0.35	0.88	1.75
❑22, Oct 88	1.75	0.35	0.88	1.75
❑23, Nov 88	1.75	0.35	0.88	1.75
❑24, Dec 88	1.75	0.35	0.88	1.75
❑25, Jan 89	1.75	0.35	0.88	1.75
❑26, Feb 89	1.95	0.35	0.88	1.75
❑27, Mar 89	1.95	0.35	0.88	1.75
❑28, Apr 89	1.95	0.39	0.98	1.95
❑29, May 89, Final Issue	1.95	0.39	0.98	1.95
❑Anl 1, Jun 89, A: Elementals	2.50	0.55	1.38	2.75

JUSTICE MACHINE, THE (INNOVATION)
INNOVATION

Value: Cover or less

❑1, Apr 90, Burn While You Learn ... 1.95
❑2, May 90 ... 1.95
❑3, Jul 90 ... 1.95
❑4, Sep 90 ... 1.95
❑5, Nov 90 ... 1.95
❑6, Jan 91 ... 2.25
❑7, Apr 91 ... 2.25

JUSTICE MACHINE, THE (MILLENNIUM)
MILLENNIUM

Value: Cover or less

❑1, The Chimera Conspiracy, Part 1; The Justice Machine: Year One, O: The Justice Machine ... 2.50
❑2, The Chimera Conspiracy, Part 2; The Justice Machine: Year Two ... 2.50

JUSTICE MACHINE (NOBLE)
NOBLE

	ORIG	GOOD	FINE	N-MINT
❑1, MGu, JBy (c)	—	0.50	1.25	2.50
❑2, MGu, TD (c)	—	0.50	1.25	2.50
❑3, Jun 81, MGu	—	0.50	1.25	2.50
❑4, MGu	—	0.50	1.25	2.50
❑5, Nov 83, MGu	—	0.50	1.25	2.50
❑Anl 1, Jan 84, 1: Elementals, THUNDER Agents	—	1.00	2.50	5.00

JUSTICE MACHINE FEATURING THE ELEMENTALS
COMICO

Value: Cover or less

❑1, May 86, MGu, The Darkforce Affair ... 2.00
❑2, Jun 86 ... 2.00
❑3, Jul 86 ... 2.00
❑4, Aug 86 ... 2.00

JUSTICE MACHINE SUMMER SPECTACULAR, THE
INNOVATION

Value: Cover or less

❑1, Machine Musings ... 2.75

JUSTICE RIDERS
DC

Value: Cover or less

❑1, nn; prestige format; Elseworlds; Justice League in old West ... 5.95

JUSTICE SOCIETY OF AMERICA
DC

	ORIG	GOOD	FINE	N-MINT
❑1, Aug 92, Home Again!	1.25	0.30	0.75	1.50
❑2, Sep 92, The Sack Of Gotham	1.25	0.30	0.75	1.50
❑3, Oct 92, Out Of The Past, V: Ultra-Humanite	1.25	0.30	0.75	1.50
❑4, Nov 92, V: Ultra-Humanite	1.25	0.30	0.75	1.50
❑5, Dec 92	1.25	0.30	0.75	1.50
❑6, Jan 93, Give Me Liberty...	1.25	0.25	0.63	1.25
❑7, Feb 93, in Bahdnesia	1.25	0.25	0.63	1.25
❑8, Mar 93	1.25	0.25	0.63	1.25
❑9, Apr 93, Alan Scott vs. Guy Gardner	1.25	0.25	0.63	1.25
❑10, May 93, Final Issue	1.25	0.25	0.63	1.25

JUSTICE SOCIETY OF AMERICA (MINI-SERIES)
DC

	ORIG	GOOD	FINE	N-MINT
❑1, Apr 91, Beware The Savage Skies!, Flash	1.00	0.40	1.00	2.00
❑2, May 91, Black Canary	1.00	0.35	0.88	1.75
❑3, Jun 91, Green Lantern	1.00	0.35	0.88	1.75
❑4, Jul 91, Hawkman	1.00	0.30	0.75	1.50
❑5, Aug 91, Flash, Hawkman	1.00	0.30	0.75	1.50
❑6, Sep 91, Green Lantern, Black Canary	1.00	0.30	0.75	1.50
❑7, Oct 91, Green Lantern, Black Canary, Hawkman, Flash, Starman	1.00	0.30	0.75	1.50
❑8, Nov 91, Green Lantern, Black Canary, Hawkman, Flash, Starman	1.00	0.30	0.75	1.50

JUSTICE SOCIETY OF AMERICA 100-PAGE SUPER SPECTACULAR
DC

Value: Cover or less

❑1, Vengeance of the Immortal Villain; The Big Super-Hero Hunt, 2000 facsimile of 1975 100-Page Super Spectacular; reprints The Flash #137 and #201, All Star Comics #57, The Brave and the Bold #62, and Adventure Comics #418 ... 6.95

JUST IMAGINE COMICS AND STORIES
JUST IMAGINE

	ORIG	GOOD	FINE	N-MINT
❑1	—	0.40	1.00	2.00
❑2	—	0.40	1.00	2.00
❑3	—	0.40	1.00	2.00
❑4	—	0.40	1.00	2.00
❑5	—	0.40	1.00	2.00
❑6	—	0.40	1.00	2.00
❑7	—	0.40	1.00	2.00
❑8	—	0.40	1.00	2.00
❑9, The Bunny of Death in SpaceFear; Tit Mouse	1.50	0.40	1.00	2.00
❑10	—	0.40	1.00	2.00
❑11	—	0.40	1.00	2.00
❑SE 1, gophers	—	0.40	1.00	2.00

JUST TWISTED
NECROMICS

Value: Cover or less

❑1 ... 2.00

JUSTY
VIZ

Value: Cover or less

❑1, Dec 88, The Tears of Astalis Part 1, b&w; Japanese ... 1.75
❑2, Dec 88, The Tears of Astalis Part 2, b&w; Japanese ... 1.75
❑3, b&w; Japanese ... 1.75
❑4, Jan 89, Hostages Part 1, b&w; Japanese ... 1.75
❑5, b&w; Japanese ... 1.75
❑6, b&w; Japanese ... 1.75
❑7, Mar 89, b&w; Japanese ... 1.75
❑8, b&w; Japanese ... 1.75
❑9, b&w; Japanese ... 1.75

K

KABOOM
AWESOME

	ORIG	GOOD	FINE	N-MINT
❑1, Sep 97, JPH (w), Sixteen Candles, 1: Kaboom	2.50	0.60	1.50	3.00
❑1/A, Sep 97, JPH (w), Sixteen Candles, Dynamic Forces variant (marked as such); Purple Awesome logo	—	0.60	1.50	3.00
❑1/GO, Sep 97, JPH (w), Sixteen Candles, 1: Kaboom, Gold edition with silver logo	—	0.80	2.00	4.00
❑2, JPH (w)	2.50	0.50	1.25	2.50
❑2/Aut, JPH (w), Signed by Jeff Matsuda	—	0.80	2.00	4.00
❑2/GO, JPH (w), Gold edition	—	0.80	2.00	4.00
❑3, JPH (w)	2.50	0.50	1.25	2.50
❑4, JPH (w)	2.50	0.50	1.25	2.50
❑5, JPH (w)	2.50	0.50	1.25	2.50
❑Ash 1, JPH (w), Preview edition	—	0.50	1.25	2.50
❑Ash 1/GO, JPH (w), Preview edition; Gold edition	—	0.80	2.00	4.00

KABUKI
IMAGE

	ORIG	GOOD	FINE	N-MINT
❑0.5, Speckle-foil Wizard variant	—	0.80	2.00	4.00
❑1, Oct 97, Separate Pieces, O: Kabuki	2.95	0.80	2.00	4.00
❑1/A, Oct 97, Separate Pieces, O: Kabuki, Jim Steranko alternate cover	2.95	1.00	2.50	5.00
❑2, Dec 97, Invisible Friends	2.95	0.70	1.75	3.50
❑3, Mar 98, Retina Escape	2.95	0.70	1.75	3.50
❑4, Jun 98, Deconstructing Akemi	2.95	0.60	1.50	3.00
❑5, Sep 98, Deeper	2.95	0.59	1.48	2.95
❑6, Nov 98	2.95	0.59	1.48	2.95
❑7, Feb 99	2.95	0.59	1.48	2.95
❑8, Jun 99	2.95	0.59	1.48	2.95
❑9, Mar 00	2.95	0.59	1.48	2.95

KABUKI AGENTS
IMAGE

Value: Cover or less

- ❑1, Aug 99, Synchronicity, Scarab 2.95
- ❑1/A, Aug 99, Scarab alternate cover 2.95
- ❑2, Oct 99, Chaos by Design, Scarab 2.95
- ❑3, Nov 99, Voodoo Doll, Scarab 2.95
- ❑4, Scarab 2.95
- ❑5, Nov 00, Tale Twp, Scarab 2.95
- ❑6, Jan 01, Scarab 2.95
- ❑7, Mar 01, Lost in Translation, Scarab 2.95
- ❑8, Scarab 2.95

KABUKI: CIRCLE OF BLOOD
CALIBER

Value: Cover or less

- ❑1, Jan 95, Ghosts In the Looking Glass, O: Kabuki, b&w 2.95
- ❑1/LE, Ghosts In the Looking Glass, O: Kabuki, Limited edition with new, painted cover 15.00
- ❑1-2, Jul 95, b&w; 2nd Printing; enhanced cover 2.95
- ❑2, Mar 95, b&w 2.95
- ❑3, May 95, b&w; reprints #1's indicia 2.95
- ❑4, Jul 95, b&w 2.95
- ❑5, Sep 95, b&w 2.95
- ❑6, Nov 95, b&w 2.95
- ❑6/LE 15.00

KABUKI CLASSICS
IMAGE

Value: Cover or less

- ❑1, Feb 99, Fear the Reaper, Squarebound; Reprints Kabuki: Fear the Reaper 3.25
- ❑2, Mar 99, Dance of Death, Reprints Kabuki: Dance of Death 3.25
- ❑3, Mar 99, Circle of Blood, Part 1, Squarebound 4.95
- ❑4, Apr 99, Circle of Blood, Part 2 3.25
- ❑5, Jul 99, Circle of Blood, Part 3 3.25
- ❑6, Jul 99, Circle of Blood, Part 4 3.25
- ❑7, Aug 99, Circle of Blood, Part 5 3.25
- ❑8, Sep 99, Circle of Blood, Part 6 3.25
- ❑9, Oct 99, Masks of the Noh, Part 1 3.25
- ❑10, Nov 99, Masks of the Noh, Part 2 3.25
- ❑11, Dec 99, Masks of the Noh, Part 3 3.25
- ❑12, Mar 00, Masks of the Noh, Part 4 3.25

KABUKI COLOR SPECIAL
CALIBER

	ORIG	GOOD	FINE	N-MINT
❑1, Jan 96	2.95	0.70	1.75	3.50

KABUKI: DANCE OF DEATH
LONDON NIGHT

	ORIG	GOOD	FINE	N-MINT
❑1	3.00	0.70	1.75	3.50

KABUKI DREAMS
IMAGE

	ORIG	GOOD	FINE	N-MINT
❑1, Jan 98, nn; b&w; reprints Kabuki Color Special and Kabuki: Dreams of the Dead	4.95	1.00	2.50	5.00

KABUKI: DREAMS OF THE DEAD
CALIBER

Value: Cover or less

- ❑1, Jul 96, nn; One-Shot 2.95

KABUKI: FEAR THE REAPER
CALIBER

Value: Cover or less

- ❑1 3.50

A descendant of OMAC emerged from a bunker after a worldwide catastrophe, dubbed The Great Disaster, to find a world run by animals where humans were kept as pets in *Kamandi, The Last Boy on Earth.*

© 1972 National Periodical Publications (DC)

KABUKI GALLERY
CALIBER

Value: Cover or less

- ❑1, Aug 95, pin-ups 2.95
- ❑1/A, Aug 95, Comic Cavalcade edition 15.00

KABUKI-IMAGES
IMAGE

Value: Cover or less

- ❑1, Jul 98, prestige format; pin-ups and story; Reprints Kabuki (Image) #1 with new pin-ups 4.95
- ❑2, Jan 99, prestige format; collects #2 and 3; Reprints Kabuki (Image) #2-3 5.95

KABUKI: MASKS OF THE NOH
IMAGE

Value: Cover or less

- ❑1 2.95
- ❑2 2.95
- ❑3 2.95
- ❑4 2.95

KABUKI REFLECTIONS
IMAGE

Value: Cover or less

- ❑1, Jul 98, no number on cover or in indicia; prestige format 4.95
- ❑2, Dec 98, prestige format 4.95
- ❑3, Jan 00 4.95

KABUKI: SKIN DEEP
CALIBER

	ORIG	GOOD	FINE	N-MINT
❑1, Oct 96	2.95	0.70	1.75	3.50
❑2, Feb 97	2.95	0.60	1.50	3.00
❑2/A, Feb 97, Alternate cover by Alex Ross; white background	2.95	0.60	1.50	3.00
❑2/LE, Wraparound cover by David Mack and Alex Ross	15.00	2.40	6.00	12.00
❑3, May 97	2.95	0.59	1.48	2.95

KAFKA
RENEGADE

	ORIG	GOOD	FINE	N-MINT
❑1, Apr 87, b&w	2.00	0.60	1.50	3.00
❑2, May 87, b&w	2.00	0.50	1.25	2.50
❑3, Jun 87, b&w	2.00	0.50	1.25	2.50
❑4, Jul 87, b&w	2.00	0.50	1.25	2.50
❑5, Aug 87, b&w	2.00	0.50	1.25	2.50
❑6, Sep 87, b&w	2.00	0.50	1.25	2.50

KAFKA: THE EXECUTION
FANTAGRAPHICS

Value: Cover or less

- ❑1, b&w; Duranona 2.95

KAKTUS
FANTAGRAPHICS

Value: Cover or less

- ❑1, b&w 2.50

KALAMAZOO COMIX
DISCOUNT HOBBY

Value: Cover or less

- ❑1 1.95
- ❑2, Win 96 1.95
- ❑3, Win 96 1.95
- ❑4, Spr 97 2.95
- ❑5, Dec 97, Blind; Mystery At The Center of The Earth 2.95

KALGAN THE GOLDEN
HARRIER

Value: Cover or less

- ❑1, Mar 88 1.95

KAMANDI: AT EARTH'S END
DC

Value: Cover or less

- ❑1, Jun 93, Dead York City 1.75
- ❑2, Jul 93 1.75
- ❑3, Aug 93, Thunder Road! 1.75
- ❑4, Sep 93 1.75
- ❑5, Oct 93 1.75
- ❑6, Nov 93 1.75

KAMANDI, THE LAST BOY ON EARTH
DC

	ORIG	GOOD	FINE	N-MINT
❑1, Nov 72, JK, JK (w), The Last Boy on Earth!, 1: Ben Boxer; 1: Dr. Canus, Ben Boxer; 1: Dr. Canus; 1: Kamandi	0.20	3.60	9.00	18.00
❑2, Jan 73, JK, JK (w)	0.20	2.00	5.00	10.00
❑3, Feb 73, JK, JK (w), in Vegas	0.20	1.60	4.00	8.00
❑4, Mar 73, JK, JK (w), 1: Prince Tuftan	0.20	1.20	3.00	6.00
❑5, Apr 73, JK, JK (w)	0.20	1.20	3.00	6.00
❑6, Jun 73, JK, JK (w)	0.20	1.00	2.50	5.00
❑7, Jul 73, JK, JK (w)	0.20	1.00	2.50	5.00
❑8, Aug 73, JK, JK (w), Return of Ben Boxer; in Washington, D.C.	0.20	1.00	2.50	5.00
❑9, Sep 73, JK, JK (w)	0.20	1.00	2.50	5.00
❑10, Oct 73, JK, JK (w)	0.20	1.00	2.50	5.00
❑11, Nov 73, JK, JK (w)	0.20	0.70	1.75	3.50

	ORIG	GOOD	FINE	N-MINT
❑12, Dec 73, JK, JK (w)	0.20	0.70	1.75	3.50
❑13, Jan 74, JK, JK (w)	0.20	0.70	1.75	3.50
❑14, Feb 74, JK, JK (w)	0.20	0.70	1.75	3.50
❑15, Mar 74, JK, JK (w)	0.20	0.70	1.75	3.50
❑16, Apr 74, JK, JK (w)	0.20	0.70	1.75	3.50
❑17, May 74, JK, JK (w)	0.20	0.70	1.75	3.50
❑18, Jun 74, JK, JK (w)	0.20	0.70	1.75	3.50
❑19, Jul 74, JK, JK (w), in Chicago	0.20	0.70	1.75	3.50
❑20, Aug 74, JK, JK (w), in Chicago	0.20	0.70	1.75	3.50
❑21, Sep 74, JK, JK (w)	0.20	0.60	1.50	3.00
❑22, Oct 74, JK, JK (w)	0.20	0.60	1.50	3.00
❑23, Nov 74, JK, JK (w)	0.20	0.60	1.50	3.00
❑24, Dec 74, JK, JK (w)	0.20	0.60	1.50	3.00
❑25, Jan 75, JK, JK (w)	0.25	0.60	1.50	3.00
❑26, Feb 75, JK, JK (w)	0.25	0.60	1.50	3.00
❑27, Mar 75, JK, JK (w)	0.25	0.60	1.50	3.00
❑28, Apr 75, JK, JK (w)	0.25	0.60	1.50	3.00
❑29, May 75, JK, JK (w), Superman's legend	0.25	0.60	1.50	3.00
❑30, Jun 75, JK, JK (w), 1: Pyra	0.25	0.60	1.50	3.00
❑31, Jul 75, JK, JK (w)	0.25	0.60	1.50	3.00
❑32, Aug 75, JK, JK (w), O: Kamandi, giant; Jack Kirby interview	0.50	0.60	1.50	3.00
❑33, Sep 75, JK, JK (w)	0.25	0.60	1.50	3.00
❑34, Oct 75, JK, JKu (c), JK (w)	0.25	0.60	1.50	3.00
❑35, Nov 75, JK, JKu (c), JK (w)	0.25	0.60	1.50	3.00
❑36, Dec 75, JK, JKu (c), JK (w)	0.25	0.60	1.50	3.00
❑37, Jan 76, JK, JKu (c), JK (w)	0.25	0.60	1.50	3.00
❑38, Feb 76, JK, JKu (c), JK (w)	0.25	0.60	1.50	3.00
❑39, Mar 76, JK, JKu (c), JK (w)	0.25	0.60	1.50	3.00
❑40, Apr 76, JK, JKu (c), JK (w)	0.30	0.60	1.50	3.00
❑41, May 76, JKu (c)	0.30	0.40	1.00	2.00
❑42, Jun 76	0.30	0.40	1.00	2.00
❑43, Jul 76, Bicentennial #4	0.30	0.40	1.00	2.00
❑44, Aug 76	0.30	0.40	1.00	2.00
❑45, Sep 76	0.30	0.40	1.00	2.00
❑46, Oct 76	0.30	0.40	1.00	2.00
❑47, Nov 76	0.30	0.40	1.00	2.00
❑48, Jan 77	0.30	0.40	1.00	2.00
❑49, Mar 77	0.30	0.40	1.00	2.00
❑50, May 77, Kamandi reverts to OMAC	0.30	0.40	1.00	2.00
❑51, Jul 77	0.35	0.40	1.00	2.00
❑52, Sep 77	0.35	0.40	1.00	2.00
❑53, Nov 77	0.35	0.40	1.00	2.00
❑54, Jan 78	0.35	0.40	1.00	2.00
❑55, Mar 78, V: Vortex Beast	0.35	0.40	1.00	2.00
❑56, May 78	0.35	0.40	1.00	2.00
❑57, Jul 78	0.35	0.40	1.00	2.00
❑58, Sep 78, A: Karate Kid	0.35	0.40	1.00	2.00
❑59, Oct 78, Final Issue; OMAC back-up begins; continues in Warlord #37	0.50	0.60	1.50	3.00

KAMA SUTRA (GIRL'S...)
BLACK LACE

Value: Cover or less

❑1 ... 2.95

KAMIKAZE CAT
PIED PIPER

Value: Cover or less

❑1, Jul 87, The Web of Cat-tastrophe?! ... 1.95

KANE
DANCING ELEPHANT

	ORIG	GOOD	FINE	N-MINT
❑1, Living in Eden	3.50	1.00	2.50	5.00
❑2	3.50	0.80	2.00	4.00
❑3	3.50	0.80	2.00	4.00
❑4	3.50	0.70	1.75	3.50
❑5	3.50	0.70	1.75	3.50
❑6	3.50	0.70	1.75	3.50
❑7	3.50	0.70	1.75	3.50
❑8	3.50	0.70	1.75	3.50
❑9	1.80	0.70	1.75	3.50
❑10	—	0.70	1.75	3.50
❑11	—	0.70	1.75	3.50
❑12	—	0.70	1.75	3.50
❑13	—	0.70	1.75	3.50
❑14	—	0.70	1.75	3.50
❑15	—	0.70	1.75	3.50
❑16	—	0.70	1.75	3.50
❑17	—	0.70	1.75	3.50
❑18	—	0.70	1.75	3.50
❑19	—	0.70	1.75	3.50
❑20	—	0.70	1.75	3.50
❑21	—	0.70	1.75	3.50
❑22	—	0.70	1.75	3.50
❑23	2.95	0.59	1.48	2.95
❑24	2.95	0.59	1.48	2.95
❑25	2.95	0.59	1.48	2.95
❑26	2.95	0.59	1.48	2.95
❑27	2.95	0.59	1.48	2.95
❑28	2.95	0.59	1.48	2.95
❑29	2.95	0.59	1.48	2.95
❑30	2.95	0.59	1.48	2.95
❑31	2.95	0.59	1.48	2.95
❑32	2.95	0.59	1.48	2.95

KANSAS THUNDER
RED MENACE

Value: Cover or less

❑1, Charm; The Romantiks, b&w ... 2.95

KAOS
TOMMY REGALADO

Value: Cover or less

❑1, Aug 94, b&w ... 2.00

KAOS MOON
CALIBER

Value: Cover or less

❑1, Full Circle Part 1 ... 2.95
❑2, Full Circle Part 2 ... 2.95
❑3 ... 2.95
❑4 ... 2.95

KAPPA EDIZIONI
KAPPA

	ORIG	GOOD	FINE	N-MINT
❑1, Piera Degli Spiriti; Animali, no cover price	—	0.40	1.00	2.00

KAPTAIN KEEN & KOMPANY
VORTEX

Value: Cover or less

❑1, Dec 86, Super Swine; Codzilla ... 1.75
❑2 ... 1.75
❑3 ... 1.75
❑4 ... 1.75
❑5 ... 1.75
❑6, Feb 88 ... 1.75

KARATE GIRL
FANTAGRAPHICS

Value: Cover or less

❑1, b&w; adult ... 2.50
❑2, b&w; adult ... 2.50

KARATE GIRL TENGU WARS
EROS

Value: Cover or less

❑1 ... 2.95
❑2 ... 2.95
❑3, Jun 95 ... 2.95

KARATE KID
DC

	ORIG	GOOD	FINE	N-MINT
❑1, Apr 76, RE; JSa, My World Begins in Yesterday	0.25	0.80	2.00	4.00
❑2, Jun 76	0.30	0.50	1.25	2.50
❑3, Aug 76	0.30	0.50	1.25	2.50
❑4, Oct 76	0.30	0.40	1.00	2.00
❑5, Dec 76	0.30	0.40	1.00	2.00
❑6, Feb 77	0.30	0.40	1.00	2.00
❑7, Apr 77, MGr	0.30	0.40	1.00	2.00
❑8, Jun 77, RE; JSa; MGr, Pandemonium...Panic...Pulsar!	0.30	0.40	1.00	2.00
❑9, Aug 77	0.35	0.40	1.00	2.00
❑10, Oct 77	0.35	0.40	1.00	2.00
❑11, Dec 77	0.35	0.40	1.00	2.00
❑12, Feb 78	0.35	0.40	1.00	2.00
❑13, Apr 78, Tomorrow's Battle...Yesterday	0.35	0.40	1.00	2.00
❑14, Jun 78	0.35	0.40	1.00	2.00
❑15, Aug 78, Final Issue	0.35	0.40	1.00	2.00

KARATE KREATURES
MA

Value: Cover or less

❑1, full color ... 2.00
❑2, full color ... 2.00

KATMANDU
ANTARCTIC

Value: Cover or less

❑1, Nov 93, b&w; adult ... 2.75
❑2, Jan 94, b&w; adult ... 2.95
❑3, Apr 94, b&w; adult ... 2.95
❑4, Mar 95, Woman of Honor Part 1, b&w; adult ... 2.75
❑5, May 95, Woman of Honor Part 2, b&w; adult ... 2.75
❑8, Jul 96, adult ... 1.95
❑9, Jul 96, adult ... 1.95
❑10, Jul 96, adult ... 1.95
❑11, Jul 96, adult ... 1.95
❑12, Jul 96, adult ... 1.95
❑13, Sep 97, b&w; adult ... 2.95
❑16, Apr 99, b&w; adult ... 2.95

KATO OF THE GREEN HORNET
NOW

Value: Cover or less

❑1, Nov 91, BA, Journey Of A Thousand Miles ... 2.50
❑2, Dec 91 ... 2.50
❑3 ... 2.50
❑4, Demon Sword ... 2.50

KATO OF THE GREEN HORNET II
NOW

Value: Cover or less

❑1, Nov 92, VM, Bad Boy ... 2.50
❑2, Dec 92 ... 2.50

KA-ZAR (1ST SERIES)
MARVEL

	ORIG	GOOD	FINE	N-MINT
❑1, Aug 70, JK; GC, SL (w), The Coming of...Ka-Zar; In His Footsteps...The Huntsman of Zeus!!, 1: Zabu; 1: Ka-Zar; A: X-Men, giant; reprints X-Men #10 (first series) and Daredevil #24; Hercules back-up	0.25	2.00	5.00	10.00
❑2, JR; JK; GT, Sightless in a Savage Land; From the Sky...Winged Wrath!, A: Daredevil; O: Ka-Zar, giant; Angel back-up	0.25	1.40	3.50	7.00
❑3, Mar 71, giant; reprints Amazing Spider-Man #57 and Daredevil #14; Angel back-up continues in Marvel Tales #30	0.25	1.40	3.50	7.00

KA-ZAR (2ND SERIES)
MARVEL

	ORIG	GOOD	FINE	N-MINT
❑1, Jan 74, Return to the Savage Land, O: Savage Land	0.20	0.60	1.50	3.00
❑2, Mar 74, DH, The Fall Of The Red Wizard!	0.20	0.50	1.25	2.50
❑3, May 74, DH	0.25	0.50	1.25	2.50
❑4, Jul 74, DH	0.25	0.50	1.25	2.50
❑5, Sep 74, DH	0.25	0.50	1.25	2.50
❑6, Nov 74, JB, Waters Of Darkness, River Of Doom!	0.25	0.40	1.00	2.00
❑7, Jan 75, JB, Revenge Of the River Gods!	0.25	0.40	1.00	2.00
❑8, Mar 75, JB	0.25	0.40	1.00	2.00
❑9, JB	0.25	0.40	1.00	2.00
❑10, JB	0.25	0.40	1.00	2.00
❑11	0.25	0.30	0.75	1.50
❑12	0.25	0.30	0.75	1.50
❑13, Dec 75	0.25	0.30	0.75	1.50
❑14, Feb 76, A: Klaw	0.25	0.30	0.75	1.50
❑15, Apr 76	0.25	0.30	0.75	1.50
❑16, Jun 76	0.30	0.30	0.75	1.50
❑17, Aug 76	0.30	0.30	0.75	1.50
❑18, Oct 76	0.30	0.30	0.75	1.50
❑19, Dec 76	0.30	0.30	0.75	1.50
❑20, Feb 77, A: Klaw	0.30	0.30	0.75	1.50

KA-ZAR (3RD SERIES)
MARVEL

Value: Cover or less

- ❑-1, Flashback 1.95
- ❑1, May 97, MWa (w) 1.99
- ❑2, Jun 97, MWa (w), Law of the Jungle 1.99
- ❑2/A, Jun 97, alternate cover 1.99
- ❑3, Jul 97 1.99
- ❑4, Aug 97, gatefold summary 1.99
- ❑5, Sep 97, V: Rhino, gatefold summary 1.99
- ❑6, Oct 97, gatefold summary 1.99
- ❑7, Nov 97, gatefold summary 1.99
- ❑8, Dec 97, gatefold summary; Spider-Man CD-ROM inserted 1.99
- ❑9, Jan 98, gatefold summary 1.99
- ❑10, Feb 98, gatefold summary 1.99
- ❑11, Mar 98, gatefold summary 1.99
- ❑12, Apr 98, V: High Evolutionary, gatefold summary 1.99
- ❑13, May 98, V: High Evolutionary, gatefold summary 1.99
- ❑14, Jun 98, gatefold summary; Flip-book 2.99
- ❑15, Jul 98, A: Punisher, gatefold summary; blinded 1.99
- ❑16, Aug 98, gatefold summary 1.99
- ❑17, Sep 98, gatefold summary 1.99
- ❑18, Oct 98, gatefold summary 1.99
- ❑19, Nov 98, gatefold summary 1.99
- ❑20, Dec 98, Final Issue; gatefold summary 1.99
- ❑Anl 1997, wraparound cover; One-Shot; gatefold summary 2.99

KAZAR OF THE SAVAGE LAND
MARVEL

Value: Cover or less

- ❑1, Feb 97, Nature of the Beasts, wraparound cover; One-Shot 2.50

KA-ZAR: SIBLING RIVALRY
MARVEL

Value: Cover or less

- ❑-1, Jul 97, O: Ka-Zar, Flashback 1.95

KA-ZAR THE SAVAGE
MARVEL

	ORIG	GOOD	FINE	N-MINT
❑1, Apr 81, BA, A New Dawn…A New World, O: Ka-Zar	0.50	0.50	1.25	2.50
❑2, May 81, BA, To Air Is Human!	0.50	0.40	1.00	2.00
❑3, Jun 81, BA	0.50	0.30	0.75	1.50
❑4, Jul 81, BA	0.50	0.30	0.75	1.50
❑5, Aug 81, BA	0.50	0.30	0.75	1.50
❑6, Sep 81, BA	0.50	0.30	0.75	1.50
❑7, Oct 81, BA	0.50	0.30	0.75	1.50
❑8, Nov 81, BA	0.50	0.30	0.75	1.50
❑9, Dec 81, BA	0.50	0.30	0.75	1.50
❑10, Jan 82, BA, direct distribution	0.75	0.30	0.75	1.50
❑11, Feb 82, GK; BA, 1: Belasco, Zabu	0.75	0.30	0.75	1.50
❑12, Mar 82, BA, panel missing	0.75	0.30	0.75	1.50
❑12-2, Reprint	0.75	0.20	0.50	1.00
❑13, Apr 82, BA	0.75	0.30	0.75	1.50
❑14, May 82, BA	0.75	0.30	0.75	1.50
❑15, Jun 82, BA	0.75	0.30	0.75	1.50
❑16, Jul 82	0.75	0.30	0.75	1.50
❑17, Aug 82	0.75	0.30	0.75	1.50
❑18, Sep 82	0.75	0.30	0.75	1.50
❑19, Oct 82, BA	0.75	0.30	0.75	1.50
❑20, Nov 82	0.75	0.30	0.75	1.50
❑21, Dec 82	0.75	0.30	0.75	1.50
❑22, Jan 83	0.75	0.30	0.75	1.50
❑23, Feb 83	0.75	0.30	0.75	1.50
❑24, Mar 83	0.75	0.30	0.75	1.50
❑25, Apr 83	0.75	0.30	0.75	1.50
❑26, May 83	0.75	0.30	0.75	1.50
❑27, Aug 83	0.75	0.30	0.75	1.50
❑28, Oct 83	0.75	0.30	0.75	1.50

Ka-Zar was the son of a British noble raised to manhood in a tropical environment where prehistoric beasts still lived.

	ORIG	GOOD	FINE	N-MINT
❑29, Dec 83, Double-size; Wedding of Ka-Zar, Shanna	1.00	0.30	0.75	1.50
❑30, Feb 84	0.75	0.30	0.75	1.50
❑31, Apr 84	1.00	0.30	0.75	1.50
❑32, Jun 84	1.00	0.30	0.75	1.50
❑33, Aug 84	1.00	0.30	0.75	1.50
❑34, Oct 84, Final Issue	1.00	0.30	0.75	1.50
❑36862, Reprint	0.75	0.20	0.50	1.00

KEIF LLAMA
ONI PRESS

Value: Cover or less

- ❑1, Mar 99, Gas War, nn 2.95

KEIF LLAMA XENO-TECH
FANTAGRAPHICS

Value: Cover or less

- ❑1 2.00
- ❑2 2.00
- ❑3 2.00
- ❑4 2.00
- ❑5 2.00
- ❑6 2.00

KELLY BELLE POLICE DETECTIVE
NEWCOMERS

Value: Cover or less

- ❑1 2.95
- ❑2, The Case of the Jeweled Scarab, Part 2 2.95
- ❑3, The Case of the Jeweled Scarab, Part 3; Kitty Smith: Hero Worship 2.95

KELVIN MACE
VORTEX

Value: Cover or less

- ❑1 3.00
- ❑2 1.75

KENDRA: LEGACY OF THE BLOOD
PERRYDOG

Value: Cover or less

- ❑1, Feb 87, b&w 2.00
- ❑2, Apr 87, b&w 2.00

KENTS, THE
DC

Value: Cover or less

- ❑1, Aug 97, Bleeding Kansas, Part 1, Clark Kent's ancestors in frontier Kansas 2.50
- ❑2, Sep 97, Bleeding Kansas, Part 2 2.50
- ❑3, Oct 97, Bleeding Kansas, Part 3 2.50
- ❑4, Nov 97, Bleeding Kansas, Part 4 2.50
- ❑5, Dec 97, Brother vs. Brother, Part 1 2.50
- ❑6, Jan 98, Brother vs. Brother, Part 2 2.50
- ❑7, Feb 98, Brother vs. Brother, Part 3 2.50
- ❑8, Mar 98, Brother vs. Brother, Part 4 2.50
- ❑9, Apr 98, To The Stars by Hard Ways, Part 1 2.50
- ❑10, May 98, To The Stars by Hard Ways, Part 2 2.50
- ❑11, Jun 98, To The Stars by Hard Ways, Part 3 2.50
- ❑12, Jul 98, To The Stars by Hard Ways, Part 4 2.50

KERRY DRAKE
BLACKTHORNE

Value: Cover or less

- ❑1, May 86 6.95
- ❑2, Jul 86 6.95
- ❑3, Dec 86 6.95
- ❑4, Feb 87 6.95
- ❑5, Jul 87 6.95

KEYHOLE
MILLENNIUM

Value: Cover or less

- ❑1, Jun 96 2.95
- ❑2, Oct 96 2.95
- ❑3 2.95
- ❑4, May 97 2.95
- ❑5, Jun 98 2.95

KICKERS, INC.
MARVEL

Value: Cover or less

- ❑1, Nov 86, This Legend Born!, 1: Kickers, Inc. 0.75
- ❑2, Dec 86 0.75
- ❑3, Jan 87 0.75
- ❑4, Feb 87 0.75
- ❑5, Mar 87 0.75
- ❑6, Apr 87 0.75
- ❑7, May 87 0.75
- ❑8, Jun 87 0.75
- ❑9, Jul 87 0.75
- ❑10, Aug 87 0.75
- ❑11, Sep 87 0.75
- ❑12, Oct 87 0.75

KID ANARCHY
FANTAGRAPHICS

Value: Cover or less

- ❑1, b&w 2.50
- ❑2, b&w 2.75
- ❑3, b&w 2.75

KID BLASTOFF
SLAVE LABOR

Value: Cover or less
- ❑1, Jun 96 .... 2.75

KID CANNIBAL
ETERNITY

Value: Cover or less
- ❑1 .... 2.50
- ❑2 .... 2.50
- ❑3 .... 2.50
- ❑4 .... 2.50

KID COLT OUTLAW
MARVEL

	ORIG	GOOD	FINE	N-MINT
❑112, Sep 63	0.12	3.60	9.00	18.00
❑113, Nov 63	0.12	3.60	9.00	18.00
❑114, Jan 64, V: Iron Mask	0.12	3.60	9.00	18.00
❑115, Mar 64	0.12	3.60	9.00	18.00
❑116, May 64	0.12	3.60	9.00	18.00
❑117, Jul 64	0.12	3.60	9.00	18.00
❑118, Sep 64, V: Doctor Danger; V: Bull Barton; V: Scorpion	0.12	3.60	9.00	18.00
❑119, Nov 64	0.12	3.60	9.00	18.00
❑120, Jan 65	0.12	3.60	9.00	18.00
❑121, Mar 65	0.12	2.80	7.00	14.00
❑122, May 65	0.12	2.80	7.00	14.00
❑123, Jul 65	0.12	2.80	7.00	14.00
❑124, Sep 65, V: Phantom Raider	0.12	2.80	7.00	14.00
❑125, Nov 65, A: Two-Gun Kid	0.12	2.80	7.00	14.00
❑126, Jan 66	0.12	2.80	7.00	14.00
❑127, Mar 66, V: Doctor Danger; V: Fat Man; V: Iron Mask	0.12	2.80	7.00	14.00
❑128, May 66	0.12	2.80	7.00	14.00
❑129, Jul 66	0.12	2.80	7.00	14.00
❑130, Sep 66, O: Kid Colt, giant	0.25	2.80	7.00	14.00
❑131, Nov 66, Reprint; giant	0.25	2.00	5.00	10.00
❑132, Jan 67, Reprint; giant	0.25	2.00	5.00	10.00
❑133, Mar 67, V: Rammer Ramkin	0.12	2.00	5.00	10.00
❑134, May 67	0.12	2.00	5.00	10.00
❑135, Jul 67	0.12	2.00	5.00	10.00
❑136, Sep 67	0.12	2.00	5.00	10.00
❑137, Nov 67	0.12	2.00	5.00	10.00
❑138, Jan 68	0.12	2.00	5.00	10.00
❑139, Mar 68, series goes on hiatus	0.12	2.00	5.00	10.00
❑140, Nov 69, Reprints begin	0.15	1.00	2.50	5.00
❑141, Dec 69	0.15	1.00	2.50	5.00
❑142, Jan 70	0.15	1.00	2.50	5.00
❑143, Feb 70	0.15	1.00	2.50	5.00
❑144, Mar 70	0.15	1.00	2.50	5.00
❑145, Apr 70	0.15	1.00	2.50	5.00
❑146, May 70	0.15	1.00	2.50	5.00
❑147, Jun 70	0.15	1.00	2.50	5.00
❑148	0.15	1.00	2.50	5.00
❑149	0.15	1.00	2.50	5.00
❑150	0.15	1.00	2.50	5.00
❑151	0.15	1.00	2.50	5.00
❑152	0.15	1.00	2.50	5.00
❑153	0.15	1.00	2.50	5.00
❑154	0.15	1.00	2.50	5.00
❑155	0.15	1.00	2.50	5.00
❑156	0.15	1.00	2.50	5.00
❑157	0.15	1.00	2.50	5.00
❑158	0.15	1.00	2.50	5.00
❑159	0.15	1.00	2.50	5.00
❑160	0.15	1.00	2.50	5.00
❑161	—	1.00	2.50	5.00
❑162	—	1.00	2.50	5.00
❑163	—	1.00	2.50	5.00
❑164	—	1.00	2.50	5.00
❑165	—	1.00	2.50	5.00
❑166	—	1.00	2.50	5.00
❑167	—	1.00	2.50	5.00
❑168	—	1.00	2.50	5.00
❑169	—	1.00	2.50	5.00
❑170	—	1.00	2.50	5.00
❑171	—	0.80	2.00	4.00
❑172	—	0.80	2.00	4.00
❑173	—	0.80	2.00	4.00
❑174	—	0.80	2.00	4.00
❑175	—	0.80	2.00	4.00
❑176	—	0.80	2.00	4.00
❑177	—	0.80	2.00	4.00
❑178	—	0.80	2.00	4.00
❑179	—	0.80	2.00	4.00
❑180	—	0.80	2.00	4.00
❑181	—	0.80	2.00	4.00
❑182	—	0.80	2.00	4.00
❑183	—	0.80	2.00	4.00
❑184	—	0.80	2.00	4.00
❑185	—	0.80	2.00	4.00
❑186	—	0.80	2.00	4.00
❑187	—	0.80	2.00	4.00
❑188	—	0.80	2.00	4.00
❑189	—	0.80	2.00	4.00
❑190	—	0.80	2.00	4.00
❑191	—	0.80	2.00	4.00
❑192	—	0.80	2.00	4.00
❑193	—	0.80	2.00	4.00
❑194	—	0.80	2.00	4.00
❑195	—	0.80	2.00	4.00
❑196	—	0.80	2.00	4.00
❑197	—	0.80	2.00	4.00
❑198	—	0.80	2.00	4.00
❑199	—	0.80	2.00	4.00
❑200	—	0.80	2.00	4.00
❑201	—	0.60	1.50	3.00
❑202	—	0.60	1.50	3.00
❑203	—	0.60	1.50	3.00
❑204, Kid Colt Helps a Lady; Trail of Disaster, Reprints Kid Colt Outlaw #72	0.25	0.60	1.50	3.00
❑205	—	0.60	1.50	3.00
❑206	—	0.60	1.50	3.00
❑207	—	0.60	1.50	3.00
❑208	—	0.60	1.50	3.00
❑209	—	0.60	1.50	3.00
❑210	—	0.60	1.50	3.00
❑211	—	0.60	1.50	3.00
❑212	—	0.60	1.50	3.00
❑213	—	0.60	1.50	3.00
❑214	—	0.60	1.50	3.00
❑215	—	0.60	1.50	3.00
❑216	—	0.60	1.50	3.00
❑217	—	0.60	1.50	3.00
❑218	—	0.60	1.50	3.00
❑219	—	0.60	1.50	3.00
❑220	—	0.60	1.50	3.00
❑221	—	0.60	1.50	3.00
❑222	—	0.60	1.50	3.00
❑223	—	0.60	1.50	3.00
❑224	—	0.60	1.50	3.00
❑225	—	0.60	1.50	3.00
❑226	—	0.60	1.50	3.00
❑227	—	0.60	1.50	3.00
❑228	—	0.60	1.50	3.00
❑229, Final Issue	—	0.60	1.50	3.00

KID DEATH & FLUFFY: HALLOWEEN SPECIAL
EVENT

Value: Cover or less
- ❑1, Slab Happy 2.95

KID DEATH & FLUFFY SPRING BREAK SPECIAL
EVENT

Value: Cover or less
- ❑1, Jun 96, Spring Break Spectacular 2.50

KID ETERNITY
DC

Value: Cover or less
- ❑1, May 93, Even Deadmen Need Friends 1.95
- ❑2, Jun 93, Stir It Up 1.95
- ❑3, Jul 93, Cupid's Folly 1.95
- ❑4, Aug 93 .... 1.95
- ❑5, Sep 93 .... 1.95
- ❑6, Oct 93 .... 1.95
- ❑7, Nov 93, Infinity 1.95
- ❑8, Dec 93 .... 1.95
- ❑9, Jan 94 .... 1.95
- ❑10, Feb 94 .... 1.95
- ❑11, Mar 94 .... 1.95
- ❑12, May 94 .... 1.95
- ❑13, Jun 94, A Date in Hell, Part 1 .... 1.95
- ❑14, Jul 94, A Date in Hell, Part 2 .... 1.95
- ❑15, Aug 94, A Date in Hell, Part 3 .... 1.95
- ❑16, Sep 94, A Date in Hell, Part 4, Final Issue 1.95

KID ETERNITY (MINI-SERIES)
DC

Value: Cover or less
- ❑1, May 91, Canto I; Canto II 4.95
- ❑2, Jul 91, Canto III; Canto IV 4.95
- ❑3, Oct 91, Canto V; Canto VI 4.95

KID 'N PLAY
MARVEL

	ORIG	GOOD	FINE	N-MINT
❑1, Feb 92	1.25	0.30	0.75	1.50
❑2, Mar 92	1.25	0.25	0.63	1.25
❑3, Apr 92	1.25	0.25	0.63	1.25
❑4, May 92	1.25	0.25	0.63	1.25
❑5, Jun 92	1.25	0.25	0.63	1.25
❑6, Jul 92	1.25	0.25	0.63	1.25
❑7, Aug 92	1.25	0.25	0.63	1.25
❑8, Sep 92	1.25	0.25	0.63	1.25
❑9, Oct 92	1.25	0.25	0.63	1.25

KID SUPREME
IMAGE

Value: Cover or less
- ❑1, Mar 96, School Daze, Kid Supreme with fist outstretched on cover 2.50
- ❑1/A, Mar 96, School Daze, Kid Supreme surounded by girls on cover 2.50

ORIG GOOD FINE N-MINT

❑2, Apr 96, Reptyle! 2.50
❑3, Jul 96, A: Glory 2.50
❑3/A, Jul 96, A: Glory, alternate cover (green background) 2.50

KID TERRIFIC
IMAGE
Value: Cover or less
❑1, Nov 98, b&w 2.95

KIDZ OF THE KING
KING
Value: Cover or less
❑1 2.95
❑2, May 94 2.95
❑3, Apr 95 2.95

KI-GORR THE KILLER
AC
Value: Cover or less
❑1, Old Thunder; Cave Girl: The Fire Pit Menace!, Reprint 3.95

KIKU SAN
AIRCEL
Value: Cover or less
❑1, Nov 88 1.95
❑2, Dec 88 1.95
❑3, Jan 89 1.95
❑4, Feb 89 1.95
❑5, Mar 89 1.95
❑6, Apr 89 1.95

KILGORE
RENEGADE
Value: Cover or less
❑1 2.00
❑2 2.00
❑3 2.00
❑4, May 88 2.00

KILL BARNY
EXPRESS
Value: Cover or less
❑1, b&w 2.50

KILL BARNY 3
EXPRESS
Value: Cover or less
❑1, b&w 2.75

KILLER FLY
SLAVE LABOR
Value: Cover or less
❑1, Mar 95 2.95
❑2, Jun 95 2.95
❑3, Sep 95, Final Issue 2.95

KILLER INSTINCT
ACCLAIM
Value: Cover or less
❑1, Jun 96, Enemy of My Enemy, based on video game 2.50
❑2, Jul 96, based on video game 2.50
❑3, Jul 96, The Price of Freedom, based on video game 2.50
❑4, Sep 96, Special, Part 1, based on video game 2.50
❑5, Oct 96, Special, Part 2, based on video game 2.50
❑6, Nov 96, Special, Part 3, based on video game 2.50

KILLER INSTINCT TOUR BOOK
IMAGE
Value: Cover or less
❑1/A, Embossed cover 5.00
❑1/B, Embossed cover 5.00
❑1/GO, Gold edition —

KILLER...TALES BY TIMOTHY TRUMAN
ECLIPSE
Value: Cover or less
❑1, Mar 85, Daral: The Savings of Sayera; Braskan Gambit 1.75

KILL IMAGE
BONEYARD

	ORIG	GOOD	FINE	N-MINT
❑1, b&w; foil cover	2.95	0.80	2.00	4.00

KILLING STROKE
ETERNITY
Value: Cover or less
❑1, b&w 2.50
❑2, b&w 2.50
❑3, b&w 2.50
❑4, b&w 2.50

KILL MARVEL
BONEYARD
Value: Cover or less
❑1/LE, Special "Marvel Can..." edition 6.95

KILLPOWER: THE EARLY YEARS
MARVEL
Value: Cover or less
❑1, Sep 93, The Gauntlet, foil cover 2.95
❑2, Oct 93 1.75
❑3, Nov 93, A: Punisher 1.75
❑4, Dec 93 1.75

KILLRAVEN
MARVEL
Value: Cover or less
❑1, Feb 01, Killraven: 2020 2.99

KILL RAZOR SPECIAL
IMAGE
Value: Cover or less
❑1, Aug 95 2.50

KILL YOUR BOYFRIEND
DC
Value: Cover or less
❑1, Jun 95, One-Shot 4.95
❑1-2, reprints 1995 one-shot with new afterword and other new material 5.95

KILROY (VOL. 2)
CALIBER
Value: Cover or less
❑1 2.95
❑1/A 2.95

KILROY IS HERE
CALIBER
Value: Cover or less
❑0, BB (c), Sympathy for the Devil; Kilroy, b&w 2.95
❑1, Reflections, b&w 2.95
❑2, b&w 2.95

Kid Eternity possessed the power to right wrongs by summoning the spirits of dead heroes.

© 1993 DC Comics (Vertigo)

ORIG GOOD FINE N-MINT

❑3, b&w 2.95
❑4, b&w 2.95

KILROY: REVELATIONS
CALIBER
Value: Cover or less
❑1, b&w; One-Shot 2.95

KILROY: THE SHORT STORIES
CALIBER
Value: Cover or less
❑1, Rosewood; Safe Haven, b&w; One-Shot 2.95

KIMBER, PRINCE OF THE FEYLONS
ANTARCTIC
Value: Cover or less
❑1, Apr 92, b&w 2.50
❑2, Jun 92, b&w 2.50

KIMURA
NIGHTWYND
Value: Cover or less
❑1, b&w 2.50
❑2, b&w 2.50
❑3, b&w 2.50
❑4, b&w 2.50

KIN
IMAGE
Value: Cover or less
❑1 2.95
❑2 2.95
❑3 2.95
❑4, Jul 00, Friendly Fire 2.95
❑5, Aug 00, A Stick in Time 2.95
❑6, Sep 00 3.95

KINDRED, THE
IMAGE
Value: Cover or less
❑1, Mar 94 2.50
❑2, Apr 94 1.95
❑3, May 94 1.95
❑3/A, May 94, alternate cover 1.95
❑4, Jul 94 2.50

KING ARTHUR AND THE KNIGHTS OF JUSTICE
MARVEL
Value: Cover or less
❑1, Opposites Attract 1.25
❑2 1.25
❑3 1.25

KING CONAN
MARVEL

	ORIG	GOOD	FINE	N-MINT
❑1, Mar 80, JB, The Witch of the Mists, V: Thoth-Amon, wife & son	0.75	0.60	1.50	3.00
❑2, Jun 80, JB	0.75	0.40	1.00	2.00
❑3, Sep 80, JB	0.75	0.40	1.00	2.00
❑4, Dec 80, V: Thoth-Amon	0.75	0.40	1.00	2.00
❑5, Mar 81	0.75	0.40	1.00	2.00
❑6, Jun 81	0.75	0.40	1.00	2.00
❑7, Sep 81	0.75	0.40	1.00	2.00
❑8, Dec 81	0.75	0.40	1.00	2.00
❑9, Mar 82	1.00	0.40	1.00	2.00
❑10, May 82	1.00	0.40	1.00	2.00
❑11, Jul 82	1.00	0.30	0.75	1.50
❑12, Sep 82	1.00	0.30	0.75	1.50
❑13, Nov 82	1.00	0.30	0.75	1.50
❑14, Jan 83	1.00	0.30	0.75	1.50
❑15, Mar 83	1.00	0.30	0.75	1.50
❑16, May 83	1.00	0.30	0.75	1.50
❑17, Jul 83	1.00	0.30	0.75	1.50
❑18, Sep 83	1.00	0.30	0.75	1.50
❑19, Nov 83, Series continued in Conan the King #20	1.00	0.30	0.75	1.50

KINGDOM, THE
DC

	ORIG	GOOD	FINE	N-MINT
❑1, Feb 99, MWa (w), Elseworlds	2.95	0.59	1.48	2.95
❑1/Aut, MWa (w), Signed by Mark Waid; Elseworlds	—	1.60	4.00	8.00
❑2, Feb 99, MZ, MWa (w), Mighty Rivers, Elseworlds	2.95	0.59	1.48	2.95
❑2/Aut, MZ, MWa (w), Signed by Mark Waid, Mike Zeck, and Terry Beatty; Elseworlds	—	2.40	6.00	12.00

KINGDOM COME
DC

	ORIG	GOOD	FINE	N-MINT
❑1, ARo, MWa (w), Truth And Justice, Elseworlds	4.95	1.20	3.00	6.00
❑1-2, 2nd Printing	4.95	0.99	2.47	4.95
❑2, ARo, MWa (w), Strange Visitor, Elseworlds	4.95	1.00	2.50	5.00
❑3, ARo, MWa (w), Up In The Sky, return of Captain Marvel; Elseworlds	4.95	1.00	2.50	5.00

	ORIG	GOOD	FINE	N-MINT
❑4, ARo, MWa (w), Never-Ending Battle, D: Captain Marvel, Elseworlds	4.95	1.00	2.50	5.00
❑Dlx 1, ARo, Deluxe slipcase edition with companion book; collects mini-series with additional material	99.95	20.00	50.00	100.00

KINGDOM, THE: KID FLASH
DC
Value: Cover or less
- ❑1, Feb 99, MWa (w), Elseworlds ... 1.99

KINGDOM, THE: NIGHTSTAR
DC
Value: Cover or less
- ❑1, Feb 99, MWa (w), A: Batman; A: Starfire; A: Green Lantern; A: Nightwing; A: Superman; A: Wonder Woman, Elseworlds 1.99

KINGDOM, THE: OFFSPRING
DC
Value: Cover or less
- ❑1, Feb 99, MWa (w), A: Plastic Man, Elseworlds ... 1.99

KINGDOM OF THE DWARFS
COMICO
Value: Cover or less
- ❑1 ... 4.95

KINGDOM OF THE WICKED
CALIBER
Value: Cover or less
- ❑1, b&w ... 2.95
- ❑2, b&w ... 2.95
- ❑3, b&w ... 2.95
- ❑4, b&w ... 2.95

KINGDOM, THE: PLANET KRYPTON
DC
Value: Cover or less
- ❑1, Feb 99, MWa (w), A: Batman; A: Gog; A: Booster Gold, Elseworlds ... 1.99

KINGDOM, THE: SON OF THE BAT
DC
Value: Cover or less
- ❑1, Feb 99, MWa (w), Convergence, A: Ibn al Xu'ffasch; A: Batman; A: Talia Al Ghul; A: Gog; A: Ra's Al Ghul; A: Superman; A: Braniac; A: Lex Luthor, Elseworlds ... 1.99

KING KONG (GOLD KEY)
GOLD KEY

	ORIG	GOOD	FINE	N-MINT
❑1, Sep 68, nn; four-color; 64pgs.; adapts 1932 film	0.25	2.40	6.00	12.00

KING KONG (MONSTER)
MONSTER

	ORIG	GOOD	FINE	N-MINT
❑1, DSt (c), b&w	2.50	0.50	1.25	2.50
❑2	1.95	0.50	1.25	2.50
❑3	1.95	0.50	1.25	2.50
❑4	1.95	0.50	1.25	2.50
❑5, Nov 91, AW (c)	2.25	0.50	1.25	2.50
❑6	2.50	0.50	1.25	2.50

KING OF THE DEAD
FANTACO
Value: Cover or less
- ❑0 ... 1.95
- ❑1 ... 1.95
- ❑2 ... 1.95
- ❑3 ... 1.95
- ❑4 ... 2.95

KINGPIN
MARVEL
Value: Cover or less
- ❑1, Nov 97, JR, SL (w), nn; One-Shot ... 5.99

KINGS IN DISGUISE
KITCHEN SINK
Value: Cover or less
- ❑1, Mar 88, SR (c), b&w ... 2.00
- ❑2, May 88, HK (c) ... 2.00
- ❑3, Jul 88 ... 2.00
- ❑4, Sep 88 ... 2.00
- ❑5, Mar 89 ... 2.00
- ❑6, Sep 89 ... 2.00

KINGS OF THE NIGHT
DARK HORSE
Value: Cover or less
- ❑1, Out of the Sunrise ... 2.25
- ❑2 ... 2.25

KING TIGER & MOTORHEAD
DARK HORSE
Value: Cover or less
- ❑1, Aug 96 ... 2.95
- ❑2, Sep 96 ... 2.95

KINKI KLITT KOMICS
RIP OFF
Value: Cover or less
- ❑1, Apr 92, b&w; adult ... 2.95
- ❑2, Jun 92, b&w; adult ... 2.50

KINKY HOOK, THE
FANTAGRAPHICS
Value: Cover or less
- ❑1, b&w; adult ... 2.50

KIP
HAMMER & ANVIL
Value: Cover or less
- ❑1, b&w ... 2.50

KIRBY KING OF THE SERIALS
BLACKTHORNE
Value: Cover or less
- ❑1, Jan 89, b&w ... 2.00

KISS
PERSONALITY

	ORIG	GOOD	FINE	N-MINT
❑1, b&w	2.95	0.70	1.75	3.50
❑2	2.95	0.60	1.50	3.00
❑3, full color	2.95	0.60	1.50	3.00

KISS & TELL
PATRICIA BREEN
Value: Cover or less
- ❑1, Dec 95, The Cage, b&w; magazine ... 2.75

KISS & TELL (VOL. 2)
SIRIUS
Value: Cover or less
- ❑1, b&w ... 2.50

KISS CLASSICS
MARVEL
Value: Cover or less
- ❑1, ME (w), O: Kiss (rock group), Reprints Marvel Super Special #1, #5 ... 10.00

KISSES
SPOOF
Value: Cover or less
- ❑1, b&w ... 2.95

KISSING CANVAS
MN DESIGN
Value: Cover or less
- ❑1, full color; photos ... 5.50

KISSNATION
MARVEL
Value: Cover or less
- ❑1, A: X-Men, One-Shot; Reprints Marvel Super Specials with new editorial ... 10.00

KISS OF DEATH
ACME
Value: Cover or less
- ❑1 ... 2.00

KISS OF THE VAMPIRE
BRAINSTORM
Value: Cover or less
- ❑1, Dark is the Night ... 2.95

KISS PRE-HISTORY
REVOLUTIONARY

	ORIG	GOOD	FINE	N-MINT
❑1, Apr 93, b&w	2.50	0.60	1.50	3.00
❑2, May 93, b&w	2.50	0.60	1.50	3.00
❑3, Jul 93, b&w	2.50	0.60	1.50	3.00

KISS: PSYCHO CIRCUS
IMAGE

	ORIG	GOOD	FINE	N-MINT
❑1, Aug 97, The Witching of Adam Moon, Part 1	1.95	0.80	2.00	4.00
❑2, Sep 97, The Witching of Adam Moon, Part 2	1.95	0.60	1.50	3.00
❑3, Oct 97	1.95	0.50	1.25	2.50
❑4, Nov 97, Smoke & Mirrors, Part 1	1.95	0.50	1.25	2.50
❑5, Dec 97, Smoke & Mirrors, Part 2	1.95	0.50	1.25	2.50
❑6, Jan 98, Smoke & Mirrors, Part 3	2.25	0.50	1.25	2.50
❑7, Mar 98, Bottle Full of Wishes	2.25	0.50	1.25	2.50
❑8, Apr 98, Forever	2.25	0.50	1.25	2.50
❑9, May 98, Four Sides to Every Story	2.25	0.50	1.25	2.50
❑10, Jun 98, Destroyer, Part 1, covers of #10-12 form quadtych	2.25	0.50	1.25	2.50
❑11, Jul 98, Destroyer, Part 2	2.25	0.50	1.25	2.50
❑12, Aug 98, Destroyer, Part 3	2.25	0.50	1.25	2.50
❑13, Oct 98, Destroyer, Part 4	2.25	0.45	1.13	2.25
❑14, Nov 98, Year of the Fox, Part 1	2.25	0.45	1.13	2.25
❑15, Dec 98, Year of the Fox, Part 2	2.25	0.45	1.13	2.25
❑16, Feb 99, World Without Heroes, Part 1	2.25	0.45	1.13	2.25
❑17, Mar 99, World Without Heroes, Part 2	2.25	0.45	1.13	2.25
❑18, Apr 99, Sunburst Finish	2.25	0.45	1.13	2.25
❑19, May 99, Fragments	2.25	0.45	1.13	2.25
❑20, Jun 99, Make Believe, Part 1	2.25	0.45	1.13	2.25
❑21, Jul 99, Make Believe, Part 2	2.25	0.45	1.13	2.25
❑22, Aug 99, Mirror Image, Part 1	2.25	0.45	1.13	2.25
❑23, Sep 99, Mirror Image, Part 2	2.25	0.45	1.13	2.25
❑24, Oct 99, Cat's Eye	2.25	0.45	1.13	2.25
❑25, Nov 99, The Devil's Tale	2.25	0.45	1.13	2.25
❑26, Jan 00	2.25	0.45	1.13	2.25
❑27, Feb 00, The Nightengale's Song	2.25	0.45	1.13	2.25
❑28, Apr 00, Perdition Blues	2.25	0.45	1.13	2.25
❑29, Apr 00, Shadow of the Moon, Part 1	—	0.45	1.13	2.25
❑30, May 00, Shadow of the Moon, Part 2	—	0.45	1.13	2.25
❑31, Jun 00, Shadow of the Moon, Part 3	—	0.50	1.25	2.50
❑SE 1, Special Wizard Edition	—	0.40	1.00	2.00

KISS: SATAN'S MUSIC?
CELEBRITY

	ORIG	GOOD	FINE	N-MINT
❑1, trading cards	—	0.80	2.00	4.00

KISSYFUR
DC

	ORIG	GOOD	FINE	N-MINT
❑1	—	0.40	1.00	2.00

KISS: YOU WANTED THE BEST, YOU GOT THE BEST
WIZARD

	ORIG	GOOD	FINE	N-MINT
❑1	—	0.20	0.50	1.00

KITCHEN SINK CLASSICS
KITCHEN SINK

	ORIG	GOOD	FINE	N-MINT
❑1, Jan 94, b&w; adult; reprints Omaha #0	3.95	0.80	2.00	4.00
❑2, b&w; adult; reprints The People's Comics	2.95	0.59	1.48	2.95
❑3, b&w; adult; reprints Death Rattle #8	2.95	0.59	1.48	2.95

KITTY PRYDE & WOLVERINE
MARVEL

	ORIG	GOOD	FINE	N-MINT
❑1, Nov 84, AM, Lies	0.75	0.70	1.75	3.50
❑2, Dec 84, AM, Terror	0.75	0.50	1.25	2.50
❑3, Jan 85, AM, Death	0.75	0.50	1.25	2.50
❑4, Feb 85, AM, Rebirth	0.75	0.50	1.25	2.50
❑5, Mar 85, AM	0.75	0.50	1.25	2.50
❑6, Apr 85, AM	0.75	0.50	1.25	2.50

KITTY PRYDE, AGENT OF SHIELD
MARVEL

Value: Cover or less

- ❑1, Dec 97, The Calling, gatefold summary ... 2.50
- ❑2, Jan 98, A: Lockheed; A: Wolverine, gatefold summary ... 2.50
- ❑3, Feb 98, gatefold summary ... 2.50

KITZ 'N' KATZ KOMIKS
PHANTASY

Value: Cover or less

- ❑1 ... 1.50
- ❑2, b&w ... 1.50
- ❑3, b&w ... 1.50
- ❑4, b&w ... 1.50
- ❑5 ... 2.00
- ❑6 ... 1.50

KIWANNI-DAUGHTER OF THE DAWN
C&T

Value: Cover or less

- ❑1, Feb 88, b&w ... 2.25

KLOR
SIRIUS

Value: Cover or less

- ❑1 ... 2.95
- ❑2 ... 2.95
- ❑3 ... 2.95

KNEWTS OF THE ROUND TABLE
PAN

Value: Cover or less

- ❑1, Jul 98, b&w ... 2.50
- ❑2, Sep 98, b&w ... 2.50
- ❑3 ... 2.50
- ❑4 ... 2.50
- ❑5 ... 2.50

KNIGHT
BEAR CLAW

Value: Cover or less

- ❑0, Oct 93 ... 2.50

KNIGHTFOOL: THE FALL OF THE SPLATMAN
PARODY PRESS

Value: Cover or less

- ❑1 ... 2.95

KNIGHTHAWK
ACCLAIM

Value: Cover or less

- ❑1, Sep 95, NA, NA (w) ... 2.50
- ❑2, Sep 95 ... 2.50
- ❑3, Oct 95 ... 2.50
- ❑4, Oct 95, NA, NA (w) ... 2.50
- ❑5, Nov 95, NA, NA (w) ... 2.50
- ❑6, Nov 95, NA, NA (w), Final Issue ... 2.50

KNIGHTMARE (ANTARCTIC)
ANTARCTIC

Value: Cover or less

- ❑1, Jul 94, b&w ... 2.75
- ❑2, Sep 94, b&w ... 2.75
- ❑3, Jan 95, Wedding Knight Part1, b&w ... 2.75
- ❑4, Mar 95, Wedding Knight Part2, b&w ... 2.75
- ❑5, Mar 95, Wedding Knight Part4, b&w ... 2.75
- ❑6, May 95, Wedding Knight Part4, b&w; Final Issue ... 2.75

KNIGHTMARE (IMAGE)
IMAGE

Value: Cover or less

- ❑0, Aug 95, RL (w), Dulcinea, 1: Knightmare, chromium cover 3.50
- ❑1, Feb 95, RL (w) ... 2.50
- ❑2, Mar 95 ... 2.50
- ❑3, Apr 95 ... 2.50
- ❑4, May 95 ... 2.50
- ❑4/A, May 95, alternate cover. 2.50
- ❑5, Jun 95, RL (w), Getting Ugly; Warcry, Flip book with Warcry #1 ... 2.50
- ❑6 ... 2.50
- ❑7 ... 2.50
- ❑8, Final Issue ... 2.50

KNIGHTS OF PENDRAGON, THE (1ST SERIES)
MARVEL

	ORIG	GOOD	FINE	N-MINT
❑1, Jul 90, Brands & Ashes	1.95	0.50	1.25	2.50
❑2, Aug 90	1.95	0.40	1.00	2.00
❑3, Oct 90	1.95	0.40	1.00	2.00
❑4, Oct 90	1.95	0.40	1.00	2.00
❑5, Nov 90	1.95	0.40	1.00	2.00
❑6, Dec 90, Once & Future	1.95	0.40	1.00	2.00
❑7, Jan 91	1.95	0.40	1.00	2.00
❑8, Feb 91, poster	1.95	0.40	1.00	2.00
❑9, Mar 91	1.95	0.40	1.00	2.00
❑10, Apr 91	1.95	0.40	1.00	2.00
❑11, May 91, A: Iron Man	1.95	0.40	1.00	2.00
❑12, Jun 91	1.95	0.40	1.00	2.00

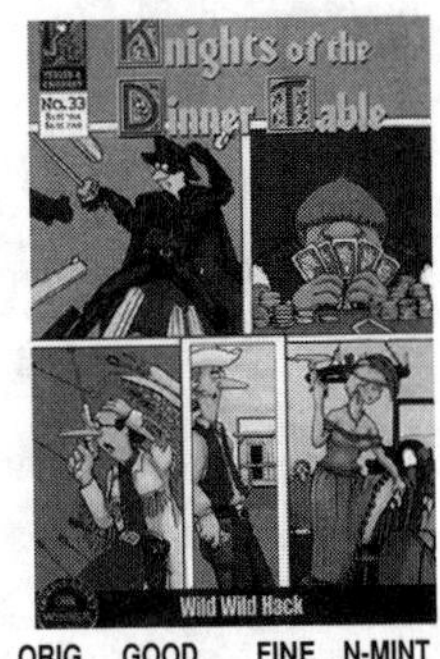

The role-playing misadventures of a group of gamers are chronicled in Kenzer & Company's *Knights of the Dinner Table.*

	ORIG	GOOD	FINE	N-MINT
❑13, Jul 91	1.95	0.40	1.00	2.00
❑14, Aug 91	1.95	0.40	1.00	2.00
❑15, Sep 91	1.95	0.40	1.00	2.00
❑16, Oct 91	1.95	0.40	1.00	2.00
❑17, Nov 91	1.95	0.40	1.00	2.00
❑18, Dec 91, A: Iron Man, Final Issue	1.95	0.40	1.00	2.00

KNIGHTS OF PENDRAGON (2ND SERIES)
MARVEL

	ORIG	GOOD	FINE	N-MINT
❑1, Jul 92, A: Iron Man	1.75	0.40	1.00	2.00
❑2, Aug 92	1.75	0.35	0.88	1.75
❑3, Sep 92	1.75	0.35	0.88	1.75
❑4, Oct 92	1.75	0.35	0.88	1.75
❑5, Nov 92, Title changes to The Knights of Pendragon; New armor	1.75	0.35	0.88	1.75
❑6, Dec 92	1.75	0.35	0.88	1.75
❑7, Jan 93	1.75	0.35	0.88	1.75
❑8, Feb 93	1.75	0.35	0.88	1.75
❑9, Mar 93, Spider-Man	1.75	0.35	0.88	1.75
❑10, Apr 93, Bloodlines, Part 1	1.75	0.35	0.88	1.75
❑11, May 93, Bloodlines, Part 2	1.75	0.35	0.88	1.75
❑12, Jun 93	1.75	0.35	0.88	1.75
❑13, Jul 93	1.75	0.35	0.88	1.75
❑14, Aug 93	1.75	0.35	0.88	1.75
❑15, Sep 93, Final Issue	1.75	0.35	0.88	1.75

KNIGHTS OF THE DINNER TABLE
KENZER & COMPANY

	ORIG	GOOD	FINE	N-MINT
❑1, Jul 94, Not Ready for Syndication	2.95	15.00	37.50	75.00
❑2, Jan 95, Gluttons for Punishment	2.95	7.60	19.00	38.00
❑3, Apr 95, License to Loot	2.95	4.40	11.00	22.00
❑4, Feb 97, Have Dice Will Travel, Gary Con issue	2.95	4.40	11.00	22.00
❑5, Mar 97, Master of the Game	2.95	4.40	11.00	22.00
❑6, Apr 97, Plays Well With Others	2.95	3.20	8.00	16.00
❑7, May 97, The Dice Man Cometh!	2.95	3.20	8.00	16.00
❑8, Jun 97, An Orc By Any Other Name	2.95	3.20	8.00	16.00
❑9, Jul 97, Two Dice for Sister Sara	2.95	3.20	8.00	16.00
❑10, Aug 97, Let the Dice Fall Where They May	2.95	3.20	8.00	16.00
❑11, Sep 97, When in Doubt: Hack!!	2.95	2.40	6.00	12.00
❑12, Oct 97, The Good The Bad and The Unlucky!	2.95	2.40	6.00	12.00
❑13, Nov 97, Men That Hack	2.95	2.40	6.00	12.00
❑14, Dec 97, A Fist Full of Dice And A Bad Attitude	2.95	2.40	6.00	12.00
❑15, Jan 98, Mama Told Me Not to Play	2.95	2.40	6.00	12.00
❑16, Feb 98, The Dice of Wrath	2.95	1.80	4.50	9.00
❑17, Mar 98, This Sword for Hire!	2.95	1.80	4.50	9.00
❑18, Apr 98, Against All Odds	2.95	1.80	4.50	9.00
❑19, May 98, Heroes of the Hack League	2.95	1.80	4.50	9.00
❑20, Jun 98, Hack in Space!	2.95	1.80	4.50	9.00
❑21, Jul 98, Home is Where You Hang Yer Dicebag, Gary Con issue	2.95	1.80	4.50	9.00
❑22, Aug 98, Opportunity Knocks	2.95	1.20	3.00	6.00
❑23, Sep 98, Dice Follies	2.95	1.20	3.00	6.00
❑24, Oct 98, Hackzilla	2.95	1.20	3.00	6.00
❑25, Nov 98, Secrets of the Hackfiles	2.95	1.20	3.00	6.00
❑26, Dec 98, The Mask of El Ravager	2.95	1.20	3.00	6.00
❑27, Jan 99, Hackburger Hill	2.95	1.20	3.00	6.00
❑28, Feb 99, Hoody Freakin' Hoo!!	2.95	1.20	3.00	6.00
❑29, Mar 99, Bad Moon Risin'	2.95	1.20	3.00	6.00
❑30, Apr 99, No Honor	2.95	1.20	3.00	6.00
❑31, May 99, Don't Fear The Reaper	2.95	0.80	2.00	4.00
❑32, Jun 99, Tales From Hog Wallers	2.95	0.80	2.00	4.00
❑33, Jul 99, Wild Wild Hack; The Night of Gaming Dangerously, Part 2, Wild Wild Hack	2.95	0.60	1.50	3.00
❑34, Aug 99, Of Dice and Men	2.95	0.59	1.48	2.95
❑35, Sep 99, Death Awaits	2.95	0.59	1.48	2.95
❑36, Oct 99, Hackmaster of Puppets	2.95	0.59	1.48	2.95
❑37, Nov 99, 15 Orcs on a Dead Dwarf's Chest	2.95	0.59	1.48	2.95
❑38, Dec 99, Hack Rogers!	2.95	0.59	1.48	2.95

	ORIG	GOOD	FINE	N-MINT
❑39, Jan 00, The Game Must Go On	2.95	0.59	1.48	2.95
❑40, Feb 00, Hack in the Saddle Again	2.95	0.59	1.48	2.95
❑41, Mar 00, 99 Gold Doubloons	2.95	0.59	1.48	2.95
❑42, Apr 00, A Hack in Time Slays Nine	2.95	0.59	1.48	2.95
❑43, May 00, Wasted Days and Wasted Knights	2.95	0.59	1.48	2.95
❑44, Jun 00, Because I'm the GM!	2.95	0.59	1.48	2.95
❑45, Jul 00, Buddy, Can You Spare a Cure?	2.95	0.59	1.48	2.95
❑46, Aug 00, Hack and Roll All Nite	2.95	0.59	1.48	2.95
❑47, Sep 00, Hooked on Psionics	2.95	0.59	1.48	2.95
❑48, Oct 00, Apocalypse Drow	2.95	0.59	1.48	2.95
❑49, Nov 00, The Six-Million Hit-Point Man	2.95	0.59	1.48	2.95
❑50, Dec 00, We've Not Yet Begun to Fight, double-sized	4.95	0.99	2.47	4.95
❑51, Jan 01, One Ring to Fool Them All	2.95	0.59	1.48	2.95
❑52	2.95	0.59	1.48	2.95
❑53	2.95	0.59	1.48	2.95
❑54	2.95	0.59	1.48	2.95
❑55	2.95	0.59	1.48	2.95
❑56	2.95	0.59	1.48	2.95
❑57	2.95	0.59	1.48	2.95

KNIGHTS OF THE DINNER TABLE/FAANS CROSSOVER SPECIAL
Six Handed Press

Value: Cover or less

❑1, b&w ... 2.95

KNIGHTS OF THE DINNER TABLE ILLUSTRATED
Kenzer & Company

Value: Cover or less

❑1, Jun 00, Lair of the Gazebo; First Impressions, b&w ... 2.95
❑2, Aug 00, Hole Lot of Trouble; Can We Talk?, b&w ... 2.95
❑3, Oct 00, Five Green Towels; A Call for Heroes, b&w ... 2.95
❑4, Dec 00, The Portal; Orcs at the Gates, b&w ... 2.95

KNIGHTS ON BROADWAY
Broadway

Value: Cover or less

❑1, Jul 96 ... 2.95
❑2, Aug 96 ... 2.95
❑3, Oct 96 ... 2.95

KNIGHT'S ROUND TABLE
Knight Press

Value: Cover or less

❑1, Oct 96, b&w; Anthology ... 2.95

KNIGHTSTRIKE
Image

Value: Cover or less

❑1, Dec 95, RL (w), Extreme Destroyer, Part 6, polybagged with Sentinel card ... 2.50

KNIGHT WATCHMAN
Image

Value: Cover or less

❑1, Jun 98, Graveyard Shift, Part 1, cover says May, indicia says Jun ... 2.95
❑2, Jul 98, Graveyard Shift, Part 2 ... 2.95
❑3, Aug 98, Graveyard Shift, Part 3 ... 2.95
❑4, Oct 98, Graveyard Shift, Part 4 ... 3.50

KNIGHT WATCHMAN: GRAVEYARD SHIFT
Caliber

Value: Cover or less

❑1, A Hard Day's Night, b&w ... 2.95
❑2, Knight Moves ... 2.95
❑3 ... 2.95
❑4 ... 2.95

KNIGHT WOLF, THE
Five Star

Value: Cover or less

❑1, Welcome to My Knightmare ... 2.50
❑2 ... 2.50
❑3 ... 2.50

KNUCKLES
Archie

	ORIG	GOOD	FINE	N-MINT
❑1, Apr 97, The Dark Legion	1.50	0.60	1.50	3.00
❑2, May 97, The Dark Legion	1.50	0.40	1.00	2.00
❑3, Jun 97, The Dark Legion	1.50	0.40	1.00	2.00
❑4, Aug 97	1.50	0.40	1.00	2.00
❑5, Sep 97	1.50	0.40	1.00	2.00
❑6, Oct 97	1.50	0.40	1.00	2.00
❑7, Dec 97	1.50	0.40	1.00	2.00
❑8, Jan 98	1.75	0.40	1.00	2.00
❑9, Feb 98	1.75	0.40	1.00	2.00
❑10, Mar 98	1.75	0.40	1.00	2.00
❑11, Apr 98	1.75	0.35	0.88	1.75
❑12, May 98	1.75	0.35	0.88	1.75
❑13, Jun 98	1.75	0.35	0.88	1.75
❑14, Jul 98	1.75	0.35	0.88	1.75
❑15, Aug 98	1.75	0.35	0.88	1.75
❑16, Sep 98	1.75	0.35	0.88	1.75
❑17, Oct 98	1.75	0.35	0.88	1.75
❑18, Nov 98, Debt of Honor!	1.75	0.35	0.88	1.75
❑19, Dec 98	1.75	0.35	0.88	1.75
❑20, Jan 99	1.75	0.35	0.88	1.75
❑21, Feb 99	1.75	0.35	0.88	1.75
❑22, Mar 99, Dark Alliance, cover forms triptych with #23 and #24	1.75	0.35	0.88	1.75
❑23, Apr 99, Dark Alliance, cover forms triptych with #22 and #24	1.79	0.36	0.89	1.79
❑24, May 99, Dark Alliance, cover forms triptych with #22 and #23	1.79	0.36	0.89	1.79
❑25, Jun 99, Childhood's End	1.79	0.36	0.89	1.79
❑26, Jul 99, The First Date	1.79	0.36	0.89	1.79
❑27, Aug 99, The First Date	1.79	0.36	0.89	1.79
❑28, Sep 99, The First Date	1.79	0.36	0.89	1.79
❑29, Oct 99, The Echidna	1.79	0.36	0.89	1.79

KNUCKLES' CHAOTIX
Archie

Value: Cover or less

❑1, Jan 96 ... 2.00

KNUCKLES THE MALEVOLENT NUN
Fantagraphics

	ORIG	GOOD	FINE	N-MINT
❑1, b&w	2.25	0.45	1.13	2.25
❑2	2.00	0.45	1.13	2.25

KOBALT
DC

Value: Cover or less

❑1, Jun 94, The Gall ... 1.75
❑2, Jul 94, Walking the Plank ... 1.75
❑3, Aug 94 ... 1.75
❑4, Sep 94, 1: Page ... 1.75
❑5, Oct 94 ... 1.75
❑6, Nov 94 ... 1.75
❑7, Dec 94, A: Static ... 1.75
❑8, Jan 95, A: Hardware ... 1.75
❑9, Feb 95 ... 1.75
❑10, Mar 95 ... 1.75
❑11, Apr 95 ... 1.75
❑12, Jun 95 ... 1.75
❑13, Jul 95 ... 2.50
❑14, Jul 95, Long Hot Summer ... 2.50
❑15, Aug 95 ... 2.50
❑16, Sep 95, Final Issue ... 2.50

KOBRA
DC

	ORIG	GOOD	FINE	N-MINT
❑1, Mar 76, Fangs of the Kobra!, 1: Kobra	0.25	0.80	2.00	4.00
❑2, May 76	0.30	0.80	2.00	4.00
❑3, Jul 76, KG, Vengeance In Ultra-Violet	0.30	0.80	2.00	4.00
❑4, Sep 76	0.30	0.80	2.00	4.00
❑5, Dec 76	0.30	0.80	2.00	4.00
❑6, Feb 77	0.30	0.80	2.00	4.00
❑7, Apr 77, Final Issue	0.30	0.80	2.00	4.00

KOGARATSU: THE LOTUS OF BLOOD
Acme

Value: Cover or less

❑1 ... 5.95

KOMODO AND THE DEFIANTS
Victory

Value: Cover or less

❑1 ... 1.50
❑2 ... 1.50

KONGA'S REVENGE
Charlton

	ORIG	GOOD	FINE	N-MINT
❑1, Reprints Konga's Revenge #3; Published out of sequence	—	1.80	4.50	9.00
❑2	—	2.80	7.00	14.00
❑3	—	2.80	7.00	14.00

KONG THE UNTAMED
DC

	ORIG	GOOD	FINE	N-MINT
❑1, Jul 75, AA, O: Kong the Untamed	0.25	0.80	2.00	4.00
❑2, Sep 75	0.25	0.60	1.50	3.00
❑3, Nov 75, AA, The Caves of Doom	0.25	0.60	1.50	3.00
❑4, Jan 76	0.25	0.60	1.50	3.00
❑5, Mar 76, Final Issue	0.25	0.60	1.50	3.00

KONNY AND CZU
Antarctic

Value: Cover or less

❑1, Sep 94, Data3, b&w ... 2.75
❑2, Nov 94, b&w ... 2.75
❑3, Jan 95, Totally an Alien Experience!, b&w ... 2.75
❑4, Mar 95, b&w ... 2.75

KOOLAU THE LEPER (JACK LONDON'S...)
Tome Press

Value: Cover or less

❑1, b&w ... 2.50

KOOSH KINS
Archie

Value: Cover or less

❑1, Oct 91, Party Time Dudes; Pardon the Eruption ... 1.00
❑2 ... 1.00
❑3 ... 1.00
❑4 ... 1.00

KORAK, SON OF TARZAN
Gold Key

	ORIG	GOOD	FINE	N-MINT
❑1, Jan 64, RM, Gold Key begins publishing	0.12	7.00	17.50	35.00
❑2, Mar 64, RM	0.12	5.00	12.50	25.00
❑3, May 64, RM	0.12	5.00	12.50	25.00
❑4, Aug 64, RM	0.12	5.00	12.50	25.00
❑5, Oct 64, RM	0.12	5.00	12.50	25.00
❑6, Dec 64, RM	0.12	4.00	10.00	20.00
❑7, Mar 65, RM	0.12	4.00	10.00	20.00
❑8, May 65, RM	0.12	4.00	10.00	20.00
❑9, Jul 65, RM	0.12	4.00	10.00	20.00
❑10, Sep 65, RM	0.12	4.00	10.00	20.00
❑11, Nov 65, RM	0.12	4.00	10.00	20.00
❑12, Mar 66	0.12	3.20	8.00	16.00

	ORIG	GOOD	FINE	N-MINT
❑13, Jun 66	0.12	3.20	8.00	16.00
❑14, Sep 66	0.12	3.20	8.00	16.00
❑15, Dec 66	0.12	3.20	8.00	16.00
❑16, Mar 67	0.12	3.20	8.00	16.00
❑17, Jun 67	0.12	3.20	8.00	16.00
❑18, Aug 67	0.12	3.20	8.00	16.00
❑19, Oct 67	0.12	3.20	8.00	16.00
❑20, Dec 67	0.12	3.20	8.00	16.00
❑21, Feb 68, RM	0.12	2.60	6.50	13.00
❑22, Apr 68	0.12	2.60	6.50	13.00
❑23, Jun 68	0.12	2.60	6.50	13.00
❑24, Aug 68	—	2.60	6.50	13.00
❑25, Oct 68	—	2.60	6.50	13.00
❑26, Dec 68	—	2.60	6.50	13.00
❑27, Feb 69	—	2.60	6.50	13.00
❑28, Apr 69	—	2.60	6.50	13.00
❑29, Jun 69	—	2.60	6.50	13.00
❑30, Aug 69	0.15	2.60	6.50	13.00
❑31, Oct 69	0.15	1.60	4.00	8.00
❑32, Dec 69	0.15	1.60	4.00	8.00
❑33	0.15	1.60	4.00	8.00
❑34	0.15	1.60	4.00	8.00
❑35	0.15	1.60	4.00	8.00
❑36	0.15	1.60	4.00	8.00
❑37, Sep 70	0.15	1.60	4.00	8.00
❑38	0.15	1.60	4.00	8.00
❑39	0.15	1.60	4.00	8.00
❑40	0.15	1.60	4.00	8.00
❑41, May 71	0.15	1.20	3.00	6.00
❑42	—	1.20	3.00	6.00
❑43	—	1.20	3.00	6.00
❑44	—	1.20	3.00	6.00
❑45	—	1.20	3.00	6.00
❑46, Jun 72, continues Gold Key numbering; DC begins publishing	0.25	0.80	2.00	4.00
❑47, Aug 72	0.20	0.40	1.00	2.00
❑48, Oct 72	0.20	0.40	1.00	2.00
❑49, Dec 72	0.20	0.40	1.00	2.00
❑50, Feb 73	0.20	0.40	1.00	2.00
❑51, Apr 73	0.20	0.40	1.00	2.00
❑52, Jul 73	0.20	0.40	1.00	2.00
❑53, Sep 73, JKu (c), Carson of Venus back-up	0.20	0.40	1.00	2.00
❑54, Nov 73, JKu (c), Carson of Venus back-up	0.20	0.40	1.00	2.00
❑55, Jan 74, JKu (c), Carson of Venus back-up	0.20	0.40	1.00	2.00
❑56, Mar 74, JKu (c), Carson of Venus back-up	0.20	0.40	1.00	2.00
❑57, Jun 74, The Most Endangered Species	0.20	0.40	1.00	2.00
❑58, Aug 74	0.25	0.40	1.00	2.00
❑59, Oct 74, Series continued in Tarzan Family #60	0.25	0.40	1.00	2.00

KORVUS
ARROW

Value: Cover or less

❑1 ... 2.95
❑2 ... 2.95
❑3, Spr 98 ... 2.95

KORVUS (VOL. 2)
ARROW

Value: Cover or less

❑1, Fal 98 ... 2.95
❑2 ... 2.95

KOSMIC KAT
IMAGE

Value: Cover or less

❑1, Aug 99 ... 2.95

KOSMIC KAT ACTIVITY BOOK
IMAGE

Value: Cover or less

❑1, Aug 99, O: Kosmic Kat ... 2.95

KREE-SKRULL WAR STARRING THE AVENGERS, THE
MARVEL

	ORIG	GOOD	FINE	N-MINT
❑1, Sep 83, NA; JB, The Kree-Skull War, Part 1; The Kree-Skull War, Part 2, Reprint	2.50	0.60	1.50	3.00
❑2, Oct 83, NA; JB, The Kree-Skull War, Part 7; The Kree-Skull War, Part 8, Reprint	2.50	0.60	1.50	3.00

KREMEN
GREY PRODUCTIONS

Value: Cover or less

❑1 ... 2.50
❑2 ... 2.50
❑3 ... 2.50

KREY
GAUNTLET

Value: Cover or less

❑1, b&w ... 2.50
❑2, b&w ... 2.50
❑3, b&w ... 2.50

KROFFT SUPERSHOW
GOLD KEY

	ORIG	GOOD	FINE	N-MINT
❑1	0.35	1.20	3.00	6.00
❑2	0.35	0.80	2.00	4.00
❑3	0.35	0.80	2.00	4.00

Bart Simpson's favorite clown attempted to open his own amusement park in the three-issue *Krusty Comics*.

© 1997 20th Century Fox Film Entertainment (Bongo)

	ORIG	GOOD	FINE	N-MINT
❑4, Some Party; Bigfoot and Wildboy: Earth Tremors	0.35	0.80	2.00	4.00
❑5	0.35	0.80	2.00	4.00
❑6	0.35	0.80	2.00	4.00

KRULL
MARVEL

	ORIG	GOOD	FINE	N-MINT
❑1, Nov 83, Photo cover	0.60	0.25	0.63	1.25
❑2, Dec 83	0.60	0.25	0.63	1.25

KRUSTY COMICS
BONGO

	ORIG	GOOD	FINE	N-MINT
❑1, The Rise and Fall of Krustyland, Part 1	2.25	0.50	1.25	2.50
❑2, The Rise and Fall of Krustyland, Part 2	2.25	0.50	1.25	2.50
❑3, The Rise and Fall of Krustyland, Part 3	2.25	0.50	1.25	2.50

KRYPTON CHRONICLES
DC

	ORIG	GOOD	FINE	N-MINT
❑1, Sep 81, CS, The Search For Superman's Roots!, A: Superman	0.50	0.30	0.75	1.50
❑2, Oct 81, CS, A: Black Flame	0.60	0.30	0.75	1.50
❑3, Nov 81, CS, O: name of Kal-El	0.60	0.30	0.75	1.50

KULL AND THE BARBARIANS
MARVEL

	ORIG	GOOD	FINE	N-MINT
❑1, May 75, b&w; magazine	1.00	1.00	2.50	5.00
❑2, Jul 75, b&w; magazine	1.00	0.60	1.50	3.00
❑3, O: Red Sonja, b&w; magazine	1.00	0.80	2.00	4.00

KULL IN 3-D
BLACKTHORNE

Value: Cover or less

❑1 ... 2.50
❑2 ... 2.50

KULL THE CONQUEROR (1ST SERIES)
MARVEL

	ORIG	GOOD	FINE	N-MINT
❑1, Jun 71, RA; WW, A King Comes Riding!, O: Kull; 1: Brule the Spear-Slayer	0.15	1.60	4.00	8.00
❑2, Sep 71, JSe, The Shadows Kingdom	0.15	0.80	2.00	4.00
❑3, Jul 72, JSe, The Death-Dance of Thulsa Doom!, A: Thulsa Doom	0.20	0.70	1.75	3.50
❑4, Sep 72, JSe	0.20	0.50	1.25	2.50
❑5, Nov 72, JSe, A Kingdom By the Sea!	0.20	0.50	1.25	2.50
❑6, Jan 73, JSe, The Lurker Beneath the Earth!	0.20	0.50	1.25	2.50
❑7, Mar 73	0.20	0.50	1.25	2.50
❑8, May 73	0.20	0.50	1.25	2.50
❑9, Jul 73	0.20	0.50	1.25	2.50
❑10, Sep 73, Continued as "Kull the Destroyer"	0.20	0.50	1.25	2.50

KULL THE CONQUEROR (2ND SERIES)
MARVEL

	ORIG	GOOD	FINE	N-MINT
❑1, JB, The Power And The Kingdom, Brule	2.00	0.50	1.25	2.50
❑2, The Blood of Kings!, Misareena	2.00	0.40	1.00	2.00

KULL THE CONQUEROR (3RD SERIES)
MARVEL

	ORIG	GOOD	FINE	N-MINT
❑1, JB, Iraina	1.25	0.40	1.00	2.00
❑2, JB	1.25	0.35	0.88	1.75
❑3, JB	1.00	0.35	0.88	1.75
❑4, Feb 84, JB	1.00	0.30	0.75	1.50
❑5, Aug 84	0.60	0.30	0.75	1.50
❑6, Oct 84	0.60	0.25	0.63	1.25
❑7, Dec 84	0.60	0.25	0.63	1.25
❑8, Feb 85	0.60	0.25	0.63	1.25
❑9, Apr 85	0.65	0.25	0.63	1.25
❑10, Jun 85, Final Issue	0.65	0.25	0.63	1.25

KULL THE DESTROYER
MARVEL

	ORIG	GOOD	FINE	N-MINT
❑11, Nov 73, Continued from Kull the Conqueror (1st Series) #10	0.20	0.40	1.00	2.00
❑12, Jan 74, MP, Moon Of Blood!	0.20	0.40	1.00	2.00
❑13, Mar 74, MP, Torches From Hell!	0.20	0.40	1.00	2.00
❑14, May 74, MP; JSn	0.25	0.40	1.00	2.00
❑15, Aug 74, MP; SD, Reprint; series goes on hiatus	0.25	0.40	1.00	2.00

	ORIG	GOOD	FINE	N-MINT
❑16, Aug 76, The Tiger In The Moon	0.25	0.40	1.00	2.00
❑17, Oct 76, AA	0.30	0.40	1.00	2.00
❑18, Dec 76, AA	0.30	0.40	1.00	2.00
❑19, Feb 77, AA	0.30	0.40	1.00	2.00
❑20, Apr 77, AA	0.30	0.40	1.00	2.00
❑21, Jun 77	0.30	0.40	1.00	2.00
❑22, Aug 77	0.30	0.40	1.00	2.00
❑23, Oct 77	0.30	0.40	1.00	2.00
❑24, Dec 77	0.35	0.40	1.00	2.00
❑25, Feb 78	0.35	0.40	1.00	2.00
❑26, Apr 78	0.35	0.40	1.00	2.00
❑27, Jun 78	0.35	0.40	1.00	2.00
❑28, Aug 78	0.35	0.40	1.00	2.00
❑29, Oct 78, A: Thulsa Doom, Final Issue	0.35	0.40	1.00	2.00

KUNG FU WARRIORS
CFW

Value: Cover or less

- ❑1 ... 2.25
- ❑2 ... 2.25
- ❑3 ... 2.25
- ❑4 ... 2.25
- ❑5 ... 2.25
- ❑6 ... 2.25
- ❑7 ... 2.25
- ❑8 ... 2.25

- ❑9 ... 2.25
- ❑10 ... 2.25
- ❑11 ... 2.25
- ❑12 ... 2.25
- ❑13 ... 2.25
- ❑14 ... 2.25
- ❑15 ... 2.25

KUNOICHI
LIGHTNING

Value: Cover or less

- ❑1, Sep 96, also contains Sinja: Resurrection #1; indicia is for Sinja: Resurrection ... 3.00

KYRA
ELSEWHERE

	ORIG	GOOD	FINE	N-MINT
❑1, b&w	1.50	0.40	1.00	2.00
❑2, Spr 86, b&w	1.75	0.40	1.00	2.00
❑3, Sum 86, b&w	1.75	0.40	1.00	2.00
❑4, Dec 86, Sister Transistor	1.75	0.40	1.00	2.00
❑5, Jun 87, Leaf in a Furnace!	1.75	0.40	1.00	2.00
❑6	1.75	0.40	1.00	2.00

K-Z COMICS PRESENTS
K-Z

Value: Cover or less

- ❑1, Jun 85, Colt; Genesis, Part 1 ... 1.50

L

LA BLUE GIRL
CPM

Value: Cover or less

- ❑1, Jul 96, b&w; adult; wraparound cover ... 2.95
- ❑2, Aug 96, b&w; adult ... 2.95
- ❑3, Sep 96, b&w; adult ... 2.95
- ❑4, Oct 96, b&w; adult ... 2.95
- ❑5, Nov 96, b&w; adult ... 2.95
- ❑6, adult ... 2.95
- ❑7, adult ... 2.95
- ❑8, adult ... 2.95
- ❑9, adult ... 2.95
- ❑10, adult ... 2.95
- ❑11, adult ... 2.95
- ❑12, adult ... 2.95

LABMAN
IMAGE

Value: Cover or less

- ❑1, Nov 96, Who Is Labman?, 1: Labman ... 3.50
- ❑1/A, Nov 96, Who Is Labman?, alternate cover ... 3.50
- ❑1/B, Nov 96, Who Is Labman?, alternate cover ... 3.50
- ❑1/C, Nov 96, Who Is Labman?, alternate cover ... 3.50
- ❑2 ... 2.95
- ❑3 ... 2.95

LABMAN SOURCEBOOK
IMAGE

	ORIG	GOOD	FINE	N-MINT
❑1, Jun 96, Limited edition giveaway from 1996 San Diego Comic-Con	—	0.20	0.50	1.00

LABOR FORCE
BLACKTHORNE

Value: Cover or less

- ❑1, Sep 86, ...But Somebody's Got to Do It! ... 1.50
- ❑2 ... 1.50
- ❑3 ... 1.75
- ❑4 ... 1.75
- ❑5 ... 1.75
- ❑6 ... 1.75
- ❑7 ... 1.75
- ❑8 ... 1.75

LABOURS OF HERCULES, THE
MALAN CLASSICAL ENTERPRISES

Value: Cover or less

- ❑1, nn; b&w ... 2.95

LABYRINTH OF MADNESS
TSR

	ORIG	GOOD	FINE	N-MINT
❑1	—	0.20	0.50	1.00

LABYRINTH: THE MOVIE
MARVEL

	ORIG	GOOD	FINE	N-MINT
❑1, RT; JB, movie Adaptation	0.75	0.30	0.75	1.50
❑2, RT; JB, movie Adaptation	0.75	0.30	0.75	1.50
❑3, RT; JB, movie Adaptation	0.75	0.30	0.75	1.50

L.A. COMICS
LOS ANGELES

	ORIG	GOOD	FINE	N-MINT
❑1, L.A. is...; Mickey Rat	0.50	0.60	1.50	3.00
❑2, Famous Lawmen Then,; Sargent Sky-watch in Nite Timey Naughties	0.50	0.60	1.50	3.00

LADY ARCANE
HERO GRAPHICS

Value: Cover or less

- ❑1, Bats!, O: Giant ... 4.95
- ❑2, b&w ... 3.50
- ❑3, b&w ... 3.50
- ❑4, b&w; Final Issue ... 2.95

LADY CRIME
AC

Value: Cover or less

- ❑1, Murder For Pennies; The Mystery Of The Underground To Oblivion, b&w; Bob Powell reprints ... 2.75

LADY DEATH
CHAOS!

Value: Cover or less

- ❑1, Feb 98, Wicked Ways; Wicked Ways, Part 1 ... 2.95
- ❑1/LE, Feb 98, Wicked Ways, Part 1, no cover price; premium limited edition ... 20.00
- ❑2, Mar 98 ... 2.95
- ❑3, Apr 98 ... 2.95
- ❑4, May 98 ... 2.95
- ❑5, Jun 98 ... 2.95
- ❑5/SC, variant cover ... 6.00
- ❑6, Jul 98, The Harrowing ... 2.95
- ❑7, Aug 98, The Harrowing ... 2.95
- ❑8, Sep 98, The Harrowing ... 2.95
- ❑9, Oct 98, The Covenant ... 2.95
- ❑10, Nov 98, The Covenant, A: Purgatori, cover says Oct, indicia says Nov ... 2.95
- ❑11, Dec 98, The Covenant ... 2.95
- ❑12, Jan 99, The Covenant ... 2.95
- ❑13, Feb 99, Inferno! ... 2.95
- ❑14, Mar 99, Inferno! ... 2.95
- ❑15, Apr 99, Inferno! ... 2.95
- ❑16, May 99, Inferno! ... 2.95

LADY DEATH (MINI-SERIES)
CHAOS!

	ORIG	GOOD	FINE	N-MINT
❑0, Nov 97, Death Becomes Her	2.95	0.60	1.50	3.00
❑0.5, Wizard mail-in promotional edition	—	1.00	2.50	5.00
❑0.5/A, Black velvet edition; Wizard mail-in promotional edition	—	1.60	4.00	8.00
❑0.5/GO, Wizard mail-in promotional edition; Gold edition	—	1.20	3.00	6.00
❑1, Feb 94	2.75	2.40	6.00	12.00
❑1/LE	—	3.00	7.50	15.00
❑1-2, Commemorative edition	2.75	0.55	1.38	2.75
❑2	2.75	2.00	5.00	10.00
❑3	2.75	1.20	3.00	6.00
❑4	2.75	0.80	2.00	4.00

LADY DEATH: DARK MILLENNIUM
CHAOS

Value: Cover or less

- ❑1, Feb 00 ... 2.95
- ❑2, Mar 00, Dark Passage ... 2.95

LADY DEATH II: BETWEEN HEAVEN & HELL
CHAOS!

	ORIG	GOOD	FINE	N-MINT
❑1, O: Lady Death, chromium cover	2.75	0.70	1.75	3.50
❑1/A, Gold edition	—	0.80	2.00	4.00
❑1/B, Black velvet limited edition	2.75	1.00	2.50	5.00
❑1/LE	—	1.00	2.50	5.00
❑1-2, Commemorative edition	2.75	0.55	1.38	2.75
❑2, Apr 95	2.75	0.60	1.50	3.00
❑3, May 95	2.75	0.60	1.50	3.00
❑4	2.75	0.60	1.50	3.00
❑4/SC, Lady Demon chase cover	2.75	1.00	2.50	5.00

LADY DEATH III: THE ODYSSEY
CHAOS!

	ORIG	GOOD	FINE	N-MINT
❑-1, Apr 96, Sneak Peek Preview; promotional piece for mini-series	1.50	0.30	0.75	1.50
❑1, Apr 96, Gold foil cover	2.95	0.70	1.75	3.50
❑1/SC, Apr 96, foil embossed cardstock wraparound cover	3.50	1.00	2.50	5.00
❑2, May 96	2.95	0.60	1.50	3.00
❑3, Jun 96	2.95	0.60	1.50	3.00
❑4, Aug 96	2.95	0.60	1.50	3.00
❑4/A, Aug 96, alternate cover by Steven Hughes	2.95	1.60	4.00	8.00

LADY DEATH IN LINGERIE
CHAOS!

	ORIG	GOOD	FINE	N-MINT
❑1, Aug 95	2.95	0.59	1.48	2.95
❑1/LE, Aug 95, no cover price; foil-stamped leather premium edition; limited to 10,000 copies	—	1.60	4.00	8.00

LADY DEATH IV: THE CRUCIBLE
CHAOS!

	ORIG	GOOD	FINE	N-MINT
❑0.5, Nov 96, Wizard promotional edition	—	1.00	2.50	5.00
❑0.5/A, Cloth alternate cover; Wizard promotional edition	—	1.60	4.00	8.00
❑1, Nov 96	2.95	0.60	1.50	3.00
❑1/A, Leather edition	—	2.00	5.00	10.00
❑1/B, All silver cover; Signed & Numbered by authors; Limited to 400; Comes with certificate of authenticity	—	3.60	9.00	18.00
❑1/SI, Nov 96, silver embossed cardstock wraparound cover	3.50	0.70	1.75	3.50
❑2, Jan 97	2.95	0.59	1.48	2.95
❑3, Mar 97	2.95	0.59	1.48	2.95
❑4	2.95	0.59	1.48	2.95
❑5, Aug 97	2.95	0.59	1.48	2.95
❑5/SC, Aug 97, no cover price; Nightmare Premium Edition	—	1.00	2.50	5.00
❑6, Oct 97	2.95	0.59	1.48	2.95

LADY DEATH: JUDGEMENT WAR
CHAOS!

Value: Cover or less

- ❑1, Nov 99 .... 2.95
- ❑2, Dec 99, A Device for Damnation 2.95
- ❑3, Jan 00, A Host for Holocaust 2.95

LADY DEATH: JUDGEMENT WAR PRELUDE
CHAOS!

Value: Cover or less

- ❑1, Oct 99, nn 2.95

LADY DEATH: RETRIBUTION
CHAOS!

	ORIG	GOOD	FINE	N-MINT
❑1, Aug 98	2.95	0.59	1.48	2.95
❑1/A, Painted alternate cover	2.95	0.70	1.75	3.50
❑1/LE, premium edition	—	0.80	2.00	4.00

LADY DEATH SWIMSUIT SPECIAL
CHAOS!

	ORIG	GOOD	FINE	N-MINT
❑1, b&w	2.50	0.50	1.25	2.50
❑1/SC, Red Velvet edition	—	1.60	4.00	8.00

LADY DEATH: THE RAPTURE
CHAOS!

Value: Cover or less

- ❑1, Jun 99 .... 2.95
- ❑2, Jul 99 .... 2.95
- ❑3, Aug 99, Fire In The Sky 2.95
- ❑4, Sep 99 .... 2.95

LADY DEATH: TRIBULATION
CHAOS!

Value: Cover or less

- ❑1, Dec 00 .... 2.95
- ❑2, Jan 01 .... 2.95

LADY DEATH/VAMPIRELLA: DARK HEARTS
CHAOS!

	ORIG	GOOD	FINE	N-MINT
❑1, Mar 99, Dark Hearts, nn; crossover with Harris	3.50	0.70	1.75	3.50
❑1/A, Premium edition (5000 printed)	—	2.00	5.00	10.00

LADY DEATH VS. PURGATORI
CHAOS!

	ORIG	GOOD	FINE	N-MINT
❑1, Dec 99, Black, White, and Red All Over!, nn; no cover price; red foil logo	—	0.60	1.50	3.00

LADY DEATH V. VAMPIRELLA
CHAOS

	ORIG	GOOD	FINE	N-MINT
❑Ash 1, Feb 00, Lady Death/Vampirella II Preview Book	—	0.20	0.50	1.00

LADY DEATH: WICKED WAYS
CHAOS!

	ORIG	GOOD	FINE	N-MINT
❑1, Feb 98	2.95	0.59	1.48	2.95
❑1/SC, Feb 98, white background cover; premium edition	—	1.00	2.50	5.00

LADY DRACULA
FANTACO

Value: Cover or less

- ❑1 .... 4.95
- ❑2, Gravy Train 4.95

LADY JUSTICE (VOL. 1) (NEIL GAIMAN'S...)
TEKNO

Value: Cover or less

- ❑1, Sep 95, Hope & Dread, 1: Lady Justice 1.95
- ❑2, Oct 95, Stepp'd in Blood... 1.95
- ❑3, Nov 95, More Wretched Than He Who Suffers 1.95
- ❑4, Dec 95, Wrong Time, Wrong Place, Part 1, begins new story-arc with new Lady Justice ... 1.95
- ❑5, Dec 95, Wrong Time, Wrong Place, Part 2 .... 1.95
- ❑6, Jan 96, Wrong Time, Wrong Place, Part 3 .... 2.25
- ❑7, Jan 96, The Chains That Cannot Bind, stand-alone story . 2.25
- ❑8, Feb 96, Ravish'd Justice... 2.25
- ❑9, Mar 96 .... 2.25
- ❑10, Apr 96 .... 2.25
- ❑11, May 96, Final Issue 2.25

LADY JUSTICE (VOL. 2) (NEIL GAIMAN'S...)
BIG

Value: Cover or less

- ❑1, Jun 96, The Big Crossover, Part 13; The Big Crossover, Part 14 .... 2.25
- ❑2, Jul 96, Control Freak Part 1 .... 2.25
- ❑3, Aug 96, Control Freak Part 2 .... 2.25
- ❑4, Sep 96, Control Freak Part 3 .... 2.25
- ❑5, Oct 96 .... 2.25
- ❑6, Nov 96, Woman About Town, Part 1; Woman About Time, Part 1 .... 2.25
- ❑7, Dec 96, Woman About Town, Part 2; Woman About Time, Part 2 .... 2.25
- ❑8, Jan 97, Woman About Town, Part 3; Woman About Time, Part 3 .... 2.25
- ❑9, Feb 97, Final Issue 2.25

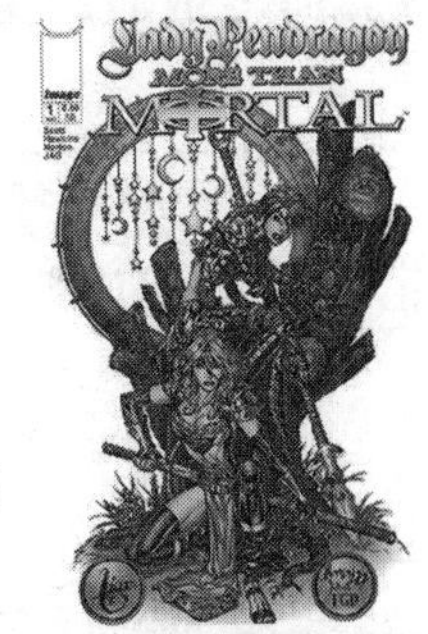

When the self-published *More than Mortal* came to Image, the characters teamed up with Matt Hawkins' *Lady Pendragon.*

© 1999 Image

LADY PENDRAGON (VOL. 1)
MAXIMUM

Value: Cover or less

- ❑1, Mar 96, Destiny Embrace, Rob Liefeld cover 2.50
- ❑1/A, Mar 96, Destiny Embrace, Alternate Cover by Joe Jusko 2.50
- ❑1/Aut, Destiny Embrace, Alternate Cover, Autographed .. 19.95
- ❑1-2, Mar 96, Destiny Embrace, Remastered edition 2.50
- ❑Ash 1, Prelude 6.95
- ❑Ash 1/Aut, Prelude, Signed by Matt Hawkins 19.95

LADY PENDRAGON (VOL. 2)
IMAGE

	ORIG	GOOD	FINE	N-MINT
❑1, Nov 98, The Journey Begins	2.50	0.60	1.50	3.00
❑1/A, Nov 98, alternate cover; castle	2.50	0.60	1.50	3.00
❑1-2, Feb 99, Lady Pendragon Remastered; reprints #1 with corrections	2.50	0.50	1.25	2.50
❑2, Dec 98, The Journey Begins, Photo cover	2.50	0.60	1.50	3.00
❑2/A, Dec 98, alternate cover; photo	2.50	0.60	1.50	3.00
❑3, Jan 99, crucified on cover	2.50	0.50	1.25	2.50
❑3/A, Jan 99, manga-style cover	2.50	0.50	1.25	2.50
❑Ash 1, Jun 98, no cover price; Convention Preview Edition	—	0.60	1.50	3.00

LADY PENDRAGON (VOL. 3)
IMAGE

	ORIG	GOOD	FINE	N-MINT
❑0, Mar 99, The Origin, flipbook with origin back-up	2.50	0.50	1.25	2.50
❑1, Mar 99	2.50	0.50	1.25	2.50
❑2, Apr 99	2.50	0.50	1.25	2.50
❑2/A, Apr 99, alternate cover; Lady Pendragon vanquished	2.50	0.50	1.25	2.50
❑3, Jul 99	2.50	0.50	1.25	2.50
❑4, Aug 99, 1: Blue	2.50	0.50	1.25	2.50
❑5, Sep 99	2.50	0.50	1.25	2.50
❑6, Oct 99	2.50	0.50	1.25	2.50
❑7, Dec 99, Future Prophecy, Part 1, Flipbook; Giant-size	3.95	0.79	1.98	3.95
❑8, Feb 00	3.95	0.50	1.25	2.50
❑9	—	0.50	1.25	2.50
❑10, Aug 00	2.50	0.50	1.25	2.50

LADY PENDRAGON GALLERY EDITION
IMAGE

Value: Cover or less

- ❑1, Oct 99 .... 2.95
- ❑1/A, Oct 99, alternate cover; photo 2.95

LADY PENDRAGON: MERLIN
IMAGE

Value: Cover or less

- ❑1, Jan 00 .... 2.95

LADY PENDRAGON/MORE THAN MORTAL
IMAGE

	ORIG	GOOD	FINE	N-MINT
❑1, May 99	2.50	0.50	1.25	2.50
❑1/A, May 99, alternate cover; white background	2.50	0.80	2.00	4.00
❑1/B, DF alternate cover (holding spear facing forward)	—	1.00	2.50	5.00
❑Ash 1, Feb 99, nn; b&w; no cover price; preview of upcoming crossover	—	0.40	1.00	2.00

LADY RAWHIDE
TOPPS

Value: Cover or less

- ❑1, Jul 95, It Can't Happen Here, Part 1 .... 2.95
- ❑2, Sep 95 .... 2.95
- ❑3, Nov 95 .... 2.95
- ❑4, Jan 96, MG (c) 2.95
- ❑5, Mar 96, Final Issue 2.95

LADY RAWHIDE (VOL. 2)
TOPPS

	ORIG	GOOD	FINE	N-MINT
❑0.5, Playing on Violent Emotions, 1: Star Wolf	—	1.00	2.50	5.00
❑1, Oct 96, Other People's Blood, Part 1, 1: Scarlet Fever	2.95	0.59	1.48	2.95

	ORIG	GOOD	FINE	N-MINT
❑2, Dec 96, Other People's Blood, Part 2, V: Scarlet Fever	2.95	0.59	1.48	2.95
❑3, Feb 97	2.95	0.59	1.48	2.95
❑4, Apr 97, b&w	2.95	0.59	1.48	2.95
❑5, Jun 97, b&w	2.95	0.59	1.48	2.95
❑6, Exists?	2.95	0.59	1.48	2.95
❑7, Exists?	2.95	0.59	1.48	2.95

LADY RAWHIDE MINI COMIC
TOPPS

	ORIG	GOOD	FINE	N-MINT
❑1, Jul 95, no cover price; Wizard supplement	—	0.20	0.50	1.00

LADY RAWHIDE: OTHER PEOPLE'S BLOOD
IMAGE

Value: Cover or less

- ❑1, Mar 99 ..... 2.95
- ❑2, Apr 99, V: Scarlet Fever ... 2.95
- ❑3, May 99, V: Ansel Plague .. 2.95
- ❑4, Jun 99, Intimate Wounds .. 2.95
- ❑5, Jul 99 ..... 2.95

LADY RAWHIDE SPECIAL EDITION
TOPPS

Value: Cover or less

- ❑1, Jun 95, reprints Zorro #2 and 3 ..... 3.95

LADY SPECTRA & SPARKY SPECIAL
J. KEVIN CARRIER

Value: Cover or less

- ❑1, Jan 95, City Held Hostage 2.50

LADY SUPREME
IMAGE

Value: Cover or less

- ❑1, May 96, Die and Let Die, Part 1, aquamarine background cover 2.50
- ❑1/A, May 96, Die and Let Die, Part 1, brown background cover. 2.50
- ❑2, Aug 96, Die and Let Die, Part 2, flip-book with New Men Special Preview Edition 2.50

LADY VAMPRÉ
BLACK OUT

	ORIG	GOOD	FINE	N-MINT
❑0	2.75	0.59	1.48	2.95
❑1	2.95	0.59	1.48	2.95

LADY VAMPRÉ: PLEASURES OF THE FLESH
BLACK OUT

Value: Cover or less

- ❑1, b&w 2.95

LADY VAMPRÉ VS. BLACK LACE
BLACK OUT

Value: Cover or less

- ❑1, Flip-book 2.95

LAFF-A-LYMPICS
MARVEL

	ORIG	GOOD	FINE	N-MINT
❑1, based on Hanna-Barbera animated series	0.35	1.60	4.00	8.00
❑2	0.35	1.20	3.00	6.00
❑3	0.35	1.20	3.00	6.00
❑4	0.35	1.20	3.00	6.00
❑5	0.35	1.20	3.00	6.00
❑6	0.35	1.00	2.50	5.00
❑7	0.35	1.00	2.50	5.00
❑8	0.35	1.00	2.50	5.00
❑9	0.35	1.00	2.50	5.00
❑10	0.35	1.00	2.50	5.00
❑11	0.35	1.00	2.50	5.00
❑12	0.35	1.00	2.50	5.00
❑13	0.35	1.00	2.50	5.00

LAFFIN' GAS
BLACKTHORNE

Value: Cover or less

- ❑1, Jun 86, Adolescent Radioactive Black Belt Hamster: The Untold Story; Radioactive Wrestling Rodents 2.00
- ❑2, The Dark Nightie!; Dork Nyte 2.00
- ❑3 ..... 2.00
- ❑4 ..... 2.00
- ❑5 ..... 2.00
- ❑6, 3-D 2.00
- ❑7 ..... 2.00
- ❑8 ..... 2.00
- ❑9 ..... 2.00
- ❑10 ..... 2.00
- ❑11 ..... 2.00
- ❑12 ..... 2.00

LANCE BARNES: POST NUKE DICK
MARVEL

Value: Cover or less

- ❑1, Apr 93, The Big Bang, Lance accidentally destroys the world 2.50
- ❑2, May 93, The Big Fit 2.50
- ❑3, Jun 93, The Big Chip 2.50
- ❑4, Jul 93 ..... 2.50

LANCELOT LINK, SECRET CHIMP
GOLD KEY

	ORIG	GOOD	FINE	N-MINT
❑1, May 71, On the Beam; Mummy's the Word	0.15	3.60	9.00	18.00
❑2, Aug 71	0.15	2.40	6.00	12.00
❑3	0.15	1.60	4.00	8.00
❑4, Feb 72	0.15	1.60	4.00	8.00
❑5, May 72	0.15	1.60	4.00	8.00
❑6, Aug 72	0.15	1.60	4.00	8.00
❑7, Nov 72	0.15	1.60	4.00	8.00
❑8, Feb 73	0.15	1.60	4.00	8.00

LANCELOT STRONG, THE SHIELD
ARCHIE

	ORIG	GOOD	FINE	N-MINT
❑1, Jun 83	1.00	0.40	1.00	2.00
❑2	1.00	0.40	1.00	2.00

LAND OF NOD, THE
DARK HORSE

Value: Cover or less

- ❑1, Jul 97, b&w 2.95
- ❑2, Nov 97, b&w 2.95
- ❑3, Feb 98, b&w 2.95
- ❑4, Jun 98, b&w 2.95

LAND OF OZ, THE
ARROW

Value: Cover or less

- ❑1, 3-D glasses 2.95
- ❑2 ..... 2.95
- ❑3 ..... 2.95
- ❑4, May 99 ..... 2.95
- ❑5, Jul 99 ..... 2.95
- ❑6, Sep 99 ..... 2.95
- ❑7, Nov 99 ..... 2.95
- ❑8, Mar 00 ..... 2.95
- ❑9, Apr 00 ..... 2.95

LANDRA SPECIAL
ALCHEMY

Value: Cover or less

- ❑1, nn; b&w 2.00

LANN
FANTAGRAPHICS

Value: Cover or less

- ❑1, b&w; adult 2.50

LA PACIFICA
DC

Value: Cover or less

- ❑1, b&w; digest 4.95
- ❑2, b&w; digest 4.95
- ❑3, b&w; digest 4.95

L.A. PHOENIX
DAVID G. BROWN STUDIOS

Value: Cover or less

- ❑1, Jul 94, Rise of the Phoenix, b&w 2.00
- ❑2, Jul 95, The Conflict, b&w .. 2.00
- ❑3, Jul 96, b&w 2.00

L.A. RAPTOR
MORBID

Value: Cover or less

- ❑1 ..... 2.95

LARS OF MARS 3-D
ECLIPSE

Value: Cover or less

- ❑1, MA, When Terrorists Die...; The Earthshaker 2.50

LASER ERASER & PRESSBUTTON
ECLIPSE

	ORIG	GOOD	FINE	N-MINT
❑1, Nov 85, Laser Eraser and Pressbutton: The Depths of Depravity; Laser Eraser and Pressbutton: The Iniquity From Antiquity	0.75	0.30	0.75	1.50
❑2, Dec 85	0.75	0.30	0.75	1.50
❑3	0.75	0.30	0.75	1.50
❑4	0.75	0.30	0.75	1.50
❑5, Laser Eraser and Pressbutton: The Gates of Hell; Ektryn: Citadel of Lost Souls	0.75	0.30	0.75	1.50
❑6	0.75	0.30	0.75	1.50
❑3D 1	2.00	0.40	1.00	2.00

LASH LARUE WESTERN
AC

Value: Cover or less

- ❑1, Reprint; some color 3.50
- ❑Anl 1, b&w; Reprint 2.95

LAST AMERICAN, THE
MARVEL

Value: Cover or less

- ❑1, Goodnight, Poughkeepsie 2.25
- ❑2 ..... 2.25
- ❑3, An American Dream 2.25
- ❑4, Twilight's Last Gleaming ... 2.25

LAST AVENGERS
MARVEL

Value: Cover or less

- ❑1, Nov 95, PD (w), A: Hawkeye; A: Hank Pym; A: Ultron; A: Cannonball; A: Wasp, Alterniverse story 5.95
- ❑2, Dec 95, PD (w), A: Hawkeye; A: Hank Pym; A: Ultron; A: Cannonball; A: Wasp, Alterniverse story 5.95

LAST DANGEROUS CHRISTMAS
AEON

Value: Cover or less

- ❑1, nn; b&w; squarebound; benefit comic for neglected and abused children 5.95

LAST DAYS OF HOLLYWOOD, U.S.A.
MORGAN

	ORIG	GOOD	FINE	N-MINT
❑1	—	0.59	1.48	2.95
❑2	—	0.59	1.48	2.95
❑3	—	0.59	1.48	2.95
❑4	—	0.59	1.48	2.95
❑5	2.95	0.59	1.48	2.95

LAST DAYS OF THE JUSTICE SOCIETY SPECIAL
DC

Value: Cover or less

- ❑1, One-Shot; JSA to Ragnarok after Crisis 2.50

LAST DAZE OF THE BAT-GUY
MYTHIC

Value: Cover or less

- ❑1, b&w 2.95

LAST DEFENDER OF CAMELOT, THE
ZIM

Value: Cover or less

- ❑1, nn; b&w 1.95

ORIG GOOD FINE N-MINT

LAST DITCH
EDGE
Value: Cover or less
- ❑1, b&w 2.50

LAST GASP COMICS AND STORIES
LAST GASP ECO-FUNNIES
Value: Cover or less
- ❑3, b&w; Anthology 3.95

LAST GENERATION, THE
BLACK TIE
Value: Cover or less
- ❑1, From Twin Fires A New Beginning 1.95
- ❑2 .... 1.95
- ❑3 .... 1.95
- ❑4 .... 1.95
- ❑5 .... 1.95

LAST KISS
ECLIPSE
Value: Cover or less
- ❑1, b&w 3.95

LAST OF THE DRAGONS
MARVEL
Value: Cover or less
- ❑1 .... 6.95

LAST OF THE VIKING HEROES, THE
GENESIS WEST
Value: Cover or less
- ❑1, Mar 87, JK (c), Last of the Viking Heroes; The Promise 1.50
- ❑2, Jun 87, GP (c) 2.00
- ❑3, JBy (c) 1.75
- ❑4, HC (c) 1.75
- ❑5/A, JK, DSt (c) 1.95
- ❑5/B 1.95
- ❑6 .... 1.95
- ❑7 .... 1.95
- ❑8 .... 1.95
- ❑9 .... 1.95
- ❑10 .... 2.50
- ❑11 .... 2.50
- ❑12, The Final Confrontation 2.50
- ❑Smr 1, FF (c), JK (w), digest; Summer Special #1 .... 2.50
- ❑Smr 2, A: Teenage Mutant Ninja Turtles, Signed, numbered edition signed by authors; Summer Special #2 .... 2.50
- ❑Smr 3, Apr 91, A: Teenage Mutant Ninja Turtles, Wizard mail-in promotional edition; Summer Special #3 .... 2.50

LAST ONE, THE
DC
Value: Cover or less
- ❑1, Jul 93, Beyond The Curtain 2.50
- ❑2, Aug 93, A Memorable Fancy 2.50
- ❑3, Sep 93 .... 2.50
- ❑4, Oct 93, Reflections 2.50
- ❑5, Nov 93, Need 2.50
- ❑6, Dec 93 .... 2.50

LAST PLANET, THE
MBS
Value: Cover or less
- ❑1, Out Of The Frying Pan; Of Madmen And Gastronomic Ghoulashness 2.50

LAST STARFIGHTER, THE
MARVEL

	ORIG	GOOD	FINE	N-MINT
❑1, Oct 84, movie Adaptation	0.75	0.40	1.00	2.00
❑2, Nov 84, movie Adaptation	0.75	0.40	1.00	2.00
❑3, Dec 84, movie Adaptation	0.75	0.40	1.00	2.00

LAST TEMPTATION, THE
MARVEL MUSIC
Value: Cover or less
- ❑1, May 94, NG (w), Bad Place Alone, A: Alice Cooper 4.95
- ❑2, Aug 94, NG (w) 4.95
- ❑3, Dec 94, NG (w), Cleanse by Fire 4.95

LATIGO KID WESTERN
AC
Value: Cover or less
- ❑1, JSe, The Bigger They Are...; Red Mask of the Rio Grande, b&w 1.95

LAUGH DIGEST MAGAZINE
ARCHIE

	ORIG	GOOD	FINE	N-MINT
❑117, Nov 94	1.75	0.35	0.88	1.75
❑118, Jan 95	1.75	0.35	0.88	1.75
❑119, Mar 95	1.75	0.35	0.88	1.75
❑120, May 95	1.75	0.35	0.88	1.75
❑121, Jul 95	1.75	0.35	0.88	1.75
❑122, Sep 95	1.75	0.35	0.88	1.75
❑123, Nov 95	1.75	0.35	0.88	1.75
❑124, Dec 95	1.75	0.35	0.88	1.75
❑125, Feb 96	1.75	0.35	0.88	1.75
❑126, Apr 96	1.75	0.35	0.88	1.75
❑127, May 96	1.75	0.35	0.88	1.75
❑128, Jul 96	1.75	0.35	0.88	1.75
❑129, Sep 96	1.79	0.36	0.89	1.79
❑130, Oct 96	1.79	0.36	0.89	1.79
❑131, Svenson Appreciation Day; Jewels and Justice	1.79	0.36	0.89	1.79
❑132, Feb 97	1.79	0.36	0.89	1.79
❑133, Apr 97	1.79	0.36	0.89	1.79
❑134, May 97	1.79	0.36	0.89	1.79
❑135, Jul 97	1.79	0.36	0.89	1.79
❑136, Sep 97	1.79	0.36	0.89	1.79
❑137, Oct 97	1.79	0.36	0.89	1.79
❑138, Dec 97	1.79	0.36	0.89	1.79
❑139, Jan 98	1.95	0.39	0.98	1.95
❑140, Mar 98	1.95	0.39	0.98	1.95

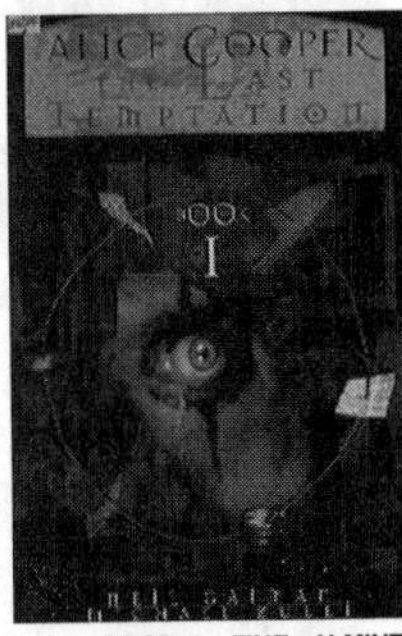

While its title is misleadingly similar to an infamous Martin Scorsese film, Marvel's *Last Temptation*, written by Neil Gaiman, featured Alice Cooper.

	ORIG	GOOD	FINE	N-MINT
❑141, May 98	1.95	0.39	0.98	1.95
❑142, Jul 98	1.95	0.39	0.98	1.95
❑143, Aug 98	1.95	0.39	0.98	1.95
❑144, Oct 98	1.95	0.39	0.98	1.95
❑145, Nov 98, DDC	1.95	0.39	0.98	1.95
❑146, Jan 99	1.95	0.39	0.98	1.95
❑147, Mar 99	1.95	0.39	0.98	1.95
❑148, Apr 99	1.99	0.40	1.00	1.99
❑149, May 99	1.99	0.40	1.00	1.99
❑150, Jul 99	1.99	0.40	1.00	1.99
❑151, Aug 99	1.99	0.40	1.00	1.99
❑152, Oct 99	1.99	0.40	1.00	1.99
❑153, Nov 99	1.99	0.40	1.00	1.99
❑154, Jan 00	1.99	0.40	1.00	1.99
❑155, Mar 00	1.99	0.40	1.00	1.99
❑156, May 00	1.99	0.40	1.00	1.99
❑157, Jul 00	2.19	0.44	1.10	2.19
❑158, Aug 00	2.19	0.44	1.10	2.19
❑159, Oct 00	2.19	0.44	1.10	2.19
❑160, Nov 00	2.19	0.44	1.10	2.19
❑161, Dec 00	2.19	0.44	1.10	2.19
❑162, Jan 01	2.19	0.44	1.10	2.19
❑163, Feb 01	2.19	0.44	1.10	2.19
❑164, Apr 01	2.19	0.44	1.10	2.19
❑165	2.19	0.44	1.10	2.19
❑166	2.19	0.44	1.10	2.19
❑167	2.19	0.44	1.10	2.19
❑168	2.19	0.44	1.10	2.19

LAUNCH!
ELSEWHERE
Value: Cover or less
- ❑1, 1: Conscience 1.75

LAUNDRYLAND
FANTAGRAPHICS
Value: Cover or less
- ❑1, b&w 2.25
- ❑2, b&w 2.50
- ❑3, b&w 2.50
- ❑4, b&w 2.50

LAUREL & HARDY IN 3-D
BLACKTHORNE
Value: Cover or less
- ❑1, Fal 87, aka Blackthorne 3-D #23 .... 2.50
- ❑2, Dec 87, aka Blackthorne 3-D #34 .... 2.50

LAVA
CROSSBREED
Value: Cover or less
- ❑1 .... 2.95

LAW, THE
ASYLUM GRAPHICS
Value: Cover or less
- ❑1, b&w; no publication date 1.75

L.A.W., THE (LIVING ASSAULT WEAPONS)
DC
Value: Cover or less
- ❑1, Sep 99, DG, BL (w), Avatar Rising 2.50
- ❑2, Oct 99, DG, BL (w), The Way of the Warrior 2.50
- ❑3, Nov 99 .... 2.50
- ❑4, Dec 99, DG, BL (w), Martial L.A.W. 2.50
- ❑5, Jan 00, DG, BL (w), To Serve and Protect 2.50
- ❑6, DG, BL (w) 2.50

LAW AND ORDER
MAXIMUM
Value: Cover or less
- ❑1, Sep 95, O: Law and Order 2.50
- ❑1/A, Sep 95, O: Law and Order, Alternate cover with women standing atop body 2.50
- ❑2, Oct 95 .... 2.50
- ❑3 .... 2.50

LAWDOG
MARVEL
Value: Cover or less
- ❑1, May 93, Lost Highway, 1: Lawdog, Embossed cover 2.50
- ❑2, Jun 93 .... 1.95
- ❑3, Jul 93 .... 1.95
- ❑4, Aug 93 .... 1.95
- ❑5, Sep 93 .... 1.95
- ❑6, Oct 93, A: 'Lina; A: Dr. Freen; A: Cleanies 1.95
- ❑7, Nov 93 .... 1.95
- ❑8, Dec 93, trading card 1.95
- ❑9, Jan 94 .... 1.95
- ❑10, Feb 94, Final Issue 1.95

LAWDOG AND GRIMROD: TERROR AT THE CROSSROADS
MARVEL
Value: Cover or less
- ❑1 .... 3.50

LAW OF DREDD, THE
FLEETWAY

	ORIG	GOOD	FINE	N-MINT
❑1, BB, Judge Dredd: Judge Death, Reprints Judge Dredd stories from 2000 A.D. #149-	1.50	0.50	1.25	2.50
❑2	1.50	0.40	1.00	2.00
❑3, V: Judge Death	1.50	0.40	1.00	2.00
❑4	1.50	0.40	1.00	2.00
❑5	1.50	0.40	1.00	2.00
❑6	1.50	0.40	1.00	2.00
❑7	1.50	0.40	1.00	2.00
❑8	1.50	0.40	1.00	2.00
❑9	1.75	0.40	1.00	2.00
❑10	1.75	0.40	1.00	2.00
❑11	1.75	0.40	1.00	2.00
❑12	1.75	0.40	1.00	2.00
❑13, A: Judge Caligula	1.75	0.40	1.00	2.00
❑14	1.75	0.40	1.00	2.00
❑15	1.75	0.40	1.00	2.00
❑16	1.75	0.35	0.88	1.75
❑17	1.75	0.35	0.88	1.75
❑18	1.75	0.35	0.88	1.75
❑19	1.75	0.35	0.88	1.75
❑20	1.75	0.35	0.88	1.75
❑21	1.75	0.35	0.88	1.75
❑22	1.75	0.35	0.88	1.75
❑23	1.75	0.35	0.88	1.75
❑24	1.75	0.35	0.88	1.75
❑25	1.75	0.35	0.88	1.75
❑26	1.75	0.35	0.88	1.75
❑27	1.75	0.35	0.88	1.75
❑28	1.75	0.35	0.88	1.75
❑29	1.75	0.35	0.88	1.75
❑30	1.75	0.39	0.98	1.95
❑31	1.95	0.39	0.98	1.95
❑32	1.95	0.39	0.98	1.95
❑33, Final Issue	1.95	0.39	0.98	1.95

LAZARUS CHURCHYARD
TUNDRA

Value: Cover or less

❑1 .... 4.50
❑2 .... 4.50
❑3 .... 4.95

LAZARUS FIVE
DC

Value: Cover or less

❑1, Jul 00 .... 2.50
❑2, Aug 00 .... 2.50
❑3, Sep 00, Prodigal Son 2.50
❑4, Oct 00, Chosen 2.50
❑5, Nov 00 .... 2.50

LAZARUS PITS, THE
BONEYARD

	ORIG	GOOD	FINE	N-MINT
❑1	2.75	0.80	2.00	4.00

LEAF
NAB

Value: Cover or less

❑1 .... 1.95
❑1/Dlx, deluxe 4.95

LEAGUE OF CHAMPIONS, THE
HERO

	ORIG	GOOD	FINE	N-MINT
❑1, Dec 90, The Gods at War; Perceptions	2.95	0.70	1.75	3.50
❑2, Feb 91, O: Malice (true origin)	2.95	0.70	1.75	3.50
❑3, Apr 91	2.95	0.70	1.75	3.50
❑4, b&w	3.50	0.70	1.75	3.50
❑5, b&w	3.50	0.70	1.75	3.50
❑6, b&w	3.50	0.70	1.75	3.50
❑7, b&w	3.50	0.70	1.75	3.50
❑8, b&w	3.50	0.70	1.75	3.50
❑9, Gargoyle!, b&w	3.50	0.70	1.75	3.50
❑10, b&w	3.50	0.70	1.75	3.50
❑11, b&w	3.95	0.79	1.98	3.95
❑12, Jul 93	2.95	0.59	1.48	2.95

LEAGUE OF EXTRAORDINARY GENTLEMEN, THE
DC

	ORIG	GOOD	FINE	N-MINT
❑1, Mar 99, AMo (w)	2.95	0.80	2.00	4.00
❑1/A, Apr 99, AMo (w), Certificate of Authenticity; DF Alternate; 5000 copies	—	1.20	3.00	6.00
❑2, Apr 99, AMo (w)	2.95	0.70	1.75	3.50
❑3, May 99, AMo (w), Mysteries of the East	2.95	0.60	1.50	3.00
❑4, Nov 99, AMo (w), Gods of Annihilation	2.95	0.59	1.48	2.95
❑5, AMo (w)	2.95	0.59	1.48	2.95
❑5/A, AMo (w), Contained fake ad for The Marvel; All but est. 200 destroyed by DC	2.95	5.00	12.50	25.00
❑6, Sep 00, AMo (w), Young Helpers League	2.95	0.59	1.48	2.95
❑Dlx 1, AMo (w), Hardcover edition, collects series	24.95	4.99	12.48	24.95

LEAGUE OF JUSTICE
DC

Value: Cover or less

❑1, Stave One: Hero Quest, prestige format; Elseworlds 5.95
❑2, Stave Two: Hero War, prestige format; Elseworlds 5.95

LEAGUE OF RATS, THE
CALIBER

Value: Cover or less

❑1, b&w 2.95

LEAGUE OF SUPER GROOVY CRIMEFIGHTERS
ANCIENT

Value: Cover or less

❑1, Jun 00, 1: Atlas (crimefighter); 1: The Ring; 1: X; 1: Mr. Phenomenal; 1: Thor (Crimefighter); 1: Cupid; 1: Black Belt 2.95
❑2 .... 2.95
❑3 .... 2.95
❑4 .... 2.95
❑5 .... 2.95

LEATHER & LACE
AIRCEL

Value: Cover or less

❑1/A, b&w; adult; Adult version 2.50
❑1/B, b&w; adult; Tame version 1.95
❑2/A, b&w; adult; Adult version 2.50
❑2/B, b&w; adult; Tame version 1.95
❑3/A, b&w; adult; Adult version 2.50
❑3/B, b&w; adult; Tame version 1.95
❑4/A, b&w; adult; Adult version 2.50
❑4/B, b&w; adult; Tame version 1.95
❑5/A, b&w; adult; Adult version 2.50
❑5/B, b&w; adult; Tame version 1.95
❑6/A, b&w; adult; Adult version 2.50
❑6/B, b&w; adult; Tame version 1.95
❑7/A, b&w; adult; Adult version 2.50
❑7/B, b&w; adult; Tame version 1.95
❑8/A, b&w; adult; Adult version 2.50
❑8/B, b&w; adult; Tame version 1.95
❑9, b&w; adult 2.50
❑10, b&w; adult 2.50
❑11, b&w; adult 2.50
❑12, Jul 90, b&w; adult 2.50
❑13, Aug 90, b&w; adult 2.50
❑14, Sep 90, b&w; adult 2.50
❑15, Oct 90, b&w; adult 2.50
❑16, Nov 90, b&w; adult 2.50
❑17, Dec 90, b&w; adult 2.50
❑18, Jan 91, b&w; adult 2.50
❑19, Feb 91, b&w; adult 2.50
❑20, Mar 91, b&w; adult 2.50
❑21, Apr 91, b&w; adult 2.50
❑22, May 91, b&w; adult 2.95
❑23, Jun 91, b&w; adult 2.95
❑24, Jul 91, b&w; adult 2.95
❑25, Aug 91, b&w; adult; Final Issue 2.95

LEATHER & LACE: BLOOD, SEX, & TEARS
AIRCEL

Value: Cover or less

❑1, Oct 91, b&w; adult 2.95
❑2, Nov 91, b&w; adult 2.95
❑3, Dec 91, b&w; adult 2.95
❑4, Jan 92, adult 2.95

LEATHER & LACE SUMMER SPECIAL
AIRCEL

Value: Cover or less

❑1, Jun 90, b&w; adult 2.50

LEATHERBOY
EROS

Value: Cover or less

❑1, Jul 94 .... 2.95
❑2, Oct 94, The Mayhem- and the Mob! 2.95
❑3, Nov 94, The Company She Keeps 2.95

LEATHERFACE
ARPAD

Value: Cover or less

❑1 .... 2.75

LEATHER UNDERWEAR
FANTAGRAPHICS

Value: Cover or less

❑1, b&w 2.50

LEAVE IT TO CHANCE
IMAGE

	ORIG	GOOD	FINE	N-MINT
❑1, Sep 96, PS, JRo (w), One Little Indian	2.50	0.60	1.50	3.00
❑1-2, PS, JRo (w), One Little Indian, 2nd Printing	2.50	0.50	1.25	2.50
❑2, Oct 96, PS, JRo (w)	2.50	0.70	1.75	3.50
❑3, Nov 96, PS, JRo (w), Rain	2.50	0.60	1.50	3.00
❑4, Feb 97, PS, JRo (w), Bad Toad Rising	2.50	0.60	1.50	3.00
❑5, May 97, PS, JRo (w)	2.50	0.60	1.50	3.00
❑6, Jul 97, PS, JRo (w)	2.50	0.50	1.25	2.50
❑7, Oct 97, PS, JRo (w), And Not a Drop to Drink	2.50	0.50	1.25	2.50
❑8, Feb 98, PS, JRo (w), The Phantom of the Mall	2.50	0.50	1.25	2.50
❑9, Apr 98, PS, JRo (w), Midnite Monster Madness	2.50	0.50	1.25	2.50
❑10, Jun 98, PS, JRo (w), Destroy All Monsters	2.50	0.50	1.25	2.50
❑11, Sep 98, PS, JRo (w), Dead Men Can't Skate	2.50	0.59	1.48	2.95
❑12, Jun 99, PS, JRo (w), The Promise	2.95	0.59	1.48	2.95

LED ZEPPELIN
PERSONALITY

Value: Cover or less

❑1, b&w 2.95
❑2, b&w 2.95
❑3, b&w 2.95
❑4, b&w 2.95

LED ZEPPELIN EXPERIENCE, THE
REVOLUTIONARY

Value: Cover or less

❑1, Aug 92, Shapes Off Things To Come, b&w 2.50
❑2, Oct 92, b&w 2.50
❑3, Dec 92, b&w 2.50
❑4, Jan 93, b&w 2.50
❑5, Feb 93, b&w 2.50

LEFT-FIELD FUNNIES
APEX NOVELTIES

	ORIG	GOOD	FINE	N-MINT
❑1, Artie Schnopp the Happy Cop; Merton:	0.50	0.80	2.00	4.00

LEGACY
MAJESTIC

	ORIG	GOOD	FINE	N-MINT
❑0, Aug 93	—	0.45	1.13	2.25
❑0/GO, Aug 93, gold	—	0.45	1.13	2.25
❑1, Oct 93, Pledge For Allegiance	2.25	0.45	1.13	2.25
❑2, Jan 94	2.25	0.45	1.13	2.25

LEGACY (FRED PERRY'S...)
ANTARCTIC

Value: Cover or less

❑1, Aug 99 ... 2.99

LEGACY OF KAIN: SOUL REAVER
TOP COW

	ORIG	GOOD	FINE	N-MINT
❑1, Oct 99	—	0.40	1.00	2.00

LEGEND LORE (ARROW)
ARROW

Value: Cover or less

❑1, Before the Storm, b&w ... 2.00
❑2, b&w ... 2.00

LEGENDLORE (CALIBER)
CALIBER

Value: Cover or less

❑1 ... 2.95
❑2 ... 2.95
❑3 ... 2.95
❑4 ... 2.95

LEGEND OF JEDIT OJANEN ON THE WORLD OF MAGIC: THE GATHERING
ACCLAIM

Value: Cover or less

❑1, Mar 96, polybagged with card ... 2.50
❑2, Apr 96, Jedits Tales, Final Issue ... 2.50

LEGEND OF KAMUI, THE
ECLIPSE

	ORIG	GOOD	FINE	N-MINT
❑1, Ichijiro (One White), Part 1, b&w; Japanese	1.50	0.60	1.50	3.00
❑1-2, Ichijiro (One White), Part 1, 2nd Printing	1.50	0.30	0.75	1.50
❑2, Ichijiro (One White), Part 2	1.50	0.40	1.00	2.00
❑2-2, Ichijiro (One White), Part 2, 2nd Printing	1.50	0.30	0.75	1.50
❑3, Red Medusas, Part 1	1.50	0.40	1.00	2.00
❑3-2, Red Medusas, Part 1	1.50	0.30	0.75	1.50
❑4, Red Medusas, Part 2	1.50	0.30	0.75	1.50
❑5	1.50	0.30	0.75	1.50
❑6	1.50	0.30	0.75	1.50
❑7	1.50	0.30	0.75	1.50
❑8	1.50	0.30	0.75	1.50
❑9	1.50	0.30	0.75	1.50
❑10	1.50	0.30	0.75	1.50
❑11	1.50	0.30	0.75	1.50
❑12	1.50	0.30	0.75	1.50
❑13	1.50	0.30	0.75	1.50
❑14	1.50	0.30	0.75	1.50
❑15, Dec 87	1.50	0.30	0.75	1.50
❑16, Jan 88, After Sunset, Part 1	1.50	0.30	0.75	1.50
❑17, Jan 88, After Sunset, Part 2	1.50	0.30	0.75	1.50
❑18, Feb 88, 48pgs	1.95	0.30	0.75	1.50
❑19, Feb 88	1.50	0.30	0.75	1.50
❑20, Mar 88	1.50	0.30	0.75	1.50
❑21, Mar 88	1.50	0.30	0.75	1.50
❑22, Apr 88	1.50	0.30	0.75	1.50
❑23, Apr 88	1.50	0.30	0.75	1.50
❑24, May 88	1.50	0.30	0.75	1.50
❑25, May 88	1.50	0.30	0.75	1.50
❑26, Jun 88	1.50	0.30	0.75	1.50
❑27, Jun 88	1.50	0.30	0.75	1.50
❑28, Jul 88	1.50	0.30	0.75	1.50
❑29, Jul 88	1.50	0.30	0.75	1.50
❑30, Aug 88	1.50	0.30	0.75	1.50
❑31, Aug 88	1.50	0.30	0.75	1.50
❑32, Sep 88	1.50	0.30	0.75	1.50
❑33, Sep 88	1.50	0.30	0.75	1.50
❑34, Oct 88	1.50	0.30	0.75	1.50
❑35, Oct 88	1.50	0.30	0.75	1.50
❑36, Nov 88	1.50	0.30	0.75	1.50
❑37, Nov 88, Final Issue	1.50	0.30	0.75	1.50

LEGEND OF LEMNEAR
CPM

	ORIG	GOOD	FINE	N-MINT
❑1, Jan 98, Legend of the Descent, wraparound cover	2.95	0.60	1.50	3.00
❑2, Feb 98, Unexpected Compassion	2.95	0.60	1.50	3.00
❑3, Mar 98, Vestiges of War	2.95	0.60	1.50	3.00
❑4, Apr 98, Impure Bronze, Part 1	2.95	0.60	1.50	3.00
❑5, May 98, Impure Bronze, Part 2	2.95	0.60	1.50	3.00
❑6, Jun 98, Pulsating Anguish, wraparound cover	2.95	0.60	1.50	3.00
❑7, Jul 98, The Face of Absurdity, wraparound cover	2.95	0.60	1.50	3.00
❑8, Aug 98, The Dilemma of Destiny	2.95	0.59	1.48	2.95
❑9, Sep 98	2.95	0.59	1.48	2.95
❑10, Oct 98	2.95	0.59	1.48	2.95
❑11, Nov 98	2.95	0.59	1.48	2.95

Aircel published adult and "tame" versions of the cover of each issue of *Leather & Lace.*

© 1989 Barry Blair (Aircel)

	ORIG	GOOD	FINE	N-MINT
❑12, Dec 98	2.95	0.59	1.48	2.95
❑13, Jan 99, wraparound cover	2.95	0.59	1.48	2.95
❑14, Feb 99	2.95	0.59	1.48	2.95

LEGEND OF LILITH
IMAGE

Value: Cover or less

❑0, no date ... 4.95

LEGEND OF MOTHER SARAH
DARK HORSE

Value: Cover or less

❑1, b&w ... 2.95
❑2, b&w ... 2.95
❑3, b&w ... 2.95
❑4, b&w ... 2.95
❑5, b&w ... 2.95
❑6, Sep 95, b&w ... 2.95
❑7, Oct 95, b&w ... 2.95
❑8, Nov 95, b&w; Final Issue .. 2.95

LEGEND OF MOTHER SARAH, THE: CITY OF THE ANGELS
DARK HORSE

Value: Cover or less

❑1, Oct 97 ... 3.95
❑2, Dec 97 ... 3.95
❑3, Jan 98 ... 3.95
❑4, Feb 98 ... 3.95
❑5, Mar 98 ... 3.95
❑6, Apr 98 ... 3.95
❑7, May 98 ... 3.95
❑8, Jun 98 ... 3.95
❑9, Jul 98 ... 3.95

LEGEND OF MOTHER SARAH, THE: CITY OF THE CHILDREN
DARK HORSE

Value: Cover or less

❑1, Jan 96 ... 3.95
❑2, Feb 96 ... 3.95
❑3, Mar 96 ... 3.95
❑4, Apr 96 ... 3.95
❑5, May 96 ... 3.95
❑6, Jun 96 ... 3.95
❑7, Jul 96 ... 3.95

LEGEND OF SLEEPY HOLLOW, THE
TUNDRA

Value: Cover or less

❑1, nn ... 6.95

LEGEND OF SUPREME
IMAGE

Value: Cover or less

❑1, Dec 94, KG (w), O: Supreme ... 2.50
❑2, Jan 95, KG (w), O: Supreme ... 2.50
❑3, Feb 95, KG (w), O: Supreme ... 2.50

LEGEND OF THE DC UNIVERSE: SUPERMAN
DC

Value: Cover or less

❑1, JRo (w), U.L.T.R.A. Humanite, Part 1, Madness and Science 1.95
❑2 ... 1.95
❑3 ... 1.95

LEGEND OF THE ELFLORD
DAVDEZ

Value: Cover or less

❑1, Jul 98 ... 2.95
❑2, Sep 98 ... 2.95
❑3 ... 2.95

LEGEND OF THE HAWKMAN
DC

Value: Cover or less

❑1 ... 4.95
❑2 ... 4.95
❑3, Flight of Faith ... 4.95

LEGEND OF THE SHIELD, THE
DC

Value: Cover or less

❑1, Jul 91, The Glory Makers, O: Shield ... 1.00
❑2, Aug 91 ... 1.00
❑3, Sep 91, 1: Millie Mazda; 1: The Black Hood (Wayne Sidmonson); 1: Bert Watson; 1: The Weapon ... 1.00
❑4, Oct 91, The Dark Mirror!!, V: Weapon ... 1.00
❑5, Nov 91, 1: Dusty Madigan 1.00
❑6, Dec 91, A: Fly; 1: Theo Carver ... 1.00
❑7, Jan 92, A: Fly ... 1.00
❑8, Feb 92, 1: The Shield I (Roger Higgins); V: Weapon ... 1.00
❑9, Mar 92 ... 1.00
❑10, Apr 92 ... 1.00
❑11, May 92, trading card ... 1.00
❑12, Jun 92 ... 1.25
❑13, Jul 92, The Glory Machine 1.25
❑14, Aug 92 ... 1.25
❑15, Sep 92 ... 1.25
❑16, Oct 92, Final Issue ... 1.25
❑Anl 1, Earth Quest, Part 2, trading card ... 2.50

LEGEND OF WONDER WOMAN, THE
DC

	ORIG	GOOD	FINE	N-MINT
❑1, May 86, KB, KB (w), Legends Live Forever	1.00	0.30	0.75	1.50
❑2, Jun 86, KB, KB (w)	1.00	0.30	0.75	1.50
❑3, Jul 86, KB, KB (w)	1.00	0.30	0.75	1.50
❑4, Aug 86, KB, KB (w)	1.00	0.30	0.75	1.50

LEGEND OF ZELDA, THE
VALIANT

Value: Cover or less

- ❑1 .... 1.95
- ❑2 .... 1.95
- ❑3 .... 1.95
- ❑4 .... 1.95
- ❑5 .... 1.95

LEGEND OF ZELDA, THE (2ND SERIES)
VALIANT

Value: Cover or less

- ❑1 .... 1.50
- ❑2 .... 1.50
- ❑3 .... 1.50
- ❑4 .... 1.50
- ❑5 .... 1.50

LEGENDS
DC

	ORIG	GOOD	FINE	N-MINT
❑1, Nov 86, JBy, Once Upon A Time...!, 1: Amanda Waller	0.75	0.40	1.00	2.00
❑2, Dec 86, JBy	0.75	0.30	0.75	1.50
❑3, Jan 87, JBy, 1: Suicide Squad (modern)	0.75	0.40	1.00	2.00
❑4, Feb 87, JBy	0.75	0.30	0.75	1.50
❑5, Mar 87, JBy	0.75	0.30	0.75	1.50
❑6, Apr 87, JBy, 1: Justice League	0.75	0.60	1.50	3.00

LEGENDS AND FOLKLORE
ZONE

Value: Cover or less

- ❑1, b&w 2.95
- ❑2, b&w 2.95

LEGENDS OF ELFINWILD, THE
WEHNER

Value: Cover or less

- ❑1, b&w 1.75

LEGENDS OF KID DEATH & FLUFFY
EVENT

Value: Cover or less

- ❑1, No Good Deed Goes Unpunished; I "Bone" New York 2.95

LEGENDS OF LUXURA
BRAINSTORM

	ORIG	GOOD	FINE	N-MINT
❑1, Feb 96, b&w; collects Luxura stories	2.95	0.59	1.48	2.95
❑1/LE, Feb 96, no cover price; Special edition; limited to 1000 copies	—	1.00	2.50	5.00

LEGENDS OF NASCAR, THE
VORTEX

Value: Cover or less

- ❑1, HT, HT (w), Bill Elliott 3.00
- ❑1-2, HT, HT (w), 2nd Printing; trading cards; Bill Elliott 3.00
- ❑, HT, HT (w), 3rd Printing; trading cards; Bill Elliott; Indicia marks it as 2nd Printing 3.00
- ❑2, Richard Petty; no indicia 2.00
- ❑2/SC, hologram 5.00
- ❑3, Ken Shrader 2.00
- ❑4, Bobby Allison 2.00
- ❑5, Sterling Marlin 2.00
- ❑6 .... 2.00
- ❑7 .... 2.00
- ❑8, DH, Benny Parsons 2.00
- ❑9, Rusty Wallace 2.00
- ❑10, Talladega Story 2.00
- ❑11, Morgan Shepherd 2.00
- ❑12 .... 2.00
- ❑13 .... 2.00
- ❑14 .... 2.00
- ❑15 .... 2.00
- ❑16, Final issue (?) 2.00

LEGENDS OF THE DARK CLAW
DC

	ORIG	GOOD	FINE	N-MINT
❑1, Apr 96, Through A Glass Darkly, O: The Dark Claw; O: The Hyena	1.95	0.40	1.00	2.00

LEGENDS OF THE DCU: CRISIS ON INFINITE EARTHS
DC

	ORIG	GOOD	FINE	N-MINT
❑1, Feb 99, The Untold Story, A: Flash II (Barry Allen, Takes place between Crisis of Infinite Earths #4 and #5; Supergirl I (Kara Zor-El)	4.95	0.99	2.47	4.95

LEGENDS OF THE DC UNIVERSE
DC

	ORIG	GOOD	FINE	N-MINT
❑1, Feb 98, Superman	1.95	0.60	1.50	3.00
❑2, Mar 98, Superman	1.95	0.50	1.25	2.50
❑3, Apr 98, Superman	1.95	0.50	1.25	2.50
❑4, May 98, Wonder Woman	1.95	0.50	1.25	2.50
❑5, Jun 98, Wonder Woman	1.95	0.50	1.25	2.50
❑6, Jul 98, Robin, Superman	1.95	0.45	1.13	2.25
❑7, Aug 98, Green Lantern/Green Arrow	1.95	0.45	1.13	2.25
❑8, Sep 98, Green Lantern/Green Arrow	1.99	0.45	1.13	2.25
❑9, Oct 98, Green Lantern/Green Arrow	1.99	0.45	1.13	2.25
❑10, Nov 98, Batgirl	1.99	0.45	1.13	2.25
❑11, Dec 98, Batgirl	1.99	0.45	1.13	2.25
❑12, Jan 99, Critical Mass, Part 1, JLA	1.99	0.45	1.13	2.25
❑13, Feb 99, Critical Mass, Part 2, JLA	1.99	0.45	1.13	2.25
❑14, Mar 99, SR, ME (w); JK (w), A: Mokkari; A: Guardian; A: Darkseid; A: Superman; A: Simyan; A: Jimmy Olsen	3.95	0.45	1.13	2.25
❑15, Apr 99, Dark Matters, Part 1, A: Flash II (Barry Allen)	1.99	0.45	1.13	2.25
❑16, May 99, Dark Matters, Part 2, A: Flash II (Barry Allen)	1.99	0.45	1.13	2.25
❑17, Jun 99, Dark Matters, Part 3, A: Flash II (Barry Allen)	1.99	0.45	1.13	2.25
❑18, Jul 99, Conflicting Emotions, Kid Flash, Raven	1.99	0.45	1.13	2.25
❑19, Aug 99, Manchester Monkey Business, Impulse; prelude to JLApe Annuals	1.99	0.45	1.13	2.25
❑20, Sep 99, MZ, The Trail of the Traitor Part 1, Green Lantern: Abin Sur	1.99	0.45	1.13	2.25
❑21, Oct 99, MZ, The Trail of the Traitor Part 2, Green Lantern: Abin Sur	1.99	0.40	1.00	1.99
❑22, Nov 99, Transilvane, Part 1; Supremum Vale	1.99	0.40	1.00	1.99
❑23, Dec 99, Dies Irae	1.99	0.40	1.00	1.99
❑24, Jan 00, The Jump, Part 1	1.99	0.40	1.00	1.99
❑25, Feb 00	1.99	0.40	1.00	1.99
❑26, Mar 00	1.99	0.40	1.00	1.99
❑27, Apr 00, TVE, Reign of the Joker!	1.99	0.40	1.00	1.99
❑28, May 00, KJ; GK, A Small Revenge	1.99	0.40	1.00	1.99
❑29, Jun 00	1.99	0.40	1.00	1.99
❑30, Jul 00	—	0.40	1.00	1.99
❑31, Aug 00	—	0.40	1.00	1.99
❑32, Sep 00, The 18th Letter	2.50	0.50	1.25	2.50
❑33, Oct 00, Destroyer of Worlds, Part 1	2.50	0.50	1.25	2.50
❑34, Nov 00, Destroyer of Worlds, Part 2	2.50	0.50	1.25	2.50
❑35, Dec 00, Destroyer of Worlds, Part 3	2.50	0.50	1.25	2.50
❑36, Jan 01, Destroyer of Worlds, Part 4	2.50	0.50	1.25	2.50
❑37, Feb 01, The Tragedy of the Traitor, Part 1	2.50	0.50	1.25	2.50
❑38, Mar 01, The Tragedy of the Traitor, Part 2	2.50	0.50	1.25	2.50
❑39, Apr 01, Sole Survivor of Earth	2.50	0.50	1.25	2.50
❑40, May 01, Lessons in Time, Part 1	2.50	0.50	1.25	2.50
❑GS 1, Sep 98, 80pgs.; Spectre, Hawkman, Teen Titans, Adam Strange, Chronos, Doom Patrol, Rip Hunter, Linear Men	4.95	0.99	2.47	4.95
❑GS 2, Jan 00, The Great Unknown; Twisted	4.95	0.99	2.47	4.95

LEGENDS OF THE DC UNIVERSE 3-D GALLERY
DC

Value: Cover or less

- ❑1, Dec 98, pin-ups 2.95

LEGENDS OF THE LEGION
DC

Value: Cover or less

- ❑1, Feb 98, O: Ultra Boy 2.25
- ❑2, Mar 98, Resistance, O: Spark 2.25
- ❑3, Apr 98, O: Umbra 2.25
- ❑4, May 98, O: Star Boy 2.25

LEGENDS OF THE LIVING DEAD
FANTACO

Value: Cover or less

- ❑1 .... 3.95

LEGENDS OF THE STARGRAZERS
INNOVATION

Value: Cover or less

- ❑1, Aug 89, Here There Be Dragons 1.95
- ❑2 .... 1.95
- ❑3 .... 1.95
- ❑4 .... 1.95
- ❑5 .... 1.95
- ❑6 .... 1.95

LEGENDS OF THE WORLD'S FINEST
DC

Value: Cover or less

- ❑1, Perchance To Dream 4.95
- ❑2 .... 4.95
- ❑3, Superman, Batman 4.95

L.E.G.I.O.N.
DC

	ORIG	GOOD	FINE	N-MINT
❑1, Feb 89, KG (w), Homecoming, 1: Stealth; O: L.E.G.I.O.N., L.E.G.I.O.N. '89 starts	1.50	0.50	1.25	2.50
❑2, Mar 89	1.50	0.40	1.00	2.00
❑3, Apr 89	1.50	0.40	1.00	2.00
❑4, May 89, A: Lobo	1.50	0.40	1.00	2.00
❑5, Jun 89, Lobo joins team	1.50	0.40	1.00	2.00
❑6, Jul 89	1.50	0.35	0.88	1.75
❑7, Aug 89	1.50	0.35	0.88	1.75
❑8, Sep 89	1.50	0.35	0.88	1.75
❑9, Nov 89, A: Phantom Girl	1.50	0.35	0.88	1.75
❑10, Dec 89	1.50	0.35	0.88	1.75
❑11, Jan 90, L.E.G.I.O.N. '90 starts	1.50	0.30	0.75	1.50
❑12, Feb 90, A: Emerald Eye	1.50	0.30	0.75	1.50
❑13, Mar 90	1.50	0.30	0.75	1.50
❑14, Apr 90	1.50	0.30	0.75	1.50
❑15, May 90	1.50	0.30	0.75	1.50
❑16, Jun 90, A: Lar Gand	1.50	0.30	0.75	1.50
❑17, Jul 90	1.50	0.30	0.75	1.50
❑18, Aug 90	1.50	0.30	0.75	1.50
❑19, Sep 90	1.50	0.30	0.75	1.50
❑20, Oct 90	1.50	0.30	0.75	1.50
❑21, Nov 90	1.50	0.30	0.75	1.50
❑22, Dec 90, A: Lady Quark	1.50	0.30	0.75	1.50
❑23, Jan 91, L.E.G.I.O.N. '91 starts	2.50	0.50	1.25	2.50
❑24, Feb 91	1.50	0.30	0.75	1.50
❑25, Mar 91	1.50	0.30	0.75	1.50
❑26, Apr 91	1.50	0.30	0.75	1.50
❑27, May 91	1.50	0.30	0.75	1.50
❑28, Jun 91, KG (w), Hard Labor	1.50	0.30	0.75	1.50
❑29, Jul 91	1.50	0.30	0.75	1.50

	ORIG	GOOD	FINE	N-MINT
❑30, Aug 91, 1: Ig'nea	1.50	0.30	0.75	1.50
❑31, Sep 91, War of the Gods, Part 5, Painted cover; Lobo vs. Captain Marvel; Lobo vs. Capt. Marvel	1.50	0.30	0.75	1.50
❑32, Oct 91, 1: Ice Man	1.50	0.30	0.75	1.50
❑33, Nov 91	1.50	0.30	0.75	1.50
❑34, Dec 91	1.50	0.30	0.75	1.50
❑35, Jan 92, L.E.G.I.O.N. '92 starts	1.50	0.30	0.75	1.50
❑36, Feb 92	1.25	0.30	0.75	1.50
❑37, Mar 92	1.25	0.30	0.75	1.50
❑38, Apr 92	1.25	0.30	0.75	1.50
❑39, May 92	1.50	0.30	0.75	1.50
❑40, Jun 92, Costs	1.50	0.30	0.75	1.50
❑41, Jul 92	1.50	0.30	0.75	1.50
❑42, Jul 92, Revolution	1.50	0.30	0.75	1.50
❑43, Aug 92	1.50	0.30	0.75	1.50
❑44, Aug 92	1.50	0.30	0.75	1.50
❑45, Sep 92	1.50	0.30	0.75	1.50
❑46, Nov 92	1.50	0.30	0.75	1.50
❑47, Dec 92, Lobo vs. Green Lantern (Hal Jordan)	1.50	0.30	0.75	1.50
❑48, Jan 93, L.E.G.I.O.N. '93 starts	1.75	0.30	0.75	1.50
❑49, Feb 93	1.75	0.35	0.88	1.75
❑50, Mar 93, Double-size; L.E.G.I.O.N. '67 back-up	3.50	0.70	1.75	3.50
❑51, Apr 93	1.75	0.35	0.88	1.75
❑52, May 93	1.75	0.35	0.88	1.75
❑53, Jun 93	1.75	0.35	0.88	1.75
❑54, Jun 93	1.75	0.35	0.88	1.75
❑55, Jul 93	1.75	0.35	0.88	1.75
❑56, Jul 93	1.75	0.35	0.88	1.75
❑57, Aug 93, Trinity	1.75	0.35	0.88	1.75
❑58, Sep 93, Trinity	1.75	0.35	0.88	1.75
❑59, Oct 93	1.75	0.35	0.88	1.75
❑60, Nov 93	1.75	0.35	0.88	1.75
❑61, Dec 93, Death of the Party!	1.75	0.35	0.88	1.75
❑62, Jan 94, L.E.G.I.O.N. '94 starts	1.75	0.35	0.88	1.75
❑63, Feb 94, We Fight and Fight and Fight	1.75	0.35	0.88	1.75
❑64, Mar 94	1.75	0.35	0.88	1.75
❑65	1.75	0.35	0.88	1.75
❑66, May 94	1.75	0.35	0.88	1.75
❑67, Jun 94	1.75	0.35	0.88	1.75
❑68, Jul 94	1.75	0.35	0.88	1.75
❑69, Aug 94, A: Ultra Boy	1.75	0.35	0.88	1.75
❑70, Sep 94, Final Issue; Giant-size; Zero Hour; story continues in R.E.B.E.L.S. '94 #0; L.E.G.I.O.N. goes renegade (becomes R.E.B.E.L.S.)	2.50	0.50	1.25	2.50
❑Anl 1, A: Superman, Vril Dox vs. Brainiac	2.95	0.59	1.48	2.95
❑Anl 2, Armageddon 2001, Part 9, Armageddon 2001	2.95	0.59	1.48	2.95
❑Anl 3, Eclipso: The Darkness Within, Part 15, Eclipso	2.95	0.59	1.48	2.95
❑Anl 4, Bloodlines, 1: Pax, Bloodlines: Deathstorm	3.50	0.70	1.75	3.50
❑Anl 5, Elseworlds; L.E.G.I.O.N. 007	3.50	0.70	1.75	3.50

LEGION ANTHOLOGY
LIMELIGHT

Value: Cover or less

❑1, Binary Angel; Atria the Grim, b&w; Anthology; manga 2.95

❑2 ...... 2.95

LEGION LOST
DC

Value: Cover or less

❑1, May 00 ...... 2.50

❑2, Jun 00, Enigma Variations 2.50

❑3, Jul 00 ...... 2.50

❑4, Aug 00 ...... 2.50

❑5, Sep 00 ...... 2.50

❑6, Oct 00, Burnout 2.50

❑7, Nov 00, Singularity 2.50

❑8, Dec 00, Lost & Found 2.50

❑9, Jan 01, Lost & Alone 2.50

❑10, Feb 01, Rosette 2.50

❑11, Mar 01, One Billion Years of Solitude 2.50

❑12, Apr 01, First & Last 2.50

LEGION MANGA ANTHOLOGY
LIMELIGHT

Value: Cover or less

❑1 ...... 2.95

❑2 ...... 2.95

❑3 ...... 2.95

❑4, Atria the Grim; Vampire Cat 2.95

LEGIONNAIRES
DC

	ORIG	GOOD	FINE	N-MINT
❑0, Oct 94, MWa (w), Close Encounters, revised Legion origin; continues in Legion of Super-Heroes #62 and Legionnaires #19	1.50	0.45	1.13	2.25
❑1, Apr 93, Baptism By Fire!, with trading card	1.25	0.60	1.50	3.00
❑2, May 93, V: Fatal Five, covers of issues #2-6 form one image	1.25	0.40	1.00	2.00
❑3, Jun 93, The Beast Below, V: Fatal Five	1.25	0.40	1.00	2.00
❑4, Jul 93, V: Fatal Five	1.25	0.40	1.00	2.00
❑5, Aug 93, V: Fatal Five	1.25	0.40	1.00	2.00
❑6, Sep 93, V: Fatal Five	1.25	0.30	0.75	1.50

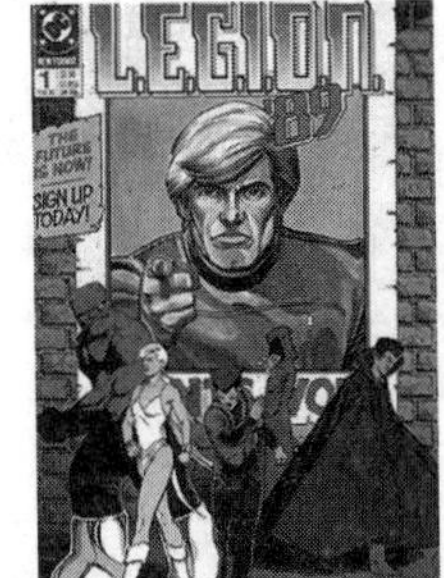

While the title changed each year in the indicia, *L.E.G.I.O.N. '89* through *'94* can be found under *L.E.G.I.O.N.*

© 1989 DC Comics

	ORIG	GOOD	FINE	N-MINT
❑7, Oct 93	1.25	0.30	0.75	1.50
❑8, Nov 93, Brainiac 5 leaves team	1.25	0.30	0.75	1.50
❑9, Dec 93	1.50	0.30	0.75	1.50
❑10, Jan 94	1.50	0.30	0.75	1.50
❑11, Feb 94, Kid Quantum joins team	1.50	0.30	0.75	1.50
❑12, Mar 94	1.50	0.30	0.75	1.50
❑13, Apr 94, Matter-Eater Lad becomes a girl	1.50	0.30	0.75	1.50
❑14, May 94	1.50	0.30	0.75	1.50
❑15, Jun 94	1.50	0.30	0.75	1.50
❑16, Jul 94, Return of Dream Girl	1.50	0.30	0.75	1.50
❑17, Aug 94, End of an Era Conclusion; End of an Era, Part 1	1.50	0.30	0.75	1.50
❑18, Sep 94, End of an Era, Part 4, Zero Hour	1.50	0.30	0.75	1.50
❑19, Nov 94	1.50	0.30	0.75	1.50
❑20, Dec 94, V: Mano	1.50	0.30	0.75	1.50
❑21, Jan 95, Enter the Workforce, 1: Work Force	1.50	0.30	0.75	1.50
❑22, Feb 95	1.50	0.30	0.75	1.50
❑23, Mar 95	1.50	0.30	0.75	1.50
❑24, Apr 95	1.50	0.30	0.75	1.50
❑25, May 95	1.50	0.30	0.75	1.50
❑26, Jun 95	1.75	0.35	0.88	1.75
❑27, Jul 95	2.25	0.45	1.13	2.25
❑28, Aug 95, 1: Legion Espionage Squad	2.25	0.45	1.13	2.25
❑29, Sep 95, 1: Dirk Morgna	2.25	0.45	1.13	2.25
❑30, Oct 95, Lightning Lad turning point	2.25	0.45	1.13	2.25
❑31, Nov 95, Future Tense, Part 3, Superboy made honorary member; Valor released into 30th century	2.25	0.45	1.13	2.25
❑32, Dec 95, A: Chronos, Underworld Unleashed	2.25	0.45	1.13	2.25
❑33, Jan 96, The Inhuman Touch, Kinetix finds Emerald Eye	2.25	0.45	1.13	2.25
❑34, Feb 96, Fallen Star	2.25	0.45	1.13	2.25
❑35, Mar 96, While You Were Out..., XS returns to 30th century; [L1996-6]	2.25	0.45	1.13	2.25
❑36, May 96	2.25	0.45	1.13	2.25
❑37, Jun 96, O: M'onel	2.25	0.45	1.13	2.25
❑38, Jul 96	2.25	0.45	1.13	2.25
❑39, Aug 96, Triad's three personalities become distinct	2.25	0.45	1.13	2.25
❑40, Sep 96, Emerald Vi	2.25	0.45	1.13	2.25
❑41, Oct 96, Aftermath	2.25	0.45	1.13	2.25
❑42, Nov 96, When Strikes the Sorceress, [L1996-20]	2.25	0.45	1.13	2.25
❑43, Dec 96, New Blood, Legion try-outs; Magno joins team; Umbra joins team; Sensor joins team; [L1996-22]	2.25	0.45	1.13	2.25
❑44, Jan 97, Taking a Licking, [L1997-1]	2.25	0.45	1.13	2.25
❑45, Feb 97, V: Mantis Morlo	2.25	0.45	1.13	2.25
❑46, Mar 97, Questions, [L1997-5]	2.25	0.45	1.13	2.25
❑47, Apr 97	2.25	0.45	1.13	2.25
❑48, May 97, V: Mordru	2.25	0.45	1.13	2.25
❑49, Jun 97, D: Atom'x; V: Mordru; A: Heroes of Xanthu; A: Workforce, poster	2.25	0.45	1.13	2.25
❑50, Jul 97, V: Mordru, Giant-size; Mysa becomes young	3.95	0.79	1.98	3.95
❑51, Aug 97	2.25	0.45	1.13	2.25
❑52, Sep 97, Vi's new powers manifest	2.25	0.45	1.13	2.25
❑53, Oct 97, Monstress joins team; Magno leaves team	2.25	0.45	1.13	2.25
❑54, Nov 97, Golden Age story; [L1997-21]	2.25	0.45	1.13	2.25
❑55, Dec 97, Control, V: Composite Man, Face cover	2.25	0.45	1.13	2.25
❑56, Jan 98, M'onel returns to Daxam	2.25	0.45	1.13	2.25
❑57, Feb 98	2.25	0.45	1.13	2.25
❑58, Mar 98	2.25	0.45	1.13	2.25
❑59, Apr 98	2.25	0.45	1.13	2.25
❑60, May 98, Chameleon leaves team; Sensor leaves team; Karate Kid joins team; Kid Quantum joins team	2.25	0.45	1.13	2.25
❑61, Jun 98, A: Superman (from Time and Time Again), Multiple time shifts	2.25	0.45	1.13	2.25

	ORIG	GOOD	FINE	N-MINT
❑62, Jul 98, Dark Circle Rising, Part 1: Crossfire	2.25	0.45	1.13	2.25
❑63, Aug 98, Dark Circle Rising, Part 3: Resignation	2.25	0.45	1.13	2.25
❑64, Sep 98, Dark Circle Rising, Part 5: Enlightenment	2.50	0.45	1.13	2.25
❑65, Oct 98, Dark Circle falls	2.50	0.50	1.25	2.50
❑66, Dec 98, 1: Charma	2.50	0.50	1.25	2.50
❑67, Jan 99, A: Kono	2.50	0.50	1.25	2.50
❑68, Feb 99, Monstress changes color	2.50	0.50	1.25	2.50
❑69, Mar 99, A: Plasma	2.50	0.50	1.25	2.50
❑70, Apr 99, Cosmic Boy vs. Domain	2.50	0.50	1.25	2.50
❑71, May 99, V: Elements of Disaster	2.50	0.50	1.25	2.50
❑72, Jun 99, Enemies of Science!, [L1999-11]	2.50	0.50	1.25	2.50
❑73, Jul 99, The Final Gathering, Star Boy solo; [L1999-13]	2.50	0.50	1.25	2.50
❑74, Aug 99, Aftershocks, [L1999-15]	2.50	0.50	1.25	2.50
❑75, Sep 99, Tyrants Three, [L1999-17]	2.50	0.50	1.25	2.50
❑76, Oct 99, The Fire This Time, O: Wildfire, [L1999-19]	2.50	0.50	1.25	2.50
❑77, Nov 99, Endless Summer!, [L1999-21]	2.50	0.50	1.25	2.50
❑78, Dec 00, Emissary, [L1999-23]	2.50	0.50	1.25	2.50
❑79, Jan 00, Legionnaires of the Damned, Part 2, [L2000-1]	2.50	0.50	1.25	2.50
❑80, Feb 00, Legionnaires of the Damned, Part 4, [L2000-3]	2.50	0.50	1.25	2.50
❑1000000, Nov 98, Come Together, set 1,000 years after events of One Million	2.50	0.50	1.25	2.50
❑Anl 1, Elseworlds	2.95	0.59	1.48	2.95
❑Anl 2, D: Apparition, Andromeda leaves team	3.95	0.79	1.98	3.95
❑Anl 3, The Long Road Home, A: Barry Allen, Legends of the Dead Earth; XS' travels in time; 1996 Annual	3.50	0.59	1.48	2.95

LEGIONNAIRES THREE
DC

	ORIG	GOOD	FINE	N-MINT
❑1, Feb 86, KG (w), Future Shock, V: Time Trapper	0.75	0.25	0.63	1.25
❑2, Mar 86	0.75	0.20	0.50	1.00
❑3, Apr 86	0.75	0.20	0.50	1.00
❑4, May 86	0.75	0.20	0.50	1.00

LEGION OF MONSTERS, THE
MARVEL

	ORIG	GOOD	FINE	N-MINT
❑1, magazine, b&w	1.00	1.20	3.00	6.00

LEGION OF NIGHT, THE
MARVEL

Value: Cover or less

- ❑1, Nov 91, Messenger From The Dead Part 1 ... 4.95
- ❑2, Dec 91, Messenger From The Dead Part 2 ... 4.95

LEGION OF STUPID HEROES
ALTERNATE CONCEPTS

Value: Cover or less

- ❑1, Jul 97, One Day at the Olympics, Jul-97; July 1997 ... 2.50
- ❑2, Sep 97, Vomit!; Once Upon a Morning Shave ... 2.50
- ❑3, Blambo and Tubs-Mariner: Play it Again Sam!; The Great Pumpkin ... 2.50
- ❑4, Mar 98, Innocent as a Baby...Rat! ... 2.50

LEGION OF STUPID KNIGHTS
ALTERNATE CONCEPTS

Value: Cover or less

- ❑SE 1, Feb 98, b&w ... 2.50

LEGION OF SUBSTITUTE HEROES SPECIAL
DC

	ORIG	GOOD	FINE	N-MINT
❑1, KG, You Can't Keep a Good Villain Down	1.25	0.40	1.00	2.00

LEGION OF SUPER-HEROES (1ST SERIES)
DC

	ORIG	GOOD	FINE	N-MINT
❑1, Feb 73, Tommy Tomorrow reprint	0.20	2.30	5.75	11.50
❑2, Mar 73	0.20	1.40	3.50	7.00
❑3, May 73, Computo The Conqueror, V: Computo	0.20	1.20	3.00	6.00
❑4, Aug 73, V: Computo	0.20	1.20	3.00	6.00

LEGION OF SUPER-HEROES, THE (2ND SERIES)
DC

	ORIG	GOOD	FINE	N-MINT
❑259, Jan 80, Superboy leaves team; Continued from "Superboy and the Legion of Super-Heroes"	0.40	0.70	1.75	3.50
❑260, Feb 80, V: Circus of Crime	0.40	0.55	1.38	2.75
❑261, Mar 80, V: Circus of Crime	0.40	0.50	1.25	2.50
❑262, Apr 80	0.40	0.50	1.25	2.50
❑263, May 80	0.40	0.50	1.25	2.50
❑264, Jun 80	0.40	0.50	1.25	2.50
❑265, Jul 80, O: Tyroc, Radio Shack computer insert; bonus Superman story	0.40	0.50	1.25	2.50
❑266, Aug 80, Return of Bouncing Boy; Return of Duo Damsel	0.40	0.50	1.25	2.50
❑267, Sep 80, O: Legion Flight Rings	0.50	0.50	1.25	2.50
❑268, Oct 80, SD	0.50	0.50	1.25	2.50
❑269, Nov 80, V: Fatal Five	0.50	0.50	1.25	2.50
❑270, Dec 80, Dark Man's identity revealed	0.50	0.50	1.25	2.50
❑271, Jan 81, O: Dark Man	0.50	0.35	0.88	1.75
❑272, Feb 81, O: Blok; 1: Dial 'H' for Hero (new), Blok joins Legion of Super-Heroes	0.50	0.35	0.88	1.75
❑273, Mar 81	0.50	0.35	0.88	1.75
❑274, Apr 81, SD, Ultra Boy becomes pirate	0.50	0.35	0.88	1.75
❑275, May 81	0.50	0.35	0.88	1.75
❑276, Jun 81	0.50	0.35	0.88	1.75
❑277, Jul 81	0.50	0.35	0.88	1.75
❑278, Aug 81, A: Reflecto; V: Grimbor	0.50	0.35	0.88	1.75
❑279, Sep 81, Reflecto's identity revealed..	0.50	0.35	0.88	1.75
❑280, Oct 81, Superboy rejoins	0.60	0.35	0.88	1.75
❑281, Nov 81, SD, V: Molecule Master	0.60	0.35	0.88	1.75
❑282, Dec 81, If Answers There Be..., O: Reflecto, Ultra Boy returns	0.60	0.35	0.88	1.75
❑283, Jan 82, O: Wildfire, Wildfire story	0.60	0.35	0.88	1.75
❑284, Feb 82	0.60	0.35	0.88	1.75
❑285, Mar 82, PB; KG, Keith Giffen plots begin	0.60	0.50	1.25	2.50
❑286, Apr 82, PB, V: Dr. Regulus; V: Doctor Regulus	0.60	0.40	1.00	2.00
❑287, May 82, KG, V: Kharlak	0.60	0.40	1.00	2.00
❑288, Jun 82, KG	0.60	0.40	1.00	2.00
❑289, Jul 82, KG	0.60	0.40	1.00	2.00
❑290, Aug 82, KG, Great Darkness Saga; Great Darkness Saga, Part 1	0.60	0.40	1.00	2.00
❑291, Sep 82, KG, Great Darkness Saga; Great Darkness Saga, Part 2	0.60	0.40	1.00	2.00
❑292, Oct 82, KG, Great Darkness Saga; Great Darkness Saga, Part 3	0.60	0.40	1.00	2.00
❑293, Nov 82, KG, Great Darkness Saga; Great Darkness Saga, Part 4	0.60	0.40	1.00	2.00
❑294, Dec 82, KG, Great Darkness Saga; Great Darkness Saga, Part 5, giant	1.00	0.40	1.00	2.00
❑295, Jan 83, O: Universo (possible origin); A: Green Lantern Corps	0.60	0.30	0.75	1.50
❑296, Feb 83	0.60	0.30	0.75	1.50
❑297, Mar 83, O: Legion of Super-Heroes, Cosmic Boy solo story	0.60	0.30	0.75	1.50
❑298, Apr 83, 1: Amethyst; 1: Dark Opal; 1: Gemworld, Amethyst, Princess of Gemworld insert	0.60	0.30	0.75	1.50
❑299, May 83, Invisible Kid II meets Invisible Kid I	0.60	0.30	0.75	1.50
❑300, Jun 83, 300th anniversary issue; Double-size; Tales of the Adult Legion; alternate futures	1.50	0.40	1.00	2.00
❑301, Jul 83	0.60	0.30	0.75	1.50
❑302, Aug 83, Lightning Lad vs. Lightning Lord	0.60	0.30	0.75	1.50
❑303, Sep 83, V: Emerald Empress	0.60	0.30	0.75	1.50
❑304, Oct 83, Legion Academy	0.60	0.30	0.75	1.50
❑305, Nov 83, Shrinking Violet revealed as Durlan; real Shrinking Violet returns	0.60	0.30	0.75	1.50
❑306, Dec 83, O: Star Boy	0.75	0.30	0.75	1.50
❑307, Jan 84, V: Prophet	0.75	0.30	0.75	1.50
❑308, Feb 84, V: Prophet	0.75	0.30	0.75	1.50
❑309, Mar 84, V: Prophet	0.75	0.30	0.75	1.50
❑310, Apr 84, V: Omen	0.75	0.30	0.75	1.50
❑311, May 84	0.75	0.30	0.75	1.50
❑312, Jun 84	0.75	0.30	0.75	1.50
❑313, Jul 84, series continues as Tales of the Legion of Super-Heroes	0.75	0.30	0.75	1.50
❑Anl 1, KG, 1: Invisible Kid II (Jacques Foccart)	1.00	0.50	1.25	2.50
❑Anl 2, KG; DaG, Whatever Gods There Be..., Wedding of Karate Kid and Princess Projectra; Karate Kid and Princess Projectra leave Legion of Super-Heroes	1.00	0.40	1.00	2.00
❑Anl 3, CS, O: Validus	1.25	0.40	1.00	2.00

LEGION OF SUPER-HEROES (3RD SERIES)
DC

	ORIG	GOOD	FINE	N-MINT
❑1, Aug 84, KG, KG (w), Here a Villain, There a Villain..., V: Legion of Super-Villains, Silver ink cover	1.25	0.60	1.50	3.00
❑2, Sep 84, KG, V: Legion of Super-Villains; 1: Kono	1.25	0.50	1.25	2.50
❑3, Oct 84, KG, V: Legion of Super-Villains	1.25	0.50	1.25	2.50
❑4, Nov 84, KG, V: Legion of Super-Villains; D: Karate Kid	1.25	0.50	1.25	2.50
❑5, Dec 84, KG, D: Nemesis Kid	1.25	0.50	1.25	2.50
❑6, Jan 85, 1: Laurel Gand	1.25	0.45	1.13	2.25
❑7, Feb 85	1.25	0.45	1.13	2.25
❑8, Mar 85	1.25	0.45	1.13	2.25
❑9, Apr 85	1.25	0.45	1.13	2.25
❑10, May 85	1.25	0.45	1.13	2.25
❑11, Jun 85, Bouncing Boy back-up	1.25	0.40	1.00	2.00
❑12, Jul 85	1.25	0.40	1.00	2.00
❑13, Aug 85	1.25	0.40	1.00	2.00
❑14, Sep 85, 1: Quislet, New members	1.25	0.40	1.00	2.00

	ORIG	GOOD	FINE	N-MINT
❑15, Oct 85	1.25	0.40	1.00	2.00
❑16, Nov 85, Crisis	1.25	0.40	1.00	2.00
❑17, Dec 85	1.25	0.40	1.00	2.00
❑18, Jan 86, Crisis	1.50	0.40	1.00	2.00
❑19, Feb 86	1.50	0.40	1.00	2.00
❑20, Mar 86, V: Tyr	1.50	0.40	1.00	2.00
❑21, Apr 86, V: Emerald Empress	1.50	0.40	1.00	2.00
❑22, May 86	1.50	0.40	1.00	2.00
❑23, Jun 86	1.50	0.40	1.00	2.00
❑24, Jul 86	1.50	0.40	1.00	2.00
❑25, Aug 86	1.50	0.40	1.00	2.00
❑26, Sep 86	1.50	0.40	1.00	2.00
❑27, Oct 86, V: Mordru	1.50	0.40	1.00	2.00
❑28, Nov 86	1.50	0.40	1.00	2.00
❑29, Dec 86, V: Starfinger	1.50	0.40	1.00	2.00
❑30, Jan 87	1.50	0.40	1.00	2.00
❑31, Feb 87, Karate Kid, Princess Projectra, Ferro Lad story	1.50	0.35	0.88	1.75
❑32, Mar 87, Universo Project	1.50	0.35	0.88	1.75
❑33, Apr 87, Universo Project	1.50	0.35	0.88	1.75
❑34, May 87, Universo Project	1.50	0.35	0.88	1.75
❑35, Jun 87, Universo Project	1.50	0.35	0.88	1.75
❑36, Jul 87, Legion elections	1.50	0.35	0.88	1.75
❑37, Aug 87, Fate of Superboy revealed; Return of Star Boy and Sun Girl	1.50	1.60	4.00	8.00
❑38, Sep 87, D: Superboy	1.50	1.60	4.00	8.00
❑39, Oct 87, CS, O: Colossal Boy	1.50	0.35	0.88	1.75
❑40, Nov 87, V: Starfinger	1.75	0.35	0.88	1.75
❑41, Dec 87, V: Starfinger	1.75	0.35	0.88	1.75
❑42, Jan 88, V: Laurel Kent, Millennium	1.75	0.35	0.88	1.75
❑43, Feb 88, V: Laurel Kent, Millennium	1.75	0.35	0.88	1.75
❑44, Mar 88, O: Quislet	1.75	0.35	0.88	1.75
❑45, Apr 88, Double-size; 30th Anniv.	2.95	0.60	1.50	3.00
❑46, May 88	1.75	0.35	0.88	1.75
❑47, Jun 88, V: Starfinger	1.75	0.35	0.88	1.75
❑48, Jul 88, V: Starfinger	1.75	0.35	0.88	1.75
❑49, Aug 88, V: Starfinger	1.75	0.35	0.88	1.75
❑50, Sep 88, D: Infinite Man; D: Time Trapper (possible death); D: Duo Damsel (half), 50th anniversary issue; Giant-size; Mon-El wounded	2.50	0.40	1.00	2.00
❑51, Oct 88	1.75	0.35	0.88	1.75
❑52, Nov 88	1.75	0.35	0.88	1.75
❑53, Dec 88	1.75	0.35	0.88	1.75
❑54, Win 88, cover says Winter; no month of publication	1.75	0.35	0.88	1.75
❑55, Hol 89, cover says Holiday; no month of publication	1.75	0.35	0.88	1.75
❑56, Jan 89	1.75	0.35	0.88	1.75
❑57, Feb 89	1.75	0.35	0.88	1.75
❑58, Mar 89, D: Emerald Empress	1.75	0.35	0.88	1.75
❑59, Apr 89	1.75	0.35	0.88	1.75
❑60, May 89, KG, The Magic Wars, Part 1	1.75	0.35	0.88	1.75
❑61, Jun 89, KG, The Magic Wars, Part 2	1.75	0.35	0.88	1.75
❑62, Jul 89, KG, The Magic Wars, Part 3, D: Magnetic Kid	1.75	0.35	0.88	1.75
❑63, Aug 89, KG, The Magic Wars, Part 4, Final Issue	1.75	0.35	0.88	1.75
❑Anl 1, KG, Who Shot Laurel Kent?	2.00	0.40	1.00	2.00
❑Anl 2, V: Validus	2.00	0.40	1.00	2.00
❑Anl 3, O: new Legion of Substitute Heroes	2.25	0.40	1.00	2.00
❑Anl 4, O: Starfinger, Private Lives; 1988 annual	2.50	0.50	1.25	2.50

LEGION OF SUPER-HEROES (4TH SERIES)
DC

	ORIG	GOOD	FINE	N-MINT
❑0, Oct 94, KG, KG (w), O: Legion of Super-Heroes (revised), continues in Legion of Super-Heroes #62 and Legionnaires #19	1.95	0.40	1.00	2.00
❑1, Nov 89, KG, KG (w), Begins five years after previous series	1.75	0.50	1.25	2.50
❑2, Dec 89	1.75	0.40	1.00	2.00
❑3, Jan 90, V: Roxxas	1.75	0.40	1.00	2.00
❑4, Feb 90, KG, KG (w), A: Mon-El	1.75	0.40	1.00	2.00
❑5, Mar 90	1.75	0.40	1.00	2.00
❑6, Apr 90	1.75	0.40	1.00	2.00
❑7, May 90	1.75	0.40	1.00	2.00
❑8, Jun 90, origin	1.75	0.40	1.00	2.00
❑9, Jul 90	1.75	0.40	1.00	2.00
❑10, Aug 90, V: Roxxas	1.75	0.40	1.00	2.00
❑11, Sep 90, A: Matter-Eater Lad	1.75	0.40	1.00	2.00
❑12, Oct 90, Legion reformed	1.75	0.40	1.00	2.00
❑13, Nov 90, poster	1.75	0.40	1.00	2.00
❑14, Jan 91	1.75	0.40	1.00	2.00
❑15, Feb 91	1.75	0.40	1.00	2.00
❑16, Mar 91	1.75	0.40	1.00	2.00
❑17, Apr 91	1.75	0.40	1.00	2.00
❑18, May 91, V: Dark Circle	1.75	0.40	1.00	2.00
❑19, Jun 91	1.75	0.40	1.00	2.00

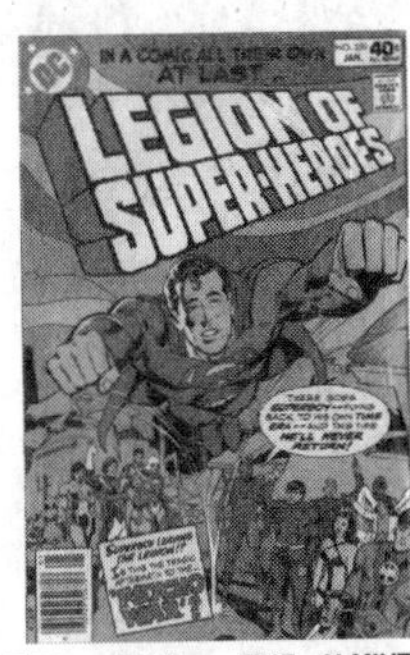

After sharing their adventures for more than 20 years, Superboy left the Legion team and returned to the 20th century in *Legion of Super-Heroes* (2nd series) #259.

	ORIG	GOOD	FINE	N-MINT
❑20, Jul 91	1.75	0.40	1.00	2.00
❑21, Aug 91, Quiet Darkness; The Quiet Darkness, Part 1	1.75	0.35	0.88	1.75
❑22, Sep 91, Quiet Darkness; The Quiet Darkness, Part 2	1.75	0.35	0.88	1.75
❑23, Oct 91, Quiet Darkness; The Quiet Darkness, Part 3, V: Lobo	1.75	0.35	0.88	1.75
❑24, Dec 91, Quiet Darkness; The Quiet Darkness, Part 4	1.75	0.35	0.88	1.75
❑25, Jan 92	1.75	0.35	0.88	1.75
❑26, Feb 92, contains map of Legion headquarters	1.75	0.35	0.88	1.75
❑27, Mar 92, V: B.I.O.N.	1.75	0.35	0.88	1.75
❑28, Apr 92, A: Sun Boy	1.75	0.35	0.88	1.75
❑29, May 92	1.75	0.35	0.88	1.75
❑30, Jun 92, The Terra Mosaic	1.75	0.35	0.88	1.75
❑31, Jul 92, The Terra Mosaic, romance cover	1.75	0.35	0.88	1.75
❑32, Aug 92, The Terra Mosaic	1.75	0.35	0.88	1.75
❑33, Sep 92, The Terra Mosaic, fate of Kid Quantum	1.75	0.35	0.88	1.75
❑34, Oct 92, The Terra Mosaic, Timber Wolf mini-series preview	1.75	0.35	0.88	1.75
❑35, Nov 92, The Terra Mosaic, Sun Boy meets Sun Boy	1.75	0.35	0.88	1.75
❑36, Nov 92, The Terra Mosaic	1.75	0.35	0.88	1.75
❑37, Dec 92, Star Boy and Dream Girl return	1.75	0.35	0.88	1.75
❑38, Dec 92, A: (of Sandman) appearance, Earth destroyed	1.75	0.50	1.25	2.50
❑39, Jan 93	1.75	0.35	0.88	1.75
❑40, Feb 93	1.75	0.35	0.88	1.75
❑41, Mar 93, 1: Legionnaires	1.75	0.35	0.88	1.75
❑42, Apr 93	1.75	0.35	0.88	1.75
❑43, May 93, White Witch returns	1.75	0.35	0.88	1.75
❑44, Jun 93, Projectra returns	1.75	0.35	0.88	1.75
❑45, Jul 93	1.75	0.35	0.88	1.75
❑46, Aug 93	1.75	0.35	0.88	1.75
❑47, Sep 93, V: dead heroes	1.75	0.35	0.88	1.75
❑48, Oct 93, V: Mordru	1.75	0.35	0.88	1.75
❑49, Nov 93	1.75	0.35	0.88	1.75
❑50, Nov 93, Wedding of Matter-Eater Lad and Saturn Queen	3.50	0.70	1.75	3.50
❑51, Dec 93	1.75	0.35	0.88	1.75
❑52, Dec 93, O: Timber Wolf retold	1.75	0.35	0.88	1.75
❑53, Jan 94, V: Glorith	1.75	0.35	0.88	1.75
❑54, Feb 94, Die-cut cover	2.95	0.59	1.48	2.95
❑55, Mar 94	1.75	0.35	0.88	1.75
❑56, Apr 94	1.75	0.35	0.88	1.75
❑57, May 94	1.75	0.35	0.88	1.75
❑58, Jun 94	1.75	0.35	0.88	1.75
❑59, Jul 94	1.95	0.39	0.98	1.95
❑60, Aug 94, End of an Era, Part 3	1.95	0.39	0.98	1.95
❑61, Sep 94, End of an Era Real Conclusion, Zero Hour; end of original Legion of Super-Heroes	1.95	0.39	0.98	1.95
❑62, Nov 94	1.95	0.39	0.98	1.95
❑63, Dec 94, 1: Athramites, new Legion headquarters, Tenzil Kem hired as chef..	1.95	0.39	0.98	1.95
❑64, Jan 95, MWa (w), Sibling Rivalry, Return of Ultra Boy	1.95	0.39	0.98	1.95
❑65, Feb 95	1.95	0.39	0.98	1.95
❑66, Mar 95, A: Laurel Gand	1.95	0.39	0.98	1.95
❑67, Apr 95	1.95	0.39	0.98	1.95
❑68, May 95	1.95	0.39	0.98	1.95
❑69, Jun 95	2.25	0.45	1.13	2.25
❑70, Jul 95	2.25	0.45	1.13	2.25
❑71, Aug 95, Trom destroyed	2.25	0.45	1.13	2.25
❑72, Sep 95	2.25	0.45	1.13	2.25
❑73, Oct 95, A: Mekt Ranz	2.25	0.45	1.13	2.25
❑74, Nov 95, Future Tense, Part 2, A: Scavenger; A: Superboy, concludes in Legionnaires #31	2.25	0.45	1.13	2.25
❑75, Dec 95, A: Chronos, Underworld Unleashed	2.25	0.45	1.13	2.25

	ORIG	GOOD	FINE	N-MINT
❑76, Jan 96, Star Boy and Gates joins team	2.25	0.45	1.13	2.25
❑77, Feb 96, Lock Up, O: Brainiac Five, [L1996-3]	2.25	0.45	1.13	2.25
❑78, Mar 96, The Gathering Doom, 1: Fatal Five, [L1996-5]	2.25	0.45	1.13	2.25
❑79, Apr 96, The Fatal Five!, V: Fatal Five, [L1996-7]	2.25	0.45	1.13	2.25
❑80, May 96	2.25	0.45	1.13	2.25
❑81, Jun 96, Dirk Morgna becomes Sun Boy; Brainiac 5 quits	2.25	0.45	1.13	2.25
❑82, Jul 96, Apparition returns	2.25	0.45	1.13	2.25
❑83, Aug 96, D: Leviathan, Violet possessed by Emerald Eye	2.25	0.45	1.13	2.25
❑84, Sep 96, Emerald Legion	2.25	0.45	1.13	2.25
❑85, Oct 96, Metropolis Now!, A: Superman, Seven Legionnaires, Inferno, and Shvaughn Erin in 20th century; [L1996-19]	2.25	0.45	1.13	2.25
❑86, Nov 96, Heart of Iron, A: Ferro, Final Night; [L1996-21]	2.25	0.45	1.13	2.25
❑87, Dec 96, She's Not There, A: Phase; A: Deadman, [L1996-23]	2.25	0.45	1.13	2.25
❑88, Jan 97, Fast Times, A: Impulse, [L1997-2]	2.25	0.45	1.13	2.25
❑89, Feb 97, A: Doctor Psycho	2.25	0.45	1.13	2.25
❑90, Mar 97, Face to Face, V: Doctor Psycho, [L1997-6]	2.25	0.45	1.13	2.25
❑91, Apr 97, Legion visits several DC eras	2.25	0.45	1.13	2.25
❑92, May 97, 20th century group lands in 1958 Happy Harbor	2.25	0.45	1.13	2.25
❑93, Jun 97, D: Douglas Nolan	2.25	0.45	1.13	2.25
❑94, Jul 97	2.25	0.45	1.13	2.25
❑95, Aug 97, A: Metal Men	2.25	0.45	1.13	2.25
❑96, Sep 97, Wedding of Ultra Boy and Apparition; Cosmic Boy revives	2.25	0.45	1.13	2.25
❑97, Oct 97, V: Mantis, Genesis; Spark gains gravity powers	2.25	0.45	1.13	2.25
❑98, Nov 97, Computo the Conqueror, Part 1, Phase meets Apparition; [L1997-22]	2.25	0.45	1.13	2.25
❑99, Dec 97, When the Reign Comes, Face cover	2.25	0.45	1.13	2.25
❑100, Jan 98, gatefold cover; Legionnaires return from 20th century	5.95	1.19	2.97	5.95
❑101, Feb 98, Spark gets her lightning powers back	2.25	0.45	1.13	2.25
❑102, Mar 98, A: Heroes of Xanthu	2.25	0.45	1.13	2.25
❑103, Apr 98, Karate Kid quits McCauley Industries	2.25	0.45	1.13	2.25
❑104, May 98, A: Kono, time shifts to 2968	2.25	0.45	1.13	2.25
❑105, Jun 98, V: Time Trapper	2.25	0.45	1.13	2.25
❑106, Jul 98, Dark Circle Rising, Part 2: Assassination	2.25	0.45	1.13	2.25
❑107, Aug 98, Dark Circle Rising, Part 4: Duplicity	2.25	0.45	1.13	2.25
❑108, Sep 98, Dark Circle Rising, Part 6: Revelation	2.50	0.45	1.13	2.25
❑109, Oct 98, V: Emerald Eye	2.50	0.50	1.25	2.50
❑110, Dec 98, Thunder joins team	2.50	0.50	1.25	2.50
❑111, Jan 99, Karate Kid vs. M'onel	2.50	0.50	1.25	2.50
❑112, Feb 99	2.50	0.50	1.25	2.50
❑113, Mar 99	2.50	0.50	1.25	2.50
❑114, Apr 99, 1: Bizarro Legion	2.50	0.50	1.25	2.50
❑115, May 99, Imperfect Strangers: Bizzaros Forever!, [L1999-10]	2.50	0.50	1.25	2.50
❑116, Jun 99, Cold Irons Bound, Thunder vs. Pernisius; [L1999-12]	2.50	0.50	1.25	2.50
❑117, Jul 99, The Machine in the Ghost, [L1999-14]	2.50	0.50	1.25	2.50
❑118, Aug 99, Shadow of the Sun, V: Pernisius, [L1999-16]	2.50	0.50	1.25	2.50
❑119, Sep 99, Eat the Poor, M'Onel and Apparition tell a L.E.G.I.O.N. story; [L1999-18]	2.50	0.50	1.25	2.50
❑120, Oct 99, The Fatal Four...Plus One!, V: Fatal Five, [L1999-20]	2.50	0.50	1.25	2.50
❑121, Nov 99, Legion of the Damned, Part 1	2.50	0.50	1.25	2.50
❑122, Dec 99, Legion of the Damned, Part 2, [L1999-24]	2.50	0.50	1.25	2.50
❑123, Jan 00, Legion of the Damned, Part 3, [L2000-2]	2.50	0.50	1.25	2.50
❑1000000, Nov 98, KG, 1, 000 Years Later, set 1, 000 years after events of One Million	2.50	0.50	1.25	2.50
❑Anl 1, O: Glorith, Ultra Boy, Legion	3.50	0.70	1.75	3.50
❑Anl 2, O: Valor	3.50	0.70	1.75	3.50
❑Anl 3, Timber Wolf goes to 20th century	3.50	0.70	1.75	3.50
❑Anl 4, Bloodlines, Part 12, 1: Jamm, Bloodlines: Earthplague; 1993 annual	3.50	0.70	1.75	3.50
❑Anl 5, Elseworlds; Legion in Oz	3.50	0.70	1.75	3.50
❑Anl 6, O: Kinetix; O: Leviathan, Year One; 0: XS	3.95	0.79	1.98	3.95
❑Anl 7, One Shot, A: Wildfire, Legends of the Dead Earth; 1996 annual	3.50	0.59	1.48	2.95

LEGION OF SUPER-HEROES INDEX
ECLIPSE

Value: Cover or less

- ❑1 ... 2.00
- ❑2, Jan 87 ... 2.00
- ❑3, Feb 87 ... 2.00
- ❑4, Mar 87 ... 2.00
- ❑5, May 87 ... 2.00

LEGION OF SUPER-HEROES SECRET FILES
DC

Value: Cover or less

- ❑1, Jan 98, Legionnaires Three; What Did the Legion Do for Money When They Were Stranded in the 20th Century?, O: Legion, bios on members and villains ... 4.95
- ❑2, Jun 99, Unknown Point of Origin, Part 2; The Legion Constitution, bios on members and villains; Legion constitution ... 4.95

LEGION OF THE STUPID-HEROES
BLACKTHORNE

Value: Cover or less

- ❑1, b&w; parody ... 1.75

LEGION: SCIENCE POLICE
DC

Value: Cover or less

- ❑1, Aug 98, Ringers, Part 1 ... 2.25
- ❑2, Sep 98, Ringers, Part 2 ... 2.25
- ❑3, Oct 98, Ringers, Part 3 ... 2.25
- ❑4, Nov 98, Ringers, Part 4 ... 2.25

LEGIONS OF LUDICROUS HEROES
C&T

Value: Cover or less

- ❑1, b&w ... 2.00

LEGION X-1 (VOL. 2)
GREATER MERCURY

Value: Cover or less

- ❑1, Aug 89, Return of the Eradicators, Part 1 ... 2.00

LEJENTIA
OPUS

Value: Cover or less

- ❑1 ... 1.95
- ❑2 ... 2.25

LEMONADE KID
AC

Value: Cover or less

- ❑1, Powell reprints ... 2.50

LENORE
SLAVE LABOR

	ORIG	GOOD	FINE	N-MINT
❑1, Feb 98, B	2.95	0.65	1.63	3.25
❑2, Jun 98, The Raven; Little Bunny Foo Foo	2.95	0.60	1.50	3.00
❑3, Sep 98, Ragamuffin; Georgie Porgie	2.95	0.59	1.48	2.95
❑4, Jan 99, The Return of Mr. Gosh; The Last Robot	2.95	0.59	1.48	2.95
❑5	2.95	0.59	1.48	2.95
❑6	2.95	0.59	1.48	2.95
❑7	2.95	0.59	1.48	2.95

LENSMAN
ETERNITY

Value: Cover or less

- ❑1, Feb 90, b&w ... 2.25
- ❑1/SC, Feb 90, b&w; cardstock cover; Special edition ... 3.95
- ❑2 ... 2.25
- ❑3 ... 2.25
- ❑4 ... 2.25
- ❑5 ... 2.25
- ❑6 ... 2.25

LENSMAN: WAR OF THE GALAXIES
ETERNITY

Value: Cover or less

- ❑1, Nov 90, Birth of a Lensman, b&w ... 2.25
- ❑2, b&w ... 2.25
- ❑3, b&w ... 2.25
- ❑4, b&w ... 2.25
- ❑5, b&w ... 2.25
- ❑6, Jun 91, b&w ... 2.25
- ❑7, Jul 91, Tregonsee, b&w ... 2.25

LEONARD NIMOY
CELEBRITY

Value: Cover or less

- ❑1, b&w ... 5.95

LEONARDO TEENAGE MUTANT NINJA TURTLE
MIRAGE

	ORIG	GOOD	FINE	N-MINT
❑1, Dec 86, continues in Teenage Mutant Ninja Turtles #10	1.50	0.40	1.00	2.00

LEOPOLD AND BRINK
FAULTLINE PRESS

Value: Cover or less

- ❑1, Jun 97, b&w ... 2.50
- ❑2, Nov 97, b&w ... 2.50
- ❑3, Jan 98, b&w ... 2.95

LESTER GIRLS: THE LIZARD'S TRAIL
ETERNITY

Value: Cover or less

- ❑1, b&w ... 2.50
- ❑2, b&w ... 2.50
- ❑3, b&w ... 2.50

LETHAL
IMAGE

Value: Cover or less

- ❑1, Feb 96 ... 2.50

LETHAL FOES OF SPIDER-MAN
MARVEL

	ORIG	GOOD	FINE	N-MINT
❑1, Sep 93, Deadly Reunion	1.75	0.40	1.00	2.00
❑2, Oct 93, Hate Is A Many Splendored Thing, A: Vulture; A: Doctor Octopus; A: Hardshell; A: Answer	1.75	0.40	1.00	2.00
❑3, Nov 93	1.75	0.40	1.00	2.00
❑4, Dec 93	1.75	0.40	1.00	2.00

LETHAL STRIKE
London Night

Value: Cover or less

- ❑0, Ice..., Commemorative edition ... 5.95
- ❑0.5, London Night ... 3.00
- ❑1, Jun 95 ... 3.00
- ❑2 ... 3.00
- ❑3 ... 3.00
- ❑Anl 1 ... 3.00

LETHAL STRIKE/DOUBLE IMPACT: LETHAL IMPACT
London Night

Value: Cover or less

- ❑1, May 96, crossover with High Impact ... 3.00

LETHARGIC COMICS
Alpha

	ORIG	GOOD	FINE	N-MINT
❑1, Lethargic Lad Is Dead!; Guy With A Gun, b&w; Spawn/Cerebus parody cover	2.50	0.70	1.75	3.50
❑2, Feb 94, Ladfall, Part 1; Guy-With-A-Gun: Interlude #1, Guy-With-A-Gun: Interlude #2, b&w	2.50	0.60	1.50	3.00
❑3, Mar 94, b&w	2.50	0.60	1.50	3.00
❑3.14, Apr 94, Suicide, Part 1; The Zit, b&w; Issue #pi	2.50	0.60	1.50	3.00
❑4, May 94, Guy-With-A-Gun; Robo-Guy, b&w; Marvels #4 parody cover	2.50	0.60	1.50	3.00
❑5, Jul 94, Lethargic Lad Returns; Roboguy, b&w; Dot-It-Yerself cover	2.50	0.60	1.50	3.00
❑6, Lethargic Lad; Guy-With-A-Gun, b&w; Sin City parody cover	2.50	0.50	1.25	2.50
❑7, b&w; Spawn/Batman parody cover	2.50	0.50	1.25	2.50
❑8, b&w	2.50	0.50	1.25	2.50
❑9, Apr 95, b&w; Bone cover; interview with Jeff Smith	2.50	0.50	1.25	2.50
❑10, b&w; Sin City parody cover	2.50	0.50	1.25	2.50
❑11, Aug 95, b&w; Milk & Cheese	2.95	0.50	1.25	2.50
❑12, A: Shi, b&w; Shi cover	2.50	0.50	1.25	2.50
❑13	2.50	0.50	1.25	2.50
❑14	2.50	0.50	1.25	2.50

LETHARGIC COMICS, WEAKLY
Lethargic

	ORIG	GOOD	FINE	N-MINT
❑1, Jun 91, 1: The Zit; 1: The Grad; 1: Him; 1: Walrus Boy; 1: Lethargic Lad; 1: No Mutants; 1: Guy with a Gun, b&w; Action Comics #601 parody cover	1.95	1.00	2.50	5.00
❑2, b&w; Detective Comics #27 parody cover	1.95	0.80	2.00	4.00
❑3, b&w; Spider-Man #1 parody cover	1.95	0.70	1.75	3.50
❑4, b&w; X-Men #1 parody cover	1.75	0.60	1.50	3.00
❑5, b&w; Dark Knight #1 parody cover	1.95	0.60	1.50	3.00
❑6, b&w; Dark Knight #4 parody cover	1.95	0.50	1.25	2.50
❑7, Crisis on Infinite Earths #12 parody cover	2.50	0.50	1.25	2.50
❑8, Avengers #4 parody cover	2.50	0.50	1.25	2.50
❑9, Spider-Man #16 parody cover; Issue reads sideways	2.50	0.50	1.25	2.50
❑10, Adventures of Captain America parody cover; Captain America parody	2.25	0.50	1.25	2.50
❑11, Youngblood #1 parody cover	2.50	0.50	1.25	2.50
❑12, b&w; Superman #75 parody cover; Alpha begins publishing	2.50	0.50	1.25	2.50

LETHARGIC LAD (1ST SERIES)
Crusade

Value: Cover or less

- ❑1 ... 2.95
- ❑2 ... 2.95
- ❑3, Sep 96, ARo (c), b&w; wrap-around cover; Kingdom Come parody ... 2.95

LETHARGIC LAD (2ND SERIES)
Crusade

Value: Cover or less

- ❑1, Oct 97, O: Guy with a Gun 2.95
- ❑2, Dec 97 ... 2.95
- ❑3, Mar 98 ... 2.95
- ❑4, Apr 98 ... 2.95
- ❑5, Jun 98, A: Lethargic Lad-Red ... 2.95
- ❑6, Sep 98, A: new Lethargic Lass ... 2.95
- ❑7, Nov 98 ... 2.95
- ❑8, Jan 99, A: past Lethargic Lads ... 2.95
- ❑9, Mar 99 ... 2.95

LEVEL X
Caliber

Value: Cover or less

- ❑1, b&w ... 3.95
- ❑2, b&w ... 3.95

LEWD MOANA
Eros

Value: Cover or less

- ❑1 ... 2.95

LEX LUTHOR: THE UNAUTHORIZED BIOGRAPHY
DC

	ORIG	GOOD	FINE	N-MINT
❑1, Jul 89, O: Luthor, Painted cover	3.95	0.80	2.00	4.00

LIAISONS DELICIEUSES
Fantagraphics

Value: Cover or less

- ❑1, b&w; adult ... 1.95
- ❑2, b&w; adult ... 1.95
- ❑3, adult ... 2.25
- ❑4, adult ... 2.25
- ❑5, adult ... 2.25

LIBBY ELLIS (ETERNITY)
Eternity

Value: Cover or less

- ❑1, Jun 88, Rocket Coaster; Sharp Stalks the Dark, Part 1 ... 1.95
- ❑2, Jul 88 ... 1.95
- ❑3, Aug 88 ... 1.95
- ❑4, Sep 88 ... 1.95

Following series published by Alpha and Lethargic, Crusade took over publication of Greg Hyland's *Lethargic Lad* in 1996.

© 1997 Greg Hyland (Crusade)

LIBBY ELLIS (MALIBU)
Malibu

Value: Cover or less

- ❑1 ... 1.95
- ❑2 ... 1.95
- ❑3 ... 1.95
- ❑4 ... 1.95

LIBERATOR
Malibu

Value: Cover or less

- ❑1, Dec 87, Looking at a Memory, 1: Liberator, b&w ... 1.95
- ❑2, Feb 88 ... 1.95
- ❑3, Mar 88 ... 1.95
- ❑4, Jun 88 ... 1.95
- ❑5, Oct 88 ... 1.95
- ❑6, Dec 88 ... 1.95

LIBERTINE, THE
Fantagraphics

Value: Cover or less

- ❑1, b&w; adult ... 2.25
- ❑2, adult ... 2.50

LIBERTY MEADOWS
Insight Studios

	ORIG	GOOD	FINE	N-MINT
❑1, Reprints first eight weeks of Liberty Meadows	2.95	1.60	4.00	8.00
❑1=2, 2nd Printing; Reprints first eight weeks of Liberty Meadows	2.95	0.80	2.00	4.00
❑2, Reprints weeks 9-16 of Liberty Meadows strip	2.95	1.00	2.50	5.00
❑3, Reprints weeks 17-24 of Liberty Meadows strip	2.95	0.80	2.00	4.00
❑4, Reprints weeks 25-32 of Liberty Meadows strip	2.95	0.80	2.00	4.00
❑5, 42 strips plus 3 Sunday strip reprints	2.95	0.80	2.00	4.00
❑6	2.95	0.70	1.75	3.50
❑7	2.95	0.70	1.75	3.50
❑8, Mar 00	2.95	0.70	1.75	3.50
❑9, Apr 00	2.95	0.70	1.75	3.50
❑10, May 00	2.95	0.70	1.75	3.50
❑11, Jun 00	2.95	0.59	1.48	2.95
❑12, Jul 00	2.95	0.59	1.48	2.95
❑13, Aug 00	2.95	0.59	1.48	2.95
❑14, Sep 00	2.95	0.59	1.48	2.95
❑15, Nov 00, reader requests	2.95	0.59	1.48	2.95
❑16, Dec 00, Wiener Dog Race	2.95	0.59	1.48	2.95
❑17, Jan 01	2.95	0.59	1.48	2.95
❑18, Feb 01	2.95	0.59	1.48	2.95
❑19	2.95	0.59	1.48	2.95
❑20	2.95	0.59	1.48	2.95
❑21	2.95	0.59	1.48	2.95

LIBERTY PROJECT, THE
Eclipse

	ORIG	GOOD	FINE	N-MINT
❑1, Jun 87, KB (w), I Fought The Law, 1: Slick; 1: The Liberty Project; 1: Crackshot; 1: Burnout; 1: Cimmaron	1.75	0.40	1.00	2.00
❑2, Jul 87, KB (w)	1.75	0.35	0.88	1.75
❑3, Aug 87, KB (w)	1.75	0.35	0.88	1.75
❑4, Sep 87, KB (w)	1.75	0.35	0.88	1.75
❑5, Oct 87, KB (w)	1.75	0.35	0.88	1.75
❑6, Nov 87, KB (w), A: Valkyrie	1.75	0.35	0.88	1.75
❑7, Dec 87, KB (w)	1.75	0.35	0.88	1.75
❑8, May 88, KB (w)	1.75	0.35	0.88	1.75

LIBRA
Eternity

Value: Cover or less

- ❑1, Apr 87 ... 1.95

LIBRARIAN, THE
Fantagraphics

Value: Cover or less

- ❑1, b&w ... 2.75

LICENSE TO KILL
Eclipse

Value: Cover or less

- ❑1, TY; MGr ... 7.95

L.I.F.E. BRIGADE, THE
Blue Comet

	ORIG	GOOD	FINE	N-MINT
❑1, L.I.F.E. Brigade: Beginning or End; Blazing Tales	2.00	0.40	1.00	2.00
❑1-2, L.I.F.E. Brigade: Beginning or End, 2nd Printing	1.80	0.40	1.00	2.00

	ORIG	GOOD	FINE	N-MINT
❑2	1.80	0.40	1.00	2.00
❑3, Title changes to New L.I.F.E. Brigade	—	0.40	1.00	2.00

LIFE OF CAPTAIN MARVEL, THE
MARVEL

	ORIG	GOOD	FINE	N-MINT
❑1, Aug 85, JSn, JSn (w), Beware The...Blood Brothers!, Baxter reprint	2.00	0.60	1.50	3.00
❑2, Sep 85, JSn, JSn (w), Betrayal!, Baxter reprint	2.00	0.50	1.25	2.50
❑3, Oct 85, JSn, Baxter reprint	2.00	0.50	1.25	2.50
❑4, Nov 85, JSn, Baxter reprint	2.00	0.50	1.25	2.50
❑5, Dec 85, JSn, Baxter reprint	2.00	0.50	1.25	2.50

LIFE OF CHRIST, THE
MARVEL

	ORIG	GOOD	FINE	N-MINT
❑1, Feb 93, The Christmas Story	2.99	0.60	1.50	3.00

LIFE OF CHRIST, THE: THE EASTER STORY
MARVEL

	ORIG	GOOD	FINE	N-MINT
❑1, The Easter Story	2.95	0.60	1.50	3.00

LIFE OF POPE JOHN PAUL II, THE
MARVEL

	ORIG	GOOD	FINE	N-MINT
❑1, Jan 83, JSt	1.50	0.50	1.25	2.50

LIFE UNDER SANCTIONS
FANTAGRAPHICS

Value: Cover or less

- ❑1, Feb 94, nn; b&w 2.95

LIFE, THE UNIVERSE AND EVERYTHING
DC

Value: Cover or less

- ❑1, prestige format; adapts Douglas Adams book 6.95
- ❑2, prestige format; adapts Douglas Adams book 6.95
- ❑3, prestige format; adapts Douglas Adams book 6.95

LIGHT AND DARKNESS WAR, THE
MARVEL

Value: Cover or less

- ❑1, Oct 88 .... 1.95
- ❑2, Nov 88 .... 1.95
- ❑3, Jan 89 .... 1.95
- ❑4, Feb 89 .... 1.95
- ❑5, Apr 89 .... 1.95
- ❑6, Sep 89 .... 1.95

LIGHT FANTASTIC, THE (TERRY PRATCHETT'S...)
INNOVATION

Value: Cover or less

- ❑0, movie Adaptation 2.50
- ❑1, Jun 92 .... 2.50
- ❑2 .... 2.50
- ❑3 .... 2.50
- ❑4 .... 2.50

LIGHTNING COMICS PRESENTS
LIGHTNING

Value: Cover or less

- ❑1, May 94, Triple Crossed 3.50

LILI
IMAGE

Value: Cover or less

- ❑0, BMB (w) 4.95

LILLITH: DEMON PRINCESS
ANTARCTIC

	ORIG	GOOD	FINE	N-MINT
❑0, Mar 98, Faith and Sin	2.95	0.39	0.98	1.95
❑0/SC, Faith and Sin, Special limited cover (Lilith flying w/green swish)	5.00	1.00	2.50	5.00
❑1, Aug 96	2.95	1.00	2.50	5.00
❑2, Oct 96	2.95	1.00	2.50	5.00
❑3, Feb 97	2.95	1.00	2.50	5.00

LIMITED COLLECTORS' EDITION
DC

	ORIG	GOOD	FINE	N-MINT
❑20, really C-20; Rudolph the Red-Nosed Reindeer	1.00	6.00	15.00	30.00
❑21, Sum 73, really C-21; Shazam!; reprints Golden Age Marvel Family stories	1.00	3.20	8.00	16.00
❑22, Fal 73, JKu; JK, really C-22; Tarzan	1.00	2.80	7.00	14.00
❑23, really C-23; House of Mystery	1.00	3.20	8.00	16.00
❑24, really C-24; Rudolph the Red-Nosed Reindeer	1.00	5.00	12.50	25.00
❑25, NA, really C-25; Batman	1.00	5.60	14.00	28.00
❑27, really C-27; Shazam!; reprints Golden Age Marvel Family stories	1.00	3.20	8.00	16.00
❑29, JK, really C-29; Tarzan	1.00	2.00	5.00	10.00
❑30, really C-30; Superman	1.00	2.40	6.00	12.00
❑31, Nov 74, really C-31; Superman	1.00	3.00	7.50	15.00
❑32, Jan 75, really C-32; Ghosts	1.00	2.00	5.00	10.00
❑33, really C-33; Rudolph the Red-Nosed Reindeer	1.00	3.00	7.50	15.00
❑34, Mar 75, really C-34; Christmas With the Super-Heroes	1.00	2.40	6.00	12.00
❑35, May 75, really C-35; Shazam!	1.00	2.00	5.00	10.00
❑36, Jul 75, JKu; JK; NR, The Creation; The Garden of Eden, really C-36; The Bible	1.00	3.00	7.50	15.00
❑37, Sep 75, really C-37; Batman	1.00	4.00	10.00	20.00
❑38, Nov 75, really C-38; Superman	1.00	2.00	5.00	10.00
❑39, Nov 75, The Man Behind the Red Hood!; How Luthor Met Superboy, really C-39; Secret Origins of Super Villains	1.00	2.00	5.00	10.00
❑40, Nov 75, really C-40; Dick Tracy	1.00	2.40	6.00	12.00
❑41, Jan 76, really C-41; Super Friends	1.00	2.00	5.00	10.00
❑42, Mar 76, really C-42; Rudolph the Red-Nosed Reindeer	1.00	2.00	5.00	10.00
❑43, Mar 76, really C-43; Christmas With the Super-Heroes	1.00	2.00	5.00	10.00
❑44, Jul 76, really C-44; Batman	1.00	2.40	6.00	12.00
❑45, Jul 76, really C-45; More Secret Origins of Super-Villains	1.00	2.00	5.00	10.00
❑46, Sep 76, really C-46; Justice League of America	1.00	2.00	5.00	10.00
❑47, Sep 76, really C-47; Superman Salutes the Bicentennial; reprints Tomahawk stories	1.00	2.00	5.00	10.00
❑48, Nov 76, really C-48; Superman vs. Flash	1.00	2.40	6.00	12.00
❑49, Nov 76, really C-49; Legion	1.00	2.00	5.00	10.00
❑50, really C-50; Rudolph the Red-Nosed Reindeer; poster	2.00	2.00	5.00	10.00
❑51, Aug 77, really C-51; Batman vs. Ra's Al Ghul	2.00	2.40	6.00	12.00
❑52, NA, really C-52; Best of DC	2.00	2.00	5.00	10.00
❑57, really C-57; Welcome Back, Kotter	2.00	2.40	6.00	12.00
❑59, Series continued in All-New Collectors' Edition; really C-59; Batman's Strangest Cases	2.00	2.80	7.00	14.00

LINCOLN-16
SKARWOOD PRODUCTIONS

Value: Cover or less

- ❑1, Aug 97 .... 2.95

LIONHEART
AWESOME

	ORIG	GOOD	FINE	N-MINT
❑1/A, Aug 99, JPH (w), Dynamic Forces variant	—	1.00	2.50	5.00
❑1/B, Aug 99, JPH (w), Women, treasure chest on cover	2.99	0.60	1.50	2.99
❑Ash 1, Jul 99, JPH (w), Wizard World '99 preview edition	—	0.60	1.50	3.00

LION KING, THE (DISNEY'S...)
MARVEL

Value: Cover or less

- ❑1, Jul 94 .... 2.50

LIPSTICK
RIP OFF

Value: Cover or less

- ❑1, May 92, b&w; adult 2.50

LISA COMICS
BONGO

Value: Cover or less

- ❑1, Lisa in Wordland; Lisa's Adventures in Wordland, One-Shot 2.25

LITA FORD: THE QUEEN OF HEAVY METAL
ROCK-IT COMICS

	ORIG	GOOD	FINE	N-MINT
❑1, guitar pick	3.95	1.00	2.50	5.00

LITTLE ARCHIE DIGEST MAGAZINE
ARCHIE

	ORIG	GOOD	FINE	N-MINT
❑1	—	0.60	1.50	3.00
❑2	—	0.40	1.00	2.00
❑3	—	0.40	1.00	2.00
❑4	—	0.40	1.00	2.00
❑5	—	0.40	1.00	2.00
❑6	—	0.40	1.00	2.00
❑7	—	0.40	1.00	2.00
❑8	—	0.40	1.00	2.00
❑9	—	0.40	1.00	2.00
❑10	—	0.40	1.00	2.00
❑11	1.75	0.35	0.88	1.75
❑12	1.75	0.35	0.88	1.75
❑13	1.75	0.35	0.88	1.75
❑14, Aug 95	1.75	0.35	0.88	1.75
❑15, Oct 95	1.75	0.35	0.88	1.75
❑16, Jun 96	1.75	0.35	0.88	1.75
❑17, Sep 96	1.79	0.36	0.89	1.79
❑18, Mar 97	1.79	0.36	0.89	1.79
❑19, Jun 97	1.79	0.36	0.89	1.79
❑20, Sep 97	1.79	0.36	0.89	1.79
❑21, Mar 98	1.95	0.39	0.98	1.95
❑22	1.95	0.39	0.98	1.95
❑23	1.95	0.39	0.98	1.95
❑24	1.95	0.39	0.98	1.95
❑25	1.95	0.39	0.98	1.95

LITTLE AUDREY (VOL. 2)
HARVEY

Value: Cover or less

- ❑1, Aug 92, It Walks Like a Man; You Make Me Laugh 1.25
- ❑2 .... 1.25
- ❑3 .... 1.25
- ❑4 .... 1.25
- ❑5 .... 1.25
- ❑6 .... 1.50
- ❑7 .... 1.50
- ❑8 .... 1.50
- ❑9 .... 1.25

LITTLE DOT (VOL. 2)
HARVEY

	ORIG	GOOD	FINE	N-MINT
❑1, Little Dot: The Dot Demon; Little Dot: Poor Old Uncle Charlie	1.25	0.30	0.75	1.50
❑2	1.25	0.30	0.75	1.50
❑3	1.25	0.30	0.75	1.50
❑4	1.25	0.30	0.75	1.50

	ORIG	GOOD	FINE	N-MINT
❑5	1.25	0.30	0.75	1.50
❑6	1.50	0.30	0.75	1.50
❑7	1.50	0.30	0.75	1.50

LITTLE DOT IN 3-D
BLACKTHORNE

Value: Cover or less
- ❑1, Sittin' Pretty; Dash It All 2.50

LITTLE GLOOMY
SLAVE LABOR

Value: Cover or less
- ❑1 .... 2.95

LITTLE GRETA GARBAGE
RIP OFF

Value: Cover or less
- ❑1, Jul 90, b&w; adult 2.50
- ❑2, Jun 91, b&w; adult 2.50

LITTLE GREY MAN
IMAGE

Value: Cover or less
- ❑1, graphic novel 6.95

LITTLE ITALY
FANTAGRAPHICS

Value: Cover or less
- ❑1, b&w 3.95

LITTLE JIM-BOB BIG FOOT
JUMP BACK PRODUCTIONS

Value: Cover or less
- ❑1, b&w; Final Issue 2.95
- ❑2, Jan 98, b&w 2.95

LITTLE LOTTA (VOL. 2)
HARVEY

	ORIG	GOOD	FINE	N-MINT
❑1, Dynamic Dot; Special Police	1.25	0.30	0.75	1.50
❑2, I Promise You a Rose Garden; The Spectator	1.25	0.30	0.75	1.50
❑3	1.25	0.30	0.75	1.50
❑4	1.25	0.30	0.75	1.50

LITTLE MERMAID, THE (DISNEY'S...)
MARVEL

	ORIG	GOOD	FINE	N-MINT
❑1, Sep 94, Sink Or Swim, movie Adaptation	1.50	0.50	1.25	2.50
❑2, Oct 94	1.50	0.40	1.00	2.00
❑3, Nov 94	1.50	0.40	1.00	2.00
❑4, Dec 94	1.50	0.40	1.00	2.00
❑5, Jan 95	1.50	0.40	1.00	2.00
❑6, Feb 95	1.50	0.40	1.00	2.00
❑7, Mar 95	1.50	0.40	1.00	2.00
❑8, Apr 95	1.50	0.40	1.00	2.00
❑9, May 95	1.50	0.40	1.00	2.00
❑10, Jun 95	1.50	0.40	1.00	2.00
❑11, Jul 95	1.50	0.40	1.00	2.00
❑12, Aug 95, Final Issue	1.50	0.40	1.00	2.00

LITTLE MERMAID (ONE-SHOT)
W.D.

Value: Cover or less
- ❑1, Under the Sea, nn 3.50

LITTLE MERMAID, THE (WALT DISNEY'S...)
DISNEY

Value: Cover or less
- ❑1, movie Adaptation; stapled 2.50
- ❑1/DM, movie Adaptation; squarebound 5.95

LITTLE MERMAID LIMITED SERIES, THE (DISNEY'S...)
DISNEY

	ORIG	GOOD	FINE	N-MINT
❑1, Feb 92	1.50	0.40	1.00	2.00
❑2, Mar 92	1.50	0.40	1.00	2.00
❑3, May 92	1.50	0.40	1.00	2.00
❑4, Jun 92	1.50	0.40	1.00	2.00

LITTLE MERMAID, THE: UNDERWATER ENGAGEMENTS (DISNEY'S...)
ACCLAIM

Value: Cover or less
- ❑1, flip-book digest set before movie 4.50

LITTLE MISS STRANGE
MILLENNIUM

Value: Cover or less
- ❑1 .... 2.95

LITTLE MISTER MAN
SLAVE LABOR

Value: Cover or less
- ❑1, Nov 95, b&w 2.95
- ❑2, Dec 95, b&w 2.95
- ❑3, Feb 96, b&w; Final Issue .. 2.95

LITTLE MONSTERS
NOW

Value: Cover or less
- ❑1, Jan 90, movie Adaptation. 1.75
- ❑2, Feb 90, Run Amuck, movie Adaptation 1.75
- ❑3, Mar 90, Pie Party, movie Adaptation 1.75
- ❑4, Apr 90, Mindwarp, movie Adaptation 1.75
- ❑5, May 90, Rampant Royalty, movie Adaptation 1.75
- ❑6, Jun 90, Sweet Revenge, movie Adaptation 1.75

LITTLE NEMO IN SLUMBERLAND 3-D
BLACKTHORNE

Value: Cover or less
- ❑1 .... 2.50

LITTLE RED HOT: CHANE OF FOOLS
IMAGE

Value: Cover or less
- ❑1, Feb 99, Chane of Fools 2.95
- ❑2, Mar 99, Rain 2.95
- ❑3, Apr 99, Prelude to a Kiss 2.95

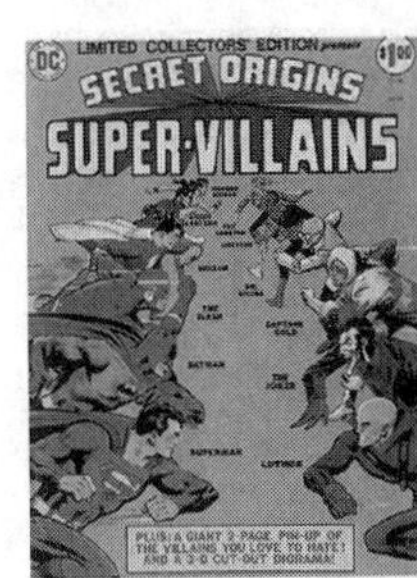

The origins of The Joker, Lex Luthor, and other super-villains were reprinted in the oversized *Limited Collectors' Edition* #C-39.

© 1975 National Periodical Publications (DC)

LITTLE RONZO IN SLUMBERLAND
SLAVE LABOR

Value: Cover or less
- ❑1, Jul 87 .... 1.75

LITTLE SHOP OF HORRORS
DC

Value: Cover or less
- ❑1, Mar 87, GC, movie Adaptation 2.00

LITTLE WHITE MOUSE
CALIBER

Value: Cover or less
- ❑1, Nov 97, A Day in the Life of a Mouse in the Field, b&w 2.95
- ❑2, Jan 98, b&w 2.95
- ❑3 .... 2.95
- ❑4 .... 2.95

LIVINGSTONE MOUNTAIN
ADVENTURE

Value: Cover or less
- ❑1, Jul 91, b&w 2.50
- ❑2, Aug 91, b&w 2.50
- ❑3, Sep 91, b&w 2.50
- ❑4, Oct 91, b&w 2.50

LIZ AND BETH (VOL. 1)
FANTAGRAPHICS

	ORIG	GOOD	FINE	N-MINT
❑1, b&w; adult	2.25	0.60	1.50	3.00
❑2, b&w; adult	2.25	0.60	1.50	3.00
❑3, b&w; adult	2.25	0.60	1.50	3.00
❑4, adult	2.50	0.60	1.50	3.00

LIZ AND BETH (VOL. 2)
FANTAGRAPHICS

Value: Cover or less
- ❑1, b&w; adult 2.50
- ❑2, b&w; adult 2.50
- ❑3, b&w; adult 2.50
- ❑4, adult 2.50

LIZ AND BETH (VOL. 3)
FANTAGRAPHICS

Value: Cover or less
- ❑1, b&w; adult 2.50
- ❑2, b&w; adult 2.50
- ❑3, b&w; adult 2.50
- ❑4, b&w; adult 2.50
- ❑5, b&w; adult 2.50
- ❑6, b&w; adult 2.50
- ❑7, b&w; adult 2.50

LIZARD LADY
AIRCEL

Value: Cover or less
- ❑1, b&w; adult 2.95
- ❑2, b&w; adult 2.95
- ❑3, b&w; adult 2.95
- ❑4, b&w; adult 2.95

LIZARDS SUMMER FUN SPECIAL
CALIBER

Value: Cover or less
- ❑1, b&w 3.50

LLOYD LLEWELLYN
FANTAGRAPHICS

Value: Cover or less
- ❑1, Apr 86 .... 2.25
- ❑2, Jun 86 .... 2.25
- ❑3, Aug 86 .... 2.25
- ❑4, Oct 86 .... 2.25
- ❑5, Jan 87 .... 2.25
- ❑6, Jun 87 .... 2.25
- ❑SE 1 .... 2.50
- ❑SE 1-2, 2nd Printing 2.95

LOBO
DC

	ORIG	GOOD	FINE	N-MINT
❑0, Oct 94, Reservoir Mooks, O: Lobo, 10/94	1.95	0.50	1.25	2.50
❑1, Dec 93, The Quigley Affair, Part 1, foil cover	2.95	0.80	2.00	4.00
❑2, Feb 94, The Quigley Affair, Part 2	1.75	0.60	1.50	3.00
❑3, Mar 94	1.75	0.60	1.50	3.00
❑4, Apr 94	1.75	0.60	1.50	3.00
❑5, May 94	1.75	0.50	1.25	2.50
❑6, Jun 94	1.75	0.50	1.25	2.50
❑7, Jul 94	1.75	0.50	1.25	2.50
❑8, Aug 94	1.75	0.50	1.25	2.50
❑9, Sep 94	1.95	0.50	1.25	2.50
❑10, Nov 94	1.95	0.50	1.25	2.50
❑11, Dec 94, Preacher Wars, Part 2	1.95	0.40	1.00	2.00
❑12, Jan 95	1.95	0.40	1.00	2.00
❑13, Feb 95	1.95	0.40	1.00	2.00
❑14, Mar 95, Lobo, P.I., Part 1	1.95	0.40	1.00	2.00
❑15, Apr 95	1.95	0.40	1.00	2.00
❑16, Jun 95	2.25	0.45	1.13	2.25

	ORIG	GOOD	FINE	N-MINT
❑17, Jul 95	2.25	0.45	1.13	2.25
❑18, Aug 95	2.25	0.45	1.13	2.25
❑19, Sep 95	2.25	0.45	1.13	2.25
❑20, Oct 95	2.25	0.45	1.13	2.25
❑21, Nov 95, A: Space Cabby	2.25	0.45	1.13	2.25
❑22, Dec 95, Underworld Unleashed	2.25	0.45	1.13	2.25
❑23, Jan 96, Stargaze Rally, Part 1	2.25	0.45	1.13	2.25
❑24, Feb 96, Stargaze Rally, Part 2	2.25	0.45	1.13	2.25
❑25, Mar 96, Lobo's Big Birfday Bash	2.25	0.45	1.13	2.25
❑26, Apr 96, The Duel	2.25	0.45	1.13	2.25
❑27, May 96	2.25	0.45	1.13	2.25
❑28, Jun 96, The Heiress, Part 1	2.25	0.45	1.13	2.25
❑29, Jul 96, The Heiress, Part 2	2.25	0.45	1.13	2.25
❑30, Aug 96, The Heiress, Part 3	2.25	0.45	1.13	2.25
❑31, Sep 96, The Heiress, Part 4	2.25	0.45	1.13	2.25
❑32, Oct 96, STance on a Wet Afternoon, Lobo's body is destroyed	2.25	0.45	1.13	2.25
❑33, Nov 96, Wetterworld	2.25	0.45	1.13	2.25
❑34, Dec 96, Bo on a Dolphin	2.25	0.45	1.13	2.25
❑35, Jan 97, Death Trek 100	2.25	0.45	1.13	2.25
❑36, Feb 97, A: Shakespeare; A: Chaucer; A: Mark Twain; A: Poe; A: Hemingway	2.25	0.45	1.13	2.25
❑37, Mar 97, Lobo's Guide to Girls	2.25	0.45	1.13	2.25
❑38, Apr 97, Last 'Bo on Earth	2.25	0.45	1.13	2.25
❑39, May 97, Lobo as a pirate	2.25	0.45	1.13	2.25
❑40, Jun 97, Lobo inside a whale	2.25	0.45	1.13	2.25
❑41, Jul 97	2.25	0.45	1.13	2.25
❑42, Aug 97	2.25	0.45	1.13	2.25
❑43, Sep 97	2.25	0.45	1.13	2.25
❑44, Oct 97, Genesis	2.25	0.45	1.13	2.25
❑45, Nov 97, The Big Brawl, Part 1, V: Jackie Chin	2.25	0.45	1.13	2.25
❑46, Dec 97, The Big Brawl, Part 2, Face cover	2.25	0.45	1.13	2.25
❑47, Jan 98	2.25	0.45	1.13	2.25
❑48, Feb 98	2.25	0.45	1.13	2.25
❑49, Mar 98, Don Alfonszo's Dinner	2.25	0.45	1.13	2.25
❑50, Apr 98, A: Keith Giffen; D: Everyone	2.25	0.45	1.13	2.25
❑51, May 98	2.25	0.45	1.13	2.25
❑52, Jun 98	2.25	0.45	1.13	2.25
❑53, Jul 98	2.25	0.45	1.13	2.25
❑54, Aug 98	2.25	0.45	1.13	2.25
❑55, Sep 98	2.50	0.45	1.13	2.25
❑56, Oct 98	2.50	0.50	1.25	2.50
❑57, Dec 98, at police convention	2.50	0.50	1.25	2.50
❑58, Jan 99, A: Superman; A: Orion	2.50	0.50	1.25	2.50
❑59, Feb 99, A: Bad Wee Bastards, in miniature world	2.50	0.50	1.25	2.50
❑60, Mar 99, The All-New, Nonviolent Adventures of Superbo, Part 1, 1: Superbo, Lobo reforms	2.50	0.50	1.25	2.50
❑61, Apr 99, The All-New, Nonviolent Adventures of Superbo, Part 2, 2: Superbo; A: Savage Six	2.50	0.50	1.25	2.50
❑62, May 99, The All-New, Nonviolent Adventures of Superbo, Part 3	2.50	0.50	1.25	2.50
❑63, Jun 99, Soul Brothers, Part 1, A: Demon	2.50	0.50	1.25	2.50
❑64, Jul 99, Soul Brothers, Part 2, A: Demon, Final Issue	2.50	0.50	1.25	2.50
❑1000000, Nov 98, Lobo's Last Job, 1: Layla	2.50	0.50	1.25	2.50
❑Anl 1, Bloodlines, Part 1, Bloodlines; Elseworlds	3.50	0.70	1.75	3.50
❑Anl 2, Elseworlds	3.50	0.70	1.75	3.50
❑Anl 3, Year One	3.95	0.79	1.98	3.95

LOBO (MINI-SERIES)
DC

	ORIG	GOOD	FINE	N-MINT
❑1, Nov 90, KG, The Last Czarnian, Part 1	0.99	0.60	1.50	3.00
❑1-2, Nov 90, 2nd Printing	0.99	0.40	1.00	2.00
❑2, Dec 90, KG, The Last Czarnian, Part 2	1.50	0.40	1.00	2.00
❑3, Jan 91, KG, The Last Czarnian, Part 3	1.50	0.40	1.00	2.00
❑4, Feb 91, KG, The Last Czarnian, Part 4	1.50	0.40	1.00	2.00

LOBO: A CONTRACT ON GAWD
DC

	ORIG	GOOD	FINE	N-MINT
❑1, Apr 94, Trouble in Paradise	1.75	0.40	1.00	2.00
❑2, May 94	1.75	0.40	1.00	2.00
❑3, Jun 94	1.75	0.40	1.00	2.00
❑4, Jul 94	1.75	0.40	1.00	2.00

LOBO: BLAZING CHAIN OF LOVE
DC

	ORIG	GOOD	FINE	N-MINT
❑1, Sep 92	1.50	0.40	1.00	2.00

LOBO: BOUNTY HUNTING FOR FUN AND PROFIT
DC

Value: Cover or less

❑1, nn; prestige format 4.95

LOBO: CHAINED
DC

Value: Cover or less

❑1, May 97, One-Shot; Lobo goes to jail 2.50

LOBO CONVENTION SPECIAL
DC

	ORIG	GOOD	FINE	N-MINT
❑1, KG (w), Lobo-Con, Set at 1993 San Diego Comic Convention	1.75	0.40	1.00	2.00

LOBOCOP
DC

	ORIG	GOOD	FINE	N-MINT
❑1, Feb 94	1.95	0.40	1.00	2.00

LOBO/DEADMAN: THE BRAVE AND THE BALD
DC

Value: Cover or less

❑1, Feb 95, Deadmen Don't Wear Plaid, nn; One-Shot 3.50

LOBO: DEATH AND TAXES
DC

Value: Cover or less

❑1, Oct 96 .... 2.25

❑2, Nov 96 .... 2.25

❑3, Dec 96 .... 2.25

❑4, Jan 97, Final Issue 2.25

LOBO/DEMON: HELLOWEEN
DC

Value: Cover or less

❑1, Dec 96, One-Shot 2.25

LOBO: FRAGTASTIC VOYAGE
DC

Value: Cover or less

❑1, nn; One-Shot; prestige format 5.95

LOBO GALLERY, THE: PORTRAITS OF A BASTICH
DC

Value: Cover or less

❑1, Sep 95, pin-ups 3.50

LOBO GOES TO HOLLYWOOD
DC

Value: Cover or less

❑1, Aug 96, One-Shot 2.25

LOBO: INFANTICIDE
DC

	ORIG	GOOD	FINE	N-MINT
❑1, Oct 92, KG, KG (w), The Theory Of Relativity	1.50	0.40	1.00	2.00
❑2, Nov 92, KG, KG (w), Your In The Army Now!	1.50	0.40	1.00	2.00
❑3, Dec 92, KG, KG (w), What Did You Do in the War, Daddy?	1.50	0.40	1.00	2.00
❑4, Jan 93, KG, KG (w), To The Devil A Daughter!	1.50	0.40	1.00	2.00

LOBO: IN THE CHAIR
DC

Value: Cover or less

❑1, Aug 94, One-Shot 1.95

LOBO: I QUIT
DC

	ORIG	GOOD	FINE	N-MINT
❑1, Dec 95, One-Shot; Lobo stops smoking	2.25	0.55	1.38	2.75

LOBO/JUDGE DREDD: PSYCHO-BIKERS VS. THE MUTANTS FROM HELL
DC

Value: Cover or less

❑1, nn; prestige format 4.95

LOBO/MASK
DC

Value: Cover or less

❑1, Feb 97, prestige format crossover with Dark Horse 5.95

❑2, Mar 97, Final Issue; prestige format crossover with Dark Horse 5.95

LOBO PARAMILITARY CHRISTMAS SPECIAL
DC

	ORIG	GOOD	FINE	N-MINT
❑1, KG, KG (w), The Lobo Xmas Sanction, D: Santa Claus	2.39	0.60	1.50	3.00

LOBO: PORTRAIT OF A VICTIM
DC

	ORIG	GOOD	FINE	N-MINT
❑1	1.75	0.40	1.00	2.00

LOBO'S BACK
DC

	ORIG	GOOD	FINE	N-MINT
❑1, May 92, KG, 1: Ramona, Variant covers exist	1.50	0.40	1.00	2.00
❑2, Jun 92, KG, Heaven Is A Four Letter Word	1.50	0.40	1.00	2.00
❑3, Oct 92, KG	1.50	0.40	1.00	2.00
❑4, Nov 92, KG	1.50	0.40	1.00	2.00

LOBO'S BIG BABE SPRING BREAK SPECIAL
DC

Value: Cover or less

❑1, Spr 95, nn 1.95

LOBO THE DUCK
DC

Value: Cover or less

❑1, Jun 97 .... 1.95

LOBO: UN-AMERICAN GLADIATORS
DC

	ORIG	GOOD	FINE	N-MINT
❑1, Jun 93, Fragituri Te Salutamus!	1.75	0.40	1.00	2.00
❑2, Jul 93, Veni, Vidi, Fragi!	1.75	0.40	1.00	2.00
❑3, Aug 93	1.75	0.40	1.00	2.00
❑4, Sep 93	1.75	0.40	1.00	2.00

LOCO VS. PULVERINE
ECLIPSE

Value: Cover or less

❑1, Jul 92, nn; b&w; wraparound cover; parody 2.50

LOGAN: PATH OF THE WARLORD
MARVEL

	ORIG	GOOD	FINE	N-MINT
❑1, Feb 96	5.95	1.20	3.00	6.00

LOGAN: SHADOW SOCIETY
MARVEL

	ORIG	GOOD	FINE	N-MINT
❑1, Dec 96, nn	5.95	1.20	3.00	6.00

LOGAN'S RUN (ADVENTURE)
ADVENTURE

	ORIG	GOOD	FINE	N-MINT
❑1, Introduction by William F. Nolan	2.25	0.50	1.25	2.50
❑2, Jul 90	2.25	0.50	1.25	2.50
❑3	2.25	0.50	1.25	2.50
❑4, Oct 90	2.25	0.50	1.25	2.50
❑5, Mar 91	2.25	0.50	1.25	2.50
❑6, Apr 91	2.25	0.50	1.25	2.50

LOGAN'S RUN (MARVEL)
MARVEL

	ORIG	GOOD	FINE	N-MINT
❑1, Jan 77, GP, movie Adaptation	0.30	0.80	2.00	4.00
❑2, Feb 77, GP, Cathedral Kill	0.30	0.60	1.50	3.00
❑3, Mar 77, GP, Sanctuary!?	0.30	0.60	1.50	3.00
❑4, Apr 77, GP, Enter the eternal Ice-World of Box	0.30	0.50	1.25	2.50
❑5, May 77, GP, End*Run	0.30	0.50	1.25	2.50
❑6, Jun 77, TS, Aftermath!, A: Thanos, New stories begin; Back-up story is first solo story featuring Thanos	0.30	0.80	2.00	4.00
❑7, Jul 77, GP, Cathedral Prime!	0.30	0.50	1.25	2.50

LOGAN'S WORLD
ADVENTURE

Value: Cover or less

- ❑1, May 91 ... 2.50
- ❑2 ... 2.50
- ❑3 ... 2.50
- ❑4 ... 2.50
- ❑5 ... 2.50
- ❑6 ... 2.50

LOIS LANE
DC

	ORIG	GOOD	FINE	N-MINT
❑1, Aug 86, GM, When It Rains, God Is Crying	1.50	0.40	1.00	2.00
❑2, Sep 86, GM, Quicksand!	1.50	0.40	1.00	2.00

LONDON'S DARK
TITAN

Value: Cover or less

- ❑1, JRo (w), Introduction by David Lloyd; 1st professional work by James Robinson ... 8.95

LONELY NIGHTS COMICS
LAST GASP

Value: Cover or less

- ❑1, Laundry Day Delight!; Fuck Story ... 2.00

LONELY WAR OF WILLY SCHULTZ, THE
AVALON

Value: Cover or less

- ❑1, b&w; Reprint ... 2.95
- ❑2 ... 2.95
- ❑3 ... 2.95
- ❑4, Escape ... 2.95

LONE RANGER, THE (PURE IMAGINATION)
PURE IMAGINATION

Value: Cover or less

- ❑1, b&w; reprints newspaper strip ... 3.00

LONE RANGER AND TONTO, THE
TOPPS

	ORIG	GOOD	FINE	N-MINT
❑1, Aug 94, It Crawls, Part 1	2.50	0.50	1.25	2.50
❑1/SC, Aug 94, It Crawls, Part 1, limited edition; foil edition	2.50	0.80	2.00	4.00
❑2, Sep 94, It Crawls, Part 2	2.50	0.50	1.25	2.50
❑2/SC, Sep 94, It Crawls, Part 2, limited edition	—	0.70	1.75	3.50
❑3, Oct 94, It Crawls, Part 3	2.50	0.50	1.25	2.50
❑3/SC, Oct 94, It Crawls, Part 3, limited edition	—	0.60	1.50	3.00
❑4, Nov 94, It Crawls, Part 4	2.50	0.50	1.25	2.50
❑4/SC, Nov 94, It Crawls, Part 4, limited edition	—	0.60	1.50	3.00

LONE WOLF AND CUB
FIRST

	ORIG	GOOD	FINE	N-MINT
❑1, May 87, FM (c), The Assassin's Road	1.95	1.20	3.00	6.00
❑1-2, The Assassin's Road, 2nd Printing	1.95	0.50	1.25	2.50
❑, The Assassin's Road, 3rd Printing	1.95	0.50	1.25	2.50
❑2, Jun 87, FM (c)	1.95	0.80	2.00	4.00
❑2-2, Jun 87, 2nd Printing	1.95	0.50	1.25	2.50
❑3, Jul 87, FM (c), The Gateless Barrier	1.95	0.80	2.00	4.00
❑3-2, The Gateless Barrier, 2nd Printing	1.95	0.50	1.25	2.50
❑4, Aug 87, FM (c)	1.95	0.60	1.50	3.00
❑5, Sep 87, FM (c)	1.95	0.60	1.50	3.00
❑6, Oct 87, FM (c), O: Lone Wolf	1.95	0.60	1.50	3.00
❑7, Nov 87, FM (c), O: Lone Wolf	1.95	0.60	1.50	3.00
❑8, Dec 87, FM (c)	1.95	0.60	1.50	3.00
❑9, Jan 88, FM (c)	1.95	0.60	1.50	3.00
❑10, Feb 88, FM (c)	1.95	0.60	1.50	3.00
❑11, Mar 88, FM (c)	2.50	0.50	1.25	2.50
❑12, Apr 88, FM (c)	2.50	0.50	1.25	2.50

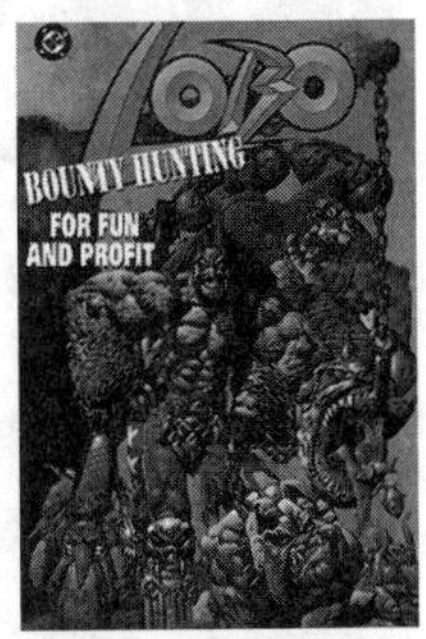

Lobo, the baddest intergalactic bounty hunter of all, gave tips on tracking down his prey in the prestige-format one-shot *Lobo: Bounty Hunting for Fun and Profit.*

© 1996 DC Comics

	ORIG	GOOD	FINE	N-MINT
❑13, May 88, BSz (c)	2.50	0.50	1.25	2.50
❑14, Jun 88, BSz (c)	2.50	0.50	1.25	2.50
❑15, Jul 88, BSz (c)	2.50	0.50	1.25	2.50
❑16, Aug 88, BSz (c)	2.50	0.50	1.25	2.50
❑17, Sep 88, BSz (c)	2.50	0.50	1.25	2.50
❑18, Oct 88, BSz (c)	2.50	0.50	1.25	2.50
❑19, Nov 88, BSz (c)	2.50	0.50	1.25	2.50
❑20, Dec 88, BSz (c)	2.50	0.50	1.25	2.50
❑21, Jan 89, BSz (c)	2.50	0.50	1.25	2.50
❑22, Feb 89, BSz (c)	2.50	0.50	1.25	2.50
❑23, Mar 89, BSz (c)	2.50	0.50	1.25	2.50
❑24, Apr 89, BSz (c)	2.50	0.50	1.25	2.50
❑25, May 89, MW (c)	2.95	0.50	1.25	2.50
❑26, Jun 89, MW (c)	2.95	0.59	1.48	2.95
❑27, Jul 89, MW (c)	2.95	0.60	1.50	3.00
❑28, Aug 89, MW (c)	2.95	0.60	1.50	3.00
❑29, Sep 89, MW (c)	2.95	0.60	1.50	3.00
❑30, Oct 89, MW (c)	2.95	0.60	1.50	3.00
❑31, Jan 90, MW (c)	3.25	0.60	1.50	3.00
❑32, Apr 90, MW (c)	3.25	0.60	1.50	3.00
❑33, May 90, MW (c)	3.25	0.60	1.50	3.00
❑34, Jun 90, MW (c)	3.25	0.65	1.63	3.25
❑35, Jun 90, MW (c)	3.25	0.65	1.63	3.25
❑36, Jul 90, MW (c)	3.25	0.65	1.63	3.25
❑37, Aug 90, MP (c)	3.25	0.65	1.63	3.25
❑38, Sep 90, MP (c)	3.25	0.65	1.63	3.25
❑39, MP (c), Giant-size	3.25	1.20	3.00	6.00
❑40, MP (c)	3.25	0.65	1.63	3.25
❑41, MP (c)	3.25	0.80	2.00	4.00
❑42, MP (c)	3.25	0.80	2.00	4.00
❑43, MP (c)	3.25	0.80	2.00	4.00
❑44, MP (c)	3.25	0.80	2.00	4.00
❑45, MP (c)	3.25	0.80	2.00	4.00
❑46	3.95	0.80	2.00	4.00
❑47	3.95	0.80	2.00	4.00
❑48	3.95	0.80	2.00	4.00
❑49	3.95	0.80	2.00	4.00

LONG, HOT SUMMER, THE
DC

Value: Cover or less

- ❑1, Jul 95, enhanced cover ... 2.95
- ❑2, Aug 95 ... 2.50
- ❑3, Sep 95 ... 2.50

LONGSHOT
MARVEL

	ORIG	GOOD	FINE	N-MINT
❑1, Sep 85, 1: Longshot	0.75	0.70	1.75	3.50
❑2, Oct 85, 1: Ricochet Rita	0.75	0.60	1.50	3.00
❑3, Nov 85, Just Let Me Die, 1: Spiral; 1: Mojo	0.75	0.50	1.25	2.50
❑4, Dec 85, Can't Give It All Away, A: Spider-Man	0.75	0.50	1.25	2.50
❑5, Jan 86, Deadly Lies	0.75	0.40	1.00	2.00
❑6, A Snake Coils..., Double-size	1.25	0.50	1.25	2.50

LONGSHOT (2ND SERIES)
MARVEL

Value: Cover or less

- ❑1, Feb 98, Fools, wraparound cover; One-Shot ... 3.99

LONGSHOT COMICS
SLAVE LABOR

Value: Cover or less

- ❑1, Jun 95, The Long and Unlearned Life of Roland Gethers ... 2.95
- ❑1-2, Feb 96, 2nd Printing ... 2.95
- ❑2, Jul 97, The Failed Promise of Bradley Gethers, b&w ... 2.95

LOOKERS
AVATAR

Value: Cover or less

- ❑1 ... 3.00
- ❑2 ... 3.00

LOOKERS: SLAVES OF ANUBIS
AVATAR

Value: Cover or less

- ❑1 ... 3.50

LOONEY TUNES (DC)
DC

	ORIG	GOOD	FINE	N-MINT
❑1, Apr 94, Earthstruck; The Shot Felt 'Round the World, A: Marvin Martian	1.50	0.45	1.13	2.25
❑2, May 94, Road Runner, Coyote	1.50	0.40	1.00	2.00

	ORIG	GOOD	FINE	N-MINT
❑3, Jun 94, Take Me Out to the Ballgame; Half-Baked Romance, Baseball issue	1.50	0.40	1.00	2.00
❑4, Jul 94, Makeover Mayhem; Peking Duck, A: Witch Hazel	1.50	0.40	1.00	2.00
❑5, Aug 94, Spaced-Out Coyote; Brawl Or Nothing, Coyote, Martians	1.50	0.35	0.88	1.75
❑6, Sep 94, Tazmanian Devil	1.50	0.30	0.75	1.50
❑7, Oct 94	1.50	0.30	0.75	1.50
❑8, Nov 94	1.50	0.30	0.75	1.50
❑9, Dec 94, If It's Tuesday, this Must be Love; The Duck with no Name	1.50	0.30	0.75	1.50
❑10, Jan 95, Christmas issue	1.50	0.30	0.75	1.50
❑11, Feb 95	1.50	0.30	0.75	1.50
❑12, Mar 95	1.50	0.30	0.75	1.50
❑13, Apr 95, Coyote	1.50	0.30	0.75	1.50
❑14, May 95	1.50	0.30	0.75	1.50
❑15, Jun 95	1.50	0.30	0.75	1.50
❑16, Jul 95, Daffy, Speedy Gonzales	1.50	0.30	0.75	1.50
❑17, Aug 95	1.50	0.30	0.75	1.50
❑18, Sep 95, Duck Dodgers	1.50	0.30	0.75	1.50
❑19, Oct 95	1.50	0.30	0.75	1.50
❑20, Nov 95, Yosemite Sam	1.50	0.30	0.75	1.50
❑21, Feb 96, Tazmanian Devil	1.50	0.30	0.75	1.50
❑22, Apr 96, Fudd Hunt; Punch 'n Tweety	1.50	0.30	0.75	1.50
❑23, Jun 96	1.75	0.35	0.88	1.75
❑24, Aug 96, Get Tweety	1.75	0.35	0.88	1.75
❑25, Oct 96, Indiana Itz Mine	1.75	0.35	0.88	1.75
❑26, Nov 96, Psylvester; Modem Operandi, indicia says Nov, cover says Dec; Sylvester, Tweety	1.75	0.35	0.88	1.75
❑27, Jan 97, One a Toon...Always a Toon, indicia says Jan, cover says Feb	1.75	0.35	0.88	1.75
❑28, Feb 97, I Love Goosey; I'll Take Manhattan, cover says Apr 96, indicia says Feb 97; Valentine's issue	1.75	0.35	0.88	1.75
❑29, May 97, Coyote	1.75	0.35	0.88	1.75
❑30, Jul 97, Twilight Zone cover	1.75	0.35	0.88	1.75
❑31, Aug 97	1.75	0.35	0.88	1.75
❑32, Sep 97, Hercules parody	1.75	0.35	0.88	1.75
❑33, Oct 97, Back to School issue	1.75	0.35	0.88	1.75
❑34, Nov 97, Sidekicked; Inherit the Windbag, Daffy versus Dinky Downunder	1.75	0.35	0.88	1.75
❑35, Dec 97, Agent Duck; Agent Daffy, Agent Daffy	1.95	0.39	0.98	1.95
❑36, Jan 98, Sylvester, Tweety	1.95	0.39	0.98	1.95
❑37, Feb 98, V: Crusher	1.95	0.39	0.98	1.95
❑38, Mar 98, The Trouble with Mars!; Puppy Love, A: Marvin Martian	1.95	0.39	0.98	1.95
❑39, Apr 98, Foghorn Leghorn	1.95	0.39	0.98	1.95
❑40, May 98, Sylvester	1.95	0.39	0.98	1.95
❑41, Jun 98, Sylvester, Porky	1.95	0.39	0.98	1.95
❑42, Jul 98, Speedy Gonzales, Sylvester	1.95	0.39	0.98	1.95
❑43, Aug 98, Bugs and Daffy do Magic	1.95	0.39	0.98	1.95
❑44, Sep 98, Tweety and Sylvester	1.99	0.40	1.00	1.99
❑45, Oct 98, Marvin Martian	1.99	0.40	1.00	1.99
❑46, Nov 98, Bugs and Taz	1.99	0.40	1.00	1.99
❑47, Dec 98, Christmas issue	1.99	0.40	1.00	1.99
❑48, Jan 99, A: Rocky and Mugsy	1.99	0.40	1.00	1.99
❑49, Feb 99, Swoon; Cityscrape, Pepe is stalked	1.99	0.40	1.00	1.99
❑50, Mar 99	1.99	0.40	1.00	1.99
❑51, Apr 99	1.99	0.40	1.00	1.99
❑52, May 99, Shake Well Before Ewes; Love's Capture	1.99	0.40	1.00	1.99
❑53, Jun 99, The Postman Always Brings Mice; One for the Books	1.99	0.40	1.00	1.99
❑54, Jul 99, Rumble on the Red Planet; Be My Pest	1.99	0.40	1.00	1.99
❑55, Aug 99, Twuce or Consequences; Trampolined Underfoot	1.99	0.40	1.00	1.99
❑56, Sep 99, Block Herds; Touchdown Tweety	1.99	0.40	1.00	1.99
❑57, Oct 99, Claws & Effect; Taking the Plunge	1.99	0.40	1.00	1.99
❑58, Nov 99, Femme Fatale; The Missing Link	1.99	0.40	1.00	1.99
❑59, Dec 99	1.99	0.40	1.00	1.99
❑60, Jan 00, Tweety Temps!; Spring Fling!	1.99	0.40	1.00	1.99
❑61, Feb 00, Roll out the Bunny; Takin' Care of Business	1.99	0.40	1.00	1.99
❑62, Mar 00	1.99	0.40	1.00	1.99
❑63, Apr 00	1.99	0.40	1.00	1.99
❑64, May 00, Moldy Locks; The Wabbit Season Pwoject	1.99	0.40	1.00	1.99
❑65, Jun 00	1.99	0.40	1.00	1.99
❑66, Jul 00	1.99	0.40	1.00	1.99
❑67, Aug 00	1.99	0.40	1.00	1.99
❑68, Sep 00	1.99	0.40	1.00	1.99
❑69, Oct 00, Image is Everything; True Hollyweird Mysteries!	1.99	0.40	1.00	1.99
❑70, Nov 00, Reach Out and Bugs Someone; So You Want a Million Bucks, Eh?	1.99	0.40	1.00	1.99
❑71, Dec 00, Hare-A 51; The Shiny	1.99	0.40	1.00	1.99
❑72, Jan 01, What Dis Country Needs; Bad News Cat	1.99	0.40	1.00	1.99
❑73, Feb 01, Looney Yule	1.99	0.40	1.00	1.99
❑74, Mar 01, The K-9 Files; Heading for Trouble	1.99	0.40	1.00	1.99
❑75, Apr 01, A Hare Gone Conclusion	1.99	0.40	1.00	1.99
❑76, May 01, Sea Monkey Business; Foes Afloat	1.99	0.40	1.00	1.99
❑77, Jun 01, Fowled Out; My Fair Doggy	1.99	0.40	1.00	1.99
❑78	1.99	0.40	1.00	1.99
❑79	1.99	0.40	1.00	1.99
❑80	1.99	0.40	1.00	1.99

LOOSE CANNON
DC

Value: Cover or less

- ❑1, Jun 95, JPH (w), Mad 1.75
- ❑2, Jul 95 .... 1.75
- ❑3, Aug 95, V: Eradicator 1.75
- ❑4, Sep 95 .... 1.75

LOOSE TEETH
FANTAGRAPHICS

Value: Cover or less

- ❑1, b&w 2.75
- ❑2, b&w 2.75
- ❑3, b&w 2.75

LORD FARRIS: SLAVEMASTER
EROS

Value: Cover or less

- ❑1, Feb 96 .... 2.95
- ❑2, May 96 .... 2.95

LORD OF THE DEAD
CONQUEST

Value: Cover or less

- ❑1, b&w 2.95

LORD PUMPKIN
MALIBU

Value: Cover or less

- ❑0, Oct 94, The Return of th Great Pumpkin 2.50

LORD PUMPKIN/NECROMANTRA
MALIBU

Value: Cover or less

- ❑1, The Last Pumpkin 2.95
- ❑2 .... 2.95

LORDS
LEGEND (NOT DARK HORSE IMPRINT)

	ORIG	GOOD	FINE	N-MINT
❑1	2.15	0.45	1.13	2.25

LORDS OF MISRULE (ATOMEKA)
ATOMEKA

Value: Cover or less

- ❑1 .... 6.95

LORDS OF MISRULE, THE (DARK HORSE)
DARK HORSE

Value: Cover or less

- ❑1, Jan 97, The Callow Heart, b&w 2.95
- ❑2, Feb 97, Far From Home, b&w 2.95
- ❑3, Mar 97, Hag Ride, b&w 2.95
- ❑4, Apr 97, b&w 2.95
- ❑5, May 97, b&w 2.95
- ❑6, Jun 97, b&w 2.95

LORDS OF THE ULTRA-REALM
DC

Value: Cover or less

- ❑1, Jun 86 .... 1.50
- ❑2, Jul 86 .... 1.50
- ❑3, Aug 86 .... 1.50
- ❑4, Sep 86 .... 1.50
- ❑5, Oct 86 .... 1.50
- ❑6, Nov 86 .... 1.50
- ❑SE 1 .... 2.25

LORELEI
STARWARP

Value: Cover or less

- ❑1, b&w 2.50

LORELEI OF THE RED MIST
CONQUEST

Value: Cover or less

- ❑1, b&w 2.95
- ❑2, b&w 2.95

LORI LOVECRAFT: MY FAVORITE REDHEAD
CALIBER

Value: Cover or less

- ❑1 .... 3.95

LORI LOVECRAFT: THE BIG COMEBACK
CALIBER

Value: Cover or less

- ❑1 .... 2.95

LORI LOVECRAFT: THE DARK LADY
CALIBER

Value: Cover or less

- ❑1 .... 2.95

LORTNOC
RADIO

Value: Cover or less

- ❑1, Aug 98, b&w 2.95

LOSERS SPECIAL
DC

	ORIG	GOOD	FINE	N-MINT
❑1, Sep 85, Crisis on Infinite Earths, O: Captain Storm; O: Johnny Cloud; D: The Losers; O: Pooch (Gunner's Dog), Crisis	1.25	0.50	1.25	2.50

ORIG GOOD FINE N-MINT

LOST, THE (CALIBER)
CALIBER

Value: Cover or less

- ❑1, Oct 96, b&w 2.95
- ❑2, b&w 2.95

LOST, THE (CHAOS)
CHAOS

Value: Cover or less

- ❑1, Dec 97, b&w 2.95
- ❑2, Jan 98, b&w 2.95
- ❑3, Feb 98, b&w; cover says Feb 97; a misprint 2.95

LOST ANGEL
CALIBER

Value: Cover or less

- ❑1, b&w 2.95

LOST CONTINENT
ECLIPSE

Value: Cover or less

- ❑1, b&w; Japanese 3.50
- ❑2, b&w; Japanese 3.50
- ❑3, b&w; Japanese 3.50
- ❑4, b&w; Japanese 3.50
- ❑5, b&w; Japanese 3.50
- ❑6, b&w; Japanese 3.50

LOST GIRLS
KITCHEN SINK

Value: Cover or less

- ❑1, Nov 95, AMo (w), adult; card-stock cover; Oversized 5.95
- ❑2, Feb 96, AMo (w), adult; card-stock cover; Oversized 5.95

LOST HEROES
DAVDEZ

Value: Cover or less

- ❑0, Mar 98 .... 2.95
- ❑1, Apr 98 .... 2.95
- ❑2, May 98 .... 2.95
- ❑3, Jun 98 .... 2.95
- ❑4, Aug 98 .... 2.95

LOST IN SPACE (DARK HORSE)
DARK HORSE

Value: Cover or less

- ❑1, Apr 98, movie Adaptation . 2.95
- ❑2, May 98, movie Adaptation 2.95
- ❑3, Jul 98, movie Adaptation .. 2.95

LOST IN SPACE (INNOVATION)
INNOVATION

	ORIG	GOOD	FINE	N-MINT
❑1, Aug 91, Seduction of the Innocent	2.50	0.60	1.50	3.00
❑2, Nov 91	2.50	0.55	1.38	2.75
❑3, Dec 91	2.50	0.55	1.38	2.75
❑4, Feb 92	2.50	0.50	1.25	2.50
❑5, Mar 92, The Perils Of Penelope	2.50	0.50	1.25	2.50
❑6, May 92, In Unity There is Strength	2.50	0.50	1.25	2.50
❑7, Jun 92, Don's Dilemma	2.50	0.50	1.25	2.50
❑8, Aug 92	2.50	0.50	1.25	2.50
❑9, Oct 92	2.50	0.50	1.25	2.50
❑10, Nov 92	2.50	0.50	1.25	2.50
❑11, Dec 92, Judy's story	2.50	0.50	1.25	2.50
❑12	2.50	0.50	1.25	2.50
❑13, Aug 93, Voyage to the Bottom of the Soul, Part 1; Journey to the Bottom of the Soul, Part 1, enhanced cardstock cover	2.50	0.99	2.47	4.95
❑13/GO, Aug 93, Voyage to the Bottom of the Soul, Part 1; Journey to the Bottom of the Soul, Part 1, enhanced cardstock cover; Gold edition	4.95	1.00	2.50	5.00
❑14, Sep 93, Voyage to the Bottom of the Soul, Part 2; Journey to the Bottom of the Soul, Part 2	2.50	0.50	1.25	2.50
❑15, Aug 93, Voyage to the Bottom of the Soul, Part 3; Journey to the Bottom of the Soul, Part 3	2.50	0.50	1.25	2.50
❑16, Sep 93, Voyage to the Bottom of the Soul, Part 4; Journey to the Bottom of the Soul, Part 4	2.50	0.50	1.25	2.50
❑17, Oct 93, Voyage to the Bottom of the Soul, Part 5; Journey to the Bottom of the Soul, Part 5	2.50	0.50	1.25	2.50
❑18, Nov 93, Voyage to the Bottom of the Soul, Part 6; Journey to the Bottom of the Soul, Part 6, Final Issue	2.50	0.50	1.25	2.50
❑Anl 1	2.95	0.59	1.48	2.95
❑Anl 2	2.95	0.59	1.48	2.95
❑SE 1, amended reprint of #1	2.50	0.50	1.25	2.50
❑SE 2	2.50	0.50	1.25	2.50

LOST IN SPACE: PROJECT ROBINSON
INNOVATION

Value: Cover or less

- ❑1, Nov 93, It's A Little Secret, Just The Robinson's Affair 2.50

LOST LAUGHTER
BAD HABIT

Value: Cover or less

- ❑1, b&w 2.50
- ❑2, b&w 2.50
- ❑3, b&w 2.50
- ❑4, Apr 94, b&w 2.50

LOST ONES, THE: FOR YOUR EYES ONLY
IMAGE

	ORIG	GOOD	FINE	N-MINT
❑1, nn; special preview; no price	—	0.20	0.50	1.00

LOST PLANET
ECLIPSE

	ORIG	GOOD	FINE	N-MINT
❑1, May 87	1.75	0.40	1.00	2.00
❑2, Jul 87	1.75	0.40	1.00	2.00

Following their deaths in *Crisis on Infinite Earths*, the team of Capt. Storm, Johnny Cloud, Gunner, and Sarge were given a final tribute in *Losers Special.*

	ORIG	GOOD	FINE	N-MINT
❑3, Sep 87	2.00	0.40	1.00	2.00
❑4, Dec 87, Through Past Darkly	2.00	0.40	1.00	2.00
❑5, Feb 88	2.00	0.40	1.00	2.00
❑6, Mar 89, My Soul to Take...	2.00	0.40	1.00	2.00

LOST UNIVERSE (GENE RODDENBERRY'S...)
TEKNO

Value: Cover or less

- ❑0, O Brave New World 2.25
- ❑1, Apr 95, O Brave New World 1.95
- ❑2, May 95, A Riddle Wrapped in an Enigma 1.95
- ❑3, Jun 95, trading card 1.95
- ❑3/A, Jun 95, variant cover 1.95
- ❑4, Jul 95, bound-in trading card 1.95
- ❑5, Aug 95, 1: Xander 1.95
- ❑6, Sep 95 .... 1.95
- ❑7, Oct 95, Final Issue 1.95

LOST WORLD, THE
MILLENNIUM

Value: Cover or less

- ❑1, Jan 96, cover says Mar, indicia says Jan 2.95
- ❑2, Mar 96 .... 2.95

LOST WORLD, THE: JURASSIC PARK
TOPPS

Value: Cover or less

- ❑1, May 97 .... 2.95
- ❑2, Jun 97 .... 2.95
- ❑3, Jul 97 .... 2.95

LOUD CANNOLI
CRAZYFISH

Value: Cover or less

- ❑1, nn 2.95

LOUDER THAN WORDS (SERGIO ARAGONÉS'...)
DARK HORSE

Value: Cover or less

- ❑1, Jul 97, SA, SA (w) 2.95
- ❑2, Aug 97, SA, SA (w) 2.95
- ❑3, Sep 97, SA, SA (w) 2.95
- ❑4, Oct 97, SA, SA (w) 2.95
- ❑5, Nov 97, SA, SA (w) 2.95
- ❑6, Dec 97, SA, SA (w) 2.95

LOUIS VS. ALI
REVOLUTIONARY

Value: Cover or less

- ❑1, Dec 93, b&w 2.95

LOVE & ROCKETS
FANTAGRAPHICS

	ORIG	GOOD	FINE	N-MINT
❑1, Fal 82	2.95	5.60	14.00	28.00
❑1-2, 2nd Printing	3.95	0.80	2.00	4.00
❑, 3rd Printing	3.95	0.79	1.98	3.95
❑1-4, 4th Printing	4.95	0.99	2.47	4.95
❑2, Spr 83	2.95	2.80	7.00	14.00
❑2-2, 2nd Printing	3.95	0.79	1.98	3.95
❑3	—	2.00	5.00	10.00
❑3-2, Apr 91, 2nd Printing	3.95	0.79	1.98	3.95
❑4	—	1.60	4.00	8.00
❑4-2, Apr 91, 2nd Printing	3.95	0.50	1.25	2.50
❑4-3, 3rd Printing	3.95	0.79	1.98	3.95
❑5	—	1.40	3.50	7.00
❑5-2, May 91, 2nd Printing	2.50	0.50	1.25	2.50
❑6	—	1.00	2.50	5.00
❑6-2, May 91, 2nd Printing	2.50	0.50	1.25	2.50
❑7, Jul 84	1.95	1.00	2.50	5.00
❑7-2, May 91, 2nd Printing	2.50	0.50	1.25	2.50
❑8	—	1.00	2.50	5.00
❑8-2, Aug 91, 2nd Printing	2.50	0.50	1.25	2.50
❑9	—	1.00	2.50	5.00
❑9-2, Oct 91, 2nd Printing	2.50	0.50	1.25	2.50
❑10	—	1.00	2.50	5.00
❑10-2, Dec 91, 2nd Printing	2.95	0.59	1.48	2.95
❑11	—	0.80	2.00	4.00
❑11-2, Feb 92, 2nd Printing	2.50	0.50	1.25	2.50
❑12, Jul 85	1.95	0.80	2.00	4.00
❑12-2, Aug 92, 2nd Printing	2.50	0.50	1.25	2.50
❑13	—	0.80	2.00	4.00
❑13-2, Oct 92, 2nd Printing	2.50	0.50	1.25	2.50
❑14, Nov 85	2.25	0.80	2.00	4.00
❑14-2, Feb 93, 2nd Printing	2.50	0.50	1.25	2.50
❑15, Jan 86	2.25	0.80	2.00	4.00
❑15-2, Aug 93, 2nd Printing	2.50	0.50	1.25	2.50
❑16, Mar 86	2.25	0.60	1.50	3.00
❑16-2, Oct 93, 2nd Printing	2.95	0.59	1.48	2.95
❑17, Jun 86	2.25	0.60	1.50	3.00

	ORIG	GOOD	FINE	N-MINT
❑18, Sep 86	2.25	0.60	1.50	3.00
❑19, Jan 87	2.25	0.60	1.50	3.00
❑20, Apr 87	2.25	0.60	1.50	3.00
❑21, Jul 87	2.25	0.45	1.13	2.25
❑22, Aug 87	2.25	0.45	1.13	2.25
❑23, Oct 87	2.25	0.45	1.13	2.25
❑24, Dec 87	2.25	0.45	1.13	2.25
❑25, Mar 88	2.25	0.45	1.13	2.25
❑26, Jun 88	2.25	0.45	1.13	2.25
❑27, Aug 88	2.25	0.45	1.13	2.25
❑28, Nov 88, 32pgs.	2.95	0.59	1.48	2.95
❑28-2, Apr 95, 2nd Printing	2.95	0.59	1.48	2.95
❑29, Mar 89	2.25	0.55	1.38	2.75
❑29-2, Mar 92, 2nd Printing	2.25	0.45	1.13	2.25
❑30, Jul 89, 40pgs.	2.25	0.59	1.48	2.95
❑30-2, Mar 92, 2nd Printing	2.95	0.59	1.48	2.95
❑31, Dec 89	2.50	0.50	1.25	2.50
❑31-2, Apr 92, 2nd Printing	2.50	0.50	1.25	2.50
❑32, May 90	2.50	0.50	1.25	2.50
❑33, Aug 90	2.50	0.50	1.25	2.50
❑34, Nov 90	2.50	0.50	1.25	2.50
❑35, Mar 91	2.75	0.55	1.38	2.75
❑36, Nov 91	2.75	0.55	1.38	2.75
❑37, Feb 92	2.75	0.55	1.38	2.75
❑38, Apr 92	2.75	0.55	1.38	2.75
❑39, Aug 92	2.75	0.55	1.38	2.75
❑40, Jan 93, 48pgs.	3.50	0.70	1.75	3.50
❑41, Apr 93	2.95	0.59	1.48	2.95
❑42, Aug 93	2.95	0.59	1.48	2.95
❑43, Nov 93	2.95	0.59	1.48	2.95
❑44, Mar 94	2.95	0.59	1.48	2.95
❑45, Jul 94	2.95	0.59	1.48	2.95
❑46, Nov 94	2.95	0.59	1.48	2.95
❑47, Apr 95	2.95	0.59	1.48	2.95
❑48, Jul 95	2.95	0.59	1.48	2.95
❑49, Nov 95	2.95	0.59	1.48	2.95
❑50, Apr 96, b&w; 56pgs.; Final Issue	4.95	0.99	2.47	4.95
❑36896, May 95, 5th Printing	4.95	0.99	2.47	4.95
❑36925, May 96, 3rd Printing	4.95	0.99	2.47	4.95

LOVE & ROCKETS BONANZA
FANTAGRAPHICS

Value: Cover or less

❑1, Mar 89, b&w; Reprint 2.95
❑1-2, Feb 92, b&w; 2nd Printing 2.95

LOVE BITES
FANTAGRAPHICS

Value: Cover or less

❑1, b&w; adult 2.25
❑2, adult 2.25

LOVE BITES (RADIO COMIX)
RADIO COMIX

Value: Cover or less

❑1, Oct 00, The Wedding 2.95

LOVE BOMB
ABACULUS

Value: Cover or less

❑1 .... 2.95
❑2, Son of Thatcher; Kurious Middle: Almost Heaven 2.95

LOVECRAFT
ADVENTURE

Value: Cover or less

❑1, The Lurking Fear 2.95
❑1/LE, limited edition 5.95
❑2 .... 2.95
❑3, The Tomb 2.95
❑4, The Alchemist 2.95

LOVE ETERNAL: A TORTURED SOUL
VLAD ENT.

Value: Cover or less

❑1, b&w 2.00

LOVE FANTASY
RENEGADE

Value: Cover or less

❑1, Check-Out Girl; The Perfect Guy, b&w 2.00

LOVE IN TIGHTS
SLAVE LABOR

Value: Cover or less

❑1, Nov 98, While You Were Sleeping; Crash Course, b&w; First heart throbbin' issue 2.95

LOVE LETTERS IN THE HAND
FANTAGRAPHICS

Value: Cover or less

❑1, b&w; adult 2.25
❑2, b&w; adult 2.25
❑3, b&w; adult 2.50

LOVELY AS A LIE
ILLUSTRATION

Value: Cover or less

❑1, Nov 94, Mortal Sins 3.25

LOVELY LADIES
CALIBER

Value: Cover or less

❑1, b&w; pin-ups 3.50

LOVELY PRUDENCE
MODERN

Value: Cover or less

❑3, b&w 2.95

LOVE SUCKS
ACE

Value: Cover or less

❑1 .... 2.95

LOWLIFE
CALIBER

Value: Cover or less

❑1, b&w 2.50
❑2, b&w 2.50
❑3, b&w 2.50
❑4, Feb 94, b&w 2.50

L.T. CAPER
SPOTLIGHT

Value: Cover or less

❑1, The Phoenix Caper 1.75

LUBA
FANTAGRAPHICS

Value: Cover or less

❑1, Feb 98, Luba in America; The Sisters, the Cousins, and the Kids 2.95
❑2, Jul 98 .... 2.95
❑3, Dec 98 .... 2.95

LUCIFER (TRIDENT)
TRIDENT

Value: Cover or less

❑1, b&w 1.95
❑2, b&w 1.95
❑3, b&w 1.95

LUCIFER (VERTIGO)
VERTIGO

	ORIG	GOOD	FINE	N-MINT
❑1, Jun 00, A Six-Card Spread	2.50	0.60	1.50	3.00
❑2, Jul 00	2.50	0.50	1.25	2.50
❑3, Aug 00	2.50	0.50	1.25	2.50
❑4, Sep 00	2.50	0.50	1.25	2.50
❑5, Oct 00, The House of Windowless Rooms, Part 1	2.50	0.50	1.25	2.50
❑6, Nov 00, The House of Windowless Rooms, Part 2	2.50	0.50	1.25	2.50
❑7, Dec 00, The House of Windowless Rooms, Part 3	2.50	0.50	1.25	2.50
❑8, Jan 01, The House of Windowless Rooms, Part 4	2.50	0.50	1.25	2.50
❑9, Feb 01, Children and Monsters	2.50	0.50	1.25	2.50
❑10, Mar 01, Children and Monsters, Part 1	2.50	0.50	1.25	2.50
❑11, Apr 01, Children and Monsters, Part 2	2.50	0.50	1.25	2.50
❑12, May 01, Children and Monsters, Part 3	2.50	0.50	1.25	2.50
❑13, Jun 01, Children and Monsters, Part 4	2.50	0.50	1.25	2.50
❑14	2.50	0.50	1.25	2.50
❑15	2.50	0.50	1.25	2.50
❑16	2.50	0.50	1.25	2.50

LUCIFER'S HAMMER
INNOVATION

Value: Cover or less

❑1, Nov 93, The Anvil 2.50
❑2, Hammer Fever 2.50
❑3 .... 2.50
❑4 .... 2.50
❑5 .... 2.50
❑6 .... 2.50

LUCK OF THE DRAW
RADIO COMIX

Value: Cover or less

❑1, Jun 00, b&w; adult 3.95

LUCKY 7
RUNAWAY GRAPHICS

Value: Cover or less

❑1, Apr 93, Martyrs & Mayhem 1.95

LUCKY LUKE: JESSE JAMES
FANTASY FLIGHT

Value: Cover or less

❑1 .... 8.95

LUCKY LUKE: THE STAGE COACH
FANTASY FLIGHT

Value: Cover or less

❑1 .... 8.95

LUDWIG VON DRAKE (WALT DISNEY'S...)
DELL

	ORIG	GOOD	FINE	N-MINT
❑1, Nov 61	0.10	4.00	10.00	20.00
❑2, Jan 62	0.10	2.40	6.00	12.00
❑3, Mar 62	0.10	2.40	6.00	12.00
❑4, Jun 62	0.10	2.40	6.00	12.00

LUFTWAFFE: 1946 (VOL. 1)
ANTARCTIC

	ORIG	GOOD	FINE	N-MINT
❑1, Jul 96, Fires of Faith, b&w	2.95	1.00	2.50	5.00
❑2, Sep 96, Clash of the Neptunes, b&w	2.95	0.80	2.00	4.00
❑3, Nov 96, Conquest of Space, b&w	2.95	0.80	2.00	4.00
❑4, Jan 97, Victory or Death, b&w; Final Issue	2.95	0.80	2.00	4.00
❑Anl 1, Apr 98, b&w	2.95	0.80	2.00	4.00

LUFTWAFFE: 1946 (VOL. 2)
ANTARCTIC

Value: Cover or less

❑1, Mar 97, Luftsturm, Part 1 .. 2.95
❑2, Apr 97, Luftsturm, Part 2, contains indicia for issue #1 ...... 2.95
❑3, May 97, Luftsturm, Part 3 .... 2.95
❑4, Jul 97, Luftsturm, Part 4 .... 2.95
❑5, Aug 97, Luftsturm, Part 5 .... 2.95

ORIG GOOD FINE N-MINT

- ❑6, Oct 97, Projekt Saucer, Part 1 .... 2.95
- ❑7, Nov 97, Projekt Saucer, Part 2 .... 2.95
- ❑8, Feb 98, index to Luftwaffe: 1946, Tigers of Terra; 50th "Families of Altered Wars" issue 2.95
- ❑9, Apr 98, Projekt Saucer, Part 3 .... 2.95
- ❑10, May 98, Projekt Saucer, Part 4 .... 2.95
- ❑11, Jun 98, Projekt Saucer, Part 5 .... 2.95
- ❑12, Jul 98, Projekt Saucer, Part 6 .... 2.95
- ❑13, Aug 98, Jagdgeschwader, Part 1 .... 2.95
- ❑14, Oct 98, Jagdgeschwader, Part 2 .... 2.95
- ❑15, Feb 99, Jagdgeschwader, Part 3 .... 2.99
- ❑16, Mar 99, Jagdgeschwader, Part 4 .... 2.99
- ❑Anl 1, Airkid; Kid War, 1998 Annual 2.95
- ❑SE 1, Apr 98, Luftwaffe 1946, Eagles of the Sky, Color Special 2.95
- ❑SE 2, Feb 97, Triebflƒgel; Triebflngel, b&w; One-Shot; Triebflƒgel Special; German rocketry; Triebflngel Special 2.95

LUFTWAFFE: 1946 TECHNICAL MANUAL
ANTARCTIC

	ORIG	GOOD	FINE	N-MINT
❑1, Feb 98, Projekt Saucer	3.95	0.80	2.00	4.00
❑2, Apr 99, Hitler's Kamikazes	3.99	0.80	2.00	4.00

LUGER
ECLIPSE

	ORIG	GOOD	FINE	N-MINT
❑1, Oct 86	1.75	0.40	1.00	2.00
❑2, Dec 86	1.75	0.40	1.00	2.00
❑3, Feb 87	1.75	0.40	1.00	2.00

LUGH, LORD OF LIGHT
FLAGSHIP

Value: Cover or less

- ❑1 .... 1.75
- ❑2, Jun 87 .... 1.75
- ❑3 .... 1.75
- ❑4 .... 1.75

LUGO
LOST BOYS

	ORIG	GOOD	FINE	N-MINT
❑0.5, Promotional edition	—	0.20	0.50	1.00

LUM URUSEI*YATSURA
VIZ

	ORIG	GOOD	FINE	N-MINT
❑1, A Good Catch; Poor Little Devil, b&w; Japanese	2.95	0.80	2.00	4.00
❑2, b&w; Japanese	2.95	0.70	1.75	3.50
❑3, b&w; Japanese	2.95	0.70	1.75	3.50
❑4, b&w; Japanese	2.95	0.65	1.63	3.25
❑5	3.25	0.65	1.63	3.25
❑6	2.95	0.65	1.63	3.25
❑7	3.25	0.65	1.63	3.25
❑8	3.25	0.65	1.63	3.25

LUNAR DONUT
LUNAR DONUT

Value: Cover or less

- ❑0, b&w; cardstock cover; says (Honey-Glazed) 2.50
- ❑1, b&w; cover says (With Sprinkles); Flip-book 2.50
- ❑2, b&w; cover says (Cherry-Filled); Flip-book 2.50
- ❑3, b&w; cover says (Jelly-Filled); Flip-book 2.50

LUNATIC BINGE
ETERNITY

	ORIG	GOOD	FINE	N-MINT
❑1	1.95	0.79	1.98	3.95
❑2, I Married Twins; Look at this Year's Horror Video	3.95	0.79	1.98	3.95

LUNATIC FRINGE, THE
INNOVATION

Value: Cover or less

- ❑1, Jul 89, O: Lunatic Fringe .. 1.75
- ❑2, Aug 89 .... 1.75

LUNATIK
MARVEL

Value: Cover or less

- ❑1, Dec 95, D: Lunatik I; 1: Lunatik II (alien) 1.95
- ❑2, Jan 96, V: Avengers 1.95
- ❑3, Feb 96, Fool's Errand, Final Issue 1.95

LURID TALES
FANTAGRAPHICS

Value: Cover or less

- ❑1, b&w; adult 2.75

LUST
EROS

Value: Cover or less

- ❑1 .... 2.95
- ❑2 .... 2.95
- ❑3 .... 2.95
- ❑4 .... 2.95
- ❑5 .... 2.95
- ❑6 .... 2.95

LUST FOR LIFE
SLAVE LABOR

Value: Cover or less

- ❑1, Feb 97, Who Am I?; Episode 415, b&w 2.95
- ❑2, May 97, b&w 2.95
- ❑3, Aug 97, Lush Life; One, b&w 2.95
- ❑4, Jan 98, I Work in a Video Store; Scary Stories 2.95

LUST OF THE NAZI WEASEL WOMEN
FANTAGRAPHICS

Value: Cover or less

- ❑1, b&w 2.25
- ❑2, b&w 2.25
- ❑3, b&w 2.25
- ❑4, b&w 2.25

The displaced master of Hell finds himself occupied with more mundane concerns in the "real" world in DC/Vertigo's *Lucifer.*

ORIG GOOD FINE N-MINT

LUX & ALBY SIGN ON AND SAVE THE UNIVERSE
DARK HORSE

Value: Cover or less

- ❑1, b&w 2.50
- ❑2, May 93, b&w 2.50
- ❑3, Jun 93, b&w 2.50
- ❑4 .... 2.50
- ❑5 .... 2.50
- ❑6 .... 2.50
- ❑7 .... 2.50
- ❑8, Oct 93 .... 2.50
- ❑9, Dec 93 .... 2.50

LUXURA & VAMPFIRE
BRAINSTORM

Value: Cover or less

- ❑1 .... 2.95

LUXURA COLLECTION (KIRK LINDO'S...)
BRAINSTORM

Value: Cover or less

- ❑1, nn; adult; cardstock cover; stories and pin-ups 4.95

LUXURA LEATHER SPECIAL
BRAINSTORM

Value: Cover or less

- ❑1, Mar 96, nn 2.95

LYCANTHROPE LEO
VIZ

Value: Cover or less

- ❑1, b&w 2.95
- ❑2, b&w 2.95
- ❑3, b&w 2.95
- ❑4, b&w 2.95
- ❑5, b&w 2.95
- ❑6, b&w 2.95
- ❑7, b&w 2.95

LYCEUM
HUNTER PRODUCTIONS

Value: Cover or less

- ❑1, Oct 96, b&w 2.95
- ❑2, Aug 97, b&w 2.95

LYCRA-WOMAN AND SPANDEX-GIRL
COMIC ZONE

Value: Cover or less

- ❑1, Dec 92, Slave 2 Fashion, b&w 2.95

LYCRA WOMAN AND SPANDEX GIRL CHRISTMAS '77 SPECIAL
COMIC ZONE

Value: Cover or less

- ❑1, b&w 2.95

LYCRA WOMAN AND SPANDEX GIRL HALLOWEEN SPECIAL
LOST CAUSE

Value: Cover or less

- ❑1, b&w 2.95

LYCRA WOMAN AND SPANDEX GIRL JURASSIC DINOSAUR SPECIAL
COMIC ZONE

Value: Cover or less

- ❑1, b&w 2.95

LYCRA WOMAN AND SPANDEX GIRL SUMMER VACATION SPECIAL
COMIC ZONE

Value: Cover or less

- ❑1, b&w 2.95

LYCRA WOMAN AND SPANDEX GIRL TIME TRAVEL SPECIAL
COMIC ZONE

Value: Cover or less

- ❑1, b&w 2.95

LYCRA WOMAN AND SPANDEX GIRL VALENTINE SPECIAL
COMIC ZONE

Value: Cover or less

- ❑1, b&w 2.95

LYNCH
IMAGE

Value: Cover or less

- ❑1, May 97, The Sword of Viracocha, One-Shot; no indicia 2.50

LYNCH MOB
CHAOS

Value: Cover or less

- ❑1, Mayhem Comes 2.50
- ❑2 .... 2.50
- ❑3 .... 2.50
- ❑4 .... 2.50

LYNX: AN ELFLORD TALE
PEREGRINE ENTERTAINMENT

Value: Cover or less

- ❑1, Mar 99, b&w 2.95

M

M
Eclipse
Value: Cover or less

- ❑1 ... 4.95
- ❑2 ... 4.95
- ❑3 ... 4.95
- ❑4 ... 5.95

MACABRE
Lighthouse
Value: Cover or less

- ❑1, b&w ... 2.00
- ❑2, b&w ... 2.00
- ❑3, b&w ... 2.00
- ❑4 ... 2.00
- ❑5 ... 2.00
- ❑6, Aug 89, Shadows; St. Peter Judgement ... 2.00

MACABRE (VOL. 2)
Lighthouse
Value: Cover or less

- ❑1 ... 2.00
- ❑2 ... 2.00

M.A.C.H. 1
Fleetway

	ORIG	GOOD	FINE	N-MINT
❑1, 1: John Probe, b&w	1.95	0.40	1.00	2.00
❑2, b&w	1.95	0.40	1.00	2.00
❑3, b&w	1.95	0.40	1.00	2.00
❑4, b&w	1.95	0.40	1.00	2.00
❑5, b&w	1.95	0.40	1.00	2.00
❑6, b&w	1.95	0.40	1.00	2.00
❑7, b&w	1.95	0.40	1.00	2.00
❑8, b&w	1.95	0.40	1.00	2.00
❑9, b&w	1.95	0.40	1.00	2.00

MACHINE, THE
Dark Horse
Value: Cover or less

- ❑1, Nov 94, Judgment Hour ... 2.50
- ❑2, Dec 94, Top of the ? Heap ... 2.50
- ❑3, Jan 95, Heaven In Hell ... 2.50
- ❑4, Feb 95 ... 2.50

MACHINE MAN
Marvel

	ORIG	GOOD	FINE	N-MINT
❑1, Apr 78, JK, JK (w), 1: Machine Man (as "Machine Man")	0.35	0.60	1.50	3.00
❑2, May 78	0.35	0.40	1.00	2.00
❑3, Jun 78	0.35	0.40	1.00	2.00
❑4, Jul 78	0.35	0.40	1.00	2.00
❑5, Aug 78	0.35	0.40	1.00	2.00
❑6, Sep 78	0.35	0.40	1.00	2.00
❑7, Oct 78	0.35	0.40	1.00	2.00
❑8, Nov 78	0.35	0.40	1.00	2.00
❑9, Dec 78	0.35	0.40	1.00	2.00
❑10, Aug 79	0.40	0.40	1.00	2.00
❑11, Oct 79	0.40	0.40	1.00	2.00
❑12, Dec 79	0.40	0.40	1.00	2.00
❑13, Feb 80	0.40	0.40	1.00	2.00
❑14, Apr 80	0.40	0.40	1.00	2.00
❑15, Jun 80, 1: Ion	0.40	0.40	1.00	2.00
❑16, Aug 80, 1: Baron Brimstone	0.40	0.40	1.00	2.00
❑17, Oct 80	0.50	0.40	1.00	2.00
❑18, Dec 80, A: Alpha Flight	0.50	0.40	1.00	2.00
❑19, Feb 81, 1: Jack O'Lantern I (Jason Macendale), Macendale becomes Hobgoblin II in Amazing Spider-Man #289	0.50	2.50	6.25	12.50

MACHINE MAN (LTD. SERIES)
Marvel

	ORIG	GOOD	FINE	N-MINT
❑1, Oct 84, He Lives Again!	0.75	0.30	0.75	1.50
❑2, Nov 84, If This Be Sanctuary?!, 1: Iron Man 2020	0.75	0.30	0.75	1.50
❑3, Dec 84, Ancient Wrecker!	0.75	0.30	0.75	1.50
❑4, Jan 85, Victory	0.75	0.30	0.75	1.50

MACHINE MAN 2020
Marvel
Value: Cover or less

- ❑1, Aug 94, Reprint ... 2.00
- ❑2, Sep 94, Reprint ... 2.00

MACHINE MAN/BASTION '98
Marvel
Value: Cover or less

- ❑1, Engines of Destruction, Part 2, A: Cable, nn; wraparound cover; gatefold summary; Marvel Annual ... 2.99

MACK BOLAN: THE EXECUTIONER (DON PENDLETON'S...)
Innovation
Value: Cover or less

- ❑1, Jul 93, enhanced cardstock cover; adapts War Against the Mafia ... 2.95
- ❑1/A, Jul 93, War Against The Mafia, Indestructible Tyvek cover ... 3.95
- ❑1/B, Jul 93, War Against The Mafia, black outer cover with red X; poster; Double-cover edition ... 3.50
- ❑2, Aug 93, Adapts War Against the Mafia ... 2.50
- ❑3, Nov 93, Adapts War Against the Mafia ... 2.50
- ❑4 ... 2.50

MACKENZIE QUEEN
Matrix
Value: Cover or less

- ❑1 ... 1.50
- ❑2, b&w ... 1.50
- ❑3 ... 1.50
- ❑4 ... 1.50
- ❑5 ... 1.50

MACK THE KNIFE: MONOCHROME MEMORIES
Caliber
Value: Cover or less

- ❑1, b&w ... 2.50

MACROSS II
Viz
Value: Cover or less

- ❑1, Contact ... 2.75
- ❑2 ... 2.75
- ❑3 ... 2.75
- ❑4 ... 2.75
- ❑5 ... 2.75
- ❑6 ... 2.75
- ❑7 ... 2.75
- ❑8 ... 2.75
- ❑9 ... 2.75
- ❑10 ... 2.75

MACROSS II: THE MICRON CONSPIRACY
Viz

	ORIG	GOOD	FINE	N-MINT
❑1, The Terrorists, b&w	2.75	0.60	1.50	3.00
❑2, b&w	2.75	0.55	1.38	2.75
❑3, b&w	2.75	0.55	1.38	2.75
❑4, b&w	2.75	0.55	1.38	2.75
❑5, b&w	2.75	0.55	1.38	2.75

MADAME XANADU
DC

	ORIG	GOOD	FINE	N-MINT
❑1, Jul 81, MR; BB, Dance for Two Demons; Falling Down to Heaven..., O: Madame Xanadu, poster of Madame Xanadu	2.00	0.60	1.50	3.00

MADBALLS
Marvel

	ORIG	GOOD	FINE	N-MINT
❑1, The Evil Dr. Frankenbeans, 1: Colonel Corn; 1: Madballs	0.75	0.20	0.50	1.00
❑2	0.75	0.20	0.50	1.00
❑3	0.75	0.20	0.50	1.00
❑4	1.00	0.20	0.50	1.00
❑5	1.00	0.20	0.50	1.00
❑6	1.00	0.20	0.50	1.00
❑7	1.00	0.20	0.50	1.00
❑8	1.00	0.20	0.50	1.00
❑9	1.00	0.20	0.50	1.00
❑10	1.00	0.20	0.50	1.00

MAD-DOG
Marvel
Value: Cover or less

- ❑1, May 93, Mad-Dog vs. The Truly Amazing Space Creatures From The Omega Galaxy ... 1.25
- ❑2, Jun 93, All-Out Action Ish, O: Mad-Dog ... 1.25
- ❑3, Jul 93 ... 1.25
- ❑4, Aug 93 ... 1.25
- ❑5, Sep 93 ... 1.25
- ❑6, Oct 93, Dogs of War, Final Issue ... 1.25

MAD DOG MAGAZINE
Blackthorne
Value: Cover or less

- ❑1 ... 1.75
- ❑2 ... 1.75
- ❑3, Mar 87 ... 1.75

MAD DOGS
Eclipse
Value: Cover or less

- ❑1 ... 2.50
- ❑2 ... 2.50
- ❑3 ... 2.50

MADMAN
Tundra

	ORIG	GOOD	FINE	N-MINT
❑1, Mar 92, Trapped By Gravity, b&w; prestige format; flip-action corners	3.95	2.00	5.00	10.00
❑1-2, Trapped By Gravity, 2nd Printing	3.95	1.00	2.50	5.00
❑, Trapped By Gravity, 3rd Printing; Kitchen Sink publishes	3.95	0.80	2.00	4.00
❑2, Apr 92	3.95	1.60	4.00	8.00
❑3, May 92	3.95	1.60	4.00	8.00

MADMAN ADVENTURES
Tundra

	ORIG	GOOD	FINE	N-MINT
❑1	2.95	1.00	2.50	5.00
❑2	2.95	0.80	2.00	4.00
❑3, Inevitability of the Impossible	2.95	0.80	2.00	4.00

MADMAN COMICS
Dark Horse

	ORIG	GOOD	FINE	N-MINT
❑1, Apr 94, The Living End, O: Madman	2.95	0.80	2.00	4.00
❑2, Jun 94	2.95	0.70	1.75	3.50
❑3, Aug 94	2.95	0.70	1.75	3.50
❑4, Oct 94	2.95	0.60	1.50	3.00
❑5, Jan 95	2.95	0.60	1.50	3.00
❑6, Mar 95	2.95	0.60	1.50	3.00
❑7, May 95	2.95	0.60	1.50	3.00
❑8, Jul 95	2.95	0.60	1.50	3.00
❑9, Oct 95	2.95	0.60	1.50	3.00
❑10, Jan 96	2.95	0.59	1.48	2.95
❑11, Oct 96, The Truth About Everything...And All the Rest!	2.95	0.59	1.48	2.95

	ORIG	GOOD	FINE	N-MINT
❑12, Apr 99, The Exit of Dr. Boiffard, Part 1, Doctor Robot back-up; Dr. Robot back-up	2.95	0.59	1.48	2.95
❑13, May 99, The Exit of Dr. Boiffard, Part 2, Doctor Robot back-up; Dr. Robot back-up	2.95	0.59	1.48	2.95
❑14, Jun 99, The Exit of Dr. Boiffard, Part 3, Doctor Robot back-up; Dr. Robot back-up	2.95	0.59	1.48	2.95
❑15, Jul 99, The Exit of Dr. Boiffard, Part 4, Doctor Robot back-up; Dr. Robot back-up	2.95	0.59	1.48	2.95
❑16, Dec 99, Frank Einstein's Holi-Daze Adventure	2.95	0.59	1.48	2.95
❑17, Aug 00, G-Men From Hell, Part 1	2.95	0.59	1.48	2.95
❑18, Sep 00, G-Men From Hell, Part 2	2.95	0.59	1.48	2.95
❑19, Oct 00, G-Men From Hell, Part 3	2.99	0.60	1.50	2.99
❑20, Dec 00, G-Men From Hell, Part 4	2.99	0.60	1.50	2.99
❑YB 1995, Jan 96, Yearbook '95; collects Madman Comics #1-5	17.95	3.59	8.98	17.95

MADMAN/THE JAM
Dark Horse

Value: Cover or less

- ❑1, Jul 98, House of Escher I 2.95
- ❑2, Aug 98, House of Escher II 2.95

MAD MONSTER PARTY ADAPTATION
Black Bear

	ORIG	GOOD	FINE	N-MINT
❑1	—	0.59	1.48	2.95
❑2	—	0.59	1.48	2.95
❑3	—	0.59	1.48	2.95
❑4	—	0.59	1.48	2.95

MADONNA
Personality

Value: Cover or less

- ❑1, b&w 2.95
- ❑1/Aut, b&w 3.95
- ❑2, b&w 2.95
- ❑2/Aut, b&w 3.95

MADONNA SEX GODDESS
Friendly

Value: Cover or less

- ❑1 .... 2.95
- ❑2 .... 2.95
- ❑3 .... 2.95

MADONNA SPECIAL
Revolutionary

Value: Cover or less

- ❑1, Aug 93, b&w 2.50

MADONNA VS. MARILYN
Celebrity

Value: Cover or less

- ❑1 .... 2.95

MAD RACCOONS
Mu

Value: Cover or less

- ❑1, Jul 91 .... 2.50
- ❑2, Sep 92 .... 2.50
- ❑3, Aug 93 .... 2.50
- ❑4, Aug 94 .... 2.95
- ❑5, Aug 95, cardstock cover 2.95
- ❑6, Jul 96, cardstock cover 2.95

MADRAVEN HALLOWEEN SPECIAL
Hamilton

Value: Cover or less

- ❑1, Oct 95, JDu; GM, Song of the Silkie, A: Wolff & Byrd, Hoo-Hah back-up, nn; One-Shot 2.95

MAEL'S RAGE
Ominous

Value: Cover or less

- ❑2, Aug 94 .... 2.50
- ❑2/SC, Aug 94, cardstock outer cover 2.50

MAELSTROM
Aircel

Value: Cover or less

- ❑1 .... 1.70
- ❑2 .... 1.70
- ❑3 .... 1.70
- ❑4 .... 1.70
- ❑5 .... 1.50
- ❑6 .... 1.50
- ❑7 .... 1.50
- ❑8 .... 1.50
- ❑9 .... 1.50
- ❑10 .... 1.50

MAGDALENA, THE
Image

Value: Cover or less

- ❑1, Apr 00, Blood Divine, Part 1 .... 2.50
- ❑2 .... 2.50
- ❑3, Jan 01 .... 2.50

MAGE
Comico

	ORIG	GOOD	FINE	N-MINT
❑1, May 84, MW, MW (w), Outrageous Slings and Arrows, 1: Kevin Matchstick	1.50	1.80	4.50	9.00
❑2, Jul 84, MW, MW (w), Too, Too Solid Flesh	1.50	1.40	3.50	7.00
❑3, Sep 84, MW, MW (w), The Mouse Trap	1.50	1.00	2.50	5.00
❑4, Nov 84, MW, MW (w), O What A Rash And Bloody Deed	1.50	1.00	2.50	5.00
❑5, Jan 85, MW, MW (w), Come What Come May	1.50	1.00	2.50	5.00
❑6, Mar 85, MW, MW (w), 1: Grendel I (Hunter Rose) (in color), Grendel	1.50	4.00	10.00	20.00
❑7, May 85, MW, MW (w), A: Grendel I (Hunter Rose)	1.50	2.00	5.00	10.00
❑8, Jul 85, MW, MW (w), A: Grendel I (Hunter Rose)	1.50	1.00	2.50	5.00
❑9, Sep 85, MW, MW (w), A: Grendel I (Hunter Rose)	1.50	0.80	2.00	4.00
❑10, Dec 85, MW, MW (w), A: Grendel I (Hunter Rose)	1.50	0.80	2.00	4.00

Innovation adapted the first of Don Pendleton's Mack Bolan novels, *War Against the Mafia*, in its short-lived comics series.

	ORIG	GOOD	FINE	N-MINT
❑11, Feb 86, MW, MW (w), A: Grendel I (Hunter Rose)	1.50	0.80	2.00	4.00
❑12, Apr 86, MW, MW (w), A: Grendel I (Hunter Rose)	1.50	0.80	2.00	4.00
❑13, Jun 86, MW, MW (w), Mark Me, D: Edsel; D: Grendel I (Hunter Rose)	1.50	1.00	2.50	5.00
❑14, Aug 86, MW, MW (w), ...Or Not to Be, A: Grendel	1.50	0.80	2.00	4.00
❑15, Dec 86, MW, MW (w), Pass With Your Best Violence, Final Issue; Giant-size	2.95	1.40	3.50	7.00

MAGE (IMAGE)
Image

	ORIG	GOOD	FINE	N-MINT
❑0, Jul 97, American Entertainment Exclusive	—	0.60	1.50	3.00
❑0/AUT, Signed by Matt Wagner	—	1.40	3.50	7.00
❑1, Jul 97, MW, MW (w), The Handle Towards My Hand	2.50	0.80	2.00	4.00
❑1/3D, Feb 98, MW, MW (w), The Handle Towards My Hand, 3-D edition; with glasses	4.95	0.99	2.47	4.95
❑2, Aug 97, MW, MW (w), When We Three Shall Meet	2.50	0.70	1.75	3.50
❑3, Sep 97, MW, MW (w), Two Truths are Told	2.50	0.70	1.75	3.50
❑4, Nov 97, MW, MW (w), Bubble, Bubble, Toil and Trouble	2.50	0.60	1.50	3.00
❑5, Jan 98, MW, MW (w), Come What Come May	2.50	0.60	1.50	3.00
❑6, Mar 98, MW, MW (w), Lay on, MacDuff	2.50	0.50	1.25	2.50
❑7, Apr 98, MW, MW (w), Infirm of Purpose	2.50	0.50	1.25	2.50
❑8, Jun 98, MW, MW (w), So Weary With Disasters	2.50	0.50	1.25	2.50
❑9, Sep 98, MW, MW (w), The Weird Sisters	2.50	0.50	1.25	2.50
❑10, Dec 98, MW, MW (w), Foul is Fair	2.50	0.50	1.25	2.50
❑11, Feb 99, MW, MW (w), Dwindle, Peak and Pine	2.50	0.50	1.25	2.50
❑12, Apr 99, MW, MW (w), A Charmed Life	2.50	0.50	1.25	2.50
❑13/A, Jun 99, covers form triptych	2.50	0.50	1.25	2.50
❑13/B, Jun 99, Mage cover	2.50	0.50	1.25	2.50
❑13/C, Jun 99, Joe Phat cover	2.50	0.50	1.25	2.50
❑14, Aug 99, MW, MW (w), When the Battle's Lost and Won	2.50	0.50	1.25	2.50
❑15, Oct 99, MW, MW (w), All that may Become a Man	2.50	0.50	1.25	2.50

MAGEBOOK
Comico

Value: Cover or less

- ❑1 .... 8.95
- ❑2 .... 7.95

MAGGIE AND HOPEY COLOR SPECIAL
Fantagraphics

Value: Cover or less

- ❑1, May 97 .... 3.50

MAGGIE THE CAT
Image

Value: Cover or less

- ❑1, Jan 96, MGr, MGr (w), Master Piece, Part 1 .... 2.50
- ❑2, Mar 96, MGr, MGr (w), Master Piece, Part 2 .... 2.50
- ❑3, MGr, MGr (w), Master Piece, Part 3, Exists? 2.50
- ❑4, MGr, MGr (w), Master Piece, Part 4, Exists? 2.50

MAGGOTS
Hamilton

Value: Cover or less

- ❑1, Nov 91, b&w 3.95
- ❑2, b&w 3.95
- ❑3, b&w 3.95

MAGICAL MATES
Antarctic

Value: Cover or less

- ❑1, Feb 96 .... 2.95
- ❑2, Apr 96 .... 2.95
- ❑3, Jun 96 .... 2.95
- ❑4, Aug 96 .... 2.95
- ❑5, Oct 96 .... 2.95
- ❑6, Dec 96 .... 2.95
- ❑7 .... 2.95
- ❑8 .... 2.95
- ❑9 .... 2.95

MAGICAL NYMPHINI, THE
Rip Off

Value: Cover or less

- ❑1, Feb 91, b&w; adult 2.50
- ❑1-2, adult; 2nd Printing 2.50
- ❑2, Apr 91, b&w; adult 2.50
- ❑2-2, adult; 2nd Printing 2.50
- ❑3, Aug 91, b&w; adult 2.50
- ❑3-2, adult; 2nd Printing 2.50

ORIG GOOD FINE N-MINT

❑4, Dec 91, b&w; adult 2.95
❑4-2, adult; 2nd Printing 2.95
❑5, Aug 92, b&w; adult............ 2.95
❑5-2, adult; 2nd Printing.......... 2.95

MAGICAL TWILIGHT
GRAPHIC VISIONS

Value: Cover or less
❑1 .... 2.95

MAGIC BOY AND GIRLFRIEND
TOP SHELF

Value: Cover or less
❑1, Jul 98, nn; b&w 8.95

MAGIC BOY & THE ROBOT ELF
SLAVE LABOR

Value: Cover or less
❑1, May 96 .... 9.95

MAGIC CARPET
SHANDA FANTASY ARTS

Value: Cover or less
❑1, Apr 99, b&w 4.50

MAGIC FLUTE, THE
ECLIPSE

Value: Cover or less
❑1 .... 4.95
❑2 .... 4.95
❑3 .... 4.95

MAGICIANS' VILLAGE
MAD MONKEY

Value: Cover or less
❑1 .... 2.45

MAGICMAN
A-PLUS

	ORIG	GOOD	FINE	N-MINT
❑1, Magicman!; The Case of the Young Old Men, b&w; Reprint	2.50	0.59	1.48	2.95

MAGIC PRIEST
ANTARCTIC

Value: Cover or less
❑1, Jun 98, A Murder of Crowe's, b&w 2.95

MAGIC: THE GATHERING-ANTIQUITIES WAR
ACCLAIM

Value: Cover or less
❑1, Nov 95, PS, O: Urza and Mishra 2.50
❑2, Dec 95, PS 2.50
❑3, Jan 96, PS 2.50
❑4, Feb 96, PS....................... 2.50

MAGIC: THE GATHERING-ELDER DRAGONS
ACCLAIM

Value: Cover or less
❑1, Apr 96, The Tikery Man 2.50
❑2, May 96 .... 2.50

MAGIC: THE GATHERING: GERARD'S QUEST
DARK HORSE

Value: Cover or less
❑1, Mar 98, MGr (w) 2.95
❑2, Apr 98, MGr (w), Legacy .. 2.95
❑3, May 98, MGr (w), Crucible.............................. 2.95
❑4, Sep 98, MGr (w), Destiny.. 2.95

MAGIC: THE GATHERING-NIGHTMARE
ACCLAIM

Value: Cover or less
❑1, Vanishing Lands............... 2.50

MAGIC: THE GATHERING-SHANDALAR
ACCLAIM

Value: Cover or less
❑1, Mar 96 .... 2.50
❑2, Apr 96, The Threshold, Final Issue.................................. 2.50

MAGIC: THE GATHERING-THE SHADOW MAGE
ACCLAIM

Value: Cover or less
❑1, bound-in Fireball card....... 2.50
❑2, Aug 95, bound-in Blue Elemental card 2.50
❑3, Sep 95, bagged with Magic: The Gathering tokens and counters 2.50
❑4, polybagged with sheet of creature tokens 2.50

MAGIC: THE GATHERING-WAYFARER
ACCLAIM

Value: Cover or less
❑1, Nov 95, VM, A Need for Monsters 2.50
❑2, Dec 95, VM...................... 2.50
❑3, Jan 96, VM 2.50
❑4, Feb 96, VM, Lovers & Comrades 2.50
❑5, Mar 96, VM 2.50

MAGIC WHISTLE
ALTERNATIVE

Value: Cover or less
❑1, b&w................................. 2.95
❑2, b&w................................. 2.95

MAGIK
MARVEL

	ORIG	GOOD	FINE	N-MINT
❑1, Dec 83, TP, Inferno	0.60	0.45	1.13	2.25
❑2, Jan 84, TP, Inferno	0.60	0.40	1.00	2.00
❑3, Feb 84, TP, Inferno	0.60	0.40	1.00	2.00
❑4, Mar 84, TP, Inferno	0.60	0.40	1.00	2.00

MAGIK (2ND SERIES)
MARVEL

Value: Cover or less
❑1, Dec 00, The Crossing Guard 2.99
❑2, Jan 01, A Gathering of Foes................................... 2.99
❑3, Feb 01, The Fall of Hades.................................. 2.99
❑4, Mar 01, Bound for Destruction 2.99

MAGNA-MAN: THE LAST SUPERHERO
COMICS INTERVIEW

Value: Cover or less
❑1, b&w................................. 1.95
❑2, Sum 88, b&w 1.95
❑3, Sum 88, b&w 1.95

MAGNESIUM ARC
ICONOGRAFIX

Value: Cover or less
❑1 .... 3.50

MAGNETIC MEN FEATURING MAGNETO
MARVEL

Value: Cover or less
❑1, Jun 97, Born Again........... 1.95

MAGNETO
MARVEL

	ORIG	GOOD	FINE	N-MINT
❑0, A Fire In The Sky; I Magneto, O: Magneto, no cover price; retailer giveaway; Promotional give-away; Reprints "A Fire in the Sky" from X-Men Classic #19; Reprints "I Magneto" From X-Men Classic #12	—	0.60	1.50	3.00

MAGNETO (LTD. SERIES)
MARVEL

Value: Cover or less
❑1, Nov 96, Return Of The Messiah............................... 1.99
❑2, Dec 96 .... 1.99
❑3, Jan 97, Killzone................ 1.99
❑4, Feb 97, Spectres, Final Issue 1.99

MAGNETO AND THE MAGNETIC MEN
MARVEL

Value: Cover or less
❑1, Apr 96, Opposites Attract................................ 1.95

MAGNETO ASCENDANT
MARVEL

Value: Cover or less
❑1, Apr 99, SL (w), The Triumph of Magneto; If Iceman Should Fail, Reprints Magneto Stories from X-Men (1st Series).............. 3.99

MAGNETO: DARK SEDUCTION
MARVEL

Value: Cover or less
❑1, Jun 00, The Masada Maneuver 2.99

MAGNETO REX
MARVEL

Value: Cover or less
❑1, May 99 .... 2.50
❑2, Jun 99 .... 2.50
❑3, Jul 99............................... 2.50

MAGNETS: ROBOT DISMANTLER
PARODY PRESS

Value: Cover or less
❑1, b&w; Foil-embossed cover.................................. 2.95

MAGNUS ROBOT FIGHTER (ACCLAIM)
ACCLAIM

	ORIG	GOOD	FINE	N-MINT
❑1, May 97, Kick the Can	2.50	0.50	1.25	2.50
❑1/SC, May 97, alternate painted cover	2.50	0.50	1.25	2.50
❑2, Jun 97, It Is Not Dying	2.50	0.50	1.25	2.50
❑3, Jul 97	2.50	0.50	1.25	2.50
❑4, Aug 97, Hell to the Chief!	2.50	0.50	1.25	2.50
❑5, Sep 97	2.50	0.50	1.25	2.50
❑6, Oct 97	2.50	0.50	1.25	2.50
❑7, Nov 97, Gold Key homage cover	2.50	0.50	1.25	2.50
❑8, Dec 97	2.50	0.50	1.25	2.50
❑9, Jan 98	2.50	0.50	1.25	2.50
❑10, Feb 98	2.50	0.50	1.25	2.50
❑11, Mar 98	2.50	0.50	1.25	2.50
❑12, Apr 98	2.50	0.50	1.25	2.50
❑13, Jan 98, no cover date; indicia says Jan	2.50	0.50	1.25	2.50
❑14, Feb 98, no cover date; indicia says Feb	2.50	0.50	1.25	2.50
❑15	2.50	0.50	1.25	2.50
❑16	2.50	0.50	1.25	2.50
❑17	2.50	0.50	1.25	2.50
❑Ash 1, Jan 97, b&w; no cover price; preview of upcoming series	—	0.20	0.50	1.00

MAGNUS, ROBOT FIGHTER (GOLD KEY)
GOLD KEY

	ORIG	GOOD	FINE	N-MINT
❑1, Feb 63, 1: Magnus; 1: Leeja Clane	0.12	20.00	50.00	100.00
❑2, May 63	0.12	12.00	30.00	60.00
❑3, Aug 63	0.12	12.00	30.00	60.00
❑4, Nov 63	0.12	7.00	17.50	35.00
❑5, Feb 64	0.12	7.00	17.50	35.00
❑6, May 64	0.12	7.00	17.50	35.00
❑7, Aug 64	0.12	7.00	17.50	35.00
❑8, Nov 64	0.12	7.00	17.50	35.00
❑9, Feb 65	0.12	7.00	17.50	35.00
❑10, May 65	0.12	7.00	17.50	35.00
❑11, Aug 65	0.12	5.00	12.50	25.00
❑12, Nov 65	0.12	5.00	12.50	25.00
❑13, Feb 66, 1: Doctor Noel	0.12	5.00	12.50	25.00
❑14, May 66	0.12	5.00	12.50	25.00
❑15, Aug 66	0.12	5.00	12.50	25.00
❑16, Nov 66	0.12	5.00	12.50	25.00
❑17, Feb 67	0.12	5.00	12.50	25.00
❑18, May 67	0.12	5.00	12.50	25.00
❑19, Aug 67	0.12	5.00	12.50	25.00
❑20, Nov 67	0.12	5.00	12.50	25.00
❑21, Feb 68	0.12	3.00	7.50	15.00
❑22, May 68, 1: Magnus; 1: Leeja Clane, reprints origin and first story; Reprints Magnus, Robot Fighter (Gold Key) #1	0.12	3.00	7.50	15.00

	ORIG	GOOD	FINE	N-MINT
❑23, Aug 68, Reprint	0.12	3.00	7.50	15.00
❑24, Nov 68, Destruction of Malev-6	0.15	3.00	7.50	15.00
❑25, Feb 69	0.15	3.00	7.50	15.00
❑26, May 69	0.15	3.00	7.50	15.00
❑27, Aug 69	0.15	3.00	7.50	15.00
❑28, Nov 69, goes on hiatus	0.15	3.00	7.50	15.00
❑29, Nov 71	0.15	1.20	3.00	6.00
❑30	0.15	1.20	3.00	6.00
❑31	0.15	1.20	3.00	6.00
❑32	0.15	1.20	3.00	6.00
❑33	0.15	1.20	3.00	6.00
❑34, The Evil Ark of Doctor Noel	0.15	1.20	3.00	6.00
❑35	—	1.20	3.00	6.00
❑36	—	1.20	3.00	6.00
❑37	0.25	1.20	3.00	6.00
❑38	—	1.20	3.00	6.00
❑39	—	1.20	3.00	6.00
❑40	—	1.20	3.00	6.00
❑41	—	1.20	3.00	6.00
❑42	—	1.20	3.00	6.00
❑43	—	1.20	3.00	6.00
❑44	—	1.20	3.00	6.00
❑45, Oct 76	0.30	1.20	3.00	6.00
❑46	—	1.20	3.00	6.00

MAGNUS ROBOT FIGHTER (VALIANT)
VALIANT

	ORIG	GOOD	FINE	N-MINT
❑0, O: Magnus, no cover price; trading card; Promotional "0" edition (from redeeming coupons in issues 1-8); sendaway	1.75	0.80	2.00	4.00
❑0/A, O: Magnus, no cover price; Promotional "0" edition without trading card; sendaway; without trading card	1.75	0.60	1.50	3.00
❑1, May 91, Steel Nation, Part 1, O: Magnus, trading card; coupon for #0 issue; trading cards	1.75	0.70	1.75	3.50
❑2, Jul 91, Steel Nation, Part 2, trading card; coupon for #0 issue	1.75	0.50	1.25	2.50
❑3, Aug 91, Steel Nation, Part 3, 1: Tekla, trading card; coupon for #0 issue	1.75	0.50	1.25	2.50
❑4, Sep 91, Steel Nation, Part 4, trading card; coupon for #0 issue	1.75	0.50	1.25	2.50
❑5, Oct 91, Invasion, Part 1, 1: Rai, trading card; coupon for #0 issue; Flip-book; Flip-book with Rai #1	1.75	0.40	1.00	2.00
❑6, Nov 91, A: Solar; A: Rai, trading card; coupon for #0 issue; Flip-book	1.75	0.40	1.00	2.00
❑7, Dec 91, V: Rai, trading card; coupon for #0 issue; Flip-book	1.75	0.40	1.00	2.00
❑8, Jan 92, A: Rai, trading card; coupon for #0 issue; Flip-book	1.95	0.40	1.00	2.00
❑9, Feb 92	1.95	0.40	1.00	2.00
❑10, Mar 92	1.95	0.40	1.00	2.00
❑11, Apr 92	1.95	0.40	1.00	2.00
❑12, May 92, Stone and Steel!, A: Turok; 1: Turok (Valiant), Giant-size	3.25	1.00	2.50	5.00
❑13, Jun 92	2.25	0.45	1.13	2.25
❑14, Jul 92	2.25	0.45	1.13	2.25
❑15, Aug 92, FM (c), Unity, Part 4, Unity	2.25	0.45	1.13	2.25
❑16, Sep 92, Unity, Part 12, Unity	2.25	0.45	1.13	2.25
❑17, Nov 92	2.25	0.45	1.13	2.25
❑18, Nov 92	2.25	0.45	1.13	2.25
❑19, Dec 92	2.25	0.45	1.13	2.25
❑20, Jan 93, Hit Or Kiss	2.25	0.45	1.13	2.25
❑21, Feb 93, Holocaust 4002, Part 1, New logo	2.25	0.45	1.13	2.25
❑21/GO, Holocaust 4002, Part 1, Gold edition; New logo	2.25	0.60	1.50	3.00
❑22, Mar 93, Holocaust 4002, Part 2	2.25	0.45	1.13	2.25
❑23, Apr 93, Holocaust 4002, Part 3	2.25	0.45	1.13	2.25
❑24, May 93, Holocaust 4002, Part 4; The Fall of North Am, Story leads into Rai and the Future Force #9	2.25	0.45	1.13	2.25
❑25, Jun 93, Flesh And Steel, Silver embossed cover	2.95	0.59	1.48	2.95
❑25/LE, Flesh And Steel, Silver embossed cover	2.95	0.60	1.50	3.00
❑26, Jul 93, Exemplar	2.25	0.45	1.13	2.25
❑27, Aug 93, The Enemy Of My Enemy, serial number coupon for contest	2.25	0.45	1.13	2.25
❑28, Sep 93, Will Of Iron, serial number coupon for contest	2.25	0.45	1.13	2.25
❑29, Oct 93, Indomitable, A: Eternal Warrior	2.25	0.45	1.13	2.25
❑30, Nov 93, The Battle For South Am, Part 2, A: X-O	2.25	0.45	1.13	2.25
❑31, Dec 93, The Battle For South Am, Part 4	2.25	0.45	1.13	2.25
❑32, Jan 94, Mal-Adjusted	2.25	0.45	1.13	2.25
❑33, Feb 94, If This Is Tuesday, This Must Be...North Am?, A: Timewalker	2.25	0.45	1.13	2.25
❑34, Mar 94, Christmas Eve: Minutes To Midnight	2.25	0.45	1.13	2.25

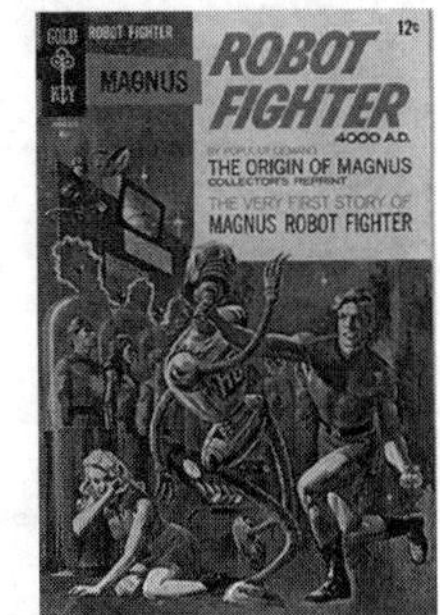

The first issue of Gold Key's *Magnus, Robot Fighter* was reprinted in #22.

© 1968 Gold Key

	ORIG	GOOD	FINE	N-MINT
❑35, Apr 94	2.25	0.45	1.13	2.25
❑36, May 94, trading card	2.25	0.45	1.13	2.25
❑37, Jun 94, A: Rai; A: Starwatchers	2.25	0.45	1.13	2.25
❑38, Aug 94	2.25	0.45	1.13	2.25
❑39, Sep 94, A: Torque	2.25	0.45	1.13	2.25
❑40, Oct 94	2.25	0.45	1.13	2.25
❑41, Nov 94, The Chaos Effect: Epsilon, Part 4, Chaos Effect	2.25	0.45	1.13	2.25
❑42, Dec 94	2.25	0.45	1.13	2.25
❑43, Jan 95, The Geomancer Quest, Part 1	2.25	0.45	1.13	2.25
❑44, Feb 95, The Geomancer Quest, Part 2	2.25	0.45	1.13	2.25
❑45, Mar 95, The Geomancer Quest, Part 3	2.25	0.45	1.13	2.25
❑46, Apr 95, The Geomancer Quest, Part 4	2.25	0.45	1.13	2.25
❑47, May 95, War & Remembrance; Cold Blooded, Part 1	2.25	0.45	1.13	2.25
❑48, Jun 95, Cold Blooded, Part 2	2.25	0.45	1.13	2.25
❑49, Jul 95	2.50	0.50	1.25	2.50
❑50, Jul 95, Birthquake	2.25	0.45	1.13	2.25
❑51, Aug 95, Birthquake	2.25	0.45	1.13	2.25
❑52, Aug 95, Birthquake	2.25	0.45	1.13	2.25
❑53, Sep 95	2.25	0.45	1.13	2.25
❑54, Sep 95	2.25	0.45	1.13	2.25
❑55, Oct 95	2.50	0.45	1.13	2.25
❑56, Oct 95	2.50	0.50	1.25	2.50
❑57, Nov 95	2.50	0.50	1.25	2.50
❑58, Nov 95	2.50	0.50	1.25	2.50
❑59, Dec 95	2.50	0.50	1.25	2.50
❑60, Dec 95	2.50	0.50	1.25	2.50
❑61, Jan 96	2.50	0.50	1.25	2.50
❑62, Jan 96, Torque becomes a Psi-Lord	2.50	0.50	1.25	2.50
❑63, Feb 96	2.50	0.50	1.25	2.50
❑64, Feb 96, D: Magnus, Robot Fighter (Valiant), Final Issue	2.50	0.45	1.13	2.25
❑YB 1, cardstock cover; 1994 Yearbook	3.95	0.79	1.98	3.95

MAGNUS ROBOT FIGHTER/NEXUS
VALIANT

	ORIG	GOOD	FINE	N-MINT
❑1, Dec 93, The Gift Horse, Part 1, covers says Mar, indicia says Dec	2.95	0.60	1.50	3.00
❑2, Apr 94, SR, The Gift Horse, Part 2	2.95	0.60	1.50	3.00

MAGUS
CALIBER

Value: Cover or less

❑1	2.95
❑1/A, Variant cover of Girl praying in foreground, Magus behind	2.95
❑2	2.95

MAINE ZOMBIE LOBSTERMEN
MAINE STREAM COMICS

Value: Cover or less

❑1, b&w	2.50
❑2, b&w	2.50
❑3, b&w	3.50

MAI, THE PSYCHIC GIRL
ECLIPSE

	ORIG	GOOD	FINE	N-MINT
❑1, May 87, Mai, The Psychic Girl, Part 1, b&w; Japanese	1.50	0.70	1.75	3.50
❑1-2, 2nd Printing	1.50	0.40	1.00	2.00
❑2, Mai, The Psychic Girl, Part 2	1.50	0.50	1.25	2.50
❑2-2, 2nd Printing	1.50	0.40	1.00	2.00
❑3, Mai, the Psychic Girl, Part 3; Mai, the Psychic Girl, Part 4	1.50	0.50	1.25	2.50
❑4, Mai, The Psychic Girl, Part 5; Mai, The Psychic Girl, Part 6	1.50	0.40	1.00	2.00
❑5, Mai, The Psychic Girl, Part 7; Mai, The Psychic Girl, Part 8	1.50	0.40	1.00	2.00
❑6, Mai, The Psychic Girl, Part 9; Mai, The Psychic Girl, Part 10	1.50	0.35	0.88	1.75
❑7, Mai, The Psychic Girl, Part 11; Mai, The Psychic Girl, Part 12	1.50	0.35	0.88	1.75
❑8, Mai, The Psychic Girl, Part 13; Mai, The Psychic Girl, Part 14	1.50	0.35	0.88	1.75
❑9, Mai, the Psychic Girl, Part 15; Mai, the Psychic Girl, Part 16	1.50	0.35	0.88	1.75
❑10	1.50	0.35	0.88	1.75
❑11	1.50	0.35	0.88	1.75
❑12	1.50	0.35	0.88	1.75
❑13	1.50	0.35	0.88	1.75

	ORIG	GOOD	FINE	N-MINT
❑14	1.50	0.35	0.88	1.75
❑15, Dec 87	1.50	0.35	0.88	1.75
❑16, Jan 88	1.50	0.35	0.88	1.75
❑17, Jan 88	1.50	0.35	0.88	1.75
❑18, Feb 88	1.50	0.35	0.88	1.75
❑19, Feb 88	1.50	0.35	0.88	1.75
❑20, Mar 88	1.50	0.35	0.88	1.75
❑21, Mar 88	1.50	0.35	0.88	1.75
❑22, Apr 88	1.50	0.35	0.88	1.75
❑23, Apr 88, Part 43, Ryu's Arrival; Part 44, Ryu's Plan	1.50	0.35	0.88	1.75
❑24, May 88	1.50	0.35	0.88	1.75
❑25, May 88	1.50	0.35	0.88	1.75
❑26, Jun 88	1.50	0.35	0.88	1.75
❑27, Jun 88	1.50	0.35	0.88	1.75
❑28, Jul 88, Final Issue	1.50	0.35	0.88	1.75

MAISON IKKOKU PART 1
VIZ

	ORIG	GOOD	FINE	N-MINT
❑1	2.95	0.80	2.00	4.00
❑2	2.95	0.70	1.75	3.50
❑3	2.95	0.70	1.75	3.50
❑4	2.95	0.70	1.75	3.50
❑5	2.95	0.70	1.75	3.50
❑6	2.95	0.70	1.75	3.50
❑7	2.95	0.70	1.75	3.50

MAISON IKKOKU PART 2
VIZ

	ORIG	GOOD	FINE	N-MINT
❑1	2.95	0.70	1.75	3.50
❑2	2.95	0.60	1.50	3.00
❑3	2.95	0.60	1.50	3.00
❑4	2.95	0.60	1.50	3.00
❑5	2.95	0.60	1.50	3.00
❑6	2.95	0.60	1.50	3.00

MAISON IKKOKU PART 3
VIZ

Value: Cover or less

❑1	2.95	❑4	2.95
❑2	2.95	❑5	2.95
❑3	2.95	❑6	2.95

MAISON IKKOKU PART 4
VIZ

Value: Cover or less

❑1, Embraced by Illness	2.95	❑6	2.95
❑2	2.75	❑7	2.95
❑3	2.75	❑8	2.95
❑4	2.95	❑9	2.95
❑5	2.95	❑10	2.95

MAISON IKKOKU PART 5
VIZ

Value: Cover or less

❑1	2.95	❑6	2.95
❑2	2.95	❑7	3.50
❑3	3.50	❑8	3.50
❑4	3.50	❑9	2.75
❑5	3.50		

MAISON IKKOKU PART 6
VIZ

Value: Cover or less

❑1	3.50	❑7	2.95
❑2	2.95	❑8	2.95
❑3	3.50	❑9	2.95
❑4	3.50	❑10	2.95
❑5	2.95	❑11	3.50
❑6	3.50		

MAISON IKKOKU PART 7
VIZ

Value: Cover or less

❑1	3.50	❑8	3.25
❑2	3.50	❑9	3.25
❑3	3.25	❑10	3.25
❑4	3.25	❑11	3.25
❑5	3.25	❑12	3.25
❑6	3.25	❑13	3.25
❑7	3.25		

MAISON IKKOKU PART 8
VIZ

Value: Cover or less

❑1	3.25	❑5	3.50
❑2	3.50	❑6	3.50
❑3	2.95	❑7	3.50
❑4	3.50	❑8	3.25

MAISON IKKOKU PART 9
VIZ

Value: Cover or less

❑1	3.25	❑5	3.25
❑2	3.25	❑6	3.25
❑3	3.25	❑7	3.25
❑4	3.25		

MAJCANS, THE
P.S.

Value: Cover or less ❑1 ..... 1.00

MAJOR BUMMER
DC

	ORIG	GOOD	FINE	N-MINT
❑1, Aug 97, What the Hell...??, 1: Major Bummer; 1: The Gecko	2.50	0.70	1.75	3.50
❑2, Sep 97	2.50	0.60	1.50	3.00
❑3, Oct 97, Alone Against the Other Guys!.	2.50	0.60	1.50	3.00
❑4, Nov 97	2.50	0.50	1.25	2.50
❑5, Dec 97, No Matter or How I Started Worrying and Saved the World, Face cover..	2.50	0.50	1.25	2.50
❑6, Jan 98	2.50	0.50	1.25	2.50
❑7, Feb 98	2.50	0.50	1.25	2.50
❑8, Mar 98	2.50	0.50	1.25	2.50
❑9, Apr 98	2.50	0.50	1.25	2.50
❑10, May 98	2.50	0.50	1.25	2.50
❑11, Jun 98	2.50	0.50	1.25	2.50
❑12, Jul 98	2.50	0.50	1.25	2.50
❑13, Aug 98	2.50	0.50	1.25	2.50
❑14, Sep 98	2.50	0.50	1.25	2.50
❑15, Oct 98	2.50	0.50	1.25	2.50

MAJOR DAMAGE
INVICTUS

Value: Cover or less

❑1, Oct 94, Above and Beyond	2.25	❑2	2.25

MAJOR POWER AND SPUNKY
EROS

Value: Cover or less ❑1, Oct 94, one shot..... 3.50

MAKEBELIEVE
LIAR

Value: Cover or less ❑1 ..... 2.95

MALCOLM-10
ONLI STUDIOS

Value: Cover or less ❑1, b&w 2.00

MALCOLM X
MILLENNIUM

Value: Cover or less ❑1 ..... 3.95

MALIBU ASHCAN: ULTRAFORCE
MALIBU

Value: Cover or less ❑1, Jun 94, nn 0.75

MALIBU SIGNATURE SERIES
MALIBU

	ORIG	GOOD	FINE	N-MINT
❑1993, autograph book giveaway	—	0.05	0.13	0.25
❑1994, autograph book giveaway	—	0.05	0.13	0.25

MALICE IN WONDERLAND
FANTAGRAPHICS

Value: Cover or less ❑1, Aug 93, WW, b&w; adult ... 2.75

MALLIMALOU
CHANCE

Value: Cover or less ❑1 ..... 1.50

MAN AGAINST TIME
IMAGE

Value: Cover or less

❑1, May 96, Every Hero	2.25	❑3, Jul 96	2.25
❑1/A, May 96	2.25	❑4, Aug 96	2.25
❑2, Jun 96, Tomorrow's Persuasion	2.25	❑5, Sep 96	2.25
		❑6	2.25

MAN-BAT (1ST SERIES)
DC

	ORIG	GOOD	FINE	N-MINT
❑1, Dec 75, SD, Beware the Eyes of Baron Tyme	0.25	1.60	4.00	8.00
❑2, Feb 76, SD, Fugitive From Blind Justice	0.25	1.00	2.50	5.00

MAN-BAT (2ND SERIES)
DC

Value: Cover or less ❑1, Dec 84, NA; DG, FR (w), Challenge of the Man-Bat; Man or Bat?, Reprint; One-Shot 2.50

MAN-BAT (MINI-SERIES)
DC

	ORIG	GOOD	FINE	N-MINT
❑1, Feb 96, Gotham Skies	2.25	0.50	1.25	2.50
❑2, Mar 96, Dark of the Moon, A: Killer Croc	2.25	0.50	1.25	2.50
❑3, Apr 96, The Deadly Sky, Final Issue	2.25	0.50	1.25	2.50

MAN CALLED A-X, THE
MALIBU

Value: Cover or less

❑0, Bedlam!	2.95	❑3, Jan 95, Silicon Skies	2.95
❑1, Nov 94	2.95	❑4	2.95
❑1/A, Nov 94	2.95	❑5	2.95
❑2, Dec 94	2.95		

MAN CALLED A-X, THE (DC)
DC

Value: Cover or less

❑1, Oct 97, A-Ten, follows events in Malibu/Bravura series	2.50	❑3, Dec 97, Battle over Bedlam	2.50
❑2, Nov 97, Massacre at Mercy General!	2.50	❑4, Jan 98	2.50
		❑5, Feb 98	2.50

	ORIG	GOOD	FINE	N-MINT

- ❑6, Mar 98, The Blight Before Christmas! 2.50
- ❑7, Apr 98 2.50
- ❑8, May 98, Final Issue 2.50

MAN CALLED LOCO, A
ACG

Value: Cover or less

- ❑1 2.50

MANDRAKE THE MAGICIAN
MARVEL

Value: Cover or less

- ❑1, Apr 95, The Quest For The 13th Scroll, cardstock cover 2.95
- ❑2, May 95, cardstock cover 2.95
- ❑3 2.95

MANDRAKE THE MAGICIAN (KING)
KING

	ORIG	GOOD	FINE	N-MINT
❑1, Sep 66, Menace of the Jungle!; The Phantom: SOS Phantom	0.12	6.00	15.00	30.00
❑2, Nov 66	0.12	3.60	9.00	18.00
❑3	0.12	2.60	6.50	13.00
❑4, Mar 67	0.12	2.40	6.00	12.00
❑5, May 67, Cape Cod Caper; The Fear Mongers, Flying saucer story	0.12	2.40	6.00	12.00
❑6, Jul 67	0.12	1.80	4.50	9.00
❑7, Aug 67	0.12	1.80	4.50	9.00
❑8, Sep 67, JJ	0.12	3.20	8.00	16.00
❑9, Oct 67	0.12	1.80	4.50	9.00
❑10, Nov 67, AR	0.12	4.80	12.00	24.00

MAN-EATING COW
NEC

	ORIG	GOOD	FINE	N-MINT
❑1, Jul 92	2.75	0.80	2.00	4.00
❑2, Nov 92	2.75	0.60	1.50	3.00
❑3, Jan 93	2.75	0.60	1.50	3.00
❑4, Apr 93, Scarcer	2.75	0.60	1.50	3.00
❑5, Jun 93	2.75	0.60	1.50	3.00
❑6, Aug 93	2.75	0.55	1.38	2.75
❑7, Nov 93, A Spooky House on a Hill Near a Graveyard	2.75	0.55	1.38	2.75
❑8, Jan 94, Hunting Heather	2.75	0.55	1.38	2.75
❑9, A: The Tick	2.75	0.60	1.50	3.00
❑10, A: The Tick	2.75	0.60	1.50	3.00

MAN-FROG
MAD DOG

Value: Cover or less

- ❑1, b&w 2.00
- ❑2, b&w 2.00

MAN FROM ATLANTIS
MARVEL

	ORIG	GOOD	FINE	N-MINT
❑1, Feb 78, TS, Birthright, Giant-size; TV series; giant	1.00	0.60	1.50	3.00
❑2, Mar 78, FR, Into the Bermuda Triangle	0.35	0.40	1.00	2.00
❑3, Apr 78	0.35	0.40	1.00	2.00
❑4, May 78, FR, The Killer Spores!	0.35	0.40	1.00	2.00
❑5, Jun 78	0.35	0.40	1.00	2.00
❑6, Jul 78	0.35	0.40	1.00	2.00
❑7, Aug 78, FR, Man Dogs And Dinosaurs, Final Issue	0.35	0.40	1.00	2.00

MAN FROM U.N.C.L.E., THE
GOLD KEY

	ORIG	GOOD	FINE	N-MINT
❑1, based on TV series	0.12	12.00	30.00	60.00
❑2	0.12	7.00	17.50	35.00
❑3	0.12	4.80	12.00	24.00
❑4	0.12	4.80	12.00	24.00
❑5, The Ten Little Uncles Affair	0.12	4.80	12.00	24.00
❑6	0.12	3.60	9.00	18.00
❑7	0.12	3.60	9.00	18.00
❑8, Sep 66, The Floating People Affair; Jet Dream: The Spider and the Spy, 10146-609	0.12	3.60	9.00	18.00
❑9	0.12	3.60	9.00	18.00
❑10	0.12	3.60	9.00	18.00
❑11	0.12	3.20	8.00	16.00
❑12	0.12	3.20	8.00	16.00
❑13	0.12	3.20	8.00	16.00
❑14	0.12	3.20	8.00	16.00
❑15	0.12	3.20	8.00	16.00
❑16	0.12	3.20	8.00	16.00
❑17	0.12	3.20	8.00	16.00
❑18	0.12	3.20	8.00	16.00
❑19	0.12	3.20	8.00	16.00
❑20	0.12	3.20	8.00	16.00
❑21, Reprint	—	2.00	5.00	10.00
❑22, Reprint; Final Issue	—	2.00	5.00	10.00

MAN FROM U.N.C.L.E., THE (2ND SERIES)
ENTERTAINMENT

	ORIG	GOOD	FINE	N-MINT
❑1, Jan 87, b&w	1.50	0.40	1.00	2.00
❑2, Feb 87	1.50	0.40	1.00	2.00
❑3, Apr 87	1.50	0.40	1.00	2.00
❑4, Aug 87	1.50	0.40	1.00	2.00
❑5, Dec 87	1.50	0.40	1.00	2.00
❑6, Feb 88	1.75	0.40	1.00	2.00
❑7, May 88	1.75	0.40	1.00	2.00
❑8, Jul 88	1.75	0.40	1.00	2.00
❑9, Aug 88	1.75	0.40	1.00	2.00
❑10, Sep 88	1.75	0.40	1.00	2.00
❑11, Sep 88	1.75	0.40	1.00	2.00

A slacker became a super-hero in DC's *Major Bummer.*

MAN FROM U.N.C.L.E., THE: THE BIRDS OF PREY AFFAIR
MILLENNIUM

Value: Cover or less

- ❑1, Mar 93, The Birds of Prey Affair, Part 1 2.95
- ❑2, Sep 93, The Birds of Prey Affair, Part 2 2.95

MANGA HORROR
AVALON

Value: Cover or less

- ❑1, The Port in the Rain; A Girl in the Castle!, b&w; reprints Ghostly Tales 2.95

MANGAPHILE
RADIO COMIX

Value: Cover or less

- ❑1, b&w 2.95
- ❑2, b&w 2.95
- ❑3, b&w 2.95
- ❑4, b&w 2.95
- ❑5, Apr 00, b&w 2.95
- ❑6, Jun 00, b&w 2.95
- ❑7, Aug 00, b&w 2.95

MANGA SHI
CRUSADE

Value: Cover or less

- ❑1, Aug 96, Shiseiji 2.95

MANGA SHI 2000
CRUSADE

Value: Cover or less

- ❑1, Feb 97, flip book with Shi: Heaven and Earth preview back-up; In the Killer Skies 2.95
- ❑2, Apr 97 2.95
- ❑3, Jun 97 2.95

MANGA SURPRISE!
MORNING & AFTERNOON, KODANSHA LTD.

	ORIG	GOOD	FINE	N-MINT
❑1, Jul 96, nn; b&w	—	0.40	1.00	2.00

MANGA VIZION
VIZ

Value: Cover or less

- ❑1, The Tragedy of P; Samurai Crusader: The Kumomaru Chronicles 4.95
- ❑2 4.95
- ❑3 4.95
- ❑4 4.95
- ❑5 4.95
- ❑6, Rumic Theater: Exrta-Large Size Happiness; Samurai Crusader: The Kumomaru Chronicles 4.95
- ❑7 4.95
- ❑8 4.95
- ❑9 4.95
- ❑10 4.95

MANGA VIZION (VOL. 2)
VIZ

Value: Cover or less

- ❑1 4.95
- ❑2 4.95
- ❑3 4.95
- ❑4 4.95
- ❑5 4.95
- ❑6 4.95
- ❑7 4.95
- ❑8 4.95
- ❑9 4.95
- ❑10 4.95
- ❑11 4.95
- ❑12 4.95

MANGA VIZION (VOL. 3)
VIZ

Value: Cover or less

- ❑1 4.95
- ❑2 4.95
- ❑3 4.95
- ❑4 4.95
- ❑5 4.95
- ❑6 4.95
- ❑7 4.95
- ❑8 4.95

MANGA VIZION (VOL. 4)
VIZ

Value: Cover or less

- ❑1 4.95
- ❑2 4.95
- ❑3 4.95
- ❑4 4.95
- ❑5 4.95
- ❑6 4.95
- ❑7 4.95
- ❑8 4.95

MANGA ZEN
ZEN COMICS

Value: Cover or less

- ❑1, b&w 2.50

MANGAZINE
ANTARCTIC

	ORIG	GOOD	FINE	N-MINT
❑1, b&w; newsprint cover; first Antarctic publication; company name misspelled throughout	1.25	0.80	2.00	4.00
❑1-2, 2nd Printing	1.50	0.40	1.00	2.00
❑2	1.50	0.70	1.75	3.50
❑3, Hedrax, Part 2; Cybersmash, Part 2	1.50	0.35	0.88	1.75
❑4	1.50	0.70	1.75	3.50
❑5	1.50	0.70	1.75	3.50

MANGAZINE (VOL. 2)
ANTARCTIC

	ORIG	GOOD	FINE	N-MINT
❑1	3.00	0.70	1.75	3.50
❑2	3.00	0.60	1.50	3.00
❑3	1.75	0.40	1.00	2.00
❑4	1.95	0.40	1.00	2.00
❑5	1.95	0.40	1.00	2.00
❑6	1.95	0.60	1.50	3.00
❑7	1.95	0.60	1.50	3.00
❑8	1.95	0.60	1.50	3.00
❑9	1.95	0.60	1.50	3.00
❑10	2.25	0.60	1.50	3.00
❑11	2.25	0.60	1.50	3.00
❑12	2.25	0.60	1.50	3.00
❑13	2.25	0.60	1.50	3.00
❑14	2.95	0.60	1.50	3.00
❑15, A View From The Castle; Machine Dog/ Part 2	2.95	0.60	1.50	3.00
❑16	2.95	0.60	1.50	3.00
❑17, Nov 92	2.95	0.60	1.50	3.00
❑18, Dec 92, Urusei Yatsura special issue	2.95	0.60	1.50	3.00
❑19, Jan 93	2.95	0.60	1.50	3.00
❑20, Feb 93	2.95	0.60	1.50	3.00
❑21, Mar 93	2.95	0.60	1.50	3.00
❑22, Apr 93	2.95	0.60	1.50	3.00
❑23, May 93	2.95	0.60	1.50	3.00
❑24, Jun 93	2.95	0.60	1.50	3.00
❑25, Jul 93	3.95	0.60	1.50	3.00
❑26, Aug 93	2.95	0.60	1.50	3.00
❑27, Sep 93	2.95	0.60	1.50	3.00
❑28, Oct 93	2.95	0.60	1.50	3.00
❑29, Nov 93	2.95	0.60	1.50	3.00
❑30, Dec 93	2.95	0.60	1.50	3.00
❑31, Jan 94	2.95	0.59	1.48	2.95
❑32, Feb 94, Super Cat Nuku-Nuku	2.95	0.59	1.48	2.95
❑33, May 94	2.95	0.59	1.48	2.95
❑34, Jul 94	2.95	0.59	1.48	2.95
❑35, Sep 94	2.95	0.59	1.48	2.95
❑36, Nov 94	2.95	0.59	1.48	2.95
❑37, Jan 95	3.95	0.59	1.48	2.95
❑38, Mar 95	2.95	0.59	1.48	2.95
❑39, May 95	2.95	0.59	1.48	2.95
❑40, Sep 95	2.95	0.59	1.48	2.95
❑41, Sep 95, Samurai Troopers	2.95	0.59	1.48	2.95
❑42, Sep 95	2.95	0.59	1.48	2.95
❑43, Sep 95, Samurai Troopers Episode Guide, Part 2	2.95	0.59	1.48	2.95
❑44, May 96	2.95	0.59	1.48	2.95

MANGLE TANGLE TALES
INNOVATION

Value: Cover or less

❑1, Harry Hart Farkule & The Crane of Thorns; Cliffed Palate, Intro by Harlan Ellison 2.95

MANHUNTER (1ST SERIES)
DC

Value: Cover or less

❑1, O: Manhunter, One-Shot; Double-size; reprints serial from Detective Comics; Archie Goodwin 2.50

MANHUNTER (2ND SERIES)
DC

	ORIG	GOOD	FINE	N-MINT
❑1, Jul 88, Visible Objects, A: appearance Manhunter II (Mark Shaw)	1.00	0.30	0.75	1.50
❑2, Aug 88	1.00	0.25	0.63	1.25
❑3, Sep 88	1.00	0.25	0.63	1.25
❑4, Oct 88	1.00	0.25	0.63	1.25
❑5, Nov 88	1.00	0.25	0.63	1.25
❑6, Dec 88	1.00	0.25	0.63	1.25
❑7, Dec 88, V: Count Vertigo	1.00	0.25	0.63	1.25
❑8, Jan 89, A: Flash, Invasion!	1.00	0.25	0.63	1.25
❑9, Jan 89, A: Flash, Invasion!	1.00	0.25	0.63	1.25
❑10, Feb 89, A: Checkmate	1.00	0.25	0.63	1.25
❑11, Mar 89	1.00	0.25	0.63	1.25
❑12, Apr 89	1.00	0.25	0.63	1.25
❑13, May 89	1.00	0.25	0.63	1.25
❑14, Jun 89, Janus Directive	1.00	0.25	0.63	1.25
❑15, Jul 89	1.00	0.25	0.63	1.25
❑16, Aug 89	1.00	0.25	0.63	1.25
❑17, Sep 89, A: Batman	1.00	0.25	0.63	1.25
❑18, Oct 89	1.00	0.25	0.63	1.25
❑19, Nov 89	1.00	0.25	0.63	1.25
❑20, Dec 89	1.00	0.25	0.63	1.25
❑21, Jan 90	1.00	0.25	0.63	1.25
❑22, Feb 90	1.00	0.25	0.63	1.25
❑23, Mar 90	1.00	0.25	0.63	1.25
❑24, Apr 90, Final Issue	1.00	0.25	0.63	1.25

MANHUNTER (3RD SERIES)
DC

	ORIG	GOOD	FINE	N-MINT
❑0, Oct 94, Here Comes The Night, 1: Manhunter III (Chase Lawler)	1.95	0.45	1.13	2.25
❑1, Nov 94, True Fiction, O: Manhunter III (Chase Lawler)	1.95	0.45	1.13	2.25
❑2, Dec 94, O: Manhunter III (Chase Lawler)	1.95	0.40	1.00	2.00
❑3, Jan 95	1.95	0.40	1.00	2.00
❑4, Feb 95	1.95	0.40	1.00	2.00
❑5, Mar 95	1.95	0.40	1.00	2.00
❑6, Apr 95	1.95	0.40	1.00	2.00
❑7, Jun 95	2.25	0.40	1.00	2.00
❑8, Jul 95	2.25	0.45	1.13	2.25
❑9, Aug 95	2.25	0.45	1.13	2.25
❑10, Sep 95	2.25	0.45	1.13	2.25
❑11, Oct 95	2.25	0.45	1.13	2.25
❑12, Nov 95, Underworld Unleashed, Final Issue; Underworld Unleashed	2.25	0.45	1.13	2.25

MANHUNTER: THE SPECIAL EDITION
DC

Value: Cover or less

❑1, nn; One-Shot; collects serial from Detective Comics plus new story 9.95

MANIK
MILLENNIUM

Value: Cover or less

❑1, Sep 95, foil cover 2.95

❑2 .... 2.95

❑3 .... 2.95

MANIMAL
RENEGADE

Value: Cover or less

❑1, Jan 86, b&w 1.70

MAN IN BLACK
RECOLLECTIONS

Value: Cover or less

❑1, b&w 2.00

❑2, Jul 91, b&w 2.00

MANKIND
CHAOS

Value: Cover or less

❑1, Sep 99 .... 2.95

MANN AND SUPERMAN
DC

Value: Cover or less

❑1 .... 5.95

MAN OF RUST
BLACKTHORNE

Value: Cover or less

❑1/A, Nov 86 .... 1.50

❑1/B, Nov 86 .... 1.50

MAN OF STEEL, THE (MINI-SERIES)
DC

	ORIG	GOOD	FINE	N-MINT
❑1, Oct 86, JBy, JBy (w), newsstand	0.75	0.60	1.50	3.00
❑1/SC, Oct 86, DG; JBy, JBy (w), direct	0.75	0.60	1.50	3.00
❑1/SI, JBy, JBy (w), silver edition	1.95	0.60	1.50	3.00
❑2, Oct 86, JBy, JBy (w)	0.75	0.50	1.25	2.50
❑2/SI, JBy, JBy (w), silver edition	1.95	0.50	1.25	2.50
❑3, Nov 86, JBy, JBy (w)	0.75	0.50	1.25	2.50
❑3/SI, JBy, JBy (w), silver edition	1.95	0.50	1.25	2.50
❑4, Nov 86, JBy, JBy (w)	0.75	0.50	1.25	2.50
❑4/SI, JBy, JBy (w), silver edition	1.95	0.50	1.25	2.50
❑5, Dec 86, JBy, JBy (w)	0.75	0.50	1.25	2.50
❑5/SI, JBy, JBy (w), silver edition	1.95	0.50	1.25	2.50
❑6, Dec 86, JBy, JBy (w)	0.75	0.50	1.25	2.50
❑6/SI, JBy, JBy (w), silver edition	1.95	0.50	1.25	2.50

MAN OF THE ATOM
ACCLAIM

	ORIG	GOOD	FINE	N-MINT
❑1, Jan 97, no cover price; preview of upcoming one-shot	—	0.20	0.50	1.00

MAN OF WAR (ECLIPSE)
ECLIPSE

Value: Cover or less

❑1, Aug 87, All This And The Big Bang Two, O: Man of War ... 1.75

❑2, Dec 87 .... 1.75

❑3, Feb 88 .... 1.75

❑4 .... 1.75

❑5 .... 1.75

MAN OF WAR (MALIBU)
MALIBU

	ORIG	GOOD	FINE	N-MINT
❑1, A Man At War	2.50	0.50	1.25	2.50
❑2	2.50	0.50	1.25	2.50
❑3	2.50	0.50	1.25	2.50
❑4	2.50	0.50	1.25	2.50
❑5, Only the Good Die Young	2.25	0.50	1.25	2.50

	ORIG	GOOD	FINE	N-MINT
❑6	2.25	0.45	1.13	2.25
❑7	2.25	0.45	1.13	2.25
❑8, Feb 94	2.25	0.45	1.13	2.25

MANOSAURS
EXPRESS

Value: Cover or less

- ❑1, The Armageddon Agenda Part 1 ... 2.95
- ❑2, The Armageddon Agenda Part 2 ... 2.95

MANTECH ROBOT WARRIORS
ARCHIE

	ORIG	GOOD	FINE	N-MINT
❑1, Sep 84, Siege Of The Renegade Robots, 1: The Mantechs	0.75	0.20	0.50	1.00
❑2	0.75	0.20	0.50	1.00
❑3	0.75	0.20	0.50	1.00
❑4, May 85, Invaders from Earth, Final Issue	0.75	0.20	0.50	1.00

MAN-THING (VOL. 1)
MARVEL

	ORIG	GOOD	FINE	N-MINT
❑1, Jan 74, JM; VM; FB, Battle for the Palace of the Gods!, A: Howard the Duck	0.20	2.40	6.00	12.00
❑2, Feb 74	0.20	1.60	4.00	8.00
❑3, Mar 74, 1: FoolKiller I (Greg Everbest), Foolkiller	0.20	1.40	3.50	7.00
❑4, Apr 74, D: FoolKiller I (Greg Everbest), Foolkiller	0.20	1.00	2.50	5.00
❑5, May 74	0.25	0.80	2.00	4.00
❑6, Jun 74, MP	0.25	0.60	1.50	3.00
❑7, Jul 74, MP	0.25	0.60	1.50	3.00
❑8, Aug 74, MP	0.25	0.60	1.50	3.00
❑9, Sep 74, MP	0.25	0.60	1.50	3.00
❑10, Oct 74, MP	0.25	0.60	1.50	3.00
❑11, Nov 74, MP	0.25	0.50	1.25	2.50
❑12, Dec 74	0.25	0.50	1.25	2.50
❑13, Jan 75	0.25	0.50	1.25	2.50
❑14, Feb 75	0.25	0.50	1.25	2.50
❑15, Mar 75	0.25	0.50	1.25	2.50
❑16, Apr 75	0.25	0.50	1.25	2.50
❑17, May 75	0.25	0.50	1.25	2.50
❑18, Jun 75	0.25	0.50	1.25	2.50
❑19, Jul 75, 1: Scavenger	0.25	0.50	1.25	2.50
❑20, Aug 75, JM	0.25	0.50	1.25	2.50
❑21, Sep 75, O: Scavenger	0.25	0.50	1.25	2.50
❑22, Oct 75, JM, A: Howard the Duck	0.25	0.60	1.50	3.00

MAN-THING (VOL. 2)
MARVEL

	ORIG	GOOD	FINE	N-MINT
❑1, Nov 79, JM, Regeneration-And Rebirth.	0.40	0.50	1.25	2.50
❑2, Jan 80, VM, Nowhere To Go But Down!	0.40	0.40	1.00	2.00
❑3, Mar 80	0.40	0.40	1.00	2.00
❑4, May 80	0.40	0.40	1.00	2.00
❑5, Jul 80	0.40	0.40	1.00	2.00
❑6, Sep 90	0.50	0.40	1.00	2.00
❑7, Nov 90	0.50	0.40	1.00	2.00
❑8, Jan 81	0.50	0.40	1.00	2.00
❑9, Mar 81	0.50	0.40	1.00	2.00
❑10, May 81	0.50	0.40	1.00	2.00
❑11, Jul 81	0.50	0.40	1.00	2.00

MAN-THING (VOL. 3)
MARVEL

Value: Cover or less

- ❑1, Dec 97, Shame, wraparound cover; gatefold summary ... 2.99
- ❑2, Jan 98, The Journey, gatefold summary ... 2.99
- ❑3, Feb 98, gatefold summary ... 2.99
- ❑4, Mar 98, Silent Night, gatefold summary ... 2.99
- ❑5, Apr 98, gatefold summary. ... 2.99
- ❑6, May 98, gatefold summary ... 2.99
- ❑7, Jun 98, A: Sub-Mariner, gatefold summary ... 2.99
- ❑8, Jul 98, A: Sub-Mariner, gatefold summary ... 2.99

MANTRA
MALIBU

	ORIG	GOOD	FINE	N-MINT
❑1, Jul 93, 1: Mantra I (Eden Blake); 1: Warstrike; 1: Boneyard, trading card, coupon; Ultraverse	1.95	0.50	1.25	2.50
❑1/Hol, Jul 93, 1: Mantra I (Eden Blake); 1: Warstrike; 1: Boneyard, Hologram cover.	—	1.00	2.50	5.00
❑1/LE, Jul 93, Ultra Limited edition	1.95	0.60	1.50	3.00
❑2, Aug 93	1.95	0.45	1.13	2.25
❑3, Sep 93, Sister Act, 1: Kismet Deadly	1.95	0.45	1.13	2.25
❑4, Oct 93, Rune, Part J, Rune	2.50	0.50	1.25	2.50
❑5, Nov 93	1.95	0.40	1.00	2.00
❑6, Dec 93, Break-Thru, Break-Thru	1.95	0.40	1.00	2.00
❑7, Jan 94	1.95	0.40	1.00	2.00
❑8, Feb 94	1.95	0.40	1.00	2.00
❑9, Mar 94	1.95	0.40	1.00	2.00
❑10, Apr 94, Flip-book with Ultraverse Premiere #2	3.50	0.70	1.75	3.50
❑11, May 94	1.95	0.39	0.98	1.95
❑12, Jun 94, The Archimage Quest, Part 3.	1.95	0.39	0.98	1.95

Introduced in *Fear* #19, Howard the Duck made several appearances with Man-Thing.

© 1974 Marvel Comics

	ORIG	GOOD	FINE	N-MINT
❑13, Aug 94, The Archimage Quest, Part 5, D: Boneyard's Wives, issue has two different covers	1.95	0.39	0.98	1.95
❑13/A, The Archimage Quest, Part 5, D: Boneyard's Wives, variant cover	1.95	0.39	0.98	1.95
❑14, Sep 94, The Archimage Quest, Part 6, D: Archimage; 1: Mantra II (Lauren)	1.95	0.39	0.98	1.95
❑15, Oct 94, The Archimage Quest, D: Notch; A: Prime	1.95	0.39	0.98	1.95
❑16, Nov 94, Wedding Knight	1.95	0.39	0.98	1.95
❑17, Dec 94, Body Building, 1: NecroMantra; V: Necro Mantra	2.50	0.39	0.98	1.95
❑18, Feb 95, Should Auld Acquaintance...!	2.50	0.39	0.98	1.95
❑19, Mar 95, Mother and Child Reunion	2.50	0.39	0.98	1.95
❑20, Apr 95, Not Without Her My Daughter, D: Overlord	2.50	0.39	0.98	1.95
❑21, May 95, Little Miss Mantras	2.50	0.50	1.25	2.50
❑22, Jun 95	2.50	0.50	1.25	2.50
❑23, Jul 95	2.50	0.50	1.25	2.50
❑24, Final Issue	2.50	0.50	1.25	2.50
❑GS 1, The Archimage Quest, Part 4, 1: Sapphire Queen; 1: Opal Queen; 1: Topaz, Giant-Size Mantra #1	3.50	0.70	1.75	3.50

MANTRA (VOL. 2)
MALIBU

	ORIG	GOOD	FINE	N-MINT
❑0, Sep 95, O: New Mantra, # Infinity	1.50	0.30	0.75	1.50
❑0/A, Sep 95, O: New Mantra, alternate cover	1.50	0.30	0.75	1.50
❑1, Oct 95, My So Called Magic Life, 1: Coven	1.50	0.40	1.00	2.00
❑2, Nov 95	1.50	0.30	0.75	1.50
❑3, Dec 95, V: Necro Mantra	1.50	0.30	0.75	1.50
❑4, Jan 96	1.50	0.30	0.75	1.50
❑5, Feb 96, V: N-ME	1.50	0.30	0.75	1.50
❑6, Mar 96, A: Rush, Final Issue; Mantra gets new costume	1.50	0.30	0.75	1.50
❑7	1.50	0.30	0.75	1.50

MANTRA: SPEAR OF DESTINY
MALIBU

Value: Cover or less

- ❑1, The Woman From Aladdin, Part 1, 1: The Herronvolk ... 2.50
- ❑2, The Woman From Aladdin, Part 2 ... 2.50

MANTUS FILES
ETERNITY

Value: Cover or less

- ❑1, b&w ... 2.50
- ❑2, b&w ... 2.50
- ❑3, b&w ... 2.50
- ❑4, b&w ... 2.50

MANY REINCARNATIONS OF LAZARUS, THE (VOL. 2)
FISHER MEDIA PUBLICATIONS

	ORIG	GOOD	FINE	N-MINT
❑1, Dec 98, The Risen and the Re-Risen: A Tale of a Restless Soul	3.00	0.60	1.50	3.00
❑Ash 1, nn; b&w; no cover price	—	0.20	0.50	1.00

MARA
AIRCEL

Value: Cover or less

- ❑1, May 91 ... 2.50
- ❑2 ... 2.50
- ❑3 ... 2.50
- ❑4, Jan 92 ... 2.95

MARA CELTIC SHAMANESS
EROS

Value: Cover or less

- ❑1, Twilight ... 2.95
- ❑2 ... 2.95
- ❑3 ... 2.95
- ❑4 ... 2.95
- ❑5 ... 2.95
- ❑6 ... 2.95

MARA CELTIC SHAMANESS BOOK 2
EROS

Value: Cover or less

- ❑1 ... 2.95
- ❑2 ... 2.95
- ❑3 ... 2.95
- ❑4 ... 2.95
- ❑5, May 97 ... 2.95

MARA OF THE CELTS BOOK 1
RIP OFF

Value: Cover or less

- ❑SE 1, Sep 93, b&w; adult ... 2.95

MARA OF THE CELTS BOOK 2
EROS

Value: Cover or less

- ❑1 ... 2.95

MARAUDER
Silverline
Value: Cover or less

	ORIG
❑1, Jan 98, Seldom an Ill Wind	2.95
❑2	2.95
❑3	2.95
❑4	2.95

MARCH HARE, THE
Lodestone
Value: Cover or less

	ORIG
❑1, KG, Home Sweet Hitman, b&w	1.50

MARC SPECTOR: MOON KNIGHT
Marvel

	ORIG	GOOD	FINE	N-MINT
❑1, Jun 89, New Moon	1.50	0.50	1.25	2.50
❑2, Jul 89	1.50	0.40	1.00	2.00
❑3, Mar 89, Butcher's Moon	1.50	0.40	1.00	2.00
❑4, Sep 89	1.50	0.40	1.00	2.00
❑5, Oct 89	1.50	0.40	1.00	2.00
❑6, Nov 89, Brother Voodoo	1.50	0.40	1.00	2.00
❑7, Nov 89, Brother Voodoo	1.50	0.40	1.00	2.00
❑8, Dec 89, Acts of Vengeance, A: Punisher, Acts of Vengeance	1.50	0.60	1.50	3.00
❑9, Dec 89, Acts of Vengeance, A: Punisher, Acts of Vengeance	1.50	0.60	1.50	3.00
❑10, Jan 90, Acts of Vengeance, 1: Ringer II, Acts of Vengeance	1.50	0.40	1.00	2.00
❑11, Feb 90	1.50	0.40	1.00	2.00
❑12, Mar 90	1.50	0.40	1.00	2.00
❑13, Apr 90	1.50	0.40	1.00	2.00
❑14, May 90	1.50	0.40	1.00	2.00
❑15, Jun 90, Trial	1.50	0.40	1.00	2.00
❑16, Jul 90, Trial	1.50	0.40	1.00	2.00
❑17, Aug 90, Trial	1.50	0.40	1.00	2.00
❑18, Sep 90, Trial	1.50	0.40	1.00	2.00
❑19, Oct 90, A: Spider-Man; A: Punisher	1.50	0.60	1.50	3.00
❑20, Nov 90, A: Spider-Man; A: Punisher	1.50	0.60	1.50	3.00
❑21, Dec 90, A: Spider-Man; A: Punisher	1.50	0.60	1.50	3.00
❑22, Jan 91	1.50	0.60	1.50	3.00
❑23, Feb 91	1.50	0.60	1.50	3.00
❑24, Mar 91	1.50	0.60	1.50	3.00
❑25, Apr 91, A: Ghost Rider, Giant-size	2.50	0.50	1.25	2.50
❑26, May 91	1.50	0.40	1.00	2.00
❑27, Jun 91	1.50	0.40	1.00	2.00
❑28, Jul 91	1.50	0.40	1.00	2.00
❑29, Aug 91	1.50	0.40	1.00	2.00
❑30, Sep 91	1.50	0.40	1.00	2.00
❑31, Oct 91	1.50	0.40	1.00	2.00
❑32, Nov 91, A: Hobgoblin	1.50	0.60	1.50	3.00
❑33, Dec 91, A: Hobgoblin	1.50	0.60	1.50	3.00
❑34, Jan 92	1.50	0.40	1.00	2.00
❑35, Feb 92, Blood Brothers, Part 1, A: Punisher	1.75	0.40	1.00	2.00
❑36, Mar 92, Blood Brothers, Part 2, A: Punisher	1.75	0.40	1.00	2.00
❑37, Apr 92, Blood Brothers, Part 3, A: Punisher	1.75	0.40	1.00	2.00
❑38, May 92, Blood Brothers, Part 4, A: Punisher	1.75	0.40	1.00	2.00
❑39, Jun 92, Impending Doom!, V: Doctor Doom	1.75	0.40	1.00	2.00
❑40, Jul 92	1.75	0.40	1.00	2.00
❑41, Aug 92	1.75	0.40	1.00	2.00
❑42, Sep 92	1.75	0.40	1.00	2.00
❑43, Oct 92, Infinity War	1.75	0.40	1.00	2.00
❑44, Nov 92, Infinity War	1.75	0.40	1.00	2.00
❑45, Dec 92	1.75	0.40	1.00	2.00
❑46, Jan 93, Death Watch	1.75	0.40	1.00	2.00
❑47, Feb 93	1.75	0.40	1.00	2.00
❑48, Mar 93	1.75	0.40	1.00	2.00
❑49, Apr 93	1.75	0.40	1.00	2.00
❑50, May 93, Die-cut cover	2.95	0.59	1.48	2.95
❑51, Jun 93	1.75	0.35	0.88	1.75
❑52, Jul 93	1.75	0.35	0.88	1.75
❑53, Aug 93	1.75	0.35	0.88	1.75
❑54, Sep 93	1.75	0.35	0.88	1.75
❑55, Oct 93, 1: Sunstreak, 1st professional Stephen Platt art	1.75	0.60	1.50	3.00
❑56, Nov 93	1.75	0.60	1.50	3.00
❑57, Dec 93	1.75	0.60	1.50	3.00
❑58, Jan 94	1.75	0.40	1.00	2.00
❑59, Feb 94	1.75	0.40	1.00	2.00
❑60, Mar 94, Final Issue	1.75	0.40	1.00	2.00
❑SE 1, Explosion At The Center Of A Madman's Crown, Team-up with Shang-Chi, Master of Kung Fu	2.50	0.50	1.25	2.50

MARILYN MONROE: SUICIDE OR MURDER?
Revolutionary
Value: Cover or less

	ORIG
❑1, Sep 93, b&w	2.50

MARIONETTE
Raven

	ORIG	GOOD	FINE	N-MINT
❑1, b&w	0.75	0.20	0.50	1.00

MARIONETTE, THE
Alpha Productions
Value: Cover or less

	ORIG
❑1, b&w	2.50
❑2, b&w	2.50

MARK, THE (1ST SERIES)
Dark Horse

	ORIG	GOOD	FINE	N-MINT
❑1, Sep 87	1.75	0.40	1.00	2.00
❑2, Dec 87	1.95	0.40	1.00	2.00
❑3, Aug 88	1.75	0.40	1.00	2.00
❑4, Sep 88	1.75	0.40	1.00	2.00
❑5, Nov 88	1.75	0.40	1.00	2.00
❑6, Jan 89, History Lesson	1.75	0.40	1.00	2.00

MARK, THE (2ND SERIES)
Dark Horse
Value: Cover or less

	ORIG
❑1, Dec 93, American Tune	2.50
❑2, Jan 94, American Success Story	2.50
❑3, Feb 94, America...Love It Or Leave	2.50
❑4, Mar 94	2.50

MARKAM
Gauntlet
Value: Cover or less

	ORIG
❑1, The Demons of Fate	2.50

MARK HAZZARD: MERC
Marvel

	ORIG	GOOD	FINE	N-MINT
❑1, Nov 86, GM, PD (w), Bad For Business, 1: Mark Hazzard	0.75	0.25	0.63	1.25
❑2, Dec 86	0.75	0.20	0.50	1.00
❑3, Jan 87	0.75	0.20	0.50	1.00
❑4, Feb 87	0.75	0.20	0.50	1.00
❑5, Mar 87	0.75	0.20	0.50	1.00
❑6, Apr 87	0.75	0.20	0.50	1.00
❑7, May 87	0.75	0.20	0.50	1.00
❑8, Jun 87	0.75	0.20	0.50	1.00
❑9, Jul 87	0.75	0.20	0.50	1.00
❑10, Aug 87, GM, Iran Slam	0.75	0.20	0.50	1.00
❑11, Sep 87	0.75	0.20	0.50	1.00
❑12, Oct 87	0.75	0.20	0.50	1.00
❑Anl 1, Nov 87, D: Hazzard	1.25	0.25	0.63	1.25

MARKSMAN, THE
Hero
Value: Cover or less

	ORIG
❑1, Jan 88, The Origin Of The Marksman, O: Marksman; O: The Marksman	1.95
❑2, Feb 88	1.95
❑3, Apr 88	1.95
❑4, Jun 88	1.95
❑5, Aug 88	1.95
❑Anl 1, Dec 88	2.75

MAROONED!
Fantagraphics
Value: Cover or less

	ORIG
❑1, b&w; adult	1.95

MARQUIS, THE: DANSE MACABRE
Oni
Value: Cover or less

	ORIG
❑1, b&w	2.95
❑2, Jul 00, b&w	2.95
❑3, Oct 00, b&w	2.95

MARRIAGE OF HERCULES AND XENA, THE
Topps
Value: Cover or less

	ORIG
❑1, Jul 98	2.95

MARRIED...WITH CHILDREN (VOL. 1)
Now

	ORIG	GOOD	FINE	N-MINT
❑1, Jun 90, The All American Family or Just Act Natural	1.75	0.50	1.25	2.50
❑1-2, The All American Family or Just Act Natural, 2nd Printing	1.75	0.40	1.00	2.00
❑2, Jul 90, Viva Las Bundys, Photo cover	1.75	0.40	1.00	2.00
❑3, Aug 90	1.75	0.40	1.00	2.00
❑4, Sep 90, Big Man Bundy	1.75	0.40	1.00	2.00
❑5, Oct 90, Shoe Zombies, Photo cover	1.75	0.40	1.00	2.00
❑6, Nov 90, TV or not TV, Photo cover	1.75	0.40	1.00	2.00
❑7, Feb 91, Final Issue	1.75	0.40	1.00	2.00

MARRIED...WITH CHILDREN (VOL. 2)
Now

	ORIG	GOOD	FINE	N-MINT
❑1, Sep 91, The Love Line, Photo cover	1.95	0.50	1.25	2.50
❑2, Oct 91, Sweet Revenge, Peggy invents bon-bon filling detector	1.95	0.45	1.13	2.25
❑3, Nov 91, Psychodad, Al turns into Psychodad	1.95	0.45	1.13	2.25
❑4, Dec 91, Photo cover	1.95	0.40	1.00	2.00
❑5, Jan 92	1.95	0.40	1.00	2.00
❑6, Mar 92, Hog Heaven!, Photo cover	1.95	0.40	1.00	2.00
❑7, Apr 92, Attack Of The Job Huntress!, Final Issue	1.95	0.40	1.00	2.00
❑Anl 1994, Annual	2.50	0.50	1.25	2.50
❑SE 1, Jul 92, Photo cover; Special; with poster	1.95	0.40	1.00	2.00

MARRIED...WITH CHILDREN: 2099
Now

	ORIG	GOOD	FINE	N-MINT
❑1, Jun 93, Recognizing Authority, Terminator spoof	1.95	0.40	1.00	2.00
❑2, Jul 93	1.95	0.40	1.00	2.00
❑3, Aug 93	1.95	0.40	1.00	2.00

MARRIED...WITH CHILDREN 3-D SPECIAL
Now

Value: Cover or less

❑1, Jun 93, The Nanny Scam, Inc. 2.95

MARRIED...WITH CHILDREN: BUCK'S TALE
Now

	ORIG	GOOD	FINE	N-MINT
❑1, Buck's Tale, O: Buck (the Bundy Family dog)	1.95	0.40	1.00	2.00

MARRIED...WITH CHILDREN: BUD BUNDY, FANBOY IN PARADISE
Now

Value: Cover or less

❑1, Fanboy In Paradise, poster 2.95

MARRIED...WITH CHILDREN: FLASHBACK SPECIAL
Now

	ORIG	GOOD	FINE	N-MINT
❑1, Jan 93, Al & Peg's First Date	1.95	0.40	1.00	2.00
❑2, Feb 93, Al & Peg's Wedding	1.95	0.40	1.00	2.00
❑3, Mar 93, Father Knows Worst	1.95	0.40	1.00	2.00

MARRIED...WITH CHILDREN: KELLY BUNDY
Now

	ORIG	GOOD	FINE	N-MINT
❑1, Aug 92, Photo cover	1.95	0.45	1.13	2.25
❑2, Sep 92, One Flew Over The Bundy's Nest, Photo cover; centerfold poster	1.95	0.45	1.13	2.25
❑3, Oct 92, Happy Birthday and Get Out!, Photo cover	1.95	0.45	1.13	2.25

MARRIED...WITH CHILDREN: KELLY GOES TO KOLLEGE
Now

Value: Cover or less

❑1, A Mind Is A Terrible Thing, poster 2.95

❑2 2.95

❑3 2.95

MARRIED...WITH CHILDREN: OFF BROADWAY
Now

	ORIG	GOOD	FINE	N-MINT
❑1, Sep 93, Off Broadway	1.95	0.40	1.00	2.00

MARRIED...WITH CHILDREN: QUANTUM QUARTET
Now

	ORIG	GOOD	FINE	N-MINT
❑1, Oct 93, parody	1.95	0.40	1.00	2.00
❑2, Nov 93, parody	1.95	0.40	1.00	2.00
❑3, Fal 94, The Big Wrap-Up; combines issues #3 and 4 into flipbook; no indicia; parody	2.95	0.59	1.48	2.95

MARS
First

	ORIG	GOOD	FINE	N-MINT
❑1, Jan 84, Rebirth	1.25	0.30	0.75	1.50
❑2, Feb 84, Mars Attacks!	1.25	0.25	0.63	1.25
❑3, Mar 84	1.25	0.25	0.63	1.25
❑4, Apr 84	1.25	0.25	0.63	1.25
❑5, May 84	1.25	0.25	0.63	1.25
❑6, Jun 84	1.25	0.25	0.63	1.25
❑7, Jul 84	1.25	0.25	0.63	1.25
❑8, Aug 84	1.25	0.25	0.63	1.25
❑9, Sep 84	1.25	0.25	0.63	1.25
❑10, Oct 84	1.25	0.25	0.63	1.25
❑11, Nov 84	1.25	0.25	0.63	1.25
❑12, Dec 84	1.25	0.25	0.63	1.25

MARS ATTACKS! (MINI-COMICS)
Pocket

Value: Cover or less

❑1, mini-comics 1.00

❑2, mini-comics 1.00

❑3, mini-comics 1.00

❑4, mini-comics 1.00

MARS ATTACKS (VOL. 1)
Topps

	ORIG	GOOD	FINE	N-MINT
❑1, May 94, KG (w), poster; Flip-book format	2.95	0.70	1.75	3.50
❑1/ACE, acetate overlay cover; Wizard Ace Edition #11; sendaway from Wizard #65	—	3.00	7.50	15.00
❑1/LE, poster; Limited edition promotional edition (5, 000 printed); Flip-book format	—	0.80	2.00	4.00
❑2, Jun 94	2.95	0.60	1.50	3.00
❑3	2.95	0.60	1.50	3.00
❑4	2.95	0.60	1.50	3.00
❑5	2.95	0.60	1.50	3.00

MARS ATTACKS (VOL. 2)
Topps

	ORIG	GOOD	FINE	N-MINT
❑1, Aug 95, KG (w), Counterstrike, Part 1	2.95	0.70	1.75	3.50
❑2, Sep 95, Counterstrike, Part 2	2.95	0.60	1.50	3.00
❑3, Oct 95, Counterstrike, Part 3	2.95	0.60	1.50	3.00
❑4, Jan 96, Counterstrike, Part 4	2.95	0.60	1.50	3.00
❑5, Jan 96, Counterstrike, Part 5	2.95	0.60	1.50	3.00
❑6, Mar 96, Claws of the Tiger, Part 1	2.95	0.60	1.50	3.00
❑7, May 96, Claws of the Tiger, Part 2	2.95	0.60	1.50	3.00
❑8	2.95	0.60	1.50	3.00

MARS ATTACKS BASEBALL SPECIAL
Topps

Value: Cover or less

❑1, Jun 96, Simon Bisley cover; One-Shot 2.95

Al Bundy channeled his favorite TV show, *Psychodad*, in *Married ... With Children* (Vol. 2) #3.

© 1991 20th Century Fox Film Corporation (Now)

MARS ATTACKS HIGH SCHOOL
Topps

Value: Cover or less

❑1, May 97 2.95

❑2, Sep 97 2.95

MARS ATTACKS IMAGE
Image

Value: Cover or less

❑1, Dec 96, BSz, KG (w), cross-over with Topps 2.50

❑2, Jan 97, BSz, KG (w), A: Spawn; A: SuperPatriot; A: Witchblade; A: Shadowhawk 2.50

❑3, Mar 97, BSz, KG (w), A: Spawn; A: SuperPatriot; A: Witchblade; A: Shadowhawk 2.50

❑4, Apr 97, BSz, KG (w), D: U.S. Male 2.50

MARS ATTACKS THE SAVAGE DRAGON
Topps

Value: Cover or less

❑1, Dec 96, crossover with Image; trading cards 2.95

❑2, Jan 97, crossover with Image 2.95

❑3, Feb 97, Killer Monday!, cross-over with Image 2.95

❑4, Mar 97, Hard Rain!, crossover with Image 2.95

MARSHAL LAW
Marvel

	ORIG	GOOD	FINE	N-MINT
❑1, Oct 87	1.95	0.70	1.75	3.50
❑2, Feb 88	1.95	0.50	1.25	2.50
❑3, Apr 88, Super Hero Messiah	1.95	0.50	1.25	2.50
❑4, Aug 88	1.95	0.50	1.25	2.50
❑5, Dec 88	1.95	0.50	1.25	2.50
❑6, Apr 89, Nemesis	1.95	0.50	1.25	2.50

MARSHAL LAW: KINGDOM OF THE BLIND
Apocalypse

Value: Cover or less

❑1, nn; newsstand 3.95

❑1/DM, nn; squarebound 5.95

MARSHAL LAW: SECRET TRIBUNAL
Dark Horse

Value: Cover or less

❑1, Sep 93, cardstock cover 2.95

❑2, Apr 94, cardstock cover 2.95

MARSHAL LAW: SUPER BABYLON
Dark Horse

Value: Cover or less

❑1, May 92, nn; prestige format 4.95

MARSHAL LAW: THE HATEFUL DEAD
Apocalypse

Value: Cover or less

❑1, nn; prestige format 5.95

M.A.R.S. PATROL TOTAL WAR
Gold Key

	ORIG	GOOD	FINE	N-MINT
❑3, WW, Series continued from Total War #2	0.12	2.00	5.00	10.00
❑4	0.12	1.60	4.00	8.00
❑5, Mystery Beachhead	0.12	1.60	4.00	8.00
❑6	0.12	1.40	3.50	7.00
❑7	0.12	1.40	3.50	7.00
❑8	0.12	1.40	3.50	7.00
❑9	0.12	1.40	3.50	7.00
❑10, Final Issue	0.12	1.40	3.50	7.00

MARTHA SPLATTERHEAD'S WEIRDEST STORIES EVER TOLD
Monster

Value: Cover or less

❑1, b&w; adult 3.50

MARTHA WASHINGTON GOES TO WAR
Dark Horse

	ORIG	GOOD	FINE	N-MINT
❑1, May 94, DaG, FM (w), The Killing Fields, cardstock cover	2.95	0.60	1.50	3.00
❑2, Jun 94, DaG, FM (w), Harmony, cardstock cover	2.95	0.60	1.50	3.00
❑3, Jul 94, DaG, FM (w), The Valley Of Death, cardstock cover	2.95	0.60	1.50	3.00
❑4, Aug 94, DaG, FM (w), cardstock cover	2.95	0.60	1.50	3.00
❑5, Nov 94, DaG, FM (w), cardstock cover	2.95	0.60	1.50	3.00

MARTHA WASHINGTON SAVES THE WORLD
Dark Horse

	ORIG	GOOD	FINE	N-MINT
❑1, Dec 97, DaG, FM (w), Comin' in on a Wing and a Prayer, cardstock cover	2.95	0.60	1.50	3.00
❑2, Jan 98, DaG, FM (w), Tomorrow, When The World is Free, cardstock cover	2.95	0.60	1.50	3.00
❑3, Feb 98, DaG, FM (w), When The Lights Go On Again All Over the World, cardstock cover	2.95	0.60	1.50	3.00

MARTHA WASHINGTON: STRANDED IN SPACE
DARK HORSE

	ORIG	GOOD	FINE	N-MINT
❑1, Nov 95, DaG, FM (w), Crossover, A: The Big Guy, nn; cardstock cover; reprints story from Dark Horse Presents	2.95	0.60	1.50	3.00

MARTIAN MANHUNTER
DC

	ORIG	GOOD	FINE	N-MINT
❑0, Oct 98, Pilgrimage	1.99	0.60	1.50	3.00
❑1, Dec 98, Duty	1.99	0.50	1.25	2.50
❑2, Jan 99	1.99	0.40	1.00	2.00
❑3, Feb 99, A: Bette Noir	1.99	0.40	1.00	2.00
❑4, Mar 99, D: Karen Smith	1.99	0.40	1.00	2.00
❑5, Apr 99, JDu	1.99	0.40	1.00	2.00
❑6, May 99, V: JLA	1.99	0.40	1.00	2.00
❑7, Jun 99, My Brother's Keeper	1.99	0.40	1.00	2.00
❑8, Jul 99, Abandon All Hope	1.99	0.40	1.00	2.00
❑9, Aug 99, The Burning Grave, A: JLA	1.99	0.40	1.00	2.00
❑10, Sep 99, Good Faith, A: Fire	1.99	0.40	1.00	2.00
❑11, Oct 99, Pilgrims	1.99	0.40	1.00	2.00
❑12, Nov 99, Past Saving, A: Vibe; A: Ice; A: Crimson Fox; A: Steel, Day of Judgment	1.99	0.40	1.00	2.00
❑13, Dec 99, Rings of Saturn, Part 1	1.99	0.40	1.00	2.00
❑14, Jan 00, Rings of Saturn, Part 2	1.99	0.40	1.00	1.99
❑15, Feb 00, Rings of Saturn, Part 3	1.99	0.40	1.00	1.99
❑16, Mar 00	1.99	0.40	1.00	1.99
❑17, Apr 00	1.99	0.40	1.00	1.99
❑18, May 00, One for All, A: JSA	1.99	0.40	1.00	1.99
❑19, Jun 00, All for One	1.99	0.40	1.00	1.99
❑20, Jul 00, Revelations, Part 1	—	0.40	1.00	1.99
❑21, Aug 00, Revelations, Part 2	—	0.40	1.00	1.99
❑22, Sep 00, Revelations, Part 3	—	0.40	1.00	1.99
❑23, Oct 00, Revelations, Part 4	2.50	0.50	1.25	2.50
❑24, Nov 00, Double Stuff	2.50	0.50	1.25	2.50
❑25, Dec 00, Renegades of Mars, Part 1	2.50	0.50	1.25	2.50
❑26, Jan 01, Renegades of Mars, Part 2	2.50	0.50	1.25	2.50
❑27, Feb 01, Renegades of Mars, Part 3	2.50	0.50	1.25	2.50
❑28, Mar 01, Torn Asunder	2.50	0.50	1.25	2.50
❑29, Apr 01, Altered Egos, Part 1	2.50	0.50	1.25	2.50
❑30, May 01, Altered Egos, Part 2	2.50	0.50	1.25	2.50
❑31, Jun 01, Altered Egos, Part 3	2.50	0.50	1.25	2.50
❑32	2.50	0.50	1.25	2.50
❑33	2.50	0.50	1.25	2.50
❑34	2.50	0.50	1.25	2.50
❑1000000, Nov 98, The Abyss of Time	1.99	0.40	1.00	2.00
❑Anl 1, Ghosts	2.95	0.59	1.48	2.95
❑Anl 2, Oct 99, Fear and Loathing on the Planet of the Apes, JLApe	2.95	0.59	1.48	2.95

MARTIAN MANHUNTER (MINI-SERIES)
DC

	ORIG	GOOD	FINE	N-MINT
❑1, May 88, Fever Dream, O: Martian Manhunter	1.25	0.30	0.75	1.50
❑2, Jun 88	1.25	0.30	0.75	1.50
❑3, Jul 88	1.25	0.30	0.75	1.50
❑4, Aug 88, Welcome Home	1.25	0.30	0.75	1.50

MARTIAN MANHUNTER: AMERICAN SECRETS
DC

Value: Cover or less

- ❑1, prestige format 4.95
- ❑2, prestige format 4.95
- ❑3, prestige format 4.95

MARTIAN MANHUNTER SPECIAL
DC

Value: Cover or less

- ❑1 3.50

MARTIN MYSTERY
DARK HORSE

Value: Cover or less

- ❑1, Mar 99 4.95
- ❑2, Apr 99 4.95
- ❑3, May 99 4.95
- ❑4, Jun 99 4.95
- ❑5, Jul 99 4.95
- ❑6, Aug 99 4.95

MARTIN THE SATANIC RACOON
GABE MARTINEZ

Value: Cover or less

- ❑1, Kiss Babies; How to Get Money out of Animal Rights Activists 1.00
- ❑2, The Shít Present; Cannibal Corpse 2.00

MARVEL 1989 - THE YEAR IN REVIEW
MARVEL

Value: Cover or less

- ❑1, overview of past year's activities in Marvel universe 3.95

MARVEL 1990 - THE YEAR IN REVIEW
MARVEL

Value: Cover or less

- ❑2, overview of past year's activities in Marvel universe 3.95

MARVEL 1991 - THE YEAR IN REVIEW
MARVEL

Value: Cover or less

- ❑3, overview of past year's activities in Marvel universe 3.95

MARVEL 1992 - THE YEAR IN REVIEW
MARVEL

Value: Cover or less

- ❑4, overview of past year's activities in Marvel universe 3.95

MARVEL 1994 - THE YEAR IN REVIEW
MARVEL

Value: Cover or less

- ❑1 2.95

MARVEL ACTION HOUR, FEATURING IRON MAN
MARVEL

Value: Cover or less

- ❑1, Nov 94, The Sea Shall Give Up Its Dead 1.50
- ❑1/CS, Nov 94, The Sea Shall Give Up Its Dead, Collector's set: includes animation cel 2.95
- ❑2, Dec 94 1.50
- ❑3, Jan 95, Ultimo 1.50
- ❑4, Feb 95 1.50
- ❑5, Mar 95, Origins, Part 1 1.50
- ❑6, Apr 95, Origins, Part 2, O: The Mandarin 1.50
- ❑7, May 95, Origins, Part 3 1.50
- ❑8, Jun 95 1.50

MARVEL ACTION HOUR, FEATURING THE FANTASTIC FOUR
MARVEL

Value: Cover or less

- ❑1, Nov 94, How It All Began.. 1.50
- ❑1/CS, Nov 94, How It All Began, Collector's set: includes animation cel 2.95
- ❑2, Dec 94 1.50
- ❑3, Jan 95 1.50
- ❑4, Feb 95 1.50
- ❑5, Mar 95 1.50
- ❑6, Apr 95 1.50
- ❑7, May 95 1.50
- ❑8, Jun 95 1.50

MARVEL ACTION UNIVERSE
MARVEL

Value: Cover or less

- ❑1, Jan 89, DS, The Triumph of the Green Goblin, Reprints Spider-Man and His Amazing Friends #1 1.00

MARVEL ADVENTURE
MARVEL

	ORIG	GOOD	FINE	N-MINT
❑1, GC, SL (w), The Tri-Man Lives!, Reprints Daredevil #22	0.25	0.60	1.50	3.00
❑2, Reprints Daredevil #23	0.25	0.40	1.00	2.00
❑3, Reprints Daredevil #24	0.25	0.40	1.00	2.00
❑4, Jun 76, Reprints Daredevil #25	0.25	0.40	1.00	2.00
❑5, Reprints Daredevil #26	0.25	0.40	1.00	2.00
❑6, Reprints Daredevil #27	0.30	0.40	1.00	2.00

MARVEL ADVENTURES
MARVEL

Value: Cover or less

- ❑1, Apr 97, A Titan in Torment!, V: Abomination; A: Hulk; V: Leader 1.50
- ❑2, May 97, The Name of the Game, V: Scorpion; A: Spider-Man 1.50
- ❑3, Jun 97, Hexed, V: Magneto; A: X-Men 1.50
- ❑4, Jul 97, V: Brotherhood of Evil Mutants; A: Hulk 1.50
- ❑5, Aug 97, V: Magneto; A: Spider-Man; V: Abomination; A: X-Men 1.50
- ❑6, Sep 97, V: Lava Men; A: Spider-Man; A: Torch 1.50
- ❑7, Oct 97, V: Tyrannus; A: Hulk 1.50
- ❑8, Nov 97, A: X-Men 1.50
- ❑9, Dec 97, A: Fantastic Four 1.50
- ❑10, Jan 98, A: Silver Surfer; V: Gladiator 1.50
- ❑11, Feb 98, V: Sandman; A: Spider-Man 1.50
- ❑12, Mar 98 1.50
- ❑13, Apr 98 1.50
- ❑14, May 98, A: Juggernaut; A: Doctor Strange; A: Hulk 1.50
- ❑15, Jun 98, A: Wolverine 1.50
- ❑16, Jul 98, V: Skrulls; A: Silver Surfer 1.50
- ❑17, Aug 98, A: Spider-Man; V: Grey Gargoyle; A: Iron Man 1.50
- ❑18, Sep 98, Final Issue 1.50

MARVEL AND DC PRESENT
MARVEL

	ORIG	GOOD	FINE	N-MINT
❑1, Nov 82, TD, Apokolips...Now., X-Men & Titans; Early Marvel/DC crossover	2.00	2.40	6.00	12.00

MARVEL BOY
MARVEL

Value: Cover or less

- ❑1, Aug 00, Hello Cruel World 2.99
- ❑2, Sep 00 2.99
- ❑3, Oct 00 2.99
- ❑4, Nov 00 2.99
- ❑5, Dec 00, Zero Zero: Year of Love 2.99
- ❑6, Mar 01, Mindless: The End 2.99

MARVEL CHILLERS
MARVEL

	ORIG	GOOD	FINE	N-MINT
❑1, Nov 75, Magic Is Alive!, 1: Modred the Mystic; 1: The Other (Chthon)	0.25	0.80	2.00	4.00
❑2, Jan 76, A: Tigra, Modred	0.25	0.60	1.50	3.00
❑3, Mar 76, O: Tigra; 1: The Darkhold, Tigra	0.25	1.00	2.50	5.00
❑4, May 76, A: Kraven; A: Tigra	0.25	0.50	1.25	2.50
❑5, Jun 76, A: Tigra	0.25	0.50	1.25	2.50
❑6, Aug 76, JBy, A: Tigra	0.25	0.50	1.25	2.50
❑7, Oct 76, A: Tigra	0.30	0.50	1.25	2.50

MARVEL CHILLERS: SHADES OF GREEN MONSTERS
MARVEL

Value: Cover or less

- ❑1, Mar 97, nn; mostly text story 2.99

MARVEL CHILLERS: THE THING IN THE GLASS CASE
MARVEL

Value: Cover or less

❑1, Mar 97, nn; mostly text story 2.99

MARVEL CLASSICS COMICS
MARVEL

	ORIG	GOOD	FINE	N-MINT
❑1, Dr. Jekyll and Mr. Hyde, Doctor Jekyll and Mr. Hyde; Dr. Jekyll and Mr. Hyde	0.50	1.20	3.00	6.00
❑2, The Time Machine, The Time Machine	0.50	0.80	2.00	4.00
❑3, The Hunchback of Notre Dame, The Hunchback of Notre Dame	0.50	0.80	2.00	4.00
❑4, 20, 000 Leagues Under the Sea, 20, 000 Leagues Under the Sea	0.50	0.80	2.00	4.00
❑5, Black Beauty, Black Beauty	0.50	0.80	2.00	4.00
❑6, Gulliver's Travels, Gulliver's Travels	0.50	0.70	1.75	3.50
❑7, Tom Sawyer, Tom Sawyer	0.50	0.70	1.75	3.50
❑8, Moby Dick, Moby Dick	0.50	0.70	1.75	3.50
❑9, Dracula, Dracula	0.50	0.70	1.75	3.50
❑10, Red Badge of Courage, Red Badge of Courage	0.50	0.70	1.75	3.50
❑11, Mysterious Island of Dr. Moreau, Mysterious Island	0.50	0.70	1.75	3.50
❑12, The Three Musketeers, Three Musketeers	0.50	0.70	1.75	3.50
❑13, Last of the Mohicans, Last of the Mohicans	0.50	0.70	1.75	3.50
❑14, War of the Worlds, War of the Worlds	0.50	0.70	1.75	3.50
❑15, Treasure Island, Treasure Island	0.50	0.70	1.75	3.50
❑16, Ivanhoe, Ivanhoe	0.50	0.70	1.75	3.50
❑17, The Count of Monte Cristo, Count of Monte Cristo	0.50	0.70	1.75	3.50
❑18, The Odyssey, Odyssey	0.50	0.70	1.75	3.50
❑19, Robinson Crusoe, Robinson Crusoe	0.50	0.70	1.75	3.50
❑20, Frankenstein, Frankenstein	0.50	0.70	1.75	3.50
❑21, Master of the World, Master of the World	0.50	0.70	1.75	3.50
❑22, Food of the Gods, Food of the Gods	0.50	0.70	1.75	3.50
❑23, The Moonstone, The Moonstone	0.50	0.70	1.75	3.50
❑24, She, She	0.50	0.70	1.75	3.50
❑25, The Invisible Man, Invisible Man	0.50	0.70	1.75	3.50
❑26, The Iliad, Iliad	0.50	0.70	1.75	3.50
❑27, Kidnapped, Kidnapped	0.60	0.70	1.75	3.50
❑28, MG, The Pit and the Pendulum, Pit & Pendulum; Mike Golden's first professional art	0.60	1.40	3.50	7.00
❑29, The Prisoner of Zenda, Prisoner of Zenda	0.60	0.70	1.75	3.50
❑30, The Arabian Nights, The Arabian Nights	0.60	0.70	1.75	3.50
❑31, The First Men In the Moon, First Man in the Moon	0.60	0.70	1.75	3.50
❑32, White Fang, White Fang	0.60	0.70	1.75	3.50
❑33, The Prince and the Pauper, The Prince and the Pauper	0.60	0.70	1.75	3.50
❑34, Robin Hood, Robin Hood	0.60	0.70	1.75	3.50
❑35, Alice In Wonderland, Alice in Wonderland	0.60	0.70	1.75	3.50
❑36, A Christmas Carol, A Christmas Carol	0.60	0.70	1.75	3.50

MARVEL COLLECTIBLE CLASSICS: AMAZING SPIDER-MAN
MARVEL

	ORIG	GOOD	FINE	N-MINT
❑300, TMc, 1: Venom, Chromium wraparound cover; Reprints Amazing Spider-Man #300	13.50	2.70	6.75	13.50
❑300/Aut, TMc, 1: Venom, Chromium wraparound cover; Signed by Bob McLeod; Reprints Amazing Spider-Man #300	—	6.00	14.99	29.99

MARVEL COLLECTIBLE CLASSICS: AVENGERS (VOL. 3)
MARVEL

Value: Cover or less

❑1, Chromium wraparound cover 13.50

MARVEL COLLECTIBLE CLASSICS: X-MEN
MARVEL

Value: Cover or less

❑1, Chromium wraparound cover; Reprints X-Men #1 .... 13.50

❑GS 1, Chromium wraparound cover; Reprints Giant Size X-Men #1 .... 13.50

MARVEL COLLECTIBLE CLASSICS: X-MEN (VOL. 2)
MARVEL

	ORIG	GOOD	FINE	N-MINT
❑1, JLee, Chromium wraparound cover	13.50	2.70	6.75	13.50
❑1/Aut, JLee, Chromium wraparound cover; Signed by Jimmy Palmiotti	—	6.00	14.99	29.99

MARVEL COLLECTOR'S EDITION
MARVEL

	ORIG	GOOD	FINE	N-MINT
❑1, RHo (w), Gimme A Break, Spider-Man, Wolverine, Ghost Rider; Charleston Chew promotion, $.50 and a candy bar wrapper; Flip-book format	1.50	0.50	1.25	2.50

MARVEL COLLECTORS' ITEM CLASSICS
MARVEL

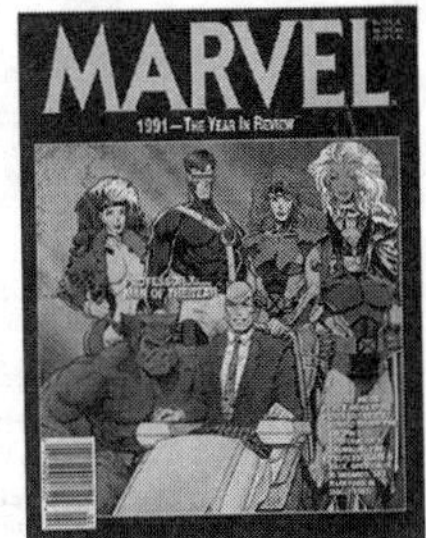

Marvel took an annual look back at the year's events in the Marvel universe in the magazine-sized *Marvel: The Year in Review*.

© 1991 Marvel Comics

	ORIG	GOOD	FINE	N-MINT
❑1, Feb 66	0.25	9.00	22.50	45.00
❑2, Apr 66	0.25	5.60	14.00	28.00
❑3, Jun 66, reprints Fantastic Four (Vol. 1) #4, Tales of Suspense #40, Incredible Hulk #3, Tales of Suspense #49, Strange Tales #110	0.25	5.00	12.50	25.00
❑4, Aug 66	0.25	5.00	12.50	25.00
❑5, Oct 66	0.25	2.80	7.00	14.00
❑6, Dec 66	0.25	2.80	7.00	14.00
❑7, Feb 67	0.25	2.80	7.00	14.00
❑8, Apr 67	0.25	2.80	7.00	14.00
❑9, Jun 67	0.25	2.80	7.00	14.00
❑10, Aug 67	0.25	2.80	7.00	14.00
❑11, Oct 67	0.25	2.40	6.00	12.00
❑12, Dec 67	0.25	2.40	6.00	12.00
❑13, Feb 68	0.25	2.40	6.00	12.00
❑14, Apr 68	0.25	2.40	6.00	12.00
❑15, Jun 68	0.25	2.40	6.00	12.00
❑16, Aug 68	0.25	2.40	6.00	12.00
❑17, Oct 68	0.25	2.40	6.00	12.00
❑18, Dec 68	0.25	2.40	6.00	12.00
❑19, Feb 69, JK; DH, SL (w), The Search For Sub-Mariner!; The Primitive	0.25	2.40	6.00	12.00
❑20, Apr 69	0.25	2.40	6.00	12.00
❑21, Jun 69	0.25	2.00	5.00	10.00
❑22, Aug 69, Series continued in Marvel's Greatest Comics #23	0.25	2.00	5.00	10.00

MARVEL COMICS PRESENTS
MARVEL

	ORIG	GOOD	FINE	N-MINT
❑1, Sep 88, JB; TS; AM, AM (w), Wolverine: Save The Tiger, Part 1; Man-Thing: Elements Of Terror, Part 1, Wolverine features begin	1.25	0.70	1.75	3.50
❑2, Sep 88, JB; TS, Wolverine: Save The Tiger, Part 2; Man-Thing: Elements Of Terror, Part 2, Wolverine	1.25	0.50	1.25	2.50
❑3, Sep 88, JB; TS, Wolverine: Save The Tiger, Part 3; Man-Thing: Elements Of Terror, Part 3, Wolverine	1.25	0.50	1.25	2.50
❑4, Oct 88, JB; TS, Wolverine: Save The Tiger, Part 4; Man-Thing: Elements Of Terror, Part 4, Wolverine	1.25	0.50	1.25	2.50
❑5, Oct 88, JB; TS, Wolverine: Save The Tiger, Part 5; Man-Thing: Elements Of Terror, Part 5, Wolverine	1.25	0.50	1.25	2.50
❑6, Nov 88, JB; TS, Wolverine: Save The Tiger, Part 6; Man-Thing: Elements Of Terror, Part 6, A: Sub-Mariner, Wolverine	1.25	0.40	1.00	2.00
❑7, Nov 88, JB; TS, SD (w), Wolverine: Save The Tiger, Part 7; Man-Thing: Elements Of Terror, Part 7, Wolverine	1.25	0.40	1.00	2.00
❑8, Dec 88, JB; TS, Wolverine: Save The Tiger, Part 8; Man-Thing: Elements Of Terror, Part 8, Wolverine	1.25	0.40	1.00	2.00
❑9, Dec 88, JB; TS, Wolverine: Save The Tiger, Part 9; Man-Thing: Elements Of Terror, Part 9, Wolverine	1.25	0.40	1.00	2.00
❑10, Jan 89, JB; TS, Wolverine: Save The Tiger, Part 10; Man-Thing: Elements Of Terror, Part 10, Wolverine; Colossus features begin	1.25	0.40	1.00	2.00
❑11, Jan 89, TS, Man-Thing: Elements Of Terror, Part 11; Colossus: God's Country, Part 2, Colossus	1.25	0.30	0.75	1.50
❑12, Feb 89, TS, Colossus, Man-Thing	1.25	0.30	0.75	1.50
❑13, Feb 89, GC, Colossus: God's Country, Part 4; Black Panther: Panther's Quest, Part 1, Colossus	1.25	0.30	0.75	1.50
❑14, Mar 89, GC, SD (w), Colossus: God's Country, Part 5; Black Panther: Panther's Quest, Part 2, Colossus	1.25	0.30	0.75	1.50
❑15, Mar 89, GC, Colossus: God's Country, Part 6; Black Panther: Panther's Quest, Part 3, Colossus	1.25	0.30	0.75	1.50
❑16, Mar 89, GC, Colossus: God's Country, Part 7; Black Panther: Panther's Quest, Part 4, Colossus	1.25	0.30	0.75	1.50
❑17, Apr 89, GC; TS, Colossus: God's Country, Part 8; Black Panther: Panther's Quest, Part 5, Cyclops: The Retribution Affair, Part 1, Cyclops features begin	1.25	0.30	0.75	1.50

	ORIG	GOOD	FINE	N-MINT
❑18, Apr 89, GC; RHo, JBy (w), Black Panther: Panther's Quest, Part 6; Cyclops: The Retribution Affair, Part 2, She-Hulk, Cyclops	1.25	0.30	0.75	1.50
❑19, May 89, Black Panther: Panther's Quest, Part 7; Cyclops: The Retribution Affair, Part 3, 1: Damage Control, Cyclops	1.25	0.30	0.75	1.50
❑20, May 89, Black Panther: Panther's Quest, Part 8; Cyclops: The Retribution Affair, Part 4, Cyclops	1.25	0.30	0.75	1.50
❑21, Jun 89, GC, Black Panther: Panther's Quest, Part 9; Cyclops: The Retribution Affair, Part 5, Cyclops	1.25	0.30	0.75	1.50
❑22, Jun 89, GC, Black Panther: Panther's Quest, Part 10; Cyclops: The Retribution Affair, Part 6, Cyclops	1.25	0.30	0.75	1.50
❑23, Jul 89, GC, Black Panther: Panther's Quest, Part 11; Cyclops: The Retribution Affair, Part 7, Cyclops	1.25	0.30	0.75	1.50
❑24, Jul 89, GC; RB, Black Panther: Panther's Quest, Part 12; Cyclops: The Retribution Affair, Part 8, Cyclops, Havok	1.25	0.30	0.75	1.50
❑25, Aug 89, RB, Black Panther: Panther's Quest, Part 13; Havok: Pharaoh's Legacy, Part 2, 1: Nth Man, Havok	1.25	0.30	0.75	1.50
❑26, Aug 89, PG; GC; RB, Black Panther: Panther's Quest, Part 14; Havok: Pharaoh's Legacy, Part 3, 1: Coldblood, Havok	1.25	0.30	0.75	1.50
❑27, Sep 89, GC; RB, Black Panther: Panther's Quest, Part 15; Havok: Pharaoh's Legacy, Part 4, Havok	1.25	0.30	0.75	1.50
❑28, Sep 89, PG; GC; RB, Black Panther: Panther's Quest, Part 16; Havok: Pharaoh's Legacy, Part 5, Havok	1.25	0.30	0.75	1.50
❑29, Sep 89, GC; RB, Black Panther: Panther's Quest, Part 17; Havok: Pharaoh's Legacy, Part 6, Havok	1.25	0.30	0.75	1.50
❑30, Oct 89, GC; RB, Black Panther: Panther's Quest, Part 18; Havok: Pharaoh's Legacy, Part 7, A: Wolverine, Havok	1.25	0.30	0.75	1.50
❑31, Oct 89, EL; PG; GC; RB, Black Panther: Panther's Quest, Part 19; Havok: Pharaoh's Legacy, Part 8, O: Coldblood, Havok, Excalibur	1.25	0.30	0.75	1.50
❑32, Nov 89, EL; PG; DH; GC, TMc (c), Black Panther: Panther's Quest, Part 20; Coldblood: Rise And Shine, Part 7, Excalibur	1.25	0.30	0.75	1.50
❑33, Nov 89, EL; JLee; PG; GC, Black Panther: Panther's Quest, Part 21; Coldblood: Rise And Shine, Part 8, Excalibur	1.25	0.30	0.75	1.50
❑34, Nov 89, EL; PG; GC, Black Panther: Panther's Quest, Part 22; Coldblood: Rise And Shine, Part 9, Excalibur	1.25	0.30	0.75	1.50
❑35, Nov 89, EL; PG; GC, Black Panther: Panther's Quest, Part 23; Coldblood: Rise And Shine, Part 10, 1: Starduster, Excalibur	1.25	0.30	0.75	1.50
❑36, Dec 89, EL; GC, Black Panther: Panther's Quest, Part 24; Excalibur: Having A Wild Weekend, Part 6, Excalibur	1.25	0.30	0.75	1.50
❑37, Dec 89, GC, Black Panther: Panther's Quest, Part 25; Excalibur: Having A Wild Weekend, Part 7, Excalibur	1.25	0.30	0.75	1.50
❑38, Dec 89, EL; JB, Excalibur: Having A Wild Weekend, Part 8; Hulk: Art For Art's Sake, Excalibur	1.25	0.40	1.00	2.00
❑39, Dec 89, BL (w), Wolverine: Black Shadow White Shadow, Part 2; Wonder Man: Stardust Miseries, Part 2, Wolverine	1.25	0.30	0.75	1.50
❑40, Dec 89, DH; BL; JB, BL (w), Wolverine: Black Shadow White Shadow, Part 3; Wonder Man: Stardust Miseries, Part 3, Wolverine	1.25	0.30	0.75	1.50
❑41, Jan 90, DC; BL; JB, BL (w), Wolverine: Black Shadow White Shadow, Part 4; Wonder Man: Stardust Miseries, Part 4, Wolverine	1.25	0.30	0.75	1.50
❑42, Jan 90, JB, Wolverine: Black Shadow White Shadow, Part 5; Wonder Man: Stardust Miseries, Part 5, Wolverine	1.25	0.30	0.75	1.50
❑43, Feb 90, Wolverine: Black Shadow White Shadow, Part 6; Wonder Man: Stardust Miseries, Part 6, Wolverine	1.25	0.30	0.75	1.50
❑44, Feb 90, JB, Wolverine: Black Shadow White Shadow, Part 7; Wonder Man: Stardust Miseries, Part 7, Wolverine	1.25	0.30	0.75	1.50
❑45, Mar 90, JB, Wolverine: Black Shadow White Shadow, Part 8; Wonder Man: Stardust Miseries, Part 8, Wolverine	1.25	0.30	0.75	1.50
❑46, Mar 90, JB, Wolverine: Black Shadow White Shadow, Part 9; Devil Slayer: Lost Souls, Part 1, Wolverine	1.25	0.30	0.75	1.50
❑47, Apr 90, JB, Wolverine: Black Shadow White Shadow, Part 10; Devil Slayer: Lost Souls, Part 2, Wolverine	1.25	0.30	0.75	1.50
❑48, Apr 90, Wolverine/Spider-Man: Life's End, Part 1; Devil Slayer: Lost Souls, Part 3, Spider-Man, Wolverine	1.25	0.40	1.00	2.00
❑49, May 90, Wolverine/Spider-Man: Life's End, Part 2; Devil Slayer: Lost Souls, Part 4, 1: Whiplash II, Spider-Man, Wolverine	1.25	0.40	1.00	2.00
❑50, May 90, Wolverine/Spider-Man: Life's End, Part 3, O: Captain Ultra, Spider-Man, Wolverine	1.25	0.40	1.00	2.00
❑51, Jun 90, RL, Wolverine	1.25	0.40	1.00	2.00
❑52, Jun 90, RL, Wolverine	1.25	0.40	1.00	2.00
❑53, Jul 90, RL, Stingray: Family Matters, Part 1, Wolverine	1.25	0.40	1.00	2.00
❑54, Jul 90, Stingray: Family Matters, Part 2; Wolverine: On The Road, Part 1, Wolverine & Hulk	1.25	0.50	1.25	2.50
❑55, Jul 90, Stingray: Family Matters, Part 3; Wolverine: On The Road, Part 2, Wolverine & Hulk	1.25	0.50	1.25	2.50
❑56, Aug 90, Stingray: Family Matters, Part 4; Wolverine: On The Road, Part 3, Wolverine & Hulk	1.25	0.50	1.25	2.50
❑57, Aug 90, Wolverine: On The Road, Part 4; Werewolf: Children Of The Beast, Part 4, Wolverine & Hulk	1.25	0.50	1.25	2.50
❑58, Sep 90, Wolverine: On The Road, Part 5; Werewolf: Children Of The Beast, Part 5, Wolverine & Hulk	1.25	0.50	1.25	2.50
❑59, Sep 90, Wolverine: On The Road, Part 6; Sub-Mariner: Neptunes Eye, Part 3, Wolverine & Hulk	1.25	0.50	1.25	2.50
❑60, Oct 90, RHo, RHo (w), Wolverine: On The Road, Part 7; Poison: Vandals Of The Heart, Part 1, Wolverine & Hulk	1.25	0.50	1.25	2.50
❑61, Oct 90, RHo, RHo (w), Wolverine: On The Road, Part 8; Poison: Vandals Of The Heart, Part 2, Wolverine & Hulk	1.25	0.50	1.25	2.50
❑62, Nov 90, RHo, Poison: Vandals Of The Heart, Part 3; Scarlet Witch: Yesterdays, Part 3, Wolverine	1.25	0.50	1.25	2.50
❑63, Nov 90, RHo, Poison: Vandals Of The Heart, Part 4; Scarlet Witch: Yesterdays, Part 4, Wolverine	1.25	0.40	1.00	2.00
❑64, Dec 90, Wolverine and Ghost Rider: Acts of Vengeance, Part 1; Poison: Vandals Of The Heart, Part 5, Wolverine, Ghost Rider	1.25	0.40	1.00	2.00
❑65, Dec 90, Wolverine and Ghost Rider: Acts of Vengeance, Part 2; Poison: Vandals Of The Heart, Part 6, Wolverine, Ghost Rider	1.25	0.40	1.00	2.00
❑66, Dec 90, Wolverine and Ghost Rider: Acts of Vengeance, Part 3; Poison: Vandals Of The Heart, Part 7, Wolverine, Ghost Rider	1.25	0.40	1.00	2.00
❑67, Jan 91, Wolverine and Ghost Rider: Acts of Vengeance, Part 4; Poison: Vandals Of The Heart, Part 8, Wolverine, Ghost Rider	1.25	0.40	1.00	2.00
❑68, Jan 91, Wolverine and Ghost Rider: Acts of Vengeance, Part 5; Fantastic Four: Deadly Dimensions, Part 5, Wolverine, Ghost Rider	1.25	0.40	1.00	2.00
❑69, Feb 91, Wolverine and Ghost Rider: Acts of Vengeance, Part 6; Shanna: The Bush Of Ghosts, Part 2, Wolverine, Ghost Rider	1.25	0.40	1.00	2.00
❑70, Feb 91, Wolverine and Ghost Rider: Acts of Vengeance, Part 7; Shanna: The Bush Of Ghosts, Part 3, Wolverine, Ghost Rider	1.25	0.40	1.00	2.00
❑71, Mar 91, Wolverine and Ghost Rider: Acts of Vengeance, Part 8; Shanna: The Bush Of Ghosts, Part 4, Warlock: Warlock And The Fleshtones, Wolverine, Ghost Rider	1.25	0.40	1.00	2.00
❑72, Mar 91, Weapon X; Shanna: The Bush Of Ghosts, Part 5, Weapon X	1.25	0.80	2.00	4.00
❑73, Mar 91, Weapon X, Part 1; Shanna: The Bush Of Ghosts, Part 6, Weapon X	1.25	0.50	1.25	2.50
❑74, Apr 91, Weapon X, Part 2; Shanna: The Bush Of Ghosts, Part 7, Weapon X	1.25	0.50	1.25	2.50
❑75, Apr 91, Weapon X, Part 3; Shanna: The Bush Of Ghosts, Part 8, Weapon X	1.25	0.50	1.25	2.50
❑76, May 91, Weapon X, Part 4; Shanna: The Bush Of Ghosts, Part 9, Weapon X	1.25	0.50	1.25	2.50
❑77, May 91, Weapon X, Part 5; Shanna: The Bush Of Ghosts, Part 10, Weapon X	1.25	0.50	1.25	2.50
❑78, Jun 91, Weapon X, Part 6; Sgt. Fury/Dracula: Rumanian Rumble, Part 2, Weapon X	1.25	0.50	1.25	2.50
❑79, Jun 91, JBy, Weapon X, Part 7; Sgt. Fury/Dracula: Rumanian Rumble, Part 3, Weapon X	1.25	0.50	1.25	2.50
❑80, Jul 91, SD, SD (w), Weapon X, Part 8; Captain America: Wargod, Part 1, Weapon X	1.25	0.50	1.25	2.50

	ORIG	GOOD	FINE	N-MINT
❑81, Jul 91, SD, SD (w), Weapon X, Part 9; Ant-Man: The Bomb, Weapon X; Daredevil	1.25	0.50	1.25	2.50
❑82, Aug 91, Weapon X, Part 10; Firestar: Life During War Time, Part 1, Weapon X.	1.25	0.50	1.25	2.50
❑83, Aug 91, SD (w), Weapon X, Part 11; Firestar: Life During War Time, Part 2, Weapon X	1.25	0.50	1.25	2.50
❑84, Sep 91, Weapon X, Part 12; Firestar: Life During War Time, Part 3, Weapon X.	1.25	0.50	1.25	2.50
❑85, Sep 91, Firestar: Life During War Time, Part 4; Wolverine: Blood Hungry, Part 1, 1: Cyber, Wolverine; 1st Kieth art on Wolverine	1.25	0.50	1.25	2.50
❑86, Oct 91, Firestar: Life During War Time, Part 5; Wolverine: Blood Hungry, Part 2, Wolverine	1.25	0.50	1.25	2.50
❑87, Oct 91, Wolverine: Blood Hungry, Part 3; Beast: Just Friends, Part 3, Wolverine	1.25	0.40	1.00	2.00
❑88, Nov 91, Wolverine: Blood Hungry, Part 4; Beast: Just Friends, Part 4, Wolverine	1.25	0.40	1.00	2.00
❑89, Nov 91, Wolverine: Blood Hungry, Part 5; Beast: Just Friends, Part 5, Wolverine	1.25	0.40	1.00	2.00
❑90, Dec 91, Ghost Rider and Cable: Servants of the Dead, Part 1; Wolverine: Blood Hungry, Part 6, A: Cable; A: Ghost Rider, Flip-book covers begin; Wolverine	1.25	0.40	1.00	2.00
❑91, Dec 91, Ghost Rider and Cable: Servants of the Dead, Part 2; Wolverine: Blood Hungry, Part 7, A: Cable; A: Ghost Rider, Wolverine	1.25	0.30	0.75	1.50
❑92, Dec 91, Ghost Rider and Cable: Servants of the Dead, Part 3; Wolverine: Blood Hungry, Part 8, A: Cable; A: Ghost Rider, Wolverine	1.25	0.30	0.75	1.50
❑93, Ghost Rider and Cable: Servants of the Dead, Part 4; Nova: And Ye Shall Remember This Day, Part 1, A: Cable; A: Ghost Rider, Wolverine	1.25	0.30	0.75	1.50
❑94, Ghost Rider and Cable: Servants of the Dead, Part 5; Thing: Grimm's Tale, A: Cable; A: Ghost Rider, Wolverine	1.25	0.30	0.75	1.50
❑95, Ghost Rider and Cable: Servants of the Dead, Part 6; Nova: And Ye Shall Remember This Day, Part 3, A: Cable; A: Ghost Rider, Wolverine	1.50	0.30	0.75	1.50
❑96, Ghost Rider and Cable: Servants of the Dead, Part 7; Nova: And Ye Shall Remember This Day, Part 4, A: Cable; A: Ghost Rider, Wolverine	1.50	0.30	0.75	1.50
❑97, Ghost Rider and Cable: Servants of the Dead, Part 8; Wolverine: Wild Frontier, Part 5, A: Cable; A: Ghost Rider, Wolverine	1.50	0.30	0.75	1.50
❑98, Wolverine: Wild Frontier, Part 6; Ghost Rider: D'Spryte Times, D'Spryte Measures, Part 1, Wolverine	1.50	0.30	0.75	1.50
❑99, RL (w), Wolverine: Hauntings; Puck: Razor's Edge, Wolverine	1.50	0.30	0.75	1.50
❑100, Dr. Doom: Dreams Of Doom; Ghost Rider: Whose Nightmare Is It Anyway, V: Doctor Doom; A: Ghost Rider, Anniversary issue; Wolverine	1.50	0.30	0.75	1.50
❑101, TS, Wolverine/Nightcrawler: Male Bonding, Part 1; Young Gods: Against A Rogue God, Part 1, Wolverine, Nightcrawler	1.50	0.30	0.75	1.50
❑102, GC; TS, Wolverine/Nightcrawler: Male Bonding, Part 2; Young Gods: Against A Rogue God, Part 2, Wolverine, Nightcrawler	1.50	0.30	0.75	1.50
❑103, GC; TS, Wolverine/Nightcrawler: Male Bonding, Part 3; Young Gods: Against A Rogue God, Part 3, Wolverine, Nightcrawler	1.50	0.30	0.75	1.50
❑104, GC; TS, Wolverine/Nightcrawler: Male Bonding, Part 4; Young Gods: Against A Rogue God, Part 4, Wolverine, Nightcrawler	1.50	0.30	0.75	1.50
❑105, GC; TS, Wolverine/Nightcrawler: Male Bonding, Part 5; Young Gods: Against A Rogue God, Part 5, Wolverine, Nightcrawler	1.50	0.30	0.75	1.50
❑106, GC; TS, Wolverine/Nightcrawler: Male Bonding, Part 6; Young Gods: Against A Rogue God, Part 6, Wolverine, Nightcrawler	1.50	0.30	0.75	1.50
❑107, GC; TS, Wolverine/Nightcrawler: Male Bonding, Part 7; Young Gods: Against A Rogue God, Part 7, Red Wolf: Fuel For The Fire, Wolverine, Nightcrawler	1.50	0.30	0.75	1.50
❑108, GC; TS, Wolverine/Nightcrawler: Male Bonding, Part 8; Young Gods: Against A Rogue God, Part 8, Wolverine, Ghost Rider	1.50	0.30	0.75	1.50
❑109, JSn (w), Young Gods: Against A Rogue God, Part 9; Typhoid's Kiss, Part 1, A: Typhoid Mary, Wolverine, Ghost Rider	1.50	0.30	0.75	1.50

Wolverine's origins were examined in Barry Windsor-Smith's "Weapon X" story, which appeared in *Marvel Comics Presents* #72-84.

© 1991 Marvel Comics

	ORIG	GOOD	FINE	N-MINT
❑110, JSn (w), Typhoid's Kiss, Part 2; Ghost Rider/Werewolf By Night: Return Of The Braineaters, Part 4, A: Typhoid Mary, Wolverine, Ghost Rider	1.50	0.30	0.75	1.50
❑111, JSn (w), Typhoid's Kiss, Part 3; Ghost Rider/Werewolf By Night: Return Of The Braineaters, Part 5, A: Typhoid Mary, Infinity War; Wolverine, Ghost Rider	1.50	0.30	0.75	1.50
❑112, GC, JSn (w), Typhoid's Kiss, Part 4; Ghost Rider/Werewolf By Night: Return Of The Braineaters, Part 6, A: Typhoid Mary, Wolverine, Ghost Rider	1.50	0.30	0.75	1.50
❑113, Typhoid's Kiss, Part 5; Giant-Man: The Third Life Of Bill Foster, Part 1, A: Typhoid Mary, Wolverine, Ghost Rider	1.50	0.30	0.75	1.50
❑114, Typhoid's Kiss, Part 6; Giant-Man: The Third Life Of Bill Foster, Part 2, A: Typhoid Mary, Wolverine, Ghost Rider	1.50	0.30	0.75	1.50
❑115, Typhoid's Kiss, Part 7; Giant-Man: The Third Life Of Bill Foster, Part 3, A: Typhoid Mary, Wolverine, Ghost Rider	1.50	0.30	0.75	1.50
❑116, Typhoid's Kiss, Part 8; Giant-Man: The Third Life Of Bill Foster, Part 4, A: Typhoid Mary, Wolverine, Ghost Rider	1.50	0.30	0.75	1.50
❑117, Giant-Man: The Third Life Of Bill Foster, Part 5; Ghost Rider/Iron Fist: The Night Has A Thousand Eyes, Part 5, 1: Ravage 2099; A: Venom, Wolverine, Ghost Rider; Ravage 2099 preview	1.50	0.30	0.75	1.50
❑118, Giant-Man: The Third Life Of Bill Foster, Part 6; Ghost Rider/Iron Fist: The Night Has A Thousand Eyes, Part 6, A: Venom; 1: Doom 2099, Wolverine; Doom 2099 preview	1.50	0.30	0.75	1.50
❑119, Ghost Rider/Cloak & Dagger: And Let There Be Light, Part 1; Wolverine/Venom: Claws And Webs, Part 3, A: Venom, Wolverine	1.50	0.30	0.75	1.50
❑120, Ghost Rider/Cloak & Dagger: And Let There Be Light, Part 2; Spider-Man: Along Came A Child, A: Venom, Wolverine	1.50	0.30	0.75	1.50
❑121, Ghost Rider/Cloak & Dagger: And Let There Be Light, Part 3; Wolverine/Venom: Claws And Webs, Part 5, Wolverine	1.50	0.30	0.75	1.50
❑122, Ghost Rider/Cloak & Dagger: And Let There Be Light, Part 4; Wolverine/Venom: Claws And Webs, Part 6, Wolverine	1.50	0.30	0.75	1.50
❑123, Ghost Rider/Typhoid Mary: The Walking Wounded, Part 1; Master Man: The Doomed Man, Wolverine	1.50	0.30	0.75	1.50
❑124, Ghost Rider/Typhoid Mary: The Walking Wounded, Part 2; Wolverine/Lynx: Passion Play, Part 2, Wolverine	1.50	0.30	0.75	1.50
❑125, Ghost Rider/Typhoid Mary: The Walking Wounded, Part 3; Wolverine/Lynx: Passion Play, Part 3, Wolverine	1.50	0.30	0.75	1.50
❑126, Ghost Rider/Typhoid Mary: The Walking Wounded, Part 4; Wolverine/Lynx: Passion Play, Part 4, Wolverine	1.50	0.30	0.75	1.50
❑127, Ghost Rider/Typhoid Mary: The Walking Wounded, Part 5; Wolverine/Lynx: Passion Play, Part 5, Wolverine	1.50	0.30	0.75	1.50
❑128, Ghost Rider/Typhoid Mary: The Walking Wounded, Part 6; Wolverine/Lynx: Passion Play, Part 6, Wolverine	1.50	0.30	0.75	1.50
❑129, Ghost Rider/Typhoid Mary: The Walking Wounded, Part 7; Wolverine/Lynx: Passion Play, Part 7, Wolverine	1.50	0.30	0.75	1.50
❑130, Ghost Rider/Typhoid Mary: The Walking Wounded, Part 8; Wolverine/Lynx: Passion Play, Part 8, Wolverine	1.50	0.30	0.75	1.50
❑131, Wolverine: These Foolish Things; Ant-Man: Late For Supper, Wolverine	1.50	0.30	0.75	1.50
❑132, Iron Fist: The Book Of Changes, Part 8;, Wolverine	1.50	0.30	0.75	1.50
❑133, Jul 93, Ghost Rider/Cage: Heart And Soul, Part 3, Wolverine	1.50	0.30	0.75	1.50
❑134, Aug 93, Ghost Rider/Cage: Heart And Soul, Part 4, Wolverine	1.50	0.30	0.75	1.50
❑135, Aug 93, Ghost Rider/Cage: Heart And Soul, Part 5, Wolverine	1.50	0.30	0.75	1.50

	ORIG	GOOD	FINE	N-MINT
❑136, Sep 93, Ghost Rider/Cage: Heart And Soul, Part 6, Wolverine	1.50	0.30	0.75	1.50
❑137, Sep 93, Wolverine	1.50	0.30	0.75	1.50
❑138, Wolverine: Rumble in the Jungle, Part 1; Spellbound, Part 1, A: Nightcrawler; A: Spellbound; A: Wusin; A: Wolverine; A: Ghost Rider; A: Masters of Silence	1.50	0.30	0.75	1.50
❑139, Wolverine: Rumble in the Jungle, Part 2; Spellbound, Part 2, A: Zxaxz; A: Spellbound; A: Foreigner; A: Wusin; A: Wolverine; A: Ghost Rider; A: Masters of Silence	1.50	0.30	0.75	1.50
❑140, Wolverine: Rumble in the Jungle, Part 3; Spellbound, Part 3, A: Zxaxz; A: Spellbound; A: Captain Universe; A: Wusin; A: Wolverine; A: Ghost Rider; A: Masters of Silence	1.50	0.30	0.75	1.50
❑141, Nov 93	1.50	0.30	0.75	1.50
❑142, Nov 93	1.50	0.30	0.75	1.50
❑143, Dec 93, Siege of Darkness, Part 2, Ghost Rider	1.75	0.35	0.88	1.75
❑144, Dec 93, Siege of Darkness, Part 6, Ghost Rider	1.75	0.35	0.88	1.75
❑145, Jan 94, Ghost Rider	1.75	0.35	0.88	1.75
❑146, Jan 94	1.75	0.35	0.88	1.75
❑147, Feb 94, Vengeance, Part 1	1.50	0.35	0.88	1.75
❑148, Feb 94, Vengeance, Part 2	1.50	0.35	0.88	1.75
❑149, Mar 94	1.50	0.35	0.88	1.75
❑150, Mar 94	1.50	0.35	0.88	1.75
❑151, Apr 94	1.50	0.35	0.88	1.75
❑152, Apr 94	1.50	0.35	0.88	1.75
❑153, May 94	1.75	0.35	0.88	1.75
❑154, May 94	1.75	0.35	0.88	1.75
❑155, May 94	1.75	0.35	0.88	1.75
❑156, Jun 94	1.75	0.35	0.88	1.75
❑157, Jun 94	1.75	0.35	0.88	1.75
❑158, Jul 94	1.75	0.35	0.88	1.75
❑159, Jul 94	1.75	0.35	0.88	1.75
❑160, Aug 94	1.75	0.35	0.88	1.75
❑161, Aug 94	1.75	0.35	0.88	1.75
❑162, Sep 94	1.75	0.35	0.88	1.75
❑163, Sep 94	1.75	0.35	0.88	1.75
❑164, Oct 94	1.75	0.35	0.88	1.75
❑165, Oct 94	1.75	0.35	0.88	1.75
❑166, Oct 94	1.75	0.35	0.88	1.75
❑167, Nov 94	1.75	0.35	0.88	1.75
❑168, Nov 94	1.75	0.35	0.88	1.75
❑169, Dec 94	1.75	0.35	0.88	1.75
❑170, Dec 94	1.75	0.35	0.88	1.75
❑171, Jan 95	1.75	0.35	0.88	1.75
❑172, Jan 95	1.75	0.35	0.88	1.75
❑173, Feb 95	1.75	0.35	0.88	1.75
❑174, Feb 95	1.75	0.35	0.88	1.75
❑175, Mar 95, Final Issue	1.75	0.35	0.88	1.75

MARVEL DOUBLE FEATURE

MARVEL

	ORIG	GOOD	FINE	N-MINT
❑1, Dec 73	0.20	1.00	2.50	5.00
❑2, Feb 74	0.20	0.80	2.00	4.00
❑3, Apr 74	0.20	0.80	2.00	4.00
❑4, Jun 74	0.25	0.60	1.50	3.00
❑5, Aug 74	0.25	0.60	1.50	3.00
❑6, Oct 74	0.25	0.60	1.50	3.00
❑7, Dec 74	0.25	0.50	1.25	2.50
❑8, Feb 75	0.25	0.50	1.25	2.50
❑9, Apr 75	0.25	0.50	1.25	2.50
❑10, Jun 75	0.25	0.50	1.25	2.50
❑11, Aug 75	0.25	0.50	1.25	2.50
❑12, Oct 75	0.25	0.50	1.25	2.50
❑13, Dec 75	0.25	0.50	1.25	2.50
❑14, Feb 76	0.25	0.50	1.25	2.50
❑15, Apr 76	0.25	0.50	1.25	2.50
❑16, Jun 76	0.25	0.50	1.25	2.50
❑17, Aug 76, Reprints Iron Man vs. Sub-Mariner #1	0.25	0.50	1.25	2.50
❑18, Oct 76, Reprints story from Iron Man #1	0.30	0.50	1.25	2.50
❑19, Dec 76	0.30	0.50	1.25	2.50
❑20, Feb 77	0.30	0.50	1.25	2.50
❑21, Apr 77	0.30	0.50	1.25	2.50

MARVEL FANFARE

MARVEL

	ORIG	GOOD	FINE	N-MINT
❑1, Mar 82, TD; MG, 1: Vertigo II, Spider-Man; Daredevil; Angel	1.25	0.90	2.25	4.50
❑2, May 82, MG, Spider-Man; Angel; Ka-Zar; Fantastic Four	1.25	0.65	1.63	3.25
❑3, Jul 82, DC, X-Men	1.25	0.65	1.63	3.25
❑4, Sep 82, TD; PS; MG, Cause and Effect, X-Men; Deathlok	1.25	0.50	1.25	2.50
❑5, Nov 82, MR; CR, To Steal The Sorcerer's Soul!, Doctor Strange	1.25	0.50	1.25	2.50
❑6, Jan 83, Switch Witch, Spider-Man; Doctor Strange; Scarlet Witch	1.25	0.40	1.00	2.00
❑7, Mar 83, DD, With Friends Like These..., Hulk; Daredevil	1.25	0.40	1.00	2.00
❑8, May 83, CI, The Light That Never Was!, Doctor Strange; Mowgli	1.50	0.40	1.00	2.00
❑9, Jul 83, Rock 'n' Soul!, Man-Thing; Mowgli	1.50	0.40	1.00	2.00
❑10, Aug 83, GP, GP (c), Widow, Black Widow; Mowgli	1.50	0.40	1.00	2.00
❑11, Nov 83, GP, Back In The USSR, Black Widow	1.50	0.40	1.00	2.00
❑12, Jan 84, GP, Black Widow	1.50	0.40	1.00	2.00
❑13, Mar 84, GP, Black Widow	1.50	0.40	1.00	2.00
❑14, May 84, Vision; Quicksilver	1.50	0.40	1.00	2.00
❑15, Jul 84, Thing	1.50	0.40	1.00	2.00
❑16, Sep 84, DC, Skywolf	1.50	0.40	1.00	2.00
❑17, Nov 84, DC, Skywolf	1.50	0.40	1.00	2.00
❑18, Jan 85, FM, Captain America	1.50	0.40	1.00	2.00
❑19, Mar 85, JSn, Cloak & Dagger	1.50	0.40	1.00	2.00
❑20, May 85, JSn, JSn (w), The Clash, Thing; Hulk; Doctor Strange	1.50	0.40	1.00	2.00
❑21, Jul 85, JSn, Thing; Hulk	1.50	0.40	1.00	2.00
❑22, Sep 85, JSn, Night Of The Octopus, Thing; Hulk; Iron Man	1.50	0.40	1.00	2.00
❑23, Nov 85, JSn, #NAME?; -From The Ashes, Thing; Hulk; Iron Man	1.50	0.40	1.00	2.00
❑24, Jan 86, Weirdworld	1.50	0.40	1.00	2.00
❑25, Mar 86, PB, Raven's Dark Sorcery, Dave Sim pin-up section; Weirdworld; Dave Sims pin-up section	1.50	0.40	1.00	2.00
❑26, May 86, PB, The Goblin Spree, Weirdworld	1.50	0.40	1.00	2.00
❑27, Jul 86, Cars, Weirdworld; Spider-Man; Daredevil	1.50	0.40	1.00	2.00
❑28, Sep 86, Murder By Numbers 1, 2, 3..., Alpha Flight	1.50	0.40	1.00	2.00
❑29, Nov 86, D: Anvil; D: Hammer, Moon Knight	1.50	0.40	1.00	2.00
❑30, Jan 87, BA, Real To Reel, Painted cover; Moon Knight	1.50	0.40	1.00	2.00
❑31, Mar 87, KGa, A Plague Of Frogs, Captain America	1.50	0.40	1.00	2.00
❑32, May 87, Captain America	1.50	0.40	1.00	2.00
❑33, Jul 87, Shadows on the Soul!, Wolverine; X-Men	1.50	0.40	1.00	2.00
❑34, Sep 87, Warriors Three	1.50	0.40	1.00	2.00
❑35, Nov 87, Hogun's Goat, Warriors Three	1.50	0.40	1.00	2.00
❑36, Jan 88, Warriors Three	1.50	0.40	1.00	2.00
❑37, Mar 88, Warriors Three	1.50	0.40	1.00	2.00
❑38, Apr 88, Moon Knight	1.50	0.40	1.00	2.00
❑39, Aug 88, Hawkeye; Moon Knight	1.95	0.40	1.00	2.00
❑40, Oct 88, Chiaroscuro, Angel; Storm	1.95	0.40	1.00	2.00
❑41, Dec 88, DG, Doctor Strange	1.95	0.40	1.00	2.00
❑42, Feb 89, Windfall!, Spider-Man	1.95	0.40	1.00	2.00
❑43, Apr 89, Sub-Mariner; Human Torch	1.95	0.40	1.00	2.00
❑44, Jun 89, Doom Bug, Iron Man; Iron Man vs. Doctor Doom	1.95	0.40	1.00	2.00
❑45, Aug 89, JBy (c), all pin-ups	1.95	0.40	1.00	2.00
❑46, Oct 89, Fantastic Four	1.95	0.40	1.00	2.00
❑47, Nov 89, Spider-Man; Hulk	1.95	0.40	1.00	2.00
❑48, Dec 89, She-Hulk	1.95	0.40	1.00	2.00
❑49, Feb 90, Doctor Strange; Dr. Strange	1.95	0.40	1.00	2.00
❑50, Apr 90, X-Factor	2.25	0.45	1.13	2.25
❑51, Jun 90, Silver Surfer	2.95	0.59	1.48	2.95
❑52, Aug 90, Black Knight; Fantastic Four	2.25	0.45	1.13	2.25
❑53, Oct 90, Black Knight; Doctor Strange	2.25	0.45	1.13	2.25
❑54, Dec 90, Black Knight; Wolverine	2.25	0.45	1.13	2.25
❑55, Feb 91, Power Pack; Wolverine	2.25	0.45	1.13	2.25
❑56, Apr 91, Shanna the She-Devil	2.25	0.45	1.13	2.25
❑57, Jun 91, Captain Marvel; Shanna the She-Devil	2.25	0.45	1.13	2.25
❑58, Aug 91, Shanna the She-Devil; Vision II (android); Scarlet Witch	2.25	0.45	1.13	2.25
❑59, Oct 91, Shanna the She-Devil	2.25	0.45	1.13	2.25
❑60, Final Issue; Black Panther; Rogue; Daredevil	2.25	0.45	1.13	2.25

MARVEL FANFARE (2ND SERIES)

MARVEL

	ORIG	GOOD	FINE	N-MINT
❑1, Sep 96, Fateful Choices, A: Falcon; A: Deathlok; A: Captain America	0.99	0.20	0.50	1.00
❑2, Oct 96, Instinct, Part 1, A: Wolverine; A: Hulk; A: Wendigo	0.99	0.20	0.50	1.00
❑3, Nov 96, Instinct, Part 2, A: Spider-Man; A: Ghost Rider	0.99	0.20	0.50	1.00
❑4, Dec 96, A: Longshot	0.99	0.20	0.50	1.00
❑5, Jan 97, Life Lessons, V: Spiral; A: Longshot; A: Dazzler	0.99	0.20	0.50	1.00
❑6, Feb 97, Second Chances, A: Iron Fist; A: Power Man; V: Sabretooth	0.99	0.20	0.50	1.00

MARVEL FEATURE (1ST SERIES)
MARVEL

	ORIG	GOOD	FINE	N-MINT
❑1, Dec 71, RA, NA (c), The Day of the Defenders!, 1: Defenders; 1: Omegatron; D: Yandroth (physical body)	0.25	15.00	37.50	75.00
❑2, Mar 72, BEv, 2: Defenders, Sub-Mariner reprint	0.25	7.20	18.00	36.00
❑3, Jun 72, BEv, A: Defenders, Defenders	0.20	7.00	17.50	35.00
❑4, Jul 72, A: Ant-Man; A: Peter Parker	0.20	2.40	6.00	12.00
❑5, Sep 72, A: Ant-Man	0.20	1.20	3.00	6.00
❑6, Nov 72, A: Ant-Man	0.20	1.20	3.00	6.00
❑7, Jan 73, GK, A: Ant-Man	0.20	1.20	3.00	6.00
❑8, Mar 73, O: Wasp; A: Ant-Man	0.20	1.20	3.00	6.00
❑9, May 73, CR, The Killer Is My Wife, A: Ant-Man; A: Iron Man	0.20	1.20	3.00	6.00
❑10, Jul 73, CR, Ant-Man No More!, A: Ant-Man	0.20	1.20	3.00	6.00
❑11, Sep 73, Thing vs. Hulk	0.20	2.20	5.50	11.00
❑12, Nov 73, A: Thanos; A: Iron Man; A: Thing	0.20	1.80	4.50	9.00

MARVEL FEATURE (2ND SERIES)
MARVEL

	ORIG	GOOD	FINE	N-MINT
❑1, Nov 75, NA; DG, The Temple Of Abomination, Red Sonja stories begin; Reprints Savage Sword of Conan #1	0.25	0.90	2.25	4.50
❑2, Jan 76, FT, Blood Of The Hunter	0.25	0.55	1.38	2.75
❑3, Mar 76, FT, Balek-Lives!	0.25	0.55	1.38	2.75
❑4, May 76, FT, Eyes Of The Gorgon	0.25	0.55	1.38	2.75
❑5, Jul 76, FT, The Bear Gold Walks!	0.25	0.55	1.38	2.75
❑6, Sep 76, Beware The Sacred Sons Of Set!, A: Conan	0.30	0.55	1.38	2.75
❑7, Nov 76, The Battle Of The Barbarians, Red Sonja vs. Conan	0.30	0.55	1.38	2.75

MARVEL FRONTIER COMICS UNLIMITED
MARVEL

Value: Cover or less

❑1, Jan 94, Immortalis: That Sleep of Death, Savage Illusions; Children of Voyager 2.95

MARVEL FUMETTI BOOK, THE
MARVEL

	ORIG	GOOD	FINE	N-MINT
❑1, Apr 84, b&w; photos with balloon captions	1.00	0.40	1.00	2.00

MARVEL GRAPHIC NOVEL
MARVEL

	ORIG	GOOD	FINE	N-MINT
❑1, JSn, JSn (w), D: Captain Marvel	5.95	2.50	6.25	12.50
❑1-2, JSn, JSn (w), D: Captain Marvel, 2nd Printing	5.95	1.20	3.00	6.00
❑, JSn, JSn (w), D: Captain Marvel, 3rd Printing	5.95	1.20	3.00	6.00
❑2, CR, Elric	4.95	1.40	3.50	7.00
❑3, JSn, JSn (w), Dreadstar	4.95	1.50	3.75	7.50
❑4, BMc, 1: New Mutants; 1: Sunspot; 1: Mirage II (Danielle "Dani" Moonstar)	4.95	2.00	5.00	10.00
❑4-2, BMc, 1: New Mutants; 1: Sunspot; 1: Mirage II (Danielle "Dani" Moonstar), 2nd Printing	4.95	1.20	3.00	6.00
❑4-3, BMc, 1: New Mutants; 1: Sunspot; 1: Mirage II (Danielle "Dani" Moonstar), 3rd Printing	4.95	1.00	2.50	5.00
❑5, BA, X-Men: God Loves, Man Kills	5.95	2.00	5.00	10.00
❑5-2, BA, 2nd Printing; X-Men: God Loves, Man Kills	5.95	1.40	3.50	7.00
❑5-3, BA, 3rd Printing; X-Men: God Loves, Man Kills	5.95	1.20	3.00	6.00
❑5-4, BA, 4th Printing; X-Men: God Loves, Man Kills	5.95	1.20	3.00	6.00
❑5-5, BA, 5th Printing; X-Men: God Loves, Man Kills	5.95	1.20	3.00	6.00
❑6, Star Slammers	5.95	1.20	3.00	6.00
❑7, CR, Killraven	5.95	1.20	3.00	6.00
❑8, JBy, Super Boxers	5.95	1.20	3.00	6.00
❑9, DC, DC (w), The Futurians	5.95	1.20	3.00	6.00
❑10, Heartburst	5.95	1.20	3.00	6.00
❑11, VM, Void Indigo	5.95	1.20	3.00	6.00
❑12, FS, Dazzler: The Movie	5.95	1.20	3.00	6.00
❑13, Starstruck	5.95	1.20	3.00	6.00
❑14, Swords of the Swashbucklers	5.95	1.20	3.00	6.00
❑15, CV, Raven Banner	5.95	1.20	3.00	6.00
❑16, Aladdin Effect	5.95	1.20	3.00	6.00
❑17, Living Monolith	5.95	1.20	3.00	6.00
❑18, JBy (w), She-Hulk	6.95	1.40	3.50	7.00
❑19, The Witch Queen of Acheron, Conan the Barbarian	6.95	1.40	3.50	7.00
❑20, Greenberg the Vampire	6.95	1.40	3.50	7.00
❑21, Marada the She-Wolf	6.95	1.40	3.50	7.00
❑22, BWr, Amazing Spider-Man	6.95	1.80	4.50	9.00
❑23, DGr, Shamballa, Dr. Strange	6.95	1.40	3.50	7.00
❑24, Daredevil	6.95	1.50	3.75	7.50
❑25, Dracula	6.95	1.40	3.50	7.00
❑26, Alien Legion	6.95	1.40	3.50	7.00
❑27, D: The Purple Man, Avengers	6.95	1.39	3.47	6.95

A four-part Black Widow story by George Pérez appeared in *Marvel Fanfare* #10-13.

	ORIG	GOOD	FINE	N-MINT
❑28, Conan the Reaver	6.95	1.39	3.47	6.95
❑29, Thing vs. Hulk	6.95	1.60	4.00	8.00
❑30, Sailor's Story	6.95	1.39	3.47	6.95
❑31, 1: Wolfpack, Wolfpack	6.95	1.39	3.47	6.95
❑32, D: Groo	6.95	2.00	5.00	10.00
❑33, Thor	6.95	1.39	3.47	6.95
❑34, Cloak & Dagger	6.95	1.39	3.47	6.95
❑35, Willow	6.95	1.39	3.47	6.95
❑36, Hard-cover; Shadow	12.95	2.59	6.47	12.95
❑37, Hercules	6.95	1.40	3.50	7.00
❑38, Silver Surfer	14.95	3.20	8.00	16.00

MARVEL GRAPHIC NOVEL: ARENA
MARVEL

Value: Cover or less

❑1 .... 5.95

MARVEL GRAPHIC NOVEL: CLOAK AND DAGGER AND POWER PACK: SHELTER FROM THE STORM
MARVEL

Value: Cover or less

❑1 .... 7.95

MARVEL GRAPHIC NOVEL: EMPEROR DOOM-STARRING THE MIGHTY AVENGERS
MARVEL

Value: Cover or less

❑1, BH 5.95

MARVEL GRAPHIC NOVEL: KA-ZAR: GUNS OF THE SAVAGE LAND
MARVEL

Value: Cover or less

❑1 .... 8.95

MARVEL GRAPHIC NOVEL: RICK MASON, THE AGENT
MARVEL

Value: Cover or less

❑1 .... 9.95

MARVEL GRAPHIC NOVEL: ROGER RABBIT IN THE RESURRECTION OF DOOM
MARVEL

Value: Cover or less

❑1, DS, The Resurrection of Doom; Tummy Trouble 8.95

MARVEL GRAPHIC NOVEL: WHO FRAMED ROGER RABBIT?
MARVEL

Value: Cover or less

❑1, DS, movie Adaptation 6.95

MARVEL GUIDE TO COLLECTING COMICS, THE
MARVEL

	ORIG	GOOD	FINE	N-MINT
❑1, Sep 82, no cover price	—	0.40	1.00	2.00

MARVEL HALLOWEEN: SUPERNATURALS TOUR BOOK
MARVEL

Value: Cover or less

❑1 .... 2.99

MARVEL: HEROES & LEGENDS
MARVEL

Value: Cover or less

❑1, Oct 96, JR2; SB; JB; GC; SD, For Better And For Worse!, wraparound cover; backstory on Reed and Sue's wedding 2.95

❑2, Nov 97, nn; untold Avengers story; Hawkeye, Quicksilver, Scarlet Witch joins team 2.99

MARVEL HOLIDAY SPECIAL
MARVEL

	ORIG	GOOD	FINE	N-MINT
❑1, A Miracle A Few Blocks Down From 34th Street; A Christmas Coda, nn; no cover date or date in indicia	2.25	0.60	1.50	3.00
❑1992, Zounds O' Silence; The Big X-Mas Blackout, nn; for 1992 holiday season	2.95	0.60	1.50	3.00
❑1993, Jan 94, nn; for 1993 holiday season	2.95	0.60	1.50	3.00
❑1994, Catastrophe on 34th Street; A Midnight Clear, nn; for 1994 holiday season	2.95	0.60	1.50	3.00
❑1996	2.95	0.59	1.48	2.95

MARVEL ILLUSTRATED: SWIMSUIT ISSUE
MARVEL

Value: Cover or less

❑1, Mar 91 .... 3.95

MARVEL KNIGHTS
MARVEL

	ORIG	GOOD	FINE	N-MINT
❑1, Jul 00, The Burrowers	2.99	0.60	1.50	2.99
❑1/A, Jul 00, The Burrowers, Daredevil close-up cover	—	1.30	3.25	6.50
❑2, Aug 00, Thunder Below, A: Ulik	2.99	0.60	1.50	2.99
❑3, Sep 00, The Destroyers, A: Ulik	2.99	0.60	1.50	2.99
❑4, Oct 00, Zaran	2.99	0.60	1.50	2.99

	ORIG	GOOD	FINE	N-MINT
❑5, Nov 00, Family and Friends	2.99	0.60	1.50	2.99
❑6, Dec 00, Maximum Security; The Reckoning	2.99	0.60	1.50	2.99
❑7, Jan 01, Strange Matters	2.99	0.60	1.50	2.99
❑8, Feb 01, Dark Matters	2.99	0.60	1.50	2.99
❑9, Mar 01, Final Matters	2.99	0.60	1.50	2.99
❑10, Apr 01, The Good with the Bad	2.99	0.60	1.50	2.99
❑11	2.99	0.60	1.50	2.99
❑12	2.99	0.60	1.50	2.99
❑13	2.99	0.60	1.50	2.99
❑14	2.99	0.60	1.50	2.99
❑15	2.99	0.60	1.50	2.99

MARVEL KNIGHTS/MARVEL BOY GENESIS EDITION
MARVEL

	ORIG	GOOD	FINE	N-MINT
❑1, Jun 00, Polybagged with Punisher (5th Series) #3	—	0.20	0.50	1.00

MARVEL KNIGHTS SKETCHBOOK
MARVEL

	ORIG	GOOD	FINE	N-MINT
❑1, Bundled with Wizard #84	—	0.20	0.50	1.00

MARVEL KNIGHTS TOUR BOOK
MARVEL

Value: Cover or less

❑1, nn; previews and interviews 2.99

MARVEL KNIGHTS WAVE 2 SKETCHBOOK
MARVEL

	ORIG	GOOD	FINE	N-MINT
❑1, Special free edition from Marvel in Wizard #90; Sketchbook	—	0.10	0.25	0.50

MARVEL MASTERPIECES 2 COLLECTION, THE
MARVEL

Value: Cover or less

❑1, Jul 94, Pin-ups 2.95
❑2, Aug 94 .... 2.95
❑3, Sep 94 .... 2.95

MARVEL MASTERPIECES COLLECTION
MARVEL

Value: Cover or less

❑1 .... 2.95
❑2 .... 2.95
❑3 .... 2.95
❑4 .... 2.95

MARVEL MILESTONE EDITION: AMAZING FANTASY
MARVEL

Value: Cover or less

❑15, Mar 92, SD, SL (w), Spider-Man!; The Bell Ringer, Reprint; Reprints of Amazing Fantasy # 15: Spider-man's Origin 2.95

MARVEL MILESTONE EDITION: AMAZING SPIDER-MAN
MARVEL

Value: Cover or less

❑1, SD, SL (w), The Chameleon Strikes!, 1: Chameleon; 1: J. Jonah Jameson; O: Spider-Man; 1: John Jameson; A: Fantastic Four, Reprints Amazing Spider-Man #1 .... 2.95
❑3, Mar 95, SD, SL (w), Spider-Man Versus Doctor Octopus, 1: Doctor Octopus, Reprints Amazing Spider-Man #3 .... 2.95
❑129, 1: Jackal; 1: the Punisher; O: Punisher, Reprints Amazing Spider-Man #129 .... 2.95
❑149, Nov 94, RA, Even If I Live, I Die!, 1: Ben Reilly (Spider-Man clone), indicia says Marvel Milestone Edition: Amazing Spider-Man #1; Reprints Amazing Spider-Man #149 .... 2.95

MARVEL MILESTONE EDITION: AVENGERS
MARVEL

Value: Cover or less

❑1, Sep 93, JK, SL (w); O: Avengers, Reprints The Avengers #1; Thor, Iron Man, Ant-man, Wasp, Hulk 2.95
❑4, Mar 95, JK, SL (w), Reprints The Avengers #4; Captain America Joins 2.95
❑16, JK, SL (w); JK (w), The Old Order Changeth, Reprints The Avengers #16; New team begins: Captain America, Hawkeye, Quicksilver, and Scarlet Witch 2.95

MARVEL MILESTONE EDITION: CAPTAIN AMERICA
MARVEL

Value: Cover or less

❑1, Mar 95, Reprints Captain America #1 .... 3.95

MARVEL MILESTONE EDITION: FANTASTIC FOUR
MARVEL

Value: Cover or less

❑1 .... 2.95
❑5 .... 2.95

MARVEL MILESTONE EDITION: GIANT-SIZE X-MEN
MARVEL

Value: Cover or less

❑1 .... 3.95

MARVEL MILESTONE EDITION: INCREDIBLE HULK
MARVEL

Value: Cover or less

❑1, Mar 91, SL; JK, SL (w); JK (w), The Coming of The Hulk; The Hulk Strikes, Reprints Incredible Hulk #1 .... 2.95

MARVEL MILESTONE EDITION: IRON FIST
MARVEL

Value: Cover or less

❑14, JBy, Snowfire, 1: Sabretooth 2.95

MARVEL MILESTONE EDITION: IRON MAN
MARVEL

Value: Cover or less

❑55, Nov 92, JSn, JSn (w), Beware the Blood Brothers!, 1: Starfox; 1: Drax; 1: Thanos, Reprints Iron Man #55 .... 2.95

MARVEL MILESTONE EDITION: TALES OF SUSPENSE
MARVEL

Value: Cover or less

❑39, Nov 94, DH; SD, Iron Man is Born; Gundar, 1: Iron Man, Reprints Tales of Suspense #39 .... 2.95

MARVEL MILESTONE EDITION: X-MEN
MARVEL

Value: Cover or less

❑1, JK, SL (w), X-Men, 1: Magneto; 1: X-Men, reprint (first series) 2.95
❑9, JK, SL (w), A: Avengers; 1: Lucifer, Reprints X-Men (1st Series) #9 .... 2.95
❑28, Nov 94, 1: Banshee, indicia says Marvel Milestone Edition: X-Men #1; Reprints X-Men (1st Series) #28 .... 2.95

MARVEL MOVIE PREMIERE
MARVEL

	ORIG	GOOD	FINE	N-MINT
❑1, The Land that Time Forgot, b&w; magazine	1.00	0.60	1.50	3.00

MARVEL MYSTERY COMICS (2ND SERIES)
MARVEL

Value: Cover or less

❑1, Dec 99, JK; BEv, Human Torch: The Parrot Strikes Back!; The Vision, Reprint 3.95

MARVEL NO-PRIZE BOOK, THE
MARVEL

	ORIG	GOOD	FINE	N-MINT
❑1, Jan 83, JK, SL (w), Lest We Should Goof...!, mistakes	1.00	0.40	1.00	2.00

MARVELOUS DRAGON CLAN
LUNAR

Value: Cover or less

❑1, Jul 94, b&w 2.50
❑2, Sep 94, b&w 2.50

MARVELOUS WIZARD OF OZ (MGM'S...)
MARVEL

	ORIG	GOOD	FINE	N-MINT
❑1, treasury-sized movie adaptation	1.50	3.00	7.50	15.00

MARVEL: PORTRAITS OF A UNIVERSE
MARVEL

Value: Cover or less

❑1, DaG 2.95
❑2 .... 2.95
❑3 .... 2.95
❑4 .... 2.95

MARVEL POSTER BOOK
MARVEL

Value: Cover or less

❑1, Jan 91, TMc 2.50

MARVEL PREMIERE
MARVEL

	ORIG	GOOD	FINE	N-MINT
❑1, Apr 72, GK, And Men Shall Call Him...Warlock!, O: Warlock; O: Counter-Earth	0.20	4.40	11.00	22.00
❑2, May 72, JK, A: Warlock, Yellow Claw	0.20	2.60	6.50	13.00
❑3, Jul 72, A: Doctor Strange	0.20	4.00	10.00	20.00
❑4, FB, A: Doctor Strange	0.20	1.80	4.50	9.00
❑5, CR; MP, A: Doctor Strange	0.20	1.40	3.50	7.00
❑6, MP; FB, A: Doctor Strange	0.20	1.40	3.50	7.00
❑7, CR; MP, A: Doctor Strange	0.20	1.40	3.50	7.00
❑8, JSn, A: Doctor Strange	0.20	1.40	3.50	7.00
❑9, Jul 73, FB, A: Doctor Strange	0.20	1.40	3.50	7.00
❑10, NA; FB, A: Doctor Strange; D: The Ancient One	0.20	1.60	4.00	8.00
❑11, NA; FB, A: Doctor Strange	0.20	1.00	2.50	5.00
❑12, NA; FB, A: Doctor Strange	0.20	1.00	2.50	5.00
❑13, Jan 74, NA; FB, 1: Sise-Neg (as Cagliostro); A: Doctor Strange	0.20	1.00	2.50	5.00
❑14, Mar 74, NA; FB, A: Doctor Strange; A: Sise-Neg	0.20	1.00	2.50	5.00
❑15, May 74, GK, 1: Iron Fist	0.25	7.00	17.50	35.00
❑16, Jul 74, 2: Iron Fist	0.25	3.60	9.00	18.00
❑17, Sep 74, A: Iron Fist	0.25	1.80	4.50	9.00
❑18, Oct 74, A: Iron Fist	0.25	1.80	4.50	9.00
❑19, Nov 74, A: Iron Fist; 1: Colleen Wing	0.25	1.80	4.50	9.00
❑20, Jan 75, A: Iron Fist	0.25	1.80	4.50	9.00
❑21, Mar 75, A: Iron Fist	0.25	1.80	4.50	9.00
❑22, Jun 75, A: Iron Fist	0.25	1.80	4.50	9.00
❑23, Aug 75, PB, A: Iron Fist	0.25	1.80	4.50	9.00
❑24, Sep 75, PB, A: Iron Fist	0.25	1.80	4.50	9.00
❑25, Oct 75, JBy, A: Iron Fist	0.25	2.80	7.00	14.00
❑26, Nov 75, JK, A: Hercules	0.25	0.80	2.00	4.00
❑27, A: Satana	0.25	0.80	2.00	4.00
❑28, Dec 75, A: Morbius; A: Legion of Monsters; A: Ghost Rider; A: Man-Thing; A: Werewolf	0.25	1.00	2.50	5.00
❑29, Apr 76, JK, O: Miss America; 1: Blue Diamond; 1: Thin Man; 1: Jack Frost I; O: Red Raven; 1: Patriot; A: Liberty Legion; O: Whizzer	0.25	0.60	1.50	3.00
❑30, Jun 76, JK, A: Liberty Legion	0.25	0.50	1.25	2.50
❑31, Aug 76, JK, 1: Woodgod	0.25	0.40	1.00	2.00
❑32, Oct 76, HC, Monark Starstalker	0.30	0.40	1.00	2.00
❑33, Dec 76, HC, A: Solomon Kane, Monark	0.30	0.40	1.00	2.00
❑34, Feb 77, HC, A: Solomon Kane	0.30	0.40	1.00	2.00

	ORIG	GOOD	FINE	N-MINT
❑35, Apr 77, The 3-D Man!, 1: 3-D Man	0.30	0.40	1.00	2.00
❑36, Jun 77, The Devil's Music, A: 3-D Man	0.30	0.40	1.00	2.00
❑37, Aug 77, Code-Name: The Cold Warrior!, A: 3-D Man	0.30	0.40	1.00	2.00
❑38, Oct 77, 1: Weirdworld	0.30	0.40	1.00	2.00
❑39, Dec 77, A: Torpedo	0.35	0.40	1.00	2.00
❑40, Feb 78, A: Torpedo; 1: Bucky II (Fred Davis)	0.35	0.40	1.00	2.00
❑41, Apr 78, TS, The Dying Sun!, A: Seeker 3000	0.35	0.40	1.00	2.00
❑42, Jun 78, Nightmare's Evolution, A: Tigra, Tigra	0.35	0.40	1.00	2.00
❑43, Aug 78, TS, In Manhattan, They Play For Keeps, 1: Paladin	0.35	0.40	1.00	2.00
❑44, Oct 78, KG, A: Jack of Hearts, Jack of Hearts	0.35	0.40	1.00	2.00
❑45, Dec 78, A: Man-Wolf, Man-Wolf	0.35	0.40	1.00	2.00
❑46, Feb 79, GP, A: Man-Wolf, War God	0.35	0.40	1.00	2.00
❑47, Apr 79, JBy, 1: Ant-Man	0.35	0.40	1.00	2.00
❑48, Jun 79, BL; JBy, The Price Of A Heart!, A: Ant-Man	0.40	0.40	1.00	2.00
❑49, Aug 79, A: The Falcon	0.40	0.40	1.00	2.00
❑50, Oct 79, From The Inside, 1: Alice Cooper	0.40	1.60	4.00	8.00
❑51, Dec 79, A: Black Panther	0.40	0.40	1.00	2.00
❑52, Feb 80, A: Black Panther	0.40	0.40	1.00	2.00
❑53, Apr 80, A: Black Panther	0.40	0.40	1.00	2.00
❑54, Jun 80, GD, 1: Caleb Hammer	0.40	0.40	1.00	2.00
❑55, Aug 80, A: Wonder Man	0.40	0.40	1.00	2.00
❑56, Oct 80, TD; HC, A: Dominic Fortune	0.50	0.40	1.00	2.00
❑57, Dec 80, 1: Doctor Who (in U.S.)	0.50	0.60	1.50	3.00
❑58, Feb 81, TD; FM, A: Doctor Who	0.50	0.50	1.25	2.50
❑59, Apr 81, A: Doctor Who	0.50	0.50	1.25	2.50
❑60, Jun 81, A: Doctor Who	0.50	0.50	1.25	2.50
❑61, Aug 81, TS, A: Star-Lord	0.50	0.40	1.00	2.00

MARVEL PRESENTS
MARVEL

	ORIG	GOOD	FINE	N-MINT
❑1, Dweller From The Depths!, 1: Bloodstone	0.25	0.80	2.00	4.00
❑2, The Hellfire Helix Hex!, O: Bloodstone	0.25	0.60	1.50	3.00
❑3, Feb 76, A: Guardians of the Galaxy	0.25	0.80	2.00	4.00
❑4, May 76, A: Guardians of the Galaxy; 1: Nikki	0.25	0.80	2.00	4.00
❑5, Jun 76, A: Guardians of the Galaxy	0.25	0.80	2.00	4.00
❑6, Aug 76, A: Guardians of the Galaxy; V: Planetary Man	0.25	0.70	1.75	3.50
❑7, Nov 76, A: Guardians of the Galaxy	0.30	0.70	1.75	3.50
❑8, Dec 76, A: Guardians of the Galaxy, reprints Silver Surfer #2	0.30	0.70	1.75	3.50
❑9, Feb 77, A: Guardians of the Galaxy; O: Starhawk II (Aleta)	0.30	0.70	1.75	3.50
❑10, Apr 77, A: Guardians of the Galaxy; O: Starhawk II (Aleta)	0.30	0.70	1.75	3.50
❑11, Jun 77, A: Guardians of the Galaxy	0.30	0.70	1.75	3.50
❑12, Aug 77, A: Guardians of the Galaxy	0.30	0.70	1.75	3.50

MARVEL PREVIEW
MARVEL

	ORIG	GOOD	FINE	N-MINT
❑1, Sum 75, Man Gods From Beyond the Stars	1.00	0.50	1.25	2.50
❑2, 1: Dominic Fortune; O: the Punisher	1.00	5.00	12.50	25.00
❑3, Sep 75, Blade the Vampire Slayer	1.00	1.00	2.50	5.00
❑4, Jan 76, 1: Star-Lord	1.00	0.80	2.00	4.00
❑5, Sherlock Holmes	1.00	0.60	1.50	3.00
❑6, Sherlock Holmes	1.00	0.60	1.50	3.00
❑7, Sep 76, 1: Rocket Raccoon, Satanna	1.00	0.60	1.50	3.00
❑8, Fal 76, A: Legion of Monsters, Morbius, Blade	1.00	1.00	2.50	5.00
❑9, Apr 77, O: Star Hawk, Man-God	1.00	0.60	1.50	3.00
❑10, Jul 77, JSn, Thor	1.00	0.60	1.50	3.00
❑11, Oct 77, Star-Lord	1.00	0.60	1.50	3.00
❑12, Jan 78, Haunt of Horror	1.00	0.60	1.50	3.00
❑13, Apr 78, UFO	1.00	0.60	1.50	3.00
❑14, Aug 78, Star-Lord	1.00	0.60	1.50	3.00
❑15, Oct 78, Star-Lord	1.00	0.60	1.50	3.00
❑16, Mar 79, Detectives	1.00	0.60	1.50	3.00
❑17, May 79, Blackmark	1.00	0.60	1.50	3.00
❑18, Aug 79, Star-Lord	1.25	0.60	1.50	3.00
❑19, Nov 79, A: Kull	1.25	0.60	1.50	3.00
❑20, Mar 80, Bizarre Adventures	1.25	0.60	1.50	3.00
❑21, May 80, A: Moon Knight	1.25	0.60	1.50	3.00
❑22, Aug 80, Merlin; King Arthur	1.25	0.60	1.50	3.00
❑23, Nov 80, FM, Bizarre Adventures	1.25	0.60	1.50	3.00
❑24, Feb 81, Paradox; Title continues as "Bizarre Adventures" with #25	1.25	0.60	1.50	3.00

MARVEL PREVIEW '93
MARVEL

Value: Cover or less

❑1 .... 3.95

MARVEL RIOT
MARVEL

Value: Cover or less

❑1, Dec 95, wraparound cover; One-Shot; parodies Age of Apocalypse 1.95

Bloodstone also appeared in Marvel's black-and-white magazine line.

MARVELS
MARVEL

	ORIG	GOOD	FINE	N-MINT
❑0, Aug 94, ARo, KB (w), Plastic dust cover; collects promo art and Human Torch story from Marvel Age; Fully painted	2.95	0.70	1.75	3.50
❑1, Jan 94, ARo, KB (w), A Time Of Marvel, wraparound acetate outer cover; Torch, Sub-Mariner, Captain America; Torch, Sub-Mariner, Capt. America; Fully painted	4.95	1.00	2.50	5.00
❑1-2, Apr 96, ARo, KB (w), 2nd Printing	2.95	0.59	1.48	2.95
❑2, Feb 94, ARo, KB (w), Monsters, wraparound acetate outer cover; Fully painted	5.95	1.00	2.50	5.00
❑2-2, May 96, ARo, KB (w), 2nd Printing	2.95	0.59	1.48	2.95
❑3, Mar 94, ARo, KB (w), Judgement Day, wraparound acetate outer cover; Coming of Galactus; Fully painted	5.95	1.00	2.50	5.00
❑3-2, May 96, ARo, KB (w), 2nd Printing; wraparound cover	2.95	1.19	2.97	5.95
❑4, Apr 94, ARo, KB (w), The Day She Died, D: Gwen Stacy, wraparound acetate outer cover; Fully painted	5.95	1.00	2.50	5.00
❑4-2, Jun 96, ARo, KB (w), 2nd Printing; wraparound cover	2.95	0.59	1.48	2.95

MARVEL SAGA
MARVEL

	ORIG	GOOD	FINE	N-MINT
❑1, Dec 85, JBy (w), The Saga Begins…!, O: Alpha Flight; O: Fantastic Four; O: X-Men	1.00	0.40	1.00	2.00
❑2, Jan 86, Transformation And Rebirth, O: Spider-Man; O: Hulk	1.00	0.30	0.75	1.50
❑3, Feb 86, O: Doom; O: Sub-Mariner	1.00	0.30	0.75	1.50
❑4, Mar 86, DC; BA; FM; JK; HT; JBy; JB; ATh, Of Gods And Mutants, O: Thor	1.00	0.30	0.75	1.50
❑5, Apr 86, O: Angel; O: Iceman	1.00	0.30	0.75	1.50
❑6, May 86, GK; JK; GT; DH; JB, Love, Hate…And Sacrifice!, O: Odin; O: Asgard; O: Iron Man	1.00	0.30	0.75	1.50
❑7, Jun 86, BL; SD, The Ties That bind!	1.00	0.30	0.75	1.50
❑8, Jul 86, JK; DH; SD, Fateful Encounters!	1.00	0.30	0.75	1.50
❑9, Aug 86, O: Vulture	1.00	0.30	0.75	1.50
❑10, Sep 86, SL (w), The Stand United!, O: Avengers; O: Beast; O: Marvel Girl	1.00	0.30	0.75	1.50
❑11, Oct 86, O: Molecule Man	1.00	0.30	0.75	1.50
❑12, Nov 86, Captain America revived	1.00	0.30	0.75	1.50
❑13, Dec 86, FM (w), Evil Dared, O: Daredevil	1.00	0.30	0.75	1.50
❑14, Jan 87, SL (w), Confrontations!, O: Quicksilver; O: Scarlet Witch	1.00	0.30	0.75	1.50
❑15, Feb 87, O: Hawkeye; O: Wonder Man	1.00	0.30	0.75	1.50
❑16, Mar 87, GK; JK; DH; PS; GC; SD, Dread Reckonings!, O: Dormammu; O: Frightful Four	1.00	0.30	0.75	1.50
❑17, Apr 87, GK; JK; DH; VM; SD, Man's Inhumanity, O: Leader; O: Ka-Zar	1.00	0.30	0.75	1.50
❑18, May 87, JK; DH; SD, SL (w); SD (w), The Triumph And The Tragedy!, O: S.H.I.E.L.D.	1.00	0.30	0.75	1.50
❑19, Jun 87, new Avengers team	1.00	0.30	0.75	1.50
❑20, Jul 87	1.00	0.30	0.75	1.50
❑21, Aug 87, X-Men	1.00	0.30	0.75	1.50
❑22, Sep 87, O: Mary Jane	1.00	0.30	0.75	1.50
❑23, Oct 87, Inhumans	1.00	0.30	0.75	1.50
❑24, Nov 87, JSt; JK; JB, SL (w); JK (w), O: Galactus	1.00	0.30	0.75	1.50
❑25, Dec 87, JSt; JK; JB, SL (w); JK (w), Reborn!, O: Silver Surfer, Final Issue	1.00	0.30	0.75	1.50

MARVELS COMICS: CAPTAIN AMERICA
MARVEL

Value: Cover or less

❑1, Jul 00, PD (w), Time Rip, Part 5 .... 2.25

MARVELS COMICS: DAREDEVIL
MARVEL

Value: Cover or less

❑1, Jun 00, Angel 2.25

MARVELS COMICS: FANTASTIC FOUR
MARVEL

Value: Cover or less

❑1, May 00, PS, The Life F antastic! 2.25

MARVELS COMICS: SPIDER-MAN
MARVEL

Value: Cover or less

❑1, Jul 00, The Menace of Spider-Man 2.25

MARVELS COMICS: THOR
MARVEL

Value: Cover or less

❑1, Jul 00, Friendly Fire 2.25

MARVELS COMICS: X-MEN
MARVEL

Value: Cover or less

❑1, Jun 00, How I Learned to Love the Bomb 2.25

MARVEL SELECTS: FANTASTIC FOUR
MARVEL

Value: Cover or less

❑1, Jan 00, JB, SL (w), And Now...The Thing! 2.75

MARVEL SELECTS: SPIDER-MAN
MARVEL

Value: Cover or less

❑1, Jan 00, GK, SL (w), The Spider or the Man?, Reprints Amazing Spider-Man #100 .... 2.75

❑2 .... 2.75

❑3 .... 2.75

MARVEL'S GREATEST COMICS
MARVEL

	ORIG	GOOD	FINE	N-MINT
❑23, Reprint; Giant-size; Title continued from "Marvel Collector's Item Classics"	0.25	1.20	3.00	6.00
❑24, Dec 69, Giant-size	0.25	1.20	3.00	6.00
❑25, Feb 70, Giant-size	0.25	1.20	3.00	6.00
❑26, Giant-size	0.25	1.20	3.00	6.00
❑27, Giant-size	0.25	1.20	3.00	6.00
❑28, Giant-size	0.25	1.20	3.00	6.00
❑29, Giant-size	0.25	1.20	3.00	6.00
❑30, Giant-size	0.25	1.20	3.00	6.00
❑31, Giant-size	0.25	1.20	3.00	6.00
❑32, Giant-size	0.25	1.20	3.00	6.00
❑33, Giant-size	0.25	1.20	3.00	6.00
❑34, Giant-size	0.25	1.20	3.00	6.00
❑35, A: Silver Surfer, Reprinted from Fantastic Four	0.20	1.00	2.50	5.00
❑36	0.20	1.00	2.50	5.00
❑37	0.20	1.00	2.50	5.00
❑38	0.20	0.70	1.75	3.50
❑39	0.20	0.70	1.75	3.50
❑40	0.20	0.70	1.75	3.50
❑41	0.20	0.70	1.75	3.50
❑42	0.20	0.70	1.75	3.50
❑43	0.20	0.70	1.75	3.50
❑44	0.20	0.70	1.75	3.50
❑45	0.20	0.70	1.75	3.50
❑46	0.20	0.70	1.75	3.50
❑47	0.20	0.70	1.75	3.50
❑48	0.20	0.70	1.75	3.50
❑49	0.25	0.70	1.75	3.50
❑50, A: Warlock (Him), Reprinted from Fantastic Four	0.25	0.80	2.00	4.00
❑51	0.25	0.60	1.50	3.00
❑52	0.25	0.50	1.25	2.50
❑53	0.25	0.50	1.25	2.50
❑54, Jan 75	0.25	0.50	1.25	2.50
❑55	0.25	0.50	1.25	2.50
❑56	0.25	0.50	1.25	2.50
❑57	0.25	0.50	1.25	2.50
❑58, Sep 75	0.25	0.50	1.25	2.50
❑59	0.25	0.50	1.25	2.50
❑60	0.25	0.50	1.25	2.50
❑61	0.25	0.50	1.25	2.50
❑62	0.25	0.50	1.25	2.50
❑63	0.25	0.50	1.25	2.50
❑64	0.25	0.50	1.25	2.50
❑65, Sep 76	0.30	0.50	1.25	2.50
❑66, Oct 76	0.30	0.50	1.25	2.50
❑67, Nov 76	0.30	0.50	1.25	2.50
❑68, Jan 77	0.30	0.50	1.25	2.50
❑69, Mar 77	0.30	0.50	1.25	2.50
❑70, May 77	0.30	0.50	1.25	2.50
❑71, Jul 77	0.30	0.40	1.00	2.00
❑72, Sep 77	0.30	0.40	1.00	2.00
❑73, Oct 77	0.30	0.40	1.00	2.00
❑74, Nov 77	0.35	0.40	1.00	2.00
❑75, Jan 78	0.35	0.40	1.00	2.00
❑76, Mar 78	0.35	0.40	1.00	2.00
❑77, May 78	0.35	0.40	1.00	2.00
❑78, Jul 78, reprints Fantastic Four #97	0.35	0.40	1.00	2.00
❑79, Sep 78	0.35	0.40	1.00	2.00
❑80, Nov 78	0.35	0.40	1.00	2.00
❑81, Jan 79	0.35	0.40	1.00	2.00
❑82, Mar 79	0.35	0.40	1.00	2.00
❑83, Dec 79	0.35	0.40	1.00	2.00
❑84, Jan 80	0.35	0.40	1.00	2.00
❑85, Feb 80	0.35	0.40	1.00	2.00
❑86, Mar 80	0.35	0.40	1.00	2.00
❑87, Apr 80	0.35	0.40	1.00	2.00
❑88, May 80	0.40	0.40	1.00	2.00
❑89, Jun 80	0.40	0.40	1.00	2.00
❑90, Jul 80	0.40	0.40	1.00	2.00
❑91, Aug 80	0.40	0.40	1.00	2.00
❑92, Sep 80, reprints Fantastic Four #112	0.50	0.40	1.00	2.00
❑93, Oct 80	0.40	0.40	1.00	2.00
❑94, Nov 80	0.40	0.40	1.00	2.00
❑95, Dec 80	0.40	0.40	1.00	2.00
❑96, Jan 81	0.40	0.40	1.00	2.00

MARVEL: SHADOWS & LIGHT
MARVEL

Value: Cover or less

❑1, Feb 97, MG, MG (w), Wolverine: The Spoon Job; Dracula: Into the Tomb, b&w; wraparound cover; Wolverine, Dracula, Doctor Strange, Captain Marvel 2.95

MARVEL SPECIAL EDITION FEATURING CLOSE ENCOUNTERS OF THE THIRD KIND
MARVEL

	ORIG	GOOD	FINE	N-MINT
❑3, treasury-sized; adapts Close Encounters of the Third Kind	1.50	1.40	3.50	7.00

MARVEL SPECIAL EDITION FEATURING SPECTACULAR SPIDER-MAN
MARVEL

	ORIG	GOOD	FINE	N-MINT
❑1, treasury-sized	1.50	2.00	5.00	10.00

MARVEL SPECIAL EDITION FEATURING STAR WARS
MARVEL

	ORIG	GOOD	FINE	N-MINT
❑1, treasury-sized adaption of Star Wars	1.00	2.40	6.00	12.00
❑2, treasury-sized adaption of Star Wars	1.00	2.00	5.00	10.00
❑3, treasury-sized; collects previous two issues	2.50	2.40	6.00	12.00

MARVEL SPECTACULAR
MARVEL

	ORIG	GOOD	FINE	N-MINT
❑1, Aug 73, JK, SL (w), reprints Thor #128	0.20	1.00	2.50	5.00
❑2, JK, SL (w), reprints Thor #129	0.20	0.60	1.50	3.00
❑3, JK, SL (w), Thunder in the Netherworld!, 1: Tana Nile (in real form), reprints Thor #130	0.20	0.60	1.50	3.00
❑4, JK, SL (w), reprints Thor #133	0.20	0.60	1.50	3.00
❑5, JK, SL (w), reprints Thor #134	0.20	0.60	1.50	3.00
❑6, JK, SL (w), reprints Tales of Asgard from Journey Into Mystery #121 and Thor #135	0.20	0.60	1.50	3.00
❑7, JK, SL (w), reprints Thor #136	0.25	0.60	1.50	3.00
❑8, Jul 74, JK, SL (w), reprints Thor #137	0.25	0.60	1.50	3.00
❑9, JK, SL (w), reprints Thor #138	0.25	0.60	1.50	3.00
❑10, JK, SL (w), reprints Thor #139	0.25	0.60	1.50	3.00
❑11, JK, SL (w), reprints Thor #140	0.25	0.40	1.00	2.00
❑12, JK, SL (w), reprints Thor #141	0.25	0.40	1.00	2.00
❑13, JK, SL (w), reprints Thor #142	0.25	0.40	1.00	2.00
❑14, JK, SL (w), reprints Thor #143	0.25	0.40	1.00	2.00
❑15, Jun 75, JK, SL (w), reprints Thor #144	0.25	0.40	1.00	2.00
❑16, JK, SL (w), reprints Thor #145	0.25	0.40	1.00	2.00
❑17, JK, SL (w), reprints Thor #146	0.25	0.40	1.00	2.00
❑18, JK, SL (w), reprints Thor #147	0.25	0.40	1.00	2.00
❑19, Nov 75, JK, SL (w), reprints Thor #148	0.25	0.40	1.00	2.00

MARVEL SPOTLIGHT (VOL. 1)
MARVEL

	ORIG	GOOD	FINE	N-MINT
❑1, Nov 71, A: Red Wolf	0.15	3.00	7.50	15.00
❑2, 1: Werewolf	0.25	7.00	17.50	35.00
❑3, A: Werewolf	0.20	3.00	7.50	15.00
❑4, A: Werewolf	0.20	3.00	7.50	15.00
❑5, MP; SD, 1: Johnny Blaze; 1: Ghost Rider I (Johnny Blaze); 1: Zarathos (Ghost Rider's Spirit of Vengeance)	0.20	10.00	25.00	50.00
❑6, A: Ghost Rider	0.20	4.00	10.00	20.00
❑7, A: Ghost Rider	0.20	3.20	8.00	16.00
❑8, FM, A: Ghost Rider	0.20	3.20	8.00	16.00
❑9, A: Ghost Rider	0.20	2.40	6.00	12.00
❑10, A: Ghost Rider	0.20	2.40	6.00	12.00
❑11, A: Ghost Rider	0.20	2.40	6.00	12.00
❑12, SD, 1: Son of Satan; 1: Son of Satan (full appearance)	0.20	2.40	6.00	12.00
❑13, A: Son of Satan; O: Satana	0.20	1.20	3.00	6.00
❑14, Mar 74, A: Son of Satan	0.20	1.00	2.50	5.00
❑15, A: Son of Satan	0.25	1.00	2.50	5.00
❑16, A: Son of Satan	0.25	0.80	2.00	4.00
❑17, A: Son of Satan	0.25	0.80	2.00	4.00
❑18, Oct 74, A: Son of Satan	0.25	0.80	2.00	4.00
❑19, Dec 74, A: Son of Satan	0.25	0.80	2.00	4.00
❑20, Feb 75, A: Son of Satan	0.25	0.80	2.00	4.00
❑21, Apr 75, A: Son of Satan	0.25	0.80	2.00	4.00
❑22, Jun 75, A: Son of Satan; A: Ghost Rider	0.25	1.00	2.50	5.00

	ORIG	GOOD	FINE	N-MINT
❑23, Aug 75, A: Son of Satan	0.25	0.80	2.00	4.00
❑24, Oct 75, A: Son of Satan, Last Son of Satan in Marvel Spotlight	0.25	0.80	2.00	4.00
❑25, Dec 75, A: Sinbad	0.25	0.60	1.50	3.00
❑26, Feb 76, A: Scarecrow (Marvel)	0.25	0.60	1.50	3.00
❑27, Apr 76, A: Sub-Mariner	0.25	0.60	1.50	3.00
❑28, Jun 76, A: Moon Knight, 1st solo story for Moon Knight	0.25	1.60	4.00	8.00
❑29, Aug 76, JK, A: Moon Knight	0.25	1.20	3.00	6.00
❑30, Oct 76, JB, A: Warriors Three	0.30	0.60	1.50	3.00
❑31, Dec 76, HC, A: Nick Fury	0.30	0.60	1.50	3.00
❑32, Feb 77, JM; SB, Dark Destiny!, 1: Spider-Woman I (Jessica Drew)	0.30	1.60	4.00	8.00
❑33, Apr 77, A: Deathlok; 1: Devil-Slayer	0.30	0.60	1.50	3.00

MARVEL SPOTLIGHT (VOL. 2)

MARVEL

	ORIG	GOOD	FINE	N-MINT
❑1, Jul 79, PB, The Saturn Storm!, A: Captain Marvel	0.40	0.60	1.50	3.00
❑2, Sep 79, TD, FM (c), A: Captain Marvel	0.40	0.40	1.00	2.00
❑3, Nov 79, PB, Blue-Red-Blue, A: Captain Marvel	0.40	0.40	1.00	2.00
❑4, Jan 80, SD, FM (c), Shadow Doom!, A: Dragon Lord	0.40	0.40	1.00	2.00
❑5, Mar 80, SD, FM (c), A Hero Is Also A Man!, A: Captain Marvel; A: Dragon Lord	0.40	0.40	1.00	2.00
❑6, May 80, TS, The Saga Of Star-Lord, O: Star-Lord	0.40	0.40	1.00	2.00
❑7, Jul 80, TS, Tears For The World Called Heaven, A: Star-Lord	0.40	0.40	1.00	2.00
❑8, Sep 80, TD; FM, A: Captain Marvel	0.50	0.40	1.00	2.00
❑9, Nov 80, SD, A: Captain Universe	0.50	0.40	1.00	2.00
❑10, Jan 81, SD, A: Captain Universe	0.50	0.40	1.00	2.00
❑11, Mar 81, SD, A: Captain Universe	0.50	0.40	1.00	2.00

MARVEL SPRING SPECIAL

MARVEL

	ORIG	GOOD	FINE	N-MINT
❑1, Nov 88, Elvira	—	0.50	1.25	2.50

MARVEL SUPER ACTION

MARVEL

	ORIG	GOOD	FINE	N-MINT
❑1, May 77, JK, reprints Captain America #100	0.30	0.80	2.00	4.00
❑2, Jul 77, JK, Reprints Captain America #101	0.30	0.50	1.25	2.50
❑3, Sep 77, JK, Reprints Captain America #102	0.30	0.50	1.25	2.50
❑4, Nov 77, JK, O: Marvel Boy, Reprints Marvel Boy #1	0.35	0.50	1.25	2.50
❑5, Jan 78, JK, Reprints Captain America #103	0.35	0.40	1.00	2.00
❑6, Mar 78, JK, Reprints Captain America #104	0.35	0.40	1.00	2.00
❑7, Apr 78, JK, Reprints Captain America #105	0.35	0.40	1.00	2.00
❑8, Jun 78, JK, Reprints Captain America #106	0.35	0.40	1.00	2.00
❑9, Aug 78, JK, Reprints Captain America #107	0.35	0.40	1.00	2.00
❑10, Oct 78, JK, Reprints Captain America #108	0.35	0.40	1.00	2.00
❑11, Dec 78, JK, Reprints Captain America #109	0.35	0.40	1.00	2.00
❑12, Feb 79, JSo, A: Hulk, Reprints Captain America #110	0.35	0.40	1.00	2.00
❑13, Apr 79, JSo, Reprints Captain America #111	0.35	0.40	1.00	2.00
❑14, Dec 79, reprints Avengers #55	0.40	0.30	0.75	1.50
❑15, Jan 80, reprints Avengers #56	0.40	0.30	0.75	1.50
❑16, Feb 80, reprints Avengers Annual #2	0.40	0.30	0.75	1.50
❑17, Mar 80, reprints Avengers Annual #2	0.40	0.30	0.75	1.50
❑18, Apr 80, reprints Avengers #57	0.40	0.30	0.75	1.50
❑19, May 80, reprints Avengers #58	0.40	0.30	0.75	1.50
❑20, Jun 80, reprints Avengers #59	0.40	0.30	0.75	1.50
❑21, Jul 80, reprints Avengers #60	0.40	0.30	0.75	1.50
❑22, Aug 80, reprints Avengers #61	0.40	0.30	0.75	1.50
❑23, Sep 80, reprints Avengers #62	0.50	0.30	0.75	1.50
❑24, Oct 80, reprints Avengers #63	0.50	0.30	0.75	1.50
❑25, Nov 80, reprints Avengers #64	0.50	0.30	0.75	1.50
❑26, Dec 80, reprints Avengers #65	0.50	0.30	0.75	1.50
❑27, Jan 81, reprints Avengers #66	0.50	0.30	0.75	1.50
❑28, Feb 81, reprints Avengers #67	0.50	0.30	0.75	1.50
❑29, Mar 81, reprints Avengers #68	0.50	0.30	0.75	1.50
❑30, Apr 81, reprints Avengers #69	0.50	0.30	0.75	1.50
❑31, May 81, reprints Avengers #70	0.50	0.30	0.75	1.50
❑32, Jun 81, reprints Avengers #71	0.50	0.30	0.75	1.50
❑33, Jul 81, reprints Avengers #72	0.50	0.30	0.75	1.50
❑34, Aug 81, reprints Avengers #73	0.50	0.30	0.75	1.50
❑35, Sep 81, reprints Avengers #74	0.50	0.30	0.75	1.50
❑36, Oct 81, reprints Avengers #75	0.50	0.30	0.75	1.50
❑37, Nov 81, reprints Avengers #76	0.50	0.30	0.75	1.50

The two treasury-sized issues of *Marvel Special Edition* adapting *Star Wars* were also collected into one treasury-sized issue.

MARVEL SUPER ACTION (MAGAZINE)

MARVEL

	ORIG	GOOD	FINE	N-MINT
❑1, Jan 76, 2: Dominic Fortune; 1: Mockingbird (as "Huntress"), b&w; One-Shot; Weird World and Punisher stories	1.00	5.60	14.00	28.00

MARVEL SUPER HERO CONTEST OF CHAMPIONS

MARVEL

	ORIG	GOOD	FINE	N-MINT
❑1, Jun 82, JR2, A Gathering of Heroes!, 1: Collective Man; 1: Talisman I; 1: Blitzkrieg; 1: Le Peregrine; 1: Shamrock, Alpha Flight	0.25	0.80	2.00	4.00
❑2, Jul 82, JR2, Frenzy In The Frozen North!, X-Men	0.25	0.70	1.75	3.50
❑3, Aug 82, JR2, Siege In The City Of The Dead!, X-Men	0.25	0.70	1.75	3.50

MARVEL SUPER-HEROES (VOL. 1)

MARVEL

	ORIG	GOOD	FINE	N-MINT
❑12, Dec 67, 1: Captain Marvel, Reprint; Title continued from "Fantasy Masterpieces"	0.25	10.00	25.00	50.00
❑13, Mar 68, 2: Captain Marvel; 1: Carol Danvers, Reprint	0.25	6.00	15.00	30.00
❑14, May 68, JK, A: Spider-Man, Reprints 1st Kirby art at Marvel	0.25	9.00	22.50	45.00
❑15, Jul 68, GC, Let The Silence Shatter!; Black Knight, Medusa	0.25	2.40	6.00	12.00
❑16, Sep 68, HT, The Phantom Eagle; The Human Torch, 1: Phantom Eagle	0.25	2.40	6.00	12.00
❑17, Nov 68, The Black Knight Reborn!; The Original Human Torch, D: Black Knight I (Sir Percy of Scandia); O: Black Knight III (Dane Whitman), Reprints All-Winners Squad #21	0.25	2.40	6.00	12.00
❑18, Jan 69, 1: Zarek; 1: Charlie-27; 1: Guardians of the Galaxy; 1: Yondu; 1: Vance Astro	0.25	5.00	12.50	25.00
❑19, Mar 69, GT, My Father, My Enemy!; The Human Torch, A: Ka-Zar, Ka-Zar	0.25	2.00	5.00	10.00
❑20, May 69, A: Doctor Doom	0.25	2.00	5.00	10.00
❑21, Jul 69, Reprint	0.25	1.20	3.00	6.00
❑22, Sep 69, Reprint	0.25	1.20	3.00	6.00
❑23, Nov 69, Reprint	0.25	1.20	3.00	6.00
❑24, Jan 69, Reprint	0.25	1.20	3.00	6.00
❑25, Mar 69, Reprint	0.25	1.20	3.00	6.00
❑26	0.25	1.20	3.00	6.00
❑27	0.25	1.20	3.00	6.00
❑28	0.25	1.20	3.00	6.00
❑29, Jan 71, WW, SL (w), Daredevil: That He May See!; The Watchers!	0.25	1.20	3.00	6.00
❑30, Apr 71	0.25	1.20	3.00	6.00
❑31, Nov 71	0.25	1.20	3.00	6.00
❑32, Reprints from Tales to Astonish begin	0.20	0.50	1.25	2.50
❑33	0.20	0.50	1.25	2.50
❑34	0.20	0.50	1.25	2.50
❑35	0.20	0.50	1.25	2.50
❑36	0.20	0.50	1.25	2.50
❑37	0.20	0.50	1.25	2.50
❑38	0.20	0.50	1.25	2.50
❑39	0.20	0.50	1.25	2.50
❑40	0.20	0.50	1.25	2.50
❑41	0.20	0.50	1.25	2.50
❑42	0.20	0.50	1.25	2.50
❑43	0.25	0.50	1.25	2.50
❑44	0.25	0.50	1.25	2.50
❑45, Sep 74, reprints Tales to Astonish #90	0.25	0.50	1.25	2.50
❑46, Oct 74, reprints Tales to Astonish #91; Hulk vs. Abomination	0.25	0.50	1.25	2.50
❑47, Nov 74, reprints Tales to Astonish #92	0.25	0.50	1.25	2.50
❑48, Jan 75, reprints Tales to Astonish #93	0.25	0.50	1.25	2.50
❑49, Mar 75, reprints Tales to Astonish #94	0.25	0.50	1.25	2.50
❑50, May 75, reprints Tales to Astonish #95	0.25	0.50	1.25	2.50
❑51, Jul 75, reprints Tales to Astonish #96	0.25	0.50	1.25	2.50
❑52, Sep 75, reprints Tales to Astonish #97	0.25	0.50	1.25	2.50
❑53, Oct 75, reprints Tales to Astonish #98	0.25	0.50	1.25	2.50
❑54, Nov 75, reprints Tales to Astonish #99	0.25	0.50	1.25	2.50
❑55, Jan 76, reprints Tales to Astonish #101	0.25	0.50	1.25	2.50

	ORIG	GOOD	FINE	N-MINT
❑56, Mar 76, reprints Incredible Hulk #102 (Tales to Astonish became Incredible Hulk)	0.25	0.50	1.25	2.50
❑57, May 76, reprints Incredible Hulk #103	0.25	0.50	1.25	2.50
❑58, Jul 76, reprints Incredible Hulk #104	0.25	0.50	1.25	2.50
❑59, Sep 76, reprints Incredible Hulk #105	0.30	0.50	1.25	2.50
❑60, Oct 76, reprints Incredible Hulk #106	0.30	0.50	1.25	2.50
❑61, Nov 76, reprints Incredible Hulk #107	0.30	0.50	1.25	2.50
❑62, Jan 77, reprints Incredible Hulk #108	0.30	0.50	1.25	2.50
❑63, Mar 77, reprints Incredible Hulk #109	0.30	0.50	1.25	2.50
❑64, May 77, reprints Incredible Hulk #110	0.30	0.50	1.25	2.50
❑65, Jun 77, reprints Incredible Hulk #111	0.30	0.50	1.25	2.50
❑66, Sep 77, reprints Incredible Hulk #112	0.30	0.50	1.25	2.50
❑67, Oct 77, reprints Incredible Hulk #113	0.30	0.50	1.25	2.50
❑68, Nov 77, reprints Incredible Hulk #114	0.30	0.50	1.25	2.50
❑69, Jan 78, reprints Incredible Hulk #115	0.30	0.50	1.25	2.50
❑70, Mar 78, reprints Incredible Hulk #116	0.30	0.50	1.25	2.50
❑71, May 78, reprints Incredible Hulk #117	0.35	0.50	1.25	2.50
❑72, Jul 78	0.35	0.50	1.25	2.50
❑73, Aug 78, reprints Incredible Hulk #120	0.35	0.50	1.25	2.50
❑74, Sep 78	0.35	0.50	1.25	2.50
❑75, Oct 78	0.35	0.50	1.25	2.50
❑76, Nov 78, reprints Incredible Hulk #124	0.35	0.50	1.25	2.50
❑77, Dec 78, reprints Incredible Hulk #125	0.35	0.50	1.25	2.50
❑78, reprints Incredible Hulk #126	0.35	0.50	1.25	2.50
❑79, Mar 79, reprints Incredible Hulk #127	0.35	0.50	1.25	2.50
❑80, May 79, reprints Incredible Hulk #128	0.40	0.50	1.25	2.50
❑81, reprints Incredible Hulk #129	0.35	0.40	1.00	2.00
❑82, reprints Incredible Hulk #130	0.35	0.40	1.00	2.00
❑83, reprints Incredible Hulk #131	0.35	0.40	1.00	2.00
❑84, Oct 79, reprints Incredible Hulk #132	0.35	0.40	1.00	2.00
❑85, reprints Incredible Hulk #133	0.35	0.40	1.00	2.00
❑86, Jan 80, reprints Incredible Hulk #134	0.35	0.40	1.00	2.00
❑87	0.35	0.40	1.00	2.00
❑88	0.35	0.40	1.00	2.00
❑89, Jul 80, reprints Incredible Hulk #139	0.40	0.40	1.00	2.00
❑90, Aug 80, SB, The Summons OF Psyklop, reprints Avengers #88	0.35	0.40	1.00	2.00
❑91, Sep 80, Brute That Shouted Love at the Heart of the Atom, reprints Incredible Hulk #140	0.50	0.40	1.00	2.00
❑92	0.40	0.40	1.00	2.00
❑93	0.40	0.40	1.00	2.00
❑94	0.40	0.40	1.00	2.00
❑95, Mar 81	0.50	0.40	1.00	2.00
❑96	0.50	0.40	1.00	2.00
❑97	0.50	0.40	1.00	2.00
❑98	0.50	0.40	1.00	2.00
❑99, Jul 81, reprints Incredible Hulk #150	0.50	0.40	1.00	2.00
❑100, Aug 81, reprints Incredible Hulk #151-152	0.75	0.40	1.00	2.00
❑101, Sep 81, reprints Incredible Hulk #153	0.50	0.40	1.00	2.00
❑102, reprints Incredible Hulk #154	0.40	0.40	1.00	2.00
❑103, Nov 81, reprints Incredible Hulk #155	0.40	0.40	1.00	2.00
❑104, Dec 81, reprints Incredible Hulk #156	0.40	0.40	1.00	2.00
❑105, Jan 82, reprints Incredible Hulk #157	0.40	0.40	1.00	2.00
❑SE 1, Oct 66, JK; BEv, SL (w), The Avengers Battle the Space Phantom; The Origin of Daredevil, 1: Daredevil, One-shot from 1966; Reprints stories from Avengers #2, Daredevil #1, Marvel Mystery Comics #8; Human Torch meets Sub-Mariner	0.25	9.00	22.50	45.00

MARVEL SUPER-HEROES (VOL. 2)
MARVEL

	ORIG	GOOD	FINE	N-MINT
❑1, May 90, FH; SD, Moon Knight: Old Business; Hercules: I Shot an Arrow Into the Sky!, O: Raptor, 80pgs.; Spring 1990	2.95	0.70	1.75	3.50
❑2, Jul 90, 80pgs.	2.95	0.65	1.63	3.25
❑3, Oct 90, 80pgs.	2.95	0.65	1.63	3.25
❑4, Dec 90, 80pgs.	2.95	0.65	1.63	3.25
❑5, Apr 91, 80pgs.	2.95	0.65	1.63	3.25
❑6, Jul 91	2.25	0.65	1.63	3.25
❑7, Oct 91	2.25	0.65	1.63	3.25
❑8, Dec 91	2.25	0.65	1.63	3.25
❑9, Apr 92, KB (w), A: Cupid	2.50	0.65	1.63	3.25
❑10, Jul 92, A: Sabretooth, 80pgs.; Oversized format	2.50	0.65	1.63	3.25
❑11, Oct 92, Ghost Rider	2.50	0.60	1.50	3.00
❑12, Jan 93, KB (w)	2.50	0.50	1.25	2.50
❑13, Apr 93, KB (w), Iron Man	2.75	0.55	1.38	2.75
❑14, Jul 93	2.75	0.55	1.38	2.75
❑15, Oct 93, DH; KP, Volstagg's Mostly Greatest Adventure; The Theft of Thor's Hammer, A: Thor; A: Iron Man, Final Issue	2.75	0.55	1.38	2.75

MARVEL SUPER-HEROES MEGAZINE
MARVEL

Value: Cover or less

	ORIG
❑1, Oct 94, FM; JR2; JBy, JBy (w), Fantastic Four: Back To The Basics!; Iron Man: Betrayal	2.95
❑2, Nov 94, FM; JR2; JBy, JBy (w), Fantastic Four: Mission For A Dead Man!; Daredevil: In The Hands Of Bullseye	2.95
❑3, Dec 94, FM	2.95
❑4, Jan 95, FM	2.95
❑5, Feb 95	2.95
❑6, Mar 95, Final Issue	2.95

MARVEL SUPER HEROES SECRET WARS
MARVEL

	ORIG	GOOD	FINE	N-MINT
❑1, May 84, MZ, 1: Beyonder (voice only), X-Men, Avengers, Fantastic Four in all	0.75	0.60	1.50	3.00
❑2, Jun 84, MZ	0.75	0.40	1.00	2.00
❑3, Jul 84, MZ, 1: Volcana	0.75	0.40	1.00	2.00
❑4, Aug 84, MZ	0.75	0.40	1.00	2.00
❑5, Sep 84, MZ	0.75	0.40	1.00	2.00
❑6, Oct 84, MZ, D: Wasp	0.75	0.40	1.00	2.00
❑7, Nov 84, MZ, 1: Spider-Woman II (Julia Carpenter)	0.75	0.60	1.50	3.00
❑8, Dec 84, MZ, 1: Alien costume (later Venom); O: Spider-Man's black costume	0.75	1.80	4.50	9.00
❑9, Jan 85, MZ	0.75	0.40	1.00	2.00
❑10, Feb 85, MZ	0.75	0.40	1.00	2.00
❑11, Mar 85, MZ	0.75	0.40	1.00	2.00
❑12, Apr 85, MZ, Giant-size; Conclusion	1.00	0.40	1.00	2.00

MARVEL SUPER SPECIAL
MARVEL

	ORIG	GOOD	FINE	N-MINT
❑1, Sep 77, O: Kiss (rock group), Group mixed drops of their blood into the printer's ink in publicity stunt	1.50	7.00	17.50	35.00
❑2, Mar 78, Conan	1.50	1.00	2.50	5.00
❑3, Jun 78, Close Encounters of the Third Kind	1.50	1.00	2.50	5.00
❑4, Aug 78, The Beatles	1.50	3.00	7.50	15.00
❑5, Dec 78, Title changes to Marvel Super Special; Jaws 2; Kiss	1.50	4.00	10.00	20.00
❑6, Dec 78, Kiss; Jaws 2	1.50	0.80	2.00	4.00
❑7, Dec 78, Nonexistent?	1.50	0.60	1.50	3.00
❑8, Battlestar Galactica; tabloid	1.50	1.00	2.50	5.00
❑9, Feb 79, Conan	1.50	1.00	2.50	5.00
❑10, Jun 79, Star-Lord	1.50	1.00	2.50	5.00
❑11, Sep 79, Warriors of Shadow Realm; Weirdworld	1.50	0.80	2.00	4.00
❑12, Nov 79, Warriors of Shadow Realm; Weirdworld	1.50	0.80	2.00	4.00
❑13, Jan 80, Warriors of Shadow Realm; Weirdworld	1.50	0.80	2.00	4.00
❑14, Feb 80, TP; GC, Meteor, Meteor	1.50	0.60	1.50	3.00
❑15, Mar 80, Star Trek: The Motion Picture	1.50	1.00	2.50	5.00
❑16, Aug 80, Empire Strikes Back	2.00	1.20	3.00	6.00
❑17, Nov 80, Xanadu	2.00	0.60	1.50	3.00
❑18, Sep 81, Raiders of the Lost Ark	2.50	0.60	1.50	3.00
❑19, Oct 81, For Your Eyes Only	2.50	0.60	1.50	3.00
❑20, Oct 81, Dragonslayer	2.50	0.60	1.50	3.00
❑21, Aug 82, Conan movie	2.50	0.60	1.50	3.00
❑22, Sep 82, Comic size; Blade Runner	2.50	0.60	1.50	3.00
❑23, Sep 82, Annie	2.50	0.60	1.50	3.00
❑24, Mar 83, Dark Crystal	2.50	0.60	1.50	3.00
❑25, Aug 83, Rock & Rule, Comic size	2.50	0.60	1.50	3.00
❑26, Sep 83, Octopussy	2.50	0.60	1.50	3.00
❑27, Sep 83, Return of the Jedi	2.50	0.60	1.50	3.00
❑28, Oct 83, Krull	2.50	0.60	1.50	3.00
❑29, Jul 84, Tarzan of the Apes	2.00	0.60	1.50	3.00
❑30, Aug 84, Indiana Jones and the Temple of Doom	2.50	0.60	1.50	3.00
❑31, Sep 84, The Last Starfighter	2.50	0.60	1.50	3.00
❑32, Oct 84, The Muppets Take Manhattan	2.50	0.60	1.50	3.00
❑33, Nov 84, Buckaroo Banzai	2.50	0.60	1.50	3.00
❑34, Nov 84, Sheena	2.50	0.60	1.50	3.00
❑35, Dec 84, Conan the Destroyer	2.50	0.60	1.50	3.00
❑36, Apr 85, Dune	2.50	0.60	1.50	3.00
❑37, Apr 85, 2010	2.00	0.60	1.50	3.00
❑38, Nov 85, Into the Realm of Darkness, Red Sonja	2.00	0.60	1.50	3.00
❑39, Mar 85, Santa Claus: the Movie	2.50	0.60	1.50	3.00
❑40, Oct 86, Labyrinth	2.50	0.60	1.50	3.00
❑41, Nov 86, Howard the Duck movie adaptation	2.50	0.60	1.50	3.00

MARVEL SWIMSUIT SPECIAL
MARVEL

	ORIG	GOOD	FINE	N-MINT
❑1, 1992; in Wakanda	3.95	0.80	2.00	4.00
❑2, 1993; on Monster Island	4.50	0.90	2.25	4.50
❑3	4.50	0.90	2.25	4.50
❑4	4.95	1.00	2.50	5.00

MARVEL TAILS
MARVEL

	ORIG	GOOD	FINE	N-MINT
❑1, Nov 83, If He Should Punch Me!, 1: Peter Porker	0.60	0.30	0.75	1.50

MARVEL TALES (2ND SERIES)
MARVEL

	ORIG	GOOD	FINE	N-MINT
❑1, Mar 66, JK; SD, SL (w), Spider-Man!; The Coming of the Hulk!, O: Giant-Man; O: The Hulk; 1: Spider-Man; O: Ant-Man; O: Iron Man, Giant-size; Amazing Fantasy #15; Listed as Marvel Tales Annual #1 in indicia	0.25	32.00	80.00	160.00
❑2, May 66, O: X-Men, Giant-size; Reprints Uncanny X-Men #1, Incredible Hulk #3, Avengers #1	0.25	15.00	37.50	75.00

	ORIG	GOOD	FINE	N-MINT
❑3, Jul 66, Giant-size; reprints Amazing Spider-Man #6	0.25	7.20	18.00	36.00
❑4, Sep 66, SD, Giant-size; Amazing Spider-Man #7	0.25	4.00	10.00	20.00
❑5, Nov 66, SD, Giant-size; Amazing Spider-Man #8	0.25	4.00	10.00	20.00
❑6, Jan 67, SD, Giant-size; Amazing Spider-Man #9	0.25	3.00	7.50	15.00
❑7, Mar 67, SD, Giant-size; Amazing Spider-Man #10	0.25	3.00	7.50	15.00
❑8, May 67, SD, Giant-size; Amazing Spider-Man #13	0.25	3.00	7.50	15.00
❑9, Jul 67, SD, Giant-size; Amazing Spider-Man #14	0.25	3.20	8.00	16.00
❑10, Sep 67, SD, Giant-size; Amazing Spider-Man #15	0.25	2.80	7.00	14.00
❑11, Nov 67, SD, Giant-size; Amazing Spider-Man #16	0.25	1.80	4.50	9.00
❑12, Jan 68, DH; SD, The Return of the Green Goblin!; The Magician and the Maiden!, 1: the Trapster ("Paste-Pot Pete"), Giant-size; Reprints stories from Amazing Spider-Man #17, Strange Tales #110, Tales to Astonish #58, Tales to Astonish #98	0.25	1.80	4.50	9.00
❑13, Mar 68, SD, O: Marvel Boy, Giant-size; Amazing Spider-Man #18; Reprints Marvel Boy #1	0.25	1.80	4.50	9.00
❑14, May 68, SD, Giant-size; Marvel Boy; Amazing Spider-Man #19	0.25	1.80	4.50	9.00
❑15, Jul 68, SD, Giant-size; Marvel Boy; Amazing Spider-Man #20	0.25	1.80	4.50	9.00
❑16, Sep 68, SD, Giant-size; Marvel Boy; Amazing Spider-Man #21	0.25	1.80	4.50	9.00
❑17, Nov 68, SD, Giant-size; Amazing Spider-Man #22	0.25	1.80	4.50	9.00
❑18, Jan 69, SD, Giant-size; Amazing Spider-Man #23	0.25	1.80	4.50	9.00
❑19, Mar 69, SD, Giant-size; Amazing Spider-Man #24	0.25	1.80	4.50	9.00
❑20, May 69, SD, Giant-size; Amazing Spider-Man #25	0.25	1.80	4.50	9.00
❑21, Jul 69, SD, Giant-size; Amazing Spider-Man #26	0.25	1.60	4.00	8.00
❑22, Sep 69, SD, Giant-size; Amazing Spider-Man #27	0.25	1.60	4.00	8.00
❑23, Nov 69, The Claws of the Cat; Every Hand Against Him!, Giant-size	0.25	1.60	4.00	8.00
❑24, Jan 70, SD, Giant-size; Amazing Spider-Man #31	0.25	1.60	4.00	8.00
❑25, Mar 70, SD, Giant-size; Amazing Spider-Man #32	0.25	1.60	4.00	8.00
❑26, SD, Giant-size; Amazing Spider-Man #33	0.25	1.60	4.00	8.00
❑27, SD, Giant-size; Amazing Spider-Man #34	0.25	1.60	4.00	8.00
❑28, Oct 70, SD, Giant-size; Amazing Spider-Man #35 and #36	0.25	1.60	4.00	8.00
❑29, Jan 71, JR, O: Green Goblin, Giant-size; Amazing Spider-Man #39 and #40	0.25	1.60	4.00	8.00
❑30, Apr 71, JR, Giant-size; Amazing Spider-Man #58 and #41; conclusion of Angel back-up from Ka-Zar #3	0.25	1.60	4.00	8.00
❑31, Jul 71, JR; SD, Giant-size; Amazing Spider-Man #37 and #42	0.25	1.60	4.00	8.00
❑32, Nov 71, JR, Amazing Spider-Man #43 and #44 Giant-size; Last giant-size issue	0.25	1.60	4.00	8.00
❑33, Feb 72, JR, Amazing Spider-Man #45 and #47	0.25	0.60	1.50	3.00
❑34, Apr 72, JR, Amazing Spider-Man #48	0.20	0.60	1.50	3.00
❑35, Jun 72, JR, Amazing Spider-Man #49	0.20	0.60	1.50	3.00
❑36, Aug 72, JR, Amazing Spider-Man #51	0.20	0.60	1.50	3.00
❑37, Sep 72, JR, Amazing Spider-Man #52	0.20	0.60	1.50	3.00
❑38, Oct 72, JR, Amazing Spider-Man #53	0.20	0.60	1.50	3.00
❑39, Nov 72, JR, Amazing Spider-Man #54	0.20	0.60	1.50	3.00
❑40, Dec 72, JR, Amazing Spider-Man #55	0.20	0.60	1.50	3.00
❑41, Feb 73, JR, Amazing Spider-Man #56	0.20	0.60	1.50	3.00
❑42, Apr 73, JR, Amazing Spider-Man #59	0.20	0.60	1.50	3.00
❑43, Jun 73, JR, Amazing Spider-Man #60	0.20	0.60	1.50	3.00
❑44, Aug 73	0.20	0.60	1.50	3.00
❑45	0.20	0.60	1.50	3.00
❑46	0.20	0.60	1.50	3.00
❑47	0.20	0.60	1.50	3.00
❑48	0.20	0.60	1.50	3.00
❑49	0.20	0.60	1.50	3.00
❑50	0.20	0.60	1.50	3.00
❑51	0.25	0.50	1.25	2.50
❑52, Aug 74	0.25	0.50	1.25	2.50
❑53, Sep 74	0.25	0.50	1.25	2.50
❑54, Oct 74	0.25	0.50	1.25	2.50
❑55, Nov 74	0.25	0.50	1.25	2.50
❑56	0.25	0.50	1.25	2.50

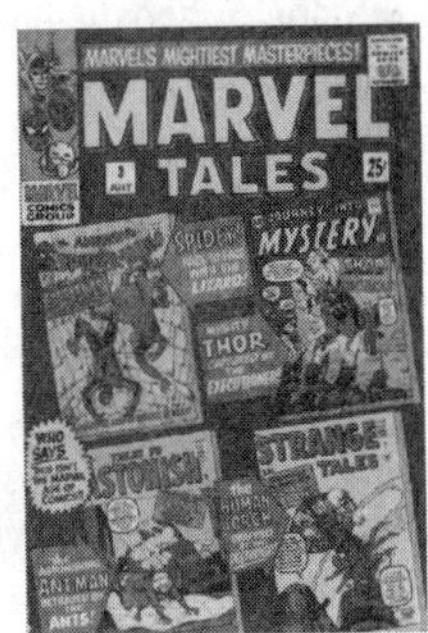

While it later devoted itself to reprints of *Amazing Spider-Man*, early issues of *Marvel Tales* also reprinted the early adventures of other Marvel characters.

	ORIG	GOOD	FINE	N-MINT
❑57	0.25	0.50	1.25	2.50
❑58	0.25	0.50	1.25	2.50
❑59	0.25	0.50	1.25	2.50
❑60	0.25	0.50	1.25	2.50
❑61, Sep 75	0.25	0.50	1.25	2.50
❑62	0.25	0.50	1.25	2.50
❑63	0.25	0.50	1.25	2.50
❑64	0.25	0.50	1.25	2.50
❑65	0.25	0.50	1.25	2.50
❑66	0.25	0.50	1.25	2.50
❑67	0.25	0.50	1.25	2.50
❑68, Jun 76	0.25	0.50	1.25	2.50
❑69, Jul 76	0.25	0.50	1.25	2.50
❑70, Aug 76	0.25	0.50	1.25	2.50
❑71, Sep 76	0.30	0.40	1.00	2.00
❑72, Oct 76	0.30	0.40	1.00	2.00
❑73, Nov 76	0.30	0.40	1.00	2.00
❑74, Dec 76	0.30	0.40	1.00	2.00
❑75, Jan 77	0.30	0.40	1.00	2.00
❑76, Feb 77	0.30	0.40	1.00	2.00
❑77, Mar 77	0.30	0.40	1.00	2.00
❑78, Apr 77	0.30	0.40	1.00	2.00
❑79, May 77	0.30	0.40	1.00	2.00
❑80, Jun 77	0.30	0.40	1.00	2.00
❑81, Jul 77	0.30	0.40	1.00	2.00
❑82, Aug 77	0.30	0.40	1.00	2.00
❑83, Sep 77	0.30	0.40	1.00	2.00
❑84, Oct 77	0.30	0.40	1.00	2.00
❑85, Nov 77	0.30	0.40	1.00	2.00
❑86, Dec 77	0.35	0.40	1.00	2.00
❑87, Jan 78	0.35	0.40	1.00	2.00
❑88, Feb 78	0.35	0.40	1.00	2.00
❑89, Mar 78	0.35	0.40	1.00	2.00
❑90, Apr 78	0.35	0.40	1.00	2.00
❑91, May 78	0.35	0.40	1.00	2.00
❑92, Jun 78	0.35	0.40	1.00	2.00
❑93, Jul 78	0.35	0.40	1.00	2.00
❑94, Aug 78	0.35	0.40	1.00	2.00
❑95, Sep 78	0.35	0.40	1.00	2.00
❑96, Oct 78	0.35	0.40	1.00	2.00
❑97, Nov 78	0.35	0.40	1.00	2.00
❑98, Dec 78, D: Gwen Stacy	0.35	0.45	1.13	2.25
❑99, Jan 79, D: Green Goblin	0.35	0.45	1.13	2.25
❑100, Feb 79, TD; GK; SD; MN	0.60	0.40	1.00	2.00
❑101, Mar 79	0.35	0.40	1.00	2.00
❑102, Apr 79	0.35	0.40	1.00	2.00
❑103, May 79	0.35	0.40	1.00	2.00
❑104, Jun 79	0.35	0.40	1.00	2.00
❑105, Jul 79	0.35	0.40	1.00	2.00
❑106, Aug 79, 1: Jackal; 1: Punisher, Reprints Amazing Spider-Man #129	0.40	0.70	1.75	3.50
❑107, Sep 79	0.40	0.40	1.00	2.00
❑108, Oct 79	0.40	0.40	1.00	2.00
❑109, Nov 79	0.40	0.40	1.00	2.00
❑110, Dec 79	0.40	0.40	1.00	2.00
❑111, Jan 80, Punisher	0.40	0.40	1.00	2.00
❑112, Feb 80, Punisher	0.40	0.40	1.00	2.00
❑113, Mar 80	0.40	0.40	1.00	2.00
❑114, Apr 80	0.40	0.40	1.00	2.00
❑115, May 80	0.40	0.40	1.00	2.00
❑116, Jun 80	0.40	0.40	1.00	2.00
❑117, Jul 80	0.40	0.40	1.00	2.00
❑118, Aug 80	0.40	0.40	1.00	2.00
❑119, Sep 80	0.50	0.40	1.00	2.00
❑120, Oct 80	0.40	0.40	1.00	2.00
❑121, Nov 80	0.50	0.40	1.00	2.00
❑122, Dec 80	0.50	0.40	1.00	2.00
❑123, Jan 81	0.50	0.40	1.00	2.00
❑124, Feb 81	0.50	0.40	1.00	2.00
❑125, Mar 81	0.50	0.40	1.00	2.00
❑126, Apr 81	0.50	0.40	1.00	2.00

	ORIG	GOOD	FINE	N-MINT
❑127, May 81	0.50	0.40	1.00	2.00
❑128, Jun 81	0.50	0.40	1.00	2.00
❑129, Jul 81	0.50	0.40	1.00	2.00
❑130, Aug 81	0.50	0.40	1.00	2.00
❑131, Sep 81	0.50	0.40	1.00	2.00
❑132, Oct 81	0.50	0.40	1.00	2.00
❑133, Nov 81	0.50	0.40	1.00	2.00
❑134, Dec 81	0.50	0.40	1.00	2.00
❑135, Jan 82	0.60	0.40	1.00	2.00
❑136, Feb 82	0.50	0.40	1.00	2.00
❑137, Mar 82, 1: Spider-Man, Reprints Amazing Fantasy #15	0.60	0.80	2.00	4.00
❑138, Apr 82, Reprints Amazing Spider-Man #1	0.60	0.80	2.00	4.00
❑139, May 82, Reprints Amazing Spider-Man #2	0.60	0.50	1.25	2.50
❑140, Jun 82, Reprints Amazing Spider-Man #3	0.60	0.50	1.25	2.50
❑141, Jul 82, Reprints Amazing Spider-Man #4	0.60	0.50	1.25	2.50
❑142, Aug 82, Reprints Amazing Spider-Man #5	0.60	0.50	1.25	2.50
❑143, Sep 82, Reprints Amazing Spider-Man #6	0.60	0.50	1.25	2.50
❑144, Oct 82, Reprints Amazing Spider-Man #7	0.60	0.50	1.25	2.50
❑145, Nov 82	0.60	0.40	1.00	2.00
❑146, Dec 82	0.60	0.40	1.00	2.00
❑147, Jan 83	0.60	0.40	1.00	2.00
❑148, Feb 83	0.60	0.40	1.00	2.00
❑149, Mar 83	0.60	0.40	1.00	2.00
❑150, Apr 83, Giant-size	0.60	0.40	1.00	2.00
❑151, May 83	0.60	0.40	1.00	2.00
❑152, Jun 83	0.60	0.40	1.00	2.00
❑153, Jul 83	0.60	0.40	1.00	2.00
❑154, Aug 83	0.60	0.40	1.00	2.00
❑155, Sep 83	0.60	0.40	1.00	2.00
❑156, Oct 83	0.60	0.40	1.00	2.00
❑157, Nov 83	0.60	0.40	1.00	2.00
❑158, Dec 83	0.60	0.40	1.00	2.00
❑159, Jan 84	0.60	0.40	1.00	2.00
❑160, Feb 84	0.60	0.40	1.00	2.00
❑161, Mar 84	0.60	0.40	1.00	2.00
❑162, Apr 84	0.60	0.40	1.00	2.00
❑163, May 84	0.60	0.40	1.00	2.00
❑164, Jun 84	0.60	0.40	1.00	2.00
❑165, Jul 84	0.60	0.40	1.00	2.00
❑166, Aug 84	0.60	0.40	1.00	2.00
❑167, Sep 84	0.60	0.40	1.00	2.00
❑168, Oct 84	0.60	0.40	1.00	2.00
❑169, Nov 84	0.60	0.40	1.00	2.00
❑170, Dec 84	0.60	0.40	1.00	2.00
❑171, Jan 85	0.60	0.40	1.00	2.00
❑172, Feb 85	0.60	0.40	1.00	2.00
❑173, Mar 85	0.60	0.40	1.00	2.00
❑174, Apr 85	0.65	0.40	1.00	2.00
❑175, May 85	0.65	0.40	1.00	2.00
❑176, Jun 85	0.65	0.40	1.00	2.00
❑177, Jul 85	0.65	0.40	1.00	2.00
❑178, Aug 85	0.65	0.40	1.00	2.00
❑179, Sep 85	0.65	0.40	1.00	2.00
❑180, Oct 85	0.65	0.40	1.00	2.00
❑181, Nov 85	0.65	0.40	1.00	2.00
❑182, Dec 85	0.65	0.40	1.00	2.00
❑183, Jan 86	0.65	0.40	1.00	2.00
❑184, Feb 86	0.75	0.40	1.00	2.00
❑185, Mar 86	0.75	0.40	1.00	2.00
❑186, Apr 86	0.75	0.40	1.00	2.00
❑187, May 86	0.75	0.40	1.00	2.00
❑188, Jun 86	0.75	0.40	1.00	2.00
❑189, Jul 86	0.75	0.40	1.00	2.00
❑190, Aug 86	0.75	0.40	1.00	2.00
❑191, Sep 86	0.75	0.40	1.00	2.00
❑192, Oct 86, Giant-size; Reprints Amazing Spider-Man #121-122	0.75	0.40	1.00	2.00
❑193, Nov 86	0.75	0.40	1.00	2.00
❑194, Dec 86	0.75	0.40	1.00	2.00
❑195, Jan 87	0.75	0.40	1.00	2.00
❑196, Feb 87	0.75	0.40	1.00	2.00
❑197, Mar 87	0.75	0.40	1.00	2.00
❑198, Apr 87	0.75	0.40	1.00	2.00
❑199, May 87	0.75	0.40	1.00	2.00
❑200, Jun 87, TMc (c), Giant-size; Reprints Amazing Spider-Man Annual #14	1.25	0.40	1.00	2.00
❑201, Jul 87, TMc (c)	0.75	0.30	0.75	1.50
❑202, Aug 87, TMc (c)	0.75	0.30	0.75	1.50
❑203, Sep 87, TMc (c)	0.75	0.30	0.75	1.50

	ORIG	GOOD	FINE	N-MINT
❑204, Oct 87, TMc (c)	0.75	0.30	0.75	1.50
❑205, Nov 87, TMc (c)	0.75	0.30	0.75	1.50
❑206, Dec 87, TMc (c)	0.75	0.30	0.75	1.50
❑207, Jan 88, TMc (c)	0.75	0.30	0.75	1.50
❑208, Feb 88, TMc (c)	0.75	0.30	0.75	1.50
❑209, Mar 88, TMc (c), 1: Jackal; 1: Punisher	0.75	0.30	0.75	1.50
❑210, Apr 88, TMc (c), A: Punisher	0.75	0.30	0.75	1.50
❑211, May 88, TMc (c), A: Punisher	0.75	0.30	0.75	1.50
❑212, Jun 88, TMc (c), A: Punisher	0.75	0.30	0.75	1.50
❑213, Jul 88, TMc (c), A: Punisher	0.75	0.30	0.75	1.50
❑214, Aug 88, TMc (c), A: Punisher	0.75	0.30	0.75	1.50
❑215, Sep 88, TMc (c), A: Punisher	0.75	0.30	0.75	1.50
❑216, Oct 88, TMc (c), A: Punisher	0.75	0.30	0.75	1.50
❑217, Nov 88, TMc (c), A: Punisher	0.75	0.30	0.75	1.50
❑218, Dec 88, TMc (c), A: Punisher	0.75	0.30	0.75	1.50
❑219, Jan 89, TMc (c), A: Punisher	0.75	0.30	0.75	1.50
❑220, Feb 89, TMc (c), A: Punisher	0.75	0.30	0.75	1.50
❑221, Mar 89, TMc (c), A: Punisher	0.75	0.30	0.75	1.50
❑222, Apr 89, TMc (c), A: Punisher	0.75	0.30	0.75	1.50
❑223, May 89, TMc (c)	0.75	0.30	0.75	1.50
❑224, Jun 89, TMc (c)	0.75	0.30	0.75	1.50
❑225, Jul 89, TMc (c)	0.75	0.30	0.75	1.50
❑226, Aug 89, TMc (c)	0.75	0.30	0.75	1.50
❑227, Sep 89, TMc (c)	1.00	0.30	0.75	1.50
❑228, Oct 89, TMc (c)	1.00	0.30	0.75	1.50
❑229, Nov 89, TMc (c)	1.00	0.30	0.75	1.50
❑230, Nov 89, TMc (c)	1.00	0.30	0.75	1.50
❑231, Dec 89, TMc (c)	1.00	0.30	0.75	1.50
❑232, Dec 89, TMc (c)	1.00	0.30	0.75	1.50
❑233, Jan 90, TMc (c)	1.00	0.30	0.75	1.50
❑234, Feb 90, TMc (c)	1.00	0.30	0.75	1.50
❑235, Mar 90, TMc (c)	1.00	0.30	0.75	1.50
❑236, Apr 90, TMc (c)	1.00	0.30	0.75	1.50
❑237, May 90, TMc (c)	1.00	0.30	0.75	1.50
❑238, Jun 90, TMc (c)	1.00	0.30	0.75	1.50
❑239, Jul 90, TMc (c)	1.00	0.30	0.75	1.50
❑240, Aug 90	1.00	0.30	0.75	1.50
❑241, Sep 90	1.00	0.30	0.75	1.50
❑242, Oct 90	1.00	0.30	0.75	1.50
❑243, Nov 90	1.00	0.30	0.75	1.50
❑244, Dec 90	1.00	0.30	0.75	1.50
❑245, Jan 91	1.00	0.30	0.75	1.50
❑246, Feb 91	1.00	0.30	0.75	1.50
❑247, Mar 91	1.00	0.30	0.75	1.50
❑248, Apr 91	1.00	0.30	0.75	1.50
❑249, May 91	1.00	0.30	0.75	1.50
❑250, Jun 91, O: Storm, Giant-size; Reprints Marvel Team-Up #100	1.50	0.30	0.75	1.50
❑251, Jul 91	1.00	0.30	0.75	1.50
❑252, Aug 91, GK, GK (w), A Monster Called Morbius, 1: Morbius, Reprints Amazing Spider-Man #101	1.00	0.30	0.75	1.50
❑253, Sep 91, GK, GK (w), Vampire at Large; The Way It Began, O: Morbius, Giant-size; Reprints Amazing Spider-Man #102	1.50	0.30	0.75	1.50
❑254, Oct 91	1.00	0.30	0.75	1.50
❑255, Nov 91, SB, Panic On Pier One!	1.00	0.30	0.75	1.50
❑256, Dec 91	1.00	0.30	0.75	1.50
❑257, Jan 92	1.00	0.30	0.75	1.50
❑258, Feb 92	1.25	0.30	0.75	1.50
❑259, Mar 92	1.25	0.30	0.75	1.50
❑260, Apr 92	1.25	0.30	0.75	1.50
❑261, May 92	1.25	0.30	0.75	1.50
❑262, Jun 92, X-Men	1.25	0.30	0.75	1.50
❑263, Jul 92	1.25	0.30	0.75	1.50
❑264, Aug 92, reprints Amazing Spider-Man Annual #5	1.25	0.30	0.75	1.50
❑265, Sep 92, reprints Amazing Spider-Man Annual #6	1.25	0.30	0.75	1.50
❑266, Oct 92	1.25	0.30	0.75	1.50
❑267, Nov 92	1.25	0.30	0.75	1.50
❑268, Dec 92	1.25	0.30	0.75	1.50
❑269, Jan 93	1.25	0.30	0.75	1.50
❑270, Feb 93	1.25	0.30	0.75	1.50
❑271, Mar 93	1.25	0.30	0.75	1.50
❑272, Apr 93	1.25	0.30	0.75	1.50
❑273, May 93	1.25	0.30	0.75	1.50
❑274, Jun 93	1.25	0.30	0.75	1.50
❑275, Jul 93	1.25	0.30	0.75	1.50
❑276, Aug 93	1.25	0.30	0.75	1.50
❑277, Sep 93, 1: Silver Sable	1.25	0.30	0.75	1.50
❑278, Oct 93, A: Beyonder; A: Kingpin, Reprints Amazing Spider-Man #268	1.25	0.30	0.75	1.50
❑279, Nov 93	1.25	0.30	0.75	1.50
❑280, Dec 93	1.25	0.30	0.75	1.50
❑281, Jan 94	1.25	0.30	0.75	1.50

	ORIG	GOOD	FINE	N-MINT
❑282, Feb 94	1.25	0.30	0.75	1.50
❑283, Mar 94, The Choice And The Challenge, O: Spider-Man, double-sized; Reprints Amazing Spider-Man #275; Hobgoblin story	1.25	0.30	0.75	1.50
❑284, Apr 94, Unmasked!, D: Fly; A: Hobgoblin, Reprints Amazing Spider-Man #276	1.25	0.30	0.75	1.50
❑285, May 94, The Rules Of The Game, Reprints Amazing Spider-Man #277	1.25	0.30	0.75	1.50
❑286, Jun 94, D: Wraith, Spider-Man, reprint; Reprints Amazing Spider-Man #278	1.50	0.30	0.75	1.50
❑286-2, Jun 94, Reprint; poster; print	2.95	0.59	1.48	2.95
❑287, Jul 94, Savage Is The Sable, Jack O'Lantern cover/story; Reprints Amazing Spider-Man #279	1.25	0.30	0.75	1.50
❑288, Aug 94, Reprints Amazing Spider-Man #280	1.25	0.30	0.75	1.50
❑289, Sep 94, Jack O'Lantern cover/story; Reprints Amazing Spider-Man #281	1.25	0.30	0.75	1.50
❑290, Oct 94, The Fury Of X-Factor, Reprints Amazing Spider-Man #282	1.50	0.30	0.75	1.50
❑291, Nov 94, Final Issue; Amazing Spider-Man #283	1.50	0.30	0.75	1.50

MARVEL TEAM-UP

MARVEL

	ORIG	GOOD	FINE	N-MINT
❑1, Mar 72, RA, GK (c), Have Yourself a Sandman Little Christmas, V: Sandman; 1: Misty Knight, Spider-Man; Human Torch	0.20	10.00	25.00	50.00
❑2, May 72, RA, GK (c), Spider-Man; Human Torch	0.20	4.80	12.00	24.00
❑3, Jul 72, RA, GK (c), A: Morbius, Spider-Man; Human Torch	0.20	5.60	14.00	28.00
❑4, Sep 72, GK, A: Morbius, Spider-Man; X-Men	0.20	5.60	14.00	28.00
❑5, Nov 72, GK, 1: Ballox ("The Monstroid"), Spider-Man; Vision	0.20	1.80	4.50	9.00
❑6, Jan 73, GK, O: Puppet Master, Spider-Man; Thing	0.20	1.80	4.50	9.00
❑7, Mar 73, RA, GK (c), 1: Kryllk the Cruel, Spider-Man; Thor	0.20	1.80	4.50	9.00
❑8, Apr 73, JM, 1: The Man-Killer, Spider-Man; The Cat	0.20	1.80	4.50	9.00
❑9, May 73, RA, JR (c), Spider-Man; Iron Man; Spider-Man, Iron Man	0.20	1.80	4.50	9.00
❑10, Jun 73, JM, JR (c), Spider-Man; Human Torch	0.20	1.80	4.50	9.00
❑11, Jul 73, JM, JR (c), Spider-Man; Inhumans	0.20	1.40	3.50	7.00
❑12, Aug 73, RA, GK (c), 1: Moondark, Spider-Man; Werewolf	0.20	1.40	3.50	7.00
❑13, Sep 73, GK, Spider-Man; Captain America	0.20	1.40	3.50	7.00
❑14, Oct 73, GK, 1: The Aquanoids, Spider-Man; Sub-Mariner	0.20	1.40	3.50	7.00
❑15, Nov 73, RA, GK (c), 1: Orb, Spider-Man; Ghost Rider	0.20	1.40	3.50	7.00
❑16, Dec 73, GK, 1: The Basilisk I (Basil Elks), Spider-Man; Captain Marvel	0.20	1.40	3.50	7.00
❑17, Jan 74, GK, V: Mole Man; V: Basilisk, Spider-Man; Mr. Fantastic	0.20	1.40	3.50	7.00
❑18, Feb 74, GK, Where Bursts The Bomb!, Human Torch; Hulk	0.20	1.40	3.50	7.00
❑19, Mar 74, GK, 1: Stegron, the Dinosaur Man, Spider-Man; Ka-Zar	0.20	1.40	3.50	7.00
❑20, Apr 74, SB, GK (c), Spider-Man; Black Panther	0.20	1.40	3.50	7.00
❑21, May 74, SB, GK (c), Spider-Man; Doctor Strange	0.25	1.20	3.00	6.00
❑22, Jun 74, SB, JR (c), The Messiah Machine, Spider-Man; Hawkeye	0.25	1.20	3.00	6.00
❑23, Jul 74, GK, A: X-Men, Human Torch; Iceman; X-Men	0.25	1.20	3.00	6.00
❑24, Aug 74, JM, GK (c), Moondog Is Another Name For Murder!, Spider-Man; Brother Voodoo	0.25	1.20	3.00	6.00
❑25, Sep 74, JM, GK (c), Three Into Two Won't Go!, Spider-Man; Daredevil	0.25	1.20	3.00	6.00
❑26, Oct 74, JM, GK (c), The Fire This Time...!, Human Torch; Thor	0.25	1.20	3.00	6.00
❑27, Nov 74, JM, JSn (c), Spider-Man; Hulk	0.25	1.20	3.00	6.00
❑28, Dec 74, JM, GK (c), The City Stealers, Spider-Man; Hercules	0.25	1.20	3.00	6.00
❑29, Jan 75, JM, JR (c), Human Torch; Iron Man	0.25	1.20	3.00	6.00
❑30, Feb 75, JM, GK (c), Spider-Man; The Falcon	0.25	1.20	3.00	6.00
❑31, Mar 75, JM, GK (c), Spider-Man; Iron Fist	0.25	1.20	3.00	6.00
❑32, Apr 75, SB, GK (c), Human Torch; Son of Satan	0.25	0.80	2.00	4.00
❑33, May 75, SB, GK (c), V: Meteor Man, Spider-Man; Nighthawk	0.25	0.80	2.00	4.00

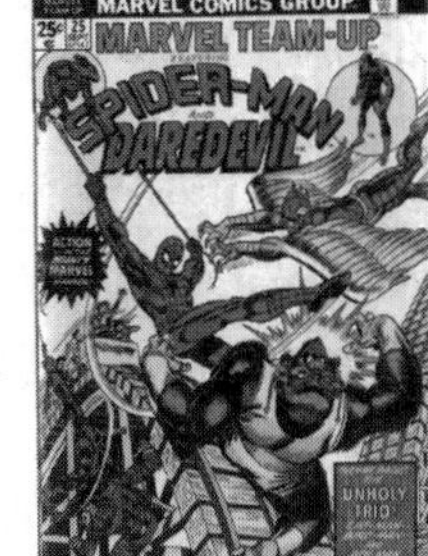

Spider-Man and Daredevil joined forces to fight a trio of DD's villains in *Marvel Team-Up* #25.

	ORIG	GOOD	FINE	N-MINT
❑34, Jun 75, SB, GK (c), V: Meteor Man, Spider-Man; Valkyrie	0.25	0.80	2.00	4.00
❑35, Jul 75, SB, GK (c), Human Torch; Doctor Strange; Doctor Strange team-up	0.25	0.80	2.00	4.00
❑36, Aug 75, SB, Spider-Man; Frankenstein	0.25	0.80	2.00	4.00
❑37, Sep 75, SB, Spider-Man; Man-Wolf	0.25	0.80	2.00	4.00
❑38, Oct 75, SB, Night Of The Griffin, Spider-Man; Beast	0.25	0.80	2.00	4.00
❑39, Nov 75, SB, Spider-Man; Human Torch	0.25	0.80	2.00	4.00
❑40, Dec 75, SB, Spider-Man; Sons of Tiger; Human Torch; Sons of the Tiger	0.25	0.80	2.00	4.00
❑41, Jan 76, SB, GK (c), Spider-Man; Scarlet Witch	0.25	0.80	2.00	4.00
❑42, Feb 76, SB, Spider-Man; Scarlet Witch; Vision	0.25	0.80	2.00	4.00
❑43, Mar 76, SB, GK (c), A: Doctor Doom, Spider-Man; Doctor Doom	0.25	0.80	2.00	4.00
❑44, Apr 76, SB, GK (c), Spider-Man; Moondragon	0.25	0.80	2.00	4.00
❑45, May 76, SB, GK (c), Spider-Man; Killraven	0.25	0.80	2.00	4.00
❑46, Jun 76, SB, RB (c), Spider-Man; Deathlok	0.25	0.80	2.00	4.00
❑47, Jul 76, GK (c), V: Basilisk, Spider-Man; Thing	0.25	0.60	1.50	3.00
❑48, Aug 76, SB, JR (c), 1: Wraith, Spider-Man; Iron Man	0.25	0.60	1.50	3.00
❑49, Sep 76, SB, JR (c), O: Wraith, Spider-Man; Iron Man; Doctor Strange	0.30	0.60	1.50	3.00
❑50, Oct 76, SB, GK (c), SB (w), The Mystery Of the Wraith!, Spider-Man; Doctor Strange; Iron Man	0.25	0.60	1.50	3.00
❑51, Nov 76, SB, GK (c), Spider-Man; Iron Man	0.30	0.60	1.50	3.00
❑52, Dec 76, SB, Danger: Demon on a Rampage!, A: Batroc, Spider-Man; Captain America	0.30	0.60	1.50	3.00
❑53, Jan 77, JBy, DC (c), A: Woodgod; A: X-Men, Spider-Man; Hulk; Woodgod; X-Men; 1st John Byrne art on X-Men	0.30	1.20	3.00	6.00
❑54, Feb 77, JBy, GK (c), A: Woodgod, Spider-Man; Hulk	0.30	0.70	1.75	3.50
❑55, Mar 77, JBy, DC (c), 1: the Gardener; V: Gardener, Spider-Man; Warlock	0.30	0.70	1.75	3.50
❑56, Apr 77, SB, JR2 (c), V: Electro; V: Blizzard, Spider-Man; Daredevil	0.30	0.40	1.00	2.00
❑57, May 77, SB, DC (c), Spider-Man; Black Widow	0.30	0.40	1.00	2.00
❑58, Jun 77, DC; SB, AM (c), Spider-Man; Ghost Rider	0.30	0.40	1.00	2.00
❑59, Jul 77, JBy, DC (c), Some Say Spidey Will Die By Fire...Some Say By Ice!, Spider-Man; Yellowjacket; The Wasp	0.30	0.40	1.00	2.00
❑60, Aug 77, JBy, AM (c), A Matter Of Love...And Death!, A: Yellowjacket, Spider-Man; The Wasp	0.30	0.40	1.00	2.00
❑61, Sep 77, JBy, RA (c), Not All The Powers Can Save Thee!, V: Super-Skrull, Spider-Man; Human Torch	0.30	0.40	1.00	2.00
❑62, Oct 77, JBy, GK (c), All This And The QE2, V: Super-Skrull, Spider-Man; Ms. Marvel	0.30	0.40	1.00	2.00
❑63, Nov 77, JBy, DC (c), Night Of The Dragon, Spider-Man; Iron Fist	0.35	0.40	1.00	2.00
❑64, Dec 77, JBy, DC (c), If Death Be My Destiny..., Spider-Man; Daughters of Dragon; Daughters of the Dragon	0.35	0.40	1.00	2.00
❑65, Jan 78, JBy, GP (c), Murder World, 1: Captain Britain (U.S.); 1: Arcade, Spider-Man	0.35	0.40	1.00	2.00
❑66, Feb 78, JBy, V: Arcade, Spider-Man; Captain Britain	0.35	0.40	1.00	2.00
❑67, Mar 78, JBy, Tigra Tigra, Burning Bright!, V: Kraven; A: Tigra, Spider-Man	0.35	0.40	1.00	2.00
❑68, Apr 78, JBy, The Measure Of A Man!, 1: D'Spayre; A: Man-Thing, Spider-Man	0.35	0.40	1.00	2.00
❑69, May 78, JBy, DC (c), Night Of The Living God!, A: Havok, Spider-Man	0.35	0.40	1.00	2.00

	ORIG	GOOD	FINE	N-MINT
❑70, Jun 78, JBy, Whom Gods Destroy!, V: Living Monolith, Spider-Man; Thor	0.35	0.40	1.00	2.00
❑71, Jul 78, Spider-Man; The Falcon	0.35	0.40	1.00	2.00
❑72, Aug 78, JM, JBy (c), Spider-Man; Iron Man	0.35	0.40	1.00	2.00
❑73, Sep 78, KP (c), Spider-Man; Daredevil	0.35	0.40	1.00	2.00
❑74, Oct 78, DC (c), A: Not Ready For Prime Time Players (Saturday Night Live), Spider-Man	0.35	0.60	1.50	3.00
❑75, Nov 78, JBy, The Smoke OF That Great Burning!, Spider-Man; Power Man	0.35	0.40	1.00	2.00
❑76, Dec 78, HC, JBy (c), If Not For Love..., Spider-Man; Doctor Strange	0.35	0.40	1.00	2.00
❑77, Jan 79, HC, JR2 (c), Spider-Man; Ms. Marvel	0.35	0.40	1.00	2.00
❑78, Feb 79, DP, AM (c), Claws!, Spider-Man; Wonder Man	0.35	0.40	1.00	2.00
❑79, Mar 79, JBy, Sword Of The She-Devil, Spider-Man; Red Sonja	0.35	0.40	1.00	2.00
❑80, Apr 79, RB (c), A Sorcerer Possessed!, Spider-Man; Doctor Strange; Clea	0.35	0.40	1.00	2.00
❑81, May 79, AM (c), D: Satana, Spider-Man; Satana	0.40	0.40	1.00	2.00
❑82, Jun 79, SB, RB (c), Spider-Man; Black Widow	0.40	0.40	1.00	2.00
❑83, Jul 79, SB, RB (c), Spider-Man; Nick Fury	0.40	0.40	1.00	2.00
❑84, Aug 79, SB, Catch A Falling Hero, Spider-Man; Shang-Chi	0.40	0.40	1.00	2.00
❑85, Sep 79, SB, AM (c), Spider-Man; Shang-Chi; Nick Fury; Black Widow	0.40	0.40	1.00	2.00
❑86, Oct 79, BMc, Story Of The Year!, Spider-Man; Guardians of Galaxy	0.40	0.40	1.00	2.00
❑87, Nov 79, GC, AM (c), 1: Hellrazor, Spider-Man; Black Panther	0.40	0.40	1.00	2.00
❑88, Dec 79, SB, RB (c), Spider-Man; Invisible Girl	0.40	0.40	1.00	2.00
❑89, Jan 80, RB; MN, Shoot Out Over Center Ring, 1: Cutthroat, Spider-Man; Nightcrawler	0.40	0.40	1.00	2.00
❑90, Feb 80, AM (c), Spider-Man; Beast	0.40	0.40	1.00	2.00
❑91, Mar 80, PB, RB (c), Spider-Man; Ghost Rider	0.40	0.40	1.00	2.00
❑92, Apr 80, CI, AM (c), Fear!, 1: Mister Fear IV (Alan Fagan), Spider-Man; Hawkeye	0.40	0.40	1.00	2.00
❑93, May 80, CI; TS, DP (c), Rags To Riches!, Spider-Man; Werewolf; Werewolf by Night	0.40	0.40	1.00	2.00
❑94, Jun 80, MZ, AM (c), Darkness, Darkness..., Spider-Man; Shroud	0.40	0.40	1.00	2.00
❑95, Jul 80, FM (c), ...And No Birds Sing!, 1: Huntress as Mockingbird; 1: Mockingbird, Spider-Man	0.40	0.40	1.00	2.00
❑96, Aug 80, Spider-Man; Howard the Duck	0.40	0.40	1.00	2.00
❑97, Sep 80, CI, Doctor Of Madness, Hulk; Spider-Woman	0.50	0.40	1.00	2.00
❑98, Oct 80, AM (c), Spider-Man; Black Widow	0.50	0.40	1.00	2.00
❑99, Nov 80, FM (c), And Machine Man Makes 3, Spider-Man; Machine Man	0.50	0.40	1.00	2.00
❑100, Dec 80, FM; JBy, FM (w), And Introducing-Karma! She Possesses People!, O: Storm; 1: Karma, double-sized; Spider-Man; Fantastic Four; Black Panther	0.75	1.00	2.50	5.00
❑101, Jan 81, To Judge A Nighthawk!, Spider-Man; Nighthawk	0.50	0.40	1.00	2.00
❑102, Feb 81, FS, FM (c), Samson And Delilah!, Spider-Man; Doc Samson	0.50	0.40	1.00	2.00
❑103, Mar 81, The Assassin Academy, Spider-Man; Ant-Man	0.50	0.40	1.00	2.00
❑104, Apr 81, AM (c), Hulk; Ka-Zar	0.50	0.40	1.00	2.00
❑105, May 81, CI, AM (c), Power Man; Iron Fist; Hulk	0.50	0.40	1.00	2.00
❑106, Jun 81, HT, FM (c), V: Scorpion, Spider-Man; Captain America	0.50	0.40	1.00	2.00
❑107, Jul 81, HT, Spider-Man; She-Hulk	0.50	0.40	1.00	2.00
❑108, Aug 81, HT, Spider-Man; Paladin	0.50	0.40	1.00	2.00
❑109, Sep 81, HT, JR2 (c), Spider-Man; Dazzler	0.50	0.40	1.00	2.00
❑110, Oct 81, HT, BL (c), Spider-Man; Iron Man	0.50	0.40	1.00	2.00
❑111, Nov 81, HT, Spider-Man; Devil-Slayer	0.50	0.40	1.00	2.00
❑112, Dec 81, HT, Spider-Man; King Kull	0.50	0.40	1.00	2.00
❑113, Jan 82, Spider-Man; Quasar	0.60	0.40	1.00	2.00
❑114, Feb 82, Spider-Man; The Falcon	0.60	0.40	1.00	2.00
❑115, Mar 82, Spider-Man; Thor	0.60	0.40	1.00	2.00
❑116, Apr 82, Spider-Man; Valkyrie	0.60	0.40	1.00	2.00
❑117, May 82, 1: Professor Power, Spider-Man; Wolverine	0.60	0.80	2.00	4.00
❑118, Jun 82, HT, Meeting Of The Minds, O: Professor Power, Spider-Man; Professor X	0.60	0.40	1.00	2.00
❑119, Jul 82, KGa, Spider-Man; Gargoyle	0.60	0.40	1.00	2.00
❑120, Aug 82, KGa, Spider-Man; Dominic Fortune	0.60	0.40	1.00	2.00
❑121, Sep 82, KGa, 1: Frog-Man II, Spider-Man; Human Torch	0.60	0.40	1.00	2.00
❑122, Oct 82, DD, Man-Thing	0.60	0.40	1.00	2.00
❑123, Nov 82, DD, Man-Thing; Daredevil	0.60	0.40	1.00	2.00
❑124, Dec 82, KGa, The Ties That Bind!, O: Professor Power, Spider-Man; The Beast	0.60	0.40	1.00	2.00
❑125, Jan 83, KGa, Tigra!, Spider-Man; Tigra	0.60	0.40	1.00	2.00
❑126, Feb 83, BH, Spider-Man; Hulk; Power Man; Son of Satan	0.60	0.40	1.00	2.00
❑127, Mar 83, KGa, Small Miracles, Spider-Man; The Watcher	0.60	0.40	1.00	2.00
❑128, Apr 83, Photo cover; Spider-Man; Captain America	0.60	0.40	1.00	2.00
❑129, May 83, KGa, ...And Much To Ponder Before The Dawn, Spider-Man; Vision; The Vision	0.60	0.40	1.00	2.00
❑130, Jun 83, SB, Till Death Do Us Part!, Spider-Man; Scarlet Witch; The Scarlet Witch	0.60	0.40	1.00	2.00
❑131, Jul 83, KGa, The Best Things In Life Are Free...But Everything Else Costs Money!, Spider-Man; Frogman	0.60	0.40	1.00	2.00
❑132, Aug 83, Spider-Man; Mr. Fantastic	0.60	0.40	1.00	2.00
❑133, Sep 83, SB, The World According To...Faustus!, Spider-Man; Fantastic Four	0.60	0.40	1.00	2.00
❑134, Oct 83, The Boy's Night Out!, Spider-Man; Jack of Hearts	0.60	0.40	1.00	2.00
❑135, Nov 83, Spider-Man; Kitty Pryde	0.60	0.40	1.00	2.00
❑136, Dec 83, Webs, Spider-Man; Wonder Man	0.60	0.40	1.00	2.00
❑137, Jan 84, O: Doctor Faustus, Spider-Man; Aunt May; Franklin Richards	0.60	0.40	1.00	2.00
❑138, Feb 84, Starting Over!, Spider-Man; Sandman (Marvel); Nick Fury	0.60	0.40	1.00	2.00
❑139, Mar 84, Spider-Man; Sandman (Marvel); Nick Fury	0.60	0.40	1.00	2.00
❑140, Apr 84, Spider-Man; Black Widow	0.60	0.40	1.00	2.00
❑141, May 84, Spider-Man new costume; Daredevil	0.60	0.40	1.00	2.00
❑142, Jun 84, Spider-Man; Captain Marvel (female, new)	0.60	0.40	1.00	2.00
❑143, Jul 84, Spider-Man; Starfox	0.60	0.40	1.00	2.00
❑144, Aug 84, Spider-Man; Moon Knight	0.60	0.40	1.00	2.00
❑145, Sep 84, Spider-Man; Iron Man	0.60	0.40	1.00	2.00
❑146, Oct 84, Spider-Man; Nomad	0.60	0.40	1.00	2.00
❑147, Nov 84, Spider-Man; Human Torch	0.60	0.40	1.00	2.00
❑148, Dec 84, A Child Shall Lead Them!, Spider-Man; Thor	0.60	0.40	1.00	2.00
❑149, Jan 85, Spider-Man; Cannonball	0.60	0.40	1.00	2.00
❑150, Feb 85, Final Issue; Giant-size; Spider-Man; X-Men	1.00	0.60	1.50	3.00
❑Anl 1, SB, DC (c), Spider-Man; X-Men	0.50	3.00	7.50	15.00
❑Anl 2, SB, AM (c), Spider-Man; Hulk	0.75	0.80	2.00	4.00
❑Anl 3, HT, FM (c), Hulk; Power Man; Iron Fist; Machine Man	0.75	0.60	1.50	3.00
❑Anl 4, FM; HT, FM (c), FM (w), Spider-Man; Iron Fist; Power Man; Daredevil; Moon Knight	0.75	0.50	1.25	2.50
❑Anl 5, Nov 81, Spider-Man; Thing; Scarlet Witch; Vision; Quasar	1.00	0.50	1.25	2.50
❑Anl 6, Oct 83, The Hunters And The Hunted!, New Mutants; Cloak & Dagger	1.00	0.50	1.25	2.50
❑Anl 7, Oct 84, Alpha Flight	1.00	0.40	1.00	2.00

MARVEL TEAM-UP (2ND SERIES)

MARVEL

	ORIG	GOOD	FINE	N-MINT
❑1, Sep 97, D.E.A.D. to Rights!, gatefold summary; Spider-Man; Generation X; Story takes place before Generation X #32	1.99	0.40	1.00	2.00
❑2, Oct 97, gatefold summary; Spider-Man; Hercules	1.99	0.40	1.00	2.00
❑3, Nov 97, A: Silver Sable, gatefold summary; Spider-Man; Sandman; Sandman (Marvel)	1.99	0.40	1.00	2.00
❑4, Dec 97, gatefold summary; Spider-Man; Man-Thing	1.99	0.40	1.00	2.00
❑5, Jan 98, V: Authority, Spider-Man	1.99	0.40	1.00	2.00
❑6, Feb 98, V: Wrecking Crew, Spider-Man; Sub-Mariner	1.99	0.40	1.00	2.00
❑7, Mar 98, Spider-Man; Blade	1.99	0.40	1.00	2.00
❑8, Apr 98, Sub-Mariner; Doctor Strange	1.99	0.40	1.00	2.00
❑9, May 98, Sub-Mariner; Captain America	1.99	0.40	1.00	2.00
❑10, Jun 98, Sub-Mariner; Thing	1.99	0.40	1.00	2.00
❑11, Jul 98, V: Wrecking Crew, Final Issue; Sub-Mariner; Iron Man	1.99	0.40	1.00	2.00

MARVEL: THE LOST GENERATION

MARVEL

Value: Cover or less

❑1, Feb 01, JBy, JBy (w), It's Starting Again, #12 in sequence. 2.99

❑2, Jan 01, JBy, JBy (w), After ..., #11 in sequence 2.99

ORIG GOOD FINE N-MINT

- ❑3, Dec 00, JBy, JBy (w), Mad to Live, A: Sub-Mariner; A: Yellow Claw, #10 in sequence 2.99
- ❑4, Nov 00, JBy, JBy (w), Lightning in the Day, #9 in sequence 2.99
- ❑5, Oct 00, JBy, JBy (w), Wild in the Streets, A: Odin; A: Thor; A: Venus, #8 in sequence 2.99
- ❑6, Sep 00, JBy, JBy (w), Crisis of Conscience, #7 in sequence 2.99
- ❑7, Aug 00, JBy, JBy (w), Highly Placed Sources, A: Sub-Mariner; A: Fantastic Four, #6 in sequence 2.99
- ❑8, JBy, JBy (w), #5 in sequence 2.95
- ❑9, JBy, JBy (w), #4 in sequence 2.95
- ❑10, Dec 00, JBy, JBy (w), Mad to Live, #3 in sequence 2.95
- ❑11, Nov 00, JBy, JBy (w), #2 in sequence 2.95
- ❑12, Oct 00, JBy, JBy (w), #1 in sequence 2.95

MARVEL TREASURY EDITION
MARVEL

	ORIG	GOOD	FINE	N-MINT
❑1, SD, The Spectacular Spider-Man	1.50	2.00	5.00	10.00
❑2, Dec 74, JK, SL (w), Captives of the Deadly Duo!; The Impossible Man, A: Sub-Mariner; 1: The Silver Surfer; 1: Galactus, The Fabulous Fantastic Four; Reprints early Fantastic Four issues	1.50	1.50	3.75	7.50
❑3, JK, SL (w), When Meet the Immortals!; Whom the Gods Would Destroy!, V: Hercules, The Mighty Thor; reprints Thor #125-130	1.50	1.50	3.75	7.50
❑4, An Informal History of the Thomas/Smith Conan; Rogues in the House, Conan	1.50	1.50	3.75	7.50
❑5, JSt; JSe; HT; JSn, The Origin of The Hulk; Let There be Battle!, reprints Hulk #3, 139, 141, Tales to Astonish #79, 100, and Marvel Feature #11	1.50	1.50	3.75	7.50
❑6, BEv; FB; GC; SD, The End...at Last!; The Origin of the Ancient One!, O: The Ancient One, Doctor Strange	1.50	1.50	3.75	7.50
❑7, Avengers	1.50	1.50	3.75	7.50
❑8, SD, Twas the Night Before Christmas; Spidey Gone Mad!, Giant Super-Hero Holiday Grab Bag; The Incredible Hulk #147, Luke Cage, Hero for Hire #7	1.50	1.50	3.75	7.50
❑9, JK; JB, JB (w), In the Rage of Battle; In Combat with Captain America!, Giant Superhero Team-up; Reprints Prince Namor, the Sub-Mariner #8, Journey into Mystery #112, Silver Surfer (Vol. 1) #14, Daredevil #43; Namor vs. Human-Torch; Daredevil vs. Captain America; Thor vs. Hulk; Silver Surfer vs. Spider-Man	1.50	1.50	3.75	7.50
❑10, JK, SL (w), To Wake the Mangog!; Now Ends the Universe, The Mighty Thor; Reprints Thor #154-157	1.50	1.50	3.75	7.50
❑11, FF, Fantastic Four	1.50	1.50	3.75	7.50
❑12, KJ; TP; SB; VM; FB, The Duck and the Defenders; The Way it All Began!, Reprints Howard the Duck #1, Giant-Size Man-Thing #4, 5, with new Defenders story; Howard the Duck	1.50	1.50	3.75	7.50
❑13, Giant Super-Hero Holiday Grab-Bag	1.50	1.50	3.75	7.50
❑14, Amazing Spider-Man; reprints Amazing Spider-Man #100-102 and Not Brand Echh #6	1.50	1.50	3.75	7.50
❑15, Conan; Red Sonja	1.50	1.50	3.75	7.50
❑16, Defenders	1.50	1.50	3.75	7.50
❑17, JSe; HT; SB, Within the Swamp, there Stirs...a Glob!; Among us Walks the Golem, The Incredible Hulk; Reprints The Incredible Hulk #121, 134, 150	1.50	1.50	3.75	7.50
❑18, Spider-Man; X-Men	2.00	1.50	3.75	7.50
❑19, Conan	2.00	1.50	3.75	7.50
❑20, Hulk; reprints Incredible Hulk #136, 137, 143, 144; pin-up gallery	2.00	1.50	3.75	7.50
❑21, FF, Fantastic Four	2.00	1.50	3.75	7.50
❑22, Spider-Man	2.00	1.50	3.75	7.50
❑23, Conan	2.00	1.50	3.75	7.50
❑24, Incredible Hulk; reprints Incredible Hulk #167-170; Wolverine and Hercules new back-up story	2.00	1.50	3.75	7.50
❑25, Spider-Man and Hulk at Winter Olympics	2.00	1.50	3.75	7.50
❑26, Hulk; Wolverine; Hercules	2.00	1.60	4.00	8.00
❑27, Marvel Team-Up; reprints MTU #9-11 and 27; new Angel story	2.00	1.50	3.75	7.50
❑28, Jul 81, V: Doctor Doom; V: Parasite; A: Hulk; A: Wonder Woman, Spider-Man and Superman	2.50	3.00	7.50	15.00

MARVEL TREASURY OF OZ
MARVEL

	ORIG	GOOD	FINE	N-MINT
❑1, adapts Baum's Land of Oz	1.50	2.00	5.00	10.00

MARVEL TREASURY SPECIAL FEATURING CAPTAIN AMERICA'S BICENTENNIAL BATTLES
MARVEL

	ORIG	GOOD	FINE	N-MINT
❑1, JK, JK (w), Captain America's Bicentennial Battles	1.50	2.80	7.00	14.00

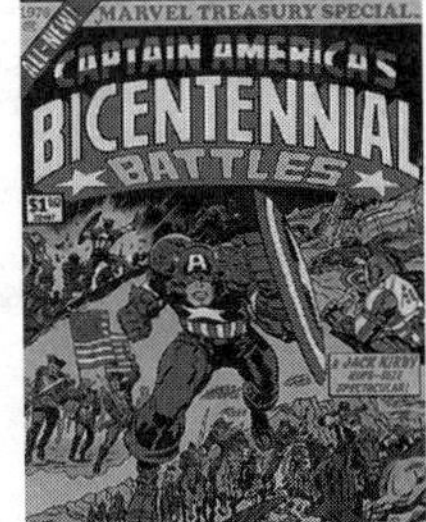

To celebrate the U.S. Bicentennial in 1976, Marvel issued a treasury edition featuring Captain America battling the forces of evil throughout America's history.

© 1976 Marvel Comics

MARVEL TREASURY SPECIAL, GIANT SUPERHERO HOLIDAY GRAB-BAG
MARVEL

	ORIG	GOOD	FINE	N-MINT
❑1, RA; WW; JK; GC, Have Yourself a Sandman, Little Christmas; In Mortal Combat with The Sub-Mariner!, Giant Super-Hero Holiday Grab Bag; reprints MTU #1, Fantastic Four #25-26, DD #7, and Amazing Adventures; reprints Marvel Team-Up #1, Fantastic Four #25-26, Daredevil #7, and Amazing Adventures	1.50	1.50	3.75	7.50

MARVEL TRIPLE ACTION
MARVEL

	ORIG	GOOD	FINE	N-MINT
❑1, reprints Avengers	0.25	1.00	2.50	5.00
❑2	0.20	0.60	1.50	3.00
❑3	0.20	0.60	1.50	3.00
❑4	0.20	0.60	1.50	3.00
❑5	0.20	0.60	1.50	3.00
❑6, Oct 72, DH, SL (w), This Hostage Earth!	0.20	0.40	1.00	2.00
❑7	0.20	0.40	1.00	2.00
❑8	0.20	0.40	1.00	2.00
❑9	0.20	0.40	1.00	2.00
❑10	0.20	0.40	1.00	2.00
❑11	0.20	0.40	1.00	2.00
❑12	0.20	0.40	1.00	2.00
❑13	0.20	0.40	1.00	2.00
❑14, Oct 73, DH, SL (w), Vengeance is Ours!	0.20	0.40	1.00	2.00
❑15	0.20	0.40	1.00	2.00
❑16	0.20	0.40	1.00	2.00
❑17	0.20	0.40	1.00	2.00
❑18	0.25	0.40	1.00	2.00
❑19	0.25	0.40	1.00	2.00
❑20	0.25	0.40	1.00	2.00
❑21, Oct 74	0.25	0.40	1.00	2.00
❑22, Nov 74, DH, SL (w), Four Against the Floodtide!, reprints Avengers #28	0.25	0.40	1.00	2.00
❑23, Jan 75	0.25	0.40	1.00	2.00
❑24	0.25	0.40	1.00	2.00
❑25	0.25	0.40	1.00	2.00
❑26, Nov 75	0.25	0.40	1.00	2.00
❑27, Jan 76	0.25	0.40	1.00	2.00
❑28, Mar 76	0.25	0.40	1.00	2.00
❑29, May 76	0.25	0.40	1.00	2.00
❑30, Jul 76	0.25	0.40	1.00	2.00
❑31, Sep 76	0.30	0.40	1.00	2.00
❑32, Nov 76	0.30	0.40	1.00	2.00
❑33, Jan 77	0.30	0.40	1.00	2.00
❑34, Mar 77	0.30	0.40	1.00	2.00
❑35, May 77	0.30	0.40	1.00	2.00
❑36, Jul 77	0.30	0.40	1.00	2.00
❑37, Sep 77	0.30	0.40	1.00	2.00
❑38, Nov 77	0.30	0.40	1.00	2.00
❑39, Jan 78	0.30	0.40	1.00	2.00
❑40, Mar 78	0.30	0.40	1.00	2.00
❑41, Apr 78	0.30	0.40	1.00	2.00
❑42, Jun 78	0.30	0.40	1.00	2.00
❑43, Aug 78	0.30	0.40	1.00	2.00
❑44, Oct 78	0.30	0.40	1.00	2.00
❑45, Dec 78, A: X-Men	0.30	0.40	1.00	2.00
❑46, Feb 79	0.30	0.40	1.00	2.00
❑47, Apr 79	0.30	0.40	1.00	2.00
❑GS 1	0.50	0.80	2.00	4.00
❑GS 2	0.50	0.80	2.00	4.00

MARVEL TWO-IN-ONE
MARVEL

	ORIG	GOOD	FINE	N-MINT
❑1, Jan 74, Man-Thing	0.20	4.40	11.00	22.00
❑2, Mar 74, Sub-Mariner; Namor	0.20	1.80	4.50	9.00
❑3, May 74, A: Black Widow, Daredevil	0.25	1.40	3.50	7.00
❑4, Jul 74, Captain America	0.25	1.40	3.50	7.00
❑5, Sep 74, Guardians of the Galaxy	0.25	1.60	4.00	8.00
❑6, Nov 74, Doctor Strange	0.25	1.60	4.00	8.00
❑7, Jan 75, A: Doctor Strange, Valkyrie	0.25	1.00	2.50	5.00

	ORIG	GOOD	FINE	N-MINT
❑8, Mar 75, Ghost Rider	0.25	1.00	2.50	5.00
❑9, May 75, Thor	0.25	1.00	2.50	5.00
❑10, Jul 75, Black Widow	0.25	1.00	2.50	5.00
❑11, Sep 75, Golem	0.25	0.60	1.50	3.00
❑12, Nov 75, Iron Man	0.25	0.60	1.50	3.00
❑13, Jan 76, I Created Braggadoom!, Power Man	0.25	0.60	1.50	3.00
❑14, Mar 76, Son of Satan	0.25	0.60	1.50	3.00
❑15, May 76, Morbius	0.25	0.60	1.50	3.00
❑16, Jun 76, Ka-Zar	0.25	0.60	1.50	3.00
❑17, Jul 76, A: Basilisk I (Basil Elks), Spider-Man	0.25	0.60	1.50	3.00
❑18, Aug 76, Scarecrow; Spider-Man	0.25	0.60	1.50	3.00
❑18/A, Aug 76, 30¢ Cover price; Scarecrow; Spider-Man	0.30	1.60	4.00	8.00
❑19, Sep 76, Tigra	0.30	0.60	1.50	3.00
❑20, Oct 76, Liberty Legion; continued from Marvel Two-In-One Annual #1	0.30	0.60	1.50	3.00
❑21, Nov 76, A: Human Torch, Doc Savage	0.30	0.60	1.50	3.00
❑22, Dec 76, Human Torch; Thor	0.30	0.60	1.50	3.00
❑23, Jan 77, Human Torch; Thor	0.30	0.60	1.50	3.00
❑24, Feb 77, SB, Black Goliath	0.30	0.60	1.50	3.00
❑25, Mar 77, Iron Fist	0.30	0.60	1.50	3.00
❑26, Apr 77, Nick Fury	0.30	0.40	1.00	2.00
❑27, May 77, Deathlok	0.30	0.40	1.00	2.00
❑28, Jun 77, Sub-Mariner	0.30	0.40	1.00	2.00
❑29, Jul 77, Two Against Hydra, Shang-Chi	0.30	0.40	1.00	2.00
❑30, Aug 77, JB, 2: Spider-Woman I (Jessica Drew)	0.30	0.40	1.00	2.00
❑31, Sep 77, Spider-Woman I (Jessica Drew)	0.30	0.40	1.00	2.00
❑32, Oct 77, Invisible Girl	0.30	0.40	1.00	2.00
❑33, Nov 77, Mordred	0.35	0.40	1.00	2.00
❑34, Dec 77, Nighthawk	0.35	0.40	1.00	2.00
❑35, Jan 78, Skull the Slayer	0.35	0.40	1.00	2.00
❑36, Feb 78, Mr. Fantastic	0.35	0.40	1.00	2.00
❑37, Mar 78, Matt Murdock	0.35	0.40	1.00	2.00
❑38, Apr 78, Daredevil	0.35	0.40	1.00	2.00
❑39, May 78, Vision; Daredevil	0.35	0.40	1.00	2.00
❑40, Jun 78, Black Panther	0.35	0.40	1.00	2.00
❑41, Jul 78, Brother Voodoo	0.35	0.40	1.00	2.00
❑42, Aug 78, Captain America	0.35	0.40	1.00	2.00
❑43, Sep 78, JBy, Man-Thing	0.35	0.40	1.00	2.00
❑44, Oct 78, GD, Hercules	0.35	0.40	1.00	2.00
❑45, Nov 78, The Andromeda Rub-Out!, Captain Marvel	0.35	0.40	1.00	2.00
❑46, Dec 78, Hulk	0.35	0.40	1.00	2.00
❑47, Jan 79, GD, 1: Machinesmith, Yancy Street Gang	0.35	0.40	1.00	2.00
❑48, Feb 79, Jack of Hearts	0.35	0.40	1.00	2.00
❑49, Mar 79, GD, Doctor Strange	0.35	0.40	1.00	2.00
❑50, Apr 79, JSt; JSe; JBy, JBy (w), Remembrance Of Things Past!, Thing vs. Thing	0.35	0.40	1.00	2.00
❑51, May 79, BMc; FM, Beast; Wonder Man; Ms. Marvel; Nick Fury	0.40	0.60	1.50	3.00
❑52, Jun 79, Moon Knight	0.40	0.40	1.00	2.00
❑53, Jul 79, JSe; JBy, Quasar	0.40	0.40	1.00	2.00
❑54, Aug 79, JSe; JBy, 1: Poundcakes; D: Deathlok I (Luther Manning); 1: Screaming Mimi, Deathlok	0.40	0.80	2.00	4.00
❑55, Sep 79, JSe; JBy, Giant Man II (Bill Foster)	0.40	0.40	1.00	2.00
❑56, Oct 79, GD; GP, 1: Letha, Thundra	0.40	0.30	0.75	1.50
❑57, Nov 79, GD; GP, Wundarr	0.40	0.30	0.75	1.50
❑58, Dec 79, GD; GP, Aquarian; Quasar	0.40	0.30	0.75	1.50
❑59, Jan 80, Trial And Error!, Human Torch	0.40	0.30	0.75	1.50
❑60, Feb 80, GD; GP, 1: Impossible Woman, Impossible Man	0.40	0.30	0.75	1.50
❑61, Mar 80, GD, 1: Her, Starhawk	0.40	0.30	0.75	1.50
❑62, Apr 80, The Taking Of Counter-Earth, Moondragon	0.40	0.30	0.75	1.50
❑63, May 80, GD, Warlock	0.40	0.30	0.75	1.50
❑64, Jun 80, GD; GP, 1: Death-Adder; 1: Anaconda; 1: Black Mamba, Stingray	0.40	0.30	0.75	1.50
❑65, Jul 80, GD; GP, Triton	0.40	0.30	0.75	1.50
❑66, Aug 80, A Congress Of Crowns!, A: Arcade, Scarlet Witch	0.40	0.30	0.75	1.50
❑67, Sep 80, Hyperion; Thundra	0.50	0.30	0.75	1.50
❑68, Oct 80, A: Arcade, Angel	0.50	0.30	0.75	1.50
❑69, Nov 80, Guardians of the Galaxy	0.50	0.30	0.75	1.50
❑70, Dec 80, Inhumans	0.50	0.30	0.75	1.50
❑71, Jan 81, 1: Helio; 1: Phobius; 1: Gronk; 1: Maelstrom, Mr. Fantastic	0.50	0.30	0.75	1.50
❑72, Feb 81, Stingray	0.50	0.30	0.75	1.50
❑73, Mar 81, Quasar	0.50	0.30	0.75	1.50
❑74, Apr 81, Puppet Master	0.50	0.30	0.75	1.50
❑75, May 81, By Blastaar Betrayed, O: Blastaar, Avengers	0.50	0.30	0.75	1.50
❑76, Jun 81, O: Ringmaster, Iceman	0.50	0.30	0.75	1.50
❑77, Jul 81, Man-Thing	0.50	0.30	0.75	1.50
❑78, Aug 81, Wonder Man	0.50	0.30	0.75	1.50
❑79, Sep 81, 1: Star-Dancer, Blue Diamond	0.50	0.30	0.75	1.50
❑80, Oct 81, Ghost Rider	0.50	0.30	0.75	1.50
❑81, Nov 81, Sub-Mariner	0.50	0.30	0.75	1.50
❑82, Dec 81, Captain America	0.50	0.30	0.75	1.50
❑83, Jan 82, Sasquatch	0.60	0.30	0.75	1.50
❑84, Feb 82, Alpha Flight	0.60	0.30	0.75	1.50
❑85, Mar 82, Giant-Man; Spider-Woman	0.60	0.30	0.75	1.50
❑86, Apr 82, Time Runs Like Sand!, Sandman (Marvel)	0.60	0.30	0.75	1.50
❑87, May 82, Menace Of The Microworld!, Ant-Man	0.60	0.30	0.75	1.50
❑88, Jun 82, She-Hulk	0.60	0.30	0.75	1.50
❑89, Jul 82, Torch; Human Torch	0.60	0.30	0.75	1.50
❑90, Aug 82, Spider-Man	0.60	0.30	0.75	1.50
❑91, Sep 82, Sphinx	0.60	0.30	0.75	1.50
❑92, Oct 82, This Evil Returning!, V: Ultron, Jocasta; Machine Man	0.60	0.30	0.75	1.50
❑93, Nov 82, D: Jocasta; A: Machine Man	0.60	0.30	0.75	1.50
❑94, Dec 82, Power Man; Iron Fist	0.60	0.30	0.75	1.50
❑95, Jan 83, Living Mummy	0.60	0.30	0.75	1.50
❑96, Feb 83, Marvel Heroes; Sandman (Marvel)	0.60	0.30	0.75	1.50
❑97, Mar 83, Iron Man	0.60	0.30	0.75	1.50
❑98, Apr 83, Franklin Richards	0.60	0.30	0.75	1.50
❑99, May 83, ROM	0.60	0.30	0.75	1.50
❑100, Jun 83, JBy (w), Final Issue; Double-size; Ben Grimm	1.00	0.50	1.25	2.50
❑Anl 1, SB, Their Name Is Legion!, Liberty Legion	0.50	0.80	2.00	4.00
❑Anl 2, Dec 77, JSn, 1: Master Order; D: Thanos; D: Warlock; 1: Champion of the Universe; 1: Lord Chaos, Thanos transformed to stone	0.60	3.00	7.50	15.00
❑Anl 3, Aug 78, Nova	0.60	0.40	1.00	2.00
❑Anl 4, Oct 79, Black Bolt	0.60	0.40	1.00	2.00
❑Anl 5, Sep 80, Hulk	0.75	0.50	1.25	2.50
❑Anl 6, Oct 81, 1: American Eagle	0.75	0.40	1.00	2.00
❑Anl 7, Oct 82, 1: Champion of the Universe, Champion	1.00	0.40	1.00	2.00

MARVEL UNIVERSE
Marvel

	ORIG	GOOD	FINE	N-MINT
❑1, Jun 98, The Spoils of War!, gatefold summary; Invaders	1.99	0.60	1.50	2.99
❑2, Jul 98, JBy (c), gatefold summary; Invaders	1.99	0.40	1.00	1.99
❑2/A, Jul 98, JBy (c), alternate cover; gatefold summary; Invaders	1.99	0.40	1.00	1.99
❑3, Aug 98, The Eve of Destruction, gatefold summary; Invaders	1.99	0.40	1.00	1.99
❑4, Sep 98, gatefold summary; Monster Hunters	1.99	0.40	1.00	1.99
❑5, Oct 98, gatefold summary; Monster Hunters	1.99	0.40	1.00	1.99
❑6, Nov 98, gatefold summary; Monster Hunters	1.99	0.40	1.00	1.99
❑7, Dec 98, O: Mole Man, Final Issue; gatefold summary; Monster Hunters	1.99	0.40	1.00	1.99

MARVEL VALENTINE SPECIAL
Marvel

	ORIG	GOOD	FINE	N-MINT
❑1, Apr 97, My Fair Spidey; Love Hurts, A: Absorbing Man; A: Phoenix; A: Spider-Man; A: Daredevil; A: Venus; A: Cyclops, One-Shot; romance anthology	1.99	0.40	1.00	2.00

MARVEL VERSUS DC/DC VERSUS MARVEL
DC

	ORIG	GOOD	FINE	N-MINT
❑1, 1: Access (out of costume), cardstock cover; crossover with Marvel; continues in Marvel versus DC #2	3.95	0.80	2.00	4.00
❑2, Mar 96, PD (w), cardstock cover; crossover with DC	3.95	0.80	2.00	4.00
❑3, Apr 96, 1: Access, cardstock cover; crossover with DC; voting results; Marvel and DC universes joined; Stories continued in Amalgam titles	3.95	0.80	2.00	4.00
❑4, PD (w), cardstock cover; Final Issue; continued from Marvel versus DC #3	3.95	0.80	2.00	4.00
❑Ash 1, nn; Consumer Preview; free preview of crossover series; with trading card and ballot	—	0.20	0.50	1.00

MARVEL X-MEN COLLECTION, THE
Marvel

Value: Cover or less

❑1, JLee, Pin-Ups	2.95
❑2, JLee	2.95
❑3, JLee	2.95

MARVEL YEAR IN REVIEW
Marvel

Value: Cover or less

❑1, TMc (c)	3.95
❑2	3.95
❑3	3.95
❑4	3.95
❑5	3.95
❑6	2.95

MASK, THE
DARK HORSE

	ORIG	GOOD	FINE	N-MINT
❑1, Feb 95, Strikes Back, Part 1; The Mask Strikes Back, Part 1	2.50	0.60	1.50	3.00
❑2, Mar 95, Strikes Back, Part 2; The Mask Strikes Back, Part 2	2.50	0.50	1.25	2.50
❑3, Apr 95, Strikes Back, Part 3; The Mask Strikes Back, Part 3	2.50	0.50	1.25	2.50
❑4, May 95, Strikes Back, Part 4; The Mask Strikes Back, Part 4	2.50	0.50	1.25	2.50
❑5, Jun 95, Strikes Back, Part 5; The Mask Strikes Back, Part 5	2.50	0.50	1.25	2.50
❑6, Jul 95, The Hunt for Green October, Part 1	2.50	0.50	1.25	2.50
❑7, Aug 95, The Hunt for Green October, Part 2	2.50	0.50	1.25	2.50
❑8, Sep 95, The Hunt for Green October, Part 3	2.50	0.50	1.25	2.50
❑9, Oct 95, The Hunt for Green October, Part 4	2.50	0.50	1.25	2.50
❑10, Dec 95, World Tour, Part 1, A: Hero Zero, King Tiger	2.50	0.50	1.25	2.50
❑11, Jan 96, World Tour, Part 2, A: Barb Wire, The Machine	2.50	0.50	1.25	2.50
❑12, Feb 96, World Tour, Part 3, A: X, Ghost, King Tiger	2.50	0.50	1.25	2.50
❑13, Mar 96, World Tour, Part 4, A: Warmaker, King Tiger, Vortex	2.50	0.50	1.25	2.50
❑14, Apr 96, Southern Discomfort, Part 1	2.50	0.50	1.25	2.50
❑15, May 96, Southern Discomfort, Part 2, A: Lt. Kellaway	2.50	0.50	1.25	2.50
❑16, Jun 96, Southern Discomfort, Part 3	2.50	0.50	1.25	2.50
❑17, Jul 96, Southern Discomfort, Part 4	2.50	0.50	1.25	2.50

MASK (1ST SERIES)
DC

Value: Cover or less

- ❑1, Dec 85, KS; CS 1.00
- ❑2, Jan 86, KS; CS 1.00
- ❑3, Feb 86, KS; CS 1.00
- ❑4, Mar 86, KS; CS 1.00

MASK (2ND SERIES)
DC

	ORIG	GOOD	FINE	N-MINT
❑1, KS; CS, MA (c), The Ice Age Cometh	1.00	0.20	0.50	1.00
❑2, Mar 87, KS; CS, MA (c), Masquerade	1.00	0.20	0.50	1.00
❑3, KS; CS, MA (c), The Switchblade Conspiracy	1.00	0.20	0.50	1.00
❑4, KS; CS, MA (c), Matt Trakker- Outlaw	1.00	0.20	0.50	1.00
❑5, KS; CS, MA (c)	1.00	0.20	0.50	1.00
❑6, KS; CS, MA (c)	1.00	0.20	0.50	1.00
❑7, KS; CS, MA (c)	1.00	0.20	0.50	1.00
❑8, KS; CS, MA (c)	1.00	0.20	0.50	1.00
❑9	—	0.20	0.50	1.00

MASK, THE (MINI-SERIES)
DARK HORSE

	ORIG	GOOD	FINE	N-MINT
❑0, Reprints Mask stories from Mayhem	4.95	0.99	2.47	4.95
❑1, Jul 94, Mask Justice	2.50	0.80	2.00	4.00
❑2, Aug 94	2.50	0.70	1.75	3.50
❑3	2.50	0.60	1.50	3.00
❑4	2.50	0.60	1.50	3.00

MASK CONSPIRACY, THE
INK & FEATHERS

Value: Cover or less

- ❑1, Big Lou back-up feature 6.95

MASKED MAN, THE
ECLIPSE

	ORIG	GOOD	FINE	N-MINT
❑1, Dec 84, The Idol, O: Masked Man, full color	1.75	0.40	1.00	2.00
❑2, Feb 85, full color	1.75	0.40	1.00	2.00
❑3, Apr 85, full color	1.75	0.40	1.00	2.00
❑4, Jun 85, full color	1.75	0.40	1.00	2.00
❑5, Aug 85, full color	1.75	0.40	1.00	2.00
❑6, Oct 85, full color	1.75	0.40	1.00	2.00
❑7, Dec 85, full color	2.00	0.40	1.00	2.00
❑8, Feb 86, full color	2.00	0.40	1.00	2.00
❑9, Apr 86, full color	2.00	0.40	1.00	2.00
❑10, b&w	2.00	0.40	1.00	2.00
❑11, b&w	2.00	0.40	1.00	2.00
❑12, Apr 88, b&w	2.00	0.40	1.00	2.00

MASKED RIDER
MARVEL

Value: Cover or less

- ❑1, Apr 96, A: Mighty Morphin Power Rangers, Ninja Rangers, based on Saban television series, one-shot 2.95

MASKED WARRIOR X
ANTARCTIC

	ORIG	GOOD	FINE	N-MINT
❑1, Apr 96, Warrior X, Part 1, b&w	2.95	0.70	1.75	3.50
❑2, Jun 96, b&w	2.95	0.59	1.48	2.95
❑3, Aug 96, b&w; 40pgs.	3.50	0.70	1.75	3.50
❑4, Oct 96, b&w	2.95	0.59	1.48	2.95

Comics fans were allowed to vote on the outcome of several of the fights in *Marvel versus DC/DC versus Marvel.*

© 1996 Marvel Characters Inc and DC Comics

MASK/MARSHAL LAW, THE
DARK HORSE

Value: Cover or less

- ❑1, Feb 98 .... 2.95
- ❑2, Mar 98, Law dons the Mask 2.95

MASK, THE: OFFICIAL MOVIE ADAPTATION
DARK HORSE

Value: Cover or less

- ❑1 .... 2.50
- ❑2 .... 2.50

MASK OF ZORRO, THE
IMAGE

Value: Cover or less

- ❑1, Aug 98 .... 2.95
- ❑2, Sep 98 .... 2.95
- ❑2/SC, Sep 98, alternate cover; photo 2.95
- ❑3, Oct 98, Photo cover; indicia says Oct 2.95
- ❑3/SC, Oct 98, alternate cover; Zorro photo 2.95
- ❑4, Dec 98, cover says Jan, indicia says Dec 2.95
- ❑4/SC, Dec 98, Photo cover 2.95

MASK RETURNS, THE
DARK HORSE

	ORIG	GOOD	FINE	N-MINT
❑1, with Mask mask	2.50	0.80	2.00	4.00
❑2	2.50	0.60	1.50	3.00
❑3	2.50	0.60	1.50	3.00
❑4, Mar 93, Walter dons Mask	2.50	0.60	1.50	3.00

MASK, THE: TOYS IN THE ATTIC
DARK HORSE

Value: Cover or less

- ❑1, Aug 98 .... 2.95
- ❑2, Sep 98, A: Kellaway, 40pgs. 2.95
- ❑3, Oct 98 .... 2.95
- ❑4, Nov 98 .... 2.95

MASK, THE: VIRTUAL SURREALITY
DARK HORSE

Value: Cover or less

- ❑1, Jul 97, The Age of Barbarians; Maskman Vs. Lavender Lass, nn; One-Shot 2.95

MASQUE OF THE RED DEATH, THE
DELL

	ORIG	GOOD	FINE	N-MINT
❑1, Oct 64, Phoo cover	0.12	4.00	10.00	20.00

MASQUERADE
MAD MONKEY

Value: Cover or less

- ❑1 .... 3.95
- ❑2 .... 3.95
- ❑Ash 1 .... 2.45

MASQUES (J.N. WILLIAMSON'S...)
INNOVATION

Value: Cover or less

- ❑1, Jul 92, Rail Rider; Nightcrawlers 4.95
- ❑2 .... 4.95

MASTER OF KUNG FU
MARVEL

	ORIG	GOOD	FINE	N-MINT
❑17, JSn, 1: Black Jack Tarr, Series continued from "Special Marvel Edition"	0.20	2.00	5.00	10.00
❑18, PG	0.25	1.10	2.75	5.50
❑19, PG, A: Man-Thing	0.25	1.10	2.75	5.50
❑20, PG	0.25	1.10	2.75	5.50
❑21	0.25	0.60	1.50	3.00
❑22, PG	0.25	0.60	1.50	3.00
❑23, Dec 74	0.25	0.60	1.50	3.00
❑24, Jan 75, JSn	0.25	0.60	1.50	3.00
❑25, Feb 75, PG	0.25	0.60	1.50	3.00
❑26, Mar 75	0.25	0.60	1.50	3.00
❑27, Apr 75	0.25	0.60	1.50	3.00
❑28, May 75	0.25	0.60	1.50	3.00
❑29, Jun 75, PG, D: Razor-Fist I	0.25	0.60	1.50	3.00
❑30, Jul 75, PG	0.25	0.60	1.50	3.00
❑31, Aug 75, PG	0.25	0.50	1.25	2.50
❑32, Sep 75	0.25	0.50	1.25	2.50
❑33, Oct 75, PG, Wicked Messenger of Madness, 1: Leiko Wu	0.25	0.50	1.25	2.50
❑34, Nov 75, PG	0.25	0.50	1.25	2.50
❑35, Dec 75, PG	0.25	0.50	1.25	2.50
❑36, Jan 76	0.25	0.50	1.25	2.50
❑37, Feb 76	0.25	0.50	1.25	2.50
❑38, Mar 76, PG	0.25	0.50	1.25	2.50
❑39, Apr 76, PG	0.25	0.50	1.25	2.50

	ORIG	GOOD	FINE	N-MINT
❑40, May 76, PG	0.25	0.50	1.25	2.50
❑41, Jun 76	0.25	0.50	1.25	2.50
❑42, Jul 76, PG, 1: Shockwave	0.25	0.50	1.25	2.50
❑43, Aug 76, PG	0.25	0.50	1.25	2.50
❑44, Sep 76, PG	0.30	0.50	1.25	2.50
❑45, Oct 76, PG	0.30	0.50	1.25	2.50
❑46, Nov 76, PG	0.30	0.50	1.25	2.50
❑47, Dec 76, PG	0.30	0.50	1.25	2.50
❑48, Jan 77, PG	0.30	0.50	1.25	2.50
❑49, Feb 77, PG, The Affair of the Agent Who Died	0.30	0.50	1.25	2.50
❑50, Mar 77, PG	0.30	0.50	1.25	2.50
❑51, Apr 77, PG	0.30	0.50	1.25	2.50
❑52, May 77	0.30	0.40	1.00	2.00
❑53, Jun 77	0.30	0.40	1.00	2.00
❑54, Jul 77	0.30	0.40	1.00	2.00
❑55, Aug 77	0.30	0.40	1.00	2.00
❑56, Sep 77	0.30	0.40	1.00	2.00
❑57, Oct 77	0.30	0.40	1.00	2.00
❑58, Nov 77	0.35	0.40	1.00	2.00
❑59, Dec 77	0.35	0.40	1.00	2.00
❑60, Jan 78, V: Doctor Doom; V: Dr. Doom	0.35	0.40	1.00	2.00
❑61, Feb 78	0.35	0.40	1.00	2.00
❑62, Mar 78	0.35	0.40	1.00	2.00
❑63, Apr 78	0.35	0.40	1.00	2.00
❑64, May 78	0.35	0.40	1.00	2.00
❑65, Jun 78	0.35	0.40	1.00	2.00
❑66, Jul 78	0.35	0.40	1.00	2.00
❑67, Aug 78	0.35	0.40	1.00	2.00
❑68, Sep 78, V: The Cat	0.35	0.40	1.00	2.00
❑69, Oct 78	0.35	0.40	1.00	2.00
❑70, Nov 78	0.35	0.40	1.00	2.00
❑71, Dec 78	0.35	0.40	1.00	2.00
❑72, Jan 79	0.35	0.40	1.00	2.00
❑73, Feb 79	0.35	0.40	1.00	2.00
❑74, Mar 79	0.35	0.40	1.00	2.00
❑75, Apr 79	0.35	0.40	1.00	2.00
❑76, May 79	0.40	0.40	1.00	2.00
❑77, Jun 79, 1: Zaran	0.40	0.40	1.00	2.00
❑78, Jul 79	0.40	0.40	1.00	2.00
❑79, Aug 79	0.40	0.40	1.00	2.00
❑80, Sep 79	0.40	0.40	1.00	2.00
❑81, Oct 79	0.40	0.40	1.00	2.00
❑82, Nov 79	0.40	0.40	1.00	2.00
❑83, Dec 79, V: Fu Manchu	0.40	0.40	1.00	2.00
❑84, Jan 80	0.40	0.40	1.00	2.00
❑85, Feb 80	0.40	0.40	1.00	2.00
❑86, Mar 80	0.40	0.40	1.00	2.00
❑87, Apr 80	0.40	0.40	1.00	2.00
❑88, May 80	0.40	0.40	1.00	2.00
❑89, Jun 80, V: Fu Manchu	0.40	0.40	1.00	2.00
❑90, Jul 80	0.40	0.40	1.00	2.00
❑91, Aug 80, GD	0.40	0.40	1.00	2.00
❑92, Sep 80, GD	0.50	0.40	1.00	2.00
❑93, Oct 80, GD	0.50	0.40	1.00	2.00
❑94, Nov 80, GD	0.50	0.40	1.00	2.00
❑95, Dec 80, GD	0.50	0.40	1.00	2.00
❑96, Jan 81, GD	0.50	0.40	1.00	2.00
❑97, Feb 81, GD	0.50	0.40	1.00	2.00
❑98, Mar 81, GD	0.50	0.40	1.00	2.00
❑99, Apr 81, GD	0.50	0.40	1.00	2.00
❑100, May 81, GD, double-sized; Giant-size	0.75	0.50	1.25	2.50
❑101, Jun 81, GD	0.50	0.30	0.75	1.50
❑102, Jul 81, GD, 1: Day pencils	0.50	0.30	0.75	1.50
❑103, Aug 81, GD	0.50	0.30	0.75	1.50
❑104, Sep 81	0.50	0.30	0.75	1.50
❑105, Oct 81, D: Razor-Fist III; 1: Razor-Fist II	0.50	0.30	0.75	1.50
❑106, Nov 81, GD, A: Velcro; O: Razor-Fist III; O: Razor-Fist II	0.50	0.30	0.75	1.50
❑107, Dec 81, GD, A: Sata	0.50	0.30	0.75	1.50
❑108, Jan 82, GD	0.60	0.30	0.75	1.50
❑109, Feb 82, GD	0.60	0.30	0.75	1.50
❑110, Mar 82, GD	0.60	0.30	0.75	1.50
❑111, Apr 82, GD	0.60	0.30	0.75	1.50
❑112, May 82, GD	0.60	0.30	0.75	1.50
❑113, Jun 82, GD	0.60	0.30	0.75	1.50
❑114, Jul 82	0.60	0.30	0.75	1.50
❑115, Aug 82, GD	0.60	0.30	0.75	1.50
❑116, Sep 82, GD	0.60	0.30	0.75	1.50
❑117, Oct 82, GD	0.60	0.30	0.75	1.50
❑118, Nov 82, GD, D: Fu Manchu, double-sized	1.00	0.30	0.75	1.50
❑119, Dec 82, GD	0.60	0.30	0.75	1.50
❑120, Jan 83, GD	0.60	0.30	0.75	1.50
❑121, Feb 83	0.60	0.30	0.75	1.50
❑122, Mar 83	0.60	0.30	0.75	1.50
❑123, Apr 83	0.60	0.30	0.75	1.50
❑124, May 83	0.60	0.30	0.75	1.50
❑125, Jun 83, Atonement, Final Issue; Double-size	1.00	0.40	1.00	2.00
❑Anl 1, KP, The Fortress of Sahra Sharn!, 1976 Annual	0.50	1.00	2.50	5.00
❑GS 1	0.50	1.60	4.00	8.00
❑GS 2	0.50	0.80	2.00	4.00
❑GS 3	0.50	0.80	2.00	4.00
❑GS 4	0.50	0.80	2.00	4.00

MASTER OF KUNG FU: BLEEDING BLACK
MARVEL

	ORIG	GOOD	FINE	N-MINT
❑1, Feb 91, Bleeding Black	2.95	0.60	1.50	3.00

MASTER OF MYSTICS: THE DEMONCRAFT
CHAKRA

Value: Cover or less

❑1 .... 1.50

❑2 .... 1.50

MASTER OF THE VOID
IRON HAMMER

Value: Cover or less

❑1, Dec 93, Surtur 2.95

MASTERS OF THE UNIVERSE
MARVEL

	ORIG	GOOD	FINE	N-MINT
❑1, May 86	0.75	0.20	0.50	1.00
❑2	0.75	0.20	0.50	1.00
❑3, The Garden Of Evil	0.75	0.20	0.50	1.00
❑4	0.75	0.20	0.50	1.00
❑5	0.75	0.20	0.50	1.00
❑6	0.75	0.20	0.50	1.00
❑7	1.00	0.20	0.50	1.00
❑8	1.00	0.20	0.50	1.00
❑9	1.00	0.20	0.50	1.00
❑10	1.00	0.20	0.50	1.00
❑11	1.00	0.20	0.50	1.00
❑12, Final Issue	1.00	0.20	0.50	1.00
❑13	1.00	0.20	0.50	1.00

MASTERS OF THE UNIVERSE (MINI-SERIES)
DC

Value: Cover or less

❑1, AA; GT, To Tempt The Gods 1.50

❑2 .... 1.00

❑3 .... 1.00

MASTER'S SERIES
AVALON

Value: Cover or less

❑1, WW, WW (w), One-Man Mission!; The Prisoner in Chateau in Beaujais, Wally Wood War 2.50

MASTERWORKS SERIES OF GREAT COMIC BOOK ARTISTS, THE
DC

	ORIG	GOOD	FINE	N-MINT
❑1, Spr 83, FF, Shining Knights, Reprints Shining Knight stories from Adventure Comics (1950-1951)	1.50	0.50	1.25	2.50
❑2, Jul 83, FF, Spores From Space	1.50	0.50	1.25	2.50
❑3, Oct 83, BWr, Molded In Evil	1.50	0.50	1.25	2.50

MATT CHAMPION
METRO

Value: Cover or less

❑1 .... 2.00

MATTERBABY
ANTARCTIC

Value: Cover or less

❑1, Feb 97, b&w 2.95

❑Anl 1, Core of Evil; Drop of Doom 2.95

MAVERICK
MARVEL

	ORIG	GOOD	FINE	N-MINT
❑1, Sep 97, Overture, wraparound cover; gatefold summary	2.99	0.60	1.50	3.00
❑2, Oct 97, wraparound cover; gatefold summary	1.99	0.39	0.98	1.95
❑2/SC, variant cover	1.95	0.39	0.98	1.95
❑3, Nov 97, A: Alpha Flight, wraparound cover; gatefold summary	1.99	0.40	1.00	1.99
❑4, Dec 97, A: Alpha Flight, wraparound cover; gatefold summary	1.99	0.40	1.00	1.99
❑5, Jan 98, gatefold summary	1.99	0.40	1.00	1.99
❑6, Feb 98, gatefold summary	1.99	0.40	1.00	1.99
❑7, Mar 98, gatefold summary	1.99	0.40	1.00	1.99
❑8, Apr 98, gatefold summary	1.99	0.40	1.00	1.99
❑9, May 98, gatefold summary	1.99	0.40	1.00	1.99
❑10, Jun 98, gatefold summary	1.99	0.40	1.00	1.99
❑11, Jul 98, gatefold summary	1.99	0.40	1.00	1.99
❑12, Aug 98, Final Issue; gatefold summary; Giant-size	1.99	0.60	1.50	2.99

MAVERICK (MINI-SERIES)
MARVEL

Value: Cover or less

❑1, Jan 97, The Sword Sung on a Barren Heath, One-Shot; Giant-size 2.95

MAVERICKS (DAGGER)
Dagger
Value: Cover or less

Issue	Price
❑1	2.50
❑2	2.50
❑3	2.50
❑4	2.50
❑5, May 94	2.50

MAVERICKS: THE NEW WAVE
Dagger
Value: Cover or less

Issue	Price
❑1	2.50
❑2	2.50
❑3	2.50

MAX BREWSTER: THE UNIVERSAL SOLDIER
Fleetway
Value: Cover or less

Issue	Price
❑1	2.95
❑2	2.95
❑3, Never Say Die	2.95

MAX BURGER PI
Graphic Image
Value: Cover or less

Issue	Price
❑1, 1: Max Burger, b&w	2.00
❑2, b&w	2.50

MAX DAMAGE: PANIC!
Head Press
Value: Cover or less

Issue	Price
❑1, Jul 95, b&w	2.75

MAXIMAGE
Image
Value: Cover or less

Issue	Price
❑1, Dec 95, RL (w), Second Coming, 1: Maximage; 1: The Ancient	2.50
❑2, Jan 96, Extreme Destroyer, Part 2, polybagged with card	2.50
❑3, Feb 96	2.50
❑4, Mar 96, Rage of Angels, Part 5, continued from Glory #10	2.50
❑5, Apr 96	2.50
❑6, May 96	2.50
❑7, Jun 96	2.50
❑8	2.50
❑9	2.50
❑10	2.50

MAXIMORTAL, THE
Tundra

Issue	ORIG	GOOD	FINE	N-MINT
❑1, Aug 92, Cheek, Chin, Knuckle, or Knee	3.95	0.80	2.00	4.00
❑2, Oct 92	3.95	0.80	2.00	4.00
❑3, Dec 92, A: Holmes	3.95	0.80	2.00	4.00
❑4, Mar 93	3.95	0.80	2.00	4.00
❑5, May 93	2.95	0.60	1.50	3.00
❑6, Jul 93	2.95	0.60	1.50	3.00
❑7, Dec 93	2.95	0.59	1.48	2.95

MAXIMUM SECURITY
Marvel
Value: Cover or less

Issue	Price
❑1, Dec 00, JOy, KB (w), Illegal Aliens	2.99
❑2, Dec 00, JOy, KB (w), A World of Hurt	2.99
❑3, Jan 01, JOy, KB (w), Whatever the Cost!	2.99

MAXIMUM SECURITY DANGEROUS PLANET
Marvel
Value: Cover or less

Issue	Price
❑1, Oct 00, JOy, KB (w), A Very Dangerous Planet, lead-in to Maximum Security	2.99

MAXIMUM SECURITY: THOR VS. EGO
Marvel
Value: Cover or less

Issue	Price
❑1, Nov 00, JK, SL (w), Behold ... The Living Planet!; And Now ... Galactus!, A: Ego; A: Recorder, reprints Thor #133, #160, and #161; Reprints Thor #133, 160, 161	2.99

MAXION
CPM Manga
Value: Cover or less

Issue	Price
❑1, Dec 99, A Beautiful Girl Suddenly Appears, b&w	2.95
❑2, Jan 00, Private Beach of Love, b&w	2.95
❑3, Feb 00, The Infinite Power of Love, b&w	2.95
❑4, Mar 00, Latent Power, b&w	2.95
❑5, Apr 00, I Want Them Both, b&w	2.95
❑6, May 00, Hold Me, b&w	2.95
❑7	2.95
❑8	2.95
❑9	2.95
❑10	2.95
❑11	2.95
❑12	2.95
❑13	2.95
❑14	2.95
❑15	2.95
❑16	2.95
❑17	2.95
❑18	2.95
❑19	2.95
❑20	2.95

MAX OF THE REGULATORS
Atlantic
Value: Cover or less

Issue	Price
❑1	1.50
❑2	1.75
❑3	1.75
❑4	1.75

MAX REP IN THE AGE OF THE ASTROTITANS
Dumbbell Press
Value: Cover or less

Issue	Price
❑1, Jun 97, b&w	2.75
❑2, Mar 98, b&w	2.75

MAX THE MAGNIFICENT
Slave Labor
Value: Cover or less

Issue	Price
❑1, Jul 87	1.50
❑2	1.50
❑3	1.50

Rick Veitch presented a different take on the Superman legend in the seven-issue *Maximortal.*

© 1992 Rick Veitch (Tundra)

MAXWELL MOUSE FOLLIES
Renegade

Issue	ORIG	GOOD	FINE	N-MINT
❑1, Feb 86, b&w	1.70	0.40	1.00	2.00
❑2, Feb 86, b&w	1.70	0.40	1.00	2.00
❑3, Jun 86, b&w	1.70	0.40	1.00	2.00
❑4, Sep 86, b&w	2.00	0.40	1.00	2.00
❑5, Dec 86	2.00	0.40	1.00	2.00
❑6, Mar 87	2.00	0.40	1.00	2.00

MAXWELL THE MAGIC CAT
Acme
Value: Cover or less

Issue	Price
❑1, AMo (w)	4.95
❑2, AMo (w)	4.95
❑3, AMo (w)	4.95
❑4, AMo (w)	5.95

MAXX
Image

Issue	ORIG	GOOD	FINE	N-MINT
❑0.5, Jun 93, Wizard promotional edition	1.95	0.80	2.00	4.00
❑0.5/GO, Jun 93, Promotional edition in slipcover with certificate of authenticity; Gold edition	1.95	2.40	6.00	12.00
❑1, Mar 93	1.95	0.60	1.50	3.00
❑1/3D, Jan 98, 3-D edition; bound-in glasses	4.95	1.00	2.50	5.00
❑1/SC, Mar 93, glow in the dark cover; Glow-in-the-dark promotional edition	1.95	1.60	4.00	8.00
❑2, Apr 93	1.95	0.50	1.25	2.50
❑3, May 93	1.95	0.50	1.25	2.50
❑4, Aug 93	1.95	0.50	1.25	2.50
❑5, Sep 93	1.95	0.50	1.25	2.50
❑6, Nov 93, cover says Oct, indicia says Nov	1.95	0.50	1.25	2.50
❑7, Mar 94, A: Pitt	1.95	0.50	1.25	2.50
❑8, May 94, A: Pitt	1.95	0.50	1.25	2.50
❑9, Jun 94	1.95	0.50	1.25	2.50
❑10, Aug 94	1.95	0.50	1.25	2.50
❑11, Oct 94	1.95	0.40	1.00	2.00
❑12, Dec 94	1.95	0.40	1.00	2.00
❑13, Jan 95	1.95	0.40	1.00	2.00
❑14, Feb 95	1.95	0.40	1.00	2.00
❑15, Apr 95, cover says February, indicia says Apr	1.95	0.40	1.00	2.00
❑16, Jun 95, cover says Feb, indicia says Jun	1.95	0.40	1.00	2.00
❑17, Jul 95	1.95	0.40	1.00	2.00
❑18, Aug 95	1.95	0.39	0.98	1.95
❑19, Sep 95	1.95	0.39	0.98	1.95
❑20, Nov 95	1.95	0.39	0.98	1.95
❑21, Jan 96	1.95	0.39	0.98	1.95
❑22, Feb 96	1.95	0.39	0.98	1.95
❑23, Mar 96	1.95	0.39	0.98	1.95
❑24, May 96	1.95	0.39	0.98	1.95
❑25, Jun 96, cover says Jul, indicia says Jun	1.95	0.39	0.98	1.95
❑26, Aug 96, O: Mr. Gone	1.95	0.39	0.98	1.95
❑27, Sep 96	1.95	0.39	0.98	1.95
❑28, Jan 97, Pool of Tears	1.95	0.39	0.98	1.95
❑29, Apr 97	1.95	0.39	0.98	1.95
❑30, Jun 97	1.95	0.39	0.98	1.95
❑31, Jul 97	1.95	0.39	0.98	1.95
❑32, Sep 97, Glorie's Story	1.95	0.39	0.98	1.95
❑33, Oct 97, The Love for Three Oranges	1.95	0.39	0.98	1.95
❑34, Dec 97	1.95	0.39	0.98	1.95
❑35, Feb 98, Endings and Beginnings, Final Issue	1.95	0.39	0.98	1.95
❑36	1.95	0.39	0.98	1.95
❑37	1.95	0.39	0.98	1.95

MAYHEM
Dark Horse

Issue	ORIG	GOOD	FINE	N-MINT
❑1, The Mask: Who's Laughing Now?; The Mark: Beyond Good and Evil, Part 1, b&w	2.50	1.00	2.50	5.00
❑2, The Mask: What Revenge Means to Me; The Mark: Beyond Good and Evil, b&w	2.50	0.80	2.00	4.00
❑3, The Mask: Have Gun, Will Use; The Mark: Beyond Good and Evil, Part 3 Mecha: Triangle, b&w	2.50	0.80	2.00	4.00
❑4, The Mask: Final Kick; The Mark: Beyond Good and Evil, Part 4, b&w	2.50	0.80	2.00	4.00

MAYHEM (KELVA)
KELVA

Value: Cover or less
❑1, Care Your Dreams Away; Planet Mars 1.25

MAZE, THE
METAPHROG

	ORIG	GOOD	FINE	N-MINT
❑1, Aug 97, Metaphrog, b&w; no indicia	3.65	0.75	1.88	3.75

MAZE AGENCY, THE
COMICO

	ORIG	GOOD	FINE	N-MINT
❑1, Dec 88, 1: The Maze Agency	1.95	0.60	1.50	3.00
❑2, Jan 89, Murder-The Lost Episodes	1.95	0.50	1.25	2.50
❑3, Feb 89	1.95	0.50	1.25	2.50
❑4, Mar 89	1.95	0.40	1.00	2.00
❑5, Apr 89	1.95	0.40	1.00	2.00
❑6, May 89	1.95	0.40	1.00	2.00
❑7, Jun 89	2.50	0.50	1.25	2.50
❑8, Dec 89	1.95	0.40	1.00	2.00
❑9, Feb 90, The English Channeler Mystery, Ellery Queen	1.95	0.40	1.00	2.00
❑10, Apr 90	1.95	0.40	1.00	2.00
❑11, Apr 90, ...Twas The Crime Before Christmas	1.95	0.40	1.00	2.00
❑12, May 90	2.50	0.40	1.00	2.00
❑13, Jun 90	1.95	0.40	1.00	2.00
❑14, Jul 90	1.95	0.40	1.00	2.00
❑15, Aug 90	1.95	0.40	1.00	2.00
❑16, Oct 90	2.50	0.50	1.25	2.50
❑17, Dec 90	2.50	0.50	1.25	2.50
❑18, Feb 91	2.50	0.50	1.25	2.50
❑19, Mar 91	2.50	0.50	1.25	2.50
❑20, May 91	2.50	0.50	1.25	2.50
❑21, Jun 91	2.50	0.50	1.25	2.50
❑22, Jul 91	2.50	0.50	1.25	2.50
❑23, Aug 91	2.50	0.50	1.25	2.50
❑Anl 1, Aug 90, MP (c), Spirit parody	2.75	0.60	1.50	3.00
❑SE 1, May 90	2.75	0.60	1.50	3.00
❑Xmas 1, Special edition	—	0.60	1.50	3.00

M.D. (GEMSTONE)
GEMSTONE

Value: Cover or less
❑1, Sep 99, JO; GE, JO (w); GE (w), The Fight for Life; Janie Some Day 2.50
❑2, Oct 99 .... 2.50
❑3, Nov 99, JO; GE, JO (w); GE (w), When You Know How; The Right Cure 2.50
❑4, Dec 99 .... 2.50
❑5, Jan 00 .... 2.50

M.D. GEIST
CPM

Value: Cover or less
❑1, Jun 95 .... 2.95
❑2, Jul 95 .... 2.95
❑3, Aug 95 .... 2.95

M.D. GEIST: GROUND ZERO
CPM

Value: Cover or less
❑1, Mar 96, prequel to M.D. Geist, Armored Trooper Votoms preview back-up 2.95
❑2, Apr 96, prequel to M.D. Geist, Armored Trooper Votoms preview back-up 2.95
❑3, May 96, prequel to M.D. Geist, Armored Trooper Votoms preview back-up 2.95

MEA CULPA
FOUR WALLS EIGHT WINDOWS

Value: Cover or less
❑1, Oct 90 .... 12.95

ME-A DAY WITH ELVIS
INVINCIBLE

	ORIG	GOOD	FINE	N-MINT
❑1	—	0.10	0.25	0.50

MEADOWLARK
PARODY PRESS

Value: Cover or less
❑1, b&w; Shadowhawksilver foil cover parody 2.95

ME AND HER
FANTAGRAPHICS

	ORIG	GOOD	FINE	N-MINT
❑1, It's Moving Day, b&w; adult	1.95	0.40	1.00	2.00
❑1-2, It's Moving Day, adult; 2nd Printing	1.95	0.40	1.00	2.00
❑2, b&w; adult	1.95	0.40	1.00	2.00
❑3, adult	1.95	0.40	1.00	2.00
❑SE 1, b&w; adult; Special edition	2.50	0.50	1.25	2.50

MEAN, GREEN BONDO MACHINE
MU PRESS

Value: Cover or less
❑1, Jul 92 .... 2.50

MEAN MACHINE
FLEETWAY

Value: Cover or less
❑1, Mean Machine: Travels with muh Shrink; Judge Dredd: The Gipper's Big Night, Judge Dredd; no date of publication; Reprints Mean Machine stories from 2000 A.D. #730-736 .... 4.95

MEANWHILE...
CROW

Value: Cover or less
❑1, Cohen and Melish; Pandora, b&w 2.95
❑2, b&w 2.95

MEASLES
FANTAGRAPHICS

Value: Cover or less
❑1, 98, The New Adventures of Venus; Little Frogs 2.95
❑2, 99 .... 2.95
❑3, Sum 99 .... 2.95
❑4, Sum 99 .... 2.95
❑5, Win 00 .... 2.95
❑6, Spr 00 .... 2.95
❑7, 01 .... 2.95

MEAT CAKE (FANTAGRAPHICS)
FANTAGRAPHICS

	ORIG	GOOD	FINE	N-MINT
❑1, b&w	2.50	0.50	1.25	2.50
❑2, b&w	2.50	0.50	1.25	2.50
❑3, b&w	2.50	0.50	1.25	2.50
❑4, b&w	2.50	0.50	1.25	2.50
❑5, Nov 95, b&w	2.95	0.59	1.48	2.95
❑6, Jan 96, b&w	2.95	0.59	1.48	2.95
❑7, b&w	2.95	0.59	1.48	2.95
❑8, Jun 98, b&w	2.95	0.59	1.48	2.95
❑9, Apr 99, AMo (w)	2.95	0.59	1.48	2.95
❑10	—	0.59	1.48	2.95
❑11	3.95	0.79	1.98	3.95

MEAT CAKE (ICONOGRAFIX)
ICONOGRAFIX

Value: Cover or less
❑1, b&w 2.50

MEATFACE THE AMAZING FLESH
MONSTER

Value: Cover or less
❑1, b&w 2.50

MECHA
DARK HORSE

	ORIG	GOOD	FINE	N-MINT
❑1, Jun 87, First Contact, full color	1.50	0.35	0.88	1.75
❑2, Aug 87, full color	1.50	0.35	0.88	1.75
❑3, b&w	1.50	0.35	0.88	1.75
❑4, b&w	1.50	0.35	0.88	1.75
❑5, b&w	1.50	0.35	0.88	1.75
❑6	1.50	0.35	0.88	1.75

MECHANIC, THE
IMAGE

Value: Cover or less
❑1, nn; One-Shot; prestige format 5.95

MECHANICAL MAN BLUES
RADIO

Value: Cover or less
❑1, Dec 98, b&w 2.95

MECHANICS
FANTAGRAPHICS

Value: Cover or less
❑1 .... 2.00
❑2 .... 2.00
❑3 .... 2.00

MECHANIMALS
NOVELLE

Value: Cover or less
❑1, b&w 3.50
❑2, b&w 2.50

MECHANIMOIDS SPECIAL X ANNIVERSARY
MU

Value: Cover or less
❑1, b&w; cardstock cover 3.50

MECHANOIDS
CALIBER

Value: Cover or less
❑1, b&w 3.50
❑2 .... 3.50
❑3 .... 3.50

MECH DESTROYER
IMAGE

Value: Cover or less
❑1, Mar 01 .... 2.95

MECHOVERSE
AIRBRUSH

Value: Cover or less
❑1, Airbrushed 1.50
❑2, Airbrushed 1.50
❑3, Airbrushed 1.50

MECHTHINGS
RENEGADE

Value: Cover or less
❑1, Jul 87, b&w 2.00
❑2, Sep 87, b&w 2.00
❑3, Nov 87, b&w 2.00
❑4, Feb 88, b&w 2.00

MEDAL OF HONOR
DARK HORSE

Value: Cover or less
❑1, Oct 94, Richard Bong: Honor Bound; Julius Langbein: The Little Drummer Boy 2.50
❑2, Nov 94, Firefly Fight; Gridiron to Glory 2.50
❑3, Dec 94, The Andrews Raid; The Black Watch 2.50
❑4, Jan 95 .... 2.50
❑5 .... 2.50
❑SE 1, Apr 94, Lt. Charles Q. Williams: Night in Hell; Sgt. Desmond Doss: The Bible Tells Me So, Special edition 2.50

MEDIA*STARR
INNOVATION

Value: Cover or less
❑1, Jul 89 .... 1.95
❑2, Aug 89 .... 1.95
❑3, Sep 89 .... 1.95

MEDIEVAL SPAWN
IMAGE

	ORIG	GOOD	FINE	N-MINT
❑1, three-part story; polybagged with Fan	—	0.40	1.00	2.00
❑2, three-part story; polybagged with Fan	—	0.40	1.00	2.00
❑3, three-part story; polybagged with Fan	—	0.40	1.00	2.00

MEDIEVAL SPAWN/WITCHBLADE
IMAGE

	ORIG	GOOD	FINE	N-MINT
❑1, May 96	2.95	0.70	1.75	3.50
❑1/AE, Gold cover; American Entertainment exclusive	—	0.90	2.25	4.50
❑1/GO, May 96, Gold edition	—	0.90	2.25	4.50
❑1/PL, Platinum edition	—	3.60	9.00	18.00
❑2, Jun 96	2.95	0.70	1.75	3.50
❑3, Jun 96, cover says Jul, indicia says Jun; Final Issue	2.95	0.60	1.50	3.00

MEDORA
LOBSTER

Value: Cover or less

❑1, Dec 99 .... 2.95

MEDUSA COMICS
TRIANGLE

Value: Cover or less

❑1 .... 1.50

MEGA DRAGON & TIGER
IMAGE

Value: Cover or less

❑1, Mar 99 .... 2.95
❑2, Apr 99 .... 2.95
❑3, May 99 .... 2.95
❑4, Jun 99 .... 2.95
❑5, Jul 99 .... 2.95

MEGAHURTZ
IMAGE

Value: Cover or less

❑1, Aug 97, Gods Born of Dreams and Demons 2.95
❑1/A, Aug 97, Gods Born of Dreams and Demons, no cover price 2.95
❑1/B, Aug 97, Gods Born of Dreams and Demons, no cover price 2.95
❑2, Sep 97, Alise in Wonderland 2.95
❑3, Oct 97, Seeing Red 2.95

MEGALITH
CONTINUITY

Value: Cover or less

❑1 .... 2.00
❑2 .... 2.00
❑3 .... 2.00
❑4, Nov 90 .... 2.00
❑5, Jan 91, Rise of Magic storyline 2.00
❑6, Jun 91 .... 2.00
❑7, Jul 91 .... 2.00
❑8, Dec 91 .... 2.00
❑9, Mar 92 .... 2.00

MEGALITH (2ND SERIES)
CONTINUITY

Value: Cover or less

❑0, Apr 93, NA (w), Deathwatch 2000, Part 1, silver foil cover; silver foil issue number; prelude to Deathwatch 2000 .... 1.00
❑0/A, Apr 93, NA (w), Deathwatch 2000, Part 1, red foil cover.. 1.00
❑1, Apr 93, NA (w), Deathwatch 2000, Part 5, trading cards.. 2.50
❑2, Jun 93, NA (w), Deathwatch 2000, Part10, trading cards 2.50
❑3, Aug 93, NA (w), Deathwatch 2000, Part16 .... 2.50
❑4, Oct 93 .... 2.50
❑5, Dec 93 .... 2.50
❑6, Dec 93 .... 2.50
❑7, Jan 94 .... 2.50

MEGATON
MEGATON

	ORIG	GOOD	FINE	N-MINT
❑1, Nov 83, Ultragirl: Sins of the Father; The City at Sunrise, A: Vanguard; 1: Megaton	2.00	0.80	2.00	4.00
❑2, Oct 85, EL	2.00	0.60	1.50	3.00
❑3, EL, EL (w), 1: Savage Dragon	2.00	1.00	2.50	5.00
❑4	2.00	0.60	1.50	3.00
❑5, Jun 86	1.50	0.60	1.50	3.00
❑6, Dec 86	1.50	0.60	1.50	3.00
❑7, Apr 87	1.50	0.60	1.50	3.00
❑8, Aug 87	1.50	0.80	2.00	4.00
❑HS 1, Vanguard: First Noel, says 1994 on cover, 1993 in indicia; unpublished cover from first Youngblood story; trading card	2.95	0.60	1.50	3.00

MEGATON MAN
KITCHEN SINK

	ORIG	GOOD	FINE	N-MINT
❑1, Nov 84, They Call the Doctor...Software!, O: Megaton Man	2.00	0.60	1.50	3.00
❑1-2, 2nd Printing	2.00	0.40	1.00	2.00
❑2, Feb 85	2.00	0.50	1.25	2.50
❑3, Apr 85, I Am Called Bad Guy, Mortal!	2.00	0.50	1.25	2.50
❑4, Jun 85, News Of The World	2.00	0.50	1.25	2.50
❑5, Aug 85, Stella's Story	2.00	0.50	1.25	2.50
❑6, Oct 85, The Death of Megaton Man; Border Worlds, Part 1, Border Worlds storyline begins	2.00	0.50	1.25	2.50
❑7, Dec 85, No Bag Guy Shall Escape My Patrol!; Border Worlds, Part 2	2.00	0.50	1.25	2.50
❑8, Feb 86, Megaton Man's All-Collegiate Issue!; Border Worlds, Part 3, Border Worlds back-up	2.00	0.50	1.25	2.50
❑9, Apr 86, Border Worlds, Part 4	2.00	0.50	1.25	2.50
❑10, Jun 86, Over-Kill!; Border Worlds, Part 5, Final Issue	2.00	0.50	1.25	2.50

MEGATON MAN: BOMBSHELL
IMAGE

Value: Cover or less

❑1, Jul 99, Megaton Man versus Unleash; Megaton Man versus Bombshell 2.95

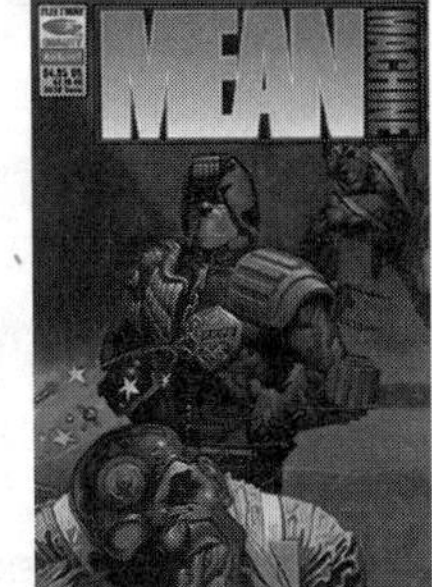

The *Mean Machine* one-shot featured a "fractured" cover where Mean had head-butted it.

© 1995 Fleetway/Quality

MEGATON MAN: HARDCOPY
IMAGE

Value: Cover or less

❑1, Feb 99, b&w; collects Internet strips 2.95
❑2, Apr 99, Mammaw Voodoo!, b&w; collects Internet strips 2.95

MEGATON MAN MEETS THE UNCATEGORIZABLE X+THEMS
KITCHEN SINK

Value: Cover or less

❑1, Apr 89, b&w; X-Men parody 2.00

MEGAZZAR DUDE
SLAVE LABOR

Value: Cover or less

❑1, Nov 91, b&w 2.95

MELISSA MOORE: BODYGUARD
DRACULINA

Value: Cover or less

❑1, b&w 2.95

MELODY
KITCHEN SINK

	ORIG	GOOD	FINE	N-MINT
❑1, b&w; adult	2.00	0.50	1.25	2.50
❑2, Lunatic Lola, b&w; adult	2.00	0.45	1.13	2.25
❑3, b&w; adult	2.00	0.40	1.00	2.00
❑4, Debauchery, b&w; adult	2.00	0.40	1.00	2.00
❑5, A Father's Ire, b&w; adult	2.00	0.40	1.00	2.00
❑6, Isosceles, b&w; adult	2.00	0.40	1.00	2.00
❑7, b&w; adult	2.25	0.45	1.13	2.25
❑8, Big City Welcome, b&w; adult	2.50	0.45	1.13	2.25

MELONPOOL CHRONICLES, THE
PARA-TROOP

Value: Cover or less

❑1, Crash Course! 2.95

MELTING POT
KITCHEN SINK

Value: Cover or less

❑1, Dec 93 .... 2.95
❑2 .... 2.95
❑3 .... 2.95
❑4, Sep 94 .... 3.50

MELTY FEELING
ANTARCTIC

Value: Cover or less

❑1, Oct 96, b&w; adult 3.50
❑2, Dec 96, The Daily Grind, b&w; adult 3.50
❑3, Jan 97, A Thief on Delight, b&w; adult 3.50
❑4, Feb 97, Summer Nana, b&w; adult 3.50

MELVIS
CHAMELEON

	ORIG	GOOD	FINE	N-MINT
❑1, Jul 94, 2, 500 copies	—	0.40	1.00	2.00
❑2	—	0.40	1.00	2.00
❑3	—	0.40	1.00	2.00
❑4	—	0.40	1.00	2.00

MEMENTO MORI
MEMENTO MORI

	ORIG	GOOD	FINE	N-MINT
❑1	—	0.40	1.00	2.00
❑2, Mar 95, b&w; no cover price; Anthology	—	0.40	1.00	2.00

MEMORIES
MARVEL

Value: Cover or less

❑1, b&w; Japanese 2.50

MEMORYMAN
DAVID MARKOFF

	ORIG	GOOD	FINE	N-MINT
❑1/Ash, 1: Memoryman, Ashcan edition given as promo at 1995 San Diego Comicon	—	0.10	0.25	0.50

MENAGERIE
CHROME TIGER

Value: Cover or less

❑1, Nov 87, Scarycat and Mousekanaut; Iron Crosses 1.95

MEN FROM EARTH
FUTURE-FUN

Value: Cover or less

❑1 .... 2.00

MEN IN BLACK, THE
AIRCEL

	ORIG	GOOD	FINE	N-MINT
❑1, Jan 90, Initiation, b&w	2.25	2.00	5.00	10.00
❑2, Feb 90, Encounter, b&w	2.25	1.60	4.00	8.00
❑3, Mar 90, Invocation, b&w	2.25	1.40	3.50	7.00

MEN IN BLACK, THE (BOOK II)
AIRCEL

	ORIG	GOOD	FINE	N-MINT
❑1, May 91, Wolf in the Fold, b&w	2.50	2.00	5.00	10.00
❑2, Jun 91, b&w	2.50	1.20	3.00	6.00
❑3, Jul 91, b&w	2.50	1.00	2.50	5.00

MEN IN BLACK: FAR CRY
MARVEL

Value: Cover or less

❑1, Aug 97, One-Shot; Jay and Kay are reunited ... 3.99

MEN IN BLACK: RETRIBUTION
MARVEL

Value: Cover or less

❑1, Dec 97 ... 3.99

MEN IN BLACK: THE MOVIE
MARVEL

Value: Cover or less

❑1, Oct 97, One-Shot; adapts movie ... 3.99

MEN OF WAR
DC

	ORIG	GOOD	FINE	N-MINT
❑1, Aug 77, Code Name: Gravedigger; Enemy Ace: Death is a Wild Beast!, 1: Gravedigger, Enemy Ace back-up	0.35	0.80	2.00	4.00
❑2, Sep 77, JKu (c), Enemy Ace back-up	0.35	0.60	1.50	3.00
❑3, Nov 77, JKu (c), Enemy Ace back-up	0.35	0.60	1.50	3.00
❑4, Jan 78, JKu (c), Dateline: Frontline back-up	0.35	0.60	1.50	3.00
❑5	—	0.60	1.50	3.00
❑6	—	0.50	1.25	2.50
❑7	—	0.50	1.25	2.50
❑8	—	0.50	1.25	2.50
❑9	—	0.50	1.25	2.50
❑10, Nov 78, JKu (c), Enemy Ace and Dateline: Frontline back-ups	0.50	0.50	1.25	2.50
❑11, Dec 78	—	0.50	1.25	2.50
❑12, Jan 79	—	0.50	1.25	2.50
❑13, Feb 79, Project Gravedigger-Plus One	0.40	0.50	1.25	2.50
❑14, Mar 79, JKu (c), Enemy Ace back-up	0.40	0.50	1.25	2.50
❑15, Apr 79, JKu (c)	0.40	0.50	1.25	2.50
❑16, May 79	—	0.50	1.25	2.50
❑17, Jun 79	—	0.50	1.25	2.50
❑18, Jul 79	—	0.50	1.25	2.50
❑19, Aug 79	—	0.50	1.25	2.50
❑20, Sep 79, JKu (c)	0.40	0.50	1.25	2.50
❑21, Oct 79	0.40	0.50	1.25	2.50
❑22, Nov 79	0.40	0.50	1.25	2.50
❑23, Dec 79	—	0.50	1.25	2.50
❑24, Jan 80	—	0.50	1.25	2.50
❑25, Feb 80	—	0.50	1.25	2.50
❑26, Mar 80, Final Issue	—	0.50	1.25	2.50

MEN'S ADVENTURE COMIX
PENTHOUSE INTERNATIONAL

	ORIG	GOOD	FINE	N-MINT
❑1, May 95, Action Figures, Part 1; Generation Sex, Part 1, 1: Miss Adventure; 1: Hericane, Comic-sized	4.95	1.20	3.00	6.00
❑2, Jul 95	4.95	1.00	2.50	5.00
❑3, Sep 95	4.95	1.00	2.50	5.00
❑4, Nov 95	4.95	1.00	2.50	5.00
❑5, Dec 95	4.95	1.00	2.50	5.00
❑6, Feb 96	4.95	1.00	2.50	5.00
❑7, Apr 96	4.95	1.00	2.50	5.00

MENTHU
BLACK INC!

Value: Cover or less

❑1, Jan 98, Tributary ... 2.95
❑2 ... 2.95
❑3 ... 2.95
❑4 ... 2.95

MENZ INSANA
DC

Value: Cover or less

❑1, Mortals and Portals; Let's Get Normal, nn; One-Shot; prestige format ... 7.95

MEPHISTO VS...
MARVEL

	ORIG	GOOD	FINE	N-MINT
❑1, Apr 87, JB, AM (w), Give The Devil His Due, Fantastic Four	1.50	0.50	1.25	2.50
❑2, May 87, JB, AM (w), Sympathy For The Devil, X-Factor	1.50	0.40	1.00	2.00
❑3, Jun 87, JB, X-Men	1.50	0.40	1.00	2.00
❑4, Jul 87, JB, Avengers	1.50	0.40	1.00	2.00

MERCEDES
ANGUS

Value: Cover or less

❑1 ... 2.95
❑2, Jan 96 ... 2.95
❑3, Feb 96 ... 2.95
❑4, Mar 96 ... 2.95
❑5, Apr 96, Six Bullets, Part 1 ... 2.95
❑6, Six Bullets, Part 2 ... 2.95
❑7, Six Bullets, Part 3 ... 2.95
❑8, Six Bullets, Part 4 ... 2.95
❑9, Six Bullets, Part 5 ... 2.95
❑10, Six Bullets, Part 6 ... 2.95
❑11, The Wicked, Part 1 ... 2.95
❑12, The Wicked, Part 2 ... 2.95

MERCHANTS OF DEATH
ECLIPSE

Value: Cover or less

❑1, Jul 88, The Hero, b&w; magazine ... 3.50
❑2, b&w; magazine ... 3.50
❑3, b&w; magazine ... 3.50
❑4, b&w; magazine ... 3.50

MERCHANTS OF VENUS, THE
DC

	ORIG	GOOD	FINE	N-MINT
❑1	5.95	1.20	3.00	6.00

MERCY
DC

	ORIG	GOOD	FINE	N-MINT
❑1, nn	5.95	1.20	3.00	6.00

MERIDIAN
CROSSGEN

Value: Cover or less

❑1, Jul 00 ... 2.95
❑2, Aug 00 ... 2.95
❑3, Sep 00 ... 2.95
❑4, Oct 00 ... 2.95
❑5 ... 2.95
❑6 ... 2.95
❑7 ... 2.95
❑8 ... 2.95
❑9 ... 2.95
❑10 ... 2.95
❑11 ... 2.95
❑12 ... 2.95
❑13 ... 2.95
❑14 ... 2.95

MERLIN
ADVENTURE

Value: Cover or less

❑1, b&w ... 2.50
❑2, b&w ... 2.50
❑3, Feb 91, Where Madness Lies, b&w ... 2.50
❑4, Mar 91, Belle du Lac, b&w ... 2.50
❑5, Apr 91, Dark Desires, b&w ... 2.50
❑6, Circle Of Fire, b&w; Final Issue ... 2.50

MERLIN: IDYLLS OF THE KING
ADVENTURE

Value: Cover or less

❑1, b&w ... 2.50
❑2, b&w ... 2.50

MERLINREALM 3-D
BLACKTHORNE

	ORIG	GOOD	FINE	N-MINT
❑1, Oct 85, When Illusions of Life Becom Deathdreams Realized	2.00	0.45	1.13	2.25

MERMAID
ALTERNATIVE

Value: Cover or less

❑1, May 98, nn; b&w ... 2.95

MERMAID FOREST
VIZ

Value: Cover or less

❑1, b&w ... 2.75
❑2, b&w ... 2.75
❑3, b&w ... 2.75
❑4, b&w ... 2.75

MERMAID'S DREAM
VIZ

Value: Cover or less

❑1, Oct 85, When Illusions of Life Become Death Dream Realized, b&w ... 2.75
❑2, The Ash Princess, b&w ... 2.75
❑3, b&w ... 2.75

MERMAID'S GAZE
VIZ

Value: Cover or less

❑1, b&w ... 2.75
❑2, b&w ... 2.75
❑3, b&w ... 2.75
❑4, b&w ... 2.75

MERMAID'S MASK
VIZ

Value: Cover or less

❑1, b&w ... 2.75
❑2, b&w ... 2.75
❑3, b&w ... 2.75
❑4 ... 2.75

MERMAID'S PROMISE
VIZ

Value: Cover or less

❑1, b&w ... 2.75
❑2, b&w ... 2.75
❑3, b&w ... 2.75
❑4, b&w ... 2.75

MERMAID'S SCAR
VIZ

Value: Cover or less

❑1, b&w ... 2.75
❑2, b&w ... 2.75
❑3, b&w ... 2.75
❑4, b&w ... 2.75

MERTON OF THE MOVEMENT
LAST GASP

	ORIG	GOOD	FINE	N-MINT
❑1, Doctor Dope; 1st Demonstration	0.50	0.70	1.75	3.50

MESSENGER, THE
IMAGE

Value: Cover or less

❑1, Jul 00, JOy, JOy (w) ... 5.95

MESSENGER 29
SEPTEMBER

	ORIG	GOOD	FINE	N-MINT
❑1, b&w	1.95	0.40	1.00	2.00

MESSIAH
PINNACLE

Value: Cover or less

❑1, b&w ... 1.50

MESSOZOIC
KITCHEN SINK

Value: Cover or less

❑1, nn ... 2.95

META-4
FIRST

Value: Cover or less

❑1, Feb 91, The Unbearable Being Of Lightness, 1: Meta-4 ... 3.95
❑2, Mar 91, Disparate Liaisons ... 2.25
❑3, Apr 91 ... 2.25

METABARONS, THE
HUMANOIDS
Value: Cover or less

	ORIG
❑1, Jan 00	2.95
❑2	2.95
❑3	2.95
❑4	2.95
❑5, Jun 00	2.95
❑6	2.95
❑7	2.95
❑8	2.95
❑9	2.95
❑10	2.95
❑11	2.95
❑12	2.95
❑13	2.95
❑14	2.95

METACOPS
FANTAGRAPHICS
Value: Cover or less

	ORIG
❑1, Feb 91, b&w	1.95
❑2, Mar 91, b&w	1.95
❑3, Jul 91, b&w	1.95

METAL BIKINI
ETERNITY
Value: Cover or less

	ORIG
❑1, Oct 90, b&w	2.25
❑2, b&w	2.25
❑3, b&w	2.25
❑4, b&w	2.25
❑5, b&w	2.25
❑6, b&w	2.25

METAL GUARDIAN FAUST
VIZ
Value: Cover or less

	ORIG
❑1, Mar 97	2.95
❑2, Apr 97	2.95
❑3, May 97	2.95
❑4, Jun 97, Dream of an Angel	2.95
❑5, Jul 97	2.95
❑6, Aug 97	2.95
❑7, Sep 97	2.95
❑8, Oct 97	2.95

METALLICA (CELEBRITY)
CELEBRITY
Value: Cover or less

	ORIG
❑1/A	2.95
❑1/B, trading cards	6.95

METALLICA (FORBIDDEN FRUIT)
FORBIDDEN FRUIT
Value: Cover or less

	ORIG
❑1, My Ferrous Lady, b&w; adult	2.95
❑2, b&w; adult	2.95

METALLICA (ROCK-IT)
ROCK-IT COMICS

	ORIG	GOOD	FINE	N-MINT
❑1, guitar pick	4.95	1.00	2.50	5.00

METALLICA'S GREATEST HITS
REVOLUTIONARY
Value: Cover or less

	ORIG
❑1, Sep 93, b&w	2.50

METAL MEN
DC

	ORIG	GOOD	FINE	N-MINT
❑1, May 63	0.12	57.00	142.50	285.00
❑2, Jul 63	0.12	25.00	62.50	125.00
❑3, Sep 63	0.12	16.00	40.00	80.00
❑4, Nov 63	0.12	16.00	40.00	80.00
❑5, Jan 64	0.12	16.00	40.00	80.00
❑6, Mar 64	0.12	10.40	26.00	52.00
❑7, May 64	0.12	10.40	26.00	52.00
❑8, Jul 64	0.12	10.40	26.00	52.00
❑9, Sep 64	0.12	10.40	26.00	52.00
❑10, Nov 64	0.12	10.40	26.00	52.00
❑11, Jan 65	0.12	7.00	17.50	35.00
❑12, Mar 65	0.12	7.00	17.50	35.00
❑13, May 65, 1: Tin's girlfriend; V: Skyscraper Robot	0.12	7.00	17.50	35.00
❑14, Jul 65	0.12	7.00	17.50	35.00
❑15, Sep 65	0.12	7.00	17.50	35.00
❑16, Nov 65	0.12	7.00	17.50	35.00
❑17, Jan 66	0.12	7.00	17.50	35.00
❑18, Mar 66	0.12	7.00	17.50	35.00
❑19, May 66	0.12	7.00	17.50	35.00
❑20, Jul 66	0.12	7.00	17.50	35.00
❑21, Sep 66	0.12	6.00	15.00	30.00
❑22, Nov 66	0.12	6.00	15.00	30.00
❑23, Jan 67	0.12	6.00	15.00	30.00
❑24, Mar 67	0.12	6.00	15.00	30.00
❑25, May 67	0.12	6.00	15.00	30.00
❑26, Jul 67	0.12	6.00	15.00	30.00
❑27, Sep 67, O: Metal Men	0.12	11.00	27.50	55.00
❑28, Nov 67	0.12	4.80	12.00	24.00
❑29, Jan 68	0.12	4.80	12.00	24.00
❑30, Mar 68	0.12	4.80	12.00	24.00
❑31, May 68	0.12	3.20	8.00	16.00
❑32, Jul 68	0.12	3.20	8.00	16.00
❑33, Sep 68	0.12	3.20	8.00	16.00
❑34, Nov 68, Death Comes Calling	0.12	3.20	8.00	16.00
❑35, Jan 69	0.12	3.20	8.00	16.00
❑36, Mar 69	0.12	3.20	8.00	16.00
❑37, May 69	0.12	3.20	8.00	16.00
❑38, Jul 69	0.12	3.20	8.00	16.00
❑39, Sep 69	0.12	3.20	8.00	16.00
❑40, Nov 69	0.15	3.20	8.00	16.00
❑41, Dec 69, series put on hiatus	0.15	3.20	8.00	16.00
❑42, Mar 73, Reprint; Series begins again (1973)	0.20	1.80	4.50	9.00
❑43, May 73, Reprint	0.20	1.80	4.50	9.00
❑44, Jul 73, V: Missile Men, Reprint; back to hiatus	0.20	1.80	4.50	9.00
❑45, May 76, Series begins again (1976)	0.30	0.80	2.00	4.00
❑46, Jul 76	0.30	0.80	2.00	4.00
❑47, Sep 76, V: Plutonium Man	0.30	0.80	2.00	4.00
❑48, Nov 76, V: Eclipso	0.30	0.80	2.00	4.00
❑49, Jan 77, V: Eclipso	0.30	0.80	2.00	4.00
❑50, Mar 77	0.30	0.80	2.00	4.00
❑51, May 77, V: Vox	0.30	0.80	2.00	4.00
❑52, Jul 77	0.35	0.80	2.00	4.00
❑53, Sep 77	0.35	0.80	2.00	4.00
❑54, Nov 77, A: Green Lantern	0.35	0.80	2.00	4.00
❑55, Jan 78, V: Missile Men	0.35	0.80	2.00	4.00
❑56, Mar 78, V: Inheritor, Final Issue	0.35	0.80	2.00	4.00

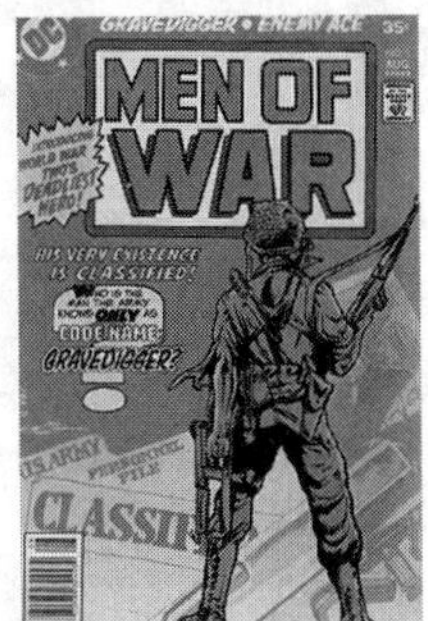

New Enemy Ace stories by Howard Chaykin ran as back-ups in *Men of War.*

METAL MEN (MINI-SERIES)
DC

	ORIG	GOOD	FINE	N-MINT
❑1, Oct 93, Thanks For The Memories, foil cover	2.50	0.50	1.25	2.50
❑2, Nov 93	1.25	0.30	0.75	1.50
❑3, Dec 93, Metalurgency	1.25	0.30	0.75	1.50
❑4, Jan 94, ThePeriodic Tables Turn!	1.25	0.30	0.75	1.50

METAL MEN OF MARS & OTHER IMPROBABLE TALES
SLAVE LABOR

	ORIG	GOOD	FINE	N-MINT
❑1, Jan 89, Metal Men of Mars; The Pharaoh of Fear, A: Captain Daring; A: Tasma, b&w	1.95	0.40	1.00	2.00

METAL MILITIA
EXPRESS
Value: Cover or less

	ORIG
❑1, Aug 95	2.50
❑2	2.50
❑3, Lost	2.50

METAMORPHO
DC

	ORIG	GOOD	FINE	N-MINT
❑1, Aug 65	0.12	8.00	20.00	40.00
❑2, Oct 65	0.12	4.00	10.00	20.00
❑3, Dec 65	0.12	3.60	9.00	18.00
❑4, Feb 66, Metamorpho in Mexico	0.12	3.00	7.50	15.00
❑5, Apr 66, Metamorpho vs. Metamorpho	0.12	3.00	7.50	15.00
❑6, Jun 66	0.12	2.40	6.00	12.00
❑7, Aug 66	0.12	2.40	6.00	12.00
❑8, Oct 66, V: Doc Dread	0.12	2.40	6.00	12.00
❑9, Dec 66	0.12	2.40	6.00	12.00
❑10, Feb 67, 1: Element Girl	0.12	2.80	7.00	14.00
❑11, Apr 67	0.12	2.00	5.00	10.00
❑12, Jun 67	0.12	2.00	5.00	10.00
❑13, Aug 67	0.12	2.00	5.00	10.00
❑14, Oct 67	0.12	2.00	5.00	10.00
❑15, Dec 67	0.12	2.00	5.00	10.00
❑16, Feb 68	0.12	2.00	5.00	10.00
❑17, Apr 68, Final Issue	0.12	2.00	5.00	10.00

METAMORPHO (MINI-SERIES)
DC
Value: Cover or less

	ORIG
❑1, Aug 93, Like Father Like Son	1.50
❑2, Sep 93, Chemical Bonds	1.50
❑3, Oct 93, Chemical Imbalance	1.50
❑4, Nov 93	1.50

METAPHYSIQUE
ECLIPSE
Value: Cover or less

	ORIG
❑1, The Path	2.50

METAPHYSIQUE (MALIBU)
MALIBU

	ORIG	GOOD	FINE	N-MINT
❑1, The Oneironauts Session One: Inner Worlds	2.95	0.59	1.48	2.95
❑2	2.95	0.59	1.48	2.95
❑3	2.95	0.59	1.48	2.95
❑4	2.95	0.59	1.48	2.95
❑5	2.95	0.59	1.48	2.95
❑6, Apocalyptic Armageddon, A: Superius	2.95	0.59	1.48	2.95
❑Ash 1	0.99	0.20	0.50	1.00

METEOR MAN
MARVEL

Value: Cover or less

- ❑1, Aug 93 — 1.25
- ❑2, Sep 93 — 1.25
- ❑3, Oct 93, A: Spider-Man — 1.25
- ❑4, Nov 93, The the Third Power!, A: Night Thrasher — 1.25
- ❑5, Dec 93 — 1.25
- ❑6, Jan 94 — 1.25

METEOR MAN: THE MOVIE
MARVEL

Value: Cover or less

- ❑1, movie Adaptation — 2.25

METROPOL (TED MCKEEVER'S...)
MARVEL

Value: Cover or less

- ❑1, Secrets and Revelations — 2.95
- ❑2, My Bones, My Pulse — 2.95
- ❑3, You Can Only Experience Death Once — 2.95
- ❑4, The Breath Of Reptiles — 2.95
- ❑5 — 2.95
- ❑6 — 2.95
- ❑7 — 2.95
- ❑8 — 2.95
- ❑9 — 2.95
- ❑10 — 2.95
- ❑11 — 2.95
- ❑12 — 2.95

METROPOL A.D. (VOL. 2, TED MCKEEVER'S...)
MARVEL

Value: Cover or less

- ❑1, Like A Babe In Arms — 3.50
- ❑2, The Smell Of Rust And Gunpowder — 3.50
- ❑3 — 3.50

METROPOLIS S.C.U.
DC

Value: Cover or less

- ❑1, Nov 94, Sawyer's Blue — 1.50
- ❑2, Dec 94, Cop Out! — 1.50
- ❑3, Jan 95 — 1.50
- ❑4, Feb 95 — 1.50

MEZ
C.A.P.

Value: Cover or less

- ❑1, May 97, b&w; Canadian cover price only — 3.00
- ❑2, Mar 98, b&w; Canadian cover price only — 3.00

MEZZ: GALACTIC TOUR 2494
DARK HORSE

Value: Cover or less

- ❑1 — 2.50

M FALLING
VAGABOND PRESS

Value: Cover or less

- ❑1, nn — 3.50

MFI: THE GHOSTS OF CHRISTMAS
IMAGE

Value: Cover or less

- ❑1, Dec 99 — 3.95

MIAMI MICE
RIP OFF

Value: Cover or less

- ❑1, Apr 86, The Mice Meet the Big Cheez; Scureface — 2.00
- ❑1-2, May 86, The Mice Meet the Big Cheez; Scureface, 2nd Printing — 2.00
- ❑, May 86, The Mice Meet the Big Cheez; Scureface, 3rd Printing — 2.00
- ❑2, Jul 86, The Deadly Cheese Dust Caper, b&w — 2.00
- ❑3, Oct 86, Pie in Der' Sky, b&w — 2.00
- ❑3/A, Pie in Der' Sky, b&w; flexi-disc; w/ soundsheet — 5.00
- ❑4, Jan 87, b&w — 2.00

MICHAELANGELO CHRISTMAS SPECIAL
MIRAGE

	ORIG	GOOD	FINE	N-MINT
❑1, Dec 90, b&w	1.75	0.40	1.00	2.00

MICHAELANGELO TEENAGE MUTANT NINJA TURTLE
MIRAGE

	ORIG	GOOD	FINE	N-MINT
❑1, The Christmas Aliens	1.50	0.50	1.25	2.50

MICHAEL JORDAN TRIBUTE
REVOLUTIONARY

Value: Cover or less

- ❑1 — 2.95

MICKEY AND DONALD (WALT DISNEY'S...)
GLADSTONE

	ORIG	GOOD	FINE	N-MINT
❑1, Mar 88, CB	0.95	0.40	1.00	2.00
❑2, CB	0.95	0.40	1.00	2.00
❑3, Jul 88, CB	0.95	0.40	1.00	2.00
❑4, Aug 88, CB	0.95	0.40	1.00	2.00
❑5, Sep 88, CB, WK (c)	0.95	0.40	1.00	2.00
❑6, Oct 88, CB	0.95	0.40	1.00	2.00
❑7, Nov 88, CB	0.95	0.40	1.00	2.00
❑8, Dec 88, CB	0.95	0.40	1.00	2.00
❑9, CB	0.95	0.40	1.00	2.00
❑10, CB	0.95	0.40	1.00	2.00
❑11, CB	0.95	0.40	1.00	2.00
❑12, Aug 89, CB	0.95	0.40	1.00	2.00
❑13, Sep 89, CB	0.95	0.40	1.00	2.00
❑14, Oct 89, CB	0.95	0.40	1.00	2.00
❑15, Nov 89, CB	0.95	0.40	1.00	2.00
❑16, Jan 90, CB, Beanstalk	0.95	0.40	1.00	2.00
❑17, Mar 90, DR; FG; CB, Mickey Mouse and Goofy; Donald Duck	1.95	0.39	0.98	1.95
❑18, May 90, FG; CB, WK (c), series continues as Donald and Mickey	1.95	0.39	0.98	1.95

MICKEY & MINNIE
W.D.

Value: Cover or less

- ❑1, Mystery in Mouseton, nn — 3.50

MICKEY MANTLE
MAGNUM

	ORIG	GOOD	FINE	N-MINT
❑1, Dec 91, JSt, The Mickey Mantle Story, Photo cover	1.75	0.40	1.00	2.00
❑2	—	0.40	1.00	2.00

MICKEY MOUSE (ONE-SHOT)
DISNEY

	ORIG	GOOD	FINE	N-MINT
❑1, nn; in Russian	—	0.80	2.00	4.00

MICKEY MOUSE (WALT DISNEY'S...)
GLADSTONE

	ORIG	GOOD	FINE	N-MINT
❑219, Oct 86, FG	0.75	0.60	1.50	3.00
❑220, Nov 86, FG	0.75	0.60	1.50	3.00
❑221, Dec 86, FG	0.75	0.50	1.25	2.50
❑222, Jan 87, FG	0.75	0.50	1.25	2.50
❑223, Feb 87, FG	0.75	0.50	1.25	2.50
❑224, Mar 87, FG	0.75	0.50	1.25	2.50
❑225, Apr 87, FG	0.75	0.50	1.25	2.50
❑226, May 87, FG	0.75	0.50	1.25	2.50
❑227, Jun 87, FG	0.95	0.50	1.25	2.50
❑228, Jul 87, FG	0.95	0.50	1.25	2.50
❑229, Aug 87, FG	0.95	0.50	1.25	2.50
❑230, Sep 87, FG	0.95	0.50	1.25	2.50
❑231, Oct 87, FG	0.95	0.50	1.25	2.50
❑232, Nov 87, FG	0.95	0.50	1.25	2.50
❑233, Dec 87, FG	0.95	0.50	1.25	2.50
❑234, Jan 88, FG	0.95	0.50	1.25	2.50
❑235, Mar 88, FG	0.95	0.50	1.25	2.50
❑236, Apr 88, FG	0.95	0.50	1.25	2.50
❑237, Jun 88, FG	0.95	0.50	1.25	2.50
❑238, Jul 88, FG	0.95	0.50	1.25	2.50
❑239, Aug 88, FG	0.95	0.50	1.25	2.50
❑240, Sep 88, FG	0.95	0.50	1.25	2.50
❑241, Oct 88, FG	0.95	0.40	1.00	2.00
❑242, Nov 88, FG	0.95	0.40	1.00	2.00
❑243, Dec 88, FG	0.95	0.40	1.00	2.00
❑244, Jan 89, FG, The Miracle Master; Society Dog Show, 60th anniversary, 100 pages; Daily Strips compilation	2.95	0.40	1.00	2.00
❑245, Mar 89, FG, Mickey Mouse and Pluto Battle the Giant Ants	0.95	0.40	1.00	2.00
❑246, Apr 89, FG	0.95	0.40	1.00	2.00
❑247, Jun 89, FG	0.95	0.40	1.00	2.00
❑248, Jul 89, FG	0.95	0.40	1.00	2.00
❑249, Aug 89, FG	0.95	0.40	1.00	2.00
❑250, FG	0.95	0.40	1.00	2.00
❑251, FG	0.95	0.40	1.00	2.00
❑252, FG	0.95	0.40	1.00	2.00
❑253, FG	0.95	0.40	1.00	2.00
❑254, FG	0.95	0.40	1.00	2.00
❑255	0.95	0.40	1.00	2.00
❑256, Final Issue	0.95	0.40	1.00	2.00

MICKEY MOUSE ADVENTURES
DISNEY

	ORIG	GOOD	FINE	N-MINT
❑1, Jun 90	1.50	0.40	1.00	2.00
❑2, Jul 90	1.50	0.30	0.75	1.50
❑3, Aug 90, V: Phantom Blot	1.50	0.30	0.75	1.50
❑4, Sep 90	1.50	0.30	0.75	1.50
❑5, Oct 90	1.50	0.30	0.75	1.50
❑6, Nov 90	1.50	0.30	0.75	1.50
❑7, Dec 90	1.50	0.30	0.75	1.50
❑8, Jan 91, JBy (c)	1.50	0.30	0.75	1.50
❑9, Feb 91, Fantasia	1.50	0.30	0.75	1.50
❑10, Mar 91	1.50	0.30	0.75	1.50
❑11, Apr 91	1.50	0.30	0.75	1.50
❑12, May 91	1.50	0.30	0.75	1.50
❑13, Jun 91	1.50	0.30	0.75	1.50
❑14, Jul 91	1.50	0.30	0.75	1.50
❑15, Aug 91	1.50	0.30	0.75	1.50
❑16, Sep 91, KB	1.50	0.30	0.75	1.50
❑17, Oct 91, Dinosaur	1.50	0.30	0.75	1.50
❑18, Nov 91, Dinosaur	1.50	0.30	0.75	1.50

MICKEY MOUSE DIGEST
GLADSTONE

	ORIG	GOOD	FINE	N-MINT
❑1	—	1.00	2.50	5.00
❑2	—	0.80	2.00	4.00
❑3	—	0.60	1.50	3.00
❑4	—	0.60	1.50	3.00
❑5	—	0.60	1.50	3.00

MICKEY RAT
LOS ANGELES COMIC BOOK CO.

	ORIG	GOOD	FINE	N-MINT
❑1, May 72, b&w; adult	0.50	1.00	2.50	5.00
❑2, Oct 72, Feelin' Kinda Disney; The Coming of the Rat-Man, b&w; adult	0.50	0.80	2.00	4.00
❑3, Jul 80, b&w; adult	1.25	0.60	1.50	3.00
❑4, ...Nothing Like a Nice Day in the Park; The Life of the Party, b&w; adult	1.50	0.60	1.50	3.00

MICRA: MIND CONTROLLED REMOTE AUTOMATON
Comics Interview
Value: Cover or less

❑1, Nov 86, The Beginning	1.75	❑5	1.75
❑2	1.75	❑6	1.75
❑3	1.75	❑7	1.75
❑4	1.75		

MICROBOTS, THE
Gold Key

	ORIG	GOOD	FINE	N-MINT
❑1, Dec 71, This is the Way the World Ends	0.15	2.00	5.00	10.00

MICRONAUTS (VOL. 1)
Marvel

	ORIG	GOOD	FINE	N-MINT
❑1, Jan 79, MG, 1: Marionette; O: Micronauts; 1: Biotron; 1: Space Glider; 1: Baron Karza; 1: The Micronauts	0.35	0.60	1.50	3.00
❑2, Feb 79, MG	0.35	0.50	1.25	2.50
❑3, Mar 79, MG	0.35	0.45	1.13	2.25
❑4, Apr 79, MG	0.35	0.45	1.13	2.25
❑5, May 79, MG	0.40	0.45	1.13	2.25
❑6, Jun 79, MG	0.40	0.40	1.00	2.00
❑7, Jul 79, MG, A: Man-Thing	0.40	0.40	1.00	2.00
❑8, Aug 79, MG, A: Captain Universe	0.40	0.45	1.13	2.25
❑9, Sep 79, MG	0.40	0.40	1.00	2.00
❑10, Oct 79, MG	0.40	0.40	1.00	2.00
❑11, Nov 79, MG	0.40	0.30	0.75	1.50
❑12, Dec 79, MG	0.40	0.30	0.75	1.50
❑13, Jan 80	0.40	0.30	0.75	1.50
❑14, Feb 80	0.40	0.30	0.75	1.50
❑15, Mar 80, A: Fantastic Four; D: Microtron	0.40	0.30	0.75	1.50
❑16, Apr 80, A: Fantastic Four	0.40	0.30	0.75	1.50
❑17, May 80, D: Jasmine; A: Fantastic Four	0.40	0.30	0.75	1.50
❑18, Jun 80	0.40	0.30	0.75	1.50
❑19, Jul 80	0.40	0.30	0.75	1.50
❑20, Aug 80, A: Ant-Man	0.40	0.30	0.75	1.50
❑21, Sep 80	0.50	0.25	0.63	1.25
❑22, Oct 80	0.50	0.25	0.63	1.25
❑23, Nov 80, V: Molecule Man	0.50	0.25	0.63	1.25
❑24, Dec 80	0.50	0.25	0.63	1.25
❑25, Jan 81, V: Mentallo; O: Baron Karza	0.50	0.25	0.63	1.25
❑26, Feb 81, PB	0.50	0.25	0.63	1.25
❑27, Mar 81, PB, D: Biotron	0.50	0.25	0.63	1.25
❑28, Apr 81, PB, A: Nick Fury	0.50	0.25	0.63	1.25
❑29, May 81, PB, A: Nick Fury	0.50	0.25	0.63	1.25
❑30, Jun 81, PB	0.50	0.25	0.63	1.25
❑31, Jul 81, PB, A: Doctor Strange	0.50	0.25	0.63	1.25
❑32, Aug 81, PB, A: Doctor Strange	0.50	0.25	0.63	1.25
❑33, Sep 81, PB, A: Doctor Strange	0.50	0.25	0.63	1.25
❑34, Oct 81, PB, A: Doctor Strange	0.50	0.25	0.63	1.25
❑35, Nov 81, A: Doctor Strange; O: Microverse, double-sized	0.75	0.25	0.63	1.25
❑36, Dec 81	0.50	0.25	0.63	1.25
❑37, Jan 82, A: Nightcrawler; A: X-Men	0.60	0.30	0.75	1.50
❑38, Feb 82, Direct sales (only) begin	0.75	0.30	0.75	1.50
❑39, Mar 82	0.75	0.25	0.63	1.25
❑40, Apr 82, A: Fantastic Four	0.75	0.25	0.63	1.25
❑41, May 82, V: Doctor Doom; V: Dr. Doom	0.75	0.25	0.63	1.25
❑42, Jun 82	0.75	0.25	0.63	1.25
❑43, Jul 82	0.75	0.25	0.63	1.25
❑44, Aug 82	0.75	0.25	0.63	1.25
❑45, Sep 82	0.75	0.25	0.63	1.25
❑46, Oct 82	0.75	0.25	0.63	1.25
❑47, Nov 82	0.75	0.25	0.63	1.25
❑48, Dec 82, 1st Guice	0.75	0.25	0.63	1.25
❑49, Jan 83	0.75	0.25	0.63	1.25
❑50, Feb 83	0.75	0.25	0.63	1.25
❑51, Mar 83	0.75	0.25	0.63	1.25
❑52, May 83	0.75	0.25	0.63	1.25
❑53, Jul 83	0.75	0.25	0.63	1.25
❑54, Sep 83	0.75	0.25	0.63	1.25
❑55, Nov 83	0.75	0.25	0.63	1.25
❑56, Jan 84	0.75	0.25	0.63	1.25
❑57, Mar 84, double-sized	1.00	0.25	0.63	1.25
❑58, May 84	0.75	0.25	0.63	1.25
❑59, Aug 84, Homeworld, Final Issue	0.75	0.25	0.63	1.25
❑Anl 1, Dec 79, SD	0.75	0.40	1.00	2.00
❑Anl 2, Oct 80, SD, V: Toymaster	0.75	0.30	0.75	1.50
❑SE 1, Dec 83	2.00	0.40	1.00	2.00
❑SE 2, Jan 84	2.00	0.40	1.00	2.00
❑SE 3, Feb 84	2.00	0.40	1.00	2.00
❑SE 4, Mar 84	2.00	0.40	1.00	2.00
❑SE 5, Apr 84	2.00	0.40	1.00	2.00

MICRONAUTS (VOL. 2)
Marvel

	ORIG	GOOD	FINE	N-MINT
❑1, Oct 84, Shadow Of The Makers, Makers	0.60	0.30	0.75	1.50
❑2, Nov 84, Life-Cycles	0.60	0.20	0.50	1.00
❑3, Dec 84	0.60	0.20	0.50	1.00
❑4, Jan 85	0.60	0.20	0.50	1.00
❑5, Feb 85	0.60	0.20	0.50	1.00
❑6, Mar 85	0.60	0.20	0.50	1.00
❑7, Apr 85	0.65	0.20	0.50	1.00
❑8, May 85	0.65	0.20	0.50	1.00
❑9, Jun 85	0.65	0.20	0.50	1.00
❑10, Jul 85	0.65	0.20	0.50	1.00
❑11, Aug 85	0.65	0.20	0.50	1.00
❑12, Sep 85	0.65	0.20	0.50	1.00
❑13, Oct 85	0.65	0.20	0.50	1.00
❑14, Nov 85	0.65	0.20	0.50	1.00
❑15, Dec 85	0.65	0.20	0.50	1.00
❑16, Jan 86, Secret Wars II	0.65	0.20	0.50	1.00
❑17, Feb 86	0.75	0.20	0.50	1.00
❑18, Mar 86, And One Clear Call for Me!	0.75	0.20	0.50	1.00
❑19, Apr 86	0.75	0.20	0.50	1.00
❑20, May 86	0.75	0.20	0.50	1.00

To celebrate Mickey Mouse's 60th anniversary, Gladstone collected a number of daily newspaper strips in a 100-page special issue.

© 1989 Walt Disney Productions (Gladstone)

MIDDLE CLASS FANTASIES
Cartoonists Co-Op

	ORIG	GOOD	FINE	N-MINT
❑1, The Frogman; A Night at Motel 6	0.50	0.60	1.50	3.00
❑2, The Return of the Frogman; chicken Noodle Goes West	1.00	0.60	1.50	3.00

MIDNIGHT
Ajax

	ORIG	GOOD	FINE	N-MINT
❑1	0.10	10.00	25.00	50.00
❑2	0.10	7.00	17.50	35.00
❑3	0.10	5.00	12.50	25.00
❑4	0.10	5.00	12.50	25.00
❑5, Feb 58, The Mightiest Force in the World!; He Sailed into Silence!	0.10	5.00	12.50	25.00
❑6	0.10	5.00	12.50	25.00

MIDNIGHT DAYS (NEIL GAIMAN'S...)
Vertigo
Value: Cover or less

❑1, Jan 00, NG (w); MW (w), Jack in the Green; Brothers, Shaggy God Stories, Hold Me, Reprints Neil Gaiman stories from Swamp Thing, Hellblazer, Sandman Midnight Theatre	17.95

MIDNIGHT EYE GOKU
Viz
Value: Cover or less

❑1	4.95	❑4	4.95
❑2	4.95	❑5	4.95
❑3	4.95	❑6	4.95

MIDNIGHT MEN
Marvel
Value: Cover or less

❑1, Jun 93, HC, HC (w), Embossed cover	2.50	❑3, HC, HC (w)	1.95
❑2, Jul 93, HC, HC (w)	1.95	❑4, HC, HC (w)	1.95

MIDNIGHT NATION
Image

	ORIG	GOOD	FINE	N-MINT
❑1/A, Oct 00, Cover A	2.50	0.60	1.50	3.00
❑1/B, Oct 00, Cover B; Dynamic Forces Exclusive	2.50	0.60	1.50	3.00
❑1/C	—	2.00	5.00	10.00
❑1/D, Convention exclusive edition	—	1.00	2.50	5.00
❑2, Nov 00	2.50	0.50	1.25	2.50
❑3, Dec 00	2.50	0.50	1.25	2.50
❑4, Jan 01	2.50	0.50	1.25	2.50
❑5, Mar 01	2.50	0.50	1.25	2.50
❑6, Apr 01	2.50	0.50	1.25	2.50

MIDNIGHT PANTHER
CPM
Value: Cover or less

❑1, Apr 97	2.95	❑7, Oct 97	2.95
❑2, May 97	2.95	❑8, Nov 97	2.95
❑3, Jun 97	2.95	❑9, Dec 97	2.95
❑4, Jul 97	2.95	❑10, Jan 98	2.95
❑5, Aug 97	2.95	❑11, Feb 98	2.95
❑6, Sep 97	2.95	❑12, Mar 98	2.95

MIDNIGHT PANTHER: FEUDAL FANTASY
CPM

Value: Cover or less

- ❑1, Sep 98, wraparound cover 2.95
- ❑2, Oct 98 2.95

MIDNIGHT PANTHER: SCHOOL DAZE
CPM

Value: Cover or less

- ❑1, Apr 98, wraparound cover 2.95
- ❑2, May 98 2.95
- ❑3, Jun 98, wraparound cover 2.95
- ❑4, Jul 98 2.95
- ❑5, Aug 98 2.95

MIDNIGHT SCREAMS
MYSTERY GRAPHIX

Value: Cover or less

- ❑1 2.50
- ❑2 2.50

MIDNIGHT SONS UNLIMITED
MARVEL

	ORIG	GOOD	FINE	N-MINT
❑1, Eyes Of The Beholder; From The Light, Darkness	3.95	0.80	2.00	4.00
❑2	3.95	0.80	2.00	4.00
❑3, A: Spider-Man	3.95	0.80	2.00	4.00
❑4	3.95	0.79	1.98	3.95
❑5, Apr 94	3.95	0.79	1.98	3.95
❑6, Jul 94	3.95	0.79	1.98	3.95
❑7, Oct 94	3.95	0.79	1.98	3.95
❑8, Jan 95	3.95	0.79	1.98	3.95
❑9, May 95, A: Blazing Skull; A: Union Jack; A: Destroyer	3.95	0.79	1.98	3.95
❑Ash 1, Previews the Midnight Sons titles	0.75	0.15	0.38	0.75

MIDNITE
BLACKTHORNE

Value: Cover or less

- ❑1 1.75
- ❑2 1.75
- ❑3 1.75

MIDNITE SKULKER, THE
TARGET

	ORIG	GOOD	FINE	N-MINT
❑1	1.50	0.35	0.88	1.75
❑2, Aug 86, Return of the Duck Knight, b&w	1.50	0.35	0.88	1.75
❑3, Oct 86, The Black Event	1.50	0.35	0.88	1.75
❑4, Dec 86	1.75	0.35	0.88	1.75
❑5, Feb 87	1.75	0.35	0.88	1.75
❑6, Apr 87	1.75	0.35	0.88	1.75
❑7, Aug 87	1.75	0.35	0.88	1.75

MIDNITE'S QUICKIES
ONE SHOT

	ORIG	GOOD	FINE	N-MINT
❑1, b&w	3.50	0.70	1.75	3.50
❑2, b&w	2.95	0.59	1.48	2.95
❑SE 1, Oct 97, b&w; no cover price; no indicia; published in Oct 97	—	0.60	1.50	3.00
❑SE 1/A, Jan 98, b&w; no cover price; center color poster	—	0.60	1.50	3.00
❑SE 1/B, Oct 97, b&w; foil variant cover	—	0.60	1.50	3.00

MIDVALE
MU PRESS

Value: Cover or less

- ❑1, b&w 2.50
- ❑2, Oct 90, b&w 2.00

MIGHTILY MURDERED POWER RINGERS
EXPRESS

Value: Cover or less

- ❑1, b&w 2.50

MIGHTY ACE, THE
OMEGA 7

Value: Cover or less

- ❑1 2.00
- ❑2, indicia indicates 1992 copyright, probably not year of publication 2.50

MIGHTY BOMB
ANTARCTIC

Value: Cover or less

- ❑1, Jul 97, Fishkill, b&w 2.95

MIGHTY BOMBSHELLS, THE
ANTARCTIC

Value: Cover or less

- ❑1, Sep 93, b&w 2.95
- ❑2, Oct 93, b&w 2.75

MIGHTY CARTOON HEROES
KARL ART

Value: Cover or less

- ❑0, Chameleon Kat; The Aquahounds 2.95

MIGHTY COMICS
ARCHIE

	ORIG	GOOD	FINE	N-MINT
❑40, Nov 66, Series continued from Fly Man #39	0.12	2.40	6.00	12.00
❑41	0.12	2.40	6.00	12.00
❑42	0.12	2.40	6.00	12.00
❑43, The Shield; The Blackhood And His Secret Ordeal, 1: The Stunner; A: The Shield; 1: The Storm King; A: The Web, Black Hood appearace	0.12	2.40	6.00	12.00
❑44	0.12	2.40	6.00	12.00
❑45	0.12	2.40	6.00	12.00
❑46	0.12	2.40	6.00	12.00
❑47	0.12	2.40	6.00	12.00
❑48	0.12	2.40	6.00	12.00
❑49	0.12	2.40	6.00	12.00
❑50, Final Issue	0.12	2.40	6.00	12.00

MIGHTY CRUSADERS, THE (1ST SERIES)
ARCHIE

	ORIG	GOOD	FINE	N-MINT
❑1, Nov 65, The Mighty Crusaders vs. The Brain Emperor; The Fly-Man's Ultra-Pals, O: The Shield	0.12	4.80	12.00	24.00
❑2, Inferno, The Destroyer, O: The Comet	0.12	3.00	7.50	15.00
❑3, O: Fly Man	0.12	2.40	6.00	12.00
❑4, "Too Many Superheroes"	0.12	1.80	4.50	9.00
❑5, 1: The Terrific Three	0.12	1.80	4.50	9.00
❑6	0.12	1.80	4.50	9.00
❑7, O: Fly Girl	0.12	1.80	4.50	9.00

MIGHTY CRUSADERS (2ND SERIES)
ARCHIE

	ORIG	GOOD	FINE	N-MINT
❑1	1.00	0.30	0.75	1.50
❑2	1.00	0.20	0.50	1.00
❑3	1.00	0.20	0.50	1.00
❑4, Nov 83	1.00	0.20	0.50	1.00
❑5, Jan 84	1.00	0.20	0.50	1.00
❑6, Mar 84	0.75	0.20	0.50	1.00
❑7, May 84	0.75	0.20	0.50	1.00
❑8, Jul 84	0.75	0.20	0.50	1.00
❑9, Sep 84	0.75	0.20	0.50	1.00
❑10, Dec 84	0.75	0.20	0.50	1.00
❑11, Mar 85	0.75	0.20	0.50	1.00
❑12, Jun 85	0.75	0.20	0.50	1.00
❑13, Sep 85	0.75	0.20	0.50	1.00

MIGHTYGUY
C&T

Value: Cover or less

- ❑1, May 87, The Origin of Mightyguy, 1: Mightyguy 1.50
- ❑2 1.50
- ❑3 1.50
- ❑4 1.50
- ❑5 1.50

MIGHTY HEROES, THE
MARVEL

Value: Cover or less

- ❑1, Jan 98, O: The Mighty Heroes, based on Terrytoons feature 2.99

MIGHTY I, THE
IMAGE

Value: Cover or less

- ❑1, May 95, Image Comics Fan Club 1.25
- ❑2, Jul 95, Image Comics Fan Club 1.25

MIGHTY MAGNOR, THE
MALIBU

	ORIG	GOOD	FINE	N-MINT
❑1, Apr 93, SA, ME (w), 1: The Mighty Magnor	1.95	0.45	1.13	2.25
❑1/SC, Apr 93, SA, ME (w), 1: The Mighty Magnor, Pop-up cover	3.95	0.79	1.98	3.95
❑2, May 93, SA, ME (w)	1.95	0.39	0.98	1.95
❑3, Jun 93, SA, ME (w)	1.95	0.39	0.98	1.95
❑4, Jul 93, SA, ME (w)	1.95	0.39	0.98	1.95
❑5, Dec 93, SA, ME (w)	1.95	0.39	0.98	1.95
❑6, Apr 94, SA, ME (w), Final Issue	1.95	0.39	0.98	1.95

MIGHTY MARVEL WESTERN, THE
MARVEL

	ORIG	GOOD	FINE	N-MINT
❑1, Oct 68, giant; Rawhide Kid, Kid Colt, Two-Gun Kid	0.25	3.60	9.00	18.00
❑2, Dec 68, giant; Rawhide Kid, Kid Colt, Two-Gun Kid	0.25	2.40	6.00	12.00
❑3, Feb 69, giant; Rawhide Kid, Kid Colt, Two-Gun Kid	0.25	2.00	5.00	10.00
❑4, Apr 69, giant; Rawhide Kid, Kid Colt, Two-Gun Kid	0.25	2.00	5.00	10.00
❑5, Jun 69, giant; Rawhide Kid, Kid Colt, Two-Gun Kid	0.25	2.00	5.00	10.00
❑6	0.25	1.60	4.00	8.00
❑7	0.25	1.60	4.00	8.00
❑8	0.25	1.60	4.00	8.00
❑9	0.25	1.60	4.00	8.00
❑10	0.25	1.20	3.00	6.00
❑11	0.25	1.20	3.00	6.00
❑12, Shoot Out With Blackjack Bordin	0.25	1.20	3.00	6.00
❑13	0.25	1.20	3.00	6.00
❑14	0.25	1.20	3.00	6.00
❑15	0.25	1.20	3.00	6.00
❑16	0.25	0.80	2.00	4.00
❑17	0.20	0.80	2.00	4.00
❑18	0.20	0.80	2.00	4.00
❑19	0.20	0.80	2.00	4.00
❑20	0.20	0.80	2.00	4.00

	ORIG	GOOD	FINE	N-MINT
❑21	0.20	0.80	2.00	4.00
❑22	0.20	0.80	2.00	4.00
❑23	0.20	0.80	2.00	4.00
❑24	0.20	0.80	2.00	4.00
❑25	0.20	0.80	2.00	4.00
❑26	0.20	0.80	2.00	4.00
❑27	0.20	0.80	2.00	4.00
❑28	0.20	0.80	2.00	4.00
❑29	0.20	0.80	2.00	4.00
❑30	0.20	0.80	2.00	4.00
❑31	0.20	0.60	1.50	3.00
❑32	0.20	0.60	1.50	3.00
❑33	0.20	0.60	1.50	3.00
❑34	0.25	0.60	1.50	3.00
❑35	0.25	0.60	1.50	3.00
❑36, Dec 74	0.25	0.60	1.50	3.00
❑37	0.25	0.60	1.50	3.00
❑38	0.25	0.60	1.50	3.00
❑39	0.25	0.60	1.50	3.00
❑40	0.25	0.60	1.50	3.00
❑41	0.25	0.60	1.50	3.00
❑42	0.25	0.60	1.50	3.00
❑43	0.25	0.60	1.50	3.00
❑44	0.25	0.60	1.50	3.00
❑45	0.25	0.60	1.50	3.00
❑46, Final Issue	0.25	0.60	1.50	3.00

MIGHTY MITES, THE (VOL. 1)
ETERNITY

	ORIG	GOOD	FINE	N-MINT
❑1, Oct 86, X-Men parody	1.80	0.40	1.00	2.00
❑2/A, Batman parody	1.80	0.40	1.00	2.00
❑2/B, Batman parody	1.80	0.40	1.00	2.00
❑3, Mar 87, b&w and color	1.95	0.40	1.00	2.00

MIGHTY MITES, THE (VOL. 2)
ETERNITY

Value: Cover or less

- ❑1, May 87, A Mite on the Town, A: Godzilla 1.95
- ❑2 ..... 1.95

MIGHTY MORPHIN POWER RANGERS (SABAN'S...)
MARVEL

	ORIG	GOOD	FINE	N-MINT
❑1, Nov 95, The Menace of Dracula, barcode card	1.75	0.50	1.25	2.50
❑2, Dec 95	1.75	0.40	1.00	2.00
❑3, Dec 95, It's Not the End of the World!, cover says Jan, indicia says Dec	1.75	0.40	1.00	2.00
❑4, Feb 96	1.75	0.40	1.00	2.00
❑5, Mar 96, Vortex	1.75	0.40	1.00	2.00
❑6, Apr 96, Elementary	1.75	0.40	1.00	2.00
❑7, May 96	1.75	0.40	1.00	2.00
❑8	1.75	0.40	1.00	2.00
❑9, Final Issue	1.75	0.40	1.00	2.00

MIGHTY MORPHIN POWER RANGERS: NINJA RANGERS/VR TROOPERS (SABAN'S...)
MARVEL

	ORIG	GOOD	FINE	N-MINT
❑1, Dec 95, Cheaters Never Prosper and Winners Never Cheat!; Father Figure, flip book with VR Troopers back-up	1.75	0.50	1.25	2.50
❑2, Jan 96, Power Rangers cover says Dec 95	1.75	0.40	1.00	2.00
❑3, Feb 96, flip book with VR Troopers back-up	1.75	0.40	1.00	2.00
❑4, Mar 96, SD, Loyalty; Ghost Of A Chance, flip book with VR Troopers back-up	1.75	0.40	1.00	2.00
❑5, Apr 96, SD, Weather Witch; The Boy Trooper, flip book with VR Troopers back-up	1.75	0.40	1.00	2.00
❑6	1.75	0.40	1.00	2.00
❑7	1.75	0.40	1.00	2.00
❑8, Final Issue	1.75	0.40	1.00	2.00

MIGHTY MORPHIN POWER RANGERS SAGA (SABAN'S...)
HAMILTON

	ORIG	GOOD	FINE	N-MINT
❑1, Dec 94, O: the Power Rangers	1.95	0.50	1.25	2.50
❑2	1.95	0.50	1.25	2.50
❑3	1.95	0.50	1.25	2.50

MIGHTY MORPHIN POWER RANGERS: THE MOVIE
MARVEL

Value: Cover or less

- ❑1, Sep 95, nn; movie Adaptation 2.95
- ❑1/SC, Sep 95, nn; cardstock cover; movie Adaptation 3.95

MIGHTY MOUSE (MARVEL)
MARVEL

	ORIG	GOOD	FINE	N-MINT
❑1, The Dark Might Returns, Dark Knight parody cover	1.00	0.40	1.00	2.00
❑2	1.00	0.30	0.75	1.50
❑3, Cooler Heads Prevail, 1: Bat-Bat, Sub-Mariner parody	1.00	0.30	0.75	1.50
❑4, GP (c), Crisis parody	1.00	0.30	0.75	1.50
❑5, Crisis parody	1.00	0.30	0.75	1.50

Marvel's *Mighty Mouse* parodied a number of other comics properties, including *The Dark Knight Returns, Crisis on Infinite Earths,* and Marvel's own Sub-Mariner.

	ORIG	GOOD	FINE	N-MINT
❑6, McFarlane parody	1.00	0.30	0.75	1.50
❑7, computer art	1.00	0.30	0.75	1.50
❑8	1.00	0.30	0.75	1.50
❑9	1.00	0.30	0.75	1.50
❑10, Letterman parody	1.00	0.30	0.75	1.50

MIGHTY MOUSE (SPOTLIGHT)
SPOTLIGHT

	ORIG	GOOD	FINE	N-MINT
❑1	1.50	0.40	1.00	2.00
❑2	1.50	0.40	1.00	2.00

MIGHTY MOUSE ADVENTURE MAGAZINE
SPOTLIGHT

Value: Cover or less

- ❑1, b&w 2.00

MIGHTY MOUSE AND FRIENDS HOLIDAY SPECIAL
SPOTLIGHT

	ORIG	GOOD	FINE	N-MINT
❑1	1.75	0.40	1.00	2.00

MIGHTY MUTANIMALS
ARCHIE

Value: Cover or less

- ❑1, Apr 92, The Mighty Mutanimals 1.25
- ❑2, Jun 92 ..... 1.25
- ❑3, Aug 92 ..... 1.25
- ❑4, Sep 92 ..... 1.25
- ❑5, Oct 92 ..... 1.25
- ❑6, Dec 92, United We Stand...Divided We Fall 1.25
- ❑7, Feb 93 ..... 1.25
- ❑8, Apr 93 ..... 1.25

MIGHTY MUTANIMALS (MINI-SERIES)
ARCHIE

	ORIG	GOOD	FINE	N-MINT
❑1, May 91, The Wild Angels, TMNT spin-off	1.25	0.30	0.75	1.50
❑2, TMNT spin-off	1.25	0.25	0.63	1.25
❑3, TMNT spin-off	1.25	0.25	0.63	1.25

MIGHTY SAMSON
GOLD KEY

	ORIG	GOOD	FINE	N-MINT
❑1, Jul 64, 1: Samson, back cover pin-up	0.12	6.00	15.00	30.00
❑2, Jun 65, 1: Terra of Jerz, back cover pin-up	0.12	3.60	9.00	18.00
❑3, Sep 65, back cover pin-up	0.12	3.60	9.00	18.00
❑4, Dec 65, back cover pin-up	0.12	2.40	6.00	12.00
❑5, Mar 66, back cover pin-up	0.12	2.40	6.00	12.00
❑6, Jun 66, The Death Geysers, back cover pin-up	0.12	2.00	5.00	10.00
❑7, Sep 66, back cover pin-up	0.12	2.00	5.00	10.00
❑8, Dec 66	0.12	2.00	5.00	10.00
❑9, Mar 67, In Washington, D.C.	0.12	2.00	5.00	10.00
❑10, Jun 67	0.12	2.00	5.00	10.00
❑11, Aug 67	0.12	1.60	4.00	8.00
❑12, Nov 67	0.12	1.60	4.00	8.00
❑13, Feb 68	0.12	1.60	4.00	8.00
❑14, May 68	0.12	1.60	4.00	8.00
❑15, Aug 68	0.12	1.60	4.00	8.00
❑16, Nov 68	0.15	1.60	4.00	8.00
❑17, Feb 69	0.15	1.60	4.00	8.00
❑18, May 69	0.15	1.60	4.00	8.00
❑19, Aug 69, N'Yark floods	0.15	1.60	4.00	8.00
❑20, Nov 69	0.15	1.60	4.00	8.00
❑21, Aug 72	0.15	1.00	2.50	5.00
❑22, Dec 73	0.20	1.00	2.50	5.00
❑23, Mar 74	0.20	1.00	2.50	5.00
❑24, Jun 74	0.20	1.00	2.50	5.00
❑25, Sep 74	0.25	1.00	2.50	5.00
❑26, Dec 74	0.25	1.00	2.50	5.00
❑27, Mar 75	0.25	1.00	2.50	5.00
❑28, Jun 75	0.25	1.00	2.50	5.00
❑29, Sep 75	0.25	1.00	2.50	5.00
❑30, Dec 75, In Macy's	0.25	1.00	2.50	5.00
❑31, Mar 76, V: giant moths	0.25	1.00	2.50	5.00
❑32, Apr 82, Peril From The Past; The Desperate Mission, Reprint; Final Issue; 1982 revival	0.60	0.60	1.50	3.00

MIGHTY TINY
ANTARCTIC

	ORIG	GOOD	FINE	N-MINT
❑1, b&w	1.75	0.40	1.00	2.00
❑2, b&w	1.75	0.40	1.00	2.00
❑3, b&w	1.75	0.40	1.00	2.00
❑4, b&w	1.75	0.40	1.00	2.00
❑5	2.50	0.50	1.25	2.50

MIGHTY TINY: THE MOUSE MARINES
ANTARCTIC

Value: Cover or less

❑1, The Wisdom Of The Poet, b&w ... 2.50

MIKE DANGER (VOL. 1) (MICKEY SPILLANE'S...)
TEKNO

Value: Cover or less

❑1, Sep 95, Danger Ahead ... 1.95
❑2, Oct 95, Danger in the Future ... 1.95
❑3, Nov 95 ... 1.95
❑4, Dec 95 ... 1.95
❑5, Dec 95 ... 1.95
❑6, Jan 96, Man Out of Time .. 2.25
❑7, Jan 96, Death in Duplicate, Part 1 ... 2.25
❑8, Feb 96 ... 2.25
❑9, Mar 96 ... 2.25
❑10, Apr 96 ... 2.25
❑11, May 96 ... 2.25

MIKE DANGER (VOL. 2) (MICKEY SPILLANE'S...)
BIG

Value: Cover or less

❑1, Jun 96, RB, The Big Crossover Chapter 11; Virtual Man ... 2.25
❑2, Jul 96, Mike's head is separated from his body ... 2.25
❑3, Aug 96 ... 2.25
❑4, Sep 96, A Woman Called Mann, V: Mann ... 2.25
❑5, Oct 96 ... 2.25
❑6, Nov 96 ... 2.25
❑7, Dec 96, Red Menace, Part 1 ... 2.25
❑8, Jan 96, Red Menace, Part 2 ... 2.25
❑9, Feb 96, Red Menace, Part 3 ... 2.25
❑10, Apr 96, Red Menace, Part 4 ... 2.25

MIKE MAUSER FILES
AVALON

Value: Cover or less

❑1, JSa, The Cayugan Curse; Dog Days ... 2.95

MIKE MIST MINUTE MIST-ERIES
ECLIPSE

Value: Cover or less

❑1, Apr 81, b&w ... 1.50

MIKE REGAN
HARDBOILED

Value: Cover or less

❑1, b&w ... 2.95

MIKE SHAYNE PRIVATE EYE
DELL

	ORIG	GOOD	FINE	N-MINT
❑1, The Gangster Era (text); The Private Practice of Michael Shayne	0.15	3.00	7.50	15.00
❑2	—	1.80	4.50	9.00
❑3, The Gangster Era: John Torrio (text); Heads...You Lose	0.12	1.80	4.50	9.00

MILIKARDO KNIGHTS
MAD BADGER

Value: Cover or less

❑1, Mar 97, b&w ... 3.00
❑2, Jan 98, b&w ... 3.00

MILK
RADIO

Value: Cover or less

❑1, Sep 97, b&w; adult ... 2.95
❑2, Nov 97, b&w; adult ... 2.95
❑3, Jan 98, b&w; adult ... 2.95
❑4, Mar 98, b&w; adult ... 2.95
❑5, May 98, b&w; adult ... 2.95
❑6, Jul 98, b&w; adult ... 2.95
❑7, Sep 98, b&w; adult ... 2.95
❑8, Nov 98, b&w; adult ... 2.95
❑9, Jan 99, b&w; adult ... 2.95
❑10, Mar 99, b&w; adult ... 2.95
❑11, May 99, b&w; adult ... 2.95
❑12, Jul 99, b&w; adult ... 2.95
❑13, Sep 99, b&w; adult ... 2.95
❑14, Nov 99, b&w; adult ... 2.95
❑15, Jan 00, b&w; adult ... 2.95
❑16, Mar 00, b&w; adult ... 2.95
❑17, May 00, b&w; adult ... 2.95
❑18, Jul 00, b&w; adult ... 2.95
❑19, Sep 00, b&w; adult ... 2.95

MILK & CHEESE
SLAVE LABOR

	ORIG	GOOD	FINE	N-MINT
❑1, Mar 91, Vas is Milk and Cheese?; Hercules of Hate!, b&w	2.50	16.00	40.00	80.00
❑1-2, Sep 91, Vas is Milk and Cheese?; Hercules of Hate!, b&w; 2nd Printing	2.50	1.20	3.00	6.00
❑, Sep 92, Vas is Milk and Cheese?; Hercules of Hate!, b&w; 3rd Printing	2.50	1.00	2.50	5.00
❑1-4, Aug 93, Vas is Milk and Cheese?; Hercules of Hate!, b&w; 4th Printing	2.50	0.60	1.50	3.00
❑1-5, Oct 94, Vas is Milk and Cheese?; Hercules of Hate!, b&w; 5th Printing	2.50	0.60	1.50	3.00
❑1-6, Sep 95, Vas is Milk and Cheese?; Hercules of Hate!, b&w; 6th Printing	2.75	0.60	1.50	3.00
❑1-7, Feb 97, Vas is Milk and Cheese?; Hercules of Hate!, b&w; 7th Printing	2.75	0.55	1.38	2.75
❑2, Mar 92, b&w; has Doctor Radium ad on back cover; Other Number One	2.50	8.00	20.00	40.00
❑2-2, Jun 93, 2nd Printing; has Fine Dairy Products ad on back cover	2.50	1.00	2.50	5.00
❑2-3, Oct 94, 3rd Printing; has APE II ad on back cover	2.50	0.80	2.00	4.00
❑2-4, Jan 96, 4th Printing	2.75	0.55	1.38	2.75
❑2-5, 5th Printing	2.75	0.55	1.38	2.75
❑3, Aug 92, b&w; has Rats ad on back cover; Third #1	2.50	6.40	16.00	32.00
❑3-2, May 93, 2nd Printing; has Fine Dairy Products ad on back cover	2.50	0.80	2.00	4.00
❑3-3, Oct 94, 3rd Printing; has APE II ad on back cover	2.50	0.60	1.50	3.00
❑3-4, Feb 96, 4th Printing	2.75	0.55	1.38	2.75
❑3-5, 5th Printing	2.75	0.55	1.38	2.75
❑4, Apr 93, b&w; has Fine Dairy Products ad on back cover; Fourth #1	2.50	4.00	10.00	20.00
❑4-2, Mar 95, 2nd Printing; has APE II ad on back cover	2.50	0.60	1.50	3.00
❑4-3, Aug 96, 3rd Printing	2.75	0.50	1.25	2.50
❑5, Apr 94, b&w; has APE ad on back cover; First Second Issue	2.50	4.00	10.00	20.00
❑5-2, Nov 94, 2nd Printing; has APE II ad on back cover	2.50	0.60	1.50	3.00
❑5-3, Feb 96, 3rd Printing	2.75	0.60	1.50	3.00
❑5-4, 4th Printing	2.75	0.55	1.38	2.75
❑6, Apr 95, b&w; Six Six Six	2.50	1.60	4.00	8.00
❑6-2, 2nd Printing	2.75	0.55	1.38	2.75
❑7, There's No Busine$$...; Alcoholics Unanimous, b&w; Latest Thing!	2.95	0.60	1.50	3.00

MILLENNIUM
DC

	ORIG	GOOD	FINE	N-MINT
❑1, Jan 88, Millennium: Week One Over	0.75	0.40	1.00	2.00
❑2, Jan 88, Millennium	0.75	0.30	0.75	1.50
❑3, Jan 88, Millennium	0.75	0.30	0.75	1.50
❑4, Jan 88, Millennium	0.75	0.30	0.75	1.50
❑5, Feb 88, Millennium	0.75	0.30	0.75	1.50
❑6, Feb 88, Millennium	0.75	0.30	0.75	1.50
❑7, Feb 88, Millennium	0.75	0.30	0.75	1.50
❑8, Feb 88, Millennium	0.75	0.30	0.75	1.50

MILLENNIUM 2.5 A.D.
AVALON

Value: Cover or less

❑1, The Saga of Buck Rogers ... 2.95

MILLENNIUM EDITION: ACTION COMICS
DC

Value: Cover or less

❑1, Feb 00, Superman; "Chuck" Dawson, 1: Superman ... 3.95

MILLENNIUM EDITION: ADVENTURE COMICS
DC

Value: Cover or less

❑61, Dec 00, Starman; Mark Lansing of Mikishawm, 1: Starman I (Ted Knight) ... 3.95
❑247, Nov 00, Otto Binder, The Legion of Super-Heroes; The 13 Superstition Arrows; Aquaman's Super Sea-Squad ... 2.50

MILLENNIUM EDITION: ALL STAR COMICS
DC

	ORIG	GOOD	FINE	N-MINT
❑3, Jun 00, 1: the Justice Society of America, Reprint	3.95	0.79	1.98	3.95
❑3/SC, Jun 00, 1: the Justice Society of America, chromium cover; Reprint	—	2.00	5.00	10.00
❑8, Feb 01, Two New Members Win Their Spurs; Introducing Wonder Woman, 1: Wonder Woman	3.95	0.79	1.98	3.95

MILLENNIUM EDITION: ALL-STAR WESTERN
DC

Value: Cover or less

❑10, Apr 00, NC; TD; GM, SA (w), Jonah Hex: Welcome to Paradise; El Diablo: The Devil's Secret, 1: Jonah Hex, Reprints All-Star Western #10 ... 2.50

MILLENNIUM EDITION: BATMAN
DC

Value: Cover or less

❑1, Feb 01, The Legend of Batman-Who He Is and How He Came to Be!; The Joker ... 3.95

MILLENNIUM EDITION: BATMAN: THE DARK KNIGHT RETURNS
DC

Value: Cover or less

❑1, Oct 00, KJ, FM (w), The Dark Knight Returns, Reprints Batman: The Dark Knight #1 ... 5.95

MILLENNIUM EDITION: CRISIS ON INFINITE EARTHS
DC

Value: Cover or less

❑1, Reprints Crisis on Infinite Earths #1 ... 2.50

MILLENNIUM EDITION: DETECTIVE COMICS
DC

Value: Cover or less

❑1, Jan 01, Speed Saunders; Cosmo, the Phantom of Disguise, Reprints Detective Comics #1 ... 3.95
❑27, Feb 00, The Bat-Man: The Case of the Chemical Syndicate; Speed Saunders Ace Investigator, 1: Batman; 1: Commissioner Gordon ... 3.95
❑38, Robin-The Boy Wonder; Spy, 1: Robin I (Dick Grayson) ... 3.95
❑225, Dec 00, If I were Batman; Roy Raymond, TV Detective: The Money that Came to Life, 1: Martian Manhunter ... 2.50
❑359, Oct 00, CI; MA, The Million Dollar Debut of Batgirl; Riddle of the Sleepytime Tax! ... 3.95

MILLENNIUM EDITION: FLASH COMICS
DC

Value: Cover or less

❑1, Sep 00, The Flash; "Cliff" Cornwall Special Agent, 1: The Flash I (Jay Garrick), Reprints Flash Comics #1 ... 3.95

ORIG GOOD FINE N-MINT

MILLENNIUM EDITION: GREEN LANTERN
DC

Value: Cover or less
❑76 .... 2.50

MILLENNIUM EDITION: HELLBLAZER
DC

Value: Cover or less
❑1, Jul 00, Hunger, Reprints Hellblazer #1 .... 2.95

MILLENNIUM EDITION: HOUSE OF MYSTERY
DC

Value: Cover or less
❑1, Sep 00, I Fell in Love With a Witch!; Man or Monster?, Reprints House of Mystery #1 .... 2.50

MILLENNIUM EDITION: HOUSE OF SECRETS
DC

Value: Cover or less
❑92, May 00, DD (w), Swamp Thing; After I Die, 1: Swamp Thing 2.50

MILLENNIUM EDITION: JLA
DC

Value: Cover or less
❑1 .... 2.50

MILLENNIUM EDITION: JUSTICE LEAGUE
DC

Value: Cover or less
❑1, Jul 00, KG, KG (w), Born Again, Reprints Justice League #1 .... 2.50

MILLENNIUM EDITION: MILITARY COMICS
DC

Value: Cover or less
❑1, Oct 00, Blackhawk; Loops and Banks 3.95

MILLENNIUM EDITION: MORE FUN COMICS
DC

Value: Cover or less
❑73, Jan 01, Doctor Fate; The Green Arrow 3.95
❑101, Nov 00, MM, Formula for Doom!; Orphans of the Sea! 2.95

MILLENNIUM EDITION: NEW GODS
DC

Value: Cover or less
❑1, Jun 00, JK, JK (w), Orion Fights for Earth! 2.50

MILLENNIUM EDITION: OUR ARMY AT WAR
DC

Value: Cover or less
❑81, Jun 00, JAb; RH; RA; JKu, The Rock of Easy Co.!; Fighting Footsteps, 1: Sgt. Rock 2.50

MILLENNIUM EDITION: PLOP!
DC

Value: Cover or less
❑1, Jul 00, AA; SA; GE, FR (w); SA (w), Plops; The Escape, Reprints Plop! #1 .... 2.50

MILLENNIUM EDITION: POLICE COMICS
DC

Value: Cover or less
❑1, Sep 00, Firebrand; 711, 1: Firebrand; 1: Plastic Man, Reprints Police Comics #1 .... 3.95

MILLENNIUM EDITION: PREACHER
DC

Value: Cover or less
❑1, Oct 00, The Time of the Preacher 2.95

MILLENNIUM EDITION: SENSATION COMICS
DC

Value: Cover or less
❑1, Oct 00, Wonder Woman; Black Pirate, Reprints Sensation Comics #1 .... 3.95

MILLENNIUM EDITION: SHOWCASE
DC

Value: Cover or less
❑4, 1: Flash II (Barry Allen), Reprints Showcase #4 .... 2.50
❑9, Jan 01, The Girl in Superman's Past; Odd Newspaper Items!, Reprints Showcase #9 .... 2.50
❑22, Dec 00, GK, SOS Green Lantern, 1: Green Lantern II (Hal Jordan), Reprints Showcase #22 .... 2.50

MILLENNIUM EDITION: SUPERBOY
DC

Value: Cover or less
❑1, Feb 01, The Man Who Could See Tomorrow!; Rocket Plane 2.95

MILLENNIUM EDITION: SUPERMAN
DC

Value: Cover or less
❑75 .... 2.95

MILLENNIUM EDITION: SUPERMAN (1ST SERIES)
DC

Value: Cover or less
❑1, Dec 00, Superman-Champion of the Oppressed!; Scientific Explanation of Superman's Amazing Strength!, Reprints Superman (1st Series) #1 .... 2.95
❑76, The Mightiest Team in the World; The Misfit Manhunter 2.95
❑233, Jan 01, Superman Breaks Loose; Super-Turtle 2.50

MILLENNIUM EDITION: SUPERMAN'S PAL JIMMY OLSEN
DC

Value: Cover or less
❑1, Apr 00, CS, The Boy of 100 Faces!; Case of the Lumberjack Jinx!, Reprints Superman's Pal Jimmy Olsen #1 .... 2.95

DC reprinted *Showcase* #4, the comic book that started the Silver Age, as part of its *Millennium Edition* series.

ORIG GOOD FINE N-MINT

MILLENNIUM EDITION: TALES CALCULATED TO DRIVE YOU MAD
DC

	ORIG	GOOD	FINE	N-MINT
❑1	—	0.59	1.48	2.95

MILLENNIUM EDITION: THE BRAVE AND THE BOLD
DC

Value: Cover or less
❑28, Feb 00, Starro the Conqueror!, 1: Snapper Carr; 1: The Justice League of America 2.50
❑85, Nov 00, NA, The Senator's Been Shot! 2.50

MILLENNIUM EDITION: THE FLASH
DC

Value: Cover or less
❑123, May 00, CI, Flash of Two Worlds!, Reprints The Flash (1st Series) #1 .... 2.50

MILLENNIUM EDITION: THE MAN OF STEEL
DC

Value: Cover or less
❑1 .... 2.50

MILLENNIUM EDITION: THE NEW TEEN TITANS
DC

Value: Cover or less
❑1, Dec 00, GP, You Can Go Home Again 2.50

MILLENNIUM EDITION: THE SAGA OF THE SWAMP THING
DC

Value: Cover or less
❑21, Feb 00, NG (w), Sleep of the Just, 1: Sanman II (Morpheus), Reprints Sandman #1 .... 2.50

MILLENNIUM EDITION: THE SANDMAN
DC

Value: Cover or less
❑1, Feb 00, NG (w), Sleep of the Just, 1: Sanman II (Morpheus), Reprints Sandman #1 .... 2.95

MILLENNIUM EDITION: THE SHADOW
DC

Value: Cover or less
❑1, Feb 01, The Doom Puzzle; The Shadow Knows (text story) 2.50

MILLENNIUM EDITION: THE SPIRIT
DC

Value: Cover or less
❑1, Jul 00, WE, WE (w), Wanted for Murder; Tony Zacco, Public Enemy No. 1, Reprints The Spirit #1 .... 2.95

MILLENNIUM EDITION: WATCHMEN
DC

Value: Cover or less
❑1, DaG, AMo (w), Reprints Watchmen #1 .... 2.50

MILLENNIUM EDITION: WHIZ COMICS
DC

Value: Cover or less
❑1 .... 3.95

MILLENNIUM EDITION: WILDC.A.T.S
DC

Value: Cover or less
❑1 .... 2.50

MILLENNIUM EDITION: WONDER WOMAN (2ND SERIES)
DC

Value: Cover or less
❑1, May 00, GP, GP (w), The Princess and the Power!, Reprints Wonder Woman (2nd Series) #1 .... 2.50

MILLENNIUM EDITION: YOUNG ROMANCE COMICS
DC

Value: Cover or less
❑1, Apr 00, I Was a Pick-Up!; The Farmer's Wife, Reprints Young Romance (DC) #1; 1st romance comic 2.95

MILLENNIUM FEVER
DC

	ORIG	GOOD	FINE	N-MINT
❑1, Oct 95	2.50	0.50	1.25	2.50
❑2, Nov 95, Fear of Rain	2.50	0.50	1.25	2.50
❑3, Dec 95	2.50	0.50	1.25	2.50
❑4, Jan 96, A Way of Seeing Things, Final Issue	2.50	0.50	1.25	2.50
❑Ash 1	—	0.15	0.38	0.75

MILLENNIUM INDEX
ECLIPSE

Value: Cover or less
❑1, Mar 88 .... 2.00
❑2, Mar 88 .... 2.00

ORIG GOOD FINE N-MINT

MINDBENDERS
MBS

Value: Cover or less

❑1, Freddies Last Dance......... 2.50

MINDGAME GALLERY, THE
MINDGAME

Value: Cover or less

❑1, Warwind; This Machine, b&w.................................... 1.95

MIND PROBE
RIP OFF

Value: Cover or less

❑1, Initiation; Ceezed, b&w..... 3.25

MINIMUM WAGE
FANTAGRAPHICS

Value: Cover or less

❑1, Oct 95.............................. 2.95
❑2, Dec 95.............................. 2.95
❑3, Mar 96.............................. 2.95
❑4, Jun 96, pin-ups................. 2.95
❑5, Nov 96.............................. 2.95
❑6, Mar 97.............................. 2.95
❑7, Aug 97.............................. 2.95
❑8, Feb 98.............................. 2.95
❑9, Jun 98.............................. 2.95
❑10, Jan 99............................ 2.95

MINISTRY OF SPACE
IMAGE

Value: Cover or less

❑1, Apr 01.............................. 2.95

MINOTAUR
LABYRINTH

Value: Cover or less

❑1, Feb 96, b&w..................... 2.50
❑2, Apr 96, b&w..................... 2.50
❑3, Jun 96, b&w; cover says Jul, indicia says Jun.................. 2.50
❑4, Sep 96, b&w; Final Issue.. 2.50

MINX, THE
DC

Value: Cover or less

❑1, Oct 98, The Chosen, Part 1................................. 2.50
❑2, Nov 98, The Chosen, Part 2................................. 2.50
❑3, Dec 98, The Chosen, Part 3................................. 2.50
❑4, Jan 99, The Monkey Quartet, Part 1................................. 2.50
❑5, Feb 99, The Monkey Quartet, Part 2, The World Service... 2.50
❑6, Mar 99, The Monkey Quartet, Part 3................................. 2.50
❑7, Apr 99, The Monkey Quartet, Part 4................................. 2.50
❑8, May 99, Eschatology and the Single Woman.................... 2.50

MIRACLEMAN
ECLIPSE

	ORIG	GOOD	FINE	N-MINT
❑1, Aug 85, AMo (w), A Dream Of Flying....	0.75	1.20	3.00	6.00
❑2, Oct 85, AMo (w), Dragons....................	0.75	0.80	2.00	4.00
❑3, Nov 85, AMo (w)...................................	0.75	0.80	2.00	4.00
❑4, Dec 85, AMo (w)...................................	0.75	0.80	2.00	4.00
❑5, Jan 86, AMo (w)...................................	0.95	0.80	2.00	4.00
❑6, Feb 86, AMo (w)...................................	0.95	0.80	2.00	4.00
❑7, Apr 86, AMo (w), Bodies; Tales of the First Empire: Soul-Stone (back-up), D: Gargunza..	0.95	0.80	2.00	4.00
❑8, Jun 86, AMo (w), 1: The New Wave, The New Wave preview..................................	0.95	0.80	2.00	4.00
❑9, Jul 86, AMo (w), birth............................	0.95	1.20	3.00	6.00
❑10, Dec 86, AMo (w).................................	0.95	1.20	3.00	6.00
❑11, May 87, AMo (w).................................	1.25	1.60	4.00	8.00
❑12, Sep 87, AMo (w).................................	1.25	1.60	4.00	8.00
❑13, Nov 87, AMo (w).................................	1.75	2.40	6.00	12.00
❑14, Apr 88, AMo (w).................................	1.75	4.00	10.00	20.00
❑15, Nov 88, AMo (w), Scarce....................	1.75	11.00	27.50	55.00
❑16, Dec 88, AMo (w), Olympus, last Moore	1.95	3.00	7.50	15.00
❑17, Jun 90, NG (w), Miracleman: The Golden Age, 1st Neil Gaiman.................	1.95	3.60	9.00	18.00
❑18, Aug 90, NG (w), Miracleman: The Golden Age; Skin Deep..........................	2.00	3.00	7.50	15.00
❑19, Nov 90, NG (w), Miracleman: The Golden Age; Notes From the Underground, cardstock cover...........................	2.50	3.00	7.50	15.00
❑20, Mar 91, NG (w), Miracleman: The Golden Age; Winter's Tale, cardstock cover..	2.50	3.00	7.50	15.00
❑21, Jul 91, NG (w), Miracleman: The Golden Age; Spy Story....................................	2.50	3.00	7.50	15.00
❑22, NG (w), Miracleman: The Golden Age; Carnival..	2.50	3.00	7.50	15.00
❑23, NG (w)..	2.50	3.40	8.50	17.00
❑24, scarcer..	2.95	4.80	12.00	24.00
❑3D 1, Dec 85, AMo (w), Miracleman and the Exiled Gods, Giant-size; 3-D Special #1.	2.25	1.00	2.50	5.00

MIRACLEMAN: APOCRYPHA
ECLIPSE

Value: Cover or less

❑1, Nov 91, MW (w); JRo (w), The Library of Olympus; Miracle Man and the Magic Monsters...... 2.50
❑2, Jan 92, NG (w); KB (w), The Library of Olympus; Prodigal.............................. 2.50
❑3, Apr 91, NG (w).................. 2.50

MIRACLEMAN FAMILY
ECLIPSE

	ORIG	GOOD	FINE	N-MINT
❑1, May 88, O: Young Miracleman.............	1.95	0.50	1.25	2.50
❑2, Sep 88, The Shadow Stealers...............	1.95	0.50	1.25	2.50

MIRACLE SQUAD
UPSHOT

Value: Cover or less

❑1, full color........................... 2.00
❑2, full color........................... 2.00
❑3, b&w.................................. 2.00
❑4, b&w.................................. 2.00

MIRACLE SQUAD, THE: BLOOD AND DUST
APPLE

Value: Cover or less

❑1, Jan 89, The Miracle Squad, Part 1, b&w.......................... 1.95
❑2, Mar 89, b&w..................... 1.95
❑3, May 89, b&w..................... 1.95
❑4, Jul 89, b&w....................... 1.95

MIRRORWALKER
NOW

Value: Cover or less

❑1, Oct 90, semi-fumetti.......... 2.95
❑2... 2.95

MIRRORWORLD: RAIN
NETCO

Value: Cover or less

❑0, Apr 97, Rain...................... 3.25
❑1, Feb 97.............................. 3.25

MISADVENTURES OF BREADMAN AND DOUGHBOY, THE
HEMLOCK PARK

	ORIG	GOOD	FINE	N-MINT
❑1, Oct 99, no cover price..........................	—	0.20	0.50	1.00

MISEROTH: AMOK HELL
NORTHSTAR

Value: Cover or less

❑1, The Big Slip Up, poster..... 4.95
❑2... 4.95
❑3... 4.95

MISERY
IMAGE

Value: Cover or less

❑1, Dec 95, Prometheus Unbound, One-Shot.......................... 2.95

MISS FURY
ADVENTURE

Value: Cover or less

❑1, Nov 91, From Generation to Generation, O: Miss Fury, full color.................................... 2.50
❑1/LE, limited edition............. 4.95
❑2, Dec 91.............................. 2.50
❑3... 2.50
❑4... 2.50

MISS FURY (AVALON)
AVALON

Value: Cover or less

❑1... 2.95
❑2... 2.95

MISSING BEINGS SPECIAL
COMICS INTERVIEW

Value: Cover or less

❑1, b&w.................................. 2.25

MISSION: IMPOSSIBLE (DELL)
DELL

	ORIG	GOOD	FINE	N-MINT
❑1, May 67..	0.12	5.00	12.50	25.00
❑2, Sep 67, The Lethal List; The Invaders..	0.12	4.00	10.00	20.00
❑3, Dec 67..	0.12	4.00	10.00	20.00
❑4, Oct 68..	0.12	4.00	10.00	20.00
❑5, Reprint..	0.12	2.40	6.00	12.00

MISSION IMPOSSIBLE (MARVEL)
MARVEL

Value: Cover or less

❑1, May 96, RL (c), Through a Mirror Darkly; Should Any of Your Agents..., prequel to movie. 2.95

MISSIONS IN TIBET
DIMENSION

Value: Cover or less

❑1, Jul 95............................... 2.50

MISSPENT YOUTHS
BRAVE NEW WORDS

Value: Cover or less

❑1, Closing Night Attitude....... 2.50
❑2... 2.50
❑3, Jul 91............................... 2.50

MISS VICTORY GOLDEN ANNIVERSARY SPECIAL
AC

Value: Cover or less

❑1, Nov 91, full color; reprint 1: Miss Victory........................ 5.00

MISTER AMERICA
ENDEAVOR

Value: Cover or less

❑1... 2.95
❑2, Apr 94............................... 2.95

MR. AVERAGE
B.S.

Value: Cover or less

❑1... 2.25
❑2... 2.25
❑3, Tales from the Rippt.......... 2.25

MR. BEAT ADVENTURES
MOORDAM

Value: Cover or less

❑1, Jan 97, Mr. Beat and Bambeano Boy; Mr. Beat Takes a Little Sip, b&w........................ 2.95

MR. BEAT'S BABES AND BONGOS ANNUAL
MOORDAM

Value: Cover or less

❑1, Instant Karma!; ...To The destruction of The Spy Girls!.................................... 2.95

MR. BEAT'S HOUSE OF BURNING JAZZ LOVE
MOORDAM

Value: Cover or less

❑1, Dec 97, b&w..................... 2.95

MR. BEAT'S TWO-FISTED ATOMIC ACTION SUPER SPECIAL
Moordam

Value: Cover or less

❑1, Sep 97, V: Roswell, b&w... 2.95

MISTER BLANK
Slave Labor

Value: Cover or less

❑0... 2.95
❑1, May 97... 2.95
❑2, May 97... 2.95
❑3, Aug 97... 2.95
❑4, Nov 97... 2.95
❑5, Feb 98... 2.95

MR. CREAM PUFF
Blackthorne

Value: Cover or less

❑1... 1.75

MR. DAY & MR. NIGHT
Slave Labor

Value: Cover or less

❑1, Apr 93... 3.95

MR. DOOM
Pied Piper

Value: Cover or less

❑1... 1.95

MISTER E
DC

	ORIG	GOOD	FINE	N-MINT
❑1, Jun 91, At The End Of Time	1.75	0.40	1.00	2.00
❑2, Jul 91	1.75	0.40	1.00	2.00
❑3, Aug 91	1.75	0.40	1.00	2.00
❑4, Sep 91, The Power!	1.75	0.40	1.00	2.00

MR. FIXITT (APPLE)
Apple

Value: Cover or less

❑1, Jan 89, It's The Thought That Counts!, b&w... 1.95
❑2, Mar 90... 2.25

MR. FIXITT (HEROIC)
Heroic

Value: Cover or less

❑1, b&w; trading card... 2.95

MR. HERO-THE NEWMATIC MAN (1ST SERIES) (NEIL GAIMAN'S...)
Tekno

	ORIG	GOOD	FINE	N-MINT
❑1, Mar 95, Toys in the Basement, 1: Mr. Hero; 1: Teknophage, game piece; trading card	1.95	0.39	0.98	1.95
❑2, Apr 95, game piece; trading card	1.95	0.39	0.98	1.95
❑3, May 95, Cain, game piece; trading card	1.95	0.39	0.98	1.95
❑4, Jun 95, coupon	1.95	0.39	0.98	1.95
❑5, Jul 95, Money	1.95	0.39	0.98	1.95
❑6, Aug 95	1.95	0.39	0.98	1.95
❑7, Sep 95, Let's Make a Deal	1.95	0.39	0.98	1.95
❑8, Oct 95	1.95	0.39	0.98	1.95
❑9, Nov 95	1.95	0.39	0.98	1.95
❑10, Dec 95	1.95	0.39	0.98	1.95
❑11, Dec 95	1.95	0.39	0.98	1.95
❑12, Jan 96	1.95	0.45	1.13	2.25
❑13, Jan 96	2.25	0.45	1.13	2.25
❑14, Feb 96	2.25	0.45	1.13	2.25
❑15, Mar 96	2.25	0.45	1.13	2.25
❑16, Apr 96	2.25	0.45	1.13	2.25
❑17, May 96, The Big Crossover, Part 3	2.25	0.45	1.13	2.25

MR. HERO-THE NEWMATIC MAN (2ND SERIES) (NEIL GAIMAN'S...)
Big

Value: Cover or less

❑1, Jun 96, The Big Crossover Chapter 10; History, D: Mr. Hero... 2.25
❑2... 2.25
❑3... 2.25
❑4... 2.25

MR. JIGSAW SPECIAL
Ocean

	ORIG	GOOD	FINE	N-MINT
❑1, Spr 88, O: Mr. Jigsaw, blue paper	1.75	0.40	1.00	2.00

MR. LIZARD 3-D
Now

Value: Cover or less

❑1, May 93, 3-D glasses; instant Mr. Lizard capsule... 3.50

MR. LIZARD ANNUAL
Now

Value: Cover or less

❑1, Sep 93, Ralph Snart capsule... 2.95

MR. MAJESTIC
DC

Value: Cover or less

❑1, Sep 99, Cosmology... 2.50
❑2, Oct 99, Repeating History 2.50
❑3, Nov 99... 2.50
❑4, Dec 99, Being & Nothingness... 2.50
❑5, Jan 00, Jailbreak!... 2.50
❑6, Feb 00... 2.50
❑7, Mar 00, Univeral Law, Part 1... 2.50
❑8, Apr 00, Univeral Law, Part 2... 2.50
❑9, May 00, Univeral Law, Part 3... 2.50

MISTER MIRACLE (1ST SERIES)
DC

	ORIG	GOOD	FINE	N-MINT
❑1, Apr 71, JK, JK (w), Murder Missile Trap, 1: Mister Miracle; 1: Oberon	0.15	5.20	13.00	26.00
❑2, Jun 71, 1: Granny Goodness; 1: Doctor Bedlam	0.15	3.20	8.00	16.00

Warren Ellis presented an alternate history where England conquered space shortly after World War II in *Ministry of Space*.

© 2001 Warren Ellis (Image)

	ORIG	GOOD	FINE	N-MINT
❑3, Aug 71, V: Dr. Bedlam; V: Doctor Bedlam, Boy Commandos reprint	0.15	2.80	7.00	14.00
❑4, Oct 71, 1: Big Barda, Boy Commandos reprint, Giant-size	0.25	2.60	6.50	13.00
❑5, Dec 71, Giant-size; Boy Commandos reprint	0.25	2.60	6.50	13.00
❑6, Feb 72, 1: Female Furies; 1: Funky Flashman, Boy Commandos reprint; 1: Lashina; 1: Funky Flashman, Giant-size; Boy Commandos reprint	0.25	2.60	6.50	13.00
❑7, Apr 72, Giant-size; Boy Commandos reprint	0.25	2.60	6.50	13.00
❑8, Jun 72, Giant-size; Boy Commandos reprint	0.25	2.60	6.50	13.00
❑9, Aug 72	0.20	2.00	5.00	10.00
❑10, Oct 72	0.20	2.00	5.00	10.00
❑11, Dec 72	0.20	1.80	4.50	9.00
❑12, Feb 73	0.20	1.80	4.50	9.00
❑13, Apr 73	0.20	1.80	4.50	9.00
❑14, Jul 73, JK, JK (w), The Quick And The Dead!, 1: Madame Evil Eye	0.20	1.80	4.50	9.00
❑15, Sep 73, 1: Mister Miracle II (Shilo Norman)	0.20	1.80	4.50	9.00
❑16, Nov 73	0.20	1.60	4.00	8.00
❑17, Jan 74	0.20	1.60	4.00	8.00
❑18, Mar 74, series goes on hiatus; Wedding of Mister Miracle and Barda	0.20	1.60	4.00	8.00
❑19, Sep 77	0.35	1.00	2.50	5.00
❑20, Oct 77	0.35	1.00	2.50	5.00
❑21, Dec 77	0.35	1.00	2.50	5.00
❑22, Feb 78	0.35	1.00	2.50	5.00
❑23, Apr 78	0.35	1.00	2.50	5.00
❑24, Jun 78	0.35	1.00	2.50	5.00
❑25, Sep 78, Final Issue	0.35	1.00	2.50	5.00
❑SE 1	1.25	0.70	1.75	3.50

MISTER MIRACLE (2ND SERIES)
DC

	ORIG	GOOD	FINE	N-MINT
❑1, Jan 89, Be It Ever So Humble, A: Dr. Bedlam; O: Mister Miracle; A: Doctor Bedlam	1.00	0.50	1.25	2.50
❑2, Feb 89	1.00	0.30	0.75	1.50
❑3, Mar 89	1.00	0.30	0.75	1.50
❑4, Apr 89	1.00	0.30	0.75	1.50
❑5, Jun 89	1.00	0.30	0.75	1.50
❑6, Jul 89	1.00	0.25	0.63	1.25
❑7, Aug 89	1.00	0.25	0.63	1.25
❑8, Sep 89	1.00	0.25	0.63	1.25
❑9, Oct 89, 1: Maxi-Man	1.00	0.25	0.63	1.25
❑10, Nov 89	1.00	0.25	0.63	1.25
❑11, Dec 89	1.00	0.25	0.63	1.25
❑12, Jan 90	1.00	0.25	0.63	1.25
❑13, Mar 90	1.00	0.25	0.63	1.25
❑14, Apr 90	1.00	0.25	0.63	1.25
❑15, May 90	1.00	0.25	0.63	1.25
❑16, Jun 90	1.00	0.25	0.63	1.25
❑17, Jul 90	1.00	0.25	0.63	1.25
❑18, Aug 90	1.00	0.25	0.63	1.25
❑19, Sep 90	1.00	0.25	0.63	1.25
❑20, Oct 90	1.00	0.25	0.63	1.25
❑21, Nov 90	1.00	0.25	0.63	1.25
❑22, Dec 90	1.00	0.25	0.63	1.25
❑23, Jan 91	1.00	0.25	0.63	1.25
❑24, Feb 91	1.00	0.25	0.63	1.25
❑25, Mar 91	1.00	0.25	0.63	1.25
❑26, Apr 91	1.00	0.25	0.63	1.25
❑27, May 91	1.25	0.25	0.63	1.25
❑28, Jun 91, Final Issue	1.25	0.25	0.63	1.25

MISTER MIRACLE (3RD SERIES)
DC

Value: Cover or less

❑1, Apr 96, Stone Walls do not a Prison Make... 1.95
❑2, May 96, V: JLA... 1.95
❑3, Jun 96... 1.95
❑4, Jul 96, V: Black Racer... 1.95
❑5, Aug 96... 1.95
❑6, Sep 96... 1.95
❑7, Oct 96, Freedom is Blind, Final Issue... 1.95

MR. MONSTER
Dark Horse

	ORIG	GOOD	FINE	N-MINT
❑1, Feb 88, Origins, Part 1; The Terror of Trezman!, O: Mr. Monster	1.75	0.40	1.00	2.00
❑2, Apr 88, Origins, Part 2	1.75	0.40	1.00	2.00
❑3, Jun 88, Origins, Part 3; Doc Stearn	1.75	0.40	1.00	2.00
❑4, Nov 88, Origins, Part 4; Cadavera	1.75	0.40	1.00	2.00
❑5, Mar 89, Origins, Part 5; Monster Boy	1.75	0.40	1.00	2.00
❑6, Oct 89, Origins, Part 6; The Secret Files of Dr. Drew, has indicia for #5	1.95	0.40	1.00	2.00
❑7, Apr 90, Origins, Part 7; Ghosts Are Dead!	1.95	0.40	1.00	2.00
❑8, Sep 90, D: Mr. Monster, Final Issue; Giant-size	4.95	1.00	2.50	5.00

MR. MONSTER ATTACKS!
Tundra

Value: Cover or less

❑1, Aug 92 ..... 3.95
❑2, Sep 92 ..... 3.95
❑3, Oct 92 ..... 3.95

MR. MONSTER PRESENTS (CRACK-A-BOOM!)
Caliber

Value: Cover or less

❑1 ..... 2.95
❑2 ..... 2.95
❑3, Sep 97 ..... 2.95

MR. MONSTER'S GAL FRIDAY...KELLY!
Image

Value: Cover or less

❑1, Jan 00, Temporary Insanity; I Married a Monser! 3.50

MR. MONSTER'S HIGH-OCTANE HORROR
Eclipse

	ORIG	GOOD	FINE	N-MINT
❑1, Aug 86, BW; GE, BW (w), The Secret Files of Dr. Drew; The Man Who Never Smiled, A.K.A. Super Duper Special #2	1.75	0.40	1.00	2.00
❑3D 1, May 86, A.K.A. Super Duper Special #1	2.00	0.50	1.25	2.50

MR. MONSTER'S HI-SHOCK SCHLOCK
Eclipse

	ORIG	GOOD	FINE	N-MINT
❑1, Mar 87, The Flat Man; Frankenstein and the Mummies, A.K.A. Super Duper Special #6	1.75	0.40	1.00	2.00
❑2, May 87, A.K.A. Super Duper Special #7	1.75	0.40	1.00	2.00

MR. MONSTER'S HI-VOLTAGE SUPER SCIENCE
Eclipse

	ORIG	GOOD	FINE	N-MINT
❑1, Jan 87, The Flying Saucer, A.K.A. Super Duper Special #5	1.75	0.40	1.00	2.00

MR. MONSTER'S TRIPLE THREAT 3-D
3-D Zone

Value: Cover or less

❑1, nn 3.95

MR. MONSTER'S TRUE CRIME
Eclipse

	ORIG	GOOD	FINE	N-MINT
❑1, Sep 86, Murder, Morphine, & Me!; Demons Dance on Galloway Moor!, A.K.A. Super Duper Special #3	1.75	0.40	1.00	2.00
❑2, Oct 86, Public Enemy #1; Vengeance of the Mounted, A.K.A. Super Duper Special #4	1.75	0.40	1.00	2.00

MR. MONSTER'S WEIRD TALES OF THE FUTURE
Eclipse

	ORIG	GOOD	FINE	N-MINT
❑1, BW, BW (w), Brain Bats of Venus; Man From the Moon, A.K.A. Super Duper Special #8	1.75	0.40	1.00	2.00

MR. MONSTER VS. GORZILLA
Image

Value: Cover or less

❑1, Jul 98, nn; One-Shot; red, white, and blue 2.95

MR. MXYZPTLK (VILLAINS)
DC

Value: Cover or less

❑1, Feb 98, New Year's Evil 1.95

MR. NATURAL
Kitchen Sink

	ORIG	GOOD	FINE	N-MINT
❑1	—	20.00	50.00	100.00
❑2	—	12.00	30.00	60.00
❑3	—	9.00	22.50	45.00
❑3-2, 2nd Printing	—	4.40	11.00	22.00
❑3-3, 3rd Printing	—	2.00	5.00	10.00
❑3-4, 4th Printing	—	0.90	2.25	4.50
❑3-5, 5th Printing; 1980	1.50	0.60	1.50	3.00
❑3-6, 6th Printing	—	0.50	1.25	2.50
❑3-7, 7th Printing	—	0.50	1.25	2.50
❑3-8, 8th Printing	2.50	0.50	1.25	2.50

MR. NIGHTMARE'S WINTER SPECIAL
Moonstone

Value: Cover or less

❑1, Dec 95, nn; b&w 3.50

MR. NIGHTMARE'S WONDERFUL WORLD
Moonstone

Value: Cover or less

❑1, Jun 95, b&w 2.95
❑2, Aug 95, A Warp Sense of Reality; Evil Man, b&w 2.95
❑3, Oct 95, b&w 2.95
❑4, Nov 95, Put on Your Party Pants, Part 1, b&w 2.95
❑5, Feb 96, Put on Your Party Pants, Part 2, b&w 2.95

MISTER PLANET
Mr. Planet

Value: Cover or less

❑1, b&w 3.00
❑2, b&w 3.00

MISTER SIXX
Imagine Nation

Value: Cover or less

❑1 ..... 1.95

MR. T AND THE T-FORCE
Now

	ORIG	GOOD	FINE	N-MINT
❑1, Jun 93, NA, NA (w), trading card; trading card	1.95	0.50	1.25	2.50
❑1/GO, NA, NA (w), Gold logo promotional edition; gold, advance	—	0.80	2.00	4.00
❑2, Sep 93, trading card	1.95	0.40	1.00	2.00
❑3, Oct 93, trading card	1.95	0.40	1.00	2.00
❑4, Nov 93, trading card	1.95	0.40	1.00	2.00
❑5, Dec 93, trading card	1.95	0.40	1.00	2.00
❑6, Jan 94, trading card	1.95	0.40	1.00	2.00
❑7, Jun 94, trading card	1.95	0.40	1.00	2.00
❑8, Jul 94, trading card	1.95	0.40	1.00	2.00
❑9, Apr 94, cover says Aug, indicia says Apr; trading card	1.95	0.40	1.00	2.00
❑10	1.95	0.40	1.00	2.00
❑11	1.95	0.40	1.00	2.00
❑12	1.95	0.40	1.00	2.00

MISTER X (VOL. 1)
Vortex

	ORIG	GOOD	FINE	N-MINT
❑1, Jun 84, 1: Mister X	1.75	0.80	2.00	4.00
❑2, Aug 84	1.75	0.55	1.38	2.75
❑3	1.75	0.55	1.38	2.75
❑4	1.75	0.50	1.25	2.50
❑5	1.75	0.50	1.25	2.50
❑6, The Revenge OF Zamora	1.75	0.50	1.25	2.50
❑7	1.75	0.50	1.25	2.50
❑8, The Secret	1.75	0.50	1.25	2.50
❑9	1.75	0.50	1.25	2.50
❑10, BSz (c)	1.75	0.50	1.25	2.50
❑11	2.25	0.50	1.25	2.50
❑12	2.25	0.50	1.25	2.50
❑13	2.25	0.50	1.25	2.50
❑14	2.25	0.50	1.25	2.50

MISTER X (VOL. 2)
Vortex

	ORIG	GOOD	FINE	N-MINT
❑1, Second Comic, Part 1, b&w	2.00	0.60	1.50	3.00
❑2, Second Comic, Part 2, b&w	2.00	0.50	1.25	2.50
❑3, Second Comic, Part 3, b&w	2.00	0.50	1.25	2.50
❑4, Second Comic, Part 4, b&w	2.00	0.50	1.25	2.50
❑5, Second Comic, Part 5, b&w	2.00	0.50	1.25	2.50
❑6, Second Comic, Part 6, b&w	2.00	0.45	1.13	2.25
❑7, b&w	2.00	0.45	1.13	2.25
❑8, b&w	2.00	0.45	1.13	2.25
❑9, Dedicated User, Part 1, b&w	2.00	0.45	1.13	2.25
❑10, Dedicated User, Part 2, b&w	2.00	0.45	1.13	2.25
❑11, Dedicated User, Part 3, b&w	2.00	0.45	1.13	2.25
❑12, Dedicated User, Part 4, b&w	2.00	0.50	1.25	2.50

MISTER X (VOL. 3)
Caliber

Value: Cover or less

❑1, The Big Picture, Part 1 ..... 2.95
❑2, The Big Picture, Part 2 ..... 2.95
❑3, The Big Picture, Part 3 ..... 2.95
❑4, The Big Picture, Part 4 ..... 2.95

MISTRESS OF BONDAGE
Fantagraphics

Value: Cover or less

❑1, b&w; adult 2.95
❑2, b&w; adult 2.95
❑3, b&w; adult 2.95

MISTY
Marvel

	ORIG	GOOD	FINE	N-MINT
❑1, Dec 85, A Day To Forget	0.65	0.20	0.50	1.00
❑2, Jan 86, Ms. Heaventeen is Ms. Understood; The Horseless Horseman of Shady Hollow	0.65	0.20	0.50	1.00
❑3, Feb 86	0.75	0.20	0.50	1.00
❑4, Mar 86	0.75	0.20	0.50	1.00
❑5, Apr 86	0.75	0.20	0.50	1.00
❑6, May 86	0.75	0.20	0.50	1.00

MISTY GIRL EXTREME
Eros

Value: Cover or less

❑1 ..... 2.95
❑2 ..... 2.95

MITES
Continum

	ORIG	GOOD	FINE	N-MINT
❑1, b&w	1.25	0.30	0.75	1.50
❑2	1.75	0.35	0.88	1.75

MOBFIRE
DC

	ORIG	GOOD	FINE	N-MINT
❑1, Dec 94, Guns And Roses	2.50	0.50	1.25	2.50
❑2, Jan 95, Petty Magicks	2.50	0.50	1.25	2.50

	ORIG	GOOD	FINE	N-MINT
❑3, Feb 95, Blood Fellas	2.50	0.50	1.25	2.50
❑4, Mar 95, A Walk Across Rooftops	2.50	0.50	1.25	2.50
❑5, Apr 95, Incommunicado, A: John Constantine	2.50	0.50	1.25	2.50
❑6, May 95, Terror Firma	2.50	0.50	1.25	2.50
❑Ash 1, Meet the Family, "Ashcan" preview given away by DC at shows	—	0.10	0.25	0.50

MOBILE POLICE PATLABOR PART 1
VIZ
Value: Cover or less

❑1, Jul 97, b&w 2.95
❑2, Aug 97, b&w 2.95
❑3, Sep 97, Mission 1, The Right Staff (such lighthearted folk), b&w 2.95
❑4, Oct 97, b&w 2.95
❑5, Nov 97, b&w 2.95
❑6, Dec 97, b&w 2.95

MOBILE POLICE PATLABOR PART 2
VIZ
Value: Cover or less

❑1, Jan 98, b&w 2.95
❑2, Feb 98, b&w 2.95
❑3, Mar 98, b&w 2.95
❑4, Apr 98, b&w 2.95
❑5, May 98, b&w 2.95
❑6, Jun 98, b&w 2.95

MOBILE SUIT GUNDAM 0079
VIZ
Value: Cover or less

❑1 .... 2.95
❑2 .... 2.95
❑3 .... 2.95
❑4 .... 2.95
❑5 .... 2.95
❑6 .... 2.95
❑7 .... 2.95
❑8 .... 2.95

MOBILE SUIT GUNDAM 0083
VIZ
Value: Cover or less

❑1 .... 4.95
❑2 .... 4.95
❑3 .... 4.95
❑4 .... 4.95
❑5 .... 4.95
❑6 .... 4.95
❑7 .... 4.95
❑8 .... 4.95
❑9 .... 4.95
❑10 .... 4.95
❑11 .... 4.95
❑12, La Vie en Rose 4.95
❑13 .... 4.95

MOBILE SUIT GUNDAM WING: GROUND ZERO
VIZ
Value: Cover or less
❑1 .... 2.95

MOBSTERS AND MONSTERS MAGAZINE
ORIGINAL SYNDICATE
Value: Cover or less
❑1, Jul 95, The Nine Lives of El Gato, Crime Mangler 3.00

MOD
KITCHEN SINK

	ORIG	GOOD	FINE	N-MINT
❑1, 1: Adventures in Limbo	—	0.80	2.00	4.00

MODEL BY DAY
RIP OFF
Value: Cover or less

❑1, Jul 90, b&w; adult 2.50
❑2, Oct 90, b&w; adult 2.50

MODERN GRIMM
SYMPTOM
Value: Cover or less
❑1, Dec 96, b&w 2.75

MODERN PULP
SPECIAL STUDIO
Value: Cover or less
❑1, Stealth, b&w 2.75

MODERN ROMANS
FANTAGRAPHICS
Value: Cover or less

❑1, b&w; adult 2.25
❑2, b&w; adult 2.25
❑3, b&w; adult 2.25

MODEST PROPOSAL, A
TOME PRESS
Value: Cover or less

❑1, b&w 2.50
❑2, b&w 2.50

MOEBIUS COMICS
CALIBER
Value: Cover or less

❑1, May 96, The Man from Ciguri; Internal Transfer 2.95
❑2, Jul 96 .... 2.95
❑3, Sep 96, The Arzach; City on Water 2.95
❑4 .... 2.95
❑5 .... 2.95
❑6 .... 2.95

MOEBIUS: EXOTICS
DARK HORSE
Value: Cover or less
❑1, nn; One-Shot; prestige format 6.95

MOEBIUS: H.P.'S ROCK CITY
DARK HORSE
Value: Cover or less
❑1, nn; One-Shot; smaller than a normal comic book; squarebound 7.95

MOEBIUS: MADWOMAN OF THE SACRED HEART
DARK HORSE
Value: Cover or less
❑1 .... 12.95

Words were matched to the pictures on an assortment of currency to produce Slave Labor's *Money Talks.*

© 1996 Slave Labor

MOEBIUS: THE MAN FROM THE CIGURI
DARK HORSE
Value: Cover or less
❑1, nn; b&w and color; One-Shot; smaller than a normal comic book; squarebound 7.95

MOGOBI DESERT RATS
STUDIO 91
Value: Cover or less
❑1, Jan 91, Waste of the World 2.25

MOJO ACTION COMPANION UNIT, THE
EXCLAIM
Value: Cover or less
❑1, Spr 97, b&w 2.75

MOJO MECHANICS
SYNDICATE PUBLISHING
Value: Cover or less

❑1, b&w 2.95
❑2 .... 2.95

MONARCHY, THE
WILDSTORM
Value: Cover or less

❑1, Apr 01, Red Shift 2.50
❑2 .... 2.50
❑3 .... 2.50
❑4 .... 2.50
❑5 .... 2.50

MONDO 3-D
3-D ZONE
Value: Cover or less
❑1, nn 3.95

MONDO BONDO
LCD
Value: Cover or less
❑1 .... 2.95

MONEY TALKS
SLAVE LABOR
Value: Cover or less

❑1, Jun 96, Paying the Piper... 3.50
❑2, Aug 96, Passing the Buck 2.95
❑3, Oct 96, Money to Burn 2.95
❑4, Dec 96, Heads or Tails 2.95
❑5, Feb 97, Dollars and Sense 2.95

MONGREL
NORTHSTAR
Value: Cover or less

❑1/A, Dec 94, Junk Yard Dog.. 3.95
❑2 .... 3.95
❑3 .... 3.95

MONICA'S STORY
ALTERNATIVE

	ORIG	GOOD	FINE	N-MINT
❑1, Feb 99, nn; b&w	2.95	0.70	1.75	3.50

MONKEES, THE
GOLD KEY

	ORIG	GOOD	FINE	N-MINT
❑1, based on TV series	—	7.00	17.50	35.00
❑2	—	5.00	12.50	25.00
❑3	—	4.00	10.00	20.00
❑4	—	3.20	8.00	16.00
❑5	—	3.20	8.00	16.00
❑6	—	2.80	7.00	14.00
❑7	—	2.80	7.00	14.00
❑8	—	2.80	7.00	14.00
❑9	—	2.80	7.00	14.00
❑10	—	2.80	7.00	14.00
❑11	—	2.00	5.00	10.00
❑12	—	2.00	5.00	10.00
❑13, Jul 68	—	2.00	5.00	10.00
❑14, Aug 68	—	2.00	5.00	10.00
❑15, Sep 68	—	2.00	5.00	10.00
❑16	—	2.00	5.00	10.00
❑17	—	2.00	5.00	10.00

MONKEY BUSINESS
PARODY
Value: Cover or less

❑1, b&w 2.50
❑2, Rank & Stinky; Mother Goose & Grimm, Ren & Stimpy parody 2.50

MONKEYMAN AND O'BRIEN
DARK HORSE

	ORIG	GOOD	FINE	N-MINT
❑1, Jul 96, Attack Of The Shrewmanoid, V: Shrewmanoid	2.95	0.70	1.75	3.50
❑2, Aug 96, The Invasion Of The Froglodytes!, V: Froglodytes	2.95	0.60	1.50	3.00

	ORIG	GOOD	FINE	N-MINT
❑3, Sep 96, Into The Terminus, A: Shrew-manoid; V: Quash, Final Issue	2.95	0.59	1.48	2.95
❑SE 1, Feb 96, Who are Monkeyman and O'Brien?, O: Monkeyman and O'Brien	2.95	0.59	1.48	2.95

MONNGA
DAIKAIJU

Value: Cover or less

❑1, Aug 95, Titanic Omega; Leviathan's Crossing ... 3.95

MONOLITH
COMICO

Value: Cover or less

❑1, Oct 91, Fugue and Variations ... 2.50
❑2, Nov 91 ... 2.50
❑3 ... 2.50

MONOLITH (LAST GASP)
LAST GASP

	ORIG	GOOD	FINE	N-MINT
❑1, The Escape from the Dead City; FøX-O	0.50	0.60	1.50	3.00

MONROE
CONQUEST

Value: Cover or less

❑1, b&w; poster; cards ... 4.95

MONSTER, THE
RING

Value: Cover or less

❑1 ... 2.00

MONSTER (BUTLER & HOGG'S...)
SLAVE LABOR

Value: Cover or less

❑1, May, Vampire Love, b&w; adult ... 2.95

MONSTER BOY
MONSTER

	ORIG	GOOD	FINE	N-MINT
❑1, b&w	2.25	0.50	1.25	2.50

MONSTER BOY COMICS
SLAVE LABOR

Value: Cover or less

❑1, Sep 97, The Collector; Sibling Snacks, b&w ... 2.95
❑2, Dec 97, b&w ... 2.95
❑3 ... 2.95

MONSTER FIGHTERS INC.
IMAGE

Value: Cover or less

❑1, Apr 99 ... 3.50

MONSTER FIGHTERS INC.: THE BLACK BOOK
IMAGE

Value: Cover or less

❑1, Sep 00, One-Shot ... 3.50

MONSTER FIGHTERS INC.: THE GHOSTS OF CHRISTMAS
IMAGE

Value: Cover or less

❑1, Dec 99, One-Shot ... 3.95

MONSTER FRAT HOUSE
ETERNITY

Value: Cover or less

❑1, Oct 89, Night on Wolf Mountain, In the Name of Science, b&w ... 2.25

MONSTER IN MY POCKET
HARVEY

	ORIG	GOOD	FINE	N-MINT
❑1, Mar 91, EC, The Convention of Terror...	1.25	0.30	0.75	1.50
❑2, May 91, The Exterminator	1.25	0.30	0.75	1.50
❑3, Jul 91, GK	1.25	0.30	0.75	1.50
❑4, Sep 91, GK	1.25	0.30	0.75	1.50

MONSTER ISLAND
COMPASS

Value: Cover or less

❑1, b&w; wraparound cover ... 3.95

MONSTER LOVE
KITCHEN SINK

Value: Cover or less

❑1, I Need to Know You; Monster's Night Out ... 2.50

MONSTERMAN
IMAGE

Value: Cover or less

❑1, Sep 97, JOy, JOy (w), Curio; The Messenger, b&w ... 2.95

MONSTER MASSACRE
ATOMEKA

Value: Cover or less

❑1, The Kingdom of Zitturk; Headcase, nn ... 7.95

MONSTER MASSACRE SPECIAL
BLACKBALL

Value: Cover or less

❑1 ... 2.50

MONSTER MATINEE
CHAOS!

Value: Cover or less

❑1, Oct 97, monster pin-ups; commentary by Forrest J. Ackerman ... 2.50
❑1/SC, Oct 97, alternate logoless cover; premium edition; monster pin-ups; commentary by Forrest J. Ackerman ... 2.50
❑2, Oct 97, monster pin-ups; commentary by Forrest J. Ackerman ... 2.50
❑3, Oct 97, monster pin-ups; commentary by Forrest J. Ackerman ... 2.50

MONSTERMEN, THE (GARY GIANNI'S...)
DARK HORSE

Value: Cover or less

❑1, Aug 99, The Skull and the Snowman; Hellboy: Goodbye, Mr. Tod ... 2.95

MONSTER MENACE
MARVEL

	ORIG	GOOD	FINE	N-MINT
❑1, Dec 93, SD, SL (w), I Spent Midnight With The Monster On Bald Mountain; The Terror Of Tim Boo Ba, Reprint	1.25	0.30	0.75	1.50
❑2, Jan 94, Reprint	1.25	0.30	0.75	1.50
❑3, Feb 94	1.25	0.30	0.75	1.50
❑4, Mar 94	1.25	0.30	0.75	1.50

MONSTER POSSE
ADVENTURE

Value: Cover or less

❑1, b&w ... 2.50
❑2, Nov 92 ... 2.50
❑3 ... 2.50

MONSTERS FROM OUTER SPACE
ADVENTURE

Value: Cover or less

❑1, Dec 92, b&w ... 2.50
❑2, b&w ... 2.50
❑3, b&w ... 2.50

MONSTERS ON THE PROWL
MARVEL

	ORIG	GOOD	FINE	N-MINT
❑9, Feb 71, Reprint; Title changes to Monsters on the Prowl; Series continued from Chamber of Darkness #8	0.15	1.20	3.00	6.00
❑10, Apr 71, Reprint	0.15	0.80	2.00	4.00
❑11, Jun 71, Reprint	0.15	0.80	2.00	4.00
❑12, Aug 71, Reprint	0.15	0.80	2.00	4.00
❑13, Oct 71	0.25	0.80	2.00	4.00
❑14, Dec 71	0.25	0.80	2.00	4.00
❑15, Feb 72	0.20	0.80	2.00	4.00
❑16, Apr 72, JSe, Forbidden Swamp; Where Walks the Ghost, King Kull	0.20	1.20	3.00	6.00
❑17	0.20	0.80	2.00	4.00
❑18	0.20	0.80	2.00	4.00
❑19	0.20	0.80	2.00	4.00
❑20, SD, Oog Lives Again; The Dangerous Doll	0.20	0.80	2.00	4.00
❑21	0.20	0.60	1.50	3.00
❑22, Apr 73, When the Monster Strikes!; The Wax People	0.20	0.60	1.50	3.00
❑23	0.20	0.60	1.50	3.00
❑24	0.20	0.60	1.50	3.00
❑25	0.20	0.60	1.50	3.00
❑26	0.20	0.60	1.50	3.00
❑27	0.20	0.60	1.50	3.00
❑28	0.25	0.60	1.50	3.00
❑29	0.25	0.60	1.50	3.00
❑30, Final Issue	0.25	0.60	1.50	3.00

MONSTERS UNLEASHED
MARVEL

	ORIG	GOOD	FINE	N-MINT
❑1, Jul 73, b&w; magazine	0.75	2.80	7.00	14.00
❑2, Frankenstein	0.75	2.00	5.00	10.00
❑3, Frankenstein, Man-Thing, Son of Satan	0.75	1.80	4.50	9.00
❑4, Frankenstein	0.75	1.80	4.50	9.00
❑5, Frankenstein, Man-Thing	0.75	1.80	4.50	9.00
❑6, Frankenstein, Werewolf	0.75	1.40	3.50	7.00
❑7, Frankenstein, Werewolf	0.75	1.40	3.50	7.00
❑8, Frankenstein, Man-Thing	0.75	1.40	3.50	7.00
❑9, Frankenstein, Man-Thing, Wendigo	0.75	1.40	3.50	7.00
❑10, Frankenstein, Tigra	0.75	1.40	3.50	7.00
❑11, Sum 75, Gabriel	0.75	1.40	3.50	7.00
❑Anl 1, Reprint	1.25	1.40	3.50	7.00

MONSTROSITY
SLAP HAPPY

Value: Cover or less

❑1, Oct 98, b&w ... 4.95

MOON BEAST
AVALON

Value: Cover or less

❑1, SD, The Night of the Werewolf; The Moon Beast ... 2.95

MOONCHILD
FORBIDDEN FRUIT

Value: Cover or less

❑1, b&w; adult ... 2.95
❑2, b&w; adult ... 2.95

MOON CHILD (VOL. 2)
FORBIDDEN FRUIT

Value: Cover or less

❑1, b&w; adult ... 3.50
❑2, b&w; adult ... 3.50
❑3, b&w; adult ... 3.50

MOONFIGHTING
HARRIER

	ORIG	GOOD	FINE	N-MINT
❑1, Mar 88, Air Warfare, b&w	1.95	0.40	1.00	2.00

MOON KNIGHT (1ST SERIES)
MARVEL

	ORIG	GOOD	FINE	N-MINT
❑1, Nov 80, BSz, Moon Knight, O: Moon Knight	0.50	0.70	1.75	3.50
❑2, Dec 80, BSz, The Slasher	0.50	0.50	1.25	2.50
❑3, Jan 81, BSz, Midnight Means Murder...	0.50	0.50	1.25	2.50
❑4, Feb 81, BSz, A Committee Of Five	0.50	0.50	1.25	2.50
❑5, Mar 81, BSz, Ghost Story	0.50	0.50	1.25	2.50
❑6, Apr 81, BSz, White Angels	0.50	0.50	1.25	2.50
❑7, May 81, BSz, The Moon Kings	0.50	0.50	1.25	2.50

	ORIG	GOOD	FINE	N-MINT
❑8, Jun 81, BSz, V: Moon Kings	0.50	0.50	1.25	2.50
❑9, Jul 81, FM; BSz, Vengeance In Reprise, V: Midnight Man	0.50	0.50	1.25	2.50
❑10, Aug 81, BSz, Too Many Midnights, V: Midnight Man	0.50	0.50	1.25	2.50
❑11, Sep 81, BSz, To Catch A Killer, V: Creed	0.50	0.50	1.25	2.50
❑12, Oct 81, FM; BSz, The Nightmare Of Morpheus	0.50	0.50	1.25	2.50
❑13, Nov 81, FM; BSz, The Cream Of The Jest, A: Daredevil	0.50	0.50	1.25	2.50
❑14, Dec 81, BSz, Stained Glass Scarlet	0.50	0.50	1.25	2.50
❑15, Jan 82, FM; BSz, FM (c), Ruling The World From His Basement, A: Thing, direct	0.75	0.50	1.25	2.50
❑16, Feb 82, Shadows Of The Moon, V: Blacksmith	0.75	0.50	1.25	2.50
❑17, Mar 82, BSz, Master Sniper's Legacy!	0.75	0.50	1.25	2.50
❑18, Apr 82, BSz, V: Slayers Elite	0.75	0.50	1.25	2.50
❑19, May 82, BSz, Assault On Island Strange, V: Arsenal	0.75	0.50	1.25	2.50
❑20, Jun 82, BSz, V: Arsenal	0.75	0.50	1.25	2.50
❑21, Jul 82, The Master Of Night Earth!	0.75	0.40	1.00	2.00
❑22, Aug 82, BSz, The Dream Demon	0.75	0.40	1.00	2.00
❑23, Sep 82, BSz	0.75	0.40	1.00	2.00
❑24, Oct 82, BSz, Scarlet Moonlight	0.75	0.40	1.00	2.00
❑25, Nov 82, BSz, Black Spectre, double-sized	1.00	0.50	1.25	2.50
❑26, Dec 82, BSz, Hit It!	0.75	0.40	1.00	2.00
❑27, Jan 83, Cop Killer!	0.75	0.40	1.00	2.00
❑28, Feb 83, BSz, Spirits In The Sand	0.75	0.40	1.00	2.00
❑29, Mar 83, BSz, Morning Star	0.75	0.40	1.00	2.00
❑30, Apr 83, BSz, The Moonwraith, Three Sixes, And A Beast	0.75	0.40	1.00	2.00
❑31, May 83, KN, A Box Of Music For Savage Studs	0.75	0.40	1.00	2.00
❑32, Jul 83, KN, When The Music Stops...	0.75	0.40	1.00	2.00
❑33, Sep 83, KN, Exploding Myths	0.75	0.40	1.00	2.00
❑34, Nov 83, Primal Scream, Scorecard	0.75	0.40	1.00	2.00
❑35, Jan 84, KN, Second Wind, A: X-Men, double-sized	1.00	0.50	1.25	2.50
❑36, Mar 84, Ghosts	0.75	0.40	1.00	2.00
❑37, May 84, Red Sins; Crawley	0.75	0.40	1.00	2.00
❑38, Jul 84, Final Rest	0.75	0.40	1.00	2.00

MOON KNIGHT (2ND SERIES)
MARVEL

	ORIG	GOOD	FINE	N-MINT
❑1, Jun 85, Knight Of The Jackal, O: Moon Knight, Double-size	1.25	0.50	1.25	2.50
❑2, Aug 85, Deadly Knowledge	0.65	0.40	1.00	2.00
❑3, Sep 85	0.65	0.40	1.00	2.00
❑4, Oct 85, Bluebeard's Castle	0.65	0.40	1.00	2.00
❑5, Nov 85, Debts And Balances	0.65	0.40	1.00	2.00
❑6, Dec 85, The Last White Knight, Painted cover	0.65	0.40	1.00	2.00

MOON KNIGHT (3RD SERIES)
MARVEL

Value: Cover or less

- ❑1, Jan 98, The Resurrection War, Part 1 ... 2.50
- ❑2, Feb 98 ... 2.50
- ❑3, Mar 98 ... 2.50
- ❑4, Apr 98 ... 2.50

MOON KNIGHT (4TH SERIES)
MARVEL

Value: Cover or less

- ❑1, Jan 99, Spector of the Past; Hole into Darkness, says Feb on cover, Jan in indicia ... 2.99
- ❑2, Feb 99 ... 2.99
- ❑3, Feb 99 ... 2.99
- ❑4, Feb 99 ... 2.99

MOON KNIGHT: DIVIDED WE FALL
MARVEL

Value: Cover or less

- ❑1, nn ... 4.95

MOON KNIGHT SPECIAL
MARVEL

Value: Cover or less

- ❑1, Shang-Chi ... 2.50

MOON KNIGHT SPECIAL EDITION
MARVEL

	ORIG	GOOD	FINE	N-MINT
❑1, Nov 83, BSz, Reprints from Hulk (magazine)	2.00	0.50	1.25	2.50
❑2, Dec 83, BSz, Reprint	2.00	0.50	1.25	2.50
❑3, Jan 84, BSz, Reprint	2.00	0.50	1.25	2.50

MOONSHADOW
MARVEL

	ORIG	GOOD	FINE	N-MINT
❑1, Songs Of Happy Chear, O: Moonshadow	1.50	0.70	1.75	3.50
❑2, A Very Uncomfortable Thing	1.50	0.50	1.25	2.50
❑3, The Crying Of The Wind	1.50	0.50	1.25	2.50
❑4, The Hoofs Of Wrath	1.50	0.40	1.00	2.00
❑5, In A Love Land	1.50	0.40	1.00	2.00
❑6, Through The Window	1.50	0.40	1.00	2.00
❑7, Counterpane	1.50	0.40	1.00	2.00
❑8, Candles	1.50	0.40	1.00	2.00
❑9	1.50	0.40	1.00	2.00

Monsters on the Prowl continued *Chamber of Darkness'* numbering.

	ORIG	GOOD	FINE	N-MINT
❑10	1.50	0.40	1.00	2.00
❑11, Contradictions, O: Moonshadow	1.50	0.40	1.00	2.00
❑12, With Joy To Hear, Final Issue	1.75	0.40	1.00	2.00

MOONSHADOW (VERTIGO)
DC

	ORIG	GOOD	FINE	N-MINT
❑1, Sep 94, Songs Of Happy Chear, O: Moonshadow	2.25	0.60	1.50	3.00
❑2, Oct 94, A Very Uncomfortable Thing	2.25	0.50	1.25	2.50
❑3, Nov 94, The Crying Of The Wind	2.25	0.50	1.25	2.50
❑4, Dec 94, The Hoofs Of Wrath	2.25	0.50	1.25	2.50
❑5, Jan 95, In A Love Land	2.25	0.50	1.25	2.50
❑6, Feb 95, Through The Window	2.25	0.45	1.13	2.25
❑7, Mar 95, Counterpane	2.25	0.45	1.13	2.25
❑8, Apr 95, Candles	2.25	0.45	1.13	2.25
❑9, May 95	2.25	0.45	1.13	2.25
❑10, Jun 95	2.25	0.45	1.13	2.25
❑11, Jul 95, Contradictions, O: Moonshadow	2.25	0.45	1.13	2.25
❑12, Aug 95, With Joy To Hear, Final Issue	2.95	0.59	1.48	2.95

MOON SHOT, THE FLIGHT OF APOLLO 12
PEPPER PIKE GRAPHIX

Value: Cover or less

- ❑1, Jun 94, One-Shot ... 2.95

MOONSTRUCK
WHITE WOLF

Value: Cover or less

- ❑1, May 87 ... 2.00

MOONTRAP
CALIBER

	ORIG	GOOD	FINE	N-MINT
❑1, b&w; movie Adaptation	1.95	0.40	1.00	2.00

MOONWALKER 3-D
BLACKTHORNE

Value: Cover or less

- ❑1 ... 2.50

MORBID ANGEL
LONDON NIGHT

Value: Cover or less

- ❑0.5, Jul 96 ... 3.00

MORBID ANGEL: PENANCE
LONDON NIGHT

Value: Cover or less

- ❑1, Sep 96 ... 3.95

MORBIUS REVISITED
MARVEL

	ORIG	GOOD	FINE	N-MINT
❑1, Aug 93, Reprints Fear #27	1.95	0.40	1.00	2.00
❑2, Sep 93, FR, The Doorway Screaming Into Hell!, Reprints Fear #28	1.95	0.40	1.00	2.00
❑3, Oct 93, DH, Through A Helleyes Darkly!, A: Simon Stroud; A: Helleyes, Reprints Fear #29	1.95	0.40	1.00	2.00
❑4, Nov 93, Reprints Fear #30	1.95	0.40	1.00	2.00
❑5, Dec 93, Reprints Fear #31	1.95	0.40	1.00	2.00

MORBIUS: THE LIVING VAMPIRE
MARVEL

Value: Cover or less

- ❑1, Sep 92, Without poster ... 2.75
- ❑1/CS, Rise of the Midnight Sons, Part 3 ... 2.75
- ❑2, Oct 92, Welcome to the Jungle ... 1.75
- ❑3, Nov 92, A: Spider-Man ... 1.75
- ❑4, Dec 92, A: Spider-Man ... 1.75
- ❑5, Jan 93, Here There Be Dragons, 1: Basilisk II ... 1.75
- ❑6, Feb 93, Tooth and Nail ... 1.75
- ❑7, Mar 93, Cemetery Dance ... 1.75
- ❑8, Apr 93 ... 1.75
- ❑9, May 93 ... 1.75
- ❑10, Jun 93 ... 1.75
- ❑11, Jul 93 ... 1.75
- ❑12, Aug 93, Midnight Massacre, Part 4, Double cover ... 2.95
- ❑13, Sep 93 ... 1.75
- ❑14, Oct 93, A: D'Spayre; A: Werewolf by Night; A: Martine ... 1.75
- ❑15, Nov 93 ... 1.75
- ❑16, Dec 93, Siege of Darkness, Part 5, Neon ink/matte finish cover ... 1.75
- ❑17, Jan 94, Siege of Darkness, Part 13, Spot-varnished cover ... 1.75
- ❑18, Feb 94 ... 1.75
- ❑19, Mar 94 ... 1.75
- ❑20, Apr 94 ... 1.75
- ❑21, May 94 ... 1.95
- ❑22, Jun 94 ... 1.95
- ❑23, Jul 94 ... 1.95
- ❑24, Aug 94 ... 1.95
- ❑25, Sep 94, Giant-size ... 2.50
- ❑26, Oct 94 ... 1.95
- ❑27, Nov 94 ... 1.95
- ❑28, Dec 94 ... 1.95
- ❑29, Jan 95 ... 1.95
- ❑30, Feb 95 ... 1.95
- ❑31, Mar 95 ... 1.95
- ❑32, Apr 95, Final Issue ... 1.95

MORE FETISH
BONEYARD

Value: Cover or less

- ❑1, Nov 93, Turning the Worm ... 2.95

MORE SECRET ORIGINS REPLICA EDITION
DC

Value: Cover or less

❑1, Dec 99, The Origin of the Justice League!; Birth of the Atom, O: Aquaman; O: The Justice League of America; O: The Atom II (Ray Palmer); O: Superman, reprints 80-Page Giant #8 ... 4.95

MORE TALES FROM GIMBLEY
HARRIER

Value: Cover or less

❑1, Feb 88, A Tale from Gimbley ... 1.95

MORE TALES FROM SLEAZE CASTLE
GRATUITOUS BUNNY

	ORIG	GOOD	FINE	N-MINT
❑1, Arrival, Part 1; Arrival, Part 2	—	0.80	2.00	4.00
❑2, Arrival, Part 4; Arrival, Part 5	—	0.60	1.50	3.00
❑3, An Ill Wind	—	0.60	1.50	3.00
❑4, Jan 91, An Ill Wind; The Adventures of Dweng & Ralph, Part 1	—	0.60	1.50	3.00
❑5, Jan 92, An Ill Wind; The Adventures of Dweng & Ralph, Part 1	—	0.60	1.50	3.00
❑6, Jan 93, An Ill Wind; The Adventures of Dweng & Ralph, Part 1	—	0.60	1.50	3.00

MORE THAN MORTAL
LIAR

	ORIG	GOOD	FINE	N-MINT
❑1, Jun 97	2.95	0.80	2.00	4.00
❑1-2, Jun 97, 2nd Printing	2.95	0.59	1.48	2.95
❑2, Sep 97	2.95	0.60	1.50	3.00
❑2/SC, Sep 97, logoless cover	2.95	0.59	1.48	2.95
❑3, Dec 97	2.95	0.60	1.50	3.00
❑4, Apr 98	2.95	0.60	1.50	3.00
❑5, Dec 99, Famine, Part 1	2.95	0.60	1.50	3.00
❑6, Mar 00, Famine, Part 2	2.95	0.59	1.48	2.95
❑Dlx 1, Collects More than Mortal #1-4	14.95	2.99	7.47	14.95

MORE THAN MORTAL/LADY PENDRAGON
IMAGE

	ORIG	GOOD	FINE	N-MINT
❑1, Jun 99, Good versus Evil	2.50	0.50	1.25	2.50
❑1/A, Jun 99, alternate cover	2.50	0.60	1.50	3.00

MORE THAN MORTAL: OTHERWORLDS
IMAGE

	ORIG	GOOD	FINE	N-MINT
❑1, Jul 99	2.95	0.60	1.50	3.00
❑1/A, Jul 99, alternate cover	2.95	0.60	1.50	3.00
❑2, Aug 99, Woman and man kneeling on cover, large figure standing behind	2.95	0.60	1.50	3.00
❑2/A, Aug 99, alternate cover	2.95	0.60	1.50	3.00
❑3, Oct 99, Woman holding sword on cover, red top left background	2.95	0.60	1.50	3.00
❑3/A, Oct 99, alternate cover	2.95	0.60	1.50	3.00
❑4, Dec 99	2.95	0.60	1.50	3.00

MORE THAN MORTAL: SAGAS
LIAR

	ORIG	GOOD	FINE	N-MINT
❑1, Aug 98, 1: Morlock	2.95	0.59	1.48	2.95
❑1/A, Aug 98, variant cover for New Dimension Comics	2.95	1.00	2.50	5.00
❑2, Oct 98	2.95	0.59	1.48	2.95
❑3, Dec 98	2.95	0.59	1.48	2.95

MORE THAN MORTAL: TRUTHS & LEGENDS
LIAR

	ORIG	GOOD	FINE	N-MINT
❑1, Jun 98, Cover has man with glowing eye at bow of ship	2.95	0.59	1.48	2.95
❑1/A, Jun 98, Variant edition	—	0.80	2.00	4.00
❑1/LE, Jun 98, Variant edition	—	1.00	2.50	5.00
❑2, Aug 98	2.95	0.59	1.48	2.95
❑3, Oct 98	2.95	0.59	1.48	2.95
❑4, Jan 99	2.95	0.59	1.48	2.95
❑5	2.95	0.59	1.48	2.95

MORLOCK 2001
ATLAS

	ORIG	GOOD	FINE	N-MINT
❑1, Feb 75, AM, The Coming Of Morlock!, O: Morlock	0.25	0.40	1.00	2.00
❑2, Apr 75, AM	0.25	0.30	0.75	1.50
❑3, Jul 75, BWr; SD; AM, O: Midnight Men	0.25	0.30	0.75	1.50

MORNING GLORY
RADIO

Value: Cover or less

❑1, Nov 98, b&w ... 2.95
❑2, Dec 98, b&w ... 2.95
❑3, Jan 99, b&w ... 2.95
❑5, May 99, b&w ... 2.95

MORNINGSTAR SPECIAL
TRIDENT

Value: Cover or less

❑1, Apr 90, The Sword in the Stone, b&w ... 2.50

MORPHOS THE SHAPECHANGER
DARK HORSE

Value: Cover or less

❑1, Jul 96, nn; One-Shot; prestige format ... 4.95

MORPHS
GRAPHXPRESS

Value: Cover or less

❑1 ... 2.00
❑2 ... 2.00
❑3 ... 2.00
❑4 ... 2.00

MORRIGAN (DIMENSION X)
DIMENSION X

Value: Cover or less

❑1, Aug 93, b&w ... 2.75

MORRIGAN (SIRIUS)
SIRIUS

Value: Cover or less

❑1 ... 2.95

MORTAL KOMBAT
MALIBU

	ORIG	GOOD	FINE	N-MINT
❑1, Jul 94, A Slow Boat To China, Blood and Thunder	2.95	0.60	1.50	3.00
❑1/A, Jul 94, variant cover (Mortal Kombat logo)	2.95	0.60	1.50	3.00
❑2, Aug 94, Blood and Thunder	2.95	0.60	1.50	3.00
❑3, Sep 94, The Art of War, Blood and Thunder	2.95	0.60	1.50	3.00
❑4, Oct 94, Blood and Thunder	2.95	0.60	1.50	3.00
❑5, Nov 94, Blood and Thunder	2.95	0.60	1.50	3.00
❑6	2.95	0.60	1.50	3.00

MORTAL KOMBAT: BARAKA
MALIBU

Value: Cover or less

❑1 ... 2.95

MORTAL KOMBAT: BATTLEWAVE
MALIBU

	ORIG	GOOD	FINE	N-MINT
❑1, Where The Wild Things Are!	2.95	0.60	1.50	3.00
❑2	2.95	0.60	1.50	3.00
❑3	2.95	0.60	1.50	3.00
❑4	2.95	0.60	1.50	3.00
❑5	2.95	0.60	1.50	3.00
❑6	2.95	0.60	1.50	3.00

MORTAL KOMBAT: GORO, PRINCE OF PAIN
MALIBU

Value: Cover or less

❑1, Sep 94, Stranger in a Strange Land ... 2.95
❑2, Oct 94 ... 2.95

MORTAL KOMBAT: KITANA & MILEENA
MALIBU

Value: Cover or less

❑1 ... 2.95

MORTAL KOMBAT: KUNG LAO
MALIBU

Value: Cover or less

❑1 ... 2.95

MORTAL KOMBAT: RAYDEN & KANO
MALIBU

Value: Cover or less

❑1 ... 2.95
❑2 ... 2.95

MORTAL KOMBAT SPECIAL EDITION
MALIBU

Value: Cover or less

❑1, Nov 94 ... 2.95
❑2 ... 2.95

MORTAL KOMBAT U.S. SPECIAL FORCES
MALIBU

Value: Cover or less

❑1, Secret Treasures ... 3.50
❑2 ... 3.50

MORTAR MAN
MARSHALL COMICS

Value: Cover or less

❑1, May 93, First Boom, b&w.. 1.95
❑2, b&w ... 1.95
❑3 ... 2.50

MORTIGAN GOTH: IMMORTALIS
MARVEL

Value: Cover or less

❑1, Sep 93, The Devil's Due, Part 1, O: Mortigan Goth ... 1.95
❑1/SC, Sep 93, The Devil's Due, Part 1, foil cover ... 2.95
❑2, Oct 93, The Devil's Due, Part 2 ... 1.95
❑3, Jan 94, The Devil's Due, Part 3 ... 1.95
❑4, Mar 94, The Devil's Due, Part 4 ... 1.95

MORT THE DEAD TEENAGER
MARVEL

Value: Cover or less

❑1, Death On The Babylon Express ... 1.75
❑2 ... 1.75
❑3 ... 1.75
❑4, Mar 93 ... 1.75

MORTY THE DOG (MU)
MU

Value: Cover or less

❑1, b&w; digest ... 3.95
❑2, Spr 91, b&w; digest ... 3.95

MORTY THE DOG (STARHEAD)
STARHEAD

	ORIG	GOOD	FINE	N-MINT
❑1, Bark And Bite!; The Big Break!	1.75	0.40	1.00	2.00

MOSAIC
SIRIUS

Value: Cover or less

❑1/A, Mar 99 ... 2.95
❑1/B, Mar 99, alternate cover; smaller logos ... 2.95

ORIG GOOD FINE N-MINT

❑2, Apr 99 ... 2.95
❑3, May 99 ... 2.95
❑4, Jun 99 ... 2.95
❑5, Jul 99 ... 2.95

MOSAIC: HELL CITY RIPPER
SIRIUS

Value: Cover or less

❑1 ... 2.95
❑1/SC, Alternate cover by Kelley Jones ... 2.95

MOSTLY WANTED
WILDSTORM

Value: Cover or less

❑1, Jul 00 ... 2.50
❑2, Aug 00 ... 2.50
❑3, Sep 00 ... 2.50
❑4, Nov 00 ... 2.50

MOTHERLESS CHILD
KITCHEN SINK

Value: Cover or less

❑1 ... 2.95

MOTHER'S OATS COMIX
RIP OFF

	ORIG	GOOD	FINE	N-MINT
❑1, The Doing of Dealer McDope; Bathroom Capers	0.50	1.00	2.50	5.00
❑2, Word Salad; The Vision	0.50	0.60	1.50	3.00

MOTHER SUPERION
ANTARCTIC

Value: Cover or less

❑1, Jul 97 ... 2.95

MOTHER TERESA OF CALCUTTA
MARVEL

	ORIG	GOOD	FINE	N-MINT
❑1	1.25	0.30	0.75	1.50

MOTLEY STORIES
DIVISION

Value: Cover or less

❑1, b&w ... 2.75

MOTORBIKE PUPPIES, THE
DARK ZULU LIES

Value: Cover or less

❑1, Jun 92, Vengeance Is Mine!, 1: The Humanals ... 2.50
❑2, Never published? ... 2.50

MOTORHEAD
DARK HORSE

Value: Cover or less

❑1, Aug 95, Hunting Party, V: Predator ... 2.50
❑2, Sep 95 ... 2.50
❑3, Oct 95 ... 2.50
❑4, Nov 95 ... 2.50
❑5, Dec 95 ... 2.50
❑6, Jan 96 ... 2.50
❑SE 1, Mar 94, Power Play ... 3.95

MOTORMOUTH
MARVEL

	ORIG	GOOD	FINE	N-MINT
❑1, 1: Motormouth	1.75	0.40	1.00	2.00
❑2	1.75	0.35	0.88	1.75
❑3, Punisher	1.75	0.35	0.88	1.75
❑4	1.75	0.35	0.88	1.75
❑5, Oct 92, War Zone, A: Punisher	1.75	0.35	0.88	1.75
❑6, Nov 92, Title changes to Motormouth & Killpower	1.75	0.35	0.88	1.75
❑7, Dec 92, A: Cable	1.75	0.35	0.88	1.75
❑8	1.75	0.35	0.88	1.75
❑9, MyS-TECH Wars	1.75	0.35	0.88	1.75
❑10, Apr 93	1.75	0.35	0.88	1.75
❑11	1.75	0.35	0.88	1.75
❑12	1.75	0.35	0.88	1.75
❑13, Final Issue	1.75	0.35	0.88	1.75

MOUNTAIN
UNDERGROUND

	ORIG	GOOD	FINE	N-MINT
❑1, Flipbook High School Funnies	0.50	0.60	1.50	3.00

MOUNTAIN WORLD
ICICLE RIDGE

Value: Cover or less

❑1, b&w ... 2.00

MOUSE ON THE MOON, THE
DELL

	ORIG	GOOD	FINE	N-MINT
❑1, Oct 63	0.12	3.00	7.50	15.00

MOVIE STAR NEWS
PURE IMAGINATION

	ORIG	GOOD	FINE	N-MINT
❑1, DSt (c), Bettie Page photos	—	1.20	3.00	6.00

MOXI
LIGHTNING

Value: Cover or less

❑1, Jul 96, Moxi; Hellina: Heart of Thorns ... 3.00

MOXI'S FRIENDS: BOBBY JOE & NITRO
LIGHTNING

Value: Cover or less

❑1, Sep 96 ... 2.75

MOXI: STRANGE DAZE
LIGHTNING

Value: Cover or less

❑1, Nov 96, b&w ... 3.00

M. REX
IMAGE

Value: Cover or less

❑1, Nov 99 ... 2.95
❑1/A, Nov 99, Exclusive cover; Large figure in background, boy, monkey on waterbike in foreground ... 2.95
❑2, Dec 99 ... 2.95
❑ASH 1/A, Jul 99, Flying car on cover ... 5.00
❑ASH 1/B, Jul 99, Blue background on cover ... 5.00

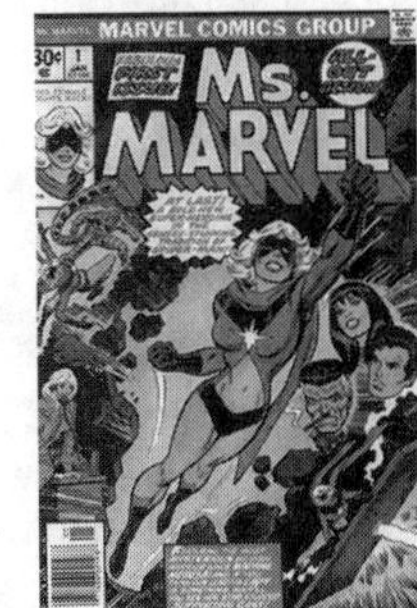

Cape Canaveral security officer Carol Danvers became Ms. Marvel after an encounter with the Kree warrior Mar-Vell.

© 1977 Marvel Comics

ORIG GOOD FINE N-MINT

MS. ANTI-SOCIAL
HELPLESS ANGER

Value: Cover or less

❑1, nn; b&w; 16pgs. ... 1.75

MS. CYANIDE & ICE
BLACK OUT

Value: Cover or less

❑0 ... 2.95
❑1, Sly & Furious preview ... 2.95

MS. FANTASTIC
CONQUEST

Value: Cover or less

❑1, b&w; adult ... 2.95
❑2, b&w; adult ... 2.95
❑3, b&w; adult ... 2.95
❑4, b&w; adult ... 2.95

MS. FANTASTIC CLASSICS
CONQUEST

Value: Cover or less

❑1, b&w; adult ... 2.95

MS. FORTUNE
IMAGE

Value: Cover or less

❑1, Jan 98, b&w ... 2.95

MS. MARVEL
MARVEL

	ORIG	GOOD	FINE	N-MINT
❑1, Jan 77, JB, This Woman, This Warrior, 1: Ms. Marvel	0.30	0.80	2.00	4.00
❑2, Feb 77	0.30	0.60	1.50	3.00
❑3, Mar 77	0.30	0.60	1.50	3.00
❑4, Apr 77	0.30	0.50	1.25	2.50
❑5, May 77, A: Vision	0.30	0.50	1.25	2.50
❑6, Jun 77	0.30	0.50	1.25	2.50
❑7, Jul 77, V: Modok	0.30	0.50	1.25	2.50
❑8, Aug 77	0.30	0.50	1.25	2.50
❑9, Sep 77, 1: Deathbird	0.30	0.50	1.25	2.50
❑10, Oct 77	0.30	0.50	1.25	2.50
❑11, Nov 77	0.35	0.40	1.00	2.00
❑12, Dec 77, V: Hecate	0.35	0.40	1.00	2.00
❑13, Jan 78, Homecoming	0.35	0.40	1.00	2.00
❑14, Feb 78, 1: Steeplejack II (Maxwell Plumm)	0.35	0.40	1.00	2.00
❑15, Mar 78	0.35	0.40	1.00	2.00
❑16, Apr 78, 1: Mystique (cameo)	0.35	1.50	3.75	7.50
❑17, May 78	0.35	0.80	2.00	4.00
❑18, Jun 78, 1: Mystique (full appearance)	0.35	2.50	6.25	12.50
❑19, Aug 78, A: Captain Marvel	0.35	0.50	1.25	2.50
❑20, Oct 78, New costume	0.35	0.40	1.00	2.00
❑21, Dec 78	0.35	0.40	1.00	2.00
❑22, Feb 79	0.35	0.40	1.00	2.00
❑23, Apr 79, Final Issue	0.35	0.40	1.00	2.00

MS. MYSTIC (CONTINUITY)
CONTINUITY

Value: Cover or less

❑1, NA, O: Ms. Mystic, reprints Ms. Mystic (Pacific) #1 ... 2.00
❑2, Jun 88, NA, reprints Ms. Mystic (Pacific) #2 ... 2.00
❑3, Jan 89, NA ... 2.00
❑4, May 89, NA ... 2.00
❑5, Aug 90, NA (c), Comics Code ... 2.00
❑6, Nov 90, NA (c), Comics Code ... 2.00
❑7, Aug 91 ... 2.00
❑8, Mar 92 ... 2.00
❑9, May 92 ... 2.00

MS. MYSTIC (PACIFIC)
PACIFIC

	ORIG	GOOD	FINE	N-MINT
❑1, Oct 82, NA, NA (w), O: Ms. Mystic, origin	1.00	0.30	0.75	1.50
❑2, Feb 84, NA, NA (w), 1: Urth 4; 1: Urth; 1: Watr; 1: Fyre; 1: Ayre	1.50	0.30	0.75	1.50

MS. MYSTIC (VOL. 2)
CONTINUITY

Value: Cover or less

❑1, Oct 93, Rise of Magic ... 2.50
❑2, Nov 93, Rise of Magic ... 2.50
❑3, Dec 93, Rise of Magic ... 2.50
❑4, Jan 94, Rise of Magic ... 2.50
❑5, Rise of Magic, Exists? ... 2.50
❑6, Rise of Magic, Exists? ... 2.50

MS. MYSTIC DEATHWATCH 2000
CONTINUITY

Value: Cover or less

❑1, May 93, NA (w), Deathwatch 2000, Part 8, Stereo diffusion cover ... 2.50
❑2, Jun 93, Deathwatch 2000, Part 12, trading card ... 2.50
❑3, Aug 93, NA (w), Deathwatch 2000, Part 17, trading card; trading card; drops Deathwatch 2000 from indicia ... 2.50

MS. PMS
Aaaahh!!

Value: Cover or less

❑1 ... 2.50

MS. QUOTED TALES
Chance

Value: Cover or less

❑1 ... 1.50

MS. TREE
Eclipse

	ORIG	GOOD	FINE	N-MINT
❑1, Eclipse publishes	1.50	0.80	2.00	4.00
❑2	1.50	0.55	1.38	2.75
❑3	1.50	0.55	1.38	2.75
❑4, Oct 83	1.50	0.50	1.25	2.50
❑5, Nov 83	1.50	0.50	1.25	2.50
❑6, Feb 84	1.50	0.40	1.00	2.00
❑7, Apr 84	1.50	0.40	1.00	2.00
❑8, May 84	1.50	0.40	1.00	2.00
❑9, Jul 84	1.75	0.40	1.00	2.00
❑10, Aug 84, Aardvark-Vanaheim begins as publisher	1.70	0.40	1.00	2.00
❑11, Sep 84	1.70	0.40	1.00	2.00
❑12, Oct 84	1.70	0.40	1.00	2.00
❑13, Nov 84	1.70	0.40	1.00	2.00
❑14, Dec 84	1.70	0.40	1.00	2.00
❑15, Jan 85	1.70	0.40	1.00	2.00
❑16, Feb 85	1.70	0.40	1.00	2.00
❑17, Apr 85	1.70	0.40	1.00	2.00
❑18, May 85	1.70	0.40	1.00	2.00
❑19, Jun 85, Renegade Press begins as publisher	1.70	0.40	1.00	2.00
❑20, Jul 85	1.70	0.40	1.00	2.00
❑21, Sep 85	1.70	0.40	1.00	2.00
❑22, Oct 85, Right to Die, Part 1, Abortion story	1.70	0.40	1.00	2.00
❑23, Nov 85, Right to Die, Part 2, Abortion story	1.70	0.40	1.00	2.00
❑24, Dec 85	1.70	0.40	1.00	2.00
❑25, Jan 86	1.70	0.40	1.00	2.00
❑26, Feb 86	1.70	0.40	1.00	2.00
❑27, Mar 86	1.70	0.40	1.00	2.00
❑28, Apr 86	1.70	0.40	1.00	2.00
❑29, May 86	1.70	0.40	1.00	2.00
❑30, Jun 86	2.00	0.40	1.00	2.00
❑31, Jul 86	2.00	0.40	1.00	2.00
❑32, Sep 86	2.00	0.40	1.00	2.00
❑33, Oct 86	2.00	0.40	1.00	2.00
❑34, Nov 86	2.00	0.40	1.00	2.00
❑35, Dec 86	2.00	0.40	1.00	2.00
❑36, Feb 87	2.00	0.40	1.00	2.00
❑37, Mar 87	2.00	0.40	1.00	2.00
❑38, Apr 87	2.00	0.40	1.00	2.00
❑39, May 87	2.00	0.40	1.00	2.00
❑40, Jun 87	2.00	0.40	1.00	2.00
❑41, Oct 87	2.00	0.40	1.00	2.00
❑42, Nov 87	2.00	0.40	1.00	2.00
❑43, Dec 87	2.00	0.40	1.00	2.00
❑44, Feb 88	2.00	0.40	1.00	2.00
❑45, Apr 88, Johnny Dynamite back-up	2.00	0.40	1.00	2.00
❑46, May 88	2.00	0.40	1.00	2.00
❑47, Aug 88	2.00	0.40	1.00	2.00
❑48, Nov 88	2.00	0.40	1.00	2.00
❑49, May 89	2.00	0.40	1.00	2.00
❑50, Jun 89, JK, Final Issue; flexi-disc	2.75	0.55	1.38	2.75
❑3D 1, Aug 85	2.00	0.50	1.25	2.50
❑3D 2, Jul 87, Ms. Tree's 1950's Three-Dimensional Crime	2.50	0.50	1.25	2.50
❑Smr 1, Aug 86, b&w; Variant edition	2.00	0.40	1.00	2.00

MS. TREE QUARTERLY
DC

	ORIG	GOOD	FINE	N-MINT
❑1, Sum 90, Gift of Death; Night Kills, Batman, Midnight	3.99	0.80	2.00	4.00
❑2, Aut 90, Butcher	3.95	0.80	2.00	4.00
❑3, Spr 91, Butcher	3.95	0.80	2.00	4.00
❑4, Sum 91	3.95	0.80	2.00	4.00
❑5, Aut 91	3.95	0.80	2.00	4.00
❑6, Win 91	3.95	0.80	2.00	4.00
❑7, Spr 92, The Family Way; Killer's Kiss, Part 2	3.95	0.80	2.00	4.00
❑8, Sum 92	3.95	0.80	2.00	4.00
❑9, One Mean Mother, Listed as Ms. Tree Special in indicia	3.95	0.80	2.00	4.00
❑10, Final Issue	3.50	0.70	1.75	3.50

MS. VICTORY SPECIAL
AC

	ORIG	GOOD	FINE	N-MINT
❑1, full color	1.75	0.40	1.00	2.00

MUKTUK WOLFSBREATH: HARD-BOILED SHAMAN
DC

Value: Cover or less

- ❑1, Aug 98, Mommy's Girl ... 2.50
- ❑2, Sep 98 ... 2.50
- ❑3, Oct 98 ... 2.50

MULLKON EMPIRE (JOHN JAKES'...)
Tekno

Value: Cover or less

- ❑1, Sep 95 ... 1.95
- ❑2, Oct 95 ... 1.95
- ❑3, Nov 95 ... 1.95
- ❑4, Dec 95 ... 1.95
- ❑5, Dec 95 ... 1.95
- ❑6, Jan 96 ... 2.25

MULTIVERSE (MICHAEL MOORCOCK'S...)
DC

Value: Cover or less

- ❑1, Nov 97, Moonbeams and Roses, Part 1; The Metaphorical Detective, Part 1 ... 2.50
- ❑2, Dec 97, Moonbeams and Roses, Part 2; The Metaphorical Detective, Part 2 ... 2.50
- ❑3, Jan 98, Moonbeams and Roses, Part 3; The Metaphorical Detective, Part 3 ... 2.50
- ❑4, Feb 98, Moonbeams and Roses, Part 4; The Metaphorical Detective, Part 4 ... 2.50
- ❑5, Mar 98, Moonbeams and Roses, Part 5; The Metaphorical Detective, Part 5 ... 2.50
- ❑6, Apr 98 ... 2.50
- ❑7, May 98 ... 2.50
- ❑8, Jun 98 ... 2.50
- ❑9, Jul 98 ... 2.50
- ❑10, Aug 98 ... 2.50
- ❑11, Sep 98 ... 2.50
- ❑12, Oct 98, Final Issue ... 2.50

MUMMY, THE (MONSTER)
Monster

Value: Cover or less

- ❑1, b&w ... 1.95
- ❑2, b&w ... 1.95
- ❑3, b&w ... 1.95
- ❑4, b&w ... 1.95

MUMMY ARCHIVES, THE
Millennium

Value: Cover or less

❑1, Jan 92 ... 2.50

MUMMY OR RAMSES THE DAMNED, THE (ANNE RICE'S...)
Millennium

Value: Cover or less

- ❑1, JM ... 5.00
- ❑2, JM ... 3.50
- ❑3, JM ... 3.50
- ❑4, JM ... 3.50
- ❑5, JM, Celeste Aida ... 3.50
- ❑6, JM ... 3.00
- ❑7, JM, The Queen of the Dead ... 3.00
- ❑8, JM ... 3.00
- ❑9, JM ... 3.00
- ❑10, JM ... 3.00
- ❑11, JM ... 3.00
- ❑12, JM ... 3.00

MUMMY'S CURSE, THE
Aircel

	ORIG	GOOD	FINE	N-MINT
❑1, Nov 90, b&w	2.25	0.50	1.25	2.50
❑2, Dec 90, b&w	2.25	0.50	1.25	2.50
❑3, Jan 91, b&w	2.25	0.50	1.25	2.50
❑4, Feb 91, b&w	2.25	0.50	1.25	2.50

MUNDEN'S BAR
First

Value: Cover or less

- ❑Anl 1, Apr 88, JSa; BB; SR; JOy, Demolition Drinking II; The Last Vampire, A: Clonezone; A: Anti-Socialman; A: Fish Police, prestige format ... 2.95
- ❑Anl 2, Mar 91, A: Teenage Mutant Ninja Turtles; A: Omaha the Cat Dancer, prestige format ... 5.95

MUNSTERS, THE (GOLD KEY)
Gold Key

	ORIG	GOOD	FINE	N-MINT
❑1, Jan 65, It's All Fright with Me; Haunted House-Cleaning, Photo cover	0.12	20.00	50.00	100.00
❑2, Apr 65	0.12	13.00	32.50	65.00
❑3, Jul 65	0.12	8.00	20.00	40.00
❑4, Oct 65	0.12	8.00	20.00	40.00
❑5, Jan 66, Screams Like Old Times!; All Haunts on Deck, back cover pin-up	0.12	8.00	20.00	40.00
❑6	0.12	5.60	14.00	28.00
❑7	0.12	5.60	14.00	28.00
❑8	0.12	5.60	14.00	28.00
❑9	0.12	5.60	14.00	28.00
❑10	0.12	5.60	14.00	28.00
❑11	0.12	4.80	12.00	24.00
❑12	0.12	4.80	12.00	24.00
❑13	0.12	4.80	12.00	24.00
❑14, Aug 67, The Shock Heard Round the World; A Bat-Time Story: The Sorcerer's Servant (text piece), Photo cover	0.12	4.80	12.00	24.00
❑15	0.12	4.80	12.00	24.00
❑16	0.12	4.80	12.00	24.00

MUNSTERS, THE (TV COMICS!)
TV Comics

	ORIG	GOOD	FINE	N-MINT
❑1, Aug 97	2.95	0.60	1.50	3.00
❑2/A, Oct 97, blue background	2.95	0.60	1.50	3.00
❑2/B, Oct 97, Alternate cover (Marilyn); red background	2.95	0.60	1.50	3.00
❑3, Dec 97	2.95	0.60	1.50	3.00
❑4, Mar 98	2.95	0.60	1.50	3.00

	ORIG	GOOD	FINE	N-MINT
❑4/SC, Mar 98, logoless	2.95	0.60	1.50	3.00
❑SE 1, Aug 97, Welcome to the Con, Comic Con 1997 Edition; red foil logo	2.95	0.60	1.50	3.00

MUPPET BABIES (HARVEY)
HARVEY

	ORIG	GOOD	FINE	N-MINT
❑1	1.25	0.30	0.75	1.50
❑2, Sep 93	1.25	0.30	0.75	1.50
❑3, Dec 93	1.50	0.30	0.75	1.50
❑4, Mar 94	1.50	0.30	0.75	1.50
❑5, May 94	1.50	0.30	0.75	1.50
❑6, Aug 94	1.50	0.30	0.75	1.50

MUPPET BABIES (STAR/MARVEL)
MARVEL

	ORIG	GOOD	FINE	N-MINT
❑1, May 85, Herman and Grandpa photo cover	0.65	0.30	0.75	1.50
❑2, The Big Space Adventure	0.65	0.20	0.50	1.00
❑3	0.65	0.20	0.50	1.00
❑4	0.65	0.20	0.50	1.00
❑5, Jan 86, The Idol of Zoom	0.65	0.20	0.50	1.00
❑6	0.65	0.20	0.50	1.00
❑7	0.75	0.20	0.50	1.00
❑8	0.75	0.20	0.50	1.00
❑9	0.75	0.20	0.50	1.00
❑10	0.75	0.20	0.50	1.00
❑11	0.75	0.20	0.50	1.00
❑12	0.75	0.20	0.50	1.00
❑13	0.75	0.20	0.50	1.00
❑14	1.00	0.20	0.50	1.00
❑15, The Magic Book	1.00	0.20	0.50	1.00
❑16	1.00	0.20	0.50	1.00
❑17	1.00	0.20	0.50	1.00
❑18, Marvel begins as publisher	1.00	0.20	0.50	1.00
❑19	1.00	0.20	0.50	1.00
❑20	1.00	0.20	0.50	1.00
❑21	1.00	0.20	0.50	1.00
❑22	1.00	0.20	0.50	1.00
❑23	1.00	0.20	0.50	1.00
❑24	1.00	0.20	0.50	1.00
❑25	1.00	0.20	0.50	1.00
❑26	1.00	0.20	0.50	1.00

MUPPET BABIES ADVENTURES
HARVEY

Value: Cover or less
❑1 ... 1.25

MUPPET BABIES BIG BOOK
HARVEY

Value: Cover or less
❑1 ... 1.95

MUPPETS TAKE MANHATTAN, THE
MARVEL

	ORIG	GOOD	FINE	N-MINT
❑1, Nov 84, movie Adaptation; Reprints Marvel Super Special #32	0.60	0.30	0.75	1.50
❑2, Dec 84, movie Adaptation; Reprints Marvel Super Special #32	0.60	0.30	0.75	1.50
❑3, Jan 85, movie Adaptation; Reprints Marvel Super Special #32	0.60	0.30	0.75	1.50

MURCIÉLAGA SHE-BAT
HEROIC

	ORIG	GOOD	FINE	N-MINT
❑1, b&w	1.50	0.59	1.48	2.95
❑2, Apr 93, A Lesson in Humility, b&w	2.95	0.59	1.48	2.95
❑3, Jul 93, b&w	2.95	0.59	1.48	2.95

MURDER
RENEGADE

Value: Cover or less
❑1, Aug 86, SD, SD (w), The Big Man; Queen of Hairy Flies .. 2.00

MURDER CAN BE FUN
SLAVE LABOR

	ORIG	GOOD	FINE	N-MINT
❑1, Feb 96, Hartford Circus Fire; Nashille Train Wreck, b&w	2.95	0.80	2.00	4.00
❑2, May 96, b&w	2.95	0.70	1.75	3.50
❑3, Aug 96, b&w	2.95	0.70	1.75	3.50
❑4, Nov 96, b&w	2.95	0.70	1.75	3.50
❑5, May 97, b&w	2.95	0.60	1.50	3.00
❑6, Jul 97, b&w	2.95	0.60	1.50	3.00
❑7, Sep 97, b&w	2.95	0.59	1.48	2.95
❑8, Jan 98, b&w	2.95	0.59	1.48	2.95
❑9, Apr 98, b&w	2.95	0.59	1.48	2.95
❑10, Aug 98, b&w	2.95	0.59	1.48	2.95
❑11, Nov 98, b&w	2.95	0.59	1.48	2.95
❑12, Feb 99, b&w	2.95	0.59	1.48	2.95

MURDER CITY
ETERNITY

Value: Cover or less
❑1, nn; b&w; Minute Movies.... 3.95

MURDER ME DEAD
EL CAPITÁN

Value: Cover or less

- ❑1 ... 2.95
- ❑2, Oct 00 ... 2.95
- ❑3 ... 2.95
- ❑4 ... 2.95
- ❑5 ... 2.95
- ❑6 ... 2.95
- ❑7 ... 2.95

While Innovation adapted Anne Rice's vampire novels, Millennium acquired the rights to her *Mummy, or Ramses the Damned.*

© 1992 Anne Rice (Millennium)

MUSIC COMICS
PERSONALITY

Value: Cover or less

- ❑2, full color ... 2.95
- ❑3, full color ... 2.95
- ❑4, b&w ... 2.50

MUSIC COMICS ON TOUR
PERSONALITY

Value: Cover or less
❑1, b&w; Beatles ... 2.95

MUTANT BOOK OF THE DEAD, THE
STARHEAD

Value: Cover or less
❑1, b&w; adult ... 2.50

MUTANT CHRONICLES
ACCLAIM

Value: Cover or less

- ❑1, May 96, Golgotha, Part 1; Golgotha, cardstock cover; polybagged with Doom Trooper card ... 2.95
- ❑2, Jun 96, Golgotha, Part 2, cardstock cover; polybagged with Doom Trooper card ... 2.95
- ❑3, Jul 96, Golgotha, Part 3, cardstock cover; polybagged with Doom Trooper card ... 2.95
- ❑4, Aug 96, Golgotha, Part 4, cardstock cover; polybagged with Doom Trooper card ... 2.95

MUTANT CHRONICLES SOURCEBOOK
ACCLAIM

Value: Cover or less
❑1, Sep 96, cardstock cover; polybagged with card ... 2.95

MUTANT MISADVENTURES OF CLOAK & DAGGER, THE
MARVEL

	ORIG	GOOD	FINE	N-MINT
❑1, Oct 88, Blind Salvation!, A: X-Factor	1.25	0.40	1.00	2.00
❑2, Dec 88	1.50	0.30	0.75	1.50
❑3, Feb 89	1.50	0.30	0.75	1.50
❑4, Apr 89, Inferno	1.50	0.30	0.75	1.50
❑5, Jun 89	1.50	0.30	0.75	1.50
❑6, Aug 89, Agony in Ecstasy	1.50	0.30	0.75	1.50
❑7, Oct 89	1.50	0.30	0.75	1.50
❑8, Dec 89	1.50	0.30	0.75	1.50
❑9, Jan 90, Acts of Vengeance, Avengers; Acts of Vengeance	2.50	0.50	1.25	2.50
❑10, Feb 90	1.50	0.30	0.75	1.50
❑11, Apr 90, The Marked Man!	1.50	0.30	0.75	1.50
❑12, Jun 90, The Devil You Know	1.50	0.30	0.75	1.50
❑13, Aug 90	1.50	0.30	0.75	1.50
❑14, Oct 90, Title changes to Cloak & Dagger	1.50	0.30	0.75	1.50
❑15, Dec 90	1.50	0.30	0.75	1.50
❑16, Feb 91	1.50	0.30	0.75	1.50
❑17, Apr 91, Spider-Man x-over	1.50	0.30	0.75	1.50
❑18, Jun 91, Infinity Gauntlet, Spider-Man, Ghost Rider	1.50	0.30	0.75	1.50
❑19, Aug 91, O: Cloak and Dagger, Final Issue	2.50	0.50	1.25	2.50

MUTANTS AND MISFITS
SILVERLINE

	ORIG	GOOD	FINE	N-MINT
❑1, full color	1.95	0.40	1.00	2.00

MUTANTS VS. ULTRAS: FIRST ENCOUNTERS
MALIBU

Value: Cover or less
❑1, Nov 95, reprints Prime vs. Hulk, Night Man vs. Wolverine, and Exiles vs. X-Men ... 6.95

MUTANT X
MARVEL

	ORIG	GOOD	FINE	N-MINT
❑1, Oct 98, In the End...As in the Beginning!, Mutant X, Iceman, Marvel Woman standing on cover; gatefold summary	2.99	0.60	1.50	3.00
❑1/A, alternate cover	2.99	0.80	2.00	4.00
❑2, Nov 98, gatefold summary	1.99	0.40	1.00	2.00
❑3, Dec 98, The Pack, gatefold summary	1.99	0.40	1.00	2.00
❑4, Jan 99, gatefold summary	1.99	0.40	1.00	2.00
❑5, Feb 99, A: Brute; A: Marvel Woman; A: Madelyne Pryor; A: Havok	1.99	0.40	1.00	2.00
❑6, Mar 99, A: Brute; A: Man-Spider; A: Madelyne Pryor	1.99	0.40	1.00	2.00
❑7, Apr 99, A: Green Goblin; A: Brute; A: Man-Spider; A: Havok	1.99	0.40	1.00	2.00
❑8, May 99, The Reign of the Queen	1.99	0.40	1.00	2.00
❑9, Jun 99, A: Mole Man; A: Elektra; A: Havok; A: Ben Grimm	1.99	0.40	1.00	2.00

	ORIG	GOOD	FINE	N-MINT
❑10, Jul 99, A: Magneto; A: X-Men	1.99	0.40	1.00	1.99
❑11, Aug 99	1.99	0.40	1.00	1.99
❑12, Sep 99	1.99	0.40	1.00	1.99
❑13, Sep 99	1.99	0.40	1.00	1.99
❑14, Nov 99	1.99	0.40	1.00	1.99
❑15, Dec 99	1.99	0.40	1.00	1.99
❑16, Jan 00	1.99	0.40	1.00	1.99
❑17	—	0.45	1.13	2.25
❑18	—	0.45	1.13	2.25
❑19	—	0.45	1.13	2.25
❑20	—	0.45	1.13	2.25
❑21	—	0.45	1.13	2.25
❑22	—	0.45	1.13	2.25
❑23	2.25	0.45	1.13	2.25
❑24	2.25	0.45	1.13	2.25
❑25	2.25	0.45	1.13	2.25
❑26, Dec 00, Long Day's Journey Through the Night!	2.25	0.45	1.13	2.25
❑27, Jan 01	2.25	0.45	1.13	2.25
❑28, Feb 01, The Hunted, Part 1	2.25	0.45	1.13	2.25
❑29, Mar 01, Logan's Running	2.25	0.45	1.13	2.25
❑30, Apr 01, Blame Canada!	2.25	0.45	1.13	2.25
❑31, May 01, You Say You Want a Resolution?	2.25	0.45	1.13	2.25
❑Anl 2001, The Key, A: Beyonder	2.99	0.60	1.50	2.99

MUTANT ZONE
AIRCEL

Value: Cover or less

❑1, Oct 91, Somewhere, Sometime..., b&w ... 2.50
❑2, b&w ... 2.50
❑3, b&w ... 2.50

MUTATIS
MARVEL

	ORIG	GOOD	FINE	N-MINT
❑1	2.25	0.50	1.25	2.50
❑2	2.25	0.50	1.25	2.50
❑3	2.25	0.50	1.25	2.50

MUTATOR
CHECKER

Value: Cover or less

❑1, Sum 98 ... 1.95
❑2 ... 1.95

MY GREATEST ADVENTURE
DC

	ORIG	GOOD	FINE	N-MINT
❑80, Jun 63, O: Robotman; O: Negative Man; O: Elastic-Girl; 1: The Doom Patrol	0.12	52.00	130.00	260.00
❑81, A: The Doom Patrol	0.12	25.00	62.50	125.00
❑82, A: The Doom Patrol	0.12	25.00	62.50	125.00
❑83, A: The Doom Patrol	0.12	25.00	62.50	125.00
❑84, A: The Doom Patrol	0.12	25.00	62.50	125.00
❑85, Feb 64, A: The Doom Patrol, Series continued in Doom Patrol (1st Series) #86	0.12	25.00	62.50	125.00

MY NAME IS CHAOS
DC

	ORIG	GOOD	FINE	N-MINT
❑1, The Song That Laid Waste To The Earth	4.95	1.00	2.50	5.00
❑2, Metamorphosis and Awakening	4.95	1.00	2.50	5.00
❑3, I Am Mars	4.95	1.00	2.50	5.00
❑4, The Power of One	4.95	1.00	2.50	5.00

MY NAME IS HOLOCAUST
DC

Value: Cover or less

❑1, May 95 ... 2.50
❑2, Jun 95 ... 2.50
❑3, Jul 95 ... 2.50
❑4, Aug 95 ... 2.50
❑5, Sep 95 ... 2.50

MY NAME IS MUD
INCOGNITO

Value: Cover or less

❑1, Incognito ... 2.50

MYRMIDON
RED HILLS PRODUCTIONS

Value: Cover or less

❑1, Jul 98, b&w ... 2.95

MY ROMANTIC ADVENTURES? (AVALON)
AVALON

Value: Cover or less

❑1, Love of a Lunatic!; Cupid is a Horse Named Bertram! ... 2.75

MYRON MOOSE FUNNIES
FANTAGRAPHICS

Value: Cover or less

❑1 ... 1.75
❑2 ... 1.75
❑3 ... 1.75

MYS-TECH WARS
MARVEL

Value: Cover or less

❑1, Mar 93, Strange Screams Of Death, Virtually all X-Men, Marvel UK characters appear ... 1.75
❑2, Apr 93, Virtually all X-Men, Marvel UK characters appear ... 1.75
❑3, May 93, Darkness Visible, Virtually all X-Men, Marvel UK characters appear ... 1.75
❑4, Jun 93, Virtually all X-Men, Marvel UK characters appear ... 1.75

MYSTERIES OF SCOTLAND YARD
MAGAZINE ENTERPRISES

	ORIG	GOOD	FINE	N-MINT
❑1, The Stone of the Dying Druid; The Trail of the Killing Kisses, Reprinted from Manhunt (5 Stories)	—	10.00	25.00	50.00

MYSTERIOUS SUSPENSE
CHARLTON

	ORIG	GOOD	FINE	N-MINT
❑1, Oct 68, SD, Question	0.12	8.00	20.00	40.00

MYSTERY DATE
LIGHTSPEED PRESS

Value: Cover or less

❑1, May 99, b&w ... 2.95

MYSTERY IN SPACE
DC

	ORIG	GOOD	FINE	N-MINT
❑53, Aug 59, CI, Adam Strange begins	0.10	250.00	625.00	1250.00
❑54, Sep 59, CI	0.10	88.00	220.00	440.00
❑55, Nov 59, CI	0.10	53.00	132.50	265.00
❑56, Dec 59, CI	0.10	35.00	87.50	175.00
❑57, Feb 60, CI	0.10	35.00	87.50	175.00
❑58, Mar 60, CI	0.10	35.00	87.50	175.00
❑59, May 60, CI	0.10	35.00	87.50	175.00
❑60, Jun 60, CI	0.10	35.00	87.50	175.00
❑61, Aug 60, CI, 1: Tornado Tyrant, Later becomes Red Tornado	0.10	24.00	60.00	120.00
❑62, Sep 60, CI	0.10	24.00	60.00	120.00
❑63, Nov 60, CI	0.10	24.00	60.00	120.00
❑64, Dec 60, CI	0.10	24.00	60.00	120.00
❑65, Feb 61, CI	0.10	24.00	60.00	120.00
❑66, Mar 61, CI, 1: The Star Rovers	0.10	24.00	60.00	120.00
❑67, May 61, CI	0.10	24.00	60.00	120.00
❑68, Jun 61, CI	0.10	24.00	60.00	120.00
❑69, Aug 61, CI	0.10	24.00	60.00	120.00
❑70, Sep 61, CI	0.10	24.00	60.00	120.00
❑71, Nov 61, CI	0.10	24.00	60.00	120.00
❑72, Dec 61, CI	0.12	19.00	47.50	95.00
❑73, Feb 62, CI	0.12	19.00	47.50	95.00
❑74, Mar 62, CI	0.12	19.00	47.50	95.00
❑75, May 62, CI, A: Justice League of America	0.12	28.00	70.00	140.00
❑76, Jun 62, CI	0.12	16.00	40.00	80.00
❑77, Aug 62, CI	0.12	16.00	40.00	80.00
❑78, Sep 62, CI	0.12	16.00	40.00	80.00
❑79, Nov 62, CI	0.12	16.00	40.00	80.00
❑80, Dec 62, CI	0.12	16.00	40.00	80.00
❑81, Feb 63, CI	0.12	12.00	30.00	60.00
❑82, Mar 63, CI	0.12	12.00	30.00	60.00
❑83, May 63, CI	0.12	12.00	30.00	60.00
❑84, Jun 63, CI	0.12	12.00	30.00	60.00
❑85, Aug 63, CI	0.12	12.00	30.00	60.00
❑86, Sep 63, CI	0.12	12.00	30.00	60.00
❑87, Nov 63, CI; MA, The Super-Brain of Adam Strange; Amazing thefts of the I.Q. Gang, A: Hawkman	0.12	25.00	62.50	125.00
❑88, Dec 63, CI; MA, The Robot Wraith of Rann; Topsy-Turvy Day in Midway City, A: Hawkman	0.12	18.00	45.00	90.00
❑89, Feb 64, CI; MA, The Super-Motorized Menace; Siren of the Space Ark, A: Hawkman	0.12	18.00	45.00	90.00
❑90, Mar 64, CI; MA, Planets in Peril, A: Hawkman	0.12	18.00	45.00	90.00
❑91, May 64, CI	0.12	5.20	13.00	26.00
❑92, Jun 64	0.12	5.20	13.00	26.00
❑93, Aug 64	0.12	5.20	13.00	26.00
❑94, Sep 64	0.12	5.20	13.00	26.00
❑95, Nov 64	0.12	5.20	13.00	26.00
❑96, Dec 64	0.12	5.20	13.00	26.00
❑97, Feb 65	0.12	5.20	13.00	26.00
❑98, Mar 65	0.12	5.20	13.00	26.00
❑99, May 65	0.12	5.20	13.00	26.00
❑100, Jun 65, The Death Of Alanna; The Planet Collectors	0.12	5.20	13.00	26.00
❑101, Aug 65	0.12	5.20	13.00	26.00
❑102, Sep 65	0.12	5.20	13.00	26.00
❑103, Nov 65	0.12	5.20	13.00	26.00
❑104, Dec 65	0.12	2.40	6.00	12.00
❑105, Feb 66	0.12	2.40	6.00	12.00
❑106, Mar 66	0.12	2.40	6.00	12.00
❑107, May 66	0.12	2.40	6.00	12.00
❑108, Jun 66	0.12	2.40	6.00	12.00
❑109, Aug 66	0.12	2.40	6.00	12.00
❑110, Sep 66, Original series ends	0.12	2.40	6.00	12.00
❑111, Sep 80, Series begins again	0.50	1.00	2.50	5.00
❑112, Oct 80	0.50	1.00	2.50	5.00
❑113, Nov 80	0.50	1.00	2.50	5.00
❑114, Dec 80	0.50	1.00	2.50	5.00
❑115, Jan 81	0.50	1.00	2.50	5.00
❑116, Feb 81	0.50	1.00	2.50	5.00
❑117, Mar 81, Final Issue	0.50	1.00	2.50	5.00

MYSTERY MAN, THE
SLAVE LABOR

Value: Cover or less

❑1, Jul 88, b&w ... 1.75
❑2, Nov 88, b&w ... 1.75

ORIG GOOD FINE N-MINT

MYSTERY MEN MOVIE ADAPTATION
DARK HORSE

Value: Cover or less

❏1, Jul 99 .... 2.95
❏2, Aug 99 .... 2.95

MYSTERYMEN STORIES
BOB BURDEN PRODUCTIONS

Value: Cover or less

❏1, Sum 96, When Stalks The Strangler..., b&w; prose story with illustrations 5.00

MYSTIC (CROSSGEN)
CROSSGEN

Value: Cover or less

❏1, Jul 00 .... 2.95
❏2, Aug 00 .... 2.95
❏3, Sep 00 .... 2.95
❏4, Oct 00 .... 2.95
❏5 .... 2.95
❏6 .... 2.95
❏7 .... 2.95
❏8 .... 2.95
❏9 .... 2.95
❏10 .... 2.95
❏11 .... 2.95
❏12 .... 2.95
❏13 .... 2.95
❏14 .... 2.95

MYSTIC EDGE
ANTARCTIC

Value: Cover or less

❏1, Oct 98, 1: Kyleen; 1: Evron; 1: Ena; 1: Risa; 1: Symattra 2.95

MYSTIC TRIGGER, THE
MAELSTROM

Value: Cover or less

❏1, Tales of the Galactic Forces preview 3.25

MYSTIQUE & SABRETOOTH
MARVEL

Value: Cover or less

❏1, Dec 96, Old Sins Cast Long Shadows 1.95
❏2, Jan 97, Torture 1.95
❏3, Feb 97, Willing Victims 1.95
❏4, Mar 97, Dead Ends 1.95

MYST: THE BOOK OF THE BLACK SHIPS
DARK HORSE

	ORIG	GOOD	FINE	N-MINT
❏0, Passages, no cover price; American Entertainment Exclusive Edition; based on video game	—	0.30	0.75	1.50
❏1, Aug 97, The Joining, based on video game	2.95	0.59	1.48	2.95
❏2	2.95	0.59	1.48	2.95
❏3	2.95	0.59	1.48	2.95
❏4	2.95	0.59	1.48	2.95

MYTH
FYGMOK

Value: Cover or less

❏1, Dec 96, b&w; wraparound cover 2.95
❏2, Feb 97, b&w 2.95

MYTHADVENTURES
WARP

	ORIG	GOOD	FINE	N-MINT
❏1, Mar 84, Warp publishes	1.50	0.40	1.00	2.00
❏2, Jun 84	1.50	0.30	0.75	1.50
❏3, Sep 84	1.50	0.30	0.75	1.50
❏4, Dec 84	1.50	0.30	0.75	1.50
❏5, Mar 85	1.50	0.30	0.75	1.50

Adam Strange was an Earthman transported to the planet Rann, which orbited Alpha Centauri, by a Zeta beam.

© 1959 National Periodical Publications

	ORIG	GOOD	FINE	N-MINT
❏6, Jun 85	1.50	0.30	0.75	1.50
❏7, Sep 85	1.50	0.30	0.75	1.50
❏8, Dec 85, PF, PF (w)	1.50	0.30	0.75	1.50
❏9, Mar 86	1.50	0.30	0.75	1.50
❏10, Apple begins as publisher	1.50	0.30	0.75	1.50
❏11	1.50	0.30	0.75	1.50
❏12, Final Issue	1.75	0.30	0.75	1.50

MYTH CONCEPTIONS
APPLE

Value: Cover or less

❏1, Nov 87 .... 1.75
❏2, Jan 88, We're off to be the Wizard 1.75
❏3, Mar 88 .... 1.75
❏4, May 88 .... 1.95
❏5, Jul 88 .... 1.95
❏6, Sep 88 .... 1.95
❏7, Nov 88 .... 1.95
❏8, Jan 89 .... 1.95

MYTHIC HEROES
CHAPTERHOUSE PRESS

Value: Cover or less

❏1, Sep 96, b&w 2.50

MYTH MAKER (ROBERT E. HOWARD'S...)
CROSS PLAINS

Value: Cover or less

❏1, Jun 99, nn 6.95

MYTHOGRAPHY
BARDIC PRESS

Value: Cover or less

❏1, Sep 96 .... 3.95
❏2, Feb 97, Oak's Daughter; Mystery Date 3.95
❏3, Apr 97 .... 3.95
❏4, Jun 97 .... 4.25
❏5, Sep 97 .... 4.25
❏6, Nov 97, Barr Girls story 3.95
❏7, Feb 98, One in a Million 4.25
❏8, May 98 .... 3.95

MYTHOS
WONDER COMIX

	ORIG	GOOD	FINE	N-MINT
❏1, Jan 87, Zakaya!	1.50	0.40	1.00	2.00
❏2, Apr 87	1.50	0.40	1.00	2.00

MYTHOS: THE FINAL TOUR
DC

Value: Cover or less

❏1, Dec 96, Shut Heaven, prestige format 5.95
❏2, Jan 97, Uncut, prestige format 5.95
❏3, Feb 97, prestige format 5.95

N

NADESICO
CPM MANGA

Value: Cover or less

❏1 .... 2.95
❏2 .... 2.95
❏3 .... 2.95
❏4 .... 2.95
❏5 .... 2.95
❏6 .... 2.95
❏7 .... 2.95
❏8 .... 2.95
❏9 .... 2.95
❏10 .... 2.95
❏11 .... 2.95
❏12 .... 2.95
❏13 .... 2.95
❏14 .... 2.95
❏15 .... 2.95
❏16 .... 2.95
❏17 .... 2.95
❏18 .... 2.95
❏19 .... 2.95
❏20 .... 2.95
❏21 .... 2.95
❏22 .... 2.95
❏23 .... 2.95
❏24 .... 2.95
❏25 .... 2.95
❏26 .... 2.95

NAIVE INTER-DIMENSIONAL COMMANDO KOALAS
ECLIPSE

Value: Cover or less

❏1, Oct 86, A: Adolescent Radioactive Black Belt Hamsters, b&w 1.50

NAKED ANGELS
EROS

Value: Cover or less

❏1 .... 2.95
❏2, May 96 .... 2.95

NAKED EYE (S.A. KING'S...)
ANTARCTIC

Value: Cover or less

❏1, Dec 94, b&w 2.75
❏2, Feb 95, Manta Ray Country; Crippled Inside, b&w 2.75
❏3, Apr 95, Sex, Drugs and E.L.O; Enquiring Mind, b&w 2.75

NAMELESS, THE
IMAGE

Value: Cover or less

❏1, May 97 .... 2.95
❏2, Jun 97 .... 2.95
❏3, Jul 97 .... 2.95
❏4, Aug 97 .... 2.95
❏5, Sep 97 .... 2.95

NAMES OF MAGIC
VERTIGO

Value: Cover or less

❏1, Feb 01, Invocation 2.50
❏2, Mar 01, Faith 2.50
❏3, Apr 01, Secrets 2.50
❏4, May 01, Flight 2.50
❏5, Jun 01 .... 2.50

NAMOR, THE SUB-MARINER
M

	ORIG	GOOD	FINE	N-MINT
❏1, Apr 90, JBy, JBy (w), Purpose!, O: Sub-Mariner	1.00	0.60	1.50	3.00
❏2, May 90, JBy, JBy (w), Eagle's Wing And Lion's Claw!	1.00	0.40	1.00	2.00
❏3, Jun 90, JBy	1.00	0.40	1.00	2.00
❏4, Jul 90, JBy	1.00	0.40	1.00	2.00
❏5, Aug 90, JBy	1.00	0.40	1.00	2.00
❏6, Sep 90, JBy	1.00	0.35	0.88	1.75
❏7, Oct 90, JBy	1.00	0.35	0.88	1.75
❏8, Nov 90, JBy	1.00	0.35	0.88	1.75
❏9, Dec 90, JBy	1.00	0.35	0.88	1.75
❏10, Jan 91, JBy	1.00	0.35	0.88	1.75
❏11, Feb 91, JBy	1.00	0.35	0.88	1.75
❏12, Mar 91, JBy, A: Captain America; A: Human Torch, Giant-size; Return of The Invaders	1.00	0.40	1.00	2.00
❏13, Apr 91, JBy	1.00	0.30	0.75	1.50
❏14, May 91, JBy	1.00	0.30	0.75	1.50

	ORIG	GOOD	FINE	N-MINT
❑15, Jun 91, JBy	1.00	0.30	0.75	1.50
❑16, Jul 91, JBy	1.00	0.30	0.75	1.50
❑17, Aug 91, JBy	1.00	0.30	0.75	1.50
❑18, Sep 91, JBy	1.00	0.30	0.75	1.50
❑19, Oct 91, JBy	1.00	0.30	0.75	1.50
❑20, Nov 91, JBy	1.00	0.30	0.75	1.50
❑21, Dec 91, JBy	1.00	0.30	0.75	1.50
❑22, Jan 92, JBy	1.00	0.30	0.75	1.50
❑23, Feb 92, JBy, A: Wolverine, Iron Fist returns	1.25	0.30	0.75	1.50
❑24, Mar 92, JBy, Wolverine; Namor fights Wolverine	1.25	0.30	0.75	1.50
❑25, Apr 92, JBy, A: Wolverine	1.25	0.30	0.75	1.50
❑26, May 92, 1st Jae Lee art	1.25	0.50	1.25	2.50
❑27, Jun 92	1.25	0.40	1.00	2.00
❑28, Jul 92, A: Iron Fist	1.25	0.40	1.00	2.00
❑29, Aug 92	1.25	0.50	1.25	2.50
❑30, Sep 92	1.25	0.50	1.25	2.50
❑31, Oct 92	1.25	0.50	1.25	2.50
❑32, Nov 92	1.25	0.50	1.25	2.50
❑33, Dec 92	1.25	0.40	1.00	2.00
❑34, Jan 93	1.25	0.40	1.00	2.00
❑35, Feb 93	1.25	0.40	1.00	2.00
❑36, Mar 93, Killing Time	1.25	0.40	1.00	2.00
❑37, Apr 93, foil cover	2.00	0.40	1.00	2.00
❑38, May 93	1.25	0.30	0.75	1.50
❑39, Jun 93	1.25	0.30	0.75	1.50
❑40, Jul 93	1.25	0.30	0.75	1.50
❑41, Aug 93	1.25	0.30	0.75	1.50
❑42, Sep 93, A: Stingray	1.25	0.30	0.75	1.50
❑43, Oct 93, A: Stingray	1.25	0.30	0.75	1.50
❑44, Nov 93	1.25	0.30	0.75	1.50
❑45, Dec 93	1.25	0.30	0.75	1.50
❑46, Jan 94, Starblast	1.25	0.30	0.75	1.50
❑47, Feb 94, Starblast, Part 5, Starblast	1.25	0.30	0.75	1.50
❑48, Mar 94, Starblast, Part 9, Starblast	1.25	0.30	0.75	1.50
❑49, Apr 94	1.25	0.30	0.75	1.50
❑50, May 94, Giant-size	1.75	0.45	1.13	2.25
❑50/SC, May 94, foil cover; Giant-size	2.95	0.60	1.50	3.00
❑51, Jun 94	1.75	0.30	0.75	1.50
❑52, Jul 94	1.50	0.30	0.75	1.50
❑53, Aug 94	1.50	0.30	0.75	1.50
❑54, Sep 94, 1: Llyron	1.50	0.30	0.75	1.50
❑55, Oct 94	1.50	0.30	0.75	1.50
❑56, Nov 94	1.50	0.30	0.75	1.50
❑57, Dec 94	1.50	0.30	0.75	1.50
❑58, Jan 95, V: Avengers	1.50	0.30	0.75	1.50
❑59, Feb 95	1.95	0.30	0.75	1.50
❑60, Mar 95	1.95	0.30	0.75	1.50
❑61, Apr 95, Atlantis Rising, Part 1	1.50	0.30	0.75	1.50
❑62, May 95, Final Issue	1.50	0.30	0.75	1.50
❑Anl 1, Subterranean Wars; Subterranean Odyssey, Part 3	2.00	0.40	1.00	2.00
❑Anl 2, Return of the Defenders, Part 3, Defenders	2.25	0.45	1.13	2.25
❑Anl 3, trading card	2.95	0.59	1.48	2.95
❑Anl 4	2.95	0.59	1.48	2.95

NANNY AND THE PROFESSOR
DELL

	ORIG	GOOD	FINE	N-MINT
❑1, Aug 70, Photo cover; based on TV show	0.15	2.80	7.00	14.00
❑2, Oct 70	0.15	1.80	4.50	9.00

NANOSOUP
MILLENNIUM

Value: Cover or less

❑1, b&w; wraparound cover ... 2.95

NARCOLEPSY DREAMS
SLAVE LABOR

Value: Cover or less

❑1, Feb 95, Big; Up and Down Career ... 2.95

❑2, Aug 95, 1973; Shakeytown ... 2.95

NARD N' PAT
CARTOONISTS' CO-OP PRESS

	ORIG	GOOD	FINE	N-MINT
❑1, b&w	0.50	0.60	1.50	3.00

NASCAR ADVENTURES
VORTEX

	ORIG	GOOD	FINE	N-MINT
❑1, DH, Welcome Back Fred; Outpost: Apocalypse, regular cover; Fred Lorenzen	2.00	0.59	1.48	2.95
❑2, Richard Petty	2.00	0.50	1.25	2.50
❑5, Ernie Irvan	2.00	0.50	1.25	2.50
❑7	2.00	0.50	1.25	2.50

NASH
IMAGE

Value: Cover or less

❑1, Jul 99, regular cover ... 2.95

❑1/A, Jul 99, Outpost: Apocalypse, Photo cover ... 2.95

❑1/B, Jul 99, Outpost: Apocalypse, no cover price ... 2.95

❑2, Jul 99, regular cover ... 2.95

❑2/A, Jul 99, Photo cover ... 2.95

❑Ash 1, Jul 99, regular cover; Preview Book ... 2.50

❑Ash 1/SC, Jul 99, Photo cover ... 2.50

NASTI: MONSTER HUNTER
SCHISM

	ORIG	GOOD	FINE	N-MINT
❑1, Don't Go Changin'...Just Die!, 1: Nasti, b&w	2.50	0.50	1.25	2.50
❑1/Aut, Don't Go Changin'...Just Die!, 1: Nasti	2.50	0.60	1.50	3.00
❑2, You Must Be..., b&w	2.50	0.50	1.25	2.50
❑3, Organized Chaos; Bru-Hed: Fast Food for Thought, b&w	2.50	0.50	1.25	2.50
❑Ash 1/LE, nn; b&w; no cover price; preview of upcoming comic book on newsprint	—	0.20	0.50	1.00

NATHANIEL DUSK
DC

	ORIG	GOOD	FINE	N-MINT
❑1, Feb 84, GC, Lovers Die At Dusk, Part 1, 1: Nathaniel Dusk	1.25	0.30	0.75	1.50
❑2, Mar 84, GC, Lovers Die at Dusk, Part 2	1.25	0.30	0.75	1.50
❑3, Apr 84, GC	1.25	0.30	0.75	1.50
❑4, May 84, GC	1.25	0.30	0.75	1.50

NATHANIEL DUSK II
DC

Value: Cover or less

❑1, Oct 85, GC ... 2.00

❑2, Nov 85, GC ... 2.00

❑3, Dec 85, GC ... 2.00

❑4, Jan 86, GC ... 2.00

NATHAN NEVER
DARK HORSE

Value: Cover or less

❑1, Mar 99 ... 4.95

❑2, Apr 99 ... 4.95

❑3, May 99 ... 4.95

❑4, Jun 99 ... 4.95

❑5, Jul 99 ... 4.95

❑6, Aug 99 ... 4.95

NATIONAL COMICS (2ND SERIES)
DC

	ORIG	GOOD	FINE	N-MINT
❑1, May 99, MWa (w), Fair Play, A: Mr. Terrific; A: Flash, Justice Society Returns	1.99	0.40	1.00	2.00

NATION OF SNITCHES, A
DC

Value: Cover or less

❑1, nn; One-Shot ... 4.95

NATURAL INQUIRER
FANTAGRAPHICS

Value: Cover or less

❑1, b&w ... 2.00

NATURAL SELECTION, THE
ATOM

Value: Cover or less

❑1, Jan 98, b&w ... 2.95

❑2, Feb 98, b&w ... 2.95

NATURE OF THE BEAST
CALIBER

Value: Cover or less

❑1, b&w ... 2.95

❑2, b&w ... 2.95

NAUGHTY BITS
FANTAGRAPHICS

	ORIG	GOOD	FINE	N-MINT
❑1, Mar 91	2.00	1.40	3.50	7.00
❑1-2, 2nd Printing	2.00	0.50	1.25	2.50
❑2	2.00	1.00	2.50	5.00
❑3	2.00	0.80	2.00	4.00
❑4	2.00	0.75	1.88	3.75
❑5	2.00	0.75	1.88	3.75
❑6, Aug 92	2.50	0.60	1.50	3.00
❑7	2.50	0.60	1.50	3.00
❑8	2.50	0.60	1.50	3.00
❑9	2.50	0.60	1.50	3.00
❑10	2.50	0.60	1.50	3.00
❑11, Jan 94	2.50	0.50	1.25	2.50
❑12, Apr 94	2.50	0.50	1.25	2.50
❑13, Jul 94	2.50	0.59	1.48	2.95
❑14, Oct 94	2.50	0.59	1.48	2.95
❑15, Feb 95	2.50	0.59	1.48	2.95
❑16	2.50	0.59	1.48	2.95
❑17	2.50	0.59	1.48	2.95
❑18, Jan 96	2.95	0.59	1.48	2.95
❑19	2.95	0.59	1.48	2.95
❑20, Aug 96	2.95	0.59	1.48	2.95
❑21, Nov 96, Bitchy Bitch & Bitsy Bitch: Fall-out; Bitchy Butch: That Time of the Year.	2.95	0.59	1.48	2.95
❑22, Mar 97	2.95	0.59	1.48	2.95
❑23, Jun 97	2.95	0.59	1.48	2.95
❑29, Jul 99	2.95	0.59	1.48	2.95

NAUSICAÄ OF THE VALLEY OF WIND PART 1
VIZ

Value: Cover or less

❑1 ... 3.25

❑2 ... 3.25

❑3 ... 3.25

❑4 ... 3.25

❑5 ... 3.25

❑6 ... 3.25

❑7 ... 3.25

NAUSICAÄ OF THE VALLEY OF WIND PART 2
VIZ

Value: Cover or less

Issue	Value
❑1	2.95
❑2	2.95
❑3	2.95
❑4	3.25

NAUSICAÄ OF THE VALLEY OF WIND PART 3
VIZ

Value: Cover or less

Issue	Value
❑1	3.95
❑2	3.95
❑3	3.95

NAUSICAÄ OF THE VALLEY OF WIND PART 4
VIZ

Value: Cover or less

Issue	Value
❑1	2.75
❑2	2.75
❑3	2.75
❑4	2.75
❑5	2.75
❑6	2.75

NAUSICAÄ OF THE VALLEY OF WIND PART 5
VIZ

Value: Cover or less

Issue	Value
❑1	2.75
❑2	2.75
❑3	2.75
❑4	2.75
❑5	2.75
❑6	2.75
❑7	2.95
❑8	2.95

NAUTILUS
SHANDA FANTASY ARTS

Value: Cover or less

Issue	Value
❑1, May 99, b&w	2.95

NAZRAT
IMPERIAL

Issue	ORIG	GOOD	FINE	N-MINT
❑1	1.80	0.40	1.00	2.00
❑2	1.80	0.40	1.00	2.00
❑3	1.80	0.40	1.00	2.00
❑4	1.95	0.40	1.00	2.00
❑5	1.95	0.40	1.00	2.00

NAZZ, THE
DC

Value: Cover or less

Issue	Value
❑1, Oct 90, BT, Michael's Book	4.95
❑2, Nov 90, BT	4.95
❑3, Dec 90, BT	4.95
❑4, Jan 91, BT	4.95

NBC SATURDAY MORNING COMICS
HARVEY

Issue	ORIG	GOOD	FINE	N-MINT
❑1, Sep 91, Wish Kid...Captain Mayhem!; Star Search (activity), Toys "R" Us give-away; Geoffrey Giraffe app	1.25	0.30	0.75	1.50

NEAR MYTHS
RIP OFF

Value: Cover or less

Issue	Value
❑1, Jul 90, b&w	2.50

NEAR TO NOW
FANDOM HOUSE

Value: Cover or less

Issue	Value
❑1, Born to Swallow; Your Sky's the Limit, b&w	2.00
❑2, b&w	2.00

NEAT STUFF
FANTAGRAPHICS

Issue	ORIG	GOOD	FINE	N-MINT
❑1	2.50	1.00	2.50	5.00
❑1-, 2nd Printing	—	0.50	1.25	2.50
❑1-2, 2nd Printing	2.50	0.50	1.25	2.50
❑2	2.50	0.80	2.00	4.00
❑2-2, 2nd Printing	2.50	0.50	1.25	2.50
❑3	2.50	0.70	1.75	3.50
❑3-2, 2nd Printing	2.50	0.50	1.25	2.50
❑4	2.50	0.60	1.50	3.00
❑4-2, 2nd Printing	2.50	0.50	1.25	2.50
❑5, Dec 86	2.25	0.50	1.25	2.50
❑6, Apr 87, all Bradley issue	2.25	0.50	1.25	2.50
❑7, Aug 87	2.25	0.50	1.25	2.50
❑8, Dec 87	2.25	0.50	1.25	2.50
❑9	2.50	0.50	1.25	2.50
❑10	2.50	0.50	1.25	2.50
❑11, Nov 88	2.50	0.50	1.25	2.50
❑12	2.50	0.50	1.25	2.50
❑13	2.50	0.50	1.25	2.50
❑14	2.50	0.50	1.25	2.50
❑15	2.50	0.50	1.25	2.50

NECROMANCER
ANARCHY

Value: Cover or less

Issue	Value
❑1, Strange Eons, b&w	3.50
❑1/Dlx, Strange Eons, Deluxe edition	3.50
❑2, b&w	3.50
❑2/Dlx, Deluxe edition	3.50
❑3, Television Snow, b&w	3.50
❑3/Dlx, Television Snow, Deluxe edition	3.50
❑4, b&w	3.50
❑4/Dlx, Deluxe edition	3.50

NECROMANCER (2ND SERIES)
ANARCHY

Value: Cover or less

Issue	Value
❑1, b&w	2.50
❑2, b&w	2.50
❑3, b&w	2.50
❑4, b&w	2.50

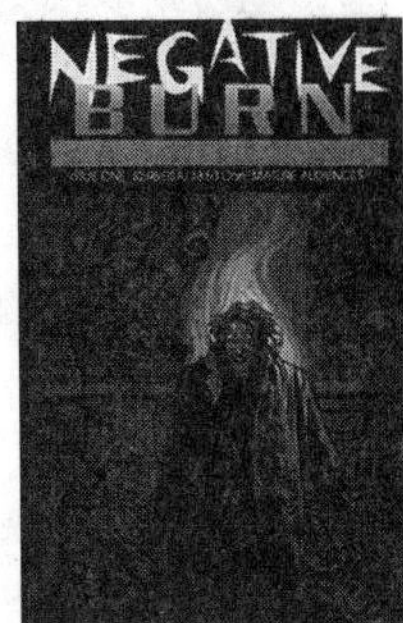

Bob Burden's Flaming Carrot made an appearance in *Negative Burn* #1.

© 1986 Caliber

NECROPOLIS
FLEETWAY

Value: Cover or less

Issue	Value
❑1, Judge Dredd	2.95
❑2, Judge Dredd	2.95
❑3, Judge Dredd	2.95
❑4	2.95
❑5	2.95
❑6	2.95
❑7	2.95
❑8	2.95
❑9	2.95

NECROSCOPE
MALIBU

Issue	ORIG	GOOD	FINE	N-MINT
❑1, Oct 92	2.95	0.60	1.50	3.00
❑1-2, Dec 92, 2nd Printing; Hologram cover	2.95	0.59	1.48	2.95
❑2, Dec 92, bagged with tattoo	2.95	0.59	1.48	2.95
❑3, Feb 93	2.95	0.59	1.48	2.95
❑4	2.95	0.59	1.48	2.95
❑5	2.95	0.59	1.48	2.95

NECROSCOPE BOOK II: WAMPHYRI
MALIBU

Value: Cover or less

Issue	Value
❑1	2.95
❑2, Nov 94, Succulents	2.95
❑3, Jan 94	2.95
❑4	2.95
❑5	2.95

NEFARISMO
EROS COMIX

Value: Cover or less

Issue	Value
❑5, May 95	2.95

NEGATIVE BURN
CALIBER

Issue	ORIG	GOOD	FINE	N-MINT
❑1, Kilroy is Here; The Flaming Carrot, b&w; Flaming Carrot	2.95	0.80	2.00	4.00
❑2, b&w	2.95	0.80	2.00	4.00
❑3, Apr 01, A: Bone, b&w	2.95	0.80	2.00	4.00
❑4, b&w	2.95	0.80	2.00	4.00
❑5, b&w	2.95	0.80	2.00	4.00
❑6, b&w	2.95	0.80	2.00	4.00
❑7, b&w	2.95	0.80	2.00	4.00
❑8, b&w	2.95	0.80	2.00	4.00
❑9, AMo (w), b&w	2.95	0.80	2.00	4.00
❑10, AMo (w), b&w	2.95	0.80	2.00	4.00
❑11, BB (w), b&w	2.95	0.80	2.00	4.00
❑12, b&w	2.95	0.80	2.00	4.00
❑13, NG (w); AMo (w); BMB (w), A: Strangers in Paradise, b&w	3.95	1.30	3.25	6.50
❑14, b&w	2.95	0.79	1.98	3.95
❑15, BB (w), Mr. Trianglehead: Canto 5; Mr. Mamoulian: Moving Things About, b&w..	2.95	0.79	1.98	3.95
❑16, b&w	2.95	0.79	1.98	3.95
❑17, b&w	2.95	0.79	1.98	3.95
❑18, b&w	2.95	0.79	1.98	3.95
❑19, b&w	2.95	0.79	1.98	3.95
❑20, b&w	2.95	0.79	1.98	3.95
❑21, b&w	2.95	0.79	1.98	3.95
❑22, b&w	2.95	0.79	1.98	3.95
❑23, b&w	2.95	0.79	1.98	3.95
❑24, b&w	2.95	0.79	1.98	3.95
❑25, b&w	3.95	0.79	1.98	3.95
❑26, b&w	3.95	0.79	1.98	3.95
❑27, b&w	3.95	0.79	1.98	3.95
❑28, b&w; Dusty Star	3.95	0.79	1.98	3.95
❑29, b&w	3.95	0.79	1.98	3.95
❑30, b&w	3.95	0.79	1.98	3.95
❑31, b&w	3.95	0.79	1.98	3.95
❑32, b&w	3.95	0.79	1.98	3.95
❑33, b&w	3.95	0.79	1.98	3.95
❑34, b&w	3.95	0.79	1.98	3.95
❑35, b&w	3.95	0.79	1.98	3.95
❑36, b&w	3.95	0.79	1.98	3.95
❑37, Dusty Star: Where the Chips Fall; Mr. Mamoulian: A Really Go, b&w; Dusty Star	3.95	0.79	1.98	3.95
❑38	3.95	0.79	1.98	3.95
❑39	3.95	0.79	1.98	3.95
❑40	3.95	0.79	1.98	3.95
❑41	3.95	0.79	1.98	3.95

	ORIG	GOOD	FINE	N-MINT
❑42	3.95	0.79	1.98	3.95
❑43	3.95	0.79	1.98	3.95
❑44	3.95	0.79	1.98	3.95
❑45	3.95	0.79	1.98	3.95
❑46	3.95	0.79	1.98	3.95
❑47	3.95	0.79	1.98	3.95
❑48	4.95	0.99	2.47	4.95
❑49	4.95	0.99	2.47	4.95
❑50, Final Issue	6.95	1.39	3.47	6.95

NEIL & BUZZ IN SPACE AND TIME
FANTAGRAPHICS

Value: Cover or less

❑1, Apr 89, b&w 2.00

NEIL THE HORSE COMICS AND STORIES
AARDVARK-VANAHEIM

	ORIG	GOOD	FINE	N-MINT
❑1, Feb 83	1.70	0.50	1.25	2.50
❑2, Apr 83	1.40	0.40	1.00	2.00
❑3, Jun 83	1.40	0.40	1.00	2.00
❑4, Aug 83	1.40	0.40	1.00	2.00
❑5, Nov 83	1.40	0.40	1.00	2.00
❑6, Feb 84	1.70	0.40	1.00	2.00
❑7, Apr 84	1.70	0.40	1.00	2.00
❑8, Jun 84	1.70	0.40	1.00	2.00
❑9, Sep 84	1.70	0.40	1.00	2.00
❑10, Dec 84	1.70	0.40	1.00	2.00
❑11, Apr 85, Title changes to Neil the Horse	2.00	0.40	1.00	2.00
❑12, Jun 85	2.00	0.40	1.00	2.00
❑13, Dec 86	2.00	0.40	1.00	2.00
❑14, Jul 88, giant	3.00	0.60	1.50	3.00
❑15, Aug 88, giant	3.00	0.60	1.50	3.00

NEMESISTER
CHEEKY PRESS

	ORIG	GOOD	FINE	N-MINT
❑1, Apr 97, The Job, b&w; cardstock cover	2.95	0.59	1.48	2.95
❑2, Jun 97, Jesusa!, b&w; cardstock cover	2.95	0.59	1.48	2.95
❑3, Sep 97, Hemi, b&w; cardstock cover	2.95	0.59	1.48	2.95
❑3/Ash, Hemi, ashcan edition	—	0.10	0.25	0.50
❑4, Nov 97, b&w; cardstock cover	2.95	0.59	1.48	2.95
❑5	2.95	0.59	1.48	2.95
❑6	2.95	0.59	1.48	2.95
❑7	2.95	0.59	1.48	2.95
❑8	2.95	0.59	1.48	2.95
❑9	2.95	0.59	1.48	2.95

NEMESIS THE WARLOCK (FLEETWAY/QUALITY)
FLEETWAY

Value: Cover or less

❑1, b&w 1.95
❑2, b&w 1.95
❑3, b&w 1.95
❑4, Nemesis the Warlock, Book II, b&w 1.95
❑5, b&w 1.95
❑6, b&w 1.95
❑7, b&w 1.95
❑8, b&w 1.95
❑9, BT, The Vengeance Of Thoth, b&w 1.95
❑10, b&w 1.95
❑11, b&w 1.95
❑12, b&w 1.95
❑13, b&w 1.95
❑14, Torquemada God, O: Torquemada, b&w 1.95
❑15, b&w 1.95
❑16, b&w 1.95
❑17, b&w 1.95
❑18, b&w 1.95
❑19, b&w 1.95

NEO
EXCALIBUR

Value: Cover or less

❑1, b&w 1.50

NEOMEN
SLAVE LABOR

Value: Cover or less

❑1, Oct 87, The Dark Age, no indicia 1.75
❑2, Jan 88 .... 1.75

NEON CITY
INNOVATION

Value: Cover or less

❑1, b&w 2.25

NEON CITY: AFTER THE FALL
INNOVATION

Value: Cover or less

❑1, Fallout, b&w 2.50

NEON CYBER
IMAGE

	ORIG	GOOD	FINE	N-MINT
❑1, Aug 99, Alliance	2.50	0.50	1.25	2.50
❑1/SC, Aug 99, Alliance, alternate cover	2.50	1.00	2.50	5.00
❑2, Sep 99, Defiance, Man facing giant on cover	2.50	0.50	1.25	2.50
❑2/SC, Sep 99, Defiance, alternate cover	2.50	0.50	1.25	2.50
❑3, Oct 99, Retaliation, alternate cover	2.50	0.50	1.25	2.50
❑4, Dec 99, Betrayal	2.50	0.50	1.25	2.50
❑5	2.50	0.50	1.25	2.50
❑6, Mar 00, Ascension	2.50	0.50	1.25	2.50
❑7	2.50	0.50	1.25	2.50
❑8, Jun 00, Redemption	2.50	0.50	1.25	2.50

NEON GENESIS EVANGELION BOOK 1
VIZ

Value: Cover or less

❑1/A 2.95
❑1/B, Special collector's edition; printed in Japanese style (back to front) 2.95
❑2/A 2.95
❑2/B, Special collector's edition; printed in Japanese style (back to front) 2.95
❑3/A 2.95
❑3/B, Special collector's edition; printed in Japanese style (back to front) 2.95
❑4/A 2.95
❑4/B, Special collector's edition; printed in Japanese style (back to front) 2.95
❑5/A 2.95
❑5/B, Special collector's edition; printed in Japanese style (back to front) 2.95
❑6/A 2.95
❑6/B, Special collector's edition; printed in Japanese style (back to front) 2.95

NEON GENESIS EVANGELION BOOK 2
VIZ

Value: Cover or less

❑1/A 3.50
❑1/B, Special collector's edition; printed in Japanese style (back to front) 3.50
❑2/A 3.25
❑2/B, Special collector's edition; printed in Japanese style (back to front) 3.25
❑3/A 2.95
❑3/B, Special collector's edition; printed in Japanese style (back to front) 2.95
❑4/A 2.95
❑4/B, Special collector's edition; printed in Japanese style (back to front) 2.95
❑5/A 2.95
❑5/B, Special collector's edition; printed in Japanese style (back to front) 2.95

NEON GENESIS EVANGELION BOOK 3
VIZ

Value: Cover or less

❑1/A 2.95
❑1/B, Special collector's edition; printed in Japanese style (back to front) 2.95
❑2/A 2.95
❑2/B, Special collector's edition; printed in Japanese style (back to front) 2.95
❑3/A 2.95
❑3/B, Special collector's edition; printed in Japanese style (back to front) 2.95
❑4/A 2.95
❑4/B, Special collector's edition; printed in Japanese style (back to front) 2.95
❑5/A 2.95
❑5/B, Special collector's edition; printed in Japanese style (back to front) 2.95
❑6/A 3.25
❑6/B, Special collector's edition; printed in Japanese style (back to front) 3.25

NEON GENESIS EVANGELION BOOK 4
VIZ

Value: Cover or less

❑1/A 2.95
❑1/B, Special collector's edition; printed in Japanese style (back to front) 2.95
❑2/A 2.95
❑2/B, Special collector's edition; printed in Japanese style (back to front) 2.95
❑3/A 2.95
❑3/B, Special collector's edition; printed in Japanese style (back to front) 2.95
❑4/A 2.95
❑4/B, Special collector's edition; printed in Japanese style (back to front) 2.95
❑5/A 2.95
❑5/B, Special collector's edition; printed in Japanese style (back to front) 2.95
❑7 .... 2.95

NERVE
NERVE

	ORIG	GOOD	FINE	N-MINT
❑1	1.50	0.40	1.00	2.00
❑2	1.50	0.30	0.75	1.50
❑3	1.50	0.30	0.75	1.50
❑4	1.50	0.30	0.75	1.50
❑5, Apr 87	1.50	0.30	0.75	1.50
❑6	1.50	0.30	0.75	1.50
❑7, Jul 87	1.50	0.30	0.75	1.50
❑8, oversize	4.00	0.80	2.00	4.00

NERVOUS REX
BLACKTHORNE

Value: Cover or less

❑1, Aug 85 .... 2.00
❑2, Oct 85 .... 2.00
❑3, Dec 85 .... 2.00
❑4, Feb 86 .... 2.00
❑5, Apr 86 .... 2.00
❑6, Jun 86 .... 2.00
❑7, Aug 86 .... 2.00
❑8, Oct 86 .... 2.00
❑9, Dec 86 .... 2.00
❑10, Feb 87 .... 2.00

NESTROBBER
BLUE SKY BLUE

Value: Cover or less

❑1, Oct 92, Nestrobber; Fast, b&w 1.95
❑2, Jun 94, b&w 1.95

NETHERWORLD
AMBITION

Value: Cover or less

❑1, b&w 1.50

NETHERWORLDS
ADVENTURE

Value: Cover or less

❑1, Aug 88, Flame and Darkness, b&w 1.95

NETMAN
INFORMATION NETWORKS

	ORIG	GOOD	FINE	N-MINT
❑0, Aug 92	—	0.10	0.25	0.50

NEURO JACK
BIG

Value: Cover or less

- ❑1, Aug 96, all-digital art 2.25

NEUROMANCER: THE GRAPHIC NOVEL
MARVEL

Value: Cover or less

- ❑1 .... 8.95

NEVADA
DC

Value: Cover or less

- ❑1, May 98, Another Damn Suck-Egg Corpse 2.50
- ❑2, Jun 98, Nibbles 2.50
- ❑3, Jul 98 .... 2.50
- ❑4, Aug 98 .... 2.50
- ❑5, Sep 98 .... 2.50
- ❑6, Oct 98, Existence is Futile 2.50

NEVERMEN, THE
DARK HORSE

Value: Cover or less

- ❑1, May 00 .... 2.95
- ❑2, Jun 00, Secrets for Dead Men 2.95
- ❑3, Jul 00, Hello, Goodbye, Good Night 2.95

NEW ADVENTURES OF ABRAHAM LINCOLN, THE
IMAGE

Value: Cover or less

- ❑1 .... 19.95

NEW ADVENTURES OF BEAUTY AND THE BEAST (DISNEY'S...)
DISNEY

Value: Cover or less

- ❑1 .... 1.50
- ❑1/DM 2.00
- ❑2 .... 1.50

NEW ADVENTURES OF CHOLLY AND FLYTRAP, THE: TILL DEATH DO US PART
MARVEL

Value: Cover or less

- ❑1, Dec 90, Till Death Do Us Part; Till Death Do Us Part, Part 1, prestige format 4.95
- ❑2, Jan 91, Till Death Do Us Part, Part 2, prestige format 4.95
- ❑3, Feb 91, Till Death Do Us Part, Part 3, prestige format 4.95

NEW ADVENTURES OF FELIX THE CAT
FELIX

	ORIG	GOOD	FINE	N-MINT
❑1, Oct 92	1.95	0.45	1.13	2.25
❑2	1.95	0.45	1.13	2.25
❑3	1.95	0.45	1.13	2.25
❑4	1.95	0.45	1.13	2.25
❑5	1.95	0.45	1.13	2.25
❑6	1.95	0.45	1.13	2.25
❑7, becomes New Adventures of Felix the Cat and Friends	1.95	0.45	1.13	2.25

NEW ADVENTURES OF HUCK FINN, THE
GOLD KEY

	ORIG	GOOD	FINE	N-MINT
❑1, The Curse of Thut	0.15	2.00	5.00	10.00

NEW ADVENTURES OF JESUS, THE
RIP OFF

	ORIG	GOOD	FINE	N-MINT
❑1, Stories from the Good Book; Jesus Gets a Ride	0.50	0.90	2.25	4.50

NEW ADVENTURES OF JUDO JOE, THE
ACE

Value: Cover or less

- ❑1, Mar 87, Streets of Terror; The Championship Bout, b&w; Reprint 1.75

NEW ADVENTURES OF RICK O'SHAY AND HIPSHOT
COTTONWOOD

Value: Cover or less

- ❑1 .... 4.95
- ❑2 .... 4.95

NEW ADVENTURES OF SHALOMAN
MARK 1

	ORIG	GOOD	FINE	N-MINT
❑1, b&w	1.95	0.40	1.00	2.00
❑2	2.50	0.50	1.25	2.50
❑3, O: Shaloman	2.50	0.50	1.25	2.50
❑4, b&w	2.50	0.50	1.25	2.50
❑5, indicia says #4	2.95	0.59	1.48	2.95
❑8, A: Y-Guys, b&w	2.50	0.50	1.25	2.50
❑SE 1, b&w	2.50	0.50	1.25	2.50

NEW ADVENTURES OF SPEED RACER, THE
NOW

Value: Cover or less

- ❑0, Nov 93, multi-dimensional cover 3.95
- ❑1, Dec 93, The Royal Race .. 1.95
- ❑2 .... 1.95
- ❑3 .... 1.95

NEW ADVENTURES OF SUPERBOY, THE
DC

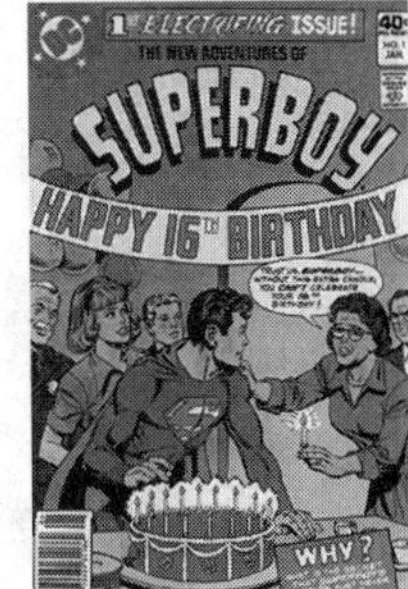

The first issue of *New Adventures of Superboy* contained a previously untold adventure from his early days.

	ORIG	GOOD	FINE	N-MINT
❑1, Jan 80, KS, The Most Important Year Of Superboy's Life!	0.40	0.40	1.00	2.00
❑2, Feb 80, KS	0.40	0.30	0.75	1.50
❑3, Mar 80, KS	0.40	0.30	0.75	1.50
❑4, Apr 80, KS	0.40	0.30	0.75	1.50
❑5, May 80, KS	0.40	0.30	0.75	1.50
❑6, Jun 80, KS	0.40	0.30	0.75	1.50
❑7, Jul 80, KS, bonus Superman story	0.40	0.30	0.75	1.50
❑8, Aug 80, KS	0.40	0.30	0.75	1.50
❑9, Sep 80, KS, V: Phantom Zone villains	0.50	0.30	0.75	1.50
❑10, Oct 80, KS, Krypto back-up	0.50	0.30	0.75	1.50
❑11, Nov 80, KS, Superbaby back-up	0.50	0.30	0.75	1.50
❑12, Dec 80, KS	0.50	0.30	0.75	1.50
❑13, Jan 81, KS	0.50	0.30	0.75	1.50
❑14, Feb 81, KS	0.50	0.30	0.75	1.50
❑15, Mar 81, KS	0.50	0.30	0.75	1.50
❑16, Apr 81, KS	0.50	0.30	0.75	1.50
❑17, May 81, KS, Krypto back-up	0.50	0.30	0.75	1.50
❑18, Jun 81, KS	0.50	0.30	0.75	1.50
❑19, Jul 81, KS	0.50	0.30	0.75	1.50
❑20, Aug 81, KS	0.50	0.30	0.75	1.50
❑21, Sep 81, KS	0.50	0.20	0.50	1.00
❑22, Oct 81, KS	0.60	0.20	0.50	1.00
❑23, Nov 81, KS	0.60	0.20	0.50	1.00
❑24, Dec 81, KS	0.60	0.20	0.50	1.00
❑25, Jan 82, KS	0.60	0.20	0.50	1.00
❑26, Feb 82, KS	0.60	0.20	0.50	1.00
❑27, Mar 82, KS	0.60	0.20	0.50	1.00
❑28, Apr 82, KS	0.60	0.20	0.50	1.00
❑29, May 82, KS	0.60	0.20	0.50	1.00
❑30, Jun 82, KS	0.60	0.20	0.50	1.00
❑31, Jul 82, KS	0.60	0.20	0.50	1.00
❑32, Aug 82, KS	0.60	0.20	0.50	1.00
❑33, Sep 82, KS	0.60	0.20	0.50	1.00
❑34, Oct 82, KS, Beware The Yellow Peri, 1: The Yellow Peril	0.60	0.20	0.50	1.00
❑35, Nov 82, KS	0.60	0.20	0.50	1.00
❑36, Dec 82, KS, Dial H for Hero back-up	0.60	0.20	0.50	1.00
❑37, Jan 83, KS	0.60	0.20	0.50	1.00
❑38, Feb 83, KS	0.60	0.20	0.50	1.00
❑39, Mar 83, KS	0.60	0.20	0.50	1.00
❑40, Apr 83, KS, Dial H for Hero back-up	0.60	0.20	0.50	1.00
❑41, May 83, KS, GK (c)	0.60	0.20	0.50	1.00
❑42, Jun 83, KS, GK (c)	0.60	0.20	0.50	1.00
❑43, Jul 83, KS, GK (c), Dial H for Hero back-up	0.60	0.20	0.50	1.00
❑44, Aug 83, KS, GK (c)	0.60	0.20	0.50	1.00
❑45, Sep 83, KS, GK (c), 1: Sunburst	0.60	0.20	0.50	1.00
❑46, Oct 83, KS	0.60	0.20	0.50	1.00
❑47, Nov 83, KS	0.60	0.20	0.50	1.00
❑48, Dec 83, KS	0.75	0.20	0.50	1.00
❑49, Jan 84, KS, Dial H for Hero back-up	0.75	0.20	0.50	1.00
❑50, Feb 84, KS; KG, A: Legion of Super-Heroes, Giant-size	1.25	0.25	0.63	1.25
❑51, Mar 84, KS, FM (c)	0.75	0.20	0.50	1.00
❑52, Apr 84, KS	0.75	0.20	0.50	1.00
❑53, May 84, KS	0.75	0.20	0.50	1.00
❑54, Jun 84, KS, Final Issue	0.75	0.20	0.50	1.00

NEW ADVENTURES OF TERRY & THE PIRATES
AVALON

Value: Cover or less

- ❑1 .... 2.95
- ❑2, The Last Garland 2.95
- ❑3 .... 2.95
- ❑4 .... 2.95
- ❑5 .... 2.95
- ❑6 .... 2.95

NEW AGE COMICS
FANTAGRAPHICS

	ORIG	GOOD	FINE	N-MINT
❑1, Independent comics sampler	0.35	0.30	0.75	1.50

NEW AMERICA
ECLIPSE

	ORIG	GOOD	FINE	N-MINT
❑1, Nov 87, TY (c), Baja, Japan	1.75	0.40	1.00	2.00
❑2, Dec 87	1.75	0.40	1.00	2.00
❑3, Jan 88, TY (c)	1.75	0.40	1.00	2.00
❑4, Feb 88	1.75	0.40	1.00	2.00

NEW BEGINNING
UNICORN

	ORIG	GOOD	FINE	N-MINT
❑1, b&w	1.50	0.40	1.00	2.00
❑2, b&w	1.75	0.40	1.00	2.00
❑3, b&w	1.75	0.40	1.00	2.00

NEW BONDAGE FAIRIES
Eros

Value: Cover or less

Issue	ORIG	Issue	ORIG
❑1	2.95	❑7	2.95
❑2	2.95	❑8	2.95
❑3	2.95	❑9	2.95
❑4	2.95	❑10	2.95
❑5	2.95	❑11	2.95
❑6	2.95	❑12	2.95

NEW CREW, THE
Personality

Issue	ORIG	GOOD	FINE	N-MINT
❑1, Patrick Stewart	2.95	0.70	1.75	3.50
❑2, Jonathan Frakes	2.95	0.60	1.50	3.00
❑3	2.95	0.60	1.50	3.00
❑4	2.95	0.60	1.50	3.00
❑5	2.95	0.60	1.50	3.00
❑6	2.95	0.60	1.50	3.00
❑7	2.95	0.60	1.50	3.00
❑8	2.95	0.60	1.50	3.00
❑9	2.95	0.60	1.50	3.00
❑10	2.95	0.60	1.50	3.00

NEW CRIME FILES OF MICHAEL MAUSER, PRIVATE EYE
Apple

Value: Cover or less

Issue	ORIG
❑1, b&w	2.50

NEW DNAGENTS, THE
Eclipse

Issue	ORIG	GOOD	FINE	N-MINT
❑1, Oct 85, ME (w), Backstory!, O: The DNAgents	0.95	0.30	0.75	1.50
❑2, Nov 85, ME (w)	0.95	0.25	0.63	1.25
❑3, Nov 85, ME (w)	0.95	0.25	0.63	1.25
❑4, Dec 85, ME (w)	0.95	0.20	0.50	1.00
❑5, Jan 86, ME (w)	0.95	0.20	0.50	1.00
❑6, Feb 86, ME (w)	0.95	0.20	0.50	1.00
❑7, Apr 86, ME (w)	0.95	0.20	0.50	1.00
❑8, Apr 86, ME (w)	0.95	0.20	0.50	1.00
❑9, Jun 86, ME (w)	0.95	0.20	0.50	1.00
❑10, Jun 86, ME (w)	0.95	0.20	0.50	1.00
❑11, Aug 86, ME (w)	0.95	0.20	0.50	1.00
❑12, Aug 86, ME (w)	0.95	0.20	0.50	1.00
❑13, Oct 86, ME (w)	1.25	0.20	0.50	1.00
❑14, Nov 86, ME (w)	1.25	0.20	0.50	1.00
❑15, Dec 86, ME (w)	1.25	0.20	0.50	1.00
❑16, Jan 87, ME (w)	1.25	0.20	0.50	1.00
❑17, Mar 87, ME (w), Final Issue	1.25	0.20	0.50	1.00

NEW ENGLAND GOTHIC
Visigoth

Value: Cover or less

Issue	ORIG
❑1, Dec 86	2.00

NEWFORCE
Image

Value: Cover or less

Issue	ORIG
❑1, Jan 96, RL (w), Extreme Destroyer, Part 8, polybagged with Kodiak card	2.50
❑2, Feb 96	2.50
❑3, Mar 96	2.50
❑4, Apr 96	2.50

NEW FRONTIER, THE
Dark Horse

Value: Cover or less

Issue	ORIG
❑1, Oct 92, b&w	2.75
❑2, Nov 92, b&w	2.75
❑3, Dec 92, b&w	2.75

NEW FRONTIERS
Evolution

Value: Cover or less

Issue	ORIG
❑1, Devil in Her Heart; Actionmaster: Life Support, b&w	1.75
❑2, Unspoken Yesterdays; Sticks and Stones and Ancient Bones, b&w	1.95

NEW GODS, THE (1ST SERIES)
DC

Issue	ORIG	GOOD	FINE	N-MINT
❑1, Mar 71, JK, JK (w), In The Beginning, 1: Lightray; 1: Highfather; 1: Kalibak; 1: Metron; 1: Apokolips; 1: Orion	0.15	7.00	17.50	35.00
❑2, May 71, JK, JK (w), 1: Deep Six	0.15	4.00	10.00	20.00
❑3, Jul 71, JK, JK (w), 1: Black Racer	0.15	3.20	8.00	16.00
❑4, Sep 71, JK, JK (w), Giant-size	0.25	2.80	7.00	14.00
❑5, Nov 71, JK, JK (w), Giant-size	0.25	2.80	7.00	14.00
❑6, Jan 72, JK, JK (w), 1: Fastbak, Giant-size	0.25	2.80	7.00	14.00
❑7, Mar 72, JK, JK (w), 1: Steppenwolf, Giant-size	0.25	2.80	7.00	14.00
❑8, May 72, JK, JK (w), Giant-size	0.25	2.00	5.00	10.00
❑9, Jul 72, JK, JK (w), 1: Forager, Giant-size	0.25	2.00	5.00	10.00
❑10, Sep 72, JK, JK (w)	0.20	1.60	4.00	8.00
❑11, Nov 72, JK, JK (w)	0.20	1.60	4.00	8.00
❑12, Jul 77, The Return of the New Gods, Series begins again (1977)	0.35	0.80	2.00	4.00
❑13, Aug 77	0.35	0.80	2.00	4.00
❑14, Oct 77	0.35	0.80	2.00	4.00
❑15, Dec 77	0.35	0.80	2.00	4.00
❑16, Feb 78	0.35	0.80	2.00	4.00
❑17, Apr 78	0.35	0.80	2.00	4.00
❑18, Jun 78	0.35	0.80	2.00	4.00
❑19, Aug 78, Final Issue	0.35	0.80	2.00	4.00

NEW GODS (2ND SERIES)
DC

Value: Cover or less

Issue	ORIG	Issue	ORIG
❑1, Jun 84, JK, Reprint	2.00	❑4, Oct 84, JK, Reprint	2.00
❑2, Jul 84, JK, Reprint	2.00	❑5, Nov 84, JK, Reprint	2.00
❑3, Aug 84, JK, Reprint	2.00	❑6, Dec 84, JK, Reprint	2.00

NEW GODS (3RD SERIES)
DC

Issue	ORIG	GOOD	FINE	N-MINT
❑1, Feb 89, Hordes	1.50	0.45	1.13	2.25
❑2, Mar 89	1.50	0.40	1.00	2.00
❑3, Apr 89	1.50	0.40	1.00	2.00
❑4, May 89	1.50	0.40	1.00	2.00
❑5, Jun 89	1.50	0.40	1.00	2.00
❑6, Jul 89	1.50	0.30	0.75	1.50
❑7, Aug 89, Bloodline, Part 1	1.50	0.30	0.75	1.50
❑8, Sep 89, Bloodline, Part 2	1.50	0.30	0.75	1.50
❑9, Oct 89, Bloodline, Part 3	1.50	0.30	0.75	1.50
❑10, Nov 89, Bloodline, Part 4	1.50	0.30	0.75	1.50
❑11, Dec 89, Bloodline, Part 5	1.50	0.30	0.75	1.50
❑12, Jan 90, Bloodline, Part 6	1.50	0.30	0.75	1.50
❑13, Feb 90	1.50	0.30	0.75	1.50
❑14, Mar 90	1.50	0.30	0.75	1.50
❑15, Apr 90	1.50	0.30	0.75	1.50
❑16, May 90	1.50	0.30	0.75	1.50
❑17, Jun 90	1.50	0.30	0.75	1.50
❑18, Jul 90	1.50	0.30	0.75	1.50
❑19, Aug 90	1.50	0.30	0.75	1.50
❑20, Sep 90	1.50	0.30	0.75	1.50
❑21, Dec 90	1.50	0.30	0.75	1.50
❑22, Jan 91	1.50	0.30	0.75	1.50
❑23, Feb 91	1.50	0.30	0.75	1.50
❑24, Mar 91	1.50	0.30	0.75	1.50
❑25, Apr 91	1.50	0.30	0.75	1.50
❑26, May 91	1.50	0.30	0.75	1.50
❑27, Jul 91	1.50	0.30	0.75	1.50
❑28, Aug 91, Final Issue	1.50	0.30	0.75	1.50

NEW GODS (4TH SERIES)
DC

Value: Cover or less

Issue	ORIG
❑1, Oct 95, Attack on the Source!	1.95
❑2, Nov 95	1.95
❑3, Dec 95, After the Fall	1.95
❑4, Jan 96	1.95
❑5, Feb 96, Descent into Madness!	1.95
❑6, Mar 96, Destruction of the Beast!	1.95
❑7, Apr 96, The End of the Gods	1.95
❑8, Jun 96, Sins of the Fathers	1.95
❑9, Jul 96	1.95
❑10, Aug 96, A: Superman	1.95
❑11, Sep 96	1.95
❑12, Nov 96, JBy, JBy (w), After the Fall	0.99
❑13, Dec 96, JBy, JBy (w), Night of the Falling Sky	1.95
❑14, Jan 97, JBy, JBy (w), The Gathering Storm!, A: Forever People	1.95
❑15, Feb 97, JBy, JBy (w)	1.95

NEW GODS SECRET FILES
DC

Value: Cover or less

Issue	ORIG
❑1, Sep 98	4.95

NEW GUARDIANS, THE
DC

Value: Cover or less

Issue	ORIG	Issue	ORIG
❑1, Sep 88, JSa, The New Guardians, Giant-size	2.00	❑7, Feb 89, Invasion!	1.25
❑2, Oct 88	1.25	❑8, Apr 89	1.25
❑3, Nov 88	1.25	❑9, Jun 89	1.25
❑4, Dec 88	1.25	❑10, Jul 89	1.25
❑5, Dec 88	1.25	❑11, Aug 89	1.25
❑6, Jan 89, Invasion!	1.25	❑12, Sep 89	1.25

NEW HAT
Black Eye

Issue	ORIG	GOOD	FINE	N-MINT
❑1	—	0.20	0.50	1.00

NEW HERO COMICS
Red Spade

Issue	ORIG	GOOD	FINE	N-MINT
❑1, b&w	—	0.20	0.50	1.00

NEW HORIZONS
Shanda Fantasy Arts

Value: Cover or less

Issue	ORIG	Issue	ORIG
❑1, b&w; Anthology	4.95	❑4, b&w; Anthology	4.50
❑2, b&w; Anthology	4.95	❑5, Apr 99, b&w; Anthology	4.50
❑3, b&w; Anthology	4.50		

NEW HUMANS, THE (ETERNITY)
Eternity

Value: Cover or less

Issue	ORIG	Issue	ORIG
❑1, Dec 87, O: New Humans	1.95	❑6	1.95
❑2, Jan 88, The Sun Never Sets; The Rovers	1.95	❑7	1.95
❑3, Feb 88	1.95	❑8, Sep 88	1.95
❑4, Mar 88, Nude cover	1.95	❑9	1.95
❑5	1.95	❑10	1.95
		❑11	1.95

	ORIG	GOOD	FINE	N-MINT

- ❑12, Mar 89 .... 1.95
- ❑13 .... 1.95
- ❑14 .... 1.95
- ❑15 .... 1.95
- ❑16 .... 1.95
- ❑17, Final Issue 1.95
- ❑Anl 1, b&w 2.95

NEW HUMANS, THE (PIED PIPER)
Pied Piper

Value: Cover or less

- ❑1, Jul 87, After the Fire, O: The New Humans, b&w 1.95
- ❑2 .... 1.95
- ❑3 .... 1.95

NEW JUSTICE MACHINE, THE
Innovation

	ORIG	GOOD	FINE	N-MINT
❑1, Nov 89, Crossroads	1.95	0.40	1.00	2.00
❑2, Jan 90	1.95	0.40	1.00	2.00
❑3, Mar 90	1.95	0.40	1.00	2.00

NEW KIDS ON THE BLOCK, THE: BACKSTAGE PASS
Harvey

Value: Cover or less

- ❑1, Sleepless Knights; A Jordan Knightmare 1.25

NEW KIDS ON THE BLOCK: CHILLIN'
Harvey

	ORIG	GOOD	FINE	N-MINT
❑1	1.25	0.30	0.75	1.50
❑2	1.25	0.25	0.63	1.25
❑3	1.25	0.25	0.63	1.25
❑4	1.25	0.25	0.63	1.25
❑5	1.25	0.25	0.63	1.25
❑6	1.25	0.25	0.63	1.25
❑7, Dec 91, The Arabian Nightmare	1.25	0.25	0.63	1.25

NEW KIDS ON THE BLOCK COMIC TOUR '90
Harvey

Value: Cover or less

- ❑1 .... 1.25

NEW KIDS ON THE BLOCK MAGIC SUMMER TOUR
Harvey

Value: Cover or less

- ❑1, nn 1.25
- ❑1/LE, nn; limited edition 3.95

NEW KIDS ON THE BLOCK, THE: NKOTB
Harvey

Value: Cover or less

- ❑1, Dec 90, Vacation Breaks; The World According to Donnie 1.25
- ❑2 .... 1.25
- ❑3 .... 1.25
- ❑4 .... 1.25
- ❑5, May 91, A Pizza Cake 1.25
- ❑6, Jul 91, on the Right Track 1.25

NEW KIDS ON THE BLOCK STEP BY STEP
Harvey

Value: Cover or less

- ❑1, nn 1.25

NEW KIDS ON THE BLOCK: VALENTINE GIRL
Harvey

Value: Cover or less

- ❑1, nn 1.25

NEW LOVE
Fantagraphics

Value: Cover or less

- ❑1, Aug 96, b&w 2.95
- ❑2, Oct 96, b&w 2.95
- ❑3, Mar 97, b&w 2.95
- ❑4, Jun 97, b&w 2.95
- ❑5, Nov 97, b&w 2.95
- ❑6, Dec 97, b&w 2.95

NEWMAN
Image

Value: Cover or less

- ❑1, Jan 96, RL (w), Extreme Destroyer, Part 3, polybagged with card; Extreme Destroyer Part 3 .... 2.50
- ❑2, Feb 96, New Beginnings 2.50
- ❑3, Apr 96 .... 2.50
- ❑4, Apr 96, Shadowhunt, Part 5, V: Youngblood 2.50

NEWMEN
Image

	ORIG	GOOD	FINE	N-MINT
❑1, Apr 94, RL (w)	1.95	0.50	1.25	2.50
❑2, May 94	1.95	0.45	1.13	2.25
❑3, Jun 94	1.95	0.45	1.13	2.25
❑4, Jul 94	1.95	0.45	1.13	2.25
❑5, Aug 94	2.50	0.50	1.25	2.50
❑6, Sep 94	2.50	0.50	1.25	2.50
❑7, Oct 94	2.50	0.50	1.25	2.50
❑8, Nov 94	2.50	0.50	1.25	2.50
❑9, Dec 94, Extreme Sacrifice	2.50	0.50	1.25	2.50
❑10, Jan 95, Extreme Sacrifice, Part 5; Extreme Sacrifice, Part 4, trading card	2.50	0.50	1.25	2.50
❑11, Feb 95, Extreme Sacrifice Aftermath, polybagged	2.50	0.50	1.25	2.50
❑11/A, Feb 95, Extreme Sacrifice Aftermath, alternate cover; polybagged	2.50	0.50	1.25	2.50
❑12, Mar 95	2.50	0.50	1.25	2.50
❑13, Apr 95, Dominion, Part 1	2.50	0.50	1.25	2.50
❑14, May 95, Dominion, Part 2	2.50	0.50	1.25	2.50
❑15, Jun 95, no indicia	2.50	0.50	1.25	2.50
❑16, Jul 95, Dominion, Part 4	2.50	0.50	1.25	2.50
❑16/A, Jul 95, Dominion, Part 4, alternate cover	2.50	0.60	1.50	3.00
❑17, Aug 95	2.50	0.50	1.25	2.50
❑18, Sep 95	2.50	0.50	1.25	2.50
❑19, Oct 95, Extreme Destroyer	2.50	0.50	1.25	2.50
❑20, Nov 95, Babewatch	2.50	0.50	1.25	2.50
❑20/A, Nov 95, Babewatch	2.50	0.50	1.25	2.50
❑21, Aug 96	2.50	0.50	1.25	2.50
❑22	2.50	0.50	1.25	2.50
❑23	2.50	0.50	1.25	2.50
❑24	2.50	0.50	1.25	2.50
❑25	2.50	0.50	1.25	2.50

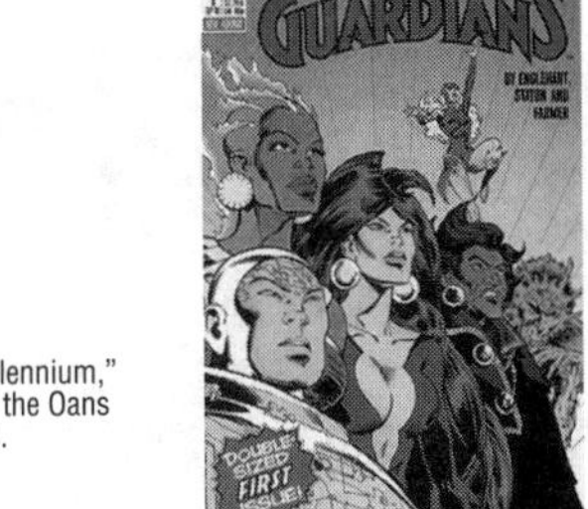

Following the events of "Millennium," ordinary humans altered by the Oans became The New Guardians.

© 1988 DC Comics

NEW MUTANTS, THE
Marvel

	ORIG	GOOD	FINE	N-MINT
❑1, Mar 83, BMc, Initiation!	0.60	0.40	1.00	2.00
❑2, Apr 83, BMc, Sentinels, V: Sentinels	0.60	0.40	1.00	2.00
❑3, May 83, BMc, Nightmare, V: Brood	0.60	0.40	1.00	2.00
❑4, Jun 83, SB, Who's Scaring Stevie?	0.60	0.30	0.75	1.50
❑5, Jul 83, SB, Heroes, A: Team America	0.60	0.30	0.75	1.50
❑6, Aug 83, SB, Road Warriors!, A: Team America	0.60	0.30	0.75	1.50
❑7, Sep 83, SB, Flying Down To Rio!	0.60	0.30	0.75	1.50
❑8, Oct 83, BMc, The Road To...Rome?, 1: Magma	0.60	0.30	0.75	1.50
❑9, Nov 83, SB, Arena, 1: Selene	0.60	0.30	0.75	1.50
❑10, Dec 83, SB, Betrayal, 1: Magma	0.60	0.30	0.75	1.50
❑11, Jan 84, SB, Magma, Assistant Editor Month	0.60	0.30	0.75	1.50
❑12, Feb 84, SB, Sunstroke	0.60	0.30	0.75	1.50
❑13, Mar 84, SB, School Daysze, 1: Cypher; A: Kitty Pryde	0.60	0.30	0.75	1.50
❑14, Apr 84, SB, Do You Believe In Magik?, V: Sy'm; A: X-Men	0.60	0.30	0.75	1.50
❑15, May 84, SB, Scaredy Cat!, X-Men	0.60	0.30	0.75	1.50
❑16, Jun 84, 1: Hellions; 1: Warpath	0.60	0.30	0.75	1.50
❑17, Jul 84, Getaway!, The New Mutants vs. The Hellions	0.60	0.30	0.75	1.50
❑18, Aug 84, BSz, Death-Hunt, 1: Warlock (machine)	0.60	0.30	0.75	1.50
❑19, Sep 84, BSz, Siege	0.60	0.30	0.75	1.50
❑20, Oct 84, BSz, Badlands	0.60	0.30	0.75	1.50
❑21, Nov 84, BSz, Slumber Party!, O: Warlock (machine), Double-size	1.00	0.30	0.75	1.50
❑22, Dec 84, BSz, The Shadow Within	0.60	0.30	0.75	1.50
❑23, Jan 85, BSz, A: Cloak & Dagger	0.60	0.30	0.75	1.50
❑24, Feb 85, BSz, The Hollow Heart, A: Cloak & Dagger	0.60	0.30	0.75	1.50
❑25, Mar 85, BSz, A: Cloak & Dagger; 1: Legion (cameo)	0.60	0.50	1.25	2.50
❑26, Apr 85, BSz, 1: Legion (psychic)	0.65	0.50	1.25	2.50
❑27, May 85, BSz, V: Legion	0.65	0.40	1.00	2.00
❑28, Jun 85, BSz, Soulwar, A: Legion	0.65	0.40	1.00	2.00
❑29, Jul 85, BSz, Meanwhile, Back At The Mansion, 1: Guido Carosella (Strong Guy)	0.65	0.40	1.00	2.00
❑30, Aug 85, BSz, Secret Wars II, Secret Wars II	0.65	0.30	0.75	1.50
❑31, Sep 85, BSz, Saturday Night Fight!	0.65	0.30	0.75	1.50
❑32, Oct 85	0.65	0.30	0.75	1.50
❑33, Nov 85, Against All Odds	0.65	0.30	0.75	1.50
❑34, Dec 85, With A Little Bit Of Luck	0.65	0.30	0.75	1.50
❑35, Jan 86, BSz, The Times, They Are A' Changin'!, A: Magneto, Magneto begins as leader of New Mutants	0.75	0.30	0.75	1.50
❑36, Feb 86, BSz, Secret Wars II, Secret Wars II	0.75	0.30	0.75	1.50
❑37, Mar 86, BSz, Secret Wars II, Secret Wars II	0.75	0.30	0.75	1.50
❑38, Apr 86, Aftermath	0.75	0.30	0.75	1.50
❑39, May 86, KP, Pawns Of The White Queen	0.75	0.30	0.75	1.50
❑40, Jun 86, A: Captain America	0.75	0.30	0.75	1.50
❑41, Jul 86	0.75	0.30	0.75	1.50
❑42, Aug 86	0.75	0.30	0.75	1.50
❑43, Sep 86	0.75	0.30	0.75	1.50
❑44, Oct 86, Runaway!, A: Legion	0.75	0.30	0.75	1.50
❑45, Nov 86, We Were Only Foolin'	0.75	0.30	0.75	1.50
❑46, Dec 86, Mutant Massacre; Bloody Sunday	0.75	0.30	0.75	1.50
❑47, Jan 87	0.75	0.30	0.75	1.50

	ORIG	GOOD	FINE	N-MINT
❑48, Feb 87, Ashes Of The Heart	0.75	0.30	0.75	1.50
❑49, Mar 87, Ashes Of The Soul	0.75	0.30	0.75	1.50
❑50, Apr 87, Father's Day!, Double-size; Professor X returns as headmaster	1.25	0.30	0.75	1.50
❑51, May 87, KN, Teacher's Choice, A: Star Jammers	0.75	0.30	0.75	1.50
❑52, Jun 87	0.75	0.30	0.75	1.50
❑53, Jul 87	0.75	0.30	0.75	1.50
❑54, Aug 87	0.75	0.30	0.75	1.50
❑55, Sep 87, Flying Wild!	0.75	0.30	0.75	1.50
❑56, Oct 87, Scavenger Hunt!	0.75	0.30	0.75	1.50
❑57, Nov 87, Birds Of A Feather	0.75	0.30	0.75	1.50
❑58, Dec 87, registration card	0.75	0.30	0.75	1.50
❑59, Jan 88, Fall of the Mutants, Fall of Mutants	0.75	0.40	1.00	2.00
❑60, Feb 88, Fall of the Mutants, D: Cypher, double-sized; Fall of the Mutants	1.25	0.40	1.00	2.00
❑61, Mar 88, Fall of the Mutants, Fall of the Mutants; new costumes; (conclusion); (conclusion)	0.75	0.40	1.00	2.00
❑62, Apr 88, To Build A Fire	0.75	0.30	0.75	1.50
❑63, May 88, A: X-Men	1.00	0.40	1.00	2.00
❑64, Jun 88, Instant Replay!	1.00	0.30	0.75	1.50
❑65, Jul 88	1.00	0.30	0.75	1.50
❑66, Aug 88	1.00	0.30	0.75	1.50
❑67, Sep 88, Promise	1.00	0.30	0.75	1.50
❑68, Oct 88, Iggusion!	1.00	0.30	0.75	1.50
❑69, Nov 88, Bad Company	1.00	0.30	0.75	1.50
❑70, Dec 88, Inferno	1.00	0.30	0.75	1.50
❑71, Jan 89, Inferno, O: N'astirh, Inferno	1.00	0.30	0.75	1.50
❑72, Feb 89, Inferno, Inferno	1.00	0.30	0.75	1.50
❑73, Mar 89, Giant-size; Inferno	1.50	0.40	1.00	2.00
❑74, Apr 89, The Right Stuff	1.00	0.30	0.75	1.50
❑75, May 89	1.00	0.30	0.75	1.50
❑76, Jun 89, RB, Splash!, A: X-Factor, Sub-Mariner; X-Terminator appear	1.00	0.30	0.75	1.50
❑77, Jul 89, RB, Strange!	1.00	0.30	0.75	1.50
❑78, Aug 89	1.00	0.30	0.75	1.50
❑79, Sep 89, Asgard!	1.00	0.30	0.75	1.50
❑80, Oct 89, Curse Of The Valkyries	1.00	0.30	0.75	1.50
❑81, Nov 89, Faith	1.00	0.30	0.75	1.50
❑82, Nov 89, The Road To Hel...	1.00	0.30	0.75	1.50
❑83, Dec 89, The Quick And The Dead	1.00	0.30	0.75	1.50
❑84, Dec 89, Acts of Vengeance, Acts of Vengeance	1.00	0.30	0.75	1.50
❑85, Jan 90, TMc (c), Acts of Vengeance, Acts of Vengeance	1.00	0.30	0.75	1.50
❑86, Feb 90, TMc (c), 1: Cable (cameo); 1: Zero, Acts of Vengeance	1.00	0.80	2.00	4.00
❑87, Mar 90, TMc (c), 1: Cable; 1: Stryfe	1.00	1.80	4.50	9.00
❑87-2, Mar 90, TMc (c), 1: Cable, 2nd printing (gold)	1.00	0.40	1.00	2.00
❑88, Apr 90, RL, TMc (c), The Great Escape, 2: Cable	1.00	0.80	2.00	4.00
❑89, May 90, TMc (c)	1.00	0.70	1.75	3.50
❑90, Jun 90, A: Sabretooth	1.00	0.70	1.75	3.50
❑91, Jul 90, A: Sabretooth	1.00	0.70	1.75	3.50
❑92, Aug 90	1.00	0.70	1.75	3.50
❑93, Sep 90, TMc (c), A: Wolverine	1.00	0.70	1.75	3.50
❑94, Oct 90, A: Wolverine	1.00	0.70	1.75	3.50
❑95, Nov 90, X-Tinction Agenda, D: Warlock (machine)	1.00	0.70	1.75	3.50
❑95-2, Nov 90, X-tinction Agenda, D: Warlock (machine), 2nd printing (gold)	1.00	0.40	1.00	2.00
❑96, Dec 90, X-Tinction Agenda	1.00	0.60	1.50	3.00
❑97, Jan 91, X-Tinction Agenda	1.00	0.60	1.50	3.00
❑98, Feb 91, RL, RL (w), The Beginning Of The End, Part 1, 1: Gideon; 1: Domino II; 1: Deadpool	1.00	1.00	2.50	5.00
❑99, Mar 91, RL, RL (w), The Beginning Of The End, Part 2, 1: Shatterstar (full appearance); 1: Feral, Sunspot leaves team	1.00	0.80	2.00	4.00
❑100, Apr 91, RL, RL (w), The Beginning Of The End, Part 3, O: Shatterstar; 1: X-Force, Giant-size	1.50	0.70	1.75	3.50
❑100-2, Apr 91, RL, RL (w), The Beginning Of The End, Part 3, 1: X-Force, 2nd printing (gold)	1.50	0.40	1.00	2.00
❑100-3, Apr 91, RL, RL (w), The Beginning Of The End, Part 3, 1: X-Force, 3rd printing (silver)	1.50	0.40	1.00	2.00
❑Anl 1, The Cosmic Cannonball Caper, 1: Lila Cheney	1.00	0.60	1.50	3.00
❑Anl 2, 1: Psylocke; 1: Meggan	1.25	1.00	2.50	5.00
❑Anl 3, A: Impossible Man	1.25	0.40	1.00	2.00
❑Anl 4, Evolutionary War, Part 4	1.75	0.40	1.00	2.00
❑Anl 5, RL, Atlantis Attacks, Part 9, Atlantis Attacks	2.00	0.40	1.00	2.00
❑Anl 6, Future Present; Days of Future Present, 1: Shatterstar (cameo)	2.00	0.50	1.25	2.50
❑Anl 7, Kings of Pain; Kings of Pain, Part 1	2.00	0.40	1.00	2.00
❑SE 1, Dec 85, Home Is Where The Heart Is	1.50	0.30	0.75	1.50
❑Smr 1, Giant-size	2.95	0.59	1.48	2.95

NEW MUTANTS, THE: TRUTH OR DEATH
MARVEL

Value: Cover or less

- ❑1, Nov 97, gatefold summary; original New Mutants travel through time and meet present-day counterparts ... 2.50
- ❑2, Dec 97, gatefold summary 2.50
- ❑3, Jan 98, gatefold summary. 2.50

NEW NIGHT OF THE LIVING DEAD
FANTACO

	ORIG	GOOD	FINE	N-MINT
❑0	1.95	0.40	1.00	2.00
❑1	3.95	0.79	1.98	3.95
❑2	3.95	0.79	1.98	3.95
❑3	3.95	0.79	1.98	3.95

NEW ORDER, THE
CREATIVE FORCE

Value: Cover or less

- ❑1, Nov 94, Rage Against the Machine, Part 1 ... 2.95

NEW PALTZ COMIX
MOODS

	ORIG	GOOD	FINE	N-MINT
❑1	1.25	0.30	0.75	1.50
❑2	1.25	0.30	0.75	1.50
❑3, Madhouse; Food	1.25	0.30	0.75	1.50

NEW PARTNERS IN PERIL
BLUE COMET

Value: Cover or less

- ❑1, b&w ... 2.25

NEW POWER STARS, THE
BLUE COMET

Value: Cover or less

- ❑1, b&w ... 2.00

NEW SHADOWHAWK, THE
IMAGE

Value: Cover or less

- ❑1, Jun 95, KB (w), Nightmares 2.50
- ❑2, Aug 95, KB (w), Monsters. 2.50
- ❑3, Sep 95 ... 2.50
- ❑4, Nov 95 ... 2.50
- ❑5, Dec 95 ... 2.50
- ❑6, Feb 96 ... 2.50
- ❑7, Mar 96 ... 2.50

NEW STATESMEN
FLEETWAY

	ORIG	GOOD	FINE	N-MINT
❑1	3.95	0.80	2.00	4.00
❑2	3.95	0.80	2.00	4.00
❑3	3.95	0.80	2.00	4.00
❑4	3.95	0.80	2.00	4.00
❑5	3.95	0.80	2.00	4.00

NEWSTIME
DC

	ORIG	GOOD	FINE	N-MINT
❑1, May 93, D: Superman magazine, nn	2.95	0.65	1.63	3.25

NEWSTRALIA
INNOVATION

	ORIG	GOOD	FINE	N-MINT
❑1, Jul 89, Eyes Of The Overlord!	1.75	0.40	1.00	2.00
❑2	1.95	0.40	1.00	2.00
❑3	1.95	0.45	1.13	2.25
❑4	2.25	0.45	1.13	2.25
❑5, b&w	2.25	0.45	1.13	2.25

NEW TALENT SHOWCASE
DC

	ORIG	GOOD	FINE	N-MINT
❑1, Jan 84	1.00	0.30	0.75	1.50
❑2, Feb 84, A Magic Carpet Ride	1.00	0.30	0.75	1.50
❑3, Mar 84	1.00	0.30	0.75	1.50
❑4, Apr 84	1.00	0.30	0.75	1.50
❑5, May 84	1.00	0.30	0.75	1.50
❑6, Jun 84	1.25	0.30	0.75	1.50
❑7, Jul 84	1.25	0.30	0.75	1.50
❑8, Aug 84	1.25	0.30	0.75	1.50
❑9, Sep 84	1.25	0.30	0.75	1.50
❑10, Oct 84	1.25	0.30	0.75	1.50
❑11, Nov 84	1.25	0.25	0.63	1.25
❑12, Dec 84	1.25	0.25	0.63	1.25
❑13, Jan 85	1.25	0.25	0.63	1.25
❑14, Feb 85	1.25	0.25	0.63	1.25
❑15, Mar 85	1.25	0.25	0.63	1.25
❑16, Apr 85, Title changes to Talent Showcase	1.25	0.25	0.63	1.25
❑17, May 85	1.25	0.25	0.63	1.25
❑18, Jun 85	1.25	0.25	0.63	1.25
❑19, Jul 85	1.25	0.25	0.63	1.25

NEW TEEN TITANS, THE (1ST SERIES)
DC

	ORIG	GOOD	FINE	N-MINT
❑1, Nov 80, RT; GP, The New Teen Titans, 1: Teen Titans	0.50	1.50	3.75	7.50
❑2, Dec 80, RT; GP, Today...The Terminator, 1: Deathstroke the Terminator; 1: Wintergreen; 1: Trigon; D: The Ravager	0.50	1.20	3.00	6.00

	ORIG	GOOD	FINE	N-MINT
❑3, Jan 81, GP, The Fearsome Five, V: Docto; 1: Psimon; 1: Fearsome Five; 1: Mammoth; 1: Gizmo; 1: Shimmer; V: Dr. Light; V: Doctor Light	0.50	0.60	1.50	3.00
❑4, Feb 81, GP, Against All Friends, A: Justice League	0.50	0.60	1.50	3.00
❑5, Mar 81, RT; CS, Trigon Lives!, 1: Trigon; O: Raven	0.50	0.60	1.50	3.00
❑6, Apr 81, GP, GP (w), Last Kill!, V: Trigon; O: Raven	0.50	0.60	1.50	3.00
❑7, May 81, RT; GP, Assault on Titans' Tower, O: Cyborg; V: Fearsome Five	0.50	0.60	1.50	3.00
❑8, Jun 81, RT; GP, GP (w), Day in the Lives; A Day in the Lives..., O: Kid Flash	0.50	0.60	1.50	3.00
❑9, Jul 81, RT; GP, Like Puppets on a String	0.50	0.60	1.50	3.00
❑10, Aug 81, RT; GP, Promethium: Unbound, A: Deathstroke the Terminator; V: Terminator; O: Changeling	0.50	0.60	1.50	3.00
❑11, Sep 81, RT; GP, When Titans Clash	0.50	0.40	1.00	2.00
❑12, Oct 81, RT; GP, Clash of the Titans	0.60	0.40	1.00	2.00
❑13, Nov 81, RT; GP, Friends and Foes Alike, Doom Patrol; Robotman returns	0.60	0.40	1.00	2.00
❑14, Dec 81, RT; GP, Revolution!, 1: Phobia; 1: Plasmus; 1: Houngan, Doom Patrol	0.60	0.40	1.00	2.00
❑15, Jan 82, RT; GP, The Brotherhood of Evil Lives Again, V: Brotherhood of Evil, Doom Patrol	0.60	0.40	1.00	2.00
❑16, Feb 82, RT; RA; GP, Starfire Unleashed!; Captain Carrot and His Amazing Zoo Crew!, 1: Alley-Kat-Abra; 1: Rubberduck; 1: Captain Carrot; 1: Fastback; 1: Pig-Iron; 1: Yankee Poodle	0.60	0.40	1.00	2.00
❑17, Mar 82, RT; GP, The Possessing of Francis Kane, A: Francis Kane	0.60	0.40	1.00	2.00
❑18, Apr 82, RT; GP, A Pretty Girl is Like a-Maladi!, A: Starfire (later Red Star); 1: Maladi Maranova	0.60	0.40	1.00	2.00
❑19, May 82, RT; GP, The Light Fantastic, A: Hawkman	0.60	0.40	1.00	2.00
❑20, Jun 82, RT; GP, Dear Mom and Dad; A Titanic Tale of Titans' Tomfoolery, 1: The Disruptor	0.60	0.40	1.00	2.00
❑21, Jul 82, RT; GP; GC, Beware the Wrath of...Brother Blood!; The Night Force, 1: Baron Winters; 1: Night Force; V: Brother Blood; 1: Harbinger; 1: Monitor	0.60	0.40	1.00	2.00
❑22, Aug 82, RT; GP, Ashes to Ashes!, V: Brother Blood	0.60	0.40	1.00	2.00
❑23, Sep 82, RT; GP, Kidnapped!, 1: Blackfire	0.60	0.40	1.00	2.00
❑24, Oct 82, RT; GP, Citadel Strike!, A: Omega Men; 1: X'Hal	0.60	0.40	1.00	2.00
❑25, Nov 82, CS; GP, War!; Fate is the Killer, A: Omega Men; 1: Masters of the Universe, Masters of the Universe preview	0.60	0.40	1.00	2.00
❑26, Dec 82, RT; GP, Runaways, 1: Terra	0.60	0.40	1.00	2.00
❑27, Jan 83, RT; GP, Runaways, Part 2, 1: Howard Rondo, Atari Force preview	0.60	0.40	1.00	2.00
❑28, Feb 83, RT; GP, Terra in the Night, A: Terra; V: Brotherhood of Evil	0.60	0.40	1.00	2.00
❑29, Mar 83, RT; GP, First Blood!, V: Brotherhood of Evil, Return of Speedy	0.60	0.40	1.00	2.00
❑30, Apr 83, RT; GP, Nightmare!, Terra joins team	0.60	0.40	1.00	2.00
❑31, May 83, RT; GP, Inferno!, V: Brotherhood of Evil	0.60	0.40	1.00	2.00
❑32, Jun 83, RT; GP, Thunder and Lightning, O: Kid Flash; A: Thunder and Lightning	0.60	0.40	1.00	2.00
❑33, Jul 83, RT; GP, Who Killed Trident?, D: Trident	0.60	0.40	1.00	2.00
❑34, Aug 83, GP, Endings...and Beginnings!, A: Deathstroke the Terminator; V: Terminator	0.60	0.40	1.00	2.00
❑35, Oct 83, GP, Siege!	0.60	0.40	1.00	2.00
❑36, Nov 83, KP, Feedback!, A: Thunder and Lightning	0.60	0.40	1.00	2.00
❑37, Dec 83, GP, Lights Out, Everyone!, A: Outsiders; V: Psimon; V: Mammoth; V: Gizmo; V: Shimmer; V: Doctor Light	0.75	0.40	1.00	2.00
❑38, Jan 84, GP, GP (w), Who is Donna Troy?, O: Wonder Girl	0.75	0.40	1.00	2.00
❑39, Feb 84, GP, GP (w), Crossroads, Dick Grayson quits as Robin; Wally West retires as Kid Flash	0.75	0.50	1.25	2.50
❑40, Mar 84, GP, GP (w), Lifeblood!, Series continued in Tales of the Teen Titans #41	0.75	0.40	1.00	2.00
❑Anl 1, GP, Final Conflict!, A: Omega Men	1.00	0.40	1.00	2.00
❑Anl 2, GP, 1: Vigilante; 1: Lyla (Harbinger); A: Monitor	1.00	0.40	1.00	2.00
❑Anl 3, The Judas Contract, Part 4, D: Terra, Published as Teen Titans Annual	1.25	0.40	1.00	2.00

NEW TEEN TITANS, THE (2ND SERIES)
DC

	ORIG	GOOD	FINE	N-MINT
❑1, Aug 84, GP, Shadows in the Dark!	1.25	0.60	1.50	3.00
❑2, Oct 84, GP, A: Trigon	1.25	0.50	1.25	2.50
❑3, Nov 84, GP, V: Trigon	1.25	0.50	1.25	2.50
❑4, Jan 85, GP, Torment!, V: Trigon	1.25	0.50	1.25	2.50

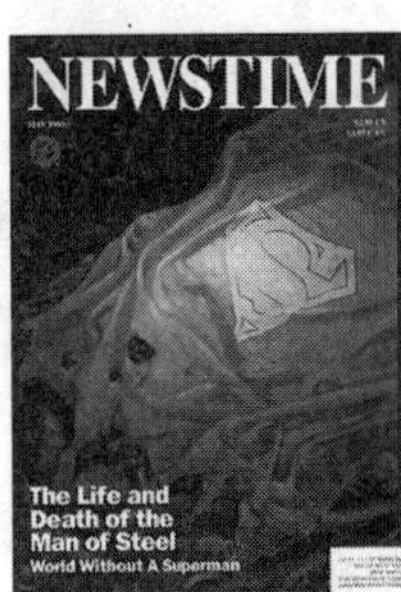

DC produced a facsimile copy of its universe's major news magazine, *Newstime*, in the wake of 1992's "Death of Superman."

© 1993 DC Comics

	ORIG	GOOD	FINE	N-MINT
❑5, Feb 85, GP, V: Trigon	1.25	0.50	1.25	2.50
❑6, Mar 85	1.25	0.40	1.00	2.00
❑7, Apr 85, O: Lilith	1.25	0.40	1.00	2.00
❑8, May 85, A: Destiny	1.25	0.40	1.00	2.00
❑9, Jun 85, 1: Kole	1.25	0.40	1.00	2.00
❑10, Jul 85	1.25	0.40	1.00	2.00
❑11, Aug 85	1.25	0.40	1.00	2.00
❑12, Sep 85, Sins of the Past	1.25	0.40	1.00	2.00
❑13, Oct 85, Crisis on Infinite Earths, Crisis	1.25	0.40	1.00	2.00
❑14, Nov 85, Crisis on Infinite Earths, Crisis	1.25	0.40	1.00	2.00
❑15, Dec 85	1.50	0.40	1.00	2.00
❑16, Jan 86, A: Omega Men	1.50	0.40	1.00	2.00
❑17, Feb 86, Wedding of Starfire	1.50	0.40	1.00	2.00
❑18, Mar 86	1.50	0.40	1.00	2.00
❑19, Apr 86	1.50	0.40	1.00	2.00
❑20, May 86, Return of original Titans; Robin II (Jason Todd) joins team	1.50	0.40	1.00	2.00
❑21, Jun 86, A: Cheshire	1.50	0.30	0.75	1.50
❑22, Jul 86	1.50	0.30	0.75	1.50
❑23, Aug 86, V: Hybrids	1.50	0.30	0.75	1.50
❑24, Oct 86, V: Hybrids	1.50	0.30	0.75	1.50
❑25, Nov 86	1.50	0.30	0.75	1.50
❑26, Dec 86	1.50	0.30	0.75	1.50
❑27, Jan 87, V: Brotherhood of Evil	1.50	0.30	0.75	1.50
❑28, Feb 87, V: Brother Blood	1.50	0.30	0.75	1.50
❑29, Mar 87, V: Brother Blood	1.50	0.30	0.75	1.50
❑30, Apr 87, V: Brother Blood	1.50	0.30	0.75	1.50
❑31, May 87, A: Batman; V: Brother Blood; A: Superman	1.50	0.30	0.75	1.50
❑32, Jun 87	1.50	0.30	0.75	1.50
❑33, Jul 87	1.50	0.30	0.75	1.50
❑34, Aug 87, V: Hybrid	1.50	0.30	0.75	1.50
❑35, Sep 87	1.50	0.30	0.75	1.50
❑36, Oct 87, V: Wildebeest	1.50	0.30	0.75	1.50
❑37, Nov 87, V: Wildebeest	1.75	0.35	0.88	1.75
❑38, Dec 87, A: Infinity Inc.; V: Ultra-Humanite	1.75	0.35	0.88	1.75
❑39, Jan 88	1.75	0.35	0.88	1.75
❑40, Feb 88, V: The Gentleman Ghost; V: Silver Fog; V: I.Q.	1.75	0.35	0.88	1.75
❑41, Mar 88, V: Wildebeest	1.75	0.35	0.88	1.75
❑42, Apr 88, Brother Blood's child born	1.75	0.35	0.88	1.75
❑43, May 88, Phobia vs. Raven	1.75	0.35	0.88	1.75
❑44, Jun 88, V: Godiva	1.75	0.35	0.88	1.75
❑45, Jul 88, A: Dial H for Hero	1.75	0.35	0.88	1.75
❑46, Aug 88, A: Dial H for Hero	1.75	0.35	0.88	1.75
❑47, Sep 88, O: Titans	1.75	0.35	0.88	1.75
❑48, Oct 88, V: Red Star	1.75	0.35	0.88	1.75
❑49, Nov 88, V: Red Star, Series continued in New Titans #50	1.75	0.35	0.88	1.75
❑Anl 1, V: Vanguard; A: Superman	2.00	0.50	1.25	2.50
❑Anl 2, Aug 86, JBy, 1: Cheshire; O: Brother Blood; A: Doctor Light	2.50	0.55	1.38	2.75
❑Anl 3, A: King Faraday; 1: Danny Chase; 1: Godiva, cover indicates '87 Annual, indicia says '86	2.25	0.50	1.25	2.50
❑Anl 4, Series continues as New Titans Annual; Private Lives	2.50	0.50	1.25	2.50

NEW TEEN TITANS (GIVEAWAYS AND PROMOS)
DC

	ORIG	GOOD	FINE	N-MINT
❑1, Beverage; DC drug issue	—	0.20	0.50	1.00
❑2, IBM/DC drug issue	—	0.20	0.50	1.00
❑3, DC; GP, Keebler; drug issue	1.00	0.20	0.50	1.00
❑4, DC, Keebler; drug issue	1.00	0.20	0.50	1.00

NEW TITANS, THE
DC

	ORIG	GOOD	FINE	N-MINT
❑0, Oct 94, The Changing Order, Impulse, Damage, Terra, Mirage joins team; Series continued in New Titans #115; Nightwing leaves team; Titans get new headquarters	1.95	0.45	1.13	2.25
❑50, Dec 88, GP, Who is Wonder Girl, Part 1, O: Wonder Girl (new origin), Series continued from New Teen Titans #49	1.75	0.50	1.25	2.50

	ORIG	GOOD	FINE	N-MINT
❑51, Dec 88, GP, Who is Wonder Girl, Part 2	1.75	0.40	1.00	2.00
❑52, Jan 89, GP, Who is Wonder Girl, Part 3	1.75	0.40	1.00	2.00
❑53, Feb 89, GP, Who is Wonder Girl, Part 4	1.75	0.40	1.00	2.00
❑54, Mar 89, GP, Who is Wonder Girl, Part 5	1.75	0.40	1.00	2.00
❑55, Jun 89, GP, GP (w), Transition, 1: Troia	1.75	0.40	1.00	2.00
❑56, Jul 89, A: Gnaark	1.75	0.40	1.00	2.00
❑57, Aug 89, GP, V: Wildebeest	1.75	0.40	1.00	2.00
❑58, Sep 89, GP	1.75	0.40	1.00	2.00
❑59, Oct 89, GP, V: Wildebeest	1.75	0.40	1.00	2.00
❑60, Nov 89, GP, GP (w), A Lonely Place of Dying, Part 2, A: Tim Drake	1.75	0.60	1.50	3.00
❑61, Dec 89, GP, GP (w), A Lonely Place of Dying, Part 4	1.75	0.50	1.25	2.50
❑62, Jan 90, A: Deathstroke the Terminator	1.75	0.40	1.00	2.00
❑63, Feb 90, A: Deathstroke the Terminator	1.75	0.40	1.00	2.00
❑64, Mar 90, A: Deathstroke the Terminator	1.75	0.40	1.00	2.00
❑65, Apr 90, A: Deathstroke the Terminator; A: Robin III	1.75	0.40	1.00	2.00
❑66, May 90, GP (w), Fatal Attraction	1.75	0.40	1.00	2.00
❑67, Jul 90, GP (w), If Looks Could Kill	1.75	0.40	1.00	2.00
❑68, Jul 90, V: Royal Flush Gang	1.75	0.40	1.00	2.00
❑69, Sep 90	1.75	0.40	1.00	2.00
❑70, Oct 90, A: Deathstroke the Terminator	1.75	0.40	1.00	2.00
❑71, Nov 90, Titans Hunt; Beginnings… Endings… and New Beginnings	1.75	0.40	1.00	2.00
❑72, Jan 91, A: Deathstroke the Terminator; D: Golden Eagle	1.75	0.40	1.00	2.00
❑73, Feb 91, A: Deathstroke the Terminator; 1: Phantasm	1.75	0.40	1.00	2.00
❑74, Mar 91, A: Deathstroke the Terminator; 1: Pantha	1.75	0.40	1.00	2.00
❑75, Apr 91, A: Deathstroke the Terminator	1.75	0.40	1.00	2.00
❑76, Jun 91, A: Deathstroke the Terminator, destruction of Titans Tower	1.75	0.40	1.00	2.00
❑77, Jul 91, A: Deathstroke the Terminator, Cyborg rebuilt	1.75	0.40	1.00	2.00
❑78, Aug 91, A: Deathstroke the Terminator	1.75	0.40	1.00	2.00
❑79, Sep 91, A: Deathstroke the Terminator; A: Team Titans	1.75	0.40	1.00	2.00
❑80, Nov 91, A: Team Titans	1.75	0.35	0.88	1.75
❑81, Dec 91, War of the Gods; War of the Gods, Part 23, A: Pariah	1.75	0.35	0.88	1.75
❑82, Jan 92, The Jericho Gambit, Part 1	1.75	0.35	0.88	1.75
❑83, Feb 92, The Jericho Gambit, Part 2, D: Jericho	1.75	0.35	0.88	1.75
❑84, Mar 92, Titans Hunt; The Jericho Gambit, Part 3, O: Phantasm; D: Raven	1.75	0.35	0.88	1.75
❑85, Apr 92, A: Team Titans, birth of baby Wildebeest	1.75	0.35	0.88	1.75
❑86, May 92, Nightwing vs. Terminator	1.75	0.35	0.88	1.75
❑87, Jun 92, Reflections	1.75	0.35	0.88	1.75
❑88, Jul 92, Bringing Up Baby	1.75	0.35	0.88	1.75
❑89, Aug 92, With Every Little Step We Take	1.75	0.35	0.88	1.75
❑90, Sep 92, Total Chaos, Part 2	1.75	0.35	0.88	1.75
❑91, Oct 92, Total Chaos, Part 5, A: Phantasm	1.75	0.35	0.88	1.75
❑92, Nov 92, Total Chaos, Part 8	1.75	0.35	0.88	1.75
❑93, Dec 92, Titans Sell-Out, Part 3, follow-up to Titans Sell-Out Special	1.75	0.35	0.88	1.75
❑94, Feb 93, covers of #94-96 form triptych	1.75	0.35	0.88	1.75
❑95, Mar 93, …Into the Fire	1.75	0.35	0.88	1.75
❑96, Apr 93, Patriot Games	1.75	0.35	0.88	1.75
❑97, May 93, The Darkening, Part 1	1.75	0.35	0.88	1.75
❑98, Jun 93, The Darkening, Part 2	1.75	0.35	0.88	1.75
❑99, Jul 93, The Darkening, Part 3, 1: Arsenal	1.75	0.35	0.88	1.75
❑100, Aug 93, Something Old, Something New, Something Borrowed, Something Dead, V: Evil Raven, pin-ups, foil cover; Giant-size; Wedding of Dick Grayson and Koriand'r	3.50	0.60	1.50	3.00
❑101, Sep 93, Aftermath	1.75	0.35	0.88	1.75
❑102, Oct 93	1.75	0.35	0.88	1.75
❑103, Nov 93	1.75	0.35	0.88	1.75
❑104, Dec 93, Terminus!, Part 1, final fate of Cyborg	1.75	0.35	0.88	1.75
❑105, Dec 93, Terminus!, Part 2	1.75	0.35	0.88	1.75
❑106, Jan 94, Terminus!, Part 3	1.75	0.35	0.88	1.75
❑107, Jan 94	1.75	0.35	0.88	1.75
❑108, Feb 94	1.75	0.35	0.88	1.75
❑109, Mar 94	1.75	0.35	0.88	1.75
❑110, May 94	1.75	0.35	0.88	1.75
❑111, Jun 94	1.75	0.35	0.88	1.75
❑112, Jul 94	1.95	0.39	0.98	1.95
❑113, Aug 94	1.95	0.39	0.98	1.95
❑114, Sep 94, new team; Series continued in The New Titans #0	1.95	0.39	0.98	1.95
❑115, Nov 94	1.95	0.39	0.98	1.95
❑116, Dec 94, A: Green Lantern, Return of Psimon	1.95	0.39	0.98	1.95
❑117, Jan 95, Psimon Didn't Psay You'd Win, V: Psimon	1.95	0.39	0.98	1.95
❑118, Feb 95, A: Thunder and Lightning	1.95	0.39	0.98	1.95
❑119, Mar 95, Forever Evil, Part 1, V: Deathwing	1.95	0.39	0.98	1.95
❑120, Apr 95, Forever Evil, Part 2, A: Supergirl	1.95	0.39	0.98	1.95
❑121, May 95	1.95	0.39	0.98	1.95
❑122, Jun 95	2.25	0.45	1.13	2.25
❑123, Jul 95	2.25	0.45	1.13	2.25
❑124, Aug 95, The Siege of The Zi Charam, Part 1	2.25	0.45	1.13	2.25
❑125, Sep 95, The Siege of The Zi Charam, Part 5, Giant-size	3.50	0.70	1.75	3.50
❑126, Oct 95, Meltdown	2.25	0.45	1.13	2.25
❑127, Nov 95, Meltdown	2.25	0.45	1.13	2.25
❑128, Dec 95, Meltdown	2.25	0.45	1.13	2.25
❑129, Jan 96, Meltdown	2.25	0.45	1.13	2.25
❑130, Feb 96, Where Nightmares End!, Final Issue	2.25	0.45	1.13	2.25
❑Anl 5, See New Teen Titans Annual for previous issues, Who's Who entries; See New Teen Titans Annual for previous issues; Who's Who entries	3.50	0.70	1.75	3.50
❑Anl 6, Stayfree's World, Chapter 1, 1: Society of Sin, Starfire	3.50	0.70	1.75	3.50
❑Anl 7, Armageddon 2001, Part 10, 1: Team Titans, Armageddon 2001	3.50	0.70	1.75	3.50
❑Anl 8, Eclipso: The Darkness Within, Part 14, Eclipso: The Darkness Within	3.50	0.60	1.50	3.00
❑Anl 9, Bloodlines; The Red Hand BluesPaul Witcover, Elizabeth Hand, 1: Anima, Bloodlines: Outbreak	3.50	0.60	1.50	3.00
❑Anl 10, Elseworlds	3.50	0.60	1.50	3.00
❑Anl 11, Year One	3.95	0.79	1.98	3.95

NEW TRIUMPH FEATURING NORTHGUARD
Matrix

	ORIG	GOOD	FINE	N-MINT
❑1, And Stand on Guard…	1.50	0.35	0.88	1.75
❑1-2, 2nd Printing	1.75	0.35	0.88	1.75
❑2	1.50	0.30	0.75	1.50
❑3, Target Red Target Blue	1.50	0.30	0.75	1.50
❑4	1.50	0.30	0.75	1.50
❑5	1.50	0.30	0.75	1.50

NEW TWO-FISTED TALES, THE
EC

	ORIG	GOOD	FINE	N-MINT
❑1, Dustoff; The Crater	4.95	1.10	2.75	5.50

NEW TWO-FISTED TALES, THE (2ND SERIES)
Dark Horse

Value: Cover or less

❑1, Oct 93, Diversion; Gettysberg, nn 4.95

NEW VAMPIRE MIYU (VOL. 1)
Ironcat

Value: Cover or less

❑1, Sep 97, Battle Against the Western Shinmas	2.95	❑4	2.95
❑2	2.95	❑5	2.95
❑3	2.95	❑6	2.95

NEW VAMPIRE MIYU (VOL. 2)
Ironcat

Value: Cover or less

❑1	2.95	❑4	2.95
❑2	2.95	❑5	2.95
❑3	2.95	❑6	2.95

NEW VAMPIRE MIYU (VOL. 4)
Ironcat

Value: Cover or less

❑1	2.95	❑4	2.95
❑2, Jan 99	2.95	❑5	2.95
❑3	2.95	❑6	2.95

NEW WARRIORS, THE
Marvel

	ORIG	GOOD	FINE	N-MINT
❑1, Jul 90, From The Ground Up!, O: New Warriors	1.00	0.40	1.00	2.00
❑1-2, Jul 90, From The Ground Up!, O: New Warriors, 2nd Printing (gold)	1.00	0.30	0.75	1.50
❑2, Aug 90, 1: Silhouette; O: Night Thrasher	1.00	0.30	0.75	1.50
❑3, Sep 90	1.00	0.30	0.75	1.50
❑4, Oct 90	1.00	0.30	0.75	1.50
❑5, Nov 90	1.00	0.30	0.75	1.50
❑6, Dec 90	1.00	0.30	0.75	1.50
❑7, Jan 91, Punisher cameo	1.00	0.30	0.75	1.50
❑8, Feb 91, O: Bengal; A: Punisher	1.00	0.30	0.75	1.50
❑9, Mar 91, Hard Choices, Part 3, A: Punisher	1.00	0.30	0.75	1.50
❑10, Apr 91	1.00	0.30	0.75	1.50
❑11, May 91, Wolverine	1.00	0.30	0.75	1.50
❑12, Jun 91	1.00	0.30	0.75	1.50
❑13, Jul 91, Forever Yesterday, Part 3	1.00	0.30	0.75	1.50
❑14, Aug 91, The Breeze of an Underwater Wind, A: Darkhawk; A: Namor	1.00	0.30	0.75	1.50

	ORIG	GOOD	FINE	N-MINT
❑15, Sep 91	1.00	0.30	0.75	1.50
❑16, Oct 91, Ground War	1.00	0.30	0.75	1.50
❑17, Nov 91, Spre Winners, A: Fantastic Four	1.00	0.30	0.75	1.50
❑18, Dec 91, Everything You Always Wanted to know About the Taylor Foundation But Were Afraid to Ask	1.00	0.30	0.75	1.50
❑19, Jan 92, Sympathy for the Devil	1.00	0.30	0.75	1.50
❑20, Feb 92, The Breaking Point	1.25	0.30	0.75	1.50
❑21, Mar 92	1.25	0.30	0.75	1.50
❑22, Apr 92, Nothing But the Truth, Part 1	1.25	0.30	0.75	1.50
❑23, May 92, Nothing But the Truth, Part 2, O: Chord; O: Silhouette; O: Night Thrasher	1.25	0.30	0.75	1.50
❑24, Jun 92, O: Chord; O: Silhouette	1.25	0.30	0.75	1.50
❑25, Jul 92, O: Chord, Die-cut cover	2.50	0.50	1.25	2.50
❑26, Aug 92, The Next Step	1.25	0.25	0.63	1.25
❑27, Sep 92	1.25	0.25	0.63	1.25
❑28, Oct 92, Heavy Turbulence, 1: Turbo I (Michiko "Mickey" Musashi); 1: Cardinal	1.25	0.25	0.63	1.25
❑29, Nov 92, World War One: This Land Must Change	1.25	0.25	0.63	1.25
❑30, Dec 92	1.25	0.25	0.63	1.25
❑31, Jan 93, Ruins	1.25	0.25	0.63	1.25
❑32, Feb 93, Forces of Light, Part 1	1.25	0.25	0.63	1.25
❑33, Mar 93, Forces of Light, Part 2, 1: Turbo II (Mike Jeffries)	1.25	0.25	0.63	1.25
❑34, Apr 93, Forces of Light, Part 3	1.25	0.25	0.63	1.25
❑35, May 93, Forces of Light, Part 4	1.25	0.25	0.63	1.25
❑36, Jun 93	1.25	0.25	0.63	1.25
❑37, Jul 93	1.25	0.25	0.63	1.25
❑38, Aug 93	1.25	0.25	0.63	1.25
❑39, Sep 93	1.25	0.25	0.63	1.25
❑40, Oct 93, A: Firelord; A: Super Nova; A: Nova, Air-Walker appearnce	1.25	0.25	0.63	1.25
❑40/SC, Oct 93, A: Firelord; A: Super Nova; A: Air-Walker; A: Nova, Gold foil on cover	2.25	0.45	1.13	2.25
❑41, Nov 93	1.25	0.25	0.63	1.25
❑42, Dec 93	1.25	0.25	0.63	1.25
❑43, Jan 94	1.25	0.25	0.63	1.25
❑44, Feb 94	1.25	0.25	0.63	1.25
❑45, Mar 94	1.25	0.25	0.63	1.25
❑46, Apr 94	1.25	0.25	0.63	1.25
❑47, May 94, Time and Time Again, Part 1	1.50	0.25	0.63	1.25
❑48, Jun 94, Time and Time Again, Part 4	1.50	0.30	0.75	1.50
❑49, Jul 94	1.50	0.30	0.75	1.50
❑50, Aug 94, Time and Time Again, Part 8, Giant-size	2.00	0.40	1.00	2.00
❑50/SC, Aug 94, Time and Time Again, Part 8, Glow-in-the-dark cover; Giant-size	2.95	0.59	1.48	2.95
❑51, Sep 94	1.50	0.30	0.75	1.50
❑52, Oct 94	1.50	0.30	0.75	1.50
❑53, Nov 94	1.50	0.30	0.75	1.50
❑54, Dec 94	1.50	0.30	0.75	1.50
❑55, Jan 95	1.50	0.30	0.75	1.50
❑56, Feb 95	1.50	0.30	0.75	1.50
❑57, Mar 95	1.50	0.30	0.75	1.50
❑58, Apr 95	1.50	0.30	0.75	1.50
❑59, May 95	1.50	0.30	0.75	1.50
❑60, Jun 95, Giant-size	2.50	0.50	1.25	2.50
❑61, Jul 95, Maximum Clonage Prologue	1.50	0.30	0.75	1.50
❑62, Aug 95, A: Scarlet Spider	1.50	0.30	0.75	1.50
❑63, Sep 95	1.50	0.30	0.75	1.50
❑64, Oct 95, return of Night Thrasher and Rage	1.50	0.30	0.75	1.50
❑65, Nov 95, return of Namorita	1.50	0.30	0.75	1.50
❑66, Dec 95, A: Speedball; A: Scarlet Spider	1.50	0.30	0.75	1.50
❑67, Jan 96, Nightmare in Scarlet, Part 2, concludes in Web of Scarlet Spider #3	1.50	0.30	0.75	1.50
❑68, Feb 96, Future Shock, Part 1, A: Guardians of the Galaxy	1.50	0.30	0.75	1.50
❑69, Mar 96, Future Shock, Part 2, D: Speedball	1.50	0.30	0.75	1.50
❑70, Apr 96, Future Shock, Part 3	1.50	0.30	0.75	1.50
❑71, May 96, Future Shock, Part 4	1.50	0.30	0.75	1.50
❑72, Jun 96, A: Avengers	1.50	0.30	0.75	1.50
❑73, Jul 96	1.50	0.30	0.75	1.50
❑74, Aug 96	1.50	0.30	0.75	1.50
❑75, Sep 96, Final Issue	2.50	0.30	0.75	1.50
❑Anl 1, Kings of Pain; Kings of Pain, Part 2, O: Night Thrasher	2.00	0.60	1.50	3.00
❑Anl 2, The Hero Killers, Part 4; Days And Nights	2.25	0.45	1.13	2.25
❑Anl 3, trading card	2.95	0.59	1.48	2.95
❑Anl 4	2.95	0.59	1.48	2.95
❑Ash 1, Team Reflections, "Ashcan" mini-comic	0.75	0.15	0.38	0.75

NEW WARRIORS, THE (VOL. 2)
MARVEL
Value: Cover or less

❑1, Oct 99, One Good Reason	2.99	❑2, Nov 99	2.99
❑3, Dec 99	2.50	❑7, Apr 00	2.50
❑4, Jan 00	2.50	❑8, May 00, Rite of Passage	2.50
❑5, Feb 00	2.50	❑9	2.50
❑6, Mar 00	2.50	❑10	2.50

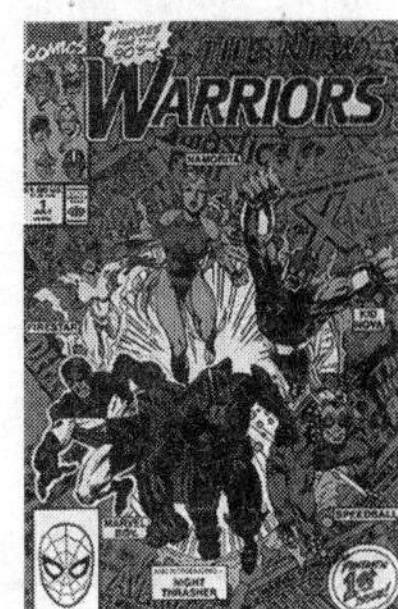

New Warriors members Firestar and Vance Astro later joined The Avengers.

NEW WAVE, THE
ECLIPSE

	ORIG	GOOD	FINE	N-MINT
❑1, Jun 86, The Man In The Corporate Booth	0.50	0.40	1.00	2.00
❑1/A, misprint	0.50	0.40	1.00	2.00
❑2, Jul 86	0.50	0.30	0.75	1.50
❑3, Jul 86, A Space Station Called Hell!	0.50	0.30	0.75	1.50
❑4, Aug 86	0.50	0.20	0.50	1.00
❑5, Aug 86	0.50	0.20	0.50	1.00
❑6, Sep 86	0.50	0.20	0.50	1.00
❑7, Sep 86	0.50	0.20	0.50	1.00
❑8, Sep 86	0.50	0.20	0.50	1.00
❑9, Oct 86	1.50	0.30	0.75	1.50
❑10, Nov 86, Breach Of Faith	1.50	0.30	0.75	1.50
❑11, Dec 86	1.50	0.30	0.75	1.50
❑12, Feb 87	1.50	0.30	0.75	1.50
❑13, Mar 87, Final Issue	1.50	0.30	0.75	1.50

NEW WAVE VERSUS THE VOLUNTEERS, THE
ECLIPSE
Value: Cover or less

❑1, Apr 87	2.50	❑2, Jun 87, You Can't Fight City Hall	2.50

NEW WORLD ORDER
BLAZER

	ORIG	GOOD	FINE	N-MINT
❑1, b&w	2.50	0.60	1.50	3.00
❑2, b&w	2.50	0.55	1.38	2.75
❑3, b&w	2.50	0.55	1.38	2.75
❑4, Aug 93, b&w	2.50	0.50	1.25	2.50
❑5, Jan 94, b&w	2.50	0.50	1.25	2.50
❑6, May 94, 1: Skinhead, b&w	2.50	0.50	1.25	2.50
❑7, Aug 94, 1: Shining, b&w	2.50	0.50	1.25	2.50
❑8, Feb 95, b&w	2.50	0.50	1.25	2.50

NEW WORLD ORDER (PIG'S EYE)
PIG'S EYE
Value: Cover or less

❑1 .... 1.00

NEW WORLDS ANTHOLOGY
CALIBER
Value: Cover or less

❑1	2.95	❑4	3.95
❑2, Jan 96, Mister X, Part 2; Little White Mouse: Dream of the Ghost, Part 1	3.95	❑5	3.95
❑3	3.95	❑6	3.95

NEW YORK CITY OUTLAWS
OUTLAW
Value: Cover or less

❑1	2.00	❑3	2.00
❑2	2.00	❑4	2.00

NEW YORK: YEAR ZERO
ECLIPSE
Value: Cover or less

❑1, Aug 88	2.00	❑3, Sep 88	2.00
❑2, Aug 88	2.00	❑4, Oct 88	2.00

NEXT MAN
COMICO

	ORIG	GOOD	FINE	N-MINT
❑1, Mar 85, 1: Next Man	1.50	0.40	1.00	2.00
❑2, Apr 85, American Pie	1.50	0.40	1.00	2.00
❑3, Jun 85	1.50	0.40	1.00	2.00
❑4, Aug 85	1.50	0.40	1.00	2.00
❑5, Oct 85	1.50	0.40	1.00	2.00

NEXT MEN (JOHN BYRNE'S...)
DARK HORSE

	ORIG	GOOD	FINE	N-MINT
❑0, Feb 92, JBy, JBy (w), Prelude, collects storyline from Dark Horse Presents; Reprints Next Men stories from Dark Horse Presents	2.50	0.60	1.50	3.00
❑1, Jan 92, JBy, JBy (w), Breakout, Embossed cover (silver logo); "Stock Certificate"	2.50	0.60	1.50	3.00
❑1-2, Jan 92, JBy, JBy (w), Breakout, 2nd Printing; Embossed cover (gold logo)	2.50	0.50	1.25	2.50

	ORIG	GOOD	FINE	N-MINT
❑2, Mar 92, JBy, JBy (w), World View, 1: Sathanus, "Stock Certificate"	2.50	0.60	1.50	3.00
❑3, Apr 92, JBy, JBy (w), Kill Factor, "Stock Certificate"	2.50	0.50	1.25	2.50
❑4, May 92, JBy, JBy (w), Boneyard, "Stock Certificate"	2.50	0.50	1.25	2.50
❑5, Jun 92, JBy, JBy (w), Survivor, "Stock Certificate"	2.50	0.50	1.25	2.50
❑6, Jul 92, JBy, JBy (w), Dominoes, "Stock Certificate"	2.50	0.50	1.25	2.50
❑7, Sep 92, JBy, JBy (w), Parallel, Part 1, 1: M4, flipbook with M4 #1 back-up story	2.50	0.50	1.25	2.50
❑8, Oct 92, JBy, JBy (w), Parallel, Part 2, flip-book with M4 #2 back-up story	2.50	0.50	1.25	2.50
❑9, Nov 92, JBy, JBy (w), Parallel, Part 3, flipbook with M4 #3 back-up story	2.50	0.50	1.25	2.50
❑10, Dec 92, JBy, JBy (w), Parallel, Interlude, flipbook with M4 #4 back-up story	2.50	0.50	1.25	2.50
❑11, Jan 93, JBy, JBy (w), Parallel, Part 4, M4 back-up story	2.50	0.50	1.25	2.50
❑12, Feb 93, JBy, JBy (w), Parallel, Part 5, M4 back-up story	2.50	0.50	1.25	2.50
❑13, Mar 93, JBy, JBy (w), Fame, Part 1, M4 back-up story	2.50	0.50	1.25	2.50
❑14, Apr 93, JBy, JBy (w), Fame, Part 2, M4 back-up story	2.50	0.50	1.25	2.50
❑15, Jun 93, JBy, JBy (w), Fame, Part 3, Photo cover; Carolyn Bickford letter; M4 back-up story	2.50	0.60	1.50	3.00
❑16, Jul 93, JBy, JBy (w), Fame, Part 4, M4 back-up story	2.50	0.50	1.25	2.50
❑17, Aug 93, JBy, FM (c), JBy (w), Fame, Part 5, M4 back-up story	2.50	0.50	1.25	2.50
❑18, Sep 93, JBy, JBy (w), Fame, Part 6, M4 back-up story	2.50	0.50	1.25	2.50
❑19, Oct 93, JBy, JBy (w), Faith, Part 1, M4 back-up story	2.50	0.50	1.25	2.50
❑20, Nov 93, JBy, JBy (w), Faith, Part 2, M4 back-up story	2.50	0.50	1.25	2.50
❑21, Dec 93, JBy, JBy (w), Faith, Part 3, A: Hellboy, M4 back-up story	2.50	0.50	1.25	2.50
❑22, Jan 94, JBy, JBy (w), Faith, Part 4, M4 back-up story	2.50	0.50	1.25	2.50
❑23, Mar 94, JBy, JBy (w), Power, Part 1, M4 back-up story	2.50	0.50	1.25	2.50
❑24, Apr 94, JBy, JBy (w), Power, Part 2, M4 back-up story	2.50	0.50	1.25	2.50
❑25, May 94, JBy, JBy (w), Power, Part 3, A: Cutter and Skywise (Elfquest characters)	2.50	0.50	1.25	2.50
❑26, Jun 94, JBy, JBy (w), Power, Part 4	2.50	0.50	1.25	2.50
❑27, Aug 94, JBy, JBy (w), Lies, Part 1	2.50	0.50	1.25	2.50
❑28, Sep 94, JBy, JBy (w), Lies, Part 2	2.50	0.50	1.25	2.50
❑29, Oct 94, JBy, JBy (w), Lies, Part 3	2.50	0.50	1.25	2.50
❑30, Dec 94, JBy, JBy (w), Lies, Part 4, series goes on hiatus	2.50	0.50	1.25	2.50

NEXT NEXUS, THE
FIRST

	ORIG	GOOD	FINE	N-MINT
❑1, SR, Three Sisters	1.95	0.40	1.00	2.00
❑2, SR	1.95	0.40	1.00	2.00
❑3, SR	1.95	0.40	1.00	2.00
❑4, SR	1.95	0.40	1.00	2.00

NEXT WAVE, THE
OVERSTREET

	ORIG	GOOD	FINE	N-MINT
❑1, Rib; Dream Walker, Sampling of Five Self-Published comics	—	0.40	1.00	2.00

NEXUS (VOL. 1)
CAPITAL

	ORIG	GOOD	FINE	N-MINT
❑1, SR, 1: Nexus, b&w	1.75	3.60	9.00	18.00
❑2, SR	1.75	2.60	6.50	13.00
❑3, Oct 82, SR, record	1.75	4.00	10.00	20.00

NEXUS (VOL. 2)
CAPITAL

	ORIG	GOOD	FINE	N-MINT
❑1, SR, Nexus begins for first time in color; Capital Comics publishes	1.50	0.80	2.00	4.00
❑2, SR, O: Nexus	1.75	0.70	1.75	3.50
❑3, SR	1.75	0.70	1.75	3.50
❑4, SR	1.75	0.70	1.75	3.50
❑5, SR	1.75	0.70	1.75	3.50
❑6, SR	1.75	0.60	1.50	3.00
❑7, SR, First Comics begins publishing	1.75	0.60	1.50	3.00
❑8, SR	1.75	0.60	1.50	3.00
❑9, SR, Teen Angel	1.75	0.50	1.25	2.50
❑10, SR	1.75	0.45	1.13	2.25
❑11, SR	1.75	0.45	1.13	2.25
❑12, SR	1.75	0.45	1.13	2.25
❑13, SR	1.75	0.45	1.13	2.25
❑14, SR	1.75	0.45	1.13	2.25
❑15, SR	1.75	0.45	1.13	2.25
❑16, SR	1.75	0.45	1.13	2.25
❑17, SR	1.75	0.45	1.13	2.25
❑18, SR	1.75	0.45	1.13	2.25
❑19, SR	1.75	0.45	1.13	2.25
❑20, SR	1.75	0.45	1.13	2.25
❑21	1.75	0.45	1.13	2.25
❑22	1.75	0.45	1.13	2.25
❑23	1.75	0.45	1.13	2.25
❑24	1.75	0.45	1.13	2.25
❑25	1.75	0.45	1.13	2.25
❑26	1.75	0.45	1.13	2.25
❑27	1.75	0.45	1.13	2.25
❑28	1.75	0.45	1.13	2.25
❑29	1.75	0.45	1.13	2.25
❑30	1.75	0.45	1.13	2.25
❑31	1.75	0.40	1.00	2.00
❑32	1.75	0.40	1.00	2.00
❑33	1.75	0.40	1.00	2.00
❑34	1.75	0.40	1.00	2.00
❑35	1.75	0.40	1.00	2.00
❑36	1.75	0.40	1.00	2.00
❑37	1.75	0.40	1.00	2.00
❑38	1.75	0.40	1.00	2.00
❑39	1.75	0.40	1.00	2.00
❑40, SR, Possession	1.75	0.40	1.00	2.00
❑41	1.75	0.40	1.00	2.00
❑42	1.75	0.40	1.00	2.00
❑43, SR, Portrait Of Death	1.75	0.40	1.00	2.00
❑44	1.75	0.40	1.00	2.00
❑45, A: Badger	1.75	0.40	1.00	2.00
❑46, A: Badger	1.75	0.40	1.00	2.00
❑47, A: Badger	1.75	0.40	1.00	2.00
❑48, A: Badger	1.75	0.40	1.00	2.00
❑49, A: Badger	1.75	0.40	1.00	2.00
❑50, A: Badger, Crossroads	1.75	0.70	1.75	3.50
❑51	1.95	0.40	1.00	2.00
❑52	1.95	0.40	1.00	2.00
❑53	1.95	0.40	1.00	2.00
❑54	1.95	0.40	1.00	2.00
❑55, Apr 89	1.95	0.40	1.00	2.00
❑56, May 89	1.95	0.40	1.00	2.00
❑57, Jun 89	1.95	0.40	1.00	2.00
❑58, Jul 89	1.95	0.40	1.00	2.00
❑59	1.95	0.40	1.00	2.00
❑60	1.95	0.40	1.00	2.00
❑61	1.95	0.40	1.00	2.00
❑62	1.95	0.40	1.00	2.00
❑63	1.95	0.40	1.00	2.00
❑64	1.95	0.40	1.00	2.00
❑65	1.95	0.40	1.00	2.00
❑66	1.95	0.40	1.00	2.00
❑67	1.95	0.40	1.00	2.00
❑68	1.95	0.40	1.00	2.00
❑69	1.95	0.40	1.00	2.00
❑70	1.95	0.40	1.00	2.00
❑71	1.95	0.40	1.00	2.00
❑72	1.95	0.40	1.00	2.00
❑73	2.25	0.45	1.13	2.25
❑74	2.25	0.45	1.13	2.25
❑75	2.25	0.45	1.13	2.25
❑76	2.25	0.45	1.13	2.25
❑77	2.25	0.45	1.13	2.25
❑78	2.25	0.45	1.13	2.25
❑79	2.25	0.45	1.13	2.25
❑80, Final issue of First series	2.25	0.45	1.13	2.25
❑81, Nexus: The Origin, Number not noted in indicia (was retroactive)	3.95	0.79	1.98	3.95
❑82, Nexus: Alien Justice, Part 1, Nexus: Alien Justice #1; Number not noted in indicia (was retroactive)	3.95	0.79	1.98	3.95
❑83, Nexus: Alien Justice, Part 2, Nexus: Alien Justice #2; Number not noted in indicia (was retroactive)	3.95	0.79	1.98	3.95
❑84, Nexus: Alien Justice, Part 3, Nexus: Alien Justice #3; Number not noted in indicia (was retroactive)	3.95	0.79	1.98	3.95
❑85, Nexus: The Wages of Sin, Part 1, Nexus: The Wages of Sin #1; Number not noted in indicia (was retroactive)	—	0.59	1.48	2.95
❑86, Nexus: The Wages of Sin, Part 2, Nexus: The Wages of Sin #2; Number not noted in indicia (was retroactive)	—	0.59	1.48	2.95
❑87, Nexus: The Wages of Sin, Part 3, Nexus: The Wages of Sin #3; Number not noted in indicia (was retroactive)	—	0.59	1.48	2.95
❑88, Nexus: The Wages of Sin, Part 4, Nexus: The Wages of Sin #4; Number not noted in indicia (was retroactive)	—	0.59	1.48	2.95
❑89, Jun 96, SR, Executioner's Song, Part 1	2.95	0.59	1.48	2.95

	ORIG	GOOD	FINE	N-MINT
❑90, Jul 96, SR, Executioner's Song, Part 2	2.95	0.59	1.48	2.95
❑91, Aug 96, SR, Executioner's Song, Part 3	2.95	0.59	1.48	2.95
❑92, Sep 96, SR, Executioner's Song, Part 4	2.95	0.59	1.48	2.95
❑93, Apr 97, SR, God Con, Part 1	2.95	0.59	1.48	2.95
❑94, May 97, SR, God Con, Part 2	2.95	0.59	1.48	2.95
❑95, Jul 97, SR, Nightmare in Blue, Part 1, b&w	2.95	0.59	1.48	2.95
❑96, Aug 97, SR, Nightmare in Blue, Part 2, b&w	2.95	0.59	1.48	2.95
❑97, Sep 97, SR, Nightmare in Blue, Part 3, b&w	2.95	0.59	1.48	2.95
❑98, Oct 97, SR, Nightmare in Blue, Part 4, b&w	2.95	0.59	1.48	2.95

NEXUS: ALIEN JUSTICE
DARK HORSE

Value: Cover or less

- ❑1 ... 3.95
- ❑2 ... 3.95
- ❑3, SR ... 3.95

NEXUS LEGENDS
FIRST

	ORIG	GOOD	FINE	N-MINT
❑1, SR	1.50	0.50	1.25	2.50
❑2, SR	1.50	0.40	1.00	2.00
❑3, SR	1.50	0.40	1.00	2.00
❑4, SR, Reprint	1.50	0.40	1.00	2.00
❑5, SR, Reprint	1.50	0.40	1.00	2.00
❑6, SR, Reprint	1.50	0.40	1.00	2.00
❑7, SR, Reprint	1.50	0.40	1.00	2.00
❑8, SR, Reprint	1.50	0.40	1.00	2.00
❑9, SR, Reprint	1.50	0.40	1.00	2.00
❑10, SR, Reprint	1.50	0.40	1.00	2.00
❑11, SR, Reprint	1.50	0.40	1.00	2.00
❑12, SR, Reprint	1.50	0.40	1.00	2.00
❑13, SR, Reprint	1.50	0.40	1.00	2.00
❑14, SR, Reprint	1.50	0.40	1.00	2.00
❑15, SR, Reprint	1.50	0.40	1.00	2.00
❑16, SR, Reprint	1.75	0.40	1.00	2.00
❑17, SR, Reprint	1.75	0.40	1.00	2.00
❑18, SR, Reprint	1.95	0.40	1.00	2.00
❑19, SR, Reprint	1.95	0.40	1.00	2.00
❑20, SR, Reprint	1.95	0.40	1.00	2.00
❑21, SR, Reprint	1.95	0.40	1.00	2.00
❑22, SR, Reprint	1.95	0.40	1.00	2.00
❑23, SR, Final Issue	1.95	0.40	1.00	2.00

NEXUS MEETS MADMAN
DARK HORSE

Value: Cover or less

- ❑1, May 96, SR, nn; One-Shot ... 2.95

NEXUS THE LIBERATOR
DARK HORSE

Value: Cover or less

- ❑1, Walking Dreams ... 2.50
- ❑2 ... 2.50
- ❑3 ... 2.50
- ❑4, The Dying of the Light ... 2.50

NEXUS: THE ORIGIN
DARK HORSE

Value: Cover or less

- ❑1, SR, O: Nexus, nn ... 3.95

NEXUS: THE WAGES OF SIN
DARK HORSE

Value: Cover or less

- ❑1, Mar 95, SR, The Client, cardstock cover ... 2.95
- ❑2, Apr 95, SR, cardstock cover ... 2.95
- ❑3, May 95, SR, cardstock cover ... 2.95
- ❑4, SR ... 2.95

NFL SUPERPRO
MARVEL

Value: Cover or less

- ❑1, Oct 91, You Bet Your Life, O: NFL SuperPro; A: Spider-Man ... 1.00
- ❑2, Nov 91, The Killer Instinct. ... 1.00
- ❑3, Dec 91, Time Out ... 1.00
- ❑4, Jan 92 ... 1.00
- ❑5, Feb 92 ... 1.25
- ❑6, Mar 92 ... 1.25
- ❑7, Apr 92 ... 1.25
- ❑8, May 92, Captain America. ... 1.25
- ❑9, Jun 92 ... 1.25
- ❑10, Jul 92 ... 1.25
- ❑11, Aug 92, Feels Like Team Spirit ... 1.25
- ❑12, Sep 92, Final Issue ... 1.25
- ❑SE 1, Sep 91, BH, Fourth and Goal to Go, 1: NFL SuperPro, Special collector's edition ... 2.00
- ❑SE 1-2, Sep 91, BH, Fourth and Goal to Go, 1: NFL SuperPro, 2nd Printing; Super Bowl Specia ... 3.95

NICK FURY, AGENT OF SHIELD (1ST SERIES)
MARVEL

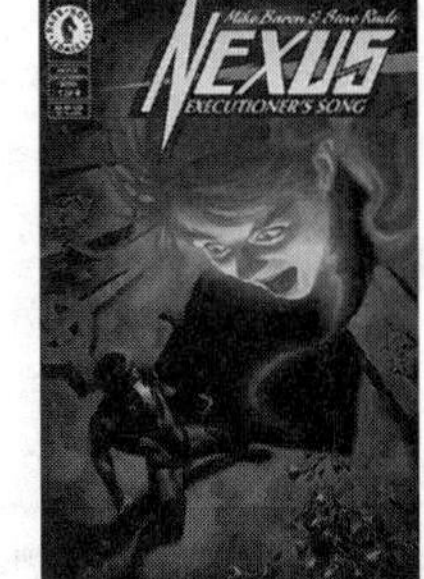

Dark Horse's run on *Nexus* included information in the indicia as to where the individual issues fit in overall continuity.

© 1996 Steve Rude (Dark Horse)

	ORIG	GOOD	FINE	N-MINT
❑1, Jun 68, JSo, JSo (w), Who is Scorpio?, 1: Scorpio	0.12	10.00	25.00	50.00
❑2, Jul 68, JSo, 1: Centurius	0.12	6.40	16.00	32.00
❑3, Aug 68, JSo, JSo (w), Dark Moon Rise, Hell Hound Kill!	0.12	5.60	14.00	28.00
❑4, Sep 68, O: Nick Fury	0.12	7.00	17.50	35.00
❑5, Oct 68, JSo	0.12	6.00	15.00	30.00
❑6, Nov 68, FS, Doom Must Fall!	0.12	3.60	9.00	18.00
❑7, Dec 68	0.12	3.60	9.00	18.00
❑8, Jan 69	0.12	2.40	6.00	12.00
❑9, Feb 69	0.12	2.40	6.00	12.00
❑10, Mar 69	0.12	2.40	6.00	12.00
❑11, The First Million Megaton Explosion	0.12	2.40	6.00	12.00
❑12	0.12	2.60	6.50	13.00
❑13	0.12	2.40	6.00	12.00
❑14	0.15	1.60	4.00	8.00
❑15, 1: Bullseye	0.15	7.00	17.50	35.00
❑16, Giant-size; Reprints from Strange Tales	0.25	1.20	3.00	6.00
❑17, Giant-size; Reprints from Strange Tales	0.25	1.20	3.00	6.00
❑18, Mar 71, Giant-size; Reprints from Strange Tales	0.25	1.20	3.00	6.00

NICK FURY, AGENT OF SHIELD (2ND SERIES)
MARVEL

	ORIG	GOOD	FINE	N-MINT
❑1, Dec 83, wraparound cover; Reprints from Nick Fury, Agent of SHIELD (1st series).	2.00	0.60	1.50	3.00
❑2, Jan 84, Reprints from Nick Fury, Agent of SHIELD (1st series)	2.00	0.60	1.50	3.00

NICK FURY, AGENT OF S.H.I.E.L.D. (3RD SERIES)
MARVEL

	ORIG	GOOD	FINE	N-MINT
❑1, Sep 89, BH, The Past Still Haunts	1.50	0.45	1.13	2.25
❑2, Oct 89, KP, A Web With Many Strands, Death's Head	1.50	0.35	0.88	1.75
❑3, Nov 89, KP, In Memory Ever Green, Death's Head	1.50	0.35	0.88	1.75
❑4, Nov 89, KP, Slips Of Memory, Sgt. Fury	1.50	0.30	0.75	1.50
❑5, Dec 89, KP, Memory And Menace!	1.50	0.30	0.75	1.50
❑6, Dec 89, KP, In Final Memory	1.50	0.30	0.75	1.50
❑7, Jan 90, KP, Chaos Serpent, Part 1; The Chaos Serpent, Part 1	1.50	0.30	0.75	1.50
❑8, Feb 90, Chaos Serpent, Part 2; The Chaos Serpent, Part 2	1.50	0.30	0.75	1.50
❑9, Mar 90, KP, Chaos Serpent, Part 3; The Chaos Serpent, Part 3	1.50	0.30	0.75	1.50
❑10, Apr 90, KP, Chaos Serpent, Part 4; The Chaos Serpent, Part 4, A: Captain America	1.50	0.30	0.75	1.50
❑11, May 90, Greetings From Scotland	1.50	0.30	0.75	1.50
❑12, Jun 90, Hydra Affair; Fears And Obsessions	1.50	0.30	0.75	1.50
❑13, Jul 90, KP, In Battle Joined!, Return of Yellow Claw	1.50	0.30	0.75	1.50
❑14, Aug 90, KP, Pyrrhic Victory	1.50	0.30	0.75	1.50
❑15, Sep 90, Apogee Of Disaster, Part 1, A: Fantastic Four	1.50	0.30	0.75	1.50
❑16, Oct 90, Apogee Of Disaster, Part 2	1.50	0.30	0.75	1.50
❑17, Nov 90, HT, Apogee Of Disaster, Part 3	1.50	0.30	0.75	1.50
❑18, Dec 90	1.50	0.30	0.75	1.50
❑19, Jan 91, HT, Downrange Of The End Of The World!	1.50	0.30	0.75	1.50
❑20, Feb 91	1.50	0.30	0.75	1.50
❑21, Mar 91, Der Totenkopf, Baron Strucker revived	1.50	0.30	0.75	1.50
❑22, Apr 91, Pledge Of Allegiance	1.50	0.30	0.75	1.50
❑23, May 91, Storm Warning	1.50	0.30	0.75	1.50
❑24, Jun 91, The Camouflaged Commemoratives Affair, A: Captain America; A: Fantastic Four	1.50	0.30	0.75	1.50
❑25, Jul 91	1.50	0.30	0.75	1.50
❑26, Aug 91, The Soldiers Of Anarchy, A: Avengers; A: Fantastic Four	1.50	0.30	0.75	1.50
❑27, Sep 91, Recruitment Drive, A: Wolverine	1.50	0.40	1.00	2.00
❑28, Oct 91, Icy Roads, A: Wolverine	1.50	0.40	1.00	2.00
❑29, Nov 91, The Cold War, A: Wolverine	1.50	0.40	1.00	2.00
❑30, Dec 91, Infinity's Not Forever, A: Deathlok	1.50	0.30	0.75	1.50
❑31, Jan 92, Infinity Is Not Forever After All!, A: Deathlok	1.50	0.30	0.75	1.50
❑32, Feb 92, Formal Wear, A: Weapon Omega	1.75	0.35	0.88	1.75
❑33, Mar 92, Man Of Action, 1: new agents (Psi-Borg, Violence, Knockabout, Ivory).	1.75	0.35	0.88	1.75
❑34, Apr 92, In The Field, V: Baron Strucker; V: Hydra	1.75	0.35	0.88	1.75
❑35, May 92, More Men Of Action	1.75	0.35	0.88	1.75
❑36, Jun 92, The Snake Who Came In From The Cold, V: Constrictor; A: Cage	1.75	0.35	0.88	1.75

	ORIG	GOOD	FINE	N-MINT
❑37, Jul 92, ...Who Killed The Changelings?!	1.75	0.35	0.88	1.75
❑38, Aug 92, Cold War of Nick Fury, Part 1.	1.75	0.35	0.88	1.75
❑39, Sep 92, Cold War of Nick Fury, Part 2.	1.75	0.35	0.88	1.75
❑40, Oct 92, Cold War of Nick Fury, Part 3..	1.75	0.35	0.88	1.75
❑41, Nov 92, Cold War of Nick Fury, Part 4.	1.75	0.35	0.88	1.75
❑42, Dec 92, The Past Recalled	1.75	0.35	0.88	1.75
❑43, Jan 93, The Dead Zone	1.75	0.35	0.88	1.75
❑44, Feb 93, Skeletons Reborn	1.75	0.35	0.88	1.75
❑45, Mar 93, The Treachery Within	1.75	0.35	0.88	1.75
❑46, Apr 93, Revelations	1.75	0.35	0.88	1.75
❑47, May 93, Final Retribution!, D: Kate Neville (Nick Fury's Girlfriend), Final Issue	1.75	0.35	0.88	1.75

NICK FURY VS. S.H.I.E.L.D.
Marvel

	ORIG	GOOD	FINE	N-MINT
❑1, Jun 88, JSo (c)	3.50	0.80	2.00	4.00
❑2, Jul 88, BSz (c)	3.50	0.70	1.75	3.50
❑3, Mar 88	3.50	0.70	1.75	3.50
❑4, Sep 88	3.50	0.70	1.75	3.50
❑5, Oct 88	3.50	0.70	1.75	3.50
❑6, Nov 88	3.50	0.70	1.75	3.50

NICK HAZARD
Harrier

Value: Cover or less

❑1, Jan 88, Invaders From Time ... 1.95

NICKI SHADOW
Relentless

Value: Cover or less

❑0, Jul 97, In the Way Back ... 1.00

❑1, Nov 97 ... 2.50

NICK NOYZ AND THE NUISANCE TOUR BOOK
Red Bullet

Value: Cover or less

❑1, b&w ... 2.50

NICK RYAN THE SKULL
Antarctic

Value: Cover or less

❑1, Dec 94, The Next Time I See You, b&w ... 2.75

❑2, Jan 95, Countdown, El Gato Negro, b&w; El Gato Negro back-up feature ... 2.75

❑3, Feb 95, Greener Grass, b&w ... 2.75

NIGHT, THE
Slave Labor

Value: Cover or less

❑0, Nov 95 ... 1.50

NIGHTBIRD
Harrier

Value: Cover or less

❑1, May 88, Compact of Fire, b&w ... 1.95

❑2, b&w ... 1.95

NIGHT BREED (CLIVE BARKER'S...)
Marvel

	ORIG	GOOD	FINE	N-MINT
❑1, ...Where The Monsters Go	1.95	0.60	1.50	3.00
❑2, Nightbreed (movie adaptation), Part 2...	1.95	0.50	1.25	2.50
❑3, Nightbreed (movie adaptation), Part 3...	1.95	0.50	1.25	2.50
❑4, Nightbreed (movie adaptation), Part 4...	1.95	0.50	1.25	2.50
❑5	2.25	0.50	1.25	2.50
❑6, The Blasphemers, Part 1	2.25	0.50	1.25	2.50
❑7	2.25	0.50	1.25	2.50
❑8	2.25	0.50	1.25	2.50
❑9	2.25	0.50	1.25	2.50
❑10	2.25	0.50	1.25	2.50
❑11	2.25	0.45	1.13	2.25
❑12	2.25	0.45	1.13	2.25
❑13, Rawhead Rex	2.25	0.45	1.13	2.25
❑14	2.25	0.45	1.13	2.25
❑15	2.25	0.45	1.13	2.25
❑16	2.25	0.45	1.13	2.25
❑17	2.25	0.45	1.13	2.25
❑18, Hunters And Trophies, Part 1	2.25	0.45	1.13	2.25
❑19, Sep 92, Hunters And Trophies, Part 2.	2.25	0.45	1.13	2.25
❑20, Hunters And Trophies, Part 3	2.50	0.50	1.25	2.50
❑21	2.50	0.50	1.25	2.50
❑22	2.50	0.50	1.25	2.50
❑23	2.50	0.50	1.25	2.50
❑24	2.50	0.50	1.25	2.50
❑25, Revelations, Final Issue	2.50	0.50	1.25	2.50

NIGHT BRIGADE
Wonder Comix

Value: Cover or less

❑1, Aug 87, b&w ... 1.95

NIGHTCAT
Marvel

Value: Cover or less

❑1, Apr 91, O: Nightcat ... 3.95

NIGHT CITY
Thorby

Value: Cover or less

❑1 ... 2.95

NIGHTCRAWLER
Marvel

	ORIG	GOOD	FINE	N-MINT
❑1, Nov 85, DC, DC (w), How Much Is That Boggie In The Window	0.75	0.40	1.00	2.00
❑2, Dec 85, DC, DC (w), A Boggie Day In L'un Dun-t'wn	0.75	0.40	1.00	2.00
❑3, Jan 86, DC, DC (w), To Bamf Or Not To Bamf!	0.75	0.40	1.00	2.00
❑4, Feb 86, DC, DC (w), The Wizard Of Oops!	0.75	0.40	1.00	2.00

NIGHTCRY
CFD

	ORIG	GOOD	FINE	N-MINT
❑1, b&w; adult; cardstock cover; Anthology	2.75	0.60	1.50	3.00
❑2, b&w; adult; cardstock cover; Anthology	2.75	0.60	1.50	3.00
❑3, b&w; adult; cardstock cover; Anthology	2.75	0.60	1.50	3.00
❑4, b&w; adult; cardstock cover; Anthology	2.75	0.60	1.50	3.00
❑5, Lycanthropos; Pick-Up #607, b&w; adult; cardstock cover; Anthology	2.75	0.60	1.50	3.00
❑6, b&w; adult; cardstock cover; Anthology	2.75	0.60	1.50	3.00

NIGHTFALL: THE BLACK CHRONICLES
Homage

Value: Cover or less

❑1, Dec 99 ... 2.95

❑2, Jan 00 ... 2.95

❑3, Feb 00 ... 2.95

NIGHT FORCE
DC

	ORIG	GOOD	FINE	N-MINT
❑1, Aug 82, GC, The Summoning, Part 1, 1: Night Force	0.60	0.50	1.25	2.50
❑2, Sep 82, GC, The Summoning, Part 2 ...	0.60	0.30	0.75	1.50
❑3, Oct 82, GC, The Summoning, Part 3 ...	0.60	0.30	0.75	1.50
❑4, Nov 82, GC, The Summoning, Part 4 ...	0.60	0.30	0.75	1.50
❑5, Dec 82, GC, The Summoning, Part 5 ...	0.60	0.30	0.75	1.50
❑6, Jan 83, GC, The Summoning, Part 6 ...	0.60	0.30	0.75	1.50
❑7, Feb 83, GC, The Summoning, Part 7 ...	0.60	0.30	0.75	1.50
❑8, Mar 83, GC, The Summoning, Epilogue	0.60	0.30	0.75	1.50
❑9, Apr 83, GC	0.60	0.30	0.75	1.50
❑10, May 83, GC	0.60	0.30	0.75	1.50
❑11, Jun 83, GC	0.60	0.30	0.75	1.50
❑12, Jul 83, GC	0.60	0.30	0.75	1.50
❑13, Aug 83, GC	0.60	0.30	0.75	1.50
❑14, Sep 83, GC, Final Issue	0.60	0.30	0.75	1.50

NIGHT FORCE (2ND SERIES)
DC

	ORIG	GOOD	FINE	N-MINT
❑1, Dec 96, BA, Millennium, Part 1	2.25	0.50	1.25	2.50
❑2, Jan 97, BA, Millennium, Part 2	2.25	0.45	1.13	2.25
❑3, Feb 97, BA, Millennium, Part 3	2.25	0.45	1.13	2.25
❑4, Mar 97	2.25	0.45	1.13	2.25
❑5, Apr 97, Dreamers of Dreams, Part 1; Dreamer of Dreams, Part 1	2.25	0.45	1.13	2.25
❑6, May 97, Dreamers of Dreams, Part 2; Dreamer of Dreams, Part 2	2.25	0.45	1.13	2.25
❑7, Jun 97, Dreamers of Dreams, Part 3; Dreamer of Dreams, Part 3	2.25	0.45	1.13	2.25
❑8, Jul 97, Convergence, Part 2, continues in Challengers of the Unknown #6	2.25	0.45	1.13	2.25
❑9, Aug 97, The Eleventh Man, Part 1	2.25	0.45	1.13	2.25
❑10, Sep 97, The Eleventh Man, Part 2	2.25	0.45	1.13	2.25
❑11, Oct 97, The Eleventh Man, Part 3	2.25	0.45	1.13	2.25
❑12, Nov 97, The Lady or the Leopard!, Final Issue	2.50	0.50	1.25	2.50

NIGHT GLIDER
Topps

Value: Cover or less

❑1, Apr 93, JK; DH, She Glides In Beauty, Like The Night, trading card, coupon for Secret City Saga #1 ... 2.95

NIGHTHAWK
Marvel

Value: Cover or less

❑1, Sep 98, Pitfall, gatefold summary ... 2.99

❑2, Oct 98, gatefold summary ... 2.99

❑3, Nov 98, gatefold summary ... 2.99

NIGHT LIFE
Strawberry Jam

Value: Cover or less

❑1, The Kingdom ... 1.50

❑2 ... 1.50

❑3 ... 1.50

❑4 ... 1.50

❑5 ... 1.50

❑6, May 87 ... 1.50

❑7 ... 1.50

❑8, Nov 91 ... 2.50

NIGHTLINGER
Gauntlet

Value: Cover or less

❑1, b&w ... 2.95

❑2, b&w ... 2.95

NIGHT MAN, THE
Malibu

Value: Cover or less

❑1, Oct 93, Rune, Part C, 1: Death Mask; O: The Night Man; 1: The Night Man (in costume), Rune ... 2.50

❑1/LE, Rune, Part C, 1: Death Mask; O: The Night Man; 1: The Night Man (in costume), Ultra-limited edition ... 25.00

❑2, Nov 93, Mangled, 1: Mangle ... 1.95

❑3, Dec 93, Break-Thru, A: Freex, Break-Thru ... 1.95

❑4, Jan 94, Who Is The Night Man?, O: Firearm ... 1.95

❑5, Feb 94, Alone ... 1.95

❑6, Mar 94 ... 1.95

❑7, Apr 94 ... 1.95

❑8, May 94 ... 1.95

❑9, Jun 94, Solitary!, D: Teknight I ... 1.95

❑10, Jul 94, Chalk, 1: Chalk; 1: Silver Daggers ... 1.95

❑11, Aug 94, Turning On, 1: Teknight II ... 1.95

❑12, Sep 94, Hostile Takeover; Hostile Takeover, Part 1, A: The Solution ... 1.95

ORIG GOOD FINE N-MINT

- ❑13, Oct 94, Life, no indicia 1.95
- ❑14, Nov 94, JRo (w), Crossfire!, D: Torso 1.95
- ❑15, Dec 94, The Night Man Before Christmas 1.95
- ❑16, Feb 95, What's In a Name; Terrible Tuesday, flipbook with Ultraverse Premiere #11 .... 3.50
- ❑17, Feb 95, BloodyFly!, 1: Blood-yFly 2.50
- ❑18, Mar 95, Sharks! 2.50
- ❑19, Apr 95, The Edge of Your Seat, D: Deathmask 2.50
- ❑20, May 95, Ashes, Ashes...We All Fall Down, D: BloodyFly 2.50
- ❑21, Jun 95 .... 2.50
- ❑22, Jul 95, A: Loki 2.50
- ❑23, Aug 95, Final Issue 2.50
- ❑Ann 1, The Pilgrim Conundrum, Part 1 .... 3.95

NIGHT MAN, THE (VOL. 2)
MALIBU
Value: Cover or less

- ❑0, Sep 95, Black September; This Is Black September, Listed as issue #Infinity 1.50
- ❑0/A, Sep 95, Black September, alternate cover 1.50
- ❑1, Oct 95, The Night's A-shine with Stars 1.50
- ❑2, Nov 95 .... 1.50
- ❑3, Dec 95, V: Lord Pumpkin .. 1.50
- ❑4, Dec 95, V: Mangle; V: Lord Pumpkin, Final Issue 1.50

NIGHT MAN/GAMBIT, THE
MALIBU
Value: Cover or less

- ❑1, Mar 96, Shedding Skin 1.95
- ❑2, Apr 96 .... 1.95
- ❑3, May 96 .... 1.95

NIGHT MAN VS. WOLVERINE
MALIBU

	ORIG	GOOD	FINE	N-MINT
❑0, Aug 95, no cover price	—	1.00	2.50	5.00

NIGHTMARE
MARVEL
Value: Cover or less

- ❑1, Dec 94, Temptation 1.95
- ❑2, Jan 95 .... 1.95
- ❑3, Feb 95 .... 1.95
- ❑4, Mar 95 .... 1.95

NIGHTMARE (ALEX NIÑO'S...)
INNOVATION
Value: Cover or less

- ❑1, Dec 89 .... 1.95

NIGHTMARE ON ELM STREET, A (FREDDY KRUEGER'S...)
MARVEL

	ORIG	GOOD	FINE	N-MINT
❑1	2.25	0.60	1.50	3.00

NIGHTMARE ON ELM STREET: THE BEGINNING
INNOVATION
Value: Cover or less

- ❑1 .... 2.50
- ❑2 .... 2.50

NIGHTMARES
ECLIPSE

	ORIG	GOOD	FINE	N-MINT
❑1, PG, Blood on Black Satin, Part 1; The Trespasser, Part 1	1.75	0.40	1.00	2.00
❑2, PG, Blood on Black Satin, Part 2; The Trespasser, Part 2	1.75	0.40	1.00	2.00

NIGHTMARES ON ELM STREET
INNOVATION
Value: Cover or less

- ❑1, Sep 91, Yours Truly, Freddy Krueger, Part 1 .... 2.50
- ❑2, Yours Truly, Freddy Krueger, Part 2 .... 2.50
- ❑3, Loose Ends, Part 1 .... 2.50
- ❑4, Loose Ends, Part 2 .... 2.50
- ❑5 .... 2.50
- ❑6 .... 2.50

NIGHTMARE THEATER
CHAOS!
Value: Cover or less

- ❑1, Nov 97, One Perfect Night; The Ballad of the Eyeball Dragster, horror anthology 2.50
- ❑2, Nov 97, horror anthology .. 2.50
- ❑3, Nov 97, horror anthology .. 2.50
- ❑4, Nov 97, horror anthology .. 2.50

NIGHTMARE WALKER
BONEYARD
Value: Cover or less

- ❑1, Jul 96, b&w 2.95

NIGHTMARK
ALPHA PRODUCTIONS
Value: Cover or less

- ❑1, b&w 2.25

NIGHTMARK: BLOOD & HONOR
ALPHA
Value: Cover or less

- ❑1, Apr 94, Midnight And Morning Black 2.50
- ❑2 .... 2.50
- ❑3 .... 2.50

NIGHTMARK MYSTERY SPECIAL
ALPHA
Value: Cover or less

- ❑1, The Devil's Brood; Kill Me In The Morning, b&w 2.50

NIGHTMASK
MARVEL

	ORIG	GOOD	FINE	N-MINT
❑1, Nov 86, The Awakening, O: Nightmask.	0.75	0.20	0.50	1.00
❑2, Dec 86	0.75	0.20	0.50	1.00
❑3, Jan 87	0.75	0.20	0.50	1.00
❑4, Feb 87	0.75	0.20	0.50	1.00
❑5, Mar 87	0.75	0.20	0.50	1.00
❑6, Apr 87	0.75	0.20	0.50	1.00
❑7, May 87	0.75	0.20	0.50	1.00
❑8, Jun 87	0.75	0.20	0.50	1.00
❑9, Jul 87	0.75	0.20	0.50	1.00
❑10, Aug 87	0.75	0.20	0.50	1.00
❑11, Sep 87	0.75	0.20	0.50	1.00
❑12, Oct 87, Final Issue	0.75	0.20	0.50	1.00

Nick Fury routed out corruption in his own spy agency in *Nick Fury vs. S.H.I.E.L.D.*

NIGHT MASTERS
CUSTOM PIC
Value: Cover or less

- ❑1 .... 1.50
- ❑2 .... 1.50
- ❑3 .... 1.50
- ❑4 .... 1.50
- ❑5 .... 1.50
- ❑6, Jan 87, Maximum Metal 1.50

NIGHT MUSIC
ECLIPSE

	ORIG	GOOD	FINE	N-MINT
❑1, Dec 84, CR, CR (w), Breakdown On The Starship Remembrance	1.75	0.40	1.00	2.00
❑2, Feb 85, CR, CR (w)	1.75	0.40	1.00	2.00
❑3, Mar 85, CR, CR (w), The King's Ankus, Rudyard Kipling adaptation	1.75	0.40	1.00	2.00
❑4, Dec 85, CR, Pelleas & Mellisande, Part 1	2.00	0.40	1.00	2.00
❑5, Dec 85, CR, Pelleas & Mellisande, Part 2	2.00	0.40	1.00	2.00
❑6, CR, Salome	1.75	0.40	1.00	2.00
❑7, Feb 88, CR, CR (w), Red Dog	2.00	0.40	1.00	2.00
❑8, Arianne and Bluebeard	3.95	0.79	1.98	3.95
❑9, CR, The Magic Flute	4.95	0.99	2.47	4.95
❑10, CR, The Magic Flute	4.95	0.99	2.47	4.95
❑11, CR, The Magic Flute	4.95	0.99	2.47	4.95

NIGHT NURSE
MARVEL

	ORIG	GOOD	FINE	N-MINT
❑1, Nov 72, The Making of a Nurse!	0.20	8.40	21.00	42.00
❑2	0.20	5.00	12.50	25.00
❑3, Murder Stalks Ward 8!	0.20	5.00	12.50	25.00
❑4, Final Issue	0.20	5.00	12.50	25.00

NIGHT OF THE LIVING DEAD
FANTACO

	ORIG	GOOD	FINE	N-MINT
❑0, b&w	1.95	0.40	1.00	2.00
❑1, b&w	4.95	0.99	2.47	4.95
❑2, Zombie Vacation, b&w	4.95	0.99	2.47	4.95
❑3, b&w	5.95	1.19	2.97	5.95
❑4, b&w	5.95	1.19	2.97	5.95

NIGHT OF THE LIVING DEAD: AFTERMATH
FANTACO
Value: Cover or less

- ❑1 .... 1.95

NIGHT OF THE LIVING DEADLINE USA
DARK HORSE
Value: Cover or less

- ❑1, Apr 92, b&w; Anthology 2.95

NIGHT OF THE LIVING DEAD: LONDON
FANTACO
Value: Cover or less

- ❑1 .... 5.95
- ❑2, Bloodline 5.95

NIGHT OF THE LIVING DEAD: PRELUDE
FANTACO
Value: Cover or less

- ❑1, b&w 1.50

NIGHT RAVEN: HOUSE OF CARDS
MARVEL
Value: Cover or less

- ❑1, Aug 91 .... 5.95

NIGHT RIDER
MARVEL

	ORIG	GOOD	FINE	N-MINT
❑1, Reprints Ghost Rider (Western) #1	0.25	1.00	2.50	5.00
❑2, The Macabre Menace Of The Tarantula!, Reprints Ghost Rider (Western) #2	0.25	0.70	1.75	3.50
❑3, Reprints Ghost Rider (Western) #3	0.25	0.70	1.75	3.50
❑4, Reprints Ghost Rider (Western) #4	0.25	0.70	1.75	3.50
❑5, Reprints Ghost Rider (Western) #5	0.25	0.70	1.75	3.50
❑6, Reprints Ghost Rider (Western) #6	0.25	0.70	1.75	3.50

NIGHT'S CHILDREN
FANTACO
Value: Cover or less

- ❑1, b&w 3.50
- ❑2, b&w 3.50
- ❑3, b&w 3.50
- ❑4, b&w 3.50

NIGHT'S CHILDREN: DOUBLE INDEMNITY
FANTACO
Value: Cover or less

- ❑1, b&w 7.95

NIGHT'S CHILDREN EROTIC FANTASIES
FANTACO

	ORIG	GOOD	FINE	N-MINT
❑1	—	0.90	2.25	4.50

NIGHT'S CHILDREN: EXOTIC FANTASIES
FANTACO

Value: Cover or less

- ❑1, b&w ... 5.95

NIGHT'S CHILDREN: FOREPLAY
FANTACO

Value: Cover or less

- ❑1, b&w ... 4.95

NIGHT'S CHILDREN: THE VAMPIRE
MILLENNIUM

Value: Cover or less

- ❑1 ... 2.95
- ❑2 ... 2.95

NIGHT'S CHILDREN: VAMPYR!
FANTACO

Value: Cover or less

- ❑1, b&w; adult ... 3.50
- ❑2, b&w; adult ... 3.50
- ❑3, b&w; adult ... 3.50

NIGHTSHADE
NO MERCY

Value: Cover or less

- ❑1, Aug 97 ... 2.50

NIGHTSHADES
LONDON NIGHT

Value: Cover or less

- ❑1, Hidden Darkness ... 2.95

NIGHTS INTO DREAMS
ARCHIE

Value: Cover or less

- ❑1, Feb 98 ... 1.75
- ❑2, Mar 98 ... 1.75
- ❑3, Apr 98 ... 1.75
- ❑4, Aug 98 ... 1.75
- ❑5, Sep 98 ... 1.75
- ❑6, Oct 98 ... 1.75

NIGHTSTALKERS
MARVEL

Value: Cover or less

- ❑1, Nov 92, Missing poster ... 2.75
- ❑1/CS, Rise of the Midnight Sons, Part 5, poster ... 2.75
- ❑2, Dec 92, Staking Claim, Part 1 ... 1.75
- ❑3, Jan 93, Staking Claim, Part 2 ... 1.75
- ❑4, Feb 93, Staking Claim, Part 3 ... 1.75
- ❑5, Mar 93, Cut to the Bone, A: Punisher ... 1.75
- ❑6, Apr 93, Comes A Pale Rider, A: Punisher ... 1.75
- ❑7, May 93, Ghosts In The Machine, A: Ghost Rider ... 1.75
- ❑8, Jun 93, A: Ghost Rider ... 1.75
- ❑9, Jul 93 ... 1.75
- ❑10, Aug 93, Midnight Massacre, Part 1, Double cover ... 1.75
- ❑11, Sep 93 ... 1.75
- ❑12, Oct 93, Portrait of Death Row, A: Row appearance, DOA appearance, Gold cover ... 1.75
- ❑13, Nov 93, Short Circuit, 1: Short Circuit ... 1.75
- ❑14, Dec 93, Siege of Darkness, Part 1, Neon ink on cover ... 1.75
- ❑15, Jan 94, Siege of Darkness, Part 8, Spot-varnish cover ... 1.75
- ❑16, Feb 94 ... 1.75
- ❑17, Mar 94 ... 1.75
- ❑18, Apr 94, All The Threads Unraveled, Final Issue ... 1.75

NIGHTSTREETS (ARROW)
ARROW

	ORIG	GOOD	FINE	N-MINT
❑1, Jul 86, Mob Rules, Part 1, 1: Mr. Katt	1.50	0.50	1.25	2.50
❑2, Oct 86	1.50	0.40	1.00	2.00
❑3, Jan 87	1.50	0.40	1.00	2.00
❑4, Apr 87	1.50	0.40	1.00	2.00
❑5, Jul 87	1.50	0.40	1.00	2.00

NIGHT THRASHER
MARVEL

Value: Cover or less

- ❑1, Aug 93, O: Night Thrasher, foil cover ... 2.95
- ❑2, Sep 93, 1: Tantrum ... 1.75
- ❑3, Oct 93, A: Tiger Tyger; A: Silhouette; A: Aardwolf ... 1.75
- ❑4, Nov 93 ... 1.75
- ❑5, Dec 93 ... 1.75
- ❑6, Jan 94 ... 1.75
- ❑7, Feb 94, Brothers in Arms, Part 1 ... 1.75
- ❑8, Mar 94, Brothers in Arms, Part 2 ... 1.75
- ❑9, Apr 94 ... 1.75
- ❑10, May 94 ... 1.95
- ❑11, Jun 94 ... 1.95
- ❑12, Jul 94 ... 1.95
- ❑13, Aug 94, Lost in the Shadows ... 1.95
- ❑14, Sep 94, Lost in the Shadows ... 1.95
- ❑15, Oct 94, KB (w), V: Hulk ... 1.95
- ❑16, Nov 94, KB (w) ... 1.95
- ❑17, Dec 94, KB (w) ... 1.95
- ❑18, Jan 95, KB (w) ... 1.95
- ❑19, Feb 95 ... 1.95
- ❑20, Mar 95, KB (w), Heart of Rage, Part 1 ... 1.95
- ❑21, Apr 95, KB (w), Heart of Rage, Part 2, Final Issue ... 1.95

NIGHT THRASHER: FOUR CONTROL
MARVEL

Value: Cover or less

- ❑1, Strength ... 2.00
- ❑2, Money ... 2.00
- ❑3 ... 2.00
- ❑4, Compassion ... 2.00

NIGHT TRIBES
DC

Value: Cover or less

- ❑1, Jul 99, A Gathering of Monsters, nn; One-Shot ... 4.95

NIGHTVEIL
AC

	ORIG	GOOD	FINE	N-MINT
❑1, Feb 84, Nightveil; Nightveil: Deathstalk!, full color	1.75	0.40	1.00	2.00
❑2	1.75	0.40	1.00	2.00
❑3	1.75	0.40	1.00	2.00
❑4	1.75	0.40	1.00	2.00
❑5	1.75	0.40	1.00	2.00
❑6	1.75	0.40	1.00	2.00
❑7, Mar 87	1.75	0.40	1.00	2.00
❑SE 1, Aug 88	1.95	0.40	1.00	2.00

NIGHTVEIL'S CAULDRON OF HORROR
AC

Value: Cover or less

- ❑1, JKu, Nightveil's Cauldron of Horror; The Ghost of Fanciful Hawkins, b&w; Reprint ... 2.50
- ❑2 ... 2.95
- ❑3, Sep 91 ... 2.95

NIGHTVENGER
AXIS

	ORIG	GOOD	FINE	N-MINT
❑Ash 1, May 94	—	0.40	1.00	2.00

NIGHTVISION
REBEL

	ORIG	GOOD	FINE	N-MINT
❑1	3.00	0.60	1.50	3.00
❑2	2.25	0.50	1.25	2.50
❑3, Love Bleeding Pictures	2.25	0.50	1.25	2.50
❑4	2.25	0.50	1.25	2.50

NIGHT VISION (ATOMEKA)
ATOMEKA

Value: Cover or less

- ❑1, nn; b&w ... 2.95

NIGHTVISION: ALL ABOUT EVE
LONDON NIGHT

Value: Cover or less

- ❑1, Expect The Unexpected...Tempest ... 3.00

NIGHT VIXEN
ABC STUDIOS

Value: Cover or less

- ❑0/A, b&w ... 3.00
- ❑0/B, Eurotika Edition ... 5.00
- ❑0/C, Manga Flux Edition ... 8.00

NIGHT WALKER
FLEETWAY

Value: Cover or less

- ❑1, Reprints Luke Kirby story from 2000 A.D. ... 2.95
- ❑2, Reprints Luke Kirby story from 2000 A.D. ... 2.95
- ❑3, Reprints Luke Kirby story from 2000 A.D. ... 2.95

NIGHT WARRIORS: DARKSTALKERS' REVENGE THE COMIC SERIES
VIZ

Value: Cover or less

- ❑1, Nov 98 ... 2.95
- ❑2 ... 3.25
- ❑3 ... 2.95
- ❑4 ... 2.95
- ❑5 ... 2.95
- ❑6 ... 2.95

NIGHTWATCH
MARVEL

Value: Cover or less

- ❑1, Apr 94, A: Spider-Man ... 1.50
- ❑1/SC, Apr 94, A: Spider-Man, foil cover ... 2.95
- ❑2, May 94 ... 1.50
- ❑3, Jun 94, AM, Mechamorph. ... 1.50
- ❑4, Jul 94 ... 1.50
- ❑5, Aug 94 ... 1.50
- ❑6, Sep 94 ... 1.50
- ❑7, Oct 94 ... 1.50
- ❑8, Nov 94 ... 1.50
- ❑9, Dec 94 ... 1.50
- ❑10, Jan 95 ... 1.50
- ❑11, Feb 95 ... 1.50
- ❑12, Mar 95, Final Issue ... 1.50

NIGHTWING
DC

	ORIG	GOOD	FINE	N-MINT
❑0.5	—	0.80	2.00	4.00
❑0.5/Pl, Signed by Chuck Dixon; Certificate of Authenticity; Platinum edition	—	1.40	3.50	7.00
❑1, Oct 96, Child Of Justice	1.95	2.00	5.00	10.00
❑2, Nov 96, Gangland Express	1.95	1.40	3.50	7.00
❑3, Dec 96, The Freebooters	1.95	1.00	2.50	5.00
❑4, Jan 97, Lady Be Deadly	1.95	0.90	2.25	4.50
❑5, Feb 97	1.95	0.90	2.25	4.50
❑6, Mar 97, The Visitor	1.95	0.70	1.75	3.50
❑7, Apr 97	1.95	0.70	1.75	3.50
❑8, May 97	1.95	0.70	1.75	3.50
❑9, Jun 97, Die Trying	1.95	0.70	1.75	3.50
❑10, Jul 97, The Neighborhood, V: Scarecrow	1.95	0.70	1.75	3.50
❑11, Aug 97, Fear Takes Flight, V: Scarecrow	1.95	0.60	1.50	3.00
❑12, Sep 97, Mutt	1.95	0.60	1.50	3.00
❑13, Oct 97, Shadows over Blƒdhaven; Shadows over Blndhaven	1.95	0.60	1.50	3.00
❑14, Nov 97, Dead Meat, A: Batman	1.95	0.60	1.50	3.00
❑15, Dec 97, Warriors Two, A: Batman; V: Two-Face, Face cover	1.95	0.60	1.50	3.00
❑16, Jan 98, Wheels	1.95	0.50	1.25	2.50
❑17, Feb 98, The Stalking Skies	1.95	0.50	1.25	2.50
❑18, Mar 98, The Hunting Moon	1.95	0.50	1.25	2.50
❑19, Apr 98, Cataclysm, Part 2, continues in Batman #553	1.95	0.50	1.25	2.50
❑20, May 98, Cataclysm, Part 11, continues in Batman #554	1.95	0.50	1.25	2.50
❑21, Jun 98, A: Blockbuster; 1: Nitewing	1.95	0.50	1.25	2.50
❑22, Jul 98, V: Brutale; V: Stallion	1.95	0.50	1.25	2.50

	ORIG	GOOD	FINE	N-MINT
❑23, Aug 98, Brotherhood of the Fist, Part 4, A: Lady Shiva, concludes in Green Arrow #135	1.95	0.50	1.25	2.50
❑24, Sep 98	1.99	0.40	1.00	2.00
❑25, Oct 98	1.99	0.40	1.00	2.00
❑26, Dec 98, A: Huntress	1.99	0.40	1.00	2.00
❑27, Jan 99, A: Huntress	1.99	0.40	1.00	2.00
❑28, Feb 99, 1: Torque; A: Huntress	1.99	0.40	1.00	2.00
❑29, Mar 99, A: Huntress	1.99	0.40	1.00	2.00
❑30, Apr 99, A: Superman	1.99	0.40	1.00	2.00
❑31, May 99, Bad Night in Bludhaven, Dick joins the Bludhaven police force	1.99	0.40	1.00	2.00
❑32, Jun 99, Double Dare	1.99	0.40	1.00	2.00
❑33, Jul 99, Acts of Violence	1.99	0.40	1.00	2.00
❑34, Aug 99, Sister Act	1.99	0.40	1.00	2.00
❑35, Sep 99, Escape to Blackgate, Part 1, No Man's Land	1.99	0.40	1.00	1.99
❑36, Oct 99, Escape to Blackgate, Part 2; Nothing But Time, No Man's Land	1.99	0.40	1.00	1.99
❑37, Nov 99, Escape to Blackgate, Part 3; Escape from Blackgate, No Man's Land	1.99	0.40	1.00	1.99
❑38, Dec 00, Ballistic Romance, Part 1, No Man's Land	1.99	0.40	1.00	1.99
❑39, Jan 00, Ballistic Romance, Part 2	1.99	0.40	1.00	1.99
❑40, Feb 00, The Devil Dies at Dawn	1.99	0.40	1.00	1.99
❑41, Mar 00	1.99	0.40	1.00	1.99
❑42, Apr 00	1.99	0.40	1.00	1.99
❑43, May 00, Improper Angles	1.99	0.40	1.00	1.99
❑44, Jun 00, The Stalkers	1.99	0.40	1.00	1.99
❑45, Jul 00	1.99	0.40	1.00	1.99
❑46, Aug 00	—	0.40	1.00	1.99
❑47, Sep 00	—	0.40	1.00	1.99
❑48, Oct 00, The Sylph, Part 1	2.25	0.45	1.13	2.25
❑49, Nov 00, Dangled	2.25	0.45	1.13	2.25
❑50, Dec 00, Big Guns	3.50	0.70	1.75	3.50
❑51, Jan 01, Tad	2.25	0.45	1.13	2.25
❑52, Feb 01, Modern Romance, A: Catwoman	2.25	0.45	1.13	2.25
❑53, Mar 01, DGry(w), Officer Down, Part 5	2.25	0.45	1.13	2.25
❑54, Apr 01, In the Middle of the Cold, Cold Night	2.25	0.45	1.13	2.25
❑55, May 01, Love & Death	2.25	0.45	1.13	2.25
❑56, Jun 01, Stalked	2.25	0.45	1.13	2.25
❑57	2.25	0.45	1.13	2.25
❑58	2.25	0.45	1.13	2.25
❑59	2.25	0.45	1.13	2.25
❑1000000, Nov 98, The Anachronism	1.99	0.40	1.00	1.99
❑Anl 1, Pulp Heroes	3.95	0.79	1.98	3.95
❑GS 1, Dec 00, Hella	5.95	1.19	2.97	5.95

NIGHTWING (MINI-SERIES)
DC

	ORIG	GOOD	FINE	N-MINT
❑1, Sep 95, The Resignation	2.25	0.70	1.75	3.50
❑2, Oct 95	2.25	0.50	1.25	2.50
❑3, Nov 95	2.25	0.50	1.25	2.50
❑4, Dec 95	2.25	0.50	1.25	2.50

NIGHTWING: ALFRED'S RETURN
DC

Value: Cover or less

❑1, Jul 95, DG, One-Shot 3.50

NIGHTWING AND HUNTRESS
DC

	ORIG	GOOD	FINE	N-MINT
❑1, May 98, DGry(w), Cosa Nostra, Part 1	1.95	0.40	1.00	2.00
❑2, Jun 98, BSz, DGry(w), Cosa Nostra, Part 2	1.95	0.40	1.00	2.00
❑3, Jul 98	1.95	0.40	1.00	2.00
❑4, Aug 98	1.95	0.40	1.00	2.00

NIGHTWING SECRET FILES
DC

Value: Cover or less

❑1, Oct 99, Taking Wing; Lost Pages: Teen Titans, background information on series 4.95

NIGHTWOLF
ENTROPY

Value: Cover or less

❑1, King of Spades 1.50

❑2 .... 1.50

NIGHT ZERO
FLEETWAY

Value: Cover or less

❑1, b&w 1.95

❑2, b&w 1.95

❑3, b&w 1.95

❑4, b&w 1.95

NIKKI BLADE SUMMER FUN
ABC STUDIOS

Value: Cover or less

❑1/A, b&w; adult 3.00

❑1/B, adult; solo figure on cover 3.00

NIMROD, THE
FANTAGRAPHICS

Value: Cover or less

❑1, Jun 98, b&w 2.95

❑2, Aug 98, b&w 2.95

Nightwing had a run-in with Catwoman during the "This Issue: Batman Dies!" crossover.

NINA'S ALL-TIME GREATEST COLLECTORS' ITEM CLASSIC COMICS
DARK HORSE

	ORIG	GOOD	FINE	N-MINT
❑1, Aug 92, A Popular Gal; Big Editor Boss-Man, b&w	2.25	0.50	1.25	2.50

NINA'S NEW & IMPROVED ALL-TIME GREATEST COLLECTORS' ITEM CLASSIC COMICS
DARK HORSE

Value: Cover or less

❑1, Feb 94, The Pet; I Was A Teen-age Hairball, b&w 2.50

NINE LIVES OF LEATHER CAT, THE
FORBIDDEN FRUIT

Value: Cover or less

❑1, 1: Leather Cat 3.50

❑2 .... 3.50

❑3 .... 3.50

❑4 .... 3.50

❑5 .... 3.50

❑6 .... 3.50

NINE RINGS OF WU-TANG, THE
IMAGE

	ORIG	GOOD	FINE	N-MINT
❑0, Nov 99, Giveaway bundled with Wizard Magazine	—	0.40	1.00	2.00
❑1/A, Nov 99, Woman with bow reclining on cover with jungle cats	2.95	0.59	1.48	2.95
❑1/B, Nov 99, Tower Records variant	2.95	0.59	1.48	2.95
❑2	2.95	0.59	1.48	2.95
❑3, Feb 00	2.95	0.59	1.48	2.95
❑4	2.95	0.59	1.48	2.95
❑5, Jul 00	2.95	0.59	1.48	2.95

NINETY-NINE GIRLS
FANTAGRAPHICS

Value: Cover or less

❑1, b&w; adult 2.25

NINE VOLT
IMAGE

Value: Cover or less

❑1, Jul 97, 1: Digit 2.50

❑1/A, Jul 97, alternate cover 2.50

❑2, Aug 97 .... 2.50

❑3, Sep 97 .... 2.50

❑4, Oct 97 .... 2.50

NINJA
ETERNITY

Value: Cover or less

❑1, Oct 86, The Dirty Game, Part 1 .... 1.80

❑2, The Dirty Game, Part 2 .... 1.80

❑3, The Dirty Game, Part 3 .... 1.80

❑4, The Dirty Game, Part 4 .... 1.80

❑5, The Dirty Game, Part 5 .... 1.95

❑6, The Dirty Game, Part 6 .... 1.95

❑7 .... 1.95

❑8 .... 1.95

❑9 .... 1.95

❑10 .... 1.95

❑11 .... 1.95

❑12, Sep 88 .... 1.95

❑13 .... 1.95

❑SE 1, b&w 2.25

NINJA-BOTS SUPER SPECIAL
PIED PIPER

Value: Cover or less

❑1 .... 1.95

NINJA BOY
WILDSTORM

	ORIG	GOOD	FINE	N-MINT
❑Ash 1, Ashcan preview; Flip book with Out There Ash #1	—	0.10	0.25	0.50

NINJA ELITE
ADVENTURE

Value: Cover or less

❑1, 7-1/2x8-1/2" version with black-and-white cover 1.50

❑1-2, 2nd Printing; 1st printing with color covers, full comic size 1.50

❑2, Jul 87 .... 1.50

❑3 .... 1.50

❑4, Dec 87 .... 1.95

❑5 .... 1.95

❑6 .... 1.95

❑7 .... 1.95

❑8 .... 1.95

NINJA FUNNIES
ETERNITY

	ORIG	GOOD	FINE	N-MINT
❑1, Jan 87	1.40	0.30	0.75	1.50
❑2	1.95	0.39	0.98	1.95
❑3	1.95	0.39	0.98	1.95
❑4	1.95	0.39	0.98	1.95
❑5	1.95	0.39	0.98	1.95

NINJA HIGH SCHOOL
ANTARCTIC

	ORIG	GOOD	FINE	N-MINT
❑0, Jan 94, b&w; Antarctic publishes	2.75	0.60	1.50	3.00
❑0/LE, Jan, b&w; foil cover edition (500 made)	2.75	0.80	2.00	4.00
❑1	1.50	1.40	3.50	7.00
❑1-2, 2nd Printing	1.50	0.50	1.25	2.50
❑2	1.95	1.00	2.50	5.00
❑2-2, 2nd Printing	—	0.40	1.00	2.00
❑3	1.95	0.80	2.00	4.00
❑3-2, 2nd Printing	—	0.40	1.00	2.00
❑4	1.95	0.80	2.00	4.00
❑4-2, 2nd Printing	—	0.40	1.00	2.00
❑5, Jun 88, b&w; Eternity begins publishing	1.95	0.80	2.00	4.00
❑6	1.95	0.70	1.75	3.50
❑6-2, 2nd Printing	1.95	0.40	1.00	2.00
❑7, Sep 88, Ben Dunn's Girls; I Only Have Bobbed for You	1.95	0.70	1.75	3.50
❑8, Dec 88	1.95	0.70	1.75	3.50
❑9, Feb 89	1.95	0.70	1.75	3.50
❑10, Mar 89	1.95	0.70	1.75	3.50
❑11, May 89	1.95	0.60	1.50	3.00
❑12	1.95	0.60	1.50	3.00
❑13	1.95	0.60	1.50	3.00
❑14	1.95	0.60	1.50	3.00
❑15	1.95	0.60	1.50	3.00
❑16, b&w	1.95	0.50	1.25	2.50
❑17, b&w	1.95	0.50	1.25	2.50
❑18, b&w	1.95	0.50	1.25	2.50
❑19, b&w	1.95	0.50	1.25	2.50
❑20, b&w	1.95	0.50	1.25	2.50
❑21, b&w	1.95	0.50	1.25	2.50
❑22, b&w	1.95	0.50	1.25	2.50
❑23	2.25	0.45	1.13	2.25
❑24	2.25	0.45	1.13	2.25
❑25	2.25	0.45	1.13	2.25
❑26	2.25	0.45	1.13	2.25
❑27	2.25	0.45	1.13	2.25
❑28	2.25	0.45	1.13	2.25
❑29	2.25	0.45	1.13	2.25
❑30	2.25	0.45	1.13	2.25
❑31	2.25	0.45	1.13	2.25
❑32, b&w	2.50	0.50	1.25	2.50
❑33, May 92, b&w	2.50	0.50	1.25	2.50
❑34, b&w	2.50	0.50	1.25	2.50
❑35, b&w	2.50	0.50	1.25	2.50
❑36, b&w	2.50	0.50	1.25	2.50
❑37, b&w	2.50	0.50	1.25	2.50
❑38, b&w	2.50	0.50	1.25	2.50
❑39, b&w	2.50	0.50	1.25	2.50
❑40, Jun 94, Aftermath, b&w	2.75	0.55	1.38	2.75
❑40/LE, Jun 94, b&w; gold foil logo edition (500 made)	2.75	0.60	1.50	3.00
❑41, Jul 94, Enter: The Y-Men, b&w	2.75	0.55	1.38	2.75
❑42, Sep 94, Secrets or Everybody's Got Something to Hide, b&w	2.75	0.55	1.38	2.75
❑43, Nov 94, What Goes Around Comes Around, b&w	2.75	0.55	1.38	2.75
❑44, Jan 95, Boy Meets-Girl...Cobra Meets Mongoose!, b&w	2.75	0.55	1.38	2.75
❑45, Mar 95, Grudge-Mismatch, b&w	2.75	0.55	1.38	2.75
❑46, May 95, The Return of the Giant Monsters, Part 1; Redeemer, Part 1, b&w; 40pgs.	2.75	0.55	1.38	2.75
❑47, Jul 95, The Return of the Giant Monsters, Part 2; Redeemer, Part 2, b&w	2.75	0.55	1.38	2.75
❑48, Sep 95, The Return of the Giant Monsters, Part 3, b&w	2.75	0.55	1.38	2.75
❑49, Nov 95, b&w	2.75	0.55	1.38	2.75
❑50, Jan 96, Crossroads; Redeemer, b&w	3.95	0.79	1.98	3.95
❑51, Apr 96, Car Wash Freakin' Monster Rally Thing!, b&w	2.95	0.59	1.48	2.95
❑52, Jun 96, b&w	2.95	0.59	1.48	2.95
❑53, Sep 96, b&w	2.95	0.59	1.48	2.95
❑54, Nov 96, Time Warp, Part 2, b&w	2.95	0.59	1.48	2.95
❑55, Jan 97, Time Warp, Part 4, b&w	2.95	0.59	1.48	2.95
❑56, Mar 97, Time Warp, Part 6, b&w	2.95	0.59	1.48	2.95
❑57, May 97, Time Warp, Part 8; Redeemer, Part 9, b&w	2.95	0.59	1.48	2.95
❑58, Aug 97, Dangerous (Diplomatic) Liasons; We're Off to Outer Space, Part 1, b&w	2.95	0.59	1.48	2.95
❑59, Oct 97, Learning Curves; We're Off to Outer Space, Part 2, b&w	2.95	0.59	1.48	2.95
❑60, Dec 97, Pet Theories, b&w	2.95	0.59	1.48	2.95
❑61, Feb 98, Humble Pie, b&w	2.95	0.59	1.48	2.95
❑62, Apr 98, Local Yokels, b&w	2.95	0.59	1.48	2.95
❑63, Jun 98, b&w	2.95	0.59	1.48	2.95
❑64, Aug 98, b&w	2.95	0.59	1.48	2.95
❑65, Oct 98, Barring the Unexpected, b&w	2.95	0.59	1.48	2.95
❑66, Dec 98, Wish in a Bottle, b&w	2.95	0.59	1.48	2.95
❑67, Mar 99, Crossed Dressed Purposes, b&w	2.95	0.60	1.50	2.99
❑68, Apr 99, Strained Nerves in Paradise, b&w	2.99	0.60	1.50	2.99
❑69, Jun 99, Prenuptial Aggrievance, b&w	2.99	0.60	1.50	2.99
❑3D 1, Jul 92, Trade Paperback	3.50	0.90	2.25	4.50
❑Smr 1, Jun 99, Hell on Wheels, Comic-sized; Summer Special (1999)	2.99	0.60	1.50	2.99
❑YB 1, b&w	—	1.20	3.00	6.00
❑YB 2, b&w; 1990 Yearbook	3.25	0.99	2.47	4.95
❑YB 3, b&w; 1991 Yearbook	3.75	0.99	2.47	4.95
❑YB 4, 8pgs.; 1992 Yearbook	3.95	0.99	2.47	4.95
❑YB 5, Oct 93, b&w; 1993 Yearbook	3.95	0.79	1.98	3.95
❑YB 6, Oct 94, b&w; 1994 Yearbook	3.95	0.79	1.98	3.95
❑YB 7, Oct 95, b&w; cover says Oct 94, indicia says Oct 95; 1995 Yearbook	3.95	0.79	1.98	3.95
❑YB 8, Oct 96, b&w; 1996 Yearbook	3.95	0.79	1.98	3.95
❑YB 9/A, Oct 97, Partners in a Strange Relationship; The Quibbler, b&w; 1997 Yearbook	3.95	0.79	1.98	3.95
❑YB 9/B, Oct 97, Partners in a Strange Relationship; The Quibbler, b&w; alternate cover; 1997 Yearbook; Star Trek	3.95	0.79	1.98	3.95
❑YB 10/A, Oct 98, Five Minutes; Wolf of the North Star 2, b&w; 1998 Yearbook	2.95	0.59	1.48	2.95
❑YB 10/B, Oct 98, Five Minutes; Wolf of the North Star 2, b&w; "Titanic" themed cover; 1998 Yearbook; Titanic	2.95	0.59	1.48	2.95

NINJA HIGH SCHOOL FEATURING SPEED RACER
ETERNITY

Value: Cover or less

❑1 .... 2.95

❑2, Dec 93 .... 2.95

NINJA HIGH SCHOOL IN COLOR
ETERNITY

	ORIG	GOOD	FINE	N-MINT
❑1, Jul 92, full color	1.95	0.50	1.25	2.50
❑2, full color	1.95	0.50	1.25	2.50
❑3, full color	1.95	0.50	1.25	2.50
❑4, full color	1.95	0.40	1.00	2.00
❑5, full color	1.95	0.40	1.00	2.00
❑6, full color	1.95	0.40	1.00	2.00
❑7, full color	1.95	0.40	1.00	2.00
❑8, full color	1.95	0.40	1.00	2.00
❑9, full color	1.95	0.40	1.00	2.00
❑10, full color	1.95	0.40	1.00	2.00
❑11, full color	1.95	0.40	1.00	2.00
❑12, full color	1.95	0.40	1.00	2.00
❑13, full color	1.95	0.40	1.00	2.00

NINJA HIGH SCHOOL PERFECT MEMORY
ANTARCTIC

	ORIG	GOOD	FINE	N-MINT
❑1, b&w; sourcebook for series	5.00	1.00	2.50	5.00
❑1-2, Jun 96, 2nd Printing	5.95	1.19	2.97	5.95
❑2, Nov 93, 96pgs.; 1996 version	4.95	1.19	2.97	5.95
❑2/PL, Nov 93, platinum	—	1.00	2.50	5.00

NINJA HIGH SCHOOL SPOTLIGHT
ANTARCTIC

Value: Cover or less

❑1, Penguin Ball; The Unreal Ghosthunters, Indicia says #29 .... 3.50

❑2, Oct 96, Marooned; Cram'n 2.95

❑3, Dec 96, Dunn Deal; Fujiko and Her Foo-Foo Bike, Ted Nomura 3.50

❑4, May 99, Flights of Fantasy;, Rod Espinosa; Indicia says #1 .... 2.99

NINJA HIGH SCHOOL SWIMSUIT SPECIAL
ANTARCTIC

	ORIG	GOOD	FINE	N-MINT
❑1, Dec 92, two different covers; Gold edition	2.95	0.80	2.00	4.00
❑2, Dec 93, 1998 Yearbook; Annual	2.95	0.79	1.98	3.95
❑3, Dec 94, Trade Paperback; Annual	2.95	0.79	1.98	3.95
❑4, Gold edition	2.95	0.79	1.98	3.95
❑1996, Dec 96, b&w; no cover price; Platinum edition; pinups	2.95	0.79	1.98	3.95

NINJA HIGH SCHOOL TALKS ABOUT COMIC BOOK PRINTING
ANTARCTIC

	ORIG	GOOD	FINE	N-MINT
❑1, full color; giveaway	—	0.20	0.50	1.00

NINJA HIGH SCHOOL TALKS ABOUT SEXUALLY TRANSMITTED DISEASES
ANTARCTIC

	ORIG	GOOD	FINE	N-MINT
❑1, full color; giveaway	—	0.40	1.00	2.00

NINJA HIGH SCHOOL: THE PROM FORMULA
ETERNITY

Value: Cover or less

❑1, full color 2.95

❑2, full color 2.95

NINJA HIGH SCHOOL: THE SPECIAL EDITION
ETERNITY

	ORIG	GOOD	FINE	N-MINT
❑1, b&w	2.25	0.50	1.25	2.50
❑2, b&w	2.25	0.50	1.25	2.50
❑3, b&w	2.25	0.50	1.25	2.50
❑4	2.25	0.50	1.25	2.50

ORIG GOOD FINE N-MINT

NINJA HIGH SCHOOL VERSION 2
ANTARCTIC

Value: Cover or less

❑1, Jul 99, I's a Family Affair!.................................. 2.50
❑2, Aug 99, Decision! Decisions!............................ 2.50

NINJAK
VALIANT

Value: Cover or less

❑0, Jun 95, Hope & Glory, Part 1, O: Ninjak; O: Doctor Silk..... 2.50
❑0/A, Jun 95, Hope & Glory, Part 2, O: Ninjak; O: Doctor Silk, cover forms diptych image with #0; #00................................ 2.50
❑1, Feb 94, Black Water, Part 1, 1: Doctor Silk, chromium cover 3.50
❑1/GO, Feb 94, Black Water, Part 1, 1: Doctor Silk, wraparound chromium cover; Gold edition................................ 3.50
❑2, Mar 94, Black Water, Part 2................................ 2.25
❑3, Apr 94.............................. 2.25
❑4, May 94, trading card......... 2.25
❑5, Jun 94, A: X-O Manowar.. 2.25
❑6, Aug 94, A: X-O Manowar.. 2.25
❑7, Sep 94............................. 2.25
❑8, Oct 94, The Chaos Effect: Gamma, Part 3, Chaos Effect 2.25
❑9, Nov 94, new uniform......... 2.25
❑10, Dec 94............................ 2.25
❑11, Jan 95............................ 2.25
❑12, Feb 95, trading card........ 2.25
❑13, Mar 95, trading card........ 2.25
❑14, Apr 95, Cry Wolf; Cry Wolf, Part 1.................................. 2.50
❑15, May 95, Cry Wolf; Cry Wolf, Part 2.................................. 2.50
❑16, Jun 95, Plague................ 2.50
❑17, Jul 95, Plague................. 2.50
❑18, Jul 95, Birthquake........... 2.50
❑19, Aug 95............................ 2.50
❑20, Aug 95............................ 2.50
❑21, Sep 95............................ 2.50
❑22, Sep 95............................ 2.50
❑23, Oct 95............................ 2.50
❑24, Oct 95............................ 2.50
❑25, Nov 95............................ 2.50
❑26, Nov 95, Final Issue......... 2.50
❑YB 1, cardstock cover........... 3.95

NINJAK (VOL. 2)
ACCLAIM

	ORIG	GOOD	FINE	N-MINT
❑1, Mar 97, KB (w), I Call on the Power of Ninjak!, 1: Ninjak II; O: Ninjak	2.50	0.50	1.25	2.50
❑1/SC, Mar 97, KB (w), I Call on the Power of Ninjak!, 1: Ninjak II, alternate painted cover	2.50	0.50	1.25	2.50
❑2, Apr 97, KB (w)	2.50	0.50	1.25	2.50
❑3, May 97, KB (w)	2.50	0.50	1.25	2.50
❑4, Jun 97, KB (w), A: Colin King, real origin of Ninjak	2.50	0.50	1.25	2.50
❑5, Jul 97, KB (w), Dark Dealings	2.50	0.50	1.25	2.50
❑6, Aug 97, KB (w), A: X-O Manowar	2.50	0.50	1.25	2.50
❑7, Sep 97, KB (w), A: X-O Manowar	2.50	0.50	1.25	2.50
❑8, Oct 97, KB (w), A: Colin King	2.50	0.50	1.25	2.50
❑9, Nov 97, KB (w)	2.50	0.50	1.25	2.50
❑10, Dec 97, KB (w)	2.50	0.50	1.25	2.50
❑11, Jan 98, KB (w)	2.50	0.50	1.25	2.50
❑12, Feb 98, KB (w), Final Issue	2.50	0.50	1.25	2.50
❑Ash 1, Nov 96, b&w; no cover price; preview of upcoming series	—	0.20	0.50	1.00

NINJUTSU, ART OF THE NINJA
SOLSON

Value: Cover or less

❑1, b&w.................................. 2.00

NINTENDO COMICS SYSTEM
VALIANT

Value: Cover or less

❑1, Anthology......................... 4.95
❑2, Anthology......................... 4.95

NINTENDO COMICS SYSTEM (2ND SERIES)
VALIANT

	ORIG	GOOD	FINE	N-MINT
❑1, Game Boy	1.50	0.40	1.00	2.00
❑2, Game Boy	1.50	0.40	1.00	2.00
❑3, Game Boy	1.50	0.40	1.00	2.00
❑4, Game Boy	1.50	0.40	1.00	2.00
❑5, Game Boy	1.50	0.40	1.00	2.00
❑6, Game Boy	1.50	0.40	1.00	2.00
❑7, Zelda	1.50	0.40	1.00	2.00
❑8, Super Mario Bros.	1.50	0.40	1.00	2.00
❑9, Super Mario Bros.	1.50	0.40	1.00	2.00

N.I.O.
ACCLAIM

Value: Cover or less

❑1, Nov 98, The Players......... 2.50

NIRA X: ANIME
ENTITY

Value: Cover or less

❑0... 2.75

NIRA X: ANNUAL
EXPRESS

Value: Cover or less

❑1/A, Sep 96, b&w; Snowman 1944 preview....................... 2.75
❑1/B, Sep 96, b&w; Snowman 1944 preview....................... 9.95

NIRA X: CYBERANGEL
EXPRESS

	ORIG	GOOD	FINE	N-MINT
❑1, Episode One, 1: Quid; 1: Paradoxx; 1: Millennia; 1: Delta-Void, Gold foil logo	2.95	0.59	1.48	2.95
❑1/LE, Episode One, 1: Quid; 1: Paradoxx; 1: Millennia; 1: Delta-Void, Limited commemorative edition; 3000 printed	2.95	0.80	2.00	4.00
❑2, Jun 96, Birth Of The Cyber Angel, 1: Solace; 1: Cyberhood; 1: Vex; 1: Talon, b&w	2.75	0.50	1.25	2.50
❑3, Jul 96, b&w	2.75	0.50	1.25	2.50
❑4, Aug 96, b&w; Final Issue	2.75	0.50	1.25	2.50

A videogame player became the new Ninjak when Acclaim revived the Valiant series.

© 1997 Acclaim

NIRA X: CYBERANGEL (3RD SERIES)
ENTITY

Value: Cover or less

❑1, Eye of the Storm, Part 1.... 2.50

NIRA X: CYBERANGEL (MINI-SERIES)
EXPRESS

	ORIG	GOOD	FINE	N-MINT
❑1, Dec 94, cardstock cover	2.95	0.60	1.50	3.00
❑2, Feb 95	2.50	0.50	1.25	2.50
❑3, Apr 95	2.50	0.50	1.25	2.50
❑4, Jun 95	2.50	0.50	1.25	2.50
❑Ash 1, Sum 94, b&w; no cover price	—	0.20	0.50	1.00

NIRA X: CYBERANGEL - CYNDER: ENDANGERED SPECIES
EXPRESS

Value: Cover or less

❑1.. 2.95
❑1/LE, cardstock cover; Commemorative edition; limited to 1500 copies......................... 12.95

NIRA X: EXODUS
AVATAR

Value: Cover or less

❑1, Oct 97................................ 3.00

NIRA X: HEATWAVE
EXPRESS

Value: Cover or less

❑1, Jul 95, enhanced wraparound cover.................................. 3.75
❑2, Aug 95............................... 2.50
❑3, Sep 95............................... 2.50

NIRA X: SOUL SKURGE
EXPRESS

Value: Cover or less

❑1, Nov 96, b&w...................... 2.75

NOBLE ARMOUR HALBERDER (JOHN AND JASON WALTRIP'S...)
ACADEMY

Value: Cover or less

❑1, Jan 97, Knight Vision 2.95

NOBODY
ONI PRESS

Value: Cover or less

❑1, Nov 98............................. 2.95
❑2, Dec 98............................. 2.95
❑3, Jan 99............................. 2.95
❑4, Feb 99............................. 2.95

NO BUSINESS LIKE SHOW BUSINESS
3-D ZONE

Value: Cover or less

❑1, b&w; not 3-D..................... 2.50

NOCTURNAL EMISSIONS
VORTEX

Value: Cover or less

❑1, b&w; adult......................... 2.50

NOCTURNALS, THE
MALIBU

	ORIG	GOOD	FINE	N-MINT
❑1, Jan 95, Black Planet, 1: The Nocturnals	2.95	0.70	1.75	3.50
❑2, Feb 95	2.95	0.60	1.50	3.00
❑3, Apr 95	2.95	0.60	1.50	3.00
❑4, Apr 95	2.95	0.60	1.50	3.00
❑5, Jun 95	2.95	0.60	1.50	3.00
❑6, Aug 95	2.95	0.60	1.50	3.00

NOCTURNALS: TROLL BRIDGE
ONI PRESS

Value: Cover or less

❑1, Oct 00, nn; One-Shot; b&w and orange.............................. 4.95

NOCTURNALS, THE: WITCHING HOUR
DARK HORSE

Value: Cover or less

❑1, May 98, nn; One-Shot....... 4.95

NOCTURNE (AIRCEL)
AIRCEL

Value: Cover or less

❑1, b&w................................. 2.50
❑2, b&w................................. 2.50
❑3, Aug 91, b&w..................... 2.50

NOCTURNE (MARVEL)
MARVEL

Value: Cover or less

❑1, Jun 95............................. 1.50
❑2, Jul 95, Through the Looking Glass, indicia says Sep 95............................... 1.50
❑3, Aug 95............................. 1.50
❑4, Sep 95............................. 1.50

NODWICK
HENCHMAN PUBLISHING

Value: Cover or less

❑1, b&w................................. 2.95
❑2, Mar 00, The Great Grave Robbery, b&w........................... 2.95

ORIG GOOD FINE N-MINT

❑3, b&w 2.95
❑4, Aug 00, The Tides of War, b&w 2.95
❑5, Oct 00, The Thirteenth Edition, b&w 2.95

NO ESCAPE
MARVEL

Value: Cover or less

❑1, Jun 94, movie Adaptation 1.50
❑2, Jul 94, movie Adaptation 1.50
❑3, Aug 94, movie Adaptation 1.50

NOG THE PROTECTOR OF THE PYRAMIDES
ONLI STUDIOS

Value: Cover or less

❑1, nn 2.00

NO GUTS OR GLORY
FANTACO

Value: Cover or less

❑1, b&w 2.95

NO HONOR
IMAGE

Value: Cover or less

❑1, Mar 01 .... 2.50
❑2, Mar 01 .... 2.50
❑3, Mar 01 .... 2.50

NO HOPE
SLAVE LABOR

Value: Cover or less

❑1, Apr 93, Life Is...; The Great Experiment or a Dangerous Idea 2.95
❑1-2, Feb 95, Life Is...; The Great Experiment or a Dangerous Idea, 2nd Printing 2.95
❑2, Aug 93, My Train Story; Wednesday 2.95
❑2-2, Apr 94, My Train Story; Wednesday, 2nd Printing 2.95
❑3, Nov 93 .... 2.95
❑3-2, Apr 94, 2nd Printing 2.95
❑4, Feb 94, Greetings Loser; A Short Walk Later 2.95
❑4-2, Oct 94, Greetings Loser; A Short Walk Later, 2nd Printing 2.95
❑5, Jun 94, Fun?; Ladies and Gentlemen Meet Mr. Sun, Part 2 .... 2.95
❑6, Sep 94, The Dresser; For the Losers 2.95
❑7, Jan 95, Freedom; Starship Earth 2.95
❑8, Apr 95, San Francisco; Happy Birthday to Me 2.95
❑9, Jul 95, Honesty is a Scary Thing; Ed Has No Brain 2.95

NOID IN 3-D, THE
BLACKTHORNE

Value: Cover or less

❑1 .... 2.50
❑2 .... 2.50

NO ILLUSIONS
COMICS DEFENCE FUND

	ORIG	GOOD	FINE	N-MINT
❑1, Drugs Scandal; Judge 45, Benefit for Comics Defence Fund (UK)	—	0.20	0.50	1.00

NOIR (ALPHA)
ALPHA

Value: Cover or less

❑1, Win 94, text & comics 3.95

NOIR (CREATIVE FORCE)
CREATIVE FORCE

Value: Cover or less

❑1, Apr 95 .... 4.95

NO JUSTICE, NO PIECE!
HEAD PRESS

Value: Cover or less

❑1, Oct 97, b&w; benefit anthology for CBLDF 2.95
❑2, Jul 98, b&w; benefit anthology for CBLDF 2.95

NOLAN RYAN
CELEBRITY

Value: Cover or less

❑1 .... 2.95

NOLAN RYAN'S 7 NO-HITTERS
REVOLUTIONARY

Value: Cover or less

❑1, Aug 93, b&w 2.95

NOMAD
MARVEL

	ORIG	GOOD	FINE	N-MINT
❑1, May 92, The Favor Banker, gatefold cover; "Want Ad" poster	2.00	0.50	1.25	2.50
❑2, Jun 92, Roadkill	1.75	0.35	0.88	1.75
❑3, Jul 92, Agents Of Questionable Ethics, Nomad vs. U.S.Agent	1.75	0.35	0.88	1.75
❑4, Aug 92, Dead Man's Hand, Part 2; Neon Knights	1.75	0.35	0.88	1.75
❑5, Sep 92, Dead Man's Hand, Part 5	1.75	0.35	0.88	1.75
❑6, Oct 92, Dead Man's Hand, Part 8	1.75	0.35	0.88	1.75
❑7, Nov 92, Infinity War; Airport Security, Infinity War	1.75	0.35	0.88	1.75
❑8, Dec 92, City of Angels, L.A riots	1.75	0.35	0.88	1.75
❑9, Jan 93	1.75	0.35	0.88	1.75
❑10, Feb 93, Raw Deals, A: Red Wolf	1.75	0.35	0.88	1.75
❑11, Mar 93, Criss Cross	1.75	0.35	0.88	1.75
❑12, Apr 93, Hidden In View, Part 1, A: Hate-Monger	1.75	0.35	0.88	1.75
❑13, May 93, Hidden In View, Part 2; If It Weren't For Love, A: Hate-Monger	1.75	0.35	0.88	1.75
❑14, Jun 93, Hidden In View, Part 3, A: Hate-Monger	1.75	0.35	0.88	1.75
❑15, Jul 93, Hidden In View, Part 4, A: Hate-Monger	1.75	0.35	0.88	1.75
❑16, Aug 93, Honor Among Thieves, A: Gambit	1.75	0.35	0.88	1.75
❑17, Sep 93	1.75	0.35	0.88	1.75
❑18, Oct 93, The Faustus Affair, Part 1, A: Dr. Faustus	1.75	0.35	0.88	1.75
❑19, Nov 93, The Faustus Affair, Part 3	1.75	0.35	0.88	1.75
❑20, Dec 93	1.75	0.35	0.88	1.75
❑21, Jan 94, A: Man-Thing	1.75	0.35	0.88	1.75
❑22, Feb 94, American Dreamers, Part 1	1.75	0.35	0.88	1.75
❑23, Mar 94, American Dreamers, Part 2	1.75	0.35	0.88	1.75
❑24, Apr 94, American Dreamers, Part 3	1.75	0.35	0.88	1.75
❑25, May 94, American Dreamers, Part 4, Final Issue	1.75	0.35	0.88	1.75

NOMAD (LTD. SERIES)
MARVEL

	ORIG	GOOD	FINE	N-MINT
❑1, Nov 90, The Big Fall Apart	1.50	0.40	1.00	2.00
❑2, Dec 90, The Wild Horses, O: Nomad	1.50	0.40	1.00	2.00
❑3, Mar 91, Cool Cats and Cry Babies	1.50	0.40	1.00	2.00
❑4, Feb 91, Melting Fire with Ice	1.50	0.40	1.00	2.00

NOMAN
TOWER

	ORIG	GOOD	FINE	N-MINT
❑1, Nov 66, WW	0.25	6.00	15.00	30.00
❑2, Mar 67, WW	0.25	4.40	11.00	22.00

NO MAN'S LAND
TUNDRA

Value: Cover or less

❑1 .... 14.95

NON
RED INK

Value: Cover or less

❑1, You can be Poor; I Am a Pineaple Pt. 1 .... 3.00
❑2 .... 3.00
❑3 .... 3.00

NO NEED FOR TENCHI!
VIZ

Value: Cover or less

❑1 .... 2.95
❑2 .... 2.95
❑3 .... 2.95
❑4 .... 2.95
❑5 .... 2.95
❑6 .... 2.95
❑7 .... 2.95

NO NEED FOR TENCHI! PART 2
VIZ

Value: Cover or less

❑1, Looking Far Beyond 2.95
❑2 .... 2.95
❑3 .... 2.95
❑4 .... 2.95
❑5 .... 2.95
❑6 .... 2.95
❑7 .... 2.95

NO NEED FOR TENCHI! PART 3
VIZ

Value: Cover or less

❑1 .... 2.95
❑2 .... 2.95
❑3 .... 2.95
❑4 .... 2.95
❑5 .... 2.95
❑6 .... 2.95

NO NEED FOR TENCHI! PART 4
VIZ

Value: Cover or less

❑1 .... 2.95
❑2 .... 2.95
❑3 .... 2.95
❑4 .... 2.95
❑5 .... 2.95
❑6 .... 2.95

NO NEED FOR TENCHI! PART 5
VIZ

Value: Cover or less

❑1 .... 3.25
❑2 .... 2.95
❑3 .... 2.95
❑4 .... 2.95
❑5 .... 2.95

NO NEED FOR TENCHI! PART 6
VIZ

Value: Cover or less

❑1, Nov 98 .... 3.25
❑2, Dec 98 .... 2.95
❑3, Jan 99 .... 3.25
❑4 .... 3.25
❑5 .... 3.25

NO NEED FOR TENCHI! PART 7
VIZ

Value: Cover or less

❑1 .... 2.95
❑2 .... 2.95
❑3 .... 2.95
❑4 .... 2.95
❑5 .... 2.95
❑6 .... 2.95

NO NEED FOR TENCHI! PART 8
VIZ

Value: Cover or less

❑1 .... 3.25

NO NINJA MAN
CUSTOM PIC

Value: Cover or less

❑1 .... 1.50
❑1-2, 2nd Printing 1.50

NO NO UFO
ANTARCTIC

Value: Cover or less

❑1, Aug 96, Male Domain Earth, adult 2.95
❑2, May 97, Mad Sisters Temple of Sex, Part 1; Male Domain Earth Part 2, b&w; adult 2.95
❑3, Sep 97, Mad Sisters Temple of Sex, Part 2; Male Domain Earth Part 3, b&w; adult 2.95
❑4, May 98, Mad Sisters Temple of Sex, Part 3, b&w; adult 2.95

NO PROFIT FOR THE WISE
CFD

Value: Cover or less

❑1, Jul 96, nn; b&w; Anthology 2.95

NORB
MU

Value: Cover or less

❑1, Jan 92 8.95

NORMALMAN
AARDVARK-VANAHEIM

	ORIG	GOOD	FINE	N-MINT
❑1, Jan 84, Not a Dream; Not a Hoax, Aardvark-Vanaheim publishes	1.70	0.50	1.25	2.50
❑2, Apr 84, ...And One Shall Slay Him!, O: Normalman	1.70	0.40	1.00	2.00
❑3, Jun 84, The Pope of Pain	1.70	0.40	1.00	2.00
❑4, Aug 84, Crisis on Earth-Twinkey	1.70	0.40	1.00	2.00
❑5, Oct 84	1.70	0.40	1.00	2.00
❑6, Dec 84, Normalman, P.I.	2.00	0.40	1.00	2.00
❑7, Feb 85, Who Killed Sgt. Fluffy This Time?	2.00	0.40	1.00	2.00
❑8, Apr 85, Misery in Space	2.00	0.40	1.00	2.00
❑9, Jun 85, Normalman Has Gaul, Renegade begins as publisher	2.00	0.40	1.00	2.00
❑10, Aug 85, Normalman for President, full color	2.00	0.40	1.00	2.00
❑11, Oct 85, Bet On It, full color	2.00	0.40	1.00	2.00
❑12, Dec 85, Love Stinks, full color	2.00	0.40	1.00	2.00
❑3D 1, Double-size	2.25	0.50	1.25	2.50

NORMALMAN 3-D
RENEGADE

Value: Cover or less

❑1, Feb 86 2.25

NORMALMAN-MEGATON MAN SPECIAL
IMAGE

Value: Cover or less

❑1, Aug 94, A: Mr. Spook; A: Flaming Carrot 2.50

NORTHERN'S HEMISPHERE
NORTHERN'S HEMISPHERE

Value: Cover or less

❑5, b&w 2.49
❑6, b&w 2.49
❑7, b&w 2.49

NORTHERN'S HEMISPHERE UNDISGUISED
NORTHERN'S HEMISPHERE

Value: Cover or less

❑1 2.50

NORTHGUARD: THE MANDES CONCLUSION
CALIBER

Value: Cover or less

❑1, Sep 89, b&w 2.50
❑2, Oct 89, b&w 2.50
❑3, Nov 89, b&w 2.50

NORTHSTAR
MARVEL

	ORIG	GOOD	FINE	N-MINT
❑1, Apr 94, Fast And Loose!	1.75	0.40	1.00	2.00
❑2, May 94, Fast and Furious!	1.75	0.40	1.00	2.00
❑3, Jun 94, Quick And The Dead!	1.75	0.40	1.00	2.00
❑4, Jul 94, Running on Empty!	1.75	0.40	1.00	2.00

NORTHSTAR PRESENTS
NORTHSTAR

Value: Cover or less

❑1, Oct 94, Zeigeist; Blood Rape of the Lust Ghouls 2.50
❑2 2.50

NORTHWEST CARTOON COOKERY
STARHEAD

Value: Cover or less

❑1, b&w; recipes from Pacific Northwest cartoonists 2.75

NOSFERATU (CALIBER)
TOME PRESS

Value: Cover or less

❑1, Jul 91, A Symphony of Shadows, b&w 2.95
❑2, Jul 91, A Symphony of Shadows, b&w 2.95

NOSFERATU (DARK HORSE)
DARK HORSE

Value: Cover or less

❑1, Mar 91, b&w 3.95

NOSFERATU, PLAGUE OF TERROR
MILLENNIUM

Value: Cover or less

❑1, b&w; duotone 2.50
❑2, b&w; duotone 2.50
❑3, b&w; duotone 2.50
❑4, Cathedral Sinister, b&w; duotone 2.50

NOSFERATU: THE DEATH MASS
ANTARCTIC

Value: Cover or less

❑1, Dec 97, b&w; adult 2.95
❑2, Jan 98, b&w; adult 2.95
❑3, Feb 98, b&w; adult 2.95
❑4, Mar 98, b&w; adult 2.95

NOSTRADAMUS CHRONICLES, THE: 1559-1821
TOME

Value: Cover or less

❑1 2.95

NOT APPROVED CRIME
AVALON

Value: Cover or less

❑1, PM, The Loot; H Is for Heroin 2.95

NOT BRAND ECHH
MARVEL

The covers of Jim Valentino's *normalman* paid tribute to famous comics series of the past, including *The Spirit*.

© 1984 Jim Valentino (Renegade)

	ORIG	GOOD	FINE	N-MINT
❑1, Aug 67, RA; JSe; JK; BEv, The Silver Burper; Too-Gone Kid: The Fastest Gums in the West!, 1: Forbush Man (on cover)	0.12	3.20	8.00	16.00
❑2, Sep 67	0.12	2.00	5.00	10.00
❑3, Oct 67, O: Bulk; O: Sore; O: Charlie America	0.12	1.80	4.50	9.00
❑4, Nov 67	0.12	1.80	4.50	9.00
❑5, Dec 67, 1: Forbush Man (full appearance); O: Forbush Man	0.12	1.80	4.50	9.00
❑6, Feb 68	0.12	1.60	4.00	8.00
❑7, Apr 68, O: Fantastical Four; O: Stupor-Man	0.12	1.60	4.00	8.00
❑8, Jun 68	0.12	1.60	4.00	8.00
❑9, Aug 68, Giant-size	0.25	2.00	5.00	10.00
❑10, Oct 68, Giant-size	0.25	2.00	5.00	10.00
❑11, Dec 68, Giant-size	0.25	2.00	5.00	10.00
❑12, Comiclot; Blechhman, Giant-size	0.25	2.00	5.00	10.00
❑13, Final Issue; Giant-size	0.25	2.00	5.00	10.00

NOT QUITE DEAD
RIP OFF

Value: Cover or less

❑1, Mar 93, b&w 2.95
❑1-2, 2nd Printing 2.95
❑2, b&w 2.95
❑3 2.95
❑4 2.95

NOVA (1ST SERIES)
MARVEL

	ORIG	GOOD	FINE	N-MINT
❑1, Sep 76, JSt; JB, 1: Nova I (Richard Ryder)	0.30	0.80	2.00	4.00
❑2, Oct 76, JSt; JB, The First Night Of...Condor!, 1: Powerhouse	0.30	0.50	1.25	2.50
❑3, Nov 76, 1: Diamondhead	0.30	0.40	1.00	2.00
❑4, Dec 76	0.30	0.40	1.00	2.00
❑5, Jan 77	0.30	0.40	1.00	2.00
❑6, Feb 77, 1: The Sphinx	0.30	0.40	1.00	2.00
❑7, Mar 77, O: The Sphinx	0.30	0.40	1.00	2.00
❑8, Apr 77	0.30	0.40	1.00	2.00
❑9, May 77	0.30	0.40	1.00	2.00
❑10, Jun 77	0.30	0.40	1.00	2.00
❑11, Jul 77	0.30	0.40	1.00	2.00
❑12, Aug 77, A: Spider-Man	0.30	0.30	0.75	1.50
❑13, Sep 77, 1: Crimebuster	0.30	0.30	0.75	1.50
❑14, Oct 77	0.30	0.30	0.75	1.50
❑15, Nov 77	0.35	0.30	0.75	1.50
❑16, Dec 77, V: Yellow Claw	0.35	0.30	0.75	1.50
❑17, Jan 78	0.35	0.30	0.75	1.50
❑18, Mar 78	0.35	0.30	0.75	1.50
❑19, May 78, 1: Blackout I (Marcus Daniels)	0.35	0.30	0.75	1.50
❑20, Jul 78	0.35	0.30	0.75	1.50
❑21, Sep 78, 1: Harris Moore (Comet), Only appears as Harris Moore	0.35	0.30	0.75	1.50
❑22, Nov 78, 1: Comet (Harris Moore)	0.35	0.30	0.75	1.50
❑23, Jan 79	0.35	0.30	0.75	1.50
❑24, Mar 79, O: Crimebuster	0.35	0.30	0.75	1.50
❑25, May 79, Final Issue	0.40	0.30	0.75	1.50

NOVA (2ND SERIES)
MARVEL

	ORIG	GOOD	FINE	N-MINT
❑1, Jan 94, Meavy Mettle	2.25	0.45	1.13	2.25
❑1/SC, Jan 94, Meavy Mettle, Special cover	2.95	0.59	1.48	2.95
❑2, Feb 94	1.75	0.40	1.00	2.00
❑3, Mar 94	1.75	0.35	0.88	1.75
❑4, Apr 94	1.75	0.35	0.88	1.75
❑5, May 94	1.95	0.35	0.88	1.75
❑6, Jun 94	1.95	0.39	0.98	1.95
❑7, Jul 94, Time and Time Again, Part 6	1.95	0.39	0.98	1.95
❑8, Aug 94	1.95	0.39	0.98	1.95
❑9, Sep 94	1.95	0.39	0.98	1.95
❑10, Oct 94	1.95	0.39	0.98	1.95
❑11, Nov 94, V: new Fantastic Four	1.95	0.39	0.98	1.95
❑12, Dec 94	1.95	0.39	0.98	1.95
❑13, Jan 95	1.95	0.39	0.98	1.95
❑14, Feb 95	1.95	0.39	0.98	1.95
❑15, Mar 95	1.95	0.39	0.98	1.95
❑16, Apr 95	1.95	0.39	0.98	1.95
❑17, May 95	1.95	0.39	0.98	1.95
❑18, Jun 95, Final Issue	1.95	0.39	0.98	1.95

ORIG GOOD FINE N-MINT

NOVA (3RD SERIES)
MARVEL
Value: Cover or less
❑1, May 99, EL, EL (w), Starting Over, wraparound cover...... 2.99
❑2, Jun 99, EL, EL (w), A: Namorita regains human; V: Diamondhead; A: Captain America... 1.99
❑3, Jul 99, EL, EL (w), V: Quintronic Man; A: Sphinx.................. 1.99
❑4, Aug 99, EL, EL (w), A: Fantastic Four 1.99
❑5, Sep 99, EL (w) 1.99
❑6, Oct 99, EL (w), The Dying Game 1.99
❑7, Nov 99 .... 1.99

NOVA HUNTER
RYAL
Value: Cover or less
❑1, coupon for trading cards... 2.50
❑1/Aut, coupon for trading cards 4.00

NOW COMICS PREVIEW
NOW

	ORIG	GOOD	FINE	N-MINT
❑1, 1: Ralph Snart; 1: Syphons; 1: Vector; 1: Valor; 1: Thunderstar	—	0.20	0.50	1.00

NOW HEPESVILLE
CALIBER
Value: Cover or less
❑1, b&w; One-Shot 3.50

NOWHERESVILLE
CALIBER
Value: Cover or less
❑1, b&w.............................. 3.50

NOWHERESVILLE: DEATH BY STARLIGHT
CALIBER
Value: Cover or less
❑1, b&w.............................. 2.95
❑2, b&w.............................. 2.95
❑3, b&w; flip book with Wordsmith #7 back-up 2.95
❑4.............................. 2.95

NOW, ON A MORE SERIOUS NOTE...
DAWN

	ORIG	GOOD	FINE	N-MINT
❑1, Sum 94, b&w; no cover price	—	0.40	1.00	2.00

NOW WHAT?!
NOW

	ORIG	GOOD	FINE	N-MINT
❑1	0.50	0.60	1.50	3.00
❑2	0.50	0.40	1.00	2.00
❑3	0.50	0.40	1.00	2.00
❑4	0.50	0.40	1.00	2.00
❑5	0.50	0.40	1.00	2.00
❑6	0.50	0.40	1.00	2.00
❑7	0.50	0.40	1.00	2.00
❑8	0.50	0.40	1.00	2.00
❑9	0.50	0.40	1.00	2.00
❑10	0.50	0.40	1.00	2.00
❑11	0.50	0.40	1.00	2.00

NTH MAN, THE ULTIMATE NINJA
MARVEL
Value: Cover or less
❑1, Aug 89, Recall 1.00
❑2, Sep 89 .... 1.00
❑3, Oct 89 .... 1.00
❑4, Nov 89 .... 1.00
❑5, Nov 89 .... 1.00
❑6, Dec 89 .... 1.00
❑7, Dec 89 .... 1.00
❑8, Jan 90 .... 1.00
❑9, Feb 90 .... 1.00
❑10, Mar 90 .... 1.00
❑11, Apr 90 .... 1.00
❑12, May 90 .... 1.00
❑13, Jun 90 .... 1.00
❑14, Jul 90 .... 1.00
❑15, Aug 90 .... 1.00
❑16, Sep 90 .... 1.00

NUANCE
MAGNETIC INK
Value: Cover or less
❑1, b&w.............................. 2.75
❑2, b&w.............................. 2.75
❑3, b&w.............................. 2.75

NUCLEAR WAR!
NEC
Value: Cover or less
❑1.............................. 3.50
❑2, Nov 00, Give me Shelter, Part 2.............................. 3.50

NULL PATROL
ESCAPE VELOCITY
Value: Cover or less
❑1.............................. 1.50
❑2, Fuel Endeavors................ 1.50

NUMIDIAN FORCE
KAMITE
Value: Cover or less
❑4.............................. 2.00

NURTURE THE DEVIL
FANTAGRAPHICS
Value: Cover or less
❑2, Jul 94, b&w...................... 2.50
❑3, Dec 94, b&w...................... 2.50

NUT RUNNERS
RIP OFF
Value: Cover or less
❑1, Sep 91, b&w.................... 2.50
❑2, Jan 92, b&w.................... 2.50

NUTS & BOTS
EXCEL GRAPHICS
Value: Cover or less
❑1, Aug 98, b&w; magazine 3.95

NYGHT SCHOOL
BRAINSTORM
Value: Cover or less
❑2, b&w; adult 2.95

O

OBERGEIST: RAGNAROK HIGHWAY
IMAGE
Value: Cover or less
❑1, May 01, Playing Pinochle with Dead Folks.......................... 2.95
❑2, Jun 01 .... 2.95
❑3, Jul 01 .... 2.95
❑4, Aug 01 .... 2.95
❑5, Sep 01 .... 2.95
❑6, Oct 01 .... 2.95

OBJECTIVE FIVE
IMAGE
Value: Cover or less
❑1, Jul 00, Index Case........... 2.95
❑2.............................. 2.95
❑3, Sep 00, Airborne.............. 2.95
❑4, Nov 00, Reunion 2.95
❑5, Dec 00, Point of No Return 2.95
❑6, Jan 01, Digging in China... 2.95

OBLIVION
COMICO
Value: Cover or less
❑1.............................. 2.50
❑2.............................. 2.50
❑3, May 96.............................. 2.95

OBLIVION CITY
SLAVE LABOR
Value: Cover or less
❑1, Mar 91, b&w 2.50
❑2, May 91, b&w.................... 2.50
❑3, Jun 91, b&w.................... 2.50
❑4, Jun 91, b&w.................... 2.50
❑5, Sep 91, b&w 2.50
❑6, Jan 92, b&w...................... 2.50
❑7, Apr 92.............................. 2.95
❑8, May 92.............................. 2.95
❑9, Jun 92.............................. 3.95

OBNOXIO THE CLOWN
MARVEL

	ORIG	GOOD	FINE	N-MINT
❑1, Apr 83, Something Slimey This Way Comes!, X-Men	0.60	0.40	1.00	2.00

OCEAN COMICS
OCEAN
Value: Cover or less
❑1, b&w.............................. 1.75

OCELOT, THE
EROS
Value: Cover or less
❑1.............................. 2.75
❑2.............................. 2.75
❑3.............................. 2.75

OCTOBER YEN
ANTARCTIC
Value: Cover or less
❑1, Jul 96, b&w...................... 3.50
❑2, Sep 96, b&w 2.95
❑3, Nov 96, b&w 2.95

OCTOBRIANA
REVOLUTION

	ORIG	GOOD	FINE	N-MINT
❑1, The Octobriana Files, Part 1; Return of Octobriana, Part 1	2.95	0.70	1.75	3.50
❑2	2.95	0.59	1.48	2.95
❑3	2.95	0.59	1.48	2.95
❑4	2.95	0.59	1.48	2.95
❑5	2.95	0.59	1.48	2.95

OCTOBRIANA: FILLING IN THE BLANKS
ARTFUL SALAMANDER
Value: Cover or less
❑1, Win 98, b&w...................... 2.95

ODD ADVENTURE-ZINE, THE
ZAMBONI PRESS
Value: Cover or less
❑1.............................. 2.95
❑2, Apr 97.............................. 2.95
❑3, Jul 97.............................. 2.95
❑4, Dec 97.............................. 2.95

ODDJOB
SLAVE LABOR
Value: Cover or less
❑1, Spr 99, Death by Gummi, b&w 2.95

OFFCASTES
MARVEL
Value: Cover or less
❑1, Embossed cover.............. 2.50
❑2.............................. 1.95
❑3.............................. 1.95

OFFERINGS
CRY FOR DAWN
Value: Cover or less
❑1, b&w; adult......................... 2.75
❑2, b&w; adult 2.50

OFFICIAL BUZ SAWYER
PIONEER
Value: Cover or less
❑1, Aug 88, b&w 2.00
❑2, Sep 88, b&w 2.00
❑3, Oct 88, b&w 2.00
❑4, Nov 88, b&w...................... 2.00
❑5, Dec 88, b&w...................... 2.00

OFFICIAL COMICS ENQUIRER SWIMSUIT PRICE GUIDE INVESTMENT ANNUAL, THE
FANTACO
Value: Cover or less
❑1 .... 4.95

OFFICIAL CRISIS CROSSOVER INDEX
ECLIPSE

	ORIG	GOOD	FINE	N-MINT
❑1, Jun 86	1.25	0.30	0.75	1.50

OFFICIAL CRISIS ON INFINITE EARTHS INDEX
ECLIPSE

	ORIG	GOOD	FINE	N-MINT
❑1, Mar 86	1.25	0.40	1.00	2.00

OFFICIAL DOOM PATROL INDEX
ECLIPSE

Value: Cover or less

❑1, Feb 86	1.50
❑2, Feb 86	1.50

OFFICIAL HANDBOOK OF THE CONAN UNIVERSE
MARVEL

	ORIG	GOOD	FINE	N-MINT
❑1	1.25	0.30	0.75	1.50
❑2, nn; no price; sold with Conan Saga #75	—	0.20	0.50	1.00

OFFICIAL HANDBOOK OF THE MARVEL UNIVERSE (VOL. 1)
MARVEL

	ORIG	GOOD	FINE	N-MINT
❑1, Jan 83, Abomination to Avengers Quinjet	1.00	0.40	1.00	2.00
❑2, Feb 83, Baron Mordo to The Collective Man	1.00	0.40	1.00	2.00
❑3, Mar 83, The Collector to Dracula	1.00	0.40	1.00	2.00
❑4, Apr 83, Dragon Man to Gypsy Moth	1.00	0.40	1.00	2.00
❑5, May 83, Hangman to Juggernaut	1.00	0.40	1.00	2.00
❑6, Jun 83, Kang to Man-Bull	1.00	0.40	1.00	2.00
❑7, Jul 83, Mandarin to Mystique	1.00	0.40	1.00	2.00
❑8, Aug 83, Namorita to Pyro	1.00	0.40	1.00	2.00
❑9, Sep 83, Quasar to She-Hulk	1.00	0.40	1.00	2.00
❑10, Oct 83, Shi'ar to Sub-Mariner	1.00	0.40	1.00	2.00
❑11, Nov 83, Subterraneans to Ursa Major	1.00	0.40	1.00	2.00
❑12, Dec 83, Valkyrie to Zzzax	1.00	0.40	1.00	2.00
❑13, Feb 84, Book of the Dead: Air-Walker to Man-Wolf	1.00	0.40	1.00	2.00
❑14, Mar 84, Book of the Dead: Marvel Boy to Zuras	1.00	0.40	1.00	2.00
❑15, May 84, Weapons, Hardware, and Paraphernalia	1.00	0.40	1.00	2.00

OFFICIAL HANDBOOK OF THE MARVEL UNIVERSE (VOL. 2)
MARVEL

	ORIG	GOOD	FINE	N-MINT
❑1, Dec 85, Abomination to Batroc's Brigade	1.50	0.40	1.00	2.00
❑2, Jan 86, Beast to Clea	1.50	0.40	1.00	2.00
❑3, Feb 86, Cloak to Doctor Octopus	1.50	0.40	1.00	2.00
❑4, Mar 86, Doctor Strange to Galactus	1.50	0.40	1.00	2.00
❑5, Apr 86, Gardener to Hulk	1.50	0.40	1.00	2.00
❑6, May 86, Human Torch to Ka-Zar	1.50	0.40	1.00	2.00
❑7, Jun 86, Khoryphos to Magneto	1.50	0.40	1.00	2.00
❑8, Jul 86, Magus to Mole Man	1.50	0.40	1.00	2.00
❑9, Aug 86, Molecule Man to Owl	1.50	0.40	1.00	2.00
❑10, Sep 86, Paladin to The Rhino	1.50	0.40	1.00	2.00
❑11, Oct 86, Richard Rider to Sidewinder	1.50	0.40	1.00	2.00
❑12, Nov 86, Sif to Sunspot	1.50	0.40	1.00	2.00
❑13, Dec 86, Super-Adaptoid to Umar	1.50	0.40	1.00	2.00
❑14, Jan 87, Unicorn to Wolverine	1.50	0.40	1.00	2.00
❑15, Mar 87, Wonder Man to Zzzax and Alien Races	1.50	0.40	1.00	2.00
❑16, Jun 87, Book of the Dead: Air-Walker to Death-Stalker	1.50	0.40	1.00	2.00
❑17, Aug 87, Book of the Dead: Destiny to Hobgoblin	1.50	0.40	1.00	2.00
❑18, Oct 87, Book of the Dead: Hyperion to Nighthawk; Book of the Dead: Hyperion II to Nighthawk II	1.50	0.40	1.00	2.00
❑19, Dec 87, Book of the Dead: Nuke to Obadiah Stane	1.50	0.40	1.00	2.00
❑20, Feb 88, Book of the Dead: Stick to Zuras	1.50	0.40	1.00	2.00

OFFICIAL HANDBOOK OF THE MARVEL UNIVERSE (VOL. 3)
MARVEL

	ORIG	GOOD	FINE	N-MINT
❑1, Jul 89, Adversary to Chameleon	1.50	0.40	1.00	2.00
❑2, Aug 89, Champion of the Universe to Ecstasy	1.50	0.40	1.00	2.00
❑3, Sep 89, Eon to Hulk	1.50	0.40	1.00	2.00
❑4, Oct 89, Human Torch I to Manikin	1.50	0.40	1.00	2.00
❑5, Nov 89, Marauders to Power Princess	1.50	0.40	1.00	2.00
❑6, Nov 89, Prowler to Serpent Society	1.50	0.40	1.00	2.00
❑7, Dec 89, Set to Tyrak	1.50	0.40	1.00	2.00
❑8, Dec 89, U-Man to Madelyne Pryor	1.50	0.40	1.00	2.00

OFFICIAL HANDBOOK OF THE MARVEL UNIVERSE MASTER EDITION
MARVEL

	ORIG	GOOD	FINE	N-MINT
❑1, Dec 90, Three-hole punched looseleaf format	3.95	0.90	2.25	4.50
❑2, Jan 91	3.95	0.90	2.25	4.50
❑3, Feb 91	3.95	0.90	2.25	4.50
❑4, Mar 91	3.95	0.90	2.25	4.50
❑5, Apr 91	3.95	0.90	2.25	4.50
❑6, May 91	3.95	0.79	1.98	3.95
❑7, Jun 91	3.95	0.79	1.98	3.95
❑8, Jul 91	3.95	0.79	1.98	3.95
❑9, Aug 91	3.95	0.79	1.98	3.95
❑10, Sep 91	3.95	0.79	1.98	3.95
❑11, Oct 91	3.95	0.79	1.98	3.95

Marvel provided readers with biographical information on its major characters in the various editions of *Official Handbook of the Marvel Universe.*

	ORIG	GOOD	FINE	N-MINT
❑12, Nov 91	4.50	0.79	1.98	3.95
❑13, Dec 91	4.50	0.90	2.25	4.50
❑14	4.50	0.90	2.25	4.50
❑15	4.50	0.90	2.25	4.50
❑16	4.50	0.90	2.25	4.50
❑17	4.50	0.90	2.25	4.50
❑18	4.50	0.90	2.25	4.50
❑19	4.50	0.90	2.25	4.50
❑20	4.50	0.90	2.25	4.50
❑21	4.50	0.90	2.25	4.50
❑22	4.50	0.90	2.25	4.50
❑23	4.50	0.90	2.25	4.50
❑24	4.50	0.90	2.25	4.50
❑25	4.50	0.90	2.25	4.50
❑26	4.50	0.90	2.25	4.50
❑27	4.50	0.90	2.25	4.50
❑28	4.95	0.99	2.47	4.95
❑29	4.95	0.99	2.47	4.95
❑30	4.95	0.99	2.47	4.95
❑31	4.95	0.99	2.47	4.95
❑32	4.95	0.99	2.47	4.95
❑33	4.95	0.99	2.47	4.95
❑34	4.95	0.99	2.47	4.95
❑35, KP, A: Avengers West Coast; A: Omega Red; A: Beyonder; A: Spider-Man 2099; A: Lilith; A: Hellstrom	4.95	0.99	2.47	4.95
❑36, Final Issue	4.95	0.99	2.47	4.95

OFFICIAL HAWKMAN INDEX, THE
ECLIPSE

Value: Cover or less

❑1, Nov 86	2.00
❑2, Dec 86	2.00

OFFICIAL HOW TO DRAW G.I. JOE
BLACKTHORNE

Value: Cover or less

❑1, Nov 87	2.00
❑2, Jan 88	2.00

OFFICIAL HOW TO DRAW ROBOTECH
BLACKTHORNE

Value: Cover or less

❑1	2.00
❑2	2.00
❑3	2.00
❑4	2.00
❑5	2.00
❑6	2.00
❑7	2.00
❑8	2.00
❑9	2.00
❑10	2.00
❑11, Dec 87	2.00
❑12	2.00
❑13	2.00
❑14	2.00

OFFICIAL HOW TO DRAW TRANSFORMERS
BLACKTHORNE

Value: Cover or less

❑1, Sep 87	2.00
❑2, Nov 87	2.00
❑3, Jan 88	2.00
❑4, Mar 88	2.00

OFFICIAL JOHNNY HAZARD
PIONEER

Value: Cover or less

❑1, Aug 88, b&w; strips	2.00

OFFICIAL JUNGLE JIM
PIONEER

Value: Cover or less

❑1, Jun 88, AR, b&w	2.00
❑2, Jul 88, AR, b&w	2.00
❑3, Aug 88, AR, b&w	2.00
❑4, Sep 88, AR, b&w	2.00
❑5, Oct 88, AR, b&w	2.00
❑6, Nov 88, AR, b&w	2.00
❑7, Dec 88, AR, b&w	2.00
❑8, Jan 89, AR, b&w	2.00
❑9, Feb 89, AR, b&w	2.00
❑10, Apr 89	2.50
❑11, Apr 89	2.50
❑12	2.50
❑13	2.50
❑14	2.50
❑15	2.50
❑16	2.50
❑Anl 1, Jan 89, AR, b&w	3.95

OFFICIAL JUSTICE LEAGUE OF AMERICA INDEX
ICG

Value: Cover or less

❑1	2.00
❑2	2.00
❑3	2.00
❑4	2.00
❑5	2.00
❑6	2.00
❑7	2.00
❑8, Covers Justice League of America #238-261, other related titles; Title changes to Justice League of America Index	2.00

OFFICIAL MANDRAKE
PIONEER
Value: Cover or less
❑1, Jun 88, b&w 2.00
❑2, Jul 88, b&w 2.00
❑3, Aug 88, b&w 2.00
❑4, Sep 88, b&w 2.00
❑5, Oct 88, b&w 2.00
❑6, Nov 88, b&w 2.00
❑7, Dec 88, b&w 2.00
❑8, Jan 89, b&w 2.00
❑9, Feb 89, b&w 2.00
❑10, Apr 89 .... 2.50
❑11, Apr 89 .... 2.50
❑12 .... 2.50
❑13 .... 2.50
❑14 .... 2.50
❑15 .... 2.50

OFFICIAL MARVEL INDEX TO AVENGERS, THE (VOL. 2)
MARVEL
Value: Cover or less
❑1, Oct 94 .... 1.95
❑2, Nov 94, Indexes issues #61-122 .... 1.95
❑3, Dec 94 .... 1.95
❑4, Jan 95, Indexes issues #177-230 .... 1.95
❑5, Feb 95 .... 1.95
❑6, Mar 95 .... 1.95

OFFICIAL MARVEL INDEX TO MARVEL TEAM-UP
MARVEL
Value: Cover or less
❑1, Jan 86 .... 1.25
❑2, Feb 86 .... 1.25
❑3, May 86 .... 1.25
❑4, Jul 86 .... 1.25
❑5, Oct 86 .... 1.25
❑6, Jul 87, Indexes Marvel Team-Up #99=112, Annual 3 .... 1.25

OFFICIAL MARVEL INDEX TO THE AMAZING SPIDER-MAN
MARVEL
Value: Cover or less
❑1, Apr 85, Indexes Amazing Fantasy #15, Amazing Spider-Man #1-29 .... 1.25
❑2, May 85 .... 1.25
❑3, Jun 85, Indexes Amazing Spider-Man#59-84, King-Size Annual #5-6, Spectacular Spider-Man #1-2 .... 1.25
❑4, Jul 85, Indexes Amazing Spider-Man#85-112, King-Size Annual #7-8 .... 1.25
❑5, Aug 85, Indexes Amazing Spider-Man#114-137, King-Size Annual #9, Giant-Sized Super-Heroes #1 .... 1.25
❑6, Sep 85, Indexes Amazing Spider-Man #138-155, Giant-Size Spider-Man #1-6 .... 1.25
❑7, Oct 85, Indexes Amazing Spider-Man #156-174; Spider-Man Annual #10-11 .... 1.25
❑8, Nov 85, Indexes issues #175-195, Annual #12 .... 1.25
❑9, Dec 85, Indexes issues #196-215, Annual #13-14 .... 1.25

OFFICIAL MARVEL INDEX TO THE AVENGERS
MARVEL
Value: Cover or less
❑1, Jun 87 .... 2.95
❑2, Aug 87 .... 2.95
❑3, Oct 87 .... 2.95
❑4, Dec 87 .... 2.95
❑5, Apr 88 .... 2.95
❑6, Jun 88 .... 2.95
❑7, Aug 88 .... 2.95

OFFICIAL MARVEL INDEX TO THE FANTASTIC FOUR
MARVEL
Value: Cover or less
❑1, Dec 85, JBy (c), Indexes Fantastic Four #1-15 .... 1.25
❑2, Jan 86, BSz (c) 1.25
❑3, Feb 86 .... 1.25
❑4, Mar 86, Indexes Fantastic Four #46-65, Annual #4 .... 1.25
❑5, Apr 86, Indexes Fantastic Four #66-84, Annual #5-6 .... 1.25
❑6, May 86, Indexes issues #85-106, Annual #7-8 .... 1.25
❑7, Jun 86, Indexes issues #107-125, Annual #9 .... 1.25
❑8, Jul 86, Indexes issues #126-141, Annual #10, Giant-Size Super-Stars #1 .... 1.25
❑9, Aug 86 .... 1.25
❑10, Sep 86, Indexes issues #161-176, Annual #11, Giant-Size Fantastic Four #4-6 .... 1.25
❑11, Oct 86, KP, Indexes issues #177-198 .... 1.25
❑12, Jan 87, Indexes issues #199-214, Annual # 12-13 .... 1.25

OFFICIAL MARVEL INDEX TO THE X-MEN
MARVEL
Value: Cover or less
❑1, May 87, cardstock cover; squarebound 2.95
❑2, Jul 87 .... 2.95
❑3, Sep 87 .... 2.95
❑4, Nov 87 .... 2.95
❑5, Mar 88 .... 2.95
❑6, May 88 .... 2.95
❑7, Jul 88 .... 2.95

OFFICIAL MARVEL INDEX TO THE X-MEN (VOL. 2)
MARVEL
Value: Cover or less
❑1, Apr 94 .... 1.95
❑2, May 94 .... 1.95
❑3, Jun 94 .... 1.95
❑4, Jul 94 .... 1.95
❑5, Aug 94 .... 1.95

OFFICIAL MODESTY BLAISE, THE
PIONEER
Value: Cover or less
❑1, Jul 88, b&w 2.00
❑2, Aug 88, b&w 2.00
❑3, Sep 88, b&w 2.00
❑4, Oct 88, b&w 2.00
❑5, Nov 88, b&w 2.00
❑6, Dec 88, b&w 2.00
❑7, Dec 88, b&w 2.00
❑8, Jan 89, b&w 2.00
❑Anl 1, Dec 88, O: Modesty, b&w 4.95

OFFICIAL PRINCE VALIANT, THE
PIONEER
Value: Cover or less
❑1, b&w; Hal Foster 2.00
❑2, b&w; Hal Foster 2.00
❑3, Aug 88, b&w; Hal Foster 2.00
❑4, Sep 88, b&w; Hal Foster 2.00
❑5, Oct 88, b&w; Hal Foster 2.00
❑6, Oct 88, b&w; Hal Foster 2.00
❑7, Nov 88, MGr (c), Foster 2.00
❑8, Dec 88, MGr (c), Foster 2.00
❑9, Jan 89, Foster 2.00
❑10, Feb 89 .... 2.50
❑11, Mar 89 .... 2.50
❑12, Apr 89 .... 2.50
❑13 .... 2.50
❑14 .... 2.50
❑15 .... 2.50
❑16 .... 2.50
❑17 .... 2.50
❑18 .... 2.50
❑Anl 1, Win 88, b&w; Hal Foster 3.95
❑KS 1, Apr 89, b&w; Foster 3.95

OFFICIAL PRINCE VALIANT MONTHLY
PIONEER
Value: Cover or less
❑1, Jun 89, b&w 3.95

OFFICIAL RIP KIRBY
PIONEER
Value: Cover or less
❑1, Aug 88, AR, b&w 2.00
❑2, Sep 88, AR, b&w 2.00
❑3, Oct 88, AR, b&w 2.00
❑4, Nov 88, AR, b&w 2.00
❑5, Dec 88, AR, b&w 2.00
❑6, Jan 89, AR, b&w 2.00

OFFICIAL SECRET AGENT, THE
PIONEER
Value: Cover or less
❑1, Jun 88, AW, b&w 2.00
❑2, Jul 88, AW, b&w 2.00
❑3, Aug 88, AW, b&w 2.00
❑4, Sep 88, AW, b&w 2.00
❑5, Oct 88, AW, b&w 2.00
❑6, Nov 88, AW, b&w 2.00
❑7, Dec 88, AW, b&w 2.00

OFFICIAL TEEN TITANS INDEX, THE
INDEPENDENT
Value: Cover or less
❑1, Aug 85 .... 1.50
❑2, Sep 85, Indexes Teen Titans #23-53, DC Super-Stars #1, Showcase #75, The Hawk and the Dove #1-6 .... 1.50
❑3, Oct 85, Indexes DC Comics Presents #26, New Teen Titans #1-25, Tales of the New Teen Titans #1-4, Marvel and DC Present #1 .... 1.50
❑4, Nov 85 .... 1.50
❑5, Dec 85 .... 1.50

OFFICIAL, AUTHORIZED ZEN INTERGALACTIC NINJA SOURCEBOOK
EXPRESS
Value: Cover or less
❑1, b&w 3.50
❑1-2, 94 revised edition 3.50

OFFWORLD
GRAPHIC IMAGE
Value: Cover or less
❑1, Return Post; The Neighborhood 3.95

OF MIND AND SOUL
RAGE
Value: Cover or less
❑1, b&w 2.25

OF MYTHS AND MEN
BLACKTHORNE
Value: Cover or less
❑1, b&w 1.75
❑2, Mar 87, b&w 1.75

OGENKI CLINIC
AKITA
Value: Cover or less
❑1 .... 3.95
❑2 .... 3.95
❑3 .... 4.50
❑4 .... 4.50
❑5 .... 4.50
❑6 .... 4.50

OGENKI CLINIC (VOL. 2)
AKITA
Value: Cover or less
❑1 .... 3.95
❑2 .... 3.95
❑3 .... 3.95
❑4 .... 3.95
❑5 .... 3.95
❑6 .... 3.95

OGENKI CLINIC (VOL. 3)
SEXY FRUIT
Value: Cover or less
❑1, Medical Record #33, Sex=Death?!?; Medical Record #34, New Year Sex Party!, A: Diane; A: Landlord; A: Iko; A: Detective Sorikomi; A: Detective Pochi, Antonio Honduras translation 3.95
❑2 .... 3.95
❑3 .... 3.95
❑4 .... 3.95
❑5 .... 3.95
❑6 .... 3.95
❑7 .... 3.95

OGENKI CLINIC (VOL. 4)
SEXY FRUIT
Value: Cover or less
❑1 .... 2.95
❑2 .... 2.95
❑3 .... 2.95
❑4, Jul 99, Medical record # 54 .... 2.95
❑5 .... 2.95
❑6 .... 2.95

OGENKI CLINIC (VOL. 5)
SEXY FRUIT
Value: Cover or less
❑1, Oct 99, Medical Record #62: Romance or Raunch?; Medical Record #63: Otenki Clinic!! . 2.95
❑2 .... 2.95
❑3 .... 2.95
❑4 .... 2.95
❑5 .... 2.95
❑6 .... 2.95
❑7 .... 2.95

OGENKI CLINIC (VOL. 6)
SEXY FRUIT
Value: Cover or less

- ❑1 .... 2.95
- ❑2 .... 2.95
- ❑3 .... 2.95
- ❑4 .... 2.95
- ❑5 .... 2.95
- ❑6, Oct 00 .... 2.95

OGRE
BLACK DIAMOND
Value: Cover or less

- ❑1, Jan 94, 1: Felony; 1: Barnacle Bill; 1: Ogre 2.95
- ❑2, Mar 94 .... 2.95
- ❑3, May 94 .... 2.95
- ❑4, Jul 94 .... 2.95

O.G. WHIZ
GOLD KEY

	ORIG	GOOD	FINE	N-MINT
❑1	0.15	5.00	12.50	25.00
❑2	0.15	3.00	7.50	15.00
❑3, Aug 71	0.15	2.00	5.00	10.00
❑4	0.15	2.00	5.00	10.00
❑5, Feb 72	0.15	2.00	5.00	10.00
❑6, May 72, Final issue of original run (1972)	0.15	2.00	5.00	10.00
❑7, Series begins again (1978)	0.15	0.60	1.50	3.00
❑8	0.15	0.60	1.50	3.00
❑9, Sep 78, A: Tubby	0.15	0.60	1.50	3.00
❑10	0.15	0.60	1.50	3.00
❑11, Stop that Mirror; Testy Testers, Final Issue	0.15	0.60	1.50	3.00

OH.
B PUBLICATIONS
Value: Cover or less

- ❑1 .... 2.95
- ❑2 .... 2.95
- ❑3 .... 2.95
- ❑4 .... 2.95
- ❑5 .... 2.95
- ❑6 .... 2.95
- ❑7 .... 2.95
- ❑8, Immola and the Luna Legion 2.95

OHM'S LAW
IMPERIAL
Value: Cover or less

- ❑1, Books of the Jihad Saga, Part 1, 1: Ohm; 1: Drakkus; 1: Black Hurrikan, full color 2.25
- ❑2, b&w; Black and White 1.95
- ❑3, b&w; Published out of sequence; Black and white . 1.95

OH MY GODDESS!
DARK HORSE

	ORIG	GOOD	FINE	N-MINT
❑1, Aug 94, The Wish, 1: Keiichi Morisato; 1: Tamiya; 1: Belldandy; 1: Otaki	2.50	1.00	2.50	5.00
❑2, Sep 94, Sexy Sister	2.50	0.60	1.50	3.00
❑3, Oct 94, Belldandy's Narrow Escape	2.50	0.60	1.50	3.00
❑4, Nov 94, The CD from Hell	2.50	0.60	1.50	3.00
❑5, Dec 94, Mara Strikes Back!!	2.50	0.60	1.50	3.00
❑6, Jan 95, The Scales of Love	2.50	0.60	1.50	3.00

OH MY GODDESS!: ADVENTURES OF THE MINI-GODDESSES
DARK HORSE
Value: Cover or less

- ❑1, May 00 .... 9.95

OH MY GODDESS! PART II
DARK HORSE

	ORIG	GOOD	FINE	N-MINT
❑1, Feb 95, Bugs	2.50	0.60	1.50	3.00
❑2, Mar 95, A Singular Sensation	2.50	0.60	1.50	3.00
❑3, Apr 95, Turkey with all the Trimmings, Oh My Cartoonist! follow-up story	2.50	0.55	1.38	2.75
❑4, May 95, Life's Just a Game of "Sugoroku Roulette",	2.50	0.55	1.38	2.75
❑5, Jun 95, Final Exam,	2.50	0.55	1.38	2.75
❑6, Jul 95, The Secret's Out,	2.50	0.55	1.38	2.75
❑7, Aug 95, Go-Kart Go,	2.95	0.60	1.50	3.00
❑8, Sep 95, What a Miracle, The Adventures of Mini-Urd story	2.95	0.60	1.50	3.00

OH MY GODDESS! PART III
DARK HORSE

	ORIG	GOOD	FINE	N-MINT
❑1, Nov 95, On a Wing and a Prayer, Cover reads "Oh My Goddess Special"	2.95	0.60	1.50	3.00
❑2, Dec 95, Love Potion #9, Cover reads "Oh My Goddess Special"	2.95	0.60	1.50	3.00
❑3, Jan 96, Sympathy for the Devil, Cover reads "Oh My Goddess Special"	2.95	0.60	1.50	3.00
❑4, Feb 96, Mystical Engine, Cover reads "Oh My Goddess Special"	2.95	0.60	1.50	3.00
❑5, Mar 96, Valentine Rhapsody, Cover reads "Oh My Goddess Special"	2.95	0.60	1.50	3.00
❑6, Apr 96, Terrible Master Urd, Part 1; Cover reads "Oh My Goddess! 1 of 6"	2.95	0.60	1.50	3.00
❑7, May 96, Terrible Master Urd, Part 2; Cover reads "Oh My Goddess! 2 of 6"	2.95	0.60	1.50	3.00
❑8, Jun 96, Terrible Master Urd, Part 3; Cover reads "Oh My Goddess! 3 of 6"	2.95	0.60	1.50	3.00
❑9, Jul 96, Terrible Master Urd, Part 4; Cover reads "Oh My Goddess! 4 of 6"	2.95	0.60	1.50	3.00
❑10, Aug 96, Terrible Master Urd, Part 5; Cover reads "Oh My Goddess, part 5 of 6"	2.95	0.60	1.50	3.00
❑11, Sep 96, Terrible Master Urd, Part 6; Cover reads "Oh My Goddess! 6 of 6"	2.95	0.60	1.50	3.00

As *Oh My Goddess!* moved into later volumes, many issues sported "Oh My Goddess! Special" on the cover with no identifying issue number. The correct information can be found in the indicia.

© 1995 Dark Horse

OH MY GODDESS! PART IV
DARK HORSE
Value: Cover or less

- ❑1, Dec 96, Robot Wars, Cover reads "Oh My Goddess Special" 2.95
- ❑2, Jan 97, Trials of Morisato, Part 1; Cover reads " Oh My Goddess! 1 of 3" 2.95
- ❑3, Feb 97, Trials of Morisato, Part 2; Cover reads " Oh My Goddess! 2 of 3" 2.95
- ❑4, Mar 97, Trials of Morisato, Part 3; Cover reads " Oh My Goddess! 3 of 3" 2.95
- ❑5, Apr 97, The Queen of Vengeance, Cover reads " Oh My Goddess Special" 2.95
- ❑6, May 97, Mara Strikes Back, Part 1; 48pgs.; Cover reads " Oh My Goddess! 1 of 3" 2.95
- ❑7, Jun 97, Mara Strikes Back, Part 2; Cover reads " Oh My Go . 2.95
- ❑8, Jul 97, Mara Strikes Back, Part 3; Cover reads " Oh My Goddess! 3 of 3" 2.95

OH MY GODDESS! PART IX
DARK HORSE
Value: Cover or less

- ❑1, Jul 00, Pretty in Scarlet 3.50
- ❑2, Aug 00, The Goddess's Apprentice 3.50
- ❑3, Sep 00, Queen Sayoko, Part 1 .... 3.50
- ❑4, Oct 00, Queen Sayoko, Part 2 .... 3.50
- ❑5, Nov 00, Queen Sayoko, Part 3 .... 3.50
- ❑6, Dec 00, Queen Sayoko, Part 4 .... 3.50
- ❑7, Jan 01, Queen Sayoko, Part 5 .... 3.50

OH MY GODDESS! PART V
DARK HORSE
Value: Cover or less

- ❑1, Sep 97, The Forgotten Promise, Cover reads " Oh My Goddess Special" 2.95
- ❑2, Oct 97, The Lunchbox of Love, Cover reads " Oh My Goddess Special" 2.95
- ❑3, Nov 97, Meet Me by the Seashore, Cover reads " Oh My Goddess Special" 3.95
- ❑4, Dec 97, You're So Bad, Cover reads " Oh My Goddess Special" 3.95
- ❑5, Jan 98, Ninja Master, Part 1; Cover reads " Oh My Goddess! 1 of 2" 2.95
- ❑6, Feb 98, Ninja Master, Part 2; The Law of the Ninja, Cover reads " Oh My Goddess! 2 of 2; 3.95
- ❑7, Mar 98, Miss Keiichi, Part 1; Cover reads " Oh My Goddess! 1 of 2" 3.95
- ❑8, Apr 98, Miss Keiichi, Part 2; Cover reads " Oh My Goddess! 2 of 2" 3.95
- ❑9, May 98, It's Lonely at the Top 3.50
- ❑10, Jun 98, Fallen Angel, Cover reads " Oh My Goddess! One-Shot" 3.95
- ❑11, Jul 98, Play the Game, Cover reads " Oh My Goddess! One-Shot" 3.95
- ❑12, Aug 98, Sorrow/ Fear Not, Cover reads " Oh My Goddess! One-Shot" 3.95

OH MY GODDESS! PART VI
DARK HORSE
Value: Cover or less

- ❑1, Oct 98, The Devil in Miss Urd, Part 1 .... 3.50
- ❑2, Dec 98, The Devil in Miss Urd, Part 2 .... 2.95
- ❑3, Jan 99, The Devil in Miss Urd, Part 3 .... 2.95
- ❑4, Feb 99, The Devil in Miss Urd, Part 4 .... 2.95
- ❑5, Mar 99, The Devil in Miss Urd, Part 5 .... 2.95
- ❑6, Apr 99, Super Urd 2.95

OH MY GODDESS! PART VII
DARK HORSE
Value: Cover or less

- ❑1, May 99, The Fourth Goddess, Part 1 .... 2.95
- ❑2, Jun 99, The Fourth Goddess, Part 2 .... 2.95
- ❑3, Jul 99, The Fourth Goddess, Part 3 .... 2.95
- ❑4, Aug 99, The Fourth Goddess, Part 4 .... 3.50
- ❑5, Sep 99, The Fourth Goddess, Part 5 .... 3.50
- ❑6, Oct 99, The Fourth Goddess, Part 6 .... 3.50
- ❑7, Nov 99, The Fourth Goddess, Part 7 .... 3.50
- ❑8, Dec 99, The Fourth Goddess, Part 8 .... 2.95

OH MY GODDESS! PART VIII
DARK HORSE
Value: Cover or less

- ❑1 .... 3.50
- ❑2 .... 3.50
- ❑3 .... 3.50
- ❑4, Hail to the Chief, Part 1 .... 3.50
- ❑5, May 00, Hail to the Chief, Part 2 .... 3.50
- ❑6, Jun 00, Hail to the Chief, Part 3 .... 3.50

OH MY GODDESS! PART X
DARK HORSE
Value: Cover or less

- ❑1 .... 3.50
- ❑2 .... 3.50
- ❑3, Apr 01, Another Me 3.50

OH MY GOTH
SIRIUS

Value: Cover or less

- ❑1 .... 2.95
- ❑2 .... 2.95
- ❑3 .... 2.95
- ❑4 .... 2.95

OH MY GOTH: HUMANS SUCK!
SIRIUS

Value: Cover or less

- ❑1, Dragon Con or Bust!, b&w 2.95
- ❑2, The Stupid Voyage of Sinbad, b&w 2.95

OINK: HEAVEN'S BUTCHER
KITCHEN SINK

Value: Cover or less

- ❑1, Dec 95 .... 4.95
- ❑2, Feb 96 .... 4.95
- ❑3, Apr 96 .... 4.95

OJ'S BIG BUST OUT
BONEYARD

	ORIG	GOOD	FINE	N-MINT
❑1, Mar 95, b&w	2.95	0.70	1.75	3.50

OKTANE
DARK HORSE

Value: Cover or less

- ❑1, Aug 95, Kicks On Route 66 2.50
- ❑2, Sep 95 .... 2.50
- ❑3, Oct 95 .... 2.50
- ❑4, Nov 95, Final Issue 2.50

OLDBLOOD
PARODY PRESS

Value: Cover or less

- ❑1 .... 2.50
- ❑1-2, 2nd Printing 2.50

OLYMPIANS, THE
MARVEL

Value: Cover or less

- ❑1, It's Not The End Of The World 3.95
- ❑2 .... 3.95

OMAC
DC

	ORIG	GOOD	FINE	N-MINT
❑1, Oct 74, JK, JK (w), Build-A-Friend, 1: Omac	0.20	1.00	2.50	5.00
❑2, Dec 74, JK, V: Mr. Big	0.20	0.70	1.75	3.50
❑3, Feb 75, JK	0.20	0.60	1.50	3.00
❑4, Apr 75, JK	0.20	0.60	1.50	3.00
❑5, Jun 75, JK, JK (w)	0.25	0.60	1.50	3.00
❑6, Aug 75, JK	0.25	0.50	1.25	2.50
❑7, Oct 75, JK	0.25	0.50	1.25	2.50
❑8, Dec 75, JK, JKu (c)	0.25	0.50	1.25	2.50

OMAC: ONE MAN ARMY CORPS
DC

Value: Cover or less

- ❑1, JBy, JBy (w), Build-A-Friend; Brother Eye and Buddy Blank, b&w; prestige format 3.95
- ❑2, JBy, JBy (w), b&w; prestige format 3.95
- ❑3, JBy, JBy (w), Mein Kampf, b&w; prestige format 3.95
- ❑4, JBy, JBy (w), b&w; prestige format 3.95

OMAHA: CAT DANCER
STEELDRAGON

	ORIG	GOOD	FINE	N-MINT
❑1	—	2.40	6.00	12.00
❑1/Ash, preview	—	0.60	1.50	3.00
❑1-2, 2nd Printing	1.75	0.80	2.00	4.00
❑2	1.75	1.60	4.00	8.00

OMAHA THE CAT DANCER (FANTAGRAPHICS)
FANTAGRAPHICS

	ORIG	GOOD	FINE	N-MINT
❑1, Jul 94	2.50	0.60	1.50	3.00
❑2, Aug 94	2.50	0.60	1.50	3.00
❑3, Nov 94	2.50	0.60	1.50	3.00
❑4, Feb 95	2.50	0.60	1.50	3.00

OMAHA THE CAT DANCER (KITCHEN SINK)
KITCHEN SINK

	ORIG	GOOD	FINE	N-MINT
❑0, 1: Omaha the Cat Dancer, Reprints early Omaha stories from Vootie, Bizarre Sex #9	2.50	0.80	2.00	4.00
❑1, Oct 86	2.00	2.00	5.00	10.00
❑1-2, 2nd Printing	2.00	0.80	2.00	4.00
❑, 3rd Printing	2.50	0.60	1.50	3.00
❑2, Oct 86	2.00	1.00	2.50	5.00
❑3, Oct 86	2.00	0.80	2.00	4.00
❑4, Jan 87	2.00	0.80	2.00	4.00
❑5, Mar 87	2.00	0.80	2.00	4.00
❑6, May 87	2.00	0.60	1.50	3.00
❑7, Jul 87	2.00	0.60	1.50	3.00
❑8, Oct 87	2.00	0.60	1.50	3.00
❑9, Feb 88	2.00	0.60	1.50	3.00
❑10, May 88	2.00	0.60	1.50	3.00
❑11, Dec 88	2.00	0.60	1.50	3.00
❑12	2.00	0.60	1.50	3.00
❑12-2, 2nd Printing	2.95	0.59	1.48	2.95
❑13, Sep 89	2.00	0.60	1.50	3.00
❑13-2, 2nd Printing	2.95	0.59	1.48	2.95
❑14, Mar 90, Wendel back-up	2.50	0.60	1.50	3.00
❑15, Jan 91	2.50	0.60	1.50	3.00
❑16, Nov 91	2.50	0.59	1.48	2.95
❑17, Feb 92	2.50	0.59	1.48	2.95
❑18, Jan 93	2.95	0.59	1.48	2.95
❑19, Jun 93	2.95	0.59	1.48	2.95
❑20, Final Kitchen Sink issue	2.95	0.59	1.48	2.95

O'MALLEY AND THE ALLEY CATS
GOLD KEY

	ORIG	GOOD	FINE	N-MINT
❑1	0.15	1.60	4.00	8.00
❑2	0.15	1.20	3.00	6.00
❑3, Jul 71	0.15	1.20	3.00	6.00
❑4	—	0.80	2.00	4.00
❑5	—	0.80	2.00	4.00
❑6	—	0.80	2.00	4.00
❑7, Jul 73	0.20	0.80	2.00	4.00
❑8, Oct 73	0.20	0.80	2.00	4.00
❑9, Jan 74, 16pgs.	0.20	0.80	2.00	4.00

OMAR LENNYX
MAGNECOM

Value: Cover or less

- ❑1, Blood Seekers, b&w 2.95

OMEGA ELITE
BLACKTHORNE

Value: Cover or less

- ❑1, b&w 3.50

OMEGA FORCE
ENTITY

Value: Cover or less

- ❑1, 1: Dual; 1: The Earon Raider; 1: Karad the Godslayer; 1: Omega Force; 1: The Drakon; 1: Flashback (Entity); 1: Archetype 2.50

OMEGA FORCE (SOUTH STAR)
SOUTH STAR

Value: Cover or less

- ❑1, Aug 92 .... 2.00

OMEGA KNIGHTS
UNDERGROUND

	ORIG	GOOD	FINE	N-MINT
❑1	2.00	0.40	1.00	2.00
❑2	—	0.40	1.00	2.00
❑3	—	0.40	1.00	2.00
❑4	—	0.40	1.00	2.00
❑5, Sundance, Part 1	—	0.40	1.00	2.00
❑6, Oct 92, Sundance, Part 2	—	0.40	1.00	2.00

OMEGA MAN
OMEGA 7

	ORIG	GOOD	FINE	N-MINT
❑0	3.00	0.60	1.50	3.00
❑1, b&w; Simpson trial; no indicia	4.00	0.80	2.00	4.00
❑Ash 1, nn; full color; no cover price; no indicia; sideways format	—	0.20	0.50	1.00

OMEGA MEN, THE
DC

	ORIG	GOOD	FINE	N-MINT
❑1, Apr 83, KG, O: Omega Men	1.00	0.40	1.00	2.00
❑2, May 83, KG, O: Broot	1.00	0.30	0.75	1.50
❑3, Jun 83, 1: Lobo	1.00	0.60	1.50	3.00
❑4, Jul 83, 1: Felicity	1.00	0.30	0.75	1.50
❑5, Aug 83, 2: Lobo	1.00	0.40	1.00	2.00
❑6, Sep 83	1.00	0.30	0.75	1.50
❑7, Oct 83, O: Citadel	1.25	0.30	0.75	1.50
❑8, Nov 83	1.25	0.30	0.75	1.50
❑9, Dec 83, A: 3rd, 3: Lobo	1.25	0.40	1.00	2.00
❑10, Jan 84, 1st Lobo Full Story	1.25	0.40	1.00	2.00
❑11, Feb 84	1.25	0.20	0.50	1.00
❑12, Mar 84	1.25	0.20	0.50	1.00
❑13, Apr 84	1.25	0.20	0.50	1.00
❑14, May 84	1.25	0.20	0.50	1.00
❑15, Jun 84	1.25	0.20	0.50	1.00
❑16, Jul 84	1.25	0.20	0.50	1.00
❑17, Aug 84	1.25	0.20	0.50	1.00
❑18, Sep 84	1.25	0.20	0.50	1.00
❑19, Oct 84, A: Lobo	1.25	0.20	0.50	1.00
❑20, Nov 84, A: Lobo	1.25	0.40	1.00	2.00
❑21, Dec 84	1.25	0.20	0.50	1.00
❑22, Jan 85	1.25	0.20	0.50	1.00
❑23, Feb 85	1.25	0.20	0.50	1.00
❑24, Mar 85	1.25	0.20	0.50	1.00
❑25, Apr 85	1.25	0.20	0.50	1.00
❑26, May 85, 1: Elu	1.25	0.20	0.50	1.00
❑27, Jun 85	1.25	0.20	0.50	1.00
❑28, Jul 85	1.25	0.20	0.50	1.00
❑29, Aug 85	1.25	0.20	0.50	1.00
❑30, Sep 85	1.25	0.20	0.50	1.00
❑31, Oct 85, Crisis On Infinite Earths, Crisis	1.50	0.20	0.50	1.00
❑32, Nov 85	1.25	0.20	0.50	1.00
❑33, Dec 85	1.25	0.20	0.50	1.00
❑34, Jan 86	1.25	0.20	0.50	1.00
❑35, Feb 86	1.25	0.20	0.50	1.00
❑36, Mar 86	1.25	0.20	0.50	1.00
❑37, Apr 86, A: Lobo	1.25	0.20	0.50	1.00
❑38, May 86	1.25	0.20	0.50	1.00
❑Anl 1	1.50	0.40	1.00	2.00
❑Anl 2, O: Primus	1.50	0.35	0.88	1.75

OMEGA THE UNKNOWN
MARVEL

	ORIG	GOOD	FINE	N-MINT
❑1, Mar 76, JM, 1: Omega the Unknown; 1: James-Michael Starling (Omega the Unknown's counterpart)	0.25	0.80	2.00	4.00
❑2, May 76, A: Hulk	0.25	0.50	1.25	2.50
❑3, Jul 76	0.25	0.40	1.00	2.00
❑4, Sep 76	0.30	0.40	1.00	2.00
❑5, Nov 76	0.30	0.40	1.00	2.00
❑6, Jan 77	0.30	0.40	1.00	2.00
❑7, Mar 77	0.30	0.40	1.00	2.00
❑8, May 77, 1: Foolkiller II (Greg Salinger)-cameo	0.30	0.40	1.00	2.00
❑9, Jul 77, 1: Foolkiller II (Greg Salinger)-full	0.30	0.60	1.50	3.00
❑10, Oct 77, D: Omega the Unknown, Final Issue	0.30	0.40	1.00	2.00

OMEN, THE (CHAOS)
CHAOS!

Value: Cover or less

- ❑1, May 98 .... 2.95
- ❑2, Jun 98 .... 2.95
- ❑3, Jul 98 .... 2.95
- ❑4, Aug 98 .... 2.95
- ❑5, Sep 98 .... 2.95

OMEN (NORTHSTAR)
NORTHSTAR

Value: Cover or less

- ❑1, b&w 2.00
- ❑2, b&w 2.00

OMEN, THE: SAVE THE CHOSEN PREVIEW
CHAOS!

Value: Cover or less

- ❑1, Sep 97, nn; preview of upcoming series 2.50

OMEN, THE: VEXED
CHAOS!

Value: Cover or less

- ❑1, Oct 98 .... 2.95

OMICRON: ASTONISHING ADVENTURES ON OTHER WORLDS
PYRAMID

Value: Cover or less

- ❑1, b&w; flexi-disc 2.25
- ❑2, Sep 87, Andromeda Space Cadet: Criss-Cross Confusion; Alexus of Vertigo: Duel, b&w; flexi-disc 2.25

OMNIBUS: MODERN PERVERSITY
BLACKBIRD

Value: Cover or less

- ❑1, nn; b&w; squarebound 3.25

OMNI COMIX
OMNI

	ORIG	GOOD	FINE	N-MINT
❑1, Mar 95, High Guard; Mission to Mars, magazine; Mar '95 issue of Omni inserted	2.95	0.80	2.00	4.00
❑2, Apr 95, insert in Apr. '95 issue of Omni with Omni Comix #2 cover; magazine	3.95	0.80	2.00	4.00
❑3, Oct 95, magazine; T.H.U.N.D.E.R. Agents story	4.95	0.99	2.47	4.95

OMNI MEN
BLACKTHORNE

Value: Cover or less

- ❑1, Apr 89, b&w 3.50

ON A PALE HORSE
INNOVATION

Value: Cover or less

- ❑1 .... 4.95
- ❑2 .... 4.95
- ❑3 .... 4.95
- ❑4 .... 4.95
- ❑5, Dec 93 .... 4.95

ONCE UPON A TIME IN THE FUTURE
PLATINUM

Value: Cover or less

- ❑1 .... 9.95

ONE, THE
MARVEL

	ORIG	GOOD	FINE	N-MINT
❑1, Jul 85, BA, The Big Sleep	1.50	0.40	1.00	2.00
❑2, Sep 85, BA	1.50	0.40	1.00	2.00
❑3, Nov 85, BA	1.50	0.40	1.00	2.00
❑4, Jan 86, BA	1.50	0.40	1.00	2.00
❑5, Mar 86, BA	1.50	0.40	1.00	2.00
❑6, May 86, BA	1.50	0.40	1.00	2.00

ONE (PACIFIC)
PACIFIC

Value: Cover or less

- ❑1, b&w; 1st Pacific title 3.00

ONE-ARM SWORDSMAN
DR. LEUNG'S

Value: Cover or less

- ❑1 .... 1.80
- ❑2 .... 1.80
- ❑3 .... 1.80
- ❑4 .... 1.80
- ❑5 .... 1.80
- ❑6 .... 1.80
- ❑7 .... 1.80

ONE-FISTED TALES
SLAVE LABOR

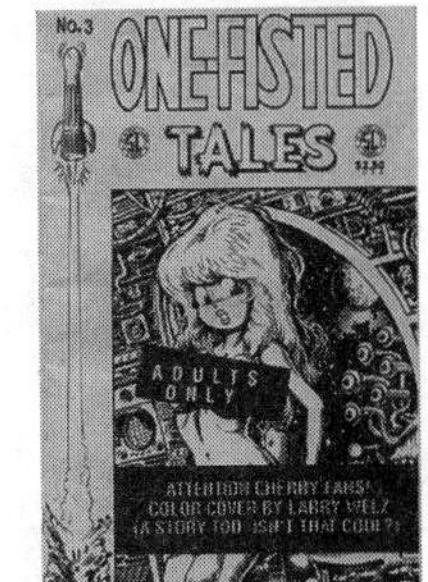

Larry Welz provided a Cherry cover and story for the third issue of Slave Labor's *One-Fisted Tales.*

© 1991 Slave Labor

	ORIG	GOOD	FINE	N-MINT
❑1, May 90, b&w; adult; brown paper wrapper	2.50	0.60	1.50	3.00
❑1-2, Nov 90, adult; 2nd Printing	2.50	0.50	1.25	2.50
❑2, Sep 90, b&w; adult; brown paper wrapper (some wrappers printed red in error)	2.50	0.60	1.50	3.00
❑2-2, Apr 93, adult; 2nd Printing; no brown paper wrapper	2.95	0.59	1.48	2.95
❑3, Feb 91, b&w; adult; Cherry cover and story; brown paper wrapper	2.50	0.50	1.25	2.50
❑3-2, Apr 93, adult; 2nd Printing; no brown paper wrapper	2.95	0.50	1.25	2.50
❑3-3, Aug 93, adult; 3rd Printing; no brown paper wrapper	2.95	0.59	1.48	2.95
❑4, Jun 91, b&w; adult	2.50	0.50	1.25	2.50
❑4-2, Jan 92, adult; 2nd Printing	2.50	0.59	1.48	2.95
❑4-3, Aug 93, adult; 3rd Printing; no brown paper wrapper	2.95	0.59	1.48	2.95
❑5, Sep 91, b&w; adult	3.95	0.79	1.98	3.95
❑5-2, Feb 92, adult; 2nd Printing	2.95	0.59	1.48	2.95
❑6, Apr 92, adult	2.95	0.59	1.48	2.95
❑7, Sep 92, b&w; adult	2.95	0.59	1.48	2.95
❑8, Mar 93, b&w; adult	2.95	0.59	1.48	2.95
❑9, Oct 93, b&w; adult	2.95	0.59	1.48	2.95
❑10, Feb 94, b&w; adult	2.95	0.59	1.48	2.95
❑11, Aug 94, b&w; adult	2.95	0.59	1.48	2.95

ONE HUNDRED AND ONE DALMATIANS (WALT DISNEY'S...)
DISNEY

Value: Cover or less

- ❑1 .... 2.50

ONE MILE UP
ECLIPSE

Value: Cover or less

- ❑1, b&w 2.50
- ❑2 .... 2.50

ONE MILLENNIUM
HUNTER PRODUCTIONS

Value: Cover or less

- ❑1, b&w 2.50
- ❑2, b&w 2.50
- ❑3, b&w 2.50
- ❑4, b&w 2.50
- ❑5, b&w 2.50

ONE-POUND GOSPEL
VIZ

	ORIG	GOOD	FINE	N-MINT
❑1	3.50	0.70	1.75	3.50
❑2	3.50	0.70	1.75	3.50
❑3	2.95	0.59	1.48	2.95
❑4	2.95	0.59	1.48	2.95

ONE-POUND GOSPEL ROUND 2
VIZ

Value: Cover or less

- ❑1 .... 2.95
- ❑2 .... 2.95
- ❑3 .... 2.95
- ❑4 .... 2.95
- ❑5 .... 2.95
- ❑6, The Fallen Lamb, Part 2 .... 2.95

ONE-SHOT PARODY
MILKY WAY

Value: Cover or less

- ❑1, X-Men 1.50

ONE-SHOT WESTERN
CALIBER

Value: Cover or less

- ❑1, b&w 2.50

ONI
DARK HORSE

Value: Cover or less

- ❑1, Feb 01 .... 2.99
- ❑2, Feb 01 .... 2.99
- ❑3, Feb 01 .... 2.99

ONI DOUBLE FEATURE
ONI PRESS

	ORIG	GOOD	FINE	N-MINT
❑1, Jan 98, MW, Jay & Silent Bob: Walt Flanagan's Dog; Secret Broadcast, 1: Jay; 1: Silent Bob, Flip-book; Jay & Silent Bob, Milk & Cheese, Secret Broadcast	2.95	1.20	3.00	6.00
❑1-2, Mar 98, 2nd Printing	2.95	0.59	1.48	2.95
❑2, Feb 98, Too Much Coffee Man, Car Crash, Secret Broadcast	2.95	0.80	2.00	4.00
❑3, Mar 98, Frumpy the Clown, Bacon, Car Crash	2.95	0.70	1.75	3.50
❑4, Apr 98, BSz (c), Bacon, A River in Egypt, Cheetahman	2.95	0.70	1.75	3.50
❑5, May 98	2.95	0.70	1.75	3.50
❑6, Jun 98, NG (w); CR (w), Only the End of the World Again, Part 1, Only The End of the World Again, Zombie Kid	2.95	0.80	2.00	4.00
❑7, Jul 98	2.95	0.59	1.48	2.95

	ORIG	GOOD	FINE	N-MINT
❑8, Aug 98, Only The End of the World Again, Satchel of Weltschmerz, Pip & Norton	2.95	0.59	1.48	2.95
❑9	2.95	0.59	1.48	2.95
❑10, Nov 98, Sam & Max, Drive-By, Road Trip	2.95	0.59	1.48	2.95
❑11, Feb 99, Usagi Yojimbo, Blue Monday, Drive-By	2.95	0.59	1.48	2.95
❑12, May 99, The Harpooner, Bluntman & Chronic, The Honor Rollers	2.95	0.59	1.48	2.95

ONIGAMI
ANTARCTIC

Value: Cover or less

- ❑1, Apr 98, In the Shadow of Every Crime ... 2.95
- ❑2, Jun 98, The Beginning of Parting ... 2.95
- ❑3, Jul 98, Revenge at an Unexpected Place, preview of Far West by Richard Moore ... 2.95

ONLY THE END OF THE WORLD AGAIN
ONI

Value: Cover or less

- ❑1, CR, NG (w) ... 6.95

ON OUR BUTTS
AEON

Value: Cover or less

- ❑1, Apr 95 ... 2.95

ON RAVEN'S WINGS
BONEYARD

Value: Cover or less

- ❑1 ... 2.95
- ❑2, Sep 94 ... 2.95

ONSLAUGHT: EPILOGUE
MARVEL

Value: Cover or less

- ❑1, Feb 97, Prisoner M-13, 1: Nina, One-Shot ... 2.95

ONSLAUGHT: MARVEL
MARVEL

	ORIG	GOOD	FINE	N-MINT
❑1, Oct 96, With Great Power..., A: di, wraparound cover	3.95	1.20	3.00	6.00

ONSLAUGHT: X-MEN
MARVEL

	ORIG	GOOD	FINE	N-MINT
❑1, Aug 96, Traitor to the Cause, wraparound cover; set-up for Onslaught crossover in Marvel titles	3.95	1.00	2.50	5.00
❑1/SC, Traitor to the Cause, variant cover	3.95	1.60	4.00	8.00

ON THE BUS
SLAVE LABOR

Value: Cover or less

- ❑1, Aug 94, The Overland Route ... 2.95

ONYX OVERLORD
MARVEL

Value: Cover or less

- ❑1, Oct 92, The Onyx Overlord, Log 1 ... 2.75
- ❑2, Nov 92, The Onyx Overlord, Log 2 ... 2.75
- ❑3, Dec 92, The Onyx Overlord, Log 3 ... 2.75
- ❑4, Jan 93, The Onyx Overlord, Log 4 ... 2.75

OOMBAH, JUNGLE MOON MAN
STRAWBERRY JAM

Value: Cover or less

- ❑1, b&w ... 2.50

OPEN SEASON
RENEGADE

Value: Cover or less

- ❑1, b&w ... 2.00
- ❑2, b&w ... 2.00
- ❑3, b&w ... 2.00
- ❑4, Oct 87, b&w ... 2.00
- ❑5, Dec 87, b&w ... 2.00
- ❑6, Apr 88, b&w; black issue ... 2.00
- ❑7, b&w ... 2.00

OPEN SORE FUNNIES
HOME-MADE EUTHANASIA

Value: Cover or less

- ❑1 ... 1.25

OPEN SPACE
MARVEL

Value: Cover or less

- ❑1, Dec 89, KB (w), Handshake; The Land Of Nod ... 4.95
- ❑2, Apr 90 ... 4.95
- ❑3, Jun 90, There Ain't No Such Thing As A Free Launch!; Dear Jenny ... 4.95
- ❑4, Aug 90 ... 4.95

OPERATION: KANSAS CITY
MOTION

Value: Cover or less

- ❑1, Win 93, b&w; Breakneck Blvd. Preview ... 2.50

OPERATION: KNIGHTSTRIKE
IMAGE

Value: Cover or less

- ❑1, May 95 ... 2.50
- ❑1/A, May 95 ... 2.50
- ❑2, Jun 95 ... 2.50
- ❑2/A, Jun 95 ... 2.50
- ❑3, Jul 95, A: Bloodstrike ... 2.50

OPERATION: STORMBREAKER
ACCLAIM

Value: Cover or less

- ❑1, Aug 97, 1: Sgt. Turok; 1: Nemesis; 1: Bravado; 1: Doctor Tomorrow, cover says Jul, indicia says Aug; One-Shot ... 3.95

OPERATIVE: SCORPIO
BLACKTHORNE

Value: Cover or less

- ❑1, Jan 89, b&w ... 3.50

OPTIC NERVE
DRAWN & QUARTERLY

	ORIG	GOOD	FINE	N-MINT
❑1	—	1.00	2.50	5.00
❑2	—	0.60	1.50	3.00
❑3	—	0.60	1.50	3.00
❑4	—	0.60	1.50	3.00
❑5	—	0.60	1.50	3.00
❑6	—	0.60	1.50	3.00
❑7, Mini-Comic	—	0.60	1.50	3.00

ORA
SON OF A TREEBOB STUDIOS

Value: Cover or less

- ❑1, Mar 99, b&w ... 2.95

ORACLE
ORACLE

	ORIG	GOOD	FINE	N-MINT
❑1, GP, b&w	—	0.60	1.50	3.00

ORACLE - A TRESPASSERS MYSTERY
AMAZING MONTAGE

Value: Cover or less

- ❑1, nn; b&w ... 4.95

ORACLE PRESENTS
ORACLE

	ORIG	GOOD	FINE	N-MINT
❑1, GP, b&w; reprint of Oracle #1	—	0.60	1.50	3.00
❑2, Aug 86, b&w; Critter Corps	1.00	0.60	1.50	3.00

ORBIT
ECLIPSE

Value: Cover or less

- ❑1, DSt (c), BA (w), Nothing for Nothing; Ginny Sweethips' Flying Circus ... 4.95
- ❑2, BA ... 4.95
- ❑3, TY (w), The Lost Garden of Enid Blyton, Beatrix Potter, Lucy Atwell and the Rest of the Lads of the 32nd Parachute Regiment; The Last Question ... 4.95

ORB MAGAZINE
ORB

Value: Cover or less

- ❑1 ... 1.25
- ❑2 ... 1.25
- ❑3, Lepers; Half-Life ... 1.25

ORIENTAL HEROES
JADEMAN

Value: Cover or less

- ❑1 ... 1.95
- ❑2 ... 1.95
- ❑3 ... 1.95
- ❑4 ... 1.95
- ❑5 ... 1.95
- ❑6 ... 1.95
- ❑7 ... 1.95
- ❑8 ... 1.95
- ❑9 ... 1.95
- ❑10 ... 1.95
- ❑11 ... 1.95
- ❑12 ... 1.95
- ❑13 ... 1.95
- ❑14 ... 1.95
- ❑15, Oct 89 ... 1.95
- ❑16 ... 1.95
- ❑17 ... 1.95
- ❑18 ... 1.95
- ❑19 ... 1.95
- ❑20 ... 1.95
- ❑21 ... 1.95
- ❑22 ... 1.95
- ❑23 ... 1.95
- ❑24 ... 1.95
- ❑25 ... 1.95
- ❑26 ... 1.95
- ❑27 ... 1.95
- ❑28 ... 1.95
- ❑29 ... 1.95
- ❑30 ... 1.95
- ❑31 ... 1.95
- ❑32 ... 1.95
- ❑33 ... 1.95
- ❑34 ... 1.95
- ❑35 ... 1.95
- ❑36 ... 1.95
- ❑37 ... 1.95
- ❑38 ... 1.95
- ❑39 ... 1.95
- ❑40 ... 1.95
- ❑41 ... 1.95
- ❑42 ... 1.95

ORIGINAL ASTRO BOY, THE
NOW

Value: Cover or less

- ❑1, Sep 87, O: Astro Boy ... 1.50
- ❑2, Oct 87 ... 1.50
- ❑3, Nov 87 ... 1.75
- ❑4, Dec 87 ... 1.75
- ❑5, Jan 88 ... 1.75
- ❑6, Feb 88 ... 1.75
- ❑7, Mar 88 ... 1.75
- ❑8, Apr 88 ... 1.75
- ❑9, May 88 ... 1.75
- ❑10, Jun 88 ... 1.75
- ❑11, Aug 88 ... 1.75
- ❑12, Sep 88 ... 1.75
- ❑13, Oct 88 ... 1.75
- ❑14, Nov 88 ... 1.75
- ❑15, Jan 89 ... 1.75
- ❑16, Feb 89 ... 1.75
- ❑17, Mar 89 ... 1.75
- ❑18, Apr 89 ... 1.75
- ❑19, May 89 ... 1.75
- ❑20, Jun 89, Final Issue ... 1.75

ORIGINAL BLACK CAT, THE
RECOLLECTIONS

Value: Cover or less

- ❑1 ... 2.00
- ❑2, Mar 89, MA (c), 1: Kit, Reprint ... 2.00
- ❑3, Sep 90 ... 2.00
- ❑4, Jun 91 ... 2.00
- ❑5, Jul 91 ... 2.00
- ❑6, Aug 91, reprints first Black Cat story from Pocket Comics #1 ... 2.00
- ❑7, Nov 91 ... 2.00
- ❑8, Title changes to Black Cat for one issue only ... 2.00
- ❑9, Title reverts to Original Black Cat ... 2.00
- ❑10, Title changes to Black Cat Comics for final issue ... 1.00

ORIGINAL BOY: DAY OF ATONEMENT
OMEGA 7

	ORIG	GOOD	FINE	N-MINT
❑1, nn; no cover price; no indicia; events deal with Million Man March on Washington	—	0.39	0.98	1.95

ORIGINAL CREW, THE
PERSONALITY

	ORIG	GOOD	FINE	N-MINT
❑1, William Shatner	2.95	0.60	1.50	3.00
❑2, Leonard Nimoy	2.95	0.60	1.50	3.00
❑3, DeForest Kelley	2.95	0.60	1.50	3.00
❑4	2.95	0.59	1.48	2.95
❑5	2.95	0.59	1.48	2.95
❑6	2.95	0.59	1.48	2.95
❑7	2.95	0.59	1.48	2.95
❑8	2.95	0.59	1.48	2.95
❑9, Bruce Hyde	2.95	0.59	1.48	2.95
❑10	2.95	0.59	1.48	2.95

ORIGINAL DICK TRACY, THE
GLADSTONE

	ORIG	GOOD	FINE	N-MINT
❑1, Sep 90, Dick Tracy vs. Mrs. Pruneface, Mrs. Pruneface	1.95	0.40	1.00	2.00
❑2, Nov 90, Influence	1.95	0.40	1.00	2.00
❑3, Jan 91, Dick Tracy Exterminates the Extortioner, Gargles	2.00	0.40	1.00	2.00
❑4, Mar 91, Dick Tracy Confronts Itchy Oliver, Itchy	2.00	0.40	1.00	2.00
❑5, May 91, Dick Tracy Rubs Shoulders, Shoulders	2.00	0.40	1.00	2.00

ORIGINAL DOCTOR SOLAR, MAN OF THE ATOM, THE
VALIANT

Value: Cover or less

❑1, Apr 95 .... 2.95

ORIGINAL E-MAN
FIRST

	ORIG	GOOD	FINE	N-MINT
❑1, Oct 85	1.75	0.40	1.00	2.00
❑2, Nov 85	1.75	0.40	1.00	2.00
❑3, Dec 85	1.75	0.40	1.00	2.00
❑4, Jan 86	1.75	0.40	1.00	2.00
❑5, Feb 86	1.75	0.40	1.00	2.00
❑6, Mar 86	1.75	0.40	1.00	2.00
❑7, Apr 86	2.00	0.40	1.00	2.00

ORIGINAL GHOST RIDER, THE
MARVEL

	ORIG	GOOD	FINE	N-MINT
❑1, Jul 92, O: Ghost Rider	1.75	0.40	1.00	2.00
❑2, Aug 92, MP, Angels from Hell, O: Ghost Rider	1.75	0.40	1.00	2.00
❑3, Sep 92	1.75	0.40	1.00	2.00
❑4, Oct 92, The Hordes of Hell; Phantom Rider: The End of the Line	1.75	0.40	1.00	2.00
❑5, Nov 92, TS, The Snakes Crawl at Night...	1.75	0.40	1.00	2.00
❑6, Dec 92	1.75	0.40	1.00	2.00
❑7, Jan 93	1.75	0.40	1.00	2.00
❑8, Feb 93	1.75	0.40	1.00	2.00
❑9, Mar 93	1.75	0.40	1.00	2.00
❑10, Apr 93	1.75	0.40	1.00	2.00
❑11, May 93, JM, Wheels On Fire	1.75	0.40	1.00	2.00
❑12, Jun 93	1.75	0.40	1.00	2.00
❑13, Jul 93	1.75	0.40	1.00	2.00
❑14, Aug 93	1.75	0.40	1.00	2.00
❑15, Sep 93, JM, ...And Lose His Own Soul!	1.75	0.40	1.00	2.00
❑16, Oct 93, JM, Satan Himself!, 1: Inferno; A: Roxanne	1.75	0.40	1.00	2.00
❑17, Nov 93	1.75	0.40	1.00	2.00
❑18, Dec 93, SB, The Desolation Run!, A: Hulk	1.75	0.40	1.00	2.00
❑19, Jan 94, Reprints Marvel Two-In-One #8	1.75	0.40	1.00	2.00
❑20, Feb 94, FR, Phantom of the Killer Skies	1.75	0.40	1.00	2.00

ORIGINAL GHOST RIDER RIDES AGAIN, THE
MARVEL

	ORIG	GOOD	FINE	N-MINT
❑1, Jul 91, The Curse Of Jonathan Blaze!, O: Ghost Rider, Reprinted from Ghost Rider #68	1.50	0.50	1.25	2.50
❑2, Aug 91	1.50	0.40	1.00	2.00
❑3, Sep 91, Temptations; Tears of a Clown	1.50	0.40	1.00	2.00
❑4, Oct 91	1.50	0.40	1.00	2.00
❑5, Nov 91	1.50	0.40	1.00	2.00
❑6, Dec 91	1.50	0.35	0.88	1.75
❑7, Jan 92	1.50	0.35	0.88	1.75

ORIGINAL MAGNUS ROBOT FIGHTER, THE
VALIANT

Value: Cover or less

❑1, Apr 92, RM, RM (w), Operation Disguise, cardstock cover; Reprints Magnus, Robot Fighter 4000 A.D. #2 .... 2.95

ORIGINAL MAN
OMEGA 7

Value: Cover or less

❑1 .... 3.50

Chester Gould foisted one of his most diabolical deathtraps on his famous detective in the "Mrs. Pruneface" sequence, reprinted in *The Original Dick Tracy* #1.

© 1990 King Features Syndicate (Gladstone)

ORIGINAL MAN: THE MOST POWERFUL MAN IN THE UNIVERSE
OMEGA 7

Value: Cover or less

❑1, Payback!, Darkforce #0 as flip-side support story 1.95

ORIGINAL MYSTERYMEN PRESENTS (BOB BURDEN'S...)
DARK HORSE

Value: Cover or less

❑1, Jul 99, Who Are the Mystery-men? 2.95

❑2, Aug 99, The Amazing Disc Man 2.95

❑3, Sep 99 .... 2.95

❑4, Oct 99 .... 3.50

ORIGINAL SAD SACK
RECOLLECTIONS

Value: Cover or less

❑1, b&w 2.00

ORIGINAL SHIELD
ARCHIE

	ORIG	GOOD	FINE	N-MINT
❑1, Apr 84	0.75	0.20	0.50	1.00
❑2, Jun 84	0.75	0.20	0.50	1.00
❑3, Aug 84	0.75	0.20	0.50	1.00
❑4, Oct 84	0.75	0.20	0.50	1.00

ORIGINAL SIN, THE
THWACK! POW!

Value: Cover or less

❑1 .... 1.00

❑2 .... 1.00

❑3 .... 1.00

ORIGINAL STREET FIGHTER, THE
ALPHA

Value: Cover or less

❑1, The Wheelman; The Lion & The Lady: The Inn At Journey's End, b&w 2.50

ORIGINAL TOM CORBETT, THE
ETERNITY

Value: Cover or less

❑1, b&w; Reprinted from Field Enterprises strips 2.95

❑2, b&w 2.95

❑3, b&w 2.95

❑4, b&w 2.95

❑5, b&w 2.95

❑6, ... 2.95

❑7, ... 2.95

❑8, ... 2.95

❑9, ... 2.95

❑10, ... 2.95

ORIGINAL TUROK, SON OF STONE, THE
VALIANT

Value: Cover or less

❑1, Apr 95, cardstock cover 2.95

❑2, May 95, The Cliff Men; Terror of the Bog, cardstock cover; Final Issue; Reprints of Turok, Son of Stone #24, #33 .... 2.95

ORIGINAL TZU, THE: SPIRITS OF DEATH
MURIM

Value: Cover or less

❑1, Dec 97, b&w; reprints manga series 2.95

ORIGIN OF GALACTUS
MARVEL

Value: Cover or less

❑1, Feb 96, JK, SL (w), O: Galactus, nn; reprints Super-Villain Classics #1 .... 2.50

ORIGIN OF THE DEFIANT UNIVERSE, THE
DEFIANT

Value: Cover or less

❑1, Feb 94, O: the Defiant Universe 1.50

ORION
DARK HORSE

	ORIG	GOOD	FINE	N-MINT
❑1, b&w; manga	3.95	0.79	1.98	3.95
❑2, b&w; manga	2.50	0.59	1.48	2.95
❑3, b&w; manga	2.50	0.59	1.48	2.95
❑4, b&w; manga	2.50	0.59	1.48	2.95
❑5, b&w; manga	2.95	0.59	1.48	2.95
❑6, Jul 93	3.95	0.79	1.98	3.95

ORION (DC)
DC

Value: Cover or less

❑1, Jun 00, O Beautiful for Spacious Skies... .... 2.50

❑2, Jul 00 .... 2.50

❑3, Aug 00 .... 2.50

❑4, Sep 00, Above the Fruited Plain... .... 2.50

❑5, Oct 00, Day of Wrath 2.50

❑6, Nov 00, EL, The King is Dead...Long Live the King!; Tales of the New Gods: The Perfect Servant 2.50
❑7, Dec 00, Tough Love! 2.50
❑8, Jan 01, The Righteous Treacheries of Desaad! Or Orion Rules! 2.50
❑9, Feb 01, The Electro Death of Honor! 2.50
❑10, Mar 01, Sirius Business! Or Dog is God Spelled Backwards! 2.50
❑11, Apr 01, Orion Rules! 2.50
❑12, May 01, Legends of Apokolips 2.50
❑13 .... 2.50
❑14 .... 2.50
❑15 .... 2.50
❑16 .... 2.50

ORLAK REDUX
CALIBER

Value: Cover or less
❑1, b&w 3.95

OSBORN JOURNALS
MARVEL

Value: Cover or less
❑1, Feb 97, Spider-man: The Osborn Journals, One-Shot; summation of Clone Saga and return of Norman Osborn as Green Goblin 2.95

OTHELLO
TOME

Value: Cover or less
❑1, nn; b&w 3.50

OTHER BIG THING (COLIN UPTON'S...)
FANTAGRAPHICS

Value: Cover or less
❑1, b&w 2.75
❑2 .... 2.25
❑3 .... 2.25
❑4, Jul 92 .... 2.50

OTHERS, THE (CORMAC)
CORMAC

Value: Cover or less
❑1 .... 1.50

OTHERS, THE (IMAGE)
IMAGE

Value: Cover or less
❑0, Mar 95, Opening Shots, Part 1; Opening Shots, Part 2, 16pgs. 1.00
❑1, Apr 95, The Mighty Fallen 2.50
❑2, May 95 .... 2.50
❑3, Jul 95 .... 2.50
❑4 .... 2.50

OTIS GOES HOLLYWOOD
DARK HORSE

Value: Cover or less
❑1, Apr 97, b&w 2.95
❑2, May 97, b&w 2.95

OTTO SPACE!
MANIFEST DESTINY

Value: Cover or less
❑1 .... 2.00
❑2, Otto Space!; Revolt 3000.. 2.00

OUR ARMY AT WAR
DC

	ORIG	GOOD	FINE	N-MINT
❑81, Dec 62, JAb; RH; RA; JKu, The Rock of Easy Co.!; Fighting Footsteps, 1: Sgt. Rock; 1: Easy Co.	0.10	440.00	1100.00	2200.00
❑82, May 59, 2: Sgt. Rock; 2: Sgt. Rock	0.10	110.00	275.00	550.00
❑83, Jun 59, JKu, 1: Easy Company, 1st Kubert Sgt. Rock	0.10	180.00	450.00	900.00
❑84, Jul 59	0.10	40.00	100.00	200.00
❑85, Aug 59, 1: The Ice Cream Soldier	0.10	48.00	120.00	240.00
❑86, Sep 59	0.10	40.00	100.00	200.00
❑87, Oct 59	0.10	40.00	100.00	200.00
❑88, Nov 59	0.10	40.00	100.00	200.00
❑89, Dec 59	0.10	40.00	100.00	200.00
❑90, Jan 60	0.10	40.00	100.00	200.00
❑91, Feb 60, 1st full-length Sgt. Rock story; All-Rock issue	0.10	100.00	250.00	500.00
❑92, Mar 60	0.10	25.00	62.50	125.00
❑93, Apr 60	0.10	25.00	62.50	125.00
❑94, May 60	0.10	25.00	62.50	125.00
❑95, Jun 60	—	25.00	62.50	125.00
❑96, Jul 60	—	25.00	62.50	125.00
❑97, Aug 60	—	25.00	62.50	125.00
❑98, Sep 60	—	25.00	62.50	125.00
❑99, Oct 60	—	25.00	62.50	125.00
❑100, Nov 60	—	25.00	62.50	125.00
❑101, Dec 60	—	15.00	37.50	75.00
❑102, Jan 61	—	15.00	37.50	75.00
❑103, Feb 61	—	15.00	37.50	75.00
❑104, Mar 61	—	15.00	37.50	75.00
❑105, Apr 61	—	15.00	37.50	75.00
❑106, May 61	—	15.00	37.50	75.00
❑107, Jun 61	—	15.00	37.50	75.00
❑108, Jul 61	—	15.00	37.50	75.00
❑109, Aug 61	—	15.00	37.50	75.00
❑110, Sep 61	—	15.00	37.50	75.00
❑111, Oct 61	—	12.00	30.00	60.00
❑112, Nov 61	—	12.00	30.00	60.00
❑113, Dec 61	—	12.00	30.00	60.00
❑114, Jan 62	—	12.00	30.00	60.00
❑115, Feb 62	—	12.00	30.00	60.00
❑116, Mar 62	—	12.00	30.00	60.00
❑117, Apr 62	—	12.00	30.00	60.00
❑118, May 62	—	12.00	30.00	60.00
❑119, Jun 62	—	12.00	30.00	60.00
❑120, Jul 62	—	12.00	30.00	60.00
❑121, Aug 62	—	9.60	24.00	48.00
❑122, Sep 62	—	9.60	24.00	48.00
❑123, Oct 62	—	9.60	24.00	48.00
❑124, Nov 62	—	9.60	24.00	48.00
❑125, Dec 62	—	9.60	24.00	48.00
❑126, Jan 63	—	9.60	24.00	48.00
❑127, Feb 63	—	9.60	24.00	48.00
❑128, Mar 63, O: Sgt. Rock	—	37.00	92.50	185.00
❑129, Apr 63	—	9.00	22.50	45.00
❑130, May 63	—	9.00	22.50	45.00
❑131, Jun 63	—	7.00	17.50	35.00
❑132, Jul 63	—	7.00	17.50	35.00
❑133, Aug 63	0.12	7.00	17.50	35.00
❑134, Sep 63	0.12	7.00	17.50	35.00
❑135, Oct 63	0.12	7.00	17.50	35.00
❑136, Nov 63	0.12	7.00	17.50	35.00
❑137, Dec 63, Too Many Sergeants	0.12	7.00	17.50	35.00
❑138, Jan 64	0.12	7.00	17.50	35.00
❑139, Feb 64	0.12	7.00	17.50	35.00
❑140, Mar 64	0.12	7.00	17.50	35.00
❑141, Apr 64	0.12	7.00	17.50	35.00
❑142, May 64	0.12	7.00	17.50	35.00
❑143, Jun 64	0.12	7.00	17.50	35.00
❑144, Jul 64	0.12	7.00	17.50	35.00
❑145, Aug 64	0.12	7.00	17.50	35.00
❑146, Sep 64	0.12	7.00	17.50	35.00
❑147, Oct 64	0.12	7.00	17.50	35.00
❑148, Nov 64	0.12	7.00	17.50	35.00
❑149, Dec 64	0.12	7.00	17.50	35.00
❑150, Jan 65	0.12	7.00	17.50	35.00
❑151, Feb 65, JKu, 1: Enemy Ace	0.12	48.00	120.00	240.00
❑152, Mar 65	0.12	4.00	10.00	20.00
❑153, Apr 65, 2: Enemy Ace	0.12	20.00	50.00	100.00
❑154, May 65	0.12	3.60	9.00	18.00
❑155, Jun 65, JKu, No Stripes for Me!; Fokker Fury!, 3: Enemy Ace (next appearance is in Showcase #57)	0.12	9.00	22.50	45.00
❑156, Jul 65	0.12	3.60	9.00	18.00
❑157, Aug 65, Nothin's Ever Lost in War!; Spotter on the Spot!, A: Enemy Ace	0.12	3.60	9.00	18.00
❑158, Sep 65, 1: Iron Major	0.12	5.60	14.00	28.00
❑159, Oct 65, The Blind Gun!; The Silent Piper!	0.12	3.60	9.00	18.00
❑160, Nov 65, What's the Color of Your Blood?	0.12	3.60	9.00	18.00
❑161, Dec 65	0.12	3.60	9.00	18.00
❑162, Jan 66, A: Viking Prince	0.12	3.60	9.00	18.00
❑163, Feb 66, A: Viking Prince	0.12	3.60	9.00	18.00
❑164, Feb 66, Giant-size (80-Page Giant #G-19)	0.25	8.00	20.00	40.00
❑165, Mar 66, V: Iron Major	0.12	3.60	9.00	18.00
❑166, Apr 66	0.12	3.60	9.00	18.00
❑167, May 66	0.12	3.60	9.00	18.00
❑168, Jun 66	0.12	3.60	9.00	18.00
❑169, Jul 66	0.12	3.60	9.00	18.00
❑170, Aug 66	0.12	3.60	9.00	18.00
❑171, Sep 66	0.12	3.20	8.00	16.00
❑172, Oct 66	0.12	3.20	8.00	16.00
❑173, Nov 66	0.12	3.20	8.00	16.00
❑174, Dec 66	0.12	3.20	8.00	16.00
❑175, Jan 67	0.12	3.20	8.00	16.00
❑176, Feb 67	0.12	3.20	8.00	16.00
❑177, Feb 67, Giant-size (80-Page Giant #G-32)	0.12	7.00	17.50	35.00
❑178, Mar 67	0.12	3.20	8.00	16.00
❑179, Apr 67	0.12	3.20	8.00	16.00
❑180, May 67	0.12	3.20	8.00	16.00
❑181, Jun 67	0.12	3.20	8.00	16.00
❑182, Jul 67, NA	0.12	4.00	10.00	20.00
❑183, Aug 67, NA	0.12	4.00	10.00	20.00
❑184, Sep 67	0.12	2.80	7.00	14.00
❑185, Oct 67	0.12	2.80	7.00	14.00
❑186, Nov 67, NA	0.12	4.00	10.00	20.00
❑187, Dec 67	0.12	2.80	7.00	14.00
❑188, Jan 68	0.12	2.80	7.00	14.00
❑189, Feb 68	0.12	2.80	7.00	14.00
❑190, Feb 68, 80pgs.	0.25	2.80	7.00	14.00
❑191, Mar 68	0.12	2.40	6.00	12.00
❑192, Apr 68	0.12	2.40	6.00	12.00
❑193, May 68	0.12	2.40	6.00	12.00
❑194, Jun 68, 1: Unit 3 (kid guerrillas)	0.12	2.40	6.00	12.00
❑195, Jul 68	0.12	2.40	6.00	12.00

	ORIG	GOOD	FINE	N-MINT
❑196, Aug 68, Stop the War I Want to Get Off	0.12	2.40	6.00	12.00
❑197, Sep 68	0.12	2.40	6.00	12.00
❑198, Oct 68	0.12	2.40	6.00	12.00
❑199, Nov 68	0.12	2.40	6.00	12.00
❑200, Dec 68, 200th issue	0.12	3.60	9.00	18.00
❑201, Jan 69	0.12	1.60	4.00	8.00
❑202, Feb 69	0.12	1.60	4.00	8.00
❑203, Feb 69, Giant-size (80-Page Giant #G-68)	0.25	4.00	10.00	20.00
❑204, Mar 69	—	1.60	4.00	8.00
❑205, Apr 69	—	1.60	4.00	8.00
❑206, May 69	—	1.60	4.00	8.00
❑207, Jun 69	—	1.60	4.00	8.00
❑208, Jul 69	—	1.60	4.00	8.00
❑209, Aug 69	—	1.60	4.00	8.00
❑210, Sep 69	—	1.60	4.00	8.00
❑211, Oct 69	0.15	1.40	3.50	7.00
❑212, Nov 69	0.15	1.40	3.50	7.00
❑213, Dec 69	0.15	1.40	3.50	7.00
❑214, Jan 70	0.15	1.40	3.50	7.00
❑215, Feb 70	0.15	1.40	3.50	7.00
❑216, Feb 70, Giant-size (80-Page Giant #G-80)	0.15	3.00	7.50	15.00
❑217, Mar 70	0.15	1.40	3.50	7.00
❑218, Apr 70	0.15	1.40	3.50	7.00
❑219, May 70	0.15	1.40	3.50	7.00
❑220, Jun 70	0.15	1.40	3.50	7.00
❑221, Jul 70	0.15	1.20	3.00	6.00
❑222, Aug 70	0.15	1.20	3.00	6.00
❑223, Sep 70	0.15	1.20	3.00	6.00
❑224, Oct 70	0.15	1.20	3.00	6.00
❑225, Nov 70	0.15	1.20	3.00	6.00
❑226, Dec 70	0.15	1.20	3.00	6.00
❑227, Jan 71	0.15	1.20	3.00	6.00
❑228, Feb 71	0.15	1.20	3.00	6.00
❑229, Mar 71, Giant-size	0.25	1.40	3.50	7.00
❑230, Mar 71	0.15	1.20	3.00	6.00
❑231, Apr 71	0.15	1.20	3.00	6.00
❑232, May 71, Three Men In A Tub; Q-Boat Of World War I	0.15	1.20	3.00	6.00
❑233, Jun 71	0.15	1.20	3.00	6.00
❑234, Jul 71	0.15	1.20	3.00	6.00
❑235, Aug 71	0.25	1.20	3.00	6.00
❑236, Sep 71	0.25	1.20	3.00	6.00
❑237, Oct 71	0.25	1.20	3.00	6.00
❑238, Nov 71	0.25	1.20	3.00	6.00
❑239, Dec 71	0.25	1.20	3.00	6.00
❑240, Jan 72	0.25	1.20	3.00	6.00
❑241, Feb 72	0.25	1.20	3.00	6.00
❑242, Feb 72, JKu (c), wraparound cover; a.k.a. DC 100-Page Super Spectacular #DC-9	0.50	2.00	5.00	10.00
❑243, Mar 72, 24 Hour Pass!; Visit To A Small War!	0.25	1.20	3.00	6.00
❑244, Apr 72	0.25	1.20	3.00	6.00
❑245, May 72	0.25	1.20	3.00	6.00
❑246, Jun 72	0.25	1.20	3.00	6.00
❑247, Jul 72	0.20	1.20	3.00	6.00
❑248, Aug 72	0.20	1.20	3.00	6.00
❑249, Sep 72	0.20	1.20	3.00	6.00
❑250, Oct 72	0.20	1.00	2.50	5.00
❑251, Nov 72	0.20	1.00	2.50	5.00
❑252, Dec 72	0.20	1.00	2.50	5.00
❑253, Jan 73	0.20	1.00	2.50	5.00
❑254, Feb 73	0.20	1.00	2.50	5.00
❑255, Mar 73	0.20	1.00	2.50	5.00
❑256, Apr 73	0.20	1.00	2.50	5.00
❑257, Jun 73	0.20	1.00	2.50	5.00
❑258, Jul 73	0.20	1.00	2.50	5.00
❑259, Aug 73	0.20	1.00	2.50	5.00
❑260, Sep 73	0.20	1.00	2.50	5.00
❑261, Oct 73	0.20	1.00	2.50	5.00
❑262, Nov 73	0.20	1.00	2.50	5.00
❑263, Dec 73	0.20	1.00	2.50	5.00
❑264, Jan 74	0.20	1.00	2.50	5.00
❑265, Feb 74	0.20	1.00	2.50	5.00
❑266, Mar 74	0.20	1.00	2.50	5.00
❑267, Apr 74	0.20	1.00	2.50	5.00
❑268, May 74	0.20	1.00	2.50	5.00
❑269, Jun 74, 100pgs.	0.60	1.00	2.50	5.00
❑270, Jul 74	—	1.00	2.50	5.00
❑271, Aug 74	0.20	1.00	2.50	5.00
❑272, Sep 74	0.20	1.00	2.50	5.00
❑273, Oct 74	0.20	1.00	2.50	5.00
❑274, Nov 74	0.20	1.00	2.50	5.00
❑275, Dec 74	0.60	1.00	2.50	5.00

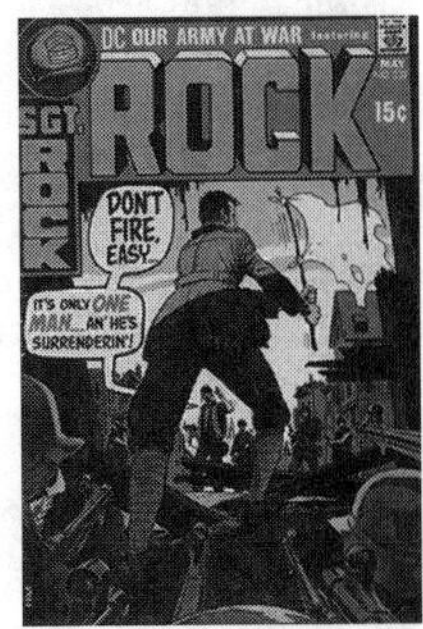

Many issues of DC's war titles, including *Our Army at War*, included an informational page or two on various weapons of war.

© 1971 National Periodical Publications (DC)

	ORIG	GOOD	FINE	N-MINT
❑276, Jan 75	0.25	1.00	2.50	5.00
❑277, Feb 75	0.25	1.00	2.50	5.00
❑278, Mar 75	0.25	1.00	2.50	5.00
❑279, Apr 75	0.25	1.00	2.50	5.00
❑280, May 75	0.25	1.00	2.50	5.00
❑281, Jun 75	0.25	1.00	2.50	5.00
❑282, Jul 75	0.25	1.00	2.50	5.00
❑283, Aug 75	0.25	1.00	2.50	5.00
❑284, Sep 75	0.25	1.00	2.50	5.00
❑285, Oct 75	0.25	1.00	2.50	5.00
❑286, Nov 75	0.25	1.00	2.50	5.00
❑287	—	1.00	2.50	5.00
❑288	—	1.00	2.50	5.00
❑289	—	1.00	2.50	5.00
❑290	—	1.00	2.50	5.00
❑291	—	1.00	2.50	5.00
❑292	—	1.00	2.50	5.00
❑293	—	1.00	2.50	5.00
❑294	—	1.00	2.50	5.00
❑295	—	1.00	2.50	5.00
❑296	—	1.00	2.50	5.00
❑297	—	1.00	2.50	5.00
❑298	—	1.00	2.50	5.00
❑299	—	1.00	2.50	5.00
❑300	—	1.00	2.50	5.00
❑301, Final Issue; Series is continued as "Sgt. Rock"	—	1.00	2.50	5.00

OUR FIGHTING FORCES
DC

	ORIG	GOOD	FINE	N-MINT
❑45, 1: Gunner & Sarge	0.10	52.00	130.00	260.00
❑46	0.10	20.00	50.00	100.00
❑47	0.10	17.00	42.50	85.00
❑48	0.10	13.00	32.50	65.00
❑49	0.10	13.00	32.50	65.00
❑50	0.10	13.00	32.50	65.00
❑51	0.10	7.60	19.00	38.00
❑52	0.10	7.60	19.00	38.00
❑53	0.10	7.60	19.00	38.00
❑54	0.10	7.60	19.00	38.00
❑55	0.10	7.60	19.00	38.00
❑56	0.10	7.60	19.00	38.00
❑57	0.10	7.60	19.00	38.00
❑58	0.10	7.60	19.00	38.00
❑59	0.10	7.60	19.00	38.00
❑60, Apr 60	0.10	7.60	19.00	38.00
❑61	0.10	6.00	15.00	30.00
❑62	0.10	6.00	15.00	30.00
❑63	0.10	6.00	15.00	30.00
❑64, Dec 60	0.10	6.00	15.00	30.00
❑65	0.12	4.00	10.00	20.00
❑66	0.12	4.00	10.00	20.00
❑67	0.12	4.00	10.00	20.00
❑68	0.12	4.00	10.00	20.00
❑69	0.12	4.00	10.00	20.00
❑70	0.12	4.00	10.00	20.00
❑71	0.12	3.20	8.00	16.00
❑72	0.12	3.20	8.00	16.00
❑73	0.12	3.20	8.00	16.00
❑74	0.12	3.20	8.00	16.00
❑75	0.12	3.20	8.00	16.00
❑76	0.12	3.20	8.00	16.00
❑77	0.12	3.20	8.00	16.00
❑78, Aug 63	0.12	3.20	8.00	16.00
❑79	0.12	3.20	8.00	16.00
❑80	0.12	3.20	8.00	16.00
❑81	0.12	2.00	5.00	10.00
❑82, Feb 64	0.12	2.00	5.00	10.00
❑83	0.12	2.00	5.00	10.00
❑84, May 64, Gunner & Sarge	0.12	2.00	5.00	10.00
❑85	0.12	2.00	5.00	10.00
❑86	0.12	2.00	5.00	10.00

	ORIG	GOOD	FINE	N-MINT
❑87	0.12	2.00	5.00	10.00
❑88	0.12	2.00	5.00	10.00
❑89	0.12	2.00	5.00	10.00
❑90	0.12	2.00	5.00	10.00
❑91, Apr 65	0.12	1.40	3.50	7.00
❑92	0.12	1.40	3.50	7.00
❑93	0.12	1.40	3.50	7.00
❑94	0.12	1.40	3.50	7.00
❑95	0.12	1.40	3.50	7.00
❑96	0.12	1.40	3.50	7.00
❑97	0.12	1.40	3.50	7.00
❑98	0.12	1.40	3.50	7.00
❑99, Feb 66, 1: Captain Phil Hunter	0.12	1.40	3.50	7.00
❑100, Apr 66, Death Also Stalks The Hunter!; The Thunderbolts, A: Captain Hunter	0.12	1.20	3.00	6.00
❑101, Jun 66	0.12	1.20	3.00	6.00
❑102, Aug 66	0.12	1.20	3.00	6.00
❑103, Oct 66	0.12	1.20	3.00	6.00
❑104, Dec 66	0.12	1.20	3.00	6.00
❑105, Feb 67	0.12	1.20	3.00	6.00
❑106, Apr 67, 1: Hunter's Hellcats; 1: Ben Hunter	0.12	1.20	3.00	6.00
❑107, Jul 67	0.12	1.20	3.00	6.00
❑108, Aug 67, A: Lt. Hunter's Hellcats	0.12	1.20	3.00	6.00
❑109, Oct 67	0.12	1.20	3.00	6.00
❑110, Dec 67	0.12	1.20	3.00	6.00
❑111, Feb 68	0.12	1.20	3.00	6.00
❑112, Apr 68	0.12	1.20	3.00	6.00
❑113, Jul 68	0.12	1.20	3.00	6.00
❑114, Aug 68	0.12	1.20	3.00	6.00
❑115, Oct 68	—	1.20	3.00	6.00
❑116, Dec 68	—	1.20	3.00	6.00
❑117, Feb 69	—	1.20	3.00	6.00
❑118, Apr 69, A: Lt. Hunter's Hellcats	—	1.20	3.00	6.00
❑119, Jun 69	—	1.20	3.00	6.00
❑120, Aug 69	—	1.20	3.00	6.00
❑121, Oct 69, 1: Heller	—	1.00	2.50	5.00
❑122, Dec 69	—	1.00	2.50	5.00
❑123, Feb 70, Losers series begins	0.15	1.00	2.50	5.00
❑124, Apr 70	0.15	1.00	2.50	5.00
❑125, Jun 70	0.15	1.00	2.50	5.00
❑126, Aug 70	0.15	1.00	2.50	5.00
❑127, Oct 70, RA, Angels over Hell's Corner; Private Buck's Army!, Losers	0.15	1.00	2.50	5.00
❑128, Dec 70	0.15	1.00	2.50	5.00
❑129, Feb 71	0.15	1.00	2.50	5.00
❑130, Apr 71	0.15	1.00	2.50	5.00
❑131, Jun 71	0.15	1.00	2.50	5.00
❑132, Aug 71, Losers	0.15	1.00	2.50	5.00
❑133, Oct 71	0.25	1.00	2.50	5.00
❑134, Dec 71	0.25	1.00	2.50	5.00
❑135, Feb 72	0.25	1.00	2.50	5.00
❑136, Apr 72	0.25	1.00	2.50	5.00
❑137, Jun 72, God Of The Losers!; Frogman Jinx!, Giant-size; Losers	0.25	1.00	2.50	5.00
❑138, Aug 72	0.20	1.00	2.50	5.00
❑139, Oct 72	0.20	1.00	2.50	5.00
❑140, Dec 72	0.20	1.00	2.50	5.00
❑141, Feb 73	0.20	1.00	2.50	5.00
❑142, Apr 73	0.20	1.00	2.50	5.00
❑143, Jul 73	0.20	1.00	2.50	5.00
❑144, Sep 73	0.20	1.00	2.50	5.00
❑145, Nov 73	0.20	1.00	2.50	5.00
❑146, Jan 74	0.20	1.00	2.50	5.00
❑147, Mar 74	0.20	1.00	2.50	5.00
❑148, May 74	0.20	1.00	2.50	5.00
❑149, Jul 74	0.20	1.00	2.50	5.00
❑150, Sep 74	0.20	1.00	2.50	5.00
❑151	—	0.80	2.00	4.00
❑152	—	0.80	2.00	4.00
❑153	—	0.80	2.00	4.00
❑154, Apr 75, JK, Losers	—	0.80	2.00	4.00
❑155, May 75	—	0.80	2.00	4.00
❑156, Jun 75	—	0.80	2.00	4.00
❑157, Jul 75	—	0.80	2.00	4.00
❑158, Aug 75, JK, Losers	0.25	0.80	2.00	4.00
❑159, Sep 75, JK, Losers	0.25	0.80	2.00	4.00
❑160, Oct 75, JK, Losers	0.25	0.80	2.00	4.00
❑161, Nov 75	0.25	0.80	2.00	4.00
❑162, Dec 75, JK, Losers	0.25	0.80	2.00	4.00
❑163	—	0.80	2.00	4.00
❑164	—	0.80	2.00	4.00
❑165	—	0.80	2.00	4.00
❑166	—	0.80	2.00	4.00
❑167	—	0.80	2.00	4.00
❑168, Aug 76	0.30	0.80	2.00	4.00
❑169, Oct 76	—	0.80	2.00	4.00
❑170, Dec 76	0.30	0.80	2.00	4.00
❑171	—	0.80	2.00	4.00
❑172	—	0.80	2.00	4.00
❑173	—	0.80	2.00	4.00
❑174	—	0.80	2.00	4.00
❑175	—	0.80	2.00	4.00
❑176	—	0.80	2.00	4.00
❑177	—	0.80	2.00	4.00
❑178	—	0.80	2.00	4.00
❑179	—	0.80	2.00	4.00
❑180	—	0.80	2.00	4.00
❑181, Final Issue	—	0.80	2.00	4.00

OUTBREED 999
BLACKOUT
Value: Cover or less

- ❑1, May 94 ... 2.95
- ❑2, Jul 94 ... 2.95
- ❑3, Aug 94 ... 2.95
- ❑4 ... 2.95
- ❑5 ... 2.95

OUTCAST, THE
ACCLAIM
Value: Cover or less

- ❑1, Dec 95, Here and Now, One-Shot ... 2.50

OUTCASTS
DC
Value: Cover or less

- ❑1, Oct 87, 1: Outcasts; 1: Kaine Salinger ... 1.75
- ❑2, Nov 87 ... 1.75
- ❑3, Dec 87 ... 1.75
- ❑4, Jan 88 ... 1.75
- ❑5, Feb 88 ... 1.75
- ❑6, Mar 88 ... 1.75
- ❑7, Apr 88, D: Kaine Salinger.. 1.75
- ❑8, May 88 ... 1.75
- ❑9, Jun 88 ... 1.75
- ❑10, Jul 88 ... 1.75
- ❑11, Aug 88 ... 1.75
- ❑12, Sep 88, The Last Outcast, Final Issue ... 1.75

OUTER EDGE
INNOVATION
Value: Cover or less

- ❑1, b&w ... 2.50

OUTER LIMITS, THE
DELL

	ORIG	GOOD	FINE	N-MINT
❑1	0.12	11.00	27.50	55.00
❑2, The Boy Who Saved the World!	0.12	6.00	15.00	30.00
❑3, They Landed First; Beyond Human Range!	0.12	4.80	12.00	24.00
❑4	0.12	4.00	10.00	20.00
❑5	0.12	4.00	10.00	20.00
❑6, The Mystery Moon; When Disasters Strike	0.12	4.00	10.00	20.00
❑7, The Space Change; Strange Masquerade	0.12	4.00	10.00	20.00
❑8	0.12	4.00	10.00	20.00
❑9, Death From the Depths!; Sea Creature Attack	0.12	4.00	10.00	20.00
❑10, Journey into the Earth; Ancient Worlds	0.12	4.00	10.00	20.00
❑11, The Prehistoric Peril; Mutations! Giants!	0.12	2.00	5.00	10.00
❑12	0.12	2.00	5.00	10.00
❑13	0.12	2.00	5.00	10.00
❑14, Mother and Child; Martian Stimulators, Inc.	0.12	2.00	5.00	10.00
❑15	0.12	2.00	5.00	10.00
❑16	0.12	2.00	5.00	10.00
❑17, Battleground of Monsters	0.12	2.00	5.00	10.00
❑18, Final Issue	0.12	2.00	5.00	10.00

OUTER SPACE BABES, THE (VOL. 3)
SILHOUETTE
Value: Cover or less

- ❑1, Dear Dad...; Big Guns ... 2.95

OUT FOR BLOOD
DARK HORSE
Value: Cover or less

- ❑1, Sep 99 ... 2.95
- ❑2, Oct 99 ... 2.95
- ❑3, Nov 99 ... 2.95
- ❑4, Dec 99 ... 2.95

OUTLANDER
MALIBU
Value: Cover or less

- ❑1 ... 1.95
- ❑2 ... 1.95
- ❑3, Dec 87, b&w ... 1.95
- ❑4, Jan 88 ... 1.95
- ❑5, Mar 88 ... 1.95
- ❑6 ... 1.95
- ❑7 ... 1.95

OUTLANDERS
DARK HORSE

	ORIG	GOOD	FINE	N-MINT
❑0, poster	2.75	0.60	1.50	3.00
❑1	2.00	0.50	1.25	2.50
❑2	2.00	0.40	1.00	2.00
❑3	2.00	0.40	1.00	2.00

	ORIG	GOOD	FINE	N-MINT
❑4	2.00	0.40	1.00	2.00
❑5	2.00	0.40	1.00	2.00
❑6	2.00	0.40	1.00	2.00
❑7	2.00	0.40	1.00	2.00
❑8	2.25	0.40	1.00	2.00
❑9	2.25	0.45	1.13	2.25
❑10	2.25	0.45	1.13	2.25
❑11	2.25	0.45	1.13	2.25
❑12	2.25	0.45	1.13	2.25
❑13	2.25	0.45	1.13	2.25
❑14	2.25	0.45	1.13	2.25
❑15	2.25	0.45	1.13	2.25
❑16	2.25	0.45	1.13	2.25
❑17	2.25	0.45	1.13	2.25
❑18	2.25	0.45	1.13	2.25
❑19	2.25	0.45	1.13	2.25
❑20	2.25	0.45	1.13	2.25
❑21	2.25	0.45	1.13	2.25
❑22	2.50	0.50	1.25	2.50
❑23	2.50	0.50	1.25	2.50
❑24	2.50	0.50	1.25	2.50
❑25, trading cards	2.50	0.50	1.25	2.50
❑26, trading cards	2.50	0.50	1.25	2.50
❑27, trading cards; Giant-size special	2.95	0.59	1.48	2.95
❑28, trading cards	2.50	0.50	1.25	2.50
❑29, trading cards	2.50	0.50	1.25	2.50
❑30	2.50	0.50	1.25	2.50
❑31	2.50	0.50	1.25	2.50
❑32	2.50	0.50	1.25	2.50
❑33, Final Issue	2.50	0.50	1.25	2.50
❑SE 1, b&w; manga; Epilogue	2.50	0.50	1.25	2.50

OUTLANDERS EPILOGUE
DARK HORSE

Value: Cover or less

- ❑1, Mar 94, nn; b&w ... 2.50

OUTLAW KID, THE (2ND SERIES)
MARVEL

	ORIG	GOOD	FINE	N-MINT
❑1, Aug 70, Hostage!; Breakthrough!	0.15	2.40	6.00	12.00
❑2, Oct 70	0.15	1.20	3.00	6.00
❑3, Dec 70	0.15	0.70	1.75	3.50
❑4, Feb 71	0.15	0.50	1.25	2.50
❑5, Apr 71	0.15	0.50	1.25	2.50
❑6, Jun 71	0.15	0.50	1.25	2.50
❑7, Aug 71	0.15	0.50	1.25	2.50
❑8, Oct 71, Giant-size	0.15	0.50	1.25	2.50
❑9, Dec 71 Series goes on hiatus	0.20	0.60	1.50	3.00
❑10, Jun 72, O: Outlaw Kid	0.20	0.40	1.00	2.00
❑11, Aug 72	0.20	0.40	1.00	2.00
❑12, Oct 72	0.20	0.40	1.00	2.00
❑13, Dec 72	0.20	0.40	1.00	2.00
❑14, Feb 73	0.20	0.40	1.00	2.00
❑15, Apr 73	0.20	0.40	1.00	2.00
❑16, Jun 73	0.20	0.40	1.00	2.00
❑17, Aug 73	0.20	0.40	1.00	2.00
❑18, Oct 73	0.20	0.40	1.00	2.00
❑19, Dec 73	0.20	0.40	1.00	2.00
❑20, Feb 74	0.20	0.40	1.00	2.00
❑21, Apr 74	0.20	0.40	1.00	2.00
❑22, Jun 74	0.20	0.40	1.00	2.00
❑23, Aug 74	0.20	0.40	1.00	2.00
❑24, Oct 74	0.20	0.40	1.00	2.00
❑25, Dec 74	0.20	0.40	1.00	2.00
❑26, Feb 75	0.20	0.40	1.00	2.00
❑27, Apr 75, O: Outlaw Kid	0.25	0.40	1.00	2.00
❑28, Jun 75	0.25	0.40	1.00	2.00
❑29, Aug 75	0.25	0.40	1.00	2.00
❑30, Oct 75	0.25	0.40	1.00	2.00

OUTLAW NATION (VERTIGO)
VERTIGO

Value: Cover or less

- ❑1, Nov 00, The End ... 2.50
- ❑2, Dec 00, Does God Look Down? ... 2.50
- ❑3, Jan 01, Too Much Force ... 2.50
- ❑4, Feb 01, Careless Love ... 2.50
- ❑5, Mar 01 ... 2.50
- ❑6, Apr 01, Two More Dead in Texas ... 2.50
- ❑7, May 01, Distant Cousins ... 2.50
- ❑8 ... 2.50
- ❑9 ... 2.50
- ❑10 ... 2.50
- ❑11 ... 2.50

OUTLAW NATION (VOL. 2)
BONEYARD

	ORIG	GOOD	FINE	N-MINT
❑1, Werewulf; Shake That Dirt Out of Your Hair, Annie Rayne	4.95	0.99	2.47	4.95
❑1/PL, Werewulf; Shake That Dirt Out of Your Hair, Annie Rayne, Tim Bradstreet cover	—	1.00	2.50	5.00

The Outlaw Kid was just one of Marvel's Western titles.

© 1970 Marvel Comics

OUTLAW OVERDRIVE
BLUE COMET

Value: Cover or less

- ❑1, Lethal Oversight, A: Deathrow, Red Edition ... 2.95

OUTLAWS, THE (DC)
DC

	ORIG	GOOD	FINE	N-MINT
❑1, Sep 91, LMc, The Wheel	1.95	0.40	1.00	2.00
❑2, Oct 91	1.95	0.40	1.00	2.00
❑3, Nov 91	1.95	0.40	1.00	2.00
❑4, Dec 91	1.95	0.40	1.00	2.00
❑5, Jan 92	1.95	0.40	1.00	2.00
❑6, Feb 92	1.95	0.40	1.00	2.00
❑7, Mar 92	1.95	0.40	1.00	2.00
❑8, Apr 92, Final Issue	1.95	0.40	1.00	2.00

OUT OF THE VORTEX (COMICS' GREATEST WORLD...)
DARK HORSE

Value: Cover or less

- ❑1, Oct 93, From The Maelstrom, Foil embossed cover ... 2.00
- ❑2, Nov 93 ... 2.00
- ❑3, Dec 93, The Final Seeker. 2.00
- ❑4, Jan 94 ... 2.00
- ❑5, Feb 94, Deep Six Death, A: Grace ... 2.00
- ❑6, Mar 94, A: Hero Zero ... 2.00
- ❑7, Apr 94, The Seventh ... 2.00
- ❑8, May 94, Trapped in the Vortex ... 2.00
- ❑9, Jun 94 ... 2.00
- ❑10, Jul 94, A: Division 13 ... 2.00
- ❑11, Sep 94 ... 2.50
- ❑12, Oct 94, Final Issue ... 2.50

OUT OF THIS WORLD (ETERNITY)
ETERNITY

Value: Cover or less

- ❑1, Ransom-One Million Decimars!; World of the Monster Brain, b&w; Reprint; Reprints stories from Strange Worlds #9, Strange Planets #16, Tomb of Terror #6, and Weird Tales of the Future #1 ... 3.50

OUTPOSTS
BLACKTHORNE

	ORIG	GOOD	FINE	N-MINT
❑1, Jun 97, The Darkling Chronicles; Mad 7	1.25	0.30	0.75	1.50

OUTSIDERS, THE (1ST SERIES)
DC

Value: Cover or less

- ❑1, Nov 85 ... 1.25
- ❑2, Dec 85, V: Nuclear Family 1.50
- ❑3, Jan 86, V: Force of July ... 1.50
- ❑4, Feb 86 ... 1.50
- ❑5, Mar 86, Christmas Carol story ... 1.50
- ❑6, Apr 86, V: Duke of Oil ... 1.50
- ❑7, May 86, V: Duke of Oil ... 1.50
- ❑8, Jun 86, JDu ... 1.50
- ❑9, Jul 86 ... 1.50
- ❑10, Aug 86 ... 1.50
- ❑11, Sep 86 ... 1.50
- ❑12, Oct 86 ... 1.50
- ❑13, Nov 86 ... 1.50
- ❑14, Dec 86 ... 1.50
- ❑15, Jan 87 ... 1.50
- ❑16, Feb 87 ... 1.50
- ❑17, Mar 87, Batman returns .. 1.50
- ❑18, Apr 87, V: Eclipso ... 1.50
- ❑19, May 87 ... 1.50
- ❑20, Jun 87 ... 1.50
- ❑21, Jul 87 ... 1.50
- ❑22, Aug 87, EC parody back-up ... 1.50
- ❑23, Sep 87 ... 1.50
- ❑24, Oct 87 ... 1.50
- ❑25, Nov 87 ... 1.50
- ❑26, Dec 87 ... 1.50
- ❑27, Jan 88, Millennium ... 1.50
- ❑28, Feb 88, Millennium ... 1.50
- ❑Anl 1 ... 2.50
- ❑SE 1, From Here To Infinity, A: Infinity, Inc., Crossover continued in Infinity Inc. SE #1 ... 1.50

OUTSIDERS (2ND SERIES)
DC

	ORIG	GOOD	FINE	N-MINT
❑0, Oct 94, From The Ashes, New team begins	1.95	0.50	1.25	2.50
❑1/A, Nov 93, Blood & Ashes, Alpha version	1.75	0.50	1.25	2.50
❑1/B, Nov 93, Omega version	1.75	0.50	1.25	2.50
❑2, Dec 93	1.75	0.40	1.00	2.00
❑3, Jan 94, A: Eradicator	1.75	0.40	1.00	2.00
❑4, Feb 94, Storming the Palace	1.75	0.40	1.00	2.00
❑5, Mar 94	1.75	0.40	1.00	2.00
❑6, Apr 94	1.75	0.40	1.00	2.00
❑7, May 94	1.75	0.40	1.00	2.00
❑8, Jun 94, JA, Shadows of Knight, A: Batman (Azrael)	1.75	0.40	1.00	2.00
❑9, Jul 94	1.75	0.40	1.00	2.00
❑10, Aug 94, Final Blood, Part 1	1.95	0.40	1.00	2.00

	ORIG	GOOD	FINE	N-MINT
❑11, Sep 94, Final Blood, Part 2; Zero Hour	1.95	0.40	1.00	2.00
❑12, Nov 94	1.95	0.40	1.00	2.00
❑13, Dec 94, A: Superman	1.95	0.40	1.00	2.00
❑14, Jan 95, Proving Ground!	1.95	0.40	1.00	2.00
❑15, Feb 95	1.95	0.40	1.00	2.00
❑16, Mar 95	1.95	0.40	1.00	2.00
❑17, Apr 95	1.95	0.40	1.00	2.00
❑18, May 95	1.95	0.40	1.00	2.00
❑19, Jun 95	2.25	0.45	1.13	2.25
❑20, Jul 95	2.25	0.45	1.13	2.25
❑21, Aug 95	2.25	0.45	1.13	2.25
❑22, Sep 95	2.25	0.45	1.13	2.25
❑23, Oct 95	2.25	0.45	1.13	2.25
❑24, Nov 95, Final Issue	2.25	0.45	1.13	2.25

OVERKILL: WITCHBLADE/ALIENS/DARKNESS/PREDATOR
IMAGE

Value: Cover or less

❑1, Dec 00 .... 5.95
❑2 .... 5.95

OVERLOAD MAGAZINE
ECLIPSE

Value: Cover or less

❑1, Apr 87, b&w 1.50

OVERMEN, THE
EXCEL

Value: Cover or less

❑1 .... 2.95

OVER THE EDGE
MARVEL

	ORIG	GOOD	FINE	N-MINT
❑1, Nov 95, ...And Fear Will Follow!, Daredevil	0.99	0.25	0.63	1.25
❑2, Dec 95, A: Doctor Strange	0.99	0.20	0.50	1.00
❑3, Jan 96, Hulk	0.99	0.20	0.50	1.00
❑4, Feb 96, Ghost Rider	0.99	0.20	0.50	1.00
❑5, Mar 96, Magdelena Black And Red, Punisher	0.99	0.20	0.50	1.00
❑6, Apr 96, Of Kings...And Bight, Shiny Things, Daredevil and Black Panther	0.99	0.20	0.50	1.00
❑7, May 96, Doctor Strange vs. Nightmare	0.99	0.20	0.50	1.00
❑8, Jun 96, Elektra	0.99	0.20	0.50	1.00
❑9, Jul 96, Ghost Rider, John Blaze	0.99	0.20	0.50	1.00
❑10, Aug 96, Final Issue; Daredevil	0.99	0.20	0.50	1.00

OVERTURE
ALL AMERICAN

Value: Cover or less

❑1, b&w 2.25
❑2, Apr 90, Hot to Trot Sky!; Spunik the Space Man, b&w 2.25

OWLHOOTS
KITCHEN SINK

Value: Cover or less

❑1, two-color 2.50
❑2, two-color 2.50

OX COW O' WAR
SPOOF

Value: Cover or less

❑1, b&w; parody 2.95

OZ
CALIBER

	ORIG	GOOD	FINE	N-MINT
❑0, Mayhem in Munchkinland!	2.95	0.80	2.00	4.00
❑1	2.95	1.20	3.00	6.00
❑2	2.95	0.80	2.00	4.00
❑3	2.95	0.80	2.00	4.00
❑4	2.95	0.80	2.00	4.00
❑5	2.95	0.70	1.75	3.50
❑6	2.95	0.70	1.75	3.50
❑7	2.95	0.70	1.75	3.50
❑8	2.95	0.70	1.75	3.50
❑9	2.95	0.70	1.75	3.50
❑10	2.95	0.70	1.75	3.50
❑11	2.95	0.60	1.50	3.00
❑12	2.95	0.60	1.50	3.00
❑13	2.95	0.60	1.50	3.00
❑14	2.95	0.60	1.50	3.00
❑15	2.95	0.60	1.50	3.00
❑16	2.95	0.60	1.50	3.00
❑17, Peace be so Fragile	2.95	0.60	1.50	3.00
❑18	2.95	0.59	1.48	2.95
❑19	2.95	0.59	1.48	2.95
❑20	2.95	0.59	1.48	2.95
❑21	2.95	0.59	1.48	2.95
❑22	2.95	0.59	1.48	2.95

OZ COLLECTION (BILL BRYAN'S...)
ARROW

Value: Cover or less

❑1 .... 2.95

OZ: DAEMONSTORM
CALIBER

Value: Cover or less

❑1, nn; b&w; One-Shot; intracompany crossover 3.95

OZ: ROMANCE IN RAGS
CALIBER

Value: Cover or less

❑1, b&w 2.95
❑2, b&w 2.95
❑3, b&w 2.95

OZ SPECIAL: FREEDOM FIGHTERS
CALIBER

Value: Cover or less

❑1, b&w 2.95

OZ SPECIAL: LION
CALIBER

Value: Cover or less

❑1, b&w; continues in Oz Special: Tin Man 2.95

OZ SPECIAL: SCARECROW
CALIBER

Value: Cover or less

❑1, b&w; continues in Oz Special: Lion 2.95

OZ SPECIAL: TIN MAN
CALIBER

Value: Cover or less

❑1, b&w; continues in Oz Special: Freedom Fighters 2.95

OZ SQUAD (1ST SERIES)
BRAVE NEW WORDS

	ORIG	GOOD	FINE	N-MINT
❑1, Oct 91	2.50	0.60	1.50	3.00
❑2, Jan 92	2.50	0.50	1.25	2.50
❑3	2.50	0.50	1.25	2.50
❑4	2.50	0.50	1.25	2.50

OZ SQUAD (2ND SERIES)
PATCHWORK PRESS

Value: Cover or less

❑1 .... 2.50
❑2 .... 2.50
❑3 .... 2.50
❑4 .... 2.50
❑5 .... 2.75
❑6 .... 2.95
❑7, Aug 95 .... 2.75
❑8, Oct 95 .... 2.75
❑9, Dec 95, O: Tin Man 2.75
❑10, O: Tin Man 2.75

OZ: STRAW & SORCERY
CALIBER

Value: Cover or less

❑1, b&w 2.95
❑2, b&w 2.95
❑3, b&w 2.95

OZ-WONDERLAND WARS
DC

	ORIG	GOOD	FINE	N-MINT
❑1, Jan 86	2.00	0.50	1.25	2.50
❑2, Feb 86, A: Hoppy the Marvel Bunny	2.00	0.50	1.25	2.50
❑3, Mar 86	2.00	0.50	1.25	2.50

OZZY OSBOURNE
ROCK-IT COMICS

	ORIG	GOOD	FINE	N-MINT
❑1, guitar pick	4.95	1.20	3.00	6.00

P

PAC (PRETER-HUMAN ASSAULT CORPS)
ARTIFACTS

Value: Cover or less

❑1, Oct 93 .... 1.95

PACIFIC PRESENTS
PACIFIC

	ORIG	GOOD	FINE	N-MINT
❑1, Oct 82, DSt; SD, Rocketeer Chapter 3; Missing Man Meets Quen Bee, Rocketeer; Missing Man	1.00	0.80	2.00	4.00
❑2, Apr 83, DSt; SD, Rocketeer Chapter 4; The Missing Man Meets The Payne Family, Rocketeer; Missing Man	1.00	0.60	1.50	3.00
❑3, Mar 84, SD, SD (w), E. Erie Smith and Walter Weary: When Ya Gotta Go-Ya Gotta Go...; The Missing Man: Am I Maro, Roma, or Raem?, Missing Man	1.50	0.30	0.75	1.50
❑4, Jun 84	1.50	0.30	0.75	1.50

PACT, THE
IMAGE

Value: Cover or less

❑1, Feb 94, Nowhere To Run, Nowhere To Hide 1.95
❑2, Apr 94, Welcome To The Big Leagues, A: Youngblood 1.95
❑3, Jun 94, 1: Atrocity, Final Issue 1.95

PAGERS COMICS ANTHOLOGY
NO TALENT

Value: Cover or less

❑1 .... 2.50
❑2 .... 2.50
❑3 .... 2.50
❑4 .... 2.50
❑5 .... 2.50
❑6, Sum 98 .... 2.50

PAINKILLER JANE
EVENT

Value: Cover or less

❑0, Jane's Addiction, O: Painkiller Jane 3.95
❑0/LE, O: Painkiller Jane, Signed by Joe Quesada, Jimmy Palmiotti, Amanda Conner, and Brian Augustyn 39.95

ORIG GOOD FINE N-MINT

❑1, Jun 97, wraparound cover 2.95
❑1/A, variant cover 2.95
❑1/B, Red foil 25.00
❑2, Jul 97, Dead in the Water, Standard cover; Jane in sunglasses close-up 2.95
❑2/A, Jul 97, Dead in the Water, variant cover; Jane running. 2.95
❑3 2.95
❑3/A, variant cover 2.95
❑4, A Place Too Bright For Dying 2.95
❑4/A, A Place Too Bright For Dying, variant cover 2.95
❑5 2.95
❑5/A, variant cover 2.95

PAINKILLER JANE/DARKCHYLDE
EVENT
Value: Cover or less

❑0, European Preview book ... 10.00
❑0/AUT, Signed by Randy Queen, Joe Quesada, and Jimmy Palmiotti; European Preview book 29.95
❑1, Lost in a Dream 2.95
❑1/A, Lost in a Dream 29.95
❑1/B, Lost in a Dream, DFE alternate cover 6.95
❑1/C, Lost in a Dream 39.95
❑Ash 1, DF Exclusive; Sketches —

PAINKILLER JANE/HELLBOY
EVENT
Value: Cover or less

❑1, Aug 98 2.95
❑1/LE 29.95

PAINKILLER JANE VS. THE DARKNESS: STRIPPER
EVENT
Value: Cover or less

❑1, Apr 97, four alternate covers 2.95
❑1/A, Jane facing forward, shooting on cover 2.95
❑1/B 2.95
❑1/C 2.95
❑1/LE 20.00

PAINTBALL UNIVERSE 2000
SPLATTOONS
Value: Cover or less
❑1 2.95

PAJAMA CHRONICLES
BLACKTHORNE
Value: Cover or less
❑1 1.75

PAKKINS' LAND
CALIBER
Value: Cover or less

❑0, Jun 97 1.95
❑1, Oct 96 2.95
❑2, Dec 96 2.95
❑3, Feb 97 2.95
❑4, May 97 2.95
❑5, Jun 97 2.95
❑6, Jul 97 2.95

PAKKINS' LAND: FORGOTTEN DREAMS
CALIBER
Value: Cover or less

❑1, Apr 98 2.95
❑2 2.95
❑3 2.95
❑4, Mar 00, published by Image 2.95

PAKKINS' LAND: QUEST FOR KINGS
CALIBER
Value: Cover or less

❑1, Quest for Kings 2.95
❑1/A, Aug 97 2.95
❑2, Sep 97 2.95
❑2/A, Aug 97, alternate cover. 2.95
❑3, Nov 97 2.95
❑4, Dec 97 2.95
❑5, Jan 98 2.95
❑6, Mar 98 2.95

PALATINE, THE
GRYPHON RAMPANT
Value: Cover or less

❑1 2.50
❑2, Oct 94, The Consort of Perun 2.50

PALESTINE
FANTAGRAPHICS
Value: Cover or less

❑1, b&w 2.50
❑2, b&w 2.50
❑3, b&w 2.50
❑4, b&w 2.95
❑5 2.50
❑6 2.50
❑7, Sep 94 2.95
❑9, Oct 95, b&w 2.95

PAL-YAT-CHEE
ADHESIVE
Value: Cover or less
❑1, b&w 2.50

PAMELA ANDERSON UNCOVERED
POP
Value: Cover or less
❑1, Thinking About Pamela Anderson 2.95

PANDA KHAN SPECIAL
ABACUS
Value: Cover or less
❑1, b&w 3.00

PANDEMONIUM
CHAOS!
Value: Cover or less
❑1, Sep 98 2.95

PANDORA PILL, THE
ACID RAIN
Value: Cover or less
❑1 2.50

PANIC (RCP)
EC
Value: Cover or less

❑1, Mar 97, Reprints Panic (EC) #1 2.50
❑2, Jun 97, African Scream; The Lady or the Tiger?, Reprints Panic (EC) #2 2.50
❑3, Sep 97, Reprints Panic (EC) #3 2.50
❑4, Dec 97, Reprints Panic (EC) #4 2.50

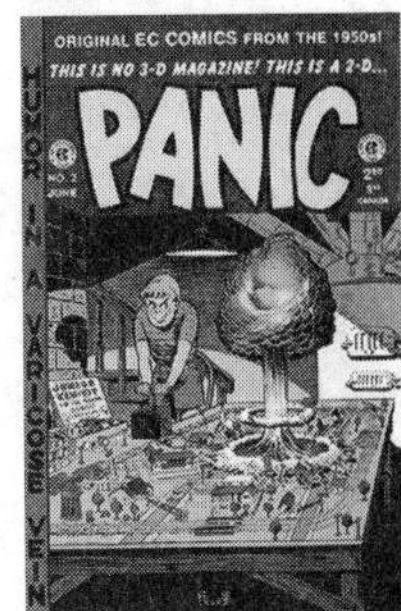

E.C.'s *Panic* was a companion title to the more successful *Mad*.

© 1997 Entertaining Comics (Russ Cochran)

ORIG GOOD FINE N-MINT

❑5, Mar 98, WW; BE; JO, WW (w); BE (w); JO (w), Tick Dracy; Baseball Jargon, Reprints Panic (EC) #5 2.50
❑6, Jun 98, WW; BE; JO, WW (w); BE (w); JO (w), The Phansom; Executive Seat, Reprints Panic (EC) #6 2.50
❑7, Sep 98, WW; BE; JO, WW (w); BE (w); JO (w), Mel Padooka; You Axed for It!, Reprints Panic (EC) #7 2.50
❑8, Dec 98, WW; BE; JO, WW (w); BE (w); JO (w), Irving Oops; Carmen, Reprints Panic (EC) #8 2.50
❑9, Mar 99 2.50
❑10, Jun 99 2.50
❑11, Sep 99 2.50
❑12, Dec 99 2.50
❑Anl 1, Collects issues #1-4 10.95
❑Anl 2, WW; BE; JO, WW (w); BE (w); JO (w), Tick Dracy; Baseball Jargon, Collects issues #5-8 10.95

PANTERA
MALIBU

❑1, Aug 94, magazine 3.95 0.80 2.00 4.00

PANTHA: HAUNTED PASSION
HARRIS
Value: Cover or less
❑1, Re-Birth; Family Ties 2.95

PANTHEON (ARCHER)
ARCHER BOOKS & GAMES
Value: Cover or less
❑1, Oct 95, b&w 2.95

PANTHEON (LONE STAR)
LONE STAR PRESS
Value: Cover or less

❑1, May 98, Comrades in Arms 2.95
❑2, Jul 98, Glory Days 2.95
❑3, Sep 98, Welcome to the Machine 2.95
❑4, Jan 99, The Final Cut 2.95
❑5, Jul 99, Under Pressure 2.95
❑6, Aug 99, Who Knows 2.95

PANTHEON: ANCIENT HISTORY
LONE STAR
Value: Cover or less
❑1, Aug 99 3.95

PAPER CINEMA: THE BOX
GREY BLOSSOM SEQUENTIALS
Value: Cover or less
❑3, Dec 98 3.55

PAPER CINEMA: WAVES IN SPACE
GREY BLOSSOM SEQUENTIALS
Value: Cover or less
❑2, Dec 98 3.55

PAPER DOLLS FROM THE CALIFORNIA GIRLS
ECLIPSE
Value: Cover or less
❑1, paper dolls 5.95

PAPER TALES
CLG COMICS
Value: Cover or less

❑1, Sum 93, b&w 2.50
❑2, Sum 94, b&w 2.50

PARA-COPS
EXCEL
Value: Cover or less
❑1 2.95

PARADAX
VORTEX
Value: Cover or less

❑1, Paradax the Insane People; Mirkin the Mystic: The Importance of Being Mirkin 1.75
❑2, Aug 87 1.75

PARADIGM
GAUNTLET
Value: Cover or less
❑1, Starts with a Bang 2.95

PARADOX PROJECT: GENESIS
PARADOX PROJECT
Value: Cover or less
❑1, Dec 98, b&w 2.95

PARAGON: DARK APOCALYPSE
AC
Value: Cover or less

❑1 2.95
❑2 2.95
❑3 2.95
❑4 2.95

PARALLAX: EMERALD NIGHT
DC
Value: Cover or less
❑1, Nov 96, The Final Night, D: Cyborg Superman, Final Night 2.95

PARANOIA (ADVENTURE)
ADVENTURE
Value: Cover or less

❑1, full color 2.95
❑2, Dec 91, full color 2.95

ORIG GOOD FINE N-MINT

❑3, full color 2.95
❑4, full color 2.95
❑5, full color 2.95
❑6, Aug 92, full color 2.95

PARANOIA (CO. & SONS)
Co. & Sons

	ORIG	GOOD	FINE	N-MINT
❑1, Tales from the Ogre's Tower; The Hunter	0.50	0.80	2.00	4.00

PARAPHERNALIA
Graphitti

Value: Cover or less
❑1, Ordering Catalogue 2.00

PARA TROOP
Comics Conspiracy

Value: Cover or less

❑0 .... 3.95
❑1, So Much Left Unsaid 2.95
❑2 .... 2.95
❑3, Oct 98 .... 2.95
❑4, Dec 98 .... 2.95
❑5, Feb 99 .... 2.95
❑Ash 1, ashcan edition 2.95

PARDNERS
Cottonwood Graphics

Value: Cover or less

❑1, b&w 7.95
❑2, b&w 7.95

PARIS THE MAN OF PLASTER
Harrier

Value: Cover or less

❑1, May 87, Paris the Man of Plaster; Temptation 1.95
❑2 .... 1.95
❑3 .... 1.95
❑4 .... 1.95
❑5 .... 1.95
❑6 .... 1.95

PARO-DEE
Parody

Value: Cover or less
❑1, The Conscientious ø-Men: Sheep of Fools!; Sam Sundae, b&w 2.50

PARODY PRESS ANNUAL SWIMSUIT SPECIAL '93
Parody Press

Value: Cover or less
❑1, Aug 93 .... 2.50

PARTICLE DREAMS
Fantagraphics

Value: Cover or less

❑1, Oct 86 .... 2.25
❑2, Jan 87 .... 2.25
❑3, Apr 87, This Fear of Gods; Make-Up Paper 2.25
❑4, Jun 87 .... 2.25
❑5 .... 2.25
❑6 .... 2.25

PARTNERS IN PANDEMONIUM
Caliber

Value: Cover or less

❑1, b&w 2.50
❑2, b&w 2.50
❑3, b&w 2.50

PARTS OF A HOLE
Caliber

Value: Cover or less
❑1, nn; b&w 2.50

PARTS UNKNOWN
Eclipse

Value: Cover or less

❑1, Aug 95, b&w 2.50
❑2, Mar 95, b&w 2.50
❑3, Jun 95, b&w 2.50
❑4, Oct 95, b&w 2.50

PARTS UNKNOWN: DARK INTENTIONS
Knight Press

Value: Cover or less

❑0, Aug 95 .... 2.95
❑1, Mar 95 .... 2.95
❑2, Jun 95 .... 2.95
❑3, Oct 95 .... 2.95
❑4 .... 2.95

PARTS UNKNOWN: HOSTILE TAKEOVER
Image

Value: Cover or less

❑1, Jun 00 .... 2.95
❑1/Ash, Preview edition 4.95
❑2, Jul 00 .... 2.95
❑2/Ash, Preview edition 4.95
❑3 .... 2.95
❑3/Ash, Preview edition 4.95
❑4, Sep 00 .... 2.95
❑4/Ash, Preview edition 4.95

PARTS UNKNOWN II: THE NEXT INVASION
Eclipse

Value: Cover or less
❑1, Dec 93, b&w 2.95

PASSOVER
Maximum

Value: Cover or less
❑1, Passover 2.99

PATHWAYS TO FANTASY
Pacific

	ORIG	GOOD	FINE	N-MINT
❑1, Jul 84, Stalking	1.50	0.40	1.00	2.00

PATRICK RABBIT
Fragments West

Value: Cover or less

❑1, Sum 88 .... 2.00
❑2 .... 2.00
❑3 .... 2.00
❑4 .... 2.00
❑5 .... 2.00
❑6 .... 2.00
❑7 .... 2.00

PATRICK STEWART
Celebrity

Value: Cover or less
❑1 .... 2.95

PATRICK STEWART VS. WILLIAM SHATNER
Celebrity

Value: Cover or less
❑1, b&w 5.95

PATRIOTS, THE
WildStorm

Value: Cover or less

❑1, Jan 00, Induction 2.50
❑2, Feb 00 .... 2.50
❑3, Mar 00 .... 2.50
❑4, Apr 00, Rebirth 2.50
❑5, May 00, Rocky Road 2.50
❑6, Jun 00 .... 2.50
❑7, Jul 00 .... 2.50
❑8, Aug 00 .... 2.50
❑9, Sep 00, Judgement Day; Judgement Day, Part 1 .... 2.50
❑10, Oct 00, Judgement Day, Part 2 .... 2.50

PAT SAVAGE: THE WOMAN OF BRONZE
Millennium

Value: Cover or less
❑1, Oct 92, Family Blood, nn... 2.50

PATTY CAKE
Permanent Press

Value: Cover or less

❑1 .... 2.95
❑2 .... 2.95
❑3 .... 2.95
❑4 .... 2.95
❑5 .... 2.95
❑6 .... 2.95

PATTY CAKE (2ND SERIES)
Caliber

Value: Cover or less

❑1 .... 2.95
❑2 .... 2.95
❑3 .... 2.95
❑HS 1, Dec 96, A Patty Cake Christmas 2.95

PATTY CAKE & FRIENDS
Slave Labor

Value: Cover or less

❑1, Nov 97, The Boob Tube; Cold-water Comfort 2.95
❑2, Dec 97, A Hard Lesson; Smell-Check 2.95
❑3, Jan 98, Told Ya So!; A Big Help 2.95
❑4, Feb 98 .... 2.95
❑5, Mar 98, The System Works; Small Wonder 2.95
❑6, Apr 98, Wiating Games 2.95
❑7, May 98, You Get What You Pay For 2.95
❑8, Jun 98, Now You See It, Now You Don't 2.95
❑9, Aug 98, Short Trip; How to Write Your Own Way-Cool Sci-Fi Script 2.95
❑10, Sep 98, Anybody Can Make a Mistake; Zip the Fox (text story) 2.95
❑11, Nov 98, It's a Fad, Fad, Fad, Fad World; The Girl With the Funny Mags 2.95
❑12, On With the Show; The Big Day 2.95
❑SE 1, Oct 97, Here There Be Monsters; Here be There Monsters, nn 3.95

PATTY CAKE & FRIENDS (VOL. 2)
Slave Labor

Value: Cover or less
❑1, Nov 00, Early to Rise; For Art's Sake, b&w; cardstock cover 4.95

PAUL THE SAMURAI
New England

	ORIG	GOOD	FINE	N-MINT
❑1, Jul 92, The Decline and Fall of the Tailfin Empire!!	2.75	0.80	2.00	4.00
❑2, Sep 92	2.75	0.60	1.50	3.00
❑3, Scarcer	2.75	1.20	3.00	6.00
❑4	2.75	0.80	2.00	4.00
❑5	2.75	0.55	1.38	2.75
❑6	2.75	0.55	1.38	2.75
❑7	2.75	0.55	1.38	2.75
❑8	2.75	0.55	1.38	2.75
❑9, A: The Tick	2.75	0.55	1.38	2.75
❑10, A: The Tick	2.75	0.55	1.38	2.75

PAUL THE SAMURAI (MINI-SERIES)
NEC

	ORIG	GOOD	FINE	N-MINT
❑1, Boiler Men: Boiler Menace!, A: The Tick	2.25	0.70	1.75	3.50
❑2, Revolt!	2.75	0.60	1.50	3.00
❑3	2.75	0.60	1.50	3.00

PAYNE
Dream Catcher Press

Value: Cover or less
❑1, Sep 95, b&w 2.50

PEACEMAKER, THE
Charlton

	ORIG	GOOD	FINE	N-MINT
❑1, Mar 67	0.12	2.40	6.00	12.00
❑2, May 67, Fightin' 5 back-up story	0.12	1.60	4.00	8.00
❑3, Jul 67, The Survivors; The Fightin' 5	0.12	1.60	4.00	8.00
❑4, Sep 67, O: The Peacemaker	0.12	2.00	5.00	10.00
❑5, Nov 67	0.12	1.60	4.00	8.00

PEACEMAKER (MINI-SERIES)
DC

	ORIG	GOOD	FINE	N-MINT
❑1, Jan 88, A Breach Of The Peace!	1.25	0.30	0.75	1.50
❑2, Feb 88, The Wages Of Tzin	1.25	0.30	0.75	1.50
❑3, Mar 88	1.25	0.30	0.75	1.50
❑4, Apr 88	1.25	0.30	0.75	1.50

PEACE PARTY
Blue Corn

Value: Cover or less
❑1, Beginnings 2.95

PEACE POSSE
Mellon Bank

Value: Cover or less
❑1, RBy, RBy (w), The End of the Violence Begins with Me! 2.95

PEANUT BUTTER AND JEREMY
ALTERNATIVE

Value: Cover or less

	ORIG
❑1, Aug 00, nn; b&w	2.95

PEBBLES AND BAMM-BAMM
CHARLTON

	ORIG	GOOD	FINE	N-MINT
❑1	0.20	3.60	9.00	18.00
❑2	0.20	2.40	6.00	12.00
❑3, Without All That...What?; A-Haunting-We-Will-Go	0.20	1.80	4.50	9.00
❑4	0.20	1.80	4.50	9.00
❑5	0.20	1.80	4.50	9.00
❑6	0.20	1.40	3.50	7.00
❑7, Oct 72	0.20	1.40	3.50	7.00
❑8	—	1.40	3.50	7.00
❑9	—	1.40	3.50	7.00
❑10	—	1.40	3.50	7.00
❑11	—	1.00	2.50	5.00
❑12	—	1.00	2.50	5.00
❑13	—	1.00	2.50	5.00
❑14	—	1.00	2.50	5.00
❑15	—	1.00	2.50	5.00
❑16	—	1.00	2.50	5.00
❑17	—	1.00	2.50	5.00
❑18	—	1.00	2.50	5.00
❑19, End of the World; The Early Riser	0.20	1.00	2.50	5.00
❑20	—	1.00	2.50	5.00
❑21	—	0.80	2.00	4.00
❑22	—	0.80	2.00	4.00
❑23	—	0.80	2.00	4.00
❑24	—	0.80	2.00	4.00
❑25	—	0.80	2.00	4.00
❑26	—	0.80	2.00	4.00
❑27	—	0.80	2.00	4.00
❑28	—	0.80	2.00	4.00
❑29	—	0.80	2.00	4.00
❑30	—	0.80	2.00	4.00
❑31	—	0.60	1.50	3.00
❑32	—	0.60	1.50	3.00
❑33	—	0.60	1.50	3.00
❑34, Aug 76	0.30	0.60	1.50	3.00
❑35, Oct 76	0.30	0.60	1.50	3.00
❑36, Dec 76	0.30	0.60	1.50	3.00

PEBBLES & BAMM-BAMM (HARVEY)
HARVEY

Value: Cover or less

	ORIG		ORIG
❑1	1.50	❑3	1.50
❑2	1.50	❑Smr 1, first edition	2.25

PEDESTRIAN VULGARITY
FANTAGRAPHICS

Value: Cover or less

	ORIG
❑1, b&w	2.50

PEEK-A-BOO 3-D
3-D ZONE

Value: Cover or less

	ORIG
❑1, BWa, nn	3.95

PEEPSHOW
DRAWN & QUARTERLY

Value: Cover or less

	ORIG		ORIG
❑1	2.50	❑6, Apr 94	2.95
❑2	2.50	❑7	2.95
❑3	2.50	❑8	2.95
❑4	2.50	❑9	2.95
❑5, Oct 93	2.95		

PELLESTAR
ETERNITY

Value: Cover or less

	ORIG		ORIG
❑1, Sep 87	1.95	❑2	1.95

PENDRAGON (AIRCEL)
AIRCEL

Value: Cover or less

	ORIG		ORIG
❑1, Nov 91, b&w; adult	2.95	❑2, Dec 91, b&w; adult	2.95

PENDULUM
ADVENTURE

Value: Cover or less

	ORIG		ORIG
❑1, b&w	2.50	❑3, b&w	2.50
❑2, b&w	2.50	❑4, b&w	2.50

PENDULUM'S ILLUSTRATED STORIES
PENDULUM

Value: Cover or less

	ORIG		ORIG
❑1, No apparent cover price; Moby Dick	4.95	❑4, 20, 000 Leagues Under the Sea	4.95
❑2, Treasure Island	4.95	❑5, Midsummer Night's Dream	4.95
❑3, Doctor Jekyll; Dr. Jekyll	4.95	❑6, Christmas Carol	4.95

PENGUIN & PENCILGUIN
FRAGMENTS WEST

Value: Cover or less

	ORIG		ORIG
❑1, Jan 87, Shoguin; Aladguin and 1001 Flavors	2.00	❑2	2.00
		❑3	2.00

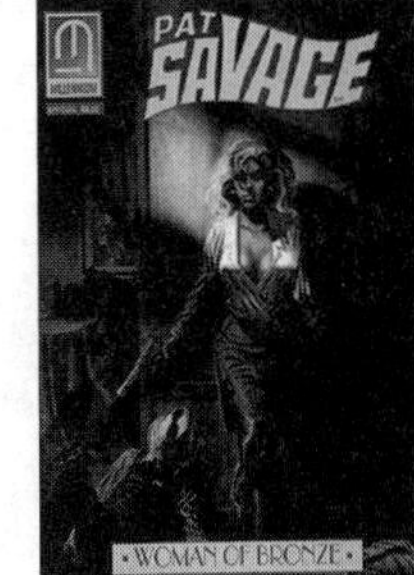

Doc Savage's cousin, Pat, often followed her adventurous relative and his side-kicks into danger.

	ORIG		ORIG
❑4	2.00	❑6	2.00
❑5	2.00		

PENGUIN BROS.
LABYRINTH STUDIOS

Value: Cover or less

	ORIG		ORIG
❑1	2.50	❑2	2.50

PENNY
AVON

	ORIG	GOOD	FINE	N-MINT
❑1, Penny's Pop!; Penny and Our Bill, Creator's Biography included	0.10	11.00	27.50	55.00
❑2	0.10	6.00	15.00	30.00
❑3	0.10	6.00	15.00	30.00
❑4	0.10	6.00	15.00	30.00
❑5	0.10	6.00	15.00	30.00
❑6, Final Issue	0.10	7.00	17.50	35.00

PENNY CENTURY
FANTAGRAPHICS

Value: Cover or less

	ORIG		ORIG
❑1, Dec 97, b&w	2.95	❑5, Jun 99, b&w	2.95
❑2, Mar 98, b&w	2.95	❑6, Nov 99, b&w	2.95
❑3, Sep 98, b&w	2.95	❑7, Jul 00, b&w	2.95
❑4, Jan 99, b&w	2.95		

PENTACLE: THE SIGN OF THE FIVE
ETERNITY

Value: Cover or less

	ORIG		ORIG
❑1, Feb 91	2.25	❑3	2.25
❑2	2.25	❑4	2.25

PENTHOUSE COMIX
PENTHOUSE INTERNATIONAL

	ORIG	GOOD	FINE	N-MINT
❑1, Jun 94	4.95	1.60	4.00	8.00
❑1-2, 14pgs.; 2nd Printing; subtitled Special Edition 1995	4.95	0.99	2.47	4.95
❑2, Jul 94	4.95	0.99	2.47	4.95
❑3, Sep 94	4.95	0.99	2.47	4.95
❑4, Nov 94	4.95	0.99	2.47	4.95
❑5, Jan 95, Man of Steel, Woman of Kleenex	4.95	0.99	2.47	4.95
❑6, Mar 95, Young Captain Adventure; Action Figures, Part 1, Comic size	4.95	0.99	2.47	4.95
❑6/A, Magazine size	4.95	0.99	2.47	4.95
❑7, May 95, Comic size	4.95	0.99	2.47	4.95
❑7/A, Magazine size	4.95	0.99	2.47	4.95
❑8, Jul 95	4.95	0.99	2.47	4.95
❑9, Sep 95	4.95	0.99	2.47	4.95
❑10, Nov 95	4.95	0.99	2.47	4.95
❑11, Jan 96	4.95	0.99	2.47	4.95
❑12, Mar 96, second anniversary issue	4.95	0.99	2.47	4.95
❑13, May 96	4.95	0.99	2.47	4.95
❑14, Jul 96	4.95	0.99	2.47	4.95
❑15, Sep 96, Denz	4.95	0.99	2.47	4.95
❑16, Oct 96	4.95	0.99	2.47	4.95
❑17, Nov 96, reprints Manara's Hidden Camera	4.95	0.99	2.47	4.95
❑18, Dec 96	4.95	0.99	2.47	4.95
❑19, Jan 97	4.95	0.99	2.47	4.95
❑20, Feb 97	4.95	0.99	2.47	4.95
❑21, Apr 97	4.95	0.99	2.47	4.95
❑22, May 97	4.95	0.99	2.47	4.95
❑23, Jun 97	4.95	0.99	2.47	4.95
❑24, Jul 97	4.95	0.99	2.47	4.95
❑25, Sep 97, Sweet Chastity reprints begin	4.95	0.99	2.47	4.95
❑26, Oct 97	4.95	0.99	2.47	4.95
❑27, Nov 97	4.95	0.99	2.47	4.95
❑28, Jan 98	4.95	0.99	2.47	4.95
❑29, Feb 98	4.95	0.99	2.47	4.95
❑30, Apr 98	4.95	0.99	2.47	4.95
❑31, May 98	4.95	0.99	2.47	4.95
❑32, Jun 98	4.95	0.99	2.47	4.95
❑33, Jul 98, Final Issue	4.95	0.99	2.47	4.95

PENTHOUSE MAX
PENTHOUSE INTERNATIONAL

Value: Cover or less

	ORIG		ORIG
❑1, Jul 96	4.95	❑2, Nov 96	4.95
		❑3, Spr 97	4.95

PEOPLE ARE PHONY
SIEGEL AND SIMON

	ORIG	GOOD	FINE	N-MINT
❑1, Will Rogers Tonight; Raw Fun!	0.75	0.80	2.00	4.00

PEOPLE'S COMICS, THE
GOLDEN GATE

	ORIG	GOOD	FINE	N-MINT
❑1, On the Street with Shuman the Human; The Confessions of Robert Crumb	0.50	0.80	2.00	4.00

PERAZIM
ANTARCTIC

Value: Cover or less
- ❑1, Sep 96, b&w 2.95
- ❑2 2.95
- ❑3 2.95

PERCEVAN: THE THREE STARS OF INGAAR
FANTASY FLIGHT

Value: Cover or less
- ❑1 8.95

PEREGRINE, THE
ALLIANCE

Value: Cover or less
- ❑1, Apr 94, b&w 2.50
- ❑2, Aug 94, b&w 2.50

PERG
LIGHTNING

Value: Cover or less
- ❑1, Oct 93, Origin of Perg, A: Dreadwolf, Glow-in the dark flip book 3.50
- ❑1/GO, Oct 93, Gold edition 3.50
- ❑1/PL, Oct 93, Origin of Perg, Platinum edition 2.50
- ❑1/SC, Oct 93, glow cover 3.50
- ❑2, Nov 93, A: Dreadwolf 2.95
- ❑2/PL, Nov 93, Platinum edition; platinum 2.95
- ❑3, Dec 93 2.95
- ❑3/PL, Platinum edition 2.50
- ❑4, Jan 94, O: Perg 2.95
- ❑4/PL, Jan 94, Platinum edition; platinum 2.95
- ❑5, Feb 94 2.95
- ❑6, Mar 94 2.95
- ❑7, Apr 94 2.95
- ❑8, May 94, Final Issue 2.95

PERIPHERY
ARCH-TYPE

Value: Cover or less
- ❑1, The Trashman; Lore: Imperfect Gentleman 2.95

PERRAMUS: ESCAPE FROM THE PAST
FANTAGRAPHICS

Value: Cover or less
- ❑1, b&w 3.50
- ❑2, b&w 3.50
- ❑3, b&w 3.50
- ❑4, b&w 3.50

PERRY
LIGHTNING

Value: Cover or less
- ❑1, Oct 97 2.95

PERSONALITY CLASSICS
PERSONALITY

Value: Cover or less
- ❑1, John Wayne 2.95
- ❑2, Marilyn Monroe 2.95
- ❑3 2.95
- ❑4 2.95

PERSONALITY COMICS PRESENTS
PERSONALITY

Value: Cover or less
- ❑1, Paulina Porizkova 2.50
- ❑2, Apr 91, Traci Lords 2.50
- ❑3, Arnold Schwarzenegger 2.50
- ❑4, Christina Applegate 2.50
- ❑5, Patrick Swayze, Demi Moore 2.95
- ❑6, Michael Jordan 2.95
- ❑7, Samantha Fox 2.95
- ❑8, Bettie Page, Jennifer Connelly 2.95
- ❑9, Kim Basinger, Michael Keaton 2.95
- ❑10, Gloria Estefan 2.95
- ❑11 2.95
- ❑12 2.95
- ❑13 2.95
- ❑14 2.95
- ❑15 2.95
- ❑16 2.95
- ❑17 2.95
- ❑18 2.95

PEST
PEST COMICS

	ORIG	GOOD	FINE	N-MINT
❑1	1.95	0.39	0.98	1.95
❑2	1.95	0.39	0.98	1.95
❑3	1.95	0.39	0.98	1.95
❑4, Pipi Soiledstockings; Bargirl	1.95	0.39	0.98	1.95
❑5, Bargirl Returns; Party Pigs at Pigstock	1.95	0.39	0.98	1.95
❑6, The Puke-O the Clown Story; Sky Cow, b&w	1.85	0.39	0.98	1.95
❑7, Fart-Force; Babushka	1.95	0.39	0.98	1.95

PET
EROS

Value: Cover or less
- ❑1, May 97 2.95

PETER CANNON-THUNDERBOLT
DC

Value: Cover or less
- ❑1, Sep 92, Rebirth, O: Thunderbolt 1.25
- ❑2, Oct 92 1.25
- ❑3, Nov 92 1.25
- ❑4, Dec 92 1.25
- ❑5, Jan 93 1.25
- ❑6, Feb 93 1.25
- ❑7, Mar 93 1.25
- ❑8, Apr 93 1.25
- ❑9, May 93 1.50
- ❑10, May 93 1.50
- ❑11, Jul 93 1.50
- ❑12, Aug 93, Final Issue 1.50

PETER KOCK
FANTAGRAPHICS

Value: Cover or less
- ❑1, b&w; adult 3.50
- ❑2, b&w; adult 2.75
- ❑3, b&w; adult 2.75
- ❑4, May 94, b&w; adult 2.75
- ❑5, Jul 94, b&w; adult 2.75
- ❑6, Aug 94, b&w; adult 2.75

PETER PAN (GOLD KEY)
GOLD KEY

	ORIG	GOOD	FINE	N-MINT
❑1, Sep 69, movie Adaptation; 10086-909	0.15	4.00	10.00	20.00
❑2	—	2.40	6.00	12.00

PETER PAN (WALT DISNEY'S...)
DISNEY

Value: Cover or less
- ❑1, Peter Pan; The Pirate Plot, Reprint; prestige format 5.95

PETER PAN AND THE WARLORDS OF OZ
HAND OF DOOM

Value: Cover or less
- ❑1 2.95

PETER PAN & THE WARLORDS OF OZ: DEAD HEAD WATER
HAND OF DOOM

Value: Cover or less
- ❑1 2.95

PETER PAN: RETURN TO NEVER-NEVER LAND
ADVENTURE

Value: Cover or less
- ❑1, full color 2.50
- ❑2, full color 2.50

PETER PARKER: SPIDER-MAN
MARVEL

Value: Cover or less
- ❑1, Jan 99, JR2, Power Without Responsibility!, V: Scorpion, wraparound cover 2.99
- ❑1/A, Jan 99, JR2, Power Without Responsibility!, sunburst variant cover 2.99
- ❑1/SC, Jan 99, JR2, Power Without Responsibility!, DFE alternate cover 6.95
- ❑2/A, Feb 99, JR2, A: Thor; A: Tocketts, Cover A 1.99
- ❑2/B, JR2, A: Thor; A: Tocketts, Cover B by Arthur Suydam 1.99
- ❑3, Mar 99, JR2, A: Mary Jane; A: Iceman; V: Shadrac, Continued from Amazing Spider-Man #3 1.99
- ❑4, Apr 99, JR2, A: Marrow 1.99
- ❑5, May 99, V: Spider-Woman; A: Black Cat 1.99
- ❑6, Jun 99, V: Bullseye; V: Kingpin 1.99
- ❑7, Jul 99, A: Blade 1.99
- ❑8, Aug 99, A: Morbius; A: Blade; A: Kingpin 1.99
- ❑9, Sep 99, V: Venom 1.99
- ❑10, Oct 99, V: Venom 1.99
- ❑11, Nov 99, Eighth Day, Part 3, continues in Juggernaut #1 1.99
- ❑12, Dec 99, Return Of The Sinister Six! 2.99
- ❑13, Jan 00 2.25
- ❑14, Feb 00 2.25
- ❑15, Mar 00 2.25
- ❑16, Apr 00 2.25
- ❑17, May 00 2.25
- ❑18, Jun 00 2.25
- ❑19, Jul 00 2.25
- ❑20, Aug 00 2.25
- ❑21, Sep 00, A Day in the Life 2.25
- ❑22, Oct 00 2.25
- ❑23, Nov 00, Read 'em and Weep 2.25
- ❑24, Dec 00 2.25
- ❑25, Jan 01 2.25
- ❑26, Feb 01, Police Story 2.25
- ❑27, Mar 01, Getting Ahead, A: Mendel Stromm 2.25
- ❑28, Apr 01, Field of Dream, A: Mendel Stromm 2.25
- ❑29, May 01, Destinations, continues in Amazing Spider-Man Annual 2001 2.25
- ❑30 2.25
- ❑31 2.25
- ❑32 2.25
- ❑33 2.25
- ❑Anl 1998, The Night They Killed Big Bear...; The Night hey Killed Big Bear..., gatefold summary; Peter Parker: Spider-Man/Elektra '98 2.99
- ❑Anl 1999, Aug 99, A: Man-Thing 3.50

PETER PORKER, THE SPECTACULAR SPIDER-HAM
MARVEL

	ORIG	GOOD	FINE	N-MINT
❑1, May 85, The Mysterious Island Of Ducktor Doom!, 1: Duck Doom; 1: Peter Porker; 1: J. Jonah Jackal; 1: Spider-Ham	0.65	0.20	0.50	1.00
❑2, Jul 85	0.65	0.20	0.50	1.00
❑3, Sep 85	0.65	0.20	0.50	1.00
❑4, Nov 85	0.65	0.20	0.50	1.00
❑5, Jan 86	0.65	0.20	0.50	1.00
❑6, Mar 86	0.65	0.20	0.50	1.00
❑7, May 86	0.75	0.20	0.50	1.00
❑8, Jul 86	0.75	0.20	0.50	1.00
❑9, Aug 86	0.75	0.20	0.50	1.00
❑10, Sep 86	0.75	0.20	0.50	1.00
❑11, Oct 86	0.75	0.20	0.50	1.00
❑12, Nov 86	0.75	0.20	0.50	1.00
❑13, Jan 87	0.75	0.20	0.50	1.00
❑14, Mar 87	0.75	0.20	0.50	1.00
❑15, May 87	0.75	0.20	0.50	1.00
❑16, Jul 87	1.00	0.20	0.50	1.00
❑17, Sep 87, Final Issue	1.00	0.20	0.50	1.00

PETER RABBIT 3-D
ETERNITY

Value: Cover or less
- ❑1, Reprints from Peter Rabbit (Avon) stories 2.95

PETER THE LITTLE PEST
MARVEL

	ORIG	GOOD	FINE	N-MINT
❑1, Peter the Little Pest; Little Pixie, 1: Little Pixie; 1: Peter, The Little Pest	0.15	3.60	9.00	18.00
❑2	0.15	2.80	7.00	14.00
❑3	0.15	2.80	7.00	14.00
❑4	0.15	2.80	7.00	14.00

PETE THE P.O.'D POSTAL WORKER
SHARKBAIT

	ORIG	GOOD	FINE	N-MINT
❑1, Oct 97	2.95	0.70	1.75	3.50
❑2, Jan 98	2.95	0.60	1.50	3.00
❑3, Mar 98	2.95	0.60	1.50	3.00
❑4, Jun 98	2.95	0.60	1.50	3.00
❑5, Aug 98, in England	2.95	0.60	1.50	3.00
❑6, Oct 98	2.95	0.59	1.48	2.95
❑7, Jan 99, V: Teddy Cougar	2.95	0.59	1.48	2.95
❑8, Apr 99, Postman on Elm Street, Part 2, V: Teddy Cougar	2.95	0.59	1.48	2.95
❑9, Jun 99, on Jerry Ringer Show	2.95	0.59	1.48	2.95
❑10, Aug 99, V: Y2K	2.95	0.59	1.48	2.95

PETWORKS VS. WILDK.A.T.S.
PARODY PRESS

Value: Cover or less

❑1, Night of the Undead Customers ... 2.50

PHAEDRA
EXPRESS

Value: Cover or less

❑1, Sep 94, nn; b&w; cardstock cover; third in series of Entity illustrated novellas with Zen Intergalactic Ninja ... 2.95

PHAGE: SHADOWDEATH (NEIL GAIMAN'S...)
BIG

Value: Cover or less

❑1, Jun 96, BT (w), Insurrection!; The Big Crossover, Part 8 ... 2.25
❑2, Aug 96, BT (w) ... 2.25
❑3, Sep 96, BT (w) ... 2.25
❑4, Sep 96, BT (w) ... 2.25
❑5, Oct 96, BT (w) ... 2.25
❑6, BT (w) ... 2.25

PHANTACEA: PHASE ONE
MCPHERSON

	ORIG	GOOD	FINE	N-MINT
❑1	1.50	1.00	2.50	5.00

PHANTASMAGORIA
TOME PRESS

Value: Cover or less

❑1, b&w ... 2.50

PHANTASY AGAINST HUNGER
TIGER

	ORIG	GOOD	FINE	N-MINT
❑1	1.50	0.40	1.00	2.00

PHANTOM, THE (2ND SERIES)
DC

	ORIG	GOOD	FINE	N-MINT
❑1, May 88, LMc, Guns, O: Phantom	1.25	0.40	1.00	2.00
❑2, Jun 88	1.25	0.40	1.00	2.00
❑3, Jul 88	1.25	0.40	1.00	2.00
❑4, Aug 88	1.25	0.40	1.00	2.00

PHANTOM, THE (3RD SERIES)
DC

	ORIG	GOOD	FINE	N-MINT
❑1, May 89	1.50	0.40	1.00	2.00
❑2, Jun 89	1.50	0.30	0.75	1.50
❑3, Jul 89	1.50	0.30	0.75	1.50
❑4, Aug 89	1.50	0.30	0.75	1.50
❑5, Sep 89	1.50	0.30	0.75	1.50
❑6, Oct 89	1.50	0.30	0.75	1.50
❑7, Nov 89	1.50	0.30	0.75	1.50
❑8, Dec 89	1.50	0.30	0.75	1.50
❑9, Jan 89	1.50	0.30	0.75	1.50
❑10, Feb 89	1.50	0.30	0.75	1.50
❑11, Mar 90	1.50	0.30	0.75	1.50
❑12, Apr 90	1.50	0.30	0.75	1.50
❑13, May 90, Final Issue	1.50	0.30	0.75	1.50

PHANTOM, THE (4TH SERIES)
WOLF

	ORIG	GOOD	FINE	N-MINT
❑0/LE, limited edition subscribers' issue	3.50	0.70	1.75	3.50
❑1	2.50	0.50	1.25	2.50
❑2	—	0.45	1.13	2.25
❑3	—	0.45	1.13	2.25
❑4	—	0.45	1.13	2.25
❑5	—	0.45	1.13	2.25
❑6	2.25	0.45	1.13	2.25
❑7	1.95	0.39	0.98	1.95
❑8	1.95	0.39	0.98	1.95

PHANTOM 2040
MARVEL

Value: Cover or less

❑1, May 95, SD, Generation Unto Generation, 1: Phantom 2040, poster ... 1.50
❑2, Jun 95, SD ... 1.50
❑3, Jul 95, SD, Poster ... 1.50
❑4, Aug 95, SD, Poster ... 1.50

PHANTOM FORCE
IMAGE

Value: Cover or less

❑0, JK, JK (w), trading card ... 2.50
❑1, Dec 93, RL; JK, JK (w), trading card ... 2.50
❑2, Apr 94 ... 3.50
❑3 ... 2.50
❑4 ... 2.50
❑5 ... 2.50
❑6 ... 2.50
❑7 ... 2.50
❑8 ... 2.50
❑Ash 1, ashcan ... 2.50

Pete the P.O.'d Postal Worker was a U.S. Postal Service employee who took "the mail must get through" to the extreme.

© 1997 Sharkbait

PHANTOM FORCE (GENESIS WEST)
GENESIS WEST

Value: Cover or less

❑0, JK (w) ... 2.50

PHANTOM GUARD
IMAGE

Value: Cover or less

❑1, Oct 97 ... 2.50
❑1/A, Oct 97, alternate cover (white background) ... 2.50
❑2, Oct 97 ... 2.50
❑3, Dec 97 ... 2.50
❑4, Jan 98 ... 2.50
❑4/SC, Jan 98, chromium cover 2.50
❑5, Feb 98 ... 2.50
❑6, Mar 98 ... 2.50

PHANTOM OF FEAR CITY
CLAYPOOL

Value: Cover or less

❑1, May 93 ... 2.50
❑2, Jul 93, Incarnation! ... 2.50
❑3, Aug 93 ... 2.50
❑4, Oct 93 ... 2.50
❑5, Nov 93 ... 2.50
❑6, Jan 94 ... 2.50
❑7 ... 2.50
❑8, Jul 94 ... 2.50
❑9, Sep 94 ... 2.50
❑10, Nov 94 ... 2.50
❑11, Feb 95 ... 2.50
❑12, May 95, Final Issue ... 2.50

PHANTOM OF THE OPERA (ETERNITY)
ETERNITY

	ORIG	GOOD	FINE	N-MINT
❑1, b&w	1.95	0.40	1.00	2.00

PHANTOM OF THE OPERA (INNOVATION)
INNOVATION

Value: Cover or less

❑1, Dec 91 ... 6.95

PHANTOM QUEST CORP.
PIONEER

Value: Cover or less

❑1, Mar 97, b&w; wraparound cover ... 2.95

PHANTOM STRANGER, THE (2ND SERIES)
DC

	ORIG	GOOD	FINE	N-MINT
❑1, Jun 69, When Ghosts Walk!; Dr. 13, The Hermit's Ghost Dog!, A: Doctor 13	0.12	10.00	25.00	50.00
❑2, Aug 69, A: Doctor 13	0.15	4.00	10.00	20.00
❑3, Oct 69, A: Doctor 13	0.15	4.00	10.00	20.00
❑4, Dec 69, NA, 1: Tala; A: Doctor 13	0.15	4.80	12.00	24.00
❑5, Feb 70, A: Doctor 13	0.15	2.40	6.00	12.00
❑6, Apr 70, A: Doctor 13	0.15	2.40	6.00	12.00
❑7, Jun 70, A: Doctor 13	0.15	2.40	6.00	12.00
❑8, Aug 70, A: Doctor 13	0.15	2.00	5.00	10.00
❑9, Oct 70, A: Doctor 13	0.15	2.00	5.00	10.00
❑10, Dec 70, A: Doctor 13	0.15	2.00	5.00	10.00
❑11, Feb 71	0.15	2.00	5.00	10.00
❑12, Apr 71, A: Doctor 13	0.15	1.60	4.00	8.00
❑13, Jun 71, A: Doctor 13	0.15	1.60	4.00	8.00
❑14, Aug 71, A: Doctor 13	0.15	1.60	4.00	8.00
❑15, Oct 71, A: Doctor 13, Giant-size	0.25	1.60	4.00	8.00
❑16, Dec 71, JA, Image In Wax, A: Mark Merlin; A: Doctor 13, Giant-size	0.25	1.60	4.00	8.00
❑17, Feb 72, A: Doctor 13, Giant-size	0.25	1.60	4.00	8.00
❑18, Apr 72, A: Mark Merlin; 1: Cassandra Craft; A: Doctor 13, Giant-size	0.25	1.60	4.00	8.00
❑19, Jun 72, A: Mark Merlin; A: Doctor 13, Giant-size	0.25	1.60	4.00	8.00
❑20, Aug 72	0.20	1.60	4.00	8.00
❑21, Oct 72, A: Doctor 13	0.20	1.20	3.00	6.00
❑22, Dec 72, A: Doctor 13	0.20	1.20	3.00	6.00
❑23, Feb 73, 1: The Spawn of Frankenstein	0.20	1.20	3.00	6.00
❑24, Apr 73, A: The Spawn of Frankenstein	0.20	1.20	3.00	6.00
❑25, Jul 73, A: The Spawn of Frankenstein	0.20	1.20	3.00	6.00
❑26, Sep 73, A: The Spawn of Frankenstein; A: Doctor 13	0.20	1.20	3.00	6.00
❑27, Nov 73, A: The Spawn of Frankenstein	0.20	1.20	3.00	6.00
❑28, Jan 74, A: The Spawn of Frankenstein	0.20	1.20	3.00	6.00
❑29, Mar 74, A: The Spawn of Frankenstein	0.20	1.20	3.00	6.00
❑30, May 74, A: The Spawn of Frankenstein	0.20	1.20	3.00	6.00
❑31, Jul 74, A: Black Orchid	0.20	1.20	3.00	6.00
❑32, Sep 74, A: Black Orchid	0.20	1.20	3.00	6.00
❑33, Nov 74, A: Deadman	0.20	1.20	3.00	6.00
❑34, Jan 75, A: Doctor 13; A: Black Orchid	0.20	1.20	3.00	6.00
❑35, Mar 75, A: Black Orchid	0.25	1.20	3.00	6.00

	ORIG	GOOD	FINE	N-MINT
❑36, May 75, A: Black Orchid	0.25	1.20	3.00	6.00
❑37, Jul 75	0.25	1.20	3.00	6.00
❑38, Sep 75, A: Black Orchid	0.25	1.20	3.00	6.00
❑39, Nov 75, A: Deadman	0.25	1.20	3.00	6.00
❑40, Jan 76, A: Deadman	0.25	1.20	3.00	6.00
❑41, Mar 76, A: Deadman, Final Issue	0.25	1.20	3.00	6.00

PHANTOM STRANGER, THE (MINI-SERIES)
DC

	ORIG	GOOD	FINE	N-MINT
❑1, Oct 87, The Heart Of A Stranger	0.75	0.60	1.50	3.00
❑2, Nov 87	0.75	0.50	1.25	2.50
❑3, Dec 87	0.75	0.50	1.25	2.50
❑4, Jan 88	0.75	0.50	1.25	2.50

PHANTOM, THE: THE GHOST WHO WALKS (LEE FALK'S...)
MARVEL

Value: Cover or less

❑1, Feb 95, cardstock cover ... 2.95
❑2, Mar 95, Heart or Darkness, cardstock cover ... 2.95
❑3, Apr 95, cardstock cover ... 2.95

PHANTOM ZONE, THE
DC

	ORIG	GOOD	FINE	N-MINT
❑1, Jan 82, GC, The Haunting of Charlie Kweskill!	0.60	0.30	0.75	1.50
❑2, Feb 82, GC	0.60	0.25	0.63	1.25
❑3, Mar 82, GC	0.60	0.25	0.63	1.25
❑4, Apr 82, GC	0.60	0.25	0.63	1.25

PHASE ONE
VICTORY

Value: Cover or less

❑1, Oct 86, Death has a Face! 1.50
❑2 ... 1.50
❑3 ... 1.50
❑4 ... 1.50
❑5 ... 1.50

PHATWARS
BON

Value: Cover or less

❑1 ... 2.00

PHAZE
ECLIPSE

Value: Cover or less

❑1, Apr 88, BSz (c), One Of Those Days ... 2.25
❑2, Oct 88, PG (c) ... 2.25

PHENOMERAMA
CALIBER

Value: Cover or less

❑1, Monkey Vato; Lifetimes ... 2.95

PHIGMENTS
AMAZING

Value: Cover or less

❑1, b&w ... 1.95
❑2 ... 1.95

PHILBERT DESANEX' DREAMS
RIP OFF

Value: Cover or less

❑1, b&w ... 2.95

PHILISTINE, THE
ONE-SHOT

Value: Cover or less

❑1, Sep 93, Into the Limelight, b&w ... 2.50
❑2, Apr 94, b&w ... 2.50
❑3, Sep 94, b&w ... 2.50
❑4 ... 2.50
❑5 ... 2.50
❑6 ... 2.50

PHINEUS: MAGICIAN FOR HIRE
PIFFLE

Value: Cover or less

❑1, Largo the Dread; Gil the Walking Dead or Vampires Suck. 2.95

PHOBOS
FLASHPOINT

Value: Cover or less

❑1, Jan 94 ... 2.50

PHOEBE: ANGEL IN BLACK
ANGEL

Value: Cover or less

❑1, City of the Spirits ... 2.95

PHOENIX
ATLAS

	ORIG	GOOD	FINE	N-MINT
❑1, Mar 75, From The Ashes, O: Phoenix (Atlas character)	0.25	0.40	1.00	2.00
❑2, Jun 75, And the Sea Ran Red!	0.25	0.40	1.00	2.00
❑3, Oct 75	0.25	0.40	1.00	2.00
❑4	0.25	0.40	1.00	2.00

PHOENIX RESTAURANT
FANDOM HOUSE

Value: Cover or less

❑1, b&w ... 3.50

PHOENIX RESURRECTION, THE: AFTERMATH
MALIBU

Value: Cover or less

❑1, Jan 96, Aftermath, continues in Foxfire #1 ... 3.95

PHOENIX RESURRECTION, THE: GENESIS
MALIBU

Value: Cover or less

❑1, Dec 95, Genesis, wraparound cover; Giant-size; continues in The Phoenix Resurrection: Revelations; Phoenix force returns ... 3.95
❑2, Red Shift Mantra ... 3.95

PHOENIX RESURRECTION, THE: RED SHIFT
MALIBU

	ORIG	GOOD	FINE	N-MINT
❑0, Mar 96, collects the seven flipbook chapters plus one new chapter	1.95	0.50	1.25	2.50
❑0/LE, Dec 95, no cover price; American Entertainment Edition	—	0.50	1.25	2.50

PHOENIX RESURRECTION, THE: REVELATIONS
MALIBU

Value: Cover or less

❑1, Dec 95, Revelations, wraparound cover; continues in The Phoenix Resurrection: Aftermath ... 3.95

PHOENIX SQUARE
SLAVE LABOR

Value: Cover or less

❑1, Aug 97, b&w ... 2.95
❑2, Nov 97 ... 2.95

PHOENIX: THE UNTOLD STORY
MARVEL

	ORIG	GOOD	FINE	N-MINT
❑1, Apr 84, JBy, The Fate Of The Phoenix, X-Men #137 with unpublished alternate ending	2.00	1.60	4.00	8.00

PHONY PAGES, THE (TERRY BEATTY'S...)
RENEGADE

Value: Cover or less

❑1, The Blue Kid; Muton Chop, Parody of Famous Comic Strips ... 2.00
❑2, Chaplain America; Capt. Mortal, Parody of Famous Comic Books ... 2.00

PICTURE TAKER, THE
SLAVE LABOR

Value: Cover or less

❑1, Jan 98, The Picture Taker, b&w ... 2.95

PIE
WOW COOL

Value: Cover or less

❑1, b&w ... 2.95

PIECE OF STEAK, A
TOME PRESS

Value: Cover or less

❑1, b&w ... 2.50

PIECES
5TH PANEL

	ORIG	GOOD	FINE	N-MINT
❑1, Apr 97, Too Much, b&w	1.95	0.50	1.25	2.50
❑2, Jul 97, b&w	1.95	0.50	1.25	2.50
❑3	2.50	0.50	1.25	2.50

PIED PIPER GRAPHIC ALBUM
PIED PIPER

Value: Cover or less

❑1, Hero Alliance ... 6.95
❑2, < Never Published > ... —
❑3, Beast Warriors ... 6.95

PIED PIPER OF HAMELIN
TOME PRESS

Value: Cover or less

❑1, b&w ... 2.95

PIGEONMAN
ABOVE & BEYOND

Value: Cover or less

❑1 ... 2.95

PIGEON-MAN, THE BIRD-BRAIN
FERRY TAIL STUDIO

Value: Cover or less

❑1, Apr 93, b&w ... 2.50

PIGHEAD
WILLIAMSON

Value: Cover or less

❑1, b&w ... 2.95

PILGRIM'S PROGRESS, THE
MARVEL

Value: Cover or less

❑1, adaptation ... 9.99

PINEAPPLE ARMY
VIZ

Value: Cover or less

❑1, Dec 88 ... 1.75
❑2 ... 1.75
❑3, Jan 89 ... 1.75
❑4 ... 1.75
❑5 ... 1.75
❑6 ... 1.75
❑7 ... 1.75
❑8, Mar 89, A Bouquet of Flowers ... 1.75
❑9 ... 1.75
❑10 ... 1.75

PINHEAD
MARVEL

Value: Cover or less

❑1, Dec 93, The Devil You Know, Embossed foil cover ... 2.95
❑2, Jan 94 ... 2.50
❑3, Feb 94 ... 2.50
❑4, Mar 94 ... 2.50
❑5, Apr 94 ... 2.50
❑6, May 94, Final Issue ... 2.50

PINHEAD VS. MARSHAL LAW: LAW IN HELL
MARVEL

Value: Cover or less

❑1, Nov 93, foil cover ... 2.95
❑2, Dec 93, foil cover ... 2.95

PINK DUST
KITCHEN SINK

Value: Cover or less

❑1, Aug 98, nn ... 3.50

PINK FLOYD
PERSONALITY

Value: Cover or less

❑1, b&w ... 2.95
❑2, b&w ... 2.95

PINK FLOYD EXPERIENCE
Revolutionary
Value: Cover or less

❑1, Jun 91, b&w 2.50
❑2, Aug 91, b&w 2.50
❑3, Oct 91, b&w 2.50
❑4, Dec 91, b&w 2.50
❑5, Feb 92, b&w 2.50

PINK PANTHER (HARVEY)
Harvey
Value: Cover or less

❑1 1.50
❑2 1.50
❑3 1.50
❑4 1.50
❑5 1.50
❑6 1.50
❑7 1.50
❑8 1.50
❑9 1.50
❑SS 1, Super Special 2.25

PINKY AND THE BRAIN
DC

	ORIG	GOOD	FINE	N-MINT
❑1, Jul 96, based on animated series	1.75	0.50	1.25	2.50
❑2, Aug 96, Excalibrain; Little Big Brain	1.75	0.40	1.00	2.00
❑3, Sep 96, Verminator	1.75	0.40	1.00	2.00
❑4, Oct 96, Pink O' The Irish; Caged Heat, Oz parody	1.75	0.35	0.88	1.75
❑5, Nov 96, Oil's Well that Ends Well, Western parody issue	1.75	0.35	0.88	1.75
❑6, Dec 96, Plan Brain from Outer Space, Photo cover; Ed Wood parody issue	1.75	0.35	0.88	1.75
❑7, Jan 97, Faust Things Faust; Clan of the Cave Mice, Faust parody	1.75	0.35	0.88	1.75
❑8, Feb 97, Mission: Impinkable	1.75	0.35	0.88	1.75
❑9, Mar 97, The Mouse who Would be King; Kappa Delta Rodent	1.75	0.35	0.88	1.75
❑10, Apr 97	1.75	0.35	0.88	1.75
❑11, May 97, Fantasia parody	1.75	0.35	0.88	1.75
❑12, Jun 97, surfing parody	1.75	0.35	0.88	1.75
❑13, Jul 97, Ali-Brain and the Forty Thieves	1.75	0.35	0.88	1.75
❑14, Aug 97, Brainlet	1.75	0.35	0.88	1.75
❑15, Sep 97, Bikers	1.75	0.35	0.88	1.75
❑16, Oct 97, Verminator 2	1.75	0.35	0.88	1.75
❑17, Nov 97, Pinkenstein	1.75	0.35	0.88	1.75
❑18, Dec 97, Braintech; Brinky 1/2, Manga parody	1.95	0.39	0.98	1.95
❑19, Jan 98, Brain plays Santa	1.95	0.39	0.98	1.95
❑20, Feb 98, Mice in Pink	1.95	0.39	0.98	1.95
❑21, Mar 98, Fantastic Voyage to the Bottom of the President's Brain; Acme Valley PTA	1.95	0.39	0.98	1.95
❑22, May 98, The Mouse in the Iron Mask	1.95	0.39	0.98	1.95
❑23, Jun 98, Jaws parody cover	1.95	0.39	0.98	1.95
❑24, Jul 98, El Cerebro; Pinky Mon Amour, Zorro parody	1.95	0.39	0.98	1.95
❑25, Aug 98, The Dark Pinky Returns	1.95	0.39	0.98	1.95
❑26, Oct 98, Demi Moore parody issue	1.99	0.39	0.98	1.95
❑27, Nov 98	1.99	0.40	1.00	1.99
❑HS 1, Jan 96, Giant-size	1.50	0.30	0.75	1.50

PINOCCHIO AND THE EMPEROR OF THE NIGHT
Marvel
Value: Cover or less

❑1, Mar 88, movie Adaptation 1.25

PINOCCHIO SPECIAL (WALT DISNEY'S...)
Gladstone

	ORIG	GOOD	FINE	N-MINT
❑1, Mar 90, WK	1.00	0.30	0.75	1.50

PINT-SIZED X-BABIES
Marvel
Value: Cover or less

❑1, Aug 98, V: Li'l Bad Guys, One-Shot; gatefold summary 2.99

PIPSQUEAK PAPERS (WALLACE WOOD'S...)
Fantagraphics
Value: Cover or less

❑1, b&w; adult 2.75

PIRACY (RCP)
EC
Value: Cover or less

❑1, Mar 98, AT; WW, WW (w); AW (w), The Privateer; The Mutineers, Reprint 2.50
❑2, Apr 98, AT; WW, WW (w); AW (w), Sea Food; Kismet, Reprint 2.50
❑3, May 98, BK; GE, BK (w); GE (w), Blackbeard; U-Boat, Reprint 2.50
❑4, Jun 98, BK; GE, BK (w); GE (w), Pirate Master; The King's Buccaneer (text story), Reprint 2.50
❑5, Jul 98, BK; GE, BK (w); GE (w), Jean Lafitte; Rag Doll, Reprint 2.50
❑6, Aug 98, GE, GE (w), Fit for a King; The Skipper, Reprint 2.50
❑7, Sep 98, BK; GE, BK (w); GE (w), Partners; Prologue (text) 2.50

PIRANHA IS LOOSE!
Special Studio
Value: Cover or less

❑1, b&w 2.75
❑2, b&w 2.75

PIRATE CORP$! (2ND SERIES)
Slave Labor

	ORIG	GOOD	FINE	N-MINT
❑1, Jun 89	1.75	0.50	1.25	2.50
❑1-2, Aug 93, 2nd Printing; has Fine Dairy Products ad on back cover	2.50	0.50	1.25	2.50
❑2, Sep 89	1.75	0.50	1.25	2.50
❑2-2, Feb 93, 2nd Printing; has Fine Dairy Products ad on back cover	2.50	0.50	1.25	2.50
❑3, Feb 91	2.50	0.50	1.25	2.50
❑3-2, Feb 93, 2nd Printing; has Fine Dairy Products ad on back cover	2.50	0.50	1.25	2.50
❑4, Apr 92	2.50	0.50	1.25	2.50
❑4-2, Sep 93, 2nd Printing; has Fine Dairy Products ad on back cover	2.50	0.50	1.25	2.50
❑5, Dec 92	2.50	0.50	1.25	2.50
❑5-2, Apr 94, 2nd Printing	2.50	0.50	1.25	2.50
❑SE 1, Mar 89, b&w; has Futurama ad on back cover	1.95	0.39	0.98	1.95
❑SE 1-2, Aug 93, 2nd Printing; has Fine Dairy Products ad on back cover	2.95	0.59	1.48	2.95

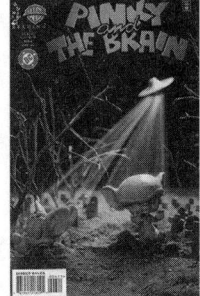

DC's *Pinky and the Brain* parodied all manner of pop-culture icons, including Ed Wood movies.

© 1996 DC Comics

PIRATE CORPS
Eternity

	ORIG	GOOD	FINE	N-MINT
❑1	1.95	0.50	1.25	2.50
❑2	1.95	0.50	1.25	2.50
❑3, Dec 87	1.95	0.50	1.25	2.50
❑4, Feb 88	1.95	0.50	1.25	2.50

PIRATE QUEEN, THE
Comax

	ORIG	GOOD	FINE	N-MINT
❑1, Lost City Of Gold, b&w; adult	2.95	0.60	1.50	3.00

PIRATES OF DARK WATER, THE
Marvel
Value: Cover or less

❑1, Nov 91 1.00
❑2, Dec 91 1.00
❑3, Jan 92 1.00
❑4, Feb 92 1.25
❑5, Mar 92 1.25
❑6, Apr 92 1.25
❑7, May 92 1.25
❑8, Jun 92 1.25
❑9, Jul 92, Final Issue 1.25

P.I.'S, THE: MICHAEL MAUSER AND MS. TREE
First

	ORIG	GOOD	FINE	N-MINT
❑1, Jan 85, JSa; MGr, The Odd Couple, Mike Hammer feature; Ms. Tree, E-Man	1.25	0.30	0.75	1.50
❑2, Mar 85, JSa	1.25	0.30	0.75	1.50
❑3, May 85, JSa	1.25	0.30	0.75	1.50

PISTOLERO
Eternity
Value: Cover or less

❑1, nn; b&w; One-Shot 3.95

PI: THE BOOK OF ANTS
Artisan Entertainment
Value: Cover or less

❑1, nn; b&w; based on movie 2.95

PITT
Image
Value: Cover or less

❑0.5, Lupe: A Nice Girl Like You 1.50
❑1, Jan 93, Fight & Flight!, 1: Pitt 1.95
❑1/GO, Jan 93, Gold edition 1.95
❑2, Jul 93, Dead Or Alive 1.95
❑3, Feb 94 1.95
❑4, Apr 94 1.95
❑5, Jun 94 1.95
❑6, Sep 94 1.95
❑7, Dec 94 1.95
❑8, Apr 94 1.95
❑9, Aug 95 1.95
❑10 1.95
❑11 1.95
❑12 1.95
❑13 1.95
❑14 2.50
❑15 2.50
❑16 2.50
❑17 2.50
❑18 2.50
❑19 2.50

PITT, THE
Marvel
Value: Cover or less

❑1, JBy; SB, JBy (w) 3.25

PIXY JUNKET
Viz
Value: Cover or less

❑1, b&w 2.75
❑2, b&w 2.75
❑3, b&w 2.75
❑4, b&w 2.75
❑5, b&w 2.75
❑6, b&w 2.75

P.J. WARLOCK
Eclipse
Value: Cover or less

❑1, Nov 86, b&w 2.00
❑2, Jan 87, b&w 2.00
❑3, b&w 2.00

PLACES THAT ARE GONE
Aeon
Value: Cover or less

❑1, Jul 94 2.75
❑2, Aug 94 2.75

PLAGUE
TOME PRESS

Value: Cover or less

- ❑1, b&w ... 2.95

PLAN 9 FROM OUTER SPACE: THIRTY YEARS LATER
ETERNITY

Value: Cover or less

- ❑1, Jan 91, b&w ... 2.50
- ❑2, b&w ... 2.50
- ❑3, b&w ... 2.50

PLANET 29
CALIBER

Value: Cover or less

- ❑1, b&w ... 2.50
- ❑2, b&w ... 2.50

PLANETARY
DC

Issue	ORIG	GOOD	FINE	N-MINT
❑1, Apr 99	2.50	0.60	1.50	3.00
❑2, May 99, Island	2.50	0.60	1.50	3.00
❑3, Jun 99, Dead Gunfighters	2.50	0.60	1.50	3.00
❑4, Jul 99, Strange Harbours	2.50	0.50	1.25	2.50
❑5, Sep 99, The Good Doctor	2.50	0.50	1.25	2.50
❑6, Nov 99	2.50	0.50	1.25	2.50
❑7, Jan 00, To be in England, in the Summertime	2.50	0.50	1.25	2.50
❑8, Feb 00	2.50	0.50	1.25	2.50
❑9, Apr 00	2.50	0.50	1.25	2.50
❑10	2.50	0.50	1.25	2.50
❑11, Sep 00, Cold World	2.50	0.50	1.25	2.50
❑12, Jan 01, Memory Cloud	2.50	0.50	1.25	2.50
❑13, Feb 01, Century	2.50	0.50	1.25	2.50
❑14, Jun 01, Zero Point	2.50	0.50	1.25	2.50

PLANET COMICS (A-LIST)
A-LIST

Value: Cover or less

- ❑1, Spr 97 ... 2.95
- ❑2, Fal 97, Flint Baker; Auro Lord of Jupiter ... 2.95

PLANET COMICS (BLACKTHORNE)
BLACKTHORNE

Value: Cover or less

- ❑1, Apr 88, DS (c), Hunt Bowman in The Lost World; Flamingo 2.00
- ❑2, Jun 88, Hunt Bowman of the Lost World; Flamingo ... 2.00
- ❑3, Aug 88 ... 2.00

PLANET OF GEEKS
STARHEAD

Value: Cover or less

- ❑1, b&w; adult ... 2.75

PLANET OF TERROR (BASIL WOLVERTON'S...)
DARK HORSE

Issue	ORIG	GOOD	FINE	N-MINT
❑1, Jul 87, BW, BW (w), Planet of Terror; End of the World	1.75	0.40	1.00	2.00

PLANET OF THE APES (ADVENTURE)
ADVENTURE

Issue	ORIG	GOOD	FINE	N-MINT
❑1, Apr 90, Beneath, extra cover in pink, yellow, or green	2.50	0.80	2.00	4.00
❑1/LE, Apr 90, Beneath, limited	5.00	0.80	2.00	4.00
❑1-2, Beneath, 2nd Printing	2.50	0.50	1.25	2.50
❑2, Jun 90, Escape!	3.50	0.60	1.50	3.00
❑3, Jul 90, Conquest	3.50	0.60	1.50	3.00
❑4, Aug 90	2.50	0.60	1.50	3.00
❑5, Sep 90, Loss	2.50	0.60	1.50	3.00
❑6, Oct 90, Welcome to Ape City	2.50	0.60	1.50	3.00
❑7, Nov 90	2.50	0.60	1.50	3.00
❑8, Dec 90, Christmas	2.50	0.60	1.50	3.00
❑9, Jan 91, Changes	2.50	0.60	1.50	3.00
❑10, Mar 91, Return to the Forbidden City	2.50	0.60	1.50	3.00
❑11, Apr 91, Warriors	2.50	0.50	1.25	2.50
❑12, May 91, Bells, Wedding of Alexander and Coure	2.50	0.50	1.25	2.50
❑13, Jun 91	2.50	0.50	1.25	2.50
❑14, Jul 91, Countdown Zero, Part 1	2.50	0.50	1.25	2.50
❑15, Aug 91, Countdown Zero, Part 2	2.50	0.50	1.25	2.50
❑16, Sep 91, Countdown Zero, Part 3	2.50	0.50	1.25	2.50
❑17, Oct 91, Countdown Zero, Part 4	2.50	0.50	1.25	2.50
❑18, Nov 91, Gorillas in the Mist	2.50	0.50	1.25	2.50
❑19, Dec 91, Quitting Time	2.50	0.50	1.25	2.50
❑20, Jan 92, Cowboys and Simians	2.50	0.50	1.25	2.50
❑21, Feb 92, The Terror Beneath	2.50	0.50	1.25	2.50
❑22, Apr 92, The Land of No Escape, sequel to Conquest of the Planet of the Apes	2.50	0.50	1.25	2.50
❑23, May 92, Final Conquest	2.50	0.50	1.25	2.50
❑24, Jul 92, Last Battle	2.50	0.50	1.25	2.50
❑Anl 1, A Day on the Planet of the Apes, b&w	3.50	0.70	1.75	3.50

PLANET OF THE APES (MARVEL)
MARVEL

Issue	ORIG	GOOD	FINE	N-MINT
❑1, Aug 74, Beneath, b&w; Special "split-cover"; magazine; adapts first movie plus new story	1.00	2.00	5.00	10.00
❑1-2, Beneath, 2nd Printing; No special cover	2.50	1.00	2.50	5.00
❑2, Oct 74, b&w; magazine; adapts first movie plus new story	1.00	1.00	2.50	5.00
❑3, Dec 74, b&w; magazine; adapts first movie plus new stories	1.00	1.00	2.50	5.00
❑4, Jan 75, b&w; magazine; adapts first movie plus new stories	1.00	1.00	2.50	5.00
❑5, Feb 75, b&w; magazine; adapts first movie plus new stories	1.00	1.00	2.50	5.00
❑6, Mar 75, b&w; magazine; concludes first movie adaptations plus new stories	1.00	1.00	2.50	5.00
❑7, Apr 75, Beneath the Planet of the Apes, b&w; magazine	1.00	0.80	2.00	4.00
❑8, May 75, Beneath the Planet of the Apes, b&w; magazine	1.00	0.80	2.00	4.00
❑9, Jun 75, Kingdom of the Apes; Beneath the Planet of the Apes, Part 3	1.00	0.80	2.00	4.00
❑10, Jul 75, Kingdom of the Apes; Beneath the Planet of the Apes, Part 4	1.00	0.80	2.00	4.00
❑11, Aug 75, Kingdom of the Apes; Beneath the Planet of the Apes, Part 5	1.00	0.80	2.00	4.00
❑12, Sep 75, Escape from the Planet of the Apes, Part 1	1.00	0.80	2.00	4.00
❑13, Aug 75, Escape from the Planet of the Apes, Part 2	1.00	0.80	2.00	4.00
❑14, Nov 75, Escape from the Planet of the Apes, Part 3	0.75	0.80	2.00	4.00
❑15, Dec 75, Escape from the Planet of the Apes, Part 4	0.75	0.80	2.00	4.00
❑16, Jan 76, Escape from the Planet of the Apes, Part 5, D: Cornelius; D: Zira	0.75	0.80	2.00	4.00
❑17, Feb 76, Conquest of the Planet of the Apes, Part 1	0.75	0.80	2.00	4.00
❑18, Mar 76, Conquest of the Planet of the Apes, Part 2	0.75	0.80	2.00	4.00
❑19, Apr 76, b&w; magazine	0.75	0.80	2.00	4.00
❑20, May 76, b&w; magazine	0.75	0.80	2.00	4.00
❑21, Jun 76, b&w; magazine	0.75	0.80	2.00	4.00
❑22, Jul 76, b&w; magazine	0.75	0.80	2.00	4.00
❑23, Aug 76, Battle for the Planet of the Apes, b&w; magazine	0.75	0.80	2.00	4.00
❑24, Sep 76, Battle for the Planet of the Apes, b&w; magazine	0.75	0.80	2.00	4.00
❑25, Oct 76, Battle for the Planet of the Apes, b&w; magazine	0.75	0.80	2.00	4.00
❑26, Nov 76, Battle for the Planet of the Apes, b&w; magazine	0.75	0.80	2.00	4.00
❑27, Dec 76, Battle for the Planet of the Apes, b&w; magazine	0.75	0.80	2.00	4.00
❑28, Jan 77, Battle for the Planet of the Apes, b&w; magazine	0.75	0.80	2.00	4.00
❑29, Feb 77, Battle for the Planet of the Apes, b&w; magazine	0.75	0.80	2.00	4.00
❑Anl 1	3.50	0.00	0.00	0.00

PLANET OF THE APES: BLOOD OF THE APES
ADVENTURE

Value: Cover or less

- ❑1, Nov 91, b&w ... 2.50
- ❑2, Dec 91, b&w ... 2.50
- ❑3, Jan 92, b&w ... 2.50
- ❑4, Feb 92, b&w ... 2.50

PLANET OF THE APES: FORBIDDEN ZONE
ADVENTURE

Value: Cover or less

- ❑1 ... 2.50
- ❑2 ... 2.50
- ❑3 ... 2.50
- ❑4 ... 2.50

PLANET OF THE APES: SINS OF THE FATHER
ADVENTURE

Value: Cover or less

- ❑1, Mar 92, b&w ... 2.50

PLANET OF THE APES: URCHAK'S FOLLY
ADVENTURE

Value: Cover or less

- ❑1, Jan 91, The Valley, b&w ... 2.50
- ❑2, Feb 91, The Bridge, b&w ... 2.50
- ❑3, Mar 91, The Savages, b&w ... 2.50
- ❑4, Apr 91, The War, b&w ... 2.50

PLANET OF VAMPIRES
ATLAS

Issue	ORIG	GOOD	FINE	N-MINT
❑1, Apr 75, PB, NA (c), The Long Road Home!	0.25	0.40	1.00	2.00
❑2, Jul 75, NA (c)	0.25	0.30	0.75	1.50
❑3, Jul 75	0.25	0.30	0.75	1.50

PLANET PATROL
EDGE

Value: Cover or less

- ❑1, Signal in Space; The Girl from Astroid Six ... 2.95

PLANET TERRY
MARVEL

Issue	ORIG	GOOD	FINE	N-MINT
❑1, Apr 84, The Search; A Clue, 1: Planet Terry	0.65	0.20	0.50	1.00
❑2, May 84	0.65	0.20	0.50	1.00
❑3	0.65	0.20	0.50	1.00
❑4	0.65	0.20	0.50	1.00
❑5	0.65	0.20	0.50	1.00
❑6	0.65	0.20	0.50	1.00
❑7	0.65	0.20	0.50	1.00
❑8	0.65	0.20	0.50	1.00
❑9	0.65	0.20	0.50	1.00
❑10	0.65	0.20	0.50	1.00

	ORIG	GOOD	FINE	N-MINT
❑11	0.65	0.20	0.50	1.00
❑12, Final Issue	0.65	0.20	0.50	1.00

PLANET-X
ETERNITY

Value: Cover or less
❑1, b&w ... 2.50

PLANET X REPRINT COMIC
PLANET X

	ORIG	GOOD	FINE	N-MINT
❑1, no cover price; reprints adaptation of The Man from Planet X	—	0.40	1.00	2.00

PLASM
DEFIANT

	ORIG	GOOD	FINE	N-MINT
❑0, bound in Diamond Previews	—	0.20	0.50	1.00

PLASMA BABY
CALIBER

Value: Cover or less
❑1, b&w ... 2.50
❑2, A: George Bush, b&w ... 2.50
❑3, b&w ... 2.50

PLASMER
MARVEL

Value: Cover or less
❑1, Nov 93, Within You...Without You!, 1: Plasmer, four trading cards ... 2.50
❑2, Dec 93 ... 1.95
❑3, Jan 94, Masters Of War! ... 1.95
❑4, Feb 94 ... 1.95

PLASTIC FORKS
MARVEL

Value: Cover or less
❑1, Trauma Humane ... 4.95
❑2, Gravity's Angel ... 4.95
❑3, Ritual Bride ... 4.95
❑4 ... 4.95
❑5 ... 4.95

PLASTIC LITTLE
CPM

Value: Cover or less
❑1, Aug 97, Prologue: Gentaro Koshigaya; Chapter 1, Tita Mu Koshigaya, 1: Roger Rogers; 1: Tita Mu Koshigaya; 1: Joshua Balboa; 1: Mei Lin Jones; O: Captain Tita Mu Koshigaya; 1: Tita Mu Koshigay, Laura Jackson and Yoko Kobayashi translation ... 2.95
❑2, Sep 97, Chapter 2, Joshua L. Balboa, 2: Roger Rogers; 2: Tita Mu Koshigaya; 2: Joshua Balboa; 2: Mei Lin Jones; 2: Joshua Balbo; 2: Mikail Diagleff, Laura Jackson and Yoko Kobayashi translation ... 2.95
❑3, Oct 97, Chapter 3, Mei Lin Jones, Laura Jackson and Yoko Kobayashi translation ... 2.95
❑4, Nov 97, Chapter 4, Roger Rogers, Laura Jackson and Yoko Kobayashi translation ... 2.95
❑5, Dec 97, Chapter 5, Mikail Diagleff, Laura Jackson and Yoko Kobayashi translation ... 2.95

PLASTIC MAN (DC)
DC

	ORIG	GOOD	FINE	N-MINT
❑1, Dec 66, GK, The Dirty Devices of Dr. Dome, O: Plastic Man	0.12	9.00	22.50	45.00
❑2, Feb 67	0.12	5.00	12.50	25.00
❑3, Apr 67, The Biggest Wheel In Town	0.12	4.00	10.00	20.00
❑4, Jun 67	0.12	4.00	10.00	20.00
❑5, Aug 67	0.12	4.00	10.00	20.00
❑6, Oct 67	0.12	2.80	7.00	14.00
❑7, Dec 67, Plastic Man's Fantastic Old Man!, A: Woozy Winks; A: Plas' father (Plastic Man 1)	0.12	2.80	7.00	14.00
❑8, Feb 68	0.12	2.80	7.00	14.00
❑9, Apr 68	0.12	2.80	7.00	14.00
❑10, Jun 68, series goes on hiatus until 1976	0.12	2.80	7.00	14.00
❑11, Mar 76, Series begins again: 1976	0.25	0.80	2.00	4.00
❑12, May 76	0.30	0.80	2.00	4.00
❑13, Jul 76	0.30	0.80	2.00	4.00
❑14, Sep 76	0.30	0.80	2.00	4.00
❑15, Nov 76	0.30	0.80	2.00	4.00
❑16, Mar 77	0.30	0.80	2.00	4.00
❑17, May 77	0.30	0.80	2.00	4.00
❑18, Jul 77	0.35	0.80	2.00	4.00
❑19, Sep 77	0.35	0.80	2.00	4.00
❑20, Nov 77, Final Issue	0.35	0.80	2.00	4.00

PLASTIC MAN (MINI-SERIES)
DC

	ORIG	GOOD	FINE	N-MINT
❑1, Nov 88, PF (w), O: Plastic Man	1.00	0.25	0.63	1.25
❑2, Dec 88, PF (w)	1.00	0.25	0.63	1.25
❑3, Jan 89, PF (w)	1.00	0.25	0.63	1.25
❑4, Feb 89, PF (w)	1.00	0.25	0.63	1.25

PLASTIC MAN SPECIAL
DC

Value: Cover or less
❑1, Aug 99, Plastic Fantastic; Plastic Facts, O: Woozy Winks ... 3.95

PLASTRON CAFÉ
MIRAGE

Value: Cover or less
❑1, Dec 92, North by Downeast; Old Times ... 2.25
❑2, Feb 93 ... 2.25
❑3, May 93, Alien Fire; North by Downeast ... 2.25
❑4, Jul 93, Spaced; North by Downeast Part IV ... 2.25

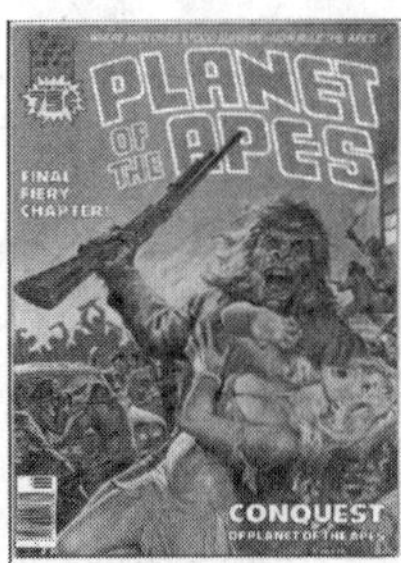

Marvel's black-and-white *Planet of the Apes* magazine adapted the second, third, and fourth Apes films.

© 1974 20th Century Fox Film Corporation (Marvel)

PLATINUM.44
COMAX

Value: Cover or less
❑1, b&w; adult ... 2.95

PLATINUM GRIT
DEAD NUMBAT

Value: Cover or less
❑1 ... 3.50
❑2 ... 3.50
❑3 ... 3.50
❑4 ... 3.50
❑5 ... 3.50
❑6, Throw That Old Thing Away Grandma; Spanky the Monkey: Spittin' Toothpaste ... 3.50

PLAYBEAR
FANTAGRAPHICS

Value: Cover or less
❑1 ... 2.95
❑2 ... 2.95
❑3, Aug 95, Lil & Jill ... 2.95

PLAYGROUND
CALIBER

Value: Cover or less
❑1, b&w ... 2.50

PLAYGROUNDS
FANTAGRAPHICS

Value: Cover or less
❑1, b&w ... 2.00

PLEASURE & PASSION (ALAZAR'S...)
BRAINSTORM

Value: Cover or less
❑1, Oct 97 ... 2.95

PLEASURE BOUND
EROS

Value: Cover or less
❑1, Feb 96 ... 2.95

PLOP!
DC

	ORIG	GOOD	FINE	N-MINT
❑1, Oct 73, BWr; SA, BW (c)	0.20	1.60	4.00	8.00
❑2, Dec 73, SA	0.20	1.20	3.00	6.00
❑3, Feb 74, SA, four-color	0.20	1.20	3.00	6.00
❑4, Apr 74, FR; BW; SA, Welcome to the Monster Convention; Now and Then	0.20	1.20	3.00	6.00
❑5, Jun 74, SA	0.20	1.20	3.00	6.00
❑6, Aug 74, SA	0.20	1.00	2.50	5.00
❑7, Oct 74, SA	0.20	1.00	2.50	5.00
❑8, Dec 74, SA	0.20	1.00	2.50	5.00
❑9, Feb 75, FR; BW; SA, Temple Of Ikka-Ka-Ka; Super Plops	0.25	1.00	2.50	5.00
❑10, Mar 75, BW; SA, JO (w), Androklutz and the Lion; A Change of Diet!	0.25	1.00	2.50	5.00
❑11, Apr 75, SA	0.25	0.80	2.00	4.00
❑12, May 75, SA	0.25	0.80	2.00	4.00
❑13, Jun 75, SA	0.25	0.80	2.00	4.00
❑14, Jul 75, SA	0.25	0.80	2.00	4.00
❑15, Aug 75, SA	0.25	0.80	2.00	4.00
❑16, Sep 75, SA	0.25	0.80	2.00	4.00
❑17, Oct 75, SA	0.25	0.80	2.00	4.00
❑18, Dec 75, SA	0.25	0.80	2.00	4.00
❑19, Feb 76, SA	0.25	0.80	2.00	4.00
❑20, Apr 76, SA	0.25	0.80	2.00	4.00
❑21, Jun 76, SA, Giant-size	0.50	1.20	3.00	6.00
❑22, Aug 76, SA, Giant-size	0.50	1.20	3.00	6.00
❑23, Oct 76, Giant-size; Wally Wood's Lord of the Rings parody	0.50	0.80	2.00	4.00
❑24, Dec 76, SA, Giant-size	0.50	1.20	3.00	6.00

POCAHONTAS (DISNEY'S...)
MARVEL

Value: Cover or less
❑1, Jul 95, movie Adaptation; prestige format one-shot ... 4.95

POE
CHEESE

	ORIG	GOOD	FINE	N-MINT
❑1, Sep 96	2.00	0.50	1.25	2.50
❑2, Oct 96	2.00	0.50	1.25	2.50
❑3, Nov 96	2.00	0.50	1.25	2.50
❑4, Dec 96, The Lords of Brass, Part 1	2.00	0.50	1.25	2.50
❑5, Feb 97, The Lords of Brass, Part 2	2.00	0.50	1.25	2.50
❑6, Apr 97, A Rough Night at Mad Meg's Tavern	2.00	0.50	1.25	2.50
❑7	2.50	0.50	1.25	2.50
❑8	2.50	0.50	1.25	2.50
❑9	2.50	0.50	1.25	2.50

	ORIG	GOOD	FINE	N-MINT
❑10	2.50	0.50	1.25	2.50
❑11	2.50	0.50	1.25	2.50

POE (VOL. 2)
SIRIUS
Value: Cover or less

- ❑1, Oct 97 ... 2.50
- ❑2, Nov 97 ... 2.50
- ❑3, Dec 97 ... 2.50
- ❑4, Jan 98 ... 2.50
- ❑5, Feb 98 ... 2.50
- ❑6, Mar 98 ... 2.50
- ❑7, May 98 ... 2.50
- ❑8, Jun 98 ... 2.50
- ❑9, Jul 98 ... 2.50
- ❑10, Aug 98 ... 2.50
- ❑11, Sep 98 ... 2.50
- ❑12, Oct 98 ... 2.50
- ❑13, Nov 98 ... 2.50
- ❑14, Jan 99 ... 2.50
- ❑15, Feb 99 ... 2.50
- ❑16, Mar 99 ... 2.50
- ❑17, Apr 99 ... 2.50
- ❑18, Aug 99 ... 2.50
- ❑19, The Balloon Hoax, A Tale of Science, Part 1 ... 2.50
- ❑20, The Balloon Hoax, A Tale of Science, Part 2; Mad Meg in Fire and Ice, Part 1 ... 2.50
- ❑21, Jan 00, The Balloon Hoax, A Tale of Science, Part 3; Mad Meg in Fire and Ice, Part 2 .. 2.95
- ❑22, Mar 00, The Balloon Hoax, A Tale of Science, Part 4; Mad Meg in Fire and Ice, Part 3 ... 2.95
- ❑23, May 00, The Balloon Hoax, A Tale of Science, Part 5; Mad Meg in Fire and Ice, Part 4 ... 2.95
- ❑24, Jul 00, The Balloon Hoax, A Tale of Science, Part 6; Mad Meg in Fire and Ice, Part 5 ... 2.95
- ❑SE 1, Dec 98, Color Special ... 2.95

POETS PROSPER: RHYME & REVELRY
TOME
Value: Cover or less

- ❑1 ... 3.50

POINT-BLANK
ECLIPSE
Value: Cover or less

- ❑1, b&w ... 2.95
- ❑2, b&w ... 2.95

POISON ELVES (MULEHIDE)
MULEHIDE

	ORIG	GOOD	FINE	N-MINT
❑8, magazine-sized; Series continued from I, Lusiphur #7	2.50	5.00	12.50	25.00
❑9, magazine-sized	2.50	4.40	11.00	22.00
❑10, magazine-sized	2.50	4.40	11.00	22.00
❑11	2.50	4.00	10.00	20.00
❑12, Oct 93	2.50	4.00	10.00	20.00
❑13, Dec 93, Desert of the Third Sin, Part 1	2.50	4.00	10.00	20.00
❑14, Feb 94, Desert of the Third Sin, Part 2	2.50	4.00	10.00	20.00
❑15, Apr 94, Scarcer	2.50	4.00	10.00	20.00
❑15-2	2.50	0.80	2.00	4.00
❑16, Jun 94	2.50	3.20	8.00	16.00
❑17	2.50	3.20	8.00	16.00
❑17-2	2.50	1.00	2.50	5.00
❑18	2.50	2.00	5.00	10.00
❑19	2.50	2.00	5.00	10.00
❑20, Final Issue	2.50	2.00	5.00	10.00

POISON ELVES (SIRIUS)
SIRIUS

	ORIG	GOOD	FINE	N-MINT
❑1, May 95	2.50	1.60	4.00	8.00
❑1-2, 2nd Printing	2.50	0.50	1.25	2.50
❑2, Jun 95	2.50	1.00	2.50	5.00
❑3, Jul 95	2.50	1.00	2.50	5.00
❑4, Aug 95	2.50	0.80	2.00	4.00
❑5	2.50	0.80	2.00	4.00
❑6	2.50	0.80	2.00	4.00
❑7	2.50	0.60	1.50	3.00
❑8	2.50	0.60	1.50	3.00
❑9	2.50	0.60	1.50	3.00
❑10	2.50	0.60	1.50	3.00
❑11	2.50	0.50	1.25	2.50
❑12	2.50	0.50	1.25	2.50
❑13, Desert Of The Third Sin, Part 1	2.50	0.50	1.25	2.50
❑14, Desert Of The Third Sin, Part 2	2.50	0.50	1.25	2.50
❑15	2.50	0.50	1.25	2.50
❑16	2.50	0.50	1.25	2.50
❑17	2.50	0.50	1.25	2.50
❑18	2.50	0.50	1.25	2.50
❑19	2.50	0.50	1.25	2.50
❑20	2.50	0.50	1.25	2.50
❑21	2.50	0.50	1.25	2.50
❑22	2.50	0.50	1.25	2.50
❑23	2.50	0.50	1.25	2.50
❑24	2.50	0.50	1.25	2.50
❑25	2.95	0.50	1.25	2.50
❑26	2.50	0.50	1.25	2.50
❑27	2.50	0.50	1.25	2.50
❑28	2.50	0.50	1.25	2.50
❑29	2.50	0.50	1.25	2.50
❑30	2.50	0.50	1.25	2.50
❑31	2.50	0.50	1.25	2.50
❑32	2.50	0.50	1.25	2.50
❑33	2.50	0.50	1.25	2.50
❑34	2.50	0.50	1.25	2.50
❑35	2.50	0.50	1.25	2.50
❑36	2.50	0.50	1.25	2.50
❑37	2.50	0.50	1.25	2.50
❑38	2.50	0.50	1.25	2.50
❑39	2.50	0.50	1.25	2.50
❑40	2.50	0.50	1.25	2.50
❑41	2.50	0.50	1.25	2.50
❑42	2.50	0.50	1.25	2.50
❑43	2.50	0.50	1.25	2.50
❑44	2.50	0.50	1.25	2.50
❑45	2.50	0.50	1.25	2.50
❑46	2.95	0.59	1.48	2.95
❑47	2.50	0.50	1.25	2.50
❑48	2.50	0.50	1.25	2.50
❑49	2.50	0.50	1.25	2.50
❑50	2.50	0.50	1.25	2.50
❑51	2.50	0.50	1.25	2.50
❑52	2.50	0.50	1.25	2.50
❑53	2.95	0.59	1.48	2.95
❑54	2.95	0.59	1.48	2.95
❑55	2.95	0.59	1.48	2.95
❑56	2.95	0.59	1.48	2.95
❑57	2.95	0.59	1.48	2.95
❑58	2.95	0.59	1.48	2.95
❑59	2.95	0.59	1.48	2.95
❑60	2.95	0.59	1.48	2.95
❑61, All the Beautiful People or: Bad Doin's at Knuckledown Lonesome	2.95	0.59	1.48	2.95
❑62, The Hunt	2.95	0.59	1.48	2.95
❑63	2.95	0.59	1.48	2.95
❑64	2.95	0.59	1.48	2.95
❑65	2.95	0.59	1.48	2.95
❑66	2.95	0.59	1.48	2.95
❑SE 1, Dec 98, Color Special	2.95	0.60	1.50	3.00

POIZON
LONDON NIGHT
Value: Cover or less

- ❑0 ... 3.00
- ❑0/Nude ... —
- ❑0.5 ... 3.00
- ❑1, Feb 96 ... 3.00
- ❑1/A, COA; Green Death edition ... 15.00
- ❑1/Nude ... 5.95
- ❑2, Apr 96, Lost Child ... 3.00
- ❑3, Jun 96 ... 3.00

POKÉMON ADVENTURES
VIZ
Value: Cover or less

- ❑1, Mysterious Mew, Mysterious Mew ... 5.95
- ❑2, Wanted: Pikachu, Wanted: Pikachu ... 5.95
- ❑3 ... 5.95
- ❑4 ... 5.95
- ❑5, The Gastly Ghosts ... 5.95

POKÉMON PART 2
VIZ
Value: Cover or less

- ❑1, Pikachu Shocks Back ... 3.25
- ❑2 ... 3.25
- ❑3 ... 3.25
- ❑4 ... 2.95

POKÉMON PART 3
VIZ
Value: Cover or less

- ❑1 ... 3.50
- ❑2 ... 3.50
- ❑3 ... 3.50
- ❑4 ... 3.50

POKÉMON: THE ELECTRIC TALE OF PIKACHU
VIZ

	ORIG	GOOD	FINE	N-MINT
❑1, Feb 09, Pikachu, I See You!, 1: Pikachu	3.25	0.70	1.75	3.50
❑1-2, 2nd Printing	3.25	0.65	1.63	3.25
❑, 3rd Printing	3.25	0.65	1.63	3.25
❑2	3.25	0.65	1.63	3.25
❑2-2, 2nd Printing	3.25	0.65	1.63	3.25
❑3	3.25	0.65	1.63	3.25
❑4	3.25	0.65	1.63	3.25

POLICE ACADEMY
MARVEL
Value: Cover or less

- ❑1 ... 1.00
- ❑2, Nov 89, The Beast from 2 1/2 Fathoms; The Cookoo Commandant ... 1.00
- ❑3 ... 1.00
- ❑4 ... 1.00
- ❑5 ... 1.00
- ❑6 ... 1.00

POLICE ACTION (2ND SERIES)
ATLAS

	ORIG	GOOD	FINE	N-MINT
❑1, Feb 75	0.25	0.40	1.00	2.00
❑2, Apr 75	0.25	0.30	0.75	1.50
❑3, Jun 75	0.25	0.30	0.75	1.50

POLIS
BRAVE NEW WORDS
Value: Cover or less

- ❑1, b&w ... 2.50
- ❑2, b&w ... 2.50

ORIG GOOD FINE N-MINT

POLLY AND HER PALS
ETERNITY
Value: Cover or less

- ❑1, Oct 90, b&w; strip reprints 2.95
- ❑2, b&w; strip reprints 2.95
- ❑3, b&w; strip reprints 2.95
- ❑4, b&w; strip reprints 2.95
- ❑5, b&w; strip reprints 2.95

POOT
FANTAGRAPHICS
Value: Cover or less

- ❑1, Win 97 2.95
- ❑2, Spr 98 2.95
- ❑3, Sum 98 2.95
- ❑4, Win 98 3.95

POPCORN!
DISCOVERY
Value: Cover or less

- ❑1, nn; b&w; cardstock cover 3.95

POPCORN PIMPS
FANTAGRAPHICS
Value: Cover or less

- ❑1, Jun 96, nn; b&w; squarebound 8.95

POPEYE (HARVEY)
HARVEY
Value: Cover or less

- ❑1 1.50
- ❑2 1.50
- ❑3 1.50
- ❑4 1.50
- ❑5 1.50
- ❑6, Jul 94 1.50
- ❑Smr 1 2.25

POPEYE SPECIAL
OCEAN

	ORIG	GOOD	FINE	N-MINT
❑1, Sum 87, Borned to the Sea, O: Popeye	1.75	0.40	1.00	2.00
❑2, Sep 88, Double Trouble Down Under	2.00	0.40	1.00	2.00

POP LIFE
FANTAGRAPHICS
Value: Cover or less

- ❑1, Oct 98, Naked Girls, Part 1; Park Life 3.95
- ❑2, Mar 99 3.95

POPPLES
MARVEL

	ORIG	GOOD	FINE	N-MINT
❑1, Dec 86, Pop Goes the Spy	0.75	0.20	0.50	1.00
❑2	0.75	0.20	0.50	1.00
❑3	0.75	0.20	0.50	1.00
❑4	1.00	0.20	0.50	1.00

PORK KNIGHT: THIS LITTLE PIGGY
SILVER SNAIL

	ORIG	GOOD	FINE	N-MINT
❑1, Pork Knight	1.70	0.40	1.00	2.00

PORNOTOPIA
RADIO
Value: Cover or less

- ❑1, Aug 99 2.95

PORT
SILVERWOLF
Value: Cover or less

- ❑1, The Egg, b&w 1.50
- ❑2, b&w 1.50

PORTABLE LOWLIFE
AEON
Value: Cover or less

- ❑1, Jul 93, nn; prestige format 4.95

PORTALS OF ELONDAR
STORYBOOK PRESS
Value: Cover or less

- ❑1, Jul 96, b&w 2.95

PORTIA PRINZ OF THE GLAMAZONS
ECLIPSE
Value: Cover or less

- ❑1, Dec 86, b&w 2.00
- ❑2, Feb 87, b&w 2.00
- ❑3, Apr 87, b&w 2.00
- ❑4, Jun 87, b&w 2.00
- ❑5, Aug 87, b&w 2.00
- ❑6, Oct 87, b&w 2.00

PORTRAIT OF A YOUNG MAN AS A CARTOONIST
HAMMER & ANVIL PRESS
Value: Cover or less

- ❑1, Oct 96 2.95
- ❑2, Dec 96 2.95
- ❑3, Feb 97 2.95
- ❑4, Apr 97 2.95
- ❑5, Jun 97 2.95
- ❑6, Aug 97 2.95
- ❑7, Oct 97 2.95
- ❑8, Jan 98 2.95

POSSIBLEMAN
BLACKTHORNE
Value: Cover or less

- ❑1, Jan 87, Revenge of the Zit Queen 1.75
- ❑2, Apr 87, Possibleman Met the Tapioca Terror 1.75

POST APOCALYPSE
SLAVE LABOR
Value: Cover or less

- ❑1, Dec 94 2.95

POST BROTHERS
RIP OFF

	ORIG	GOOD	FINE	N-MINT
❑19, Apr 91, b&w; Series continued from Those Annoying Post Brothers #18	2.00	0.50	1.25	2.50
❑20, Jun 91, b&w	2.50	0.50	1.25	2.50
❑21, Aug 91, b&w	2.50	0.50	1.25	2.50
❑22, Oct 91, b&w	2.50	0.50	1.25	2.50
❑23, Oct 91, b&w	2.50	0.50	1.25	2.50

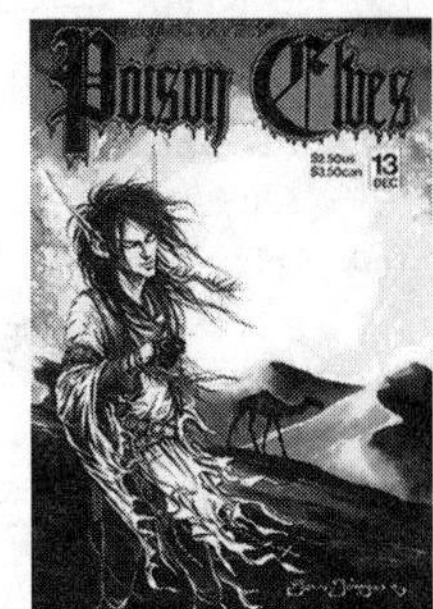

Drew Hayes changed the name of *I, Lusiphur* to *Poison Elves* with #8.

© 1993 Drew Hayes (Mulehide)

	ORIG	GOOD	FINE	N-MINT
❑24, Dec 91, b&w	2.50	0.50	1.25	2.50
❑25, Feb 92, b&w	2.50	0.50	1.25	2.50
❑26, Apr 92, b&w	2.50	0.50	1.25	2.50
❑27, Jun 92, b&w	2.50	0.50	1.25	2.50
❑28, Aug 92, b&w	2.50	0.50	1.25	2.50
❑29, Oct 92, b&w	2.50	0.50	1.25	2.50
❑30, Dec 92, b&w	2.50	0.50	1.25	2.50
❑31, Feb 93, b&w	2.50	0.50	1.25	2.50
❑32, Apr 93, b&w	2.50	0.50	1.25	2.50
❑33, Jun 93, Distorion for All, b&w; Listed as "Those Annoying Post Brothers"	2.50	0.50	1.25	2.50
❑34, Aug 93, b&w	2.50	0.50	1.25	2.50
❑35, Oct 93, b&w	2.50	0.50	1.25	2.50
❑36, Dec 93, b&w	2.50	0.50	1.25	2.50
❑37, Feb 94, b&w	2.50	0.50	1.25	2.50
❑38, Apr 94, b&w; series continues as Those Annoying Post Bros.	2.50	0.50	1.25	2.50

POTENTIAL
SLAVE LABOR
Value: Cover or less

- ❑1, Mar 98, Unit One: The Cell, b&w; magazine-sized 3.50
- ❑2 3.50
- ❑3, Sep 98, Unit Three: Mechanisms of Evolution 4.95
- ❑4, Feb 99, Unit Four: Plants Form and Function 3.50

POUND, THE
RADIO COMIX
Value: Cover or less

- ❑1, Mar 00, b&w 2.95

POWDER BURN
ANTARCTIC
Value: Cover or less

- ❑1, Mar 99, b&w 2.99
- ❑1/A, Mar 99, b&w; wraparound cover 2.99
- ❑1/CS, Mar 99, poster; Collector's Set 5.99

POWER, THE
AIRCEL
Value: Cover or less

- ❑1, Mar 91, The Power, Part 1; the Power, b&w 2.25
- ❑2, Apr 91, The Power, Part 2, b&w 2.25
- ❑3, May 91, The Power, Part 3, b&w 2.25
- ❑4, Jun 91, The Power, Part 4, b&w 2.25

POWER & GLORY
BRAVURA

	ORIG	GOOD	FINE	N-MINT
❑1LE, serigraph cover	—	0.60	1.50	3.00
❑1/A, Feb 94, HC, HC (w), Alternate cover (marked); Bravura Gold Stamp coupon	2.50	0.50	1.25	2.50
❑1/B, Feb 94, HC, HC (w), Alternate cover (marked); Bravura Gold Stamp coupon	2.50	0.50	1.25	2.50
❑1/LE, serigraph cover	—	0.50	1.25	2.50
❑1/SC, blue foil	—	0.60	1.50	3.00
❑2, Mar 94, HC, HC (w), Bravura Gold Stamp coupon	2.50	0.50	1.25	2.50
❑3, Apr 94, HC, HC (w), Bravura Gold Stamp coupon	2.50	0.50	1.25	2.50
❑4, May 94, HC, HC (w), Bravura Gold Stamp coupon	2.50	0.50	1.25	2.50
❑WS 1, Dec 94, HC, HC (w), Giant-size; Winter Special #1	2.95	0.59	1.48	2.95

POWER BRIGADE
MOVING TARGET
Value: Cover or less

- ❑1 1.75

POWER COMICS (ECLIPSE)
ECLIPSE
Value: Cover or less

- ❑1, Mar 88, BB; DaG, Powerbolt; Invasion of the Robots, b&w 2.00
- ❑2, May 88, BB; DaG, The All-Africa Wrestling Championship; The return of Dr. Crime, b&w 2.00
- ❑3, Jul 88, BB; DaG, b&w 2.00
- ❑4, Sep 88, BB; DaG, b&w 2.00

POWER COMICS (POWER)
POWER
Value: Cover or less

- ❑1, Aug 77, O: Nightwitch, 1st Dave Sim aardvark; 1st Dave Sims aardvark 2.00
- ❑1-2, 2nd Printing 2.00

- ❑2, Sep 77, MGu, 1: Cobalt Blue 2.00
- ❑3, Oct 77, Who Serves the Gentle Lady? 2.00
- ❑4, Nov 77 .... 2.00
- ❑5, Dec 77, MGu 2.00

POWER DEFENSE
Miller

Value: Cover or less

- ❑1, b&w 2.50

POWER FACTOR (1ST SERIES)
Wonder

Value: Cover or less

- ❑1, May 86, Wonder Color Publisher 1.95
- ❑2, Jun 86, Pied Piper Publisher 1.95

POWER FACTOR (2ND SERIES)
Innovation

Value: Cover or less

- ❑1, Oct 90, A Factor of One 1.95
- ❑2, Dec 90 .... 2.25
- ❑3, Feb 91 .... 2.25
- ❑SE 1, Jan 91, Who Runs This Town, Anyway? 2.75

POWER GIRL
DC

Value: Cover or less

- ❑1, Jun 88, Threads! 1.00
- ❑2, Jul 88 .... 1.00
- ❑3, Aug 88 .... 1.00
- ❑4, Sep 88 .... 1.00

POWER LINE
Marvel

	ORIG	GOOD	FINE	N-MINT
❑1, May 88	1.25	0.30	0.75	1.50
❑2, Jul 88	1.25	0.30	0.75	1.50
❑3, Sep 88	1.25	0.30	0.75	1.50
❑4, Nov 88	1.50	0.30	0.75	1.50
❑5, Jan 89	1.50	0.30	0.75	1.50
❑6, Mar 89	1.50	0.30	0.75	1.50
❑7, May 89, GM, Hidden Cargo	1.50	0.30	0.75	1.50
❑8, Jul 89	1.50	0.30	0.75	1.50

POWER LORDS
DC

Value: Cover or less

- ❑1, Dec 83, To The Victor...The Universe!, 1: Power Lords... 1.00
- ❑2, Jan 84, The Dimension Of Doom! 1.00
- ❑3, Feb 85, All Hail Arkus, Lord Of The Universe 1.00

POWER MAN & IRON FIST
Marvel

	ORIG	GOOD	FINE	N-MINT
❑17, Feb 74, GT, A: Iron Man, Title continued from "Hero For Hire"	0.20	1.00	2.50	5.00
❑18, Apr 74	0.20	0.60	1.50	3.00
❑19, Jun 74	0.25	0.60	1.50	3.00
❑20, Aug 74	0.25	0.60	1.50	3.00
❑21, Oct 74, V: Power Man	0.25	0.50	1.25	2.50
❑22, Dec 74	0.25	0.50	1.25	2.50
❑23, Feb 75	0.25	0.50	1.25	2.50
❑24, Apr 75, V: Circus of Crime; 1: Black Goliath	0.25	0.50	1.25	2.50
❑25, Jun 75, V: Circus of Crime	0.25	0.50	1.25	2.50
❑26, Aug 75	0.25	0.50	1.25	2.50
❑27, Oct 75, GP	0.25	0.50	1.25	2.50
❑28, Dec 75	0.25	0.50	1.25	2.50
❑29, Feb 76	0.25	0.50	1.25	2.50
❑30, Apr 76	0.25	0.50	1.25	2.50
❑31, May 76, NA	0.25	0.50	1.25	2.50
❑32, Jun 76	0.25	0.40	1.00	2.00
❑33, Jul 76	0.25	0.40	1.00	2.00
❑34, Aug 76	0.25	0.40	1.00	2.00
❑35, Sep 76	0.30	0.40	1.00	2.00
❑36, Oct 76	0.30	0.40	1.00	2.00
❑37, Nov 76, 1: Chemistro II (Archibald "Arch" Morton)	0.30	0.40	1.00	2.00
❑38, Dec 76	0.30	0.40	1.00	2.00
❑39, Jan 77	0.30	0.40	1.00	2.00
❑40, Feb 77	0.30	0.40	1.00	2.00
❑41, Mar 77, 1: Thunderbolt (William Carver as...)	0.30	0.40	1.00	2.00
❑42, Apr 77	0.30	0.40	1.00	2.00
❑43, May 77	0.30	0.40	1.00	2.00
❑44, Jun 77	0.30	0.40	1.00	2.00
❑45, Jul 77, JSn, A: Mace	0.30	0.40	1.00	2.00
❑46, Aug 77, GT, 1: Zzax	0.30	0.40	1.00	2.00
❑47, Oct 77, A: Iron Fist	0.30	0.40	1.00	2.00
❑48, Dec 77, JBy, 1: Power Man and Iron Fist	0.35	0.40	1.00	2.00
❑49, Feb 78, JBy, A: Iron Fist, series continues as Power Man & Iron Fist	0.35	0.40	1.00	2.00
❑50, Apr 78, JBy	0.35	0.40	1.00	2.00
❑51, Jun 78	0.35	0.30	0.75	1.50
❑52, Aug 78	0.35	0.30	0.75	1.50
❑53, Oct 78, O: Nightshade	0.35	0.30	0.75	1.50
❑54, Dec 78, O: Iron Fist	0.35	0.30	0.75	1.50
❑55, Feb 79	0.35	0.30	0.75	1.50
❑56, Apr 79, 1: Señor Suerte II (Jaime Garcia)	0.35	0.30	0.75	1.50
❑57, Jun 79, A: X-Men	0.40	0.50	1.25	2.50
❑58, Aug 79, 1: El Aguila	0.40	0.30	0.75	1.50
❑59, Oct 79, BL	0.40	0.30	0.75	1.50
❑60, Dec 79, BL	0.40	0.30	0.75	1.50
❑61, Feb 80, BL	0.40	0.20	0.50	1.00
❑62, Apr 80, BL, D: Thunderbolt	0.40	0.20	0.50	1.00
❑63, Jun 80, BL	0.40	0.20	0.50	1.00
❑64, Aug 80, BL	0.40	0.20	0.50	1.00
❑65, Oct 80, BL, V: El Aguila	0.50	0.20	0.50	1.00
❑66, Dec 80, FM (c), 2: Sabretooth; 2: Sabretooth	0.50	2.40	6.00	12.00
❑67, Feb 81	0.50	0.20	0.50	1.00
❑68, Apr 81, FM, FM (c)	0.50	0.20	0.50	1.00
❑69, May 81	0.50	0.20	0.50	1.00
❑70, Jun 81, FM (c), O: Colleen Wing	0.50	0.20	0.50	1.00
❑71, Jul 81, FM (c)	0.50	0.20	0.50	1.00
❑72, Aug 81, FM (c)	0.50	0.20	0.50	1.00
❑73, Sep 81, FM (c), A: ROM	0.50	0.20	0.50	1.00
❑74, Oct 81, FM (c)	0.50	0.20	0.50	1.00
❑75, Nov 81, origins	0.75	0.20	0.50	1.00
❑76, Dec 81, FM	0.50	0.20	0.50	1.00
❑77, Jan 82, A: Daredevil	0.60	0.20	0.50	1.00
❑78, Feb 82, V: El Aguila; A: Sabretooth	0.60	1.20	3.00	6.00
❑79, Mar 82	0.60	0.20	0.50	1.00
❑80, Apr 82, V: Montenegro	0.60	0.20	0.50	1.00
❑81, May 82	0.60	0.20	0.50	1.00
❑82, Jun 82	0.60	0.20	0.50	1.00
❑83, Jul 82	0.60	0.20	0.50	1.00
❑84, Aug 82, A: Sabretooth	0.60	1.00	2.50	5.00
❑85, Sep 82	0.60	0.20	0.50	1.00
❑86, Oct 82, A: Moon Knight	0.60	0.20	0.50	1.00
❑87, Nov 82, A: Moon Knight	0.60	0.20	0.50	1.00
❑88, Dec 82	0.60	0.20	0.50	1.00
❑89, Jan 83	0.60	0.20	0.50	1.00
❑90, Feb 83, KB (w), V: Unus; A: Unus the Untouchable	0.60	0.20	0.50	1.00
❑91, Mar 83	0.60	0.20	0.50	1.00
❑92, Apr 83, KB (w), V: Hammerhead; 1: Eel II (Edward Lavell)	0.60	0.20	0.50	1.00
❑93, May 83, KB (w), V: Chemistro	0.60	0.20	0.50	1.00
❑94, Jun 83, KB (w), 1: Chemistro III (Calvin Carr)	0.60	0.20	0.50	1.00
❑95, Jul 83, KB (w)	0.60	0.20	0.50	1.00
❑96, Aug 83, KB (w), V: Chemistro	0.60	0.20	0.50	1.00
❑97, Sep 83, KB (w), V: Fera	0.60	0.20	0.50	1.00
❑98, Oct 83, KB (w)	0.60	0.20	0.50	1.00
❑99, Nov 83, KB (w), V: Fera	0.60	0.20	0.50	1.00
❑100, Dec 83, KB (w), V: Khan, Giant-size	1.00	0.20	0.50	1.00
❑101, Jan 84	0.60	0.20	0.50	1.00
❑102, Feb 84, KB (w)	0.60	0.20	0.50	1.00
❑103, Mar 84	0.60	0.20	0.50	1.00
❑104, Apr 84	0.60	0.20	0.50	1.00
❑105, May 84, KB (w)	0.60	0.20	0.50	1.00
❑106, Jun 84	0.60	0.20	0.50	1.00
❑107, Jul 84	0.60	0.20	0.50	1.00
❑108, Aug 84	0.60	0.20	0.50	1.00
❑109, Sep 84, V: Reaper	0.60	0.20	0.50	1.00
❑110, Oct 84	0.60	0.20	0.50	1.00
❑111, Nov 84	0.60	0.20	0.50	1.00
❑112, Dec 84	0.60	0.20	0.50	1.00
❑113, Jan 85, D: Solarr	0.60	0.20	0.50	1.00
❑114, Feb 85	0.60	0.20	0.50	1.00
❑115, Mar 85	0.60	0.20	0.50	1.00
❑116, Apr 85	0.65	0.20	0.50	1.00
❑117, May 85	0.65	0.20	0.50	1.00
❑118, Jul 85	0.65	0.20	0.50	1.00
❑119, Sep 85	0.65	0.20	0.50	1.00
❑120, Nov 85	0.65	0.20	0.50	1.00
❑121, Jan 86, Secret Wars II	0.65	0.20	0.50	1.00
❑122, Mar 86	0.75	0.20	0.50	1.00
❑123, May 86	0.75	0.20	0.50	1.00
❑124, Jul 86	0.75	0.20	0.50	1.00
❑125, Sep 86, D: Iron Fist (H'yithri double)	1.25	0.50	1.25	2.50
❑Anl 1	0.50	0.70	1.75	3.50
❑GS 1	0.50	0.80	2.00	4.00

POWER OF PRIME
Malibu

Value: Cover or less

- ❑1, Jul 95, Primal Mysteries, O: Prime, story continues in Prime #25 and #26 .... 2.50
- ❑2, Aug 95, O: Prime 2.50
- ❑3, Sep 95, O: Prime 2.50
- ❑4, Nov 95, O: Prime 2.50

POWER OF SHAZAM, THE
DC

	ORIG	GOOD	FINE	N-MINT
❑1, Mar 95, JOy (w), Things Change	1.50	0.60	1.50	3.00
❑2, Apr 95, JOy (w), V: Arson Fiend	1.50	0.40	1.00	2.00
❑3, May 95, JOy (w)	1.75	0.40	1.00	2.00
❑4, Jun 95, JOy (w), Family Values, Return of Mary Marvel, Tawky Tawny	1.75	0.40	1.00	2.00

	ORIG	GOOD	FINE	N-MINT
❑5, Jul 95, JOy (w)	1.75	0.40	1.00	2.00
❑6, Aug 95, JOy (w), Return of Captain Nazi; Freddy Freeman and grandfather injured	1.75	0.40	1.00	2.00
❑7, Sep 95, JOy (w), Return of Captain Marvel Jr.	1.75	0.40	1.00	2.00
❑8, Oct 95, CS, JOy (w), A: Spy Smasher; A: Bulletman; A: Minuteman	1.75	0.40	1.00	2.00
❑9, Nov 95, JOy (w)	1.75	0.40	1.00	2.00
❑10, Dec 95, JOy (w), O: Shazam; O: Rock of Eternity; O: Black Adam; O: Blaze; O: Satanus	1.75	0.40	1.00	2.00
❑11, Jan 96, JOy (w), A: Bulletman, Return of Ibis; Return of Uncle Marvel; Return of Marvel Family; Return of Ibis, Uncle Marvel, Marvel Family	1.75	0.35	0.88	1.75
❑12, Feb 96, JOy (w), End Game, O: Seven Deadly Foes of Man	1.75	0.35	0.88	1.75
❑13, Mar 96, JOy (w), The Worm Turns	1.75	0.35	0.88	1.75
❑14, Apr 96, GK, JOy (w), Chain Lightning, 1: Chain Lightning, Captain Marvel Jr. solo story	1.75	0.35	0.88	1.75
❑15, Jun 96, JOy (w)	1.75	0.35	0.88	1.75
❑16, Jul 96, JOy (w)	1.75	0.35	0.88	1.75
❑17, Aug 96, JOy (w)	1.75	0.35	0.88	1.75
❑18, Sep 96, JOy (w)	1.75	0.35	0.88	1.75
❑19, Oct 96, JSa; GK, JOy (w), The Wall, A: Minuteman, Captain Marvel Jr. vs. Captain Nazi	1.75	0.35	0.88	1.75
❑20, Nov 96, JOy (w), Shelter from the Storm, A: Superman, Final Night	1.75	0.35	0.88	1.75
❑21, Dec 96, JOy (w), The Big Rubout!, A: Plastic Man	1.75	0.35	0.88	1.75
❑22, Jan 97, JOy (w), Of Shadows and Fog..., A: Batman	1.75	0.35	0.88	1.75
❑23, Feb 97, JOy (w), Child of the Atom, V: Mr. Atom	1.75	0.35	0.88	1.75
❑24, Mar 97, JOy (w), The Trail of the Scorpion, A: Spy Smasher; A: Baron Blitzkrieg; A: C.C. Batson	1.75	0.35	0.88	1.75
❑25, Apr 97, V: Ibac, C.C. Batson as Captain Marvel	1.75	0.35	0.88	1.75
❑26, May 97, Shazam attempts to set time right again	1.75	0.35	0.88	1.75
❑27, Jun 97, A: Waverider, time is restored to proper course	1.75	0.35	0.88	1.75
❑28, Jul 97	1.75	0.35	0.88	1.75
❑29, Aug 97, A: Hoppy the Marvel Bunny	1.75	0.35	0.88	1.75
❑30, Sep 97, V: Mr. Finish, Mary receives new costume	1.75	0.35	0.88	1.75
❑31, Oct 97, Genesis; Billy and Mary reveal their identities to the Bromfields	1.75	0.39	0.98	1.95
❑32, Nov 97, 1: Windshear	1.95	0.39	0.98	1.95
❑33, Dec 97, JOy (w), Face cover	1.95	0.39	0.98	1.95
❑34, Jan 98, JOy (w), With Friends Like These..., A: Gangbuster	1.95	0.39	0.98	1.95
❑35, Feb 98, Lightning and Stars, Part 2, A: Starman, continues in Starman #40	1.95	0.39	0.98	1.95
❑36, Mar 98, Lightning and Stars, Part 4, A: Starman	1.95	0.39	0.98	1.95
❑37, Apr 98, JOy (w), CM3, CM3 vs. Doctor Morpheus; CM3 vs. Dr. Morpheus	1.95	0.39	0.98	1.95
❑38, May 98, The Monster Society of Evil!, Part 1	1.95	0.39	0.98	1.95
❑39, Jun 98, The Monster Society of Evil!, Part 2	1.95	0.39	0.98	1.95
❑40, Jul 98, The Monster Society of Evil!, Part 3	1.95	0.39	0.98	1.95
❑41, Aug 98, The Monster Society of Evil!, Part 4, D: Mr. Mind	1.95	0.39	0.98	1.95
❑42, Sep 98, A: Chain Lightning	2.50	0.39	0.98	1.95
❑43, Oct 98, kids on life support	2.50	0.50	1.25	2.50
❑44, Dec 98, A: Thunder; A: Black Adam	2.50	0.50	1.25	2.50
❑45, Jan 99, A: Justice League of America	2.50	0.50	1.25	2.50
❑46, Feb 99, JOy, JOy (w), A: Black Adam; V: Superman	2.50	0.50	1.25	2.50
❑47, Mar 99, JOy, JOy (w), A: Black Adam, Final Issue	2.50	0.50	1.25	2.50
❑1000000, Nov 98, JOy, JOy (w), Between the Rock and a Hot Place	2.50	0.50	1.25	2.50
❑Anl 1, JOy (w), Legends of the Dead Earth; True Believers, 1996; Legends of the Dead Earth	2.95	0.59	1.48	2.95

POWER OF STRONG MAN
AC

Value: Cover or less ❑1, b&w; Reprint ... 2.50

POWER OF THE ATOM
DC

Value: Cover or less

	ORIG		ORIG
❑1, Aug 88, Home Is The Hero	1.00	❑5, Dec 88, A: Elongated Man	1.00
❑2, Sep 88	1.00	❑6, Win 88, V: Chronos	1.00
❑3, Oct 88, V: Strobe	1.00	❑7, Hol 88, Invasion!	1.00
❑4, Nov 88, Bonus Book #8	1.00	❑8, Jan 89, Invasion!	1.00

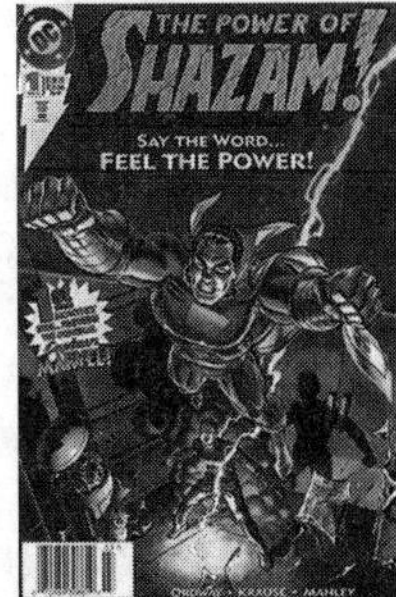

Jerry Ordway paid homage to Captain Marvel's history when he revamped The Big Red Cheese and his supporting cast with new adventures beginning in 1995.

	ORIG		ORIG
❑9, Feb 89, A: Justice League International	1.00	❑14, Jul 89, V: Humbug	1.00
❑10, Mar 89, V: Humbug	1.00	❑15, Aug 89	1.00
❑11, Apr 89	1.00	❑16, Sep 89	1.00
❑12, May 89	1.00	❑17, Oct 89	1.00
❑13, Jun 89	1.00	❑18, Nov 89	1.00

POWER PACHYDERMS
MARVEL

Value: Cover or less ❑1, one-shot parody ... 1.25

POWER PACK
MARVEL

	ORIG	GOOD	FINE	N-MINT
❑1, Aug 84, 1: Lightspeed; 1: Power Pack; 1: Mass Master; O: of; V: Snarks, Giant-size	1.00	0.40	1.00	2.00
❑2, Sep 84	0.60	0.30	0.75	1.50
❑3, Oct 84	0.60	0.20	0.50	1.00
❑4, Nov 84	0.60	0.20	0.50	1.00
❑5, Dec 84	0.60	0.20	0.50	1.00
❑6, Jan 85, A: Spider-Man	0.60	0.20	0.50	1.00
❑7, Feb 85, A: Cloak & Dagger	0.60	0.20	0.50	1.00
❑8, Mar 85, A: Cloak & Dagger	0.60	0.20	0.50	1.00
❑9, Apr 85, BA	0.65	0.20	0.50	1.00
❑10, May 85, BA	0.65	0.20	0.50	1.00
❑11, Jun 85	0.65	0.20	0.50	1.00
❑12, Jul 85, A: X-Men	0.65	0.20	0.50	1.00
❑13, Aug 85, BA	0.65	0.20	0.50	1.00
❑14, Sep 85	0.65	0.20	0.50	1.00
❑15, Oct 85	0.65	0.20	0.50	1.00
❑16, Nov 85, 1: Kofi	0.65	0.20	0.50	1.00
❑17, Dec 85	0.65	0.20	0.50	1.00
❑18, Jan 86, BA, Secret Wars II, Secret Wars II	0.65	0.20	0.50	1.00
❑19, Feb 86, BA, A: Wolverine, Giant-size	1.25	0.30	0.75	1.50
❑20, Mar 86, A: New Mutants	0.75	0.20	0.50	1.00
❑21, Apr 86, BA	0.75	0.20	0.50	1.00
❑22, May 86	0.75	0.20	0.50	1.00
❑23, Jun 86	0.75	0.20	0.50	1.00
❑24, Jul 86	0.75	0.20	0.50	1.00
❑25, Aug 86	1.25	0.20	0.50	1.00
❑26, Oct 86, A: Cloak & Dagger	1.00	0.20	0.50	1.00
❑27, Dec 86, Mutant Massacre, A: Sabretooth; A: Wolverine, Mutant Massacre	1.00	0.30	0.75	1.50
❑28, Feb 87, A: Avengers; A: Fantastic Four	1.00	0.20	0.50	1.00
❑29, Apr 87, A: Spider-Man; A: Hobgoblin, Giant-size	1.00	0.20	0.50	1.00
❑30, Jun 87	1.00	0.20	0.50	1.00
❑31, Aug 87, 1: Trash	1.00	0.20	0.50	1.00
❑32, Oct 87	1.00	0.20	0.50	1.00
❑33, Nov 87	1.00	0.20	0.50	1.00
❑34, Jan 88	1.00	0.20	0.50	1.00
❑35, Feb 88, Fall of Mutants	1.00	0.20	0.50	1.00
❑36, Apr 88	1.00	0.20	0.50	1.00
❑37, May 88	1.00	0.20	0.50	1.00
❑38, Jul 88	1.00	0.20	0.50	1.00
❑39, Aug 88	1.25	0.20	0.50	1.00
❑40, Sep 88	1.25	0.20	0.50	1.00
❑41, Nov 88	1.25	0.20	0.50	1.00
❑42, Dec 88, Inferno; Revenge of the Boogy Man, Part 1, Inferno	1.25	0.20	0.50	1.00
❑43, Jan 89, Revenge of the Boogy Man, Part 2, Inferno	1.50	0.20	0.50	1.00
❑44, Mar 89, Revenge of the Boogy Man, Part 3, Inferno	1.50	0.30	0.75	1.50
❑45, Apr 89, Revenge of the Boogy Man	1.50	0.30	0.75	1.50
❑46, May 89, A: Punisher	1.50	0.30	0.75	1.50
❑47, Jul 89	1.50	0.30	0.75	1.50
❑48, Sep 89	1.50	0.30	0.75	1.50
❑49, Oct 89	1.50	0.30	0.75	1.50
❑50, Nov 89, Giant-size	1.95	0.40	1.00	2.00
❑51, Dec 89, 1: Numinus	1.50	0.30	0.75	1.50
❑52, Dec 89	1.50	0.30	0.75	1.50
❑53, Jan 90, Acts of Vengeance, Acts of Vengeance	1.50	0.30	0.75	1.50
❑54, Feb 90	1.50	0.30	0.75	1.50

	ORIG	GOOD	FINE	N-MINT
❑55, Apr 90	1.50	0.30	0.75	1.50
❑56, Jun 90	1.50	0.30	0.75	1.50
❑57, Jul 90	1.50	0.30	0.75	1.50
❑58, Sep 90, Galactus	1.50	0.30	0.75	1.50
❑59, Oct 90	1.50	0.30	0.75	1.50
❑60, Nov 90	1.50	0.30	0.75	1.50
❑61, Dec 90	1.50	0.30	0.75	1.50
❑62, Jan 91, Final Issue	1.50	0.40	1.00	2.00
❑HS 1, Feb 92, Small Changes; Aaw, Christmas!, magazine-sized	2.25	0.50	1.25	2.50

POWER PACK (VOL. 2)
MARVEL

Value: Cover or less

❑1, Aug 00, Power Re-Play 2.99

POWER PLAYS (AC)
AC

Value: Cover or less

❑1, b&w 1.75

❑2, Fal 85, b&w 1.75

POWER PLAYS (EXTRAVA-GANDT)
EXTRAVA-GANDT

Value: Cover or less

❑1, b&w 2.00

❑3, b&w 2.00

POWERPUFF GIRLS, THE
DC

	ORIG	GOOD	FINE	N-MINT
❑1, May 00, Squirrelly Burly	1.99	1.70	4.25	8.50
❑2, Jun 00	1.99	0.90	2.25	4.50
❑3, Jul 00	1.99	0.80	2.00	4.00
❑4, Aug 00	1.99	0.60	1.50	3.00
❑5, Sep 00, Holy Molar!	1.99	0.50	1.25	2.50
❑6, Oct 00, Dial "M" for Mojo	1.99	0.40	1.00	1.99
❑7, Nov 00, Remote Controller	1.99	0.40	1.00	1.99
❑8, Dec 00, Mayor, May I?	1.99	0.40	1.00	1.99
❑9, Jan 01, Creature at Large!	1.99	0.40	1.00	1.99
❑10, Feb 01, Rogue Clowns	1.99	0.40	1.00	1.99
❑11	1.99	0.40	1.00	1.99
❑12, Apr 01, Snow Day	1.99	0.40	1.00	1.99
❑13, May 01, Paranoid Puffs	1.99	0.40	1.00	1.99
❑14	1.99	0.40	1.00	1.99
❑15	1.99	0.40	1.00	1.99
❑16	1.99	0.40	1.00	1.99
❑17	1.99	0.40	1.00	1.99

POWERPUFF GIRLS DOUBLE WHAMMY, THE
DC

	ORIG	GOOD	FINE	N-MINT
❑1, Dec 00, Squirrelly Burly, Collects stories from Powerpuff Girls #1-2, Dexter's Laboratory #7	3.95	1.00	2.50	5.00

POWER RANGERS TURBO: INTO THE FIRE
ACCLAIM

Value: Cover or less

❑1, Into The Fire; 90 Miles Per Horror 4.50

POWER RANGERS ZEO
IMAGE

Value: Cover or less

❑1, Aug 96, With Friends Like These... .... 2.50

❑2 .... 2.50

POWERS
IMAGE

	ORIG	GOOD	FINE	N-MINT
❑1, BMB (w)	2.95	1.00	2.50	5.00
❑2, BMB (w)	2.95	1.60	4.00	8.00
❑3, Jun 00, BMB (w), #1 in indicia	2.95	0.80	2.00	4.00
❑4, BMB (w)	2.95	0.70	1.75	3.50
❑5, BMB (w)	2.95	0.59	1.48	2.95
❑6, BMB (w)	2.95	0.59	1.48	2.95
❑7, BMB (w)	2.95	0.59	1.48	2.95
❑8, BMB (w)	2.95	0.59	1.48	2.95
❑9, BMB (w)	2.95	0.59	1.48	2.95
❑10, BMB (w)	2.95	0.59	1.48	2.95
❑11, BMB (w)	2.95	0.59	1.48	2.95
❑12, BMB (w)	2.95	0.59	1.48	2.95
❑13, BMB (w)	2.95	0.59	1.48	2.95
❑14, BMB (w)	2.95	0.59	1.48	2.95

POWERS COLORING/ACTIVITY BOOK
IMAGE

Value: Cover or less

❑1, BMB (w) 1.50

POWERS THAT BE
BROADWAY

	ORIG	GOOD	FINE	N-MINT
❑1, Nov 95, Because I Can, 1: Star Seed; 1: Fatale, Fatale and Star Seed; 1st comic from Broadway Comics	2.50	0.45	1.13	2.25
❑2, Dec 95, Star Seed	2.50	0.50	1.25	2.50
❑2/Ash, Sep 95, b&w; giveaway preview edition; Star Seed	—	0.20	0.50	1.00
❑3, Jan 96, Star Seed	2.50	0.50	1.25	2.50
❑3/Ash, Oct 95, b&w; giveaway preview edition; Star Seed	—	0.20	0.50	1.00
❑4, Feb 96, Star Seed	2.50	0.50	1.25	2.50
❑5, Apr 96, V: Gina and Charlotte; 1: Marnie, Star Seed	2.50	0.50	1.25	2.50
❑6, May 96, 1: Ajax, Star Seed	2.95	0.59	1.48	2.95
❑7, Jul 96, Title changes to Star Seed	2.95	0.59	1.48	2.95
❑8	2.95	0.59	1.48	2.95
❑9, Oct 96	2.95	0.59	1.48	2.95

PRAIRIE MOON AND OTHER STORIES
DARK HORSE

Value: Cover or less

❑1, nn; b&w; Rick Geary 2.25

PREACHER
DC

	ORIG	GOOD	FINE	N-MINT
❑1, Apr 95, 1: Jesse Custer	2.95	2.00	5.00	10.00
❑2, May 95, 1: The Saint of Killers	2.50	1.00	2.50	5.00
❑3, Jun 95	2.50	0.80	2.00	4.00
❑4, Jul 95	2.50	0.80	2.00	4.00
❑5, Aug 95	2.50	0.80	2.00	4.00
❑6, Sep 95	2.50	0.70	1.75	3.50
❑7, Oct 95	2.50	0.70	1.75	3.50
❑8, Nov 95, All in the Family, Part 1	2.50	0.70	1.75	3.50
❑9, Dec 95, All in the Family, Part 2	2.50	0.70	1.75	3.50
❑10, Jan 96, All in the Family, Part 3	2.50	0.70	1.75	3.50
❑11, Feb 96, All in the Family, Part 4	2.50	0.60	1.50	3.00
❑12, Mar 96, All in the Family, Part 5	2.50	0.60	1.50	3.00
❑13, Apr 96, Hunters, Part 1	2.50	0.60	1.50	3.00
❑14, Jun 96, Hunters, Part 2; Hunters, Part 1	2.50	0.60	1.50	3.00
❑15, Jul 96, Hunters, Part 3; Hunters, Part 2	2.50	0.60	1.50	3.00
❑16, Aug 96, Hunters, Part 4; Hunters, Part 3	2.50	0.50	1.25	2.50
❑17, Sep 96, Hunters Epilogue; Hunters, Part 4	2.50	0.50	1.25	2.50
❑18, Oct 96, Texas and the Spaceman	2.50	0.50	1.25	2.50
❑19, Nov 96, Crusaders, Part 1	2.50	0.50	1.25	2.50
❑20, Dec 96, Crusaders, Part 2	2.50	0.50	1.25	2.50
❑21, Jan 97, Crusaders, Part 3	2.50	0.50	1.25	2.50
❑22, Feb 97, Crusaders, Part 4	2.50	0.50	1.25	2.50
❑23, Mar 97, Crusaders, Part 5	2.50	0.50	1.25	2.50
❑24, Apr 97, Crusaders, Part 6	2.50	0.50	1.25	2.50
❑25, May 97, O: Cassidy	2.50	0.50	1.25	2.50
❑26, Jun 97, To the Streets of Manhattan I Wandered Away, O: Cassidy	2.50	0.50	1.25	2.50
❑27, Jul 97, Gunchicks	2.50	0.50	1.25	2.50
❑28, Aug 97, Rumors of War	2.50	0.50	1.25	2.50
❑29, Sep 97, A: You-Know-Who	2.50	0.50	1.25	2.50
❑30, Oct 97, A: You-Know-Who	2.50	0.50	1.25	2.50
❑31, Nov 97	2.50	0.50	1.25	2.50
❑32, Dec 97, Snakes in the Grass	2.50	0.50	1.25	2.50
❑33, Jan 98	2.50	0.50	1.25	2.50
❑34, Feb 98, War in the Sun, Part 1	2.50	0.50	1.25	2.50
❑35, Mar 98, War in the Sun, Part 2	2.50	0.50	1.25	2.50
❑36, Apr 98, War in the Sun, Part 3	2.50	0.50	1.25	2.50
❑37, May 98, War in the Sun, Part 4	2.50	0.50	1.25	2.50
❑38, Jun 98, A: You-Know-Who	2.50	0.50	1.25	2.50
❑39, Jul 98, Jesse loses an eye; Starr loses a leg	2.50	0.50	1.25	2.50
❑40, Aug 98	2.50	0.50	1.25	2.50
❑41, Sep 98, six months later; Jesse becomes sheriff of Salvation, Texas	2.50	0.50	1.25	2.50
❑42, Oct 98, 1: Odin Quincannon	2.50	0.50	1.25	2.50
❑43, Nov 98, Jesse's mother's story	2.50	0.50	1.25	2.50
❑44, Dec 98	2.50	0.50	1.25	2.50
❑45, Jan 99, Southern Cross	2.50	0.50	1.25	2.50
❑46, Feb 99, White Mischief	2.50	0.50	1.25	2.50
❑47, Mar 99, Jesse Get Your Gun	2.50	0.50	1.25	2.50
❑48, Apr 99, Salvation, D: Odin Quincannon	2.50	0.50	1.25	2.50
❑49, May 99, First Contact	2.50	0.50	1.25	2.50
❑50, Jun 99, The Land of Bad Things, Giant-size	3.75	0.75	1.88	3.75
❑51, Jul 99, Freedom's Just Another Word for Nothing Left to Lose, 100 Bullets preview	2.50	0.50	1.25	2.50
❑52, Aug 99, Even Hitgirls get the Blues	2.50	0.50	1.25	2.50
❑53, Sep 99, Too Dumb for New York City and Too Ugly for L.A.	2.50	0.50	1.25	2.50
❑54, Oct 99	2.50	0.50	1.25	2.50
❑55, Nov 99, Harbinger	2.50	0.50	1.25	2.50
❑56, Dec 99	2.50	0.50	1.25	2.50
❑57, Jan 00, Of the Irish in America	2.50	0.50	1.25	2.50
❑58, Feb 00, Dot the I's and Cross the T's	2.50	0.50	1.25	2.50
❑59, Mar 00, Alamo, Part 1	2.50	0.50	1.25	2.50
❑60, Apr 00, Alamo, Part 2	2.50	0.50	1.25	2.50
❑61, May 00, Alamo, Part 3	2.50	0.50	1.25	2.50
❑62, Jun 00, Alamo, Part 4	2.50	0.50	1.25	2.50
❑63, Jul 00, Alamo, Part 5	2.50	0.50	1.25	2.50
❑64, Aug 00, Alamo, Part 6	2.50	0.50	1.25	2.50
❑65, Sep 00, Alamo, Part 7	2.50	0.50	1.25	2.50
❑66, Oct 00, A Hell of a Vision, Final Issue; Giant-size	3.75	0.75	1.88	3.75

PREACHER SPECIAL: CASSIDY: BLOOD & WHISKEY
DC

Value: Cover or less

❑1, Feb 98, One-Shot; prestige format 5.95

PREACHER SPECIAL: ONE MAN'S WAR
DC

	ORIG	GOOD	FINE	N-MINT
❑1, Mar 98, O: Starr	4.95	1.00	2.50	5.00

PREACHER SPECIAL: SAINT OF KILLERS
DC

	ORIG	GOOD	FINE	N-MINT
❑1, Aug 96	2.50	0.80	2.00	4.00
❑2, Sep 96	2.50	0.70	1.75	3.50
❑3, Oct 96	2.50	0.60	1.50	3.00
❑4, Nov 96	2.50	0.60	1.50	3.00

PREACHER SPECIAL: TALL IN THE SADDLE
VERTIGO

	ORIG	GOOD	FINE	N-MINT
❑1	—	0.99	2.47	4.95

PREACHER SPECIAL: THE GOOD OLD BOYS
DC

Value: Cover or less

❑1, A: T.C.; A: Jody, One-Shot ... 4.95

PREACHER SPECIAL: THE STORY OF YOU-KNOW-WHO
DC

Value: Cover or less

❑1, Dec 96, O: You-Know-Who, One-Shot ... 4.95

PRECIOUS METAL
ARTS INDUSTRIA

Value: Cover or less

❑1, b&w; adult ... 2.50

PREDATOR
DARK HORSE

	ORIG	GOOD	FINE	N-MINT
❑1, Jun 89, full color	2.25	1.00	2.50	5.00
❑1-2, 2nd Printing	2.25	0.50	1.25	2.50
❑2	2.25	0.70	1.75	3.50
❑3	2.25	0.60	1.50	3.00
❑4	2.25	0.60	1.50	3.00

PREDATOR 2
DARK HORSE

	ORIG	GOOD	FINE	N-MINT
❑1, Feb 91, Photo cover; trading cards	2.50	0.60	1.50	3.00
❑2, Jun 91, Photo cover; trading cards	2.50	0.60	1.50	3.00

PREDATOR: BAD BLOOD
DARK HORSE

Value: Cover or less

❑1, Dec 93 ... 2.50
❑2, Feb 94 ... 2.50
❑3, May 94 ... 2.50
❑4, Jun 94 ... 2.50

PREDATOR: BIG GAME
DARK HORSE

Value: Cover or less

❑1, Mar 91, trading cards ... 2.50
❑2, Apr 91, no trading cards despite cover advisory ... 2.50
❑3, May 91, trading cards ... 2.50
❑4, Jun 91 ... 2.50

PREDATOR: CAPTIVE
DARK HORSE

Value: Cover or less

❑1, Apr 98, nn; One-Shot ... 2.95

PREDATOR: COLD WAR
DARK HORSE

Value: Cover or less

❑1, Sep 91 ... 2.50
❑2, Oct 91 ... 2.50
❑3, Nov 91 ... 2.50
❑4, Dec 91 ... 2.50

PREDATOR: DARK RIVER
DARK HORSE

Value: Cover or less

❑1, Jul 96 ... 2.95
❑2, Aug 96 ... 2.95
❑3, Sep 96 ... 2.95
❑4, Oct 96 ... 2.95

PREDATOR: HELL & HOT WATER
DARK HORSE

Value: Cover or less

❑1, Apr 97, GC, uninked pencils 2.95
❑2, May 97, GC, uninked pencils ... 2.95
❑3, Jun 97, GC, uninked pencils 2.95

PREDATOR: HELL COME A WALKIN'
DARK HORSE

Value: Cover or less

❑1, Feb 98, Predator in Civil War ... 2.95
❑2, Mar 98, Predator in Civil War ... 2.95

PREDATOR: HOMEWORLD
DARK HORSE

Value: Cover or less

❑1, Mar 99 ... 2.95
❑2, Apr 99 ... 2.95
❑3, May 99 ... 2.95
❑4, Jun 99 ... 2.95

PREDATOR: INVADERS FROM THE FOURTH DIMENSION
DARK HORSE

Value: Cover or less

❑1, Jul 94, nn; One-Shot ... 3.95

PREDATOR: JUNGLE TALES
DARK HORSE

Value: Cover or less

❑1, Mar 95, Predator: Rite of Passage; Predator: The Pride at Nghasa, nn; collects Predator: Rite of Passage from DHC #1 and 2; Predator: The Pride of Nghasa from DHC #10-12... 2.95

PREDATOR: KINDRED
DARK HORSE

Value: Cover or less

❑1, Dec 96, Kindred, Part 1 ... 2.50
❑2, Jan 97, Kindred, Part 2 ... 2.50
❑3, Feb 97, Kindred, Part 3 ... 2.50
❑4, Mar 97 ... 2.50

A World War I-based adventure was chronicled in the two-issue *Predator: The Bloody Sands of Time.*

© 1992 20th Century Fox Film Corporation (Dark Horse)

PREDATOR: NEMESIS
DARK HORSE

Value: Cover or less

❑1, Dec 97, Predator Nemesis, Part 1 ... 2.95
❑2, Jan 98 ... 2.95

PREDATOR: PRIMAL
DARK HORSE

Value: Cover or less

❑1, Jul 97, Predator vs. bears ... 2.95
❑2, Aug 97, Predator vs. bears ... 2.95

PREDATOR: RACE WAR
DARK HORSE

Value: Cover or less

❑0, Apr 93 ... 2.50
❑1, Feb 93 ... 2.50
❑2, Mar 93 ... 2.50
❑3, Aug 93 ... 2.50
❑4, Oct 93 ... 2.50

PREDATOR: STRANGE ROUX
DARK HORSE

Value: Cover or less

❑1, Nov 96, nn; One-Shot; recipe for Strange Roux in back ... 2.95

PREDATOR: THE BLOODY SANDS OF TIME
DARK HORSE

	ORIG	GOOD	FINE	N-MINT
❑1, Feb 92, Predator in WW I	2.50	0.55	1.38	2.75
❑2, Feb 92, Predator in WW I	2.50	0.55	1.38	2.75

PREDATOR VERSUS JUDGE DREDD
DARK HORSE

Value: Cover or less

❑1, Oct 97 ... 2.50
❑2, Nov 97 ... 2.50
❑3, Dec 97 ... 2.50

PREDATOR VS. MAGNUS ROBOT FIGHTER
DARK HORSE

	ORIG	GOOD	FINE	N-MINT
❑1, Nov 92, Sport	2.95	0.60	1.50	3.00
❑1/PL, Sport, Platinum promotional edition	—	0.80	2.00	4.00
❑2, Spoils, trading cards	2.95	0.60	1.50	3.00

PREDATOR: XENOGENESIS
DARK HORSE

Value: Cover or less

❑1, Aug 99 ... 2.95
❑2, Sep 99 ... 2.95
❑3, Oct 99 ... 2.95
❑4, Nov 99 ... 2.95

PREMIERE
DIVERSITY

Value: Cover or less

❑1, Kolmec the Savage: When a Stranger Calls, Part 1, 1500 printed ... 2.75
❑1/GO, Kolmec the Savage: When a Stranger Calls, Part 1, Gold limited edition (175 printed). 10.00
❑1/LE, Kolmec the Savage: When a Stranger Calls, Part 1, Limited edition (175 printed) ... 5.00
❑2, Kolmec the Savage: When a Stranger Calls, Part 2; Lifer: Guilty as Sin, Part 2, poster ... 2.75

PRESERVATION OF OBSCURITY, THE
LUMP OF SQUID

Value: Cover or less

❑1 ... 2.75
❑2 ... 2.75

PRESSED TONGUE (DAVE COOPER'S...)
FANTAGRAPHICS

Value: Cover or less

❑1, b&w; adult ... 2.95
❑3, Dec 94, b&w; adult ... 2.95

PRESTO KID, THE
AC

Value: Cover or less

❑1, b&w; Reprint ... 2.50

PRE-TEEN DIRTY-GENE KUNG-FU KANGAROOS
BLACKTHORNE

	ORIG	GOOD	FINE	N-MINT
❑1, Aug 86, A: TMNT	1.50	0.40	1.00	2.00
❑2, Nov 86	1.50	0.40	1.00	2.00
❑3	1.75	0.40	1.00	2.00

PREY
MONSTER

Value: Cover or less

❑1, b&w ... 2.25
❑2, b&w ... 2.25
❑3, b&w ... 2.25

PREY FOR US SINNERS
FANTACO

Value: Cover or less

❑1, nn ... 4.95

PREZ
DC

	ORIG	GOOD	FINE	N-MINT
❑1, Sep 73, Oh Say Does That Star Spangled Banner Yet Wave?	0.20	1.60	4.00	8.00
❑2, Nov 73	0.20	0.80	2.00	4.00
❑3, Jan 74	0.20	0.80	2.00	4.00
❑4, Mar 74	0.20	0.80	2.00	4.00

PRIDE & JOY
DC

Value: Cover or less

- ❑1, Jul 97 ... 2.50
- ❑2, Aug 97 ... 2.50
- ❑3, Sep 97 ... 2.50
- ❑4, Oct 97 ... 2.50

PRIEST
MAXIMUM

Value: Cover or less

- ❑1, Aug 96, RL (w), 1: Priest .. 2.99
- ❑2, RL (w) ... 2.99
- ❑3, RL (w) ... 2.99

PRIMAL
DARK HORSE

Value: Cover or less

- ❑1 ... 2.50
- ❑2 ... 2.50

PRIMAL FORCE
DC

	ORIG	GOOD	FINE	N-MINT
❑0, Oct 94, The Call, 1: Primal Force	1.95	0.45	1.13	2.25
❑1, Nov 94, Water Signs, O: the Leymen	1.95	0.45	1.13	2.25
❑2, Dec 94	1.95	0.39	0.98	1.95
❑3, Jan 95, Histories	1.95	0.39	0.98	1.95
❑4, Feb 95	1.95	0.39	0.98	1.95
❑5, Mar 95	1.95	0.39	0.98	1.95
❑6, Apr 95	1.95	0.39	0.98	1.95
❑7, May 95	1.95	0.39	0.98	1.95
❑8, Jun 95	2.25	0.39	0.98	1.95
❑9, Jul 95	2.25	0.45	1.13	2.25
❑10, Aug 95	2.25	0.45	1.13	2.25
❑11, Sep 95	2.25	0.45	1.13	2.25
❑12, Oct 95	2.25	0.45	1.13	2.25
❑13, Nov 95, Underworld Unleashed, A: Lord Satanus, Underworld Unleashed	2.25	0.45	1.13	2.25
❑14, Dec 95, Final Issue	2.25	0.45	1.13	2.25

PRIMAL RAGE
SIRIUS

	ORIG	GOOD	FINE	N-MINT
❑1, b&w	2.50	0.59	1.48	2.95
❑2, b&w	2.50	0.59	1.48	2.95
❑3, b&w	2.50	0.59	1.48	2.95
❑4, b&w	2.50	0.59	1.48	2.95

PRIME (VOL. 1)
MALIBU

	ORIG	GOOD	FINE	N-MINT
❑0.5, Wizard promotional edition	—	0.50	1.25	2.50
❑1, Jun 93, The King Of Beasts, 1: Doctor Gross; 1: Prime, Ultraverse	1.95	0.60	1.50	3.00
❑1/Hol, The King Of Beasts, 1: Doctor Gross; 1: Prime, Holographic promotional edition	—	1.00	2.50	5.00
❑1/LE, Jun 93, The King Of Beasts, 1: Doctor Gross; 1: Prime, $1.95 on cover; give-away; "Ultra-Limited" edition; foil stamped	1.95	0.60	1.50	3.00
❑2, Jul 93, card; Ultraverse; trading card	1.95	0.40	1.00	2.00
❑3, Aug 93, Dead Again...And Again, O: Prime	1.95	0.40	1.00	2.00
❑4, Sep 93, 1: Maxi-Man; V: Prototype; A: Prototype II (Jimmy Ruiz), two different covers	1.95	0.40	1.00	2.00
❑5, Oct 93, Rune, Part B, Rune	2.50	0.40	1.00	2.00
❑6, Nov 93	1.95	0.40	1.00	2.00
❑7, Dec 93, Break-Thru, Break-Thru	1.95	0.40	1.00	2.00
❑8, Jan 94, The Return Of Doctor Gross, A: Mantra; O: Freex	1.95	0.39	0.98	1.95
❑9, Feb 94, Atomic Lies!	1.95	0.39	0.98	1.95
❑10, Mar 94, The Men From The Boys, A: Firearm	1.95	0.39	0.98	1.95
❑11, Apr 94, Heroes Of Sunset Strip	1.95	0.39	0.98	1.95
❑12, May 94, flip-book with Ultraverse Premiere #3	3.50	0.70	1.75	3.50
❑13, Jul 94, Double Dangerous, two different covers; Freex preview	2.95	0.39	0.98	1.95
❑13/A, Double Dangerous, variant cover	1.95	0.39	0.98	1.95
❑14, Sep 94, Age of Rebellion, 1: Papa VeritT	1.95	0.39	0.98	1.95
❑15, Oct 94, GP, House of Horrors	1.95	0.39	0.98	1.95
❑16, Nov 94, Up Against the Wall!, 1: Turbo-Charge	1.95	0.39	0.98	1.95
❑17, Dec 94, Hungry for Heroes	1.95	0.39	0.98	1.95
❑18, Dec 94, One-Two Punch	1.95	0.39	0.98	1.95
❑19, Jan 95, Prime Season	1.95	0.39	0.98	1.95
❑20, Mar 95, Cupid's Arrow, 1: Phade	2.50	0.39	0.98	1.95
❑21, Apr 95, JSa, A Hero Dies!, A: Chelsea Clinton	2.50	0.39	0.98	1.95
❑22, May 95, Getting Weird	2.50	0.39	0.98	1.95
❑23, Jun 95	2.50	0.39	0.98	1.95
❑24, Jun 95	2.50	0.39	0.98	1.95
❑25, Jul 95, O: Prime, continued from Power of Prime #1	2.50	0.39	0.98	1.95
❑26, Aug 95, O: Prime, continues in Power of Prime #2	2.50	0.39	0.98	1.95
❑Anl 1, Oct 94, Gross and Disgusting, Part 1, A: Hardcase; 1: new Prime, Prime: Gross and Disgusting	3.95	0.79	1.98	3.95
❑Ash 1, ashcan edition	0.75	0.20	0.50	1.00

PRIME (VOL. 2)
MALIBU

Value: Cover or less

- ❑0, Sep 95, A: Spider-Man, Black September; #Infinity ... 1.50
- ❑0/A, Sep 95, A: Spider-Man, alternate cover; Black September 1.50
- ❑1, Oct 95, A Matter of Soul, A: Lizard, Spider-Prime ... 1.50
- ❑2, Nov 95 ... 1.50
- ❑3, Dec 95 ... 1.50
- ❑4, Jan 96, Kevin rejoins Prime body ... 1.50
- ❑5, Feb 96 ... 1.50
- ❑6, Mar 96, A: Solitaire ... 1.50
- ❑7, Apr 96 ... 1.50
- ❑8 ... 1.50
- ❑9, Jun 96 ... 1.50
- ❑10, Jul 96 ... 1.50
- ❑11, Aug 96 ... 1.50
- ❑12, Sep 96 ... 1.50
- ❑13, Oct 96 ... 1.50
- ❑14, Nov 96, Monster Mash ... 1.50
- ❑15, Dec 96, V: Lord Pumpkin, Final Issue ... 1.50

PRIME/CAPTAIN AMERICA
MALIBU

Value: Cover or less

- ❑1, Mar 96 ... 3.95

PRIME CUTS
FANTAGRAPHICS

Value: Cover or less

- ❑1, Jan 87 ... 3.50
- ❑2, Mar 87 ... 3.50
- ❑3, May 87 ... 3.50
- ❑4 ... 3.50
- ❑5 ... 3.50
- ❑6 ... 3.50
- ❑7 ... 3.95
- ❑8 ... 3.95
- ❑9 ... 3.95
- ❑10 ... 3.95

PRIME CUTS (MIKE DEODATO'S...)
CALIBER

Value: Cover or less

- ❑1, Jack; Lycanthropos ... 2.95

PRIMER
COMICO

	ORIG	GOOD	FINE	N-MINT
❑1, 1: Az; 1: Skrog; 1: Slaughterman, b&w.	1.50	1.20	3.00	6.00
❑2, MW, MW (w), My Brother's Keeper?; Judas Kiss, 1: Grendel I (Hunter Rose); 1: Argent	1.50	13.00	32.50	65.00
❑3	1.50	1.00	2.50	5.00
❑4, Victor; The Power, 1: Laserman; 1: Firebringer, b&w	1.50	1.00	2.50	5.00
❑5, 1: The Maxx (original), 1st professional art by Sam Kieth	1.50	4.00	10.00	20.00
❑6, 1: Evangeline	1.50	1.20	3.00	6.00

PRIMER (VOL. 2)
COMICO

Value: Cover or less

- ❑1, May 96, Lady Bathory: The Assassin's Song ... 2.95

PRIME SLIME TALES
MIRAGE

Value: Cover or less

- ❑1, Slime after Slime, Published By Mirage Studio ... 1.50
- ❑2, Having the Slime of Their Lives..., Published By Mirage Studio ... 1.50
- ❑3, Nov 86, Roach Wars, Published By Now Comics ... 1.50
- ❑4, Jan 87, Published By Now Comics ... 1.50

PRIME VS. THE INCREDIBLE HULK
MALIBU

	ORIG	GOOD	FINE	N-MINT
❑0, Jul 95, no cover price	—	1.00	2.50	5.00

PRIMITIVES
SPARETIME STUDIOS

Value: Cover or less

- ❑1, Jan 95, 1: Primitives, b&w 2.50
- ❑2, May 95, b&w ... 2.50
- ❑3, Oct 95, b&w ... 2.50

PRIMORTALS (VOL. 1) (LEONARD NIMOY'S...)
TEKNO

Value: Cover or less

- ❑1, Mar 95, Escape to Earth, trading card ... 1.95
- ❑2, Apr 95 ... 1.95
- ❑3, May 95, The Approaching Storm, trading card ... 1.95
- ❑4, Jun 95 ... 1.95
- ❑5, Jul 95 ... 1.95
- ❑6, Aug 95 ... 1.95
- ❑7, Sep 95 ... 1.95
- ❑8, Oct 95 ... 1.95
- ❑9, Nov 95 ... 1.95
- ❑10, Dec 95 ... 1.95
- ❑11, Dec 95 ... 1.95
- ❑12, Jan 96 ... 2.25
- ❑13, Mar 96 ... 2.25
- ❑14, Apr 96 ... 2.25
- ❑15, May 96, Final Issue ... 2.25
- ❑16, Final Issue ... 2.25

PRIMORTALS (VOL. 2) (LEONARD NIMOY'S...)
BIG

Value: Cover or less

- ❑0, Jun 96, The Big Crossover, Part 9; Cross Country: World in Flames ... 2.25
- ❑1, Jul 96 ... 2.25
- ❑2, Aug 96 ... 2.25
- ❑3, Sep 96 ... 2.25

ORIG GOOD FINE N-MINT

- ❑4, Oct 96 .... 2.25
- ❑5, Nov 96 .... 2.25
- ❑6, Dec 96 .... 2.25
- ❑7, Jan 97, Final Issue 2.25

PRIMORTALS ORIGINS (LEONARD NIMOY'S...)
TEKNO

Value: Cover or less

- ❑1, Jun 95, O: the Primortals .. 2.25
- ❑2, O: the Primortals 2.25

PRIMUS
CHARLTON

	ORIG	GOOD	FINE	N-MINT
❑1, Feb 72	0.20	1.40	3.50	7.00
❑2	0.20	0.80	2.00	4.00
❑3	0.20	0.80	2.00	4.00
❑4, Jun 72	0.20	0.80	2.00	4.00
❑5	0.20	0.60	1.50	3.00
❑6	0.20	0.60	1.50	3.00
❑7, Oct 72	0.20	0.60	1.50	3.00

PRINCE: ALTER EGO
PIRANHA MUSIC

Value: Cover or less

- ❑1, Dec 91, BB (c) 2.00

PRINCE AND THE NEW POWER GENERATION: THREE CHAINS OF GOLD
DC

Value: Cover or less

- ❑1, nn 3.50

PRINCE AND THE PAUPER
DELL

	ORIG	GOOD	FINE	N-MINT
❑1, Jul 62, movie Adaptation; 01-654-207	0.15	3.00	7.50	15.00

PRINCE AND THE PAUPER, THE (DISNEY'S...)
DISNEY

Value: Cover or less

- ❑1, movie Adaptation; square-bound 5.95

PRINCE NAMOR, THE SUB-MARINER
MARVEL

	ORIG	GOOD	FINE	N-MINT
❑1, Sep 84	0.75	0.30	0.75	1.50
❑2, Oct 84	0.75	0.30	0.75	1.50
❑3, Nov 84	0.75	0.30	0.75	1.50
❑4, Dec 84, The Road Not Taken!	0.75	0.30	0.75	1.50

PRINCE NIGHTMARE
AAAARGH!

Value: Cover or less

- ❑1 .... 2.95

PRINCESS KARANAM AND THE DJINN OF THE GREEN JUG
MU PRESS

Value: Cover or less

- ❑1, nn; b&w 2.50

PRINCESS PRINCE
CPM MANGA

Value: Cover or less

- ❑1, Oct 00 .... 2.95
- ❑1/A, Oct 00, alternate wrap-around cover 2.95
- ❑2 .... 2.95
- ❑3 .... 2.95
- ❑4 .... 2.95
- ❑5 .... 2.95
- ❑6 .... 2.95
- ❑7 .... 2.95
- ❑8 .... 2.95
- ❑9 .... 2.95
- ❑10 .... 2.95

PRINCESS SALLY
ARCHIE

Value: Cover or less

- ❑1, Apr 95 .... 1.50
- ❑2, May 95 .... 1.50
- ❑3, Jun 95 .... 1.50

PRINCE VALIANT (MARVEL)
MARVEL

Value: Cover or less

- ❑1, Dec 94, CV (w), The Sword in the Stone, cardstock cover 3.95
- ❑2, Jan 95, CV (w), cardstock cover 3.95
- ❑3, Feb 95, CV (w), cardstock cover 3.95
- ❑4, Mar 95, cardstock cover.... 3.95

PRINCE VALIANT MONTHLY
PIONEER

Value: Cover or less

- ❑1, b&w 4.95
- ❑2, b&w 4.95
- ❑3, b&w 4.95
- ❑4, b&w 4.95

PRINCE VANDAL
TRIUMPHANT

Value: Cover or less

- ❑1, Interference, Unleashed! .. 2.50
- ❑2, Unleashed! 2.50
- ❑3 .... 2.50
- ❑4 .... 2.50
- ❑5 .... 2.50
- ❑6 .... 2.50

PRIORITY: WHITE HEAT
AC

Value: Cover or less

- ❑1, Mar 87, The Blitz of vengeance!: Two Riddles to Recife 1.75
- ❑2 .... 1.75

PRISONER, THE
DC

Value: Cover or less

- ❑1, Dec 88, Arrival, a 3.50
- ❑2, Jan 89, By Hook Or By Crook, b 3.50
- ❑3, Jan 89, Confrontation, c.... 3.50
- ❑4, Feb 89, Departure, d 3.50

PRISONER OF CHILLON
TOME PRESS

Value: Cover or less

- ❑1, b&w 2.95

DC's four-issue The Prisoner mini-series was denoted, not by issue numbers, but by letters.

© 1988 DC Comics

ORIG GOOD FINE N-MINT

PRISONOPOLIS
MEDIAWARP

Value: Cover or less

- ❑1, Feb 97, b&w 2.75
- ❑2, Apr 97, b&w 2.75

PRIVATE BEACH: FUN AND PERILS IN THE TRUDYVERSE
ANTARCTIC

Value: Cover or less

- ❑1, Jan 95, b&w 2.75
- ❑2, Mar 95, b&w 2.75
- ❑3, May 95, b&w 2.75

PRIVATE COMMISSIONS (GRAY MORROW'S...)
FORBIDDEN FRUIT

Value: Cover or less

- ❑1, b&w; adult 2.95
- ❑2, b&w; adult 2.95

PRIVATEERS
VANGUARD

Value: Cover or less

- ❑1 .... 1.50
- ❑2 .... 1.50

PRIVATE EYES
ETERNITY

Value: Cover or less

- ❑1, Sep 88, b&w; Saint reprints 1.95
- ❑2, Nov 88, b&w; Saint reprints 1.95
- ❑3, Jan 89, b&w; Saint reprints 1.95
- ❑4, May 89 .... 2.95
- ❑5, Aug 89 .... 3.50
- ❑6 .... 3.95

PRO ACTION MAGAZINE (VOL. 2)
MARVEL

Value: Cover or less

- ❑1, Jul 94 .... 2.95
- ❑2, Sep 94 .... 2.95
- ❑3, Nov 94, magazine with bound-in Spider-Man comjc book... 2.95

PROBE
IMPERIAL

	ORIG	GOOD	FINE	N-MINT
❑1, Earth Case	1.80	0.40	1.00	2.00
❑2	1.95	0.40	1.00	2.00
❑3	1.95	0.40	1.00	2.00

PROF. COFFIN
CHARLTON

	ORIG	GOOD	FINE	N-MINT
❑19, Oct 85, WH; JAb; JSa, The Midnight Philosopher; Weave Me a Web	0.75	0.40	1.00	2.00
❑20	0.75	0.40	1.00	2.00
❑21, Feb 86, WH; JSa; TS, The Midnight Philosopher: The Fortune teller; Game Preserve	0.75	0.40	1.00	2.00

PROFESSIONAL, THE: GOLGO 13
VIZ

Value: Cover or less

- ❑1, full color; Japanese 4.95
- ❑2, full color; Japanese 4.95
- ❑3, full color; Japanese 4.95

PROFESSOR OM
INNOVATION

Value: Cover or less

- ❑1, May 90 .... 2.50

PROFESSOR XAVIER AND THE X-MEN
MARVEL

	ORIG	GOOD	FINE	N-MINT
❑1, Nov 95, JDu, Trial by Fire!, retells origin of team and first mission	0.99	0.30	0.75	1.50
❑2, Dec 95, JDu, A: Vanisher, retells first Vanisher story	0.99	0.30	0.75	1.50
❑3, Jan 96, retells first Blob story	0.99	0.30	0.75	1.50
❑4, Feb 96, retells first meeting with Brotherhood of Evil Mutants	0.99	0.25	0.63	1.25
❑5, Mar 96, The Brotherhood, retells first meeting with Brotherhood of Evil Mutants	0.99	0.25	0.63	1.25
❑6, Apr 96, Fallen Angel	0.99	0.25	0.63	1.25
❑7, May 96, Sub-Mariner vs. Magneto	0.99	0.25	0.63	1.25
❑8, Jun 96	0.99	0.25	0.63	1.25
❑9, Jul 96	0.99	0.25	0.63	1.25
❑10, Aug 96, V: Avengers	0.99	0.25	0.63	1.25
❑11, Sep 96, A: Ka-Zar	0.99	0.20	0.50	1.00
❑12, Oct 96, V: Juggernaut	0.99	0.20	0.50	1.00
❑13, Nov 96, V: Juggernaut	0.99	0.20	0.50	1.00
❑14, Dec 96, Living Dangerously	0.99	0.20	0.50	1.00
❑15, Jan 97, Dangerous Convictions, V: Stranger; V: Magneto	0.99	0.20	0.50	1.00
❑16, Feb 97, Enter the Sentinels, V: Sentinels	0.99	0.20	0.50	1.00

	ORIG	GOOD	FINE	N-MINT
❑17, Mar 97, Probes	0.99	0.20	0.50	1.00
❑18, Apr 97, Final Sanction, V: Sentinels, Final Issue	0.99	0.20	0.50	1.00

PROFOLIO
ALCHEMY

Value: Cover or less

- ❑1, b&w ... 1.50
- ❑2, some color ... 2.50
- ❑3, b&w ... 2.50

PROFOLIO (VOL. 3)
ALCHEMY

Value: Cover or less

- ❑1 ... 5.95

PROGENY
CALIBER

Value: Cover or less

- ❑1, nn; b&w ... 4.95

PROGRAM ERROR: BATTLEBOT
PHANTASY

Value: Cover or less

- ❑1 ... 2.00

PROJECT, THE
DC

Value: Cover or less

- ❑1, b&w; digest; short story collection ... 5.95
- ❑2, b&w; digest; short story collection ... 5.95

PROJECT A-KO
MALIBU

Value: Cover or less

- ❑1, Mar 94, It Came Form A-Ko Space ... 2.95
- ❑2, Mar 94, The Rivals ... 2.95
- ❑3, May 94, Dual Duel ... 2.95
- ❑4, Jun 94, Hit And Rum ... 2.95

PROJECT A-KO 2
CPM

Value: Cover or less

- ❑1, Apr 95, The Plot Of The Daitokuji Financial Group! ... 2.95
- ❑2, Jun 95, Off The Ground ... 2.95
- ❑3, Aug 95, Like Father, Like Daughter ... 2.95

PROJECT A-KO VERSUS
CPM

Value: Cover or less

- ❑1, Oct 95, Project A-Ko Versus the Universe ... 2.95
- ❑2, Dec 95 ... 2.95
- ❑3, Feb 96 ... 2.95
- ❑4, Apr 96 ... 2.95
- ❑5, Jun 96, Final Issue ... 2.95

PROJECT: DARK MATTER
DIMM COMICS

Value: Cover or less

- ❑1, Apr 96, Project: Dark Matter; Fishbone, b&w ... 2.50
- ❑2, Jun 96, b&w; cardstock cover ... 2.50
- ❑3, b&w; cardstock cover ... 2.50
- ❑4, Sep 97, b&w ... 2.50

PROJECT: GENERATION
TRUTH

	ORIG	GOOD	FINE	N-MINT
❑1, Jun 00, Distributed at San Diego Comic-Con	—	0.20	0.50	1.00

PROJECT: HERO
VANGUARD

Value: Cover or less

- ❑1, Aug 87 ... 1.50
- ❑2 ... 1.50

PROJECT SEX
FANTAGRAPHICS

Value: Cover or less

- ❑1, b&w; adult ... 2.50

PROJECT X
KITCHEN SINK

Value: Cover or less

- ❑1, nn; Eastman/Bisley; bagged Thump'n Guts; poster; trading card ... 4.95

PROMETHEA
DC

Value: Cover or less

- ❑1, Aug 99, AMo (w), Promethea: The Radiant, Heavenly City, O: Promethea ... 3.50
- ❑2, Sep 99, AMo (w), The Judgment of Solomon ... 2.95
- ❑3, Oct 99, AMo (w), Misty Magicians ... 2.95
- ❑4, Nov 99, AMo (w), A Faerie Romance ... 2.95
- ❑5, AMo (w) ... 2.95
- ❑6, Mar 00, AMo (w), The 5 Swell Guys: Firefight on 5th Avenue! ... 2.95
- ❑7, Apr 00, AMo (w), Rocks and Hard Places ... 2.95
- ❑8, AMo (w) ... 2.95
- ❑9, AMo (w) ... 2.95
- ❑10, Oct 00, AMo (w), Sex, Stars & Serpents ... 2.95
- ❑11, Dec 00, AMo (w), Promethea Under Attack! ... 2.95
- ❑12, Feb 01, AMo (w) ... 2.95
- ❑13, Apr 01, AMo (w), The Fields we Know ... 2.95

PROMETHEUS (VILLAINS)
DC

Value: Cover or less

- ❑1, Feb 98, New Year's Evil ... 1.95

PROMETHEUS' GIFT
CAT-HEAD

Value: Cover or less

- ❑1, nn; b&w ... 2.25

PROMISE
VIZ

Value: Cover or less

- ❑1, nn; b&w; squarebound ... 5.95

PROPELLERMAN
DARK HORSE

Value: Cover or less

- ❑1 ... 2.95
- ❑2, trading cards ... 2.95
- ❑3 ... 2.95
- ❑4 ... 2.95
- ❑5 ... 2.95
- ❑6 ... 2.95
- ❑7 ... 2.95
- ❑8 ... 2.95

PROPHECY OF THE SOUL SORCERER
ARCANE

	ORIG	GOOD	FINE	N-MINT
❑1	—	0.59	1.48	2.95
❑2	—	0.59	1.48	2.95
❑3	2.95	0.59	1.48	2.95
❑Ash 1, Oct 98	1.99	0.40	1.00	2.00

PROPHECY OF THE SOUL SORCERER (VOL. 2)
ARCANE

Value: Cover or less

- ❑1, Oct 98 ... 2.95
- ❑2 ... 2.95
- ❑3, Today, Tomorrow and Yesterday, Part 1 ... 2.95

PROPHECY OF THE SOUL SORCERER PREVIEW ISSUE
ARCANE

	ORIG	GOOD	FINE	N-MINT
❑1	1.99	0.40	1.00	2.00

PROPHET
IMAGE

	ORIG	GOOD	FINE	N-MINT
❑0, Jul 94	2.50	0.60	1.50	3.00
❑0/A, Jul 94, San Diego Comic-Con edition	2.50	0.60	1.50	3.00
❑1, Oct 93, RL (w), O: Prophet	2.50	0.60	1.50	3.00
❑1/GO, Oct 93, Gold edition	—	0.60	1.50	3.00
❑2, Nov 93	1.95	0.50	1.25	2.50
❑3, Jan 94	1.95	0.50	1.25	2.50
❑4, Feb 94	1.95	0.50	1.25	2.50
❑4/SC, Feb 94, Variant cover by Platt	1.95	0.60	1.50	3.00
❑5, Apr 94	1.95	0.50	1.25	2.50
❑6, Jun 94	1.95	0.50	1.25	2.50
❑7, Sep 94	2.50	0.50	1.25	2.50
❑8, Nov 94, War Games part 2	2.50	0.50	1.25	2.50
❑9, Dec 94	2.50	0.50	1.25	2.50
❑10, Jan 95, Extreme Sacrifice, Part 7; Extreme Sacrifice, Part 6, trading card	2.50	0.50	1.25	2.50

PROPHET (VOL. 2)
IMAGE

Value: Cover or less

- ❑1/A, Aug 95 ... 3.50
- ❑1/B, Aug 95 ... 3.50
- ❑1/C, Aug 95, enhanced wrap-around cover ... 3.50
- ❑2/A, Sep 95, FM (c) ... 2.50
- ❑2/B, Sep 95, alternate cover ... 2.50
- ❑3, Nov 95 ... 2.50
- ❑4, Feb 96, A: NewMen ... 2.50
- ❑5, Feb 96 ... 2.50
- ❑6, Apr 96 ... 2.50
- ❑7, May 96, A: Youngblood ... 2.50
- ❑8, Jul 96 ... 2.50
- ❑Anl 1/A, Sep 95, polybagged with PowerCardz ... 2.50
- ❑Anl 1/B, Sep 95, polybagged with PowerCardz ... 2.50

PROPHET (VOL. 3)
AWESOME

Value: Cover or less

- ❑1, Mar 00, RL (w), Flip cover (McFarlane cover on back side) ... 2.99
- ❑1/A, Mar 00, RL (w), Red background, woman standing with sword, large man in background ... 2.99

PROPHET BABEWATCH
IMAGE

Value: Cover or less

- ❑1, Dec 95, cover says #1; indicia says #2 ... 2.50

PROPHET/CABLE
MAXIMUM

Value: Cover or less

- ❑1, Jan 97, RL (w), crossover with Marvel ... 3.50
- ❑2, Mar 97, RL (w), cover says #1, indicia says #2; crossover with Marvel ... 3.50

PROPHET/CHAPEL: SUPER SOLDIERS
IMAGE

Value: Cover or less

- ❑1/A, May 96 ... 2.50
- ❑1/B, May 96, alternate cover (b&w) ... 2.50
- ❑2, Jun 96 ... 2.50

PROPOSITION PLAYER
VERTIGO

Value: Cover or less

- ❑1, Dec 99, A New Player or the Truth About Cat and Dog Owners! ... 2.50
- ❑2, Jan 00, High Stakes Game, or The Man Who Could Bullsh*t his Way Out of Trouble, Twice (But not Thrice) ... 2.50
- ❑3, Feb 00 ... 2.50
- ❑4, Mar 00 ... 2.50
- ❑5, Apr 00, Full House or No Way to Treat a Lady ... 2.50
- ❑6, May 00, Stacking the Deck or A Clean Well-Lit Place ... 2.50

PROTECTORS, THE (MALIBU)
MALIBU

Value: Cover or less

- ❑1, When Heroes Gather, O: Protectors, Split cover (in various colors) ... 1.95
- ❑1/CS, O: Protectors, with poster and wrapper ... 2.50
- ❑2, with poster ... 2.50
- ❑3 ... 2.50
- ❑4 ... 2.50
- ❑5/A, bullet hole; bagged ... 2.50
- ❑5/B, Embossed cover; bullet hole ... 2.95
- ❑5/C, Die-cut cover; bullet hole 4.50

	ORIG	GOOD	FINE	N-MINT

❑6 .... 2.50
❑6/CS, with poster 2.50
❑7, Prelude To Chaos 2.50
❑8 .... 2.50
❑9 .... 2.50
❑10 .... 2.50
❑11 .... 2.50
❑12 .... 2.50
❑13, Genesis 2.25
❑14 .... 2.25
❑15 .... 2.25
❑16, Dec 93 .... 2.25
❑17, Jan 94 .... 2.25
❑18, Feb 94 .... 2.25
❑19, Mar 94, Genesis 2.50
❑20, Final Issue 2.50

PROTECTORS, THE (NEW YORK)
NEW YORK

Value: Cover or less
❑1 .... 1.70
❑2 .... 1.70

PROTECTORS HANDBOOK
MALIBU

Value: Cover or less
❑1 .... 2.50

PROTHEUS (MIKE DEODATO'S...)
CALIBER

Value: Cover or less
❑1, Leo Protheus and the Last Defense 2.95
❑2 .... 2.95

PROTISTA CHRONICLES, THE
XULU

	ORIG	GOOD	FINE	N-MINT
❑1, no cover price	—	0.40	1.00	2.00

PROTOTYKES HOLIDAY SPECIAL/HERO ILLUSTRATED HOLIDAY SPECIAL
DARK HORSE

	ORIG	GOOD	FINE	N-MINT
❑1	—	0.20	0.50	1.00
❑2, JBy, JBy (w), Clause and Effect	—	0.20	0.50	1.00

PROTOTYPE
MALIBU

	ORIG	GOOD	FINE	N-MINT
❑0, Aug 94, First...and Foremost; Buena Sera, Mrs. Campbell, O: Prototype I (Bob Campbell), Reprints origin story from Malibu Sun plus new story	2.50	0.39	0.98	1.95
❑1, Aug 93, Budget Cuts, 1: Veil; 1: Glare; 1: Prototype I (Bob Campbell); 1: Prototype II (Jimmy Ruiz), Ultraverse; 1st appear	1.95	0.50	1.25	2.50
❑1/Hol, Budget Cuts, 1: Veil; 1: Glare; 1: Prototype I (Bob Campbell); 1: Prototype II (Jimmy Ruiz), Hologram cover limited edition; hologram	1.95	1.00	2.50	5.00
❑2, Sep 93, Games Of Death, 1: Backstabber; A: Prime	1.95	0.39	0.98	1.95
❑3, Oct 93, Rune, Part F, Giant-size; Rune	2.50	0.50	1.25	2.50
❑4, Nov 93, Wrathful Moon, 1: Wrath	1.95	0.39	0.98	1.95
❑5, Dec 93, Break-Thru, A: Strangers, Break-Thru; Continued in Strangers #7	1.95	0.39	0.98	1.95
❑6, Jan 94, 1: Arena	1.95	0.39	0.98	1.95
❑7, Feb 94	1.95	0.39	0.98	1.95
❑8, Mar 94	1.95	0.39	0.98	1.95
❑9, Apr 94	1.95	0.39	0.98	1.95
❑10, May 94	1.95	0.39	0.98	1.95
❑11, Jun 94, I'm on Fire	1.95	0.39	0.98	1.95
❑12, Jul 94, Assault on the Dark Tower	1.95	0.39	0.98	1.95
❑13, Aug 94, KB (w), Hostile Takeover; A Firm Hand, flipbook with Ultraverse Premiere #6	3.50	0.70	1.75	3.50
❑14, Oct 94, Bent, Folded, Spindled and Mutilated	1.95	0.39	0.98	1.95
❑15, Nov 94, Burning Commitment	1.95	0.39	0.98	1.95
❑16, Dec 94, Driven to Kill, 1: Wild Popes	1.95	0.39	0.98	1.95
❑17, Jan 95, On the Trail of the Techuza	1.95	0.39	0.98	1.95
❑18, Feb 95, Friendly Fire	2.50	0.50	1.25	2.50
❑GS 1, Hostile Takeover, Part 4, Giant-Size edition	2.50	0.50	1.25	2.50

PROWLER (ECLIPSE)
ECLIPSE

Value: Cover or less
❑1, Jul 87, Blood And Magic, 1: Prowler 1.75
❑2, Aug 87 .... 1.75
❑3, Sep 87 .... 1.75
❑4, Oct 87 .... 1.75

PROWLER (MARVEL)
MARVEL

Value: Cover or less
❑1, Nov 94, Approaching Dust 1.75
❑2, Dec 94 .... 1.75
❑3, Jan 95 .... 1.75
❑4, Feb 95 .... 1.75

PROWLER IN "WHITE ZOMBIE", THE
ECLIPSE

Value: Cover or less
❑1, Oct 88, White Zombie, b&w 2.00

PRO WRESTLING'S TRUE FACTS
DAN PETTIGLIO

Value: Cover or less
❑1, Apr 94, nn; b&w 2.95

PRUDENCE & CAUTION
DEFIANT

Value: Cover or less
❑1, May 94, A'Hunting We Will GO, Double-size; English and Spanish versions 3.25
❑2 .... 2.50
❑3 .... 2.50

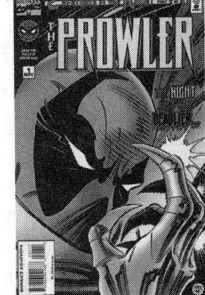

Hobie Brown became The Prowler in *Amazing Spider-Man* #78.

	ORIG	GOOD	FINE	N-MINT

❑4 .... 2.50
❑5 .... 2.50
❑6, Final Issue 2.50

PRYDE & WISDOM
MARVEL

Value: Cover or less
❑1, Sep 96, Mystery School 1.95
❑2, Oct 96 .... 1.95
❑3, Nov 96, Mystery Train, Final Issue 1.95

PSI-FORCE
MARVEL

	ORIG	GOOD	FINE	N-MINT
❑1, Nov 86, Hour Of The Wolf!	0.75	0.20	0.50	1.00
❑2, Dec 86	0.75	0.20	0.50	1.00
❑3, Jan 87	0.75	0.20	0.50	1.00
❑4, Feb 87	0.75	0.20	0.50	1.00
❑5, Mar 87	0.75	0.20	0.50	1.00
❑6, Apr 87	0.75	0.20	0.50	1.00
❑7, May 87	0.75	0.20	0.50	1.00
❑8, Jun 87	0.75	0.20	0.50	1.00
❑9, Jul 87	0.75	0.20	0.50	1.00
❑10, Aug 87	0.75	0.20	0.50	1.00
❑11, Sep 87	0.75	0.20	0.50	1.00
❑12, Oct 87	0.75	0.20	0.50	1.00
❑13, Nov 87	0.75	0.20	0.50	1.00
❑14, Dec 87	0.75	0.20	0.50	1.00
❑15, Jan 88	0.75	0.20	0.50	1.00
❑16, Feb 88	0.75	0.20	0.50	1.00
❑17, Mar 88	0.75	0.20	0.50	1.00
❑18, Apr 88	0.75	0.20	0.50	1.00
❑19, May 88	1.25	0.25	0.63	1.25
❑20, Jun 88	1.25	0.25	0.63	1.25
❑21, Jul 88	1.25	0.25	0.63	1.25
❑22, Aug 88	1.25	0.25	0.63	1.25
❑23, Sep 88	1.25	0.25	0.63	1.25
❑24, Oct 88	1.25	0.25	0.63	1.25
❑25, Nov 88	1.25	0.25	0.63	1.25
❑26, Dec 88	1.50	0.25	0.63	1.25
❑27, Jan 89	1.50	0.25	0.63	1.25
❑28, Feb 89	1.50	0.25	0.63	1.25
❑29, Mar 89	1.50	0.25	0.63	1.25
❑30, Apr 89	1.50	0.25	0.63	1.25
❑31, May 89	1.50	0.25	0.63	1.25
❑32, Jun 89, Final Issue	1.50	0.25	0.63	1.25
❑Anl 1	1.25	0.25	0.63	1.25

PSI-JUDGE ANDERSON
FLEETWAY

	ORIG	GOOD	FINE	N-MINT
❑1, Revenge	1.95	0.40	1.00	2.00
❑2	1.95	0.40	1.00	2.00
❑3	1.95	0.40	1.00	2.00
❑4	1.95	0.40	1.00	2.00
❑5	1.95	0.40	1.00	2.00
❑6	1.95	0.40	1.00	2.00
❑7	1.95	0.40	1.00	2.00
❑8	1.95	0.40	1.00	2.00
❑9	1.95	0.40	1.00	2.00
❑10	1.95	0.40	1.00	2.00
❑11	1.95	0.40	1.00	2.00
❑12	1.95	0.40	1.00	2.00
❑13	1.95	0.40	1.00	2.00
❑14	1.95	0.40	1.00	2.00
❑15, Final Issue	1.95	0.40	1.00	2.00

PSI-JUDGE ANDERSON: ENGRAMS
FLEETWAY

Value: Cover or less
❑1, Anderson, Psi Division: Engram, b&w 1.95
❑2, Anderson, Psi Division: Engram, b&w 1.95

PSI-JUDGE ANDERSON: PSIFILES
FLEETWAY

Value: Cover or less
❑1 .... 2.95

PSI-LORDS
VALIANT

	ORIG	GOOD	FINE	N-MINT
❑1, Sep 94, Postcard From Olympus, chromium wrap-around cover; Valiant Vision.	3.50	0.70	1.75	3.50
❑1/GO, Sep 94, Postcard From Olympus, no cover price; Gold edition	3.50	1.00	2.50	5.00

	ORIG	GOOD	FINE	N-MINT
❑2, Oct 94, Valiant Vision	2.25	0.45	1.13	2.25
❑3, Nov 94, The Chaos Effect: Epsilon, Part 3, Valiant Vision; Chaos Effect	2.25	0.45	1.13	2.25
❑4, Dec 94	2.25	0.45	1.13	2.25
❑5, Jan 95	2.25	0.45	1.13	2.25
❑6, Feb 95, Infection, Part 1	2.25	0.45	1.13	2.25
❑7, Mar 95, Infection, Part 2	2.25	0.45	1.13	2.25
❑8, Apr 95, V: Destroyer	2.25	0.45	1.13	2.25
❑9, May 95	2.25	0.45	1.13	2.25
❑10, Jun 95, Final Issue	2.25	0.45	1.13	2.25

PSYBA-RATS, THE
DC

	ORIG	GOOD	FINE	N-MINT
❑1, Apr 95, They Byte, D: Channelman	2.50	0.50	1.25	2.50
❑2, May 95	1.50	0.50	1.25	2.50
❑3, Jun 95	1.50	0.50	1.25	2.50

PSYCHO, THE
DC

Value: Cover or less

- ❑1, Sep 91 ... 4.95
- ❑2, Oct 91 ... 4.95
- ❑3, Dec 91 ... 4.95

PSYCHO (ALFRED HITCHCOCK'S...)
INNOVATION

Value: Cover or less

- ❑1 ... 2.50
- ❑2 ... 2.50
- ❑3 ... 2.50

PSYCHOANALYSIS (GEMSTONE)
GEMSTONE

Value: Cover or less

- ❑1, JKa, JKa (w), Freddy Carter; Ellen Lyman ... 2.50
- ❑2, JKa, JKa (w), Freddy Carter; Ellen Lyman ... 2.50
- ❑3, JKa, JKa (w), Freddy Carter; Ellen Lyman ... 2.50
- ❑4, JKa, JKa (w), Freddy Carter; Mark Stone ... 2.50
- ❑Anl 1, JKa, JKa (w), Collects series ... 10.95

PSYCHOBLAST
FIRST

Value: Cover or less

- ❑1, Nov 87, Coming Back, 1: Psychoblast ... 1.75
- ❑2, Dec 87 ... 1.75
- ❑3, Jan 88, Forever Yours! ... 1.75
- ❑4, Feb 88 ... 1.75
- ❑5, Mar 88 ... 1.75
- ❑6, Apr 88 ... 1.75
- ❑7, May 88 ... 1.75
- ❑8, Jun 88 ... 1.75
- ❑9, Jul 88, Final Issue ... 1.75

PSYCHO KILLERS
COMIC ZONE

	ORIG	GOOD	FINE	N-MINT
❑1, b&w; Charles Manson	2.75	0.80	2.00	4.00
❑1-2, 2nd Printing; Charles Manson	2.95	0.60	1.50	3.00
❑2, b&w; David Berkowitz ("The Son of Sam")	2.75	0.70	1.75	3.50
❑2-2, 2nd Printing; David Berkowitz ("The Son of Sam")	2.95	0.60	1.50	3.00
❑3, b&w; Ed Gein	2.75	0.70	1.75	3.50
❑3-2, 2nd Printing; Ed Gein	2.95	0.59	1.48	2.95
❑4, Henry Lee Lucas	2.95	0.59	1.48	2.95
❑5, Jeffrey Dahmer	2.95	0.65	1.63	3.25
❑6, Richard Ramirez ("The Nightstalker")	2.95	0.59	1.48	2.95
❑7, Judias Buenoano	2.95	0.59	1.48	2.95
❑8, John Wayne Gacy	2.95	0.59	1.48	2.95
❑9, Ted Bundy	2.95	0.59	1.48	2.95
❑10, Dean Corll ("The Candy Man")	2.95	0.59	1.48	2.95
❑11, The Hillside Strangler; A lawsuit was filed and resulted in this book being taken off the market	2.95	0.70	1.75	3.50
❑12, The Boston Strangler	2.95	0.59	1.48	2.95
❑13, Andrei Chikatilo	2.95	0.59	1.48	2.95
❑14, Aileen Wuornos	2.95	0.59	1.48	2.95
❑15, Charles Starkweather	2.95	0.59	1.48	2.95

PSYCHO KILLERS PMS SPECIAL
ZONE

	ORIG	GOOD	FINE	N-MINT
❑1	2.95	0.65	1.63	3.25

PSYCHOMAN
REVOLUTIONARY

Value: Cover or less

- ❑1, 1: Psychoman ... 2.50

PSYCHONAUT
FANTAGRAPHICS

Value: Cover or less

- ❑1, Mar 96, b&w ... 3.95
- ❑3, b&w; flipbook with The Pursuers ... 3.50

PSYCHONAUTS
MARVEL

Value: Cover or less

- ❑1 ... 4.95
- ❑2 ... 4.95
- ❑3 ... 4.95
- ❑4 ... 4.95

PSYCHO-PATH
VENUSIAN

	ORIG	GOOD	FINE	N-MINT
❑1, Gang Bang, Part 2	—	0.40	1.00	2.00
❑2, Sep 90, Gang Bang, Part 2	2.00	0.40	1.00	2.00

PSYCHOTIC ADVENTURES ILLUSTRATED
LAST GASP

	ORIG	GOOD	FINE	N-MINT
❑1, The Book of Zee; The Dreamer	0.50	0.60	1.50	3.00
❑2	0.50	0.60	1.50	3.00
❑3, The Wreck of the Ship John B.; Women of the Wood	0.50	0.60	1.50	3.00

PSYENCE FICTION
ABACULUS

	ORIG	GOOD	FINE	N-MINT
❑0.5, Sum 98, Truth & Bone, Part 1; The Fallen, b&w; Ashcan preview edition	0.99	0.20	0.50	1.00
❑1, Truth & Bone, Part 1; The Fallen	2.95	0.59	1.48	2.95

PSYLOCKE & ARCHANGEL: CRIMSON DAWN
MARVEL

Value: Cover or less

- ❑1, Aug 97, gatefold cover; gatefold summary ... 2.50
- ❑2, Sep 97, gatefold summary ... 2.50
- ❑3, Oct 97, gatefold summary ... 2.50
- ❑4, Nov 97, gatefold summary ... 2.50

PTERANOMAN
KITCHEN SINK

Value: Cover or less

- ❑1, Aug 90, Donald Simpson ... 2.00

PUBLIC ENEMIES (ETERNITY)
ETERNITY

Value: Cover or less

- ❑1, b&w; Reprint ... 3.95
- ❑2, b&w; Reprint ... 3.95

PUKE & EXPLODE
NORTHSTAR

Value: Cover or less

- ❑1 ... 2.50
- ❑2 ... 2.50

PULP (VOL. 1)
VIZ

Value: Cover or less

- ❑1, Dec 97 ... 5.95

PULP (VOL. 2)
VIZ

Value: Cover or less

- ❑1, Jan 98 ... 5.95
- ❑2, Feb 98 ... 5.95
- ❑3, Mar 98 ... 5.95
- ❑4, Apr 98 ... 5.95
- ❑5, May 98 ... 5.95
- ❑6, Jun 98 ... 5.95
- ❑7, Jul 98 ... 5.95
- ❑8, Aug 98 ... 5.95
- ❑9, Sep 98, Dance Till Tomorrow, Part 16; Dance Till Tomorrow, Part 17 ... 5.95
- ❑10, Oct 98 ... 5.95
- ❑11, Nov 98 ... 5.95
- ❑12, Dec 98 ... 5.95

PULP (VOL. 3)
VIZ

Value: Cover or less

- ❑1, Jan 99, Strain, Part 14; Voyeurs, Inc.: Case One, Part 3 ... 5.95
- ❑2, Feb 99 ... 5.95
- ❑3, Mar 99 ... 5.95
- ❑4, Apr 99 ... 5.95
- ❑5, May 99 ... 5.95
- ❑6, Jun 99 ... 5.95
- ❑7, Jul 99 ... 5.95
- ❑8, Aug 99 ... 5.95
- ❑9, Sep 99 ... 5.95
- ❑10, Oct 99 ... 5.95
- ❑11, Nov 99 ... 5.95
- ❑12, Dec 99 ... 5.95

PULP (VOL. 4)
VIZ

Value: Cover or less

- ❑1, Jan 00 ... 5.95
- ❑2, Feb 00 ... 5.95
- ❑3, Mar 00 ... 5.95
- ❑4, Apr 00 ... 5.95
- ❑5, May 00 ... 5.95
- ❑6, Jun 00 ... 5.95

PULP ACTION
AVALON

Value: Cover or less

- ❑1 ... 2.95
- ❑2 ... 2.95
- ❑3 ... 2.95
- ❑4 ... 2.95
- ❑5, Remember Me?; One Lone Man ... 2.95
- ❑6, Safe Behind Bars ... 2.95
- ❑7 ... 2.95
- ❑8, SD, Any Stranger; Grim Reaper's Wax Museum ... 2.95

PULP DREAMS
FANTAGRAPHICS

Value: Cover or less

- ❑1, b&w; adult ... 2.50

PULP FANTASTIC
VERTIGO

Value: Cover or less

- ❑1, Feb 00, HC (w), The Father ... 2.50
- ❑2, Mar 00, HC (w), The Son ... 2.50
- ❑3, Apr 00, HC (w), And the Holy S*it ... 2.50

PULP FICTION
A LIST

	ORIG	GOOD	FINE	N-MINT
❑1, Spr 97, The Hawk; The vengeful Corpse, b&w; reprints Golden Age material	2.50	0.50	1.25	2.50
❑2, Fal 97, b&w; reprints Golden Age material	2.50	0.50	1.25	2.50
❑3, Win 97, b&w; reprints Golden Age material	2.50	0.50	1.25	2.50
❑4	—	0.50	1.25	2.50
❑5, Spencer Steel; Wine, Women and-Sign!	2.95	0.59	1.48	2.95
❑6	2.95	0.59	1.48	2.95

PULP WESTERN
AVALON

Value: Cover or less ❑1 .... 2.95

PULSE, THE
BLACKJACK

	ORIG	GOOD	FINE	N-MINT
❑1, Jun 97, Lab Rat 7; Project: Gotterdammerung, b&w; no cover price; Anthology	—	0.40	1.00	2.00

PUMA BLUES, THE
AARDVARK ONE

	ORIG	GOOD	FINE	N-MINT
❑1, Jun 86, 10, 000 copies printed; Aardvark One International Publisher	2.00	0.40	1.00	2.00
❑1-2, 2nd Printing	1.70	0.40	1.00	2.00
❑2, Sep 86, 10, 000 copies printed	1.70	0.40	1.00	2.00
❑3, Dec 86, 19, 000 copies printed	1.70	0.40	1.00	2.00
❑4, Feb 87, 13, 000 copies printed	1.70	0.34	0.85	1.70
❑5, Mar 87, 13, 000 copies printed	1.70	0.34	0.85	1.70
❑6, Apr 87, 13, 000 copies printed	1.70	0.34	0.85	1.70
❑7, May 87, 12, 000 copies printed	1.70	0.34	0.85	1.70
❑8, May 87	1.70	0.34	0.85	1.70
❑9, Jul 87	1.70	0.34	0.85	1.70
❑10, Aug 87	1.70	0.34	0.85	1.70
❑11, Sep 87	1.70	0.34	0.85	1.70
❑12, Oct 87	1.70	0.34	0.85	1.70
❑13, Dec 87	1.70	0.34	0.85	1.70
❑14, Jan 88	1.70	0.34	0.85	1.70
❑15	1.70	0.34	0.85	1.70
❑16	1.70	0.34	0.85	1.70
❑17	1.70	0.34	0.85	1.70
❑18, self-published	1.70	0.34	0.85	1.70
❑19, self-published	1.70	0.34	0.85	1.70
❑20, AMo (w), self-published	1.70	0.34	0.85	1.70
❑21, b&w; Mirage Studio Publisher	1.70	0.34	0.85	1.70
❑22, b&w	1.70	0.34	0.85	1.70
❑23, b&w	1.70	0.34	0.85	1.70

PUMMELER
PARODY PRESS

Value: Cover or less ❑1, b&w; Foil embossed cover; Punisher parody 2.95

PUMMELER $2099
PARODY PRESS

Value: Cover or less ❑1, Gold Trimmed Foil Cover .. 2.95

PUMPKINHEAD: THE RITES OF EXORCISM
DARK HORSE

Value: Cover or less

❑1 .... 2.50 ❑3 .... 2.50

❑2 .... 2.50 ❑4 .... 2.50

PUNISHER (1ST SERIES)
MARVEL

	ORIG	GOOD	FINE	N-MINT
❑1, Jan 86, Double-size	1.25	1.60	4.00	8.00
❑2, Feb 86, MZ, Back To The War	0.75	1.00	2.50	5.00
❑3, Mar 86, MZ, Slaughterday	0.75	0.80	2.00	4.00
❑4, Apr 86, MZ, Final Solution, Part 1	0.75	0.80	2.00	4.00
❑5, May 86, MZ, Final Solution, Part 2	0.75	0.80	2.00	4.00

PUNISHER, THE (2ND SERIES)
MARVEL

	ORIG	GOOD	FINE	N-MINT
❑1, Jul 87	0.75	0.80	2.00	4.00
❑2, Aug 87, KJ, Bolivia	0.75	0.60	1.50	3.00
❑3, Oct 87, KJ, The Devil Came From Kansas!	0.75	0.50	1.25	2.50
❑4, Nov 87	0.75	0.40	1.00	2.00
❑5, Jan 88	0.75	0.40	1.00	2.00
❑6, Feb 88	0.75	0.40	1.00	2.00
❑7, Mar 88	0.75	0.40	1.00	2.00
❑8, May 88	1.00	0.40	1.00	2.00
❑9, Jun 88	1.00	0.40	1.00	2.00
❑10, Aug 88, A: Daredevil	1.00	0.60	1.50	3.00
❑11, Sep 88	1.00	0.40	1.00	2.00
❑12, Oct 88	1.00	0.40	1.00	2.00
❑13, Nov 88	1.00	0.40	1.00	2.00
❑14, Dec 88, A: Kingpin	1.00	0.40	1.00	2.00
❑15, Jan 89, To Topple The Kingpin, A: Kingpin	1.00	0.40	1.00	2.00
❑16, Feb 89, Escalation, A: Kingpin	1.00	0.40	1.00	2.00
❑17, Mar 89	1.00	0.40	1.00	2.00
❑18, Apr 89, V: Kingpin	1.00	0.40	1.00	2.00
❑19, May 89, The Spider	1.00	0.40	1.00	2.00
❑20, Jun 89, Bad Tip	1.00	0.40	1.00	2.00
❑21, Jul 89, EL, The Boxer	1.00	0.40	1.00	2.00
❑22, Aug 89, EL, Ninja Training Camp	1.00	0.40	1.00	2.00
❑23, Sep 89, EL, Capture The Flag	1.00	0.40	1.00	2.00
❑24, Oct 89, EL, Land Of The Eternal Sun, 1: Shadowmasters	1.00	0.40	1.00	2.00
❑25, Nov 89, EL, Sunset In Kansas, A: Shadowmasters, Giant-sized	1.75	0.40	1.00	2.00
❑26, Nov 89, RH, The Whistle Blower	1.00	0.40	1.00	2.00
❑27, Dec 89	1.00	0.40	1.00	2.00

The Punisher faced Dr. Doom during "Acts of Vengeance."

	ORIG	GOOD	FINE	N-MINT
❑28, Dec 89, Acts of Vengeance, Acts of Vengeance	1.00	0.40	1.00	2.00
❑29, Jan 90, Acts of Vengeance, Acts of Vengeance	1.00	0.40	1.00	2.00
❑30, Feb 90, Confession	1.00	0.40	1.00	2.00
❑31, Mar 90, Crankin'	1.00	0.40	1.00	2.00
❑32, Apr 90, Speedy Solution	1.00	0.40	1.00	2.00
❑33, May 90, Reaver Fever	1.00	0.40	1.00	2.00
❑34, Jun 90, Exo-Skeleton	1.00	0.40	1.00	2.00
❑35, Jul 90, Jigsaw Puzzle, Part 1, Jigsaw Puzzle	1.00	0.40	1.00	2.00
❑36, Aug 90, Jigsaw Puzzle, Part 2, Jigsaw Puzzle	1.00	0.40	1.00	2.00
❑37, Aug 90, Jigsaw Puzzle, Part 3, Jigsaw Puzzle	1.00	0.40	1.00	2.00
❑38, Sep 90, Jigsaw Puzzle, Part 4, Jigsaw Puzzle	1.00	0.40	1.00	2.00
❑39, Sep 90, Jigsaw Puzzle, Part 5, Jigsaw Puzzle	1.00	0.40	1.00	2.00
❑40, Oct 90, Jigsaw Puzzle, Part 6, Jigsaw Puzzle	1.00	0.40	1.00	2.00
❑41, Oct 90, Should A Gentleman Offer A Tiparillo To A Lady?	1.00	0.30	0.75	1.50
❑42, Nov 90, The Punisher In St. Paradine's	1.00	0.30	0.75	1.50
❑43, Dec 90, Border Run	1.00	0.30	0.75	1.50
❑44, Jan 91, Flag Burner	1.00	0.30	0.75	1.50
❑45, Feb 91, One Way Fare	1.00	0.30	0.75	1.50
❑46, Mar 91, Cold Cache	1.00	0.30	0.75	1.50
❑47, Apr 91, The Brattle Gun, Part 1	1.00	0.30	0.75	1.50
❑48, May 91, The Brattle Gun, Part 2	1.00	0.30	0.75	1.50
❑49, Jun 91, Death Below Zero	1.00	0.30	0.75	1.50
❑50, Jul 91, Bark Like A Dog; Yo Yo, double-sized	1.50	0.40	1.00	2.00
❑51, Aug 91, Golden Buddha	1.00	0.30	0.75	1.50
❑52, Sep 91, Lupe	1.00	0.30	0.75	1.50
❑53, Oct 91, Final Days, Part 1	1.00	0.30	0.75	1.50
❑54, Nov 91, Final Days, Part 2	1.00	0.30	0.75	1.50
❑55, Nov 91, Final Days, Part 3	1.00	0.30	0.75	1.50
❑56, Dec 91, Final Days, Part 4	1.00	0.30	0.75	1.50
❑57, Dec 91, Final Days, Part 5, photo cover with paper overlay	1.00	0.40	1.00	2.00
❑58, Jan 92, Final Days, Part 6	1.00	0.30	0.75	1.50
❑59, Jan 92, Final Days, Part 7, Punisher becomes black	1.00	0.30	0.75	1.50
❑60, Feb 92, VM, Escape from New York, A: Luke Cage	1.25	0.30	0.75	1.50
❑61, Mar 92, VM, Crackdown, A: Luke Cage	1.25	0.30	0.75	1.50
❑62, Apr 92, VM, Fade to White, Punisher becomes white again	1.25	0.30	0.75	1.50
❑63, May 92, The Big Check-Out	1.25	0.25	0.63	1.25
❑64, Eurohit, Part 1	1.25	0.25	0.63	1.25
❑65, Eurohit, Part 2	1.25	0.25	0.63	1.25
❑66, Eurohit, Part 3	1.25	0.25	0.63	1.25
❑67, Eurohit, Part 4	1.25	0.25	0.63	1.25
❑68, Eurohit, Part 5	1.25	0.25	0.63	1.25
❑69, Eurohit, Part 6	1.25	0.25	0.63	1.25
❑70, Eurohit, Part 7	1.25	0.25	0.63	1.25
❑71, Oct 92, Loose Ends	1.25	0.25	0.63	1.25
❑72, Nov 92, Life During Wartime	1.25	0.25	0.63	1.25
❑73, Dec 92, Police Action, Part 1	1.25	0.25	0.63	1.25
❑74, Jan 93, Police Action, Part 2	1.25	0.25	0.63	1.25
❑75, Feb 93, Police Action, Part 3, Embossed cover	2.75	0.55	1.38	2.75
❑76, Mar 93, Lava	1.25	0.30	0.75	1.50
❑77, Apr 93, Survival, Part 1	1.25	0.30	0.75	1.50
❑78, May 93, VM, Survival, Part 2	1.25	0.30	0.75	1.50
❑79, Jun 93, Survival, Part 3	1.25	0.30	0.75	1.50
❑80, Jul 93, Last Confession	1.25	0.30	0.75	1.50
❑81, Aug 93, Bodies Of Evidence	1.25	0.25	0.63	1.25
❑82, Sep 93, Firefight, Part 1	1.25	0.25	0.63	1.25

	ORIG	GOOD	FINE	N-MINT
❑83, Oct 93, Firefight, Part 2	1.25	0.25	0.63	1.25
❑84, Nov 93, Firefight, Part 3	1.25	0.25	0.63	1.25
❑85, Dec 93, Suicide Run Prelude	1.25	0.25	0.63	1.25
❑86, Jan 94, Suicide Run, Part 3, Giant-size	2.95	0.59	1.48	2.95
❑87, Feb 94, Suicide Run, Part 6	1.25	0.25	0.63	1.25
❑88, Mar 94, Suicide Run, Part 9	1.25	0.25	0.63	1.25
❑89, Apr 94, Fortress: Miami, Part 1	1.25	0.25	0.63	1.25
❑90, May 94, Fortress: Miami, Part 2	1.50	0.25	0.63	1.25
❑91, Jun 94, RH, Fortress: Miami, Part 3	1.50	0.30	0.75	1.50
❑92, Jul 94, RH, Fortress: Miami, Part 4	1.50	0.30	0.75	1.50
❑93, Aug 94	1.50	0.30	0.75	1.50
❑94, Sep 94, No Rules, Part 1	1.50	0.30	0.75	1.50
❑95, Oct 94, No Rules, Part 2	1.50	0.30	0.75	1.50
❑96, Nov 94, Raving Beauty	1.50	0.30	0.75	1.50
❑97, Dec 94, The Devil's Secret Name	1.50	0.30	0.75	1.50
❑98, Jan 95	1.50	0.30	0.75	1.50
❑99, Feb 95	1.50	0.30	0.75	1.50
❑100, Mar 95, The Cage!, Giant-size	2.95	0.59	1.48	2.95
❑100/SC, Mar 95, The Cage!, foil cover; Giant-size	3.95	0.79	1.98	3.95
❑101, Apr 95	1.50	0.30	0.75	1.50
❑102, May 95	1.50	0.30	0.75	1.50
❑103, Jun 95, Countdown, Part 1 (4)	1.50	0.30	0.75	1.50
❑104, Jul 95, Countdown, Part 4 (1), Final Issue	1.50	0.30	0.75	1.50
❑Anl 1, Evolutionary War, Part 2	1.75	0.70	1.75	3.50
❑Anl 2, Atlantis Attacks, Part 5, V: Moon Knight, Atlantis Attacks	2.00	0.50	1.25	2.50
❑Anl 3, Lifeform; Lifeform, Part 1	2.00	0.50	1.25	2.50
❑Anl 4, JLee, Von Strucker Gambit; The Von Strucker Gambit	2.00	0.40	1.00	2.00
❑Anl 5, The System Bytes, Part 1, System Bytes	2.25	0.45	1.13	2.25
❑Anl 6, trading card; Polybagged	2.95	0.59	1.48	2.95
❑Anl 7	2.95	0.59	1.48	2.95

PUNISHER (3RD SERIES)
MARVEL

Value: Cover or less

- ❑1, Nov 95, Condemned, foil cover ... 2.95
- ❑2, Dec 95, A: Hatchetman ... 1.95
- ❑3, Dec 95 ... 1.95
- ❑4, Feb 96, V: Jigsaw; A: Daredevil ... 1.95
- ❑5, Mar 96, PB, Firepower! ... 1.95
- ❑6, Apr 96, PB, Hostage to the Devil ... 1.95
- ❑7, May 96 ... 1.95
- ❑8, Jun 96 ... 1.95
- ❑9, Jul 96 ... 1.95
- ❑10, Aug 96, V: Jigsaw ... 1.95
- ❑11, Sep 96, Onslaught: Impact 2, S.H.I.E.L.D. helicarrier crashes ... 1.95
- ❑12, Oct 96, Total X-Tinction, Part 1, V: X-Cutioner ... 1.95
- ❑13, Nov 96, Total X-Tinction, Part 2, V: X-Cutioner ... 1.95
- ❑14, Dec 96, Total X-Tinction, Part 3, V: X-Cutioner ... 1.95
- ❑15, Jan 97, Total X-Tinction, Part 4, V: X-Cutioner ... 1.95
- ❑16, Feb 97, Total X-Tinction, Part 5, V: X-Cutioner ... 1.50
- ❑17, Mar 97, Dead Man Walking 1.95
- ❑18, Apr 97, Double Cross, Final Issue ... 1.95

PUNISHER, THE (4TH SERIES)
MARVEL

Value: Cover or less

- ❑1, Nov 98, BWr, Purgatory, Part 1, gatefold summary ... 2.99
- ❑1/SC, Nov 98, BWr, Purgatory, Part 1, DFE alternate cover 6.95
- ❑2, Dec 98, BWr, Purgatory, Part 2, gatefold summary ... 2.99
- ❑3, Jan 99, BWr, Purgatory, Part 3 ... 2.99
- ❑4, Feb 99, BWr, Purgatory, Part 4, A: Oliver ... 2.99

PUNISHER (5TH SERIES)
MARVEL

	ORIG	GOOD	FINE	N-MINT
❑1, Apr 00, Welcome Back, Frank	2.99	0.80	2.00	4.00
❑1/SC, Apr 00, Welcome Back, Frank, White background on cover	—	1.70	4.25	8.50
❑2, May 00, Badaboom, Badabing	2.99	0.70	1.75	3.50
❑2/SC, May 00, Badaboom, Badabing, White background on cover	—	1.20	3.00	6.00
❑3, Jun 00, The Devil by the Horns, Polybagged with Marvel Knights/Marvel Boy Genesis Edition	2.99	0.70	1.75	3.50
❑4, Jul 00, Wild Kingdom	2.99	0.60	1.50	3.00
❑5, Aug 00, Even Worse Things	2.99	0.60	1.50	3.00
❑6, Sep 00, Spit Out of Luck	2.99	0.60	1.50	2.99
❑7, Oct 00, Bring Out Your Dead	2.99	0.60	1.50	2.99
❑8, Nov 00, Desperate Measures, 1: The Russian	2.99	0.60	1.50	2.99
❑9, Dec 00, From Russia with Love	2.99	0.60	1.50	2.99
❑10, Jan 01, Glutton for Punishment	2.99	0.60	1.50	2.99
❑11, Feb 01, Any Which Way You Can, 1: The Vigilante Squad; D: The Russian	2.99	0.60	1.50	2.99
❑12, Mar 01, Go Frank Go, D: Ma Gnucci	2.99	0.60	1.50	2.99

PUNISHER 2099
MARVEL

Value: Cover or less

- ❑1, Feb 93, Deadly Genesis, 1: Punisher 2099, foil cover ... 1.75
- ❑2, Mar 93, The Morning After, 1: Fearmaster ... 1.25
- ❑3, Apr 93 ... 1.25
- ❑4, May 93, Heroes Day ... 1.25
- ❑5, Jun 93, Punishment Hotel. 1.25
- ❑6, Jul 93 ... 1.25
- ❑7, Aug 93, Love 'n' Bullets, Part 1 ... 1.25
- ❑8, Sep 93, Love 'n' Bullets, Part 2 ... 1.25
- ❑9, Oct 93, Love 'n' Bullets, Part 3, D: Kerry Dowen ... 1.25
- ❑10, Nov 93 ... 1.25
- ❑11, Dec 93 ... 1.25
- ❑12, Jan 94 ... 1.25
- ❑13, Feb 94, Fall of the Hammer, Part 5 ... 1.25
- ❑14, Mar 94 ... 1.25
- ❑15, Apr 94 ... 1.25
- ❑16, May 94 ... 1.50
- ❑17, Jun 94 ... 1.50
- ❑18, Jul 94 ... 1.50
- ❑19, Aug 94 ... 1.50
- ❑20, Sep 94 ... 1.50
- ❑21, Oct 94, Punisher Versus Punisher! ... 1.50
- ❑22, Nov 94 ... 1.50
- ❑23, Dec 94 ... 1.50
- ❑24, Jan 95 ... 1.50
- ❑25, Feb 95 ... 2.25
- ❑25/SC, Feb 95, Special cover 2.95
- ❑26, Mar 95 ... 1.50
- ❑27, Apr 95 ... 1.50
- ❑28, May 95 ... 1.95
- ❑29, Jun 95 ... 1.95
- ❑30, Jul 95 ... 1.95
- ❑31, Aug 95 ... 1.95
- ❑32, Sep 95 ... 1.95
- ❑33, Oct 95 ... 1.95
- ❑34, Nov 95, Final Issue; continues in 2099 A.D. Apocalypse #1 ... 1.95

PUNISHER, THE: A MAN NAMED FRANK
MARVEL

Value: Cover or less

- ❑1, Jun 94, nn; One-Shot ... 6.95

PUNISHER ANNIVERSARY MAGAZINE, THE
MARVEL

Value: Cover or less

- ❑1 ... 4.95

PUNISHER ARMORY, THE
MARVEL

	ORIG	GOOD	FINE	N-MINT
❑1, Jul 90, weapons	1.50	0.40	1.00	2.00
❑2, Jun 91	1.75	0.40	1.00	2.00
❑3	1.75	0.40	1.00	2.00
❑4	2.00	0.40	1.00	2.00
❑5	2.00	0.40	1.00	2.00
❑6	2.00	0.40	1.00	2.00
❑7	2.00	0.40	1.00	2.00
❑8	2.00	0.40	1.00	2.00
❑9	2.00	0.40	1.00	2.00
❑10, Nov 94	2.00	0.40	1.00	2.00

PUNISHER BACK TO SCHOOL SPECIAL
MARVEL

	ORIG	GOOD	FINE	N-MINT
❑1, Nov 92, The Sinner	2.95	0.70	1.75	3.50
❑2, No Pain, 1993	2.95	0.60	1.50	3.00
❑3, Oct 94, 1994	2.95	0.60	1.50	3.00

PUNISHER/BATMAN: DEADLY KNIGHTS
MARVEL

Value: Cover or less

- ❑1, Oct 94, KJ; JR, nn ... 4.95

PUNISHER/BLACK WIDOW: SPINNING DOOMSDAY'S WEB
MARVEL

Value: Cover or less

- ❑1 ... 9.95

PUNISHER: BLOODLINES
MARVEL

Value: Cover or less

- ❑1, DC, nn; prestige format ... 5.95

PUNISHER: DIE HARD IN THE BIG EASY
MARVEL

Value: Cover or less

- ❑1, nn; prestige format one-shot ... 4.95

PUNISHER, THE: EMPTY QUARTER
MARVEL

Value: Cover or less

- ❑1, Nov 94, nn; prestige format one-shot ... 6.95

PUNISHER: G-FORCE
MARVEL

Value: Cover or less

- ❑1, nn; squarebound with cardstock cover; One-Shot ... 4.95

PUNISHER HOLIDAY SPECIAL
MARVEL

	ORIG	GOOD	FINE	N-MINT
❑1, foil cover	2.95	0.60	1.50	3.00
❑2, The Killing Season	2.95	0.60	1.50	3.00
❑3, Jan 95	2.95	0.60	1.50	3.00

PUNISHER: INTRUDER
MARVEL

Value: Cover or less

- ❑1 ... 9.95
- ❑1/HC ... 14.95

PUNISHER INVADES THE 'NAM: FINAL INVASION
MARVEL

Value: Cover or less

- ❑1, Feb 94, nn ... 6.95

PUNISHER KILLS THE MARVEL UNIVERSE
MARVEL

	ORIG	GOOD	FINE	N-MINT
❑1, Nov 95	5.95	5.00	12.50	25.00
❑36893, Mar 00, 2nd Printing	5.95	1.19	2.97	5.95

PUNISHER MAGAZINE, THE
MARVEL

	ORIG	GOOD	FINE	N-MINT
❑1, Sep 89, b&w; Reprints Punisher (Ltd. Series) #1 in black & white	2.25	0.60	1.50	3.00
❑2, Oct 89, b&w; Reprints Punisher (Ltd. Series) #2-3 in black & white	2.25	0.50	1.25	2.50
❑3, Nov 89, b&w; Reprints Punisher (Ltd. Series) #4-5 in black & white	2.25	0.50	1.25	2.50
❑4, Dec 89, b&w; Reprints Punisher #1-2 in black & white	2.25	0.50	1.25	2.50
❑5, Dec 89, b&w; Reprints Punisher #3-4 in black & white	2.25	0.50	1.25	2.50
❑6, Jan 90, Garbage; Wild Rose, b&w; Reprints Punisher #5-6 in black & white	2.25	0.50	1.25	2.50
❑7, Feb 90, b&w; Reprints Punisher #7-8 in black & white	2.25	0.50	1.25	2.50
❑8, Mar 90, b&w; Reprint	2.25	0.50	1.25	2.50
❑9, Apr 90, b&w; Reprint	2.25	0.50	1.25	2.50
❑10, May 90, b&w; Reprint	2.25	0.50	1.25	2.50
❑11, Jun 90, b&w; Reprint	2.25	0.50	1.25	2.50
❑12, Jul 90, b&w; Reprint	2.25	0.50	1.25	2.50
❑13, Aug 90, b&w; Reprint	2.25	0.50	1.25	2.50
❑14, Sep 90, b&w; Reprints Punisher War Journal #1-2	2.25	0.50	1.25	2.50
❑15, Oct 90, b&w; Reprint	2.25	0.50	1.25	2.50
❑16, Nov 90, b&w; Reprint	2.25	0.50	1.25	2.50

PUNISHER MEETS ARCHIE, THE
MARVEL

	ORIG	GOOD	FINE	N-MINT
❑1, Aug 94, enhanced cover	3.95	0.80	2.00	4.00
❑1/SC, Die-cut cover	3.95	0.90	2.25	4.50

PUNISHER MOVIE SPECIAL, THE
MARVEL

Value: Cover or less ❑1, Jun 90, BA, nn 5.95

PUNISHER, THE: NO ESCAPE
MARVEL

Value: Cover or less ❑1, nn; prestige format 4.95

PUNISHER, THE: ORIGIN MICRO CHIP
MARVEL

	ORIG	GOOD	FINE	N-MINT
❑1, Over The Edge, O: Micro Chip	1.75	0.40	1.00	2.00
❑2	1.75	0.40	1.00	2.00

PUNISHER/PAINKILLER JANE
MARVEL

Value: Cover or less ❑1, Jan 01, Lovesick, cardstock cover; One-Shot 3.50

PUNISHER: P.O.V.
MARVEL

	ORIG	GOOD	FINE	N-MINT
❑1, BW; BWr, JSn (w), Foresight	4.95	1.00	2.50	5.00
❑2, BW; BWr, JSn (w), Extro-Spection	4.95	1.00	2.50	5.00
❑3, BW; BWr, JSn (w), Intro-Spection	4.95	1.00	2.50	5.00
❑4, BW; BWr, JSn (w), Hindsight	4.95	1.00	2.50	5.00

PUNISHER SUMMER SPECIAL
MARVEL

	ORIG	GOOD	FINE	N-MINT
❑1, Aug 91	2.95	0.60	1.50	3.00
❑2, Aug 92, Rough Cut; High Risk	2.95	0.60	1.50	3.00
❑3, Dead Man Coming Through; Faster, Faster	2.50	0.50	1.25	2.50
❑4, Jul 94, Soiled Legacy; Killing An After-noon	2.95	0.59	1.48	2.95

PUNISHER: THE GHOSTS OF INNOCENTS
MARVEL

Value: Cover or less

❑1, JSn (w) 5.95

❑2, JSn (w) 5.95

PUNISHER: THE PRIZE
MARVEL

Value: Cover or less ❑1, nn; prestige format 4.95

PUNISHER VS. DAREDEVIL
MARVEL

Value: Cover or less ❑1, Jun 00, KJ; FM; JR2, FM (w), Child's Play; Good Guys Wear Red, Reprint 3.50

PUNISHER WAR JOURNAL, THE
MARVEL

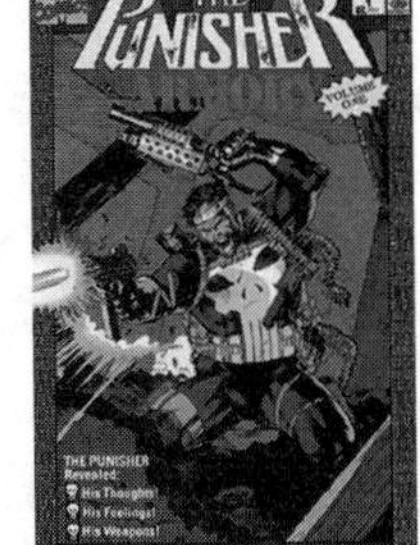

Detailed information on The Punisher's weaponry was given in the occasional issues of *Punisher Armory.*

	ORIG	GOOD	FINE	N-MINT
❑1, Nov 88, JLee, A Eye for an Eye, Part 1, O: Punisher	1.50	0.40	1.00	2.00
❑2, Dec 88, JLee, A Eye for an Eye, Part 2, A: Daredevil	1.50	0.30	0.75	1.50
❑3, Feb 89, A Eye for an Eye, Part 3, A: Daredevil	1.50	0.30	0.75	1.50
❑4, Mar 89, JLee	1.50	0.30	0.75	1.50
❑5, May 89, JLee, Crucible	1.50	0.30	0.75	1.50
❑6, Jun 89, JLee, A: Wolverine	1.50	0.30	0.75	1.50
❑7, Jul 89, JLee, Endangered Species, A: Wolverine	1.50	0.30	0.75	1.50
❑8, Sep 89, JLee	1.50	0.30	0.75	1.50
❑9, Oct 89, JLee, Guilt Trip	1.50	0.30	0.75	1.50
❑10, Nov 89, JLee, Second Shot	1.50	0.30	0.75	1.50
❑11, Dec 89, JLee, Shock Treatment	1.50	0.30	0.75	1.50
❑12, Dec 89, JLee, Acts of Vengeance, Acts of Vengeance	1.50	0.30	0.75	1.50
❑13, Dec 89, JLee, Acts of Vengeance, Acts of Vengeance	1.50	0.30	0.75	1.50
❑14, Jan 90, RH, Blind Faith, A: Spider-Man	1.50	0.30	0.75	1.50
❑15, Feb 90, RH, Headlines!, A: Spider-Man	1.50	0.30	0.75	1.50
❑16, Mar 90, Panhandle	1.50	0.30	0.75	1.50
❑17, Apr 90, JLee, Topical Trouble	1.50	0.30	0.75	1.50
❑18, May 90, JLee, Kahuna	1.50	0.30	0.75	1.50
❑19, Jun 90, JLee, Trauma In Paradise	1.50	0.30	0.75	1.50
❑20, Jul 90, The Debt	1.50	0.30	0.75	1.50
❑21, Aug 90, Deep Water	1.50	0.30	0.75	1.50
❑22, Sep 90, Snowstorm	1.50	0.30	0.75	1.50
❑23, Oct 90, Firepower Among The Ruins, Part 1	1.75	0.35	0.88	1.75
❑24, Nov 90, Firepower Among The Ruins, Part 2	1.75	0.35	0.88	1.75
❑25, Dec 90, Sicilian Saga, Part 1	1.75	0.35	0.88	1.75
❑26, Jan 91, Sicilian Saga, Part 2	1.75	0.35	0.88	1.75
❑27, Feb 91, Sicilian Saga, Part 3	1.75	0.35	0.88	1.75
❑28, Mar 91, Meat	1.75	0.35	0.88	1.75
❑29, Apr 91, Crash And Burn, A: Ghost Rider	1.75	0.35	0.88	1.75
❑30, May 91, Spin Cycle, A: Ghost Rider	1.75	0.35	0.88	1.75
❑31, Jun 91, Pipeline, Painted cover	1.75	0.35	0.88	1.75
❑32, Jul 91, Blow Out	1.75	0.35	0.88	1.75
❑33, Aug 91, Fire In The Hole	1.75	0.35	0.88	1.75
❑34, Sep 91, Blackout	1.75	0.35	0.88	1.75
❑35, Oct 91, Motivation	1.75	0.35	0.88	1.75
❑36, Nov 91, Let Them Eat Cake, Photo cover	1.75	0.35	0.88	1.75
❑37, Dec 91, Controversy	1.75	0.35	0.88	1.75
❑38, Jan 92, Terminal Velocity	1.75	0.35	0.88	1.75
❑39, Feb 92, Slay Ride	1.75	0.35	0.88	1.75
❑40, Mar 92, Good Money After Bad	1.75	0.35	0.88	1.75
❑41, Apr 92, Armageddon Express	1.75	0.35	0.88	1.75
❑42, May 92, Ten To One	1.75	0.35	0.88	1.75
❑43, Jun 92, VM, Adirondack Haunts	1.75	0.35	0.88	1.75
❑44, Jul 92, VM, Home Sweet Home	1.75	0.35	0.88	1.75
❑45, Aug 92, Dead Man's Hand, Part 3	1.75	0.35	0.88	1.75
❑46, Sep 92, Dead Man's Hand, Part 6	1.75	0.35	0.88	1.75
❑47, Oct 92, Dead Man's Hand, Part 9	1.75	0.35	0.88	1.75
❑48, Nov 92, Walk Through Fire, Part 1	1.75	0.35	0.88	1.75
❑49, Dec 92, Walk Through Fire, Part 2	1.75	0.35	0.88	1.75
❑50, Jan 93, Payback!, Part 1, 1: Punisher 2099, Embossed cover; Punisher 2099 Preview	2.95	0.59	1.48	2.95
❑51, Feb 93, Payback!, Part 2	1.75	0.35	0.88	1.75
❑52, Mar 93, Heart of Ice	1.75	0.35	0.88	1.75
❑53, Apr 93, Heart Of Stone	1.75	0.35	0.88	1.75
❑54, May 93, Surface Thrill	1.75	0.35	0.88	1.75
❑55, Jun 93, Conviction, Part 3	1.75	0.35	0.88	1.75
❑56, Jul 93, 24 Hours of Power!	1.75	0.35	0.88	1.75
❑57, Aug 93, Blood Money, A: Daredevil; A: Ghost Rider	1.75	0.35	0.88	1.75
❑58, Sep 93, Hideout, Part 6, A: Daredevil; A: Ghost Rider	1.75	0.35	0.88	1.75
❑59, Oct 93, The House That Hate Built, A: Max	1.75	0.35	0.88	1.75
❑60, Nov 93, A: Cage	1.75	0.35	0.88	1.75
❑61, Dec 93, Suicide Run, Part 1, Embossed foil cover; Giant-size	2.95	0.59	1.48	2.95
❑62, Jan 94, Suicide Run, Part 4	1.75	0.35	0.88	1.75
❑63, Feb 94, Suicide Run, Part 7	1.75	0.35	0.88	1.75
❑64, Mar 94, Suicide Run, Part 10, regular cover	2.25	0.45	1.13	2.25

	ORIG	GOOD	FINE	N-MINT
❑64/SC, Mar 94, Suicide Run, Part 10, Die-cut cover	2.95	0.59	1.48	2.95
❑65, Apr 94, Pariah, Part 1	1.75	0.35	0.88	1.75
❑66, May 94, BA, Pariah, Part 2	1.75	0.39	0.98	1.95
❑67, Jun 94, Pariah, Part 3; Trouble, Part 1	1.95	0.39	0.98	1.95
❑68, Jul 94, Pariah, Part 4; Trouble, Part 2	1.95	0.39	0.98	1.95
❑69, Aug 94, Pariah, Part 5	1.95	0.39	0.98	1.95
❑70, Sep 94	1.95	0.39	0.98	1.95
❑71, Oct 94, Last Entry, Part 1	1.95	0.39	0.98	1.95
❑72, Nov 94, Last Entry, Part 2	1.95	0.39	0.98	1.95
❑73, Dec 94, Last Entry, Part 3	1.95	0.39	0.98	1.95
❑74, Jan 95, Last Entry, Part 4	1.95	0.39	0.98	1.95
❑75, Feb 95, Last Entry, Part 5	2.50	0.39	0.98	1.95
❑76, Mar 95, First Entry, Part 1, New Punisher (Lynn Michaels) begins	1.95	0.39	0.98	1.95
❑77, Apr 95	1.95	0.39	0.98	1.95
❑78, May 95	1.95	0.39	0.98	1.95
❑79, Jun 95, Countdown, Part 2 (3), D: Microchip	1.95	0.39	0.98	1.95
❑80, Jul 95, Countdown, Part 5 (0), D: Stone Cold, Final Issue	1.95	0.39	0.98	1.95

PUNISHER, THE: WAR ZONE
MARVEL

Value: Cover or less

- ❑1, Mar 92, JR2, Only the Dead Know Brooklyn, Die-cut cover 2.25
- ❑2, Apr 92, JR2, Blood in the Water 1.75
- ❑3, May 92, JR2, The Frame.. 1.75
- ❑4, Jun 92, JR2, Closer to the Frame 1.75
- ❑5, Jul 92, JR2, Feeding Frenzy 1.75
- ❑6, Aug 92, JR2, The Carrion Eaters 1.75
- ❑7, Sep 92, JR2, Mugger's Picnic 1.75
- ❑8, Oct 92, JR2, The Hunting Ground 1.75
- ❑9, Nov 92, Goners 1.75
- ❑10, Dec 92, Tight Spot 1.75
- ❑11, Jan 93, In a Deadly Place 1.75
- ❑12, Feb 93, Psychoville, Part 1 .... 1.75
- ❑13, Mar 93, Psychoville, Part 2 .... 1.75
- ❑14, Apr 92, Psychoville, Part 3 .... 1.75
- ❑15, May 93, Psychoville, Part 4 .... 1.75
- ❑16, Jun 93, Psychoville, Part 5 .... 1.75
- ❑17, Jul 93, The Jericho Syndrome, Part 1 .... 1.75
- ❑18, Aug 93, The Jericho Syndrome, Part 2 .... 1.75
- ❑19, Sep 93, The Jericho Syndrome, Part 3, A: Wolverine 1.75
- ❑20, Oct 93, Numbah One Boom Boom 1.75
- ❑21, Nov 93, 2 Mean 2 Die!.... 1.75
- ❑22, Dec 93, Taking Tiger Mountain 1.75
- ❑23, Jan 94, VM, Suicide Run, Part 2, D: Rapido, Embossed foil cover; Giant-size 2.95
- ❑24, Feb 94, VM; JB, Suicide Run, Part 5 .... 1.75
- ❑25, Mar 94, VM; JB, Suicide Run, Part 8 .... 2.25
- ❑26, Apr 94, JB, Conan with a Gun, Part 1 .... 1.75
- ❑27, May 94, Conan with a Gun, Part 2 .... 1.95
- ❑28, Jun 94, JB, Conan with a Gun, Part 3 .... 1.95
- ❑29, Jul 94, JB, Conan with a Gun, Part 4 .... 1.95
- ❑30, Aug 94, Conan with a Gun, Part 5 .... 1.95
- ❑31, Sep 94, River of Blood; River of Blood, Part 1 .... 1.95
- ❑32, Oct 94, River of Blood; River of Blood, Part 2 .... 1.95
- ❑33, Nov 94, JKu, River of Blood, Part 3 .... 1.95
- ❑34, Dec 94, JKu, River of Blood, Part 4 .... 1.95
- ❑35, Jan 95, River of Blood, Part 5 .... 1.95
- ❑36, Feb 95, River of Blood, Part 6 .... 1.95
- ❑37, Mar 95, Dark Judgment, Part 1, O: Max (The Punisher's dog) 1.95
- ❑38, Apr 95, Dark Judgment, Part 2 .... 1.95
- ❑39, May 95, Dark Judgment, Part 3 .... 1.95
- ❑40, Jun 95, Dark Judgment, Part 4 .... 1.95
- ❑41, Jul 95, Countdown, Part 3 (2), Final Issue 1.95
- ❑Anl 1, card 2.95
- ❑Anl 2, Hurt So Good; Second Chance, D: Roc 2.95

PUNISHER/WOLVERINE AFRICAN SAGA
MARVEL

Value: Cover or less

- ❑1, nn 5.95

PUNISHER, THE: YEAR ONE
MARVEL

Value: Cover or less

- ❑1, Dec 94, Family Business, O: the Punisher 2.50
- ❑2, Jan 95, O: the Punisher.... 2.50
- ❑3, Feb 95, O: the Punisher.... 2.50
- ❑4, Mar 95, Fire With Fire, O: the Punisher 2.50

PUNX
ACCLAIM

Value: Cover or less

- ❑1, Nov 95, KG, KG (w), Street Smarrts 2.50
- ❑2, Dec 95, KG, KG (w) 2.50
- ❑3, Jan 96, KG, KG (w) 2.50

PUNX (MANGA) SPECIAL
ACCLAIM

Value: Cover or less

- ❑1, Mar 96, nn; to be read from back to front 2.50

PUPPET MASTER
ETERNITY

Value: Cover or less

- ❑1, full color 2.50
- ❑2, full color 2.50
- ❑3, full color 2.50
- ❑4, full color 2.50

PUPPET MASTER: CHILDREN OF THE PUPPET MASTER
ETERNITY

Value: Cover or less

- ❑1, full color 2.50
- ❑2, full color 2.50

PURE IMAGES
PURE IMAGINATION

Value: Cover or less

- ❑1, some color 2.50
- ❑2, some color 2.50
- ❑3, monsters; some color........ 2.50
- ❑4, monsters; some color........ 2.50

PURGATORI
CHAOS!

	ORIG	GOOD	FINE	N-MINT
❑0.5, Dec 00	2.95	0.59	1.48	2.95
❑1, Oct 98, Revelations	2.95	0.60	1.50	3.00
❑2, Nov 98, V: Lady Death	2.95	0.59	1.48	2.95
❑3, Dec 98	2.95	0.59	1.48	2.95
❑4, Jan 99	2.95	0.59	1.48	2.95
❑5, Feb 99, Karmilla	2.95	0.59	1.48	2.95
❑6, Mar 99, Jade	2.95	0.59	1.48	2.95
❑7, Apr 99, Blood Finale!, V: Dracula	2.95	0.59	1.48	2.95
❑Ash 1, nn; no cover price; ashcan preview	—	0.60	1.50	3.00

PURGATORI: EMPIRE
CHAOS

Value: Cover or less

- ❑1, May 00, Reign of Blood 2.95
- ❑2 .... 2.95
- ❑3 .... 2.95

PURGATORI: GODDESS RISING
CHAOS!

Value: Cover or less

- ❑1, Jul 99 .... 2.95
- ❑2, Aug 99 .... 2.95
- ❑3, Sep 99 .... 2.95
- ❑4, Dec 99 .... 2.95

PURGATORI: THE DRACULA GAMBIT
CHAOS!

	ORIG	GOOD	FINE	N-MINT
❑1, Aug 97	2.95	0.59	1.48	2.95
❑1/SC, Aug 97, no cover price; Centennial Premium Edition	—	0.60	1.50	3.00

PURGATORI: THE DRACULA GAMBIT SKETCHBOOK
CHAOS!

Value: Cover or less

- ❑1, Jul 97, nn; b&w preliminary sketches 2.95

PURGATORI: THE VAMPIRES MYTH
CHAOS!

	ORIG	GOOD	FINE	N-MINT
❑-1, Aug 96	1.50	0.30	0.75	1.50
❑1, Aug 96, Red foil embossed	3.50	0.70	1.75	3.50
❑1/LE, Aug 96, wraparound acetate cover; premium edition; limited to 10, 000 copies	—	1.00	2.50	5.00
❑1/SC, Oct 96, "Krome" edition (color)	—	1.60	4.00	8.00
❑2, Oct 96	2.95	0.60	1.50	3.00
❑3, Dec 96	2.95	0.59	1.48	2.95
❑4	2.95	0.59	1.48	2.95
❑5	2.95	0.59	1.48	2.95
❑6	2.95	0.59	1.48	2.95

PURGATORY USA
SLAVE LABOR

	ORIG	GOOD	FINE	N-MINT
❑1, Mar 89, Welcome to Maynardville; Chicken, b&w; Ed Brubaker's first published work	1.75	0.40	1.00	2.00

PURGE
ANIA

Value: Cover or less

- ❑0, Purification Agenda........ 1.95
- ❑1, Aug 93, Codeblock, Part 1 .... 1.95

PURGE (AMARA)
AMARA

Value: Cover or less

- ❑0, Preview edition........ 1.50

PURPLE CLAW MYSTERIES
AC

Value: Cover or less

- ❑1, b&w; Reprint........ 2.95

PURPLE HOOD, THE
JOHN SPENCER & CO.

	ORIG	GOOD	FINE	N-MINT
❑1	—	1.00	2.50	5.00
❑2, Destroy the World!; Deep Danger	—	1.00	2.50	5.00

PURR
BLUE EYED DOG

	ORIG	GOOD	FINE	N-MINT
❑1, Harry Clarke; Angel with a Gun	5.00	1.60	4.00	8.00

PUSSYCAT
MARVEL

	ORIG	GOOD	FINE	N-MINT
❑1, WW; BWa, b&w; magazine	0.35	30.00	75.00	150.00

Q

Q-LOC
CHIASMUS

Value: Cover or less

❑1, Aug 94 ... 2.50

QUACK!
STAR*REACH

	ORIG	GOOD	FINE	N-MINT
❑1, Jul 76, Duckaneer; The Wraith!, b&w	1.25	0.50	1.25	2.50
❑2, Jan 77, Newton the Rabbit Wonder!; The Cure	1.25	0.50	1.25	2.50
❑3, Apr 77, The Beavers; The Wraith: Duck Death	1.25	0.50	1.25	2.50
❑4, Jun 77, Home on the Range, Rabbit!; The Beavers	1.25	0.50	1.25	2.50
❑5, Sep 77, The Reality Wraith; Tales of the Oregon Bobcat: At Last, Long Love!	1.25	0.50	1.25	2.50
❑6, Dec 77, The Quark: Son of Quack; Into the Motherlode!	1.25	0.50	1.25	2.50

QUADRANT
QUADRANT

Value: Cover or less

❑1, adult ... 1.95
❑2, adult ... 1.95
❑3, adult ... 1.95
❑4, adult ... 1.95
❑5, adult ... 1.95
❑6, adult; no cover date ... 1.95
❑7, adult ... 1.95
❑8, b&w; adult ... 1.95

QUADRO GANG, THE
NONSENSE UNLIMITED

Value: Cover or less

❑1, b&w ... 1.25

QUAGMIRE
KITCHEN SINK

	ORIG	GOOD	FINE	N-MINT
❑1, Sum 70, b&w; adult	0.50	0.60	1.50	3.00

QUAGMIRE U.S.A.
ANTARCTIC

Value: Cover or less

❑1, Mar 94, b&w ... 2.75
❑2, May 94, b&w ... 2.75
❑3, Jul 94, b&w ... 2.75

QUALITY SPECIAL
FLEETWAY

	ORIG	GOOD	FINE	N-MINT
❑1, Strontium Dog	1.50	0.40	1.00	2.00
❑2, Midnight Surfer	1.50	0.40	1.00	2.00

QUANTUM & WOODY
ACCLAIM

	ORIG	GOOD	FINE	N-MINT
❑0/AE, American Entertainment exclusive	—	0.60	1.50	3.00
❑1, Jun 97, Klang	2.50	0.50	1.25	2.50
❑1/A, Klang, Painted cover	2.50	0.50	1.25	2.50
❑2, Jul 97	2.50	0.50	1.25	2.50
❑3, Aug 97, 1: The Goat	2.50	0.50	1.25	2.50
❑4, Sep 97	2.50	0.50	1.25	2.50
❑5, Oct 97, Bad Haircut at Table Six	2.50	0.50	1.25	2.50
❑6, Nov 97	2.50	0.50	1.25	2.50
❑7, Dec 97	2.50	0.50	1.25	2.50
❑8, Jan 98	2.50	0.50	1.25	2.50
❑9, Feb 98, A: Troublemakers	2.50	0.50	1.25	2.50
❑10, Mar 98	2.50	0.50	1.25	2.50
❑11, Apr 98	2.50	0.50	1.25	2.50
❑12, Jan 98, no cover date; indicia says Jan	2.50	0.50	1.25	2.50
❑13, Feb 98, no cover date; indicia says Feb	2.50	0.50	1.25	2.50
❑14	2.50	0.50	1.25	2.50
❑15	2.50	0.50	1.25	2.50
❑16	2.50	0.50	1.25	2.50
❑17, Final Issue	2.50	0.50	1.25	2.50
❑Ash 1, Feb 97, no cover price; b&w preview of series	—	0.20	0.50	1.00

QUANTUM CREEP
PARODY PRESS

Value: Cover or less

❑1, b&w ... 2.50

QUANTUM LEAP
INNOVATION

	ORIG	GOOD	FINE	N-MINT
❑1, Sep 91, First There Was A Mountain, Then There Was No Mountain, Then There Was, 1: Doctor Sam Beckett (Quantum Leap)	2.50	1.20	3.00	6.00
❑2, Dec 91	2.50	1.00	2.50	5.00
❑3, Mar 92, Sam as Santa	2.50	1.00	2.50	5.00
❑4, Apr 92, The 50, 000 Quest, Sam on game show	2.50	1.00	2.50	5.00
❑5, May 92, Seeing is Believing, Superman theme cover	2.50	1.00	2.50	5.00
❑6, Sep 92, A Tale of Two Cindys	2.50	0.80	2.00	4.00
❑7, Oct 92, Lives on the Fringe	2.50	0.80	2.00	4.00
❑8, Dec 92, Getaway	2.50	0.80	2.00	4.00
❑9, Feb 93, Up Against a Stonewall	2.50	0.80	2.00	4.00
❑10, Apr 93, Too Funny for Words	2.50	0.60	1.50	3.00
❑11, May 93, For the Good of the Nation	2.50	0.60	1.50	3.00
❑12, Jun 93, Waiting...	2.50	0.60	1.50	3.00
❑13, Aug 93, One Giant Leap, foil-enhanced cardstock cover; Time and Space Special #1	2.95	0.60	1.50	3.00

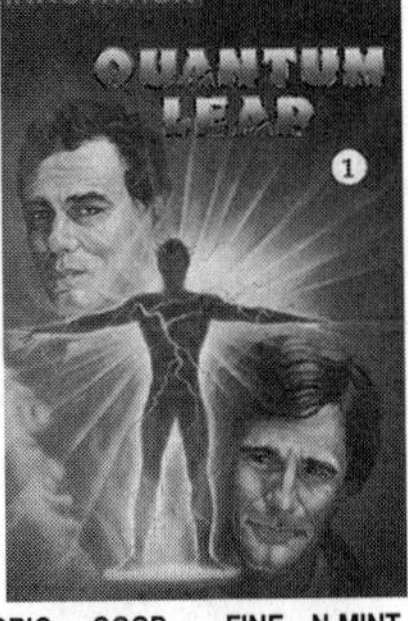

Dr. Sam Beckett's time-travel adventures occurred within his own lifetime for the most part.

© 1991 Belsarius Productions (Innovation)

	ORIG	GOOD	FINE	N-MINT
❑Anl 1	2.95	0.60	1.50	3.00
❑SE 1, Oct 92, First There Was A Mountain, Then There Was No Mountain, Then There Was, reprints #1	2.50	0.60	1.50	3.00

QUASAR
MARVEL

Value: Cover or less

❑1, Oct 89, The Price of Power!, O: Quasar ... 1.00
❑2, Nov 89 ... 1.00
❑3, Nov 89 ... 1.00
❑4, Dec 89, O: Quantum ... 1.00
❑5, Dec 89, Acts of Vengeance, Part 10, V: Absorbing Man, Acts of Vengeance ... 1.00
❑6, Jan 90, Acts of Vengeance, Part 19, V: Venom; V: Living Laser; V: Red Ghost, Acts of Vengeance ... 1.00
❑7, Feb 90, A: Spider-Man, Spider-Man has cosmic powers ... 1.00
❑8, Mar 90 ... 1.00
❑9, Apr 90, 1: Captain Atlas ... 1.00
❑10, May 90, O: Captain Atlas ... 1.00
❑11, Jun 90, Phoenix ... 1.00
❑12, Jul 90 ... 1.00
❑13, Aug 90 ... 1.00
❑14, Sep 90, TMc (c) ... 1.00
❑15, Oct 90 ... 1.00
❑16, Nov 90, 48pgs ... 1.50
❑17, Dec 90 ... 1.00
❑18, Jan 91 ... 1.50
❑19, Feb 91, 1: Starlight ... 1.00
❑20, Mar 91, Fantastic Four ... 1.00
❑21, Apr 91 ... 1.00
❑22, May 91 ... 1.00
❑23, Jun 91, A: Ghost Rider ... 1.00
❑24, Jul 91, 1: Infinity (physical) 1.00
❑25, Aug 91, new costume ... 1.00
❑26, Sep 91, Infinity Gauntlet, Infinity Gauntlet ... 1.00
❑27, Oct 91, Infinity Gauntlet, 1: Epoch, Infinity Gauntlet ... 1.00
❑28, Nov 91 ... 1.00
❑29, Dec 91 ... 1.00
❑30, Jan 92 ... 1.00
❑31, Feb 92, A: D.P.7, New Universe ... 1.25
❑32, Mar 92, Operation: Galactic Storm, Part 3, A: Starfox; 1: Korath the Pursuer; A: Imperial Guard, Galactic Storm ... 1.25
❑33, Apr 92, Operation: Galactic Storm, Part 10, Galactic Storm ... 1.25
❑34, May 92, Operation: Galactic Storm, Part 17, A: Binary, Galactic Storm ... 1.25
❑35, Jun 92, Operation: Galactic Storm aftermath, Galactic Storm ... 1.25
❑36, Jul 92, A: Makkari; V: Souleater; A: Her ... 1.25
❑37, Aug 92 ... 1.25
❑38, Sep 92, Infinity War, Infinity War ... 1.25
❑39, Oct 92, Infinity War, Infinity War ... 1.25
❑40, Nov 92, Infinity War, Infinity War ... 1.25
❑41, Dec 92, 1: Kismet ... 1.25
❑42, Jan 93 ... 1.25
❑43, Feb 93 ... 1.25
❑44, Mar 93 ... 1.25
❑45, Apr 93 ... 1.25
❑46, May 93 ... 1.25
❑47, Jun 93, 1: Thunderstrike ... 1.25
❑48, Jul 93 ... 1.25
❑49, Aug 93 ... 1.25
❑50, Sep 93, Horizon Of Holes, A: Silver Surfer, Holo-grafix cover; Giant-size ... 2.95
❑51, Oct 93, A: Anglemen; A: Squadron Supreme ... 1.25
❑52, Nov 93 ... 1.25
❑53, Dec 93 ... 1.25
❑54, Jan 94 ... 1.25
❑55, Feb 94, Starblast, Part 6 ... 1.25
❑56, Mar 94, Starblast, Part 10 ... 1.25
❑57, Apr 94 ... 1.25
❑58, May 94 ... 1.25
❑59, Jun 94 ... 1.25
❑60, Jul 94, Final Issue ... 1.25
❑SE 1, Mar 92, reprints Quasar #32 ... 1.25
❑SE 2, Apr 92, reprints Quasar #33 ... 1.25
❑SE 3, May 92, reprints Quasar #34 ... 1.25

QUEEN & COUNTRY
ONI

Value: Cover or less

❑1, Mar 01 ... 2.95

QUEEN OF THE DAMNED (ANNE RICE'S...)
INNOVATION

Value: Cover or less

❑1, 91, On the Road to the Vampire Lestat ... 2.50
❑2, 92 ... 2.50
❑3, 92 ... 2.50
❑4, 92 ... 2.50
❑5, 92 ... 2.50
❑6, 93, All Hallow's Eve, Part 1 ... 2.50
❑7, 93, All Hallow's Eve, Part 2 ... 2.50
❑8, Jul 93 ... 2.50
❑9, Sep 93 ... 2.50
❑10, Nov 93 ... 2.50
❑11, Dec 93 ... 2.50
❑12 ... 2.50

QUEEN'S GREATEST HITS
REVOLUTIONARY

Value: Cover or less

❑1, Nov 93, b&w ... 2.50

QUEST FOR CAMELOT
DC

Value: Cover or less

❑1, Jul 98, movie Adaptation ... 4.95

QUEST FOR DREAMS LOST
LITERACY VOLUNTEERS

Value: Cover or less

- ❑1, The Quest for Dreams Lost; Teenage Mutant Ninja Turtles, A: Teenage Mutant Ninja Turtles; A: Trollords; A: Eb'nn the Raven; A: Reacto Man; A: Falterous; A: J.B. Space, b&w; The Realm story 2.00

QUESTION, THE
DC

Value: Cover or less

- ❑1, Feb 87, The Bad News, Painted cover 1.50
- ❑2, Mar 87 .... 1.50
- ❑3, Apr 87 .... 1.50
- ❑4, May 87 .... 1.50
- ❑5, Jun 87 .... 1.50
- ❑6, Jul 87 .... 1.50
- ❑7, Aug 87 .... 1.50
- ❑8, Sep 87 .... 1.50
- ❑9, Oct 87 .... 1.50
- ❑10, Nov 87 .... 1.50
- ❑11, Dec 87 .... 1.50
- ❑12, Jan 88 .... 1.50
- ❑13, Feb 88 .... 1.75
- ❑14, Mar 88 .... 1.75
- ❑15, Apr 88 .... 1.75
- ❑16, May 88 .... 1.75
- ❑17, Jun 88, Rorschach, Green Arrow 1.75
- ❑18, Jul 88, Green Arrow 1.75
- ❑19, Aug 88 .... 1.75
- ❑20, Oct 88 .... 1.75
- ❑21, Nov 88 .... 1.75
- ❑22, Dec 88 .... 1.75
- ❑23, Win 88 .... 1.75
- ❑24, Jan 89 .... 1.75
- ❑25, Feb 89 .... 1.75
- ❑26, Mar 89, A: Riddler 1.75
- ❑27, Jun 89 .... 1.75
- ❑28, Jul 89 .... 1.75
- ❑29, Aug 89 .... 1.75
- ❑30, Sep 89 .... 1.75
- ❑31, Oct 89 .... 1.75
- ❑32, Nov 89 .... 1.75
- ❑33, Dec 89 .... 1.75
- ❑34, Jan 90 .... 1.75
- ❑35, Mar 90 .... 1.75
- ❑36, Apr 90, Final Issue 1.75
- ❑Anl 1, Batman, Green Arrow 2.50
- ❑Anl 2, Green Arrow 3.50

QUESTION QUARTERLY, THE
DC

Value: Cover or less

- ❑1, Aut 90, Any Man's Death 2.50
- ❑2, Sum 91, Gomorrah Homecoming 2.50
- ❑3, Aut 91 .... 2.50
- ❑4, Win 91 .... 2.95
- ❑5, Spr 92, Outrage, Final Issue 2.95

QUESTION RETURNS, THE
DC

Value: Cover or less

- ❑1, Feb 97, One-Shot 3.50

QUEST OF THE TIGER WOMAN, THE
MILLENNIUM

Value: Cover or less

- ❑1, The Sky Devil 2.95

QUEST PRESENTS
QUEST

	ORIG	GOOD	FINE	N-MINT
❑1, Jul 83	1.00	0.30	0.75	1.50
❑2, Sep 83	1.25	0.30	0.75	1.50
❑3, Nov 83	1.50	0.30	0.75	1.50

QUESTPROBE
MARVEL

	ORIG	GOOD	FINE	N-MINT
❑1, Aug 84, JR, 1: Chief Examiner, Hulk	0.75	0.30	0.75	1.50
❑2, Jan 85, JM; AM, AM (w), Mysterio Times Two!, Spider-Man	0.75	0.30	0.75	1.50
❑3, Nov 85, Human Torch; Thing	0.75	0.30	0.75	1.50

QUICK DRAW MCGRAW
CHARLTON

	ORIG	GOOD	FINE	N-MINT
❑1, Nov 70	0.15	2.00	5.00	10.00
❑2, Jan 71	0.15	1.40	3.50	7.00
❑3, Mar 71	0.15	1.00	2.50	5.00
❑4, May 71	0.15	1.00	2.50	5.00
❑5, Jul 71	0.15	1.00	2.50	5.00
❑6, Sep 71	0.15	0.80	2.00	4.00
❑7, Nov 71	0.15	0.80	2.00	4.00
❑8, Jan 72	0.15	0.80	2.00	4.00

QUICKEN FORBIDDEN
CRYPTIC PRESS

	ORIG	GOOD	FINE	N-MINT
❑1, b&w	—	0.65	1.63	3.25
❑2, b&w	—	0.60	1.50	3.00
❑3, b&w	—	0.60	1.50	3.00
❑4, b&w	—	0.60	1.50	3.00
❑5, b&w	—	0.60	1.50	3.00
❑6, b&w	—	0.60	1.50	3.00
❑7, b&w	—	0.60	1.50	3.00
❑8, b&w	—	0.60	1.50	3.00
❑9, Anxiety Disorder, Part 1, b&w	2.95	0.60	1.50	3.00

QUICKSILVER
MARVEL

Value: Cover or less

- ❑1, Nov 97, The Beast in Me, wrap-around cover; gatefold summary 2.99
- ❑2, Dec 97, gatefold summary 1.99
- ❑3, Jan 98, gatefold summary 1.99
- ❑4, Feb 98, gatefold summary 1.99
- ❑5, Mar 98, gatefold summary 1.99
- ❑6, Apr 98, A: Inhumans, gatefold summary 1.99
- ❑7, May 98, A: Black Knight, gatefold summary 1.99
- ❑8, Jun 98, gatefold summary; in Savage Land 1.99
- ❑9, Jul 98, gatefold summary 1.99
- ❑10, Aug 98, Live Kree or Die, Part 3, gatefold summary; concludes in Avengers #7 .... 1.99
- ❑11, Sep 98, The Siege of Wundagore, Part 2, A: Heroes for Hire, gatefold summary 1.99
- ❑12, Oct 98, The siege of Wundagore, Part 4, V: Exodus, gatefold summary; double-sized 2.99
- ❑13, Nov 98, gatefold summary 1.99

QUINCY LOOKS INTO HIS FUTURE
GENERAL ELECTRIC

	ORIG	GOOD	FINE	N-MINT
❑1, nn; giveaway; King Features strip	—	0.40	1.00	2.00

QUIT YOUR JOB
ALTERNATIVE

Value: Cover or less

- ❑1, nn; b&w 6.95

QUIVERS
CALIBER

Value: Cover or less

- ❑1, BMB, BMB (w), b&w 2.95
- ❑2, b&w 2.95

Q-UNIT
HARRIS

Value: Cover or less

- ❑1, 1: Q-Unit, trading card; Polybagged with "layered reality cybercard" 2.95

R

RABBIT
SHARKBAIT

Value: Cover or less

- ❑1, The Serpent's Agenda, Part 1 .... 2.50

RABID
FANTACO

Value: Cover or less

- ❑1, nn 5.95

RABID ANIMAL KOMIX
KRANKIN' KOMIX

Value: Cover or less

- ❑1, Another Day, Another 12-Pack 2.95
- ❑2, Laff Riot 2.95

RABID RACHEL
MILLER

Value: Cover or less

- ❑1, b&w 2.00

RACE AGAINST TIME
DARK ANGEL

Value: Cover or less

- ❑1, Jun 97 .... 2.50
- ❑2, Aug 97 .... 2.50

RACE OF SCORPIONS
DARK HORSE

Value: Cover or less

- ❑1, Jul 91, The Big Lizards, b&w 2.25
- ❑2, Aug 91 .... 2.50
- ❑3, Sep 92 .... 2.50
- ❑4, Oct 91 .... 2.50

RACE OF SCORPIONS (MINI-SERIES)
DARK HORSE

Value: Cover or less

- ❑1, Mar 90, b&w 4.50
- ❑2, Sep 90, b&w 4.95

RACER X
NOW

	ORIG	GOOD	FINE	N-MINT
❑1, Sep 88	1.75	0.40	1.00	2.00
❑2, Oct 88	1.75	0.35	0.88	1.75
❑3, Nov 88	1.75	0.35	0.88	1.75
❑4, Jan 89	1.75	0.35	0.88	1.75
❑5, Feb 89	1.75	0.35	0.88	1.75
❑6, Mar 89	1.75	0.35	0.88	1.75
❑7, Apr 89	1.75	0.35	0.88	1.75
❑8, May 89, Comics Code	1.75	0.35	0.88	1.75
❑9, Jun 89, Comics Code	1.75	0.35	0.88	1.75
❑10, Jul 89, Comics Code	1.75	0.35	0.88	1.75
❑11, Aug 89, Comics Code	1.75	0.35	0.88	1.75

RACER X (3RD SERIES)
WILDSTORM

Value: Cover or less

- ❑1, Oct 00, The Prince 2.95
- ❑2, Nov 00, The ProtTgT 2.95
- ❑3, Dec 00, The Mark of Death 2.95

RACER X (VOL. 2)
NOW

	ORIG	GOOD	FINE	N-MINT
❑1, Sep 89	1.75	0.40	1.00	2.00
❑2, Oct 89, Death Drives a rented Car!	1.75	0.35	0.88	1.75
❑3, Nov 89	1.75	0.35	0.88	1.75
❑4, Dec 89	1.75	0.35	0.88	1.75
❑5, Jan 90	1.75	0.35	0.88	1.75
❑6, Feb 90	1.75	0.35	0.88	1.75
❑7, Mar 90	1.75	0.35	0.88	1.75
❑8, Apr 90	1.75	0.35	0.88	1.75
❑9, May 90	1.75	0.35	0.88	1.75
❑10, Jun 90	1.75	0.35	0.88	1.75

RACER X PREMIERE
Now

Value: Cover or less

- ❑1, Aug 88, nn 3.50

RACK & PAIN
Dark Horse

Value: Cover or less

- ❑1, Mar 94, Death & Deception, Dark Horse 2.50
- ❑2, Apr 94 .... 2.50
- ❑3, May 94, Why the Gods Kill 2.50
- ❑4, Jun 94 .... 2.50

RACK & PAIN: KILLERS
Chaos

Value: Cover or less

- ❑1, Death & Deception, Chaos 2.95
- ❑2 .... 2.95
- ❑3 .... 2.95
- ❑4 .... 2.95

RADICAL DREAMER
Blackball

	ORIG	GOOD	FINE	N-MINT
❑0, May 94, Dreams Cannot Die!, poster comic	1.99	0.50	1.25	2.50
❑1, Jun 94, Dreamnet Mainline, poster comic	1.99	0.40	1.00	2.00
❑2, Jul 94, poster comic	1.99	0.59	1.48	2.95
❑3, poster comic	1.99	0.50	1.25	2.50
❑4, Nov 94, foldout comic on cardstock	2.50	0.50	1.25	2.50

RADICAL DREAMER (VOL. 2)
Mark's Giant Economy Size

Value: Cover or less

- ❑1, Jun 95, b&w 2.95
- ❑2, Jul 95, b&w 2.95
- ❑3, Aug 95, b&w 2.95
- ❑4, Sep 95, b&w 2.95
- ❑5, Dec 95, b&w 2.95

RADIOACTIVE MAN
Bongo

	ORIG	GOOD	FINE	N-MINT
❑1, The Origin Of Radioactive Man, O: Radioactive Man, glow cover	2.95	0.80	2.00	4.00
❑88, The Molten Menace Of Magmom The Lava Man, 2nd issue	1.95	0.50	1.25	2.50
❑216, See No Evil, Hear No Evil, 3rd issue	1.95	0.45	1.13	2.25
❑412, In Ze Clutches of Doctor Crab!, trading card; 4th issue	2.25	0.45	1.13	2.25
❑679, 5th issue	2.25	0.45	1.13	2.25
❑1000, Jan 95, In his own Image, 6th issue	2.25	0.45	1.13	2.25

RADIOACTIVE MAN (VOL. 2)
Bongo

Value: Cover or less

- ❑1, #100 on cover 2.50

RADIOACTIVE MAN 80 PAGE COLOSSAL
Bongo

Value: Cover or less

- ❑1, To Betroth a Foe; Radioactive Man, Teen Idol 4.95

RADIO BOY
Eclipse

Value: Cover or less

- ❑1, b&w 1.50

RADREX
Bullet

Value: Cover or less

- ❑1 .... 2.25

RAGAMUFFINS
Eclipse

	ORIG	GOOD	FINE	N-MINT
❑1, Jan 85, GC	1.75	0.40	1.00	2.00

RAGE
Anarchy Bridgeworks

Value: Cover or less

- ❑1, Enemy of the People 2.95

RAGGEDYMAN
Cult

	ORIG	GOOD	FINE	N-MINT
❑1, b&w	2.50	0.50	1.25	2.50
❑1/SC, b&w; Prism cover	2.75	0.55	1.38	2.75
❑2, Corporate Entity, Part 1, b&w	2.50	0.39	0.98	1.95
❑3, Corporate Entity, Part 2, b&w	2.50	0.39	0.98	1.95
❑4, Corporate Entity, Part 3, b&w	2.50	0.50	1.25	2.50
❑5, Jul 93, b&w	2.50	0.50	1.25	2.50
❑6	—	0.50	1.25	2.50

RAGING ANGELS
Classic Hippie

Value: Cover or less

- ❑1, b&w 2.50

RAGMAN
DC

	ORIG	GOOD	FINE	N-MINT
❑1, Sep 76, Origin Of The Tatterdemalion, 1: Ragman	0.30	1.00	2.50	5.00
❑2, Nov 76	0.30	0.60	1.50	3.00
❑3, Jan 77, JKu	0.30	0.60	1.50	3.00
❑4, Mar 77, JKu	0.30	0.60	1.50	3.00
❑5, Jul 77, JKu	0.30	0.60	1.50	3.00

RAGMAN (MINI-SERIES)
DC

	ORIG	GOOD	FINE	N-MINT
❑1, Oct 91, PB, KG (w), Bones Of The Defenseless	1.50	0.40	1.00	2.00
❑2, Nov 91, PB, A Ragged Revenge	1.50	0.40	1.00	2.00
❑3, Dec 91	1.50	0.40	1.00	2.00
❑4, Jan 92	1.50	0.40	1.00	2.00
❑5, Feb 92	1.50	0.40	1.00	2.00
❑6, Mar 92	1.25	0.40	1.00	2.00
❑7, Apr 92, RT; PB; KG, KG (w), The Summit	1.25	0.40	1.00	2.00
❑8, May 92, Final Issue	1.25	0.40	1.00	2.00

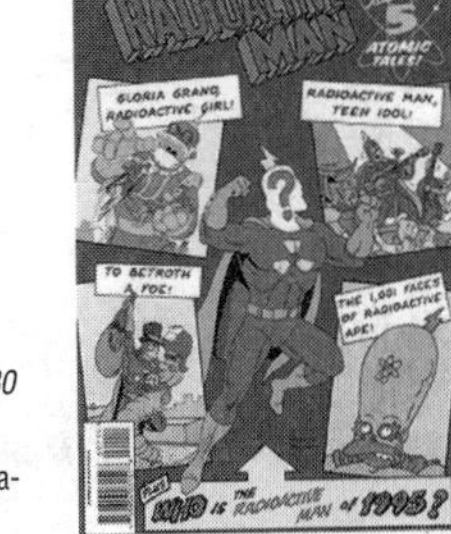

Bongo paid tribute to DC's 80-Page Giants with its own *Radioactive Man 80 Page Colossal* in 1996.

© 1996 20th Century Fox Film Corporation (Bongo)

RAGMAN: CRY OF THE DEAD
DC

	ORIG	GOOD	FINE	N-MINT
❑1, Aug 93	1.75	0.40	1.00	2.00
❑2, Sep 93, Child's Play	1.75	0.35	0.88	1.75
❑3, Oct 93, Mange Moun!	1.75	0.35	0.88	1.75
❑4, Nov 93, Blood Sacrifice	1.75	0.35	0.88	1.75
❑5, Dec 93	1.75	0.35	0.88	1.75
❑6, Jan 94, Cheval Blanc!	1.75	0.35	0.88	1.75

RAGMOP
Planet Lucy

Value: Cover or less

- ❑1 .... 2.75
- ❑1-2, Dec 95, 2nd Printing 3.10
- ❑2 .... 2.75
- ❑2-2, Dec 95, 2nd Printing 2.95
- ❑3, Oct 95 .... 2.95
- ❑4, Dec 95 .... 2.95
- ❑5, Feb 96 .... 2.95
- ❑6, Apr 96 .... 2.95
- ❑7, Jun 96 .... 2.95

RAGMOP (VOL. 2)
Image

Value: Cover or less

- ❑1, Sep 97, O: Thrill Kitten, b&w; synopsis of first series 2.95
- ❑2, Nov 97, b&w 2.95
- ❑3 .... 2.95

RAGNAROK GUY
Sun

Value: Cover or less

- ❑1 .... 2.50

RAHRWL
Northstar

	ORIG	GOOD	FINE	N-MINT
❑1, Limited edition original print (1988). 32 pages. 500 copies produced	2.25	0.50	1.25	2.50
❑1-2, 2nd Printing; New edition with redrawn art, 2 additional pages; Splash page identifies it as a new printing	2.25	0.45	1.13	2.25

RAI
Valiant

Value: Cover or less

- ❑0, Nov 92, BL (w), The Blood Of Heroes, 1: Rai (new); 1: Bloodshot; O: Rai, series continues as Rai and the Future Force; Foretells future of Valiant Universe 2.25
- ❑1, Mar 92, Invasion, Part 2, trading cards; Flip-book with Magnus Robot Fighter (Valiant) #5 .... 1.95
- ❑2, Apr 92 .... 1.95
- ❑3, May 92 .... 1.95
- ❑4, Jun 92, Scarcer 1.95
- ❑5, Jul 92 .... 2.25
- ❑6, Aug 92, FM (c), Unity, Part 7, Unity 2.25
- ❑7, Sep 92, Unity, Part 15, D: Rai (original), Unity 2.25
- ❑8, Oct 92, Unity epilogue; Series continued in Rai and the Future Force #9 .... 2.25
- ❑25, Oct 94, Series continued from Rai and the Future Force #24 .... 2.25
- ❑26, Nov 94, The Chaos Effect: Epsilon, Part 3, Chaos Effect 2.25
- ❑27, Dec 94 .... 2.25
- ❑28, Jan 95 .... 2.25
- ❑29, Feb 95 .... 2.25
- ❑30, Mar 95 .... 2.25
- ❑31, Apr 95, Bad Penny; Bad Penny, Part 1 .... 2.25
- ❑32, May 95, Bad Penny; Bad Penny, Part 2 .... 2.25
- ❑33, Jun 95, Final Issue 2.25

RAI AND THE FUTURE FORCE
Valiant

	ORIG	GOOD	FINE	N-MINT
❑9, May 93, A: Magnus; A: Eternal Warrior; A: X-O Commando, Series continued from Rai #8	2.50	0.50	1.25	2.50
❑9/GO, Gold	—	0.70	1.75	3.50
❑9/LE, Series continued from Rai #8	2.50	0.60	1.50	3.00
❑10, Jun 93, The Death of Japan	2.25	0.45	1.13	2.25
❑11, Jul 93	2.25	0.45	1.13	2.25
❑12, Aug 93, serial number coupon for contest	2.25	0.45	1.13	2.25
❑13, Sep 93	2.25	0.45	1.13	2.25
❑14, Oct 93, A: X-O Manowar armor	2.25	0.45	1.13	2.25
❑15, Nov 93, The Battle For South Am, Part 1	2.25	0.45	1.13	2.25
❑16, Dec 93	2.25	0.45	1.13	2.25
❑17, Jan 94	2.25	0.45	1.13	2.25
❑18, Feb 94	2.25	0.45	1.13	2.25
❑19, Mar 94	2.25	0.45	1.13	2.25
❑20, Apr 94, Spylocke revealed as spider-alien	2.25	0.45	1.13	2.25

Issue	ORIG	GOOD	FINE	N-MINT
❑21, May 94, trading card; series continues as Rai	2.25	0.45	1.13	2.25
❑22, Jun 94, D: Rai	2.25	0.45	1.13	2.25
❑23, Aug 94	2.25	0.45	1.13	2.25
❑24, Sep 94, new Rai; Series continued in Rai #25	2.25	0.45	1.13	2.25

RAI COMPANION
VALIANT

Issue	ORIG	GOOD	FINE	N-MINT
❑1, no cover price	—	0.20	0.50	1.00

RAIDER 3000
GAUNTLET

Value: Cover or less

- ❑1, Lethal Enforcement!, b&w ... 2.95
- ❑2, b&w ... 2.95

RAIDERS OF THE LOST ARK
MARVEL

Issue	ORIG	GOOD	FINE	N-MINT
❑1, Sep 81, KJ; JB	0.50	0.40	1.00	2.00
❑2, Oct 81, KJ; JB	0.50	0.40	1.00	2.00
❑3, Nov 81, KJ; JB	0.50	0.40	1.00	2.00

RAIN
TUNDRA

Value: Cover or less

- ❑1, Moments In The Rain, Introduction by Stephen R. Bissette ... 1.95
- ❑2 ... 1.95
- ❑3 ... 1.95
- ❑4 ... 1.95
- ❑5 ... 1.95
- ❑6 ... 1.95

RAINBOW BRITE AND THE STAR STEALER
DC

Value: Cover or less

- ❑1, Rainbow Brite and the Star Stealer, Official movie adaption ... 1.00

RAK
RAK GRAPHICS

Value: Cover or less

- ❑1, b&w ... 5.00

RAKEHELL
DRACULINA

Value: Cover or less

- ❑1 ... 2.50

RALFY ROACH
BUGGED OUT

Value: Cover or less

- ❑1, Jun 93, nn ... 2.95

RALPH SNART ADVENTURES (VOL. 1)
NOW

Issue	ORIG	GOOD	FINE	N-MINT
❑1, Jun 86, 1: Ralph Snart	1.00	0.60	1.50	3.00
❑2, Jul 86	1.00	0.40	1.00	2.00
❑3, Aug 86	1.00	0.40	1.00	2.00

RALPH SNART ADVENTURES (VOL. 2)
NOW

Issue	ORIG	GOOD	FINE	N-MINT
❑1, Nov 86, Ralph Snart: Derelict Bum!	1.25	0.40	1.00	2.00
❑2, Dec 86	1.25	0.30	0.75	1.50
❑3, Jan 87	1.50	0.30	0.75	1.50
❑4, Feb 87	1.50	0.30	0.75	1.50
❑5, Mar 87	1.50	0.30	0.75	1.50
❑6, Apr 87	1.50	0.30	0.75	1.50
❑7, May 87	1.50	0.30	0.75	1.50
❑8, Jun 87	1.50	0.30	0.75	1.50
❑9, Jul 87	1.50	0.30	0.75	1.50

RALPH SNART ADVENTURES (VOL. 3)
NOW

Value: Cover or less

- ❑1, Sep 88 ... 1.75
- ❑1/3D, Nov 92, bagged with no cards ... 2.95
- ❑1/CS, Nov 92, 3-D; bagged with 12 cards ... 3.50
- ❑2, Oct 88 ... 1.75
- ❑3, Nov 88 ... 1.75
- ❑4, Jan 89 ... 1.75
- ❑5, Feb 89 ... 1.75
- ❑6, Mar 89 ... 1.75
- ❑7, Apr 89 ... 1.75
- ❑8, May 89 ... 1.75
- ❑9, Jun 89 ... 1.75
- ❑10, Jul 89 ... 1.75
- ❑11, Aug 89 ... 1.75
- ❑12, Sep 89 ... 1.75
- ❑13, Oct 89 ... 1.75
- ❑14, Nov 89 ... 1.75
- ❑15, Dec 89 ... 1.75
- ❑16, Jan 90 ... 1.75
- ❑17, Feb 90 ... 1.75
- ❑18, Mar 90 ... 1.75
- ❑19, Apr 90 ... 1.75
- ❑20, May 90 ... 1.75
- ❑21, Jun 90 ... 1.75
- ❑22, Jul 90, posters ... 1.75
- ❑23, Aug 90, cover says May, indicia says Aug ... 1.75
- ❑24, Sep 90, Three-Dimensional Ralph Snart, prestige format; with glasses ... 2.95
- ❑25, Oct 90, The Early Years ... 1.75
- ❑26, Nov 90 ... 1.75

RALPH SNART ADVENTURES (VOL. 4)
NOW

Value: Cover or less

- ❑1, May 92 ... 2.50
- ❑2, Jun 92 ... 2.50
- ❑3, Jul 92 ... 2.50

RALPH SNART ADVENTURES (VOL. 5)
NOW

Value: Cover or less

- ❑1, Jul 93 ... 2.50
- ❑2, Aug 93, trading card ... 2.50
- ❑3, Sep 93, trading card ... 2.50
- ❑4, Oct 93, trading card ... 2.50
- ❑5, Nov 93, trading card ... 2.50

RALPH SNART: THE LOST ISSUES
NOW

Value: Cover or less

- ❑1, Apr 93 ... 2.50
- ❑2, May 93 ... 2.50
- ❑3, Jun 93 ... 2.50

RAMBLIN' DAWG
EDGE

Value: Cover or less

- ❑1, Jul 94 ... 2.95

RAMBO
BLACKTHORNE

Value: Cover or less

- ❑1, Oct 88, b&w ... 2.00

RAMBO III
BLACKTHORNE

Value: Cover or less

- ❑1, movie Adaptation ... 2.00
- ❑3D 1, movie Adaptation ... 2.50

RAMM
MEGATON

Value: Cover or less

- ❑1, May 87, Rammifications ... 1.50
- ❑2 ... 1.50

RAMPAGING HULK
MARVEL

Value: Cover or less

- ❑1, Aug 98, b&w; Giant-size ... 1.99
- ❑2, Sep 98, 1: Ravage, gatefold summary ... 1.99
- ❑2/A, Sep 98, variant cover; gatefold summary ... 1.99
- ❑3, Oct 98, V: Ravage, gatefold summary ... 1.99
- ❑4, Nov 98, gatefold summary ... 1.99
- ❑5, Dec 98, V: Fantastic Four, gatefold summary ... 1.99
- ❑6, Jan 99, V: Puma, Final Issue; gatefold summary ... 1.99

RAMPAGING HULK (MAGAZINE)
MARVEL

Issue	ORIG	GOOD	FINE	N-MINT
❑1, Jan 77, The Monster or the Man?; Outsiders, b&w	1.00	1.30	3.25	6.50
❑2, Apr 77, AA, And Then ... the X-Men; Bloodstone: Scream, the Shrike!, O: the X-Men	1.00	1.50	3.75	7.50
❑3, Jun 77, AA, The Monster and The Metal Master; Bloodstone: And There Shall Come Death!, Bloodstone/Iron Man back-up story	1.00	0.70	1.75	3.50
❑4, Aug 77, 1: Exo-Mind, Bloodstone/Iron Man back-up story	1.00	0.70	1.75	3.50
❑5, Oct 77, AA; KP, Lo, The Sub-Mariner Strikes; Bloodstone: Suite Fear, A: Sub-Mariner	1.00	0.70	1.75	3.50
❑6, Dec 77	1.00	0.60	1.50	3.00
❑7, Feb 78, JM; KP, Night of the Wraith; Man-Thing: Beyond the Great Divide, A: Man-Thing	1.00	0.60	1.50	3.00
❑8, Apr 78, AA; HT, A Gathering of Doom; Earth Shall Have a New Master, A: Avengers	1.00	0.60	1.50	3.00
❑9, Jun 78	1.00	0.60	1.50	3.00
❑10	1.00	0.60	1.50	3.00

RANA 7
NGNG

Value: Cover or less

- ❑1 ... 2.95
- ❑2 ... 2.95
- ❑3 ... 2.95
- ❑4 ... 2.95

RANA 7: WARRIORS OF VENGEANCE
NGNG STUDIOS

Value: Cover or less

- ❑1, Dec 95, Warriors of Vengeance, Part 1 ... 2.50
- ❑2, Mar 96, Warriors of Vengeance, Part 2 ... 2.50

RANK & STINKY
PARODY PRESS

Value: Cover or less

- ❑1, b&w ... 2.50
- ❑1-2, Rank & Stinky Eencore Edition ... 2.50
- ❑SE 1, b&w ... 2.75

RANMA 1/2
VIZ

Issue	ORIG	GOOD	FINE	N-MINT
❑1, Here's Ranma; Ranma's Secret, Comic in color	4.95	5.00	12.50	25.00
❑2, I Hate Men; Never, Never, Never,	4.95	2.00	5.00	10.00
❑3, To the Tree-Borne Kettle-Girl; Body and Soul	4.95	1.60	4.00	8.00
❑4, You'll Understand Soon Enough; Because There's a Girl He Likes, Comics become B&W	2.95	1.20	3.00	6.00
❑5, You're Cute When You Smile; The Hunter	2.95	1.20	3.00	6.00
❑6, Bread Feud; Showdown,	2.95	1.00	2.50	5.00
❑7, A Bad Cut; Who Says You're Cute,	2.95	1.00	2.50	5.00

RANMA 1/2 PART 2
VIZ

Issue	ORIG	GOOD	FINE	N-MINT
❑1, The Transformation of Ryoga; He's Got a Beef,	2.95	1.40	3.50	7.00
❑2, Kodachi, the Black Rose; The Love of the Black Rose	2.95	1.00	2.50	5.00
❑3, Take Care of My Sister; I'll See That You Lose,	2.95	0.80	2.00	4.00
❑4, Hot Competition; I Give Up	2.95	0.80	2.00	4.00

	ORIG	GOOD	FINE	N-MINT
❑5, Darling Charlotte; A Kiss in the Rink, A: Akane Tendo;	2.95	0.80	2.00	4.00
❑6, Lips at a Loss; Lips at War	2.95	0.70	1.75	3.50
❑7, I'll Never Let Go; Burning the Bridges ...	2.95	0.70	1.75	3.50
❑8, Ryoga Explodes!; The Waters of Love, 1: Shampoo	2.95	0.70	1.75	3.50
❑9, Kiss of Death; You I Love,	2.95	0.70	1.75	3.50
❑10, Akane Gets Shampooed; Shampoo Cleans Up	2.95	0.70	1.75	3.50
❑11, Formula #911; Bie Liao (Goodbye)	2.75	0.70	1.75	3.50

RANMA 1/2 PART 3
VIZ

	ORIG	GOOD	FINE	N-MINT
❑1, Looking for a Weak Spot; Weak Spot - Found!,	2.75	0.60	1.50	3.00
❑2, Cat Hell; Cat-Fu,	2.75	0.60	1.50	3.00
❑3, You'd Have Kissed Anybody?; Shampoo Rides Again,	2.75	0.60	1.50	3.00
❑4, Attack of the Wild Mousse; The Martial Arts Magic Show	2.75	0.60	1.50	3.00
❑5, Cat's Tongue Got You?; The Phoenix Pill,	2.75	0.60	1.50	3.00
❑6, All's Fair at the Fair; War of the Melons,	2.75	0.60	1.50	3.00
❑7, Naval Engagement; Kitten of the Sea, .	2.75	0.60	1.50	3.00
❑8, Care to Join Me?; Training Meals	2.75	0.60	1.50	3.00
❑9, The Breaking Point; The Immortal Man,	2.75	0.60	1.50	3.00
❑10, Fast Break; The Way of Tea,	2.75	0.60	1.50	3.00
❑11, Meet Miss Satsuki; Proposal Accepted,	2.75	0.60	1.50	3.00
❑12, It's Fast or It's Free; Eyes on the Prize,	2.75	0.60	1.50	3.00
❑13, Noodles, Anyone?; I Won't Eat It!, A: Cologne;	2.75	0.60	1.50	3.00

RANMA 1/2 PART 4
VIZ

	ORIG	GOOD	FINE	N-MINT
❑1, The Evil Wakes; He's Something Else, 1: Happosai	2.75	0.60	1.50	3.00
❑2, Bathhouse Battle; Moonlight Serenade,	2.75	0.60	1.50	3.00
❑3, The Wrath of Happosai; The Scent of a Woman,	2.75	0.60	1.50	3.00
❑4, Fathers Know Best; Instant Spring,	2.75	0.60	1.50	3.00
❑5, No Need for Ranma; The Destroyer Strikes,	2.75	0.60	1.50	3.00
❑6, Just One More Kiss; Wherefore Art Thou, Romeo?,	2.75	0.60	1.50	3.00
❑7, Romeo? Romeo? Romeo?; Not Your Typical Juliet,	2.75	0.60	1.50	3.00
❑8, A Kiss to the Victor; Quest for the Hidden Spring,	2.75	0.60	1.50	3.00
❑9, The Trouble with Girls' Locker Rooms; From the Spring, Springs a Message, ...	2.75	0.60	1.50	3.00
❑10, The Way the Cookie Crumbles; Negative Feelings,	2.75	0.60	1.50	3.00
❑11, Take Me Out to the Bathtub; ...I Ate the Whole Thing,	2.75	0.60	1.50	3.00

RANMA 1/2 PART 5
VIZ

	ORIG	GOOD	FINE	N-MINT
❑1, Okonomiyaki Means "I Love You"; Saucy Reply,	2.75	0.60	1.50	3.00
❑2, Ukyo's Secret; Ryoga vs. Ukyo,	2.95	0.60	1.50	3.00
❑3, Love Letters in the Sauce; Ryoga's What!?,	2.95	0.60	1.50	3.00
❑4, At Long Last...The Date!; Happosai Days Are Here Again,	2.95	0.60	1.50	3.00
❑5, One Moment to Love; I Won't Fall in Love!,	2.95	0.60	1.50	3.00
❑6, The Abduction of...Akane?; Duck, Ranma, Duck!,	2.95	0.60	1.50	3.00
❑7, Akane Becomes a Duck; Fowl Play	2.95	0.60	1.50	3.00
❑8, The Happiest Mousse; Tsubasa Kurenai Busts Loose!	2.95	0.60	1.50	3.00
❑9, Lunchtime Lunacy; The Perfect Match,	2.95	0.60	1.50	3.00
❑10, Ryoga, Come Home; Oh, Brother!, A: Kasumi Tendo	2.95	0.60	1.50	3.00
❑11, Get Lost, Yoiko!; The Ultimate Technique,	2.75	0.60	1.50	3.00
❑12, Get The Secret Scroll!; The Fire-Burst of Terror!	2.75	0.60	1.50	3.00

RANMA 1/2 PART 6
VIZ

Value: Cover or less

❑1, Embraceable You; Hold Me Close, ... 2.95
❑2, Akane's Power-Up!; Super Badminton 2.95
❑3, Serious Side Effects; The Return of the Principal 2.95
❑4, Journey into the Principal's Office; The Principal of the Thing, ... 2.95
❑5, One Hairy Day; Shear Folly, A: Akane Tendo; 2.95
❑6, Gonna Make You Tardy!; The Soap of Happiness 2.95
❑7, Cupids, Draw Back Your Bow; Don't Follow Me, ... 2.95
❑8 .... 2.95
❑9, The Legendary Moxibustion of Evil; The World's Weakest Man, ... 2.95
❑10, Weak for Life?; The Valley of Moxibustion, ... 2.95
❑11, Training in the Spiral of Hell; The Inflammable Man, ... 2.95
❑12, The Roar of Heaven; The Great Rematch, ... 2.95
❑13, St. Happosai; Burn, Happy, Burn!, ... 2.95
❑14, The Paper Chase; Ranma Reborn, ... 2.95

Blackthorne adapted both the first and third Rambo films.

© 1988 Blackthorne

RANMA 1/2 PART 7
VIZ

Value: Cover or less

❑1, Who Will Bell the Cat?; Kitty Takes a Bride, ... 2.95
❑2, Swim Like a Hammer; Courage Under Water 2.95
❑3, Step Outside!; The Mark of the Gods 2.95
❑4 .... 2.95
❑5 .... 2.95
❑6 .... 2.95
❑7 .... 2.95
❑8 .... 2.95
❑9 .... 2.95
❑10 .... 2.95
❑11 .... 2.95
❑12 .... 2.95
❑13 .... 2.95
❑14 .... 2.95

RANMA 1/2 PART 8
VIZ

Value: Cover or less

❑1, Kung Fu Stew 2.95
❑2 .... 2.95
❑3 .... 2.95
❑4 .... 2.95
❑5 .... 2.95
❑7 .... 2.95

RANMA 1/2 PART 9
VIZ

Value: Cover or less

❑1, Melonhead 2.95

RANT
BONEYARD

	ORIG	GOOD	FINE	N-MINT
❑1, Nov 94, JJ, b&w	2.95	0.59	1.48	2.95
❑2, Feb 95, JJ, b&w	2.95	0.59	1.48	2.95
❑3, JJ	2.95	0.59	1.48	2.95
❑Ash 1, JJ, Ashcan version of issue #1. Black and white cover	—	0.50	1.25	2.50

RAPHAEL TEENAGE MUTANT NINJA TURTLE
MIRAGE

	ORIG	GOOD	FINE	N-MINT
❑1, Nov 87, Oversized	1.50	0.40	1.00	2.00
❑1-2, 2nd Printing	1.50	0.30	0.75	1.50

RARE BREED
CHRYSALIS STUDIOS

Value: Cover or less

❑1, Nov 95, 1: Ambush; 1: Swede; 1: Buffalo Soldier; 1: Ammo; 1: The Ravager 2.50
❑2, Mar 96 .... 2.50

RASCALS IN PARADISE
DARK HORSE

	ORIG	GOOD	FINE	N-MINT
❑1, Aug 94, magazine	3.95	0.80	2.00	4.00
❑2, Oct 94, magazine	3.95	0.80	2.00	4.00
❑3, Dec 94, Final Issue; magazine	3.95	0.80	2.00	4.00

RAT BASTARD
CRUCIAL

	ORIG	GOOD	FINE	N-MINT
❑1, Jun 97, Fix for a King	1.95	0.50	1.25	2.50
❑1/Ash, Jun 97, Fix for a King, Black and white ashcan edition	1.95	0.50	1.25	2.50
❑2, Nov 97, Fix for a King	1.95	0.40	1.00	2.00
❑3, Apr 98, Fix for a King	1.95	0.40	1.00	2.00
❑4, Jul 98, Fix for a King	1.95	0.40	1.00	2.00
❑5, Oct 98, Vengeance Day	1.95	0.39	0.98	1.95
❑6, Jul 99, Vengeance Day	1.95	0.39	0.98	1.95

RATED X
AIRCEL

Value: Cover or less

❑1, Apr 91, The Non-Entity, b&w; adult 2.95
❑2, b&w; adult 2.95
❑3, b&w; adult 2.95
❑SE 1, b&w; adult 2.95

RAT FINK COMICS
WORLD OF FANDOM

Value: Cover or less

❑1, b&w 2.50
❑2, b&w 2.50
❑3, b&w 2.50

RAT FINK COMIX (ED "BIG DADDY" ROTH'S...)
STARHEAD

Value: Cover or less

❑1, Life with Rat F 2.00

RATFOO
SPIT WAD

Value: Cover or less

❑1, Sep 97, b&w 2.95

RAT PREVIEW (JUSTIN HAMPTON'S...)
AEON

	ORIG	GOOD	FINE	N-MINT
❑1, May 97, b&w; no cover price; ashcan-sized	—	0.20	0.50	1.00

RATS!
SLAVE LABOR

Value: Cover or less

- ❑1, Aug 92, b&w 2.50

RAVAGE 2099
MARVEL

Value: Cover or less

- ❑1, Dec 92, SL (w), Metallic ink cover 1.75
- ❑2, Jan 93, SL (w), The Madness Unleashed 1.25
- ❑3, Feb 93, SL (w), Horror in Hell-rock 1.25
- ❑4, Mar 93, SL (w), The Mark of the Mutroid 1.25
- ❑5, Apr 93 .... 1.25
- ❑6, May 93 .... 1.25
- ❑7, Jun 93 .... 1.25
- ❑8, Jul 93 .... 1.25
- ❑9, Aug 93 .... 1.25
- ❑10, Sep 93 .... 1.25
- ❑11, Oct 93, The Stigmata Effect 1.25
- ❑12, Nov 93 .... 1.25
- ❑13, Dec 93 .... 1.25
- ❑14, Jan 94 .... 1.25
- ❑15, Feb 94, Fall of the Hammer, Part 2 .... 1.25
- ❑16, Mar 94 .... 1.25
- ❑17, Apr 94 .... 1.25
- ❑18, May 94 .... 1.25
- ❑19, Jun 94 .... 1.50
- ❑20, Jul 94 .... 1.50
- ❑21, Aug 94 .... 1.50
- ❑22, Sep 94 .... 1.50
- ❑23, Oct 94 .... 1.50
- ❑24, Nov 94 .... 1.50
- ❑25, Dec 94 .... 2.25
- ❑25/SC, Dec 94, enhanced cover 2.95
- ❑26, Jan 95 .... 1.50
- ❑27, Feb 95 .... 1.50
- ❑28, Mar 95 .... 1.50
- ❑29, Apr 95 .... 1.50
- ❑30, May 95 .... 1.50
- ❑31, Jun 95 .... 1.95
- ❑32, Jul 95 .... 1.95
- ❑33, Aug 95, Final Issue 1.95

RAVEN
RENAISSANCE

Value: Cover or less

- ❑1, Sep 93, 1: Ian Macauley; 1: Raven 2.50
- ❑2, Nov 93 .... 2.50
- ❑3, Apr 94 .... 2.50
- ❑4, Aug 94 .... 2.75

RAVEN CHRONICLES
CALIBER

Value: Cover or less

- ❑1, Jul 95, Prelude; The Bloodfire, b&w 2.95
- ❑2, b&w 2.95
- ❑3, b&w 2.95
- ❑4, b&w 2.95

RAVENS AND RAINBOWS
PACIFIC

Value: Cover or less

- ❑1, Dec 83, JJ, JJ (w), Union; Bias 1.50

RAVENWIND
PARIAH

Value: Cover or less

- ❑1, Jun 96, b&w 2.50

RAVER
MALIBU

Value: Cover or less

- ❑1, Apr 93, 1: Raver, foil cover 2.95
- ❑2 .... 1.95
- ❑3 .... 1.95

RAWHIDE KID
MARVEL

	ORIG	GOOD	FINE	N-MINT
❑17, Aug 60, JK, O: Rawhide Kid	0.10	60.00	150.00	300.00
❑18, Oct 60	0.10	16.00	40.00	80.00
❑19, Dec 60	0.10	16.00	40.00	80.00
❑20, Feb 61	0.10	16.00	40.00	80.00
❑21, Apr 61	0.10	15.00	37.50	75.00
❑22, Jun 61	0.10	15.00	37.50	75.00
❑23, Aug 61, JK, O: Rawhide Kid	0.10	33.00	82.50	165.00
❑24, Oct 61	0.10	15.00	37.50	75.00
❑25, Dec 61	0.10	15.00	37.50	75.00
❑26, Feb 62	0.10	15.00	37.50	75.00
❑27, Apr 62	0.12	15.00	37.50	75.00
❑28, Jun 62	0.12	15.00	37.50	75.00
❑29, Aug 62	0.12	15.00	37.50	75.00
❑30, Oct 62	0.12	15.00	37.50	75.00
❑31, Dec 62	0.12	12.00	30.00	60.00
❑32, Feb 63	0.12	12.00	30.00	60.00
❑33, Apr 63	0.12	12.00	30.00	60.00
❑34, Jun 63	0.12	12.00	30.00	60.00
❑35, Aug 63	0.12	12.00	30.00	60.00
❑36, Oct 63	0.12	11.00	27.50	55.00
❑37, Dec 63	0.12	11.00	27.50	55.00
❑38, Feb 64	0.12	11.00	27.50	55.00
❑39, Apr 64	0.12	11.00	27.50	55.00
❑40, Jun 64, A: Two-Gun Kid	0.12	11.00	27.50	55.00
❑41, Aug 64	0.12	11.00	27.50	55.00
❑42, Oct 64	0.12	11.00	27.50	55.00
❑43, Dec 64	0.12	11.00	27.50	55.00
❑44, Feb 65	0.12	11.00	27.50	55.00
❑45, Apr 65, JK, O: Rawhide Kid	0.12	17.00	42.50	85.00
❑46, Jun 65	0.12	11.00	27.50	55.00
❑47, Aug 65	0.12	6.00	15.00	30.00
❑48, Oct 65, V: Marko the Manhunter	0.12	6.00	15.00	30.00
❑49, Dec 65, V: Masquerader	0.12	6.00	15.00	30.00
❑50, Feb 66, A: Kid Colt; V: Masquerader	0.12	6.00	15.00	30.00
❑51, Apr 66, V: Aztecs	0.12	6.00	15.00	30.00
❑52, Jun 66	0.12	6.00	15.00	30.00
❑53, Aug 66	0.12	6.00	15.00	30.00
❑54, Oct 66	0.12	6.00	15.00	30.00
❑55, Dec 66, V: Plunderers	0.12	6.00	15.00	30.00
❑56, Feb 67, V: Peacemaker	0.12	6.00	15.00	30.00
❑57, Apr 67, V: Enforcerers (not Spider-Man villains)	0.12	6.00	15.00	30.00
❑58, Jun 67	0.12	6.00	15.00	30.00
❑59, Aug 67, V: Drako	0.12	6.00	15.00	30.00
❑60, Oct 67	0.12	6.00	15.00	30.00
❑61, Dec 67, A: Calamity Jane; A: Wild Bill Hickock	0.12	4.40	11.00	22.00
❑62, Feb 68, V: Drako	0.12	4.40	11.00	22.00
❑63, Apr 68	0.12	4.40	11.00	22.00
❑64, Jun 68, Kid Colt back-up	0.12	4.40	11.00	22.00
❑65, Aug 68	0.12	4.40	11.00	22.00
❑66, Oct 68, Two-Gun Kid back-up	0.12	4.40	11.00	22.00
❑67, Dec 68	0.12	4.40	11.00	22.00
❑68, Feb 69, V: Cougar	0.12	4.40	11.00	22.00
❑69, Apr 69	0.12	4.40	11.00	22.00
❑70, Jun 69	0.12	4.40	11.00	22.00
❑71, Aug 69	0.15	2.80	7.00	14.00
❑72, Oct 69	0.15	2.80	7.00	14.00
❑73, Dec 69	0.15	2.80	7.00	14.00
❑74, Feb 70	0.15	2.80	7.00	14.00
❑75, Apr 70	0.15	2.80	7.00	14.00
❑76, May 70	0.15	2.80	7.00	14.00
❑77, Jun 70	0.15	2.80	7.00	14.00
❑78, Jul 70	0.15	2.80	7.00	14.00
❑79, Aug 70	0.15	2.80	7.00	14.00
❑80, Oct 70	0.15	2.80	7.00	14.00
❑81, Nov 70, Range War	0.15	2.80	7.00	14.00
❑82, Dec 70	0.15	2.80	7.00	14.00
❑83, Jan 71	0.15	2.80	7.00	14.00
❑84, Feb 71	0.15	2.80	7.00	14.00
❑85, Mar 71	0.15	2.80	7.00	14.00
❑86, Apr 71, JK, O: Rawhide Kid	0.15	2.80	7.00	14.00
❑87, May 71	0.15	2.00	5.00	10.00
❑88, Jun 71	0.15	2.00	5.00	10.00
❑89, Jul 71	0.15	2.00	5.00	10.00
❑90, Aug 71	0.15	2.00	5.00	10.00
❑91, Sep 71	0.15	2.00	5.00	10.00
❑92, Oct 71	0.25	2.00	5.00	10.00
❑93, Nov 71	0.25	2.00	5.00	10.00
❑94, Dec 71	0.20	2.00	5.00	10.00
❑95, Jan 72	0.20	2.00	5.00	10.00
❑96, Feb 72	0.20	2.00	5.00	10.00
❑97, Mar 72	0.25	2.00	5.00	10.00
❑98, Apr 72	0.25	2.00	5.00	10.00
❑99, May 72	0.20	2.00	5.00	10.00
❑100, Jun 72, O: Rawhide Kid	0.20	2.80	7.00	14.00
❑101, Jul 72	0.20	1.40	3.50	7.00
❑102, Aug 72	0.20	1.40	3.50	7.00
❑103, Sep 72	0.20	1.40	3.50	7.00
❑104, Oct 72	0.20	1.40	3.50	7.00
❑105, Nov 72	0.20	1.40	3.50	7.00
❑106, Dec 72	0.20	1.40	3.50	7.00
❑107, Jan 73	0.20	1.40	3.50	7.00
❑108, Feb 73	0.20	1.40	3.50	7.00
❑109, Mar 73	0.20	1.40	3.50	7.00
❑110, Apr 73	0.20	1.40	3.50	7.00
❑111, May 73	0.20	1.40	3.50	7.00
❑112, Jun 73	0.20	1.40	3.50	7.00
❑113, Jul 73	0.20	1.40	3.50	7.00
❑114, Aug 73	0.20	1.40	3.50	7.00
❑115, Sep 73	0.20	1.40	3.50	7.00
❑116, Oct 73	0.20	1.20	3.00	6.00
❑117, Nov 73	0.20	1.20	3.00	6.00
❑118, Jan 74	0.20	1.20	3.00	6.00
❑119, Mar 74	0.20	1.20	3.00	6.00
❑120, May 74	0.20	1.20	3.00	6.00
❑121, Jul 74	0.25	1.20	3.00	6.00
❑122, Sep 74	0.25	1.20	3.00	6.00
❑123, Nov 74	0.25	1.20	3.00	6.00
❑124, Jan 75	0.25	1.20	3.00	6.00
❑125, Mar 75	0.25	1.20	3.00	6.00
❑126, May 75	0.25	1.20	3.00	6.00
❑127, Jul 75	0.25	1.20	3.00	6.00
❑128, Sep 75	0.25	1.20	3.00	6.00
❑129, Oct 75	0.25	1.20	3.00	6.00
❑130, Nov 75	0.25	1.20	3.00	6.00
❑131, Jan 76	0.25	1.20	3.00	6.00
❑132, Mar 76	0.25	1.20	3.00	6.00

	ORIG	GOOD	FINE	N-MINT
❑133, May 76	0.25	1.20	3.00	6.00
❑134, Jul 76	0.25	1.20	3.00	6.00
❑135, Sep 76	0.30	1.20	3.00	6.00
❑136, Nov 76	0.30	1.20	3.00	6.00
❑137, Jan 77	0.30	1.20	3.00	6.00
❑138, Mar 77	0.30	1.20	3.00	6.00
❑139, May 77	0.30	1.20	3.00	6.00
❑140, Jul 77	0.30	1.20	3.00	6.00
❑141, Sep 77	0.30	1.20	3.00	6.00
❑142, Nov 77	0.30	1.20	3.00	6.00
❑143, Jan 78	0.35	1.20	3.00	6.00
❑144, Mar 78	0.35	1.20	3.00	6.00
❑145, May 78	0.35	1.20	3.00	6.00
❑146, Jul 78	0.35	1.20	3.00	6.00
❑147, Sep 78	0.35	1.20	3.00	6.00
❑148, Nov 78	0.35	1.20	3.00	6.00
❑149, Jan 79	0.35	1.20	3.00	6.00
❑150, Mar 79	0.35	1.20	3.00	6.00
❑151, May 79	0.35	1.20	3.00	6.00
❑SE 1, Reprint	0.25	2.40	6.00	12.00

RAWHIDE KID (LTD. SERIES)
MARVEL

	ORIG	GOOD	FINE	N-MINT
❑1, Aug 85, JSe; HT; JBy, The Living Legend, O: Rawhide Kid	0.75	0.30	0.75	1.50
❑2, Sep 85, JSe; HT; JBy, The Not-so-Wild-West	0.75	0.30	0.75	1.50
❑3, Oct 85, JSe; HT; JBy	0.75	0.30	0.75	1.50
❑4, Nov 85, JSe; HT; JBy	0.75	0.30	0.75	1.50

RAW MEDIA ILLUSTRATED
ABC STUDIOS

Value: Cover or less

- ❑1, May 98, wet T-shirt cover ... 3.25
- ❑1/Nude, May 98, nude photo cover ... 3.25

RAW MEDIA MAGS
REBEL

Value: Cover or less

- ❑1, b&w; adult ... 5.00
- ❑2, b&w; adult ... 5.00
- ❑3, b&w; adult ... 5.00
- ❑4, May 94, b&w; adult ... 5.00

RAW PERIPHERY
SLAVE LABOR

Value: Cover or less

- ❑1, Dear Reader; Jazebel's Virtue, b&w; adult; Anthology ... 2.95

RAY, THE
DC

	ORIG	GOOD	FINE	N-MINT
❑0, Oct 94, Missing, O: The Ray II (Ray Terrill)	1.95	0.45	1.13	2.25
❑1, May 94, Rebirth	1.75	0.45	1.13	2.25
❑1/SC, May 94, Rebirth, foil cover	2.95	0.60	1.50	3.00
❑2, Jun 94, Juice, O: The Ray II (Ray Terrill)	1.75	0.40	1.00	2.00
❑3, Jul 94	1.75	0.40	1.00	2.00
❑4, Aug 94	1.95	0.40	1.00	2.00
❑5, Sep 94	1.95	0.40	1.00	2.00
❑6, Nov 94	1.95	0.40	1.00	2.00
❑7, Dec 94, A: Black Canary	1.95	0.40	1.00	2.00
❑8, Jan 95, The Main Man, V: Lobo	1.95	0.40	1.00	2.00
❑9, Feb 95	1.95	0.40	1.00	2.00
❑10, Mar 95	1.95	0.40	1.00	2.00
❑11, Apr 95	1.95	0.40	1.00	2.00
❑12, May 95	1.95	0.40	1.00	2.00
❑13, Jun 95	2.25	0.45	1.13	2.25
❑14, Jul 95	2.25	0.45	1.13	2.25
❑15, Aug 95, V: Deathmasque	2.25	0.45	1.13	2.25
❑16, Sep 95	2.25	0.45	1.13	2.25
❑17, Oct 95	2.25	0.45	1.13	2.25
❑18, Nov 95, Underworld Unleashed, Underworld Unleashed	2.25	0.45	1.13	2.25
❑19, Dec 95, Underworld Unleashed, Underworld Unleashed	2.25	0.45	1.13	2.25
❑20, Jan 96, The Tide, A: Golden Age Black Condor	2.25	0.45	1.13	2.25
❑21, Feb 96, It, V: Black Condor	2.25	0.45	1.13	2.25
❑22, Mar 96, Masks	2.25	0.45	1.13	2.25
❑23, May 96	2.25	0.45	1.13	2.25
❑24, Jun 96	2.25	0.45	1.13	2.25
❑25, Jul 96, Time and Tempest!, Part 1, A: Triumph; A: Bart Allen, Ray in the future	3.50	0.45	1.13	2.25
❑26, Aug 96, Time and Tempest!, Part 2, continued from events in JLA Annual #10	2.25	0.45	1.13	2.25
❑27, Sep 96, Time and Tempest!, Part 3	2.25	0.45	1.13	2.25
❑28, Oct 96, Disclosure, O: Joshua, Final Issue; secrets of both Ray's pasts revealed	2.25	0.45	1.13	2.25
❑Anl 1	3.95	0.79	1.98	3.95

RAY, THE (MINI-SERIES)
DC

	ORIG	GOOD	FINE	N-MINT
❑1, Feb 92, Grander than Fire, O: The Ray II (Ray Terrill)	1.00	0.80	2.00	4.00
❑2, Mar 92	1.00	0.60	1.50	3.00
❑3, Apr 92	1.00	0.40	1.00	2.00
❑4, May 92	1.00	0.40	1.00	2.00
❑5, Jun 92, Emerson Must Die	1.00	0.40	1.00	2.00
❑6, Jul 92	1.00	0.40	1.00	2.00

John Byrne presented the last adventure of an aged Rawhide Kid in this four-issue mini-series.

© 1985 Marvel Comics

RAY BRADBURY COMICS
TOPPS

	ORIG	GOOD	FINE	N-MINT
❑1, Feb 93, AW (w), Dinosaurs, 3 trading cards	2.95	0.70	1.75	3.50
❑2, Apr 93, HK; MW, HK (w); MW (w), Horror, 3 trading cards	2.95	0.70	1.75	3.50
❑3, Jun 93, Dinosaurs, 3 trading cards	2.95	0.70	1.75	3.50
❑4, Aug 93, Alien Terror	2.95	0.70	1.75	3.50
❑5, Oct 93, 3 trading cards; Final issue (#6 canceled)	2.95	0.70	1.75	3.50
❑SE 1, The Illustrated Man, Illustrated Man	2.95	0.70	1.75	3.50

RAY BRADBURY COMICS: MARTIAN CHRONICLES
TOPPS

	ORIG	GOOD	FINE	N-MINT
❑1, Jun 94, The Off Season; Kaleidoscope	2.50	0.65	1.63	3.25

RAY BRADBURY COMICS: TRILOGY OF TERROR
TOPPS

	ORIG	GOOD	FINE	N-MINT
❑1, May 94, WW	2.50	0.65	1.63	3.25

RAY-MOND
DEEP-SEA

Value: Cover or less

- ❑1 ... 2.95
- ❑2 ... 2.95

RAYNE
SHEET HAPPIES

Value: Cover or less

- ❑1, Jul 95, b&w ... 2.50
- ❑2, Apr 96, b&w; cover says Mar, indicia says Apr ... 2.50
- ❑3, Aug 96, b&w ... 2.50
- ❑4, Jul 97, b&w ... 2.95

RAZOR
LONDON NIGHT

	ORIG	GOOD	FINE	N-MINT
❑0, Torture	3.00	0.60	1.50	3.00
❑0/A, Direct Market edition	3.95	0.80	2.00	4.00
❑0-2, 2nd Printing	—	0.60	1.50	3.00
❑0.5, 1: Poizon, Promotional giveaway	—	0.60	1.50	3.00
❑1, The Suffering	2.50	0.80	2.00	4.00
❑1-2, The Suffering, 2nd Printing; Photo cover	3.00	0.60	1.50	3.00
❑2	2.50	0.60	1.50	3.00
❑2/PL, Platinum edition	—	0.80	2.00	4.00
❑2/SC	3.95	1.00	2.50	5.00
❑3	2.50	0.60	1.50	3.00
❑3/CS, posters	—	0.80	2.00	4.00
❑4	2.50	0.60	1.50	3.00
❑4/PL	—	0.80	2.00	4.00
❑5	—	0.60	1.50	3.00
❑5/PL, Platinum edition	—	0.80	2.00	4.00
❑6	—	0.60	1.50	3.00
❑7	—	0.60	1.50	3.00
❑8	2.95	0.60	1.50	3.00
❑9	—	0.60	1.50	3.00
❑10, O: Stryke	3.00	0.60	1.50	3.00
❑11, Sep 94, b&w	3.00	0.60	1.50	3.00
❑12, b&w; Series continued in Razor Uncut #13	3.00	0.60	1.50	3.00
❑Anl 1, 1: Shi	2.95	4.00	10.00	20.00
❑Anl 1/GO, 1: Shi, Gold limited edition	2.95	5.00	12.50	25.00
❑Anl 2, b&w	3.00	0.70	1.75	3.50

RAZOR (VOL. 2)
LONDON NIGHT

Value: Cover or less

- ❑1 ... 3.00
- ❑2 ... 3.00
- ❑3 ... 3.00
- ❑4 ... 3.00
- ❑5 ... 3.00
- ❑6, May 97 ... 3.00
- ❑7, Jun 97, Money for Hire, Final Issue ... 3.00

RAZOR & SHI SPECIAL
LONDON NIGHT

	ORIG	GOOD	FINE	N-MINT
❑1, Crossover with Crusade	—	0.60	1.50	3.00
❑1/PL, Platinum edition	—	0.80	2.00	4.00

RAZOR ARCHIVES
London Night
Value: Cover or less

❑1, May 97, Angel in Black 3.95
❑2, Jun 97, Angel in Black 5.00
❑3 ..... 5.00
❑4, Jul 97 ..... 5.00

RAZOR: BURN
London Night
Value: Cover or less

❑1 ..... 3.00
❑2 ..... 3.00
❑3 ..... 3.00
❑4 ..... 3.00

RAZOR/CRY NO MORE
London Night
Value: Cover or less

❑1, nn 3.95

RAZOR: DARK ANGEL/FINAL NAIL
London Night
Value: Cover or less

❑1 ..... 3.00

RAZORGUTS
Monster
Value: Cover or less

❑1, b&w 2.25
❑2, Feb 92, b&w 2.25
❑3, b&w 2.25
❑4, b&w 2.25

RAZORLINE: THE FIRST CUT
Marvel

	ORIG	GOOD	FINE	N-MINT
❑1, Have You Heard The One About Felon Bale?, sampler; Previews Hokum & Hex, Hyperkind, Saint Sinner, and Ectokid	0.75	0.20	0.50	1.00

RAZOR/MORBID ANGEL
London Night
Value: Cover or less

❑1 ..... 3.00
❑2 ..... 3.00
❑3, Dec 96 ..... 3.00

RAZOR'S EDGE
Innovation
Value: Cover or less

❑1, b&w 2.50

RAZOR: THE SUFFERING
London Night
Value: Cover or less

❑1 ..... 3.00
❑1/A, "Director's Cut" 3.00
❑2 ..... 3.00
❑2/A, "Director's Cut" 3.00
❑3 ..... 3.00

RAZOR: TORTURE
London Night

	ORIG	GOOD	FINE	N-MINT
❑0, enhanced wraparound cover; polybagged with card and catalog	3.95	0.79	1.98	3.95
❑1	3.00	0.60	1.50	3.00
❑1/SC, alternate cover with no cover price	—	0.60	1.50	3.00
❑2	3.00	0.60	1.50	3.00
❑2/SC, no cover price	—	0.60	1.50	3.00
❑3, Apr 96	3.00	0.60	1.50	3.00

RAZOR: UNCUT
London Night

	ORIG	GOOD	FINE	N-MINT
❑13, Series continued from Razor #12	—	0.60	1.50	3.00
❑14	—	0.60	1.50	3.00
❑15	—	0.60	1.50	3.00
❑16	—	0.60	1.50	3.00
❑17	—	0.60	1.50	3.00
❑18, Dec 95	3.00	0.60	1.50	3.00
❑19	—	0.60	1.50	3.00
❑20, b&w	3.00	0.60	1.50	3.00
❑21, May 96, b&w	3.00	0.60	1.50	3.00
❑22, b&w	3.00	0.60	1.50	3.00
❑23	—	0.60	1.50	3.00
❑24	—	0.60	1.50	3.00
❑25	—	0.60	1.50	3.00
❑26	—	0.60	1.50	3.00
❑27	—	0.60	1.50	3.00
❑28	—	0.60	1.50	3.00
❑29	—	0.60	1.50	3.00
❑30	—	0.60	1.50	3.00
❑31	—	0.60	1.50	3.00
❑32	—	0.60	1.50	3.00
❑33	—	0.60	1.50	3.00
❑34	—	0.60	1.50	3.00
❑35	—	0.60	1.50	3.00
❑36	—	0.60	1.50	3.00
❑37	—	0.60	1.50	3.00
❑38	—	0.60	1.50	3.00
❑39	—	0.60	1.50	3.00
❑40	—	0.60	1.50	3.00
❑41	—	0.60	1.50	3.00
❑42	—	0.60	1.50	3.00
❑43	—	0.60	1.50	3.00
❑44	—	0.60	1.50	3.00
❑45	—	0.60	1.50	3.00
❑46	—	0.60	1.50	3.00
❑47	—	0.60	1.50	3.00
❑48	—	0.60	1.50	3.00
❑49	—	0.60	1.50	3.00
❑50	—	0.60	1.50	3.00
❑51	—	0.60	1.50	3.00

RAZOR/WARRIOR NUN AREALA-FAITH
London Night
Value: Cover or less

❑1, May 96, nn; one-shot crossover with Antarctic 3.95

RAZORWIRE
5th Panel
Value: Cover or less

❑1, Jun 96, All Parts Being Equal, Run Amok, Pieces, Bite, b&w 1.50
❑2, Jul 97, Bite 2; All Parts Being Equal Part 2, b&w 1.95

REACTION: THE ULTIMATE MAN
Studio Archein
Value: Cover or less

❑1, nn 2.95

REACTO-MAN
B-Movie
Value: Cover or less

❑1, Shock Value 1.50
❑2 ..... 1.50
❑3, 1: Warhead 1.50

REACTOR GIRL
Tragedy Strikes
Value: Cover or less

❑1, b&w 2.50
❑2 ..... 2.95
❑3 ..... 2.95
❑4 ..... 2.95
❑5 ..... 2.95

REAGAN'S RAIDERS
Solson
Value: Cover or less

❑1, RB 2.00
❑2, RB 2.00
❑3, RB 2.00

REAL ADVENTURES OF JONNY QUEST, THE
Dark Horse

	ORIG	GOOD	FINE	N-MINT
❑1, Sep 96, Net of Chaos, Part 1, based on 1996 animated series	2.95	0.60	1.50	3.00
❑2, Oct 96, Net of Chaos, Part 2	2.95	0.59	1.48	2.95
❑3, Nov 96	2.95	0.59	1.48	2.95
❑4, Dec 96	2.95	0.59	1.48	2.95
❑5, Jan 97	2.95	0.59	1.48	2.95
❑6, Feb 97	2.95	0.59	1.48	2.95
❑7, Mar 97	2.95	0.59	1.48	2.95
❑8, May 97	2.95	0.59	1.48	2.95
❑9, Jun 97	2.95	0.59	1.48	2.95
❑10, Jul 97	2.95	0.59	1.48	2.95
❑11, Aug 97	2.95	0.59	1.48	2.95
❑12, Sep 97, Final Issue	2.95	0.59	1.48	2.95

REAL DEAL MAGAZINE
Real Deal
Value: Cover or less

❑5, b&w; magazine 2.00

REAL GHOSTBUSTERS, THE (VOL. 1)
Now

	ORIG	GOOD	FINE	N-MINT
❑1, Aug 88, Ghostbusters movie adaptation	1.75	0.40	1.00	2.00
❑2, Sep 88	1.75	0.35	0.88	1.75
❑3, Oct 88	1.75	0.35	0.88	1.75
❑4, Nov 88	1.75	0.35	0.88	1.75
❑5, Jan 89	1.75	0.35	0.88	1.75
❑6, Feb 89	1.75	0.35	0.88	1.75
❑7, Mar 89	1.75	0.35	0.88	1.75
❑8, Apr 89, Toad Island	1.75	0.35	0.88	1.75
❑9, May 89	1.75	0.35	0.88	1.75
❑10, Jun 89	1.75	0.35	0.88	1.75
❑11, Jul 89	1.75	0.35	0.88	1.75
❑12, Aug 89	1.75	0.35	0.88	1.75
❑13, Sep 89	1.75	0.35	0.88	1.75
❑14, Oct 89	1.75	0.35	0.88	1.75
❑15, Nov 89	1.75	0.35	0.88	1.75
❑16, Dec 89	1.75	0.35	0.88	1.75
❑17, Jan 90	1.75	0.35	0.88	1.75
❑18, Feb 90	1.75	0.35	0.88	1.75
❑19, Mar 90	1.75	0.35	0.88	1.75
❑20, Apr 90, ...At the Earth's Core!, pin-up poster	1.75	0.35	0.88	1.75
❑21, May 90, Ecto-X!; The Spooked Suit!	1.75	0.35	0.88	1.75
❑22, Jun 90	1.75	0.35	0.88	1.75
❑23, Jul 90	1.75	0.35	0.88	1.75
❑24, Aug 90, Carnival	1.75	0.35	0.88	1.75
❑25, Sep 90	1.75	0.35	0.88	1.75
❑26, Oct 90	1.75	0.35	0.88	1.75
❑27, Nov 90, The Last Voyage of the Lady Anne, Pin-up	1.75	0.35	0.88	1.75
❑28, Dec 90, Final issue?	1.75	0.35	0.88	1.75
❑3D 1, Slimer's Unbirthday; It's Slimer!, glasses; gatefold summary	2.95	0.59	1.48	2.95

REAL GHOSTBUSTERS (VOL. 2)
Now
Value: Cover or less

❑1, Nov 91 ..... 1.75
❑1/3D, Oct 91, polybagged; w/ glasses 2.95
❑2, Dec 91 ..... 1.75
❑3, Jan 92 ..... 1.75
❑4, Feb 92 ..... 1.75
❑Anl 1992, Mar 92 ..... 1.00
❑Anl 1993, Dec 92, 3-D 2.95

REAL GHOSTBUSTERS SUMMER SPECIAL
Now
Value: Cover or less

- ❑1, Sum 93, nn 2.95

REAL GIRL
Fantagraphics
Value: Cover or less

- ❑1, b&w; adult 2.50
- ❑2, b&w; adult 2.50
- ❑3, b&w; adult 2.95
- ❑4, b&w; adult 2.95
- ❑5, b&w; adult 3.50
- ❑6, b&w; adult 3.50
- ❑7, Aug 94, b&w; adult 3.50

REAL LIFE
Fantagraphics
Value: Cover or less

- ❑1, b&w 2.50

REALLY FANTASTIC ALIEN SEX FRENZY (CYNTHIA PETAL'S...)
Fantagraphics
Value: Cover or less

- ❑1, b&w; adult 3.95

REALM, THE (VOL. 1)
Arrow

	ORIG	GOOD	FINE	N-MINT
❑1	1.50	0.60	1.50	3.00
❑2, repeats indicia for #1	1.50	0.40	1.00	2.00
❑3	1.50	0.40	1.00	2.00
❑4, Sep 86, Of Damsels and Darklords; It's a Small World, 1: Deadworld	1.50	0.80	2.00	4.00
❑5	1.50	0.35	0.88	1.75
❑6	1.50	0.35	0.88	1.75
❑7	1.50	0.35	0.88	1.75
❑8	1.50	0.35	0.88	1.75
❑9	1.50	0.35	0.88	1.75
❑10	1.50	0.35	0.88	1.75
❑11, A Night on the Town	1.50	0.35	0.88	1.75
❑12	1.50	0.35	0.88	1.75
❑13	1.95	0.39	0.98	1.95
❑14, Feb 89, b&w	1.95	0.39	0.98	1.95
❑15, Apr 89, b&w	1.95	0.39	0.98	1.95
❑16, May 89, b&w	1.95	0.50	1.25	2.50
❑17	2.50	0.50	1.25	2.50
❑18	2.50	0.50	1.25	2.50
❑19, no publication date	2.50	0.50	1.25	2.50
❑20, Dec 90, Demonstorm	2.50	0.50	1.25	2.50
❑21, Demonstorm, no publication date	2.50	0.50	1.25	2.50

REALM, THE (VOL. 2)
Caliber
Value: Cover or less

- ❑1, BMB, b&w 2.95
- ❑2, b&w 2.95
- ❑3, b&w 2.95
- ❑4, b&w 2.95
- ❑5, b&w 2.95
- ❑6, b&w 2.95
- ❑7, b&w 2.95
- ❑8, b&w 2.95
- ❑9, b&w 2.95
- ❑10, b&w 2.95
- ❑11, b&w 2.95
- ❑12, b&w 2.95
- ❑13, b&w 2.95

REALM HANDBOOK, THE
Caliber
Value: Cover or less

- ❑1 .... 2.95

REALM OF THE DEAD
Caliber
Value: Cover or less

- ❑1 .... 2.95
- ❑2 .... 2.95
- ❑3 .... 2.95

REAL SCHMUCK
Starhead
Value: Cover or less

- ❑1, Near Death Of A Mail-Man; First Date, b&w 2.95

REAL SMUT
Fantagraphics
Value: Cover or less

- ❑1, b&w; adult 2.50
- ❑2, b&w; adult 2.50
- ❑3, b&w; adult 2.50
- ❑4, b&w; adult 2.75
- ❑5, b&w; adult 2.75
- ❑6, b&w; adult 2.50

REAL STUFF
Fantagraphics

	ORIG	GOOD	FINE	N-MINT
❑1, b&w; adult	2.00	0.60	1.50	3.00
❑2, b&w; adult	2.00	0.55	1.38	2.75
❑3, b&w; adult	2.25	0.50	1.25	2.50
❑4, Death Of A Junkie; Our Thing, b&w; adult	2.25	0.50	1.25	2.50
❑5, b&w; adult	2.25	0.50	1.25	2.50
❑6, b&w; adult	2.25	0.50	1.25	2.50
❑7, b&w; adult	2.25	0.50	1.25	2.50
❑8, b&w; adult	2.25	0.50	1.25	2.50
❑9, b&w; adult	2.25	0.50	1.25	2.50
❑10, b&w; adult	2.95	0.59	1.48	2.95
❑11, b&w; adult	2.50	0.50	1.25	2.50
❑12, The Surprise; Flashback, b&w; adult	2.50	0.50	1.25	2.50
❑13, b&w; adult	2.50	0.50	1.25	2.50
❑14, b&w; adult	2.50	0.50	1.25	2.50
❑15, b&w; adult	2.50	0.50	1.25	2.50
❑16, b&w; adult	2.50	0.50	1.25	2.50
❑17, b&w; adult	2.50	0.50	1.25	2.50
❑18, adult	2.50	0.50	1.25	2.50
❑19, Jul 94, b&w; adult	2.50	0.50	1.25	2.50
❑20, Oct 94, b&w; adult	2.95	0.59	1.48	2.95

A group of friends who shared adventures when they were younger are reunited in *Realworlds: Justice League of America.*

© 1999 DC Comics

REAL WAR STORIES
Eclipse
Value: Cover or less

- ❑1, BB; TY, BSz (c), The Elite of the Fleet; Tapestries Part1, False Note 2.00
- ❑2, BSz 4.95

REAL WEIRD WAR
Avalon
Value: Cover or less

- ❑1, The Last Kamikaze; Theatre of Fear, "Real Weird War" on cover 2.95

REAL WEIRD WEST
Avalon
Value: Cover or less

- ❑1, JA, Water, Water, Everywhere; Valley of Death 2.95

REALWORLDS: JUSTICE LEAGUE OF AMERICA
DC
Value: Cover or less

- ❑1, The Return of the Justice League 5.95

REALWORLDS: WONDER WOMAN
DC
Value: Cover or less

- ❑1, Wonder Woman versus the Red Menace! 5.95

RE-ANIMATOR (AIRCEL)
Aircel
Value: Cover or less

- ❑1, full color; movie Adaptation 2.95
- ❑2, full color; movie Adaptation 2.95
- ❑3, full color; movie Adaptation 2.95

RE-ANIMATOR: DAWN OF THE RE-ANIMATOR
Adventure
Value: Cover or less

- ❑1, Dead and Buried, b&w 2.50
- ❑2, Apr 92, Creatures of the Night 2.95
- ❑3, May 92, The Dead in Their Masquerade 2.50
- ❑4 .... 2.50

RE-ANIMATOR IN FULL COLOR
Adventure
Value: Cover or less

- ❑1, Nov 91 .... 2.95
- ❑2 .... 2.95
- ❑3, Apr 92 .... 2.95

R.E.B.E.L.S.
DC
Value: Cover or less

- ❑0, Oct 94, Less Than Zero, O: Vril Dox II; O: L.E.G.I.O.N.; O: Yril Dox, story continued from L.E.G.I.O.N. '94 #70 .... 1.95
- ❑1, Nov 94, Escape To Nowhere 1.95
- ❑2, Dec 94, Title changes to R.E.B.E.L.S. '95 .... 1.95
- ❑3, Jan 95, Brains 1.95
- ❑4, Feb 95 .... 1.95
- ❑5, Mar 95 .... 1.95
- ❑6, Apr 95 .... 1.95
- ❑7, May 95 .... 1.95
- ❑8, Jun 95 .... 2.25
- ❑9, Jul 95 .... 2.25
- ❑10, Aug 95 .... 2.25
- ❑11, Sep 95, return of Captain Comet 2.25
- ❑12, Oct 95 .... 2.25
- ❑13, Nov 95, Underworld Unleashed, Underworld Unleashed 2.25
- ❑14, Dec 95, Title changes to R.E.B.E.L.S. '96 .... 2.25
- ❑15, Jan 96, Nerves 2.25
- ❑16, Feb 96, Expiring Minds 2.25
- ❑17, Mar 96, Deliverance, Final Issue 2.25

REBEL SWORD
Dark Horse
Value: Cover or less

- ❑1, Oct 94, b&w 2.50
- ❑2, Nov 94, b&w 2.50
- ❑3, Dec 94, b&w 2.50
- ❑4, Jan 95, b&w 2.50
- ❑5, Feb 95, b&w 2.50

RECOLLECTIONS SAMPLER
Recollections

	ORIG	GOOD	FINE	N-MINT
❑1, b&w; 16pgs.; Reprint	0.50	0.20	0.50	1.00

RECORD OF LODOSS WAR: CHRONICLES OF THE HEROIC KNIGHT
CPM Manga
Value: Cover or less

- ❑1, Sep 00, b&w 2.95
- ❑2, Oct 00, b&w 2.95
- ❑3 .... 2.95
- ❑4 .... 2.95
- ❑5 .... 2.95
- ❑6 .... 2.95

	ORIG	GOOD	FINE	N-MINT

❑7 .... 2.95
❑8 .... 2.95
❑9 .... 2.95
❑10 .... 2.95
❑11 .... 2.95

RECORD OF LODOSS WAR: THE GREY WITCH
CPM

Value: Cover or less

❑1, Nov 98, wraparound cover 2.95
❑2, Dec 98 .... 2.95
❑3, Jan 99, wraparound cover 2.95
❑4, Feb 99 .... 2.95
❑5, Mar 99 .... 2.95
❑6, Apr 99 .... 2.95
❑7, May 99 .... 2.95
❑8, Jun 99 .... 2.95
❑9, Jul 99 .... 2.95
❑10, Aug 99 .... 2.95
❑11, Sep 99 .... 2.95
❑12, Oct 99 .... 2.95
❑13, Nov 99 .... 2.95
❑14, Dec 99 .... 2.95
❑15, Jan 00 .... 2.95
❑16, Feb 00 .... 2.95
❑17, Mar 00 .... 2.95
❑18, Apr 00 .... 2.95
❑19, May 00 .... 2.95
❑20, Jun 00 .... 2.95
❑21, Jul 00 .... 2.95
❑22, Aug 00 .... 2.95

RECTUM ERRRECTUM
BONEYARD

Value: Cover or less

❑1, Catamite's Anal RevengeThe Penile Colony 3.95

REDBLADE
DARK HORSE

Value: Cover or less

❑1, The Death Factory, gatefold cover 2.50
❑2 .... 2.50
❑3 .... 2.50

RED CIRCLE SORCERY
RED CIRCLE

	ORIG	GOOD	FINE	N-MINT
❑6, Series continued from Chilling Adventures in Sorcery #5	0.25	0.30	0.75	1.50
❑7	0.25	0.30	0.75	1.50
❑8, Aug 74, FT; GM, The Highwayman's Escape; Die in the name of the Law!	0.25	0.30	0.75	1.50
❑9	0.25	0.30	0.75	1.50
❑10	0.25	0.30	0.75	1.50
❑11	0.25	0.30	0.75	1.50

REDDEVIL
AC

Value: Cover or less

❑1, Clutches of the Claws Part 1; Claw, b&w and red; no indicia 2.95

RED DRAGON
COMICO

Value: Cover or less

❑1, Jun 96 .... 2.95

REDEEMER, THE
IMAGES & REALITIES

Value: Cover or less

❑1 .... 2.95

REDEEMERS, THE
ANTARCTIC

Value: Cover or less

❑1, Dec 97, Phatasms, b&w 2.95

RED FLANNEL SQUIRREL, THE
SIRIUS

Value: Cover or less

❑1, Oct 97, David Quinn, b&w 2.95

REDFOX
HARRIER

	ORIG	GOOD	FINE	N-MINT
❑1, Treasure Of Pthud, 1: Redfox, Harrier publishes	1.75	0.80	2.00	4.00
❑1-2, Treasure Of Pthud, 1: Redfox, 2nd Printing; Harrier publishes	1.75	0.35	0.88	1.75
❑2	1.75	0.60	1.50	3.00
❑3, May 86	1.75	0.50	1.25	2.50
❑4, Jul 86	1.75	0.35	0.88	1.75
❑5, Sep 86	1.75	0.35	0.88	1.75
❑6, Nov 86, The Captain's Story; White Lies	1.75	0.35	0.88	1.75
❑7	1.75	0.35	0.88	1.75
❑8, Mar 87, White Company	1.75	0.35	0.88	1.75
❑9, May 87, Welcom to the Darkside	1.75	0.35	0.88	1.75
❑10, Jul 87, Never Forever, Last Harrier issue	2.00	0.35	0.88	1.75
❑11, Sep 87, Life After Death, Valkyrie begins publishing	2.00	0.40	1.00	2.00
❑12, Nov 87, Requiem; Cantata	2.00	0.40	1.00	2.00
❑13, Jan 88, Thorns	2.00	0.40	1.00	2.00
❑14, Mar 88, White Waves	2.00	0.40	1.00	2.00
❑15, May 88, To Market, To Market..., Luther Arkwright cameo	2.00	0.40	1.00	2.00
❑16, Jun 88, Road to Mulhaarn	2.00	0.40	1.00	2.00
❑17, Aug 88, Raid on Pthud: A Bespoke Fantasy	2.00	0.40	1.00	2.00
❑18, Oct 88, Lyssa the Axe...Csárdás; Lyssa the Axe...Csárdás	2.00	0.40	1.00	2.00
❑19, Feb 89	2.00	0.40	1.00	2.00
❑20, Jun 89, Fragments, Final Issue	2.00	0.40	1.00	2.00

RED HEAT
BLACKTHORNE

Value: Cover or less

❑1, Jul 88, b&w; movie Adaptation 2.00
❑1/3D, Jul 88, movie Adaptation 2.50

REDMASK OF THE RIO GRANDE
AC

Value: Cover or less

❑1, full color; Reprint 2.95
❑2 .... 2.95
❑3, 3-D effects 2.95

RED MOON
MILLENNIUM

Value: Cover or less

❑1, Mar 95, The Tale of Terror; Lycanthropos, b&w 2.95
❑2 .... 2.95

RED PLANET PIONEER
INESCO

Value: Cover or less

❑1 .... 2.95

RED RAZORS: A DREDDWORLD ADVENTURE
FLEETWAY

Value: Cover or less

❑1, Red Razors; Strange Cases 2.95
❑2 .... 2.95
❑3 .... 2.95

RED REVOLUTION, THE
CALIBER

Value: Cover or less

❑1, b&w 2.95

RED ROCKET 7
DARK HORSE

Value: Cover or less

❑1, Aug 97 .... 3.95
❑2, Sep 97 .... 3.95
❑3, Oct 97 .... 3.95
❑4, Nov 97 .... 3.95
❑5, Jan 98 .... 3.95
❑6, Mar 98, All Apologies 3.95
❑7, Jun 98 .... 3.95

RED SONJA (VOL. 1)
MARVEL

	ORIG	GOOD	FINE	N-MINT
❑1, Nov 76, FT, O: Red Sonja	0.30	0.60	1.50	3.00
❑2, Jan 77, FT	0.30	0.40	1.00	2.00
❑3, May 77, FT, The Games of Gita	0.30	0.40	1.00	2.00
❑4, Jul 77, FT, The Lake of the Unknownb.	0.30	0.40	1.00	2.00
❑5, Sep 77, FT, Master Of The Bells!	0.30	0.40	1.00	2.00
❑6, Nov 77, FT, WP (w), The Singing Tower	0.35	0.30	0.75	1.50
❑7, Jan 78, FT, Throne of Blood!	0.35	0.30	0.75	1.50
❑8, Mar 78, FT, Vengeance of the Golden Circle	0.35	0.30	0.75	1.50
❑9, May 78, FT, Chariot of the Fire Stallions	0.35	0.30	0.75	1.50
❑10, Jul 78, FT, Red Lace	0.35	0.30	0.75	1.50
❑11, Sep 78, FT, Sightless in a Strage Land!	0.35	0.30	0.75	1.50
❑12, Nov 78	0.35	0.30	0.75	1.50
❑13, Jan 79	0.35	0.30	0.75	1.50
❑14, Mar 79	0.35	0.30	0.75	1.50
❑15, May 79	0.40	0.30	0.75	1.50

RED SONJA (VOL. 2)
MARVEL

	ORIG	GOOD	FINE	N-MINT
❑1, Feb 83, The Blood That Binds!	0.60	0.20	0.50	1.00
❑2, Mar 83	0.60	0.20	0.50	1.00

RED SONJA (VOL. 3)
MARVEL

	ORIG	GOOD	FINE	N-MINT
❑1, Aug 83, While Lovers Embrace- Demons Feed!, giant	1.00	0.30	0.75	1.50
❑2, Oct 83, Blood Debt, giant	1.00	0.30	0.75	1.50
❑3, Dec 83, giant	1.00	0.30	0.75	1.50
❑4, Feb 84, giant	1.00	0.30	0.75	1.50
❑5, Jan 85, PB, The Armies Of The Inland Sea	0.60	0.30	0.75	1.50
❑6, Feb 85, PB, The Endless Swamp!	0.60	0.30	0.75	1.50
❑7, Mar 85, Harvest!	0.60	0.30	0.75	1.50
❑8, Apr 85	0.65	0.30	0.75	1.50
❑9, May 85, The Queen Of Hearts!	0.65	0.30	0.75	1.50
❑10, Aug 85, Strangers!	0.65	0.30	0.75	1.50
❑11, Nov 85, Buried Alive	0.65	0.30	0.75	1.50
❑12, Feb 86, Descent!	0.75	0.30	0.75	1.50
❑13, The Demon's Tooth, Final Issue	0.75	0.30	0.75	1.50

RED SONJA: SCAVENGER HUNT
MARVEL

Value: Cover or less

❑1, Dec 95, One-Shot 2.95

RED SONJA: THE MOVIE
MARVEL

	ORIG	GOOD	FINE	N-MINT
❑1, Nov 85, Into the Realm of Darkness!, movie Adaptation	0.75	0.25	0.63	1.25
❑2, Dec 85, movie Adaptation	0.75	0.25	0.63	1.25

RED STAR, THE
IMAGE

	ORIG	GOOD	FINE	N-MINT
❑1, Jun 00	2.95	0.70	1.75	3.50
❑2, Jul 00	2.95	0.60	1.50	3.00
❑3, Oct 00	2.95	0.59	1.48	2.95
❑4, Jan 01	2.95	0.59	1.48	2.95
❑5, Feb 01	2.95	0.59	1.48	2.95

RED TORNADO
DC

	ORIG	GOOD	FINE	N-MINT
❑1, Jul 85, CI, KB (w), Storm Warning	0.75	0.20	0.50	1.00
❑2, Aug 85, CI, KB (w), Shattered	0.75	0.20	0.50	1.00
❑3, Sep 85, CI, KB (w), The Eye of the Storm	0.75	0.20	0.50	1.00
❑4, Oct 85, CI, KB (w), Ghost in the Machine	0.75	0.20	0.50	1.00

RED WOLF
Marvel

	ORIG	GOOD	FINE	N-MINT
❑1, May 72, 1: Lobo (Marvel); 1: Red Wolf	0.20	0.80	2.00	4.00
❑2, Jul 72	0.20	0.40	1.00	2.00
❑3, Sep 72	0.20	0.40	1.00	2.00
❑4, Nov 72, V: Man-Bear	0.20	0.40	1.00	2.00
❑5, Jan 73	0.20	0.40	1.00	2.00
❑6, Mar 73	0.20	0.40	1.00	2.00
❑7, May 73	0.20	0.40	1.00	2.00
❑8, Jul 73	0.20	0.40	1.00	2.00
❑9, Sep 73, Final Issue	0.20	0.40	1.00	2.00

REESE'S PIECES
Eclipse

Value: Cover or less

- ❑1 ... 1.75
- ❑2 ... 1.75

RE:GEX
Awesome

Value: Cover or less

- ❑0, Dec 98, RL, RL (w); JPH (w), Re:Gex, Woman with swords standing over figures ... 2.50
- ❑0/A, Jan 99, RL, RL (w); JPH (w), Re:Gex, Man with swords standing over figures ... 2.50
- ❑1, RL, RL (w); JPH (w) ... 2.50
- ❑1/A, RL, RL (w); JPH (w), Two women with swords on cover; White background ... 2.50

REGGIE'S REVENGE
Archie

Value: Cover or less

- ❑1, Spr 94 ... 2.00
- ❑2, Fal 94 ... 2.00
- ❑3, Spr 95 ... 2.00

REGISTRY OF DEATH
Kitchen Sink

Value: Cover or less

- ❑1, Nov 96, nn; oversized tpb ... 15.95

REGULATORS
Image

Value: Cover or less

- ❑1, Jun 95, KB (w), A Touch Of Scandal ... 2.50
- ❑2, Jul 95, KB (w), A: Vortex... 2.50
- ❑3, Aug 95, KB (w) ... 2.50
- ❑4, KB (w) ... 2.50

REID FLEMING
Boswell

	ORIG	GOOD	FINE	N-MINT
❑1, 1: Reid Fleming	—	2.00	5.00	10.00
❑1-2, 2nd Printing	—	0.80	2.00	4.00

REID FLEMING, WORLD'S TOUGHEST MILKMAN
Eclipse

	ORIG	GOOD	FINE	N-MINT
❑1, Oct 86, Rogue to Riches; A Day Like Any Other	2.00	1.60	4.00	8.00
❑1-2, A Day Like Any Other; Monday Morning, 2nd Printing	2.00	0.80	2.00	4.00
❑, A Day Like Any Other; Monday Morning, 3rd Printing	2.00	0.60	1.50	3.00
❑1-4, A Day Like Any Other; Monday Morning, 4th Printing	2.00	0.60	1.50	3.00
❑1-5, A Day Like Any Other; Monday Morning, 5th Printing	2.00	0.50	1.25	2.50
❑1-6, A Day Like Any Other; Monday Morning, 6th Printing; 1996	2.95	0.59	1.48	2.95
❑2, Rogue to Riches	2.00	0.80	2.00	4.00
❑2-2, 2nd Printing	2.00	0.40	1.00	2.00
❑2-3, Mar 89, 3rd Printing	2.00	0.40	1.00	2.00
❑3, Dec 88, Rogue to Riches	2.00	0.60	1.50	3.00
❑4, Nov 89, Rogue to Riches	2.00	0.60	1.50	3.00
❑5, Nov 90, Rogue to Riches	2.00	0.60	1.50	3.00
❑6	—	0.40	1.00	2.00
❑7, Jan 97, Another Dawn	2.95	0.40	1.00	2.00
❑8, Aug 97, Another Dawn	2.95	0.40	1.00	2.00
❑9, Apr 98, Another Dawn	2.95	0.59	1.48	2.95

REIGN OF THE DRAGONLORD
Eternity

Value: Cover or less

- ❑1, Oct 86 ... 1.80
- ❑2 ... 1.80

REIKI WARRIORS
Revolutionary

Value: Cover or less

- ❑1, Aug 93, Never a Good Time to Die; Guilt by Association, b&w ... 2.95

RELATIVE HEROES
DC

Value: Cover or less

- ❑1, Mar 00, DGry(w) ... 2.50
- ❑2, Apr 00, DGry(w) ... 2.50
- ❑3, May 00, DGry(w), Free Lunch ... 2.50
- ❑4, Jun 00, DGry(w), Visibility. 2.50
- ❑5, Jul 00, DGry(w) ... 2.50
- ❑6, Aug 00, DGry(w) ... 2.50

RELENTLESS PURSUIT
Slave Labor

Value: Cover or less

- ❑1, Jan 89, b&w ... 1.75
- ❑2, May 89, The Battle of White Bird Canyon, b&w ... 1.75
- ❑3, Sep 89, The Nez Perce Flight, b&w ... 2.95
- ❑4, Jan 90, b&w ... 3.95

The Red Star features the United Republics of the Red Star and their space-based defense system.

© 2000 Team Red Star (Image)

REMARKABLE WORLDS OF PHINEAS B. FUDDLE, THE
Paradox

Value: Cover or less

- ❑1 ... 5.95
- ❑2 ... 5.95
- ❑3 ... 5.95
- ❑4 ... 5.95

REN & STIMPY SHOW
Marvel

	ORIG	GOOD	FINE	N-MINT
❑1/A, Dec 92, Ren scratch&sniff card	2.25	0.50	1.25	2.50
❑1/B, Dec 92, Stimpy scratch&sniff card	2.25	0.50	1.25	2.50
❑1-2, Ren & Stimpy Go Bad!; Powdered Toast Man vs The Kings of Crim!, 2nd Printing; No air fouler	2.25	0.45	1.13	2.25
❑, Ren & Stimpy Go Bad!; Powdered Toast Man vs The Kings of Crim!, 3rd Printing; No air fouler	2.25	0.45	1.13	2.25
❑2, Jan 93	1.75	0.40	1.00	2.00
❑2-2, 2nd Printing	1.75	0.35	0.88	1.75
❑3, Feb 93	1.75	0.40	1.00	2.00
❑3-2, 2nd Printing	1.75	0.35	0.88	1.75
❑4, Mar 93, A: Muddy Mudskipper	1.75	0.40	1.00	2.00
❑5, Apr 93, The Croco-Men From Planet Zed!, in space	1.75	0.40	1.00	2.00
❑6, May 93, Clash Of Titans: Break-Fest Of Champions, A: Spider-Man	1.75	0.35	0.88	1.75
❑7, Jun 93, Kid Stimpy, Kid Stimpy	1.75	0.35	0.88	1.75
❑8, Jul 93, The Maltese Stimpy, Maltese Stimpy	1.75	0.35	0.88	1.75
❑9, Aug 93, Wakka Makka Ho'k, Mekka Stimpy Ho!; Wakka Makka Hodk, Mekka Stimpy Ho!	1.75	0.35	0.88	1.75
❑10, Sep 93, Bug Out	1.75	0.35	0.88	1.75
❑11, Oct 93, Ren's Peaceful Place	1.75	0.35	0.88	1.75
❑12, Nov 93, Stimpy cloned	1.75	0.35	0.88	1.75
❑13, Dec 93, Eencredeebly Pathetic Excuse For A Halloween Eesue!, Halloween issue	1.75	0.35	0.88	1.75
❑14, Jan 94, Mars Needs Velcro	1.75	0.35	0.88	1.75
❑15, Feb 94, Black Mail, White Christmas, Green Moulah, Christmas issue	1.75	0.35	0.88	1.75
❑16, Mar 94, The King And We!, Elvis parody	1.75	0.35	0.88	1.75
❑17, Apr 94	1.75	0.35	0.88	1.75
❑18, May 94, Powdered Toast Man	1.95	0.35	0.88	1.75
❑19, Jun 94, Minimalist Issue	1.95	0.39	0.98	1.95
❑20, Jul 94, Late Night With Muddy Mudskipper, A: Muddy Mudskipper	1.95	0.39	0.98	1.95
❑21, Aug 94	1.95	0.39	0.98	1.95
❑22, Sep 94	1.95	0.39	0.98	1.95
❑23, Oct 94, wrestling	1.95	0.39	0.98	1.95
❑24, Nov 94, Box Tops, box top collecting	1.95	0.39	0.98	1.95
❑25, Dec 94, Obedience School, V: Dogzilla	1.95	0.39	0.98	1.95
❑25/SC, Dec 94, enhanced cover	2.95	0.59	1.48	2.95
❑26, Jan 95, A: Sven Hoek	1.95	0.39	0.98	1.95
❑27, Feb 95, Raiders of the Lost Yak	1.95	0.39	0.98	1.95
❑28, Mar 95, Bath Time, A: Filthy the monkey	1.95	0.39	0.98	1.95
❑29, Apr 95, Sherlock Ho'k; Sherlock Hodk	1.95	0.39	0.98	1.95
❑30, May 95, Ren's birthday	1.95	0.39	0.98	1.95
❑31, Jun 95, From Vienna With Love	1.95	0.39	0.98	1.95
❑32, Jul 95	1.95	0.39	0.98	1.95
❑33, Aug 95	1.95	0.39	0.98	1.95
❑34, Sep 95	1.95	0.39	0.98	1.95
❑35, Oct 95	1.95	0.39	0.98	1.95
❑36, Nov 95	1.95	0.39	0.98	1.95
❑37, Dec 95, aliens	1.95	0.39	0.98	1.95
❑38, Jan 96	1.95	0.39	0.98	1.95
❑39, Feb 96	1.95	0.39	0.98	1.95
❑40, Mar 96	1.95	0.39	0.98	1.95
❑41, Apr 96, Stockboy Ren; It's a Joyful Life	1.95	0.39	0.98	1.95
❑42, May 96	1.95	0.39	0.98	1.95
❑43, Jun 96	1.95	0.39	0.98	1.95
❑44, Jul 96, Final Issue	1.95	0.39	0.98	1.95
❑HS 1, Feb 95, nn	2.95	0.59	1.48	2.95
❑SE 1, Jul 94	2.95	0.59	1.48	2.95
❑SE 2, Oct 94, Want Ads; Quarterback Sneaks, Summer Jobs	2.95	0.60	1.50	3.00

ORIG GOOD FINE N-MINT

REN & STIMPY SHOW, THE: RADIO DAZE
MARVEL

Value: Cover or less

❑1, Nov 95, based on audio release of same name......... 1.95

REN & STIMPY SHOW SPECIAL, THE: AROUND THE WORLD IN A DAZE
MARVEL

Value: Cover or less

❑1, Jan 96, nn; One-Shot........ 2.95

REN & STIMPY SHOW SPECIAL: EENTERACTIVE
MARVEL

Value: Cover or less

❑1, Jul 95, nn.......................... 2.95

REN & STIMPY SHOW SPECIAL: FOUR SWERKS
MARVEL

Value: Cover or less

❑1, Jan 95, nn.......................... 2.95

REN & STIMPY SHOW SPECIAL: POWDERED TOAST MAN
MARVEL

	ORIG	GOOD	FINE	N-MINT
❑1, Apr 94, Leave Everything To Me!, Powdered Toast Man	2.95	0.60	1.50	3.00

REN & STIMPY SHOW SPECIAL: POWDERED TOASTMAN'S CEREAL
MARVEL

Value: Cover or less

❑1, Apr 95, nn.......................... 2.95

REN & STIMPY SHOW SPECIAL: SPORTS
MARVEL

Value: Cover or less

❑1, Oct 95, nn.......................... 2.95

RENEGADE, THE
RIP OFF

Value: Cover or less

❑1, Aug 91, b&w; adult............ 2.50

RENEGADE!, THE (MAGNECOM)
MAGNECOM

Value: Cover or less

❑1, Dec 93, Night Slayer......... 2.95

RENEGADE RABBIT
PRINTED MATTER

	ORIG	GOOD	FINE	N-MINT
❑1, The Good, The Bad-and The Furry	1.75	0.35	0.88	1.75
❑2	1.75	0.35	0.88	1.75
❑3	1.75	0.35	0.88	1.75
❑4	1.75	0.35	0.88	1.75
❑5, Cerebus parody	1.50	0.35	0.88	1.75

RENEGADE ROMANCE
RENEGADE

Value: Cover or less

❑1, b&w.................................. 3.50

❑2, b&w.................................. 3.50

RENEGADES, THE
AGE OF HEROES

Value: Cover or less

❑1.. 1.00

❑2.. 1.00

RENEGADES OF JUSTICE, THE
BLUE MASQUE

Value: Cover or less

❑1, b&w.................................. 2.50

❑2, b&w.................................. 2.50

RENFIELD
CALIBER

	ORIG	GOOD	FINE	N-MINT
❑1, The Patient	2.95	0.59	1.48	2.95
❑1/LE, The Patient, Limited "special edition" with second cover	5.95	1.19	2.97	5.95
❑2	2.95	0.59	1.48	2.95
❑3	2.95	0.59	1.48	2.95
❑Ash 1, nn; b&w; no cover price	—	0.20	0.50	1.00

RENNIN COMICS (JIM CHADWICK'S...)
RESTLESS MUSE

Value: Cover or less

❑1, Sum 97, b&w.................... 2.95

REPLACEMENT GOD
HANDICRAFT

Value: Cover or less

❑6, Dec 98, 80pgs.................. 6.95

REPLACEMENT GOD, THE
SLAVE LABOR

	ORIG	GOOD	FINE	N-MINT
❑1, Jun 95, Freedom	2.95	1.20	3.00	6.00
❑1-2, Dec 95, Freedom, 2nd Printing	2.95	0.60	1.50	3.00
❑2, Sep 95, I of Knute	2.95	0.70	1.75	3.50
❑3, Dec 95, Bravery	2.95	0.60	1.50	3.00
❑4, Apr 96	2.95	0.59	1.48	2.95
❑5, Jul 96	2.95	0.59	1.48	2.95
❑6	2.95	0.59	1.48	2.95
❑7	2.95	0.59	1.48	2.95
❑8	2.95	0.59	1.48	2.95

REPLACEMENT GOD AND OTHER STORIES, THE
IMAGE

Value: Cover or less

❑1, May 97, b&w; flip-book with Knute's Escapes back-up ... 2.95

❑2, Jul 97, b&w; flip-book with Harris Thermidor back-up......... 2.95

❑3, Sep 97, Replacement God; Knute's Escapes, b&w; flip-book with Knute's Escapes back-up............................. 2.95

❑4, Nov 97, Replacement God; Knute's Escapes, b&w; flip-book with Knute's Escapes back-up.............................. 2.95

❑5, Jan 98, Replacement God; Knute's Escapes, b&w; flip-book with Knute's Escapes back-up.............................. 2.95

REPORTER
REPORTER

Value: Cover or less

❑1.. 3.00

REQUIEM FOR DRACULA
MARVEL

Value: Cover or less

❑1, GC, Batwings Over Transylvania!, Reprints Tomb of Dracula #69, 70............................... 2.00

RESCUEMAN
BEST

Value: Cover or less

❑1, b&w.................................. 2.95

RESCUERS DOWN UNDER, THE (DISNEY'S...)
DISNEY

Value: Cover or less

❑1.. 2.95

RESIDENT EVIL
IMAGE

	ORIG	GOOD	FINE	N-MINT
❑1, Mar 98, S.T.A.R.S. Files; Who Are These Guys?	4.95	1.10	2.75	5.50
❑2, Jun 98, A New Chapter of Evil; Mutant Menagerie	4.95	1.00	2.50	5.00
❑3, Sep 98, Wolf Hunt; Danger Island	4.95	1.00	2.50	5.00
❑4, Dec 98	4.95	1.00	2.50	5.00
❑5, Feb 99	4.95	1.00	2.50	5.00

RESIDENT EVIL: FIRE AND ICE
WILDSTORM

Value: Cover or less

❑1, Dec 00............................. 2.50

❑2, Jan 01.............................. 2.50

❑3, Feb 01.............................. 2.50

❑4, May 01.............................. 2.50

RESTAURANT AT THE END OF THE UNIVERSE, THE
DC

Value: Cover or less

❑1, prestige format.................. 6.95

❑2, prestige format.................. 6.95

❑3, Final Issue; prestige format................................. 6.95

RESURRECTION MAN
DC

	ORIG	GOOD	FINE	N-MINT
❑1, May 97, Lenticular disc on cover	2.50	0.60	1.50	3.00
❑2, Jun 97, A: Justice League of America	2.50	0.50	1.25	2.50
❑3, Jul 97	2.50	0.50	1.25	2.50
❑4, Aug 97	2.50	0.50	1.25	2.50
❑5, Sep 97	2.50	0.50	1.25	2.50
❑6, Oct 97, Genesis; Resurrection Man powerless	2.50	0.50	1.25	2.50
❑7, Nov 97, BG, Gotham D.O.A., A: Batman	2.50	0.50	1.25	2.50
❑8, Dec 97, BG, Tricks or Treats, Face cover	2.50	0.50	1.25	2.50
❑9, Jan 98, A: Hitman	2.50	0.50	1.25	2.50
❑10, Feb 98, A: Hitman	2.50	0.50	1.25	2.50
❑11, Mar 98, BG, Origin of the Species, Part 1, O: Resurrection Man	2.50	0.50	1.25	2.50
❑12, Apr 98	2.50	0.50	1.25	2.50
❑13, May 98	2.50	0.50	1.25	2.50
❑14, Jun 98	2.50	0.50	1.25	2.50
❑15, Jul 98	2.50	0.50	1.25	2.50
❑16, Aug 98, A: Supergirl	2.50	0.50	1.25	2.50
❑17, Sep 98, A: Supergirl	2.50	0.50	1.25	2.50
❑18, Oct 98, A: Phantom Stranger; A: Deadman	2.50	0.50	1.25	2.50
❑19, Dec 98	2.50	0.50	1.25	2.50
❑20, Jan 99	2.50	0.50	1.25	2.50
❑21, Feb 99, V: Major Force; A: Justice League of America	2.50	0.50	1.25	2.50
❑22, Mar 99	2.50	0.50	1.25	2.50
❑23, Apr 99, Mitch as a woman	2.50	0.50	1.25	2.50
❑24, May 99, Forgotten but not Gone, A: Vigilante; A: Vandal Savage; A: Ballistic; A: Cave Carson; A: Ray; A: Animal Man	2.50	0.50	1.25	2.50
❑25, Jun 99, Millennium then, A: Forgotten Heroes	2.50	0.50	1.25	2.50
❑26, Jul 99, Millennium Now!, A: Immortal Man	2.50	0.50	1.25	2.50
❑27, Aug 99, The Ends of the Earth, D: Immortal Man	2.50	0.50	1.25	2.50
❑1000000, Nov 98, A Handful of Dust	2.50	0.50	1.25	2.50

RETALIATOR, THE
ECLIPSE

Value: Cover or less

❑1, Avenging Angel, b&w; game card.................................... 2.50

❑2, My Little Sunshine, b&w; game card.................................... 2.50

❑3, b&w.................................. 2.50

❑4, b&w.................................. 2.50

❑5.. 2.50

RETIEF
ADVENTURE

Value: Cover or less

❑1, b&w.................................. 2.25

❑2, b&w.................................. 2.25

❑3, b&w.................................. 2.25

❑4, b&w.................................. 2.25

❑5, b&w.................................. 2.25

❑6, b&w.................................. 2.25

RETIEF (KEITH LAUMER'S...)
MAD DOG

Value: Cover or less

- ❑1, Apr 87, Policy 2.00
- ❑2, Jun 87 ..... 2.00
- ❑3, Aug 87 ..... 2.00
- ❑4, Oct 87 ..... 2.00
- ❑5, Jan 88 ..... 2.00
- ❑6, Mar 88 ..... 2.00

RETIEF AND THE WARLORDS
ADVENTURE

Value: Cover or less

- ❑1, b&w 2.50
- ❑2, b&w 2.50
- ❑3, b&w 2.50
- ❑4, b&w 2.50

RETIEF: DIPLOMATIC IMMUNITY
ADVENTURE

Value: Cover or less

- ❑1, b&w 2.50
- ❑2, b&w 2.50

RETIEF: GRIME AND PUNISHMENT
ADVENTURE

Value: Cover or less

- ❑1, Nov 91, Grime and Punishment, b&w 2.50

RETIEF OF THE C.D.T.
MAD DOG

Value: Cover or less

- ❑1, b&w 2.00

RETIEF: THE GARBAGE INVASION
ADVENTURE

Value: Cover or less

- ❑1, b&w 2.50

RETIEF: THE GIANT KILLER
ADVENTURE

Value: Cover or less

- ❑1, b&w 2.50

RETRO 50'S COMIX
EDGE

Value: Cover or less

- ❑1, b&w 2.95
- ❑2, b&w 2.95
- ❑3, b&w; free fly 3.50

RETRO COMICS
AC

Value: Cover or less

- ❑0, b&w; cardstock cover; Cat-Man 5.95
- ❑1, b&w; cardstock cover; Fighting Yank 5.95
- ❑2, b&w; cardstock cover; Miss Victory 5.95
- ❑3, The League of the Rotting Dead; Hog Wild!, Original Cat-Man and Kitten 5.95

RETRO-DEAD
BLAZER

Value: Cover or less

- ❑1, Nov 95, b&w 2.95

RETROGRADE
ETERNITY

Value: Cover or less

- ❑1 ..... 1.95
- ❑2 ..... 1.95
- ❑3 ..... 1.95

RETURN OF DISNEY'S ALADDIN, THE
DISNEY

Value: Cover or less

- ❑1, More Arabian Nights, Part 1 ..... 1.50
- ❑2, More Arabian Nights, Part 2 ..... 1.50

RETURN OF GIRL SQUAD X
FANTACO

Value: Cover or less

- ❑1, nn 4.95

RETURN OF HAPPY THE CLOWN, THE
CALIBER

Value: Cover or less

- ❑1, b&w 3.50
- ❑2, b&w 2.95

RETURN OF HERBIE, THE
AVALON

Value: Cover or less

- ❑1, b&w; reprints and new story (originally scheduled for Dark Horse's Herbie #3) 2.50

RETURN OF LUM URUSEI*YATSURA, THE
VIZ

	ORIG	GOOD	FINE	N-MINT
❑1, b&w	2.95	0.60	1.50	3.00
❑2, b&w	2.75	0.60	1.50	3.00
❑3, b&w	2.75	0.60	1.50	3.00
❑4, b&w	2.95	0.60	1.50	3.00
❑5, b&w	2.95	0.60	1.50	3.00
❑6, b&w	2.95	0.60	1.50	3.00

RETURN OF LUM URUSEI*YATSURA, PART 2, THE
VIZ

	ORIG	GOOD	FINE	N-MINT
❑1, b&w	2.75	0.60	1.50	3.00
❑2, b&w	2.75	0.60	1.50	3.00
❑3, b&w	2.75	0.60	1.50	3.00
❑4, b&w	2.75	0.60	1.50	3.00
❑5, b&w	2.75	0.60	1.50	3.00
❑6, b&w	2.75	0.60	1.50	3.00
❑7, b&w	2.75	0.60	1.50	3.00
❑8, b&w	2.75	0.60	1.50	3.00
❑9, b&w	2.75	0.60	1.50	3.00
❑10, b&w	2.75	0.60	1.50	3.00
❑11, b&w	2.75	0.60	1.50	3.00
❑12, b&w	2.75	0.60	1.50	3.00
❑13, b&w	2.75	0.60	1.50	3.00

The Forgotten Heroes reappeared as *Resurrection Man* neared its end.

RETURN OF LUM URUSEI*YATSURA, PART 3, THE
VIZ

Value: Cover or less

- ❑1, b&w 2.95
- ❑2, b&w 2.95
- ❑3, b&w 2.95
- ❑4, b&w 2.95
- ❑5, b&w 2.95
- ❑6, b&w 2.95
- ❑7, b&w 2.95
- ❑8, b&w 2.95
- ❑9, b&w 2.95
- ❑10, b&w 2.95
- ❑11, b&w 2.95

RETURN OF LUM URUSEI*YATSURA, PART 4, THE
VIZ

Value: Cover or less

- ❑1, b&w 2.95
- ❑2, b&w 2.95
- ❑3, b&w 2.95
- ❑4, b&w 2.95
- ❑5, b&w 2.95
- ❑6, b&w 2.95
- ❑7, b&w 2.95
- ❑8, b&w 2.95
- ❑9, b&w 2.95
- ❑10, b&w 2.95
- ❑11, b&w 2.95

RETURN OF MEGATON MAN, THE
KITCHEN SINK

	ORIG	GOOD	FINE	N-MINT
❑1, Jul 88, Returns!	2.00	0.50	1.25	2.50
❑2, Revamp Relive!!!	2.00	0.50	1.25	2.50
❑3, Reborn-Redeemed!	2.00	0.50	1.25	2.50

RETURN OF TARZAN, THE (EDGAR RICE BURROUGHS'...)
DARK HORSE

Value: Cover or less

- ❑1, Apr 97, TY, TY (w), adapts Burroughs novel 2.95
- ❑2, May 97, TY, TY (w), adapts Burroughs novel 2.95
- ❑3, Jun 97, TY, TY (w), back cover has reproductions of New Story Magazine covers; adapts Burroughs novel 2.95

RETURN OF THE SKYMAN
ACE

Value: Cover or less

- ❑1, Sep 87, SD 1.75

RETURN OF VALKYRIE, THE
ECLIPSE

Value: Cover or less

- ❑1, The Heap; On Wings of Death 9.95

RETURN TO JURASSIC PARK
TOPPS

Value: Cover or less

- ❑1, JSa, No Man's Land 2.50
- ❑2 ..... 2.50
- ❑3, Jun 95, JSa, No Wimps Land 2.95
- ❑4, Jul 95, JSa 2.95
- ❑5, Aug 95 ..... 2.95
- ❑6, Sep 95 ..... 2.95
- ❑7, Nov 95, Inquiring Minds, Part 1 ..... 2.95
- ❑8, Jan 96, Inquiring Minds, Part 2 ..... 2.95
- ❑9 ..... 2.95

RETURN TO THE EVE
MONOLITH

Value: Cover or less

- ❑1, The Hanging Garden 2.50

REVELATIONS (CLIVE BARKER'S...)
ECLIPSE

Value: Cover or less

- ❑1 ..... 7.95

REVELATIONS (DARK HORSE)
DARK HORSE

	ORIG	GOOD	FINE	N-MINT
❑1/Ash, Mar 95, KG (w)	—	0.20	0.50	1.00

REVELATIONS (GOLDEN REALM)
GOLDEN REALM UNLIMITED

Value: Cover or less

- ❑1 ..... 2.75

REVELATION: THE COMIC BOOK
DRAW NEAR ART STUDIOS

	ORIG	GOOD	FINE	N-MINT
❑1, b&w; no cover price; based on Book of Revelation	—	0.71	1.78	3.56
❑2, b&w; based on Book of Revelation	3.50	0.71	1.78	3.56
❑3, b&w; based on Book of Revelation	3.50	0.71	1.78	3.56
❑4, b&w; based on Book of Revelation	3.50	0.71	1.78	3.56

REVELRY IN HELL
FANTAGRAPHICS

Value: Cover or less

- ❑1, b&w; adult 2.50

REVENGE OF THE PROWLER
ECLIPSE

	ORIG	GOOD	FINE	N-MINT
❑1, Feb 88, Slow Burn	1.75	0.40	1.00	2.00
❑2, Mar 88, Search and Destroy, flexi-disc	2.50	0.50	1.25	2.50
❑3, Apr 88, If I Should Die Before I Wake, Part 1	1.95	0.40	1.00	2.00
❑4, Jun 88, If I Should Die Before I Wake, Part 2	1.95	0.40	1.00	2.00

REVENGERS, THE
CONTINUITY
Value: Cover or less

❑1, Sep 85, NA, NA (w), Revengers Featuring Armor and Silver Streak, The ... 2.00
❑2, Jun 86, NA, NA (w), Revengers Featuring Megalith ... 2.00
❑3, Feb 87 ... 2.00
❑SE 1, Nov 93, NA (w) ... 4.95

REVENGERS FEATURING MEGALITH
CONTINUITY
Value: Cover or less

❑1, newsstand ... 2.00
❑1/DM, Apr 85 ... 2.00
❑2, Sep 85 ... 2.00
❑3, Nov 86 ... 2.00
❑4, Mar 88 ... 2.00
❑5, Mar 88 ... 2.00
❑6, Mar 88 ... 2.00

REVENGERS: HYBRIDS SPECIAL
CONTINUITY
Value: Cover or less

❑1, Jul 92, continues in Hybrids: The Origin #2 ... 4.95

REVEREND ABLACK: ADVENTURES OF THE ANTICHRIST
CREATIVEFORCE DESIGNS
Value: Cover or less

❑1 ... 2.50
❑2, Jul 96, b&w ... 2.50

REVOLVER
FLEETWAY
Value: Cover or less

❑1, O: Dan Dare ... 2.50
❑2 ... 2.50
❑3 ... 2.50
❑4 ... 2.50
❑5, Purple Days; Happenstance & Kismet ... 2.50
❑6 ... 2.50
❑7, Purple Days; Happenstance & Kismet ... 2.50

REVOLVER (ROBIN SNYDER'S...)
RENEGADE

	ORIG	GOOD	FINE	N-MINT
❑1, Nov 85, Star Guide; Cookie for the Bear, Sci-Fi Adventure	1.70	0.40	1.00	2.00
❑2, Dec 85, Sci-Fi Adventure	1.70	0.40	1.00	2.00
❑3, Jan 86, SD (w), The Expert; Marshal of the Zodiac: The Icarus Assigment, Sci-Fi Adventure	1.70	0.40	1.00	2.00
❑4, Feb 86, Fantastic Fables	1.70	0.40	1.00	2.00
❑5, Mar 86, Fantastic Fables	1.70	0.40	1.00	2.00
❑6, Fantastic Fables	1.70	0.40	1.00	2.00
❑7, Ditko's World: Static	1.70	0.40	1.00	2.00
❑8, Ditko's World: Static	1.70	0.40	1.00	2.00
❑9, Ditko's World: Static	1.70	0.40	1.00	2.00
❑10, Murder	1.70	0.40	1.00	2.00
❑11, Murder	1.70	0.40	1.00	2.00
❑12, Murder	1.70	0.40	1.00	2.00
❑Anl 1, ATh (c), b&w	2.00	0.40	1.00	2.00

REVOLVING DOORS
BLACKTHORNE
Value: Cover or less

❑1, Oct 86 ... 1.75
❑2 ... 1.75
❑3 ... 1.75

RHAJ
MU
Value: Cover or less

❑1, b&w ... 2.00
❑2, b&w ... 2.00
❑3, b&w ... 2.00
❑4 ... 2.25

RHANES OF TERROR, THE
BUFFALO NICKEL
Value: Cover or less

❑1, Oct 99 ... 2.99
❑2 ... 2.99
❑3 ... 2.99
❑4 ... 2.99

RHUDIPRRT, PRINCE OF FUR
MU
Value: Cover or less

❑1, b&w ... 2.00
❑2, b&w ... 2.00
❑3 ... 2.25
❑4, Nov 90 ... 2.50
❑5, Jun 91 ... 2.25
❑6, Nov 91 ... 2.50
❑7, b&w ... 2.50
❑8, Jan 94 ... 2.50

RIB
DILEMMA
Value: Cover or less

❑1, Apr 96, b&w ... 1.95

RIBIT!
COMICO
Value: Cover or less

❑1, FT, FT (w) ... 1.95
❑2, FT, FT (w) ... 1.95
❑3, FT, FT (w) ... 1.95
❑4, FT, FT (w) ... 1.95

RICHARD DRAGON, KUNG-FU FIGHTER
DC

	ORIG	GOOD	FINE	N-MINT
❑1, Apr 75, Coming Of A Dragon!, 1: Richard Dragon, Kung Fu Fighter	0.25	0.60	1.50	3.00
❑2, JSn	0.25	0.40	1.00	2.00
❑3	0.25	0.40	1.00	2.00
❑4	0.25	0.40	1.00	2.00
❑5	0.25	0.40	1.00	2.00
❑6	0.25	0.40	1.00	2.00
❑7	0.25	0.40	1.00	2.00
❑8	0.25	0.40	1.00	2.00
❑9	0.25	0.40	1.00	2.00
❑10	0.25	0.40	1.00	2.00
❑11	0.25	0.30	0.75	1.50
❑12	0.25	0.30	0.75	1.50
❑13	0.25	0.30	0.75	1.50
❑14	0.25	0.30	0.75	1.50
❑15	0.25	0.30	0.75	1.50
❑16	0.25	0.30	0.75	1.50
❑17	0.25	0.30	0.75	1.50
❑18, Nov 77, Final Issue	0.25	0.30	0.75	1.50

RICHARD SPECK
BONEYARD
Value: Cover or less

❑1, Mar 93 ... 2.75

RICHIE RICH (2ND SERIES)
HARVEY
Value: Cover or less

❑1, Mar 91 ... 1.25
❑2, May 91 ... 1.25
❑3, Jul 91 ... 1.25
❑4, Sep 91 ... 1.25
❑5, Nov 91 ... 1.25
❑6, Jan 92 ... 1.25
❑7, Mar 92 ... 1.25
❑8, May 92 ... 1.25
❑9, Jul 92 ... 1.25
❑10, Sep 92 ... 1.25
❑11, Nov 92, EC, The $1, 000, 000 Pool Party; Reggie ... 1.25
❑12, Jan 93 ... 1.25
❑13, Mar 93 ... 1.25
❑14, May 93 ... 1.25
❑15, Jul 93 ... 1.25
❑16, Sep 93 ... 1.50
❑17, Nov 93 ... 1.50
❑18, Jan 94 ... 1.50
❑19, Feb 94 ... 1.50
❑20, Mar 94 ... 1.50
❑21, Apr 94 ... 1.50
❑22, May 94 ... 1.50
❑23, Jun 94 ... 1.50
❑24, Jul 94 ... 1.50
❑25, Aug 94 ... 1.50
❑26, Sep 94 ... 1.50
❑27, Oct 94 ... 1.50
❑28, Nov 94 ... 1.50

RICHIE RICH (MOVIE ADAPTATION)
MARVEL
Value: Cover or less

❑1, Feb 95, movie Adaptation . 2.95

RICHIE RICH ADVENTURE DIGEST MAGAZINE
HARVEY

	ORIG	GOOD	FINE	N-MINT
❑1, May 92	1.75	0.40	1.00	2.00
❑2, Feb 93	1.75	0.35	0.88	1.75
❑3, Jun 93	1.75	0.35	0.88	1.75
❑4, Oct 93	1.75	0.35	0.88	1.75
❑5, Feb 94	1.75	0.35	0.88	1.75
❑6, Jun 94	1.75	0.35	0.88	1.75

RICHIE RICH AND CASPER IN 3-D
BLACKTHORNE
Value: Cover or less

❑1/A ... 2.50
❑1/B, Spanish; Burger King ... 2.50

RICHIE RICH AND THE NEW KIDS ON THE BLOCK
HARVEY

	ORIG	GOOD	FINE	N-MINT
❑1	1.25	0.30	0.75	1.50

RICHIE RICH BIG BOOK (VOL. 2)
HARVEY
Value: Cover or less

❑1, Keep It Cool; Always Courteous ... 1.95
❑2 ... 1.95

RICHIE RICH DIGEST MAGAZINE
HARVEY

	ORIG	GOOD	FINE	N-MINT
❑1	1.75	0.80	2.00	4.00
❑2	1.75	0.60	1.50	3.00
❑3	1.75	0.60	1.50	3.00
❑4	1.75	0.60	1.50	3.00
❑5	1.75	0.60	1.50	3.00
❑6	1.75	0.60	1.50	3.00
❑7	1.75	0.60	1.50	3.00
❑8	1.75	0.60	1.50	3.00
❑9	1.75	0.60	1.50	3.00
❑10	1.75	0.60	1.50	3.00
❑11	1.75	0.40	1.00	2.00
❑12	1.75	0.40	1.00	2.00
❑13	1.75	0.40	1.00	2.00
❑14	1.75	0.40	1.00	2.00
❑15	1.75	0.40	1.00	2.00
❑16	1.75	0.40	1.00	2.00
❑17	1.75	0.40	1.00	2.00
❑18	1.75	0.40	1.00	2.00
❑19	1.75	0.40	1.00	2.00

	ORIG	GOOD	FINE	N-MINT
❑20, Apr 90, Kops 'n' Krooks Special	1.75	0.40	1.00	2.00
❑21, Jun 90	1.75	0.40	1.00	2.00
❑22, Aug 90	1.75	0.40	1.00	2.00
❑23	1.75	0.40	1.00	2.00
❑24	1.75	0.40	1.00	2.00
❑25	1.75	0.40	1.00	2.00
❑26	1.75	0.40	1.00	2.00
❑27	1.75	0.40	1.00	2.00
❑28	1.75	0.40	1.00	2.00
❑29, May 91	1.75	0.40	1.00	2.00
❑30	1.75	0.40	1.00	2.00
❑31	1.75	0.40	1.00	2.00
❑32	1.75	0.40	1.00	2.00
❑33	1.75	0.40	1.00	2.00
❑34, Jun 92	1.75	0.40	1.00	2.00
❑35, Sep 92	1.75	0.40	1.00	2.00
❑36, Jan 93	1.75	0.40	1.00	2.00
❑37, May 93	1.75	0.40	1.00	2.00
❑38, Sep 93	1.75	0.40	1.00	2.00
❑39	1.75	0.40	1.00	2.00
❑40	1.75	0.40	1.00	2.00
❑41, Jul 94	1.75	0.40	1.00	2.00
❑42, Oct 94	1.75	0.40	1.00	2.00

RICHIE RICH GIANT SIZE
HARVEY

Value: Cover or less

- ❑1 2.25
- ❑2 2.25
- ❑3 2.25
- ❑4 2.25

RICHIE RICH GOLD NUGGETS DIGEST MAGAZINE
HARVEY

	ORIG	GOOD	FINE	N-MINT
❑1	—	0.40	1.00	2.00
❑2	—	0.40	1.00	2.00
❑3, Apr 91	1.75	0.40	1.00	2.00
❑4	—	0.40	1.00	2.00

RICHIE RICH HOLIDAY DIGEST
HARVEY

	ORIG	GOOD	FINE	N-MINT
❑1	—	0.60	1.50	3.00
❑2	—	0.40	1.00	2.00
❑3	—	0.40	1.00	2.00
❑4	—	0.40	1.00	2.00
❑5	—	0.40	1.00	2.00
❑6	—	0.40	1.00	2.00
❑7	—	0.40	1.00	2.00
❑8	—	0.40	1.00	2.00
❑9	—	0.40	1.00	2.00
❑10	—	0.40	1.00	2.00
❑11	—	0.40	1.00	2.00
❑12	—	0.40	1.00	2.00
❑13	—	0.40	1.00	2.00
❑14	—	0.40	1.00	2.00
❑15	—	0.40	1.00	2.00
❑16	—	0.40	1.00	2.00
❑17	—	0.40	1.00	2.00
❑18	—	0.40	1.00	2.00
❑19	1.75	0.35	0.88	1.75

RICHIE RICH MILLION DOLLAR DIGEST
HARVEY

	ORIG	GOOD	FINE	N-MINT
❑1	1.75	1.00	2.50	5.00
❑2	1.75	0.60	1.50	3.00
❑3	1.75	0.60	1.50	3.00
❑4	1.75	0.60	1.50	3.00
❑5	1.75	0.60	1.50	3.00
❑6	1.75	0.60	1.50	3.00
❑7	1.75	0.60	1.50	3.00
❑8	1.75	0.60	1.50	3.00
❑9	1.75	0.60	1.50	3.00
❑10	1.75	0.60	1.50	3.00
❑11	1.75	0.40	1.00	2.00
❑12	1.75	0.40	1.00	2.00
❑13, Aug 89	1.75	0.40	1.00	2.00
❑14	1.75	0.40	1.00	2.00
❑15	1.75	0.40	1.00	2.00
❑16	1.75	0.40	1.00	2.00
❑17	1.75	0.40	1.00	2.00
❑18	1.75	0.40	1.00	2.00
❑19	1.75	0.40	1.00	2.00
❑20	1.75	0.40	1.00	2.00
❑21	1.75	0.40	1.00	2.00
❑22	1.75	0.40	1.00	2.00
❑23	1.75	0.40	1.00	2.00
❑24	1.75	0.40	1.00	2.00
❑25	1.75	0.40	1.00	2.00
❑26, Jul 92	1.75	0.40	1.00	2.00
❑27, Nov 92	1.75	0.40	1.00	2.00
❑28, Mar 93	1.75	0.40	1.00	2.00
❑29, Jul 93	1.75	0.40	1.00	2.00
❑30, Nov 93	1.75	0.40	1.00	2.00
❑31, Mar 94	1.75	0.40	1.00	2.00

Harvey revived the adventures of "The Poor Little Rich Boy" in 1991.

	ORIG	GOOD	FINE	N-MINT
❑32, May 94	1.75	0.40	1.00	2.00
❑33, Aug 94	1.75	0.40	1.00	2.00
❑34, Nov 94	1.75	0.40	1.00	2.00

RICHIE RICH MONEY WORLD DIGEST
HARVEY

	ORIG	GOOD	FINE	N-MINT
❑1	1.75	0.40	1.00	2.00
❑2	1.75	0.35	0.88	1.75
❑3, Apr 92	1.75	0.35	0.88	1.75
❑4, Aug 92	1.75	0.35	0.88	1.75
❑5, Dec 92	1.75	0.35	0.88	1.75
❑6, Apr 93	1.75	0.35	0.88	1.75
❑7, Aug 93	1.75	0.35	0.88	1.75
❑8	1.75	0.35	0.88	1.75

RICHIE RICH VACATION DIGEST
HARVEY

Value: Cover or less

- ❑1992, Oct 92, #1 on cover 1.75
- ❑1993, Oct 93, #1 on cover 1.75

RIMA, THE JUNGLE GIRL
DC

	ORIG	GOOD	FINE	N-MINT
❑1, May 74, Spirit Of The Woods, O: Rima, the Jungle Girl	0.20	0.60	1.50	3.00
❑2, Jul 74, NR, Flight From Eden, O: Rima, the Jungle Girl	0.20	0.40	1.00	2.00
❑3, Sep 74, NR, Rio Lama; Space Voyagers: The Hot Spot, O: Rima, the Jungle Girl	0.20	0.40	1.00	2.00
❑4, Nov 74, The Flaming Forest, O: Rima, the Jungle Girl	0.20	0.40	1.00	2.00
❑5, Jan 75	0.20	0.40	1.00	2.00
❑6, Mar 75	0.25	0.40	1.00	2.00
❑7, May 75, Final Issue	0.25	0.40	1.00	2.00

RIME OF THE ANCIENT MARINER, THE (TOME)
TOME PRESS

Value: Cover or less

- ❑1, nn; b&w 3.95

RIMSHOT
RIP OFF

Value: Cover or less

- ❑1, Jun 90, b&w; adult 2.00
- ❑2, Feb 91, b&w; adult 2.00
- ❑3, Jul 91, b&w; adult 2.50

RING OF ROSES
DARK HORSE

Value: Cover or less

- ❑1, b&w 2.50
- ❑2, b&w 2.50
- ❑3, b&w 2.50
- ❑4, b&w 2.50

RING OF THE NIBELUNG, THE
DC

Value: Cover or less

- ❑1, GK, Rhinegold; The Rhinegold 4.95
- ❑2, GK, Valkyrie; The Valkyrie 4.95
- ❑3, GK, Siegfried 4.95
- ❑4, GK, Twilight of Gods 4.95

RING OF THE NIBELUNG, THE (DARK HORSE)
DARK HORSE

Value: Cover or less

- ❑1, Feb 00, CR, CR (w), The Rape of the Gold 2.95
- ❑2, Mar 00, CR, CR (w) 2.95
- ❑3, Apr 00, CR, CR (w) 2.95
- ❑4, May 00, CR, CR (w), The First Murder 2.95

RING OF THE NIBELUNG, THE (VOL. 2)
DARK HORSE

Value: Cover or less

- ❑1, Aug 00, CR, CR (w), The Valkyrie 2.95
- ❑2, Sep 00, CR, CR (w), The Valkyrie 2.95
- ❑3, Oct 00, CR, CR (w), The Valkyrie 2.99

RING OF THE NIBELUNG, THE (VOL. 3)
DARK HORSE

Value: Cover or less

- ❑1, Dec 00, CR, CR (w), Siegfried 2.99
- ❑2, Jan 01, CR, CR (w), Siegfried 2.99
- ❑3, Feb 01, CR, CR (w), Siegfried 2.99

RINGO KID, THE
MARVEL

	ORIG	GOOD	FINE	N-MINT
❑1, Jan 70, AW, SL (w), The Hostage; Stranger in Town, Reprint from Ringo Kid Western	0.15	1.60	4.00	8.00
❑2, Mar 70, JSe, The Sheriff's Star!; Deadly Ambush, reprints from Ringo Kid Western #9	0.15	1.00	2.50	5.00

	ORIG	GOOD	FINE	N-MINT
❑3, May 70	0.15	0.80	2.00	4.00
❑4, Jul 70	0.15	0.80	2.00	4.00
❑5, Sep 70	0.15	0.80	2.00	4.00
❑6, Nov 70	0.15	0.80	2.00	4.00
❑7, Jan 71	0.15	0.80	2.00	4.00
❑8, Mar 71	0.15	0.80	2.00	4.00
❑9, May 71	0.15	0.80	2.00	4.00
❑10, Jul 71	0.15	0.80	2.00	4.00
❑11, Sep 71	0.15	0.60	1.50	3.00
❑12, Nov 71	0.25	0.60	1.50	3.00
❑13, Jan 72	0.25	0.60	1.50	3.00
❑14, Mar 72	0.20	0.60	1.50	3.00
❑15, May 72	0.20	0.60	1.50	3.00
❑16, Jul 72	0.20	0.60	1.50	3.00
❑17, Sep 72	0.20	0.60	1.50	3.00
❑18, Nov 72	0.20	0.60	1.50	3.00
❑19, Jan 73	0.20	0.60	1.50	3.00
❑20, Mar 73	0.20	0.60	1.50	3.00
❑21, May 73	0.20	0.60	1.50	3.00
❑22, Jul 73	0.20	0.60	1.50	3.00
❑23, Sep 73	0.20	0.60	1.50	3.00
❑24, Nov 73	0.20	0.60	1.50	3.00
❑25, Nov 75	0.20	0.60	1.50	3.00
❑26, Jan 76	0.20	0.60	1.50	3.00
❑27, Mar 76	0.20	0.60	1.50	3.00
❑28, May 76	0.20	0.60	1.50	3.00
❑29, Jul 76	0.20	0.60	1.50	3.00
❑30, Sep 76, Final Issue	0.20	0.60	1.50	3.00

RIO AT BAY
DARK HORSE

Value: Cover or less

- ❑1, Aug 92, Hot Lead For Jonny Hardluck ... 2.95
- ❑2, Aug 92 ... 2.95

RIO GRAPHIC NOVEL
COMICO

Value: Cover or less

- ❑1, May 87 ... 8.95

RIO KID
ETERNITY

Value: Cover or less

- ❑1, b&w ... 2.50
- ❑2, b&w ... 2.50
- ❑3, b&w ... 2.50

RION 2990
RION

Value: Cover or less

- ❑1, Despair, b&w ... 1.50
- ❑2, b&w ... 1.50
- ❑3 ... 1.50
- ❑4 ... 1.50

RIOT, ACT 1
VIZ

Value: Cover or less

- ❑1 ... 2.75
- ❑2 ... 2.75
- ❑3 ... 2.75
- ❑4 ... 2.95
- ❑5 ... 2.95
- ❑6 ... 2.95

RIOT, ACT 2
VIZ

Value: Cover or less

- ❑1 ... 2.95
- ❑2 ... 2.95
- ❑3 ... 2.95
- ❑4 ... 2.95
- ❑5 ... 2.95
- ❑6 ... 2.95
- ❑7 ... 2.95

RIOT GEAR
TRIUMPHANT

Value: Cover or less

- ❑1 ... 2.50
- ❑1/Ash, Escape, Ashcan edition (color) ... 2.50
- ❑2 ... 2.50
- ❑3 ... 2.50
- ❑4, D: Captain Tich, Unleashed! 2.50
- ❑5, Jan 94, Retribution ... 2.50
- ❑6, Feb 94, Retribution ... 2.50
- ❑7, Mar 94 ... 2.50
- ❑8, Apr 94, One Last Exit ... 2.50
- ❑9 ... 2.50
- ❑10 ... 2.50
- ❑11, Final issue? ... 2.50
- ❑Ash 1, full color; ashcan ... 2.50

RIOT GEAR: VIOLENT PAST
TRIUMPHANT

Value: Cover or less

- ❑1, Feb 94 ... 2.50
- ❑2, Feb 94, 14, 000 printed ... 2.50

RIPCLAW (VOL. 1)
IMAGE

	ORIG	GOOD	FINE	N-MINT
❑0.5, Wizard promotional edition	—	0.40	1.00	2.00
❑0.5/GO, Wizard promotional edition; Gold edition	—	0.50	1.25	2.50
❑1, Apr 95	2.50	0.50	1.25	2.50
❑2, Jun 95	2.50	0.50	1.25	2.50
❑3, Jul 95	2.50	0.50	1.25	2.50
❑4	2.50	0.50	1.25	2.50

RIPCLAW (VOL. 2)
IMAGE

Value: Cover or less

- ❑1, Dec 95 ... 2.50
- ❑2, Jan 96 ... 2.50
- ❑3, Feb 96 ... 2.50
- ❑4, Mar 96 ... 2.50
- ❑5, Apr 96 ... 2.50
- ❑6, Jun 96 ... 2.50
- ❑SE 1, Oct 95, Special Edition #1 ... 2.50

R.I.P. COMICS MODULE
TSR

Value: Cover or less

- ❑1 ... 2.95
- ❑2 ... 2.95
- ❑3 ... 2.95
- ❑4 ... 2.95
- ❑5, Brasher ... 2.95
- ❑6, Brasher ... 2.95
- ❑7, Brasher ... 2.95
- ❑8, Brasher ... 2.95

R.I.P.D.
DARK HORSE

Value: Cover or less

- ❑1, Oct 99 ... 2.95
- ❑2, Nov 99 ... 2.95
- ❑3, Dec 99 ... 2.95
- ❑4, Jan 00 ... 2.95

RIPFIRE
MALIBU

Value: Cover or less

- ❑0, Jan 95, Genesis ... 2.50

RIP HUNTER...TIME MASTER
DC

	ORIG	GOOD	FINE	N-MINT
❑1	0.12	65.00	162.50	325.00
❑2	0.12	25.00	62.50	125.00
❑3	0.12	20.00	50.00	100.00
❑4	0.12	17.00	42.50	85.00
❑5	0.12	17.00	42.50	85.00
❑6, ATh	0.12	15.00	37.50	75.00
❑7, Apr 62, ATh	0.12	15.00	37.50	75.00
❑8, Jun 62	0.12	12.00	30.00	60.00
❑9, Aug 62	0.12	12.00	30.00	60.00
❑10, Oct 62	0.12	12.00	30.00	60.00
❑11, Dec 62	0.12	12.00	30.00	60.00
❑12, Feb 63	0.12	12.00	30.00	60.00
❑13, Apr 63	0.12	12.00	30.00	60.00
❑14, Jun 63	0.12	12.00	30.00	60.00
❑15, Aug 63	0.12	12.00	30.00	60.00
❑16, Oct 63	0.12	10.00	25.00	50.00
❑17, Dec 63	0.12	10.00	25.00	50.00
❑18, Feb 64	0.12	10.00	25.00	50.00
❑19, Apr 64, Cleopatra's Deadly Trap; Rip Caesar-Conqueror of Egypt	0.12	10.00	25.00	50.00
❑20, Jun 64	0.12	10.00	25.00	50.00
❑21, Aug 64	0.12	8.40	21.00	42.00
❑22, Oct 64	0.12	8.40	21.00	42.00
❑23, Dec 64	0.12	8.40	21.00	42.00
❑24, Feb 65	0.12	8.40	21.00	42.00
❑25, Apr 65	0.12	8.40	21.00	42.00
❑26, Jun 65, Bring Back The Cosmic Key	0.12	7.00	17.50	35.00
❑27, Aug 65	0.12	7.00	17.50	35.00
❑28, Oct 65	0.12	7.00	17.50	35.00
❑29, Dec 65, Final Issue	0.12	7.00	17.50	35.00

RIP IN TIME
FANTAGOR

	ORIG	GOOD	FINE	N-MINT
❑1, b&w	1.50	0.40	1.00	2.00
❑2, Rip in Time; Going Home, b&w	1.50	0.40	1.00	2.00
❑3, Rip in Time; The Secret of Zokma, b&w	1.50	0.40	1.00	2.00
❑4, Rip in Time, b&w	1.50	0.40	1.00	2.00
❑5, Rip in Time; The Awakening, b&w	1.50	0.40	1.00	2.00

RIPLEY'S BELIEVE IT OR NOT!: BEAUTY & GROOMING
SCHANES

Value: Cover or less

- ❑1 ... 2.50

RIPLEY'S BELIEVE IT OR NOT!: CHILD PRODIGIES
SCHANES

Value: Cover or less

- ❑1 ... 2.50

RIPLEY'S BELIEVE IT OR NOT!: CRUELTY
SCHANES PRODUCTS

Value: Cover or less

- ❑1, Jun 93, b&w; says Crime & Murder on cover; reprints newspaper cartoons ... 2.50
- ❑2, Jun 93, b&w; says Crime & Murder on cover; reprints newspaper cartoons ... 2.50

RIPLEY'S BELIEVE IT OR NOT!: FAIRY TALES & LITERATURE
SCHANES

Value: Cover or less

- ❑1 ... 2.50

RIPLEY'S BELIEVE IT OR NOT!: FEATS OF WONDER
SCHANES

Value: Cover or less

- ❑1 ... 2.50

RIPLEY'S BELIEVE IT OR NOT!: SPORTS FEATS
SCHANES PRODUCTS

Value: Cover or less

- ❑1, Jun 93, b&w; reprints newspaper cartoons ... 2.50

RIPLEY'S BELIEVE IT OR NOT!: STRANGE DEATHS
SCHANES PRODUCTS

Value: Cover or less

- ❑1, Jun 93, b&w; reprints newspaper cartoons ... 2.50

RIPLEY'S BELIEVE IT OR NOT TRUE WAR STORIES
GOLD KEY

	ORIG	GOOD	FINE	N-MINT
❑1, The Red Knight of Germany; The Incredible Sea Hunt of Sub E-11, #3 in overall series; Continued in Ripley's Believe It or Not #4	0.12	4.80	12.00	24.00

RIP OFF COMIX
Rip Off

	ORIG	GOOD	FINE	N-MINT
❑1	0.75	4.00	10.00	20.00
❑2	1.50	2.40	6.00	12.00
❑3	1.50	1.60	4.00	8.00
❑4, Nov 78, Kangaroo Court; Freak Brothers: the 4th Freak Brother!	1.50	1.20	3.00	6.00
❑5, Sep 79, Think Eighties; Freak Brothers: Take Out…	2.00	1.00	2.50	5.00
❑6, Mar 80, The Adventures of Fat Freddy's Cat; Freak Brothers: Death of Fat Freddy	2.00	1.00	2.50	5.00
❑6-2, Jan 80, The Adventures of Fat Freddy's Cat; Freak Brothers: Death of Fat Freddy, 2nd printing (1980)	1.50	0.50	1.25	2.50
❑7, Nov 80	1.50	1.00	2.50	5.00
❑8, May 81, 1981	2.00	0.80	2.00	4.00
❑9, Sep 81, 1981	2.00	0.80	2.00	4.00
❑10, Mar 82	2.00	0.80	2.00	4.00
❑11, Oct 82	2.95	0.60	1.50	3.00
❑12, Apr 83	2.95	0.60	1.50	3.00
❑13	2.95	0.60	1.50	3.00
❑14, Apr 87	2.95	0.60	1.50	3.00
❑15, Jul 87	2.95	0.60	1.50	3.00
❑16, Oct 87	2.95	0.60	1.50	3.00
❑17, Jan 88	2.95	0.60	1.50	3.00
❑18, Apr 88	2.95	0.60	1.50	3.00
❑19, Jul 88	2.95	0.60	1.50	3.00
❑20, Oct 88	2.95	0.60	1.50	3.00
❑21, Jan 89, 20th Anniversary	3.50	0.60	1.50	3.00
❑22, Apr 89	2.95	0.60	1.50	3.00
❑23, Jul 89	2.95	0.60	1.50	3.00
❑24, Oct 89, San Diego Con	3.25	0.65	1.63	3.25
❑25, Jan 90	3.25	0.65	1.63	3.25
❑26, Apr 90	3.25	0.65	1.63	3.25
❑27, Jul 90	3.25	0.79	1.98	3.95
❑28, Oct 90	3.50	0.70	1.75	3.50
❑29, Jan 91	3.50	0.70	1.75	3.50
❑30, Apr 91	3.50	0.70	1.75	3.50
❑31, Mar 92	3.50	0.70	1.75	3.50

RIPPER
Aircel

Value: Cover or less

- ❑1, 1: Ripper 2.50
- ❑2 .... 2.50
- ❑3 .... 2.50
- ❑4 .... 2.50
- ❑5 .... 2.50
- ❑6 .... 2.50

RIPPER LEGACY, THE
Caliber

Value: Cover or less

- ❑1 .... 2.95
- ❑2 .... 2.95
- ❑3 .... 2.95

RIPTIDE
Image

Value: Cover or less

- ❑1, Sep 95, Ugly Little Dreams 2.50
- ❑2, Oct 95 .... 2.50

RISE OF APOCALYPSE
Marvel

Value: Cover or less

- ❑1, Oct 96, Hammer & Chisel, O: Apocalypse, wraparound cover 1.95
- ❑2, Nov 96, O: Apocalypse, wraparound cover 1.95
- ❑3, Dec 96, Face of the Gods, O: Apocalypse, wraparound cover 1.95
- ❑4, Jan 97, O: Apocalypse, wraparound cover; Final Issue 1.95

RISING STARS
Image

	ORIG	GOOD	FINE	N-MINT
❑0, Wizard promotional edition	—	1.60	4.00	8.00
❑0/GO, Gold logo variant from Wizard promotion	—	4.00	10.00	20.00
❑1, Aug 99, Standard edition; Team standing over coffin	2.50	0.70	1.75	3.50
❑1/A, Aug 99, Holofoil edition	2.50	3.00	7.50	15.00
❑1/B, Aug 99, chromium cover	2.50	4.00	10.00	20.00
❑1/C, Aug 99, Gold "Monster Edition"; Team with burning figure kneeling in foreground	—	2.50	6.25	12.50
❑1/D, Aug 99, Gold "Monster Edition"; Children running to house	—	2.50	6.25	12.50
❑1/E, Aug 99, Gold "Monster Edition"; Battle scene with blonde woman in foreground.	—	2.50	6.25	12.50
❑1/F, Aug 99, Gold "Monster Edition"; Team standing over coffin	—	2.50	6.25	12.50
❑1/G, Aug 99, Another Universe/Wizard World variant (boy standing in foreground looking at large glowing sphere, Wizard World/AU markings)	—	1.00	2.50	5.00
❑1/H, Aug 99, No "Monster Edition" logo; Battle scene with blonde woman in foreground	—	1.00	2.50	5.00
❑2, Oct 99	2.50	0.50	1.25	2.50
❑2/A, Dec 99, Dymamic Forces variant cover	—	1.00	2.50	5.00
❑2/B, Dec 99, Dymamic Forces gold variant cover (Dynamic Forces seal on cover)	—	2.00	5.00	10.00

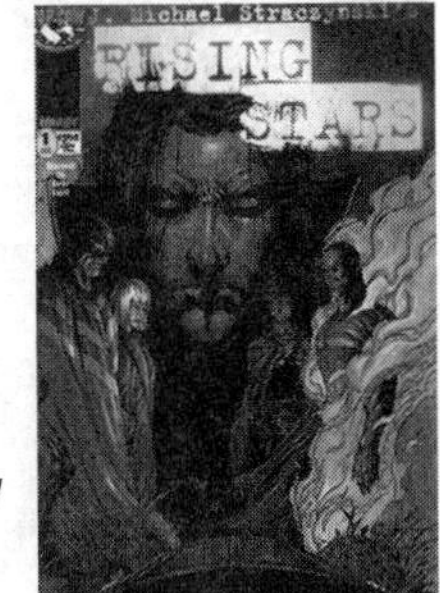

At least nine cover variants were produced for J. Michael Straczynski's *Rising Stars* #1.

© 1999 J. Michael Straczynski (Image)

	ORIG	GOOD	FINE	N-MINT
❑3, Dec 99	2.50	0.50	1.25	2.50
❑4	2.50	0.50	1.25	2.50
❑5, Mar 00, The World Between	2.50	0.50	1.25	2.50
❑6	2.50	0.50	1.25	2.50
❑7	2.50	0.50	1.25	2.50
❑8	2.50	0.50	1.25	2.50
❑9, Aug 00, Choices Made	2.50	0.50	1.25	2.50
❑10, Oct 00, Reversals of Fortune	2.50	0.50	1.25	2.50
❑11, Nov 00, What Goes Around	2.50	0.50	1.25	2.50
❑12, Jan 01, A, B, C, and D	2.50	0.50	1.25	2.50
❑13, Mar 01, Stalingrad	2.50	0.50	1.25	2.50
❑14, May 01, Things Change	2.50	0.50	1.25	2.50
❑Ash 1, Oct 00, Variations & Midnight Thoughts, Convention Exclusive preview	5.00	1.20	3.00	6.00
❑ASH 1/A, Prelude edition	2.95	0.59	1.48	2.95

RIVERDALE HIGH
Archie

	ORIG	GOOD	FINE	N-MINT
❑1, Aug 90	1.00	0.30	0.75	1.50
❑2	1.00	0.20	0.50	1.00
❑3	1.00	0.20	0.50	1.00
❑4	1.00	0.20	0.50	1.00
❑5	1.00	0.20	0.50	1.00

RIVETS & RUBY
Radio

Value: Cover or less

- ❑1, Feb 98 .... 2.95
- ❑2, Apr 98 .... 2.95
- ❑3, Jul 98 .... 2.95
- ❑4 .... 2.95

RIVIT
Blackthorne

Value: Cover or less

- ❑1, A Rivit in Time: Saves None!!!; Bare Bones 1.75

ROACHMILL (BLACKTHORNE)
Blackthorne

	ORIG	GOOD	FINE	N-MINT
❑1, Dec 86	1.75	0.40	1.00	2.00
❑2, Feb 87	1.75	0.40	1.00	2.00
❑3, Apr 87	1.75	0.40	1.00	2.00
❑4, Jun 87	1.75	0.40	1.00	2.00
❑5, Sep 87	1.75	0.40	1.00	2.00
❑6, Oct 87	1.75	0.40	1.00	2.00

ROACHMILL (DARK HORSE)
Dark Horse

Value: Cover or less

- ❑1, May 88 .... 1.75
- ❑2, Jun 88 .... 1.75
- ❑3, Sep 88 .... 1.75
- ❑4, Nov 88 .... 1.75
- ❑5, Apr 89, Hot Sex 1.75
- ❑6, Jun 89 .... 1.75
- ❑7, Oct 89 .... 1.75
- ❑8, Jan 90, indicia says Jan 89; a misprint 1.75
- ❑9, Apr 90, The Hunt for Miss October 1.95
- ❑10, Dec 90, Final Issue; trading cards 1.95

ROADKILL
Lighthouse

Value: Cover or less

- ❑1, b&w 2.00
- ❑2, b&w 2.00

ROADKILL: A CHRONICLE OF THE DEADWORLD
Caliber

Value: Cover or less

- ❑1, nn; text 2.95

ROAD TRIP
Oni

Value: Cover or less

- ❑1, Aug 00, nn; b&w; collects story from Oni Double Feature #9 and #10 .... 2.95

ROADWAYS
Cult Press

Value: Cover or less

- ❑1, May 94, The Road to Nowhere, b&w 2.75
- ❑2, Jun 94, b&w 2.75
- ❑3 .... 2.75
- ❑4 .... 2.75

ROARIN' RICK'S RARE BIT FIENDS
King Hell

Value: Cover or less

- ❑1, Jul 94 .... 2.95
- ❑2, Aug 94 .... 2.95
- ❑3, Sep 94 .... 2.95
- ❑4, Oct 94 .... 2.95

- ❏5, Nov 94 ... 2.95
- ❏6, Dec 94 ... 2.95
- ❏7, Jan 95 ... 2.95

ROBBIN' $3000
PARODY

Value: Cover or less

- ❏1, b&w ... 2.50

ROB HANES
WCG

Value: Cover or less

- ❏1, Jan 91, The Care Package, b&w ... 2.50

ROB HANES ADVENTURES
WCG

Value: Cover or less

- ❏1, Oct 00, Where in the World is Rob Hanes? ... 2.50

ROBIN
DC

	ORIG	GOOD	FINE	N-MINT
❏0, Oct 94, O: Robin II (Jason Todd); O: Robin III (Timothy Drake); O: Robin I (Dick Grayson)	1.50	0.40	1.00	2.00
❏1, Nov 93, Outcast, 1: Shotgun Smith	1.50	0.50	1.25	2.50
❏1/SC, Nov 93, Embossed cover	2.95	0.70	1.75	3.50
❏2, Jan 94	1.50	0.40	1.00	2.00
❏3, Feb 94	1.50	0.40	1.00	2.00
❏4, Mar 94, Clueless, A: Spoiler	1.50	0.40	1.00	2.00
❏5, Apr 94	1.50	0.40	1.00	2.00
❏6, May 94, A: Huntress	1.50	0.40	1.00	2.00
❏7, Jun 94, KnightQuest Conclusion	1.50	0.40	1.00	2.00
❏8, Jul 94, KnightsEnd, Part 5	1.50	0.40	1.00	2.00
❏9, Aug 94, KnightsEnd Aftermath; KnightsEnd Aftermath, Part 1	1.50	0.40	1.00	2.00
❏10, Sep 94, Zero Hour; Tim Drake Robin teams with Dick Grayson Robin	1.50	0.40	1.00	2.00
❏11, Nov 94, Prodigal, Part 4	1.50	0.35	0.88	1.75
❏12, Dec 94, Prodigal, Part 8	1.50	0.35	0.88	1.75
❏13, Jan 95, Prodigal Conclusion	1.50	0.35	0.88	1.75
❏14, Feb 95, Troika, Part 4	1.50	0.35	0.88	1.75
❏14/SC, Feb 95, Troika, Part 4, enhanced cardstock cover	2.50	0.50	1.25	2.50
❏15, Mar 95	1.50	0.35	0.88	1.75
❏16, Apr 95, All Fall Down	1.50	0.35	0.88	1.75
❏17, Jun 95	1.95	0.40	1.00	2.00
❏18, Jul 95	1.95	0.40	1.00	2.00
❏19, Aug 95, V: Ulysses	1.95	0.40	1.00	2.00
❏20, Sep 95, V: Ulysses	1.95	0.40	1.00	2.00
❏21, Oct 95, Ninja camp	1.95	0.40	1.00	2.00
❏22, Nov 95, Ninja camp	1.95	0.40	1.00	2.00
❏23, Dec 95, V: Killer Moth a.k.a. Charaxes, Underworld Unleashed	1.95	0.40	1.00	2.00
❏24, Jan 96, V: Killer Moth a.k.a. Charaxes, Underworld Unleashed	1.95	0.40	1.00	2.00
❏25, Feb 96, Sophomore Lethal, anti-guns issue	1.95	0.40	1.00	2.00
❏26, Mar 96, The Hard Lessons	1.95	0.40	1.00	2.00
❏27, Mar 96, Contagion, Part 3	1.95	0.40	1.00	2.00
❏28, Apr 96, Contagion, Part 11	1.95	0.40	1.00	2.00
❏29, May 96	1.95	0.40	1.00	2.00
❏30, Jun 96	1.95	0.40	1.00	2.00
❏31, Jul 96, A: Wildcat	1.95	0.40	1.00	2.00
❏32, Aug 96, Legacy, Part 3	1.95	0.40	1.00	2.00
❏33, Sep 96, Legacy, Part 7	1.95	0.40	1.00	2.00
❏34, Oct 96, Situations and Comedies, self-contained story	1.95	0.40	1.00	2.00
❏35, Nov 96, Iced!, A: Spoiler, Final Night...	1.95	0.40	1.00	2.00
❏36, Dec 96, War Toy Story, V: Ulysses; V: Toyman	1.95	0.40	1.00	2.00
❏37, Jan 97, Who Dies With the Most Toys..., V: Ulysses; V: Toyman	1.95	0.40	1.00	2.00
❏38, Feb 97	1.95	0.40	1.00	2.00
❏39, Mar 97, Gotaway Gone	1.95	0.40	1.00	2.00
❏40, Apr 97	1.95	0.39	0.98	1.95
❏41, May 97	1.95	0.39	0.98	1.95
❏42, Jun 97	1.95	0.39	0.98	1.95
❏43, Jul 97	1.95	0.39	0.98	1.95
❏44, Aug 97, A: Spoiler	1.95	0.39	0.98	1.95
❏45, Sep 97, self-contained story	1.95	0.39	0.98	1.95
❏46, Oct 97, self-contained story	1.95	0.39	0.98	1.95
❏47, Nov 97, Warchild, A: Batman; V: Ulysses; A: Nightwing	1.95	0.39	0.98	1.95
❏48, Dec 97, Mission Creep, Face cover	1.95	0.39	0.98	1.95
❏49, Jan 98, A: King Snake	1.95	0.39	0.98	1.95
❏50, Feb 98, A: Lady Shiva; A: King Snake	2.95	0.39	0.98	1.95
❏51, Mar 98, Kiss and Kill	1.95	0.39	0.98	1.95
❏52, Apr 98, Cataclysm, Part 7, continues in Batman: Blackgate-Isle of Men #1	1.95	0.39	0.98	1.95
❏53, May 98, Cataclysm Conclusion	1.95	0.39	0.98	1.95
❏54, Jun 98, A: Spoiler, Aftershock	1.95	0.39	0.98	1.95
❏55, Jul 98, Brotherhood of the Fist, Part 3, continues in Nightwing #23	1.95	0.39	0.98	1.95
❏56, Aug 98, A: Spoiler, Tim breaks up with Ariana	1.95	0.39	0.98	1.95
❏57, Sep 98, Spoiler and Robin date	1.99	0.40	1.00	1.99
❏58, Oct 98, V: Steeljacket	1.99	0.40	1.00	1.99
❏59, Dec 98, V: Steeljacket	1.99	0.40	1.00	1.99
❏60, Jan 99	1.99	0.40	1.00	1.99
❏61, Feb 99	1.99	0.40	1.00	1.99
❏62, Mar 99, A: Flash III (Wally West), Tim relocates to Keystone City	1.99	0.40	1.00	1.99
❏63, Apr 99, A: Captain Boomerang; A: Flash III (Wally West); A: Superman; A: Riddler	1.99	0.40	1.00	1.99
❏64, May 99, Stop Me If You've Heard This One, V: Captain Boomerang; A: Flash III (Wally West); V: Riddler	1.99	0.40	1.00	1.99
❏65, Jun 99, A Blessed Event, Spoiler's child is born	1.99	0.40	1.00	1.99
❏66, Jul 99, Tim returns to Gotham	1.99	0.40	1.00	1.99
❏67, Aug 99, Way Dark, A: Nightwing, No Man's Land	1.99	0.40	1.00	1.99
❏68, Sep 99, War Beneath the Streets! Part 1, V: Ratcatcher, No Man's Land	1.99	0.40	1.00	1.99
❏69, Oct 99, War Beneath the Streets! Part 2, V: Ratcatcher, No Man's Land	1.99	0.40	1.00	1.99
❏70, Nov 99	1.99	0.40	1.00	1.99
❏71, Dec 99, The Lizard King	1.99	0.40	1.00	1.99
❏72, Jan 00, Stand on Grand Avenue	1.99	0.40	1.00	1.99
❏73, Feb 00	1.99	0.40	1.00	1.99
❏74, Mar 00	1.99	0.40	1.00	1.99
❏75, Apr 00, Thrashed, Giant-size	2.95	0.59	1.48	2.95
❏76, May 00, Wings over Brentwood	1.99	0.40	1.00	1.99
❏77, Jun 00	—	0.40	1.00	1.99
❏78, Jul 00	—	0.40	1.00	1.99
❏79, Aug 00	—	0.40	1.00	1.99
❏80, Sep 00, The Girl	2.25	0.45	1.13	2.25
❏81, Oct 00, The Obtuse Conundrum	2.25	0.45	1.13	2.25
❏82, Nov 00, The New Kid	2.25	0.45	1.13	2.25
❏83, Dec 00, Wrong Place, Wrong Time	2.25	0.45	1.13	2.25
❏84, Jan 01, UnFathomable	2.25	0.45	1.13	2.25
❏85, Feb 01, Fool's Errand, A: Joker	2.25	0.45	1.13	2.25
❏86, Mar 01, Officer Down, Part 2	2.25	0.45	1.13	2.25
❏87, Apr 01, Secrets Revealed	2.25	0.45	1.13	2.25
❏88, May 01, Secrets & Lies	2.25	0.45	1.13	2.25
❏89	2.25	0.45	1.13	2.25
❏90	2.25	0.45	1.13	2.25
❏91	2.25	0.45	1.13	2.25
❏92	2.25	0.45	1.13	2.25
❏1000000, Nov 98, Dark Planet, A: Robin the Toy Wonder	1.99	0.40	1.00	1.99
❏Anl 3, Elseworlds	2.95	0.59	1.48	2.95
❏Anl 4, Year One	2.95	0.79	1.98	3.95
❏Anl 5, Legends of the Dead Earth	2.95	0.59	1.48	2.95
❏Anl 6, Pulp Heroes	3.95	0.79	1.98	3.95
❏GS 1, Sep 00, Nature's Bride: A Tale of Robin and Marital Bliss, Eighty Page Giant	5.95	1.19	2.97	5.95

ROBIN (MINI-SERIES)
DC

	ORIG	GOOD	FINE	N-MINT
❏1, Jan 91, Big Bad World, 1: King Snake, poster; poster	1.00	0.60	1.50	3.00
❏1-2, Jan 91, 1: King Snake, 2nd Printing; (no poster); (no poster)	1.00	0.30	0.75	1.50
❏, 1: King Snake, 3rd Printing; (no poster); (no poster)	1.00	0.30	0.75	1.50
❏2, Feb 91	1.00	0.50	1.25	2.50
❏2-2, Feb 91, 2nd Printing	1.00	0.30	0.75	1.50
❏3, Mar 91	1.00	0.40	1.00	2.00
❏4, Apr 91, V: Lady Shiva	1.00	0.40	1.00	2.00
❏5, May 91, V: King Shark	1.00	0.40	1.00	2.00
❏Anl 1, Eclipso: The Darkness Within, Part 12, Eclipso	2.50	0.50	1.25	2.50
❏Anl 2, Bloodlines, 1: Razorsharp, Bloodlines	2.50	0.50	1.25	2.50

ROBIN 3000
DC

Value: Cover or less

- ❏1, CR ... 4.95
- ❏2, CR ... 4.95

ROBIN/ARGENT DOUBLE-SHOT
DC

Value: Cover or less

- ❏1, Feb 98 ... 1.95

ROBIN HOOD (ECLIPSE)
ECLIPSE

Value: Cover or less

- ❏1 ... 2.50
- ❏2 ... 2.50
- ❏3 ... 2.50

ROBIN HOOD (ETERNITY)
ETERNITY

Value: Cover or less

- ❏1, Aug 89, b&w ... 2.25
- ❏2, b&w ... 2.25
- ❏3, b&w ... 2.25
- ❏4, b&w ... 2.25

	ORIG	GOOD	FINE	N-MINT

ROBIN II
DC

	ORIG	GOOD	FINE	N-MINT
❑1, Oct 91, CR, newsstand; no hologram	1.00	0.20	0.50	1.00
❑1/A, CR, Robin Hologram; Joker in straight jacket	1.50	0.35	0.88	1.75
❑1/B, CR, Joker Holding cover; Robin Hologram	1.50	0.35	0.88	1.75
❑1/C, CR, Batman cover; Robin Hologram	1.50	0.35	0.88	1.75
❑1/CS, Oct 91, set of all covers; all variations of #1; extra hologram	10.00	2.00	5.00	10.00
❑1/D, CR, Joker Standing cover; Robin Hologram	1.50	0.35	0.88	1.75
❑2, Nov 91, Normal cover; newsstand; no hologram	1.00	0.20	0.50	1.00
❑2/A, Joker w/mallet cover; Batman Hologram	1.50	0.35	0.88	1.75
❑2/B, Joker w/dart board cover; Batman Hologram	1.50	0.35	0.88	1.75
❑2/C, Joker w/dagger cover; Batman Hologram	1.00	0.35	0.88	1.75
❑2/CS, all variations of #2	8.00	1.80	4.50	9.00
❑3, Nov 91, Normal cover; newsstand; no hologram	1.00	0.20	0.50	1.00
❑3/A, Robin Swinging cover; Joker Hologram	1.50	0.30	0.75	1.50
❑3/B, Joker Hologram; Robin perched	1.50	0.30	0.75	1.50
❑3/CS, all variations of #3	6.00	1.20	3.00	6.00
❑4, Dec 91, Normal cover; newsstand, no hologram	1.00	0.20	0.50	1.00
❑4/A, Bat signal hologram	1.50	0.30	0.75	1.50
❑4/CS, all variations of #4	4.00	0.85	2.13	4.25
❑Dlx 1, boxed with hologram cards (limited to 25,000); Deluxe set; Contains all issues and variations in bookshelf binder	30.00	6.00	15.00	30.00

ROBIN III: CRY OF THE HUNTRESS
DC
Value: Cover or less

- ❑1, Dec 92, Cry of the Huntress, Part 1, newsstand 1.25
- ❑1/SC, Dec 92, Cry of the Huntress, Part 1, moving cover 2.50
- ❑2, Jan 93, Cry of the Huntress, Part 2, newsstand 1.25
- ❑2/SC, Jan 93, Cry of the Huntress, Part 2, moving cover 2.50
- ❑3, Jan 93, Cry of the Huntress, Part 3, newsstand 1.25
- ❑3/SC, Jan 93, Cry of the Huntress, Part 3, moving cover 2.50
- ❑4, Feb 93, Cry of the Huntress, Part 4, newsstand 1.25
- ❑4/SC, Feb 93, Cry of the Huntress, Part 4, moving cover 2.50
- ❑5, Feb 93, Cry of the Huntress, Part 5, newsstand 1.25
- ❑5/SC, Feb 93, Cry of the Huntress, Part 5, moving cover 2.50
- ❑6, Mar 93, Cry of the Huntress, Part 6, newsstand 1.25
- ❑6/SC, Mar 93, Cry of the Huntress, Part 6, moving cover 2.50

ROBIN PLUS
DC
Value: Cover or less

- ❑1, Dec 96, Dashing Through the Storm, A: Impulse 2.95
- ❑2, Dec 97, A: Fang, continues in Scare Tactics #10 2.95

ROBIN RED AND THE LUTINS
ACE
Value: Cover or less

- ❑1, Nov 86 1.75
- ❑2 1.75

ROBIN: YEAR ONE
DC
Value: Cover or less

- ❑1 4.95
- ❑2 4.95
- ❑3 4.95
- ❑4 4.95

ROBOCOP (MAGAZINE)
MARVEL

	ORIG	GOOD	FINE	N-MINT
❑1, Oct 87, movie Adaptation	2.00	0.50	1.25	2.50

ROBOCOP (MARVEL)
MARVEL

	ORIG	GOOD	FINE	N-MINT
❑1, Mar 90, Kombat Zone	1.50	0.60	1.50	3.00
❑2, Apr 90	1.50	0.40	1.00	2.00
❑3, May 90, Dreamerama	1.50	0.30	0.75	1.50
❑4, Jun 90	1.50	0.30	0.75	1.50
❑5, Jul 90	1.50	0.30	0.75	1.50
❑6, Aug 90	1.50	0.30	0.75	1.50
❑7, Sep 90	1.50	0.30	0.75	1.50
❑8, Oct 90	1.50	0.30	0.75	1.50
❑9, Nov 90	1.50	0.30	0.75	1.50
❑10, Dec 90	1.50	0.30	0.75	1.50
❑11, Jan 91	1.50	0.30	0.75	1.50
❑12, Feb 91	1.50	0.30	0.75	1.50
❑13, Mar 91	1.50	0.30	0.75	1.50
❑14, Apr 91	1.50	0.30	0.75	1.50
❑15, May 91	1.50	0.30	0.75	1.50
❑16, Jun 91	1.50	0.30	0.75	1.50
❑17, Jul 91	1.50	0.30	0.75	1.50
❑18, Aug 91	1.50	0.30	0.75	1.50
❑19, Sep 91	1.50	0.30	0.75	1.50
❑20, Oct 91	1.50	0.30	0.75	1.50
❑21, Nov 91	1.50	0.30	0.75	1.50

The third Robin's training began in earnest in the first *Robin* mini-series.

	ORIG	GOOD	FINE	N-MINT
❑22, Dec 91	1.50	0.30	0.75	1.50
❑23, Jan 92, Final Issue	1.50	0.30	0.75	1.50

ROBOCOP (MOVIE ADAPTATION)
MARVEL
Value: Cover or less

- ❑1, Jul 90, movie Adaptation; prestige format 4.95

ROBOCOP 2
MARVEL

	ORIG	GOOD	FINE	N-MINT
❑1, Kid's Stuff, movie Adaptation; comic book	1.00	0.30	0.75	1.50
❑2, movie Adaptation; comic book	1.00	0.30	0.75	1.50
❑3, movie Adaptation; comic book	1.00	0.30	0.75	1.50

ROBOCOP 2 (MAGAZINE)
MARVEL

	ORIG	GOOD	FINE	N-MINT
❑1, b&w; movie Adaptation; magazine	2.25	0.50	1.25	2.50

ROBOCOP 3
DARK HORSE
Value: Cover or less

- ❑1, Jul 93, movie Adaptation 2.50
- ❑2, Sep 93, movie Adaptation 2.50
- ❑3, Nov 93, movie Adaptation 2.50

ROBOCOP: MORTAL COILS
DARK HORSE
Value: Cover or less

- ❑1, Sep 93 2.50
- ❑2, Oct 93 2.50
- ❑3, Nov 93 2.50
- ❑4, Dec 93 2.50

ROBOCOP: PRIME SUSPECT
DARK HORSE
Value: Cover or less

- ❑1, Oct 92 2.50
- ❑2, Nov 92 2.50
- ❑3, Dec 92 2.50
- ❑4, Jan 93 2.50

ROBOCOP: ROULETTE
DARK HORSE
Value: Cover or less

- ❑1, Dec 93 2.50
- ❑2, Jan 94 2.50
- ❑3, Feb 94 2.50
- ❑4, Mar 94 2.50

ROBOCOP VERSUS THE TERMINATOR
DARK HORSE

	ORIG	GOOD	FINE	N-MINT
❑1, FM (w), RoboCop cut-out	2.50	0.60	1.50	3.00
❑1/PL, FM (w), RoboCop cut-out; Platinum promotional edition	—	0.80	2.00	4.00
❑2, FM (w), Includes Terminator cut-out, Terminator cut-out	2.50	0.50	1.25	2.50
❑3, FM (w), Flo cut-out	2.50	0.50	1.25	2.50
❑4, FM (w), ED-209 cut-out	2.50	0.50	1.25	2.50

ROBO-HUNTER
EAGLE

	ORIG	GOOD	FINE	N-MINT
❑1	1.00	0.30	0.75	1.50
❑2, DaG, Robo-Hunter; Harlem Heroes	1.00	0.25	0.63	1.25
❑3, DaG, Robo-Hunter; Harlem Heroes	1.00	0.25	0.63	1.25
❑4, DaG, Robo-Hunter; Harlem Heroes	1.00	0.25	0.63	1.25
❑5, Robo-Hunter	1.00	0.25	0.63	1.25

ROBOTECH
ANTARCTIC
Value: Cover or less

- ❑1, Mar 97, Megastorm, Part 1 2.95
- ❑2, May 97, Megastorm, Part 2 2.95
- ❑3, Jul 97, Megastorm, Part 3. 2.95
- ❑4, Sep 97, Rolling Thunder, Part 1 2.95
- ❑5, Nov 97, Rolling Thunder, Part 2 2.95
- ❑6, Jan 98, Rolling Thunder, Part 3 2.95
- ❑7, Mar 98, Rolling Thunder, Part 4 2.95
- ❑8, May 98, Variants, Part 1 2.95
- ❑9, Jul 98, Variants, Part 2 2.95
- ❑10, Sep 98, Variants, Part 3 2.95
- ❑11, Nov 98, Variants, Part 4 2.95
- ❑Anl 1, Apr 98, The First Person; Shop Talk or Why You Should Never Ride Without a Helmet, b&w 2.95

ROBOTECH: AMAZON WORLD-ESCAPE FROM PRAXIS
ACADEMY
Value: Cover or less

- ❑1, Dec 94 2.95

ROBOTECH: CLASS REUNION
ANTARCTIC
Value: Cover or less

- ❑1, Dec 98, b&w 3.95

ROBOTECH: CLONE
ACADEMY

Value: Cover or less

Issue	ORIG
❑0	2.95
❑1, The Dialect Of Duality, Part 2	2.95
❑2	2.95
❑3	2.95
❑4	2.95
❑5	2.95
❑SE 1	3.50

ROBOTECH: COVERT-OPS
ANTARCTIC

Value: Cover or less

Issue	ORIG
❑1, Aug 98, b&w	2.95
❑2, Sep 98, b&w	2.95

ROBOTECH: CYBER WORLD-SECRETS OF HAYDON IV
ACADEMY

Value: Cover or less

Issue	ORIG
❑1	2.95

ROBOTECH DEFENDERS
DC

Issue	ORIG	GOOD	FINE	N-MINT
❑1, Jan 85, MA, The Gathering	0.75	0.40	1.00	2.00
❑2, Apr 85, MA, three-issue series was finished in two issues	0.75	0.40	1.00	2.00

ROBOTECH: ESCAPE
ANTARCTIC

Value: Cover or less

Issue	ORIG
❑1, May 98, b&w	2.95

ROBOTECH: FINAL FIRE
ANTARCTIC

Value: Cover or less

Issue	ORIG
❑1, Dec 98, b&w	2.95

ROBOTECH: FIREWALKERS
ETERNITY

Value: Cover or less

Issue	ORIG
❑1	2.50

ROBOTECH GENESIS
ETERNITY

Value: Cover or less

Issue	ORIG
❑1, full color; trading cards	2.50
❑1/LE, limited	5.95
❑2	2.50
❑3	2.50
❑4, trading cards	2.50
❑5, trading cards	2.50
❑6	2.50

ROBOTECH II: INVID WORLD, ASSAULT ON OPTERA
ACADEMY

Value: Cover or less

Issue	ORIG
❑1, Oct 94	2.95

ROBOTECH II: THE SENTINELS
ETERNITY

Issue	ORIG	GOOD	FINE	N-MINT
❑1, Nov 88, A New Threat	1.95	0.70	1.75	3.50
❑1-2, 2nd Printing	1.95	0.40	1.00	2.00
❑2, Dec 88	1.95	0.50	1.25	2.50
❑3, Jan 89	1.95	0.50	1.25	2.50
❑3-2, Feb 89, 2nd Printing	1.95	0.40	1.00	2.00
❑4, Mar 89	1.95	0.45	1.13	2.25
❑5, Apr 89	1.95	0.45	1.13	2.25
❑6, May 89	1.95	0.40	1.00	2.00
❑7, Jun 89	1.95	0.40	1.00	2.00
❑8, Jul 89	1.95	0.40	1.00	2.00
❑9, Sep 89	1.95	0.40	1.00	2.00
❑10, Oct 89	1.95	0.40	1.00	2.00
❑11, Oct 89	1.95	0.40	1.00	2.00
❑12, Nov 89	1.95	0.40	1.00	2.00
❑13, Dec 89	1.95	0.40	1.00	2.00
❑14, Jan 90	1.95	0.40	1.00	2.00
❑15	1.95	0.40	1.00	2.00
❑16, Apr 90, Final Issue	1.95	0.39	0.98	1.95

ROBOTECH II: THE SENTINELS BOOK II
ETERNITY

Value: Cover or less

Issue	ORIG
❑1, May 90	2.25
❑2	2.25
❑3	2.25
❑4	2.25
❑5	2.25
❑6	2.25
❑7	2.25
❑8	2.25
❑9	2.25
❑10	2.25
❑11	2.25
❑12	2.50
❑13, Mar 92	2.50
❑14	2.50
❑15	2.50
❑16	2.50
❑17	2.50
❑18	2.50
❑19	2.50
❑20	2.50

ROBOTECH II: THE SENTINELS BOOK III
ETERNITY

Value: Cover or less

Issue	ORIG
❑1	2.50
❑2	2.50
❑3	2.50
❑4	2.50
❑5	2.50
❑6	2.50

ROBOTECH II: THE SENTINELS BOOK IV
ACADEMY

Value: Cover or less

Issue	ORIG
❑1	2.95
❑2	2.95
❑3	2.95
❑4	2.95
❑5	2.95
❑6, May 96, Clockwork of Doom!	2.95

ROBOTECH II: THE SENTINELS CYBERPIRATES
ETERNITY

Value: Cover or less

Issue	ORIG
❑1	2.25
❑2	2.25
❑3	2.25
❑4	2.25

ROBOTECH II: THE SENTINELS SCRIPT BOOK
ETERNITY

Value: Cover or less

Issue	ORIG
❑1, b&w	9.95

ROBOTECH II: THE SENTINELS SPECIAL
ETERNITY

Value: Cover or less

Issue	ORIG
❑1, Apr 89	1.95
❑2	1.95

ROBOTECH II: THE SENTINELS SWIMSUIT SPECTACULAR
ETERNITY

Value: Cover or less

Issue	ORIG
❑1	2.95

ROBOTECH II: THE SENTINELS: THE ILLUSTRATED HANDBOOK
ETERNITY

Value: Cover or less

Issue	ORIG
❑1	2.50
❑2	2.50
❑3	2.50

ROBOTECH II: THE SENTINELS THE MALCONTENT UPRISINGS
ETERNITY

Value: Cover or less

Issue	ORIG
❑1	1.95
❑2, Sep 89	1.95
❑3	1.95
❑4, Dec 89	1.95
❑5	1.95
❑6	1.95
❑7	1.95
❑8	1.95
❑9	1.95
❑10	1.95
❑11	1.95
❑12	1.95

ROBOTECH II: THE SENTINELS: THE UNTOLD STORY
ETERNITY

Value: Cover or less

Issue	ORIG
❑1, b&w	2.50

ROBOTECH II: THE SENTINELS WEDDING SPECIAL
ETERNITY

Issue	ORIG	GOOD	FINE	N-MINT
❑1, Apr 89	1.95	0.40	1.00	2.00
❑2, May 89	1.95	0.40	1.00	2.00

ROBOTECH IN 3-D
COMICO

Value: Cover or less

Issue	ORIG
❑1	2.50

ROBOTECH: INVID WAR
ETERNITY

Value: Cover or less

Issue	ORIG
❑1, May 92, b&w	2.50
❑2, b&w	2.50
❑3, b&w	2.50
❑4, b&w	2.50
❑5, b&w	2.50
❑6, b&w	2.50
❑7, b&w	2.50
❑8, b&w	2.50
❑9, b&w	2.50
❑10, b&w	1.25
❑11, b&w	1.25
❑12, b&w	1.25
❑13, b&w	1.25
❑14	2.50
❑15	2.50
❑16	2.50
❑17	2.50
❑18	2.50

ROBOTECH: INVID WAR AFTERMATH
ETERNITY

Value: Cover or less

Issue	ORIG
❑1, b&w	2.50
❑2, b&w	2.50

ROBOTECH MASTERS
COMICO

Value: Cover or less

Issue	ORIG
❑1, Jul 85, False Start	2.50
❑2	1.50
❑3, Nov 85, Volunteers!	1.50
❑4, Nov 85	1.50
❑5	1.50
❑6	1.50
❑7	1.50
❑8	1.50
❑9	1.50
❑10, Aug 86	1.50
❑11	1.50
❑12	1.50
❑13	1.50
❑14	1.50
❑15	1.50
❑16	1.50
❑17	1.50
❑18	1.50
❑19	1.50
❑20	1.50
❑21	1.50
❑22	1.50
❑23	1.50

ROBOTECH: MECHANGEL
ACADEMY

Value: Cover or less

Issue	ORIG
❑1	2.95
❑2	2.95
❑3, War in the Wastelands, O: Mechangel	2.95

ROBOTECH: MEGASTORM
ANTARCTIC

Value: Cover or less

Issue	ORIG
❑1, Aug 98, wraparound cover	7.95

ROBOTECH: RETURN TO MACROSS
ETERNITY

Issue	ORIG	GOOD	FINE	N-MINT
❑1, Mar 93, b&w	2.50	0.60	1.50	3.00
❑2, b&w	2.50	0.50	1.25	2.50
❑3, b&w	2.50	0.50	1.25	2.50
❑4, b&w	2.50	0.50	1.25	2.50
❑5, b&w	2.50	0.50	1.25	2.50
❑6, b&w	2.50	0.50	1.25	2.50
❑7, b&w	2.50	0.50	1.25	2.50
❑8, b&w	2.50	0.50	1.25	2.50
❑9, b&w	2.50	0.50	1.25	2.50
❑10, Jan 94, b&w	2.50	0.50	1.25	2.50
❑11	—	0.50	1.25	2.50

	ORIG	GOOD	FINE	N-MINT
❑12	—	0.50	1.25	2.50
❑13	—	0.50	1.25	2.50
❑14	—	0.50	1.25	2.50
❑15	—	0.50	1.25	2.50
❑16	—	0.50	1.25	2.50
❑17	—	0.50	1.25	2.50
❑18	—	0.50	1.25	2.50
❑19	—	0.50	1.25	2.50
❑20	—	0.50	1.25	2.50
❑21	—	0.50	1.25	2.50
❑22	—	0.50	1.25	2.50
❑23	—	0.50	1.25	2.50
❑24	—	0.50	1.25	2.50
❑25	—	0.50	1.25	2.50
❑26	—	0.50	1.25	2.50
❑27	—	0.50	1.25	2.50
❑28	—	0.50	1.25	2.50
❑29	—	0.50	1.25	2.50
❑30	—	0.50	1.25	2.50
❑31	—	0.50	1.25	2.50
❑32, May 96	2.95	0.59	1.48	2.95

ROBOTECH: SENTINELS - RUBICON
ANTARCTIC
Value: Cover or less

- ❑1, Jun 98, A Sort of Homecoming, b&w ... 2.95
- ❑2 ... 2.95
- ❑3 ... 2.95
- ❑4 ... 2.95
- ❑5 ... 2.95
- ❑6 ... 2.95
- ❑7 ... 2.95

ROBOTECH SPECIAL
COMICO
Value: Cover or less

- ❑1, May 88, O: Dana Sterling ... 2.50

ROBOTECH THE GRAPHIC NOVEL
COMICO
Value: Cover or less

- ❑1 ... 5.95

ROBOTECH: THE MACROSS SAGA
COMICO

	ORIG	GOOD	FINE	N-MINT
❑1, "Macross" this issue	15.00	1.60	4.00	8.00
❑2, Title changes to Robotech: The Macross Saga	1.50	0.80	2.00	4.00
❑3	1.50	0.60	1.50	3.00
❑4	1.50	0.60	1.50	3.00
❑5	1.50	0.60	1.50	3.00
❑6, Sep 85	1.50	0.40	1.00	2.00
❑7, Nov 85	1.50	0.40	1.00	2.00
❑8	1.50	0.40	1.00	2.00
❑9	1.50	0.40	1.00	2.00
❑10	1.50	0.40	1.00	2.00
❑11	1.50	0.40	1.00	2.00
❑12	1.50	0.40	1.00	2.00
❑13	1.50	0.40	1.00	2.00
❑14	1.50	0.40	1.00	2.00
❑15	1.50	0.40	1.00	2.00
❑16	1.50	0.40	1.00	2.00
❑17	1.50	0.40	1.00	2.00
❑18	1.50	0.40	1.00	2.00
❑19	1.50	0.40	1.00	2.00
❑20	1.50	0.40	1.00	2.00
❑21	1.50	0.40	1.00	2.00
❑22	1.50	0.40	1.00	2.00
❑23	1.50	0.40	1.00	2.00
❑24	1.50	0.40	1.00	2.00
❑25	1.50	0.40	1.00	2.00
❑26	1.75	0.40	1.00	2.00
❑27	1.75	0.40	1.00	2.00
❑28	1.75	0.40	1.00	2.00
❑29	1.75	0.40	1.00	2.00
❑30	1.75	0.40	1.00	2.00
❑31	1.75	0.40	1.00	2.00
❑32	1.75	0.40	1.00	2.00
❑33	1.75	0.40	1.00	2.00
❑34	1.75	0.40	1.00	2.00
❑35	1.75	0.40	1.00	2.00
❑36, Final Issue	1.95	0.40	1.00	2.00

ROBOTECH: THE NEW GENERATION
COMICO
Value: Cover or less

- ❑1, Jul 85, RBy, The Invid Invasion ... 2.50
- ❑2, Sep 85, The Lost City ... 1.50
- ❑3 ... 1.50
- ❑4 ... 1.50
- ❑5, Jan 86 ... 1.50
- ❑6, Mar 86 ... 1.50
- ❑7 ... 1.50
- ❑8 ... 1.50
- ❑9, Jul 86 ... 1.50
- ❑10 ... 1.50
- ❑11 ... 1.50
- ❑12 ... 1.50
- ❑13 ... 1.50
- ❑14 ... 1.50
- ❑15 ... 1.50

Peter David wrote both the novelization and the comics adaptation of *The Rocketeer.*

© 1990 Dave Stevens and Disney Pictures

- ❑16 ... 1.50
- ❑17 ... 1.50
- ❑18 ... 1.50
- ❑19 ... 1.50
- ❑20 ... 1.50
- ❑21 ... 1.50
- ❑22 ... 1.75
- ❑23 ... 1.75
- ❑24 ... 1.75
- ❑25, last ... 1.75

ROBOTECH: VERMILION
ANTARCTIC
Value: Cover or less

- ❑1, Aug 97 ... 2.95
- ❑2, Oct 97 ... 2.95
- ❑3, Dec 97 ... 2.95
- ❑4, Feb 97 ... 2.95

ROBOTECH WARRIORS
ACADEMY
Value: Cover or less

- ❑1, Feb 95 ... 2.95

ROBOTECH: WINGS OF GIBRALTAR
ANTARCTIC
Value: Cover or less

- ❑1, Aug 98 ... 2.95
- ❑2, Sep 98 ... 2.95

ROBOTIX
MARVEL

	ORIG	GOOD	FINE	N-MINT
❑1, Feb 86, HT, HT (w), A World In Chaos, 1: The Protectons; 1: The Terrokors	0.75	0.20	0.50	1.00

ROBO WARRIORS
CFW
Value: Cover or less

- ❑1, A: Sifu; 1: Reiki ... 1.75
- ❑2, 0: Citation; Origin of Citation 1.95
- ❑3, A: Soldiers of Reiki; A: Solilo-quy Jones; 1: She-Bat ... 1.95
- ❑4 ... 1.95
- ❑5 ... 1.95
- ❑6 ... 1.95
- ❑7, 1: Mr. Slimey ... 1.95
- ❑8, Reiki becomes Mister No .. 1.95

ROBYN OF SHERWOOD
CALIBER
Value: Cover or less

- ❑1, b&w ... 2.95

ROCKERS
RIP OFF
Value: Cover or less

- ❑1, Jul 88, b&w; adult ... 2.00
- ❑2, Oct 88, A Night of Spinning Stars, Pink Elephants and the Midnite Man; Kick Me, b&w; adult ... 2.00
- ❑3, Jan 89, Confessions; Mister Rectumy, b&w; adult ... 2.00
- ❑4, Feb 89, b&w; adult ... 2.00
- ❑5, May 89, b&w; adult ... 2.00
- ❑6, Jun 89, b&w; adult ... 2.00
- ❑7, Sep 89, b&w; adult ... 2.00
- ❑8, Feb 90, b&w; adult ... 2.00

ROCKETEER 3-D COMIC, THE
DISNEY
Value: Cover or less

- ❑1, Jun 91, NA, NA (w), nn; with audiotape; Based on The Rocketeer movie ... 5.00

ROCKETEER ADVENTURE MAGAZINE, THE
COMICO

	ORIG	GOOD	FINE	N-MINT
❑1, Jul 88, Cliff's New York Adventure; Brucilla The Muscle Galactic girl Guide, Comico publishes	2.00	1.00	2.50	5.00
❑2, Jul 89, Nightmare at Large; Sitting Duck	2.75	0.70	1.75	3.50
❑3, Jan 95, DSt, DSt (w), Death Stalks The Midway, Dark Horse publishes	2.95	0.60	1.50	3.00

ROCKETEER SPECIAL EDITION, THE
ECLIPSE
Value: Cover or less

- ❑1, Nov 84, DSt, DSt (w) ... 1.50

ROCKETEER, THE: THE OFFICIAL MOVIE ADAPTATION
DISNEY
Value: Cover or less

- ❑1, RH, DSt (c), PD (w), nn; no cover date; stapled ... 2.95
- ❑1/DM, RH, DSt (c), PD (w), nn; no cover date; movie Adaptation; squarebound ... 5.95

ROCKETMAN: KING OF THE ROCKET MEN
INNOVATION
Value: Cover or less

- ❑1 ... 2.50
- ❑2 ... 2.50
- ❑3 ... 2.50
- ❑4 ... 2.50

ROCKET RACCOON
MARVEL

	ORIG	GOOD	FINE	N-MINT
❑1, May 85, Animal Crackers	0.75	0.20	0.50	1.00
❑2, Jun 85	0.75	0.20	0.50	1.00
❑3, Jul 85	0.75	0.20	0.50	1.00
❑4, Aug 85	0.75	0.20	0.50	1.00

ROCKET RANGER
ADVENTURE
Value: Cover or less

- ❑1, Sep 91, full color 2.95
- ❑2, Dec 91, b&w 2.95
- ❑3, b&w 2.95
- ❑4, b&w 2.95
- ❑5, Jul 92, Arrested!, b&w 2.95
- ❑6 2.95

ROCK FANTASY
ROCK FANTASY
Value: Cover or less

- ❑1, Pink Floyd 3.00
- ❑2, Rolling Stones 3.00
- ❑3, Led Zeppelin 3.00
- ❑4, New Kids on the Block; Stevie Nicks 3.00
- ❑5, Guns 'n Roses 3.00
- ❑6, Monstrosities of Rock 3.00
- ❑7, The Sex Pistols 3.00
- ❑8, Alice Cooper 3.00
- ❑9, Van Halen 3.00
- ❑10, Kiss 3.00
- ❑11, Jimi Hendrix 3.00
- ❑12, Def Leppard 3.00
- ❑13, David Bowie 3.00
- ❑14, The Doors 3.00
- ❑15, Pink Floyd II 3.00
- ❑16, Double-size; The Great Gig in the Sky 5.00
- ❑17, Send me An Angel, Rock Vixens 3.00

ROCKHEADS
SOLSON
Value: Cover or less

- ❑1 1.95

ROCKIN' BONES
NEW ENGLAND
Value: Cover or less

- ❑1, b&w 2.75
- ❑2, b&w 2.75
- ❑3, b&w 2.75
- ❑HS 1, Xmas Special 2.75

ROCKINFREAKAPOTAMUS PRESENTS THE RED HOT CHILI PEPPERS ILLUSTRATED LYRICS
TELLTALE PUBLICATIONS
Value: Cover or less

- ❑1, Jul 97, nn; b&w; magazine-sized 3.95

ROCKMEEZ, THE
JZINK COMICS
Value: Cover or less

- ❑1 2.50
- ❑2, Nov 92 2.50
- ❑3 2.50
- ❑4 2.50

ROCK 'N' ROLL COMICS
REVOLUTIONARY

	ORIG	GOOD	FINE	N-MINT
❑1, Jun 89, Guns 'N' Roses	1.50	1.60	4.00	8.00
❑1-2, Jul 89, 2nd Printing	1.50	1.20	3.00	6.00
❑, Aug 89, 3rd Printing	1.95	0.40	1.00	2.00
❑1-4, Sep 89, 4th Printing	1.95	0.40	1.00	2.00
❑1-5, Oct 89, 5th Printing	1.95	0.40	1.00	2.00
❑1-6, Nov 89, 6th Printing	1.95	0.40	1.00	2.00
❑1-7, Dec 89, 7th Printing; Color, completely different than first six printings	1.95	0.40	1.00	2.00
❑2, Aug 89, Metallica	1.50	1.00	2.50	5.00
❑2-2, Sep 89, 2nd Printing; Metallica	1.95	0.60	1.50	3.00
❑2-3, Sep 89, 3rd Printing; Metallica	1.95	0.40	1.00	2.00
❑2-4, Sep 89, 4th Printing; Metallica	1.95	0.40	1.00	2.00
❑2-5, Sep 89, 5th Printing; Metallica	1.95	0.40	1.00	2.00
❑2-6, full color; 6th Printing; Metallica; 50% new material added	1.50	0.40	1.00	2.00
❑3, Sep 89, Bon Jovi; Banned by Great Southern Co.; Rare	1.95	3.00	7.50	15.00
❑3-2, Oct 89	1.95	0.39	0.98	1.95
❑4, Oct 89, Motley Crue; Banned by Great Southern Co.; 15, 000 copies burned by Great Southern	1.95	12.00	30.00	60.00
❑4-2, Oct 89, 2nd printing (no Ace Back-words); Banned by Great Southern Co.	1.95	0.80	2.00	4.00
❑5, Nov 89, Def Leppard	1.95	0.50	1.25	2.50
❑5-2, Nov 89, 2nd Printing; Def Leppard	1.95	0.30	0.75	1.50
❑6, Dec 89, Rolling Stones	1.95	0.60	1.50	3.00
❑6-2, Jan 90, 2nd Printing; Rolling Stones	1.95	0.30	0.75	1.50
❑6-3, Jan 90, 3rd Printing; Rolling Stones	1.95	0.30	0.75	1.50
❑6-4, Feb 90, 4th Printing; Rolling Stones	1.95	0.30	0.75	1.50
❑7, Jan 90, The Who	1.95	0.50	1.25	2.50
❑7-2, Feb 90, 2nd Printing; The Who	1.95	0.30	0.75	1.50
❑7-3, Mar 90, 3rd Printing; The Who	1.95	0.30	0.75	1.50
❑8, Skid Row; Never published: banned by injunction from Great Southern Company	1.50	0.00	0.00	0.00
❑9, Mar 90, Kiss	1.95	1.20	3.00	6.00
❑9-2, Apr 90, 2nd Printing; Kiss	1.95	0.40	1.00	2.00
❑9-3, May 90, 3rd Printing; Kiss	1.95	0.40	1.00	2.00
❑10, Apr 90, Two different versions printed, one with Whitesnake on cover, one with Warrant; Warrant, Whitesnake	1.95	0.50	1.25	2.50
❑10-2, May 90, 2nd Printing; Whitesnake only on cover	1.95	0.30	0.75	1.50
❑11, May 90, Aerosmith	1.95	0.50	1.25	2.50
❑12, Jun 90, New Kids on the Block	1.95	0.60	1.50	3.00
❑12-2, Aug 90, 2nd Printing; New Kids On the Block	1.95	0.30	0.75	1.50
❑13, Jul 90, Led Zeppelin	1.95	0.50	1.25	2.50
❑14, Aug 90, Sex Pistols	1.95	0.50	1.25	2.50
❑15, Sep 90, full color; Poison	1.95	0.50	1.25	2.50
❑16, Oct 90, full color; Van Halen	1.95	0.50	1.25	2.50
❑17, Nov 90, full color; Madonna	1.95	0.80	2.00	4.00
❑18, Dec 90, Alice Cooper; Full color	1.95	0.50	1.25	2.50
❑19, Apr 91, Fight For The Right To Fight; 2 Live Crew, 1 Brave Mother, b&w; rather vicious anti-Tipper Gore/PMRC back-up story; Public Enemy, 2 Live Crew	2.50	0.50	1.25	2.50
❑20, Apr 91, b&w; Queensryche	2.50	0.50	1.25	2.50
❑21, Jan 91, b&w; Prince	2.50	0.50	1.25	2.50
❑22, Feb 91, full color; AC/DC	2.50	0.50	1.25	2.50
❑23, Mar 91, b&w; Living Colour	2.50	0.50	1.25	2.50
❑24, Mar 91, Anthrax b&w	2.50	0.50	1.25	2.50
❑25, May 91, b&w; ZZ Top	2.50	0.50	1.25	2.50
❑26, May 91, Doors	2.50	0.50	1.25	2.50
❑27, Jun 91, Doors	2.50	0.50	1.25	2.50
❑28, Jun 91, Ozzy Osbourne; Black Sabbath	2.50	0.50	1.25	2.50
❑29, Jul 91, Ozzy Osbourne; Black Sabbath	2.50	0.50	1.25	2.50
❑30, Jul 91, The Cure, The Cure	2.50	0.50	1.25	2.50
❑31, Aug 91, A New Ice Age, Vanilla Ice	2.50	0.50	1.25	2.50
❑32, Aug 91, Frank Zappa	2.50	0.50	1.25	2.50
❑33, Sep 91, Guns 'N' Roses II	2.50	0.50	1.25	2.50
❑34, Sep 91, Black Crowes	2.50	0.50	1.25	2.50
❑35, Oct 91, R.E.M.	2.50	0.50	1.25	2.50
❑36, Oct 91, Michael Jackson	2.50	0.50	1.25	2.50
❑37, Nov 91, Ice-T	2.50	0.50	1.25	2.50
❑38, Nov 91, Rod Stewart	2.50	0.50	1.25	2.50
❑39, Dec 91, The Fall of the New Kids	2.50	0.50	1.25	2.50
❑40, Dec 91, NWA; Ice Cube	2.50	0.50	1.25	2.50
❑41, Jan 92, Paula Abdul	2.50	0.50	1.25	2.50
❑42, Jan 92, Metallica II	2.50	0.50	1.25	2.50
❑43, Feb 92, Guns N' Roses: Tales from the Tour	2.50	0.50	1.25	2.50
❑44, Feb 92, Scorpions	2.50	0.50	1.25	2.50
❑45, Mar 92, Grateful Dead	2.50	0.50	1.25	2.50
❑46, Apr 92, Grateful Dead II	2.50	0.50	1.25	2.50
❑47, May 92, Grateful Dead III	2.50	0.50	1.25	2.50
❑48, Jun 92, Queen	2.50	0.50	1.25	2.50
❑49, Jul 92, Rush	2.50	0.50	1.25	2.50
❑50, Aug 92, Bob Dylan	2.50	0.50	1.25	2.50
❑51, Sep 92, Bob Dylan II	2.50	0.50	1.25	2.50
❑52, Oct 92, Bob Dylan III	2.50	0.50	1.25	2.50
❑53, Nov 92, Bruce Springsteen	2.50	0.50	1.25	2.50
❑54, Dec 92, U2	2.50	0.50	1.25	2.50
❑55, Jan 93, U2 II	2.50	0.50	1.25	2.50
❑56, Feb 93, David Bowie	2.50	0.50	1.25	2.50
❑57, Mar 93, Aerosmith	2.50	0.50	1.25	2.50
❑58, Apr 93, Kate Bush	2.50	0.50	1.25	2.50
❑59, May 93, Eric Clapton	2.50	0.50	1.25	2.50
❑60, Jun 93, Genesis	2.50	0.50	1.25	2.50
❑61, Jul 93, Yes	2.50	0.50	1.25	2.50
❑62, Aug 93, Elton John	2.50	0.50	1.25	2.50
❑63, Sep 93, Janis Joplin	2.50	0.50	1.25	2.50
❑64, Oct 93, '60s San Francisco	2.50	0.50	1.25	2.50
❑65, Nov 93, Sci-Fi Space Rockers	2.50	0.50	1.25	2.50

ROCK N' ROLL COMICS MAGAZINE
REVOLUTIONARY

	ORIG	GOOD	FINE	N-MINT
❑1	—	0.59	1.48	2.95
❑2	—	0.59	1.48	2.95
❑3	—	0.59	1.48	2.95
❑4	—	0.59	1.48	2.95
❑5, Oct 90, Rock This Way!; Satisfaction, Aerosmith/Rolling Stones	2.95	0.59	1.48	2.95

ROCKOLA
MIRAGE
Value: Cover or less

- ❑1 1.50

ROCKO'S MODERN LIFE
MARVEL
Value: Cover or less

- ❑1, Jun 94, Dental Hyjinks; This is a Test!, TV cartoon 1.95
- ❑2, Jul 94 1.95
- ❑3, Aug 94 1.95
- ❑4, Sep 94 1.95
- ❑5, Oct 94 1.95
- ❑6, Nov 94 1.95
- ❑7, Dec 94 1.95

ROCKY HORROR PICTURE SHOW, THE: THE COMIC BOOK
CALIBER

	ORIG	GOOD	FINE	N-MINT
❑1, Jul 90, full color	2.95	1.40	3.50	7.00
❑1-2, 2nd Printing; new cover	2.95	0.60	1.50	3.00
❑2, Aug 90, full color	2.95	0.80	2.00	4.00
❑3, Sep 90, full color	2.95	0.80	2.00	4.00

ROCKY LANE WESTERN (AC)
AC
Value: Cover or less

- ❑1, b&w; Reprint 2.50
- ❑2, b&w; Reprint 5.95
- ❑Anl 1, b&w; Reprint 2.95

ROEL
SIRIUS
Value: Cover or less

- ❑1, Feb 97, b&w; cardstock cover; One-Shot 2.95

	ORIG	GOOD	FINE	N-MINT

ROG-2000
PACIFIC

Value: Cover or less — ❑1, JBy 2.00

ROGAN GOSH
DC

Value: Cover or less — ❑1, nn 6.95

ROGER FNORD
RIP OFF

Value: Cover or less — ❑1, Apr 92, b&w; adult 2.50

ROGER RABBIT
DISNEY

	ORIG	GOOD	FINE	N-MINT
❑1, Jun 90, The Trouble with Toons!; Good Neighbor Roger, 1: Dick Flint	1.50	0.70	1.75	3.50
❑2, Jul 90, The Color of Trouble!; Gym Dandy	1.50	0.50	1.25	2.50
❑3, Aug 90, Rollercoaster Rabbit; Roller Coaster Riot	1.50	0.50	1.25	2.50
❑4, Sep 90, Little China in Big Trouble; Cot-ton-Tailspin	1.50	0.50	1.25	2.50
❑5, Oct 90, Justifiable Hamicide!; Nuts 'n' Volts	1.50	0.50	1.25	2.50
❑6, Nov 90, Taxi Turmoil; The Candy Cane Mutiny	1.50	0.40	1.00	2.00
❑7, Dec 90, Djinn Game; Dial M for Roger	1.50	0.40	1.00	2.00
❑8, Jan 91, The Spies of Life; Top Bun	1.50	0.40	1.00	2.00
❑9, Feb 91	1.50	0.40	1.00	2.00
❑10, Mar 91	1.50	0.40	1.00	2.00
❑11, Apr 91	1.50	0.30	0.75	1.50
❑12, May 91	1.50	0.30	0.75	1.50
❑13, Jun 91, Stork Raving Mad!; Hare Appar-ent	1.50	0.30	0.75	1.50
❑14, Jul 91	1.50	0.30	0.75	1.50
❑15, Aug 91	1.50	0.30	0.75	1.50
❑16, Sep 91	1.50	0.30	0.75	1.50
❑17, Oct 91	1.50	0.30	0.75	1.50
❑18, Nov 91, Final Issue	1.50	0.30	0.75	1.50
❑SE 1, Who Framed Rick Flint?, nn	3.50	0.70	1.75	3.50

ROGER RABBIT IN 3-D
DISNEY

Value: Cover or less — ❑1, with glasses; 3-D Zone reprints 2.50

ROGER RABBIT'S TOONTOWN
DISNEY

Value: Cover or less

- ❑1, Aug 91, Well, You Name It!; Baby Herman: Shopping Spree 1.50
- ❑2, Sep 91, Winsor McCay tribute 1.50
- ❑3, Oct 91 .... 1.50
- ❑4, Nov 91, 1: Winnie Weasel 1.50
- ❑5, Dec 91, Weasels solo story 1.50

ROGER WILCO
ADVENTURE

Value: Cover or less

- ❑1, full color 2.95
- ❑2, Apr 92, Death to the Deltaur, b&w 2.95

ROGUE (MARVEL)
MARVEL

Value: Cover or less

- ❑1, Jan 95, enhanced cover 2.95
- ❑2, Feb 95, enhanced cover 2.95
- ❑3, Mar 95, The Gauntlet, enhanced cover 2.95
- ❑4, Apr 95, enhanced cover 2.95

ROGUE (MONSTER)
MONSTER

Value: Cover or less — ❑1, b&w 1.95

ROGUES, THE (VILLAINS)
DC

Value: Cover or less — ❑1, Feb 98, New Year's Evil 1.95

ROGUE SATELLITE COMICS
SLAVE LABOR

Value: Cover or less

- ❑1, Aug 96, b&w 2.95
- ❑2, b&w 2.95
- ❑3, Mar 97, b&w 2.95
- ❑SE 1, A: Flaming Carrot, nn; b&w 2.95

ROGUES GALLERY
DC

Value: Cover or less — ❑1, BSz; MW, One-Shot; pin-ups 3.50

ROGUE TROOPER (1ST SERIES)
FLEETWAY

	ORIG	GOOD	FINE	N-MINT
❑1, DaG, Rogue Trooper; Rogue Trooper: Tower of Death	0.75	0.40	1.00	2.00
❑2, DaG, Rogue Trooper: Moving Target; Rogue Trooper: Triple Cross	0.75	0.40	1.00	2.00
❑3, DaG, Rogue Trooper: The Decapitators; Rogue Trooper: The Rookies	0.75	0.40	1.00	2.00
❑4, Rogue Trooper: Eraser Evaders!; Rogue Trooper: War of Nerves	0.75	0.40	1.00	2.00
❑5, DaG, Rogue Trooper: Menace of the Dream Weavers; Rogue Trooper: Bagman Blues	0.75	0.40	1.00	2.00
❑6	1.50	0.35	0.88	1.75

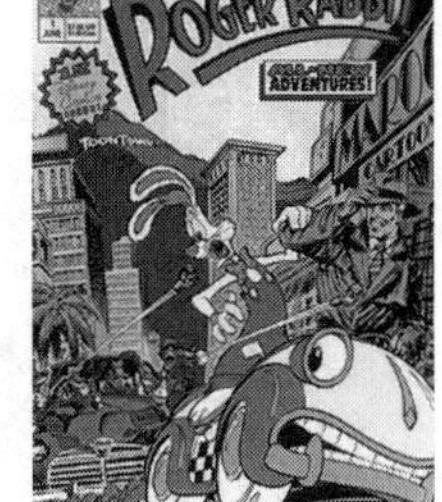

Roger Rabbit teamed up with a new detective, Dick Flint, in the first issue of his ongoing series.

	ORIG	GOOD	FINE	N-MINT
❑7, AMo (w), Rogue Trooper: Pray for War	0.95	0.35	0.88	1.75
❑8	1.25	0.35	0.88	1.75
❑9, Rogue Trooper: Fort Neuro; Rogue Trooper: Bio Wire!	1.25	0.35	0.88	1.75
❑10	1.25	0.35	0.88	1.75
❑11	1.25	0.30	0.75	1.50
❑12, Rogue Trooper: Major Magnum, Part 2; Rogue Trooper: Milli-Com Memories	1.25	0.30	0.75	1.50
❑13, Rogue Trooper: The Vid Vultures; Rogue Trooper: Eye of the Traitor	1.25	0.30	0.75	1.50
❑14, Rogue Trooper: Eye of the Traitor; Rogue Trooper: Mega-Minefield	1.25	0.30	0.75	1.50
❑15	1.25	0.30	0.75	1.50
❑16, Rogue Trooper: You Only Die Twice; Rogue Trooper: Message From Milli-Com	1.25	0.30	0.75	1.50
❑17, Rogue Trooper: Rank and Vile!	1.25	0.30	0.75	1.50
❑18, Rogue Trooper: Death Valley!	1.25	0.30	0.75	1.50
❑19, Rogue Trooper: To the Ends of Nu Earth; Rogue Trooper: Return of a Hero?	1.25	0.30	0.75	1.50
❑20	1.50	0.30	0.75	1.50
❑21, double issue #21/22	1.50	0.30	0.75	1.50
❑23, double issue #23/24	1.50	0.30	0.75	1.50
❑25	1.50	0.30	0.75	1.50
❑26	1.50	0.30	0.75	1.50
❑27	1.50	0.30	0.75	1.50
❑28	1.50	0.30	0.75	1.50
❑29	1.50	0.30	0.75	1.50
❑30, Rogue Trooper: Testing, Testing...; Tyr-anny Rex	1.50	0.35	0.88	1.75
❑31	1.50	0.35	0.88	1.75
❑32, Rogue Trooper: Hit One; Thirst	1.50	0.35	0.88	1.75
❑33	1.50	0.35	0.88	1.75
❑34, Rogue Trooper: Hit One; Chopper: Soul on Fire	1.50	0.35	0.88	1.75
❑35, Rogue Trooper: Hit One; Chopper: Soul on Fire	1.50	0.35	0.88	1.75
❑36, Rogue Trooper: The Hit Parade; Ace Trucking Co.: Last Lug to Abbo Dabbo	1.50	0.35	0.88	1.75
❑37	1.50	0.35	0.88	1.75
❑38, Rogue Trooper: Hit Two; Rogue Trooper: Hit Three	1.50	0.35	0.88	1.75
❑39	1.75	0.35	0.88	1.75
❑40	1.75	0.35	0.88	1.75
❑41	1.75	0.35	0.88	1.75
❑42	1.75	0.35	0.88	1.75
❑43	1.75	0.35	0.88	1.75
❑44, Rogue Trooper: Nu Earth Flashback; Visible Man	1.75	0.35	0.88	1.75
❑45, Rogue Trooper: Nu Earth Flashback; Strontium Dog: Tales From the Doghouse	1.75	0.35	0.88	1.75
❑46	1.75	0.35	0.88	1.75
❑47	1.75	0.35	0.88	1.75
❑48, Rogue Trooper; Ace Trucking Co.: On the Dangle	1.75	0.35	0.88	1.75
❑49	1.75	0.35	0.88	1.75

ROGUE TROOPER (2ND SERIES)
FLEETWAY

Value: Cover or less

- ❑1, O: Rogue Trooper 2.95
- ❑2 .... 2.95
- ❑3 .... 2.95
- ❑4 .... 2.95
- ❑5 .... 2.95
- ❑6 .... 2.95
- ❑7 .... 2.95
- ❑8, Apocalypse Dreadnought Part 6-10 .... 2.95
- ❑9 .... 2.95

ROJA FUSION
ANTARCTIC

Value: Cover or less — ❑1, Apr 95 .... 2.95

ROLAND: DAYS OF WRATH
TERRA MAJOR

Value: Cover or less — ❑1, Jul 99 .... 2.95

ROLLERCOASTER
FANTAGRAPHICS

Value: Cover or less — ❑1, Sep 96, b&w; cardstock cover; magazine 3.95

ROLLERCOASTERS SPECIAL EDITION
BLUE COMET

	ORIG	GOOD	FINE	N-MINT
❑1	1.80	0.40	1.00	2.00

ROLLING STONES
PERSONALITY

Value: Cover or less

❑1, b&w ... 2.95
❑2, b&w ... 2.95
❑3, b&w ... 2.95

ROLLING STONES: VOODOO LOUNGE
MARVEL

Value: Cover or less

❑1, nn; prestige format one-shot ... 6.95

ROM
MARVEL

	ORIG	GOOD	FINE	N-MINT
❑1, Dec 79, SB, Arrival!, 1: ROM	0.40	0.40	1.00	2.00
❑2, Jan 80, SB, FM (c)	0.40	0.40	1.00	2.00
❑3, Feb 80, SB, FM (c), 1: Firefall	0.40	0.40	1.00	2.00
❑4, Mar 80, SB	0.40	0.30	0.75	1.50
❑5, Apr 80, SB	0.40	0.30	0.75	1.50
❑6, May 90, SB	0.40	0.30	0.75	1.50
❑7, Jun 90, SB	0.40	0.30	0.75	1.50
❑8, Jul 90, SB, Deathwing!	0.40	0.30	0.75	1.50
❑9, Aug 90, SB, The Stalker In The Night!	0.40	0.30	0.75	1.50
❑10, Sep 90, SB, Warrior Over Washington	0.50	0.30	0.75	1.50
❑11, Oct 90, SB	0.50	0.25	0.63	1.25
❑12, Nov 90, SB	0.50	0.25	0.63	1.25
❑13, Dec 80, SB	0.50	0.25	0.63	1.25
❑14, Jan 81, SB, Ultimate Android	0.50	0.25	0.63	1.25
❑15, Feb 81, SB	0.50	0.25	0.63	1.25
❑16, Mar 81, SB	0.50	0.25	0.63	1.25
❑17, Apr 81, SB, Hybrid!, A: X-Men	0.50	0.30	0.75	1.50
❑18, May 81, SB, A: X-Men	0.50	0.30	0.75	1.50
❑19, Jun 81, JSt; SB, A: X-Men	0.50	0.25	0.63	1.25
❑20, Jul 81, JSt; SB, Mindgames	0.50	0.25	0.63	1.25
❑21, Aug 81, JSt; SB, Move Over Rom-There's A New Hero In Town!	0.50	0.25	0.63	1.25
❑22, Sep 81, JSt; SB	0.50	0.25	0.63	1.25
❑23, Oct 81, JSt; SB, A: Power Man	0.50	0.25	0.63	1.25
❑24, Nov 81, JSt; SB, D: Protector; D: Comet (Harris Moore); D: Nova-Prime; D: Powerhouse; D: Crimebuster	0.50	0.30	0.75	1.50
❑25, Dec 81, JSt; SB, Giant-size	0.75	0.30	0.75	1.50
❑26, Jan 82	0.60	0.25	0.63	1.25
❑27, Feb 82	0.60	0.25	0.63	1.25
❑28, Mar 82	0.60	0.25	0.63	1.25
❑29, Apr 82	0.60	0.25	0.63	1.25
❑30, May 82	0.60	0.25	0.63	1.25
❑31, Jun 82	0.60	0.25	0.63	1.25
❑32, Jul 82	0.60	0.25	0.63	1.25
❑33, Aug 82	0.60	0.25	0.63	1.25
❑34, Sep 82	0.60	0.25	0.63	1.25
❑35, Oct 82	0.60	0.25	0.63	1.25
❑36, Nov 82	0.60	0.25	0.63	1.25
❑37, Dec 82	0.60	0.25	0.63	1.25
❑38, Jan 83	0.60	0.25	0.63	1.25
❑39, Feb 83	0.60	0.25	0.63	1.25
❑40, Mar 83	0.60	0.25	0.63	1.25
❑41, Apr 83	0.60	0.25	0.63	1.25
❑42, May 83	0.60	0.25	0.63	1.25
❑43, Jun 83	0.60	0.25	0.63	1.25
❑44, Jul 83, 1: Devastator II	0.60	0.25	0.63	1.25
❑45, Aug 83	0.60	0.25	0.63	1.25
❑46, Sep 83	0.60	0.25	0.63	1.25
❑47, Oct 83	0.60	0.25	0.63	1.25
❑48, Nov 83	0.60	0.25	0.63	1.25
❑49, Dec 83	0.60	0.25	0.63	1.25
❑50, Jan 84, SB, Extraterrestrials!, A: Skrulls; D: Torpedo, double-sized	1.00	0.25	0.63	1.25
❑51, Feb 84	0.60	0.25	0.63	1.25
❑52, Mar 84	0.60	0.25	0.63	1.25
❑53, Apr 84	0.60	0.25	0.63	1.25
❑54, May 84	0.60	0.25	0.63	1.25
❑55, Jun 84	0.60	0.25	0.63	1.25
❑56, Jul 84, A: Alpha Flight	0.60	0.25	0.63	1.25
❑57, Aug 84, A: Alpha Flight	0.60	0.25	0.63	1.25
❑58, Sep 84, Dire Wraiths	0.60	0.25	0.63	1.25
❑59, Oct 84, SD	0.60	0.25	0.63	1.25
❑60, Nov 84, SD	0.60	0.25	0.63	1.25
❑61, Dec 84, SD	0.60	0.25	0.63	1.25
❑62, Jan 85, SD	0.60	0.25	0.63	1.25
❑63, Feb 85, SD	0.60	0.25	0.63	1.25
❑64, Mar 85	0.60	0.25	0.63	1.25
❑65, Apr 85	0.65	0.25	0.63	1.25
❑66, May 85	0.65	0.25	0.63	1.25
❑67, Jun 85	0.65	0.25	0.63	1.25
❑68, Jul 85	0.65	0.25	0.63	1.25
❑69, Aug 85	0.65	0.25	0.63	1.25
❑70, Sep 85	0.65	0.25	0.63	1.25
❑71, Oct 85, D: The Unseen	0.65	0.25	0.63	1.25
❑72, Nov 85, Secret Wars II, Secret Wars II	0.65	0.25	0.63	1.25
❑73, Dec 85	0.75	0.25	0.63	1.25
❑74, Jan 86, D: Seeker	0.75	0.25	0.63	1.25
❑75, Feb 86, D: Scanner; D: Trapper	0.75	0.25	0.63	1.25
❑Anl 1, Stardust	1.00	0.30	0.75	1.50
❑Anl 2	1.00	0.25	0.63	1.25
❑Anl 3, A: New Mutants	1.00	0.30	0.75	1.50
❑Anl 4, D: Pulsar; A: Gladiator	1.25	0.25	0.63	1.25

ROMANCER
MOONSTONE

Value: Cover or less

❑1, Dec 96, nn; b&w ... 2.95

ROMANTIC TAILS
HEAD PRESS

Value: Cover or less

❑1, Aug 98, b&w ... 2.95

RONALD MCDONALD
CHARLTON

	ORIG	GOOD	FINE	N-MINT
❑1, Sep 70	0.15	6.00	15.00	30.00
❑2, Nov 70	0.15	4.00	10.00	20.00
❑3, Jan 71	0.15	4.00	10.00	20.00
❑4, Mar 71	0.15	4.00	10.00	20.00

RONIN
DC

	ORIG	GOOD	FINE	N-MINT
❑1, Jul 83, FM, FM (w)	2.50	1.00	2.50	5.00
❑2, Sep 83, FM, FM (w)	2.50	0.80	2.00	4.00
❑3, Nov 83, FM, FM (w)	2.50	0.80	2.00	4.00
❑4, Jan 84, FM, FM (w)	2.50	0.80	2.00	4.00
❑5, Jan 84, FM, FM (w)	2.50	0.80	2.00	4.00
❑6, Aug 84, FM, FM (w), Scarcer	2.50	1.20	3.00	6.00

ROOK, THE
HARRIS

Value: Cover or less

❑1, Jun 95, Fist Full of Chaos, nn ... 2.95
❑2, The Good, The Bad and The Chaotic ... 2.95

ROOK MAGAZINE, THE
WARREN

	ORIG	GOOD	FINE	N-MINT
❑1	1.75	0.80	2.00	4.00
❑2, May 79, The Man Whom Time Forgot; Day Before Tomorrow	—	0.50	1.25	2.50
❑3, Jun 80	2.00	0.50	1.25	2.50
❑4, Aug 80	2.00	0.50	1.25	2.50
❑5	—	0.50	1.25	2.50
❑6	—	0.50	1.25	2.50
❑7	—	0.50	1.25	2.50
❑8	—	0.50	1.25	2.50
❑9	—	0.50	1.25	2.50
❑10	—	0.50	1.25	2.50
❑11	—	0.40	1.00	2.00
❑12	—	0.40	1.00	2.00
❑13	—	0.40	1.00	2.00
❑14	—	0.40	1.00	2.00

ROOTER
CUSTOM

Value: Cover or less

❑1, Aug 96, Sweatin' Bullets ... 2.95
❑2, Dec 96, Big Bad Beaver ... 2.95
❑3, Feb 97, The Big Izzy ... 2.95
❑4, May 97, Da Voodoo Blues ... 2.95
❑5, Jul 97 ... 2.95
❑6, Oct 97 ... 2.95

ROOTER (VOL. 2)
CUSTOM

Value: Cover or less

❑1, Da Voodoo Blues, b&w ... 2.95

ROOTS OF THE OPPRESSOR
NORTHSTAR

Value: Cover or less

❑1, b&w ... 2.95

ROOTS OF THE SWAMP THING
DC

Value: Cover or less

❑1, BWr, Reprint ... 2.00
❑2, BWr, Reprint ... 2.00
❑3, Sep 86, BWr, The Last of the Ravenwind Witches; A Clockwork Horror, Reprint; reprints Swamp Thing #5 and #6 and House of Mystery #191 ... 2.00
❑4, Oct 86, BWr, Night of the Bat; The Lurker in Tunnel 13!, A: Batman, Reprint; reprints Swamp Thing #7 and #8 and House of Mystery #221 ... 2.00
❑5, Nov 86, BWr, The Stalker From Beyond; The Man Who Would Not Die, O: Swamp Thing, reprints Swamp Thing #9 and #10 and House of Mystery #92; Reprints stories from Swamp Thing #9, #10, House of Mystery #92 ... 2.00

ROSCOE! THE DAWG, ACE DETECTIVE
RENEGADE

Value: Cover or less

❑1, Jul 87, b&w ... 2.00
❑2, Oct 87, b&w ... 2.00
❑3, Nov 87, b&w ... 2.00
❑4, Jan 88, b&w ... 2.00

ORIG GOOD FINE N-MINT

ROSE
HERO

Value: Cover or less

- ❑1 ... 3.50
- ❑2 ... 2.95
- ❑3 ... 3.95
- ❑4 ... 3.95
- ❑5, Dec 93 ... 2.95

ROSE & GUNN
BISHOP

Value: Cover or less

- ❑3, May 95, b&w ... 2.95
- ❑4, Jun 95, b&w ... 2.95
- ❑5, Aug 95, b&w ... 2.95

ROSE & GUNN CREATOR'S CHOICE
BISHOP

Value: Cover or less

- ❑1, Sep 95, b&w ... 2.95

ROSWELL: LITTLE GREEN MAN
BONGO

Issue	ORIG	GOOD	FINE	N-MINT
❑1, The Untold Story	2.95	0.70	1.75	3.50
❑2	2.95	0.60	1.50	3.00
❑3, V: Professor Von Sphinkter	2.95	0.60	1.50	3.00
❑4, D: Shorty George	2.95	0.60	1.50	3.00
❑5	2.95	0.60	1.50	3.00
❑6	2.95	0.60	1.50	3.00

ROUGH RAIDERS
BLUE COMET

Issue	ORIG	GOOD	FINE	N-MINT
❑1	1.80	0.40	1.00	2.00
❑2	1.80	0.40	1.00	2.00
❑3	1.80	0.40	1.00	2.00
❑Anl 1	2.50	0.50	1.25	2.50

ROULETTE
CALIBER

Value: Cover or less

- ❑1, b&w ... 2.50

ROVERS, THE
MALIBU

Value: Cover or less

- ❑1, Sep 87, I Don't Like Mondays ... 1.95
- ❑2 ... 1.95
- ❑3 ... 1.95
- ❑4 ... 1.95
- ❑5 ... 1.95
- ❑6, b&w ... 1.95
- ❑7, b&w ... 1.95

ROYAL ROY
MARVEL

Issue	ORIG	GOOD	FINE	N-MINT
❑1, The Mystery Of The Missing Crown, 1: Royal Roy	0.65	0.20	0.50	1.00
❑2	0.65	0.20	0.50	1.00
❑3	0.65	0.20	0.50	1.00
❑4	0.65	0.20	0.50	1.00
❑5	0.65	0.20	0.50	1.00
❑6, Final Issue	0.65	0.20	0.50	1.00

ROY ROGERS WESTERN
AC

Value: Cover or less

- ❑1, RM, Roy Rogers: The Vengeance Trail; Dale Evans: The Old Cowboy, b&w; Reprint .. 4.95

ROY ROGERS WESTERN CLASSICS
AC

Value: Cover or less

- ❑1, Reprint; some color ... 2.95
- ❑2, Reprint; some color ... 2.95
- ❑3, Reprint; some color ... 3.95
- ❑4, Reprint; some color ... 3.95
- ❑5, Reprint; photos ... 2.95

RUBBER BLANKET
RUBBER BLANKET

Value: Cover or less

- ❑1, b&w ... 5.75
- ❑2 ... 7.75
- ❑3 ... 7.95

RUBES REVUE, THE
FRAGMENTS WEST

Value: Cover or less

- ❑1, b&w ... 2.00

RUBY SHAFT'S TALES OF THE UNEXPURGATED
FANTAGRAPHICS

Value: Cover or less

- ❑1, b&w; adult ... 2.50

RUCK BUD WEBSTER AND HIS SCREECHING COMMANDOS
PYRAMID

Value: Cover or less

- ❑1, b&w ... 1.60

RUDE AWAKENING
DENNIS MCMILLAN

Value: Cover or less

- ❑1, Apr 96, b&w ... 12.95

RUGRATS COMIC ADVENTURES
NICKELODEON MAGAZINES

Issue	ORIG	GOOD	FINE	N-MINT
❑1	—	0.70	1.75	3.50
❑2	—	0.60	1.50	3.00
❑3	—	0.60	1.50	3.00
❑4	—	0.60	1.50	3.00
❑5	—	0.60	1.50	3.00
❑6	—	0.60	1.50	3.00
❑7	—	0.60	1.50	3.00
❑8, Jun 98, no cover price; magazine	—	0.60	1.50	3.00
❑9	—	0.60	1.50	3.00
❑10, Aug 98, no cover price; magazine	—	0.60	1.50	3.00

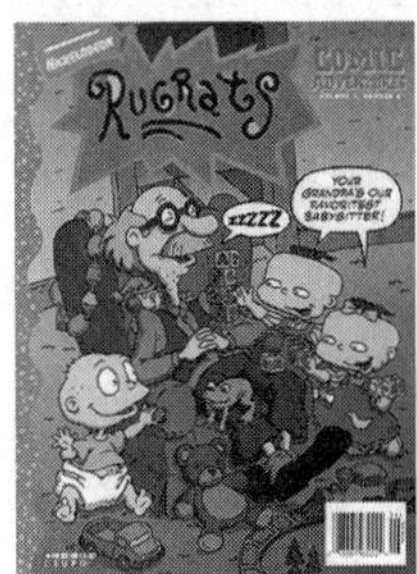

The *Sugar & Spike*-like antics of a group of toddlers are captured in Nickelodeon's *Rugrats Comics Adventures.*

© 1998 Klasky-Csupo (Nickelodeon)

ORIG GOOD FINE N-MINT

RUGRATS COMIC ADVENTURES (VOL. 2)
NICKELODEON MAGAZINES

Issue	ORIG	GOOD	FINE	N-MINT
❑1, Sep 98, Tales from the Crib!; Most Valuable Baby, no cover price; magazine	—	0.60	1.50	3.00

RUINS
MARVEL

Value: Cover or less

- ❑1, Aug 95, Men On Fire, Acetate cover overlaying cardstock inner cover ... 4.95
- ❑2, Sep 95, Women In Flight, Acetate cover overlaying cardstock inner cover ... 4.95

RUMBLE GIRLS: SILKY WARRIOR TANSIE
IMAGE

Value: Cover or less

- ❑1 ... 3.50
- ❑2, Jun 00, Speed! Candy! ... 3.50
- ❑3, Jul 00, Sugar and Wax ... 3.50
- ❑4, Sapphire Bullets ... 3.50
- ❑5, It's Not Romantic ... 3.50
- ❑6, Boy, Girl, Boy, Girl ... 3.50

RUMIC WORLD
VIZ

Value: Cover or less

- ❑1, b&w; Fire Tripper ... 3.25
- ❑2, b&w; Laughing Target ... 3.50

RUMMAGE $2099
PARODY PRESS

Value: Cover or less

- ❑1, Spirits of Whispers of the Dark Miniseries of Vengeance, Part 2, foil cover ... 2.95

RUNAWAY-A KNOWN ASSOCIATES MYSTERY
KNOWN ASSOCIATES

Value: Cover or less

- ❑1, nn; b&w; One-Shot ... 2.50

RUNE
MALIBU

Issue	ORIG	GOOD	FINE	N-MINT
❑0, Jan 94, no cover price; Promotional edition (from redeeming coupons in early Ultraverse comics)	—	0.60	1.50	3.00
❑1, Jan 94, trading card	1.95	0.40	1.00	2.00
❑1/SC, Jan 94, Foil limited edition; silver foil logo	1.95	0.40	1.00	2.00
❑2, Feb 94, The Source	1.95	0.39	0.98	1.95
❑3, Mar 94, The Spoils Of War; Ripfire, 1: Elven; 1: Ripfire, Ultraverse Premiere #1; Flip-book with Ultraverse Premiere #1	3.50	0.70	1.75	3.50
❑4, Jun 94	1.95	0.39	0.98	1.95
❑5, Sep 94, Gemini	1.95	0.39	0.98	1.95
❑6, Dec 94	1.95	0.39	0.98	1.95
❑7, Feb 95, Rise of the Gods, Part 1	1.95	0.39	0.98	1.95
❑8, Feb 95, Rise of the Gods, Part 2	1.95	0.39	0.98	1.95
❑9, Apr 95, Rise of the Gods, Part 3, D: Tantalus; D: Master Oshi; D: Sybil	1.95	0.39	0.98	1.95
❑GS 1, O: Rune; 1: Tantalus; D: El Gato; 1: Master Oshi; 1: Sybil, Giant-size Rune #1	2.50	0.50	1.25	2.50

RUNE (VOL. 2)
MALIBU

Issue	ORIG	GOOD	FINE	N-MINT
❑0, Sep 95, Curse Of Rune: Day For Night, black cover; Black September; Rune # (Infinity)	1.50	0.30	0.75	1.50
❑0/SC, Sep 95, Curse Of Rune: Day For Night, alternate cover; Rune # (Infinity)..	1.50	0.40	1.00	2.00
❑1, Oct 95, A: Annihilus; A: Adam Warlock; A: Gemini	1.50	0.30	0.75	1.50
❑2, Nov 95, The Quality of Mercy	1.50	0.30	0.75	1.50
❑3, Dec 95, Tooth and Claw	1.50	0.30	0.75	1.50
❑4, Jan 96	1.50	0.30	0.75	1.50
❑5, Feb 96	1.50	0.30	0.75	1.50
❑6, Mar 96	1.50	0.30	0.75	1.50
❑7, Apr 96, Final Issue	1.50	0.30	0.75	1.50

RUNE: HEARTS OF DARKNESS
MALIBU

Value: Cover or less

- ❑1, Sep 96, Flip-book ... 1.50
- ❑2, Oct 96, Flip-book ... 1.50
- ❑3, Nov 96, Flip-book ... 1.50

RUNE/SILVER SURFER
MARVEL

Issue	ORIG	GOOD	FINE	N-MINT
❑1, Apr 95, Into Infinity, newsstand edition; crossover	2.95	0.60	1.50	3.00
❑1/DM, Apr 95, Direct Market edition; crossover; Squarebound with glossier paper ..	5.95	1.20	3.00	6.00

RUNE VS. VENOM
MALIBU

Value: Cover or less

❑1, Dec 95, Rune-Venom 3.95

RUNE/WRATH
MALIBU

	ORIG	GOOD	FINE	N-MINT
❑1, gold foil ashcan	—	0.20	0.50	1.00

RUSH LIMBAUGH MUST DIE
BONEYARD

	ORIG	GOOD	FINE	N-MINT
❑1, Nov 93, nn; b&w; adult	3.95	1.00	2.50	5.00

RUST
NOW

	ORIG	GOOD	FINE	N-MINT
❑1, Jul 87	1.50	0.40	1.00	2.00
❑2, Aug 87	1.50	0.40	1.00	2.00
❑3, Sep 87	1.50	0.40	1.00	2.00
❑4, Nov 87	1.75	0.40	1.00	2.00
❑5, Dec 87	1.75	0.40	1.00	2.00
❑6, Jan 88	1.50	0.40	1.00	2.00
❑7, Feb 88	1.75	0.40	1.00	2.00
❑8, Mar 88	1.50	0.40	1.00	2.00
❑9, Apr 88	1.75	0.40	1.00	2.00
❑10, May 88	1.75	0.40	1.00	2.00
❑11, Jul 88	1.75	0.40	1.00	2.00
❑12, Aug 88, Terminator preview	1.75	0.40	1.00	2.00
❑13, Sep 88	1.75	0.40	1.00	2.00

RUST (2ND SERIES)
NOW

	ORIG	GOOD	FINE	N-MINT
❑1, Feb 89	1.75	0.40	1.00	2.00
❑2, Mar 89	1.75	0.40	1.00	2.00
❑3, Apr 89	1.75	0.40	1.00	2.00
❑4, May 89	1.75	0.40	1.00	2.00
❑5, Jun 89	1.75	0.40	1.00	2.00
❑6, Aug 89	1.75	0.40	1.00	2.00
❑7, Sep 89	1.75	0.40	1.00	2.00

RUST (3RD SERIES)
ADVENTURE

Value: Cover or less

❑1, Apr 92, O: Rust, full color; Adventure Comics.............. 2.95

❑1/LE, Apr 92, cardstock cover; limited edition; rust-colored foil logo 4.95

❑2 .... 2.95

❑3, Aug 92, Sandblasting, full color.................................... 2.95

❑4, Sep 92, Recycled............. 2.95

RUST (4TH SERIES)
CALIBER

Value: Cover or less

❑1, Hazing Part 1 .... 2.95

❑2, Hazing Part 2 .... 2.95

S

SABAN POWERHOUSE
ACCLAIM

Value: Cover or less

❑1, digest; Power Rangers Turbo, Masked Rider, Samurai Pizza Cats; no indicia 4.50

❑2, digest; Power Rangers Turbo, Masked Rider, Samurai Pizza Cats, BettleBorgs 4.50

SABAN PRESENTS POWER RANGERS TURBO VS. BEETLEBORGS METALLIX
ACCLAIM

Value: Cover or less

❑1, nn; digest 4.50

SABINA
EROS

	ORIG	GOOD	FINE	N-MINT
❑1	—	0.59	1.48	2.95
❑2	—	0.59	1.48	2.95
❑3	—	0.59	1.48	2.95
❑4	—	0.59	1.48	2.95
❑5	—	0.59	1.48	2.95
❑6	—	0.59	1.48	2.95
❑7, Jul 96, The Rivals	2.95	0.59	1.48	2.95

SABLE
FIRST

	ORIG	GOOD	FINE	N-MINT
❑1, Mar 88, Resting Place	1.75	0.40	1.00	2.00
❑2, Apr 88	1.75	0.40	1.00	2.00
❑3, May 88	1.75	0.40	1.00	2.00
❑4, Jun 88	1.75	0.40	1.00	2.00
❑5, Jul 88, Fatal Mistakes	1.75	0.40	1.00	2.00
❑6, Aug 88, ...Painful To Get As Well As Keep	1.75	0.40	1.00	2.00
❑7, Sep 88, ...Into The Toxic Wasteland	1.75	0.40	1.00	2.00
❑8, Oct 88	1.95	0.40	1.00	2.00
❑9, Nov 88, Into The Heart Of Darkness	1.95	0.40	1.00	2.00
❑10, Dec 88	1.95	0.40	1.00	2.00
❑11, Jan 89, Word Of Honor	1.95	0.40	1.00	2.00
❑12, Feb 89	1.95	0.40	1.00	2.00
❑13, Mar 89	1.95	0.40	1.00	2.00
❑14, Apr 89, And The Creatures Were Stirring	1.95	0.40	1.00	2.00
❑15, May 89, Art In The Blood, Part 1	1.95	0.40	1.00	2.00
❑16, Jun 89, Art In The Blood, Part 2	1.95	0.40	1.00	2.00
❑17, Jul 89	1.95	0.40	1.00	2.00
❑18, Aug 89	1.95	0.40	1.00	2.00
❑19, Sep 89	1.95	0.40	1.00	2.00
❑20, Oct 89	1.95	0.40	1.00	2.00
❑21, Nov 89	1.95	0.40	1.00	2.00
❑22, Dec 89	1.95	0.40	1.00	2.00
❑23, Jan 90	1.95	0.40	1.00	2.00
❑24, Feb 90	1.95	0.40	1.00	2.00
❑25, Mar 90	1.95	0.40	1.00	2.00
❑26, Apr 90	1.95	0.40	1.00	2.00
❑27, May 90	1.95	0.40	1.00	2.00

SABLE (MIKE GRELL'S...)
F

	ORIG	GOOD	FINE	N-MINT
❑1, Mar 90, MGr, MGr (w), The Iron Monster, Reprint; Reprints Jon Sable, Freelance #1	1.75	0.40	1.00	2.00
❑2, Apr 90, MGr, MGr (w), Reprint	1.75	0.40	1.00	2.00
❑3, May 90, MGr, MGr (w), Reprint	1.75	0.40	1.00	2.00
❑4, Jun 90, MGr, MGr (w), Reprint	1.75	0.40	1.00	2.00
❑5, Jul 90, MGr, MGr (w), Reprint	1.75	0.40	1.00	2.00
❑6, Aug 90, MGr, MGr (w), Reprint	1.75	0.40	1.00	2.00
❑7, Sep 90, MGr, MGr (w), Reprint	1.75	0.40	1.00	2.00
❑8, Oct 90, MGr, MGr (w), Reprint	1.75	0.40	1.00	2.00
❑9, Nov 90, MGr, MGr (w), Reprint	1.75	0.40	1.00	2.00
❑10, Dec 90, MGr, MGr (w), Reprint	1.75	0.40	1.00	2.00

SABRA BLADE
DRACULINA

Value: Cover or less

❑1, Dec 94, b&w 2.50

❑1/SC, Dec 94, b&w; alternate two-color cover.................... 2.50

SABRE
ECLIPSE

	ORIG	GOOD	FINE	N-MINT
❑1, Aug 82, PG, Slow Fade Of An Endangered Species, 1: Sabre	1.00	0.50	1.25	2.50
❑2, Oct 82, PG, Slow Fade Of An Endangered Species	1.00	0.40	1.00	2.00
❑3, Dec 82, PG, Exploitation Of Everything Dear, Part 1	1.00	0.40	1.00	2.00
❑4, Mar 83, Exploitation Of Everything Dear, Part 2	1.50	0.40	1.00	2.00
❑5, Jul 83, Exploitation Of Everything Dear, Part 3	1.50	0.40	1.00	2.00
❑6, Oct 83, Exploitation Of Everything Dear, Part 4	1.50	0.40	1.00	2.00
❑7, Dec 83, Exploitation Of Everything Dear, Part 5	1.50	0.40	1.00	2.00
❑8, Feb 84, Exploitation Of Everything Dear, Part 6	1.50	0.40	1.00	2.00
❑9, Apr 84, Exploitation Of Everything Dear, Part 7	1.50	0.40	1.00	2.00
❑10, Jun 84, The Decadence Indoctrination, Part 1	1.50	0.35	0.88	1.75
❑11, Aug 84, The Decadence Indoctrination, Part 2	1.75	0.35	0.88	1.75
❑12, Jan 85, The Decadence Indoctrination, Part 3	1.75	0.35	0.88	1.75
❑13, Apr 85, The Decadence Indoctrination, Part 4	1.75	0.35	0.88	1.75
❑14, Aug 85, The Decadence Indoctrination, Part 5	2.00	0.35	0.88	1.75

SABRETOOTH
MARVEL

Value: Cover or less

❑1, Aug 93, Home Is The Hunter, Die-cut cover....................... 2.95

❑2, Sep 93 .... 2.95

❑3, Oct 93, City Of Light, City Of Night!, A: Mystique, cardstock cover 2.95

❑4, Nov 93.............................. 2.95

❑SE 1, Jan 95, In the Red Zone, enhanced wraparound cover; One-Shot; Special edition.... 4.95

SABRETOOTH CLASSIC
MARVEL

	ORIG	GOOD	FINE	N-MINT
❑1, May 94, reprints Power Man & Iron Fist #66	1.50	0.40	1.00	2.00
❑2, Jun 94, KGa, Slasher, reprints Power Man & Iron Fist #78	1.50	0.30	0.75	1.50
❑3, Jul 94, reprints Power Man & Iron Fist #84	1.50	0.30	0.75	1.50
❑4, Aug 94, reprints Peter Parker; The Spectacular Spider-Man #116; reprints Peter Parker, The Spectacular Spider-Man #116	1.50	0.30	0.75	1.50
❑5, Sep 94, reprints Peter Parker; The Spectacular Spider-Man #119; reprints Peter Parker, The Spectacular Spider-Man #119	1.50	0.30	0.75	1.50
❑6, Oct 94, reprints X-Factor #10	1.50	0.30	0.75	1.50
❑7, Nov 94, reprints The Mighty Thor #374	1.50	0.30	0.75	1.50
❑8, Dec 94, reprints Power Pack #27	1.50	0.30	0.75	1.50
❑9, Jan 95, reprints Uncanny X-Men #212	1.50	0.30	0.75	1.50
❑10, Feb 95, reprints Uncanny X-Men #213	1.50	0.30	0.75	1.50
❑11, Mar 95, reprints Daredevil #238	1.50	0.30	0.75	1.50
❑12, Apr 95, reprints back-up stories from Classic X-Men #10 and Marvel Super-Heroes (no issue given)	1.50	0.30	0.75	1.50
❑13, May 95, reprints Uncanny X-Men #219	1.50	0.30	0.75	1.50
❑14, Jun 95, reprints Uncanny X-Men #221	1.50	0.30	0.75	1.50
❑15, Jul 95, reprints Uncanny X-Men #222	1.50	0.30	0.75	1.50

SABRINA
Archie

	ORIG	GOOD	FINE	N-MINT
❑1, May 97, DDC, The Cleopatra Chronicles, Part 1; Queen of Denial	1.50	0.50	1.25	2.50
❑2, Jun 97, The Cleopatra Chronicles, Part 2	1.50	0.40	1.00	2.00
❑3, Jul 97, The Cleopatra Chronicles, Part 3	1.50	0.40	1.00	2.00
❑4, Aug 97	1.50	0.30	0.75	1.50
❑5, Sep 97	1.50	0.30	0.75	1.50
❑6, Oct 97	1.50	0.30	0.75	1.50
❑7, Nov 97	1.50	0.30	0.75	1.50
❑8, Dec 97	1.50	0.30	0.75	1.50
❑9, Jan 98	1.75	0.35	0.88	1.75
❑10, Feb 98	1.75	0.35	0.88	1.75
❑11, Mar 98	1.75	0.35	0.88	1.75
❑12, Apr 98	1.75	0.35	0.88	1.75
❑13, May 98	1.75	0.35	0.88	1.75
❑14, Jun 98	1.75	0.35	0.88	1.75
❑15, Jul 98	1.75	0.35	0.88	1.75
❑16, Aug 98	1.75	0.35	0.88	1.75
❑17, Sep 98, A: Josie & the Pussycats	1.75	0.35	0.88	1.75
❑18, Oct 98	1.75	0.35	0.88	1.75
❑19, Nov 98, DDC, Photo cover; back to the '60s	1.75	0.35	0.88	1.75
❑20, Dec 98	1.75	0.35	0.88	1.75
❑21, Jan 99	1.75	0.35	0.88	1.75
❑22, Feb 99	1.75	0.35	0.88	1.75
❑23, Mar 99	1.75	0.35	0.88	1.75
❑24, Apr 99	1.79	0.36	0.89	1.79
❑25, May 99	1.79	0.36	0.89	1.79
❑26, Jun 99	1.79	0.36	0.89	1.79
❑27, Jul 99	1.79	0.36	0.89	1.79
❑28, Aug 99, A: Sonic, continues in Sonic Super Special #10	1.79	0.36	0.89	1.79
❑29, Sep 99	1.79	0.36	0.89	1.79
❑30, Oct 99	1.79	0.36	0.89	1.79
❑31, Nov 99	1.79	0.36	0.89	1.79

SABRINA (VOL. 2)
Archie

Value: Cover or less

❑1, Jan 00, based on the animated series	1.99	❑12, Dec 00	1.99
❑2, Feb 00	1.99	❑13, Jan 01	1.99
❑3, Mar 00	1.99	❑14, Feb 01	1.99
❑4, Apr 00	1.99	❑15	1.99
❑5, May 00	1.99	❑16	1.99
❑6, Jun 00	1.99	❑17	1.99
❑7, Jul 00	1.99	❑18	1.99
❑8, Aug 00	1.99	❑19	1.99
❑9, Sep 00	1.99	❑20	1.99
❑10, Oct 00	1.99	❑21	1.99
❑11, Nov 00	1.99	❑22	1.99

SABRINA THE TEENAGE WITCH
Archie

	ORIG	GOOD	FINE	N-MINT
❑1, Giant-size	—	9.00	22.50	45.00
❑2, Giant-size	—	4.00	10.00	20.00
❑3, Giant-size	—	2.40	6.00	12.00
❑4, Giant-size	—	2.40	6.00	12.00
❑5, Giant-size	—	2.40	6.00	12.00
❑6, Giant-size	—	2.00	5.00	10.00
❑7, Giant-size	—	2.00	5.00	10.00
❑8, Giant-size	—	2.00	5.00	10.00
❑9, Giant-size	—	2.00	5.00	10.00
❑10, Giant-size	—	2.00	5.00	10.00
❑11, Giant-size	—	1.60	4.00	8.00
❑12, Giant-size	—	1.60	4.00	8.00
❑13, Giant-size	—	1.60	4.00	8.00
❑14, Giant-size	—	1.60	4.00	8.00
❑15, Giant-size	—	1.60	4.00	8.00
❑16, Giant-size	—	1.60	4.00	8.00
❑17, Giant-size	—	1.60	4.00	8.00
❑18	—	1.20	3.00	6.00
❑19	—	1.20	3.00	6.00
❑20	—	1.20	3.00	6.00
❑21	—	1.00	2.50	5.00
❑22	—	1.00	2.50	5.00
❑23	—	1.00	2.50	5.00
❑24	—	1.00	2.50	5.00
❑25	—	1.00	2.50	5.00
❑26	—	1.00	2.50	5.00
❑27	—	1.00	2.50	5.00
❑28	—	1.00	2.50	5.00
❑29	—	1.00	2.50	5.00
❑30	—	1.00	2.50	5.00
❑31	—	0.80	2.00	4.00
❑32	—	0.80	2.00	4.00
❑33, Aug 76	0.30	0.80	2.00	4.00

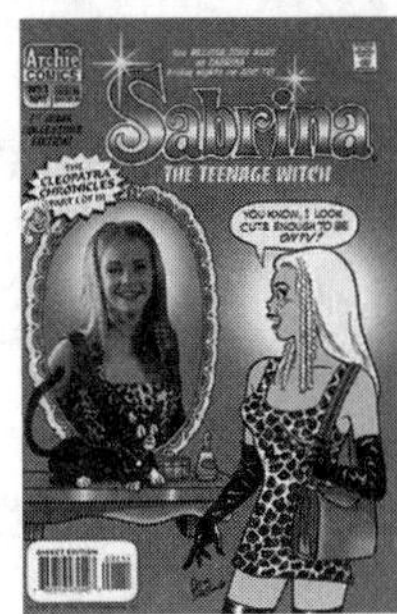

Sabrina summoned Cleopatra to the present, where the Queen of the Nile promptly took over as the school's most popular girl, in the first issue of *Sabrina*.

	ORIG	GOOD	FINE	N-MINT
❑34	—	0.80	2.00	4.00
❑35, An Emotion Potion; Li'l Jinx...It Adds Up!, A: Veronica; A: Jughead; A: Ethel; A: Betty	0.30	0.80	2.00	4.00
❑36	—	0.80	2.00	4.00
❑37, Feb 77	0.30	0.80	2.00	4.00
❑38	—	0.80	2.00	4.00
❑39	—	0.80	2.00	4.00
❑40	—	0.80	2.00	4.00
❑41	—	0.80	2.00	4.00
❑42	—	0.80	2.00	4.00
❑43	—	0.80	2.00	4.00
❑44	—	0.80	2.00	4.00
❑45	—	0.80	2.00	4.00
❑46	—	0.80	2.00	4.00
❑47	—	0.80	2.00	4.00
❑48	—	0.80	2.00	4.00
❑49	—	0.80	2.00	4.00
❑50	—	0.80	2.00	4.00
❑51	—	0.60	1.50	3.00
❑52	—	0.60	1.50	3.00
❑53	—	0.60	1.50	3.00
❑54	—	0.60	1.50	3.00
❑55	—	0.60	1.50	3.00
❑56, Oct 78	0.40	0.60	1.50	3.00
❑57	—	0.60	1.50	3.00
❑58	—	0.60	1.50	3.00
❑59	—	0.60	1.50	3.00
❑60	—	0.60	1.50	3.00
❑61	—	0.40	1.00	2.00
❑62	—	0.40	1.00	2.00
❑63	—	0.40	1.00	2.00
❑64	—	0.40	1.00	2.00
❑65	—	0.40	1.00	2.00
❑66	—	0.40	1.00	2.00
❑67	—	0.40	1.00	2.00
❑68	—	0.40	1.00	2.00
❑69	—	0.40	1.00	2.00
❑70	—	0.40	1.00	2.00
❑71	—	0.40	1.00	2.00
❑72	—	0.40	1.00	2.00
❑73	—	0.40	1.00	2.00
❑74	—	0.40	1.00	2.00
❑75	—	0.40	1.00	2.00
❑76	—	0.40	1.00	2.00
❑77	—	0.40	1.00	2.00
❑HS 1, "Sabrina's Halloween Spoook-Tacular"	2.00	0.40	1.00	2.00
❑HS 2	2.00	0.40	1.00	2.00
❑HS 3	2.00	0.40	1.00	2.00

SABRINA THE TEENAGE WITCH (2ND SERIES)
Archie

Value: Cover or less

❑1, One-Shot 2.00

SACHS & VIOLENS
Marvel

	ORIG	GOOD	FINE	N-MINT
❑1, Nov 93, GP, PD (w), Sachs and the Single Girl, Part 1, Embossed cover	2.75	0.60	1.50	3.00
❑1/PL, Nov 93, GP, PD (w), Sachs and the Single Girl, Part 1, Embossed cover; Platinum promotional edition	—	0.60	1.50	3.00
❑2, May 94, GP, PD (w), Sachs and the Single Girl, Part 2, trading card	2.25	0.45	1.13	2.25
❑3, Jun 94, GP, PD (w), Sachs and the Single Girl, Part 3, Sex, nudity	2.25	0.45	1.13	2.25
❑4, Jul 94, GP, PD (w), Sachs and the Single Girl, Part 4, trading card	2.25	0.45	1.13	2.25

SACRIFICED TREES
Mansion

Value: Cover or less

❑1, Zakiriah: The Raven Sleeps Tonight 3.00

SAD SACK AT HOME FOR THE HOLIDAYS
Lorne-Harvey

Value: Cover or less

❑1 2.00

SAD SACK IN 3-D
Blackthorne

Value: Cover or less

- ❑1 ... 2.50

SAFEST PLACE IN THE WORLD, THE
Dark Horse

Value: Cover or less

- ❑1, SD, SD (w), Biette Person, nn ... 2.50

SAFETY-BELT MAN
Sirius

Value: Cover or less

- ❑1, Jun 94, Why Did the Dummy cross the Road?; A Day in the Death of Bill Bardo ... 2.50
- ❑2, Oct 94 ... 2.50
- ❑3, Feb 95 ... 2.50
- ❑4, Jun 95, The Videon Truth, Part 2; Lady Def, color centerfold ... 2.50
- ❑5 ... 2.50
- ❑6 ... 2.50

SAFETY-BELT MAN: ALL HELL
Sirius

Value: Cover or less

- ❑1 ... 2.95
- ❑2, Jun 96 ... 2.95
- ❑3 ... 2.95
- ❑4 ... 2.95
- ❑5, Jan 97 ... 2.95
- ❑6, Aug 97 ... 2.95

SAFFIRE
Image

Value: Cover or less

- ❑1 ... 2.95
- ❑2, Dec 00 ... 2.95
- ❑3, Feb 01 ... 2.95

SAGA
Odyssey

Value: Cover or less

- ❑1, The Apatian Chronicles, b&w ... 1.95

SAGA OF CRYSTAR, THE CRYSTAL WARRIOR
Marvel

	ORIG	GOOD	FINE	N-MINT
❑1, May 83, The Sundered Throne, 1: Crystar	2.00	0.40	1.00	2.00
❑2, Jul 83, Ika, 1: Ika	0.60	0.20	0.50	1.00
❑3, Sep 83, In The Sanctum Sanctorum Of Doctor Strange!, A: Doctor Strange	0.60	0.20	0.50	1.00
❑4, Nov 83	0.60	0.20	0.50	1.00
❑5, Jan 84	0.60	0.20	0.50	1.00
❑6, Mar 84, A: Nightcrawler	0.60	0.20	0.50	1.00
❑7, May 84	0.60	0.20	0.50	1.00
❑8, Jul 84	0.60	0.20	0.50	1.00
❑9, Sep 84	0.60	0.20	0.50	1.00
❑10, Nov 84	0.60	0.20	0.50	1.00
❑11, Feb 85, A: Alpha Flight, Final Issue; Double-size	1.00	0.20	0.50	1.00

SAGA OF RA'S AL GHUL
DC

Value: Cover or less

- ❑1, Jan 88 ... 2.50
- ❑2, Feb 88 ... 2.50
- ❑3, Mar 88 ... 2.50
- ❑4, Apr 88 ... 2.50

SAGA OF THE MAN ELF, THE
Trident

Value: Cover or less

- ❑1, Aug 89, Reigns of Power ... 2.25
- ❑2 ... 2.25
- ❑3 ... 2.25
- ❑4 ... 2.25
- ❑5 ... 2.25

SAGA OF THE ORIGINAL HUMAN TORCH
Marvel

Value: Cover or less

- ❑1, Apr 90, RB, The Lighted Torch, O: The Human Torch I (android) ... 1.50
- ❑2, May 90, RB, O: Toro ... 1.50
- ❑3, Jun 90, RB, Out Of The Ashes, D: Hitler ... 1.50
- ❑4, Jul 90, RB ... 1.50

SAGA OF THE SUB-MARINER
Marvel

	ORIG	GOOD	FINE	N-MINT
❑1, Nov 88, RB, A Legend A-Borning, O: Sub-Mariner	1.25	0.30	0.75	1.50
❑2, Dec 88	1.50	0.30	0.75	1.50
❑3, Jan 89	1.50	0.30	0.75	1.50
❑4, Feb 89, A: Human Torch	1.50	0.30	0.75	1.50
❑5, Mar 89, A: Invaders; A: Captain America; A: Human Torch	1.50	0.30	0.75	1.50
❑6, Apr 89, A: Invaders; A: Captain America; A: Human Torch; A: Torch	1.50	0.30	0.75	1.50
❑7, May 89, A: Fantastic Four	1.50	0.30	0.75	1.50
❑8, Jun 89, A: Avengers; A: Fantastic Four	1.50	0.30	0.75	1.50
❑9, Jul 89, A: Avengers; A: Fantastic Four	1.50	0.30	0.75	1.50
❑10, Aug 89	1.50	0.30	0.75	1.50
❑11, Sep 89	1.50	0.30	0.75	1.50
❑12, Oct 89	1.50	0.30	0.75	1.50

SAGA OF THE SWAMP THING, THE
DC

	ORIG	GOOD	FINE	N-MINT
❑1, May 82, TY, What Peace There May Be in Silence, O: Swamp Thing	0.60	0.60	1.50	3.00
❑2, Jun 82	0.60	0.40	1.00	2.00
❑3, Jul 82	0.60	0.40	1.00	2.00
❑4, Aug 82	0.60	0.40	1.00	2.00
❑5, Sep 82	0.60	0.40	1.00	2.00
❑6, Oct 82	0.60	0.40	1.00	2.00
❑7, Nov 82	0.60	0.40	1.00	2.00
❑8, Dec 82	0.60	0.40	1.00	2.00
❑9, Jan 83	0.60	0.40	1.00	2.00
❑10, Feb 83	0.60	0.40	1.00	2.00
❑11, Mar 83	0.60	0.40	1.00	2.00
❑12, Apr 83	0.60	0.40	1.00	2.00
❑13, May 83	0.60	0.40	1.00	2.00
❑14, Jun 83	0.60	0.40	1.00	2.00
❑15, Jul 83	0.60	0.40	1.00	2.00
❑16, Aug 83	0.60	0.40	1.00	2.00
❑17, Oct 83	0.60	0.40	1.00	2.00
❑18, Nov 83	0.60	0.40	1.00	2.00
❑19, Dec 83	0.60	0.40	1.00	2.00
❑20, Jan 84, AMo (w), Alan Moore scripts begin	0.75	2.40	6.00	12.00
❑21, Feb 84, AMo (w), O: Swamp Thing (new origin)	0.75	2.00	5.00	10.00
❑22, Mar 84, AMo (w)	0.75	1.20	3.00	6.00
❑23, Apr 84, AMo (w)	0.75	1.20	3.00	6.00
❑24, May 84, AMo (w), A: Justice League	0.75	1.20	3.00	6.00
❑25, Jun 84, AMo (w)	0.75	1.20	3.00	6.00
❑26, Jul 84, AMo (w)	0.75	0.80	2.00	4.00
❑27, Aug 84, AMo (w)	0.75	0.80	2.00	4.00
❑28, Sep 84, AMo (w)	0.75	0.80	2.00	4.00
❑29, Oct 84, AMo (w)	0.75	0.80	2.00	4.00
❑30, Nov 84, AMo (w)	0.75	0.80	2.00	4.00
❑31, Dec 84, AMo (w)	0.75	0.80	2.00	4.00
❑32, Jan 85, AMo (w)	0.75	0.80	2.00	4.00
❑33, Feb 85	0.75	0.60	1.50	3.00
❑34, Mar 85, AMo (w)	0.75	1.00	2.50	5.00
❑35, Apr 85, AMo (w)	0.75	0.60	1.50	3.00
❑36, May 85, AMo (w)	0.75	0.60	1.50	3.00
❑37, Jun 85, AMo (w), Growth Patterns, 1: John Constantine	0.75	3.20	8.00	16.00
❑38, Jul 85, AMo (w), Still Waters, 2: John Constantine, Series continues as Swamp Thing	0.75	1.60	4.00	8.00
❑39, AMo (w), Fish Story, A: John Constantine	0.75	1.40	3.50	7.00
❑40, AMo (w), The Curse, A: John Constantine	0.75	1.40	3.50	7.00
❑41, AMo (w)	—	0.60	1.50	3.00
❑42, AMo (w)	—	0.60	1.50	3.00
❑43, AMo (w)	—	0.60	1.50	3.00
❑44, AMo (w)	—	0.60	1.50	3.00
❑45, AMo (w), Series continued as "Swamp Thing (2nd Series) #46"	—	0.60	1.50	3.00
❑Anl 1, movie Adaptation; 1982	1.00	0.40	1.00	2.00
❑Anl 2, AMo (w), A: Phantom Stranger; A: Deadman; A: Spectre; A: Demon	1.25	0.80	2.00	4.00
❑Anl 3, Distant Cousins, A: Congorilla, 1987	2.00	0.50	1.25	2.50

SAIGON CHRONICLES
Avalon

Value: Cover or less

- ❑1, This Crummy War; The Enemy Within ... 2.95

SAILOR MOON COMIC
Mixxzine

	ORIG	GOOD	FINE	N-MINT
❑1, Continued from MixxZine	2.95	3.00	7.50	15.00
❑1/A, San Diego limited edition version	2.95	2.40	6.00	12.00
❑2	2.95	1.60	4.00	8.00
❑3, D: Kunzite, Destruction of the Moon Kingdom (flashback)	2.95	1.60	4.00	8.00
❑4	2.95	1.60	4.00	8.00
❑5	2.95	1.20	3.00	6.00
❑6	—	1.20	3.00	6.00
❑7	—	1.20	3.00	6.00
❑8	—	1.00	2.50	5.00
❑9	—	0.80	2.00	4.00
❑10	—	0.60	1.50	3.00
❑11	—	0.60	1.50	3.00
❑12	—	0.60	1.50	3.00
❑13	—	0.60	1.50	3.00
❑14	—	0.60	1.50	3.00
❑15	—	0.60	1.50	3.00
❑16	—	0.60	1.50	3.00
❑17	—	0.60	1.50	3.00
❑18	—	0.60	1.50	3.00
❑19	—	0.60	1.50	3.00
❑20	—	0.60	1.50	3.00
❑21	—	0.60	1.50	3.00
❑22	—	0.60	1.50	3.00
❑23	—	0.60	1.50	3.00
❑24	—	0.60	1.50	3.00
❑25	—	0.60	1.50	3.00
❑26	—	0.60	1.50	3.00
❑27	—	0.60	1.50	3.00
❑28	—	0.60	1.50	3.00

	ORIG	GOOD	FINE	N-MINT
❑29	—	0.60	1.50	3.00
❑30	—	0.60	1.50	3.00
❑31	—	0.59	1.48	2.95
❑32	—	0.59	1.48	2.95
❑33	2.95	0.59	1.48	2.95

SAILOR MOON SUPERS
MIXX

Value: Cover or less
❑1 .... 9.95

SAILOR'S STORY, A
MARVEL

Value: Cover or less
❑1 .... 5.95

SAILOR'S STORY, A: WINDS, DREAMS, AND DRAGONS
MARVEL

Value: Cover or less
❑1 .... 6.95

SAINT ANGEL
IMAGE

Value: Cover or less

❑0, Mar 00 .... 2.95
❑1, Jun 00 .... 3.95
❑2, Oct 00 .... 3.95
❑3, Dec 00 .... 3.95
❑4, Mar 01 .... 3.95

SAINT GERMAINE
CALIBER

Value: Cover or less
❑1 .... 2.95

SAINTS, THE
SATURN

Value: Cover or less
❑0, Apr 95, b&w 2.50
❑1, Fal 96, b&w 2.50

SAINT SINNER
MARVEL

Value: Cover or less

❑1, Oct 93, World Without End, O: Saint Sinner, foil cover 2.50
❑2, Nov 93 .... 1.75
❑3, Dec 93 .... 1.75
❑4, Jan 94 .... 1.75
❑5, Feb 94 .... 1.75
❑6, Apr 94, The Child Stealer, Part 1 .... 1.75
❑7, Apr 94, The Child Stealer, Part 2 .... 1.75
❑8 .... 1.75

SALIMBA
BLACKTHORNE

Value: Cover or less
❑1, b&w 3.50
❑3D 1, Aug 86, Pirate's Heart!, b&w 2.50
❑3D 2, Sep 86, Well of Night 2.50

SALLY FORTH
FANTAGRAPHICS

Value: Cover or less

❑1 .... 2.95
❑1-2, Jun 95, 2nd Printing 2.95
❑2, Oct 93 .... 2.95
❑3, Feb 94 .... 2.95
❑4, Apr 94 .... 2.95
❑5, Jul 94 .... 2.95
❑6, Sep 94 .... 2.95
❑7, Nov 94 .... 2.95
❑8, Jan 95 .... 2.95

SAM & MAX, FREELANCE POLICE
MARVEL

Value: Cover or less
❑1, nn 2.25

SAM & MAX FREELANCE POLICE SPECIAL
COMICO

Value: Cover or less
❑1 .... 2.75

SAM AND MAX, FREELANCE POLICE SPECIAL, THE
FISHWRAP

Value: Cover or less
❑1, b&w 1.75

SAM & MAX FREELANCE POLICE SPECIAL COLOR COLLECTION
MARVEL

Value: Cover or less
❑1, nn 4.95

SAM AND TWITCH
IMAGE

Value: Cover or less

❑1, Aug 99, BMB (w), Udaku, Part 1 .... 2.50
❑2, Sep 99, BMB (w), Udaku, Part 2 .... 2.50
❑3, Oct 99, BMB (w), Udaku, Part 3 .... 2.50
❑4, Nov 99, BMB (w), Udaku, Part 4 .... 2.50
❑5, Dec 99, BMB (w), Udaku, Part 5 .... 2.50
❑6, Jan 00, BMB (w) 2.50
❑7, Feb 00, BMB (w) 2.50
❑8, Mar 00, BMB (w) 2.50
❑9, Apr 00, BMB (w) 2.50
❑10, May 00, BMB (w), Witchcraft, Part 1 .... 2.50
❑11, Jun 00, BMB (w), Witchcraft, Part 2 .... 2.50
❑12, Jul 00, BMB (w), Witchcraft, Part 3 .... 2.50
❑13, Aug 00, BMB (w), Witchcraft, Part 4 .... 2.50
❑14, Sep 00, BMB (w), Dumb Laws and Eggs 2.50
❑15, Oct 00, BMB (w), Bounty Hunter Wars, Part 1 .... 2.50
❑16, Nov 00, BMB (w), Bounty Hunter Wars, Part 2 .... 2.50
❑17, Dec 00, BMB (w), Bounty Hunter Wars, Part 3 .... 2.50
❑18, Jan 01, BMB (w), Bounty Hunter Wars, Part 4 .... 2.50
❑19, Feb 01, BMB (w), Bounty Hunter Wars, Part 5 .... 2.50
❑20, Mar 01, TMc (w), The John Doe Affair, Part 1 .... 2.50
❑21 .... 2.50
❑22 .... 2.50
❑23 .... 2.50
❑24 .... 2.50

SAM BRONX AND THE ROBOTS
ECLIPSE

	ORIG	GOOD	FINE	N-MINT
❑1, hardcover	—	1.39	3.47	6.95

Written by Alan Moore, John Constantine was introduced as a supporting character in *Saga of the Swamp Thing* #37.

© 1985 DC Comics

SAMBU GASSHO (A CHORUS IN THREE PARTS)
BODO GENKI STUDIOS

	ORIG	GOOD	FINE	N-MINT
❑1, Aug 94, nn; b&w; no cover price; Anthology	—	0.20	0.50	1.00

SAM SLADE, ROBO-HUNTER
FLEETWAY

	ORIG	GOOD	FINE	N-MINT
❑1, Robo-Hunter: The Beast Of Blackheart Manor	0.75	0.40	1.00	2.00
❑2, DaG, Robo-Hunter: The Beast Of Blackheart Manor; Ro-Busters: Death on the Orient Express!, Part 2	0.75	0.30	0.75	1.50
❑3, DaG, Robo-Hunter: The Filby Case;	0.75	0.30	0.75	1.50
❑4, DaG, Robo-Hunter: The Filby Case; Ro-Busters: The Terra-Meks!	0.75	0.30	0.75	1.50
❑5, DaG, Robo-Hunter: Day of the Droids; Ro-Busters: The Terra-Meks!	0.75	0.30	0.75	1.50
❑6, Ro-Busters: Bax the Burner; ABC Warriors: The Tournament of the Damned, 52pgs.	1.25	0.30	0.75	1.50
❑7, Robo-Hunter; ABC Warriors	1.25	0.30	0.75	1.50
❑8, DaG, Robo-Hunter; ABC Warriors	1.25	0.30	0.75	1.50
❑9, Robo-Hunter: Day of the Droids; ABC Warriors	1.25	0.30	0.75	1.50
❑10, Robo-Hunter: Day of the Droids; ABC Warriors	1.25	0.30	0.75	1.50
❑11, Oct, Robo-Hunter: Day of the Droids; ABC Warriors, no year of publication	1.25	0.30	0.75	1.50
❑12, DaG, Robo-Hunter: Killing of Kidd; Harlem Heroes	1.25	0.30	0.75	1.50
❑13, DaG, Robo-Hunter: Killing of Kidd; Harlem Heroes	1.25	0.30	0.75	1.50
❑14, DaG, Robo-Hunter: Football Crazy; Harlem Heroes	1.25	0.30	0.75	1.50
❑15, Robo-Hunter: Play it Again, Sam; Harlem Heroes	1.25	0.30	0.75	1.50
❑16, Robo-Hunter; Harlem Heroes	1.25	0.30	0.75	1.50
❑17, DaG, Robo-Hunter: Play it Again, Sam; Harlem Heroes	1.25	0.30	0.75	1.50
❑18, DaG, Robo-Hunter: Teeny-Mek Attack; Judge Dredd: The Academy of Law	1.25	0.30	0.75	1.50
❑19, Robo-Hunter: The Slaying of Slade; Ace Trucking Co.	1.25	0.30	0.75	1.50
❑20	1.50	0.30	0.75	1.50
❑21, double issue #21/22	1.50	0.30	0.75	1.50
❑22	—	0.30	0.75	1.50
❑23, double issue #23/24	1.50	0.30	0.75	1.50
❑24	—	0.30	0.75	1.50
❑25	1.50	0.30	0.75	1.50
❑26, Robo-Hunter: Sam Slade's Last Case; The Great Detective Caper: Hemlock Bones-Who He?	1.50	0.30	0.75	1.50
❑27, Robo-Hunter: Sam Slade's Last Case; Ulysses Sweet: Fruitcake and Veg!	1.50	0.30	0.75	1.50
❑28, Robo-Hunter: Farewell, My Billions; Ace Trucking Co.	1.50	0.30	0.75	1.50
❑29, Hap Hazzard; Mirror, Mirror, on the Wall…	1.50	0.30	0.75	1.50
❑30, Robo-Hunter; Ace Trucking Co.: The Great Mush Rush	1.50	0.30	0.75	1.50
❑31, Robo-Hunter! Tharg the Mighty: The Shedding	1.50	0.30	0.75	1.50
❑32	1.50	0.30	0.75	1.50
❑33, Final Issue	1.50	0.30	0.75	1.50

SAMSON
SAMSON

Value: Cover or less
❑0.5, Jan 95, no indicia 2.50

SAM STORIES: LEGS
IMAGE

Value: Cover or less
❑1, Dec 99 .... 2.50

SAMURAI
AIRCEL

	ORIG	GOOD	FINE	N-MINT
❑1	1.70	0.60	1.50	3.00
❑1-2, 2nd Printing	1.70	0.40	1.00	2.00
❑, 3rd Printing	1.70	0.40	1.00	2.00
❑2	1.70	0.40	1.00	2.00

	ORIG	GOOD	FINE	N-MINT
❑3	1.70	0.40	1.00	2.00
❑4	1.70	0.40	1.00	2.00
❑5	—	0.40	1.00	2.00
❑6	—	0.40	1.00	2.00
❑7	—	0.40	1.00	2.00
❑8	—	0.40	1.00	2.00
❑9	—	0.40	1.00	2.00
❑10	—	0.40	1.00	2.00
❑11	—	0.40	1.00	2.00
❑12	—	0.40	1.00	2.00
❑13, 1st Dale Keown art	—	0.60	1.50	3.00
❑14	—	0.60	1.50	3.00
❑15	—	0.60	1.50	3.00
❑16	—	0.60	1.50	3.00
❑17	—	0.40	1.00	2.00
❑18	—	0.40	1.00	2.00
❑19	—	0.40	1.00	2.00
❑20	—	0.40	1.00	2.00
❑21	—	0.40	1.00	2.00
❑22	—	0.40	1.00	2.00
❑23, Final Issue	—	0.40	1.00	2.00

SAMURAI (VOL. 2)
AIRCEL

Value: Cover or less

- ❑1 ... 2.00
- ❑2 ... 2.00
- ❑3 ... 2.00

SAMURAI (VOL. 3)
AIRCEL

Value: Cover or less

- ❑1 ... 1.95
- ❑2 ... 1.95
- ❑3 ... 1.95
- ❑4 ... 1.95
- ❑5 ... 1.95
- ❑6 ... 1.95
- ❑7 ... 1.95

SAMURAI (VOL. 4)
WARP

Value: Cover or less

- ❑1, May 97, b&w ... 2.95

SAMURAI 7
GAUNTLET

Value: Cover or less

- ❑1, b&w ... 2.50
- ❑2, Something Wickeder This Way Comes, b&w ... 2.50
- ❑3, b&w ... 2.50

SAMURAI CAT
MARVEL

Value: Cover or less

- ❑1, Jun 91 ... 2.25
- ❑2, Aug 91 ... 2.25
- ❑3, Sep 91 ... 2.25

SAMURAI COMPILATION BOOK
AIRCEL

Value: Cover or less

- ❑1, b&w ... 4.95
- ❑2, b&w ... 4.95

SAMURAI: DEMON SWORD
NIGHT WYND

Value: Cover or less

- ❑1 ... 2.50
- ❑2 ... 2.50
- ❑3 ... 2.50
- ❑4 ... 2.50

SAMURAI FUNNIES
SOLSON

Value: Cover or less

- ❑1, Texas chainsaw ... 2.00
- ❑2, Samurai 13th ... 2.00

SAMURAI GUARD
COLBURN

	ORIG	GOOD	FINE	N-MINT
❑1, Nov 99	2.50	0.50	1.25	2.50
❑2, Jun 00	2.50	0.50	1.25	2.50
❑Ash 1	—	0.20	0.50	1.00

SAMURAI JAM
SLAVE LABOR

Value: Cover or less

- ❑1, Jan 94 ... 2.95
- ❑2, Apr 94 ... 2.95
- ❑3, Jun 94, Board Walk ... 2.95
- ❑4, Sep 94 ... 2.95

SAMURAI: MYSTIC CULT
NIGHTWYND

Value: Cover or less

- ❑1, b&w ... 2.50
- ❑2, b&w ... 2.50
- ❑3, b&w ... 2.50
- ❑4, b&w ... 2.50

SAMURAI PENGUIN
SLAVE LABOR

Value: Cover or less

- ❑1, Jun 86, b&w ... 1.50
- ❑2, Aug 86, b&w ... 1.50
- ❑3, Feb 87, b&w; pink logo version also exist ... 1.50
- ❑4, May 87, b&w ... 1.50
- ❑5, Sep 87, b&w ... 1.50
- ❑6, Mar 88, D: Samurai Penguin ... 1.95
- ❑7, Jul 88 ... 1.75
- ❑8, May 89 ... 1.75

SAMURAI PENGUIN: FOOD CHAIN FOLLIES
SLAVE LABOR

Value: Cover or less

- ❑1, Apr 91, nn; One-Shot ... 5.95

SAMURAI SQUIRREL
SPOTLIGHT

Value: Cover or less

- ❑1, Into The Lair ... 1.75
- ❑2 ... 1.75

SAMURAI: VAMPIRE'S HUNT
NIGHTWYND

Value: Cover or less

- ❑1, b&w ... 2.50
- ❑2, b&w ... 2.50
- ❑3, b&w ... 2.50
- ❑4, b&w ... 2.50

SAMUREE (1ST SERIES)
CONTINUITY

Value: Cover or less

- ❑1, May 87 ... 2.00
- ❑2, Aug 87 ... 2.00
- ❑3, May 88 ... 2.00
- ❑4, Jan 89 ... 2.00
- ❑5, Apr 89 ... 2.00
- ❑6, Aug 89 ... 2.00
- ❑7, Feb 90 ... 2.00
- ❑8, Nov 90 ... 2.00
- ❑9, Jan 91 ... 2.00

SAMUREE (2ND SERIES)
CONTINUITY

Value: Cover or less

- ❑1, May 93, NA (w), Rise of Magic ... 2.50
- ❑2, Sep 93, NA (w), Rise of Magic ... 2.50
- ❑3, Dec 93 ... 2.50
- ❑4, Jan 94 ... 2.50

SAMUREE (3RD SERIES)
ACCLAIM

Value: Cover or less

- ❑1, Oct 95 ... 2.50
- ❑2, Nov 95 ... 2.50

SANCTUARY PART 1
VIZ

	ORIG	GOOD	FINE	N-MINT
❑1, b&w	4.95	1.20	3.00	6.00
❑2, b&w	4.95	1.00	2.50	5.00
❑3	4.95	1.00	2.50	5.00
❑4	4.95	1.00	2.50	5.00
❑5	4.95	1.00	2.50	5.00
❑6	4.95	1.00	2.50	5.00
❑7	4.95	1.00	2.50	5.00
❑8	4.95	1.00	2.50	5.00
❑9	4.95	1.00	2.50	5.00

SANCTUARY PART 2
VIZ

Value: Cover or less

- ❑1 ... 4.95
- ❑2 ... 4.95
- ❑3 ... 4.95
- ❑4 ... 4.95
- ❑5, Yakuza ... 4.95
- ❑6 ... 4.95
- ❑7 ... 4.95
- ❑8 ... 4.95
- ❑9 ... 4.95

SANCTUARY PART 3
VIZ

Value: Cover or less

- ❑1, Oath Of Brotherhood, b&w ... 3.25
- ❑2, Strategy; Reorganization, b&w ... 3.25
- ❑3, b&w ... 3.25
- ❑4, b&w ... 3.25
- ❑5, b&w ... 3.25
- ❑6, b&w ... 3.25
- ❑7, b&w ... 3.25
- ❑8, b&w ... 3.25

SANCTUARY PART 4
VIZ

Value: Cover or less

- ❑1, Offense and Defense; Ruthless Pursuit ... 3.25
- ❑2 ... 3.25
- ❑3 ... 3.25
- ❑4 ... 3.25
- ❑5 ... 3.25
- ❑6 ... 3.50
- ❑7 ... 3.50

SANCTUARY PART 5
VIZ

	ORIG	GOOD	FINE	N-MINT
❑1	3.50	0.70	1.75	3.50
❑2	3.50	0.70	1.75	3.50
❑3	3.50	0.70	1.75	3.50
❑4	3.50	0.70	1.75	3.50
❑5	3.50	0.70	1.75	3.50
❑6	3.50	0.70	1.75	3.50
❑7	3.50	0.70	1.75	3.50
❑8	3.50	0.70	1.75	3.50
❑9	3.50	0.70	1.75	3.50
❑10	3.50	0.70	1.75	3.50
❑11	3.50	0.70	1.75	3.50
❑12	2.95	0.70	1.75	3.50
❑13	2.95	0.70	1.75	3.50

SANCTUM
BLACKSHOE

Value: Cover or less

- ❑1/LE, Limited edition from 1999 San Diego Comic-Con ... 3.95

SAN DIEGO COMIC-CON COMICS
DARK HORSE

	ORIG	GOOD	FINE	N-MINT
❑1, con giveaway	2.95	0.65	1.63	3.25
❑2, Aug 93, MW, Danger Unlimited; Concrete: Steel Rain, 1: Danger Unlimited, con giveaway; 1993 Comic-Con	2.95	0.59	1.48	2.95
❑3, Aug 94, con giveaway; 1994 Comic-Con	2.50	0.50	1.25	2.50
❑4, Aug 95, FM (w), The Mask in San Diego; Foot Soldiers, 1995 Comic-Con	2.50	0.50	1.25	2.50

SANDMADAM
SPOOF

Value: Cover or less ❑1, b&w 2.95

SANDMAN
DC

	ORIG	GOOD	FINE	N-MINT
❑1, Jan 89, NG (w), 1: Sandman III (Morpheus), Giant-size	2.00	4.40	11.00	22.00
❑2, Feb 89, NG (w), A: Cain; A: Abel	1.50	1.40	3.50	7.00
❑3, Mar 89, NG (w), A: John Constantine	1.50	1.20	3.00	6.00
❑4, Apr 89, NG (w), A: Demon	1.50	0.90	2.25	4.50
❑5, May 89, NG (w)	1.50	0.90	2.25	4.50
❑6, Jun 89, NG (w)	1.50	0.80	2.00	4.00
❑7, Jul 89, NG (w)	1.50	0.80	2.00	4.00
❑8, Aug 89, NG (w), The Sound of her Wings, 1: Death (Sandman), Regular edition, no indicia in inside front cover	1.50	2.00	5.00	10.00
❑8/LE, NG (w), The Sound of her Wings, 1: Death (Sandman), Has indicia in inside front cover, editorial by Karen Berger; limited edition; 1000 copies	1.50	8.00	20.00	40.00
❑9, Sep 89, NG (w)	1.50	0.80	2.00	4.00
❑10, Nov 89, NG (w), A Doll's House, Part 1	1.50	0.80	2.00	4.00
❑11, Dec 89, NG (w), A Doll's House, Part 2	1.50	0.80	2.00	4.00
❑12, Jan 90, NG (w), A Doll's House, Part 3	1.50	0.80	2.00	4.00
❑13, Feb 90, NG (w), A Doll's House, Part 4	1.50	0.80	2.00	4.00
❑14, Mar 90, NG (w), A Doll's House, Part 5	1.50	0.80	2.00	4.00
❑15, Apr 90, NG (w), A Doll's House, Part 6	1.50	0.60	1.50	3.00
❑16, Jun 90, NG (w), A Doll's House, Part 7	1.50	0.60	1.50	3.00
❑17, Jul 90, NG (w), Dream Country; Calliope	1.50	0.60	1.50	3.00
❑18, Aug 90, NG (w), Dream Country; Dream of 1000 Cats	1.50	0.60	1.50	3.00
❑19, Sep 90, CV, NG (w), Dream Country, properly printed; Midsummer Night's Dream	1.50	0.60	1.50	3.00
❑19/A, Sep 90, CV, NG (w), Dream Country, pages out of order; Midsummer Night's Dream	1.50	0.60	1.50	3.00
❑20, Oct 90, NG (w), Dream Country; Facade, D: Element Girl	1.50	0.60	1.50	3.00
❑21, Nov 90, NG (w), Season of Mists prelude	1.50	0.60	1.50	3.00
❑22, Jan 91, NG (w), Season of Mists, Part 1, 1: Daniel (new Sandman)	1.50	0.80	2.00	4.00
❑23, Feb 91, NG (w), Season of Mists, Part 2	1.50	0.50	1.25	2.50
❑24, Mar 91, NG (w), Season of Mists, Part 3	1.50	0.50	1.25	2.50
❑25, Apr 91, NG (w), Season of Mists, Part 4	1.50	0.50	1.25	2.50
❑26, May 91, NG (w), Season of Mists, Part 5	1.50	0.50	1.25	2.50
❑27, Jun 91, NG (w), Season of Mists, Part 6	1.50	0.50	1.25	2.50
❑28, Jul 91, NG (w), Season of Mists, Part 7	1.50	0.50	1.25	2.50
❑29, Aug 91, NG (w), Distant Mirrors	1.50	0.50	1.25	2.50
❑30, Sep 91, NG (w), Distant Mirrors	1.50	0.50	1.25	2.50
❑31, Oct 91, NG (w), Distant Mirrors	1.50	0.50	1.25	2.50
❑32, Nov 91, NG (w), A Game of You, Part 1	1.50	0.50	1.25	2.50
❑33, Dec 91, NG (w), A Game of You, Part 2	1.50	0.50	1.25	2.50
❑34, Jan 92, NG (w), A Game of You, Part 3	1.50	0.50	1.25	2.50
❑35, Feb 92, NG (w), A Game of You, Part 4	1.50	0.50	1.25	2.50
❑36, Apr 92, NG (w), A Game of You, Part 5, Giant-size	1.50	0.60	1.50	3.00
❑37, May 92, NG (w), A Game of You, Part 6	1.50	0.50	1.25	2.50
❑38, Jun 92, NG (w), Convergence	1.50	0.50	1.25	2.50
❑39, Jul 92, NG (w), Convergence	1.50	0.50	1.25	2.50
❑40, Aug 92, NG (w), Convergence	1.50	0.50	1.25	2.50
❑41, Sep 92, NG (w), Brief Lives, Part 1	1.50	0.50	1.25	2.50
❑42, Oct 92, NG (w), Brief Lives, Part 2	1.50	0.50	1.25	2.50
❑43, Nov 92, NG (w), Brief Lives, Part 3	1.50	0.50	1.25	2.50
❑44, Dec 92, NG (w), Brief Lives, Part 4	1.50	0.50	1.25	2.50
❑45, Jan 93, NG (w), Brief Lives, Part 5	1.75	0.50	1.25	2.50
❑46, Feb 93, NG (w), Brief Lives, Part 6, AIDS informational insert; Brief Lives	1.75	0.50	1.25	2.50
❑47, Mar 93, NG (w), Brief Lives, Part 7	1.75	0.50	1.25	2.50
❑48, Apr 93, NG (w), Brief Lives, Part 8	1.75	0.50	1.25	2.50
❑49, May 93, NG (w), Brief Lives, Part 9	1.75	0.50	1.25	2.50
❑50, Jun 93, CR, NG (w), Distant Mirrors; Ramadan, Double-size; Bronze ink	2.95	0.90	2.25	4.50
❑50/GO, Jun 93, CR, NG (w), Distant Mirrors; Ramadan, Gold edition	—	4.00	10.00	20.00
❑51, Jul 93, DG; BT, NG (w), World's End	1.95	0.50	1.25	2.50
❑52, Aug 93, BT, NG (w), World's End	1.95	0.50	1.25	2.50
❑53, Sep 93, BT, NG (w), World's End	1.95	0.50	1.25	2.50
❑54, Oct 93, BT, NG (w), World's End; The Golden Boy, O: Prez Rickard	1.95	0.50	1.25	2.50
❑55, Nov 93, NG (w), World's End	1.95	0.50	1.25	2.50
❑56, Dec 93, BT, NG (w), World's End	1.95	0.50	1.25	2.50
❑57, Feb 94, NG (w), The Kindly Ones, Part 1, preview of American Freak: A Tale of the Un-Men	1.95	0.50	1.25	2.50
❑58, Mar 94, NG (w), The Kindly Ones, Part 2	1.95	0.50	1.25	2.50
❑59, Apr 94, NG (w), The Kindly Ones, Part 3	1.95	0.50	1.25	2.50
❑60, Jun 94, NG (w), The Kindly Ones, Part 4	1.95	0.50	1.25	2.50
❑61, Jul 94, NG (w), The Kindly Ones, Part 5	1.95	0.50	1.25	2.50

MARTIN • BYRNE • MILLER • DARROW • CHADWICK • ADAMS
GEARY • GIBBONS • MIGNOLA • WAGNER • ALLRED • O'BARR

For several years, Dark Horse produced a giveaway comic book for the San Diego Comic-Con.

© 1993 Dark Horse

	ORIG	GOOD	FINE	N-MINT
❑62, Aug 94, NG (w), The Kindly Ones, Part 6	1.95	0.50	1.25	2.50
❑63, Sep 94, NG (w), The Kindly Ones, Part 7	1.95	0.50	1.25	2.50
❑64, Nov 94, NG (w), The Kindly Ones, Part 8	1.95	0.50	1.25	2.50
❑65, Dec 94, NG (w), The Kindly Ones, Part 9	1.95	0.50	1.25	2.50
❑66, Jan 95, NG (w), The Kindly Ones, Part 10	1.95	0.50	1.25	2.50
❑67, Mar 95, NG (w), The Kindly Ones, Part 11	1.95	0.50	1.25	2.50
❑68, May 95, NG (w), The Kindly Ones, Part 12	1.95	0.50	1.25	2.50
❑69, Jul 95, NG (w), The Kindly Ones, Part 13, D: Sandman III (Morpheus)	2.50	0.60	1.50	3.00
❑70, Aug 95, NG (w), The Wake, Part 1	2.50	0.50	1.25	2.50
❑71, Sep 95, NG (w), The Wake, Part 2	2.50	0.50	1.25	2.50
❑72, Nov 95, NG (w), The Wake, Part 3, burial of Dream	2.50	0.50	1.25	2.50
❑73, Dec 95, NG (w), The Wake, Part 4, A: Hob Gadling	2.50	0.50	1.25	2.50
❑74, Jan 96, NG (w), Exiles	2.50	0.50	1.25	2.50
❑75, Mar 96, CV, NG (w), The Tempest, A: William Shakespeare, Final Issue; contains timeline	3.95	0.80	2.00	4.00
❑SE 1, BT, NG (w), The Song Of The Orpheus, Glow-in-the-dark cover; Orpheus special edition	3.50	1.00	2.50	5.00

SANDMAN, THE
DC

	ORIG	GOOD	FINE	N-MINT
❑1, Win 74	0.20	1.20	3.00	6.00
❑2, May 75, JK	0.25	0.80	2.00	4.00
❑3, Jul 75, JK	0.25	0.80	2.00	4.00
❑4, Sep 75, JK, Panic In The Dream Stream, A: Demon	0.25	0.80	2.00	4.00
❑5, Nov 75, JK	0.25	0.80	2.00	4.00
❑6, Jan 76, JK, Final Issue	0.25	0.80	2.00	4.00

SANDMAN, THE: A GALLERY OF DREAMS
DC

Value: Cover or less ❑1, nn 2.95

SANDMAN MIDNIGHT THEATRE
DC

Value: Cover or less ❑1, Sep 95, NG (w); MW (w), nn; prestige format; Morpheus meets Wesley Dodds 6.95

SANDMAN MYSTERY THEATRE
DC

	ORIG	GOOD	FINE	N-MINT
❑1, Apr 93, MW (w), The Tarantula, Part 1; Tarantula, Part 1	1.95	0.80	2.00	4.00
❑2, May 93, MW (w), The Tarantula, Part 2; Tarantula, Part 2	1.95	0.60	1.50	3.00
❑3, Jun 93, MW (w), The Tarantula, Part 3; Tarantula, Part 3	1.95	0.60	1.50	3.00
❑4, Jul 93, MW (w), The Tarantula, Part 4; Tarantula, Part 4	1.95	0.60	1.50	3.00
❑5, Aug 93, MW (w), The Face, Part 1	1.95	0.60	1.50	3.00
❑6, Sep 93, MW (w), The Face, Part 2	1.95	0.60	1.50	3.00
❑7, Oct 93, MW (w), The Face, Part 3	1.95	0.60	1.50	3.00
❑8, Nov 93, MW (w), The Face, Part 4	1.95	0.60	1.50	3.00
❑9, Dec 93, MW (w), The Brute, Part 1	1.95	0.60	1.50	3.00
❑10, Jan 94, MW (w), The Brute, Part 2	1.95	0.60	1.50	3.00
❑11, Feb 94, MW (w), The Brute, Part 3	1.95	0.55	1.38	2.75
❑12, Mar 94, MW (w), The Brute, Part 4	1.95	0.55	1.38	2.75
❑13, Apr 94, MW (w), The Vamp, Part 1	1.95	0.55	1.38	2.75
❑14, May 94, MW (w), The Vamp, Part 2	1.95	0.55	1.38	2.75
❑15, Jun 94, MW (w), The Vamp, Part 3	1.95	0.55	1.38	2.75
❑16, Jul 94, MW (w), The Vamp, Part 4	1.95	0.55	1.38	2.75
❑17, Aug 94, MW (w), The Scorpion, Part 1	1.95	0.55	1.38	2.75
❑18, Sep 94, MW (w), The Scorpion, Part 2	1.95	0.55	1.38	2.75
❑19, Oct 94, MW (w), The Scorpion, Part 3	1.95	0.55	1.38	2.75
❑20, Nov 94, MW (w), The Scorpion, Part 4	1.95	0.55	1.38	2.75
❑21, Dec 94, MW (w), Dr. Death, Part 1	1.95	0.50	1.25	2.50
❑22, Jan 95, MW (w), Dr. Death, Part 2	1.95	0.50	1.25	2.50
❑23, Feb 95, MW (w), Dr. Death, Part 3	1.95	0.50	1.25	2.50
❑24, Mar 95, MW (w), Dr. Death, Part 4	1.95	0.50	1.25	2.50
❑25, Apr 95, MW (w), Night of the Butcher, Part 1	1.95	0.50	1.25	2.50

	ORIG	GOOD	FINE	N-MINT
❑26, May 95, MW (w), Night of the Butcher, Part 2	2.25	0.50	1.25	2.50
❑27, Jun 95, MW (w), Night of the Butcher, Part 3	2.25	0.50	1.25	2.50
❑28, Jul 95, MW (w), Night of the Butcher, Part 4	2.25	0.50	1.25	2.50
❑29, Aug 95, MW (w), The Hourman, Part 1	2.25	0.50	1.25	2.50
❑30, Sep 95, MW (w), The Hourman, Part 2	2.25	0.50	1.25	2.50
❑31, Oct 95, MW (w), The Hourman, Part 3	2.25	0.50	1.25	2.50
❑32, Nov 95, MW (w), The Hourman, Part 4	2.25	0.50	1.25	2.50
❑33, Dec 95, MW (w), The Python, Part 1	2.25	0.50	1.25	2.50
❑34, Jan 96, MW (w), The Python, Part 2	2.25	0.50	1.25	2.50
❑35, Feb 96, MW (w), The Python, Part 3	2.25	0.50	1.25	2.50
❑36, Mar 96, MW (w), The Python, Part 4	2.25	0.50	1.25	2.50
❑37, Apr 96, MW (w), The Mist, Part 1	2.25	0.50	1.25	2.50
❑38, May 96, MW (w), The Mist, Part 2	2.25	0.50	1.25	2.50
❑39, Jun 96, MW (w), The Mist, Part 3	2.25	0.50	1.25	2.50
❑40, Jul 96, MW (w), The Mist, Part 4	2.25	0.50	1.25	2.50
❑41, Aug 96, MW (w), Phantom of the Fair, Part 1; The Phantom of the Fair, Part 1	2.25	0.50	1.25	2.50
❑42, Sep 96, MW (w), Phantom of the Fair, Part 2; The Phantom of the Fair, Part 2	2.25	0.50	1.25	2.50
❑43, Oct 96, MW (w), Phantom of the Fair, Part 3; The Phantom of the Fair, Part 3, A: Crimson Avenger	2.25	0.50	1.25	2.50
❑44, Nov 96, MW (w), Phantom of the Fair, Part 4; The Phantom of the Fair, Part 4	2.50	0.50	1.25	2.50
❑45, Dec 96, MW (w), The Blackhawk, Part 1, A: Blackhawk, Photo cover	2.50	0.50	1.25	2.50
❑46, Jan 97, MW (w), The Blackhawk, Part 2	2.50	0.50	1.25	2.50
❑47, Feb 97, MW (w), The Blackhawk, Part 3	2.50	0.50	1.25	2.50
❑48, Mar 97, MW (w), The Blackhawk, Part 4, Photo cover	2.50	0.50	1.25	2.50
❑49, Apr 97, MW (w), Return of the Scarlet Ghost, Part 1	2.50	0.50	1.25	2.50
❑50, May 97, MW (w), Return of the Scarlet Ghost, Part 2, Giant-size	2.50	0.70	1.75	3.50
❑51, Jun 97, MW (w), Return of the Scarlet Ghost, Part 3	2.50	0.50	1.25	2.50
❑52, Jul 97, MW (w), Return of the Scarlet Ghost, Part 4	2.50	0.50	1.25	2.50
❑53, Aug 97, MW (w), The Crone, Part 1	2.50	0.50	1.25	2.50
❑54, Sep 97, MW (w), The Crone, Part 2	2.50	0.50	1.25	2.50
❑55, Oct 97, MW (w), The Crone, Part 3	2.50	0.50	1.25	2.50
❑56, Nov 97, MW (w), The Crone, Part 4	2.50	0.50	1.25	2.50
❑57, Dec 97, MW (w), The Cannon, Part 1	2.50	0.50	1.25	2.50
❑58, Jan 98, MW (w), The Cannon, Part 2	2.50	0.50	1.25	2.50
❑59, Feb 98, MW (w), The Cannon, Part 3	2.50	0.50	1.25	2.50
❑60, Mar 98, MW (w), The Cannon, Part 4	2.50	0.50	1.25	2.50
❑61, Apr 98, The City, Part 1	2.50	0.50	1.25	2.50
❑62, May 98, The City, Part 2	2.50	0.50	1.25	2.50
❑63, Jul 98, The City, Part 3	2.50	0.50	1.25	2.50
❑64, Aug 98, The City, Part 4	2.50	0.50	1.25	2.50
❑65, Sep 98, The Goblin, Part 1	2.50	0.50	1.25	2.50
❑66, Oct 98, The Goblin, Part 2	2.50	0.50	1.25	2.50
❑67, Nov 98, The Goblin, Part 3	2.50	0.50	1.25	2.50
❑68, Dec 98, The Goblin, Part 4	2.50	0.50	1.25	2.50
❑69, Jan 99, The Hero; The Hero, Part 1	2.50	0.50	1.25	2.50
❑70, Feb 99, The Hero; The Hero, Part 2, Final Issue	2.50	0.50	1.25	2.50
❑Anl 1, MW (w)	3.95	0.80	2.00	4.00

SANDMAN PRESENTS, THE: LOVE STREET
DC

Value: Cover or less

❑1, Jul 99, John Constantine in the '60s 2.95

❑2, Aug 99 .... 2.95

❑3, Sep 99 .... 2.95

SANDMAN PRESENTS: LUCIFER
DC

Value: Cover or less

❑1, Mar 99, The Morningstar Option, Part 1 .... 2.95

❑2, Apr 99, The Morningstar Option, Part 2 .... 2.95

❑3, May 99, The Morningstar Option, Part 3 .... 2.95

SANDMAN PRESENTS: PETREFAX
VERTIGO

Value: Cover or less

❑1, Mar 00, Travels in Malegrise, Part 1 .... 2.95

❑2, Apr 00, Travels in Malegrise, Part 2 .... 2.95

❑3, May 00, Travels in Malegrise, Part 3 .... 2.95

❑4, Jun 00, Travels in Malegrise, Part 4 .... 2.95

SANDS, THE
BLACK EYE

Value: Cover or less

❑1, b&w; smaller than a normal comic book 2.50

❑2, b&w; smaller than a normal comic book 2.50

❑3, Feb 97, b&w; smaller than a normal comic book 2.50

SAN FRANCISCO COMIC BOOK, THE
SAN FRANCISCO COMIC BOOK CO.

	ORIG	GOOD	FINE	N-MINT
❑1	0.50	1.00	2.50	5.00
❑2, The Adventures o	0.50	0.60	1.50	3.00
❑3, Sacred Goose Thrills; Surreal Comics	0.50	0.60	1.50	3.00

	ORIG	GOOD	FINE	N-MINT
❑4	—	0.60	1.50	3.00
❑5	—	0.60	1.50	3.00
❑6	—	0.60	1.50	3.00
❑7	—	0.60	1.50	3.00

SANTA CLAUS ADVENTURES (WALT KELLY'S...)
INNOVATION

Value: Cover or less

❑1, WK, nn; Reprint 6.95

SANTA CLAWS (ETERNITY)
ETERNITY

Value: Cover or less

❑1, b&w 2.95

SANTA CLAWS (THORBY)
THORBY

Value: Cover or less

❑1 .... 2.95

SANTANA
MALIBU

	ORIG	GOOD	FINE	N-MINT
❑1, May 94, TY, The Story of Santana; The Guitars of Santana, magazine	3.95	1.00	2.50	5.00

SANTA THE BARBARIAN
MAXIMUM

Value: Cover or less

❑1, The Big Red Slay; The Night Before X-Mas 2.99

SAPPHIRE
AIRCEL

	ORIG	GOOD	FINE	N-MINT
❑1, Feb 90, adult	2.50	0.59	1.48	2.95
❑2, Mar 90, adult	2.50	0.59	1.48	2.95
❑3, Apr 90, adult	2.50	0.50	1.25	2.50
❑4, May 90, adult	2.50	0.50	1.25	2.50
❑5, Jun 90, adult	2.50	0.50	1.25	2.50
❑6, Jul 90, adult	2.50	0.50	1.25	2.50
❑7, Aug 90, adult	2.50	0.50	1.25	2.50
❑8, adult	2.50	0.50	1.25	2.50
❑9, Sep 90, adult	2.50	0.50	1.25	2.50

SAP TUNES
FANTAGRAPHICS

Value: Cover or less

❑1, b&w 2.50

❑2, b&w 2.50

SARAH-JANE HAMILTON PRESENTS SUPERSTARS OF EROTICA
RE-VISIONARY

Value: Cover or less

❑1, Savannah: Piercing the Veil 2.95

SARGE STEEL
CHARLTON

	ORIG	GOOD	FINE	N-MINT
❑1, Dec 64	0.12	3.00	7.50	15.00
❑2, Feb 65	0.12	2.00	5.00	10.00
❑3, May 65	0.12	1.60	4.00	8.00
❑4, Jul 65	0.12	1.60	4.00	8.00
❑5, Sep 65	0.12	1.60	4.00	8.00
❑6, Nov 65	0.12	1.20	3.00	6.00
❑7, Apr 66	0.12	1.20	3.00	6.00
❑8, Oct 66	0.12	1.20	3.00	6.00
❑9, becomes Secret Agent	0.12	1.20	3.00	6.00

SATANIKA
VEROTIK

	ORIG	GOOD	FINE	N-MINT
❑0	2.95	0.80	2.00	4.00
❑1, Jan 95	2.95	1.00	2.50	5.00
❑2	2.95	0.80	2.00	4.00
❑3	2.95	0.80	2.00	4.00
❑4	2.95	0.60	1.50	3.00
❑5, Oct 96	2.95	0.60	1.50	3.00
❑6, Jan 97	2.95	0.59	1.48	2.95
❑7, Apr 97	2.95	0.59	1.48	2.95
❑8	2.95	0.59	1.48	2.95
❑9, Mar 98	2.95	0.59	1.48	2.95
❑10	—	0.59	1.48	2.95
❑11	3.95	0.79	1.98	3.95

SATANIKA ILLUSTRATIONS, THE
VEROTIK

Value: Cover or less

❑1, Sep 96, adult; cardstock cover; pin-ups 3.95

SATAN PLACE
THUNDERHILL

Value: Cover or less

❑1, Disposable Love; Say Goodnight, Sophie 3.50

SATAN'S SIX
TOPPS

Value: Cover or less

❑1, Apr 93, FM; JK, JK (c); TMc (c), JK (w), 1: Satan's Six, trading card; Wolff and Byrd, Counselors of the Macabre backup story 2.95

❑2, Idol hands, trading cards 2.95

❑3, trading cards 2.95

❑4, KB (w), trading cards 2.95

SATAN'S SIX: HELLSPAWN
TOPPS

Value: Cover or less

❑1, A Hell of a Town, Inside index lists it as issue #2 .... 2.50

❑2, Jun 94 .... 2.50

❑3, Jul 94 .... 2.50

SATURDAY MORNING: THE COMIC
MARVEL

Value: Cover or less

❑1, Apr 96, A: Liz Phair, Matthew Sweet, Ramones, Collective Soul 1.95

SATURDAY NITE
ANSON JEW

Value: Cover or less

❑1, The Samaritan; Youth, b&w 2.95

SAUCY LITTLE TART
EROS

Value: Cover or less

❑1, Dec 95 .... 2.95

SAVAGE COMBAT TALES
ATLAS

	ORIG	GOOD	FINE	N-MINT
❑1, Feb 75, Reborn In Battle; Bounty, O: Sgt. Stryker's Death Squad	0.25	0.40	1.00	2.00
❑2, Apr 75	0.25	0.30	0.75	1.50
❑3, Jul 75	0.25	0.30	0.75	1.50

SAVAGE DRAGON, THE
IMAGE

	ORIG	GOOD	FINE	N-MINT
❑0.5, EL, EL (w)	—	0.60	1.50	3.00
❑0.5/Pl, EL, EL (w)	—	0.80	2.00	4.00
❑1, Jun 93, EL, EL (w)	1.95	0.60	1.50	3.00
❑2, Jul 93, EL, EL (w), A: Teenage Mutant Ninja Turtles, Flip book with Vanguard #0	2.95	0.60	1.50	3.00
❑3, Aug 93, EL, EL (w), Mighty Man back-up feature	1.95	0.50	1.25	2.50
❑4, Sep 93, EL, EL (w)	1.95	0.45	1.13	2.25
❑5, Oct 93, EL, EL (w)	1.95	0.45	1.13	2.25
❑6, Nov 93, EL, EL (w)	1.95	0.45	1.13	2.25
❑7, Jan 94, EL, EL (w)	1.95	0.45	1.13	2.25
❑8, Mar 94, EL, EL (w)	1.95	0.40	1.00	2.00
❑9, Apr 94, EL, EL (w)	1.95	0.40	1.00	2.00
❑10, May 94, EL, EL (w), alternate cover; newsstand version	1.95	0.40	1.00	2.00
❑10/DM, May 94, EL, EL (w)	1.95	0.40	1.00	2.00
❑11, Jul 94, EL, EL (w)	1.95	0.40	1.00	2.00
❑12, Aug 94, EL, EL (w), She Dragon	1.95	0.40	1.00	2.00
❑13, EL, EL (w), 1: Condition Red	2.50	0.50	1.25	2.50
❑13/A, Jun 95, EL; JLee, JLee(w), Image X month version	1.95	0.50	1.25	2.50
❑14, Oct 94, EL, EL (w)	1.95	0.39	0.98	1.95
❑15, Dec 94, EL, EL (w)	2.50	0.50	1.25	2.50
❑16, Jan 95, EL, EL (w), Savage Dragon on cover	2.50	0.50	1.25	2.50
❑17/A, Feb 95, EL, EL (w), Two women on cover; two different interior pages; nudity	2.50	0.50	1.25	2.50
❑18, Mar 95, EL, EL (w)	2.50	0.50	1.25	2.50
❑19, Apr 95, EL, EL (w)	2.50	0.50	1.25	2.50
❑20, Jul 95, EL, EL (w)	2.50	0.50	1.25	2.50
❑21, Aug 95, EL, EL (w)	2.50	0.50	1.25	2.50
❑22, Sep 95, EL, EL (w), A: Teenage Mutant Ninja Turtles	2.50	0.50	1.25	2.50
❑23, Oct 95, EL, EL (w)	2.50	0.50	1.25	2.50
❑24, Dec 95, EL, EL (w)	2.50	0.50	1.25	2.50
❑25, Jan 96, EL, EL (w), double-sized	3.95	0.79	1.98	3.95
❑25/A, Jan 96, EL, EL (w), alternate cover; double-sized	3.95	0.79	1.98	3.95
❑26, Mar 96, EL, EL (w)	2.50	0.50	1.25	2.50
❑27, Apr 96, EL, EL (w)	2.50	0.50	1.25	2.50
❑27/A, Apr 96, EL, EL (w), alternate cover only available at WonderCon	2.50	0.50	1.25	2.50
❑28, May 96, EL, EL (w), A: Maxx	2.50	0.50	1.25	2.50
❑29, Jul 96, EL, EL (w), A: Wildstar	2.50	0.50	1.25	2.50
❑30, Aug 96, EL, EL (w), A: Spawn	2.50	0.50	1.25	2.50
❑31, Sep 96, EL, EL (w), censored version says God is good inside Image logo on cover; God vs. The Devil	2.50	0.50	1.25	2.50
❑31/A, Sep 96, EL, EL (w), God vs. The Devil; uncensored version	2.50	0.50	1.25	2.50
❑32, Oct 96, EL, EL (w)	2.50	0.50	1.25	2.50
❑33, Nov 96, EL, EL (w), Birth of Dragon's son	2.50	0.50	1.25	2.50
❑34, Dec 96, A: Hellboy	2.50	0.50	1.25	2.50
❑35, Feb 97, EL, EL (w), A: Hellboy	2.50	0.50	1.25	2.50
❑36, Mar 97, EL, EL (w), 1: Zeek	2.50	0.50	1.25	2.50
❑37, Apr 97, EL, EL (w)	2.50	0.50	1.25	2.50
❑38, May 97, EL, EL (w)	2.50	0.50	1.25	2.50
❑39, Jun 97, EL, EL (w)	2.50	0.50	1.25	2.50
❑40, Jul 97, EL, EL (w)	2.50	0.50	1.25	2.50
❑40/A, Jul 97, EL, EL (w)	2.50	0.50	1.25	2.50
❑41, Sep 97, EL, EL (w), A: DNAgents; A: Hellboy; A: Vampirella; A: Madman; A: Megaton; A: Zot; A: E-Man; A: Femforce; A: Monkeyman; A: Wildstar	2.50	0.50	1.25	2.50
❑42, Oct 97, EL, EL (w)	2.50	0.50	1.25	2.50
❑43, Nov 97, EL, EL (w)	2.50	0.50	1.25	2.50
❑44, Dec 97, EL, EL (w)	2.50	0.50	1.25	2.50
❑45, Jan 98, EL, EL (w)	2.50	0.50	1.25	2.50
❑46, Feb 98, EL, EL (w)	2.50	0.50	1.25	2.50

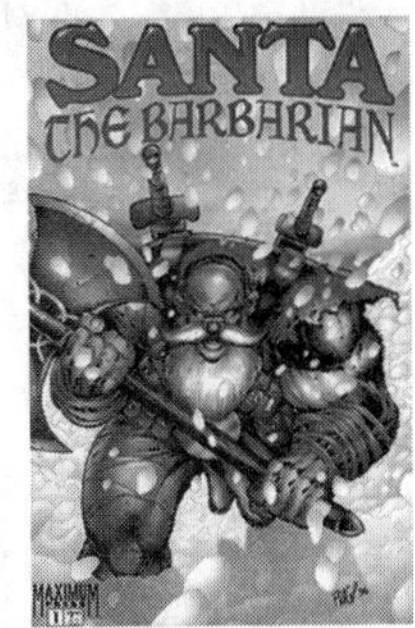

The jolly old elf got a new attitude in Maximum's *Santa the Barbarian*.

	ORIG	GOOD	FINE	N-MINT
❑47, Mar 98, EL, EL (w)	2.50	0.50	1.25	2.50
❑48, Apr 98, EL, EL (w)	2.50	0.50	1.25	2.50
❑49, May 98, EL, EL (w)	2.50	0.50	1.25	2.50
❑50, Jun 98, JPH (w), Mighty Man: Critter Crime Wave; Mighty Man: Wicked Worm's Circus of Evil, 100pgs.	5.95	1.19	2.97	5.95
❑51/A, Jul 98, EL, EL (w), red logo	2.50	0.50	1.25	2.50
❑51/B, Jul 98, EL, EL (w), yellow logo	2.50	0.50	1.25	2.50
❑52, Aug 98, EL, EL (w)	2.50	0.50	1.25	2.50
❑53, Sep 98, EL, EL (w)	2.50	0.50	1.25	2.50
❑54, Oct 98, EL, EL (w)	2.50	0.50	1.25	2.50
❑55, Nov 98, EL, EL (w)	2.50	0.50	1.25	2.50
❑56, Dec 98, EL, EL (w)	2.50	0.50	1.25	2.50
❑57, Jan 99, EL, EL (w)	2.50	0.50	1.25	2.50
❑58, Feb 99, EL, EL (w)	2.50	0.50	1.25	2.50
❑59, Mar 99, EL, EL (w)	2.50	0.50	1.25	2.50
❑60, Apr 99, EL, EL (w)	2.50	0.50	1.25	2.50
❑61, May 99, EL, EL (w)	2.50	0.50	1.25	2.50
❑62, Jun 99, EL, EL (w)	2.50	0.50	1.25	2.50
❑63, Jun 99, EL, EL (w)	2.50	0.50	1.25	2.50
❑64, Jul 99, EL, EL (w)	2.50	0.50	1.25	2.50
❑65, Aug 99, EL, EL (w)	2.50	0.50	1.25	2.50
❑66, Aug 99, EL, EL (w)	2.50	0.50	1.25	2.50
❑67, Sep 99, EL, EL (w)	2.50	0.50	1.25	2.50
❑68, Oct 99, EL, EL (w)	2.50	0.50	1.25	2.50
❑69, Nov 99, EL, EL (w)	2.50	0.50	1.25	2.50
❑70, Dec 99, EL, EL (w)	2.50	0.50	1.25	2.50
❑71, Jan 00, EL, EL (w)	2.50	0.50	1.25	2.50
❑72, Feb 00, EL, EL (w)	—	0.50	1.25	2.50
❑73, Mar 00, EL, EL (w)	—	0.50	1.25	2.50
❑74, Apr 00, EL, EL (w)	—	0.50	1.25	2.50
❑75, May 00, EL, EL (w), Giant-size	5.95	1.19	2.97	5.95
❑76, Jun 00, EL, EL (w), This Savage World!	2.95	0.59	1.48	2.95
❑77, Jul 00, EL, EL (w), Something Wild!!	2.95	0.59	1.48	2.95
❑78, Aug 00, EL, EL (w), Mind-Slaves of the Brainchild!	2.95	0.59	1.48	2.95
❑79, Sep 00, EL, EL (w), The Attack of the 60-Foot Woman!	2.95	0.59	1.48	2.95
❑80, Oct 00, EL, EL (w), The Lurkers Beneath Lake Fear!	2.95	0.59	1.48	2.95
❑81, Nov 00, EL, EL (w), The Land Down Under	2.95	0.59	1.48	2.95
❑82, Dec 00, EL, EL (w), The Bug Riders!	2.95	0.59	1.48	2.95
❑83, Jan 01, EL, EL (w), The Arena of Death!, A: Madman	2.95	0.59	1.48	2.95
❑84, Feb 01, EL, EL (w), Breakout from Command "D"	2.95	0.59	1.48	2.95
❑85, EL, EL (w)	2.95	0.59	1.48	2.95
❑86, EL, EL (w)	2.95	0.59	1.48	2.95
❑87, EL, EL (w)	2.95	0.59	1.48	2.95
❑88, EL, EL (w)	2.95	0.59	1.48	2.95

SAVAGE DRAGON, THE (MINI-SERIES)
IMAGE

Value: Cover or less

❑1, Jul 92, EL, EL (w), Baptism of Fire, A: Spawn; 1: Savage Dragon; 1: SuperPatriot, four cover logo variants (bottom of logo is white, blue, green, or yellow); poster by Larsen 1.95

❑2, Oct 92, EL, EL (w), Born Again Patriot, Centerfold Savage Dragon poster 1.95

❑3, Dec 92, EL, EL (w), Rock This Town, coupon for Image Comics #0; Centerfold Savage Dragon poster 1.95

SAVAGE DRAGON ARCHIVES
IMAGE

Value: Cover or less

❑1, Sep 98, EL, EL (w) 2.95

❑2, Oct 98, EL, EL (w), Possessed, 2: Savage Dragon, Reprints Graphic Fantasy #2 .... 2.95

❑3, Dec 98, EL, EL (w), Dead Line; To Battle the Dragon 2.95

❑4, Jan 99, EL, EL (w), Dungeons & Dragons; The Dragon in Angel Fueled Quake 2.95

SAVAGE DRAGON/DESTROYER DUCK, THE
IMAGE

Value: Cover or less

❑1, Nov 96, A: Teenage Mutant Ninja Turtles 3.95

SAVAGE DRAGON/MARSHAL LAW, THE
IMAGE

Value: Cover or less

❑1, Jul 97, b&w; indicia says Savage Dragon/Marshall Law 2.95

❑2, Aug 97, b&w 2.95

SAVAGE DRAGON: RED HORIZON
IMAGE

Value: Cover or less

❑1, Feb 97 ... 2.50
❑2, Apr 97 ... 2.50
❑3, May 97 ... 2.50

SAVAGE DRAGON: SEX & VIOLENCE
IMAGE

Value: Cover or less

❑1, Aug 97, EL (w) ... 2.50
❑2, Sep 97, EL (w) ... 2.50

SAVAGE DRAGON/TEENAGE MUTANT NINJA TURTLES CROSSOVER
MIRAGE

Value: Cover or less

❑1, Sep 93, EL (w), Enter the Savage Dragon! ... 2.75

SAVAGE DRAGON VS. THE SAVAGE MEGATON MAN, THE
IMAGE

	ORIG	GOOD	FINE	N-MINT
❑1, Mar 93, Savage Brawl	1.95	0.40	1.00	2.00
❑1/GO, Mar 93, EL, Gold foil cover	1.95	0.60	1.50	3.00

SAVAGE FISTS OF KUNG FU
MARVEL

	ORIG	GOOD	FINE	N-MINT
❑1, The Master Plan of Fu Manchu; The Sons of the Tiger!, O: The Sons of the Dragon.	1.50	1.60	4.00	8.00

SAVAGE FUNNIES
VISION

Value: Cover or less

❑1, Jul 96 ... 1.95
❑2, Jul 96 ... 1.95

SAVAGE HENRY
VORTEX

	ORIG	GOOD	FINE	N-MINT
❑1, Jan 87	1.75	0.40	1.00	2.00
❑2, Going Interactive	1.75	0.40	1.00	2.00
❑3	1.75	0.40	1.00	2.00
❑4	1.75	0.40	1.00	2.00
❑5	1.75	0.40	1.00	2.00
❑6	1.75	0.40	1.00	2.00
❑7, Sep 88, b&w	1.75	0.40	1.00	2.00
❑8	1.75	0.40	1.00	2.00
❑9	1.75	0.40	1.00	2.00
❑10	1.75	0.40	1.00	2.00
❑11	2.00	0.40	1.00	2.00
❑12	2.00	0.40	1.00	2.00
❑13, Last Vortex issue	2.00	0.40	1.00	2.00
❑14, Mar 91, b&w; Rip Off begins as publisher	2.00	0.50	1.25	2.50
❑15, May 91, b&w	2.00	0.50	1.25	2.50
❑16, Jul 91, b&w	2.50	0.50	1.25	2.50
❑17, Sep 91, b&w	2.50	0.50	1.25	2.50
❑18, Nov 91, b&w	2.50	0.50	1.25	2.50
❑19, Jan 92, b&w	2.50	0.50	1.25	2.50
❑20, Mar 92, b&w	2.50	0.50	1.25	2.50
❑21, May 92, b&w	2.50	0.50	1.25	2.50
❑22, Jul 92, b&w	2.50	0.50	1.25	2.50
❑23, Sep 92, b&w	2.50	0.50	1.25	2.50
❑24, Nov 92, b&w	2.50	0.50	1.25	2.50
❑25, Jan 93, b&w	2.50	0.50	1.25	2.50
❑26, Mar 93, b&w	2.50	0.50	1.25	2.50
❑27, May 93	2.50	0.50	1.25	2.50
❑28, Jul 93, b&w	2.50	0.50	1.25	2.50
❑29, Sep 93, b&w	2.50	0.50	1.25	2.50
❑30, Nov 93, b&w; Final Issue; 1993	2.50	0.50	1.25	2.50

SAVAGE HENRY (ICONOGRAFIX)
CALIBER

Value: Cover or less

❑1, b&w ... 2.95
❑2, A: Moby, b&w ... 2.95
❑3, b&w ... 2.95

SAVAGE HENRY: HEADSTRONG
CALIBER

Value: Cover or less

❑1, Headstand, A: Fraser Geesin; A: Ron Geesin, b&w ... 2.95
❑2, b&w ... 2.95
❑3, b&w ... 2.95

SAVAGE HULK, THE
MARVEL

Value: Cover or less

❑1, Jan 96, Courtroom Sequence; Old Friends, nn; prestige format ... 6.95

SAVAGE NINJA
CADILLAC

Value: Cover or less

❑1 ... 1.00

SAVAGE RETURN OF DRACULA, THE
MARVEL

Value: Cover or less

❑1, GC, Dracula; The Fear Within, Reprints Tomb of Dracula #1, 2 ... 2.00

SAVAGES
COMAX

Value: Cover or less

❑1, b&w ... 2.50

SAVAGE SHE-HULK, THE
MARVEL

	ORIG	GOOD	FINE	N-MINT
❑1, Feb 80, JB, SL (w), The She-Hulk Lives, 1: She-Hulk	0.40	0.80	2.00	4.00
❑2, Mar 80, Deathrace!, 1: Dan "Zapper" Ridge; 1: Morris Walters	0.40	0.60	1.50	3.00
❑3, Apr 80	0.40	0.50	1.25	2.50
❑4, May 80	0.40	0.50	1.25	2.50
❑5, Jun 80	0.40	0.50	1.25	2.50
❑6, Jul 80, A: Iron Man	0.40	0.40	1.00	2.00
❑7, Aug 80	0.40	0.40	1.00	2.00
❑8, Sep 80, A: Man-Thing	0.50	0.40	1.00	2.00
❑9, Oct 80	0.50	0.40	1.00	2.00
❑10, Nov 80	0.50	0.40	1.00	2.00
❑11, Dec 80	0.50	0.40	1.00	2.00
❑12, Jan 81, V: Gemini	0.50	0.40	1.00	2.00
❑13, Feb 81, Through The Crystal!, A: Man-Wolf	0.50	0.40	1.00	2.00
❑14, Mar 81, Life In The Bloodstream, A: Hellcat; A: Man-Wolf	0.50	0.40	1.00	2.00
❑15, Apr 81, Delusions	0.50	0.40	1.00	2.00
❑16, May 81, The Zapping Of The She-Hulk	0.50	0.40	1.00	2.00
❑17, Jun 81, V: Man-Elephant	0.50	0.40	1.00	2.00
❑18, Jul 81, V: Grappler	0.50	0.40	1.00	2.00
❑19, Aug 81	0.50	0.40	1.00	2.00
❑20, Sep 81	0.50	0.40	1.00	2.00
❑21, Oct 81	0.50	0.40	1.00	2.00
❑22, Nov 81, V: Radius	0.50	0.40	1.00	2.00
❑23, Dec 81	0.50	0.40	1.00	2.00
❑24, Jan 82	0.60	0.40	1.00	2.00
❑25, Feb 82, Transmutations, Final Issue; Giant-size	1.00	0.40	1.00	2.00

SAVAGE SWORD OF CONAN
MARVEL

	ORIG	GOOD	FINE	N-MINT
❑1, Aug 74, GK; NA; JB, GK (w), Curse of the Undead-Man; Red Sonja, O: Blackmark; O: Red Sonja, b&w	1.00	8.00	20.00	40.00
❑2, Oct 74	1.00	3.60	9.00	18.00
❑3, Dec 74	1.00	2.00	5.00	10.00
❑4, Feb 75	1.00	1.60	4.00	8.00
❑5, Apr 75	1.00	1.60	4.00	8.00
❑6, Jun 75	1.00	1.60	4.00	8.00
❑7, Aug 75	1.00	1.60	4.00	8.00
❑8, Oct 75	1.00	1.60	4.00	8.00
❑9, Dec 75	1.00	1.60	4.00	8.00
❑10, Feb 76	1.00	1.60	4.00	8.00
❑11, Apr 76	1.00	1.20	3.00	6.00
❑12, Jun 76	1.00	1.20	3.00	6.00
❑13, Aug 76	1.00	1.20	3.00	6.00
❑14, Sep 76, Shadows of Zamboula	1.00	1.20	3.00	6.00
❑15, Oct 76	1.00	1.20	3.00	6.00
❑16, Dec 76	1.00	1.20	3.00	6.00
❑17, Feb 77	1.00	1.20	3.00	6.00
❑18, Apr 77	1.00	1.20	3.00	6.00
❑19, Jun 77	1.00	1.20	3.00	6.00
❑20, Jul 77	1.00	1.20	3.00	6.00
❑21, Aug 77	1.00	1.00	2.50	5.00
❑22, Sep 77	1.00	1.00	2.50	5.00
❑23, Oct 77	1.00	1.00	2.50	5.00
❑24, Nov 77	1.00	1.00	2.50	5.00
❑25, Dec 77	1.00	1.00	2.50	5.00
❑26, Jan 78	1.00	1.00	2.50	5.00
❑27, Mar 78	1.00	1.00	2.50	5.00
❑28, Apr 78	1.00	1.00	2.50	5.00
❑29, May 78	1.00	1.00	2.50	5.00
❑30, Jun 78	1.00	0.80	2.00	4.00
❑31, Jul 78	1.00	0.80	2.00	4.00
❑32, Aug 78	1.00	0.80	2.00	4.00
❑33, Sep 78	1.00	0.80	2.00	4.00
❑34, Oct 78, 1: Garth	1.00	0.80	2.00	4.00
❑35, Nov 78	1.00	0.80	2.00	4.00
❑36, Dec 78	1.00	0.80	2.00	4.00
❑37, Feb 79	1.00	0.80	2.00	4.00
❑38, Mar 79, TD; JB, The Road of the Eagles; A Gazetteer of the Hyborian Age, Part 6	1.00	0.80	2.00	4.00
❑39, Apr 79	1.00	0.80	2.00	4.00
❑40, May 79	1.00	0.80	2.00	4.00
❑41, Jun 79, Conan the Buccaneer; The Ballad of BTlit	1.00	0.80	2.00	4.00
❑42, Jul 79, TD; JB, Conan the Buccaneer; A Gazetteer of the Hyborian Age, Part 9	1.00	0.80	2.00	4.00
❑43, Aug 79	1.00	0.80	2.00	4.00
❑44, Sep 79, TD; SB, The Star of Khorala; Hyborian Heraldry and Cartography	1.00	0.80	2.00	4.00
❑45, Oct 79	1.25	0.80	2.00	4.00
❑46, Nov 79, TD, Moon of Blood; The Savage Swordbooks of Conan	1.25	0.80	2.00	4.00

	ORIG	GOOD	FINE	N-MINT
❑47, Dec 79, GK; JB, The Treasure of Trancios; The Secret of the Black Stranger	1.25	0.80	2.00	4.00
❑48, Jan 80, TD; JB, Conan the Liberator, Part 1; Chains and Fetters, Part 2	1.25	0.80	2.00	4.00
❑49, Feb 80	1.25	0.80	2.00	4.00
❑50, Mar 80, TD; JB, Conan the Liberator, part 3; Conan at Fifty	1.25	0.80	2.00	4.00
❑51, Apr 80	1.25	0.60	1.50	3.00
❑52, May 80, Conan the Liberator, Part 5; The Chan Barbarians	1.25	0.60	1.50	3.00
❑53, Jun 80, Conan and the Sorcerer, Part 1; The Hyborian Reporter	1.25	0.60	1.50	3.00
❑54, Jul 80, Conan and the Sorcerer, Part 2; Satan's Swordbearers	1.25	0.60	1.50	3.00
❑55, Aug 80, Conan and the Sorcerer, Part 3; Havoc in Hyboria	1.25	0.60	1.50	3.00
❑56, Sep 80, GD; TD; JB, The Sword of Skelos, Part 1; To Kush and Beyond	1.25	0.60	1.50	3.00
❑57, Oct 80, TD; JB, The Sword of Skelos, Part 2; Surgeons and Scars	1.25	0.60	1.50	3.00
❑58, Nov 80, KGa; TD; JB, The Sword of Skelos, Part 3; Reh: Bard From the Shadows	1.25	0.60	1.50	3.00
❑59, Dec 80, The City of Skulls; The Kozaks Ride	1.25	0.60	1.50	3.00
❑60, Jan 81, JB, The Ivory Goddess; Conan of the Storyboards	1.25	0.60	1.50	3.00
❑61, Feb 81, JB, GD (w), The Wizard Fiend of Zingara!; Barbarians by Day	1.25	0.60	1.50	3.00
❑62, Mar 81, Temple of the Tiger; The One Black Stain	1.25	0.60	1.50	3.00
❑63, Apr 81, GK (w), Moat of Blood; Andrax, the Last	1.25	0.60	1.50	3.00
❑64, May 81, GK (w); ATh (w), Children of Rhan; The Devil's Bait	1.25	0.60	1.50	3.00
❑65, Jun 81, GK; JB, Fangs of the Serpent; Bront	1.25	0.60	1.50	3.00
❑66, Jul 81, The Sea of No Return; Bront, Part 2	1.25	0.60	1.50	3.00
❑67, Aug 81, AA; GK; JB, GK (w), Plunder of Death Island; In the Desert of Dreams	1.25	0.60	1.50	3.00
❑68, Sep 81, Black Cloaks of Ophir; The Lost Race	1.25	0.60	1.50	3.00
❑69, Oct 81, Eye of the Sorcerer; A Romas Kukalis Portfolio	1.25	0.60	1.50	3.00
❑70, Nov 81, JB, Dwellers in the Depths; A Cimmerian in Hollywood, article on Conan movie	1.25	0.60	1.50	3.00
❑71, Dec 81, Lurker in the Labyrinth; Cimmerian and the Conjeress	1.50	0.60	1.50	3.00
❑72, Jan 82, The Colossus of Shem	1.25	0.60	1.50	3.00
❑73, Feb 82, JB, The Changeling Quest; Island of Pirates' Doom, Part 1	1.25	0.60	1.50	3.00
❑74, Mar 82, GD; VM; JB, Lady of the Silver Snows; The Black Stone	1.25	0.60	1.50	3.00
❑75, Apr 82, Temple of the Twelve-Eyed Thing; Conan By Chiodo	1.25	0.60	1.50	3.00
❑76, May 82, Dominion of the Bat; Demons of Ghost Swamp	1.25	0.60	1.50	3.00
❑77, Jun 82, The Cave Dwellers; Islands of Pirates' Doom, Part 4	1.25	0.60	1.50	3.00
❑78, Jul 82, Demons of the Firelight, Part 1; Day of the Sword	1.25	0.60	1.50	3.00
❑79, Aug 82, Demons of the Firelight, Part 2; Bront: In The Halls of Shilme	1.25	0.60	1.50	3.00
❑80, Sep 82, AA; JB, The Colossus of Argos; Bront: The Pact	1.25	0.60	1.50	3.00
❑81, Oct 82, The Palace of Pleasure; Bront: The Conclusion	1.25	0.60	1.50	3.00
❑82, Nov 82, Devil in the Dark, Part 1; Song of Red Sonja	1.25	0.60	1.50	3.00
❑83, Dec 82, Devil in the Dark, Part 2; Hunters and the Hunted, A: Red Sonja	1.25	0.60	1.50	3.00
❑84, Jan 83, The Darsome Demon of Rabba Than!; Bonus Pin-Ups	1.25	0.60	1.50	3.00
❑85, Feb 83, Daughter of the God King; The Illuminated Hyborian Age Map	1.25	0.60	1.50	3.00
❑86, Mar 83, GK, Revenge of the Sorcerer; Lion of the Waves	1.25	0.60	1.50	3.00
❑87, Apr 83, The Armor of Zulda Thaal!; Escape From the Temple	1.25	0.60	1.50	3.00
❑88, May 83, JB, Isle of the Hunter; The Dark Stranger	1.25	0.60	1.50	3.00
❑89, Jun 83, GK (w), Gamesmen of Asgalun; Rite of Blood	1.25	0.60	1.50	3.00
❑90, Jul 83, Devourer of Souls!	1.25	0.60	1.50	3.00
❑91, Aug 83, VM; JB, Forest of Fiends!; The Beast	1.25	0.60	1.50	3.00
❑92, Sep 83, The Jeweled Bird	1.25	0.60	1.50	3.00
❑93, Oct 83, The World Beyond the Mists!; Challenge	1.25	0.60	1.50	3.00
❑94, Nov 83, Death Dwarves of Stygia!	1.25	0.60	1.50	3.00
❑95, Dec 83, Night of the Rat!; The Hill of Horror	1.25	0.60	1.50	3.00

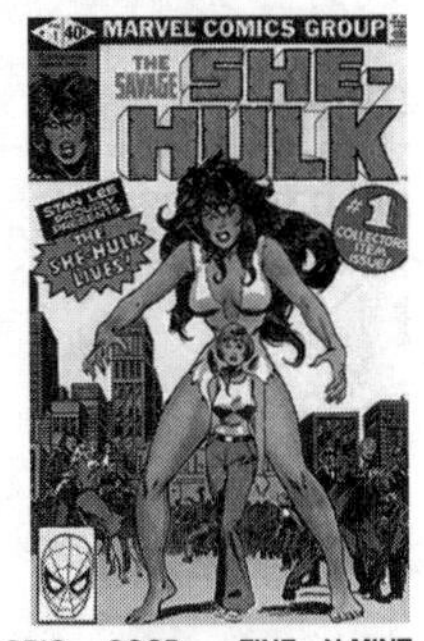

A blood transfusion from her gamma-irradiated cousin Bruce Banner gave lawyer Jennifer Walters super-human strength and green skin as She-Hulk.

© 1980 Marvel Comics

	ORIG	GOOD	FINE	N-MINT
❑96, Jan 84, JB, The Ape-Bat of Marmet Tarn!	1.25	0.60	1.50	3.00
❑97, Feb 84, The Leopard Men of Darfar!	1.25	0.60	1.50	3.00
❑98, Mar 84, JB, The Blood Ruby of Death!; The Lady of the Tower!	1.25	0.60	1.50	3.00
❑99, Apr 84, JB, The Informer!; One Night At The Maul	1.25	0.60	1.50	3.00
❑100, May 84, JB, When a God Lives!; The Gift	1.50	0.60	1.50	3.00
❑101, Jun 84, JB, The Siren!	1.50	0.50	1.25	2.50
❑102, Jul 84, The Iron Lions of the Kharamun!	1.50	0.50	1.25	2.50
❑103, Aug 84, The White Tiger of Vendhya!; Men of the Shadows!, Part 1	1.50	0.50	1.25	2.50
❑104, Sep 84, Treachery of the Gray Wolf!; Men of the Shadows!, Part 2	1.50	0.50	1.25	2.50
❑105, Oct 84, The Mill; The Crypt	1.50	0.50	1.25	2.50
❑106, Nov 84, GD, Feud of Blood; Men of the Shadows!, Part 3	1.50	0.50	1.25	2.50
❑107, Dec 84, The Eyes of G'Bharr R'Jinn; Deepest Devotion	1.50	0.50	1.25	2.50
❑108, Jan 85, The Claws of the Osprey; Fear of Crom	1.50	0.50	1.25	2.50
❑109, Feb 85, The Shatterer of Worlds; The Vezek Inn	1.50	0.50	1.25	2.50
❑110, Mar 85, The Army of the Dead; The Dinner Guest	1.50	0.50	1.25	2.50
❑111, Apr 85, Mud Men of Keshan; In the Eye of the Beholder	1.50	0.50	1.25	2.50
❑112, May 85, A Dream of Empire; Mitra Defend Us	1.50	0.50	1.25	2.50
❑113, Jun 85, Quest for the Shrine of Luma; A Quiet Place	1.50	0.50	1.25	2.50
❑114, Jul 85, The Riddle of the Demuzaar; The Toll	1.50	0.50	1.25	2.50
❑115, Aug 85, VM, Isle of the Faceless Ones; The Warlord of the Castle	1.50	0.50	1.25	2.50
❑116, Sep 85, Lords of the Falcon; The Boon	1.50	0.50	1.25	2.50
❑117, Oct 85, The Winds of Aka-Gaar; The Opponents	1.50	0.50	1.25	2.50
❑118, Nov 85, Valley of Howling Shadows; Alchemy	1.50	0.50	1.25	2.50
❑119, Dec 85, The Homecoming; Kull the Conqueror: From Beyond the Grave!	1.50	0.50	1.25	2.50
❑120, Jan 86, Star of Thamazhu; Kull the Conqueror	1.50	0.50	1.25	2.50
❑121, Feb 86, The Fountain of Umir; Kull the Conqueror: Pieces of Horror	1.50	0.50	1.25	2.50
❑122, Mar 86, The Blossoms of the Black Lotus; One Against All	1.50	0.50	1.25	2.50
❑123, Apr 86, Secret of the Great Stone; The Debt of the Warrior	1.50	0.50	1.25	2.50
❑124, May 86	1.50	0.50	1.25	2.50
❑125, Jun 86	1.50	0.50	1.25	2.50
❑126, Jul 86	1.50	0.50	1.25	2.50
❑127, Aug 86	1.50	0.50	1.25	2.50
❑128, Sep 86	1.50	0.50	1.25	2.50
❑129, Oct 86	1.50	0.50	1.25	2.50
❑130, Nov 86	1.50	0.50	1.25	2.50
❑131, Dec 86	2.00	0.50	1.25	2.50
❑132, Jan 87, Master of the Broadsword; The Sea King	1.50	0.50	1.25	2.50
❑133, Feb 87	1.50	0.50	1.25	2.50
❑134, Mar 87	1.50	0.50	1.25	2.50
❑135, Apr 87	1.50	0.50	1.25	2.50
❑136, May 87, The Lost Legion, Part 1; The Brawl	1.50	0.50	1.25	2.50
❑137, Jun 87, The Lost Legion, Part 2; The Brawl	1.50	0.50	1.25	2.50
❑138, Jul 87, Lair of the Lizard; The Mine	1.50	0.50	1.25	2.50
❑139, Aug 87	1.50	0.50	1.25	2.50
❑140, Sep 87, The Girl of the Haunted Wood; Nightmare	1.50	0.50	1.25	2.50
❑141, Oct 87	1.50	0.50	1.25	2.50
❑142, Nov 87	1.50	0.50	1.25	2.50
❑143, Dec 87	1.50	0.50	1.25	2.50
❑144, Jan 88	1.50	0.50	1.25	2.50
❑145, Feb 88, Feast of the Stag, A: Red Sonja	1.50	0.50	1.25	2.50

	ORIG	GOOD	FINE	N-MINT
❑146, Mar 88	1.50	0.50	1.25	2.50
❑147, Apr 88, Vulture's Shadow; Rites of Passage	1.50	0.50	1.25	2.50
❑148, May 88	1.50	0.50	1.25	2.50
❑149, Jun 88	1.50	0.50	1.25	2.50
❑150, Jul 88, Call to the Slain; Trial by Fear	1.50	0.50	1.25	2.50
❑151, Aug 88, Fury of the Near-Men; A Bond of Blood	2.00	0.50	1.25	2.50
❑152, Sep 88, Valley Beyond the Stars; Invictus	2.00	0.50	1.25	2.50
❑153, Oct 88, LMc, Phantasm; Blood on the Sand, A: Red Sonja	2.00	0.50	1.25	2.50
❑154, Nov 88, Return of the Iron Damsels; To Fight Another Day!	2.00	0.50	1.25	2.50
❑155, Dec 88	2.00	0.50	1.25	2.50
❑156, Jan 89, Rogue's Honor; Dave Simons Portfolio	2.00	0.50	1.25	2.50
❑157, Feb 89	2.00	0.50	1.25	2.50
❑158, Mar 89, Bane of the Dark Brotherhood; Caresses of Mine Enemy	2.00	0.50	1.25	2.50
❑159, Apr 89	2.00	0.50	1.25	2.50
❑160, May 89	2.00	0.50	1.25	2.50
❑161, Jun 89	2.00	0.50	1.25	2.50
❑162, Jul 89	2.00	0.50	1.25	2.50
❑163, Aug 89	2.00	0.50	1.25	2.50
❑164, Sep 89	2.25	0.50	1.25	2.50
❑165, Oct 89, City of Rats; Siege!	2.25	0.50	1.25	2.50
❑166, Nov 89	2.25	0.50	1.25	2.50
❑167, Dec 89	2.25	0.50	1.25	2.50
❑168, Jan 90	2.25	0.50	1.25	2.50
❑169, Feb 90	2.25	0.50	1.25	2.50
❑170, Mar 90	2.25	0.50	1.25	2.50
❑171, Apr 90	2.25	0.50	1.25	2.50
❑172, May 90	2.25	0.50	1.25	2.50
❑173, Jun 90	2.25	0.50	1.25	2.50
❑174, Jul 90, Series continues as Savage Sword of Conan the Barbarian	2.25	0.45	1.13	2.25
❑175, Aug 90	2.25	0.45	1.13	2.25
❑176, Sep 90	2.25	0.45	1.13	2.25
❑177, Oct 90	2.25	0.45	1.13	2.25
❑178, Nov 90	2.25	0.45	1.13	2.25
❑179, Dec 90, Fury of the Iron Damsels, A: Red Sonja	2.25	0.45	1.13	2.25
❑180, Jan 91	2.25	0.45	1.13	2.25
❑181, Feb 91	2.25	0.45	1.13	2.25
❑182, Mar 91	2.25	0.45	1.13	2.25
❑183, Apr 91	2.25	0.45	1.13	2.25
❑184, May 91, Disciple	2.25	0.45	1.13	2.25
❑185, Jun 91	2.25	0.45	1.13	2.25
❑186, Jul 91	2.25	0.45	1.13	2.25
❑187, Aug 91, Red Sonja Quells the Song of the Siren, A: Red Sonja	2.25	0.45	1.13	2.25
❑188, Sep 91	2.25	0.45	1.13	2.25
❑189, Oct 91	2.25	0.45	1.13	2.25
❑190, Nov 91	2.25	0.45	1.13	2.25
❑191, Dec 91	2.25	0.45	1.13	2.25
❑192, Jan 92	2.25	0.45	1.13	2.25
❑193, Feb 92	2.25	0.45	1.13	2.25
❑194, Mar 92	2.25	0.45	1.13	2.25
❑195, Apr 92	2.25	0.45	1.13	2.25
❑196, May 92	2.25	0.45	1.13	2.25
❑197, Jun 92	2.25	0.45	1.13	2.25
❑198, Jul 92	2.25	0.45	1.13	2.25
❑199, Aug 92	2.25	0.45	1.13	2.25
❑200, Sep 92	2.25	0.45	1.13	2.25
❑201, Oct 92	2.25	0.45	1.13	2.25
❑202, Nov 92	2.25	0.45	1.13	2.25
❑203, Dec 92	2.25	0.45	1.13	2.25
❑204, Jan 93	2.25	0.45	1.13	2.25
❑205, Feb 93	2.25	0.45	1.13	2.25
❑206, Mar 93	2.25	0.45	1.13	2.25
❑207, Apr 93, JB, Conan and the Spider God, Part 1	2.25	0.45	1.13	2.25
❑208, May 93, JB, Conan and the Spider God, Part 2	2.25	0.45	1.13	2.25
❑209, Jun 93, JB, Conan and the Spider God, Part 3	2.25	0.45	1.13	2.25
❑210, Jul 93, JB, Conan and the Spider God, Part 4	2.25	0.45	1.13	2.25
❑211, Aug 93	2.25	0.45	1.13	2.25
❑212, Sep 93	2.25	0.45	1.13	2.25
❑213, Oct 93	2.25	0.45	1.13	2.25
❑214, Nov 93, Adapted from Robert E. Howard's "Red Nails"	2.25	0.45	1.13	2.25
❑215, Dec 93	2.25	0.45	1.13	2.25
❑216, Jan 94	2.25	0.45	1.13	2.25
❑217, Feb 94	2.25	0.45	1.13	2.25
❑218, Mar 94	2.25	0.45	1.13	2.25
❑219, Apr 94	2.25	0.45	1.13	2.25
❑220, May 94	2.25	0.45	1.13	2.25
❑221, May 94, b&w	2.25	0.45	1.13	2.25
❑222, Jun 94, b&w	2.25	0.45	1.13	2.25
❑223, Jul 94, b&w	2.25	0.45	1.13	2.25
❑224, Aug 94, b&w	2.25	0.45	1.13	2.25
❑225, Sep 94, b&w	2.25	0.45	1.13	2.25
❑226, Oct 94, b&w	2.25	0.45	1.13	2.25
❑227, Nov 94, b&w	2.25	0.45	1.13	2.25
❑228, Dec 94, b&w	2.25	0.45	1.13	2.25
❑229, Jan 95, b&w	2.25	0.45	1.13	2.25
❑230, Feb 95, b&w	2.25	0.45	1.13	2.25
❑231, Mar 95, b&w	2.25	0.45	1.13	2.25
❑232, Apr 95, b&w	2.25	0.45	1.13	2.25
❑233, May 95, b&w	2.25	0.45	1.13	2.25
❑234, Jun 95, b&w	2.25	0.45	1.13	2.25
❑235, Jul 95, b&w; Final Issue	2.25	0.45	1.13	2.25
❑Anl 1, b&w	1.25	0.25	0.63	1.25
❑SE 1	—	1.20	3.00	6.00

SAVAGE SWORD OF MIKE
Fandom House

Value: Cover or less

- ❑1, b&w 2.00

SAVAGE TALES (1ST SERIES)
Marvel

	ORIG	GOOD	FINE	N-MINT
❑1, May 71, JB; GC; GM, Conan the Barbarian; The Fury of the Femizons, 1: Man-Thing; A: Conan, b&w magazine	0.50	12.00	30.00	60.00
❑2, Oct 73, FB; GM; AW	0.75	4.80	12.00	24.00
❑3, Feb 74, FB; AW	0.75	3.00	7.50	15.00
❑4, May 74, GK; NA	0.75	2.00	5.00	10.00
❑5, Jul 74, GK; NA	0.75	2.00	5.00	10.00
❑6, Sep 74	0.75	1.60	4.00	8.00
❑7, Nov 74	0.75	1.60	4.00	8.00
❑8, Jan 75	1.00	1.60	4.00	8.00
❑9, Mar 75	1.00	1.60	4.00	8.00
❑10, May 75	1.00	1.60	4.00	8.00
❑11, Jul 75	1.00	1.60	4.00	8.00
❑12, Sum 75	1.25	1.20	3.00	6.00
❑Anl 1, GK, O: Ka-Zar, b&w	1.25	1.40	3.50	7.00

SAVAGE TALES (2ND SERIES)
Marvel

	ORIG	GOOD	FINE	N-MINT
❑1, Oct 85, MG, b&w; magazine; 1st 'Nam story	1.50	0.80	2.00	4.00
❑2, Dec 85, JSe, 2nd 'Nam story	1.50	0.60	1.50	3.00
❑3	1.50	0.50	1.25	2.50
❑4, 'Nam	1.50	0.50	1.25	2.50
❑5, Jun 96, JSe	1.50	0.50	1.25	2.50
❑6	1.50	0.40	1.00	2.00
❑7	1.50	0.40	1.00	2.00
❑8	1.50	0.40	1.00	2.00
❑9, Final Issue	1.50	0.40	1.00	2.00

SAVANT GARDE
Image

	ORIG	GOOD	FINE	N-MINT
❑1, Mar 97	2.50	0.50	1.25	2.50
❑2, Apr 97, 1: Innuendo	2.50	0.50	1.25	2.50
❑3, May 97	2.50	0.50	1.25	2.50
❑4, Jun 97	2.50	0.50	1.25	2.50
❑5, Jul 97	2.50	0.50	1.25	2.50
❑6, Aug 97	2.50	0.50	1.25	2.50
❑7, Sep 97	2.50	0.50	1.25	2.50
❑FAN 1, Feb 97	—	0.20	0.50	1.00
❑FAN 2, Mar 97	—	0.20	0.50	1.00
❑FAN 3, Apr 97	—	0.20	0.50	1.00

SAVED BY THE BELL
Harvey

Value: Cover or less

- ❑1, May 92, A Chillin' Holiday; The Bayside Bugler 1.95
- ❑2 ..... 1.95
- ❑3 ..... 1.95
- ❑4 ..... 1.95
- ❑5 ..... 1.95

SAVIOUR
Trident

Value: Cover or less

- ❑1, b&w; adult 4.00
- ❑2, Feb 90, b&w; adult 1.95
- ❑3, b&w; adult 2.50
- ❑4, b&w; adult 2.50
- ❑5, b&w; adult 2.50

SB NINJA HIGH SCHOOL
Antarctic

Value: Cover or less

- ❑1/A, Aug 92, b&w 2.95
- ❑1/B, Aug 92, b&w; trading card 4.95
- ❑2/A, b&w 2.95
- ❑2/B, b&w; trading card 4.95
- ❑3/A, Sep 94, b&w 2.75
- ❑3/B, Sep 94, b&w; trading card 4.95
- ❑4, Feb 95, b&w 2.75
- ❑5, May 95, b&w 2.75
- ❑6, Aug 95, b&w 2.75
- ❑7, Nov 95, b&w 2.75

ORIG GOOD FINE N-MINT

SCAB
FANTACO
Value: Cover or less

❑1, b&w 3.50
❑2, b&w 3.50

SCALES OF THE DRAGON
SUNDRAGON
Value: Cover or less

❑1, Mar 97, b&w; Flip-book 1.95

SCAN
ICONOGRAFIX
Value: Cover or less

❑1, b&w 2.95
❑2, b&w 2.95

SCANDALS
THORBY
Value: Cover or less

❑1 .... 2.95

SCANDAL SHEET
ARRIBA
Value: Cover or less

❑1, b&w 2.50

SCARAB
DC
Value: Cover or less

❑0, Mar 94, Paradise Defiled 1.95
❑1, Nov 93, All Roads Lead to the Minotaur 1.95
❑2, Dec 93, Lost and Found, A: Phantom Stranger 1.95
❑3, Jan 94, Moveable Feasts 1.95
❑4, Feb 94, A Dawn Chorus 1.95
❑5, Mar 94 .... 1.95
❑6, Apr 94 .... 1.95
❑7, May 94, The Power and the Glory 1.95
❑8, Jun 94, What the Rabbit Saw 1.95

SCARAMOUCH
INNOVATION
Value: Cover or less

❑1, Death Warmed Over, b&w 2.25
❑2, b&w 2.25

SCARECROW (VILLAINS)
DC
Value: Cover or less

❑1, Feb 98, Mistress of Fear, New Year's Evil 1.95

SCARE TACTICS
DC
Value: Cover or less

❑1, Dec 96, Blitzkrieg Bop, 1: Grossout; O: Scare Tactics; 1: Arnold Burnsteel; 1: F; 1: Fang (Jake); 1: Slither (Jim); 1: Screamqueen (Nina Skorzeny) 2.25
❑2, Jan 97, Haunting Season, 2: Grossout; 1: Scaremobile; 2: Arnold Burnsteel; 2: Fang (Jake); 2: Slither (Jim); 2: Screamqueen (Nina Skorzeny); 2: Slit, Road Trip 2.25
❑3, Feb 97 .... 2.25
❑4, Mar 97, Big for his Age, O: Phil 2.25
❑5, Apr 97, Morbid Fascination, Valentine's Day Nightmare 2.25
❑6, May 97 .... 2.25
❑7, Jun 97 .... 2.25
❑8, Jul 97, Convergenge, Part 4 .... 2.25
❑9, Aug 97, O: Slither, series goes on hiatus; story continues in Impulse Plus #1 .... 2.25
❑10, Jan 98, A: Batman 2.25
❑11, Feb 98, D: Slither 2.25
❑12, Mar 98, Final Issue; Phil transforms 2.25

SCARLET CRUSH
AWESOME
Value: Cover or less

❑1, Jan 98 .... 2.50
❑2 .... 2.50

SCARLET IN GASLIGHT
ETERNITY
Value: Cover or less

❑1, b&w; Sherlock Holmes vs. Dracula 1.95
❑2 .... 1.95
❑3 .... 1.95
❑4, Jun 88 .... 1.95

SCARLET KISS: THE VAMPYRE
ALL AMERICAN
Value: Cover or less

❑1, Dawne Burnes Vampire, b&w 2.95

SCARLET SCORPION/DARKSHADE
AC
Value: Cover or less

❑1, Jul 95, Ghost 3.50
❑2 .... 3.50

SCARLET SPIDER
MARVEL

	ORIG	GOOD	FINE	N-MINT
❑1, Nov 95, GK, Virtual Mortality, Part 3	1.95	0.40	1.00	2.00
❑2, Dec 95, JR2, Cyberwar, Part 3, concludes in Spectacular Scarlet Spider #2	1.95	0.40	1.00	2.00

SCARLET SPIDER UNLIMITED
MARVEL
Value: Cover or less

❑1, Nov 95, You Say You Want An Evolution! 3.95

SCARLETT
DC
Value: Cover or less

❑1, Jan, Blood Of Innocence, 1: Scarlett, 48pgs. 2.95
❑2, Feb 93 .... 2.95
❑3, Mar 93 .... 1.75
❑4, Apr 93 .... 1.75
❑5, May 93 .... 1.75
❑6, Jun 93, GM, Blood Of The Damned, Part 1 .... 1.75
❑7, Jul 93 .... 1.75
❑8, Aug 93 .... 1.75
❑9, Sep 93 .... 1.75
❑10, Oct 93 .... 1.75
❑11, Nov 93 .... 1.75
❑12, Dec 93 .... 1.75
❑13, Jan 94 .... 1.75
❑14, Feb 94, Final Issue 1.75

When *Scare Tactics* went on hiatus in 1997, the story continued in several of DC's *Plus* titles, beginning with *Impulse Plus*.

© 1997 DC Comics

ORIG GOOD FINE N-MINT

SCARLET THUNDER
SLAVE LABOR
Value: Cover or less

❑1, Nov 95, 1: Dot; O: Blue Streak; 1: Jason Pine; 1: Adam Garrison; 1: Red Bolt, 1st a 1.50
❑2, Feb 96, 2: Dot; 2: Jason Pine; 2: Adam Garrison; 2: Red Bolt, 1st apperance Blue Streak 1.50
❑3, May 96, 2: Blue Streak; 1: Oskar (cameo); 1: Betty Joseph 2.50
❑4, Dec 96, 1: Lady Liberty; 1: Oskar (full); 2: Betty Joseph 2.50

SCARLETT PILGRIM
LAST GASP
Value: Cover or less

❑1 .... 1.00

SCARLET WITCH
MARVEL
Value: Cover or less

❑1, Dark Designs 1.75
❑2 .... 1.75
❑3 .... 1.75
❑4 .... 1.75

SCARLET ZOMBIE, THE
COMAX
Value: Cover or less

❑1, b&w; adult 2.95

SCARY BOOK, THE
CALIBER

	ORIG	GOOD	FINE	N-MINT
❑1, b&w	2.50	0.50	1.25	2.50
❑2, b&w	1.75	0.50	1.25	2.50

SCARY GODMOTHER
SIRIUS
Value: Cover or less

❑1, The Search for Mister Boogeylegs 2.95

SCARY GODMOTHER: BLOODY VALENTINE
SIRIUS
Value: Cover or less

❑1, Feb 98, The Fright Side 3.95

SCARY GODMOTHER HOLIDAY SPOOKTACULAR
SIRIUS
Value: Cover or less

❑1, Nov 98, The Fright Side; The Search for Mister Boogeylegs, b&w; wraparound cover 2.95

SCARY GODMOTHER REVENGE OF JIMMY
SIRIUS
Value: Cover or less

❑1, hardcover 19.95

SCARY GODMOTHER: WILD ABOUT HARRY
SIRIUS
Value: Cover or less

❑1, b&w 2.95
❑2, b&w 2.95

SCATTERBRAIN
DARK HORSE
Value: Cover or less

❑1, Jun 98, Abu Gung and the Beanstalk; Bring on the Robots 2.95
❑2, Jul 98 .... 2.95
❑3, Aug 98 .... 2.95
❑4, Sep 98, SA (c) 2.95

SCAVENGERS (FLEETWAY/QUALITY)
FLEETWAY

	ORIG	GOOD	FINE	N-MINT
❑1, Judge Dredd	1.25	0.30	0.75	1.50
❑2, Flesh; Judge Dredd: Bob & Carol & Ted & Ringo, Judge Dredd	1.25	0.30	0.75	1.50
❑3, Judge Dredd	1.25	0.30	0.75	1.50
❑4, Judge Dredd	1.25	0.30	0.75	1.50
❑5	1.25	0.30	0.75	1.50
❑6	1.50	0.30	0.75	1.50
❑7	1.50	0.30	0.75	1.50
❑8	1.50	0.30	0.75	1.50
❑9	1.50	0.30	0.75	1.50
❑10	1.50	0.30	0.75	1.50
❑11	1.50	0.30	0.75	1.50
❑12	1.50	0.30	0.75	1.50
❑13	1.50	0.30	0.75	1.50
❑14	1.50	0.30	0.75	1.50

SCAVENGERS (TRIUMPHANT)
TRIUMPHANT

	ORIG	GOOD	FINE	N-MINT
❑0, Mar 94, 30, 000-copy edition; giveaway	—	0.20	0.50	1.00
❑0/A, Mar 94, 18, 000-copy edition	2.50	0.50	1.25	2.50
❑0/B, Mar 94, 5000-copy edition	2.50	0.50	1.25	2.50

	ORIG	GOOD	FINE	N-MINT
❑1, Mar 94	2.50	0.50	1.25	2.50
❑1/Ash, Redemption, ashcan edition	2.50	0.50	1.25	2.50
❑2	2.50	0.50	1.25	2.50
❑3, Counter Strike	2.50	0.50	1.25	2.50
❑4	2.50	0.50	1.25	2.50
❑5, D: Jack Hanal, Unleashed!	2.50	0.50	1.25	2.50
❑6, Unleashed!	2.50	0.50	1.25	2.50
❑7, Jan 94	2.50	0.50	1.25	2.50
❑8, Feb 94	2.50	0.50	1.25	2.50
❑9, Mar 94	2.50	0.50	1.25	2.50
❑10, Apr 94, Snowblind	2.50	0.50	1.25	2.50
❑11, May 94	2.50	0.50	1.25	2.50

SCC CONVENTION SPECIAL
SUPER CREW

Value: Cover or less

Issue	Price
❑1, 1994 Convention Special	2.25

SCENARIO A
ANTARCTIC

Value: Cover or less

Issue	Price
❑1, Jul 98, b&w	2.95
❑2, Sep 98, b&w	2.95

SCENE OF THE CRIME
DC

Value: Cover or less

Issue	Price
❑1, May 99, A Little Piece of Goodnight, Part 1	2.50
❑2, Jun 99, A Little Piece of Goodnight, Part 2	2.50
❑3, Jul 99, A Little Piece of Goodnight, Part 3	2.50
❑4, Aug 99, A Little Piece of Goodnight, Part 4	2.50

SCHIZO
ANTARCTIC

Value: Cover or less

Issue	Price
❑1, Dec 94, b&w	3.50
❑2, Jan 96, b&w	3.95
❑3, Mar 98, b&w	3.95

SCIENCE AFFAIR, A
ANTARCTIC

	ORIG	GOOD	FINE	N-MINT
❑1, Mar 94, b&w	2.75	0.55	1.38	2.75
❑1/GO, Mar 94, Gold edition	—	0.60	1.50	3.00
❑2, May 94, b&w	2.75	0.55	1.38	2.75

SCIENCE FICTION CLASSICS
DRAGON LADY

Value: Cover or less

Issue	Price
❑1, Twin Earths	5.95

SCI-FI
ROUGH COPY

Value: Cover or less

Issue	Price
❑1, Volcanic Partners; Martian Chronicles	2.95

SCIMIDAR
ETERNITY

	ORIG	GOOD	FINE	N-MINT
❑1, Jun 88, b&w	1.95	0.50	1.25	2.50
❑2, Bloody Mary, b&w	1.95	0.50	1.25	2.50
❑3, b&w	1.95	0.50	1.25	2.50
❑4/A, mild cover	1.95	0.40	1.00	2.00
❑4/B, hot cover	1.95	0.40	1.00	2.00

SCIMIDAR (CFD)
CFD

Value: Cover or less

Issue	Price
❑1, b&w	2.95
❑3	2.75

SCIMIDAR BOOK II
ETERNITY

	ORIG	GOOD	FINE	N-MINT
❑1, b&w; adult	—	0.60	1.50	3.00
❑1-2, adult; 2nd Printing	—	0.60	1.50	3.00
❑2, b&w; adult	—	0.60	1.50	3.00
❑3, b&w; adult	—	0.60	1.50	3.00
❑4, b&w; adult	—	0.60	1.50	3.00

SCIMIDAR BOOK III
ETERNITY

	ORIG	GOOD	FINE	N-MINT
❑1, b&w; adult	—	0.60	1.50	3.00
❑1-2, adult; 2nd Printing	—	0.60	1.50	3.00
❑2, b&w; adult	—	0.60	1.50	3.00
❑3, b&w; adult	—	0.60	1.50	3.00
❑4, b&w; adult	—	0.60	1.50	3.00

SCIMIDAR BOOK IV: "WILD THING"
ETERNITY

	ORIG	GOOD	FINE	N-MINT
❑1, adult	—	0.60	1.50	3.00
❑1/Nude, adult; Nude cover	—	0.60	1.50	3.00
❑2, b&w; adult	—	0.60	1.50	3.00
❑3, b&w; adult	—	0.60	1.50	3.00
❑4, b&w; adult	—	0.60	1.50	3.00

SCIMIDAR BOOK V: "LIVING COLOR"
ETERNITY

	ORIG	GOOD	FINE	N-MINT
❑1, b&w; adult	—	0.60	1.50	3.00
❑1/Nude, b&w; adult; Nude cover	—	0.60	1.50	3.00
❑2, b&w; adult	—	0.60	1.50	3.00
❑3, b&w; adult	—	0.60	1.50	3.00
❑4, b&w; adult	—	0.60	1.50	3.00

SCIMIDAR PIN-UP BOOK
ETERNITY

Value: Cover or less

Issue	Price
❑1, full color; unstapled	3.75

SCION
CROSSGEN

Value: Cover or less

Issue	Price
❑1, Jul 00	2.95
❑2, Aug 00	2.95
❑3, Sep 00	2.95
❑4, Oct 00	2.95
❑5	2.95
❑6	2.95
❑7	2.95
❑8	2.95
❑9	2.95
❑10	2.95
❑11	2.95
❑12	2.95
❑13	2.95
❑14	2.95

SCI-TECH
DC

Value: Cover or less

Issue	Price
❑1, Sep 99, ...And Then There Was Light	2.50
❑2, Oct 99, The Deep Blue Sea	2.50
❑3, Nov 99	2.50
❑4, Dec 99, Reunion	2.50

SCOOBY-DOO (ARCHIE)
ARCHIE

Value: Cover or less

Issue	Price
❑1, Oct 95	1.50
❑2, Nov 95	1.50
❑3, Dec 95	1.50
❑4, Jan 96	1.50
❑5, Feb 96	1.50
❑6, Mar 96	1.50
❑7, Apr 96	1.50
❑8, May 96	1.50
❑10, Jul 96, DS, ME (w)	1.50
❑11, Aug 96	1.50
❑12, Sep 96	1.50
❑14, Nov 96	1.50
❑15, Dec 96	1.50
❑16, Jan 97	1.50
❑17, Feb 97	1.50
❑18, Mar 97	1.50
❑19, Apr 97	1.50
❑20, May 97	1.50
❑21, Jun 97	1.50

SCOOBY-DOO (DC)
DC

	ORIG	GOOD	FINE	N-MINT
❑1, Aug 97	1.75	0.50	1.25	2.50
❑2, Sep 97, The Roswell Riddle; Stubble trouble	1.75	0.40	1.00	2.00
❑3, Oct 97, JSa, The Truth; Wax Attacks	1.75	0.40	1.00	2.00
❑4, Nov 97, The Old Ways; How I Spent my Winter Break	1.75	0.40	1.00	2.00
❑5, Dec 97, Legend of the Silver Scream; The Best Laid Plans...	1.95	0.40	1.00	2.00
❑6, Jan 98, A: Stetson Rogers (Shaggy's cousin)	1.95	0.40	1.00	2.00
❑7, Feb 98	1.95	0.40	1.00	2.00
❑8, Mar 98, EC, Kung Fu Month!; Like a Cracked Mirror	1.95	0.40	1.00	2.00
❑9, Apr 98	1.95	0.40	1.00	2.00
❑10, May 98	1.95	0.40	1.00	2.00
❑11, Jun 98	1.95	0.40	1.00	2.00
❑12, Jul 98, mystery at a comic-book convention	1.95	0.40	1.00	2.00
❑13, Aug 98	1.95	0.40	1.00	2.00
❑14, Sep 98	1.99	0.40	1.00	2.00
❑15, Oct 98	1.99	0.40	1.00	2.00
❑16, Nov 98, A: Groovy Ghoulie	1.99	0.40	1.00	2.00
❑17, Dec 98	1.99	0.40	1.00	2.00
❑18, Jan 99	1.99	0.40	1.00	2.00
❑19, Feb 99, JSa, The Ghost of Holiday Presents	1.99	0.40	1.00	2.00
❑20, Mar 99, JSa, Revenge of the Mudman; Revenge, Inc., A: Mystery, Inc.	1.99	0.40	1.00	2.00
❑21, Apr 99, JSa, A: Mystery, Inc.	1.99	0.40	1.00	1.99
❑22, May 99	1.99	0.40	1.00	1.99
❑23, Jun 99, The Big Lake Fake; The Haunted Halibut	1.99	0.40	1.00	1.99
❑24, Jul 99, DP, Don't Believe What You See!; Surf's Up, Monster's Down	1.99	0.40	1.00	1.99
❑25, Aug 99, DP, The Phantom of the Mosh Pit; Caves of Castle Finn	1.99	0.40	1.00	1.99
❑26, Sep 99, JSa, One Night in Roswell, Part 1	1.99	0.40	1.00	1.99
❑27, Oct 99, JSa, One Night in Roswell, Part 3	1.99	0.40	1.00	1.99
❑28, Nov 99, Lst of the Mugwumps; High School Ghoul	1.99	0.40	1.00	1.99
❑29, Dec 99, DP; JSa, Three Shears for Shaggy; The Oceanarium Horror	1.99	0.40	1.00	1.99
❑30, Jan 00, JSa, Spring-Heeled Jack; Dog Gone Ghost	1.99	0.40	1.00	1.99
❑31, Feb 00	1.99	0.40	1.00	1.99
❑32, Mar 00	1.99	0.40	1.00	1.99
❑33, Apr 00	1.99	0.40	1.00	1.99
❑34, May 00, JSa, The Hound of the Basket Cases; Return of the King	1.99	0.40	1.00	1.99
❑35, Jun 00, JSa, Phast Phood Phantom; The Weeping Bride of Lover's Leap!	1.99	0.40	1.00	1.99
❑36, Jul 00	1.99	0.40	1.00	1.99
❑37, Aug 00	1.99	0.40	1.00	1.99
❑38, Sep 00	1.99	0.40	1.00	1.99

	ORIG	GOOD	FINE	N-MINT
❑39, Oct 00, JSa, Two Heads Are Better than None; The Chocalatier Chortled!	1.99	0.40	1.00	1.99
❑40, Nov 00, Roc Around the Clock; Ghost Tour	1.99	0.40	1.00	1.99
❑41, Dec 00, JSa, Trolley Molly; Down in the Dumps	1.99	0.40	1.00	1.99
❑42, Jan 01, Dig Them Bones; Good Ghost Haunting	1.99	0.40	1.00	1.99
❑43, Feb 01, JSa, Nutcracker Not-So-Sweet; Mascot Madness	1.99	0.40	1.00	1.99
❑44, Mar 01, JSa, Planet-Terrorium	1.99	0.40	1.00	1.99
❑45, Apr 01, JSa, Diamond Dog; Rest in Pizza	1.99	0.40	1.00	1.99
❑46, May 01, JSa, DDC (w), Ghost Writer; The Ex-Verminators	1.99	0.40	1.00	1.99
❑47, Jun 01, JSa, Bats What I'm Afraid Of; Tune Goon	1.99	0.40	1.00	1.99
❑48	1.99	0.40	1.00	1.99
❑49	1.99	0.40	1.00	1.99
❑50	1.99	0.40	1.00	1.99
❑SE 1, Oct 99, EC; JSa, Spooky Spectacular; The Comic Book Convention Affair, 64pgs.; Spooky Spectacular	3.95	0.79	1.98	3.95
❑SE 2, Oct 00, JSa, Welcome to Monsterville; The Jersey Devil	3.95	0.79	1.98	3.95

SCOOBY-DOO (HARVEY)
HARVEY

	ORIG	GOOD	FINE	N-MINT
❑1	1.25	0.30	0.75	1.50
❑2, Witches' Night Out; The Skeleton Speaks!	1.25	0.30	0.75	1.50
❑3	1.25	0.30	0.75	1.50
❑GS 1	2.25	0.45	1.13	2.25
❑GS 2	2.25	0.45	1.13	2.25
❑SE 1	1.95	0.39	0.98	1.95
❑SE 2	1.95	0.39	0.98	1.95

SCOOBY-DOO (MARVEL)
MARVEL

	ORIG	GOOD	FINE	N-MINT
❑1, Oct 77	0.30	1.20	3.00	6.00
❑2	—	0.80	2.00	4.00
❑3	—	0.60	1.50	3.00
❑4	0.35	0.60	1.50	3.00
❑5	—	0.60	1.50	3.00
❑6	—	0.60	1.50	3.00
❑7	—	0.60	1.50	3.00
❑8	—	0.60	1.50	3.00
❑9	—	0.60	1.50	3.00

SCOOBY-DOO BIG BOOK
HARVEY

Value: Cover or less

❑1 .... 1.95
❑2 .... 1.95

SCOOBY DOO, WHERE ARE YOU? (CHARLTON)
CHARLTON

	ORIG	GOOD	FINE	N-MINT
❑1	—	3.00	7.50	15.00
❑2	—	2.00	5.00	10.00
❑3	—	1.40	3.50	7.00
❑4	—	1.40	3.50	7.00
❑5	—	1.40	3.50	7.00
❑6	—	1.20	3.00	6.00
❑7	—	1.20	3.00	6.00
❑8	—	1.20	3.00	6.00
❑9	—	1.20	3.00	6.00
❑10, It's Dynamite!; Giant-Size (text story)	0.30	1.20	3.00	6.00
❑11	0.30	1.00	2.50	5.00

SCOOTERMAN
WELLZEE

Value: Cover or less

❑1, Apr 96, b&w 2.75
❑2, Dec 96, b&w; poster 2.75
❑3, Jul 97, b&w 2.75

SCORCHED EARTH
TUNDRA

Value: Cover or less

❑1, Apr 91 .... 2.95
❑2, Jun 91 .... 2.95
❑3, Aug 91 .... 2.95

SCORCHY
FORBIDDEN FRUIT

Value: Cover or less

❑1, b&w; adult 3.50

SCORE, THE
DC

Value: Cover or less

❑1, adult 4.95
❑2, adult 4.95
❑3, adult 4.95
❑4, adult 4.95

SCORN: DEADLY REBELLION
SCC ENTERTAINMENT

Value: Cover or less

❑0, Jul 96, b&w 2.95

SCORN: HEATWAVE
SCC ENTERTAINMENT

Value: Cover or less

❑1, Jan 97, b&w; follows events in Scorn: Deadly Rebellion 3.95

The Scooby gang visited Roswell, N.M., in *Scooby-Doo (DC)* #26 and #27.

© 1999 Hanna-Barbera (DC)

SCORPIA
MILLER

Value: Cover or less

❑1 .... 2.50
❑2 .... 2.50

SCORPION
ANNRUEL STUDIOS

Value: Cover or less

❑1, b&w 2.50

SCORPION, THE
ATLAS

	ORIG	GOOD	FINE	N-MINT
❑1, Feb 75, HC, HC (c), HC (w), The Death's Gemini Commission, 1: The Scorpion I (Moro Frost)	0.25	0.40	1.00	2.00
❑2, Apr 75, BWr	0.25	0.30	0.75	1.50
❑3, Jul 75, 1: The Scorpion II (David Harper), Final Issue	0.25	0.30	0.75	1.50

SCORPION CORPS
DAGGER

Value: Cover or less

❑1, Nov 93, 1: Streik, coupon for Dagger Universe #0 .... 2.50
❑2, coupon for Dagger Universe #0 .... 2.50
❑3 .... 2.50
❑4 .... 2.50
❑5 .... 2.50
❑6, Parting Shots 2.50
❑7 .... 2.50
❑8 .... 2.50
❑9 .... 2.50
❑10 .... 2.50

SCORPION MOON
EXPRESS

Value: Cover or less

❑1, Oct 94, nn; b&w; cardstock cover; 4th in a series of Entity illustrated novellas with Zen Intergalactic Ninja 2.95

SCORPIO RISING
MARVEL

Value: Cover or less

❑1, Oct 94, HC (w), nn; prestige format one-shot 5.95

SCORPIO ROSE
ECLIPSE

	ORIG	GOOD	FINE	N-MINT
❑1, Jan 83, MR, 1: Doctor Orient; 1: Scorpio Rose	1.50	0.40	1.00	2.00
❑2, Oct 83	1.50	0.40	1.00	2.00

SCOUT
ECLIPSE

	ORIG	GOOD	FINE	N-MINT
❑1, Nov 85	1.75	0.40	1.00	2.00
❑2, Dec 85	1.75	0.40	1.00	2.00
❑3, Jan 85	1.75	0.40	1.00	2.00
❑4, Feb 86	1.75	0.40	1.00	2.00
❑5, Mar 86	1.75	0.40	1.00	2.00
❑6, Apr 86	1.75	0.40	1.00	2.00
❑7, May 86	1.75	0.40	1.00	2.00
❑8, Jun 86	1.75	0.40	1.00	2.00
❑9, Jul 86, Airboy preview	1.25	0.40	1.00	2.00
❑10, Aug 86	1.25	0.40	1.00	2.00
❑11, Sep 86	1.75	0.35	0.88	1.75
❑12, Oct 86, Me and the Devil	1.75	0.35	0.88	1.75
❑13, Nov 86	1.75	0.35	0.88	1.75
❑14, Dec 86	1.75	0.35	0.88	1.75
❑15, Jan 87	1.75	0.35	0.88	1.75
❑16, Feb 87, 3-D	2.50	0.50	1.25	2.50
❑17, Mar 87	1.75	0.35	0.88	1.75
❑18, Apr 87	1.75	0.35	0.88	1.75
❑19, May 87, flexidisc	2.50	0.60	1.50	3.00
❑20, Jun 87	1.75	0.35	0.88	1.75
❑21, Jul 87	1.75	0.35	0.88	1.75
❑22, Aug 87	1.75	0.35	0.88	1.75
❑23, Sep 87	1.75	0.35	0.88	1.75
❑24, Oct 87	1.75	0.35	0.88	1.75

SCOUT HANDBOOK
ECLIPSE

Value: Cover or less

❑1, nn 1.75

SCOUT: WAR SHAMAN
ECLIPSE

	ORIG	GOOD	FINE	N-MINT
❑1, Mar 88, Down in the Bottom	1.95	0.40	1.00	2.00
❑2, May 88	1.95	0.40	1.00	2.00

	ORIG	GOOD	FINE	N-MINT
❑3, Jun 88	1.95	0.40	1.00	2.00
❑4, Jul 88	1.95	0.40	1.00	2.00
❑5, Wooly Bully•War Movie!!, Part 1	—	0.40	1.00	2.00
❑6, Sep 88, Wooly Bully•War Movie!!, Part 2	1.95	0.40	1.00	2.00
❑7	—	0.40	1.00	2.00
❑8	—	0.40	1.00	2.00
❑9	—	0.40	1.00	2.00
❑10	—	0.40	1.00	2.00
❑11	—	0.40	1.00	2.00
❑12	—	0.40	1.00	2.00
❑13	—	0.40	1.00	2.00
❑14	—	0.40	1.00	2.00
❑15	—	0.40	1.00	2.00
❑16, D: Scout	—	0.40	1.00	2.00

SCRAP CITY PACK RATS
Out of the Blue
Value: Cover or less

- ❑1, Lightning Strikes, b&w 1.50
- ❑2, b&w 1.50
- ❑3, b&w 1.50
- ❑4, b&w 1.75
- ❑5, Clam on the Lam, b&w 1.75

SCRATCH
Outside
Value: Cover or less

- ❑1 ...... 1.75
- ❑2 ...... 1.75
- ❑3 ...... 1.75
- ❑4 ...... 1.75
- ❑5 ...... 1.75
- ❑6 ...... 1.75

SCREAMERS
Eros

	ORIG	GOOD	FINE	N-MINT
❑1	—	0.59	1.48	2.95
❑2	—	0.59	1.48	2.95
❑3, Oct 95, Rock Hard	2.95	0.59	1.48	2.95

SCREEN MONSTERS
Zone
Value: Cover or less

- ❑1 ...... 2.95

SCREENPLAY
Slave Labor
Value: Cover or less

- ❑1, Jun 89, b&w 1.75

SCREWBALL SQUIRREL
Dark Horse
Value: Cover or less

- ❑1, Jul 95, Mauled At The Mall, Wolf & Red back-up 2.50
- ❑2, Aug 95, Droopy back-up 2.50
- ❑3, Sep 95, Final Issue; Wolf & Red back-up 2.50

SCREW COMICS
Fantagraphics
Value: Cover or less

- ❑1, Juden Creature; The Adventures of Truli Godawful, Secretary at, b&w; adult 3.50

SCRUBS IN SCRUBLAND: THE REFLEX
Scrubland Prod.
Value: Cover or less

- ❑1, b&w; Anthology 2.50

SCUD: TALES FROM THE VENDING MACHINE
Fireman

	ORIG	GOOD	FINE	N-MINT
❑1	2.50	0.60	1.50	3.00
❑2	2.50	0.50	1.25	2.50
❑3	2.50	0.50	1.25	2.50
❑4, Rhythmic Metaphor	2.50	0.50	1.25	2.50

SCUD: THE DISPOSABLE ASSASSIN
Fireman Press

	ORIG	GOOD	FINE	N-MINT
❑1, Feb 94, 1: Scud, b&w; trading card	2.95	2.40	6.00	12.00
❑1-2, 1: Scud, 2nd Printing; trading card	2.95	0.60	1.50	3.00
❑, 1: Scud, 3rd Printing; trading card	2.95	0.60	1.50	3.00
❑2, May 94, b&w	2.95	1.20	3.00	6.00
❑3, b&w	2.95	1.00	2.50	5.00
❑4, b&w	2.95	1.00	2.50	5.00
❑5, b&w	2.95	1.00	2.50	5.00
❑6, b&w	2.95	0.80	2.00	4.00
❑7, b&w	2.95	0.80	2.00	4.00
❑8, b&w	2.95	0.80	2.00	4.00
❑9, b&w	2.95	0.80	2.00	4.00
❑10, b&w	2.95	0.80	2.00	4.00
❑11	2.95	0.60	1.50	3.00
❑12	2.95	0.60	1.50	3.00
❑13	2.95	0.60	1.50	3.00
❑14	2.95	0.60	1.50	3.00
❑15	2.95	0.60	1.50	3.00
❑16	2.95	0.59	1.48	2.95
❑17	2.95	0.59	1.48	2.95
❑18	2.95	0.59	1.48	2.95
❑19	2.95	0.59	1.48	2.95
❑20	2.95	0.59	1.48	2.95

SCUM OF THE EARTH
Aircel
Value: Cover or less

- ❑1, b&w; movie Adaptation 2.50
- ❑2, b&w; movie Adaptation 2.50

SEA DEVILS
DC

	ORIG	GOOD	FINE	N-MINT
❑1, Oct 61	0.10	65.00	162.50	325.00
❑2, Dec 61	0.10	37.00	92.50	185.00
❑3, Feb 62	0.12	25.00	62.50	125.00
❑4, Apr 62	0.12	18.00	45.00	90.00
❑5, Jun 62	0.12	18.00	45.00	90.00
❑6, Aug 62	0.12	12.00	30.00	60.00
❑7, Oct 62	0.12	12.00	30.00	60.00
❑8, Dec 62	0.12	12.00	30.00	60.00
❑9, Feb 63	0.12	12.00	30.00	60.00
❑10, Apr 63	0.12	12.00	30.00	60.00
❑11, Jun 63	0.12	8.00	20.00	40.00
❑12, Aug 63	0.12	8.00	20.00	40.00
❑13, Oct 63, JKu; GC	0.12	9.00	22.50	45.00
❑14, Dec 63	0.12	8.00	20.00	40.00
❑15, Feb 64	0.12	8.00	20.00	40.00
❑16, Apr 64	0.12	8.00	20.00	40.00
❑17, Jun 64	0.12	8.00	20.00	40.00
❑18, Aug 64	0.12	8.00	20.00	40.00
❑19, Oct 64	0.12	8.00	20.00	40.00
❑20, Dec 64, The Menace Of the Reptile Men	0.12	8.00	20.00	40.00
❑21, Feb 65	0.12	6.00	15.00	30.00
❑22, Apr 65	0.12	6.00	15.00	30.00
❑23, Jun 65	0.12	6.00	15.00	30.00
❑24, Aug 65	0.12	6.00	15.00	30.00
❑25, Oct 65	0.12	6.00	15.00	30.00
❑26, Dec 65	0.12	6.00	15.00	30.00
❑27, Feb 66	0.12	6.00	15.00	30.00
❑28, Apr 66	0.12	6.00	15.00	30.00
❑29, Jun 66	0.12	6.00	15.00	30.00
❑30, Aug 66	0.12	6.00	15.00	30.00
❑31, Oct 66	0.12	6.00	15.00	30.00
❑32, Dec 66	0.12	6.00	15.00	30.00
❑33, Feb 67	0.12	6.00	15.00	30.00
❑34, Apr 67	0.12	6.00	15.00	30.00
❑35, Jun 67, Final Issue	0.12	6.00	15.00	30.00

SEADRAGON, THE
Elite
Value: Cover or less

- ❑1, May 86, Beward the World of Shadows! 1.75
- ❑2, Jun 86 ...... 1.75
- ❑3, Aug 86 ...... 1.75
- ❑4 ...... 1.75
- ❑5 ...... 1.75
- ❑6 ...... 1.75

SEA HUNT
Dell

	ORIG	GOOD	FINE	N-MINT
❑4, Mar 60, Photo cover; numbering continues from Dell Four Color	0.10	7.00	17.50	35.00
❑5, Jun 60, Photo cover	0.10	7.00	17.50	35.00
❑6, Sep 60, Photo cover	0.10	7.00	17.50	35.00
❑7, Dec 60, Photo cover	0.10	6.00	15.00	30.00
❑8, Mar 61, no cover price	—	6.00	15.00	30.00
❑9, Jun 61, Underwater Cover-Up; Suspicious Waters, Photo cover	0.15	6.00	15.00	30.00
❑10, Sep 61, Photo cover	0.15	5.00	12.50	25.00
❑11, Dec 61, Photo cover	0.15	5.00	12.50	25.00
❑12, Mar 62, Photo cover	0.15	5.00	12.50	25.00
❑13, Jun 62, Photo cover	0.15	5.00	12.50	25.00

SEALS
Studio Aries

	ORIG	GOOD	FINE	N-MINT
❑Ash 1, May 00, b&w; preview	—	0.20	0.50	1.00

SEAQUEST
Nemesis

	ORIG	GOOD	FINE	N-MINT
❑1, Mar 94, KP, Deep Faith, cardstock cover; based on TV show	2.25	0.50	1.25	2.50
❑2	2.25	0.45	1.13	2.25
❑3	2.25	0.45	1.13	2.25

SEARCHERS, THE
Caliber
Value: Cover or less

- ❑1 ...... 2.95
- ❑2 ...... 2.95
- ❑3 ...... 2.95
- ❑4 ...... 2.95

SEARCHERS, THE: APOSTLE OF MERCY
Caliber
Value: Cover or less

- ❑1, Giant-size 2.95
- ❑2 ...... 3.95

SEBASTIAN (WALT DISNEY'S...)
Disney

	ORIG	GOOD	FINE	N-MINT
❑1, Fiddling Around; Sebastian In Scotland	1.50	0.40	1.00	2.00
❑2	1.50	0.40	1.00	2.00

SEBASTIAN O
DC

	ORIG	GOOD	FINE	N-MINT
❑1, May 93, The Yellow Book, 1: Sebastian O	1.95	0.40	1.00	2.00
❑2, Jun 93, Against Nature	1.95	0.40	1.00	2.00
❑3, Jul 93, The Queen Is Dead	1.95	0.40	1.00	2.00

SECOND CITY
HARRIER
Value: Cover or less

- ❑1 ... 1.95
- ❑2 ... 1.95
- ❑3 ... 1.95
- ❑4 ... 1.95

SECOND LIFE OF DOCTOR MIRAGE, THE
VALIANT

	ORIG	GOOD	FINE	N-MINT
❑1, Nov 93, BL (w), Darque Passage, A: Master Darque; D: Gwen Mirage; O: Doctor Mirage	2.50	0.50	1.25	2.50
❑1/GO, Nov 93, Gold edition	—	0.60	1.50	3.00
❑2, Dec 93	2.50	0.50	1.25	2.50
❑3, Jan 94	2.50	0.50	1.25	2.50
❑4, Feb 94	2.50	0.50	1.25	2.50
❑5, Mar 94, A: Shadowman	2.50	0.50	1.25	2.50
❑6, Apr 94	2.50	0.50	1.25	2.50
❑7, May 94, V: Doctor Eclipse, trading card	2.50	0.50	1.25	2.50
❑8, Jun 94	2.50	0.50	1.25	2.50
❑9, Aug 94	2.50	0.50	1.25	2.50
❑10, Sep 94	2.50	0.50	1.25	2.50
❑11, Oct 94, The Chaos Effect: Beta, Part 2, Chaos Effect	2.50	0.50	1.25	2.50
❑12, Nov 94	2.50	0.50	1.25	2.50
❑13, Dec 94, A: Walt Willey	2.50	0.50	1.25	2.50
❑14, Jan 95	2.50	0.50	1.25	2.50
❑15, Feb 95	2.50	0.50	1.25	2.50
❑16, Mar 95, Building the Perfect Beast, Part 1	2.50	0.50	1.25	2.50
❑17, Apr 95, Building the Perfect Beast, Part 2	2.50	0.50	1.25	2.50
❑18, May 95, Building the Perfect Beast, Part 3, Final Issue	2.50	0.50	1.25	2.50

SECOND RATE HEROES
FOUNDATION
Value: Cover or less

- ❑1, b&w ... 2.50
- ❑2, b&w ... 2.50

SECRET AGENT (CHARLTON)
CHARLTON

	ORIG	GOOD	FINE	N-MINT
❑9, Oct 66, The Warmaker!, 1: Mr. Ize!, Series continued from Sarge Steel #8	0.25	1.60	4.00	8.00
❑10, Oct 67	0.12	1.20	3.00	6.00

SECRET AGENT (GOLD KEY)
GOLD KEY

	ORIG	GOOD	FINE	N-MINT
❑1, Nov 66, The Panic Package, Photo cover	0.12	8.00	20.00	40.00
❑2, Jan 68, Photo cover	0.12	5.00	12.50	25.00

SECRET AGENTS
PERSONALITY
Value: Cover or less

- ❑1, b&w ... 2.95
- ❑2, b&w ... 2.95
- ❑3, b&w ... 2.95

SECRET CITY SAGA (JACK KIRBY'S...)
TOPPS
Value: Cover or less

- ❑0, Apr 93, Amemoto: Mephistopheles ... 2.95
- ❑1, May 93, SD, SD (w), In Battle Joined, trading cards ... 2.95
- ❑2, Jun 93, JBy; BSz; SD, trading cards ... 2.95
- ❑3, Jul 93, SD, trading cards ... 2.95
- ❑4, Aug 93, SD, trading cards ... 2.95

SECRET DEFENDERS
MARVEL

	ORIG	GOOD	FINE	N-MINT
❑1, Mar 93, foil cover; Story continued from Doctor Strange #50	2.50	0.50	1.25	2.50
❑2, Apr 93	1.75	0.35	0.88	1.75
❑3, May 93	1.75	0.35	0.88	1.75
❑4, Jun 93	1.75	0.35	0.88	1.75
❑5, Jul 93	1.75	0.35	0.88	1.75
❑6, Aug 93	1.75	0.35	0.88	1.75
❑7, Sep 93	1.75	0.35	0.88	1.75
❑8, Oct 93, A: Xanadu; A: Doctor Strange; A: Scarlet Witch; A: Spider-Man; A: Captain America	1.75	0.35	0.88	1.75
❑9, Nov 93, Revenge, Part 1	1.75	0.35	0.88	1.75
❑10, Dec 93	1.75	0.35	0.88	1.75
❑11, Jan 94	1.75	0.35	0.88	1.75
❑12, Feb 94, foil cover	2.50	0.50	1.25	2.50
❑13, Mar 94	1.75	0.35	0.88	1.75
❑14, Apr 94	1.75	0.35	0.88	1.75
❑15, May 94	1.95	0.35	0.88	1.75
❑16, Jun 94	1.95	0.39	0.98	1.95
❑17, Jul 94	1.95	0.39	0.98	1.95
❑18, Aug 94	1.95	0.39	0.98	1.95
❑19, Sep 94	1.95	0.39	0.98	1.95
❑20, Oct 94	1.95	0.39	0.98	1.95
❑21, Nov 94	1.95	0.39	0.98	1.95
❑22, Dec 94	1.95	0.39	0.98	1.95
❑23, Jan 95	1.95	0.39	0.98	1.95
❑24, Feb 95, V: original Defenders	1.95	0.39	0.98	1.95
❑25, Mar 95, Final Issue; Giant-size	1.95	0.50	1.25	2.50

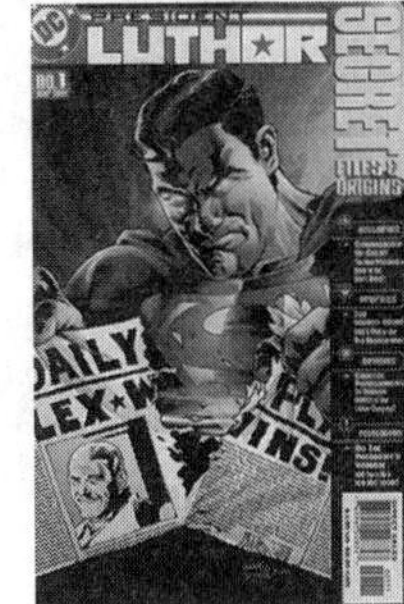

The secrets of the DC universe's U.S. President, Lex Luthor, were revealed in *Secret Files President Luthor.*

© 2001 DC Comics

SECRET DOORS
DIMENSION
Value: Cover or less

- ❑1, b&w ... 1.50

SECRET FANTASIES
BULLSEYE
Value: Cover or less

- ❑1, b&w and red; digest ... 2.25
- ❑2, b&w; cardstock cover; normal-sized ... 2.95

SECRET FILES
ANGEL
Value: Cover or less

- ❑0, Jun 96, b&w ... 2.95
- ❑0/Nude, Jun 96, b&w; cardstock cover; nude cover edition ... 10.00
- ❑1, Fal 96, b&w ... 2.95

SECRET FILES AND ORIGINS GUIDE TO THE DC UNIVERSE 2000
DC
Value: Cover or less

- ❑1 ... 4.95

SECRET FILES: INVASION DAY
ANGEL
Value: Cover or less

- ❑1 ... 5.00
- ❑1/Nude ... 5.00
- ❑2 ... 5.00
- ❑2/Nude ... 5.00

SECRET FILES PRESIDENT LUTHOR
DC
Value: Cover or less

- ❑1, Mar 01, JPH (w), The Why; Most Suitable Person ... 4.95

SECRET FILES: THE STRANGE CASE
ANGEL
Value: Cover or less

- ❑1, Pretty Little Secrets ... 2.95

SECRET KILLERS, THE
BRONZE MAN
Value: Cover or less

- ❑1, Oct 97, Where Dragons Roam, Part 1, b&w ... 2.95
- ❑2, Where Dragons Roam, Part 2, b&w ... 2.95
- ❑3, b&w ... 2.95
- ❑4, b&w; cover doesn't; becomes Exit from Shadow; indicia indicates name change ... 2.95

SECRET ORIGINS (1ST SERIES)
DC

	ORIG	GOOD	FINE	N-MINT
❑Anl 1, Aug 61, second issue published as 80 Page Giant #8; reprints Silver Age origins	0.12	90.00	225.00	450.00

SECRET ORIGINS (2ND SERIES)
DC

	ORIG	GOOD	FINE	N-MINT
❑1, Mar 73, JKu; CI, The Ghost; Mystery of the Human Thunderbolt!, O: Batman; O: Flash; O: Superman	0.20	2.80	7.00	14.00
❑2, May 73	0.20	1.60	4.00	8.00
❑3, Aug 73, O: Wildcat; O: Wonder Woman	0.20	1.40	3.50	7.00
❑4, Oct 73, O: Vigilante; O: Kid Eternity	0.20	1.40	3.50	7.00
❑5, Dec 73	0.20	1.20	3.00	6.00
❑6, Feb 74	0.20	1.20	3.00	6.00
❑7, Oct 74, O: Aquaman; O: Robin I (Dick Grayson)	0.20	1.20	3.00	6.00

SECRET ORIGINS (3RD SERIES)
DC

	ORIG	GOOD	FINE	N-MINT
❑1, Apr 86, O: Superman	0.75	0.60	1.50	3.00
❑2, May 86, O: Blue Beetle	0.75	0.40	1.00	2.00
❑3, Jun 86, O: Captain Marvel	0.75	0.40	1.00	2.00
❑4, Jul 86, O: Firestorm	0.75	0.40	1.00	2.00
❑5, Aug 86, O: The Crimson Avenger	0.75	0.40	1.00	2.00
❑6, Sep 86, O: Batman (Golden Age); O: Halo	1.25	0.40	1.00	2.00
❑7, Oct 86, O: Green Lantern (Guy Gardner); O: Sandman II (Dr. Garrett Sanford)	1.25	0.40	1.00	2.00
❑8, Nov 86, O: Shadow Lass; O: Doll Man.	1.25	0.40	1.00	2.00
❑9, Dec 86, O: Stripsey; O: Skyman; O: Flash I (Jay Garrick)	1.25	0.40	1.00	2.00
❑10, Jan 87, O: Phantom Stranger, Legends	1.25	0.40	1.00	2.00
❑11, Feb 87, JOy (c), O: Hawkman (Golden Age); O: Power Girl	1.25	0.40	1.00	2.00
❑12, Mar 87, O: Challengers of the Unknown; O: The Fury (Golden Age)	1.25	0.40	1.00	2.00
❑13, Apr 87, O: Whip; O: Nightwing; O: Johnny Thunder	1.25	0.40	1.00	2.00
❑14, May 87, O: Suicide Squad, Legends..	1.25	0.40	1.00	2.00
❑15, Jun 87, O: Deadman; O: Spectre	1.25	0.40	1.00	2.00
❑16, Jul 87, O: Warlord; O: Hourman I (Rex Tyler)	1.25	0.40	1.00	2.00

	ORIG	GOOD	FINE	N-MINT
❑17, Aug 87, O: Doctor Occult; O: Adam Strange	1.25	0.40	1.00	2.00
❑18, Sep 87, O: Green Lantern I (Alan Scott); O: Creeper	1.25	0.40	1.00	2.00
❑19, Oct 87, MA, JK (c), O: Guardian; O: Uncle Sam	1.25	0.40	1.00	2.00
❑20, Nov 87, O: Batgirl; O: Doctor Mid-Nite (Golden Age)	1.25	0.40	1.00	2.00
❑21, Dec 87, O: Jonah Hex; O: Black Condor	1.25	0.40	1.00	2.00
❑22, Jan 88, O: Manhunters, Millennium	1.25	0.40	1.00	2.00
❑23, Feb 88, O: Guardians of the Universe; O: Floronic Man, Millennium	1.25	0.40	1.00	2.00
❑24, Mar 88, O: Doctor Fate; O: Blue Devil	1.25	0.40	1.00	2.00
❑25, Apr 88, O: the Legion of Super-Heroes; O: The Atom (Golden Age)	1.25	0.40	1.00	2.00
❑26, May 88, O: Black Lightning; O: Miss America	1.25	0.40	1.00	2.00
❑27, Jun 88, O: Zatanna; O: Zatara	1.50	0.40	1.00	2.00
❑28, Jul 88, O: Midnight; O: Nightshade	1.50	0.40	1.00	2.00
❑29, Aug 88, O: Mr. America; O: Red Tornado (Golden Age); O: The Atom (Silver Age)	1.50	0.40	1.00	2.00
❑30, Sep 88, O: Elongated Man; O: Plastic Man	1.50	0.40	1.00	2.00
❑31, Oct 88, O: Justice Society of America	1.50	0.40	1.00	2.00
❑32, Nov 88, O: Justice League of America	1.50	0.40	1.00	2.00
❑33, Dec 88, O: Mr. Miracle; O: Green Flame; O: Icemaiden	1.50	0.40	1.00	2.00
❑34, Dec 88, O: Captain Atom; O: G'Nort; O: Rocket Red	1.50	0.40	1.00	2.00
❑35, Jan 89, O: Max Lord; O: Martian Manhunter; O: Booster Gold	1.50	0.40	1.00	2.00
❑36, Jan 89, O: Poison Ivy; O: Green Lantern (Silver Age)	1.50	0.40	1.00	2.00
❑37, Feb 89, O: Legion of Substitute Heroes; O: Doctor Light	1.50	0.40	1.00	2.00
❑38, Mar 89, O: Green Arrow; O: Speedy	1.50	0.40	1.00	2.00
❑39, Apr 89, O: Man-Bat; O: Animal Man	1.50	0.40	1.00	2.00
❑40, May 89, O: Detective Chimp; O: Congorilla; O: Gorilla Grodd	1.50	0.40	1.00	2.00
❑41, Jun 89, O: Flash's Rogue's Gallery	1.50	0.40	1.00	2.00
❑42, Jul 89, O: Phantom Girl; O: Grim Ghost	1.50	0.40	1.00	2.00
❑43, Aug 89, O: Cave Carson; O: Dove; O: Hawk; O: Chris KL-99	1.50	0.40	1.00	2.00
❑44, Sep 89, O: Clayface II; O: Clayface IV; O: Clayface I; O: Clayface III	1.50	0.40	1.00	2.00
❑45, Oct 89, O: El Diablo; O: Blackhawk	1.50	0.40	1.00	2.00
❑46, Dec 89, Blueprints of Teen Titans Headquarters, Legion of Super-Heroes Headquarters	1.75	0.40	1.00	2.00
❑47, Feb 90, O: Ferro Lad; O: Chemical King; O: Karate Kid	1.75	0.40	1.00	2.00
❑48, Apr 90, O: Stanley and His Monster; O: Trigger Twins; O: Ambush Bug; O: Rex the Wonder Dog	1.75	0.40	1.00	2.00
❑49, Jun 90, O: Silent Knight; O: Bouncing Boy; O: Newsboy Legion	1.75	0.40	1.00	2.00
❑50, Aug 90, O: Dolphin; O: Earth-2; O: Black Canary; O: Space Museum; O: Johnny Thunder (cowboy); O: Robin I (Dick Grayson), 100pgs.; Final Issue	3.95	0.40	1.00	2.00
❑Anl 1, JBy (c), O: The Doom Patrol	2.00	0.40	1.00	2.00
❑Anl 2, O: Flash II (Barry Allen); O: Flash III (Wally West)	2.00	0.40	1.00	2.00
❑Anl 3, 1: Flamebird; O: Teen Titans	2.95	0.40	1.00	2.00
❑GS 1, Dec 98, O: Secret; O: Arrowette; O: Spoiler; O: Impulse; O: Superboy; O: Robin III (Tim Drake); O: Wonder Girl, 80pgs.	4.95	0.99	2.47	4.95
❑SE 1, Oct 89, O: Penguin; O: Two-Face; O: Riddler	2.00	0.40	1.00	2.00

SECRET ORIGINS OF KRANKIN' KOMIX
KRANKIN' KOMIX

Value: Cover or less

❑1, Nov 96 .... 1.00

SECRET ORIGINS OF SUPER-VILLAINS
DC

Value: Cover or less

❑GS 1, Dec 99, Random Choice; The Rise of Tartarus, O: Granny Goodness; O: Encantadora; O: Tartarus; O: Sinestro; O: Johnny Sorrow; O: Echo; O: Amazo 4.95

SECRET ORIGINS OF THE WORLD'S GREATEST SUPER HEROES
DC

Value: Cover or less

❑1 .... 4.95

SECRET ORIGINS REPLICA EDITION
DC

Value: Cover or less

❑1, cardstock fold-out cover; reprints Secret Origins #1 (1st series) 4.95

SECRET PLOT
EROS

Value: Cover or less

❑1, Oct 97, Junkie Teacher..... 2.95

❑2 .... 2.95

SECRET SIX
DC

	ORIG	GOOD	FINE	N-MINT
❑1, May 68, 1: The Secret Six, splash page is cover	0.12	6.00	15.00	30.00
❑2, Jul 68, Plunder the Pentagon!	0.12	3.60	9.00	18.00
❑3, Sep 68	0.12	2.40	6.00	12.00
❑4, Nov 68	0.12	2.40	6.00	12.00
❑5, Jan 69	0.12	2.40	6.00	12.00
❑6, Mar 69	0.12	2.40	6.00	12.00
❑7, May 69, Final Issue	0.12	2.40	6.00	12.00

SECRET SOCIETY OF SUPER-VILLAINS
DC

	ORIG	GOOD	FINE	N-MINT
❑1, Jun 76, O: Secret Society	0.30	1.00	2.50	5.00
❑2, Aug 76, A: Captain Comet	0.30	0.70	1.75	3.50
❑3, Oct 76	0.30	0.70	1.75	3.50
❑4, Dec 76	0.30	0.70	1.75	3.50
❑5, Feb 77	0.30	0.70	1.75	3.50
❑6, Apr 77	0.30	0.50	1.25	2.50
❑7, Jun 77	0.30	0.50	1.25	2.50
❑8, Aug 77	0.35	0.50	1.25	2.50
❑9, Sep 77	0.35	0.50	1.25	2.50
❑10, Oct 77	0.35	0.50	1.25	2.50
❑11, Dec 77	0.35	0.50	1.25	2.50
❑12, Jan 78	0.35	0.50	1.25	2.50
❑13, Mar 78	0.35	0.50	1.25	2.50
❑14, May 78	0.35	0.50	1.25	2.50
❑15, Jul 78, Final Issue	0.35	0.50	1.25	2.50

SECRETS OF DRAWING COMICS (RICH BUCKLER'S...)
SHOWCASE

Value: Cover or less

❑1, Jan 94, RB, RB (w) 2.50

❑2, RB, RB (w) 2.50

❑3, RB, RB (w) 2.50

❑4, RB, RB (w) 2.50

SECRETS OF SINISTER HOUSE
DC

	ORIG	GOOD	FINE	N-MINT
❑5, Continues from Sinister House of Secret Love #4	0.20	1.00	2.50	5.00
❑6	0.20	0.80	2.00	4.00
❑7	0.20	0.80	2.00	4.00
❑8	0.20	0.80	2.00	4.00
❑9	0.20	0.80	2.00	4.00
❑10, NA	0.20	1.20	3.00	6.00
❑11	0.20	0.80	2.00	4.00
❑12	0.20	0.80	2.00	4.00
❑13	0.20	0.80	2.00	4.00
❑14	0.20	0.80	2.00	4.00
❑15	0.20	0.80	2.00	4.00
❑16	0.20	0.80	2.00	4.00
❑17	0.20	0.80	2.00	4.00
❑18, GK, The Strange Shop on Demon Street; Mad to Order, Final Issue	0.20	0.80	2.00	4.00

SECRETS OF THE LEGION OF SUPER-HEROES
DC

	ORIG	GOOD	FINE	N-MINT
❑1, Jan 81, O: the Legion of Super-Heroes	0.50	0.40	1.00	2.00
❑2, Feb 81	0.50	0.40	1.00	2.00
❑3, Mar 81	0.50	0.40	1.00	2.00

SECRETS OF THE VALIANT UNIVERSE
VALIANT

	ORIG	GOOD	FINE	N-MINT
❑1, May 94, BH (w); BL (w), Wizard Magazine promo; no price; bagged with Wizard Special	—	0.40	1.00	2.00
❑2, Oct 94, BH (w), The Chaos Effect: Beta, Part 4, Chaos Effect	2.25	0.45	1.13	2.25
❑3, Oct 95, BL (w), Torn Between Two Mothers, cover says Feb; future Rai; indicia says Oct	2.25	0.45	1.13	2.25

SECRETUM SECRETORUM
TWILIGHT TWINS

Value: Cover or less

❑0 .... 3.50

SECRET WARS II
MARVEL

	ORIG	GOOD	FINE	N-MINT
❑1, Jul 85, A: New Mutants; A: X-Men	0.75	0.40	1.00	2.00
❑2, Aug 85, A: Iron Fist; A: Power Man; D: Hate-Monger III ("H.M. Unger"); A: Spider-Man; A: Fantastic Four	0.75	0.30	0.75	1.50
❑3, Sep 85	0.75	0.30	0.75	1.50
❑4, Oct 85, V: Avengers; 1: Kurse; A: Kursei	0.75	0.30	0.75	1.50
❑5, Nov 85, V: Avengers; 1: Boomer (Boom Boom); V: New Mutants; V: Fantastic Four; V: X-Men	0.75	0.50	1.25	2.50
❑6, Dec 85	0.75	0.30	0.75	1.50
❑7, Jan 86, V: All villains	0.75	0.30	0.75	1.50
❑8, Feb 86, O: Beyonder	0.75	0.30	0.75	1.50
❑9, Mar 86, D: Beyonder, double-sized	1.25	0.30	0.75	1.50

SECRET WEAPONS
VALIANT

	ORIG	GOOD	FINE	N-MINT
❑1, Sep 93, 1: Doctor Eclipse, Serial number contest	2.25	0.50	1.25	2.50
❑1/GO, Sep 93, Gold edition	—	0.60	1.50	3.00

	ORIG	GOOD	FINE	N-MINT
❑2, Oct 93	2.25	0.45	1.13	2.25
❑3, Nov 93, Empirical Dynasty, Part 1	2.25	0.45	1.13	2.25
❑4, Dec 93	2.25	0.45	1.13	2.25
❑5, Jan 94, A: Ninjak	2.25	0.45	1.13	2.25
❑6, Feb 94, The Horror Below, Part 1	2.25	0.45	1.13	2.25
❑7, Mar 94, The Horror Below, Part 2, A: Turok; A: X-O Manowar	2.25	0.45	1.13	2.25
❑8, Apr 94, V: Harbinger	2.25	0.45	1.13	2.25
❑9, May 94, A: Bloodshot, trading card	2.25	0.45	1.13	2.25
❑10, Jun 94	2.25	0.45	1.13	2.25
❑11, Aug 94, A: Bloodshot, Enclosed in manila envelope "For Your Eyes Only" cover; bagged top secret	2.50	0.45	1.13	2.25
❑12, Sep 94, A: Bloodshot	2.25	0.45	1.13	2.25
❑13, Oct 94, The Chaos Effect: Gamma, Part 2, Chaos Effect	2.25	0.45	1.13	2.25
❑14, Nov 94	2.25	0.45	1.13	2.25
❑15, Dec 94	2.25	0.45	1.13	2.25
❑16, Jan 95	2.25	0.45	1.13	2.25
❑17, Feb 95	2.25	0.45	1.13	2.25
❑18, Mar 95, A: Ninjak	2.25	0.45	1.13	2.25
❑19, Apr 95	2.25	0.45	1.13	2.25
❑20, May 95, Rampage, Part 2; Bloodshot Rampage, Part 2, (see Bloodshot #28)	2.25	0.45	1.13	2.25
❑21, May 95, Rampage, Part 4; Bloodshot Rampage, Part 4, Final Issue	2.25	0.45	1.13	2.25

SECTAURS
MARVEL

	ORIG	GOOD	FINE	N-MINT
❑1	0.75	0.20	0.50	1.00
❑2, Aug 85	0.75	0.20	0.50	1.00
❑3	0.75	0.20	0.50	1.00
❑4	0.75	0.20	0.50	1.00
❑5	0.75	0.20	0.50	1.00
❑6	0.75	0.20	0.50	1.00
❑7	0.75	0.20	0.50	1.00
❑8	0.75	0.20	0.50	1.00

SECTION 12
MYTHIC

Value: Cover or less

❑1, Awakenings!, b&w 2.95

SECTION ZERO
IMAGE

Value: Cover or less

❑1, Jun 00, Ground Zero, Part 1 .... 2.50

❑2, Jul 00, Ground Zero, Part 2 .... 2.50

❑3, Sep 00, Ground Zero, Part 3 .... 2.50

SEDUCTION
ETERNITY

	ORIG	GOOD	FINE	N-MINT
❑1, Second Stringer; In Site, b&w	0.25	0.50	1.25	2.50

SEDUCTION OF THE INNOCENT (ECLIPSE)
ECLIPSE

	ORIG	GOOD	FINE	N-MINT
❑1, MM, DSt (w), Adventures into Darkness; Death Dives Deep, Reprints from Adventures into Darkness #6, Out of the Shadows #7, Fantastic Worlds #7, Out of the Shadows #9	1.75	0.50	1.25	2.50
❑2, Was he Death-Proof?; More Deadly Than the Male	1.75	0.40	1.00	2.00
❑3, ATh, The Crushed Gardenia; The Cup of the Dead	1.75	0.40	1.00	2.00
❑4, ATh, ATh (w), Images of Sand; The Beast From the Deep	1.75	0.40	1.00	2.00
❑5, TY; ATh, ATh (w), Phantom Ship; Death Drum	1.75	0.40	1.00	2.00
❑6, RA (w); FF (w); GT (w); ATh (w), The Hands of Don Jose; Your Grave is Ready	1.75	0.40	1.00	2.00
❑3D 1, MM, DSt (c), DSt (w), Adventures into Darkness; Death Dives Deep	2.25	0.50	1.25	2.50
❑3D 2, BWr (c), Was He Death-Proof?; More Deadly Than the Male	2.25	0.50	1.25	2.50

SEEKER
CALIBER

Value: Cover or less

❑1, Apr 94, b&w 2.95

❑2, b&w 2.95

SEEKER 3000
MARVEL

	ORIG	GOOD	FINE	N-MINT
❑1, Jun 98, A New Beginning..., wraparound cover	2.99	0.60	1.50	2.99
❑2, Jul 98, wraparound cover	2.50	0.60	1.50	2.99
❑3, Aug 98, wraparound cover	2.50	0.60	1.50	2.99
❑4, Sep 98, wraparound cover	2.50	0.60	1.50	2.99

SEEKER 3000 PREMIERE
MARVEL

Value: Cover or less

❑1, Jun 98, reprints Marvel Premiere #41 .... 1.50

SEEKERS INTO THE MYSTERY
DC

	ORIG	GOOD	FINE	N-MINT
❑1, Jan 96, The Pilgrimage of Lucas Hart, Part 1	2.50	0.50	1.25	2.50
❑2, Feb 96, The Pilgrimage of Lucas Hart, Part 2	2.50	0.50	1.25	2.50

Eclipse reprinted a number of pre-Comics Code horror stories in its short-lived *Seduction of the Innocent* series.

	ORIG	GOOD	FINE	N-MINT
❑3, Mar 96, The Pilgrimage of Lucas Hart, Part 3	2.50	0.50	1.25	2.50
❑4, Apr 96, The Pilgrimage of Lucas Hart, Part 4	2.50	0.50	1.25	2.50
❑5, Jun 96, The Pilgrimage of Lucas Hart, Part 5	2.50	0.50	1.25	2.50
❑6, Jul 96, Falling Down to Heaven, Part 1	2.50	0.50	1.25	2.50
❑7, Aug 96, Falling Down to Heaven, Part 2, Gently Stealing	2.50	0.50	1.25	2.50
❑8, Sep 96, Falling Down to Heaven, Part 3	2.50	0.50	1.25	2.50
❑9, Oct 96, Falling Down to Heaven, Part 4	2.50	0.50	1.25	2.50
❑10, Nov 96, Falling Down to Heaven, Part 5	2.50	0.50	1.25	2.50
❑11, Dec 96, God's Shadow, Part 1	2.50	0.50	1.25	2.50
❑12, Jan 97, God's Shadow, Part 2	2.50	0.50	1.25	2.50
❑13, Feb 97, God's Shadow, Part 3	2.50	0.50	1.25	2.50
❑14, Mar 97, God's Shadow, Part 4	2.50	0.50	1.25	2.50
❑15, Apr 97, The Death of Lucas Hart, Final Issue	2.50	0.59	1.48	2.95

SEEKER: VENGEANCE
SKY

	ORIG	GOOD	FINE	N-MINT
❑1, Nov 93	2.50	0.50	1.25	2.50
❑1/GO, Nov 93, Gold edition	2.50	0.60	1.50	3.00
❑2	2.50	0.50	1.25	2.50

SELF-LOATHING COMICS
FANTAGRAPHICS

Value: Cover or less

❑1, A Day in the Life; A Day in the Life of Aline Kominsky-Crumb-Crumb 3.50

❑2 .... 3.50

SEMPER FI
MARVEL

	ORIG	GOOD	FINE	N-MINT
❑1, Dec 88, JSe	0.75	0.25	0.63	1.25
❑2, Jan 89, JSe	0.75	0.25	0.63	1.25
❑3, Feb 89, JSe	0.75	0.25	0.63	1.25
❑4, Mar 89, JSe	0.75	0.25	0.63	1.25
❑5, Apr 89, JSe	0.75	0.25	0.63	1.25
❑6, May 89, JSe	0.75	0.25	0.63	1.25
❑7, Jun 89, JSe	0.75	0.25	0.63	1.25
❑8, Jul 89, JSe	0.75	0.25	0.63	1.25
❑9, Aug 89, JSe	0.75	0.25	0.63	1.25

SENSATIONAL SHE-HULK, THE
MARVEL

	ORIG	GOOD	FINE	N-MINT
❑1, May 89, JBy, JBy (w)	1.50	0.50	1.25	2.50
❑2, Jun 89, JBy, JBy (w), V: Toad Men	1.50	0.40	1.00	2.00
❑3, Jul 89, JBy, JBy (w), A: Spider-Man	1.50	0.40	1.00	2.00
❑4, Aug 89, JBy, JBy (w), A: Blonde Phantom	1.50	0.40	1.00	2.00
❑5, Sep 89, JBy, JBy (w)	1.50	0.40	1.00	2.00
❑6, Oct 89, JBy, JBy (w), A: Razorback	1.50	0.40	1.00	2.00
❑7, Nov 89, JBy, JBy (w), A: Razorback	1.50	0.40	1.00	2.00
❑8, Nov 89, JBy, JBy (w), A: Nick St. Christopher	1.50	0.40	1.00	2.00
❑9, Dec 89, V: Madcap	1.50	0.35	0.88	1.75
❑10, Dec 89	1.50	0.35	0.88	1.75
❑11, Jan 90	1.50	0.35	0.88	1.75
❑12, Feb 90	1.50	0.35	0.88	1.75
❑13, Mar 90	1.50	0.35	0.88	1.75
❑14, Apr 90, A: Howard the Duck	1.50	0.35	0.88	1.75
❑15, May 90, A: Howard the Duck	1.50	0.35	0.88	1.75
❑16, Jun 90, A: Howard the Duck	1.50	0.35	0.88	1.75
❑17, Jul 90, A: Howard the Duck	1.50	0.35	0.88	1.75
❑18, Aug 90, The Dentist in the Iron Mask	1.50	0.35	0.88	1.75
❑19, Sep 90, Year Zero, A: Nosferata the She-Bat	1.50	0.35	0.88	1.75
❑20, Oct 90	1.50	0.35	0.88	1.75
❑21, Nov 90, Blonde Phantom	1.50	0.35	0.88	1.75
❑22, Dec 90, Blonde Phantom	1.50	0.35	0.88	1.75
❑23, Jan 91, Blonde Phantom	1.50	0.35	0.88	1.75
❑24, Feb 91, Death's Head	1.50	0.35	0.88	1.75
❑25, Mar 91, Hercules	1.50	0.35	0.88	1.75
❑26, Apr 91	1.50	0.35	0.88	1.75
❑27, May 91, white inside covers	1.50	0.35	0.88	1.75
❑28, Jun 91	1.50	0.35	0.88	1.75

	ORIG	GOOD	FINE	N-MINT
❑29, Jul 91	1.50	0.35	0.88	1.75
❑30, Aug 91	1.50	0.35	0.88	1.75
❑31, Sep 91, JBy, JBy (w)	1.50	0.35	0.88	1.75
❑32, Oct 91, JBy, JBy (w)	1.50	0.35	0.88	1.75
❑33, Nov 91, JBy, JBy (w)	1.50	0.35	0.88	1.75
❑34, Dec 91, JBy, JBy (w)	1.50	0.35	0.88	1.75
❑35, Jan 92, JBy, JBy (w)	1.50	0.35	0.88	1.75
❑36, Feb 92, JBy, JBy (w), A: Wyatt Wingfoot	1.75	0.35	0.88	1.75
❑37, Mar 92, JBy, JBy (w)	1.75	0.35	0.88	1.75
❑38, Apr 92, JBy, JBy (w), V: Mahkizmo	1.75	0.35	0.88	1.75
❑39, May 92, JBy, JBy (w), V: Mahkizmo; A: Thing	1.75	0.35	0.88	1.75
❑40, Jun 92, JBy, JBy (w)	1.75	0.35	0.88	1.75
❑41, Jul 92, JBy, JBy (w)	1.75	0.35	0.88	1.75
❑42, Aug 92, JBy, JBy (w)	1.75	0.35	0.88	1.75
❑43, Sep 92, JBy, JBy (w)	1.75	0.35	0.88	1.75
❑44, Oct 92, JBy, JBy (w)	1.75	0.35	0.88	1.75
❑45, Nov 92, JBy, JBy (w)	1.75	0.35	0.88	1.75
❑46, Dec 92, JBy, JBy (w)	1.75	0.35	0.88	1.75
❑47, Jan 93, JBy, JBy (w)	1.75	0.35	0.88	1.75
❑48, Feb 93, JBy, JBy (w)	1.75	0.35	0.88	1.75
❑49, Mar 93, JBy, JBy (w)	1.75	0.35	0.88	1.75
❑50, Apr 93, FM; DG; HC; JBy; WP, FM (w); JBy (w), Green foil cover; Double-size	2.95	0.59	1.48	2.95
❑51, May 93, Savage She-Hulk vs. Sensational She-Hulk	1.75	0.35	0.88	1.75
❑52, Jun 93, To Die and Live in L.A., Part 1	1.75	0.35	0.88	1.75
❑53, Jul 93, To Die and Live in L.A., Part 2	1.75	0.35	0.88	1.75
❑54, Aug 93, To Die and Live in L.A., Part 3	1.75	0.35	0.88	1.75
❑55, Sep 93, To Die and Live in L.A., Part 4	1.75	0.35	0.88	1.75
❑56, Oct 93, To Die and Live in L.A., Part 5, A: Hulk	1.75	0.35	0.88	1.75
❑57, Nov 93, To Die and Live in L.A., Part 6, A: Hulk	1.75	0.35	0.88	1.75
❑58, Dec 93, V: Electro; A: Tommy the Gopher	1.75	0.35	0.88	1.75
❑59, Jan 94	1.75	0.35	0.88	1.75
❑60, Feb 94, A: Millie the Model, Final Issue	1.75	0.35	0.88	1.75

SENSATIONAL SHE-HULK IN CEREMONY, THE
MARVEL

Value: Cover or less

❑1, leg shaving ... 3.95
❑2 ... 3.95

SENSATIONAL SPIDER-MAN, THE
MARVEL

	ORIG	GOOD	FINE	N-MINT
❑-1, Jul 97, Flashback	1.99	0.40	1.00	2.00
❑0, Jan 96, Ultimate Commitment, O: Spider-Man; 1: Armada, enhanced wraparound cardstock cover with lenticular animation card attached; new costume	4.95	1.00	2.50	5.00
❑1, Feb 96, Media Blizzard, Part 1	1.95	0.40	1.00	2.00
❑2, Mar 96	1.95	0.40	1.00	2.00
❑2/CS, Feb 96, Media Blizzard, Part 1, cassette	2.95	0.59	1.48	2.95
❑3, Apr 96, Web of Carnage, Part 1	1.95	0.40	1.00	2.00
❑4, May 96, Blood Brothers, Part 1, Ben Reilly revealed as Spider-Man	1.95	0.40	1.00	2.00
❑5, Jun 96, Blood Brothers, Part 5, V: Molten Man	1.95	0.40	1.00	2.00
❑6, Jul 96	1.95	0.40	1.00	2.00
❑7, Aug 96	1.95	0.40	1.00	2.00
❑8, Sep 96, V: Looter	1.95	0.40	1.00	2.00
❑9, Oct 96, A: Swarm	1.99	0.40	1.00	2.00
❑10, Nov 96	1.99	0.40	1.00	2.00
❑11, Dec 96, Revelations, Part 2	1.99	0.40	1.00	2.00
❑11/CS, Dec 96, Revelations, Part 2, card, checklist	—	0.60	1.50	3.00
❑12, Jan 97, V: Trapster	1.99	0.40	1.00	2.00
❑13, Feb 97, Deluge, Part 1, A: Shanna; A: Ka-Zar	1.99	0.40	1.00	2.00
❑14, Mar 97, Deluge, Part 2, A: Hulk; A: Shanna; A: Ka-Zar	1.99	0.40	1.00	2.00
❑15, Apr 97, Deluge, Part 3, A: Hulk; A: Shanna; A: Ka-Zar	1.99	0.40	1.00	2.00
❑16, May 97, Paralyzed!, V: Prowler	1.99	0.40	1.00	2.00
❑17, Jun 97, Helpless!, V: Vulture	1.99	0.40	1.00	2.00
❑18, Aug 97, gatefold summary	1.99	0.40	1.00	2.00
❑19, Sep 97, V: Living Pharaoh, gatefold summary	1.99	0.40	1.00	2.00
❑20, Oct 97, gatefold summary	1.99	0.40	1.00	2.00
❑21, Nov 97, gatefold summary	1.99	0.40	1.00	1.99
❑22, Dec 97, A: Doctor Strange, gatefold summary	1.99	0.40	1.00	1.99
❑23, Jan 98, gatefold summary	1.99	0.40	1.00	1.99
❑24, Feb 98, V: Hydro-Man, gatefold summary	1.99	0.40	1.00	1.99
❑25, Mar 98, Spider-Hunt, Part 1, gatefold summary; double-sized	2.99	0.40	1.00	1.99
❑26, Apr 98, V: Sandman; V: Hydro-Man, gatefold summary; Identity Crisis	1.99	0.40	1.00	1.99
❑27, May 98, Identity Crisis, gatefold summary	1.99	0.40	1.00	1.99
❑28, Jun 98, Identity Crisis, A: Hornet, gatefold summary	1.99	0.40	1.00	1.99
❑29, Jul 98, A: Black Cat, gatefold summary	1.99	0.40	1.00	1.99
❑30, Aug 98, gatefold summary	1.99	0.40	1.00	1.99
❑31, Sep 98, V: Rhino, gatefold summary	1.99	0.40	1.00	1.99
❑32, Oct 98, The Gathering of Five, Part 1, gatefold summary	1.99	0.40	1.00	1.99
❑33, Nov 98, The Gathering of Five, Part 5, V: Override, Final Issue; gatefold summary	1.99	0.40	1.00	1.99
❑Anl 1996, Kraven's First Hunt, O: Kraven the Hunter	2.99	0.60	1.50	3.00

SENSATION COMICS (2ND SERIES)
DC

Value: Cover or less

❑1, May 99, JRo (w), Womanly Deeds and Manly Words, A: Speed Saunders; A: Hawkgirl; A: Wonder Woman, Justice Society Returns; Hawkgirl; Speed Saunders ... 1.99

SENSEI
FIRST

Value: Cover or less

❑1, May 89 ... 2.75
❑2 ... 2.75
❑3 ... 2.75
❑4, Dec 89 ... 2.75

SENTAI
ANTARCTIC

Value: Cover or less

❑1, Feb 94, b&w; The Journal of Asian SF and Fantasy ... 2.95
❑2, Apr 94, b&w; The Journal of Asian SF and Fantasy ... 2.95
❑3, Jul 94, b&w; The Journal of Asian SF and Fantasy ... 2.95
❑4, Sep 94, b&w; The Journal of Asian SF and Fantasy ... 2.95
❑5, Nov 94, The Journal of Asian SF and Fantasy ... 3.95
❑6, Feb 95, b&w; The Journal of Asian SF and Fantasy ... 2.95
❑7, Apr 95, b&w; The Journal of Asian SF and Fantasy ... 2.95

SENTINEL
HARRIER

Value: Cover or less

❑1 ... 1.95
❑2 ... 1.95
❑3 ... 1.95
❑4 ... 1.95

SENTINELS OF JUSTICE (2ND SERIES)
AC

	ORIG	GOOD	FINE	N-MINT
❑1, Avenger	—	0.80	2.00	4.00
❑2, Jet Girl	—	0.80	2.00	4.00
❑3, Yankee Girl	—	0.80	2.00	4.00

SENTINELS OF JUSTICE COMPACT
AC

Value: Cover or less

❑1 ... 3.95
❑2 ... 3.95
❑3 ... 3.95

SENTINELS PRESENTS...CRYSTAL WORLD, THE: PRISONERS OF SPHERIS
ACADEMY

Value: Cover or less

❑1 ... 2.95

SENTRY, THE
MARVEL

Value: Cover or less

❑1, Sep 00, The Suit ... 2.99
❑2, Oct 00, The Unicorn ... 2.99
❑3, Nov 00, The Photograph, A: Spider-Man; A: Hulk ... 2.99
❑4, Dec 00, The Conspiracy, A: Doctor Strange ... 2.99
❑5, Jan 01, The Betrayal, A: Avengers; A: Spider-Man; A: Hulk; A: Fantastic Four ... 2.99

SENTRY/FANTASTIC FOUR
MARVEL

Value: Cover or less

❑1, Feb 01, The Sentry and Fantastic Four ... 2.99

SENTRY/HULK
MARVEL

Value: Cover or less

❑1, Feb 01, BSz, The Sentry and Hulk ... 2.99

SENTRY SPECIAL
INNOVATION

Value: Cover or less

❑1, Jun 91 ... 2.75

SENTRY/SPIDER-MAN
MARVEL

Value: Cover or less

❑1, Feb 01, The Sentry and Spider-Man ... 2.99

SENTRY/THE VOID
MARVEL

Value: Cover or less

❑1, Feb 01, The Sentry and the Truth ... 2.99

SENTRY/X-MEN
MARVEL

Value: Cover or less

❑1, Feb 01, The Sentry and Angel of The X-Men ... 2.99

SEPULCHER
ILLUSTRATION

Value: Cover or less

❑1, Mar 00, Hell's Choice ... 2.99
❑2, May 00, Eyes of Doom ... 2.99

SEQUENTIAL
I Don't Get It

Value: Cover or less

Issue	ORIG
❑1	2.95
❑2	2.95
❑3, Jun 99	2.95

SERAPHIM
Innovation

Value: Cover or less

Issue	ORIG
❑1, May 90	2.50
❑2	2.50
❑3	2.50

SGT. FURY
Marvel

Issue	ORIG	GOOD	FINE	N-MINT
❑1, Dec 63, 1: Sgt. Nick Fury; 1: Dum Dum Dugan; 1: General Samuel "Happy Sam" Sawyer	0.12	185.00	462.50	925.00
❑2, Jan 64	0.12	65.00	162.50	325.00
❑3, Feb 64, A: Reed Richards	0.12	35.00	87.50	175.00
❑4, Mar 64, D: Junior Juniper	0.12	35.00	87.50	175.00
❑5, Apr 64, JK, SL (w), At the Mercy of Baron Strucker, 1: Baron Strucker	0.12	35.00	87.50	175.00
❑6, May 64	0.12	23.00	57.50	115.00
❑7, Jun 64, JK, SL (w), The Court-Martial of Sergeant Fury	0.12	23.00	57.50	115.00
❑8, Jul 64, 1: Percival Pinkerton; V: Doctor Zemo (later Baron Zemo)	0.12	23.00	57.50	115.00
❑9, Aug 64	0.12	23.00	57.50	115.00
❑10, Sep 64, 1: Captain Savage	0.12	23.00	57.50	115.00
❑11, Oct 64	0.12	12.00	30.00	60.00
❑12, Nov 64	0.12	12.00	30.00	60.00
❑13, Dec 64, JK, SL (w), Fighting Side-By-Side With Captain America and Bucky!, A: Captain America	0.12	57.00	142.50	285.00
❑13-2, JK, SL (w), Fighting Side-By-Side With Captain America and Bucky!, A: Captain America, 2nd Printing	0.12	0.40	1.00	2.00
❑14, Jan 65, A: Baron Strucker	0.12	12.00	30.00	60.00
❑15, Feb 65, 1: Hans Rooten	0.12	12.00	30.00	60.00
❑16, Mar 65	0.12	12.00	30.00	60.00
❑17, Apr 65	0.12	12.00	30.00	60.00
❑18, May 65	0.12	12.00	30.00	60.00
❑19, Jun 65	0.12	12.00	30.00	60.00
❑20, Jul 65	0.12	12.00	30.00	60.00
❑21, Aug 65	0.12	9.60	24.00	48.00
❑22, Sep 65	0.12	9.60	24.00	48.00
❑23, Oct 65	0.12	9.60	24.00	48.00
❑24, Nov 65, SL (w), When the Howlers Hit the Home Front!	0.12	9.60	24.00	48.00
❑25, Dec 65	0.12	9.60	24.00	48.00
❑26, Jan 66	0.12	9.60	24.00	48.00
❑27, Feb 66, Explanation of Sgt. Fury's eye patch	0.12	9.60	24.00	48.00
❑28, Mar 66, V: Baron Strucker	0.12	9.60	24.00	48.00
❑29, Apr 66, Armageddon!, V: Baron Strucker	0.12	9.60	24.00	48.00
❑30, May 66	0.12	9.60	24.00	48.00
❑31, Jun 66	0.12	6.00	15.00	30.00
❑32, Jul 66	0.12	6.00	15.00	30.00
❑33, Aug 66	0.12	6.00	15.00	30.00
❑34, Sep 66, O: General Samuel "Happy Sam" Sawyer; O: Howling Commandos	0.12	6.00	15.00	30.00
❑35, Oct 66, Eric Koenig joins Howling Commandos	0.12	6.00	15.00	30.00
❑36, Nov 66	0.12	6.00	15.00	30.00
❑37, Dec 66	0.12	6.00	15.00	30.00
❑38, Jan 67	0.12	6.00	15.00	30.00
❑39, Feb 67	0.12	6.00	15.00	30.00
❑40, Mar 67	0.12	6.00	15.00	30.00
❑41, Apr 67	0.12	4.80	12.00	24.00
❑42, May 67	0.12	4.80	12.00	24.00
❑43, Jun 67	0.12	4.80	12.00	24.00
❑44, Jul 67	0.12	4.80	12.00	24.00
❑45, Aug 67	0.12	4.80	12.00	24.00
❑46, Sep 67	0.12	4.80	12.00	24.00
❑47, Oct 67, Fury on furlough	0.12	4.80	12.00	24.00
❑48, Nov 67, JSe, return of Blitz Squad	0.12	4.80	12.00	24.00
❑49, Dec 67, JSe, Howlers in Pacific	0.12	4.80	12.00	24.00
❑50, Jan 68, JSe, Howlers in Pacific	0.12	4.80	12.00	24.00
❑51, Feb 68	0.12	3.60	9.00	18.00
❑52, Mar 68, in Treblinka	0.12	3.60	9.00	18.00
❑53, Apr 68	0.12	3.60	9.00	18.00
❑54, May 68	0.12	3.60	9.00	18.00
❑55, Jun 68	0.12	3.60	9.00	18.00
❑56, Jul 68, Gabriel, Blow Your Horn!	0.12	3.60	9.00	18.00
❑57, Aug 68, JSe; TS, The Informer	0.12	3.60	9.00	18.00
❑58, Sep 68	0.12	3.60	9.00	18.00
❑59, Oct 68	0.12	3.60	9.00	18.00
❑60, Nov 68	0.12	3.60	9.00	18.00
❑61, Dec 68	0.12	3.60	9.00	18.00
❑62, Jan 69, The Name is...Bass...Sergeant Bass!, O: Sgt. Fury	0.12	3.60	9.00	18.00
❑63, Feb 69	0.12	3.60	9.00	18.00

The adventures of a Marvel super-hero nobody remembered working with were chronicled in the five-issue *The Sentry* and a series of spin-offs.

Issue	ORIG	GOOD	FINE	N-MINT
❑64, Mar 69, The Peacemonger!, Story continued from Captain Savage and his Leatherneck Raiders #11	0.12	3.60	9.00	18.00
❑65, Apr 69, Blood is Thicker!	0.12	3.60	9.00	18.00
❑66, May 69	0.12	3.60	9.00	18.00
❑67, Jun 69, JSe (c), With a Little Help From my Friends	0.12	3.60	9.00	18.00
❑68, Jul 69, Fury goes home on leave	0.15	3.60	9.00	18.00
❑69, Aug 69, 1: Jacob Fury (later becomes Scorpio)	0.15	3.60	9.00	18.00
❑70, Sep 69, 1: Missouri Marauders	0.15	3.60	9.00	18.00
❑71, Oct 69	0.15	3.00	7.50	15.00
❑72, Nov 69	0.15	3.00	7.50	15.00
❑73, Dec 69	0.15	3.00	7.50	15.00
❑74, Jan 70	0.15	3.00	7.50	15.00
❑75, Feb 70	0.15	3.00	7.50	15.00
❑76, Mar 70, Fury's father vs. The Red Baron	0.15	3.00	7.50	15.00
❑77, Apr 70	0.15	3.00	7.50	15.00
❑78, May 70	0.15	3.00	7.50	15.00
❑79, Jun 70	0.15	3.00	7.50	15.00
❑80, Sep 70	0.15	3.00	7.50	15.00
❑81, Nov 70	0.15	2.40	6.00	12.00
❑82, Dec 70	0.15	2.40	6.00	12.00
❑83, Jan 71, Dum-Dum Dugan vs. Man-Mountain McCoy	0.15	2.40	6.00	12.00
❑84, Feb 71	0.15	2.40	6.00	12.00
❑85, Mar 71	0.15	2.40	6.00	12.00
❑86, Apr 71	0.15	2.40	6.00	12.00
❑87, May 71	0.15	2.40	6.00	12.00
❑88, Jun 71, A: Patton	0.15	2.40	6.00	12.00
❑89, Jul 71	0.15	2.40	6.00	12.00
❑90, Aug 71, ...And One Must Die!	0.15	2.40	6.00	12.00
❑91, Sep 71	0.15	2.00	5.00	10.00
❑92, Oct 71, Giant-size	0.25	2.00	5.00	10.00
❑93, Dec 71, A Traitor in Our Midsts!	0.20	2.00	5.00	10.00
❑94, Jan 72, Who'll Stop The Rain?	0.20	2.00	5.00	10.00
❑95, Feb 72, JK, Reprint	0.20	2.00	5.00	10.00
❑96, Mar 72, This Ravaged Land!	0.20	2.00	5.00	10.00
❑97, Apr 72	0.20	2.00	5.00	10.00
❑98, May 72, 1: Dugan's Deadly Dozen	0.20	2.00	5.00	10.00
❑99, Jun 72	0.20	2.00	5.00	10.00
❑100, Jul 72, A: Stan Lee; A: Captain America; A: Martin Goodman; A: Dick Ayers; A: Gary Friedrich	0.20	2.00	5.00	10.00
❑101, Sep 72, O: the Howling Commandos	0.20	1.60	4.00	8.00
❑102, Sep 72, Death for a Dollar!	0.20	1.40	3.50	7.00
❑103, Oct 72	0.20	1.40	3.50	7.00
❑104, Nov 72, The Tanks are Coming!, A: Combat Kelly and Deadly Dozen	0.20	1.40	3.50	7.00
❑105, Dec 72	0.20	1.40	3.50	7.00
❑106, Jan 73	0.20	1.40	3.50	7.00
❑107, Feb 73	0.20	1.40	3.50	7.00
❑108, Mar 73	0.20	1.40	3.50	7.00
❑109, Apr 73	0.20	1.40	3.50	7.00
❑110, May 73	0.20	1.40	3.50	7.00
❑111, Jun 73	0.20	1.20	3.00	6.00
❑112, Jul 73, V: Baron Strucker	0.20	1.20	3.00	6.00
❑113, Aug 73	0.20	1.20	3.00	6.00
❑114, Sep 73	0.20	1.20	3.00	6.00
❑115, Oct 73	0.20	1.20	3.00	6.00
❑116, Nov 73	0.20	1.20	3.00	6.00
❑117, Jan 74	0.20	1.20	3.00	6.00
❑118, Mar 74, The War Machine, V: Rommel	0.20	1.20	3.00	6.00
❑119, May 74	0.20	1.20	3.00	6.00
❑120, Jul 74	0.20	1.20	3.00	6.00
❑121, Sep 74	0.25	1.00	2.50	5.00
❑122, Oct 74	0.25	1.00	2.50	5.00
❑123, Nov 74	0.25	1.00	2.50	5.00
❑124, Jan 75	0.25	1.00	2.50	5.00
❑125, Mar 75	0.25	1.00	2.50	5.00
❑126, May 75	0.25	1.00	2.50	5.00
❑127, Jul 75	0.25	1.00	2.50	5.00

	ORIG	GOOD	FINE	N-MINT
❑128, Sep 75	0.25	1.00	2.50	5.00
❑129, Oct 75	0.25	1.00	2.50	5.00
❑130, Nov 75	0.25	1.00	2.50	5.00
❑131, Jan 76	0.25	0.80	2.00	4.00
❑132, Mar 76	0.25	0.80	2.00	4.00
❑133, May 76	0.25	0.80	2.00	4.00
❑134, Jul 76	0.25	0.80	2.00	4.00
❑135, Sep 76	0.30	0.80	2.00	4.00
❑136, Oct 76	0.30	0.80	2.00	4.00
❑137, Nov 76	0.30	0.80	2.00	4.00
❑138, Jan 77	0.30	0.80	2.00	4.00
❑139, Mar 77	0.30	0.80	2.00	4.00
❑140, May 77	0.30	0.80	2.00	4.00
❑141, Jul 77	0.30	0.80	2.00	4.00
❑142, Sep 77	0.30	0.80	2.00	4.00
❑143, Nov 77	0.30	0.80	2.00	4.00
❑144, Jan 78	0.30	0.80	2.00	4.00
❑145, Mar 78	0.30	0.80	2.00	4.00
❑146, May 78	0.30	0.80	2.00	4.00
❑147, Jul 78	0.30	0.80	2.00	4.00
❑148, Sep 78	0.30	0.80	2.00	4.00
❑149, Nov 78	0.30	0.80	2.00	4.00
❑150, Jan 79	0.30	0.80	2.00	4.00
❑151, Mar 79	0.30	0.60	1.50	3.00
❑152, Jun 79	0.30	0.60	1.50	3.00
❑153, Aug 79	0.30	0.60	1.50	3.00
❑154, Oct 79	0.30	0.60	1.50	3.00
❑155, Dec 79	0.30	0.60	1.50	3.00
❑156, Feb 80	0.30	0.60	1.50	3.00
❑157, Apr 80	0.30	0.60	1.50	3.00
❑158, Jun 80	0.30	0.60	1.50	3.00
❑159, Aug 80	0.30	0.60	1.50	3.00
❑160, Oct 80	0.30	0.60	1.50	3.00
❑161, Dec 80	0.30	0.60	1.50	3.00
❑162, Feb 81	0.30	0.60	1.50	3.00
❑163, Apr 81	0.30	0.60	1.50	3.00
❑164, Jun 81	0.30	0.60	1.50	3.00
❑165, Aug 81	0.30	0.60	1.50	3.00
❑166, Oct 81	0.30	0.60	1.50	3.00
❑167, Dec 81	0.30	0.60	1.50	3.00
❑Anl 1, Korea	0.25	25.00	62.50	125.00
❑Anl 2, O: S.H.I.E.L.D., Reprint; D-Day	0.25	11.00	27.50	55.00
❑Anl 3, Cover reads "King-Size Special"; Vietnam	0.25	6.00	15.00	30.00
❑Anl 4, Apr 68, The Battle of the Bulge; Gary and Dick Up Front!, Cover reads "King-Size Special"; Battle of the Bulge	0.25	4.40	11.00	22.00
❑Anl 5, Cover reads "King-Size Special"	0.25	2.00	5.00	10.00
❑Anl 6, Cover reads "King-Size Special"	0.25	1.80	4.50	9.00
❑Anl 7, Cover reads "King-Size Special"	0.25	1.80	4.50	9.00

SGT. ROCK
DC

	ORIG	GOOD	FINE	N-MINT
❑302, Mar 77, Series continued from "Our Army At War"	—	2.80	7.00	14.00
❑303, Apr 77	—	1.80	4.50	9.00
❑304, May 77	—	1.80	4.50	9.00
❑305, Jun 77	—	1.80	4.50	9.00
❑306, Jul 77	—	1.80	4.50	9.00
❑307, Aug 77	0.35	1.80	4.50	9.00
❑308, Sep 77	0.35	1.80	4.50	9.00
❑309, Oct 77	0.35	1.80	4.50	9.00
❑310, Nov 77	0.35	1.80	4.50	9.00
❑311, Dec 77	0.35	1.60	4.00	8.00
❑312, Jan 78	0.35	1.60	4.00	8.00
❑313, Feb 78	0.35	1.60	4.00	8.00
❑314, Mar 78	0.35	1.60	4.00	8.00
❑315, Apr 78	0.35	1.60	4.00	8.00
❑316, May 78	0.35	1.60	4.00	8.00
❑317, Jun 78	0.35	1.60	4.00	8.00
❑318, Jul 78	—	1.60	4.00	8.00
❑319, Aug 78	—	1.60	4.00	8.00
❑320, Sep 78	—	1.60	4.00	8.00
❑321, Oct 78	0.50	1.20	3.00	6.00
❑322, Nov 78	0.50	1.20	3.00	6.00
❑323, Dec 78	—	1.20	3.00	6.00
❑324, Jan 79	—	1.20	3.00	6.00
❑325, Feb 79	0.40	1.20	3.00	6.00
❑326, Mar 79	—	1.20	3.00	6.00
❑327, Apr 79	—	1.20	3.00	6.00
❑328, May 79	—	1.20	3.00	6.00
❑329, Jun 79	—	1.20	3.00	6.00
❑330, Jul 79	—	1.20	3.00	6.00
❑331, Aug 79	0.40	1.00	2.50	5.00
❑332, Sep 79	0.40	1.00	2.50	5.00
❑333, Oct 79	—	1.00	2.50	5.00
❑334, Nov 79	—	1.00	2.50	5.00
❑335, Dec 79	—	1.00	2.50	5.00
❑336, Jan 80	—	1.00	2.50	5.00
❑337, Feb 80	—	1.00	2.50	5.00
❑338, Mar 80	—	1.00	2.50	5.00
❑339, Apr 80	—	1.00	2.50	5.00
❑340, May 80	—	1.00	2.50	5.00
❑341, Jun 80	—	1.00	2.50	5.00
❑342, Jul 80	—	0.80	2.00	4.00
❑343, Aug 80	—	0.80	2.00	4.00
❑344, Sep 80	—	0.80	2.00	4.00
❑345, Oct 80	—	0.80	2.00	4.00
❑346, Nov 80	—	0.80	2.00	4.00
❑347, Dec 80	—	0.80	2.00	4.00
❑348, Jan 81	—	0.80	2.00	4.00
❑349, Feb 81	—	0.80	2.00	4.00
❑350, Mar 81	—	0.80	2.00	4.00
❑351, Apr 81	—	0.60	1.50	3.00
❑352, May 81	—	0.60	1.50	3.00
❑353, Jun 81	—	0.60	1.50	3.00
❑354, Jul 81	—	0.60	1.50	3.00
❑355, Aug 81	—	0.60	1.50	3.00
❑356, Sep 81	—	0.60	1.50	3.00
❑357, Oct 81	—	0.60	1.50	3.00
❑358, Nov 81	—	0.60	1.50	3.00
❑359, Dec 81	—	0.60	1.50	3.00
❑360, Jan 82	—	0.60	1.50	3.00
❑361, Feb 82	—	0.60	1.50	3.00
❑362, Mar 82	—	0.60	1.50	3.00
❑363, Apr 82	—	0.60	1.50	3.00
❑364, May 82	—	0.60	1.50	3.00
❑365, Jun 82	—	0.60	1.50	3.00
❑366, Jul 82	—	0.60	1.50	3.00
❑367, Aug 82	—	0.60	1.50	3.00
❑368, Sep 82, JKu, 30 Years Of Dogtags	—	0.60	1.50	3.00
❑369, Oct 82, Too Easy To Die	—	0.60	1.50	3.00
❑370, Nov 82	—	0.60	1.50	3.00
❑371, Dec 82	—	0.50	1.25	2.50
❑372, Jan 83	—	0.50	1.25	2.50
❑373, Feb 83, Burning Soldier	0.60	0.50	1.25	2.50
❑374, Mar 83, Trust Me	0.60	0.50	1.25	2.50
❑375, Apr 83	0.60	0.50	1.25	2.50
❑376, May 83	0.60	0.50	1.25	2.50
❑377, Jun 83, A: Worry Wart	0.60	0.50	1.25	2.50
❑378, Jul 83, Christmas	0.60	0.50	1.25	2.50
❑379, Aug 83	0.60	0.50	1.25	2.50
❑380, Sep 83	0.60	0.50	1.25	2.50
❑381, Oct 83	0.60	0.50	1.25	2.50
❑382, Nov 83	—	0.50	1.25	2.50
❑383, Dec 83	0.75	0.50	1.25	2.50
❑384, Jan 84	0.75	0.50	1.25	2.50
❑385, Feb 84	0.75	0.50	1.25	2.50
❑386, Mar 84	0.75	0.50	1.25	2.50
❑387, Apr 84	0.75	0.50	1.25	2.50
❑388, May 84	0.75	0.50	1.25	2.50
❑389, Jun 84	0.75	0.50	1.25	2.50
❑390, Jul 84	0.75	0.50	1.25	2.50
❑391, Aug 84	0.75	0.40	1.00	2.00
❑392, Sep 84	0.75	0.40	1.00	2.00
❑393, Oct 84	0.75	0.40	1.00	2.00
❑394, Nov 84	0.75	0.40	1.00	2.00
❑395, Dec 84	0.75	0.40	1.00	2.00
❑396, Jan 85	0.75	0.40	1.00	2.00
❑397, Feb 85	0.75	0.40	1.00	2.00
❑398, Mar 85	0.75	0.40	1.00	2.00
❑399, Apr 85	0.75	0.40	1.00	2.00
❑400, May 85	0.75	0.40	1.00	2.00
❑401, Jun 85	0.75	0.40	1.00	2.00
❑402, Jul 85	0.75	0.40	1.00	2.00
❑403, Aug 85	0.75	0.40	1.00	2.00
❑404, Sep 85, V: Iron Major	0.75	0.40	1.00	2.00
❑405, Oct 85, Angels with Black Wings; Angels With Black Wings, Part 1	0.75	0.40	1.00	2.00
❑406, Nov 85, Angels with Black Wings; Angels With Black Wings, Part 2	0.75	0.40	1.00	2.00
❑407, Dec 85	0.75	0.40	1.00	2.00
❑408, Feb 86, Shelly Mayer tribute	0.75	0.40	1.00	2.00
❑409, Apr 86	0.75	0.40	1.00	2.00
❑410, Jun 86	0.75	0.40	1.00	2.00
❑411, Aug 86	0.75	0.40	1.00	2.00
❑412, Oct 86	0.75	0.40	1.00	2.00
❑413, Dec 86	0.75	0.40	1.00	2.00
❑414, Feb 87, Christmas	0.75	0.40	1.00	2.00
❑415, Apr 87	0.75	0.40	1.00	2.00
❑416, Jun 87	0.75	0.40	1.00	2.00
❑417, Aug 87, looking into future	0.75	0.40	1.00	2.00
❑418, Oct 87, looking into future	0.75	0.40	1.00	2.00
❑419, Dec 87	1.00	0.40	1.00	2.00
❑420, Feb 88	1.00	0.40	1.00	2.00
❑421, Apr 88	1.00	0.40	1.00	2.00
❑422, Jul 88, Final Issue	1.00	0.40	1.00	2.00
❑Anl 1	—	0.80	2.00	4.00
❑Anl 2, Sep 82	—	0.80	2.00	4.00

	ORIG	GOOD	FINE	N-MINT
❑Anl 3, Aug 83	—	0.60	1.50	3.00
❑Anl 4, Aug 84	—	0.60	1.50	3.00

SGT. ROCK (2ND SERIES)
DC
Value: Cover or less

❑14, Jul 91, Series continued from Sgt. Rock Special #13......... 2.00
❑15, Aug 91 .... 2.00
❑16, Sep 91 .... 2.00
❑17, Oct 91 .... 2.00
❑18, Nov 91, JKu; MG, Half a Sergeant!; Enemy Ace: Death Whispers-Death Screams!.. 2.00
❑19, Dec 91 .... 2.00
❑20, Jan 92 .... 2.00
❑21, Feb 92 .... 2.00
❑22, Final Issue 2.00
❑SE 1, Oct 92, 1992 Special... 2.95
❑SE 2, HC, The Angel; Hammer and Anvil, Commemorates 50th anniversary of the Battle of the Bulge; 1994 Special 2.95

SGT. ROCK SPECIAL
DC

	ORIG	GOOD	FINE	N-MINT
❑1, A: Viking Prince	2.00	0.60	1.50	3.00
❑2	2.00	0.50	1.25	2.50
❑3, Mar 89	2.00	0.50	1.25	2.50
❑4, Jun 89	2.00	0.50	1.25	2.50
❑5, Sep 89	2.00	0.50	1.25	2.50
❑6, Dec 89	2.00	0.50	1.25	2.50
❑7, Mar 90	2.00	0.50	1.25	2.50
❑8, Jun 90	2.00	0.50	1.25	2.50
❑9, Sep 90	2.00	0.50	1.25	2.50
❑10, Dec 90	2.00	0.50	1.25	2.50
❑11, Mar 91	2.00	0.50	1.25	2.50
❑12, May 91	2.00	0.50	1.25	2.50
❑13, Jun 91	2.00	0.50	1.25	2.50

SGT. ROCK'S PRIZE BATTLE TALES REPLICA EDITION
DC
Value: Cover or less

❑1, IN; RH; RA; JKu, The D.I. And the Sand Fleas!; Silent Fish! 5.95

SERGIO ARAGONÉS DESTROYS DC
DC
Value: Cover or less

❑1, Jun 96, SA, ME (w), One-Shot 3.50

SERGIO ARAGONÉS MASSACRES MARVEL
MARVEL
Value: Cover or less

❑1, Jun 96, wraparound cover; One-Shot 3.50

SERINA
ANTARCTIC
Value: Cover or less

❑1, Mar 96, Upheaval, b&w.... 2.95
❑2, May 96, b&w 2.95
❑3, Jul 96 .... 2.95

SERIUS BOUNTY HUNTER
BLACKTHORNE
Value: Cover or less

❑1, Nov 87, b&w 1.75
❑2, Jan 88, b&w 1.75
❑3, b&w 1.75

SERPENTINA
LIGHTNING
Value: Cover or less

❑1/A, Feb 98, b&w 2.95
❑1/B, Feb 98, alternate cover 2.95

SERPENTYNE
NIGHTWYND
Value: Cover or less

❑1, b&w 2.50
❑2, b&w 2.50
❑3, b&w 2.50

SERRA ANGEL ON THE WORLD OF MAGIC: THE GATHERING
ACCLAIM
Value: Cover or less

❑1, Aug 96, One-Shot; prestige format; polybagged with oversized Serra Angel card 5.95

SETH THROB UNDERGROUND ARTIST
SLAVE LABOR
Value: Cover or less

❑1, Mar 94 .... 2.95
❑2, May 94 .... 2.95
❑3, Aug 94 .... 2.95
❑4, Dec 94 .... 2.95
❑5, Mar 95 .... 2.95
❑6, Jun 95 .... 2.95
❑7, Sep 95 .... 2.95

SETTEI
ANTARCTIC
Value: Cover or less

❑1, Feb 93, b&w 7.95
❑2, Apr 93, b&w 7.95

SETTEI SUPER SPECIAL FEATURING: PROJECT A-KO
ANTARCTIC
Value: Cover or less

❑1, Feb 94, full color 2.95

SEVEN BLOCK
MARVEL
Value: Cover or less

❑1, nn; prestige format 4.50

SEVEN GUYS OF JUSTICE, THE
FALSE IDOL
Value: Cover or less

❑1, Apr 00 .... 2.00
❑2 .... 2.00
❑3 .... 2.00
❑4 .... 2.00
❑5 .... 2.00
❑6 .... 2.00
❑7 .... 2.00
❑8 .... 2.00
❑9 .... 2.00
❑10 .... 2.00

To commemorate the 50th anniversary of The Battle of the Bulge, Sgt. Rock's involvement in the World War II fight was covered in *Sgt. Rock Special* #2.

ORIG GOOD FINE N-MINT

SEVEN MILES A SECOND
DC
Value: Cover or less

❑1, nn; One-Shot; prestige format 7.95

SEWAGE DRAGOON, THE
PARODY PRESS
Value: Cover or less

❑1 .... 2.50
❑1-2, 2nd Printing 2.50

SEX & DEATH
ACID RAIN

	ORIG	GOOD	FINE	N-MINT
❑1, Pwdre Ser; The Flea, b&w	2.50	0.79	1.98	3.95

SEXCAPADES
EROS
Value: Cover or less

❑1 .... 2.95
❑2 .... 2.95
❑3 .... 2.95

SEX DRIVE
M.A.I.N.
Value: Cover or less

❑1, Demi the Demoness Meets Capt. Fortune Preview; Maid Service 3.00

SEXECUTIONER
FANTAGRAPHICS
Value: Cover or less

❑1, b&w; adult 2.50
❑2, b&w; adult 2.50
❑3, b&w; adult 2.50

SEXHIBITION
FANTAGRAPHICS
Value: Cover or less

❑1 .... 2.95
❑2 .... 2.95
❑3 .... 2.95
❑4, Feb 96 .... 2.95

SEX IN THE SINEMA
COMIC ZONE
Value: Cover or less

❑1, b&w; adult 2.95
❑2, b&w; adult 2.95
❑3, b&w; adult 2.95
❑4, b&w; adult 2.95

SEX, LIES AND MUTUAL FUNDS OF THE YUPPIES FROM HELL
MARVEL
Value: Cover or less

❑1, Priorities; Getting Serious 2.95

SEX MACHINE
FANTAGRAPHICS

	ORIG	GOOD	FINE	N-MINT
❑1, b&w; adult	2.50	0.50	1.25	2.50
❑2, b&w; adult	—	0.59	1.48	2.95
❑3, Dec 97, b&w; adult	2.95	0.59	1.48	2.95

SEXPLOITATION CINEMA: A CARTOON HISTORY
REVISIONARY
Value: Cover or less

❑1, Nov 98, b&w; adult 3.50

SEX TREK: THE NEXT INFILTRATION
FRIENDLY
Value: Cover or less

❑1, b&w; adult 2.95

SEX WAD
EROS
Value: Cover or less

❑1 .... 2.95
❑2, The Rite of Puberty; Modern Lust 2.95

SEX WARRIOR
DARK HORSE
Value: Cover or less

❑1 .... 2.50
❑2 .... 2.50

SEXX WARS
IMMORTAL
Value: Cover or less

❑1, Once Upon a Time 2.95

SEXY STORIES FROM THE WORLD RELIGIONS
LAST GASP
Value: Cover or less

❑1, Marozias Secret, The Curse of Saint Dymphna, Divine Anarchy, The Gospel According to Father Phlem, Fits of Passion, Saint Agnes, Ecclesiasticus 9, 1-9, Santa and New Year's.. 2.50

SEXY SUPERSPY
FORBIDDEN FRUIT
Value: Cover or less

❑1, b&w; adult 2.95
❑2, b&w; adult 2.95
❑3, b&w; adult 2.95
❑4, b&w; adult 2.95
❑5, b&w; adult 2.95
❑6, b&w; adult 2.95
❑7, b&w; adult 2.95

SEXY WOMEN
CELEBRITY

Value: Cover or less

Issue	ORIG
❑1	2.95
❑2	2.95

SFA SPOTLIGHT
SHANDA FANTASY ARTS

Issue	ORIG	GOOD	FINE	N-MINT
❑1	—	0.59	1.48	2.95
❑2	—	0.59	1.48	2.95
❑3	—	0.59	1.48	2.95
❑4, May 99, Tales of the Morphing Period, b&w	2.95	0.59	1.48	2.95
❑5, May 99, b&w; Zebra Comics	4.50	0.90	2.25	4.50

SHADE, THE
DC

Issue	ORIG	GOOD	FINE	N-MINT
❑1, Apr 97, JRo (w), A Family Affair	2.25	0.50	1.25	2.50
❑2, May 97, JRo (w)	2.25	0.50	1.25	2.50
❑3, Jun 97, JRo (w), A: Jay Garrick	2.25	0.50	1.25	2.50
❑4, Jul 97, JRo (w), Shade: Finale	2.25	0.50	1.25	2.50

SHADE, THE CHANGING MAN (1ST SERIES)
DC

Issue	ORIG	GOOD	FINE	N-MINT
❑1, Jul 77, SD, SD (w), Escape to Battleground Earth!, 1: Shade	0.35	0.60	1.50	3.00
❑2, Sep 77, SD	0.35	0.40	1.00	2.00
❑3, Nov 77, SD	0.35	0.40	1.00	2.00
❑4, Jan 78, SD	0.35	0.40	1.00	2.00
❑5, Mar 78, SD	0.35	0.40	1.00	2.00
❑6, May 78, SD, V: Khaos	0.35	0.40	1.00	2.00
❑7, Jul 78, SD	0.35	0.40	1.00	2.00
❑8, Sep 78, SD	0.35	0.40	1.00	2.00

SHADE, THE CHANGING MAN (2ND SERIES)
DC

Issue	ORIG	GOOD	FINE	N-MINT
❑1, Jul 90, Execution Day, 1: American Scream; 1: Kathy George	2.50	0.60	1.50	3.00
❑2, Aug 90	1.50	0.40	1.00	2.00
❑3, Sep 90	1.50	0.40	1.00	2.00
❑4, Oct 90	1.50	0.40	1.00	2.00
❑5, Nov 90	1.50	0.40	1.00	2.00
❑6, Dec 90	1.50	0.40	1.00	2.00
❑7, Jan 91	1.50	0.40	1.00	2.00
❑8, Feb 91, Love and Haight	1.50	0.40	1.00	2.00
❑9, Mar 91	1.50	0.40	1.00	2.00
❑10, Apr 91	1.50	0.40	1.00	2.00
❑11, May 91	1.50	0.40	1.00	2.00
❑12, Jun 91	1.50	0.40	1.00	2.00
❑13, Jul 91	1.50	0.40	1.00	2.00
❑14, Aug 91	1.50	0.40	1.00	2.00
❑15, Sep 91	1.50	0.40	1.00	2.00
❑16, Oct 91	1.50	0.40	1.00	2.00
❑17, Nov 91	1.75	0.40	1.00	2.00
❑18, Dec 91	1.75	0.40	1.00	2.00
❑19, Jan 92	1.75	0.40	1.00	2.00
❑20, Jan 92	1.75	0.40	1.00	2.00
❑21, Mar 92, Off the Road, Part 1; Of The Road	1.75	0.40	1.00	2.00
❑22, Apr 92, Off the Road, Part 2	1.75	0.40	1.00	2.00
❑23, May 92, Off the Road, Part 3; The Invisible Loom	1.75	0.40	1.00	2.00
❑24, Jun 92, The Road	1.75	0.40	1.00	2.00
❑25, Jul 92, The End of the Road	1.75	0.40	1.00	2.00
❑26, Aug 92	1.75	0.40	1.00	2.00
❑27, Sep 92	1.75	0.40	1.00	2.00
❑28, Oct 92	1.75	0.40	1.00	2.00
❑29, Nov 92	1.75	0.40	1.00	2.00
❑30, Dec 92	1.75	0.40	1.00	2.00
❑31, Jan 93, Ernest And Jim, Part 1	1.75	0.40	1.00	2.00
❑32, Feb 93, Ernest And Jim, Part 2, D: Talks About Aids insert	1.75	0.40	1.00	2.00
❑33, Mar 93, Birth Pains, Part 1, Vertigo line starts	1.75	0.40	1.00	2.00
❑34, Apr 93, Birth Pains, Part 2	1.75	0.40	1.00	2.00
❑35, May 93	1.75	0.40	1.00	2.00
❑36, Jun 93, The Passion Child, Part 1	1.95	0.40	1.00	2.00
❑37, Jul 93, The Passion Child, Part 2	1.95	0.40	1.00	2.00
❑38, Aug 93, The Great American Novel	1.95	0.40	1.00	2.00
❑39, Sep 93, Pond Life	1.95	0.40	1.00	2.00
❑40, Oct 93, In Bed With Shade	1.95	0.40	1.00	2.00
❑41, Nov 93, Angel Dust	1.95	0.40	1.00	2.00
❑42, Dec 93, History Lesson, Part 1	1.95	0.40	1.00	2.00
❑43, Jan 94, History Lesson, Part 2	1.95	0.40	1.00	2.00
❑44, Feb 94, History Lesson, Part 3	1.95	0.40	1.00	2.00
❑45, Mar 94, A Season in Hell, Part 1	1.95	0.40	1.00	2.00
❑46, Apr 94, A Season in Hell, Part 2	1.95	0.40	1.00	2.00
❑47, May 94, A Season in Hell, Part 3	1.95	0.40	1.00	2.00
❑48, Jun 94, A Season in Hell, Part 4	1.95	0.40	1.00	2.00
❑49, Jul 94, A Season in Hell, Part 5	1.95	0.40	1.00	2.00
❑50, Aug 94, A Season in Hell, Part 6, Giant-size	2.95	0.60	1.50	3.00
❑51, Sep 94, The Morning of the Masks, Part 1	1.95	0.40	1.00	2.00
❑52, Oct 94, The Morning of the Masks, Part 2	1.95	0.40	1.00	2.00
❑53, Nov 94, The Morning of the Masks, Part 3	1.95	0.40	1.00	2.00
❑54, Dec 94	1.95	0.40	1.00	2.00
❑55, Jan 95, Life is Short, Part 1	1.95	0.40	1.00	2.00
❑56, Feb 95	1.95	0.40	1.00	2.00
❑57, Mar 95	1.95	0.40	1.00	2.00
❑58, Apr 95	1.95	0.40	1.00	2.00
❑59, May 95	2.25	0.45	1.13	2.25
❑60, Jun 95	2.25	0.45	1.13	2.25
❑61, Jul 95	2.25	0.45	1.13	2.25
❑62, Aug 95	2.25	0.45	1.13	2.25
❑63, Sep 95	2.25	0.45	1.13	2.25
❑64, Oct 95	2.25	0.45	1.13	2.25
❑65, Nov 95	2.25	0.45	1.13	2.25
❑66, Dec 95	2.25	0.45	1.13	2.25
❑67, Jan 96	2.25	0.45	1.13	2.25
❑68, Feb 96, After Kathy, Part 1	2.25	0.45	1.13	2.25
❑69, Mar 96, After Kathy, Part 2	2.25	0.45	1.13	2.25
❑70, Apr 96, Final Issue	2.25	0.45	1.13	2.25

SHADES AND ANGELS
CANDLE LIGHT PRESS

Value: Cover or less

Issue	ORIG
❑1, The Shade Pool, b&w	2.95

SHADES OF BLUE
AMP

Value: Cover or less

Issue	ORIG
❑1, Jul 99, b&w	2.50

SHADES OF GRAY
LADY LUCK

Value: Cover or less

Issue	ORIG
❑1	2.50
❑2	2.50
❑3	2.50
❑4	2.50
❑5	2.50
❑6	2.50
❑7	2.50
❑8	2.50
❑9	2.50
❑10	2.50
❑11	2.50

SHADES OF GRAY COMICS AND STORIES
TAPESTRY

Value: Cover or less

Issue	ORIG
❑1	2.95
❑2	2.95
❑3	2.95
❑4	2.95

SHADE SPECIAL
AC

Value: Cover or less

Issue	ORIG
❑1, Oct 84	1.50

SHADO: SONG OF THE DRAGON
DC

Value: Cover or less

Issue	ORIG
❑1, MGr (w), Souvenirs	4.95
❑2, MGr (w)	4.95
❑3, MGr (w)	4.95
❑4, MGr (w), The Black Dragon	4.95

SHADOW, THE (1ST SERIES)
ARCHIE

Issue	ORIG	GOOD	FINE	N-MINT
❑1, Aug 64, The Menace Of Radiation Rogue	0.12	6.00	15.00	30.00
❑2, Sep 64, Shiwan Khan's Murderous Master-Plan!; The Triangle of Terror!	0.12	3.60	9.00	18.00
❑3	0.12	3.60	9.00	18.00
❑4	0.12	3.60	9.00	18.00
❑5, Mar 65, The Menace of Radiation Rogue!; The Sinister Triumph of Shiwan Khan!, 1: Radiation Rogue	0.12	3.60	9.00	18.00
❑6	0.12	3.60	9.00	18.00
❑7	0.12	3.60	9.00	18.00
❑8, Final Issue	0.12	3.60	9.00	18.00

SHADOW, THE (2ND SERIES)
DC

Issue	ORIG	GOOD	FINE	N-MINT
❑1, Nov 73, The Doom Puzzle!	0.20	4.00	10.00	20.00
❑2, Jan 74	0.20	2.00	5.00	10.00
❑3, Mar 74, BWr	0.20	2.40	6.00	12.00
❑4, May 74	0.20	1.80	4.50	9.00
❑5, Jul 74	0.20	1.20	3.00	6.00
❑6, Sep 74, Night Of The Ninja	0.20	1.80	4.50	9.00
❑7, Nov 74	0.20	1.20	3.00	6.00
❑8, Jan 75	0.20	1.20	3.00	6.00
❑9, Mar 75	0.25	1.20	3.00	6.00
❑10, May 75	0.25	1.20	3.00	6.00
❑11, Jul 75, A: The Avenger	0.25	1.20	3.00	6.00
❑12, Sep 75	0.20	1.20	3.00	6.00

SHADOW, THE (3RD SERIES)
DC

Issue	ORIG	GOOD	FINE	N-MINT
❑1, May 86, HC, HC (w), Blood & Judgment, The Shadow returns	1.50	0.60	1.50	3.00
❑2, Jun 86, HC, HC (w)	1.50	0.40	1.00	2.00
❑3, Jul 86, HC, HC (w)	1.50	0.40	1.00	2.00
❑4, Aug 86, HC, HC (w)	1.50	0.40	1.00	2.00

SHADOW, THE (4TH SERIES)
DC

Issue	ORIG	GOOD	FINE	N-MINT
❑1, Aug 87, BSz	1.50	0.50	1.25	2.50
❑2, Sep 87, BSz	1.50	0.40	1.00	2.00
❑3, Oct 87, BSz	1.50	0.40	1.00	2.00
❑4, Nov 87, BSz	1.50	0.40	1.00	2.00
❑5, Dec 87, BSz	1.50	0.40	1.00	2.00

	ORIG	GOOD	FINE	N-MINT
❑6, Jan 88, BSz	1.50	0.40	1.00	2.00
❑7, Feb 88	1.75	0.40	1.00	2.00
❑8, Mar 88, Seven Deadly Finns, Part 1	1.75	0.40	1.00	2.00
❑9, Apr 88, Seven Deadly Finns, Part 2	1.75	0.40	1.00	2.00
❑10, May 88, Seven Deadly Finns, Part 3	1.75	0.40	1.00	2.00
❑11, Jun 88, Seven Deadly Finns, Part 4	1.75	0.40	1.00	2.00
❑12, Jul 88, Seven Deadly Finns, Part 5	1.75	0.40	1.00	2.00
❑13, Aug 88, Seven Deadly Finns, Part 6, D: Shadow	1.75	0.40	1.00	2.00
❑14, Sep 88	1.75	0.40	1.00	2.00
❑15, Oct 88	1.75	0.40	1.00	2.00
❑16, Nov 88	1.75	0.40	1.00	2.00
❑17, Dec 88, A: Avenger	1.75	0.40	1.00	2.00
❑18, Dec 88, A: Avenger	1.75	0.40	1.00	2.00
❑19, Jan 89, Shadow alive again	1.75	0.40	1.00	2.00
❑Anl 1, EC parody	2.25	0.50	1.25	2.50
❑Anl 2	2.50	0.50	1.25	2.50

SHADOW, THE (MOVIE ADAPTATION)
DARK HORSE

Value: Cover or less

❑1 ... 2.50
❑2 ... 2.50

SHADOW AGENTS
ARMAGEDDON

Value: Cover or less

❑1, May 91, Call to Arms ... 2.50

SHADOW AND DOC SAVAGE, THE
DARK HORSE

Value: Cover or less

❑1, Jul 95, The Case of the Shrieking Skeletons, Part 1 ... 2.95
❑2, Aug 95, The Case of the Shrieking Skeletons, Part 2 ... 2.95

SHADOW AND THE MYSTERIOUS 3, THE
DARK HORSE

Value: Cover or less

❑1, Sep 94, Fate's Free Fall; Cold Day in Hell, nn ... 2.95

SHADOWBLADE
HOT

Value: Cover or less

❑1 ... 1.75

SHADOW, THE: BLOOD AND JUDGMENT
DC

Value: Cover or less

❑1, HC ... 12.95

SHADOW CABINET
DC

Value: Cover or less

❑0, Jan 94, Shadow War, Part 6, A: Blood Syndicate; A: Hardware; A: Icon; A: Static; A: Xombi, Giant-size ... 2.50
❑1, Jun 94, A Handful Of S.A.N.D., D: Corpsicle; O: Sideshow; O: Iron Butterfly ... 1.75
❑2, Jul 94 ... 1.75
❑3, Aug 94, 1: Telesthene ... 1.75
❑4, Sep 94 ... 1.75
❑5, Oct 94 ... 1.75
❑6, Nov 94, Red Death, Part 1 ... 1.75
❑7, Dec 94, Red Death, Part 2 ... 1.75
❑8, Jan 95, Red Death, Part 3 ... 1.75
❑9, Feb 95 ... 1.75
❑10, Mar 95 ... 1.75
❑11, Apr 95 ... 1.75
❑12, May 95 ... 1.75
❑13, Jun 95 ... 2.50
❑14, Jul 95 ... 2.50
❑15, Aug 95, Long Hot Summer ... 2.50
❑16, Sep 95, The Long Hot Summer ... 2.50
❑17, Oct 95, Final Issue ... 2.50

SHADOW COMIX SHOWCASE
SHADOW COMIX

Value: Cover or less

❑1, May 96, Outlander 0.1; Darkblade ... 2.95

SHADOW CROSS
DARKSIDE

Value: Cover or less

❑1, Oct 95 ... 2.75

SHADOW EMPIRES: FAITH CONQUERS
DARK HORSE

	ORIG	GOOD	FINE	N-MINT
❑1, Aug 94	2.95	0.65	1.63	3.25
❑2, Sep 94	2.95	0.60	1.50	3.00
❑3, Oct 94	2.95	0.60	1.50	3.00
❑4, Nov 94	2.95	0.60	1.50	3.00

SHADOWGEAR
ANTARCTIC

Value: Cover or less

❑1, Feb 99, Hardwired, Part 1 ... 2.99
❑2, Mar 99, Hardwired, Part 2 ... 2.99
❑3, Apr 99, Hardwired, Part 3 ... 2.99

SHADOWHAWK (VOL. 1)
IMAGE

	ORIG	GOOD	FINE	N-MINT
❑1, Aug 92, A Knightmare Walking, 1: Shadowhawk, Embossed cover; coupon for Image Comics #0	2.50	0.60	1.50	3.00
❑1/A, 1: Shadowhawk, Embossed cover; coupon for Image Comics #0; Newsstand edition (no gold stamp)	1.95	0.40	1.00	2.00
❑2, Oct 92, Good Night For Arson, A: Spawn; 1: Arson, poster	1.95	0.50	1.25	2.50
❑3, Dec 92, Liquid Fire; Opening Shots, 1: Liquefier; 1: The Others, Glow-in-the-dark cover	1.95	0.50	1.25	2.50
❑4, Mar 93, Enter: The Dragon, A: Savage Dragon	1.95	0.40	1.00	2.00

Michael W. Kaluta was the writer and artist on DC's first *Shadow* series.

SHADOWHAWK (VOL. 2)
IMAGE

	ORIG	GOOD	FINE	N-MINT
❑1, May 93, The Shadow Of The Hawk, diecut foil cover	3.50	0.70	1.75	3.50
❑1/GO, May 93, Gold	—	0.60	1.50	3.00
❑2, Jul 93, The Secret Revealed, 1: Hawk's Shadow, Foil-embossed cover; ShadowHawk's identity revealed	1.95	0.40	1.00	2.00
❑2/GO, Jul 93, Gold edition	—	0.60	1.50	3.00
❑3, Aug 93, Like Lambs To The..., 1: J.P. Slaughter; 1: The Pact, Cover perforated to allow folding out into poster	2.95	0.59	1.48	2.95

SHADOWHAWK (VOL. 3)
IMAGE

	ORIG	GOOD	FINE	N-MINT
❑0, Oct 94, RL, A: Mars Gunther; A: Bloodstrike; A: Mist; O: Shadowhawk, cover says September	1.95	0.50	1.25	2.50
❑1, Nov 93, Through The Past, Darkly, 1: Valentine, Foil-embossed cover	1.95	0.50	1.25	2.50
❑2, Dec 93, The Needle And The Damage Done, 1: U.S. Male, U.S. Male bonus book (bound-in)	1.95	0.40	1.00	2.00
❑3, Feb 94, Fold-up cover	1.95	0.59	1.48	2.95
❑4, Mar 94	1.95	0.59	1.48	2.95
❑12, The Monster Within, Part 1, (Numbering sequence follows from total of all ShadowHawk books published to this point)	1.95	0.39	0.98	1.95
❑13, Sep 94, The Monster Within, Part 2, A: WildC.A.T.s	1.95	0.39	0.98	1.95
❑14, Oct 94, Monster Within, Part 3; The Monster Within, Part 3, A: 1963 heroes	2.50	0.50	1.25	2.50
❑15, Nov 94, Monster Within, Part 4; The Monster Within, Part 4, A: The Others	2.50	0.50	1.25	2.50
❑16, Jan 95, Monster Within, Part 5; The Monster Within, Part 5, A: Supreme	2.50	0.50	1.25	2.50
❑17, Mar 95, Monster Within, Part 6, A: Spawn	2.50	0.50	1.25	2.50
❑18, May 95, D: Shadowhawk, Final Issue	2.50	0.50	1.25	2.50
❑SE 1, Dec 94, Images of Tomorrow; Images of Yesterday, Special edition; Flip-book	3.50	0.70	1.75	3.50

SHADOWHAWK GALLERY
IMAGE

	ORIG	GOOD	FINE	N-MINT
❑1, Apr 94	1.95	0.40	1.00	2.00

SHADOWHAWKS OF LEGEND
IMAGE

Value: Cover or less

❑1, Nov 95, KB (w), A journey ThroughShadows; The Shadow of Justice ... 4.95

SHADOWHAWK-VAMPIRELLA
IMAGE

Value: Cover or less

❑2, Feb 95, crossover; continued from Vampirella - Shadowhawk #1 ... 4.95

SHADOW, THE: HELL'S HEAT WAVE
DARK HORSE

Value: Cover or less

❑1, Apr 95 ... 2.95
❑2, May 95 ... 2.95
❑3, Jun 95 ... 2.95

SHADOW HOUSE
SHADOW HOUSE PRESS

Value: Cover or less

❑1, Aug 97, PB, Autumn's Arrival, The Revenant, Fetid Matter, Nightmark, Dark Streets, b&w ... 2.95
❑2, Oct 97, b&w ... 2.95
❑3, Dec 97, b&w ... 2.95
❑4, Feb 98, b&w ... 2.95

SHADOWHUNT SPECIAL
IMAGE

Value: Cover or less

❑1/A, Apr 96, Part 1 of five-part crossover ... 2.50
❑1/B, Apr 96, alternate cover; Part 1 of five-part crossover ... 2.50

SHADOW, THE: IN THE COILS OF LEVIATHAN
DARK HORSE

Value: Cover or less

❑1, Oct 93 ... 2.95
❑2, Dec 93 ... 2.95
❑3, Feb 94 ... 2.95
❑4, Apr 94 ... 2.95

SHADOW LADY (MASAKAZU KATSURA'S...)
DARK HORSE

	ORIG	GOOD	FINE	N-MINT
❑1, Oct 98, Dangeous Love, Part 1; Dangerous Love, 1: Shadow Lady	2.50	0.60	1.50	3.00
❑2, Nov 98, Dangeous Love, Part 2; Dangerous Love, 2: De-Mo; 2: Shadow Lady; 1: Bright Honda; 2: Aimi	2.50	0.50	1.25	2.50
❑3, Dec 98, Dangeous Love, Part 3; Dangerous Love	2.50	0.50	1.25	2.50
❑4, Jan 99, Dangeous Love, Part 4; Dangerous Love	2.50	0.50	1.25	2.50
❑5, Feb 99, Dangeous Love, Part 5; Dangerous Love	2.50	0.50	1.25	2.50
❑6, Mar 99, Dangeous Love, Part 6; Dangerous Love	2.50	0.50	1.25	2.50
❑7, Apr 99, The Eyes of a Stranger, Part 1; Dangerous Love	2.50	0.50	1.25	2.50
❑8, May 99, The Eyes of a Stranger, Part 2; The Eyes Of A Stranger	2.50	0.50	1.25	2.50
❑9, Jun 99, The Eyes Of A Stranger, Part 3; The Eyes Of A Stranger	2.50	0.50	1.25	2.50
❑10, Jul 99, The Eyes of a Stranger, Part 4; The Eyes Of A Stranger	2.50	0.50	1.25	2.50
❑11, Aug 99, The Eyes Of A Stranger, Part 5; The Eyes Of A Stranger	2.50	0.50	1.25	2.50
❑12, Sep 99, The Eyes Of A Stranger, Part 6; The Eyes Of A Stranger	2.50	0.50	1.25	2.50
❑13, Oct 99, The Awakening	2.50	0.50	1.25	2.50
❑14, Nov 99, The Awakening	2.50	0.50	1.25	2.50
❑15, Dec 99, The Awakening	2.50	0.50	1.25	2.50
❑16, Jan 00, The Awakening	2.50	0.50	1.25	2.50
❑17, Feb 00, The Awakening	2.50	0.50	1.25	2.50
❑18, Mar 00, The Awakening	2.50	0.50	1.25	2.50
❑19, Apr 00, The Awakening	2.50	0.50	1.25	2.50
❑20, May 00, Sudden Death, Part 1	2.50	0.50	1.25	2.50
❑21, Jun 00, Sudden Death, Part 2	2.50	0.50	1.25	2.50
❑22, Jul 00, Sudden Death, Part 3	2.50	0.50	1.25	2.50
❑23, Aug 00, Sudden Death, Part 4	2.50	0.50	1.25	2.50
❑24, Sep 00, Sudden Death, Part 5	2.50	0.50	1.25	2.50
❑SE 1, Oct 00	3.99	0.80	2.00	3.99

SHADOWLAND
FANTAGRAPHICS

Value: Cover or less

❑1, b&w 2.25

❑2, b&w 2.25

SHADOWLINE SPECIAL
IMAGE

	ORIG	GOOD	FINE	N-MINT
❑1	—	0.20	0.50	1.00

SHADOWLORD/TRIUNE
JET CITY

Value: Cover or less

❑1, Win 86 .... 1.50

SHADOWMAN
VALIANT

	ORIG	GOOD	FINE	N-MINT
❑0, Apr 94, O: Shadowman I (Maxim St. James); O: Shadowman II (Jack Boniface)	2.50	0.50	1.25	2.50
❑0/GO, Gold edition	—	0.80	2.00	4.00
❑0/SC, Apr 94, O: Shadowman I (Maxim St. James); O: Shadowman II (Jack Boniface), chromium cover	3.50	0.79	1.98	3.95
❑1, May 92, 1: Shadowman II (Jack Boniface)	2.50	0.60	1.50	3.00
❑2, Jun 92	2.50	0.60	1.50	3.00
❑3, Jul 92	2.50	0.50	1.25	2.50
❑4, Aug 92, FM (c), Unity, Part 6, Unity	2.50	0.50	1.25	2.50
❑5, Sep 92, Unity, Part 14, Unity	2.50	0.50	1.25	2.50
❑6, Oct 92	2.50	0.50	1.25	2.50
❑7, Nov 92	2.50	0.50	1.25	2.50
❑8, Dec 92, V: Master Darque	2.50	0.50	1.25	2.50
❑9, Jan 93	2.50	0.50	1.25	2.50
❑10, Feb 93	2.50	0.50	1.25	2.50
❑11, Mar 93	2.50	0.50	1.25	2.50
❑12, Apr 93, BH, BH (w), Dark Rapture, V: Master Darque	2.50	0.50	1.25	2.50
❑13, May 93	2.50	0.50	1.25	2.50
❑14, Jun 93, BH, BH (w), Crosses	2.50	0.50	1.25	2.50
❑15, Jul 93, BH, BH (w), April Visions	2.50	0.50	1.25	2.50
❑16, Aug 93, 1: Doctor Mirage	2.50	0.60	1.50	3.00
❑17, Sep 93, A: Archer & Armstrong, Serial number contest	2.50	0.50	1.25	2.50
❑18, Oct 93	2.50	0.50	1.25	2.50
❑19, Nov 93, A: Aerosmith, Aerosmith	2.50	0.50	1.25	2.50
❑20, Dec 93	2.50	0.50	1.25	2.50
❑21, Jan 94, V: Master Darque	2.50	0.50	1.25	2.50
❑22, Feb 94	2.50	0.50	1.25	2.50
❑23, Mar 94, A: Doctor Mirage	2.50	0.50	1.25	2.50
❑24, Apr 94	2.50	0.50	1.25	2.50
❑25, Apr 94, trading card	2.50	0.50	1.25	2.50
❑26, Jun 94	2.50	0.50	1.25	2.50
❑27, Aug 94	2.50	0.50	1.25	2.50
❑28, Sep 94	2.50	0.50	1.25	2.50
❑29, Oct 94, The Chaos Effect: Beta, Part 1, Chaos Effect	2.50	0.50	1.25	2.50
❑30, Nov 94	2.50	0.50	1.25	2.50
❑31, Dec 94	2.50	0.50	1.25	2.50
❑32, Jan 94	2.50	0.50	1.25	2.50
❑33, Feb 94	2.50	0.50	1.25	2.50
❑34, Mar 94	2.50	0.50	1.25	2.50
❑35, Apr 95	2.50	0.50	1.25	2.50
❑36, May 95	2.50	0.50	1.25	2.50
❑37, Jun 95, BH	2.50	0.50	1.25	2.50
❑38, Jul 95, BH	2.50	0.50	1.25	2.50
❑39, Aug 95, BH	2.50	0.50	1.25	2.50
❑40, Sep 95, BH	2.50	0.50	1.25	2.50
❑41, Oct 95, BH	2.50	0.50	1.25	2.50
❑42, Nov 95, BH	2.50	0.50	1.25	2.50
❑43, Dec 95, BH	2.50	0.50	1.25	2.50
❑YB 1, Dec 94, Yearbook 1	3.95	0.79	1.98	3.95

SHADOWMAN (VOL. 2)
ACCLAIM

	ORIG	GOOD	FINE	N-MINT
❑1, Mar 97, Deadside, Part 1	2.50	0.50	1.25	2.50
❑1/SC, Mar 97, Deadside, Part 1, Painted cover	2.50	0.50	1.25	2.50
❑2, Apr 97, Deadside, Part 2	2.50	0.50	1.25	2.50
❑3, May 97, Deadside, Part 3	2.50	0.50	1.25	2.50
❑4, Jun 97, Deadside, Part 4	2.50	0.50	1.25	2.50
❑5, Jul 97	2.50	0.50	1.25	2.50
❑5/Ash, Mar 97, b&w; no cover price; preview of upcoming issue	—	0.20	0.50	1.00
❑6, Aug 97	2.50	0.50	1.25	2.50
❑7, Sep 97	2.50	0.50	1.25	2.50
❑8, Oct 97	2.50	0.50	1.25	2.50
❑9, Nov 97	2.50	0.50	1.25	2.50
❑10, Dec 97	2.50	0.50	1.25	2.50
❑11, Jan 98	2.50	0.50	1.25	2.50
❑12, Feb 98	2.50	0.50	1.25	2.50
❑13, Mar 98, Goat Month	2.50	0.50	1.25	2.50
❑14, Apr 98	2.50	0.50	1.25	2.50
❑15, Jan 98, no cover date; indicia says Jan	2.50	0.50	1.25	2.50
❑16, Feb 98, no cover date; indicia says Feb	2.50	0.50	1.25	2.50
❑Ash 1, Nov 96, b&w; no cover price; preview of upcoming series	—	0.20	0.50	1.00

SHADOWMAN (VOL. 3)
ACCLAIM

Value: Cover or less

❑1, Jul 99, Mission Unspeakable 3.95

❑2, Aug 99 .... 3.95

❑3, Sep 99 .... 3.95

❑4, Oct 99, Soul Survivor 3.95

SHADOW MASTER
PSYGNOSIS

	ORIG	GOOD	FINE	N-MINT
❑0, Preview	—	0.20	0.50	1.00

SHADOWMASTERS
MARVEL

	ORIG	GOOD	FINE	N-MINT
❑1, Oct 89, Shadows Of The Past, O: Shadowmasters	3.95	0.80	2.00	4.00
❑2, Nov 89	3.95	0.80	2.00	4.00
❑3, Dec 89	3.95	0.80	2.00	4.00
❑4, Jan 90, Into The Void	3.95	0.80	2.00	4.00

SHADOWMEN
TRIDENT

Value: Cover or less

❑1, b&w; adult 2.25

❑2, b&w; adult 2.25

SHADOW OF THE BATMAN
DC

	ORIG	GOOD	FINE	N-MINT
❑1, Dec 85, By Death's Eerie Light!; The Master Plan of Dr. Phosphorus	1.75	0.60	1.50	3.00
❑2, Jan 86	1.75	0.40	1.00	2.00
❑3, Feb 86	1.75	0.40	1.00	2.00
❑4, Mar 86	1.75	0.40	1.00	2.00
❑5, Apr 86	1.75	0.40	1.00	2.00

SHADOW OF THE TORTURER, THE (GENE WOLFE'S...)
INNOVATION

Value: Cover or less

❑1, Resurrection and Death, movie Adaptation 2.50

❑2, movie Adaptation 2.50

❑3, movie Adaptation 2.50

❑4 .... 2.50

❑5 .... 2.50

❑6 .... 2.50

SHADOW RAVEN
POC-IT

Value: Cover or less

❑1, Jun 95, Fangs Of The Serpent, 1: Shadow Raven 2.50

SHADOW REIGNS
AIX C.C.

Value: Cover or less

❑0, Dec 97 .... 2.95

SHADOW RIDERS
Marvel

Value: Cover or less

- ❑1, The Screaming Man!, 1: Shadow Riders, Embossed cover ... 2.50
- ❑2 ... 1.75
- ❑3 ... 1.75
- ❑4 ... 1.75

SHADOWS & LIGHT
Marvel

Value: Cover or less

- ❑1, Feb 98, BWr (w); SD (w), Free Fall; A Man's Reach, b&w ... 2.99
- ❑2, Apr 98, b&w ... 2.99
- ❑3, Jul 98, b&w ... 2.99

SHADOW'S EDGE, THE
Lion

Value: Cover or less

- ❑1 ... 3.95

SHADOWS FALL
DC

Value: Cover or less

- ❑1, Nov 94, Absence Makes The Heart ... 2.95
- ❑2, Dec 94, Toys for the Play of Ghosts ... 2.95
- ❑3, Jan 95, Windows for the Dark ... 2.95
- ❑4, Feb 95, Echoes of Who You Are ... 2.95
- ❑5, Mar 95, Dreamling Alice ... 2.95
- ❑6, Apr 95, Alone With Mirrors ... 2.95

SHADOWS FROM THE GRAVE
Renegade

Value: Cover or less

- ❑1, b&w ... 2.00
- ❑2, Mar 88, Blood Will Tell; Creeping Up with the Joneses!, b&w ... 2.00

SHADOW SLASHER
Pocket Change

Value: Cover or less

- ❑1, Blood of The City, 1: Riplash ... 2.50

SHADOW SLAYER
Eternity

Value: Cover or less

- ❑0 ... 1.95

SHADOWSTAR
Shadowstar

	ORIG	GOOD	FINE	N-MINT
❑1	1.50	0.40	1.00	2.00
❑2, Nov 85	1.50	0.40	1.00	2.00
❑3, Dec 85, first Slave Labor comic book	1.50	0.40	1.00	2.00

SHADOW STATE
Broadway

	ORIG	GOOD	FINE	N-MINT
❑1, Dec 95, DC, BloodS.C.R.E.A.M.: Scream 'em Down; Till Death Do Us Part: Image Isn't Everything, Part 1, 1: BloodS.C.R.E.A.M., enhanced cardstock cover; BloodS.C.R.E.A.M., Fatale	2.50	0.50	1.25	2.50
❑2, Jan 96, Till Death Do Us Part: Image Isn't Everything, Part 2, Till Death Do Us Part; Fatale	2.50	0.50	1.25	2.50
❑3, Mar 96, Till Death Do Us Part	2.50	0.50	1.25	2.50
❑4, Apr 96, Till Death Do Us Part	2.50	0.50	1.25	2.50
❑5, May 96, Till Death Do Us Part	2.50	0.50	1.25	2.50
❑6	2.95	0.59	1.48	2.95
❑7	2.95	0.59	1.48	2.95
❑Ash 1, Sep 95, b&w; giveaway preview edition; Till Death Do Us Part, Fatale	—	0.20	0.50	1.00

SHADOW STRIKES!, THE
DC

	ORIG	GOOD	FINE	N-MINT
❑1, Sep 89, Death's Head	1.75	0.50	1.25	2.50
❑2, Oct 89	1.75	0.45	1.13	2.25
❑3, Nov 89	1.75	0.40	1.00	2.00
❑4, Dec 89	1.75	0.40	1.00	2.00
❑5, Jan 90, A: Doc Savage	1.75	0.40	1.00	2.00
❑6, Feb 90, A: Doc Savage	1.75	0.40	1.00	2.00
❑7, Mar 90	1.75	0.40	1.00	2.00
❑8, Apr 90, V: Shiwan Khan	1.75	0.40	1.00	2.00
❑9, May 90, V: Shiwan Khan	1.75	0.40	1.00	2.00
❑10, Jun 90, V: Shiwan Khan	1.75	0.40	1.00	2.00
❑11, Aug 90	1.75	0.40	1.00	2.00
❑12, Sep 90	1.75	0.40	1.00	2.00
❑13, Oct 90	1.75	0.40	1.00	2.00
❑14, Dec 90	1.75	0.40	1.00	2.00
❑15, Jan 91	1.75	0.40	1.00	2.00
❑16, Feb 91	1.75	0.40	1.00	2.00
❑17, Mar 91	1.75	0.40	1.00	2.00
❑18, Apr 91	1.75	0.40	1.00	2.00
❑19, May 91	2.00	0.40	1.00	2.00
❑20, Jun 91	2.00	0.40	1.00	2.00
❑21, Jul 91	2.00	0.40	1.00	2.00
❑22, Aug 91	2.00	0.40	1.00	2.00
❑23, Sep 91	2.00	0.40	1.00	2.00
❑24, Oct 91	2.00	0.40	1.00	2.00
❑25, Nov 91	2.00	0.40	1.00	2.00
❑26, Dec 91	2.00	0.40	1.00	2.00
❑27, Jan 92	2.00	0.40	1.00	2.00
❑28, Feb 92	2.00	0.40	1.00	2.00
❑29, Mar 92	2.00	0.40	1.00	2.00

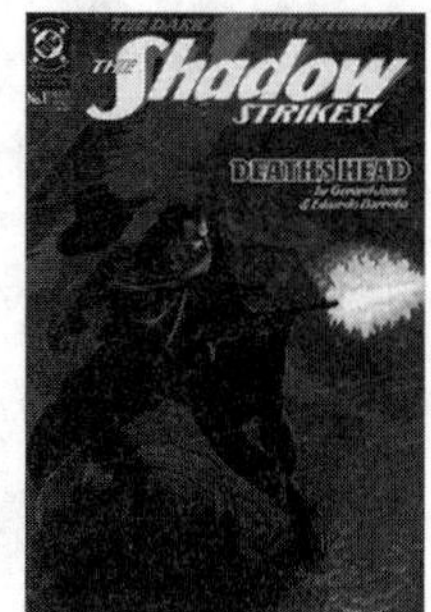

Depression-era adventures of The Shadow and his operatives were told in *The Shadow Strikes!*

	ORIG	GOOD	FINE	N-MINT
❑30, Apr 92, Disillusions & Illusions	2.00	0.40	1.00	2.00
❑31, May 92, Disillusions & Illusions	2.00	0.40	1.00	2.00
❑Anl 1, Dec 89, DS	3.50	0.70	1.75	3.50

SHADOWTOWN
Iconografix

Value: Cover or less

- ❑1, Break-Out ... 2.50

SHADOWTOWN: BLACK FIST RISING
Madheart

Value: Cover or less

- ❑1, b&w ... 2.50

SHADOW WAR OF HAWKMAN, THE
DC

	ORIG	GOOD	FINE	N-MINT
❑1, May 85, AA; RHo, The Shadow War of Hawkman	0.75	0.30	0.75	1.50
❑2, Jun 85, RHo, Fallen Angels	0.75	0.25	0.63	1.25
❑3, Jul 85, RHo, My Worlds Opposed, A: Aquaman; A: Elongated Man	0.75	0.25	0.63	1.25
❑4, Aug 85, RHo, No Sound of Clashing Wars	0.75	0.25	0.63	1.25

SHADOW WARRIOR
Gateway

Value: Cover or less

- ❑1, b&w ... 1.95

SHAIANA
Express

Value: Cover or less

- ❑1, enhanced cover ... 3.75
- ❑2 ... 2.50
- ❑3 ... 2.50

SHALOMAN
Mark 1

Value: Cover or less

- ❑1, b&w ... 1.75
- ❑2, b&w ... 1.75
- ❑3, b&w ... 1.75
- ❑4, b&w ... 1.75
- ❑5, b&w ... 1.75
- ❑6, b&w ... 1.75
- ❑7, b&w ... 1.75
- ❑8, b&w ... 1.75
- ❑9, b&w ... 1.75

SHAMAN
Continuity

	ORIG	GOOD	FINE	N-MINT
❑0, One-Shot	—	0.40	1.00	2.00

SHAMAN'S TEARS
Image

	ORIG	GOOD	FINE	N-MINT
❑0, Dec 95, MGr, MGr (w), says 1996 indicia; meant 1995	1.95	0.50	1.25	2.50
❑1, May 93, MGr, MGr (w), Warcry, foil cover	2.50	0.50	1.25	2.50
❑1/PL, May 93, MGr, Platinum edition	2.50	0.80	2.00	4.00
❑2, Jul 93, MGr, MGr (w), cover says Aug; indicia says Jul	2.50	0.50	1.25	2.50
❑3, Nov 94, MGr, MGr (w)	1.95	0.39	0.98	1.95
❑3/Ash, MGr, MGr (w), Limited "ashcan" run of Shaman's Tears #3	—	0.60	1.50	3.00
❑4, Dec 94, MGr, MGr (w), Title moves back to Image	1.95	0.39	0.98	1.95
❑5, Jan 95, MGr, MGr (w)	1.95	0.39	0.98	1.95
❑6, Feb 95, MGr, MGr (w)	1.95	0.39	0.98	1.95
❑7, May 95, MGr, MGr (w)	1.95	0.39	0.98	1.95
❑8, May 95, MGr, MGr (w)	1.95	0.39	0.98	1.95
❑9, Jun 95, MGr, MGr (w)	1.95	0.39	0.98	1.95
❑10, Jul 95, MGr, MGr (w)	1.95	0.39	0.98	1.95
❑11, Aug 95, MGr, MGr (w)	2.50	0.39	0.98	1.95
❑12, Aug 95, MGr, MGr (w)	2.50	0.39	0.98	1.95

SHANDA THE PANDA
Mu

Value: Cover or less

- ❑1, May 92, b&w ... 2.50
- ❑2 ... 2.50
- ❑3 ... 2.75
- ❑4 ... 2.75
- ❑5 ... 2.75
- ❑6 ... 2.75
- ❑7 ... 2.75
- ❑8, Birthday Suite ... 2.75
- ❑9, Rings and Things ... 2.75
- ❑10 ... 2.75
- ❑11, Raccoon's Tune ... 2.75
- ❑12 ... 2.75
- ❑13 ... 2.75
- ❑14, Christmas Presence ... 2.95
- ❑15 ... 2.95
- ❑16 ... 2.95

SHANDA THE PANDA (2ND SERIES)
Antarctic

Value: Cover or less

- ❑1, Jun 93 ... 2.50
- ❑2, Aug 93 ... 2.50
- ❑3, Oct 93 ... 2.75
- ❑4, Dec 93 ... 2.75

	ORIG	GOOD	FINE	N-MINT

- ❑5, Aug 94 ... 2.75
- ❑6, Oct 94 ... 2.75
- ❑7, Jan 95 ... 2.75
- ❑8, Feb 95 ... 2.75
- ❑9, May 95 ... 2.75
- ❑10, Jul 95 ... 2.75
- ❑11, Sep 95 ... 2.75
- ❑12, Nov 95 ... 2.75
- ❑13, Jan 96 ... 2.75
- ❑14, Mar 96 ... 2.75
- ❑15, May 96 ... 2.75
- ❑16, Jul 96 ... 1.95
- ❑17 ... 1.95
- ❑18 ... 1.95
- ❑19 ... 1.95
- ❑20 ... 1.95
- ❑21, Sep 97 ... 2.95
- ❑24, Apr 99 ... 2.95

SHANGHAI: BIG MACHINE
Brick House Digital

Value: Cover or less

- ❑1 ... 2.95

SHANGHAIED: THE SAGA OF THE BLACK KITE
Eternity

Issue	ORIG	GOOD	FINE	N-MINT
❑1	1.80	0.40	1.00	2.00
❑2	1.95	0.40	1.00	2.00
❑3	1.95	0.40	1.00	2.00

SHANNA THE SHE-DEVIL
Marvel

Issue	ORIG	GOOD	FINE	N-MINT
❑1, 1: Shanna the She-Devil	0.20	1.60	4.00	8.00
❑2	0.20	1.00	2.50	5.00
❑3	0.20	0.70	1.75	3.50
❑4	0.20	0.70	1.75	3.50
❑5	0.20	0.70	1.75	3.50

SHAOLIN
Black Tiger

Value: Cover or less

- ❑1, 1: The Tiger ... 2.95
- ❑2 ... 2.95
- ❑3 ... 2.95
- ❑4 ... 2.95
- ❑5 ... 2.95

SHAQUILLE O'NEAL VS. MICHAEL JORDAN
Personality

Value: Cover or less

- ❑1 ... 2.95
- ❑2 ... 2.95

SHARDS
Ascension

Value: Cover or less

- ❑1, Apr 94 ... 2.50

SHARKY
Image

Value: Cover or less

- ❑1/A, Feb 98, Lo, He Shall Walk Among Us! ... 2.50
- ❑1/B, Feb 98, Lo, He Shall Walk Among Us!, back cover pin-up ... 2.50
- ❑1/C, Feb 98, Lo, He Shall Walk Among Us!, signing tour edition ... 2.50
- ❑1/D, Feb 98, Lo, He Shall Walk Among Us!, no cover price; The $1, 000, 000 variant ... 2.50
- ❑2/A, Apr 98, Back to School!. 2.50
- ❑2/B, Apr 98, Back to School!, alternate wraparound cover (with Savage Dragon) ... 2.50
- ❑3, May 98, Blazin' Glory ... 2.50
- ❑4, 98, I Get by With a Little Help From my Friends!, Group charging on cover, "The Bad Guy!" inset; gives date of publication as Late ... 2.50
- ❑4/A, variant cover ... 2.50

SHATTER (1ST SERIES)
First

Issue	ORIG	GOOD	FINE	N-MINT
❑1, Jun 85, Headhunters, 1: Shatter, This is the first computer-generated comic book	1.75	0.50	1.25	2.50
❑1-2, Headhunters, 1: Shatter, 2nd Printing; This is the first computer-generated comic book	1.75	0.40	1.00	2.00

SHATTER (2ND SERIES)
First

Issue	ORIG	GOOD	FINE	N-MINT
❑1, Dec 85, first computer-drawn comic book; Continued from Shatter one-shot	1.75	0.50	1.25	2.50
❑2, Feb 86, Avenues of Escape	1.75	0.40	1.00	2.00
❑3, Jun 86	1.75	0.40	1.00	2.00
❑4, Aug 86, A Man Named Shatter	1.75	0.40	1.00	2.00
❑5, Oct 86, The Third World War, Part 1	1.75	0.40	1.00	2.00
❑6, Dec 86	1.75	0.40	1.00	2.00
❑7, Feb 87, Bringing Up Baby!	1.75	0.40	1.00	2.00
❑8, Apr 87, Red Dawns, White Nights and blue Mondays	1.75	0.40	1.00	2.00
❑9, Jun 87	1.75	0.40	1.00	2.00
❑10, Aug 87	1.75	0.40	1.00	2.00
❑11, Oct 87	1.75	0.40	1.00	2.00
❑12, Dec 87	1.75	0.40	1.00	2.00
❑13, Feb 88	1.75	0.40	1.00	2.00
❑14, Apr 88	1.75	0.40	1.00	2.00

SHATTERED EARTH
Eternity

Value: Cover or less

- ❑1, Nov 88, For Her I Serve; Exten-Four ... 1.95
- ❑2 ... 1.95
- ❑3 ... 1.95
- ❑4, Mar 89 ... 1.95
- ❑5 ... 1.95
- ❑6 ... 1.95
- ❑7 ... 1.95
- ❑8 ... 1.95
- ❑9 ... 1.95

SHATTERED IMAGE
Image

Value: Cover or less

- ❑1, Aug 96, KB (w), A: Spawn; A: Gen13; A: Savage Dragon; A: Deathblow ... 2.50
- ❑2, Oct 96, KB (w), A: Spawn; A: Gen13; A: Savage Dragon; A: Deathblow, incorrect cover date ... 2.50
- ❑3, Nov 96, KB (w), A: Spawn; A: Gen13; A: Savage Dragon; A: Deathblow, cover says Oct, indicia says Nov ... 2.50
- ❑4, Dec 96, KB (w), A: Spawn; A: Youngblood; A: Gen13; A: Savage Dragon; A: Knight Watchman; A: Ultiman; A: Shadowhawk, Final Issue ... 2.50

SHATTERPOINT
Eternity

Value: Cover or less

- ❑1, b&w; Broid ... 2.25
- ❑2, b&w; Broid ... 2.25
- ❑3, b&w; Broid ... 2.25
- ❑4, b&w; Broid ... 2.25

SHAZAM!
DC

Issue	ORIG	GOOD	FINE	N-MINT
❑1, Feb 73, CCB, In The Beginning..., O: Captain Marvel (Golden Age)	0.20	1.60	4.00	8.00
❑2, Apr 73, CCB	0.20	1.00	2.50	5.00
❑3, Jun 73, CCB	0.20	0.80	2.00	4.00
❑4, Jul 73, CCB	0.20	0.80	2.00	4.00
❑5, Sep 73, CCB	0.20	0.60	1.50	3.00
❑6, Oct 73, CCB, Photo cover	0.20	0.60	1.50	3.00
❑7, Nov 73, CCB	0.20	0.60	1.50	3.00
❑8, Dec 73, CCB, 100pgs.; scheduled as DC 100-Page Super-Spectacular #DC-23	0.50	2.00	5.00	10.00
❑9, Jan 74, CCB	0.20	0.50	1.25	2.50
❑10, Feb 74, CCB, V: Aunt Minerva, Mary Marvel back-up	0.20	0.50	1.25	2.50
❑11, Mar 74	0.20	0.40	1.00	2.00
❑12, Jun 74, 100pgs.	0.60	1.60	4.00	8.00
❑13, Aug 74, 100pgs.	0.60	1.60	4.00	8.00
❑14, Oct 74, KS, A: Monster Society, 100pgs.	0.60	1.60	4.00	8.00
❑15, Dec 74, A: Lex Luthor, 100pgs.	0.60	1.60	4.00	8.00
❑16, Feb 75, V: Seven Deadly Sins, 100pgs.	0.60	1.60	4.00	8.00
❑17, Apr 75, 100pgs.	0.60	1.60	4.00	8.00
❑18, Jun 75	0.25	0.40	1.00	2.00
❑19, Aug 75	0.25	0.40	1.00	2.00
❑20, Oct 75	0.25	0.40	1.00	2.00
❑21, Dec 75, Captain Marvel	0.25	0.40	1.00	2.00
❑22, Feb 76, V: King Kull	0.25	0.40	1.00	2.00
❑23, Win 76	0.30	0.40	1.00	2.00
❑24, Spr 76	0.30	0.40	1.00	2.00
❑25, Oct 76, 1: Isis	0.30	0.60	1.50	3.00
❑26, Dec 76	0.30	0.40	1.00	2.00
❑27, Feb 77	0.30	0.40	1.00	2.00
❑28, Apr 77, V: Black Adam	0.30	0.40	1.00	2.00
❑29, Jun 77, V: Ibac	0.30	0.40	1.00	2.00
❑30, Aug 77	0.35	0.40	1.00	2.00
❑31, Oct 77, A: Minute Man	0.35	0.40	1.00	2.00
❑32, Dec 77	0.35	0.40	1.00	2.00
❑33, Feb 78, V: Mr. Atom	0.35	0.40	1.00	2.00
❑34, Apr 78, O: Captain Marvel Jr., Captain Marvel Jr. vs. Captain Nazi	0.35	0.40	1.00	2.00
❑35, Jun 78	0.35	0.40	1.00	2.00

SHAZAM! POWER OF HOPE
DC

Value: Cover or less

- ❑1, ARo ... 9.95

SHAZAM: THE NEW BEGINNING
DC

Issue	ORIG	GOOD	FINE	N-MINT
❑1, Apr 87, O: Captain Marvel (Golden Age)-new origin	0.75	0.40	1.00	2.00
❑2, May 87, "S" is for Wisdom... "H" is for Strength, V: Black Adam	0.75	0.40	1.00	2.00
❑3, Jun 87	0.75	0.40	1.00	2.00
❑4, Jul 87	0.75	0.40	1.00	2.00

SHEBA
Sick Mind

Value: Cover or less

- ❑1, Jul 96, b&w ... 2.95
- ❑2, Nov 96, b&w ... 2.95
- ❑3 ... 2.50
- ❑4 ... 2.50

SHEBA (2ND SERIES)
Sirius

Value: Cover or less

- ❑1, Dec 97, b&w ... 2.50
- ❑2, Mar 98, b&w ... 2.50
- ❑3, Jun 98, b&w ... 2.50
- ❑4, Sep 98, b&w ... 2.50
- ❑5, b&w ... 2.50
- ❑6, May 99, Reunions, b&w ... 2.95

SHEBA PANTHEON
Sirius

Value: Cover or less

- ❑1, Aug 98, b&w; collects strips and character bios ... 2.50

SHE BUCCANEER
Monster

Value: Cover or less

- ❑1, b&w ... 2.25
- ❑2, b&w ... 2.25

ORIG GOOD FINE N-MINT

SHE-CAT
AC
Value: Cover or less

❑1, Jun 89, Stray Cat!, b&w.... 2.50
❑2, Apr 90, b&w 2.50
❑3, May 90, b&w 2.50
❑4, Jun 90, b&w 2.50

SHEEDEVA
FANTAGRAPHICS
Value: Cover or less

❑1, Aug 94, b&w; adult 2.95
❑2, Nov 94, b&w; adult 2.95

SHEENA
MARVEL

❑1, Dec 84, GM, movie Adaptation 0.75 0.40 1.00 2.00
❑2, Feb 85, GM, movie Adaptation 0.75 0.40 1.00 2.00

SHEENA 3-D SPECIAL
BLACKTHORNE
Value: Cover or less

❑1, May 85 .... 2.00

SHEENA-QUEEN OF THE JUNGLE
LONDON NIGHT
Value: Cover or less

❑1/A, Alligator cover 5.00
❑1/B, Leopard cover 5.00
❑1/C, Zebra cover 5.00
❑1/D, Ministry Edition 3.00
❑1/LE, White leather edition.... 15.00

SHEENA, QUEEN OF THE JUNGLE 3-D
BLACKTHORNE
Value: Cover or less

❑1, May 85, DSt 2.50

SHEILA TRENT: VAMPIRE HUNTER
DRACULINA
Value: Cover or less

❑1, 1: Sheila Trent 2.50
❑2 .... 2.50

SHELL SHOCK
MIRAGE
Value: Cover or less

❑1, Anthology 12.95

SHERLOCK HOLMES (AVALON)
AVALON
Value: Cover or less

❑1, b&w 2.95

SHERLOCK HOLMES (DC)
DC

❑1, Oct 75, The Final Problem 0.25 0.80 2.00 4.00

SHERLOCK HOLMES (ETERNITY)
ETERNITY
Value: Cover or less

❑1, b&w; strip reprints 1.95
❑2, b&w; strip reprints 1.95
❑3, b&w; strip reprints 1.95
❑4, b&w; strip reprints 1.95
❑5, b&w; strip reprints 1.95
❑6, b&w; strip reprints 1.95
❑7, b&w; strip reprints 1.95
❑8, b&w; strip reprints 1.95
❑9, b&w; strip reprints 1.95
❑10, b&w; strip reprints 1.95
❑11, A Case of Blind Fear, b&w; strip reprints 1.95
❑12, b&w; strip reprints 1.95
❑13, b&w; strip reprints 1.95
❑14, b&w; strip reprints 1.95
❑15, b&w; strip reprints 1.95
❑16 .... 2.25
❑17 .... 2.25
❑18 .... 2.25
❑19 .... 2.25
❑20 .... 2.25
❑21 .... 2.50
❑22 .... 2.50
❑23, Final Issue 2.75

SHERLOCK HOLMES: ADVENTURES OF THE OPERA GHOST
CALIBER
Value: Cover or less

❑1 .... 2.95
❑2 .... 2.95

SHERLOCK HOLMES CASEBOOK
ETERNITY
Value: Cover or less

❑1, The Deadly Inheritance; The Tunnel Scheme, Originally published as New Adventures of Sherlock Holmes 2.25
❑2, The Derelict Ship; The Safe Robber, Originally published as New Adventures of Sherlock Holmes 2.25

SHERLOCK HOLMES: DR. JEKYLL & MR. HOLMES
CALIBER
Value: Cover or less

❑1, nn; b&w; One-Shot 2.95

SHERLOCK HOLMES IN THE CASE OF THE MISSING MARTIAN
ETERNITY
Value: Cover or less

❑1, Jul 90, b&w 2.25
❑2, Aug 90, b&w 2.25
❑3, Sep 90, b&w 2.25
❑4, Oct 90, b&w 2.25

SHERLOCK HOLMES IN THE CURIOUS CASE OF THE VANISHING VILLAIN
ATOMEKA
Value: Cover or less

❑1, nn 4.50

SHERLOCK HOLMES MYSTERIES
MOONSTONE
Value: Cover or less

❑1, The Scorned Mistress; Memories of an Angel 2.95

SHERLOCK HOLMES OF THE '30S
ETERNITY
Value: Cover or less

❑1, b&w; strip reprints 2.95
❑2, b&w; strip reprints 2.95
❑3, b&w; strip reprints 2.95
❑4, b&w; strip reprints 2.95
❑5, b&w; strip reprints 2.95
❑6, b&w; strip reprints 2.95
❑7, b&w; Final Issue; strip reprints 2.95

The worlds of Sir Arthur Conan Doyle and H.G. Wells crossed in *Sherlock Holmes and the Case of the Missing Martian.*

ORIG GOOD FINE N-MINT

SHERLOCK HOLMES READER
TOME
Value: Cover or less

❑1, The Loch Ness Horror, Part 1 .... 3.95

SHERLOCK HOLMES: RETURN OF THE DEVIL
ADVENTURE
Value: Cover or less

❑1, Sep 92, b&w 2.50
❑2, b&w 2.50

SHERLOCK JR.
ETERNITY
Value: Cover or less

❑1, b&w; strip reprints 2.50
❑2, b&w; strip reprints 2.50
❑3, b&w; strip reprints 2.50

SHERMAN'S MARCH THROUGH ATLANTA TO THE SEA
HERITAGE COLLECTION
Value: Cover or less

❑1, nn; wraparound cover; One-Shot; retells Civil War story 3.50

SHEVA'S WAR
DC
Value: Cover or less

❑1, Oct 98 .... 2.95
❑2, Nov 98 .... 2.95
❑3, Dec 98 .... 2.95
❑4, Jan 99 .... 2.95
❑5, Feb 99 .... 2.95

SHI
CRUSADE

❑0, Flipbook with Wolverine/Shi Night of Justice Preview 2.99 0.60 1.50 2.99
❑0.5, Wizard promotional edition with COA — 0.60 1.50 3.00

SHI: ART OF WAR TOUR BOOK
CRUSADE
Value: Cover or less

❑1 .... 4.95

SHI: BLACK, WHITE, AND RED
CRUSADE
Value: Cover or less

❑1, May 98, b&w and red 2.95
❑2, May 98, b&w and red 2.95

SHI/CYBLADE: THE BATTLE FOR INDEPENDENTS
CRUSADE

❑1, Sep 95, A: Bone; A: Cerebus; 1: The Atomik Angels, crossover; concludes Image's Cyblade/Shi: The Battle for Independents #1; Numerous other independent characters appear 2.95 0.80 2.00 4.00
❑1/SC, Sep 95, alternate cover; crossover; concludes Image's Cyblade/Shi: The Battle for Independents #1 .... 2.95 1.00 2.50 5.00

SHI/DAREDEVIL: HONOR THY MOTHER
CRUSADE
Value: Cover or less

❑1, Jan 97, flipbook with TCB Sneak Attack Edition #1; crossover with Marvel 2.95
❑1/LE, "Banzai" edition 10.00

SHIDIMA
IMAGE
Value: Cover or less

❑1/A, Jan 01, Outlaws Return, Many figures on cover, man center holding rope 2.95
❑1/B, Jan 01, Outlaws Return, Four figures on cover, man front holding sword 2.95
❑2, Mar 01, Reunion 2.95

SHI: EAST WIND RAIN
CRUSADE

❑1, Nov 97, East Wind Rain, Painted cover 3.50 0.70 1.75 3.50
❑2, Feb 98 .... 3.50 0.70 1.75 3.50
❑Ash 1, Jul 97, no cover price; Sneak Teaser Preview .... — 0.20 0.50 1.00

SHIELD
MARVEL

❑1, Feb 73, JK; DH, SL (w), When the Unliving Strike!, Nick Fury reprints from Strange Tales 0.20 1.60 4.00 8.00
❑2, Apr 73, Nick Fury reprints from Strange Tales 0.20 1.00 2.50 5.00
❑3, Jun 73, Nick Fury reprints from Strange Tales 0.20 1.00 2.50 5.00
❑4, Aug 73, JK, SL (w), The Power Of Shield!, Nick Fury reprints from Strange Tales..... 0.20 1.00 2.50 5.00
❑5, Oct 73, Nick Fury reprints from Strange Tales 0.20 1.00 2.50 5.00

SHIELD (ARCHIE)
ARCHIE
Value: Cover or less

- ❑1, Jun 83, RB 1.00
- ❑2, Aug 83, RB (c) 1.00
- ❑3, Dec 83, Title changes to Steel Sterling 1.00

SHI: HEAVEN & EARTH
CRUSADE
Value: Cover or less

- ❑1, Jul 97 .... 2.95
- ❑1/A, Jul 97, alternate cover 2.95
- ❑2, Nov 97 .... 2.95
- ❑2/A, Nov 97, logoless cover 2.95
- ❑3, Jan 98 .... 2.95
- ❑4/A, Apr 98, alternate cover (Shi facing right) 2.95
- ❑Ash 1, Special Teaser Preview 2.95

SHI: KAIDAN
CRUSADE

	ORIG	GOOD	FINE	N-MINT
❑1, Oct 96, The Soul of the Sword!; The Mad Monk, b&w; Japanese ghost stories	2.95	0.59	1.48	2.95
❑1/A, Oct 96, The Soul of the Sword!; The Mad Monk, b&w; alternate wraparound cover with no cover copy; Japanese ghost stories	2.95	0.60	1.50	3.00

SHILOH: THE DEVIL'S OWN DAY
HERITAGE COLLECTION
Value: Cover or less

- ❑1, nn; wraparound cover; One-Shot; retells Civil War battle 3.50

SHI: MASQUERADE
CRUSADE
Value: Cover or less

- ❑1, Mar 98, wraparound painted cover 3.50

SHIMMER
AVATAR
Value: Cover or less

- ❑1 .... 3.50

SHI: NIGHTSTALKERS
CRUSADE
Value: Cover or less

- ❑1, Sep 97, VM, T. C. B. 3.50

SHION: BLADE OF THE MINSTREL
VIZ
Value: Cover or less

- ❑1, Sep 90, b&w 9.95

SHIP OF FOOLS (CALIBER)
CALIBER
Value: Cover or less

- ❑1, b&w 2.95
- ❑2, Dante's Compass 2.95
- ❑3, Bowling for $$$, b&w 2.95
- ❑4 .... 2.95
- ❑5 .... 2.95
- ❑6 .... 2.95

SHIP OF FOOLS (IMAGE)
IMAGE
Value: Cover or less

- ❑0, Aug 97, b&w 2.95
- ❑1, Oct 97, Doesn't Anybody Care, Part 1, b&w 2.95
- ❑2, Dec 97, b&w 2.95
- ❑3, Feb 98, Zombie, b&w 2.95

SHIPWRECKED!
DISNEY
Value: Cover or less

- ❑1, DS, nn; movie Adaptation 5.95

SHI: REKISHI
CRUSADE
Value: Cover or less

- ❑1, Jan 97, flipbook with Shi: East Wind Rain Sneak Attack Edition #1 .... 2.95
- ❑2, Apr 97 .... 2.95

SHI: SENRYAKU
CRUSADE
Value: Cover or less

- ❑1, Aug 95 .... 2.95
- ❑1/SC, Aug 95, 1: 4 cover mix, Variant "virgin" cover with no type 2.95
- ❑2, Oct 95 .... 2.95
- ❑3, Dec 95 .... 2.95

SHI: THE BLOOD OF SAINTS
CRUSADE

	ORIG	GOOD	FINE	N-MINT
❑1, Nov 96	2.95	0.59	1.48	2.95
❑FAN 1, Nov 96, Promotional edition from FAN magazine	—	0.40	1.00	2.00

SHI: THE SERIES
CRUSADE

	ORIG	GOOD	FINE	N-MINT
❑1, Aug 97	2.95	0.70	1.75	3.50
❑1/A, Sneak preview edition with photo cover with Tia Carrera	2.95	0.70	1.75	3.50
❑2, Sep 97	2.95	0.60	1.50	3.00
❑3, Oct 97	2.95	0.60	1.50	3.00
❑4, Nov 97	2.95	0.60	1.50	3.00
❑5, Dec 97	2.95	0.60	1.50	3.00
❑6, Jan 98	2.95	0.59	1.48	2.95
❑7, Feb 98, manga-style cover	2.95	0.59	1.48	2.95
❑8, Mar 98	2.95	0.59	1.48	2.95
❑9, Apr 98	2.95	0.59	1.48	2.95
❑9/A, Apr 98, alternate cover (full moon in background)	2.95	0.59	1.48	2.95
❑9/B, Apr 98, alternate cover (Shi on her back)	2.95	0.59	1.48	2.95
❑9/C, Apr 98, alternate cover (manga-style)	2.95	0.59	1.48	2.95
❑10, May 98	2.95	0.59	1.48	2.95
❑10/A, May 98, alternate cover (in water)	2.95	0.59	1.48	2.95
❑10/B, May 98, alternate cover (cherry blossoms)	2.95	0.59	1.48	2.95
❑10/C, May 98, alternate cover (drawing sword)	2.95	0.59	1.48	2.95
❑11, Jun 98, b&w	2.95	0.59	1.48	2.95
❑12, Jul 98	2.95	0.59	1.48	2.95
❑13	2.95	0.59	1.48	2.95
❑14	2.95	0.59	1.48	2.95
❑15	2.95	0.59	1.48	2.95
❑16	2.95	0.59	1.48	2.95

SHI: THE WAY OF THE WARRIOR
CRUSADE

	ORIG	GOOD	FINE	N-MINT
❑0.5	5.00	0.60	1.50	3.00
❑0.5/Pl	20.00	0.80	2.00	4.00
❑1, Mar 94	2.50	1.20	3.00	6.00
❑1/A	2.50	1.00	2.50	5.00
❑1/B, "Fan Appreciation Edition" #1 with no logo on cover	1.95	1.60	4.00	8.00
❑1/C, Gold logo on cover; Commemorative edition from the 1994 San Diego Comic Con	—	1.60	4.00	8.00
❑2	2.50	1.00	2.50	5.00
❑2/A, Fan appreciation edition #2	2.50	0.60	1.50	3.00
❑2/Ash, Ashcan promotional edition of Shi: The Way of the Warrior #2	—	1.00	2.50	5.00
❑2/B, San Diego Comicon edition	2.50	1.20	3.00	6.00
❑3	2.50	0.80	2.00	4.00
❑4	2.50	0.80	2.00	4.00
❑5, Apr 95, 1: Tomoe	2.50	0.60	1.50	3.00
❑5/SC, Apr 95, 1: Tomoe, Silvestri variant cover	2.50	1.00	2.50	5.00
❑6	2.95	0.60	1.50	3.00
❑6/A, Fan Appreciation Edition	2.95	0.60	1.50	3.00
❑6/Ash, Commemorative edition from 1995 San Diego Comic Con	—	0.80	2.00	4.00
❑7, Mar 96, back-up crossover with Lethargic Lad	2.50	0.60	1.50	3.00
❑7/SC, Mar 96, no cover price; chromium edition; back-up crossover with Lethargic Lad; limited to 5, 000 copies	—	0.80	2.00	4.00
❑8	2.95	0.60	1.50	3.00
❑8/A, Combo Gold Club version; 5000 publisher; With certificate of Authenticity	—	1.00	2.50	5.00
❑9, Sep 96	2.95	0.60	1.50	3.00
❑10, Oct 96, wraparound cover	2.95	0.60	1.50	3.00
❑11, Dec 96	2.95	0.60	1.50	3.00
❑12, Apr 97, contains Angel Fire preview	2.95	0.60	1.50	3.00
❑FAN 1, The Blood of Saints, Overstreet Fan promotional edition #1; Included with Fan magazine	—	0.20	0.50	1.00
❑FAN 2, Included with Fan magazine; Overstreet Fan promotional edition #2	—	0.20	0.50	1.00
❑FAN 3, Included with Fan magazine; Overstreet Fan promotional edition #3	—	0.20	0.50	1.00

SHI/VAMPIRELLA
CRUSADE
Value: Cover or less

- ❑1, Oct 97, In Rashomon, crossover with Harris 2.95

SHI VS. TOMOE
CRUSADE
Value: Cover or less

- ❑1, Foil wrap-around cover, color 3.95
- ❑1/LE, Preview sold at San Diego Comic Con, black and white 5.00

SHI: YEAR OF THE DRAGON
CRUSADE
Value: Cover or less

- ❑1 .... 2.99

SHOCK & SPANK THE MONKEYBOYS SPECIAL
ARROW
Value: Cover or less

- ❑1, b&w 2.50

SHOCKING FUTURES (ALAN MOORE'S...)
TITAN
Value: Cover or less

- ❑1, AMo (w) 9.95

SHOCKROCKETS
IMAGE
Value: Cover or less

- ❑1, KB (w) 2.50
- ❑2, KB (w) 2.50
- ❑3, Jun 00, KB (w), The Triangle Trade 2.50
- ❑4, Jul 00, KB (w), Rocket Science 2.50
- ❑5, Aug 00, KB (w), Base Treachery 2.50
- ❑6, Oct 00, KB (w), The Darkest Hour... .... 2.50

SHOCK SUSPENSTORIES (RCP)
EC

	ORIG	GOOD	FINE	N-MINT
❑1, Sep 92, JKa; JO, The Neat Job; Yellow, Electrocution cover; Reprints Shock SuspenStories #1; Ray Bradbury adaptation	1.50	0.40	1.00	2.00
❑2, Dec 92, Kickback; Gee, Dad...It's a Daisy, Reprints Shock SuspenStories #2	1.50	0.40	1.00	2.00

	ORIG	GOOD	FINE	N-MINT
❑3, Mar 93, Just Desserts; The Guilty, Reprints Shock SuspenStories #3	1.50	0.40	1.00	2.00
❑4, Jun 93, JKa; WW; JO, Split Second; Confession, Reprints Shock SuspenStories #4	2.00	0.40	1.00	2.00
❑5, Sep 93, JKa; WW; JO, Well-Traveled; Hate, Reprints Shock SuspenStories #5	2.00	0.40	1.00	2.00
❑6, Dec 93, GI; JKa; WW; JO, GI (w); JKa (w); WW (w); JO (w), Dead Right!; Under Cover!, Reprints Shock SuspenStories #6	2.00	0.40	1.00	2.00
❑7, Mar 94, GI; JKa; WW; JK; JO; GE, AF (c), GI (w); JKa (w); WW (w); JO (w), Beauty at the Beach!; The Bribe!, Reprints Shock SuspenStories #7	2.00	0.40	1.00	2.00
❑8, Jun 94, JKa; WW; AW; GE, AF (c), JKa (w); WW (w); AW (w); GE (w), Piecemeal; The Assault!, Reprints Shock SuspenStories #8	2.00	0.40	1.00	2.00
❑9, Sep 94, WW; JO, WW (w); JO (w), The October Game; Came the Dawn!, Reprints Shock SuspenStories #9	2.00	0.40	1.00	2.00
❑10, Dec 94, WW; JO, WW (w); JO (w), The Sacrifice; ...So Shall Ye Reap!, Reprints Shock SuspenStories #10	2.00	0.40	1.00	2.00
❑11, Mar 95, The Tryst; In Gratitude..., Reprints Shock SuspenStories #11	2.00	0.40	1.00	2.00
❑12, Jun 95, Deadline; The Monkey, Reprints Shock SuspenStories #12	2.00	0.40	1.00	2.00
❑13, Sep 95, Only Skin-Deep; Blood-Brothers, Reprints Shock SuspenStories #13	2.00	0.40	1.00	2.00
❑14, The Orphan; The Whipping, Reprints Shock SuspenStories #14	2.00	0.40	1.00	2.00
❑15, WW; GE, WW (w); GE (w), Raw Deal; The Confidant, Reprints Shock SuspenStories #15; Cannibalism story	2.00	0.40	1.00	2.00
❑16, JO; GE, JO (w); GE (w), ...My Brother's Keeper; The Hazing, Reprints Shock SuspenStories #16	2.00	0.40	1.00	2.00
❑17, JO; GE, JO (w); GE (w), 4-Sided Triangle; In Character, Reprints Shock SuspenStories #17	2.50	0.50	1.25	2.50
❑18, BK; GE, BK (w); GE (w), Cadillac Fever; The Trap, Reprints Shock SuspenStories #18	2.50	0.50	1.25	2.50
❑Anl 1, The Neat Job; Yellow, Reprints Shock SuspenStories #1-5	8.95	1.79	4.47	8.95
❑Anl 2, GI; JKa; WW; JO, GI (w); JKa (w); WW (w); JO (w), Dead Right!; Under Cover!, Reprints Shock SuspenStories #6-10	9.95	1.99	4.97	9.95
❑Anl 3, The Tryst; In Gratitude..., Reprints Shock SuspenStories #11-14	8.95	1.79	4.47	8.95
❑Anl 4, BK; GE, BK (w); GE (w), Reprints Shock SuspenStories #15-18	9.95	1.99	4.97	9.95

SHOCK THE MONKEY
MILLENNIUM

Value: Cover or less

❑1 .... 2.95
❑2, b&w 3.95

SHOCK THERAPY
HARRIER

Value: Cover or less

❑1, Frog Part 1; Epitaph 1.95
❑2 .... 1.95
❑3, Frog Part 3; Chance of a Ghost 1.95
❑4 .... 1.95
❑5 .... 1.95

SHOCKWAVE
LONDON EDITIONS

	ORIG	GOOD	FINE	N-MINT
❑1	0.95	0.60	1.50	3.00
❑2	0.95	0.50	1.25	2.50
❑3	0.95	0.50	1.25	2.50
❑4, Final issue?	0.95	0.50	1.25	2.50

SHOGUN WARRIORS
MARVEL

	ORIG	GOOD	FINE	N-MINT
❑1, Feb 79, HT, Raydeen!, 1: Shogun Warriors	0.35	0.50	1.25	2.50
❑2, Mar 79	0.35	0.40	1.00	2.00
❑3, Apr 79	0.35	0.40	1.00	2.00
❑4, May 79	0.40	0.40	1.00	2.00
❑5, Jun 79	0.40	0.40	1.00	2.00
❑6, Jul 79	0.40	0.40	1.00	2.00
❑7, Aug 79	0.40	0.40	1.00	2.00
❑8, Sep 79	0.40	0.40	1.00	2.00
❑9, Oct 79	0.40	0.40	1.00	2.00
❑10, Nov 79	0.40	0.40	1.00	2.00
❑11, Dec 79	0.40	0.30	0.75	1.50
❑12, Jan 80	0.40	0.30	0.75	1.50
❑13, Feb 80	0.40	0.30	0.75	1.50
❑14, Mar 80	0.40	0.30	0.75	1.50
❑15, Apr 80	0.40	0.30	0.75	1.50
❑16, May 80, D: Followers	0.40	0.30	0.75	1.50
❑17, Jun 80	0.40	0.30	0.75	1.50
❑18, Jul 80	0.40	0.30	0.75	1.50

While it started with the adventures of Fireman Farrell, it wasn't until #4 that a feature in *Showcase*, the revival of The Flash, caught on with readers.

© 1956 National Periodical Publications (DC)

	ORIG	GOOD	FINE	N-MINT
❑19, Aug 80, A: Fantastic Four	0.40	0.30	0.75	1.50
❑20, Sep 80, A: Fantastic Four	0.50	0.30	0.75	1.50

SHOJO ZEN
ZEN

Value: Cover or less

❑1, Love and Zen 2.50

SHOOTY BEAGLE
FANTAGRAPHICS

Value: Cover or less

❑1, b&w; adult 2.25
❑2, b&w; adult 2.25
❑3, b&w; adult 2.25

SHORT ON PLOT!
MU

Value: Cover or less

❑1, nn; b&w 2.50

SHORT ORDER
HEAD

	ORIG	GOOD	FINE	N-MINT
❑1	—	4.00	10.00	20.00
❑2, Jan 74, Don't Get Around Much Anymore; The Shlockpeople	0.75	3.00	7.50	15.00

SHORTS (PAT KELLEY'S...)
ANTARCTIC

Value: Cover or less

❑1, Oct 97, A B-Movie Primer; As Mr. Ology!: How Does Gravity Work? 2.95
❑2 .... 2.95

SHORTSTOP SQUAD
ULTIMATE SPORTS FORCE

Value: Cover or less

❑1, A: Barry Larkin; A: Derek Jeter; A: Alex Rodriguez; A: Cal Ripken, Jr., Barry Larkin apperance 3.95

SHOTGUN MARY (1ST SERIES)
ANTARCTIC

	ORIG	GOOD	FINE	N-MINT
❑1, Sep 95	2.95	0.80	2.00	4.00
❑1/CS, Sep 95, CD of music; CD edition	8.95	1.99	4.97	9.95
❑1/SC, Sep 95, alternate cover	2.95	0.59	1.48	2.95
❑2	2.95	0.60	1.50	3.00
❑3, Exists?	2.95	0.60	1.50	3.00
❑Ash 1, Sep 95, ashcan edition	2.95	0.59	1.48	2.95

SHOTGUN MARY (2ND SERIES)
ANTARCTIC

	ORIG	GOOD	FINE	N-MINT
❑1, Mar 98, Fall	2.95	0.59	1.48	2.95
❑1/SC, Fall, Limited edition cover (purple)	2.95	0.80	2.00	4.00
❑2, May 98, Impact	2.95	0.59	1.48	2.95
❑3, Jul 98, Consciousness, Final Issue	2.95	0.59	1.48	2.95

SHOTGUN MARY: BLOOD LORE
ANTARCTIC

Value: Cover or less

❑1, Feb 97, Visceral Portent 2.95
❑2, Apr 97, Strange Terrain 2.95
❑3, Jun 97, Surprises 2.95
❑4, Aug 97, Reversals 2.95

SHOTGUN MARY: DEVILTOWN
ANTARCTIC

Value: Cover or less

❑1, Jul 96 .... 2.95
❑1/LE, Commemorative edition 5.40

SHOTGUN MARY SHOOTING GALLERY
ANTARCTIC

Value: Cover or less

❑1, Jun 96, Anthology 2.95

SHOTGUN MARY: SON OF THE BEAST
ANTARCTIC

Value: Cover or less

❑1, Oct 97 .... 2.95

SHOWCASE
DC

	ORIG	GOOD	FINE	N-MINT
❑1, Apr 56, Fire Fighters	0.10	570.00	1425.00	2850.00
❑2, Jun 56, JKu, Kings of Wild	0.10	155.00	387.50	775.00
❑3, Aug 56, Frogmen	0.10	150.00	375.00	750.00
❑4, Oct 56, JKu; CI, 1: Flash II (Barry Allen)	0.10	5000.00	12500.00	25000.00
❑5, Dec 56, Manhunters	0.10	180.00	450.00	900.00
❑6, Feb 57, JK (c), 1: Challengers of the Unknown	0.10	700.00	1750.00	3500.00
❑7, Apr 57, JK (c), 2: Challengers of the Unknown; 2: Challengers of the Unknown	0.10	350.00	875.00	1750.00
❑8, Jun 57, CI, 1: Captain Cold; 2: Flash II (Barry Allen)	0.10	2200.00	5500.00	11000.00
❑9, Aug 57, A: Lois Lane	0.10	1200.00	3000.00	6000.00

	ORIG	GOOD	FINE	N-MINT
❑10, Oct 57, A: Lois Lane	0.10	500.00	1250.00	2500.00
❑11, Dec 57, JK (c), A: Challengers of the Unknown	0.10	320.00	800.00	1600.00
❑12, Feb 58, JK (c), A: Challengers of the Unknown	0.10	320.00	800.00	1600.00
❑13, Apr 58, A: Flash II (Barry Allen); 1: Mr. Element	0.10	800.00	2000.00	4000.00
❑14, Jun 58, O: Dr. Alchemy; 1: Doctor Alchemy; A: Flash II (Barry Allen)	0.10	840.00	2100.00	4200.00
❑15, Aug 58, 1: Space Ranger	0.10	330.00	825.00	1650.00
❑16, Oct 58, Space Ranger	0.10	180.00	450.00	900.00
❑17, Dec 58, GK (c), 1: Adam Strange	0.10	440.00	1100.00	2200.00
❑18, Feb 59, GK (c), 1: Rann, Adam Strange	0.10	220.00	550.00	1100.00
❑19, Apr 59, GK (c), Adam Strange	0.10	220.00	550.00	1100.00
❑20, Jun 59, 1: Rip Hunter	0.10	170.00	425.00	850.00
❑21, Aug 59, 2: Rip Hunter	0.10	90.00	225.00	450.00
❑22, Oct 59, GK, 1: Carol Ferris; 1: Green Lantern II (Hal Jordan)	0.10	950.00	2375.00	4750.00
❑23, Dec 59, GK, 1: Invisible Destroyer, Green Lantern	0.10	310.00	775.00	1550.00
❑24, Feb 60, GK, Green Lantern	0.10	290.00	725.00	1450.00
❑25, Apr 60, JKu, Rip Hunter	0.10	55.00	137.50	275.00
❑26, Jun 60, JKu, Rip Hunter	0.10	55.00	137.50	275.00
❑27, Aug 60, RH, 1: Sea Devils	0.10	140.00	350.00	700.00
❑28, Oct 60, RH, Sea Devils	0.10	70.00	175.00	350.00
❑29, Dec 60, RH, Sea Devils	0.10	70.00	175.00	350.00
❑30, Feb 61, O: Aquaman	0.10	130.00	325.00	650.00
❑31, Apr 61, Aquaman	0.10	65.00	162.50	325.00
❑32, Jun 61, Aquaman	0.10	65.00	162.50	325.00
❑33, Aug 61, Aquaman	0.10	65.00	162.50	325.00
❑34, Oct 61, GK, 1: Atom II (Ray Palmer)	0.10	250.00	625.00	1250.00
❑35, Dec 61, GK, 2: Atom II (Ray Palmer); 2: Atom II (Ray Palmer)	0.10	140.00	350.00	700.00
❑36, Feb 62, GK, A: Atom II (Ray Palmer)	0.12	105.00	262.50	525.00
❑37, Apr 62, 1: Metal Men	0.12	100.00	250.00	500.00
❑38, Jun 62, A: Metal Men	0.12	70.00	175.00	350.00
❑39, Aug 62, 1: Chemo; A: Metal Men	0.12	60.00	150.00	300.00
❑40, Oct 62, A: Metal Men	0.12	60.00	150.00	300.00
❑41, Dec 62, Tommy Tomorrow	0.12	30.00	75.00	150.00
❑42, Feb 63, Tommy Tomorrow	0.12	30.00	75.00	150.00
❑43, Apr 63, Doctor No/007; Dr. No/007	0.12	80.00	200.00	400.00
❑44, Jun 63, Tommy Tomorrow	0.12	20.00	50.00	100.00
❑45, Aug 63, JKu, O: Sgt. Rock	0.12	45.00	112.50	225.00
❑46, Oct 63, Tommy Tomorrow	0.12	19.00	47.50	95.00
❑47, Dec 63, Tommy Tomorrow	0.12	19.00	47.50	95.00
❑48, Feb 64, Cave Carson	0.12	13.00	32.50	65.00
❑49, Apr 64, Cave Carson	0.12	13.00	32.50	65.00
❑50, Jun 64, CI; MA, I Spy	0.12	13.00	32.50	65.00
❑51, Aug 64, CI; MA, I Spy	0.12	13.00	32.50	65.00
❑52, Oct 64, Cave Carson	0.12	13.00	32.50	65.00
❑53, Dec 64, JKu, G.I. Joe	0.12	16.00	40.00	80.00
❑54, Feb 65, JKu, G.I. Joe	0.12	16.00	40.00	80.00
❑55, Apr 65, MA, O: Doctor Fate	0.12	55.00	137.50	275.00
❑56, Jun 65, MA, 1: Psycho-Pirate II (Roger Hayden), Doctor Fate	0.12	20.00	50.00	100.00
❑57, Aug 65, JKu, Killer of the Skies!, Enemy Ace	0.12	24.00	60.00	120.00
❑58, Oct 65, JKu, Enemy Ace	0.12	24.00	60.00	120.00
❑59, Dec 65, A: Teen Titans	0.12	18.00	45.00	90.00
❑60, Feb 66, MA, O: The Spectre	0.12	45.00	112.50	225.00
❑61, Apr 66, MA, Spectre	0.12	25.00	62.50	125.00
❑62, Jun 66, JO, 1: Inferior Five; 1: White Feather; 1: Blimp; 1: Awkwardman; 1: Merryman; 1: Dumb Bunny; 1: Earth-12	0.12	14.00	35.00	70.00
❑63, Aug 66, JO, Inferior Five	0.12	7.00	17.50	35.00
❑64, Oct 66, MA, Spectre	0.12	25.00	62.50	125.00
❑65, Dec 66, Inferior Five	0.12	7.00	17.50	35.00
❑66, Feb 67, 1: B'wana Beast	0.12	4.00	10.00	20.00
❑67, Apr 67, B'wana Beast	0.12	4.00	10.00	20.00
❑68, Jun 67, Maniaks	0.12	4.00	10.00	20.00
❑69, Aug 67, Maniaks	0.12	4.00	10.00	20.00
❑70, Oct 67, A: Binky	0.12	4.00	10.00	20.00
❑71, Dec 67, Maniaks	0.12	4.00	10.00	20.00
❑72, Feb 68, JKu; ATh, Top Gun	0.12	4.00	10.00	20.00
❑73, Apr 68, SD, 1: Creeper	0.12	22.00	55.00	110.00
❑74, May 68, 1: Anthro	0.12	13.00	32.50	65.00
❑75, Jun 68, SD, DG (w); SD (w), The Hawk and the Dove, 1: Hawk I (Hank Hall); 1: Dove I (Don Hall)	0.12	17.00	42.50	85.00
❑76, Aug 68, 1: Bat Lash	0.12	8.00	20.00	40.00
❑77, Sep 68, 1: Angel & Ape	0.12	9.00	22.50	45.00
❑78, Nov 68, 1: Jonny Double	0.12	6.00	15.00	30.00
❑79, Dec 68, 1: Dolphin	0.12	9.00	22.50	45.00
❑80, Feb 69, NA (c), Phantom Stranger	0.12	7.00	17.50	35.00
❑81, Mar 69, Windy & Willy	0.12	2.40	6.00	12.00
❑82, May 69, 1: Nightmaster	0.12	9.00	22.50	45.00
❑83, Jun 69, BWr, Nightmaster	0.12	8.00	20.00	40.00
❑84, Aug 69, BWr, Nightmaster	0.15	8.00	20.00	40.00
❑85, Sep 69, JKu, Firehair	0.15	2.40	6.00	12.00
❑86, Nov 69, JKu, Firehair	0.15	2.40	6.00	12.00
❑87, Dec 69, JKu, Firehair	0.15	2.40	6.00	12.00
❑88, Feb 70, Jason's Quest	0.15	1.60	4.00	8.00
❑89, Mar 70, Jason's Quest	0.15	1.60	4.00	8.00
❑90, May 70, Manhunter 2070	0.15	1.40	3.50	7.00
❑91, Jun 70, Manhunter 2070	0.15	1.40	3.50	7.00
❑92, Aug 70, Manhunter 2070	0.15	1.40	3.50	7.00
❑93, Sep 70, Manhunter 2070	0.15	1.40	3.50	7.00
❑94, Aug 77, JA; JSa, 1: Doom Patrol II; 1: Celsius	0.35	2.00	5.00	10.00
❑95, Oct 77, JA; JSa, A: The Doom Patrol, Doom Patrol	0.35	1.60	4.00	8.00
❑96, Dec 77, JA; JSa, A: The Doom Patrol, Doom Patrol	0.35	1.60	4.00	8.00
❑97, Feb 78, Power Girl	0.35	1.00	2.50	5.00
❑98, Mar 78, JSa, When The Symbioship Strikes!, O: Power Girl	0.35	1.00	2.50	5.00
❑99, Apr 78, Power Girl	0.35	1.00	2.50	5.00
❑100, May 78, Double-size; all-star issue	0.60	1.00	2.50	5.00
❑101, Jun 78, MA; AM, JK (c), Mystery in Space, Hawkman	0.35	1.00	2.50	5.00
❑102, Jul 78, MA; AM, JK (c), Strange Adventures, Hawkman	0.35	1.00	2.50	5.00
❑103, Aug 78, MA; AM, JK (c), Adventures on Other Worlds, Hawkman	0.35	1.00	2.50	5.00
❑104, Sep 78, Final Issue; OSS Spies	0.50	1.00	2.50	5.00

SHOWCASE '93
DC

	ORIG	GOOD	FINE	N-MINT
❑1, Jan 93, Catwoman: Sorrow Street; Blue Devil: Speak of the Devil, Catwoman, Cyborg, Blue Devil	1.95	0.45	1.13	2.25
❑2, Feb 93, Catwoman, Cyborg, Blue Devil	1.95	0.45	1.13	2.25
❑3, Mar 93, Catwoman, Flash, Blue Devil	1.95	0.45	1.13	2.25
❑4, Apr 93, Catwoman, Geo-Force, Blue Devil	1.95	0.40	1.00	2.00
❑5, May 93, Robin, Peacemaker, Blue Devil	1.95	0.40	1.00	2.00
❑6, Jun 93, Robin, Peacemaker, Blue Devil	1.95	0.40	1.00	2.00
❑7, Jul 93, Knightfall; Knightfall, Part 13, Two-Face, Deathstroke, Jade, Obsidian, Peacemaker	1.95	0.50	1.25	2.50
❑8, Aug 93, KJ, Knightfall; Knightfall, Part 14, Two-Face, Batman, Deadshot, Fire and Ice	1.95	0.50	1.25	2.50
❑9, Sep 93, JRo (w), The Huntress: Survival; The Kobra Kronicles, Part 4, Huntress, Peacemaker, Shining Knight	1.95	0.40	1.00	2.00
❑10, Oct 93, Huntress, Deathstroke, Katana	1.95	0.40	1.00	2.00
❑11, Nov 93, Nightwing, Robin, Kobra Kronicles	1.95	0.40	1.00	2.00
❑12, Dec 93, Nightwing, Robin, Green Lantern, Creeper	1.95	0.40	1.00	2.00

SHOWCASE '94
DC

Value: Cover or less

- ❑1, Jan 94, JRo (w), The Great Pretender, Joker, New Gods, Gunfire ... 1.95
- ❑2, Feb 94, Joker ... 1.95
- ❑3, Mar 94, Arkham Asylum, Blue Beetle, Psyba-Rats ... 1.95
- ❑4, Apr 94, Arkham Asylum, Blue Beetle, Psyba-Rats ... 1.95
- ❑5, May 94, Huntress, Loose Cannon, Bloodwynd ... 1.95
- ❑6, Jun 94, Robin ... 1.95
- ❑7, Jul 94, KB (w), Penguin, Arsenal, Terrorsmith ... 1.95
- ❑8, Aug 94, Scarface, Zero Hour Prelude ... 1.95
- ❑9, Sep 94, Scarface, Zero Hour Prelude ... 1.95
- ❑10, Oct 94, Azrael, Zero Hour, Black Condor ... 1.95
- ❑11, Nov 94, Man-Bat, Starfire, Black Condor ... 1.95
- ❑12, Dec 94 ... 1.95

SHOWCASE '95
DC

Value: Cover or less

- ❑1, Jan 95, Supergirl, Alan Scott, Argus ... 2.50
- ❑2, Feb 95, Supergirl, Metal Men, Argus ... 2.50
- ❑3, Mar 95, Eradicator: No Mercy; Claw: Reunions, Eradicator, Claw, The Question ... 2.50
- ❑4, Apr 95 ... 2.50
- ❑5, Jun 95 ... 2.50
- ❑6, Jul 95, Bibbo, Lobo, Science Police, Legionnaires ... 2.95
- ❑7, Aug 95, Mongul, Arion, New Gods ... 2.95
- ❑8, Sep 95, Mongul, Spectre, Arsenal ... 2.95
- ❑9, Oct 95, Lois Lane, Lobo, Martian Manhunter ... 2.95
- ❑10, Nov 95, Gangbuster, Ferrin Colos, Hi-Tech ... 2.95
- ❑11, Nov 95, Agent Liberty; Arkham Asylum; Hi-Tech ... 2.95
- ❑12, Dec 95, Supergirl, Maitresse, The Shade ... 2.95

SHOWCASE '96
DC

Value: Cover or less

- ❑1, Jan 96, Steel and Guy Gardner: Warrior, Aqualad, Metropolis S.C.U. ... 2.95
- ❑2, Feb 96, Steel: Good Guy, Bad Buy, and Other Guys; Flesh and Bone, Steel and Guy Gardner: Warrior, Circe, Metallo ... 2.95
- ❑3, Mar 96, Birds of a Feather; Mercy Killing, Lois Lane and Black Canary, Doctor Fate and The Shade, Lightray ... 2.95
- ❑4, Apr 96, JRo (w), The Devil's Own; The Shade and Dr. Fate: Day & Night, Night & Bright, Guardian and Firebrand, Doctor Fate and The Shade, The Demon ... 2.95
- ❑5, Jun 96, Green Arrow and Thorn, Doctor Fate and The Shade, New Gods ... 2.95
- ❑6, Jul 96, Superboy and The Demon, Firestorm, The Atom ... 2.95

ORIG GOOD FINE N-MINT

❑7, Aug 96, Gangbuster and The Power of Shazam!, Fire, Firestorm ... 2.95
❑8, Sep 96, Superboy and Superman, Legionnaires, Supergirl ... 2.95
❑9, Oct 96, Shadow Dragon: Honor Bound; Illumination, Shadowdragon and Lady Shiva, Doctor Light, Martian Manhunter ... 2.95
❑10, Nov 96, The Bridges of Metropolis County; Captain Comet: The Future, Bibbo, Ultra Boy, Captain Comet ... 2.95
❑11, Dec 96, Legion of Super-Heroes: Brain in Vain; Scare Tactics: In the Road, Brainiac vs. Legion, Wildcat, Scare Tactics ... 2.95
❑12, Win 96, Roots; Overrun, Final Issue; Brainiac vs. Legion, Jesse Quick, King Faraday ... 2.95

SHRED
CFW
Value: Cover or less

❑1 ... 2.25
❑2 ... 2.25
❑3 ... 2.25
❑4 ... 2.25
❑5 ... 2.25
❑6 ... 2.25
❑7 ... 2.25
❑8 ... 2.25

SHRIEK
FANTACO
Value: Cover or less

❑1, b&w ... 4.95
❑2, b&w ... 4.95
❑SE 1, b&w ... 3.50
❑SE 2, b&w; Dangerbrain ... 3.50
❑SE 3, b&w ... 3.50

SHRIKE
VICTORY
Value: Cover or less

❑1, May 87, Death and a Little Depression, b&w ... 1.50
❑2 ... 1.50

SHROUD, THE
MARVEL
Value: Cover or less

❑1, Mar 94, The Deadly Past, Part 1, O: The Shroud ... 1.75
❑2, Apr 94 ... 1.75
❑3, May 94 ... 1.75
❑4, Jun 94 ... 1.75

SHUGGA
FANTAGRAPHICS
Value: Cover or less

❑1, b&w; adult ... 2.50
❑2, b&w; adult ... 2.50

SHURIKEN (BLACKTHORNE)
BLACKTHORNE
Value: Cover or less

❑1 ... 7.95

SHURIKEN (ETERNITY)
ETERNITY
Value: Cover or less

❑1, Jun 91, b&w ... 2.50
❑2, b&w ... 2.50
❑3, b&w ... 2.50
❑4, b&w ... 2.50
❑5, b&w ... 2.50
❑6, b&w ... 2.50

SHURIKEN (VICTORY)
VICTORY
Value: Cover or less

❑1, Win 85, RBy, RBy (w), The Enemy, Win-85 ... 1.50
❑2, Fal 85, RBy, RBy (w), Scratched!, Fal-85 ... 1.50
❑3 ... 1.50
❑4, Nov 86 ... 1.50
❑5 ... 1.50
❑6 ... 1.50
❑7 ... 1.50
❑8 ... 1.50

SHURIKEN: COLD STEEL
ETERNITY
Value: Cover or less

❑1, Jul 89, Welcome to Dangertemps, Part 1, b&w; 16 pgs. ... 1.50
❑2 ... 1.95
❑3 ... 1.95
❑4 ... 1.95
❑5 ... 1.95
❑6 ... 1.95

SHURIKEN TEAM-UP
ETERNITY
Value: Cover or less

❑1, b&w; Shuriken, Libra, Kokutai ... 1.95

SHUT UP AND DIE!
IMAGE
Value: Cover or less

❑1, Temptation ... 2.95
❑2, A. W. M. (Angry White Man) ... 2.95
❑3, The Bad Week ... 2.95
❑4 ... 2.95
❑5 ... 2.95

SICK SMILES
AIIIE!
Value: Cover or less

❑1, Jun 94 ... 2.50
❑2, Jul 94 ... 2.50
❑3 ... 2.50
❑4 ... 2.50
❑5 ... 2.50
❑6 ... 2.50
❑7 ... 2.50
❑8, Apr 95 ... 2.95

SIDEKICKS
FANBOY
Value: Cover or less

❑1, Jun 00, The New Teen Titan, Part 1 ... 2.75

A soldier of fortune acquires a symbol of power and uses it to fight for intergalactic justice in CrossGen's *Sigil.*

ORIG GOOD FINE N-MINT

SIDE SHOW
MATURE MAGIC
Value: Cover or less

❑1 ... 1.75

SIDESHOW COMICS
PAN GRAPHICS

	ORIG	GOOD	FINE	N-MINT
❑1, b&w	2.00	0.35	0.88	1.75
❑2, b&w	2.00	0.35	0.88	1.75
❑3	1.25	0.35	0.88	1.75
❑4	1.25	0.35	0.88	1.75
❑5, Bad Foot Dealin'	1.25	0.35	0.88	1.75

SIEGE
IMAGE
Value: Cover or less

❑1, Jan 97, The Ultimate Conspiracy ... 2.50
❑2, Feb 97, The Road Less Traveled ... 2.50
❑3, Mar 97 ... 2.50
❑4, Apr 97 ... 2.50

SIEGEL AND SHUSTER: DATELINE 1930S
ECLIPSE

	ORIG	GOOD	FINE	N-MINT
❑1, Nov 84	1.50	0.35	0.88	1.75
❑2, Sep 85, Snoopy and Smiley; Kay	1.50	0.35	0.88	1.75

SIEGE OF THE ALAMO
TOME PRESS
Value: Cover or less

❑1, Jul 91, b&w ... 2.50

SIGHT UNSEEN
FANTAGRAPHICS
Value: Cover or less

❑1, Apr 97, nn; b&w; wraparound cover; collects story from The Stranger and The Philadelphia Weekly ... 2.95

SIGIL
CROSSGEN
Value: Cover or less

❑1, Jul 00 ... 2.95
❑2, Aug 00 ... 2.95
❑3, Sep 00 ... 2.95
❑4, Oct 00 ... 2.95
❑5 ... 2.95
❑6 ... 2.95
❑7 ... 2.95
❑8 ... 2.95
❑9 ... 2.95
❑10 ... 2.95
❑11 ... 2.95
❑12 ... 2.95
❑13 ... 2.95
❑14 ... 2.95

SIGMA
IMAGE
Value: Cover or less

❑1, Fire From Heaven ... 2.50
❑2, May 96, Fire from Heaven, Part 6 ... 2.50
❑3, Jun 96, Fire from Heaven, Part 14 ... 2.50

SILBUSTER
ANTARCTIC
Value: Cover or less

❑1, Jan 94, Wandering Siblings ... 2.95
❑2, Feb 94 ... 2.95
❑3, Mar 94 ... 2.95
❑4, Apr 94 ... 2.95
❑5, Oct 94 ... 2.95
❑6, Nov 94 ... 2.95
❑7, Dec 94 ... 2.95
❑8, Jan 95 ... 2.95
❑9, Feb 95 ... 2.95
❑10, Aug 95 ... 2.95
❑11, Oct 95 ... 2.95
❑12, Oct 95 ... 2.95
❑13, Oct 95 ... 2.95
❑14, Oct 95 ... 2.95
❑15, May 96 ... 2.95
❑16, Jul 96 ... 2.95
❑17, Sep 96 ... 2.95
❑18, Sep 96 ... 2.95
❑19, Jan 97 ... 2.95

SILENCERS
CALIBER
Value: Cover or less

❑1, Jul 91, Damage, b&w ... 2.50
❑2, Damage Control, b&w ... 2.50
❑3, Stories, b&w ... 2.50
❑4, b&w ... 2.50

SILENT CITY, THE
KITCHEN SINK
Value: Cover or less

❑1, Oct 95, b&w; oversized graphic novel ... 24.95

SILENT INVASION, THE
RENEGADE

	ORIG	GOOD	FINE	N-MINT
❑1, Apr 86, The Stubbinsville Connection, Part 1, b&w	1.70	0.40	1.00	2.00
❑2, Jun 86, The Stubbinsville Connection, Part 2, b&w	1.70	0.40	1.00	2.00

	ORIG	GOOD	FINE	N-MINT
❑3, Aug 86, b&w	1.70	0.55	1.38	2.75
❑4, Oct 86, A Pink Slip for a Pinko, b&w	2.00	0.55	1.38	2.75
❑5, Dec 86, b&w	2.00	0.55	1.38	2.75
❑6, Feb 87, b&w	2.00	0.55	1.38	2.75
❑7, May 87, b&w	2.00	0.55	1.38	2.75
❑8, Jul 87, b&w	2.00	0.55	1.38	2.75
❑9, Sep 87, b&w	2.00	0.55	1.38	2.75
❑10, Nov 87, b&w	2.00	0.55	1.38	2.75
❑11, Jan 88, b&w	2.00	0.55	1.38	2.75
❑12, Mar 88, b&w	2.00	0.55	1.38	2.75

SILENT INVASION, THE: ABDUCTIONS
CALIBER

Value: Cover or less

❑1, May 98, b&w ... 2.95

SILENT MÖBIUS: INTO THE LABYRINTH
VIZ

Value: Cover or less

❑1 ... 2.95
❑2 ... 2.95
❑3 ... 2.95
❑4 ... 2.95
❑5 ... 2.95
❑6 ... 2.95

SILENT MÖBIUS PART 1
VIZ

Value: Cover or less

❑1, Cyber Psychic City, Part 1, full color ... 4.95
❑2, Cyber Psychic City, Part 2, full color ... 4.95
❑3, Cyber Psychic City, Part 3, full color ... 4.95
❑4, full color ... 4.95
❑5, full color ... 4.95
❑6, full color ... 4.95

SILENT MÖBIUS PART 2
VIZ

Value: Cover or less

❑1, Katsumi Liquer, Part 1 ... 4.95
❑2 ... 4.95
❑3 ... 4.95
❑4 ... 4.95
❑5 ... 4.95

SILENT MÖBIUS PART 3
VIZ

Value: Cover or less

❑1 ... 4.95
❑2 ... 4.95
❑3 ... 2.75
❑4 ... 2.75
❑5 ... 2.75

SILENT MÖBIUS PART 4
VIZ

Value: Cover or less

❑1 ... 2.75
❑2 ... 2.75
❑3 ... 2.75
❑4 ... 2.75
❑5 ... 2.75

SILENT RAPTURE
AVATAR

Value: Cover or less

❑1 ... 3.00
❑2 ... 3.00

SILENT SCREAMERS: NOSFERATU
IMAGE

Value: Cover or less

❑1, Oct 00 ... 4.95

SILENT WINTER/PINEAPPLEMAN
LIMELIGHT

Value: Cover or less

❑1 ... 2.95

SILKE
DARK HORSE

Value: Cover or less

❑1, Jan 01, Playing God ... 2.95
❑2, Feb 01, The Chameleon ... 2.99

SILLY-CAT
JOE CHIAPPETTA

Value: Cover or less

❑1, Dec 97, Pickin' an' Grabbin'; Chuck Taylor ... 1.00

SILLY DADDY
JOE CHIAPPETTA

	ORIG	GOOD	FINE	N-MINT
❑1	—	0.80	2.00	4.00
❑2, Sep 95, b&w; flipbook with King Cat back-up	2.75	0.60	1.50	3.00
❑3	—	0.60	1.50	3.00
❑4	—	0.60	1.50	3.00
❑5	—	0.60	1.50	3.00
❑6	—	0.60	1.50	3.00
❑7	—	0.60	1.50	3.00
❑8	—	0.60	1.50	3.00
❑9	—	0.60	1.50	3.00
❑10, Mar 96, b&w	2.75	0.60	1.50	3.00
❑11, A Death in The Family, b&w	2.75	0.55	1.38	2.75
❑12, b&w	2.75	0.55	1.38	2.75
❑13, b&w	2.75	0.55	1.38	2.75
❑14, b&w; no cover price	2.75	0.55	1.38	2.75
❑15	2.75	0.55	1.38	2.75
❑16, A Death in The Family interlude	2.75	0.55	1.38	2.75
❑17	2.75	0.55	1.38	2.75
❑18, Hit Parade, Baby	2.75	0.55	1.38	2.75

SILVER
COMICOLOR

Value: Cover or less

❑1 ... 2.00

SILVER AGE
DC

Value: Cover or less

❑1, Jul 00, MWa (w), Pawns of the Invincible Immortal! ... 2.50
❑GS 1, Jul 00, S.O.S. to Nowhere; The Mad Hatter's Hat Crimes, O: Super-Turtle, 80pgs. ... 5.95

SILVER AGE: CHALLENGERS OF THE UNKNOWN
DC

Value: Cover or less

❑1, Jul 00, A Small Matter of Time ... 2.50

SILVER AGE: DIAL H FOR HERO
DC

Value: Cover or less

❑1, Jul 00, MWa (w), The One-Man Justice League ... 2.50

SILVER AGE: DOOM PATROL
DC

Value: Cover or less

❑1, Jul 00, The War of the Super-Weapons ... 2.50

SILVER AGE: FLASH
DC

Value: Cover or less

❑1, Jul 00, The Flash's Big Day ... 2.50

SILVER AGE: GREEN LANTERN
DC

Value: Cover or less

❑1, Jul 00, BA, KB (w), Alone...Against Injustice! ... 2.50

SILVER AGE: JUSTICE LEAGUE OF AMERICA
DC

Value: Cover or less

❑1, Jul 00, The League Without Justice! ... 2.50

SILVER AGE SECRET FILES
DC

Value: Cover or less

❑1, Jul 00, The Silver Age; Justi ... 4.95

SILVER AGE: SHOWCASE
DC

Value: Cover or less

❑1, Jul 00, DG, The 7 Soldiers of Victory ... 2.50

SILVER AGE: TEEN TITANS
DC

Value: Cover or less

❑1, Jul 00, The Tyrannical Terror of Sheriff Law ... 2.50

SILVER AGE: THE BRAVE AND THE BOLD
DC

Value: Cover or less

❑1, Jul 00, The Great Gotham Switcheroo! ... 2.50

SILVERBACK
COMICO

Value: Cover or less

❑1, The Dreamer, O: Argent ... 2.50
❑2, Cold Memories, O: Argent. 2.50
❑3, O: Argent ... 2.50

SILVERBLADE
DC

Value: Cover or less

❑1, Sep 87, GC, The Lord Of Sunset Boulevard, 1: Silverblade, poster ... 1.25
❑2, Oct 87, GC, Son Of Silverblade ... 1.25
❑3, Nov 87, GC ... 1.25
❑4, Dec 87, GC ... 1.25
❑5, Jan 88, GC ... 1.25
❑6, Feb 88, GC, One Through The Heart ... 1.25
❑7, Mar 88, GC ... 1.25
❑8, May 88, GC ... 1.25
❑9, Jun 88, GC ... 1.25
❑10, Jul 88, GC ... 1.25
❑11, Aug 88, GC ... 1.25
❑12, Sep 88, GC ... 1.25

SILVER CROSS
ANTARCTIC

Value: Cover or less

❑1, Nov 97 ... 2.95
❑2, Jan 98 ... 2.95
❑3, Mar 98 ... 2.95

SILVERFAWN
CALIBER

Value: Cover or less

❑1, Wings Of Freedom ... 1.95

SILVERHAWKS
MARVEL

Value: Cover or less

❑1, The Origin Story ... 1.00
❑2 ... 1.00
❑3 ... 1.00
❑4 ... 1.00
❑5 ... 1.00
❑6, A Few Laughs With the Old Crowd, Final Issue ... 1.00
❑7 ... 1.00

SILVERHEELS
PACIFIC

Value: Cover or less

❑1 ... 1.50
❑2 ... 1.50
❑3 ... 1.50

SILVER SABLE
MARVEL

	ORIG	GOOD	FINE	N-MINT
❑1, Jun 92, Personal Stakes, Embossed cover	2.00	0.40	1.00	2.00
❑2, Jul 92, Gattling's Big Guns, Part 1	1.25	0.30	0.75	1.50
❑3, Aug 92, Gattling's Big Guns, Part 2	1.25	0.30	0.75	1.50
❑4, Sep 92, Infinity War	1.25	0.30	0.75	1.50
❑5, Oct 92, Infinity War	1.25	0.25	0.63	1.25

	ORIG	GOOD	FINE	N-MINT
❑6, Nov 92, Museum of Theft, A: Deathlok..	1.25	0.25	0.63	1.25
❑7, Dec 92, Welcome To My Museum, A: Deathlok	1.25	0.25	0.63	1.25
❑8, Jan 93, War Criminal	1.25	0.25	0.63	1.25
❑9, Feb 93, Origins, O: Wild Pack	1.25	0.25	0.63	1.25
❑10, Mar 93, Crossed Purposes, A: Punisher	1.25	0.25	0.63	1.25
❑11, Apr 93	1.25	0.25	0.63	1.25
❑12, May 93	1.25	0.25	0.63	1.25
❑13, Jun 93	1.25	0.25	0.63	1.25
❑14, Jul 93	1.25	0.25	0.63	1.25
❑15, Aug 93	1.25	0.25	0.63	1.25
❑16, Sep 93	1.25	0.25	0.63	1.25
❑17, Oct 93, A: Crippler; A: Baron Von Strucker; A: New Outlaws, Infinity Crusade crossover	1.25	0.25	0.63	1.25
❑18, Nov 93	1.25	0.25	0.63	1.25
❑19, Dec 93	1.25	0.25	0.63	1.25
❑20, Jan 94	1.25	0.25	0.63	1.25
❑21, Feb 94	1.25	0.25	0.63	1.25
❑22, Mar 94	1.25	0.25	0.63	1.25
❑23, Apr 94, V: Deadpool; A: Daredevil	1.25	0.25	0.63	1.25
❑24, May 94	1.50	0.30	0.75	1.50
❑25, Jun 94, Giant-size	2.00	0.40	1.00	2.00
❑26, Jul 94	1.50	0.30	0.75	1.50
❑27, Aug 94	1.50	0.30	0.75	1.50
❑28, Sep 94	1.50	0.30	0.75	1.50
❑29, Oct 94	1.50	0.30	0.75	1.50
❑30, Nov 94	1.50	0.30	0.75	1.50
❑31, Dec 94	1.50	0.30	0.75	1.50
❑32, Jan 95	1.50	0.30	0.75	1.50
❑33, Feb 95	1.50	0.30	0.75	1.50
❑34, Mar 95	1.50	0.30	0.75	1.50
❑35, Apr 95, Final Issue	1.50	0.30	0.75	1.50

SILVER SCREAM
RECOLLECTIONS

Value: Cover or less

- ❑1, b&w; Reprint 2.00
- ❑2, b&w; Reprint 2.00
- ❑3, b&w; Reprint 2.00

SILVER STAR
PACIFIC

Value: Cover or less

- ❑1, Feb 83, JK, JK (w), 1: Last of the Viking Heroes 1.00
- ❑2, Apr 83, JK, JK (w) 1.00
- ❑3, Jun 83, JK, JK (w), The Others; Flynn, Part 1 .... 1.00
- ❑4, Aug 83, JK, JK (w) 1.00
- ❑5, Nov 83, JK, JK (w) 1.00
- ❑6, Jan 84, JK, JK (w) 1.00

SILVER STAR (JACK KIRBY'S...)
TOPPS

Value: Cover or less

- ❑1, Oct 93, KB (w), The Job, trading cards; trading cards 2.95
- ❑2 .... 2.50
- ❑3 .... 2.50
- ❑4 .... 2.50

SILVERSTORM (AIRCEL)
AIRCEL

Value: Cover or less

- ❑1, Luck, a Storm-Tossed Coin, 1: Silver Dollar; 1: Tempest, b&w 2.25
- ❑2, b&w 2.25
- ❑3, Jul 90, b&w 2.25
- ❑4, b&w 2.25

SILVERSTORM (SILVERLINE)
SILVERLINE

Value: Cover or less

- ❑1, Oct 98 .... 2.95
- ❑2 .... 2.95
- ❑3 .... 2.95
- ❑4 .... 2.95

SILVER SURFER (FIRESIDE)
MARVEL

Value: Cover or less

- ❑1, JK, SL (w), (Fireside; 1978) 4.95

SILVER SURFER, THE (VOL. 1)
MARVEL

	ORIG	GOOD	FINE	N-MINT
❑1, Aug 68, JB; GC, SL (w), The Origin of the Silver Surfer!; The Wonder of The Watcher!, O: Silver Surfer, Giant-size	0.25	90.00	225.00	450.00
❑2, Oct 68, JB, SL (w), Giant-size	0.25	35.00	87.50	175.00
❑3, Dec 68, JB, SL (w), A: Thor; 1: Mephisto, Giant-size	0.25	30.00	75.00	150.00
❑4, Feb 69, JB, SL (w), Giant-size; Scarce .	0.25	75.00	187.50	375.00
❑5, Apr 69, JB, SL (w), Giant-size	0.25	20.00	50.00	100.00
❑6, Jun 69, JB, SL (w), Giant-size	0.25	20.00	50.00	100.00
❑7, Aug 69, JB, SL (w), Giant-size	0.25	18.00	45.00	90.00
❑8, Sep 69, JB, SL (w)	0.15	13.00	32.50	65.00
❑9, Oct 69, JB, SL (w), To Steal The Surfer's Soul	0.15	13.00	32.50	65.00
❑10, Nov 69, JB, SL (w), A World He Never Made	0.15	13.00	32.50	65.00
❑11, Dec 69, JB, SL (w)	0.15	11.60	29.00	58.00
❑12, Jan 70, JB, SL (w)	0.15	11.60	29.00	58.00
❑13, Feb 70, JB, SL (w)	0.15	11.60	29.00	58.00
❑14, Mar 70, JB, SL (w), A: Spider-Man	0.15	15.00	37.50	75.00

The members of the Justice League and their arch-enemies exchanged minds in DC's "Silver Age" event.

	ORIG	GOOD	FINE	N-MINT
❑15, Apr 70, JB, SL (w)	0.15	9.00	22.50	45.00
❑16, May 70, JB, SL (w)	0.15	9.00	22.50	45.00
❑17, Jun 70, JB, SL (w)	0.15	9.00	22.50	45.00
❑18, Sep 70, JB, SL (w), A: Inhumans, Final Issue	0.15	9.00	22.50	45.00

SILVER SURFER (VOL. 2)
MARVEL

	ORIG	GOOD	FINE	N-MINT
❑1, Jun 82, JBy, SL (w); JBy (w), Escape-To Terror!	1.00	2.40	6.00	12.00

SILVER SURFER, THE (VOL. 2)
MARVEL

	ORIG	GOOD	FINE	N-MINT
❑1, Dec 88, SL (w), Parable	1.00	0.60	1.50	3.00
❑2, Jan 89, SL (w)	1.00	0.50	1.25	2.50

SILVER SURFER, THE (VOL. 3)
MARVEL

	ORIG	GOOD	FINE	N-MINT
❑-1, Jul 97, A: Stan Lee, Flashback	1.99	0.45	1.13	2.25
❑0.5, Wizard promotional edition (mail-in) ..	—	0.60	1.50	3.00
❑0.5/Pl, Platinum edition; Wizard promotional edition (mail-in)	—	1.20	3.00	6.00
❑1, Jul 87, MR, Free, Double-size	1.25	1.60	4.00	8.00
❑2, Aug 87	0.75	1.00	2.50	5.00
❑3, Sep 87	0.75	0.80	2.00	4.00
❑4, Oct 87, A: Mantis	0.75	0.80	2.00	4.00
❑5, Nov 87, O: Skrulls; A: Mantis	0.75	0.80	2.00	4.00
❑6, Dec 87	0.75	0.70	1.75	3.50
❑7, Jan 88	0.75	0.70	1.75	3.50
❑8, Feb 88	0.75	0.70	1.75	3.50
❑9, Mar 88	0.75	0.70	1.75	3.50
❑10, Apr 88	0.75	0.70	1.75	3.50
❑11, May 88, 1: Reptyl	1.00	0.60	1.50	3.00
❑12, Jun 88	1.00	0.60	1.50	3.00
❑13, Jul 88	1.00	0.60	1.50	3.00
❑14, Aug 88	1.00	0.60	1.50	3.00
❑15, Sep 88	1.00	0.80	2.00	4.00
❑16, Oct 88, A: Fantastic Four	1.00	0.60	1.50	3.00
❑17, Nov 88	1.00	0.60	1.50	3.00
❑18, Dec 88	1.00	0.60	1.50	3.00
❑19, Jan 89	1.00	0.60	1.50	3.00
❑20, Feb 89	1.00	0.60	1.50	3.00
❑21, Mar 89	1.00	0.60	1.50	3.00
❑22, Apr 89	1.00	0.60	1.50	3.00
❑23, May 89	1.00	0.60	1.50	3.00
❑24, Jun 89	1.00	0.60	1.50	3.00
❑25, Jul 89, V: new Super-Skrull, Giant-size	1.50	0.70	1.75	3.50
❑26, Aug 89	1.00	0.50	1.25	2.50
❑27, Sep 89	1.00	0.50	1.25	2.50
❑28, Oct 89	1.00	0.50	1.25	2.50
❑29, Nov 89	1.00	0.50	1.25	2.50
❑30, Nov 89	1.00	0.50	1.25	2.50
❑31, Dec 89, Giant-size	1.50	0.60	1.50	3.00
❑32, Dec 89	1.00	0.40	1.00	2.00
❑33, Jan 90	1.00	0.40	1.00	2.00
❑34, Feb 90, A: Thanos	1.00	0.70	1.75	3.50
❑35, Mar 90, A: Thanos, Drax the Destroyer resurrected	1.00	0.70	1.75	3.50
❑36, Apr 90, A: Thanos	1.00	0.60	1.50	3.00
❑37, May 90, A: Thanos	1.00	0.60	1.50	3.00
❑38, Jun 90, A: Silver Surfer vs. Thanos; A: Thanos	1.00	0.60	1.50	3.00
❑39, Jul 90, A: Thanos	1.00	0.60	1.50	3.00
❑40, Aug 90	1.00	0.40	1.00	2.00
❑41, Sep 90	1.00	0.40	1.00	2.00
❑42, Oct 90	1.00	0.40	1.00	2.00
❑43, Nov 90	1.00	0.40	1.00	2.00
❑44, Dec 90	1.00	0.40	1.00	2.00
❑45, Jan 91	1.00	0.40	1.00	2.00
❑46, Feb 91, Return of Adam Warlock	1.00	0.50	1.25	2.50
❑47, Mar 91, A: Warlock	1.00	0.50	1.25	2.50
❑48, Apr 91	1.00	0.40	1.00	2.00
❑49, May 91	1.00	0.40	1.00	2.00
❑50, Jun 91, JSn (w), Deeply Buried Secrets, O: Silver Surfer, Silver embossed cover.	1.50	1.00	2.50	5.00

	ORIG	GOOD	FINE	N-MINT
❑50-2, Jun 91, JSn (w), Deeply Buried Secrets, O: Silver Surfer, 2nd Printing; Silver embossed cover	1.50	0.40	1.00	2.00
❑50-3, JSn (w), Deeply Buried Secrets, O: Silver Surfer, 3rd Printing; Silver embossed cover	1.50	0.40	1.00	2.00
❑51, Jul 91, Infinity Gauntlet, Infinity Gauntlet	1.00	0.40	1.00	2.00
❑52, Aug 91, Infinity Gauntlet, A: Drax; A: Firelord, Infinity Gauntlet	1.00	0.40	1.00	2.00
❑53, Aug 91, Infinity Gauntlet, Infinity Gauntlet	1.00	0.40	1.00	2.00
❑54, Sep 91, Infinity Gauntlet, Infinity Gauntlet	1.00	0.40	1.00	2.00
❑55, Sep 91, Infinity Gauntlet, Infinity Gauntlet	1.00	0.40	1.00	2.00
❑56, Oct 91, Infinity Gauntlet, Infinity Gauntlet	1.00	0.40	1.00	2.00
❑57, Oct 91, Infinity Gauntlet, A: Thanos, Infinity Gauntlet	1.00	0.40	1.00	2.00
❑58, Nov 91, Infinity Gauntlet, Infinity Gauntlet	1.00	0.40	1.00	2.00
❑59, Nov 91, Infinity Gauntlet, Infinity Gauntlet	1.00	0.40	1.00	2.00
❑60, Dec 91	1.00	0.40	1.00	2.00
❑61, Jan 92, Carrier	1.00	0.40	1.00	2.00
❑62, Feb 92, Battlelines	1.25	0.40	1.00	2.00
❑63, Mar 92	1.00	0.40	1.00	2.00
❑64, Apr 92, Inner Turmoil	1.00	0.40	1.00	2.00
❑65, May 92, Cold Blooded	1.00	0.40	1.00	2.00
❑66, Jun 92, Conflicting Emotions, 1: Avatar	1.00	0.40	1.00	2.00
❑67, Jul 92, Infinity war	1.25	0.40	1.00	2.00
❑68, Aug 92, Infinity war, Infinity War	1.00	0.40	1.00	2.00
❑69, Aug 92, Infinity war, 1: Morg	1.00	0.40	1.00	2.00
❑70, Sep 92, Herald Ordeal, Part 1, O: Morg	1.00	0.40	1.00	2.00
❑71, Sep 92, Herald Ordeal, Part 2	1.00	0.40	1.00	2.00
❑72, Oct 92, Herald Ordeal, Part 3	1.00	0.40	1.00	2.00
❑73, Oct 92, Herald Ordeal, Part 4	1.00	0.40	1.00	2.00
❑74, Nov 92, Herald Ordeal, Part 5	1.00	0.40	1.00	2.00
❑75, Nov 92, Herald Ordeal, Part 6, D: Nova (female), silver foil cover	2.50	0.70	1.75	3.50
❑76, Dec 92, Prisoners	1.25	0.30	0.75	1.50
❑77, Jan 93	1.25	0.30	0.75	1.50
❑78, Feb 93, Armored And Dangerous	1.25	0.30	0.75	1.50
❑79, Mar 93	1.25	0.30	0.75	1.50
❑80, Apr 93	1.25	0.30	0.75	1.50
❑81, May 93	1.25	0.30	0.75	1.50
❑82, Jun 93	1.75	0.35	0.88	1.75
❑83, Jul 93	1.75	0.30	0.75	1.50
❑84, Aug 93	1.75	0.30	0.75	1.50
❑85, Sep 93, A: Goddess; A: Storm; A: Wonder Man, Infinity Crusade	1.75	0.30	0.75	1.50
❑85/CS, A: Goddess; A: Storm; A: Wonder Man, "Dirtbag special"; Polybagged with Dirt #4; Infinity Crusade crossover	2.95	0.59	1.48	2.95
❑86, Oct 93	1.75	0.30	0.75	1.50
❑87, Nov 93	1.75	0.30	0.75	1.50
❑88, Jan 94	1.75	0.30	0.75	1.50
❑89, Feb 94	1.25	0.30	0.75	1.50
❑90, Mar 94, Giant-size	1.95	0.39	0.98	1.95
❑91, Apr 94	1.25	0.25	0.63	1.25
❑92, May 94	1.50	0.30	0.75	1.50
❑93, Jun 94	1.50	0.30	0.75	1.50
❑94, Jul 94	1.50	0.30	0.75	1.50
❑95, Aug 94	1.50	0.30	0.75	1.50
❑96, Sep 94	1.50	0.30	0.75	1.50
❑97, Oct 94	1.50	0.30	0.75	1.50
❑98, Nov 94	1.50	0.30	0.75	1.50
❑99, Dec 94	1.50	0.30	0.75	1.50
❑100, Jan 95, Giant-size	2.25	0.50	1.25	2.50
❑100/SC, Jan 95, enhanced cover; Giant-size	3.95	0.79	1.98	3.95
❑101, Feb 95	1.50	0.30	0.75	1.50
❑102, Mar 95	1.50	0.30	0.75	1.50
❑103, Apr 95	1.50	0.30	0.75	1.50
❑104, May 95	1.50	0.30	0.75	1.50
❑105, Jun 95, V: Super-Skrull	1.50	0.30	0.75	1.50
❑106, Jul 95, Relinquishes Power Cosmic	1.50	0.30	0.75	1.50
❑107, Aug 95	1.50	0.30	0.75	1.50
❑108, Sep 95, regains Power Cosmic	1.50	0.30	0.75	1.50
❑109, Oct 95	1.50	0.30	0.75	1.50
❑110, Nov 95	1.50	0.30	0.75	1.50
❑111, Dec 95, GP (w)	1.50	0.30	0.75	1.50
❑112, Jan 96	1.95	0.39	0.98	1.95
❑113, Feb 96	1.95	0.39	0.98	1.95
❑114, Mar 96, GP (w), Deja Vu?	1.95	0.39	0.98	1.95
❑115, Apr 96	1.95	0.39	0.98	1.95
❑116, May 96	1.95	0.39	0.98	1.95
❑117, Jun 96	1.95	0.39	0.98	1.95
❑118, Jul 96	1.95	0.39	0.98	1.95
❑119, Aug 96	1.95	0.39	0.98	1.95
❑120, Sep 96	1.50	0.39	0.98	1.95
❑121, Oct 96	1.50	0.39	0.98	1.95
❑122, Nov 96, GP (w), It's The End Of The World As We Know It!, V: Captain Marvel	1.50	0.39	0.98	1.95
❑123, Dec 96, Surfer returns to Earth	1.50	0.39	0.98	1.95
❑124, Jan 97, A Place Called Home, A: Kymaera	1.50	0.30	0.75	1.50
❑125, Feb 97, The Heart of the Beast, V: Hulk, wraparound cover; Giant-size	2.99	0.60	1.50	2.99
❑126, Mar 97, The Barrier, A: Doctor Strange	1.99	0.40	1.00	1.99
❑127, Apr 97, Puppets	1.99	0.39	0.98	1.95
❑128, May 97, Beneath the Silver Skin, A: Spider-Man, Daredevil	1.99	0.40	1.00	1.99
❑129, Jun 97	1.99	0.40	1.00	1.99
❑130, Aug 97, gatefold summary	1.99	0.40	1.00	1.99
❑131, Sep 97, gatefold summary	1.99	0.40	1.00	1.99
❑132, Oct 97, gatefold summary	1.99	0.40	1.00	1.99
❑133, Nov 97, A: Puppet Master, gatefold summary	1.99	0.40	1.00	1.99
❑134, Dec 97, gatefold summary	1.99	0.40	1.00	1.99
❑135, Jan 98, A: Agatha Harkness, gatefold summary	1.99	0.40	1.00	1.99
❑136, Feb 98, gatefold summary	1.99	0.40	1.00	1.99
❑137, Mar 98, A: Agatha Harkness, gatefold summary	1.99	0.40	1.00	1.99
❑138, Apr 98, A: Thing, gatefold summary	1.99	0.40	1.00	1.99
❑139, May 98, gatefold summary	1.99	0.40	1.00	1.99
❑140, Jun 98, gatefold summary	1.99	0.40	1.00	1.99
❑141, Jul 98, gatefold summary	1.99	0.40	1.00	1.99
❑142, Aug 98, gatefold summary	1.99	0.40	1.00	1.99
❑143, Sep 98, V: Psycho-Man, gatefold summary	1.99	0.40	1.00	1.99
❑144, Oct 98, gatefold summary	1.99	0.40	1.00	1.99
❑145, Oct 98, gatefold summary	1.99	0.40	1.00	1.99
❑146, Nov 98, Final Issue; gatefold summary	1.99	0.40	1.00	1.99
❑Anl 1, Evolutionary War, Part 3	1.75	0.80	2.00	4.00
❑Anl 2, Atlantis Attacks, Part 1, Atlantis Attacks	2.00	0.60	1.50	3.00
❑Anl 3, Lifeform; Lifeform, Part 4	2.00	0.50	1.25	2.50
❑Anl 4, Korvac Quest; Korvac Quest, Part 3	2.00	0.50	1.25	2.50
❑Anl 5, Return of Defenders; Return of the Defenders, Part 3, O: Nebula	2.25	0.50	1.25	2.50
❑Anl 6, A: Ganymede; A: Ronan the Accuser; 1: Legacy; A: Jack of Hearts; A: Terrax, trading card; Polybagged	2.95	0.59	1.48	2.95
❑Anl 7	2.95	0.59	1.48	2.95
❑Anl 1997, wraparound cover	2.99	0.60	1.50	2.99
❑Anl 1998, Millennius!, V: Millennius, wraparound cover; gatefold summary; Silver Surfer/Thor '98	2.99	0.60	1.50	2.99

SILVER SURFER: DANGEROUS ARTIFACTS
MARVEL

Value: Cover or less

❑1, Jun 96, One-Shot 3.95

SILVER SURFER: INNER DEMONS
MARVEL

Value: Cover or less

❑1, Apr 98, One-Shot; collects Silver Surfer #123, 125, 126 .... 3.50

SILVER SURFER: JUDGMENT DAY
MARVEL

Value: Cover or less

❑1, Oct 88, hardcover 14.95

SILVER SURFER: LOFTIER THAN MORTALS
MARVEL

Value: Cover or less

❑1, Oct 99 .... 2.50

❑2 .... 2.50

SILVER SURFER/SUPERMAN
MARVEL

Value: Cover or less

❑1, Nov 96, GP (w), Pop!, nn; prestige format; crossover with DC 5.95

SILVER SURFER: THE ENSLAVERS
MARVEL

Value: Cover or less

❑1, Mar 90, hardcover 16.95

SILVER SURFER VS. DRACULA
MARVEL

Value: Cover or less

❑1, Reprint; stories from Venus #19, others; Reprints Tomb of Dracula #50 .... 1.75

SILVER SURFER/WARLOCK: RESURRECTION
MARVEL

Value: Cover or less

❑1, Mar 93, JSn, JSn (w), The Pact 2.50

❑2, Apr 93 .... 2.50

❑3, May 93, JSn, JSn (w), Welcome To Hades! 2.50

❑4, Jun 93, JSn, JSn (w), End Game 2.50

SILVER SURFER/WEAPON ZERO
MARVEL

Value: Cover or less

❑1, Apr 97, Devil's Reign, Chapter 8; Devil's Reign, crossover with Image 2.95

SILVER SWEETIE, THE
SPOOF

Value: Cover or less

- ❑1, b&w ... 2.95

SILVERWING SPECIAL
NOW

	ORIG	GOOD	FINE	N-MINT
❑1, Jan 87	0.95	0.20	0.50	1.00

SIMON AND KIRBY CLASSICS
PURE IMAGINATION

Value: Cover or less

- ❑1, Nov 86 ... 2.00

SIMON CAT IN TAXI
SLAB-O-CONCRETE

	ORIG	GOOD	FINE	N-MINT
❑1, Post card comics	—	0.30	0.75	1.50

SIMPSONS COMICS
BONGO

Value: Cover or less

- ❑1, The Amazing Colossal Homer, Fantastic Four #1 homage cover; poster; Bart Simpsons' Creepy Crawly Tales back-up 2.25
- ❑2, Cool Hand Bart, V: Sideshow Bob, Patty & Selma's Ill-Fated Romance Comics back-up .. 1.95
- ❑3, The Perplexing Puzzle of the Springfield Puma; Krusty, Agent of K.L.O.W.N., Krusty, Agent of K.L.O.W.N. back-up ... 1.95
- ❑4, It's In The Cards; Busman, infinity cover; trading card; Gnarly Adventures of Busman back-up ... 2.25
- ❑5, When Bongos Collide; When Bongos Collide, Part 2, wrap-around cover ... 2.25
- ❑6, Be-Bop-A-Lisa, Chief Wiggum's Pre-Code Crime Comics back-up ... 2.25
- ❑7, McBain Comics back-up... 2.25
- ❑8, I Shrink, Therefore I'm Small, Edna; Queen of the Jungle back-up ... 2.25
- ❑9, The Purple Prose Of Springfield, Lisa's diary; Barney Gumble back-up ... 2.25
- ❑10, Apu's Kwik-E Comics back-up ... 2.25
- ❑11, evil Flanders; Homer on the Range back-up ... 2.25
- ❑12, White-Knuckled War Stories back-up ... 2.25
- ❑13, Jimbo Jones' Wedgie Comics back-up ... 2.25
- ❑14, Cantankerous Coot Classics back-up ... 2.25
- ❑15, Heinous Funnies back-up 2.25
- ❑16, Waitresses In The Sky, Bongo Grab Bag back-up ... 2.25
- ❑17, Headlight Comics back-up 2.25
- ❑18, Milhouse Comics back-up 2.25
- ❑19, Roswell back-up ... 2.25
- ❑20, Bad homage cover; Roswell back-up ... 2.25
- ❑21, Roswell back-up ... 2.25
- ❑22, Burns and Apu team up; Roswell back-up ... 2.25
- ❑23, Reverend Lovejoy's Hellfire Comics back-up ... 2.25
- ❑24, Li'l Homey back-up ... 2.25
- ❑25, Marge gets her own talk show; Itchy & Scratchy back-up ... 2.25
- ❑26, Speed parody ... 2.25
- ❑27, Homer gets smart ... 2.25
- ❑28, Krusty founds his own country ... 2.25
- ❑29, Homer becomes a pro wrestler ... 2.25
- ❑30, Burns clones Smithers.... 2.25
- ❑31, Homer thinks he's Radioactive Man ... 2.25
- ❑32, Krusty's coffee bar ... 2.25
- ❑33, Alternate Springfield ... 2.25
- ❑34, Burns sponsors Bart as a snowboarder ... 2.25
- ❑35, Marge opens a daycare .. 2.25
- ❑36, The return of the geeks... 2.25
- ❑37, El Grampo ... 2.25
- ❑38, Burns makes addictive donuts ... 2.25
- ❑39, Homer and Comic Book Guy on trial ... 2.25
- ❑40, Krusty does live show from Simpsons house; Lard Lad back-up ... 2.50
- ❑41, Bart Simpson & The Krusty Brand Fun Factory ... 2.50
- ❑42, The Homer Show; Slobberwacky back-up ... 2.50
- ❑43, story told backwards; Poochie back-up ... 2.50
- ❑44, Lisa substitutes; Bartman back-up ... 2.50
- ❑45, Hot Dog On A Schtick, Hot Dog On A Schtick ... 2.50
- ❑46, Angels with Yellow Faces, A: Sideshow Bob ... 2.50
- ❑47 ... 2.50
- ❑48 ... 2.50
- ❑49 ... 2.50
- ❑50, Wall or Nothing; The 1001 Costumes of Bartman, Giant-size ... 5.95
- ❑51, Bart and Lisa and Marge and Homer and Maggie (to a lesser extent) vs. Thanksgiving!; What Would Possibly Happen If Cletus Went to College, Cletus back-up ... 2.50
- ❑52, Worst Christmas Ever!; A Springfield Christmas Carol 2.50
- ❑53, The Beer Boys; Around Town with Ned Flanders, Ned Flanders back-up ... 2.50
- ❑54 ... 2.50
- ❑55 ... 2.50
- ❑56 ... 2.50
- ❑57 ... 2.50
- ❑58 ... 2.50
- ❑59 ... 2.50
- ❑60 ... 2.50

SIMPSONS COMICS (MAGAZINE)
BONGO

	ORIG	GOOD	FINE	N-MINT
❑1, Mar 97	2.00	0.80	2.00	4.00
❑2, Apr 97	2.00	0.65	1.63	3.25
❑3, May 97, The Perplexing Puzzle of the Springfield Puma; Krusty, Agent of K.L.O.W.N.	2.00	0.65	1.63	3.25
❑4, Jun 97	2.00	0.65	1.63	3.25
❑5, Jul 97	2.00	0.65	1.63	3.25
❑6, Aug 97	2.00	0.65	1.63	3.25
❑7, Sep 97	2.00	0.65	1.63	3.25
❑8, Oct 97	2.00	0.65	1.63	3.25
❑9, Nov 97	2.00	0.65	1.63	3.25
❑10, Dec 97	2.00	0.65	1.63	3.25
❑11, Jan 98	2.00	0.65	1.63	3.25
❑12, Feb 98	2.00	0.65	1.63	3.25
❑13, Mar 98, Give Me Merchandising or Give Me Death!; Cabin Fervor	2.00	0.65	1.63	3.25
❑14, Apr 98	2.00	0.65	1.63	3.25
❑15, May 98	2.00	0.65	1.63	3.25
❑16, Jun 98	2.00	0.65	1.63	3.25
❑17, Jul 98	2.00	0.65	1.63	3.25
❑18, Aug 98	2.00	0.65	1.63	3.25
❑19, Sep 98	2.00	0.65	1.63	3.25
❑20, Oct 98	2.00	0.65	1.63	3.25
❑21, Nov 98	2.00	0.65	1.63	3.25
❑22, Dec 98	2.00	0.65	1.63	3.25
❑23, Jan 99	2.00	0.65	1.63	3.25
❑24, Feb 99	2.00	0.65	1.63	3.25
❑25, Mar 99, Get off the Bus!; The Comic Cover Caper!, Reprints Bartman #1	2.00	0.65	1.63	3.25

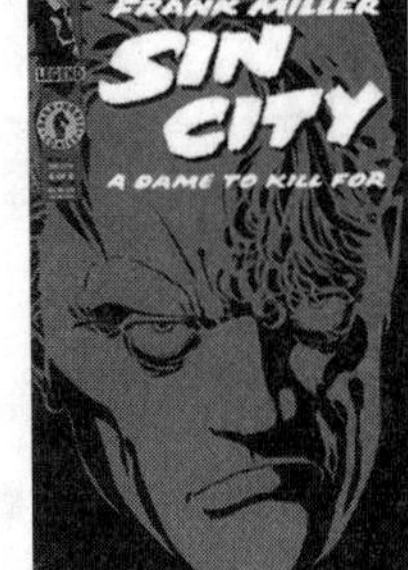

Sin City: A Dame to Kill For is just one of Frank Miller's many crime noir series set in a corrupt city.

© 1994 Frank Miller (Dark Horse)

SIMPSONS COMICS AND STORIES
WELSH

	ORIG	GOOD	FINE	N-MINT
❑1, Lo, There Shall Come...A Bartman, 1: The Simpsons; O: Bartman, with poster	2.50	0.80	2.00	4.00

SIMPSONS COMICS PRESENTS BART SIMPSON
BONGO

Value: Cover or less

- ❑1, Big Fat Trouble in Little Springfield; Grrrl-Whirl ... 2.50
- ❑2, DDC, Bart's Day at the Zoo; Talent Hunt, A: Bartman ... 2.50

SIN
TRAGEDY STRIKES

Value: Cover or less

- ❑1, b&w ... 2.95
- ❑2, b&w ... 2.95
- ❑3, b&w ... 2.95

SINBAD
ADVENTURE

Value: Cover or less

- ❑1, Nov 89, The Four Trials of Sinbad, b&w; cardstock cover .. 2.25
- ❑2, Dec 89, b&w; cardstock cover ... 2.25
- ❑3, Jan 90, b&w; cardstock cover ... 2.25
- ❑4, Mar 90, b&w ... 2.25

SINBAD BOOK II
ADVENTURE

Value: Cover or less

- ❑1, Mar 91, House of God; In the House of God, b&w ... 2.50
- ❑2, Apr 91, House of God, b&w ... 2.50
- ❑3, May 91, House of God, b&w ... 2.50
- ❑4, Jun 91, House of God, b&w ... 2.50

SIN CITY (COZMIC)
COZMIC

	ORIG	GOOD	FINE	N-MINT
❑1, 2001 A Haze Odyssey; Sin City Suicide	0.75	0.30	0.75	1.50

SIN CITY: A DAME TO KILL FOR
DARK HORSE

	ORIG	GOOD	FINE	N-MINT
❑1, FM, FM (w), b&w	2.95	0.70	1.75	3.50
❑2, FM, FM (w), b&w	2.95	0.65	1.63	3.25
❑3, FM, FM (w), b&w	2.95	0.60	1.50	3.00
❑4, Mar 94, FM, FM (w), b&w	2.95	0.60	1.50	3.00
❑5, Apr 94, FM, FM (w), b&w	2.95	0.60	1.50	3.00
❑6, May 94, FM, FM (w), b&w	2.95	0.60	1.50	3.00

SIN CITY: FAMILY VALUES
DARK HORSE

	ORIG	GOOD	FINE	N-MINT
❑1, Oct 97, FM, FM (w), nn; b&w; One-Shot	10.00	3.00	7.50	15.00
❑1/A, FM, FM (w), Cover has Roller-skating girl	—	3.00	7.50	15.00
❑1/LE, FM, FM (w), Limited edition hardcover	75.00	15.00	37.50	75.00

SIN CITY: HELL AND BACK
DARK HORSE

Value: Cover or less

- ❑1, Jul 99, FM, FM (w), b&w; cardstock cover ... 2.95
- ❑2, Aug 99, FM, FM (w), b&w; cardstock cover ... 2.95
- ❑3, Sep 99, FM, FM (w), b&w; cardstock cover ... 2.95
- ❑4, Oct 99, FM, FM (w), b&w; cardstock cover ... 2.95
- ❑5, Nov 99, FM, FM (w), b&w; cardstock cover ... 2.95
- ❑6, Dec 99, FM, FM (w), b&w; cardstock cover ... 2.95
- ❑7, Jan 00, FM, FM (w), b&w; cardstock cover ... 2.95
- ❑8, FM, FM (w), b&w; cardstock cover ... 2.95
- ❑9, FM, FM (w), b&w; cardstock cover ... 2.95

SIN CITY: JUST ANOTHER SATURDAY NIGHT
DARK HORSE

	ORIG	GOOD	FINE	N-MINT
❑0.5, FM, FM (w), Wizard promotional edition	—	0.60	1.50	3.00
❑1, Oct 98, FM, FM (w), nn; b&w; One-Shot	2.50	0.50	1.25	2.50

ORIG GOOD FINE N-MINT

SIN CITY: LOST, LONELY, & LETHAL
DARK HORSE

Value: Cover or less

❑1, Dec 96, FM, FM (w), nn; cardstock cover; One-Shot; b&w and blue 2.95

SIN CITY: SEX & VIOLENCE
DARK HORSE

Value: Cover or less

❑1, Mar 97, FM, FM (w), Wrong Turn; Wrong Track, nn; b&w; cardstock cover; One-Shot.. 2.95

SIN CITY: SILENT NIGHT
DARK HORSE

Value: Cover or less

❑1, Nov 95, FM, FM (w), nn; b&w; cardstock cover; One-Shot.. 2.95

SIN CITY: THAT YELLOW BASTARD
DARK HORSE

Value: Cover or less

❑1, Feb 96, FM, FM (w) 2.95
❑2, Feb 96, FM, FM (w) 2.95
❑3, Apr 96, FM, FM (w) 2.95
❑4, May 96, FM, FM (w) 2.95
❑5, Jun 96, FM, FM (w) 2.95
❑6, Jul 96, FM, FM (w) 2.95

SIN CITY: THE BABE WORE RED AND OTHER STORIES
DARK HORSE

Value: Cover or less

❑1, Nov 94, FM, FM (w), nn; b&w and red 2.95

SIN CITY: THE BIG FAT KILL
DARK HORSE

Value: Cover or less

❑1, Nov 94, FM, FM (w), b&w 2.95
❑2, Dec 94, FM, FM (w), b&w; cardstock cover 2.95
❑3, Jan 95, FM, FM (w), b&w; cardstock cover 2.95
❑4, Feb 95, FM, FM (w), b&w; cardstock cover 2.95
❑5, Mar 95, FM, FM (w), b&w; cardstock cover 2.95

SINDY
FORBIDDEN FRUIT

Value: Cover or less

❑1, b&w; adult 2.95
❑2, b&w; adult 2.95
❑3, b&w; adult 2.95
❑4, b&w; adult 2.95
❑5, b&w; adult 2.95

SINERGY
CALIBER

Value: Cover or less

❑1, b&w 2.95
❑1/LE, limited edition 5.95
❑2, b&w 2.95
❑2/LE, limited edition 5.95
❑3, b&w 2.95
❑3/LE, limited edition 5.95
❑4, b&w 2.95
❑4/LE, limited edition 5.95
❑5, b&w 2.95
❑5/LE, limited edition 5.95

SINISTER HOUSE OF SECRET LOVE, THE
DC

	ORIG	GOOD	FINE	N-MINT
❑1	0.25	2.40	6.00	12.00
❑2, TD, JO (w), To Wed the Devil; Shattered Dreams	0.25	1.60	4.00	8.00
❑3	0.25	1.60	4.00	8.00
❑4, TD, Kiss Of The Serpent, Series continued in Secrets of Sinister House #5	0.25	1.60	4.00	8.00

SINISTER ROMANCE
HARRIER

	ORIG	GOOD	FINE	N-MINT
❑1, The Isis Syndrome!; You Put a Spell on Me!, b&w	1.95	0.40	1.00	2.00
❑2, b&w	1.95	0.40	1.00	2.00
❑3, b&w	1.95	0.39	0.98	1.95
❑4, b&w	1.95	0.39	0.98	1.95

SINJA: DEADLY SINS
LIGHTNING

Value: Cover or less

❑1 ..... 3.00
❑1/A, Commemorative edition. 5.95
❑1/B, Nude edition 9.95

SINJA: RESURRECTION
LIGHTNING

Value: Cover or less

❑1, Aug 96, cover says Kunoichi; flipbook with Kunoichi #1; indicia says Sinja: Resurrection 3.00

SINNAMON (VOL. 1)
CATFISH

Value: Cover or less

❑1, Dec 95, Girls Will be Girls, 1: Sinnamon 2.50

SINNAMON (VOL. 2)
CATFISH

	ORIG	GOOD	FINE	N-MINT
❑1	2.75	0.55	1.38	2.75
❑2	2.75	0.55	1.38	2.75
❑3	2.75	0.55	1.38	2.75
❑4	2.75	0.55	1.38	2.75
❑4/SC, Variant cover edition (500 printed)	—	1.00	2.50	5.00
❑5	2.75	0.55	1.38	2.75
❑5/SC, Certificate of Authenticity; Variant cover edition (500 printed)	—	0.80	2.00	4.00
❑6	2.75	0.55	1.38	2.75
❑7, The Pyre-Anna Saga, Part 1	2.75	0.55	1.38	2.75
❑8, Sinnamon vs. Aerobica	2.75	0.55	1.38	2.75

ORIG GOOD FINE N-MINT

SINNER
FANTAGRAPHICS

Value: Cover or less

❑1 ..... 2.95
❑2 ..... 2.95
❑3 ..... 2.95
❑4 ..... 2.95
❑5 ..... 2.95

SINNERS, THE
DC

Value: Cover or less

❑1 ..... 9.95

SINNIN!
FANTAGRAPHICS

Value: Cover or less

❑1, b&w; adult 2.25
❑2, b&w; adult 2.25

SIN OF THE MUMMY
FANTAGRAPHICS

Value: Cover or less

❑1, b&w; adult 2.50

SINS OF YOUTH: AQUABOY/LAGOON MAN
DC

Value: Cover or less

❑1, May 00, Turning Back the Tides of Time 2.50

SINS OF YOUTH: BATBOY AND ROBIN
DC

Value: Cover or less

❑1, May 00, Big Magic 2.50

SINS OF YOUTH: JLA, JR.
DC

Value: Cover or less

❑1, May 00, You Gotta Be Kidding! 2.50

SINS OF YOUTH: KID FLASH/IMPULSE
DC

Value: Cover or less

❑1, May 00, Media Blitz 2.50

SINS OF YOUTH SECRET FILES
DC

Value: Cover or less

❑1, May 00, Disaffected Youth; CD-TV ad 4.95

SINS OF YOUTH: STARWOMAN AND THE JSA (JUNIOR SOCIETY)
DC

Value: Cover or less

❑1, May 00, Stars and Tykes 2.50

SINS OF YOUTH: SUPERMAN, JR./SUPERBOY, SR.
DC

Value: Cover or less

❑1, May 00, The Adventures of Superboy when he wa a Man! 2.50

SINS OF YOUTH: THE SECRET/DEADBOY
DC

Value: Cover or less

❑1, May 00, Looking for Trouble 2.50

SINS OF YOUTH: WONDER GIRLS
DC

Value: Cover or less

❑1, May 00, Coming of Age..... 2.50

SINTHIA
LIGHTNING

Value: Cover or less

❑1/A, Oct 97 ..... 2.95
❑1/B, Oct 97, alternate cover .. 2.95
❑1/PL, Oct 97, Platinum edition 9.95
❑2/A, Jan 98 ..... 3.00
❑2/B, Jan 98 ..... 3.00

SIR CHARLES BARKLEY AND THE REFEREE MURDERS
HAMILTON

Value: Cover or less

❑1, JSn 9.95

SIREN (MALIBU)
MALIBU

Value: Cover or less

❑0, Sep 95, Black September; #Infinity 1.50
❑0/A, Sep 95, alternate cover . 1.50
❑1, Oct 95, V: War Machine 1.50
❑2, Nov 95, V: War Machine ... 1.50
❑3, Dec 95, Choosing Sides, Final Issue; continues in Siren Special #1 ..... 1.50
❑SE 1, Feb 96, O: Siren 1.95

SIREN: SHAPES
IMAGE

Value: Cover or less

❑1, May 98, Shapes, Part 1 .... 2.95
❑2, Sep 98, Shapes, Part 2 ..... 2.95
❑3, Nov 98, Shapes, Part 3 ..... 2.95

SIRENS OF THE LOST WORLD
COMAX

Value: Cover or less

❑1, b&w; adult 2.95

SIRIUS GALLERY 1999
SIRIUS

	ORIG	GOOD	FINE	N-MINT
❑1, Apr 99, cardstock cover; pin-ups	—	0.40	1.00	2.00

SISTER ARMAGEDDON
DRACULINA

	ORIG	GOOD	FINE	N-MINT
❑1, 1: Sister Armageddon	2.75	0.55	1.38	2.75
❑2, b&w	2.50	0.55	1.38	2.75
❑3, b&w	2.95	0.60	1.50	3.00
❑4	3.00	0.60	1.50	3.00

SISTERHOOD OF STEEL
MARVEL

	ORIG	GOOD	FINE	N-MINT
❑1, Dec 84	1.50	0.40	1.00	2.00
❑2, Feb 85	1.50	0.40	1.00	2.00

	ORIG	GOOD	FINE	N-MINT
❑3, Apr 85	1.50	0.40	1.00	2.00
❑4, Jun 85	1.50	0.40	1.00	2.00
❑5, Aug 85, Passion, Pain, And Politics	1.50	0.40	1.00	2.00
❑6, Oct 85, Loyalties	1.50	0.40	1.00	2.00
❑7, Dec 85, Vows And Vengeances	1.50	0.40	1.00	2.00
❑8, Feb 86, Judgement And Justice	1.50	0.40	1.00	2.00

SISTERS OF DARKNESS
ILLUSTRATION

Value: Cover or less

- ❑1/A, Adult cover 3.25
- ❑1/B, tame cover 3.25
- ❑2/A, Adult cover 3.25
- ❑2/B, tame cover 3.25
- ❑3, Aug 97 .... 3.25

SISTERS OF MERCY
MAXIMUM

Value: Cover or less

- ❑1, Dec 95, 1: Doctor Vincent Casey; 1: Sisters of Mercy (super-heroes) 2.50
- ❑1/A, Dec 95, alternate cover 2.50
- ❑2 .... 2.50
- ❑3 .... 2.50
- ❑4 .... 2.50
- ❑5 .... 2.50

SISTERS OF MERCY (VOL. 2)
LONDON NIGHT

Value: Cover or less

- ❑0, Mar 97 .... 1.50

SISTERS OF MERCY: WHEN RAZORS CRY CRIMSON TEARS
NO MERCY

Value: Cover or less

- ❑1, Oct 96 .... 2.50

SISTER VAMPIRE
ANGEL

Value: Cover or less

- ❑1, A World of Gray 2.95

SIX DEGREES
HERETIC PRESS

	ORIG	GOOD	FINE	N-MINT
❑1, b&w	2.95	0.70	1.75	3.50
❑1/Aut, print, certificate of authenticity	2.95	1.20	3.00	6.00
❑2, b&w	2.95	0.59	1.48	2.95
❑3, b&w	2.95	0.59	1.48	2.95
❑4, b&w	2.95	0.59	1.48	2.95
❑5, b&w	2.95	0.59	1.48	2.95

SIX FROM SIRIUS
MARVEL

	ORIG	GOOD	FINE	N-MINT
❑1, Jul 84, PG, Phaedrea	1.50	0.40	1.00	2.00
❑2, Aug 84, PG, Masterfax	1.50	0.40	1.00	2.00
❑3, Sep 84, PG, Heavenstone	1.50	0.40	1.00	2.00
❑4, Oct 84, PG, Mind-Prime	1.50	0.40	1.00	2.00

SIX FROM SIRIUS 2
MARVEL

	ORIG	GOOD	FINE	N-MINT
❑1, PG	1.75	0.40	1.00	2.00
❑2, PG	1.75	0.40	1.00	2.00
❑3, PG	1.75	0.40	1.00	2.00
❑4, PG	1.75	0.40	1.00	2.00

SIX-GUN HEROES
A-PLUS

Value: Cover or less

- ❑1, b&w; Reprint 2.50

SIX-GUN WESTERN (TROJAN)
TROJAN

	ORIG	GOOD	FINE	N-MINT
❑1, Six-Gun Rampage (text story), Pulp	0.25	10.00	25.00	50.00

SIX MILLION DOLLAR MAN, THE
CHARLTON

	ORIG	GOOD	FINE	N-MINT
❑1, JSa, The Beginning of The Six Million Dollar Man, O: The Six Million Dollar Man; 1: The Six Million Dollar Man (in comics)	0.30	1.00	2.50	5.00
❑2, Aug 76, JSa, The Effigy	0.30	0.70	1.75	3.50
❑3, Oct 76, Marketing tie-in for action figure	0.30	0.60	1.50	3.00
❑4	0.30	0.60	1.50	3.00
❑5, Oct 77	0.35	0.60	1.50	3.00
❑6	0.35	0.40	1.00	2.00
❑7, Mar 78	0.35	0.40	1.00	2.00
❑8	0.35	0.40	1.00	2.00
❑9	0.35	0.40	1.00	2.00

SIX MILLION DOLLAR MAN, THE (MAGAZINE)
CHARLTON

	ORIG	GOOD	FINE	N-MINT
❑1	—	1.20	3.00	6.00
❑2	—	1.00	2.50	5.00
❑3	—	0.80	2.00	4.00
❑4	—	0.80	2.00	4.00
❑5	—	0.80	2.00	4.00
❑6	—	0.80	2.00	4.00
❑7	—	0.80	2.00	4.00

SIX STRING SAMURAI
AWESOME

Value: Cover or less

- ❑1, RL (w) 2.95

SIXTY NINE
EROS

Value: Cover or less

- ❑1 .... 2.75
- ❑2 .... 2.75
- ❑3 .... 2.75
- ❑4, Jul 94, Primed & Cut 2.75

Neal Adams' *Skateman* featured the heroic actions of a roller-skating expert.

© 1983 Neal Adams (Pacific)

SIZZLE THEATRE
SLAVE LABOR

Value: Cover or less

- ❑1, Aug 91, b&w; adult 2.50

SIZZLIN' SISTERS
EROS

Value: Cover or less

- ❑1 .... 2.95
- ❑2, Aug 97 .... 2.95

SKATEMAN
PACIFIC

Value: Cover or less

- ❑1, Nov 83, NA, NA (w), Skateman; Futureworld, 1: Skateman ... 1.50

SKELETON GIRL
SLAVE LABOR

Value: Cover or less

- ❑1, Dec 95, Today I; Stacy pinup, 1: Stacy the Maniacal, Angst-Filled Hate Girl; 1: J.J., Ske; 1: Skeleton Girl; 1: J.J., Skeleton Boy 2.95
- ❑2, Apr 96, The Stitch; Utterly, Ridiculously Inane and Frustrating Couple Fight #1, 2: Skeleton Girl; 2: J.J., Skeleton Boy 2.95
- ❑3, Sep 96, Confessions of and X-Phile!!; Space! The Conclusion!!! 2.95

SKELETON HAND
AVALON

Value: Cover or less

- ❑1, Deathless Mortal; Sea of Retribution 2.99

SKELETON KEY
AMAZE INK

	ORIG	GOOD	FINE	N-MINT
❑1, Jul 95	1.50	0.40	1.00	2.00
❑2, Aug 95	1.50	0.40	1.00	2.00
❑3, Sep 95	1.50	0.40	1.00	2.00
❑4, Oct 95	1.50	0.40	1.00	2.00
❑5, Nov 95	1.50	0.40	1.00	2.00
❑6, Dec 95	1.50	0.40	1.00	2.00
❑7, Jan 96	1.50	0.40	1.00	2.00
❑8, Feb 96	1.50	0.40	1.00	2.00
❑9, Mar 96	1.50	0.40	1.00	2.00
❑10, Apr 96	1.75	0.40	1.00	2.00
❑11, May 96	1.75	0.35	0.88	1.75
❑12, Jun 96	1.75	0.35	0.88	1.75
❑13, Jul 96	1.75	0.35	0.88	1.75
❑14, Aug 96	1.75	0.35	0.88	1.75
❑15, Sep 96, cover says Aug, indicia says Sep	1.75	0.35	0.88	1.75
❑16, Oct 96	1.75	0.35	0.88	1.75
❑17, Nov 96	1.75	0.35	0.88	1.75
❑18, Dec 96	1.75	0.35	0.88	1.75
❑19, Jan 97	1.75	0.35	0.88	1.75
❑20, Feb 97	1.75	0.35	0.88	1.75
❑21, Mar 97	1.75	0.35	0.88	1.75
❑22, Apr 97	1.75	0.35	0.88	1.75
❑23, May 97	1.75	0.35	0.88	1.75
❑24, Jun 97	1.75	0.35	0.88	1.75
❑25	1.75	0.35	0.88	1.75
❑26	1.75	0.35	0.88	1.75
❑27	1.75	0.35	0.88	1.75
❑28	1.75	0.35	0.88	1.75
❑29	1.75	0.35	0.88	1.75
❑30	1.75	0.35	0.88	1.75

SKELETON WARRIORS
MARVEL

Value: Cover or less

- ❑1, Apr 95, Dark Dawn, O: The Skeleton Warriors; 1: Baron Dark; 1: Talyn; 1: Grimskull; 1: Doctor Cyborn; 1: Prince Lightstar 1.50
- ❑2, May 95 .... 1.50
- ❑3, Jun 95 .... 1.50
- ❑4, Jul 95, Final Issue 1.50

SKETCHBOOK SERIES, THE
TUNDRA

Value: Cover or less

- ❑1, Melting Pot 3.95
- ❑2, Totleben 3.95
- ❑3, Zulli 3.95
- ❑4 .... 3.95
- ❑5, CV 3.95
- ❑6, Screaming Masks 3.95
- ❑7 .... 3.95
- ❑8, Forg 3.95
- ❑9 .... 3.95
- ❑10 .... 4.95

ORIG GOOD FINE N-MINT

SKIDMARKS
TUNDRA
Value: Cover or less
- ❑1, b&w.......... 2.95
- ❑2, b&w.......... 2.95
- ❑3, b&w.......... 2.95

SKIM LIZARD
PUPPY TOSS
Value: Cover or less
- ❑1, Fil.......... 2.95

SKIN
TUNDRA
Value: Cover or less
- ❑1.......... 8.95

SKIN13
EXPRESS
Value: Cover or less
- ❑0.5/A, Oct 95, b&w; Amazing SKIN Thir-Teen; reprints Skin13 #1.......... 2.50
- ❑0.5/B, Oct 95, b&w; Barbari-SKIN; reprints Skin13 #1..... 2.50
- ❑0.5/C, Oct 95, b&w; SKIN-et Jackson; reprints Skin13 #1 2.50
- ❑0.5/A-2, 2nd Printing.......... 2.50
- ❑0.5/B-2, 2nd Printing.......... 2.50
- ❑0.5/C-2, 2nd Printing.......... 2.50
- ❑1/A, b&w.......... 2.50
- ❑1/B, b&w; Heavy Metal-style cover.......... 2.50
- ❑1/C, b&w; Spider-Man #1-style cover.......... 2.50

SKIN GRAFT
ICONOGRAFIX
Value: Cover or less
- ❑1, b&w.......... 3.50

SKIN GRAFT: THE ADVENTURES OF A TATTOOED MAN
DC
Value: Cover or less
- ❑1, Jul 93, Blood And Ink.......... 2.50
- ❑2, Aug 93, Skin And Bone.... 2.50
- ❑3, Sep 93, Body and Soul..... 2.50
- ❑4, Oct 93, Dissolve And Combine.......... 2.50

SKINHEADS IN LOVE
FANTAGRAPHICS
Value: Cover or less
- ❑1, b&w; adult.......... 2.25

SKIZZ
FLEETWAY
Value: Cover or less
- ❑1, AMo (w).......... 1.95
- ❑2.......... 1.95
- ❑3.......... 1.95

SKREEMER
DC
Value: Cover or less
- ❑1, May 89.......... 2.00
- ❑2, Jun 89.......... 2.00
- ❑3, Jul 89.......... 2.00
- ❑4, Aug 89, His Corpse To Wake.......... 2.00
- ❑5, Sep 89.......... 2.00
- ❑6, Oct 89, Finnegan's Wake.. 2.00

SKROG
COMICO
Value: Cover or less
- ❑1, b&w.......... 3.50

SKROG (YIP, YIP, YAY) SPECIAL
CRYSTAL
Value: Cover or less
- ❑1, b&w.......... 2.50

SKRULL KILL KREW
MARVEL
Value: Cover or less
- ❑1, Sep 95, Skrull Meat, cardstock cover.......... 2.95
- ❑2, Oct 95, Goin' Krazy!, A: Captain America, cardstock cover.......... 2.95
- ❑3, Nov 95, A: Captain America, cardstock cover.......... 2.95
- ❑4, Dec 95, A: Fantastic Four, cardstock cover.......... 2.95
- ❑5, Jan 96, cardstock cover; Final Issue.......... 2.95

SKULKER, THE
THORBY
Value: Cover or less
- ❑1.......... 2.95

SKULL & BONES
DC
Value: Cover or less
- ❑1, Revolution Day.......... 4.95
- ❑2, Evil Empire.......... 4.95
- ❑3, Iron Curtain.......... 4.95

SKULL COMICS
LAST GASP

	ORIG	GOOD	FINE	N-MINT
❑1	—	2.00	5.00	10.00
❑2, Jan 70, Lame Lem's Love; Tall Tail	0.50	1.20	3.00	6.00
❑3	0.50	0.80	2.00	4.00
❑4	0.50	0.80	2.00	4.00
❑5, Jan 72, The Rats in the Walls; Wilfred Kreel and the Hand of KaS	0.50	0.80	2.00	4.00
❑6, Jun 72, A Gothic Tale	0.50	0.80	2.00	4.00

SKULL THE SLAYER
MARVEL

	ORIG	GOOD	FINE	N-MINT
❑1, Apr 75, The Coming Of Skull The Slayer!, O: Skull the Slayer	0.25	0.50	1.25	2.50
❑2	0.25	0.30	0.75	1.50
❑3	0.25	0.30	0.75	1.50
❑4	0.25	0.30	0.75	1.50
❑5	0.25	0.30	0.75	1.50
❑6	0.25	0.30	0.75	1.50
❑7, Sep 76	0.30	0.30	0.75	1.50
❑8, Nov 76	0.30	0.30	0.75	1.50

SKUNK
MU PRESS
Value: Cover or less
- ❑1, Dec 93, nn; b&w; adult...... 2.50

ORIG GOOD FINE N-MINT

SKUNK, THE
EXPRESS
Value: Cover or less
- ❑3, Jul 96, b&w; cover says #tree.......... 2.75
- ❑4, Sep 96, b&w.......... 2.75
- ❑5, Sep 96, b&w; cover says Cinco de Mayo.......... 2.75
- ❑6, Oct 96, b&w; cover says #sick.......... 2.75

SKY APE (LES ADVENTURES)
SLAVE LABOR
Value: Cover or less
- ❑1, Jun 97, b&w.......... 2.95
- ❑2, Sep 97, b&w.......... 2.95
- ❑3, Jan 98, b&w.......... 2.95

SKY COMICS PRESENTS MONTHLY
SKY COMICS
Value: Cover or less
- ❑1, b&w.......... 2.50

SKYE BLUE
MU PRESS
Value: Cover or less
- ❑1, b&w.......... 2.50
- ❑2, b&w.......... 2.50
- ❑3.......... 2.50

SKY GAL
AC
Value: Cover or less
- ❑1, MB, MB (w), Ginger And The Gremlins!; Blood On The Type-writer!, 1: Sky Gal, some reprint; Reprints Sky Gal stories from Jumbo Comics #68, others plus new story.......... 3.95
- ❑2, MB, some color; some reprint; Reprints Sky Gal stories from Jumbo Comics plus new story.......... 3.95
- ❑3, MB, some color; some reprint; Reprints Sky Gal stories from Jumbo Comics plus new story.......... 3.95

SKY MASTERS
PURE IMAGINATION
Value: Cover or less
- ❑1, WW; JK, b&w; strip reprints.......... 7.95

SKYNN & BONES
BRAINSTORM
Value: Cover or less
- ❑1, Red Zone; Assault.......... 2.95

SKYWOLF
ECLIPSE

	ORIG	GOOD	FINE	N-MINT
❑1, Mar 88, The War Garden	1.75	0.40	1.00	2.00
❑2, May 88, Bamboo Gauntlet	1.75	0.40	1.00	2.00
❑3, Oct 88, Breakout	1.95	0.40	1.00	2.00

SLACKER COMICS
SLAVE LABOR
Value: Cover or less
- ❑1, Aug 94.......... 2.95
- ❑1-2, Apr 95, 2nd Printing.......... 2.95
- ❑2, Nov 94.......... 2.95
- ❑3, Feb 95.......... 2.95
- ❑4, May 95.......... 2.95
- ❑5, Sep 95.......... 2.95
- ❑6, Dec 95, What's Wrong with Wak?!?; Today Is the Worst Day of the Rest of Your Life.......... 2.95
- ❑7, Feb 96, Randy, the Heart-breaker; Randy, the Angry Little Grunge Puppy.......... 2.95
- ❑8, May 96.......... 2.95
- ❑9, Aug 96, A List of Things that Jus.......... 2.95
- ❑10, Randy's Pals 'n' Gals; If You Will Be so Kind as to Indulge Me for a Minute.......... 2.95
- ❑11, Jan 97, Hang the D.J.; Lil' Frank, Jr. Detective.......... 2.95
- ❑12, Randy; The Slacker Fun Page.......... 2.95
- ❑13, Apr 97, Popular Alternative Mu.......... 2.95
- ❑14, May 97, Wotta' Rip!; I Was a Teenage Singing Banana, Slacker Annual; Also titled "Annual #1".......... 2.95
- ❑15, Patricia, the Happy Little Goth Chick; Epilogue..., no indicia 2.95
- ❑16, Apr 98, Retaility Bites; A Gag Reflex Cartoon.......... 2.95
- ❑17, Jul 98, Slacker's Soapbox; Baptism of Fire.......... 2.95
- ❑18, Oct 98, Slacker Asks More of the Hard Questions; The Wake, Pt. I.......... 2.95

SLÁINE THE BERSERKER
FLEETWAY

	ORIG	GOOD	FINE	N-MINT
❑1	1.25	0.30	0.75	1.50
❑2	1.25	0.30	0.75	1.50
❑3	1.25	0.30	0.75	1.50
❑4	1.25	0.30	0.75	1.50
❑5	1.25	0.30	0.75	1.50
❑6	1.25	0.30	0.75	1.50
❑7	1.25	0.30	0.75	1.50
❑8	1.25	0.30	0.75	1.50
❑9	1.25	0.30	0.75	1.50
❑10	1.25	0.30	0.75	1.50
❑11	1.25	0.30	0.75	1.50
❑12	1.25	0.30	0.75	1.50
❑13	1.50	0.30	0.75	1.50
❑14, double issue #14/15	1.50	0.30	0.75	1.50
❑16, double issue #16/17	1.50	0.30	0.75	1.50
❑18	1.50	0.30	0.75	1.50
❑19	1.50	0.30	0.75	1.50
❑20	1.50	0.30	0.75	1.50

SLÁINE THE HORNED GOD
FLEETWAY

	ORIG	GOOD	FINE	N-MINT
❑1	2.95	0.70	1.75	3.50
❑2	2.95	0.60	1.50	3.00
❑3	2.95	0.60	1.50	3.00
❑4	2.95	0.60	1.50	3.00
❑5	2.95	0.60	1.50	3.00
❑6	2.95	0.60	1.50	3.00

SLÁINE THE KING
FLEETWAY
Value: Cover or less

	ORIG		ORIG
❑21	1.50	❑25	1.50
❑22	1.50	❑26	1.50
❑23	1.50	❑27	1.50
❑24	1.50	❑28	1.50

SLAM DUNK KINGS
PERSONALITY
Value: Cover or less

- ❑1, Mar 92, b&w; Michael Jordan ... 2.95
- ❑2, b&w ... 2.95
- ❑3, b&w ... 2.95
- ❑4, b&w ... 2.95

SLAPSTICK
MARVEL
Value: Cover or less

- ❑1, Nov 92, The Totally Awesome Origin Of Slapstick!, 1: Slapstick ... 1.25
- ❑2, Dec 92 ... 1.25
- ❑3, Jan 93 ... 1.25
- ❑4, Feb 93, A: Ghost Rider ... 1.25

SLASH
NORTHSTAR
Value: Cover or less

- ❑1, Aug 93, Blood Rape of the Lust Ghouls; Night City: Music on the Bridge, b&w; adult ... 2.95
- ❑1/SE, Aug 93, Blood Rape of the Lust Ghouls; Night City: Music on the Bridge, adult ... 4.95
- ❑2, b&w; adult ... 2.95
- ❑3, b&w; adult ... 2.95
- ❑4, b&w; adult ... 2.95
- ❑5, Oct 93, Burn; A Mission From God, adult ... 2.95

SLASH MARAUD
DC

	ORIG	GOOD	FINE	N-MINT
❑1, Nov 87, PG, Beautiful Blues!	1.75	0.45	1.13	2.25
❑2, Dec 87, PG	1.75	0.40	1.00	2.00
❑3, Jan 88, PG	1.75	0.40	1.00	2.00
❑4, Feb 88, PG, Halfway To Hyde On The Mulloid Express	1.75	0.40	1.00	2.00
❑5, Mar 88, PG	1.75	0.40	1.00	2.00
❑6, Apr 88, PG	1.75	0.40	1.00	2.00

SLAUGHTERMAN
COMICO
Value: Cover or less

- ❑1, b&w ... 3.50
- ❑2, b&w ... 3.50

SLAVE GIRL
ETERNITY
Value: Cover or less

- ❑1, Mar 89, b&w; Reprint ... 2.25

SLAVE LABOR STORIES
SLAVE LABOR
Value: Cover or less

- ❑1, Feb 92, Stretching; Do Scientists Dream of Electric Sheep?, b&w; Doctor Radium; Dr. Radium ... 2.95
- ❑2, Apr 92, Milk and Cheese: Con Job!; Eating Elvis, b&w; Milk & Cheese ... 2.95
- ❑3, Jul 92, Biill the Clown; Frozen Embryo, b&w; Bill the Clown 2.95
- ❑4, Nov 92, Why We Hate the French; A Letter, b&w; Samurai Penguin ... 2.95

SLAVE PIT FUNNIES
SLAVE PIT
Value: Cover or less

- ❑1, Salve Escape; Tales of the Toolbox ... 4.95

SLAYERS
CPM MANGA
Value: Cover or less

- ❑1, Oct 98 ... 2.95
- ❑2, Nov 98, The Black Fox ... 2.95
- ❑3, Dec 98 ... 2.95
- ❑4, Jan 99 ... 2.95
- ❑5, Feb 99 ... 2.95

SLEAZY SCANDALS OF THE SILVER SCREEN
KITCHEN SINK
Value: Cover or less

- ❑1, Fatty's Fatal Fling; The Suicide of Lupe Velez ... 2.50

SLEDGE HAMMER
MARVEL
Value: Cover or less

- ❑1, Feb 88, Creephouse!, 1: Sledge Hammer; A: Satana, TV tie-in ... 1.00
- ❑2, Mar 88, A: Spider-Man, TV tie-in ... 1.00

SLEEPWALKER
MARVEL

	ORIG	GOOD	FINE	N-MINT
❑1, Jun 91, To Sleep Perchance To Scream!, 1: Sleepwalker	1.00	0.30	0.75	1.50
❑2, Jul 91, 1: 8-Ball	1.00	0.20	0.50	1.00
❑3, Aug 91	1.00	0.20	0.50	1.00
❑4, Sep 91	1.00	0.20	0.50	1.00
❑5, Oct 91, A: Spider-Man	1.00	0.20	0.50	1.00
❑6, Nov 91, A: Spider-Man	1.00	0.20	0.50	1.00
❑7, Dec 91, Infinity Gauntlet	1.00	0.20	0.50	1.00
❑8, Jan 92, A: Deathlok	1.25	0.25	0.63	1.25
❑9, Feb 92	1.25	0.25	0.63	1.25
❑10, Mar 92	1.25	0.25	0.63	1.25
❑11, Apr 92	1.25	0.25	0.63	1.25

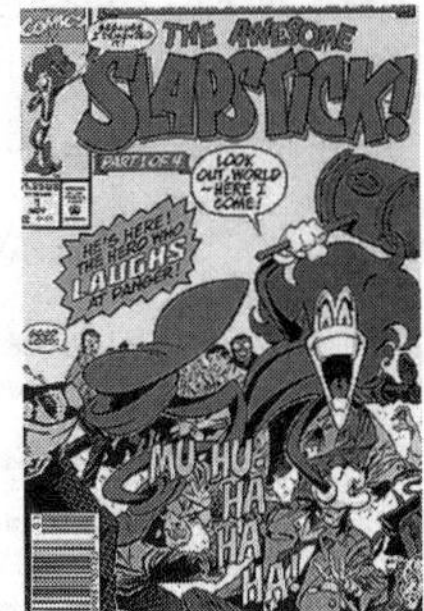

Marvel's Slapstick was introduced in a trading-card set in 1992.

	ORIG	GOOD	FINE	N-MINT
❑12, May 92	1.25	0.25	0.63	1.25
❑13, Jun 92, Color Blindness, Part 1, 1: Spectra	1.25	0.25	0.63	1.25
❑14, Jul 92, Color Blindness, Part 2	1.25	0.25	0.63	1.25
❑15, Aug 92, Color Blindness, Part 3	1.25	0.25	0.63	1.25
❑16, Sep 92, Color Blindness, Part 4	1.25	0.25	0.63	1.25
❑17, Oct 92	1.25	0.25	0.63	1.25
❑18, Nov 92	1.25	0.25	0.63	1.25
❑19, Dec 92, Mindfield, Part 1, Die-cut cover	2.00	0.40	1.00	2.00
❑20, Jan 93, Mindfield, Part 2	1.25	0.25	0.63	1.25
❑21, Feb 93, Mindfield, Part 3	1.25	0.25	0.63	1.25
❑22, Mar 93, Mindfield, Part 4	1.25	0.25	0.63	1.25
❑23, Apr 93, Mindfield, Part 5	1.25	0.25	0.63	1.25
❑24, May 93, Mindfield, Part 6	1.25	0.25	0.63	1.25
❑25, Jun 93, Holo-grafix cover	2.95	0.59	1.48	2.95
❑26, Jul 93	1.25	0.25	0.63	1.25
❑27, Aug 93	1.25	0.25	0.63	1.25
❑28, Sep 93	1.25	0.25	0.63	1.25
❑29, Oct 93, A: Spectra	1.25	0.25	0.63	1.25
❑30, Nov 93	1.25	0.25	0.63	1.25
❑31, Dec 93	1.25	0.25	0.63	1.25
❑32, Jan 94	1.25	0.25	0.63	1.25
❑33, Feb 94, Final Issue	1.25	0.25	0.63	1.25
❑HS 1	2.00	0.40	1.00	2.00

SLEEPWALKING
HALL OF HEROES
Value: Cover or less

- ❑1, Jan 96, b&w ... 2.50
- ❑1/SC, Jan 96, b&w; alternate logoless cover; Black Magic edition ... 9.95
- ❑2, Jun 97, b&w ... 2.50
- ❑2/SC, Jun 97, b&w; alternate logoless cover ... 2.50

SLEEPY HOLLOW
VERTIGO
Value: Cover or less

- ❑1, Jan 00 ... 7.95

SLEEZE BROTHERS
MARVEL
Value: Cover or less

- ❑1, Aug 89, Nice 'N' Sleazy ... 1.75
- ❑2, Sep 89 ... 1.75
- ❑3, Oct 89 ... 1.75
- ❑4, Nov 89 ... 1.75
- ❑5, Dec 89 ... 1.75
- ❑6, Jan 90 ... 1.75

SLEEZE BROTHERS, THE (2ND SERIES)
MARVEL
Value: Cover or less

- ❑1, nn ... 3.95

SLICE
EXPRESS
Value: Cover or less

- ❑1, Oct 96, b&w ... 2.75

SLIDERS
ACCLAIM

	ORIG	GOOD	FINE	N-MINT
❑1, Jun 96, based on TV series	2.50	0.60	1.50	3.00
❑2, Jul 96, based on TV series	2.50	0.50	1.25	2.50
❑3, Sep 96, Ultimatum, Part 1	2.50	0.50	1.25	2.50
❑4, Sep 96, Ultimatum, Part 2	2.50	0.50	1.25	2.50
❑5, Oct 96, Darkest Hour, Part 1	2.50	0.50	1.25	2.50
❑6, Nov 96, Darkest Hour, Part 2	2.50	0.50	1.25	2.50
❑7, Dec 96, VM, Darkest Hour, Part 3	2.50	0.50	1.25	2.50
❑SE 1, Nov 96, Narcotica, Narcotica	3.95	0.79	1.98	3.95
❑SE 2, Jan 97, Blood & Splendor	3.95	0.79	1.98	3.95
❑SE 3, Mar 97, Deadly Secrets	3.95	0.79	1.98	3.95

SLIGHTLY BENT COMICS
SLIGHTLY BENT
Value: Cover or less

- ❑1, Fal 98, Dude-Guy, Earth's Best Pal; Those Dang Gnats!, b&w ... 3.00
- ❑2, Win 99, b&w ... 3.00

SLIMER!
NOW

	ORIG	GOOD	FINE	N-MINT
❑1, May 89, A Kindly Ghost; Ghostly Plumbing	1.75	0.40	1.00	2.00
❑2, Jun 89	1.75	0.40	1.00	2.00
❑3, Jul 89	1.75	0.40	1.00	2.00
❑4, Aug 89	1.75	0.35	0.88	1.75
❑5, Sep 89	1.75	0.35	0.88	1.75

	ORIG	GOOD	FINE	N-MINT
❑6, Oct 89	1.75	0.35	0.88	1.75
❑7, Nov 89	1.75	0.35	0.88	1.75
❑8, Dec 89	1.75	0.35	0.88	1.75
❑9, Jan 90	1.75	0.35	0.88	1.75
❑10, Feb 90, Thanksgiving Nightmares; Sleepless Nights	1.75	0.35	0.88	1.75
❑11, Mar 90	1.75	0.35	0.88	1.75
❑12, Apr 90, Supernatural Bowl; Fooled for Love	1.75	0.35	0.88	1.75
❑13, May 90, Stupid Cupid; Car-Wash Spook	1.75	0.35	0.88	1.75
❑14, Jun 90, Art For Slimer's Sake; Trans-Mutant Terror	1.75	0.35	0.88	1.75
❑15, Jul 90, Genie With the Light Green Slime; Monster Movie	1.75	0.35	0.88	1.75
❑16, Aug 90, The Ghostly Egg; Ray's From the Grave	1.75	0.35	0.88	1.75
❑17, Sep 90	1.75	0.35	0.88	1.75
❑18, Oct 90, A Bird in the Slime; Surgical Spirit	1.75	0.35	0.88	1.75
❑19, Nov 90, Rind Around the Slime; Doomsday Mask!	1.75	0.35	0.88	1.75

SLINGERS
MARVEL

	ORIG	GOOD	FINE	N-MINT
❑0, The Learning Curve, Wizard promotional edition	—	0.20	0.50	1.00
❑1/A, Dec 98, So Whose Idea Was this Anyway?, A: Black Marvel; A: Prodigy; A: Hornet; A: Dusk; A: Ricochet, variant cover with caption "Prodigy: Prepare for Justice!"; gatefold summary	2.99	0.60	1.50	2.99
❑1/B, Dec 98, So Whose Idea Was this Anyway?, A: Black Marvel; A: Prodigy; A: Hornet; A: Dusk; A: Ricochet, Caption "Dusk Falls Over Manhattan" on cover; gatefold summary	2.99	0.60	1.50	2.99
❑1/C, Dec 98, So Whose Idea Was this Anyway?, variant cover with caption "Hornet: Feel the Sting!"; gatefold summary	2.99	0.60	1.50	2.99
❑1/D, Dec 98, So Whose Idea Was this Anyway?, variant cover with caption "Ricochet Springs into Action!"; gatefold summary	2.99	0.60	1.50	2.99
❑2, Jan 99, Cover A; gatefold summary	1.99	0.40	1.00	2.00
❑2/SC, Cover B	1.99	0.40	1.00	2.00
❑3, Feb 99, A: Prodigy; A: Spider-Man	1.99	0.40	1.00	1.99
❑4, Mar 99, A: Prodigy	1.99	0.40	1.00	1.99
❑5, Apr 99, A: Black Marvel	1.99	0.40	1.00	1.99
❑6, May 99	1.99	0.40	1.00	1.99
❑7, Jun 99, V: Griz	1.99	0.40	1.00	1.99
❑8, Jul 99	1.99	0.40	1.00	1.99
❑9, Aug 99, Ricochet vs. Nanny and Orphan-maker	1.99	0.40	1.00	1.99
❑10, Sep 99	1.99	0.40	1.00	1.99
❑12, Nov 99	1.99	0.40	1.00	1.99

SLOTH PARK
BLATANT

Value: Cover or less

- ❑1 ... 2.95

SLOW BURN
EROS

Value: Cover or less

- ❑1 ... 2.95

SLOW DEATH
LAST GASP

	ORIG	GOOD	FINE	N-MINT
❑1	—	2.00	5.00	10.00
❑2, Jan 70, The Sex Evolsors of Tecnicus	—	1.20	3.00	6.00
❑3	—	1.00	2.50	5.00
❑4, Jan 72, Eyes of the Beholder; Ecotopia 2001	0.50	1.00	2.50	5.00
❑5, Jan 73, Last Gasp; Recycled	0.75	1.00	2.50	5.00
❑6	—	0.60	1.50	3.00
❑7, Dec 76, Nits Make Lice; Armistace: 1918	—	0.60	1.50	3.00
❑8, Jul 77, The Honour & Glory of Whaling; The Bengal Blues, Greenpeace issue	1.00	0.60	1.50	3.00
❑9	—	0.60	1.50	3.00
❑10	—	0.60	1.50	3.00
❑11	—	0.60	1.50	3.00

SLOWPOKE COMIX
ALTERNATIVE

Value: Cover or less

- ❑1, Nov 98, The Umbrella; The Giraffe Quandary, b&w ... 2.95

SLUDGE
MALIBU

Value: Cover or less

- ❑1, Oct 93, Rune, Part A, 1: Sludge, Rune ... 2.50
- ❑1/LE, Rune, Part A, 1: Sludge, Ultra Ltd. ... 5.00
- ❑2, Nov 93, 1: Bloodstorm ... 1.95
- ❑3, Dec 93, Break-Thru, 1: Lord Pumpkin, Break-Thru ... 1.95
- ❑4, Jan 94, Cold Blood, O: Mantra ... 1.95
- ❑5, Feb 94, Creatures Of The Night ... 1.95
- ❑6, Mar 94, V: Lord Pumpkin ... 1.95
- ❑7, Jun 94 ... 1.95
- ❑8, Jul 94, V: Bloodstorm ... 1.95
- ❑9, Sep 94, Zuke 'em Till They Glow!, V: Lord Pumpkin ... 1.95
- ❑10, Oct 94, Form Follows Unction, 1: Vinaigrette; 1: Organism 0.9B; 1: Bash Brothers ... 1.95
- ❑11, Nov 94, Intellectual Exercise!, V: Bash Brothers ... 1.95
- ❑12, Dec 94, Neverland Blues, Part 2; Grenade and Electrocute: Soldiers of Fortune, 1: Mr. Mischief; 1: Witch; A: Prime, flip-book with Ultraverse Premiere #8 ... 3.50
- ❑13, Final Issue ... 1.95

SLUG 'N' GINGER
FANTAGRAPHICS

Value: Cover or less

- ❑1, b&w; adult ... 2.25

SLUTBURGER STORIES
RIP OFF

Value: Cover or less

- ❑1, Jul 90, b&w; adult ... 2.50
- ❑2, Jul 91, b&w; adult ... 2.50

SMALL PRESS EXPO
INSIGHT

Value: Cover or less

- ❑1995, Swimsuit Pin-ups, Benefit Comic for American Cancer Society ... 2.95
- ❑1996 ... 2.95
- ❑1997, The Staros Report...SPX; Silly Daddy: Actual Thoughts, Benefit comic for Comic Legal Defense Fund ... 2.95

SMALL PRESS SWIMSUIT SPECTACULAR
ALLIED

Value: Cover or less

- ❑1, Jun 95, b&w; pin-ups; benefit comic for American Cancer Society ... 2.95

SMASH COMICS (2ND SERIES)
DC

Value: Cover or less

- ❑1, May 99, Name Your Poison, A: Hourman; A: Doctor Mid-Nite, Justice Society Returns ... 1.99

SMILE (KITCHEN SINK)
KITCHEN SINK

	ORIG	GOOD	FINE	N-MINT
❑1, Fang; Humble There a Rocky Start!	0.50	0.60	1.50	3.00

SMILE (MIXX)
MIXX

Value: Cover or less

- ❑1, Dec 98, Sailor Moon ... 3.99
- ❑2 ... 3.99
- ❑3 ... 3.99
- ❑4 ... 3.99
- ❑5 ... 3.99
- ❑6 ... 3.99
- ❑7, Dec 99 ... 3.99
- ❑8 ... 3.99

SMILEY
CHAOS

Value: Cover or less

- ❑1 ... 2.95

SMILEY ANTI-HOLIDAY SPECIAL
CHAOS!

Value: Cover or less

- ❑1, Jan 99 ... 2.95

SMILEY'S SPRING BREAK
CHAOS!

Value: Cover or less

- ❑1, Apr 99 ... 2.95

SMILEY WRESTLING SPECIAL
CHAOS!

Value: Cover or less

- ❑1, May 99, nn; One-Shot ... 2.95

SMILIN' ED
FANTACO

Value: Cover or less

- ❑1, FH, b&w ... 1.25
- ❑2, FH, b&w ... 1.25
- ❑3, FH, b&w ... 1.25
- ❑4, FH, b&w ... 1.25

SMITH BROWN JONES
KIWI STUDIOS

	ORIG	GOOD	FINE	N-MINT
❑1	2.95	0.80	2.00	4.00
❑2, All Mirth & No Matter	2.95	0.59	1.48	2.95
❑3	2.95	0.59	1.48	2.95
❑4, We Have Met the Enemy and He is You!	2.95	0.59	1.48	2.95
❑5	2.95	0.59	1.48	2.95

SMITH BROWN JONES: ALIEN ACCOUNTANT
SLAVE LABOR

Value: Cover or less

- ❑1, May 98, The Hero & The Sidekick ... 2.95
- ❑2, Aug 98, The Troll ... 2.95
- ❑3, Nov 98, The Vampire Unicorn ... 2.95
- ❑4, Feb 99, The Brother ... 2.95

SMITH BROWN JONES: HALLOWEEN SPECIAL
SLAVE LABOR

Value: Cover or less

- ❑1, Oct 98, b&w; Anthology ... 2.95

SMOOT
SKIP WILLIAMSON

Value: Cover or less

- ❑1, Snappy Sammy Smoot; Citizen Smoot ... 2.95

SMURFS
MARVEL

	ORIG	GOOD	FINE	N-MINT
❑1	0.60	0.40	1.00	2.00
❑2	0.60	0.40	1.00	2.00
❑3	0.60	0.40	1.00	2.00

SMUT THE ALTERNATIVE COMIC
WILTSHIRE

	ORIG	GOOD	FINE	N-MINT
❑1	0.80	0.60	1.50	3.00

SNACK BAR
BIG TOWN

Value: Cover or less

- ❑1 ... 2.95

SNAKE, THE
SPECIAL STUDIO

Value: Cover or less

❑1, Dec 89, The Den of Madame Joy, b&w 3.50

SNAKE EYES
FANTAGRAPHICS

Value: Cover or less

❑1, b&w 7.95
❑2, b&w 7.95
❑3, b&w 7.95

SNAK POSSE
HCOM

Value: Cover or less

❑1, Jun 94, 1: Carrot Ship; 1: Banana Bolt; 1: Kernel; 1: Blush; 1: Flash; 1: Snak Posse; 1: Silky Stalker, 1st ap 1.95
❑2, Jul 94 .... 1.95

SNAP THE PUNK TURTLE
SUPER CREW

Value: Cover or less

❑0.5 .... 2.25

SNARF
KITCHEN SINK

	ORIG	GOOD	FINE	N-MINT
❑1, Feb 72, adult	0.50	1.00	2.50	5.00
❑2, Aug 72, adult	0.50	0.80	2.00	4.00
❑3, Nov 72, WE (c), adult	0.50	0.80	2.00	4.00
❑4, Mar 73, adult	0.50	0.80	2.00	4.00
❑5, Mar 74, HK (c), adult	0.65	0.60	1.50	3.00
❑6, Feb 76, Life in the Ice and Salt Works; Crutch or Cure?, adult	0.75	0.60	1.50	3.00
❑7, Feb 77, adult	1.00	0.60	1.50	3.00
❑8, Oct 78, adult	1.00	0.60	1.50	3.00
❑9, Feb 81, adult	1.50	0.60	1.50	3.00
❑10, Feb 87, A: Omaha the Cat Dancer, adult	2.00	0.60	1.50	3.00
❑11, Latex Love; Mr. Ned the Talking Gila Monster, adult	2.00	0.40	1.00	2.00
❑12, Raising Nancies; Uncle Mud, adult	2.00	0.40	1.00	2.00
❑13, adult	2.00	0.40	1.00	2.00
❑14, adult	2.00	0.40	1.00	2.00
❑15, adult	2.50	0.50	1.25	2.50

SNARL
CALIBER

Value: Cover or less

❑1, Eaters; The Dog, b&w 2.50
❑2, b&w 2.50
❑3, b&w 2.50

SNOID COMICS
KITCHEN SINK

Value: Cover or less

❑1, This Cartooning is Tricky Busu-ness; The Snoid Goes Bohemian 2.00

S'NOT FOR KIDS
VORTEX

Value: Cover or less

❑1, b&w 6.95

SNOWMAN
EXPRESS

	ORIG	GOOD	FINE	N-MINT
❑1, Terror Eyes, 1: Snowman	2.50	1.00	2.50	5.00
❑1/A, Terror Eyes, 1: Snowman, variant cover	—	1.20	3.00	6.00
❑1-2, Jul 96, 1: Snowman, b&w; 2nd Printing; no cover price; given out at 1996 Comic Con International: San Diego	2.50	0.50	1.25	2.50
❑2	2.50	0.80	2.00	4.00
❑2/A, variant cover	—	1.00	2.50	5.00
❑2-2, 2nd Printing	2.50	0.50	1.25	2.50
❑3	2.50	0.60	1.50	3.00
❑3/A, variant cover	—	0.60	1.50	3.00

SNOW WHITE
MARVEL

	ORIG	GOOD	FINE	N-MINT
❑1, Jan 95, nn; movie Adaptation; lead story is reprint of Dell Four Color #49	1.95	0.40	1.00	2.00

SNOW WHITE AND THE SEVEN DWARFS (WALT DISNEY'S...)
GLADSTONE

	ORIG	GOOD	FINE	N-MINT
❑1, The Many Faces f Snow White; Three Faces of Snow White and Tenggren's Evil Witch, poster	2.95	0.70	1.75	3.50

SNUFF
BONEYARD

Value: Cover or less

❑1, May 97, b&w; adult 2.95

SOB: SPECIAL OPERATIONS BRANCH
PROMETHEAN

Value: Cover or less

❑1, May 94, D: Bandwidth; 1: Orion (Major James T. Greene); 1: Ferret (Prometheus); 1: Polymorph; 1: SOB, b&w 2.25

SOCKETEER, THE
KARDIA

Value: Cover or less

❑1, b&w; parody 2.25

SOCK MONKEY
DARK HORSE

Value: Cover or less

❑1, Sep 98, b&w 2.95
❑2, Oct 98, b&w 2.95

SOCK MONKEY (TONY MILLIONAIRE'S...)
DARK HORSE

Value: Cover or less

❑1, Jul 99, b&w 2.95
❑2, Aug 99, b&w 2.95

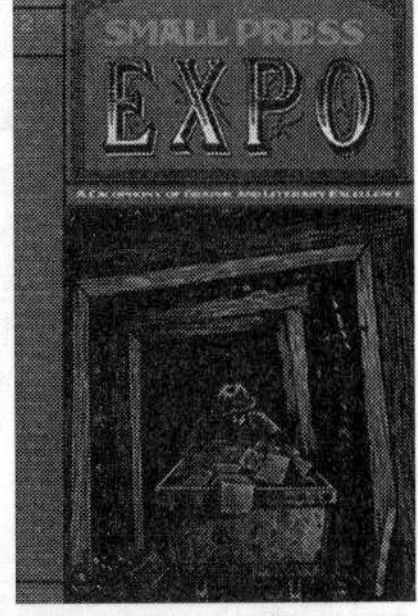

The *Small Press Expo* comics showcase work by creators attending the show. Proceeds from the sale of the comics benefit the Comic Book Legal Defense Fund.

SOCK MONKEY (VOL. 3) (TONY MILLIONAIRE'S...)
DARK HORSE

Value: Cover or less

❑1, Nov 00 .... 2.99
❑2 .... 2.99

SO DARK THE ROSE
CFD

Value: Cover or less

❑1, nn 2.95

SOFA JET CITY CRISIS
VISUAL ASSAULT

Value: Cover or less

❑1, nn; b&w 6.95

S.O.F.T. CORPS
SPOOF

Value: Cover or less

❑1 .... 2.95

SOJOURN
DREAMER

	ORIG	GOOD	FINE	N-MINT
❑1, May 98	2.95	0.42	1.05	2.10
❑2	—	0.42	1.05	2.10
❑3	—	0.42	1.05	2.10
❑4	—	0.42	1.05	2.10
❑5	2.10	0.42	1.05	2.10
❑6	3.15	0.63	1.58	3.15
❑7	3.15	0.63	1.58	3.15
❑8	3.15	0.63	1.58	3.15
❑9	3.15	0.63	1.58	3.15
❑10	3.15	0.63	1.58	3.15

SOLAR LORD
IMAGE

Value: Cover or less

❑1, Mar 99 .... 2.50
❑2, Apr 99 .... 2.50
❑3, May 99 .... 2.50
❑4, Jun 99 .... 2.50
❑5, Jul 99 .... 2.50
❑6, Aug 99 .... 2.50
❑7, Sep 99 .... 2.50

SOLARMAN
MARVEL

Value: Cover or less

❑1, Jan 89, JM, SL (w), Star Burst!, O: Solarman 1.00
❑2, May 90, MZ, SL (w), This Silent Death, This Hostage Earth 1.00

SOLAR, MAN OF THE ATOM
VALIANT

	ORIG	GOOD	FINE	N-MINT
❑1, Sep 91, Second Death, Part 1, O: Solar	1.75	0.60	1.50	3.00
❑2, Oct 91, Second Death, Part 2, O: Solar	1.75	0.40	1.00	2.00
❑3, Nov 91, Second Death, Part 3, 1: Harbinger Foundation; O: Solar; 1: Toyo Harada	1.75	0.40	1.00	2.00
❑4, Dec 91, Second Death, Part 4, O: Solar	1.75	0.40	1.00	2.00
❑5, Jan 92	1.95	0.40	1.00	2.00
❑6, Feb 92, V: Spider-Aliens	1.95	0.40	1.00	2.00
❑7, Mar 92, V: X-O armor	1.95	0.40	1.00	2.00
❑8, Apr 92	2.25	0.40	1.00	2.00
❑9, May 92	2.25	0.40	1.00	2.00
❑10, Jun 92, 1: Eternal Warrior (cameo), All-black embossed cover	3.95	0.80	2.00	4.00
❑10-2, 2nd Printing	3.95	0.79	1.98	3.95
❑11, Jul 92, 1: Eternal Warrior (full appearance)	2.25	0.50	1.25	2.50
❑12, Aug 92, FM (c), Unity, Part 9, Unity	2.25	0.50	1.25	2.50
❑13, Sep 92, Unity, Part 17, Unity	2.25	0.50	1.25	2.50
❑14, Oct 92, 1: Fred Bender	2.25	0.45	1.13	2.25
❑15, Nov 92	2.25	0.45	1.13	2.25
❑16, Dec 92, D: Lyja (Valiant)	2.25	0.45	1.13	2.25
❑17, Jan 93, Seed of Destruction, Part 3, A: X-O Manowar	2.25	0.45	1.13	2.25
❑18, Feb 93	2.25	0.45	1.13	2.25
❑19, Mar 93, Virtually Real	2.25	0.45	1.13	2.25
❑20, Apr 93	2.25	0.45	1.13	2.25
❑21, May 93, Afraid of the Darque, Part 1, V: Master Darque	2.25	0.45	1.13	2.25
❑22, Jun 93, Afraid of the Darque, Part 2; Where Do Gods Go to Pray?, V: Master Darque	2.25	0.45	1.13	2.25
❑23, Jul 93, Afraid of the Darque, Part 3; Split Decision, 1: Solar the Destroyer	2.25	0.45	1.13	2.25
❑24, Aug 93, Half a Man	2.25	0.45	1.13	2.25

	ORIG	GOOD	FINE	N-MINT
❑25, Sep 93, Solar Eclipse, V: Doctor Eclipse, Secret Weapons x-over	2.25	0.45	1.13	2.25
❑26, Oct 93	2.25	0.45	1.13	2.25
❑27, Nov 93, Awake in the Dreamtime	2.25	0.45	1.13	2.25
❑28, Dec 93, Solar the Destroyer vs. spiders	2.25	0.45	1.13	2.25
❑29, Jan 94, Valiant Vision	2.25	0.45	1.13	2.25
❑30, Feb 94	2.25	0.45	1.13	2.25
❑31, Mar 94	2.25	0.45	1.13	2.25
❑32, Apr 94	2.25	0.45	1.13	2.25
❑33, May 94, Valiant Vision; trading card	2.25	0.45	1.13	2.25
❑34, Jun 94, Valiant Vision	2.25	0.45	1.13	2.25
❑35, Aug 94, Valiant Vision	2.25	0.45	1.13	2.25
❑36, Sep 94, Revenge Times Two, Part 1, V: Doctor Eclipse; V: Ravenus	2.25	0.45	1.13	2.25
❑37, Oct 94, Revenge Times Two, Part 2, V: Doctor Eclipse; V: Ravenus	2.25	0.45	1.13	2.25
❑38, Nov 94, The Chaos Effect: Epsilon, Part 1, Chaos Effect	2.25	0.45	1.13	2.25
❑39, Dec 94	2.25	0.45	1.13	2.25
❑40, Jan 95	2.25	0.45	1.13	2.25
❑41, Feb 95	2.25	0.45	1.13	2.25
❑42, Mar 95, Elements of Evil, Part 1	2.25	0.45	1.13	2.25
❑43, Apr 95, Elements of Evil, Part 2	2.25	0.45	1.13	2.25
❑44, May 95	2.25	0.45	1.13	2.25
❑45, Jun 95	2.25	0.45	1.13	2.25
❑46, Jul 95, DG	2.50	0.50	1.25	2.50
❑47, Aug 95, DG	2.50	0.50	1.25	2.50
❑48, Sep 95, DG	2.50	0.50	1.25	2.50
❑49, Sep 95, DG	2.50	0.50	1.25	2.50
❑50, Oct 95, DG	2.50	0.50	1.25	2.50
❑51, Nov 95, DG	2.50	0.50	1.25	2.50
❑52, Nov 95, DG	2.50	0.50	1.25	2.50
❑53, Dec 95, DG	2.50	0.50	1.25	2.50
❑54, Dec 95, DG	2.50	0.50	1.25	2.50
❑55, Jan 96	2.50	0.50	1.25	2.50
❑56, Jan 96	2.50	0.50	1.25	2.50
❑57, Feb 96	2.50	0.50	1.25	2.50
❑58, Feb 96	2.50	0.50	1.25	2.50
❑59, Mar 96, Texas destroyed	2.50	0.50	1.25	2.50
❑60, Apr 96	2.50	0.50	1.25	2.50
❑36801, 2nd Printing	3.95	0.79	1.98	3.95

SOLAR, MAN OF THE ATOM (VOL. 2)
ACCLAIM

Value: Cover or less

❑1, May 97, nn; One-Shot; lays groundwork for second Valiant universe 3.95

SOLAR, MAN OF THE ATOM-HELL ON EARTH
ACCLAIM

Value: Cover or less

❑1, Jan 98, Domino 2.50
❑2, Feb 98 .... 2.50
❑3, Mar 98 .... 2.50
❑4 .... 2.50

SOLAR, MAN OF THE ATOM-REVELATIONS
ACCLAIM

Value: Cover or less

❑1, Nov 97, One-Shot 3.95

SOLAR STELLA
SIRIUS

Value: Cover or less

❑1, Aug 00, Solar Stella meets the Dark Master, b&w; One-Shot 2.95

SOLDIERS OF FREEDOM
AC

Value: Cover or less

❑1, Jul 87 .... 1.75
❑2, Aug 87 .... 1.95

SOLD OUT
FANTACO

Value: Cover or less

❑1 .... 1.50
❑2 .... 1.50

SOLITAIRE
MALIBU

	ORIG	GOOD	FINE	N-MINT
❑1, Nov 93, The Pleasure Principle, 1: Solitaire, Comes polybagged with one of 4 "ace" trading cards	1.95	0.40	1.00	2.00
❑1/CS, Nov 93, trading card	2.50	0.50	1.25	2.50
❑2, Dec 93, Break-Thru, Break-Thru	1.95	0.40	1.00	2.00
❑3, Feb 94, Curse of the Monkey Woman, O: Night Man	1.95	0.40	1.00	2.00
❑4, Mar 94, Bad Monkey, O: Solitaire	1.95	0.40	1.00	2.00
❑5, Apr 94, Even In Death	1.95	0.40	1.00	2.00
❑6, May 94	1.95	0.39	0.98	1.95
❑7, Sep 94, On the Edge, 1: Double Edge	1.95	0.39	0.98	1.95
❑8, Sep 94, Criss-Cross, 1: The Degenerate	1.95	0.39	0.98	1.95
❑9, Sep 94, Talkin' 'Bout My Degeneration, D: The Degenerate	1.95	0.39	0.98	1.95
❑10, Oct 94, Hostile Takeover; Hostile Takeover, Part 2	1.95	0.39	0.98	1.95
❑11, Nov 94, Whose Life is It?	1.95	0.39	0.98	1.95
❑12, Dec 94, Womb of Fire, D: Anton Lone; D: Jinn, Final Issue	1.95	0.39	0.98	1.95

SOLO (DARK HORSE)
DARK HORSE

Value: Cover or less

❑1, Jul 96, movie Adaptation .. 2.50
❑2, Aug 96, Final Issue; movie Adaptation 2.50

SOLO (MARVEL)
MARVEL

Value: Cover or less

❑1, Sep 94, Blood Of The Hunted, Part 1, O: Solo 1.75
❑2, Oct 94, Blood Of The Hunted, Part 2 .... 1.75
❑3, Nov 94, Blood Of The Hunted, Part 3 .... 1.75
❑4, Dec 94, Blood Of The Hunted, Part 4, Final Issue 1.75

SOLO AVENGERS
MARVEL

	ORIG	GOOD	FINE	N-MINT
❑1, Dec 87, Here Comes Hawkeye, I.D. card; 1st solo Mockingbird story	0.75	0.20	0.50	1.00
❑2, Jan 88, Captain Marvel	0.75	0.20	0.50	1.00
❑3, Feb 88, V: Batroc, Moon Knight vs. Shroud	0.75	0.20	0.50	1.00
❑4, Mar 88, Black Knight	0.75	0.20	0.50	1.00
❑5, Apr 88, Scarlet Witch	0.75	0.20	0.50	1.00
❑6, May 88, Falcon	0.75	0.20	0.50	1.00
❑7, Jun 88, Black Widow	0.75	0.20	0.50	1.00
❑8, Jul 88, Hank Pym	0.75	0.20	0.50	1.00
❑9, Aug 88, Hellcat	0.75	0.20	0.50	1.00
❑10, Sep 88, Doctor Druid	0.75	0.20	0.50	1.00
❑11, Oct 88, Hercules	0.75	0.20	0.50	1.00
❑12, Nov 88	0.75	0.20	0.50	1.00
❑13, Dec 88, Wonder Man	0.75	0.20	0.50	1.00
❑14, Jan 89, Black Widow	0.75	0.20	0.50	1.00
❑15, Feb 89	0.75	0.20	0.50	1.00
❑16, Mar 89, Moondragon	0.75	0.20	0.50	1.00
❑17, Apr 89, Sub-Mariner	0.75	0.20	0.50	1.00
❑18, May 89, Moondragon	0.75	0.20	0.50	1.00
❑19, Jun 89, Black Panther	0.75	0.20	0.50	1.00
❑20, Jul 89, Moondragon; series continues as Avengers Spotlight	0.75	0.20	0.50	1.00

SOLO EX-MUTANTS
ETERNITY

	ORIG	GOOD	FINE	N-MINT
❑1	1.95	0.40	1.00	2.00
❑2, Feb 88	1.95	0.40	1.00	2.00
❑3, Jun 88	1.95	0.40	1.00	2.00
❑4	1.95	0.40	1.00	2.00
❑5	1.95	0.40	1.00	2.00
❑6	1.95	0.40	1.00	2.00

SOLOMON KANE
MARVEL

	ORIG	GOOD	FINE	N-MINT
❑1, Sep 85, Red Shadows, Double-size	1.25	0.30	0.75	1.50
❑2, Nov 85, And Faith, Undying...	0.65	0.25	0.63	1.25
❑3, Jan 86, Blades Of The Brotherhood	0.65	0.25	0.63	1.25
❑4, Mar 86, The Prophet	0.75	0.25	0.63	1.25
❑5, May 86, Hills Of The Dead	0.75	0.25	0.63	1.25
❑6, Jul 86, AW	0.75	0.25	0.63	1.25

SOLOMON KANE IN 3-D
BLACKTHORNE

Value: Cover or less

❑1 .... 2.50

SOLSON CHRISTMAS SPECIAL
SOLSON

	ORIG	GOOD	FINE	N-MINT
❑1, JLee, Samurai Santa; 1st Jim Lee art...	—	0.60	1.50	3.00

SOLSON'S COMIC TALENT STARSEARCH
SOLSON

Value: Cover or less

❑1 .... 1.50
❑2 .... 1.50

SOLUTION, THE
MALIBU

	ORIG	GOOD	FINE	N-MINT
❑0, Jan 94, no cover price; Promotional (coupon redemption) edition	—	0.50	1.25	2.50
❑1, Sep 93, The Problem, 1: Shadowmage; 1: Tech; 1: Dropkick; 1: Outrage; 1: The Solution; 1: Quattro	1.95	0.40	1.00	2.00
❑1/LE, Sep 93, The Problem, 1: Shadowmage; 1: Tech; 1: Dropkick; 1: Outrage; 1: The Solution; 1: Quattro, Ultra-Limited foil edition	1.95	0.60	1.50	3.00
❑2, Oct 93, Rune, Part K, 40pgs.; Rune	2.50	0.50	1.25	2.50
❑3, Nov 93, The Hunted	1.95	0.40	1.00	2.00
❑4, Dec 93, Break-Thru, Break-Thru	1.95	0.40	1.00	2.00
❑5, Jan 94, It's A Hard World, O: The Strangers, Dropkick solo story	1.95	0.39	0.98	1.95
❑6, Feb 94, O: Tech; O: The Solution	1.95	0.39	0.98	1.95
❑7, Mar 94, O: The Solution	1.95	0.39	0.98	1.95
❑8, Apr 94, O: The Solution	1.95	0.39	0.98	1.95
❑9, Jun 94	1.95	0.39	0.98	1.95
❑10, Jul 94, Backtrack, Part 1	1.95	0.39	0.98	1.95
❑11, Aug 94, Backtrack, Part 2	1.95	0.39	0.98	1.95
❑12, Oct 94, Backtrack, Part 3	1.95	0.39	0.98	1.95
❑13, Oct 94, Hostile Takeover; Hostile Takeover, Part 3	1.95	0.39	0.98	1.95

	ORIG	GOOD	FINE	N-MINT
❑14, Dec 94, Killing Spree	1.95	0.39	0.98	1.95
❑15, Jan 95, The Trap, Part 1	1.95	0.39	0.98	1.95
❑16, Jan 95, The Trap, Part 2; Manic Monday, flipbook with Ultraverse Premiere #10	3.50	0.70	1.75	3.50
❑17, Feb 95, The Trap, Part 3	2.50	0.50	1.25	2.50

SOMEPLACE STRANGE
MARVEL

Value: Cover or less

❑1 .... 6.95

SOMERSET HOLMES
PACIFIC

	ORIG	GOOD	FINE	N-MINT
❑1, Sep 83, BA	1.50	0.50	1.25	2.50
❑2, Nov 83, BA	1.50	0.40	1.00	2.00
❑3, Feb 84, BA	1.50	0.40	1.00	2.00
❑4, Apr 84, BA	1.50	0.40	1.00	2.00
❑5, Nov 84, BA	1.50	0.40	1.00	2.00
❑6, Dec 84, BA	1.50	0.40	1.00	2.00

SOME TALES FROM GIMBLEY
HARRIER

Value: Cover or less

❑1, Jun 87, A Tale from Gimbley 1.95

SOMETHING
STRICTLY UNDERGROUND

Value: Cover or less

❑1, The Eighth Seal 2.95

SOMETHING AT THE WINDOW IS SCRATCHING
SLAVE LABOR

Value: Cover or less

❑1 .... 9.95

SOMETHING DIFFERENT
WOOGA CENTRAL

Value: Cover or less

❑1, b&w; adult 2.00

❑2, Spr 92, Mark Twain's 1601, adult; flexidisc 2.00

SOMNAMBULO: SLEEP OF THE JUST
9TH CIRCLE STUDIOS

Value: Cover or less

❑1, Aug 96, b&w 2.95

SONGBOOK (ALAN MOORE'S...)
CALIBER

Value: Cover or less

❑1, AMo (w), Rose Madder; Me and Dorothy Parker, Collected from issues of Negative Burn 5.95

SONG OF THE CID
TOME PRESS

Value: Cover or less

❑1, b&w 2.95

❑2, b&w 2.95

SONG OF THE SIRENS
MILLENNIUM

Value: Cover or less

❑1, b&w 2.95

❑2, b&w 2.95

SONGS OF BASTARDS
CONQUEST

Value: Cover or less

❑1, b&w 2.95

SONIC & KNUCKLES: MECHA MADNESS SPECIAL
ARCHIE

Value: Cover or less

❑1 .... 2.00

SONIC & KNUCKLES SPECIAL
ARCHIE

Value: Cover or less

❑1, Aug 95 .... 2.00

SONIC BLAST SPECIAL
ARCHIE

Value: Cover or less

❑1 .... 2.00

SONIC DISRUPTORS
DC

Value: Cover or less

❑1, Dec 87, Are You Ready To Rock? 1.75

❑2, Jan 88 .... 1.75

❑3, Feb 88 .... 1.75

❑4, Mar 88 .... 1.75

❑5, May 88 .... 1.75

❑6, Jun 88 .... 1.75

❑7, Jul 88, Final Issue; series goes on hiatus with unresolved storyline; Series cancelled 1.75

SONIC LIVE SPECIAL
ARCHIE

Value: Cover or less

❑1, One-Shot; Knuckles back-up continues in Sonic the Hedgehog #45 .... 2.00

SONIC QUEST - THE DEATH EGG SAGA
ARCHIE

Value: Cover or less

❑2, Jan 97 .... 1.50

SONIC'S FRIENDLY NEMESIS KNUCKLES
ARCHIE

	ORIG	GOOD	FINE	N-MINT
❑1, Jul 96	1.50	0.60	1.50	3.00
❑2, Aug 96	1.50	0.40	1.00	2.00
❑3, Sep 96	1.50	0.40	1.00	2.00

SONIC THE HEDGEHOG
ARCHIE

	ORIG	GOOD	FINE	N-MINT
❑0, Meet Me at the Corner of Hedgehog & Vine!; You Bet My Life!	1.25	0.80	2.00	4.00
❑1, Feb 93, Meet Me at the Corner of Hedgehog & Vine!; You Bet My Life!	1.25	2.00	5.00	10.00
❑2	1.25	1.20	3.00	6.00

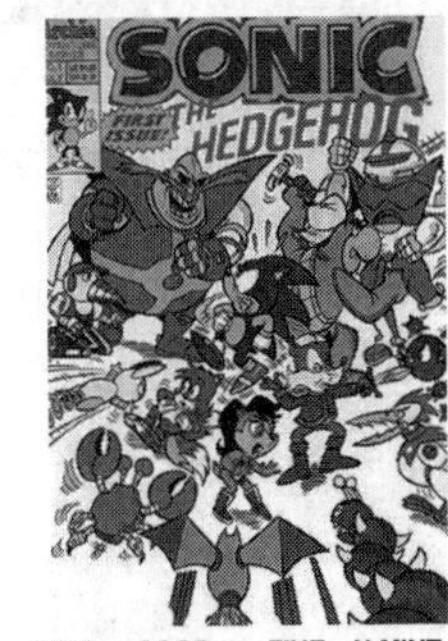

The adventures of videogame character Sonic the Hedgehog have high appeal with younger readers.

© 1993 Sega (Archie)

	ORIG	GOOD	FINE	N-MINT
❑3	1.25	1.00	2.50	5.00
❑4	1.25	1.00	2.50	5.00
❑5	1.25	1.00	2.50	5.00
❑6	1.25	0.80	2.00	4.00
❑7	1.25	0.80	2.00	4.00
❑8	1.25	0.80	2.00	4.00
❑9	1.25	0.80	2.00	4.00
❑10	1.25	0.80	2.00	4.00
❑11, Jun 94	1.25	0.60	1.50	3.00
❑12, Jul 94	1.25	0.60	1.50	3.00
❑13, Aug 94	1.50	0.60	1.50	3.00
❑14, Sep 94	1.50	0.60	1.50	3.00
❑15, Oct 94	1.50	0.60	1.50	3.00
❑16, Nov 94	1.50	0.60	1.50	3.00
❑17, Dec 94	1.50	0.60	1.50	3.00
❑18, Jan 95	1.50	0.60	1.50	3.00
❑19	1.50	0.60	1.50	3.00
❑20, Mar 95	1.50	0.60	1.50	3.00
❑21, Apr 95	1.50	0.40	1.00	2.00
❑22, May 95	1.50	0.40	1.00	2.00
❑23, Jun 95, Ivo Robotnik, Freedom Fighter; Sonic's Pal, Antoine: The Vol-Ant-Teer!	1.50	0.40	1.00	2.00
❑24, Jul 95	1.50	0.40	1.00	2.00
❑25, Aug 95	1.50	0.40	1.00	2.00
❑26, Sep 95	1.50	0.40	1.00	2.00
❑27, Oct 95	1.50	0.40	1.00	2.00
❑28, Nov 95	1.50	0.40	1.00	2.00
❑29, Dec 95	1.50	0.40	1.00	2.00
❑30, Jan 96	1.50	0.40	1.00	2.00
❑31, Jan 96	1.50	0.40	1.00	2.00
❑32, Mar 96	1.50	0.40	1.00	2.00
❑33	1.50	0.40	1.00	2.00
❑34, May 96	1.50	0.40	1.00	2.00
❑35	1.50	0.40	1.00	2.00
❑36, Jul 96	1.50	0.40	1.00	2.00
❑37, Aug 96, Bunnie Rabbot back-up story	1.50	0.40	1.00	2.00
❑38, Sep 96, Tails solo story	1.50	0.40	1.00	2.00
❑39, Oct 96, Mecha Madness	1.50	0.40	1.00	2.00
❑40, Nov 96	1.50	0.40	1.00	2.00
❑41, Nov 96	1.50	0.40	1.00	2.00
❑42, Jan 97	1.50	0.40	1.00	2.00
❑43, Feb 97	1.50	0.40	1.00	2.00
❑44, Mar 97	1.50	0.40	1.00	2.00
❑45, Apr 97	1.50	0.40	1.00	2.00
❑46, May 97	1.50	0.40	1.00	2.00
❑47, Jun 97, End Game, Part 1	1.50	0.40	1.00	2.00
❑48, Jul 97, End Game, Part 2	1.50	0.40	1.00	2.00
❑49, Aug 97, End Game, Part 3	1.50	0.40	1.00	2.00
❑50, Sep 97, End Game, Part 4	1.50	0.40	1.00	2.00
❑51, Oct 97	1.50	0.30	0.75	1.50
❑52, Nov 97, noir issue	1.50	0.30	0.75	1.50
❑53, Dec 97	1.50	0.30	0.75	1.50
❑54, Jan 98	1.75	0.30	0.75	1.50
❑55, Feb 98	1.75	0.30	0.75	1.50
❑56, Mar 98	1.75	0.30	0.75	1.50
❑57, Apr 98	1.75	0.30	0.75	1.50
❑58, May 98	1.75	0.30	0.75	1.50
❑59, Jun 98	1.75	0.30	0.75	1.50
❑60, Jul 98	1.75	0.30	0.75	1.50
❑61, Aug 98	1.75	0.30	0.75	1.50
❑62, Sep 98	1.75	0.30	0.75	1.50
❑63, Oct 98	1.75	0.30	0.75	1.50
❑64, Nov 98, The Naugus Trilogy, Part 1; On His Majesty's Secret Service	1.75	0.35	0.88	1.75
❑65, Dec 98, The Naugus Trilogy, Part 2	1.75	0.35	0.88	1.75
❑66, Jan 99, The Naugus Trilogy, Part 3	1.75	0.35	0.88	1.75
❑67, Feb 99	1.75	0.35	0.88	1.75
❑68, Mar 99	1.75	0.35	0.88	1.75
❑69, Apr 99	1.79	0.36	0.89	1.79
❑70, May 99	1.79	0.36	0.89	1.79
❑71, Jun 99	1.79	0.36	0.89	1.79

	ORIG	GOOD	FINE	N-MINT
❑72, Jul 99	1.79	0.36	0.89	1.79
❑73, Aug 99	1.79	0.36	0.89	1.79
❑74, Sep 99	1.79	0.36	0.89	1.79
❑75, Oct 99	1.79	0.36	0.89	1.79
❑76, Nov 99	1.79	0.36	0.89	1.79
❑77, Dec 99	1.79	0.36	0.89	1.79
❑78, Jan 00	1.79	0.36	0.89	1.79
❑79, Feb 00	1.79	0.36	0.89	1.79
❑80, Mar 00	1.79	0.36	0.89	1.79
❑81, Apr 00	1.79	0.36	0.89	1.79
❑82, May 00	1.79	0.36	0.89	1.79
❑83, Jun 00	1.99	0.40	1.00	1.99
❑84, Jul 00	1.99	0.40	1.00	1.99
❑85, Aug 00	1.99	0.40	1.00	1.99
❑86, Sep 00	1.99	0.40	1.00	1.99
❑87, Oct 00	1.99	0.40	1.00	1.99
❑88, Nov 00	1.99	0.40	1.00	1.99
❑89, Dec 00	1.99	0.40	1.00	1.99
❑90, Jan 01	1.99	0.40	1.00	1.99
❑91, Feb 01	1.99	0.40	1.00	1.99
❑92, Mar 01	1.99	0.40	1.00	1.99
❑93, Apr 01	1.99	0.40	1.00	1.99
❑94	1.99	0.40	1.00	1.99
❑95	1.99	0.40	1.00	1.99
❑96	1.99	0.40	1.00	1.99
❑97	1.99	0.40	1.00	1.99
❑98	1.99	0.40	1.00	1.99
❑99	1.99	0.40	1.00	1.99
❑100	1.99	0.40	1.00	1.99
❑SS 1	2.00	0.40	1.00	2.00
❑SS 2, Brave New World	2.00	0.40	1.00	2.00
❑SS 3, Firsts	2.25	0.45	1.13	2.25
❑SS 4, Return of the King	2.25	0.45	1.13	2.25
❑SS 5, Sonic Kids	2.25	0.45	1.13	2.25
❑SS 6, Director's Cut; expanded version of Sonic #50	2.25	0.45	1.13	2.25
❑SS 7, crossover with Image	2.25	0.45	1.13	2.25
❑SS 8	2.25	0.45	1.13	2.25
❑SS 9	2.29	0.46	1.14	2.29
❑SS 10, A: Sabrina	2.29	0.46	1.14	2.29
❑SS 11	2.29	0.46	1.14	2.29
❑SS 12	2.29	0.46	1.14	2.29
❑SS 13	2.29	0.46	1.14	2.29
❑SS 14	2.29	0.46	1.14	2.29
❑SS 15, Feb 01	2.49	0.50	1.25	2.49

SONIC THE HEDGEHOG (MINI-SERIES)
ARCHIE

	ORIG	GOOD	FINE	N-MINT
❑1	—	4.00	10.00	20.00
❑2	—	2.00	5.00	10.00
❑3	—	2.00	5.00	10.00

SONIC THE HEDGEHOG IN YOUR FACE SPECIAL
ARCHIE

Value: Cover or less ❑1 .... 2.00

SONIC THE HEDGEHOG TRIPLE TROUBLE SPECIAL
ARCHIE

Value: Cover or less ❑1, Oct 95 .... 2.00

SONIC VS. KNUCKLES BATTLE ROYAL SPECIAL
ARCHIE

Value: Cover or less ❑1 .... 2.00

SON OF AMBUSH BUG
DC

	ORIG	GOOD	FINE	N-MINT
❑1, Jul 86, KG, How Come You Do Me Like You Do Do Do?	0.75	0.30	0.75	1.50
❑2, Aug 86, KG	0.75	0.30	0.75	1.50
❑3, Sep 86, KG	0.75	0.30	0.75	1.50
❑4, Oct 86, KG	0.75	0.30	0.75	1.50
❑5, Nov 86, KG	0.75	0.30	0.75	1.50
❑6, Dec 86, KG	0.75	0.30	0.75	1.50

SON OF MUTANT WORLD
FANTAGOR

	ORIG	GOOD	FINE	N-MINT
❑1, Targets; The Small World of Lewis Stillman, full color	2.00	0.60	1.50	3.00
❑2, Watching You; Inna Pit, full color	2.00	0.50	1.25	2.50
❑3, Dead Run; Twilight of the Dogs, b&w; Black and white issues begin	1.75	0.40	1.00	2.00
❑4, Afterthought; Different, b&w	1.75	0.40	1.00	2.00
❑5, Flypaper; Silver, Emeralds and Rubies, b&w	1.75	0.40	1.00	2.00

SON OF SATAN
MARVEL

	ORIG	GOOD	FINE	N-MINT
❑1, Dec 75	0.25	2.00	5.00	10.00
❑2, Feb 76, The Possession!	0.25	1.60	4.00	8.00
❑3, Apr 76	0.25	1.20	3.00	6.00
❑4, Jun 76, CR, Cloud of Witness!	0.25	1.20	3.00	6.00
❑5, Aug 76	0.25	1.20	3.00	6.00
❑6, Oct 76	0.30	1.00	2.50	5.00
❑7, Dec 76	0.30	1.00	2.50	5.00
❑8, Feb 77	0.30	1.00	2.50	5.00

SON OF SUPERMAN
DC

Value: Cover or less ❑1, HC (w) 14.95

SON OF YUPPIES FROM HELL
MARVEL

Value: Cover or less ❑1 .... 3.50

SOPHISTIKATS KATCH-UP KOLLECTION, THE
SILK PURRS PRESS

Value: Cover or less ❑1, Jul 95, nn; b&w 5.95

SORCERER'S CHILDREN, THE
SILLWILL PRESS

Value: Cover or less

❑1, Dec 98 .... 2.95
❑2, Feb 99 .... 2.95
❑3, Apr 99 .... 2.95
❑4, Jul 99 .... 2.95

S.O.S.
FANTAGRAPHICS

Value: Cover or less ❑1, nn; b&w; adult 2.75

SOUL
FLASHPOINT

	ORIG	GOOD	FINE	N-MINT
❑1, Mar 94, The Wakening	2.50	0.50	1.25	2.50
❑1/GO, The Wakening, Gold edition	2.50	0.60	1.50	3.00

SOULQUEST
INNOVATION

Value: Cover or less ❑1, Apr 89, Unfinished Portraits 3.95

SOUL SAGA
TOP COW

Value: Cover or less

❑1 .... 5.95
❑2 .... 2.50
❑3, Aug 00 .... 2.50
❑4, Oct 00 .... 2.95
❑5, Apr 01 .... 2.95

SOULSEARCHERS AND COMPANY
CLAYPOOL

	ORIG	GOOD	FINE	N-MINT
❑1, PD (w); RHo (w), Puppet Dictatorship	2.50	0.80	2.00	4.00
❑2, PD (w)	2.50	0.60	1.50	3.00
❑3, Aug 93, PD (w), Sandman parody	2.50	0.60	1.50	3.00
❑4, Sep 93, PD (w)	2.50	0.60	1.50	3.00
❑5, Oct 93, PD (w)	2.50	0.60	1.50	3.00
❑6, Feb 94, PD (w)	2.50	0.50	1.25	2.50
❑7, May 94, PD (w)	2.50	0.50	1.25	2.50
❑8, Jul 94, PD (w)	2.50	0.50	1.25	2.50
❑9, PD (w)	2.50	0.50	1.25	2.50
❑10, Jan 95, PD (w)	2.50	0.50	1.25	2.50
❑11, Feb 95, RHo, PD (w), Liquid Assets	2.50	0.50	1.25	2.50
❑12, May 95, PD (w)	2.50	0.50	1.25	2.50
❑13, Jul 95, PD (w)	2.50	0.50	1.25	2.50
❑14, Oct 95, PD (w)	2.50	0.50	1.25	2.50
❑15, Dec 95, PD (w)	2.50	0.50	1.25	2.50
❑16, Feb 96, PD (w)	2.50	0.50	1.25	2.50
❑17, Apr 96, PD (w)	2.50	0.50	1.25	2.50
❑18, Jun 96, PD (w)	2.50	0.50	1.25	2.50
❑19, Aug 96, PD (w)	2.50	0.50	1.25	2.50
❑20, Oct 96, PD (w)	2.50	0.50	1.25	2.50
❑21, Dec 96, PD (w)	2.50	0.50	1.25	2.50
❑22, Feb 97, PD (w)	2.50	0.50	1.25	2.50
❑23, Apr 97, PD (w)	2.50	0.50	1.25	2.50
❑24, Jun 97, PD (w)	2.50	0.50	1.25	2.50
❑25, Aug 97, PD (w)	2.50	0.50	1.25	2.50
❑26, Oct 97, PD (w)	2.50	0.50	1.25	2.50
❑27, Dec 97, PD (w)	2.50	0.50	1.25	2.50
❑28, Feb 98, PD (w)	2.50	0.50	1.25	2.50
❑29, Apr 98, JM; DC, PD (w), Animal Crackers!	2.50	0.50	1.25	2.50
❑30, Jun 98, PD (w)	2.50	0.50	1.25	2.50
❑31, Aug 98, PD (w), Li'l Soulsearchers	2.50	0.50	1.25	2.50
❑32, Sep 98, PD (w)	2.50	0.50	1.25	2.50
❑33, Nov 98, PD (w)	2.50	0.50	1.25	2.50
❑34, Jan 99, PD (w)	2.50	0.50	1.25	2.50
❑35, Mar 99, PD (w)	2.50	0.50	1.25	2.50
❑36, May 99, PD (w)	2.50	0.50	1.25	2.50
❑37, Jul 99, PD (w)	2.50	0.50	1.25	2.50
❑38, Sep 99, PD (w)	2.50	0.50	1.25	2.50
❑39, Nov 99, PD (w), Festival of Lights	2.50	0.50	1.25	2.50
❑40, Jan 00, PD (w)	2.50	0.50	1.25	2.50
❑41, Mar 00, PD (w)	2.50	0.50	1.25	2.50
❑42, May 00, PD (w), Kelly the Demon Slayer	2.50	0.50	1.25	2.50
❑43, Jul 00, DC, PD (w), It's in the Bag	2.50	0.50	1.25	2.50
❑44, Sep 00, PD (w), Town 4 Sale!	2.50	0.50	1.25	2.50
❑45	2.50	0.50	1.25	2.50
❑46	2.50	0.50	1.25	2.50
❑47	2.50	0.50	1.25	2.50
❑48	2.50	0.50	1.25	2.50
❑49	2.50	0.50	1.25	2.50

ORIG GOOD FINE N-MINT

SOUL TREK
SPOOF

Value: Cover or less

❑1, b&w; parody...................... 2.95
❑2, b&w; parody...................... 2.95

SOULWIND
IMAGE

Value: Cover or less

❑1, Mar 97, b&w..................... 2.95
❑2, Apr 97, b&w..................... 2.95
❑3, May 97, b&w..................... 2.95
❑4, Jun 97, b&w..................... 2.95
❑5, Oct 97, The Day I Tried to Live, Part 1, b&w........................ 2.95
❑6, Dec 97, The Day I Tried to Live, Part 2, b&w........................ 2.95
❑7, Feb 98, The Day I Tried to Live, Part 3, b&w........................ 2.95
❑8, Apr 98, The Day I Tried to Live, Part 4, b&w........................ 2.95

SOUTHERN BLOOD
JM COMICS

Value: Cover or less

❑1, b&w.................................. 2.50
❑2, b&w.................................. 2.50

SOUTHERN COMFORT
CEROS

Value: Cover or less

❑1, adult................................ 2.95

SOUTHERN-FRIED HOMICIDE
CREMO

Value: Cover or less

❑1, nn; b&w; cardstock cover................................ 7.95

SOUTHERN KNIGHTS
GUILD

	ORIG	GOOD	FINE	N-MINT
❑2, Title changes to Southern Knights	—	0.40	1.00	2.00
❑3, Jul 83	1.50	0.40	1.00	2.00
❑4	—	0.40	1.00	2.00
❑5	—	0.40	1.00	2.00
❑6, Jun 84	—	0.40	1.00	2.00
❑7, Sep 84	—	0.40	1.00	2.00
❑8, Apr 85	—	0.40	1.00	2.00
❑9, Jun 85	—	0.40	1.00	2.00
❑10, Aug 85	—	0.40	1.00	2.00
❑11, Oct 85	—	0.40	1.00	2.00
❑12, Dec 85	—	0.40	1.00	2.00
❑13, Feb 86	—	0.40	1.00	2.00
❑14, Apr 86	—	0.40	1.00	2.00
❑15, Jun 86	—	0.40	1.00	2.00
❑16, Aug 86	1.75	0.40	1.00	2.00
❑17, Oct 86	1.75	0.40	1.00	2.00
❑18, Dec 86	1.75	0.40	1.00	2.00
❑19, Feb 87	1.75	0.40	1.00	2.00
❑20, Apr 87	1.75	0.40	1.00	2.00
❑21, Jun 87	1.75	0.40	1.00	2.00
❑22, Aug 87	1.75	0.40	1.00	2.00
❑23, Dec 87	1.75	0.40	1.00	2.00
❑24, Dec 87	1.75	0.40	1.00	2.00
❑25, Feb 88	1.75	0.40	1.00	2.00
❑26, Apr 88	1.75	0.40	1.00	2.00
❑27, Jun 88	1.75	0.40	1.00	2.00
❑28, Aug 88	1.95	0.40	1.00	2.00
❑29, Aug 88	1.95	0.40	1.00	2.00
❑30, Sep 88	1.95	0.40	1.00	2.00
❑31, Oct 88	1.95	0.40	1.00	2.00
❑32, Jan 89	1.95	0.40	1.00	2.00
❑33, Sep 89	1.95	0.40	1.00	2.00
❑34	2.25	0.45	1.13	2.25
❑35, b&w	3.50	0.70	1.75	3.50
❑36, b&w	3.50	0.70	1.75	3.50
❑HS 1, Oct 88, Wizard promotional edition; Dread Halloween Special; b&w Reprint	2.25	0.45	1.13	2.25
❑SE 1, Apr 89, b&w; Reprint	2.25	0.45	1.13	2.25

SOUTHERN KNIGHTS PRIMER
COMICS INTERVIEW

Value: Cover or less

❑1, b&w; Reprint...................... 2.25

SOUTHERN SQUADRON (2ND SERIES)
ETERNITY

Value: Cover or less

❑1.. 2.50
❑2.. 2.50
❑3.. 2.50
❑4.. 2.50

SOUTHERN SQUADRON, THE (AIRCEL)
AIRCEL

Value: Cover or less

❑1, Aug 90, MGr (c), Moving Home, 1: The Dingo; 1: Southern Squadron; 1: Nightlifter. 2.25
❑2, Sep 90............................ 2.25
❑3, Sep 90............................ 2.25
❑4, Nov 90, PG (c)................... 2.25

SOUTHERN SQUADRON: THE FREEDOM OF INFORMATION ACT
ETERNITY

Value: Cover or less

❑1, Jan 92, Fantastic Four #1 homage cover.......................... 2.50
❑2, Feb 92............................ 2.50
❑3, Mar 92............................ 2.50

SOVEREIGN SEVEN
DC

Value: Cover or less

❑1, Jul 95, It Was a Dark and Stormy Night..., 1: Cascade; 1: Rampart; 1: Indigo; 1: Reflex; 1: Network; 1: Cruiser; 1: Sovereign Seven; 1: Conal.......... 1.95
❑1/SC, Jul 95, no cover price; foil edition................................ 10.00
❑2, Aug 95............................ 1.95
❑3, Sep 95, Costume Drama.. 1.95

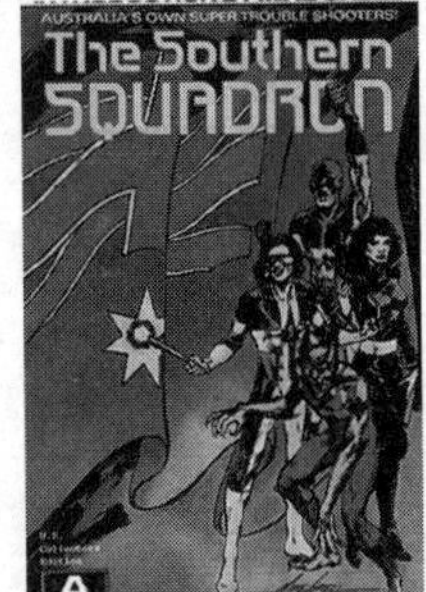

The Southern Squadron was an Australian group of super-powered trouble-shooters.

© 1990 Aircel

ORIG GOOD FINE N-MINT

❑4, Oct 95.............................. 1.95
❑5, Nov 95.............................. 1.95
❑6, Dec 95.............................. 1.95
❑7, Jan 96.............................. 1.95
❑8, Feb 96, The Wild Hunt...... 1.95
❑9, Mar 96, 12th Night........... 1.95
❑10, Apr 96, Road Trip, Part 1 1.95
❑11, Jun 96, Road Trip, Part 2 1.95
❑12, Jul 96, Road Trip, Part 3. 1.95
❑13, Aug 96, Lost Souls, Part 1 1.95
❑14, Sep 96, Lost Souls, Part 2 1.95
❑15, Oct 96, Prom Night......... 1.95
❑16, Nov 96, Final Night......... 1.95
❑17, Dec 96, Hot Pursuit......... 1.95
❑18, Jan 97, Meridian: Force Twenty, Cascade quits........ 1.95
❑19, Feb 97, Bolo, A: Clark Kent.................................... 1.95
❑20, Mar 97, Q&A.................. 1.95
❑21, Apr 97, Casey the Spy!... 1.95
❑22, May 97........................... 1.95
❑23, Jun 97........................... 1.95
❑24, Jul 97, A: Superman........ 1.95
❑25, Aug 97, A: Power Girl...... 1.95
❑26, Sep 97, A: Hitman........... 2.25
❑27, Oct 97, Genesis.............. 2.25
❑28, Nov 97, Whatever Happened to Power Girl?, A: Impulse... 2.25
❑29, Dec 97, Busted!, Face cover..................................... 2.25
❑30, Jan 98........................... 2.25
❑31, Feb 98........................... 2.25
❑32, Mar 98, Night of the Hunters................................ 2.25
❑33, Apr 98........................... 2.25
❑34, May 98........................... 2.25
❑35, Jun 98........................... 2.25
❑36, Jul 98, Final Issue........... 2.25
❑Anl 1, A: Lobo, Year One; Big Barda................................... 3.95
❑Anl 2, Memento Mori, Legends of the Dead Earth; 1996 Annual.................................. 2.95

SOVEREIGN SEVEN PLUS
DC

Value: Cover or less

❑1, Feb 97, A: Legion............. 2.95

SOVIET SUPER SOLDIERS
MARVEL

Value: Cover or less

❑1, Nov 92, The Red Triangle Agenda................................ 2.00

SPACE: 1999
CHARLTON

	ORIG	GOOD	FINE	N-MINT
❑1, JSa, Moonless Night, O: Moonbase Alpha	0.25	1.00	2.50	5.00
❑2	—	0.60	1.50	3.00
❑3, JBy	—	0.80	2.00	4.00
❑4, JBy	—	0.80	2.00	4.00
❑5, JBy	—	0.80	2.00	4.00
❑6, JBy	—	0.80	2.00	4.00
❑7	—	0.50	1.25	2.50

SPACE: 34-24-34
MN DESIGN

Value: Cover or less

❑1, b&w; photos..................... 4.50

SPACE: ABOVE AND BEYOND
TOPPS

Value: Cover or less

❑1, Jan 96, Out of the Silent Space................................ 2.95
❑2, Feb 96, Mars Ain't the Kind of Place to Raise Your Kids.... 2.95
❑3, Mar 96............................ 2.95

SPACE: ABOVE AND BEYOND-THE GAUNTLET
TOPPS

Value: Cover or less

❑1, May 96, Running the Gauntlet............................ 2.95
❑2, Jun 96, A Gauntlet Hurled................................ 2.95

SPACE ADVENTURES
CHARLTON

	ORIG	GOOD	FINE	N-MINT
❑33, SD, 1: Captain Atom	0.10	65.00	162.50	325.00
❑34, SD, 2: Captain Atom	0.10	30.00	75.00	150.00
❑35, SD, A: Captain Atom	0.10	25.00	62.50	125.00
❑36, SD, A: Captain Atom	0.10	25.00	62.50	125.00
❑37, SD, A: Captain Atom	0.10	25.00	62.50	125.00
❑38, SD, A: Captain Atom	0.10	25.00	62.50	125.00
❑39, SD, A: Captain Atom	0.10	25.00	62.50	125.00
❑40, SD, A: Captain Atom	0.10	25.00	62.50	125.00
❑41	0.10	5.00	12.50	25.00
❑42, Oct 61, SD, A: Captain Atom	0.10	15.00	37.50	75.00
❑43	—	5.00	12.50	25.00
❑44	—	5.00	12.50	25.00
❑45	—	5.00	12.50	25.00
❑46	—	5.00	12.50	25.00
❑47	—	5.00	12.50	25.00
❑48, A True Friend; The Ambassador From Earth	0.12	5.00	12.50	25.00
❑49	—	5.00	12.50	25.00
❑50	—	5.00	12.50	25.00

	ORIG	GOOD	FINE	N-MINT
❑51	—	3.60	9.00	18.00
❑52	—	3.60	9.00	18.00
❑53	—	3.60	9.00	18.00
❑54	—	3.60	9.00	18.00
❑55	—	3.60	9.00	18.00
❑56	—	3.60	9.00	18.00
❑57	—	3.60	9.00	18.00
❑58	—	3.60	9.00	18.00
❑59	—	3.60	9.00	18.00
❑60, Oct 67	0.12	3.60	9.00	18.00
❑61	—	2.40	6.00	12.00
❑62	—	2.40	6.00	12.00
❑63	—	2.40	6.00	12.00
❑64	—	2.40	6.00	12.00
❑65	—	2.40	6.00	12.00
❑66	—	2.40	6.00	12.00
❑67	—	2.40	6.00	12.00
❑68	—	2.40	6.00	12.00
❑69	—	2.40	6.00	12.00
❑70	—	2.40	6.00	12.00
❑71, Jan 79	0.35	2.40	6.00	12.00
❑72	—	2.40	6.00	12.00

SPACE ARK
AC

Value: Cover or less

- ❑1, No Time for Space Ark! 1.75
- ❑2, Cattycornered 1.75
- ❑3, b&w 1.75
- ❑4, b&w 1.75
- ❑5, b&w 1.75

SPACE BANANAS
KARL ART

Value: Cover or less

- ❑0, The Shrinking Gas Strikes!, Captain Action #0 as i nsert 1.95

SPACE BEAVER
TEN-BUCK

Value: Cover or less

- ❑1, Oct 86 .... 1.50
- ❑2 .... 1.50
- ❑3, Feb 87 .... 1.50
- ❑4 .... 1.50
- ❑5 .... 1.50
- ❑6, Sep 87 .... 1.50
- ❑7 .... 1.50
- ❑8 .... 1.50
- ❑9 .... 1.50
- ❑10 .... 1.50
- ❑11 .... 1.50

SPACE CIRCUS
DARK HORSE

Value: Cover or less

- ❑1, Jul 00, SA, ME (w) 2.95
- ❑2, Aug 00, SA, ME (w) 2.95
- ❑3, Sep 00, SA, ME (w) 2.95
- ❑4, Oct 00, SA, ME (w) 2.95

SPACED
UNBRIDLED AMBITION

	ORIG	GOOD	FINE	N-MINT
❑1	—	0.40	1.00	2.00
❑2	—	0.40	1.00	2.00
❑3	—	0.40	1.00	2.00
❑4	—	0.40	1.00	2.00
❑5	—	0.40	1.00	2.00
❑6	—	0.40	1.00	2.00
❑7	1.60	0.40	1.00	2.00
❑8, Beer, Wine & Set-Ups	1.60	0.40	1.00	2.00
❑9	1.60	0.40	1.00	2.00
❑10, b&w; Eclipse publisher	1.50	0.40	1.00	2.00
❑11, b&w	1.50	0.40	1.00	2.00
❑12, b&w	1.50	0.40	1.00	2.00
❑13, b&w	1.50	0.40	1.00	2.00

SPACED (COMICS AND COMIX)
COMICS AND COMIX

	ORIG	GOOD	FINE	N-MINT
❑1	1.00	0.80	2.00	4.00

SPACED OUT (FORBIDDEN FRUIT)
FORBIDDEN FRUIT

Value: Cover or less

- ❑1, Jul 92, Cyborg 28-H; Downed 2.95

SPACED OUT (PRINT MINT)
PRINT MINT

	ORIG	GOOD	FINE	N-MINT
❑1, Run!; Perish the Thought	0.50	0.60	1.50	3.00

SPACE FAMILY ROBINSON
GOLD KEY

	ORIG	GOOD	FINE	N-MINT
❑1, Low circulation	0.12	30.00	75.00	150.00
❑2, Robinson's become lost in space	0.12	15.00	37.50	75.00
❑3	0.12	10.00	25.00	50.00
❑4	0.12	10.00	25.00	50.00
❑5	0.12	10.00	25.00	50.00
❑6	0.12	8.00	20.00	40.00
❑7	0.12	8.00	20.00	40.00
❑8	0.12	8.00	20.00	40.00
❑9	0.12	8.00	20.00	40.00
❑10	0.12	8.00	20.00	40.00
❑11	0.12	5.00	12.50	25.00
❑12, The Iron Dwarfs	0.12	5.00	12.50	25.00
❑13	0.12	5.00	12.50	25.00
❑14	0.12	5.00	12.50	25.00
❑15, Title changes to "Space Family Robinson Lost in Space"	0.12	5.00	12.50	25.00
❑16	0.12	4.00	10.00	20.00
❑17	0.12	4.00	10.00	20.00
❑18	0.12	4.00	10.00	20.00
❑19	0.12	4.00	10.00	20.00
❑20	0.12	4.00	10.00	20.00
❑21, Apr 67, Operation Survival!	0.12	3.60	9.00	18.00
❑22	0.12	3.60	9.00	18.00
❑23	0.12	3.60	9.00	18.00
❑24, Oct 67, The Savage Earth; captain Venture: The Big Wave	0.12	3.60	9.00	18.00
❑25	0.12	3.60	9.00	18.00
❑26	0.12	3.60	9.00	18.00
❑27	0.12	3.60	9.00	18.00
❑28, Jun 68, When Suns Collide	0.12	3.60	9.00	18.00
❑29, Aug 68, four-color; 32pgs.	0.15	3.60	9.00	18.00
❑30	0.15	3.60	9.00	18.00
❑31	0.15	3.60	9.00	18.00
❑32	0.15	3.60	9.00	18.00
❑33	0.15	3.60	9.00	18.00
❑34	0.15	3.60	9.00	18.00
❑35, Aug 69	0.15	3.60	9.00	18.00
❑36, Oct 69, Final issue of original run	—	3.60	9.00	18.00
❑37, Oct 73, Series begins again	—	3.60	9.00	18.00
❑38, Title changes to "Space Family Robinson, Lost in Space on Space Station One"	—	3.60	9.00	18.00
❑39	—	3.60	9.00	18.00
❑40	—	3.60	9.00	18.00
❑41	—	3.60	9.00	18.00
❑42	—	3.60	9.00	18.00
❑43	—	3.60	9.00	18.00
❑44, Aug 75	—	3.60	9.00	18.00
❑45	—	1.60	4.00	8.00
❑46	—	1.60	4.00	8.00
❑47	—	1.60	4.00	8.00
❑48	—	1.60	4.00	8.00
❑49	—	1.60	4.00	8.00
❑50	—	1.60	4.00	8.00
❑51	—	1.60	4.00	8.00
❑52	—	1.60	4.00	8.00
❑53	—	1.60	4.00	8.00
❑54	—	1.60	4.00	8.00
❑55, Series begins again	—	1.00	2.50	5.00
❑56	—	1.00	2.50	5.00
❑57	—	1.00	2.50	5.00
❑58	—	1.00	2.50	5.00
❑59, Final Issue	—	1.00	2.50	5.00

SPACE FUNNIES
ARCHIVAL

Value: Cover or less

- ❑1, BW 5.95

SPACEGAL COMICS
THORBY

Value: Cover or less

- ❑1 .... 2.95
- ❑2, O: Spacegal, Flip-Book with Johnny Cosmic #1 .... 2.95

SPACE GHOST (COMICO)
COMICO

Value: Cover or less

- ❑1, Dec 87, SR, ME (w); SR (w), The Sinister Spectre 3.50

SPACE GHOST (GOLD KEY)
GOLD KEY

	ORIG	GOOD	FINE	N-MINT
❑1	0.12	30.00	75.00	150.00

SPACE GIANTS, THE
BONEYARD

Value: Cover or less

- ❑1 .... 2.75

SPACEGIRL COMICS
BILL JONES GRAPHICS

Value: Cover or less

- ❑1, Nov 95, b&w 2.50
- ❑2, Nov 95, b&w 2.50

SPACEHAWK
DARK HORSE

	ORIG	GOOD	FINE	N-MINT
❑1, BW, BW (w), Spacehawk vs. The Brain Bats of Venus	2.00	0.40	1.00	2.00
❑2, BW, BW (w), Vulture Men from the Void; The Superhuman Enemy of Crime	2.00	0.40	1.00	2.00
❑3, BW, BW (w), Visit to the Planet of Terror	2.00	0.45	1.13	2.25
❑4, BW, BW (w), Spacehawk: Superhuman Enemy of Crime; Spacehawk: Lone Wolf of the Void	2.25	0.45	1.13	2.25
❑5, Jan 93, BW, BW (w)	2.50	0.50	1.25	2.50

SPACE HUSTLERS
SLAVE LABOR

Value: Cover or less

- ❑1, Mar 97, Sewercide, b&w 2.95

SPACE JAM
DC

Value: Cover or less

- ❑1, nn; movie Adaptation; prestige format 5.95

SPACEKNIGHTS
MARVEL
Value: Cover or less

- ❑1, Oct 00, JSn (w), Ebon Tidings 2.99
- ❑2, Nov 00, JSn (w), Dishonor! 2.99
- ❑3, Dec 00, JSn (w), Redemption! 2.99
- ❑4, Jan 01, JSn (w), ... Retreat and Regroup! 2.99
- ❑5, Feb 01, JSn (w), War! 2.99

SPACEMAN
DELL

	ORIG	GOOD	FINE	N-MINT
❑2	0.12	7.00	17.50	35.00
❑3	0.12	5.60	14.00	28.00
❑4, Our Solar System: Venus; Space Man	0.12	4.40	11.00	22.00
❑5, Our Solar System: Jupiter; Space Man	0.12	4.40	11.00	22.00
❑6	0.12	4.40	11.00	22.00
❑7, Space Man: Space Battle; The Time Niche (text)	0.12	4.00	10.00	20.00
❑8, The Moon; Space Man: The Soulless One	0.12	4.00	10.00	20.00
❑9, Reprints Space Man #1	—	1.00	2.50	5.00
❑10, Reprints Space Man #2	—	1.00	2.50	5.00

SPACE PATROL (ADVENTURE)
ADVENTURE
Value: Cover or less

- ❑1 2.50
- ❑2, b&w 2.50
- ❑3 2.50

SPACE SLUTZ
COMIC ZONE
Value: Cover or less

- ❑1, b&w; adult 3.95

SPACE TIME SHUFFLE A TRILOGY
ALPHA PRODUCTIONS
Value: Cover or less

- ❑1, b&w 1.95
- ❑2, b&w 1.95

SPACE TRIP TO THE MOON
AVALON
Value: Cover or less

- ❑1, b&w; adapts Destination: Moon 2.95

SPACE USAGI
MIRAGE

	ORIG	GOOD	FINE	N-MINT
❑1, Jun 92, b&w	2.00	0.60	1.50	3.00
❑2, Jul 92, b&w	2.00	0.60	1.50	3.00
❑3, Aug 92, b&w	2.00	0.60	1.50	3.00

SPACE USAGI (VOL. 2)
MIRAGE

	ORIG	GOOD	FINE	N-MINT
❑1, Nov 93, White Star Rising, Part 1	2.75	0.60	1.50	3.00
❑2, Jan 94, White Star Rising, Part 2	2.75	0.60	1.50	3.00
❑3, Mar 94, White Star Rising, Part 3	2.75	0.60	1.50	3.00

SPACE USAGI (VOL. 3)
DARK HORSE
Value: Cover or less

- ❑1, Jan 96, Warrior, Part 1, b&w 2.95
- ❑2, Feb 96, Warrior, Part 2, b&w 2.95
- ❑3, Mar 96, Warrior, Part 3, b&w 2.95

SPACE WAR
CHARLTON

	ORIG	GOOD	FINE	N-MINT
❑1	0.10	17.00	42.50	85.00
❑2	0.10	10.00	25.00	50.00
❑3	0.10	10.00	25.00	50.00
❑4, SD	0.10	18.00	45.00	90.00
❑5, SD	0.10	18.00	45.00	90.00
❑6, SD	0.10	18.00	45.00	90.00
❑7	0.10	5.60	14.00	28.00
❑8, SD	0.10	18.00	45.00	90.00
❑9	—	5.60	14.00	28.00
❑10, SD	—	18.00	45.00	90.00
❑11	—	5.60	14.00	28.00
❑12	—	5.60	14.00	28.00
❑13, The Snail From Uranus; Earth's Deadly Weapon	—	5.60	14.00	28.00
❑14	—	5.60	14.00	28.00
❑15	—	5.60	14.00	28.00
❑16, Rescue in Space; The Greatest Adventure	0.12	3.00	7.50	15.00
❑17	0.12	3.00	7.50	15.00
❑18, The Great Powers of Space; The Peacemakers	0.12	3.00	7.50	15.00
❑19, The Long Orbit!; The Imitators	0.12	3.00	7.50	15.00
❑20, Underworld; The Beginning	0.12	3.00	7.50	15.00
❑21, An Ugly World; Easy Victory	0.12	3.00	7.50	15.00
❑22, The Raiders; The Mercenaries	0.12	3.00	7.50	15.00
❑23, The War Mongers; The End of Time	0.12	3.00	7.50	15.00
❑24, The Emerald Moon; Assault Force	0.12	3.00	7.50	15.00
❑25, Action At Station 4!; Darken The Sun	0.12	3.00	7.50	15.00
❑26	—	3.00	7.50	15.00
❑27, Series continued in Fightin' 5 #28	—	3.00	7.50	15.00
❑28, Series begins again (1978)	—	0.70	1.75	3.50
❑29	—	0.70	1.75	3.50
❑30, Lifelong Companion; The Anywhere Machine	0.35	0.70	1.75	3.50
❑31	—	0.70	1.75	3.50
❑32	—	0.70	1.75	3.50

Stan Sakai's rabbit ronin headed into orbit for three *Space Usagi* series.

SPACE WAR CLASSICS
AVALON
Value: Cover or less

- ❑1, b&w 2.95

SPACE WOLF
ANTARCTIC
Value: Cover or less

- ❑1, b&w 2.50
- ❑2, b&w 2.50

SPAM
ALPHA PRODUCTIONS
Value: Cover or less

- ❑1, b&w 1.50
- ❑2, b&w 1.50

SPANDEX TIGHTS
LOST CAUSE

	ORIG	GOOD	FINE	N-MINT
❑1, Sep 94, Couched Terms, b&w	1.95	0.50	1.25	2.50
❑2, Nov 94, b&w	2.25	0.45	1.13	2.25
❑3, b&w	2.25	0.45	1.13	2.25
❑4, Mar 95, b&w	2.25	0.45	1.13	2.25
❑5, May 95, b&w	2.25	0.45	1.13	2.25
❑6, Jul 95, V: Mighty Awful Sour Rangers, b&w; false cover for Mighty Awful Sour Rangers #1	2.50	0.50	1.25	2.50

SPANDEX TIGHTS (VOL. 2)
LOST CAUSE
Value: Cover or less

- ❑1, Jan 97, b&w 2.95
- ❑2, Mar 97, The Strange Secret of Huggy Love, b&w 2.95
- ❑3, May 97, Space Opera, Part 1, b&w 2.95

SPANISH FLY
EROS
Value: Cover or less

- ❑1 2.95
- ❑2 2.95
- ❑3 2.95
- ❑4 2.95
- ❑5, May 96, Ursula 2.95

SPANK
FANTAGRAPHICS
Value: Cover or less

- ❑2, b&w; adult 2.25
- ❑3, b&w; adult 2.25
- ❑4, b&w; adult 2.25

SPANK THE MONKEY
ARROW
Value: Cover or less

- ❑1, Jul 99, b&w 2.95

SPANNER'S GALAXY
DC
Value: Cover or less

- ❑1, Dec 84, Castling, mini-series 2.00
- ❑2, Jan 85 1.00
- ❑3, Feb 85 1.00
- ❑4, Mar 85 1.00
- ❑5, Apr 85 1.00
- ❑6, May 85 1.00

SPARKPLUG
HEROIC
Value: Cover or less

- ❑1, Once Upon A Time In Deutschland, b&w 2.95
- ❑2, b&w; trading card 3.95
- ❑3 2.95

SPARKY & TIM
AARON WARNER
Value: Cover or less

- ❑1, Feb 99 5.95

SPARROW (MILLENNIUM)
MILLENNIUM
Value: Cover or less

- ❑1, Where Demons Dwell, b&w 2.95
- ❑2, Apr 95, b&w 2.95
- ❑3, May 95, b&w 2.95
- ❑4, Jul 95, b&w 2.95

SPARTAN: WARRIOR SPIRIT
IMAGE
Value: Cover or less

- ❑1, Jul 95, KB (w) 2.50
- ❑2, Sep 95, KB (w) 2.50
- ❑3, Oct 95, KB (w) 2.50
- ❑4, Nov 95, KB (w) 2.50

SPARTAN X: HELL-BENT-HERO-FOR-HIRE (JACKIE CHAN'S...)
IMAGE
Value: Cover or less

- ❑1, Mar 98, MG, MG (w), The Armor of Heaven, Part 1 2.95
- ❑2, Apr 98, MG, MG (w), The Armor of Heaven, Part 2 2.95

❑3, May 98, MG, MG (w), The Armor of Heaven, Part 3, cover says Jun, indicia says May . 2.95

❑4, Jul 98, MG, MG (w), The Armor of Heaven, Part 4, cover says Aug, indicia says Jul........... 2.95

SPARTAN X: THE ARMOUR OF HEAVEN (JACKIE CHAN'S...)

TOPPS

Value: Cover or less

❑1, May 97............................. 2.95

SPASM (PARODY PRESS)

PARODY PRESS

Value: Cover or less

❑1... 9.95

SPASM (ROUGH COPY)

ROUGH COPY

Value: Cover or less

❑1.. 2.95

❑2.. 2.95

❑3.. 2.95

❑4.. 2.95

❑5, Meet Oomori: Full Time Student/Part Time Assassin; Ode to a Grecian Formula 2.95

SPAWN

IMAGE

	ORIG	GOOD	FINE	N-MINT
❑1, May 92, TMc, TMc (w), Questions, 1: Spawn	1.95	1.80	4.50	9.00
❑1/A, Sep 97, TMc, b&w; promo with Spawn #65	1.95	0.39	0.98	1.95
❑2, Jul 92, TMc, TMc (w), 1: Violator, cover says Jun, indicia says Jul	1.95	1.20	3.00	6.00
❑3, Aug 92, TMc, TMc (w)	1.95	1.00	2.50	5.00
❑4, Sep 92, TMc, TMc (w), coupon for Image Comics #0; with coupon	1.95	1.00	2.50	5.00
❑5, Oct 92, TMc, TMc (w)	1.95	0.80	2.00	4.00
❑6, Nov 92, TMc, TMc (w), Payback, Part 1, 1: Overt-Kill	1.95	0.60	1.50	3.00
❑7, Jan 93, TMc, TMc (w), Payback, Part 2	1.95	0.60	1.50	3.00
❑8, Mar 93, TMc, AMo (w), In Heaven, cover says Feb, indicia says Mar; poster	1.95	0.60	1.50	3.00
❑9, Mar 93, TMc, NG (w), Angela, 1: Angela, poster	1.95	0.80	2.00	4.00
❑10, May 93, TMc, Crossing Over, A: Cerebus	1.95	0.65	1.63	3.25
❑11, Jun 93, TMc, FM (w), Home	1.95	0.60	1.50	3.00
❑12, Jul 93, TMc, TMc (w), Flashback	1.95	0.60	1.50	3.00
❑13, Aug 93, TMc, TMc (w), Spawn vs. Chapel	1.95	0.60	1.50	3.00
❑14, Sep 93, TMc, TMc (w), Myths, Part 1, A: Violator	1.95	0.60	1.50	3.00
❑15, Nov 93, TMc, TMc (w)	1.95	0.60	1.50	3.00
❑16, Dec 93, TMc, Reflections, Part 1, 1: Anti-Spawn	1.95	0.60	1.50	3.00
❑17, Jan 94, TMc, Reflections, Part 2, 1: Anti-Spawn, Spawn vs. Anti-Spawn	1.95	0.50	1.25	2.50
❑18, Feb 94, TMc, Reflections, Part 3	1.95	0.50	1.25	2.50
❑19, Oct 94, TMc, Published out of sequence with fill-in art	1.95	0.40	1.00	2.00
❑20, Nov 94, TMc, Published out of sequence with fill-in art	1.95	0.40	1.00	2.00
❑21, May 94, TMc	1.95	0.50	1.25	2.50
❑22, Jun 94, TMc	1.95	0.45	1.13	2.25
❑23, Aug 94, TMc	1.95	0.45	1.13	2.25
❑24, Sep 94, TMc	1.95	0.45	1.13	2.25
❑25, Oct 94, TMc	1.95	0.45	1.13	2.25
❑26, Dec 94, TMc	1.95	0.45	1.13	2.25
❑27, Jan 95, TMc	1.95	0.45	1.13	2.25
❑28, Feb 95, TMc	1.95	0.45	1.13	2.25
❑29, Mar 95, TMc	1.95	0.45	1.13	2.25
❑30, Apr 95, TMc	1.95	0.45	1.13	2.25
❑31, May 95, TMc, TMc (w), The Homecoming	1.95	0.45	1.13	2.25
❑32, Jun 95, TMc, TMc (w), Appearances	1.95	0.45	1.13	2.25
❑33, Jul 95, TMc, TMc (w), Shadows, Part 1	1.95	0.45	1.13	2.25
❑34, Aug 95, TMc, TMc (w), Shadows, Part 2	1.95	0.45	1.13	2.25
❑35, Sep 95, TMc, TMc (w)	1.95	0.45	1.13	2.25
❑36, Oct 95, TMc, TMc (w)	1.95	0.45	1.13	2.25
❑37, Nov 95, TMc, TMc (w)	1.95	0.45	1.13	2.25
❑38, Dec 95, TMc, TMc (w), 1: Cy-Gor, cover says Aug, indicia says Dec	1.95	0.45	1.13	2.25
❑39, Dec 95, TMc, TMc (w), Noel, Christmas story	1.95	0.45	1.13	2.25
❑40, Jan 96, TMc (w), Fugitives, Part 1	1.95	0.45	1.13	2.25
❑41, Jan 96, TMc (w), Fugitives, Part 2	1.95	0.40	1.00	2.00
❑42, Feb 96, TMc (w), Fanboy	1.95	0.40	1.00	2.00
❑43, Feb 96, TMc (w)	1.95	0.40	1.00	2.00
❑44, Mar 96, TMc (w)	1.95	0.40	1.00	2.00
❑45, Mar 96, TMc (w)	1.95	0.40	1.00	2.00
❑46, Apr 96, TMc (w)	1.95	0.40	1.00	2.00
❑47, Apr 96, TMc (w)	1.95	0.40	1.00	2.00
❑48, May 96, TMc (w)	1.95	0.40	1.00	2.00
❑49, May 96, TMc (w)	1.95	0.40	1.00	2.00
❑50, Jun 96, TMc (w)	3.95	0.59	1.48	2.95
❑51, Aug 96, TMc (w), cover says Jul, indicia says Aug	1.95	0.39	0.98	1.95
❑52, Aug 96, TMc (w)	1.95	0.39	0.98	1.95
❑53, Sep 96, TMc (w)	1.95	0.39	0.98	1.95
❑54, Oct 96, TMc (w)	1.95	0.39	0.98	1.95
❑55, Nov 96, TMc (w), Sabotage	1.95	0.39	0.98	1.95
❑56, Dec 96, TMc (w), Kahn	1.95	0.39	0.98	1.95
❑57, Jan 97, TMc (w), The Beast	1.95	0.39	0.98	1.95
❑58, Feb 97, TMc (w)	1.95	0.39	0.98	1.95
❑59, Mar 97, TMc (w)	1.95	0.39	0.98	1.95
❑60, Apr 97, TMc (w)	1.95	0.39	0.98	1.95
❑61, May 97, TMc (w)	1.95	0.39	0.98	1.95
❑62, Jun 97, TMc (w), A: Angela	1.95	0.39	0.98	1.95
❑63, Jul 97, TMc (w)	1.95	0.39	0.98	1.95
❑64, Aug 97, TMc (w), polybagged with McFarlane Toys catalog	1.95	0.39	0.98	1.95
❑65, Sep 97, TMc (w), The Past, Photo cover	1.95	0.39	0.98	1.95
❑66, Oct 97, TMc (w), Demons	1.95	0.39	0.98	1.95
❑67, Nov 97, TMc (w), Homeland	1.95	0.39	0.98	1.95
❑68, Jan 98, TMc (w), Intersection	1.95	0.39	0.98	1.95
❑69, Jan 98, TMc (w), Freaky	1.95	0.39	0.98	1.95
❑70, Feb 98, TMc (w), Darkness	1.95	0.39	0.98	1.95
❑71, Apr 98, TMc (w), Apparitions	1.95	0.39	0.98	1.95
❑72, May 98, TMc (w), Bloodless	1.95	0.39	0.98	1.95
❑73, Jun 98, TMc (w), The Heap	1.95	0.39	0.98	1.95
❑74, Jul 98, TMc (w), The Void	1.95	0.39	0.98	1.95
❑75, Aug 98, TMc (w), Sacred Ground	1.95	0.39	0.98	1.95
❑76, Sep 98, TMc (w), Farewell Dance	1.95	0.39	0.98	1.95
❑77, Oct 98, TMc (w), Relics	1.95	0.39	0.98	1.95
❑78, Nov 98	1.95	0.39	0.98	1.95
❑79, Jan 99, TMc (w)	1.95	0.39	0.98	1.95
❑80, Feb 99, TMc (w)	1.95	0.39	0.98	1.95
❑81, Mar 99, TMc (w), Devil Inside, Part 1	1.95	0.39	0.98	1.95
❑82, Apr 99, TMc (w), Devil Inside, Part 2	1.95	0.39	0.98	1.95
❑83, May 99, TMc (w), The Conqueror	1.95	0.39	0.98	1.95
❑84, Jun 99, TMc (w), The Waiting	1.95	0.39	0.98	1.95
❑85, Jul 99, TMc (w), EndGame	1.95	0.39	0.98	1.95
❑86, Aug 99, TMc (w), Abdication	1.95	0.39	0.98	1.95
❑87, Sep 99, TMc (w), Folklore	1.95	0.39	0.98	1.95
❑88, Oct 99, TMc (w), Seasons of Change.	1.95	0.39	0.98	1.95
❑89, Nov 99, TMc (w), The Devil You Know	1.95	0.39	0.98	1.95
❑90, Dec 99, TMc (w), Three Uses of the Knife	1.95	0.39	0.98	1.95
❑91, Jan 00	1.95	0.39	0.98	1.95
❑92, Feb 00	1.95	0.39	0.98	1.95
❑93, Mar 00, TMc (w), The Devil's Banquet	1.95	0.39	0.98	1.95
❑94, Apr 00, TMc (w), The Children's Hour	1.95	0.39	0.98	1.95
❑95, May 00	1.95	0.39	0.98	1.95
❑96, Jun 00	1.95	0.39	0.98	1.95
❑97, Jul 00, TMc (w), Heaven's Folly	1.95	0.39	0.98	1.95
❑98, Aug 00, TMc (w), The Trouble With Angels	2.50	0.50	1.25	2.50
❑99, Sep 00, TMc (w), The Edge of Darkness	2.50	0.50	1.25	2.50
❑100/A, Nov 00, TMc (w), Milestone, Todd McFarlane cover; Giant-size	4.95	0.99	2.47	4.95
❑100/B, Nov 00, TMc (w), Milestone, Ashley Wood cover; Giant-size	4.95	0.99	2.47	4.95
❑100/C, Nov 00, TMc (w), Milestone, Frank Miller cover; Giant-size	4.95	0.99	2.47	4.95
❑100/D, Nov 00, TMc (w), Milestone, Mike Mignola Cover; Giant-size	4.95	0.99	2.47	4.95
❑100/E, Nov 00, TMc (w), Milestone, Alex Ross cover; Giant-size	4.95	0.99	2.47	4.95
❑100/F, Nov 00, TMc (w), Milestone, Greg Capullo cover; Giant-size	4.95	0.99	2.47	4.95
❑101, Dec 00, TMc (w), Aftermath	2.50	0.50	1.25	2.50
❑102, Jan 01, TMc (w), Cautionary Tales, Part 1	2.50	0.50	1.25	2.50
❑103, Feb 01, TMc (w), Cautionary Tales, Part 2	2.50	0.50	1.25	2.50
❑104, Feb 01, TMc (w), Cautionary Tales, Part 3	2.50	0.50	1.25	2.50
❑105, Feb 01, TMc (w), Retribution Overdrive, Part 1	2.50	0.50	1.25	2.50
❑106, Mar 01, TMc (w), Retribution Overdrive, Part 2	2.50	0.50	1.25	2.50
❑107, Apr 01, TMc (w), The Kingdom, Part 1	2.50	0.50	1.25	2.50
❑108	2.50	0.50	1.25	2.50
❑109	2.50	0.50	1.25	2.50
❑110	2.50	0.50	1.25	2.50
❑111	2.50	0.50	1.25	2.50
❑112	2.50	0.50	1.25	2.50
❑Anl 1, Blood and Shadows; Blood & Shadow, squarebound	4.95	0.99	2.47	4.95
❑FAN 1, Promotional edition included in Overstreet Fan	—	0.20	0.50	1.00
❑FAN 2, Promotional edition included in Overstreet Fan	—	0.20	0.50	1.00
❑FAN 3, Oct 96, Promotional edition included in Overstreet Fan	—	0.20	0.50	1.00

SPAWN-BATMAN
IMAGE

	ORIG	GOOD	FINE	N-MINT
❑1, TMc, FM (w), nn	3.95	0.80	2.00	4.00

SPAWN BIBLE
IMAGE

Value: Cover or less

❑1, Aug 96, TMc (w), background on series ... 1.95

SPAWN BLOOD AND SALVATION
IMAGE

Value: Cover or less

❑1, Nov 99 ... 4.95

SPAWN BLOOD FEUD
IMAGE

Value: Cover or less

❑1, Jun 95, AMo (w), Part 1 ... 2.25
❑2, Jul 95, AMo (w), Part 2 ... 2.25
❑3, Aug 95, AMo (w), Part 3 ... 2.25
❑4, Sep 95, AMo (w) ... 2.25

SPAWN MOVIE ADAPTATION
IMAGE

Value: Cover or less

❑1, Dec 97, nn; movie Adaptation; prestige format ... 4.95

SPAWN: THE DARK AGES
IMAGE

	ORIG	GOOD	FINE	N-MINT
❑1, Mar 99, Devil's Knight	2.50	0.60	1.50	3.00
❑1/SC, Mar 99, Devil's Knight, Variant cover by McFarlane	2.50	0.50	1.25	2.50
❑2, Apr 99, Forsaken	2.50	0.50	1.25	2.50
❑3, May 99, Unward	2.50	0.50	1.25	2.50
❑4, Jun 99, Death and Glory	2.50	0.50	1.25	2.50
❑5, Jul 99, Crimson Shadow	2.50	0.50	1.25	2.50
❑6, Aug 99, Benediction	2.50	0.50	1.25	2.50
❑7, Sep 99, Providence	2.50	0.50	1.25	2.50
❑8, Oct 99, Acts of Contrition	2.50	0.50	1.25	2.50
❑9, Nov 99, A Merry Round of Cheer	2.50	0.50	1.25	2.50
❑10, Dec 99, A Child's Crusade, Part 1	2.50	0.50	1.25	2.50
❑11, Jan 00	2.50	0.50	1.25	2.50
❑12, Feb 00	2.50	0.50	1.25	2.50
❑13, Mar 00	2.50	0.50	1.25	2.50
❑14, Apr 00	2.50	0.50	1.25	2.50
❑15, May 00	2.50	0.50	1.25	2.50
❑16, Jun 00, Heart of the Hellspawn	2.50	0.50	1.25	2.50
❑17, Jul 00, The Circle and the Worm	2.50	0.50	1.25	2.50
❑18, Aug 00, Crucified	2.50	0.50	1.25	2.50
❑19, Sep 00, Like Any Other Man	2.50	0.50	1.25	2.50
❑20, Oct 00, Voices in the Dark	2.50	0.50	1.25	2.50
❑21, Nov 00, Sins of the Hellspawn	2.50	0.50	1.25	2.50
❑22, Jan 01, The Seeding	2.50	0.50	1.25	2.50
❑23, Feb 01, The Beast	2.50	0.50	1.25	2.50
❑24, Mar 01, Bleed, Pagan Bleed	2.50	0.50	1.25	2.50

SPAWN THE IMPALER
IMAGE

Value: Cover or less

❑1, Oct 96, MGr, MGr (w) ... 2.95
❑2, Nov 96, MGr, MGr (w) ... 2.95
❑3, Dec 96, MGr, MGr (w) ... 2.95

SPAWN THE UNDEAD
IMAGE

	ORIG	GOOD	FINE	N-MINT
❑1, Jun 99, A face in the Crowd	1.95	0.40	1.00	2.00
❑2, Jul 99, The Door to Nowhere	1.95	0.39	0.98	1.95
❑3, Aug 99, My Soul to Keep	1.95	0.39	0.98	1.95
❑4, Sep 99, Song Sung Bloo	1.95	0.39	0.98	1.95
❑5, Oct 99, The Wind that Shakes the Barley, Part 1	1.95	0.39	0.98	1.95
❑6, Nov 99, The Wind that Shakes the Barley, Part 2	1.95	0.39	0.98	1.95
❑7, Dec 99, Up the Down Stairs	1.95	0.39	0.98	1.95

SPAWN/WILDC.A.T.S
IMAGE

	ORIG	GOOD	FINE	N-MINT
❑1, Jan 96, AMo (w), Devilday, Part 1	2.50	0.60	1.50	3.00
❑2, Feb 96, AMo (w), Devilday, Part 2	2.50	0.50	1.25	2.50
❑3, Mar 96, AMo (w), Devilday, Part 3	2.50	0.50	1.25	2.50
❑4, Apr 96, AMo (w), Devilday, Part 4	2.50	0.50	1.25	2.50

SPECIAL HUGGING AND OTHER CHILDHOOD TALES
SLAVE LABOR

Value: Cover or less

❑1, Apr 89, b&w ... 1.95

SPECIAL MARVEL EDITION
MARVEL

	ORIG	GOOD	FINE	N-MINT
❑1, Jan 71, JK, SL (w), Into the Blaze of Battle!; To Kill a Thunder God!, reprints Thor stories from Journey into Mystery #117-119; Thor reprints begin	0.25	1.20	3.00	6.00
❑2, reprints Thor stories from Journey into Mystery #120-122	0.25	0.80	2.00	4.00
❑3, reprints Thor stories from Journey into Mystery #123-125	0.25	0.80	2.00	4.00
❑4, reprints Thor #126 and #127; Thor reprints end	0.25	0.80	2.00	4.00
❑5, Jul 72, Sgt. Fury reprints begin	0.20	0.60	1.50	3.00
❑6, Sep 72	0.20	0.60	1.50	3.00
❑7, Nov 72, Sgt. Fury	0.20	0.60	1.50	3.00

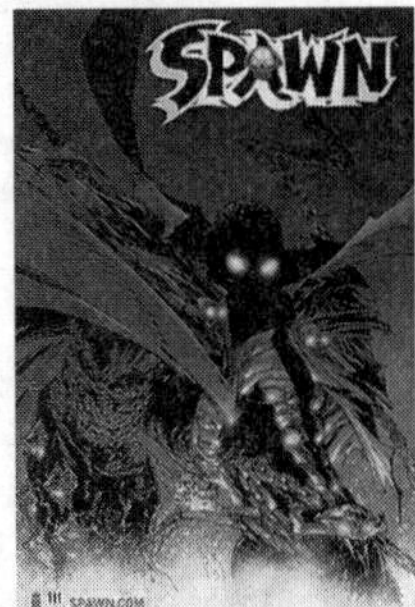

With *Savage Dragon*, Todd McFarlane's *Spawn* is one of Image's longest-running series.

	ORIG	GOOD	FINE	N-MINT
❑8	0.20	0.60	1.50	3.00
❑9	0.20	0.60	1.50	3.00
❑10	0.20	0.60	1.50	3.00
❑11, A: Captain America	0.20	0.60	1.50	3.00
❑12	0.20	0.60	1.50	3.00
❑13, Oct 73, SD, Too Small to Fight, Too Young to Die!	0.20	0.60	1.50	3.00
❑14, Sgt. Fury reprints end	0.20	0.60	1.50	3.00
❑15, Dec 73, JSn, 1: Nayland Smith; 1: Shang-Chi, Master of Kung Fu	0.20	4.00	10.00	20.00
❑16, Feb 74, JSn, 1: Midnight; 2: Shang-Chi, Master of Kung Fu, series continues as Master of Kung Fu	0.20	2.00	5.00	10.00

SPECIAL WAR SERIES
CHARLTON

	ORIG	GOOD	FINE	N-MINT
❑1	0.12	2.00	5.00	10.00
❑2	0.12	1.60	4.00	8.00
❑3, Terror in the Caves; Special Service 3X (text story), War and Attack	0.12	1.60	4.00	8.00
❑4, 1: Judomaster	0.12	3.20	8.00	16.00

SPECIES
DARK HORSE

Value: Cover or less

❑1, Jun 95, Species, movie Adaptation ... 2.50
❑2, Jul 95, movie Adaptation ... 2.50
❑3, Aug 95, movie Adaptation ... 2.50
❑4, Sep 95, movie Adaptation ... 2.50

SPECIES: HUMAN RACE
DARK HORSE

Value: Cover or less

❑1, Nov 96 ... 2.95
❑2, Dec 96 ... 2.95
❑3, Jan 97 ... 2.95
❑4, Feb 97 ... 2.95

SPECTACLES
ALTERNATIVE PRESS

Value: Cover or less

❑1, Feb 97, The Frost Chances; Land of The Early Bird, b&w ... 2.95
❑2, May 97, b&w ... 2.95
❑3, Sep 97, Deeper than your Strangest Dreams; Shell Men, b&w ... 2.95
❑4, Jan 98, b&w ... 2.95

SPECTACULAR SCARLET SPIDER
MARVEL

Value: Cover or less

❑1, Nov 95, Virtual Mortality, Part 4 ... 1.95
❑2, Dec 95, SB, Cyberwar, Part 4 ... 1.95

SPECTACULAR SPIDER-MAN, THE
MARVEL

	ORIG	GOOD	FINE	N-MINT
❑-1, Jul 97, Flashback	1.99	0.40	1.00	2.00
❑1, Dec 76, JR; SB, SL (w); JR (w), Lo, This Monster; In the Beginning, Tarantula	0.30	3.20	8.00	16.00
❑2, Jan 77, JM; JR; SB, SL (w); JR (w), The Goblin Lives, Kraven	0.30	1.20	3.00	6.00
❑3, Feb 77, SB, 1: Lightmaster	0.30	0.80	2.00	4.00
❑4, Mar 77, SB, V: Vulture	0.30	0.80	2.00	4.00
❑5, Apr 77, SB, V: Vulture	0.30	0.80	2.00	4.00
❑6, May 77, V: Morbius	0.30	0.70	1.75	3.50
❑7, Jun 77, V: Morbius	0.30	0.70	1.75	3.50
❑8, Jul 77, V: Morbius	0.30	0.70	1.75	3.50
❑9, Aug 77, A: White Tiger	0.30	0.60	1.50	3.00
❑10, Sep 77, A: White Tiger	0.30	0.60	1.50	3.00
❑11, Oct 77, SB	0.35	0.60	1.50	3.00
❑12, Nov 77, SB, A: Brother Power; 1: Razorback (partial)	0.35	0.60	1.50	3.00
❑13, Dec 77, SB, O: Razorback; 1: Razorback (full)	0.35	0.60	1.50	3.00
❑14, Jan 78, SB, V: Hatemonger	0.35	0.60	1.50	3.00
❑15, Feb 78, SB, A: Razorback	0.35	0.60	1.50	3.00
❑16, Mar 78, SB, V: Beetle	0.35	0.60	1.50	3.00
❑17, Apr 78, A: Angel; A: Iceman	0.35	0.60	1.50	3.00
❑18, May 78, A: Angel; A: Iceman	0.35	0.60	1.50	3.00
❑19, Jun 78, V: Enforcers	0.35	0.60	1.50	3.00
❑20, Jul 78, V: Light Master	0.35	0.60	1.50	3.00
❑21, Aug 78, A: Moon Knight	0.35	0.50	1.25	2.50
❑22, Sep 78, A: Moon Knight	0.35	0.50	1.25	2.50

	ORIG	GOOD	FINE	N-MINT
❑23, Oct 78, A: Moon Knight	0.35	0.50	1.25	2.50
❑24, Nov 78	0.35	0.50	1.25	2.50
❑25, Dec 78, 1: Carrion I	0.35	0.50	1.25	2.50
❑26, Jan 79, A: Daredevil	0.35	0.50	1.25	2.50
❑27, Feb 79, DC; FM, A: Daredevil, Frank Miller's first Daredevil art	0.35	1.00	2.50	5.00
❑28, Mar 79, FM, A: Daredevil	0.35	0.80	2.00	4.00
❑29, Apr 79, V: Carrion	0.35	0.50	1.25	2.50
❑30, May 79, V: Carrion	0.40	0.50	1.25	2.50
❑31, Jun 79, D: Carrion I	0.40	0.50	1.25	2.50
❑32, Jul 79	0.40	0.50	1.25	2.50
❑33, Aug 79, O: Iguana	0.40	0.50	1.25	2.50
❑34, Sep 79, V: Lizard	0.40	0.50	1.25	2.50
❑35, Oct 79	0.40	0.50	1.25	2.50
❑36, Nov 79, V: Swarm	0.40	0.50	1.25	2.50
❑37, Dec 79, V: Swarm	0.40	0.50	1.25	2.50
❑38, Jan 80, V: Morbius	0.40	0.50	1.25	2.50
❑39, Feb 80, V: Schizoid Man	0.40	0.50	1.25	2.50
❑40, Mar 80, V: Lizard	0.40	0.50	1.25	2.50
❑41, Apr 80, V: Meteor Man	0.40	0.50	1.25	2.50
❑42, May 80, A: Human Torch	0.40	0.50	1.25	2.50
❑43, Jun 80, 1: Belladonna	0.40	0.50	1.25	2.50
❑44, Jul 80	0.40	0.50	1.25	2.50
❑45, Aug 80, Vulture	0.40	0.50	1.25	2.50
❑46, Sep 80, FM (c), Cobra	0.50	0.50	1.25	2.50
❑47, Oct 80	0.50	0.50	1.25	2.50
❑48, Nov 80, Double Defeat!	0.50	0.50	1.25	2.50
❑49, Dec 80, A: Prowler, Title changes to Peter Parker, The Spectacular Spider-Man	0.50	0.50	1.25	2.50
❑50, Jan 81, JM; JR2, Smuggler	0.50	0.50	1.25	2.50
❑51, Feb 81, FM (c), V: Mysterio	0.50	0.50	1.25	2.50
❑52, Mar 81, FM (c), A: White Tiger	0.50	0.50	1.25	2.50
❑53, Apr 81, FS; JM, V: Tinkerer	0.50	0.50	1.25	2.50
❑54, May 81, FM (c)	0.50	0.50	1.25	2.50
❑55, Jun 81, V: Nitro	0.50	0.50	1.25	2.50
❑56, Jul 81, FM (c), V: Jack O'Lantern II	0.50	0.80	2.00	4.00
❑57, Aug 81	0.50	0.50	1.25	2.50
❑58, Sep 81, JBy, Ring Out The Old, Ring In The New, V: Ringer	0.50	0.50	1.25	2.50
❑59, Oct 81, JM	0.50	0.50	1.25	2.50
❑60, Nov 81, JM (c); FM (c), O: Spider-Man; V: Beetle, Giant-size	0.75	0.50	1.25	2.50
❑61, Dec 81, By The Light Of The Silvery Moonstone...!, A: Moonstone	0.50	0.50	1.25	2.50
❑62, Jan 82, V: Gold Bug	0.60	0.50	1.25	2.50
❑63, Feb 82, V: Molten Man	0.60	0.50	1.25	2.50
❑64, Mar 82, 1: Cloak & Dagger	0.60	0.90	2.25	4.50
❑65, Apr 82, V: Kraven	0.60	0.40	1.00	2.00
❑66, May 82, V: Electro	0.60	0.40	1.00	2.00
❑67, Jun 82, V: Kingpin	0.60	0.40	1.00	2.00
❑68, Jul 82, V: Robot Master	0.60	0.40	1.00	2.00
❑69, Aug 82, A: Cloak & Dagger	0.60	0.40	1.00	2.00
❑70, Sep 82, A: Cloak & Dagger	0.60	0.40	1.00	2.00
❑71, Oct 82, Gun control story	0.60	0.40	1.00	2.00
❑72, Nov 82, V: Doctor Octopus	0.60	0.40	1.00	2.00
❑73, Dec 82, V: Owl	0.60	0.40	1.00	2.00
❑74, Jan 83, BH, Fantasia!, A: Black Cat	0.60	0.40	1.00	2.00
❑75, Feb 83, A: Black Cat, Giant-size	1.00	0.50	1.25	2.50
❑76, Mar 83, A: Black Cat	0.60	0.40	1.00	2.00
❑77, Apr 83, A: Gladiator	0.60	0.40	1.00	2.00
❑78, May 83, V: Doctor Octopus	0.60	0.40	1.00	2.00
❑79, Jun 83, V: Doctor Octopus	0.60	0.40	1.00	2.00
❑80, Jul 83, J. Jonah Jameson solo story	0.60	0.40	1.00	2.00
❑81, Aug 83, JM; AM, Stalkers In The Shadows, A: Cloak & Dagger; A: Punisher	0.60	0.40	1.00	2.00
❑82, Sep 83, A: Cloak & Dagger; A: Punisher	0.60	0.50	1.25	2.50
❑83, Oct 83, A: Punisher	0.60	0.60	1.50	3.00
❑84, Nov 83	0.60	0.40	1.00	2.00
❑85, Dec 83, A: Hobgoblin (Ned Leeds); V: Hobgoblin	0.60	0.80	2.00	4.00
❑86, Jan 84, A: Fred Hembeck, Asst. Editor Month	0.60	0.40	1.00	2.00
❑87, Feb 84, AM, Mistaken Identities, reveals identity	0.60	0.40	1.00	2.00
❑88, Mar 84, A: Black Cat; V: Cobra; V: Mr. Hyde	0.60	0.40	1.00	2.00
❑89, Apr 84, A: Kingpin; A: Fantastic Four, Fantastic Four apperance	0.60	0.40	1.00	2.00
❑90, May 84, AM, new costume; Black Cat's new powers	0.60	0.40	1.00	2.00
❑91, Jun 84, V: Blob	0.60	0.40	1.00	2.00
❑92, Jul 84, 1: The Answer; V: Answer	0.60	0.40	1.00	2.00
❑93, Aug 84, V: Answer	0.60	0.40	1.00	2.00
❑94, Sep 84, V: Silvermane; A: Cloak & Dagger	0.60	0.40	1.00	2.00
❑95, Oct 84, V: Silvermane; A: Cloak & Dagger	0.60	0.40	1.00	2.00
❑96, Nov 84, V: Silvermane; A: Cloak & Dagger	0.60	0.40	1.00	2.00
❑97, Dec 84, V: Hermit	0.60	0.40	1.00	2.00
❑98, Jan 85, 1: Spot; V: Kingpin	0.60	0.40	1.00	2.00
❑99, Feb 85, V: Spot	0.60	0.40	1.00	2.00
❑100, Mar 85, V: Spot, 100th anniversary issue; Giant-size	1.00	0.80	2.00	4.00
❑101, Apr 85, V: Blacklash	0.65	0.40	1.00	2.00
❑102, May 85, V: Killer Shrike	0.65	0.40	1.00	2.00
❑103, Jun 85	0.65	0.40	1.00	2.00
❑104, Jul 85, V: Rocket Racer	0.65	0.40	1.00	2.00
❑105, Aug 85, A: Wasp	0.65	0.40	1.00	2.00
❑106, Sep 85, A: Wasp	0.65	0.40	1.00	2.00
❑107, Oct 85, D: Jean DeWolff	0.65	0.40	1.00	2.00
❑108, Nov 85	0.65	0.40	1.00	2.00
❑109, Dec 85	0.65	0.40	1.00	2.00
❑110, Jan 86, A: Daredevil	0.65	0.40	1.00	2.00
❑111, Feb 86, Secret Wars II, Secret Wars II	0.75	0.40	1.00	2.00
❑112, Mar 86, Christmas story	0.75	0.40	1.00	2.00
❑113, Apr 86	0.75	0.40	1.00	2.00
❑114, May 86	0.75	0.40	1.00	2.00
❑115, Jun 86, A: Doctor Strange	0.75	0.40	1.00	2.00
❑116, Jul 86, A: Sabretooth	0.75	0.60	1.50	3.00
❑117, Aug 86, A: Doctor Strange	0.75	0.40	1.00	2.00
❑118, Sep 86	0.75	0.40	1.00	2.00
❑119, Oct 86, A: Sabretooth	0.75	0.60	1.50	3.00
❑120, Nov 86	0.75	0.40	1.00	2.00
❑121, Dec 86	0.75	0.40	1.00	2.00
❑122, Jan 87	0.75	0.40	1.00	2.00
❑123, Feb 87, PD (w), With Friends Like These, V: Blaze	0.75	0.40	1.00	2.00
❑124, Mar 87, V: Doctor Octopus	0.75	0.40	1.00	2.00
❑125, Apr 87, A: Spider Woman	0.75	0.40	1.00	2.00
❑126, May 87, A: Spider Woman	0.75	0.40	1.00	2.00
❑127, Jun 87, Among Us Lurks...A Lizard!, V: Lizard	0.75	0.40	1.00	2.00
❑128, Jul 87, A: Silver Sable	0.75	0.40	1.00	2.00
❑129, Aug 87, V: Foreigner	0.75	0.40	1.00	2.00
❑130, Sep 87, V: Hobgoblin	0.75	0.60	1.50	3.00
❑131, Oct 87, MZ, Kraven's Last Hunt, Part 3, Kraven	0.75	1.00	2.50	5.00
❑132, Nov 87, Kraven's Last Hunt, Part 6, Kraven	0.75	0.80	2.00	4.00
❑133, Dec 87, BSz	0.75	0.60	1.50	3.00
❑134, Jan 88, V: Sin Eater	0.75	0.40	1.00	2.00
❑135, Feb 88, V: Electro; V: Sin Eater, Title returns to The Spectacular Spider-Man	0.75	0.40	1.00	2.00
❑136, Mar 88, V: Sin Eater	0.75	0.40	1.00	2.00
❑137, Apr 88, V: Tarantula	0.75	0.40	1.00	2.00
❑138, May 88, V: Tarantula; A: Captain America	1.00	0.40	1.00	2.00
❑139, Jun 88, O: Tombstone	1.00	0.60	1.50	3.00
❑140, Jul 88, A: Punisher	1.00	0.40	1.00	2.00
❑141, Aug 88, A: Punisher	1.00	0.40	1.00	2.00
❑142, Sep 88, A: Punisher	1.00	0.40	1.00	2.00
❑143, Oct 88, A: Punisher	1.00	0.40	1.00	2.00
❑144, Nov 88, V: Boomerang, in San Diego	1.00	0.40	1.00	2.00
❑145, Dec 88	1.00	0.40	1.00	2.00
❑146, Jan 89, SB, Inferno, Inferno	1.00	0.40	1.00	2.00
❑147, Feb 89, 1: Hobgoblin III, Inferno	1.00	2.00	5.00	10.00
❑148, Mar 89, Inferno	1.00	0.40	1.00	2.00
❑149, Apr 89, 1: Carrion II (Malcolm McBride)	1.00	0.60	1.50	3.00
❑150, May 89, V: Tombstone	1.00	0.40	1.00	2.00
❑151, Jun 89, V: Tombstone	1.00	0.40	1.00	2.00
❑152, Jul 89, SB, A Wolf's Tale..., V: Lobo Brothers	1.00	0.40	1.00	2.00
❑153, Aug 89, V: Tombstone	1.00	0.40	1.00	2.00
❑154, Sep 89, V: Puma	1.00	0.40	1.00	2.00
❑155, Oct 89, V: Tombstone	1.00	0.40	1.00	2.00
❑156, Nov 89, V: Banjo	1.00	0.40	1.00	2.00
❑157, Nov 89, V: Electro	1.00	0.40	1.00	2.00
❑158, Dec 89, Acts of Vengeance, V: Trapster, Acts of Vengeance; Spider-Man gets cosmic powers	1.00	1.000	2.50	5.00
❑159, Dec 89, Acts of Vengeance, V: Brothers Grimm, Acts of Vengeance; Cosmic-powered Spider-Man	1.00	0.80	2.00	4.00
❑160, Jan 90, Acts of Vengeance, V: Doctor Doom, Acts of Vengeance; Cosmic-powered Spider-Man	1.00	0.30	0.75	1.50
❑161, Feb 90, V: Hobgoblin III	1.00	0.30	0.75	1.50
❑162, Mar 90, V: Carrion; A: Hobgoblin III	1.00	0.30	0.75	1.50
❑163, Apr 90, V: Carrion; V: Hobgoblin III	1.00	0.30	0.75	1.50
❑164, May 90, V: Beetle	1.00	0.30	0.75	1.50
❑165, Jun 90, D: Arranger	1.00	0.30	0.75	1.50
❑166, Jul 90, SB, The Deadly Lads From Liverpool	1.00	0.30	0.75	1.50
❑167, Aug 90, SB, A Misty Kind Of Memory	1.00	0.30	0.75	1.50

	ORIG	GOOD	FINE	N-MINT
❑168, Sep 90, Avengers	1.00	0.30	0.75	1.50
❑169, Oct 90, Avengers	1.00	0.30	0.75	1.50
❑170, Nov 90, Avengers	1.00	0.30	0.75	1.50
❑171, Dec 90, SB, Ordeal, Part 1, V: Puma	1.00	0.30	0.75	1.50
❑172, Jan 91, V: Puma	1.00	0.30	0.75	1.50
❑173, Feb 91, SB, Creatures Stirring, Doctor Octopus	1.00	0.30	0.75	1.50
❑174, Mar 91, SB, Dedication (Or Jonah Goes TO Pieces!, Doctor Octopus	1.00	0.30	0.75	1.50
❑175, Apr 91, SB, Spouse Trap, Doctor Octopus	1.00	0.30	0.75	1.50
❑176, May 91, SB, KB (w), The Love Of Power, 1: Corona	1.00	0.30	0.75	1.50
❑177, Jun 91, SB, KB (w), Fever Pitch	1.00	0.30	0.75	1.50
❑178, Jul 91, SB, The Child Within, Part 1, V: Vermin	1.00	0.30	0.75	1.50
❑179, Aug 91, SB, The Child Within, Part 2, V: Vermin	1.00	0.30	0.75	1.50
❑180, Sep 91, SB, The Child Within, Part 3, V: Green Goblin	1.00	0.30	0.75	1.50
❑181, Oct 91, SB, The Child Within, Part 4, V: Green Goblin	1.00	0.30	0.75	1.50
❑182, Nov 91, SB, The Child Within, Part 5, O: Vermin; V: Green Goblin	1.00	0.30	0.75	1.50
❑183, Dec 91, SB, The Child Within, Part 6, V: Green Goblin	1.00	0.30	0.75	1.50
❑184, Jan 92, SB, A: Green Goblin	1.00	0.30	0.75	1.50
❑185, Feb 92, SB, A: Frogman	1.25	0.30	0.75	1.50
❑186, Mar 92, SB, Funeral Arrangements, Part 1, V: Vulture	1.25	0.30	0.75	1.50
❑187, Apr 92, SB, Funeral Arrangements, Part 2, V: Vulture	1.25	0.30	0.75	1.50
❑188, May 92, SB, Funeral Arrangements, Part 3, V: Vulture	1.25	0.30	0.75	1.50
❑189, Jun 92, SB, The Osborn Legacy, O: Spider-Man, Hologram cover; Double-size; 30th Anniversary Issue; Gatefold painted poster	2.95	0.80	2.00	4.00
❑189-2, Jun 92, SB, 2nd Printing; Hologram cover	2.95	0.60	1.50	3.00
❑190, Jul 92, SB, The Horns Of A Dilemma	1.25	0.30	0.75	1.50
❑191, Aug 92, SB, Eye of the Puma, Part 1	1.25	0.30	0.75	1.50
❑192, Sep 92, SB, Eye of the Puma, Part 2	1.25	0.30	0.75	1.50
❑193, Oct 92, SB, Eye of the Puma, Part 3, V: Puma	1.25	0.30	0.75	1.50
❑194, Nov 92, SB, Death of Vermin, Part 1, V: Vermin	1.25	0.30	0.75	1.50
❑195, Dec 92, SB, Death of Vermin, Part 2, V: Vermin	1.25	0.30	0.75	1.50
❑195/CS, SB, Death of Vermin, Part 2, Polybagged with Dirt Magazine #2, cassette sampler tape; "Dirtbag Special"	2.50	0.50	1.25	2.50
❑196, Jan 93, SB, Death of Vermin, Part 3, D: Vermin	1.25	0.30	0.75	1.50
❑197, Feb 93, SB, Power Play!	1.25	0.30	0.75	1.50
❑198, Mar 93, SB, A: X-Men	1.25	0.30	0.75	1.50
❑199, Apr 93, SB, Falling!, A: X-Men	1.25	0.30	0.75	1.50
❑200, May 93, SB, Best Of Enemies, D: Green Goblin, foil cover	2.95	0.60	1.50	3.00
❑201, Jun 93, SB, Maximum Carnage, Part 5, A: Venom; A: Carnage	1.25	0.30	0.75	1.50
❑202, Jul 93, SB, Maximum Carnage, Part 9, A: Venom; A: Carnage	1.25	0.30	0.75	1.50
❑203, Aug 93, SB, Maximum Carnage, Part 15; Maximum Carnage, Part 13, A: Venom; A: Carnage	1.25	0.30	0.75	1.50
❑204, Sep 93, SB, Death by Tombstone, Part 1, V: Tombstone	1.25	0.30	0.75	1.50
❑205, Oct 93, SB, Death by Tombstone, Part 2, V: Tombstone	1.25	0.30	0.75	1.50
❑206, Nov 93, V: Tombstone	1.25	0.30	0.75	1.50
❑207, Dec 93, V: Shroud	1.25	0.30	0.75	1.50
❑208, Jan 94, SB, V: Shroud	1.25	0.30	0.75	1.50
❑209, Feb 94, SB, V: Foreigner	1.25	0.30	0.75	1.50
❑210, Mar 94, SB, V: Foreigner	1.25	0.30	0.75	1.50
❑211, Apr 94, Pursuit, Part 2	1.25	0.30	0.75	1.50
❑212, May 94	1.25	0.30	0.75	1.50
❑213, Jun 94, Hail Mary, Part 1, V: Typhoid Mary	1.50	0.30	0.75	1.50
❑213/CS, Jun 94, Hail Mary, Part 1, V: Typhoid Mary, TV preview; print	2.95	0.59	1.48	2.95
❑214, Jul 94, V: Bloody Mary	1.50	0.30	0.75	1.50
❑215, Aug 94	1.50	0.30	0.75	1.50
❑216, Sep 94, V: Scorpion	1.50	0.30	0.75	1.50
❑217, Oct 94, Power & Responsibility; Power and Responsibility, Part 4, A: Ben Reilly	2.95	0.30	0.75	1.50
❑217/SC, Oct 94, Power and Responsibility, Part 4; The Double, Part 4, A: Ben Reilly, enhanced cover; Giant-size; flip-book with back-up story	2.95	0.59	1.48	2.95
❑218, Nov 94, Back from the Edge, Part 2, V: Puma	1.50	0.30	0.75	1.50

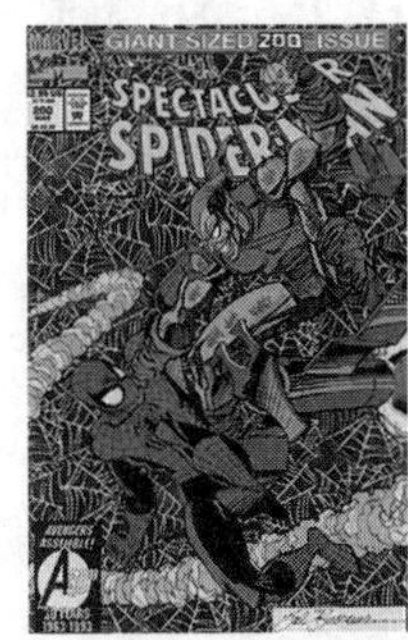

The second Green Goblin, Harry Osborn, met his end in *Spectacular Spider-Man* #200.

© 1993 Marvel Comics

	ORIG	GOOD	FINE	N-MINT
❑219, Dec 94, Back from the Edge, Part 4	1.50	0.30	0.75	1.50
❑220, Jan 95, Giant-size; flip book with illustrated story from The Ultimate Spider-Man back-up	2.25	0.50	1.25	2.50
❑221, Feb 95, Web of Death, Part 4, D: Doctor Octopus	1.50	0.60	1.50	3.00
❑222, Mar 95, The Price of Truth, Part 1	1.50	0.30	0.75	1.50
❑223, Apr 95, Giant-size	2.50	0.50	1.25	2.50
❑223/SC, Apr 95, enhanced cover; Giant-size	2.95	0.59	1.48	2.95
❑224, May 95	1.50	0.30	0.75	1.50
❑225, Jun 95, SB, Return of the Green Goblin; He was Such a Nice Boy, 1: Green Goblin IV, Giant-size	2.95	0.79	1.98	3.95
❑225/SC, Jun 95, Hologram on cover	3.95	0.79	1.98	3.95
❑226, Jul 95, The Trial of Peter Parker, Part 4, identity of clone revealed	1.50	0.30	0.75	1.50
❑227, Aug 95	1.50	0.30	0.75	1.50
❑228, Sep 95, Time Bomb, Part 1, continues in Web of Spider-Man #129	1.50	0.30	0.75	1.50
❑229, Oct 95, SB; BSz, The Greatest Responsibility, Part 3, wraparound cover; Giant-size; the clone retires	2.50	0.50	1.25	2.50
❑229/SC, Oct 95, The Greatest Responsibility, Part 3, enhanced acetate outer cover; the clone retires	3.95	0.79	1.98	3.95
❑230, Jan 96, Vengeance Is Mine-Sayeth The Sword, V: D.K., Special cover; Giant-size	1.50	0.79	1.98	3.95
❑231, Feb 96, SB, The Return of Kaine, Part 1	1.50	0.30	0.75	1.50
❑232, Mar 96, SB, A Show of Force, New Doctor Octopus returns	1.50	0.30	0.75	1.50
❑233, Apr 96, SB, Web of Carnage, Part 4	1.50	0.30	0.75	1.50
❑234, May 96, Blood Brothers, Part 4	1.50	0.30	0.75	1.50
❑235, Jun 96, return of Will o' the Wisp	1.50	0.30	0.75	1.50
❑236, Jul 96, V: Dragon-Man	1.50	0.30	0.75	1.50
❑237, Aug 96, V: Lizard	1.50	0.30	0.75	1.50
❑238, Sep 96, O: second Lizard	1.50	0.30	0.75	1.50
❑239, Oct 96, V: Lizard	1.50	0.30	0.75	1.50
❑240, Nov 96, Revelations, Part 1	1.50	0.30	0.75	1.50
❑241, Dec 96, A New Day Dawning	1.50	0.30	0.75	1.50
❑242, Jan 97, Facedancing, V: Chameleon	1.50	0.30	0.75	1.50
❑243, Feb 97, Who Am I?, V: Chameleon	1.50	0.30	0.75	1.50
❑244, Mar 97, Backlash, 1: Kangaroo II; V: Kraven	1.99	0.40	1.00	1.99
❑245, Apr 97, Kravinov's Revenge, V: Chameleon	1.99	0.40	1.00	1.99
❑246, May 97, The Legion of Losers!, V: Legion of Losers (Gibbon, Spot, Kangaroo, Grizzly)	1.99	0.40	1.00	1.99
❑247, Jun 97	1.99	0.40	1.00	1.99
❑248, Aug 97, gatefold summary	1.99	0.40	1.00	1.99
❑249, Sep 97, gatefold summary; Norman Osborn buys Daily Bugle	1.99	0.40	1.00	1.99
❑250, Oct 97, wraparound cover; gatefold summary; Giant-size	3.25	0.60	1.50	2.99
❑251, Nov 97, V: Kraven, gatefold summary	1.99	0.40	1.00	1.99
❑252, Dec 97, V: Kraven, gatefold summary	1.99	0.40	1.00	1.99
❑253, Jan 98, V: Calypso; V: Kraven, gatefold summary	1.99	0.40	1.00	1.99
❑254, Feb 98, gatefold summary	1.99	0.40	1.00	1.99
❑255, Mar 98, Spider-Hunt, Part 4, gatefold summary	2.99	0.40	1.00	1.99
❑256, Apr 98, V: White Rabbit, gatefold summary	1.99	0.40	1.00	1.99
❑257, May 98, has second cover with The Spectacular Prodigy #1; gatefold summary; Identity Crisis	1.99	0.40	1.00	1.99
❑258, Jun 98, Identity Crisis, gatefold summary	1.99	0.40	1.00	1.99
❑259, Jul 98, Goblins at the Gate, Part 1, gatefold summary	1.99	0.40	1.00	1.99
❑260, Aug 98, Goblins at the Gate, Part 2, gatefold summary	1.99	0.40	1.00	1.99
❑261, Sep 98, Goblins at the Gate, Part 3, gatefold summary	1.99	0.40	1.00	1.99

	ORIG	GOOD	FINE	N-MINT
❑262, Oct 98, The Gathering of Five, Part 4, gatefold summary	1.99	0.40	1.00	1.99
❑263, Nov 98, JBy (c), The Final Chapter, Part 3, Final Issue; gatefold summary	1.99	0.40	1.00	1.99
❑Anl 1, Dec 79, JM; RB, Doctor Octopus	0.75	1.00	2.50	5.00
❑Anl 2, Sep 80, JM, Vengeance Is Mine-Sayeth The Sword, 1: Rapier	0.75	0.80	2.00	4.00
❑Anl 3, Nov 81, Dark Side Of The Moon	0.75	0.60	1.50	3.00
❑Anl 4, Nov 84, O: Ben Parker ("Uncle Ben"), Title changes to Peter Parker, The Spectacular Spider-Man Annual	1.00	0.60	1.50	3.00
❑Anl 5, Oct 85	1.25	0.60	1.50	3.00
❑Anl 6, Oct 86, series continues as Spectacular Spider-Man Annual	1.25	0.60	1.50	3.00
❑Anl 7, V: Puma, Title returns to Spectacular Spider-Man Annual	1.25	0.60	1.50	3.00
❑Anl 8, Evolutionary War, Part 10	1.75	0.80	2.00	4.00
❑Anl 9, Atlantis attacks, Part 6, Atlantis Attacks	2.00	0.50	1.25	2.50
❑Anl 10, SL (w), Spidey's Totally Tiny Adventure, Part 2, tiny Spider-Man	2.00	0.50	1.25	2.50
❑Anl 11, FH (w), Vibranium Vendetta; The Vibranium Vendetta	2.00	0.50	1.25	2.50
❑Anl 12, Hero Killers; Hero Killers, Part 2, A: New Warriors, Venom back-up story	2.25	0.50	1.25	2.50
❑Anl 13, trading card	2.95	0.59	1.48	2.95
❑Anl 14, V: Green Goblin	2.95	0.59	1.48	2.95
❑Anl 1997, Dead Men Walking, Peter Parker Spider-Man '97	2.99	0.60	1.50	2.99
❑SE 1, Planet of the Symbiotes, Part 4, Invasion!; Growing Pains, Part 4, Party Monster, A: Venom; A: Carnage; A: The Lizard; A: Scarlet Spider, Flip-book; Super special	3.95	0.79	1.98	3.95

SPECTACULAR SPIDER-MAN (MAGAZINE)
MARVEL

	ORIG	GOOD	FINE	N-MINT
❑1, Jul 68, JR, 1: Richard Raleigh, Man Monster, b&w; magazine	0.35	7.00	17.50	35.00
❑2, Nov 68, JR, V: Green Goblin, color magazine	0.40	10.00	25.00	50.00

SPECTACULAR SPIDER-MAN SUPER SPECIAL, THE
MARVEL

Value: Cover or less

❑1, Sep 95, Planet of the Symbiotes, Part 4, Flip-book; two of the stories conclude in Web of Spider-Man Super Special #1 3.95

SPECTRE, THE (1ST SERIES)
DC

	ORIG	GOOD	FINE	N-MINT
❑1, Dec 67, GC; MA	0.12	18.00	45.00	90.00
❑2, Feb 68, NA	0.12	12.00	30.00	60.00
❑3, Apr 68, NA	0.12	12.00	30.00	60.00
❑4, Jun 68, NA	0.12	12.00	30.00	60.00
❑5, Aug 68, NA	0.12	12.00	30.00	60.00
❑6, Oct 68, MA	0.12	7.00	17.50	35.00
❑7, Dec 68, MA	0.12	7.00	17.50	35.00
❑8, Feb 69, MA	0.12	7.00	17.50	35.00
❑9, Apr 69, BWr	0.12	7.00	17.50	35.00
❑10, Jun 69	0.12	7.00	17.50	35.00

SPECTRE, THE (2ND SERIES)
DC

	ORIG	GOOD	FINE	N-MINT
❑1, Apr 87, GC, Vessels	1.00	0.60	1.50	3.00
❑2, May 87	1.00	0.50	1.25	2.50
❑3, Jun 87	1.00	0.50	1.25	2.50
❑4, Jul 87	1.00	0.50	1.25	2.50
❑5, Aug 87	1.00	0.50	1.25	2.50
❑6, Sep 87, GC, Murder Of My Mystery	1.00	0.45	1.13	2.25
❑7, Oct 87, A: Zatanna	1.00	0.45	1.13	2.25
❑8, Nov 87	1.00	0.45	1.13	2.25
❑9, Dec 87	1.25	0.45	1.13	2.25
❑10, Jan 88, Millennium	1.25	0.45	1.13	2.25
❑11, Feb 88, Millennium	1.25	0.40	1.00	2.00
❑12, Mar 88	1.25	0.40	1.00	2.00
❑13, Apr 88	1.25	0.40	1.00	2.00
❑14, May 88	1.25	0.40	1.00	2.00
❑15, Jun 88	1.25	0.40	1.00	2.00
❑16, Jul 88, Secret Weapon	1.25	0.40	1.00	2.00
❑17, Aug 88	1.25	0.35	0.88	1.75
❑18, Sep 88	1.25	0.35	0.88	1.75
❑19, Oct 88	1.25	0.35	0.88	1.75
❑20, Nov 88	1.25	0.35	0.88	1.75
❑21, Dec 88	1.25	0.30	0.75	1.50
❑22, Dec 88	1.25	0.30	0.75	1.50
❑23, Jan 89, Invasion!	1.25	0.30	0.75	1.50
❑24, Feb 89, Ghosts in the Machine, Part 1	1.25	0.30	0.75	1.50
❑25, Apr 89, Ghosts in the Machine, Part 2	1.50	0.30	0.75	1.50
❑26, May 89, Ghosts in the Machine, Part 3	1.50	0.30	0.75	1.50
❑27, Jun 89, Ghosts in the Machine, Part 4	1.50	0.30	0.75	1.50
❑28, Aug 89, Ghosts in the Machine, Part 5	1.50	0.30	0.75	1.50
❑29, Sep 89, Ghosts in the Machine, Part 6	1.50	0.30	0.75	1.50
❑30, Oct 89	1.50	0.30	0.75	1.50
❑31, Nov 89	1.50	0.30	0.75	1.50
❑Anl 1, Ghost, Dead Man, Devil-Child ..., A: Deadman	2.00	0.50	1.25	2.50

SPECTRE, THE (3RD SERIES)
DC

	ORIG	GOOD	FINE	N-MINT
❑0, Oct 94, The Temptation Of The Spectre, O: The Spectre	1.95	0.50	1.25	2.50
❑1, Dec 92, Crimes Of Violence, O: The Spectre, Glow-in-the-dark cover	1.75	1.20	3.00	6.00
❑2, Jan 93	1.75	1.00	2.50	5.00
❑3, Feb 93	1.75	0.80	2.00	4.00
❑4, Mar 93, Crime And Judgement	1.75	0.60	1.50	3.00
❑5, Apr 93, CV (c)	1.75	0.60	1.50	3.00
❑6, May 93, The Bleeding Gun	1.75	0.60	1.50	3.00
❑7, Jun 93	1.75	0.60	1.50	3.00
❑8, Jul 93, Glow-in-the-dark cover	2.50	0.70	1.75	3.50
❑9, Aug 93, No Good Deed Goes Unpunished	1.75	0.60	1.50	3.00
❑10, Sep 93	1.75	0.60	1.50	3.00
❑11, Oct 93, The Deepest Cut	1.75	0.60	1.50	3.00
❑12, Nov 93	1.75	0.60	1.50	3.00
❑13, Dec 93, Righteousness, Glow-in-the-dark cover	1.75	0.60	1.50	3.00
❑14, Jan 94	1.75	0.50	1.25	2.50
❑15, Feb 94	1.75	0.50	1.25	2.50
❑16, Mar 94, JA, Call for Blood	1.75	0.50	1.25	2.50
❑17, Apr 94	1.75	0.50	1.25	2.50
❑18, May 94	1.75	0.50	1.25	2.50
❑19, Jun 94	1.75	0.50	1.25	2.50
❑20, Jul 94	1.75	0.50	1.25	2.50
❑21, Aug 94	1.95	0.40	1.00	2.00
❑22, Sep 94, A: Spear of Destiny; V: Superman	1.95	0.40	1.00	2.00
❑23, Nov 94	1.95	0.40	1.00	2.00
❑24, Dec 94	1.95	0.40	1.00	2.00
❑25, Jan 95, Malicious	1.95	0.40	1.00	2.00
❑26, Feb 95	1.95	0.40	1.00	2.00
❑27, Mar 95	1.95	0.40	1.00	2.00
❑28, Apr 95	1.95	0.40	1.00	2.00
❑29, May 95	1.95	0.40	1.00	2.00
❑30, Jun 95	2.25	0.45	1.13	2.25
❑31, Jul 95	2.25	0.45	1.13	2.25
❑32, Aug 95	2.25	0.45	1.13	2.25
❑33, Sep 95	2.25	0.45	1.13	2.25
❑34, Oct 95	2.25	0.45	1.13	2.25
❑35, Nov 95, Underworld Unleashed	2.25	0.45	1.13	2.25
❑36, Dec 95, Underworld Unleashed	2.25	0.45	1.13	2.25
❑37, Jan 96, The Haunting of America, Part 1	2.25	0.50	1.25	2.50
❑38, Feb 96, The Haunting of America, Part 2, O: Uncle Sam	2.25	0.50	1.25	2.50
❑39, Mar 96, The Haunting of America, Part 3, O: Shadrach	2.25	0.50	1.25	2.50
❑40, Apr 96, The Haunting of America, Part 4, O: Captain Fear	2.25	0.50	1.25	2.50
❑41, May 96, The Haunting of America, Part 5	2.25	0.50	1.25	2.50
❑42, Jun 96, The Haunting of America, Part 6	2.25	0.50	1.25	2.50
❑43, Jul 96, The Haunting of America, Part 7	2.25	0.50	1.25	2.50
❑44, Aug 96, The Haunting of America, Part 8	2.25	0.50	1.25	2.50
❑45, Sep 96, The Haunting of America, Part 9, homosexuality issues	2.25	0.50	1.25	2.50
❑46, Oct 96, The Haunting of America, Part 10, National Interest acquires Spear of Destiny	2.25	0.50	1.25	2.50
❑47, Nov 96, The Haunting of America, Part 11, Final Night	2.25	0.50	1.25	2.50
❑48, Dec 96, The Haunting of America, Part 12	2.25	0.50	1.25	2.50
❑49, Jan 97, The Haunting of America, Part 13	2.50	0.50	1.25	2.50
❑50, Feb 97, The Haunting of America, Part 14 (Conclusion); The Haunting of America, Part 14	2.50	0.50	1.25	2.50
❑51, Mar 97, The Haunting of Jim Corrigan; A Savage Innocence	2.50	0.50	1.25	2.50
❑52, Apr 97, The Haunting of Jim Corrigan	2.50	0.50	1.25	2.50
❑53, May 97, The Haunting of Jim Corrigan	2.50	0.50	1.25	2.50
❑54, Jun 97, The Haunting of Jim Corrigan	2.50	0.50	1.25	2.50
❑55, Jul 97, The Haunting of Jim Corrigan	2.50	0.50	1.25	2.50
❑56, Aug 97, The Haunting of Jim Corrigan	2.50	0.50	1.25	2.50
❑57, Sep 97	2.50	0.50	1.25	2.50
❑58, Oct 97	2.50	0.50	1.25	2.50
❑59, Nov 97, True Believers	2.50	0.50	1.25	2.50
❑60, Dec 97, Within, Face cover	2.50	0.50	1.25	2.50
❑61, Jan 98	2.50	0.50	1.25	2.50
❑62, Feb 98, Final Issue; funeral of Jim Corrigan	2.50	0.50	1.25	2.50
❑Anl 1, A: Doctor Fate, Year One	3.95	0.79	1.98	3.95

SPECTRE, THE (4TH SERIES)
DC

Value: Cover or less

- ❑1, Mar 01 ... 2.50
- ❑2, Apr 01, Redeeming the Demon, Part 1 ... 2.50
- ❑3, May 01, Redeeming the Demon, Part 2 ... 2.50
- ❑4, Jun 01, Redeeming the Demon, Part 3 ... 2.50
- ❑5 ... 2.50
- ❑6 ... 2.50
- ❑7 ... 2.50

SPECTRESCOPE
SPECTRE

	ORIG	GOOD	FINE	N-MINT
❑1, Mar 94, no cover price; giveaway	—	0.20	0.50	1.00

SPECTRUM
NEW HORIZONS

Value: Cover or less

- ❑1, Jul 87, b&w ... 1.50

SPECTRUM COMICS PREVIEWS
SPECTRUM

Value: Cover or less

- ❑1, Feb 83, In the Beginning..., 1: Survivors ... 3.00

SPEEDBALL
MARVEL

	ORIG	GOOD	FINE	N-MINT
❑1, Sep 88, SD, SD (w), O: Speedball	0.75	0.20	0.50	1.00
❑2, Oct 88, SD, SD (w), Stuck on You!	0.75	0.20	0.50	1.00
❑3, Nov 88, SD	0.75	0.20	0.50	1.00
❑4, Dec 88, SD	0.75	0.20	0.50	1.00
❑5, Jan 89, SD	0.75	0.20	0.50	1.00
❑6, Feb 89, SD	0.75	0.20	0.50	1.00
❑7, Mar 89, SD	0.75	0.20	0.50	1.00
❑8, Apr 89, SD	0.75	0.20	0.50	1.00
❑9, May 89, SD	0.75	0.20	0.50	1.00
❑10, Jun 89, SD	0.75	0.20	0.50	1.00

SPEED BUGGY
CHARLTON

	ORIG	GOOD	FINE	N-MINT
❑1	0.25	2.40	6.00	12.00
❑2, Sep 75	0.25	1.60	4.00	8.00
❑3	0.25	1.60	4.00	8.00
❑4	0.25	1.60	4.00	8.00
❑5, Safari Nice Place to Visit But...; Old Timers Day	0.25	1.60	4.00	8.00
❑6	0.25	1.60	4.00	8.00
❑7	0.25	1.60	4.00	8.00
❑8	0.25	1.60	4.00	8.00
❑9	0.25	1.60	4.00	8.00

SPEED DEMON
MARVEL

	ORIG	GOOD	FINE	N-MINT
❑1, Apr 96, AM, Demon's Night	1.95	0.40	1.00	2.00

SPEED FORCE
DC

Value: Cover or less

- ❑1, Nov 97, JBy, Burning Secrets; Like Straws in a Hurricane, anthology series with stories of the various Flashes ... 3.95

SPEED RACER (1ST SERIES)
NOW

	ORIG	GOOD	FINE	N-MINT
❑1, Aug 87, Death of a Racer, O: Speed Racer	1.50	0.50	1.25	2.50
❑1-2, O: Speed Racer, 2nd Printing	1.50	0.30	0.75	1.50
❑2, Sep 87	1.50	0.40	1.00	2.00
❑3, Oct 87	1.50	0.40	1.00	2.00
❑4, Nov 87	1.75	0.35	0.88	1.75
❑5, Dec 87, Dead Heat	1.75	0.35	0.88	1.75
❑6, Jan 88	1.75	0.35	0.88	1.75
❑7, Mar 88	1.75	0.35	0.88	1.75
❑8, Apr 88	1.75	0.35	0.88	1.75
❑9, May 88	1.75	0.35	0.88	1.75
❑10, Jun 88	1.75	0.35	0.88	1.75
❑11, Jul 88	1.75	0.35	0.88	1.75
❑12, Aug 88	1.75	0.35	0.88	1.75
❑13, Sep 88	1.75	0.35	0.88	1.75
❑14, Oct 88	1.75	0.35	0.88	1.75
❑15, Nov 88	1.75	0.35	0.88	1.75
❑16, Dec 88	1.75	0.35	0.88	1.75
❑17, Jan 89	1.75	0.35	0.88	1.75
❑18, Mar 89	1.75	0.35	0.88	1.75
❑19, Apr 89	1.75	0.35	0.88	1.75
❑20, May 89	1.75	0.35	0.88	1.75
❑21, Jun 89	1.75	0.35	0.88	1.75
❑22, Jul 89	1.75	0.35	0.88	1.75
❑23, Aug 89, poster	1.75	0.35	0.88	1.75
❑24, Sep 89	1.75	0.35	0.88	1.75
❑25, Oct 89	1.75	0.35	0.88	1.75
❑26, Nov 89	1.75	0.35	0.88	1.75
❑27, Dec 89	1.75	0.35	0.88	1.75
❑28, Jan 90	1.75	0.35	0.88	1.75
❑29, Feb 90	1.75	0.35	0.88	1.75
❑30, Mar 90	1.75	0.35	0.88	1.75

After housing The Spectre's spirit for nearly 60 years, Jim Corrigan was finally allowed to go to his reward in *The Spectre* (3rd series) #62.

	ORIG	GOOD	FINE	N-MINT
❑31, Apr 90	1.75	0.35	0.88	1.75
❑32, May 90	1.75	0.35	0.88	1.75
❑33, Jun 90	1.75	0.35	0.88	1.75
❑34, Jul 90	1.75	0.35	0.88	1.75
❑35, Aug 90	1.75	0.35	0.88	1.75
❑36, Sep 90	1.75	0.35	0.88	1.75
❑37, Oct 90	1.75	0.35	0.88	1.75
❑38, Nov 90, Final Issue	1.75	0.35	0.88	1.75
❑SE 1, Mar 88, O: the Mach 5 (Speed Racer's Car)	2.00	0.50	1.25	2.50
❑SE 1-2, Sep 88, 2nd Printing	1.75	0.35	0.88	1.75

SPEED RACER (2ND SERIES)
DC

Value: Cover or less

- ❑1, Oct 99, Born to Race ... 2.50
- ❑2, Nov 99 ... 2.50
- ❑3, Dec 99, Enter the Mach 5 ... 2.50

SPEED RACER 3-D SPECIAL
NOW

Value: Cover or less

- ❑1, Jan 93 ... 2.95

SPEED RACER CLASSICS
NOW

Value: Cover or less

- ❑1, Oct 88, b&w ... 3.75
- ❑2, Feb 89, b&w ... 3.95

SPEED RACER FEATURING NINJA HIGH SCHOOL
NOW

Value: Cover or less

- ❑1, Aug 93, Quandary In Quagmire, trading card ... 2.50
- ❑2, Sep 93, two trading cards ... 2.50

SPEED RACER: RETURN OF THE GRX
NOW

Value: Cover or less

- ❑1, Mar 94, The Haunted Engine ... 1.95
- ❑2, Apr 94 ... 1.95

SPEED TRIBES
NEMICRON

Value: Cover or less

- ❑1, Aug 98, The Beginning ... 2.95

SPELLBINDERS
FLEETWAY

	ORIG	GOOD	FINE	N-MINT
❑1, Dec 86, Sláine: The Beast in the Broch; Nemesis: The Gothic Empire	1.25	0.30	0.75	1.50
❑2	1.25	0.30	0.75	1.50
❑3	1.25	0.30	0.75	1.50
❑4	1.25	0.30	0.75	1.50
❑5	1.25	0.30	0.75	1.50
❑6	1.25	0.30	0.75	1.50
❑7	1.25	0.30	0.75	1.50
❑8	1.25	0.30	0.75	1.50
❑9	1.25	0.30	0.75	1.50
❑10	1.25	0.30	0.75	1.50
❑11	1.25	0.30	0.75	1.50
❑12	1.25	0.30	0.75	1.50

SPELLBOUND
MARVEL

Value: Cover or less

- ❑1, Jan 88, Power! ... 1.50
- ❑2, Feb 88 ... 1.50
- ❑3, Feb 88 ... 1.50
- ❑4, Mar 88 ... 1.50
- ❑5, Apr 88 ... 1.50
- ❑6, Apr 88, Double Size ... 2.25

SPELLCASTER
MEDUSA

Value: Cover or less

- ❑1, The Past ... 2.95
- ❑2 ... 2.95
- ❑3 ... 2.95

SPELLJAMMER
DC

Value: Cover or less

- ❑1, Sep 90, Journey's Song, Kirstig's Tale ... 1.75
- ❑2 ... 1.75
- ❑3 ... 1.75
- ❑4 ... 1.75
- ❑5 ... 1.75
- ❑6, Circle Of Fear ... 1.75
- ❑7 ... 1.75
- ❑8 ... 1.75
- ❑9 ... 1.75
- ❑10 ... 1.75
- ❑11 ... 1.75
- ❑12 ... 1.75
- ❑13 ... 1.75
- ❑14, Nimone ... 1.75
- ❑15 ... 1.75
- ❑16 ... 1.75
- ❑17 ... 1.75
- ❑18 ... 1.75

SPEX-7
SHADOW SHOCK
Value: Cover or less

- ❑1, Sum 94, b&w ... 1.50

SPICECAPADES
FANTAGRAPHICS
Value: Cover or less

- ❑1, Spr 99, Why I'm Ga-Ga Over Baby Spice; The Spice Girls Forget the Words, nn; wraparound cover; magazine-sized; Spice Girls parody ... 4.95

SPICY ADULT STORIES
AIRCEL
Value: Cover or less

- ❑1, Mar 91, pulp reprints ... 2.50
- ❑2, Apr 91, pulp reprints ... 2.50
- ❑3, May 91, pulp reprints ... 2.50
- ❑4, pulp reprints ... 2.50

SPICY TALES
ETERNITY
Value: Cover or less

- ❑1, b&w; Reprint ... 1.95
- ❑2, b&w; Reprint ... 1.95
- ❑3, b&w; Reprint ... 1.95
- ❑4, b&w; Reprint ... 1.95
- ❑5, b&w; Reprint ... 1.95
- ❑6, b&w; Reprint ... 1.95
- ❑7, b&w; Reprint ... 1.95
- ❑8, b&w; Reprint ... 1.95
- ❑9, b&w; Reprint ... 1.95
- ❑10 ... 2.25
- ❑11 ... 2.25
- ❑12 ... 2.25
- ❑13 ... 2.25
- ❑14 ... 2.25
- ❑15 ... 2.25
- ❑16 ... 2.50
- ❑17, The Hidden Murder; News Ace ... 2.50
- ❑18 ... 2.95
- ❑19 ... 2.95
- ❑20 ... 2.95
- ❑SE 1, b&w; Reprint ... 2.25
- ❑SE 2, b&w; Reprint ... 2.25

SPIDER, THE
ECLIPSE
Value: Cover or less

- ❑1, Jun 91, Blood Dance ... 4.95
- ❑2, Aug 91 ... 4.95
- ❑3, Oct 91 ... 4.95

SPIDERBABY COMIX (S.R. BISSETTE'S...)
SPIDERBABY
Value: Cover or less

- ❑1, Cell Food; Cries from the Vegetable Kingdom ... 3.95

SPIDER-BOY
MARVEL

	ORIG	GOOD	FINE	N-MINT
❑1, Apr 96, Big Trouble!	1.95	0.50	1.25	2.50

SPIDER-BOY TEAM-UP
MARVEL
Value: Cover or less

- ❑1, Jun 97, Too Many Heroes...Too Little Time! ... 1.95

SPIDER-FEMME
SPOOF
Value: Cover or less

- ❑1, parody ... 2.50

SPIDER-GIRL
MARVEL

	ORIG	GOOD	FINE	N-MINT
❑0, Oct 98, O: Spider-Girl, reprints What If? #105	2.99	0.60	1.50	3.00
❑0.5, Wizard promotional edition	—	0.60	1.50	3.00
❑1, Oct 98, Choices, White cover with Spider-Girl facing forward	1.99	0.60	1.50	3.00
❑1/A, Oct 98, Choices, variant cover	1.99	0.60	1.50	3.00
❑2, Nov 98, A: Darkdevil, gatefold summary	1.99	0.40	1.00	2.00
❑3, Dec 98, A: Fantastic Five, gatefold summary	1.99	0.40	1.00	2.00
❑4, Jan 99, V: Dragon King	1.99	0.40	1.00	2.00
❑5, Feb 99, Ghosts of the Past, 1: Spider-Venom; A: Venom	1.99	0.40	1.00	2.00
❑6, Mar 99, Majority Rules!, A: Green Goblin; A: Ladyhawk	1.99	0.40	1.00	1.99
❑7, Apr 99, The Last Days of Spider-Man, A: Mary Jane Parker; A: Nova	1.99	0.40	1.00	1.99
❑8, May 99, V: Crazy Eight; V: Mr. Nobody; A: Kingpin	1.99	0.40	1.00	1.99
❑9, Jun 99, V: Killer Watt	1.99	0.40	1.00	1.99
❑10, Jul 99, A: Spider-Man	1.99	0.40	1.00	1.99
❑11, Aug 99, V: Spider-Slayer; A: Spider-Man; A: Human Torch	1.99	0.40	1.00	1.99
❑12, Sep 99	1.99	0.40	1.00	1.99
❑13, Oct 99	1.99	0.40	1.00	1.99
❑14	1.99	0.40	1.00	1.99
❑15, Dec 99, Swingin 'n' Slammin' With Speedball	1.99	0.40	1.00	1.99
❑16	—	0.45	1.13	2.25
❑17	—	0.45	1.13	2.25
❑18	—	0.45	1.13	2.25
❑19	—	0.45	1.13	2.25
❑20	—	0.45	1.13	2.25
❑21	—	0.45	1.13	2.25
❑22	—	0.45	1.13	2.25
❑23	—	0.45	1.13	2.25
❑24	—	0.45	1.13	2.25
❑25	2.99	0.60	1.50	2.99
❑26, Nov 00, Passages!	2.25	0.45	1.13	2.25
❑27, Dec 00, End Game	2.25	0.45	1.13	2.25
❑28, Jan 01, Unfinished Business!	2.25	0.45	1.13	2.25
❑29, Feb 01, Strange Allies!	2.25	0.45	1.13	2.25
❑30, Mar 01, The Winds of War!	2.25	0.45	1.13	2.25
❑31, Apr 01, With Friends Like These	2.25	0.45	1.13	2.25
❑32	2.25	0.45	1.13	2.25
❑33	2.25	0.45	1.13	2.25
❑34	2.25	0.45	1.13	2.25
❑35	2.25	0.45	1.13	2.25
❑36	2.25	0.45	1.13	2.25
❑Anl 1999	3.99	0.80	2.00	3.99

SPIDER-MAN
MARVEL

	ORIG	GOOD	FINE	N-MINT
❑-1, Jul 97, Flashback	1.99	0.40	1.00	2.00
❑0.5	—	0.80	2.00	4.00
❑0.5/Pl, Signed by Michael Lopez; Platinum edition	—	1.20	3.00	6.00
❑1, Aug 90, TMc, TMc (w), Torment, Part 1, Green cover (newsstand)	1.75	0.60	1.50	3.00
❑1/CG, TMc, TMc (w), Torment, Part 1, bagged newsstand (green)	1.75	0.80	2.00	4.00
❑1/CS, TMc, TMc (w), Torment, Part 1, bagged silver cover	2.00	1.20	3.00	6.00
❑1/PL, Aug 90, TMc, TMc (w), Torment, Part 1, Platinum edition; giveaway	1.75	12.00	30.00	60.00
❑1/SI, Aug 90, TMc, TMc (w), Torment, Part 1, silver cover	1.75	0.60	1.50	3.00
❑1-2, TMc, TMc (w), Torment, Part 1, 2nd Printing; Gold cover; UPC box	1.75	0.50	1.25	2.50
❑1/DM-2, Aug 90, TMc, 2nd Printing; Gold cover; direct sale	1.75	0.50	1.25	2.50
❑2, Sep 90, TMc, TMc (w), Torment, Part 2, Lizard	1.75	0.60	1.50	3.00
❑3, Oct 90, TMc, TMc (w), Torment, Part 3, Lizard	1.75	0.60	1.50	3.00
❑4, Nov 90, TMc, TMc (w), Torment, Part 4, Lizard	1.75	0.60	1.50	3.00
❑5, Dec 90, TMc, TMc (w), Torment, Part 5, Lizard	1.75	0.60	1.50	3.00
❑6, Jan 91, TMc, TMc (w), Masques, Part 1, A: Ghost Rider; V: Hobgoblin	1.75	0.60	1.50	3.00
❑7, Feb 91, TMc, TMc (w), Masques, Part 2, A: Ghost Rider; V: Hobgoblin	1.75	0.60	1.50	3.00
❑8, Mar 91, TMc, TMc (w), Perceptions, Part 1, A: Wolverine; V: Wendigo	1.75	0.50	1.25	2.50
❑9, Apr 91, TMc, TMc (w), Perceptions, Part 2, A: Wolverine; V: Wendigo	1.75	0.50	1.25	2.50
❑10, May 91, TMc, TMc (w), Perceptions, Part 3, A: Wolverine; V: Wendigo	1.75	0.50	1.25	2.50
❑11, Jun 91, TMc, TMc (w), Perceptions, Part 4, A: Wolverine; V: Wendigo	1.75	0.50	1.25	2.50
❑12, Jul 91, TMc, TMc (w), Perceptions, Part 5, A: Wolverine; V: Wendigo	1.75	0.50	1.25	2.50
❑13, Aug 91, TMc, TMc (w), Sub City, Part 1, Spider-Man wears black costume	1.75	0.50	1.25	2.50
❑14, Sep 91, TMc, TMc (w), Sub City, Part 2	1.75	0.50	1.25	2.50
❑15, Oct 91, EL, EL (w), The Mutant Factor, A: Beast	1.75	0.40	1.00	2.00
❑16, Nov 91, TMc, TMc (w), Sabotage, Part 1, X-Force; Sideways printing	1.75	0.40	1.00	2.00
❑17, Dec 91, AW, No One Gets Outta Here Alive!, V: Thanos	1.75	0.40	1.00	2.00
❑18, Jan 92, EL, EL (w), Revenge of the Sinister Six, Part 1; Revenge of Sinister Six, Part 1, Ghost Rider	1.75	0.40	1.00	2.00
❑19, Feb 92, EL, EL (w), Revenge of the Sinister Six, Part 2; Revenge of Sinister Six, Part 2, A: Hulk	1.75	0.40	1.00	2.00
❑20, Mar 92, EL, EL (w), Revenge of the Sinister Six, Part 3; Revenge of Sinister Six, Part 3, A: Deathlok; A: Solo; A: Hulk; A: Nova	1.75	0.40	1.00	2.00
❑21, Apr 92, EL, EL (w), Revenge of the Sinister Six, Part 4; Revenge of Sinister Six, Part 4, A: Deathlok; A: Solo, Deathlok appearnace	1.75	0.40	1.00	2.00
❑22, May 92, EL, EL (w), Revenge of the Sinister Six, Part 5; Revenge of Sinister Six, Part 5, A: Deathlok; A: Ghost Rider; A: Hulk; A: Sleepwalker	1.75	0.40	1.00	2.00
❑23, Jun 92, EL, EL (w), Revenge of the Sinister Six, Part 6; Revenge of Sinister Six, Part 6, A: Deathlok; A: Ghost Rider; A: Hulk; A: Fantastic Four	1.75	0.40	1.00	2.00
❑24, Jul 92, Infinity War, Infinity War	1.75	0.40	1.00	2.00
❑25, Aug 92, Why Me?, A: Phoenix	1.75	0.40	1.00	2.00
❑26, Sep 92, With Great Responsibility-!, O: Spider-Man, Hologram cover; 30th Anniversary Edition; Gatefold poster	3.50	0.80	2.00	4.00
❑27, Oct 92, MR, There's Something About a Gun, Part 1	1.75	0.40	1.00	2.00

	ORIG	GOOD	FINE	N-MINT
❑28, Nov 92, There's Something About a Gun, Part 2	1.75	0.40	1.00	2.00
❑29, Dec 92, Return to the Mad Dog Ward, Part 1	1.75	0.40	1.00	2.00
❑30, Jan 93, Return to the Mad Dog Ward, Part 2	1.75	0.40	1.00	2.00
❑31, Feb 93, Return to the Mad Dog Ward, Part 3	1.75	0.40	1.00	2.00
❑32, Mar 93, BMc, Vengeance, Part 1	1.75	0.40	1.00	2.00
❑33, Apr 93, BMc, Vengeance, Part 2, A: Punisher	1.75	0.40	1.00	2.00
❑34, May 93, BMc, Vengeance, Part 3, A: Punisher	1.75	0.40	1.00	2.00
❑35, Jun 93, Maximum Carnage, Part 4, A: Venom; A: Carnage	1.75	0.40	1.00	2.00
❑36, Jul 93, Maximum Carnage, Part 8, A: Venom; A: Carnage	1.75	0.40	1.00	2.00
❑37, Aug 93, Maximum Carnage, Part 12, A: Venom; A: Carnage	1.75	0.40	1.00	2.00
❑38, Sep 93, KJ, Light the Night, Part 1	1.75	0.40	1.00	2.00
❑39, Oct 93, KJ, Light the Night, Part 2, A: Electro	1.75	0.40	1.00	2.00
❑40, Nov 93, KJ, Light the Night, Part 3, V: Electro	1.75	0.40	1.00	2.00
❑41, Dec 93, Storm Warnings, Part 1	1.75	0.40	1.00	2.00
❑42, Jan 94, Storm Warnings, Part 2	1.75	0.40	1.00	2.00
❑43, Feb 94	1.75	0.40	1.00	2.00
❑44, Mar 94	1.75	0.40	1.00	2.00
❑45, Apr 94, Pursuit, Part 1	1.75	0.40	1.00	2.00
❑46, May 94, Beware the Rage of a Desperate Man, Part 1	1.95	0.40	1.00	2.00
❑46/CS, May 94, Beware the Rage of a Desperate Man, Part 1, animation cel; with print	2.75	0.60	1.50	3.00
❑47, Jun 94, Beware the Rage of a Desperate Man, Part 2, V: Hobgoblin	1.95	0.40	1.00	2.00
❑48, Jul 94, V: Hobgoblin	1.95	0.40	1.00	2.00
❑49, Aug 94	1.95	0.40	1.00	2.00
❑50, Sep 94	2.50	0.50	1.25	2.50
❑50/SC, Sep 94, Holo-grafix cover	3.95	0.79	1.98	3.95
❑51, Oct 94, Power and Responsibility, Part 3, A: Ben Reilly	1.95	0.50	1.25	2.50
❑51/SC, Oct 94, Power and Responsibility, Part 3; The Double, Part 3, A: Ben Reilly, enhanced cover; Giant-size; flip-book with back-up	2.95	0.59	1.48	2.95
❑52, Nov 94, The clone vs. Venom	1.95	0.40	1.00	2.00
❑53, Dec 94, The clone defeats Venom	1.95	0.40	1.00	2.00
❑54, Jan 95, Web of Life, Part 2, flip book with illustrated story from The Ultimate Spider-Man back-up	2.75	0.40	1.00	2.00
❑55, Feb 95, Web of Life, Part 4	1.95	0.40	1.00	2.00
❑56, Mar 95	1.95	0.40	1.00	2.00
❑57, Apr 95, JR2, Aftershocks, Part 1; The Parker Legacy, Part 2, Giant-size	2.50	0.50	1.25	2.50
❑57/SC, Apr 95, Aftershocks, Part 1; The Parker Legacy, Part 2, enhanced cardstock cover; Giant-size	2.95	0.59	1.48	2.95
❑58, May 95	1.95	0.40	1.00	2.00
❑59, Jun 95	1.95	0.40	1.00	2.00
❑60, Jul 95, The Trial of Peter Parker, Part 3, Kaine's identity revealed	1.95	0.40	1.00	2.00
❑61, Aug 95, Maximum Clonage, Part 4	1.95	0.40	1.00	2.00
❑62, Sep 95, Exiled, Part 3	1.95	0.40	1.00	2.00
❑63, Oct 95, The Greatest Responsibility, Part 2, OverPower game cards bound-in	1.95	0.40	1.00	2.00
❑64, Jan 96, V: Poison	1.95	0.40	1.00	2.00
❑65, Feb 96, Media Blizzard, Part 3	1.95	0.40	1.00	2.00
❑66, Mar 96, JR2, The Return of Kaine, Part 4	1.95	0.40	1.00	2.00
❑67, Apr 96, JR2, JR2 (w), Web of Carnage, Part 3	1.95	0.40	1.00	2.00
❑68, May 96, Blood Brothers, Part 3	1.95	0.40	1.00	2.00
❑69, Jun 96	1.95	0.40	1.00	2.00
❑70, Jul 96, A: Hammerhead	1.95	0.40	1.00	2.00
❑71, Aug 96, JR2, V: Hammerhead	1.95	0.40	1.00	2.00
❑72, Sep 96, JR2, Onslaught: Impact 2, V: Sentinels	1.95	0.40	1.00	2.00
❑73, Oct 96, JR2	1.99	0.40	1.00	2.00
❑74, Nov 96, JR2, A: Daredevil	1.99	0.40	1.00	2.00
❑75, Dec 96, JR2, Revelations, Part 4, D: Ben Reilly, wraparound cover; Giant-size; return of original Green Goblin	2.99	0.70	1.75	3.50
❑76, Jan 97, JR2, SHOC, V: S.H.O.C.	1.99	0.40	1.00	2.00
❑77, Feb 97, V: Morbius	1.95	0.40	1.00	2.00
❑78, Mar 97, JR2, The Love of a Woman, V: Morbius	1.99	0.40	1.00	2.00
❑79, Apr 97, JR2, After the Fall, A: Morbius; V: S.H.O.C.	1.99	0.40	1.00	2.00
❑80, May 97, JR2, Blood Simple, A: Morbius; V: Hammerhead	1.99	0.40	1.00	2.00
❑81, Jun 97, JR2, Shadow of the Cat	1.99	0.40	1.00	2.00

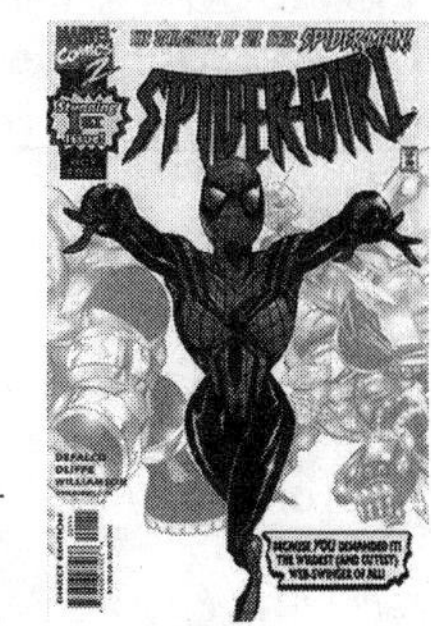

In an alternate future, Peter Parker's daughter discovers she has inherited her father's super-powers and dons a spider-themed costume in *Spider-Girl.*

	ORIG	GOOD	FINE	N-MINT
❑82, Aug 97, gatefold summary	1.99	0.40	1.00	2.00
❑83, Sep 97, gatefold summary	1.99	0.40	1.00	2.00
❑84, Oct 97, V: Juggernaut, gatefold summary	1.99	0.40	1.00	2.00
❑85, Nov 97, V: Shocker, gatefold summary	1.99	0.40	1.00	2.00
❑86, Dec 97, A: Trapster; V: Shocker, gatefold summary	1.99	0.40	1.00	2.00
❑87, Jan 98, V: Shocker, gatefold summary	1.99	0.40	1.00	2.00
❑88, Feb 98, gatefold summary	1.99	0.40	1.00	2.00
❑89, Mar 98, Spider-Hunt, Part 3, V: Shotgun; V: Punisher, gatefold summary	1.99	0.40	1.00	2.00
❑90, Apr 98, Identity Crisis, V: Blastaar; 1: Spidey as Dusk, gatefold summary	1.99	0.40	1.00	2.00
❑91, May 98, Identity Crisis, Part 3, gatefold summary; Identity Crisis	1.99	0.40	1.00	2.00
❑92, Jun 98, gatefold summary; Identity Crisis	1.99	0.40	1.00	2.00
❑93, Jul 98, A: Ghost Rider, gatefold summary	1.99	0.40	1.00	2.00
❑94, Aug 98, gatefold summary	1.99	0.40	1.00	2.00
❑95, Sep 98, V: Nitro, gatefold summary	1.99	0.40	1.00	2.00
❑96, Oct 98, The Gathering of Five, Part 3, A: Madame Web, gatefold summary	1.99	0.40	1.00	2.00
❑97, Nov 98, JBy (c), The Final Chapter, Part 2, gatefold summary	1.99	0.40	1.00	2.00
❑98/A, Nov 98, The Final Chapter, Part 4, Final Issue; gatefold summary	1.99	0.40	1.00	2.00
❑98/B, Nov 98, JBy (c), The Final Chapter, Part 4, alternate cover; Final Issue; gatefold summary; series begins again as Peter Parker: Spider-Man	1.99	0.40	1.00	2.00
❑Anl 1997, 1997 Annual	2.99	0.60	1.50	2.99
❑Anl 1998, A: Moon Boy; A: Devil Dinosaur, wraparound cover; gatefold summary	2.99	0.60	1.50	2.99
❑GS 1, Giant-Sized Spider-Man	3.99	0.80	2.00	3.99
❑HS 1995, A: Venom; A: Human Torch, nn; One-Shot; Trade Paperback; 1995 Holiday Special	2.95	0.59	1.48	2.95

SPIDER-MAN 2099
MARVEL

	ORIG	GOOD	FINE	N-MINT
❑1, Nov 92, PD (w), O: Spider-Man 2099; 1: Tyler Stone, foil cover	1.75	0.35	0.88	1.75
❑1/Aut, Nov 92, AW, foil cover; with certificate of authenticity	1.75	0.35	0.88	1.75
❑2, Dec 92, PD (w), O: Spider-Man 2099	1.25	0.25	0.63	1.25
❑3, Jan 93, PD (w), Nothing Gained, O: Spider-Man 2099	1.25	0.25	0.63	1.25
❑4, Feb 93, PD (w), The Specialist, 1: The Specialist	1.25	0.25	0.63	1.25
❑5, Mar 93, PD (w)	1.25	0.25	0.63	1.25
❑6, Apr 93, PD (w), 1: Vulture 2099	1.25	0.25	0.63	1.25
❑7, May 93, PD (w), Wing And A Prayer	1.25	0.25	0.63	1.25
❑8, Jun 93, PD (w)	1.25	0.25	0.63	1.25
❑9, Jul 93, PD (w)	1.25	0.25	0.63	1.25
❑10, Aug 93, PD (w)	1.25	0.25	0.63	1.25
❑11, Sep 93, PD (w)	1.25	0.25	0.63	1.25
❑12, Oct 93, PD (w)	1.25	0.25	0.63	1.25
❑13, Nov 93, PD (w)	1.25	0.25	0.63	1.25
❑14, Dec 93, PD (w)	1.25	0.25	0.63	1.25
❑15, Jan 94, PD (w)	1.25	0.25	0.63	1.25
❑16, Feb 94, PD (w), Fall of the Hammer, Part 1	1.25	0.25	0.63	1.25
❑17, Mar 94, PD (w)	1.25	0.25	0.63	1.25
❑18, Apr 94, PD (w)	1.25	0.25	0.63	1.25
❑19, May 94, PD (w)	1.50	0.30	0.75	1.50
❑20, Jun 94, PD (w)	1.50	0.30	0.75	1.50
❑21, Jul 94, PD (w)	1.50	0.30	0.75	1.50
❑22, Aug 94, PD (w)	1.50	0.30	0.75	1.50
❑23, Sep 94, PD (w)	1.50	0.30	0.75	1.50
❑24, Oct 94, PD (w)	1.50	0.30	0.75	1.50
❑25, Nov 94, PD (w), Giant-size	2.25	0.45	1.13	2.25
❑25/SC, Nov 94, PD (w), enhanced cover; Giant-size	2.95	0.59	1.48	2.95
❑26, Dec 94, PD (w)	1.50	0.30	0.75	1.50
❑27, Jan 95, PD (w)	1.50	0.30	0.75	1.50

	ORIG	GOOD	FINE	N-MINT
❑28, Feb 95, PD (w)	1.50	0.30	0.75	1.50
❑29, Mar 95, PD (w)	1.50	0.30	0.75	1.50
❑30, Apr 95, PD (w)	1.50	0.30	0.75	1.50
❑31, May 95, PD (w)	1.50	0.30	0.75	1.50
❑32, Jun 95, PD (w)	1.50	0.39	0.98	1.95
❑33, Jul 95, PD (w), A: Strange 2099	1.95	0.39	0.98	1.95
❑34, Aug 95, PD (w)	1.95	0.39	0.98	1.95
❑35, Sep 95, PD (w)	1.95	0.39	0.98	1.95
❑35/SC, Sep 95, PD (w), alternate cover	1.95	0.39	0.98	1.95
❑36, Oct 95, PD (w), Spiderman 2099 on cover	1.95	0.39	0.98	1.95
❑36/SC, Oct 95, PD (w), alternate cover; says Venom 2099; forms diptych	1.95	0.39	0.98	1.95
❑37, Nov 95, PD (w)	1.95	0.39	0.98	1.95
❑37/SC, Nov 95, alternate cover; says Venom 2099	1.95	0.39	0.98	1.95
❑38, Dec 95, PD (w), Spiderman 2099 on cover	1.95	0.39	0.98	1.95
❑38/SC, Dec 95, PD (w), alternate cover; says Venom 2099; forms diptych	1.95	0.39	0.98	1.95
❑39, Jan 96, PD (w)	1.95	0.39	0.98	1.95
❑40, Feb 96, PD (w), V: Goblin 2099	1.95	0.39	0.98	1.95
❑41, Mar 96, PD (w)	1.95	0.39	0.98	1.95
❑42, Apr 96, PD (w), Earth	1.95	0.39	0.98	1.95
❑43, May 96, PD (w), Water	1.95	0.39	0.98	1.95
❑44, Jun 96	1.95	0.39	0.98	1.95
❑45, Jul 96, V: Goblin 2099	1.95	0.39	0.98	1.95
❑46, Aug 96, V: Vulture 2099, Final Issue; story continues in Fantastic Four 2099 #8	1.95	0.39	0.98	1.95
❑Anl 1, 1994 Annual	2.95	0.59	1.48	2.95
❑SE 1, Nov 95	3.95	0.79	1.98	3.95

SPIDER-MAN 2099 MEETS SPIDER-MAN
MARVEL

Value: Cover or less

❑1, Nov 95, PD (w), nn 5.95

SPIDER-MAN ADVENTURES
MARVEL

Value: Cover or less

❑1, Dec 94, Night of the Lizard, adapts animated series....... 1.50
❑1/SC, Dec 94, Night of the Lizard, enhanced cover; Adapts animated series 2.95
❑2, Jan 95, adapts animated series 1.50
❑3, Feb 95, V: Spider-Slayer, adapts animated series....... 1.50
❑4, Mar 95, adapts animated series 1.50
❑5, Apr 95, V: Mysterio, adapts animated series 1.50
❑6, May 95, adapts animated series 1.50
❑7, Jun 95, adapts animated series 1.50
❑8, Jul 95, Adapts animated series....... 1.50
❑9, Aug 95, V: Shocker, Adapts animated series....... 1.50
❑10, Sep 95, V: Venom, Adapts animated series....... 1.50
❑11, Oct 95, V: Hobgoblin, Adapts animated series....... 1.50
❑12, Nov 95, V: Hobgoblin, Adapts animated series....... 1.50
❑13, Dec 95, A: Nick Fury; V: Chameleon; A: S.H.I.E.L.D., Adapts animated series....... 1.50
❑14, Jan 96, V: Doctor Octopus, Adapts animated series....... 1.50
❑15, Feb 96, V: Lizard, Final Issue; Adapts animated series; Continues in Adventures of Spider-Man #1 .... 1.50

SPIDER-MAN AND BATMAN
MARVEL

Value: Cover or less

❑1, Sep 95, nn; prestige format....... 5.95

SPIDER-MAN AND DAREDEVIL SPECIAL EDITION
MARVEL

Value: Cover or less

❑1, Mar 84....... 2.00

SPIDER-MAN AND HIS AMAZING FRIENDS
MARVEL

	ORIG	GOOD	FINE	N-MINT
❑1, Dec 81, DS, The Triumph of the Green Goblin, A: Green Goblin; A: Iceman; 1: Firestar, Adapted from television show	0.50	0.50	1.25	2.50

SPIDER-MAN AND MYSTERIO
MARVEL

Value: Cover or less

❑1, Jan 01, Jack's Back, A: Daredevil, says Spider-Man: The Mysterio Manifesto on the cover....... 2.99
❑2, Feb 01, Even the Dead Can Lie!, A: Daredevil, says Spider-Man: The Mysterio Manifesto on the cover....... 2.99
❑3, Mar 01, False Truths!, A: Daredevil, says Spider-Man: The Mysterio Manifesto on the cover....... 2.99

SPIDER-MAN AND THE DALLAS COWBOYS
MARVEL

	ORIG	GOOD	FINE	N-MINT
❑1, Sep 83, nn; Danger in Dallas giveaway.	—	2.00	5.00	10.00

SPIDER-MAN AND THE INCREDIBLE HULK
MARVEL

	ORIG	GOOD	FINE	N-MINT
❑1, Sep 81, nn; Chaos in Kansas City giveaway	—	2.00	5.00	10.00

SPIDER-MAN & THE NEW MUTANTS
MARVEL

	ORIG	GOOD	FINE	N-MINT
❑1, nn; giveaway; child abuse	—	0.60	1.50	3.00

SPIDER-MAN AND X-FACTOR: SHADOWGAMES
MARVEL

	ORIG	GOOD	FINE	N-MINT
❑1, May 94, PB, KB (w), Shadow-Games, Part 1, 1: Shadow Force	1.95	0.45	1.13	2.25
❑2, Jun 94, PB, KB (w), Shadow-Games, Part 2	1.95	0.45	1.13	2.25
❑3, Jul 94, PB, KB (w), Shadow-Games, Part 3	1.95	0.45	1.13	2.25

SPIDER-MAN ANNUAL
MARVEL

Value: Cover or less

❑1, hardcover....... 3.95

SPIDER-MAN/BADROCK
MAXIMUM

Value: Cover or less

❑1/A, Mar 97, first part of story....... 2.99
❑1/B, Mar 97, second part of story....... 2.99

SPIDER-MAN: CHAPTER ONE
MARVEL

Value: Cover or less

❑0, May 99, JBy, JBy (w), Where Walks the Lizard, O: Sandman; O: Vulture; O: Lizard....... 2.50
❑1, Dec 98, JBy, JBy (w), Bitter Lesson, O: Spider-Man; O: Doctor Octopus....... 2.50
❑1/A, Dec 98, JBy, JBy (w), Bitter Lesson, O: Spider-Man; O: Doctor Octopus, DFE alternate cover 6.95
❑1/B, Dec 98, JBy, JBy (w), Bitter Lesson, O: Spider-Man; O: Doctor Octopus....... 19.63
❑1/C, Dec 98, JBy, JBy (w), Bitter Lesson, O: Spider-Man; O: Doctor Octopus....... 19.63
❑2, Dec 98, V: Chameleon; A: J. Jonah Jameson; A: Fantastic Four....... 2.50
❑2/A, JBy, JBy (w), Cover A.... 2.50
❑2/B, JBy, JBy (w), Cover B.... 2.50
❑2/C, JBy, JBy (w), Cover forms diptych with issue #1 DFE cover 6.95
❑3, Jan 99, JBy, JBy (w), A: Mad Thinker; O: Vulture 2.50
❑4, Feb 99, JBy, JBy (w), V: Doctor Doom; V: Doctor Octopus.... 2.50
❑5, Mar 99, JBy, JBy (w), A: Doctor Doom; V: Lizard....... 2.50
❑6, Apr 99, JBy, JBy (w), V: Electro; A: Human Torch....... 2.50
❑7, May 99, JBy, JBy (w), V: Mysterio 2.50
❑8, Jun 99, JBy, JBy (w), V: Green Goblin; A: Hulk 2.50
❑9, Jul 99, JBy, JBy (w), A: Daredevil; V: Kraven 2.50
❑10, Aug 99, JBy, JBy (w), V: Green Goblin....... 2.50
❑11, Sep 99, JBy, JBy (w), A: Giant-Man 2.50
❑12, Oct 99, JBy, JBy (w), V: Sandman, Final Issue....... 3.50
❑13, JBy, JBy (w) 2.50
❑Dlx 1, JBy, JBy (w)....... 29.95
❑Dlx 1/LE, JBy, JBy (w)....... 29.95

SPIDER-MAN: CHRISTMAS IN DALLAS
MARVEL

	ORIG	GOOD	FINE	N-MINT
❑1, Dec 83, nn; giveaway	—	2.00	5.00	10.00

SPIDER-MAN CLASSICS
MARVEL

	ORIG	GOOD	FINE	N-MINT
❑1, Apr 93, SD, SL (w), The Origin Of Doctor Strange, O: Doctor Strange; 1: Spider-Man, Reprints Amazing Fantasy #15 & Strange Tales #115	1.25	0.40	1.00	2.00
❑2, May 93, SD, SL (w); SD (w), Spider-Man; Spider-Man vs. the Chameleon, 1: Chameleon; 1: J. Jonah Jameson; O: Spider-Man; A: Fantastic Four, record; Reprints Amazing Spider-Man #1	1.25	0.30	0.75	1.50
❑3, Jun 93, SD, SL (w); SD (w), Duel to the Death with the Vulture; The Uncanny Threat of the Terrible Tinkerer, 1: Vulture; 1: Tinkerer; 1: Mysterio (as "alien"), Reprints Amazing Spider-Man #2	1.25	0.30	0.75	1.50
❑4, Jul 93, SD, SL (w); SD (w), Spider-Man Versus Doctor Octopus, 1: Doctor Octopus, Reprints Amazing Spider-Man #3	1.25	0.30	0.75	1.50
❑5, Aug 93, SD, SL (w); SD (w), Nothing Can Stop the Sandman, 1: Sandman (Marvel); 1: Betty Brant, Reprints Amazing Spider-Man #4	1.25	0.30	0.75	1.50
❑6, Sep 93, SD, SL (w); SD (w), Marked for Destruction by Dr. Doom, A: Doctor Doom, Reprints Amazing Spider-Man #5	1.25	0.30	0.75	1.50
❑7, Oct 93, SD, SL (w); SD (w), Face-to-Face with the Lizard, 1: The Lizard, Reprints Amazing Spider-Man #6	1.25	0.30	0.75	1.50
❑8, Nov 93, SD, SL (w); SD (w), Return of the Vulture, 2: The Vulture, Reprints Amazing Spider-Man #7	1.25	0.30	0.75	1.50
❑9, Dec 93, SD, SL (w); SD (w), The Terrible Threat of the Living Brain, A: Human Torch; 1: The Living Brain, Reprints Amazing Spider-Man #8	1.25	0.30	0.75	1.50
❑10, Jan 94, SD, SL (w); SD (w), The Man Called Electro, 1: Electro, Reprints Amazing Spider-Man #9	1.25	0.30	0.75	1.50
❑11, Feb 94, SD, SL (w); SD (w), The Enforcers, 1: Enforcers; 1: Big Man, Reprints Amazing Spider-Man #10	1.25	0.30	0.75	1.50
❑12, Mar 94, SD, SL (w); SD (w), Turning Point, 2: Doctor Octopus, Reprints Amazing Spider-Man #11	1.25	0.30	0.75	1.50
❑13, Apr 94	1.25	0.25	0.63	1.25
❑14, May 94	1.25	0.25	0.63	1.25
❑15, Jun 94, 1: Green Goblin I (Norman Osborn)	1.25	0.25	0.63	1.25

ORIG GOOD FINE N-MINT

❑15/CS, Jun 94, 1: Green Goblin I (Norman Osborn), polybagged with animation print 2.95 0.59 1.48 2.95
❑16, Jul 94 1.25 0.25 0.63 1.25

SPIDER-MAN COLLECTORS' PREVIEW
MARVEL

Value: Cover or less
❑1, Dec 94 1.50

SPIDER-MAN COMICS MAGAZINE
MARVEL

Value: Cover or less

❑1, Jan 87, digest 1.50
❑2, Mar 87, digest 1.50
❑3, May 87, digest 1.50
❑4, Jul 87, digest 1.50
❑5, Sep 87, digest 1.50
❑6, Nov 87, digest 1.50
❑7, Jan 88, digest 1.50
❑8, Mar 88, digest 1.50
❑9, May 88, digest 1.50
❑10, Jul 88, digest 1.50
❑11, Sep 88, digest 1.50
❑12, Nov 88, JM; JR, SL (w), digest 1.50
❑13, Jan 89, digest 1.50

SPIDER-MAN: DEAD MAN'S HAND
MARVEL

Value: Cover or less
❑1, Apr 97, wraparound cover 2.99

SPIDER-MAN: DEATH AND DESTINY
MARVEL

Value: Cover or less
❑1, Aug 00, Focus 2.99
❑2, Sep 00, The Camera Doesn't Lie 2.99
❑3, Oct 00, D...ja Vu All Over Again 2.99

SPIDER-MAN/DR. STRANGE: THE WAY TO DUSTY DEATH
MARVEL

Value: Cover or less
❑1, graphic novel 6.95

SPIDER-MAN: FEAR ITSELF
MARVEL

Value: Cover or less
❑1, Feb 92, RA, SL (w) 12.95

SPIDER-MAN: FRIENDS & ENEMIES
MARVEL

Value: Cover or less

❑1, Jan 95, 1: The Metahumes 1.95
❑2, Feb 95 1.95
❑3, Mar 95 1.95
❑4, Apr 95, Fire Of Freedom 1.95

SPIDER-MAN: FUNERAL FOR AN OCTOPUS
MARVEL

Value: Cover or less

❑1, Mar 95, Eight Arms Beyond the Grave 1.50
❑2, Apr 95 1.50
❑3, May 95 1.50
❑4, Jun 95 1.50

SPIDER-MAN/GEN13
MARVEL

Value: Cover or less
❑1, Nov 96, PD (w), Crossed Generations, nn; prestige format 4.95

SPIDER-MAN: HOBGOBLIN LIVES
MARVEL

Value: Cover or less
❑1, Jan 97, Victims, D: Jason Macendale, wraparound cover 2.50
❑2, Feb 97, Back In Business, wraparound cover 2.50
❑3, Apr 97, Secrets, wraparound cover; Final Issue; identity of Hobgoblin revealed; True identity of Hobgoblin I revealed 2.50

SPIDER-MAN/KINGPIN: TO THE DEATH
MARVEL

Value: Cover or less
❑1, A: Daredevil, nn; prestige format 5.95

SPIDER-MAN: LEGACY OF EVIL
MARVEL

Value: Cover or less
❑1, Jun 96, KB (w), One-Shot; retells history of Green Goblin 3.95

SPIDER-MAN: LIFELINE
MARVEL

Value: Cover or less
❑1, Apr 01, SR, Pieces of Fate, A: Doctor Strange 2.99
❑2, May 01, SR, Snakes in the Grass, A: Doctor Strange; A: Lizard 2.99
❑3, Jun 01, SR, A Taste of Infinity, A: Doctor Strange; A: Lizard 2.99

SPIDER-MAN: MADE MEN
MARVEL

Value: Cover or less
❑1, Aug 99 5.99

SPIDER-MAN MAGAZINE
MARVEL

Value: Cover or less

❑1, Win 94, nn 1.95
❑2, Jun 94 1.95
❑3, Jul 94 1.95
❑4, Aug 94, X-Men 1.95
❑5, Sep 94 1.95
❑6, Oct 94, X-Men 1.95
❑7, Nov 94 1.95
❑8, Dec 94 1.95
❑9, Jan 95, flip book with Iron Man back-up 1.95
❑10, Feb 95, flip book with X-Men back-up 1.95

SPIDER-MAN MAGAZINE (2ND SERIES)
MARVEL

Value: Cover or less
❑1, Spr 95, nn 2.50

SPIDER-MAN: MAXIMUM CLONAGE ALPHA
MARVEL

❑1, Aug 95, and the Jackal Cries, "Death", Acetate wraparound cover overlay 4.95 1.00 2.50 5.00

Steve Rude teamed Spider-Man and Doctor Strange for a three-issue mini-series featuring appearances by The Lizard and Man Mountain Marko in *Spider-Man: Lifeline*.

ORIG GOOD FINE N-MINT

SPIDER-MAN: MAXIMUM CLONAGE OMEGA
MARVEL

❑1, Aug 95, D: The Jackal, enhanced wraparound cover 4.95 1.00 2.50 5.00

SPIDER-MAN MEGAZINE
MARVEL

Value: Cover or less

❑1, Oct 94 2.50
❑2, Nov 94, JM; RA; JR2; SD, But the Cat Came Back...; Goin' Straight! 2.95
❑3, Dec 94 2.95
❑4, Jan 95 2.95
❑5, Feb 95 2.95
❑6, Mar 95, Final Issue 2.95

SPIDER-MAN MYSTERIES
MARVEL

❑1, Aug 98, nn; no cover price; prototype for children's comic — 0.20 0.50 1.00

SPIDER-MAN: POWER OF TERROR
MARVEL

Value: Cover or less

❑1, Jan 95, Beneficial Alliances 1.95
❑2, Feb 95 1.95
❑3, Mar 95 1.95
❑4, Apr 95 1.95

SPIDER-MAN, POWER PACK
MARVEL

❑1, Aug 84, JM, Secrets, no cover price; Giveaway from the National Committee for Prevention of Child Abuse; sexual abuse — 0.20 0.50 1.00

SPIDER-MAN/PUNISHER: FAMILY PLOT
MARVEL

Value: Cover or less
❑1, Feb 96, DG, The Fall 2.95
❑2, Feb 96, Redemption 2.95

SPIDER-MAN, PUNISHER, SABRETOOTH: DESIGNER GENES
MARVEL

Value: Cover or less
❑1, nn 8.95

SPIDER-MAN: REDEMPTION
MARVEL

Value: Cover or less

❑1, Sep 96, MZ, no ads 1.50
❑2, Oct 96, MZ 1.50
❑3, Nov 96, MZ 1.50
❑4, Dec 96, MZ, Burning Bright 1.50

SPIDER-MAN: REVENGE OF THE GREEN GOBLIN
MARVEL

Value: Cover or less
❑1, Oct 00, Madness Takes Its Toll 2.99
❑2, Nov 00, Lives in the Balance! 2.99
❑3, Dec 00, Surrender to the Dark!, events lead in to Amazing Spider-Man #25 and Peter Parker, Spider-Man #25 2.99

SPIDER-MAN SAGA
MARVEL

Value: Cover or less

❑1, Nov 91 2.95
❑2, Dec 91 2.95
❑3, Jan 92 2.95
❑4, Feb 92 2.95

SPIDER-MAN SPECIAL EDITION
MARVEL

❑1, PD (w), The Trial Of Venom, A: Venom, Embossed cover; poster; "The Trial of Venom" special edition to benefit Unicef. 1.25 0.60 1.50 3.00

SPIDER-MAN, STORM AND POWER MAN
MARVEL

❑1, Apr 82, nn; Smokescreen giveaway — 0.40 1.00 2.00

SPIDER-MAN SUPER SPECIAL
MARVEL

Value: Cover or less
❑1, Jul 95, Flip-book; two of the stories continue in Venom Super Special #1 3.95

SPIDER-MAN TEAM-UP
MARVEL

❑1, Dec 95, MWa (w), A: Psylocke; A: Phoenix; A: Beast; A: Hellfire Club; A: Archangel; A: Cyclops; A: X-Men 2.95 0.60 1.50 3.00
❑2, Mar 96, GP (w), Ambush, A: Silver Surfer 2.95 0.60 1.50 3.00
❑3, Jun 96, A: Fantastic Four 2.95 0.60 1.50 3.00
❑4, Sep 96, A: Avengers 2.95 0.60 1.50 3.00
❑5, Dec 96, A: Gambit; A: Howard the Duck 2.99 0.60 1.50 3.00

	ORIG	GOOD	FINE	N-MINT
❑6, Mar 97, BMc; TP, Breaking And Entering; Lost Souls, A: Doctor Strange; A: Hulk; A: Aquarian; A: Dracula	2.99	0.60	1.50	3.00
❑7, Jun 97, DG; SB, KB (w), Old Scores, A: Thunderbolts	2.99	0.60	1.50	3.00

SPIDER-MAN: THE ARACHNIS PROJECT
MARVEL

	ORIG	GOOD	FINE	N-MINT
❑1, Aug 94	1.75	0.40	1.00	2.00
❑2, Sep 94	1.75	0.40	1.00	2.00
❑3, Oct 94	1.75	0.40	1.00	2.00
❑4, Nov 94	1.75	0.40	1.00	2.00
❑5, Dec 94	1.75	0.40	1.00	2.00
❑6, Jan 95	1.75	0.40	1.00	2.00

SPIDER-MAN: THE CLONE JOURNAL
MARVEL

	ORIG	GOOD	FINE	N-MINT
❑1, Mar 95, Puppet, O: Ben Reilly, One-Shot	2.95	0.60	1.50	3.00

SPIDER-MAN: THE DEATH OF CAPTAIN STACY
MARVEL

Value: Cover or less

❑1, Aug 00, JR; GK, SL (w), The Arms of Doctor Octopus!; Doc Ock Lives!, D: Captain Stacy, Reprint; Reprints Amazing Spider-Man #88-90 .... 3.50

SPIDER-MAN: THE FINAL ADVENTURE
MARVEL

	ORIG	GOOD	FINE	N-MINT
❑1, Dec 95, Destiny's Web, enhanced cardstock cover; clone returns to action one last time	2.95	0.60	1.50	3.00
❑2, Jan 96, enhanced cardstock cover	2.95	0.60	1.50	3.00
❑3, Feb 96, Skin Deep, enhanced cardstock cover	2.95	0.60	1.50	3.00
❑4, Mar 96, To End The Begin, enhanced cardstock cover; Peter loses his powers	2.95	0.60	1.50	3.00

SPIDER-MAN: THE JACKAL FILES
MARVEL

Value: Cover or less

❑1, Aug 95, One-Shot; files on main Spider-Man characters and equipment 1.95

SPIDER-MAN: THE LOST YEARS
MARVEL

	ORIG	GOOD	FINE	N-MINT
❑0, Jan 96, The Double; The Parker Legacy, collects clone origin back-up stories; Collects prologue chapters to series	3.95	0.79	1.98	3.95
❑1, Aug 95, JR2, enhanced cardstock cover	2.95	0.60	1.50	3.00
❑2, Sep 95, JR2, Intimacies, enhanced cardstock cover	2.95	0.60	1.50	3.00
❑3, Oct 95, JR2, enhanced cardstock cover	2.95	0.60	1.50	3.00

SPIDER-MAN: THE MANGA
MARVEL

Value: Cover or less

❑1, Dec 97	3.99	❑17, Aug 98	2.99
❑2, Jan 98, V: Electro	2.99	❑18, Sep 98	2.99
❑3, Feb 98	2.99	❑19, Sep 98	2.99
❑4, Feb 98	2.99	❑20, Oct 98	2.99
❑5, Mar 98	2.99	❑21, Oct 98	2.99
❑6	2.99	❑22	2.99
❑7	2.99	❑23	2.99
❑8, Apr 98	2.99	❑24	2.99
❑9, Apr 98	2.99	❑25	2.99
❑10, May 98	2.99	❑26, A: Mitsuo Kitano	2.99
❑11, May 98	2.99	❑27, A: Mitsuo Kitano	2.99
❑12, Jun 98	2.99	❑28, A: Mitsuo Kitano	2.99
❑13, Jun 98	2.99	❑29, A: Mitsuo Kitano	2.99
❑14, Jul 98, V: Mysterio	2.99	❑30, A: Mitsuo Kitano	2.99
❑15, Jul 98	2.99	❑31	2.99
❑16, Aug 98, V: Mysterio	2.99		

SPIDER-MAN: THE MUTANT AGENDA
MARVEL

Value: Cover or less

❑0, Mar 94, A: Beast; O: Spider-Man; V: Hobgoblin, cover says Feb, indicia says Mar; strip reprints; Spaces to paste in newspaper strip 1.25

❑1, Mar 94, A: Beast; V: Hobgoblin, Ties in with daily Spider-Man newspaper strip 1.75

❑2, Apr 94, A: Beast; V: Hobgoblin 1.75

❑3, May 94, A: Beast; V: Hobgoblin 1.75

SPIDER-MAN: THE PARKER YEARS
MARVEL

Value: Cover or less

❑1, Nov 95, One-Shot; retells events in the clone's life from Amazing Spider-Man #150 to the present 2.50

SPIDER-MAN UNIVERSE
MARVEL

Value: Cover or less

❑1, Mar 00, JBy (w), Living in Oblivion; The Time Before, D: Mary Jane (revealed), Reprints Peter Parker: Spider-Man #13, Web-spinners #13, Spider-Woman (2nd Series) #8 .... 4.99

SPIDER-MAN UNLIMITED
MARVEL

	ORIG	GOOD	FINE	N-MINT
❑1, May 93, Maximum Carnage, Part 1, A: Venom; A: Carnage	3.95	1.00	2.50	5.00
❑2, Aug 93, KB (w), Maximum Carnage; Maximum Carnage, Part 14, A: Venom; A: Carnage	3.95	0.90	2.25	4.50
❑3, Nov 93, KB (w), Doctor Octopus	3.95	0.90	2.25	4.50
❑4, Feb 94, KB (w), Still Living In Fear; Just A Joe Named Guy, Mysterio	3.95	0.90	2.25	4.50
❑5, May 94, KB (w), Human Torch	3.95	0.90	2.25	4.50
❑6, Aug 94	3.95	0.80	2.00	4.00
❑7, Nov 94, Spider-Man and clone	3.95	0.80	2.00	4.00
❑8, Feb 95, Spider-Man and clone	3.95	0.80	2.00	4.00
❑9, May 95, Mark of Kaine, Part 5	3.95	0.80	2.00	4.00
❑10, Sep 95, Exiled, Part 4, V: Vulture	3.95	0.80	2.00	4.00
❑11, Jan 96, SB, The Skull Jackets; Night Work, A: Black Cat; 1: Skull Jacket	3.95	0.80	2.00	4.00
❑12, May 96, V: Scorpia; V: Beetle; V: Jack O'Lantern; V: Boomerang; V: Shocker	3.95	0.80	2.00	4.00
❑13, Aug 96, A: Iron Fist; A: Luke Cage; V: Scorpion	3.95	0.59	1.48	2.95
❑14, Dec 96, Game's End, D: Nightwatch; D: Polestar	2.99	0.60	1.50	2.99
❑15, Feb 97, Facing the Void, V: Puma	2.99	0.60	1.50	2.99
❑16, May 97, The Wages of Conquest, A: Silver Sable	2.99	0.60	1.50	2.99
❑17, Aug 97, V: Robot Master, gatefold summary	2.99	0.60	1.50	2.99
❑18, Nov 97, O: Doctor Octopus, gatefold summary	2.99	0.60	1.50	2.99
❑19, Feb 98, V: Lizard, gatefold summary	2.99	0.60	1.50	2.99
❑20, May 98, A: Hannibal King, gatefold summary	2.99	0.60	1.50	2.99
❑21, Aug 98, A: Frankenstein's Monster, gatefold summary	2.99	0.60	1.50	2.99
❑22, Nov 98, V: Scorpion, Final Issue; gatefold summary	2.99	0.60	1.50	2.99
❑23	2.99	0.60	1.50	2.99

SPIDER-MAN UNLIMITED (2ND SERIES)
MARVEL

Value: Cover or less

❑1, Dec 99, Worlds Apart, based on animated television show 2.99

SPIDER-MAN UNMASKED
MARVEL

Value: Cover or less

❑1, Nov 96, nn 5.95

SPIDER-MAN: VENOM AGENDA
MARVEL

Value: Cover or less

❑1, Jan 98, One-Shot; gatefold summary 2.99

SPIDER-MAN VS. DRACULA
MARVEL

	ORIG	GOOD	FINE	N-MINT
❑1, RA, Ship Of Fiends!, Reprint	1.75	0.40	1.00	2.00

SPIDER-MAN VS. PUNISHER
MARVEL

Value: Cover or less

❑1, Jul 00, No One Here Gets Out Alive 2.99

SPIDER-MAN VS. THE HULK
MARVEL

	ORIG	GOOD	FINE	N-MINT
❑1, nn; giveaway	—	0.20	0.50	1.00

SPIDER-MAN VS. WOLVERINE
MARVEL

Value: Cover or less

❑1, Feb 87, D: Ned Leeds....... 2.50

❑1-2, Aug 90, D: Ned Leeds, cardstock cover 4.95

SPIDER-MAN: WEB OF DOOM
MARVEL

	ORIG	GOOD	FINE	N-MINT
❑1, Aug 94	1.75	0.40	1.00	2.00
❑2, Sep 94	1.75	0.40	1.00	2.00
❑3, Oct 94	1.75	0.40	1.00	2.00

SPIDER, THE: REIGN OF THE VAMPIRE KING
ECLIPSE

Value: Cover or less

❑1 .... 4.95

❑2 .... 5.95

❑3 .... 5.95

SPIDER'S WEB, THE
BLAZING

Value: Cover or less

❑1, Web-Man in The Web of Time; G-8 and His Battle Aces, Flipbook 1.50

SPIDER-WOMAN
MARVEL

	ORIG	GOOD	FINE	N-MINT
❑1, Apr 78, CI, ...A Future Uncertain!, O: Spider-Woman I (Jessica Drew)	0.35	0.80	2.00	4.00
❑2, May 78, 1: Morgan LeFay	0.35	0.60	1.50	3.00
❑3, Jun 78, 1: Brothers Grimm	0.35	0.50	1.25	2.50
❑4, Jul 78	0.35	0.40	1.00	2.00
❑5, Aug 78	0.35	0.40	1.00	2.00
❑6, Sep 78	0.35	0.35	0.88	1.75
❑7, Oct 78	0.35	0.35	0.88	1.75

	ORIG	GOOD	FINE	N-MINT
❑8, Nov 78	0.35	0.35	0.88	1.75
❑9, Dec 78, 1: Needle	0.35	0.35	0.88	1.75
❑10, Jan 79	0.35	0.35	0.88	1.75
❑11, Feb 79	0.35	0.30	0.75	1.50
❑12, Mar 79, D: Brothers Grimm	0.35	0.30	0.75	1.50
❑13, Apr 79	0.35	0.30	0.75	1.50
❑14, May 79	0.40	0.30	0.75	1.50
❑15, Jun 79	0.40	0.30	0.75	1.50
❑16, Jul 79	0.40	0.30	0.75	1.50
❑17, Aug 79	0.40	0.30	0.75	1.50
❑18, Sep 79	0.40	0.30	0.75	1.50
❑19, Oct 79, V: Werewolf	0.40	0.30	0.75	1.50
❑20, Nov 79, A: Spider-Man	0.40	0.30	0.75	1.50
❑21, Dec 79	0.40	0.30	0.75	1.50
❑22, Jan 80	0.40	0.30	0.75	1.50
❑23, Feb 80	0.40	0.30	0.75	1.50
❑24, Mar 80, TVE, Trapped-In The Dooms-day Room!	0.40	0.30	0.75	1.50
❑25, Apr 80, To Free A Felon!	0.40	0.30	0.75	1.50
❑26, May 80, JBy (c)	0.40	0.30	0.75	1.50
❑27, Jun 80	0.40	0.30	0.75	1.50
❑28, Jul 80, A: Spider-Man	0.40	0.30	0.75	1.50
❑29, Aug 80, A: Spider-Man	0.40	0.30	0.75	1.50
❑30, Sep 80, 1: Doctor Karl Malus	0.50	0.30	0.75	1.50
❑31, Oct 80	0.50	0.30	0.75	1.50
❑32, Nov 80	0.50	0.30	0.75	1.50
❑33, Dec 80, 1: Turner D. Century	0.50	0.30	0.75	1.50
❑34, Jan 81	0.50	0.30	0.75	1.50
❑35, Feb 81	0.50	0.30	0.75	1.50
❑36, Mar 81, The Wanderer!	0.50	0.30	0.75	1.50
❑37, Apr 81, 1: Siryn; A: X-Men	0.50	0.80	2.00	4.00
❑38, Jun 81, A: X-Men	0.50	0.60	1.50	3.00
❑39, Aug 81	0.50	0.25	0.63	1.25
❑40, Oct 81	0.50	0.25	0.63	1.25
❑41, Dec 81	0.50	0.25	0.63	1.25
❑42, Feb 82	0.60	0.25	0.63	1.25
❑43, Apr 82	0.60	0.25	0.63	1.25
❑44, Jun 82	0.60	0.25	0.63	1.25
❑45, Aug 82	0.60	0.25	0.63	1.25
❑46, Oct 82	0.60	0.25	0.63	1.25
❑47, Dec 82	0.60	0.25	0.63	1.25
❑48, Feb 83	0.60	0.25	0.63	1.25
❑49, Apr 83	0.60	0.25	0.63	1.25
❑50, Jun 83, D: Spider-Woman I (Jessica Drew), Photo cover; Final Issue; Giant-size	1.00	0.80	2.00	4.00

SPIDER-WOMAN (2ND SERIES)

MARVEL

Value: Cover or less

❑1, Nov 93	1.75	❑3, Jan 94	1.75
❑2, Dec 93	1.75	❑4, Feb 94	1.75

SPIDER-WOMAN (3RD SERIES)

MARVEL

	ORIG	GOOD	FINE	N-MINT
❑1, Jul 99, JBy (w), Spider Spider	2.99	0.60	1.50	2.99
❑2, Aug 99	1.99	0.60	1.50	2.99
❑3, Sep 99	1.99	0.40	1.00	1.99
❑4, Oct 99	1.99	0.40	1.00	1.99
❑5, Nov 99	1.99	0.40	1.00	1.99
❑6, Dec 99	1.99	0.40	1.00	1.99
❑7	1.99	0.40	1.00	1.99
❑8	1.99	0.40	1.00	1.99
❑9	1.99	0.40	1.00	1.99
❑10	—	0.45	1.13	2.25
❑11	—	0.45	1.13	2.25
❑12	—	0.45	1.13	2.25
❑13	—	0.45	1.13	2.25
❑14	—	0.45	1.13	2.25
❑15	2.25	0.45	1.13	2.25
❑16	2.25	0.45	1.13	2.25
❑17	2.25	0.45	1.13	2.25
❑18, Dec 00, JBy (w), Dry Bones, Final Issue	2.25	0.45	1.13	2.25

SPIDERY-MON: MAXIMUM CARCASS

PARODY PRESS

Value: Cover or less

❑1/A, Covers of the three variants join together to form a mural; Variant edition A	3.25
❑1/B, Covers of the three variants join together to form a mural; Variant edition B	3.25
❑1/C, Covers of the three variants join together to form a mural; Variant edition C	3.25

SPIDEY SUPER STORIES

MARVEL

	ORIG	GOOD	FINE	N-MINT
❑1, Oct 74, Spider-Man is Born!; Spidey Signs Up!, O: Spider-Man	0.35	1.20	3.00	6.00
❑2, Nov 74	0.35	0.80	2.00	4.00
❑3, Dec 74, V: Circus of Crime	0.35	0.60	1.50	3.00
❑4, Jan 75	0.35	0.60	1.50	3.00

Marvel tied its comics and newspaper presence together in *Spider-Man: The Mutant Agenda.*

© 1994 Marvel Comics

	ORIG	GOOD	FINE	N-MINT
❑5, Feb 75	0.35	0.60	1.50	3.00
❑6, Mar 75	0.35	0.50	1.25	2.50
❑7, Apr 75	0.35	0.50	1.25	2.50
❑8, May 75	0.35	0.50	1.25	2.50
❑9, Jun 75, V: Doctor Doom; V: Dr. Doom	0.35	0.50	1.25	2.50
❑10	0.35	0.50	1.25	2.50
❑11	0.35	0.50	1.25	2.50
❑12	0.35	0.50	1.25	2.50
❑13	0.35	0.50	1.25	2.50
❑14, Dec 75, A: Shanna	0.35	0.50	1.25	2.50
❑15, Feb 76, A: Storm	0.35	0.50	1.25	2.50
❑16, Apr 76	0.35	0.50	1.25	2.50
❑17, Jun 76	0.35	0.50	1.25	2.50
❑18, Aug 76	0.35	0.50	1.25	2.50
❑19, Oct 76	0.35	0.50	1.25	2.50
❑20, Dec 76	0.35	0.50	1.25	2.50
❑21, Feb 77	0.35	0.50	1.25	2.50
❑22, Apr 77	0.35	0.50	1.25	2.50
❑23, Jun 77, The Amazing Shrinking Spidey	0.35	0.50	1.25	2.50
❑24, Jul 77, A: Thundra	0.35	0.50	1.25	2.50
❑25, Aug 77	0.35	0.50	1.25	2.50
❑26, Sep 77	0.35	0.50	1.25	2.50
❑27, Oct 77	0.35	0.50	1.25	2.50
❑28, Nov 77	0.35	0.50	1.25	2.50
❑29, Dec 77, V: Kingpin	0.35	0.50	1.25	2.50
❑30, Jan 78, V: Kang the Conqueror	0.35	0.50	1.25	2.50
❑31, Feb 78	0.35	0.50	1.25	2.50
❑32, Mar 78	0.35	0.50	1.25	2.50
❑33, Apr 78, A: Hulk	0.35	0.50	1.25	2.50
❑34, May 78	0.35	0.50	1.25	2.50
❑35, Jul 78, A: Shanna	0.35	0.50	1.25	2.50
❑36, Sep 78	0.35	0.50	1.25	2.50
❑37, Nov 78	0.35	0.50	1.25	2.50
❑38, Jan 79	0.35	0.50	1.25	2.50
❑39, Mar 79, A: Hellcat; A: Thanos	0.35	0.50	1.25	2.50
❑40, May 79	0.40	0.50	1.25	2.50
❑41, Jul 79	0.40	0.50	1.25	2.50
❑42, Sep 79	0.40	0.50	1.25	2.50
❑43, Nov 79	0.40	0.50	1.25	2.50
❑44, Jan 80	0.40	0.50	1.25	2.50
❑45, Mar 80, A: Silver Surfer; A: Doctor Doom	0.40	0.50	1.25	2.50
❑46, May 80	0.50	0.50	1.25	2.50
❑47, Jul 80	0.50	0.50	1.25	2.50
❑48, Sep 80	0.50	0.50	1.25	2.50
❑49, Nov 80	0.50	0.50	1.25	2.50
❑50, Jan 81	0.50	0.50	1.25	2.50
❑51, Mar 81	0.50	0.50	1.25	2.50
❑52, May 81	0.50	0.50	1.25	2.50
❑53, Jul 81	0.50	0.50	1.25	2.50
❑54, Sep 81	0.50	0.50	1.25	2.50
❑55, Nov 81, V: Kingpin	0.50	0.50	1.25	2.50
❑56, Jan 82	0.60	0.50	1.25	2.50
❑57, Mar 82, Final Issue	0.60	0.50	1.25	2.50

SPINELESS-MAN $2099

PARODY PRESS

Value: Cover or less

❑1 ... 2.50

SPINE-TINGLING TALES (DR. SPEKTOR PRESENTS...)

GOLD KEY

	ORIG	GOOD	FINE	N-MINT
❑1	0.25	0.60	1.50	3.00
❑2	0.25	0.40	1.00	2.00
❑3	0.25	0.40	1.00	2.00
❑4	0.25	0.40	1.00	2.00

SPINWORLD

SLAVE LABOR

Value: Cover or less

❑1, Jul 97, BA, The Snake and the Staff, b&w	2.95
❑2, Aug 97, BA, Spacing Dutch-man, b&w	2.95
❑3, Oct 97, BA, Spacing Dutch-man, b&w	2.95
❑4, Jan 98, BA, Politics of Plenty, b&w	3.95

SPIRAL PATH, THE
Eclipse

	ORIG	GOOD	FINE	N-MINT
❑1	1.50	0.35	0.88	1.75
❑2	1.50	0.35	0.88	1.75

SPIRAL ZONE
DC

Value: Cover or less

- ❑1, Feb 88, DG; CI, Colossus Of Doom 1.00
- ❑2, Mar 88, DG; CI 1.00
- ❑3, Apr 88, DG; CI 1.00
- ❑4, May 88, DG; CI 1.00

SPIRIT, THE (5TH SERIES)
Harvey

	ORIG	GOOD	FINE	N-MINT
❑1, WE, WE (w), O: The Spirit, Harvey	0.25	10.00	25.00	50.00
❑2, WE, WE (w)	0.25	8.40	21.00	42.00

SPIRIT, THE (6TH SERIES)
Kitchen Sink

	ORIG	GOOD	FINE	N-MINT
❑1, Jan 73, b&w; adult; Krupp/Kitchen Sink publishes	0.50	2.80	7.00	14.00
❑2, adult	—	2.80	7.00	14.00

SPIRIT, THE (7TH SERIES)
Ken Pierce

	ORIG	GOOD	FINE	N-MINT
❑1	3.95	3.60	9.00	18.00
❑2	5.95	3.60	9.00	18.00
❑3	5.95	3.60	9.00	18.00
❑4	6.95	3.60	9.00	18.00

SPIRIT, THE (8TH SERIES)
Kitchen Sink

	ORIG	GOOD	FINE	N-MINT
❑1, Oct 83, WE, WE (w), The Christmas Spirit; The Return of the Villains of '42, O: The Spirit, full color; Kitchen Sink publishes; #291, 292, 293, 294	1.75	1.00	2.50	5.00
❑2, Dec 83, WE, WE (w), Hildie and Satin; The Siberian Dagger, full color; #295, 296, 297, 298	1.75	0.80	2.00	4.00
❑3, Feb 84, WE, WE (w), Introducing Blubber; Rockhead Stone, full color; #299, 300, 301, 302	1.75	0.80	2.00	4.00
❑4, Mar 84, WE, WE (w), Nylon Rose; The Last Trolley, full color; #303, 304; Reprints Police Comics #98 Spirit Story	2.00	0.70	1.75	3.50
❑5, Jun 84, WE, WE (w)	2.00	0.70	1.75	3.50
❑6, Aug 84, WE, WE (w), Welcome Home, Ebony!; Carrion's Rock	2.00	0.70	1.75	3.50
❑7, Oct 84, WE, WE (w)	2.95	0.70	1.75	3.50
❑8, Feb 85, WE, WE (w)	2.95	0.70	1.75	3.50
❑9, Apr 85, WE, WE (w)	2.95	0.70	1.75	3.50
❑10, Jun 85, WE, WE (w)	2.95	0.59	1.48	2.95
❑11, Aug 85, WE, WE (w)	2.95	0.59	1.48	2.95
❑12, Oct 85, WE, WE (w)	1.95	0.40	1.00	2.00
❑13, Nov 85, WE, WE (w)	1.95	0.40	1.00	2.00
❑14, Dec 85, WE, WE (w)	1.95	0.40	1.00	2.00
❑15, Jan 86, WE, WE (w), Hoagy the Yogi; April Fool, #356, 357, 358, 359	1.95	0.40	1.00	2.00
❑16, Feb 86, WE, WE (w)	1.95	0.40	1.00	2.00
❑17, Mar 86, WE, WE (w)	1.95	0.40	1.00	2.00
❑18, Apr 86, WE, WE (w)	1.95	0.40	1.00	2.00
❑19, May 86, WE, WE (w), Black Gold; Hangly Hollyer Mansion	1.95	0.40	1.00	2.00
❑20, Jun 86, WE, WE (w), Hanzel and Gretel; Li'l Adam	1.95	0.40	1.00	2.00
❑21, Jul 86, WE, WE (w)	1.95	0.40	1.00	2.00
❑22, Aug 86, WE, WE (w), A Killer At Large; Into the Light	1.95	0.40	1.00	2.00
❑23, Sep 86, WE, WE (w), Cinderella; Mr. McDool	1.95	0.40	1.00	2.00
❑24, Oct 86, WE, WE (w)	1.95	0.40	1.00	2.00
❑25, Nov 86, WE, WE (w)	1.95	0.40	1.00	2.00
❑26, Dec 86, WE, WE (w)	1.95	0.40	1.00	2.00
❑27, Jan 87, WE, WE (w), Montabaldo; Blackmail	2.00	0.40	1.00	2.00
❑28, Feb 87, WE, WE (w)	2.00	0.40	1.00	2.00
❑29, Mar 87, WE, WE (w)	2.00	0.40	1.00	2.00
❑30, Apr 87, WE, WE (w)	2.00	0.40	1.00	2.00
❑31, May 87, WE, WE (w)	2.00	0.40	1.00	2.00
❑32, Jun 87, WE, WE (w), Cheap is Cheap; Murder, ...Bloodless Type	2.00	0.40	1.00	2.00
❑33, Jul 87, WE, WE (w)	2.00	0.40	1.00	2.00
❑34, Aug 87, WE, WE (w)	2.00	0.40	1.00	2.00
❑35, Sep 87, WE, WE (w)	2.00	0.40	1.00	2.00
❑36, Oct 87, WE, WE (w)	2.00	0.40	1.00	2.00
❑37, Nov 87, WE, WE (w)	2.00	0.40	1.00	2.00
❑38, Dec 88, WE, WE (w)	2.00	0.40	1.00	2.00
❑39, Jan 88, WE, WE (w), Almanac of the Year 1948; Ice	2.00	0.40	1.00	2.00
❑40, Feb 88, WE, WE (w)	2.00	0.40	1.00	2.00
❑41, Mar 88, WE, WE (w), Wertham parody	2.00	0.40	1.00	2.00
❑42, Apr 88, WE, WE (w)	2.00	0.40	1.00	2.00
❑43, May 88, WE, WE (w)	2.00	0.40	1.00	2.00
❑44, Jun 88, WE, WE (w)	2.00	0.40	1.00	2.00
❑45, Jul 88, WE, WE (w)	2.00	0.40	1.00	2.00
❑46, Aug 88, WE, WE (w)	2.00	0.40	1.00	2.00
❑47, Sep 88, WE, WE (w), Matua; The Return	2.00	0.40	1.00	2.00
❑48, Oct 88, WE, WE (w), Rat-Tat The Toy Machine Gun; Ten Minutes	2.00	0.40	1.00	2.00
❑49, Nov 88, WE, WE (w), Crime; Death of Autumn Mews	2.00	0.40	1.00	2.00
❑50, Dec 88, WE, WE (w), Elect Miss Rhinemaiden; The Inner Voice	2.00	0.40	1.00	2.00
❑51, Jan 89, WE, WE (w), The Embezzler; Winter Haven	2.00	0.40	1.00	2.00
❑52, Feb 89, WE, WE (w), The Christmas Spirit; Fan Mail	2.00	0.40	1.00	2.00
❑53, Mar 89, WE, WE (w), The Predictions of Druid Peer; Nickless Nerser	2.00	0.40	1.00	2.00
❑54, Apr 89, WE, WE (w)	2.00	0.40	1.00	2.00
❑55, May 89, WE, WE (w), Carrion; The Island	2.00	0.40	1.00	2.00
❑56, Jun 89, WE, WE (w), Taxes; A Day At the Zoo	2.00	0.40	1.00	2.00
❑57, Jul 89, WE, WE (w)	2.00	0.40	1.00	2.00
❑58, Aug 89, WE, WE (w), Sammy the Explorer; Willum and the Baron	2.00	0.40	1.00	2.00
❑59, Sep 89, WE, WE (w), The Ship vs. darling O'Shea; The Desert	2.00	0.40	1.00	2.00
❑60, Oct 89, WE, WE (w), Investigation; The Wreck of Old 78, #532, 533, 534, 535	2.00	0.40	1.00	2.00
❑61, Nov 89, WE, WE (w), Cape Cod Vacation; Teacher's Pet!, #536, 537, 538, 539	2.00	0.40	1.00	2.00
❑62, Dec 89, WE, WE (w), The Big Win; O'Shea's Uncle	2.00	0.40	1.00	2.00
❑63, Jan 90, WE, WE (w), Halloween; Vietnam '50	2.00	0.40	1.00	2.00
❑64, Feb 90, WE, WE (w), Little Willum; The Winnah	2.00	0.40	1.00	2.00
❑65, Mar 90, WE, WE (w), The Christmas Spirit; Happy New Year	2.00	0.40	1.00	2.00
❑66, Apr 90, WE, WE (w), Future Death; The Meanest Man in the World	2.00	0.40	1.00	2.00
❑67, May 90, WE, WE (w), To the Spirit With Love; Portier Fortune	2.00	0.40	1.00	2.00
❑68, Jun 90, WE, WE (w)	2.00	0.40	1.00	2.00
❑69, Jul 90, WE, WE (w), Time Bomb; Hobart	2.00	0.40	1.00	2.00
❑70, Aug 90, WE, WE (w), The Hero; The 7th Husband	2.00	0.40	1.00	2.00
❑71, Sep 90, WE, WE (w), Wanchu; Khyber Bill	2.00	0.40	1.00	2.00
❑72, Oct 90, WE, WE (w), The Loot of Robinson Crusoe; Heat	2.00	0.40	1.00	2.00
❑73, Nov 90, The Return of the Narcissus; The Foxtrot Poll	2.00	0.40	1.00	2.00
❑74, Dec 90, Dance of the Bullfighter; Dr. Schyzoid	2.00	0.40	1.00	2.00
❑75, Jan 91, Roamin Umpire; The Suicide Town	2.00	0.40	1.00	2.00
❑76, Feb 91, A Perfect Crime Plot; Claymore Castle's Curse	2.00	0.40	1.00	2.00
❑77, Mar 91, The League of Liars; The Man From Mars	2.00	0.40	1.00	2.00
❑78, Apr 91, Joe Fix; Joshua Blows His Horn	2.00	0.40	1.00	2.00
❑79, May 91, A Witness to Murder; The First Man on Mars, #608, 609, 610, 611	2.00	0.40	1.00	2.00
❑80, Jun 91, Leap Year; It Kills by Dark, #612, 613, 614, 615	2.00	0.40	1.00	2.00
❑81, Jul 91, Dolan Walks a Beat; Staple Springs, #616, 617, 618, 619	2.00	0.40	1.00	2.00
❑82, Aug 91, Ellen Dolan for Mayor!; The Great Galactic Mystery, #620, 621, 622, 623	2.00	0.40	1.00	2.00
❑83, Sep 91, The Incident of the Sitting Duck; Assassins Incorporated, #625, 626, 627, 628	2.00	0.40	1.00	2.00
❑84, Oct 91, What Are You Really Like?; 500 Papers	2.00	0.40	1.00	2.00
❑85, Nov 91, The Ballad of Greenly Sleeve; Matt Slugg, #632, 633, 634, 635	2.00	0.40	1.00	2.00
❑86, Dec 91	2.00	0.40	1.00	2.00
❑87, Jan 92, Final Issue	2.00	0.40	1.00	2.00

SPIRIT, THE (MAGAZINE)
Warren

	ORIG	GOOD	FINE	N-MINT
❑1, Apr 74, WE, WE (w), The Last Trolley; Escape	1.00	3.00	7.50	15.00
❑2, Jun 74, WE, WE (w)	1.00	1.60	4.00	8.00
❑3, Aug 74, WE, WE (w)	1.00	1.40	3.50	7.00
❑4, Oct 74, WE, WE (w)	1.00	1.00	2.50	5.00
❑5, Dec 74, WE, WE (w)	1.00	1.00	2.50	5.00
❑6, Feb 75, WE, WE (w)	1.25	1.00	2.50	5.00
❑7, Apr 75, WE, WE (w)	1.25	1.00	2.50	5.00
❑8, Jun 75, WE, WE (w)	1.25	1.00	2.50	5.00
❑9, Aug 75, WE, WE (w)	1.25	1.00	2.50	5.00

	ORIG	GOOD	FINE	N-MINT
❑10, Oct 75, WE, WE (w)	1.25	1.00	2.50	5.00
❑11, Dec 75, WE, WE (w)	1.25	0.60	1.50	3.00
❑12, Feb 76, WE, WE (w)	1.25	0.60	1.50	3.00
❑13, Apr 76, WE, WE (w)	1.25	0.60	1.50	3.00
❑14, Jun 76, WE, WE (w)	1.25	0.60	1.50	3.00
❑15, Aug 76, WE, WE (w)	1.25	0.60	1.50	3.00
❑16, Oct 76, WE, WE (w)	1.25	0.60	1.50	3.00
❑17, Nov 77, WE, WE (w)	1.50	0.60	1.50	3.00
❑18, May 78, WE, WE (w)	1.50	0.60	1.50	3.00
❑19, Oct 78, WE, WE (w)	1.50	0.60	1.50	3.00
❑20, Mar 79, WE, WE (w)	1.50	0.60	1.50	3.00
❑21, Jul 79, WE, WE (w)	1.75	0.60	1.50	3.00
❑22, Dec 79, WE, WE (w)	1.75	0.60	1.50	3.00
❑23, Feb 80, WE, WE (w)	1.75	0.60	1.50	3.00
❑24, May 80, WE, WE (w)	1.75	0.60	1.50	3.00
❑25, Aug 80, WE, WE (w)	1.75	0.60	1.50	3.00
❑26, Dec 80, WW; WE, WW (w); WE (w), The Public Interest; The Confessions of Monks Mallon	2.00	0.60	1.50	3.00
❑27, Feb 81, WE, WE (w)	2.00	0.60	1.50	3.00
❑28, Apr 81, WE, WE (w)	2.00	0.60	1.50	3.00
❑29, Jun 81, WE, WE (w)	2.00	0.60	1.50	3.00
❑30, Jul 81, WE, WE (w)	2.00	0.60	1.50	3.00
❑31, Oct 81, WE, WE (w)	2.00	0.60	1.50	3.00
❑32, Dec 81, WE, WE (w)	2.50	0.60	1.50	3.00
❑33, Feb 82, WE, WE (w)	2.50	0.60	1.50	3.00
❑34, Apr 82, WE, WE (w)	2.50	0.60	1.50	3.00
❑35, Jun 82, WE, WE (w)	2.50	0.60	1.50	3.00
❑36, Aug 82, WE, WE (w)	2.95	0.60	1.50	3.00
❑37, Oct 82, WE, WE (w)	2.95	0.60	1.50	3.00
❑38, Dec 82, WE, WE (w)	2.95	0.60	1.50	3.00
❑39, Feb 83, WE, WE (w)	2.95	0.60	1.50	3.00
❑40, Apr 83, WE, WE (w)	2.95	0.60	1.50	3.00
❑41, Jun 83, WE, WE (w)	2.95	0.60	1.50	3.00

SPIRIT JAM
KITCHEN SINK

Value: Cover or less

❑1 ... 5.95

SPIRIT OF THE TAO, THE
IMAGE

	ORIG	GOOD	FINE	N-MINT
❑1, Jun 98	2.50	0.80	2.00	4.00
❑2, Jul 98, Ta Chuan (The Great Commentary), Part1	2.50	0.60	1.50	3.00
❑3, Aug 98	2.50	0.60	1.50	3.00
❑4, Sep 98	2.50	0.50	1.25	2.50
❑5, Nov 98	2.50	0.50	1.25	2.50
❑6, Dec 98	2.50	0.50	1.25	2.50
❑7, Feb 99	2.50	0.50	1.25	2.50
❑8, Apr 99	2.50	0.50	1.25	2.50
❑9, May 99	2.50	0.50	1.25	2.50
❑10, Jun 99	2.50	0.50	1.25	2.50
❑11, Aug 99	2.50	0.50	1.25	2.50
❑12	2.50	0.50	1.25	2.50
❑13, Nov 99	2.50	0.50	1.25	2.50
❑Ash 1, 1: Lance; 1: Jasmine	—	1.60	4.00	8.00

SPIRIT OF THE WIND
CHOCOLATE MOUSE

Value: Cover or less

❑1, b&w ... 2.00

SPIRIT OF WONDER
DARK HORSE

Value: Cover or less

- ❑1, Apr 96, b&w ... 2.95
- ❑2, May 96, b&w ... 2.95
- ❑3, Jun 96, b&w ... 2.95
- ❑4, Jul 96, China Strikes Back, Part 1, b&w ... 2.95
- ❑5, Aug 96, China Strikes Back, Part 2, b&w; Final Issue ... 2.95

SPIRITS
MIND WALKER

Value: Cover or less

❑3, Sep 95, b&w ... 2.95

SPIRITS OF VENOM
MARVEL

Value: Cover or less

❑1, Storm Shadows; Chasing Shadows ... 9.95

SPIRIT, THE: THE NEW ADVENTURES
KITCHEN SINK

Value: Cover or less

- ❑1, Mar 98, DaG, AMo (w), The Most Important Meal; Force of Arms ... 3.50
- ❑2, Apr 98, The Return of Mink Stole; Sunday in the Park with St. George ... 3.50
- ❑3, May 98, AMo (w), Last Night I Dreamed of Dr. Cobra; Ellen's Stalker ... 3.50
- ❑4, Jun 98, The Samovar of Shooshnipoor; The Weapon ... 3.50
- ❑5, Jul 98, Cursed Beauty ... 3.50
- ❑6, Sep 98, Swami Vashtibubu; Baby Eichberg ... 3.50
- ❑7, Oct 98, Golf Anyone?; The Pacifist ... 3.50
- ❑8, Nov 98, Sweetheart ... 3.50

SPIRIT: THE ORIGIN YEARS
KITCHEN SINK

Value: Cover or less

- ❑1, May 92, WE, WE (w), The Origin of the Spirit; The Return of Dr. Cobra, O: The Spirit ... 2.95
- ❑2, Jul 92, WE, WE (w) ... 2.95
- ❑3, Sep 92, WE, WE (w) ... 2.95
- ❑4, Nov 92, WE, WE (w) ... 2.95
- ❑5, Jan 93, WE, WE (w) ... 2.95
- ❑6, Mar 93, WE, WE (w) ... 2.95
- ❑7, May 93, WE, WE (w) ... 2.95
- ❑8, Jul 93, WE, WE (w) ... 2.95
- ❑9, Sep 93, WE, WE (w) ... 2.95
- ❑10, Dec 93, WE, WE (w) ... 2.95

Kitchen Sink's black-and-white reprints of Will Eisner's *Spirit* began in 1983 and ended in 1992.

© 1983 Will Eisner (Kitchen Sink Press)

SPIRIT WORLD
DC

	ORIG	GOOD	FINE	N-MINT
❑1, Jul 71, JK, JK (w), poster	0.25	7.00	17.50	35.00

SPIROU & FANTASIO: Z IS FOR ZORGLUB
FANTASY FLIGHT

Value: Cover or less

❑1, graphic novel ... 8.95

SPITFIRE AND THE TROUBLESHOOTERS
MARVEL

	ORIG	GOOD	FINE	N-MINT
❑1, Oct 86, HT, Beginnings	0.75	0.20	0.50	1.00
❑2, Nov 86	0.75	0.20	0.50	1.00
❑3, Dec 86	0.75	0.20	0.50	1.00
❑4, Jan 87, TMc	0.75	0.20	0.50	1.00
❑5, Feb 87	0.75	0.20	0.50	1.00
❑6, Mar 87	0.75	0.20	0.50	1.00
❑7, Apr 87	0.75	0.20	0.50	1.00
❑8, May 87, Down And Dirty	0.75	0.20	0.50	1.00
❑9, Jun 87, Series continued in "Code Name: Spitfire"	0.75	0.20	0.50	1.00

SPITTIN' IMAGE
ECLIPSE

Value: Cover or less

❑1, Fred Schiller, nn; b&w parody ... 2.50

SPIT WAD COMICS
SPIT WAD PRESS

Value: Cover or less

❑1, Jun 83, b&w ... 2.50

SPLAT!
MAD DOG

Value: Cover or less

- ❑1, b&w ... 2.50
- ❑2, Mar 87, Cartoon Man's Best Friend; Steroids ... 2.50
- ❑3 ... 2.50

SPLATTER (ARPAD)
ARPAD

Value: Cover or less

❑1, b&w ... 2.50

SPLATTER (NORTHSTAR)
NORTHSTAR

	ORIG	GOOD	FINE	N-MINT
❑1, b&w; adult	2.75	0.99	2.47	4.95
❑2, b&w; adult	2.75	0.55	1.38	2.75
❑3, b&w; adult	2.75	0.55	1.38	2.75
❑4, b&w; adult	2.75	0.55	1.38	2.75
❑5, b&w; adult	2.75	0.55	1.38	2.75
❑6, b&w; adult	2.75	0.55	1.38	2.75
❑7, Klownshock: Through the Looking Glass; Conversation O'er a Corpse, b&w; adult.	2.75	0.55	1.38	2.75
❑8, adult	2.75	0.55	1.38	2.75
❑Anl 1, adult	4.95	0.99	2.47	4.95

SPLITTING IMAGE
IMAGE

Value: Cover or less

- ❑1, Mar 93, Based On A True Story!, parody ... 1.95
- ❑2, Apr 93, parody ... 1.95

SPOOF
MARVEL

	ORIG	GOOD	FINE	N-MINT
❑1, Darn Shadows!; Marooned	0.15	1.20	3.00	6.00
❑2	0.20	0.80	2.00	4.00
❑3	0.20	0.80	2.00	4.00
❑4	0.20	0.80	2.00	4.00
❑5, Nut Gallery; 177 Sick, Final Issue	0.20	0.80	2.00	4.00

SPOOF COMICS
SPOOF

Value: Cover or less

- ❑0, b&w; Imp-Unity ... 2.50
- ❑1, b&w; Spider-Femme ... 2.50
- ❑1-2, full color; 2nd Printing; Spider-Femme ... 2.50
- ❑2, b&w; Batbabe ... 2.50
- ❑2-2, full color; Batbabe ... 2.50
- ❑3, Aug 92, b&w; Wolverbroad ... 2.95
- ❑4, Sep 92, b&w; Superbabe ... 2.95
- ❑5, Oct 92, b&w; Daredame ... 2.95
- ❑6, b&w; X-Babes ... 2.95
- ❑7, b&w; Justice Broads ... 2.95
- ❑8, b&w; Fantastic Femmes ... 2.95
- ❑9, b&w; Hobo ... 2.95
- ❑10, b&w ... 2.95
- ❑11, b&w ... 2.95
- ❑12, Mar 93, b&w; Deathlocks ... 2.95

SPOOK CITY
MYTHIC

Value: Cover or less

❑1, Nov 97, b&w ... 2.95

SPOOKGIRL
SLAVE LABOR

Value: Cover or less

❑1 ... 2.95

SPOOKY (VOL. 2)
HARVEY

Value: Cover or less

❑1 ... 1.25
❑2 ... 1.25
❑3 ... 1.25
❑4, No Boos are Good Boos; Nightmare The Galloping Ghost .. 1.25

SPOOKY DIGEST
HARVEY

	ORIG	GOOD	FINE	N-MINT
❑1	1.75	0.40	1.00	2.00
❑2	1.75	0.40	1.00	2.00

SPOOKY THE DOG CATCHER
PAW PRINTS

Value: Cover or less

❑1, Oct 94, b&w ... 2.50

SPORTS CLASSICS
PERSONALITY

Value: Cover or less

❑1 ... 2.95
❑1/LE, limited edition ... 5.95
❑2 ... 2.95
❑3 ... 2.95
❑4 ... 2.95
❑5 ... 2.95

SPORTS COMICS
PERSONALITY

Value: Cover or less

❑1 ... 2.50
❑2 ... 2.50
❑3 ... 2.50
❑4 ... 2.50

SPORTS HALL OF SHAME IN 3-D
BLACKTHORNE

Value: Cover or less

❑1, baseball ... 2.50

SPORTS LEGENDS
REVOLUTIONARY

Value: Cover or less

❑1, Sep 92, b&w; Joe Namath 2.50
❑2, Oct 92, b&w; Gordie Howe 2.50
❑3, Nov 92, b&w; Arthur Ashe 2.50
❑4, Dec 92, full color; Muhammad Ali ... 2.50
❑5, Jan 93, full color; O.J. Simpson ... 2.50
❑6, Feb 93, full color; K.A. Jabbar ... 2.50
❑7, Mar 93, b&w; Walter Payton 2.95
❑8, Apr 93, b&w; Wilt Chamberlain ... 2.95
❑9, May 93, b&w; Joe Louis 2.95

SPORTS LEGENDS SPECIAL - BREAKING THE COLOR BARRIER
REVOLUTIONARY

Value: Cover or less

❑1, Oct 93, b&w ... 2.95

SPORTS PERSONALITIES
PERSONALITY

Value: Cover or less

❑1, Bo Jackson ... 2.95
❑2, Nolan Ryan ... 2.95
❑3, Rickey Henderson ... 2.95
❑4, Magic Johnson ... 2.95
❑5 ... 2.95
❑6 ... 2.95
❑7 ... 2.95
❑8 ... 2.95
❑9 ... 2.95
❑10 ... 2.95
❑11 ... 2.95
❑12 ... 2.95
❑13 ... 2.95

SPORTS SUPERSTARS
REVOLUTIONARY

Value: Cover or less

❑1, Apr 92, b&w; Michael Jordan ... 2.50
❑2, May 92, b&w; Wayne Gretzsky ... 2.50
❑3, Jun 92, b&w; Magic Johnson ... 2.50
❑4, Jul 92, b&w; Joe Montana 2.50
❑5, Aug 92, b&w; Mike Tyson. 2.50
❑6, Sep 92, b&w; Larry Bird.... 2.50
❑7, Oct 92, b&w; John Elway.. 2.50
❑8, Nov 92, b&w; Julius Erving 2.50
❑9, Dec 92, full color; Barry Sanders ... 2.75
❑10, Jan 93, full color; Isiah Thomas ... 2.75
❑11, Feb 92, full color; Mario Lemieux ... 2.95
❑12, Mar 93, b&w; Dan Marino 2.95
❑13, Apr 93, b&w; Deion Sanders ... 2.95
❑14, May 93, b&w; Patrick Ewing ... 2.95
❑15, Jun 93, b&w; Charles Barkley ... 2.95
❑16, Aug 93, b&w; Shaquille O'neal, Christian Laettner.... 2.95
❑Anl 1, Feb 93, full color; Michael Jordan II ... 2.75

SPOTLIGHT
MARVEL

	ORIG	GOOD	FINE	N-MINT
❑1, Sep 78, Huckleberry Hound	0.35	1.60	4.00	8.00
❑2	—	1.20	3.00	6.00
❑3	—	1.20	3.00	6.00
❑4	—	1.20	3.00	6.00

SPOTLIGHT ON THE GENIUS THAT IS JOE SACCO
FANTAGRAPHICS

Value: Cover or less

❑1, nn; b&w ... 4.95

SPRING BREAK COMICS
AC

	ORIG	GOOD	FINE	N-MINT
❑1, Mar 87, b&w	1.00	0.30	0.75	1.50

SPRING-HEEL JACK
REBEL

Value: Cover or less

❑1, b&w ... 2.25
❑2, b&w ... 2.25

SPRINGTIME TALES (WALT KELLY'S...)
ECLIPSE

Value: Cover or less

❑1, WK, Peter Wheat ... 2.50

SPUD
SPUD PRESS

Value: Cover or less

❑1, Sum 96, b&w ... 3.50

SPUNKY KNIGHT
FANTAGRAPHICS

Value: Cover or less

❑1, May 96 ... 2.95
❑2, Jun 96 ... 2.95
❑3, Jul 96 ... 2.95

SPUNKY TODD: THE PSYCHIC BOY
CALIBER

Value: Cover or less

❑1, b&w ... 2.95

SPYBOY
DARK HORSE

	ORIG	GOOD	FINE	N-MINT
❑1, Oct 99, PD (w)	2.50	0.80	2.00	4.00
❑2, Nov 99, PD (w), Live and Let Fry	2.50	0.60	1.50	3.00
❑3, Dec 99, PD (w), From Russia With Fries and a Coke	2.50	0.60	1.50	3.00
❑4, Jan 00, PD (w)	2.50	0.60	1.50	3.00
❑5, Feb 00, PD (w)	2.50	0.60	1.50	3.00
❑6, Mar 00, PD (w)	2.50	0.50	1.25	2.50
❑7, Apr 00, PD (w)	2.50	0.50	1.25	2.50
❑8, May 00, PD (w)	2.50	0.50	1.25	2.50
❑9, Jun 00, PD (w), Boldfinger	2.50	0.50	1.25	2.50
❑10, Jul 00, PD (w)	2.50	0.50	1.25	2.50
❑11, Aug 00, PD (w)	2.50	0.50	1.25	2.50
❑12, Sep 00, PD (w), Spygirl!	2.95	0.59	1.48	2.95
❑13, Oct 00, PD (w)	—	0.59	1.48	2.95
❑14, Nov 00, PD (w), The Beer and the Dragon	2.99	0.60	1.50	2.99
❑15, Jan 01, PD (w), The Deadly Gourmet Affair	2.99	0.60	1.50	2.99
❑16, Mar 01, PD (w), Fatal Election!	2.99	0.60	1.50	2.99

SPYKE
MARVEL

Value: Cover or less

❑1, Jul 93, 1: Spyke Jones, Embossed cover ... 2.50
❑2, Aug 93 ... 1.95
❑3, Sep 93 ... 1.95
❑4, Oct 93, A: Sonia; A: Muffy ... 1.95

SQUADRON SUPREME
MARVEL

	ORIG	GOOD	FINE	N-MINT
❑1, Sep 85, BH, The Utopia Principle	1.25	0.30	0.75	1.50
❑2, Oct 85, V: Scarlet Centurion	0.75	0.20	0.50	1.00
❑3, Nov 85	0.75	0.20	0.50	1.00
❑4, Dec 85	0.75	0.20	0.50	1.00
❑5, Jan 86, V: Institute of Evil	0.75	0.20	0.50	1.00
❑6, Feb 86	0.75	0.20	0.50	1.00
❑7, Mar 86	0.75	0.20	0.50	1.00
❑8, Apr 86	0.75	0.20	0.50	1.00
❑9, May 86, D: Tom Thumb	0.75	0.20	0.50	1.00
❑10, Jun 86	0.75	0.20	0.50	1.00
❑11, Jul 86	0.75	0.20	0.50	1.00
❑12, Aug 86	1.25	0.25	0.63	1.25

SQUALOR
FIRST

Value: Cover or less

❑1, Dec 89, TS, Quiet Island, 1st comics work by Stefan Petrucha ... 2.75
❑2, Jun 90, TS ... 2.75
❑3, Jul 90, TS ... 2.75
❑4, Aug 90, TS ... 2.75

SQUEE!
SLAVE LABOR

	ORIG	GOOD	FINE	N-MINT
❑1, Apr 97, A Walk to School; Tickle Me Hellmo!	2.95	1.40	3.50	7.00
❑1-2, A Walk to School; Tickle Me Hellmo!, 2nd Printing	2.95	0.59	1.48	2.95
❑2	2.95	1.00	2.50	5.00
❑3, Nov 97, Just Before Bedtime; The Space Monkey	2.95	0.70	1.75	3.50
❑4	2.95	0.70	1.75	3.50

SRI KRISHNA
CHAKRA

Value: Cover or less

❑1, The Advent ... 3.50

STACIA STORIES
KITCHEN SINK PRESS

Value: Cover or less

❑1, Jun 95, b&w ... 2.95

STAIN
FATHOM

	ORIG	GOOD	FINE	N-MINT
❑1	—	0.59	1.48	2.95

STAINLESS STEEL ARMADILLO
ANTARCTIC
Value: Cover or less

- ❑1, Feb 95, b&w ... 2.95
- ❑2, Apr 95, b&w ... 2.95
- ❑3, Jun 95, b&w ... 2.95
- ❑4, Aug 95, b&w ... 2.95
- ❑5, Oct 95, b&w ... 2.95

STAINLESS STEEL RAT
EAGLE

	ORIG	GOOD	FINE	N-MINT
❑1, Oct 85, Reprinted from 2000 A.D. #140-145	2.25	0.50	1.25	2.50
❑2, Nov 85, Reprinted from 2000 A.D. #146-151	1.50	0.50	1.25	2.50
❑3, Dec 85	1.50	0.50	1.25	2.50
❑4, Jan 86	1.75	0.50	1.25	2.50
❑5, Feb 86	1.75	0.50	1.25	2.50
❑6, Mar 86	1.75	0.50	1.25	2.50

STALKER
DC

	ORIG	GOOD	FINE	N-MINT
❑1, Jul 75, WW; SD, 1: Stalker	0.25	0.30	0.75	1.50
❑2, Sep 75	0.25	0.30	0.75	1.50
❑3, Nov 75	0.25	0.30	0.75	1.50
❑4, Jan 76	0.25	0.30	0.75	1.50

STALKERS
MARVEL
Value: Cover or less

- ❑1, Apr 90, Motown Madness. 1.50
- ❑2, May 90 ... 1.50
- ❑3, Jun 90 ... 1.50
- ❑4, Jul 90 ... 1.50
- ❑5, Aug 90 ... 1.50
- ❑6, Sep 90 ... 1.50
- ❑7 ... 1.50
- ❑8 ... 1.50
- ❑9, Inside Out ... 1.50
- ❑10 ... 1.50
- ❑11 ... 1.50
- ❑12 ... 1.50

STALKING RALPH
AEON
Value: Cover or less

- ❑1, Oct 95, nn; cardstock cover; One-Shot ... 4.95

STAND UP COMIX (BOB RUMBA'S...)
GREY
Value: Cover or less

- ❑1, b&w ... 2.50

STANLEY AND HIS MONSTER
DC

	ORIG	GOOD	FINE	N-MINT
❑1, Feb 93, PF, PF (w), How To Build A Tree Fort	1.50	0.50	1.25	2.50
❑2, Mar 93, PF, PF (w), Old Friends	1.50	0.40	1.00	2.00
❑3, Apr 93, PF, PF (w), Parental Discretion.	1.50	0.40	1.00	2.00
❑4, May 93, PF, PF (w), Going Down	1.50	0.40	1.00	2.00

STANLEY THE SNAKE WITH THE OVERACTIVE IMAGINATION
EMERALD
Value: Cover or less

- ❑1, b&w ... 1.50
- ❑2, b&w ... 1.50

STAR
IMAGE
Value: Cover or less

- ❑1, Jun 95 ... 2.50
- ❑2, Jul 95 ... 2.50
- ❑3, Aug 95 ... 2.50
- ❑4, Oct 95, cover says Aug, indicia says Oct ... 2.50

STARBIKERS
RENEGADE
Value: Cover or less

- ❑1, b&w ... 2.00

STARBLAST
MARVEL
Value: Cover or less

- ❑1, Jan 94, HT, Once in a Blue Moon ... 2.00
- ❑2, Feb 94 ... 1.75
- ❑3, Mar 94 ... 1.75
- ❑4, Apr 94 ... 1.75

STAR BLAZERS
COMICO

	ORIG	GOOD	FINE	N-MINT
❑1	1.75	0.40	1.00	2.00
❑2	1.75	0.40	1.00	2.00
❑3	1.75	0.40	1.00	2.00
❑4	1.75	0.40	1.00	2.00

STAR BLAZERS (VOL. 2)
COMICO

	ORIG	GOOD	FINE	N-MINT
❑1, The Jackals Come To Feed!	1.95	0.40	1.00	2.00
❑2	1.95	0.40	1.00	2.00
❑3	2.50	0.50	1.25	2.50
❑4	2.50	0.50	1.25	2.50
❑5	2.50	0.50	1.25	2.50

STAR BLAZERS: THE MAGAZINE OF SPACE BATTLESHIP YAMATO
ARGO
Value: Cover or less

- ❑0, Scarlet Scarf ... 2.95
- ❑1, Mar 95, nn ... 2.95

STAR BLECCH: DEEP SPACE DINER
PARODY PRESS
Value: Cover or less

- ❑1/A, Star Blecch: Deep Space Diner cover ... 2.50
- ❑1/B, Star Blecch: The Degeneration cover ... 2.50

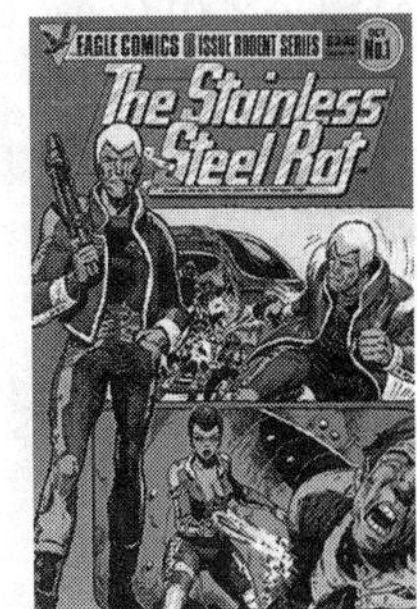

Eagle adapted Harry Harrison's stories of Slippery Jim DeGriz in the six-issue *Stainless Steel Rat.*

© 1985 Harry Harrison (Eagle)

STAR BRAND, THE
MARVEL

	ORIG	GOOD	FINE	N-MINT
❑1, Oct 86, JR2, 1: Star Brand	0.75	0.20	0.50	1.00
❑2, Nov 86	0.75	0.20	0.50	1.00
❑3, Dec 86	0.75	0.20	0.50	1.00
❑4, Jan 87	0.75	0.20	0.50	1.00
❑5, Feb 87	0.75	0.20	0.50	1.00
❑6, Mar 87	0.75	0.20	0.50	1.00
❑7, Apr 87	0.75	0.20	0.50	1.00
❑8, May 87	0.75	0.20	0.50	1.00
❑9, Jun 87	0.75	0.20	0.50	1.00
❑10, Jul 87	0.75	0.20	0.50	1.00
❑11, Jan 88, JBy, Title changes to The Star Brand	0.75	0.20	0.50	1.00
❑12, Mar 88, JBy, O: New Universe (explains "White Event"); O: Star Brand, Prelude to The Pitt	0.75	0.20	0.50	1.00
❑13, May 88, JBy	1.25	0.20	0.50	1.00
❑14, Jul 88, JBy	1.25	0.20	0.50	1.00
❑15, Sep 88, JBy	1.25	0.20	0.50	1.00
❑16, Nov 88, JBy	1.25	0.20	0.50	1.00
❑17, Jan 89, JBy	1.50	0.20	0.50	1.00
❑18, Mar 89, JBy	1.50	0.20	0.50	1.00
❑19, May 89, JBy, Final Issue	1.50	0.20	0.50	1.00
❑Anl 1	1.25	0.25	0.63	1.25

STARCHILD
TALIESEN PRESS
Value: Cover or less

- ❑0, Apr 93, b&w ... 2.50
- ❑1, Awakenings, Part 1, b&w; wraparound cover ... 2.25
- ❑1-2, 2nd Printing ... —
- ❑2, Awakenings, Part 2; Children Of The Storm, b&w; wraparound cover ... 2.25
- ❑2-2, Feb 94, Awakenings, Part 2, b&w; 2nd Printing; wraparound cover ... 2.50
- ❑2-3, Feb 94, Awakenings, Part 2, b&w; 2nd Printing; wraparound cover ... 2.50
- ❑3, Awakenings, Part 3, b&w; wraparound cover ... 2.50
- ❑4, Awakenings, Part 4, b&w; wraparound cover ... 2.50
- ❑5, Jan 94, Awakenings, Part 5, b&w; wraparound cover ... 2.50
- ❑6, Feb 94, Awakenings, Part 6, b&w; wraparound cover ... 2.50
- ❑7, Mar 94, Awakenings, Part 7, b&w; wraparound cover ... 2.50
- ❑8, Apr 94, Awakenings, Part 8, b&w; wraparound cover ... 2.50
- ❑9, May 94, Awakenings, Part 9, b&w; wraparound cover ... 2.50
- ❑10, Awakenings, Part 10, b&w; wraparound cover ... 2.50
- ❑11, Awakenings, Part 11, b&w; wraparound cover ... 2.50
- ❑12, Jun 95, Awakenings, Part 12, b&w; wraparound cover ... 2.50
- ❑13 ... 2.50
- ❑14, Final Issue ... 2.50

STARCHILD: CROSSROADS
COPPERVALE
Value: Cover or less

- ❑1, Nov 95, The Weaver's Tale, b&w ... 2.95
- ❑2, Jan 96, The Innkeeper's Tale, b&w ... 2.95
- ❑3, Mar 96, The Wanderer's Tale, b&w ... 2.95

STARCHILD: MYTHOPOLIS
IMAGE
Value: Cover or less

- ❑0, Jul 97, b&w ... 2.95
- ❑1, Sep 97, Pinehead, Part 1, b&w ... 2.95
- ❑2, Nov 97, Pinehead, Part 2, b&w ... 2.95
- ❑3, Jan 98, Pinehead, Part 3, b&w ... 2.95
- ❑4, Apr 93, The Fisher King, Part 1, b&w ... 2.95
- ❑5, The Fisher King, Part 2 ... 2.95
- ❑6 ... 2.95

STARCHY
EXCEL
Value: Cover or less

- ❑1 ... 1.95

STAR COMICS MAGAZINE
MARVEL

	ORIG	GOOD	FINE	N-MINT
❑1, Reprint; digest	1.50	0.60	1.50	3.00
❑2, Reprint; digest	1.50	0.40	1.00	2.00
❑3, Reprint; digest	1.50	0.40	1.00	2.00
❑4, Reprint; digest	1.50	0.40	1.00	2.00
❑5, Reprint; digest	1.50	0.40	1.00	2.00
❑6, Reprint; digest	1.50	0.40	1.00	2.00
❑7, Reprint; digest	1.50	0.40	1.00	2.00
❑8, Reprint; digest	1.50	0.40	1.00	2.00

	ORIG	GOOD	FINE	N-MINT
❑9, Reprint; digest	1.50	0.40	1.00	2.00
❑10, Reprint; digest	1.50	0.40	1.00	2.00
❑11, Reprint; digest	1.50	0.40	1.00	2.00
❑12, Reprint; digest	1.50	0.40	1.00	2.00
❑13, Reprint; digest	1.50	0.40	1.00	2.00

S.T.A.R. CORPS
DC

Value: Cover or less

- ❑1, Nov 93 .... 1.50
- ❑2, Dec 93 .... 1.50
- ❑3, Jan 94, Star Pupil 1.50
- ❑4, Feb 94 .... 1.50
- ❑5, Mar 94, Trauma 1.50
- ❑6, Apr 94 .... 1.50

STAR CROSSED
DC

Value: Cover or less

- ❑1, Jun 97, The Black Holes of Logic 2.50
- ❑2, Jul 97 .... 2.50
- ❑3, Aug 97 .... 2.50

STARDUST (NEIL GAIMAN AND CHARLES VESS'...)
DC

Value: Cover or less

- ❑1, CV, NG (w), Being a Romance Within the Realms of Faerie, prestige format 5.95
- ❑2, CV, NG (w), prestige format 5.95
- ❑3, CV, NG (w), prestige format 5.95
- ❑4, CV, NG (w), prestige format 6.95

STARDUSTERS
NIGHTWYND

Value: Cover or less

- ❑1, b&w 2.50
- ❑2, b&w 2.50
- ❑3, b&w 2.50
- ❑4, b&w 2.50

STARFIRE
DC

	ORIG	GOOD	FINE	N-MINT
❑1, Sep 76, A World Made Of War, 1: Starfire I	0.30	0.30	0.75	1.50
❑2, Nov 76	0.30	0.20	0.50	1.00
❑3, Jan 77	0.30	0.20	0.50	1.00
❑4, Mar 77	0.30	0.20	0.50	1.00
❑5, May 77	0.30	0.20	0.50	1.00
❑6, Jul 77	0.30	0.20	0.50	1.00
❑7, Sep 77	0.30	0.20	0.50	1.00
❑8, Nov 77	0.30	0.20	0.50	1.00

STAR FORCES
THE OTHER FACULTY

	ORIG	GOOD	FINE	N-MINT
❑1, The First Encounter	0.50	0.60	1.50	3.00

STARFORCE SIX SPECIAL
AC

Value: Cover or less

- ❑1, Nov 84 .... 1.50

STARGATE
EXPRESS

Value: Cover or less

- ❑1 .... 2.95
- ❑1/SC, Photo cover 3.50
- ❑2, Aug 96, movie Adaptation; photo section back-up 2.95
- ❑2/SC, Aug 96, Photo cover; movie Adaptation; photo section back-up 3.50
- ❑3, Sep 96, movie Adaptation; photo section back-up 2.95
- ❑3/SC, Sep 96, Photo cover; movie Adaptation; photo section back-up 3.50
- ❑4, Oct 96, Final Issue; movie Adaptation; photo section back-up 2.95
- ❑4/SC, Oct 96, Photo cover; Final Issue; movie Adaptation; photo section back-up 3.50

STARGATE DOOMSDAY WORLD
ENTITY

Value: Cover or less

- ❑1, Nov 96 .... 2.95
- ❑2 .... 2.95
- ❑3 .... 2.95

STARGATE: THE NEW ADVENTURES COLLECTION
ENTITY

Value: Cover or less

- ❑1, Collects Stargate: One Nation Under Ra; Stargate: Underworld 5.95

STARGATE UNDERWORLD
ENTITY

	ORIG	GOOD	FINE	N-MINT
❑1	—	0.59	1.48	2.95

STARGODS
ANTARCTIC

Value: Cover or less

- ❑1, Jul 98, Anachron 2.95
- ❑1/CS, Jul 98, Anachron, alternate cover; poster 5.95
- ❑2, Sep 98, The Golden Bow .. 2.95
- ❑2/CS, Sep 98, The Golden Bow, alternate cover; poster 5.95

STARGODS: VISIONS
ANTARCTIC

Value: Cover or less

- ❑1, Dec 98, pin-ups 2.95

STARHEAD PRESENTS
STARHEAD

	ORIG	GOOD	FINE	N-MINT
❑1	0.95	0.20	0.50	1.00
❑2, Curse Of The Baby Monster	0.95	0.20	0.50	1.00
❑3, Bad Teens	0.95	0.20	0.50	1.00

STAR HUNTERS
DC

	ORIG	GOOD	FINE	N-MINT
❑1, Nov 77	0.35	0.20	0.50	1.00
❑2, Jan 78, BL, The Annihilist Factor	0.35	0.20	0.50	1.00
❑3, Mar 78, BL; MN, The Sowers Of Holocaust	0.35	0.20	0.50	1.00
❑4, May 78	0.35	0.20	0.50	1.00
❑5, Jul 78	0.35	0.20	0.50	1.00
❑6, Sep 78	0.35	0.20	0.50	1.00
❑7, Nov 78, Final Issue	0.35	0.20	0.50	1.00

STAR JACKS
ANTARCTIC

Value: Cover or less

- ❑1, Jun 94, b&w 2.75

STAR JAM COMICS
REVOLUTIONARY

Value: Cover or less

- ❑1, Apr 92, b&w; M.C. Hammer story 2.50
- ❑2, Jun 92, b&w; Janet Jackson story 2.50
- ❑3, Aug 92, Genesis and Revelation, b&w; Beverly Hills 90210 story 2.50
- ❑4, Sep 92, b&w; Beverly Hills 90210 story 2.50
- ❑5, Oct 92, b&w; Beverly Hills 90210 story 2.50
- ❑6, Nov 92, b&w; Kriss Kross story 2.50
- ❑7, Dec 92, b&w; Marky Mark story 2.50
- ❑8, Jan 93, b&w; Madonna story 2.50
- ❑9, Feb 93, b&w; Jennie Garth story 2.50
- ❑10, Mar 93, b&w; Melrose Place story 2.50

STARJAMMERS
MARVEL

Value: Cover or less

- ❑1, Oct 95, Cepheid Variable, enhanced cardstock cover; OverPower cards bound-in . 2.95
- ❑2, Nov 95, enhanced cardstock cover 2.95
- ❑3, Dec 95, enhanced cardstock cover 2.95
- ❑4, Jan 96, enhanced cardstock cover; Final Issue 2.95

STARJONGLEUR, THE
TRYLVERTEL

Value: Cover or less

- ❑1, Aug 86, Plots Primeval, b&w 2.00
- ❑2, Win 87, b&w 2.00

STARKID
DARK HORSE

Value: Cover or less

- ❑1, Jan 98, Brood Storm, nn; prequel to movie 2.95

STARK RAVEN
ENDLESS HORIZONS

Value: Cover or less

- ❑1, Sep 00, The Screaming Rain, Part 1 .... 2.95

STARLIGHT
ETERNITY

Value: Cover or less

- ❑1, Oct 87, The Outer Space Babes, A: Outer Space Babes 1.95

STARLIGHT AGENCY, THE
ANTARCTIC

	ORIG	GOOD	FINE	N-MINT
❑1, Jun 91, b&w	1.95	0.50	1.25	2.50
❑2, Aug 91, b&w	1.95	0.50	1.25	2.50
❑3, Sep 91, b&w	1.95	0.50	1.25	2.50

STARLION: A PAWN'S GAME
STORM

Value: Cover or less

- ❑1, Feb 93, Puppet Strings and Captain's Chairs 2.25

STARLORD
MARVEL

Value: Cover or less

- ❑1, Dec 96 .... 2.50
- ❑2, Jan 97, Time Quake; Strontium Dog 2.50
- ❑3, Feb 97, Final Issue 2.50

STARLORD MEGAZINE
MARVEL

Value: Cover or less

- ❑1, Nov 96, JBy; MG, back cover pin-up; Reprint; preview of new Starlord series; Reprints Star-Lord, The Special Edition #1 2.95

STAR-LORD, THE SPECIAL EDITION
MARVEL

	ORIG	GOOD	FINE	N-MINT
❑1, Feb 82, JBy; MG	1.50	0.40	1.00	2.00

STARLOVE
FORBIDDEN FRUIT

Value: Cover or less

- ❑1, b&w; adult 2.95
- ❑2, b&w; adult 3.50

STARMAN (1ST SERIES)
DC

	ORIG	GOOD	FINE	N-MINT
❑1, Oct 88, Grassroots Hero, 1: Starman IV (William Payton)	1.00	0.40	1.00	2.00
❑2, Nov 88	1.00	0.30	0.75	1.50
❑3, Dec 88, V: Bolt	1.00	0.30	0.75	1.50
❑4, Win 88, V: Power Elite	1.00	0.30	0.75	1.50
❑5, Hol 89, Invasion!	1.00	0.30	0.75	1.50
❑6, Jan 89, Invasion!	1.00	0.30	0.75	1.50
❑7, Feb 89	1.00	0.30	0.75	1.50
❑8, Mar 89, A: Lady Quark	1.00	0.30	0.75	1.50
❑9, Apr 89, O: Blockbuster; A: Batman	1.00	0.30	0.75	1.50
❑10, May 89, O: Blockbuster; A: Batman	1.00	0.30	0.75	1.50
❑11, Jun 89	1.00	0.25	0.63	1.25

	ORIG	GOOD	FINE	N-MINT
❑12, Jul 89	1.00	0.25	0.63	1.25
❑13, Aug 89	1.00	0.25	0.63	1.25
❑14, Sep 89, Superman	1.00	0.25	0.63	1.25
❑15, Oct 89, 1: Deadline	1.00	0.25	0.63	1.25
❑16, Nov 89	1.00	0.25	0.63	1.25
❑17, Dec 89, Power Girl	1.00	0.25	0.63	1.25
❑18, Jan 90	1.00	0.25	0.63	1.25
❑19, Feb 90	1.00	0.25	0.63	1.25
❑20, Mar 90	1.00	0.25	0.63	1.25
❑21, Apr 90	1.00	0.25	0.63	1.25
❑22, May 90, V: Deadline	1.00	0.25	0.63	1.25
❑23, Jun 90	1.00	0.25	0.63	1.25
❑24, Jul 90	1.00	0.25	0.63	1.25
❑25, Aug 90	1.00	0.25	0.63	1.25
❑26, Sep 90, 1: David Knight	1.00	0.40	1.00	2.00
❑27, Oct 90, Riders On The Storm, O: Starman III (David Knight)	1.00	0.25	0.63	1.25
❑28, Nov 90, Superman	1.00	0.25	0.63	1.25
❑29, Dec 90	1.00	0.25	0.63	1.25
❑30, Jan 91	1.00	0.25	0.63	1.25
❑31, Feb 91	1.00	0.25	0.63	1.25
❑32, Mar 91	1.00	0.25	0.63	1.25
❑33, Apr 91	1.00	0.25	0.63	1.25
❑34, May 91	1.00	0.25	0.63	1.25
❑35, Jun 91	1.00	0.25	0.63	1.25
❑36, Jul 91, Intruder Alert!	1.00	0.25	0.63	1.25
❑37, Aug 91	1.00	0.25	0.63	1.25
❑38, Sep 91, War of the Gods, Part 6, War of the Gods	1.00	0.25	0.63	1.25
❑39, Oct 91	1.00	0.25	0.63	1.25
❑40, Nov 91	1.00	0.25	0.63	1.25
❑41, Dec 91	1.00	0.25	0.63	1.25
❑42, Jan 92	1.00	0.25	0.63	1.25
❑43, Feb 92	1.00	0.25	0.63	1.25
❑44, Mar 92, Lobo	1.25	0.25	0.63	1.25
❑45, Apr 92, Lobo	1.25	0.25	0.63	1.25

STARMAN (2ND SERIES)
DC

	ORIG	GOOD	FINE	N-MINT
❑0, Oct 94, JRo (w), Sins of the Father, Part 1	1.95	1.00	2.50	5.00
❑1, Nov 94, JRo (w), Sins of the Father, Part 2	1.95	1.00	2.50	5.00
❑2, Dec 94, JRo (w), Sins of the Father, Part 3	1.95	0.80	2.00	4.00
❑3, Jan 95, JRo (w), Night Flight	1.95	0.80	2.00	4.00
❑4, Feb 95, JRo (w)	1.95	0.60	1.50	3.00
❑5, Mar 95, JRo (w)	1.95	0.60	1.50	3.00
❑6, Apr 95, JRo (w)	1.95	0.60	1.50	3.00
❑7, May 95, JRo (w), A Knight at the Circus, Part 1	1.95	0.60	1.50	3.00
❑8, Jun 95, JRo (w), A Knight at the Circus, Part 2	2.25	0.60	1.50	3.00
❑9, Jul 95, JRo (w), Shards	2.25	0.60	1.50	3.00
❑10, Aug 95, JRo (w), The Day Before the Day to Come, V: Solomon Grundy	2.25	0.60	1.50	3.00
❑11, Sep 95, JRo (w)	2.25	0.50	1.25	2.50
❑12, Oct 95, JRo (w), Sins of the Child, Part 1	2.25	0.50	1.25	2.50
❑13, Nov 95, JRo (w), Sins of the Child, Part 2, Underworld Unleashed	2.25	0.50	1.25	2.50
❑14, Dec 95, JRo (w), Sins of the Child, Part 3	2.25	0.50	1.25	2.50
❑15, Jan 96, JRo (w), Sins of the Child, Part 4	2.25	0.50	1.25	2.50
❑16, Feb 96, JRo (w), Sins of the Child, Part 5	2.25	0.50	1.25	2.50
❑17, Mar 96, JRo (w), Beyond Sins	2.25	0.50	1.25	2.50
❑18, Apr 96, JRo (w), First Joust, Original Starman versus The Mist	2.25	0.50	1.25	2.50
❑19, Jun 96, JRo (w), Talking with David '96, Times Past	2.25	0.50	1.25	2.50
❑20, Jul 96, JRo (w), Sand and Stars, Part 1; Sand of the Stars, Part 1, A: Dian Belmont; A: Wesley Dodds	2.25	0.50	1.25	2.50
❑21, Aug 96, JRo (w), Sand and Stars, Part 2; Sand of the Stars, Part 2	2.25	0.50	1.25	2.50
❑22, Sep 96, JRo (w), Sand and Stars, Part 3; Sand of the Stars, Part 3	2.25	0.50	1.25	2.50
❑23, Oct 96, JRo (w), Sand and Stars, Part 4; Sand of the Stars, Part 4	2.25	0.50	1.25	2.50
❑24, Nov 96, JRo (w), Demon Quest, Part 1; Hell & Back, Part 1	2.25	0.50	1.25	2.50
❑25, Dec 96, JRo (w), Demon Quest, Part 2; Hell & Back, Part 2	2.25	0.50	1.25	2.50
❑26, Jan 97, JRo (w), Demon Quest, Part 3; Hell & Back, Part 3	2.25	0.50	1.25	2.50
❑27, Feb 97, JRo (w), Christmas Knight	2.25	0.50	1.25	2.50
❑28, Mar 97, JRo (w), Superfreaks & Backstabbers	2.25	0.50	1.25	2.50
❑29, Apr 97, JRo (w)	2.25	0.50	1.25	2.50
❑30, May 97, JRo (w), Infernal Devices, Part 1	2.25	0.50	1.25	2.50
❑31, Jun 97, JRo (w), Infernal Devices, Part 2	2.25	0.50	1.25	2.50
❑32, Jul 97, JRo (w), Infernal Devices, Part 3	2.25	0.50	1.25	2.50
❑33, Aug 97, JRo (w), Dark Knights, A: Batman; A: Sentinel; A: Solomon Grundy	2.25	0.50	1.25	2.50
❑34, Sep 97, JRo (w), A: Jason Woodrue; A: Batman; A: Sentinel; A: Solomon Grundy; A: Ted Knight	2.25	0.50	1.25	2.50

Jack Knight, the son of the original Starman, took up his father's mantle during "Zero Hour."

	ORIG	GOOD	FINE	N-MINT
❑35, Oct 97, JRo (w), Genesis	2.25	0.50	1.25	2.50
❑36, Nov 97, JRo (w), A: Will Payton	2.25	0.50	1.25	2.50
❑37, Dec 97, JRo (w), Talking with David '97, Face cover	2.25	0.50	1.25	2.50
❑38, Jan 98, JRo (w), ...La Fraternite De Justice Et Liberte!, 1: Baby Starman, Mist vs. Justice League Europe	2.25	0.50	1.25	2.50
❑39, Feb 98, JRo (w), Lightning and Stars, Part 1, cover forms diptych with Starman #40; continues in Power of Shazam! #35	2.25	0.50	1.25	2.50
❑40, Mar 98, JRo (w), Lightning and Stars, Part 3, cover forms diptych with Starman #39	2.25	0.50	1.25	2.50
❑41, Apr 98, JRo (w), Villain's Redemption, V: Doctor Phosphorus	2.25	0.45	1.13	2.25
❑42, May 98, JRo (w), Science and Sorcery 1944, A: Demon	2.25	0.45	1.13	2.25
❑43, Jun 98, JRo (w), A: Justice League of America	2.25	0.45	1.13	2.25
❑44, Jul 98, JRo (w), Things That Go Bump in the Night 1944, A: Phantom Lady	2.25	0.45	1.13	2.25
❑45, Aug 98, JRo (w), Journey to the Stars	2.25	0.45	1.13	2.25
❑46, Sep 98, JRo (w), Times Past: Good Men and Bad 1954	2.25	0.45	1.13	2.25
❑47, Oct 98, JRo (w), City Without Light, Part 1	2.50	0.50	1.25	2.50
❑48, Dec 98, JRo (w), Stars My Destination: A Blue World, A: Solomon Grundy	2.50	0.50	1.25	2.50
❑49, Jan 99, JRo (w), Stars My Destination: Talking with David '99	2.50	0.50	1.25	2.50
❑50, Feb 99, JRo (w), Stars My Destination, A: Legion	3.95	0.79	1.98	3.95
❑51, Mar 99, JRo (w), Stars My Destination, A: Jor-El, on Krypton	2.50	0.50	1.25	2.50
❑52, Apr 99, JRo (w), Stars My Destination, A: Adam Strange; A: Turran Kha, on Rann	2.50	0.50	1.25	2.50
❑53, May 99, JRo (w), Stars My Destination, A: Adam Strange, on Rann	2.50	0.50	1.25	2.50
❑54, Jun 99, JRo (w), Times Past; 1899: A Rich Man's Family, Times Past	2.50	0.50	1.25	2.50
❑55, Jul 99, JRo (w), Stars My Destination; Taxicab Confessions, A: Space Cabbie	2.50	0.50	1.25	2.50
❑56, Aug 99, JRo (w), City Without Light, Part 2	2.50	0.50	1.25	2.50
❑57, Sep 99, JRo (w), Stars My Destination; The Welcome Wagon, A: Tigorr; A: Fastbak, on Throneworld	2.50	0.50	1.25	2.50
❑58, Oct 99, JRo (w), Stars My Destination; Familiar Faces, Some Forgotten, A: Will Payton	2.50	0.50	1.25	2.50
❑59, Nov 99, JRo (w), Stars My Destination; The Secret of Will Payton	2.50	0.50	1.25	2.50
❑60, Dec 99, Stars My Destination, Jack returns to Earth	2.50	0.50	1.25	2.50
❑61, Jan 00, JRo (w), In Tranquility and Fire	2.50	0.50	1.25	2.50
❑62, Feb 00, JRo (w), Grand Guignol, Part 1	2.50	0.50	1.25	2.50
❑63, Mar 00, JRo (w), Grand Guignol, Part 2	2.50	0.50	1.25	2.50
❑64, Apr 00, JRo (w), Grand Guignol, Part 3	2.50	0.50	1.25	2.50
❑65, May 00, JRo (w), Grand Guignol, Part 4	2.50	0.50	1.25	2.50
❑66, Jun 00, JRo (w), Grand Guignol, Part 5	2.50	0.50	1.25	2.50
❑67, Jul 00, JRo (w), Grand Guignol, Part 6	2.50	0.50	1.25	2.50
❑68, Aug 00, JRo (w), Grand Guignol, Part 7	2.50	0.50	1.25	2.50
❑69, Sep 00, JRo (w), Grand Guignol, Part 8	2.50	0.50	1.25	2.50
❑70, Oct 00, JRo (w), Grand Guignol, Part 9	2.50	0.50	1.25	2.50
❑71, Nov 00, JRo (w), Grand Guignol, Part 10	2.50	0.50	1.25	2.50
❑72, Dec 00, JRo (w), Grand Guignol, Part 11	2.50	0.50	1.25	2.50
❑73, Jan 01, JRo (w), Grand Guignol, Part 12	2.50	0.50	1.25	2.50
❑74, Feb 01, RH, JRo (w), His Death and the Dying of It, Times Past	2.50	0.50	1.25	2.50
❑75, Mar 01, JRo (w), Sons and Fathers	2.50	0.50	1.25	2.50
❑76, Apr 01, JRo (w), Talking with David (and Ted)	2.50	0.50	1.25	2.50
❑77, May 01, JRo (w), 1951, Part 1	2.50	0.50	1.25	2.50
❑78, Jun 01, JRo (w), 1951, Part 2	2.50	0.50	1.25	2.50
❑1000000, Nov 98, JRo (w), All the Starlight Shining	2.50	0.50	1.25	2.50

	ORIG	GOOD	FINE	N-MINT
❑Anl 1, JRo (w), Legends of the Dead Earth; Shade tells stories of Ted Knight and Gavyn; 1996 Annual	3.50	0.70	1.75	3.50
❑Anl 2, JRo (w), Stars in my Eyes!, Pulp Heroes; 1997 annual	3.95	0.79	1.98	3.95
❑GS 1, Jan 99, JRo (w), 80pgs.	4.95	0.99	2.47	4.95

STARMAN: SECRET FILES
DC

Value: Cover or less

❑1, Apr 98, background on series........ 4.95

STARMAN: THE MIST
DC

Value: Cover or less

❑1, Jun 98, JRo (w), Good Girls and Bad, One-Shot; Girlfrenzy1.95

STARMASTERS (AC)
AC

Value: Cover or less

❑1, The Women of W.O.S.P.; Breed........ 1.50

STAR MASTERS (MARVEL)
MARVEL

Value: Cover or less

❑1, Dec 95, The Stars, My Desperation, A: Silver Surfer; A: Beta Ray Bill; A: The Silver Surfer; A: Quasar........ 1.95

❑2, Jan 96, The Cauldron of Conversion, A: Silver Surfer; A: Beta Ray Thor; A: Quasar........ 1.95

❑3, Feb 96, A: Silver Surfer; A: Beta Ray Thor; A: Quasar, Final Issue; continues in Cosmic Powers Unlimited #4........ 1.95

STAR RANGERS
ADVENTURE

Value: Cover or less

❑1, Oct 87, JM, Community of Victims........ 1.95

❑2........ 1.95

❑3, Dec 87, Pilots of the Purple Twilight, Part 2........ 1.95

STAR*REACH
STAR*REACH

	ORIG	GOOD	FINE	N-MINT
❑1, HC; JSn, HC (w); JSn (w), ...The Birth of Death!; Fish Myths	0.75	0.40	1.00	2.00
❑2, DG, "In the Light of Future Days..."	1.00	0.40	1.00	2.00
❑3	—	0.40	1.00	2.00
❑4	—	0.40	1.00	2.00
❑5	—	0.30	0.75	1.50
❑6, Oct 76, AN; GD; JSa, Elric: The Prisoner of Pan-Pang; Childsong	1.25	0.30	0.75	1.50
❑7	—	0.30	0.75	1.50
❑8	—	0.30	0.75	1.50
❑9	—	0.30	0.75	1.50
❑10	—	0.30	0.75	1.50
❑11	—	0.30	0.75	1.50
❑12	—	0.30	0.75	1.50
❑13	—	0.30	0.75	1.50
❑14	—	0.30	0.75	1.50
❑15	—	0.30	0.75	1.50
❑16	—	0.30	0.75	1.50
❑17	—	0.30	0.75	1.50
❑18	—	0.30	0.75	1.50

STAR*REACH CLASSICS
ECLIPSE

	ORIG	GOOD	FINE	N-MINT
❑1, DG	—	0.40	1.00	2.00
❑2	—	0.40	1.00	2.00
❑3	—	0.40	1.00	2.00
❑4	—	0.40	1.00	2.00
❑5, Jul 84, HC	1.75	0.40	1.00	2.00
❑6, CR	—	0.40	1.00	2.00

STARRIORS
MARVEL

	ORIG	GOOD	FINE	N-MINT
❑1, Nov 84, Discovery	0.75	0.20	0.50	1.00
❑2, Dec 84, Under Fire!	0.75	0.20	0.50	1.00
❑3, Jan 85, Assault!	0.75	0.20	0.50	1.00
❑4, Feb 85, Quest's End!	0.75	0.20	0.50	1.00

STAR ROVERS
COMAX

Value: Cover or less

❑1, b&w; adult........ 2.95

STARS AND S.T.R.I.P.E.
DC

	ORIG	GOOD	FINE	N-MINT
❑0, Jul 99, JRo (w), A Chilly Day in Opal, A: Starman	2.95	0.59	1.48	2.95
❑1, Aug 99, New Kid on the Block	2.50	0.59	1.48	2.95
❑2, Sep 99, True Colors	2.50	0.59	1.48	2.95
❑3, Oct 99, Bloodrush, 1: Skeeter	2.50	0.59	1.48	2.95
❑4, Nov 99, Waking the Dead!, A: Captain Marvel, Day of Judgment	2.50	0.59	1.48	2.95
❑5, Dec 99, The Subs, Part 1, A: Young Justice	2.95	0.59	1.48	2.95
❑6, Jan 00, The Subs, Part 2	2.95	0.59	1.48	2.95
❑7, Feb 00, You Kids Today!	2.95	0.59	1.48	2.95
❑8, Mar 00	—	0.59	1.48	2.95
❑9, Apr 00	—	0.59	1.48	2.95
❑10, May 00, Shortcuts	2.50	0.50	1.25	2.50
❑11, Jun 00, Knight Time	2.50	0.50	1.25	2.50

STAR SEED
BROADWAY

Value: Cover or less

❑7, Jul 96, Series continued from Powers That Be #6........ 2.95

❑8, Aug 96........ 2.95

❑9, Sep 96, It's the End of the World as we Know It, Part 5, Final Issue........ 2.95

STARSHIP TROOPERS
DARK HORSE

Value: Cover or less

❑1, movie Adaptation........ 2.95

❑2, movie Adaptation........ 2.95

STARSHIP TROOPERS (MAGAZINE)
TITAN

	ORIG	GOOD	FINE	N-MINT
❑1	1.50	0.60	1.50	3.00

STARSHIP TROOPERS: BRUTE CREATIONS
DARK HORSE

Value: Cover or less

❑1, nn; One-Shot........ 2.95

STARSHIP TROOPERS: DOMINANT SPECIES
DARK HORSE

Value: Cover or less

❑1, Aug 98........ 2.95

❑2, Sep 98........ 2.95

❑3, Oct 98........ 2.95

❑4, Nov 98........ 2.95

STARSHIP TROOPERS: INSECT TOUCH
DARK HORSE

Value: Cover or less

❑1, cardstock cover........ 2.95

❑2, cardstock cover........ 2.95

❑3, cardstock cover........ 2.95

STAR SLAMMERS (MALIBU)
MALIBU

Value: Cover or less

❑1, May 94, The Minoan Agendas, Part 1, coupon........ 2.50

❑2, Jun 94, The Minoan Agendas, Part 2, coupon........ 2.50

❑3, Aug 94, The Minoan Agendas, Part 3, coupon........ 2.50

❑4, Feb 95, The Minoan Agendas, Part 4, coupon........ 2.50

❑5, The Minoan Agendas, Part 5, coupon........ 2.50

STAR SLAMMERS SPECIAL
DARK HORSE

Value: Cover or less

❑1, Jun 96, nn; One-Shot........ 2.95

STARSLAYER
PACIFIC

	ORIG	GOOD	FINE	N-MINT
❑1, Feb 82, MGr, MGr (w), 1: Rocketeer (cameo); O: Starslayer	1.00	0.40	1.00	2.00
❑2, Apr 82, DSt; MGr; SA, MGr (w), 1: Rocketeer (full appearance); O: Rocketeer, Groo	1.00	1.00	2.50	5.00
❑3, Jun 82, DSt; MGr, MGr (w), A: Rocketeer	1.00	0.60	1.50	3.00
❑4, Aug 82, MGr, MGr (w)	1.00	0.30	0.75	1.50
❑5, Nov 82, MGr; SA, ME (w); MGr (w), A: Groo	1.00	0.60	1.50	3.00
❑6, Apr 83, MGr, MGr (w)	1.00	0.30	0.75	1.50
❑7, Aug 83, First Comics begins publishing	1.00	0.30	0.75	1.50
❑8, Sep 83	1.00	0.30	0.75	1.50
❑9, Oct 83	1.00	0.30	0.75	1.50
❑10, Nov 83, 1: Grimjack	1.00	0.40	1.00	2.00
❑11, Dec 83, A: Grimjack	1.00	0.30	0.75	1.50
❑12, Jan 84, A: Grimjack	1.00	0.30	0.75	1.50
❑13, Feb 84, A: Grimjack	1.00	0.30	0.75	1.50
❑14, Mar 84, A: Grimjack	1.00	0.30	0.75	1.50
❑15, Apr 84, A: Grimjack	1.00	0.30	0.75	1.50
❑16, May 84, A: Grimjack	1.00	0.30	0.75	1.50
❑17, Jun 84, A: Grimjack	1.00	0.30	0.75	1.50
❑18, Jul 84, A: Grimjack	1.00	0.30	0.75	1.50
❑19, Aug 84	1.00	0.30	0.75	1.50
❑20, Sep 84	1.00	0.30	0.75	1.50
❑21, Oct 84	1.00	0.25	0.63	1.25
❑22, Nov 84	1.25	0.25	0.63	1.25
❑23, Dec 84	1.25	0.25	0.63	1.25
❑24, Jan 85	1.25	0.25	0.63	1.25
❑25, Feb 85, The Black Flame back-up story	1.25	0.25	0.63	1.25
❑26, Mar 85	1.25	0.25	0.63	1.25
❑27, Apr 85	1.25	0.25	0.63	1.25
❑28, May 85	1.25	0.25	0.63	1.25
❑29, Jun 85	1.25	0.25	0.63	1.25
❑30, Jul 85	1.25	0.25	0.63	1.25
❑31, Aug 85	1.25	0.25	0.63	1.25
❑32, Sep 85	1.25	0.25	0.63	1.25
❑33, Oct 85	1.25	0.25	0.63	1.25
❑34, Nov 85, Final Issue	1.25	0.25	0.63	1.25

STARSLAYER: THE DIRECTOR'S CUT
ACCLAIM

Value: Cover or less

❑1, Jun 95, MGr, MGr (w), New story and artwork........ 2.50

❑2, Jun 95, MGr, MGr (w), Reprints Starslayer #1........ 2.50

❑3, Jul 95, MGr, MGr (w), Reprints Starslayer #2........ 2.50

❑4, Jul 95, MGr, MGr (w), Reprints Starslayer #3........ 2.50

❑5, Aug 95, MGr, MGr (w), Reprints Starslayer #4........ 2.50

❑6, Sep 95, MGr, MGr (w), cover says Aug, indicia says Sep; Reprints Starslayer #5........ 2.50

❑7, Sep 95, MGr, MGr (w), Reprints Starslayer #6........ 2.50

❑8, Dec 95, MGr, MGr (w), New story and artwork........ 2.50

STAR SPANGLED COMICS (2ND SERIES)
DC

	ORIG	GOOD	FINE	N-MINT
❑1, May 99, ...A Terrifying Hour!, A: Sandman; A: Star Spangled Kid, Justice Society Returns	1.99	0.40	1.00	2.00

STAR SPANGLED WAR STORIES
DC

	ORIG	GOOD	FINE	N-MINT
❑90, May 60, 1: Dinosaur Island, Island of Armored Giants (dinosaur) story	0.10	65.00	162.50	325.00
❑91, Jul 60	0.10	9.00	22.50	45.00
❑92, Sep 60, Dinosaurs	0.10	22.00	55.00	110.00
❑93, Nov 60	0.10	9.00	22.50	45.00
❑94, Jan 61, Dinosaurs	0.10	22.00	55.00	110.00
❑95, Mar 61, Dinosaurs	0.10	22.00	55.00	110.00
❑96, May 61, Dinosaurs	0.10	22.00	55.00	110.00
❑97, Jul 61, Dinosaurs	0.10	22.00	55.00	110.00
❑98, Sep 61, Dinosaurs	0.10	22.00	55.00	110.00
❑99, Nov 61, Dinosaurs	0.10	22.00	55.00	110.00
❑100, Jan 62, Dinosaurs	0.12	29.00	72.50	145.00
❑101, Mar 62, Dinosaurs	0.12	15.00	37.50	75.00
❑102, May 62, Dinosaurs	0.12	15.00	37.50	75.00
❑103, Jul 62, Dinosaurs	0.12	15.00	37.50	75.00
❑104, Sep 62, Dinosaurs	0.12	15.00	37.50	75.00
❑105, Nov 62, Dinosaurs	0.12	15.00	37.50	75.00
❑106, Jan 63, Dinosaurs	0.12	15.00	37.50	75.00
❑107, Mar 63, Dinosaurs	0.12	15.00	37.50	75.00
❑108, May 63, Dinosaurs	0.12	15.00	37.50	75.00
❑109, Jul 63, Dinosaurs	0.12	15.00	37.50	75.00
❑110, Sep 63, Dinosaurs	0.12	15.00	37.50	75.00
❑111, Nov 63, War That Time Forgot, Dinosaurs	0.12	15.00	37.50	75.00
❑112, Jan 64, Dinosaurs	0.12	15.00	37.50	75.00
❑113, Mar 64, Dinosaurs	0.12	15.00	37.50	75.00
❑114, May 64, Dinosaurs	0.12	15.00	37.50	75.00
❑115, Jul 64, Dinosaurs	0.12	15.00	37.50	75.00
❑116, Sep 64, War That Time Forgot, Dinosaurs	0.12	15.00	37.50	75.00
❑117, Nov 64, Dinosaurs	0.12	15.00	37.50	75.00
❑118, Jan 65, Dinosaurs	0.12	15.00	37.50	75.00
❑119, Mar 65, Dinosaurs	0.12	15.00	37.50	75.00
❑120, Apr 65, Dinosaurs	0.12	15.00	37.50	75.00
❑121, Jun 65, Dinosaurs	0.12	15.00	37.50	75.00
❑122, Aug 65, Dinosaurs	0.12	15.00	37.50	75.00
❑123, Oct 65, Dinosaurs	0.12	15.00	37.50	75.00
❑124, Dec 65, Dinosaurs	0.12	15.00	37.50	75.00
❑125, Feb 66, War That Time Forgot, Dinosaurs	0.12	15.00	37.50	75.00
❑126, Apr 66, 1: Sgt. Gorilla	0.12	15.00	37.50	75.00
❑127, Jun 66, Dinosaurs	0.12	15.00	37.50	75.00
❑128, Aug 66, Dinosaurs	0.12	15.00	37.50	75.00
❑129, Oct 66, Dinosaurs	0.12	15.00	37.50	75.00
❑130, Dec 66, War That Time Forgot, Dinosaurs	0.12	15.00	37.50	75.00
❑131, Mar 67, Dinosaurs	0.12	15.00	37.50	75.00
❑132, May 67, Dinosaurs	0.12	15.00	37.50	75.00
❑133, Jul 67, Dinosaurs	0.12	15.00	37.50	75.00
❑134, Sep 67, NA, War That Time Forgot, Dinosaurs	0.12	16.00	40.00	80.00
❑135, Nov 67, War That Time Forgot, Dinosaurs	0.12	15.00	37.50	75.00
❑136, Jan 68, Dinosaurs	0.12	15.00	37.50	75.00
❑137, Mar 68, War That Time Forgot, Dinosaurs	0.12	15.00	37.50	75.00
❑138, May 68, Enemy Ace stories begin	0.12	15.00	37.50	75.00
❑139, Jul 68, O: Enemy Ace	0.12	12.00	30.00	60.00
❑140, Sep 68, Enemy Ace	0.12	7.00	17.50	35.00
❑141, Nov 68, Enemy Ace	0.12	7.00	17.50	35.00
❑142, Jan 69, Enemy Ace	0.12	7.00	17.50	35.00
❑143, Mar 69, Enemy Ace	0.12	7.00	17.50	35.00
❑144, May 69, NA; JKu, Enemy Ace	0.12	8.00	20.00	40.00
❑145, Jul 69, Enemy Ace	0.12	7.00	17.50	35.00
❑146, Sep 69, Enemy Ace; Brother Enemy, Enemy Ace	0.15	4.80	12.00	24.00
❑147, Nov 69, JKu, Enemy Ace	0.15	4.80	12.00	24.00
❑148, Jan 70, Enemy Ace	0.15	4.80	12.00	24.00
❑149, Mar 70	0.15	4.80	12.00	24.00
❑150, May 70, JKu, Enemy Ace, Viking Prince	0.15	4.80	12.00	24.00
❑151, Jul 70, JKu, 1: Unknown Soldier	0.15	20.00	50.00	100.00
❑152, Sep 70, Instant Glory!; Battle Album: Lafayette Escadrille, 2: The Unknown Soldier	0.15	5.00	12.50	25.00
❑153, Nov 70, JKu, Everybody Dies; Enemy Ace: Fokker Fury	0.15	5.00	12.50	25.00
❑154, Jan 71, JKu, O: Unknown Soldier	0.15	14.00	35.00	70.00
❑155, Mar 71, reprints Enemy Ace story	0.15	3.20	8.00	16.00
❑156, May 71, Unknown Soldier; Enemy Ace back-up	0.15	2.80	7.00	14.00

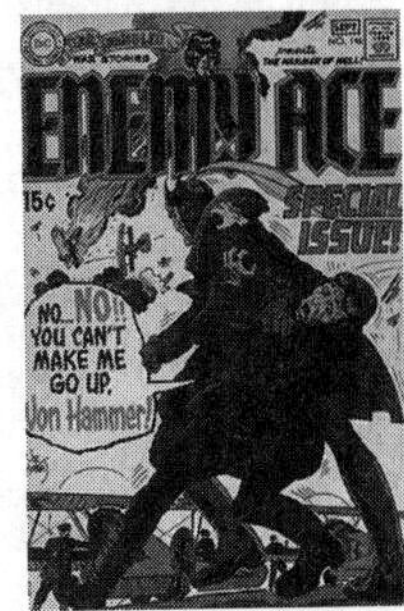

After appearing in *Showcase*, Joe Kubert's Enemy Ace moved to *Star Spangled War Stories*.

	ORIG	GOOD	FINE	N-MINT
❑157, Jul 71, Unknown Soldier meets Easy Co.; Enemy Ace back-up	0.15	2.80	7.00	14.00
❑158, Sep 71	0.25	2.80	7.00	14.00
❑159, Nov 71	0.25	2.80	7.00	14.00
❑160, Jan 72	0.25	2.80	7.00	14.00
❑161, Mar 72, Regular Enemy Ace stories end	0.25	2.80	7.00	14.00
❑162, May 72	0.25	1.20	3.00	6.00
❑163, Jul 72, JKu; CI, Kill the General!; The Ace who Died Twice!	0.25	1.20	3.00	6.00
❑164, Sep 72, ATh, Remittance Man!; Battle Album: Hannibal	0.20	1.20	3.00	6.00
❑165, Nov 72, Witness For A Coward; Shot'n'Shell	0.20	1.20	3.00	6.00
❑166, Jan 73	0.20	1.20	3.00	6.00
❑167, Feb 73	0.20	1.20	3.00	6.00
❑168, Mar 73, TS (w), The Glory Hound!; The Last Raid	0.20	1.20	3.00	6.00
❑169, Apr 73, Destroy the Devil's Broomstick!; Battle Album: The Little Big Horn!.	0.20	1.20	3.00	6.00
❑170, Jun 73	0.20	1.20	3.00	6.00
❑171, Jul 73, Appointment in Prague!; Who to Believe!, O: The Unknown Soldier	0.20	1.20	3.00	6.00
❑172, Aug 73	0.20	1.20	3.00	6.00
❑173, Sep 73	0.20	1.20	3.00	6.00
❑174, Oct 73, FR (w), Operation Snafu!; King of the Hill	0.20	1.20	3.00	6.00
❑175, Nov 73	0.20	1.20	3.00	6.00
❑176, Dec 73, FT, FR (w), Target: The Unknown Soldier; Charge!	0.20	1.20	3.00	6.00
❑177, Jan 74	0.20	1.20	3.00	6.00
❑178, Feb 74	0.20	1.20	3.00	6.00
❑179, Mar 74, A Town Called Hate!; Warrior!	0.20	1.20	3.00	6.00
❑180, Jun 74	0.20	1.20	3.00	6.00
❑181, Aug 74, FT, FR (w), One Guy in the Right Place...; The Balloon Buster: Hell's Angels	0.20	1.00	2.50	5.00
❑182, Oct 74, FR (w), A Thirst for Death! ...	0.20	1.00	2.50	5.00
❑183, Dec 74	0.25	1.00	2.50	5.00
❑184, Feb 75, SA (w), A Sense of Obligation; War Games	0.25	1.00	2.50	5.00
❑185, Mar 75	0.25	1.00	2.50	5.00
❑186, Apr 75, Man of God...Man of War; The Last Kill	0.25	1.00	2.50	5.00
❑187, May 75, A Death in the Chapel; Waiting for a Legend	0.25	1.00	2.50	5.00
❑188, Jun 75, Encounter	0.25	1.00	2.50	5.00
❑189, Jul 75, The Cadaver Gap Massacres; Midway!	0.25	1.00	2.50	5.00
❑190, Aug 75, Project: Omega	0.25	1.00	2.50	5.00
❑191, Sep 75	0.25	1.00	2.50	5.00
❑192, Oct 75, Vendetta	0.25	1.00	2.50	5.00
❑193, Nov 75, Save the Children!; There Are No Guns on a Showboat, pre-CBG Alan Light newsletter ad	0.25	1.00	2.50	5.00
❑194, Dec 75	0.25	1.00	2.50	5.00
❑195, Jan 76, The Deathmasters; Duel in the Desert	0.25	1.00	2.50	5.00
❑196, Feb 76, Target Red; Just One More .	0.25	1.00	2.50	5.00
❑197, Mar 76	0.25	1.00	2.50	5.00
❑198, Apr 76, The Unknown Soldier: Traitor!; The Last Battle	0.30	1.00	2.50	5.00
❑199, May 76, The Crime Of Sgt. Schepke; Killing Machine	0.30	1.00	2.50	5.00
❑200, Jul 76, JKu, Deathride; Enemy Ace: Shooting Star, A: Mademoiselle Marie....	0.30	1.00	2.50	5.00
❑201, Sep 76, The Back-Alley War	0.30	1.00	2.50	5.00
❑202, Nov 76, The Cure	0.30	1.00	2.50	5.00
❑203, Jan 77, Curtain Call	0.30	1.00	2.50	5.00
❑204, Mar 77, The Unknown Soldier Must Die!; A Walk Up a Hill, Series continues as Unknown Soldier	0.30	1.00	2.50	5.00

STARSTONE
AIRCEL

Value: Cover or less

❑1, b&w	1.70
❑2, b&w	1.70
❑3, b&w	1.70

STARSTREAM
Gold Key

Issue	ORIG	GOOD	FINE	N-MINT
❑1	0.79	0.60	1.50	3.00
❑2	0.79	0.60	1.50	3.00
❑3	0.79	0.60	1.50	3.00
❑4, Call Me Joe; Ben Franklin, Martian	0.79	0.60	1.50	3.00

STARSTRUCK (DARK HORSE)
Dark Horse

Value: Cover or less

Issue	Value
❑1, Aug 90, Silver Bells and Cockle Shells, b&w	2.95
❑2, b&w	2.95
❑3, Jan 90, The Right Bait, b&w	2.95
❑4, Mar 91, Mother's Little Helpers, trading cards	2.95

STARSTRUCK (EPIC)
Marvel

Issue	ORIG	GOOD	FINE	N-MINT
❑1, Feb 85, Liar's Poker	1.50	0.50	1.25	2.50
❑2, Apr 85, Conspicuous By Their Absence	1.50	0.40	1.00	2.00
❑3, Jun 85	1.50	0.40	1.00	2.00
❑4, Aug 85	1.50	0.40	1.00	2.00
❑5, Oct 85	1.50	0.40	1.00	2.00
❑6, Feb 86	1.50	0.40	1.00	2.00

STARTLING CRIME ILLUSTRATED
Caliber

Value: Cover or less

Issue	Value
❑1, b&w	2.95

STAR TREK (1ST SERIES)
Gold Key

Issue	ORIG	GOOD	FINE	N-MINT
❑1, Oct 67, wraparound photo cover	0.12	57.00	142.50	285.00
❑2, Jun 68, Photo cover	0.12	37.00	92.50	185.00
❑3, Dec 68, Photo cover	0.15	28.00	70.00	140.00
❑4, Jun 69, Photo cover	0.15	28.00	70.00	140.00
❑5, Sep 69, Photo cover	0.15	28.00	70.00	140.00
❑6, Dec 69, Photo cover	0.15	23.00	57.50	115.00
❑7, Mar 70, Photo cover	0.15	23.00	57.50	115.00
❑8, Sep 70, Photo cover	0.15	23.00	57.50	115.00
❑9, Feb 71, last photo cover	0.15	23.00	57.50	115.00
❑10, May 71	0.15	12.00	30.00	60.00
❑11, Aug 71	0.15	12.00	30.00	60.00
❑12, Nov 71	0.15	12.00	30.00	60.00
❑13, Feb 72	0.15	12.00	30.00	60.00
❑14, May 72	0.15	12.00	30.00	60.00
❑15, Aug 72	0.15	12.00	30.00	60.00
❑16, Nov 72	0.15	12.00	30.00	60.00
❑17, Feb 73	0.15	12.00	30.00	60.00
❑18, May 73	0.15	12.00	30.00	60.00
❑19, Jul 73	0.15	12.00	30.00	60.00
❑20, Sep 73	0.20	12.00	30.00	60.00
❑21, Nov 73	0.20	9.00	22.50	45.00
❑22, Jan 74	0.20	9.00	22.50	45.00
❑23, Mar 74	0.20	9.00	22.50	45.00
❑24, May 74	0.20	9.00	22.50	45.00
❑25, Jul 74	0.25	9.00	22.50	45.00
❑26, Sep 74, The Perfect Dream	0.25	9.00	22.50	45.00
❑27, Nov 74	0.25	9.00	22.50	45.00
❑28, Jan 75	0.25	9.00	22.50	45.00
❑29, Mar 75	0.25	9.00	22.50	45.00
❑30, May 75	0.25	9.00	22.50	45.00
❑31, Jul 75	0.25	7.00	17.50	35.00
❑32, Aug 75	—	7.00	17.50	35.00
❑33, Sep 75	—	7.00	17.50	35.00
❑34, Oct 75	—	7.00	17.50	35.00
❑35, Nov 75	—	7.00	17.50	35.00
❑36, Mar 76	—	7.00	17.50	35.00
❑37, May 76	—	7.00	17.50	35.00
❑38, Jul 76	—	7.00	17.50	35.00
❑39, Aug 76	—	7.00	17.50	35.00
❑40, Sep 76	—	7.00	17.50	35.00
❑41, Nov 76	—	4.80	12.00	24.00
❑42, Jan 77	—	4.80	12.00	24.00
❑43, Feb 77	—	4.80	12.00	24.00
❑44, May 77	—	4.80	12.00	24.00
❑45, Jul 77	—	4.80	12.00	24.00
❑46, Aug 77	—	4.80	12.00	24.00
❑47, Sep 77	—	4.80	12.00	24.00
❑48, Oct 77	—	4.80	12.00	24.00
❑49, Nov 77	—	4.80	12.00	24.00
❑50, Jan 78	—	4.80	12.00	24.00
❑51, Mar 78, A: Professor Whipple	0.35	4.80	12.00	24.00
❑52, May 78	—	4.80	12.00	24.00
❑53, Jul 78	—	4.80	12.00	24.00
❑54, Aug 78	—	4.80	12.00	24.00
❑55, Sep 78	—	4.80	12.00	24.00
❑56, Oct 78	—	4.80	12.00	24.00
❑57, Nov 78	—	4.80	12.00	24.00
❑58, Dec 78	—	4.80	12.00	24.00
❑59, Jan 79	—	4.80	12.00	24.00
❑60, Feb 79	—	4.00	10.00	20.00
❑61, Mar 79, Final Issue	—	4.00	10.00	20.00

STAR TREK (2ND SERIES)
Marvel

Issue	ORIG	GOOD	FINE	N-MINT
❑1, Apr 80, KJ; DC, Star Trek: The Motion Picture, adapts Star Trek: The Motion Picture	0.40	0.80	2.00	4.00
❑2, May 80, KJ; DC, adapts Star Trek: The Motion Picture	0.40	0.60	1.50	3.00
❑3, Jun 80, KJ; DC, adapts Star Trek: The Motion Picture	0.40	0.40	1.00	2.00
❑4, Jul 80	0.40	0.40	1.00	2.00
❑5, Aug 80	0.40	0.40	1.00	2.00
❑6, Sep 80	0.50	0.40	1.00	2.00
❑7, Oct 80	0.50	0.40	1.00	2.00
❑8, Nov 80	0.50	0.40	1.00	2.00
❑9, Dec 80	0.50	0.40	1.00	2.00
❑10, Jan 81, Starfleet files	0.50	0.40	1.00	2.00
❑11, Feb 81	0.50	0.40	1.00	2.00
❑12, Mar 81	0.50	0.40	1.00	2.00
❑13, Apr 81, A: McCoy's daughter	0.50	0.40	1.00	2.00
❑14, Jun 81	0.50	0.40	1.00	2.00
❑15, Aug 81	0.50	0.40	1.00	2.00
❑16, Oct 81	0.50	0.40	1.00	2.00
❑17, Dec 81	0.50	0.40	1.00	2.00
❑18, Feb 82, Final Issue	0.60	0.40	1.00	2.00

STAR TREK (3RD SERIES)
DC

Issue	ORIG	GOOD	FINE	N-MINT
❑1, Feb 84, TS, The Wormhole Connection, 1: Bearclaw	0.75	0.80	2.00	4.00
❑2, Mar 84, TS	0.75	0.60	1.50	3.00
❑3, Apr 84, TS	0.75	0.60	1.50	3.00
❑4, May 84, TS	0.75	0.60	1.50	3.00
❑5, Jun 84, TS	0.75	0.60	1.50	3.00
❑6, Jul 84, TS	0.75	0.50	1.25	2.50
❑7, Aug 84, TS, O: Saavik	0.75	0.50	1.25	2.50
❑8, Nov 84, TS, V: Romulans	0.75	0.50	1.25	2.50
❑9, Dec 84, TS, Return of Mirror Universe	0.75	0.50	1.25	2.50
❑10, Jan 85, TS	0.75	0.50	1.25	2.50
❑11, Feb 85, TS, The two Spocks mind-meld	0.75	0.40	1.00	2.00
❑12, Mar 85, TS, Mirror Universe Enterprise's engineering hull destroyed	0.75	0.40	1.00	2.00
❑13, Apr 85, TS	0.75	0.40	1.00	2.00
❑14, May 85, TS	0.75	0.40	1.00	2.00
❑15, Jun 85, TS	0.75	0.40	1.00	2.00
❑16, Jul 85, TS, Kirk receives command of Excelsior	0.75	0.40	1.00	2.00
❑17, Aug 85, TS	0.75	0.40	1.00	2.00
❑18, Sep 85, TS	0.75	0.40	1.00	2.00
❑19, Oct 85, DS; TS	0.75	0.40	1.00	2.00
❑20, Nov 85, TS	0.75	0.40	1.00	2.00
❑21, Dec 85, TS	0.75	0.40	1.00	2.00
❑22, Jan 86, TS, return of Redjac	0.75	0.40	1.00	2.00
❑23, Feb 86, TS, return of Redjac	0.75	0.40	1.00	2.00
❑24, Mar 86, TS	0.75	0.40	1.00	2.00
❑25, Apr 86, TS	0.75	0.40	1.00	2.00
❑26, May 86, TS	0.75	0.40	1.00	2.00
❑27, Jun 86, TS	0.75	0.40	1.00	2.00
❑28, Jul 86, GM; TS	0.75	0.40	1.00	2.00
❑29, Aug 86, TS	0.75	0.40	1.00	2.00
❑30, Sep 86, TS	0.75	0.40	1.00	2.00
❑31, Oct 86, TS	0.75	0.40	1.00	2.00
❑32, Nov 86, TS	0.75	0.40	1.00	2.00
❑33, Dec 86, Giant-size; 20th Anniversary of Star Trek issue; original Enterprise meets Excelsior	1.25	0.40	1.00	2.00
❑34, Jan 87	0.75	0.40	1.00	2.00
❑35, Feb 87, GM	0.75	0.40	1.00	2.00
❑36, Mar 87, returns to Vulcan	0.75	0.40	1.00	2.00
❑37, Apr 87, CS, follows events of Star Trek IV	0.75	0.40	1.00	2.00
❑38, May 87	0.75	0.40	1.00	2.00
❑39, Jun 87, return of Harry Mudd	0.75	0.40	1.00	2.00
❑40, Jul 87, A: Harry Mudd	0.75	0.40	1.00	2.00
❑41, Aug 87, V: Orion pirates	0.75	0.40	1.00	2.00
❑42, Sep 87	0.75	0.40	1.00	2.00
❑43, Oct 87	0.75	0.40	1.00	2.00
❑44, Nov 87	0.75	0.40	1.00	2.00
❑45, Dec 87	0.75	0.40	1.00	2.00
❑46, Jan 88	0.75	0.40	1.00	2.00
❑47, Feb 88	0.75	0.40	1.00	2.00
❑48, Mar 88, PD (w), 1: Moron, first Peter David script	0.75	0.40	1.00	2.00
❑49, Apr 88, PD (w)	1.00	0.40	1.00	2.00
❑50, May 88, PD (w), Giant-size	1.50	0.40	1.00	2.00
❑51, Jun 88, PD (w)	1.00	0.40	1.00	2.00
❑52, Jul 88, PD (w)	1.00	0.40	1.00	2.00

	ORIG	GOOD	FINE	N-MINT
❑53, Aug 88, PD (w)	1.00	0.40	1.00	2.00
❑54, Sep 88, PD (w), Return of Finnegan	1.00	0.40	1.00	2.00
❑55, Oct 88, PD (w)	1.00	0.40	1.00	2.00
❑56, Nov 88, PD (w), Final Issue; set during first five-year mission	1.00	0.40	1.00	2.00
❑Anl 1, Kirk's first mission on The Enterprise	1.25	0.40	1.00	2.00
❑Anl 2, A: Captain Pike, The final mission of the first five-year mission	1.25	0.40	1.00	2.00
❑Anl 3, CS, Scotty's romances	1.25	0.40	1.00	2.00

STAR TREK (4TH SERIES)
DC

	ORIG	GOOD	FINE	N-MINT
❑1, Oct 89, PD (w), The Return!	1.50	1.00	2.50	5.00
❑2, Nov 89	1.50	0.80	2.00	4.00
❑3, Dec 89	1.50	0.60	1.50	3.00
❑4, Jan 90, 1: R.J. Blaise	1.50	0.60	1.50	3.00
❑5, Feb 90	1.50	0.50	1.25	2.50
❑6, Mar 90	1.50	0.50	1.25	2.50
❑7, Apr 90	1.50	0.50	1.25	2.50
❑8, May 90, V: Sweeney	1.50	0.50	1.25	2.50
❑9, Jun 90, V: Sweeney	1.50	0.50	1.25	2.50
❑10, Jul 90, The Trial of James T. Kirk, A: Samuel Cogsley; A: Areel Shaw	1.50	0.50	1.25	2.50
❑11, Aug 90, The Trial of James T. Kirk, A: Leonard James Akaar; A: Bella Oxmyx	1.50	0.40	1.00	2.00
❑12, Sep 90, The Trial of James T. Kirk	1.50	0.40	1.00	2.00
❑13, Oct 90, The Worthy	1.50	0.40	1.00	2.00
❑14, Dec 90, The Worthy	1.50	0.40	1.00	2.00
❑15, Jan 91, PD (w), The Worthy, The Worthy; final Peter David issue	1.50	0.40	1.00	2.00
❑16, Feb 91	1.50	0.40	1.00	2.00
❑17, Mar 91	1.50	0.40	1.00	2.00
❑18, Apr 91	1.50	0.40	1.00	2.00
❑19, May 91	1.50	0.40	1.00	2.00
❑20, Jun 91	1.50	0.40	1.00	2.00
❑21, Jul 91	1.75	0.40	1.00	2.00
❑22, Aug 91, Return of Harry Mudd	1.75	0.40	1.00	2.00
❑23, Sep 91, A: Harry Mudd	1.75	0.40	1.00	2.00
❑24, Oct 91, A: Harry Mudd, double-sized; 25th anniversary of Star Trek	2.95	0.60	1.50	3.00
❑25, Nov 91, A: Captain Styles; A: Saavik	1.75	0.40	1.00	2.00
❑26, Dec 91	1.75	0.40	1.00	2.00
❑27, Jan 92	1.75	0.40	1.00	2.00
❑28, Feb 92	1.75	0.40	1.00	2.00
❑29, Mar 92	1.75	0.40	1.00	2.00
❑30, Apr 92	1.75	0.40	1.00	2.00
❑31, May 92	1.75	0.40	1.00	2.00
❑32, Jun 92	1.75	0.40	1.00	2.00
❑33, Jul 92	1.75	0.40	1.00	2.00
❑34, Aug 92	1.75	0.40	1.00	2.00
❑35, Sep 92, The Tabukan Syndrome, Part 1; Tabukan Syndrome, Part 1	1.75	0.40	1.00	2.00
❑36, Sep 92, The Tabukan Syndrome, Part 2; Tabukan Syndrome, Part 2	1.75	0.40	1.00	2.00
❑37, Oct 92, The Tabukan Syndrome, Part 3; Tabukan Syndrome, Part 3	1.75	0.40	1.00	2.00
❑38, Oct 92, The Tabukan Syndrome, Part 4; Tabukan Syndrome, Part 4	1.75	0.40	1.00	2.00
❑39, Nov 92, The Tabukan Syndrome, Part 5; Tabukan Syndrome, Part 5	1.75	0.40	1.00	2.00
❑40, Nov 92, The Tabukan Syndrome, Part 6; Tabukan Syndrome, Part 6	1.75	0.40	1.00	2.00
❑41, Dec 92	1.75	0.40	1.00	2.00
❑42, Jan 93, A Little Adventure...Goes a Long Way, Part 1	1.75	0.40	1.00	2.00
❑43, Feb 93, A Little Adventure...Goes a Long Way, Part 2	1.75	0.40	1.00	2.00
❑44, Mar 93	1.75	0.40	1.00	2.00
❑45, Apr 93, Return of Trelane	1.75	0.40	1.00	2.00
❑46, May 93	1.75	0.40	1.00	2.00
❑47, May 93	1.75	0.40	1.00	2.00
❑48, Jun 93	1.75	0.40	1.00	2.00
❑49, Jun 93	1.75	0.40	1.00	2.00
❑50, Jul 93, A: Gary Seven, Giant-size anniversary special	3.50	0.70	1.75	3.50
❑51, Aug 93	1.75	0.40	1.00	2.00
❑52, Sep 93	1.75	0.40	1.00	2.00
❑53, Oct 93	1.75	0.40	1.00	2.00
❑54, Nov 93, Time Crime, Part 2	1.75	0.40	1.00	2.00
❑55, Dec 93	1.75	0.40	1.00	2.00
❑56, Jan 94	1.75	0.40	1.00	2.00
❑57, Feb 94	1.75	0.40	1.00	2.00
❑58, Mar 94, cover forms triptych with issues #59 and 60; Chekov's first days on the Enterprise	1.75	0.40	1.00	2.00
❑59, Apr 94, cover forms triptych with issues #58 and 60; Chekov's first days on the Enterprise	1.75	0.40	1.00	2.00
❑60, Jun 94, cover forms triptych with issues #57 and 58; Chekov's first days on the Enterprise	1.75	0.40	1.00	2.00
❑61, Jul 94, return to Talos IV	1.95	0.40	1.00	2.00

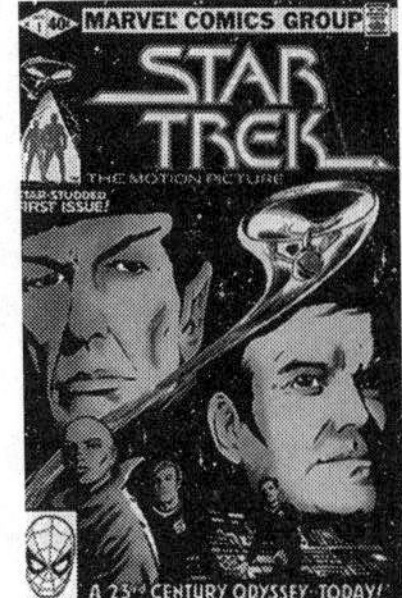

Marvel's *Star Trek* series began with an adaptation of the first *Star Trek* movie.

© 1980 Paramount (Marvel)

	ORIG	GOOD	FINE	N-MINT
❑62, Aug 94, The Lone Alone	1.95	0.40	1.00	2.00
❑63, Sep 94	1.95	0.40	1.00	2.00
❑64, Oct 94, follows events of Where No Man Has Gone Before	1.95	0.40	1.00	2.00
❑65, Nov 94	1.95	0.40	1.00	2.00
❑66, Dec 94	1.95	0.40	1.00	2.00
❑67, Jan 95	1.95	0.40	1.00	2.00
❑68, Feb 95	1.95	0.40	1.00	2.00
❑69, Mar 95, Wolf in Cheap Clothing, Part 1	1.95	0.40	1.00	2.00
❑70, Apr 95	1.95	0.40	1.00	2.00
❑71, May 95	2.50	0.50	1.25	2.50
❑72, Jun 95	2.50	0.50	1.25	2.50
❑73, Jul 95, Star-Crossed, Part 1	2.50	0.50	1.25	2.50
❑74, Aug 95, Star-Crossed, Part 2	2.50	0.50	1.25	2.50
❑75, Sep 95	3.95	0.79	1.98	3.95
❑76, Oct 95	2.50	0.50	1.25	2.50
❑77, Nov 95	2.50	0.50	1.25	2.50
❑78, Dec 95, The Chosen, Part 1	2.50	0.50	1.25	2.50
❑79, Jan 96, The Chosen, Part 2	2.50	0.50	1.25	2.50
❑80, Feb 96, The Chosen, Part 3, Final Issue	2.50	0.50	1.25	2.50
❑Anl 1	2.95	0.70	1.75	3.50
❑Anl 2, Kirk at Starfleet Academy	2.95	0.65	1.63	3.25
❑Anl 3, Homeworld	3.50	0.70	1.75	3.50
❑Anl 4, Spock on Enterprise with Captain Pike	3.50	0.70	1.75	3.50
❑Anl 5, 1994 Annual	3.95	0.79	1.98	3.95
❑Anl 6, Convergence, Part 1, D: Gary Seven, continues in Star Trek: TNG Annual #6; 1995 Annual	3.95	0.79	1.98	3.95
❑SE 1, Spr 94, Blaise of Glory	3.50	0.70	1.75	3.50
❑SE 2, Win 94, Raise the Defiant	3.95	0.70	1.75	3.50
❑SE 3, Win 95, Unforgiven	3.95	0.79	1.98	3.95

STAR TREK: DEEP SPACE NINE (MALIBU)
MALIBU

Value: Cover or less

	Value
❑0, premium limited edition; QVC offer	28.00
❑1, Stowaway	2.50
❑1/A, Aug 93, Stowaway, photo cover (newsstand)	2.50
❑1/B, Aug 93, Stowaway, line-drawing cover	2.50
❑1/C, Aug 93, Stowaway, deluxe edition (black/foil)	19.95
❑2, Sep 93, trading card	2.50
❑3, Oct 93	2.50
❑4, Nov 93	2.50
❑5, Dec 93	2.50
❑6, Jan 94	2.50
❑7, Feb 94	2.50
❑8, May 94	2.50
❑9, Jun 94	2.50
❑10, Jun 94	2.50
❑11, Jul 94	2.50
❑12, Jul 94	2.50
❑13, Aug 94	2.50
❑14, Sep 94	2.50
❑15, Sep 94	2.50
❑16, Nov 94	2.50
❑17, Dec 94	2.50
❑18, Jan 95	2.50
❑19, Feb 95	2.50
❑20, Mar 95	2.50
❑21, Apr 95	2.50
❑22, May 95	2.50
❑23, May 95	2.50
❑24, Jun 95	2.50
❑25, Jul 95	3.50
❑26, Jul 95	2.50
❑27, Aug 95	2.50
❑28, Sep 95	2.50
❑29, Oct 95, A: Bashir; A: Will Riker; A: Captain Sisko; A: Thomas Riker; A: Mirror Universe Tuvok	2.50
❑30	2.50
❑31	—
❑32, Final Issue	—
❑Anl 1	3.95
❑Ash 1, limited edition ashcan	—
❑SE 1	3.50

STAR TREK: DEEP SPACE NINE (MARVEL)
MARVEL

	ORIG	GOOD	FINE	N-MINT
❑1, Nov 96, Judgment Day, DS9 is drawn into the wormhole	1.99	0.40	1.00	2.00
❑2, Dec 96	1.99	0.40	1.00	2.00
❑3, Jan 97, The Cancer Within, Part 1	1.99	0.40	1.00	2.00
❑4, Feb 97, The Cancer Within, Part 2	1.99	0.40	1.00	2.00
❑5, Mar 97, The Shadow Group	1.99	0.40	1.00	2.00
❑6, Apr 97, Risk	1.99	0.40	1.00	2.00
❑7, May 97	1.99	0.40	1.00	2.00
❑8, Aug 97	1.99	0.40	1.00	2.00
❑9, Sep 97	1.99	0.40	1.00	2.00
❑10, Oct 97	1.99	0.40	1.00	2.00
❑11, Nov 97, gatefold summary	1.99	0.40	1.00	2.00
❑12, Dec 97, Telepathy War, Part 2, gatefold summary	1.99	0.40	1.00	2.00

	ORIG	GOOD	FINE	N-MINT
❑13, Jan 98, gatefold summary	1.99	0.40	1.00	2.00
❑14, Feb 98, A: Tribbles, gatefold summary	1.99	0.40	1.00	2.00
❑15, Mar 98, Final Issue; gatefold summary	1.99	0.40	1.00	2.00

STAR TREK: DEEP SPACE NINE, THE CELEBRITY SERIES: BLOOD AND HONOR
MALIBU
Value: Cover or less

❑1, May 95 .... 2.95

STAR TREK: DEEP SPACE NINE HEARTS AND MINDS
MALIBU
Value: Cover or less

❑1, Jun 94, For the Glory of the Empire, Part 1, an original Deep Space Nine mini series 2.50
❑2, Jul 94 .... 2.50
❑3, Aug 94 .... 2.50
❑4, Sep 94 .... 2.50

STAR TREK: DEEP SPACE NINE: LIGHTSTORM
MALIBU
Value: Cover or less

❑1, Dec 94 .... 3.50

STAR TREK: DEEP SPACE NINE, THE MAQUIS
MALIBU
Value: Cover or less

❑1, Feb 95, The Maquis: Soldier of Peace, Part 1 .... 2.50
❑2, Mar 95, The Maquis: Soldier of Peace, Part 2 .... 2.50
❑3, Apr 95, The Maquis: Soldier of Peace, Part 3 .... 2.50

STAR TREK: DEEP SPACE NINE-N-VECTOR
DC
Value: Cover or less

❑1, Aug 00 .... 2.50
❑2, Sep 00 .... 2.50
❑3, Oct 00 .... 2.50
❑4, Nov 00 .... 2.50

STAR TREK: DEEP SPACE NINE: RULES OF DIPLOMACY
MALIBU
Value: Cover or less

❑1, Aug 95, Rules Of Diplomacy, Co-Author Aron Eisenberg plays "Nog" in series 2.95

STAR TREK: DEEP SPACE NINE/STAR TREK: THE NEXT GENERATION
MALIBU

	ORIG	GOOD	FINE	N-MINT
❑1, Oct 94, The Wormhole Trap!, part two of a four-part crossover with DC; Deep Space Nine/The Next Generation crossover, Part 2; Continued from Star Trek: The Next Generation/Star Trek: Deep Space Nine #1; Continues in Star Trek: The Next Generation/Star Trek: Deep Space Nine #2	2.50	0.50	1.25	2.50
❑2, Nov 94, The Enemy Unseen, part three of a four-part crossover with DC; Deep Space Nine/The Next Generation crossover, Part 4; Continued from Star Trek: The Next Generation/Star Trek: Deep Space Nine #2	2.50	0.50	1.25	2.50
❑Ash 1, no cover price; Ashcan preview; flip-book with DC's Star Trek: The Next Generation/Star Trek: Deep Space Nine Ashcan	—	0.20	0.50	1.00

STAR TREK: DEEP SPACE NINE: TEROK NOR
MALIBU
Value: Cover or less

❑0, Jan 95, O: Deep Space Nine 2.95

STAR TREK: DEEP SPACE NINE, ULTIMATE ANNUAL
MALIBU
Value: Cover or less

❑1, No Time Like The Present 5.95

STAR TREK: DEEP SPACE NINE, WORF SPECIAL
MALIBU
Value: Cover or less

❑0, Bonds of Honor 3.95

STAR TREK: EARLY VOYAGES
MARVEL
Value: Cover or less

❑1, Feb 97, Flesh of My Flesh, Christopher Pike as Enterprise captain 2.99
❑2, Mar 97, The Fires of Pharos, V: Klingons 1.99
❑3, Apr 97, Our Dearest Blood, prequel to The Cage 1.99
❑4, May 97, Nor Iron Bars a Cage, Yeoman Colt's POV on The Cage 1.99
❑5, Jun 97 .... 1.99
❑6, Jul 97 .... 1.99
❑7, Aug 97, gatefold summary; Pike vs. Kaaj 1.99
❑8, Sep 97, gatefold summary 1.99
❑9, Oct 97, gatefold summary 1.99
❑10, Nov 97, V: Chakuun, gatefold summary 1.99
❑11, Dec 97, gatefold summary 1.99
❑12, Jan 98, A: Robert April, gatefold summary 1.99
❑13, Feb 98, A: Scotty; A: Kirk, gatefold summary 1.99
❑14, Mar 98, A: Scotty; A: Kirk, gatefold summary 1.99
❑15, Apr 98, A: Scotty; A: Kirk, gatefold summary 1.99
❑16, May 98, Pike goes undercover; gatefold summary 1.99
❑17, Jun 98, Final Issue; gatefold summary 1.99

STAR TREK: ENTER THE WOLVES
WILDSTORM
Value: Cover or less

❑1 .... 5.99

STAR TREK: FIRST CONTACT
MARVEL
Value: Cover or less

❑1, Nov 96, cardstock cover; movie Adaptation; prestige format 5.99

STAR TREK GENERATIONS
DC
Value: Cover or less

❑1, One-Shot; movie Adaptation 3.95
❑1/PR, movie Adaptation; prestige format one-shot 5.95

STAR TREKKER
ANTARCTIC
Value: Cover or less

❑1, Dec 92, b&w; parody (never distributed) 2.95

STAR TREK: MIRROR MIRROR
MARVEL
Value: Cover or less

❑1, Feb 97, Fragile Class, one-shot sequel to original series episode 3.99

STAR TREK MOVIE SPECIAL
DC

	ORIG	GOOD	FINE	N-MINT
❑3, Star Trek III	1.50	0.40	1.00	2.00
❑4, Star Trek IV	2.00	0.40	1.00	2.00
❑5, Star Trek V	2.00	0.40	1.00	2.00

STAR TREK: NEW FRONTIER-DOUBLE TIME
DC
Value: Cover or less

❑1, Nov 00, PD (w) 5.95

STAR TREK: OPERATION ASSIMILATION
MARVEL
Value: Cover or less

❑1, Apr 97, One-Shot; Romulans as Borg 2.99

STAR TREK SPECIAL
WILDSTORM
Value: Cover or less

❑1, Bloodline; A Rolling Stone Gathers No Nanoprobes...... 6.95

STAR TREK: STARFLEET ACADEMY
MARVEL
Value: Cover or less

❑1, Dec 96, Prime Directives, A: Nog 1.99
❑2, Jan 97, Liberty 1.99
❑3, Feb 97, Loyalty Test 1.99
❑4, Mar 97, War and Peace, Part 1 .... 1.99
❑5, Apr 97, Love and Death, D: Kamilah 1.99
❑6, May 97, Passages 1.99
❑7, Jun 97 .... 1.99
❑8, Jul 97, return of Charlie X. 1.99
❑9, Aug 97, A: Pike, gatefold summary; on Talos IV 1.99
❑10, Sep 97, gatefold summary 1.99
❑11, Oct 97, gatefold summary; cadets on trial for going to Talos IV 1.99
❑12, Nov 97, Telepathy War, Part 1, gatefold summary 1.99
❑13, Dec 97, gatefold summary 1.99
❑14, Jan 98, T'Priell Revealed, Part 1, gatefold summary 1.99
❑15, Feb 98, T'Priell Revealed, Part 2, gatefold summary 1.99
❑16, Mar 98, T'Priell Revealed, Part 3, gatefold summary 1.99
❑17, Apr 98, gatefold summary 1.99
❑18/A, May 98, gatefold summary; English language edition 1.99
❑18/B, May 98, gatefold summary; Klingon language edition 1.99
❑19, Jun 98, Final Issue; gatefold summary 1.99

STAR TREK: TELEPATHY WAR
MARVEL
Value: Cover or less

❑1, Nov 97, One-Shot; concludes storyline crossing over the various titles 2.99

STAR TREK-THE MODALA IMPERATIVE
DC

	ORIG	GOOD	FINE	N-MINT
❑1, Jul 91	1.75	0.50	1.25	2.50
❑2, Aug 91, Tools of Tyranny	1.75	0.40	1.00	2.00
❑3, Aug 91	1.75	0.40	1.00	2.00
❑4, Sep 91	1.75	0.40	1.00	2.00

STAR TREK: THE NEXT GENERATION
DC

	ORIG	GOOD	FINE	N-MINT
❑1, Oct 89, The Gift	1.50	1.00	2.50	5.00
❑2, Nov 89	1.50	0.80	2.00	4.00
❑3, Dec 89	1.50	0.60	1.50	3.00
❑4, Jan 90	1.50	0.60	1.50	3.00
❑5, Feb 90	1.50	0.60	1.50	3.00
❑6, Mar 90	1.50	0.50	1.25	2.50
❑7, Apr 90	1.50	0.50	1.25	2.50
❑8, May 90	1.50	0.50	1.25	2.50
❑9, Jun 90	1.50	0.50	1.25	2.50
❑10, Jul 90	1.50	0.50	1.25	2.50
❑11, Aug 90	1.50	0.50	1.25	2.50
❑12, Sep 90	1.50	0.50	1.25	2.50
❑13, Oct 90	1.50	0.50	1.25	2.50
❑14, Dec 90, Holiday on Ice	1.50	0.50	1.25	2.50
❑15, Jan 91, V: Ferengi	1.50	0.50	1.25	2.50
❑16, Feb 91	1.50	0.50	1.25	2.50
❑17, Mar 91	1.50	0.50	1.25	2.50
❑18, Apr 91	1.50	0.50	1.25	2.50
❑19, May 91	1.50	0.50	1.25	2.50
❑20, Jun 91	1.50	0.50	1.25	2.50
❑21, Jul 91	1.75	0.40	1.00	2.00
❑22, Aug 91	1.75	0.40	1.00	2.00
❑23, Sep 91	1.75	0.40	1.00	2.00
❑24, Oct 91, double-sized	2.50	0.40	1.00	2.00
❑25, Nov 91, Giant-size	1.50	0.40	1.00	2.00
❑26, Dec 91	1.50	0.40	1.00	2.00
❑27, Jan 92	1.50	0.40	1.00	2.00
❑28, Feb 92, Return of K'ehleyr	1.50	0.40	1.00	2.00
❑29, Mar 92	1.50	0.40	1.00	2.00

	ORIG	GOOD	FINE	N-MINT
❑30, Apr 92	1.50	0.40	1.00	2.00
❑31, May 92	1.75	0.40	1.00	2.00
❑32, Jun 92	1.75	0.40	1.00	2.00
❑33, Jul 92, Q turns the crew into Klingons	1.75	0.40	1.00	2.00
❑34, Jul 92	1.75	0.40	1.00	2.00
❑35, Aug 92	1.75	0.40	1.00	2.00
❑36, Aug 92	1.75	0.40	1.00	2.00
❑37, Sep 92	1.75	0.40	1.00	2.00
❑38, Sep 92	1.75	0.40	1.00	2.00
❑39, Oct 92	1.75	0.40	1.00	2.00
❑40, Nov 92	1.75	0.40	1.00	2.00
❑41, Dec 92	1.75	0.40	1.00	2.00
❑42, Jan 93	1.75	0.40	1.00	2.00
❑43, Feb 93	1.75	0.40	1.00	2.00
❑44, Mar 93	1.75	0.40	1.00	2.00
❑45, Apr 93	1.75	0.40	1.00	2.00
❑46, May 93	1.75	0.40	1.00	2.00
❑47, Jun 93, Worst of Both Worlds	1.75	0.40	1.00	2.00
❑48, Jul 93, Worst of Both Worlds	1.75	0.40	1.00	2.00
❑49, Aug 93, Worst of Both Worlds	1.75	0.40	1.00	2.00
❑50, Sep 93, Worst of Both Worlds, Giant-size	3.50	0.70	1.75	3.50
❑51, Oct 93	1.75	0.40	1.00	2.00
❑52, Oct 93, The Rich and the Dead!, Dixon Hill story	1.75	0.40	1.00	2.00
❑53, Nov 93	1.75	0.40	1.00	2.00
❑54, Nov 93	1.75	0.40	1.00	2.00
❑55, Dec 93	1.75	0.40	1.00	2.00
❑56, Jan 94, Companionship	1.75	0.40	1.00	2.00
❑57, Mar 94	1.75	0.40	1.00	2.00
❑58, Apr 94	1.75	0.40	1.00	2.00
❑59, May 94	1.75	0.40	1.00	2.00
❑60, Jun 94	1.75	0.40	1.00	2.00
❑61, Jul 94, Brothers in Darkness	1.95	0.40	1.00	2.00
❑62, Aug 94	1.95	0.40	1.00	2.00
❑63, Sep 94	1.95	0.40	1.00	2.00
❑64, Oct 94	1.95	0.40	1.00	2.00
❑65, Nov 94	1.95	0.40	1.00	2.00
❑66, Dec 94	1.95	0.40	1.00	2.00
❑67, Jan 95, Friends and Other Strangers, Part 1	1.95	0.40	1.00	2.00
❑68, Feb 95, Friends and Other Strangers, Part 2	1.95	0.40	1.00	2.00
❑69, Mar 95, Friends and Other Strangers, Part 3	1.95	0.40	1.00	2.00
❑70, Apr 95, Friends and Other Strangers, Part 4	1.95	0.40	1.00	2.00
❑71, May 95	1.95	0.40	1.00	2.00
❑72, Jun 95, War and Madness, Part 1	2.50	0.50	1.25	2.50
❑73, Jul 95, War and Madness, Part 2	2.50	0.50	1.25	2.50
❑74, Aug 95, War and Madness, Part 3	2.50	0.50	1.25	2.50
❑75, Sep 95, V: Borg, Giant-size	3.95	0.79	1.98	3.95
❑76, Oct 95	2.50	0.50	1.25	2.50
❑77, Nov 95	2.50	0.50	1.25	2.50
❑78, Dec 95	2.50	0.50	1.25	2.50
❑79, Jan 96, Artificiality, Q transforms the crew into androids	2.50	0.50	1.25	2.50
❑80, Feb 96, The Abandoned, Final Issue	2.50	0.50	1.25	2.50
❑Anl 1, 1990 Annual	2.95	0.70	1.75	3.50
❑Anl 2, 1991 Annual	3.50	0.70	1.75	3.50
❑Anl 3, 1992 Annual	3.50	0.70	1.75	3.50
❑Anl 4, 1993 Annual	3.50	0.70	1.75	3.50
❑Anl 5, Brother's Keeper, 1994 Annual	3.95	0.70	1.75	3.50
❑Anl 6, Convergence, Part 2, continued from Star Trek Annual #6; 1995 Annual	3.95	0.79	1.98	3.95
❑SE 1	3.50	0.70	1.75	3.50
❑SE 2, Sum 94, 1994 Special	3.95	0.79	1.98	3.95
❑SE 3, Win 95, Pandora's Prodigy, 1995 Special	3.95	0.79	1.98	3.95

STAR TREK: THE NEXT GENERATION (MINI-SERIES)
DC

	ORIG	GOOD	FINE	N-MINT
❑1, Feb 88	1.50	0.60	1.50	3.00
❑2, Mar 88	1.00	0.40	1.00	2.00
❑3, Apr 88	1.00	0.40	1.00	2.00
❑4, May 88	1.00	0.40	1.00	2.00
❑5, Jun 88, Q Affects, D: Geordi	1.00	0.40	1.00	2.00
❑6, Jul 88, Here Today	1.00	0.40	1.00	2.00

STAR TREK: THE NEXT GENERATION/DEEP SPACE NINE
DC

	ORIG	GOOD	FINE	N-MINT
❑1, Dec 94, Prophets and Losses, crossover with Malibu; Deep Space Nine/The Next Generation crossover, Part 1; Continues in Star Trek: Deep Space Nine/The Next Generation #1	2.50	0.50	1.25	2.50
❑2, Jan 95, Encounter with...The Othersiders!, crossover with Malibu; Deep Space Nine/The Next Generation crossover, Part 3; Continued from Star Trek: Deep Space Nine/The Next Generation #1; Continues in Star Trek: Deep Space Nine/The Next Generation #2	2.50	0.50	1.25	2.50
❑Ash 1, no cover price; flip-book with Malibu's Deep Space Nine/Star Trek: The Next Generation Ashcan	—	0.20	0.50	1.00

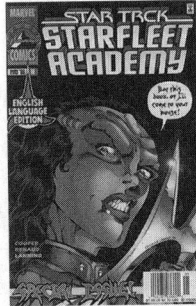

Star Trek: Starfleet Academy #18 featured versions printed in English and Klingon.

© 1998 Paramount (Marvel)

STAR TREK: THE NEXT GENERATION-ILL WIND
DC

Value: Cover or less

- ❑1, Nov 95 — 2.50
- ❑2, Dec 95 — 2.50
- ❑3, Jan 96 — 2.50
- ❑4, Feb 96 — 2.50

STAR TREK: THE NEXT GENERATION-PERCHANCE TO DREAM
DC

Value: Cover or less

- ❑1, Feb 00 — 2.50
- ❑2, Mar 00 — 2.50
- ❑3, Apr 00 — 2.50
- ❑4, May 00 — 2.50

STAR TREK: THE NEXT GENERATION: RIKER
MARVEL

Value: Cover or less

- ❑1, Jul 98, The Enemy of My Enemy, One-Shot — 3.50

STAR TREK:THE NEXT GENERATION-SHADOWHEART
DC

Value: Cover or less

- ❑1, Dec 94, The Lion and the Lamb — 1.95
- ❑2, Jan 95 — 1.95
- ❑3, Feb 95 — 1.95
- ❑4, Mar 95 — 1.95

STAR TREK: THE NEXT GENERATION-THE GORN CRISIS
DC

Value: Cover or less

- ❑1/HC — 29.95

STAR TREK: THE NEXT GENERATION-THE KILLING SHADOWS
DC

Value: Cover or less

- ❑1, Nov 00, The Trap — 2.50
- ❑2, Dec 00, The Hunted — 2.50
- ❑3, Jan 01, The Trap — 2.50
- ❑4, Feb 01, The Secret — 2.50

STAR TREK: THE NEXT GENERATION-THE SERIES FINALE
DC

Value: Cover or less

- ❑1, nn; adapts final TV episode — 3.95

STAR TREK: THE NEXT GENERATION/X-MEN
MARVEL

	ORIG	GOOD	FINE	N-MINT
❑1	4.95	0.99	2.47	4.95
❑1/SC, Cover has Wolverine, Data, Riker, Sentinel in background	—	1.60	4.00	8.00

STAR TREK UNLIMITED
MARVEL

	ORIG	GOOD	FINE	N-MINT
❑1, Nov 96, Directives; Dying of the Light, Anthology; Original crew story; Next Generation story	2.99	0.60	1.50	3.00
❑2, Jan 97, Action of the Tiger; The Unkindest Cut, Anthology; Original crew story; Next Generation story	2.99	0.60	1.50	3.00
❑3, Apr 97, Anthology; Original crew story; Next Generation story	2.99	0.60	1.50	3.00
❑4, May 97, Anthology; Original crew story; Next Generation story; Original series and Next Generation stories crossover	2.99	0.60	1.50	3.00
❑5, Sep 97, Anthology; Original series and Next Generation stories crossover; Original crew story; Next Generation story	2.99	0.60	1.50	3.00
❑6, Nov 97, Telepathy War, Part 4	2.99	0.60	1.50	3.00
❑7, Jan 98	2.99	0.60	1.50	3.00
❑8, Mar 98, Kang vs. Sulu	2.99	0.60	1.50	3.00
❑9, May 98, Chekov wins a Klingon cruiser	2.99	0.60	1.50	3.00
❑10, Jul 98, A Piece of Reaction	2.99	0.60	1.50	3.00

STAR TREK: UNTOLD VOYAGES
MARVEL

Value: Cover or less

- ❑1, Mar 98, Renewal — 2.50
- ❑2, Apr 98, A: Saavik — 2.50
- ❑3, May 98, A: Onlies — 2.50
- ❑4, Jun 98, Sulu takes command — 2.50
- ❑5, Jul 98, Final Issue — 3.50

STAR TREK VI: THE UNDISCOVERED COUNTRY
DC

Value: Cover or less

- ❑1, The Undiscovered Country; newsstand — 2.95
- ❑1/DM, The Undiscovered Country; prestige format — 5.95

STAR TREK: VOYAGER
MARVEL

	ORIG	GOOD	FINE	N-MINT
❑1, Nov 96	1.95	0.40	1.00	2.00
❑2, Dec 96, Under Ion Skies	1.95	0.40	1.00	2.00
❑3, Jan 97, Repercussions	1.99	0.40	1.00	2.00
❑4, Feb 97, Homeostasis, Part 1	1.99	0.40	1.00	2.00
❑5, Mar 97, Homeostasis, Part 2	1.99	0.40	1.00	2.00
❑6, Apr 97, RelicQuest, Part 1	1.99	0.40	1.00	2.00
❑7, May 97, RelicQuest, Part 2	1.99	0.40	1.00	2.00
❑8, Jun 97	1.99	0.40	1.00	2.00
❑9, Sep 97, gatefold summary	1.99	0.40	1.00	2.00
❑10, Oct 97, gatefold summary; replays events at Wolf 359	1.99	0.40	1.00	2.00
❑11, Nov 97, V: Leviathan, gatefold summary	1.99	0.40	1.00	2.00
❑12, Dec 97, gatefold summary	1.99	0.40	1.00	2.00
❑13, Jan 98, Telepathy War, Part 5, gatefold summary	1.99	0.40	1.00	2.00
❑14, Feb 98, 1: Seven of Nine, gatefold summary	1.99	0.40	1.00	2.00
❑15, Mar 98, Final Issue; gatefold summary	1.99	0.40	1.00	2.00

STAR TREK: VOYAGER-FALSE COLORS
DC

Value: Cover or less

- ❑1, Jan 00 ... 5.95

STAR TREK: VOYAGER: SPLASHDOWN
MARVEL

Value: Cover or less

- ❑1, Apr 98, gatefold summary 2.50
- ❑2, May 98, gatefold summary 2.50
- ❑3, Jun 98, gatefold summary 2.50
- ❑4, Jul 98, gatefold summary; final Marvel Star Trek comic book ... 2.50

STAR TREK: VOYAGER-THE PLANET KILLER
DC

Value: Cover or less

- ❑1, Mar 01, Ultimate Weapon. 2.95
- ❑2, Apr 01, Old Tricks ... 2.95
- ❑3, May 01, Death ... 2.95

STAR TREK/X-MEN
MARVEL

	ORIG	GOOD	FINE	N-MINT
❑1, Dec 96, Star Trex, One-Shot; X-Men meet original Enterprise crew	4.95	1.00	2.50	5.00

STAR TREK/X-MEN: SECOND CONTACT
MARVEL

	ORIG	GOOD	FINE	N-MINT
❑1, May 98, A: Kang, One-Shot; X-Men meet Next Generation crew; Sentinels; continues in Star Trek: The Next Generation/X-Men: Planet X novel	4.99	1.00	2.50	5.00

STAR WARS
MARVEL

	ORIG	GOOD	FINE	N-MINT
❑1, Jul 77, HC, Star Wars, Part 1, movie Adaptation	0.30	5.00	12.50	25.00
❑1/A, Jul 77, HC, Star Wars, Part 1, movie Adaptation; 35 cent variation; Rare variation; Price is in a square area, and UPC code appears with a line drawn through it	0.35	50.00	125.00	250.00
❑1-2, HC, Star Wars, Part 1, 2nd Printing; "Reprint" in upper-left corner	0.30	0.80	2.00	4.00
❑2, Aug 77, HC, Star Wars, Part 2, movie Adaptation	0.30	3.00	7.50	15.00
❑2-2, HC, Star Wars, Part 2, 2nd Printing; Has blank square where UPC code would go	0.35	0.70	1.75	3.50
❑3, Sep 77, HC, Star Wars, Part 3, movie Adaptation	0.30	3.00	7.50	15.00
❑3-2, HC, Star Wars, Part 3, 2nd Printing; Has blank square where UPC code would go	0.35	0.70	1.75	3.50
❑4, Oct 77, HC, Star Wars, Part 4, movie Adaptation; low distribution	0.30	3.00	7.50	15.00
❑4-2, HC, Star Wars, Part 4, 2nd Printing; Has blank square where UPC code would go	0.35	0.70	1.75	3.50
❑5, Nov 77, HC, Star Wars, Part 5, movie Adaptation	0.35	3.00	7.50	15.00
❑5-2, HC, Star Wars, Part 5, 2nd Printing; Has blank square where UPC code would go	0.35	0.70	1.75	3.50
❑6, Dec 77, HC, Star Wars, Part 6, movie Adaptation	0.35	3.00	7.50	15.00
❑6-2, HC, Star Wars, Part 6, 2nd Printing; Has blank square where UPC code would go	0.35	0.70	1.75	3.50
❑7, Jan 78, HC	0.35	2.40	6.00	12.00
❑7-2, HC, 2nd Printing; Has blank square where UPC code would go	0.35	0.60	1.50	3.00
❑8, Feb 78, HC, Eight For Aduba-3	0.35	2.40	6.00	12.00
❑8-2, HC, Eight For Aduba-3, 2nd Printing; Has blank square where UPC code would go	0.35	0.60	1.50	3.00
❑9, Mar 78, HC, Showdown On A Wasteland World!	0.35	2.40	6.00	12.00
❑9-2, HC, 2nd Printing; Has blank square where UPC code would go	0.35	0.60	1.50	3.00
❑10, Apr 78, Behemoth From The World Below	0.35	1.60	4.00	8.00
❑11, May 78	0.35	1.40	3.50	7.00
❑12, Jun 78	0.35	1.40	3.50	7.00
❑13, Jul 78, CI	0.35	1.40	3.50	7.00
❑14, Aug 78, CI, The Sound Of Armageddon!	0.35	1.40	3.50	7.00
❑15, Sep 78, CI, Star Duel!, D: Crimson Jack	0.35	1.40	3.50	7.00
❑16, Oct 78, 1: Valance the bounty hunter..	0.35	1.40	3.50	7.00
❑17, Nov 78, HT; AM, Crucible!, low distribution; Tatooine adventure set before first movie	0.35	1.40	3.50	7.00
❑18, Dec 78, low distribution	0.35	1.40	3.50	7.00
❑19, Jan 79, BWi; CI, The Ultimate Gamble!, low distribution	0.35	1.40	3.50	7.00
❑20, Feb 79, BWi; CI, Deathgame	0.35	1.40	3.50	7.00
❑21, Mar 79	0.35	1.00	2.50	5.00
❑22, Apr 79	0.35	1.00	2.50	5.00
❑23, May 79, BWi; CI, Flight Into Fury!	0.40	1.00	2.50	5.00
❑24, Jun 79, BWi; CI, Silent Drifting, flashback to before first movie	0.40	1.00	2.50	5.00
❑25, Jul 79	0.40	1.00	2.50	5.00
❑26, Aug 79	0.40	1.00	2.50	5.00
❑27, Sep 79, BWi; CI, Return Of The Hunter	0.40	1.00	2.50	5.00
❑28, Oct 79, BWi; CI, What Ever Happened To Jabba The Hut, A: Jabba the Hutt (not movie version)	0.40	1.00	2.50	5.00
❑29, Nov 79, BWi; CI, Dark Encounter, A: Darth Vader	0.40	1.00	2.50	5.00
❑30, Dec 79, GD; CI, A Princess Alone!	0.40	1.00	2.50	5.00
❑31, Jan 80, BWi; CI, Return To Tatooine!, return to Tatooine	0.40	0.80	2.00	4.00
❑32, Feb 80, BWi; CI, The Jawa Express	0.40	0.80	2.00	4.00
❑33, Mar 80, GD; CI, Saber Clash!	0.40	0.80	2.00	4.00
❑34, Apr 80, D: Baron Tagge	0.40	0.80	2.00	4.00
❑35, May 80, A: Luke Skywalker; A: Darth Vader	0.40	0.80	2.00	4.00
❑36, Jun 80	0.40	0.80	2.00	4.00
❑37, Jul 80, GD; CI, In Mortal Combat, 1st Vader/Luke duel	0.40	0.80	2.00	4.00
❑38, Aug 80, MG, living spaceship	0.40	0.80	2.00	4.00
❑39, Sep 80, AW, Empire Strikes Back; The Empire Strikes Back, Part 1	0.50	0.80	2.00	4.00
❑40, Oct 80, AW, Empire Strikes Back; The Empire Strikes Back, Part 2	0.50	0.80	2.00	4.00
❑41, Nov 80, AW, Empire Strikes Back; The Empire Strikes Back, Part 3	0.50	0.80	2.00	4.00
❑42, Dec 80, AW, Empire Strikes Back; The Empire Strikes Back, Part 4	0.50	0.80	2.00	4.00
❑43, Jan 81, AW, Empire Strikes Back; The Empire Strikes Back, Part 5	0.50	0.80	2.00	4.00
❑44, Feb 81, AW, Empire Strikes Back; The Empire Strikes Back, Part 6	0.50	0.80	2.00	4.00
❑45, Mar 81, first post-Empire Strikes Back story	0.50	0.60	1.50	3.00
❑46, Apr 81	0.50	0.60	1.50	3.00
❑47, May 81	0.50	0.60	1.50	3.00
❑48, Jun 81	0.50	0.60	1.50	3.00
❑49, Jul 81, low distribution	0.50	0.60	1.50	3.00
❑50, Aug 81, TP; AW, Crimson Forever, double-sized	0.75	0.60	1.50	3.00
❑51, Sep 81, A: Star II appearance; A: Tarkin	0.50	0.60	1.50	3.00
❑52, Oct 81, A: Star II appearance; A: Tarkin	0.50	0.60	1.50	3.00
❑53, Nov 81	0.50	0.60	1.50	3.00
❑54, Dec 81	0.50	0.60	1.50	3.00
❑55, Jan 82	0.60	0.60	1.50	3.00
❑56, Feb 82	0.60	0.60	1.50	3.00
❑57, Mar 82	0.60	0.60	1.50	3.00
❑58, Apr 82, Return to Cloud City	0.60	0.60	1.50	3.00
❑59, May 82	0.60	0.60	1.50	3.00
❑60, Jun 82	0.60	0.60	1.50	3.00
❑61, Jul 82	0.60	0.60	1.50	3.00
❑62, Aug 82, Luke kicked out of Alliance	0.60	0.60	1.50	3.00
❑63, Sep 82	0.60	0.60	1.50	3.00
❑64, Oct 82	0.60	0.60	1.50	3.00
❑65, Nov 82	0.60	0.60	1.50	3.00
❑66, Dec 82	0.60	0.60	1.50	3.00
❑67, Jan 83	0.60	0.60	1.50	3.00
❑68, Feb 83	0.60	0.60	1.50	3.00
❑69, Mar 83	0.60	0.60	1.50	3.00
❑70, Apr 83	0.60	0.60	1.50	3.00
❑71, May 83	0.60	0.60	1.50	3.00
❑72, Jun 83	0.60	0.60	1.50	3.00
❑73, Jul 83	0.60	0.60	1.50	3.00
❑74, Aug 83	0.60	0.60	1.50	3.00
❑75, Sep 83	0.60	0.60	1.50	3.00
❑76, Oct 83	0.60	0.60	1.50	3.00
❑77, Nov 83	0.60	0.60	1.50	3.00
❑78, Dec 83	0.60	0.60	1.50	3.00
❑79, Jan 84	0.60	0.60	1.50	3.00
❑80, Feb 84	0.60	0.60	1.50	3.00
❑81, Mar 84, Photo cover; first post-Return of the Jedi story	0.60	0.60	1.50	3.00
❑82, Apr 84	0.60	0.60	1.50	3.00
❑83, May 84	0.60	0.60	1.50	3.00
❑84, Jun 84	0.60	0.60	1.50	3.00
❑85, Jul 84	0.60	0.60	1.50	3.00

	ORIG	GOOD	FINE	N-MINT
❑86, Aug 84	0.60	0.60	1.50	3.00
❑87, Sep 84	0.60	0.60	1.50	3.00
❑88, Oct 84	0.60	0.60	1.50	3.00
❑89, Nov 84	0.60	0.60	1.50	3.00
❑90, Dec 84	0.60	0.60	1.50	3.00
❑91, Jan 85	0.60	0.60	1.50	3.00
❑92, Feb 85, Giant-size	1.00	0.60	1.50	3.00
❑93, Mar 85	0.60	0.60	1.50	3.00
❑94, Apr 85	0.65	0.60	1.50	3.00
❑95, May 85	0.65	0.60	1.50	3.00
❑96, Jun 85	0.65	0.60	1.50	3.00
❑97, Jul 85	0.65	0.60	1.50	3.00
❑98, Aug 85	0.65	0.60	1.50	3.00
❑99, Sep 85	0.65	0.60	1.50	3.00
❑100, Oct 85, Giant-size	1.25	0.60	1.50	3.00
❑101, Nov 85	0.65	0.60	1.50	3.00
❑102, Dec 85	0.65	0.60	1.50	3.00
❑103, Jan 86	0.65	0.60	1.50	3.00
❑104, Mar 86	0.75	0.60	1.50	3.00
❑105, May 86	0.75	0.60	1.50	3.00
❑106, Jul 86	0.75	0.60	1.50	3.00
❑107, Sep 86, Final Issue	0.75	5.00	12.50	25.00
❑Anl 1, Dec 79	0.75	1.60	4.00	8.00
❑Anl 2	1.00	1.00	2.50	5.00
❑Anl 3	1.00	1.00	2.50	5.00

STAR WARS (DARK HORSE)
DARK HORSE

	ORIG	GOOD	FINE	N-MINT
❑0, HC, American Entertainment exclusive	—	2.00	5.00	10.00
❑1, Dec 98, Prelude to Rebellion, Part 1	2.50	0.80	2.00	4.00
❑2, Jan 99, Prelude to Rebellion, Part 2	2.50	0.60	1.50	3.00
❑3, Feb 99, Prelude to Rebellion, Part 3	2.50	0.60	1.50	3.00
❑4, Mar 99, Prelude to Rebellion, Part 4	2.50	0.60	1.50	3.00
❑5, Apr 99, Prelude to Rebellion, Part 5	2.50	0.60	1.50	3.00
❑6, May 99, Prelude to Rebellion, Part 6	2.50	0.60	1.50	3.00
❑7, Jun 99, Outlander, Part 1	2.50	0.50	1.25	2.50
❑8, Jul 99, Outlander, Part 2	2.50	0.50	1.25	2.50
❑9, Aug 99, Outlander, Part 3	2.50	0.50	1.25	2.50
❑10, Sep 99, Outlander, Part 4	2.50	0.50	1.25	2.50
❑11, Oct 99, Outlander, Part 5	2.50	0.50	1.25	2.50
❑12, Nov 99, Outlander, Part 6	2.50	0.50	1.25	2.50
❑13, Dec 99, Emissaries to Malastare, Part 1	2.50	0.50	1.25	2.50
❑14, Jan 00, Emissaries to Malastare, Part 2	2.50	0.50	1.25	2.50
❑15, Feb 00, Emissaries to Malastare, Part 3	2.50	0.50	1.25	2.50
❑16, Mar 00, Emissaries to Malastare, Part 4	2.50	0.50	1.25	2.50
❑17, Apr 00, Emissaries to Malastare, Part 5	2.50	0.50	1.25	2.50
❑18, May 00, Emissaries to Malastare, Part 6	2.50	0.50	1.25	2.50
❑19, Jun 00, JDu, Twilight, Part 1	2.50	0.50	1.25	2.50
❑20, Jul 00, JDu, Twilight, Part 2	2.50	0.50	1.25	2.50
❑21, Aug 00, JDu, Twilight, Part 3	2.50	0.50	1.25	2.50
❑22, Sep 00, JDu, Twilight, Part 4	2.50	0.50	1.25	2.50
❑23, Oct 00, Infinity's End, Part 1	2.50	0.50	1.25	2.50
❑24, Nov 00, Infinity's End, Part 2	2.50	0.50	1.25	2.50
❑25, Dec 00, Infinity's End, Part 3	2.50	0.50	1.25	2.50
❑26, Jan 01, Infinity's End, Part 4	2.50	0.50	1.25	2.50
❑27, Feb 01, Starcrash	—	0.60	1.50	2.99
❑28, Mar 01, The Hunt for Aurra Sing, Part 1	—	0.60	1.50	2.99
❑29, Apr 01, The Hunt for Aurra Sing, Part 2	2.99	0.60	1.50	2.99
❑30	2.99	0.60	1.50	2.99
❑31	2.99	0.60	1.50	2.99
❑32	2.99	0.60	1.50	2.99

STAR WARS (MAGAZINE)
DARK HORSE

	ORIG	GOOD	FINE	N-MINT
❑1, Oct 92, Star Wars: Dark Empire; Indiana Jones and the Fate of Atlantis, trading cards	2.50	1.00	2.50	5.00
❑2	2.50	0.80	2.00	4.00
❑3	2.50	0.60	1.50	3.00
❑4	2.50	0.60	1.50	3.00
❑5	2.50	0.60	1.50	3.00
❑6	2.50	0.60	1.50	3.00
❑7	2.50	0.60	1.50	3.00
❑8	2.50	0.60	1.50	3.00
❑9	2.50	0.60	1.50	3.00
❑10	2.50	0.60	1.50	3.00

STAR WARS: A NEW HOPE MANGA
DARK HORSE
Value: Cover or less

- ❑1, Jul 98 .... 9.95
- ❑2, Jul 98 .... 9.95
- ❑3, Sep 98 .... 9.95
- ❑4, Oct 98 .... 9.95

STAR WARS: A NEW HOPE-THE SPECIAL EDITION
DARK HORSE
Value: Cover or less

- ❑1, Jan 97 .... 2.95
- ❑2, Feb 97 .... 2.95
- ❑3, Mar 97 .... 2.95
- ❑4, Apr 97 .... 2.95

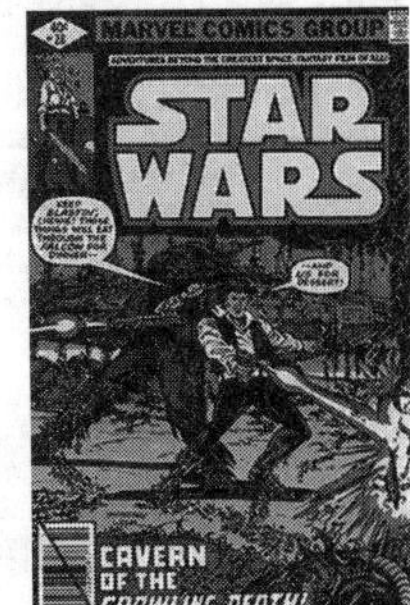

Before he was introduced in *Return of the Jedi*, a radically different version of Jabba the Hutt appeared in Marvel's *Star Wars* #28.

STAR WARS: BOBA FETT
DARK HORSE
Value: Cover or less

- ❑0.5, Wizard mail-in edition 5.00
- ❑0.5/GO, Wizard promotional edition; Gold edition 10.00
- ❑1, Dec 95, Bounty on Bar-Kooda, cardstock cover 3.95
- ❑2, Sep 96, When the Fat Lady Sings, cardstock cover 3.95
- ❑3, Aug 97, Murder Most Foul, cardstock cover 3.95

STAR WARS: BOBA FETT-AGENT OF DOOM
DARK HORSE
Value: Cover or less

- ❑1, Nov 00 .... 2.99

STAR WARS: BOBA FETT: ENEMY OF THE EMPIRE
DARK HORSE
Value: Cover or less

- ❑1, Jan 99 .... 2.95
- ❑2, Feb 99 .... 2.95
- ❑3, Mar 99 .... 2.95
- ❑4, Apr 99 .... 2.95

STAR WARS: BOBA FETT-TWIN ENGINES OF DESTRUCTION
DARK HORSE
Value: Cover or less

- ❑1, Jan 97, nn 2.95

STAR WARS: CHEWBACCA
DARK HORSE
Value: Cover or less

- ❑1, Jan 00, BA 2.95
- ❑2, Feb 00, BA 2.95
- ❑3, Mar 00, BA 2.95
- ❑4, Apr 00, BA 2.95

STAR WARS: CRIMSON EMPIRE
DARK HORSE

	ORIG	GOOD	FINE	N-MINT
❑1, Dec 97, PG	2.95	1.20	3.00	6.00
❑2, Jan 98, PG	2.95	1.00	2.50	5.00
❑3, Feb 98, PG	2.95	1.00	2.50	5.00
❑4, Mar 98, PG	2.95	1.00	2.50	5.00
❑5, Apr 98, PG, Crimson Empire, Part 5	2.95	1.00	2.50	5.00
❑6, May 98, PG, Council of blood	2.95	1.00	2.50	5.00

STAR WARS: CRIMSON EMPIRE II: COUNCIL OF BLOOD
DARK HORSE

	ORIG	GOOD	FINE	N-MINT
❑1, Nov 98, PG	2.95	0.80	2.00	4.00
❑2, Dec 98, PG	2.95	0.59	1.48	2.95
❑3, Jan 99, PG	2.95	0.59	1.48	2.95
❑4, Feb 99, PG	2.95	0.59	1.48	2.95
❑5, Mar 99, PG	2.95	0.59	1.48	2.95
❑6, Apr 99, PG	2.95	0.59	1.48	2.95

STAR WARS: DARK EMPIRE
DARK HORSE

	ORIG	GOOD	FINE	N-MINT
❑1, Dec 91, cardstock cover	2.95	1.20	3.00	6.00
❑1-2, Aug 92, 2nd Printing	2.95	0.60	1.50	3.00
❑2, Feb 92, cardstock cover	2.95	0.80	2.00	4.00
❑2-2, Aug 92, 2nd Printing	2.95	0.60	1.50	3.00
❑3, Apr 92, The Battle for Calamari, cardstock cover	2.95	0.80	2.00	4.00
❑3-2, The Battle for Calamari, 2nd Printing	2.95	0.60	1.50	3.00
❑4, Apr 92, cardstock cover	2.95	0.80	2.00	4.00
❑5, Aug 92, cardstock cover	2.95	0.60	1.50	3.00
❑6, Oct 92, cardstock cover; Final Issue	2.95	0.60	1.50	3.00
❑Ash 1, Mar 96, nn; wraparound cover; newsprint preview of trade paperback collection of mini-series	0.99	0.20	0.50	1.00

STAR WARS: DARK EMPIRE II
DARK HORSE
Value: Cover or less

- ❑1, Dec 94, cardstock cover 2.95
- ❑2, Jan 95, Uel on Nar Shaddaa, cardstock cover 2.95
- ❑3, Feb 95, cardstock cover 2.95
- ❑4, Mar 95, cardstock cover 2.95
- ❑5, Apr 95, cardstock cover 2.95
- ❑6, May 95, cardstock cover 2.95

STAR WARS: DARK FORCE RISING
DARK HORSE
Value: Cover or less

- ❑1, May 97, cardstock cover; adapts Timothy Zahn novel. 2.95
- ❑2, Jun 97, cardstock cover; adapts Timothy Zahn novel. 2.95
- ❑3, Jul 97, cardstock cover; adapts Timothy Zahn novel 2.95
- ❑4, Aug 97, cardstock cover; adapts Timothy Zahn novel. 2.95
- ❑5, Sep 97, cardstock cover; adapts Timothy Zahn novel. 2.95
- ❑6, Oct 97, cardstock cover; adapts Timothy Zahn novel. 2.95

STAR WARS: DARTH MAUL
DARK HORSE
Value: Cover or less

- ❑1, Sep 00, JDu ... 2.95
- ❑1/SC, Sep 00, JDu, Photo cover ... 2.95
- ❑2, Oct 00, JDu ... 2.99
- ❑2/SC, Oct 00, JDu, Photo cover ... 2.99
- ❑3, Nov 00, JDu ... 2.99
- ❑3/SC, Nov 00, JDu, Photo cover ... 2.99
- ❑4, Dec 00, JDu ... 2.99
- ❑4/SC, Dec 00, JDu, Photo cover ... 2.99

STAR WARS: DROIDS (VOL. 1)
DARK HORSE

	ORIG	GOOD	FINE	N-MINT
❑1, Apr 94, enhanced cover	2.95	0.60	1.50	3.00
❑2, May 94	2.50	0.55	1.38	2.75
❑3, Jun 94, The Scarlet Pirate; End of the Game	2.50	0.55	1.38	2.75
❑4, Jul 94	2.50	0.50	1.25	2.50
❑5, Aug 94	2.50	0.50	1.25	2.50
❑6, Sep 94	2.50	0.50	1.25	2.50
❑SE 1, Jan 95, Special edition; Reprints serial from Dark Horse Comics	2.50	0.50	1.25	2.50

STAR WARS: DROIDS (VOL. 2)
DARK HORSE
Value: Cover or less

- ❑1, Apr 95, Rebellion, Part 1 ... 2.50
- ❑2, May 95, Rebellion, Part 2 ... 2.50
- ❑3, Jun 95, Rebellion, Part 3 ... 2.50
- ❑4, Jul 95, Rebellion, Part 4 ... 2.50
- ❑5, Sep 95 ... 2.50
- ❑6, Oct 95 ... 2.50
- ❑7, Nov 95 ... 2.50
- ❑8, Dec 95 ... 2.50

STAR WARS: EMPIRE'S END
DARK HORSE
Value: Cover or less

- ❑1, Oct 95, cardstock cover ... 2.95
- ❑2, Nov 95, cardstock cover ... 2.95

STAR WARS: EPISODE I ANAKIN SKYWALKER
DARK HORSE
Value: Cover or less

- ❑1, May 99, cardstock cover ... 2.95
- ❑1/SC, May 99, Photo cover ... 2.95

STAR WARS: EPISODE I OBI-WAN KENOBI
DARK HORSE
Value: Cover or less

- ❑1, May 99, cardstock cover ... 2.95
- ❑1/SC, May 99, Photo cover ... 2.95

STAR WARS: EPISODE I QUEEN AMIDALA
DARK HORSE
Value: Cover or less

- ❑1, May 99, cardstock cover ... 2.95
- ❑1/SC, May 99, Photo cover ... 2.95

STAR WARS: EPISODE I QUI-GON JINN
DARK HORSE
Value: Cover or less

- ❑1, May 99, cardstock cover ... 2.95
- ❑1/SC, May 99, Photo cover ... 2.95

STAR WARS: EPISODE I THE PHANTOM MENACE
DARK HORSE
Value: Cover or less

- ❑1, May 99, cardstock cover ... 2.95
- ❑1/SC, May 99, Photo cover ... 2.95
- ❑2, May 99, cardstock cover ... 2.95
- ❑2/SC, May 99, Photo cover ... 2.95
- ❑3, May 99, cardstock cover ... 2.95
- ❑3/SC, May 99, Photo cover ... 2.95
- ❑4, May 99, cardstock cover ... 2.95
- ❑4/SC, May 99, Photo cover ... 2.95

STAR WARS HANDBOOK
DARK HORSE
Value: Cover or less

- ❑1, Jul 98, X-Wing Rogue Squadron profiles ... 2.95
- ❑2, Jul 99, Crimson Empire profiles ... 2.95

STAR WARS: HEIR TO THE EMPIRE
DARK HORSE
Value: Cover or less

- ❑1, Oct 95 ... 2.95
- ❑2, Nov 95 ... 2.95
- ❑3, Dec 95 ... 2.95
- ❑4, Jan 96 ... 2.95
- ❑5, Mar 96 ... 2.95
- ❑6, Apr 96 ... 2.95

STAR WARS IN 3-D
BLACKTHORNE
Value: Cover or less

- ❑1, Dec 87, a.k.a. Blackthorne in 3-D #30 ... 2.50

STAR WARS: JABBA THE HUTT
DARK HORSE
Value: Cover or less

- ❑1, Apr 95, The Gaar Suppoon Hit ... 2.50
- ❑2, Jun 95, The Hunger of Princess Nampi ... 2.50
- ❑3, Aug 95, The Dynasty Trap ... 2.50
- ❑4, Feb 96, The Betrayal ... 2.50

STAR WARS: JEDI ACADEMY-LEVIATHAN
DARK HORSE
Value: Cover or less

- ❑1, Oct 98 ... 2.95
- ❑2, Nov 98 ... 2.95
- ❑3, Dec 98 ... 2.95
- ❑4, Jan 99 ... 2.95

STAR WARS: JEDI COUNCIL: ACTS OF WAR
DARK HORSE
Value: Cover or less

- ❑1, Jun 00 ... 2.95
- ❑2, Jul 00 ... 2.95
- ❑3, Aug 00 ... 2.95
- ❑4, Sep 00 ... 2.95

STAR WARS: JEDI VS. SITH
DARK HORSE
Value: Cover or less

- ❑1, Apr 01 ... 2.99
- ❑2, Apr 01 ... 2.99
- ❑3, Apr 01 ... 2.99
- ❑4, Apr 01 ... 2.99
- ❑5, Apr 01 ... 2.99
- ❑6, Apr 01 ... 2.99

STAR WARS: MARA JADE
DARK HORSE

	ORIG	GOOD	FINE	N-MINT
❑1, Aug 98, By the Emperor's Hand, Part 1	2.95	0.60	1.50	3.00
❑2, Sep 98, By the Emperor's Hand, Part 2, 2: Mara Jade	2.95	0.59	1.48	2.95
❑3, Oct 98, By the Emperor's Hand, Part 3	2.95	0.59	1.48	2.95
❑4, Nov 98, By the Emperor's Hand, Part 4, Darth Vader cameo; Luke Skywalker cameo; Emperor cameo	2.95	0.59	1.48	2.95
❑5, Dec 98, By the Emperor's Hand, Part 5	2.95	0.59	1.48	2.95
❑6, Jan 99, By the Emperor's Hand, Part 6	2.95	0.59	1.48	2.95

STAR WARS: QUI-GON & OBI-WAN-LAST STAND ON ORD MANTELL
DARK HORSE
Value: Cover or less

- ❑1/A, Dec 00, Obi-Wan leaping on cover, Qui-Gon standing ... 2.99
- ❑1/B, Dec 00, Qui-gon and Obi-Wan standing on cover, Obi-Wan has light sabre out ... 2.99
- ❑1/C, Dec 00, Photo cover ... 2.99
- ❑2/A, Feb 01, Drawn cover ... 2.99
- ❑2/B, Feb 01, Photo cover ... 2.99
- ❑3/A, Mar 01, Drawn cover ... 2.99
- ❑3/B, Mar 01, Photo cover ... 2.99

STAR WARS: RETURN OF THE JEDI
MARVEL

	ORIG	GOOD	FINE	N-MINT
❑1, AW, At The Hands Of Jabba The Hut, Reprints Marvel Super Special #27	0.60	0.80	2.00	4.00
❑2, AW, Reprints Marvel Super Special #27	0.60	0.80	2.00	4.00
❑3, AW, Mission To Endor, Reprints Marvel Super Special #27	0.60	0.80	2.00	4.00
❑4, Jan 84, AW, Reprints Marvel Super Special #27	0.60	0.80	2.00	4.00

STAR WARS: RIVER OF CHAOS
DARK HORSE
Value: Cover or less

- ❑1, Jun 95 ... 2.50
- ❑2, Jul 95 ... 2.50
- ❑3, Sep 95 ... 2.50
- ❑4, Nov 95 ... 2.50

STAR WARS: SHADOWS OF EMPIRE-EVOLUTION
DARK HORSE
Value: Cover or less

- ❑1, Feb 98 ... 2.95
- ❑2, Mar 98, The Journey of a Thousand Light-Years ... 2.95
- ❑3, Apr 98 ... 2.95
- ❑4, May 98 ... 2.95
- ❑5, Jun 98 ... 2.95

STAR WARS: SHADOWS OF THE EMPIRE
DARK HORSE
Value: Cover or less

- ❑1, May 96 ... 2.95
- ❑2, Jun 96 ... 2.95
- ❑3, Jul 96 ... 2.95
- ❑4, Aug 96 ... 2.95
- ❑5, Sep 96 ... 2.95
- ❑6, Oct 96 ... 2.95

STAR WARS: SHADOW STALKER
DARK HORSE
Value: Cover or less

- ❑1, Sep 97, nn; One-Shot ... 2.95

STAR WARS: SPLINTER OF THE MIND'S EYE
DARK HORSE
Value: Cover or less

- ❑1, Dec 95, After the Fall ... 2.50
- ❑2, Feb 96 ... 2.50
- ❑3, Apr 96 ... 2.95
- ❑4, Jun 96, Final Issue ... 2.95

STAR WARS TALES
DARK HORSE
Value: Cover or less

- ❑1, Sep 99, Life, Death, and the Living Force; Mara Jade: A Night On the Town ... 4.95
- ❑2, Dec 99, Routine; Darth Vader: Extinction, Part 2 ... 4.95
- ❑3 ... 4.95
- ❑4 ... 4.95
- ❑5, Sep 00, Yaddle's Tale: The One Below; What They Called Me ... 4.95

STAR WARS: TALES FROM MOS EISLEY
DARK HORSE
Value: Cover or less

- ❑1, Mar 96, Light Duty, nn ... 2.95

STAR WARS: TALES OF THE JEDI
DARK HORSE

	ORIG	GOOD	FINE	N-MINT
❑1, Oct 93, Ulic Qel-Droma And The Beast Wars Of Onderon	2.50	0.80	2.00	4.00
❑2, Nov 93	2.50	0.70	1.75	3.50
❑3, Dec 93	2.50	0.65	1.63	3.25
❑4, Jan 94	2.50	0.50	1.25	2.50
❑5, Feb 94	2.50	0.50	1.25	2.50

STAR WARS: TALES OF THE JEDI-DARK LORDS OF THE SITH
DARK HORSE

	ORIG	GOOD	FINE	N-MINT
❑1, Oct 94	2.50	0.60	1.50	3.00
❑2, Nov 94	2.50	0.60	1.50	3.00
❑3, Dec 94	2.50	0.60	1.50	3.00
❑4, Jan 95	2.50	0.60	1.50	3.00

	ORIG	GOOD	FINE	N-MINT
❑5, Feb 95	2.50	0.60	1.50	3.00
❑6, Mar 95	2.50	0.60	1.50	3.00

STAR WARS: TALES OF THE JEDI-FALL OF THE SITH EMPIRE
Dark Horse
Value: Cover or less

- ❑1, Jun 97, Man with marionettes on cover 2.95
- ❑1/A, Variant cover, flame in background 2.95
- ❑2, Jul 97 2.95
- ❑3, Aug 97 2.95
- ❑4, Sep 97 2.95
- ❑5, Oct 97 2.95

STAR WARS: TALES OF THE JEDI-REDEMPTION
Dark Horse
Value: Cover or less

- ❑1, Jul 98, A Gathering of Jedi 2.95
- ❑2, Aug 98 2.95
- ❑3, Sep 98, Homecoming 2.95
- ❑4, Oct 98, The Trials of a Jedi 2.95
- ❑5, Nov 98 2.95

STAR WARS: TALES OF THE JEDI-THE FREEDON NADD UPRISING
Dark Horse
Value: Cover or less

- ❑1, Aug 94 2.50
- ❑2, Sep 94, Final Issue 2.50

STAR WARS: TALES OF THE JEDI-THE GOLDEN AGE OF THE SITH
Dark Horse
Value: Cover or less

- ❑0, Conquest And Unification 0.99
- ❑1, Oct 96, Into The Unknown 2.95
- ❑2, Nov 96, Funeral for a Dark Lord 2.95
- ❑3, Dec 96, The Fabric of an Empire 2.95
- ❑4, Jan 97, Pawns of the Sith Lord 2.95
- ❑5, Feb 97, The Flight of Starbreaker 12 2.95

STAR WARS: TALES OF THE JEDI-THE SITH WAR
Dark Horse
Value: Cover or less

- ❑1, Aug 95 2.50
- ❑2, Sep 95 2.50
- ❑3, Oct 95 2.50
- ❑4, Nov 95 2.50
- ❑5, Dec 95 2.50
- ❑6, Jan 96 2.50

STAR WARS: THE BOUNTY HUNTERS-AURRA SING
Dark Horse
Value: Cover or less

- ❑1, Jul 99, nn; One-Shot 2.95

STAR WARS: THE BOUNTY HUNTERS-KENIX KIL
Dark Horse
Value: Cover or less

- ❑1, Oct 99, one shot 2.95

STAR WARS: THE BOUNTY HUNTERS-SCOUNDREL'S WAGES
Dark Horse
Value: Cover or less

- ❑1, Aug 99, nn; One-Shot 2.95

STAR WARS: THE EMPIRE STRIKES BACK-MANGA
Dark Horse
Value: Cover or less

- ❑1, Jan 99 9.95
- ❑2, Feb 99 9.95
- ❑3, Mar 99 9.95
- ❑4, Apr 99 9.95

STAR WARS: THE JABBA TAPE
Dark Horse
Value: Cover or less

- ❑1, Dec 98, nn 2.95

STAR WARS: THE LAST COMMAND
Dark Horse

	ORIG	GOOD	FINE	N-MINT
❑1, Nov 97	2.95	0.70	1.75	3.50
❑2, Dec 97	2.95	0.60	1.50	3.00
❑3, Feb 98	2.95	0.60	1.50	3.00
❑4, Mar 98	2.95	0.60	1.50	3.00
❑5, Apr 98	2.95	0.60	1.50	3.00
❑6, Jul 98	2.95	0.59	1.48	2.95

STAR WARS: THE PROTOCOL OFFENSIVE
Dark Horse
Value: Cover or less

- ❑1, Sep 97, nn; One-Shot; prestige format; Co-written by actor who played C-3PO 4.95

STAR WARS: UNDERWORLD-THE YAVIN VASSILIKA
Dark Horse
Value: Cover or less

- ❑1/A, Dec 00, Drawn cover with Hand Solo, Lando Calrisian, and Boba Fett 2.99
- ❑1/B, Dec 00, Painted cover with Jabba the Hutt 2.99
- ❑2/A, Jan 01 2.99
- ❑2/B, Jan 01, Photo cover 2.99
- ❑3/A, Feb 01, Drawn cover with Hand Solo, Lando Calrisian, and Boba Fett 2.99
- ❑3/B, Feb 01, Photo cover featuring Harrison Ford 2.99
- ❑4/A, Mar 01 2.99
- ❑4/B, Mar 01, Photo cover with bounty hunters 2.99
- ❑5/A, Apr 01 2.99
- ❑5/B, Apr 01 2.99

STAR WARS: UNION
Dark Horse

	ORIG	GOOD	FINE	N-MINT
❑1, Nov 99	2.95	2.80	7.00	14.00
❑2, Dec 99	2.95	2.00	5.00	10.00
❑3, Jan 00	2.95	1.40	3.50	7.00
❑4, Feb 00, Wedding of Luke Skywalker & Mara Jade	2.95	1.00	2.50	5.00

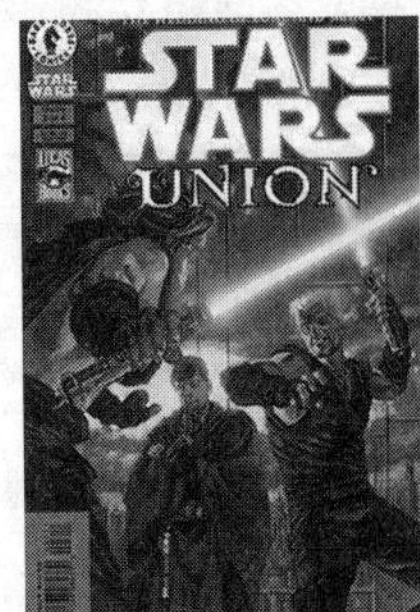

Luke Skywalker and Mara Jade were wed in *Star Wars: Union.*

STAR WARS: VADER'S QUEST
Dark Horse
Value: Cover or less

- ❑1, Feb 99, DaG 2.95
- ❑2, Mar 99, DaG 2.95
- ❑3, Apr 99, DaG 2.95
- ❑4, May 99, DaG 2.95

STAR WARS: X-WING ROGUE SQUADRON
Dark Horse

	ORIG	GOOD	FINE	N-MINT
❑0.5, Wizard mail-in edition	—	0.60	1.50	3.00
❑0.5/Pl, Platinum edition	10.00	1.00	2.50	5.00
❑1, Jul 95, Rebel Opposition, Part 1; The Rebel Opposition, Part 1	2.95	0.80	2.00	4.00
❑2, Aug 95, Rebel Opposition, Part 2; The Rebel Opposition, Part 2	2.95	0.70	1.75	3.50
❑3, Sep 95, Rebel Opposition, Part 3; The Rebel Opposition, Part 3	2.95	0.70	1.75	3.50
❑4, Oct 95, Rebel Opposition, Part 4; The Rebel Opposition, Part 4	2.95	0.70	1.75	3.50
❑5, Feb 96, The Phantom Affair, Part 1	2.95	0.60	1.50	3.00
❑6, Mar 96, The Phantom Affair, Part 2	2.95	0.60	1.50	3.00
❑7, Apr 96, The Phantom Affair, Part 3	2.95	0.60	1.50	3.00
❑8, Jun 96, The Phantom Affair, Part 4	2.95	0.60	1.50	3.00
❑9, Jul 96, Battleground: Tatooine, Part 1	2.95	0.60	1.50	3.00
❑10, Jul 96, Battleground: Tatooine, Part 2	2.95	0.60	1.50	3.00
❑11, Aug 96, Battleground: Tatooine, Part 3	2.95	0.60	1.50	3.00
❑12, Sep 96, Battleground: Tatooine, Part 4	2.95	0.60	1.50	3.00
❑13, Oct 96, The Warrior Princess, Part 1	2.95	0.60	1.50	3.00
❑14, Dec 96, The Warrior Princess, Part 2	2.95	0.60	1.50	3.00
❑15, Jan 97, The Warrior Princess, Part 3	2.95	0.60	1.50	3.00
❑16, Feb 97, The Warrior Princess, Part 4	2.95	0.60	1.50	3.00
❑17, Mar 97, Requiem for a Rogue, Part 1	2.95	0.60	1.50	3.00
❑18, Apr 97, Requiem for a Rogue, Part 2	2.95	0.60	1.50	3.00
❑19, May 97, Requiem for a Rogue, Part 3	2.95	0.60	1.50	3.00
❑20, Jun 97, Requiem for a Rogue, Part 4	2.95	0.60	1.50	3.00
❑21, Aug 97, In the Empire's Service, Part 1	2.95	0.60	1.50	3.00
❑22, Sep 97, In the Empire's Service, Part 2	2.95	0.60	1.50	3.00
❑23, Oct 97, In the Empire's Service, Part 3	2.95	0.60	1.50	3.00
❑24, Nov 97, In the Empire's Service, Part 4	2.95	0.60	1.50	3.00
❑25, Dec 97, The Making of Baron Fel, O: Baron Fel, Giant-size	3.95	0.80	2.00	4.00
❑26, Jan 98, Family Ties, Part 1	2.95	0.59	1.48	2.95
❑27, Feb 98, Family Ties, Part 2	2.95	0.59	1.48	2.95
❑28, Mar 98, Masquerade, Part 1	2.95	0.59	1.48	2.95
❑29, Apr 98, Masquerade, Part 2	2.95	0.59	1.48	2.95
❑30, May 98, Masquerade, Part 3	2.95	0.59	1.48	2.95
❑31, Jun 98, Masquerade, Part 4	2.95	0.59	1.48	2.95
❑32, Jul 98, Mandatory Retirement, Part 1	2.95	0.59	1.48	2.95
❑33, Aug 98, Mandatory Retirement, Part 2	2.95	0.59	1.48	2.95
❑34, Sep 98, Mandatory Retirement, Part 3	2.95	0.59	1.48	2.95
❑35, Nov 98, Mandatory Retirement, Part 4	2.95	0.59	1.48	2.95
❑SE 1, Aug 95, nn; promotional giveaway with Kellogg's Apple Jacks	—	0.20	0.50	1.00

STAR WEEVILS
Rip Off
Value: Cover or less

- ❑1 1.00

STAR WESTERN
Avalon
Value: Cover or less

- ❑1, Jingles and Wil 5.95
- ❑2, Tom Mix: Blackmail!; Wyatt Earp: Gun-Crazy Marshal, John Wayne feature 5.95
- ❑3, Lash Larue: King of the Camp; Black Jack, Clint Eastwood feature 5.95
- ❑4 5.95
- ❑5 5.95

S.T.A.T.
Majestic
Value: Cover or less

- ❑1, Dec 93 2.25
- ❑1/SC, foil cover 2.25

STATIC
DC

	ORIG	GOOD	FINE	N-MINT
❑1, Jun 93, Trail By Fire, 1: Static; 1: Frieda Goren; 1: Hotstreak	1.50	0.40	1.00	2.00
❑1/CS, Jun 93, Trail By Fire, 1: Static; 1: Frieda Goren; 1: Hotstreak, poster; trading card; Collector's Set	2.95	0.60	1.50	3.00

	ORIG	GOOD	FINE	N-MINT
❑1/SI, Trail By Fire, 1: Static; 1: Frieda Goren; 1: Hotstreak, Silver (limited promotional) edition	—	0.60	1.50	3.00
❑2, Jul 93, Everything But The Girl, 1: Tarmack; O: Static	1.50	0.30	0.75	1.50
❑3, Aug 93, Pounding The Pavement	1.50	0.30	0.75	1.50
❑4, Sep 93, 1: Don Giacomo Cornelius	1.50	0.30	0.75	1.50
❑5, Oct 93, Megablast, 1: Commando X	1.50	0.30	0.75	1.50
❑6, Nov 93	1.50	0.30	0.75	1.50
❑7, Dec 93	1.50	0.30	0.75	1.50
❑8, Jan 94, Shadow War, Part 5, Shadow War	1.50	0.30	0.75	1.50
❑9, Feb 94, Static Needs A New Pair Of Shoes, 1: Virus	1.50	0.30	0.75	1.50
❑10, Mar 94, 1: Coil; 1: Puff	1.50	0.30	0.75	1.50
❑11, Apr 94	1.50	0.30	0.75	1.50
❑12, May 94, Full Yellow Jacket, 1: Snakefinger	1.50	0.30	0.75	1.50
❑13, Jun 94	1.50	0.30	0.75	1.50
❑14, Aug 94, Worlds Collide; Worlds Collide, Part 14, Giant-size	2.50	0.50	1.25	2.50
❑15, Sep 94	1.75	0.35	0.88	1.75
❑16, Oct 94, What are Little Boys Made Of?, 1: Joyride	1.75	0.35	0.88	1.75
❑17, Nov 94, What are Little Boys Made Of?	1.75	0.35	0.88	1.75
❑18, Dec 94, What are Little Boys Made Of?	1.75	0.35	0.88	1.75
❑19, Jan 95, What are Little Boys Made Of?	1.75	0.35	0.88	1.75
❑20, Feb 95, What are Little Boys Made Of?	1.75	0.35	0.88	1.75
❑21, Mar 95, A: Blood Syndicate	1.75	0.35	0.88	1.75
❑22, Apr 95	1.75	0.35	0.88	1.75
❑23, Jun 95	1.75	0.35	0.88	1.75
❑24, Jul 95	1.75	0.35	0.88	1.75
❑25, Jul 95, Long Hot Summer, Double-size	3.95	0.79	1.98	3.95
❑26, Aug 95, Long Hot Summer	2.50	0.50	1.25	2.50
❑27, Sep 95, Long Hot Summer	0.99	0.50	1.25	2.50
❑28, Oct 95	2.50	0.50	1.25	2.50
❑29, Nov 95, The Long Hot Summer	2.50	0.50	1.25	2.50
❑30, Dec 95, D: Larry	2.50	0.50	1.25	2.50
❑31, Jan 96, GK, Cape Fear	0.99	0.20	0.50	0.99
❑32, Feb 96	2.50	0.50	1.25	2.50
❑33, Mar 96, Bee, My Love	2.50	0.50	1.25	2.50
❑34, Apr 96, Blame it on Picasso	2.50	0.50	1.25	2.50
❑35, May 96	2.50	0.50	1.25	2.50
❑36, Jun 96	2.50	0.50	1.25	2.50
❑37, Jul 96	2.50	0.50	1.25	2.50
❑38, Aug 96	2.50	0.50	1.25	2.50
❑39, Sep 96	2.50	0.50	1.25	2.50
❑40, Oct 96, KP, Boyz Night Out	2.50	0.50	1.25	2.50
❑41, Nov 96, Love Bites, Part 1; Love ites, Part 1	2.50	0.50	1.25	2.50
❑42, Dec 96, Love Bites, Part 2; Love ites, Part 2	2.50	0.50	1.25	2.50
❑43, Jan 97, Power Struggle; Power Strugge	2.50	0.50	1.25	2.50
❑44, Feb 97	2.50	0.50	1.25	2.50
❑45, Mar 97	2.50	0.50	1.25	2.50
❑46	2.50	0.50	1.25	2.50
❑47, Final Issue	2.50	0.50	1.25	2.50

STATIC SHOCK!: REBIRTH OF THE COOL
MILESTONE

Value: Cover or less

- ❑1, Jan 01, As I Was Saying Before I Was Interrupted... 2.50
- ❑2, Feb 01, Standing on the Verge of Getting it On 2.50
- ❑3, May 01, The Story So Far... 2.50
- ❑4 2.50

STEALTH FORCE
MALIBU

Value: Cover or less

- ❑1 1.95
- ❑2 1.95
- ❑3 1.95
- ❑4 1.95
- ❑5 1.95
- ❑6, Dec 87 1.95
- ❑7 1.95
- ❑8, Eternity begins as publisher 1.95

STEALTH SQUAD
PETRA

Value: Cover or less

- ❑0, O: Stealth Squad 2.50
- ❑1, All Fall Down!, 1: Stealth Squad; 1: Strikeforce Champion; 1: Stealth One; 1: Solar Blade; 1: Kid Mammoth; 1: Swoop; 1: Fire Flare 2.50
- ❑2 2.50
- ❑3 2.50
- ❑4 2.50

STEAMPUNK
WILDSTORM

Value: Cover or less

- ❑1, Apr 00, Birth Pangs 2.50
- ❑2, May 00, 100 Dragons 2.50
- ❑3 2.50
- ❑4 2.50
- ❑5, Oct 00, Contrition 2.50
- ❑6, Jan 01, Mechanica Sundown, Part 1 2.50
- ❑7, Apr 01, Mechanica Sundown, Part 2 2.50
- ❑8 2.50
- ❑9 2.50

STEAMPUNK: CATECHISM
WILDSTORM

Value: Cover or less

- ❑1, Jan 00 2.50

STECH
SILVERWOLF

Value: Cover or less

- ❑1, Dec 86, Triad, Part 1, b&w 1.50

STEED AND MRS. PEEL
ECLIPSE

	ORIG	GOOD	FINE	N-MINT
❑1, Dec 90, Crown And Anchor	4.95	1.00	2.50	5.00
❑2, May 91	4.95	1.00	2.50	5.00
❑3	4.95	1.00	2.50	5.00

STEEL
DC

	ORIG	GOOD	FINE	N-MINT
❑0, Oct 94, In The Beginning!	1.50	0.40	1.00	2.00
❑1, Feb 94, Wrought Iron	1.50	0.40	1.00	2.00
❑2, Mar 94, Turf War!	1.50	0.30	0.75	1.50
❑3, Apr 94	1.50	0.30	0.75	1.50
❑4, May 94	1.50	0.30	0.75	1.50
❑5, Jun 94, Retaliation	1.50	0.30	0.75	1.50
❑6, Jul 94, Worlds Collide, Part 5, A: Hardware	1.50	0.30	0.75	1.50
❑7, Aug 94, Worlds Collide, Part 12, A: Hardware; A: Icon	1.50	0.30	0.75	1.50
❑8, Sep 94	1.50	0.30	0.75	1.50
❑9, Nov 94	1.50	0.30	0.75	1.50
❑10, Dec 94	1.50	0.30	0.75	1.50
❑11, Jan 95, Maximum Orbit, Part 1	1.50	0.30	0.75	1.50
❑12, Feb 95, Maximum Orbit, Part 2	1.50	0.30	0.75	1.50
❑13, Mar 95, Maximum Orbit, Part 3	1.50	0.30	0.75	1.50
❑14, Apr 95	1.50	0.30	0.75	1.50
❑15, May 95	1.50	0.30	0.75	1.50
❑16, Jun 95	1.95	0.39	0.98	1.95
❑17, Jul 95	1.95	0.39	0.98	1.95
❑18, Aug 95	1.95	0.39	0.98	1.95
❑19, Sep 95	1.95	0.39	0.98	1.95
❑20, Oct 95	1.95	0.39	0.98	1.95
❑21, Nov 95, Underworld Unleashed	1.95	0.39	0.98	1.95
❑22, Dec 95, A: Eradicator; A: Supergirl	1.95	0.39	0.98	1.95
❑23, Jan 96, Wired!	1.95	0.39	0.98	1.95
❑24, Feb 96, Countdown to Destiny	1.95	0.39	0.98	1.95
❑25, Mar 96, Family Feud, Part 1	1.95	0.39	0.98	1.95
❑26, May 96	1.95	0.39	0.98	1.95
❑27, Jun 96	1.95	0.39	0.98	1.95
❑28, Jul 96, V: Plasmus	1.95	0.39	0.98	1.95
❑29, Aug 96	1.95	0.39	0.98	1.95
❑30, Sep 96	1.95	0.39	0.98	1.95
❑31, Oct 96, Possession	1.95	0.39	0.98	1.95
❑32, Nov 96, Herculean Labors, V: Blockbuster	1.95	0.39	0.98	1.95
❑33, Dec 96, Withdrawal Symptoms	1.95	0.39	0.98	1.95
❑34, Jan 97, Bang, A: Margot, new armor	1.95	0.39	0.98	1.95
❑35, Feb 97	1.95	0.39	0.98	1.95
❑36, Mar 97, Home	1.95	0.39	0.98	1.95
❑37, Apr 97	1.95	0.39	0.98	1.95
❑38, May 97	1.95	0.39	0.98	1.95
❑39, Jun 97	1.95	0.39	0.98	1.95
❑40, Jul 97, The Never Ending Story, 1: new hammer	1.95	0.45	1.13	2.25
❑41, Aug 97	1.95	0.39	0.98	1.95
❑42, Sep 97	1.95	0.39	0.98	1.95
❑43, Oct 97, A: Superman, Genesis	1.95	0.39	0.98	1.95
❑44, Nov 97	1.95	0.39	0.98	1.95
❑45, Dec 97, Fire, Face cover	1.95	0.39	0.98	1.95
❑46, Jan 98, Bori, A: Superboy	1.95	0.39	0.98	1.95
❑47, Feb 98	1.95	0.50	1.25	2.50
❑48, Mar 98	2.50	0.50	1.25	2.50
❑49, Apr 98, Heart	2.50	0.50	1.25	2.50
❑50, May 98, A: Superman, Millennium Giants	2.50	0.50	1.25	2.50
❑51, Jun 98	2.50	0.50	1.25	2.50
❑52, Jul 98, Final Issue	2.50	0.50	1.25	2.50
❑Anl 1, Elseworlds	2.95	0.59	1.48	2.95
❑Anl 2, Year One	3.95	0.79	1.98	3.95

STEEL ANGEL
GAUNTLET

Value: Cover or less

- ❑1 2.50

STEEL CLAW, THE
FLEETWAY

	ORIG	GOOD	FINE	N-MINT
❑1, Dec 86	0.75	0.30	0.75	1.50
❑2	0.75	0.30	0.75	1.50
❑3	0.75	0.30	0.75	1.50
❑4	1.25	0.30	0.75	1.50
❑5	1.25	0.30	0.75	1.50

STEELDRAGON STORIES
STEELDRAGON

Value: Cover or less

- ❑1 1.50

STEELE DESTINIES
NIGHTSCAPES

Value: Cover or less

- ❑1, Apr 95, b&w 2.95
- ❑2, Jun 95, b&w 2.95
- ❑3, Sep 95, b&w 2.95

STEELGRIP STARKEY
MARVEL

	ORIG	GOOD	FINE	N-MINT
❑1, Jun 86, Working Man's Myth!	1.50	0.35	0.88	1.75
❑2, Aug 86	1.50	0.35	0.88	1.75
❑3, Nov 86	1.50	0.35	0.88	1.75
❑4, Dec 86	1.50	0.35	0.88	1.75
❑5, Jan 87	1.50	0.35	0.88	1.75
❑6, May 87	1.75	0.35	0.88	1.75

STEEL, THE INDESTRUCTIBLE MAN
DC

	ORIG	GOOD	FINE	N-MINT
❑1, Mar 78, DH, From Hell Is Forged...A Hero!, 1: Steel	0.35	0.60	1.50	3.00
❑2, Apr 78	0.35	0.40	1.00	2.00
❑3, Jun 78	0.35	0.40	1.00	2.00
❑4, Sep 78	0.35	0.40	1.00	2.00
❑5, Nov 78	0.50	0.40	1.00	2.00

STEEL PULSE
TRUE FICTION

Value: Cover or less

- ❑1, Mar 86, This Belt is Mine!; Arthur "Sherlock" Jones Wrestling Detective: Death Grip, b&w 2.00
- ❑2, b&w 2.00
- ❑3, b&w 2.00
- ❑4 .... 3.50

STEEL STERLING
ARCHIE

Value: Cover or less

- ❑4, Jan 84, A License to Kill, Red Circle publishes 1.00
- ❑5, Mar 84, The Young Steelers: Too Easy to Kill, Archie publishes 1.00
- ❑6, May 84 .... 1.00
- ❑7, Jul 84 .... 1.00

STEEL: THE OFFICIAL COMIC ADAPTATION OF THE WARNER BROS. MOTION PICTURE
DC

Value: Cover or less

- ❑1, nn; movie Adaptation; prestige format 4.95

STEELTOWN ROCKERS
MARVEL

Value: Cover or less

- ❑1, Apr 90, Held For Ransom. 1.00
- ❑2, May 90 .... 1.00
- ❑3, Jun 90 .... 1.00
- ❑4, Jul 90 .... 1.00
- ❑5, Aug 90 .... 1.00
- ❑6, Sep 90 .... 1.00

STELLAR COMICS
STELLAR

Value: Cover or less

- ❑1, Noble: The Jungle; Hello, Goodbye, Part 1 .... 2.50

STELLAR LOSERS
ANTARCTIC

Value: Cover or less

- ❑1, Feb 93, b&w 2.50
- ❑2, Apr 93, b&w 2.50
- ❑3, Jun 93, b&w 2.50

STEPHEN DARKLORD
RAK

Value: Cover or less

- ❑1, b&w 1.75
- ❑2, b&w 1.75
- ❑3, b&w 1.75

STEPS TO A DRUG FREE LIFE
DAVID G. BROWN STUDIOS

	ORIG	GOOD	FINE	N-MINT
❑1, Feb 98, nn; promotional comic done for the Alcohol and Drug Council of Greater L.A. and Share Inc.	—	0.20	0.50	1.00

STERN WHEELER
SPOTLIGHT

Value: Cover or less

- ❑1 .... 1.75

STEVEN
KITCHEN SINK

	ORIG	GOOD	FINE	N-MINT
❑1, b&w	2.95	0.60	1.50	3.00
❑2, b&w	2.95	0.60	1.50	3.00
❑3, b&w	2.95	0.60	1.50	3.00
❑4, b&w	2.95	0.60	1.50	3.00
❑5	3.50	0.70	1.75	3.50
❑6, b&w	3.50	0.70	1.75	3.50
❑7	3.50	0.70	1.75	3.50
❑8, Dec 96, b&w; cardstock cover; over-sized	3.50	0.70	1.75	3.50

STEVEN PRESENTS DUMPY
FANTAGRAPHICS

Value: Cover or less

- ❑1, May 99, b&w 2.95

STEVEN'S COMICS
DK PRESS

Value: Cover or less

- ❑3, b&w 3.00

ST. GEORGE
MARVEL

	ORIG	GOOD	FINE	N-MINT
❑1, Jun 88, KJ, When Mercy Seasons Justice	1.25	0.30	0.75	1.50
❑2, Aug 88	1.25	0.30	0.75	1.50
❑3, Oct 88	1.50	0.30	0.75	1.50
❑4, Dec 88	1.50	0.30	0.75	1.50
❑5, Feb 89	1.50	0.30	0.75	1.50
❑6, Apr 89	1.50	0.30	0.75	1.50
❑7, Jun 89	1.50	0.30	0.75	1.50
❑8, Aug 89	1.50	0.30	0.75	1.50

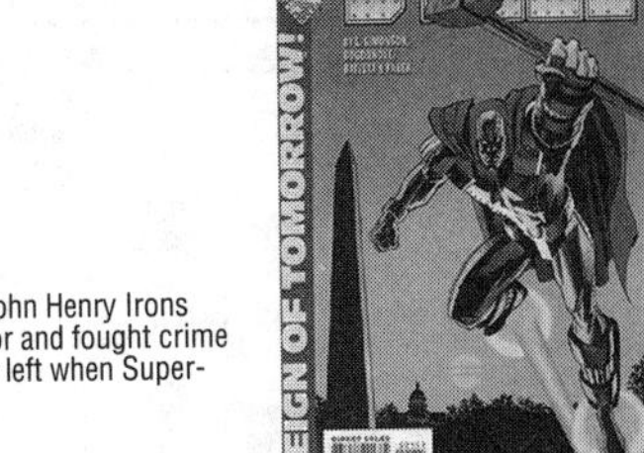

Former steelworker John Henry Irons donned a suit of armor and fought crime as Steel to fill the gap left when Superman died.

© 1994 DC Comics

STICKBOY (FANTAGRAPHICS)
FANTAGRAPHICS

Value: Cover or less

- ❑1, b&w 2.50
- ❑1-2, 2nd Printing 2.75
- ❑2, b&w 2.50
- ❑3, b&w 2.50
- ❑4, Nov 90, b&w 2.95
- ❑5, Feb 92, b&w 2.50

STICKBOY (STARHEAD)
STARHEAD

Value: Cover or less

- ❑1, b&w 2.50
- ❑2, b&w 2.50
- ❑3, b&w 2.50
- ❑4, b&w 2.50
- ❑5, b&w 2.50
- ❑6, b&w 2.50

STIG'S INFERNO
VORTEX

	ORIG	GOOD	FINE	N-MINT
❑1	1.95	0.40	1.00	2.00
❑2	1.95	0.40	1.00	2.00
❑3	3.50	0.70	1.75	3.50
❑4	3.50	0.70	1.75	3.50
❑5	1.75	0.35	0.88	1.75
❑6, b&w	1.50	0.30	0.75	1.50
❑7, b&w	1.50	0.30	0.75	1.50

STIMULATOR
FANTAGRAPHICS

Value: Cover or less

- ❑1, b&w; adult 2.50

STING
ARTLINE STUDIOS

Value: Cover or less

- ❑1, flip book with Killer Synthetic Toads 2.50

STING OF THE GREEN HORNET
NOW

Value: Cover or less

- ❑1, Jun 92, Out of the Shadows, A: Adolf Hitler, bagged with poster 2.50
- ❑1/CS, Out of the Shadows, A: Adolf Hitler, poster and trading card 2.75
- ❑2, Jul 92 .... 2.50
- ❑2/CS, Jul 92, bagged with poster 2.75
- ❑3, Aug 92, The Terror Express 2.50
- ❑3/CS, Aug 92, The Terror Express, bagged with poster 2.75
- ❑4, Sep 92 .... 2.50
- ❑4/CS, Sep 92, stitched with poster 2.75

STINZ (1ST SERIES)
FANTAGRAPHICS

	ORIG	GOOD	FINE	N-MINT
❑1, b&w	2.00	0.80	2.00	4.00
❑2, b&w	2.00	0.60	1.50	3.00
❑3, b&w	2.00	0.60	1.50	3.00
❑4, b&w	2.00	0.50	1.25	2.50
❑5	2.50	0.50	1.25	2.50

STINZ (2ND SERIES)
BRAVE NEW WORDS

Value: Cover or less

- ❑1, On a Pale Horse, b&w 2.50
- ❑2, b&w 2.50

STINZ (3RD SERIES)
MU

Value: Cover or less

- ❑1, Family Values 2.50
- ❑2, Old Man Out 2.50
- ❑3, The Bob War 2.50
- ❑4, Bum Steer 2.50
- ❑5, A Stranger to Our Kind 4.95
- ❑6, A Marvelous Resistance ... 5.50
- ❑7, A Dog's Life 4.95

STINZ: BUM STEER
MU

Value: Cover or less

- ❑1, Oct 95, nn; b&w; One-Shot 2.95

STINZ: FAMILY VALUES
MU

Value: Cover or less

- ❑1, nn; b&w 2.50

STINZ: OLD MAN OUT
MU

Value: Cover or less

- ❑1, Oct 94, nn 2.95

STINZ: THE BOBWAR
Mu

Value: Cover or less

- ❑1, Feb 95, nn; b&w; One-Shot ... 2.95

STONE
Image

	ORIG	GOOD	FINE	N-MINT
❑1, Aug 98, The Awakening, part 1	2.50	0.50	1.25	2.50
❑1/A, Aug 98, The Awakening, part 1, Variant cover with white background	2.50	0.50	1.25	2.50
❑1/B, Aug 98, The Awakening, part 1, Variant cover with side view of Stone, jewel showing in armband	2.50	0.50	1.25	2.50
❑2, Sep 98, The Awakening, part 2	2.50	0.50	1.25	2.50
❑2/A, Sep 98, The Awakening, part 2, DFE chrome cover; reprints indicia from #1	2.50	1.20	3.00	6.00
❑2/B, Sep 98, The Awakening, part 2, alternate cover (white border); Signed by Brian Haberlin	2.50	0.80	2.00	4.00
❑3, Nov 98, The Awakening, part 3	2.50	0.50	1.25	2.50
❑4, Apr 99, The Awakening, part 4	2.50	0.50	1.25	2.50

STONE (VOL. 2)
Image

Value: Cover or less

- ❑1, Aug 99 ... 2.50
- ❑1/SC, Aug 99, Chrome cover 6.95
- ❑2, Sep 99 ... 2.50
- ❑3, Dec 99 ... 2.50

STONE COLD STEVE AUSTIN
Chaos

Value: Cover or less

- ❑1, Oct 99, Tougher than the Rest, cover says Nov, indicia says Oct ... 2.95
- ❑2 ... 2.95
- ❑3 ... 2.95
- ❑4 ... 2.95

STONE PROTECTORS
Harvey

Value: Cover or less

- ❑1, May 94, The Legend of the Stone Protectors, 1: the Stone Protectors ... 1.50
- ❑2 ... 1.50
- ❑3, Sep 94, The Mystic of Myth-randir ... 1.50

STONEWALL IN THE SHENANDOAH
Heritage Collection

Value: Cover or less

- ❑1, nn; wraparound cover ... 3.50

STORIES FROM BOSNIA
Drawn and Quarterly

Value: Cover or less

- ❑1, b&w; cardstock cover; Oversized ... 3.95

STORM
Marvel

Value: Cover or less

- ❑1, Feb 96, Sunburst And Snow-blind, enhanced cardstock cover ... 2.95
- ❑2, Mar 96, The Ghost Has No Home, enhanced cardstock cover ... 2.95
- ❑3, Apr 96, The Tinderbox Of A Heart, enhanced cardstock cover ... 2.95
- ❑4, May 96, enhanced cardstock cover; Final Issue ... 2.95

STORMQUEST
Caliber

Value: Cover or less

- ❑1, Nov 94 ... 1.95
- ❑2, Dec 94 ... 1.95
- ❑3 ... 1.95
- ❑4 ... 1.95
- ❑5 ... 1.95
- ❑6 ... 1.95

STORMWATCH
Image

	ORIG	GOOD	FINE	N-MINT
❑0, Aug 93, JLee(w), 1: Warguard; 1: Nautica; 1: Flashpoint; 1: Backlash, Polybagged	2.50	0.50	1.25	2.50
❑1, Mar 93, 1: Fuji; 1: Deathtrap; 1: Synergy; 1: StormWatch; 1: Strafe; 1: Winter; 1: Diva; 1: Battalion; 1: Hellstrike	1.95	0.50	1.25	2.50
❑1/GO, Mar 93, Gold foil cover	1.95	0.80	2.00	4.00
❑2, May 93, 1: Ion & Lance; 1: Fahrenheit; 1: Cannon; 1: Regent	1.95	0.40	1.00	2.00
❑3, Jul 93, 1: LaSalle; A: Backlash	1.95	0.40	1.00	2.00
❑4, Aug 93, V: Warguard, cover says Oct	1.95	0.39	0.98	1.95
❑5, Nov 93	1.95	0.39	0.98	1.95
❑6, Dec 93	1.95	0.39	0.98	1.95
❑7, 1: Sunburst	1.95	0.39	0.98	1.95
❑8, 1: Rainmaker	1.95	0.39	0.98	1.95
❑9, Apr 94	2.50	0.50	1.25	2.50
❑10	1.95	0.39	0.98	1.95
❑10/A, Jun 94, Variant edition cover	1.95	1.00	2.50	5.00
❑10/B, Jun 94, variant cover	1.95	1.00	2.50	5.00
❑11, Aug 94	1.95	0.39	0.98	1.95
❑12, Aug 94	1.95	0.39	0.98	1.95
❑13, Sep 94	1.95	0.39	0.98	1.95
❑14, Sep 94	1.95	0.39	0.98	1.95
❑15, Oct 94	1.95	0.39	0.98	1.95
❑16, Nov 94	1.95	0.39	0.98	1.95
❑17, Dec 94	2.50	0.50	1.25	2.50
❑18, Jan 95	2.50	0.50	1.25	2.50
❑19, Feb 95	2.50	0.50	1.25	2.50
❑20, Mar 95	2.50	0.50	1.25	2.50
❑21, Apr 95, 1: Tao, cover says #1	2.50	0.50	1.25	2.50
❑22, May 95, WildStorm Rising Chapter 9; Wildstorm Rising, Part 9, bound-in trading cards	2.50	0.50	1.25	2.50
❑23, Jun 95	2.50	0.50	1.25	2.50
❑24, Jul 95	2.50	0.50	1.25	2.50
❑25, May 94, cover says Jun 95; Images of Tomorrow; Shipped out of sequence as preview to future events (after #9)	2.50	0.50	1.25	2.50
❑25-2, Aug 95, 2nd Printing	2.50	0.50	1.25	2.50
❑26, Aug 95	2.50	0.50	1.25	2.50
❑27, Aug 95	2.50	0.50	1.25	2.50
❑28, Sep 95, 1: Flint; 1: Storm Force; 1: Swift, cover forms right half of diptych with issue #29	2.50	0.50	1.25	2.50
❑29, Oct 95, cover says Nov; indicia says Oct	2.50	0.50	1.25	2.50
❑30, Nov 95	2.50	0.50	1.25	2.50
❑31, Dec 95	2.50	0.50	1.25	2.50
❑32, Jan 96	2.50	0.50	1.25	2.50
❑33, Feb 96	2.50	0.50	1.25	2.50
❑34, Mar 96	2.50	0.50	1.25	2.50
❑35, Apr 96, Fire from Heaven, Part 5	2.50	0.50	1.25	2.50
❑36, Jun 96, Fire from Heaven, Part 12	2.50	0.50	1.25	2.50
❑37, Jul 96, 1: Jenny Sparks; 1: Hawksmoor, Giant-size	3.50	0.70	1.75	3.50
❑38, Aug 96	2.50	0.50	1.25	2.50
❑39, Aug 96	2.50	0.50	1.25	2.50
❑40, Oct 96	2.50	0.50	1.25	2.50
❑41, Oct 96	2.50	0.50	1.25	2.50
❑42, Nov 96	2.50	0.50	1.25	2.50
❑43, Dec 96	2.50	0.50	1.25	2.50
❑44/A, Jan 97, O: Jenny Sparks, Torrid Tales cover; homages to various comics eras	2.50	0.50	1.25	2.50
❑44/B, Jan 97, GK (c), O: Jenny Sparks, Pop Art Masterpiece cover	2.50	0.50	1.25	2.50
❑44/C, Jan 97, O: Jenny Sparks, Who Watches The Weathermen cover	2.50	0.50	1.25	2.50
❑45, Feb 97	2.50	0.50	1.25	2.50
❑46, Mar 97	2.50	0.50	1.25	2.50
❑47, Apr 97	2.50	0.50	1.25	2.50
❑48, May 97	2.50	0.50	1.25	2.50
❑49, Jun 97	2.50	0.50	1.25	2.50
❑50, Jul 97, Final Issue; Giant-size	4.50	0.90	2.25	4.50
❑SE 1, Jan 94, 1: Argos	3.50	0.70	1.75	3.50
❑SE 2, May 95	3.50	0.50	1.25	2.50

STORMWATCH (2ND SERIES)
Image

Value: Cover or less

- ❑1, Oct 97, Strange Weather, Part 1 ... 2.50
- ❑1/A, Oct 97, alternate cover (white background) ... 2.50
- ❑1/B, Oct 97, Voyager pack ... 2.50
- ❑2, Nov 97, Strange Weather, Part 2 ... 2.50
- ❑3, Dec 97, Strange Weather, Part 3 ... 2.50
- ❑4, Feb 98, A Finer World, Part 1 ... 2.50
- ❑5, Mar 98, A Finer World, Part 2 ... 2.50
- ❑5/A, Mar 98, alternate cover; group flying ... 2.50
- ❑6, Apr 98, A Finer World, Part 3 ... 2.50
- ❑7, May 98, Bleed, Part 1 ... 2.50
- ❑8, Jun 98, Bleed, Part 2 ... 2.50
- ❑9, Jul 98, Bleed, Part 3 ... 2.50
- ❑10, Aug 98, Bleed, Part 2; No Reason ... 2.50
- ❑11, Sep 98, No Direction Home ... 2.50

STORMWATCHER
Eclipse

Value: Cover or less

- ❑1, Apr 89, Back in Business, b&w ... 2.00
- ❑2, May 89, b&w ... 2.00
- ❑3, b&w ... 2.00
- ❑4, b&w ... 2.00

STORMWATCH SOURCEBOOK
Image

Value: Cover or less

- ❑1, Jan 94 ... 2.50

STRAND
Trident

Value: Cover or less

- ❑1, Nov 90, Strand Episode 1; Where Angels Fear to Tread, b&w ... 2.50
- ❑2, b&w ... 2.50

STRANDED ON PLANET X
Radio

Value: Cover or less

- ❑1, Jun 99 ... 2.95

STRANGE ADVENTURES
DC

	ORIG	GOOD	FINE	N-MINT
❑125, Feb 61	0.10	11.00	27.50	55.00
❑126, Mar 61	0.10	11.00	27.50	55.00
❑127	0.10	11.00	27.50	55.00
❑128	0.10	11.00	27.50	55.00
❑129, Jun 61	0.10	11.00	27.50	55.00
❑130, Jul 61	0.10	11.00	27.50	55.00
❑131, Aug 61	0.10	9.60	24.00	48.00

	ORIG	GOOD	FINE	N-MINT
❑132, Sep 61	0.10	9.60	24.00	48.00
❑133, Oct 61	0.10	9.60	24.00	48.00
❑134, Nov 61	0.10	9.60	24.00	48.00
❑135	0.10	7.00	17.50	35.00
❑136, Jan 62	0.12	7.00	17.50	35.00
❑137, Feb 62	0.12	7.00	17.50	35.00
❑138, Mar 62, A: The Atomic Knights	0.12	7.00	17.50	35.00
❑139, Apr 62	0.12	7.00	17.50	35.00
❑140, May 62	0.12	7.00	17.50	35.00
❑141, Jun 62	0.12	7.00	17.50	35.00
❑142, Jul 62	0.12	7.00	17.50	35.00
❑143, Aug 62	0.12	7.00	17.50	35.00
❑144, Sep 62, A: The Atomic Knights	0.12	7.00	17.50	35.00
❑145, Oct 62	0.12	7.00	17.50	35.00
❑146, Nov 62	0.12	7.00	17.50	35.00
❑147, Dec 62, A: The Atomic Knights	0.12	7.00	17.50	35.00
❑148, Jan 63	0.12	7.00	17.50	35.00
❑149, Feb 63	0.12	7.00	17.50	35.00
❑150, Mar 63, A: The Atomic Knights	0.12	7.00	17.50	35.00
❑151, Apr 63	0.12	6.00	15.00	30.00
❑152, May 63	0.12	6.00	15.00	30.00
❑153, Jun 63, A: The Atomic Knights	0.12	6.00	15.00	30.00
❑154, Jul 63	0.12	6.00	15.00	30.00
❑155, Aug 63	0.12	6.00	15.00	30.00
❑156, Sep 63, A: The Atomic Knights	0.12	6.00	15.00	30.00
❑157, Oct 63	0.12	6.00	15.00	30.00
❑158, Nov 63	0.12	6.00	15.00	30.00
❑159, Dec 63	0.12	6.00	15.00	30.00
❑160, Jan 64, A: The Atomic Knights	0.12	6.00	15.00	30.00
❑161, Feb 64	0.12	3.60	9.00	18.00
❑162, Mar 64	0.12	3.60	9.00	18.00
❑163, Apr 64	0.12	3.60	9.00	18.00
❑164, May 64	0.12	3.60	9.00	18.00
❑165, Jun 64	0.12	3.60	9.00	18.00
❑166, Jul 64	0.12	3.60	9.00	18.00
❑167, Aug 64	0.12	3.60	9.00	18.00
❑168	0.12	3.60	9.00	18.00
❑169, Oct 64	0.12	3.60	9.00	18.00
❑170, Nov 64	0.12	3.60	9.00	18.00
❑171, Dec 64	0.12	3.60	9.00	18.00
❑172, Jan 65	0.12	3.60	9.00	18.00
❑173, Feb 65	0.12	3.60	9.00	18.00
❑174, Mar 65	0.12	3.60	9.00	18.00
❑175	0.12	3.60	9.00	18.00
❑176, May 65	0.12	3.60	9.00	18.00
❑177, 1: Immortal Man	0.12	3.60	9.00	18.00
❑178, Jul 65	0.12	3.60	9.00	18.00
❑179, Aug 65	0.12	3.60	9.00	18.00
❑180, Sep 65, 1: Animal Man (no costume)	0.12	20.00	50.00	100.00
❑181, Oct 65	0.12	2.60	6.50	13.00
❑182, Nov 65	0.12	2.60	6.50	13.00
❑183, Dec 65	0.12	2.60	6.50	13.00
❑184, Jan 66, A: Animal Man	0.12	14.00	35.00	70.00
❑185, Feb 66, A: Star Hawkins; A: Immortal Man	0.12	2.60	6.50	13.00
❑186, Mar 66	0.12	2.60	6.50	13.00
❑187, Apr 66, 1: The Enchantress	0.12	2.60	6.50	13.00
❑188, May 66	0.12	2.60	6.50	13.00
❑189, Jun 66	0.12	2.60	6.50	13.00
❑190, Jul 66, 1: Animal Man (in costume)	0.12	15.00	37.50	75.00
❑191, Aug 66	0.12	2.00	5.00	10.00
❑192, Sep 66	0.12	2.00	5.00	10.00
❑193, Oct 66	0.12	2.00	5.00	10.00
❑194, Nov 66	0.12	2.00	5.00	10.00
❑195, Dec 66, A: Animal Man	0.12	9.00	22.50	45.00
❑196, Jan 67	0.12	2.00	5.00	10.00
❑197, Feb 67	0.12	2.00	5.00	10.00
❑198, Mar 67	0.12	2.00	5.00	10.00
❑199, Apr 67	0.12	2.00	5.00	10.00
❑200, May 67	0.12	2.00	5.00	10.00
❑201, Jun 67, A: Animal Man	0.12	6.00	15.00	30.00
❑202, Jul 67	0.12	1.80	4.50	9.00
❑203, Aug 67, The Winged Beasts Of Nightmare Swamp!; The Split Man!	0.12	1.80	4.50	9.00
❑204, Sep 67	0.12	1.80	4.50	9.00
❑205, Oct 67, 1: Deadman	0.12	14.00	35.00	70.00
❑206, Nov 67, 2: Deadman	0.12	9.00	22.50	45.00
❑207, Dec 67, Deadman	0.12	6.40	16.00	32.00
❑208, Jan 68, Deadman	0.12	6.40	16.00	32.00
❑209, Feb 68, Deadman	0.12	6.40	16.00	32.00
❑210, Mar 68, Deadman	0.12	6.40	16.00	32.00
❑211, Apr 68, Deadman	0.12	5.60	14.00	28.00
❑212, Jun 68, Deadman	0.12	5.60	14.00	28.00
❑213, Aug 68, Deadman	0.12	5.60	14.00	28.00
❑214, Oct 68, Deadman	0.12	5.60	14.00	28.00

Adam Strange stories from *Mystery in Space* were later reprinted in *Strange Adventures.*

© 1967 National Periodical Publications (DC)

	ORIG	GOOD	FINE	N-MINT
❑215, Dec 68, 1: Sensei; 1: League of Assassins, Deadman	0.12	5.60	14.00	28.00
❑216, Feb 69, Deadman	0.12	5.60	14.00	28.00
❑217, Apr 69	0.12	1.40	3.50	7.00
❑218, Jun 69	0.12	1.40	3.50	7.00
❑219, Aug 69	0.15	1.40	3.50	7.00
❑220, Oct 69	0.15	1.40	3.50	7.00
❑221, Dec 69	0.15	1.40	3.50	7.00
❑222, Feb 70, NA, New Adam Strange story	0.15	2.00	5.00	10.00
❑223, Apr 70	0.15	1.40	3.50	7.00
❑224, Jun 70	0.15	1.40	3.50	7.00
❑225, Aug 70	0.15	1.40	3.50	7.00
❑226, Oct 70, giant series begins	0.25	1.40	3.50	7.00
❑227, Dec 70, JKu (c)	0.25	1.40	3.50	7.00
❑228, Feb 71	0.25	1.40	3.50	7.00
❑229, Apr 71	0.25	1.40	3.50	7.00
❑230, Jun 71	0.25	1.40	3.50	7.00
❑231, Aug 71	0.25	0.80	2.00	4.00
❑232, Oct 71	0.25	0.80	2.00	4.00
❑233, Dec 71	0.25	0.80	2.00	4.00
❑234, Feb 72	0.25	0.80	2.00	4.00
❑235, Apr 72	0.25	0.80	2.00	4.00
❑236, Jun 72	0.25	0.80	2.00	4.00
❑237, Jun 72, The Skyscraper That Came To Life!; Ray-Gun In The Sky!	0.20	0.80	2.00	4.00
❑238, Oct 72, CI; MA, The Secret of the Tomb Thumb Spacemen!; The Man Who Killed Himself!	0.20	0.80	2.00	4.00
❑239, Dec 72	0.20	0.80	2.00	4.00
❑240, Feb 73	0.20	0.80	2.00	4.00
❑241, Apr 73	0.20	0.80	2.00	4.00
❑242, Jul 73	0.20	0.80	2.00	4.00
❑243, Sep 73	0.20	0.80	2.00	4.00
❑244, Nov 73, Final Issue	0.20	0.80	2.00	4.00

STRANGE ADVENTURES (MINI-SERIES)

VERTIGO

Value: Cover or less

- ❑1, Nov 99 ... 2.50
- ❑2, Dec 99, Third Toe, Left Boot; Ice Cream Comes to Wharftown ... 2.50
- ❑3, Jan 00, The Split; Driving Miss 134 ... 2.50
- ❑4, Feb 00 ... 2.50

STRANGE ATTRACTORS

RETROGRAFIX

	ORIG	GOOD	FINE	N-MINT
❑1, May 93, The Sorrows of Young Sophie	2.50	0.80	2.00	4.00
❑1-2, Jul 94, The Sorrows of Young Sophie, 2nd Printing	2.50	0.55	1.38	2.75
❑2, Aug 93, I Went to See the Gypsy	2.50	0.70	1.75	3.50
❑2-2, Jul 93, I Went to See the Gypsy, 2nd Printing	2.50	0.55	1.38	2.75
❑3, Nov 93, Dear Diary	2.50	0.70	1.75	3.50
❑3-2, Jun 93, Dear Diary, 2nd Printing	2.50	0.55	1.38	2.75
❑4, Feb 94, Heart Of Stone	2.50	0.60	1.50	3.00
❑4-2, Jun 94, Heart Of Stone, 2nd Printing	2.50	0.55	1.38	2.75
❑5, May 94	2.50	0.60	1.50	3.00
❑6, Aug 94	2.50	0.50	1.25	2.50
❑7, Nov 94	2.50	0.50	1.25	2.50
❑8, Jan 95	2.50	0.50	1.25	2.50
❑9, Apr 95	2.50	0.50	1.25	2.50
❑10, Jun 95	2.50	0.50	1.25	2.50
❑11, Sep 95	2.50	0.50	1.25	2.50
❑12, Nov 95	2.50	0.50	1.25	2.50
❑13, Feb 96	2.95	0.50	1.25	2.50
❑14, Jul 96	2.95	0.50	1.25	2.50
❑15, Feb 97	2.95	0.50	1.25	2.50

STRANGE ATTRACTORS: MOON FEVER

CALIBER

Value: Cover or less

- ❑1, Feb 97, b&w ... 2.95
- ❑2 ... 2.95
- ❑3 ... 2.95

STRANGE AVENGING TALES (STEVE DITKO'S...)

FANTAGRAPHICS

Value: Cover or less

- ❑1, Feb 97, SD, SD (w), The Baffler in All Mine; The Spoiler Files ... 2.95

STRANGE BREW
AARDVARK-VANAHEIM

	ORIG	GOOD	FINE	N-MINT
1	—	0.60	1.50	3.00

STRANGE COMBAT TALES
MARVEL

Value: Cover or less

- 1, Oct 93, March Of The Dead, A: Julian Drake 2.50
- 2, Nov 83 2.50
- 3 2.50
- 4, Midnight Crusade 2.50

STRANGE DAYS
ECLIPSE

Value: Cover or less

- 1, Freakwave; Tales from the 4th Dimesion 1.50
- 2 1.50
- 3 1.50

STRANGE EMBRACE
ATOMEKA

Value: Cover or less

- 1, b&w 3.95
- 2, b&w 3.95
- 3, b&w 3.95

STRANGEHAVEN
ABIOGENESIS PRESS

	ORIG	GOOD	FINE	N-MINT
1, Jun 95	2.95	1.00	2.50	5.00
2	2.95	0.80	2.00	4.00
3, Dec 95, Call No Man Happy; My Alien Retina	2.95	0.80	2.00	4.00
4, Jun 96	2.95	0.59	1.48	2.95
5, Nov 96	2.95	0.59	1.48	2.95
6, May 97	2.95	0.59	1.48	2.95
7	2.95	0.59	1.48	2.95
8, 97	2.95	0.59	1.48	2.95
9, Jun 98	2.95	0.59	1.48	2.95
10, Nov 98	2.95	0.59	1.48	2.95
11, Apr 99	2.95	0.59	1.48	2.95
12, Oct 99	2.95	0.59	1.48	2.95

STRANGE HEROES
LONE STAR

Value: Cover or less

- 1, Jun 00, Spellbinder; Otherland 2.95

STRANGELOVE
EXPRESS

Value: Cover or less

- 1, b&w 2.50
- 2, b&w 2.50

STRANGER IN A STRANGE LAND
RIP OFF

Value: Cover or less

- 1, Jun 89, Stranger in a Strange Land; What Wine Goes with Face...?, b&w; adult 2.00
- 2, May 90, Inside Every Fat Man There's a Thin Man Dying; Brilliant Finish, b&w; adult 2.00
- 3, Sep 91, b&w; adult 2.50

STRANGERS, THE
MALIBU

	ORIG	GOOD	FINE	N-MINT
1, Jun 93, Jumpstart!, 1: The Night Man (out of costume); 1: The Strangers	1.95	0.40	1.00	2.00
1/Hol, Jun 93, hologram edition	—	1.00	2.50	5.00
1/LE, Jun 93, Ultra-limited edition	1.95	0.80	2.00	4.00
2, Jul 93, card	1.95	0.40	1.00	2.00
3, Aug 93, 1: TNTNT	1.95	0.40	1.00	2.00
4, Sep 93, A: Hardcase	1.95	0.40	1.00	2.00
5, Oct 93, Dynamic Tension!; Rune, Part G, 40pgs.; Rune	2.50	0.50	1.25	2.50
6, Nov 93	1.95	0.39	0.98	1.95
7, Dec 93, Break-Thru, Break-Thru	1.95	0.39	0.98	1.95
8, Jan 94, Taken By The Sky!, O: The Solution	1.95	0.39	0.98	1.95
9, Feb 94	1.95	0.39	0.98	1.95
10, Mar 94	1.95	0.39	0.98	1.95
11, Apr 94	1.95	0.39	0.98	1.95
12, May 94	1.95	0.39	0.98	1.95
13, Jun 94, MGu, KB (w), This Space Still Available; Anatomy of a Hero, Part 2, 1: Pilgrim, contains Ultraverse Premiere #4	3.50	0.70	1.75	3.50
14, Jul 94, the Man of Power, 1: Byter	1.95	0.39	0.98	1.95
15, Aug 94, Homeboy, 1: Rodent; 1: Generator X; 1: Lightshow	1.95	0.39	0.98	1.95
16, Sep 94, Party Time	1.95	0.39	0.98	1.95
17, Oct 94, Blood of an Ultra, A: Rafferty	1.95	0.39	0.98	1.95
18, Nov 94, The Pitch	1.95	0.39	0.98	1.95
19, Dec 94, The Teknight Before Christmas	1.95	0.39	0.98	1.95
20, Jan 95, The Name of the Game is Fear, 1: M.C. Zed; 1: Beater	1.95	0.39	0.98	1.95
21, Feb 95, Life in Wartime!	2.50	0.39	0.98	1.95
22, Mar 95, Machines in Wartime!	2.50	0.39	0.98	1.95
23, Apr 95, The Subject is...Taboo!	2.50	0.39	0.98	1.95
24, May 95, The Subject is...TNTNT II!, Final Issue	2.50	0.39	0.98	1.95
Anl 1, The Pilgrim Conundrum, Part 2	3.95	0.79	1.98	3.95

STRANGERS IN PARADISE
ANTARCTIC

	ORIG	GOOD	FINE	N-MINT
0, b&w	—	14.00	35.00	70.00
1, Nov 93, b&w	2.75	12.00	30.00	60.00
1-2, Mar 94, b&w; 2nd Printing	2.75	1.00	2.50	5.00
, Apr 94, b&w; 3rd Printing	2.75	0.60	1.50	3.00
2, Dec 93, b&w	2.75	3.00	7.50	15.00
3, Feb 94, b&w	2.75	3.00	7.50	15.00

STRANGERS IN PARADISE (2ND SERIES)
ABSTRACT

	ORIG	GOOD	FINE	N-MINT
1, Sep 94, b&w	2.75	5.00	12.50	25.00
1/SC, Gold logo edition	2.75	0.80	2.00	4.00
1-2, Apr 95, b&w; 2nd Printing	2.75	0.55	1.38	2.75
2, Nov 94, b&w	2.75	2.40	6.00	12.00
2/SC, Gold logo edition	2.75	0.60	1.50	3.00
3, Jan 95, b&w	2.75	2.00	5.00	10.00
3/SC, Gold logo edition	2.75	0.60	1.50	3.00
4, Mar 95, b&w	2.75	1.60	4.00	8.00
4/SC, Gold logo edition	2.75	0.55	1.38	2.75
5, Jun 95, b&w	2.75	1.60	4.00	8.00
5/SC, Gold logo edition	2.75	0.55	1.38	2.75
6, Jul 95, b&w	2.75	1.20	3.00	6.00
6/SC, Gold logo edition	2.75	0.55	1.38	2.75
7, Sep 95, b&w	2.75	1.20	3.00	6.00
7/SC, Gold logo edition	2.75	0.55	1.38	2.75
8, Nov 95, b&w	2.75	1.20	3.00	6.00
8/SC, Gold logo edition	2.75	0.55	1.38	2.75
9, Jan 96, b&w	2.75	1.20	3.00	6.00
9/SC, Gold logo edition	2.75	0.55	1.38	2.75
10, Feb 96, b&w	2.75	1.20	3.00	6.00
10/SC, Gold logo edition	2.75	0.55	1.38	2.75
11, b&w	2.75	0.80	2.00	4.00
11/SC, Gold logo edition	2.75	0.55	1.38	2.75
12, May 96, b&w	2.75	0.80	2.00	4.00
12/SC, Gold logo edition	2.75	0.55	1.38	2.75
13, Jun 96, b&w	2.75	0.60	1.50	3.00
14, Jul 96, Molly & Poo, continues in 3rd series (Image); Titled: Terry Moore's Strangers in Paradise	2.75	0.55	1.38	2.75
SE 1, Molly & Poo Special	2.75	0.60	1.50	3.00

STRANGERS IN PARADISE (3RD SERIES)
HOMAGE

	ORIG	GOOD	FINE	N-MINT
1, Oct 96, b&w	2.75	0.80	2.00	4.00
2, Dec 96, b&w	2.75	0.60	1.50	3.00
3, Jan 97, b&w	2.75	0.60	1.50	3.00
4, Feb 97, b&w	2.75	0.60	1.50	3.00
5, Apr 97, b&w; cover says Mar, indicia says Apr	2.75	0.60	1.50	3.00
6, May 97, b&w	2.75	0.60	1.50	3.00
7, Jul 97, b&w	2.75	0.60	1.50	3.00
8, Aug 97, b&w; returns to Abstract	2.75	0.60	1.50	3.00
9	2.75	0.60	1.50	3.00
10	2.75	0.60	1.50	3.00
11	2.75	0.60	1.50	3.00
12	2.75	0.60	1.50	3.00
13	2.75	0.60	1.50	3.00
14	2.75	0.60	1.50	3.00
15	2.75	0.60	1.50	3.00
16	—	0.60	1.50	3.00
17	—	0.60	1.50	3.00
18	—	0.60	1.50	3.00
19	—	0.60	1.50	3.00
20	—	0.60	1.50	3.00
21	—	0.60	1.50	3.00
22	—	0.60	1.50	3.00
23	—	0.60	1.50	3.00
24	—	0.60	1.50	3.00
25	—	0.60	1.50	3.00
26	—	0.60	1.50	3.00
27	—	0.60	1.50	3.00
28	—	0.60	1.50	3.00
29	—	0.60	1.50	3.00
30	—	0.60	1.50	3.00
31	—	0.59	1.48	2.95
32	—	0.59	1.48	2.95
33	—	0.59	1.48	2.95
34	—	0.59	1.48	2.95
35	—	0.59	1.48	2.95
36	—	0.59	1.48	2.95
37	—	0.59	1.48	2.95
38	—	0.59	1.48	2.95
39	—	0.59	1.48	2.95
40	—	0.59	1.48	2.95
41	—	0.59	1.48	2.95
42	2.95	0.59	1.48	2.95
SE 1, Feb 99, Lyrics and Poems	2.75	0.60	1.50	3.00

STRANGER'S TALE, A
VINEYARD

Value: Cover or less

- 1, Temple; Spork, b&w; cardstock cover 2.00

STRANGER THAN FICTION
IMPACT STUDIOS

Value: Cover or less

Issue	Price
❑1, b&w	1.99
❑2, Jul 98, b&w	1.99
❑3	1.99
❑4	1.99

STRANGE SPORTS STORIES
DC

Issue	ORIG	GOOD	FINE	N-MINT
❑1, Oct 73, CS; DG; BO, FR (w), To Beat The Devil; A Tall Tale Of Tenpins	0.20	2.00	5.00	10.00
❑2, Dec 73, IN; CS; DG; MA, FR (w), Karate on the Moon!; Volley of Death	0.20	1.40	3.50	7.00
❑3, Feb 74, CS; DG, FR (w), Gridiron Knight-mare!; Man Who Leaped Over the Earth!	0.20	1.00	2.50	5.00
❑4, Apr 74, DG, The Challenge of the Face-less Five; Man with the Golden Gloves!	0.20	1.00	2.50	5.00
❑5, Jun 74	0.20	1.00	2.50	5.00
❑6, Aug 74	0.20	1.00	2.50	5.00

STRANGE SPORTS STORIES (ADVENTURE)
ADVENTURE

Value: Cover or less

Issue	Price
❑1	2.50

STRANGE STORIES
AVALON

Value: Cover or less

Issue	Price
❑1, b&w; reprints John Force and Magic Man stories	2.95

STRANGE TALES (1ST SERIES)
MARVEL

Issue	ORIG	GOOD	FINE	N-MINT
❑89, Oct 61, JK, 1: Fin Fang Foom	0.10	50.00	125.00	250.00
❑90, Nov 61	0.10	23.00	57.50	115.00
❑91, Dec 61	0.10	23.00	57.50	115.00
❑92, Jan 62	0.10	23.00	57.50	115.00
❑93, Feb 62	0.10	21.00	52.50	105.00
❑94, Mar 62	0.10	21.00	52.50	105.00
❑95, Apr 62	0.10	21.00	52.50	105.00
❑96, May 62	0.10	21.00	52.50	105.00
❑97, Jun 62, Aunt May & Uncle Ben prototype characters (?)	0.10	65.00	162.50	325.00
❑98, Jul 62	0.10	21.00	52.50	105.00
❑99, Aug 62	0.10	21.00	52.50	105.00
❑100, Sep 62	0.12	21.00	52.50	105.00
❑101, Oct 62, JK; SD, Human Torch features begin	0.12	165.00	412.50	825.00
❑102, Nov 62, JK; SD, A: Human Torch	0.12	60.00	150.00	300.00
❑103, Dec 62, JK; SD, A: Human Torch	0.12	48.00	120.00	240.00
❑104, Jan 63, JK; SD, 1: Paste-Pot Pete; A: Human Torch	0.12	48.00	120.00	240.00
❑105, Feb 63, JK; SD, A: Human Torch	0.12	48.00	120.00	240.00
❑106, Mar 63, SD, A: Human Torch; A: Fantastic Four	0.12	35.00	87.50	175.00
❑107, Apr 63, SD, Human Torch vs. Sub-Mariner	0.12	38.00	95.00	190.00
❑108, May 63, JK; SD, A: Human Torch	0.12	35.00	87.50	175.00
❑109, Jun 63, JK; SD, 1: Circe (later becomes Sersi); A: Human Torch	0.12	35.00	87.50	175.00
❑110, Jul 63, SD, 1: Wong (Doctor Strange's manservant); 1: Doctor Strange; 1: The Ancient One; A: Human Torch	0.12	200.00	500.00	1000.00
❑111, Aug 63, SD, 2: Doctor Strange; 1: Eel I (Leopold Stryke); 1: Baron Mordo; 1: Asbestos; A: Human Torch	0.12	60.00	150.00	300.00
❑112, Sep 63, SD, A: Human Torch	0.12	22.00	55.00	110.00
❑113, Oct 63, SD, A: Human Torch; 1: Plant-man	0.12	22.00	55.00	110.00
❑114, Nov 63, JK; SD, A: Human Torch, Villain (The Acrobat) appears, dressed as Captain America	0.12	50.00	125.00	250.00
❑115, Dec 63, SD, O: Doctor Strange; A: Human Torch	0.12	75.00	187.50	375.00
❑116, Jan 64, Human Torch vs. Thing	0.12	17.00	42.50	85.00
❑117, Feb 64, A: Human Torch	0.12	14.00	35.00	70.00
❑118, Mar 64, A: Human Torch	0.12	14.00	35.00	70.00
❑119, Apr 64, A: Spider-Man; A: Human Torch	0.12	18.00	45.00	90.00
❑120, May 64, A: Iceman; A: Human Torch	0.12	17.00	42.50	85.00
❑121, Jun 64, A: Human Torch	0.12	9.60	24.00	48.00
❑122, Jul 64, A: Human Torch	0.12	9.60	24.00	48.00
❑123, Aug 64, A: Thor; 1: The Beetle; A: Human Torch; A: Thing	0.12	9.60	24.00	48.00
❑124, Sep 64, A: Human Torch; A: Thing	0.12	9.60	24.00	48.00
❑125, Oct 64, A: Human Torch	0.12	9.60	24.00	48.00
❑126, Nov 64, 1: Clea; A: Human Torch; 1: Dormammu	0.12	11.00	27.50	55.00
❑127, Dec 64, A: Human Torch	0.12	8.40	21.00	42.00
❑128, Jan 65, A: Human Torch	0.12	8.40	21.00	42.00
❑129, Feb 65, A: Human Torch	0.12	8.40	21.00	42.00
❑130, Mar 65, SD, A: Beatles; A: Human Torch	0.12	9.60	24.00	48.00
❑131, Apr 65, SD, A: Human Torch; A: Thing	0.12	8.40	21.00	42.00
❑132, May 65, SD, A: Human Torch; A: Thing	0.12	8.40	21.00	42.00
❑133, Jun 65, SD, A: Human Torch; A: Thing	0.12	8.40	21.00	42.00

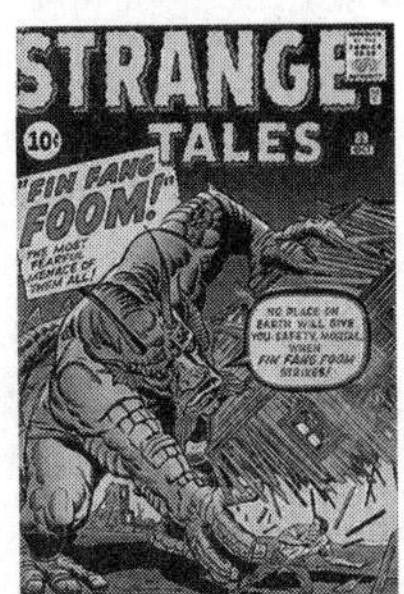

The dragon-like monster Fin Fang Foom made his first appearance in *Strange Tales* (1st series) #89.

Issue	ORIG	GOOD	FINE	N-MINT
❑134, Jul 65, SD, A: Watcher; A: Human Torch; A: Torch, Last Human Torch issue	0.12	8.40	21.00	42.00
❑135, Aug 65, JK; SD, SL (w), Nick Fury, Agent of S.H.I.E.L.D.: The Man for the Job!; Dr. Strange: Eternity Beckons!, 1: Hydra; 1: Nick Fury, Agent of SHIELD; 1: S.H.I.E.L.D.	0.12	17.00	42.50	85.00
❑136, Sep 65, JK; SD, Doctor Strange	0.12	5.60	14.00	28.00
❑137, Oct 65	0.12	5.60	14.00	28.00
❑138, Nov 65, 1: Eternity	0.12	5.60	14.00	28.00
❑139, Dec 65	0.12	5.60	14.00	28.00
❑140, Jan 66	0.12	5.60	14.00	28.00
❑141, Feb 66, 1: Mentallo; 1: The Fixer	0.12	5.60	14.00	28.00
❑142, Mar 66	0.12	5.60	14.00	28.00
❑143, Apr 66	0.12	5.60	14.00	28.00
❑144, May 66, 1: Jasper Sitwell (SHIELD agent); 1: The Druid	0.12	5.60	14.00	28.00
❑145, Jun 66	0.12	5.60	14.00	28.00
❑146, Jul 66, 1: Advanced Idea Mechanics (A.I.M.)	0.12	6.00	15.00	30.00
❑147, Aug 66, 1: Kaluu	0.12	5.60	14.00	28.00
❑148, Sep 66, JK; BEv, O: The Ancient One	0.12	10.00	25.00	50.00
❑149, Oct 66, JK; BEv	0.12	5.60	14.00	28.00
❑150, Nov 66, JK; BEv; JB, 1: Umar, 1st John Buscema art at Marvel	0.12	6.40	16.00	32.00
❑151, Dec 66, JSo; JK; BEv, 1st Jim Steranko art at Marvel	0.12	8.40	21.00	42.00
❑152, Jan 67	0.12	5.00	12.50	25.00
❑153, Feb 67	0.12	5.00	12.50	25.00
❑154, Mar 67, 1: Dreadnought (original)	0.12	5.00	12.50	25.00
❑155, Apr 67	0.12	5.00	12.50	25.00
❑156, May 67, A: Daredevil	0.12	5.00	12.50	25.00
❑157, Jun 67, 1: Living Tribunal	0.12	5.00	12.50	25.00
❑158, Jul 67, D: Baron Strucker	0.12	5.00	12.50	25.00
❑159, Aug 67, JSo, O: Fury; A: Captain America; O: Nick Fury, Agent of SHIELD; 1: Val Fontaine	0.12	6.40	16.00	32.00
❑160, Sep 67, A: Captain America	0.12	5.00	12.50	25.00
❑161, Oct 67, A: Captain America	0.12	5.00	12.50	25.00
❑162, Nov 67, A: Captain America	0.12	5.00	12.50	25.00
❑163, Dec 67	0.12	5.00	12.50	25.00
❑164, Jan 68, 1: Yandroth	0.12	5.00	12.50	25.00
❑165, Feb 68	0.12	5.00	12.50	25.00
❑166, Mar 68	0.12	5.00	12.50	25.00
❑167, Apr 68, DA; JSo	0.12	5.00	12.50	25.00
❑168, May 68, DA; JSo, O: Brother Voodoo, original series continues as Doctor Strange; Nick Fury, Agent of SHIELD series ends	0.12	5.00	12.50	25.00
❑169, Jun 73, second series begins; Brother Voodoo	0.20	0.70	1.75	3.50
❑170, Aug 73, Brother Voodoo	0.20	0.70	1.75	3.50
❑171, Oct 73, 1: Baron Samedi, Brother Voodoo	0.20	0.70	1.75	3.50
❑172, Dec 73, Brother Voodoo	0.20	0.70	1.75	3.50
❑173, Feb 74, GC, Sacrifice Play!, 1: Black Talon I (Desmond Drew), Brother Voodoo	0.20	0.70	1.75	3.50
❑174, Jun 74, JM; JB, There Walks The Golem!, O: Golem	0.25	0.70	1.75	3.50
❑175, Aug 74, SD, Rep-Torr	0.25	0.70	1.75	3.50
❑176, Oct 74, Golem	0.25	0.70	1.75	3.50
❑177, Dec 74, TD, There Comes Now Raging Fire!, Golem	0.25	0.70	1.75	3.50
❑178, Feb 75, JSn, 1: Magus; O: Warlock	0.25	3.00	7.50	15.00
❑179, Apr 75, JSn, A: Warlock; 1: Pip	0.25	2.00	5.00	10.00
❑180, Jun 75, JSn, A: Warlock; 1: Gamora.	0.25	2.00	5.00	10.00
❑181, Aug 75, JSn, A: Warlock	0.25	2.00	5.00	10.00
❑182, Oct 75, Reprint	0.25	0.60	1.50	3.00
❑183, Dec 75, Reprint	0.25	0.60	1.50	3.00
❑184, Feb 76, Reprint	0.25	0.60	1.50	3.00
❑185, Apr 76, Reprint	0.25	0.60	1.50	3.00
❑186, Jun 76, Reprint	0.25	0.60	1.50	3.00
❑187, Aug 76, Reprint	0.30	0.60	1.50	3.00
❑188, Oct 76, Reprint	0.30	0.60	1.50	3.00
❑Anl 1, Reprint	0.25	65.00	162.50	325.00
❑Anl 2, A: Spider-Man; A: Human Torch	0.25	70.00	175.00	350.00

STRANGE TALES (2ND SERIES)
MARVEL

	ORIG	GOOD	FINE	N-MINT
❑1, Apr 87, Cloak & Dagger; And Have Not Charity, Doctor Strange, Cloak & Dagger	0.75	0.30	0.75	1.50
❑2, May 87, All In The Family; The World Well Lost For Love-!	0.75	0.25	0.63	1.25
❑3, Jun 87	0.75	0.25	0.63	1.25
❑4, Jul 87	0.75	0.25	0.63	1.25
❑5, Aug 87	0.75	0.25	0.63	1.25
❑6, Sep 87	0.75	0.25	0.63	1.25
❑7, Oct 87, Defenders	0.75	0.25	0.63	1.25
❑8, Nov 87	0.75	0.25	0.63	1.25
❑9, Dec 87	0.75	0.25	0.63	1.25
❑10, Jan 88	0.75	0.25	0.63	1.25
❑11, Feb 88	0.75	0.25	0.63	1.25
❑12, Mar 88, Black Cat	0.75	0.25	0.63	1.25
❑13, Apr 88, A: Punisher	0.75	0.35	0.88	1.75
❑14, May 88, A: Punisher	0.75	0.35	0.88	1.75
❑15, Jun 88	0.75	0.25	0.63	1.25
❑16, Jul 88	0.75	0.25	0.63	1.25
❑17, Aug 88	0.75	0.30	0.75	1.50
❑18, Sep 88, A: X-Factor, X-Factor	0.75	0.25	0.63	1.25
❑19, Oct 88, Final Issue	0.75	0.25	0.63	1.25

STRANGE TALES (3RD SERIES)
MARVEL

Value: Cover or less

- ❑1, Nov 94, KB (w), 1: Khlog; 1: Golden Gator; 1: Orrgo the Unconquerable, acetate overlay cover; prestige format 6.95

STRANGE TALES (4TH SERIES)
MARVEL

Value: Cover or less

- ❑1, Sep 98, Man-Thing: Destroyer of Worlds; Werewolf: Love is Colder Than Death, Part 2, A: Man-Thing; A: Werewolf, gatefold summary 4.99
- ❑2, Oct 98, A: Man-Thing; A: Werewolf, gatefold summary 4.99
- ❑3 .... 4.99
- ❑4 .... 4.99

STRANGE TALES: DARK CORNERS
MARVEL

Value: Cover or less

- ❑1, May 98, Cloak & Dagger: Expressway to Hell; Morbius the Living Vampire: Desiring Martine, gatefold summary 3.99

STRANGE WEATHER LATELY
METAPHROG

Value: Cover or less

- ❑1 .... 3.50
- ❑2, Dec 97 .... 3.50
- ❑3, Feb 98 .... 3.50
- ❑4 .... 3.50
- ❑5, Jun 98 .... 3.50
- ❑6, Aug 98 .... 3.50
- ❑7, Oct 98 .... 3.00
- ❑8 .... 3.00
- ❑9 .... 3.00
- ❑10, May 99 .... 3.50

STRANGE WINK (JOHN BOLTON'S...)
DARK HORSE

Value: Cover or less

- ❑1, Mar 98, b&w; Anthology ... 2.95
- ❑2, Apr 98, b&w; Anthology ... 2.95
- ❑3, May 98, b&w; Anthology ... 2.95

STRANGE WORLDS (ETERNITY)
ETERNITY

Value: Cover or less

- ❑1, b&w; Reprint 3.95

STRANGE WORLDS (NORTH COAST)
NORTH COAST STUDIOS

Value: Cover or less

- ❑1, b&w; cardstock cover; magazine 4.00

STRANGLING DESDEMONA
NINGEN MANGA

Value: Cover or less

- ❑1, b&w 2.95

STRAPPED (DERRECK WAYNE JACKSON'S...)
GOTHIC IMAGES

Value: Cover or less

- ❑1, The Confrontation Factor, Part 1 .... 2.00
- ❑2, The Confrontation Factor, Part 2 .... 2.00
- ❑3, The Confrontation Factor, Part 3 .... 2.00
- ❑4, The Confrontation Factor, Part 4 .... 2.00

STRATA
RENEGADE

	ORIG	GOOD	FINE	N-MINT
❑1, Jan 86, b&w	2.00	0.40	1.00	2.00
❑2, b&w	1.70	0.40	1.00	2.00
❑3	2.00	0.40	1.00	2.00
❑4	2.00	0.40	1.00	2.00
❑5	2.00	0.40	1.00	2.00

STRATONAUT
NIGHTWYND

Value: Cover or less

- ❑1, b&w 2.50
- ❑2, b&w 2.50
- ❑3, b&w 2.50
- ❑4, b&w 2.50

STRATOSFEAR
CALIBER

Value: Cover or less

- ❑1 .... 2.95

STRAWBERRY SHORTCAKE
MARVEL

	ORIG	GOOD	FINE	N-MINT
❑1, Apr 85, The Great Pie Baking Contest; Secret Land	0.65	0.20	0.50	1.00
❑2, Goblin' Goblin; Bigger and Bigger	0.65	0.20	0.50	1.00
❑3	0.65	0.20	0.50	1.00
❑4	0.65	0.20	0.50	1.00
❑5, Who's Your Really, Really Best Friend?	0.65	0.20	0.50	1.00
❑6	0.65	0.20	0.50	1.00
❑7	—	0.20	0.50	1.00

STRAW MEN
ALL AMERICAN

Value: Cover or less

- ❑1, b&w 1.95
- ❑2, b&w 1.95
- ❑3, b&w 1.95
- ❑4, Jan 90, The New Geneticists, b&w 1.95
- ❑5, b&w 1.95
- ❑6, b&w 1.95
- ❑7, b&w 1.95
- ❑8, b&w 1.95

STRAY BULLETS
EL CAPITAN

	ORIG	GOOD	FINE	N-MINT
❑1, The Look Of Love	2.95	1.00	2.50	5.00
❑1-2, The Look Of Love, 2nd Printing	2.95	0.60	1.50	3.00
❑, The Look Of Love, 3rd Printing; indicia says #3; third print	2.95	0.60	1.50	3.00
❑1-4, The Look Of Love, 4th Printing	2.95	0.60	1.50	3.00
❑2, Apr 95, Victimology	2.95	0.80	2.00	4.00
❑2-2, Victimology, 2nd Printing	2.95	0.60	1.50	3.00
❑2-3, Victimology, 3rd Printing	2.95	0.60	1.50	3.00
❑2-4, Victimology, 4th Printing	2.95	0.60	1.50	3.00
❑3, May 95, The Party	2.95	0.60	1.50	3.00
❑3-2, The Party, 2nd Printing	2.95	0.60	1.50	3.00
❑4, indicia contains information for issue #3	2.95	0.60	1.50	3.00
❑5, indicia contains information for issue #4	2.95	0.60	1.50	3.00
❑6, Sep 95, How I Spent My Summer Vacation or The Rocket Ship Of Life Is Goin My Way or Three Cheers For God-He's Certainly A Swell Guy or Home Is Where Mom Lives or I Don't Care, As Long As I Gots Me Space Munchies	2.95	0.60	1.50	3.00
❑7, Nov 95	2.95	0.60	1.50	3.00
❑8, Feb 96	2.95	0.60	1.50	3.00
❑9, May 96	2.95	0.60	1.50	3.00
❑10, Aug 96	2.95	0.60	1.50	3.00
❑11, Oct 96	2.95	0.59	1.48	2.95
❑12, Jan 97	2.95	0.59	1.48	2.95
❑13, Apr 97	2.95	0.59	1.48	2.95
❑14	2.95	0.59	1.48	2.95
❑15, Jul 98, Sex and Violence, part 1	2.95	0.59	1.48	2.95
❑16, Aug 98, Two-Week Vacation	2.95	0.59	1.48	2.95
❑17, Nov 98, While Ricky Fish Was Sleeping...	2.95	0.59	1.48	2.95
❑18, Feb 99	2.95	0.59	1.48	2.95
❑19, Apr 99	2.95	0.59	1.48	2.95
❑20, Jul 99	2.95	0.59	1.48	2.95

STRAY CATS
TWILIGHT TWINS

Value: Cover or less

- ❑1, Jan 99, b&w 2.50

STRAY TOASTERS
MARVEL

	ORIG	GOOD	FINE	N-MINT
❑1, BSz, BSz (w)	3.50	0.90	2.25	4.50
❑2, BSz, BSz (w)	3.50	0.90	2.25	4.50
❑3, BSz, BSz (w), Sicker Here...Than Over There	3.50	0.90	2.25	4.50
❑4, BSz, BSz (w)	3.50	0.90	2.25	4.50

STREET FIGHTER (MALIBU)
MALIBU

Value: Cover or less

- ❑1, Battle Scars 2.95
- ❑1/GO, Battle Scars, gold foil edition 15.00
- ❑2 .... 2.95
- ❑2/GO, gold foil edition 15.00
- ❑3 .... 2.95
- ❑3/GO, gold foil edition 15.00

STREETFIGHTER (OCEAN)
OCEAN

	ORIG	GOOD	FINE	N-MINT
❑1, Aug 86, Flame in the Night, 1: Streetfighter	1.75	0.40	1.00	2.00
❑2, Nov 86, The Sacrifice, 2: Streetfighter..	1.75	0.40	1.00	2.00
❑3, Feb 87	1.75	0.40	1.00	2.00
❑4, May 87	1.75	0.40	1.00	2.00

STREET FIGHTER II (TOKUMA SHOTEN)
TOKUMA SHOTEN

Value: Cover or less

- ❑1, Apr 94 .... 2.95

STREET FIGHTER II (VIZ)
VIZ

Value: Cover or less

- ❑1, Apr 94 .... 2.95
- ❑2, May 94 .... 2.95
- ❑3 .... 2.95
- ❑4 .... 2.95
- ❑5 .... 2.95
- ❑6 .... 2.95
- ❑7 .... 2.95
- ❑8 .... 2.95

ORIG GOOD FINE N-MINT

STREET FIGHTER II: THE ANIMATED MOVIE
VIZ
Value: Cover or less

❑1 .... 2.95
❑2 .... 2.95
❑3 .... 2.95
❑4 .... 2.95
❑5 .... 2.95

STREET FIGHTER: THE BATTLE FOR SHADALOO
DC
Value: Cover or less

❑1, nn; movie Adaptation; polybagged with trading card and temporary tattoos 3.95

STREET HEROES 2005
ETERNITY
Value: Cover or less

❑1, Jan 89, Night Shift, b&w ... 1.95
❑2, b&w 1.95
❑3, b&w 1.95

STREET MUSIC
FANTAGRAPHICS
Value: Cover or less

❑1, b&w 2.95
❑2, b&w 2.95
❑3, b&w 2.95
❑4, b&w 2.95
❑5, b&w 2.95
❑6, b&w 2.95

STREET POET RAY (BLACKTHORNE)
BLACKTHORNE
Value: Cover or less

❑1, Apr 89, b&w 2.00
❑2, b&w 2.00

STREETS
DC
Value: Cover or less

❑1, Tenderloin 4.95
❑2 .... 4.95
❑3 .... 4.95

STREET SHARKS
ARCHIE
Value: Cover or less

❑1, May 96 .... 1.50
❑3, Aug 96 .... 1.50

STREET SHARKS (MINI-SERIES)
ARCHIE
Value: Cover or less

❑1, Jan 96, 1: Doctor Pirahnoid; 1: The Street Sharks, based on toy line and animated series 1.50
❑2, Feb 96 .... 1.50
❑3, Mar 96, Sharkstorm 1.50

STREET WOLF
BLACKTHORNE
Value: Cover or less

❑1, Jul 86, When Angels Cry, b&w 2.00
❑2, Sep 86, Black Rain, b&w .. 2.00
❑3, b&w 2.00

STRICTLY INDEPENDENT!
ONE SHOT PRESS
Value: Cover or less

❑1, Jan 96, b&w 2.50
❑2, b&w; Flip-book; Flip Book, Elvira, Killer Clowns 2.50

STRIKE!
ECLIPSE
Value: Cover or less

❑1, Aug 87, The Inheritance, 1: Strike; O: Sgt. Strike 1.75
❑2, Sep 87, O: Sgt. Strike 1.75
❑3, Oct 87, O: Sgt. Strike 1.75
❑4, Nov 87, O: Sgt. Strike 1.75
❑5, Dec 87, O: Sgt. Strike 1.75
❑6, Feb 88, O: Sgt. Strike, Final Issue 1.75

STRIKEBACK! (IMAGE)
IMAGE
Value: Cover or less

❑1, Jan 96, Reprints Strikeback (Malibu) #1 with new cover. 2.50
❑2, Feb 96, Reprints Strikeback (Malibu) #2 with new cover. 2.50
❑3, Mar 96, Reprints Strikeback (Malibu) #3 with new cover. 2.50
❑4, Apr 96 .... 2.50
❑5, Jun 96, Final Issue 2.50
❑6 .... 2.50

STRIKEBACK! (MALIBU)
MALIBU
Value: Cover or less

❑1, Oct 94 .... 2.95
❑2, Nov 94 .... 2.95
❑3, Dec 94 .... 2.95

STRIKE FORCE AMERICA
COMICO
Value: Cover or less

❑1, Aug 92, Black Dog 2.50

STRIKE FORCE LEGACY
COMICO
Value: Cover or less

❑1 .... 3.95

STRIKEFORCE: MORITURI
MARVEL

	ORIG	GOOD	FINE	N-MINT
❑1, Dec 86, We Who Are About To Die, 1: Strikeforce: Morituri, Whilce Portacio's 1st pro work	0.75	0.40	1.00	2.00
❑2, Jan 87, BA	0.75	0.30	0.75	1.50
❑3, Feb 87, BA	0.75	0.30	0.75	1.50
❑4, Mar 87	0.75	0.35	0.88	1.75
❑5, Apr 87, BA	0.75	0.25	0.63	1.25
❑6, May 87, BA	0.75	0.25	0.63	1.25
❑7, Jun 87, BA	0.75	0.25	0.63	1.25
❑8, Jul 87, BA	0.75	0.25	0.63	1.25
❑9, Aug 87, BA	0.75	0.25	0.63	1.25
❑10, Sep 87, 1st full story by Whilce Portacio	0.75	0.25	0.63	1.25
❑11, Oct 87, BA	0.75	0.25	0.63	1.25
❑12, Nov 87, BA	0.75	0.25	0.63	1.25

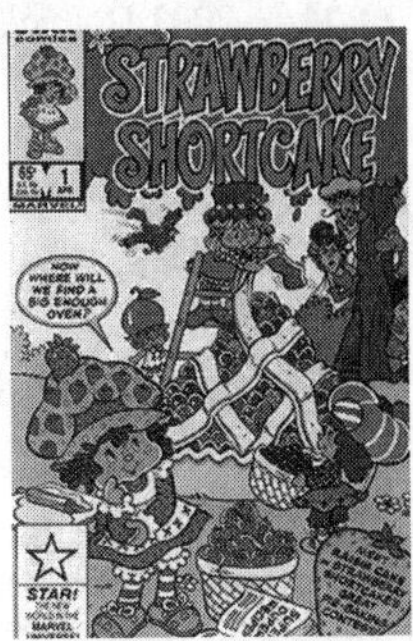

While some retailers are reporting prices of up to $10 for individual issues of *Strawberry Shortcake*, these appear to be isolated cases of collectors completing runs. The average collector has little to no interest in the title.

	ORIG	GOOD	FINE	N-MINT
❑13, Dec 87, BA, Giant-size	1.25	0.30	0.75	1.50
❑14, Jan 88, BA	0.75	0.25	0.63	1.25
❑15, Feb 88, BA	1.00	0.25	0.63	1.25
❑16, Mar 88	1.00	0.25	0.63	1.25
❑17, Apr 88	1.00	0.25	0.63	1.25
❑18, May 88, BA	1.00	0.25	0.63	1.25
❑19, Jun 88, BA	1.00	0.25	0.63	1.25
❑20, Jul 88, BA	1.00	0.25	0.63	1.25
❑21, Sep 88	1.25	0.25	0.63	1.25
❑22, Oct 88	1.25	0.25	0.63	1.25
❑23, Nov 88	1.25	0.25	0.63	1.25
❑24, Dec 88	1.50	0.30	0.75	1.50
❑25, Jan 89	1.25	0.30	0.75	1.50
❑26, Feb 89	1.50	0.30	0.75	1.50
❑27, Mar 89	1.50	0.30	0.75	1.50
❑28, Apr 89	1.50	0.30	0.75	1.50
❑29, May 89	1.50	0.30	0.75	1.50
❑30, Jun 89	1.50	0.30	0.75	1.50
❑31, Jul 89, Final Issue	1.50	0.30	0.75	1.50

STRIKEFORCE: MORITURI: ELECTRIC UNDERTOW
MARVEL
Value: Cover or less

❑1, Dec 89, Street Moves, Strikeforce: Morituri 3.95
❑2, Dec 89, Strikeforce: Morituri 3.95
❑3, Strikeforce: Morituri 3.95
❑4, Strikeforce: Morituri 3.95
❑5, Mar 90, The Battle, Strikeforce: Morituri 3.95

STRIKER
VIZ
Value: Cover or less

❑1, Overture, b&w 2.75
❑2, b&w 2.75
❑3, b&w 2.75
❑4, b&w 2.75

STRIKER: SECRET OF THE BERSERKER
VIZ
Value: Cover or less

❑1, b&w 2.75
❑2, b&w 2.75
❑3, b&w 2.75
❑4, b&w 2.75

STRIKE! VERSUS SGT. STRIKE SPECIAL
ECLIPSE
Value: Cover or less

❑1, May 88, The Man 1.95

STRIPPERS AND SEX QUEENS OF THE EXOTIC WORLD
FANTAGRAPHICS
Value: Cover or less

❑1, adult 3.95
❑2, adult 3.95
❑3, Jun 94, b&w; adult; cardstock cover 3.95
❑4, Oct 94, b&w; adult; Final Issue 3.95

STRIPS
RIP OFF
Value: Cover or less

❑1, Dec 89, b&w; adult 2.50
❑2, Feb 90, b&w; adult 2.50
❑3, Apr 90, b&w; adult 2.50
❑4, Jun 90, b&w; adult 2.50
❑5, Nov 90, b&w; adult 2.50
❑6, Dec 90, b&w; adult 2.50
❑7, Feb 91, b&w; adult 2.50
❑8, Mar 91, b&w; adult 2.50
❑9, Jun 91, b&w; adult; series goes on hiatus 2.50
❑10, b&w; adult; wraparound cover; series returns (1997). 2.95
❑11, b&w; adult; wraparound cover 2.95
❑12, b&w; adult 2.95
❑SE 1, adult; reprints Rip Off issues with additional mat erial 2.95
❑SE 2, adult; reprints Rip Off issues with additional mat erial 2.95

STRONG GUY REBORN
MARVEL
Value: Cover or less

❑1, Sep 97, The Heart of the Matter, One-Shot; gatefold summary 2.99

STRONTIUM BITCH
FLEETWAY
Value: Cover or less

❑1, AMo (w), Island of the Damned Part 1-6 .... 2.95
❑2, AMo (w), Island of the Damned Part 7-12 .... 2.95

STRONTIUM DOG
FLEETWAY

	ORIG	GOOD	FINE	N-MINT
❑1, Only The Best Survive	1.25	0.30	0.75	1.50
❑2	1.25	0.25	0.63	1.25

	ORIG	GOOD	FINE	N-MINT
❑3	1.25	0.25	0.63	1.25
❑4, The Moses Incident, Part 1	1.25	0.25	0.63	1.25
❑5	1.25	0.25	0.63	1.25
❑6, The Killing	1.25	0.25	0.63	1.25
❑7, Strontium Dog: The Killing; Strontium Dog: The Two-Faced Terror	1.25	0.25	0.63	1.25
❑8	1.25	0.25	0.63	1.25
❑9, Strontium Dog: Outlaw; Tharg's Future Shocks: With a Bang	1.25	0.25	0.63	1.25
❑10, Strontium Dog: Outlaw	1.25	0.25	0.63	1.25
❑11, Strontium Dog; Strontium Dog: The Slavers of Drule	1.25	0.25	0.63	1.25
❑12	1.25	0.25	0.63	1.25
❑13	1.50	0.30	0.75	1.50
❑14, double issue #14/15	1.50	0.30	0.75	1.50
❑15	1.50	0.30	0.75	1.50
❑16, double issue #16/17	1.50	0.30	0.75	1.50
❑17	1.50	0.30	0.75	1.50
❑18	1.50	0.30	0.75	1.50
❑19	1.50	0.30	0.75	1.50
❑20	1.50	0.30	0.75	1.50
❑21	1.50	0.30	0.75	1.50
❑22	1.50	0.30	0.75	1.50
❑23	1.50	0.30	0.75	1.50
❑24	1.50	0.30	0.75	1.50
❑25	1.50	0.30	0.75	1.50
❑26	1.50	0.30	0.75	1.50
❑27	1.50	0.30	0.75	1.50
❑28	1.50	0.30	0.75	1.50
❑29	1.50	0.30	0.75	1.50
❑SE 1, AMo (w), Strontium Dog: The Wolrogs; Grawks Bearing Gifts, Special Edition #1; Reprints from 2000 A.D. #87-94.	1.50	0.30	0.75	1.50

STRONTIUM DOG (MINI-SERIES)
EAGLE

	ORIG	GOOD	FINE	N-MINT
❑1, Strontium Dog: Portrait of a Mutant, O: Johnny Alpha	1.25	0.30	0.75	1.50
❑2, Strontium Dog: Portrait of a Mutant	1.25	0.30	0.75	1.50
❑3, Strontium Dog: Portrait of a Mutant	1.25	0.30	0.75	1.50
❑4	1.25	0.30	0.75	1.50

STRÜDEL WAR
ROUGH COPY

Value: Cover or less

- ❑1, I Am a Chimpazee; Frida and Friends: The Metallic Necklace, Flip-book ... 2.95

STRYFE'S STRIKE FILE
MARVEL

Value: Cover or less

- ❑1, Jan 93, Follows X-Cutioner's Song x-over series ... 1.75
- ❑1-2, Jan 93, 2nd Printing; Gold cover ... 1.75

STRYKE
LONDON NIGHT

	ORIG	GOOD	FINE	N-MINT
❑0, Ice...	2.95	0.60	1.50	3.00
❑0/A, Ice..., alternate cover	2.95	0.80	2.00	4.00
❑1	2.95	0.60	1.50	3.00

ST. SWITHIN'S DAY
TRIDENT

	ORIG	GOOD	FINE	N-MINT
❑1, b&w; One-Shot	2.50	0.60	1.50	3.00
❑1-2, Mar 98, b&w; 2nd Printing; One-Shot.	2.95	0.59	1.48	2.95

ST. SWITHIN'S DAY (ONI)
ONI

Value: Cover or less

- ❑1, Mar 98 ... 2.95

STUDIO COMICS PRESENTS
STUDIO

Value: Cover or less

- ❑1, May 95, Lion's Mayne, Battle Bunnies ... 2.50

STUNT DAWGS
HARVEY

Value: Cover or less

- ❑1, Mar 93, Rom Russia with Like! ... 1.25

STUPID
IMAGE

Value: Cover or less

- ❑1, May 93, Spewn, parody ... 1.95

STUPID COMICS
ONI

Value: Cover or less

- ❑1, Jul 00, nn; b&w; collects Mahfood's strips from Java Magazine ... 2.95

STUPID HEROES
MIRAGE

Value: Cover or less

- ❑1, Aug 94, Super Crooks, 1: Cinder; 1: Scott Poundstone; 1: Rock Boy; 1: Muscle Master, trading cards ... 2.75
- ❑2, Oct 94, Wall Crawling Weirdos!, 1: MISTer, trading cards ... 2.75
- ❑3, Dec 94, Betrayal!, trading cards ... 2.75

STUPIDMAN
PARODY

Value: Cover or less

- ❑1 ... 2.50

STUPIDMAN: BURIAL FOR A BUDDY
PARODY

Value: Cover or less

- ❑1/A, Gloomsday, b&w ... 2.50
- ❑1/B, b&w ... 2.50

STUPIDMAN: RAIN ON THE STUPIDMEN
PARODY

Value: Cover or less

- ❑1/A, I Am...Stupidman, b&w . 2.95
- ❑1/B, b&w ... 2.95

STUPID, STUPID RAT TAILS
CARTOON BOOKS

Value: Cover or less

- ❑1, Dec 99 ... 2.95
- ❑2 ... 2.95
- ❑3 ... 2.95

STYGMATA
EXPRESS

Value: Cover or less

- ❑0, O: Stygmata ... 2.95
- ❑1, Jul 94, b&w; enhanced cover ... 2.95
- ❑2, Paradise Remembered, 1: Savanna; 1: The Sieger; O: Stygmata, Foil-stamped cover ... 2.95
- ❑3, Oct 94, b&w ... 2.95

SUBHUMAN
DARK HORSE

Value: Cover or less

- ❑1, Nov 98 ... 2.95
- ❑2, Dec 98 ... 2.95
- ❑3, Jan 99 ... 2.95
- ❑4, Feb 99 ... 2.95

SUB-MARINER, THE (VOL. 2)
MARVEL

	ORIG	GOOD	FINE	N-MINT
❑1, May 68, JB, O: Sub-Mariner	0.12	18.00	45.00	90.00
❑2, Jun 68, JB, A: Triton	0.12	8.00	20.00	40.00
❑3, Jul 68, JB, A: Triton	0.12	4.40	11.00	22.00
❑4, Aug 68, JB	0.12	4.40	11.00	22.00
❑5, Sep 68, JB, 1: Tiger Shark	0.12	4.80	12.00	24.00
❑6, Oct 68, JB	0.12	4.40	11.00	22.00
❑7, Nov 68, JB, For President - The Man Called Destiny!, 1: Ikthon, photo background cover	0.12	4.40	11.00	22.00
❑8, Dec 68, JB, In the Rage of Battle!, V: Thing	0.12	4.40	11.00	22.00
❑8-2, JB, In the Rage of Battle!, V: The Thing, 2nd Printing	0.12	0.30	0.75	1.50
❑9, Jan 69, The Spell of the Serpent!, 1: Naga; 1: Lemuria	0.12	4.40	11.00	22.00
❑10, Feb 69, O: Naga	0.12	4.40	11.00	22.00
❑11, Mar 69	0.12	3.20	8.00	16.00
❑12, Apr 69	0.12	3.20	8.00	16.00
❑13, May 69	0.12	3.20	8.00	16.00
❑14, Jun 69, A: Human Torch; D: Toro	0.12	6.00	15.00	30.00
❑15, Jul 69	0.12	2.40	6.00	12.00
❑16, Aug 69, 1: Thakos	0.15	2.00	5.00	10.00
❑17, Sep 69, 1: Kormok	0.15	2.00	5.00	10.00
❑18, Oct 69	0.15	2.00	5.00	10.00
❑19, Nov 69, 1: Stingray	0.15	2.00	5.00	10.00
❑20, Dec 69	0.15	2.00	5.00	10.00
❑21, Jan 70	0.15	1.40	3.50	7.00
❑22, Feb 70, A: Doctor Strange	0.15	1.40	3.50	7.00
❑23, Mar 70, 1: Orka	0.15	1.40	3.50	7.00
❑24, Apr 70	0.15	1.40	3.50	7.00
❑25, May 70, O: Atlantis	0.15	1.40	3.50	7.00
❑26, Jun 70, D: Red Raven	0.15	1.40	3.50	7.00
❑27, Jul 70, SB, 1: Commander Kraken	0.15	1.40	3.50	7.00
❑28, Aug 70	0.15	1.40	3.50	7.00
❑29, Sep 70, SB, V: Hercules	0.15	1.40	3.50	7.00
❑30, Oct 70, SB, A: Captain Marvel	0.15	1.40	3.50	7.00
❑31, Nov 70	0.15	1.40	3.50	7.00
❑32, Dec 70, 1: Llyra	0.15	1.40	3.50	7.00
❑33, Jan 71, JM; SB, 1: Namora	0.15	1.40	3.50	7.00
❑34, Feb 71, JM; SB, A: Silver Surfer; A: Hulk, Leads into Defenders #1	0.15	3.00	7.50	15.00
❑35, Mar 71, JM; SB, A: Silver Surfer; A: Hulk	0.15	3.00	7.50	15.00
❑36, Apr 71, SB; BWr, 1: The Octo-Meks, Wedding of Lady Dorma	0.15	1.40	3.50	7.00
❑37, May 71, RA, The Way to Dusty Death!, D: Lady Dorma	0.15	1.40	3.50	7.00
❑38, Jun 71, RA; JSe, Namor Agonistes!, O: Sub-Mariner	0.15	1.40	3.50	7.00
❑39, Jul 71, JM; RA, ...And Here I'll Stand.	0.15	1.40	3.50	7.00
❑40, Aug 71, A: Spider-Man	0.15	1.40	3.50	7.00
❑41, Sep 71, GT	0.15	0.80	2.00	4.00
❑42, Oct 71, GT, And a House Whose Name ... is Death!	0.15	0.80	2.00	4.00
❑43, Nov 71, Giant-size	0.25	0.80	2.00	4.00
❑44, Dec 71, A: Human Torch	0.20	0.80	2.00	4.00
❑45, Jan 72	0.20	0.80	2.00	4.00
❑46, Feb 72, GC	0.20	0.80	2.00	4.00
❑47, Mar 72, GC	0.20	0.80	2.00	4.00

	ORIG	GOOD	FINE	N-MINT
❑48, Apr 72, GC	0.20	0.80	2.00	4.00
❑49, May 72, GC	0.20	0.80	2.00	4.00
❑50, Jun 72, BEv, 1: Namorita	0.20	1.40	3.50	7.00
❑51, Jul 72, BEv	0.20	0.80	2.00	4.00
❑52, Aug 72, BEv	0.20	0.80	2.00	4.00
❑53, Sep 72, BEv	0.20	0.80	2.00	4.00
❑54, Oct 72, BEv, 1: Lorvex	0.20	0.80	2.00	4.00
❑55, Nov 72, BEv	0.20	0.80	2.00	4.00
❑56, Dec 72, 1: Tamara Rahn	0.20	0.80	2.00	4.00
❑57, Jan 73	0.20	0.80	2.00	4.00
❑58, Feb 73, BEv	0.20	0.80	2.00	4.00
❑59, Mar 73, BEv	0.20	0.80	2.00	4.00
❑60, BEv	0.20	0.80	2.00	4.00
❑61	0.20	0.80	2.00	4.00
❑62	0.20	0.80	2.00	4.00
❑63, 1: Volpan; 1: Arkus	0.20	0.80	2.00	4.00
❑64, 1: Madoxx	0.20	0.80	2.00	4.00
❑65	0.20	0.80	2.00	4.00
❑66, 1: Raman	0.20	0.80	2.00	4.00
❑67	0.20	0.80	2.00	4.00
❑68	0.20	0.80	2.00	4.00
❑69	0.20	0.80	2.00	4.00
❑70	0.25	0.80	2.00	4.00
❑71	0.25	0.80	2.00	4.00
❑72, Sep 74, DA, From the Void it Came..., Final Issue	0.25	0.80	2.00	4.00
❑36740, JB, In the Rage of Battle!, V: The Thing, 2nd Printing	0.12	0.30	0.75	1.50
❑SE 1, SB, Reprint; Sub-Mariner Special Edition #1	0.25	1.20	3.00	6.00
❑SE 2, BEv, Reprint; Sub-Mariner Special Edition #2	0.25	1.20	3.00	6.00

SUBMISSIVE SUZANNE
FANTAGRAPHICS

	ORIG	GOOD	FINE	N-MINT
❑1, b&w; adult	2.50	0.50	1.25	2.50
❑2, b&w; adult	2.50	0.50	1.25	2.50
❑3, b&w; adult	—	0.59	1.48	2.95
❑4, b&w; adult	—	0.59	1.48	2.95
❑5, b&w; adult	—	0.59	1.48	2.95
❑6, Aug 98, b&w; adult	2.95	0.59	1.48	2.95

SUBSPECIES
ETERNITY

Value: Cover or less

- ❑1, May 91, Blood Feud 2.50
- ❑2 .... 2.50
- ❑3 .... 2.50
- ❑4 .... 2.50

SUBSTANCE AFFECT
CRAZYFISH

Value: Cover or less

- ❑1, Dare You Resist The Magic Pickle; Grrrl Scout 2.95

SUBSTANCE QUARTERLY
SUBSTANCE

Value: Cover or less

- ❑1, Spr 94, 1: Misfits, b&w 3.00
- ❑2, Sum 94, 1: Faerie King, b&w 3.00
- ❑3, Fal 94, The Faerie King; Misfits, 1: Platt; 1: Nash; O: Faerie King, b&w; Nash sneak peek 3.00

SUBTLE VIOLENTS
CRY FOR DAWN

	ORIG	GOOD	FINE	N-MINT
❑1, Rhyder; Ahryssia	2.50	3.00	7.50	15.00
❑1/A, Rhyder; Ahryssia, San Diego Comic-Con edition	2.50	32.00	80.00	160.00

SUBURBAN HIGH LIFE
SLAVE LABOR

Value: Cover or less

- ❑1, Jun 87, Amazing 2-D Glasses; Scientific Novelty Company 1.75
- ❑1-2, Feb 88, 2nd Printing; blue circle on front cover a darker blue 1.75
- ❑2, Aug 87, Audience Participation; House of Floyd 1.75
- ❑3, Oct 87, The Happy Homemaker; Javatown 1.75

SUBURBAN HIGH LIFE (VOL. 2)
SLAVE LABOR

Value: Cover or less

- ❑1, May 88, Oversized 5.95

SUBURBAN NIGHTMARES
RENEGADE

Value: Cover or less

- ❑1, Jul 88, Dark Secrets of Green Valley, Part 1, b&w 2.00
- ❑2, Jul 88, Dark Secrets of Green Valley, Part 2, b&w 2.00
- ❑3, Aug 88, Dark Secrets of Green Valley, Part 3; Just Another Joe, b&w 2.00
- ❑4, Aug 88, b&w 2.00

SUBURBAN SHE-DEVILS
MARVEL

Value: Cover or less

- ❑1, Jagged Image, Cover reads Suburban Jersey Ninja She-Devils 1.50

SUBURBAN VOODOO
FANTAGRAPHICS

Value: Cover or less

- ❑1, b&w 2.50

Sheldon Mayer wrote and drew the adventures of a pair of toddlers who had their own language (shared with all other babies, human and otherwise) in *Sugar & Spike*.

© 1961 National Periodical Publications (DC)

SUCCUBUS
FANTAGRAPHICS

Value: Cover or less

- ❑1, b&w; adult 2.50

SUCKER THE COMIC
TROMA

Value: Cover or less

- ❑1 .... 2.50

SUCKLE
FANTAGRAPHICS

Value: Cover or less

- ❑1, Jan 96, nn; b&w; adult; digest 14.95

SUGAR & SPIKE
DC

	ORIG	GOOD	FINE	N-MINT
❑1, May 56	0.10	230.00	575.00	1150.00
❑2, Jul 56	0.10	100.00	250.00	500.00
❑3, Sep 56	0.10	82.00	205.00	410.00
❑4, Nov 56	0.10	82.00	205.00	410.00
❑5, Jan 57	0.10	82.00	205.00	410.00
❑6, Mar 57	0.10	53.00	132.50	265.00
❑7, May 57	0.10	53.00	132.50	265.00
❑8, Jun 57	0.10	53.00	132.50	265.00
❑9, Aug 57	0.10	53.00	132.50	265.00
❑10, Sep 57	0.10	53.00	132.50	265.00
❑11, Oct 57	0.10	42.00	105.00	210.00
❑12, Dec 57	0.10	42.00	105.00	210.00
❑13, Feb 58	0.10	42.00	105.00	210.00
❑14, Mar 58	0.10	42.00	105.00	210.00
❑15, Apr 58, left-handedness	0.10	42.00	105.00	210.00
❑16, Jun 58	0.10	42.00	105.00	210.00
❑17, Aug 58	0.10	42.00	105.00	210.00
❑18, Sep 58	0.10	42.00	105.00	210.00
❑19, Oct 58	0.10	42.00	105.00	210.00
❑20, Dec 58	0.10	42.00	105.00	210.00
❑21, Mar 59	0.10	27.00	67.50	135.00
❑22, May 59	0.10	27.00	67.50	135.00
❑23, Jul 59	0.10	27.00	67.50	135.00
❑24, Sep 59	0.10	27.00	67.50	135.00
❑25, Nov 59, Halloween issue	0.10	27.00	67.50	135.00
❑26, Jan 60, Christmas issue	0.10	27.00	67.50	135.00
❑27, Mar 60, Valentine's issue	0.10	27.00	67.50	135.00
❑28, May 60	0.10	27.00	67.50	135.00
❑29, Jul 60	0.10	27.00	67.50	135.00
❑30, Sep 60	0.10	27.00	67.50	135.00
❑31, Nov 60, Halloween issue	0.10	20.00	50.00	100.00
❑32, Jan 61, Christmas issue	0.10	20.00	50.00	100.00
❑33, Mar 61	0.10	20.00	50.00	100.00
❑34, May 61	0.10	20.00	50.00	100.00
❑35, Jul 61, A: Grampa Plumm	0.10	20.00	50.00	100.00
❑36, Sep 61, The Big Yacht Race; Small War	0.10	20.00	50.00	100.00
❑37, Nov 61, Halloween issue	0.10	20.00	50.00	100.00
❑38, Jan 62, Christmas issue with Christmas cards	0.12	20.00	50.00	100.00
❑39, Mar 62, Valentine's issue with valentines	0.12	20.00	50.00	100.00
❑40, May 62, 1: Space Sprout	0.12	20.00	50.00	100.00
❑41, Jul 62	0.12	14.00	35.00	70.00
❑42, Sep 62, Vacation issue	0.12	14.00	35.00	70.00
❑43, Nov 62, Halloween issue	0.12	14.00	35.00	70.00
❑44, Jan 63, Christmas issue with Christmas cards	0.12	14.00	35.00	70.00
❑45, Mar 63, Valentine's issue with valentines	0.12	14.00	35.00	70.00
❑46, May 63, Wedding cover	0.12	14.00	35.00	70.00
❑47, Jul 63	0.12	14.00	35.00	70.00
❑48, Sep 63	0.12	14.00	35.00	70.00
❑49, Nov 63, Halloween issue	0.12	14.00	35.00	70.00
❑50, Jan 64, Christmas issue with Christmas cards	0.12	14.00	35.00	70.00
❑51, Mar 64, Valentine's issue with valentines	0.12	11.00	27.50	55.00
❑52, May 64	0.12	11.00	27.50	55.00
❑53, Jul 64	0.12	11.00	27.50	55.00
❑54, Sep 64	0.12	11.00	27.50	55.00
❑55, Nov 64, Halloween issue	0.12	11.00	27.50	55.00
❑56, Jan 65, Christmas issue with Christmas cards	0.12	11.00	27.50	55.00

	ORIG	GOOD	FINE	N-MINT
❑57, Mar 65, Valentine's issue with valentines	0.12	11.00	27.50	55.00
❑58, May 65	0.12	11.00	27.50	55.00
❑59, Jul 65	0.12	11.00	27.50	55.00
❑60, Sep 65	0.12	11.00	27.50	55.00
❑61, Nov 65, A: Uncle Charley, Halloween issue	0.12	9.00	22.50	45.00
❑62, Jan 66, Christmas issue with Christmas cards	0.12	9.00	22.50	45.00
❑63, Mar 66, Valentine's issue with valentines	0.12	9.00	22.50	45.00
❑64, May 66	0.12	9.00	22.50	45.00
❑65, Jul 66, Summer issue	0.12	9.00	22.50	45.00
❑66, Sep 66	0.12	9.00	22.50	45.00
❑67, Nov 66, Halloween issue	0.12	9.00	22.50	45.00
❑68, Jan 67, Christmas issue	0.12	9.00	22.50	45.00
❑69, Mar 67, 1: Tornado Tot	0.12	9.00	22.50	45.00
❑70, May 67, Sugar & Spike become giants	0.12	9.00	22.50	45.00
❑71, Jul 67	0.12	9.00	22.50	45.00
❑72, Sep 67, 1: Bernie the Brain	0.12	9.00	22.50	45.00
❑73, Nov 67	0.12	9.00	22.50	45.00
❑74, Jan 68	0.12	9.00	22.50	45.00
❑75, Mar 68, The Mystery of the Mischevious Marble!, 1: M.C.P. pellet	0.12	9.00	22.50	45.00
❑76, May 68	0.12	9.00	22.50	45.00
❑77, Jul 68, A: Bernie the Brain	0.12	9.00	22.50	45.00
❑78, Sep 68	0.12	9.00	22.50	45.00
❑79, Nov 68	0.12	9.00	22.50	45.00
❑80, Jan 69, A: Bernie the Brain	0.12	9.00	22.50	45.00
❑81, Mar 69	0.12	6.40	16.00	32.00
❑82, May 69, Sugar & Spike as grown-ups	0.12	6.40	16.00	32.00
❑83, Jul 69, super-powers	0.12	6.40	16.00	32.00
❑84, Sep 69, Bernie the Brain's Biggest Blunder!; Mayhem by Machine	0.15	6.40	16.00	32.00
❑85, Oct 69	0.25	6.40	16.00	32.00
❑86, Nov 69	0.15	6.40	16.00	32.00
❑87, Jan 70, 1: Marvin the Midget	0.15	6.40	16.00	32.00
❑88, Mar 70	0.15	6.40	16.00	32.00
❑89, May 70	0.15	6.40	16.00	32.00
❑90, Jul 70, 1: Flumsh	0.15	6.40	16.00	32.00
❑91, Sep 70	0.15	6.40	16.00	32.00
❑92, Nov 70	0.15	6.40	16.00	32.00
❑93, Jan 71	0.15	6.40	16.00	32.00
❑94, Mar 71, 1: Raymond	0.15	6.40	16.00	32.00
❑95, May 71	0.15	6.40	16.00	32.00
❑96, Jul 71	0.25	6.40	16.00	32.00
❑97, Sep 71	0.25	6.40	16.00	32.00
❑98, Nov 71, Final Issue	0.25	6.40	16.00	32.00

SUGAR BUZZ
SLAVE LABOR

Value: Cover or less

- ❑1, Jan 98, Valenteen in Bad Hair Day!; Mr. Extra the Super Evolved Man, b&w 2.95
- ❑2 ..... 2.95
- ❑3 ..... 2.95
- ❑4 ..... 2.95

SUGAR RAY FINHEAD
WOLF PRESS

Value: Cover or less

- ❑1 ..... 2.50
- ❑2 ..... 2.95
- ❑3 ..... 2.95
- ❑4 ..... 2.95
- ❑5 ..... 2.95
- ❑6, Jul 94 ..... 2.95
- ❑7 ..... 2.95
- ❑8 ..... 2.95
- ❑9 ..... 2.95
- ❑10, Sep 97 ..... 2.95
- ❑11, Oct 98 ..... 2.95

SUGARVIRUS
ATOMEKA

Value: Cover or less

- ❑1, nn; b&w 3.95

SUICIDE SQUAD
DC

	ORIG	GOOD	FINE	N-MINT
❑1, May 87, HC (c), Trial By Blood	0.75	0.30	0.75	1.50
❑2, Jun 87	0.75	0.25	0.63	1.25
❑3, Jul 87, V: Female Furies; D: Mindboggler	0.75	0.25	0.63	1.25
❑4, Aug 87	0.75	0.25	0.63	1.25
❑5, Sep 87	0.75	0.25	0.63	1.25
❑6, Oct 87	0.75	0.25	0.63	1.25
❑7, Nov 87	0.75	0.25	0.63	1.25
❑8, Dec 87	0.75	0.25	0.63	1.25
❑9, Jan 88, 1: Duchess, Millennium Week 4	0.75	0.25	0.63	1.25
❑10, Feb 88, A: Batman	0.75	0.25	0.63	1.25
❑11, Mar 88, A: Speedy, Vixen	0.75	0.25	0.63	1.25
❑12, Apr 88	0.75	0.25	0.63	1.25
❑13, May 88, A: Justice League International, continued from Justice League International #13; Suicide Squad view of Justice League	0.75	0.25	0.63	1.25
❑14, Jun 88, Nightshade Odyssey, Part 1	0.75	0.25	0.63	1.25
❑15, Jul 88, Nightshade Odyssey, Part 2	0.75	0.25	0.63	1.25
❑16, Aug 88, Nightshade Odyssey, Part 3, A: Shade, the Changing Man	1.00	0.20	0.50	1.00
❑17, Sep 88, V: Jihad	1.00	0.20	0.50	1.00
❑18, Oct 88, Ravan vs. Bronze Tiger	1.00	0.20	0.50	1.00
❑19, Nov 88	1.00	0.20	0.50	1.00
❑20, Dec 88	1.00	0.20	0.50	1.00
❑21, Dec 88	1.00	0.20	0.50	1.00
❑22, Jan 89	1.00	0.20	0.50	1.00
❑23, Jan 89	1.00	0.20	0.50	1.00
❑24, Feb 89	1.00	0.20	0.50	1.00
❑25, Mar 89	1.00	0.20	0.50	1.00
❑26, Apr 89	1.00	0.20	0.50	1.00
❑27, May 89, Janus Directive	1.00	0.20	0.50	1.00
❑28, May 89, Janus Directive, V: Force of July	1.00	0.20	0.50	1.00
❑29, Jun 89, Janus Directive	1.00	0.20	0.50	1.00
❑30, Jun 89, Janus Directive	1.00	0.20	0.50	1.00
❑31, Jul 89	1.00	0.20	0.50	1.00
❑32, Aug 89	1.00	0.20	0.50	1.00
❑33, Sep 89	1.00	0.20	0.50	1.00
❑34, Oct 89	1.00	0.20	0.50	1.00
❑35, Nov 89	1.00	0.20	0.50	1.00
❑36, Dec 89	1.00	0.20	0.50	1.00
❑37, Jan 90	1.00	0.20	0.50	1.00
❑38, Feb 90	1.00	0.20	0.50	1.00
❑39, Mar 90	1.00	0.20	0.50	1.00
❑40, Apr 90, Phoenix Gambit, Batman poster	1.00	0.20	0.50	1.00
❑41, May 90, Phoenix Gambit	1.00	0.20	0.50	1.00
❑42, Jun 90, Phoenix Gambit	1.00	0.20	0.50	1.00
❑43, Jul 90, Phoenix Gambit	1.00	0.20	0.50	1.00
❑44, Aug 90, Flash	1.00	0.20	0.50	1.00
❑45, Sep 90	1.00	0.20	0.50	1.00
❑46, Oct 90	1.00	0.20	0.50	1.00
❑47, Nov 90, choice Of Dooms	1.00	0.20	0.50	1.00
❑48, Dec 90, Joker	1.00	0.20	0.50	1.00
❑49, Jan 91	1.00	0.20	0.50	1.00
❑50, Feb 91	2.00	0.30	0.75	1.50
❑51, Mar 91	1.00	0.20	0.50	1.00
❑52, Apr 91	1.00	0.20	0.50	1.00
❑53, May 91	1.00	0.20	0.50	1.00
❑54, Jun 91	1.00	0.20	0.50	1.00
❑55, Jul 91	1.00	0.20	0.50	1.00
❑56, Aug 91	1.00	0.20	0.50	1.00
❑57, Sep 91	1.00	0.20	0.50	1.00
❑58, Oct 91, War of the Gods; War of the Gods, Part 16, A: Black Adam	1.00	0.20	0.50	1.00
❑59, Nov 91	1.25	0.20	0.50	1.00
❑60, Dec 91	1.25	0.20	0.50	1.00
❑61, Jan 92	1.25	0.20	0.50	1.00
❑62, Feb 92	1.25	0.20	0.50	1.00
❑63, Mar 92	1.25	0.20	0.50	1.00
❑64, Apr 92, Nasty As They Want To Be!	1.25	0.25	0.63	1.25
❑65, May 92	1.25	0.25	0.63	1.25
❑66, Jun 92, Final Issue	1.25	0.25	0.63	1.25
❑Anl 1, A: Manhunter, secret of Argent revealed	1.50	0.30	0.75	1.50

SUIT, THE
VIRTUAL

Value: Cover or less

- ❑1, May 96, digest; Invasion 3.99
- ❑2, Jun 97, Countdown, digest 3.99

SULTRY TEENAGE SUPER FOXES
SOLSON

Value: Cover or less

- ❑1, b&w 2.00
- ❑2, b&w 2.00

SUNBURN
ALTERNATIVE

Value: Cover or less

- ❑1, Aug 00, nn; b&w; smaller than normal comic book 2.95

SUN DEVILS
DC

	ORIG	GOOD	FINE	N-MINT
❑1, Jul 84, Planet Kill	1.25	0.30	0.75	1.50
❑2, Aug 84	1.50	0.30	0.75	1.50
❑3, Sep 84	1.50	0.30	0.75	1.50
❑4, Oct 84	1.50	0.30	0.75	1.50
❑5, Nov 84	1.50	0.30	0.75	1.50
❑6, Dec 84	1.50	0.30	0.75	1.50
❑7, Jan 85	1.50	0.30	0.75	1.50
❑8, Feb 85	1.50	0.30	0.75	1.50
❑9, Mar 85	1.50	0.30	0.75	1.50
❑10, Apr 85	1.50	0.30	0.75	1.50
❑11, May 85	1.50	0.30	0.75	1.50
❑12, Jun 85	1.50	0.30	0.75	1.50

SUNFIRE & BIG HERO SIX
MARVEL

Value: Cover or less

- ❑1, Sep 98, Land of the Rising Sun, Part 1, A: Silver Samurai; A: Hiro; A: Baymax; A: Gogo Tomago; A: Honey Lemon 2.50
- ❑2, Oct 98, Land of the Rising Sun, Part 2, A: Silver Samurai; A: Hiro; A: Baymax; A: Gogo Tomago; A: Honey Lemon 2.50
- ❑3, Nov 98, Land of the Rising Sun, Part 3, A: Silver Samurai; A: Hiro; A: Baymax; A: Gogo Tomago; A: Honey Lemon 2.50

SUNGLASSES AFTER DARK
VEROTIK

Value: Cover or less

Issue	Value
❑1	5.00
❑2	3.50
❑3	3.50

SUNRISE
HARRIER

Value: Cover or less

Issue	Value
❑1	1.95
❑2, May 87	1.95

SUN-RUNNERS
PACIFIC

Value: Cover or less

Issue	Value
❑1, Feb 84, PB	1.50
❑2, Mar 84, PB	1.50
❑3, May 84, PB	1.50
❑4	1.75
❑5	1.75
❑6	1.75
❑7, Final Issue	1.75
❑HS 1, Double-size	1.95
❑SE 1, Special edition	1.95

SUPERBOY (1ST SERIES)
DC

	ORIG	GOOD	FINE	N-MINT
❑86, Jan 61, A: Legion of Super-Heroes; 1: Pete Ross	0.10	25.00	62.50	125.00
❑87, Mar 61	0.10	10.40	26.00	52.00
❑88, Apr 61	0.10	10.40	26.00	52.00
❑89, Jun 61, 1: Mon-El	0.10	44.00	110.00	220.00
❑90, Jul 61	0.10	9.60	24.00	48.00
❑91, Sep 61	0.10	9.60	24.00	48.00
❑92, Oct 61	0.10	9.60	24.00	48.00
❑93, Dec 61, A: Legion of Super-Heroes	0.12	9.60	24.00	48.00
❑94, Jan 62	0.12	7.00	17.50	35.00
❑95, Mar 62	0.12	7.00	17.50	35.00
❑96, Apr 62	0.12	7.00	17.50	35.00
❑97, Jun 62	0.12	7.00	17.50	35.00
❑98, Jul 62, 1: Ultra Boy; A: Legion of Super-Heroes	0.12	9.00	22.50	45.00
❑99, Sep 62	0.12	7.00	17.50	35.00
❑100, Oct 62, A: Legion of Super-Heroes; 1: Phantom Zone villains, 100th anniversary issue	0.12	35.00	87.50	175.00
❑101, Dec 62	0.12	3.20	8.00	16.00
❑102, Jan 63, Superbaby back-up	0.12	3.20	8.00	16.00
❑103, Mar 63, Red K story	0.12	3.20	8.00	16.00
❑104, Apr 63, O: Phantom Zone	0.12	3.20	8.00	16.00
❑105, Jun 63	0.12	3.20	8.00	16.00
❑106, Jul 63	0.12	3.20	8.00	16.00
❑107, Sep 63	0.12	3.20	8.00	16.00
❑108, Oct 63	0.12	3.20	8.00	16.00
❑109, Dec 63	0.12	3.20	8.00	16.00
❑110, Jan 64	0.12	3.20	8.00	16.00
❑111, Mar 64	0.12	3.00	7.50	15.00
❑112, Apr 64	0.12	3.00	7.50	15.00
❑113, Jun 64	0.12	3.00	7.50	15.00
❑114, Jul 64	0.12	3.00	7.50	15.00
❑115, Sep 64, Atomic Superboy	0.12	3.00	7.50	15.00
❑116, Oct 64, Superboy, King of the Wolf-Pack!; The False Superboy of Smallville!	0.12	3.00	7.50	15.00
❑117, Dec 64, A: Legion	0.12	3.00	7.50	15.00
❑118, Jan 65	0.12	3.00	7.50	15.00
❑119, Mar 65	0.12	3.00	7.50	15.00
❑120, Apr 65	0.12	3.00	7.50	15.00
❑121, Jun 65, Clark loses his super-powers; Jor-El back-up	0.12	2.00	5.00	10.00
❑122, Jul 65	0.12	2.00	5.00	10.00
❑123, Sep 65	0.12	2.00	5.00	10.00
❑124, Oct 65, 1: Insect Queen	0.12	2.00	5.00	10.00
❑125, Dec 65, 1: Kid Psycho	0.12	2.00	5.00	10.00
❑126, Jan 66, O: Krypto	0.12	2.00	5.00	10.00
❑127, Mar 66	0.12	2.00	5.00	10.00
❑128, Apr 66, A: Kryptonite Kid; A: Dev-Em, Imaginary Story	0.12	2.00	5.00	10.00
❑129, May 66, Giant-size	0.25	2.60	6.50	13.00
❑130, Jun 66, Superbaby	0.12	1.60	4.00	8.00
❑131, Jul 66	0.12	1.60	4.00	8.00
❑132, Sep 66	0.12	1.60	4.00	8.00
❑133, Oct 66, A: Robin	0.12	1.60	4.00	8.00
❑134, Dec 66, Krypto back-up	0.12	1.60	4.00	8.00
❑135, Jan 67	0.12	1.60	4.00	8.00
❑136, Mar 67	0.12	1.60	4.00	8.00
❑137, Apr 67	0.12	1.60	4.00	8.00
❑138, Jun 67, Giant-size	0.25	2.60	6.50	13.00
❑139, Jun 67	0.12	1.40	3.50	7.00
❑140, Jul 67	0.12	1.40	3.50	7.00
❑141, Sep 67	0.12	1.20	3.00	6.00
❑142, Oct 67, A: Beppo	0.12	1.20	3.00	6.00
❑143, Dec 67, NA (c)	0.12	1.20	3.00	6.00
❑144, Jan 68, CS (c)	0.12	1.20	3.00	6.00
❑145, Mar 68, NA (c)	0.12	1.20	3.00	6.00
❑146, Apr 68, NA (c)	0.12	1.20	3.00	6.00

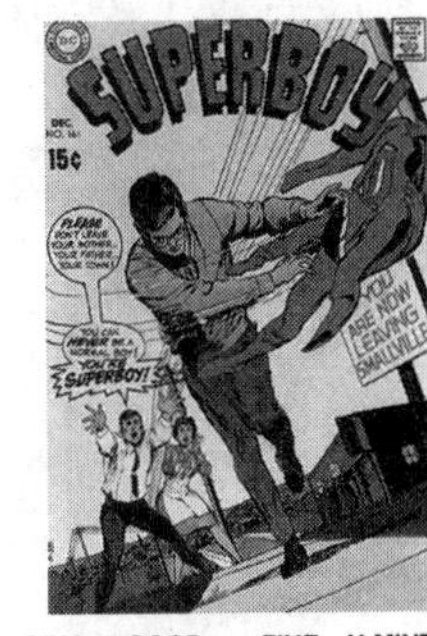

To become a "normal" teen-ager, Clark Kent stripped himself of his super-powers in *Superboy* (1st series) #161.

© 1969 National Periodical Publications (DC)

	ORIG	GOOD	FINE	N-MINT
❑147, Jun 68, O: Cosmic Boy; O: Saturn Girl, Giant-size	0.25	2.00	5.00	10.00
❑148, Jun 68, NA (c)	0.12	1.20	3.00	6.00
❑149, Jul 68, NA (c)	0.12	1.20	3.00	6.00
❑150, Sep 68, NA (c), V: Mr. Cipher	0.12	1.20	3.00	6.00
❑151, Oct 68, NA (c)	0.12	1.20	3.00	6.00
❑152, Dec 68, WW, NA (c)	0.12	1.20	3.00	6.00
❑153, Jan 69, WW, NA (c), FR (w), Challenge of the Cosmic Invaders!	0.12	1.20	3.00	6.00
❑154, Mar 69, WW, NA (c)	0.12	1.20	3.00	6.00
❑155, Apr 69, WW, NA (c)	0.12	1.20	3.00	6.00
❑156, Jun 69, Giant-size	0.25	1.80	4.50	9.00
❑157, Jun 69, WW	0.12	1.20	3.00	6.00
❑158, Jul 69, WW	0.15	1.20	3.00	6.00
❑159, Sep 69, WW	0.15	1.20	3.00	6.00
❑160, Oct 69, WW	0.15	1.20	3.00	6.00
❑161, Dec 69, WW, FR (w), The Strange Death Of Superboy!	0.15	1.20	3.00	6.00
❑162, Jan 70	0.15	1.20	3.00	6.00
❑163, Mar 70, NA (c)	0.15	1.20	3.00	6.00
❑164, Apr 70, NA (c)	0.15	1.20	3.00	6.00
❑165, Jun 70, Giant-size	0.25	1.80	4.50	9.00
❑166, Jun 70, NA (c)	0.15	1.20	3.00	6.00
❑167, Jul 70, NA (c)	0.15	1.20	3.00	6.00
❑168, Sep 70, NA (c)	0.15	1.20	3.00	6.00
❑169, Oct 70	0.15	1.20	3.00	6.00
❑170, Dec 70	0.15	1.20	3.00	6.00
❑171, Jan 71	0.15	0.80	2.00	4.00
❑172, Mar 71, A: Legion of Super-Heroes	0.15	1.00	2.50	5.00
❑173, Apr 71, DG; GT, NA (c), O: Cosmic Boy	0.15	0.80	2.00	4.00
❑174, Jun 71, Giant-size; reprints Adventure #219, #225, and #262, Superboy #53 and #105	0.25	1.40	3.50	7.00
❑175, Jun 71, MA, NA (c)	0.15	0.80	2.00	4.00
❑176, Jul 71, WW; GT; MA, NA (c), A: Legion of Super-Heroes	0.15	0.80	2.00	4.00
❑177, Sep 71, MA, Giant-size	0.25	0.80	2.00	4.00
❑178, Oct 71, MA, NA (c), Giant-size	0.25	0.80	2.00	4.00
❑179, Nov 71, Giant-size	0.25	0.80	2.00	4.00
❑180, Dec 71, Giant-size	0.25	0.80	2.00	4.00
❑181, Jan 72, Giant-size; reprints Adventure #355	0.25	0.80	2.00	4.00
❑182, Feb 72, Giant-size	0.25	0.80	2.00	4.00
❑183, Mar 72, Giant-size	0.25	0.80	2.00	4.00
❑184, Apr 72, O: Dial "H" For Hero, Giant-size	0.25	0.80	2.00	4.00
❑185, May 72, A: Legion of Super-Heroes, wraparound cover; a.k.a. DC 100-Page Super Spectacular #185	0.50	0.80	2.00	4.00
❑186, May 72	0.25	0.80	2.00	4.00
❑187, Jun 72	0.25	0.80	2.00	4.00
❑188, Jul 72, O: Karkan	0.20	0.80	2.00	4.00
❑189, Aug 72	0.20	0.80	2.00	4.00
❑190, Sep 72	0.20	0.80	2.00	4.00
❑191, Oct 72, O: Sunboy	0.20	0.80	2.00	4.00
❑192, Dec 72, Superbaby	0.20	0.80	2.00	4.00
❑193, Feb 73	0.20	0.80	2.00	4.00
❑194, Apr 73	0.20	0.80	2.00	4.00
❑195, Jun 73, 1: Wildfire; A: Legion of Super-Heroes, Wildfire joins team	0.20	0.80	2.00	4.00
❑196, Jul 73, last Superboy solo story	0.20	0.80	2.00	4.00
❑197, Sep 73, MA, Legion of Super-Heroes stories begin	0.20	1.20	3.00	6.00
❑198, Oct 73, V: Fatal Five	0.20	0.80	2.00	4.00
❑199, Nov 73	0.20	0.80	2.00	4.00
❑200, Feb 74, Wedding of Bouncing Boy and Duo Damsel	0.20	1.20	3.00	6.00
❑201, Apr 74	0.20	0.60	1.50	3.00
❑202, Jun 74, 100pgs.	0.60	0.60	1.50	3.00
❑203, Aug 74, D: Invisible Kid I (Lyle Norg); V: Validus	0.20	0.60	1.50	3.00
❑204, Oct 74, 1: Anti Lad	0.20	0.60	1.50	3.00
❑205, Dec 74, 100pgs.; reprints Superboy #88, Adventure #350 and #351	0.60	0.60	1.50	3.00

	ORIG	GOOD	FINE	N-MINT
❑206, Jan 75	0.25	0.60	1.50	3.00
❑207, Feb 75	0.25	0.60	1.50	3.00
❑208, Apr 75	0.50	0.60	1.50	3.00
❑209, Jun 75	0.25	0.60	1.50	3.00
❑210, Aug 75, O: Karate Kid	0.25	0.60	1.50	3.00
❑211, Sep 75, A: Legion Subs	0.25	0.60	1.50	3.00
❑212, Oct 75, Matter-Eater Lad leaves team	0.25	0.60	1.50	3.00
❑213, Dec 75, A: Miracle Machine	0.25	0.60	1.50	3.00
❑214, Jan 76	0.25	0.60	1.50	3.00
❑215, Mar 76	0.25	0.60	1.50	3.00
❑216, Apr 76, 1: Tyroc	0.30	0.60	1.50	3.00
❑217, Jun 76, 1: Laurel Kent	0.30	0.60	1.50	3.00
❑218, Jul 76, Tyroc joins team	0.30	0.60	1.50	3.00
❑219, Sep 76, V: Fatal Five	0.30	0.60	1.50	3.00
❑220, Oct 76	0.30	0.60	1.50	3.00
❑221, Nov 76, 1: Grimbor; 1: Charma	0.30	0.40	1.00	2.00
❑222, Dec 76	0.30	0.40	1.00	2.00
❑223, Jan 77, 1: Pulsar Stargrave; V: Time Trapper	0.30	0.40	1.00	2.00
❑224, Feb 77, V: Stargrave	0.30	0.40	1.00	2.00
❑225, Mar 77, 1: Dawnstar	0.30	0.40	1.00	2.00
❑226, Apr 77, Dawnstar joins team; Stargrave's identity revealed	0.30	0.40	1.00	2.00
❑227, May 77	0.30	0.40	1.00	2.00
❑228, Jun 77, D: Chemical King	0.35	0.40	1.00	2.00
❑229, Jul 77	0.35	0.40	1.00	2.00
❑230, Aug 77, Bouncing Boy's powers restored; series continues as Superboy and the Legion of Super-Heroes	0.35	0.40	1.00	2.00
❑Anl 1, Sum 64	0.25	27.00	67.50	135.00
❑SP 1, pin-up back cover; Reprint; Superboy Spectacular; giant	1.00	0.60	1.50	3.00

SUPERBOY (2ND SERIES)
DC

	ORIG	GOOD	FINE	N-MINT
❑1, Jan 90, JM, The Superboy, Photo cover from TV show	1.00	0.40	1.00	2.00
❑2, Feb 90	1.00	0.30	0.75	1.50
❑3, Mar 90	1.00	0.30	0.75	1.50
❑4, Apr 90	1.00	0.30	0.75	1.50
❑5, May 90	1.00	0.30	0.75	1.50
❑6, Jun 90	1.00	0.30	0.75	1.50
❑7, Jul 90	1.00	0.30	0.75	1.50
❑8, Aug 90, Bizarro	1.00	0.30	0.75	1.50
❑9, Sep 90, CS	1.00	0.30	0.75	1.50
❑10, Oct 90, CS	1.00	0.30	0.75	1.50
❑11, Nov 90, CS	1.00	0.30	0.75	1.50
❑12, Dec 90, CS	1.00	0.30	0.75	1.50
❑13, Jan 91, Mxyzptlk	1.00	0.30	0.75	1.50
❑14, Feb 91, V: Brimstone	1.00	0.30	0.75	1.50
❑15, Mar 91	1.00	0.30	0.75	1.50
❑16, Apr 91, A: Superman	1.25	0.30	0.75	1.50
❑17, May 91	1.25	0.30	0.75	1.50
❑18, Jun 91, Series continued in Adventures of Superboy #19	1.25	0.30	0.75	1.50
❑19, Aug 91, Title changes to The Adventures of Superboy	1.25	0.20	0.50	1.00

SUPERBOY (3RD SERIES)
DC

	ORIG	GOOD	FINE	N-MINT
❑0, Oct 94, O: Superboy (clone)	1.50	0.40	1.00	2.00
❑1, Feb 94, Trouble In Paradise	1.50	0.50	1.25	2.50
❑2, Mar 94, 1: Knockout; 1: Scavenger	1.50	0.40	1.00	2.00
❑3, Apr 94, V: Scavenger	1.50	0.40	1.00	2.00
❑4, May 94	1.50	0.40	1.00	2.00
❑5, Jun 94	1.50	0.40	1.00	2.00
❑6, Jul 94, Worlds Collide, Part 3; Worlds Collide, Part 1, crossover with Milestone Media	1.50	0.40	1.00	2.00
❑7, Aug 94, Worlds Collide, Part 8; Menace 2 Societies!, crossover with Milestone Media	1.50	0.40	1.00	2.00
❑8, Sep 94, Zero Hour; meets original Superboy	1.50	0.40	1.00	2.00
❑9, Nov 94	1.50	0.40	1.00	2.00
❑10, Dec 94	1.50	0.40	1.00	2.00
❑11, Jan 95, Reality Bites!	1.50	0.40	1.00	2.00
❑12, Feb 95	1.50	0.40	1.00	2.00
❑13, Mar 95, Watery Grave, Part 1	1.50	0.40	1.00	2.00
❑14, Apr 95, Watery Grave, Part 2	1.50	0.40	1.00	2.00
❑15, May 95, Watery Grave, Part 3	1.50	0.40	1.00	2.00
❑16, Jun 95, V: Loose Cannon	1.95	0.40	1.00	2.00
❑17, Jul 95	1.95	0.40	1.00	2.00
❑18, Aug 95, V: Valor	1.95	0.40	1.00	2.00
❑19, Sep 95, Valor enters Phantom Zone	1.95	0.40	1.00	2.00
❑20, Oct 95, A: Green Lantern	1.95	0.40	1.00	2.00
❑21, Nov 95, Future Tense, Part 1, continues in Legion of Super-Heroes #74	1.95	0.40	1.00	2.00
❑22, Dec 95, A: Killer Frost, Underworld Unleashed	1.95	0.40	1.00	2.00
❑23, Jan 96	1.95	0.40	1.00	2.00
❑24, Feb 96, Like Damocles' Sword, V: Silver Sword, Knockout's past revealed	1.95	0.40	1.00	2.00
❑25, Mar 96, Losin' It, Part 1, Giant-size	2.95	0.60	1.50	3.00
❑26, Apr 96, Losin' It, Part 2	1.95	0.40	1.00	2.00
❑27, May 96, Losin' It, Part 3	1.95	0.40	1.00	2.00
❑28, Jun 96, Losin' It, Part 4, A: Supergirl	1.95	0.40	1.00	2.00
❑29, Jul 96, Losin' It, Part 5	1.95	0.40	1.00	2.00
❑30, Aug 96, Losin' It, Part 6, Knockout captured	1.95	0.40	1.00	2.00
❑31, Sep 96	1.95	0.40	1.00	2.00
❑32, Oct 96, So, Tell me about Superboy, O: Superboy	1.95	0.40	1.00	2.00
❑33, Nov 96, Running Hot and Cold, Final Night	1.95	0.40	1.00	2.00
❑34, Dec 96, Going Mental, Dubbilex regains powers	1.95	0.40	1.00	2.00
❑35, Jan 97, Kidnapped!, 1: The Agenda	1.95	0.40	1.00	2.00
❑36, Feb 97, Grudge Match, V: Match	1.95	0.40	1.00	2.00
❑37, Mar 97, SB, Sledge-Hammered!	1.95	0.40	1.00	2.00
❑38, Apr 97, Meltdown, Part 1	1.95	0.40	1.00	2.00
❑39, May 97, Meltdown, Part 2	1.95	0.40	1.00	2.00
❑40, Jun 97, Meltdown, Part 3, continues in Superboy & the Ravers #10	1.95	0.40	1.00	2.00
❑41, Jul 97, Meltdown: The Cure	1.95	0.40	1.00	2.00
❑42, Aug 97	1.95	0.40	1.00	2.00
❑43, Sep 97	1.95	0.40	1.00	2.00
❑44, Oct 97, Superboy goes to timeless island	1.95	0.40	1.00	2.00
❑45, Nov 97, Invaders from the Future!, A: Legion of Super-Heroes; V: Silver Sword	1.95	0.40	1.00	2.00
❑46, Dec 97, Sword Play, Face cover	1.95	0.40	1.00	2.00
❑47, Jan 98, A: Green Lantern	1.95	0.40	1.00	2.00
❑48, Feb 98	1.95	0.40	1.00	2.00
❑49, Mar 98	1.95	0.40	1.00	2.00
❑50, Apr 98, Last Boy on Earth, Part 1	1.95	0.40	1.00	2.00
❑51, May 98, Last Boy on Earth, Part 2	1.95	0.39	0.98	1.95
❑52, Jun 98, Last Boy on Earth, Part 3, Superboy returns to Hawaii	1.95	0.39	0.98	1.95
❑53, Jul 98, Last Boy on Earth, Part 4	1.95	0.39	0.98	1.95
❑54, Aug 98, A: Guardian	1.95	0.39	0.98	1.95
❑55, Sep 98, 1: new Hex; V: Grokk	1.99	0.39	0.98	1.95
❑56, Oct 98, Mechanic takes over Cadmus	1.99	0.39	0.98	1.95
❑57, Dec 98, Demolition Run	1.99	0.40	1.00	1.99
❑58, Jan 99, Demolition Run	1.99	0.40	1.00	1.99
❑59, Feb 99, A: Project: Cadmus; A: Superman, on Krypton	1.99	0.40	1.00	1.99
❑60, Mar 99, Hyper-Tension, Part 1	1.99	0.40	1.00	1.99
❑61, Apr 99, Hyper-Tension, Part 2, learns Superman's identity	1.99	0.40	1.00	1.99
❑62, May 99, Hyper-Tension, Part 3, O: Black Zero	1.99	0.40	1.00	1.99
❑63, Jun 99, Hyper-Tension, Part 4, V: Doomsdays	1.99	0.40	1.00	1.99
❑64, Jul 99, Hyper-Tension, Part 5	1.99	0.40	1.00	1.99
❑65, Aug 99, Hyper-Tension, Part 6, A: Damage; A: Hero Hotline; A: Robin; A: Creeper; A: Impulse; A: Green Lantern; A: Inferno; A: Steel; A: Metal Men	1.99	0.40	1.00	1.99
❑66, Sep 99, Wild Hunt, back to Wild Lands	1.99	0.40	1.00	1.99
❑67, Oct 99, Tooth & Claw, V: King Shark	1.99	0.40	1.00	1.99
❑68, Nov 99	1.99	0.40	1.00	1.99
❑69, Dec 99, Hawaii-Hana Hou!	1.99	0.40	1.00	1.99
❑70, Jan 00, The Evil Factory, Part 1	1.99	0.40	1.00	1.99
❑71, Feb 00, The Evil Factory, Part 2	1.99	0.40	1.00	1.99
❑72, Mar 00, The Evil Factory, Part 3	1.99	0.40	1.00	1.99
❑73, Apr 00, The Evil Factory, Part 4	1.99	0.40	1.00	1.99
❑74, May 00, Game, Set & Match!, Sins of Youth	1.99	0.40	1.00	1.99
❑75, Jun 00	—	0.40	1.00	1.99
❑76, Jul 00	—	0.40	1.00	1.99
❑77, Aug 00	—	0.40	1.00	1.99
❑78, Sep 00, Give Me Liberty...!	2.25	0.45	1.13	2.25
❑79, Oct 00, The Power & The Prize!	2.25	0.45	1.13	2.25
❑80, Nov 00, Boiling Point	2.25	0.45	1.13	2.25
❑81, Dec 00, Fever Pitch	2.25	0.45	1.13	2.25
❑82, Jan 01, Power Lunch	2.25	0.45	1.13	2.25
❑83, Feb 01, How Kon-El Got His Groove Back	2.25	0.45	1.13	2.25
❑84, Mar 01, Smells Like Rage	2.25	0.45	1.13	2.25
❑85, Apr 01, Silent, But Deadly	2.25	0.45	1.13	2.25
❑86, May 01, Southern Cookin'	2.25	0.45	1.13	2.25
❑87	2.25	0.45	1.13	2.25
❑88	2.25	0.45	1.13	2.25
❑89	2.25	0.45	1.13	2.25
❑90	2.25	0.45	1.13	2.25
❑1000000, Nov 98, Omac: One Million and Counting	1.99	0.40	1.00	2.00

	ORIG	GOOD	FINE	N-MINT
❑Anl 1, Elseworlds; concludes story from Adventures of Superman Annual #6	2.95	0.60	1.50	3.00
❑Anl 2, Year One; Identity of being who Superboy was cloned from is revealed	3.95	0.80	2.00	4.00
❑Anl 3, Legends of the Dead Earth	2.95	0.59	1.48	2.95
❑Anl 4, Pulp Heroes	3.95	0.79	1.98	3.95

SUPERBOY AND THE LEGION OF SUPER-HEROES
DC

	ORIG	GOOD	FINE	N-MINT
❑231, Sep 77, V: Fatal Five	0.60	0.40	1.00	2.00
❑232, Oct 77	0.60	0.40	1.00	2.00
❑233, Nov 77, 1: Infinite Man	0.60	0.40	1.00	2.00
❑234, Dec 77	0.60	0.40	1.00	2.00
❑235, Jan 78	0.60	0.40	1.00	2.00
❑236, Feb 78	0.60	0.40	1.00	2.00
❑237, Mar 78, Saturn Girl leaves team; Lightning Lad leaves team	0.60	0.40	1.00	2.00
❑238, Apr 78, wraparound cover; reprints Adventure Comics #359 and 360	0.60	0.40	1.00	2.00
❑239, May 78	0.60	0.40	1.00	2.00
❑240, Jun 78, O: Dawnstar; V: Grimbor	0.60	0.40	1.00	2.00
❑241, Jul 78	0.60	0.40	1.00	2.00
❑242, Aug 78	0.60	0.40	1.00	2.00
❑243, Sep 78, A: Legion Subs	0.50	0.40	1.00	2.00
❑244, Oct 78, Mordru returns	0.50	0.40	1.00	2.00
❑245, Nov 78, Lightning Lad and Saturn Girl rejoin	0.50	0.40	1.00	2.00
❑246, Dec 78	0.40	0.40	1.00	2.00
❑247, Jan 79	0.40	0.40	1.00	2.00
❑248, Feb 79	0.40	0.40	1.00	2.00
❑249, Mar 79	0.40	0.40	1.00	2.00
❑250, Apr 79	0.40	0.40	1.00	2.00
❑251, May 79	0.40	0.30	0.75	1.50
❑252, Jun 79	0.40	0.30	0.75	1.50
❑253, Jul 79, V: League of Super-Assassins; 1: Blok	0.40	0.30	0.75	1.50
❑254, Aug 79	0.40	0.30	0.75	1.50
❑255, Sep 79, Legion visits Krypton before it's destroyed	0.40	0.30	0.75	1.50
❑256, Oct 79, O: Brainiac 5	0.40	0.30	0.75	1.50
❑257, Nov 79, SD, Return of Bouncing Boy; Return of Duo Damsel	0.40	0.30	0.75	1.50
❑258, Dec 79, V: Psycho Warrior, series continues as Legion of Super-Heroes	0.40	0.30	0.75	1.50

SUPERBOY & THE RAVERS
DC

	ORIG	GOOD	FINE	N-MINT
❑1, Sep 96, House Rules, Part 1	1.95	0.50	1.25	2.50
❑2, Oct 96, House Rules, Part 2	1.95	0.40	1.00	2.00
❑3, Nov 96, House Rules, Part 3, 1: Half-Life	1.95	0.40	1.00	2.00
❑4, Dec 96, House Rules, Part 4	1.95	0.40	1.00	2.00
❑5, Jan 97, Dial "X" for X-Mas, V: Scavenger	1.95	0.40	1.00	2.00
❑6, Feb 97, Truth or Dare	1.95	0.40	1.00	2.00
❑7, Mar 97, Road Trip, Part 1, A: Impulse	1.95	0.40	1.00	2.00
❑8, Apr 97, Road Trip, Part 2, A: Warrior	1.95	0.40	1.00	2.00
❑9, May 97, Road Trip, Part 3, A: Superman	1.95	0.40	1.00	2.00
❑10, Jun 97, Meltdown, Part 4, continued from Superboy #40	1.95	0.40	1.00	2.00
❑11, Jul 97	1.95	0.40	1.00	2.00
❑12, Aug 97	1.95	0.40	1.00	2.00
❑13, Sep 97	1.95	0.40	1.00	2.00
❑14, Oct 97, V: Female Furies, Genesis	1.95	0.40	1.00	2.00
❑15, Nov 97, Edge of the Event Horizon	1.95	0.40	1.00	2.00
❑16, Dec 97, Half-Life of the Party!	1.95	0.40	1.00	2.00
❑17, Jan 98	1.95	0.40	1.00	2.00
❑18, Feb 98	1.95	0.40	1.00	2.00
❑19, Mar 98, Final Issue	1.95	0.40	1.00	2.00

SUPERBOY PLUS
DC

Value: Cover or less

❑1, Jan 97, Junior Partners, A: Captain Marvel Jr. 2.95

❑2, Fal 97, A: Slither, continues in Catwoman Plus #1 .... 2.95

SUPERBOY/RISK DOUBLE-SHOT
DC

Value: Cover or less

❑1, Feb 98 .... 1.95

SUPERBOY/ROBIN: WORLD'S FINEST THREE
DC

Value: Cover or less

❑1, V: Poison Ivy; V: Metallo, prestige format 4.95

❑2, V: Poison Ivy; V: Metallo, prestige format 4.95

SUPERBOY'S LEGION
DC

Value: Cover or less

❑1 .... 5.95

❑2 .... 5.95

SUPERCOPS
NOW

Value: Cover or less

❑1, Sep 90, double-sized 2.75

❑2, Oct 90, 2nd Generation 1.75

❑3, Nov 90 .... 1.75

❑4, Feb 91 .... 1.75

The two-issue Elseworlds series *Superboy's Legion* featured R.J. Brande finding Superboy's rocket in the 30th century.

© 2001 DC Comics

SUPER COPS, THE
RED CIRCLE

	ORIG	GOOD	FINE	N-MINT
❑1, GM, Crime Is Out Of Fashion	0.25	0.40	1.00	2.00

SUPER DC GIANT
DC

	ORIG	GOOD	FINE	N-MINT
❑13, Oct 70, really S-13; Binky	—	15.00	37.50	75.00
❑14, Oct 70, really S-14; Westerns	0.25	6.00	15.00	30.00
❑15, Oct 70, really S-15; Westerns	0.25	6.00	15.00	30.00
❑16, Oct 70, really S-16; Brave & the Bold	0.25	6.00	15.00	30.00
❑17, really S-17; Romance	—	20.00	50.00	100.00
❑18, really S-18; Three Mouseketeers	—	10.00	25.00	50.00
❑19, really S-19; Jerry Lewis	—	10.00	25.00	50.00
❑20, really S-20; House of Mystery	—	8.00	20.00	40.00
❑21, really S-21; Romance	—	30.00	75.00	150.00
❑22, Mar 71, really S-22; Westerns	0.25	5.00	12.50	25.00
❑23, really S-23; Unexpected	—	6.00	15.00	30.00
❑24, May 71, really S-24; Supergirl	0.25	6.00	15.00	30.00
❑25, Aug 71, really S-25; Challengers of the Unknown	0.25	5.00	12.50	25.00
❑26, Aug 71, really S-26; Aquaman	0.25	5.00	12.50	25.00
❑27, Sum 76, Flying Saucers	—	3.00	7.50	15.00

SUPERFAN
MARK 1

Value: Cover or less

❑1, b&w 1.95

SUPERFIST AYUMI
EROS

Value: Cover or less

❑1 .... 2.95

❑2 .... 2.95

SUPER FRIENDS
DC

	ORIG	GOOD	FINE	N-MINT
❑1, Nov 76	0.30	1.00	2.50	5.00
❑2, Dec 76	0.30	0.40	1.00	2.00
❑3, Feb 77	0.30	0.40	1.00	2.00
❑4, Apr 77	0.30	0.40	1.00	2.00
❑5, Jun 77	0.35	0.40	1.00	2.00
❑6, Aug 77	0.35	0.40	1.00	2.00
❑7, Oct 77, 1: Tasmanian Devil; 1: Wonder Twins	0.35	0.40	1.00	2.00
❑8, Nov 77	0.35	0.40	1.00	2.00
❑9, Dec 77, 1: Iron Maiden	0.35	0.40	1.00	2.00
❑10, Mar 78	0.35	0.40	1.00	2.00
❑11, May 78	0.35	0.30	0.75	1.50
❑12, Jul 78, 1: Doctor Mist	0.35	0.30	0.75	1.50
❑13, Sep 78	0.35	0.30	0.75	1.50
❑14, Nov 78	0.50	0.30	0.75	1.50
❑15, Dec 78	0.40	0.30	0.75	1.50
❑16, Jan 79	0.40	0.30	0.75	1.50
❑17, Feb 79	0.40	0.30	0.75	1.50
❑18, Mar 79	0.40	0.30	0.75	1.50
❑19, Apr 79	0.40	0.30	0.75	1.50
❑20, May 79	0.40	0.30	0.75	1.50
❑21, Jun 79	0.40	0.30	0.75	1.50
❑22, Jul 79	0.40	0.30	0.75	1.50
❑23, Aug 79	0.40	0.30	0.75	1.50
❑24, Sep 79	0.40	0.30	0.75	1.50
❑25, Oct 79, 1: Fire	0.40	0.30	0.75	1.50
❑26, Nov 79	0.40	0.30	0.75	1.50
❑27, Dec 79	0.40	0.30	0.75	1.50
❑28, Jan 80	0.40	0.30	0.75	1.50
❑29, Feb 80	0.40	0.30	0.75	1.50
❑30, Mar 80	0.40	0.30	0.75	1.50
❑31, Apr 80, A: Black Orchid	0.40	0.30	0.75	1.50
❑32, May 80	0.40	0.30	0.75	1.50
❑33, Jun 80	0.40	0.30	0.75	1.50
❑34, Jul 80	0.40	0.30	0.75	1.50
❑35, Aug 80	0.40	0.30	0.75	1.50
❑36, Sep 80	0.50	0.30	0.75	1.50
❑37, Oct 80	0.50	0.30	0.75	1.50
❑38, Nov 80	0.50	0.30	0.75	1.50
❑39, Dec 80	0.50	0.30	0.75	1.50
❑40, Jan 81	0.50	0.30	0.75	1.50

	ORIG	GOOD	FINE	N-MINT
❑41, Feb 81	0.50	0.30	0.75	1.50
❑42, Mar 81, 1: Green Flame	0.50	0.30	0.75	1.50
❑43, Apr 81	0.50	0.30	0.75	1.50
❑44, May 81	0.50	0.30	0.75	1.50
❑45, Jun 81	0.50	0.30	0.75	1.50
❑46, Jul 81	0.50	0.30	0.75	1.50
❑47, Aug 81, Final Issue	0.50	0.30	0.75	1.50
❑SE 1, says A TV Comic on cover; giveaway	—	0.40	1.00	2.00

SUPERGIRL (1ST SERIES)
DC

	ORIG	GOOD	FINE	N-MINT
❑1	0.20	3.00	7.50	15.00
❑2	0.20	2.00	5.00	10.00
❑3, Feb 73, The Garden of Death	0.20	1.60	4.00	8.00
❑4	0.20	1.60	4.00	8.00
❑5, Jun 73, The Devil's Brother	0.20	1.60	4.00	8.00
❑6	0.20	1.60	4.00	8.00
❑7	0.20	1.60	4.00	8.00
❑8, Nov 73	0.20	1.60	4.00	8.00
❑9, Jan 74	0.20	1.60	4.00	8.00
❑10, Sep 74, A: Prez, Final Issue	0.20	1.60	4.00	8.00

SUPERGIRL (2ND SERIES)
DC

	ORIG	GOOD	FINE	N-MINT
❑14, Dec 83, Title changes to Supergirl; Series continued from "Daring New Adventures of Supergirl"	—	0.60	1.50	3.00
❑15, Jan 84	—	0.60	1.50	3.00
❑16, Feb 84, CI, Bug-Out!, A: Ambush Bug	0.75	0.60	1.50	3.00
❑17, Mar 84	—	0.60	1.50	3.00
❑18, Apr 84	—	0.60	1.50	3.00
❑19, May 84	—	0.60	1.50	3.00
❑20, Jun 84, A: Justice League of America; A: Teen Titans	—	0.60	1.50	3.00
❑21, Jul 84, CI	—	0.60	1.50	3.00
❑22, Aug 84, CI	—	0.60	1.50	3.00
❑23, Sep 84, CI, Final Issue	—	0.60	1.50	3.00
❑DOT 1, AT, JO (w), Department of Transportation giveaway	—	0.60	1.50	3.00

SUPERGIRL (3RD SERIES)
DC

	ORIG	GOOD	FINE	N-MINT
❑1, Sep 96, PD (w), Body & Soul, Matrix merges with Linda Danvers	1.95	1.20	3.00	6.00
❑1-2, Sep 96, PD (w), 2nd Printing	1.95	0.60	1.50	3.00
❑2, Oct 96, PD (w), Cat's Paw, Matrix learns more of Linda Danvers' past	1.95	0.80	2.00	4.00
❑3, Nov 96, PD (w), And No Dawn to Follow the Darkness, V: Gorilla Grodd, Final Night	1.95	0.70	1.75	3.50
❑4, Dec 96, PD (w), Belly of the Beast, V: Gorilla Grodd	1.95	0.60	1.50	3.00
❑5, Jan 97, PD (w), Chemical Imbalance, V: Chemo	1.95	0.60	1.50	3.00
❑6, Feb 97, PD (w), Trust Fund, V: Rampage; A: Superman	1.95	0.50	1.25	2.50
❑7, Mar 97, Art History	1.95	0.50	1.25	2.50
❑8, Apr 97, PD (w)	1.95	0.40	1.00	2.00
❑9, May 97, PD (w), V: Tempus	1.95	0.40	1.00	2.00
❑10, Jun 97, PD (w)	1.95	0.40	1.00	2.00
❑11, Jul 97, PD (w), V: Silver Banshee	1.95	0.40	1.00	2.00
❑12, Aug 97, PD (w)	1.95	0.40	1.00	2.00
❑13, Sep 97, PD (w)	1.95	0.40	1.00	2.00
❑14, Oct 97, PD (w), Genesis	1.95	0.40	1.00	2.00
❑15, Nov 97, PD (w), Gods of the Twilight, V: Extremists	1.95	0.40	1.00	2.00
❑16, Dec 97, PD (w), Blonde Justice, V: Extremists, Face cover	1.95	0.40	1.00	2.00
❑17, Jan 98, PD (w), V: Despero	1.95	0.40	1.00	2.00
❑18, Feb 98, PD (w), V: Despero	1.95	0.40	1.00	2.00
❑19, Mar 98, PD (w), Middle-Aged Crisis, V: Blastoff	1.95	0.40	1.00	2.00
❑20, Apr 98, PD (w), Millennium Giants	1.95	0.40	1.00	2.00
❑21, May 98, PD (w)	1.95	0.40	1.00	2.00
❑22, Jun 98, PD (w)	1.95	0.40	1.00	2.00
❑23, Jul 98, PD (w), A: Steel	1.95	0.40	1.00	2.00
❑24, Aug 98, PD (w), A: Resurrection Man	1.95	0.40	1.00	2.00
❑25, Sep 98, PD (w)	1.99	0.40	1.00	2.00
❑26, Oct 98, PD (w), O: Comet	1.99	0.40	1.00	2.00
❑27, Dec 98, PD (w), V: Female Furies	1.99	0.40	1.00	2.00
❑28, Jan 99, PD (w), V: Female Furies	1.99	0.40	1.00	2.00
❑29, Feb 99, PD (w), A: Granny Goodness; A: Female Furies; A: Twilight	1.99	0.40	1.00	2.00
❑30, Mar 99, PD (w), V: Matrix	1.99	0.40	1.00	2.00
❑31, Apr 99, PD (w), V: Matrix	1.99	0.40	1.00	1.99
❑32, May 99, PD (w), The Quality of Mercy	1.99	0.40	1.00	1.99
❑33, Jun 99, PD (w), Above a Murmur	1.99	0.40	1.00	1.99
❑34, Jul 99, PD (w), We'll Always Have Parasite, V: Parasite	1.99	0.40	1.00	1.99
❑35, Aug 99, PD (w), For Those Who Came Late..., V: Parasite	1.99	0.40	1.00	1.99
❑36, Sep 99, PD (w), Justice Delayed, A: Young Justice	1.99	0.40	1.00	1.99
❑37, Oct 99, PD (w), Heck's Angels, Part 4, A: Young Justice	1.99	0.40	1.00	1.99
❑38, Nov 99, PD (w), A: Zauriel, Day of Judgment	1.99	0.40	1.00	1.99
❑39, Dec 99, PD (w), On Ice	1.99	0.40	1.00	1.99
❑40, Feb 00, PD (w), Fading Ember	1.99	0.40	1.00	1.99
❑41, PD (w)	1.99	0.40	1.00	1.99
❑42, PD (w)	1.99	0.40	1.00	1.99
❑43, Apr 00, PD (w), Damned if you do...	1.99	0.40	1.00	1.99
❑44, May 00, PD (w), Shadows of Doubt	1.99	0.40	1.00	1.99
❑45, Jun 00, PD (w)	—	0.40	1.00	1.99
❑46, Jul 00, PD (w)	—	0.40	1.00	1.99
❑47, Aug 00, PD (w)	—	0.40	1.00	1.99
❑48, Sep 00, PD (w), Fallen Angel	2.25	0.45	1.13	2.25
❑49, Oct 00, PD (w), Through a Mirror Darkly	2.25	0.45	1.13	2.25
❑50, Nov 00, PD (w), Wally's Angels, Giant-size	3.95	0.79	1.98	3.95
❑51, Dec 00, PD (w), Making a Splash	2.25	0.45	1.13	2.25
❑52, Jan 01, PD (w), Supergirl, Interrupted	2.25	0.45	1.13	2.25
❑53, Feb 01, PD (w), Art for Art's Sake	2.25	0.45	1.13	2.25
❑54, Mar 01, PD (w), Statue of Limitations	2.25	0.45	1.13	2.25
❑55, Apr 01, PD (w), Dale of the Mule	2.25	0.45	1.13	2.25
❑56, May 01, PD (w), Demon Rum	2.25	0.45	1.13	2.25
❑57	2.25	0.45	1.13	2.25
❑58	2.25	0.45	1.13	2.25
❑59	2.25	0.45	1.13	2.25
❑60	2.25	0.45	1.13	2.25
❑1000000, Nov 98, PD (w), When She Was Good..., A: R'E'L	1.99	0.40	1.00	1.99
❑Anl 1, Legends of the Dead Earth	2.95	0.59	1.48	2.95
❑Anl 2, Pulp Heroes	3.95	0.79	1.98	3.95

SUPERGIRL (MINI-SERIES)
DC

	ORIG	GOOD	FINE	N-MINT
❑1, Feb 94, Trial Run	1.50	0.60	1.50	3.00
❑2, Mar 94, Demands	1.50	0.50	1.25	2.50
❑3, Apr 94	1.50	0.50	1.25	2.50
❑4, May 94	1.50	0.50	1.25	2.50

SUPERGIRL/LEX LUTHOR SPECIAL
DC

Value: Cover or less ❑1, cover says Supergirl and Team Luthor; One-Shot 2.50

SUPERGIRL MOVIE SPECIAL
DC

Value: Cover or less ❑1, GM, movie Adaptation 1.25

SUPERGIRL PLUS
DC

Value: Cover or less ❑1, Feb 97, A: Mary Marvel 2.95

SUPERGIRL/PRYSM DOUBLE SHOT
DC

Value: Cover or less ❑1, Feb 98, One-Shot 1.95

SUPER GOOF (WALT DISNEY...)
GOLD KEY

	ORIG	GOOD	FINE	N-MINT
❑1	—	4.80	12.00	24.00
❑2	—	2.40	6.00	12.00
❑3	—	2.40	6.00	12.00
❑4	—	2.00	5.00	10.00
❑5	—	2.00	5.00	10.00
❑6	—	2.00	5.00	10.00
❑7	—	2.00	5.00	10.00
❑8	—	2.00	5.00	10.00
❑9	—	2.00	5.00	10.00
❑10	—	2.00	5.00	10.00
❑11	—	1.40	3.50	7.00
❑12	—	1.40	3.50	7.00
❑13	—	1.40	3.50	7.00
❑14	—	1.40	3.50	7.00
❑15	—	1.40	3.50	7.00
❑16, Feb 71	—	1.40	3.50	7.00
❑17, May 71	0.15	1.40	3.50	7.00
❑18, Aug 71	—	1.40	3.50	7.00
❑19, Nov 71	—	1.40	3.50	7.00
❑20, Feb 72	—	1.40	3.50	7.00
❑21, May 72	0.15	1.00	2.50	5.00
❑22, Aug 72	—	1.00	2.50	5.00
❑23, Nov 72	—	1.00	2.50	5.00
❑24	—	1.00	2.50	5.00
❑25	—	1.00	2.50	5.00
❑26	—	1.00	2.50	5.00
❑27	—	1.00	2.50	5.00
❑28	—	1.00	2.50	5.00
❑29	—	1.00	2.50	5.00
❑30	—	1.00	2.50	5.00
❑31	—	0.60	1.50	3.00
❑32, Nov 74	0.25	0.60	1.50	3.00

	ORIG	GOOD	FINE	N-MINT
❑33	—	0.60	1.50	3.00
❑34	—	0.60	1.50	3.00
❑35	—	0.60	1.50	3.00
❑36, Dec 75	0.25	0.60	1.50	3.00
❑37, Feb 76	—	0.60	1.50	3.00
❑38, Jun 76	—	0.60	1.50	3.00
❑39, Sep 76	—	0.60	1.50	3.00
❑40, Nov 76, The Crystal Egg Affair; The Worlds Strongest Weakling	0.30	0.60	1.50	3.00
❑41, Feb 77	—	0.60	1.50	3.00
❑42, Jun 77	—	0.60	1.50	3.00
❑43, Sep 77	0.30	0.60	1.50	3.00
❑44, Nov 77	—	0.60	1.50	3.00
❑45	—	0.60	1.50	3.00
❑46	—	0.60	1.50	3.00
❑47	—	0.60	1.50	3.00
❑48, Aug 78	0.35	0.60	1.50	3.00
❑49, Oct 78	0.35	0.60	1.50	3.00
❑50	—	0.60	1.50	3.00
❑51	—	0.50	1.25	2.50
❑52	—	0.50	1.25	2.50
❑53, Jun 79	0.40	0.50	1.25	2.50
❑54	—	0.50	1.25	2.50
❑55	—	0.50	1.25	2.50
❑56	—	0.50	1.25	2.50
❑57	—	0.50	1.25	2.50
❑58, Mar 80	0.40	0.50	1.25	2.50
❑59	—	0.50	1.25	2.50
❑60	—	0.50	1.25	2.50
❑61	—	0.50	1.25	2.50
❑62	—	0.50	1.25	2.50
❑63	—	0.50	1.25	2.50
❑64	—	0.50	1.25	2.50
❑65	—	0.50	1.25	2.50
❑66	—	0.50	1.25	2.50
❑67, Mini But Mighty; The Runaway Planet	0.60	0.50	1.25	2.50
❑68	—	0.50	1.25	2.50
❑69	—	0.50	1.25	2.50
❑70	—	0.50	1.25	2.50
❑71	—	0.50	1.25	2.50
❑72	—	0.50	1.25	2.50
❑73	—	0.50	1.25	2.50
❑74, Final Issue	—	0.50	1.25	2.50

SUPER GREEN BERET
MILSON

	ORIG	GOOD	FINE	N-MINT
❑1, Apr 67, Super Green Beret; True Combat Action	0.25	6.00	15.00	30.00
❑2	0.25	4.80	12.00	24.00

SUPER HEROES BATTLE SUPER GORILLAS
DC

	ORIG	GOOD	FINE	N-MINT
❑1, Win 76	0.50	1.40	3.50	7.00

SUPER HEROES PUZZLES AND GAMES
MARVEL

	ORIG	GOOD	FINE	N-MINT
❑1, Apr 80, O: Spider-Woman; O: The Hulk; O: Spider-Man; O: Captain America, nn; giveaway	—	0.40	1.00	2.00

SUPER HEROES STAMP ALBUM
USPS

Value: Cover or less

❑1, 1900-1909	2.95
❑2, 1910-1919	2.95
❑3, 1920-1929	2.95
❑4, no Snow White coverage; 1930-1939	2.95
❑5, 1940-1949	2.95
❑6, 1950-1959; 3-D stamp	2.95
❑7, 1960-1969	2.95
❑8, 1970-1979	2.95
❑9, 1980-1989	2.95
❑10, 1990-1999	2.95

SUPER INFORMATION HIJINKS: REALITY CHECK
TAVICAT

Value: Cover or less

❑1, Oct 95, Insomniacs!, b&w	2.95
❑2, Dec 95, b&w	2.95
❑3	2.95
❑4	2.95
❑5	2.95

SUPER INFORMATION HIJINKS: REALITY CHECK! (2ND SERIES)
SIRIUS

Value: Cover or less

❑1	2.95
❑2	2.95
❑3	2.95
❑4	2.95
❑5	2.95
❑6	2.95
❑7	2.95
❑8, Jan 98, When Kittens Collide!	2.95
❑9, Mar 98	2.95
❑10, May 98	2.95
❑11, Jul 98	2.95
❑12, Oct 98	2.95

SUPERIOR SEVEN
IMAGINE THIS PRODUCTIONS

Value: Cover or less

❑1, The Starcore Saga, Part 1	2.95
❑2, The Starcore Saga, Part 2	2.95
❑3, The Starcore Saga, Part 3	2.95
❑4, Somebodies Gonna Get a Punchn' Da Head	1.95
❑5	1.95

Due to licensing issues, there was no information on the Snow White stamp in *Super Heroes Stamp Album #4*.

SUPERMAN (1ST SERIES)
DC

	ORIG	GOOD	FINE	N-MINT
❑142, Jan 61	0.10	22.00	55.00	110.00
❑143, Feb 61	0.10	22.00	55.00	110.00
❑144, Apr 61, A: Lex Luthor	0.10	22.00	55.00	110.00
❑145, May 61	0.10	22.00	55.00	110.00
❑146, Jul 61, O: Superman, Superman's life	0.10	30.00	75.00	150.00
❑147, Aug 61, CS, 1: Legion of Super-Villains; 1: Legion of Super-Heroes (adult)	0.10	27.00	67.50	135.00
❑148, Oct 61, CS, V: Mxyzptlk	0.10	22.00	55.00	110.00
❑149, Nov 61, CS, A: Legion of Super-Heroes	0.10	25.00	62.50	125.00
❑150, Jan 62	0.12	13.00	32.50	65.00
❑151, Feb 62	0.12	13.00	32.50	65.00
❑152, Apr 62, A: Legion of Super-Heroes	0.12	13.00	32.50	65.00
❑153, May 62	0.12	13.00	32.50	65.00
❑154, Jul 62, CS	0.12	13.00	32.50	65.00
❑155, Aug 62	0.12	13.00	32.50	65.00
❑156, Oct 62	0.12	13.00	32.50	65.00
❑157, Nov 62, 1: Gold Kryptonite	0.12	13.00	32.50	65.00
❑158, Jan 63, CS, 1: Flamebird; 1: Nightwing	0.12	13.00	32.50	65.00
❑159, Feb 63	0.12	13.00	32.50	65.00
❑160, Apr 63	0.12	13.00	32.50	65.00
❑161, May 63, D: Ma & Pa Kent	0.12	13.00	32.50	65.00
❑162, Jul 63, CS	0.12	10.00	25.00	50.00
❑163, Aug 63	0.12	10.00	25.00	50.00
❑164, Oct 63, CS	0.12	10.00	25.00	50.00
❑165, Nov 63	0.12	10.00	25.00	50.00
❑166, Jan 64	0.12	10.00	25.00	50.00
❑167, Feb 64, CS, O: Braniac 5 (new origin); O: Brainiac (new origin)	0.12	10.00	25.00	50.00
❑168, Apr 64	0.12	10.00	25.00	50.00
❑169, May 64	0.12	10.00	25.00	50.00
❑170, Jul 64, A: John F. Kennedy	0.12	10.00	25.00	50.00
❑171, Aug 64, CS	0.12	10.00	25.00	50.00
❑172, Oct 64	0.12	10.00	25.00	50.00
❑173, Nov 64	0.12	10.00	25.00	50.00
❑174, Jan 65	0.12	10.00	25.00	50.00
❑175, Feb 65, Imaginary Story	0.12	10.00	25.00	50.00
❑176, Apr 65, CS	0.12	10.00	25.00	50.00
❑177, May 65	0.12	10.00	25.00	50.00
❑178, Jul 65	0.12	10.00	25.00	50.00
❑179, Aug 65, Tales of Kryptonite, Part 4	0.12	10.00	25.00	50.00
❑180, Oct 65	0.12	10.00	25.00	50.00
❑181, Nov 65, CS	0.12	7.00	17.50	35.00
❑182, Jan 66, V: Toyman	0.12	7.00	17.50	35.00
❑183, Jan 66, Giant-size; Golden Age reprints	0.25	9.00	22.50	45.00
❑184, Feb 66	0.12	7.00	17.50	35.00
❑185, Apr 66	0.12	7.00	17.50	35.00
❑186, May 66, CS	0.12	7.00	17.50	35.00
❑187, Jun 66, Giant-size; Fortress stories	0.25	9.00	22.50	45.00
❑188, Jul 66, CS	0.12	7.00	17.50	35.00
❑189, Aug 66	0.12	7.00	17.50	35.00
❑190, Oct 66	0.12	7.00	17.50	35.00
❑191, Nov 66, V: D.E.M.O.N.	0.12	6.00	15.00	30.00
❑192, Jan 67, CS, Imaginary Story	0.12	6.00	15.00	30.00
❑193, Feb 67, Giant-size; reprints Action #223 and Superman #149	0.25	8.00	20.00	40.00
❑194, Feb 67, CS	0.12	6.00	15.00	30.00
❑195, Apr 67, CS	0.12	6.00	15.00	30.00
❑196, May 67	0.12	6.00	15.00	30.00
❑197, Jul 67, Giant-size; All Clark Kent issue	0.25	8.00	20.00	40.00
❑198, Jul 67, CS	0.12	6.00	15.00	30.00
❑199, Aug 67, 1st Flash/Superman race; 1st Superman/Flash race	0.12	40.00	100.00	200.00
❑200, Oct 67	0.12	6.00	15.00	30.00
❑201, Nov 67, CS	0.12	4.00	10.00	20.00
❑202, Dec 67, Giant-size; Bizarro issue	0.25	6.00	15.00	30.00

	ORIG	GOOD	FINE	N-MINT
❑203, Jan 68, CS (c)	0.12	4.00	10.00	20.00
❑204, Feb 68, NA (c), 1: Q-energy	0.12	4.00	10.00	20.00
❑205, Apr 68	0.12	4.00	10.00	20.00
❑206, May 68	0.12	4.00	10.00	20.00
❑207, Jul 68, 30th anniversary; Giant-size	0.25	6.00	15.00	30.00
❑208, Jul 68	0.12	4.00	10.00	20.00
❑209, Aug 68	0.12	4.00	10.00	20.00
❑210, Oct 68	0.12	4.00	10.00	20.00
❑211, Nov 68	0.12	4.00	10.00	20.00
❑212, Jan 69, Giant-size; Superbabies	0.25	6.00	15.00	30.00
❑213, Jan 69, The Most Dangerous Door in the World!; The Orphans of Space!, A: Lex Luthor	0.12	4.00	10.00	20.00
❑214, Feb 69	0.12	4.00	10.00	20.00
❑215, Apr 69, Lois Lane ... Dead ... Yet Alive; Superman's First Exploit, Imaginary Story; Superman as widower	0.12	4.00	10.00	20.00
❑216, May 69, in Vietnam	0.12	4.00	10.00	20.00
❑217, Jul 69, CS (c), Giant-size	0.25	6.00	15.00	30.00
❑218, Jul 69	0.15	4.00	10.00	20.00
❑219, Aug 69	0.15	4.00	10.00	20.00
❑220, Oct 69	0.15	4.00	10.00	20.00
❑221, Nov 69	0.15	4.00	10.00	20.00
❑222, Jan 70, Giant-size	0.25	6.00	15.00	30.00
❑223, Jan 70	0.15	4.00	10.00	20.00
❑224, Feb 70, Imaginary Story	0.15	4.00	10.00	20.00
❑225, Apr 70	0.15	4.00	10.00	20.00
❑226, May 70	0.15	4.00	10.00	20.00
❑227, Jul 70, Giant-size	0.25	6.00	15.00	30.00
❑228, Jul 70, DA; CS	0.15	4.00	10.00	20.00
❑229, Aug 70, DA; CS, The Ex-Superman; Clark Kent, Assassin!	0.15	4.00	10.00	20.00
❑230, Oct 70, DA; CS, Imaginary Story	0.15	4.00	10.00	20.00
❑231, Nov 70, CS; NA, Imaginary Story	0.15	4.00	10.00	20.00
❑232, Jan 71, Giant-size	0.25	6.00	15.00	30.00
❑233, Jan 71, Kryptonite No More	0.15	4.00	10.00	20.00
❑234, Feb 71, A: Sand Superman	0.15	4.00	10.00	20.00
❑235, Mar 71	0.15	4.00	10.00	20.00
❑236, Apr 71, World of Krypton back-up	0.15	4.00	10.00	20.00
❑237, May 71	0.15	4.00	10.00	20.00
❑238, Jun 71, A: Sand Superman	0.15	4.00	10.00	20.00
❑239, Jul 71, CS; GM; MA, Giant-size; reprints Action #267 and #268, Superman #127 and #164	0.25	6.00	15.00	30.00
❑240, Jul 71, A: I-Ching	0.15	1.60	4.00	8.00
❑241, Aug 71, A: Sand Superman; A: I-Ching, giant	0.25	1.40	3.50	7.00
❑242, Sep 71, A: final	0.25	1.40	3.50	7.00
❑243, Oct 71	0.25	1.40	3.50	7.00
❑244, Nov 71	0.25	1.40	3.50	7.00
❑245, Jan 72, MR; CS, back cover pin-up; a.k.a. DC 100-Page Super-Spectacular #DC-7; reprints from All-Star Western #117, The Atom #3, Detective #66, Kid Eternity #3, Mystery in Space #89, and Superman #87, and #167	0.50	2.40	6.00	12.00
❑246, Dec 71	0.25	1.20	3.00	6.00
❑247, Jan 72, Must There Be a Superman?, A: Guardians of the Universe, 1st Private Life of Clark Kent; Superman of Tomorrow back-up	0.25	1.20	3.00	6.00
❑248, Feb 72	0.25	1.20	3.00	6.00
❑249, Mar 72, CS; NA, 1: Terra-Man	0.25	2.00	5.00	10.00
❑250, Apr 72	0.25	1.20	3.00	6.00
❑251, May 72, CS; MA	0.25	1.20	3.00	6.00
❑252, Jun 72, CS; MA, wraparound cover; a.k.a. DC 100-Page Super Spectacular #DC-13	0.50	2.40	6.00	12.00
❑253, Jun 72, CS; MA, Reprint	0.25	1.20	3.00	6.00
❑254, Jul 72, CS; NA	0.20	2.40	6.00	12.00
❑255, Aug 72	0.20	0.60	1.50	3.00
❑256, Sep 72	0.20	0.60	1.50	3.00
❑257, Oct 72	0.20	0.60	1.50	3.00
❑258, Nov 72	0.20	0.60	1.50	3.00
❑259, Dec 72	0.20	0.60	1.50	3.00
❑260, Jan 73	0.20	0.60	1.50	3.00
❑261, Feb 73	0.20	0.60	1.50	3.00
❑262, Mar 73	0.20	0.60	1.50	3.00
❑263, Apr 73	0.20	0.60	1.50	3.00
❑264, Jun 73, 1: Steve Lombard	0.20	0.80	2.00	4.00
❑265, Jul 73	0.20	0.60	1.50	3.00
❑266, Aug 73	0.20	0.60	1.50	3.00
❑267, Sep 73	0.20	0.60	1.50	3.00
❑268, Oct 73	0.20	0.60	1.50	3.00
❑269, Nov 73	0.20	0.60	1.50	3.00
❑270, Dec 73	0.20	0.60	1.50	3.00
❑271, Jan 74	0.20	0.60	1.50	3.00
❑272, Feb 74, CS; BO, 100pgs.; Reprint	0.50	1.40	3.50	7.00
❑273, Mar 74, CS; BO	0.20	0.60	1.50	3.00
❑274, Apr 74, CS; BO	0.20	0.60	1.50	3.00
❑275, May 74, CS; BO	0.20	0.60	1.50	3.00
❑276, Jun 74, CS; BO, 1: Captain Thunder	0.20	0.60	1.50	3.00
❑277, Jul 74, CS; BO	0.20	0.60	1.50	3.00
❑278, Aug 74, CS; BO, 100pgs.	0.60	1.20	3.00	6.00
❑279, Sep 74, A: Batgirl	0.20	0.60	1.50	3.00
❑280, Oct 74	0.20	0.60	1.50	3.00
❑281, Nov 74	0.20	0.60	1.50	3.00
❑282, Dec 74	0.20	0.60	1.50	3.00
❑283, Jan 75	0.20	0.60	1.50	3.00
❑284, Feb 75, CS; BO, 100pgs.	0.60	1.20	3.00	6.00
❑285, Mar 75, A: Roy Raymond	0.25	0.50	1.25	2.50
❑286, Apr 75, V: Parasite; V: Luthor	0.25	0.50	1.25	2.50
❑287, May 75, Return of Krypto	0.25	0.50	1.25	2.50
❑288, Jun 75	0.25	0.50	1.25	2.50
❑289, Jul 75	0.25	0.50	1.25	2.50
❑290, Aug 75	0.25	0.50	1.25	2.50
❑291, Sep 75	0.25	0.50	1.25	2.50
❑292, Oct 75, CS; BO, O: Lex Luthor	0.25	0.80	2.00	4.00
❑293, Nov 75	0.25	0.50	1.25	2.50
❑294, Dec 75	0.25	0.50	1.25	2.50
❑295, Jan 76	0.25	0.50	1.25	2.50
❑296, Feb 76, Superman loses powers when not in costume	0.25	0.50	1.25	2.50
❑297, Mar 76	0.25	0.50	1.25	2.50
❑298, Apr 76	0.30	0.50	1.25	2.50
❑299, May 76	0.30	0.50	1.25	2.50
❑300, Jun 76, CS; BO, O: Superman of 2001, 300th anniversary issue	0.30	1.20	3.00	6.00
❑301, Jul 76	0.30	0.50	1.25	2.50
❑302, Aug 76	0.30	0.50	1.25	2.50
❑303, Sep 76	0.30	0.50	1.25	2.50
❑304, Oct 76	0.30	0.50	1.25	2.50
❑305, Nov 76	0.30	0.50	1.25	2.50
❑306, Dec 76, V: Bizarro	0.30	0.50	1.25	2.50
❑307, Jan 77, FS, NA (c)	0.30	0.50	1.25	2.50
❑308, Feb 77, FS, NA (c)	0.30	0.50	1.25	2.50
❑309, Mar 77	0.30	0.50	1.25	2.50
❑310, Apr 77	0.30	0.50	1.25	2.50
❑311, May 77	0.30	0.50	1.25	2.50
❑312, Jun 77	0.35	0.50	1.25	2.50
❑313, Jul 77, DA; CS, NA (c)	0.35	0.50	1.25	2.50
❑314, Aug 77	0.35	0.50	1.25	2.50
❑315, Sep 77	0.35	0.50	1.25	2.50
❑316, Oct 77	0.35	0.50	1.25	2.50
❑317, Nov 77, NA (c), Return of Lana Lang	0.35	0.50	1.25	2.50
❑318, Dec 77, CS	0.35	0.50	1.25	2.50
❑319, Jan 78, CS	0.35	0.50	1.25	2.50
❑320, Feb 78, CS	0.35	0.50	1.25	2.50
❑321, Mar 78	0.35	0.50	1.25	2.50
❑322, Apr 78, V: Parasite	0.35	0.50	1.25	2.50
❑323, May 78, V: Atomic Skull	0.35	0.50	1.25	2.50
❑324, Jun 78, V: Titano	0.35	0.50	1.25	2.50
❑325, Jul 78	0.35	0.50	1.25	2.50
❑326, Aug 78	0.35	0.50	1.25	2.50
❑327, Sep 78	0.50	0.50	1.25	2.50
❑328, Oct 78	0.50	0.50	1.25	2.50
❑329, Nov 78	0.50	0.50	1.25	2.50
❑330, Dec 78	0.40	0.50	1.25	2.50
❑331, Jan 79	0.40	0.50	1.25	2.50
❑332, Feb 79	0.40	0.50	1.25	2.50
❑333, Mar 79	0.40	0.50	1.25	2.50
❑334, Apr 79	0.40	0.50	1.25	2.50
❑335, May 79, V: Mxyzptlk	0.40	0.50	1.25	2.50
❑336, Jun 79	0.40	0.50	1.25	2.50
❑337, Jul 79	0.40	0.50	1.25	2.50
❑338, Aug 79, Kandor enlarged	0.40	0.50	1.25	2.50
❑339, Sep 79	0.40	0.50	1.25	2.50
❑340, Oct 79	0.40	0.50	1.25	2.50
❑341, Nov 79, A: J. Wilbur Wolfingham	0.40	0.50	1.25	2.50
❑342, Dec 79	0.40	0.50	1.25	2.50
❑343, Jan 80	0.40	0.50	1.25	2.50
❑344, Feb 80	0.40	0.50	1.25	2.50
❑345, Mar 80	0.40	0.50	1.25	2.50
❑346, Apr 80	0.40	0.50	1.25	2.50
❑347, May 80	0.40	0.50	1.25	2.50
❑348, Jun 80	0.40	0.50	1.25	2.50
❑349, Jul 80	0.40	0.50	1.25	2.50
❑350, Aug 80	0.40	0.50	1.25	2.50
❑351, Sep 80	0.50	0.40	1.00	2.00
❑352, Oct 80	0.50	0.40	1.00	2.00
❑353, Nov 80	0.50	0.40	1.00	2.00
❑354, Dec 80	0.50	0.40	1.00	2.00
❑355, Jan 81, JSn	0.50	0.40	1.00	2.00

	ORIG	GOOD	FINE	N-MINT
❑356, Feb 81	0.50	0.40	1.00	2.00
❑357, Mar 81	0.50	0.40	1.00	2.00
❑358, Apr 81	0.50	0.40	1.00	2.00
❑359, May 81	0.50	0.40	1.00	2.00
❑360, Jun 81	0.50	0.40	1.00	2.00
❑361, Jul 81	0.50	0.40	1.00	2.00
❑362, Aug 81, Lana and Lois contract deadly virus that killed Kents	0.50	0.40	1.00	2.00
❑363, Sep 81, A: Lex Luthor	0.50	0.40	1.00	2.00
❑364, Oct 81	0.50	0.40	1.00	2.00
❑365, Nov 81, A: Supergirl, Superboy back-up	0.50	0.40	1.00	2.00
❑366, Dec 81	0.50	0.40	1.00	2.00
❑367, Jan 82	0.60	0.40	1.00	2.00
❑368, Feb 82	0.60	0.40	1.00	2.00
❑369, Mar 82, V: Parasite	0.60	0.40	1.00	2.00
❑370, Apr 82	0.60	0.40	1.00	2.00
❑371, May 82	0.60	0.40	1.00	2.00
❑372, Jun 82	0.60	0.40	1.00	2.00
❑373, Jul 82	0.60	0.40	1.00	2.00
❑374, Aug 82	0.60	0.40	1.00	2.00
❑375, Sep 82	0.60	0.40	1.00	2.00
❑376, Oct 82	0.60	0.40	1.00	2.00
❑377, Nov 82, Masters of the Universe Preview	0.60	0.40	1.00	2.00
❑378, Dec 82	0.60	0.40	1.00	2.00
❑379, Jan 83, A: Bizarro	0.60	0.40	1.00	2.00
❑380, Feb 83	0.60	0.40	1.00	2.00
❑381, Mar 83	0.60	0.40	1.00	2.00
❑382, Apr 83	0.60	0.40	1.00	2.00
❑383, May 83	0.60	0.40	1.00	2.00
❑384, Jun 83	0.60	0.40	1.00	2.00
❑385, Jul 83	0.60	0.40	1.00	2.00
❑386, Aug 83	0.60	0.40	1.00	2.00
❑387, Sep 83	0.60	0.40	1.00	2.00
❑388, Oct 83	0.60	0.40	1.00	2.00
❑389, Nov 83	0.60	0.40	1.00	2.00
❑390, Dec 83	0.75	0.40	1.00	2.00
❑391, Jan 84	0.75	0.40	1.00	2.00
❑392, Feb 84	0.75	0.40	1.00	2.00
❑393, Mar 84	0.75	0.40	1.00	2.00
❑394, Apr 84	0.75	0.40	1.00	2.00
❑395, May 84	0.75	0.40	1.00	2.00
❑396, Jun 84	0.75	0.40	1.00	2.00
❑397, Jul 84	0.75	0.40	1.00	2.00
❑398, Aug 84	0.75	0.40	1.00	2.00
❑399, Sep 84	0.75	0.40	1.00	2.00
❑400, Oct 84, FM; JK; MGr; WE; JOy; SD; AW; JD, 400th anniversary issue; Giant-size	1.50	1.00	2.50	5.00
❑401, Nov 84	0.75	0.40	1.00	2.00
❑402, Dec 84	0.75	0.40	1.00	2.00
❑403, Jan 85	0.75	0.40	1.00	2.00
❑404, Feb 85	0.75	0.40	1.00	2.00
❑405, Mar 85	0.75	0.40	1.00	2.00
❑406, Apr 85	0.75	0.40	1.00	2.00
❑407, May 85, powers passed along	0.75	0.40	1.00	2.00
❑408, Jun 85, nuclear nightmare	0.75	0.40	1.00	2.00
❑409, Jul 85	0.75	0.40	1.00	2.00
❑410, Aug 85	0.75	0.40	1.00	2.00
❑411, Sep 85, Julius Schwartz' birthday	0.75	0.40	1.00	2.00
❑412, Oct 85	0.75	0.40	1.00	2.00
❑413, Nov 85	0.75	0.40	1.00	2.00
❑414, Dec 85, Crisis on Infinite Earths, Crisis	0.75	0.40	1.00	2.00
❑415, Jan 86, Crisis on Infinite Earths, Crisis	0.75	0.40	1.00	2.00
❑416, Feb 86, Superman learns Luthor's connection to Einstein	0.75	0.40	1.00	2.00
❑417, Mar 86, What if Kal-El's rocket landed on Mars?	0.75	0.40	1.00	2.00
❑418, Apr 86	0.75	0.40	1.00	2.00
❑419, May 86	0.75	0.40	1.00	2.00
❑420, Jun 86	0.75	0.40	1.00	2.00
❑421, Jul 86	0.75	0.40	1.00	2.00
❑422, Aug 86	0.75	0.40	1.00	2.00
❑423, Sep 86, AMo (w), Final Issue; series continues as Adventures of Superman	0.75	1.60	4.00	8.00
❑Anl 1, 1: Supergirl reprinted; 1: Supergirl, Reprints Action Comics #252	0.25	110.00	275.00	550.00
❑Anl 2, O: Titano	0.25	60.00	150.00	300.00
❑Anl 3, Sum 61, Strange Lives of Superman	0.25	40.00	100.00	200.00
❑Anl 4, A: Legion of Super-Heroes	0.25	35.00	87.50	175.00
❑Anl 5, Krypton	0.25	20.00	50.00	100.00
❑Anl 6, 1: Legion of Super-Heroes, Reprints Adventure Comics #247	0.25	17.00	42.50	85.00
❑Anl 7, Sum 63, O: Superman-Batman team, 25th anniversary	0.25	12.00	30.00	60.00

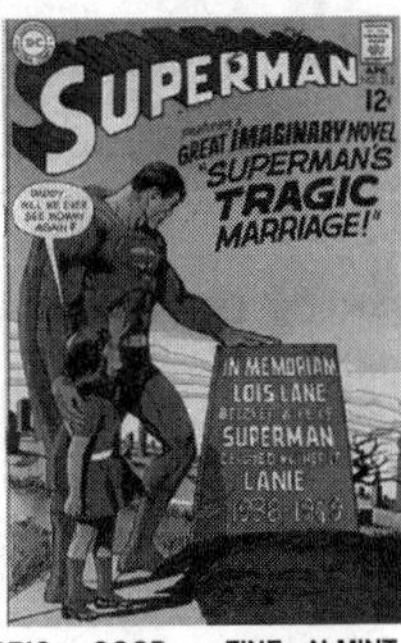

Superman became a single parent when Lois was killed by one of his enemies in an imaginary story in *Superman* (1st series) #215.

	ORIG	GOOD	FINE	N-MINT
❑Anl 8, 80pgs.; Untold Stories and Secret Origins	0.25	9.00	22.50	45.00
❑Anl 9	1.00	1.00	2.50	5.00
❑Anl 10, CS, Sword of Superman	1.25	1.00	2.50	5.00
❑Anl 11, DaG, AMo (w), A: Batman; A: Robin; A: Wonder Woman; V: Mongul	1.25	0.80	2.00	4.00
❑Anl 12, V: Luthor's Warsuit	1.25	0.60	1.50	3.00
❑SE 1, GK	1.00	0.80	2.00	4.00
❑SE 2, Apr 84	1.25	0.80	2.00	4.00
❑SE 3, Apr 85, V: Amazo	1.25	0.80	2.00	4.00

SUPERMAN (2ND SERIES) DC

	ORIG	GOOD	FINE	N-MINT
❑0, Oct 94, Peer Pressure, Part 2, ▲1994-38	1.50	0.60	1.50	3.00
❑1, Jan 87, JBy, JBy (w), Heart Of Stone, 1: Metallo (new)	0.75	1.00	2.50	5.00
❑2, Feb 87, JBy	0.75	0.70	1.75	3.50
❑3, Mar 87, JBy, Legends, 1: Amazing Grace	0.75	0.60	1.50	3.00
❑4, Apr 87, JBy, 1: Bloodsport	0.75	0.50	1.25	2.50
❑5, May 87, JBy	0.75	0.50	1.25	2.50
❑6, Jun 87, JBy	0.75	0.40	1.00	2.00
❑7, Jul 87, JBy, 1: Rampage (DC)	0.75	0.40	1.00	2.00
❑8, Aug 87, JBy, A: Legion of Super-Heroes; A: Superboy	0.75	0.40	1.00	2.00
❑9, Sep 87, JBy, V: Luthor; V: Joker	0.75	0.70	1.75	3.50
❑10, Oct 87, JBy	0.75	0.40	1.00	2.00
❑11, Nov 87, JBy, O: Mr. Mxyzptlk	0.75	0.40	1.00	2.00
❑12, Dec 87, JBy, O: Lori Lemaris	0.75	0.40	1.00	2.00
❑13, Jan 88, JBy, Millennium	0.75	0.40	1.00	2.00
❑14, Feb 88, JBy, A: Green Lantern, Millennium	0.75	0.40	1.00	2.00
❑15, Mar 88, JBy	0.75	0.40	1.00	2.00
❑16, Apr 88, JBy, V: Prankster	0.75	0.40	1.00	2.00
❑17, May 88, JBy, V: Silver Banshee	0.75	0.40	1.00	2.00
❑18, Jun 88, JBy, return to Krypton	0.75	0.40	1.00	2.00
❑19, Jul 88, JBy, 1: Psi-Phon; 1: Dreadnaught	0.75	0.40	1.00	2.00
❑20, Aug 88, JBy, A: Doom Patrol	0.75	0.40	1.00	2.00
❑21, Sep 88, JBy, Supergirl	0.75	0.40	1.00	2.00
❑22, Oct 88, JBy, Supergirl	0.75	0.40	1.00	2.00
❑23, Nov 88, A: Batman	0.75	0.40	1.00	2.00
❑24, Dec 88	0.75	0.40	1.00	2.00
❑25, Dec 88	0.75	0.40	1.00	2.00
❑26, Jan 89, Invasion!	0.75	0.40	1.00	2.00
❑27, Jan 89, Invasion!	0.75	0.40	1.00	2.00
❑28, Feb 89, in space	0.75	0.40	1.00	2.00
❑29, Mar 89, in space	0.75	0.40	1.00	2.00
❑30, Apr 89, in space	0.75	0.40	1.00	2.00
❑31, May 89, Mxyzptlk vs. Luthor	0.75	0.40	1.00	2.00
❑32, Jun 89, V: Mongul	0.75	0.40	1.00	2.00
❑33, Jul 89	0.75	0.40	1.00	2.00
❑34, Aug 89, V: Skyhook	0.75	0.40	1.00	2.00
❑35, Sep 89, A: Black Racer	0.75	0.40	1.00	2.00
❑36, Oct 89, V: Prankster	0.75	0.40	1.00	2.00
❑37, Nov 89, A: Newsboys	0.75	0.40	1.00	2.00
❑38, Dec 89	0.75	0.40	1.00	2.00
❑39, Jan 90	0.75	0.40	1.00	2.00
❑40, Feb 90	0.75	0.40	1.00	2.00
❑41, Mar 90, Day of the Krypton Man, Part 1, A: Lobo	0.75	0.40	1.00	2.00
❑42, Apr 90, Day of the Krypton Man, Part 4	0.75	0.40	1.00	2.00
❑43, May 90, V: Kryptonite Man	0.75	0.40	1.00	2.00
❑44, Jun 90, Dark Knight over Metropolis, A: Batman	0.75	0.40	1.00	2.00
❑45, Jul 90	0.75	0.40	1.00	2.00
❑46, Aug 90, A: Obsidian; V: Terraman; A: Jade	0.75	0.40	1.00	2.00
❑47, Sep 90, V: Blaze	0.75	0.40	1.00	2.00
❑48, Oct 90, A: Sinbad	0.75	0.40	1.00	2.00
❑49, Nov 90, Krisis of the Krimson Kryptonite, Part 1	0.75	0.40	1.00	2.00
❑50, Dec 90, JOy (w), Krisis of the Krimson Kryptonite, Part 4; The Human Factor, Clark Kent proposes to Lois Lane	1.50	1.00	2.50	5.00

	ORIG	GOOD	FINE	N-MINT
❑50-2, Dec 90, JOy (w), Krisis of the Krimson Kryptonite, Part 4; The Human Factor, 2nd Printing; Clark Kent proposes to Lois Lane	1.50	0.35	0.88	1.75
❑51, Jan 91, JOy, JOy (w), Mister Z!, 1: Mister Z; V: Mr. Z, ▲1991-1	1.00	0.40	1.00	2.00
❑52, Feb 91, V: Terraman	1.00	0.40	1.00	2.00
❑52-2, Feb 91, 2nd Printing	1.00	0.30	0.75	1.50
❑53, Mar 91, JOy (w), Truth, Justice, And The American Way, Lois reacts to Superman disclosing identity	1.00	0.50	1.25	2.50
❑53-2, Mar 91, JOy (w), Truth, Justice, And The American Way, 2nd Printing; Lois reacts to Superman disclosing identity	1.00	0.30	0.75	1.50
❑54, Apr 91, Time & Time Again, Part 3, in 40s	1.00	0.35	0.88	1.75
❑55, May 91, Time & Time Again, Part 6, A: Demon, in Middle Ages	1.00	0.35	0.88	1.75
❑56, Jun 91, Red Glass	1.00	0.35	0.88	1.75
❑57, Jul 91, Return Of The Krypton Man, Double-size; Krypton Man	1.75	0.40	1.00	2.00
❑58, Aug 91, V: Bloodhounds	1.00	0.30	0.75	1.50
❑59, Sep 91, Blackout, Part 1	1.00	0.30	0.75	1.50
❑60, Oct 91, Blackout, Part 2, V: Intergang; 1: Agent Liberty	1.00	0.40	1.00	2.00
❑61, Nov 91, Blackout, Part 3, A: Waverider; A: Linear Men	1.00	0.30	0.75	1.50
❑62, Dec 91, Blackout, Part 4	1.00	0.30	0.75	1.50
❑63, Jan 92, A: Aquaman	1.00	0.30	0.75	1.50
❑64, Feb 92, Christmas issue	1.00	0.30	0.75	1.50
❑65, Mar 92, Panic in the Sky Second Strike, A: Aquaman; A: Batman; A: Captain Marvel; A: Deathstroke; A: Guy Gardner	1.00	0.30	0.75	1.50
❑66, Apr 92, Panic in the Sky Final Strike, A: Aquaman; A: Batman; A: Captain Marvel; A: Deathstroke; A: Guy Gardner	1.00	0.30	0.75	1.50
❑67, May 92	1.00	0.30	0.75	1.50
❑68, Jun 92, Deathstroke	1.25	0.30	0.75	1.50
❑69, Jul 92	1.25	0.30	0.75	1.50
❑70, Aug 92, Robin	1.25	0.30	0.75	1.50
❑71, Sep 92	1.25	0.30	0.75	1.50
❑72, Oct 92	1.25	0.30	0.75	1.50
❑73, Nov 92, Doomsday, A: Waverider; A: Doomsday	1.25	0.60	1.50	3.00
❑73-2	1.25	0.35	0.88	1.75
❑74, Dec 92, Countdown to Doomsday!, Doomsday; ▲1992-74	1.25	0.80	2.00	4.00
❑74-2, Dec 92, Countdown to Doomsday!, ▲1992-74	1.25	0.30	0.75	1.50
❑75, Jan 93, Doomsday!, D: Superman, newsstand; unbagged	1.25	0.80	2.00	4.00
❑75/CS, Jan 93, Doomsday!, D: Superman, poster, stamps, arm band, trading card, obituary	2.50	2.00	5.00	10.00
❑75/PL, Jan 93, Doomsday!, D: Superman, poster, stamps, arm band, trading card, obituary; Platinum edition	1.25	7.00	17.50	35.00
❑75-2, Jan 93, Doomsday!, D: Superman, 2nd Printing	1.25	0.40	1.00	2.00
❑75-3, Jan 93, Doomsday!, D: Superman, 3rd Printing	1.25	0.30	0.75	1.50
❑75-4, Jan 93, Doomsday!, D: Superman, 4th Printing	1.25	0.30	0.75	1.50
❑76, Feb 93, Funeral for a Friend, Part 4	1.25	0.50	1.25	2.50
❑77, Mar 93, Funeral for a Friend, Part 8	1.25	0.50	1.25	2.50
❑78, Jun 93, Reign of the Supermen, 1: Cyborg Superman, poster	1.50	0.40	1.00	2.00
❑78/CS, 1: Cyborg Superman, Die-cut cover; poster	1.95	0.50	1.25	2.50
❑79, Jul 93, Reign of the Supermen	1.50	0.40	1.00	2.00
❑80, Aug 93, Reign of the Supermen, V: Mongul, Coast City destroyed; Cyborg Superman revealed as evil	1.50	0.40	1.00	2.00
❑81, Sep 93, Reign of the Supermen; Resurrections	1.50	0.40	1.00	2.00
❑82, Oct 93, Reign of the Supermen, return of Superman; Reign of the Superman ends; True Superman revealed	1.50	0.40	1.00	2.00
❑82/SC, chromium cover; with poster; Reign of the Superman ends; True Superman revealed	2.00	0.70	1.75	3.50
❑83, Nov 93, Funeral for a Friend Epilogue.	1.50	0.40	1.00	2.00
❑84, Dec 93, V: Toyman; D: Adam Grant	1.50	0.40	1.00	2.00
❑85, Jan 94	1.50	0.40	1.00	2.00
❑86, Feb 94	1.50	0.40	1.00	2.00
❑87, Mar 94, Bizarro's World, Part 1, Bizarro	1.50	0.40	1.00	2.00
❑88, Apr 94, Bizarro	1.50	0.40	1.00	2.00
❑89, May 94	1.50	0.40	1.00	2.00
❑90, Jun 94, BA	1.50	0.40	1.00	2.00
❑91, Jul 94, BA	1.50	0.40	1.00	2.00
❑92, Aug 94, Massacre in Metropolis, Part 1	1.50	0.40	1.00	2.00
❑93, Sep 94, Zero Hour, Zero Hour	1.50	0.40	1.00	2.00
❑94, Nov 94, Dead Again	1.50	0.40	1.00	2.00

	ORIG	GOOD	FINE	N-MINT
❑95, Dec 94, Dead Again, A: Atom	1.50	0.40	1.00	2.00
❑96, Jan 95, Dead Again, ▲1995-2	1.50	0.40	1.00	2.00
❑97, Feb 95, 1: Shadowdragon	1.50	0.40	1.00	2.00
❑98, Mar 95	1.50	0.40	1.00	2.00
❑99, Apr 95, A: Agent Liberty	1.50	0.40	1.00	2.00
❑100, May 95, Death of Clark Kent, Part 1; The Death Of Clark Kent, Giant-size; 100th anniversary edition; ▲1995-18	2.95	0.60	1.50	3.00
❑100/SC, May 95, The Death Of Clark Kent, enhanced cover; Giant-size; 100th anniversary edition; ▲1995-18	3.95	0.80	2.00	4.00
❑101, Jun 95, Grief, ▲1995-22	1.95	0.40	1.00	2.00
❑102, Jul 95, V: Captain Marvel	1.95	0.40	1.00	2.00
❑103, Aug 95, V: Arclight	1.95	0.40	1.00	2.00
❑104, Sep 95, Cyborg is released by Darkseid	1.95	0.40	1.00	2.00
❑105, Oct 95, A: Green Lantern	1.95	0.40	1.00	2.00
❑106, Nov 95, Trial of Superman	1.95	0.40	1.00	2.00
❑107, Dec 95, Trial of Superman	1.95	0.40	1.00	2.00
❑108, Jan 96, Trial of Superman, D: Mope.	1.95	0.40	1.00	2.00
❑109, Feb 96, The Kill Fee!, Christmas story; return of Lori Lemaris; ▲1996-7	1.95	0.40	1.00	2.00
❑110, Mar 96, The Treasure Hunt Caper, A: Plastic Man, ▲1996-11	1.95	0.40	1.00	2.00
❑111, Apr 96, Divisions, ▲1996-16	1.95	0.40	1.00	2.00
❑112, Jun 96	1.95	0.40	1.00	2.00
❑113, Jul 96	1.95	0.40	1.00	2.00
❑114, Aug 96	1.95	0.40	1.00	2.00
❑115, Sep 96, Lois becomes foreign correspondent	1.95	0.40	1.00	2.00
❑116, Oct 96, The Bottle City, Part 3, Teen Titans preview	1.95	0.40	1.00	2.00
❑117, Nov 96, Sanctuary, Final Night; ▲1996-42	1.95	0.40	1.00	2.00
❑118, Dec 96, From the Heart, A: Wonder Woman, Lois decides to return to Metropolis; ▲1996-46	1.95	0.40	1.00	2.00
❑119, Jan 97, Power Struggle; Subburned!, A: Legion, ▲1997-1	1.95	0.40	1.00	2.00
❑120, Feb 97, To Be a Superman	1.95	0.40	1.00	2.00
❑121, Mar 97, They Call It Suicide Slum, ▲1997-10	1.95	0.40	1.00	2.00
❑122, Apr 97, energy powers begin to manifest	1.95	0.40	1.00	2.00
❑123, May 97, Superman...Reborn!, New costume	1.95	0.60	1.50	3.00
❑123/SC, May 97, Superman...Reborn!, glow-in-the-dark cardstock cover; New costume	1.95	1.00	2.50	5.00
❑124, Jun 97, A: Booster Gold	1.95	0.40	1.00	2.00
❑125, Jul 97, A: Atom, in Kandor	1.95	0.40	1.00	2.00
❑126, Aug 97, A: Batman	1.95	0.40	1.00	2.00
❑127, Sep 97, Superman Revenge Squad leader's identity revealed	1.95	0.40	1.00	2.00
❑128, Oct 97, V: Cyborg Superman, Genesis	1.95	0.40	1.00	2.00
❑129, Nov 97, Within Human Reach, A: Scorn, ▲1997-44	1.95	0.40	1.00	2.00
❑130, Dec 97, the Longest Halloween, Face cover	1.95	0.40	1.00	2.00
❑131, Jan 98, D: Mayor Berkowitz, birth of Lena Luthor	1.95	0.40	1.00	2.00
❑132, Feb 98	1.95	0.40	1.00	2.00
❑133, Mar 98	1.95	0.40	1.00	2.00
❑134, Apr 98, Millennium Giants	1.95	0.40	1.00	2.00
❑135, May 98, leads into Superman Forever #1; End of Superman Red/Blue	1.95	0.40	1.00	2.00
❑136, Jul 98, Superman 2999	1.95	0.40	1.00	2.00
❑137, Aug 98, Superman 2999, V: Muto	1.95	0.40	1.00	2.00
❑138, Sep 98, V: Dominus; A: Kismet	1.99	0.40	1.00	2.00
❑139, Oct 98, V: Dominus	1.99	0.40	1.00	1.99
❑140, Dec 98, in Kandor; Inventor's identity revealed	1.99	0.40	1.00	1.99
❑141, Jan 99, 1: Outburst	1.99	0.40	1.00	1.99
❑142, Feb 99, A: Outburst	1.99	0.40	1.00	1.99
❑143, Mar 99, A: Superman Robots; A: Supermen of America	1.99	0.40	1.00	1.99
❑144, Apr 99, Fortress destroyed	1.99	0.40	1.00	1.99
❑145, Jun 99, Public Hearing, ▲1999-23	1.99	0.40	1.00	1.99
❑146, Jul 99, Rough Day at the Office, A: Toyman	1.99	0.40	1.00	1.99
❑147, Aug 99, One-Man JLA; Secret Origin Part 1: The Knight, Superman as Green Lantern	1.99	0.40	1.00	1.99
❑148, Sep 99, Champions	1.99	0.40	1.00	1.99
❑149, Oct 99, SB, Who is Strange Visitor?, Part 1, ▲1999-40	1.99	0.40	1.00	1.99
❑150, Nov 99	1.99	0.40	1.00	1.99
❑150/SC, Nov 99, Special cover	3.95	0.79	1.98	3.95
❑151, Dec 99, Daily Planet reopens	1.99	0.40	1.00	1.99
❑152, Jan 00, JPH (w), Deadline U.S.A., ▲2000-1	1.99	0.40	1.00	1.99

	ORIG	GOOD	FINE	N-MINT
❑153, Feb 00, JPH (w), Say Goodbye, ▲2000-5	1.99	0.40	1.00	1.99
❑154, Mar 00	1.99	0.40	1.00	1.99
❑155, Apr 00	1.99	0.40	1.00	1.99
❑156, May 00, JPH (w), The Tender Trap, ▲2000-18	1.99	0.40	1.00	1.99
❑157, Jun 00, JPH (w), Superman's Enemy Lois Lane, ▲2000-22	1.99	0.40	1.00	1.99
❑158, Jul 00	1.99	0.40	1.00	1.99
❑159, Aug 00	—	0.40	1.00	1.99
❑160, Sep 00	—	0.40	1.00	1.99
❑161, Oct 00, JPH (w), The Reign of Emperor Joker, Part 2, ▲2000-39	2.25	0.45	1.13	2.25
❑162, Nov 00, JPH (w), American Dream, ▲2000-43	2.25	0.45	1.13	2.25
❑163, Dec 00, JPH (w), Where Monsters Lurk!, ▲2000-47	2.25	0.45	1.13	2.25
❑164, Jan 01, JPH (w), Tales From the Bizarro World, ▲2001-1	2.25	0.45	1.13	2.25
❑165, Feb 01, JPH (w), Help!, ▲2001-6	2.25	0.45	1.13	2.25
❑166, Mar 01, JPH (w), Fathers..., ▲2001-10	2.25	0.45	1.13	2.25
❑167, Apr 01, JPH (w), Return to Krypton, Part 1, ▲2001-14	2.25	0.45	1.13	2.25
❑168, May 01, JPH (w), With This Ring..., ▲2001-18	2.25	0.45	1.13	2.25
❑169, Jun 01, Infestation, Part 1, ▲2001-22	2.25	0.45	1.13	2.25
❑170	2.25	0.45	1.13	2.25
❑171	2.25	0.45	1.13	2.25
❑172, JPH (w)	2.25	0.45	1.13	2.25
❑1000000, Nov 98, Down to Earth	1.99	0.40	1.00	1.99
❑1000000/LE, Down to Earth	14.99	3.00	7.49	14.99
❑3D 1	3.95	0.79	1.98	3.95
❑Anl 1, O: Titano	1.25	0.80	2.00	4.00
❑Anl 2, Private Lives	1.50	0.60	1.50	3.00
❑Anl 3, Armageddon 2001, Part 2, Armageddon 2001	2.00	0.50	1.25	2.50
❑Anl 3-2, 2nd Printing	2.00	0.40	1.00	2.00
❑Anl 3-3, 3rd Printing; silver	2.00	0.40	1.00	2.00
❑Anl 4, Eclipso: The Darkness Within, Part 5, Eclipso: The Darkness Within	2.50	0.50	1.25	2.50
❑Anl 5, Bloodlines, 1: Myriad, Bloodlines	2.50	0.50	1.25	2.50
❑Anl 6, Elseworlds	2.95	0.59	1.48	2.95
❑Anl 7, A: Doctor Occult; A: Dr. Occult, Year One	3.95	0.79	1.98	3.95
❑Anl 8, Legends of the Dead Earth; The League of Supermen	2.95	0.59	1.48	2.95
❑Anl 9, A: Doc Savage, Pulp Heroes	3.95	0.59	1.48	2.95
❑Anl 10, A: Phantom Zone villains, Ghosts	2.95	0.59	1.48	2.95
❑Anl 11, Oct 99, The Apes of Wrath, JLApe	2.95	0.59	1.48	2.95
❑GS 1, Feb 99, 80pgs.	4.95	0.99	2.47	4.95
❑GS 2, Jun 99, Under Control; If I Had a Hammer, 80pgs.	4.95	0.99	2.47	4.95
❑GS 3, Nov 00, I, Witness, 80pgs.	4.95	0.99	2.47	4.95
❑SE 1, The Sand Man, 1992 Special	3.50	0.80	2.00	4.00

SUPERMAN (GIVEAWAYS)
DC

	ORIG	GOOD	FINE	N-MINT
❑1, game giveaway	—	0.20	0.50	1.00
❑2, Pizza Hut	—	0.20	0.50	1.00
❑3, Jul 80, Radio Shack	—	0.20	0.50	1.00
❑4, Radio Shack	—	0.20	0.50	1.00
❑5, Radio Shack	—	0.20	0.50	1.00

SUPERMAN 3-D
DC

	ORIG	GOOD	FINE	N-MINT
❑1, Dec 98, Bad Trip to Nowhere, glasses	3.95	0.80	2.00	4.00

SUPERMAN ADVENTURES
DC

Based on the animated series, *Superman Adventures* had its own version of "Kryptonite No More!"

© 2001 DC Comics

	ORIG	GOOD	FINE	N-MINT
❑1, Nov 96, Men of Steel, based on animated series; follow-up to pilot episode	1.75	0.60	1.50	3.00
❑2, Dec 96, Be Careful What You Wish For, V: Metallo	1.75	0.50	1.25	2.50
❑3, Jan 97, Distant Thunder, V: Brainiac	1.75	0.50	1.25	2.50
❑4, Feb 97, Eye to Eye	1.75	0.40	1.00	2.00
❑5, Mar 97, Balance of Power, V: Livewire	1.75	0.40	1.00	2.00
❑6, Apr 97	1.75	0.40	1.00	2.00
❑7, May 97, All Creatures Great and Small, Part 1, V: Jax-ur, Mala; V: Jax-ur; V: Mala	1.75	0.40	1.00	2.00
❑8, Jun 97, All Creatures Great and Small, Part 2, V: Jax-ur, Mala; V: Jax-ur; V: Mala	1.75	0.40	1.00	2.00
❑9, Jul 97, Return of the Hero	1.75	0.40	1.00	2.00
❑10, Aug 97, V: Toyman	1.75	0.40	1.00	2.00
❑11, Sep 97	1.75	0.40	1.00	2.00
❑12, Oct 97, The War Within, Part 2	1.75	0.40	1.00	2.00
❑13, Nov 97	1.75	0.40	1.00	2.00
❑14, Dec 97, ME (w), Stop the Presses!, Face cover	1.75	0.40	1.00	2.00
❑15, Jan 98, ME (w), Maximum Effort!, A: Bibbo	1.95	0.40	1.00	2.00
❑16, Feb 98, Clark Kent, You're a Nobody!	1.95	0.40	1.00	2.00
❑17, Mar 98	1.95	0.40	1.00	2.00
❑18, Apr 98, It's a Super Life	1.95	0.40	1.00	2.00
❑19, May 98, The Bodyguard of Steel	1.95	0.40	1.00	2.00
❑20, Jun 98	1.95	0.40	1.00	2.00
❑21, Jul 98, double-sized; adapts Supergirl episode	3.95	0.79	1.98	3.95
❑22, Aug 98	1.95	0.40	1.00	2.00
❑23, Sep 98, V: Brainiac; A: Livewire	1.99	0.40	1.00	2.00
❑24, Oct 98, V: Parasite	1.99	0.40	1.00	2.00
❑25, Nov 98, A: Batgirl	1.99	0.40	1.00	2.00
❑26, Dec 98, V: Mxyzptlk	1.99	0.40	1.00	2.00
❑27, Jan 99, 1: Superior-Man	1.99	0.40	1.00	2.00
❑28, Feb 99, A: Jimmy Olsen, Jimmy and Superman switch bodies	1.99	0.40	1.00	2.00
❑29, Mar 99, A: Lobo; A: Bizarro, Lobo appearance	1.99	0.40	1.00	2.00
❑30, Apr 99	1.99	0.40	1.00	2.00
❑31, May 99	1.99	0.40	1.00	2.00
❑32, Jun 99, Sullivan's Girl Friend, Lois Lane	1.99	0.40	1.00	2.00
❑33, Jul 99, Clark Kent is Superman and I Can Prove It!	1.99	0.40	1.00	2.00
❑34, Aug 99, Sanctuary, A: Doctor Fate	1.99	0.40	1.00	2.00
❑35, Sep 99, Never Play with the Toyman's Toys!, V: Toyman	1.99	0.40	1.00	2.00
❑36, Oct 99, This is a Job for Superman	1.99	0.40	1.00	2.00
❑37, Nov 99, Clark Kent: Public Enemy, V: Multi-Face	1.99	0.40	1.00	2.00
❑38, Dec 99, If I Ruled the World!	1.99	0.40	1.00	2.00
❑39, Jan 00, Reunion	1.99	0.40	1.00	2.00
❑40, Feb 00, Old Wounds	1.99	0.40	1.00	2.00
❑41, Mar 00	1.99	0.40	1.00	1.99
❑42, Apr 00	1.99	0.40	1.00	1.99
❑43, May 00, Are You My Mother Box?	1.99	0.40	1.00	1.99
❑44, Jun 00, Law and Orders	1.99	0.40	1.00	1.99
❑45, Jul 00	1.99	0.40	1.00	1.99
❑46, Aug 00	1.99	0.40	1.00	1.99
❑47, Sep 00	1.99	0.40	1.00	1.99
❑48, Oct 00, The Believer	1.99	0.40	1.00	1.99
❑49, Nov 00, The Challenge	1.99	0.40	1.00	1.99
❑50, Dec 00	1.99	0.40	1.00	1.99
❑51, Jan 01, How Many Miles to Nowhere Atoll...?	1.99	0.40	1.00	1.99
❑52, Feb 01, A Death in the Family	1.99	0.40	1.00	1.99
❑53, Mar 01, ME (w), The Greatest Escape!	1.99	0.40	1.00	1.99
❑54, Apr 01, Kryptonite No More!, Part 1	1.99	0.40	1.00	1.99
❑55, May 01, Kryptonite No More!, Part 2	1.99	0.40	1.00	1.99
❑56	1.99	0.40	1.00	1.99
❑57	1.99	0.40	1.00	1.99
❑58	1.99	0.40	1.00	1.99
❑59	1.99	0.40	1.00	1.99
❑Anl 1, JSa, Dark Planes Drifter, ties in with Adventures in the DC Universe Annual #1 and Batman and Robin Adventures Annual #2	3.95	0.79	1.98	3.95
❑SE 1, Feb 98, V: Lobo	2.95	0.59	1.48	2.95

SUPERMAN: A NATION DIVIDED
DC

Value: Cover or less

❑1, nn; prestige format; Elseworlds; Superman in Civil War 4.95

SUPERMAN & BATMAN: GENERATIONS
DC

Value: Cover or less

❑1, JBy, JBy (w), 1939, The Vigilantes, V: Joker; V: Lex Luthor; V: Ultra-Humanite, Elseworlds story 4.95

❑2, JBy, JBy (w), V: Mxyzptlk; V: Joker Junior; V: Bat-Mite, Elseworlds story 4.95

❑3, JBy, JBy (w), A: Ra's Al Ghul; D: Luthor, Elseworlds story 4.95

❑4, JBy, JBy (w), A: Lana Lang, Elseworlds story 4.95

SUPERMAN & BATMAN MAGAZINE
WELSH

	ORIG	GOOD	FINE	N-MINT
❑1, Sum 93, bagged with poster	2.95	0.60	1.50	3.00
❑2	1.95	0.40	1.00	2.00

	ORIG	GOOD	FINE	N-MINT
❑3, trading cards	2.95	0.60	1.50	3.00
❑4, Spr 94	1.95	0.40	1.00	2.00
❑5, Sum 94, magazine	1.95	0.40	1.00	2.00
❑7, Win 95, magazine	1.95	0.40	1.00	2.00
❑8, Spr 95, magazine	1.95	0.40	1.00	2.00

SUPERMAN AND BATMAN: WORLD'S FUNNEST
DC

Value: Cover or less

❑1, FM; BB, Last Imp Standing ... 6.95

SUPERMAN & BUGS BUNNY
DC

Value: Cover or less

❑1, Jul 00, TP; JSa, ME (w) ... 2.50
❑2, Aug 00, TP; JSa, ME (w) ... 2.50
❑3, Sep 00, TP; JSa, ME (w), The Duck Knight Returns! ... 2.50
❑4, Oct 00, TP; JSa, ME (w), Cwisis on Infinite Earths ... 2.50

SUPERMAN ARCHIVES
DC

Value: Cover or less

❑1, Dec 89, reprint #1-4; 1939-1940 ... 39.95
❑2, Dec 90, reprint #5-8; 1940 39.95
❑3, Dec 91, reprint #9-12; 194139.95
❑4, reprint #13-16; 1941-42 ... 49.95
❑5, reprint #17-20 ... 49.95

SUPERMAN: DISTANT FIRES
DC

Value: Cover or less

❑1, nn; prestige format; Elseworlds ... 5.95

SUPERMAN/DOOMSDAY: HUNTER/PREY
DC

	ORIG	GOOD	FINE	N-MINT
❑1, prestige format	4.95	1.20	3.00	6.00
❑2, O: Doomsday, prestige format	4.95	1.20	3.00	6.00
❑3, D: Doomsday, prestige format	4.95	1.20	3.00	6.00

SUPERMAN: EMPEROR JOKER
DC

Value: Cover or less

❑1, Oct 00, JPH (w), It's a Joker World, Baby, We Just Live in It! ... 3.50

SUPERMAN: END OF THE CENTURY
DC

	ORIG	GOOD	FINE	N-MINT
❑1	—	1.19	2.97	5.95

SUPERMAN FAMILY, THE
DC

	ORIG	GOOD	FINE	N-MINT
❑164, May 74, 100pgs.; Series continued from "Superman's Pal Jimmy Olsen"	0.60	3.00	7.50	15.00
❑165, Jul 74, 100pgs.; reprints from Action #296, Jimmy Olsen #59, Lois Lane #47, Superboy #111, #133, and Superman #186	0.60	2.40	6.00	12.00
❑166, Sep 74, 100pgs.	0.60	2.40	6.00	12.00
❑167, Nov 74, 100pgs.	0.60	2.40	6.00	12.00
❑168, Jan 75, 100pgs.	0.60	2.40	6.00	12.00
❑169, Mar 75, 100pgs.	0.60	2.40	6.00	12.00
❑170, May 75, 100pgs.	0.50	2.40	6.00	12.00
❑171, Jul 75, 100pgs.	0.50	2.00	5.00	10.00
❑172, Sep 75, 100pgs.	0.50	2.00	5.00	10.00
❑173, Nov 75, 100pgs.	0.50	2.00	5.00	10.00
❑174, Jan 75, 100pgs.	0.50	2.00	5.00	10.00
❑175, Mar 76, 100pgs.	0.50	2.00	5.00	10.00
❑176, May 76, 100pgs.	0.50	2.00	5.00	10.00
❑177, Jul 76, reprints from Jimmy Olsen #74 and Lois Lane #53	0.50	2.00	5.00	10.00
❑178, Sep 76	0.50	1.00	2.50	5.00
❑179, Oct 76	0.50	1.00	2.50	5.00
❑180, Nov 76	0.50	1.00	2.50	5.00
❑181, Jan 77	0.50	0.70	1.75	3.50
❑182, Apr 77	1.00	0.70	1.75	3.50
❑183, Jun 77	1.00	0.70	1.75	3.50
❑184, Aug 77, V: Prankster	1.00	0.70	1.75	3.50
❑185, Oct 77	1.00	0.70	1.75	3.50
❑186, Dec 77, A: Earth-2 Superman	1.00	0.70	1.75	3.50
❑187, Feb 78, A: Earth-2 Superman	1.00	0.70	1.75	3.50
❑188, Apr 78	1.00	0.70	1.75	3.50
❑189, Jun 78	1.00	0.70	1.75	3.50
❑190, Aug 78	1.00	0.70	1.75	3.50
❑191, Oct 78	1.00	0.70	1.75	3.50
❑192, Dec 78	1.00	0.70	1.75	3.50
❑193, Feb 79	1.00	0.70	1.75	3.50
❑194, Apr 79, MR, V: Jimmy clones	1.00	0.70	1.75	3.50
❑195, Jun 79	1.00	0.70	1.75	3.50
❑196, Aug 79	1.00	0.70	1.75	3.50
❑197, Oct 79	1.00	0.70	1.75	3.50
❑198, Dec 79	1.00	0.70	1.75	3.50
❑199, Feb 80	1.00	0.70	1.75	3.50
❑200, Apr 80, Imaginary Story	1.00	0.70	1.75	3.50
❑201, Jun 80	1.00	0.60	1.50	3.00
❑202, Aug 80	1.00	0.60	1.50	3.00
❑203, Oct 80, 1: Lana Lang	1.00	0.60	1.50	3.00
❑204, Dec 80, V: Enchantress	1.00	0.60	1.50	3.00
❑205, Feb 81, 1: H.I.V.E.; V: Enchantress	1.00	0.60	1.50	3.00
❑206, Apr 81, A: Lesla-Lar	1.00	0.60	1.50	3.00
❑207, Jun 81, A: Legion; V: Universo	1.00	0.60	1.50	3.00
❑208, Jul 81, Supergirl relocates to New York	1.00	0.60	1.50	3.00
❑209, Aug 81	1.00	0.60	1.50	3.00
❑210, Sep 81	1.00	0.60	1.50	3.00
❑211, Oct 81	1.00	0.60	1.50	3.00
❑212, Nov 81	1.00	0.60	1.50	3.00
❑213, Dec 81, 1: Insect Queen (Lana Lang)	1.00	0.60	1.50	3.00
❑214, Jan 82	1.00	0.60	1.50	3.00
❑215, Feb 82	1.00	0.60	1.50	3.00
❑216, Mar 82	1.00	0.60	1.50	3.00
❑217, Apr 82	1.00	0.60	1.50	3.00
❑218, May 82	1.00	0.60	1.50	3.00
❑219, Jun 82, V: Master Jailer	1.00	0.60	1.50	3.00
❑220, Jul 82, V: Master Jailer	1.00	0.60	1.50	3.00
❑221, Aug 82, V: Master Jailer	1.00	0.60	1.50	3.00
❑222, Sep 82, Final Issue	1.00	0.60	1.50	3.00

SUPERMAN/FANTASTIC FOUR
DC

Value: Cover or less

❑1 ... 9.95

SUPERMAN FOR ALL SEASONS
DC

Value: Cover or less

❑1, JPH (w), Spring, prestige format; Spring ... 4.95
❑2, JPH (w), Summer, prestige format; Summer ... 4.95
❑3, JPH (w), Fall, prestige format; Fall ... 4.95
❑4, JPH (w), Winter, prestige format; Winter ... 4.95

SUPERMAN FOR EARTH
DC

Value: Cover or less

❑1, Apr 91, JO (c), nn ... 4.95

SUPERMAN FOREVER
DC

	ORIG	GOOD	FINE	N-MINT
❑1, Jun 98, prestige format; newsstand edition; Superman returns to normal powers	4.95	1.10	2.75	5.50
❑1/Aut, Signed by Alex Ross, Dan Jurgens, Joe Rubinstein, Bret Breeding, Jon Bogdanove, Stuart Immonen	—	6.00	15.00	30.00
❑1/SC, Jun 98, lenticular animation cover; prestige format; Superman returns to normal powers	5.95	1.40	3.50	7.00

SUPER MANGA BLAST!
DARK HORSE

	ORIG	GOOD	FINE	N-MINT
❑1	4.95	0.99	2.47	4.95
❑2	4.95	0.99	2.47	4.95
❑3	4.95	0.99	2.47	4.95
❑4, Jun 00, 3x3 Eyes; What's Michael	4.95	0.99	2.47	4.95
❑5	—	0.99	2.47	4.95
❑6	—	0.99	2.47	4.95
❑7	—	0.99	2.47	4.95
❑8	—	0.99	2.47	4.95
❑9	—	0.99	2.47	4.95
❑10, Feb 01, Seraphic Feather; Oh My Goddess!	4.99	1.00	2.49	4.99
❑11	4.99	1.00	2.49	4.99
❑12, May 01, Club 9; 3x3 Eyes	4.99	1.00	2.49	4.99
❑13	4.99	1.00	2.49	4.99
❑14	4.99	1.00	2.49	4.99

SUPERMAN GALLERY, THE
DC

Value: Cover or less

❑1 ... 2.95

SUPERMAN/GEN13
WILDSTORM

Value: Cover or less

❑1, Jun 00, The Never-Ending Prattle ... 2.50
❑1/A, Jun 00, The Never-Ending Prattle, Fairchild opening shirt to show Supergirl costume on cover ... 2.50
❑2, Jul 00, Supergirl/Fairchild cover ... 2.50
❑2/A, Jul 00, Large figures looking down on cover ... 2.50
❑3, Aug 00 ... 2.50

SUPERMAN, INC.
DC

Value: Cover or less

❑1 ... 6.95

SUPERMAN IV MOVIE SPECIAL
DC

Value: Cover or less

❑1, Oct 87, movie Adaptation .. 2.00

SUPERMAN: KAL
DC

Value: Cover or less

❑1, nn; prestige format one-shot 5.95

SUPERMAN: KING OF THE WORLD
DC

Value: Cover or less

❑1, Jun 99, King of the World, ▲1999-22 ... 3.95
❑1/GO, Jun 99, King of the World, enhanced cardstock cover; ▲1999-22 ... 4.95

SUPERMAN: LAST SON OF EARTH
DC

Value: Cover or less

❑1 ... 5.95
❑2 ... 5.95

SUPERMAN: LEX 2000
DC

Value: Cover or less

❑1, Jan 01, JPH (w), Triumph over Tragedy; One or the Other .. 3.50

SUPERMAN: LOIS LANE
DC

Value: Cover or less

❑1, Jun 98, One-Shot; Girlfrenzy 1.95

SUPERMAN/MADMAN HULLABALOO, THE
DARK HORSE

Value: Cover or less

❑1, Jun 97, Man and Super-Madman!, crossover with DC 2.95

❑2, Jul 97, Hot Dang! Yin Yang!, crossover with DC 2.95

❑3, Aug 97, crossover with DC 2.95

SUPERMAN MEETS THE QUIK BUNNY
DC

	ORIG	GOOD	FINE	N-MINT
❑1, DG; CI, Quik Thinking, nn; promotional giveaway from Nestle	—	0.20	0.50	1.00

SUPERMAN METROPOLIS SECRET FILES
DC

Value: Cover or less

❑1, Jul 00, JPH (w), Metropolica; Fortress of Solitude 4.95

SUPERMAN MOVIE SPECIAL
DC

	ORIG	GOOD	FINE	N-MINT
❑1	1.00	0.40	1.00	2.00

SUPERMAN MOVIE SPECIAL, THE
DC

	ORIG	GOOD	FINE	N-MINT
❑1, Sep 83, CS; GM, Photo cover; movie Adaptation; adapts Superman III	1.00	0.40	1.00	2.00

SUPERMAN: PEACE ON EARTH
DC

Value: Cover or less

❑1, ARo, Peace on Earth, Oversized 9.95

❑1/Aut, ARo, Peace on Earth, Signed by Alex Ross; Oversized 22.95

SUPERMAN PLUS
DC

Value: Cover or less

❑1, Feb 97, Yesterday, Today, and Tomorrow, A: Legion 2.95

SUPERMAN RED/SUPERMAN BLUE
DC

Value: Cover or less

❑1, Superman Red/Superman Blue, 1: Superman Red, 3-D glasses 3.95

❑Dlx 1, Feb 98, nn; one-shot with 3-D cover; polybagged with reprint of Superman 3-D and 3-D glasses; Superman splits into two beings 4.95

SUPERMAN: SAVE THE PLANET
DC

Value: Cover or less

❑1, Oct 98, Daily Planet sold to Lex Luthor 2.95

❑1/SC, Oct 98, acetate overlay 3.95

SUPERMAN: SECRET FILES
DC

Value: Cover or less

❑1, Jan 98, Secret Origin; Jimmy Olsen's Past Lives, O: Superman, background material .. 4.95

❑2, May 99, background material 4.95

SUPERMAN'S GIRL FRIEND LOIS LANE
DC

	ORIG	GOOD	FINE	N-MINT
❑22, Jan 61	0.10	18.00	45.00	90.00
❑23, Feb 61	0.10	18.00	45.00	90.00
❑24, Apr 61	0.10	18.00	45.00	90.00
❑25, May 61	0.10	18.00	45.00	90.00
❑26, Jul 61	0.10	18.00	45.00	90.00
❑27, Aug 61	0.10	18.00	45.00	90.00
❑28, Oct 61	0.10	18.00	45.00	90.00
❑29, Nov 61	0.10	18.00	45.00	90.00
❑30, Jan 62	0.10	10.00	25.00	50.00
❑31, Feb 62	0.12	10.00	25.00	50.00
❑32, Apr 62	0.12	10.00	25.00	50.00
❑33, May 62, A: Mon-El; A: Phantom Zone .	0.12	10.00	25.00	50.00
❑34, Jul 62	0.12	10.00	25.00	50.00
❑35, Aug 62, CS	0.12	10.00	25.00	50.00
❑36, Oct 62	0.12	10.00	25.00	50.00
❑37, Nov 62	0.12	10.00	25.00	50.00
❑38, Jan 63	0.12	10.00	25.00	50.00
❑39, Feb 63, CS	0.12	10.00	25.00	50.00
❑40, Apr 63	0.12	10.00	25.00	50.00
❑41, May 63, CS	0.12	10.00	25.00	50.00
❑42, Jul 63	0.12	10.00	25.00	50.00
❑43, Aug 63	0.12	10.00	25.00	50.00
❑44, Oct 63	0.12	10.00	25.00	50.00
❑45, Nov 63	0.12	10.00	25.00	50.00
❑46, Jan 64	0.12	10.00	25.00	50.00
❑47, Feb 64	0.12	10.00	25.00	50.00
❑48, Apr 64	0.12	10.00	25.00	50.00
❑49, May 64	0.12	10.00	25.00	50.00
❑50, Jul 64	0.12	10.00	25.00	50.00
❑51, Aug 64	0.12	7.00	17.50	35.00
❑52, Oct 64	0.12	7.00	17.50	35.00

"What's Michael?," a popular Japanese comic strip featuring a cat, is reprinted in English in Dark Horse's *Super Manga Blast!*

	ORIG	GOOD	FINE	N-MINT
❑53, Nov 64, KS, How Lois Lane Fell in Love with Superman!; Superman's Home-town Sweetheart, How Lois fell in love with Superman	0.12	7.00	17.50	35.00
❑54, Jan 65	0.12	7.00	17.50	35.00
❑55, Feb 65	0.12	7.00	17.50	35.00
❑56, Apr 65	0.12	7.00	17.50	35.00
❑57, May 65	0.12	7.00	17.50	35.00
❑58, Jul 65	0.12	7.00	17.50	35.00
❑59, Aug 65	0.12	7.00	17.50	35.00
❑60, Oct 65	0.12	7.00	17.50	35.00
❑61, Nov 65	0.12	7.00	17.50	35.00
❑62, Jan 66	0.12	7.00	17.50	35.00
❑63, Feb 66, V: S.K.U.L., Noel Neill interview	0.12	7.00	17.50	35.00
❑64, Apr 66	0.12	7.00	17.50	35.00
❑65, May 66	0.12	7.00	17.50	35.00
❑66, Jul 66	0.12	7.00	17.50	35.00
❑67, Aug 66	0.12	7.00	17.50	35.00
❑68, Sep 66, Giant-size	0.12	9.00	22.50	45.00
❑69, Oct 66	0.12	7.00	17.50	35.00
❑70, Nov 66, A: Catwoman, 1st Catwoman in Silver Age	0.12	45.00	112.50	225.00
❑71, Jan 67, A: Catwoman	0.12	26.00	65.00	130.00
❑72, Feb 67	0.12	3.20	8.00	16.00
❑73, Apr 67	0.12	3.20	8.00	16.00
❑74, May 67, 1: Bizarro-Flash; 1: Bizarro Flash	0.12	7.00	17.50	35.00
❑75, Jul 67	0.12	3.20	8.00	16.00
❑76, Aug 67	0.12	3.20	8.00	16.00
❑77, Sep 67, Giant-size	0.12	5.00	12.50	25.00
❑78, Oct 67	0.12	3.20	8.00	16.00
❑79, Nov 67	0.12	2.00	5.00	10.00
❑80, Jan 68	0.12	2.00	5.00	10.00
❑81, Feb 68	0.12	2.00	5.00	10.00
❑82, Apr 68	0.12	2.00	5.00	10.00
❑83, May 68	0.12	2.00	5.00	10.00
❑84, Jul 68	0.12	2.00	5.00	10.00
❑85, Aug 68	0.12	2.00	5.00	10.00
❑86, Sep 68, NA, Giant-size	0.25	3.60	9.00	18.00
❑87, Oct 68	0.12	2.00	5.00	10.00
❑88, Nov 68	0.12	2.00	5.00	10.00
❑89, Jan 69, Imaginary Story; Lois marries Batman	0.12	2.00	5.00	10.00
❑90, Feb 69	0.12	2.00	5.00	10.00
❑91, Apr 69	0.12	2.00	5.00	10.00
❑92, May 69	0.12	2.00	5.00	10.00
❑93, Jul 69, A: Wonder Woman	0.15	2.00	5.00	10.00
❑94, Aug 69	0.15	2.00	5.00	10.00
❑95, Sep 69, Giant-size	0.15	3.60	9.00	18.00
❑96, Oct 69	0.15	1.60	4.00	8.00
❑97, Nov 69	0.15	1.60	4.00	8.00
❑98, Jan 70	0.15	1.60	4.00	8.00
❑99, Feb 70	0.15	1.60	4.00	8.00
❑100, Apr 70	0.15	1.60	4.00	8.00
❑101, May 70	0.15	1.60	4.00	8.00
❑102, Jul 70	0.15	1.60	4.00	8.00
❑103, Aug 70	0.15	1.60	4.00	8.00
❑104, Sep 70, Giant-size	0.15	3.60	9.00	18.00
❑105, Oct 70, 1: The 1,000; 1: Rose & Thorn II (Rose Forrest)	0.15	3.00	7.50	15.00
❑106, Nov 70	0.15	1.20	3.00	6.00
❑107, Dec 70	0.15	1.20	3.00	6.00
❑108	0.15	1.20	3.00	6.00
❑109	0.15	1.20	3.00	6.00
❑110	0.15	1.20	3.00	6.00
❑111	0.15	1.20	3.00	6.00
❑112	0.15	1.20	3.00	6.00
❑113, Giant-size	0.15	3.00	7.50	15.00
❑114	0.15	1.20	3.00	6.00
❑115	—	1.20	3.00	6.00
❑116	—	1.20	3.00	6.00
❑117	—	1.20	3.00	6.00

	ORIG	GOOD	FINE	N-MINT
❑118	—	1.20	3.00	6.00
❑119	—	1.20	3.00	6.00
❑120	—	1.20	3.00	6.00
❑121, Feb 72	—	1.00	2.50	5.00
❑122, Apr 72	—	1.00	2.50	5.00
❑123, May 72	—	1.00	2.50	5.00
❑124, Jun 72	—	1.00	2.50	5.00
❑125, Aug 72	—	1.00	2.50	5.00
❑126, Sep 72	—	1.00	2.50	5.00
❑127, Oct 72	0.20	1.00	2.50	5.00
❑128, Dec 72	—	1.00	2.50	5.00
❑129, Feb 73, Serpent in Paradise; Rose and the Thorn: The Million Dollar Night!	—	1.00	2.50	5.00
❑130, Apr 73	—	1.00	2.50	5.00
❑131, Jun 73	0.20	1.00	2.50	5.00
❑132, Jul 73	—	1.00	2.50	5.00
❑133, Sep 73	—	1.00	2.50	5.00
❑134, Oct 73	—	1.00	2.50	5.00
❑135, Nov 73	—	1.00	2.50	5.00
❑136, Jan 74, A: Wonder Woman	0.20	1.00	2.50	5.00
❑137	0.20	1.00	2.50	5.00
❑Anl 1, Sum 62	0.25	20.00	50.00	100.00
❑Anl 2	—	12.00	30.00	60.00

SUPERMAN: SILVER BANSHEE
DC

Value: Cover or less

❑1, Dec 98, Superman: Silver Banshee 2.25

❑2, Jan 99 ..... 2.25

SUPERMAN'S METROPOLIS
DC

Value: Cover or less

❑1, nn; prestige format; Elseworlds 5.95

SUPERMAN'S NEMESIS: LEX LUTHOR
DC

Value: Cover or less

❑1, Mar 99, Dark Victory, Part 1 ..... 2.50

❑2, Apr 99, Dark Victory, Part 2, V: Demolitia 2.50

❑3, May 99, Dark Victory, Part 3 ..... 2.50

❑4, Jun 99, Dark Victory, Part 4 ..... 2.50

SUPERMAN'S PAL JIMMY OLSEN
DC

	ORIG	GOOD	FINE	N-MINT
❑50, Jan 61	0.10	15.00	37.50	75.00
❑51, Mar 61	0.10	10.00	25.00	50.00
❑52, Apr 61	0.12	10.00	25.00	50.00
❑53, Jun 61	0.12	10.00	25.00	50.00
❑54, Jul 61	0.12	10.00	25.00	50.00
❑55, Sep 61	0.12	10.00	25.00	50.00
❑56, Oct 61	0.12	10.00	25.00	50.00
❑57, Dec 61, CS, A: Supergirl	0.12	6.00	15.00	30.00
❑58, Jan 62	0.12	6.00	15.00	30.00
❑59, Mar 62, CS	0.12	6.00	15.00	30.00
❑60, Apr 62	0.12	6.00	15.00	30.00
❑61, Jun 62	0.12	6.00	15.00	30.00
❑62, Jul 62, Elastic Lad in Phantom Zone	0.12	6.00	15.00	30.00
❑63, Sep 62	0.12	6.00	15.00	30.00
❑64, Oct 62	0.12	6.00	15.00	30.00
❑65, Dec 62	0.12	6.00	15.00	30.00
❑66, Jan 63	0.12	6.00	15.00	30.00
❑67, Mar 63	0.12	6.00	15.00	30.00
❑68, Apr 63	0.12	6.00	15.00	30.00
❑69, Jun 63, CS	0.12	6.00	15.00	30.00
❑70, Jul 63, Silver Kryptonite	0.12	6.00	15.00	30.00
❑71, Sep 63	0.12	5.00	12.50	25.00
❑72, Oct 63, CS, A: Legion of Super-Heroes	0.12	6.00	15.00	30.00
❑73, Dec 63	0.12	6.00	15.00	30.00
❑74, Jan 64, CS, A: Lex Luthor	0.12	5.00	12.50	25.00
❑75, Mar 64, A: Supergirl	0.12	5.00	12.50	25.00
❑76, Apr 64, A: Saturn Girl; A: Triplicate Girl; A: Saturn Girl, Lightning Lass, Triplicate Girl; A: Lightning Lass	0.12	6.00	15.00	30.00
❑77, Jun 64	0.12	5.00	12.50	25.00
❑78, Jul 64	0.12	5.00	12.50	25.00
❑79, Sep 64, Jimmy as Beatle	0.12	5.00	12.50	25.00
❑80, Oct 64, 1: Bizarro-Jimmy Olsen	0.12	5.00	12.50	25.00
❑81, Dec 64	0.12	5.00	12.50	25.00
❑82, Jan 65	0.12	5.00	12.50	25.00
❑83, Mar 65	0.12	5.00	12.50	25.00
❑84, Apr 65, CS	0.12	5.00	12.50	25.00
❑85, Jun 65, CS	0.12	5.00	12.50	25.00
❑86, Jul 65	0.12	5.00	12.50	25.00
❑87, Sep 65, A: Bizarro Jimmy; A: Legion of Super-Villains	0.12	5.00	12.50	25.00
❑88, Oct 65	0.12	4.00	10.00	20.00
❑89, Dec 65	0.12	4.00	10.00	20.00
❑90, Jan 66	0.12	4.00	10.00	20.00
❑91, Mar 66	0.12	3.20	8.00	16.00
❑92, Apr 66, A: Batman	0.12	3.20	8.00	16.00
❑93, Jun 66	0.12	3.20	8.00	16.00
❑94, Jul 66	0.12	3.20	8.00	16.00
❑95, Aug 66, Giant-size	0.12	5.00	12.50	25.00
❑96, Sep 66	0.12	3.20	8.00	16.00
❑97, Oct 66	0.12	3.20	8.00	16.00
❑98, Dec 66	0.12	3.20	8.00	16.00
❑99, Jan 67, Jimmy as one-man Legion	0.12	3.20	8.00	16.00
❑100, Mar 67, Wedding of Jimmy and Lucy Lane	0.12	5.00	12.50	25.00
❑101, Apr 67	—	2.40	6.00	12.00
❑102, Jun 67	—	2.40	6.00	12.00
❑103, Jul 67	—	2.40	6.00	12.00
❑104, Aug 67, Giant-size; giant; Weird Adventures	0.25	5.00	12.50	25.00
❑105, Sep 67, World of 1, 000 Olsens	0.12	2.40	6.00	12.00
❑106, Oct 67	—	2.40	6.00	12.00
❑107, Dec 67, CS	—	2.40	6.00	12.00
❑108, Jan 68, CS	—	2.40	6.00	12.00
❑109, Mar 68, A: Luthor	0.12	2.40	6.00	12.00
❑110, Apr 68, CS	—	2.40	6.00	12.00
❑111, Jun 68	—	2.40	6.00	12.00
❑112, Jul 68	—	2.40	6.00	12.00
❑113, Aug 68, 80pgs.; Anti-Superman issue	0.25	5.00	12.50	25.00
❑114, Sep 68	—	2.40	6.00	12.00
❑115, Oct 68, A: Aquaman	0.12	2.40	6.00	12.00
❑116, Dec 68	0.12	2.40	6.00	12.00
❑117, Jan 69	—	2.40	6.00	12.00
❑118, Mar 69	—	2.40	6.00	12.00
❑119, Apr 69	—	2.40	6.00	12.00
❑120, Jun 69	—	2.00	5.00	10.00
❑121, Jul 69	—	2.00	5.00	10.00
❑122, Aug 69, 80pgs.	—	2.00	5.00	10.00
❑123, Sep 69	0.15	2.00	5.00	10.00
❑124, Oct 69	0.15	2.00	5.00	10.00
❑125, Dec 69, Superman's Saddest Day!; The Spendthrift and the Miser	0.15	2.00	5.00	10.00
❑126, Jan 70, A: Kryptonite Plus	0.15	2.00	5.00	10.00
❑127, Mar 70	0.15	2.00	5.00	10.00
❑128, Apr 70	0.15	2.00	5.00	10.00
❑129, Jun 70	0.15	2.00	5.00	10.00
❑130, Jul 70	0.15	2.00	5.00	10.00
❑131, Aug 70, 80pgs.	0.15	1.60	4.00	8.00
❑132, Sep 70	0.15	1.60	4.00	8.00
❑133, Oct 70, JK, 1: Habitat; A: Newsboy Legion	0.15	2.00	5.00	10.00
❑134, Dec 70, 1: Darkseid	0.15	5.00	12.50	25.00
❑135, Jan 71, 1: Project Cadmus	0.15	2.40	6.00	12.00
❑136, Mar 71, O: Guardian (new)	0.15	2.40	6.00	12.00
❑137, Apr 71	0.15	2.40	6.00	12.00
❑138, Jun 71	0.15	2.40	6.00	12.00
❑139, Jul 71, A: Don Rickles	0.15	2.40	6.00	12.00
❑140, Aug 71, reprints Jimmy Olsen #69, #72, and Superman #158	0.35	2.40	6.00	12.00
❑141, Sep 71	0.25	2.00	5.00	10.00
❑142, Oct 71	0.25	2.00	5.00	10.00
❑143, Nov 71, JK	0.25	2.00	5.00	10.00
❑144, Dec 71, JK	0.25	2.00	5.00	10.00
❑145, Jan 72	0.25	2.00	5.00	10.00
❑146, Feb 72	0.25	2.00	5.00	10.00
❑147, Mar 72	0.25	2.00	5.00	10.00
❑148, Apr 72	0.25	2.00	5.00	10.00
❑149, May 72	0.25	2.00	5.00	10.00
❑150, Jun 72	0.25	2.00	5.00	10.00
❑151, Jul 72	0.20	1.60	4.00	8.00
❑152	0.20	1.40	3.50	7.00
❑153	0.20	1.40	3.50	7.00
❑154	0.20	1.40	3.50	7.00
❑155, Jan 73	0.20	1.40	3.50	7.00
❑156	0.20	1.40	3.50	7.00
❑157	0.20	1.40	3.50	7.00
❑158	0.20	1.40	3.50	7.00
❑159	0.20	1.40	3.50	7.00
❑160	0.20	1.40	3.50	7.00
❑161, Nov 73	0.20	1.40	3.50	7.00
❑162, Dec 73	0.20	1.40	3.50	7.00
❑163, Feb 74, Final Issue; Series continues as The Superman Family	0.20	1.40	3.50	7.00

SUPERMAN SPECTACULAR
DC

	ORIG	GOOD	FINE	N-MINT
❑1, V: Brainiac; V: Luthor, nn	1.00	0.60	1.50	3.00

SUPERMAN: SPEEDING BULLETS
DC

Value: Cover or less

❑1, nn; prestige format; Elseworlds 4.95

ORIG GOOD FINE N-MINT

SUPERMAN: THE DARK SIDE
DC

Value: Cover or less

❑1 .... 4.95
❑2 .... 4.95
❑3 .... 4.95

SUPERMAN: THE DOOMSDAY WARS
DC

Value: Cover or less

❑1, Birth, A: Lana Lang; A: Pete Ross; A: Justice League of America 4.95
❑1/LE 24.95
❑2 .... 4.95
❑3 .... 4.95

SUPERMAN: THE EARTH STEALERS
DC

Value: Cover or less

❑1, May 88, CS; JOy, JBy (w), nn; One-Shot 2.95

SUPERMAN: THE LAST GOD OF KRYPTON
DC

Value: Cover or less

❑1, nn; prestige format 4.95

SUPERMAN: THE LEGACY OF SUPERMAN
DC

Value: Cover or less

❑1, CS, The Guardians Of Metropolis; Gangbuster Of Suicidal Slum, 64pgs.; Follows up after Superman's demise 2.50

SUPERMAN: THE MAN OF STEEL
DC

	ORIG	GOOD	FINE	N-MINT
❑0, Oct 94, Peer Pressure, Part 1, ▲1994-37	1.50	0.50	1.25	2.50
❑1, Jul 91, Man of Steel/Man of Fire!, 1: Cerberus, ▲1991-19	1.75	0.70	1.75	3.50
❑2, Aug 91, V: Rorc; V: Sgt. Belcher	1.00	0.50	1.25	2.50
❑3, Sep 91, War of the Gods, Part 2, War of the Gods	1.00	0.50	1.25	2.50
❑4, Oct 91, V: Angstrom	1.00	0.40	1.00	2.00
❑5, Nov 91, V: Atomic Skull	1.00	0.40	1.00	2.00
❑6, Dec 91, Blackout, Part 3	1.00	0.40	1.00	2.00
❑7, Jan 92, V: Jolt; V: Blockhouse	1.00	0.40	1.00	2.00
❑8, Feb 92, V: Jolt; V: Blockhouse	1.00	0.40	1.00	2.00
❑9, Mar 92, Panic in the Sky First Strike	1.00	0.40	1.00	2.00
❑10, Apr 92, Panic in the Sky Fifth Strike	1.00	0.40	1.00	2.00
❑11, May 92	1.25	0.30	0.75	1.50
❑12, Jun 92	1.25	0.30	0.75	1.50
❑13, Jul 92	1.25	0.30	0.75	1.50
❑14, Aug 92, A: Robin	1.25	0.30	0.75	1.50
❑15, Sep 92, A: Blaze; A: Satanus	1.25	0.30	0.75	1.50
❑16, Oct 92	1.25	0.30	0.75	1.50
❑17, Nov 92, Doomsday!, 1: Doomsday (cameo)	1.25	0.60	1.50	3.00
❑18, Dec 92, Doomsday!, 1: Doomsday (full appearance), ▲1992-18	1.25	0.80	2.00	4.00
❑18-2, Dec 92, Doomsday!, A: Doomsday, 2nd Printing; ▲1992-18	1.25	0.40	1.00	2.00
❑18-3, Dec 92, Doomsday!, A: Doomsday, 3rd Printing; ▲1992-18	1.25	0.30	0.75	1.50
❑19, Jan 93, Doomsday is Here!, V: Doomsday, ▲1993-1	1.25	0.60	1.50	3.00
❑20, Feb 93, Funeral for a Friend, Part 3	1.25	0.50	1.25	2.50
❑21, Mar 93, Funeral for a Friend, Part 7, Pa Kent has heart attack	1.25	0.50	1.25	2.50
❑22, Jun 93, Reign of the Supermen; Steel, 1: Steel (John Henry Irons)	1.50	0.40	1.00	2.00
❑22/SC, Jun 93, Steel, Die-cut cover	1.95	0.50	1.25	2.50
❑23, Jul 93, Reign of the Supermen, Steel vs. Superboy	1.50	0.40	1.00	2.00
❑24, Aug 93, Reign of the Supermen; Impact!, Steel vs. Last Son of Krypton	1.50	0.40	1.00	2.00
❑25, Sep 93, Reign of the Supermen	1.50	0.40	1.00	2.00
❑26, Oct 93, Reign of the Supermen; Blast Off!	1.50	0.40	1.00	2.00
❑27, Nov 93	1.50	0.40	1.00	2.00
❑28, Dec 93	1.50	0.40	1.00	2.00
❑29, Jan 94, Spilled Blood	1.50	0.40	1.00	2.00
❑30, Feb 94, Lobo	1.50	0.40	1.00	2.00
❑30/SC, Feb 94, vinyl clings cover	2.50	0.60	1.50	3.00
❑31, Mar 94, Obsessions!	1.50	0.40	1.00	2.00
❑32, Apr 94, Bizarro	1.50	0.40	1.00	2.00
❑33, May 94	1.50	0.40	1.00	2.00
❑34, Jun 94, Battle for Metropolis	1.50	0.40	1.00	2.00
❑35, Jul 94, Worlds Collide, Part 1, crossover with Milestone Media	1.50	0.40	1.00	2.00
❑36, Aug 94, Worlds Collide, Part 10, A: Hardware; A: Icon; A: Static, ▲1994-29	1.50	0.40	1.00	2.00
❑37, Sep 94, Zero Hour	1.50	0.40	1.00	2.00
❑38, Nov 94, Dead Again	1.50	0.40	1.00	2.00
❑39, Dec 94, Dead Again	1.50	0.40	1.00	2.00
❑40, Jan 95, Dead Again, ▲1995-1	1.50	0.40	1.00	2.00
❑41, Feb 95	1.50	0.40	1.00	2.00
❑42, Mar 95	1.50	0.40	1.00	2.00
❑43, Apr 95, A: Mr. Miracle	1.50	0.40	1.00	2.00
❑44, May 95	1.50	0.40	1.00	2.00
❑45, Jun 95	1.95	0.40	1.00	2.00
❑46, Jul 95	1.95	0.40	1.00	2.00
❑47, Aug 95	1.95	0.40	1.00	2.00
❑48, Sep 95, A: Aquaman	1.95	0.40	1.00	2.00
❑49, Oct 95	1.95	0.40	1.00	2.00
❑50, Nov 95, Trial of Superman, Giant-size	2.95	0.60	1.50	3.00
❑51, Dec 95, Trial of Superman, V: Freelance	1.95	0.40	1.00	2.00
❑52, Jan 96, Trial of Superman, V: Cyborg	1.95	0.40	1.00	2.00
❑53, Feb 96, The Game, V: Brawl	1.95	0.40	1.00	2.00
❑54, Mar 96, Ghosts, A: Spectre, ▲1996-10	1.95	0.40	1.00	2.00
❑55, Apr 96, Something Fishy, D: Jeb Friedman, ▲1996-15	1.95	0.40	1.00	2.00
❑56, May 96, V: Mxyzptlk	1.95	0.40	1.00	2.00
❑57, Jun 96, A: Golden Age Flash	1.95	0.40	1.00	2.00
❑58, Jul 96	1.95	0.40	1.00	2.00
❑59, Aug 96, V: Parasite	1.95	0.40	1.00	2.00
❑60, Sep 96, The Bottle City, Part 2	1.95	0.40	1.00	2.00
❑61, Oct 96, Losin' It, polybagged with On the Edge; ▲1996-41	1.95	0.40	1.00	2.00
❑62, Oct 96, To Build a Fire, O: Superman, Final Night; ▲1996-45	1.95	0.40	1.00	2.00
❑63, Dec 96, Hawaiian Honeymoon; Fireworks, Lois rescues Clark from terrorists; ▲1996-50	1.95	0.40	1.00	2.00
❑64, Jan 97, Power Struggle; Into the Fire!, ▲1997-4	1.95	0.40	1.00	2.00
❑65, Mar 97, SB, Losers, V: Superman Revenge Squad, ▲1997-9	1.95	0.40	1.00	2.00
❑66, Apr 97	1.95	0.40	1.00	2.00
❑67, May 97, A: Scorn, destruction of old costume	1.95	0.40	1.00	2.00
❑68, Jun 97, V: Metallo	1.95	0.40	1.00	2.00
❑69, Jul 97, A: Atom, in Kandor	1.95	0.40	1.00	2.00
❑70, Aug 97, V: Saviour; A: Scorn	1.95	0.40	1.00	2.00
❑71, Sep 97, 1: Baud	1.95	0.40	1.00	2.00
❑72, Oct 97, V: Mainframe, Genesis	1.95	0.40	1.00	2.00
❑73, Nov 97, V: Parademons	1.95	0.40	1.00	2.00
❑74, Dec 97, Subterranean Terror, V: Rajiv; A: Sam Lane, Face cover; ▲1997-47	1.95	0.40	1.00	2.00
❑75, Jan 98, The Death of Mr. Mxyptlk, A: Mike Carlin; D: Mr. Mxyzptlk, ▲1998-1	1.95	0.40	1.00	2.00
❑76, Feb 98, A: Mokkari; A: Morgan Edge; A: Simyan	1.95	0.40	1.00	2.00
❑77, Mar 98, Triangles, cover forms diptych with Action Comics #742	1.95	0.40	1.00	2.00
❑78, Apr 98, Millennium Giants	1.95	0.40	1.00	2.00
❑79, May 98, Millennium Giants aftermath	1.95	0.40	1.00	2.00
❑80, Jun 98, set in late '30s	1.95	0.40	1.00	2.00
❑81, Jul 98, set in late '30s	1.95	0.40	1.00	2.00
❑82, Aug 98, V: Dominus; A: Kismet	1.95	0.40	1.00	2.00
❑83, Sep 98, A: Waverider	1.99	0.40	1.00	2.00
❑84, Dec 98, 1: Inventor, in Kandor	1.99	0.40	1.00	2.00
❑85, Jan 99, V: Mokkari; V: Simyan	1.99	0.40	1.00	2.00
❑86, Feb 99	1.99	0.40	1.00	2.00
❑87, Mar 99, A: Supergirl; A: Superboy; A: Steel	1.99	0.40	1.00	2.00
❑88, May 99, V: Robots	1.99	0.40	1.00	2.00
❑89, Jun 99, Prelude to a Coronation, V: Dominus, ▲1999-21	1.99	0.40	1.00	2.00
❑90, Jul 99, A Girl and her Robot, ▲1999-26	1.99	0.40	1.00	2.00
❑91, Aug 99, Nemesis, ▲1999-31	1.99	0.40	1.00	1.99
❑92, Sep 99, One-Man JLA; Secret Origins, Part 4, Superman as Martian Manhunter; ▲1999-35	1.99	0.40	1.00	1.99
❑93, Oct 99, The Sea Beast of Metropolis!, ▲1999-39	1.99	0.40	1.00	1.99
❑94, Nov 99, A: Strange Visitor; V: Parasite	1.99	0.40	1.00	1.99
❑95, 00, Krypton Lives, ▲1999-48	1.99	0.40	1.00	1.99
❑96, Jan 00, Home, ▲2000-3	1.99	0.40	1.00	1.99
❑97, Feb 00	1.99	0.40	1.00	1.99
❑98, Mar 00	1.99	0.40	1.00	1.99
❑99, Apr 00, All that Dwell in Dark Waters, ▲2000-16	1.99	0.40	1.00	1.99

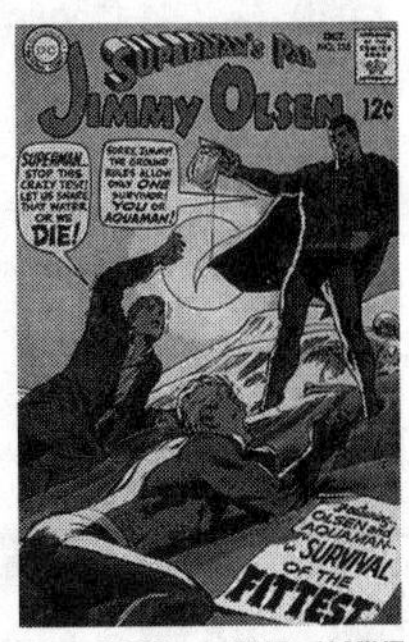

Aquaman made an appearance in *Superman's Pal Jimmy Olsen* #115.

© 1968 National Periodical Publications (DC)

	ORIG	GOOD	FINE	N-MINT
❑100, May 00, Creation Story, Giant-size; ▲2000-20	2.99	0.60	1.50	2.99
❑100/SC, May 00, Creation Story, Special fold-out cover; Giant-size; ▲2000-20	3.99	0.80	2.00	3.99
❑101, Jun 00	1.99	0.40	1.00	1.99
❑102, Jul 00	—	0.40	1.00	1.99
❑103, Aug 00	—	0.40	1.00	1.99
❑104, Sep 00, No Axioms, ▲2000-36	2.25	0.45	1.13	2.25
❑105, Oct 00, Emperor Joker, Part 3, (c)2000-41	2.25	0.45	1.13	2.25
❑106, Nov 00, Under the Waterfront, ▲2000-45	2.25	0.45	1.13	2.25
❑107, Dec 00, In the Zone, ▲2000-49	2.25	0.45	1.13	2.25
❑108, Jan 01, Metropolis is Burning, ▲2001-4	2.25	0.45	1.13	2.25
❑109, Feb 01, World Without Superman, ▲2001-8	2.25	0.45	1.13	2.25
❑110, Mar 01, Saints, A: Stars and S.T.R.I.P.E., ▲2001-12	2.25	0.45	1.13	2.25
❑111, Apr 01, The Most Dangerous Kryptonian Game, ▲2001-16	2.25	0.45	1.13	2.25
❑112, May 01, The Adventures of...Krypto!, ▲2001-20	2.25	0.45	1.13	2.25
❑113	2.25	0.45	1.13	2.25
❑114	2.25	0.45	1.13	2.25
❑115	2.25	0.45	1.13	2.25
❑116	2.25	0.45	1.13	2.25
❑1000000, Nov 98, JOy, Fear & Loathing	1.99	0.40	1.00	1.99
❑Anl 1, Eclipso: The Darkness Within, Part 2, A: Eclipso	2.50	0.60	1.50	3.00
❑Anl 2, Bloodlines, 1: Edge, Bloodlines	2.50	0.60	1.50	3.00
❑Anl 3, Elseworlds	2.95	0.60	1.50	3.00
❑Anl 4, Superman: Year One, A: Justice League, Year One	2.95	0.60	1.50	3.00
❑Anl 5, KB (w), The Never-Ending Battle, 1: Kaleb, Legends of the Dead Earth	2.95	0.60	1.50	3.00
❑Anl 6, Pulp Heroes	3.95	0.79	1.98	3.95

SUPERMAN: THE MAN OF STEEL GALLERY
DC

Value: Cover or less

❑1, Dec 95, pin-ups 3.50

SUPERMAN: THE MAN OF TOMORROW
DC

	ORIG	GOOD	FINE	N-MINT
❑1, Sum 95	1.95	0.40	1.00	2.00
❑2, Fal 95, A: Alpha Centurion	1.95	0.40	1.00	2.00
❑3, Win 95, Trial of Superman, A: how Luthor regained strength and, Underworld Unleashed	1.95	0.40	1.00	2.00
❑4, Spr 96, ...The World's Mightiest Mortals!, A: Captain Marvel, ▲1996-13	1.95	0.40	1.00	2.00
❑5, Sum 96, Wedding of Lex Luthor and Contessa	1.95	0.40	1.00	2.00
❑6, Fal 96, Going to Extremes, V: Jackal, ▲1996-38	1.95	0.40	1.00	2.00
❑7, Win 97, V: Maxima	1.95	0.40	1.00	2.00
❑8, Sum 97, V: Rock	1.95	0.40	1.00	2.00
❑9, Fal 97, Ma and Pa Kent remember Superman's career	1.95	0.40	1.00	2.00
❑10, Win 98, Obsession vs. Maxima	1.95	0.40	1.00	2.00
❑11, Fal 98, Timewar	1.99	0.40	1.00	2.00
❑12, Win 98	1.99	0.40	1.00	2.00
❑13, Spr 98	1.99	0.40	1.00	2.00
❑14, Sum 98, V: Riot	1.99	0.40	1.00	2.00
❑15, Fal 98, V: Neron, Day of Judgment	2.95	0.60	1.50	3.00
❑1000000, Nov 98	1.99	0.40	1.00	2.00

SUPERMAN: THE ODYSSEY
DC

Value: Cover or less

❑1, Jul 99, nn; One-Shot; prestige format 4.95

SUPERMAN: THE SECRET YEARS
DC

	ORIG	GOOD	FINE	N-MINT
❑1, Feb 85, CS	0.75	0.30	0.75	1.50
❑2, Mar 85, CS, A: Lori Lemaris, Clark reveals his secret to Billy Cramer	0.75	0.30	0.75	1.50
❑3, Apr 85, CS, Terminus, D: Billy Cramer	0.75	0.30	0.75	1.50
❑4, May 85, CS, Superboy becomes Superman; Clark Kent meets Perry White	0.75	0.30	0.75	1.50

SUPERMAN: THE WEDDING ALBUM
DC

Value: Cover or less

❑1, Dec 96, newsstand edition with gatefold back cover; Wedding of Clark Kent and Lois Lane; ▲1996-47 .... 4.95

❑1/DM, Dec 96, white cardstock wraparound cover with gatefold back cover; Wedding of Clark Kent and Lois Lane 4.95

SUPERMAN/TOYMAN
DC

Value: Cover or less

❑1, One-Shot; promo for toy line 1.95

SUPERMAN: UNDER A YELLOW SUN
DC

Value: Cover or less

❑1, nn; prestige format one-shot 5.95

SUPERMAN VS. ALIENS
DC

Value: Cover or less

❑1, Jul 95, prestige format; crossover with Dark Horse 4.95

❑2, Aug 95, prestige format; crossover with Dark Horse 4.95

❑3, Sep 95, prestige format; crossover with Dark Horse 4.95

SUPERMAN VS. PREDATOR
DC

Value: Cover or less

❑1 .... 4.95

❑2 .... 4.95

❑3 .... 4.95

SUPERMAN VS. THE AMAZING SPIDER-MAN
DC

	ORIG	GOOD	FINE	N-MINT
❑1, RA; DG, V: Lex Luthor, Doc Ock; V: Doctor Octopus; V: Lex Luthor, treasury-sized; first DC/Marvel crossover	2.00	4.00	10.00	20.00

SUPERMAN VS. THE TERMINATOR: DEATH TO THE FUTURE
DARK HORSE

Value: Cover or less

❑1, Dec 99 .... 2.95

❑2, Jan 00 .... 2.95

❑3, Feb 00 .... 2.95

❑4, Mar 00 .... 2.95

SUPERMAN VILLAINS SECRET FILES
DC

Value: Cover or less

❑1, Jun 98, biographical info on Superman's Rogues Gallery 4.95

SUPERMAN: WAR OF THE WORLDS
DC

Value: Cover or less

❑1, nn; prestige format one-shot; Elseworlds 5.95

❑1/LE 18.95

SUPERMAN: "WHATEVER HAPPENED TO THE MAN OF TOMORROW?"
DC

Value: Cover or less

❑1, AMo (w), nn; prestige format collection of Action Comics #583 and Superman #423... 5.95

SUPERMAN/WONDER WOMAN: WHOM GODS DESTROY
DC

Value: Cover or less

❑1, TheDream, prestige format; Elseworlds 4.95

❑2, The Hunt, prestige format; Elseworlds 4.95

❑3, prestige format; Elseworlds 4.95

❑4, The Price, Final Issue; prestige format; Elseworlds 4.95

SUPER MARIO BROS. (1ST SERIES)
VALIANT

Value: Cover or less

❑1 .... 1.95

❑2 .... 1.95

❑3 .... 1.95

❑4 .... 1.95

❑5, Dug Stoopid Bomb! 1.95

❑6, The Buddy System; Weight Up 1.95

❑SE 1, The Legend; Mutiny on the Fungi 1.95

SUPER MARIO BROS. (2ND SERIES)
VALIANT

Value: Cover or less

❑1 .... 1.50

❑2 .... 1.50

❑3 .... 1.50

❑4 .... 1.50

❑5 .... 1.50

SUPERMEN OF AMERICA
DC

Value: Cover or less

❑1, Mar 99, Fire From Heaven, O: Supermen of America 3.95

❑1/CS, Mar 99, Fire From Heaven, O: Supermen of America, Gatefold cardstock cover; membership kit for Supermen of America; Collector's edition 4.95

❑2, Apr 99 .... 2.50

❑3, May 99, A Piece of the Action 2.50

❑4, Jun 99, Up, Up, and Away... .... 2.50

SUPERMODELS IN THE RAINFOREST
SIRIUS

Value: Cover or less

❑1, Welcome to the Amazon; The Lost World, b&w 2.95

❑2, b&w 2.95

❑3 .... 2.95

SUPERNATURAL LAW
EXHIBIT A PRESS

Value: Cover or less

❑24, Oct 99, You'll Never Suck Blood in This Town Again, was Wolff & Byrd, Counselors of the Macabre 2.50

❑25 .... 2.50

❑26, May 00, Black Market Souls! 2.50

❑27, Jul 00, Bright Lights, Big Feet; Jury Duty 2.50

❑28, Oct 00, Is Everyone Courting Disaster? 2.50

❑29, Jul 00, The Inevitable Hank 2.50

❑30 .... 2.50

❑31 .... 2.50

SUPERNATURALS, THE
MARVEL

	ORIG	GOOD	FINE	N-MINT
❑1/A, Dec 98, Design Demons, Satana mask	3.99	0.80	2.00	3.99
❑1/B, Dec 98, Design Demons	3.99	0.80	2.00	3.99
❑1/C, Dec 98, Design Demons	3.99	0.80	2.00	3.99
❑1/D, Dec 98, Design Demons	3.99	0.80	2.00	3.99
❑1/E, Dec 98, Design Demons, Ghost Rider mask	3.99	0.90	2.25	4.50

	ORIG	GOOD	FINE	N-MINT
❑1/LE, Dec 98, Design Demons	14.95	6.00	14.99	29.99
❑2, Dec 98	3.99	0.80	2.00	3.99
❑3, Dec 98	3.99	0.80	2.00	3.99
❑4, Dec 98	3.99	0.80	2.00	3.99
❑Ash 1, Character bios, sketches, creator bios	2.99	0.60	1.50	2.99

SUPERNATURALS TOUR BOOK, THE
MARVEL

Value: Cover or less

❑1, Oct 98, nn; cardstock cover; preview of series ... 2.99

SUPERNATURAL THRILLERS
MARVEL

	ORIG	GOOD	FINE	N-MINT
❑1, Dec 72, It! (Theodore Sturgeon adaptation)	0.20	1.60	4.00	8.00
❑2, Feb 73, Invisible Man	0.20	1.00	2.50	5.00
❑3, Apr 73, GK, The Valley of the Worm, The Valley of the Worm	0.20	0.80	2.00	4.00
❑4, Dr. Jekyll and Mr. Hyde	0.20	0.80	2.00	4.00
❑5, 1: Living Mummy	0.20	0.80	2.00	4.00
❑6, The Headless Horseman	0.20	0.70	1.75	3.50
❑7, A: Living Mummy	0.25	0.70	1.75	3.50
❑8, A: Living Mummy	0.25	0.70	1.75	3.50
❑9, A: Living Mummy	0.25	0.70	1.75	3.50
❑10, A: Living Mummy	0.25	0.70	1.75	3.50
❑11, A: Living Mummy	0.25	0.70	1.75	3.50
❑12, A: Living Mummy	0.25	0.70	1.75	3.50
❑13, A: Living Mummy	0.25	0.70	1.75	3.50
❑14, A: Living Mummy	0.25	0.70	1.75	3.50
❑15, Oct 75, TS, Armageddon At The Aleph!, A: Living Mummy	0.25	0.70	1.75	3.50

SUPERPATRIOT
IMAGE

	ORIG	GOOD	FINE	N-MINT
❑1, Jul 93, EL (w); KG (w), Liberty & Justice	1.95	0.40	1.00	2.00
❑2, Sep 93	1.95	0.40	1.00	2.00
❑3, Oct 93	1.95	0.40	1.00	2.00
❑4, Nov 93, cover says Dec, indicia says Nov	1.95	0.40	1.00	2.00

SUPERPATRIOT: LIBERTY & JUSTICE
IMAGE

Value: Cover or less

❑1, Jun 95 ... 2.50
❑2, Aug 95 ... 2.50
❑3, Sep 95 ... 2.50
❑4, Oct 95 ... 2.50

SUPER POWERS (1ST SERIES)
DC

	ORIG	GOOD	FINE	N-MINT
❑1, Jul 84, JK (c)	0.75	0.20	0.50	1.00
❑2, Aug 84, JK (c)	0.75	0.20	0.50	1.00
❑3, Sep 84, JK (c)	0.75	0.20	0.50	1.00
❑4, Oct 84, JK (c)	0.75	0.20	0.50	1.00
❑5, Nov 84, JK, JK (c), JK (w)	0.75	0.20	0.50	1.00

SUPER POWERS (2ND SERIES)
DC

	ORIG	GOOD	FINE	N-MINT
❑1, Sep 85, JK, Seeds Of Doom!	0.75	0.20	0.50	1.00
❑2, Oct 85, JK	0.75	0.20	0.50	1.00
❑3, Nov 85, JK	0.75	0.20	0.50	1.00
❑4, Dec 85, JK	0.75	0.20	0.50	1.00
❑5, Jan 86, JK	0.75	0.20	0.50	1.00
❑6, Feb 86, JK	0.75	0.20	0.50	1.00

SUPER POWERS (3RD SERIES)
DC

	ORIG	GOOD	FINE	N-MINT
❑1, Sep 86, CI, Threshold	0.75	0.20	0.50	1.00
❑2, Oct 86, CI	0.75	0.20	0.50	1.00
❑3, Nov 86, CI	0.75	0.20	0.50	1.00
❑4, Dec 86, CI	0.75	0.20	0.50	1.00

SUPER SEXXX
FANTAGRAPHICS

Value: Cover or less

❑1, b&w; adult ... 3.25

SUPER SHARK HUMANOIDS
FISH TALES

Value: Cover or less

❑1, Apr 92 ... 2.75

SUPER SOLDIER
DC

Value: Cover or less

❑1, Apr 96, DaG, MWa (w), Secret Of The K-Bombs, O: Super Soldier ... 1.95

SUPER SOLDIER: MAN OF WAR
DC

Value: Cover or less

❑1, Jun 97, DaG, MWa (w); DaG (w), Deadly Cargo ... 1.95

SUPER SOLDIERS
MARVEL

Value: Cover or less

❑1, Apr 93, Memories, Part 1, foil cover ... 2.50
❑2, May 93, Memories, Part 2 ... 1.75
❑3, Jun 93 ... 1.75
❑4, Jul 93 ... 1.75
❑5, Aug 93 ... 1.75
❑6, Sep 93 ... 1.75
❑7, Oct 93, A: Nick Fury, X-Men cameo ... 1.75
❑8, Nov 93 ... 1.75
❑9 ... 1.75
❑10, Final Issue ... 1.75

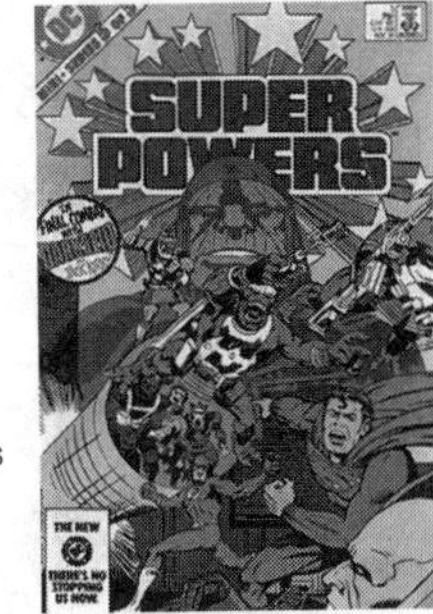

To promote Kenner's toy line based on its characters, DC published several *Super Powers* mini-series.

© 1984 DC Comics

SUPERSONIC SOUL PUDDIN COMICS & STORIES
FOUR CATS FUNNY BOOKS

Value: Cover or less

❑1, Jun 95 ... 3.50

SUPER SONIC VS. HYPER KNUCKLES
ARCHIE

Value: Cover or less

❑1, One-Shot ... 2.00

SUPERSWINE
CALIBER

Value: Cover or less

❑1, b&w ... 2.50
❑2, b&w ... 2.50

SUPER TABOO
FANTAGRAPHICS

Value: Cover or less

❑1, Dec 95 ... 2.95
❑2, Jan 96 ... 2.95

SUPER-TEAM FAMILY
DC

	ORIG	GOOD	FINE	N-MINT
❑1, Nov 75	0.50	1.20	3.00	6.00
❑2, Jan 76, Showdown in San Lorenzo!; The Track of the Hook!, A: Batman; A: Creeper; A: Green Arrow; A: Superman; A: Deadman; A: Wildcat; A: Speedy	0.50	0.80	2.00	4.00
❑3, Mar 76	0.50	0.80	2.00	4.00
❑4, May 76, The Revenge of Solomon Grundy!; The Menace of the Moonman!, A: Batman; A: Robin; A: Solomon Grundy; A: Superman; A: Justice Society of America	0.50	0.80	2.00	4.00
❑5, Jul 76	0.50	0.60	1.50	3.00
❑6, Sep 76	0.50	0.60	1.50	3.00
❑7, Nov 76, Teen Titans	0.50	0.60	1.50	3.00
❑8, Jan 77, A: Challengers of the Unknown, New stories begin	0.50	0.80	2.00	4.00
❑9, Mar 77, A: Challengers of the Unknown	0.50	0.80	2.00	4.00
❑10, May 77, A: Challengers of the Unknown	0.50	0.80	2.00	4.00
❑11, Jul 77, Flash, Atom, Supergirl	0.60	0.60	1.50	3.00
❑12, Sep 77	0.60	0.60	1.50	3.00
❑13, Nov 77, Atom, Aquaman, Captain Comet	0.60	0.60	1.50	3.00
❑14, Jan 78	0.60	0.60	1.50	3.00
❑15, Apr 78	0.60	0.60	1.50	3.00

SUPER-VILLAIN CLASSICS
MARVEL

	ORIG	GOOD	FINE	N-MINT
❑1, May 83, O: Galactus, Reprint	0.60	0.60	1.50	3.00

SUPER-VILLAIN TEAM-UP
MARVEL

	ORIG	GOOD	FINE	N-MINT
❑1, Aug 75, GT; BEv; GE, Slayers from the Sea!, A: Sub-Mariner; A: Doctor Doom	0.25	1.40	3.50	7.00
❑2, Oct 75, SB, In the Midst of Life...!, A: Sub-Mariner; A: Doctor Doom	0.25	1.00	2.50	5.00
❑3, Dec 75, A: Sub-Mariner; A: Doctor Doom	0.25	0.80	2.00	4.00
❑4, Feb 76, A: Sub-Mariner; A: Doctor Doom	0.25	0.80	2.00	4.00
❑5, Apr 76, A: Sub-Mariner; A: Doctor Doom; 1: Shroud	0.25	0.80	2.00	4.00
❑6, Jun 76, A: Sub-Mariner; A: Doctor Doom	0.25	0.60	1.50	3.00
❑7, Aug 76, A: Sub-Mariner; A: Doctor Doom; O: Shroud	0.25	0.60	1.50	3.00
❑8, Oct 76, A: Sub-Mariner; A: Doctor Doom; 1: Rajah	0.30	0.60	1.50	3.00
❑9, Dec 76, A: Sub-Mariner; A: Doctor Doom	0.30	0.60	1.50	3.00
❑10, Feb 77, A: Sub-Mariner; A: Doctor Doom	0.30	0.60	1.50	3.00
❑11, Apr 77	0.30	0.60	1.50	3.00
❑12, Jun 77	0.30	0.60	1.50	3.00
❑13, Aug 77	0.30	0.60	1.50	3.00
❑14, Oct 77	0.30	0.60	1.50	3.00
❑15, Nov 77, A: Doctor Doom; A: Red Skull	0.30	0.60	1.50	3.00
❑16, May 79, A: Doctor Doom; A: Red Skull	0.40	0.60	1.50	3.00
❑17, Jun 80, A: Doctor Doom; A: Red Skull	0.40	0.60	1.50	3.00
❑GS 1	0.50	1.00	2.50	5.00
❑GS 2	0.50	1.00	2.50	5.00

SUPPRESSED!
TOME PRESS

Value: Cover or less

❑1, Columbus; Pilgrims, b&w ... 2.95

SUPREME
IMAGE

	ORIG	GOOD	FINE	N-MINT
❑0, Aug 95, The Weight	2.50	0.50	1.25	2.50
❑1, Nov 92, RL (w), Second Coming, silver foil-embossed cover	1.95	0.50	1.25	2.50
❑1/GO, Nov 92, Second Coming, Embossed cover; Gold promotional edition	—	0.50	1.25	2.50
❑2, Feb 93, 1: Grizlock, covers says May, indicia says Feb	1.95	0.40	1.00	2.00
❑3, Jun 93, 1: Khrome	1.95	0.40	1.00	2.00
❑4, Jul 93	1.95	0.40	1.00	2.00
❑5, Aug 93, 1: Thor (Image)	1.95	0.40	1.00	2.00
❑6, Oct 93, 1: the Starguard	1.95	0.40	1.00	2.00
❑7, Nov 93	1.95	0.40	1.00	2.00
❑8, Dec 93	1.95	0.40	1.00	2.00
❑9, Jan 94	1.95	0.40	1.00	2.00
❑10, Feb 94	1.95	0.40	1.00	2.00
❑11, Mar 94, Extreme Prejudice, Part 4	1.95	0.40	1.00	2.00
❑12, Apr 94	1.95	0.40	1.00	2.00
❑13, Jun 94, Supreme Madness, Part 1	2.50	0.50	1.25	2.50
❑14, Jun 94, Supreme Madness, Part 2	2.50	0.50	1.25	2.50
❑15, Jul 94, Supreme Madness, Part 3	2.50	0.50	1.25	2.50
❑16, Jul 94, Supreme Madness, Part 4	2.50	0.50	1.25	2.50
❑17, Aug 94, Supreme Madness, Part 5, V: Pitt	2.50	0.50	1.25	2.50
❑18, Aug 94, Supreme Madness, Part 6	2.50	0.50	1.25	2.50
❑19, Sep 94	2.50	0.50	1.25	2.50
❑20, Oct 94, A: Kid Supreme	2.50	0.50	1.25	2.50
❑21, Nov 94, God War, Part 1	2.50	0.50	1.25	2.50
❑22, Dec 94, God War, Part 2	2.50	0.50	1.25	2.50
❑23, Jan 95, Extreme Sacrifice, Part 2; Extreme Sacrifice, Part 1, polybagged with trading card	2.50	0.50	1.25	2.50
❑24, Feb 95, Extreme Sacrifice Aftermath	2.50	0.50	1.25	2.50
❑25, May 94, Images of Tomorrow; Shipped out of sequence after #12 to give preview of future	1.95	0.50	1.25	2.50
❑26, Mar 95, V: Kid Supreme	2.50	0.50	1.25	2.50
❑27, Apr 95	2.50	0.50	1.25	2.50
❑28	2.50	0.50	1.25	2.50
❑28/A, May 95, A: Glory	2.50	0.50	1.25	2.50
❑28/B, May 95, A: Glory	2.50	0.50	1.25	2.50
❑29, Jun 95, Supreme Apocalypse, Part 1, polybagged with Power Cardz	2.50	0.50	1.25	2.50
❑30, Jul 95, Supreme Apocalypse, Part 5, polybagged with Power Cardz	2.50	0.50	1.25	2.50
❑31, Aug 95	2.50	0.50	1.25	2.50
❑32, Oct 95	2.50	0.50	1.25	2.50
❑33, Nov 95, Babewatch	2.50	0.50	1.25	2.50
❑34, Dec 95	2.50	0.50	1.25	2.50
❑35, Jan 96, Extreme Destroyer, Part 7, polybagged with Lady Supreme card	2.50	0.50	1.25	2.50
❑36, Feb 96	2.50	0.50	1.25	2.50
❑37, Mar 96	2.50	0.50	1.25	2.50
❑37/A, Mar 96, alternate cover	2.50	0.50	1.25	2.50
❑37/B, Mar 96, alternate cover	2.50	0.50	1.25	2.50
❑38, Apr 96	2.50	0.50	1.25	2.50
❑39, May 96, V: Loki	2.50	0.50	1.25	2.50
❑40, Jul 96	2.50	0.50	1.25	2.50
❑41, Aug 96, AMo (w), Newmen Special Preview Edition back-up	2.50	0.70	1.75	3.50
❑41/A, Aug 96, AMo (w), alternate cover (Superman homage); Newmen Special Preview Edition back-up	2.50	0.70	1.75	3.50
❑41/B, Aug 96, alternate cover (Superman homage); Signed by Alan Moore; limited edition	2.50	3.00	7.50	15.00
❑41/C, Aug 96, alternate cover (American Entertainment exclusive)	2.50	1.80	4.50	9.00
❑41-2, 2nd Printing	2.50	0.50	1.25	2.50
❑42, Sep 96, AMo (w), Superman homage; moves to Maximum Press	2.50	0.60	1.50	3.00
❑43, Oct 96, AMo (w), Superman homage	2.50	0.60	1.50	3.00
❑44, Jan 97, AMo (w)	2.50	0.60	1.50	3.00
❑45, Jan 97, AMo (w)	2.50	0.50	1.25	2.50
❑46, Feb 97, AMo (w), 1: Suprema	2.50	0.50	1.25	2.50
❑47, Mar 97, AMo (w), 1: Twilight	2.50	0.50	1.25	2.50
❑48, Apr 97, AMo (w)	2.50	0.50	1.25	2.50
❑49, May 97, AMo (w), cover says Jun, indicia says May	2.50	0.50	1.25	2.50
❑50, AMo (w), Giant-size	2.50	0.50	1.25	2.50
❑51, AMo (w)	2.50	0.50	1.25	2.50
❑52/A, Sep 97, AMo (w)	2.50	0.70	1.75	3.50
❑52/B, Sep 97, AMo (w)	2.50	0.50	1.25	2.50
❑53, Sep 97, AMo (w)	2.50	0.50	1.25	2.50
❑54, Nov 97, AMo (w)	2.50	0.50	1.25	2.50
❑55, Nov 97, AMo (w), Silence at Gettysburg, cover says Dec, indicia says Nov	2.50	0.50	1.25	2.50
❑56, Feb 98	2.50	0.50	1.25	2.50
❑Anl 1, May 95, A: The Allies	2.95	0.59	1.48	2.95

SUPREME: GLORY DAYS
IMAGE

	ORIG	GOOD	FINE	N-MINT
❑1, Oct 94, RL (w)	2.95	0.60	1.50	3.00
❑2, Dec 94, RL (w), Final Issue	2.50	0.50	1.25	2.50

SUPREME: THE RETURN
AWESOME

Value: Cover or less

❑1, May 99, continues story from Supreme #56 ... 2.99
❑2, Jun 99, infinite Darius Daxes ... 2.99
❑3 ... 2.99
❑4 ... 2.99
❑5, May 00, AMo (w), Suddenly ... The Supremium Man!, A: Master Meteor; A: Supremium Man ... 2.99
❑6, Jun 00, RL, AMo (w), New Jack City! ... 2.99

SUPREMIE
PARODY

Value: Cover or less

❑1, The Babe of Steel, b&w ... 2.50

SURFCRAZED COMICS
PACIFICA

Value: Cover or less

❑1 ... 2.50
❑3, 3-D ... 3.95
❑4 ... 2.50

SURF SUMO
STAR TIGER

Value: Cover or less

❑1, Clone Wars ... 2.95
❑1-2, Clone Wars, 2nd printing with insert noting rights had reverted to Mighty Graphics; June 1997 ... 2.95

SURGE
ECLIPSE

	ORIG	GOOD	FINE	N-MINT
❑1, Jul 84, ME (w), Human Hunt	1.50	0.35	0.88	1.75
❑2, Aug 84, ME (w)	1.50	0.35	0.88	1.75
❑3, Oct 84, ME (w)	1.50	0.35	0.88	1.75
❑4, Jan 85, ME (w)	1.50	0.35	0.88	1.75

SURROGATE SAVIOUR
HOT BRAZEN COMICS

Value: Cover or less

❑1, Sep 95, b&w ... 2.50
❑2, Nov 95, b&w ... 2.75
❑3, Jun 96, b&w ... 2.95

SURVIVE!
APPLE

Value: Cover or less

❑1, b&w ... 2.75

SURVIVORS, THE (BURNSIDE)
BURNSIDE

Value: Cover or less

❑1 ... 1.95

SURVIVORS (FANTAGRAPHICS)
FANTAGRAPHICS

Value: Cover or less

❑1 ... 2.50
❑2 ... 2.50

SURVIVORS, THE (PRELUDE)
PRELUDE

Value: Cover or less

❑1, Oct 86, Destinies ... 1.95
❑2 ... 1.95

SURVIVORS (SPECTRUM)
SPECTRUM

Value: Cover or less

❑1 ... 2.00
❑2 ... 2.00
❑3 ... 2.00
❑4 ... 2.00

SUSHI
SHUNGA

	ORIG	GOOD	FINE	N-MINT
❑1, b&w; adult	2.50	0.60	1.50	3.00
❑1-2, adult; 2nd Printing	2.50	0.50	1.25	2.50
❑2, b&w; adult	2.50	0.60	1.50	3.00
❑3, b&w; adult	2.50	0.60	1.50	3.00
❑4, b&w; adult	2.50	0.60	1.50	3.00
❑5, b&w; adult	2.50	0.60	1.50	3.00
❑6, b&w; adult	2.50	0.60	1.50	3.00
❑7, adult	2.50	0.50	1.25	2.50
❑8, adult	2.50	0.50	1.25	2.50

SUSPIRA: THE GREAT WORKING
CHAOS

Value: Cover or less

❑1 ... 2.95
❑2 ... 2.95
❑3 ... 2.95
❑4 ... 2.95

SUSSEX VAMPIRE, THE
CALIBER

Value: Cover or less

❑1 ... 2.95

SUSTAH-GIRL: QUEEN OF THE BLACK AGE
ONLI STUDIOS

Value: Cover or less

❑1, b&w ... 2.00

SWAMP FEVER
BIG MUDDY

	ORIG	GOOD	FINE	N-MINT
❑1, Split! Splat!; The Real Dope on Drugs	0.50	0.60	1.50	3.00

SWAMP THING (1ST SERIES)
DC

	ORIG	GOOD	FINE	N-MINT
❑1, Nov 72, BWr, O: Swamp Thing	0.20	10.00	25.00	50.00
❑2, Jan 73, BWr	0.20	5.00	12.50	25.00
❑3, Mar 73, BWr, 1: Patchwork Man	0.20	3.20	8.00	16.00
❑4, May 73, BWr	0.20	3.20	8.00	16.00
❑5, Aug 73, BWr	0.20	2.40	6.00	12.00
❑6, Oct 73, BWr	0.20	2.40	6.00	12.00
❑7, Dec 73, BWr, A: Batman, Batman	0.20	2.00	5.00	10.00
❑8, Feb 74, BWr	0.20	1.60	4.00	8.00
❑9, Apr 74, BWr	0.20	1.60	4.00	8.00
❑10, Jun 74, BWr	0.20	1.60	4.00	8.00
❑11, Aug 74, NR, The Conqueror Worms!	0.20	0.90	2.25	4.50
❑12, Oct 74, NR	0.20	0.90	2.25	4.50
❑13, Dec 74, NR	0.20	0.90	2.25	4.50
❑14, Feb 75, NR	0.25	0.90	2.25	4.50
❑15, Apr 75, NR	0.25	0.90	2.25	4.50
❑16, May 75, NR	0.25	0.90	2.25	4.50
❑17, Jul 75, NR	0.25	0.90	2.25	4.50
❑18, Sep 75, NR	0.25	0.90	2.25	4.50
❑19, Oct 75, NR	0.25	0.90	2.25	4.50
❑20, Jan 76, NR	0.25	0.90	2.25	4.50
❑21, Mar 76, NR	0.25	0.90	2.25	4.50
❑22, May 76, NR	0.30	0.90	2.25	4.50
❑23, Jul 76, NR	0.30	0.90	2.25	4.50
❑24, Sep 76, NR, Final Issue	0.30	0.90	2.25	4.50

SWAMP THING (2ND SERIES)
DC

	ORIG	GOOD	FINE	N-MINT
❑46, Mar 86, AMo (w), A: John Constantine, Crisis; Series continued from "Saga of the Swamp Thing"	0.75	0.80	2.00	4.00
❑47, Apr 86, AMo (w)	0.75	0.60	1.50	3.00
❑48, May 86, AMo (w)	0.75	0.60	1.50	3.00
❑49, Jun 86, AMo (w), 1: The Parliament of Trees	0.75	0.60	1.50	3.00
❑50, Jul 86, AMo (w), D: Sargon, Giant-size	1.25	0.80	2.00	4.00
❑51, Aug 86, AMo (w)	0.75	0.60	1.50	3.00
❑52, Sep 86, AMo (w), A: Joke; A: Arkham Asylum, Joker	0.75	0.80	2.00	4.00
❑53, Oct 86, AMo (w), A: Batman, Arkham Asylum story	0.75	0.90	2.25	4.50
❑54, Nov 86, AMo (w)	0.75	0.60	1.50	3.00
❑55, Dec 86, AMo (w)	0.75	0.60	1.50	3.00
❑56, Jan 87, AA, AMo (w), My Blue Heaven	0.75	0.60	1.50	3.00
❑57, Feb 87, AMo (w)	0.75	0.60	1.50	3.00
❑58, Mar 87, AMo (w), Spectre preview	0.75	0.60	1.50	3.00
❑59, Apr 87, AMo (w)	0.75	0.60	1.50	3.00
❑60, May 87, AMo (w), new format	0.75	0.60	1.50	3.00
❑61, Jun 87, AMo (w)	1.00	0.60	1.50	3.00
❑62, Jul 87, AMo (w)	1.00	0.60	1.50	3.00
❑63, Aug 87, AMo (w)	1.00	0.60	1.50	3.00
❑64, Sep 87, AMo (w), last with Moore	1.00	0.60	1.50	3.00
❑65, Oct 87, 1: Sprout, Arkham Asylum	1.00	0.60	1.50	3.00
❑66, Nov 87, Arkham Asylum	1.00	0.50	1.25	2.50
❑67, Dec 87, 1: Hellblazer	1.25	0.50	1.25	2.50
❑68, Jan 88	1.25	0.50	1.25	2.50
❑69, Feb 88	1.25	0.50	1.25	2.50
❑70, Mar 88	1.25	0.50	1.25	2.50
❑71, Apr 88	1.25	0.50	1.25	2.50
❑72, May 88	1.25	0.50	1.25	2.50
❑73, Jun 88	1.25	0.50	1.25	2.50
❑74, Jul 88	1.25	0.50	1.25	2.50
❑75, Aug 88	1.25	0.50	1.25	2.50
❑76, Sep 88	1.25	0.50	1.25	2.50
❑77, Oct 88, Infernal Triangles	1.25	0.50	1.25	2.50
❑78, Nov 88, To Sow One's Seed in the Wind	1.25	0.50	1.25	2.50
❑79, Dec 88, A: Superman	1.25	0.50	1.25	2.50
❑80, Win 88	1.25	0.50	1.25	2.50
❑81, Hol 89, Invasion!; Widows Weed, Invasion!	1.25	0.50	1.25	2.50
❑82, Jan 89, Sgt. Rock	1.25	0.45	1.13	2.25
❑83, Feb 89, Enemy Ace	1.25	0.45	1.13	2.25
❑84, Mar 89, A: Sandman	1.25	1.00	2.50	5.00
❑85, Apr 89, Jonah Hex, Bat Lash	1.25	0.45	1.13	2.25
❑86, May 89, Tomahawk, Rip Hunter, Demon	1.50	0.45	1.13	2.25
❑87, Jun 89, Shining Knight, Demon	1.50	0.45	1.13	2.25
❑88, Sep 89, Survival of the Fittest	1.50	0.45	1.13	2.25
❑89, Oct 89, Founding Fathers	1.50	0.45	1.13	2.25
❑90, Dec 89, Journeys, 1: TefT Holland, Formerly known as Sprout	1.50	0.50	1.25	2.50
❑91, Jan 90, A: Woodgod	1.50	0.45	1.13	2.25
❑92, Feb 90	1.50	0.45	1.13	2.25
❑93, Mar 90	1.50	0.45	1.13	2.25
❑94, Apr 90	1.50	0.45	1.13	2.25
❑95, May 90	1.50	0.45	1.13	2.25
❑96, Jun 90	1.50	0.45	1.13	2.25

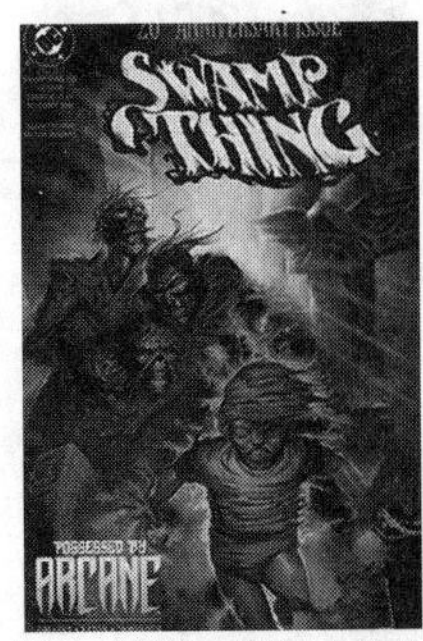

Swamp Thing celebrated the character's 20th anniversary in 1992 with "Family Reunion" in *Swamp Thing* (2nd series) #125.

	ORIG	GOOD	FINE	N-MINT
❑97, Jul 90	1.50	0.45	1.13	2.25
❑98, Aug 90	1.50	0.45	1.13	2.25
❑99, Sep 90	1.50	0.45	1.13	2.25
❑100, Oct 90, Giant-size	2.50	0.60	1.50	3.00
❑101, Nov 90	1.50	0.45	1.13	2.25
❑102, Dec 90	1.50	0.45	1.13	2.25
❑103, Jan 91	1.50	0.45	1.13	2.25
❑104, Feb 91	1.50	0.45	1.13	2.25
❑105, Mar 91	1.50	0.45	1.13	2.25
❑106, Apr 91	1.50	0.45	1.13	2.25
❑107, May 91	1.50	0.45	1.13	2.25
❑108, Jun 91	1.50	0.45	1.13	2.25
❑109, Jul 91	1.50	0.45	1.13	2.25
❑110, Aug 91	1.75	0.45	1.13	2.25
❑111, Sep 91	1.75	0.45	1.13	2.25
❑112, Oct 91	1.75	0.45	1.13	2.25
❑113, Nov 91	1.75	0.45	1.13	2.25
❑114, Dec 91	1.75	0.45	1.13	2.25
❑115, Jan 92	1.75	0.45	1.13	2.25
❑116, Feb 92	1.75	0.45	1.13	2.25
❑117, Mar 92	1.75	0.45	1.13	2.25
❑118, Apr 92	1.75	0.45	1.13	2.25
❑119, May 92, 1: Lady Jane	1.75	0.45	1.13	2.25
❑120, Jun 92	1.75	0.45	1.13	2.25
❑121, Jul 92	1.75	0.40	1.00	2.00
❑122, Aug 92, The Eye Of The Needleman	1.75	0.40	1.00	2.00
❑123, Sep 92, Punctures	1.75	0.40	1.00	2.00
❑124, Oct 92	1.75	0.40	1.00	2.00
❑125, Nov 92, Family Reunion, 20th Anniversary Issue; Arcane	2.95	0.65	1.63	3.25
❑126, Dec 92, The Big Picture	1.75	0.40	1.00	2.00
❑127, Jan 93, Project Proteus, Part 1	1.75	0.40	1.00	2.00
❑128, Feb 93, Project Proteus, Part 2, Vertigo line begins	1.75	0.40	1.00	2.00
❑129, Mar 93, Swamp Fever	1.75	0.40	1.00	2.00
❑130, Apr 93	1.75	0.40	1.00	2.00
❑131, May 93, Folk Remedy	1.75	0.40	1.00	2.00
❑132, Jun 93	1.95	0.40	1.00	2.00
❑133, Jul 93	1.95	0.40	1.00	2.00
❑134, Aug 93	1.95	0.40	1.00	2.00
❑135, Sep 93	1.95	0.40	1.00	2.00
❑136, Oct 93	1.95	0.40	1.00	2.00
❑137, Nov 93	1.95	0.40	1.00	2.00
❑138, Dec 93, And in the End…	1.95	0.40	1.00	2.00
❑139, Jan 94, The Mind Fields, Part 2	1.95	0.40	1.00	2.00
❑140, Mar 94, Bad Gumbo, Part 1	1.95	0.40	1.00	2.00
❑140/PL, Mar 94, platinum	—	1.20	3.00	6.00
❑141, Apr 94	1.95	0.40	1.00	2.00
❑142, May 94	1.95	0.40	1.00	2.00
❑143, Jun 94, Desert Hearts	1.95	0.40	1.00	2.00
❑144, Jul 94	1.95	0.40	1.00	2.00
❑145, Aug 94	1.95	0.40	1.00	2.00
❑146, Sep 94	1.95	0.40	1.00	2.00
❑147, Oct 94	1.95	0.40	1.00	2.00
❑148, Nov 94	1.95	0.40	1.00	2.00
❑149, Dec 94	1.95	0.40	1.00	2.00
❑150, Jan 95, Illumination, The, Giant-size	2.95	0.60	1.50	3.00
❑151, Feb 95	2.95	0.40	1.00	2.00
❑152, Mar 95, River Run, Part 1	2.95	0.40	1.00	2.00
❑153, Apr 95	1.95	0.40	1.00	2.00
❑154, May 95	2.25	0.45	1.13	2.25
❑155, Jun 95	2.25	0.45	1.13	2.25
❑156, Jul 95	2.25	0.45	1.13	2.25
❑157, Aug 95	2.25	0.45	1.13	2.25
❑158, Sep 95	2.25	0.45	1.13	2.25
❑159, Oct 95, Photo cover	2.25	0.50	1.25	2.50
❑160, Nov 95	2.25	0.50	1.25	2.50
❑161, Dec 95	2.25	0.50	1.25	2.50
❑162, Jan 96	2.25	0.50	1.25	2.50
❑163, Feb 96, Trees of Knowledge	2.25	0.50	1.25	2.50
❑164, Mar 96, The Parliament of Vapors	2.25	0.50	1.25	2.50

	ORIG	GOOD	FINE	N-MINT
❑165, Apr 96, CS, Chester Williams: American Cop	2.25	0.50	1.25	2.50
❑166, May 96	2.25	0.50	1.25	2.50
❑167, Jun 96	2.25	0.50	1.25	2.50
❑168, Jul 96	2.25	0.50	1.25	2.50
❑169, Aug 96	2.25	0.50	1.25	2.50
❑170, Sep 96	2.25	0.50	1.25	2.50
❑171, Oct 96, Trial by Fire, Final Issue	2.25	0.50	1.25	2.50
❑Anl 4, A: Batman	2.00	0.70	1.75	3.50
❑Anl 5, A: Brother Power	2.95	0.70	1.75	3.50
❑Anl 6	2.95	0.59	1.48	2.95
❑Anl 7, The Children's Crusade, Part 4, Children's Crusade	3.95	0.79	1.98	3.95

SWAMP THING (3RD SERIES)
VERTIGO

	ORIG	GOOD	FINE	N-MINT
❑1, May 00, In Lieu of Flowers	2.50	0.60	1.50	3.00
❑2, Jun 00, A Tree Falls in the Forest	2.50	0.50	1.25	2.50
❑3, Jul 00	2.50	0.50	1.25	2.50
❑4, Aug 00, Killing Time, Part 1	2.50	0.50	1.25	2.50
❑5, Sep 00, Killing Time, Part 2	2.50	0.50	1.25	2.50
❑6, Oct 00, Killing Time, Part 3	2.50	0.50	1.25	2.50
❑7, Nov 00, Concrete Jungle, Part 1	2.50	0.50	1.25	2.50
❑8, Dec 00, Concrete Jungle, Part 2	2.50	0.50	1.25	2.50
❑9, Jan 01, Concrete Jungle, Part 3	2.50	0.50	1.25	2.50
❑10, Feb 01, Silk Cut	2.50	0.50	1.25	2.50
❑11, Mar 01, Red Harvest, Part 1	2.50	0.50	1.25	2.50
❑12, Apr 01, Red Harvest, Part 2	2.50	0.50	1.25	2.50
❑13, May 01, Red Harvest, Part 3	2.50	0.50	1.25	2.50
❑14, Jun 01, Red Harvest, Part 4	2.50	0.50	1.25	2.50
❑15	2.50	0.50	1.25	2.50
❑16	2.50	0.50	1.25	2.50
❑17	2.50	0.50	1.25	2.50

SWAMP THING: ROOTS
DC

Value: Cover or less

❑1, nn; prestige format one-shot 7.95

SWAN
LITTLE IDYLLS

Value: Cover or less

❑1, Jun 95, b&w 2.95

❑2, Jun 95, b&w 2.95

SWEET
ADEPT

Value: Cover or less

❑1 .... 3.95

SWEETCHILDE
NEW MOON

Value: Cover or less

❑1, b&w; adult 2.95

SWEET CHILDE: LOST CONFESSIONS
ANARCHY BRIDGEWORKS

Value: Cover or less

❑1 .... 2.95

SWEET LUCY
BRAINSTORM

Value: Cover or less

❑1, Jun 93, b&w 2.95

❑2, b&w 2.95

SWEET LUCY: BLONDE STEELE
BRAINSTORM

Value: Cover or less

❑1, Blonde Steel; Technophelia 2.95

SWEET LUCY COMMEMORATIVE EDITION
BRAINSTORM

Value: Cover or less

❑1 .... 3.95

SWEETMEATS
ATOMEKA

Value: Cover or less

❑1, nn; b&w one-shot 3.95

SWEET XVI
MARVEL

Value: Cover or less

❑1, The Invitation; How to Make a Roman Braid 1.00

❑2 .... 1.00

❑3 .... 1.00

❑4 .... 1.00

❑5 .... 1.00

❑6 .... 1.00

❑SE 1, Back to School Special 2.25

SWERVE
SLAVE LABOR

Value: Cover or less

❑1, Dec 95, False Start 1.50

❑2, Mar 96 .... 1.50

SWIFTSURE
HARRIER

	ORIG	GOOD	FINE	N-MINT
❑1, May 85, Arrival; A Fall From Grace	1.75	0.40	1.00	2.00
❑2	1.75	0.40	1.00	2.00
❑3, Aug 85	1.75	0.40	1.00	2.00
❑4	1.75	0.40	1.00	2.00
❑5, Nov 85	1.75	0.40	1.00	2.00
❑6, Jan 86	1.75	0.40	1.00	2.00
❑7, Mar 86	1.75	0.40	1.00	2.00
❑8, May 86	1.75	0.40	1.00	2.00
❑9, Jul 86, Redfox	1.75	0.40	1.00	2.00
❑10	1.50	0.40	1.00	2.00
❑11	1.50	0.40	1.00	2.00
❑12	1.50	0.40	1.00	2.00
❑13	1.95	0.40	1.00	2.00
❑14	1.95	0.40	1.00	2.00
❑15	1.95	0.40	1.00	2.00
❑16	1.95	0.40	1.00	2.00
❑17	1.95	0.40	1.00	2.00
❑18	1.95	0.40	1.00	2.00

SWIFTSURE & CONQUEROR
HARRIER

	ORIG	GOOD	FINE	N-MINT
❑1	1.75	0.40	1.00	2.00
❑2	1.75	0.35	0.88	1.75
❑3	1.75	0.35	0.88	1.75
❑4	1.75	0.35	0.88	1.75
❑5	1.75	0.35	0.88	1.75
❑6	1.75	0.35	0.88	1.75
❑7	1.75	0.35	0.88	1.75
❑8	1.75	0.35	0.88	1.75
❑9, A: Redfox	1.75	0.50	1.25	2.50
❑10	1.50	0.30	0.75	1.50
❑11	1.50	0.30	0.75	1.50
❑12	1.50	0.30	0.75	1.50
❑13, Tales of the Rugged Reptile: One Too Many; Lieutenant Fl'ff: Nowhere to Run..	1.95	0.39	0.98	1.95
❑14	1.95	0.39	0.98	1.95
❑15	1.95	0.39	0.98	1.95
❑16	1.95	0.39	0.98	1.95
❑17	1.95	0.39	0.98	1.95
❑18	1.95	0.39	0.98	1.95

SWITCHBLADE
SILVERLINE

Value: Cover or less

❑1, Dec 97 .... 2.95

SWORD OF DAMOCLES
IMAGE

Value: Cover or less

❑1, Mar 96, Fire from Heaven Prelude 1, 1: Fire From Heaven; 1: Sword of Damocles 2.50

❑2, Jul 96, Fire from Heaven Finale 1; Fire From Heaven Finale, Part 1 .... 2.50

SWORD OF SORCERY
DC

	ORIG	GOOD	FINE	N-MINT
❑1, Mar 73, NA; HC, Fafhrd and The Gray Mouser	0.20	0.60	1.50	3.00
❑2, May 73, HC, Fafhrd and The Gray Mouser	0.20	0.40	1.00	2.00
❑3, Aug 73, HC, Fafhrd and The Gray Mouser	0.20	0.40	1.00	2.00
❑4, Oct 73, HC, Fafhrd and The Gray Mouser	0.20	0.40	1.00	2.00
❑5, Dec 73, JSe, Final Issue; Fafhrd and The Gray Mouser	0.20	0.40	1.00	2.00

SWORD OF THE ATOM
DC

	ORIG	GOOD	FINE	N-MINT
❑1, Sep 83, GK, Stormy Passage	0.60	0.30	0.75	1.50
❑2, Oct 83, GK	0.60	0.30	0.75	1.50
❑3, Nov 83, GK	0.60	0.30	0.75	1.50
❑4, Dec 83, GK	0.60	0.30	0.75	1.50
❑SE 1, GK	1.25	0.30	0.75	1.50
❑SE 2, GK	1.25	0.30	0.75	1.50
❑SE 3, PB	1.25	0.30	0.75	1.50

SWORD OF THE SAMURAI
ACG

Value: Cover or less

❑1, b&w; Reprint 2.50

SWORD OF VALOR
A+

Value: Cover or less

❑1, JA; GD; DG; JB, GD (w); DG (w); TS (w), Kuno: Son of Steel; The Tower Maiden 2.50

❑2, Thane of Bagarth, Part 2 .. 2.50

❑3, The Promise; Thane of Bagarth, Part 3 .... 2.50

❑4 .... 2.50

SWORDSMEN AND SAURIANS
ECLIPSE

Value: Cover or less

❑1, b&w 19.95

SWORDS OF CEREBUS
AARDVARK-VANAHEIM

Value: Cover or less

❑1 .... 5.00

❑1-2, 2nd Printing 5.00

❑, 3rd Printing 5.00

❑2 .... 5.00

❑2-2, 2nd Printing 5.00

❑3 .... 6.00

❑3-2, 2nd Printing 6.00

❑3-3, 3rd Printing 6.00

❑4 .... 6.00

❑4-2, 2nd Printing 6.00

❑5 .... 5.00

❑6, first printing omitted issue #25 .... 5.00

SWORDS OF CEREBUS SUPPLEMENT
AARDVARK-VANAHEIM

	ORIG	GOOD	FINE	N-MINT
❑1, giveaway to buyers of Swords of Cerebus #6 first printing; reprinted issue #25	—	0.20	0.50	1.00

SWORDS OF SHAR-PEI
CALIBER

Value: Cover or less

❑1, Path of Freedom, b&w 2.50

❑2, b&w 2.50

	ORIG	GOOD	FINE	N-MINT

SWORDS OF TEXAS
ECLIPSE
Value: Cover or less

- ❑1, Oct 87, Lost Highway 1.75
- ❑2 .... 1.75
- ❑3, Jan 88 .... 1.75
- ❑4, Mar 88 .... 1.75

SWORDS OF THE SWASHBUCKLERS
MARVEL

	ORIG	GOOD	FINE	N-MINT
❑1, May 85, Shockwaves	1.50	0.40	1.00	2.00
❑2, Jul 85	1.50	0.35	0.88	1.75
❑3, Sep 85	1.50	0.35	0.88	1.75
❑4, Nov 85, The Wierdling	1.50	0.30	0.75	1.50
❑5, Jan 86	1.50	0.30	0.75	1.50
❑6, Mar 86	1.50	0.30	0.75	1.50
❑7, May 86	1.50	0.30	0.75	1.50
❑8, Jul 86	1.50	0.30	0.75	1.50
❑9, Sep 86	1.50	0.30	0.75	1.50
❑10, Nov 86	1.50	0.30	0.75	1.50
❑11, Jan 87	1.50	0.30	0.75	1.50
❑12, Mar 87	1.75	0.30	0.75	1.50

SWORDS OF VALOR
A-PLUS
Value: Cover or less

- ❑1, b&w 2.50
- ❑2, b&w 2.50
- ❑3, b&w 2.50
- ❑4, b&w 2.50

SYMBOLS OF JUSTICE
HIGH IMPACT
Value: Cover or less

- ❑1, Jun 95 .... 2.95

SYNN, THE GIRL FROM LSD
AC
Value: Cover or less

- ❑1, Aug 90, b&w 3.95

SYNTHETIC ASSASSIN, THE
NIGHT REALM
Value: Cover or less

- ❑1 .... 1.50

SYPHONS
NOW

	ORIG	GOOD	FINE	N-MINT
❑1, Jul 86, Night Moves, 1: Syphons	1.50	0.40	1.00	2.00
❑2, Sep 86	1.50	0.30	0.75	1.50
❑3, Nov 86	1.50	0.30	0.75	1.50

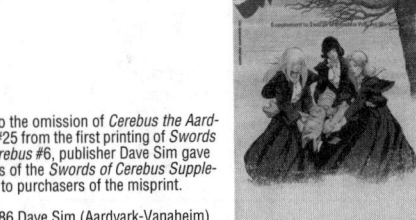

Due to the omission of *Cerebus the Aardvark* #25 from the first printing of *Swords of Cerebus* #6, publisher Dave Sim gave copies of the *Swords of Cerebus Supplement* to purchasers of the misprint.

© 1986 Dave Sim (Aardvark-Vanaheim)

	ORIG	GOOD	FINE	N-MINT
❑4, Jan 87	1.50	0.30	0.75	1.50
❑5, Mar 87	1.50	0.30	0.75	1.50
❑6, Jul 87	1.50	0.30	0.75	1.50
❑7, Aug 87	1.50	0.30	0.75	1.50

SYPHONS (VOL. 2)
NOW

	ORIG	GOOD	FINE	N-MINT
❑0, Dec 93, Load and Run, Part 1, Preview edition	—	0.20	0.50	1.00
❑1, May 94, Load and Run, Part 1	2.95	0.50	1.25	2.50
❑2, Jun 94, Drag and Drop	2.50	0.50	1.25	2.50
❑3, Jul 94	2.50	0.50	1.25	2.50

SYPHONS: THE SYGATE STRATAGEM
NOW
Value: Cover or less

- ❑1 .... 2.95
- ❑2 .... 2.95
- ❑3 .... 2.95

SYSTEM, THE
DC
Value: Cover or less

- ❑1, May 96 .... 2.95
- ❑2, Jun 96 .... 2.95
- ❑3, Jul 96 .... 2.95

SYSTEM SEVEN
ARROW
Value: Cover or less

- ❑1, Dec 87, T.E.S.T. Results 1.50
- ❑2 .... 1.50
- ❑3 .... 1.50

T

T2: CYBERNETIC DAWN
MALIBU

	ORIG	GOOD	FINE	N-MINT
❑0, Apr 96, Flip-Book with T2 Nuclear Twilight #0	2.95	0.60	1.50	3.00
❑1, Nov 95, Lost & Found, immediately follows events of T2 Judgment Day	2.50	0.50	1.25	2.50
❑2, Dec 95, Search Mode	2.50	0.50	1.25	2.50
❑3, Jan 96, Judgement Impaired	2.50	0.50	1.25	2.50
❑4, Feb 96	2.50	0.50	1.25	2.50

T2: NUCLEAR TWILIGHT
MALIBU

	ORIG	GOOD	FINE	N-MINT
❑0, Apr 96, The Programming Of Fate, Flip-book with T2 Cybernetic Dawn #0	2.95	0.60	1.50	3.00
❑1, Nov 95, prequel to first Terminator movie	2.50	0.50	1.25	2.50
❑2, Dec 95, Suicide Mission	2.50	0.50	1.25	2.50
❑3, Jan 96, Dead Men Walking	2.50	0.50	1.25	2.50
❑4, Father's Day	2.50	0.50	1.25	2.50

TABOO
SPIDERBABY
Value: Cover or less

- ❑1, b&w 9.95
- ❑2, b&w 9.95
- ❑3, b&w 9.95
- ❑4, b&w 14.95
- ❑5 .... 14.95
- ❑6, with booklet 14.95
- ❑7, with booklet 14.95
- ❑8, Jun 95, b&w 14.95
- ❑9, In the Garden; Worms 14.95

TABOUX
ANTARCTIC
Value: Cover or less

- ❑1, Aug 96, The Evil Legacy... 3.95
- ❑2, Aug 96, Just Deserts 3.95

TAILGUNNER JO
DC
Value: Cover or less

- ❑1, Sep 88, The Curve Of Binding Energy 1.25
- ❑2, Oct 88 .... 1.25
- ❑3, Nov 88 .... 1.25
- ❑4, Dec 88 .... 1.25
- ❑5, Win 88 .... 1.25
- ❑6, Jan 89 .... 1.25

TAILS
ARCHIE
Value: Cover or less

- ❑1, Dec 95 .... 1.50
- ❑2, Jan 96 .... 1.50
- ❑3, Feb 96 .... 1.50

TAINTED
DC
Value: Cover or less

- ❑1, Feb 95 .... 4.95

TAINTED BLOOD
WEIRDLING
Value: Cover or less

- ❑1, Apr 96, Bury My Lovely 2.95

TAKEN UNDER COMPENDIUM
CALIBER
Value: Cover or less

- ❑1, A Faint Smell of Violet; Only Say the Word, nn; b&w 2.95

TAKION
DC
Value: Cover or less

- ❑1, Jun 96, Birth Pains 1.75
- ❑2, Jul 96, V: Captain Atom; V: Green Lantern; V: Flash 1.75
- ❑3, Aug 96 .... 1.75
- ❑4, Sep 96, Blind Faith 1.75
- ❑5, Oct 96, Homecoming 1.75
- ❑6, Nov 96, Dark Dawn 1.75
- ❑7, Dec 96, Moonlight, Final Issue; Lightray returns 1.75

TALE OF HALIMA, THE
FANTAGRAPHICS
Value: Cover or less

- ❑1, b&w; adult 2.75
- ❑2, b&w; adult 2.75

TALE OF MYA ROM, THE
AIRCEL
Value: Cover or less

- ❑1, b&w 1.70

TALE OF ONE BAD RAT, THE
DARK HORSE

	ORIG	GOOD	FINE	N-MINT
❑1, Oct 94, BT, NG (w); BT (w), Town, Introduction by Neil Gaiman	2.95	0.80	2.00	4.00
❑2, Nov 94, BT, BT (w)	2.95	0.60	1.50	3.00
❑3, Dec 94, BT, BT (w)	2.95	0.60	1.50	3.00
❑4, Jan 95, BT, BT (w)	2.95	0.60	1.50	3.00

TALE OF THE BODY THIEF, THE (ANNE RICE'S...)
SICILIAN DRAGON
Value: Cover or less

- ❑1 .... 2.95
- ❑2, Oct 99 .... 2.95
- ❑3 .... 2.95
- ❑4 .... 2.95
- ❑5 .... 2.95
- ❑6 .... 2.95
- ❑7 .... 2.95
- ❑8 .... 2.95
- ❑9 .... 2.95
- ❑10 .... 2.95
- ❑11 .... 2.95
- ❑12 .... 2.95

TALES CALCULATED TO DRIVE YOU MAD
EC
Value: Cover or less

- ❑1 .... 3.99
- ❑2 .... 3.99
- ❑3 .... 3.99
- ❑4 .... 3.99
- ❑5 .... 3.99
- ❑6, Reprints Mad #16-18 .... 3.99
- ❑7 .... 3.99
- ❑8, Reprints Mad #22, 23 .... 3.99

TALES FROM GROUND ZERO
EXCEL

Value: Cover or less

- ❑1, b&w ... 4.95

TALES FROM NECROPOLIS
BRAINSTORM

Value: Cover or less

- ❑1, Wood Werk; Ghost in the Machine, b&w ... 2.95

TALES FROM SLEAZE CASTLE
GRATUITOUS BUNNY

	ORIG	GOOD	FINE	N-MINT
❑1	—	0.50	1.25	2.50
❑2	—	0.50	1.25	2.50
❑3, Rest and Recuperation	—	0.50	1.25	2.50

TALES FROM THE AGE OF APOCALYPSE: SINISTER BLOODLINES
MARVEL

Value: Cover or less

- ❑1, Dec 97, nn ... 5.99

TALES FROM THE ANIVERSE (ARROW)
ARROW

	ORIG	GOOD	FINE	N-MINT
❑1	1.50	0.40	1.00	2.00
❑2	1.50	0.30	0.75	1.50
❑3, The Politics of Piracy; Retro Ram and his Rocket Rangers	1.50	0.30	0.75	1.50
❑4, Ms. Chevious and Ganda: A Matter of Style; J.B. Space: Much to Stew About Nothing	1.50	0.30	0.75	1.50
❑5	1.50	0.30	0.75	1.50
❑6	1.50	0.30	0.75	1.50

TALES FROM THE ANIVERSE (MASSIVE)
MASSIVE

Value: Cover or less

- ❑1, b&w ... 2.25
- ❑2 ... 2.75
- ❑3 ... 2.25

TALES FROM THE BOG
ABERRATION

Value: Cover or less

- ❑1, Nov 95, b&w ... 2.95
- ❑2, Feb 96, b&w ... 2.95
- ❑3, Jun 96, b&w ... 2.95
- ❑4, Sep 96, b&w ... 2.95
- ❑5, Apr 97, b&w ... 2.95
- ❑6, Jun 97, b&w ... 2.95
- ❑7, Nov 97, b&w ... 3.95

TALES FROM THE BOG (DIRECTOR'S CUT)
ABERRATION

Value: Cover or less

- ❑1, b&w ... 2.95

TALES FROM THE CLONEZONE
DARK HORSE

Value: Cover or less

- ❑1 ... 1.75

TALES FROM THE CRYPT (COCHRAN)
COCHRAN

Value: Cover or less

- ❑1, JKa; JCr; AW ... 2.00
- ❑2, Oct 91, JKa; JCr; AW ... 2.00
- ❑3, Dec 91, JKa; JCr; AW ... 2.00
- ❑4, Feb 92, JKa; JCr; AW ... 2.00
- ❑5, Mar 92, JKa; JCr; AW ... 2.00
- ❑6, May 92, JKa; JCr; AW ... 2.00
- ❑7, Jul 92, JKa; JCr; AW ... 2.00

TALES FROM THE CRYPT (COCHRAN ONE-SHOT)
COCHRAN

Value: Cover or less

- ❑1, Jul 91, over-sized reprint of Tales #31 and Crime SuspenStories #12 ... 3.95

TALES FROM THE CRYPT (GLADSTONE)
GLADSTONE

	ORIG	GOOD	FINE	N-MINT
❑1, Jul 90, JKa; BE; FF; JCr; AW; GE, BE (w); FF (w); AW (w); GE (w), Lower Birth!; This Trick'll Kill You, O: Crypt-Keeper, "Touch and Go", a Ray Bradbury adaptation; Reprints Tales From the Crypt #33, Crime SuspenStories #17	1.95	0.60	1.50	3.00
❑2, Sep 90, JKa; JCr; JO, JKa (w); JCr (w); JO (w), By the Fright of the Silvery Moon!; Midnight Mess,Reprints Tales From the Crypt #35, Crime SuspenStories #18	1.95	0.50	1.25	2.50
❑3, Nov 90, JKa; WW; JCr; JO; HK, JKa (w); WW (w); JO (w); HK (w), Undertaking Pallor; The Craving Grave,Reprints Tales From the Crypt #39, Crime SuspenStories #1	1.95	0.50	1.25	2.50
❑4, Jan 91, JKa; JCr; JO; HK; AW; AF ,Reprints Tales From the Crypt #18, Crime SuspenStories #16	2.00	0.50	1.25	2.50
❑5, Mar 91, JKa; BK; JCr ,Reprints Tales From the Crypt #45, Crime SuspenStories #5	2.00	0.50	1.25	2.50
❑6, May 91, JKa; BK; JCr ,Reprints Tales From the Crypt #42, Crime SuspenStories #27	2.00	0.50	1.25	2.50

TALES FROM THE CRYPT (RCP)
EC

	ORIG	GOOD	FINE	N-MINT
❑1, Sep 92, JCr; AF, Death Must Come; The Man Who Was Death,Reprints Crypt of Terror (EC) #17	1.50	0.40	1.00	2.00
❑2, Dec 92, The Maestro's Hand; The Living Corpse,Reprints Crypt of Terror (EC) #18	1.50	0.40	1.00	2.00
❑3, Mar 93, Ghost Ship; The Hungry Grave,Reprints Crypt of Terror (EC) #19.	1.50	0.40	1.00	2.00
❑4, Jun 93, GI; JKa; JCr; AF, The Thing From the Sea!; End of the Search (text story),Reprints Tales From the Crypt (EC) #20	2.00	0.40	1.00	2.00
❑5, Sep 93, GI; WW; HK; AF, A Shocking Way to Die!; Terror Ride!,Reprints Tales From the Crypt (EC) #21	2.00	0.40	1.00	2.00
❑6, Dec 93, GI; JCr; AF, The Thing From The Grave!; Blood Type 'V'!,Reprints Tales From the Crypt (EC) #22	2.00	0.40	1.00	2.00
❑7, Mar 94, JCr; AF ,Reprints Tales From the Crypt (EC) #23	2.00	0.40	1.00	2.00
❑8, Jun 94, WW; JCr, AF (c),Reprints Tales From the Crypt (EC) #24	2.00	0.40	1.00	2.00
❑9, Sep 94,Reprints Tales From the Crypt (EC) #25	2.00	0.40	1.00	2.00
❑10, Dec 94,Reprints Tales From the Crypt (EC) #26	2.00	0.40	1.00	2.00
❑11, Mar 95, JKa; JO, JKa (w); JO (w), Well-Cooked Hams!; Madame Bluebeard,Reprints Tales From the Crypt (EC) #27	2.00	0.40	1.00	2.00
❑12, Jun 95, JKa; JO, JKa (w); JO (w), Bargain in Death!; Ants in Her Trance!,Reprints Tales From the Crypt (EC) #28	2.00	0.40	1.00	2.00
❑13, Sep 95, JKa; JO, JKa (w); JO (w), Grounds…For Horror!,Reprints Tales From the Crypt (EC) #29	2.00	0.40	1.00	2.00
❑14, Dec 95, JKa; JO, JKa (w); JO (w), Gastly Prospects!; A Hollywood Ending!,Reprints Tales From the Crypt (EC) #30	2.00	0.40	1.00	2.00
❑15, Mar 96, JKa; AW, JKa (w); AW (w), Survival…Or Death!; The Thing in the 'Glades!,Reprints Tales From the Crypt (EC) #31	2.00	0.40	1.00	2.00
❑16, Jun 96, GE, GE (w), T Ain't the Meat…It's the Humanity!; Roped In!,Reprints Tales From the Crypt (EC) #32	2.00	0.50	1.25	2.50
❑17, Sep 96, JKa; GE, JKa (w); GE (w), Lower Berth!; This Trick'll Kill You!, O: the The Crypt Keeper,Reprints Tales From the Crypt (EC) #33	2.50	0.50	1.25	2.50
❑18, Dec 96, JKa; GE, JKa (w); GE (w), Mirror, Mirror, on the Wall!; Oil's Well that Ends Well!,Reprints Tales From the Crypt (EC) #34	2.50	0.50	1.25	2.50
❑19, Mar 97, JKa; JO, JKa (w); JO (w), By the Fright of the Silvery Moon!; Midnight Mess!,Reprints Tales From the Crypt (EC) #35	2.50	0.50	1.25	2.50
❑20, Jun 97, JKa; GE, JKa (w); GE (w), Fare Tonight, Followed by Increasing Clottiness…; Curiousity Killed…,Reprints Tales From the Crypt (EC) #36	2.50	0.50	1.25	2.50
❑21, Sep 97, BE; JO, BE (w); JO (w), Dead Right!; Pleasant Screams,Reprints Tales From the Crypt (EC) #37	2.50	0.50	1.25	2.50
❑22, Dec 97, BE, BE (w), Tight Grip!; …Only Skin Deep!,Reprints Tales From the Crypt (EC) #38	2.50	0.50	1.25	2.50
❑23, Mar 98, JKa; JO, JKa (w); JO (w), Undertaking Palor; The Craving Grave,Reprints Tales From the Crypt (EC) #39	2.50	0.50	1.25	2.50
❑24, Jun 98, BK; GE, BK (w); GE (w), Food for Though; Pearly to Dead,Reprints Tales From the Crypt (EC) #40	2.50	0.50	1.25	2.50
❑25, Sep 98, JKa; GE, JKa (w); GE (w), Operation Friendship; Come Back, Little Linda!,Reprints Tales From the Crypt (EC) #41	2.50	0.50	1.25	2.50
❑26, Dec 98,Reprints Tales From the Crypt (EC) #42	2.50	0.50	1.25	2.50
❑27, Mar 99,Reprints Tales From the Crypt (EC) #43	2.50	0.50	1.25	2.50
❑28, Jun 99,Reprints Tales From the Crypt (EC) #44	2.50	0.50	1.25	2.50
❑29, Sep 99,Reprints Tales From the Crypt (EC) #45	2.50	0.50	1.25	2.50
❑30, Dec 99, Upon Reflection; Blind Alleys,Reprints Tales From the Crypt (EC) #46; material originally prepared for Crypt of Terror #1	2.50	0.50	1.25	2.50
❑Anl 1,Collects Tales From the Crypt #1-5	8.95	1.79	4.47	8.95
❑Anl 2	9.95	1.99	4.97	9.95
❑Anl 3	10.95	2.19	5.47	10.95
❑Anl 4	12.95	2.59	6.47	12.95
❑Anl 5,Collects Tales From the Crypt #37-41	13.50	2.70	6.75	13.50

TALES FROM THE EDGE!
VANGUARD

	ORIG	GOOD	FINE	N-MINT
❑1, Jun 93, b&w	2.95	0.70	1.75	3.50
❑2, Sep 93, b&w	2.95	2.00	5.00	10.00
❑3, Dec 93, b&w	2.95	0.60	1.50	3.00
❑4, Jul 94, b&w	2.95	0.60	1.50	3.00

	ORIG	GOOD	FINE	N-MINT
❑5	2.95	0.60	1.50	3.00
❑6	2.95	0.60	1.50	3.00
❑7, Jul 95, b&w	2.95	0.60	1.50	3.00
❑8, b&w	2.95	1.20	3.00	6.00
❑9, b&w	2.95	2.00	5.00	10.00
❑10, b&w	2.95	1.20	3.00	6.00
❑11	—	1.00	2.50	5.00
❑12, Sacred Monkey Man	4.00	0.80	2.00	4.00
❑13	—	0.60	1.50	3.00
❑14	—	1.00	2.50	5.00
❑15, BSz ,Bill Sienkiewicz Special	5.55	1.11	2.78	5.55
❑Smr 1, Aug 94, b&w; cardstock cover	3.50	0.70	1.75	3.50

TALES FROM THE FRIDGE
KITCHEN SINK

	ORIG	GOOD	FINE	N-MINT
❑1, Jun 73, b&w	0.75	0.60	1.50	3.00

TALES FROM THE HEART
ENTROPY

	ORIG	GOOD	FINE	N-MINT
❑1,no cover date	1.50	0.80	2.00	4.00
❑2	1.50	0.65	1.63	3.25
❑3, Dec 88, b&w	1.75	0.60	1.50	3.00
❑4, Jan 89, b&w	1.75	0.60	1.50	3.00
❑5, May 89, b&w	1.75	0.59	1.48	2.95
❑6, Oct 89, b&w	1.75	0.59	1.48	2.95
❑7, Nov 90	2.95	0.59	1.48	2.95
❑8, Apr 91, Monkey Business	2.50	0.59	1.48	2.95
❑9, Aug 92, A Day in the Life	2.50	0.59	1.48	2.95
❑10, Mar 93, Mawa, b&w	2.95	0.59	1.48	2.95
❑11, May 94, Taking It, b&w	2.95	0.59	1.48	2.95

TALES FROM THE HEART OF AFRICA: THE TEMPORARY NATIVES
MARVEL

Value: Cover or less

❑1, Aug 90, nn; One-Shot 3.95

TALES FROM THE KIDS
DAVID G. BROWN STUDIOS

	ORIG	GOOD	FINE	N-MINT
❑1, Apr 96, b&w; no cover price; anthology by children; produced for L.A. Cultural Affairs Dept.	—	0.40	1.00	2.00

TALES FROM THE LEATHER NUN
LAST GASP

	ORIG	GOOD	FINE	N-MINT
❑1, Tales of the Leather Nun; The Adventures of Robert Crumb Himself	0.50	2.80	7.00	14.00

TALES FROM THE MAHABHARATA
AMAR CHITRA KATHA

Value: Cover or less

❑16, The Golden Mongoose; The Pigeon's Sacrifice 3.50

TALES FROM THE OUTER BOROUGHS
FANTAGRAPHICS

Value: Cover or less

❑1, b&w 2.25
❑2, b&w 2.25
❑3, b&w 2.25
❑4, b&w 2.50
❑5, b&w 2.50

TALES FROM THE PLAGUE
ECLIPSE

Value: Cover or less

❑1 .... 3.95

TALES FROM THE RAVAGED LANDS
MAGI STUDIOS

Value: Cover or less

❑0, nn; no indicia; b&w introduction to series 2.00
❑1, b&w; no indicia or cover date 2.50
❑2, b&w; no indicia or cover date 2.50
❑3, Jan 96, b&w 2.50
❑4, b&w; no indicia or cover date 2.50

TALES FROM THE STONE TROLL CAFÉ
PLANET X

Value: Cover or less

❑1 .... 1.75

TALES OF A CHECKERED MAN
D.W. BRUBAKER PRODUCTIONS

	ORIG	GOOD	FINE	N-MINT
❑1, b&w; no cover price	—	0.40	1.00	2.00

TALES OF ASGARD (VOL. 1)
MARVEL

	ORIG	GOOD	FINE	N-MINT
❑1, JK, SL (w), Odin Battles Ymir, King of the Ice Giants; Surtur the Fire Demon!	0.25	6.00	15.00	30.00

TALES OF ASGARD (VOL. 2)
MARVEL

	ORIG	GOOD	FINE	N-MINT
❑1, Feb 84, JK, SL (w), The Hordes of Harokin!; The Fateful Change!	1.25	0.30	0.75	1.50

TALES OF BEATRIX FARMER
MU

Value: Cover or less

❑1, Feb 96, nn; b&w 2.95

TALES OF BLUE & GREY
AVALON

Value: Cover or less

❑1, b&w 2.95

TALES OF EVIL
ATLAS

	ORIG	GOOD	FINE	N-MINT
❑1, Feb 75, Spawn Of The Devil!; A Matter Of Breeding, Stake Out	0.25	0.40	1.00	2.00
❑2, Apr 75, TS, The Fifty Dollar Body!; The Last Train	0.25	0.30	0.75	1.50
❑3, Jul 75, RB, RB (w), Man-Monster!	0.25	0.30	0.75	1.50

Tony Stark first donned his Iron Man armor in *Tales of Suspense* #39.

TALES OF GHOST CASTLE
DC

	ORIG	GOOD	FINE	N-MINT
❑1, May 75, NR, A Child's Garden Of Graves; A Soul A Day Keeps The Devil Away	0.25	0.40	1.00	2.00
❑2, Jul 75, Snake-Eyes; The Inheritors, The Fate Of The Fortune Hunter	0.25	0.40	1.00	2.00
❑3, Sep 75	0.25	0.40	1.00	2.00

TALES OF G.I. JOE
MARVEL

Value: Cover or less

❑1, Jan 88, DP; HT, Operation: Last Doomsday; Hot Potato!,Reprint; Reprints G.I. Joe, A Real America Hero #1 .... 2.25
❑2, Feb 88,Reprint; Reprints G.I. Joe, A Real America Hero #2 .... 1.50
❑3, Mar 88,Reprint; Reprints G.I. Joe, A Real America Hero #3 .... 1.50
❑4, Apr 88,Reprint; Reprints G.I. Joe, A Real America Hero #4 .... 1.50
❑5, May 88,Reprint; Reprints G.I. Joe, A Real America Hero #5 .... 1.50
❑6, Jun 88,Reprint; Reprints G.I. Joe, A Real America Hero #6 .... 1.50
❑7, Jul 88,Reprint; Reprints G.I. Joe, A Real America Hero #7 .... 1.50
❑8, Aug 88,Reprint; Reprints G.I. Joe, A Real America Hero #8 .... 1.50
❑9, Sep 88,Reprint; Reprints G.I. Joe, A Real America Hero #9 .... 1.50
❑10, Oct 88,Reprint; Reprints G.I. Joe, A Real America Hero #10 .... 1.50
❑11, Nov 88,Reprint; Reprints G.I. Joe, A Real America Hero #11 .... 1.50
❑12, Dec 88,Reprint; Reprints G.I. Joe, A Real America Hero #12 .... 1.50
❑13, Jan 89,Reprint; Reprints G.I. Joe, A Real America Hero #13 .... 1.50
❑14, Feb 89,Reprint; Reprints G.I. Joe, A Real America Hero #14 .... 1.50
❑15, Mar 89,Reprint; Reprints G.I. Joe, A Real America Hero #15 .... 1.50

TALES OF JERRY
HACIENDA

Value: Cover or less

❑1, b&w 2.50
❑2 .... 2.50
❑3 .... 2.50
❑4 .... 2.50
❑5 .... 2.50
❑6 .... 2.50
❑7 .... 2.50
❑8 .... 2.50
❑9 .... 2.50
❑10 .... 2.50

TALES OF LETHARGY
ALPHA

Value: Cover or less

❑1, Guy With A Gun; The Evil Thumb, b&w 2.50
❑2, Guy With A Gun; Dream Date, b&w 2.50
❑3, Guy With A Gun; Spider-San, b&w 2.50

TALES OF ORDINARY MADNESS
DARK HORSE

Value: Cover or less

❑1, b&w 2.50
❑2, b&w 2.50
❑3, b&w 2.50
❑4, b&w 2.50

TALES OF SCREAMING HORROR
FANTACO

Value: Cover or less

❑1, b&w 3.50

TALES OF SEX AND DEATH
PRINT MINT

	ORIG	GOOD	FINE	N-MINT
❑1, Apr 71, Soupygoy; God Takes Him From Me	0.50	0.60	1.50	3.00
❑2, The Greening of America; If Brains Were Muscles	0.75	0.60	1.50	3.00

TALES OF SHAUNDRA
RIP OFF

Value: Cover or less

❑1 .... 12.95

TALES OF SUSPENSE
MARVEL

	ORIG	GOOD	FINE	N-MINT
❑39, Mar 63, JK, 1: Iron Man,Grey armor; Iron Man stories begin	0.12	720.00	1800.00	3600.00
❑40, Apr 63, JK, 2: Iron Man; 1: Iron Man gold armor	0.12	270.00	675.00	1350.00
❑41, May 63, JK	0.12	130.00	325.00	650.00
❑42, Jun 63, DH; SD, 1: Mad Pharoah	0.12	60.00	150.00	300.00
❑43, Jul 63, 1: Kala	0.12	60.00	150.00	300.00
❑44, Aug 63	0.12	60.00	150.00	300.00

	ORIG	GOOD	FINE	N-MINT
❑45, Sep 63, V: Jack Frost II (Gregor Shapanka); 1: Happy Hogan; 1: Pepper Potts	0.12	60.00	150.00	300.00
❑46, Oct 63, 1: Crimson Dynamo	0.12	37.00	92.50	185.00
❑47, Nov 63, 1: Melter	0.12	37.00	92.50	185.00
❑48, Dec 63, SD ,New armor for Iron Man (red and gold)	0.12	43.00	107.50	215.00
❑49, Jan 64, SD, A: Angel II	0.12	33.00	82.50	165.00
❑50, Feb 64, DH, 1: The Mandarin	0.12	23.00	57.50	115.00
❑51, Mar 64, DH, 1: Scarecrow (Marvel)	0.12	18.00	45.00	90.00
❑52, Apr 64, DH, 1: The Black Widow; 1: Black Widow	0.12	27.00	67.50	135.00
❑53, May 64, DH, O: Watcher; O: The Watcher	0.12	23.00	57.50	115.00
❑54, Jun 64, DH, 1: Black Knight II (Nathan Garrett)	0.12	12.00	30.00	60.00
❑55, Jul 64	0.12	12.00	30.00	60.00
❑56, Aug 64, DH, 1: Unicorn I (Milos Masaryk)	0.12	12.00	30.00	60.00
❑57, Sep 64, DH, 1: Hawkeye; A: Black Widow	0.12	32.00	80.00	160.00
❑58, Oct 64, DH, A: Captain America	0.12	53.00	132.50	265.00
❑59, Nov 64, JK; DH, 1: Jarvis; V: Black Knight,Captain America second-feature begins	0.12	53.00	132.50	265.00
❑60, Dec 64, JK, Assassins	0.12	23.00	57.50	115.00
❑61, Jan 65, JK; DH, Assassins	0.12	13.00	32.50	65.00
❑62, Feb 65, JK; DH, Assassins, O: Mandarin,redesign of Iron Man's helmet	0.12	13.00	32.50	65.00
❑63, Mar 65, A: Sgt. Duffy; A: General Phillips; A: Dr. Erskine; O: Captain America; O: Bucky; A: Doctor Erskine	0.12	35.00	87.50	175.00
❑64, Apr 65, 1: Agent 13 (Peggy Carter)	0.12	14.00	35.00	70.00
❑65, May 65, A: Red Skull	0.12	24.00	60.00	120.00
❑66, Jun 65, O: Red Skull,Red Skull returns	0.12	24.00	60.00	120.00
❑67, Jul 65	0.12	10.00	25.00	50.00
❑68, Aug 65	0.12	10.00	25.00	50.00
❑69, Sep 65, 1: Titanium Man I (Boris Bullski)	0.12	10.00	25.00	50.00
❑70, Oct 65	0.12	10.00	25.00	50.00
❑71, Nov 65	0.12	9.00	22.50	45.00
❑72, Dec 65	0.12	9.00	22.50	45.00
❑73, Jan 66, D: Black Knight II (Nathan Garrett)	0.12	9.00	22.50	45.00
❑74, Feb 66	0.12	9.00	22.50	45.00
❑75, Mar 66, 1: Batroc; 1: Second Agent 13 (Sharon Carter)	0.12	9.00	22.50	45.00
❑76, Apr 66, 1: Ultimo (cameo)	0.12	9.00	22.50	45.00
❑77, May 66, O: Ultimo; 1: Peggy Carter; 1: Ultimo (full appearance)	0.12	9.00	22.50	45.00
❑78, Jun 66, A: Nick Fury	0.12	9.00	22.50	45.00
❑79, Jul 66, 1: Cosmic Cube (Kubik)	0.12	9.00	22.50	45.00
❑80, Aug 66,Cosmic Cube; Sub-Mariner vs. Iron Man	0.12	9.00	22.50	45.00
❑81, Sep 66	0.12	8.00	20.00	40.00
❑82, Oct 66, 1: Adaptoid	0.12	8.00	20.00	40.00
❑83, Nov 66	0.12	8.00	20.00	40.00
❑84, Dec 66, 1: Super-Adaptoid	0.12	8.00	20.00	40.00
❑85, Jan 67, GK; GC, V: Mandarin,Happy substitutes as Iron Man	0.12	8.00	20.00	40.00
❑86, Feb 67, JK; GC, SL (w), Death Duel For The Life Of Happy Hogan; The Secret!	0.12	8.00	20.00	40.00
❑87, Mar 67	0.12	8.00	20.00	40.00
❑88, Apr 67, GK; GC	0.12	8.00	20.00	40.00
❑89, May 67, GK; GC	0.12	8.00	20.00	40.00
❑90, Jun 67, GK; GC, O: Byrrah	0.12	8.00	20.00	40.00
❑91, Jul 67, GK; GC	0.12	8.00	20.00	40.00
❑92, Aug 67, GK; GC	0.12	8.00	20.00	40.00
❑93, Sep 67, GK; GC	0.12	8.00	20.00	40.00
❑94, Oct 67, 1: Modok	0.12	8.00	20.00	40.00
❑95, Nov 67, GK; GC, 1: Walter Newell (later becomes Stingray),Captain America's identity revealed	0.12	8.00	20.00	40.00
❑96, Dec 67, GK; GC	0.12	8.00	20.00	40.00
❑97, Jan 68, GK; JK; GC, SL (w), The Coming of Whiplash!; And So It Begins..., A: Black Panther; 1: Whiplash	0.12	8.00	20.00	40.00
❑98, Feb 68, GK; GC, 1: Whitney Frost	0.12	8.00	20.00	40.00
❑99, Mar 68, GK; GC, V: Red Skull,series continues as Captain America; Series continued in Captain America #100, Iron Man #1	0.12	8.00	20.00	40.00

TALES OF SUSPENSE (VOL. 2)
MARVEL

Value: Cover or less

❑1, Jan 95, JRo (w), Men And Machines,acetate outer cover; prestige format one-shot 6.95

TALES OF TERROR
ECLIPSE

	ORIG	GOOD	FINE	N-MINT
❑1, Jul 85	1.75	0.40	1.00	2.00
❑2, Sep 85	1.75	0.40	1.00	2.00
❑3, Nov 85	1.75	0.40	1.00	2.00
❑4, Jan 86	1.75	0.40	1.00	2.00
❑5, Mar 86	1.75	0.40	1.00	2.00
❑6, May 86, Change of Scene; Good Neighbors	1.75	0.40	1.00	2.00
❑7, Jul 86	1.75	0.40	1.00	2.00
❑8, Sep 86	1.75	0.40	1.00	2.00
❑9, Nov 86, The Dark Man; The Cubicle	1.75	0.40	1.00	2.00
❑10, Jan 87	2.00	0.40	1.00	2.00
❑11, Mar 87	2.00	0.40	1.00	2.00
❑12, May 87	2.00	0.40	1.00	2.00
❑13, Jul 87	2.00	0.40	1.00	2.00

TALES OF THE ARMORKINS
CO. & SONS

	ORIG	GOOD	FINE	N-MINT
❑1, Prisoners of Love; the Amazing Liver	0.50	0.60	1.50	3.00

TALES OF THE BEANWORLD
ECLIPSE

	ORIG	GOOD	FINE	N-MINT
❑1	1.50	0.80	2.00	4.00
❑2	1.50	0.60	1.50	3.00
❑3	1.50	0.60	1.50	3.00
❑4	1.50	0.60	1.50	3.00
❑5	1.50	0.60	1.50	3.00
❑6	2.00	0.60	1.50	3.00
❑7	2.00	0.60	1.50	3.00
❑8	2.00	0.60	1.50	3.00
❑9	2.00	0.60	1.50	3.00
❑10	2.00	0.60	1.50	3.00
❑11	2.00	0.40	1.00	2.00
❑12	2.00	0.40	1.00	2.00
❑13	2.00	0.40	1.00	2.00
❑14	2.00	0.40	1.00	2.00
❑15	2.00	0.40	1.00	2.00
❑16	2.00	0.40	1.00	2.00
❑17, The Mystery Pods Must Go!	2.00	0.40	1.00	2.00
❑18, Tale Of The Goofy Jerks	2.00	0.40	1.00	2.00
❑19	2.00	0.40	1.00	2.00
❑20	2.50	0.50	1.25	2.50
❑21, The First Time Professor Garbanzo Discovered The Four Realities	2.95	0.59	1.48	2.95

TALES OF THE CLOSET
HETRICMARTIN

Value: Cover or less

❑1, b&w 2.50
❑2, b&w 2.50
❑3, b&w 2.50
❑4, b&w 2.50
❑5, b&w 2.50
❑6, b&w 2.50

TALES OF THE CYBORG GERBILS
HARRIER

Value: Cover or less

❑1, Nov 87, The Prof; Shopping 1.95

TALES OF THE DARKNESS
IMAGE

Value: Cover or less

❑0.5, Apr 98 ..... 2.95
❑1, Apr 98 ..... 2.95
❑2, Jun 98 ..... 2.95
❑3, Aug 98 ..... 2.95
❑4, Dec 98 ..... 2.95

TALES OF THE FEHNNIK (ANTARCTIC)
ANTARCTIC

Value: Cover or less

❑1, Aug 95, b&w 2.95

TALES OF THE FEHNNIK (RADIO)
RADIO

Value: Cover or less

❑1, Jun 98, b&w 2.95

TALES OF THE GREAT UNSPOKEN
TOP SHELF

	ORIG	GOOD	FINE	N-MINT
❑1, nn; b&w; no cover price	—	0.20	0.50	1.00

TALES OF THE GREEN BERET
DELL

	ORIG	GOOD	FINE	N-MINT
❑1	0.12	6.00	15.00	30.00
❑2	0.12	4.00	10.00	20.00
❑3, Jun 67, The Charlie Trap; Don't Call me Chicken	0.12	4.00	10.00	20.00
❑4	0.12	4.00	10.00	20.00
❑5	0.12	4.00	10.00	20.00

TALES OF THE GREEN BERETS
AVALON

Value: Cover or less

❑1, JKu ,"The Green Berets" in the indicia 2.95
❑2, JKu ,"The Green Berets" in the indicia 2.95
❑3, JKu ,"The Green Berets" in the indicia 2.95
❑4, JKu 2.95
❑5, JKu 2.95
❑6, JKu 2.95
❑7, JKu ,"Green Berets" in the indicia 2.95

TALES OF THE GREEN HORNET (1ST SERIES)
NOW

	ORIG	GOOD	FINE	N-MINT
❑1, Sep 90	1.75	0.40	1.00	2.00
❑2, Oct 90	1.75	0.40	1.00	2.00

TALES OF THE GREEN HORNET (2ND SERIES)
Now

Value: Cover or less

- ❑1, Jan 92, Destiny, Part 1 ..... 1.95
- ❑2, Feb 92, Destiny, Part 2, O: The Green Hornet 1.95
- ❑3, Mar 92 ..... 1.95
- ❑4, Apr 92 ..... 1.95

TALES OF THE GREEN HORNET (3RD SERIES)
Now

Value: Cover or less

- ❑1, Sep 92, bagged with hologram card 2.75
- ❑2, Oct 92 ..... 2.50
- ❑3, Nov 92 ..... 2.50

TALES OF THE GREEN LANTERN CORPS
DC

	ORIG	GOOD	FINE	N-MINT
❑1, May 81, JSe; FMc, Challenge, O: Green Lantern	0.50	0.30	0.75	1.50
❑2, Jun 81, JSe; FMc	0.50	0.25	0.63	1.25
❑3, Jul 81, JSe; JSa; FMc, Triumph!	0.50	0.25	0.63	1.25
❑Anl 1	1.25	0.25	0.63	1.25

TALES OF THE JACKALOPE
Blackthorne

Value: Cover or less

- ❑1 ..... 2.00
- ❑2 ..... 2.00
- ❑3 ..... 2.00
- ❑4 ..... 2.00
- ❑5 ..... 2.00
- ❑6, Throwing Continuity To The Wind; The One That Got Away 2.00
- ❑7 ..... 2.00

TALES OF THE KUNG FU WARRIORS
CFW

	ORIG	GOOD	FINE	N-MINT
❑1, 1: Squamous; 1: Ethereal Black	1.95	0.40	1.00	2.00
❑2	—	0.40	1.00	2.00
❑3	—	0.40	1.00	2.00
❑4	—	0.40	1.00	2.00
❑5	—	0.40	1.00	2.00
❑6	—	0.40	1.00	2.00
❑7	—	0.40	1.00	2.00
❑8	—	0.40	1.00	2.00
❑9	—	0.40	1.00	2.00
❑10	2.25	0.45	1.13	2.25
❑11	2.25	0.45	1.13	2.25
❑12	2.25	0.45	1.13	2.25
❑13	2.25	0.45	1.13	2.25
❑14, 1: Sumo	2.25	0.45	1.13	2.25

TALES OF THE LEGION
DC

	ORIG	GOOD	FINE	N-MINT
❑314, Aug 84, O: White Witch	0.75	0.30	0.75	1.50
❑315, Sep 84, KG (w), Judgement!, V: Dark Circle	0.75	0.30	0.75	1.50
❑316, Oct 84, O: White Witch	0.75	0.30	0.75	1.50
❑317, Nov 84	0.75	0.30	0.75	1.50
❑318, Dec 84, V: Persuader	0.75	0.30	0.75	1.50
❑319, Jan 85	0.75	0.30	0.75	1.50
❑320, Feb 85	0.75	0.30	0.75	1.50
❑321, Mar 85	0.75	0.30	0.75	1.50
❑322, Apr 85	0.75	0.30	0.75	1.50
❑323, May 85	0.75	0.30	0.75	1.50
❑324, Jun 85, V: Dark Circle	0.75	0.30	0.75	1.50
❑325, Jul 85, 5 to the Infinite Power	0.75	0.30	0.75	1.50
❑326, Aug 85, V: Legion of Super-Villains, begins reprints of Legion of Super-Heroes (3rd series); Reprints begin	0.75	0.25	0.63	1.25
❑327, Sep 85, V: Legion of Super-Villains	0.75	0.25	0.63	1.25
❑328, Oct 85, V: Legion of Super-Villains	0.75	0.25	0.63	1.25
❑329, Nov 85, V: Legion of Super-Villains; D: Karate Kid	0.75	0.25	0.63	1.25
❑330, Dec 85, V: Legion of Super-Villains	0.75	0.25	0.63	1.25
❑331, Jan 86, O: Lightning Lad; O: Lightning Lass; O: Lightning Lord	0.75	0.25	0.63	1.25
❑332, Feb 86	0.75	0.25	0.63	1.25
❑333, Mar 86	0.75	0.25	0.63	1.25
❑334, Apr 86	0.75	0.25	0.63	1.25
❑335, May 86	0.75	0.25	0.63	1.25
❑336, Jun 86	0.75	0.25	0.63	1.25
❑337, Jul 86	0.75	0.25	0.63	1.25
❑338, Aug 86	0.75	0.25	0.63	1.25
❑339, Sep 86, Magnetic Kid joins team; Tellus joins team; Polar Boy joins team; Quislet joins team; Sensor Girl joins team	0.75	0.25	0.63	1.25
❑340, Oct 86, V: Doctor Regulus	0.75	0.25	0.63	1.25
❑341, Nov 86	0.75	0.25	0.63	1.25
❑342, Dec 86	0.75	0.25	0.63	1.25
❑343, Jan 87, O: Wildfire	0.75	0.25	0.63	1.25
❑344, Feb 87	0.75	0.25	0.63	1.25
❑345, Mar 87	0.75	0.25	0.63	1.25
❑346, Apr 87	0.75	0.25	0.63	1.25
❑347, May 87, V: Universo	0.75	0.25	0.63	1.25
❑348, Jun 87, in Phantom Zone	0.75	0.25	0.63	1.25
❑349, Jul 87	0.75	0.25	0.63	1.25

The Legion of Super-Heroes faced The Dark Circle yet again in *Tales of the Legion* #315.

	ORIG	GOOD	FINE	N-MINT
❑350, Aug 87, Sensor Girl's identity revealed	0.75	0.25	0.63	1.25
❑351, Sep 87, V: Fatal Five	0.75	0.25	0.63	1.25
❑352, Oct 87	0.75	0.25	0.63	1.25
❑353, Nov 87	1.00	0.25	0.63	1.25
❑354, Dec 87, Final Issue	1.00	0.25	0.63	1.25
❑Anl 4	1.25	0.30	0.75	1.50
❑Anl 5, O: Validus	1.25	0.30	0.75	1.50

TALES OF THE MARVELS: BLOCKBUSTER
Marvel

Value: Cover or less

- ❑1, Apr 95, acetate overlay outer cover; One-Shot; prestige format 5.95

TALES OF THE MARVELS: INNER DEMONS
Marvel

Value: Cover or less

- ❑1, nn; acetate overlay outer cover; One-Shot 5.95

TALES OF THE MARVELS: WONDER YEARS
Marvel

Value: Cover or less

- ❑1, Aug 95, wraparound acetate outer cover 4.95
- ❑2, Sep 95, wraparound acetate outer cover 4.95

TALES OF THE MARVEL UNIVERSE
Marvel

Value: Cover or less

- ❑1, Feb 97, KB (w), Onslaught epilogue, A: Thunderbolts; A: Kristoff; A: Doctor Strange; A: Ka-Zar, wraparound cover; Ka-Zar appearace; Doctor Strange apperance 2.99

TALES OF THE NEW TEEN TITANS
DC

	ORIG	GOOD	FINE	N-MINT
❑1, Jun 82, GP, Cyborg, O: Cyborg	0.60	0.30	0.75	1.50
❑2, Jul 82, GP, Raven, O: Raven	0.60	0.20	0.50	1.00
❑3, Aug 82, GD; GP, The Changeling, O: Changeling	0.60	0.20	0.50	1.00
❑4, Sep 82, EC; GP, Starfire, 1: Ryand'r; O: Starfire II (Koriand'r)	0.60	0.20	0.50	1.00

TALES OF THE NINJA WARRIORS
CFW

Value: Cover or less

- ❑1, b&w 2.25
- ❑2, b&w 2.25
- ❑3, b&w 2.25
- ❑4, b&w 2.25
- ❑5, b&w 2.25
- ❑6, b&w 2.25
- ❑7, b&w 2.25
- ❑8, b&w 2.25
- ❑9, b&w 2.25
- ❑10, b&w 2.25
- ❑11, b&w 2.25
- ❑12, b&w 2.25
- ❑13, b&w 2.25
- ❑14, b&w 2.25
- ❑15, Parallax: The Third Wave; Kabuki Kid, Part 2, b&w 2.25
- ❑16, b&w 2.25

TALES OF THE SUN RUNNERS
Sirius

Value: Cover or less

- ❑1, Jul 86, Dancing in the Dark 1.50
- ❑2 ..... 1.95
- ❑3 ..... 1.95

TALES OF THE TEENAGE MUTANT NINJA TURTLES
Mirage

	ORIG	GOOD	FINE	N-MINT
❑1, May 87	1.50	0.60	1.50	3.00
❑2, Jul 87	1.50	0.40	1.00	2.00
❑3, Oct 87	1.50	0.40	1.00	2.00
❑4, Feb 88, cover says Jan, indicia says Feb	1.50	0.40	1.00	2.00
❑5, May 88	1.50	0.40	1.00	2.00
❑6, Aug 88	1.50	0.40	1.00	2.00
❑7, Aug 89, cover says Apr, indicia says Aug; Final Issue	1.50	0.40	1.00	2.00

TALES OF THE TEEN TITANS
DC

	ORIG	GOOD	FINE	N-MINT
❑41, Apr 84, GP, Baptism of Blood, A: Brother Blood, Series continued from New Teen Titans (1st Series) #40	0.75	0.40	1.00	2.00
❑42, May 84, GP, Judas Contract, Part 1; The Judas Contract, Part 1, The Eyes of Tara Markov, V: Deathstroke	0.75	0.40	1.00	2.00

	ORIG	GOOD	FINE	N-MINT
❑43, Jun 84, GP, Judas Contract, Part 2; The Judas Contract, Part 2, Betrayal, V: H.I.V.E.; V: Deathstroke	0.75	0.40	1.00	2.00
❑44, Jul 84, GP, Judas Contract, Part 3; The Judas Contract, O: Jericho; 1: Nightwing	0.75	1.20	3.00	6.00
❑45, Aug 84, GP, A: Aqualad; A: Aquagirl	0.75	0.30	0.75	1.50
❑46, Sep 84, GP, Showdown!, V: H.I.V.E.	0.75	0.30	0.75	1.50
❑47, Oct 84, GP, Final Conflict!, V: H.I.V.E.	0.75	0.30	0.75	1.50
❑48, Nov 84, SR; GP, The Recombatants, V: Recombatants	0.75	0.30	0.75	1.50
❑49, Dec 84, GP; CI, The Light That Failed, V: Dr. Light; V: Doctor Light	0.75	0.30	0.75	1.50
❑50, Feb 85, GP, We Are Gathered Here Today..., Giant-size; Wedding of Wonder Girl	1.25	0.40	1.00	2.00
❑51, Mar 85, 1: Azrael (not Batman character); V: Cheshire	0.75	0.30	0.75	1.50
❑52, Apr 85, V: Cheshire	0.75	0.30	0.75	1.50
❑53, May 85, A: Deathstroke	0.75	0.30	0.75	1.50
❑54, Jun 85, DG; RB, Blind Justice!, A: Deathstroke,Trial of Deathstroke	0.75	0.30	0.75	1.50
❑55, Jul 85,Changeling vs. Deathstroke	0.75	0.30	0.75	1.50
❑56, Aug 85, V: Fearsome Five	0.75	0.30	0.75	1.50
❑57, Sep 85, V: Fearsome Five,Cyborg transformed	0.75	0.30	0.75	1.50
❑58, Oct 85, A: Harbinger; V: Fearsome Five; A: Monitor	0.75	0.30	0.75	1.50
❑59, Nov 85,reprints DC Comics Presents #26	0.75	0.30	0.75	1.50
❑60, Dec 85, V: Trigon,series begins reprinting New Teen Titans (second series)	0.75	0.20	0.50	1.00
❑61, Jan 86, V: Trigon	0.75	0.20	0.50	1.00
❑62, Feb 86, V: Trigon	0.75	0.20	0.50	1.00
❑63, Mar 86, V: Trigon	0.75	0.20	0.50	1.00
❑64, Apr 86, V: Trigon	0.75	0.20	0.50	1.00
❑65, May 86	0.75	0.20	0.50	1.00
❑66, Jun 86, O: Lilith	0.75	0.20	0.50	1.00
❑67, Jul 86	0.75	0.20	0.50	1.00
❑68, Aug 86, A: Kole	0.75	0.20	0.50	1.00
❑69, Sep 86	0.75	0.20	0.50	1.00
❑70, Oct 86, O: Kole	0.75	0.20	0.50	1.00
❑71, Nov 86	0.75	0.20	0.50	1.00
❑72, Dec 86, A: Outsiders	0.75	0.20	0.50	1.00
❑73, Jan 87	0.75	0.20	0.50	1.00
❑74, Feb 87	0.75	0.20	0.50	1.00
❑75, Mar 87, A: Omega Men	0.75	0.20	0.50	1.00
❑76, Apr 87,Wedding of Starfire	0.75	0.20	0.50	1.00
❑77, May 87	0.75	0.20	0.50	1.00
❑78, Jun 87,new team	0.75	0.20	0.50	1.00
❑79, Jul 87	0.75	0.20	0.50	1.00
❑80, Aug 87, A: Cheshire, Lian	0.75	0.20	0.50	1.00
❑81, Sep 87	0.75	0.20	0.50	1.00
❑82, Oct 87	0.75	0.20	0.50	1.00
❑83, Nov 87	0.75	0.20	0.50	1.00
❑84, Dec 87	0.75	0.20	0.50	1.00
❑85, Jan 88	0.75	0.20	0.50	1.00
❑86, Feb 88, V: Twister	0.75	0.20	0.50	1.00
❑87, Mar 88, V: Brotherhood of Evil	0.75	0.20	0.50	1.00
❑88, Apr 88, V: Brother Blood	0.75	0.20	0.50	1.00
❑89, May 88, V: Brother Blood	1.35	0.20	0.50	1.00
❑90, Jun 88	0.75	0.20	0.50	1.00
❑91, Jul 88,Final Issue	0.75	0.20	0.50	1.00
❑Anl 3, The Judas Contract, Part 4	—	0.40	1.00	2.00
❑Anl 4, V: Vanguard; A: Superman,reprints New Teen Titans Annual #1	1.25	0.25	0.63	1.25
❑Anl 5	—	0.25	0.63	1.25

TALES OF THE UNEXPECTED
DC

	ORIG	GOOD	FINE	N-MINT
❑40, Aug 59,Space Ranger stories begin	0.10	130.00	325.00	650.00
❑41, A: Space Ranger	0.10	55.00	137.50	275.00
❑42, A: Space Ranger	0.10	55.00	137.50	275.00
❑43, A: Space Ranger,Space Ranger cover	0.10	90.00	225.00	450.00
❑44, A: Space Ranger	0.10	40.00	100.00	200.00
❑45, A: Space Ranger	0.10	40.00	100.00	200.00
❑46, A: Space Ranger	0.10	30.00	75.00	150.00
❑47, A: Space Ranger	0.10	30.00	75.00	150.00
❑48, A: Space Ranger	0.10	30.00	75.00	150.00
❑49, A: Space Ranger	0.10	30.00	75.00	150.00
❑50, A: Space Ranger	0.10	30.00	75.00	150.00
❑51, A: Space Ranger	0.10	25.00	62.50	125.00
❑52, A: Space Ranger	0.10	25.00	62.50	125.00
❑53, A: Space Ranger	0.10	25.00	62.50	125.00
❑54, A: Space Ranger	0.10	25.00	62.50	125.00
❑55, A: Space Ranger	0.10	25.00	62.50	125.00
❑56, A: Space Ranger	0.10	20.00	50.00	100.00
❑57, A: Space Ranger	0.10	20.00	50.00	100.00
❑58, A: Space Ranger	0.10	20.00	50.00	100.00
❑59, A: Space Ranger	0.10	20.00	50.00	100.00
❑60, A: Space Ranger	0.10	20.00	50.00	100.00
❑61, A: Space Ranger	0.10	17.00	42.50	85.00
❑62, A: Space Ranger	0.10	17.00	42.50	85.00
❑63, A: Space Ranger	0.10	17.00	42.50	85.00
❑64, A: Space Ranger	0.10	17.00	42.50	85.00
❑65, A: Space Ranger	0.10	17.00	42.50	85.00
❑66, A: Space Ranger	0.10	17.00	42.50	85.00
❑67, A: Space Ranger	0.10	17.00	42.50	85.00
❑68, A: Space Ranger	—	17.00	42.50	85.00
❑69, A: Space Ranger	—	17.00	42.50	85.00
❑70, A: Space Ranger	—	17.00	42.50	85.00
❑71, A: Space Ranger	—	12.00	30.00	60.00
❑72, A: Space Ranger	0.12	12.00	30.00	60.00
❑73, A: Space Ranger	0.12	12.00	30.00	60.00
❑74, Jan 63, A: Space Ranger	0.12	12.00	30.00	60.00
❑75, Feb 63, A: Space Ranger	0.12	10.00	25.00	50.00
❑76, A: Space Ranger	0.12	10.00	25.00	50.00
❑77, A: Space Ranger	0.12	10.00	25.00	50.00
❑78, A: Space Ranger	0.12	10.00	25.00	50.00
❑79, A: Space Ranger	0.12	10.00	25.00	50.00
❑80, A: Space Ranger	0.12	10.00	25.00	50.00
❑81, A: Space Ranger	0.12	10.00	25.00	50.00
❑82, A: Space Ranger	0.12	10.00	25.00	50.00
❑83	0.12	6.00	15.00	30.00
❑84, Sep 64	0.12	6.00	15.00	30.00
❑85, Nov 64	0.12	6.00	15.00	30.00
❑86, Jan 65	0.12	6.00	15.00	30.00
❑87, Mar 65	0.12	6.00	15.00	30.00
❑88, May 65	0.12	6.00	15.00	30.00
❑89, Jul 65	0.12	6.00	15.00	30.00
❑90, Sep 65	0.12	6.00	15.00	30.00
❑91, Nov 65	0.12	4.40	11.00	22.00
❑92, Jan 66	0.12	4.40	11.00	22.00
❑93, Mar 66	0.12	4.40	11.00	22.00
❑94, May 66	0.12	4.40	11.00	22.00
❑95, Jul 66	0.12	4.40	11.00	22.00
❑96, Sep 66	0.12	4.40	11.00	22.00
❑97, Nov 66, One Month to Die!; The Human Stallion, A: Automan	0.12	4.40	11.00	22.00
❑98, Jan 67	0.12	4.40	11.00	22.00
❑99, Mar 67	0.12	4.40	11.00	22.00
❑100	0.12	4.40	11.00	22.00
❑101	0.12	4.00	10.00	20.00
❑102	0.12	4.00	10.00	20.00
❑103	0.12	4.00	10.00	20.00
❑104, Dec 67,Series continues as The Unexpected	0.12	4.00	10.00	20.00

TALES OF THE WITCHBLADE
IMAGE

	ORIG	GOOD	FINE	N-MINT
❑0.5, Jun 97,Wizard promotional item	2.95	1.00	2.50	5.00
❑0.5/A,Signed by Nathan Cabrera; Wizard "Certified Authentic" exclusive	—	2.00	5.00	10.00
❑0.5/GO, Jun 97,Wizard promotional item; gold logo	2.95	1.00	2.50	5.00
❑1, Anne Bonny	2.95	0.80	2.00	4.00
❑1/A, Nov 96, Anne Bonny,alternate cover; Green background with Witchblade front, arms behind back	2.95	1.00	2.50	5.00
❑1/B, Nov 96,alternate cover (blue background with black panther)	2.95	0.59	1.48	2.95
❑1/GO, Nov 96, Gold edition	2.95	1.00	2.50	5.00
❑1/PL, Nov 96, Platinum edition	2.95	1.60	4.00	8.00
❑2, Jun 97, Annabella Altavista	2.95	0.60	1.50	3.00
❑3, Oct 97	2.95	0.60	1.50	3.00
❑4, Jan 98, Selena	2.95	0.59	1.48	2.95
❑5, May 98, Maitea	2.95	0.59	1.48	2.95
❑6, Sep 98, Samantha	2.95	0.59	1.48	2.95
❑7/A, Jun 99, Raquel,Woman turning around, eyes in background on cover	2.95	0.59	1.48	2.95
❑7/B, Jun 99, Raquel,Alternate cover (woman standing before pyramid)	2.95	0.59	1.48	2.95
❑8, Oct 99	2.95	0.59	1.48	2.95
❑9, Jan 01, Raquel	2.95	0.59	1.48	2.95

TALES OF THE ZOMBIE
MARVEL

	ORIG	GOOD	FINE	N-MINT
❑1, Aug 73, O: Zombie, b&w; magazine	0.75	1.60	4.00	8.00
❑2	0.75	1.00	2.50	5.00
❑3	0.75	0.80	2.00	4.00
❑4	0.75	0.80	2.00	4.00
❑5	0.75	0.80	2.00	4.00
❑6	0.75	0.80	2.00	4.00
❑7	0.75	0.80	2.00	4.00
❑8	0.75	0.80	2.00	4.00
❑9	0.75	0.80	2.00	4.00
❑10, Mar 75	0.75	0.80	2.00	4.00
❑Anl 1,Reprint	1.25	0.80	2.00	4.00

TALE SPIN
DISNEY

Value: Cover or less

Issue	Price
❑1, Jun 91	1.50
❑2	1.50
❑3	1.50
❑4	1.50
❑5	1.50
❑6	1.50
❑7	1.50

TALESPIN (ONE-SHOT)
DISNEY

Value: Cover or less

Issue	Price
❑1, nn; Sky-Raker	3.50

TALE SPIN LIMITED SERIES
DISNEY

Value: Cover or less

Issue	Price
❑1, Jan 91, Take Off, Part 1	1.50
❑2, Take Off, Part 2	1.50
❑3, Take Off, Part 3	1.50
❑4, Take Off, Part 4	1.50

TALES TO ASTONISH (VOL. 1)
MARVEL

Issue	ORIG	GOOD	FINE	N-MINT
❑27, Jan 62, JK; SD, 1: Hijacker; 1: Ant-Man (out of costume)	0.10	600.00	1500.00	3000.00
❑28, Feb 62, JK; SD	0.12	30.00	75.00	150.00
❑29, Mar 62, JK; SD	0.12	30.00	75.00	150.00
❑30, Apr 62, JK; SD	0.12	30.00	75.00	150.00
❑31, May 62, JK; SD	0.12	30.00	75.00	150.00
❑32, Jun 62, JK; SD	0.12	30.00	75.00	150.00
❑33, Jul 62, JK; SD	0.12	30.00	75.00	150.00
❑34, Aug 62, JK; SD	0.12	30.00	75.00	150.00
❑35, Sep 62, JK; SD, 2: Ant-Man; 1: Ant-Man (in costume)	0.12	290.00	725.00	1450.00
❑36, Oct 62, JK; SD	0.12	110.00	275.00	550.00
❑37, Nov 62, JK; SD	0.12	62.00	155.00	310.00
❑38, Dec 62, 1: Egghead	0.12	62.00	155.00	310.00
❑39, Jan 63	0.12	62.00	155.00	310.00
❑40, Feb 63	0.12	62.00	155.00	310.00
❑41, Mar 63, DH; SD	0.12	40.00	100.00	200.00
❑42, Apr 63, DH; SD, 1: The Voice	0.12	40.00	100.00	200.00
❑43, May 63, DH; SD	0.12	40.00	100.00	200.00
❑44, Jun 63, JK; SD, 1: Wasp	0.12	50.00	125.00	250.00
❑45, Jul 63, DH; SD	0.12	25.00	62.50	125.00
❑46, Aug 63, DH; SD, A: Crimson Dynamo	0.12	25.00	62.50	125.00
❑47, Sep 63, DH; SD	0.12	25.00	62.50	125.00
❑48, Oct 63, DH; SD, 1: Porcupine	0.12	25.00	62.50	125.00
❑49, Nov 63, JK; DH; AM, 1: Giant Man, Ant-Man becomes Giant Man	0.12	35.00	87.50	175.00
❑50, Dec 63, JK; SD, 1: Human Top (later becomes Whirlwind)	0.12	17.00	42.50	85.00
❑51, Jan 64, JK	0.12	17.00	42.50	85.00
❑52, Feb 64, 1: Black Knight II (Nathan Garrett)	0.12	17.00	42.50	85.00
❑53, Mar 64	0.12	17.00	42.50	85.00
❑54, Apr 64	0.12	17.00	42.50	85.00
❑55, May 64	0.12	17.00	42.50	85.00
❑56, Jun 64, V: Magician	0.12	17.00	42.50	85.00
❑57, Jul 64, A: Spider-Man	0.12	22.00	55.00	110.00
❑58, Aug 64	0.12	17.00	42.50	85.00
❑59, Sep 64, Giant-Man vs. Hulk	0.12	25.00	62.50	125.00
❑60, Oct 64, Giant Man/Hulk double feature begins	0.12	30.00	75.00	150.00
❑61, Nov 64	0.12	11.20	28.00	56.00
❑62, Dec 64, 1: The Leader	0.12	11.20	28.00	56.00
❑63, Jan 65, 1: The Wrecker II; O: The Leader	0.12	11.20	28.00	56.00
❑64, Feb 65	0.12	11.20	28.00	56.00
❑65, Mar 65, Giant-Man's new costume	0.12	11.20	28.00	56.00
❑66, Apr 65	0.12	11.20	28.00	56.00
❑67, May 65	0.12	11.20	28.00	56.00
❑68, Jun 65, V: Leader	0.12	11.20	28.00	56.00
❑69, Jul 65, Giant Man feature ends	0.12	11.20	28.00	56.00
❑70, Aug 65, Sub-Mariner begins	0.12	17.00	42.50	85.00
❑71, Sep 65, 1: Vashti	0.12	8.80	22.00	44.00
❑72, Oct 65	0.12	8.80	22.00	44.00
❑73, Nov 65	0.12	8.80	22.00	44.00
❑74, Dec 65	0.12	8.80	22.00	44.00
❑75, Jan 66, 1: Behemoth	0.12	8.80	22.00	44.00
❑76, Feb 66	0.12	8.80	22.00	44.00
❑77, Mar 66, Banner revealed as Hulk	0.12	8.80	22.00	44.00
❑78, Apr 66	0.12	8.80	22.00	44.00
❑79, May 66	0.12	8.80	22.00	44.00
❑80, Jun 66, JK; GC	0.12	8.80	22.00	44.00
❑81, Jul 66, JK; GC, 1: Boomerang	0.12	8.80	22.00	44.00
❑82, Aug 66, JK; GC, Iron Man vs. Sub-Mariner	0.12	13.00	32.50	65.00
❑83, Sep 66	0.12	8.80	22.00	44.00
❑84, Oct 66	0.12	8.80	22.00	44.00
❑85, Nov 66	0.12	8.80	22.00	44.00
❑86, Dec 66	0.12	8.80	22.00	44.00
❑87, Jan 67	0.12	8.80	22.00	44.00
❑88, Feb 67	0.12	8.80	22.00	44.00
❑89, Mar 67	0.12	8.80	22.00	44.00
❑90, Apr 67, 1: Byrrah; 1: The Abomination	0.12	8.80	22.00	44.00
❑91, May 67	0.12	8.40	21.00	42.00
❑92, Jun 67, A: Silver Surfer	0.12	11.00	27.50	55.00
❑93, Jul 67, A: Silver Surfer	0.12	11.00	27.50	55.00
❑94, Aug 67	0.12	8.40	21.00	42.00
❑95, Sep 67	0.12	8.40	21.00	42.00
❑96, Oct 67	0.12	8.40	21.00	42.00
❑97, Nov 67	0.12	8.40	21.00	42.00
❑98, Dec 67, 1: Seth (Namor's advisor)	0.12	8.40	21.00	42.00
❑99, Jan 68	0.12	8.40	21.00	42.00
❑100, Feb 68, Hulk vs. Sub-Mariner	0.12	11.60	29.00	58.00
❑101, Mar 68, Hulk feature continued in Incredible Hulk #102; Sub-Mariner feature continued in Iron Man & Sub-Mariner #1	0.12	15.00	37.50	75.00

New England Comics reprinted several horror stories originally published before the establishment of the Comics Code in *Tales Too Terrible to Tell.*

© 1991 New England Comics

TALES TO ASTONISH (VOL. 2)
MARVEL

Issue	ORIG	GOOD	FINE	N-MINT
❑1, Dec 79, JB	0.40	0.40	1.00	2.00
❑2, Jan 80, JB	0.40	0.30	0.75	1.50
❑3, Feb 80, JB	0.40	0.30	0.75	1.50
❑4, Mar 80, JB	0.40	0.30	0.75	1.50
❑5, Apr 80, JB	0.40	0.30	0.75	1.50
❑6, May 80, JB	0.40	0.30	0.75	1.50
❑7, Jun 80, JB	0.40	0.30	0.75	1.50
❑8, Jul 80, JB	0.40	0.30	0.75	1.50
❑9, Aug 80, JB	0.40	0.30	0.75	1.50
❑10, Sep 80, JB	0.40	0.30	0.75	1.50
❑11, Oct 80, JB	0.40	0.30	0.75	1.50
❑12, Nov 80, JB	0.40	0.30	0.75	1.50
❑13, Dec 80, JB	0.50	0.30	0.75	1.50
❑14, Jan 81, JB	0.50	0.30	0.75	1.50

TALES TO ASTONISH (VOL. 3)
MARVEL

Value: Cover or less

Issue	Price
❑1, Dec 94, PD (w), Loki's Dream, acetate outer cover; prestige format one-shot	6.95

TALES TO OFFEND
DARK HORSE

Value: Cover or less

Issue	Price
❑1, Jul 97, FM, FM (w), Lance Blastoff; Daddy's Little Girl, Lance Blastoff	2.95

TALES TOO TERRIBLE TO TELL
NEC

Value: Cover or less

Issue	Price
❑1, Vampire; Clumsy, b&w; Reprints from Mister Mystery #13, Weird Chills #1, Weird Chills #3, Mister Mystery #16, Purple Claw #1, Strange Mysteries #7, Mister Mystery #17	2.95
❑1-2, May 93, Horror of Mixed Torsos!, 2nd printing with new cover; Reprints from Mister Mystery #13, Weird Chills #1, Weird Chills #3, Mister Mystery #16, Purple Claw #1, Strange Mysteries #7, Mister Mystery #17	3.50
❑2, Mar 91, Head of Horror; The Door, b&w; Reprints from Strange Mysteries #6, Weird Mysteries #11, Unseen #14, Black Cat Mystery #45, Journey into Fear #5, Ghoul Tales #3, Dark Mysteries #13	3.50
❑3, Jun 91, Voice of Doom; The Disguise, b&w; Reprints from Weird Chills #3, Weird Mysteries #10, Weird Chills #1, Adventures into Darkness #13, Horrific #5	3.50
❑4, Dec 91, The Gossips!; Fiends From the Crypt, b&w; Reprints from Mister Mystery #13, Fantastic Fears #8, Unseen #14, Journey into Fear #12, Fantastic Fears #6, Purple Claw #1, Fantastic Fears #4, Dark Mysteries #19	3.50
❑5, b&w; Reprint	3.50
❑6, b&w; Reprint	3.50
❑7, b&w; Reprint	3.50

TALISMEN: SCSI VOODOO
BLINK

Value: Cover or less

Issue	Price
❑1	2.75
❑2	2.75
❑3	2.75

TALK DIRTY
FANTAGRAPHICS

Value: Cover or less

Issue	Price
❑1, b&w; adult	2.50
❑2, b&w; adult	2.50
❑3, b&w; adult	2.95

TALKING ORANGUTANS IN BORNEO
GT-LABS

Value: Cover or less

❑1, nn; b&w; efforts to educate orangutans to communicate via sign language ... 3.50

TALL TAILS
GOLDEN REALM

	ORIG	GOOD	FINE	N-MINT
❑1, b&w	1.50	0.40	1.00	2.00
❑2, Firequest	1.50	0.40	1.00	2.00
❑3	2.95	0.59	1.48	2.95
❑4	2.95	0.59	1.48	2.95
❑5	2.95	0.59	1.48	2.95
❑6	2.95	0.59	1.48	2.95
❑7	2.95	0.59	1.48	2.95

TALONZ
STOP DRAGON

Value: Cover or less

❑1, Jan 87, b&w ... 1.50

TALOS OF THE WILDERNESS SEA
DC

Value: Cover or less

❑1, GK, GK (w), To the Wilderness Sea ... 2.00

TAMMAS
PANDEMONIUM

Value: Cover or less

❑1, Dec 86, Hail and Farewell ... 1.50

TANGENT COMICS/DOOM PATROL
DC

Value: Cover or less

❑1, Dec 97, Saving Time,One-Shot; alternate universe ... 2.95

TANGENT COMICS/GREEN LANTERN
DC

Value: Cover or less

❑1, Dec 97, JRo (w), From Beyond the Unknown,One-Shot; alternate universe ... 2.95

TANGENT COMICS/JLA
DC

Value: Cover or less

❑1, Sep 98,One-Shot; alternate universe ... 1.95

TANGENT COMICS/METAL MEN
DC

Value: Cover or less

❑1, Dec 97, Secrets & Lies,One-Shot; alternate universe ... 2.95

TANGENT COMICS/NIGHTWING
DC

Value: Cover or less

❑1, Dec 97, JDu, The Most Dangerous Man in the World,One-Shot; alternate universe ... 2.95

TANGENT COMICS/NIGHTWING: NIGHT FORCE
DC

Value: Cover or less

❑1, Sep 98,One-Shot; alternate universe ... 1.95

TANGENT COMICS/POWERGIRL
DC

Value: Cover or less

❑1, Sep 98,One-Shot; alternate universe ... 1.95

TANGENT COMICS/SEA DEVILS
DC

Value: Cover or less

❑1, Dec 97, KB (w), Devils and the Deep,One-Shot; alternate universe ... 2.95

TANGENT COMICS/SECRET SIX
DC

Value: Cover or less

❑1, Dec 97, Bad Moon,One-Shot; alternate universe ... 2.95

TANGENT COMICS/TALES OF THE GREEN LANTERN
DC

Value: Cover or less

❑1, Sep 98,One-Shot; alternate universe ... 1.95

TANGENT COMICS/THE ATOM
DC

Value: Cover or less

❑1, Dec 97, Truth,One-Shot; alternate universe ... 2.95

TANGENT COMICS/THE BATMAN
DC

Value: Cover or less

❑1, Sep 98,One-Shot; alternate universe ... 1.95

TANGENT COMICS/THE FLASH
DC

Value: Cover or less

❑1, Dec 97, Premiere,One-Shot; alternate universe ... 2.95

TANGENT COMICS/THE JOKER
DC

Value: Cover or less

❑1, Dec 97, Laugh 'Till it Hurts,One-Shot; alternate universe ... 2.95

TANGENT COMICS/THE JOKER'S WILD
DC

Value: Cover or less

❑1, Sep 98,One-Shot; alternate universe ... 1.95

TANGENT COMICS/THE SUPERMAN
DC

Value: Cover or less

❑1, Sep 98,One-Shot; alternate universe ... 1.95

TANGENT COMICS/THE TRIALS OF THE FLASH
DC

Value: Cover or less

❑1, Sep 98,One-Shot; alternate universe ... 1.95

TANGENT COMICS/WONDER WOMAN
DC

Value: Cover or less

❑1, Sep 98,One-Shot; alternate universe ... 1.95

TANK GIRL
DARK HORSE

	ORIG	GOOD	FINE	N-MINT
❑1, May 91, 1: Tank Girl (in American comics), b&w; trading cards; British	2.25	0.70	1.75	3.50
❑2, Jun 91, b&w; British	2.25	0.60	1.50	3.00
❑3, Jul 91, b&w; British	2.25	0.60	1.50	3.00
❑4, Aug 91, b&w; British	2.25	0.60	1.50	3.00

TANK GIRL 2
DARK HORSE

	ORIG	GOOD	FINE	N-MINT
❑1, Jun 93, I've Got Friends At Bells End..., b&w and color; British	2.50	0.60	1.50	3.00
❑2, Jul 93, b&w and color; British	2.50	0.60	1.50	3.00
❑3, Aug 93, b&w and color; British	2.50	0.60	1.50	3.00
❑4, Sep 93, b&w and color; British	2.50	0.60	1.50	3.00

TANK GIRL: APOCALYPSE
DC

Value: Cover or less

❑1, Nov 95,Tank Girl becomes pregnant ... 2.25
❑2, Dec 95 ... 2.25
❑3, Jan 96 ... 2.25
❑4, Feb 96, So Long, It's Been Good To Know Ya,Tank Girl gives birth ... 2.25

TANK GIRL MOVIE ADAPTATION
DC

Value: Cover or less

❑1, nn; prestige format one-shot ... 5.95

TANK GIRL: THE ODYSSEY
DC

Value: Cover or less

❑1, Jun 95 ... 2.25
❑2, Jul 95 ... 2.25
❑3, Aug 95 ... 2.25
❑4, Oct 95 ... 2.25

TANK VIXENS
ANTARCTIC

Value: Cover or less

❑1, Jan 94 ... 2.95
❑2, Mar 94 ... 2.95
❑3 ... 2.95
❑4, Mar 96 ... 2.95

TANTALIZING STORIES
TUNDRA

Value: Cover or less

❑1, Oct 92 ... 2.25
❑2, Dec 92 ... 2.25
❑3, Feb 93 ... 2.25
❑4, Apr 93 ... 2.25
❑6 ... 2.50

TAOLAND
SUMITEK

	ORIG	GOOD	FINE	N-MINT
❑1, Nov 94, Yingpeng's Friends, b&w; cardstock cover	1.50	0.40	1.00	2.00
❑2, Aug 95, b&w; cardstock cover	2.95	1.19	2.97	5.95
❑3, Sep 95, b&w; cardstock cover	3.25	1.19	2.97	5.95
❑4, Feb 96, b&w	3.25	1.19	2.97	5.95
❑5, Dec 96, Night & Day, prestige format	5.95	1.19	2.97	5.95

TAOLAND ADVENTURES
ANTARCTIC

Value: Cover or less

❑1, Mar 99 ... 3.50
❑2, May 99 ... 3.50

TAP
PROMETHEAN

Value: Cover or less

❑1, Sep 94 ... 2.95
❑2, Jan 95 ... 2.95
❑3, Jan 95,indicia is for issue #2 2.95

TAPESTRY
SUPERIOR JUNK

Value: Cover or less

❑1, b&w ... 1.50
❑1-2, Apr 95,2nd Printing ... 1.50
❑2, Apr 94, b&w ... 1.95
❑3, Jun 94, b&w ... 1.95
❑4, Oct 94, b&w ... 2.25
❑5, b&w ... 2.25

TAPPING THE VEIN
ECLIPSE

	ORIG	GOOD	FINE	N-MINT
❑1, prestige format; foil-embossed logo	6.95	1.50	3.75	7.50
❑2, Skins of the Fathers; In the Hills, the Cities, prestige format; foil-embossed logo	6.95	1.40	3.50	7.00
❑3, prestige format; foil-embossed logo	6.95	1.40	3.50	7.00
❑4, prestige format; foil-embossed logo	7.95	1.59	3.97	7.95
❑5	7.95	1.59	3.97	7.95

TARGET: AIRBOY
ECLIPSE

	ORIG	GOOD	FINE	N-MINT
❑1, Mar 88, A: Clint from A.R.B.B.H.,cardstock cover	1.95	0.40	1.00	2.00

TARGITT
ATLAS

	ORIG	GOOD	FINE	N-MINT
❑1, Mar 75, Boston Tea Party, O: Targitt	0.25	0.40	1.00	2.00
❑2, Jun 75	0.25	0.30	0.75	1.50
❑3, Jul 75	0.25	0.30	0.75	1.50

TAROT: WITCH OF THE BLACK ROSE
BROADSWORD

Value: Cover or less

Issue	Cover	Issue	Cover
❑1	2.95	❑6	2.95
❑2	2.95	❑7	2.95
❑3	2.95	❑8	2.95
❑4, Sep 00	2.95	❑9	2.95
❑5	2.95		

TARZAN (DARK HORSE)
DARK HORSE

	ORIG	GOOD	FINE	N-MINT
❑1, Jul 96, Tarzan's Jungle Fury, Part 1	2.95	0.60	1.50	3.00
❑2, Aug 96, Tarzan's Jungle Fury, Part 2	2.95	0.60	1.50	3.00
❑3, Aug 96, Tarzan's Jungle Fury, Part 3	2.95	0.60	1.50	3.00
❑4, Sep 96, Tarzan's Jungle Fury, Part 4	2.95	0.60	1.50	3.00
❑5, Nov 96, Tarzan's Jungle Fury, Part 5	2.95	0.60	1.50	3.00
❑6, Nov 96, Tarzan's Jungle Fury, Part 6	2.95	0.60	1.50	3.00
❑7, Jan 97, Legion of Hate, Part 1; Friend of Foe?	2.95	0.60	1.50	3.00
❑8, Feb 97, Legion of Hate, Part 2; Flesh and Mud	2.95	0.60	1.50	3.00
❑9, Mar 97, Legion of Hate, Part 3; Today Your Love Tomorrow The World	2.95	0.60	1.50	3.00
❑10, Apr 97, Legion of Hate, Part 4	2.95	0.60	1.50	3.00
❑11, May 97, Le Monstre, Part 1; Le Monstre	2.95	0.60	1.50	3.00
❑12, Jun 97, Le Monstre, Part 2; Le Monstre	2.95	0.59	1.48	2.95
❑13, Aug 97, The Modern Prometheus, Part 1	2.95	0.59	1.48	2.95
❑14, Sep 97, The Modern Prometheus, Part 2	2.95	0.59	1.48	2.95
❑15, Sep 97, Tooth and Nail, Part 1	2.95	0.59	1.48	2.95
❑16, Oct 97, Tooth and Nail, Part 2	2.95	0.59	1.48	2.95
❑17, Dec 97, TY, Versus The Moon Men, Part 1; Tarzan vs. The Moon Men	2.95	0.59	1.48	2.95
❑18, Jan 98, Versus The Moon Men, Part 2	2.95	0.59	1.48	2.95
❑19, Feb 98, Versus The Moon Men, Part 3	2.95	0.59	1.48	2.95
❑20, Mar 98, Versus The Moon Men, Part 4	2.95	0.59	1.48	2.95

TARZAN (DC)
DC

	ORIG	GOOD	FINE	N-MINT
❑207, Apr 72, JKu, Origin Of The Ape-Man, O: Tarzan, Giant-size; John Carter of Mars back-up; Series continued from Tarzan (Dell)	0.25	1.60	4.00	8.00
❑208, May 72, JKu, O: Tarzan,John Carter of Mars back-up	0.25	0.80	2.00	4.00
❑209, Jun 72, JKu, O: Tarzan,John Carter of Mars back-up continues in Weird Worlds #1	0.25	0.80	2.00	4.00
❑210, Jul 72, JKu, O: Tarzan	0.20	0.80	2.00	4.00
❑211, Aug 72, JKu	0.20	0.60	1.50	3.00
❑212, Sep 72, JKu	0.20	0.60	1.50	3.00
❑213, Oct 72, JKu	0.20	0.60	1.50	3.00
❑214, Nov 72, JKu ,Beyond the Farthest Star back-up	0.20	0.60	1.50	3.00
❑215, Dec 72, JKu ,Beyond the Farthest Star back-up	0.20	0.60	1.50	3.00
❑216, Jan 73, JKu ,Beyond the Farthest Star back-up	0.20	0.60	1.50	3.00
❑217, Feb 73, JKu ,Beyond the Farthest Star back-up	0.20	0.60	1.50	3.00
❑218, Mar 73, JKu ,Beyond the Farthest Star back-up	0.20	0.60	1.50	3.00
❑219, May 73, JKu	0.20	0.60	1.50	3.00
❑220, Jun 73, JKu	0.20	0.60	1.50	3.00
❑221, Jul 73, JKu	0.20	0.60	1.50	3.00
❑222, Aug 73, JKu	0.20	0.60	1.50	3.00
❑223, Sep 73, JKu	0.20	0.60	1.50	3.00
❑224, Oct 73, JKu	0.20	0.60	1.50	3.00
❑225, Nov 73, JKu	0.20	0.60	1.50	3.00
❑226, Dec 73, JKu	0.20	0.60	1.50	3.00
❑227, Jan 74, JKu	0.20	0.60	1.50	3.00
❑228, Feb 74, JKu	0.20	0.60	1.50	3.00
❑229, Mar 74	0.20	0.60	1.50	3.00
❑230, May 74,100pgs.	0.60	1.00	2.50	5.00
❑231, Jul 74,100pgs.	0.60	1.00	2.50	5.00
❑232, Sep 74,100pgs.	0.60	1.00	2.50	5.00
❑233, Nov 74,100pgs.	0.60	1.00	2.50	5.00
❑234, Jan 75,100pgs.	0.60	1.00	2.50	5.00
❑235, Mar 75,100pgs.	0.60	1.00	2.50	5.00
❑236, Apr 75	0.25	0.50	1.25	2.50
❑237, May 75, RM, JKu (c)	0.25	0.50	1.25	2.50
❑238, Jun 75	0.50	0.50	1.25	2.50
❑239, Jul 75, JKu	0.50	0.50	1.25	2.50
❑240, Aug 75, JKu ,adapts The Castaways	0.25	0.50	1.25	2.50
❑241, Sep 75	0.25	0.50	1.25	2.50
❑242, Oct 75	0.25	0.50	1.25	2.50
❑243, Nov 75	0.25	0.50	1.25	2.50
❑244, Dec 75	0.25	0.50	1.25	2.50
❑245, Jan 76	0.25	0.50	1.25	2.50
❑246, Feb 76	0.25	0.50	1.25	2.50
❑247, Mar 76	0.30	0.50	1.25	2.50
❑248, Apr 76	0.30	0.50	1.25	2.50
❑249, May 76	0.30	0.50	1.25	2.50
❑250, Jun 76	0.30	0.50	1.25	2.50
❑251, Jul 76	0.30	0.50	1.25	2.50
❑252, Aug 76	0.30	0.50	1.25	2.50
❑253, Sep 76	0.30	0.50	1.25	2.50
❑254, Oct 76	0.30	0.50	1.25	2.50
❑255, Nov 76	0.30	0.50	1.25	2.50
❑256, Dec 76, JKu ,adapts Tarzan the Untamed	0.30	0.50	1.25	2.50
❑257, Jan 77, JKu, JKu (w), The Nightmare!	0.30	0.50	1.25	2.50
❑258, Feb 77,Final Issue	0.30	0.50	1.25	2.50

The characters in DC's Tangent universe shared their names, but little else, with characters in the mainstream DC universe.

TARZAN (DISNEY'S...)
DARK HORSE

Value: Cover or less

Issue	Cover	Issue	Cover
❑1	2.95	❑2, Jul 99	2.95

TARZAN (GOLD KEY)
GOLD KEY

	ORIG	GOOD	FINE	N-MINT
❑132, Nov 62, RM ,Continued from Tarzan (Dell) #131	0.12	2.80	7.00	14.00
❑133, Jan 63	0.12	2.80	7.00	14.00
❑134, Mar 63	0.12	2.80	7.00	14.00
❑135, May 63	0.12	2.80	7.00	14.00
❑136, Jul 63	0.12	2.80	7.00	14.00
❑137, Aug 63	0.12	2.80	7.00	14.00
❑138, Oct 63	0.12	2.80	7.00	14.00
❑139, Dec 63	0.12	2.80	7.00	14.00
❑140, Feb 64	0.12	2.80	7.00	14.00
❑141, Apr 64	0.12	2.80	7.00	14.00
❑142, Jun 64	0.12	2.80	7.00	14.00
❑143, Jul 64	0.12	2.80	7.00	14.00
❑144, Aug 64	0.12	2.80	7.00	14.00
❑145, Sep 64	0.12	2.80	7.00	14.00
❑146, Oct 64	0.12	2.80	7.00	14.00
❑147, Dec 64	0.12	2.80	7.00	14.00
❑148, Feb 65	0.12	2.80	7.00	14.00
❑149, Apr 65	0.12	2.80	7.00	14.00
❑150, Jun 65	0.12	2.80	7.00	14.00
❑151, Aug 65	0.12	2.80	7.00	14.00
❑152, Sep 65	0.12	2.80	7.00	14.00
❑153, Oct 65	0.12	2.80	7.00	14.00
❑154, Nov 65	0.12	2.80	7.00	14.00
❑155, Dec 65, RM, O: Tarzan,adapts Tarzan of the Apes	0.12	3.60	9.00	18.00
❑156, Feb 66, RM ,adapts Return of Tarzan	0.12	2.00	5.00	10.00
❑157, Apr 66, RM, The Beasts Of Tarzan,adapts Beasts of Tarzan	0.12	2.00	5.00	10.00
❑158, Jun 66, RM ,adapts Son of Tarzan	0.12	2.00	5.00	10.00
❑159, Aug 66, RM ,adapts Jewels of Opar	0.12	2.00	5.00	10.00
❑160, Sep 66, RM ,adapts Jewels of Opar	0.12	2.00	5.00	10.00
❑161, Oct 66, RM ,adapts Jewels of Opar	0.12	2.00	5.00	10.00
❑162, Dec 66,TV Adventures on cover	0.12	2.00	5.00	10.00
❑163, Jan 67, RM ,adapts Tarzan the Untamed	0.12	1.60	4.00	8.00
❑164, Feb 67, RM ,adapts Tarzan the Untamed	0.12	1.60	4.00	8.00
❑165, Mar 67,Photo cover	0.12	2.00	5.00	10.00
❑166, Apr 67, RM ,adapts Tarzan the Terrible	0.12	1.60	4.00	8.00
❑167, May 67, RM ,adapts Tarzan the Terrible	0.12	1.60	4.00	8.00
❑168, Jun 67,Photo cover	0.12	2.00	5.00	10.00
❑169, Jul 67,adapts Jungle Tales of Tarzan	0.12	1.60	4.00	8.00
❑170, Aug 67,adapts Jungle Tales of Tarzan	0.12	1.60	4.00	8.00
❑171, Sep 67,Photo cover	0.12	2.00	5.00	10.00
❑172, Oct 67, RM ,adapts Tarzan and the Golden Lion	0.12	1.40	3.50	7.00

	ORIG	GOOD	FINE	N-MINT
❑173, Dec 67, RM ,adapts Tarzan and the Golden Lion	0.12	1.40	3.50	7.00
❑174, Feb 68, RM ,adapts Tarzan and the Ant Men	0.12	1.40	3.50	7.00
❑175, Apr 68, RM ,adapts Tarzan and the Ant Men	0.12	1.40	3.50	7.00
❑176, Jun 68, RM ,adapts Tarzan; Lord of the Jungle	0.12	1.40	3.50	7.00
❑177, Jul 68, RM ,adapts Tarzan; Lord of the Jungle	0.12	1.40	3.50	7.00
❑178, Aug 68,reprints issue #155	0.15	1.40	3.50	7.00
❑179, Sep 68,adapts Tarzan at the Earth's Core	0.15	1.40	3.50	7.00
❑180, Oct 68,adapts Tarzan at the Earth's Core	0.15	1.40	3.50	7.00
❑181, Dec 68,adapts Tarzan at the Earth's Core	0.15	1.40	3.50	7.00
❑182, Feb 69,adapts Tarzan the Invincible	0.15	1.40	3.50	7.00
❑183, Apr 69,adapts Tarzan the Invincible	0.15	1.40	3.50	7.00
❑184, Jun 69,adapts Tarzan Triumphant	0.15	1.40	3.50	7.00
❑185, Jul 69,adapts Tarzan Triumphant	0.15	1.40	3.50	7.00
❑186, Aug 69,adapts Tarzan and the City of Gold	0.15	1.40	3.50	7.00
❑187, Sep 69,adapts Tarzan and the City of Gold	0.15	1.40	3.50	7.00
❑188, Oct 69,adapts Tarzan's Quest	0.15	1.40	3.50	7.00
❑189, Dec 69,adapts Tarzan's Quest	0.15	1.40	3.50	7.00
❑190, Feb 70,adapts Tarzan ahd the Forbidden City; adapts Tarzan and the Forbidden City	0.15	1.40	3.50	7.00
❑191, Apr 70,adapts Tarzan ahd the Forbidden City; adapts Tarzan and the Forbidden City	0.15	1.40	3.50	7.00
❑192, Jun 70,adapts Tarzan and the Foreign Legion	0.15	1.40	3.50	7.00
❑193, Jul 70,adapts Tarzan and the Foreign Legion	0.15	1.40	3.50	7.00
❑194, Aug 70,adapts Tarzan and the Lost Empire	0.15	1.40	3.50	7.00
❑195, Sep 70,adapts Tarzan and the Lost Empire	0.15	1.40	3.50	7.00
❑196, Oct 70,adapts Tarzan and the Tarzan Twins	0.15	1.40	3.50	7.00
❑197, Dec 70	0.15	1.40	3.50	7.00
❑198, Feb 71	0.15	1.40	3.50	7.00
❑199, Apr 71	0.15	1.40	3.50	7.00
❑200, Jun 71	0.15	1.40	3.50	7.00
❑201, Jul 71	0.15	1.20	3.00	6.00
❑202, Aug 71, RM ,astronauts land in jungle	0.15	1.20	3.00	6.00
❑203, Sep 71	0.15	1.20	3.00	6.00
❑204, Oct 71	0.15	1.20	3.00	6.00
❑205, Dec 71	0.15	1.20	3.00	6.00
❑206, Feb 72, Tarzan and the Lion Man,moves to DC; Series continued in Tarzan (DC) #207	0.15	1.20	3.00	6.00

TARZAN (MARVEL)
MARVEL

	ORIG	GOOD	FINE	N-MINT
❑1, Jun 77, JB, Tarzan And The Jewels Of Opar	0.30	0.60	1.50	3.00
❑2, Jul 77	0.30	0.40	1.00	2.00
❑3, Aug 77	0.30	0.40	1.00	2.00
❑4, Sep 77	0.30	0.40	1.00	2.00
❑5, Oct 77	0.30	0.40	1.00	2.00
❑6, Nov 77	0.35	0.30	0.75	1.50
❑7, Dec 77	0.35	0.30	0.75	1.50
❑8, Jan 78	0.35	0.30	0.75	1.50
❑9, Feb 78	0.35	0.30	0.75	1.50
❑10, Mar 78	0.35	0.30	0.75	1.50
❑11, Apr 78	0.35	0.30	0.75	1.50
❑12, May 78	0.35	0.30	0.75	1.50
❑13, Jun 78	0.35	0.30	0.75	1.50
❑14, Jul 78	0.35	0.30	0.75	1.50
❑15, Aug 78	0.35	0.30	0.75	1.50
❑16, Sep 78	0.35	0.30	0.75	1.50
❑17, Oct 78	0.35	0.30	0.75	1.50
❑18, Nov 78	0.35	0.30	0.75	1.50
❑19, Dec 78	0.35	0.30	0.75	1.50
❑20, Jan 79	0.35	0.30	0.75	1.50
❑21, Feb 79	0.35	0.30	0.75	1.50
❑22, Mar 79	0.35	0.30	0.75	1.50
❑23, Apr 79	0.35	0.30	0.75	1.50
❑24, May 79	0.40	0.30	0.75	1.50
❑25, Jun 79	0.40	0.30	0.75	1.50
❑26, Jul 79	0.40	0.30	0.75	1.50
❑27, Aug 79	0.40	0.30	0.75	1.50
❑28, Sep 79	0.40	0.30	0.75	1.50
❑29, Oct 79	0.40	0.30	0.75	1.50
❑Anl 1	0.50	0.40	1.00	2.00
❑Anl 2	0.60	0.30	0.75	1.50
❑Anl 3	0.60	0.30	0.75	1.50

TARZAN AND THE JEWELS OF OPAR (EDGAR RICE BURROUGHS'...)
DARK HORSE

Value: Cover or less

❑1, Jun 99, RM, nn; digest; collects stories from Dell's Tarzan #159-161 plus pin-ups 10.95

TARZAN: A TALE OF MUGAMBI (EDGAR RICE BURROUGHS'...)
DARK HORSE

Value: Cover or less

❑1, Jun 95, nn; One-Shot 2.95

TARZAN/CARSON OF VENUS
DARK HORSE

Value: Cover or less

❑1, May 98 .... 2.95
❑2, Jun 98 .... 2.95
❑3, Jul 98 .... 2.95
❑4, Aug 98 .... 2.95

TARZAN DIGEST
DC

	ORIG	GOOD	FINE	N-MINT
❑1, Aut 72	0.50	0.60	1.50	3.00

TARZAN FAMILY, THE
DC

	ORIG	GOOD	FINE	N-MINT
❑60, Feb 76	0.50	1.00	2.50	5.00
❑61, Feb 76	0.50	1.00	2.50	5.00
❑62, Apr 76	0.50	0.80	2.00	4.00
❑63, Jun 76	0.50	0.80	2.00	4.00
❑64, Aug 76	0.50	0.80	2.00	4.00
❑65, Sep 76	0.50	0.80	2.00	4.00
❑66, Nov 76	0.50	0.80	2.00	4.00

TARZAN/JOHN CARTER: WARLORDS OF MARS
DARK HORSE

Value: Cover or less

❑1, Jan 96, Red Awakening 2.50
❑2, Apr 96, A: Cathoris; A: Tars Tarkas; A: Cathoris, Tars Tarkas, Dejah Thoris; A: Dejah Thoris,indicia says #3, cover says #2 .... 2.50
❑3, May 96, V: John Carter 2.50
❑4, Jul 96, D: Taka,Final Issue 2.50

TARZAN, LORD OF THE JUNGLE (GOLD KEY)
GOLD KEY

	ORIG	GOOD	FINE	N-MINT
❑1, Sep 65	0.25	8.00	20.00	40.00

TARZAN: LOVE, LIES AND THE LOST CITY
MALIBU

	ORIG	GOOD	FINE	N-MINT
❑1, Aug 92, MW (w), Tarzan's First Love, Tarzan: The Scar, Flip-book	3.95	0.79	1.98	3.95
❑2, Sep 92	2.50	0.79	1.98	3.95
❑3, Oct 92	2.50	0.79	1.98	3.95

TARZAN OF THE APES
MARVEL

	ORIG	GOOD	FINE	N-MINT
❑1, Jul 84, DS, ME (w), O: Tarzan	0.60	0.60	1.50	3.00
❑2, Aug 84, DS, ME (w), O: Tarzan	0.60	0.60	1.50	3.00

TARZAN OF THE APES (EDGAR RICE BURROUGHS'...)
DARK HORSE

Value: Cover or less

❑1, May 99, RM, nn; digest; collects stories from Dell's Tarzan #155-158 and spot illustrations from Tarzan #154-156 .... 12.95

TARZAN: THE BECKONING
MALIBU

Value: Cover or less

❑1, Nov 92, TY, TY (w) 2.50
❑2, Dec 92, TY, TY (w) 2.50
❑3, Jan 93, TY, TY (w) 2.50
❑4, Feb 93, TY, TY (w) 2.50
❑5, Mar 93, TY, TY (w) 2.50
❑6, Apr 93, TY, TY (w) 2.50
❑7, Jun 93, TY, TY (w) 2.50

TARZAN: THE LOST ADVENTURE (EDGAR RICE BURROUGHS'...)
DARK HORSE

Value: Cover or less

❑1, Jan 95, TY, Tarzan: The Lost Adventure; John Carter Of Mars, b&w; squarebound 2.95
❑2, Feb 95, TY, b&w; squarebound 2.95
❑3, Mar 95, TY, b&w; squarebound 2.95
❑4, Apr 95, TY, b&w; squarebound 2.95

TARZAN: THE RIVERS OF BLOOD (EDGAR RICE BURROUGHS' ...)
DARK HORSE

Value: Cover or less

❑1, Nov 99 .... 2.95
❑2, Dec 99 .... 2.95
❑3, Jan 00 .... 2.95
❑4, Feb 00,final issue of eight-issue mini-series 2.95

TARZAN: THE SAVAGE HEART
DARK HORSE

Value: Cover or less

❑1, Apr 99, MGr 2.95
❑2, May 99, MGr 2.95
❑3, Jun 99, MGr 2.95
❑4, Jul 99, MGr 2.95

TARZAN THE WARRIOR
MALIBU
Value: Cover or less

❑1, Mar 92 .... 2.50
❑2, May 92 .... 2.50
❑3, Jun 92 .... 2.50
❑4, Aug 92 .... 2.50
❑5, Sep 92 .... 2.50

TARZAN VS. PREDATOR AT THE EARTH'S CORE
DARK HORSE
Value: Cover or less

❑1, Jan 96, Worlds Within Worlds 2.50
❑2, Feb 96 .... 2.50
❑3, Mar 96 .... 2.50
❑4, Jun 96, D: Mahar Queen, Final Issue 2.50

TARZAN WEEKLY
BYBLOS

	ORIG	GOOD	FINE	N-MINT
❑1	0.12	1.00	2.50	5.00

T.A.S.E.R.
COMICREATIONS
Value: Cover or less

❑1, Sep 92, b&w 2.00
❑2, Jun 93, b&w 2.00

TASTY BITS
AVALON
Value: Cover or less

❑1, Frame 137; Shadows 2.95

TATTERED BANNERS
DC
Value: Cover or less

❑1, Nov 98, KG (w), Real Men Don't Klik 2.95
❑2, Dec 98, KG (w) 2.95
❑3, Jan 99, Escape From New York 2.95
❑4, Feb 99, KG (w) 2.95

TATTOO
CALIBER
Value: Cover or less

❑1, Zombie Slayer 2.95
❑2 .... 2.95

TATTOO MAN
FANTAGRAPHICS
Value: Cover or less

❑1, b&w 2.75

TAXX, THE
EXPRESS
Value: Cover or less

❑0.5 .... 1.50
❑1, b&w 2.75

T-BIRD CHRONICLES
ME COMIX
Value: Cover or less

❑1, b&w 1.50
❑2, b&w 1.50

TEAM 7
IMAGE

	ORIG	GOOD	FINE	N-MINT
❑1, Oct 94, Gone Animal	2.50	0.60	1.50	3.00
❑1/A, Oct 94, Gone Animal, Variant cover by Whilce Portacio	2.50	0.60	1.50	3.00
❑2, Nov 94	2.50	0.50	1.25	2.50
❑3, Dec 94	2.50	0.50	1.25	2.50
❑4, Feb 95	2.50	0.50	1.25	2.50
❑Ash 1, Oct 94, b&w; ashcan promo edition	—	0.20	0.50	1.00

TEAM 7: DEAD RECKONING
IMAGE
Value: Cover or less

❑1, Jan 96, Don't Look Back... 2.50
❑2, Feb 96 .... 2.50
❑3, Mar 96 .... 2.50
❑4, Apr 96 .... 2.50

TEAM 7-OBJECTIVE: HELL
IMAGE
Value: Cover or less

❑1, May 95, The Wolves, with card 2.50
❑2, Jun 95 .... 2.50
❑3, Jul 95 .... 2.50

TEAM AMERICA
MARVEL

	ORIG	GOOD	FINE	N-MINT
❑1, Jun 82, The Origin Of Team America, O: Team America	0.60	0.20	0.50	1.00
❑2, Jul 82, LMc	0.60	0.20	0.50	1.00
❑3, Aug 82, LMc	0.60	0.20	0.50	1.00
❑4, Sep 82, LMc	0.60	0.20	0.50	1.00
❑5, Oct 82	0.60	0.20	0.50	1.00
❑6, Nov 82	0.60	0.20	0.50	1.00
❑7, Dec 82	0.60	0.20	0.50	1.00
❑8, Jan 83	0.60	0.20	0.50	1.00
❑9, Feb 83, A: Iron Man	0.60	0.20	0.50	1.00
❑10, Mar 83	0.60	0.20	0.50	1.00
❑11, Apr 83, A: Ghost Rider	0.60	0.20	0.50	1.00
❑12, May 83, DP, Double-size; Marauder unmasked	1.00	0.20	0.50	1.00

TEAM ANARCHY
DAGGER
Value: Cover or less

❑1 .... 2.75
❑2 .... 2.50
❑3 .... 2.50
❑4 .... 2.50
❑5 .... 2.50
❑6 .... 2.50
❑7, May 94 .... 2.50

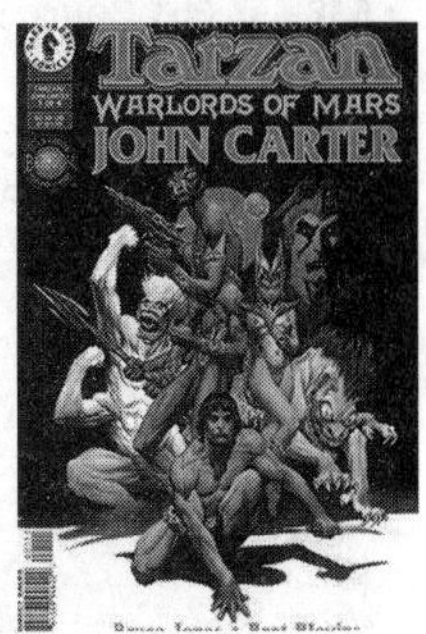

Two of Edgar Rice Burroughs' literary worlds collided when Tarzan was stranded on John Carter's Mars in *Tarzan/John Carter: Warlords of Mars.*

TEAM NIPPON
AIRCEL
Value: Cover or less

❑1, 1: Team Nippon, b&w 1.95
❑2, b&w 1.95
❑3, b&w 1.95
❑4, b&w 1.95
❑5, b&w 1.95
❑6, b&w 1.95
❑7, b&w; Final Issue 1.95

TEAM ONE: STORMWATCH
IMAGE
Value: Cover or less

❑1, Jun 95, cover says Jul, indicia says Jun 2.50
❑2, Aug 95 .... 2.50

TEAM ONE: WILDC.A.T.S
IMAGE
Value: Cover or less

❑1, Jul 95, JRo (w) 2.50
❑2, Sep 95, JRo (w) 2.50

TEAM SUPERMAN
DC
Value: Cover or less

❑1, Jul 99, They Died With Their Capes On 2.95

TEAM SUPERMAN SECRET FILES
DC
Value: Cover or less

❑1, May 98, biographical info on Superboy, Supergirl, Steel, and respective villains 4.95

TEAM TITANS
DC

	ORIG	GOOD	FINE	N-MINT
❑1/A, Sep 92, Total Chaos, Part 3, O: Killowat, Comes in five different covers	1.75	0.40	1.00	2.00
❑1/B, Sep 92, Total Chaos, Part 3, O: Mirage, Comes in five different covers	1.75	0.40	1.00	2.00
❑1/C, Sep 92, Total Chaos, Part 3, O: Nightrider, Comes in five different covers	1.75	0.40	1.00	2.00
❑1/D, Sep 92, Total Chaos, Part 3, O: Redwing, Comes in five different covers	1.75	0.40	1.00	2.00
❑1/E, Sep 92, Total Chaos, Part 3, O: Terra, Comes in five different covers	1.75	0.40	1.00	2.00
❑2, Oct 92, Total Chaos, Part 6, 1: Battalion	1.75	0.35	0.88	1.75
❑3, Nov 92, Total Chaos, Part 9	1.75	0.35	0.88	1.75
❑4, Dec 92, Titans Sell-Out, Part 4, 1: Judge & Jury	1.75	0.35	0.88	1.75
❑5, Feb 93	1.75	0.35	0.88	1.75
❑6, Mar 93	1.75	0.35	0.88	1.75
❑7, Apr 93	1.75	0.35	0.88	1.75
❑8, May 93, 1: Deathwing	1.75	0.35	0.88	1.75
❑9, Jun 93	1.75	0.35	0.88	1.75
❑10, Jul 93	1.75	0.35	0.88	1.75
❑11, Aug 93	1.75	0.35	0.88	1.75
❑12, Sep 93	1.75	0.35	0.88	1.75
❑13, Oct 93	1.75	0.35	0.88	1.75
❑14, Nov 93	1.75	0.35	0.88	1.75
❑15, Dec 93, The Hardest Copy or Truth and Consequences	1.75	0.35	0.88	1.75
❑16, Jan 94, To Sleep, Perchance to Dream...	1.75	0.35	0.88	1.75
❑17, Feb 94, You Can't Go Home Again, Part 1	1.75	0.35	0.88	1.75
❑18, Mar 94	1.75	0.35	0.88	1.75
❑19, Apr 94	1.75	0.35	0.88	1.75
❑20, May 94	1.75	0.35	0.88	1.75
❑21, Jun 94, Facing the Future	1.75	0.35	0.88	1.75
❑22, Jul 94	1.95	0.35	0.88	1.75
❑23, Aug 94	1.95	0.39	0.98	1.95
❑24, Sep 94, Final Issue; Zero Hour	1.95	0.39	0.98	1.95
❑Anl 1, Bloodlines, 1: Chimera, Bloodlines	3.50	0.70	1.75	3.50
❑Anl 2, Elseworlds	3.50	0.59	1.48	2.95

TEAM X
MARVEL
Value: Cover or less

❑2000, A: Deathbird; A: Morlocks; A: Shi'Ar; A: Bishop 3.50

TEAM X/TEAM 7
MARVEL
Value: Cover or less

❑1, All Sold Out, nn; crossover with Image; squarebound 4.95

TEAM YANKEE
FIRST
Value: Cover or less

- ❑1, Jan 89, Zero Hour 1.95
- ❑2, Jan 89 .... 1.95
- ❑3, Jan 89, Spearhead 1.95
- ❑4, Feb 89 .... 1.95
- ❑5, Feb 89 .... 1.95
- ❑6, Feb 89 .... 1.95

TEAM YOUNGBLOOD
IMAGE
Value: Cover or less

- ❑1, Sep 93, RL (w), Blackout, 1: Masada; 1: Dutch 1.95
- ❑2, Oct 93 .... 1.95
- ❑3, Nov 93 .... 1.95
- ❑4, Dec 93 .... 1.95
- ❑5, Jan 94, 1: Lynx 1.95
- ❑6, Feb 94 .... 1.95
- ❑7, Mar 94, Extreme Prejudice, Part 1, 1: Quantum 1.95
- ❑8, Apr 94, Extreme Prejudice, Part 5 .... 1.95
- ❑9, May 94 .... 1.95
- ❑10, Jun 94 .... 2.50
- ❑11, Jul 94 .... 2.50
- ❑12, Aug 94 .... 2.50
- ❑13, Sep 94 .... 2.50
- ❑14, Oct 94,Riptide poses nude 2.50
- ❑15, Nov 94, New Blood part 2 2.50
- ❑16, Dec 94,polybagged with trading card 2.50
- ❑17, Jan 95, Extreme Sacrifice, Part 7; Extreme Sacrifice, Part 5,polybagged with trading card 2.50
- ❑18, May 95, Extreme 3000 .... 2.50
- ❑19, Jun 95 .... 2.50
- ❑20, Jul 95 .... 2.50
- ❑21, Mar 96, A: Angela and Glory 2.50
- ❑22, Apr 96, Shadowhunt,Final Issue 2.50

TEARS
BONEYARD PRESS
Value: Cover or less

- ❑1, Oct 92, Symphony of Pain, b&w 2.95
- ❑2, Dec 92, Journey of the Holy, b&w 2.95

TEASER AND THE BLACKSMITH
FANTAGRAPHICS
Value: Cover or less

- ❑1, b&w; adult 3.50

TECH HIGH
VIRTUALLY REAL ENTERPRISES
Value: Cover or less

- ❑1, Fal 96, b&w 2.50
- ❑2, Win 96, b&w 2.50
- ❑3, Spr 97, b&w 2.50

TECHNO MANIACS
INDEPENDENT
Value: Cover or less

- ❑1 .... 1.95

TECHNOPOLIS
CALIBER
Value: Cover or less

- ❑1, Inceptum 2.95
- ❑2 .... 2.95
- ❑3 .... 2.95
- ❑4 .... 2.95

TEENAGE MUTANT NINJA TURTLES (1ST SERIES)
MIRAGE

	ORIG	GOOD	FINE	N-MINT
❑1, 1: Teenage Mutant Ninja Turtles, ad for Gobbledygook #1 & 2; 1st printing-Beware of counterfeits	1.50	30.00	75.00	150.00
❑1/CF,Counterfeit of first printing; Most counterfeit copies have streak or scratch marks across center of back cover, black part of cover is slightly bluish instead of black-Info from Overstreet guide	1.50	0.00	0.00	0.00
❑1-2, 1: Teenage Mutant Ninja Turtles,2nd Printing	1.50	3.00	7.50	15.00
❑, Feb 85, 1: Teenage Mutant Ninja Turtles,3rd Printing	1.50	1.60	4.00	8.00
❑1-4, 1: Teenage Mutant Ninja Turtles,4th Printing; says Reprinting the first issue on cover	1.50	0.80	2.00	4.00
❑1-5, Aug 88, 1: Teenage Mutant Ninja Turtles,5th Printing; fifth printing	1.50	0.60	1.50	3.00
❑2,1st printing-Beware of counterfeits	1.50	4.00	10.00	20.00
❑2/CF,Counterfeit: Uses glossy cover stock	1.50	0.00	0.00	0.00
❑2-2,2nd Printing	1.50	1.20	3.00	6.00
❑2-3,3rd Printing	1.50	0.60	1.50	3.00
❑2-4,3rd Printing	1.50	0.80	2.00	4.00
❑3,first printing; correct	1.50	1.60	4.00	8.00
❑3/A, Giveaway, rare; first printing; misprints; Laird's photo appears in white instead of blue	1.50	3.00	7.50	15.00
❑3-2,2nd Printing	1.50	0.60	1.50	3.00
❑4	1.50	0.80	2.00	4.00
❑4-2,2nd Printing	1.50	0.40	1.00	2.00
❑5	1.50	0.80	2.00	4.00
❑5-2,2nd Printing	1.50	0.40	1.00	2.00
❑6	1.50	0.60	1.50	3.00
❑6-2,2nd Printing	1.50	0.40	1.00	2.00
❑7,First color Teenage Mutant Ninja Turtles (color insert)	1.75	1.00	2.50	5.00
❑7-2,2nd Printing; No color story	1.75	0.40	1.00	2.00
❑8, A: Cerebus	1.50	0.80	2.00	4.00
❑9, Sep 86	1.50	0.60	1.50	3.00
❑10, Apr 87, b&w	1.50	0.60	1.50	3.00
❑11, Jun 87, b&w	1.50	0.80	2.00	4.00
❑12, Sep 87	1.50	0.60	1.50	3.00
❑13, Feb 88	1.50	0.60	1.50	3.00
❑14, May 88,cover says Feb, indicia says May	1.50	0.60	1.50	3.00
❑15, Sum 88	1.50	0.60	1.50	3.00
❑16, Sep 88,cover says Jul, indicia says Sep	1.50	0.40	1.00	2.00
❑17, Jan 89,cover says Nov, indicia says Jan	1.50	0.40	1.00	2.00
❑18, Feb 89, b&w	1.50	0.40	1.00	2.00
❑18-2, full color; 2nd Printing	1.50	0.40	1.00	2.00
❑19, Mar 89,Return to NY	1.75	0.40	1.00	2.00
❑20, Apr 89,Return to NY	1.75	0.40	1.00	2.00
❑21, May 89,Return to NY	1.75	0.40	1.00	2.00
❑22, Jun 89	1.75	0.40	1.00	2.00
❑23, Aug 89,cover says Jul, indicia says Aug	1.75	0.40	1.00	2.00
❑24	1.75	0.40	1.00	2.00
❑25	1.75	0.40	1.00	2.00
❑26, Dec 89,cover says Oct, indicia says Dec	1.75	0.40	1.00	2.00
❑27, Dec 89,cover says Nov, indicia says Dec	1.75	0.40	1.00	2.00
❑28	1.75	0.40	1.00	2.00
❑29, May 90,cover says Mar, indicia says May	1.75	0.40	1.00	2.00
❑30, Jun 90,cover says Apr, indicia says Jun	1.75	0.40	1.00	2.00
❑31, Jul 90	1.75	0.40	1.00	2.00
❑32, Aug 90	1.75	0.40	1.00	2.00
❑33, full color	1.95	0.40	1.00	2.00
❑34	1.75	0.40	1.00	2.00
❑35, Mar 91	2.00	0.40	1.00	2.00
❑36, Aug 91	2.00	0.40	1.00	2.00
❑37, Jun 91	2.00	0.40	1.00	2.00
❑38, Jul 91	2.00	0.40	1.00	2.00
❑39, Sep 91	2.00	0.40	1.00	2.00
❑40, Oct 91	2.00	0.40	1.00	2.00
❑41, Nov 91	2.00	0.40	1.00	2.00
❑42, Dec 91	2.00	0.40	1.00	2.00
❑43, Jan 92	2.00	0.40	1.00	2.00
❑44, Feb 92	2.00	0.40	1.00	2.00
❑45, Mar 92	2.00	0.40	1.00	2.00
❑46, Apr 92	2.00	0.40	1.00	2.00
❑47, May 92	2.00	0.40	1.00	2.00
❑48, Jun 92	2.00	0.40	1.00	2.00
❑49, Jul 92	2.00	0.40	1.00	2.00
❑50, Aug 92, b&w; City At War	2.00	0.40	1.00	2.00
❑51, Sep 92, City At War; City At War, Part 1, b&w	2.00	0.40	1.00	2.00
❑52, Oct 92, City At War; City At War, Part 2, b&w	2.25	0.45	1.13	2.25
❑53, Nov 92, City At War; City At War, Part 3, b&w	2.25	0.45	1.13	2.25
❑54, Dec 92, City At War; City At War, Part 4, b&w	2.25	0.45	1.13	2.25
❑55, Jan 93, City At War; City At War, Part 5, b&w	2.25	0.45	1.13	2.25
❑56, Feb 93, City At War; City At War, Part 6, b&w	2.25	0.45	1.13	2.25
❑57, Mar 93, City At War; City At War, Part 7, b&w	2.25	0.45	1.13	2.25
❑58, Apr 93, City At War; City At War, Part 8, b&w	2.25	0.45	1.13	2.25
❑59, May 93, City At War; City At War, Part 9, b&w	2.25	0.45	1.13	2.25
❑60, Jun 93, City At War; City At War, Part 10, b&w	2.25	0.45	1.13	2.25
❑61, Jul 93, City At War; City At War, Part 11, b&w	2.25	0.45	1.13	2.25
❑62, Aug 93, City At War; City At War, Part 12, b&w; Final Issue	2.25	0.45	1.13	2.25

TEENAGE MUTANT NINJA TURTLES (2ND SERIES)
MIRAGE

	ORIG	GOOD	FINE	N-MINT
❑1, Oct 93, full color	2.75	0.60	1.50	3.00
❑2, Dec 93, full color	2.75	0.60	1.50	3.00
❑3, Feb 94, full color	2.75	0.60	1.50	3.00
❑4, Apr 94	2.75	0.60	1.50	3.00
❑5, Jun 94	2.75	0.60	1.50	3.00
❑6, Aug 94	2.75	0.55	1.38	2.75
❑7, Oct 94	2.75	0.55	1.38	2.75
❑8, Nov 94, Bog, Part 1	2.75	0.55	1.38	2.75
❑9, Aug 95	2.75	0.55	1.38	2.75
❑10, Aug 95, Bog, Part 2	2.75	0.55	1.38	2.75
❑11, Sep 95, Bog, Part 3	2.75	0.55	1.38	2.75
❑12, Sep 95, Bog, Part 4	2.75	0.55	1.38	2.75
❑13, Oct 95,Final Issue	2.75	0.55	1.38	2.75
❑SE 1, Jan 93, The Maltese Turtle,Special.	2.95	0.59	1.48	2.95

TEENAGE MUTANT NINJA TURTLES (3RD SERIES)
IMAGE

	ORIG	GOOD	FINE	N-MINT
❑1, Jun 96	1.95	0.70	1.75	3.50
❑2, Jul 96	1.95	0.65	1.63	3.25
❑3, Sep 96	1.95	0.65	1.63	3.25
❑4, Oct 96	1.95	0.60	1.50	3.00
❑5, Dec 96	2.50	0.60	1.50	3.00

	ORIG	GOOD	FINE	N-MINT
❑6, Jan 97	2.50	0.60	1.50	3.00
❑7, Feb 97	2.50	0.60	1.50	3.00
❑8	2.50	0.60	1.50	3.00
❑9, May 97, A: Knight Watchman	2.95	0.60	1.50	3.00
❑10	2.95	0.60	1.50	3.00
❑11, Oct 97	2.95	0.59	1.48	2.95
❑12, Dec 97	2.95	0.59	1.48	2.95
❑13, Feb 98	2.95	0.59	1.48	2.95
❑14, Apr 98	2.95	0.59	1.48	2.95
❑15, May 98	2.95	0.59	1.48	2.95
❑16, Jul 98	2.95	0.59	1.48	2.95
❑17, Sep 98	2.95	0.59	1.48	2.95
❑18, Oct 98	2.95	0.59	1.48	2.95
❑19, Jan 99	2.95	0.59	1.48	2.95
❑20, Mar 99	2.95	0.59	1.48	2.95
❑21, May 99	2.95	0.59	1.48	2.95
❑22, Jul 99	2.95	0.59	1.48	2.95
❑23, Oct 99	2.95	0.59	1.48	2.95

TEENAGE MUTANT NINJA TURTLES ADVENTURES (1ST SERIES)
ARCHIE

	ORIG	GOOD	FINE	N-MINT
❑1, Aug 88, Heroes in a Half-Shell!	1.00	0.60	1.50	3.00
❑2, Oct 88	1.00	0.50	1.25	2.50
❑3, Dec 88	1.00	0.50	1.25	2.50

TEENAGE MUTANT NINJA TURTLES ADVENTURES (2ND SERIES)
ARCHIE

	ORIG	GOOD	FINE	N-MINT
❑1, Mar 89, Return of the Shredder	1.00	0.60	1.50	3.00
❑2, May 89, Return of the Shredder	1.00	0.50	1.25	2.50
❑3, Jul 89	1.00	0.50	1.25	2.50
❑4, Sep 89	1.00	0.40	1.00	2.00
❑5, Oct 89	1.00	0.40	1.00	2.00
❑6, Nov 89, Something Fishy Goes Down...	1.00	0.40	1.00	2.00
❑7, Dec 89	1.00	0.40	1.00	2.00
❑8, Feb 90	1.00	0.40	1.00	2.00
❑9, Mar 90	1.00	0.40	1.00	2.00
❑10, May 90	1.00	0.40	1.00	2.00
❑11, Jun 90	1.00	0.30	0.75	1.50
❑12, Jul 90	1.00	0.30	0.75	1.50
❑13, Oct 90	1.00	0.30	0.75	1.50
❑14, Nov 90	1.00	0.30	0.75	1.50
❑15, Dec 90, The Howling of Distant Shadows	1.00	0.30	0.75	1.50
❑16	1.00	0.30	0.75	1.50
❑17	1.00	0.30	0.75	1.50
❑18	1.00	0.30	0.75	1.50
❑19, 1: Mighty Mutanimals	1.25	0.30	0.75	1.50
❑20	1.25	0.30	0.75	1.50
❑21	1.25	0.30	0.75	1.50
❑22	1.25	0.30	0.75	1.50
❑23	1.25	0.30	0.75	1.50
❑24	1.25	0.30	0.75	1.50
❑25	1.25	0.30	0.75	1.50
❑26	1.25	0.30	0.75	1.50
❑27	1.25	0.30	0.75	1.50
❑28	1.25	0.30	0.75	1.50
❑29	1.25	0.30	0.75	1.50
❑30	1.25	0.30	0.75	1.50
❑31	1.25	0.30	0.75	1.50
❑32	1.25	0.30	0.75	1.50
❑33	1.25	0.30	0.75	1.50
❑34	1.25	0.30	0.75	1.50
❑35	1.25	0.30	0.75	1.50
❑36	1.25	0.30	0.75	1.50
❑37	1.25	0.30	0.75	1.50
❑38	1.25	0.30	0.75	1.50
❑39	1.25	0.30	0.75	1.50
❑40	1.25	0.30	0.75	1.50
❑41	1.25	0.30	0.75	1.50
❑42	1.25	0.30	0.75	1.50
❑43	1.25	0.30	0.75	1.50
❑44	1.25	0.30	0.75	1.50
❑45, Jun 93	1.25	0.30	0.75	1.50
❑46, Jul 93	1.25	0.30	0.75	1.50
❑47, Aug 93	1.25	0.30	0.75	1.50
❑48, Sep 93	1.25	0.30	0.75	1.50
❑49, Oct 93	1.25	0.30	0.75	1.50
❑50, Nov 93	1.25	0.30	0.75	1.50
❑51, Dec 93	1.25	0.30	0.75	1.50
❑52, Jan 94	1.25	0.30	0.75	1.50
❑53, Feb 94	1.25	0.30	0.75	1.50
❑54, Mar 94	1.25	0.30	0.75	1.50
❑55, Apr 94, Terracide, Part 1	1.25	0.30	0.75	1.50
❑56, May 94	1.25	0.30	0.75	1.50
❑57, Jun 94	1.25	0.30	0.75	1.50

The Teenage Mutant Ninja Turtles were the creation of Kevin Eastman and Peter Laird.

© 1990 Kevin Eastman and Peter Laird (Mirage)

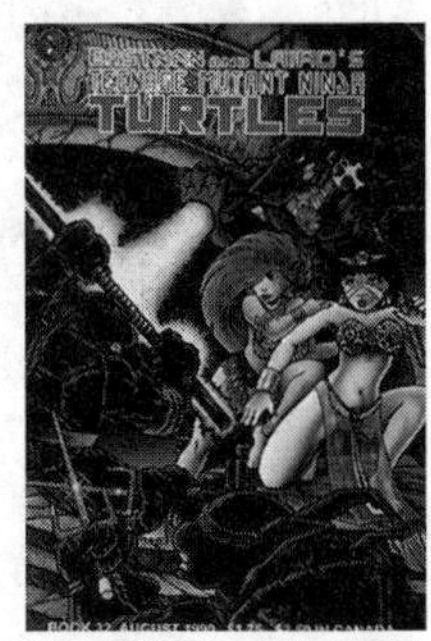

	ORIG	GOOD	FINE	N-MINT
❑58, Jul 94	1.25	0.30	0.75	1.50
❑59, Aug 94	1.50	0.30	0.75	1.50
❑60, Sep 94	1.50	0.30	0.75	1.50
❑61, Oct 94	1.50	0.30	0.75	1.50
❑62, Nov 94, poster	1.75	0.30	0.75	1.50
❑63, Dec 94	1.50	0.30	0.75	1.50
❑64, Jan 95	1.50	0.30	0.75	1.50
❑65, Feb 95	1.50	0.30	0.75	1.50
❑66, Mar 95	1.50	0.30	0.75	1.50
❑67, Apr 95	1.50	0.30	0.75	1.50
❑68, May 95	1.50	0.30	0.75	1.50
❑69, Jun 95	1.50	0.30	0.75	1.50
❑70, Jul 95	1.50	0.30	0.75	1.50
❑71, Sep 95, The Early Years, Part 1	1.50	0.30	0.75	1.50
❑72, Oct 95, The Early Years, Part 2,Final Issue	1.50	0.30	0.75	1.50
❑SE 1, Spr 91, Green Legs and Gams; Red Sails in the Sunset, nn; Teenage Mutant Ninja Turtles Meet Archie	2.50	0.50	1.25	2.50
❑SE 2	2.50	0.50	1.25	2.50
❑SE 3	2.50	0.50	1.25	2.50
❑SE 4	2.50	0.50	1.25	2.50
❑SE 5	2.50	0.50	1.25	2.50
❑SE 6, Giant-Size Special #6	1.95	0.40	1.00	2.00
❑SE 7	1.95	0.40	1.00	2.00
❑SE 8	1.95	0.40	1.00	2.00
❑SE 9	1.95	0.40	1.00	2.00
❑SE 10	2.00	0.40	1.00	2.00
❑SE 11,Teenage Mutant Ninja Turtles Special #11	2.00	0.40	1.00	2.00

TEENAGE MUTANT NINJA TURTLES ADVENTURES (3RD SERIES)
ARCHIE

Value: Cover or less

❑1, Jan 96, The Year of the Turtle	1.50
❑2, Feb 96, The Year of the Turtle	1.50
❑3, Mar 96, The Year of the Turtle	1.50

TEENAGE MUTANT NINJA TURTLES AUTHORIZED MARTIAL ARTS TRAINING MANUAL
SOLSON

	ORIG	GOOD	FINE	N-MINT
❑1, RB, RB (w)	2.25	0.50	1.25	2.50
❑2	2.25	0.50	1.25	2.50
❑3	2.25	0.50	1.25	2.50
❑4	2.25	0.50	1.25	2.50

TEENAGE MUTANT NINJA TURTLES CLASSICS DIGEST
ARCHIE

	ORIG	GOOD	FINE	N-MINT
❑1	1.75	0.40	1.00	2.00
❑2	1.75	0.35	0.88	1.75
❑3	1.75	0.35	0.88	1.75
❑4	1.75	0.35	0.88	1.75
❑5	1.75	0.35	0.88	1.75
❑6	1.75	0.35	0.88	1.75
❑7, Dec 94, digest	1.75	0.35	0.88	1.75
❑8	1.75	0.35	0.88	1.75

TEENAGE MUTANT NINJA TURTLES/FLAMING CARROT CROSSOVER
MIRAGE

	ORIG	GOOD	FINE	N-MINT
❑1, Nov 93, Land Of Green Fire	2.75	0.60	1.50	3.00
❑2, Dec 93	2.75	0.60	1.50	3.00
❑3, Jan 94	2.75	0.60	1.50	3.00
❑4, Feb 94	2.75	0.60	1.50	3.00

TEENAGE MUTANT NINJA TURTLES III THE MOVIE: THE TURTLES ARE BACK...IN TIME
ARCHIE

Value: Cover or less

❑1, nn; newsstand	2.50
❑1/PR, Prestige edition	4.95

TEENAGE MUTANT NINJA TURTLES II: THE SECRET OF THE OOZE
MIRAGE

Value: Cover or less

❑1	5.95

TEENAGE MUTANT NINJA TURTLES MEET THE CONSERVATION CORPS

ARCHIE

Value: Cover or less

- ❑1 ... 2.50

TEENAGE MUTANT NINJA TURTLES MICHAELANGELO CHRISTMAS SPECIAL

MIRAGE

Value: Cover or less

- ❑1, Michaelangelo: The Christmas Aliens; Raphael: A Christmas Carol ... 1.75

TEENAGE MUTANT NINJA TURTLES MOVIE II

ARCHIE

Value: Cover or less

- ❑1, Jun 91, The Secret of the Ooze, nn ... 2.50

TEENAGE MUTANT NINJA TURTLES MUTANT UNIVERSE SOURCEBOOK

ARCHIE

	ORIG	GOOD	FINE	N-MINT
❑1	1.95	0.40	1.00	2.00
❑2	1.95	0.40	1.00	2.00
❑3	1.95	0.40	1.00	2.00

TEENAGE MUTANT NINJA TURTLES PRESENTS: APRIL O'NEIL

ARCHIE

Value: Cover or less

- ❑1, Apr 93, May East Saga; The May East Saga, Part 1, You're Fired! ... 1.25
- ❑2, May East Saga; The May East Saga, Part 2 ... 1.25
- ❑3, May East Saga; The May East Saga, Part 3 ... 1.25

TEENAGE MUTANT NINJA TURTLES PRESENTS: DONATELLO AND LEATHERHEAD

ARCHIE

Value: Cover or less

- ❑1, Jul 93, Hassles in Hollow Earth! ... 1.25
- ❑2, Aug 93, Found-One Lost World! ... 1.25
- ❑3, Sep 93 ... 1.25

TEENAGE MUTANT NINJA TURTLES PRESENTS MERDUDE AND MICHAELANGELO

ARCHIE

Value: Cover or less

- ❑1, Oct 93 ... 1.25
- ❑2, Nov 93 ... 1.25
- ❑3, Dec 93 ... 1.25

TEENAGE MUTANT NINJA TURTLES-SAVAGE DRAGON CROSSOVER

MIRAGE

	ORIG	GOOD	FINE	N-MINT
❑1, Aug 95	2.75	0.60	1.50	3.00

TEENAGE MUTANT NINJA TURTLES: THE MOVIE (ARCHIE)

ARCHIE

Value: Cover or less

- ❑1, Sum 90,newsstand ... 2.50
- ❑1/DM, Sum 90, prestige format ... 4.95
- ❑1/PR, Prestige edition ... 5.95

TEENAGE MUTANT NINJA TURTLES: THE MOVIE (MIRAGE)

MIRAGE

Value: Cover or less

- ❑1, nn; b&w ... 5.95

TEENAGENTS (JACK KIRBY'S...)

TOPPS

Value: Cover or less

- ❑1, Aug 93, KB (w), Here be Monsters!,three trading cards ... 2.95
- ❑2, Sep 93, KB (w),trading cards ... 2.95
- ❑3, Oct 93, KB (w), A: Liberty Project,trading cards ... 2.95
- ❑4, Nov 93, KB (w),cards; Zorro preview ... 2.95

TEEN COMICS

PERSONALITY

Value: Cover or less

- ❑1 ... 2.50
- ❑2 ... 2.50
- ❑3 ... 2.50
- ❑4 ... 2.50

TEEN TALES: THE LIBRARY COMIC

DAVID G. BROWN STUDIOS

	ORIG	GOOD	FINE	N-MINT
❑1, Oct 97, nn; promotional comic book done for the L.A. Public Library	—	0.20	0.50	1.00

TEEN TITANS, THE

DC

	ORIG	GOOD	FINE	N-MINT
❑1, Feb 66, NC ,Peace Corps	0.12	30.00	75.00	150.00
❑2, Apr 66, NC	0.12	16.00	40.00	80.00
❑3, Jun 66, NC	0.12	9.00	22.50	45.00
❑4, Aug 66, NC	0.12	9.00	22.50	45.00
❑5, Oct 66, NC	0.12	9.00	22.50	45.00
❑6, Dec 66	0.12	6.00	15.00	30.00
❑7, Feb 67, The Mad Mod, Merchant of Menace!	0.12	6.00	15.00	30.00
❑8, Apr 67	0.12	6.00	15.00	30.00
❑9, Jun 67	0.12	6.00	15.00	30.00
❑10, Aug 67	0.12	6.00	15.00	30.00
❑11, Oct 67	0.12	4.40	11.00	22.00
❑12, Dec 67	0.12	4.40	11.00	22.00
❑13, Feb 68	0.12	4.40	11.00	22.00
❑14, Apr 68	0.12	4.40	11.00	22.00
❑15, Jun 68	0.12	4.40	11.00	22.00
❑16, Aug 68	0.12	4.40	11.00	22.00
❑17, Oct 68	0.12	4.40	11.00	22.00
❑18, Dec 68, 1: Starfire	0.12	5.00	12.50	25.00
❑19, Feb 69	0.12	4.40	11.00	22.00
❑20, Apr 69, NC; NA	0.12	5.00	12.50	25.00
❑21, Jun 69, NC; NA	0.12	5.00	12.50	25.00
❑22, Aug 69, NC; NA, O: Wonder Girl	0.15	5.00	12.50	25.00
❑23, Oct 69, GK, DG (w), The Rock 'n' Roll Rogue	0.15	2.80	7.00	14.00
❑24, Dec 69, GK, DG (w), Skis of Death	0.15	2.80	7.00	14.00
❑25, Feb 70, NC, DG (w), The Titans Kill a Saint?, 1: Lilith	0.15	2.80	7.00	14.00
❑26, Apr 70, NC, DG (w), A Penny for a Black Star	0.15	2.40	6.00	12.00
❑27, Jun 70, GT; CI, DG (w), Nightmare in Space,in space	0.15	2.40	6.00	12.00
❑28, Aug 70, NC, DG (w), Blindspot	0.15	2.40	6.00	12.00
❑29, Oct 70, NC, DG (w), Captives!, A: Hawk & Dove	0.15	2.40	6.00	12.00
❑30, Dec 70, CI, DG (w), Greed...Kills!; Whirl-wind, A: Aquagirl	0.15	2.40	6.00	12.00
❑31, Feb 71, GT, DG (w), To Order is to Destroy; From One to Twenty	0.15	2.00	5.00	10.00
❑32, Apr 71, NC, DG (w), A Mystical Realm, a World Gone Mad	0.15	2.00	5.00	10.00
❑33, Jun 71, GT, DG (w), Less than Human?,Robin returns	0.15	2.00	5.00	10.00
❑34, Aug 71, GT, The Demon of Dog Island	0.15	2.00	5.00	10.00
❑35, Oct 71, GT, Intruders of the Forbidden Crypt; A Titan is Born, 1: Think Freak, reprints; Giant-size	0.25	2.00	5.00	10.00
❑36, Dec 71, JA; NC; GT, The Tomb Be Their Destiny; The Girl of the Shadows, reprints; Giant-size	0.25	2.00	5.00	10.00
❑37, Feb 72, GT, Scourge of the Skeletal Riders; Superboy Meets the Young Green Arrow, reprints; Giant-size	0.25	2.00	5.00	10.00
❑38, Apr 72, GT, Through These Doors Pass the Bravest Titans of Them All; Nameless, Wader I, reprints; Giant-size	0.25	2.00	5.00	10.00
❑39, Jun 72, GT, Awake, Barbaric Titan; After the Cat, reprints; Giant-size	0.25	2.00	5.00	10.00
❑40, Aug 72, The Spawn of the Sinister Sea, A: Aqualad; 1: Black Moray	0.20	2.00	5.00	10.00
❑41, Oct 72, What Lies in Litchburg Grave-yard?; Her Brother's Keeper	0.20	2.00	5.00	10.00
❑42, Dec 72, Slaves of the Emperor Bug	0.20	2.00	5.00	10.00
❑43, Feb 73, Inherit the Howling Night; Please Tell Me My Name,series goes on hiatus	0.20	2.00	5.00	10.00
❑44, Nov 76, JO (w), The Man Who Toppled the Titans, 1: Guardian; V: Doctor Light,Series begins again (1976); New team: Kid Flash, Wonder Girl, Robin, Speedy, Mal	0.30	1.60	4.00	8.00
❑45, Dec 76, IN, You Cant Say No The To Angel Of Death! (Or Can You?)	0.30	1.60	4.00	8.00
❑46, Feb 77, IN, The Fiddler's Concert of Crime, V: Fiddler	0.30	1.60	4.00	8.00
❑47, Apr 77, Trouble-Which Rhymes with Double, 1: Sizematic II; 1: Flamesplasher II; 1: Darklight II; 1: Sizematic I; 1: Flames-plasher I; 1: Darklight I	0.30	1.60	4.00	8.00
❑48, Jun 77, Daddy's Little Crimefighter, 1: The Bumblebee; 1: Harlequin	0.35	3.00	7.50	15.00
❑49, Aug 77, Raid of the Rocket-Rollers, 1: Bryan the Brain	0.35	1.60	4.00	8.00
❑50, Oct 77, DH, The Coast-to-Coast Calamities,Bat-Girl returns	0.35	3.60	9.00	18.00
❑51, Nov 77, DH, Titans East! Titans West! And Never (?) the Teens Shall Meet!, A: Titans West	0.35	1.60	4.00	8.00
❑52, Dec 77, DH, When Titans Clash, A: Titans West	0.35	1.60	4.00	8.00
❑53, Feb 78, In the Beginning..., 1: The Antithesis; O: Teen Titans,Final Issue	0.35	1.60	4.00	8.00

TEEN TITANS (2ND SERIES)

DC

	ORIG	GOOD	FINE	N-MINT
❑1, Oct 96, GP, Titan's Children, Part 1, O: New team of four teen-agers led by Atom	1.95	0.80	2.00	4.00
❑2, Nov 96, GP, Titan's Children, Part 2	1.95	0.60	1.50	3.00
❑3, Dec 96, GP, Titan's Children, Part 3, A: Mad Mod; V: Jugular; A: Mr. Jupiter,team gets new costumes	1.95	0.60	1.50	3.00
❑4, Jan 97, Coming Out, Part 1, A: Robin; A: Nightwing; A: Captain Marvel Jr.	1.95	0.50	1.25	2.50
❑5, Feb 97, Coming Out, Part 2, A: Robin; A: Nightwing; A: Supergirl; A: Captain Marvel Jr.	1.95	0.50	1.25	2.50
❑6, Mar 97, GP, Moving Daze	1.95	0.50	1.25	2.50
❑7, Apr 97	1.95	0.50	1.25	2.50
❑8, May 97	1.95	0.50	1.25	2.50
❑9, Jun 97, A: Warlord	1.95	0.50	1.25	2.50
❑10, Jul 97,in Skartaris	1.95	0.50	1.25	2.50
❑11, Aug 97	1.95	0.40	1.00	2.00

	ORIG	GOOD	FINE	N-MINT
❑12, Sep 97, Then & Now, Part 1,48pgs.; flashback with original Titans	2.95	0.40	1.00	2.00
❑13, Oct 97, Then & Now, Part 2,flashback with original Titans	1.95	0.40	1.00	2.00
❑14, Nov 97, GP, Then & Now, Part 3,identity of Omen revealed	1.95	0.40	1.00	2.00
❑15, Jan 98, GP, Then & Now, Part 4, D: Joto,real identity of Omen revealed	1.95	0.40	1.00	2.00
❑16, Feb 98, Then & Now Aftermath	1.95	0.40	1.00	2.00
❑17, Mar 98,new members join	1.95	0.40	1.00	2.00
❑18, Apr 98, Night of the Beast	1.95	0.40	1.00	2.00
❑19, Apr 98, A: Superman,Millennium Giants	1.95	0.40	1.00	2.00
❑20, May 98	1.95	0.40	1.00	2.00
❑21, Jun 98, Titans Hunt, Part 1	1.95	0.40	1.00	2.00
❑22, Jul 98, Titans Hunt, Part 2, A: Changeling	1.95	0.40	1.00	2.00
❑23, Aug 98, Titans Hunt, Part 3, A: Superman	1.95	0.39	0.98	1.95
❑24, Sep 98, Titans Hunt, Part 4,Final Issue	1.95	0.39	0.98	1.95
❑Anl 1,Pulp Heroes	3.95	0.79	1.98	3.95
❑Anl 1999,80pgs.; cardstock cover; Reprint; published in 1999 in style of '60s Annual.	4.95	0.99	2.47	4.95

TEEN TITANS SPOTLIGHT
DC

	ORIG	GOOD	FINE	N-MINT
❑1, Aug 86, Starfire: Black and White,Starfire	0.75	0.25	0.63	1.25
❑2, Sep 86,Starfire	0.75	0.25	0.63	1.25
❑3, Oct 86, RA, Jericho: The Past is Prologue,Jericho	0.75	0.25	0.63	1.25
❑4, Nov 86,Jericho	0.75	0.25	0.63	1.25
❑5, Dec 86,Jericho	0.75	0.25	0.63	1.25
❑6, Jan 87, Conflagration!,Jericho	0.75	0.20	0.50	1.00
❑7, Feb 87	0.75	0.20	0.50	1.00
❑8, Mar 87, Queen of Hives,Hawk	0.75	0.20	0.50	1.00
❑9, Apr 87, A: Robotman,Changeling	0.75	0.20	0.50	1.00
❑10, May 87,Aqualad	0.75	0.20	0.50	1.00
❑11, Jun 87,Brotherhood of Evil	0.75	0.20	0.50	1.00
❑12, Jul 87,Wonder Girl	0.75	0.20	0.50	1.00
❑13, Aug 87	0.75	0.20	0.50	1.00
❑14, Sep 87,Nightwing, Batman	0.75	0.20	0.50	1.00
❑15, Oct 87,Omega Men	0.75	0.20	0.50	1.00
❑16, Nov 87	0.75	0.20	0.50	1.00
❑17, Dec 87	0.75	0.20	0.50	1.00
❑18, Jan 88, Millennium: Week 4,Millennium; Aqualad	0.75	0.20	0.50	1.00
❑19, Feb 88, Millennium: Week 8,Millennium; Starfire	0.75	0.20	0.50	1.00
❑20, Mar 88,Cyborg; Changeling	0.75	0.20	0.50	1.00
❑21, Apr 88,Final Issue; original Titans	0.75	0.20	0.50	1.00

TEK KNIGHTS
ARTLINE

Value: Cover or less

❑1, b&w 2.95

TEKNO*COMIX HANDBOOK
TEKNO

Value: Cover or less

❑1, May 96,information on various Tekno characters 3.95

TEKNOPHAGE (NEIL GAIMAN'S...)
TEKNO

	ORIG	GOOD	FINE	N-MINT
❑1, Aug 95	1.95	0.39	0.98	1.95
❑1/SC, Jul 95,enhanced cover; Steel Edition	—	0.60	1.50	3.00
❑2, Sep 95	1.95	0.39	0.98	1.95
❑3, Oct 95, BT, Feed the Machine	1.95	0.39	0.98	1.95
❑4, Nov 95	1.95	0.39	0.98	1.95
❑5, Dec 95	1.95	0.39	0.98	1.95
❑6, Dec 95	1.95	0.39	0.98	1.95
❑7, Jan 96	2.25	0.45	1.13	2.25
❑8, Feb 96	2.25	0.45	1.13	2.25
❑9, Feb 96	2.25	0.45	1.13	2.25
❑10, Mar 96	2.25	0.45	1.13	2.25

TEKNOPHAGE VERSUS ZEERUS
BIG

Value: Cover or less

❑1, Jul 96,One-Shot 3.25

TEKQ
GAUNTLET

Value: Cover or less

❑1, b&w 2.95
❑2, b&w 2.95
❑3, b&w 2.95
❑4, b&w 2.95

TEKWORLD
MARVEL

	ORIG	GOOD	FINE	N-MINT
❑1, Sep 92	1.75	0.50	1.25	2.50
❑2, Oct 92	1.75	0.40	1.00	2.00
❑3, Nov 92	1.75	0.40	1.00	2.00
❑4, Dec 92	1.75	0.40	1.00	2.00
❑5, Jan 93	1.75	0.40	1.00	2.00
❑6, Feb 93	1.75	0.40	1.00	2.00
❑7, Mar 93	1.75	0.40	1.00	2.00
❑8, Apr 93	1.75	0.40	1.00	2.00

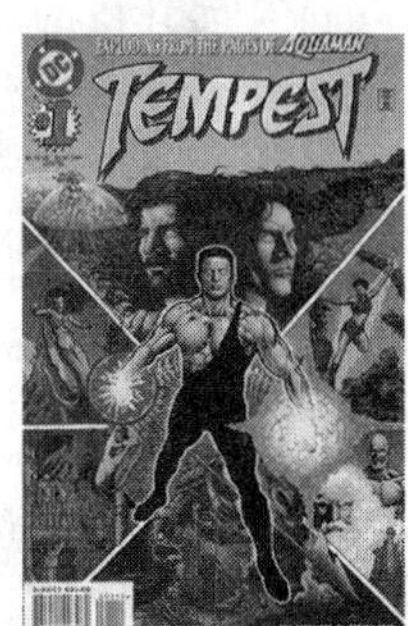

Aqualad acquired new powers and a facial scar in DC's *Tempest* mini-series.

© 1996 DC Comics

	ORIG	GOOD	FINE	N-MINT
❑9, May 93	1.75	0.40	1.00	2.00
❑10, Jun 93	1.75	0.40	1.00	2.00
❑11, Jul 93	1.75	0.35	0.88	1.75
❑12, Aug 93	1.75	0.35	0.88	1.75
❑13, Sep 93	1.75	0.35	0.88	1.75
❑14, Oct 93, A: Jake Cardigan,Begins adaptation of TekLords	1.75	0.35	0.88	1.75
❑15, Nov 93	1.75	0.35	0.88	1.75
❑16, Dec 93	1.75	0.35	0.88	1.75
❑17, Jan 94	1.75	0.35	0.88	1.75
❑18, Feb 94	1.75	0.35	0.88	1.75
❑19, Mar 94	1.75	0.35	0.88	1.75
❑20, Apr 94	1.75	0.35	0.88	1.75
❑21, May 94	1.75	0.35	0.88	1.75
❑22, Jun 94	1.75	0.35	0.88	1.75
❑23, Jul 94	1.75	0.35	0.88	1.75
❑24, Aug 94,Final Issue	1.75	0.35	0.88	1.75

TELLOS
IMAGE

Value: Cover or less

❑1, May 99 ..... 2.50
❑2, Jun 99 ..... 2.50
❑3, Jul 99 ..... 2.50
❑4, Oct 99 ..... 2.50
❑4/A, Oct 99,alternate cover w/ moon in background 2.50
❑4/B, Oct 99,alternate cover w/ skeletons in bottom left 2.50
❑5 ..... 2.50
❑6 ..... 2.50
❑7 ..... 2.50
❑8, Aug 00, The Sleeping Giant 2.50
❑9, Sep 00, Rites of Darkness 2.50
❑10, Nov 00 ..... 2.50
❑Ash 1,Dynamic Forces preview 2.50

TELL TALE HEART AND OTHER STORIES
FANTAGRAPHICS

Value: Cover or less

❑1, b&w 2.50

TELLURIA
ZUB

Value: Cover or less

❑1, Yonna 2.50
❑2, The Orb, Part 1 ..... 2.50
❑3, The Orb, Part 2 ..... 2.50

TEMPEST
DC

Value: Cover or less

❑1, Nov 96, Prophets And Kings, Part 1,Tula returns 1.75
❑2, Dec 96, Prophets And Kings, Part 2 ..... 1.75
❑3, Jan 97, Prophets And Kings, Part 3,Aqualad's true origin revealed 1.75
❑4, Feb 97, Prophets And Kings, Part 4 ..... 1.75

TEMPLATE
HEAD PRESS

Value: Cover or less

❑0,flip-book with Max Damage #0 ..... 2.95
❑1, Dec 95, A Mind is a Terrible Thing, b&w 2.50
❑2, Feb 96, b&w 2.50
❑3, Apr 96, b&w 2.50
❑4, Jun 96, b&w 2.50
❑5, Aug 96, b&w 2.50
❑6, Nov 96, Ism By Thy Name, Part 2, b&w 2.50
❑7, Jul 97, b&w 2.50
❑SE 1, Feb 97, b&w 2.95
❑SE 1/Ash, Feb 97,Ashcan preview of special #1 ..... 1.00
❑SE 1/SC, Feb 97,alternate cover 2.95

TEMPLE SNARE
MU

Value: Cover or less

❑1, nn; b&w 2.25

TEMPTRESS: THE BLOOD OF EVE
CALIBER

Value: Cover or less

❑1, Forever and a Day, Part 1 ..... 2.95

TEMPUS FUGITIVE
DC

Value: Cover or less

❑1 ..... 4.95
❑2 ..... 4.95
❑3 ..... 5.95
❑4 ..... 5.95

TENCHI MUYO!
PIONEER

Value: Cover or less

❑1, Mar 97 ..... 2.95
❑2, Mar 97 ..... 2.95
❑3, May 97 ..... 2.95
❑4, Jul 97 ..... 2.95
❑5, Aug 97 ..... 2.95

TENTH, THE
IMAGE

	ORIG	GOOD	FINE	N-MINT
❑0, Aug 97,American Entertainment exclusive	—	0.60	1.50	3.00
❑0.5, Aug 97, Wizard promotional edition with certificate of authenticity	—	1.00	2.50	5.00
❑1, Jan 97,cover says Mar, indicia says Jan	2.50	0.60	1.50	3.00
❑1/A, Jan 97,American Entertainment exclusive cover	2.50	0.80	2.00	4.00
❑2, Feb 97,cover says Apr, indicia says Feb	2.50	0.50	1.25	2.50
❑3, May 97	2.50	0.50	1.25	2.50
❑4, Jun 97	2.50	0.50	1.25	2.50

TENTH, THE (2ND SERIES)
IMAGE

	ORIG	GOOD	FINE	N-MINT
❑0, O: The Tenth	2.95	0.60	1.50	3.00
❑0/A, O: The Tenth,Signed by Tony Daniel..	—	1.60	4.00	8.00
❑0/AE, O: The Tenth,American Entertainment exclusive	—	0.80	2.00	4.00
❑1, Sep 97, Abuse of Humanity	2.50	0.60	1.50	3.00
❑1/AE, Sep 97, Abuse of Humanity,American Entertainment exclusive cover (logo at bottom right)	2.50	0.80	2.00	4.00
❑2, Oct 97	2.50	0.60	1.50	3.00
❑3	2.50	0.50	1.25	2.50
❑3/A, Nov 97,Alternate "Adrenalyn" cover	2.50	0.60	1.50	3.00
❑3/B, Nov 97,Signed by Tony Daniel; Wizard "Certified Authentic" limited edition	2.50	1.60	4.00	8.00
❑4, Dec 97	2.50	0.50	1.25	2.50
❑5, Jan 98	2.50	0.50	1.25	2.50
❑6, Feb 98	2.50	0.50	1.25	2.50
❑7, Mar 98	2.50	0.50	1.25	2.50
❑8, Apr 98	2.50	0.50	1.25	2.50
❑9, Jun 98, No Sweets After Dark	2.50	0.50	1.25	2.50
❑10, Jul 98, Killcrow	2.50	0.50	1.25	2.50
❑10/A, Jul 98,alternate cover (logo on right)	2.50	0.50	1.25	2.50
❑11, Aug 98, Gathering of the Children	2.50	0.50	1.25	2.50
❑11/A, Aug 98,alternate cover (white background)	2.50	0.50	1.25	2.50
❑12, Oct 98	2.50	0.50	1.25	2.50
❑13, Nov 98	2.50	0.50	1.25	2.50
❑14, Jan 99	2.50	0.50	1.25	2.50
❑14/A, Jan 99,alternate cover (solo face)	2.50	0.50	1.25	2.50

TENTH, THE (3RD SERIES)
IMAGE

	ORIG	GOOD	FINE	N-MINT
❑1	2.95	0.59	1.48	2.95
❑1/A, Feb 99, The Black Embrace,alternate cover	2.95	0.59	1.48	2.95
❑1/B, Feb 99,alternate cover; DFE chromium edition	2.95	2.00	5.00	10.00
❑2, Apr 99	2.95	0.50	1.25	2.50
❑3, May 99	2.95	0.50	1.25	2.50
❑4, Jun 99	2.95	0.50	1.25	2.50

TENTH, THE (4TH SERIES)
IMAGE

	ORIG	GOOD	FINE	N-MINT
❑1, Sep 99	2.95	0.50	1.25	2.50
❑1/A, Sep 99,Girl wearing shirt and panties on cover	2.95	1.20	3.00	6.00
❑1/B, Sep 99,Another Universe exclusive cover	2.95	0.60	1.50	3.00
❑2, Oct 99, Evil's Child	2.50	0.50	1.25	2.50
❑3	2.50	0.50	1.25	2.50
❑4	2.50	0.50	1.25	2.50

TENTH CONFIGURATION, THE
IMAGE

Value: Cover or less

- ❑1, Aug 98 .... 2.50

TENTH, THE: RESURRECTED
DARK HORSE

Value: Cover or less

- ❑1/A, Jul 01,Lady standing in front of glowing skulls in background on cover 2.99
- ❑1/B, Jul 01,Hulking figure on cover 2.99

TEN YEARS OF LOVE & ROCKETS
FANTAGRAPHICS

Value: Cover or less

- ❑1, Sep 92, Heart Break Soup: Space Case; Is It 10 Years Already?, nn; b&w 1.50

TERMINAL CITY
DC

	ORIG	GOOD	FINE	N-MINT
❑1, Jul 96, On the Wall	2.50	0.70	1.75	3.50
❑1/Aut, Jul 96, On the Wall,Limited to 75 copies	—	1.00	2.50	5.00
❑2, Aug 96, On the Wall	2.50	0.60	1.50	3.00
❑3, Sep 96, On the Wall	2.50	0.60	1.50	3.00
❑4, Oct 96, On the Wall	2.50	0.50	1.25	2.50
❑5, Nov 96, On the Wall	2.50	0.50	1.25	2.50
❑6, Dec 96, On the Wall	2.50	0.50	1.25	2.50
❑7, Jan 97, On the Wall	2.50	0.50	1.25	2.50
❑8, Feb 97, On the Wall	2.50	0.50	1.25	2.50
❑9, Mar 97, On the Wall,Final Issue	2.50	0.50	1.25	2.50

TERMINAL CITY: AERIAL GRAFFITI
DC

Value: Cover or less

- ❑1, Nov 97 .... 2.50
- ❑2, Dec 97 .... 2.50
- ❑3, Jan 98 .... 2.50
- ❑4, Feb 98 .... 2.50
- ❑5, Mar 98 .... 2.50

TERMINAL POINT
DARK HORSE

Value: Cover or less

- ❑1, Feb 93, b&w 2.50
- ❑2, Mar 93, b&w 2.50
- ❑3, Apr 93, b&w 2.50

TERMINATOR, THE (1ST SERIES)
NOW

	ORIG	GOOD	FINE	N-MINT
❑1, Sep 88,movie tie-in	1.75	0.40	1.00	2.00
❑2, Oct 88	1.75	0.35	0.88	1.75
❑3, Nov 88	1.75	0.35	0.88	1.75
❑4, Jan 89	1.75	0.35	0.88	1.75
❑5, Feb 89, The Bee Stings	1.75	0.35	0.88	1.75
❑6, Mar 89, Goin' Back to Miami	1.75	0.35	0.88	1.75
❑7, Apr 89	1.75	0.35	0.88	1.75
❑8, May 89, In The Belly Of The Beast,Comics Code	1.75	0.35	0.88	1.75
❑9, Jun 89,Comics Code	1.75	0.35	0.88	1.75
❑10, Jul 89,Comics Code	1.75	0.35	0.88	1.75
❑11, Aug 89,Comics Code	1.75	0.35	0.88	1.75
❑12, Sep 89,Comics Code	1.75	0.35	0.88	1.75
❑13, Oct 89,Comics Code	1.75	0.35	0.88	1.75
❑14, Nov 89, Into The Deep Blue Sea,Comics Code	1.75	0.35	0.88	1.75
❑15, Dec 89,Comics Code	1.75	0.35	0.88	1.75
❑16, Jan 90,Comics Code	1.75	0.35	0.88	1.75
❑17, Feb 90,Final Issue; Comics Code	1.75	0.35	0.88	1.75

TERMINATOR, THE (2ND SERIES)
DARK HORSE

	ORIG	GOOD	FINE	N-MINT
❑1, Aug 90, Tempest, Part 1	2.50	0.60	1.50	3.00
❑2, Sep 90, Tempest, Part 2	2.50	0.60	1.50	3.00
❑3, Oct 90, Tempest, Part 3	2.50	0.60	1.50	3.00
❑4, Nov 90, Tempest, Part 4	2.50	0.60	1.50	3.00

TERMINATOR, THE (3RD SERIES)
DARK HORSE

Value: Cover or less

- ❑1, nn; leads into 1998 series 2.95

TERMINATOR, THE (4TH SERIES)
DARK HORSE

Value: Cover or less

- ❑1,no month of publication 2.95
- ❑2, Oct 98 .... 2.95
- ❑3, Nov 98, The Kiss of Death! 2.95
- ❑4, Dec 98, Cyborg Showdown 2.95

TERMINATOR, THE (MAGAZINE)
TRIDENT

	ORIG	GOOD	FINE	N-MINT
❑1	1.00	0.60	1.50	3.00
❑2	1.00	0.60	1.50	3.00
❑3	1.00	0.60	1.50	3.00
❑4	1.00	0.60	1.50	3.00

TERMINATOR 2: JUDGMENT DAY
MARVEL

	ORIG	GOOD	FINE	N-MINT
❑1, Sep 91, KJ, Arrival,movie Adaptation	1.00	0.40	1.00	2.00
❑2, Oct 91, KJ ,movie Adaptation	1.00	0.40	1.00	2.00
❑3, Oct 91, KJ, Departure,movie Adaptation	1.00	0.40	1.00	2.00

TERMINATOR 2: JUDGMENT DAY (MAGAZINE)
MARVEL

	ORIG	GOOD	FINE	N-MINT
❑1, Sep 91, nn; b&w; movie Adaptation; magazine	2.25	0.60	1.50	3.00

TERMINATOR, THE: ALL MY FUTURES PAST
NOW

	ORIG	GOOD	FINE	N-MINT
❑1	1.75	0.50	1.25	2.50
❑2	1.75	0.50	1.25	2.50

TERMINATOR: ENDGAME
DARK HORSE

Value: Cover or less

- ❑1, Sep 92, JRo (w) 2.50
- ❑2, Oct 92, JRo (w) 2.50
- ❑3, Oct 92, JRo (w) 2.50

TERMINATOR: HUNTERS AND KILLERS
DARK HORSE

	ORIG	GOOD	FINE	N-MINT
❑1, Mar 92	2.50	0.50	1.25	2.50
❑2, Apr 92	2.50	0.50	1.25	2.50
❑3, May 92	2.50	0.50	1.25	2.50

TERMINATOR, THE: ONE SHOT
DARK HORSE

Value: Cover or less

- ❑1, Jul 91, MW, JRo (w), nn; prestige format; pop-up 5.95

TERMINATOR: SECONDARY OBJECTIVES
DARK HORSE

Value: Cover or less

- ❑1, Jul 91, PG, JRo (w) 2.50
- ❑2, Aug 91, PG, JRo (w) 2.50
- ❑3, Sep 91, PG, JRo (w) 2.50
- ❑4, Oct 91, PG, JRo (w) 2.50

TERMINATOR, THE: THE BURNING EARTH
NOW

	ORIG	GOOD	FINE	N-MINT
❑1, Mar 90, ARo ,1st comics work by Alex Ross	1.75	1.50	3.75	7.50
❑2, Apr 90, ARo	1.75	1.00	2.50	5.00
❑3, May 90, ARo	1.75	1.00	2.50	5.00
❑4, Jun 90, ARo	1.75	1.20	3.00	6.00
❑5, Jul 90, ARo	1.75	1.20	3.00	6.00

TERMINATOR, THE: THE DARK YEARS
DARK HORSE
Value: Cover or less

- ❑1, Aug 99 ... 2.95
- ❑2, Oct 99 ... 2.95
- ❑3, Nov 99 ... 2.95
- ❑4, Nov 99 ... 2.95

TERMINATOR, THE: THE ENEMY WITHIN
DARK HORSE
Value: Cover or less

- ❑1, Nov 91 ... 2.50
- ❑2, Dec 91 ... 2.50
- ❑3, Jan 92 ... 2.50
- ❑4, Feb 92 ... 2.50

TERRAFORMERS
WONDER COLOR
Value: Cover or less

- ❑1, Apr 87, ...and on the Eighth Day... ... 1.95
- ❑2 ... 1.95

TERRANAUTS
FANTASY GENERAL
Value: Cover or less

- ❑1 ... 1.75

TERRARISTS
MARVEL
Value: Cover or less

- ❑1, Nov 93, Summertime Blues ... 2.50
- ❑2, Dec 93, Sign O'the Times ... 2.50
- ❑3, Jan 94 ... 2.50
- ❑4, Feb 94, Death and the Maiden ... 2.50

TERRITORY, THE
DARK HORSE
Value: Cover or less

- ❑1, Jan 99 ... 2.95
- ❑2, Feb 99 ... 2.95
- ❑3, Mar 99 ... 2.95
- ❑4, Apr 99 ... 2.95

TERROR, THE
LEADSLINGER
Value: Cover or less

- ❑1, b&w ... 2.50

TERRORESS
HELPLESS ANGER
Value: Cover or less

- ❑1, Dec 90, An Act of Insanity, b&w; adult ... 2.50

TERROR, INC.
MARVEL

	ORIG	GOOD	FINE	N-MINT
❑1, Jul 92, Caveat Emptor, 1: Terror	1.75	0.40	1.00	2.00
❑2, Aug 92, Deal With the Devil, 1: Hellfire	1.75	0.35	0.88	1.75
❑3, Sep 92	1.75	0.35	0.88	1.75
❑4, Oct 92, Hostile Takeover	1.75	0.35	0.88	1.75
❑5, Nov 92	1.75	0.35	0.88	1.75
❑6, Dec 92, A: Punisher	1.75	0.35	0.88	1.75
❑7, Jan 93, A: Punisher	1.75	0.35	0.88	1.75
❑8, Feb 93	1.75	0.35	0.88	1.75
❑9, Mar 93, A: Wolverine	1.75	0.35	0.88	1.75
❑10, Apr 93, A: Wolverine	1.75	0.35	0.88	1.75
❑11, May 93, For Love Nor Money, Part 1, A: Silver Sable; A: Punisher	1.75	0.35	0.88	1.75
❑12, Jun 93, For Love Nor Money, Part 4	1.75	0.35	0.88	1.75
❑13, Jul 93, Infinity Crusade, A: Ghost Rider,Final Issue	1.75	0.35	0.88	1.75

TERROR ON THE PLANET OF THE APES
ADVENTURE
Value: Cover or less

- ❑1, MP, The Lawgiver, b&w ... 2.50
- ❑2, b&w ... 2.50
- ❑3, Aug 91, MP, Spawn Of The Mutant-Pits, b&w; reprints Planet of the Apes (Marvel) #3 ... 2.50
- ❑4, Dec 91, A Riverboat Named Simian, b&w; reprints Planet of the Apes (Marvel) #4 ... 2.50

TERROR TALES
ETERNITY
Value: Cover or less

- ❑1, b&w ... 2.50

TERRY AND THE PIRATES (AVALON)
AVALON
Value: Cover or less

- ❑1, b&w; strip reprints ... 2.95
- ❑2 ... 2.95

TERRY AND THE PIRATES (FEUCHTWANGER)
SIG. FEUCHTWANGER

	ORIG	GOOD	FINE	N-MINT
❑1	—	5.00	12.50	25.00

TEST DIRT
FANTAGRAPHICS
Value: Cover or less

- ❑1, b&w ... 2.50

Dark Horse's first *Terminator* mini-series featured a new group of T-800s coming to the present to hunt down and kill Sarah Conner.

TEST DRIVE
M.A.I.N.
Value: Cover or less

- ❑1, (Side A)Symbol; Night Storm,Flip Book Previews (Side A & B) ... 3.00

TEX BENSON (3-D ZONE)
3-D ZONE
Value: Cover or less

- ❑1,b&w (not 3-D) ... 2.50
- ❑2,b&w (not 3-D) ... 2.50

TEX BENSON (METRO)
METRO
Value: Cover or less

- ❑1, The World Within The Mirror, Part 1, b&w ... 2.00
- ❑2, The World Within The Mirror, Part 2 ... 2.00
- ❑3 ... 2.00
- ❑4 ... 2.00

TEYKWA
GEMSTONE
Value: Cover or less

- ❑1, Oct 88, b&w ... 1.75

THACKER'S REVENGE
EXPLORER
Value: Cover or less

- ❑1, b&w; Archie parody ... 2.95

THANE OF BAGARTH
AVALON
Value: Cover or less

- ❑1, JA ... 2.95

THANOS QUEST, THE
MARVEL
Value: Cover or less

- ❑1, Sep 90, JSn (w), Schemes and Dreams ... 4.95
- ❑1-2, JSn (w), Schemes and Dreams,2nd Printing ... 4.95
- ❑2, Oct 90 ... 4.95

THAT CHEMICAL REFLEX
CFD
Value: Cover or less

- ❑1 ... 2.50
- ❑2 ... 2.50
- ❑3 ... 2.50

THB
HORSE PRESS

	ORIG	GOOD	FINE	N-MINT
❑1, b&w	2.95	1.60	4.00	8.00
❑1-2, b&w; reprints THB #1 with revised and additional material	5.50	1.10	2.75	5.50
❑2, b&w	2.95	1.20	3.00	6.00
❑3, Jan 95, b&w	2.95	1.00	2.50	5.00
❑4, Feb 95, b&w	2.95	1.00	2.50	5.00
❑5, Mar 95, b&w	2.95	0.80	2.00	4.00
❑6	—	0.80	2.00	4.00
❑69, Oct 94, nn; b&w; no cover price; Promotional edition with 12-page story; promo edition	—	0.60	1.50	3.00

T.H.E. CAT
GOLD KEY

	ORIG	GOOD	FINE	N-MINT
❑1,Photo cover	—	2.40	6.00	12.00
❑2,Photo cover	—	2.00	5.00	10.00
❑3,Photo cover	—	2.00	5.00	10.00
❑4,Photo cover	—	2.00	5.00	10.00

THECOMICSTORE.COM PRESENTS
THECOMICSTORE.COM

	ORIG	GOOD	FINE	N-MINT
❑1	—	0.20	0.50	1.00

THERE'S A MADMAN IN MY MIRROR
BENCH PRESS
Value: Cover or less

- ❑1, Mar 99, nn; cardstock cover ... 3.50

THESPIAN
DARK MOON
Value: Cover or less

- ❑1, Apr 95 ... 2.50

THEY CALL ME...THE SKUL
VIRTUAL
Value: Cover or less

- ❑1, May 96, From the Depths, Chapter 1, 1: Skul, digest; Only issue published ... 3.99
- ❑1/A, Oct 96, digest ... 2.50

THEY CAME FROM THE 50S
ETERNITY
Value: Cover or less

- ❑1, De, b&w; Reprint ... 9.95

THEY WERE 11
Viz
Value: Cover or less

- ❑1, b&w 2.75
- ❑2, b&w 2.75
- ❑3, b&w 2.75
- ❑4, b&w 2.75

THEY WERE CHOSEN TO BE THE SURVIVORS
Spectrum

	ORIG	GOOD	FINE	N-MINT
❑1, Jun 83, Siege	0.60	0.40	1.00	2.00
❑2, Sep 83, A Hunter's Rage	1.00	0.40	1.00	2.00
❑3	1.00	0.40	1.00	2.00
❑4	1.00	0.40	1.00	2.00

THIEF
Penguin Palace
Value: Cover or less

- ❑1, Jul 95, b&w 2.50

THIEF OF SHERWOOD
A-Plus
Value: Cover or less

- ❑1, b&w; Reprint 2.25

THIEVES
Silverwolf
Value: Cover or less

- ❑1 .... 1.50

THIEVES & KINGS
I Box Publishing

	ORIG	GOOD	FINE	N-MINT
❑1, Sep 94	2.35	0.80	2.00	4.00
❑1-2,2nd Printing	2.35	0.50	1.25	2.50
❑2, Nov 94	2.35	0.60	1.50	3.00
❑2-2,2nd Printing	2.35	0.50	1.25	2.50
❑3, Jan 95	2.35	0.60	1.50	3.00
❑3-2,2nd Printing	2.35	0.47	1.17	2.35
❑4, Mar 95	2.35	0.60	1.50	3.00
❑5, May 95	2.35	0.60	1.50	3.00
❑6, Jul 95	2.35	0.55	1.38	2.75
❑7, Sep 95	2.35	0.55	1.38	2.75
❑8	2.35	0.55	1.38	2.75
❑9	2.35	0.55	1.38	2.75
❑10	2.35	0.55	1.38	2.75
❑11	2.35	0.50	1.25	2.50
❑12	2.35	0.50	1.25	2.50
❑13	2.35	0.50	1.25	2.50
❑14	2.35	0.50	1.25	2.50
❑15	2.35	0.50	1.25	2.50
❑16	2.35	0.50	1.25	2.50
❑17	2.35	0.50	1.25	2.50
❑18	2.35	0.50	1.25	2.50
❑19	2.35	0.50	1.25	2.50
❑20	2.35	0.50	1.25	2.50
❑21	2.35	0.47	1.17	2.35
❑22	2.35	0.47	1.17	2.35
❑23	2.35	0.47	1.17	2.35
❑24	2.35	0.47	1.17	2.35
❑25	2.50	0.50	1.25	2.50
❑26	2.50	0.50	1.25	2.50
❑27	2.50	0.50	1.25	2.50
❑28	2.50	0.50	1.25	2.50
❑29	2.50	0.50	1.25	2.50
❑30	2.50	0.50	1.25	2.50
❑31	2.50	0.50	1.25	2.50
❑32	2.50	0.50	1.25	2.50
❑33	2.50	0.50	1.25	2.50
❑34	2.50	0.50	1.25	2.50
❑35	2.50	0.50	1.25	2.50
❑36	2.50	0.50	1.25	2.50

THING, THE
Marvel

	ORIG	GOOD	FINE	N-MINT
❑1, Jul 83, JBy (w), Lifelines, O: The Thing.	0.60	0.40	1.00	2.00
❑2, Aug 83, JBy (w), For Beauty Passed Away, O: The Thing	0.60	0.30	0.75	1.50
❑3, Sep 83, JBy (w), Turning Point, A: Inhumans	0.60	0.30	0.75	1.50
❑4, Oct 83, JBy (w), I, Monster!, A: Inhumans	0.60	0.30	0.75	1.50
❑5, Nov 83, JBy (w), With Friends Like These, A: Spider-Man; A: She-Hulk	0.60	0.30	0.75	1.50
❑6, Dec 83, JBy (w), Mindscape, V: Puppet Master,all-black issue	0.60	0.30	0.75	1.50
❑7, Jan 84,Asst. Editor Month	0.60	0.30	0.75	1.50
❑8, Feb 84, JBy (w), Ancient Evenings Ancient Pain!	0.60	0.30	0.75	1.50
❑9, Mar 84, JBy (w), What Price A Soul?	0.60	0.30	0.75	1.50
❑10, Apr 84, JBy (w), Marking Time,Secret Wars	0.60	0.30	0.75	1.50
❑11, May 84, JBy (w), Rocky Grimm, Part 1,Secret Wars aftermath	0.60	0.25	0.63	1.25
❑12, Jun 84, JBy (w), Rocky Grimm, Part 2	0.60	0.25	0.63	1.25
❑13, Jul 84, JBy (w), Rocky Grimm, Part 3..	0.60	0.25	0.63	1.25
❑14, Aug 84, Rocky Grimm, Part 4	0.60	0.25	0.63	1.25
❑15, Sep 84, Rocky Grimm, Part 5	0.60	0.25	0.63	1.25
❑16, Oct 84, Rocky Grimm, Part 6	0.60	0.25	0.63	1.25
❑17, Nov 84, Rocky Grimm, Part 7	0.60	0.25	0.63	1.25
❑18, Dec 84, Rocky Grimm, Part 8	0.60	0.25	0.63	1.25
❑19, Jan 85, JBy (w), Rocky Grimm, Part 9	0.60	0.25	0.63	1.25
❑20, Feb 85, JBy (w), Rocky Grimm, Part 10	0.60	0.25	0.63	1.25
❑21, Mar 85, JBy (w), Revelations	0.60	0.25	0.63	1.25
❑22, Apr 85, Remembrances,returns to Earth	0.65	0.25	0.63	1.25
❑23, May 85,quits Fantastic Four	0.65	0.25	0.63	1.25
❑24, Jun 85, V: Rhino; D: Miracle Man (Marvel)	0.65	0.25	0.63	1.25
❑25, Jul 85, Legends	0.65	0.25	0.63	1.25
❑26, Aug 85, Runaways, V: Taskmaster	0.65	0.25	0.63	1.25
❑27, Sep 85, The Thing And The Thunderiders	0.65	0.25	0.63	1.25
❑28, Oct 85, 1: Demolition Dunphy (later becomes D-Man)	0.65	0.25	0.63	1.25
❑29, Nov 85	0.65	0.25	0.63	1.25
❑30, Dec 85, Secret Wars II,Secret Wars II	0.65	0.25	0.63	1.25
❑31, Jan 86	0.75	0.25	0.63	1.25
❑32, Feb 86	0.75	0.25	0.63	1.25
❑33, Mar 86, D: Titania	0.75	0.25	0.63	1.25
❑34, Apr 86, D: The Sphinx	0.75	0.25	0.63	1.25
❑35, May 86	0.75	0.25	0.63	1.25
❑36, Jun 86,Final Issue	0.75	0.25	0.63	1.25

THING FROM ANOTHER WORLD, THE
Dark Horse
Value: Cover or less

- ❑1,cardstock cover 2.95
- ❑2,cardstock cover 2.95

THING FROM ANOTHER WORLD: CLIMATE OF FEAR
Dark Horse
Value: Cover or less

- ❑1 .... 2.50
- ❑2 .... 2.50
- ❑3 .... 2.50
- ❑4 .... 2.50

THING FROM ANOTHER WORLD, THE: ETERNAL VOWS
Dark Horse
Value: Cover or less

- ❑1, Dec 93, PG, From This Day Forth 2.50
- ❑2, Jan 94, PG, In Sickness Or In Health 2.50
- ❑3, Feb 94, Climate of Fear 2.50
- ❑4, Mar 94 .... 2.50

THIRD EYE (DARK ONE'S...)
Sirius
Value: Cover or less

- ❑1, nn; prestige format; pin-ups 4.95
- ❑2, Dec 98,cardstock cover; pin-ups and stories 4.95

THIRD WORLD WAR
Fleetway
Value: Cover or less

- ❑1 .... 2.50
- ❑2 .... 2.50
- ❑3, The Killing Yields 2.50
- ❑4 .... 2.50
- ❑5 .... 2.50
- ❑6 .... 2.50

THIRTEEN O'CLOCK
Dark Horse
Value: Cover or less

- ❑1, nn; b&w 2.95

THIRTEEN SOMETHING!
Global
Value: Cover or less

- ❑1 .... 1.95

THIS IS HEAT
Aeon
Value: Cover or less

- ❑1, nn; b&w 2.50

THIS IS NOT AN EXIT
Draculina
Value: Cover or less

- ❑1 .... 2.95
- ❑2, Food 2.95

THIS IS SICK!
Silver Skull
Value: Cover or less

- ❑1, b&w; foil cover; Zen 2.95
- ❑2 .... 2.95

THOR
Marvel

	ORIG	GOOD	FINE	N-MINT
❑126, Mar 66, SL; JK, SL (w); JK (w), V: Hercules	0.12	22.00	55.00	110.00
❑127, Apr 66, SL; JK, SL (w); JK (w), 1: Pluto; 1: Midgard Serpent; 1: Volla	0.12	9.00	22.50	45.00
❑128, May 66, SL; JK, SL (w); JK (w)	0.12	9.00	22.50	45.00
❑129, Jun 66, SL; JK, SL (w); JK (w), 1: Tana Nile (disguised); 1: Hela; 1: Ares	0.12	9.00	22.50	45.00
❑130, Jul 66, SL; JK, SL (w); JK (w), Thunder in the Netherworld!, 1: Tana Nile (in real form)	0.12	9.00	22.50	45.00
❑131, Aug 66, SL; JK, SL (w); JK (w)	0.12	9.00	22.50	45.00
❑132, Sep 66, SL; JK, SL (w); JK (w), Rigel Where Gods May Fear to Tread!, V: Ego, the Living Planet; 1: Ego; 1: Recorder	0.12	9.00	22.50	45.00
❑133, Oct 66, SL; JK, SL (w); JK (w)	0.12	9.00	22.50	45.00
❑134, Nov 66, SL; JK, SL (w); JK (w), 1: High Evolutionary; 1: Man-Beast	0.12	10.00	25.00	50.00
❑135, Dec 66, SL; JK, SL (w); JK (w), O: High Evolutionary	0.12	9.00	22.50	45.00

	ORIG	GOOD	FINE	N-MINT
❑136, Jan 67, SL; JK, SL (w); JK (w), 1: Sif,Jane Foster denied immortality	0.12	9.00	22.50	45.00
❑137, Feb 67, SL; JK, SL (w); JK (w), 1: Ulik	0.12	9.00	22.50	45.00
❑138, Mar 67, SL; JK, SL (w); JK (w)	0.12	9.00	22.50	45.00
❑139, Apr 67, SL; JK, SL (w); JK (w)	0.12	9.00	22.50	45.00
❑140, May 67, SL; JK, SL (w); JK (w), V: Growing Man	0.12	9.00	22.50	45.00
❑141, Jun 67, SL; JK, SL (w); JK (w)	0.12	5.60	14.00	28.00
❑142, Jul 67, SL; JK, SL (w); JK (w)	0.12	5.60	14.00	28.00
❑143, Aug 67, SL; JK, SL (w); JK (w)	0.12	5.60	14.00	28.00
❑144, Sep 67, SL; JK, SL (w); JK (w)	0.12	5.60	14.00	28.00
❑145, Oct 67, SL; JK, SL (w); JK (w), Abandoned On Earth,Tales of Asgard back-up story	0.12	5.60	14.00	28.00
❑146, Oct 67, SL; JK, SL (w); JK (w), If The Thunder Be Gone; The Origin of the Incomparable Inhumans, A: Circus of Crime; O: Inhumans; A: Ringmaster	0.12	5.60	14.00	28.00
❑147, Dec 67, SL; JK, SL (w); JK (w), O: Inhumans	0.12	5.60	14.00	28.00
❑148, Jan 68, SL; JK, SL (w); JK (w), O: Black Bolt; 1: The Wrecker III	0.12	5.60	14.00	28.00
❑149, Feb 68, SL; JK, SL (w); JK (w), O: Black Bolt; O: Medusa; O: Maximus	0.12	5.60	14.00	28.00
❑150, Mar 68, SL; JK, SL (w); JK (w), A: Inhumans	0.12	5.60	14.00	28.00
❑151, Apr 68, SL; JK, SL (w); JK (w), A: Inhumans	0.12	5.60	14.00	28.00
❑152, May 68, SL; JK, SL (w); JK (w)	0.12	5.60	14.00	28.00
❑153, Jun 68, SL; JK, SL (w); JK (w)	0.12	5.60	14.00	28.00
❑154, Jul 68, SL; JK, SL (w); JK (w), V: Mangog	0.12	5.60	14.00	28.00
❑155, Aug 68, SL; JK, SL (w); JK (w)	0.12	5.60	14.00	28.00
❑156, Sep 68, SL; JK, SL (w); JK (w)	0.12	5.60	14.00	28.00
❑157, Oct 68, SL; JK, SL (w); JK (w), Behind Him...Ragnarok!	0.12	5.60	14.00	28.00
❑158, Nov 68, SL; JK, SL (w); JK (w), The Way it Was, O: Thor; O: Don Blake	0.12	11.00	27.50	55.00
❑159, Dec 68, SL; JK	0.12	5.60	14.00	28.00
❑160, Jan 69, SL; JK, V: Galactus	0.12	5.60	14.00	28.00
❑161, Feb 69, SL; JK, V: Galactus	0.12	3.60	9.00	18.00
❑162, Mar 69, SL; JK, O: Galactus	0.12	6.40	16.00	32.00
❑163, Apr 69, SL; JK	0.12	3.60	9.00	18.00
❑164, May 69, SL; JK	0.12	3.60	9.00	18.00
❑165, Jun 69, SL; JK, A: Him (Warlock)	0.15	6.00	15.00	30.00
❑166, Jul 69, SL; JK, A: Him (Warlock)	0.15	5.00	12.50	25.00
❑167, Aug 69, SL; JK, A: Sif	0.15	3.00	7.50	15.00
❑168, Sep 69, SL; JK, O: Galactus	0.15	6.00	15.00	30.00
❑169, Oct 69, SL; JK, O: Galactus	0.15	6.00	15.00	30.00
❑170, Nov 69	0.15	3.00	7.50	15.00
❑171, Dec 69	0.15	3.00	7.50	15.00
❑172, Jan 70	0.15	3.00	7.50	15.00
❑173, Feb 70	0.15	3.00	7.50	15.00
❑174, Mar 70	0.15	3.00	7.50	15.00
❑175, Apr 70	0.15	3.00	7.50	15.00
❑176, May 70, V: Surtur the Fire Demon	0.15	3.00	7.50	15.00
❑177, Jun 70	0.15	3.00	7.50	15.00
❑178, Jul 70	0.15	3.00	7.50	15.00
❑179, Aug 70	0.15	3.00	7.50	15.00
❑180, Sep 70, NA, V: Mephisto	0.15	2.60	6.50	13.00
❑181, Oct 70, NA, V: Loki; V: Mephisto	0.15	2.60	6.50	13.00
❑182, Nov 70	0.15	1.20	3.00	6.00
❑183, Dec 70	0.15	1.20	3.00	6.00
❑184, Jan 71, 1: Infinity (as force)	0.15	1.20	3.00	6.00
❑185, Feb 71	0.15	1.20	3.00	6.00
❑186, Mar 71	0.15	1.20	3.00	6.00
❑187, Apr 71	0.15	1.20	3.00	6.00
❑188, May 71	0.15	1.20	3.00	6.00
❑189, Jun 71	0.15	1.20	3.00	6.00
❑190, Jul 71	0.15	1.20	3.00	6.00
❑191, Aug 71	0.15	1.20	3.00	6.00
❑192, Sep 71	0.15	1.20	3.00	6.00
❑193, Oct 71, SB; JB, A: Silver Surfer	0.25	7.00	17.50	35.00
❑194, Nov 71	0.20	0.80	2.00	4.00
❑195, Dec 71	0.20	0.80	2.00	4.00
❑196, Jan 72	0.20	0.80	2.00	4.00
❑197, Feb 72	0.20	0.80	2.00	4.00
❑198, Mar 72	0.20	0.80	2.00	4.00
❑199, Apr 72	0.20	0.80	2.00	4.00
❑200, Jun 72, JB ,Ragnarok	0.20	1.60	4.00	8.00
❑201, Jul 72, JB	0.20	0.60	1.50	3.00
❑202, Aug 72, JB	0.20	0.60	1.50	3.00
❑203, Sep 72, JB	0.20	0.60	1.50	3.00
❑204, Oct 72, JB	0.20	0.60	1.50	3.00
❑205, Nov 72, JB	0.20	0.60	1.50	3.00
❑206, Dec 72, JB	0.20	0.60	1.50	3.00
❑207, Jan 73, JB	0.20	0.60	1.50	3.00
❑208, Feb 73, JB	0.20	0.60	1.50	3.00

"Tales of Asgard," a back-up series featuring adventures of the other Norse gods, ran in several issues of *Thor*.

	ORIG	GOOD	FINE	N-MINT
❑209, Mar 73, JB, 1: Ultimus	0.20	0.60	1.50	3.00
❑210, Apr 73, JB	0.20	0.60	1.50	3.00
❑211, May 73, JB	0.20	0.60	1.50	3.00
❑212, Jun 73, JB	0.20	0.60	1.50	3.00
❑213, Jul 73, JB	0.20	0.60	1.50	3.00
❑214, Aug 73	0.20	0.60	1.50	3.00
❑215, Sep 73	0.20	0.60	1.50	3.00
❑216, Oct 73	0.20	0.60	1.50	3.00
❑217, Nov 73	0.20	0.60	1.50	3.00
❑218, Dec 73	0.20	0.60	1.50	3.00
❑219, Jan 74	0.20	0.60	1.50	3.00
❑220, Feb 74	0.20	0.60	1.50	3.00
❑221, Mar 74	0.20	0.60	1.50	3.00
❑222, Apr 74	0.20	0.60	1.50	3.00
❑223, May 74	0.25	0.60	1.50	3.00
❑224, Jun 74	0.25	0.60	1.50	3.00
❑225, Jul 74, 1: Firelord	0.25	0.80	2.00	4.00
❑226, Aug 74	0.25	0.50	1.25	2.50
❑227, Sep 74	0.25	0.50	1.25	2.50
❑228, Oct 74	0.25	0.50	1.25	2.50
❑229, Nov 74	0.25	0.50	1.25	2.50
❑230, Dec 74	0.25	0.50	1.25	2.50
❑231, Jan 75	0.25	0.50	1.25	2.50
❑232, Feb 75	0.25	0.50	1.25	2.50
❑233, Mar 75	0.25	0.50	1.25	2.50
❑234, Apr 75	0.25	0.50	1.25	2.50
❑235, May 75, 1: The Possessor	0.25	0.50	1.25	2.50
❑236, Jun 75	0.25	0.50	1.25	2.50
❑237, Jul 75	0.25	0.50	1.25	2.50
❑238, Aug 75, JSt; JB	0.25	0.50	1.25	2.50
❑239, Sep 75, 1: Horus; 1: Osiris	0.25	0.50	1.25	2.50
❑240, Oct 75, 1: Seth; 1: Isis (Marvel)	0.25	0.50	1.25	2.50
❑241, Nov 75, JB	0.25	0.50	1.25	2.50
❑242, Dec 75, JB	0.25	0.50	1.25	2.50
❑243, Jan 76, JB	0.25	0.50	1.25	2.50
❑244, Feb 76, JB	0.25	0.50	1.25	2.50
❑245, Mar 76, JB	0.25	0.50	1.25	2.50
❑246, Apr 76, JB, A: Firelord	0.25	0.50	1.25	2.50
❑247, May 76, JB	0.25	0.50	1.25	2.50
❑248, Jun 76, JB	0.25	0.50	1.25	2.50
❑249, Jul 76, JB ,Sif trades places with Jane	0.25	0.50	1.25	2.50
❑250, Aug 76, JB	0.25	0.50	1.25	2.50
❑251, Sep 76	0.30	0.50	1.25	2.50
❑252, Oct 76	0.30	0.50	1.25	2.50
❑253, Nov 76	0.30	0.50	1.25	2.50
❑254, Dec 76	0.30	0.50	1.25	2.50
❑255, Jan 77	0.30	0.50	1.25	2.50
❑256, Feb 77	0.30	0.50	1.25	2.50
❑257, Mar 77	0.30	0.50	1.25	2.50
❑258, Apr 77	0.30	0.50	1.25	2.50
❑259, May 77	0.30	0.50	1.25	2.50
❑260, Jun 77	0.30	0.50	1.25	2.50
❑261, Jul 77	0.30	0.50	1.25	2.50
❑262, Aug 77, TD, Even An Immortal Can Die!	0.30	0.50	1.25	2.50
❑263, Sep 77	0.30	0.50	1.25	2.50
❑264, Oct 77	0.30	0.50	1.25	2.50
❑265, Nov 77	0.35	0.50	1.25	2.50
❑266, Dec 77	0.35	0.50	1.25	2.50
❑267, Jan 78	0.35	0.50	1.25	2.50
❑268, Feb 78	0.35	0.50	1.25	2.50
❑269, Mar 78	0.35	0.50	1.25	2.50
❑270, Apr 78	0.35	0.50	1.25	2.50
❑271, May 78, A: Iron Man	0.35	0.50	1.25	2.50
❑272, Jun 78	0.35	0.50	1.25	2.50
❑273, Jul 78, 1: Red Norvell	0.35	0.50	1.25	2.50
❑274, Aug 78, 1: Frigga; 1: Sigyn; D: Balder	0.35	0.50	1.25	2.50
❑275, Sep 78, 1: Hermod	0.35	0.50	1.25	2.50
❑276, Oct 78,Red Norvell named Thor	0.35	0.50	1.25	2.50
❑277, Nov 78	0.35	0.50	1.25	2.50
❑278, Dec 78	0.35	0.50	1.25	2.50

	ORIG	GOOD	FINE	N-MINT
❑279, Jan 79	0.35	0.50	1.25	2.50
❑280, Feb 79	0.35	0.50	1.25	2.50
❑281, Mar 79, A: Immortus	0.35	0.40	1.00	2.00
❑282, Apr 79	0.35	0.40	1.00	2.00
❑283, May 79, A: Celestials	0.40	0.40	1.00	2.00
❑284, Jun 79, A: Externals	0.40	0.40	1.00	2.00
❑285, Jul 79	0.40	0.40	1.00	2.00
❑286, Aug 79	0.40	0.40	1.00	2.00
❑287, Sep 79	0.40	0.40	1.00	2.00
❑288, Oct 79	0.40	0.40	1.00	2.00
❑289, Nov 79	0.40	0.40	1.00	2.00
❑290, Dec 79, V: El Toro Rojo	0.40	0.40	1.00	2.00
❑291, Jan 80	0.40	0.40	1.00	2.00
❑292, Feb 80	0.40	0.40	1.00	2.00
❑293, Mar 80	0.40	0.40	1.00	2.00
❑294, Apr 80, KP, O: Odin; O: Asgard; 1: Frey	0.40	0.40	1.00	2.00
❑295, May 80, KP	0.40	0.40	1.00	2.00
❑296, Jun 80, KP	0.40	0.40	1.00	2.00
❑297, Jul 80, KP ,Thor as Siegfried	0.40	0.40	1.00	2.00
❑298, Aug 80, KP	0.40	0.40	1.00	2.00
❑299, Sep 80, KP	0.50	0.40	1.00	2.00
❑300, Oct 80, KP, O: Odin; O: The Destroyer; D: Zuras (physical death),giant; Balder revived	0.75	1.00	2.50	5.00
❑301, Nov 80,Thor meets other pantheons	0.50	0.40	1.00	2.00
❑302, Dec 80	0.50	0.40	1.00	2.00
❑303, Jan 81	0.50	0.40	1.00	2.00
❑304, Feb 81, V: Wrecking Crew	0.50	0.40	1.00	2.00
❑305, Mar 81, KP, Hark, The Herald Angel Lives!	0.50	0.40	1.00	2.00
❑306, Apr 81, KP, Fury Of The Firelord!, O: Firelord; D: Air-Walker (real form)	0.50	0.40	1.00	2.00
❑307, May 81, Wings In The Night!	0.50	0.40	1.00	2.00
❑308, Jun 81, KP, The Snow Giant	0.50	0.40	1.00	2.00
❑309, Jul 81, Beware The Bombardiers!	0.50	0.40	1.00	2.00
❑310, Aug 81, V: Mephisto	0.50	0.40	1.00	2.00
❑311, Sep 81	0.50	0.40	1.00	2.00
❑312, Oct 81, KP, The Judgement Of Tyr, V: Tyr	0.50	0.40	1.00	2.00
❑313, Nov 81	0.50	0.40	1.00	2.00
❑314, Dec 81, KP, Acts Of Destruction, 1: Shawna Lynde	0.50	0.40	1.00	2.00
❑315, Jan 82, KP, The Thunderbolt God And The Bi-Beast	0.60	0.40	1.00	2.00
❑316, Feb 82	0.60	0.40	1.00	2.00
❑317, Mar 82, KP, Chaos At Canaveral	0.60	0.40	1.00	2.00
❑318, Apr 82, GK, A Kingdom Lost	0.60	0.40	1.00	2.00
❑319, May 82, KP, The Zaniac Craves Blood!	0.60	0.40	1.00	2.00
❑320, Jun 82, KP, Blake's Menagerie	0.60	0.40	1.00	2.00
❑321, Jul 82, Magick's Menace!	0.60	0.40	1.00	2.00
❑322, Aug 82, The Wrath And The Power!, D: Darkoth	0.60	0.40	1.00	2.00
❑323, Sep 82	0.60	0.40	1.00	2.00
❑324, Oct 82	0.60	0.40	1.00	2.00
❑325, Nov 82	0.60	0.40	1.00	2.00
❑326, Dec 82	0.60	0.40	1.00	2.00
❑327, Jan 83	0.60	0.40	1.00	2.00
❑328, Feb 83, 1: Megatak	0.60	0.40	1.00	2.00
❑329, Mar 83	0.60	0.40	1.00	2.00
❑330, Apr 83, BH, The Coming Of The Crusader!, 1: Crusader II (Arthur Blackwood)	0.60	0.40	1.00	2.00
❑331, May 83	0.60	0.40	1.00	2.00
❑332, Jun 83	0.60	0.40	1.00	2.00
❑333, Jul 83, ...Like A Bat Out Of Heaven, V: Dracula	0.60	0.40	1.00	2.00
❑334, Aug 83	0.60	0.40	1.00	2.00
❑335, Sep 83, Runequest's End!, 1: The Possessor	0.60	0.40	1.00	2.00
❑336, Oct 83, HT, Of Gods And Men	0.60	0.40	1.00	2.00
❑337, Nov 83, 1: Beta Ray Bill,1st Simonson Thor	0.60	0.80	2.00	4.00
❑338, Dec 83, A: Beta Ray Bill	0.60	0.60	1.50	3.00
❑339, Jan 84, 1: Lorelei; A: Beta Ray Bill	0.60	0.50	1.25	2.50
❑340, Feb 84, A: Beta Ray Bill	0.60	0.50	1.25	2.50
❑341, Mar 84, 1: Sigurd Jarlson	0.60	0.40	1.00	2.00
❑342, Apr 84	0.60	0.40	1.00	2.00
❑343, May 84	0.60	0.40	1.00	2.00
❑344, Jun 84, 1: Malekith the Dark Elf	0.60	0.40	1.00	2.00
❑345, Jul 84	0.60	0.40	1.00	2.00
❑346, Aug 84	0.60	0.40	1.00	2.00
❑347, Sep 84, 1: Algrim	0.60	0.40	1.00	2.00
❑348, Oct 84	0.60	0.40	1.00	2.00
❑349, Nov 84, O: Odin	0.60	0.40	1.00	2.00
❑350, Dec 84, A: Beta Ray Bill	0.60	0.40	1.00	2.00
❑351, Jan 85, A: Fantastic Four	0.60	0.40	1.00	2.00
❑352, Feb 85, A: Avengers; A: Beta Ray Bill; A: Fantastic Four	0.60	0.40	1.00	2.00

	ORIG	GOOD	FINE	N-MINT
❑353, Mar 85	0.60	0.40	1.00	2.00
❑354, Apr 85	0.65	0.40	1.00	2.00
❑355, May 85	0.65	0.40	1.00	2.00
❑356, Jun 85	0.65	0.40	1.00	2.00
❑357, Jul 85	0.65	0.40	1.00	2.00
❑358, Aug 85,Beta Ray Bill vs. Titanium Man	0.65	0.40	1.00	2.00
❑359, Sep 85, A: Loki; D: Megatak	0.65	0.40	1.00	2.00
❑360, Oct 85	0.65	0.40	1.00	2.00
❑361, Nov 85	0.65	0.40	1.00	2.00
❑362, Dec 85	0.65	0.40	1.00	2.00
❑363, Jan 86, Secret Wars II,Secret Wars II; Thor's face scarred	0.65	0.40	1.00	2.00
❑364, Feb 86	0.75	0.40	1.00	2.00
❑365, Mar 86,Thor turned into frog	0.75	0.40	1.00	2.00
❑366, Apr 86	0.75	0.40	1.00	2.00
❑367, May 86	0.75	0.40	1.00	2.00
❑368, Jun 86	0.75	0.40	1.00	2.00
❑369, Jul 86	0.75	0.40	1.00	2.00
❑370, Aug 86	0.75	0.40	1.00	2.00
❑371, Sep 86, A: Justice Peace	0.75	0.40	1.00	2.00
❑372, Oct 86	0.75	0.40	1.00	2.00
❑373, Nov 86,Mutant Massacre	0.75	0.40	1.00	2.00
❑374, Dec 86, Mutant Massacre, A: X-Factor,Mutant Massacre	0.75	0.60	1.50	3.00
❑375, Jan 87	0.75	0.40	1.00	2.00
❑376, Feb 87	0.75	0.40	1.00	2.00
❑377, Mar 87	0.75	0.40	1.00	2.00
❑378, Apr 87	0.75	0.40	1.00	2.00
❑379, May 87	0.75	0.40	1.00	2.00
❑380, Jun 87	0.75	0.40	1.00	2.00
❑381, Jul 87	0.75	0.30	0.75	1.50
❑382, Aug 87,300th Thor issue	1.25	0.40	1.00	2.00
❑383, Sep 87,Secret Wars II	0.75	0.30	0.75	1.50
❑384, Oct 87, 1: Dargo (future Thor)	0.75	0.30	0.75	1.50
❑385, Nov 87, A: Hulk	0.75	0.30	0.75	1.50
❑386, Dec 87, 1: Leir	0.75	0.30	0.75	1.50
❑387, Jan 88	0.75	0.30	0.75	1.50
❑388, Feb 88	0.75	0.30	0.75	1.50
❑389, Mar 88	0.75	0.30	0.75	1.50
❑390, Apr 88	0.75	0.30	0.75	1.50
❑391, May 88, A: Spider-Man; 1: Eric Masterson	0.75	0.40	1.00	2.00
❑392, Jun 88, 1: Quicksand	0.75	0.30	0.75	1.50
❑393, Jul 88	0.75	0.30	0.75	1.50
❑394, Aug 88	0.75	0.30	0.75	1.50
❑395, Sep 88, 1: Wind Warrior; 1: Earth-Lord	0.75	0.30	0.75	1.50
❑396, Oct 88	0.75	0.30	0.75	1.50
❑397, Nov 88	0.75	0.30	0.75	1.50
❑398, Dec 88, 1: Caber	0.75	0.30	0.75	1.50
❑399, Jan 89	0.75	0.30	0.75	1.50
❑400, Feb 89, A: Avengers; V: Seth and Surtur,giant	1.75	0.40	1.00	2.00
❑401, Mar 89	0.75	0.20	0.50	1.00
❑402, Apr 89	0.75	0.20	0.50	1.00
❑403, May 89	0.75	0.20	0.50	1.00
❑404, Jun 89	0.75	0.20	0.50	1.00
❑405, Jul 89	0.75	0.20	0.50	1.00
❑406, Aug 89	0.75	0.20	0.50	1.00
❑407, Sep 89	1.00	0.20	0.50	1.00
❑408, Oct 89,Eric Masterson absorbs Thor's essence; series continues as The Mighty Thor through #490	1.00	0.20	0.50	1.00
❑409, Nov 89,Title changes to The Mighty Thor	1.00	0.20	0.50	1.00
❑410, Nov 89	1.00	0.20	0.50	1.00
❑411, Dec 89, Acts of Vengeance, Part 4, 1: Chord; V: Juggernaut; 1: New Warriors (cameo); 1: New Warriors (cameo appearance); 1: Night Thrasher,Acts of Vengeance	1.00	0.60	1.50	3.00
❑412, Dec 89, Acts of Vengeance, Part 13, V: Juggernaut; 1: New Warriors (full appearance),Acts of Vengeance	1.00	0.40	1.00	2.00
❑413, Jan 90, Acts of Vengeance	1.00	0.20	0.50	1.00
❑414, Feb 90	1.00	0.20	0.50	1.00
❑415, Mar 90, O: Thor	1.00	0.20	0.50	1.00
❑416, Apr 90	1.00	0.20	0.50	1.00
❑417, May 90	1.00	0.20	0.50	1.00
❑418, Jun 90	1.00	0.20	0.50	1.00
❑419, Jul 90, 1: Black Galaxy; 1: Stellaris	1.00	0.20	0.50	1.00
❑420, Aug 90, Black Galaxy, 1: Nobilus (partial appearance); O: Nobilus	1.00	0.20	0.50	1.00
❑421, Aug 90, Black Galaxy	1.00	0.20	0.50	1.00
❑422, Sep 90, Black Galaxy, 1: Analyzer; O: Nobilus	1.00	0.20	0.50	1.00
❑423, Sep 90, Black Galaxy, 1: Nobilus (full appearance)	1.00	0.20	0.50	1.00
❑424, Oct 90, Black Galaxy	1.00	0.20	0.50	1.00

	ORIG	GOOD	FINE	N-MINT
❑425, Oct 90	1.00	0.20	0.50	1.00
❑426, Nov 90	1.00	0.20	0.50	1.00
❑427, Dec 90, A: Excalibur	1.00	0.20	0.50	1.00
❑428, Jan 91, A: Excalibur	1.00	0.20	0.50	1.00
❑429, Feb 91, A: Ghost Rider	1.00	0.20	0.50	1.00
❑430, Mar 91, A: Ghost Rider	1.00	0.20	0.50	1.00
❑431, Apr 91	1.00	0.20	0.50	1.00
❑432, May 91, JK, D: Loki; 1: Thor; 1: Thor II (Eric Masterson); A: 300th, Giant size	1.00	0.40	1.00	2.00
❑433, Jun 91	1.00	0.40	1.00	2.00
❑434, Jul 91	1.00	0.20	0.50	1.00
❑435, Aug 91	1.00	0.20	0.50	1.00
❑436, Sep 91	1.00	0.20	0.50	1.00
❑437, Oct 91	1.00	0.20	0.50	1.00
❑438, Nov 91, Thor War, Part 1, V: Zarrko	1.00	0.20	0.50	1.00
❑439, Nov 91, Thor War, Part 2	1.00	0.20	0.50	1.00
❑440, Dec 91, Thor War, Part 3, 1: Thor Corps (Dargo, Beta Ray Bill, Eric Masterson)	1.00	0.20	0.50	1.00
❑441, Dec 91, Thor War, Part 4	1.00	0.20	0.50	1.00
❑442, Jan 92, Return of Don Blake	1.00	0.20	0.50	1.00
❑443, Jan 92, A: Silver Surfer; A: Doctor Strange; V: Mephisto	1.00	0.20	0.50	1.00
❑444, Feb 92	1.25	0.25	0.63	1.25
❑445, Mar 92, Operation: Galactic Storm, Part 7, V: Gladiator, Galactic Storm	1.25	0.25	0.63	1.25
❑446, Apr 92, Operation: Galactic Storm, Part 14, A: Avengers, Galactic Storm	1.25	0.25	0.63	1.25
❑447, May 92, A: Absorbing Man; A: Spider-Man	1.25	0.25	0.63	1.25
❑448, Jun 92, A: Spider-Man	1.25	0.25	0.63	1.25
❑449, Jul 92, 1: Bloodaxe	1.25	0.25	0.63	1.25
❑450, Aug 92, O: Loki, Giant-size anniversary special	2.50	0.50	1.25	2.50
❑451, Sep 92, V: Bloodaxe	1.25	0.25	0.63	1.25
❑452, Oct 92	1.25	0.25	0.63	1.25
❑453	1.25	0.25	0.63	1.25
❑454	1.25	0.25	0.63	1.25
❑455	1.25	0.25	0.63	1.25
❑456	1.25	0.25	0.63	1.25
❑457, Final Gauntlet!, Original Thor returns	1.25	0.25	0.63	1.25
❑458	1.25	0.25	0.63	1.25
❑459	1.25	0.25	0.63	1.25
❑460, JSn (w), Fragments, Painted cover	1.25	0.25	0.63	1.25
❑461	1.25	0.25	0.63	1.25
❑462	1.25	0.25	0.63	1.25
❑463, Jun 93	1.25	0.25	0.63	1.25
❑464, Jul 93	1.25	0.25	0.63	1.25
❑465, Aug 93	1.25	0.25	0.63	1.25
❑466, Sep 93	1.25	0.25	0.63	1.25
❑467, Oct 93, A: Pluto; A: Valkyrie; A: Lady Sif, Infinity Crusade crossover	1.25	0.25	0.63	1.25
❑468, Nov 93	1.25	0.25	0.63	1.25
❑469, Dec 93	1.25	0.25	0.63	1.25
❑470, Jan 94	1.25	0.25	0.63	1.25
❑471, Feb 94, Blood and Thunder; Blood and Thunder, Part 13	1.25	0.25	0.63	1.25
❑472, Mar 94	1.25	0.25	0.63	1.25
❑473, Apr 94	1.25	0.25	0.63	1.25
❑474, May 94	1.50	0.30	0.75	1.50
❑475, Jun 94, Survival Of The Fiercest, O: Thor, Giant-size	2.00	0.40	1.00	2.00
❑475/SC, Jun 94, Survival Of The Fiercest, O: Thor, foil cover; Giant-size	2.50	0.50	1.25	2.50
❑476, Jul 94	1.50	0.30	0.75	1.50
❑477, Aug 94	1.50	0.30	0.75	1.50
❑478, Sep 94, A: Red Norvell	1.50	0.30	0.75	1.50
❑479, Oct 94	1.50	0.30	0.75	1.50
❑480, Nov 94	1.50	0.30	0.75	1.50
❑481, Dec 94, V: Grotesk	1.50	0.30	0.75	1.50
❑482, Jan 95, Giant-size	2.95	0.59	1.48	2.95
❑483, Feb 95	1.50	0.30	0.75	1.50
❑484, Mar 95	1.50	0.30	0.75	1.50
❑485, Apr 95	1.50	0.30	0.75	1.50
❑486, May 95	1.50	0.30	0.75	1.50
❑487, Jun 95	1.50	0.30	0.75	1.50
❑488, Jul 95	1.50	0.30	0.75	1.50
❑489, Aug 95, V: Hulk	1.50	0.30	0.75	1.50
❑490, Sep 95, V: Absorbing Man	1.50	0.30	0.75	1.50
❑491, Oct 95, Title returns to Thor	1.50	0.30	0.75	1.50
❑492, Nov 95, A: Enchantress	1.50	0.30	0.75	1.50
❑493, Dec 95, A: Enchantress	1.50	0.30	0.75	1.50
❑494, Jan 96	1.50	0.30	0.75	1.50
❑495, Feb 96	1.50	0.30	0.75	1.50
❑496, Mar 96, First Sign; First Sign, Part 2, A: Captain America	1.50	0.30	0.75	1.50
❑497, Apr 96, Thor Must Die	1.50	0.30	0.75	1.50
❑498, May 96	1.50	0.30	0.75	1.50

Thor acquired a new civilian identity, a New York paramedic, in the first issue of *Thor* (Vol. 2).

	ORIG	GOOD	FINE	N-MINT
❑499, Jun 96	1.50	0.30	0.75	1.50
❑500, Jul 96, wraparound cover; Giant-size	2.50	0.50	1.25	2.50
❑501, Aug 96, A: Red Norvell	1.50	0.30	0.75	1.50
❑502, Sep 96, O: Thor	1.50	0.30	0.75	1.50
❑Anl 2, JK, SL (w), If Asgard Falls...; Defying the Magic of Mad Merlin!, Cover reads "King Size Special"; reprints from Journey into Mystery #96 and #103	0.25	9.00	22.50	45.00
❑Anl 3, Jan 71, JK, A World Gone Mad!; Balder Must Die!, A: Absorbing Man; A: Grey Gargoyle, reprints Thor stories from Journey into Mystery #113 and #114; reprints Tales of Asgard from Journey into Mystery #107-110	0.25	2.00	5.00	10.00
❑Anl 4, JK, Reprint; Cover reads "King Size Special"	0.25	1.80	4.50	9.00
❑Anl 5, JK; JB, 1: Apollo	0.50	1.50	3.75	7.50
❑Anl 6, JK; JB	0.50	1.50	3.75	7.50
❑Anl 7	0.60	1.50	3.75	7.50
❑Anl 8	0.75	1.20	3.00	6.00
❑Anl 9, LMc, The Great Game!	0.75	0.70	1.75	3.50
❑Anl 10, BH, A Time To Die!, 1: Yama; O: Chthon; 1: Erishkegal; 1: Ahpuch	1.00	0.70	1.75	3.50
❑Anl 11	1.00	0.70	1.75	3.50
❑Anl 12, 1: Vidar	1.00	0.70	1.75	3.50
❑Anl 13, V: Mephisto	1.25	0.60	1.50	3.00
❑Anl 14, Atlantis Attacks, Part 13, Title changes to The Mighty Thor Annual	2.00	0.50	1.25	2.50
❑Anl 15, The Terminus Factor, Part 3, O: Terminus	2.00	0.50	1.25	2.50
❑Anl 16, Korvac Quest; Korvac Quest, Part 2	2.50	0.50	1.25	2.50
❑Anl 17, Citizen Kang, Part 2; The Ten Most Heinous Enemies of the Mighty Thor, Citizen Kang	2.25	0.50	1.25	2.50
❑Anl 18, trading card	2.95	0.59	1.48	2.95
❑Anl 19	2.95	0.59	1.48	2.95
❑GS 1	0.50	1.00	2.50	5.00

THOR (VOL. 2)
MARVEL

	ORIG	GOOD	FINE	N-MINT
❑1, JR2, Giant-size	3.50	0.70	1.75	3.50
❑1/A, Jul 98, JR2, sketch cover; gatefold summary	2.99	4.00	10.00	20.00
❑1/B, Jul 98, JR2, Sunburst cover; gatefold summary	2.99	1.00	2.50	5.00
❑1/C, JR2, DFE alternate cover	10.00	1.00	2.50	5.00
❑1/D, JR2, DFE alternate cover; Signed by Dan Jurgens and John Romita Jr.	24.95	1.60	4.00	8.00
❑2, Aug 98, JR2, gatefold summary; Thor receives new mortal identity	1.99	0.50	1.25	2.50
❑2/A, JR2, variant cover	1.99	0.50	1.25	2.50
❑3, Sep 98, JR2, V: Sedna, gatefold summary	1.99	0.40	1.00	2.00
❑4, Oct 98, JR2, A: Namor, gatefold summary	1.99	0.40	1.00	2.00
❑5, Nov 98, JR2, gatefold summary	1.99	0.40	1.00	2.00
❑6, Dec 98, JR2, A: Hercules, gatefold summary	1.99	0.40	1.00	2.00
❑7, Jan 99, JR2, A: Hercules, gatefold summary	1.99	0.40	1.00	2.00
❑8, Feb 99, JR2, A: Spider-Man, gatefold summary; concludes in Peter Parker; Spider-Man #2	1.99	0.40	1.00	2.00
❑9, Mar 99, JB	1.99	0.40	1.00	2.00
❑10, Apr 99, JR2, V: Perrikus	1.99	0.40	1.00	2.00
❑11, May 99, A: Volstagg; V: Perrikus	1.99	0.40	1.00	1.99
❑12, Jun 99, A: Replicus; V: Perrikus; A: Warriors Three; A: Destroyer; A: Hercules, wraparound cover	2.99	0.60	1.50	2.99
❑13, Jul 99, V: Marnot	1.99	0.40	1.00	1.99
❑14, Aug 99, V: Absorbing Man; A: Iron Man	1.99	0.40	1.00	1.99
❑15, Sep 99, A: Warriors Three	1.99	0.40	1.00	1.99
❑16, Oct 99	1.99	0.40	1.00	1.99
❑17, Nov 99, The Eighth Day	1.99	0.40	1.00	1.99
❑18, Dec 99	1.99	0.40	1.00	1.99
❑19, Jan 00	1.99	0.40	1.00	1.99
❑20, Feb 00	—	0.45	1.13	2.25

	ORIG	GOOD	FINE	N-MINT
❑21, Mar 00	—	0.45	1.13	2.25
❑22, Apr 00	—	0.45	1.13	2.25
❑23, May 00	—	0.45	1.13	2.25
❑24, Jun 00	—	0.45	1.13	2.25
❑25, Jul 00	—	0.45	1.13	2.25
❑26, Aug 00	—	0.45	1.13	2.25
❑27, Sep 00	—	0.45	1.13	2.25
❑28, Oct 00	2.25	0.45	1.13	2.25
❑29, Nov 00, Whence Comes Death, A: Wrecking Crew	2.25	0.45	1.13	2.25
❑30, Dec 00, Maximum Security; Winter's Edge, A: Beta Ray Bill; A: Malekith	2.25	0.45	1.13	2.25
❑31, Jan 01	2.25	0.45	1.13	2.25
❑32, Feb 01, Forever Kursed,100pgs.	3.50	0.70	1.75	3.50
❑33, Mar 01, The Million Dollar Debut of Thor Girl!, 1: Thor Girl	2.25	0.45	1.13	2.25
❑34, Apr 01, Man of Tomorrow, A: Gladiator	2.25	0.45	1.13	2.25
❑35, May 01, Across All Worlds, A: Gladiator	2.99	0.60	1.50	2.99
❑36	2.25	0.45	1.13	2.25
❑37	2.25	0.45	1.13	2.25
❑38	2.25	0.45	1.13	2.25
❑39	2.25	0.45	1.13	2.25
❑Anl 1999, Mar 99, Tears of a God, V: Doom,wraparound cover; set between Heroes Reborn and Heroes Return	3.50	0.70	1.75	3.50
❑Anl 2001, When Fall the Gods!, A: Beta Ray Bill; A: Hercules	3.50	0.70	1.75	3.50

THOR CORPS
MARVEL

Value: Cover or less

❑1, Sep 93, A Gathering Of Heroes-! 1.75
❑2, Oct 93, Gather Chaos!, A: Machine Man 2020; A: Invaders; A: Franklin Richards; A: Midnight Wreckers 1.75
❑3, Nov 93 .... 1.75
❑4, Dec 93 .... 1.75

THORION OF THE NEW ASGODS
MARVEL

Value: Cover or less

❑1, Jun 97, JR2, KG (w), Thorion The Hunter! 1.95

THORR-SVERD
VINCENT

Value: Cover or less

❑1, b&w 1.00
❑2, b&w 1.00
❑3, b&w 1.00

THOR: THE LEGEND
MARVEL

Value: Cover or less

❑1, Sep 96,wraparound cover; One-Shot; information on Thor's career and supporting cast.. 3.95

THOSE ANNOYING POST BROS.
VORTEX

	ORIG	GOOD	FINE	N-MINT
❑1, Dopplekiller; Bugtown Is Anywhere It Wants to Be!	1.75	0.60	1.50	3.00
❑2	1.75	0.40	1.00	2.00
❑3	1.75	0.40	1.00	2.00
❑4, Consummation Day	1.75	0.40	1.00	2.00
❑5	1.75	0.40	1.00	2.00
❑6	1.75	0.40	1.00	2.00
❑7	1.75	0.40	1.00	2.00
❑8	1.75	0.40	1.00	2.00
❑9	1.75	0.40	1.00	2.00
❑10	1.75	0.40	1.00	2.00
❑11	1.75	0.40	1.00	2.00
❑12	1.75	0.40	1.00	2.00
❑13	1.75	0.40	1.00	2.00
❑14	1.75	0.40	1.00	2.00
❑15	2.00	0.40	1.00	2.00
❑16	2.00	0.40	1.00	2.00
❑17	2.00	0.40	1.00	2.00
❑18,Series continues as Post Brothers	2.00	0.40	1.00	2.00
❑39, Aug 94, b&w; Series continued from "Post Brothers" #38	2.50	0.50	1.25	2.50
❑40, Oct 94, b&w	2.50	0.50	1.25	2.50
❑41, Dec 94, b&w	2.50	0.50	1.25	2.50
❑42, Feb 95, b&w	2.50	0.50	1.25	2.50
❑43, Jun 95, Turf, b&w	2.50	0.50	1.25	2.50
❑44, Jul 95, b&w	2.50	0.50	1.25	2.50
❑45, Aug 95, b&w	2.95	0.50	1.25	2.50
❑46, Oct 95, b&w	2.95	0.50	1.25	2.50
❑47, Nov 95, b&w	2.95	0.50	1.25	2.50
❑48, Feb 96, b&w	2.95	0.50	1.25	2.50
❑Anl 1, Aug 95, b&w; cardstock cover	4.95	0.99	2.47	4.95

THOSE CRAZY PECKERS
U.S.COMICS

Value: Cover or less

❑1, Feb 87, Hard Days Night .. 2.00

THOSE UNSTOPPABLE ROGUES
ORIGINAL SYNDICATE

Value: Cover or less

❑1, Mar 95 .... 3.95

THRAX
EVENT

Value: Cover or less

❑1, Nov 96, Hardwired for Action 2.95
❑2 .... 2.95

THREAT!
FANTAGRAPHICS

Value: Cover or less

❑1, b&w 2.25
❑2 .... 2.25
❑3 .... 2.25
❑4 .... 2.25
❑5 .... 2.25
❑6 .... 2.25
❑7 .... 2.25
❑8, Jan 87, Zone: As the Crow Flies; The Holo Brothers: Blue Brawls 2.25
❑9 .... 2.25
❑10 .... 2.25

THREE
INVINCIBLE

Value: Cover or less

❑1, Love; City of Assassins, Part 1 .... 2.00
❑2 .... 2.00
❑3 .... 2.00
❑4, City of Assassins-Chapter 4; Griffons 2.00

THREE MUSKETEERS (ETERNITY)
ETERNITY

Value: Cover or less

❑1, b&w 1.95
❑2, b&w 1.95
❑3, b&w 1.95

THREE MUSKETEERS (MARVEL)
MARVEL

Value: Cover or less

❑1,movie Adaptation 1.50
❑2,movie Adaptation 1.50

THREE STOOGES IN 3-D
ETERNITY

Value: Cover or less

❑1 .... 3.95

THREE STOOGES IN FULL COLOR
ETERNITY

Value: Cover or less

❑1,Reprint 5.95

THRESHOLD (1ST SERIES)
SLEEPING GIANT

Value: Cover or less

❑1, Oct 96, b&w 2.50
❑2, Nov 96, b&w; Final Issue .. 2.50

THRESHOLD (2ND SERIES)
SLEEPING GIANT

Value: Cover or less

❑1, Dec 97, Nico-Teen, b&w ... 2.50
❑2, Mar 98, The Hair Club, b&w 2.50
❑3, The Demolition 2.50
❑3/Aut, The Demolition,Signed by David Yurkovich 2.50

THRESHOLD (3RD SERIES)
AVATAR

Value: Cover or less

❑1 .... 4.95
❑2 .... 4.95
❑3 .... 4.95
❑4, Donna Mia; Black Reign ... 4.95
❑5 .... 4.95
❑6 .... 4.95
❑7 .... 4.95
❑8 .... 4.95
❑9 .... 4.95
❑10 .... 4.95
❑11 .... 4.95
❑12 .... 4.95
❑13 .... 4.95
❑14 .... 4.95
❑15 .... 4.95
❑16 .... 4.95
❑17 .... 4.95
❑18 .... 4.95
❑19 .... 4.95
❑20 .... 4.95
❑21 .... 4.95
❑22 .... 4.95
❑23 .... 4.95
❑24 .... 4.95
❑25 .... 4.95
❑26 .... 4.95
❑27 .... 4.95
❑28 .... 4.95
❑29 .... 4.95
❑30 .... 4.95
❑31 .... 4.95
❑32 .... 4.95
❑33 .... 4.95
❑34 .... 4.95
❑35 .... 4.95
❑36 .... 4.95
❑37 .... 4.95
❑38 .... 4.95
❑39 .... 4.95
❑40 .... 4.95
❑41 .... 4.95
❑42 .... 4.95

THRESHOLD OF REALITY
MAINTECH

Value: Cover or less

❑1, Sep 86 .... 1.00
❑2 .... 1.00
❑3 .... 1.00

THRESHOLD: THE STAMP COLLECTOR
SLEEPING GIANT

Value: Cover or less

❑1, Mar 97, b&w 2.50
❑2, May 97, b&w 2.50

THRILLER
DC

	ORIG	GOOD	FINE	N-MINT
❑1, Nov 83, TVE, TVE (c), Downtime, Part 1	1.25	0.40	1.00	2.00
❑2, Dec 83, O: Thriller	1.25	0.35	0.88	1.75
❑3, Jan 84	1.25	0.35	0.88	1.75
❑4, Feb 84	1.25	0.30	0.75	1.50
❑5, Mar 84,Elvis satire	1.25	0.30	0.75	1.50
❑6, Apr 84,Elvis satire	1.25	0.30	0.75	1.50
❑7, May 84	1.25	0.30	0.75	1.50
❑8, Jun 84	1.25	0.30	0.75	1.50
❑9, Jul 84	1.25	0.30	0.75	1.50

	ORIG	GOOD	FINE	N-MINT
❑10, Aug 84	1.25	0.30	0.75	1.50
❑11, Sep 84	1.25	0.30	0.75	1.50
❑12, Oct 84	1.25	0.30	0.75	1.50

THRILLING ADVENTURE STORIES
ATLAS

	ORIG	GOOD	FINE	N-MINT
❑1, Feb 75, RH; EC; FT, RH (w), Tigerman and the Flesh Peddlers; The Sting of Death, b&w; magazine	0.75	1.00	2.50	5.00
❑2, Aug 75	0.75	0.80	2.00	4.00

THRILLING ADVENTURE STRIPS
DRAGON LADY
Value: Cover or less

- ❑5,(formerly Best of Tribune Company) ... 2.95
- ❑6 ... 2.95
- ❑7 ... 2.95
- ❑8 ... 2.95
- ❑9 ... 2.95
- ❑10 ... 2.95

THRILLING COMICS (2ND SERIES)
DC

	ORIG	GOOD	FINE	N-MINT
❑1, May 99, RH, No More Tomorrows, A: Hawkman; A: Tigress; A: Wildcat,Manhunter apperance	1.99	0.40	1.00	2.00

THRILL KILL
CALIBER
Value: Cover or less

- ❑1, b&w ... 2.50

THRILLKILLER
DC
Value: Cover or less

- ❑1, Jan 97, HC (w),Elseworlds story ... 2.50
- ❑2, Feb 97, HC (w),Elseworlds story ... 2.50
- ❑3, Mar 97, HC (w),Elseworlds story ... 2.50

THRILLKILLER '62
DC
Value: Cover or less

- ❑1, nn; One-Shot; prestige format; Elseworlds; sequel to Thrillkiller ... 4.95

THRILLOGY
PACIFIC
Value: Cover or less

- ❑1, Prometheus Primeval; All That Glitters... ... 1.50

THUMB SCREW
CALIBER
Value: Cover or less

- ❑1, b&w ... 3.50
- ❑2, b&w ... 3.50

THUMP'N GUTS
KITCHEN SINK
Value: Cover or less

- ❑1,Poly-bag reads Project X, includes poster and trading card ... 2.95

THUN'DA, KING OF THE CONGO
AC
Value: Cover or less

- ❑1, b&w; Reprint ... 2.50

THUN'DA TALES (FRANK FRAZETTA'S...)
FANTAGRAPHICS
Value: Cover or less

- ❑1, FF, King of the Lost Lands; The Monsters from the Mists, O: Thun'da ... 2.00

T.H.U.N.D.E.R.
SOLSON
Value: Cover or less

- ❑1, Rumble! ... 1.95

THUNDER AGENTS
TOWER

	ORIG	GOOD	FINE	N-MINT
❑1, Nov 65, WW, Dynamo, 1: NoMan; 1: Menthor; 1: The THUNDER Squad; 1: Iron Maiden; 1: Dynamo	0.25	22.00	55.00	110.00
❑2, Jan 66, WW, 1: Lightning; D: Egghead..	0.25	13.00	32.50	65.00
❑3, Mar 66, WW	0.25	9.00	22.50	45.00
❑4, Apr 66, WW, O: Lightning	0.25	8.00	20.00	40.00
❑5, Jun 66, WW	0.25	8.00	20.00	40.00
❑6, Jul 66, WW	0.25	6.00	15.00	30.00
❑7, Aug 66, WW, D: Menthor	0.25	6.00	15.00	30.00
❑8, Sep 66, WW, 1: Raven	0.25	6.00	15.00	30.00
❑9, Oct 66	0.25	4.80	12.00	24.00
❑10, Nov 66	0.25	4.80	12.00	24.00
❑11, Mar 67, WW	0.25	5.20	13.00	26.00
❑12, Apr 67, WW	0.25	5.20	13.00	26.00
❑13, Jun 67, WW, A: Undersea Agent	0.25	5.20	13.00	26.00
❑14, Jul 67, WW	0.25	5.20	13.00	26.00
❑15, Sep 67, WW	0.25	5.20	13.00	26.00
❑16, Oct 67, WW	0.25	3.00	7.50	15.00
❑17, Dec 67, WW	0.25	3.00	7.50	15.00
❑18, Sep 68, WW	0.25	3.00	7.50	15.00
❑19, Nov 68, WW	0.25	3.00	7.50	15.00
❑20, Jan 66, WW, O: Dynamo,Reprint; Final Issue	0.25	2.00	5.00	10.00

T.H.U.N.D.E.R. AGENTS (VOL. 2)
J.C.

	ORIG	GOOD	FINE	N-MINT
❑1, May 83, The Invasion Begins	1.00	0.40	1.00	2.00
❑2, Jan 84	1.00	0.40	1.00	2.00

A selection of Frank Frazetta's Golden Age work on *Thun'da* was reprinted by Fantagraphics as *Frank Frazetta's Thun'da Tales.*

© 1989 Frank Frazetta (Fantagraphics)

THUNDER AGENTS (WALLY WOOD'S...)
DELUXE
Value: Cover or less

- ❑1, Nov 84, DC; GP; KG ... 2.00
- ❑2, Jan 85, DC; GP; KG ... 2.00
- ❑3, Nov 85, DC; GP; KG ... 2.00
- ❑4, Feb 86, DC; GP; KG ... 2.00
- ❑5, Oct 86, JOy; KG ... 2.00

THUNDERBOLT
CHARLTON

	ORIG	GOOD	FINE	N-MINT
❑1, Jan 66, 1: Thunderbolt	0.12	3.20	8.00	16.00
❑51, Mar 66,Series continues after hiatus (Son of Vulcan #50?)	0.12	2.00	5.00	10.00
❑52, Jun 66	0.12	1.80	4.50	9.00
❑53, Aug 66	0.12	1.80	4.50	9.00
❑54, Oct 66, This One's for Tabu!; Behold...The Sentinels	0.12	1.80	4.50	9.00
❑55, Dec 66	0.12	1.80	4.50	9.00
❑56, Feb 67	0.12	1.80	4.50	9.00
❑57, May 67	0.12	1.80	4.50	9.00
❑58, Jul 67	0.12	1.80	4.50	9.00
❑59, Sep 67	0.12	1.80	4.50	9.00
❑60, Nov 67,Final Issue	0.12	1.80	4.50	9.00

THUNDERBOLTS
MARVEL

	ORIG	GOOD	FINE	N-MINT
❑-1, Jul 97, KB (w), Distant Rumblings!, A: Namor; A: Baron Zemo,Flashback	1.99	0.40	1.00	2.00
❑0, KB (w), A Rare Niight Off,Free	—	0.20	0.50	1.00
❑1, Apr 97, KB (w), Justice...Like Lightning!, Giant-size; Identities of Thunderbolts revealed	2.99	0.80	2.00	4.00
❑2, May 97, KB (w), Deceiving Appearances, V: Mad Thinker	1.99	0.60	1.50	3.00
❑3, Jun 97, KB (w)	1.99	0.60	1.50	3.00
❑4, Jul 97, KB (w), 1: Jolt,Jolt joins team; 1st appearace of Jolt	1.99	0.50	1.25	2.50
❑5, Aug 97, KB (w), gatefold summary; Atlas vs. Growing Man	1.99	0.50	1.25	2.50
❑6, Sep 97, KB (w), gatefold summary	1.99	0.40	1.00	2.00
❑7, Oct 97, KB (w), V: Elements of Doom, gatefold summary	1.99	0.40	1.00	2.00
❑8, Nov 97, KB (w), gatefold summary	1.99	0.40	1.00	2.00
❑9, Dec 97, KB (w), A: Black Widow, gatefold summary	1.99	0.40	1.00	2.00
❑10, Jan 98, KB (w), gatefold summary; Thunderbolts revealed as Masters of Evil	1.99	0.40	1.00	2.00
❑11, Feb 98, KB (w), gatefold summary	1.99	0.40	1.00	2.00
❑12, Mar 98, KB (w), A: Avengers; A: Fantastic Four,wraparound cover; gatefold summary	2.99	1.20	3.00	6.00
❑13, Apr 98, KB (w), gatefold summary	1.99	0.40	1.00	2.00
❑14, May 98, KB (w), gatefold summary	1.99	0.40	1.00	2.00
❑15, Jun 98, KB (w), gatefold summary	1.99	0.40	1.00	2.00
❑16, Jul 98, KB (w), Thunder & Lightning, V: Lightning Rods (formerly Great Lakes Avengers), gatefold summary	1.99	0.40	1.00	2.00
❑17, Aug 98, KB (w), V: Graviton, gatefold summary	1.99	0.40	1.00	2.00
❑18, Sep 98, KB (w), gatefold summary	1.99	0.40	1.00	2.00
❑19, Oct 98, KB (w), 1: Charcoal, gatefold summary	1.99	0.40	1.00	2.00
❑20, Nov 98, KB (w), V: new Masters of Evil, gatefold summary	1.99	0.40	1.00	2.00
❑21, Dec 98, KB (w), A: Hawkeye, gatefold summary	1.99	0.40	1.00	2.00
❑22, Jan 99, KB (w), gatefold summary; Hercules vs. Atlas	1.99	0.40	1.00	2.00
❑23, Feb 99, KB (w), A: U.S. Agent	1.99	0.40	1.00	2.00
❑24, Mar 99, KB (w), The Eye of the Storm, A: Citizen V	1.99	0.40	1.00	2.00
❑25, Apr 99, KB (w), V: Masters of Evil,wraparound cover; double-sized	2.99	0.60	1.50	2.99
❑25/Aut, KB (w), A: Masters of Evil,Signed by Mark Bagley	—	2.40	6.00	12.00
❑26, May 99,Mach-1 in prison	1.99	0.40	1.00	1.99
❑27, Jun 99, A: Archangel	1.99	0.40	1.00	1.99
❑28, Jul 99, A: Archangel; V: Graviton	1.99	0.40	1.00	1.99

	ORIG	GOOD	FINE	N-MINT
❑29, Aug 99, A: Machine Man; V: Graviton	1.99	0.40	1.00	1.99
❑30, Sep 99,Hawkeye and Moonstone caught in clinch	1.99	0.40	1.00	1.99
❑31, Oct 99	1.99	0.40	1.00	1.99
❑32, Nov 99	1.99	0.40	1.00	1.99
❑33, Dec 99	1.99	0.40	1.00	1.99
❑34, Jan 00	1.99	0.40	1.00	1.99
❑35, Feb 00	—	0.45	1.13	2.25
❑36, Mar 00	—	0.45	1.13	2.25
❑37, Apr 00	—	0.45	1.13	2.25
❑38, May 00	—	0.45	1.13	2.25
❑39, Jun 00	—	0.45	1.13	2.25
❑40, Jul 00	—	0.45	1.13	2.25
❑41, Aug 00, Tug of War!, A: Sandman	2.25	0.45	1.13	2.25
❑42, Sep 00, Two Ships, A: Wonder Man	2.25	0.45	1.13	2.25
❑43, Oct 00, Chasing Your Own Tail!, A: Black Widow	2.25	0.45	1.13	2.25
❑44, Nov 00, Keeping an Ion the Crowd!, A: Avengers; A: Nefaria	2.25	0.45	1.13	2.25
❑45, Dec 00, Maximum Security; Heroic Tendencies, Part 1: The Inside Job	2.25	0.45	1.13	2.25
❑46, Jan 01, Heroic Tendencies, Part 2: Heart and Soul,return of Jolt	2.25	0.45	1.13	2.25
❑47, Feb 01, Heroic Tendencies, Part 3: Big Problems!, A: Captain Marvel	2.25	0.45	1.13	2.25
❑48, Mar 01, Revelations! The Beginning of the End	2.25	0.45	1.13	2.25
❑49, Apr 01, Explanations! The End of the Beginning	2.25	0.45	1.13	2.25
❑50, May 01, Redemption?, A: Citizen V, double-sized	2.99	0.60	1.50	2.99
❑51	2.25	0.45	1.13	2.25
❑52	2.25	0.45	1.13	2.25
❑53	2.25	0.45	1.13	2.25
❑54	2.25	0.45	1.13	2.25
❑Anl 1997, KB (w), O: Thunderbolts,wrap-around cover; 1997 Annual	2.99	0.60	1.50	3.00
❑Ash 1,Ashcan preview; American Entertainment	—	0.50	1.25	2.50
❑Ash 1/Aut,Signed by Mark Bagley; Ashcan preview	—	0.80	2.00	4.00

THUNDERBUNNY (1ST SERIES)
ARCHIE

	ORIG	GOOD	FINE	N-MINT
❑1, Jan 84, Rabbit Trapped!	1.00	0.40	1.00	2.00

THUNDERBUNNY (2ND SERIES)
WARP

	ORIG	GOOD	FINE	N-MINT
❑1, Jun 85, O: retold,Warp publishes	1.50	0.40	1.00	2.00
❑2, Aug 85	1.50	0.40	1.00	2.00
❑3, Oct 85	1.50	0.40	1.00	2.00
❑4, Dec 85	1.50	0.40	1.00	2.00
❑5, Feb 86	1.50	0.40	1.00	2.00
❑6, Thunderbunny Vs. Thunderrabbit, b&w; Apple begins publishing	1.50	0.40	1.00	2.00
❑7, b&w	1.50	0.40	1.00	2.00
❑8	1.75	0.35	0.88	1.75
❑9	1.75	0.35	0.88	1.75
❑10, Jul 87	1.75	0.35	0.88	1.75
❑11, Sep 87, A: THUNDER Agents	1.75	0.35	0.88	1.75
❑12, Nov 87,last	1.75	0.35	0.88	1.75

THUNDERCATS
MARVEL

	ORIG	GOOD	FINE	N-MINT
❑1	0.65	0.50	1.25	2.50
❑2	0.65	0.30	0.75	1.50
❑3	0.75	0.30	0.75	1.50
❑4	0.75	0.30	0.75	1.50
❑5	0.75	0.30	0.75	1.50
❑6	0.75	0.30	0.75	1.50
❑7	0.75	0.20	0.50	1.00
❑8	0.75	0.20	0.50	1.00
❑9	0.75	0.20	0.50	1.00
❑10	0.75	0.20	0.50	1.00
❑11	1.00	0.20	0.50	1.00
❑12	1.00	0.20	0.50	1.00
❑13	1.00	0.20	0.50	1.00
❑14	1.00	0.20	0.50	1.00
❑15	1.00	0.20	0.50	1.00
❑16	1.00	0.20	0.50	1.00
❑17	1.00	0.20	0.50	1.00
❑18	1.00	0.20	0.50	1.00
❑19	1.00	0.20	0.50	1.00
❑20	1.00	0.20	0.50	1.00
❑21	1.00	0.20	0.50	1.00
❑22	1.00	0.20	0.50	1.00
❑23	1.00	0.20	0.50	1.00
❑24,Final Issue	1.00	0.20	0.50	1.00

THUNDER GIRLS
PIN & INK PRESS

Value: Cover or less

- ❑1, Sum 97 .... 2.95
- ❑2, Sum 99 .... 2.95
- ❑3, Fal 99 .... 2.95

THUNDERGOD
CRUSADE

Value: Cover or less

- ❑1, Aug 96, b&w 2.95
- ❑2, Oct 96, b&w 2.95
- ❑3, Dec 96, b&w 2.95

THUNDERMACE
RAK

	ORIG	GOOD	FINE	N-MINT
❑1, Mar 86, Origin, b&w	1.50	0.40	1.00	2.00
❑2	1.75	0.35	0.88	1.75
❑3	1.75	0.35	0.88	1.75
❑4	1.75	0.35	0.88	1.75
❑5	2.00	0.40	1.00	2.00
❑6	2.00	0.40	1.00	2.00
❑7	2.00	0.40	1.00	2.00

THUNDERSAURS: THE BODACIOUS ADVENTURES OF BIFF THUNDERSAUR
INNOVATION

Value: Cover or less

- ❑1, b&w 2.75

THUNDERSKULL! (SIDNEY MELLON'S...)
SLAVE LABOR

Value: Cover or less

- ❑1, Aug 89, b&w 1.95

THUNDERSTRIKE
MARVEL

Value: Cover or less

- ❑1, Jun 93, Blood Without Glory!, 1: Carjack; A: Bloodaxe,Prism cover 2.95
- ❑2, Nov 93 .... 1.25
- ❑3, Dec 93 .... 1.25
- ❑4, Jan 94 .... 1.25
- ❑5, Feb 94 .... 1.25
- ❑6, Mar 94 .... 1.25
- ❑7, Apr 94 .... 1.25
- ❑8, May 94 .... 1.50
- ❑9, Jun 94 .... 1.50
- ❑10, Jul 94, A: Thor 1.50
- ❑11, Aug 94 .... 1.50
- ❑12, Sep 94 .... 1.50
- ❑13 .... 1.50
- ❑13/A, Oct 94 .... 1.50
- ❑13/B, Oct 94,flip-book with Code Blue back-up; second indicia gives title as Marvel Double Feature ... Thunderstrike/Code Blue 2.50
- ❑14, Home-Wrecker; Up From Below 1.50
- ❑14/A, Nov 94 .... 1.50
- ❑14/B, Nov 94,flip-book with Code Blue back-up; second indicia gives title as Marvel Double Feature ... Thunderstrike/Code Blue 2.50
- ❑15 .... 1.50
- ❑15/A, Dec 94 .... 1.50
- ❑15/B, Dec 94,flip-book with Code Blue back-up; second indicia gives title as Marvel Double Feature ... Thunderstrike/Code Blue 2.50
- ❑16 .... 1.50
- ❑16/A, Jan 95, 25 .... 1.50
- ❑16/B, Jan 95,flip-book with Code Blue back-up; second indicia gives title as Marvel Double Feature ... Thunderstrike/Code Blue 2.50
- ❑17, Feb 95 .... 1.50
- ❑18, Mar 95 .... 1.50
- ❑19, Apr 95 .... 1.50
- ❑20, May 95 .... 1.50
- ❑21, Jun 95,Avengers #1 homage cover 1.50
- ❑22, Jul 95,Identity of Bloodaxe revealed 1.50
- ❑23, Aug 95, V: Seth, Avengers, Thor; V: Avengers; V: Thor; V: Seth 1.50
- ❑24, Sep 95, D: Eric Masterson,Final Issue 1.50

TICK, THE
NEC

	ORIG	GOOD	FINE	N-MINT
❑1, Jun 88,Black background on cover	1.75	3.00	7.50	15.00
❑1-2,2nd Printing	1.95	0.60	1.50	3.00
❑,3rd Printing	1.95	0.50	1.25	2.50
❑1-4,4th Printing	2.25	0.45	1.13	2.25
❑1-5	2.75	0.55	1.38	2.75
❑2, Sep 88,Die-cut cover	1.75	1.60	4.00	8.00
❑2/SC,Without die-cut cover	—	3.00	7.50	15.00
❑2-2,2nd Printing	1.95	0.60	1.50	3.00
❑2-3,3rd Printing	2.25	0.45	1.13	2.25
❑2-4,4th Printing	2.25	0.45	1.13	2.25
❑2-5	2.75	0.55	1.38	2.75
❑3	1.95	1.20	3.00	6.00
❑3-2, Nov 89,2nd Printing; Yellow stripe on cover saying "Encore Presentation"	2.25	0.60	1.50	3.00
❑3-3	2.75	0.55	1.38	2.75
❑3-4	2.75	0.55	1.38	2.75
❑4, Apr 89, 1: Paul the Samurai	1.95	1.60	4.00	8.00
❑4-2, 1: Paul the Samurai,2nd Printing	2.25	0.45	1.13	2.25
❑4-3, 1: Paul the Samurai	2.75	0.55	1.38	2.75
❑4-4, 1: Paul the Samurai	2.75	0.55	1.38	2.75
❑4-5, 1: Paul the Samurai	2.75	0.55	1.38	2.75
❑5, Aug 89,Scarcer	1.95	1.60	4.00	8.00
❑5-2	2.75	0.55	1.38	2.75
❑6, Nov 89	2.25	1.00	2.50	5.00
❑6-2	2.75	0.55	1.38	2.75
❑6-3	2.75	0.55	1.38	2.75
❑7, Feb 90	2.25	1.00	2.50	5.00
❑7-2	2.75	0.55	1.38	2.75
❑8, Jul 90,Has logo	2.25	1.60	4.00	8.00
❑8/SC,No logo on cover	—	1.60	4.00	8.00

	ORIG	GOOD	FINE	N-MINT
❑8-2	2.75	0.55	1.38	2.75
❑9, Mar 91, 1: The Chainsaw Vigilante	2.75	0.60	1.50	3.00
❑10, Oct 91	2.75	0.60	1.50	3.00
❑11, Aug 92	2.75	0.60	1.50	3.00
❑12, May 93	2.75	0.60	1.50	3.00
❑12/LE,Gold spider foil on front	—	4.00	10.00	20.00
❑13, Nov 00, Pseudo-Tick edition	3.50	0.70	1.75	3.50
❑SE 1, 1: The Tick, Special edition	—	10.00	25.00	50.00
❑SE 2, 2: The Tick, Special edition	—	5.00	12.50	25.00

TICK & ARTHUR, THE
NEC

Value: Cover or less

❑1 ... 3.50

TICK BIG BLUE DESTINY, THE
NEC

Value: Cover or less

❑1, 1: The Impressionist,Arthur and Tick with #1 posing on cover; Keen Edition ... 2.95
❑1/A, Fear No Art (Unless It's Out To Get You), 1: The Impressionist,Die-cut cover; Wicked Keen Edition ... 4.95
❑1/Ash, 1: The Impressionist, ashcan edition ... 2.95
❑1/B, Fear No Art (Unless It's Out To Get You), 1: The Impressionist, Wicked Keen Edition without Die-Cut Cover; (500 printed); (500 printed) ... 19.00
❑2 ... 2.95
❑2/SC,Tick-buster cover ... 2.95
❑3 ... 3.50
❑4,Justice Cover ... 3.50
❑4/A,Ocean cover ... 3.50
❑5 ... 3.50

TICK BIG SUMMER ANNUAL, THE
NEC

Value: Cover or less

❑1, Jul 99, The Enemy of My Enemy is My Enemy! ... 3.50

TICK, THE: CIRCUS MAXIMUS
NEC

Value: Cover or less

❑1 ... 3.50
❑2 ... 3.50
❑3 ... 3.50
❑4 ... 3.50

TICK, THE: HEROES OF THE CITY
NEC

Value: Cover or less

❑1, Feb 99, Prologue; Arthur ... 3.50

TICK, THE: KARMA TORNADO
NEC

	ORIG	GOOD	FINE	N-MINT
❑1, Oct 93, trading cards	3.25	0.80	2.00	4.00
❑1-2, Jan 97,2nd Printing	2.95	0.59	1.48	2.95
❑2, Jan 94, Electric Boogaloo	2.75	0.70	1.75	3.50
❑2-2, Feb 97, Electric Boogaloo,2nd Printing	2.95	0.59	1.48	2.95
❑3, May 94,Scarce	2.75	1.00	2.50	5.00
❑3-2, Mar 97,2nd Printing; flip book with The Tick's Back back-up	2.95	0.59	1.48	2.95
❑4, Jul 94,Scarce	2.75	1.00	2.50	5.00
❑4-2, Apr 97,2nd Printing; flip book with The Tick's Back back-up	2.95	0.59	1.48	2.95
❑5, Aug 94,Scarce	2.75	1.00	2.50	5.00
❑5-2,2nd Printing	2.95	0.59	1.48	2.95
❑6, Oct 94	2.75	0.80	2.00	4.00
❑6-2,2nd Printing	2.95	0.59	1.48	2.95
❑7	2.75	0.80	2.00	4.00
❑7-2,2nd Printing	2.95	0.59	1.48	2.95
❑8	2.75	0.80	2.00	4.00
❑8-2,2nd Printing	2.95	0.59	1.48	2.95
❑9	2.75	0.60	1.50	3.00
❑9-2,2nd Printing	2.95	0.59	1.48	2.95

TICK: LUNY BIN TRILOGY
NEC

Value: Cover or less

❑1 ... 3.50

TICK'S BACK, THE
NEC

Value: Cover or less

❑0, Aug 97,Red cover ... 2.95
❑0/A,Green Cover ... 5.00
❑0/B,Gold Tick Cover ... 7.50
❑0/C,No logo, Gold cover ... 10.00

TICK'S BIG BACK TO SCHOOL SPECIAL, THE
NEC

Value: Cover or less

❑1, Back to School! ... 3.50

TICK'S BIG CRUISE SHIP VACATION SPECIAL, THE
NEC

Value: Cover or less

❑1, Sep 00 ... 3.50

TICK'S BIG FATHER'S DAY SPECIAL, THE
NEC

Value: Cover or less

❑1, Jun 00, Enter: Kid Tick!, 1: Kid Tick ... 3.50

TICK'S BIG HALLOWEEN SPECIAL, THE
NEC

Value: Cover or less

❑1, Oct 99, Haunted Halloween Hootenanny ... 3.50

TICK'S BIG ROMANTIC ADVENTURE, THE
NEC

Value: Cover or less

❑1, Bad Chemistry ... 2.95

TICK'S BIG YULE LOG SPECIAL
NEC

Value: Cover or less

❑1, Dec 97, b&w ... 3.50
❑1998 ... 3.50
❑1999 ... 3.50

The Thunderbolts turned out to be the former Masters of Evil masquerading as heroes in the wake of "Onslaught," during which a number of major heroes, including the Fantastic Four, had disappeared.

TICK'S GIANT CIRCUS OF THE MIGHTY, THE
NEC

Value: Cover or less

❑1, Sum 92 ... 2.75
❑2, Sum 92 ... 2.75

TICK-TOCK FOLLIES
SLAVE LABOR

Value: Cover or less

❑1, Dec 96 ... 2.95

TIC TOC TOM
DETONATOR CANADA

Value: Cover or less

❑1, Aut 95, b&w ... 2.95
❑2, Win 95, b&w ... 2.95
❑3, Spr 96, b&w ... 2.95

TIGERMAN
ATLAS

	ORIG	GOOD	FINE	N-MINT
❑1, Sep 75, 1: Tigerman	0.25	0.40	1.00	2.00
❑2, Jun 75, SD	0.25	0.30	0.75	1.50
❑3, Sep 75, SD	0.25	0.30	0.75	1.50

TIGERS OF TERRA
MIND-VISIONS

Value: Cover or less

❑1 ... 3.00
❑2 ... 3.00
❑3 ... 3.00
❑4 ... 3.50
❑5 ... 3.50
❑6 ... 3.50
❑7 ... 3.50
❑8 ... 3.75
❑9,two covers: a and b ... 3.75
❑10, b&w ... 3.75
❑11, b&w ... 3.95
❑12, Jul 93, b&w ... 3.95

TIGERS OF TERRA (VOL. 2)
ANTARCTIC

	ORIG	GOOD	FINE	N-MINT
❑0, Aug 93	2.95	0.59	1.48	2.95
❑1, Oct 93, Tigers of Burma	2.75	0.60	1.50	3.00
❑2, Dec 93, Roses of Red Phoenix	2.75	0.60	1.50	3.00
❑3, Feb 94	2.75	0.60	1.50	3.00
❑4, Apr 94	2.75	0.60	1.50	3.00
❑5, Jul 94, The Third Yamato	2.75	0.60	1.50	3.00
❑6, Sep 94	2.75	0.60	1.50	3.00
❑7, Dec 94	2.75	0.60	1.50	3.00
❑8, Jan 95, Projekt: Mars	2.75	0.60	1.50	3.00
❑9, Mar 95, Tiger III, Part 1	2.75	0.60	1.50	3.00
❑10, Apr 95, Tiger III, Part 2	2.75	0.60	1.50	3.00
❑11, May 95, Tiger III, Part 3	2.75	0.55	1.38	2.75
❑12, Jun 95	2.75	0.55	1.38	2.75
❑13, Jul 95	2.75	0.55	1.38	2.75
❑14, Aug 95	2.75	0.55	1.38	2.75
❑15	2.75	0.55	1.38	2.75
❑16	2.75	0.55	1.38	2.75
❑17	2.75	0.55	1.38	2.75
❑18	2.75	0.59	1.48	2.95
❑19	2.75	0.59	1.48	2.95
❑20, Mar 96	2.95	0.59	1.48	2.95
❑21, May 96	2.95	0.59	1.48	2.95
❑22, Jul 96	2.95	0.59	1.48	2.95
❑23, Sep 96	2.95	0.59	1.48	2.95
❑24, Nov 96, The Flying Cosmotigers	3.95	0.79	1.98	3.95
❑25, Jan 97, Revelation	2.95	0.59	1.48	2.95

TIGERS OF TERRA (VOL. 3)
ANTARCTIC

Value: Cover or less

❑1, Jul 00, War Against the Sun ... 2.95

TIGERS OF TERRA: TECHNICAL MANUAL
ANTARCTIC

Value: Cover or less

❑1, b&w ... 2.95
❑2, Jun 96, b&w ... 2.95

TIGER WOMAN, THE
MILLENNIUM

Value: Cover or less

❑1, Sep 94,no indicia ... 2.95
❑2, Apr 95,cover says Quest of the Tiger Woman #1; no indicia; but title page says Tiger Woman #2 ... 2.95

TIGER-X
ETERNITY

Value: Cover or less

❑1, b&w; Story continued from Tiger-X Special #1 ... 1.95
❑2, b&w ... 1.95
❑3, b&w ... 1.95
❑SE 1, b&w ... 2.25
❑SE 1-2,2nd Printing ... 2.25

TIGER-X BOOK II
ETERNITY

	ORIG	GOOD	FINE	N-MINT
❑1, Stalking Horse, b&w	1.95	0.40	1.00	2.00
❑2, b&w	1.95	0.40	1.00	2.00
❑3, b&w	1.95	0.40	1.00	2.00
❑4, b&w	1.95	0.40	1.00	2.00

TIGRESS, THE
HERO

Value: Cover or less

- ❑1, Aug 92, The Return of the Tigress, A: Flare, b&w ... 2.95
- ❑2, A: Flare, b&w ... 2.95
- ❑3, 1: Mudpie, b&w ... 2.95
- ❑4, b&w ... 2.95
- ❑5, b&w ... 2.95
- ❑6, Jun 93 ... 3.95

TIGRESS (BASEMENT)
BASEMENT

Value: Cover or less

- ❑1 ... 2.95

TIJUANA BIBLE, THE
STARHEAD

Value: Cover or less

- ❑1, b&w; adult ... 3.95
- ❑2, Blondie; Clock For Sale, b&w; adult ... 3.95
- ❑3, b&w; adult ... 3.95
- ❑4, The Traveling Salesman And The Farmers Daughter; Schnazle Durante, b&w; adult; Bluesie Toons ... 3.95
- ❑5, The Sensation Of The Aquacade; It Happened On The Flying Trapeze,adult; World's Fair ... 2.50
- ❑6, The Adventures Of A Fuller Brush Man; Obliging Lady,adult; Fuller Brush Man ... 2.50
- ❑7, Wally And The King; Wally And The Sultan,adult; Royalty issue ... 2.50
- ❑8, Get A Li'l Like The Fishes Do; Filling A Large Cavity,adult; Hollywood women ... 2.50
- ❑9,adult; An Artist's Affaire ... 2.50

TILAZEUS MEETS THE MESSIAH
AIIIE

Value: Cover or less

- ❑1 ... 2.50

TIMBER WOLF
DC

	ORIG	GOOD	FINE	N-MINT
❑1, Nov 92, Twentieth Century Wolf	1.25	0.30	0.75	1.50
❑2, Dec 92	1.25	0.30	0.75	1.50
❑3, Jan 93, V: Creeper	1.25	0.30	0.75	1.50
❑4, Feb 93	1.25	0.30	0.75	1.50
❑5, Mar 93	1.25	0.30	0.75	1.50

TIME BANDITS
MARVEL

	ORIG	GOOD	FINE	N-MINT
❑1, Feb 82,movie Adaptation	1.00	0.30	0.75	1.50

TIME BREAKERS
DC

Value: Cover or less

- ❑1, Jan 97, Lives of Our Time ... 2.25
- ❑2, Feb 97, Mind Out of Time ... 2.25
- ❑3, Mar 97, Again and Again Time ... 2.25
- ❑4, Apr 97, Challenge for a Time ... 2.25
- ❑5, May 97, The Day has Come to Time ... 2.25

TIMECOP
DARK HORSE

Value: Cover or less

- ❑1, Sep 94,movie Adaptation . 2.50
- ❑2, Sep 94,movie Adaptation .. 2.50

TIMEDRIFTER (GERARD JONES'...)
INNOVATION

Value: Cover or less

- ❑1, Dec 90, Right Place, Wrong Time, b&w ... 2.25
- ❑2, b&w ... 2.25
- ❑3, b&w ... 2.25

TIME GATES
DOUBLE EDGE

Value: Cover or less

- ❑1 ... 1.95
- ❑2 ... 1.95
- ❑3 ... 1.95

TIMEJUMP WAR, THE
APPLE

Value: Cover or less

- ❑1, Oct 89, b&w ... 2.25
- ❑2, b&w ... 2.25
- ❑3, b&w ... 2.25

TIME KILLERS
FLEETWAY

Value: Cover or less

- ❑1, Killing Time,Tales From Beyond Space: The Men In Red ... 2.95
- ❑2 ... 2.95
- ❑3 ... 2.95
- ❑4 ... 2.95
- ❑5 ... 2.95
- ❑6, Tales From Beyond Science: Secrets of the Organism; Shadows ... 2.95
- ❑7 ... 2.95

TIMELESS TALES (BOB POWELL'S...)
ECLIPSE

Value: Cover or less

- ❑1, Mar 89, Gotta Match?; Supreme Penalty, b&w ... 2.00

TIMELY PRESENTS: ALL-WINNERS
MARVEL

Value: Cover or less

- ❑1, Dec 99, The Crime of the Ages!, nn; Reprint; Reprints All-Winners Comics #19 ... 3.99

TIMELY PRESENTS: HUMAN TORCH
MARVEL

Value: Cover or less

- ❑1, Feb 99, BEv, Human Torch, Part 1; Human Torch, Part 2, A: Sub-Mariner,Painted cover by Ray Lago; Reprinted from Human Torch Comics #5 ... 3.99

TIME MACHINE, THE
ETERNITY

Value: Cover or less

- ❑1, Apr 90, b&w; Based on the story by H.G. Wells ... 2.50
- ❑2, b&w ... 2.50
- ❑3, b&w ... 2.50

TIME MASTERS
DC

	ORIG	GOOD	FINE	N-MINT
❑1, Feb 90, Time Won't Let Me	1.75	0.40	1.00	2.00
❑2, Mar 90, No Time To Live	1.75	0.35	0.88	1.75
❑3, Apr 90	1.75	0.35	0.88	1.75
❑4, May 90, Time is on my Side	1.75	0.35	0.88	1.75
❑5, Jun 90, A: Viking Prince	1.75	0.35	0.88	1.75
❑6, Jul 90, A: Doctor Fate; A: Dr. Fate	1.75	0.35	0.88	1.75
❑7, Aug 90, A: Arion	1.75	0.35	0.88	1.75
❑8, Sep 90	1.75	0.35	0.88	1.75

TIME OUT OF MIND
GRAPHIC SERIALS

	ORIG	GOOD	FINE	N-MINT
❑1	1.85	0.40	1.00	2.00
❑2	1.75	0.35	0.88	1.75
❑3	1.75	0.35	0.88	1.75

TIMESLIP COLLECTION
MARVEL

Value: Cover or less

- ❑1, Nov 98,wraparound cover; collects short features from Marvel Vision ... 2.99

TIMESLIP SPECIAL
MARVEL

Value: Cover or less

- ❑1, Oct 98, The Coming of the Avengers,cardstock cover ... 5.99

TIMESPELL
CLUB 408 GRAPHICS

	ORIG	GOOD	FINE	N-MINT
❑0, b&w; cardstock cover	2.95	0.59	1.48	2.95
❑1, Blood on the Moon, b&w; cardstock cover	2.95	0.59	1.48	2.95
❑2, Domestic Oblivion, b&w; cardstock cover	2.95	0.59	1.48	2.95
❑3, The Soul Cage, b&w; cardstock cover	2.95	0.59	1.48	2.95
❑4, Childermas, b&w; cardstock cover	2.95	0.59	1.48	2.95
❑Ash 1, nn; no cover price; ashcan preview of upcoming series	—	0.20	0.50	1.00

TIMESPELL: THE DIRECTOR'S CUT
CLUB 408 GRAPHICS

Value: Cover or less

- ❑1, Blood on the Moon, b&w; no price on cover; reprints #1 with revisions and additions ... 2.95

TIMESPIRITS
MARVEL

	ORIG	GOOD	FINE	N-MINT
❑1, Oct 84, TY, Indian Spring	1.50	0.40	1.00	2.00
❑2, Dec 84	1.50	0.35	0.88	1.75
❑3, Feb 85	1.50	0.35	0.88	1.75
❑4, Apr 85, AW	1.50	0.35	0.88	1.75
❑5, Jul 85	1.50	0.35	0.88	1.75
❑6, Sep 85	1.50	0.35	0.88	1.75
❑7, Dec 85	1.50	0.35	0.88	1.75
❑8, Mar 86	1.50	0.35	0.88	1.75

TIME TRAVELER AI
CPM MANGA

Value: Cover or less

- ❑1, b&w ... 2.95
- ❑2, b&w ... 2.95
- ❑3, b&w ... 2.95
- ❑4, b&w ... 2.95
- ❑5, b&w ... 2.95
- ❑6, b&w ... 2.95

TIME TRAVELER HERBIE
AVALON

Value: Cover or less

- ❑1, Herbie goes Nap-Happy; Christopher Columbus Popnecker! ... 2.95

TIME TUNNEL, THE
GOLD KEY

	ORIG	GOOD	FINE	N-MINT
❑1, The Assassins; Mars Countdown	0.12	5.00	12.50	25.00
❑2	0.12	5.00	12.50	25.00

TIME TWISTED TALES
RIP OFF

Value: Cover or less

- ❑1, The Year is 3711(2nd story) ... 2.00

TIME TWISTERS
FLEETWAY

	ORIG	GOOD	FINE	N-MINT
❑1, DaG, AMo (w), Tharg's Time Twisters: The Hyper-Historic Headbang; Tharg'	1.25	0.30	0.75	1.50
❑2, DaG, Tharg's Fu	1.25	0.30	0.75	1.50
❑3, Tharg's Future Shocks The Wages of Sin; Tharg's Future Shocks Salad Days	1.25	0.30	0.75	1.50
❑4, DaG, Tharg's Future Shocks Bad Timing; Tharg's Future Shocks The End of the Universe	1.25	0.30	0.75	1.50

	ORIG	GOOD	FINE	N-MINT
❑5, Tharg's Future Shocks: Bad Maxwell; Extra! Extra!	1.25	0.30	0.75	1.50
❑6, Dr. Dales Diary; The Pioneer	1.25	0.30	0.75	1.50
❑7, AMo (w), Tharg's Future Shocks: Twist Ending; Superbean	1.25	0.30	0.75	1.50
❑8, DaG, Eureka; Horn of Plenty	1.25	0.30	0.75	1.50
❑9, AMo (w), The Big Clock; Tharg's	1.25	0.30	0.75	1.50
❑10, The Message; Tharg's Future Shocks: Fair's Fare	1.25	0.30	0.75	1.50
❑11, Tharg's Future Shocks: Sid; Tharg's F	1.50	0.30	0.75	1.50
❑12, Time Twisters: The Avenging Kong Meets Laur	1.50	0.30	0.75	1.50
❑13, T.R.A.I.N.; Tharg's Future Shocks: And So to Bed…	1.50	0.30	0.75	1.50
❑14, BB, Tharg the Mighty: The D	1.50	0.30	0.75	1.50
❑15, DaG, T	1.50	0.30	0.75	1.50
❑16, Exit the Wally; Tharg's Future Shocks Car Wars	1.50	0.30	0.75	1.50
❑17, Curse Your Lucky Star; Tharg's Future Shocks Daffy Daffid	1.50	0.30	0.75	1.50
❑18, Wally Saves the Day; Tharg's Future Shocks Disconnected	1.50	0.30	0.75	1.50
❑19, It's the Thought that Counts!; Tharg's Time Twisters	1.50	0.30	0.75	1.50
❑20, Bill Tompkins meets…Bill Tompkins; The Real Right Stuff	1.50	0.30	0.75	1.50
❑21, It's a Mad, Mad, Mad, World; Tharg's Future Shocks Sud's Law,Final Issue	1.50	0.30	0.75	1.50

TIMEWALKER
ACCLAIM
Value: Cover or less

- ❑0, Mar 96, DP, BH (w), Child of Time, O: Ivar 2.50
- ❑1, Jan 95, DP, BH (w), Ivar The Traveler,cover has Dec 94 coverdate 2.50
- ❑2, Feb 95, DP, BH (w), The Enemy is There,cover has Jan coverdate 2.50
- ❑3, Mar 95,cover has Feb coverdate 2.50
- ❑4, Apr 95, DP, BH (w), Mac!,cover has Mar coverdate 2.50
- ❑5, Apr 95 .... 2.50
- ❑6, May 95, Harbinger Wars Pt 1 .... 2.50
- ❑7, Jun 95, Harbinger Wars Pt 2 .... 2.50
- ❑8, Jul 95, Harbinger Wars Pt 3,Birthquake 2.50
- ❑9, Jul 95, DP ,Birthquake 2.50
- ❑10, Aug 95, The Last God Of Dura Europus 2.50
- ❑11, Aug 95 .... 2.50
- ❑12, Sep 95, DP 2.50
- ❑13, Sep 95 .... 2.50
- ❑14, Oct 95 .... 2.50
- ❑15, Oct 95,Final Issue 2.50
- ❑YB 1, May 95, A: H.A.R.D. Corps,wraparound cover; Yearbook 2.95

TIME WANKERS
FANTAGRAPHICS
Value: Cover or less

- ❑1, Sep 96, b&w; adult 2.25
- ❑2, b&w; adult 2.25
- ❑3, b&w; adult 2.25
- ❑4, b&w; adult 2.25
- ❑5, b&w; adult 2.25

TIME WARP
DC

	ORIG	GOOD	FINE	N-MINT
❑1, Nov 79, DA; JA; DG; SD; RB; TS; DN, If The World Had To End Twice…; The Mating Game	1.00	0.25	0.63	1.25
❑2, Jan 80	1.00	0.25	0.63	1.25
❑3, Mar 80	1.00	0.25	0.63	1.25
❑4, May 80	1.00	0.25	0.63	1.25
❑5, Jul 80,Final Issue	1.00	0.25	0.63	1.25

TIME WARRIOR
BLAZING
Value: Cover or less

- ❑1 .... 2.50

TIME WARRIORS: THE BEGINNING
FANTASY GENERAL
Value: Cover or less

- ❑1 .... 1.50

TIM HOLT WESTERN ANNUAL
AC
Value: Cover or less

- ❑1, b&w; Reprint 2.95

TINCAN MAN
IMAGE
Value: Cover or less

- ❑1, Jan 00 .... 2.95
- ❑2, Feb 00 .... 2.95
- ❑Ash 1, Dec 99, Hitting Bottom,Preview issue 2.95

TINY DEATHS
YUGP
Value: Cover or less

- ❑1 .... 1.75
- ❑2, Jan 97, Wrench in my Monkey; My Brain 1.75

TIPPER GORE'S COMICS AND STORIES
REVOLUTIONARY
Value: Cover or less

- ❑1, Oct 89, b&w 1.95
- ❑2, Jan 90, Think or Die; Coaster Maniac!, b&w 1.95
- ❑3, Mar 90, b&w 1.95
- ❑4, May 90, b&w 1.95
- ❑5, Jul 90, Rhoads Beyond; Behind Blue Eyes, b&w 1.95

TITAN A.E.
DARK HORSE
Value: Cover or less

- ❑1, May 00 .... 2.95
- ❑2, Jun 00 .... 2.95
- ❑3, Jul 00 .... 2.95

Tipper Gore's lobbying efforts for music labeling led to Revolutionary's *Tipper Gore's Comics and Stories.*

© 1989 Revolutionary

TITANS, THE
DC

	ORIG	GOOD	FINE	N-MINT
❑1, Mar 99, DGry(w), That Strange Buzzing Sound, A: H.I.V.E.,new team	2.50	0.60	1.50	3.00
❑1/Aut, Mar 99, DGry(w), That Strange Buzzing Sound, A: H.I.V.E.,Signed by Devin Grayson	—	3.19	7.97	15.95
❑2, Apr 99, DGry(w), A: H.I.V.E.; A: Superman	2.50	0.50	1.25	2.50
❑3, May 99, DGry(w), V: Goth	2.50	0.50	1.25	2.50
❑4, Jun 99, DGry(w), The Dissing, V: Goth.	2.50	0.50	1.25	2.50
❑5, Jul 99, DGry(w), Hydrophobia	2.50	0.50	1.25	2.50
❑6, Aug 99, DGry(w), Heritage, V: Red Panzer; A: Green Lantern	2.50	0.50	1.25	2.50
❑7, Sep 99, DGry(w), Need for Speed Part 1	2.50	0.50	1.25	2.50
❑8, Oct 99, DGry(w), Need for Speed Part 2	2.50	0.50	1.25	2.50
❑9, Nov 99, DGry(w)	2.50	0.50	1.25	2.50
❑10, Dec 99, DGry(w), The Immortal Coil, Part 1	2.50	0.50	1.25	2.50
❑11, Jan 00, DGry(w), The Immortal Coil, Part 2	2.50	0.50	1.25	2.50
❑12, Feb 00	2.50	0.50	1.25	2.50
❑13, Mar 00	2.50	0.50	1.25	2.50
❑14, Apr 00, Chain of Command	2.50	0.50	1.25	2.50
❑15, May 00, DGry(w), Survival	2.50	0.50	1.25	2.50
❑16, Jun 00	2.50	0.50	1.25	2.50
❑17, Jul 00	2.50	0.50	1.25	2.50
❑18, Aug 00	2.50	0.50	1.25	2.50
❑19, Sep 00, DGry(w), The Price of Victory	2.50	0.50	1.25	2.50
❑20, Oct 00, DGry(w), Transitions	2.50	0.50	1.25	2.50
❑21, Nov 00, The Trial of Cheshire, Part 1 .	2.50	0.50	1.25	2.50
❑22, Dec 00, The Trial of Cheshire, Part 2 .	2.50	0.50	1.25	2.50
❑23, Jan 01, Who is Troia?, Part 1	2.50	0.50	1.25	2.50
❑24, Feb 01, Who is Troia?, Part 2	2.50	0.50	1.25	2.50
❑25, Mar 01, Who is Troia?, Part 3, Giant-size	3.95	0.79	1.98	3.95
❑26, Apr 01, Nothing Personal,Just Business	2.50	0.50	1.25	2.50
❑27, May 01, Desperate Measures	2.50	0.50	1.25	2.50
❑28	2.50	0.50	1.25	2.50
❑29	2.50	0.50	1.25	2.50
❑30	2.50	0.50	1.25	2.50
❑31	2.50	0.50	1.25	2.50

TITANS/LEGION OF SUPER-HEROES: UNIVERSE ABLAZE
DC
Value: Cover or less

- ❑1 .... 4.95
- ❑2 .... 4.95
- ❑3 .... 4.95
- ❑4 .... 4.95

TITAN SPECIAL
DARK HORSE
Value: Cover or less

- ❑1, Jun 94, Chosen People, D: Golden Boy,One-Shot 3.95

TITANS: SCISSORS, PAPER, STONE
DC
Value: Cover or less

- ❑1, nn; prestige format; manga-style; Elseworlds 4.95

TITANS SECRET FILES, THE
DC
Value: Cover or less

- ❑1, Mar 99, DGry(w) 4.95
- ❑2, Oct 00, Interludes; Shifting Gears 4.95

TITANS SELL-OUT! SPECIAL
DC
Value: Cover or less

- ❑1, Nov 92,One-Shot 3.50

TIYU
EXPRESS

	ORIG	GOOD	FINE	N-MINT
❑1, Oct 96,Special picture-only cover	2.95	1.99	4.97	9.95

T-MINUS-1
RENEGADE
Value: Cover or less

- ❑1, b&w 2.00

TMNT MUTANT UNIVERSE SOURCEBOOK
ARCHIE

	ORIG	GOOD	FINE	N-MINT
❑1,A-M	1.95	0.40	1.00	2.00
❑2,N-Z	1.95	0.40	1.00	2.00

TO BE ANNOUNCED
STRAWBERRY JAM

Value: Cover or less

Issue	ORIG	GOOD	FINE	N-MINT
❑1				1.50
❑2				1.50
❑3				1.50
❑4				1.50
❑5				1.50
❑6				1.50
❑7				1.50

TODD MCFARLANE PRESENTS: KISS PSYCHO CIRCUS
IMAGE

Value: Cover or less

Issue	ORIG	GOOD	FINE	N-MINT
❑1, Oct 98, magazine; reprints #1-3 of comic book				6.95
❑2, Apr 99, Kiss: Psycho Circus #4, 5				4.95
❑3, Aug 99, Kiss: Psycho Circus #6, 7				4.95
❑4, Nov 99, Kiss: Psycho Circus #8, 9				4.95
❑5, Apr 00, Destroyer, Part 1; Destroyer, Part 2				4.95

TODD MCFARLANE PRESENTS: OZZY OSBOURNE
IMAGE

Value: Cover or less

Issue	ORIG	GOOD	FINE	N-MINT
❑1, Jun 99, Picking the Brain of Ozzy Osbourne; Biography of a Madman, magazine				4.95

TODD MCFARLANE PRESENTS: THE CROW MAGAZINE
IMAGE

Value: Cover or less

Issue	ORIG	GOOD	FINE	N-MINT
❑1, Mar 00, Resurrection; Shadows, James O'Barr interview				4.95

TO DIE FOR
BLACKTHORNE

Value: Cover or less

Issue	ORIG	GOOD	FINE	N-MINT
❑1, b&w; movie Adaptation				2.50
❑1/3D,movie Adaptation				2.50

TOMAHAWK
DC

Issue	ORIG	GOOD	FINE	N-MINT
❑76, Sep 61	0.10	6.80	17.00	34.00
❑77, Nov 61	0.10	6.80	17.00	34.00
❑78, Jan 62	0.10	6.80	17.00	34.00
❑79, Mar 62	0.10	6.80	17.00	34.00
❑80, May 62	0.10	6.80	17.00	34.00
❑81, Jul 62, 1: Miss Liberty	0.12	5.20	13.00	26.00
❑82, Sep 62	0.12	5.20	13.00	26.00
❑83, Nov 62	0.12	5.20	13.00	26.00
❑84, Jan 63	0.12	5.20	13.00	26.00
❑85, Mar 63	0.12	5.20	13.00	26.00
❑86, May 63	0.12	5.20	13.00	26.00
❑87, Jul 63	0.12	5.20	13.00	26.00
❑88, Sep 63	0.12	5.20	13.00	26.00
❑89, Nov 63	0.12	5.20	13.00	26.00
❑90, Jan 64	0.12	5.20	13.00	26.00
❑91, Mar 64	0.12	3.20	8.00	16.00
❑92, May 64	0.12	3.20	8.00	16.00
❑93, Jul 64	0.12	3.20	8.00	16.00
❑94, Sep 64	0.12	3.20	8.00	16.00
❑95, Nov 64	0.12	3.20	8.00	16.00
❑96, Jan 65	0.12	3.20	8.00	16.00
❑97, Mar 65	0.12	3.20	8.00	16.00
❑98, May 65	0.12	3.20	8.00	16.00
❑99, Jul 65	0.12	3.20	8.00	16.00
❑100, Sep 65	0.12	3.20	8.00	16.00
❑101, Nov 65	0.12	2.00	5.00	10.00
❑102, Jan 66	0.12	2.00	5.00	10.00
❑103, Mar 66	0.12	2.00	5.00	10.00
❑104, May 66	0.12	2.00	5.00	10.00
❑105, Jul 66	0.12	2.00	5.00	10.00
❑106, Sep 66	0.12	2.00	5.00	10.00
❑107, Nov 66	0.12	2.00	5.00	10.00
❑108, Jan 67	0.12	2.00	5.00	10.00
❑109, Mar 67	0.12	2.00	5.00	10.00
❑110, May 67	0.12	2.00	5.00	10.00
❑111, Jul 67	0.12	1.60	4.00	8.00
❑112, Sep 67	0.12	1.60	4.00	8.00
❑113, Nov 67	0.12	1.60	4.00	8.00
❑114, Jan 68	0.12	1.60	4.00	8.00
❑115, Mar 68	0.12	1.60	4.00	8.00
❑116, May 68	0.12	1.60	4.00	8.00
❑117, Jul 68	0.12	1.60	4.00	8.00
❑118, Sep 68	0.12	1.60	4.00	8.00
❑119, Nov 68	0.12	1.60	4.00	8.00
❑120, Jan 69	0.12	1.60	4.00	8.00
❑121, Mar 69	0.12	1.20	3.00	6.00
❑122	—	1.20	3.00	6.00
❑123	—	1.20	3.00	6.00
❑124	—	1.20	3.00	6.00
❑125	—	1.20	3.00	6.00
❑126	—	1.20	3.00	6.00
❑127	—	1.20	3.00	6.00
❑128	—	1.20	3.00	6.00
❑129	—	1.20	3.00	6.00
❑130	—	1.20	3.00	6.00
❑131, FF ,Series becomes "Son of Tomahawk"	—	1.20	3.00	6.00
❑132	—	1.20	3.00	6.00
❑133, FT, Scalp Hunter; The Way It Was!	—	0.90	2.25	4.50
❑134	—	0.90	2.25	4.50
❑135, FT, Death On Ghost Mountain	0.15	0.90	2.25	4.50
❑136	—	0.90	2.25	4.50
❑137	—	0.90	2.25	4.50
❑138	—	0.90	2.25	4.50
❑139, Mar 72, FF ,says Son of Tomahawk on cover	0.25	0.90	2.25	4.50
❑140, May 72,says Son of Tomahawk on cover; Final Issue	0.25	0.90	2.25	4.50

TOM & JERRY (VOL. 2)
HARVEY

Issue	ORIG	GOOD	FINE	N-MINT
❑1,Reprint	1.25	0.30	0.75	1.50
❑2, Nov 91, At the Circus; What a Parrot,Reprint	1.25	0.25	0.63	1.25
❑3,Reprint	1.25	0.25	0.63	1.25
❑4,Reprint	1.25	0.25	0.63	1.25
❑5,Reprint	1.25	0.25	0.63	1.25
❑6, Jan 93, The Karate Mouse; The Mixed - Up,Reprint	1.25	0.25	0.63	1.25
❑7,Reprint	1.25	0.25	0.63	1.25
❑8,Reprint	1.25	0.25	0.63	1.25
❑9	1.50	0.30	0.75	1.50
❑10	1.50	0.30	0.75	1.50
❑11	1.50	0.30	0.75	1.50
❑12	1.50	0.30	0.75	1.50
❑13	1.50	0.30	0.75	1.50
❑14	1.50	0.30	0.75	1.50
❑15	1.50	0.30	0.75	1.50
❑16	1.50	0.30	0.75	1.50
❑17, Jul 94	1.50	0.30	0.75	1.50
❑18, Aug 94	1.50	0.30	0.75	1.50
❑Anl 1, Sep 94	2.25	0.45	1.13	2.25

TOM & JERRY 50TH ANNIVERSARY SPECIAL
HARVEY

Value: Cover or less

Issue	ORIG	GOOD	FINE	N-MINT
❑1, CB ,Reprint				2.50

TOM & JERRY ADVENTURES
HARVEY

Value: Cover or less

Issue	ORIG	GOOD	FINE	N-MINT
❑1,Reprint				1.25

TOM & JERRY AND FRIENDS
HARVEY

Value: Cover or less

Issue	ORIG	GOOD	FINE	N-MINT
❑1,Reprint				1.25
❑2,Reprint				1.25
❑3,Reprint				1.25
❑4,Reprint				1.25

TOM & JERRY BIG BOOK
HARVEY

Value: Cover or less

Issue	ORIG	GOOD	FINE	N-MINT
❑1				1.95
❑2				1.95

TOM & JERRY DIGEST
HARVEY

Value: Cover or less

Issue	ORIG	GOOD	FINE	N-MINT
❑1,Reprint				1.75

TOM & JERRY GIANT SIZE
HARVEY

Value: Cover or less

Issue	ORIG	GOOD	FINE	N-MINT
❑1,Reprint				1.95
❑2				2.25

TOMATO
STARHEAD

Value: Cover or less

Issue	ORIG	GOOD	FINE	N-MINT
❑1, Apr 94, My Date with Camille Paglia, b&w; adult				2.75
❑2, Feb 95, b&w; adult				2.75

TOMB OF DARKNESS
MARVEL

Issue	ORIG	GOOD	FINE	N-MINT
❑9,Series continued from Beware #8	0.25	0.80	2.00	4.00
❑10	0.25	0.80	2.00	4.00
❑11	0.25	0.80	2.00	4.00
❑12	0.25	0.80	2.00	4.00
❑13	0.25	0.80	2.00	4.00
❑14	0.25	0.80	2.00	4.00
❑15	0.25	0.80	2.00	4.00
❑16, Back From The Dead!; The Last Of Mr. Mordeaux	0.25	0.80	2.00	4.00
❑17	0.25	0.80	2.00	4.00
❑18	0.25	0.80	2.00	4.00
❑19	0.25	0.80	2.00	4.00
❑20	0.25	0.80	2.00	4.00
❑21, The Day Before Doomsday!; Five Fingers	0.25	0.80	2.00	4.00
❑22	0.25	0.80	2.00	4.00
❑23,Final Issue	0.25	0.80	2.00	4.00

TOMB OF DRACULA
MARVEL

Issue	ORIG	GOOD	FINE	N-MINT
❑1, Apr 72, GC, Dracula, 1: Dracula (Marvel); 1: Frank Drake,Dracula revived	0.20	8.00	20.00	40.00
❑2, May 72, GC	0.20	3.60	9.00	18.00

	ORIG	GOOD	FINE	N-MINT
❑3, Jul 72, GC, Who Stalks The Vampire?, 1: Rachel Van Helsing	0.20	2.80	7.00	14.00
❑4, Sep 72, GC, Through A Mirror Darkly!	0.20	2.80	7.00	14.00
❑5, Nov 72, GC, Death To A Vampire Slayer!	0.20	2.80	7.00	14.00
❑6, Jan 73, GC	0.20	2.00	5.00	10.00
❑7, Mar 73, GC, 1: Edith Harker	0.20	2.00	5.00	10.00
❑8, May 73, GC	0.20	2.00	5.00	10.00
❑9, Jun 73, GC, Death From The Sea!, 1: Lucas Brand	0.20	2.00	5.00	10.00
❑10, Jul 73, GC, 1: Blade the Vampire Slayer	0.20	8.00	20.00	40.00
❑11, Aug 73, GC, The Voodoo-Man	0.20	1.60	4.00	8.00
❑12, Sep 73, GC, Night Of The Screaming House!, A: Blade the Vampire Slayer; A: Blade	0.20	2.00	5.00	10.00
❑13, Oct 73, GC, To Kill A Vampire, O: Blade the Vampire Slayer; 1: Deacon Frost	0.20	4.00	10.00	20.00
❑14, Nov 73, GC, Dracula Is Dead!, A: Blade the Vampire Slayer	0.20	2.00	5.00	10.00
❑15, Dec 73, GC, Fear Is The Name Of The Game!	0.20	1.60	4.00	8.00
❑16, Jan 74, GC, Return From The Grave!	0.20	1.60	4.00	8.00
❑17, Feb 74, GC, Death Rides The Rails!, A: Blade the Vampire Slayer	0.20	2.00	5.00	10.00
❑18, Mar 74, GC, Enter: Werewolf By Night, V: Werewolf by Night	0.20	1.60	4.00	8.00
❑19, Apr 74, GC, Snowbound In Hell!, A: Blade the Vampire Slayer	0.20	2.00	5.00	10.00
❑20, May 74, GC, The Coming Of Doctor Sun, 1: Doctor Sun	0.25	1.60	4.00	8.00
❑21, Jun 74, GC, Deathknell, A: Blade the Vampire Slayer; O: Doctor Sun	0.25	1.60	4.00	8.00
❑22, Jul 74, GC, ...In Death Do We Join	0.25	1.40	3.50	7.00
❑23, Aug 74, GC, Shadows In The Night	0.25	1.40	3.50	7.00
❑24, Sep 74, GC, A Night For The Living...A Morning For The Dead	0.25	1.40	3.50	7.00
❑25, Oct 74, GC, Night of the Blood Stalker, 1: Hannibal King	0.25	1.40	3.50	7.00
❑25-2, GC, 1: Hannibal King,2nd Printing; (part of Marvel Value Pack); (part of Marvel Value Pack)	—	0.30	0.75	1.50
❑26, Nov 74, GC, Where Lurks The Chimera!	0.25	1.40	3.50	7.00
❑27, Dec 74, TP; GC, Night-Fire!	0.25	1.40	3.50	7.00
❑28, Jan 75, TP; GC, Madness In the Mind!, 1: Adri Nitall	0.25	1.40	3.50	7.00
❑29, Feb 75, TP; GC, Vengeance Is Mine! Sayeth The Vampire	0.25	1.40	3.50	7.00
❑30, Mar 75, GC, A: Blade the Vampire Slayer	0.25	1.60	4.00	8.00
❑31, Apr 75, TP; GC, Ten Lords A Dying!	0.25	1.20	3.00	6.00
❑32, May 75, GC	0.25	1.20	3.00	6.00
❑33, Jun 75, TP; GC, Blood On My Hands!	0.25	1.20	3.00	6.00
❑34, Jul 75, TP; GC, Showdown Of Blood!, A: Brother Voodoo	0.25	1.20	3.00	6.00
❑35, Aug 75, TP; GC, Hell Hath No Fury, A: Brother Voodoo	0.25	1.20	3.00	6.00
❑36, Sep 75, GC, A: Brother Voodoo	0.25	1.20	3.00	6.00
❑37, Oct 75, TP; GC, The Vampire Is Coming!, 1: Harold H. Harold	0.25	1.20	3.00	6.00
❑38, Nov 75, TP; GC, Blood-Rush!, A: Doctor Sun	0.25	1.20	3.00	6.00
❑39, Dec 75, TP; GC, The Death Of Dracula, D: Dracula	0.25	1.20	3.00	6.00
❑40, Jan 76, TP; GC, Nightmares Of A Living Deadman!	0.25	1.20	3.00	6.00
❑41, Feb 76, GC, A: Blade the Vampire Slayer	0.25	1.20	3.00	6.00
❑42, Mar 76, GC, A: Blade the Vampire Slayer; V: Doctor Sun	0.25	1.00	2.50	5.00
❑43, Apr 76, GC	0.25	1.00	2.50	5.00
❑44, May 76, GC, A: Blade the Vampire Slayer; V: Doctor Strange; A: Hannibal King	0.25	1.00	2.50	5.00
❑45, Jun 76, GC, A: Hannibal King,Blade vs. Hannibal King	0.25	1.00	2.50	5.00
❑46, Jul 76, GC, A: Blade the Vampire Slayer; A: Blade,Wedding of Dracula	0.25	1.00	2.50	5.00
❑47, Aug 76, GC, A: Blade the Vampire Slayer	0.25	1.00	2.50	5.00
❑48, Sep 76, GC, A: Blade the Vampire Slayer; A: Hannibal King	0.30	1.00	2.50	5.00
❑49, Oct 76, GC, A: Blade the Vampire Slayer; A: Blade; A: Frankenstein; A: D'Artagnan; A: Tom Sawyer; A: Zorro	0.30	1.00	2.50	5.00
❑50, Nov 76, GC, A: Silver Surfer; A: Blade the Vampire Slayer	0.30	1.60	4.00	8.00
❑51, Dec 76, TP; GC, The Wildest Party, 1: Janus,Blade vs. Hannibal King	0.30	1.00	2.50	5.00
❑52, Jan 77, GC	0.30	1.00	2.50	5.00
❑53, Feb 77, GC, A: Son of Satan,Blade vs. Hannibal King and Deacon Frost	0.30	1.00	2.50	5.00

Blade the Vampire Slayer was a frequent adversary of the Prince of Darkness.

© 1973 Marvel Comics

	ORIG	GOOD	FINE	N-MINT
❑54, Mar 77, TP; GC, 'Twas The Night Before Christmas, A: Blade; O: Janus,birth of Dracula's son	0.30	1.00	2.50	5.00
❑55, Apr 77, GC	0.30	1.00	2.50	5.00
❑56, May 77, GC	0.30	1.00	2.50	5.00
❑57, Jun 77, TP; GC, The Forever Man	0.30	1.00	2.50	5.00
❑58, Jul 77, GC	0.30	1.00	2.50	5.00
❑59, Aug 77, GC	0.30	1.00	2.50	5.00
❑60, Sep 77, TP; GC, The Wrath Of Dracula!	0.30	1.00	2.50	5.00
❑61, Nov 77, GC, O: Janus	0.35	0.80	2.00	4.00
❑62, Jan 78, GC	0.35	0.80	2.00	4.00
❑63, Mar 78, GC	0.35	0.80	2.00	4.00
❑64, May 78, TP; GC, Life After Undeath	0.35	0.80	2.00	4.00
❑65, Jul 78, TP; GC, Where No Vampire Has Gone Before!	0.35	0.80	2.00	4.00
❑66, Sep 78, TP; GC, Showdown Greenwich Village!	0.35	0.80	2.00	4.00
❑67, Nov 78, TP; GC, At Long Last Lilith!, A: Lilith	0.35	0.80	2.00	4.00
❑68, Feb 79, GC	0.35	0.80	2.00	4.00
❑69, Apr 79, TP; GC, Batwings Over Transylvania!	0.35	0.80	2.00	4.00
❑70, Aug 79, D: Dracula, Double-size	0.60	1.20	3.00	6.00
❑GS 2	0.50	1.00	2.50	5.00
❑GS 3,Reprints Uncanny Tales #6	0.50	1.00	2.50	5.00

TOMB OF DRACULA (LTD. SERIES)
MARVEL

	ORIG	GOOD	FINE	N-MINT
❑1, Nov 91, GC; AW, Day Of Blood! Night Of Redemption!, Part 1	4.95	1.00	2.50	5.00
❑2, Dec 91, GC; AW, Day Of Blood! Night Of Redemption!, Part 2	4.95	1.00	2.50	5.00
❑3, Jan 92, GC; AW, Day Of Blood! Night Of Redemption!, Part 3	4.95	1.00	2.50	5.00
❑4, Feb 92, GC; AW, Day Of Blood! Night Of Redemption!, Part 4	4.95	1.00	2.50	5.00

TOMB OF DRACULA (MAGAZINE)
MARVEL

	ORIG	GOOD	FINE	N-MINT
❑1, Oct 79, GC, Black Genesis; The Newest Dracula, b&w; magazine	1.25	0.80	2.00	4.00
❑2, Dec 79, SD	1.25	0.60	1.50	3.00
❑3, Feb 80, TP; FM; GC	1.25	0.60	1.50	3.00
❑4, Apr 80, TP; GC	1.25	0.60	1.50	3.00
❑5, Jun 80, TP; JB; GC	1.25	0.60	1.50	3.00
❑6, Aug 80, GC, A House Divided; Violets for a Vampire	1.25	0.60	1.50	3.00

TOMB RAIDER GALLERY, THE
IMAGE

Value: Cover or less ❑1, Dec 00 .... 2.95

TOMB RAIDER: THE SERIES
IMAGE

	ORIG	GOOD	FINE	N-MINT
❑1/A,Lara Croft crouching on rock with setting sun	2.50	0.50	1.25	2.50
❑1/B,Lara in tree with temple in background	2.50	0.50	1.25	2.50
❑1/C,Lara climbing mountain	2.50	0.50	1.25	2.50
❑1/D,Lara standing in front of ruins	2.50	0.50	1.25	2.50
❑1/E,Holofoil cover; Lara on rock, no sun in background	—	1.40	3.50	7.00
❑1/F,Another Universe Exclusive	—	1.00	2.50	5.00
❑1/G,Tower Records exclusive; Gold foil Tomb Raider logo; Lara on rock, no sun in background	—	0.60	1.50	3.00
❑1/H,Tower records exclusive w/o gold logo	—	1.00	2.50	5.00
❑2	2.50	0.50	1.25	2.50
❑2/A,Santa cover with blue background; Tower records	—	1.00	2.50	5.00
❑2/B,Santa cover with yellowish holo-foil background; Tower Records	—	1.30	3.25	6.50
❑3	2.50	0.50	1.25	2.50
❑3/A, Monster Mart Edition; Lara kneeling on ruins, Monster Mart logo in lower right	—	1.40	3.50	7.00
❑3/B, Gold Monster Mart edition; Lara kneeling on ruins, Monster Mart logo in lower right	—	1.20	3.00	6.00

	ORIG	GOOD	FINE	N-MINT
❑4, Apr 00,Lara sitting on troot of tree, man standing, flames behind	2.50	0.50	1.25	2.50
❑4/A,Lara in tree, DF logo at bottom left	—	0.80	2.00	4.00
❑4/B,Similar cover to 4, with Certificate of Authenticity	—	1.60	4.00	8.00
❑5, May 00,Lara standing, dinosaur skeleton in background	2.50	0.50	1.25	2.50
❑5/A,Dynamic Forces variant, Tomb Raider logo in upper right, DF logo below, Lara standing on Triceratops skull	—	1.20	3.00	6.00
❑6, Jul 00	2.50	0.50	1.25	2.50
❑7, Jul 00, Dead Center, Part 1	2.50	0.50	1.25	2.50
❑7/A, Museum edition, limited to 25 copies.	—	25.00	62.50	125.00
❑8, Oct 00, Dead Center, Part 2	2.50	0.50	1.25	2.50
❑9, Dec 00,Lara sitting, faces in background	2.50	0.50	1.25	2.50
❑9/A,White background, holding two guns	—	0.80	2.00	4.00
❑9/B,Lara fighting crocodile, DF logo at top left	—	1.20	3.00	6.00
❑9/C,Lara fighting crocodile, blue foil around DF logo at top left	—	1.20	3.00	6.00
❑9/D,Sketch cover, black and white	—	2.00	5.00	10.00
❑10, Jan 01	2.50	0.50	1.25	2.50
❑10/A,Gold foil around Tomb Raider logo, includes Certificate of Authenticity	—	2.00	5.00	10.00
❑10/B,Red foil around Tomb Raider logo, includes Certificate of Authenticity	—	2.00	5.00	10.00
❑11, Mar 01	2.50	0.50	1.25	2.50
❑12, Apr 01	2.50	0.50	1.25	2.50
❑13, May 01	2.50	0.50	1.25	2.50
❑14	2.50	0.50	1.25	2.50
❑15	2.50	0.50	1.25	2.50
❑15/A,DFE red foil cover	14.99	3.00	7.49	14.99
❑Ash 1, Preview edition	—	1.00	2.50	5.00
❑ASH 1/A, Convention edition; Preview cover, with second outer cover (black & white) with Lara Croft on front, logo with white space on back	—	1.00	2.50	5.00

TOMB RAIDER/WITCHBLADE
IMAGE

	ORIG	GOOD	FINE	N-MINT
❑1,Green Cover	—	1.20	3.00	6.00
❑1/A,Brown cover	—	1.20	3.00	6.00
❑1/B,Signed by Michael Turner; Certificate of Authenticity	—	4.00	10.00	20.00

TOMB RAIDER/WITCHBLADE REVISITED
IMAGE

Value: Cover or less

❑1, Dec 98 ... 2.95

TOMB TALES
CRYPTIC ENTERTAINMENT

Value: Cover or less

❑1, b&w; cardstock cover ... 3.00
❑2, Jun 97, b&w; cardstock cover ... 3.00

TOM CORBETT
ETERNITY

Value: Cover or less

❑1, b&w ... 2.25
❑2, b&w ... 2.25
❑3, b&w ... 2.25
❑4, b&w ... 2.25

TOM CORBETT BOOK TWO
ETERNITY

Value: Cover or less

❑1, b&w ... 2.25
❑2, b&w ... 2.25
❑3, b&w ... 2.25
❑4, b&w ... 2.25

TOM LANDRY
SPIRE

	ORIG	GOOD	FINE	N-MINT
❑1, nn	0.49	0.60	1.50	3.00

TOMMI GUNN
LONDON NIGHT

Value: Cover or less

❑1, May 96 ... 3.00

TOMMI GUNN: KILLER'S LUST
LONDON NIGHT

Value: Cover or less

❑1, Feb 97 ... 3.00
❑1/Nude, Feb 97,chromium cover ... 3.00

TOM MIX WESTERN
AC

Value: Cover or less

❑1,Reprint ... 2.95
❑2, b&w; Reprint ... 2.50

TOMMY AND THE MONSTERS
NEW COMICS

Value: Cover or less

❑1, The Gibbering Thralls, b&w ... 1.95

TOMOE
CRUSADE

	ORIG	GOOD	FINE	N-MINT
❑0, Mar 96	2.95	0.60	1.50	3.00
❑0/LE, Limited edition (5,000 printed)	—	0.80	2.00	4.00
❑0/SC,variant cover	2.95	0.60	1.50	3.00
❑1, Apr 96	2.95	0.60	1.50	3.00
❑1/LE, Limited edition (5,000 printed)	—	0.80	2.00	4.00
❑1-2, Fan Appreciation Edition; contains preview of Manga Shi 2000	2.95	0.60	1.50	3.00
❑2, May 96	2.95	0.60	1.50	3.00
❑3	2.95	0.60	1.50	3.00

TOMOE: UNFORGETTABLE FIRE
CRUSADE

	ORIG	GOOD	FINE	N-MINT
❑1, Jun 97,prequel to Shi: The Series	2.95	0.59	1.48	2.95
❑1/LE, Jun 97,no cover price; American Entertainment Exclusive Edition; prequel to Shi: The Series	—	0.70	1.75	3.50

TOMOE/WITCHBLADE: FIRE SERMON
CRUSADE

Value: Cover or less

❑1, Sep 96, Fire Sermon,one-shot crossover with Image ... 3.95
❑1/A, Sep 96,no cover price; Avalon edition ... 5.00

TOMORROW KNIGHTS
MARVEL

Value: Cover or less

❑1, Jun 90, Working Class Stiffs ... 1.95
❑2, Jul 90 ... 1.50
❑3, Sep 90 ... 1.50
❑4, Nov 90 ... 1.50
❑5 ... 1.50
❑6 ... 1.50

TOMORROW MAN
ANTARCTIC

Value: Cover or less

❑1, Aug 93, b&w; foil cover ... 2.95

TOMORROW MAN & KNIGHT HUNTER: LAST RITES
ANTARCTIC

Value: Cover or less

❑1, Jul 94, b&w ... 2.75
❑2, Oct 94, b&w ... 2.75
❑3, Dec 94, b&w ... 2.75
❑4, Feb 95, Resurrection, b&w ... 2.75
❑5, Apr 95, b&w ... 2.75
❑6, Jun 95, Vendetta, b&w ... 2.75

TOMORROW STORIES
DC

	ORIG	GOOD	FINE	N-MINT
❑1, Oct 99, AMo (w), Smalltown Stardom, Amnesia, The First American and U.S.Angel, The Cobweb	3.50	0.80	2.00	4.00
❑2, Nov 99, AMo (w), How Things Work Out; Jack B. Quick: The Unbearableness of Being Light	2.95	0.60	1.50	3.00
❑3, Dec 99, AMo (w), Jack B. Quick: Pet Theory; The Cobweb	2.95	0.59	1.48	2.95
❑4, Jan 00, AMo (w), The First American and U.S.Angel: the bitter Crumbs of Defeat!?!; Li'l Cobweb	2.95	0.59	1.48	2.95
❑5	2.95	0.59	1.48	2.95
❑6	2.95	0.59	1.48	2.95
❑7, Jun 00, AMo (w), A Bigger Splash!; Grooveweb	2.95	0.59	1.48	2.95
❑8, Jan 01, Justice in Tights!; Cobweb	2.95	0.59	1.48	2.95
❑9, Feb 01, AMo (w), Farewell, My Lullabye; The Origin of The First American, O: The First American	2.95	0.59	1.48	2.95
❑10	2.95	0.59	1.48	2.95
❑11	2.95	0.59	1.48	2.95
❑12	2.95	0.59	1.48	2.95

TOM STRONG
DC

	ORIG	GOOD	FINE	N-MINT
❑1, Jun 99, AMo (w), How Tom Strong Got Started, O: Tom Strong	2.95	0.80	2.00	4.00
❑2, Jul 99, AMo (w), Return of the Modular Man	2.95	0.60	1.50	3.00
❑3, Aug 99, AMo (w), Aztech Nights	2.95	0.59	1.48	2.95
❑4, Oct 99, AMo (w), Swastika Girls!	2.95	0.59	1.48	2.95
❑5, Dec 99, Memories of Pangaea	2.95	0.59	1.48	2.95
❑6, AMo (w)	2.95	0.59	1.48	2.95
❑7, Mar 00, AMo (w), Sons and Heirs	2.95	0.59	1.48	2.95
❑8, AMo (w)	2.95	0.59	1.48	2.95
❑9, Sep 00, AMo (w), Terror Temple of Tayasal!	2.95	0.59	1.48	2.95
❑10, Nov 00, AMo (w), Tom Strong and his Phantom Autogyro; Funnyland!	2.95	0.59	1.48	2.95
❑11, Jan 01, AMo (w), Strange Reunion	2.95	0.59	1.48	2.95

TONGUE*LASH
DARK HORSE

Value: Cover or less

❑1, Aug 96, The Serpent's Tooth, Part 1 ... 2.95
❑2, Sep 96, The Serpent's Tooth, Part 2 ... 2.95

TONGUE*LASH II
DARK HORSE

Value: Cover or less

❑1, Feb 99 ... 2.95
❑2, Mar 99 ... 2.95

TONY BRAVADO, TROUBLE-SHOOTER
RENEGADE

Value: Cover or less

❑1, b&w ... 2.00
❑2, b&w ... 2.00
❑3, b&w ... 2.50
❑4, b&w ... 2.50

TOOL & DIE
FLASHPOINT

Value: Cover or less

❑1, Mar 94 ... 2.50

TOO MUCH COFFEE MAN
ADHESIVE

	ORIG	GOOD	FINE	N-MINT
❑1, Too Much Coffee Man vs. Trademark Copyright Man, b&w	2.50	2.40	6.00	12.00
❑2, ClichT, b&w	2.50	1.60	4.00	8.00
❑3, b&w	2.50	1.20	3.00	6.00
❑4, b&w	2.50	1.00	2.50	5.00
❑5, The Death of Too Much Coffee Man, b&w	2.50	1.00	2.50	5.00
❑6	—	0.60	1.50	3.00
❑7	—	0.60	1.50	3.00
❑8	—	0.60	1.50	3.00
❑MC 1,Mini-comic	1.00	2.00	5.00	10.00
❑MC 1-2,2nd Printing; Mini-comic	1.00	0.60	1.50	3.00
❑MC 2,Mini-comic	1.00	1.60	4.00	8.00
❑MC 2-2,2nd Printing; Mini-comic	1.00	0.60	1.50	3.00
❑MC 3,Mini-comic	1.00	1.60	4.00	8.00
❑MC 3-2,2nd Printing; Mini-comic	1.00	0.60	1.50	3.00
❑MC 4,Mini-comic	1.00	1.20	3.00	6.00
❑MC 4-2,2nd Printing; Mini-comic	1.00	0.60	1.50	3.00
❑SE 1, Jul 97, Too Much Coffee Man Meets His Coffee Maker, nn; b&w	2.95	0.60	1.50	3.00
❑SE 2, Full-Color Special Edition	2.95	0.60	1.50	3.00

TOON WARZ: THE FANDOM MENACE
SIRIUS

Value: Cover or less

- ❑1/A, Jul 99,Believe This Man cover 2.95
- ❑1/B, Jul 99,Vain Affair cover.. 2.95
- ❑1/C, Jul 99,Newspeak cover. 2.95
- ❑1/D, Jul 99,Primear cover 2.95

TOOTH AND CLAW
IMAGE

Value: Cover or less

- ❑1, Aug 99 .... 2.95
- ❑2, Sep 99,Woman-cat holding skull on cover 2.95
- ❑2/A, Sep 99,alternate cover.. 2.95
- ❑3 .... 2.95
- ❑Ash 1,DF Exclusive preview book 5.00

TOP 10
DC

Value: Cover or less

- ❑1, Sep 99, AMo (w) 3.50
- ❑2, Oct 99, AMo (w) 2.95
- ❑3, Nov 99, AMo (w), Eight Miles High 2.95
- ❑4, Dec 99, AMo (w), Great Infestations 2.95
- ❑5, Jan 00, AMo (w) 2.95
- ❑6, AMo (w) 2.95
- ❑7, Apr 00, AMo (w), Mythdemeanors 2.95
- ❑8, AMo (w) 2.95
- ❑9, Oct 00, AMo (w), Rules of Engagement 2.95
- ❑10, Jan 01, AMo (w), Music for the Dead 2.95
- ❑11, May 01, AMo (w), His First Day on the New Job 2.95
- ❑12 .... 2.95

TOP CAT
CHARLTON

	ORIG	GOOD	FINE	N-MINT
❑1	—	3.60	9.00	18.00
❑2	—	2.00	5.00	10.00
❑3	—	1.20	3.00	6.00
❑4, May 71	0.15	1.20	3.00	6.00
❑5, Jul 71	—	1.20	3.00	6.00
❑6, Sep 71	—	0.80	2.00	4.00
❑7, Nov 71	0.20	0.80	2.00	4.00
❑8	—	0.80	2.00	4.00
❑9	—	0.80	2.00	4.00
❑10	—	0.80	2.00	4.00
❑11	—	0.60	1.50	3.00
❑12	—	0.60	1.50	3.00
❑13	—	0.60	1.50	3.00
❑14	—	0.60	1.50	3.00
❑15	—	0.60	1.50	3.00
❑16	—	0.60	1.50	3.00
❑17	—	0.60	1.50	3.00
❑18	—	0.60	1.50	3.00
❑19	—	0.60	1.50	3.00
❑20	—	0.60	1.50	3.00

TOP COW CLASSICS IN BLACK AND WHITE: APHRODITE IX
IMAGE

	ORIG	GOOD	FINE	N-MINT
❑1, Sep 00	—	0.59	1.48	2.95

TOP COW CLASSICS IN BLACK AND WHITE: ASCENSCION
IMAGE

Value: Cover or less

- ❑1 .... 2.95

TOP COW CLASSICS IN BLACK AND WHITE: FATHOM
IMAGE

Value: Cover or less

- ❑1 .... 2.95

TOP COW CLASSICS IN BLACK AND WHITE: MIDNIGHT NATION
IMAGE

	ORIG	GOOD	FINE	N-MINT
❑1, Sep 00	—	0.59	1.48	2.95

TOP COW CLASSICS IN BLACK AND WHITE: RISING STARS
IMAGE

Value: Cover or less

- ❑1, Jul 00, Nova Placenta 2.95

Alan Moore's *Top 10* features a super-powered police force in a world where everyone has super-powers.

© 1999 Alan Moore/America's Best Comics (DC)

TOP COW CLASSICS IN BLACK AND WHITE: THE DARKNESS
IMAGE

Value: Cover or less

- ❑1, Mar 00, Coming of Age 2.95

TOP COW CLASSICS IN BLACK AND WHITE: TOMB RAIDER
IMAGE

Value: Cover or less

- ❑1, Dec 00 .... 2.95

TOP COW CLASSICS IN BLACK AND WHITE: WITCHBLADE
IMAGE

Value: Cover or less

- ❑1 .... 2.95

TOP COW PRODUCTIONS INC./BALLISTIC STUDIOS SWIMSUIT SPECIAL
IMAGE

Value: Cover or less

- ❑1, May 95 .... 2.95

TOP COW SECRETS
IMAGE

Value: Cover or less

- ❑WS 1, Jan 96, Blind Justice, Special Winter Lingerie Edition; pin-ups 2.95

TOP DOG
MARVEL

	ORIG	GOOD	FINE	N-MINT
❑1, Apr 85, The Dog-Gone Beginning, 1: Top Dog	0.65	0.20	0.50	1.00
❑2	0.65	0.20	0.50	1.00
❑3, The Mad Biter; Caged	0.65	0.20	0.50	1.00
❑4	0.65	0.20	0.50	1.00
❑5	0.65	0.20	0.50	1.00
❑6, Feb 86, Frank 'n' Stein	0.65	0.20	0.50	1.00
❑7	0.75	0.20	0.50	1.00
❑8	0.75	0.20	0.50	1.00
❑9	0.75	0.20	0.50	1.00
❑10	0.75	0.20	0.50	1.00
❑11	0.75	0.20	0.50	1.00
❑12	0.75	0.20	0.50	1.00
❑13	0.75	0.20	0.50	1.00
❑14,Final Issue	1.00	0.20	0.50	1.00

TOPPS COMICS PRESENTS
TOPPS

	ORIG	GOOD	FINE	N-MINT
❑0,Previewed Teenagents, Silver Star, Jack Kirby's Secret City Saga, Bill the Galactic Hero, etc.	—	0.30	0.75	1.50
❑1, giveaway	—	0.20	0.50	1.00

TOP SHELF (PRIMAL GROOVE)
PRIMAL GROOVE PRESS

Value: Cover or less

- ❑1, Win 95, b&w; Anthology.... 5.00

TOP SHELF (TOP SHELF)
TOP SHELF

Value: Cover or less

- ❑1 .... 6.95
- ❑2 .... 6.95
- ❑3 .... 6.95
- ❑4 .... 6.95
- ❑5 .... 6.95
- ❑6 .... 6.95
- ❑7, On Parade 6.95

TOR (DC)
DC

	ORIG	GOOD	FINE	N-MINT
❑1, Jun 75, JKu, JKu (w), The Beating, O: Tor	0.25	0.60	1.50	3.00
❑2, Aug 75, JKu, JKu (w)	0.25	0.40	1.00	2.00
❑3, Oct 75, JKu, JKu (w)	0.25	0.40	1.00	2.00
❑4, Dec 75, JKu, JKu (w)	0.25	0.40	1.00	2.00
❑5, Feb 76, JKu, JKu (w)	0.25	0.40	1.00	2.00
❑6, Apr 76, JKu, JKu (w),Final Issue	0.25	0.40	1.00	2.00

TOR (EPIC)
MARVEL

Value: Cover or less

- ❑1, Jun 93, JKu, JKu (w), O: Tor, large size 5.95
- ❑2, Jul 93, JKu, JKu (w), The Chosen One, large size 5.95
- ❑3, JKu, JKu (w), large size 5.95
- ❑4, JKu, JKu (w), large size 5.95

TOR 3-D
ECLIPSE

	ORIG	GOOD	FINE	N-MINT
❑1, JKu, JKu (w), Tor; Animals of 1,000,000 Years Ago-Triceratops, 3-D glasses	1.50	0.50	1.25	2.50
❑2, JKu, JKu (w), Killer-man!; The Story of Evolution!, 3-D glasses	1.50	0.50	1.25	2.50

ORIG GOOD FINE N-MINT

TORCH OF LIBERTY SPECIAL
DARK HORSE
Value: Cover or less
❑1, Jan 95, JBy (w), nn; One-Shot 2.50

TORCHY (INNOVATION)
INNOVATION
Value: Cover or less
❑1, BWa, b&w; Reprint 2.50
❑2, BWa, b&w; Reprint 2.50
❑3, BWa, b&w; Reprint 2.50
❑4, BWa, b&w; Reprint 2.50
❑5, BWa, b&w; Reprint 2.50
❑9, BWa, b&w; 1st Olivia cover; Reprint 2.50
❑Smr 1, b&w; Reprint; Summer Fun Special 2.50

TORG
ADVENTURE
Value: Cover or less
❑1, b&w 2.50
❑2, Mar 92, b&w 2.50
❑3, Apr 92, b&w 2.50
❑4, May 92, b&w 2.50

TORI DO
PENGUIN PALACE
Value: Cover or less
❑1, Aug 94, b&w 2.25
❑1-2, Mar 95,2nd Printing 2.25

TO RIVERDALE AND BACK AGAIN
ARCHIE
Value: Cover or less
❑1, GC, JBy (c), nn 2.50

TOR JOHNSON: HOLLYWOOD STAR
MONSTER
Value: Cover or less
❑1, b&w 2.50

TOR LOVE BETTY
FANTAGRAPHICS
Value: Cover or less
❑1, b&w; adult 2.75

TORMENT
AIRCEL
Value: Cover or less
❑1, b&w; adult 2.95
❑2, b&w; adult 2.95
❑3, b&w; adult 2.95

TORPEDO
HARD BOILED
Value: Cover or less
❑1, Triple Cross, b&w; Reprint 2.95
❑2, b&w; Reprint 2.95
❑3, b&w; Reprint 2.95
❑4, b&w; Reprint 2.95

TORRID AFFAIRS
ETERNITY
Value: Cover or less
❑1, b&w; Reprint 2.25
❑2/A,tame cover 2.25
❑2/B,sexy cover 2.25
❑3 .... 2.95
❑4 .... 2.95
❑5 .... 2.95

TORSO
IMAGE

	ORIG	GOOD	FINE	N-MINT
❑1, BMB (w)	3.95	0.79	1.98	3.95
❑2, BMB (w)	3.95	0.79	1.98	3.95
❑3, BMB (w)	3.95	0.99	2.47	4.95
❑4, BMB (w)	4.95	0.99	2.47	4.95
❑5, BMB, BMB (w)	4.95	0.99	2.47	4.95
❑6, BMB, BMB (w),48pgs.	4.95	0.99	2.47	4.95

TORTOISE AND THE HARE, THE
LAST GASP

	ORIG	GOOD	FINE	N-MINT
❑1, Back-up stories: The Phantom Roar-Shock's; The Early Adventures of Roger Rabbit	0.50	0.60	1.50	3.00

TOTAL ECLIPSE
ECLIPSE
Value: Cover or less
❑1, May 88, BA, BSz (c), Zzed, A: Valkyrie; V: Misery; V: Z; A: Prowler; A: Strike; A: New Wave; A: Skywolf; A: Airboy; A: Black Angel; A: Sgt. Strike 3.95
❑2, Aug 88, JKu, BSz (c), Danny Dreams, A: Valkyrie; A: Prowler; A: Strike; A: New Wave; A: Skywolf; A: Airboy; A: Liberty Project; A: Sgt. Strike; A: Miracle 3.95
❑3, Dec 88, BSz (c), A: Valkyrie; A: Prowler; A: Beanish; A: Strike; A: New Wave; A: Skywolf; A: Airboy; A: Liberty Project; A: Sgt. Strike 3.95
❑4, Jan 89, BSz (c), A: Valkyrie; 1: Dr. Eclipse; A: Prowler; A: Beanish; 1: Doctor Eclipse; A: New Wave; A: Skywolf; A: Airboy; D: Strike!; A: Sgt. Strike 3.95
❑5, Apr 89, BSz (c), A: Valkyrie; V: Misery; A: Aztec Ace; A: Heap; A: Prowler; A: Beanish; A: New Wave; A: Skywolf; A: Airboy; A: Sgt. Strike 3.95

TOTAL ECLIPSE: THE SERAPHIM OBJECTIVE
ECLIPSE
Value: Cover or less
❑1, Nov 88, KB (w), A: Heap; A: Airboy; A: Liberty Project 1.95

TOTAL JUSTICE
DC
Value: Cover or less
❑1, Oct 96, Tim,based on Kenner action figures 2.25
❑2, Nov 96, Mike,based on Kenner action figures 2.25
❑3, Nov 96, Kyle,based on Kenner action figures 2.25

TOTALLY ALIEN
TRIGON
Value: Cover or less
❑1, b&w 2.50
❑2, b&w 2.50
❑3, b&w 2.50
❑4, b&w 2.50
❑5, b&w 2.50

TOTALLY HORSES!
PAINTED PONY
Value: Cover or less
❑1, magazine; horse stories 1.95
❑2, Spr 97, magazine; horse stories 1.95
❑3, magazine; horse stories 1.95
❑4, magazine; horse stories 1.95
❑5, Sum 98, magazine; horse stories 1.95

TOTAL RECALL
DC
Value: Cover or less
❑1,movie Adaptation 2.95

TOTAL WAR
GOLD KEY

	ORIG	GOOD	FINE	N-MINT
❑1, Jul 65	—	4.00	10.00	20.00
❑2, Oct 65,Series continued in M.A.R.S. Patrol #3	—	3.00	7.50	15.00

TOTEMS (CARTOON FROLICS)
CARTOON FROLICS
Value: Cover or less
❑1 .... 2.95
❑2 .... 2.95
❑3, Pawns 2.95

TOTEMS (VERTIGO)
VERTIGO
Value: Cover or less
❑1, Feb 00 .... 5.95

TOTEM: SIGN OF THE WARDOG (1ST SERIES)
ALPHA PRODUCTIONS
Value: Cover or less
❑1, b&w 2.25
❑2, b&w 2.25

TOTEM: SIGN OF THE WARDOG (2ND SERIES)
ALPHA PRODUCTIONS
Value: Cover or less
❑1, b&w 2.50
❑2, b&w 2.50
❑Anl 1, No Safe Haven; The Mother Of Mayhem, Databank, Boys Will Be Boys 3.50

TO THE HEART OF THE STORM (DC)
DC
Value: Cover or less
❑1, Sep 00, WE, WE (w) 14.95

TOUCH OF SILK, A TASTE OF LEATHER, A
BONEYARD
Value: Cover or less
❑1, Mar 94, nn; b&w 2.95

TOUCH OF SILVER, A
IMAGE
Value: Cover or less
❑1, Jan 97, Birthday, b&w; semi-autobiographical 2.95
❑2, Mar 97, Dance, b&w; semi-autobiographical 2.95
❑3, May 97, Bullies, b&w; semi-autobiographical 2.95
❑4, Jul 97, Separation, b&w; semi-autobiographical 2.95
❑5, Sep 97, Fantasy,b&w with color section; semi-autobiographical 2.95
❑6, Nov 97, b&w; semi-autobiographical 2.95

TOUGH GUYS AND WILD WOMEN
ETERNITY
Value: Cover or less
❑1, Mar 89, The Saint Dective Cases: Suite 13; Blackmail Beauty, b&w; Saint reprints 2.25
❑2, b&w; Saint reprints 2.25

TOWER OF SHADOWS
MARVEL

	ORIG	GOOD	FINE	N-MINT
❑1, Sep 69, JSo; JCr; JB, SL (w); JSo (w); JCr (w), At the Stroke of Midnight!; From Beyond the Brink!	0.15	3.00	7.50	15.00
❑2, NA	0.15	2.00	5.00	10.00
❑3, Jan 70	0.15	2.00	5.00	10.00
❑4, Jan 70	0.15	1.60	4.00	8.00
❑5, May 70	0.15	1.60	4.00	8.00
❑6, Jul 70, WW; GC; SD; TS, SL (w); TS (w), Man in the Rat-Hole!; The Ghost-Beast!.	0.15	1.60	4.00	8.00
❑7, Sep 70, I Was Trapped By Titano The Monster That Time Forgot!; The Scream Of Things	0.15	1.60	4.00	8.00
❑8, Nov 70, WW; SD	0.15	1.60	4.00	8.00
❑9, Nov 70,Series continued in Creatures On the Loose #10	0.15	1.20	3.00	6.00
❑SE 1	—	1.60	4.00	8.00

TOXIC!
APOCALYPSE
Value: Cover or less
❑1,Marshal Law 2.50
❑2,Marshal Law 2.50
❑3,Marshal Law 2.50
❑4,Marshal Law 2.50
❑5, Accident Man: Confessions of a Teenage Sociopath, O: Accident Man; A: The Bogie Man,Marshal Law; Mutomatic; The Driver 2.50
❑6,Marshal Law 2.50
❑7,Marshal Law 2.50
❑8,Marshal Law 2.50
❑9,Marshal Law 2.50
❑10,Marshal Law 2.50
❑11,Marshal Law 2.50
❑12,Marshal Law 2.50
❑13,Marshal Law 2.50

	ORIG	GOOD	FINE	N-MINT
❑14,Marshal Law				2.50
❑15,Marshal Law				2.50
❑16,Marshal Law				2.50
❑17,Marshal Law				2.50
❑18,Marshal Law				2.50
❑19,Marshal Law				2.50

TOXIC AVENGER
MARVEL

	ORIG	GOOD	FINE	N-MINT
❑1, Apr 91, A Hideously Deformed Creature of Superhuman Size and Strength is Born, 1: Toxic Avenger	1.50	0.40	1.00	2.00
❑2, May 91	1.50	0.30	0.75	1.50
❑3, Jun 91	1.50	0.30	0.75	1.50
❑4, Jul 91, Lethal Linda And The Legend Of Sludgeface	1.50	0.30	0.75	1.50
❑5, Aug 91	1.50	0.30	0.75	1.50
❑6, Sep 91	1.50	0.30	0.75	1.50
❑7, Oct 91	1.50	0.30	0.75	1.50
❑8, Nov 91, The Souvlaki Sewer Syndrome Part II: Oooze Brute	1.50	0.30	0.75	1.50
❑9, Dec 91	1.50	0.30	0.75	1.50
❑10, Jan 92, Die Yuppie Scum,Photo cover	1.50	0.30	0.75	1.50
❑11, Feb 92, VM, Nukin' Weasels	1.50	0.30	0.75	1.50

TOXIC CRUSADERS
MARVEL

Value: Cover or less

- ❑1, The Making of Toxie, O: Toxic Avenger 1.25
- ❑2, JSa, The Big Broadcast of 1992 .... 1.25
- ❑3 .... 1.25
- ❑4 .... 1.25
- ❑5 .... 1.25
- ❑6 .... 1.25
- ❑7 .... 1.25
- ❑8 .... 1.25

TOXIC GUMBO
DC

Value: Cover or less

- ❑1, nn; One-Shot; prestige format 5.95

TOXIC PARADISE
SLAVE LABOR

Value: Cover or less

- ❑1, Love and Romance; Loser, b&w; cardstock cover; Love & Romance 4.95

TOXINE
NOSE

Value: Cover or less

- ❑1 .... 3.00

TOYBOY
CONTINUITY

Value: Cover or less

- ❑1, Oct 86, NA, NA (w) 2.00
- ❑2, Aug 87, NA, NA (w) 2.00
- ❑3, Nov 87, NA, NA (w) 2.00
- ❑4, Feb 88, NA, NA (w) 2.00
- ❑5, Jun 88, NA, NA (w) 2.00
- ❑6, NA, NA (w) 2.00
- ❑7, Mar 89, NA, NA (w) 2.00

TOY STORY (DISNEY'S...)
MARVEL

Value: Cover or less

- ❑1 .... 4.95

TRACI LORDS: THE OUTLAW YEARS
BONEYARD

	ORIG	GOOD	FINE	N-MINT
❑1	2.75	0.60	1.50	3.00

TRACKER
BLACKTHORNE

Value: Cover or less

- ❑1, May 88, b&w 2.00
- ❑2, b&w 2.00

TRAGG AND THE SKY GODS
WHITMAN

	ORIG	GOOD	FINE	N-MINT
❑1, DS, Death-Duel	—	1.00	2.50	5.00
❑2	—	0.60	1.50	3.00
❑3	—	0.50	1.25	2.50
❑4	—	0.50	1.25	2.50
❑5	—	0.50	1.25	2.50
❑6	0.25	0.50	1.25	2.50
❑7	—	0.50	1.25	2.50
❑8	—	0.50	1.25	2.50
❑9	—	0.50	1.25	2.50

TRAILER TRASH
TUNDRA

Value: Cover or less

- ❑1, b&w; adult 2.00
- ❑4, b&w; adult 2.95
- ❑7, Jun 96, b&w; adult 2.95
- ❑8, Nov 96, b&w; adult 2.95

TRANCERS
ETERNITY

Value: Cover or less

- ❑1, Aug 91, full color; movie Adaptation 2.50
- ❑2, full color; movie Adaptation 2.50

TRANQUILITY
DREAMSMITH

Value: Cover or less

- ❑1, b&w 2.50
- ❑2, Oct 98, b&w 2.50
- ❑3, Nov 98, b&w 2.50

TRANQUILIZER
LUXURIOUS

Value: Cover or less

- ❑1 .... 2.95
- ❑2 .... 2.95

Fan nostalgia and low print runs have caused an increase in prices for the last few issues of *The Transformers.*

TRANSFORMERS, THE
MARVEL

	ORIG	GOOD	FINE	N-MINT
❑1, Sep 84, 1: Transformers,"Limited Series #1"	0.75	0.50	1.25	2.50
❑2, Nov 84,"Limited Series #2"	0.75	0.40	1.00	2.00
❑3, Jan 85,Spider-Man; "Limited Series #3"	0.75	0.40	1.00	2.00
❑4, Mar 85,"Limited Series #4"	0.75	0.30	0.75	1.50
❑5, Jun 85	0.75	0.30	0.75	1.50
❑6, Jul 85	0.75	0.30	0.75	1.50
❑7, Aug 85	0.75	0.30	0.75	1.50
❑8, Sep 85, A: Dinobots	0.75	0.30	0.75	1.50
❑9, Oct 85	0.75	0.30	0.75	1.50
❑10, Nov 85, V: Devastator	0.75	0.30	0.75	1.50
❑11, Dec 85, V: Jetfire	0.75	0.30	0.75	1.50
❑12, Jan 86	0.75	0.30	0.75	1.50
❑13, Feb 86	0.75	0.30	0.75	1.50
❑14, Mar 86	0.75	0.30	0.75	1.50
❑15, Apr 86	0.75	0.30	0.75	1.50
❑16, May 86	0.75	0.30	0.75	1.50
❑17, Jun 86	0.75	0.30	0.75	1.50
❑18, Jul 86	0.75	0.30	0.75	1.50
❑19, Aug 86	0.75	0.30	0.75	1.50
❑20, Sep 86	0.75	0.30	0.75	1.50
❑21, Oct 86, 1: Aerialbots	0.75	0.25	0.63	1.25
❑22, Nov 86	0.75	0.25	0.63	1.25
❑23, Dec 86	0.75	0.25	0.63	1.25
❑24, Jan 87	0.75	0.25	0.63	1.25
❑25, Feb 87	0.75	0.25	0.63	1.25
❑26, Mar 87	0.75	0.25	0.63	1.25
❑27, Apr 87	0.75	0.25	0.63	1.25
❑28, May 87	1.00	0.25	0.63	1.25
❑29, Jun 87	1.00	0.25	0.63	1.25
❑30, Jul 87	1.00	0.25	0.63	1.25
❑31, Aug 87	1.00	0.25	0.63	1.25
❑32, Sep 87	1.00	0.25	0.63	1.25
❑33, Oct 87	1.00	0.25	0.63	1.25
❑34, Nov 87	1.00	0.25	0.63	1.25
❑35, Dec 87	1.00	0.25	0.63	1.25
❑36, Jan 88	1.00	0.25	0.63	1.25
❑37, Feb 88	1.00	0.25	0.63	1.25
❑38, Mar 88	1.00	0.25	0.63	1.25
❑39, Apr 88	1.00	0.25	0.63	1.25
❑40, May 88	1.00	0.25	0.63	1.25
❑41, Jun 88	1.00	0.20	0.50	1.00
❑42, Jul 88	1.00	0.20	0.50	1.00
❑43, Aug 88	1.00	0.20	0.50	1.00
❑44, Sep 88	1.00	0.20	0.50	1.00
❑45, Oct 88	1.00	0.20	0.50	1.00
❑46, Nov 88	1.00	0.20	0.50	1.00
❑47, Dec 88	1.00	0.20	0.50	1.00
❑48, Jan 89	1.00	0.20	0.50	1.00
❑49, Feb 89	1.00	0.20	0.50	1.00
❑50, Mar 89	1.50	0.20	0.50	1.00
❑51, Apr 89	1.00	0.20	0.50	1.00
❑52, May 89	1.00	0.20	0.50	1.00
❑53, Jun 89	1.00	0.20	0.50	1.00
❑54, Jul 89	1.00	0.20	0.50	1.00
❑55, Aug 89	1.00	0.20	0.50	1.00
❑56, Sep 89	1.00	0.20	0.50	1.00
❑57, Oct 89	1.00	0.20	0.50	1.00
❑58, Nov 89	1.00	0.20	0.50	1.00
❑59, Nov 89	1.00	0.20	0.50	1.00
❑60, Dec 89	1.00	0.20	0.50	1.00
❑61, Dec 89	1.00	0.20	0.50	1.00
❑62, Jan 90	1.00	0.20	0.50	1.00
❑63, Feb 90	1.00	0.20	0.50	1.00
❑64, Mar 90	1.00	0.20	0.50	1.00
❑65, Apr 90	1.00	0.20	0.50	1.00
❑66, May 90	1.00	0.20	0.50	1.00
❑67, Jun 90	1.00	0.20	0.50	1.00
❑68, Jul 90	1.00	0.20	0.50	1.00

	ORIG	GOOD	FINE	N-MINT
❏69, Aug 90	1.00	0.20	0.50	1.00
❏70, Sep 90	1.00	0.20	0.50	1.00
❏71, Oct 90	1.00	0.20	0.50	1.00
❏72, Nov 90	1.00	0.20	0.50	1.00
❏73, Dec 90	1.00	0.20	0.50	1.00
❏74, Jan 91	1.00	0.20	0.50	1.00
❏75, Feb 91, Double-size	1.50	0.30	0.75	1.50
❏76, Mar 91	1.00	0.20	0.50	1.00
❏77, Apr 91	1.00	0.20	0.50	1.00
❏78, May 91	1.00	3.00	7.50	15.00
❏79, Jun 91	1.00	3.00	7.50	15.00
❏80, Jul 91,Final Issue	1.00	5.00	12.50	25.00

TRANSFORMERS COMICS MAGAZINE
MARVEL

Value: Cover or less

❏1, Jan 87, digest	1.50	❏6, Nov 87	1.50
❏2, Mar 87	1.50	❏7, Jan 88	1.50
❏3, May 87	1.50	❏8, Mar 88	1.50
❏4, Jul 87	1.50	❏9, May 88	1.50
❏5, Sep 87	1.50	❏10, Jul 88	1.50

TRANSFORMERS: GENERATION 2
MARVEL

Value: Cover or less

❏1, Nov 93, O: Transformers	1.75	❏6, Apr 94	1.75
❏1/SC, Nov 93, O: Transformers,foil fold-out cover	2.95	❏7, May 94	1.75
❏2, Dec 93	1.75	❏8, Jun 94	1.75
❏3, Jan 94	1.75	❏9, Jul 94	1.75
❏4, Feb 94, A: Dinobots	1.75	❏10, Aug 94	1.75
❏5, Mar 94	1.75	❏11, Sep 94	1.75
		❏12, Oct 94,Final Issue; double-sized	2.25

TRANSFORMERS, THE: HEADMASTERS
MARVEL

	ORIG	GOOD	FINE	N-MINT
❏1, Jul 87	1.00	0.20	0.50	1.00
❏2, Sep 87, FS, Broken Glass	1.00	0.20	0.50	1.00
❏3, Nov 87	1.00	0.20	0.50	1.00
❏4, Jan 88	0.75	0.20	0.50	1.00

TRANSFORMERS IN 3-D, THE
BLACKTHORNE

Value: Cover or less

❏1, The Test	2.50	❏2, Dec 87	2.50
		❏3, Apr 88	2.50

TRANSFORMERS MOVIE
MARVEL

	ORIG	GOOD	FINE	N-MINT
❏1, Dec 86	0.75	0.20	0.50	1.00
❏2, Jan 87	0.75	0.20	0.50	1.00
❏3, Feb 87	0.75	0.20	0.50	1.00

TRANSFORMERS UNIVERSE
MARVEL

Value: Cover or less

❏1, Dec 86	1.25	❏3, Feb 87	1.25
❏2, Jan 87	1.25	❏4, Mar 87	1.25

TRANSIT
VORTEX

Value: Cover or less

❏1	1.75	❏4	1.75
❏2	1.75	❏5	1.75
❏3	1.75		

TRANSMETROPOLITAN
DC

	ORIG	GOOD	FINE	N-MINT
❏1, Sep 97	2.50	1.20	3.00	6.00
❏2, Oct 97	2.50	1.00	2.50	5.00
❏3, Nov 97, Up on the Roof	2.50	0.80	2.00	4.00
❏4, Dec 97, On the Stump	2.50	0.80	2.00	4.00
❏5, Jan 98	2.50	0.80	2.00	4.00
❏6, Feb 98	2.50	0.60	1.50	3.00
❏7, Mar 98	2.50	0.60	1.50	3.00
❏8, Apr 98	2.50	0.60	1.50	3.00
❏9, May 98	2.50	0.60	1.50	3.00
❏10, Jun 98	2.50	0.60	1.50	3.00
❏11, Jul 98	2.50	0.60	1.50	3.00
❏12, Aug 98	2.50	0.60	1.50	3.00
❏13, Sep 98, Year of the Bastard, Part 1	2.50	0.50	1.25	2.50
❏14, Oct 98, Year of the Bastard, Part 2	2.50	0.50	1.25	2.50
❏15, Nov 98, Year of the Bastard, Part 3	2.50	0.50	1.25	2.50
❏16, Dec 98, Year of the Bastard, Part 4	2.50	0.50	1.25	2.50
❏17, Jan 99, Year of the Bastard, Part 5	2.50	0.50	1.25	2.50
❏18, Feb 99, Year of the Bastard, Part 6	2.50	0.50	1.25	2.50
❏19, Mar 99, The New Scum, Part 1	2.50	0.50	1.25	2.50
❏20, Apr 99, The New Scum, Part 2	2.50	0.50	1.25	2.50
❏21, May 99, The New Scum, Part 3	2.50	0.50	1.25	2.50
❏22, Jun 99, The New Scum, Part 4, New Streets	2.50	0.50	1.25	2.50
❏23, Jul 99, The New Scum, Part 5, New Boss,100 Bullets preview	2.50	0.50	1.25	2.50
❏24, Aug 99	2.50	0.50	1.25	2.50
❏25, Sep 99, Here To Go	2.50	0.50	1.25	2.50
❏26, Oct 99, 21 Days in the City	2.50	0.50	1.25	2.50
❏27, Nov 99	2.50	0.50	1.25	2.50
❏28, Dec 99, Lonely Ciy, Part 1	2.50	0.50	1.25	2.50
❏29, Jan 00, Lonely Ciy, Part 2	2.50	0.50	1.25	2.50
❏30, Feb 00, Lonely Ciy, Part 3	2.50	0.50	1.25	2.50
❏31, Mar 00	2.50	0.50	1.25	2.50
❏32, Apr 00	2.50	0.50	1.25	2.50
❏33, May 00, Dancing in the Here and Now	2.50	0.50	1.25	2.50
❏34	2.50	0.50	1.25	2.50
❏35	2.50	0.50	1.25	2.50
❏36	2.50	0.50	1.25	2.50
❏37, Oct 00, Back to Basics, Part 1	2.50	0.50	1.25	2.50
❏38, Nov 00, Back to Basics, Part 2	2.50	0.50	1.25	2.50
❏39, Dec 00, Back to Basics, Part 3	2.50	0.50	1.25	2.50
❏40, Jan 01, Business	2.50	0.50	1.25	2.50
❏41, Feb 01, There is a Reason	2.50	0.50	1.25	2.50
❏42, Mar 01, Spider's Thrash	2.50	0.50	1.25	2.50
❏43, Apr 01, Dirge, Part 1	2.50	0.50	1.25	2.50
❏44, May 01, Dirge, Part 2	2.50	0.50	1.25	2.50
❏45, Jun 01, Dirge, Part 3	2.50	0.50	1.25	2.50
❏46	2.50	0.50	1.25	2.50
❏47	2.50	0.50	1.25	2.50

TRANSMETROPOLITAN: I HATE IT HERE
VERTIGO

Value: Cover or less

❏1, Jun 00	5.95

TRANSMUTATION OF IKE GARUDA, THE
MARVEL

Value: Cover or less

❏1	3.95	❏2	3.95

TRANS NUBIANS
ADEOLA

Value: Cover or less

❏1	2.95

TRASH
FLEETWAY

Value: Cover or less

❏1, How Green Is My Computer	2.95	❏2	2.95

TRAUMA CORPS
ANUBIS

Value: Cover or less

❏1, Feb 94	2.75

TRAVELERS, THE
SOUTH JERSEY REBELLION PRODUCTIONS

Value: Cover or less

❏1, b&w; no indicia	2.25

TRAVELLER'S TALE, A
ANTARCTIC

Value: Cover or less

❏1, b&w	2.50	❏2, Aug 92, b&w	2.50
		❏3, Oct 92, b&w	2.50

TREASURE CHESTS
EROS

	ORIG	GOOD	FINE	N-MINT
❏1	—	0.59	1.48	2.95
❏2	—	0.59	1.48	2.95
❏3	—	0.59	1.48	2.95
❏4	—	0.59	1.48	2.95
❏5, Jul 00, Dental Men Prefer Blondes; I See London, I See France	2.95	0.59	1.48	2.95

TREEHOUSE OF HORROR (BART SIMPSON'S...)
BONGO

	ORIG	GOOD	FINE	N-MINT
❏1, 95, JRo (w), Call Me Homer; Little Shop of Homers,Halloween stories	2.95	0.70	1.75	3.50
❏2, 96,infinity cover; Halloween stories	2.50	0.50	1.25	2.50
❏3, 97, The Immigration of the Body Snatchers; Fatal Reception,Halloween story	2.50	0.50	1.25	2.50
❏4, 98,Halloween stories	2.50	0.50	1.25	2.50
❏5, SA ,Halloween stories; Eisner award winner	3.50	0.70	1.75	3.50
❏6, Hell-o-Ween; Metamorphsimpsons,Halloween stories	4.50	0.90	2.25	4.50

TREKKER (DARK HORSE)
DARK HORSE

Value: Cover or less

❏1, May 87, Smuggler's Blues, b&w	1.50	❏6, Mar 88	1.50
❏2, Jul 87, b&w	1.50	❏7	1.50
❏3, Sep 87	1.75	❏8	1.50
❏4, Nov 87	1.75	❏9	1.50
❏5, Jan 88	1.75	❏SE 1, Sins Of The Fathers,Color Special	2.95

TREKKER (IMAGE)
IMAGE

Value: Cover or less

❏SE 1, Jun 99, Trial by Fire	2.95

TREK TEENS
PARODY PRESS

Value: Cover or less

❏1, Feb 93, b&w	2.50	❏1/A, Feb 93, b&w; alternate cover	2.50

TRENCHCOAT BRIGADE
DC
Value: Cover or less

- ❑1, Mar 99 ..... 2.50
- ❑2, Apr 99 ..... 2.50
- ❑3, May 99 ..... 2.50
- ❑4, Jun 99 ..... 2.50

TRENCHER
IMAGE

	ORIG	GOOD	FINE	N-MINT
❑1, May 93, KG, KG (w), Life Sucks...And Then You Come Back	1.95	0.40	1.00	2.00
❑2, Jun 93, KG	1.95	0.40	1.00	2.00
❑3, Jul 93, KG	1.95	0.40	1.00	2.00
❑4, Oct 93, KG	1.95	0.40	1.00	2.00

TRENCHER X-MAS BITES HOLIDAY BLOW-OUT
BLACKBALL
Value: Cover or less

- ❑1, Dec 93, KG 2.50

TRESPASSERS, THE
AMAZING MONTAGE
Value: Cover or less

- ❑1 ..... 2.50
- ❑2 ..... 2.50
- ❑3 ..... 2.50
- ❑4 ..... 2.50
- ❑5 ..... 2.50

TRIAD UNIVERSE
TRIAD
Value: Cover or less

- ❑1, Jul 94 ..... 2.25
- ❑2, Aug 94, b&w 2.25

TRIAL RUN
MILLER
Value: Cover or less

- ❑1, b&w 2.00
- ❑2, b&w 2.00
- ❑3, b&w 2.00
- ❑4, b&w 2.00
- ❑5, b&w 2.00
- ❑6, b&w 2.00
- ❑7, b&w 2.00
- ❑14 ..... 2.50
- ❑15 ..... 2.50

TRIARCH
CALIBER
Value: Cover or less

- ❑1, b&w 2.50
- ❑2, b&w 2.50

TRIBE
IMAGE
Value: Cover or less

- ❑1, Mar 93, Blindspot,Embossed cover; Only issue published by Image 2.95
- ❑1/A, Mar 93,foil cover; Special edition 2.95
- ❑1/B, Mar 93,cover says Apr, indicia says Mar; Special edition; gold logo 2.95
- ❑1/C, Mar 93,White cover; gold logo 2.95
- ❑2,Axis begins publishing 1.95
- ❑3, Apr 94,Final Issue 1.95

TRIBE (VOL. 2)
GOOD
Value: Cover or less

- ❑0, Oct 96 ..... 2.95

TRICKSTER KING MONKEY
EASTERN
Value: Cover or less

- ❑1 ..... 1.75

TRIDENT
TRIDENT
Value: Cover or less

- ❑1, b&w; adult 3.50
- ❑2, b&w; adult 3.50
- ❑3, b&w; adult 3.50
- ❑4, b&w; adult 3.50
- ❑5, Apr 90, b&w; adult 3.50
- ❑6, b&w; adult 3.50
- ❑7, b&w; adult 3.50
- ❑8, b&w; adult 3.50

TRIGGERMAN
CALIBER
Value: Cover or less

- ❑1 ..... 2.95
- ❑2 ..... 2.95

TRIGGER TWINS
DC

	ORIG	GOOD	FINE	N-MINT
❑1, Mar 73, RA; CI, Code of the Trigger Twins!; Pow-Wow Smith: The Bandit and the Bracelet!,Reprints from All-Star Western #94, 81, 103	0.20	1.00	2.50	5.00

TRILOGY TOUR
CARTOON
Value: Cover or less

- ❑1, Sum 97, b&w; promotional comic for Summer 1997 tour 1.50

TRILOGY TOUR II
CARTOON
Value: Cover or less

- ❑1, Jun 98, b&w and color; promotional comic for Summer 1998 tour 4.95

TRINITY ANGELS
ACCLAIM

	ORIG	GOOD	FINE	N-MINT
❑1, Jul 97, Trinity Angels, 1: Maria Barbella; 1: Gianna Barbella; 1: Trenchmouth; 1: Teresa Angelina Barbella; 1: Rubberneck	2.50	0.50	1.25	2.50
❑1/SC, Jul 97,alternate painted cover	2.50	0.50	1.25	2.50
❑2, Aug 97, V: Prick	2.50	0.50	1.25	2.50

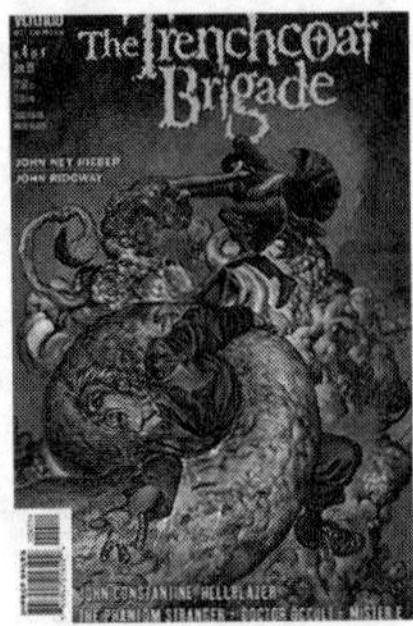

The overcoat-wearing magic users of the DC universe — John Constantine, Mr. E, The Phantom Stranger, and Dr. Occult — joined forces to stop a magical threat in *The Trenchcoat Brigade*.

© 1999 DC Comics

	ORIG	GOOD	FINE	N-MINT
❑3, Sep 97,Justice League America #1 homage cover	2.50	0.50	1.25	2.50
❑4, Oct 97	2.50	0.50	1.25	2.50
❑5, Nov 97,new costumes	2.50	0.50	1.25	2.50
❑6, Dec 97, Song of the Lounge Lizard, 1: The Lounge Lizard	2.50	0.50	1.25	2.50
❑7, Jan 98,Showgirls tribute cover	2.50	0.50	1.25	2.50
❑8, Feb 98	2.50	0.50	1.25	2.50
❑9, Mar 98	2.50	0.50	1.25	2.50
❑10, Apr 98	2.50	0.50	1.25	2.50
❑11, Jan 98,no cover date; indicia says Jan	2.50	0.50	1.25	2.50
❑12, Feb 98,no cover date; Final Issue; indicia says Feb	2.50	0.50	1.25	2.50
❑Ash 1, Mar 97, b&w; no cover price; preview of upcoming series	—	0.20	0.50	1.00

TRIPLE DARE
ALTERNATIVE
Value: Cover or less

- ❑1, May 98, b&w; Anthology 2.95

TRIPLE•X
DARK HORSE
Value: Cover or less

- ❑1, Dec 94, Amsterdam, Part 1 ..... 3.95
- ❑2, Jan 95, Amsterdam, Part 2 ..... 3.95
- ❑3, Feb 95 ..... 3.95
- ❑4, Mar 95 ..... 3.95
- ❑5, Apr 95 ..... 3.95
- ❑6, May 95 ..... 4.95
- ❑7, Jul 95 ..... 4.95

TRIPLE-X CINEMA: A CARTOON HISTORY
RE-VISIONARY
Value: Cover or less

- ❑1, Mar 97, b&w; adult 3.50
- ❑2, Apr 97, b&w; adult 3.50
- ❑3, May 97, b&w; adult 3.50

TRIUMPH
DC
Value: Cover or less

- ❑1, Jun 95 ..... 1.75
- ❑2, Jul 95 ..... 1.75
- ❑3, Aug 95 ..... 1.75
- ❑4, Sep 95 ..... 1.75

TRIUMPHANT UNLEASHED
TRIUMPHANT
Value: Cover or less

- ❑0,Unleashed Prologue 2.50
- ❑0/A,free; Unleashed Prologue 2.50
- ❑0/SC,no cover price; Mail-in special-cover edition. Given as promo from coupons in first 9 Triumphant books; Unleashed Prologue; red logo; mail-away version 2.50
- ❑1 ..... 2.50

TRIUMVIRATE
CATACOMB
Value: Cover or less

- ❑1, b&w; flipbook with Pinnacle #1 ..... 2.50

TROLL
IMAGE
Value: Cover or less

- ❑1, Dec 93 ..... 2.50

TROLL: HALLOWEEN SPECIAL
IMAGE
Value: Cover or less

- ❑1, Oct 94, A: The Maxx 2.95

TROLL II
IMAGE
Value: Cover or less

- ❑1, Jul 94 ..... 3.95

TROLL: ONCE A HERO
IMAGE
Value: Cover or less

- ❑1, Aug 94 ..... 2.50

TROLLORDS (VOL. 1)
TRU STUDIOS

	ORIG	GOOD	FINE	N-MINT
❑1, 1: Trollords, b&w	1.50	0.40	1.00	2.00
❑1-2, 1: Trollords,2nd Printing	1.50	0.30	0.75	1.50
❑2	1.50	0.30	0.75	1.50
❑3	1.50	0.30	0.75	1.50
❑4	1.50	0.30	0.75	1.50
❑5	1.50	0.30	0.75	1.50
❑6	1.50	0.30	0.75	1.50
❑7	1.50	0.30	0.75	1.50
❑8	1.50	0.30	0.75	1.50
❑9	1.50	0.30	0.75	1.50
❑10	1.50	0.30	0.75	1.50

	ORIG	GOOD	FINE	N-MINT
❑11	1.50	0.30	0.75	1.50
❑12	1.50	0.30	0.75	1.50
❑13	1.50	0.30	0.75	1.50
❑14	1.50	0.30	0.75	1.50
❑15	1.50	0.30	0.75	1.50
❑SE 1, Feb 87, One Fearful Night; Remember Me, full color; Jerry's Big Fun Book	1.75	0.40	1.00	2.00

TROLLORDS (VOL. 2)
COMICO

	ORIG	GOOD	FINE	N-MINT
❑1	1.95	0.40	1.00	2.00
❑2	1.95	0.40	1.00	2.00
❑3	1.95	0.40	1.00	2.00
❑4	1.95	0.50	1.25	2.50

TROLLORDS: DEATH AND KISSES
APPLE

Value: Cover or less

- ❑1, b&w 2.25
- ❑2, b&w 2.25
- ❑3, b&w 2.25
- ❑4, b&w 2.25
- ❑5, b&w 2.25
- ❑6 .... 2.50

TROLL PATROL
HARVEY

Value: Cover or less

- ❑1, Jan 93, The Legend of Troll Town; The Great Troll Hunt. 1.95

TROMBONE
KNOCKABOUT

Value: Cover or less

- ❑1,adult 2.50

TROPO
BLACKBIRD

Value: Cover or less

- ❑1, b&w 2.75
- ❑2, b&w 2.75
- ❑3, b&w 2.75
- ❑4, b&w 2.75
- ❑5, b&w 2.75

TROUBLE EXPRESS
RADIO

Value: Cover or less

- ❑1, Nov 98, The Hustler 2.95
- ❑1/A, Nov 98, The Hustler,Adam Warren cover 2.95
- ❑2, Jan 99 .... 2.95

TROUBLE MAGNET
DC

Value: Cover or less

- ❑1, Feb 00 .... 2.50
- ❑2, Mar 00 .... 2.50
- ❑3, Apr 00 .... 2.50
- ❑4, May 00, The Memory Conflict 2.50

TROUBLEMAKERS
ACCLAIM

	ORIG	GOOD	FINE	N-MINT
❑1, Apr 97, The Age of Innocence, 1: Blur; 1: Rebound; 1: XL; 1: Calamity; 1: Troublemakers,cover says Mar, indicia says Apr	2.50	0.50	1.25	2.50
❑1/SC, Apr 97,indicia and cover dates match	2.50	0.50	1.25	2.50
❑2, May 97,cover says Apr, indicia says May	2.50	0.50	1.25	2.50
❑3, Jun 97	2.50	0.50	1.25	2.50
❑4, Jun 97	2.50	0.50	1.25	2.50
❑5, Aug 97	2.50	0.50	1.25	2.50
❑6, Sep 97	2.50	0.50	1.25	2.50
❑7, Oct 97	2.50	0.50	1.25	2.50
❑8, Nov 97, Controled Chaos,Cover swipe from X-Men (1st Series) #100	2.50	0.50	1.25	2.50
❑9, Dec 97,teen sex issue	2.50	0.50	1.25	2.50
❑10, Jan 98	2.50	0.50	1.25	2.50
❑11, Feb 98	2.50	0.50	1.25	2.50
❑12, Mar 98	2.50	0.50	1.25	2.50
❑13, Apr 98	2.50	0.50	1.25	2.50
❑14, Jan 98,no cover date; indicia says Jan	2.50	0.50	1.25	2.50
❑15, Feb 98,no cover date; Final Issue; indicia says Feb	2.50	0.50	1.25	2.50
❑16, Mar 98,month of publication repeated	2.50	0.50	1.25	2.50
❑17, Mar 98,month of publication repeated	2.50	0.50	1.25	2.50
❑18, Mar 98,month of publication repeated	2.50	0.50	1.25	2.50
❑19, Jun 98	2.50	0.50	1.25	2.50
❑Ash 1, Nov 96, b&w; no cover price; preview of upcoming series	—	0.20	0.50	1.00

TROUBLEMAN
IMAGE

Value: Cover or less

- ❑1, Jun 96 .... 2.25
- ❑2, Jul 96 .... 2.25
- ❑3, Aug 96 .... 2.25

TROUBLESHOOTERS INC.
NIGHTWOLF GRAPHICS

Value: Cover or less

- ❑1, Win 95, b&w 2.50
- ❑2, Spr 95, b&w 2.50

TROUBLE WITH GIRLS, THE (VOL. 1)
MALIBU

	ORIG	GOOD	FINE	N-MINT
❑1, Aug 87, b&w	1.95	0.50	1.25	2.50
❑2	1.95	0.45	1.13	2.25
❑3	1.95	0.45	1.13	2.25
❑4	1.95	0.45	1.13	2.25
❑5	1.95	0.45	1.13	2.25
❑6	1.95	0.40	1.00	2.00
❑7, b&w	1.95	0.40	1.00	2.00
❑8, b&w	1.95	0.40	1.00	2.00
❑9, b&w	1.95	0.40	1.00	2.00
❑10, b&w	1.95	0.40	1.00	2.00
❑11, b&w	1.95	0.40	1.00	2.00
❑12, b&w	1.95	0.40	1.00	2.00
❑13, b&w	1.95	0.40	1.00	2.00
❑14, b&w	1.95	0.40	1.00	2.00
❑Anl 1, b&w	2.95	0.65	1.63	3.25
❑HS 1, b&w; Mail-in special-cover edition. Given as promo from coupons in first 9 Triumphant books	2.95	0.59	1.48	2.95

TROUBLE WITH GIRLS, THE (VOL. 2)
COMICO

	ORIG	GOOD	FINE	N-MINT
❑1, Glamour Girls, full color; Comico begins publishing	1.95	0.50	1.25	2.50
❑2, full color	1.95	0.40	1.00	2.00
❑3, full color	1.95	0.40	1.00	2.00
❑4, full color	1.95	0.40	1.00	2.00
❑5, b&w; Eternity begins publishing; Black & white format begins	1.95	0.39	0.98	1.95
❑6, b&w	1.95	0.39	0.98	1.95
❑7, b&w	1.95	0.39	0.98	1.95
❑8, b&w	1.95	0.39	0.98	1.95
❑9, b&w	1.95	0.39	0.98	1.95
❑10, Dreaming of a White Girls, b&w	1.95	0.39	0.98	1.95
❑11, b&w	1.95	0.39	0.98	1.95
❑12, b&w	1.95	0.39	0.98	1.95
❑13, The Lost City of Girls, Part 1, b&w	1.95	0.39	0.98	1.95
❑14, The Lost City of Girls, Part 2, b&w	1.95	0.39	0.98	1.95
❑15, The Lost City of Girls, Part 3, b&w	1.95	0.45	1.13	2.25
❑16, The Lost City of Girls, Part 4	2.25	0.45	1.13	2.25
❑17	2.25	0.45	1.13	2.25
❑18	2.25	0.45	1.13	2.25
❑19	2.25	0.45	1.13	2.25
❑20	2.25	0.45	1.13	2.25
❑21	2.25	0.45	1.13	2.25
❑22	2.25	0.45	1.13	2.25
❑23	2.25	0.45	1.13	2.25

TROUBLE WITH GIRLS, THE: THE NIGHT OF THE LIZARD
MARVEL

	ORIG	GOOD	FINE	N-MINT
❑1, Jun 93,Embossed cover	2.50	0.50	1.25	2.50
❑2, Jul 93	1.95	0.45	1.13	2.25
❑3, Aug 93	1.95	0.45	1.13	2.25
❑4, Sep 93	1.95	0.45	1.13	2.25

TROUBLE WITH TIGERS
ANTARCTIC

Value: Cover or less

- ❑1, Jan 92, b&w 2.50
- ❑2, Feb 92, b&w 2.50

TROUT FISSION
TALL TALE

Value: Cover or less

- ❑1, Jul 98, b&w 1.95
- ❑2, Oct 98, b&w 2.95

TROY
TOME

Value: Cover or less

- ❑1 .... 2.95

TRS-80 COMPUTER WHIZ KIDS
ARCHIE

	ORIG	GOOD	FINE	N-MINT
❑1, nn; giveaway	—	0.40	1.00	2.00

TRUE ADVENTURES OF ADAM AND BRYON, THE
AMERICAN MULE

Value: Cover or less

- ❑1, May 98, b&w 2.50
- ❑2 .... 2.50
- ❑3 .... 2.50

TRUE CONFUSIONS
FANTAGRAPHICS

Value: Cover or less

- ❑1, b&w 2.50

TRUE FAITH
DC

Value: Cover or less

- ❑1, nn; squarebound; reprints Garth Ennis' first story from 1990 .... 12.95

TRUE GEIN
BONEYARD

	ORIG	GOOD	FINE	N-MINT
❑1, May 93, Ed!	2.75	0.60	1.50	3.00

TRUE GLITZ
RIP OFF

Value: Cover or less

- ❑1, Life in the Bagel Belt with Didi Glitz; Rubberware 2.50

TRUE LOVE
ECLIPSE

	ORIG	GOOD	FINE	N-MINT
❑1, NC; ATh, DSt (c), Stars in my Eyes; Wrong Way to Happiness,Reprints stories from New Romances #17, Thrilling Romances #22, #24, and Intimate Love #20	1.50	0.40	1.00	2.00
❑2, NC; ATh, Blinded by Love; Unwanted Love,Reprints stories from Popular Romance #22, New Romances #13, #15, and Thrilling Romances #24	1.50	0.40	1.00	2.00

TRUE NORTH, THE
Comic Legends Defense Fund

Value: Cover or less

- ❑1, nn; b&w; cardstock cover; benefit comic 3.50

TRUE NORTH II, THE
Comic Legends Defense Fund

Value: Cover or less

- ❑1, nn; cardstock foldout cover 4.50

TRUE SIN
Boneyard

Value: Cover or less

- ❑1 ..... 2.95

TRUE SPY STORIES
Caliber

Value: Cover or less

- ❑1, b&w; bios 2.95

TRUE SWAMP
Peristaltic Press

	ORIG	GOOD	FINE	N-MINT
❑1, b&w	2.50	0.50	1.25	2.50
❑2, May 94, b&w	2.50	0.50	1.25	2.50
❑3	2.50	0.50	1.25	2.50
❑4, Oct 94, Even Daisies Could Use More White, b&w	3.00	0.50	1.25	2.50
❑5, Feb 95, b&w	2.95	0.59	1.48	2.95

TRUFAN ADVENTURES THEATRE
Paragraphics

Value: Cover or less

- ❑1, b&w 1.95
- ❑2, 3-D 1.95

TRULY TASTELESS AND TACKY
Caliber

Value: Cover or less

- ❑1, b&w 2.50

TRYPTO THE ACID DOG
Renegade

Value: Cover or less

- ❑1, b&w 2.00

TSC JAMS
TSC

Value: Cover or less

- ❑0, TB7 and the Technobeetles; Bushmaster 3.95
- ❑1, nn 3.95

TSR WORLDS
DC

Value: Cover or less

- ❑Anl 1, 1: Meredith; 1: The Spelljammers 3.95

TSUNAMI GIRL
Image

Value: Cover or less

- ❑1,no month of publication 2.95
- ❑2, Even Gods Cry,no month of publication 2.95
- ❑3 ..... 2.95

TSUNAMI, THE IRRESISTIBLE FORCE
Epoch

Value: Cover or less

- ❑1 ..... 2.00

TUG & BUSTER (ART & SOUL)
Art & Soul

	ORIG	GOOD	FINE	N-MINT
❑1, Nov 95	2.95	0.60	1.50	3.00
❑2, Jan 96	2.95	0.60	1.50	3.00
❑3, Mar 96, Soiree, Wrong Number	2.95	0.60	1.50	3.00
❑4, May 96	2.95	0.60	1.50	3.00
❑5, Aug 96	2.95	0.60	1.50	3.00
❑6	2.95	0.60	1.50	3.00
❑7, Feb 98	2.95	0.60	1.50	3.00

TUG & BUSTER (IMAGE)
Image

Value: Cover or less

- ❑1, Aug 98, Now Museum, Now You Don't!, b&w 2.95

TUMBLING BOXES
Fantagraphics

Value: Cover or less

- ❑1, Dec 94, b&w; adult 2.95

TUROK ADON'S CURSE
Acclaim

Value: Cover or less

- ❑1 ..... 4.95

TUROK: CHILD OF BLOOD
Acclaim

Value: Cover or less

- ❑1, Jan 98,One-Shot 3.95

TUROK, DINOSAUR HUNTER
Acclaim

Value: Cover or less

- ❑0, Nov 95, Domini Canes, O: Turok; O: Andar; O: Lost Land 2.50
- ❑1, Jul 93, Cold Blood Blazing,chromium cover 3.50
- ❑1/GO,chromium cover; Gold logo edition; Gold edition 40.00
- ❑2, Aug 93 ..... 2.50
- ❑3, Sep 93 ..... 2.50
- ❑4, Oct 93 ..... 2.50
- ❑5, Nov 93 ..... 2.50
- ❑6, Dec 93 ..... 2.50
- ❑7, Jan 94 ..... 2.50
- ❑8, Feb 94 ..... 2.50
- ❑9, Mar 94 ..... 2.50
- ❑10, Apr 94 ..... 2.50
- ❑11, May 94,trading card 2.50
- ❑12, Jun 94 ..... 2.50
- ❑13, Aug 94, Return of Captain Red, Part 1, V: Captain Red 2.50
- ❑14, Sep 94, Return of Captain Red, Part 2, V: Captain Red 2.50
- ❑15, Oct 94, Return of Captain Red, Part 3, V: Captain Red 2.50
- ❑16, Oct 94, The Chaos Effect: Beta, Part 3,Chaos Effect 2.50

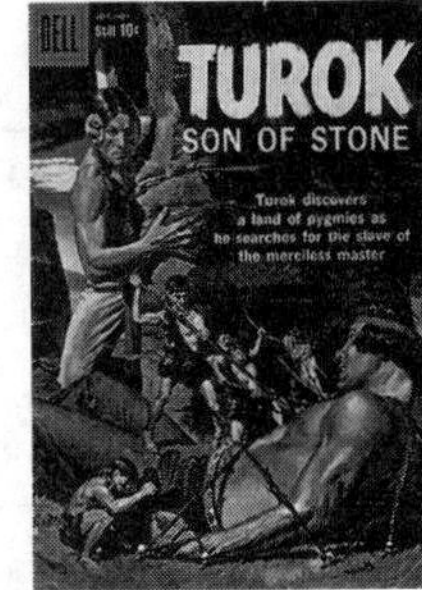

Native Americans Turok and Andar wandered into a lost valley where prehistoric creatures and cavemen survived in *Turok, Son of Stone*.

© 1962 Western Publishing (Dell)

- ❑17, Nov 94 ..... 2.50
- ❑18, Dec 94 ..... 2.50
- ❑19, Jan 95, A: X-O Manowar 2.50
- ❑20, Feb 95 ..... 2.50
- ❑21, Mar 95 ..... 2.50
- ❑22, Apr 95 ..... 2.50
- ❑23, May 95 ..... 2.50
- ❑24, Jun 95,back to the Lost Land 2.50
- ❑25, Jul 95 ..... 2.50
- ❑26, Jul 95, A: Captain Red,Birthquake 2.50
- ❑27, Aug 95 ..... 2.50
- ❑28, Aug 95 ..... 2.50
- ❑29, Sep 95 ..... 2.50
- ❑30, Sep 95 ..... 2.50
- ❑31, Oct 95, PG 2.50
- ❑32, Oct 95, PG 2.50
- ❑33, Nov 95 ..... 2.50
- ❑34, Nov 95 ..... 2.50
- ❑35, Dec 95,Painted cover 2.50
- ❑36, Dec 95 ..... 2.50
- ❑37, Jan 96 ..... 2.50
- ❑38, Jan 96 ..... 2.50
- ❑39, Feb 96 ..... 2.50
- ❑40, Mar 96 ..... 2.50
- ❑41, Apr 96 ..... 2.50
- ❑42, Apr 96 ..... 2.50
- ❑43, May 96 ..... 2.50
- ❑44, May 96 ..... 2.50
- ❑45, Jun 96 ..... 2.50
- ❑46, Aug 96 ..... 2.50
- ❑47, Aug 96,Final Issue 2.50
- ❑YB 1, Yearbook 1 ..... 3.95

TUROK: SEEDS OF EVIL
Acclaim

Value: Cover or less

- ❑1, newsstand edition 4.99
- ❑1/DM,Direct cover 4.99

TUROK/SHADOWMAN
Acclaim

Value: Cover or less

- ❑1, Feb 99, Army of One 3.95

TUROK, SON OF STONE
Dell

	ORIG	GOOD	FINE	N-MINT
❑1,a.k.a. Dell Four-Color #596	0.10	115.00	287.50	575.00
❑2,a.k.a. Dell Four-Color #656	0.10	65.00	162.50	325.00
❑3,Series continued from appearances in Four-Color Comics	0.10	25.00	62.50	125.00
❑4	0.10	20.00	50.00	100.00
❑5	0.10	20.00	50.00	100.00
❑6	0.10	18.00	45.00	90.00
❑7	0.10	18.00	45.00	90.00
❑8	—	18.00	45.00	90.00
❑9	—	18.00	45.00	90.00
❑10	—	18.00	45.00	90.00
❑11	—	12.00	30.00	60.00
❑12	—	12.00	30.00	60.00
❑13	—	12.00	30.00	60.00
❑14	—	12.00	30.00	60.00
❑15	—	12.00	30.00	60.00
❑16	—	12.00	30.00	60.00
❑17	—	12.00	30.00	60.00
❑18	—	12.00	30.00	60.00
❑19	—	12.00	30.00	60.00
❑20	—	12.00	30.00	60.00
❑21	—	7.20	18.00	36.00
❑22	—	7.20	18.00	36.00
❑23	—	7.20	18.00	36.00
❑24	—	7.20	18.00	36.00
❑25	—	7.20	18.00	36.00
❑26	—	7.20	18.00	36.00
❑27	—	7.20	18.00	36.00
❑28	—	7.20	18.00	36.00
❑29	0.12	7.20	18.00	36.00
❑30	0.12	7.20	18.00	36.00
❑31	0.12	5.60	14.00	28.00
❑32	0.12	5.60	14.00	28.00
❑33	0.12	5.60	14.00	28.00
❑34, Jul 63, The Ghostly Terror; Young Earth: The Dinosaur's Day,10030-307	0.12	5.60	14.00	28.00
❑35, Sep 63	0.12	5.60	14.00	28.00
❑36, Nov 63	0.12	5.60	14.00	28.00
❑37, Jan 64	0.12	5.60	14.00	28.00
❑38, Mar 64	0.12	5.60	14.00	28.00
❑39, May 64	0.12	5.60	14.00	28.00
❑40, Jul 64	0.12	5.60	14.00	28.00
❑41, Sep 64	0.12	4.00	10.00	20.00
❑42, Nov 64	0.12	4.00	10.00	20.00
❑43, Jan 65	0.12	4.00	10.00	20.00

	ORIG	GOOD	FINE	N-MINT
❑44, Mar 65	0.12	4.00	10.00	20.00
❑45, May 65	0.12	4.00	10.00	20.00
❑46, Jul 65	0.12	4.00	10.00	20.00
❑47, Sep 65, Outcasts of the Flood; Young Earth: The Cro-Magnon Come,10030-509	0.12	4.00	10.00	20.00
❑48	0.12	4.00	10.00	20.00
❑49	0.12	4.00	10.00	20.00
❑50	0.12	4.00	10.00	20.00
❑51	0.12	3.20	8.00	16.00
❑52	0.12	3.20	8.00	16.00
❑53	0.12	3.20	8.00	16.00
❑54	0.12	3.20	8.00	16.00
❑55	0.12	3.20	8.00	16.00
❑56	0.12	3.20	8.00	16.00
❑57	0.12	3.20	8.00	16.00
❑58	0.12	3.20	8.00	16.00
❑59	0.12	3.20	8.00	16.00
❑60	0.12	3.20	8.00	16.00
❑61	0.12	2.40	6.00	12.00
❑62	0.12	2.40	6.00	12.00
❑63	—	2.40	6.00	12.00
❑64	—	2.40	6.00	12.00
❑65	—	2.40	6.00	12.00
❑66	—	2.40	6.00	12.00
❑67	—	2.40	6.00	12.00
❑68	—	2.40	6.00	12.00
❑69	—	2.40	6.00	12.00
❑70	—	2.40	6.00	12.00
❑71	—	1.60	4.00	8.00
❑72, Jan 71	0.15	1.60	4.00	8.00
❑73	—	1.60	4.00	8.00
❑74	—	1.60	4.00	8.00
❑75	—	1.60	4.00	8.00
❑76	—	1.60	4.00	8.00
❑77	—	1.60	4.00	8.00
❑78	—	1.60	4.00	8.00
❑79	—	1.60	4.00	8.00
❑80	—	1.60	4.00	8.00
❑81	—	1.60	4.00	8.00
❑82	—	1.60	4.00	8.00
❑83	—	1.60	4.00	8.00
❑84	—	1.60	4.00	8.00
❑85	—	1.60	4.00	8.00
❑86	—	1.60	4.00	8.00
❑87	—	1.60	4.00	8.00
❑88	—	1.60	4.00	8.00
❑89	—	1.60	4.00	8.00
❑90	—	1.60	4.00	8.00
❑91	—	1.20	3.00	6.00
❑92	—	1.20	3.00	6.00
❑93	—	1.20	3.00	6.00
❑94	—	1.20	3.00	6.00
❑95	—	1.20	3.00	6.00
❑96	—	1.20	3.00	6.00
❑97	—	1.20	3.00	6.00
❑98	—	1.20	3.00	6.00
❑99, Sep 75	0.20	1.20	3.00	6.00
❑100	—	1.20	3.00	6.00
❑101	0.25	1.20	3.00	6.00
❑102	—	1.20	3.00	6.00
❑103	—	1.20	3.00	6.00
❑104	—	1.20	3.00	6.00
❑105	—	1.20	3.00	6.00
❑106	—	1.20	3.00	6.00
❑107	—	1.20	3.00	6.00
❑108	—	1.20	3.00	6.00
❑109	—	1.20	3.00	6.00
❑110	—	1.20	3.00	6.00
❑111	—	1.00	2.50	5.00
❑112	—	1.00	2.50	5.00
❑113	—	1.00	2.50	5.00
❑114	—	1.00	2.50	5.00
❑115	—	1.00	2.50	5.00
❑116	—	1.00	2.50	5.00
❑117	—	1.00	2.50	5.00
❑118	—	1.00	2.50	5.00
❑119	—	1.00	2.50	5.00
❑120	—	1.00	2.50	5.00
❑121	—	1.00	2.50	5.00
❑122	—	1.00	2.50	5.00
❑123	—	1.00	2.50	5.00
❑124	—	1.00	2.50	5.00
❑125	—	1.00	2.50	5.00
❑126	—	1.00	2.50	5.00
❑127	—	1.00	2.50	5.00
❑128	—	1.00	2.50	5.00
❑129	—	1.00	2.50	5.00
❑130,Final Issue	—	1.00	2.50	5.00
❑GS 1	—	13.00	32.50	65.00

TUROK: SPRING BREAK IN THE LOST LAND

ACCLAIM

Value: Cover or less

- ❑1, Jul 97,One-Shot ... 3.95

TUROK: THE EMPTY SOULS

ACCLAIM

	ORIG	GOOD	FINE	N-MINT
❑1, Apr 97	3.95	0.79	1.98	3.95
❑1/SC, Apr 97,alternate painted cover	3.95	0.79	1.98	3.95
❑Ash 1, Nov 96, b&w; no cover price; preview of upcoming series	—	0.20	0.50	1.00

TUROK THE HUNTED

ACCLAIM

Value: Cover or less

- ❑1, Mar 96, MGr (w) ... 2.50
- ❑2, Mar 96, MGr (w) ... 2.50

TUROK, TIMEWALKER: SEVENTH SABBATH

ACCLAIM

Value: Cover or less

- ❑1, Aug 97,covers form diptych ... 2.50
- ❑2, Sep 97,covers form diptych ... 2.50

TURTLE SOUP

MIRAGE

	ORIG	GOOD	FINE	N-MINT
❑1, Nov 91, Toyoduh: The Naked City; Turtles Attack	2.50	1.00	2.50	5.00

TURTLE SOUP (2ND SERIES)

MIRAGE

Value: Cover or less

- ❑1, Nov 91 ... 2.50
- ❑2, Dec 91 ... 2.50
- ❑3, Jan 92 ... 2.50
- ❑4, Feb 92 ... 2.50

TV STARS

MARVEL

	ORIG	GOOD	FINE	N-MINT
❑1, 1: Grape Ape (in comics); 1: Captain Caveman (in comics)	0.35	1.20	3.00	6.00
❑2	0.35	0.80	2.00	4.00
❑3	0.35	0.80	2.00	4.00
❑4,Final Issue	0.35	0.80	2.00	4.00

TWICE-TOLD TALES OF UNSUPERVISED EXISTENCE

RIP OFF

Value: Cover or less

- ❑1, Apr 89, Sunny and Danny; After Annadette, b&w ... 2.00

TWILIGHT (AVATAR)

AVATAR

Value: Cover or less

- ❑1 ... 3.00
- ❑2 ... 3.00

TWILIGHT (DC)

DC

Value: Cover or less

- ❑1, HC (w), Last Frontier ... 4.95
- ❑2, HC (w), Blood on the Stars ... 4.95
- ❑3, HC (w), Lords of the Long Shadow ... 4.95

TWILIGHT AVENGER, THE (ELITE)

ELITE

Value: Cover or less

- ❑1, Jul 86 ... 1.75
- ❑2, Oct 86 ... 1.75

TWILIGHT AVENGER, THE (ETERNITY)

ETERNITY

Value: Cover or less

- ❑1, Jul 88, b&w ... 1.95
- ❑2, Aug 88, b&w ... 1.95
- ❑3, Sep 88, b&w ... 1.95
- ❑4, Nov 88, b&w ... 1.95
- ❑5, Feb 89, b&w ... 1.95
- ❑6, May 89, b&w ... 1.95
- ❑7, Aug 89, b&w ... 1.95
- ❑8, Feb 90, b&w ... 1.95

TWILIGHT GIRL

CROSS PLAINS

Value: Cover or less

- ❑1 ... 2.95
- ❑2 ... 2.95
- ❑3, Jan 01 ... 2.95

TWILIGHT MAN

FIRST

Value: Cover or less

- ❑1, Jun 89, Wind From the East ... 2.75
- ❑2, Jul 89, Bedtime Story ... 2.75
- ❑3, Aug 89, Nightmare World .. 2.75
- ❑4, Sep 89, Wind Fall ... 2.75

TWILIGHT PEOPLE

CALIBER

Value: Cover or less

- ❑1, b&w ... 2.95
- ❑2, b&w ... 2.95

TWILIGHT X

PORK CHOP PRESS

	ORIG	GOOD	FINE	N-MINT
❑1, b&w	—	0.40	1.00	2.00
❑2, b&w	—	0.40	1.00	2.00
❑3, b&w	—	0.40	1.00	2.00

TWILIGHT X (VOL. 2)

ANTARCTIC

Value: Cover or less

- ❑1, b&w ... 2.50
- ❑2, b&w ... 2.50
- ❑3, b&w ... 2.50
- ❑4, Sep 93, b&w ... 2.50
- ❑5, Feb 94, b&w ... 2.75

TWILIGHT-X: INTERLUDE
ANTARCTIC

Value: Cover or less

Issue	Price
❑1, Jul 92, b&w	2.50
❑2, Sep 92, b&w	2.50
❑3, Nov 92, b&w	2.50
❑4, Jan 93, b&w	2.50
❑5, Mar 93, b&w	2.50
❑6, May 93, b&w	2.50

TWILIGHT-X: INTERLUDE (VOL. 2)
ANTARCTIC

Value: Cover or less

Issue	Price
❑1, Jun 93, b&w	2.50
❑2, Jul 93, b&w	2.50
❑3, Aug 93, b&w	2.50
❑4, Sep 93, b&w	2.50
❑5, Oct 93, b&w	2.75

TWILIGHT X QUARTERLY
ANTARCTIC

Value: Cover or less

Issue	Price
❑1, Sep 94, b&w	2.95
❑2, Nov 94, b&w	2.95
❑3, Feb 95, Ascension 8: Whirlwind Part II; Twilight Knights, b&w	2.95

TWILIGHT ZONE, THE (VOL. 1)
DELL

Issue	ORIG	GOOD	FINE	N-MINT
❑1,published as Dell Four-Color #1173	0.10	15.00	37.50	75.00
❑2,published as Dell Four-Color #1174	0.10	9.00	22.50	45.00
❑3, May 62, The Man from Nowhere; Hard Luck Harvey,01-860-207	0.10	7.00	17.50	35.00
❑4,01-860-210	0.10	6.00	15.00	30.00
❑5	—	6.00	15.00	30.00
❑6	—	6.00	15.00	30.00
❑7	—	6.00	15.00	30.00
❑8	—	6.00	15.00	30.00
❑9	—	6.00	15.00	30.00
❑10	—	6.00	15.00	30.00
❑11	—	5.20	13.00	26.00
❑12, The Shadow With Claws; The Haunted Sentry Box (text story)	0.12	5.20	13.00	26.00
❑13	0.12	5.20	13.00	26.00
❑14, Feb 66, The Day That Vanished; The Death Car,10016-602	0.12	5.20	13.00	26.00
❑15, Moment of Decision; Wipe Out The Future	0.12	5.20	13.00	26.00
❑16	0.12	5.20	13.00	26.00
❑17	0.12	5.20	13.00	26.00
❑18	0.12	5.20	13.00	26.00
❑19	0.12	5.20	13.00	26.00
❑20	0.12	5.20	13.00	26.00
❑21, May 67	0.12	2.60	6.50	13.00
❑22	0.12	2.60	6.50	13.00
❑23	0.12	2.60	6.50	13.00
❑24	0.12	2.60	6.50	13.00
❑25, Tombstone Valley; The Ghost in the Drifting Tomb (text story)	0.12	2.60	6.50	13.00
❑26, Jul 68, The Bridgegroom; Journeys Into Oblivion,10016-807	0.12	2.60	6.50	13.00
❑27, Dec 68	0.15	2.60	6.50	13.00
❑28	0.15	1.60	4.00	8.00
❑29, Jun 69, Captain Clegg's Treasure; The Curse of Amne Machen (text story),10016-906	0.15	1.60	4.00	8.00
❑30, Tall Timber; In The Cards	0.15	1.60	4.00	8.00
❑31	0.15	1.20	3.00	6.00
❑32, Voice in the Wind!; Secret of the Death-Ship (text story)	0.15	1.20	3.00	6.00
❑33	0.15	1.20	3.00	6.00
❑34, Beware the Kewpie Dolls; Dream of Gold (text story)	0.15	1.20	3.00	6.00
❑35	0.15	1.20	3.00	6.00
❑36	0.15	1.20	3.00	6.00
❑37	0.15	1.20	3.00	6.00
❑38	0.15	1.20	3.00	6.00
❑39	0.15	1.20	3.00	6.00
❑40	0.15	1.20	3.00	6.00
❑41, Guilt Has A Thousand Eyes; Harbinger of Death	0.15	1.00	2.50	5.00
❑42, Mar 72, The Haunted Taxi; Torture Revisited (text story),90016-203	0.15	1.00	2.50	5.00
❑43	0.15	1.00	2.50	5.00
❑44, The Camera Doesn't Lie; The Call	0.15	1.00	2.50	5.00
❑45	0.15	1.00	2.50	5.00
❑46, Dream of the Devil; Passage of the Doomed	0.15	1.00	2.50	5.00
❑47, Jan 73	0.15	1.00	2.50	5.00
❑48, Mar 73, Nightmare in Miniature; Fiery Death (text story)	0.15	1.00	2.50	5.00
❑49, May 73	0.20	1.00	2.50	5.00
❑50, Jul 73	0.20	1.00	2.50	5.00
❑51, Aug 73	—	1.00	2.50	5.00
❑52, Sep 73	—	0.80	2.00	4.00
❑53, Nov 73	—	0.80	2.00	4.00
❑54, Jan 74	—	0.80	2.00	4.00
❑55, Mar 74	—	0.80	2.00	4.00

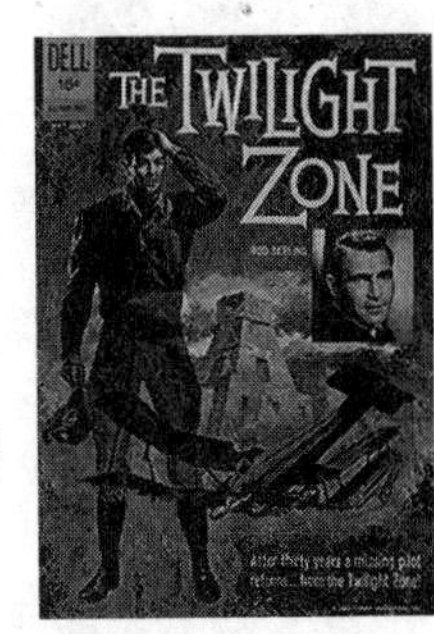

Just as he did on TV, Rod Serling hosted the stories in the comics version of *Twilight Zone.*

© 1962 Rod Serling/CBS Television (Dell)

Issue	ORIG	GOOD	FINE	N-MINT
❑56, May 74	—	0.80	2.00	4.00
❑57, Jul 74	—	0.80	2.00	4.00
❑58	—	0.80	2.00	4.00
❑59	—	0.80	2.00	4.00
❑60	—	0.80	2.00	4.00
❑61	—	0.80	2.00	4.00
❑62	—	0.80	2.00	4.00
❑63	—	0.80	2.00	4.00
❑64	—	0.80	2.00	4.00
❑65, The Unseen; Over My Dead Body	—	0.80	2.00	4.00
❑66	—	0.80	2.00	4.00
❑67	—	0.80	2.00	4.00
❑68	—	0.80	2.00	4.00
❑69	—	0.80	2.00	4.00
❑70	—	0.80	2.00	4.00
❑71	—	0.60	1.50	3.00
❑72, Cave of the Time-Mists; Your Daily Hor-ror-Scope	0.25	0.60	1.50	3.00
❑73	—	0.60	1.50	3.00
❑74	—	0.60	1.50	3.00
❑75	—	0.60	1.50	3.00
❑76	—	0.60	1.50	3.00
❑77	—	0.60	1.50	3.00
❑78	—	0.60	1.50	3.00
❑79	—	0.60	1.50	3.00
❑80	—	0.60	1.50	3.00
❑81	—	0.60	1.50	3.00
❑82	—	0.60	1.50	3.00
❑83	—	0.60	1.50	3.00
❑84	—	0.60	1.50	3.00
❑85	—	0.60	1.50	3.00
❑86	—	0.60	1.50	3.00
❑87	0.35	0.60	1.50	3.00
❑88	—	0.60	1.50	3.00
❑89	—	0.60	1.50	3.00
❑90	—	0.60	1.50	3.00
❑91	—	0.60	1.50	3.00
❑92,Final Issue	0.60	0.60	1.50	3.00

TWILIGHT ZONE, THE (VOL. 2)
NOW

Issue	ORIG	GOOD	FINE	N-MINT
❑1, Nov 91, The Big Dry,two covers	1.95	0.50	1.25	2.50
❑1/DM, The Big Dry, Direct Market edition	1.95	0.50	1.25	2.50
❑2, Dec 91, Blind Alley	1.95	0.45	1.13	2.25
❑3, Jan 92, Big Shot	1.95	0.45	1.13	2.25
❑4, Feb 92	1.95	0.40	1.00	2.00
❑5, Mar 92	1.95	0.40	1.00	2.00
❑6, Apr 92	1.95	0.40	1.00	2.00
❑7, May 92	1.95	0.40	1.00	2.00
❑8, Jun 92	1.95	0.40	1.00	2.00
❑9, Jul 92,Holographic cover; 3-D glasses; 3-D; bagged; hologram; Partial 3-D art	2.95	0.59	1.48	2.95
❑9/PR, Jul 92,Holographic cover; 3-D glasses; prestige format; 3-D; with glasses; hologram; Partial 3-D art; Extra stories	4.95	0.99	2.47	4.95
❑10, Aug 92	1.95	0.39	0.98	1.95
❑11, Sep 92	1.95	0.39	0.98	1.95
❑12	1.95	0.39	0.98	1.95
❑13	1.95	0.39	0.98	1.95
❑14	1.95	0.39	0.98	1.95
❑15	1.95	0.39	0.98	1.95
❑16	1.95	0.39	0.98	1.95
❑SF 1, Mar 93, button; hologram button; Science-Fiction Special	3.50	0.70	1.75	3.50

TWILIGHT ZONE, THE (VOL. 3)
NOW

Value: Cover or less

Issue	Price
❑1, May 93, Mother, May I Go Out to Play?	2.50
❑2, Jun 93, Pull the Plug,two different covers; computer special	2.50
❑3, Jul 93	2.50
❑4, Aug 93	2.50
❑Anl 1993, Apr 93	2.50

TWILIGHT ZONE 3-D SPECIAL, THE
Now

Value: Cover or less
❑1, Apr 93,glasses 2.95

TWILIGHT ZONE PREMIERE, THE
Now

Value: Cover or less

❑1, Oct 91, NA, BSz (c), Crazy as a Soup Sandwich, nn; Introduction by Harlan Ellison 2.50
❑1/CS, Crazy as a Soup Sandwich,Collector's Set (poly-bagged, gold logo); Not code approved; Introduction by Harlan Ellison 2.50
❑1/DM, Oct 91, NA, Crazy as a Soup Sandwich; Wishing Book,Introduction by Harlan Ellison 2.95
❑1/PR, Crazy as a Soup Sandwich; Darkness Upon the Face of the Deep (text story), Prestige edition; Introduction by Harlan Ellison 4.95
❑1-2, Crazy as a Soup Sandwich,2nd Printing; Introduction by Harlan Ellison 2.50
❑1/DM-2, NA, Crazy as a Soup Sandwich,Not code-approved; Introduction by Harlan Ellison 2.50

TWIN EARTHS
R. Susor

Value: Cover or less
❑1, b&w; strip reprints 5.95
❑2, b&w; strip reprints 5.95

TWIST
Kitchen Sink

Value: Cover or less
❑1, BW, b&w 2.00
❑2, May 88, Greatest Story Ever; The Dope Peddler 2.00
❑3 .... 2.00

TWISTED
Alchemy

Value: Cover or less
❑1, b&w 3.95

TWISTED 3-D TALES
Blackthorne

Value: Cover or less
❑1 .... 2.50

TWISTED SISTERS
Kitchen Sink

	ORIG	GOOD	FINE	N-MINT
❑1, Boogie Chillun; Impasse, b&w	3.50	0.70	1.75	3.50
❑2	3.50	0.70	1.75	3.50
❑3	3.50	0.70	1.75	3.50
❑4	3.50	0.70	1.75	3.50

TWISTED TALES
Pacific

	ORIG	GOOD	FINE	N-MINT
❑1, Nov 82, Infected; Out of His Depth,Pacific publishes	1.50	0.70	1.75	3.50
❑2, Apr 83, Over His Head; Nightwatch	1.50	0.50	1.25	2.50
❑3, Jun 83, Me an' Ol' Rex; Off Key	1.50	0.50	1.25	2.50
❑4, Aug 83, The Well; Nick of Time	1.50	0.50	1.25	2.50
❑5, Terminated; Scritch...Scritch...Scritch...	1.50	0.50	1.25	2.50
❑6, You, Illusion; Evening Walk	1.50	0.50	1.25	2.50
❑7	1.50	0.50	1.25	2.50
❑8, Way Down There Below the Dark; First Impressions,Eclipse publishes	1.50	0.50	1.25	2.50
❑9, Warped Panels; Deadlights	1.50	0.50	1.25	2.50
❑10, Dec 84, Beer; One for the Money...Two for the Show	1.50	0.50	1.25	2.50
❑3D 1, Aug 86, Terminated; Way Down there Below in the Dark	2.50	0.50	1.25	2.50

TWISTED TALES OF BRUCE JONES, THE
Eclipse

	ORIG	GOOD	FINE	N-MINT
❑1	1.50	0.40	1.00	2.00
❑2	1.50	0.40	1.00	2.00
❑3, Mar 86, Morgan; Nudels	1.50	0.40	1.00	2.00
❑4	1.50	0.40	1.00	2.00

TWISTED TANTRUMS OF THE PURPLE SNIT, THE
Blackthorne

Value: Cover or less
❑1, A: Hammy Hamster 1.75
❑2 .... 1.75

TWISTED TIMES (ALAN MOORE'S...)
Titan

Value: Cover or less
❑1 .... 8.95

TWISTER
Harris

	ORIG	GOOD	FINE	N-MINT
❑1, poster, trading cards; trading card	2.95	0.60	1.50	3.00

TWITCH (JUSTIN HAMPTON'S...)
Aeon

Value: Cover or less
❑1 .... 2.75

TWO FACES OF TOMORROW, THE
Dark Horse

Value: Cover or less

❑1, Aug 97, b&w 2.95
❑2, Sep 97, b&w; wraparound cover 3.95
❑3, Oct 97, b&w 3.95
❑4, Nov 97, b&w 3.95
❑5, Dec 97, b&w 3.95
❑6, Jan 98, b&w 3.95
❑7, Feb 98, b&w 3.95
❑8, Mar 98, b&w 3.95
❑9, Apr 98, b&w 3.95
❑10, May 98, b&w 3.95
❑11, Jun 98, b&w 3.95
❑12, Jul 98, b&w 3.95
❑13, Aug 98, b&w 3.95

TWO-FISTED SCIENCE
General Tektronics Labs

Value: Cover or less
❑1, b&w 2.50

TWO-FISTED TALES (RCP)
EC

	ORIG	GOOD	FINE	N-MINT
❑1, Oct 92, WW; JCr; HK; AF, Conquest; Hong Kong Intrigue!,Reprints Two-Fisted Tales (EC) #18	2.00	0.40	1.00	2.00
❑2, WW; JSe; JCr; HK, War Story!; Escape (text story),Reprints Two-Fisted Tales (EC) #19	1.50	0.40	1.00	2.00
❑3, WW; JSe; HK, Massacred!; Devils in Baggy Pants!,Reprints Two-Fisted Tales (EC) #20	1.50	0.40	1.00	2.00
❑4, Jul 93, WW; JSe; HK, Ambush!; Pigs of the Roman Empire,Reprints Two-Fisted Tales (EC) #21	2.00	0.40	1.00	2.00
❑5, AT; WW; JSe; HK, Enemy Contact!; Dying City!,Reprints Two-Fisted Tales (EC) #22	2.00	0.40	1.00	2.00
❑6, WW; JSe; HK, Death Stand!; Old Soldiers Never Die!,Reprints Two-Fisted Tales (EC) #23	2.00	0.40	1.00	2.00
❑7, WW; JSe; HK, Hill 203!; Bug Out!,Reprints Two-Fisted Tales (EC) #24	2.00	0.40	1.00	2.00
❑8, Mud!; Bunker Hill!,Reprints Two-Fisted Tales (EC) #25	2.00	0.40	1.00	2.00
❑9, The Trap!; Hagaru-Ri!,Reprints Two-Fisted Tales (EC) #26	2.00	0.40	1.00	2.00
❑10, Luck!; Custer's Last Stand,Reprints Two-Fisted Tales (EC) #27	2.00	0.40	1.00	2.00
❑11,Reprints Two-Fisted Tales (EC) #28	2.00	0.40	1.00	2.00
❑12,Reprints Two-Fisted Tales (EC) #29	2.00	0.40	1.00	2.00
❑13, Oct 95,Reprints Two-Fisted Tales (EC) #30	2.00	0.40	1.00	2.00
❑14,Reprints Two-Fisted Tales (EC) #31	2.00	0.40	1.00	2.00
❑15,Reprints Two-Fisted Tales (EC) #32	2.00	0.40	1.00	2.00
❑16,Reprints Two-Fisted Tales (EC) #33	2.50	0.50	1.25	2.50
❑17,Reprints Two-Fisted Tales (EC) #34	2.50	0.50	1.25	2.50
❑18,Reprints Two-Fisted Tales (EC) #35	2.50	0.50	1.25	2.50
❑19,Reprints Two-Fisted Tales (EC) #36	2.50	0.50	1.25	2.50
❑20,Reprints Two-Fisted Tales (EC) #37	2.50	0.50	1.25	2.50
❑21, JSe, JSe (w), Lost City!; War-path!,Reprints Two-Fisted Tales (EC) #38	2.50	0.50	1.25	2.50
❑22,Reprints Two-Fisted Tales (EC) #39	2.50	0.50	1.25	2.50
❑23,Reprints Two-Fisted Tales (EC) #40	2.50	0.50	1.25	2.50
❑24,Reprints Two-Fisted Tales (EC) #41	2.50	0.50	1.25	2.50
❑Anl 1,Collects Two-Fisted Tales #1-5	8.95	1.79	4.47	8.95
❑Anl 2,Collects Two-Fisted Tales #6-10	9.95	1.99	4.97	9.95
❑Anl 3	10.95	2.19	5.47	10.95
❑Anl 4	12.95	2.59	6.47	12.95
❑Anl 5	13.50	2.70	6.75	13.50

TWO-GUN KID
Marvel

	ORIG	GOOD	FINE	N-MINT
❑58, O: Two-Gun Kid	0.10	4.00	10.00	20.00
❑59	0.10	4.00	10.00	20.00
❑60, O: Two-Gun Kid	0.12	6.00	15.00	30.00
❑61	0.12	2.40	6.00	12.00
❑62	0.12	2.40	6.00	12.00
❑63	0.12	2.40	6.00	12.00
❑64	0.12	2.40	6.00	12.00
❑65	0.12	2.40	6.00	12.00
❑66	0.12	2.40	6.00	12.00
❑67	0.12	2.40	6.00	12.00
❑68	0.12	2.40	6.00	12.00
❑69	0.12	2.40	6.00	12.00
❑70	0.12	2.40	6.00	12.00
❑71	0.12	2.40	6.00	12.00
❑72, Nov 64, V: Geronimo	0.12	2.40	6.00	12.00
❑73, Jan 65	0.12	2.40	6.00	12.00
❑74, Mar 65	0.12	2.40	6.00	12.00
❑75, May 65	0.12	2.40	6.00	12.00
❑76, Jul 65	0.12	2.40	6.00	12.00
❑77, Sep 65	0.12	2.40	6.00	12.00
❑78, Nov 65	0.12	2.40	6.00	12.00
❑79, Jan 66, V: Joe Goliath	0.12	2.40	6.00	12.00
❑80, Mar 66, V: Billy the Kid	0.12	2.40	6.00	12.00
❑81, May 66	0.12	1.60	4.00	8.00
❑82, Jul 66	0.12	1.60	4.00	8.00
❑83, Sep 66, V: Durango	0.12	1.60	4.00	8.00
❑84, Nov 66	0.12	1.60	4.00	8.00
❑85, Jan 67	0.12	1.60	4.00	8.00
❑86, Mar 67, V: Cole Younger	0.12	1.60	4.00	8.00
❑87, May 67	0.12	1.60	4.00	8.00
❑88, Jul 67, V: Rattler	0.12	1.60	4.00	8.00
❑89, Sep 67, A: Kid Colt; A: Rawhide Kid...	0.12	1.60	4.00	8.00
❑90, Nov 67	0.12	1.60	4.00	8.00
❑91, Jan 68, V: Silver Sidewinder	0.12	1.60	4.00	8.00
❑92, Mar 68,series goes on hiatus	0.12	1.60	4.00	8.00

	ORIG	GOOD	FINE	N-MINT
❑93, Jul 70,Reprints begin	0.15	0.80	2.00	4.00
❑94, Sep 70	0.15	0.80	2.00	4.00
❑95, Nov 70	0.15	0.80	2.00	4.00
❑96	0.15	0.80	2.00	4.00
❑97	0.15	0.80	2.00	4.00
❑98	0.15	0.80	2.00	4.00
❑99	0.15	0.80	2.00	4.00
❑100	—	0.80	2.00	4.00
❑101, O: Two Gun Kid	—	0.80	2.00	4.00
❑102	—	0.80	2.00	4.00
❑103	—	0.80	2.00	4.00
❑104	—	0.80	2.00	4.00
❑105	—	0.80	2.00	4.00
❑106	—	0.80	2.00	4.00
❑107	—	0.80	2.00	4.00
❑108	—	0.80	2.00	4.00
❑109	—	0.80	2.00	4.00
❑110	—	0.80	2.00	4.00
❑111	—	0.80	2.00	4.00
❑112	—	0.80	2.00	4.00
❑113	—	0.80	2.00	4.00
❑114	—	0.80	2.00	4.00
❑115	—	0.80	2.00	4.00
❑116	—	0.80	2.00	4.00
❑117	—	0.80	2.00	4.00
❑118	—	0.80	2.00	4.00
❑119	—	0.80	2.00	4.00
❑120	—	0.80	2.00	4.00
❑121	—	0.80	2.00	4.00
❑122	—	0.80	2.00	4.00
❑123	—	0.80	2.00	4.00
❑124	—	0.80	2.00	4.00
❑125	—	0.80	2.00	4.00
❑126	—	0.80	2.00	4.00
❑127	—	0.80	2.00	4.00
❑128	—	0.80	2.00	4.00
❑129	—	0.80	2.00	4.00
❑130	—	0.80	2.00	4.00
❑131	—	0.80	2.00	4.00
❑132	—	0.80	2.00	4.00
❑133	—	0.80	2.00	4.00
❑134	—	0.80	2.00	4.00
❑135	—	0.80	2.00	4.00
❑136,Final Issue	—	0.80	2.00	4.00

TWO-GUN KID: SUNSET RIDERS
MARVEL

Value: Cover or less

- ❑1, Nov 95, Biting the Bullet,Painted cover ... 6.95
- ❑2, Dec 95, Crossing the Golden Gate Bridge,Painted cover ... 6.95

The real-life stories of famous scientists are chronicled in *Two-Fisted Science.*

© 1996 General Tektronics Labs

TWO THOUSAND MANIACS
AIRCEL

Value: Cover or less

- ❑1, b&w; movie Adaptation ... 2.50
- ❑2, b&w; movie Adaptation ... 2.50
- ❑3, b&w; movie Adaptation ... 2.50

TWO X JUSTICE
GRAPHIC SERIALS

Value: Cover or less

- ❑1 ... 2.00

TYKES
ALTERNATIVE

Value: Cover or less

- ❑1, Nov 97 ... 2.95
- ❑Ash 1, Jul 97, nn; b&w and pink; smaller than normal comic book ... 2.95

TYPHOID
MARVEL

Value: Cover or less

- ❑1, Nov 95,wraparound cardstock cover ... 3.95
- ❑2, Dec 95, A: Cinemaniacs,wraparound cardstock cover ... 3.95
- ❑3, Jan 96,wraparound cardstock cover ... 3.95
- ❑4, Feb 96, Red Riding Hood,wraparound cardstock cover ... 3.95

TYRANNOSAURUS TEX
MONSTER

Value: Cover or less

- ❑1, b&w ... 2.50
- ❑2, b&w ... 2.50

TYRANT (S.R. BISSETTE'S...)
SPIDER BABY

	ORIG	GOOD	FINE	N-MINT
❑1, Sep 94, Knock Knock	2.95	0.60	1.50	3.00
❑2	2.95	0.60	1.50	3.00
❑3, Feb 95	2.95	0.60	1.50	3.00
❑3/GO	—	0.70	1.75	3.50
❑4	2.95	0.60	1.50	3.00
❑5	2.95	0.60	1.50	3.00
❑6	2.95	0.60	1.50	3.00

TZU THE REAPER
MURIM

Value: Cover or less

- ❑1, Sep 97 ... 2.95
- ❑2, Oct 97 ... 2.95
- ❑3, Dec 97 ... 2.95

U

UBERDUB
CALIBER

Value: Cover or less

- ❑1, Sep 91 ... 2.50
- ❑2, Sep 91, In the Wake of the Call ... 2.50
- ❑3, Jan 92 ... 2.50

UFO & OUTER SPACE
WHITMAN

	ORIG	GOOD	FINE	N-MINT
❑14,Reprints UFO Flying Saucers #3	—	1.20	3.00	6.00
❑15,Reprints UFO Flying Saucers #4	0.35	0.80	2.00	4.00
❑16,Reprint	—	0.80	2.00	4.00
❑17	—	0.80	2.00	4.00
❑18	—	0.80	2.00	4.00
❑19	—	0.80	2.00	4.00
❑20	—	0.80	2.00	4.00
❑21	—	0.60	1.50	3.00
❑22	—	0.60	1.50	3.00
❑23	—	0.60	1.50	3.00
❑24	—	0.60	1.50	3.00
❑25,Reprints UFO Flying Saucers #2	—	0.60	1.50	3.00

UFO ENCOUNTERS
GOLDEN PRESS

Value: Cover or less

- ❑1, The UFOs and Flying Saucers; The UFO R ... 1.95

UFO FLYING SAUCERS
GOLD KEY

	ORIG	GOOD	FINE	N-MINT
❑1, Oct 68,giant	0.25	4.00	10.00	20.00
❑2	0.15	2.40	6.00	12.00
❑3	—	2.40	6.00	12.00
❑4	0.25	2.40	6.00	12.00
❑5	0.25	1.40	3.50	7.00
❑6	0.25	1.40	3.50	7.00
❑7	0.25	1.40	3.50	7.00
❑8	0.25	1.40	3.50	7.00
❑9	0.25	1.40	3.50	7.00
❑10, The Phantom Bat Machines; Town in Terror!	0.25	1.40	3.50	7.00
❑11	—	1.40	3.50	7.00
❑12	—	1.40	3.50	7.00
❑13, Jan 77,series continues as UFO & Outer Space	—	1.40	3.50	7.00

ULTIMATE MARVEL MAGAZINE
MARVEL

	ORIG	GOOD	FINE	N-MINT
❑1, Feb 01,reprints Ultimate Spider-Man #1 and #2	3.99	1.20	3.00	6.00
❑2, Mar 01,reprints Ultimate Spider-Man #3 and Ultimate X-Men #1	3.99	0.80	2.00	4.00
❑3, Apr 01,reprints Ultimate Spider-Man #4 and Ultimate X-Men #2	3.99	0.80	2.00	4.00
❑4	3.99	0.80	2.00	3.99
❑5	3.99	0.80	2.00	3.99
❑6	3.99	0.80	2.00	3.99
❑7	3.99	0.80	2.00	3.99

ULTIMATE MARVEL TEAM-UP
MARVEL

Value: Cover or less

- ❑1, Apr 01, MW, BMB (w), A: Spider-Man; A: Sabretooth; A: Wolverine,cardstock cover; Listed in indicia as Ultimate Spider-Man and Wolverine ... 2.99
- ❑2, May 01, BMB (w), A: Spider-Man; A: Hulk ... 2.99
- ❑3 ... 2.99
- ❑4 ... 2.99
- ❑5 ... 2.99
- ❑6 ... 2.99

ULTIMATE SPIDER-MAN
MARVEL

	ORIG	GOOD	FINE	N-MINT
❑1, Oct 00, BMB (w), Powerless, A: Norman Osborn; A: Mary Jane Watson; O: Spider-Man	2.99	6.00	15.00	30.00
❑1/A, BMB (w),White background on cover-otherwise same as #1	2.50	12.00	30.00	60.00
❑1/B, BMB (w),Dynamic Forces cover	—	8.00	20.00	40.00
❑2, Dec 00, BMB (w), Growing Pains,cardstock cover	2.50	5.00	12.50	25.00
❑3, Jan 01, BMB (w), Wannabe, O: Green Goblin,cardstock cover; Spider-Man gets his costume	2.50	4.00	10.00	20.00
❑4, Feb 01, BMB (w), With Great Power, D: Uncle Ben (off-panel),cardstock cover	2.50	3.00	7.50	15.00
❑5, Mar 01, BMB (w), Life Lessons, D: Uncle Ben (revealed),cardstock cover	2.25	3.00	7.50	15.00
❑6, Apr 01, BMB (w), Big Time Super Hero, 1: Green Goblin (full),cardstock cover	2.25	0.45	1.13	2.25
❑7, May 01, BMB (w), Secret Identity, A: Green Goblin,cardstock cover	2.25	0.45	1.13	2.25
❑8	2.25	0.45	1.13	2.25
❑9	2.25	0.45	1.13	2.25
❑10	2.25	0.45	1.13	2.25
❑11	2.25	0.45	1.13	2.25

ULTIMATE X-MEN
MARVEL

	ORIG	GOOD	FINE	N-MINT
❑1, Feb 01, The Tomorrow People, Part 1,cardstock cover	2.25	2.40	6.00	12.00
❑1/A, Feb 01, The Tomorrow People, Part 1	2.25	2.00	5.00	10.00
❑1/B, Feb 01, The Tomorrow People, Part 1,sketch cover	—	8.00	20.00	40.00
❑1/C, Feb 01, The Tomorrow People, Part 1,DF alternate (color) cover; 7000 printed	—	6.00	15.00	30.00
❑2, Mar 01, The Tomorrow People, Part 2,cardstock cover	2.25	1.20	3.00	6.00
❑3, Apr 01, The Tomorrow People, Part 3,cardstock cover	2.25	0.80	2.00	4.00
❑4, May 01, The Tomorrow People, Part 4	2.25	0.80	2.00	4.00
❑5, Jun 01, The Tomorrow People, Part 5	2.25	0.80	2.00	4.00
❑6, Jul 01, The Tomorrow People, Part 6	2.25	0.45	1.13	2.25
❑7	2.25	0.45	1.13	2.25
❑8	2.25	0.45	1.13	2.25

ULTRAFORCE (VOL. 1)
MALIBU

	ORIG	GOOD	FINE	N-MINT
❑0, Sep 94, GP, Ultra Madness/UltraForce	2.50	0.50	1.25	2.50
❑0/SC, Jul 94, GP ,no cover price; ashcan-sized	—	0.20	0.50	1.00
❑1, Aug 94, GP, The Force Be With You, 1: Atalon, trading card	2.50	0.50	1.25	2.50
❑1/Hol, GP, The Force Be With You,Hologram cover	—	1.00	2.50	5.00
❑2, Oct 94, GP, Collision Course	1.95	0.39	0.98	1.95
❑3, Nov 94, GP, Head to Head	1.95	0.39	0.98	1.95
❑4, Jan 95, GP, Ghosts	1.95	0.39	0.98	1.95
❑5, Feb 95, GP, Last Stand	1.95	0.39	0.98	1.95
❑6, Mar 95, GP, Final Blow	2.50	0.50	1.25	2.50
❑7, Apr 95, Mosh Pit	2.50	0.50	1.25	2.50
❑8, May 95, GP, Black September, Part 1; Heaven on Earth	2.50	0.50	1.25	2.50
❑9	2.50	0.50	1.25	2.50
❑10	2.50	0.50	1.25	2.50
❑Ash 1,Ashcan	0.75	0.15	0.38	0.75

ULTRAFORCE (VOL. 2)
MALIBU

	ORIG	GOOD	FINE	N-MINT
❑0,#Infinity	1.50	0.30	0.75	1.50
❑0/A, Sep 95, Black September,#infinity on cover	1.50	0.30	0.75	1.50
❑0/B, Sep 95,alternate cover	1.50	0.70	1.75	3.50
❑0/SC,alternate cover; #Infinity	1.50	0.30	0.75	1.50
❑1, Oct 95, Shot Down, Part 1	1.50	0.30	0.75	1.50
❑2, Nov 95, Shot Down, Part 2,contains reprint of UltraForce #1	1.50	0.30	0.75	1.50
❑3, Dec 95, Shot Down, Part 3	1.50	0.30	0.75	1.50
❑4, Jan 96	1.50	0.30	0.75	1.50
❑5, Feb 96	1.50	0.30	0.75	1.50
❑6, Mar 96	1.50	0.30	0.75	1.50
❑7, Apr 96	1.50	0.30	0.75	1.50
❑8, May 96	1.50	0.30	0.75	1.50
❑9, Jun 96	1.50	0.30	0.75	1.50
❑10	1.50	0.30	0.75	1.50
❑11, Aug 96	1.50	0.30	0.75	1.50
❑12, Sep 96, A: Exiles	1.50	0.30	0.75	1.50
❑13, Oct 96	1.50	0.30	0.75	1.50
❑14	1.50	0.30	0.75	1.50
❑15, Dec 96, D: Ripfire,Final Issue	1.50	0.30	0.75	1.50

ULTRAFORCE/AVENGERS
MALIBU

Value: Cover or less

	ORIG
❑1, Fal 95, GP, GP (w), Countdown to Black September, Part 5	3.95

ULTRAFORCE/AVENGERS PRELUDE
MALIBU

Value: Cover or less

	ORIG
❑1, Jul 95, The Sword is Drawn…,a.k.a. UltraForce #11	2.50

ULTRAFORCE/SPIDER-MAN
MALIBU

Value: Cover or less

	ORIG
❑1, Jan 96,alternate covers: 1A and 1B	3.95

ULTRAGIRL
MARVEL

Value: Cover or less

	ORIG
❑1, Nov 96, Powerhouse of Style	1.50
❑2, Dec 96, Playing With Fire..	1.50
❑3, Mar 97, Rock My World, A: New Warriors	1.50

ULTRAHAWK
D.M.S.

Value: Cover or less

	ORIG
❑1, The Avenger	1.50

ULTRA KLUTZ
ONWARD

	ORIG	GOOD	FINE	N-MINT
❑1, Jun 86, Exile; Deputy Day-shift: Mayhem at the Mall	1.50	0.40	1.00	2.00
❑2	—	0.40	1.00	2.00
❑3	—	0.40	1.00	2.00
❑4	—	0.40	1.00	2.00
❑5	—	0.40	1.00	2.00
❑6	—	0.40	1.00	2.00
❑7	—	0.40	1.00	2.00
❑8	—	0.40	1.00	2.00
❑9	—	0.40	1.00	2.00
❑10	—	0.40	1.00	2.00
❑11	—	0.40	1.00	2.00
❑12	—	0.40	1.00	2.00
❑13	—	0.40	1.00	2.00
❑14	—	0.40	1.00	2.00
❑15	—	0.40	1.00	2.00
❑16	—	0.30	0.75	1.50
❑17	—	0.30	0.75	1.50
❑18	—	0.35	0.88	1.75
❑19	—	0.35	0.88	1.75
❑20	—	0.35	0.88	1.75
❑21	—	0.35	0.88	1.75
❑22	—	0.35	0.88	1.75
❑23	—	0.40	1.00	2.00
❑24	—	0.40	1.00	2.00
❑25	—	0.40	1.00	2.00
❑26, Nov 88, Problem Solving; Hope for the Galaxy	2.00	0.40	1.00	2.00
❑27	—	0.40	1.00	2.00
❑28	—	0.40	1.00	2.00
❑29	—	0.40	1.00	2.00
❑30	—	0.40	1.00	2.00
❑31	—	0.40	1.00	2.00

ULTRA KLUTZ '81
ONWARD

	ORIG	GOOD	FINE	N-MINT
❑1	1.50	0.40	1.00	2.00

ULTRAMAN (NEMESIS)
NEMESIS

	ORIG	GOOD	FINE	N-MINT
❑-1, Mar 94,negative image on cover	1.75	0.50	1.25	2.50
❑1,Split cover	1.75	0.50	1.25	2.50
❑1/A,alternate cover	2.25	0.45	1.13	2.25
❑2	1.75	0.39	0.98	1.95
❑3, Aug 94	1.95	0.39	0.98	1.95
❑4, Sep 94	1.95	0.39	0.98	1.95
❑5	1.95	0.39	0.98	1.95

ULTRAMAN (ULTRACOMICS)
HARVEY

	ORIG	GOOD	FINE	N-MINT
❑1, Jul 93, Revenge of the Gudis, Part 1, O: Ultraman,newsstand	1.75	0.40	1.00	2.00
❑1/CS, Jul 93, Revenge of the Gudis, Part 1, trading card	2.50	0.50	1.25	2.50
❑1/DM, Jul 93,no type on cover; trading card	2.50	0.70	1.75	3.50
❑2, Revenge of the Gudis, Part 2,newsstand	1.75	0.35	0.88	1.75
❑2/CS, Revenge of the Gudis, Part 2, trading card	2.50	0.50	1.25	2.50
❑2/DM,no cover type; direct sale; trading card	2.50	0.50	1.25	2.50
❑3,newsstand	1.75	0.35	0.88	1.75
❑3/CS, trading card	2.50	0.50	1.25	2.50
❑3/DM,trading cards	2.50	0.50	1.25	2.50

ULTRAMAN CLASSIC: BATTLE OF THE ULTRA-BROTHERS
VIZ

Value: Cover or less

	ORIG
❑1, b&w	4.95
❑2, b&w	4.95
❑3, b&w	4.95
❑4, b&w	4.95
❑5, b&w	4.95

ULTRA MONTHLY
MALIBU

Value: Cover or less

- ❑1, Jun 93, actually giveaway. 0.50
- ❑2, Jul 93, actually giveaway.. 0.50
- ❑3, Aug 93, cover says Sep, indicia says Aug; actually giveaway 0.50
- ❑4 0.50
- ❑5 0.50
- ❑6 0.50

ULTRAVERSE/AVENGERS PRELUDE
MALIBU

Value: Cover or less

- ❑1, Jul 95, The Swords are Drawn... 2.50

ULTRAVERSE DOUBLE FEATURE: PRIME AND SOLITAIRE
MALIBU

Value: Cover or less

- ❑1, Jan 95, Prime: The King of Beasts; Solitaire: No Place Like Home 3.95

ULTRAVERSE: FUTURE SHOCK
MALIBU

Value: Cover or less

- ❑1, Feb 97, Future Shock, final Ultraverse adventure 2.50

ULTRAVERSE ORIGINS
MALIBU

	ORIG	GOOD	FINE	N-MINT
❑1, Jan 94, O: Prime, Origin	0.99	0.25	0.63	1.25

ULTRAVERSE PREMIERE
MALIBU

	ORIG	GOOD	FINE	N-MINT
❑0, Nov 93, Primal Appearance; From on High	—	0.20	0.50	1.00

ULTRAVERSE UNLIMITED
MALIBU

Value: Cover or less

- ❑1, Jun 96, A: Warlock 2.50

ULTRAVERSE YEAR ONE
MALIBU

Value: Cover or less

- ❑1, Sep 94 4.95

ULTRAVERSE YEAR TWO
MALIBU

Value: Cover or less

- ❑1 4.95

ULTRAVERSE YEAR ZERO: THE DEATH OF THE SQUAD
MALIBU

Value: Cover or less

- ❑1, Apr 95, O: Hardcase; O: The Squad 2.95
- ❑2, May 95 2.95
- ❑3, Jun 95 2.95
- ❑4, Jul 95 2.95

UNBOUND
IMAGE

Value: Cover or less

- ❑1, Jan 98, Chapter One, b&w 2.95

UNCANNY ORIGINS
MARVEL

	ORIG	GOOD	FINE	N-MINT
❑1, O: Cyclops	0.99	0.25	0.63	1.25
❑1/A, Sep 96, O: Cyclops, variant cover	0.99	0.25	0.63	1.25
❑2, Oct 96, O: Quicksilver	0.99	0.20	0.50	1.00
❑3, Nov 96, O: Archangel	0.99	0.20	0.50	1.00
❑4, Dec 96, Forged in Fire, O: Firelord	0.99	0.20	0.50	1.00
❑5, Jan 97, O: Hulk	0.99	0.20	0.50	1.00
❑6, Feb 97, Lo! A Beast is Born!, O: Beast..	0.99	0.20	0.50	1.00
❑7, Mar 97, O: Venom	0.99	0.20	0.50	1.00
❑8, Apr 97, O: Nightcrawler	0.99	0.20	0.50	1.00
❑9, May 97, O: Storm	0.99	0.20	0.50	1.00
❑10, Jun 97, O: Black Cat	0.99	0.20	0.50	1.00
❑11, Jul 97, O: Black Knight	0.99	0.20	0.50	1.00
❑12, Aug 97, O: Doctor Strange	0.99	0.20	0.50	1.00
❑13, Sep 97, O: Daredevil	0.99	0.20	0.50	1.00
❑14, Oct 97, O: Iron Fist	0.99	0.20	0.50	1.00

UNCANNY TALES (2ND SERIES)
MARVEL

	ORIG	GOOD	FINE	N-MINT
❑1	0.10	1.00	2.50	5.00
❑2	0.10	0.70	1.75	3.50
❑3	0.10	0.70	1.75	3.50
❑4	0.10	0.70	1.75	3.50
❑5	0.10	0.70	1.75	3.50
❑6	0.10	0.70	1.75	3.50
❑7	0.10	0.70	1.75	3.50
❑8	0.10	0.70	1.75	3.50
❑9	0.10	0.70	1.75	3.50
❑10	0.10	0.70	1.75	3.50
❑11	0.10	0.70	1.75	3.50
❑12	0.10	0.70	1.75	3.50

UNCANNY X-MEN, THE
MARVEL

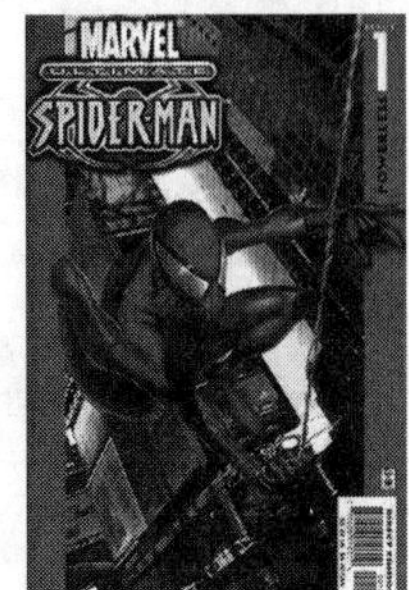

Brian Michael Bendis presented an updated origin for Spider-Man in *Ultimate Spider-Man* #1.

	ORIG	GOOD	FINE	N-MINT
❑-1, Jul 97, Flashback	1.99	0.40	1.00	2.00
❑142, Feb 81, JBy, Mind Out of Time, D: Wolverine (future); D: Storm (future); A: Rachel Summers (Phoenix III); D: Colossus (future), Series continued from X-Men (1st Series) #141	0.50	4.00	10.00	20.00
❑143, Mar 81, JBy, Demon, Last Byrne art on X-Men	0.50	1.80	4.50	9.00
❑144, Apr 81, BA, Even in Death, A: Man-Thing	0.50	1.40	3.50	7.00
❑145, May 81, DC, Kidnapped	0.50	1.40	3.50	7.00
❑146, Jun 81, DC, Murderworld	0.50	1.40	3.50	7.00
❑147, Jul 81, DC, Rogue Storm	0.50	1.40	3.50	7.00
❑148, Aug 81, DC, Cry, Mutant, A: Spider-Woman; 1: Caliban; A: Dazzler	0.50	1.40	3.50	7.00
❑149, Sep 81, DC, And the Dead Shall Bury the Living	0.50	1.40	3.50	7.00
❑150, Oct 81, DC, I, Magneto, V: Magneto, double-sized; Cyclops rejoins the X-Men	0.75	1.60	4.00	8.00
❑151, Nov 81, BMc, X-Men Minus One	0.50	1.00	2.50	5.00
❑152, Dec 81, BMc, The Hellfire Gambit	0.50	1.00	2.50	5.00
❑153, Jan 82, DC, Kitty's Fairy Tale	0.60	1.00	2.50	5.00
❑154, Feb 82, DC, Reunion	0.60	1.00	2.50	5.00
❑155, Mar 82, DC, First Blood	0.60	1.00	2.50	5.00
❑156, Apr 82, DC, Pursuit	0.60	1.00	2.50	5.00
❑157, May 82, DC, Hide-'N-Seek, A: Phoenix	0.60	1.00	2.50	5.00
❑158, Jun 82, DC, The Life That Late I Led, A: Rogue	0.60	1.80	4.50	9.00
❑159, Jul 82, BSz, Night Screams, A: Dracula	0.60	1.20	3.00	6.00
❑160, Aug 82, BA, Chutes and Ladders, 1: Magik (Illyana Rasputin as teenager)	0.60	1.20	3.00	6.00
❑161, Sep 82, DC, Gold Rush, O: Magneto; O: Professor X	0.60	1.20	3.00	6.00
❑162, Oct 82, DC, Beyond the Farthest Star, Wolverine solo story	0.60	1.60	4.00	8.00
❑163, Nov 82, DC, Rescue Mission	0.60	1.00	2.50	5.00
❑164, Dec 82, DC, Binary Star, 1: Binary	0.60	1.00	2.50	5.00
❑165, Jan 83, PS, Transfigurations	0.60	1.00	2.50	5.00
❑166, Feb 83, PS, Live Free or Die, 1: Lockheed, Double-size	1.00	1.00	2.50	5.00
❑167, Mar 83, PS, The Goldilocks Syndrome, A: New Mutants	0.60	1.00	2.50	5.00
❑168, Apr 83, PS, Professor Xavier is a Jerk!, 1: Madelyne Pryor	0.60	1.00	2.50	5.00
❑169, May 83, PS, Catacombs, 1: Sunder; 1: Morlocks	0.60	1.00	2.50	5.00
❑170, Jun 83, PS, Dancin' in the Dark	0.60	1.00	2.50	5.00
❑171, Jul 83, PS, Rogue, Rogue joins team	0.60	1.60	4.00	8.00
❑172, Aug 83, PS, Scarlet in Glory	0.60	1.00	2.50	5.00
❑173, Sep 83, PS, To Have and Have Not, O: Silver Samurai	0.60	1.00	2.50	5.00
❑174, Oct 83, PS, Romances	0.60	1.00	2.50	5.00
❑175, Nov 83, PS, Phoenix, double-sized	1.00	1.20	3.00	6.00
❑176, Dec 83, JR2, Decisions, 1: Valerie Cooper	0.60	1.00	2.50	5.00
❑177, Jan 84, JR2, Sanction	0.60	0.80	2.00	4.00
❑178, Feb 84, JR2, Hell Hath No Fury...	0.60	0.80	2.00	4.00
❑179, Mar 84, JR2, What Happened to Kitty	0.60	0.80	2.00	4.00
❑180, Apr 84, JR2, Whose Life is it, Anyway?	0.60	0.80	2.00	4.00
❑181, May 84, JR2, Tokyo Story	0.60	0.80	2.00	4.00
❑182, Jun 84, JR2, Madness	0.60	0.80	2.00	4.00
❑183, Jul 84, JR2, He'll Never Make Me Cry	0.60	0.80	2.00	4.00
❑184, Aug 84, JR2, The Past...of Future Days, A: Selene; A: Rachel; 1: Forge	0.60	1.00	2.50	5.00
❑185, Sep 84, JR2, Public Enemy, Storm loses powers	0.60	0.80	2.00	4.00
❑186, Oct 84, Lifedeath, double-sized; Storm	1.00	1.00	2.50	5.00
❑187, Nov 84, JR2, Wraithkill	0.60	0.60	1.50	3.00
❑188, Dec 84, JR2, Legacy of the Lost	0.60	0.60	1.50	3.00
❑189, Jan 85, JR2, Two Girls Out to Have Fun	0.60	0.60	1.50	3.00
❑190, Feb 85, JR2, An Age Undreamed Of, A: Avengers; A: Spider-Man	0.60	0.60	1.50	3.00
❑191, Mar 85, JR2, Raiders of the Lost Temple, A: Avengers; A: Spider-Man; A: Captain America	0.60	0.60	1.50	3.00
❑192, Apr 85, JR2, Fun'n'Games, Magus	0.60	0.60	1.50	3.00
❑193, May 85, JR2, Warhunt 2, double-sized; 20th anniv.; 100th New X-Men	1.25	1.20	3.00	6.00
❑194, Jun 85, JR2, Juggernaut's Back in Town, V: Juggernaut	0.65	0.60	1.50	3.00
❑195, Jul 85, JR2, It Was a Dark and Stormy Night, A: Power Pack	0.65	0.60	1.50	3.00
❑196, Aug 85, JR2, What Was That?, Secret Wars II	0.65	0.60	1.50	3.00
❑197, Sep 85, JR2, To Save Arcade?	0.65	0.60	1.50	3.00
❑198, Oct 85, Lifedeath II	0.65	0.60	1.50	3.00
❑199, Nov 85, JR2, The Spiral Path, 1: Phoenix III (Rachel Summers)	0.65	0.80	2.00	4.00

	ORIG	GOOD	FINE	N-MINT
❑200, Dec 85, JR2, Trial of Magneto; The Trial of Magneto, Double-size	1.25	1.40	3.50	7.00
❑201, Jan 86, Duel, 1: Cable (as baby),1st Portacio art in X-Men	0.65	1.00	2.50	5.00
❑202, Feb 86, JR2, X-Men…I've Gone to Kill-The Beyonder!,Secret Wars II	0.75	0.60	1.50	3.00
❑203, Mar 86, JR2, Crossroads,Secret Wars II	0.75	0.60	1.50	3.00
❑204, Apr 86, What Happened to Nightcrawler?,Nightcrawler solo story	0.75	0.60	1.50	3.00
❑205, May 86, Wounded Wolf, A: Power Pack,Wolverine solo story	0.75	1.60	4.00	8.00
❑206, Jun 86, JR2, Freedom is a Four Letter Word, V: Freedom Force	0.75	0.60	1.50	3.00
❑207, Jul 86, JR2, Ghosts,Wolverine vs. Phoenix	0.75	0.60	1.50	3.00
❑208, Aug 86, JR2, Retribution	0.75	0.60	1.50	3.00
❑209, Sep 86, JR2, Salvation	0.75	0.60	1.50	3.00
❑210, Oct 86, JR2, Mutant Massacre; The Morning After, 1: Marauders	0.75	1.40	3.50	7.00
❑211, Nov 86, JR2, Mutant Massacre	0.75	1.40	3.50	7.00
❑212, Dec 86, Mutant Massacre; The Last Run, A: Sabretooth,Wolverine vs. Sabretooth	0.75	1.60	4.00	8.00
❑213, Jan 87, Psylocke,Wolverine vs. Sabretooth	0.75	1.60	4.00	8.00
❑214, Feb 87, With Malice Toward All	0.75	0.60	1.50	3.00
❑215, Mar 87, Old Soldiers, 1: Crimson Commando	0.75	0.60	1.50	3.00
❑216, Apr 87, Crucible	0.75	0.60	1.50	3.00
❑217, May 87, Folly's Gambit, A: Juggernaut	0.75	0.60	1.50	3.00
❑218, Jun 87, Charge of the Light Brigade, V: Juggernaut	0.75	0.60	1.50	3.00
❑219, Jul 87, Where Duty Lies,Havok joins X-Men	0.75	0.60	1.50	3.00
❑220, Aug 87, Unfinished Business	0.75	0.60	1.50	3.00
❑221, Sep 87, Death by Drowning, V: Mr. Sinister; 1: Mister Sinister	0.75	1.00	2.50	5.00
❑222, Oct 87, Heartbreak, V: Sabretooth	0.75	1.20	3.00	6.00
❑223, Nov 87, KGa, Omens and Portents	0.75	0.60	1.50	3.00
❑224, Dec 87, The Dark Before the Dawn,registration card	0.75	0.60	1.50	3.00
❑225, Jan 88, False Dawn,Fall of Mutants	0.75	1.00	2.50	5.00
❑226, Feb 88, Go Tell the Spartans, Double-size; Fall of Mutants; Storm regains powers	1.25	1.00	2.50	5.00
❑227, Mar 88, The Belly of the Beast,Fall of Mutants	0.75	1.00	2.50	5.00
❑228, Apr 88, Deadly Games	0.75	0.60	1.50	3.00
❑229, May 88, Down Under, 1: The Reavers	1.00	0.60	1.50	3.00
❑230, Jun 88, Twas the Night…	1.00	0.60	1.50	3.00
❑231, Jul 88, … Dressed For Dinner	1.00	0.60	1.50	3.00
❑232, Aug 88, Earthfall	1.00	0.60	1.50	3.00
❑233, Sep 88, Dawn of Blood	1.00	0.60	1.50	3.00
❑234, Sep 88, Glory Day	1.00	0.60	1.50	3.00
❑235, Oct 88, Welcome to Genosha	1.00	0.60	1.50	3.00
❑236, Oct 88, Busting Loose	1.00	0.60	1.50	3.00
❑237, Nov 88, Who's Human	1.00	0.60	1.50	3.00
❑238, Nov 88, Gonna Be a Revolution	1.00	0.60	1.50	3.00
❑239, Dec 88, Vanities,Inferno	1.00	0.60	1.50	3.00
❑240, Jan 89, Strike the Match, A: Sabretooth,Inferno	1.00	0.60	1.50	3.00
❑241, Feb 89, Fan the Flame,Inferno	1.00	0.60	1.50	3.00
❑242, Mar 89, Burn!, Double-size; Inferno	1.00	0.60	1.50	3.00
❑243, Apr 89, Ashes,Inferno	1.00	0.60	1.50	3.00
❑244, May 89, Ladies' Night, 1: Jubilee	1.00	1.80	4.50	9.00
❑245, Jun 89, RL, Men!	1.00	0.60	1.50	3.00
❑246, Jul 89, The Day of Other Lights	1.00	0.60	1.50	3.00
❑247, Aug 89, The Light That Failed	1.00	0.60	1.50	3.00
❑248, Sep 89, JLee, The Cradle Will Fall,1st Jim Lee art on X-Men	1.00	1.60	4.00	8.00
❑248-2, JLee,2nd Printing; Reprint; 1st Jim Lee art on X-Men	1.25	0.30	0.75	1.50
❑249, Oct 89, The Dane Curse	1.00	0.60	1.50	3.00
❑250, Oct 89, The Shattered Star	1.00	0.60	1.50	3.00
❑251, Nov 89, Fever Dream	1.00	0.60	1.50	3.00
❑252, Nov 89, Where's Wolverine	1.00	0.50	1.25	2.50
❑253, Nov 89, Storm Warnings	1.00	0.50	1.25	2.50
❑254, Dec 89, All-New, All-Different-Here We Go Again, D: Sunder	1.00	0.50	1.25	2.50
❑255, Dec 89, Crash and Burn	1.00	0.50	1.25	2.50
❑256, Dec 89, JLee, The Key That Breaks the Locks,Acts of Vengeance	1.00	1.00	2.50	5.00
❑257, Jan 90, JLee, I am Lady Mandarin,Acts of Vengeance	1.00	1.00	2.50	5.00
❑258, Feb 90, JLee, Broken Chains,Acts of Vengeance	1.00	1.00	2.50	5.00
❑259, Mar 90, Dream a Little Dream	1.00	0.60	1.50	3.00
❑260, Apr 90, Star 90	1.00	0.60	1.50	3.00
❑261, May 90, Harriers Hunt	1.00	0.50	1.25	2.50

	ORIG	GOOD	FINE	N-MINT
❑262, Jun 90, Scary Monsters	1.00	0.50	1.25	2.50
❑263, Jul 90, The Lower Depths	1.00	0.50	1.25	2.50
❑264, Jul 90, Hot Pursuit	1.00	0.50	1.25	2.50
❑265, Aug 90, Storm	1.00	0.50	1.25	2.50
❑266, Aug 90, Gambit: Out of the Frying Pan, 1: Gambit (full appearance)	1.00	5.00	12.50	25.00
❑267, Sep 90, JLee, Nanny: Into the Fire,Captain America, Wolverine, Black Widow team-up	1.00	2.00	5.00	10.00
❑268, Sep 90, JLee, Madripoor Knights	1.00	2.00	5.00	10.00
❑269, Oct 90, JLee, Rogue Redux	1.00	0.80	2.00	4.00
❑270, Nov 90, JLee, X-Tinction; X-Tinction Agenda, Part 1	1.00	1.20	3.00	6.00
❑270-2, Nov 90, JLee, X-Tinction; X-Tinction Agenda, Part 1,2nd Printing; Gold cover	1.00	0.40	1.00	2.00
❑271, Dec 90, JLee, X-Tinction; X-Tinction Agenda, Part 4	1.00	0.80	2.00	4.00
❑272, Jan 91, JLee, X-Tinction; X-Tinction Agenda, Part 7	1.00	0.80	2.00	4.00
❑273, Feb 91, JBy; MG, Too Many Mutants	1.00	0.60	1.50	3.00
❑274, Mar 91, JLee, Crossroads, A: Nick Fury; A: Magneto; A: Ka-Zar	1.00	0.60	1.50	3.00
❑275, Apr 91, JLee, The Path Not Taken, Double-size	1.50	0.80	2.00	4.00
❑275-2, Apr 91, JLee,2nd Printing; Double-size; gold logo	1.50	0.40	1.00	2.00
❑276, May 91, JLee, Double Death	1.00	0.50	1.25	2.50
❑277, Jun 91, JLee, Free Charley	1.00	0.50	1.25	2.50
❑278, Jul 91, PS, The Battle of Muir Isle	1.00	0.50	1.25	2.50
❑279, Aug 91, Bad to the Bone	1.00	0.50	1.25	2.50
❑280, Sep 91, One Step Back-Two Steps Forward,X-Factor crossover	1.00	0.50	1.25	2.50
❑281, Oct 91, JBy (w), Fresh Upstart, 1: Fitzroy,wraparond cover; new team	1.00	0.40	1.00	2.00
❑281-2, Oct 91, 1: Fitzroy,wraparound cover; 2nd printing (red); New team begins	1.00	0.30	0.75	1.50
❑282, Nov 91, JBy (w), Payback, 1: Bishop (cameo)	1.00	0.60	1.50	3.00
❑282-2, Nov 91, 1: Bishop (cameo),2nd Printing; Gold cover	1.00	0.25	0.63	1.25
❑283, Dec 91, JBy (w), Bishop's Crossing, 1: Bishop (full)	1.00	0.80	2.00	4.00
❑284, Jan 92, JBy (w), Into the Void	1.00	0.50	1.25	2.50
❑285, Feb 92, JBy (w), Down the Rabbit Hole, 1: Mikhail Rasputin	1.25	0.50	1.25	2.50
❑286, Mar 92, Close Call	1.25	0.40	1.00	2.00
❑287, Apr 92, JR2, Bishop to King's Five, O: Bishop	1.25	0.50	1.25	2.50
❑288, May 92	1.25	0.40	1.00	2.00
❑289, Jun 92,Bishop joins X-Men	1.25	0.40	1.00	2.00
❑290, Jul 92	1.25	0.40	1.00	2.00
❑291, Aug 92	1.25	0.40	1.00	2.00
❑292, Sep 92	1.25	0.40	1.00	2.00
❑293, Oct 92	1.25	0.40	1.00	2.00
❑294/CS, Nov 92, X-Cutioner's Song; X-Cutioner's Song, Part 1, trading card	1.50	0.40	1.00	2.00
❑295/CS, Dec 92, X-Cutioner's Song; X-Cutioner's Song, Part 5, trading card	1.50	0.40	1.00	2.00
❑296/CS, Jan 93, X-cutioner's Song, Part 9, trading card	1.50	0.40	1.00	2.00
❑297, Feb 93, X-Cutioner's Song aftermath	1.25	0.30	0.75	1.50
❑298, Mar 93	1.25	0.30	0.75	1.50
❑299, Apr 93	1.25	0.30	0.75	1.50
❑300, May 93,holo-foil cover; Double-size	3.95	1.00	2.50	5.00
❑301, Jun 93	1.25	0.30	0.75	1.50
❑302, Jul 93	1.25	0.30	0.75	1.50
❑303, Aug 93, D: Illyana Rasputin	1.25	0.40	1.00	2.00
❑304, Sep 93, 30th Anniversary Issue; hologram	3.95	1.00	2.50	5.00
❑305, Oct 93, JR2	1.25	0.30	0.75	1.50
❑306, Nov 93	1.25	0.30	0.75	1.50
❑307, Dec 93	1.25	0.30	0.75	1.50
❑308, Jan 94	1.25	0.30	0.75	1.50
❑309, Feb 94	1.25	0.30	0.75	1.50
❑310, Mar 94, trading cards	1.95	0.30	0.75	1.50
❑311, Apr 94	1.25	0.30	0.75	1.50
❑312, May 94, Marvel-Mart supplement	1.50	0.30	0.75	1.50
❑313, Jun 94	1.50	0.30	0.75	1.50
❑314, Jul 94	1.50	0.30	0.75	1.50
❑315, Aug 94	1.50	0.30	0.75	1.50
❑316, Sep 94, Generation Next, Part 1	1.50	0.30	0.75	1.50
❑316/SC, Sep 94, Generation Next, Part 1,enhanced cover	2.95	0.60	1.50	3.00
❑317, Oct 94, Generation Next, Part 3	1.50	0.30	0.75	1.50
❑317/SC, Oct 94, Generation Next, Part 3,enhanced cover	2.95	0.60	1.50	3.00
❑318, Nov 94	1.50	0.30	0.75	1.50
❑318/Dlx, Nov 94, Deluxe edition	1.95	0.40	1.00	2.00
❑319, Dec 94	1.50	0.30	0.75	1.50

	ORIG	GOOD	FINE	N-MINT
❑319/Dlx, Dec 94, Deluxe edition	1.95	0.40	1.00	2.00
❑320, Jan 95, Legion Quest, Part 1	1.50	0.30	0.75	1.50
❑320/Dlx, Jan 95, Legion Quest, Part 1, Deluxe edition	1.95	0.40	1.00	2.00
❑320/GO, Jan 95,no cover price; Wizard edition; gold logo	—	0.40	1.00	2.00
❑321, Feb 95, Legion Quest, Part 3	1.50	0.30	0.75	1.50
❑321/Dlx, Feb 95, Deluxe edition	1.95	0.40	1.00	2.00
❑322, Jul 95, V: Juggernaut; V: Onslaught	1.95	0.40	1.00	2.00
❑323, Aug 95, 1: Sack and Vessel	1.95	0.40	1.00	2.00
❑324, Sep 95	1.95	0.40	1.00	2.00
❑325, Oct 95,enhanced gatefold cardstock cover	3.95	0.80	2.00	4.00
❑326, Nov 95	1.95	0.40	1.00	2.00
❑327, Dec 95, The Fate of Magneto Is Revealed, A: Magneto	1.95	0.40	1.00	2.00
❑328, Jan 96,Psylocke vs. Sabretooth	1.95	0.40	1.00	2.00
❑329, Feb 96	1.95	0.40	1.00	2.00
❑330, Mar 96, JPH (w), Quest for the Crimson Dawn	1.95	0.40	1.00	2.00
❑331, Apr 96, The Splinter of our Discontent,Iceman vs. White Queen	1.95	0.40	1.00	2.00
❑332, May 96, V: Ozymandias	1.95	0.40	1.00	2.00
❑333, Jun 96	1.95	0.40	1.00	2.00
❑334, Jul 96, A: Juggernaut	1.95	0.40	1.00	2.00
❑335, Aug 96, Onslaught: Phase 1, A: Apocalypse; A: Uatu	1.95	0.40	1.00	2.00
❑336, Sep 96, Onslaught: Phase 2	1.95	0.40	1.00	2.00
❑337, Oct 96	1.95	0.40	1.00	2.00
❑338, Nov 96,Angel regains his wings	1.95	0.40	1.00	2.00
❑339, Dec 96, A: Spider-Man,Cyclops vs. Havok	1.95	0.40	1.00	2.00
❑340, Jan 97	1.95	0.40	1.00	2.00
❑341, Feb 97, When Strikes a Gladiator!,Cannonball vs. Gladiator	1.95	0.40	1.00	2.00
❑342, Mar 97	1.95	0.40	1.00	2.00
❑342/A,Variant cover (Rogue)	1.95	2.40	6.00	12.00
❑343, Apr 97, Where No X-Man Has Gone Before!	1.95	0.40	1.00	2.00
❑344, May 97, Casualties of War	1.95	0.40	1.00	2.00
❑345, Jun 97, Moving On	1.99	0.40	1.00	2.00
❑346, Aug 97, Operation Zero Tolerance, A: Spider-Man, gatefold summary	1.99	0.40	1.00	2.00
❑347, Sep 97, gatefold summary	1.99	0.40	1.00	2.00
❑348, Oct 97, gatefold summary	1.99	0.40	1.00	2.00
❑349, Nov 97, V: Maggot, gatefold summary	1.99	0.40	1.00	2.00
❑350, Dec 97, gatefold summary	1.99	0.40	1.00	1.99
❑350/SC, Dec 97,enhanced cover; gatefold summary	2.99	0.60	1.50	2.99
❑351, Jan 98, V: Pyro, gatefold summary; Cecilia joins team	1.99	0.40	1.00	1.99
❑352, Feb 98, gatefold summary	1.99	0.40	1.00	1.99
❑353, Mar 98, gatefold summary; Rogue vs. Wolverine	1.99	0.40	1.00	1.99
❑354, Apr 98, V: Sauron, gatefold summary	1.99	0.40	1.00	1.99
❑355, May 98, A: Alpha Flight, gatefold summary	1.99	0.40	1.00	1.99
❑356, Jun 98, gatefold summary	1.99	0.40	1.00	1.99
❑357, Jul 98, gatefold summary	1.99	0.40	1.00	1.99
❑358, Aug 98, gatefold summary	1.99	0.40	1.00	1.99
❑359, Sep 98, gatefold summary	1.99	0.40	1.00	1.99
❑360, Oct 98, gatefold summary; double-sized; Kitty Pryde, Colossus, Nightcrawler rejoin team	2.99	0.60	1.50	2.99
❑360/SC,Special cover; Kitty Pryde, Colossus, Nightcrawler rejoin team	3.99	0.80	2.00	3.99
❑361, Nov 98, gatefold summary; Return of Gambit	1.99	0.40	1.00	1.99
❑362, Dec 98, The Hunt for Xavier, Part 1, gatefold summary	1.99	0.40	1.00	1.99
❑363, Jan 99, The Hunt for Xavier, Part 3, gatefold summary	1.99	0.40	1.00	1.99
❑364, Jan 99, The Hunt for Xavier, Part 5, gatefold summary	1.99	0.40	1.00	1.99
❑365, Mar 99,cover says Feb, indicia says Mar; gatefold summary	1.99	0.40	1.00	1.99
❑366, Apr 99	1.99	0.40	1.00	1.99
❑367, Apr 99	1.99	0.40	1.00	1.99
❑368, Jun 99,cover says May, indicia says Jun; Wolverine vs. Magneto	1.99	0.40	1.00	1.99
❑369, Jun 99, V: Juggernaut	1.99	0.40	1.00	1.99
❑370, Jul 99	1.99	0.40	1.00	1.99
❑371, Aug 99, A: Warlock	1.99	0.40	1.00	1.99
❑372, Sep 99	1.99	0.40	1.00	1.99
❑373, Oct 99	1.99	0.40	1.00	1.99
❑374, Nov 99	1.99	0.40	1.00	1.99
❑375, Dec 99, I am Not Now, Nor Have I Ever Been..., Giant-size	2.99	0.60	1.50	2.99
❑376, Jan 00	1.99	0.40	1.00	1.99

Bishop, a mutant from the future, made his first full appearance in *Uncanny X-Men* #283.

© 1991 Marvel Comics

	ORIG	GOOD	FINE	N-MINT
❑377, Feb 00	—	0.45	1.13	2.25
❑378, Mar 00	—	0.45	1.13	2.25
❑379, Apr 00	—	0.45	1.13	2.25
❑380, May 00	—	0.45	1.13	2.25
❑381, Jun 00	—	0.45	1.13	2.25
❑382, Jul 00	—	0.45	1.13	2.25
❑383, Aug 00, Moscow Knights, Giant-size	2.99	0.60	1.50	2.99
❑384, Sep 00	2.25	0.45	1.13	2.25
❑385, Oct 00	2.25	0.45	1.13	2.25
❑386, Nov 00	2.25	0.45	1.13	2.25
❑387, Dec 00, Maximum Security; Cry Justice, Cry Vengeance!	2.25	0.45	1.13	2.25
❑388, Jan 01	2.25	0.45	1.13	2.25
❑389, Feb 01, The Good Shepherd	2.25	0.45	1.13	2.25
❑390, Feb 01, The Cure, D: Colossus	2.25	0.45	1.13	2.25
❑391, Mar 01, Dad	2.25	0.45	1.13	2.25
❑392, Apr 01, Eve of Destruction, Part 1	2.25	0.45	1.13	2.25
❑393	2.25	0.45	1.13	2.25
❑394	2.25	0.45	1.13	2.25
❑395	2.25	0.45	1.13	2.25
❑396	2.25	0.45	1.13	2.25
❑Anl 1, Dec 70,listed as X-Men in indicia, X-Men Special on cover; Cover reads "King Size Special"; reprints X-Men #9 and 11.	0.25	12.00	30.00	60.00
❑Anl 2, Nov 71, GK (c), Cover reads "King Size Special"; reprints X-Men #22 and 23	0.12	9.00	22.50	45.00
❑Anl 3, Jan 80, FM; GP, 1: Arkon	0.75	4.00	10.00	20.00
❑Anl 4, Nov 80, JR2, A: Doctor Strange,series continues as Uncanny X-Men Annual	0.75	1.80	4.50	9.00
❑Anl 5, Nov 81, BMc; BA, Ou, La La-Badoon; The Sundered Realm, A: Fantastic Four	0.75	1.40	3.50	7.00
❑Anl 6, Nov 82, BSz, Blood Feud, D: Rachel Van Helsing; A: Dracula	1.00	1.40	3.50	7.00
❑Anl 7, MG, Scavenger Hunt	1.00	1.00	2.50	5.00
❑Anl 8, The Adventures of Lockheed the Space Dragon and his Pet Girl, Kitty	1.00	1.00	2.50	5.00
❑Anl 9, There's No Place Like Home	1.25	2.40	6.00	12.00
❑Anl 10, Performance, 1: X-babies; 1: Longshot	1.25	2.00	5.00	10.00
❑Anl 11, Lost in the Funhouse	1.25	0.80	2.00	4.00
❑Anl 12, Resurrection	1.75	0.80	2.00	4.00
❑Anl 13, Double Cross,Atlantis Attacks	2.00	0.60	1.50	3.00
❑Anl 14, Future Present; You Must Remember This, 1: Gambit (cameo)	2.00	2.40	6.00	12.00
❑Anl 15, Kings of Pain; Kings of Pain, Part 3	2.00	0.80	2.00	4.00
❑Anl 16, Shattershot, Part 2,Shattershot	2.25	0.45	1.13	2.25
❑Anl 17,trading card	2.95	0.59	1.48	2.95
❑Anl 18	2.95	0.59	1.48	2.95
❑Anl 1995, Nov 95,wraparound cover	3.95	0.79	1.98	3.95
❑Anl 1996,wraparound cover	2.99	0.59	1.48	2.95
❑Anl 1997,wraparound cover	2.99	0.60	1.50	2.99
❑Anl 1998,wraparound cover; Uncanny X-Men/Fantastic Four '98	2.99	0.60	1.50	2.99
❑Anl 2000, Share	3.50	0.70	1.75	3.50
❑GS 1, 1: Illyana Rasputin; 1: Nightcrawler; 1: Storm; 1: Colossus; 1: Thunderbird; 1: X-Men (new)	0.50	120.00	300.00	600.00
❑GS 2	0.50	15.00	37.50	75.00

UNCENSORED MOUSE, THE
ETERNITY

Value: Cover or less

❑1, Apr 89, FG, FG (w), b&w; 40pgs.; Mickey Mouse 2.50

❑2, FG, FG (w),Mickey Mouse 2.50

UNCLE JOE'S COMMIE BOOK FEATURING CUTEY BUNNY
RIP OFF

Value: Cover or less

❑1, b&w 2.95

UNCLE SAM
DC

	ORIG	GOOD	FINE	N-MINT
❑1, ARo, prestige format	4.95	1.00	2.50	5.00
❑2, ARo, prestige format	4.95	1.00	2.50	5.00

UNCLE SCROOGE (WALT DISNEY...)
DELL

	ORIG	GOOD	FINE	N-MINT
❑210, Oct 86, CB	0.75	1.20	3.00	6.00
❑211, Nov 86, CB	0.75	1.20	3.00	6.00
❑212, Dec 86, CB	0.75	1.20	3.00	6.00
❑213, Jan 86	0.75	1.20	3.00	6.00
❑214, Feb 87	0.75	1.20	3.00	6.00
❑215, Mar 87	0.75	1.20	3.00	6.00
❑216, Apr 87, CB	0.75	1.20	3.00	6.00
❑217, May 87	0.75	1.20	3.00	6.00
❑218, Jun 87, CB	0.95	1.20	3.00	6.00
❑219, Jul 87, DR ,1st Rosa Disney story	0.95	1.20	3.00	6.00
❑220, Aug 87, DR; CB	0.95	1.00	2.50	5.00
❑221, Sep 87, CB	0.95	1.00	2.50	5.00
❑222, Oct 87, CB	0.95	1.00	2.50	5.00
❑223, Nov 87, CB	0.95	1.00	2.50	5.00
❑224, Dec 87, DR; CB	0.95	1.00	2.50	5.00
❑225, Feb 88, CB	0.95	1.00	2.50	5.00
❑226, May 88, DR; CB	0.95	1.00	2.50	5.00
❑227, Jul 88, CB	0.95	1.00	2.50	5.00
❑228, Aug 88, CB	0.95	1.00	2.50	5.00
❑229, Sep 88, CB	0.95	1.00	2.50	5.00
❑230, Oct 88, CB	0.95	1.00	2.50	5.00
❑231, Nov 88, CB, DR (c)	0.95	1.00	2.50	5.00
❑232, Dec 88, CB	0.95	1.00	2.50	5.00
❑233, Feb 89, CB	0.95	1.00	2.50	5.00
❑234, May 89, CB	0.95	1.00	2.50	5.00
❑235, Jul 89, DR	0.95	1.00	2.50	5.00
❑236, Aug 89, CB	0.95	1.00	2.50	5.00
❑237, Sep 89, CB	0.95	1.00	2.50	5.00
❑238, Oct 89, CB	0.95	1.00	2.50	5.00
❑239, Nov 89, CB	0.95	1.00	2.50	5.00
❑240, Dec 89, CB	0.95	1.00	2.50	5.00
❑241, Feb 90, DR; CB	1.95	0.80	2.00	4.00
❑242, Apr 90, CB, double-sized	1.95	0.80	2.00	4.00
❑243, Jun 90, Pie in the Sky; The Carpocanth	1.50	0.80	2.00	4.00
❑244, Jul 90	1.50	0.80	2.00	4.00
❑245, Aug 90	1.50	0.80	2.00	4.00
❑246, Sep 90	1.50	0.80	2.00	4.00
❑247, Oct 90	1.50	0.80	2.00	4.00
❑248, Nov 90	1.50	0.80	2.00	4.00
❑249, Dec 90	1.50	0.80	2.00	4.00
❑250, Jan 91, CB	2.25	0.80	2.00	4.00
❑251, Feb 91, CB	1.50	0.80	2.00	4.00
❑252, Mar 91	1.50	0.80	2.00	4.00
❑253, Apr 91, CB, The Fabulous Philosopher's Stone	1.50	0.80	2.00	4.00
❑254, May 91, CB	1.50	0.80	2.00	4.00
❑255, Jun 91, CB	1.50	0.80	2.00	4.00
❑256, Jul 91, CB	1.50	0.80	2.00	4.00
❑257, Aug 91	1.50	0.80	2.00	4.00
❑258, Sep 91, CB	1.50	0.80	2.00	4.00
❑259, Oct 91, Time Tetrad, Part 3	1.50	0.80	2.00	4.00
❑260, Nov 91	1.50	0.80	2.00	4.00
❑261, Dec 91, DR, Return to Xanadu	1.50	0.50	1.25	2.50
❑262, Jan 92, DR, Return to Xanadu	1.50	0.50	1.25	2.50
❑263, Feb 92, DR	1.50	0.50	1.25	2.50
❑264, Mar 92	1.50	0.50	1.25	2.50
❑265, Apr 92, CB	1.50	0.50	1.25	2.50
❑266, May 92, CB	1.50	0.50	1.25	2.50
❑267, Jun 92, CB ,contains Duckburg map piece 3 of 9	1.50	0.50	1.25	2.50
❑268, Jul 92, CB ,contains Duckburg map piece 6 of 9	1.50	0.50	1.25	2.50
❑269, Aug 92, CB ,contains Duckburg map piece 9 of 9	1.50	0.50	1.25	2.50
❑270, Sep 92, CB ,Olympics	1.50	0.50	1.25	2.50
❑271, Oct 92, CB	1.50	0.50	1.25	2.50
❑272, Nov 92, CB	1.50	0.50	1.25	2.50
❑273, Dec 92, CB	1.50	0.50	1.25	2.50
❑274, Jan 93, CB, Hall of the Mermaid Queen	1.50	0.50	1.25	2.50
❑275, Feb 93, CB	1.50	0.50	1.25	2.50
❑276, Mar 93, DR	1.50	0.50	1.25	2.50
❑277, Apr 93, CB	1.50	0.50	1.25	2.50
❑278, May 93, CB	1.50	0.50	1.25	2.50
❑279, Jun 93, CB	1.50	0.50	1.25	2.50
❑280, Jul 93	1.50	0.50	1.25	2.50
❑281, Aug 93, CB, DR (c)	1.50	0.50	1.25	2.50
❑282, Oct 93, CB	1.50	0.50	1.25	2.50
❑283, Dec 93, CB	1.50	0.50	1.25	2.50
❑284, Feb 94, CB	1.50	0.50	1.25	2.50
❑285, Apr 94, DR, Life and Times of Scrooge McDuck, Part 1	1.50	0.50	1.25	2.50
❑286, Jun 94, DR, Life and Times of Scrooge McDuck, Part 2	1.50	0.50	1.25	2.50
❑287, Aug 94, DR, Life and Times of Scrooge McDuck, Part 3	1.50	0.50	1.25	2.50
❑288, Oct 94, DR, Life and Times of Scrooge McDuck, Part 4	1.50	0.50	1.25	2.50
❑289, Dec 94, DR, Life and Times of Scrooge McDuck, Part 5	1.50	0.50	1.25	2.50
❑290, Feb 95, DR, Life and Times of Scrooge McDuck, Part 6	1.50	0.50	1.25	2.50
❑291, Apr 95, DR, Life and Times of Scrooge McDuck, Part 7	1.50	0.50	1.25	2.50
❑292, Jun 95, DR, Life and Times of Scrooge McDuck, Part 8	1.50	0.50	1.25	2.50
❑293, Aug 95, DR, Life and Times of Scrooge McDuck, Part 9	1.95	0.50	1.25	2.50
❑294, Oct 95, DR, Life and Times of Scrooge McDuck, Part 10,newsprint covers begin	1.50	0.50	1.25	2.50
❑295, Dec 95, DR, Life and Times of Scrooge McDuck, Part 11	1.50	0.50	1.25	2.50
❑296, Feb 96, DR, Life and Times of Scrooge McDuck, Part 12	1.50	0.50	1.25	2.50
❑297, Apr 96, DR, Life and Times of Scrooge McDuck, Part 0	1.50	0.50	1.25	2.50
❑298, Jun 96	1.50	0.50	1.25	2.50
❑299, Aug 96	1.50	0.50	1.25	2.50
❑300, Oct 96	2.25	0.45	1.13	2.25
❑301, Dec 96	1.50	0.30	0.75	1.50
❑302, Feb 97, CB, Monkey Business,reprints from WDC&S #297	1.50	0.30	0.75	1.50
❑303, Apr 97,newsprint covers end	1.50	0.30	0.75	1.50
❑304, Jun 97, CB, Mr. Private Eye,Reprint.	1.95	0.30	0.75	1.50
❑305, Aug 97, CB, Flour Follies; A Matter of Factory,Reprint	1.95	0.30	0.75	1.50
❑306, Oct 97, DR, DR (c), DR (w), Life and Times of Scrooge McDuck, Part 6.5: The Vigilante of Pizen Bluff	1.95	0.30	0.75	1.50
❑307, Dec 97	1.95	0.30	0.75	1.50
❑308, Feb 98	1.95	0.30	0.75	1.50
❑309, May 98,prestige format begins	6.95	1.39	3.47	6.95
❑310, Jun 98	6.95	1.39	3.47	6.95
❑311, Jul 98	6.95	1.39	3.47	6.95
❑312, Aug 98	6.95	1.39	3.47	6.95
❑313, Sep 98	6.95	1.39	3.47	6.95
❑314, Oct 98	6.95	1.39	3.47	6.95
❑315, Nov 98	6.95	1.39	3.47	6.95
❑316, Dec 98	6.95	1.39	3.47	6.95
❑317, Jan 99	6.95	1.39	3.47	6.95
❑318, Feb 99,Final Issue	6.95	1.39	3.47	6.95

UNCLE SCROOGE ADVENTURES
GLADSTONE

	ORIG	GOOD	FINE	N-MINT
❑1, Nov 87, CB	0.95	1.00	2.50	5.00
❑2, Dec 87, CB	0.95	0.60	1.50	3.00
❑3, Jan 88, CB	0.95	0.40	1.00	2.00
❑4, Apr 88, CB	0.95	0.40	1.00	2.00
❑5, Jun 88, DR	0.95	1.20	3.00	6.00
❑6, Aug 88, CB	0.95	0.40	1.00	2.00
❑7, Sep 88, CB	0.95	0.40	1.00	2.00
❑8, Oct 88, CB	0.95	0.40	1.00	2.00
❑9, Nov 88, DR	0.95	1.00	2.50	5.00
❑10, Dec 88, CB	0.95	0.40	1.00	2.00
❑11, Jan 89, CB	0.95	0.40	1.00	2.00
❑12, Mar 89, CB	0.95	0.40	1.00	2.00
❑13, Jun 89, CB, DR (c)	0.95	0.40	1.00	2.00
❑14, Aug 89, DR	0.95	1.00	2.50	5.00
❑15, Sep 89, CB	0.95	0.40	1.00	2.00
❑16, Oct 89, CB	0.95	0.40	1.00	2.00
❑17, Nov 89, CB	0.95	0.40	1.00	2.00
❑18, Dec 89, CB	0.95	0.40	1.00	2.00
❑19, Jan 90, CB, DR (c)	0.95	0.40	1.00	2.00
❑20, Mar 90, DR; CB, double-sized	1.95	1.00	2.50	5.00
❑21, May 90, DR; CB, double-sized	1.95	1.00	2.50	5.00
❑22, Sep 93, CB ,Reprint	1.50	0.30	0.75	1.50
❑23, Nov 93, CB ,64pgs.; Reprint	2.95	0.59	1.48	2.95
❑24, Jan 94, CB ,Reprint	1.50	0.30	0.75	1.50
❑25, Mar 94, CB, DR (c),Reprint	1.50	0.30	0.75	1.50
❑26, May 94, CB, Back to the Klondike,Reprint	2.95	0.59	1.48	2.95
❑27, Jul 94, DR, O: Junior Woodchucks Handbook	1.50	0.30	0.75	1.50
❑28, Sep 94, CB, A: Terries and Fermies,64pgs.; Reprint	2.95	0.59	1.48	2.95
❑29, Nov 94	1.50	0.30	0.75	1.50
❑30, Jan 95,64pgs.	2.95	0.59	1.48	2.95
❑31, Mar 95	1.50	0.30	0.75	1.50
❑32, May 95	1.50	0.30	0.75	1.50
❑33, Jul 95, CB, CB (w), Horsing Around with History,new story	2.95	0.59	1.48	2.95
❑34, Sep 95	1.95	0.39	0.98	1.95
❑35, Nov 95	1.95	0.39	0.98	1.95

	ORIG	GOOD	FINE	N-MINT
❑36, Jan 96	1.95	0.39	0.98	1.95
❑37, Mar 96,newprint covers begin	1.50	0.30	0.75	1.50
❑38, May 96	1.50	0.30	0.75	1.50
❑39, Aug 96	1.50	0.30	0.75	1.50
❑40, Sep 96	1.50	0.30	0.75	1.50
❑41, Nov 96	1.95	0.39	0.98	1.95
❑42, Jan 97	1.95	0.39	0.98	1.95
❑43, Feb 97, CB ,reprints The Queen of the Wild Dog Pack from US #62	1.50	0.30	0.75	1.50
❑44, Mar 97	1.50	0.30	0.75	1.50
❑45, Apr 97	1.50	0.30	0.75	1.50
❑46, May 97,newprint covers end	1.95	0.39	0.98	1.95
❑47, Jun 97, CB, The Menehune Mystery,Reprint	1.95	0.39	0.98	1.95
❑48, Jul 97	1.95	0.39	0.98	1.95
❑49, Aug 97	1.95	0.39	0.98	1.95
❑50, Sep 97, CB, The Secret of Atlantis,Reprint	1.95	0.39	0.98	1.95
❑51, Oct 97, DR, The Treasure of the Ten Avatars	1.95	0.39	0.98	1.95
❑52, Nov 97	1.95	0.39	0.98	1.95
❑53, Dec 97, Secret of the Incas, Part 1	1.95	0.39	0.98	1.95
❑54, Feb 98, Secret of the Incas, Part 2	1.95	0.39	0.98	1.95

UNCLE SCROOGE & DONALD DUCK (WALT DISNEY'S...)
GLADSTONE

	ORIG	GOOD	FINE	N-MINT
❑1, Jan 98, Ten-Penny Opera; The Crocodile Collector	1.95	0.40	1.00	2.00
❑2, Mar 98	1.95	0.40	1.00	2.00

UNCLE SCROOGE COMICS DIGEST
GLADSTONE

	ORIG	GOOD	FINE	N-MINT
❑1, Dec 86, CB	1.50	0.60	1.50	3.00
❑2, Feb 87, CB	1.50	0.40	1.00	2.00
❑3, Apr 87, CB	1.50	0.40	1.00	2.00
❑4, Jun 87, CB	1.50	0.40	1.00	2.00
❑5, Aug 87, CB	1.50	0.40	1.00	2.00

UNCLE SCROOGE GOES TO DISNEYLAND (WALT DISNEY'S...)
GLADSTONE

	ORIG	GOOD	FINE	N-MINT
❑1, CB ,Dell Giant	2.50	55.00	137.50	275.00
❑1/A, digest	1.50	1.00	2.50	5.00
❑1-2/A, CB, digest	1.50	1.00	2.50	5.00
❑1-2, CB	2.50	1.20	3.00	6.00

UNCLE SLAM & FIRE DOG
ACTION PLANET

Value: Cover or less

- ❑1, Visiting Yesterday; My Dream Date with Uncle Slam 2.95
- ❑2, The Origin of Me; The Terror of President Binky Dinky Doo.. 2.95

UNCUT COMICS
UNCUT COMICS

	ORIG	GOOD	FINE	N-MINT
❑1, Apr 97, nn; b&w; free handout; Origins .	—	0.20	0.50	1.00
❑1/A, Feb 97, b&w; non-slick cover	1.50	0.30	0.75	1.50
❑1/B, Feb 97, b&w; non-slick alternate cover	1.50	0.30	0.75	1.50
❑2, May 97, b&w; flip-book with alternate cover back-up	1.95	0.39	0.98	1.95

UNDERDOG (CHARLTON)
CHARLTON

	ORIG	GOOD	FINE	N-MINT
❑1, Jul 70,poster	0.15	8.00	20.00	40.00
❑2, Sep 70	0.15	4.80	12.00	24.00
❑3, Nov 70	0.15	3.60	9.00	18.00
❑4, Jan 71	0.15	3.60	9.00	18.00
❑5, Mar 71	0.15	3.60	9.00	18.00
❑6, May 71	0.15	3.00	7.50	15.00
❑7, Jul 71	—	3.00	7.50	15.00
❑8, Sep 71	—	3.00	7.50	15.00
❑9, Nov 71	0.20	3.00	7.50	15.00
❑10, Jan 72	0.20	3.00	7.50	15.00
❑11	—	2.00	5.00	10.00
❑12	—	2.00	5.00	10.00
❑13	—	2.00	5.00	10.00
❑14	—	2.00	5.00	10.00
❑15	—	2.00	5.00	10.00
❑16	—	2.00	5.00	10.00
❑17	—	2.00	5.00	10.00
❑18	—	2.00	5.00	10.00
❑19	—	2.00	5.00	10.00
❑20	—	2.00	5.00	10.00
❑21	—	2.00	5.00	10.00
❑22	—	1.60	4.00	8.00
❑23	—	1.60	4.00	8.00

UNDERDOG (HARVEY)
HARVEY

Value: Cover or less

- ❑1, Nov 93 .... 1.50
- ❑2, Jan 93 .... 1.50
- ❑3, Mar 94 .... 1.50
- ❑4, May 94 .... 1.50
- ❑5, Jul 94 .... 1.50
- ❑Smr 1 .... 2.25

Uncle Scrooge recounted his early adventures in Don Rosa's "The Life and Times of Scrooge McDuck."

© 1994 Walt Disney Productions (Gladstone)

UNDERDOG (SPOTLIGHT)
SPOTLIGHT

	ORIG	GOOD	FINE	N-MINT
❑1	1.50	0.40	1.00	2.00
❑2	1.50	0.40	1.00	2.00

UNDERDOG 3-D
BLACKTHORNE

Value: Cover or less

- ❑1 .... 2.50

UNDERGROUND
AIRCEL

Value: Cover or less

- ❑1, nn; b&w 1.70

UNDERGROUND (ANDREW VACHSS'...)
DARK HORSE

Value: Cover or less

- ❑1, Feb 94, Into the Underground; There is no Dog 3.95
- ❑2, Mar 94 .... 3.95
- ❑3, Apr 94 .... 3.95
- ❑4, May 94 .... 3.95

UNDERGROUND CLASSICS
RIP OFF

	ORIG	GOOD	FINE	N-MINT
❑1, Dec 85,Fabulous Furry Freak Brothers.	1.50	0.60	1.50	3.00
❑2, Feb 86,Dealer McDope	2.00	0.50	1.25	2.50
❑2-2,2nd Printing	2.00	0.40	1.00	2.00
❑2-3,3rd Printing	2.00	0.50	1.25	2.50
❑3, Mar 86,Dealer McDope	2.00	0.50	1.25	2.50
❑3-2,2nd Printing	2.00	0.40	1.00	2.00
❑4, Sep 87	2.50	0.50	1.25	2.50
❑5, Nov 87,Wonder Warthog	2.00	0.50	1.25	2.50
❑6, Feb 88	2.00	0.50	1.25	2.50
❑7, Apr 88	2.50	0.50	1.25	2.50
❑8, Jun 88, The Forty Year Old Hippie: Talks to the Whales; A different Drummer	2.50	0.50	1.25	2.50
❑9, Feb 89,Art of Greg Irons	2.50	0.50	1.25	2.50
❑10,Jesus	2.50	0.50	1.25	2.50
❑11,Jesus	2.50	0.50	1.25	2.50
❑12, Jul 90,Shelton 3-D	2.95	0.50	1.25	2.50
❑12-2,2nd Printing	2.95	0.59	1.48	2.95
❑13,Jesus	2.50	0.50	1.25	2.50
❑14,Jesus	2.50	0.50	1.25	2.50
❑15	2.50	0.50	1.25	2.50

UNDERSEA AGENT
TOWER

	ORIG	GOOD	FINE	N-MINT
❑1, Jan 66	0.25	5.60	14.00	28.00
❑2, Apr 66,Lt. Jones gains electrical powers	0.25	4.00	10.00	20.00
❑3, Jun 66	0.25	3.20	8.00	16.00
❑4, Aug 66	0.25	3.20	8.00	16.00
❑5, Oct 66	0.25	3.20	8.00	16.00
❑6, Mar 67,Final Issue	0.25	3.20	8.00	16.00

UNDERSIDE
CALIBER

Value: Cover or less

- ❑1 .... 2.95

UNDERTAKER
CHAOS

	ORIG	GOOD	FINE	N-MINT
❑0,Collector's issue; Wizard	—	0.60	1.50	3.00
❑0.5	—	0.80	2.00	4.00
❑1, Apr 99, Prophecy of the Dead,Drawn cover	2.95	0.80	2.00	4.00
❑1/A, Prophecy of the Dead,DFE red foil cover	—	1.20	3.00	6.00
❑1/B, Prophecy of the Dead,DFE red foil cover	—	1.60	4.00	8.00
❑1/SC, Apr 99,Photo cover	2.95	0.80	2.00	4.00
❑2, May 99	2.95	0.59	1.48	2.95
❑3, Jun 99	2.95	0.59	1.48	2.95
❑4, Jul 99	2.95	0.59	1.48	2.95
❑5, Aug 99	2.95	0.59	1.48	2.95
❑6, Sep 99	2.95	0.59	1.48	2.95
❑7, Oct 99	2.95	0.59	1.48	2.95
❑8, Nov 99, Streets Paved with Blood	2.95	0.59	1.48	2.95
❑9, Dec 99, Honeymoon in Hell	2.95	0.59	1.48	2.95
❑10, Jan 00, Broken Vows. Broken Hearts. Broken Bones.	2.95	0.59	1.48	2.95
❑HS 1, Oct 99, digest	2.95	0.59	1.48	2.95

UNDER TERRA
PREDAWN

Value: Cover or less

❑2, b&w	2.45
❑3, b&w	2.45
❑4, b&w	2.45
❑5, b&w	2.45
❑6, b&w	1.75

UNDERWORLD (DC)
DC

	ORIG	GOOD	FINE	N-MINT
❑1, Dec 87	1.25	0.25	0.63	1.25
❑2, Jan 88	1.00	0.25	0.63	1.25
❑3, Feb 88, Saving Grace	1.00	0.25	0.63	1.25
❑4, Mar 88	1.00	0.25	0.63	1.25

UNDERWORLD (DEATH)
DEATH

Value: Cover or less

❑1, b&w ... 2.00

UNDERWORLD UNLEASHED
DC

	ORIG	GOOD	FINE	N-MINT
❑1, Nov 95, MWa (w), D: Captain Cold; D: Heat Wave; 1: Neron; D: Mirror Master; D: Weather Wizard; D: Boomerang; D: Mongul	2.95	0.70	1.75	3.50
❑2, Dec 95, MWa (w)	2.95	0.65	1.63	3.25
❑3, Dec 95, MWa (w)	2.95	0.65	1.63	3.25

UNDERWORLD UNLEASHED: ABYSS-HELL'S SENTINEL
DC

Value: Cover or less

❑1, Dec 95,One-Shot ... 2.95

UNDERWORLD UNLEASHED: APOKOLIPS-DARK UPRISING
DC

Value: Cover or less

❑1, Nov 95,One-Shot ... 1.95

UNDERWORLD UNLEASHED: BATMAN-DEVIL'S ASYLUM
DC

Value: Cover or less

❑1,One-Shot ... 2.95

UNDERWORLD UNLEASHED: PATTERNS OF FEAR
DC

Value: Cover or less

❑1, Dec 95, A: Oracle, One-Shot ... 2.95

UNDIE DOG
HALLEY'S

	ORIG	GOOD	FINE	N-MINT
❑1, b&w	1.00	0.30	0.75	1.50

UNEXPECTED, THE
DC

	ORIG	GOOD	FINE	N-MINT
❑105, Feb 68,Series continued from Tales of the Unexpected #104	0.12	5.20	13.00	26.00
❑106, Apr 68	0.12	3.00	7.50	15.00
❑107	0.12	3.00	7.50	15.00
❑108	0.12	3.00	7.50	15.00
❑109	0.12	3.00	7.50	15.00
❑110	0.12	3.00	7.50	15.00
❑111	0.12	3.00	7.50	15.00
❑112, Apr 69	0.12	3.00	7.50	15.00
❑113	0.12	3.00	7.50	15.00
❑114	0.15	2.00	5.00	10.00
❑115	—	2.00	5.00	10.00
❑116	—	2.00	5.00	10.00
❑117	—	2.00	5.00	10.00
❑118, Apr 70	0.15	2.00	5.00	10.00
❑119, BWr	0.15	2.40	6.00	12.00
❑120	0.15	2.00	5.00	10.00
❑121, BWr	0.15	2.80	7.00	14.00
❑122	0.15	2.00	5.00	10.00
❑123	0.15	2.00	5.00	10.00
❑124, Apr 71	0.15	2.00	5.00	10.00
❑125	—	2.00	5.00	10.00
❑126	—	2.00	5.00	10.00
❑127	—	2.00	5.00	10.00
❑128, BWr	—	2.40	6.00	12.00
❑129	—	1.20	3.00	6.00
❑130	—	1.20	3.00	6.00
❑131, DD, Run For Your Death; The Beast of Bristol	—	1.20	3.00	6.00
❑132	—	1.20	3.00	6.00
❑133	—	1.20	3.00	6.00
❑134	—	1.20	3.00	6.00
❑135	—	1.20	3.00	6.00
❑136	—	1.20	3.00	6.00
❑137	—	1.20	3.00	6.00
❑138	—	1.20	3.00	6.00
❑139	—	1.20	3.00	6.00
❑140	—	1.20	3.00	6.00
❑141	—	1.20	3.00	6.00
❑142	—	1.20	3.00	6.00
❑143	—	1.20	3.00	6.00
❑144	—	1.20	3.00	6.00
❑145, Mar 73	0.20	1.20	3.00	6.00
❑146	—	1.20	3.00	6.00
❑147	—	1.20	3.00	6.00
❑148	—	1.20	3.00	6.00
❑149	—	1.20	3.00	6.00
❑150	—	1.20	3.00	6.00
❑151	—	1.20	3.00	6.00
❑152	—	1.20	3.00	6.00
❑153	—	1.20	3.00	6.00
❑154	—	1.20	3.00	6.00
❑155	—	1.20	3.00	6.00
❑156	—	1.20	3.00	6.00
❑157,100pgs.	—	2.00	5.00	10.00
❑158,100pgs.	—	2.00	5.00	10.00
❑159, Oct 74,100pgs.	0.60	2.00	5.00	10.00
❑160, MM, The Death of an Exorcist; Over My Dead Body,100pgs.	—	2.00	5.00	10.00
❑161,100pgs.	—	2.00	5.00	10.00
❑162,100pgs.	—	2.00	5.00	10.00
❑163	—	0.80	2.00	4.00
❑164	—	0.80	2.00	4.00
❑165	—	0.80	2.00	4.00
❑166	—	0.80	2.00	4.00
❑167	—	0.80	2.00	4.00
❑168	—	0.80	2.00	4.00
❑169	—	0.80	2.00	4.00
❑170	—	0.80	2.00	4.00
❑171	—	0.80	2.00	4.00
❑172	—	0.80	2.00	4.00
❑173	—	0.80	2.00	4.00
❑174	—	0.80	2.00	4.00
❑175	—	0.80	2.00	4.00
❑176	—	0.80	2.00	4.00
❑177, Feb 77	0.30	0.80	2.00	4.00
❑178	—	0.80	2.00	4.00
❑179	—	0.80	2.00	4.00
❑180	—	0.80	2.00	4.00
❑181	—	0.80	2.00	4.00
❑182	—	0.80	2.00	4.00
❑183	—	0.80	2.00	4.00
❑184	—	0.80	2.00	4.00
❑185	—	0.80	2.00	4.00
❑186	—	0.80	2.00	4.00
❑187	—	0.80	2.00	4.00
❑188	—	0.80	2.00	4.00
❑189	1.00	0.80	2.00	4.00
❑190	1.00	0.80	2.00	4.00
❑191, MR	1.00	1.00	2.50	5.00
❑192	1.00	0.60	1.50	3.00
❑193	1.00	0.60	1.50	3.00
❑194	1.00	0.60	1.50	3.00
❑195	—	0.60	1.50	3.00
❑196	—	0.60	1.50	3.00
❑197	—	0.60	1.50	3.00
❑198	—	0.60	1.50	3.00
❑199	—	0.60	1.50	3.00
❑200	—	0.60	1.50	3.00
❑201, Aug 80	0.40	0.60	1.50	3.00
❑202, Death Trap; The Creature of the Park	—	0.60	1.50	3.00
❑203	—	0.60	1.50	3.00
❑204	—	0.60	1.50	3.00
❑205	—	0.60	1.50	3.00
❑206	—	0.60	1.50	3.00
❑207	—	0.60	1.50	3.00
❑208	—	0.60	1.50	3.00
❑209	—	0.60	1.50	3.00
❑210	—	0.60	1.50	3.00
❑211	—	0.60	1.50	3.00
❑212	—	0.60	1.50	3.00
❑213	—	0.60	1.50	3.00
❑214	—	0.60	1.50	3.00
❑215	—	0.60	1.50	3.00
❑216	—	0.60	1.50	3.00
❑217	0.60	0.60	1.50	3.00
❑218	—	0.60	1.50	3.00
❑219	—	0.60	1.50	3.00
❑220, Mar 82	0.60	0.60	1.50	3.00
❑221	—	0.60	1.50	3.00
❑222,Final Issue	—	0.60	1.50	3.00

UNFORGIVEN, THE
MYTHIC

	ORIG	GOOD	FINE	N-MINT
❑1	—	0.55	1.38	2.75

UNFUNNY X-CONS, THE
PARODY PRESS

Value: Cover or less

❑1, Sep 92,three variant covers (X, Y, Z)	2.50
❑1-2,2nd Printing with trading card	2.50

UNICORN ISLE
APPLE

	ORIG	GOOD	FINE	N-MINT
❑1, Oct 86, b&w	1.50	0.40	1.00	2.00
❑2, b&w	1.50	0.40	1.00	2.00
❑3, b&w	1.50	0.40	1.00	2.00

	ORIG	GOOD	FINE	N-MINT
❑4	1.75	0.40	1.00	2.00
❑5	1.75	0.40	1.00	2.00
❑6	1.50	0.40	1.00	2.00
❑7	1.50	0.40	1.00	2.00
❑8	1.50	0.40	1.00	2.00
❑9	1.50	0.40	1.00	2.00
❑10	1.50	0.40	1.00	2.00
❑11	1.50	0.40	1.00	2.00
❑12	1.50	0.40	1.00	2.00

UNICORN KING
Kz Comics

	ORIG	GOOD	FINE	N-MINT
❑1, Dec 86, b&w	0.95	0.40	1.00	2.00

UNION
Image
Value: Cover or less

- ❑1, Feb 95 ... 2.50
- ❑2, Mar 95 ... 2.50
- ❑3, Apr 95 ... 2.50
- ❑4, May 95,with cards ... 2.50
- ❑5, Jun 95, 1: Rhiannon ... 2.50
- ❑6, Jul 95, A: Fairchild ... 2.50
- ❑7, Aug 95 ... 2.50
- ❑8, Oct 95 ... 2.50
- ❑9, Feb 96,covers says Dec, indicia says Feb; Final Issue; Story continued in Union: Final Vengeance ... 2.50

UNION (MINI-SERIES)
Image
Value: Cover or less

- ❑0, Jul 94 ... 2.50
- ❑0/A, Jul 94,alternate cover; Variant edition cover ... 2.50
- ❑1, Jun 93,Foil-embossed cover ... 2.95
- ❑2, Oct 93 ... 1.95
- ❑3, Dec 93 ... 1.95
- ❑4, Mar 94 ... 1.95

UNION: FINAL VENGEANCE
Image
Value: Cover or less

- ❑1, Oct 97, Knight of Faith,concludes story from Union #9 ... 2.50

UNION JACK
Marvel
Value: Cover or less

- ❑1, Dec 98, Tradition, gatefold summary ... 2.99
- ❑2, Jan 99, gatefold summary ... 2.99
- ❑3, A: Baron Blood ... 2.99

UNION JACKS
Anacom
Value: Cover or less

- ❑1, b&w ... 2.00

UNITY
Valiant

	ORIG	GOOD	FINE	N-MINT
❑0, Aug 92, Unity, Part 1, giveaway; Blue cover (regular edition)	—	0.20	0.50	1.00
❑0/LE, Aug 92, Unity, Part 1, Red cover (limited promotional edition)	—	0.60	1.50	3.00
❑1, Oct 92, Unity, Part 18	1.50	0.40	1.00	2.00
❑1/GO, Unity, Part 18, Gold edition	—	0.60	1.50	3.00
❑1/PL, Platinum edition	—	0.60	1.50	3.00
❑YB 1, Yearbook #1; The Lost Chapter, A: Solar; A: X-O Manowar,cardstock cover; Yearbook 1; a.k.a. Unity: The Lost Chapter	3.95	0.79	1.98	3.95

UNITY 2000
Acclaim
Value: Cover or less

- ❑1, Nov 99, JSn, Absent Friends ... 2.50
- ❑2, Dec 99, JSn ... 2.50
- ❑3, Jan 00, JSn, Painful Truth or Apocalyptic Conse-quences,series canceled ... 2.50

UNIVERSAL MONSTERS: DRACULA
Dark Horse
Value: Cover or less

- ❑1, nn; Based on the classic Universal pictures film ... 4.95

UNIVERSAL MONSTERS: FRANKENSTEIN
Dark Horse
Value: Cover or less

- ❑1, nn; Based on the classic Universal pictures film ... 3.95

UNIVERSAL MONSTERS: THE CREATURE FROM THE BLACK LAGOON
Dark Horse
Value: Cover or less

- ❑1, Aug 93, nn; movie Adaptation ... 4.95

UNIVERSAL MONSTERS: THE MUMMY
Dark Horse
Value: Cover or less

- ❑1, nn; movie Adaptation; Based on the classic Universal pictures film ... 4.95

UNIVERSAL SOLDIER (NOW)
Now
Value: Cover or less

- ❑1, Sep 92, The Quick and the Undead, O: Universal Soldiers,newsstand ... 1.95
- ❑1/DM, Sep 92, The Quick and the Undead, O: Universal Soldiers,Hologram cover; direct sale ... 2.50
- ❑1/SC, Sep 92,Waldenbooks; has UPC box and hologram ... 2.50
- ❑2, Oct 92,newsstand ... 1.95
- ❑2/DM, Oct 92,direct-sale ... 2.50
- ❑3, Nov 92,Photo cover; newsstand ... 1.95
- ❑3/DM, Nov 92,uncensored ... 2.50

While protecting the new Captain Marvel, an alternate history Captain America died in *Universe X: Cap.*

UNIVERSE X
Marvel
Value: Cover or less

- ❑0, Sep 00, ARo (c), ARo (w),cardstock cover; follows events of Earth X ... 3.99
- ❑1, Oct 00, ARo (c), ARo (w),cardstock cover ... 3.50
- ❑2, Nov 00, ARo (c), ARo (w),cardstock cover ... 3.50
- ❑3, Dec 00, ARo (c), ARo (w),cardstock cover ... 3.50
- ❑4, Jan 01, ARo (c),cardstock cover ... 3.50
- ❑5, Feb 01, ARo (c),cardstock cover ... 3.50
- ❑6, Mar 01, ARo (c),cardstock cover ... 3.50
- ❑7, Apr 01, ARo (c),cardstock cover ... 3.50
- ❑8, May 01, ARo (c),cardstock cover ... 3.50
- ❑9 ... 3.50
- ❑10 ... 3.50
- ❑11 ... 3.50
- ❑12 ... 3.50

UNIVERSE X: CAP
Marvel
Value: Cover or less

- ❑1, Feb 01, ARo (c), D: Captain America ... 3.99

UNIVERSE X: SPIDEY
Marvel

	ORIG	GOOD	FINE	N-MINT
❑1, Jan 01, ARo (c)	3.99	0.80	2.00	3.99
❑1/A, Jan 01, ARo (c),Dynamic Forces variant	—	1.20	3.00	6.00
❑1/B, Jan 01, ARo (c),Dynamic Forces variant sketch cover	—	2.00	5.00	10.00
❑1/C, Jan 01, ARo (c), recalled edition with potentially libelous statement in background of one panel	3.99	12.00	30.00	60.00

UNKNOWN SOLDIER
DC

	ORIG	GOOD	FINE	N-MINT
❑205, May 77	0.30	1.20	3.00	6.00
❑206, Jul 77	0.35	1.20	3.00	6.00
❑207, Sep 77, Kill the King!; Lt. Larry Rock: Killers All!	0.35	1.20	3.00	6.00
❑208, Oct 77	0.35	1.20	3.00	6.00
❑209, Nov 77, FT, Tattered Glory!; Real Estate	0.35	1.20	3.00	6.00
❑210, Dec 77, Sparrows Can't Sing!	0.35	1.20	3.00	6.00
❑211, Jan 78, RH, Man of War; In Country	0.35	1.00	2.50	5.00
❑212, Feb 78, The Traitor in Wolf's Clothing!	0.35	1.00	2.50	5.00
❑213, Mar 78, The Ten Year Old Secret Weapon!; Across the Staked Plains!	0.35	1.00	2.50	5.00
❑214, Apr 78, Deadly Reunion, A: Mademoiselle Marie	0.35	1.00	2.50	5.00
❑215, May 78, JKu, The Savage Sea!; Casualty List	0.35	1.00	2.50	5.00
❑216, Jun 78, Taps at Arlington; The Silk Umbrella of Death!	0.35	1.00	2.50	5.00
❑217, Jul 78, Dictators Never Sleep!; Ants	0.35	1.00	2.50	5.00
❑218, Aug 78, The Unknown Soldier Must Die!	0.35	1.00	2.50	5.00
❑219, Sep 78, FM; JKu, Laughter in Hell!; The Edge of History	0.50	1.00	2.50	5.00
❑220, Oct 78, JKu, The Rubber Band Heroes; Of Blood and Roses	0.50	1.00	2.50	5.00
❑221, Nov 78, Sunset for a Samurai!; The Burning Man!	0.50	1.00	2.50	5.00
❑222, Dec 78, JKu, No Exit From Stalag 19!	0.40	1.00	2.50	5.00
❑223, Jan 79, Mission: Incredible!	0.40	1.00	2.50	5.00
❑224, Feb 79, Welcome to Valhalla!; At the Mercy of Tigers!	0.40	1.00	2.50	5.00
❑225, Mar 79	0.40	1.00	2.50	5.00
❑226, Apr 79, Sink the Kronhorst!; Andy Stewart Combat Nurse: Rendevous	0.40	1.00	2.50	5.00
❑227, May 79, The Blind Eye of God!; Andy Stewart Combat Nurse: The Iron Fist	0.40	1.00	2.50	5.00
❑228, Jun 79, Heroes Don't Have Crowns; Andy Stewart Combat Nurse: Coward's Debt	0.40	1.00	2.50	5.00
❑229, Jul 79, Get the Desert Fox!	0.40	1.00	2.50	5.00
❑230, Aug 79	0.40	0.80	2.00	4.00
❑231, Sep 79, JKu, Bridge of No Return!	0.40	0.80	2.00	4.00
❑232, Oct 79, The Invisible Traitor!	0.40	0.80	2.00	4.00
❑233, Nov 79, JKu, Destroy Wolf Lair-And Die!	0.40	0.80	2.00	4.00

	ORIG	GOOD	FINE	N-MINT
❑234, Dec 79	0.40	0.80	2.00	4.00
❑235, Jan 80, Death in Blue and Grey!; Return to Beach Red	0.40	0.80	2.00	4.00
❑236, Feb 80, An Honorable Betrayal?	0.40	0.80	2.00	4.00
❑237, Mar 80, No God in St. Just!	0.40	0.80	2.00	4.00
❑238, Apr 80, Operation: Pied Piper!	0.40	0.80	2.00	4.00
❑239, May 80, The 20 Mile Rabbit Hole!	0.40	0.80	2.00	4.00
❑240, Jun 80, The Hammer of Glory!	0.40	0.80	2.00	4.00
❑241, Jul 80, Shall Heroes Prevail?	0.40	0.80	2.00	4.00
❑242, Aug 80, Red Flows the Don!	0.40	0.80	2.00	4.00
❑243, Sep 80, Double Switch!; Dateline: Frontline: The Yanks are Comin'	0.50	0.80	2.00	4.00
❑244, Oct 80, JKu, A: Captain Storm	0.50	0.80	2.00	4.00
❑245, Nov 80, Crack of Doom!; The Vanishing American	0.50	0.80	2.00	4.00
❑246, Dec 80, Only the Desert Wins	0.50	0.80	2.00	4.00
❑247, Jan 81, JKu, Season in Hell!	0.50	0.80	2.00	4.00
❑248, Feb 81, O: Unknown Soldier	0.50	1.20	3.00	6.00
❑249, Mar 81, Doorway of Destiny!, Mask of a Maqui, O: Unknown Soldier	0.50	1.20	3.00	6.00
❑250, Apr 81	0.50	0.80	2.00	4.00
❑251, May 81	0.50	0.80	2.00	4.00
❑252, Jun 81, JSe, Bomber's Moon!; War Games	0.50	0.80	2.00	4.00
❑253, Jul 81	0.50	0.80	2.00	4.00
❑254, Aug 81	0.50	0.80	2.00	4.00
❑255, Sep 81	0.50	0.80	2.00	4.00
❑256, Oct 81	0.60	0.80	2.00	4.00
❑257, Nov 81, JKu, Til Armageddon Do Us Part!; Blood Brothers!, O: Capt. Storm; A: John F. Kennedy	0.60	0.80	2.00	4.00
❑258, Dec 81, His Eye is on the Sparrow!; Swan Song!, A: John F. Kennedy	0.60	0.80	2.00	4.00
❑259, Jan 82, We Who Are About to Die...; Bob Kanigher's Gallery of War:Voices, A: John F. Kennedy	0.60	0.80	2.00	4.00
❑260, Feb 82, The Rustbucket Mutiny!; The Fleet That Failed	0.60	0.80	2.00	4.00
❑261, Mar 82, Hour of the Beast!; They Rode to the Sound of The Guns	0.60	0.80	2.00	4.00
❑262, Apr 82	0.60	0.80	2.00	4.00
❑263, May 82	0.60	0.80	2.00	4.00
❑264, Jun 82, Hell is a Cold Place!; Killers of the Sky!, Part 3	0.60	0.80	2.00	4.00
❑265, Jul 82	0.60	0.80	2.00	4.00
❑266, Aug 82	0.60	0.80	2.00	4.00
❑267, Sep 82	0.60	0.80	2.00	4.00
❑268, Oct 82, A Farewell to War, D: The Unknown Soldier; D: Hitler; D: Chat Noir,Final Issue; Fall of Berlin	0.60	1.00	2.50	5.00

UNKNOWN SOLDIER (MINI-SERIES)
DC

	ORIG	GOOD	FINE	N-MINT
❑1, Apr 97	2.50	0.80	2.00	4.00
❑2, May 97	2.50	0.60	1.50	3.00
❑3, Jun 97	2.50	0.60	1.50	3.00
❑4, Jul 97	2.50	0.60	1.50	3.00

UNKNOWN SOLDIER, THE (MINI-SERIES)
DC

	ORIG	GOOD	FINE	N-MINT
❑1, Win 88, O: Unknown Soldier	1.50	0.60	1.50	3.00
❑2, Hol 88	1.50	0.60	1.50	3.00
❑3, Jan 89	1.50	0.60	1.50	3.00
❑4, Mar 89	1.50	0.60	1.50	3.00
❑5, Apr 89	1.50	0.60	1.50	3.00
❑6, May 89, The Replacement	1.50	0.60	1.50	3.00
❑7, Jul 89	1.50	0.60	1.50	3.00
❑8, Aug 89	1.75	0.60	1.50	3.00
❑9, Sep 89	1.75	0.60	1.50	3.00
❑10, Oct 89	1.75	0.60	1.50	3.00
❑11, Nov 89	1.75	0.60	1.50	3.00
❑12, Dec 89	1.75	0.60	1.50	3.00

UNKNOWN WORLDS OF FRANK BRUNNER, THE
ECLIPSE

Value: Cover or less

- ❑1, Aug 85, FB, FB (w), Harvest of Horror!; What Rough Beast ... 1.75
- ❑2, Aug 85, FB, FB (w), Sword of Dragonus; The Wizard's Venom ... 1.75

UNKNOWN WORLDS OF SCIENCE FICTION
MARVEL

	ORIG	GOOD	FINE	N-MINT
❑1, Jan 75, b&w; magazine	1.00	0.60	1.50	3.00
❑2, Mar 75, b&w; magazine	1.00	0.60	1.50	3.00
❑3, May 75, b&w; magazine	1.00	0.60	1.50	3.00
❑4, Jul 75, b&w; magazine	1.00	0.60	1.50	3.00
❑5, Sep 75, b&w; magazine	1.00	0.60	1.50	3.00
❑6, Nov 75, b&w; magazine	1.00	0.60	1.50	3.00
❑SE 1,Reprint	1.25	0.60	1.50	3.00

UNLEASHED!
TRIUMPHANT

Value: Cover or less

- ❑1 ... 2.50

UNLIMITED ACCESS
MARVEL

	ORIG	GOOD	FINE	N-MINT
❑1, Dec 97, A: Juggernaut; A: Spider-Man; A: Wonder Woman,crossover with DC	1.99	0.50	1.25	2.50
❑2, Jan 98, Let's Do the Time Warp Again!, A: Legion of Super-Heroes; A: X-Men,crossover with DC	1.99	0.40	1.00	2.00
❑3, Feb 98, A: Avengers; A: Justice League of America,crossover with DC	1.99	0.40	1.00	2.00
❑4, Mar 98,crossover with DC; new Amalgams	2.99	0.60	1.50	3.00

UNSUPERVISED EXISTENCE
FANTAGRAPHICS

Value: Cover or less

- ❑1, b&w ... 2.00
- ❑2, b&w ... 2.00
- ❑3 ... 2.50
- ❑4 ... 2.50
- ❑5 ... 2.00
- ❑6 ... 2.25
- ❑7 ... 2.25
- ❑7-2,2nd Printing ... 2.00
- ❑36709,2nd Printing ... 2.00

UNTAMED
MARVEL

Value: Cover or less

- ❑1, Jun 93, Wounds of Equal People, Part 1,Embossed cover ... 2.50
- ❑2, Jul 93, Wounds of Equal People, Part 2 ... 1.95
- ❑3, Aug 93, Wounds of Equal People, Part 3 ... 1.95

UNTAMED LOVE (FRANK FRAZETTA'S...)
FANTAGRAPHICS

Value: Cover or less

- ❑1, FF, Too Late for Love; The Wrong Road ... 2.00

UNTOLD LEGEND OF CAPTAIN MARVEL, THE
MARVEL

Value: Cover or less

- ❑1, Apr 97, Soldier, A: Silver Surfer; A: Galactus ... 2.50
- ❑2, May 97, Hero, V: Imperial Guard ... 2.50
- ❑3, Jun 97, Legend, V: Brood ... 2.50

UNTOLD LEGEND OF THE BATMAN, THE
DC

	ORIG	GOOD	FINE	N-MINT
❑1, Jul 80, JA; JBy, In The Beginning, O: Batman	0.40	0.60	1.50	3.00
❑2, Aug 80, JA	0.40	0.40	1.00	2.00
❑3, Sep 80, JA	0.50	0.40	1.00	2.00

UNTOLD ORIGIN OF FEMFORCE
AC

Value: Cover or less

- ❑1, O: Femforce ... 4.95

UNTOLD ORIGIN OF MS. VICTORY
AC

Value: Cover or less

- ❑1, Dec 89, O: Ms. Victory, b&w ... 2.50

UNTOLD TALES OF CHASTITY
CHAOS

Value: Cover or less

- ❑1, Nov 00 ... 2.95

UNTOLD TALES OF LADY DEATH
CHAOS

Value: Cover or less

- ❑1, Nov 00, O: Lady Death ... 2.95

UNTOLD TALES OF PURGATORI
CHAOS

Value: Cover or less

- ❑1, Nov 00 ... 2.95

UNTOLD TALES OF SPIDER-MAN
MARVEL

	ORIG	GOOD	FINE	N-MINT
❑-1, Jul 97,Flashback	0.99	0.20	0.50	1.00
❑1, Sep 95, KB (w), O: Spider-Man	0.99	0.30	0.75	1.50
❑2, Oct 95, KB (w)	0.99	0.25	0.63	1.25
❑3, Nov 95, KB (w), V: Sandman	0.99	0.25	0.63	1.25
❑4, Dec 95, KB (w), J. Jonah Jameson vs. Spider-Man	0.99	0.20	0.50	1.00
❑5, Jan 96, KB (w), V: Vulture	0.99	0.20	0.50	1.00
❑6, Feb 96, KB (w), A: Human Torch	0.99	0.20	0.50	1.00
❑7, Mar 96, KB (w), On the Trail of the Amazing Spider-Man, O: Electro	0.99	0.20	0.50	1.00
❑8, Apr 96, KB (w), V: Enforcers	0.99	0.20	0.50	1.00
❑9, May 96, KB (w), V: Lizard	0.99	0.20	0.50	1.00
❑10, Jun 96, KB (w)	0.99	0.20	0.50	1.00
❑11, Jul 96, KB (w)	0.99	0.20	0.50	1.00
❑12, Aug 96, KB (w), O: Betty Brant	0.99	0.20	0.50	1.00
❑13, Sep 96, KB (w), V: Black Knight; D: Bluebird	0.99	0.20	0.50	1.00
❑14, Oct 96, KB (w)	0.99	0.20	0.50	1.00
❑15, Nov 96, KB (w)	0.99	0.20	0.50	1.00
❑16, Dec 96, KB (w), The Boy Next Door, A: Mary Jane	0.99	0.20	0.50	1.00
❑17, Jan 97, KB (w), Spidey Battles Hawkeye the Marksman!, V: Hawkeye	0.99	0.20	0.50	1.00
❑18, Feb 97, KB (w), Unseen Dangers, V: Headsman	0.99	0.20	0.50	1.00
❑19, Mar 97, KB (w), V: Doctor Octopus	0.99	0.20	0.50	1.00
❑20, Apr 97, KB (w), Wings of Hatred, V: Vulture; O: The Vulture	0.99	0.20	0.50	1.00
❑21, May 97, A: X-Men	0.99	0.20	0.50	1.00
❑22, Jun 97	0.99	0.20	0.50	1.00

	ORIG	GOOD	FINE	N-MINT
❑23, Aug 97, V: Crime Master	0.99	0.20	0.50	1.00
❑24, Sep 97	0.99	0.20	0.50	1.00
❑25, Oct97, V: Green Goblin, cover says Sep, indicia says Oct; Final Issue	0.99	0.20	0.50	1.00
❑Anl 1996, GK, KB (w), How Kurt Busiek and Patrick Olliffe Re-Create Untold Tales!; A Guided Tour to the World of Untold Tales!, A: Fantastic Four; A: Namor, Untold Tales of Spider-Man '96	1.99	0.39	0.98	1.95
❑Anl 1997, Untold Tales of Spider-Man '97	1.95	0.39	0.98	1.95

UNTOUCHABLES
CALIBER

Value: Cover or less

❑1, Aug 97, A New Beginning. 2.95
❑2, Sep 97 2.95
❑3, Oct 97 2.95
❑4, Nov 97 2.95

UNTOUCHABLES (EASTERN)
EASTERN

	ORIG	GOOD	FINE	N-MINT
❑1	0.75	0.20	0.50	1.00
❑2	0.75	0.20	0.50	1.00

UP FROM BONDAGE
FANTAGRAPHICS

Value: Cover or less

❑1, b&w; adult 2.95

UP FROM THE DEEP
RIP OFF

	ORIG	GOOD	FINE	N-MINT
❑1, The Black Saint and the Sinner Lady; When Dreams Collide	1.00	0.60	1.50	3.00

URBAN HIPSTER
ALTERNATIVE

Value: Cover or less

❑1, Oct 98, 411 UH; Lost in Space, b&w 2.95

URBAN LEGENDS
DARK HORSE

	ORIG	GOOD	FINE	N-MINT
❑1, b&w	2.95	0.60	1.50	3.00

UROTSUKIDOJI: LEGEND OF THE OVERFIEND
CPM

Value: Cover or less

❑1, Jul 98 2.95
❑2, Aug 98 2.95
❑3, Sep 98 2.95

URTH 4
CONTINUITY

Value: Cover or less

❑1, May 89, NA, NA (w) 2.00
❑2, Apr 90, NA, NA (w) 2.00
❑3, Oct 90, NA, NA (w) 2.00
❑4, Dec 90, NA, NA (w) 2.00

URZA-MISHRA WAR ON THE WORLD OF MAGIC: THE GATHERING
ACCLAIM

Value: Cover or less

❑1, Sep 96, squarebound; polybagged with Soldevi Steam Beast card 5.95
❑2, Sep 96, squarebound; polybagged with Soldevi Steam Beast and Phyrexian War Beast cards 5.95

U.S. 1
MARVEL

	ORIG	GOOD	FINE	N-MINT
❑1, May 83, HT, O: U.S. 1	0.60	0.20	0.50	1.00
❑2, Jun 83, HT	0.60	0.20	0.50	1.00
❑3, Jul 83, FS	0.60	0.20	0.50	1.00
❑4, Aug 83, FS	0.60	0.20	0.50	1.00
❑5, Sep 83, FS	0.60	0.20	0.50	1.00
❑6, Oct 83, FS	0.60	0.20	0.50	1.00
❑7, Dec 83, FS	0.60	0.20	0.50	1.00
❑8, Feb 84, FS	0.60	0.20	0.50	1.00
❑9, Apr 84	0.60	0.20	0.50	1.00
❑10, Jun 84, FS	0.60	0.20	0.50	1.00
❑11, Aug 84, FS	0.60	0.20	0.50	1.00
❑12, Oct 84, SD	0.60	0.20	0.50	1.00

U.S.AGENT
MARVEL

	ORIG	GOOD	FINE	N-MINT
❑1, Jun 93	1.75	0.40	1.00	2.00
❑2, Jul 93	1.75	0.40	1.00	2.00
❑3, Aug 93	1.75	0.40	1.00	2.00
❑4, Sep 93	1.75	0.40	1.00	2.00

USAGI YOJIMBO (VOL. 1)
FANTAGRAPHICS

	ORIG	GOOD	FINE	N-MINT
❑1, Jul 87, b&w	2.00	1.60	4.00	8.00
❑1-2, Jul 87, 2nd Printing	2.00	0.50	1.25	2.50
❑2, Sep 87, b&w	2.00	1.00	2.50	5.00
❑3, Oct 87, b&w	2.00	1.00	2.50	5.00
❑4, Nov 87, Bats, The Cat, and The Rabbit, b&w	2.00	0.70	1.75	3.50
❑5, Jan 88, b&w	2.00	0.70	1.75	3.50
❑6, Feb 88, b&w	2.00	0.60	1.50	3.00
❑7, Mar 88, The Withered Field, b&w	2.00	0.60	1.50	3.00
❑8, May 88, The Promise in the Snow, b&w	2.00	0.60	1.50	3.00
❑9, Jul 88, The Conspiracy of Eight, b&w	2.00	0.60	1.50	3.00
❑10, Aug 88, A: Teenage Mutant Ninja Turtles, b&w	2.00	0.60	1.50	3.00
❑10-2, Aug 88, 2nd Printing	2.00	0.40	1.00	2.00
❑11, Sep 88, SA, b&w	2.00	0.50	1.25	2.50
❑12, Oct 88, b&w	2.00	0.50	1.25	2.50

John Byrne and Jim Aparo examined Batman's origins in *Untold Legend of the Batman.*

	ORIG	GOOD	FINE	N-MINT
❑13, Jan 89, b&w; indicia says Jan 88; a misprint	2.00	0.50	1.25	2.50
❑14, Jan 89, b&w; indicia says Jan 89	2.00	0.50	1.25	2.50
❑15, Mar 89, b&w	2.00	0.50	1.25	2.50
❑16, May 89, b&w	2.00	0.50	1.25	2.50
❑17, Jul 89, b&w	2.00	0.50	1.25	2.50
❑18, Oct 89, b&w	2.00	0.50	1.25	2.50
❑19, Dec 89, b&w	2.00	0.50	1.25	2.50
❑20, Feb 90, b&w	2.00	0.50	1.25	2.50
❑21, Apr 90, b&w	2.00	0.50	1.25	2.50
❑22, May 90, b&w	2.00	0.50	1.25	2.50
❑23, Jul 90, b&w	2.00	0.50	1.25	2.50
❑24, Sep 90, b&w; Lone Goat & Kid	2.00	0.50	1.25	2.50
❑25, Nov 90, b&w	2.00	0.50	1.25	2.50
❑26, Jan 91, b&w; indicia says Jan 90; another misprint	2.00	0.50	1.25	2.50
❑27, Mar 91, b&w	2.00	0.50	1.25	2.50
❑28, May 91, b&w	2.00	0.50	1.25	2.50
❑29, Jul 91, b&w	2.00	0.50	1.25	2.50
❑30, Sep 91, b&w; back cover reproduces front cover without logos	2.25	0.50	1.25	2.50
❑31, Nov 91, b&w	2.25	0.50	1.25	2.50
❑32, Feb 92, b&w	2.25	0.50	1.25	2.50
❑33, Apr 92, b&w	2.25	0.50	1.25	2.50
❑34, Jun 92, b&w	2.25	0.50	1.25	2.50
❑35, Aug 92, b&w	2.25	0.50	1.25	2.50
❑36, Nov 92, b&w	2.25	0.50	1.25	2.50
❑37, Feb 93, b&w	2.25	0.50	1.25	2.50
❑38, Mar 93, b&w; Final Issue	2.25	0.50	1.25	2.50
❑36801, Aug 88, 2nd Printing	2.00	0.40	1.00	2.00
❑SE 1, Color special #1	—	0.70	1.75	3.50
❑SE 2, Color special #2	—	0.70	1.75	3.50
❑SE 3, Color special #3	—	0.70	1.75	3.50
❑SE 4, Jul 97	3.50	0.70	1.75	3.50
❑Smr 1, Oct 86, SA, b&w; introduction by Mark Evanier	2.75	0.80	2.00	4.00

USAGI YOJIMBO (VOL. 2)
MIRAGE

	ORIG	GOOD	FINE	N-MINT
❑1, Mar 93, A: Teenage Mutant Ninja Turtles, full color	2.75	0.90	2.25	4.50
❑2, May 93, A: Teenage Mutant Ninja Turtles	2.75	0.70	1.75	3.50
❑3, Jul 93, A: Teenage Mutant Ninja Turtles	2.75	0.70	1.75	3.50
❑4, Sep 93	2.75	0.70	1.75	3.50
❑5, Nov 93	2.75	0.70	1.75	3.50
❑6, Jan 94, Battlefield, Part 1	2.75	0.60	1.50	3.00
❑7, Apr 94, Battlefield, Part 2	2.75	0.60	1.50	3.00
❑8, Jun 94	2.75	0.60	1.50	3.00
❑9, Aug 94, Slavers, Part 1	2.75	0.60	1.50	3.00
❑10, Oct 94, Slavers, Part 2; The Nature of the Serpent	2.75	0.60	1.50	3.00
❑11, Dec 94, Daisho, Part 1; Mongrels, Part 1	2.75	0.55	1.38	2.75
❑12, Feb 95, Daisho, Part 2; Mongrels, Part 2	2.75	0.55	1.38	2.75
❑13, Apr 95, Runaways, Part 1; Black Soul	2.75	0.55	1.38	2.75
❑14, Jun 95, Runaways, Part 2	2.75	0.55	1.38	2.75
❑15, Aug 95, Lionheart: Real Heroes, Part 1, 1: Lionheart (in color)	2.75	0.55	1.38	2.75
❑16, Oct 95, A Meeting of Strangers; Lionheart: Real Heroes, Part 2, Final Issue	2.75	0.55	1.38	2.75

USAGI YOJIMBO (VOL. 3)
DARK HORSE

	ORIG	GOOD	FINE	N-MINT
❑1, Apr 96	2.95	0.80	2.00	4.00
❑2, May 96	2.95	0.60	1.50	3.00
❑3, Jun 96	2.95	0.60	1.50	3.00
❑4, Jul 96	2.95	0.60	1.50	3.00
❑5, Aug 96, The Chrysanthemum Pass	2.95	0.60	1.50	3.00
❑6, Oct 96	2.95	0.60	1.50	3.00
❑7, Nov 96	2.95	0.60	1.50	3.00
❑8, Dec 96	2.95	0.60	1.50	3.00
❑9, Jan 97	2.95	0.60	1.50	3.00
❑10, Feb 97	2.95	0.60	1.50	3.00
❑11, Mar 97, The Lord of Owls; The First Tenet	2.95	0.60	1.50	3.00

	ORIG	GOOD	FINE	N-MINT
❑12, The Obakeneko of Geishu Clan	2.95	0.60	1.50	3.00
❑13, Aug 97, Grasscutter	2.95	0.60	1.50	3.00
❑14, Sep 97, Grasscutter	2.95	0.59	1.48	2.95
❑15, Oct 97, Grasscutter	2.95	0.59	1.48	2.95
❑16, Nov 97, Grasscutter	2.95	0.59	1.48	2.95
❑17, Jan 98, Grasscutter	2.95	0.59	1.48	2.95
❑18, Feb 98, Grasscutter	2.95	0.59	1.48	2.95
❑19, Mar 98, Grasscutter	2.95	0.59	1.48	2.95
❑20, Grasscutter	2.95	0.59	1.48	2.95
❑21, Jun 98, Grasscutter	2.95	0.59	1.48	2.95
❑22, Jul 98, Grasscutter	2.95	0.59	1.48	2.95
❑23, Sep 98, My Father's Swords	2.95	0.59	1.48	2.95
❑24, Oct 98, The Demon Flute	2.95	0.59	1.48	2.95
❑25, Nov 98, Momo-Usagi-Taro,Momo-Usagi-Taro	2.95	0.59	1.48	2.95
❑26, Jan 99, The Hairpin Murders	2.95	0.59	1.48	2.95
❑27, Feb 99, The Hairpin Murders	2.95	0.59	1.48	2.95
❑28, Apr 99, The Courtesan	2.95	0.59	1.48	2.95
❑29, May 99, The Courtesan	2.95	0.59	1.48	2.95
❑30, Jul 99	2.95	0.59	1.48	2.95
❑31, Sep 99	2.95	0.59	1.48	2.95
❑32, Oct 99	2.95	0.59	1.48	2.95
❑33, Nov 99	2.95	0.59	1.48	2.95
❑34	2.95	0.59	1.48	2.95
❑35	2.95	0.59	1.48	2.95
❑36	2.95	0.59	1.48	2.95
❑37	2.95	0.59	1.48	2.95
❑38	2.95	0.59	1.48	2.95
❑39, Jul 00, Grasscutter II, Part 1	2.95	0.59	1.48	2.95
❑40, Aug 00	—	0.59	1.48	2.95
❑41, Sep 00	—	0.59	1.48	2.95
❑42, Oct 00	—	0.59	1.48	2.95
❑43, Nov 00	—	0.59	1.48	2.95
❑44, Dec 00	—	0.59	1.48	2.95
❑45, Jan 01, Grasscutter II, Part 6	2.99	0.60	1.50	2.99
❑46, Mar 01, Showdown, Part 1	2.99	0.60	1.50	2.99
❑47, Apr 01, Showdown, Part 2	2.99	0.60	1.50	2.99

V

V
DC

	ORIG	GOOD	FINE	N-MINT
❑1, Feb 85, CI ,Based on TV series	0.75	0.30	0.75	1.50
❑2, Mar 85, CI	0.75	0.20	0.50	1.00
❑3, Apr 85, CI, Encounter!	0.75	0.20	0.50	1.00
❑4, May 85, CI	0.75	0.20	0.50	1.00
❑5, Jun 85, The Price of Peace	0.75	0.20	0.50	1.00
❑6, Jul 85, CI, Shatterday	0.75	0.20	0.50	1.00
❑7, Aug 85, CI	0.75	0.20	0.50	1.00
❑8, Sep 85, CI	0.75	0.20	0.50	1.00
❑9, Oct 85, CI	0.75	0.20	0.50	1.00
❑10, Nov 85, CI	0.75	0.20	0.50	1.00
❑11, Dec 85, CI	0.75	0.20	0.50	1.00
❑12, Jan 86, CI	0.75	0.20	0.50	1.00
❑13, Feb 86, CI	0.75	0.20	0.50	1.00
❑14, Mar 86, CI	0.75	0.20	0.50	1.00
❑15, Apr 86, CI	0.75	0.20	0.50	1.00
❑16, May 86, CI	0.75	0.20	0.50	1.00
❑17, Jun 86, DG	0.75	0.20	0.50	1.00
❑18, Jul 86, DG ,Final Issue	0.75	0.20	0.50	1.00

VAGABOND
IMAGE

Value: Cover or less

❑1/A, Aug 00,Pat Lee cover.... 2.95

❑1/B, Aug 00,Ryan Benjamin cover 2.95

VALENTINE
REDEYE PRESS

Value: Cover or less

❑1, Sep 97, b&w 2.95

VALENTINO
RENEGADE

	ORIG	GOOD	FINE	N-MINT
❑1, Apr 85, Drafted!; Party!, nn; b&w	1.70	0.40	1.00	2.00
❑2, Apr 87, b&w; Valentino Too	1.70	0.40	1.00	2.00
❑3, Apr 88, b&w; Valentino the 3rd	2.00	0.40	1.00	2.00

VALERIAN
FANTASY FLIGHT

Value: Cover or less

❑1, Jul 96, Heroes of the Equinox, b&w; Heroes of the Equinox 2.95

VALERIA, THE SHE-BAT (CONTINUITY)
CONTINUITY

	ORIG	GOOD	FINE	N-MINT
❑1, May 93, NA, NA (w), Deathwatch 2000,no cover price; Promotional edition, never available for ordering	—	0.60	1.50	3.00
❑2, Promotional edition, never available for ordering	—	0.60	1.50	3.00
❑3,Published out of sequence (after #5)	2.50	0.50	1.25	2.50
❑4,Published out of sequence	2.50	0.50	1.25	2.50
❑5, Nov 93, Rise of Magic, A: Knight-hawk,Tyvek wraparound cover	2.50	0.40	1.00	2.00

VALERIA THE SHE-BAT (WINDJAMMER)
ACCLAIM

Value: Cover or less

❑1, Sep 95, NA, NA (w) 2.50

❑2, Sep 95, NA, NA (w) 2.50

VALHALLA
ANTARCTIC

Value: Cover or less

❑1, Feb 99 .... 2.99

VALIANT EFFORTS (VOL. 2)
VALIANT COMICS

Value: Cover or less

❑1, May 91, Street Fury 1.95

VALIANT READER
VALIANT

Value: Cover or less

❑1,background 0.75

VALIANT VARMINTS
SHANDA FANTASY ARTS

Value: Cover or less

❑1, b&w 4.50

VALIANT VISION STARTER KIT
VALIANT

Value: Cover or less

❑1, Jan 94, NA (c),comic book, glasses, poster 2.95

VALKYR
IRONCAT

Value: Cover or less

❑1 .... 2.95

❑2 .... 2.95

❑3 .... 2.95

VALKYRIE (1ST SERIES)
ECLIPSE

	ORIG	GOOD	FINE	N-MINT
❑1, May 87, PG	1.75	0.40	1.00	2.00
❑2, Jun 87, BA; PG	1.75	0.40	1.00	2.00
❑3, Aug 87, BA; PG	1.75	0.40	1.00	2.00

VALKYRIE (2ND SERIES)
ECLIPSE

	ORIG	GOOD	FINE	N-MINT
❑1, Jul 88, BA	1.75	0.40	1.00	2.00
❑2, Aug 88, BA	1.75	0.40	1.00	2.00
❑3, Sep 88, BA	1.75	0.40	1.00	2.00

VALKYRIE (3RD SERIES)
MARVEL

Value: Cover or less

❑1, Jan 97, Without Wings 2.95

VALLEY OF THE DINOSAURS
HARVEY

	ORIG	GOOD	FINE	N-MINT
❑1, Oct 93, Fight the Angry Mountain; Engine Trouble in Space! (text story)	2.25	1.20	3.00	6.00
❑2	0.25	0.60	1.50	3.00
❑3	0.25	0.60	1.50	3.00
❑4	0.25	0.60	1.50	3.00
❑5	0.25	0.60	1.50	3.00
❑6	0.25	0.50	1.25	2.50
❑7	0.25	0.50	1.25	2.50
❑8	0.25	0.50	1.25	2.50
❑9	0.25	0.50	1.25	2.50
❑10	0.25	0.50	1.25	2.50
❑11,Final Issue	0.25	0.50	1.25	2.50

VALOR (DC)
DC

	ORIG	GOOD	FINE	N-MINT
❑1, Nov 92, Eclipso: The Darkness Within aftermath	1.25	0.40	1.00	2.00
❑2, Dec 92, A: Supergirl	1.25	0.30	0.75	1.50
❑3, Jan 93	1.25	0.30	0.75	1.50
❑4, Feb 93,Lobo	1.25	0.30	0.75	1.50
❑5, Mar 93	1.25	0.30	0.75	1.50
❑6, Apr 93	1.25	0.30	0.75	1.50
❑7, May 93	1.25	0.30	0.75	1.50
❑8, Jun 93	1.25	0.30	0.75	1.50
❑9, Jul 93	1.25	0.30	0.75	1.50
❑10, Aug 93	1.25	0.30	0.75	1.50
❑11, Sep 93	1.25	0.30	0.75	1.50
❑12, Oct 93, D.O.A., Part 1	1.25	0.30	0.75	1.50
❑13, Nov 93, D.O.A., Part 2	1.50	0.30	0.75	1.50
❑14, Dec 93, D.O.A., Part 3	1.50	0.30	0.75	1.50
❑15, Jan 94, D.O.A., Part 4	1.50	0.30	0.75	1.50
❑16, Feb 94, MWa (w), D.O.A., Part 5	1.50	0.30	0.75	1.50
❑17, Mar 94, D.O.A., Part 6	1.50	0.30	0.75	1.50
❑18, Apr 94, D.O.A. Aftermath	1.50	0.30	0.75	1.50
❑19, May 94	1.50	0.30	0.75	1.50
❑20, Jun 94, KB (w)	1.50	0.30	0.75	1.50
❑21, Jul 94, KB (w)	1.50	0.30	0.75	1.50
❑22, Aug 94, KB (w), End of an Era, Part 2	1.50	0.30	0.75	1.50
❑23, Sep 94, KB (w), Zero Hour; End of an Era, Part 5,Final Issue	1.50	0.30	0.75	1.50

ORIG GOOD FINE N-MINT

VALOR (RCP)
GEMSTONE
Value: Cover or less

- ❑1, Oct 98, GI; BK; AT; WW; AW, GI (w); BK (w); AT (w); WW (w); AW (w), The Arena; The Guardians of Empire (text story)... 2.50
- ❑2, Nov 98 ... 2.50
- ❑3, Dec 98 ... 2.50
- ❑4, Jan 99 ... 2.50
- ❑5, Feb 99 ... 2.50

VALOR THUNDERSTAR AND HIS FIREFLIES
NOW
Value: Cover or less

- ❑1, Dec 86 ... 1.50
- ❑2 ... 1.50
- ❑3 ... 1.50

VAMPEROTICA
BRAINSTORM

	ORIG	GOOD	FINE	N-MINT
❑1, Deadly Desire; God's Chariot, b&w; adult	2.95	1.60	4.00	8.00
❑1/GO,adult; Gold edition	—	2.00	5.00	10.00
❑1/PL,adult; Platinum edition	—	2.00	5.00	10.00
❑1-2, Sep 94,adult; 2nd Printing	2.95	0.80	2.00	4.00
❑, Dec 94,adult; 3rd Printing	2.95	0.60	1.50	3.00
❑2, b&w; adult	2.95	1.00	2.50	5.00
❑3, b&w; adult	2.95	0.60	1.50	3.00
❑4, b&w; adult	2.95	0.60	1.50	3.00
❑5, b&w; adult	2.95	0.60	1.50	3.00
❑6, Baptism; Sight of Blood, b&w; adult	2.95	0.60	1.50	3.00
❑7, b&w; adult	2.95	0.60	1.50	3.00
❑8, b&w; adult	2.95	0.60	1.50	3.00
❑9, b&w; adult	2.95	0.60	1.50	3.00
❑10, b&w; adult	2.95	0.60	1.50	3.00
❑11, b&w; adult	2.95	0.60	1.50	3.00
❑12, Feb 96, b&w; adult	2.95	0.60	1.50	3.00
❑13, b&w; adult	2.95	0.60	1.50	3.00
❑14, b&w; adult	2.95	0.60	1.50	3.00
❑15, b&w; adult	2.95	0.60	1.50	3.00
❑16,adult	2.95	0.60	1.50	3.00
❑16/Nude,adult; Nude cover	—	1.00	2.50	5.00
❑17,adult	—	0.59	1.48	2.95
❑17/A,adult; chromium cover	—	0.99	2.47	4.95
❑18,adult	—	0.59	1.48	2.95
❑18/Nude,adult; Nude cover	—	1.00	2.50	5.00
❑19,adult	—	0.59	1.48	2.95
❑19/A,adult; variant cover	—	0.59	1.48	2.95
❑19/Nude,adult; Nude cover	—	1.00	2.50	5.00
❑20,adult	—	0.59	1.48	2.95
❑20/Nude,adult; Nude cover	—	1.00	2.50	5.00
❑21,adult	—	0.59	1.48	2.95
❑22,adult	—	0.59	1.48	2.95
❑22/Nude,adult; Nude cover	—	1.00	2.50	5.00
❑23,adult	—	0.60	1.50	3.00
❑24,adult	—	0.60	1.50	3.00
❑24/Nude, Bad Lands,adult; Nude cover	2.95	1.00	2.50	5.00
❑25,adult	—	0.60	1.50	3.00
❑26,adult	—	0.60	1.50	3.00
❑27,adult	—	0.60	1.50	3.00
❑28,adult	—	0.60	1.50	3.00
❑29,adult	—	0.60	1.50	3.00
❑30,adult	—	0.60	1.50	3.00
❑31,adult	—	0.60	1.50	3.00
❑32,adult	—	0.60	1.50	3.00
❑33,adult	—	0.60	1.50	3.00
❑34,adult	—	0.60	1.50	3.00
❑35,adult	—	0.60	1.50	3.00
❑36,adult	—	0.60	1.50	3.00
❑37,adult	—	0.60	1.50	3.00
❑38,adult	—	0.60	1.50	3.00
❑39,adult	—	0.60	1.50	3.00
❑40,adult	—	0.60	1.50	3.00
❑41,adult	—	0.60	1.50	3.00
❑42,adult	—	0.60	1.50	3.00
❑43,adult	—	0.60	1.50	3.00
❑44,adult	3.00	0.60	1.50	3.00
❑45,adult	3.00	0.60	1.50	3.00
❑45/SC,adult; Photo cover	4.00	0.80	2.00	4.00
❑46,adult	3.00	0.60	1.50	3.00
❑47,adult	3.00	0.60	1.50	3.00
❑48,adult	3.00	0.60	1.50	3.00
❑49,adult	3.00	0.60	1.50	3.00
❑Anl 1,adult; Annual #1	—	0.79	1.98	3.95
❑Anl 1/GO,adult; Annual #1-Gold Edition	—	1.60	4.00	8.00
❑SS 1,adult; Blue cover (regular edition)	2.95	0.80	2.00	4.00

VAMPEROTICA MAGAZINE
BRAINSTORM

	ORIG	GOOD	FINE	N-MINT
❑1, Legend of Ichor; Murder Most Fowl	4.95	0.99	2.47	4.95
❑1/Nude,Nude cover	—	1.20	3.00	6.00
❑1/SC,Julie Strain Commemorative cover	10.00	2.00	5.00	10.00
❑2	4.95	0.99	2.47	4.95
❑2/Nude,Nude cover	—	1.20	3.00	6.00
❑2/SC,Photo cover	5.95	1.19	2.97	5.95

Following the events of "Eclipso: The Darkness Within," a Daxamite arrived on Earth and decided to stay and fight crime with his newly acquired super-powers.

© 1992 DC Comics

	ORIG	GOOD	FINE	N-MINT
❑3	4.95	0.99	2.47	4.95
❑3/Nude,Nude cover	—	1.20	3.00	6.00
❑3/SC,Photo cover	—	1.20	3.00	6.00
❑4	5.95	1.19	2.97	5.95
❑4/Nude,Nude cover	—	1.20	3.00	6.00
❑4/SC,Photo cover	5.95	1.19	2.97	5.95
❑5	5.95	1.19	2.97	5.95
❑5/Nude,Nude cover	—	1.20	3.00	6.00
❑6	5.95	1.19	2.97	5.95
❑6/SC,Photo cover	5.95	1.19	2.97	5.95
❑7	—	1.19	2.97	5.95
❑7/SC,Photo cover	—	1.19	2.97	5.95
❑8	—	1.19	2.97	5.95
❑8/SC,Photo cover	—	1.19	2.97	5.95
❑9	—	1.19	2.97	5.95
❑9/SC,Photo cover	—	1.19	2.97	5.95
❑10	—	1.19	2.97	5.95
❑10/SC,Photo cover	—	1.19	2.97	5.95
❑11	2.50	0.50	1.25	2.50
❑11/Nude,Nude cover	3.00	0.60	1.50	3.00
❑12	2.50	0.50	1.25	2.50
❑12/Nude,Nude cover	3.00	0.60	1.50	3.00

VAMPEROTICA PRESENTS COUNTESS VLADIMIRA
BRAINSTORM

	ORIG	GOOD	FINE	N-MINT
❑1	—	0.59	1.48	2.95

VAMPFIRE
BRAINSTORM
Value: Cover or less

- ❑1, Sep 96, b&w; adult ... 2.95

VAMPFIRE: EROTIC ECHO
BRAINSTORM
Value: Cover or less

- ❑1 ... 2.95
- ❑2, Feb 97 ... 2.95
- ❑2/Nude, Feb 97 ... 2.95

VAMPFIRE: NECROMANTIQUE
BRAINSTORM
Value: Cover or less

- ❑1, Aug 97 ... 2.95
- ❑2 ... 2.95

VAMPIRE COMPANION, THE
INNOVATION
Value: Cover or less

- ❑1,cardstock cover ... 2.50
- ❑2, The Last Sunrise,cardstock cover ... 2.50
- ❑3 ... 2.50

VAMPIRE GIRLS: BUBBLE GUM & BLOOD
ANGEL
Value: Cover or less

- ❑1 ... 2.95
- ❑2 ... 2.95

VAMPIRE GIRLS: CALIFORNIA 1969
ANGEL ENTERTAINMENT
Value: Cover or less

- ❑0, May 96, b&w ... 2.95
- ❑0/A, nn; b&w; nude embossed foil cardstock cover; no indicia.. 20.00
- ❑0/Nude, May 96, b&w; Nude cover ... 10.00
- ❑1, Aug 96, b&w ... 2.95

VAMPIRE GIRLS, POETS OF BLOOD: SAN FRANCISCO
ANGEL
Value: Cover or less

- ❑1, The Surreal World ... 5.00
- ❑1/Nude, The Surreal World ... 5.00
- ❑2,Flipbook Previews of Angel ... 5.00
- ❑2/Nude,Flipbook Previews of Angel ... 5.00

VAMPIRE LESTAT, THE (ANNE RICE'S...)
INNOVATION

	ORIG	GOOD	FINE	N-MINT
❑1, Jan 90	2.50	1.20	3.00	6.00
❑1-2,2nd Printing	2.50	0.60	1.50	3.00
❑2	2.50	0.80	2.00	4.00
❑2-2,2nd Printing	2.50	0.50	1.25	2.50
❑2-3,3rd Printing	2.50	0.50	1.25	2.50
❑3, May 90	2.50	0.80	2.00	4.00
❑3-2,2nd Printing	2.50	0.50	1.25	2.50
❑4, Jun 90, Vitaicum for the Maquise	2.50	0.60	1.50	3.00
❑5, Sep 90	2.50	0.60	1.50	3.00
❑6, Nov 90	2.50	0.50	1.25	2.50
❑7, Jan 91	2.50	0.50	1.25	2.50
❑8, Mar 91	2.50	0.50	1.25	2.50

	ORIG	GOOD	FINE	N-MINT
❑9, May 91	2.50	0.50	1.25	2.50
❑10, 91	2.50	0.50	1.25	2.50
❑11, 91	2.50	0.50	1.25	2.50
❑12, 91	2.50	0.50	1.25	2.50

VAMPIRELLA
HARRIS

	ORIG	GOOD	FINE	N-MINT
❑0, Dec 94,enhanced cover; contains Vampirella timeline	2.95	1.00	2.50	5.00
❑0/A,Blue logo	2.95	1.00	2.50	5.00
❑0/GO, Gold edition	—	3.00	7.50	15.00
❑0/SI,Silver logo	2.95	1.00	2.50	5.00
❑1, Nov 92, full color	2.95	3.00	7.50	15.00
❑1-2,2nd Printing	2.95	1.00	2.50	5.00
❑2, A: Dracula, full color	2.95	2.40	6.00	12.00
❑3, full color	2.95	2.00	5.00	10.00
❑4, full color	2.95	1.60	4.00	8.00
❑5, full color	2.95	1.60	4.00	8.00

VAMPIRELLA 25TH ANNIVERSARY SPECIAL
HARRIS

	ORIG	GOOD	FINE	N-MINT
❑1, Oct 96, nn; One-Shot; prestige format	5.95	1.19	2.97	5.95
❑1/A, Oct 96,Silver logo with no words on cover	—	1.20	3.00	6.00

VAMPIRELLA & THE BLOOD RED QUEEN OF HEARTS
HARRIS

Value: Cover or less

❑1, Sep 96, The Blood Red Queen of Hearts; The Return of the Blood Red Queen, Collects stories from Vampirella (Magazine) #49, 60, 61, 62, 65, 66, 101, and 102 .... 9.95

VAMPIRELLA: ASCENDING EVIL
HARRIS

	ORIG	GOOD	FINE	N-MINT
❑1	2.95	0.59	1.48	2.95
❑1/AE,American Entertainment variant cover	—	1.00	2.50	5.00
❑2	2.95	0.59	1.48	2.95
❑3	2.95	0.59	1.48	2.95
❑4	2.95	0.59	1.48	2.95

VAMPIRELLA: BLOOD LUST
HARRIS

	ORIG	GOOD	FINE	N-MINT
❑1, Jul 97, JRo (w),cardstock cover	4.95	1.00	2.50	5.00
❑2, Aug 97, JRo (w),cardstock cover	4.95	1.00	2.50	5.00

VAMPIRELLA CLASSIC
HARRIS

Value: Cover or less

❑1, Feb 95,Reprints Vampirella #12 in color 2.95
❑2, Apr 95 .... 2.95
❑3, Jun 95 .... 2.95
❑4 .... 2.95
❑5 .... 2.95

VAMPIRELLA COMMEMORATIVE EDITION
HARRIS

Value: Cover or less

❑1, Nov 96, KB (w) 2.95

VAMPIRELLA: CROSSOVER GALLERY
HARRIS

Value: Cover or less

❑1, Sep 97,wraparound cover; pin-ups; 2.95

VAMPIRELLA: DEATH & DESTRUCTION
HARRIS

	ORIG	GOOD	FINE	N-MINT
❑1, Jul 96	2.95	0.59	1.48	2.95
❑1/A,Vampirella sitting on cover	—	0.60	1.50	3.00
❑1/LE,Vampirella logo only on cover	—	1.00	2.50	5.00
❑2, Aug 96	2.95	0.59	1.48	2.95
❑3, Sep 96	2.95	0.59	1.48	2.95
❑Ash 1	—	0.60	1.50	3.00

VAMPIRELLA/DRACULA & PANTHA SHOWCASE
HARRIS

Value: Cover or less

❑1, Aug 97, JRo (w),Vampirella on cover; flip-book with previews of Vampirella/Dracula and Pantha 1.50
❑1/A, Aug 97, JRo (w),Pantha on cover; flip-book with previews of Vampirella/Dracula and Pantha 1.50

VAMPIRELLA/DRACULA: THE CENTENNIAL
HARRIS

Value: Cover or less

❑1, Oct 97 .... 5.95
❑1/A,David Mack cover 5.95
❑1/B,Gary Frank cover 5.95
❑2, Oct 97 .... 5.95

VAMPIRELLA/LADY DEATH
HARRIS

	ORIG	GOOD	FINE	N-MINT
❑1, Feb 99	3.50	0.70	1.75	3.50
❑1/A, Valentine edition; Red foil	—	1.00	2.50	5.00
❑1/LE	—	2.00	5.00	10.00

VAMPIRELLA LIVES
HARRIS

	ORIG	GOOD	FINE	N-MINT
❑1, Dec 96,white cardstock outer cover with cutout	3.50	0.70	1.75	3.50
❑1/A, Dec 96,Photo cover with Vampirella leaning forward	—	0.80	2.00	4.00
❑1/B, Dec 96,Photo cover with Vampirella side view	—	0.80	2.00	4.00
❑1/C, Dec 96,Die-cut linen cover	—	2.00	5.00	10.00
❑2, Jan 97,Vampirella bathing in blood	2.95	0.59	1.48	2.95
❑2/A, Jan 97,Blue background	—	0.60	1.50	3.00
❑2/B, Jan 97,Photo cover	—	0.80	2.00	4.00
❑3, Feb 97,Drawn cover	2.95	0.59	1.48	2.95
❑3/A, Feb 97,Photo cover	—	0.80	2.00	4.00

VAMPIRELLA MONTHLY
HARRIS

	ORIG	GOOD	FINE	N-MINT
❑0,Vampirella standing, two figures in background	—	0.80	2.00	4.00
❑0/A,Vampirella bathing in blood	—	0.80	2.00	4.00
❑1, Nov 97, Ascending Evil, Part 1,Gold foil logo on cover	2.95	0.80	2.00	4.00
❑1/A, Ascending Evil, Part 1,Vampirella eating something bloody on cover	—	1.00	2.50	5.00
❑1/B, Ascending Evil, Part 1,Vampirella eating something bloody on cover; Gold marking	—	1.00	2.50	5.00
❑1/C, Ascending Evil, Part 1,Vampirella staing on cover, demon-eyed figures in background	—	1.00	2.50	5.00
❑1/D, Ascending Evil, Part 1,Vampirella standing on cover, black background, blue logo	—	1.00	2.50	5.00
❑1/E, Ascending Evil, Part 1, American Entertainment Edition; Vampirella reclining on skull	—	1.00	2.50	5.00
❑1/F, Ascending Evil, Part 1,Vampirella standing on cover, black background with foil logo	—	1.00	2.50	5.00
❑2, Dec 97, Ascending Evil, Part 2	2.95	0.60	1.50	3.00
❑2/A, Ascending Evil, Part 2,Man shooting gun at Vampirella	—	0.60	1.50	3.00
❑3, Jan 98, Ascending Evil, Part 3	2.95	0.60	1.50	3.00
❑3/A, Ascending Evil, Part 3,Vampirella on motorcycle (only figure on cover)	—	0.60	1.50	3.00
❑4, Feb 98, Holy War, Part 1	2.95	0.60	1.50	3.00
❑4/A, Holy War, Part 1, Crimson edition	—	0.80	2.00	4.00
❑4/B, Holy War, Part 1,Vampirella holding gun	—	0.60	1.50	3.00
❑5, Mar 98, Holy War, Part 2	2.95	0.60	1.50	3.00
❑6, Apr 98, Holy War, Part 3	2.95	0.60	1.50	3.00
❑7, Jun 98, Queen's Gambit, Part 1, A: Shi	2.95	0.60	1.50	3.00
❑7/A, Queen's Gambit, Part 1,Vampirella with finger to mouth	—	0.80	2.00	4.00
❑7/B, Queen's Gambit, Part 1,Shi on cover in foreground, Vampirella in background	—	0.80	2.00	4.00
❑7/C, Queen's Gambit, Part 1,Shi in background, Vampirella in foreground	—	0.80	2.00	4.00
❑7/D, Queen's Gambit, Part 1,Vampirella and Shi on checkerboard floor, foil logo	—	1.20	3.00	6.00
❑7/E, Queen's Gambit, Part 1,Vampirella and Shi on checkerboard floor	—	0.80	2.00	4.00
❑8, Jul 98, Queen's Gambit, Part 2, A: Shi	2.95	0.60	1.50	3.00
❑9, Aug 98, Queen's Gambit, Part 3, A: Shi	2.95	0.60	1.50	3.00
❑10, Sep 98, Hell on Earth, Part 1	2.95	0.60	1.50	3.00
❑10/A, Hell on Earth, Part 1,Black-and-white cover	—	1.20	3.00	6.00
❑10/B, Hell on Earth, Part 1,Color cover with no words	—	1.00	2.50	5.00
❑11, Oct 98, Hell on Earth, Part 2	2.95	0.60	1.50	3.00
❑12, Nov 98, Hell on Earth, Part 3	2.95	0.60	1.50	3.00
❑12/A,Vampirella in spiky bodysuit	—	0.60	1.50	3.00
❑12/B, Nov 98, Hell on Earth, Part 3,Vampirella hurling woman	2.95	0.60	1.50	3.00
❑12/SC, Nov 98, Hell on Earth, Part 3,Like B cover	2.95	1.20	3.00	6.00
❑13, Mar 99, World's End, Part 1	2.95	0.60	1.50	3.00
❑13/A, World's End, Part 1,Vampirella holding heart	—	0.60	1.50	3.00
❑14, Apr 99, World's End, Part 2	2.95	0.59	1.48	2.95
❑14/A, World's End, Part 2,Vampirella standing, figure in background	—	0.60	1.50	3.00
❑15, May 99, World's End, Part 3	2.95	0.59	1.48	2.95
❑15/A, May 99, World's End, Part 3	2.95	0.59	1.48	2.95
❑15/B, May 99, World's End, Part 3,alternate cover (facing away)	2.95	0.59	1.48	2.95
❑16, Jun 99	2.95	0.59	1.48	2.95
❑16/A,Vampirella ø 4 other similarly clad women on cover	—	0.60	1.50	3.00
❑16/B,Pantha photo cover (standing), orange/red background	—	0.80	2.00	4.00
❑16/C,Vampirella photo cover	—	1.00	2.50	5.00
❑16/D,Patha drawn cover	—	0.60	1.50	3.00
❑16/E,Patha photo cover (crawling), white background	—	0.80	2.00	4.00
❑16/F, blue background,Pantha photo cover (standing), blue background	—	0.80	2.00	4.00
❑17, Jul 99, Rebirth, Part 1	2.95	0.59	1.48	2.95

	ORIG	GOOD	FINE	N-MINT
❑17/A,Vampirella bound on cover	—	0.60	1.50	3.00
❑17/B,Pantha photo cover (standiing), blue background	—	0.80	2.00	4.00
❑17/C,Vampirella photo cover	—	0.80	2.00	4.00
❑17/D,Two women with giant serpent in background on cover	—	0.60	1.50	3.00
❑17/E,Pantha photo cover (sitting with arm outstretched), blue background	—	0.80	2.00	4.00
❑18, Aug 99, JPH (w), Rebirth, Part 2	2.95	0.59	1.48	2.95
❑18/A,Vampirella with arms outstretched on cover	—	0.60	1.50	3.00
❑18/B,"Chesty" close-up Vampirella cover	—	0.60	1.50	3.00
❑19, Sep 99, Rebirth, Part 3; Kust for Life, Two Vampirellas on cover	2.95	0.59	1.48	2.95
❑19/A,Vampirella holding skull on cover	—	0.60	1.50	3.00
❑20, Oct 99,Vampirella with gun	2.95	0.59	1.48	2.95
❑20/A,Vampirella standing with fangs present	—	0.60	1.50	3.00
❑21, Nov 99,Photo cover, tinted background	2.95	0.59	1.48	2.95
❑21/A,Drawn cover	—	0.60	1.50	3.00
❑21/B,Photo cover, white background	—	0.80	2.00	4.00
❑22, Dec 99,Photo cover, red tinted background	2.95	0.80	2.00	4.00
❑22/A,Drawn cover	—	0.60	1.50	3.00
❑22/B,Photo cover, white background	—	0.80	2.00	4.00
❑23, Jan 00,Vampirella fighting Lady Death, cover has words	2.95	0.59	1.48	2.95
❑23/A,Wordless cover with Vampirella on knees	—	1.40	3.50	7.00
❑23/B,Red-logo cover with Vampirella on knees	—	1.00	2.50	5.00
❑23/C,Silver logo cover with Vampirella on knees	—	0.60	1.50	3.00
❑23/D,Wordless cover with Vampirella fighting Lady Death	—	1.20	3.00	6.00
❑24, Feb 00,Vampirella with gun, fishnet stockings in foreground on cover	2.95	0.59	1.48	2.95
❑24/A,Reflections in sunglasses on cover	—	0.60	1.50	3.00
❑24/B,Vampirella on motorcycle, other female figure at top	—	0.60	1.50	3.00
❑25, Mar 00,Vampirella in chains with male figure	2.95	0.59	1.48	2.95
❑25/A,Two women on motorcycles	—	0.60	1.50	3.00
❑26, Apr 00, Vampirella vs. Lady Death: The End,Vampirella facing Lady Death on cover	2.95	0.59	1.48	2.95
❑26/A,Vampirella in foreground, Lady Death in background	—	0.60	1.50	3.00
❑Ash 1, Aug 97,"Ascending Evil" on cover	—	1.00	2.50	5.00
❑ASH 1/A,"Holy War" on cover	—	1.00	2.50	5.00
❑Ash 2	—	1.00	2.50	5.00
❑Ash 3	—	1.00	2.50	5.00
❑Ash 3/A,Leather cover; Convention exclusive limited to 1000 copies	—	3.00	7.50	15.00
❑Ash 4	—	0.60	1.50	3.00
❑Ash 5	—	0.60	1.50	3.00
❑Ash 6	—	0.60	1.50	3.00

VAMPIRELLA: MORNING IN AMERICA
HARRIS

Value: Cover or less

- ❑1, b&w; distributed by Dark Horse; squarebound 3.95
- ❑2, Nov 91, b&w; squarebound 3.95
- ❑3, Jan 92, b&w; squarebound 3.95
- ❑4, Apr 92, b&w; squarebound 3.95

VAMPIRELLA OF DRAKULON
HARRIS

Value: Cover or less

- ❑0, The Origin of Vampirella; The High Gloss Egyptian Junk Peddler 2.95
- ❑1, Jan 95, Beware, Dreamers 2.95
- ❑2 2.95
- ❑3,Poly-bagged 2.95

VAMPIRELLA/PAINKILLER JANE
HARRIS

Value: Cover or less

- ❑1, May 98,foil-enhanced cover; crossover with Event 3.50
- ❑1/A,Variant cover, Vampirella and Painkiller Jane on rooftop 5.00
- ❑1/B,Blue cover, Vampirella and Painkiller posing (in mid-air!) 24.95
- ❑1/GO, Gold edition 24.95
- ❑Ash 1, Jan 98,no cover price —

VAMPIRELLA PIN-UP SPECIAL
HARRIS

Value: Cover or less

- ❑1, Oct 95 2.95
- ❑1/A,White background and snake on cover 2.95

VAMPIRELLA: SAD WINGS OF DESTINY
HARRIS

	ORIG	GOOD	FINE	N-MINT
❑1, Sep 96, nn; cardstock cover; One-Shot; gold edition limited to 5000	3.95	0.79	1.98	3.95
❑1/GO, Sep 96,Gold mark on cover	—	1.00	2.50	5.00

Harris and Chaos' primary female characters, Vampirella and Lady Death, met for a Valentine's adventure in February 1999.

© 1999 Harris and Chaos

VAMPIRELLA/SHADOWHAWK: CREATURES OF THE NIGHT
HARRIS

Value: Cover or less

- ❑1, Feb 95,crossover with Image; concludes in Shadowhawk - Vampirella #2 4.95
- ❑2,"ShadowHawk/Vampirella". 4.95

VAMPIRELLA/SHI
HARRIS

Value: Cover or less

- ❑1, Nine Kinds of Dirt,no cover price; crossover with Crusade 2.95

VAMPIRELLA: SILVER ANNIVERSARY COLLECTION
HARRIS

Value: Cover or less

- ❑1/A, Jan 97, The Glorious Return of Sweet Baby Theda,Good Girl cover 2.50
- ❑1/B, Jan 97, The Glorious Return of Sweet Baby Theda,Bad Girl cover 2.50
- ❑2/A, The Beauty and the Behemoth; The Blob Beast of Blighter's Boy,Good Girl cover 2.50
- ❑2/B, The Beauty and the Behemoth; The Blob Beast of Blighter's Boy,Bad Girl cover 2.50
- ❑3/A, Curse of the Pasha's Princess; Down the Earth,Good Girl cover 2.50
- ❑3/B, Curse of the Pasha's Princess; Down the Earth,Bad Girl cover 2.50
- ❑4/A, Salves of the Alien Amazon; Vampirella and the Alien Amazon,Good Girl cover 2.50
- ❑4/B, Salves of the Alien Amazon; Vampirella and the Alien Amazon,Bad Girl cover 2.50

VAMPIRELLA'S SUMMER NIGHTS
HARRIS

Value: Cover or less

- ❑1, KB (w), Vampirella Meets Creepy and Eerie; The Reach of the Dead, nn; b&w 3.95

VAMPIRELLA STRIKES
HARRIS

	ORIG	GOOD	FINE	N-MINT
❑1, Oct 95, The Prize, Part 1,Photo cover	2.95	0.60	1.50	3.00
❑1/A, The Prize, Part 1,Alternate Photo cover; Marble background	2.95	0.60	1.50	3.00
❑1/B,Photo cover, Vampirella with moon in background	—	0.60	1.50	3.00
❑1/C,Photo cover, Vampirella against blue background	—	0.60	1.50	3.00
❑1/LE, The Prize, Part 1	—	2.00	5.00	10.00
❑2, Dec 95, The Prize, Part 2	2.95	0.60	1.50	3.00
❑3, Feb 96	2.95	0.60	1.50	3.00
❑4, Apr 96	2.95	0.60	1.50	3.00
❑5, Jun 96, A: Eudaemon	2.95	0.60	1.50	3.00
❑6, Aug 96	2.95	0.60	1.50	3.00
❑7, Oct 96,Final Issue	2.95	0.60	1.50	3.00
❑Anl 1	2.95	0.60	1.50	3.00
❑Anl 1/A, Dec 96	2.95	0.60	1.50	3.00
❑Anl 1/B, Dec 96	2.95	0.60	1.50	3.00

VAMPIRELLA VS HEMORRHAGE
HARRIS

	ORIG	GOOD	FINE	N-MINT
❑1, Apr 97, The Red Death part 1	3.50	0.70	1.75	3.50
❑1/A, Mar 97, The Red Death part 1,Vampirella with red hand on cover	—	0.70	1.75	3.50
❑1/Ash, Mar 97,no cover price; ashcan	—	0.20	0.50	1.00
❑2, May 97, The Red Death part 2	3.50	0.70	1.75	3.50
❑3, Jun 97, The Red Death part 3	3.50	0.70	1.75	3.50

VAMPIRELLA VS PANTHA
HARRIS

	ORIG	GOOD	FINE	N-MINT
❑1/A, Mar 97,cardstock cover; Vampirella standing over body in street with police cars in background	3.50	0.70	1.75	3.50
❑1/B, Mar 97,cardstock cover	3.50	0.70	1.75	3.50
❑1/C, Mar 97,Pantha on cover with black background	3.50	0.70	1.75	3.50
❑Ash 1, "Special Showcase Edition" on cover	—	0.70	1.75	3.50

VAMPIRELLA/WETWORKS
HARRIS

	ORIG	GOOD	FINE	N-MINT
❑1, Jun 97	—	0.60	1.50	3.00

VAMPIRE MIYU
ANTARCTIC

	ORIG	GOOD	FINE	N-MINT
❑1	2.95	0.70	1.75	3.50
❑2	2.95	0.60	1.50	3.00

	ORIG	GOOD	FINE	N-MINT
❑3	2.95	0.60	1.50	3.00
❑4	2.95	0.60	1.50	3.00
❑5	2.95	0.60	1.50	3.00
❑6	2.95	0.60	1.50	3.00
❑Ash 1, Spectral Time, 1: Vampire Miyu, Ash-can promotional edition from 1995 San Diego Comic-Con	—	0.10	0.25	0.50

VAMPIRES LUST
CFD

Value: Cover or less

- ❑1, Sep 96, b&w; adult ... 2.95
- ❑1/Nude, Sep 96,adult; nude photo cover ... 3.95

VAMPIRE'S PRANK
ACID RAIN

Value: Cover or less

- ❑1, Morbinjaw ... 2.95

VAMPIRE TALES
MARVEL

	ORIG	GOOD	FINE	N-MINT
❑1, Aug 73, ME (w), Morbius; To Kill a Were-wolf, A: Morbius,1st full Morbius story	0.75	3.00	7.50	15.00
❑2, Oct 73, 1: Satana	0.75	0.70	1.75	3.50
❑3	0.75	0.70	1.75	3.50
❑4, Apr 74	0.75	0.70	1.75	3.50
❑5, Jun 74	0.75	0.70	1.75	3.50
❑6, Aug 74, A: Lilith	0.75	0.70	1.75	3.50
❑7, Oct 74	0.75	0.70	1.75	3.50
❑8, Dec 74, A: Blade	0.75	0.70	1.75	3.50
❑9, Feb 75, A: Blade	0.75	0.70	1.75	3.50
❑10, Apr 75, A: Blade	0.75	0.70	1.75	3.50
❑11, Jun 75,Final Issue	0.75	0.70	1.75	3.50
❑Anl 1,Reprint	1.25	0.40	1.00	2.00

VAMPIRE VERSES, THE
CFD

Value: Cover or less

- ❑1, Aug 95, b&w ... 2.95
- ❑2, b&w ... 2.95
- ❑3, Jun 96, b&w ... 2.95
- ❑3/LE, Jun 96,alternate nude cover; limited edition of 1000 copies ... 10.00

VAMPIRE VIXENS
ACID RAIN

Value: Cover or less

- ❑1 ... 2.75

VAMPIRE WORLD
ACID RAIN

Value: Cover or less

- ❑1, Upon a Black Spire ... 2.75

VAMPIRE YUI
IRONCAT

Value: Cover or less

- ❑1, Jul 00 ... 2.95

VAMPIRIC JIHAD
APPLE

Value: Cover or less

- ❑1, nn; b&w; cardstockcover; reprints material from Blood of Dracula #14-19 ... 4.95

VAMPORNELLA
ADAM POST

Value: Cover or less

- ❑1, Amori Taylor ... 2.95

VAMPRESS LUXURA, THE
BRAINSTORM

Value: Cover or less

- ❑1, Connoisseur,wraparound cover ... 2.95
- ❑1/GO, Connoisseur ... 10.00

VAMPS
DC

	ORIG	GOOD	FINE	N-MINT
❑1, Aug 94	1.95	0.50	1.25	2.50
❑2, Sep 94	1.95	0.50	1.25	2.50
❑3, Oct 94	1.95	0.50	1.25	2.50
❑4, Nov 94	1.95	0.50	1.25	2.50
❑5, Dec 94	1.95	0.50	1.25	2.50
❑6, Jan 95	1.95	0.50	1.25	2.50

VAMPS: HOLLYWOOD & VEIN
DC

	ORIG	GOOD	FINE	N-MINT
❑1, Feb 96	2.25	0.50	1.25	2.50
❑2, Mar 96	2.25	0.50	1.25	2.50
❑3, Apr 96, Undeath in Venice	2.25	0.50	1.25	2.50
❑4, May 96, Surfing the Red Wave	2.25	0.50	1.25	2.50
❑5, Jun 96	2.25	0.50	1.25	2.50
❑6, Jul 96, Fire...Earth...Water...Metal...Wood,Final Issue	2.25	0.50	1.25	2.50

VAMPS: PUMPKIN TIME
DC

Value: Cover or less

- ❑1, Dec 98, Midnight Ride ... 2.50
- ❑2, Jan 99 ... 2.50
- ❑3, Feb 99 ... 2.50

VAMPURADA
TAVICAT

Value: Cover or less

- ❑1, Jul 95 ... 1.95

VAMPYRES
ETERNITY

Value: Cover or less

- ❑1, The End of All Vampires; Creatures in the NightThe God of the Dead, b&w; Reprint ... 2.25
- ❑2, b&w; Reprint ... 2.25
- ❑3, Mar 89, My Flesh Claws; The Voodoo Dead, b&w; Reprint ... 2.25
- ❑4, b&w; Reprint ... 2.25

VAMPYRE'S KISS
AIRCEL

Value: Cover or less

- ❑1, Jun 90, b&w; adult ... 2.50
- ❑2, Jul 90, b&w; adult ... 2.50
- ❑3, Aug 90, b&w; adult ... 2.50
- ❑4, Sep 90, b&w; adult ... 2.50

VAMPYRE'S KISS, BOOK II
AIRCEL

Value: Cover or less

- ❑1, b&w; adult ... 2.50
- ❑2, Dec 90, b&w; adult ... 2.50
- ❑3, Feb 91, b&w; adult ... 2.50
- ❑4, Mar 91, b&w; adult ... 2.50

VAMPYRE'S KISS, BOOK III
AIRCEL

Value: Cover or less

- ❑1, Aug 91, b&w; adult ... 2.50
- ❑2, b&w; adult ... 2.50
- ❑3, b&w; adult ... 2.50
- ❑4, b&w; adult ... 2.50

VANDALA
CHAOS!

Value: Cover or less

- ❑1, Aug 00, Wings of Fate ... 2.95

VANGUARD
IMAGE

	ORIG	GOOD	FINE	N-MINT
❑1, Oct 93, EL, EL (w)	1.95	0.40	1.00	2.00
❑2, Nov 93, EL, EL (w)	1.95	0.40	1.00	2.00
❑3, Dec 93, EL, EL (w), A: Savage Dragon	1.95	0.40	1.00	2.00
❑4, Feb 94, EL, EL (w)	1.95	0.40	1.00	2.00
❑5, Apr 94, EL, EL (w)	1.95	0.40	1.00	2.00
❑6, May 94, EL, EL (w)	1.95	0.40	1.00	2.00

VANGUARD (2ND SERIES)
IMAGE

Value: Cover or less

- ❑1, Oct 96, Strange Visitors, b&w ... 2.95
- ❑2, Oct 96, Strange Visitors, b&w ... 2.95
- ❑3, Dec 96, Strange Visitors, A: Supreme, b&w ... 2.95
- ❑4, Jan 97, Strange Visitors, A: Savage Dragon; A: Super Patriot, b&w; cover says Feb, indicia says Jan ... 2.95

VANGUARD: ETHEREAL WARRIORS
IMAGE

Value: Cover or less

- ❑1, Aug 00 ... 5.95

VANGUARD ILLUSTRATED
PACIFIC

	ORIG	GOOD	FINE	N-MINT
❑1, TY; SR, Libretto; Encyclopedias	1.50	0.30	0.75	1.50
❑2, DSt	1.50	0.30	0.75	1.50
❑3, TY; SR, Freak Wave!; Duel With: Dorf Dishware, Part 3	1.50	0.30	0.75	1.50
❑4, Quark; Success, Part 4	1.50	0.30	0.75	1.50
❑5, Friend in Need; Adventures in Art	1.50	0.30	0.75	1.50
❑6, Jun 84, The Struggle's End; The God Run	1.50	0.30	0.75	1.50
❑7, GE, The Ballad of Hardcase Bradley; Goldyn, 1: Mr. Monster	1.50	0.80	2.00	4.00
❑8,Exists?	1.50	0.30	0.75	1.50
❑9,Exists?	1.50	0.30	0.75	1.50
❑10,Exists?	1.50	0.30	0.75	1.50
❑11,Exists?	1.50	0.30	0.75	1.50

VANITY
PACIFIC

Value: Cover or less

- ❑1, Jun 84, Vanity; Escape From Fire ... 1.50
- ❑2, Aug 84, A Scent of Lilac; Avalone ... 1.50

VANITY ANGEL
ANTARCTIC

	ORIG	GOOD	FINE	N-MINT
❑1, Sep 94, b&w; adult	3.50	0.70	1.75	3.50
❑1-2, May 95,adult; 2nd Printing	3.50	0.70	1.75	3.50
❑2, Oct 94, b&w; adult	3.50	0.70	1.75	3.50
❑2-2, Jun 95,adult; 2nd Printing	3.50	0.70	1.75	3.50
❑3, Nov 94, b&w; adult	2.95	0.70	1.75	3.50
❑4, Dec 94, b&w; adult	2.95	0.70	1.75	3.50
❑5, Jan 95, b&w; adult	2.95	0.70	1.75	3.50
❑6, Feb 95, b&w; adult	2.95	0.70	1.75	3.50

VARCEL'S VIXENS
CALIBER

Value: Cover or less

- ❑1, b&w ... 2.50
- ❑2, b&w ... 2.50
- ❑3, b&w ... 2.50

VARIATIONS ON THE THEME
SCARLET ROSE

Value: Cover or less

- ❑1 ... 2.75
- ❑2 ... 2.75
- ❑3 ... 2.75
- ❑4 ... 2.75

VARIOGENESIS
DAGGER

Value: Cover or less

- ❑0, Jun 94 ... 3.50

VARLA VORTEX
BONEYARD

Value: Cover or less

- ❑1, Babes of Blood ... 2.95

VARMINTS
BLUE COMET

	ORIG	GOOD	FINE	N-MINT
❑1	1.80	0.40	1.00	2.00
❑SE 1,Panda Khan	2.50	0.50	1.25	2.50

VAST KNOWLEDGE OF GENERAL SUBJECTS, A
FANTAGRAPHICS

Value: Cover or less
❑1, Sep 94, b&w 4.95

VAULT OF DOOMNATION, THE
B-MOVIE

Value: Cover or less
❑1, Zombie; Valentine's Day, b&w 1.70

VAULT OF EVIL
MARVEL

	ORIG	GOOD	FINE	N-MINT
❑1	0.20	1.00	2.50	5.00
❑2	0.20	0.60	1.50	3.00
❑3	0.20	0.60	1.50	3.00
❑4, The Old Mill; The Face That Followed	0.20	0.50	1.25	2.50
❑5	—	0.50	1.25	2.50
❑6	—	0.50	1.25	2.50
❑7	—	0.50	1.25	2.50
❑8	—	0.50	1.25	2.50
❑9	—	0.50	1.25	2.50
❑10	—	0.50	1.25	2.50
❑11	—	0.40	1.00	2.00
❑12	—	0.40	1.00	2.00
❑13	—	0.40	1.00	2.00
❑14	—	0.40	1.00	2.00
❑15	—	0.40	1.00	2.00
❑16	—	0.40	1.00	2.00
❑17	—	0.40	1.00	2.00
❑18	—	0.40	1.00	2.00
❑19	—	0.40	1.00	2.00
❑20	—	0.40	1.00	2.00
❑21	—	0.40	1.00	2.00
❑22	—	0.40	1.00	2.00
❑23,Final Issue	—	0.40	1.00	2.00

VAULT OF HORROR, THE (GLADSTONE)
GLADSTONE

	ORIG	GOOD	FINE	N-MINT
❑1, Aug 90,Reprints The Vault of Horror #34, The Haunt of Fear #1	1.95	0.50	1.25	2.50
❑2, Oct 90,Reprints The Vault of Horror #27, The Haunt of Fear #17	1.95	0.50	1.25	2.50
❑3, Dec 90,Reprints The Vault of Horror #13, The Haunt of Fear #22	1.95	0.50	1.25	2.50
❑4, Feb 91,Reprints The Vault of Horror #23, The Haunt of Fear #13	2.00	0.50	1.25	2.50
❑5, Apr 91, JKa; WW; JCr; AF, Southern Hospitality!; The Jelly Fish!,Reprints The Vault of Horror #19, The Haunt of Fear #5	2.00	0.50	1.25	2.50
❑6, Jun 91,Reprints The Vault of Horror #32, Weird Fantasy #6	2.00	0.50	1.25	2.50
❑7,Reprints The Vault of Horror #26, Weird Fantasy #7	2.00	0.50	1.25	2.50

VAULT OF HORROR (RCP)
COCHRAN

Value: Cover or less

❑1, Sep 91 .... 2.00
❑2, Nov 91 .... 2.00
❑3, Jan 92, JKa; WW; JCr; AF, Two of a Kind!; Graft in Concrete!,Reprints Vault of Horror #26, Weird Science #7........ 2.00
❑4, Mar 92.............................. 2.00
❑5, May 92 .... 2.00

VAULT OF HORROR, THE (RCP)
GEMSTONE

Value: Cover or less

❑1, Oct 92, WW; JCr; HK; AF, WW (w); JCr (w); HK (w); AF (w), Portrait in Wax!; The Werewolf Legend,Reprints The Vault of Horror #12 .... 2.00
❑2, Jan 93,Reprints The Vault of Horror #13........................... 2.00
❑3, Apr 93,Reprints The Vault of Horror #14........................... 2.00
❑4, Jul 93,Reprints The Vault of Horror #15........................... 2.00
❑5, Oct 93,Reprints The Vault of Horror #16........................... 2.00
❑6, Jan 94, Terror on the Moors!; Baby...It's Cold Inside!,Reprints The Vault of Horror #17....... 2.00
❑7, Apr 94, Sink-Hole!; Lend me a Hand!,Reprints The Vault of Horror #18........................... 2.00
❑8, Jul 94, Southern Hospitality!; The Jellyfish!,Reprints The Vault of Horror #19 .... 2.00
❑9, Oct 94, About Face; The Reluctant Vampire,Reprints The Vault of Horror #20....................... 2.00
❑10, Jan 95, One Last Fling!; That's a 'Croc'!,Reprints The Vault of Horror #20............. 2.00
❑11, Apr 95,Reprints The Vault of Horror #21........................... 2.00
❑12, Jul 95,Reprints The Vault of Horror #22........................... 2.00
❑13, Oct 95,Reprints The Vault of Horror #23........................... 2.00
❑14, Jan 96,Reprints The Vault of Horror #24........................... 2.00
❑15, Apr 96,Reprints The Vault of Horror #25........................... 2.00
❑16, Jul 96,Reprints The Vault of Horror #26........................... 2.50
❑17, Oct 96,Reprints The Vault of Horror #27........................... 2.50
❑18, Jan 97,Reprints The Vault of Horror #28........................... 2.50
❑19, Apr 97,Reprints The Vault of Horror #29........................... 2.50
❑20, Jul 97,Reprints The Vault of Horror #30........................... 2.50
❑21, Oct 97, JCr; GE, JCr (w); GE (w), Whirlpool; Out of His Head!,Reprints The Vault of Horror #31........................... 2.50
❑22, Jan 98,Reprints The Vault of Horror #32........................... 2.50
❑23, Apr 98,Reprints The Vault of Horror #33........................... 2.50
❑24, Jul 98,Reprints The Vault of Horror #34........................... 2.50
❑25, Oct 98.............................. 2.50
❑26, Jan 99.............................. 2.50

DC had its own group of female vampires in the three *Vamps* mini-series.

© 1994 DC Comics

❑27, Apr 99 .... 2.50
❑28, Jul 99 .... 2.50
❑29, Oct 99 .... 2.50
❑Anl 1,Collects The Vault of Horror #1-5 .... 8.95
❑Anl 2,Collects The Vault of Horror #6-10 .... 9.95
❑Anl 3, Fountains of Youth!; The Monster in the Ice!,Collects The Vault of Horror #11-15 .... 10.95
❑Anl 4 .... 12.95
❑Anl 5, Road Hog; Night of the Ghouls 13.50

VAULT OF SCREAMING HORROR
FANTACO

Value: Cover or less
❑1, Dead Heat!; Mistress of Whorla House 3.50

VAULT OF WHORES
EROS

Value: Cover or less
❑1 .... 2.95

VECTOR
NOW

Value: Cover or less

❑1, Jul 86, Happy Birthday from Dimension V........................ 1.50
❑2, Sep 86, The Menace of Modem 1.50
❑3, Nov 86, Nite-Flite 1.50
❑4, Jan 87, Last Stand at Stonehenge 1.75

VEGAS KNIGHTS
PIONEER

Value: Cover or less
❑1, MGr (c)............................. 1.95

VEGETABLE LOVER
FANTAGRAPHICS

Value: Cover or less
❑1, b&w; adult 2.75

VEGMAN
CHECKER

Value: Cover or less
❑1, Spr 98, b&w 2.95
❑2, Sum 98, b&w; indicia for #1 repeated inside.................... 2.95

VELOCITY (ECLIPSE)
ECLIPSE

Value: Cover or less
❑5, b&w 2.95

VELOCITY (IMAGE)
IMAGE

Value: Cover or less
❑1, Nov 95, KB (w).................. 2.50
❑2, Dec 95, KB (w).................. 2.50
❑3, Jan 96, KB (w).................. 2.50

VELVET
ADVENTURE

Value: Cover or less

❑1, b&w.................................. 2.50
❑2, b&w.................................. 2.50
❑3, b&w 2.50
❑4, b&w 2.50

VELVET ARTICHOKE THEATRE
VELVET ARTICHOKE PRESS

Value: Cover or less
❑1, Sum 98, b&w..................... 2.00

VELVET TOUCH
ANTARCTIC

Value: Cover or less

❑1, Oct 93, Dino Goddess; Gilligan's Island,adult 3.95
❑1/PL, Oct 93, Dino Goddess; Gilligan's Island, full color; adult; platinum.............................. 10.00
❑1-2, Apr 95, Dino Goddess; Gilligan's Island,adult; 2nd Printing 3.95
❑2, Jan 94,adult....................... 2.95
❑3, Jul 94,adult........................ 2.95
❑4, Aug 94,adult....................... 2.95
❑5, Oct 94,adult....................... 2.95
❑6, Jan 95, The Naked Individual's; The B-Squad,adult 2.95

VENDETTA: HOLY VINDICATOR
RED BULLET

Value: Cover or less

❑1, b&w; first printing limited to 500 copies.................................. 2.50
❑2, b&w; first printing limited to 500 copies.................................. 2.50
❑3, b&w; first printing limited to 3000 copies 2.50
❑4, b&w; Final Issue................ 2.50

VENGEANCE OF THE AZTECS
CALIBER

	ORIG	GOOD	FINE	N-MINT
❑1, b&w	2.95	0.59	1.48	2.95
❑2, b&w	2.95	0.59	1.48	2.95
❑3, b&w	2.50	0.59	1.48	2.95
❑4	2.95	0.59	1.48	2.95
❑5	2.95	0.59	1.48	2.95

VENGEANCE OF VAMPIRELLA
HARRIS

	ORIG	GOOD	FINE	N-MINT
❑0, Nov 95, The Mystery Walk, Part 0	2.95	0.59	1.48	2.95
❑0.5	—	0.00	0.00	0.00
❑0.5/A	—	0.00	0.00	0.00
❑1, Apr 94,red foil wraparound cover	2.95	0.70	1.75	3.50
❑1/A,Blue foil	—	0.60	1.50	3.00
❑1/GO, Gold promotional edition	2.95	2.00	5.00	10.00
❑1-2,2nd Printing; blue foil wraparound cover	2.95	0.60	1.50	3.00
❑2, full color	2.95	0.60	1.50	3.00
❑3	2.95	0.60	1.50	3.00
❑4, Jul 94, Danse with the Undead, Part 1	2.95	0.60	1.50	3.00
❑5, Aug 94, Danse with the Undead, Part 2, 1: The Undead	2.95	0.60	1.50	3.00
❑6, Sep 94	2.95	0.60	1.50	3.00
❑6/A, Special Limited Edition on cover	—	0.80	2.00	4.00
❑7	2.95	0.60	1.50	3.00
❑8, trading card	2.95	0.60	1.50	3.00
❑9	2.95	0.60	1.50	3.00
❑10	2.95	0.60	1.50	3.00
❑11, Feb 95,polybagged with trading card	2.95	0.60	1.50	3.00
❑12, Mar 95, 1: Passion,cover date Feb 95	2.95	0.60	1.50	3.00
❑13, Apr 95	2.95	0.60	1.50	3.00
❑14	2.95	0.60	1.50	3.00
❑14/A,Vampirella sitting, man at top	—	0.60	1.50	3.00
❑15, Jun 95	2.95	0.60	1.50	3.00
❑15/A,Back-to-back with man holding gun	—	0.60	1.50	3.00
❑16	2.95	0.60	1.50	3.00
❑16/A,Vampirella springing, fingernails outstretched	—	0.60	1.50	3.00
❑17	2.95	0.60	1.50	3.00
❑17/A,Woman with sword at right swinging at Vampirella	—	0.60	1.50	3.00
❑18	2.95	0.60	1.50	3.00
❑18/A,Vampirella against purple-red background	—	0.60	1.50	3.00
❑19	2.95	0.60	1.50	3.00
❑19/A,Vampirella holding heart	—	0.60	1.50	3.00
❑20	2.95	0.60	1.50	3.00
❑21	2.95	0.60	1.50	3.00
❑22	2.95	0.60	1.50	3.00
❑23, Strange Days Coming	2.95	0.60	1.50	3.00
❑24, Hell in a Handbasket	2.95	0.60	1.50	3.00
❑25, Apr 96, The End,cardstock cover with red foil; Final Issue	2.95	0.60	1.50	3.00
❑25/A,Vampirella with candles on cover	—	0.60	1.50	3.00
❑25/Ash, Mar 95,Preview Ashcan	—	1.00	2.50	5.00
❑25/B,Blue foil on cover	—	1.00	2.50	5.00
❑25/GO,Gold logo	—	1.00	2.50	5.00
❑25/PL,Platinum logo	—	1.20	3.00	6.00

VENGEFUL SKYE, THE
DAVDEZ

Value: Cover or less

- ❑1, Sum 98 ... 2.95

VENGER ROBO
VIZ

Value: Cover or less

- ❑1 ... 2.75
- ❑2 ... 2.75
- ❑3 ... 2.75
- ❑4 ... 2.75
- ❑5 ... 2.75
- ❑6 ... 2.75
- ❑7 ... 2.75

VENOM: ALONG CAME A SPIDER
MARVEL

Value: Cover or less

- ❑1, Jan 96 ... 2.95
- ❑2, Feb 96 ... 2.95
- ❑3, Mar 96 ... 2.95
- ❑4, Apr 96 ... 2.95

VENOM: CARNAGE UNLEASHED
MARVEL

Value: Cover or less

- ❑1, Apr 95,cardstock cover ... 2.95
- ❑2, May 95,cardstock cover ... 2.95
- ❑3, Jun 95,cardstock cover ... 2.95
- ❑4, Jul 95,cardstock cover ... 2.95

VENOM: DEATHTRAP-THE VAULT
MARVEL

Value: Cover or less

- ❑1, D: Trap: the Vault), nn; one-shot (also published as Avengers ... 6.95

VENOM: FINALE
MARVEL

	ORIG	GOOD	FINE	N-MINT
❑1, Nov 97, The Spider Stratagem, gatefold summary	1.99	0.40	1.00	2.00
❑2, Dec 97, V: Spider-Man, gatefold summary	1.99	0.40	1.00	2.00
❑3, Jan 98, V: Spider-Man, gatefold summary	1.99	0.40	1.00	2.00

VENOM: FUNERAL PYRE
MARVEL

Value: Cover or less

- ❑1, Aug 93, A: Punisher,foil cover ... 2.95
- ❑2, Sep 93 ... 2.95
- ❑3, Oct 93, A: Pyre; A: Punisher ... 2.95

VENOM: LETHAL PROTECTOR
MARVEL

	ORIG	GOOD	FINE	N-MINT
❑1, Feb 93,Metallic ink cover	2.95	0.60	1.50	3.00
❑1/A, Feb 93,black cover	2.95	15.00	37.50	75.00
❑1/GO, Feb 93, Gold edition	—	1.00	2.50	5.00
❑2, Mar 93	2.95	0.60	1.50	3.00
❑3, Apr 93	2.95	0.60	1.50	3.00
❑4, May 93, A: Spider-Man	2.95	0.60	1.50	3.00
❑5, Jun 93, A: Spider-Man	2.95	0.60	1.50	3.00
❑6, Jul 93, A: Spider-Man	2.95	0.60	1.50	3.00

VENOM: LICENSE TO KILL
MARVEL

	ORIG	GOOD	FINE	N-MINT
❑1, Jun 97, Dr. Yes!	1.99	0.40	1.00	2.00
❑2, Jul 97	1.99	0.40	1.00	2.00
❑3, Aug 97, gatefold summary	1.99	0.40	1.00	2.00

VENOM: NIGHTS OF VENGEANCE
MARVEL

Value: Cover or less

- ❑1, Aug 94,red foil cover ... 2.95
- ❑2, Sep 94,cardstock cover ... 2.95
- ❑3, Oct 94,cardstock cover ... 2.95
- ❑4, Nov 94,cardstock cover ... 2.95

VENOM: ON TRIAL
MARVEL

	ORIG	GOOD	FINE	N-MINT
❑1, Mar 97, A: Spider-Man; A: Daredevil	1.99	0.40	1.00	2.00
❑2, Apr 97, Disorder in the Court!, A: Spider-Man; A: Daredevil	1.99	0.40	1.00	2.00
❑3, May 97, Trial and Error!, A: Spider-Man; A: Carnage; A: Daredevil	1.99	0.40	1.00	2.00

VENOM: SEED OF DARKNESS
MARVEL

	ORIG	GOOD	FINE	N-MINT
❑-1, Jul 97,Flashback	1.95	0.40	1.00	2.00

VENOM: SEPARATION ANXIETY
MARVEL

Value: Cover or less

- ❑1, Dec 94, Apart,Embossed cover ... 2.95
- ❑2, Jan 95 ... 2.95
- ❑3, Feb 95 ... 2.95
- ❑4, Mar 95 ... 2.95

VENOM: SIGN OF THE BOSS
MARVEL

	ORIG	GOOD	FINE	N-MINT
❑1, Sep 97, gatefold summary	1.99	0.40	1.00	2.00
❑2, Oct 97, gatefold summary	1.99	0.40	1.00	2.00

VENOM: SINNER TAKES ALL
MARVEL

Value: Cover or less

- ❑1, Aug 95, Venom: Sinner Takes All, Part 1; The Jury: Trial Run, Part 1, 1: Sin-Eater III ... 2.95
- ❑2, Sep 95, Venom: Sinner Takes All, Part 2; The Jury: Trial Run, Part 2 ... 2.95
- ❑3, Oct 95, Venom: Sinner Takes All, Part 3; The Jury: Trial Run, Part 3 ... 2.95
- ❑4, Nov 95, Venom: Sinner Takes All, Part 4; The Jury: Trial Run, Part 4 ... 2.95
- ❑5, Dec 95, Venom: Sinner Takes All, Part 4; The Jury: Trial Run, Part 5 ... 2.95

VENOM SUPER SPECIAL
MARVEL

Value: Cover or less

- ❑1, Aug 95, Flip-book; two of the stories continue in Spectacular Spider-Man Super Special #1 ... 3.95

VENOM: THE ENEMY WITHIN
MARVEL

Value: Cover or less

- ❑1, Feb 94,Glow-in-the-dark cover ... 2.95
- ❑2, Mar 94 ... 2.95
- ❑3, Apr 94 ... 2.95

VENOM: THE HUNGER
MARVEL

	ORIG	GOOD	FINE	N-MINT
❑1, Aug 96	1.95	0.40	1.00	2.00
❑2, Sep 96	1.95	0.40	1.00	2.00
❑3, Oct 96	1.95	0.40	1.00	2.00
❑4, Nov 96	1.95	0.40	1.00	2.00

VENOM: THE HUNTED
MARVEL

Value: Cover or less

- ❑1, May 96 ... 2.95
- ❑2, Jun 96 ... 2.95
- ❑3, Jul 96 ... 2.95

VENOM: THE MACE
MARVEL

Value: Cover or less

- ❑1, May 94 ... 2.95
- ❑2, Jun 94 ... 2.95
- ❑3, Jul 94 ... 2.95

VENOM: THE MADNESS
MARVEL

Value: Cover or less

- ❑1, Nov 93, V: Juggernaut,Embossed cover ... 2.95
- ❑2, Dec 93, V: Juggernaut ... 2.95
- ❑3, Jan 94, V: Juggernaut ... 2.95

VENOM: TOOTH AND CLAW
MARVEL

	ORIG	GOOD	FINE	N-MINT
❑1, Nov 96, Into the Jaws of Death, V: Wolverine	1.99	0.40	1.00	2.00
❑2, Dec 96, V: Wolverine	1.99	0.40	1.00	2.00
❑3, Jan 97, V: Wolverine,Final Issue	1.99	0.40	1.00	2.00

VENTURE
AC

Value: Cover or less

- ❑1 ... 1.75
- ❑2 ... 1.75
- ❑3 ... 1.75

VENTURE SAN DIEGO COMIC-CON SPECIAL EDITION
Venture
Value: Cover or less

Issue	Price
❑1, Jul 94, b&w	2.50

VENUMB
Parody Press
Value: Cover or less

Issue	Price
❑1, b&w	2.50

VENUS DOMINA
Verotik
Value: Cover or less

Issue	Price
❑1	4.95
❑2	4.95
❑3, Mar 97	4.95

VENUS INTERFACE, THE (HEAVY METAL'S...)
HM Communications

Issue	ORIG	GOOD	FINE	N-MINT
❑1	4.50	1.20	3.00	6.00

VENUS WARS, THE
Dark Horse
Value: Cover or less

Issue	Price
❑1, Apr 91, 1: Ken Seno, b&w; Japanese; trading cards	2.25
❑2, b&w; Japanese; trading cards	2.25
❑3, b&w; Japanese; trading cards	2.25
❑4	2.25
❑5	2.25
❑6	2.25
❑7	2.50
❑8	2.25
❑9	2.25
❑10	2.50
❑11	2.50
❑12	2.75
❑13	2.25
❑14	2.25

VENUS WARS II, THE
Dark Horse

Issue	ORIG	GOOD	FINE	N-MINT
❑1, Jun 92	2.50	0.50	1.25	2.50
❑2, Jul 92	2.50	0.50	1.25	2.50
❑3, Aug 92	2.50	0.50	1.25	2.50
❑4, Sep 92	2.50	0.50	1.25	2.50
❑5, Oct 92, b&w	2.25	0.50	1.25	2.50
❑6, Nov 92, b&w	2.25	0.50	1.25	2.50
❑7, Dec 92, b&w	2.25	0.50	1.25	2.50
❑8, Jan 93, b&w	2.75	0.50	1.25	2.50
❑9, Feb 93, b&w	2.95	0.50	1.25	2.50
❑10, Mar 93, b&w	2.95	0.50	1.25	2.50
❑11, Apr 93, b&w	2.95	0.59	1.48	2.95
❑12, May 93, b&w	2.95	0.59	1.48	2.95
❑13, Jun 93	2.50	0.59	1.48	2.95
❑14, Jul 93	2.50	0.59	1.48	2.95
❑15, Aug 93	2.50	0.59	1.48	2.95

VERBATIM
Fantagraphics
Value: Cover or less

Issue	Price
❑1, Apr 93, b&w	2.75
❑2, b&w	2.75

VERDICT, THE
Eternity
Value: Cover or less

Issue	Price
❑1, HC (c)	1.95
❑2	1.95
❑3	1.95
❑4	1.95

VERMILLION
DC
Value: Cover or less

Issue	Price
❑1, Oct 96, Starlight Drive, Part 1	2.25
❑2, Nov 96, Starlight Drive, Part 2	2.25
❑3, Dec 96, Starlight Drive, Part 3	2.25
❑4, Jan 97, Starlight Drive, Part 4	2.25
❑5, Feb 97, Starlight Drive, Part 5	2.25
❑6, Mar 97, Starlight Drive, Part 6	2.25
❑7, Apr 97	2.25
❑8, May 97	2.25
❑9, Jun 97	2.25
❑10, Jul 97	2.25
❑11, Aug 97	2.25
❑12, Sep 97	2.25

VERONICA
Archie

Issue	ORIG	GOOD	FINE	N-MINT
❑1, Apr 89	0.75	0.40	1.00	2.00
❑2	0.75	0.30	0.75	1.50
❑3	0.95	0.30	0.75	1.50
❑4	0.95	0.30	0.75	1.50
❑5	0.95	0.30	0.75	1.50
❑6	—	0.30	0.75	1.50
❑7	—	0.30	0.75	1.50
❑8	—	0.30	0.75	1.50
❑9	—	0.30	0.75	1.50
❑10	—	0.30	0.75	1.50
❑11	—	0.30	0.75	1.50
❑12	—	0.30	0.75	1.50
❑13	—	0.30	0.75	1.50
❑14	—	0.30	0.75	1.50
❑15	—	0.30	0.75	1.50
❑16	—	0.30	0.75	1.50
❑17	1.00	0.30	0.75	1.50
❑18	1.00	0.30	0.75	1.50
❑19	1.00	0.30	0.75	1.50
❑20	1.00	0.30	0.75	1.50
❑21	1.25	0.25	0.63	1.25
❑22	1.25	0.25	0.63	1.25
❑23	1.25	0.25	0.63	1.25

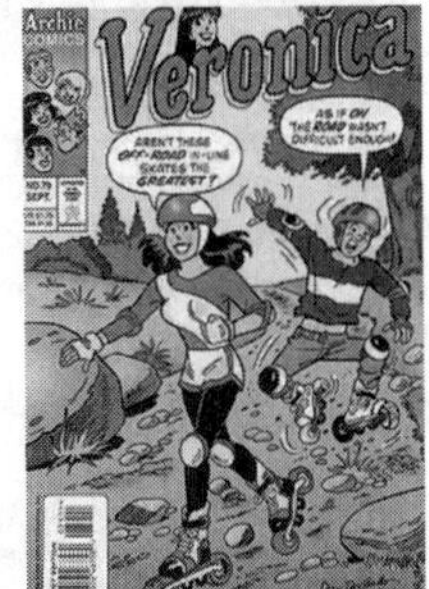

Both of Archie's girlfriends have had their own series for several years.

© 1998 Archie Comic Publications

Issue	ORIG	GOOD	FINE	N-MINT
❑24	1.25	0.25	0.63	1.25
❑25	1.25	0.25	0.63	1.25
❑26	1.25	0.25	0.63	1.25
❑27, Apr 93	1.25	0.25	0.63	1.25
❑28, Jun 93, The Genie is a Teen-i.e.; Mr. Lodge: Jest Request	1.25	0.25	0.63	1.25
❑29, Aug 93	1.25	0.25	0.63	1.25
❑30, Sep 93	1.25	0.25	0.63	1.25
❑31, Oct 93	1.25	0.25	0.63	1.25
❑32, Dec 93	1.25	0.25	0.63	1.25
❑33, Feb 94	1.25	0.25	0.63	1.25
❑34, Apr 94	1.25	0.25	0.63	1.25
❑35, Jun 94	1.25	0.25	0.63	1.25
❑36, Aug 94	1.50	0.30	0.75	1.50
❑37, Sep 94	1.50	0.30	0.75	1.50
❑38, Oct 94	1.50	0.30	0.75	1.50
❑39, Dec 94, Love Showdown, Part 4	1.50	0.30	0.75	1.50
❑40, Jan 95	1.50	0.30	0.75	1.50
❑41, Mar 95	1.50	0.30	0.75	1.50
❑42, Apr 95	1.50	0.30	0.75	1.50
❑43, Jun 95	1.50	0.30	0.75	1.50
❑44, Jul 95	1.50	0.30	0.75	1.50
❑45, Aug 95	1.50	0.30	0.75	1.50
❑46, Sep 95	1.50	0.30	0.75	1.50
❑47, Oct 95	1.50	0.30	0.75	1.50
❑48, Nov 95	1.50	0.30	0.75	1.50
❑49, Jan 96	1.50	0.30	0.75	1.50
❑50, Feb 96	1.50	0.30	0.75	1.50
❑51, Apr 96	1.50	0.30	0.75	1.50
❑52, Jun 96	1.50	0.30	0.75	1.50
❑53, Jul 96	1.50	0.30	0.75	1.50
❑54, Aug 96	1.50	0.30	0.75	1.50
❑55, Sep 96	1.50	0.30	0.75	1.50
❑56, Oct 96	1.50	0.30	0.75	1.50
❑57, Nov 96	1.50	0.30	0.75	1.50
❑58, Future Shock; Tooth-Fully Speaking...	1.50	0.30	0.75	1.50
❑59, Jan 97	1.50	0.30	0.75	1.50
❑60, Feb 97	1.50	0.30	0.75	1.50
❑61, Mar 97	1.50	0.30	0.75	1.50
❑62, Apr 97	1.50	0.30	0.75	1.50
❑63, May 97	1.50	0.30	0.75	1.50
❑64, Jun 97	1.50	0.30	0.75	1.50
❑65, Jul 97	1.50	0.30	0.75	1.50
❑66, Aug 97	1.50	0.30	0.75	1.50
❑67, Sep 97	1.50	0.30	0.75	1.50
❑68, Oct 97	1.50	0.30	0.75	1.50
❑69, Nov 97	1.50	0.30	0.75	1.50
❑70, Dec 97	1.50	0.30	0.75	1.50
❑71, Jan 98	1.75	0.30	0.75	1.50
❑72, Feb 98	1.75	0.30	0.75	1.50
❑73, Mar 98	1.75	0.30	0.75	1.50
❑74, Apr 98, Veronica markets Jughead's beanie	1.75	0.30	0.75	1.50
❑75, May 98	1.75	0.30	0.75	1.50
❑76, Jun 98	1.75	0.30	0.75	1.50
❑77, Jul 98	1.75	0.30	0.75	1.50
❑78, Aug 98	1.75	0.30	0.75	1.50
❑79, Sep 98, Shop Around the World; All Washed Up!	1.75	0.35	0.88	1.75
❑80, Oct 98	1.75	0.35	0.88	1.75
❑81, Nov 98, Another Brilliant Idea, Veronica in Oz	1.75	0.35	0.88	1.75
❑82, Dec 98	1.75	0.35	0.88	1.75
❑83, Jan 99	1.75	0.35	0.88	1.75
❑84, Feb 99	1.75	0.35	0.88	1.75
❑85, Mar 99	1.75	0.35	0.88	1.75
❑86, Apr 99, Dressed to Chill	1.79	0.36	0.89	1.79
❑87, May 99, Flash in the Pan	1.79	0.36	0.89	1.79
❑88, Jun 99	1.79	0.36	0.89	1.79
❑89, Jul 99	1.79	0.36	0.89	1.79
❑90, Aug 99	1.79	0.36	0.89	1.79
❑91, Aug 99	1.79	0.36	0.89	1.79
❑92, Oct 99	1.79	0.36	0.89	1.79
❑93, Nov 99	1.79	0.36	0.89	1.79

	ORIG	GOOD	FINE	N-MINT
❑94, Dec 99	1.79	0.36	0.89	1.79
❑95, Jan 00	1.79	0.36	0.89	1.79
❑96, Feb 00	1.79	0.36	0.89	1.79
❑97, Mar 00	1.79	0.36	0.89	1.79
❑98, Apr 00	1.79	0.36	0.89	1.79
❑99, May 00	1.99	0.40	1.00	1.99
❑100, Jun 00	1.99	0.40	1.00	1.99
❑101, Jul 00	1.99	0.40	1.00	1.99
❑102, Aug 00	1.99	0.40	1.00	1.99
❑103, Sep 00	1.99	0.40	1.00	1.99
❑104, Oct 00	1.99	0.40	1.00	1.99
❑105, Nov 00	1.99	0.40	1.00	1.99
❑106, Dec 00	1.99	0.40	1.00	1.99
❑107, Jan 01	1.99	0.40	1.00	1.99
❑108, Feb 01	1.99	0.40	1.00	1.99
❑109, Mar 01	1.99	0.40	1.00	1.99
❑110, Apr 01	1.99	0.40	1.00	1.99
❑111	1.99	0.40	1.00	1.99
❑112	1.99	0.40	1.00	1.99
❑113	1.99	0.40	1.00	1.99
❑114	1.99	0.40	1.00	1.99
❑115	1.99	0.40	1.00	1.99
❑116	1.99	0.40	1.00	1.99
❑117	1.99	0.40	1.00	1.99

VERONICA'S DIGEST MAGAZINE
ARCHIE

	ORIG	GOOD	FINE	N-MINT
❑1	1.75	0.40	1.00	2.00
❑2	1.75	0.35	0.88	1.75
❑3	1.75	0.35	0.88	1.75
❑4, Sep 95	1.75	0.35	0.88	1.75
❑5, Sep 96	1.75	0.35	0.88	1.75
❑6, Oct 97	1.79	0.36	0.89	1.79

VEROTIKA
VEROTIK

	ORIG	GOOD	FINE	N-MINT
❑1,adult	2.95	0.80	2.00	4.00
❑2, Jan 95,adult	2.95	0.60	1.50	3.00
❑3,adult	2.95	0.60	1.50	3.00
❑4,adult	2.95	0.60	1.50	3.00
❑5,adult	2.95	0.60	1.50	3.00
❑6,adult	2.95	0.60	1.50	3.00
❑7,adult	2.95	0.60	1.50	3.00
❑8, Feb 96, Grub-Girl; Rococco,adult	2.95	0.60	1.50	3.00
❑9,adult	2.95	0.60	1.50	3.00
❑10,adult	2.95	0.60	1.50	3.00
❑11,adult	2.95	0.60	1.50	3.00
❑12,adult	2.95	0.60	1.50	3.00
❑13,adult	2.95	0.60	1.50	3.00
❑14,adult	2.95	0.60	1.50	3.00
❑15,adult	3.95	0.79	1.98	3.95

VEROTIK ILLUSTRATED
VEROTIK

Value: Cover or less

❑1, Aug 97 .... 6.95
❑2, Dec 97 .... 6.95
❑3, Apr 98 .... 6.95

VEROTIK ROGUES GALLERY OF VILLAINS
VEROTIK

Value: Cover or less

❑1, Nov 97, nn; adult; pin-ups 3.95

VERSION
DARK HORSE

Value: Cover or less

❑1.1 .... 2.50
❑1.2 .... 2.50
❑1.3 .... 2.50
❑1.4 .... 2.50
❑1.5 .... 2.50
❑1.6 .... 2.50
❑1.7 .... 2.50
❑1.8 .... 2.50
❑2.1 .... 2.95
❑2.2 .... 2.95
❑2.3 .... 2.95
❑2.4 .... 2.95
❑2.5 .... 2.95
❑2.6 .... 2.95
❑2.7 .... 2.95

VERTIGO GALLERY, THE: DREAMS AND NIGHTMARES
DC

	ORIG	GOOD	FINE	N-MINT
❑1,pin-ups	3.50	0.80	2.00	4.00

VERTIGO JAM
DC

Value: Cover or less

❑1, Aug 93 .... 3.95

VERTIGO PREVIEW
VERTIGO

	ORIG	GOOD	FINE	N-MINT
❑1, new Sandman story; Previews DC Vertigo titles	0.75	0.30	0.75	1.50

VERTIGO RAVE
DC

	ORIG	GOOD	FINE	N-MINT
❑1, Aut 94, previews of Vertigo line, plus new Books of Magic story	0.99	0.30	0.75	1.50

VERTIGO SECRET FILES & ORIGINS: SWAMP THING
VERTIGO

Value: Cover or less

❑1, Nov 00, Bitter Fruit: How TefT's Adventures Began; The DDI Secret Files 4.95

VERTIGO VERITÉ: THE UNSEEN HAND
VERTIGO

Value: Cover or less

❑1, Sep 96 .... 2.50
❑2, Oct 96, Ruin, Rape, and Rock 'n' Roll 2.50
❑3, Nov 96, Moscow Underground 2.50
❑4, Dec 96, Hand's Up 2.50

VERTIGO VISIONS: DOCTOR OCCULT
DC

Value: Cover or less

❑1, Jul 94,One-Shot 3.95

VERTIGO VISIONS: DR. THIRTEEN
DC

Value: Cover or less

❑1, Sep 98, Do Als Dream of Electric Sleep?,One-Shot 5.95

VERTIGO VISIONS: PREZ
DC

Value: Cover or less

❑1, Sep 95, ES, Smells Like Teen President,One-Shot 3.95

VERTIGO VISIONS: THE GEEK
DC

Value: Cover or less

❑1 .... 3.95

VERTIGO VISIONS: THE PHANTOM STRANGER
DC

Value: Cover or less

❑1, Oct 93 .... 3.50

VERTIGO VISIONS: TOMAHAWK
DC

Value: Cover or less

❑1, Jul 98,One-Shot 4.95

VERTIGO VOICES: THE EATERS
VERTIGO

Value: Cover or less

❑1 .... 4.95

VERTIGO: WINTER'S EDGE
DC

Value: Cover or less

❑1, Jan 98, MW (w), House of Secrets; The Sandman: The Flowers,wraparound cover; prestige format anthology.... 7.95
❑2, Jan 99, The Minx: Stories; Death: Winter's Tale,wraparound cover; Anthology 6.95
❑3, Jan 00, DaG, DaG (w); JPH (w), The Sandman: Desire: How They Met Themselves; 100 Bullets: Silencer Night 6.95

VERY BEST OF DENNIS THE MENACE
MARVEL

	ORIG	GOOD	FINE	N-MINT
❑1	1.25	0.60	1.50	3.00
❑2	1.25	0.40	1.00	2.00
❑3, Aug 82	1.25	0.40	1.00	2.00

VERY MU CHRISTMAS, A
MU

Value: Cover or less

❑1, Nov 92, nn 2.95

VERY VICKY
ICONOGRAFIX

Value: Cover or less

❑1, b&w 2.95
❑1-2,2nd Printing 2.50
❑2, b&w 2.50
❑3, b&w 2.50
❑4, b&w 2.50
❑5, b&w 2.50
❑6, b&w 2.50
❑7, b&w 2.50
❑8, b&w 2.50

VESPERS
MARS MEDIA GROUP

Value: Cover or less

❑1, Aug 95 .... 2.50

VEXT
DC

Value: Cover or less

❑1, Mar 99, KG (w), In the Beginning, A: Zauriel; A: Superman; O: Vext 2.50
❑2, Apr 99, KG (w), 1: Road Rage 2.50
❑3, May 99, KG (w) 2.50
❑4, Jun 99, KG (w), Love Hurts!, A: Paramour 2.50
❑5, Jul 99, KG (w), Love Stinks! 2.50
❑6, Aug 99, KG (w) 2.50

V FOR VENDETTA
DC

	ORIG	GOOD	FINE	N-MINT
❑1, Sep 88, AMo (w), The Villain; The Voice	2.00	0.60	1.50	3.00
❑2, Oct 88, AMo (w)	2.00	0.50	1.25	2.50
❑3, Nov 88, AMo (w)	2.00	0.50	1.25	2.50
❑4, Dec 88	2.00	0.50	1.25	2.50
❑5, Win 88, AMo (w), A Vocational Viewpoint; The Vacation	2.00	0.50	1.25	2.50
❑6, Hol 88, AMo (w), Vengeance; Vicissitude	2.00	0.50	1.25	2.50
❑7, Jan 89, AMo (w)	2.00	0.50	1.25	2.50
❑8, Feb 89, AMo (w)	2.00	0.50	1.25	2.50
❑9, Mar 89, AMo (w)	2.00	0.50	1.25	2.50
❑10, May 89, AMo (w)	2.00	0.50	1.25	2.50

VIC & BLOOD
MAD DOG

Value: Cover or less

❑1, Oct 87, b&w 2.00
❑2, Feb 88, b&w 2.00

VICIOUS
BRAINSTORM

Value: Cover or less

❑1, b&w; adult 2.95

	ORIG	GOOD	FINE	N-MINT

VICKI
ATLAS

	ORIG	GOOD	FINE	N-MINT
❑1,reprints Tippy Teen	—	4.00	10.00	20.00
❑2,reprints Tippy Teen	—	2.80	7.00	14.00
❑3,reprints Tippy Teen	—	2.00	5.00	10.00
❑4,reprints Tippy Teen	—	2.00	5.00	10.00

VICKI VALENTINE
RENEGADE
Value: Cover or less

- ❑1, Jul 85, b&w 1.70
- ❑2, Nov 85, b&w 1.70
- ❑3, b&w 1.70
- ❑4, b&w 1.70

VICTIM
SILVERWOLF
Value: Cover or less

- ❑1, Feb 87, Deathborg II 1.50

VICTIMS
ETERNITY

	ORIG	GOOD	FINE	N-MINT
❑1, b&w; Reprint	1.95	0.40	1.00	2.00
❑2, b&w; Reprint	1.95	0.40	1.00	2.00
❑3, b&w; Reprint	1.95	0.40	1.00	2.00
❑4, Jan 89, b&w; Reprint	1.95	0.40	1.00	2.00
❑5, Feb 89, b&w; Reprint	1.95	0.40	1.00	2.00
❑6	1.95	0.40	1.00	2.00

VICTORIAN, THE
PENNY-FARTHING

	ORIG	GOOD	FINE	N-MINT
❑0.5, Aug 98,preview of upcoming series; Sketches and notes for series	1.00	0.20	0.50	1.00
❑1, Mar 99, Self-Realization, Part 1	2.95	0.60	1.50	3.00
❑2, Apr 99	2.95	0.59	1.48	2.95
❑3, May 99	2.95	0.59	1.48	2.95
❑4, Jun 99	2.95	0.59	1.48	2.95
❑5, Jul 99	2.95	0.59	1.48	2.95
❑6, Aug 99, Ain De Si...cle	2.95	0.59	1.48	2.95

VICTORY (TOPPS)
TOPPS
Value: Cover or less

- ❑1, Jun 94, KG, KB (w),First and final issue (series cancelled) 2.50

VIDEO CLASSICS
ETERNITY
Value: Cover or less

- ❑1, b&w; Mighty Mouse 3.50
- ❑2, b&w; Mighty Mouse 3.50

VIDEO HIROSHIMA
AEON
Value: Cover or less

- ❑1, Aug 95, nn; b&w; One-Shot 2.50

VIDEO JACK
MARVEL
Value: Cover or less

- ❑1, Sep 87, KG, KG (w), Pilot Error 1.25
- ❑2, Nov 87, KG, KG (w) 1.25
- ❑3, Mar 88, KG, KG (w) 1.25
- ❑4, May 88, KG, KG (w) 1.25
- ❑5, Jul 88, KG, KG (w) 1.25
- ❑6, Sep 88, This is Your Life & Death; Space Trek 1.25

VIETNAM JOURNAL
APPLE

	ORIG	GOOD	FINE	N-MINT
❑1, Nov 87, The Field Jacket, b&w	1.75	0.40	1.00	2.00
❑1-2,2nd Printing	1.75	0.40	1.00	2.00
❑2, Jan 88	1.75	0.40	1.00	2.00
❑3, Mar 88	1.75	0.40	1.00	2.00
❑4, May 88	1.75	0.40	1.00	2.00
❑5, Jul 88	1.75	0.40	1.00	2.00
❑6, Sep 88	1.95	0.40	1.00	2.00
❑7, Nov 88	1.95	0.40	1.00	2.00
❑8, Jan 89, To Face the Beast	1.95	0.40	1.00	2.00
❑9, Mar 89	1.95	0.40	1.00	2.00
❑10, May 89	1.95	0.40	1.00	2.00
❑11, Jul 89	2.25	0.45	1.13	2.25
❑12, Sep 89	2.25	0.45	1.13	2.25
❑13, Nov 89	2.25	0.45	1.13	2.25
❑14, Jan 90	2.25	0.45	1.13	2.25
❑15, Mar 90	2.25	0.45	1.13	2.25
❑16, May 90,Final Issue	2.25	0.45	1.13	2.25

VIETNAM JOURNAL: BLOODBATH AT KHE SANH
APPLE
Value: Cover or less

- ❑1, b&w 2.75
- ❑2, b&w 2.75
- ❑3, b&w 2.75
- ❑4, b&w 2.75

VIETNAM JOURNAL: TET '68
APPLE
Value: Cover or less

- ❑1, b&w 2.75
- ❑2, b&w 2.75
- ❑3, b&w 2.75
- ❑4, b&w 2.75
- ❑5, b&w 2.75
- ❑6, b&w 2.75

VIETNAM JOURNAL: VALLEY OF DEATH
APPLE
Value: Cover or less

- ❑1, Jun 94, b&w 2.75

Brother Power the Geek returned for one more adventure in *Vertigo Visions: The Geek.*

© 1994 DC Comics

	ORIG	GOOD	FINE	N-MINT

VIGILANTE, THE
DC
Value: Cover or less

- ❑1, Nov 83, DG; KP, A Fable For Our Times!, 1: Vigilante II (Adrian Chase) 1.25
- ❑2, Jan 84, KP 1.25
- ❑3, Feb 84, V: Cyborg 1.25
- ❑4, Mar 84, A: The Exterminator 1.25
- ❑5, Apr 84, 1: Cannon; 1: Saber 1.25
- ❑6, May 84, O: Vigilante II (Adrian Chase) 1.25
- ❑7, Jun 84, O: Vigilante II (Adrian Chase) 1.25
- ❑8, Jul 84 .... 1.25
- ❑9, Aug 84, D: J.J. Davis 1.25
- ❑10, Sep 84 .... 1.25
- ❑11, Oct 84 .... 1.25
- ❑12, Nov 84 .... 1.25
- ❑13, Dec 84 .... 1.25
- ❑14, Feb 85 .... 1.25
- ❑15, Mar 85 .... 1.25
- ❑16, Apr 85 .... 1.25
- ❑17, May 85, AMo (w) 1.25
- ❑18, Jun 85, AMo (w) 1.25
- ❑19, Jul 85 .... 1.25
- ❑20, Aug 85, A: Nightwing 1.25
- ❑21, Sep 85 .... 1.25
- ❑22, Oct 85,Crisis 1.25
- ❑23, Nov 85 .... 1.25
- ❑24, Dec 85 .... 1.50
- ❑25, Jan 86 .... 1.50
- ❑26, Feb 86 .... 1.50
- ❑27, Mar 86 .... 1.50
- ❑28, Apr 86 .... 1.50
- ❑29, May 86 .... 1.50
- ❑30, Jun 86 .... 1.50
- ❑31, Jul 86 .... 1.50
- ❑32, Aug 86 .... 1.50
- ❑33, Sep 86 .... 1.50
- ❑34, Oct 86 .... 1.50
- ❑35, Nov 86, O: Mad Bomber . 1.50
- ❑36, Dec 86, A: Peacemaker .. 1.50
- ❑37, Jan 87 .... 1.50
- ❑38, Feb 87 .... 1.50
- ❑39, Mar 87 .... 1.50
- ❑40, Apr 87 .... 1.50
- ❑41, May 87 .... 1.50
- ❑42, Jun 87, A: Peacemaker ... 1.50
- ❑43, Jul 87, A: Peacemaker 1.50
- ❑44, Aug 87 .... 1.50
- ❑45, Sep 87, 1: Blackthorn 1.50
- ❑46, Oct 87 .... 1.50
- ❑47, Nov 87, A: Batman 1.50
- ❑48, Dec 87 .... 1.50
- ❑49, Jan 88 .... 1.50
- ❑50, Feb 88, D: Vigilante II (Adrian Chase),Vigilante commits suicide 1.50
- ❑Anl 1 .... 2.00
- ❑Anl 2 .... 2.00

VIGILANTE 8: SECOND OFFENSE
CHAOS
Value: Cover or less

- ❑1, Dec 99 .... 2.95

VIGILANTE: CITY LIGHTS, PRAIRIE JUSTICE
DC
Value: Cover or less

- ❑1, Nov 95, JRo (w) 2.50
- ❑2, Dec 95, JRo (w) 2.50
- ❑3, Jan 96, JRo (w) 2.50
- ❑4, Feb 96, JRo (w) 2.50

VIGIL: BLOODLINE
DUALITY
Value: Cover or less

- ❑1, Baby Steps 2.95
- ❑2 .... 2.95
- ❑3, Slash ø Burn 2.95
- ❑4, Dirt 2.95
- ❑5, Nov 98, Desertion 2.95
- ❑6 .... 2.95
- ❑7 .... 2.95
- ❑8, Jul 99, Daddy's Little Girl .. 2.95

VIGIL: DESERT FOXES
MILLENNIUM
Value: Cover or less

- ❑1, Jul 95, b&w 3.95
- ❑2, Aug 95, b&w 3.95

VIGIL: ERUPTION
MILLENNIUM
Value: Cover or less

- ❑1, Aug 96, b&w 3.95
- ❑2 .... 2.95

VIGIL: FALL FROM GRACE
INNOVATION
Value: Cover or less

- ❑1, Mar 92, 1: Greg Tonelli; 1: Grace Kimble, b&w 2.95
- ❑2, b&w 2.95

VIGIL: KUKULKAN
INNOVATION
Value: Cover or less

- ❑1 .... 2.95

VIGIL: REBIRTH
MILLENNIUM
Value: Cover or less

- ❑1, Nov 94, O: Grace Kimble, b&w 3.95
- ❑2, Dec 94, O: Grace Kimble, b&w 3.95

VIGIL: SCATTERSHOTS
DUALITY PRESS
Value: Cover or less

- ❑1, Jul 97, b&w 3.95
- ❑2 .... 3.95

VIGIL: THE GOLDEN PARTS
INNOVATION

Value: Cover or less

❑1, b&w 2.95

VIGIL: VAMPORUM ANIMATURI
MILLENNIUM

Value: Cover or less

❑1, May 94, nn; b&w 3.95

VIGNETTE COMICS
HARRIER

Value: Cover or less

❑1, b&w 1.95

VILE
RAGING RHINO

Value: Cover or less

❑1 .... 2.95

VILLAINS & VIGILANTES
ECLIPSE

Value: Cover or less

❑1, Dec 86, A Charge of Mayhem, 1: Shadowman (Eclipse); 1: Condor 1.50
❑2, Mar 87 .... 1.50
❑3, Apr 87 .... 1.50
❑4, Apr 87 .... 1.50

VILLA OF THE MYSTERIES
FANTAGRAPHICS

Value: Cover or less

❑1, b&w 3.95
❑2, b&w 3.95
❑3, Jul 98, b&w 3.95

VINCENT J. MIELCAREK JR. MEMORIAL COMIC
COOPER UNION

Value: Cover or less

❑1, nn; b&w 3.00

VINTAGE COMIC CLASSICS
RECOLLECTIONS

	ORIG	GOOD	FINE	N-MINT
❑1, Feb 90,Red Demon reprint	—	0.40	1.00	2.00

VINTAGE MAGNUS ROBOT FIGHTER
VALIANT

	ORIG	GOOD	FINE	N-MINT
❑1, Jan 92, RM, RM (w), O: Magnus Robot Fighter,Reprint	1.95	0.40	1.00	2.00
❑2, Feb 92, RM, RM (w),Reprint	1.95	0.40	1.00	2.00
❑3, Mar 92, RM, RM (w),Reprint	1.95	0.40	1.00	2.00
❑4, Apr 92, RM, RM (w),Reprint	1.95	0.40	1.00	2.00

VIOLATOR
IMAGE

	ORIG	GOOD	FINE	N-MINT
❑1, May 94, AMo (w), 1: The Admonisher	1.95	0.50	1.25	2.50
❑2, Jun 94, AMo (w)	1.95	0.50	1.25	2.50
❑3, Jul 94, AMo (w)	1.95	0.50	1.25	2.50

VIOLATOR VS. BADROCK
IMAGE

Value: Cover or less

❑1, May 95, AMo (w) 2.50
❑1/A, May 95, AMo (w) 2.50
❑2, Jun 95, AMo (w) 2.50
❑3, Jul 95, AMo (w) 2.50
❑4, Aug 95, AMo (w) 2.50

VIOLENT CASES
TITAN

	ORIG	GOOD	FINE	N-MINT
❑1, NG (w)	4.95	3.00	7.50	15.00
❑1-2, NG (w),2nd Printing; In color, with new forward by Neil Gaiman	4.95	2.00	5.00	10.00
❑, NG (w),New cover (red) by Dave McKean; Kitchen Sink publishes	12.95	2.59	6.47	12.95

VIOLENT MESSIAHS
HURRICANE

Value: Cover or less

❑1, Jul 97, b&w 2.95
❑2 .... 2.95
❑3 .... 2.95

VIOLENT MESSIAHS (2ND SERIES)
IMAGE

Value: Cover or less

❑1, Jun 00 .... 2.95
❑2, Aug 00 .... 2.95
❑3, Sep 00 .... 2.95
❑4, Nov 00 .... 2.95
❑5, Jan 01 .... 2.95

VIOLENT TALES
DEATH

Value: Cover or less

❑1, Nov 97, b&w 2.95

VIPER
DC

Value: Cover or less

❑1, Aug 94 .... 1.95
❑2, Sep 94 .... 1.95
❑3, Oct 94 .... 1.95
❑4, Nov 94 .... 1.95

VIRTEX
OKTOMICA

	ORIG	GOOD	FINE	N-MINT
❑0, Oct 98	1.50	0.30	0.75	1.50
❑1, Dec 98, Divine Intervention, Part 1	2.50	0.50	1.25	2.50
❑2, Jan 99, Divine Intervention, Part 2	2.50	0.50	1.25	2.50
❑3, Divine Intervention, Part 3	2.50	0.50	1.25	2.50
❑Ash 1	—	0.20	0.50	1.00

VIRTUA FIGHTER
MARVEL

Value: Cover or less

❑1, Aug 95 .... 2.95

VIRTUAL BANG
IRONCAT

Value: Cover or less

❑1 .... 2.95
❑2 .... 2.95

VIRUS
DARK HORSE

Value: Cover or less

❑1 .... 2.50
❑2 .... 2.50
❑3 .... 2.50
❑4 .... 2.50

VISAGE SPECIAL EDITION
ILLUSION STUDIOS

	ORIG	GOOD	FINE	N-MINT
❑1, Aug 96, b&w	1.95	0.40	1.00	2.00

VISION, THE
MARVEL

Value: Cover or less

❑1, Nov 94, Dreams and Madmen 1.75
❑2, Dec 94 .... 1.75
❑3, Jan 95, Visionary Dreams 1.75
❑4, Feb 95 .... 1.75

VISION & SCARLET WITCH (VOL. 1)
MARVEL

	ORIG	GOOD	FINE	N-MINT
❑1, Nov 82	0.60	0.30	0.75	1.50
❑2, Dec 82, A: Whizzer	0.60	0.30	0.75	1.50
❑3, Jan 83, A: Wonder Man	0.60	0.30	0.75	1.50
❑4, Feb 83, A: Magneto	0.60	0.30	0.75	1.50

VISION & SCARLET WITCH (VOL. 2)
MARVEL

	ORIG	GOOD	FINE	N-MINT
❑1, Oct 85	1.25	0.30	0.75	1.50
❑2, Nov 85, D: Whizzer	0.75	0.25	0.63	1.25
❑3, Dec 85	0.75	0.25	0.63	1.25
❑4, Jan 86	0.75	0.25	0.63	1.25
❑5, Feb 86	0.75	0.25	0.63	1.25
❑6, Mar 86	0.75	0.25	0.63	1.25
❑7, Apr 86	0.75	0.25	0.63	1.25
❑8, May 86	0.75	0.25	0.63	1.25
❑9, Jun 86	0.75	0.25	0.63	1.25
❑10, Jul 86	0.75	0.25	0.63	1.25
❑11, Aug 86, A: Spider-Man	0.75	0.25	0.63	1.25
❑12, Sep 86	1.25	0.25	0.63	1.25

VISIONARIES
MARVEL

Value: Cover or less

❑1, Jan 88 .... 1.50
❑2, Feb 88 .... 1.00
❑3, Mar 88 .... 1.00
❑4, Apr 88 .... 1.00
❑5, May 88 .... 1.00
❑6, Jun 88 .... 1.00

VISIONS
CALIBER

Value: Cover or less

❑1 .... 4.95

VISIONS: DAVID MACK
CALIBER

Value: Cover or less

❑1 .... 5.95

VISIONS OF CURVES
FANTAGRAPHICS

Value: Cover or less

❑1, Apr 94, b&w 4.95
❑2 .... 4.95
❑3, May 95,Sketchbook 4.95

VISIONS: R.G. TAYLOR
CALIBER

Value: Cover or less

❑1, nn; b&w 2.50

VISITATIONS
IMAGE

Value: Cover or less

❑1, nn; b&w; squarebound 6.95

VISITOR, THE
VALIANT

Value: Cover or less

❑1, Apr 95, Layers Upon Layers 2.50
❑2, May 95, V: Harbinger 2.50
❑3, Jun 95,Acclaim begins publishing 2.50
❑4, Jul 95 .... 2.50
❑5, Jul 95 .... 2.50
❑6, Aug 95 .... 2.50
❑7, Aug 95 .... 2.50
❑8, Sep 95,The Harbinger's identity is revealed 2.50
❑9, Sep 95 .... 2.50
❑10, Oct 95 .... 2.50
❑11, Oct 95 .... 2.50
❑12, Nov 95 .... 2.50
❑13, Nov 95 .... 2.50

VISITOR VS. THE VALIANT UNIVERSE, THE
VALIANT

Value: Cover or less

❑1, Feb 95, A Stranger in a Strange Land,cardstock cover 2.95
❑2, Mar 95,cardstock cover 2.95

VISUAL ASSAULT OMNIBUS
VISUAL ASSAULT

Value: Cover or less

❑1, b&w 2.50
❑2, b&w 2.50
❑3, b&w; Flip-book 3.00

VIXEN 9
SAMSON

Value: Cover or less

❑1, Flip-book; no indicia 2.50

VIXEN WARRIOR DIARIES
RAGING RHINO

Value: Cover or less

❑1, b&w; adult 2.95

VIXEN WARS: VENGEANCE MANIFESTO
RAGING RHINO

Value: Cover or less

❑1, b&w; adult 2.95
❑2, b&w; adult 2.95
❑3, b&w; adult 2.95
❑4, b&w; adult 2.95
❑5, b&w; adult 2.95

VIXEN WARS, WAR WITHOUT WALLS, THE
RAGING RHINO

Value: Cover or less

- ❑1 ... 2.95
- ❑2 ... 2.95
- ❑3, War Without Walls ... 2.95

VOGUE
IMAGE

Value: Cover or less

- ❑1, Oct 95 ... 2.50
- ❑1/A, Oct 95,alternate cover ... 2.50
- ❑2, Nov 95 ... 2.50
- ❑3, Dec 95 ... 2.50
- ❑4 ... 2.50

VOID INDIGO
MARVEL

	ORIG	GOOD	FINE	N-MINT
❑1,Continued from Marvel Graphic Novel	1.50	0.40	1.00	2.00
❑2	1.50	0.40	1.00	2.00

VOLCANIC NIGHTS
PALLIARD

Value: Cover or less

- ❑1, b&w; adult ... 2.95

VOLCANIC REVOLVER
ONI

Value: Cover or less

- ❑1, Jan 99, b&w ... 2.95
- ❑2, Jan 99, b&w ... 2.95
- ❑3, Mar 99, b&w ... 2.95

VOLTRON
SOLSON

	ORIG	GOOD	FINE	N-MINT
❑1	0.75	0.20	0.50	1.00
❑2	0.75	0.20	0.50	1.00
❑3	0.75	0.20	0.50	1.00

VOLUNTEER COMICS SUMMER LINE-UP '96
VOLUNTEER

Value: Cover or less

- ❑1, Sum 96, nn; b&w; previews ... 2.95

VOLUNTEERS QUEST FOR DREAMS LOST
LITERACY

Value: Cover or less

- ❑1, b&w; Turtles; Trollords ... 2.00

VON FANGE BROTHERS-GREEN HAIR AND RED "S'S", THE
MIKEY-SIZED COMICS

Value: Cover or less

- ❑1, Jul 96, nn; b&w ... 1.75

VON FANGE BROTHERS-THE UNCOMMONS, THE
MIKEY-SIZED COMICS

Value: Cover or less

- ❑1, Oct 96, nn; b&w ... 1.75

VONPYRE
EYEFUL

Value: Cover or less

- ❑1, VonPyre; The Lindy Jax and the Old Tin Box ... 2.95

VOODOO (IMAGE)
IMAGE

Value: Cover or less

- ❑1, Nov 97, AMo (w), Legba ... 2.50
- ❑2, Dec 97, AMo (w), Erzulie ... 2.50
- ❑3, Jan 98, AMo (w), Samedi ... 2.50
- ❑4, Mar 98, AMo (w), Damballa ... 2.50

VOODOO INK
DEJA-VU

Value: Cover or less

- ❑0, b&w ... 1.95
- ❑1, b&w ... 1.95
- ❑2, b&w ... 1.95
- ❑3, b&w ... 1.95
- ❑4, b&w ... 1.95
- ❑5, b&w ... 1.95

VOODOOM
ONI

Value: Cover or less

- ❑1, Jun 00, nn; b&w; smaller than regular comic book ... 4.95

VOODOO•ZEALOT: SKIN TRADE
IMAGE

Value: Cover or less

- ❑1, Aug 95, nn; One-Shot ... 4.95

VORTEX (COMICO)
COMICO

Value: Cover or less

- ❑1 ... 2.50
- ❑2 ... 2.50
- ❑3,Exists? ... 2.50
- ❑4,Exists? ... 2.50

VORTEX (ENTITY)
ENTITY

Value: Cover or less

- ❑1, Jan 96 ... 2.95

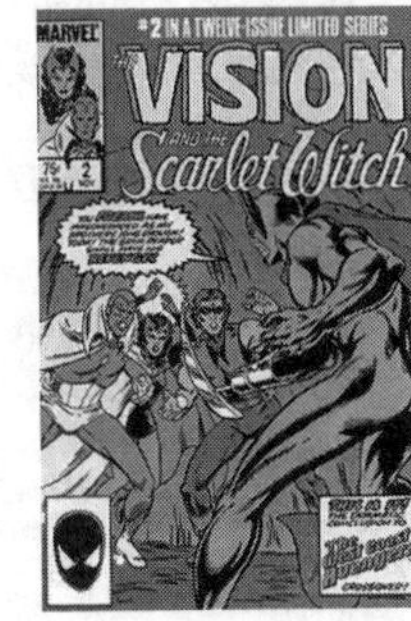

Golden Age hero The Whizzer breathed his last in *Vision & Scarlet Witch* (Vol. 2) #2.

VORTEX (HALL OF HEROES)
HALL OF HEROES

Value: Cover or less

- ❑1, b&w ... 2.50
- ❑2 ... 2.50
- ❑3, Dec 93, Run for Cover ... 2.50
- ❑4, Feb 94, Drx Kilbourne ... 2.50
- ❑5, Apr 94, Into The Dark ... 2.50
- ❑6, Dec 94, Machine Gun Messiah ... 2.50

VORTEX (VORTEX)
VORTEX

	ORIG	GOOD	FINE	N-MINT
❑1, Nov 82, In the Lion's Den; Trip to Glory	1.75	0.40	1.00	2.00
❑2	1.75	0.40	1.00	2.00
❑3, May 83, The Magus; Fantastic Fear	1.95	0.40	1.00	2.00
❑4	1.75	0.40	1.00	2.00
❑5	1.75	0.40	1.00	2.00
❑6, The Studio; Public Interest	1.75	0.40	1.00	2.00
❑7	1.75	0.40	1.00	2.00
❑8	1.75	0.40	1.00	2.00
❑9	1.75	0.40	1.00	2.00
❑10, Sep 84, Elderberry Down; New Ruins for Old	1.75	0.40	1.00	2.00
❑11	1.75	0.35	0.88	1.75
❑12	1.75	0.35	0.88	1.75
❑13	1.75	0.35	0.88	1.75
❑14	1.75	0.35	0.88	1.75
❑15	1.75	0.35	0.88	1.75

VORTEX THE WONDER MULE
CUTTING EDGE

Value: Cover or less

- ❑1, b&w ... 2.95
- ❑2, b&w ... 2.95

VOX
APPLE

	ORIG	GOOD	FINE	N-MINT
❑1, Jun 89, JBy (c), Hypehopper, b&w	1.95	0.40	1.00	2.00
❑2	2.25	0.45	1.13	2.25
❑3	2.25	0.45	1.13	2.25
❑4	2.25	0.45	1.13	2.25
❑5	2.25	0.45	1.13	2.25
❑6	2.25	0.45	1.13	2.25
❑7	2.25	0.45	1.13	2.25

VOYEUR, THE
AIRCEL

Value: Cover or less

- ❑1, b&w; adult ... 2.50
- ❑2, b&w; adult ... 2.50
- ❑3, b&w; adult ... 2.50
- ❑4,adult ... 2.95

VROOM SOCKO
SLAVE LABOR

Value: Cover or less

- ❑1, Nov 93,reprints strips from Deadline U.K. ... 2.50

VULGAR VINCE
THROB

Value: Cover or less

- ❑1, Professor Groinwauld's Robot of Death! ... 1.75

VULTURES OF WHAPETON
CONQUEST

Value: Cover or less

- ❑1, b&w ... 2.95

W
GOOD

Value: Cover or less

- ❑1, Nov 96 ... 2.95

W

WABBIT WAMPAGE
AMAZING

Value: Cover or less

- ❑1 ... 1.95

WACKY RACES
GOLD KEY

	ORIG	GOOD	FINE	N-MINT
❑1	0.15	7.00	17.50	35.00
❑2, Feb 71	0.15	4.40	11.00	22.00
❑3	0.15	3.60	9.00	18.00
❑4, Aug 71, Beat the Clock Through Yellow-rock; Follow Through to Yoo Hoo	0.15	3.60	9.00	18.00
❑5	0.15	3.60	9.00	18.00
❑6	0.15	3.60	9.00	18.00
❑7	0.15	3.60	9.00	18.00

WACKY SQUIRREL
DARK HORSE

	ORIG	GOOD	FINE	N-MINT
❑1, b&w	2.00	0.40	1.00	2.00
❑2	1.75	0.40	1.00	2.00
❑3	1.75	0.40	1.00	2.00
❑4, Oct 88	1.75	0.40	1.00	2.00
❑SE 1, Oct 87, A: Mr. Monster, Flip-book; Halloween Adventure Special	1.75	0.40	1.00	2.00
❑Smr 1, Jul 87,Summer Fun Special	2.00	0.40	1.00	2.00

WAHH
FRANK & HANK

Value: Cover or less

- ❑1, b&w; cardstock cover; no indicia ... 2.95
- ❑2, b&w; cardstock cover ... 2.95

WAHOO MORRIS
Too Hip Gott Go Graphics

Value: Cover or less

- ❑1, Jun 98, b&w ... 2.75

WAITING FOR THE END OF THE WORLD
Rodent

	ORIG	GOOD	FINE	N-MINT
❑1	—	0.20	0.50	1.00
❑2	—	0.20	0.50	1.00
❑3, On the Road to Ragnorak	—	0.20	0.50	1.00

WAITING PLACE, THE
Slave Labor

Value: Cover or less

- ❑1, Apr 97 ... 2.95
- ❑2, May 97 ... 2.95
- ❑3, Jun 97 ... 2.95
- ❑4, Jul 97 ... 2.95
- ❑5, Aug 97 ... 2.95
- ❑6, Sep 97 ... 2.95

WALDO WORLD
Fantagraphics

Value: Cover or less

- ❑1, Milton in College ... 2.50
- ❑2 ... 2.50

WALKING DEAD, THE
Aircel

Value: Cover or less

- ❑1 ... 2.25
- ❑2 ... 2.25
- ❑3 ... 2.25
- ❑4 ... 2.25
- ❑SE 1, Zombie Special, b&w .. 2.25

WALK THROUGH OCTOBER
Caliber

Value: Cover or less

- ❑1, b&w ... 2.95

WALL OF FLESH
AC

	ORIG	GOOD	FINE	N-MINT
❑1, b&w; Reprint	2.95	0.70	1.75	3.50

WALLY THE WIZARD
Marvel

	ORIG	GOOD	FINE	N-MINT
❑1, Apr 85	0.65	0.20	0.50	1.00
❑2, May 85	0.65	0.20	0.50	1.00
❑3, Jun 85	0.65	0.20	0.50	1.00
❑4, Jul 85	0.65	0.20	0.50	1.00
❑5, Aug 85	0.65	0.20	0.50	1.00
❑6, Sep 85	0.65	0.20	0.50	1.00
❑7, Oct 85	0.65	0.20	0.50	1.00
❑8, Nov 85	0.65	0.20	0.50	1.00
❑9, Dec 85	0.65	0.20	0.50	1.00
❑10, Jan 86	0.65	0.20	0.50	1.00
❑11, Feb 86	0.65	0.20	0.50	1.00
❑12, Mar 86, Final Issue	0.65	0.20	0.50	1.00

WALT DISNEY GIANT
Gladstone

Value: Cover or less

- ❑1, Sep 95, DR, Hearts of the Yukon, newsprint cover ... 2.25
- ❑2, Nov 95, CB, Mines of King Solomon, newsprint cover ... 2.25
- ❑3, Jan 96, CB, Super Snooper, newsprint cover ... 2.25
- ❑4, Mar 96, The Mysterious Stranger, newsprint cover; Mickey Mouse ... 2.25
- ❑5, May 96, newsprint cover; Mickey and Donald ... 2.25
- ❑6, Jul 96, newsprint cover; Uncle Scrooge and the Junior Woodchucks ... 2.25
- ❑7, Sep 96, CB, Micro-Ducks from Outer Space, newsprint cover ... 2.25

WALT DISNEY'S AUTUMN ADVENTURES
Disney

Value: Cover or less

- ❑1, CB ... 2.95
- ❑2, CB ... 2.95

WALT DISNEY'S CHRISTMAS PARADE
Gladstone

Value: Cover or less

- ❑1, Win 88, CB, 100pgs.; card-stock cover; Reprint ... 2.95
- ❑2, CB, Reprint ... 2.95

WALT DISNEY'S COMICS AND STORIES
Dell

	ORIG	GOOD	FINE	N-MINT
❑244, Jan 61, CB	—	4.40	11.00	22.00
❑245, Feb 61, CB	—	4.40	11.00	22.00
❑246, Mar 61, CB	—	4.40	11.00	22.00
❑247, Apr 61, CB	—	4.40	11.00	22.00
❑248, May 61, CB	—	4.40	11.00	22.00
❑249, Jun 61, CB	—	4.40	11.00	22.00
❑250, Jul 61, CB	—	4.40	11.00	22.00
❑251, Aug 61, CB	—	4.40	11.00	22.00
❑252, Sep 61, CB	—	4.40	11.00	22.00
❑253, Oct 61, CB	—	4.40	11.00	22.00
❑254, Nov 61, CB	—	4.40	11.00	22.00
❑255, Dec 61, CB	—	4.40	11.00	22.00
❑256, Jan 62, CB	—	4.40	11.00	22.00
❑257, Feb 62, CB	—	4.40	11.00	22.00
❑258, Mar 62, CB	—	4.40	11.00	22.00
❑259, Apr 62, CB	—	4.40	11.00	22.00
❑260, May 62, CB	—	4.40	11.00	22.00
❑261, Jun 62, CB	—	4.00	10.00	20.00
❑262, Jul 62, CB	—	4.00	10.00	20.00
❑263, Aug 62, CB	—	4.00	10.00	20.00
❑264, Sep 62, CB	—	4.00	10.00	20.00
❑265, Oct 62, CB	—	4.00	10.00	20.00
❑266, Nov 62, CB	—	4.00	10.00	20.00
❑267, Dec 62, CB	—	4.00	10.00	20.00
❑268, Jan 63, CB	—	4.00	10.00	20.00
❑269, Feb 63, CB	—	4.00	10.00	20.00
❑270, Mar 63, CB	—	4.00	10.00	20.00
❑271, Apr 63, CB	—	4.00	10.00	20.00
❑272, May 63, CB	—	4.00	10.00	20.00
❑273, Jun 63, CB	—	4.00	10.00	20.00
❑274, Jul 63, CB	—	4.00	10.00	20.00
❑275, Aug 63, CB	—	4.00	10.00	20.00
❑276, Sep 63, CB	—	4.00	10.00	20.00
❑277, Oct 63, CB	—	4.00	10.00	20.00
❑278, Nov 63, CB	—	4.00	10.00	20.00
❑279, Dec 63, CB	—	4.00	10.00	20.00
❑280, Jan 64, CB	—	4.00	10.00	20.00
❑281, Feb 64, CB	—	4.00	10.00	20.00
❑282, Mar 64, CB	—	4.00	10.00	20.00
❑283, Apr 64, CB	—	4.00	10.00	20.00
❑284, May 64	—	2.40	6.00	12.00
❑285, Jun 64	—	2.40	6.00	12.00
❑286, Jul 64, CB	—	3.20	8.00	16.00
❑287, Aug 64	—	2.40	6.00	12.00
❑288, Sep 64, CB	—	3.20	8.00	16.00
❑289, Oct 64, CB	—	3.20	8.00	16.00
❑290, Nov 64	—	2.40	6.00	12.00
❑291, Dec 64, CB	—	3.20	8.00	16.00
❑292, Jan 65, CB	—	3.20	8.00	16.00
❑293, Feb 65, CB	—	3.20	8.00	16.00
❑294, Mar 65	—	2.40	6.00	12.00
❑295, Apr 65	—	2.40	6.00	12.00
❑296, May 65	—	2.40	6.00	12.00
❑297, Jun 65, CB	—	3.20	8.00	16.00
❑298, Jul 65, CB	—	3.20	8.00	16.00
❑299, Aug 65, CB	—	3.20	8.00	16.00
❑300, Sep 65, CB	—	3.20	8.00	16.00
❑301, Oct 65, CB	—	3.20	8.00	16.00
❑302, Nov 65, CB	—	3.20	8.00	16.00
❑303, Dec 65, CB	—	3.20	8.00	16.00
❑304, Jan 66, CB	—	3.20	8.00	16.00
❑305, Feb 66, CB	—	3.20	8.00	16.00
❑306, Mar 66, CB	—	3.20	8.00	16.00
❑307, Apr 66, CB	—	3.20	8.00	16.00
❑308, May 66, CB	—	3.20	8.00	16.00
❑309, Jun 66	—	2.40	6.00	12.00
❑310, Jul 66	—	2.40	6.00	12.00
❑311, Aug 66	—	2.40	6.00	12.00
❑312, Sep 66, CB, The Big Fetch; The Chipmunk Mobile	—	3.20	8.00	16.00
❑313, Oct 66	—	1.60	4.00	8.00
❑314, Nov 66	—	1.60	4.00	8.00
❑315, Dec 66	—	1.60	4.00	8.00
❑316, Jan 67	—	1.60	4.00	8.00
❑317, Feb 67	—	1.60	4.00	8.00
❑318, Mar 67	—	1.60	4.00	8.00
❑319, Apr 67	—	1.60	4.00	8.00
❑320, May 67	—	1.60	4.00	8.00
❑321, Jun 67	—	1.60	4.00	8.00
❑322, Jul 67	—	1.60	4.00	8.00
❑323, Aug 67	—	1.60	4.00	8.00
❑324, Sep 67	—	1.60	4.00	8.00
❑325, Oct 67	—	1.60	4.00	8.00
❑326, Nov 67	—	1.60	4.00	8.00
❑327, Dec 67	—	1.60	4.00	8.00
❑328, Jan 68, CB	—	1.60	4.00	8.00
❑329, Feb 68	—	1.60	4.00	8.00
❑330, Mar 68	—	1.60	4.00	8.00
❑331, Apr 68	—	1.60	4.00	8.00
❑332, May 68	—	1.60	4.00	8.00
❑333, Jun 68	—	1.60	4.00	8.00
❑334, Jul 68	—	1.60	4.00	8.00
❑335, Aug 68, CB	—	2.40	6.00	12.00
❑336, Sep 68	—	1.60	4.00	8.00
❑337, Oct 68	—	1.60	4.00	8.00
❑338, Nov 68	—	1.60	4.00	8.00
❑339, Dec 68	—	1.60	4.00	8.00
❑340, Jan 69	—	1.60	4.00	8.00
❑341, Feb 69	—	1.60	4.00	8.00
❑342, Mar 69, CB	—	2.40	6.00	12.00
❑343, Apr 69, CB	—	2.40	6.00	12.00
❑344, May 69, CB	—	2.40	6.00	12.00
❑345, Jun 69, CB	—	2.40	6.00	12.00
❑346, Jul 69, CB	—	2.40	6.00	12.00

	ORIG	GOOD	FINE	N-MINT
❑347, Aug 69, CB	—	2.40	6.00	12.00
❑348, Sep 69, CB	—	2.40	6.00	12.00
❑349, Oct 69, CB	—	2.40	6.00	12.00
❑350, Nov 69, CB	—	2.40	6.00	12.00
❑351, Dec 69, CB	—	2.40	6.00	12.00
❑351/A, CB, poster	—	3.20	8.00	16.00
❑352, Jan 70, CB	—	2.40	6.00	12.00
❑352/A, CB, poster	—	3.20	8.00	16.00
❑353, Feb 70, CB	—	2.40	6.00	12.00
❑353/A, CB, poster	—	3.20	8.00	16.00
❑354, Mar 70, CB	—	2.40	6.00	12.00
❑354/A, CB, poster	—	3.20	8.00	16.00
❑355, Apr 70, CB	—	2.40	6.00	12.00
❑355/A, CB, poster	—	3.20	8.00	16.00
❑356, May 70, CB	—	2.40	6.00	12.00
❑356/A, CB, poster	—	3.20	8.00	16.00
❑357, Jun 70, CB	—	2.40	6.00	12.00
❑357/A, CB, poster	—	3.20	8.00	16.00
❑358, Jul 70, CB	—	2.40	6.00	12.00
❑358/A, CB, poster	—	3.20	8.00	16.00
❑359, Aug 70, CB	—	2.40	6.00	12.00
❑359/A, CB, poster	—	3.20	8.00	16.00
❑360, Sep 70, CB	—	2.40	6.00	12.00
❑360/A, CB, poster	—	3.20	8.00	16.00
❑361, Oct 70, CB	0.15	2.40	6.00	12.00
❑362, Nov 70, CB	0.15	2.40	6.00	12.00
❑363, Dec 70, CB	0.15	2.40	6.00	12.00
❑364, Jan 71, CB	0.15	2.40	6.00	12.00
❑365, Feb 71, CB	0.15	2.40	6.00	12.00
❑366, Mar 71, CB	0.15	2.40	6.00	12.00
❑367, Apr 71, CB	0.15	2.40	6.00	12.00
❑368, May 71, CB	0.15	2.40	6.00	12.00
❑369, Jun 71, CB	0.15	2.40	6.00	12.00
❑370, Jul 71, CB	0.15	2.40	6.00	12.00
❑371, Aug 71, CB	0.15	2.40	6.00	12.00
❑372, Sep 71, CB	0.15	2.40	6.00	12.00
❑373, Oct 71, CB	0.15	2.40	6.00	12.00
❑374, Nov 71, CB	0.15	2.40	6.00	12.00
❑375, Dec 71, CB	0.15	2.40	6.00	12.00
❑376, Jan 72, CB	0.15	2.40	6.00	12.00
❑377, Feb 72, CB	0.15	2.40	6.00	12.00
❑378, Mar 72, CB	0.15	2.40	6.00	12.00
❑379, Apr 72, CB	0.15	2.40	6.00	12.00
❑380, May 72, CB	0.15	2.40	6.00	12.00
❑381, Jun 72, CB	0.15	2.40	6.00	12.00
❑382, Jul 72, CB	0.15	2.40	6.00	12.00
❑383, Aug 72, CB	0.15	2.40	6.00	12.00
❑384, Sep 72, CB	0.15	2.40	6.00	12.00
❑385, Oct 72, CB	0.15	2.40	6.00	12.00
❑386, Nov 72, CB	0.15	2.40	6.00	12.00
❑387, Dec 72, CB ,16pgs.	0.15	2.40	6.00	12.00
❑388, Jan 73, CB	0.15	2.40	6.00	12.00
❑389, Feb 73, CB	0.15	2.40	6.00	12.00
❑390, Mar 73, CB	0.15	2.40	6.00	12.00
❑391, Apr 73, CB	0.15	2.40	6.00	12.00
❑392, May 73, CB	0.20	2.40	6.00	12.00
❑393, Jun 73, CB	0.20	2.40	6.00	12.00
❑394, Jul 73, CB	0.20	2.40	6.00	12.00
❑395, Aug 73, CB	0.20	2.40	6.00	12.00
❑396, Sep 73, CB	0.20	2.40	6.00	12.00
❑397, Oct 73, CB	0.20	2.40	6.00	12.00
❑398, Nov 73, CB	0.20	2.40	6.00	12.00
❑399, Dec 73, CB	0.20	2.40	6.00	12.00
❑400, Jan 74, CB	0.20	2.40	6.00	12.00
❑401, Feb 74, CB	0.20	1.60	4.00	8.00
❑402, Mar 74, CB	—	1.60	4.00	8.00
❑403, Apr 74, CB	—	1.60	4.00	8.00
❑404, May 74, CB	—	1.60	4.00	8.00
❑405, Jun 74, CB	—	1.60	4.00	8.00
❑406, Jul 74, CB	—	1.60	4.00	8.00
❑407, Aug 74, CB	—	1.60	4.00	8.00
❑408, Sep 74, CB	—	1.60	4.00	8.00
❑409, Oct 74, CB	—	1.60	4.00	8.00
❑410, Nov 74, CB	—	1.60	4.00	8.00
❑411, Dec 74, CB	—	1.60	4.00	8.00
❑412, Jan 75, CB	—	1.60	4.00	8.00
❑413, Feb 75, CB	—	1.60	4.00	8.00
❑414, Mar 75, CB	—	1.60	4.00	8.00
❑415, Apr 75, CB	—	1.60	4.00	8.00
❑416, May 75, CB	—	1.60	4.00	8.00
❑417, Jun 75, CB	—	1.60	4.00	8.00
❑418, Jul 75, CB	—	1.60	4.00	8.00
❑419, Aug 75, CB	0.25	1.60	4.00	8.00
❑420, Sep 75, CB	—	1.60	4.00	8.00
❑421, Oct 75, CB	—	1.60	4.00	8.00

Gladstone's *Walt Disney Giant* reprinted earlier Disney stories and had newsprint covers as a cost-saving measure.

	ORIG	GOOD	FINE	N-MINT
❑422, Nov 75, CB	—	1.60	4.00	8.00
❑423, Dec 75, CB	—	1.60	4.00	8.00
❑424, Jan 76, CB	—	1.60	4.00	8.00
❑425, Feb 76, CB	—	1.60	4.00	8.00
❑426, Mar 76, CB	—	1.60	4.00	8.00
❑427, Apr 76, CB	—	1.60	4.00	8.00
❑428, May 76, CB	—	1.60	4.00	8.00
❑429, Jun 76, CB	—	1.60	4.00	8.00
❑430, Jul 76	—	0.80	2.00	4.00
❑431, Aug 76, CB	—	1.20	3.00	6.00
❑432, Sep 76, CB	—	1.20	3.00	6.00
❑433, Oct 76	—	0.80	2.00	4.00
❑434, Nov 76, CB	—	1.20	3.00	6.00
❑435, Dec 76, CB	—	1.20	3.00	6.00
❑436, Jan 77, CB	—	1.20	3.00	6.00
❑437, Feb 77	—	0.80	2.00	4.00
❑438, Mar 77	—	0.80	2.00	4.00
❑439, Apr 77, CB	—	1.20	3.00	6.00
❑440, May 77, CB	—	1.20	3.00	6.00
❑441, Jun 77	—	0.80	2.00	4.00
❑442, Jul 77, CB	0.30	1.00	2.50	5.00
❑443, Aug 77, CB	—	1.00	2.50	5.00
❑444, Sep 77	—	0.60	1.50	3.00
❑445, Oct 77	—	0.60	1.50	3.00
❑446, Nov 77, CB	—	1.00	2.50	5.00
❑447, Dec 77, CB	—	1.00	2.50	5.00
❑448, Jan 78, CB	—	1.00	2.50	5.00
❑449, Feb 78, CB	—	1.00	2.50	5.00
❑450, Mar 78, CB	—	1.00	2.50	5.00
❑451, Apr 78, CB	—	0.80	2.00	4.00
❑452, May 78, CB	—	0.80	2.00	4.00
❑453, Jun 78, CB	—	0.80	2.00	4.00
❑454, Jul 78, CB	—	0.80	2.00	4.00
❑455, Aug 78, CB	—	0.80	2.00	4.00
❑456, Sep 78, CB	—	0.80	2.00	4.00
❑457, Oct 78, CB	—	0.80	2.00	4.00
❑458, Nov 78, CB	—	0.80	2.00	4.00
❑459, Dec 78, CB	—	0.80	2.00	4.00
❑460, Jan 79, CB	—	0.80	2.00	4.00
❑461, Feb 79, CB	—	0.80	2.00	4.00
❑462, Mar 79, CB	—	0.80	2.00	4.00
❑463, Apr 79, CB	—	0.80	2.00	4.00
❑464, May 79, CB	—	0.80	2.00	4.00
❑465, Jun 79, CB	—	0.80	2.00	4.00
❑466, Jul 79	—	0.60	1.50	3.00
❑467, Aug 79, CB	—	0.80	2.00	4.00
❑468, Sep 79, CB	0.40	0.80	2.00	4.00
❑469, Oct 79, CB	—	0.80	2.00	4.00
❑470, Nov 79, CB	—	0.80	2.00	4.00
❑471, Dec 79, CB	—	0.80	2.00	4.00
❑472, Jan 80, CB	—	0.80	2.00	4.00
❑473, Feb 80, CB	—	0.80	2.00	4.00
❑474, Mar 80, CB ,Whitman begins publishing	—	0.80	2.00	4.00
❑475, Apr 80, CB	—	0.80	2.00	4.00
❑476, May 80, CB	—	0.80	2.00	4.00
❑477, Jun 80, CB	—	0.80	2.00	4.00
❑478, Jul 80, CB	—	0.80	2.00	4.00
❑479, Aug 80, CB	—	0.80	2.00	4.00
❑480, Sep 80, CB	—	0.80	2.00	4.00
❑481, Oct 80, CB	—	0.80	2.00	4.00
❑482, Nov 80, CB	—	0.80	2.00	4.00
❑483, Dec 80, CB	—	0.80	2.00	4.00
❑484, CB	—	0.80	2.00	4.00
❑485, CB	—	0.80	2.00	4.00
❑486, CB	—	0.80	2.00	4.00
❑487, CB	—	0.80	2.00	4.00
❑488, CB	—	0.80	2.00	4.00
❑489, CB	—	0.80	2.00	4.00
❑490, CB	—	0.80	2.00	4.00
❑491, CB	—	0.80	2.00	4.00

	ORIG	GOOD	FINE	N-MINT
❑492, CB	—	0.80	2.00	4.00
❑493, CB	—	0.80	2.00	4.00
❑494, CB	—	0.80	2.00	4.00
❑495, CB	—	0.80	2.00	4.00
❑496, CB	—	0.80	2.00	4.00
❑497, CB	—	0.80	2.00	4.00
❑498, CB	—	0.80	2.00	4.00
❑499, CB	—	0.80	2.00	4.00
❑500, CB	—	0.80	2.00	4.00
❑501, CB	—	0.80	2.00	4.00
❑502, CB	—	0.80	2.00	4.00
❑503, CB	—	0.80	2.00	4.00
❑504, CB	—	0.80	2.00	4.00
❑505, CB, Battle of Petras; The Tragic Magic Touch	—	0.80	2.00	4.00
❑506	—	0.80	2.00	4.00
❑507, CB	—	0.80	2.00	4.00
❑508, CB	—	0.80	2.00	4.00
❑509, CB	0.60	0.80	2.00	4.00
❑510, CB	0.60	0.80	2.00	4.00
❑511, Oct 86, CB ,Gladstone begins publishing	0.75	1.80	4.50	9.00
❑512, Nov 86	0.75	1.40	3.50	7.00
❑513, Dec 86	0.75	1.40	3.50	7.00
❑514, Jan 87	0.75	1.00	2.50	5.00
❑515, Feb 87	0.75	1.00	2.50	5.00
❑516, Mar 87, CB	0.75	1.00	2.50	5.00
❑517, Apr 87	0.75	0.60	1.50	3.00
❑518, May 87	0.75	0.60	1.50	3.00
❑519, Jun 87, CB	0.75	1.60	4.00	8.00
❑520, Jul 87, CB	0.95	0.80	2.00	4.00
❑521, Aug 87, WK; CB	0.95	0.80	2.00	4.00
❑522, WK; CB, O: Huey, Dewey, Louie	0.95	0.80	2.00	4.00
❑523, Oct 87, DR; CB ,1st Rosa 10-page story	0.95	0.80	2.00	4.00
❑524, Nov 87, CB	0.95	0.80	2.00	4.00
❑525, Dec 87, CB	0.95	0.80	2.00	4.00
❑526, Jan 88, CB	0.95	0.80	2.00	4.00
❑527, Mar 88, CB	0.95	0.80	2.00	4.00
❑528, May 88, CB	0.95	0.80	2.00	4.00
❑529, Jun 88, CB	0.95	0.80	2.00	4.00
❑530, Aug 88, CB	0.95	0.80	2.00	4.00
❑531, DR; CB, WK (c)	0.95	0.80	2.00	4.00
❑532, DR; CB	0.95	0.80	2.00	4.00
❑533, CB	0.95	0.80	2.00	4.00
❑534, CB	0.95	0.80	2.00	4.00
❑535, CB	0.95	0.80	2.00	4.00
❑536, CB	0.95	0.80	2.00	4.00
❑537, CB ,1st Wm. Van Horn 10-page story	0.95	0.80	2.00	4.00
❑538, CB, WK (c)	0.95	0.80	2.00	4.00
❑539, Jun 89, CB	0.95	0.80	2.00	4.00
❑540, Jul 89, CB	0.95	0.80	2.00	4.00
❑541, Aug 89, CB, WK (c),48 pgs.	1.50	0.80	2.00	4.00
❑542, Sep 89, CB	1.50	0.80	2.00	4.00
❑543, Oct 89, CB, WK (c)	1.50	0.80	2.00	4.00
❑544, Nov 89, CB, WK (c)	1.50	0.80	2.00	4.00
❑545, Dec 89, CB	1.50	0.80	2.00	4.00
❑546, Feb 90, WK; CB	1.95	0.80	2.00	4.00
❑547, Apr 90, DR; CB	1.95	0.80	2.00	4.00
❑548, Jun 90, CB, Home is the Hero,Disney begins publishing	1.50	0.80	2.00	4.00
❑549, Jul 90, CB	1.50	0.80	2.00	4.00
❑550, Aug 90, CB ,Milkman story	2.25	0.60	1.50	3.00
❑551, Sep 90, CB	1.50	0.40	1.00	2.00
❑552, Oct 90, CB	1.50	0.40	1.00	2.00
❑553, Nov 90, CB	1.50	0.40	1.00	2.00
❑554, Dec 90, CB	1.50	0.40	1.00	2.00
❑555, Jan 91	1.50	0.30	0.75	1.50
❑556, Feb 91	1.50	0.30	0.75	1.50
❑557, Mar 91, CB	1.50	0.40	1.00	2.00
❑558, Apr 91, CB	1.50	0.40	1.00	2.00
❑559, May 91, CB	1.50	0.40	1.00	2.00
❑560, Jun 91, CB	1.50	0.40	1.00	2.00
❑561, Jul 91, CB	1.50	0.40	1.00	2.00
❑562, Aug 91, CB	1.50	0.40	1.00	2.00
❑563, Sep 91, CB	1.50	0.40	1.00	2.00
❑564, Oct 91, CB, Time Tetrad, Part 2	1.50	0.40	1.00	2.00
❑565, Nov 91, CB	1.50	0.40	1.00	2.00
❑566, Dec 91, CB	2.95	0.40	1.00	2.00
❑567, Jan 92, CB	1.50	0.40	1.00	2.00
❑568, Feb 92, CB	1.50	0.40	1.00	2.00
❑569, Mar 92, CB	1.50	0.40	1.00	2.00
❑570, Apr 92, CB ,Valentine centerfold	1.50	0.40	1.00	2.00
❑571, May 92, CB ,64pgs.	2.95	0.40	1.00	2.00
❑572, Jun 92, CB ,map piece	1.50	0.40	1.00	2.00
❑573, Jul 92, CB ,map piece	1.50	0.40	1.00	2.00
❑574, Aug 92, CB ,map piece	2.95	0.59	1.48	2.95
❑575, Sep 92	2.95	0.59	1.48	2.95
❑576, Oct 92, CB	2.95	0.59	1.48	2.95
❑577, Nov 92, CB ,Reprint	1.50	0.59	1.48	2.95
❑578, Dec 92, CB ,Reprint	1.50	0.30	0.75	1.50
❑579, Jan 93, CB	1.50	0.30	0.75	1.50
❑580, Feb 93, CB ,strip reprint	2.95	0.59	1.48	2.95
❑581, Mar 93, CB ,Reprint	1.50	0.30	0.75	1.50
❑582, Apr 93, WK; FG, Sky Island	2.95	0.30	0.75	1.50
❑583, May 93, WK; FG, Sky Island	2.95	0.30	0.75	1.50
❑584, Jun 93, CB ,Reprint	1.50	0.30	0.75	1.50
❑585, Jul 93, FG; CB ,Reprint	2.50	0.50	1.25	2.50
❑586, Aug 93	1.50	0.30	0.75	1.50
❑587, Oct 93	1.50	0.30	0.75	1.50
❑588, Dec 93	1.50	0.30	0.75	1.50
❑589, Feb 94	1.50	0.30	0.75	1.50
❑590, Apr 94	1.50	0.30	0.75	1.50
❑591, Jun 94	1.50	0.30	0.75	1.50
❑592, Aug 94	1.50	0.30	0.75	1.50
❑593, Oct 94	1.50	0.30	0.75	1.50
❑594, Dec 94	1.50	0.30	0.75	1.50
❑595, Feb 95	1.50	0.30	0.75	1.50
❑596, Apr 95	1.50	0.30	0.75	1.50
❑597, Jun 95	1.50	0.30	0.75	1.50
❑598, Aug 95	1.50	0.40	1.00	2.00
❑599, Oct 95	1.95	0.40	1.00	2.00
❑600, Dec 95, DR; CB, Giant-size; reprints first Donald Duck stories by trio	2.95	0.59	1.48	2.95
❑601, Feb 96,upgrades to prestige format	5.95	1.19	2.97	5.95
❑602, Apr 96	5.95	1.19	2.97	5.95
❑603, Jun 96	5.95	1.19	2.97	5.95
❑604, Aug 96	5.95	1.19	2.97	5.95
❑605, Oct 96	5.95	1.19	2.97	5.95
❑606, Dec 96	5.95	1.19	2.97	5.95
❑607, Jan 96	5.95	1.19	2.97	5.95
❑608, Feb 97	5.95	1.19	2.97	5.95
❑609, Mar 97	5.95	1.19	2.97	5.95
❑610, Mar 97	6.95	1.19	2.97	5.95
❑611, Apr 97	6.95	1.19	2.97	5.95
❑612, May 97	6.95	1.39	3.47	6.95
❑613, Jun 97	6.95	1.39	3.47	6.95
❑614, Jul 97	6.95	1.39	3.47	6.95
❑615, Aug 97	6.95	1.39	3.47	6.95
❑616, Sep 97	6.95	1.39	3.47	6.95
❑617, Oct 97	6.95	1.39	3.47	6.95
❑618, Nov 97	6.95	1.39	3.47	6.95
❑619, Dec 97,Pinocchio features	6.95	1.39	3.47	6.95
❑620, Jan 98	6.95	1.39	3.47	6.95
❑621, Feb 98	6.95	1.39	3.47	6.95
❑622, Mar 98	6.95	1.39	3.47	6.95
❑623, Apr 98	6.95	1.39	3.47	6.95
❑624, May 98	6.95	1.39	3.47	6.95
❑625, Jun 98	6.95	1.39	3.47	6.95
❑626, Jul 98	6.95	1.39	3.47	6.95
❑627, Aug 98	6.95	1.39	3.47	6.95
❑628, Sep 98	6.95	1.39	3.47	6.95
❑629, Oct 98	6.95	1.39	3.47	6.95
❑630, Nov 98	6.95	1.39	3.47	6.95
❑631, Dec 98	6.95	1.39	3.47	6.95
❑632, Jan 99	6.95	1.39	3.47	6.95
❑633, Feb 99,Final Issue	6.95	1.39	3.47	6.95

WALT DISNEY'S COMICS AND STORIES PENNY PINCHER

GLADSTONE

	ORIG	GOOD	FINE	N-MINT
❑1, May 97, CB, The Purloined Putty,Reprint	0.99	0.20	0.50	1.00
❑2, Jun 97, CB, Feud and Far Between,reprints Barks' Feud and Far Between	0.99	0.20	0.50	1.00
❑3, Jul 97	0.99	0.20	0.50	1.00
❑4, Aug 97	0.99	0.20	0.50	1.00

WALT DISNEY'S COMICS DIGEST

GLADSTONE

	ORIG	GOOD	FINE	N-MINT
❑1, WK; CB	—	1.20	3.00	6.00
❑2, CB	—	0.80	2.00	4.00
❑3, CB	—	0.80	2.00	4.00
❑4, CB	—	0.80	2.00	4.00
❑5, CB	—	0.80	2.00	4.00
❑6, CB	—	0.80	2.00	4.00
❑7, CB	—	0.80	2.00	4.00

WALT DISNEY'S HOLIDAY PARADE

DISNEY

Value: Cover or less

	Value
❑1, CB, CB (w), Three Good Little Ducks; Don We Now Our Prey Apparel	2.95
❑2, CB	2.95

WALT DISNEY SHOWCASE

GOLD KEY

	ORIG	GOOD	FINE	N-MINT
❑1,Boatniks	—	3.20	8.00	16.00
❑2,Moby Duck	—	2.00	5.00	10.00

	ORIG	GOOD	FINE	N-MINT
❑3,Bongo & Lumpjaw	—	1.80	4.50	9.00
❑4	—	1.80	4.50	9.00
❑5,$1,000,000 Duck	—	2.40	6.00	12.00
❑6,Bedknobs & Broomsticks	—	2.40	6.00	12.00
❑7	—	1.80	4.50	9.00
❑8, Jun 72,Daisy and Donald; Goofy and Clarabelle	0.15	1.80	4.50	9.00
❑9,101 Dalmations	0.15	2.00	5.00	10.00
❑10, Sep 72, DS, Napoleon and Samantha,Napoleon and Samantha movie adaptation	0.15	2.40	6.00	12.00
❑11	—	1.60	4.00	8.00
❑12	—	1.60	4.00	8.00
❑13, Feb 73	—	1.60	4.00	8.00
❑14, Apr 73,World's Greatest Athlete	—	2.40	6.00	12.00
❑15, Jun 73,Three Little Pigs	0.20	1.60	4.00	8.00
❑16, Jul 73,Aristocats movie adaptation reprint	0.20	2.40	6.00	12.00
❑17, Aug 73	—	2.40	6.00	12.00
❑18, Oct 73,Gyro Gearloose	0.20	2.40	6.00	12.00
❑19, Dec 73,That Darn Cat	—	2.00	5.00	10.00
❑20	—	1.80	4.50	9.00
❑21	—	1.60	4.00	8.00
❑22	—	1.60	4.00	8.00
❑23	—	1.60	4.00	8.00
❑24,Herbie Rides Again	—	1.40	3.50	7.00
❑25,Old Yeller	—	1.40	3.50	7.00
❑26,Lt. Robin Crusoe, USN	—	1.40	3.50	7.00
❑27,Island at the Top of the World	—	1.40	3.50	7.00
❑28	—	1.40	3.50	7.00
❑29,Escape to Witch Mountain	—	1.40	3.50	7.00
❑30,Magica De Spell	0.25	3.00	7.50	15.00
❑31	—	1.80	4.50	9.00
❑32	—	1.80	4.50	9.00
❑33	—	1.40	3.50	7.00
❑34	—	1.40	3.50	7.00
❑35	—	1.40	3.50	7.00
❑36	—	1.40	3.50	7.00
❑37	—	1.40	3.50	7.00
❑38, Apr 77	0.30	1.40	3.50	7.00
❑39	—	1.40	3.50	7.00
❑40,The Rescuers	—	1.60	4.00	8.00
❑41,Herbie Goes to Monte Carlo	—	1.60	4.00	8.00
❑42, Jan 78	0.30	1.40	3.50	7.00
❑43,Pete's Dragon	—	2.40	6.00	12.00
❑44,Return From Witch Mountain; Castaways	—	1.40	3.50	7.00
❑45	—	1.40	3.50	7.00
❑46,The Cat From Outer Space	—	1.40	3.50	7.00
❑47	—	1.40	3.50	7.00
❑48	—	1.40	3.50	7.00
❑49	—	1.40	3.50	7.00
❑50,Bedknobs & Broomsticks reprint	—	1.40	3.50	7.00
❑51,101 Dalmations	—	1.40	3.50	7.00
❑52,Unidentified Flying Oddball	0.60	1.40	3.50	7.00
❑53	—	1.40	3.50	7.00
❑54,Final Issue; The Black Hole	—	1.40	3.50	7.00

WALT DISNEY'S SPRING FEVER
DISNEY

Value: Cover or less ❑1, Spr 91, CB 2.95

WALT DISNEY'S SUMMER FUN
DISNEY

Value: Cover or less ❑1 .... 2.95

WALTER
DARK HORSE

Value: Cover or less

❑1, Feb 96, Campaign of Teror 2.50
❑2, Mar 96 .... 2.50
❑3, Apr 96 .... 2.50
❑4, May 96,Final Issue 2.50

WALTER KITTY IN...THE HOLLOW EARTH
VISION

Value: Cover or less
❑1, Jul 96 .... 1.95
❑2, Jul 96 .... 1.95

WALT THE WILDCAT
MOTION COMICS

Value: Cover or less ❑1, Sep 95 .... 2.50

WANDA LUWAND & THE PIRATE GIRLS
FANTAGRAPHICS

Value: Cover or less ❑1, b&w; adult 2.50

WANDERERS, THE
DC

	ORIG	GOOD	FINE	N-MINT
❑1, Jun 88, From Graves of Nothing, 1: Re-Animage; 1: The Elvar; 1: The Wanderers; 1: Aviax	1.25	0.30	0.75	1.50
❑2, Jul 88, The First Mission	1.25	0.30	0.75	1.50
❑3, Aug 88, A Dream of Monsters	1.25	0.30	0.75	1.50
❑4, Sep 88	1.25	0.30	0.75	1.50
❑5, Oct 88	1.25	0.30	0.75	1.50
❑6, Nov 88	1.25	0.30	0.75	1.50

A group of Legion of Super-Heroes wannabes were killed in a space accident and then resurrected by a Controller in *Wanderers* #1.

© 1988 DC Comics

	ORIG	GOOD	FINE	N-MINT
❑7, Dec 88	1.25	0.30	0.75	1.50
❑8, Dec 88	1.25	0.30	0.75	1.50
❑9, Jan 89	1.25	0.30	0.75	1.50
❑10, Jan 89	1.25	0.30	0.75	1.50
❑11, Feb 89	1.25	0.30	0.75	1.50
❑12, Mar 89	1.25	0.30	0.75	1.50
❑13, Apr 89,Final Issue	1.25	0.30	0.75	1.50

WANDERING STAR
PEN AND INK

	ORIG	GOOD	FINE	N-MINT
❑1, b&w	2.00	1.60	4.00	8.00
❑1-2,2nd Printing	2.00	0.80	2.00	4.00
❑,3rd Printing	2.00	0.60	1.50	3.00
❑2, b&w	2.00	1.00	2.50	5.00
❑3, b&w	2.00	0.80	2.00	4.00
❑4, b&w	2.00	0.80	2.00	4.00
❑5, b&w	2.00	0.80	2.00	4.00
❑6, Mar 94, b&w	2.00	0.60	1.50	3.00
❑7, b&w	2.00	0.60	1.50	3.00
❑8, Oct 94, b&w	2.00	0.60	1.50	3.00
❑9, Aug 95, b&w	2.50	0.60	1.50	3.00
❑10, Oct 95, b&w	2.50	0.60	1.50	3.00
❑11, b&w	2.50	0.50	1.25	2.50
❑12, b&w	2.50	0.50	1.25	2.50
❑13, b&w	2.50	0.50	1.25	2.50
❑14, b&w	2.50	0.50	1.25	2.50
❑15, b&w	2.50	0.50	1.25	2.50
❑16, b&w	2.50	0.50	1.25	2.50
❑17, b&w	2.50	0.50	1.25	2.50
❑18, b&w	2.50	0.50	1.25	2.50
❑19, b&w	2.50	0.50	1.25	2.50
❑20, b&w	2.50	0.50	1.25	2.50
❑21, b&w	2.50	0.50	1.25	2.50

WANDERING STARS
FANTAGRAPHICS

Value: Cover or less ❑1, The Wanderer 2.00

WANTED, THE WORLD'S MOST DANGEROUS VILLAINS
DC

	ORIG	GOOD	FINE	N-MINT
❑1, Aug 72,reprints stories from Batman #112, World's Finest #111, and Green Lantern #1	0.20	2.00	5.00	10.00
❑2, Oct 72,reprints stories from Batman #25 and Flash #121	0.20	1.60	4.00	8.00
❑3, Nov 72,reprints stories from Action #69, More Fun #65, and Flash #100	0.20	1.60	4.00	8.00
❑4, Dec 72, 1: Solomon Grundy,reprints stories from All-American #61 and Kid Eternity #15	0.20	1.20	3.00	6.00
❑5, Jan 73,reprints stories from Green Lantern #33 and Doll Man #15	0.20	1.20	3.00	6.00
❑6, Feb 73,reprints stories from Adventure #77 and Sensation Comics #66 and 71	0.20	1.20	3.00	6.00
❑7, Apr 73,reprints stories from More Fun #76, Flash #90, and Adventure #72	0.20	1.20	3.00	6.00
❑8, Jul 73,reprints stories from Flash #114 and More Fun #73	0.20	1.20	3.00	6.00
❑9, Sep 73,Reprint; Final Issue	0.20	1.20	3.00	6.00

WAR, THE
MARVEL

Value: Cover or less

❑1, Jun 89,Series continued from story in "The Draft" 3.50
❑2, Jul 89 .... 3.50
❑3, Aug 89 .... 3.50
❑4, Feb 90 .... 3.50

WAR AGAINST CRIME (GEMSTONE)
GEMSTONE

Value: Cover or less

❑1, Apr 00, JCr, JCr (w), Public Enemy...the Story of Machine-Gun Kelley!; Portfolio of Death!,Reprints War Against Crime #1 .... 2.50
❑2, May 00, Hank "Two-Gun" Corley!; The Crystal Ball Killer,Reprints War Against Crime #2 .... 2.50
❑3, Jun 00, AF, AF (w), Frisco Florrie; Savage Strongboy,Reprints War Against Crime #3 .... 2.50
❑4, Jul 00, AF, AF (w), The Machine-Gun Mad Mobsters; Choo-Choo Jones,Reprints War Against Crime #4 .... 2.50

❑5, GI; JCr; AF, GI (w); JCr (w); AF (w), Little Miss Mob Marker; Curse of the Pharaoh,Reprints War Against Crime #5 ... 2.50

❑Anl 1,Collects issues #1-5 ... 13.50

WARBLADE: ENDANGERED SPECIES
IMAGE

Value: Cover or less

- ❑1, Jan 95,Tri-fold cover ... 2.50
- ❑2, Feb 95, A: Ripclaw ... 2.50
- ❑3, Mar 95 ... 2.50
- ❑4, Apr 95 ... 2.50

WARCAT
COCONUT

Value: Cover or less

- ❑Ash 1, Oct 97, nn; b&w; preview of issues #1 and 2; no indicia ... 2.95
- ❑SE 1 ... 2.95

WARCHILD
MAXIMUM PRESS

Value: Cover or less

- ❑1/A, Dec 94,Warchild charging on cover ... 2.50
- ❑1/B,Variant cover with Warchild standing, red background ... 2.50
- ❑2/A, Jan 95,Warchild and woman on cover ... 2.50
- ❑2/B, Jan 95,Warchild alone on cover ... 2.50
- ❑3/A, Jun 95,Warchild crouching on cover ... 2.50
- ❑3/B, Jun 95,Warchild standing on cover, white background ... 2.50
- ❑3/C,Warchild standing on cover, red background ... 2.50
- ❑4, Aug 95 ... 2.50

WAR CRIMINALS
COMIC ZONE

Value: Cover or less

- ❑1, b&w ... 2.95

WARCRY
IMAGE

Value: Cover or less

- ❑1 ... 2.50

WAR DANCER
DEFIANT

	ORIG	GOOD	FINE	N-MINT
❑1, Feb 94, 1: War Dancer	2.50	0.50	1.25	2.50
❑2, Mar 94	2.50	0.50	1.25	2.50
❑3, Apr 94	2.50	0.50	1.25	2.50
❑4, May 94, A: Charlemagne; O: War Dancer, Giant-size	2.50	0.65	1.63	3.25
❑5, Jun 94	2.50	0.50	1.25	2.50
❑6,Final Issue	2.50	0.50	1.25	2.50

WAR GAMES
BISHOP PRESS

Value: Cover or less

- ❑1, b&w ... 2.50

WARHAMMER MONTHLY
GAMES WORKSHOP

	ORIG	GOOD	FINE	N-MINT
❑0, Feb 98, The Bridge; Bloodquest	—	0.20	0.50	1.00
❑1, DarkBlade, Part 1; Predator & Prey	2.95	0.59	1.48	2.95
❑2, DarkBlade, Part 2; Titan: Baptism	2.95	0.59	1.48	2.95
❑3	2.95	0.59	1.48	2.95
❑4	2.95	0.59	1.48	2.95
❑5	2.95	0.59	1.48	2.95
❑6	2.95	0.59	1.48	2.95
❑7	2.95	0.59	1.48	2.95
❑8	2.95	0.59	1.48	2.95
❑9	2.95	0.59	1.48	2.95
❑10	2.95	0.59	1.48	2.95
❑11	2.95	0.59	1.48	2.95
❑12	2.95	0.59	1.48	2.95
❑13	2.95	0.59	1.48	2.95
❑14	2.95	0.59	1.48	2.95
❑15	2.95	0.59	1.48	2.95
❑16	2.95	0.59	1.48	2.95
❑17	2.95	0.59	1.48	2.95
❑18	2.95	0.59	1.48	2.95
❑19	2.95	0.59	1.48	2.95
❑20	2.95	0.59	1.48	2.95
❑21	2.95	0.59	1.48	2.95
❑22	2.95	0.59	1.48	2.95
❑23	2.95	0.59	1.48	2.95
❑24	2.95	0.59	1.48	2.95
❑25	2.95	0.59	1.48	2.95
❑26	2.95	0.59	1.48	2.95
❑27	2.95	0.59	1.48	2.95
❑28	2.95	0.59	1.48	2.95
❑29	2.95	0.59	1.48	2.95
❑30	2.95	0.59	1.48	2.95
❑31	2.95	0.59	1.48	2.95
❑32	2.95	0.59	1.48	2.95
❑33	2.95	0.59	1.48	2.95
❑34	2.95	0.59	1.48	2.95
❑35	2.95	0.59	1.48	2.95
❑36	2.95	0.59	1.48	2.95
❑37	2.95	0.59	1.48	2.95
❑38	2.95	0.59	1.48	2.95
❑39	2.95	0.59	1.48	2.95
❑40	2.95	0.59	1.48	2.95
❑41	2.95	0.59	1.48	2.95
❑42	2.95	0.59	1.48	2.95
❑43	2.95	0.59	1.48	2.95
❑44	2.95	0.59	1.48	2.95

WARHAWKS COMICS MODULE
TSR

Value: Cover or less

- ❑1, ...And Let Slip the Hawks of War ... 2.95
- ❑2 ... 2.95
- ❑3 ... 2.95
- ❑4 ... 2.95
- ❑5, Court-Martial,Warhawks 2050 ... 2.95
- ❑6,Warhawks 2050 ... 2.95
- ❑7, Battle of Britain, Part 1,Warhawks 2050 ... 2.95
- ❑8, Battle of Britain, Part 2,Warhawks 2050 ... 2.95
- ❑9, Battle of Britain, Part 3,Warhawks 2050 ... 2.95

WARHEADS
MARVEL

Value: Cover or less

- ❑1, Jun 92, 1: Warheads,Wolverine ... 1.75
- ❑2, Jul 92 ... 1.75
- ❑3, Aug 92 ... 1.75
- ❑4, Sep 92 ... 1.75
- ❑5, Oct 92 ... 1.75
- ❑6,Death's Head II cameo ... 1.75
- ❑7 ... 1.75
- ❑8, A: Silver Surfer; A: X-Men ... 1.75
- ❑9, A: X-Men ... 1.75
- ❑10, Apr 93, A: X-Men ... 1.75
- ❑11, May 93 ... 1.75
- ❑12, Jun 93 ... 1.75
- ❑13, Jul 93 ... 1.75
- ❑14, Aug 93,Final Issue ... 1.75

WARHEADS: BLACK DAWN
MARVEL

	ORIG	GOOD	FINE	N-MINT
❑1, Jul 93,foil cover	2.95	0.59	1.48	2.95
❑2	1.75	0.59	1.48	2.95

WAR HEROES CLASSICS
RECOLLECTIONS

Value: Cover or less

- ❑1, b&w; Reprint ... 2.00

WAR IS HELL
MARVEL

	ORIG	GOOD	FINE	N-MINT
❑1, Jan 73, AW ,Reprint	0.20	1.60	4.00	8.00
❑2, Mar 73,Reprint	0.20	1.00	2.50	5.00
❑3, May 73,Reprint	0.20	1.00	2.50	5.00
❑4, Jul 73,Reprint	0.20	1.00	2.50	5.00
❑5, Sep 73,Reprint	0.20	1.00	2.50	5.00
❑6, Nov 73,Reprint	0.20	0.80	2.00	4.00
❑7, Jun 74, SL (w), While the Jungle Sleeps, A: Sgt. Fury,Reprint; Reprints Sgt. Fury #17	0.25	0.80	2.00	4.00
❑8, Aug 74, A: Sgt. Fury,Reprint	0.25	0.80	2.00	4.00
❑9, Oct 74	0.25	0.60	1.50	3.00
❑10, Dec 74	0.25	0.60	1.50	3.00
❑11, Feb 75	0.25	0.60	1.50	3.00
❑12, Apr 75	0.25	0.60	1.50	3.00
❑13, Jun 75	0.25	0.60	1.50	3.00
❑14, Aug 75	0.25	0.60	1.50	3.00
❑15, Oct 75,Final Issue	0.25	0.60	1.50	3.00

WARLANDS
IMAGE

	ORIG	GOOD	FINE	N-MINT
❑1, Aug 99, The Fall of Shal 'Hazar	2.50	0.60	1.50	3.00
❑1/A, Aug 99, The Fall of Shal 'Hazar,alternate cover	2.50	0.60	1.50	3.00
❑1/B, Aug 99, The Fall of Shal 'Hazar,alternate cover	2.50	0.60	1.50	3.00
❑2, Sep 99, Homecoming	2.50	0.50	1.25	2.50
❑2/A, Sep 99, Homecoming,alternate cover	2.50	0.50	1.25	2.50
❑3, Nov 99, Dataran Rising	2.50	0.50	1.25	2.50
❑4	2.50	0.50	1.25	2.50
❑5, Mar 00, A Call to Arms	2.50	0.50	1.25	2.50
❑6	2.50	0.50	1.25	2.50
❑7, Jun 00, Fallen Comrades	2.50	0.50	1.25	2.50
❑8, Jul 00, Fallen Comrades	2.50	0.50	1.25	2.50
❑9, Aug 00, Aalok's Reckoning	2.50	0.50	1.25	2.50
❑10, Oct 00, Vampire's Reckoning	2.50	0.50	1.25	2.50
❑11, Nov 00, Into the Teeth of Darkness	2.50	0.50	1.25	2.50
❑12, Feb 01, Reckoning	2.50	0.50	1.25	2.50

WARLANDS EPILOGUE: THREE STORIES
IMAGE

Value: Cover or less

- ❑1, Mar 01 ... 5.95

WARLASH
CFD

Value: Cover or less

- ❑1, Apr 95, The Hardfire Syndrome, Part 1 ... 2.95

WARLOCK (1ST SERIES)
MARVEL

	ORIG	GOOD	FINE	N-MINT
❑1, Aug 72, GK, GK (c), The Day of the Prophet, O: Warlock	0.20	2.00	5.00	10.00
❑2, Oct 72	0.20	1.00	2.50	5.00
❑3, Dec 72	0.20	0.80	2.00	4.00
❑4, Feb 73, GK	0.20	0.80	2.00	4.00
❑5, Apr 73	0.20	0.80	2.00	4.00
❑6, Jun 73	0.20	0.80	2.00	4.00

	ORIG	GOOD	FINE	N-MINT
❑7, Aug 73	0.20	0.80	2.00	4.00
❑8, Oct 73	0.20	0.80	2.00	4.00
❑9, Oct 75, JSn, A: Thanos	0.25	0.80	2.00	4.00
❑10, Dec 75, JSn, O: Thanos	0.25	1.60	4.00	8.00
❑11, Feb 76, JSn, A: Thanos	0.25	1.60	4.00	8.00
❑12, Apr 76, JSn	0.25	1.00	2.50	5.00
❑13, Jun 76, JSn	0.25	1.00	2.50	5.00
❑14, Aug 76, JSn	0.25	1.00	2.50	5.00
❑15, Nov 76, JSn, A: Thanos	0.30	1.20	3.00	6.00

WARLOCK (2ND SERIES)
MARVEL

	ORIG	GOOD	FINE	N-MINT
❑1, Dec 82, JSn ,Reprint	2.00	0.70	1.75	3.50
❑2, Jan 83, JSn ,Reprint	2.00	0.60	1.50	3.00
❑3, Feb 83, JSn ,Reprint	2.00	0.60	1.50	3.00
❑4, Mar 83, JSn ,Reprint	2.00	0.60	1.50	3.00
❑5, Apr 83, JSn ,Reprint	2.00	0.60	1.50	3.00
❑6, May 83, JSn ,Reprint	2.00	0.60	1.50	3.00
❑SE 1	2.00	0.50	1.25	2.50

WARLOCK (3RD SERIES)
MARVEL

Value: Cover or less

- ❑1, May 92,Reprint; Reprints Warlock Special Edition #1 .... 2.50
- ❑2, Jun 92,Reprint; Reprints Warlock Special Edition #2 .... 2.50
- ❑3, Jul 92,Reprint; Reprints Warlock Special Edition #3 .... 2.50
- ❑4, Aug 92,Reprint; Reprints Warlock Special Edition #4 .... 2.50
- ❑5, Sep 92,Reprint; Reprints Warlock Special Edition #5 .... 2.50
- ❑6, Oct 92,Reprint; Reprints Warlock Special Edition #6 .... 2.50

WARLOCK (4TH SERIES)
MARVEL

	ORIG	GOOD	FINE	N-MINT
❑1, Nov 98, gatefold summary	2.99	0.60	1.50	3.00
❑2, Dec 98, V: Captain Marvel, gatefold summary	2.99	0.60	1.50	3.00
❑3, Jan 99, V: Drax, gatefold summary	2.99	0.60	1.50	3.00
❑4, Feb 99, A: Annihilus; A: Blastaar; A: Syphonn	2.99	0.60	1.50	3.00

WARLOCK (5TH SERIES)
MARVEL

	ORIG	GOOD	FINE	N-MINT
❑1, Oct 99, Cipher	1.99	0.40	1.00	2.00
❑2, Nov 99	1.99	0.40	1.00	1.99
❑3, Nov 99	1.99	0.40	1.00	1.99
❑4, Dec 99	1.99	0.40	1.00	1.99

WARLOCK 5
AIRCEL

	ORIG	GOOD	FINE	N-MINT
❑1, b&w	1.70	0.40	1.00	2.00
❑2, b&w	1.70	0.40	1.00	2.00
❑3, b&w	1.70	0.40	1.00	2.00
❑4, b&w	1.70	0.40	1.00	2.00
❑5,robot skull cover	1.70	0.40	1.00	2.00
❑6,woman's face on cover	1.70	0.40	1.00	2.00
❑7	1.70	0.40	1.00	2.00
❑8	1.70	0.40	1.00	2.00
❑9	1.70	0.40	1.00	2.00
❑10	1.70	0.40	1.00	2.00
❑11	1.70	0.40	1.00	2.00
❑12	1.70	0.40	1.00	2.00
❑13	1.70	0.40	1.00	2.00
❑14	1.70	0.40	1.00	2.00
❑15	1.70	0.40	1.00	2.00
❑16	1.95	0.40	1.00	2.00
❑17	1.95	0.40	1.00	2.00
❑18	1.95	0.40	1.00	2.00
❑19	1.95	0.40	1.00	2.00
❑20	1.95	0.40	1.00	2.00
❑21	1.95	0.40	1.00	2.00
❑22	1.95	0.40	1.00	2.00

WARLOCK 5 (SIRIUS)
SIRIUS

Value: Cover or less

- ❑1, Jan 98 .... 2.50
- ❑2, Feb 98 .... 2.50
- ❑3, Mar 98 .... 2.50
- ❑4, Apr 98 .... 2.50

WARLOCK 5 BOOK II
AIRCEL

Value: Cover or less

- ❑1, b&w 2.00
- ❑2, b&w 2.00
- ❑3, b&w 2.00
- ❑4, b&w 2.00
- ❑5, b&w 2.00
- ❑6, b&w 2.00
- ❑7, b&w 2.00

WARLOCK AND THE INFINITY WATCH
MARVEL

	ORIG	GOOD	FINE	N-MINT
❑1, Feb 92, JSn (w),follows events of The Infinity Gauntlet	1.75	0.50	1.25	2.50
❑2, Mar 92, JSn (w), Gathering the Watch!	1.75	0.40	1.00	2.00
❑3, Apr 92, JSn (w), A: High Evolutionary	1.75	0.40	1.00	2.00
❑4, May 92, JSn (w), They	1.75	0.40	1.00	2.00
❑5, Jun 92, JSn (w), Old Foes	1.75	0.40	1.00	2.00

Significant Marvel war stories were reprinted in *War is Hell.*

© 1973 Marvel Comics

	ORIG	GOOD	FINE	N-MINT
❑6, Jul 92, JSn (w), Revenge of the Beast	1.75	0.40	1.00	2.00
❑7, Aug 92, JSn (w)	1.75	0.40	1.00	2.00
❑8, Sep 92, JSn (w)	1.75	0.40	1.00	2.00
❑9, Oct 92, JSn (w), Infinity War, O: Gamora,Infinity War	1.75	0.40	1.00	2.00
❑10, Nov 92, JSn (w), Self-Destructive Tendencies	1.75	0.40	1.00	2.00
❑11, Dec 92, JSn (w), The Appeal	1.75	0.35	0.88	1.75
❑12, Jan 93	1.75	0.35	0.88	1.75
❑13, Feb 93	1.75	0.35	0.88	1.75
❑14, Mar 93	1.75	0.35	0.88	1.75
❑15, Apr 93	1.75	0.35	0.88	1.75
❑16, May 93	1.75	0.35	0.88	1.75
❑17, Jun 93	1.75	0.35	0.88	1.75
❑18, Jul 93	1.75	0.35	0.88	1.75
❑19, Aug 93	1.75	0.35	0.88	1.75
❑20, Sep 93	1.75	0.35	0.88	1.75
❑21, Oct 93, JSn (w), A: Goddess; A: Thor; A: Drax the Destroyer,Infinity Crusade crossover	1.75	0.35	0.88	1.75
❑22, Nov 93	1.75	0.35	0.88	1.75
❑23, Dec 93	1.75	0.35	0.88	1.75
❑24, Jan 94	1.75	0.35	0.88	1.75
❑25, Feb 94, Blood and Thunder, Part 12,diecut cover	2.95	0.59	1.48	2.95
❑26, Mar 94	1.75	0.35	0.88	1.75
❑27, Apr 94	1.75	0.35	0.88	1.75
❑28, May 94	1.95	0.35	0.88	1.75
❑29, Jun 94	1.95	0.39	0.98	1.95
❑30, Jul 94	1.95	0.39	0.98	1.95
❑31, Aug 94	1.95	0.39	0.98	1.95
❑32, Sep 94	1.95	0.39	0.98	1.95
❑33, Oct 94	1.95	0.39	0.98	1.95
❑34, Nov 94	1.95	0.39	0.98	1.95
❑35, Dec 94	1.95	0.39	0.98	1.95
❑36, Jan 95	1.95	0.39	0.98	1.95
❑37, Feb 95	1.95	0.39	0.98	1.95
❑38, Mar 95	1.95	0.39	0.98	1.95
❑39, Apr 95	1.95	0.39	0.98	1.95
❑40, May 95	1.95	0.39	0.98	1.95
❑41, Jun 95, Atlantis Rising, Part 3	1.95	0.39	0.98	1.95
❑42, Jul 95,Final Issue	1.95	0.39	0.98	1.95

WARLOCK CHRONICLES
MARVEL

Value: Cover or less

- ❑1, Jul 93, Infinity Crusade,Prism cover 2.95
- ❑2, Aug 93 .... 2.00
- ❑3, Sep 93 .... 2.00
- ❑4, Oct 93, JSn (w), A: Magus; A: Goddess,Infinity Crusade crossover 2.00
- ❑5, Nov 93 .... 2.00
- ❑6, Dec 93 .... 2.00
- ❑7, Jan 94 .... 2.00
- ❑8, Feb 94, Blood and Thunder, Part 11,Final Issue 2.00

WARLOCKS
AIRCEL

	ORIG	GOOD	FINE	N-MINT
❑1, Anarchy Unbound, b&w	1.95	0.40	1.00	2.00
❑2, Warlocks in New York, b&w	1.95	0.40	1.00	2.00
❑3, Where Angels Fear to Tread, b&w	1.95	0.40	1.00	2.00
❑4, b&w	1.95	0.40	1.00	2.00
❑5, b&w	1.95	0.40	1.00	2.00
❑6, b&w	1.95	0.40	1.00	2.00
❑7, b&w	1.95	0.40	1.00	2.00
❑8, b&w	1.95	0.40	1.00	2.00
❑9, b&w	1.95	0.40	1.00	2.00
❑10, b&w	1.95	0.40	1.00	2.00
❑11, Mar 90, b&w	1.95	0.40	1.00	2.00
❑12, b&w	1.95	0.40	1.00	2.00
❑SE 1, b&w	2.25	0.45	1.13	2.25

WARLORD
DC

	ORIG	GOOD	FINE	N-MINT
❑1, Feb 76, MGr, O: Warlord	0.25	1.60	4.00	8.00
❑2, Apr 76, MGr, 1: Machiste	0.25	0.80	2.00	4.00
❑3, Nov 76, MGr	0.30	0.60	1.50	3.00

	ORIG	GOOD	FINE	N-MINT
❑4, Jan 77, MGr	0.30	0.60	1.50	3.00
❑5, Mar 77, MGr, 1: Dragonsword	0.30	0.60	1.50	3.00
❑6, May 77, MGr, 1: Mariah Romanola; 1: Mariah	0.30	0.60	1.50	3.00
❑7, Jul 77, MGr, O: Machiste	0.35	0.40	1.00	2.00
❑8, Sep 77, MGr	0.35	0.40	1.00	2.00
❑9, Nov 77, MGr	0.35	0.40	1.00	2.00
❑10, Jan 78, MGr ,Deimos	0.35	0.40	1.00	2.00
❑11, Mar 78, MGr ,reprints 1st Issue Special	0.35	0.30	0.75	1.50
❑12, May 78, MGr, 1: Aton	0.35	0.30	0.75	1.50
❑13, Jul 78, MGr	0.35	0.30	0.75	1.50
❑14, Sep 78, MGr	0.35	0.30	0.75	1.50
❑15, Nov 78, MGr, 1: Joshua Morgan(Warlord's son)	0.50	0.30	0.75	1.50
❑16, Dec 78, MGr	0.40	0.30	0.75	1.50
❑17, Jan 79, MGr	0.40	0.30	0.75	1.50
❑18, Feb 79, MGr	0.40	0.30	0.75	1.50
❑19, Mar 79, MGr	0.40	0.30	0.75	1.50
❑20, Apr 79, MGr	0.40	0.30	0.75	1.50
❑21, May 79, MGr	0.40	0.30	0.75	1.50
❑22, Jun 79, MGr	0.40	0.30	0.75	1.50
❑23, Jul 79, MGr	0.40	0.30	0.75	1.50
❑24, Aug 79, MGr	0.40	0.30	0.75	1.50
❑25, Sep 79, MGr	0.40	0.30	0.75	1.50
❑26, Oct 79, MGr	0.40	0.30	0.75	1.50
❑27, Nov 79, MGr	0.40	0.30	0.75	1.50
❑28, Dec 79, MGr, 1: Wizard World; 1: Mongo Ironhand	0.40	0.30	0.75	1.50
❑29, Jan 80, MGr	0.40	0.30	0.75	1.50
❑30, Feb 80, MGr	0.40	0.20	0.50	1.00
❑31, Mar 80, MGr	0.40	0.20	0.50	1.00
❑32, Apr 80, MGr, 1: Shakira	0.40	0.20	0.50	1.00
❑33, May 80, MGr	0.40	0.20	0.50	1.00
❑34, Jun 80, MGr	0.40	0.20	0.50	1.00
❑35, Jul 80, MGr	0.40	0.20	0.50	1.00
❑36, Aug 80, MGr	0.40	0.20	0.50	1.00
❑37, Sep 80, MGr, O: Omac (new origin),Omac back-up	0.50	0.20	0.50	1.00
❑38, Oct 80, MGr, 1: Jennifer Morgan (Warlord's daughter),Omac back-up	0.50	0.20	0.50	1.00
❑39, Nov 80, MGr ,Omac back-up	0.50	0.20	0.50	1.00
❑40, Dec 80, MGr	0.50	0.20	0.50	1.00
❑41, Jan 81, MGr	0.50	0.20	0.50	1.00
❑42, Feb 81, MGr, A: Omac	0.50	0.20	0.50	1.00
❑43, Mar 81, MGr, A: Omac	0.50	0.20	0.50	1.00
❑44, Apr 81, MGr	0.50	0.20	0.50	1.00
❑45, May 81, MGr	0.50	0.20	0.50	1.00
❑46, Jun 81, MGr	0.50	0.20	0.50	1.00
❑47, Jul 81, MGr, 1: Rostov,Omac back-up	0.50	0.20	0.50	1.00
❑48, Aug 81, EC; MGr, 1: Claw the Unconquered; 1: Arak; 1: Arak, Son of Thunder, Giant-size	0.50	0.30	0.75	1.50
❑49, Sep 81, MGr, 1: The Evil One,Claw back-up	0.50	0.20	0.50	1.00
❑50, Oct 81, MGr	0.60	0.20	0.50	1.00
❑51, Nov 81, MGr ,reprints Warlord #1; Dragonsword back-up	0.60	0.20	0.50	1.00
❑52, Dec 81, MGr ,Dragonsword back-up	0.60	0.20	0.50	1.00
❑53, Jan 82,Dragonsword back-up	0.60	0.20	0.50	1.00
❑54, Feb 82	0.60	0.20	0.50	1.00
❑55, Mar 82, MGr (c), 1: Arion; 1: Lady Chian,Arion back-up	0.60	0.20	0.50	1.00
❑56, Apr 82, MGr (c),Arion back-up	0.60	0.20	0.50	1.00
❑57, May 82, MGr (c),Arion back-up	0.60	0.20	0.50	1.00
❑58, Jun 82, MGr (c),Arion back-up	0.60	0.20	0.50	1.00
❑59, Jul 82, MGr (c), 1: Garn Daanuth,Arion back-up	0.60	0.20	0.50	1.00
❑60, Aug 82, MGr (c),Arion back-up	0.60	0.20	0.50	1.00
❑61, Sep 82, MGr (c),Arion back-up	0.60	0.20	0.50	1.00
❑62, Oct 82, MGr (c),Arion back-up	0.60	0.20	0.50	1.00
❑63, Nov 82, MGr (c), 1: Conqueror of the Barren Earth,Arion back-up	0.60	0.20	0.50	1.00
❑64, Dec 82,Barren Earth back-up; Masters of the Universe preview	0.60	0.20	0.50	1.00
❑65, Jan 83	0.60	0.20	0.50	1.00
❑66, Feb 83	0.60	0.20	0.50	1.00
❑67, Mar 83	0.60	0.20	0.50	1.00
❑68, Apr 83	0.60	0.20	0.50	1.00
❑69, May 83	0.60	0.20	0.50	1.00
❑70, Jun 83	0.60	0.20	0.50	1.00
❑71, Jul 83	0.60	0.20	0.50	1.00
❑72, Aug 83	0.60	0.20	0.50	1.00
❑73, Sep 83	0.60	0.20	0.50	1.00
❑74, Oct 83	0.60	0.20	0.50	1.00
❑75, Nov 83	0.60	0.20	0.50	1.00
❑76, Dec 83	0.75	0.20	0.50	1.00
❑77, Jan 84	0.75	0.20	0.50	1.00
❑78, Feb 84	0.75	0.20	0.50	1.00
❑79, Mar 84	0.75	0.20	0.50	1.00
❑80, Apr 84	0.75	0.20	0.50	1.00
❑81, May 84	0.75	0.20	0.50	1.00
❑82, Jun 84	0.75	0.20	0.50	1.00
❑83, Jul 84	0.75	0.20	0.50	1.00
❑84, Aug 84	0.75	0.20	0.50	1.00
❑85, Sep 84	0.75	0.20	0.50	1.00
❑86, Oct 84	0.75	0.20	0.50	1.00
❑87, Nov 84	0.75	0.20	0.50	1.00
❑88, Dec 84	0.75	0.20	0.50	1.00
❑89, Jan 85	0.75	0.20	0.50	1.00
❑90, Feb 85	0.75	0.20	0.50	1.00
❑91, Mar 85, O: Warlord; O: Travis Morgan	0.75	0.20	0.50	1.00
❑92, Apr 85	0.75	0.20	0.50	1.00
❑93, May 85	0.75	0.20	0.50	1.00
❑94, Jun 85	0.75	0.20	0.50	1.00
❑95, Jul 85	0.75	0.20	0.50	1.00
❑96, Aug 85	0.75	0.20	0.50	1.00
❑97, Sep 85	0.75	0.20	0.50	1.00
❑98, Oct 85	0.75	0.20	0.50	1.00
❑99, Nov 85	0.75	0.20	0.50	1.00
❑100, Dec 85, MGr (c), Skartaris Unchained, Giant-size	1.25	0.20	0.50	1.00
❑101, Jan 86, MGr (c)	0.75	0.20	0.50	1.00
❑102, Feb 86, MGr (c)	0.75	0.20	0.50	1.00
❑103, Mar 86, MGr (c)	0.75	0.20	0.50	1.00
❑104, Apr 86, MGr (c)	0.75	0.20	0.50	1.00
❑105, May 86	0.75	0.20	0.50	1.00
❑106, Jun 86	0.75	0.20	0.50	1.00
❑107, Jul 86	0.75	0.20	0.50	1.00
❑108, Aug 86	0.75	0.20	0.50	1.00
❑109, Sep 86	0.75	0.20	0.50	1.00
❑110, Oct 86	0.75	0.20	0.50	1.00
❑111, Nov 86	0.75	0.20	0.50	1.00
❑112, Dec 86, MGr (c)	0.75	0.20	0.50	1.00
❑113, Jan 87	0.75	0.20	0.50	1.00
❑114, Feb 87,Legends	0.75	0.20	0.50	1.00
❑115, Mar 87,Legends	0.75	0.20	0.50	1.00
❑116, Apr 87	0.75	0.20	0.50	1.00
❑117, May 87, MGr (c)	0.75	0.20	0.50	1.00
❑118, Jun 87	0.75	0.20	0.50	1.00
❑119, Jul 87	0.75	0.20	0.50	1.00
❑120, Aug 87	0.75	0.20	0.50	1.00
❑121, Sep 87	0.75	0.20	0.50	1.00
❑122, Oct 87	0.75	0.20	0.50	1.00
❑123, Nov 87	1.00	0.20	0.50	1.00
❑124, Dec 87	1.00	0.20	0.50	1.00
❑125, Jan 88, D: Tara	1.00	0.20	0.50	1.00
❑126, Feb 88	1.00	0.20	0.50	1.00
❑127, Mar 88	1.00	0.20	0.50	1.00
❑128, Apr 88	1.00	0.20	0.50	1.00
❑129, May 88, Maddox's Revenge, Part 1	1.00	0.20	0.50	1.00
❑130, Jul 88, Maddox's Revenge, Part 2	1.00	0.20	0.50	1.00
❑131, Sep 88, RL, Maddox's Revenge, Part 3,Bonus Book #6; Rob Liefeld's first work at DC	1.00	0.40	1.00	2.00
❑132, Nov 88	1.00	0.20	0.50	1.00
❑133, Dec 88, JDu ,Final Issue; Giant-size	1.50	0.30	0.75	1.50
❑Anl 1, MGr	1.00	0.40	1.00	2.00
❑Anl 2	1.00	0.20	0.50	1.00
❑Anl 3	1.25	0.20	0.50	1.00
❑Anl 4	1.25	0.20	0.50	1.00
❑Anl 5	1.25	0.20	0.50	1.00
❑Anl 6	1.25	0.20	0.50	1.00

WARLORD (MINI-SERIES)
DC

	ORIG	GOOD	FINE	N-MINT
❑1, Jan 92, MGr (c)	1.75	0.40	1.00	2.00
❑2, Feb 92, MGr (c)	1.75	0.40	1.00	2.00
❑3, Mar 92, MGr (c)	1.75	0.40	1.00	2.00
❑4, Apr 92, MGr (c)	1.75	0.40	1.00	2.00
❑5, May 92, MGr (c)	1.75	0.40	1.00	2.00
❑6, Jun 92, MGr (c)	1.75	0.40	1.00	2.00

WAR MACHINE
MARVEL

Value: Cover or less

- ❑1, Apr 94, Something to Believe In, Giant-size; newsstand.... 2.00
- ❑1/SC, Apr 94, Something to Believe In,Embossed cover; Giant-size.... 2.95
- ❑2, May 94, Something to Believe In.... 1.50
- ❑3, Jun 94, Contents Under Pressure.... 1.50
- ❑4, Jul 94.... 1.50
- ❑5, Aug 94, V: Deathtoll.... 1.50
- ❑6, Sep 94, V: Deathtoll.... 1.50
- ❑7, Oct 94, A: Hawkeye.... 1.50
- ❑8, Nov 94, A: Iron Man.... 1.50
- ❑8/CS, Nov 94,polybagged with 16-page Marvel Action Hour preview, acetate print, coupon, sweepstakes entry form.... 2.95
- ❑9, Dec 94.... 1.50
- ❑10, Jan 95.... 1.50
- ❑11, Feb 95.... 1.50

ORIG GOOD FINE N-MINT

- ❑12, Mar 95 .... 1.50
- ❑13, Apr 95 .... 1.50
- ❑14, May 95 .... 1.50
- ❑15, Jun 95,flip book with War Machine: Brothers in Arms part 2 .... 2.50
- ❑16, Jul 95 .... 1.50
- ❑17, Aug 95 .... 1.50
- ❑18, Sep 95 .... 1.50
- ❑19, Oct 95 .... 1.50
- ❑20, Nov 95 .... 1.50
- ❑21, Dec 95, The Crossing, A: U.S.Agent; A: Hawkeye; A: Anachronauts; A: Black Widow 1.50
- ❑22, Jan 96 .... 1.50
- ❑23, Feb 96 .... 1.50
- ❑24, Mar 96, Time Will Tell 1.50
- ❑25, Apr 96, The Kiss Off!,Final Issue 1.50
- ❑Ash 1, ashcan edition 0.75

WAR MAN
Marvel
Value: Cover or less
- ❑1, trading cards 2.50
- ❑2, trading cards 2.50

WAR OF THE GODS
DC
Value: Cover or less
- ❑1, Sep 91, GP, War of the Gods, Part 1, mini-posters 1.75
- ❑2, Oct 91, GP, War of the Gods, Part 9,newsstand cover 1.75
- ❑2/DM, Oct 91, GP ,direct sale cover 1.75
- ❑3, Nov 91, GP, War of the Gods, Part 17,newsstand cover 1.75
- ❑3/DM, Nov 91, GP ,direct sale cover 1.75
- ❑4, Dec 91, GP, War of the Gods, Part 21,newsstand cover 1.75
- ❑4/DM, Dec 91, GP ,direct sale cover 1.75

WAR OF THE WORLDS, THE (CALIBER)
Caliber
Value: Cover or less
- ❑1 .... 2.95
- ❑2 .... 2.95
- ❑3 .... 2.95
- ❑4 .... 2.95
- ❑5 .... 2.95

WAR OF THE WORLDS (ETERNITY)
Eternity

	ORIG	GOOD	FINE	N-MINT
❑1	1.95	0.40	1.00	2.00
❑2	1.95	0.40	1.00	2.00
❑3	1.95	0.40	1.00	2.00
❑4	1.95	0.40	1.00	2.00
❑5	1.95	0.40	1.00	2.00
❑6	1.95	0.40	1.00	2.00

WAR OF THE WORLDS, THE: THE MEMPHIS FRONT
Arrow
Value: Cover or less
- ❑1, b&w; wrapraound cover 2.95
- ❑1/A, b&w; expanded page count 2.95
- ❑2 .... 2.95
- ❑3 .... 2.95
- ❑4 .... 2.95
- ❑5 .... 2.95

WARP
First
Value: Cover or less
- ❑1, Mar 83, FB, 1: Chaos; 1: Lord Cumulus,This is the first comic published by First Comics 2.00
- ❑2, Apr 83, FB 1.50
- ❑3, May 83, FB 1.50
- ❑4, Jun 83, FB 1.50
- ❑5, Aug 83, FB 1.50
- ❑6, Sep 83, FB 1.50
- ❑7, Oct 83, FB 1.50
- ❑8, Nov 83 .... 1.25
- ❑9, Dec 83 .... 1.25
- ❑10, Feb 84 .... 1.25
- ❑11, Mar 84 .... 1.25
- ❑12, Apr 84 .... 1.25
- ❑13, May 84 .... 1.25
- ❑14, Jul 84 .... 1.25
- ❑15, Aug 84 .... 1.25
- ❑16, Sep 84 .... 1.25
- ❑17, Oct 84 .... 1.25
- ❑18, Dec 84 .... 1.25
- ❑19, Feb 85,Final Issue 1.25
- ❑SE 1, Jul 83, O: Chaos 1.50
- ❑SE 2, Jan 84 .... 1.00
- ❑SE 3, Jun 84,Chaos 1.00

WARP-3
Equinox
Value: Cover or less
- ❑1, Mar 90, b&w 1.50

WAR PARTY
Lightning
Value: Cover or less
- ❑1, Oct 94 .... 2.95

WARP GRAPHICS ANNUAL
Warp

	ORIG	GOOD	FINE	N-MINT
❑1, WP (w), Elfquest: Courage, b, full color; Elfquest, Panda Khan, Unicorn Isle, Captain Obese, Thunderbunny, MythAdventures	2.95	0.60	1.50	3.00

WARPWALKING
Caliber
Value: Cover or less
- ❑1, b&w 2.50
- ❑2, The Quick and the Dead, b&w 2.50
- ❑3, b&w 2.50
- ❑4, b&w 2.50

WARRIOR (ULTIMATE CREATIONS)
Ultimate Creations
Value: Cover or less
- ❑1 .... 2.95
- ❑2 .... 2.95
- ❑3 .... 2.95
- ❑4 .... 2.95

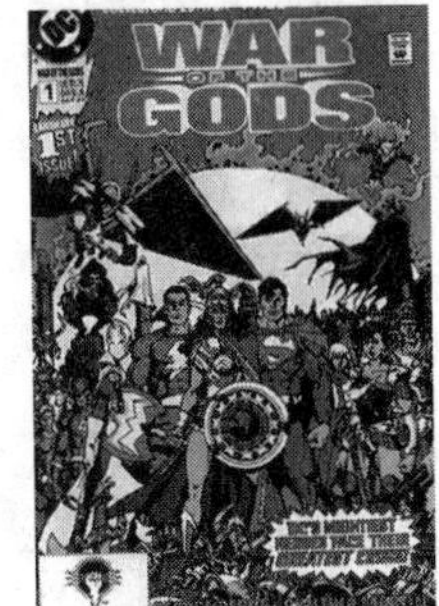

The members of various pantheons, including the gods that gave Wonder Woman and Captain Marvel their unique powers, vied for control of the DC universe in *War of the Gods.*

ORIG GOOD FINE N-MINT

WARRIOR NUN AREALA (VOL. 1)
Antarctic

	ORIG	GOOD	FINE	N-MINT
❑1, Dec 94, Gods and Beasts, 1: Warrior Nun Areala; 1: Shotgun Mary	2.95	1.00	2.50	5.00
❑1/LE, Dec 94, Gods and Beasts,no cover price; collector's edition of 5000; Limited edition (5000 made)	—	1.00	2.50	5.00
❑1-2, Mar 95, Gods and Beasts,2nd Printing	2.95	0.60	1.50	3.00
❑2, Feb 95	2.95	0.80	2.00	4.00
❑3, Apr 95, Redemption	2.95	0.80	2.00	4.00
❑3/CS, Redemption, CD	—	1.60	4.00	8.00
❑3/Dlx, Apr 95,cardstock cover; polybagged with CD	7.95	1.59	3.97	7.95
❑3/LE, Apr 95, Redemption,no cover price; silver foil cover edition (1000 made); Limited edition (1000 made)	8.00	1.00	2.50	5.00

WARRIOR NUN AREALA (VOL. 2)
Antarctic

	ORIG	GOOD	FINE	N-MINT
❑1, Jun 97, The Hammer & The Holocaust, Part 1	2.95	0.60	1.50	3.00
❑1/SC, Jun 97, The Hammer & The Holocaust, Part 1, Leather edition; Print run of 700	—	1.20	3.00	6.00
❑2, Sep 97, The Hammer & The Holocaust, Part 2	2.95	0.60	1.50	3.00
❑3, Nov 97	2.95	0.60	1.50	3.00
❑4, Jan 98, Holy Man, Holy Terror, Part 1	2.95	0.60	1.50	3.00
❑5, Mar 98, Holy Man, Holy Terror, Part 2	2.95	0.60	1.50	3.00
❑6, May 98, Nor a Liar Run, Aware	2.95	0.60	1.50	3.00

WARRIOR NUN AREALA (VOL. 3)
Antarctic
Value: Cover or less
- ❑1, Jul 99 .... 2.50
- ❑2, Aug 99 .... 2.50

WARRIOR NUN AREALA AND AVENGELYNE
Antarctic
Value: Cover or less
- ❑1/A, Dec 96,crossover with Maximum Press 2.95
- ❑1/B, Dec 96,logoless cover and poster insert; poster edition 5.95

WARRIOR NUN AREALA AND GLORY
Antarctic
Value: Cover or less
- ❑1, Sep 97,crossover with Awesome 2.95
- ❑1/CS, Sep 97, limited poster edition; crossover with Awesome 5.95

WARRIOR NUN AREALA/RAZOR: REVENGE
Antarctic
Value: Cover or less
- ❑1, Jan 99, Promises to Keep 2.99
- ❑1/Dlx, Jan 99, Promises to Keep, Deluxe Edition with painted cover 5.99

WARRIOR NUN AREALA: RESURRECTION
Antarctic
Value: Cover or less
- ❑1, Nov 98 .... 2.95
- ❑1/SC, Sum 98,alternate logoless cover 5.95
- ❑2, Jan 99, Hands of Fate, Fists of Fury 2.95
- ❑3, Mar 99 .... 2.95
- ❑4 .... 2.99
- ❑5 .... 2.99
- ❑6 .... 2.99
- ❑Ash 1, Nov 98, nn; b&w preview 1.00

WARRIOR NUN AREALA: RHEINTÖCHTER
Antarctic
Value: Cover or less
- ❑1, Dec 97, b&w 2.95
- ❑2, Apr 98, b&w 2.95

WARRIOR NUN AREALA: RITUALS
Antarctic

	ORIG	GOOD	FINE	N-MINT
❑1, Aug 95, Conspiracy	2.95	0.59	1.48	2.95
❑1/SC, Aug 95, Conspiracy,no cover price	—	0.80	2.00	4.00
❑2, Oct 95, Masques	2.95	0.59	1.48	2.95
❑3, Dec 95	2.95	0.59	1.48	2.95
❑4, Feb 96	2.95	0.59	1.48	2.95
❑5, Apr 96, Treacherous Liaison	2.95	0.59	1.48	2.95
❑6, Jun 96,40pgs.	3.50	0.59	1.48	2.95

WARRIOR NUN: BLACK & WHITE
Antarctic

	ORIG	GOOD	FINE	N-MINT
❑1, Feb 97, Sea Demons, Part 1	2.95	0.60	1.50	3.00
❑2, Apr 97, Sea Demons, Part 2,cover says Jan, indicia says Apr	2.95	0.60	1.50	3.00

	ORIG	GOOD	FINE	N-MINT
❑3, Jun 97, Nemesis	2.95	0.60	1.50	3.00
❑4, Aug 97, Winter Jade, Part 1	2.95	0.60	1.50	3.00
❑5, Oct 97, Winter Jade, Part 2	2.95	0.60	1.50	3.00
❑6, Dec 97, Winter Jade, Part 3	2.95	0.60	1.50	3.00
❑7, Feb 98	2.95	0.60	1.50	3.00
❑8, Mar 98, Ninja Nun	2.95	0.60	1.50	3.00
❑9, Apr 98, Breaking & Entering	2.95	0.60	1.50	3.00
❑10, May 98, Dismissal	2.95	0.60	1.50	3.00
❑11, Jun 98, The Scenic Route	2.95	0.60	1.50	3.00
❑12, Jul 98, Sister Trinity	2.95	0.60	1.50	3.00
❑13, Sep 98, Far West	2.95	0.60	1.50	3.00
❑14, Oct 98, Cryptopolis	2.95	0.60	1.50	3.00
❑15, Nov 98, Sister Trinity	2.95	0.59	1.48	2.95
❑16, Jan 99, Redeemers, Part 5, End Game	2.99	0.60	1.50	2.99
❑17, Feb 99, Sister Trinity	2.99	0.60	1.50	2.99
❑18, Mar 99, Reaction	2.99	0.60	1.50	2.99
❑19, Apr 99	2.99	0.60	1.50	2.99
❑20, A Solemn Duty	—	0.60	1.50	2.99
❑21, Jul 99	2.50	0.50	1.25	2.50

WARRIOR NUN DEI
ANTARCTIC
Value: Cover or less

❑1, Comics Cavalcade Commemorative Edition 5.95

WARRIOR NUN DEI: AFTERTIME
ANTARCTIC

	ORIG	GOOD	FINE	N-MINT
❑1, Jan 97	2.95	0.60	1.50	3.00
❑2	2.95	0.60	1.50	3.00
❑3, Mar 99	2.95	0.60	1.50	3.00

WARRIOR NUN: FRENZY
ANTARCTIC
Value: Cover or less

❑1, Jan 98 ..... 2.95
❑2, Jun 98 ..... 2.95

WARRIOR NUN: SCORPIO ROSE
ANTARCTIC
Value: Cover or less

❑1, Sep 96 ..... 2.95
❑2, Nov 96 ..... 2.95
❑3, Jan 97 ..... 2.95
❑4, Mar 97,Final Issue 2.95

WARRIOR NUN VS RAZOR
ANTARCTIC
Value: Cover or less

❑1, May 96, Deceiver,crossover with London Night Studios .. 3.95

WARRIOR OF WAVERLY STREET, THE
DARK HORSE
Value: Cover or less

❑1, Nov 96 ..... 2.95
❑2, Dec 96,Final Issue 2.95

WARRIORS
ADVENTURE

	ORIG	GOOD	FINE	N-MINT
❑1, Two Sides of Man; The Twelfth Cup	1.95	0.40	1.00	2.00
❑2, Dec 87	1.95	0.40	1.00	2.00
❑3	1.95	0.40	1.00	2.00

WARRIORS OF PLASM
DEFIANT

	ORIG	GOOD	FINE	N-MINT
❑1, Aug 93, The Sedition Agenda, Part 1, 1: Warriors of Plasm; 1: Lorca,First Defiant Comic (not including Warriors of Plasm #0 promotion)	2.95	0.59	1.48	2.95
❑2, Sep 93	2.95	0.59	1.48	2.95
❑3, Oct 93	2.95	0.59	1.48	2.95
❑4, Nov 93	2.95	0.59	1.48	2.95
❑5, Dec 93	2.50	0.50	1.25	2.50
❑6, Jan 94, 1: Prudence	2.50	0.50	1.25	2.50
❑7, Feb 94	2.50	0.50	1.25	2.50
❑8, Mar 94,40pgs.	2.75	0.55	1.38	2.75
❑9, Apr 94,40pgs.	2.50	0.55	1.38	2.75
❑10, May 94	2.50	0.50	1.25	2.50
❑11, Jun 94	2.50	0.50	1.25	2.50
❑12	2.50	0.50	1.25	2.50
❑13,Final issue?	2.50	0.50	1.25	2.50

WARRIORS OF PLASM GRAPHIC NOVEL
DEFIANT
Value: Cover or less

❑1,Home for the Holidays 6.95

WARRIOR'S WAY
BENCH PRESS
Value: Cover or less

❑1 ..... 2.99
❑2, Aug 98 ..... 2.99
❑2/A, Aug 98,alternate cover .. 2.99
❑3 ..... 2.99

WAR SIRENS AND LIBERTY BELLES
RECOLLECTIONS
Value: Cover or less

❑1, b&w; cardstock cover; Reprint 4.95

WAR SLUTS
PRETTY GRAPHIC
Value: Cover or less

❑1, b&w; adult 3.95
❑2, b&w; adult; cardstock cover 3.95

WARSTRIKE
MALIBU
Value: Cover or less

❑1, May 94 ..... 1.95
❑2, Jun 94, The Darkness, 1: Backlash (Ultraverse); 1: Gaunt; 1: Domingo; 1: Quixote 1.95
❑3, Jul 94, The Politics of Greed 1.95
❑4, Aug 94, Games, 1: Captain U.S.A. 1.95
❑5, Sep 94, The Symphony of the Damned, 1: Aeon 1.95
❑6, Oct 94, Fear, Hate, Hope, A: Rafferty 1.95
❑7, Nov 94, A Lonely Place of Dying,Final Issue 1.95
❑GS 1, Dec 94, Faith No More; Godwheel (Prelude), Giant-size; Lord Pumpkin reborn... 2.50

WARWORLD!
DARK HORSE
Value: Cover or less

❑1, b&w 1.75

WARZONE
EXPRESS
Value: Cover or less

❑1, b&w; enhanced cardstock cover 2.95
❑2, b&w; enhanced cardstock cover 2.95
❑3, b&w; enhanced cardstock cover 2.95

WASHMEN
NEW YORK
Value: Cover or less

❑1 ..... 1.70

WASH TUBBS QUARTERLY
DRAGON LADY
Value: Cover or less

❑1 ..... 4.95
❑2 ..... 5.95
❑3 ..... 5.95
❑4 ..... 5.95
❑5 ..... 5.95

WASTE L.A.: DESCENT
JOHN GAUSHELL
Value: Cover or less

❑1, Jan 96, b&w; fumetti 2.50
❑2, Mar 96, b&w; fumetti 2.50
❑3, May 96, b&w; fumetti 2.50

WASTELAND
DC

	ORIG	GOOD	FINE	N-MINT
❑1, Dec 87, Foo Goo; R.ab.	1.75	0.40	1.00	2.00
❑2, Jan 88, That's Entertainment; Ghengis Sings!!	1.75	0.40	1.00	2.00
❑3, Feb 88, American Squalor; Dies Illa	1.75	0.40	1.00	2.00
❑4, Mar 88, Sonnet LXVI; A Safe Place	1.75	0.40	1.00	2.00
❑5, Apr 88,correct cover	1.75	0.40	1.00	2.00
❑5/A, Apr 88,cover of #6	1.75	0.40	1.00	2.00
❑6, May 88,correct cover	1.75	0.40	1.00	2.00
❑6/A, May 88,blank cover	1.75	0.40	1.00	2.00
❑7, Jun 88	1.75	0.40	1.00	2.00
❑8, Jul 88	1.75	0.40	1.00	2.00
❑9, Aug 88	1.75	0.40	1.00	2.00
❑10, Sep 88	1.75	0.40	1.00	2.00
❑11, Oct 88, Embryo; Revenge of the Swamp Creature!	1.75	0.40	1.00	2.00
❑12, Nov 88, After the Dead Detective; Passing Grade	1.75	0.40	1.00	2.00
❑13, Dec 88, Tipped Toes; Astigmata	1.75	0.40	1.00	2.00
❑14, Win 88, Metamorphfloozie; Whistling Past the Graveyard	1.75	0.40	1.00	2.00
❑15, Hol 88, Crocophagia, or Hamlet in Aegypt; Zero Hour	1.75	0.40	1.00	2.00
❑16, Feb 89, The Woman Who Tried to Find God; All I Want for Christmas is the Head of Idi Amin!	1.75	0.40	1.00	2.00
❑17, Apr 89	2.00	0.40	1.00	2.00
❑18, May 89, The Casebook of the Dead Detective: "86",Final Issue	2.00	0.40	1.00	2.00

WATCHCATS
HARRIER
Value: Cover or less

❑1 ..... 1.95

WATCHMEN
DC

	ORIG	GOOD	FINE	N-MINT
❑1, Sep 86, DaG, AMo (w), 1: Ozymandias; 1: Doctor Manhattan; D: The Comedian; 1: Rorshach	1.50	1.20	3.00	6.00
❑2, Oct 86, DaG, AMo (w)	1.50	0.80	2.00	4.00
❑3, Nov 86, DaG, AMo (w)	1.50	0.80	2.00	4.00
❑4, Dec 86, DaG, AMo (w), O: Doctor Manhattan	1.50	0.60	1.50	3.00
❑5, Jan 87, DaG, AMo (w)	1.50	0.60	1.50	3.00
❑6, Feb 87, DaG, AMo (w), O: Rorshach	1.50	0.60	1.50	3.00
❑7, Mar 87, DaG, AMo (w)	1.50	0.60	1.50	3.00
❑8, Apr 87, DaG, AMo (w)	1.50	0.60	1.50	3.00
❑9, May 87, DaG, AMo (w)	1.50	0.60	1.50	3.00
❑10, Jul 87, DaG, AMo (w)	1.50	0.60	1.50	3.00
❑11, Aug 87, DaG, AMo (w), O: Ozymandias	1.50	0.60	1.50	3.00
❑12, Oct 87, DaG, AMo (w), D: Rorshach	1.50	0.60	1.50	3.00

WATERWORLD: CHILDREN OF LEVIATHAN
ACCLAIM
Value: Cover or less

❑1, Aug 97,no indicia 2.50
❑2 ..... 2.50
❑3 ..... 2.50
❑4 ..... 2.50

WAVEMAKERS
BLIND BAT

Value: Cover or less
- ❑1 ... 3.00

WAVE WARRIORS
ASTROBOYS

	ORIG	GOOD	FINE	N-MINT
❑1, full color	1.00	0.40	1.00	2.00

WAXWORK
BLACKTHORNE

Value: Cover or less
- ❑1, b&w; movie Adaptation ... 2.00
- ❑3D 1,movie Adaptation ... 2.50

WAY OUT STRIPS (FANTAGRAPHICS)
FANTAGRAPHICS

Value: Cover or less
- ❑1, b&w ... 2.50
- ❑2, May 94, b&w ... 2.75
- ❑3, Aug 94, b&w ... 2.75

WAY OUT STRIPS (TRAGEDY STRIKES)
TRAGEDY STRIKES

Value: Cover or less
- ❑1, b&w ... 2.95
- ❑2, b&w ... 2.95
- ❑3, b&w ... 2.95

WAYWARD WARRIOR
ALPHA PRODUCTIONS

Value: Cover or less
- ❑1, b&w ... 1.95
- ❑2, b&w ... 1.95
- ❑3, b&w ... 1.95

WCW WORLD CHAMPIONSHIP WRESTLING
MARVEL

	ORIG	GOOD	FINE	N-MINT
❑1, Apr 92	1.25	0.40	1.00	2.00
❑2, May 92	1.25	0.30	0.75	1.50
❑3, Jun 92	1.25	0.30	0.75	1.50
❑4, Jul 92	1.25	0.30	0.75	1.50
❑5, Aug 92	1.25	0.30	0.75	1.50
❑6, Sep 92	1.25	0.30	0.75	1.50
❑7, Oct 92	1.25	0.30	0.75	1.50
❑8, Nov 92	1.25	0.30	0.75	1.50
❑9, Dec 92	1.25	0.30	0.75	1.50
❑10, Jan 93	1.25	0.30	0.75	1.50
❑11, Feb 93	1.25	0.30	0.75	1.50
❑12, Mar 93, Bombed!	1.25	0.30	0.75	1.50

WEAPON X
MARVEL

	ORIG	GOOD	FINE	N-MINT
❑1, Mar 95, Unforgiven Trespasses,Age of Apocalypse	1.95	0.40	1.00	2.00
❑2, Apr 95, Fire in the Sky!,Age of Apocalypse	1.95	0.40	1.00	2.00
❑3, May 95,Age of Apocalypse	1.95	0.40	1.00	2.00
❑4, Jun 95,Age of Apocalypse	1.95	0.40	1.00	2.00

WEAPON ZERO
IMAGE

	ORIG	GOOD	FINE	N-MINT
❑1, Jun 95, 1: Weapon Zero,Issue #T-4	2.50	0.60	1.50	3.00
❑1/GO, Jun 95, Gold edition; Issue #T-4; 1000 copies produced for Chicago Comicon	—	0.50	1.25	2.50
❑2, Aug 95,Issue #T-3	2.50	0.50	1.25	2.50
❑3, Sep 95,Issue #T-2	2.50	0.50	1.25	2.50
❑4, Oct 95,Issue #T-1	2.50	0.50	1.25	2.50
❑5, Dec 95,Issue #T-O; Issue #T-0	2.50	0.50	1.25	2.50

WEAPON ZERO (VOL. 2)
IMAGE

	ORIG	GOOD	FINE	N-MINT
❑1, Mar 96,indicia gives year of publication as 1995	2.50	0.60	1.50	3.00
❑2, Apr 96,indicia gives year of publication as 1995	2.50	0.60	1.50	3.00
❑3, May 96	2.50	0.60	1.50	3.00
❑4, Jun 96,indicia gives year of publication as 1995	2.50	0.60	1.50	3.00
❑5, Jul 96,indicia gives year of publication as 1995	2.50	0.60	1.50	3.00
❑6, Aug 96	2.50	0.50	1.25	2.50
❑7, Sep 96	2.50	0.50	1.25	2.50
❑8, Nov 96	2.50	0.50	1.25	2.50
❑9, Dec 96	2.50	0.50	1.25	2.50
❑10, Feb 97, Family Feuds	2.50	0.50	1.25	2.50
❑11, Apr 97	2.50	0.50	1.25	2.50
❑12, May 97	2.50	0.50	1.25	2.50
❑13, Jun 97	2.50	0.50	1.25	2.50
❑14, Sep 97	2.50	0.50	1.25	2.50
❑15, Dec 97	3.50	0.70	1.75	3.50

WEAPON ZERO/SILVER SURFER
TOP COW

Value: Cover or less
- ❑1, Jan 97, Devil's Reign, Part 1; Devil's Reign,crossover with Marvel; continues in Cyblade/ Ghost Rider ... 2.95
- ❑1/A, Jan 97,alternate cover ... 2.95

WEASEL GUY: ROAD TRIP
IMAGE

Value: Cover or less
- ❑1, Aug 99, Moving Day ... 2.95
- ❑1/A, Aug 99, Moving Day,alternate cover ... 2.95
- ❑2, Oct 99, Barn Razing ... 3.50

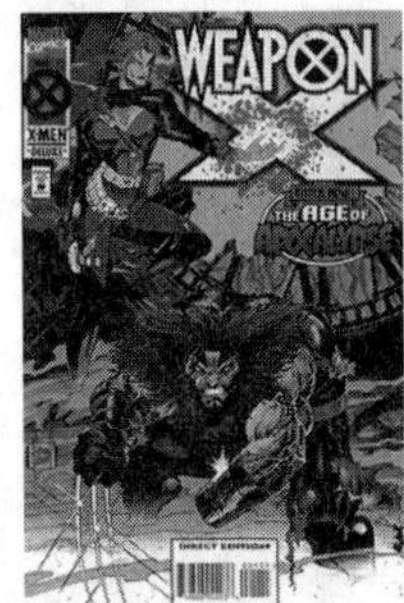

The "Age of Apocalypse" version of Wolverine retained his Weapon X name, but was short a hand.

WEASEL PATROL, THE
ECLIPSE

Value: Cover or less
- ❑1, b&w ... 2.00

WEATHER WOMAN
CPM MANGA

Value: Cover or less
- ❑1, Aug 00, b&w ... 2.95
- ❑1/A, Aug 00, b&w; alternate cover; Weather Woman smoking ... 2.95

WEAVEWORLD
MARVEL

Value: Cover or less
- ❑1, prestige format ... 4.95
- ❑2, prestige format ... 4.95
- ❑3, prestige format ... 4.95

WEB, THE
DC

	ORIG	GOOD	FINE	N-MINT
❑1, Sep 91, 1: Templar; 1: Bill Grady; 1: The Web (full appearance)	1.00	0.25	0.63	1.25
❑2, Oct 91, 1: Jump; 1: Powell Jennings; O: The Web; 1: Brew; 1: The Sunshine Kid; 1: Gunny	1.00	0.20	0.50	1.00
❑3, Nov 91, 1: Meridian; 1: St. James	1.00	0.20	0.50	1.00
❑4, Dec 91, 1: Silver	1.00	0.20	0.50	1.00
❑5, Jan 92	1.00	0.20	0.50	1.00
❑6, Feb 92	1.00	0.20	0.50	1.00
❑7, Apr 92	1.00	0.20	0.50	1.00
❑8, Apr 92, 1: Studs	1.00	0.20	0.50	1.00
❑9, May 92, The Coming Of The Crusaders, Part 5,trading card	1.00	0.20	0.50	1.00
❑10, Jun 92	1.25	0.25	0.63	1.25
❑11, Jul 92	1.25	0.25	0.63	1.25
❑12, Aug 92	1.25	0.25	0.63	1.25
❑13, Sep 92	1.25	0.25	0.63	1.25
❑14, Oct 92,Final Issue	1.25	0.25	0.63	1.25
❑Anl 1,trading card	2.50	0.50	1.25	2.50

WEBBER'S WORLD
ALLSTAR

Value: Cover or less
- ❑1 ... 4.95

WEB-MAN
ARGOSY

Value: Cover or less
- ❑1, The Tentacles of Dr. Kraken,gatefold cover ... 2.50

WEB OF SCARLET SPIDER
MARVEL

	ORIG	GOOD	FINE	N-MINT
❑1, Nov 95, Virtual Mortality, Part 1, O: Scarlet Spider	1.95	0.40	1.00	2.00
❑2, Dec 95, Cyberwar, Part 1, A: Cyber-Slayers	1.95	0.40	1.00	2.00
❑3, Jan 96, Nightmare in Scarlet, Part 1, A: Firestar,continues in New Warriors #67	1.95	0.40	1.00	2.00
❑4, Feb 96, Nightmare in Scarlet, Part 3,Final Issue	1.95	0.40	1.00	2.00

WEB OF SPIDER-MAN, THE
MARVEL

	ORIG	GOOD	FINE	N-MINT
❑1, Apr 85	0.65	1.00	2.50	5.00
❑2, May 85	0.65	0.60	1.50	3.00
❑3, Jun 85	0.65	0.60	1.50	3.00
❑4, Jul 85, V: Doctor Octopus	0.65	0.60	1.50	3.00
❑5, Aug 85, V: Doctor Octopus	0.65	0.60	1.50	3.00
❑6, Sep 85,Secret Wars II	0.65	0.60	1.50	3.00
❑7, Oct 85, V: Hulk	0.65	0.60	1.50	3.00
❑8, Nov 85	0.65	0.60	1.50	3.00
❑9, Dec 85	0.65	0.60	1.50	3.00
❑10, Jan 86, A: Dominic Fortune	0.65	0.60	1.50	3.00
❑11, Feb 86	0.75	0.50	1.25	2.50
❑12, Mar 86	0.75	0.50	1.25	2.50
❑13, Apr 86	0.75	0.50	1.25	2.50
❑14, May 86	0.75	0.50	1.25	2.50
❑15, Jun 86, 1: Chance I (Nicholas Powell); 1: The Foreigner	0.75	0.50	1.25	2.50
❑16, Jul 86	0.75	0.50	1.25	2.50
❑17, Aug 86, V: Magma,red suit destroyed.	0.75	0.50	1.25	2.50
❑18, Sep 86,Venom cameo	0.75	0.50	1.25	2.50
❑19, Oct 86, 1: Solo	0.75	0.50	1.25	2.50
❑20, Nov 86	0.75	0.50	1.25	2.50

	ORIG	GOOD	FINE	N-MINT
❑21, Dec 86	0.75	0.50	1.25	2.50
❑22, Jan 87	0.75	0.50	1.25	2.50
❑23, Feb 87	0.75	0.50	1.25	2.50
❑24, Mar 87	0.75	0.50	1.25	2.50
❑25, Apr 87	0.75	0.50	1.25	2.50
❑26, May 87	0.75	0.50	1.25	2.50
❑27, Jun 87	0.75	0.50	1.25	2.50
❑28, Jul 87	0.75	0.50	1.25	2.50
❑29, Aug 87, A: Hobgoblin II (Jason Macendale); A: Wolverine	0.75	0.80	2.00	4.00
❑30, Sep 87, O: The Rose	0.75	0.60	1.50	3.00
❑31, Oct 87, Kraven's Last Hunt, Part 1, V: Kraven	0.75	0.80	2.00	4.00
❑32, Nov 87, Kraven's Last Hunt, Part 4, V: Kraven	0.75	0.80	2.00	4.00
❑33, Dec 87, BSz (c)	0.75	0.50	1.25	2.50
❑34, Jan 88	0.75	0.50	1.25	2.50
❑35, Feb 88, 1: Tarantula II (Luis Alvarez)	0.75	0.50	1.25	2.50
❑36, Mar 88, O: Tarantula II (Luis Alvarez)	0.75	0.60	1.50	3.00
❑37, Apr 88	0.75	0.50	1.25	2.50
❑38, May 88, A: Hobgoblin II (Jason Macendale); V: Hobgoblin	1.00	0.80	2.00	4.00
❑39, Jun 88, Cult of Love	1.00	0.50	1.25	2.50
❑40, Jul 88, Cult of Love	1.00	0.50	1.25	2.50
❑41, Aug 88, Cult of Love	1.00	0.50	1.25	2.50
❑42, Sep 88, Cult of Love	1.00	0.50	1.25	2.50
❑43, Oct 88, Cult of Love	1.00	0.50	1.25	2.50
❑44, Nov 88, A: Hulk	1.00	0.40	1.00	2.00
❑45, Dec 88, V: Vulture	1.00	0.40	1.00	2.00
❑46, Jan 89	1.00	0.40	1.00	2.00
❑47, Feb 89, V: Hobgoblin,Inferno	1.00	0.40	1.00	2.00
❑48, Mar 89, O: Demogoblin; V: Hobgoblin,Inferno	1.00	1.20	3.00	6.00
❑49, Apr 89	1.00	0.30	0.75	1.50
❑50, May 89, Giant-sized	1.50	0.40	1.00	2.00
❑51, Jun 89	1.00	0.30	0.75	1.50
❑52, Jul 89, V: Chameleon	1.00	0.30	0.75	1.50
❑53, Aug 89	1.00	0.30	0.75	1.50
❑54, Sep 89, V: Chameleon	1.00	0.30	0.75	1.50
❑55, Oct 89, V: Chameleon	1.00	0.30	0.75	1.50
❑56, Nov 89, V: Rocket Racer	1.00	0.30	0.75	1.50
❑57, Nov 89, V: Skinhead	1.00	0.30	0.75	1.50
❑58, Dec 89,Acts of Vengeance	1.00	0.40	1.00	2.00
❑59, Dec 89, Acts of Vengeance,Acts of Vengeance; Spider-Man with cosmic powers	1.00	1.00	2.50	5.00
❑60, Jan 90, Acts of Vengeance,Acts of Vengeance	1.00	0.40	1.00	2.00
❑61, Feb 90, Acts of Vengeance,Acts of Vengeance	1.00	0.40	1.00	2.00
❑62, Mar 90	1.00	0.30	0.75	1.50
❑63, Apr 90	1.00	0.30	0.75	1.50
❑64, May 90,Acts of Vengeance	1.00	0.30	0.75	1.50
❑65, Jun 90,Acts of Vengeance	1.00	0.30	0.75	1.50
❑66, Jul 90, A: Green Goblin	1.00	0.30	0.75	1.50
❑67, Aug 90, A: Green Goblin	1.00	0.30	0.75	1.50
❑68, Sep 90	1.00	0.30	0.75	1.50
❑69, Oct 90	1.00	0.30	0.75	1.50
❑70, Nov 90,Spider-Hulk	1.00	0.30	0.75	1.50
❑71, Dec 90	1.00	0.30	0.75	1.50
❑72, Jan 91	1.00	0.30	0.75	1.50
❑73, Feb 91	1.00	0.30	0.75	1.50
❑74, Mar 91	1.00	0.30	0.75	1.50
❑75, Apr 91	1.00	0.30	0.75	1.50
❑76, May 91, A: Fantastic Four	1.00	0.30	0.75	1.50
❑77, Jun 91	1.00	0.30	0.75	1.50
❑78, Jul 91, A: Cloak & Dagger	1.00	0.30	0.75	1.50
❑79, Aug 91	1.00	0.30	0.75	1.50
❑80, Sep 91, V: Silvermane	1.00	0.30	0.75	1.50
❑81, Oct 91, KB (w)	1.00	0.30	0.75	1.50
❑82, Nov 91, KB (w)	1.00	0.30	0.75	1.50
❑83, Dec 91, KB (w)	1.00	0.30	0.75	1.50
❑84, Jan 92, Name of the Rose, Part 1; The Name of the Rose, Part 1, A: Hobgoblin	1.00	0.30	0.75	1.50
❑85, Feb 92, Name of the Rose, Part 2; The Name of the Rose, Part 2	1.25	0.30	0.75	1.50
❑86, Mar 92, Name of the Rose, Part 3; The Name of the Rose, Part 3	1.25	0.30	0.75	1.50
❑87, Apr 92, Name of the Rose, Part 4; The Name of the Rose, Part 4	1.25	0.30	0.75	1.50
❑88, May 92, Name of the Rose, Part 5; The Name of the Rose, Part 5	1.25	0.30	0.75	1.50
❑89, Jun 92, Name of the Rose, Part 6; The Name of the Rose, Part 6	1.25	0.30	0.75	1.50
❑90, Jul 92, Double-size; hologram; Poster.	2.95	0.80	2.00	4.00
❑90-2, Jul 92,2nd Printing; Double-size; hologram; Poster	1.25	0.59	1.48	2.95
❑91, Aug 92	1.25	0.30	0.75	1.50
❑92, Sep 92	1.25	0.30	0.75	1.50
❑93, Oct 92, Hobgoblin Reborn, Part 1	1.25	0.30	0.75	1.50
❑94, Nov 92, Hobgoblin Reborn, Part 2, V: Hobgoblin	1.25	0.30	0.75	1.50
❑95, Dec 92, Spirits of Venom, Part 1, V: Venom; A: Johnny Blaze; A: Ghost Rider	1.25	0.30	0.75	1.50
❑96, Jan 93, Spirits of Venom, Part 3, V: Venom; A: Johnny Blaze; A: Ghost Rider	1.25	0.30	0.75	1.50
❑97, Feb 93, My Enemy's Enemy, Part 1	1.25	0.30	0.75	1.50
❑98, Mar 93, My Enemy's Enemy, Part 2	1.25	0.30	0.75	1.50
❑99, Apr 93, V: New Enforcers	1.25	0.30	0.75	1.50
❑100, May 93, 1: Spider-Armor,foil cover	2.95	0.60	1.50	3.00
❑101, Jun 93, Maximum Carnage, Part 2	1.25	0.30	0.75	1.50
❑102, Jul 93, Maximum Carnage, Part 6	1.25	0.30	0.75	1.50
❑103, Aug 93, Maximum Carnage, Part 10	1.25	0.30	0.75	1.50
❑104, Sep 93	1.25	0.30	0.75	1.50
❑105, Oct 93, A: Archangel,Infinity Crusade	1.25	0.30	0.75	1.50
❑106, Nov 93,Infinity Crusade	1.25	0.30	0.75	1.50
❑107, Dec 93, A: Sandman; A: Quicksand.	1.25	0.30	0.75	1.50
❑108, Jan 94, A: Sandman; A: Quicksand.	1.25	0.30	0.75	1.50
❑109, Feb 94	1.25	0.30	0.75	1.50
❑110, Mar 94	1.25	0.30	0.75	1.50
❑111, Apr 94, V: Lizard	1.25	0.30	0.75	1.50
❑112, May 94, Pursuit, Part 3	1.50	0.30	0.75	1.50
❑113, Jun 94, Live and Let Die, Part 1, A: Black Cat; A: Gambit	1.50	0.30	0.75	1.50
❑113/CS, Jun 94, Live and Let Die, Part 1, A: Black Cat; A: Gambit, animation cel; TV preview; print	2.95	0.60	1.50	3.00
❑114, Jul 94	1.50	0.30	0.75	1.50
❑115, Aug 94	1.50	0.30	0.75	1.50
❑116, Sep 94	1.50	0.30	0.75	1.50
❑117, Oct 94, Power & Responsibility; Power and Responsibility, Part 1, A: Ben Reilly, Flip-book	1.50	0.50	1.25	2.50
❑117/SC, Oct 94, Power & Responsibility; Power and Responsibility, Part 1, A: Ben Reilly,foil cover; Flip-book	2.95	0.80	2.00	4.00
❑118, Nov 94	1.50	0.50	1.25	2.50
❑119, Dec 94,Scarlet Spider vs. Venom	1.50	0.30	0.75	1.50
❑119/CS, Dec 94, polybagged with Marvel Milestone Edition: Amazing Spider-Man #150 and POP card for Amazing Spider-Ma; Scarlet Spider vs. Venom	6.45	1.29	3.22	6.45
❑120, Jan 95, A: Morbius, Flip-book; Giant-size	2.25	0.60	1.50	3.00
❑121, Feb 95, Web of Life, Part 3, V: Kaine	1.50	0.30	0.75	1.50
❑122, Mar 95, Smoke & Mirrors, Part 1, A: Jackal	1.50	0.30	0.75	1.50
❑123, Apr 95, Players & Pawns, Part 2, A: Jackal	1.50	0.30	0.75	1.50
❑124, May 95, The Mark of Kaine, Part 1	1.50	0.30	0.75	1.50
❑125, Jun 95, Lives Unlived; Shining Armor, Giant-size	2.95	0.59	1.48	2.95
❑125/SC, Jun 95, Lives Unlived; Shining Armor,Hologram on cover; Giant-size	3.95	0.79	1.98	3.95
❑126, Jul 95, The Trial of Peter Parker, Part 1	1.50	0.30	0.75	1.50
❑127, Aug 95, Maximum Clonage, Part 2	1.50	0.30	0.75	1.50
❑128, Sep 95, Exiled, Part 1	1.50	0.30	0.75	1.50
❑129, Oct 95, Time Bomb, Part 2, A: New Warriors,Final Issue	1.50	0.30	0.75	1.50
❑Anl 1, A: 4th,Painted cover	1.25	1.00	2.50	5.00
❑Anl 2, A: New Mutants	1.25	1.20	3.00	6.00
❑Anl 3,pin-ups	1.25	0.60	1.50	3.00
❑Anl 4, Evolutionary War, Part 8, 1: Poison	1.75	0.60	1.50	3.00
❑Anl 5, Atlantis Attacks, Part 11, O: Silver Sable; A: Fantastic Four,Atlantis Attacks	2.00	0.50	1.25	2.50
❑Anl 6, V: Psycho-Man,Tiny Spidey	2.00	0.50	1.25	2.50
❑Anl 7, Vibranium Vendetta, O: Green Goblin; V: Ultron; O: Venom; A: Black Panther; A: Iron Man; O: Hobgoblin	2.00	0.50	1.25	2.50
❑Anl 8, Hero Killers; The Hero Killers, Part 3, V: Rhino; V: Constrictor; A: Venom; V: Beetle; V: Whiplash; A: New Warriors	2.25	0.60	1.50	3.00
❑Anl 9, 1: The Cadre,trading card	2.95	0.59	1.48	2.95
❑Anl 10, V: Shriek	2.95	0.59	1.48	2.95
❑SS 1, Planet of the Symbiotes, Part 5; Black Cat: Cat & Robbers, Flip-book; Super Special	3.95	0.79	1.98	3.95

WEBSPINNERS: TALES OF SPIDER-MAN

MARVEL

Value: Cover or less

❑1, Jan 99, Webspinners Spider-Man, V: Mysterio, gatefold summary	2.99
❑1/Aut, Jan 99, A: Mysterio,Signed by Michael Zuli	19.63
❑2/A, Feb 99,Cover A	2.99
❑2/B,Cover B by Steve Rude	2.50
❑3, Mar 99, V: Mysterio; A: Betsy Schneider	2.50
❑4, Apr 99, KG, A: Silver Surfer	2.50
❑5, May 99	2.50
❑6, Jun 99, A: Silver Surfer	2.50
❑7, Jul 99, V: Sandman	2.50
❑8, Aug 99, V: Sandman	2.50
❑9, Sep 99	2.50
❑11, Nov 99	2.50

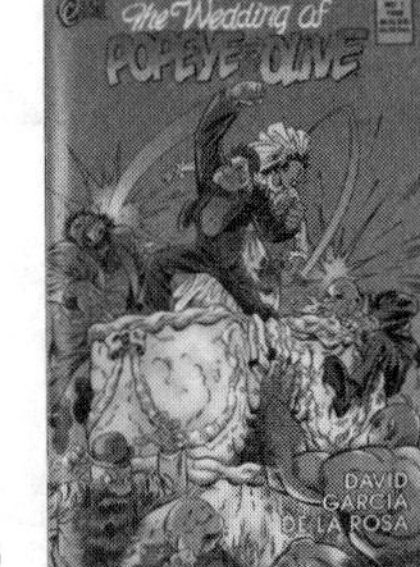

Peter David wrote *The Wedding of Popeye and Olive Oyl.*

WEDDING OF DRACULA
MARVEL

Value: Cover or less

	ORIG	GOOD	FINE	N-MINT
❑1,Reprints Tomb of Dracula 30,45, & 46				2.00

WEDDING OF POPEYE AND OLIVE, THE
OCEAN

Value: Cover or less

	ORIG	GOOD	FINE	N-MINT
❑1, b&w				2.75

WEEZUL
LIGHTNING

Value: Cover or less

	ORIG	GOOD	FINE	N-MINT
❑1/A, Aug 96				2.75
❑1/B, Aug 96,alternate cover				3.00

WEIRD
AVALON

Value: Cover or less

	ORIG	GOOD	FINE	N-MINT
❑1				2.99
❑2				2.99
❑3				2.99
❑4				2.99

WEIRD, THE
DC

Value: Cover or less

	ORIG	GOOD	FINE	N-MINT
❑1, Apr 88, BWr, A: Justice League International				1.50
❑2, May 88, BWr, A: Justice League International				1.50
❑3, Jun 88, BWr, A: Justice League International				1.50
❑4, Jul 88, BWr, A: Justice League International				1.50

WEIRD (MAGAZINE)
DC

Value: Cover or less

	ORIG	GOOD	FINE	N-MINT
❑1, Sum 97, The Ones That Got Away; Other Oswalds, b&w; magazine; reprints material from Big Book of Conspiracies; Summer 1997				2.99

WEIRDFALL
ANTARCTIC

Value: Cover or less

	ORIG	GOOD	FINE	N-MINT
❑1, Jul 95, Murphy's War, b&w				2.75
❑2, Sep 95, b&w				2.75
❑3, Nov 95, b&w				2.75

WEIRD FANTASY (RCP)
EC

	ORIG	GOOD	FINE	N-MINT
❑1, Oct 92, JKa; WW; HK; AF ,Reprint	2.00	0.50	1.25	2.50
❑2, Jan 93, JKa; WW; HK; AF ,Reprints Weird Fantasy #14	1.50	0.40	1.00	2.00
❑3, Apr 93, JKa; WW; HK; AF ,Reprint	1.50	0.40	1.00	2.00
❑4, Jul 93, JKa; WW; HK; AF ,Reprint	2.00	0.40	1.00	2.00
❑5, Oct 93, JKa; WW; HK; AF, JKa (w); WW (w); HK (w); AF (w), Child of Tomorrow!; The Time Machine and the Shmoe!,Reprint	2.00	0.40	1.00	2.00
❑6, Jan 94, JKa; WW; HK; AF, Space-Warp; The Dimension Translator,Reprint	2.00	0.40	1.00	2.00
❑7, Apr 94, JKa; WW; AF, 7 Year Old Genius; Come Into My Parlor,Reprint	2.00	0.40	1.00	2.00
❑8, Jul 94, The Origin of the Species; It Didn't Matter,Reprint	2.00	0.40	1.00	2.00
❑9, Oct 94, Spawn of Mars; The Duplicates,Reprint	2.00	0.40	1.00	2.00
❑10, Jan 95, The Secret of Saturn's Ring; A Timely Shock,Reprint	2.00	0.40	1.00	2.00
❑11, Apr 95,Reprint	2.00	0.50	1.25	2.50
❑12, Jul 95,Reprint	2.00	0.50	1.25	2.50
❑13, Oct 95,Reprint	2.00	0.50	1.25	2.50
❑14, Jan 96, FF ,Reprint	2.00	0.50	1.25	2.50
❑15, Apr 96, AW ,Reprint	2.00	0.50	1.25	2.50
❑16, Jul 96, AW ,Reprint	2.00	0.50	1.25	2.50
❑17, Oct 96, AW ,Reprint	2.00	0.50	1.25	2.50
❑18, Jan 97,Reprint	2.50	0.50	1.25	2.50
❑19, JKa; BE; JSe; JO; AW, JKa (w); BE (w); JSe (w); JO (w); AW (w), King of the Grey Spaces!; Hot-Rod!,Reprints Weird Fantasy (EC) #19	2.50	0.50	1.25	2.50
❑20, JKa; BE; JSe; JO; AW, JKa (w); BE (w); JSe (w); JO (w); AW (w), ...For Us the Living; I, Rocket,Reprints Weird Fantasy (EC) #20	2.50	0.50	1.25	2.50
❑21, JKa; BE; JSe; JO; AW, JKa (w); BE (w); JSe (w); JO (w); AW (w), My Home...; Saved,Reprints Weird Fantasy (EC) #21.	2.50	0.50	1.25	2.50
❑22, BK; JO, BK (w); JO (w), The Silent Towns; The Freaks,Reprints Weird Fantasy (EC) #22	2.50	0.50	1.25	2.50
❑Anl 1,Reprints Weird Fantasy #1-5	8.95	1.79	4.47	8.95
❑Anl 2,Reprints Weird Fantasy #6-10	9.95	1.99	4.97	9.95
❑Anl 3	8.95	1.79	4.47	8.95
❑Anl 4	9.95	1.99	4.97	9.95
❑Anl 5,Reprints Weird Fantasy #19-22	10.95	2.19	5.47	10.95

WEIRD MELVIN
MARC HANSEN STUFF!

Value: Cover or less

	ORIG	GOOD	FINE	N-MINT
❑1, Feb 95, O: Weird Melvin, b&w				2.95
❑2, Apr 95, b&w				2.95
❑3, Jun 95, b&w				2.95
❑4, Aug 95, b&w				2.95
❑5, Oct 95, b&w				2.95

WEIRD MYSTERY TALES
DC

	ORIG	GOOD	FINE	N-MINT
❑1, Jul 72, JK	0.20	1.80	4.50	9.00
❑2, Sep 72	0.20	1.20	3.00	6.00
❑3, Nov 72	0.20	1.00	2.50	5.00
❑4, Jan 73, The Devil to Pay; The Secret of Bat Island	0.20	1.00	2.50	5.00
❑5, Apr 73	0.20	1.00	2.50	5.00
❑6, Jul 73	0.20	0.80	2.00	4.00
❑7, Sep 73	0.20	0.80	2.00	4.00
❑8, Nov 73	0.20	0.80	2.00	4.00
❑9, Dec 73	0.20	0.80	2.00	4.00
❑10, Mar 74	0.20	0.80	2.00	4.00
❑11, Apr 74	0.20	0.80	2.00	4.00
❑12, Jul 74	0.20	0.80	2.00	4.00
❑13, Aug 74	0.20	0.80	2.00	4.00
❑14, Oct 74	0.20	0.80	2.00	4.00
❑15, Jan 75	0.20	0.80	2.00	4.00
❑16, Mar 75	0.25	0.80	2.00	4.00
❑17, Apr 75	0.25	0.80	2.00	4.00
❑18, May 75	0.25	0.80	2.00	4.00
❑19, Jun 75	0.25	0.80	2.00	4.00
❑20, Jul 75	0.25	0.80	2.00	4.00
❑21, Aug 75	0.25	0.80	2.00	4.00
❑22, Sep 75	0.25	0.80	2.00	4.00
❑23, Oct 75	0.25	0.80	2.00	4.00
❑24, Nov 75,Final Issue	0.25	0.80	2.00	4.00

WEIRD ROMANCE
ECLIPSE

Value: Cover or less

	ORIG	GOOD	FINE	N-MINT
❑1, b&w				2.00

WEIRD SCIENCE (GLADSTONE)
GLADSTONE

	ORIG	GOOD	FINE	N-MINT
❑1, Sep 90, JKa; WW; JO; HK; AW; GE; AF, JKa (w); WW (w); JO (w); HK (w); AW (w); GE (w); AF (w), A New Beginning; The Headhunters, Ray Bradbury Adaptation ("Outcast of the Stars"); Reprints Weird Science (EC) #22; Weird Fantasy (EC) #1	1.95	0.40	1.00	2.00
❑2, Nov 90, JKa; WW; JO; AW ,Reprint	1.95	0.40	1.00	2.00
❑3, Jan 91, JKa; WW; HK; AF, The Gray Cloud of Death; The Martian Monster,Reprints Weird Science (EC) #9, Weird Fantasy (EC) #14	2.00	0.40	1.00	2.00
❑4, Mar 91, WW; JO; AF ,Reprint	2.00	0.40	1.00	2.00

WEIRD SCIENCE (RCP)
EC

	ORIG	GOOD	FINE	N-MINT
❑1, Sep 92, JKa; WW; HK; AF, JKa (w); WW (w); HK (w); AF (w), Lost in the Microcosm; Dream of Doom,Reprints Weird Science (EC) #1	1.50	0.50	1.25	2.50
❑2, Dec 92, The Flying Saucer Invasion; The Meteor Monster,Reprints Weird Science (EC) #2	1.50	0.40	1.00	2.00
❑3, Mar 93, Destruction of the Earth!; The Sounds From Another World!,Reprints Weird Science (EC) #3	1.50	0.40	1.00	2.00
❑4, Jun 93, GI; JKa; HK; AF, Panic!; The Radioactive Child!,Reprints Weird Science (EC) #4	2.00	0.40	1.00	2.00
❑5, Sep 93, JKa; WW; HK; AF, Made of the Future!; Return,Reprints Weird Science (EC) #5	2.00	0.40	1.00	2.00
❑6, Dec 93, JKa; WW; HK; AF, Spawn of Venus; Man and Superman!,Reprints Weird Science (EC) #6	2.00	0.40	1.00	2.00
❑7, Mar 94, JKa; WW; HK; AF, AF (c), It Was the Monster From the Fourth Dimension; Something Missing!,Reprints Weird Science (EC) #7	2.00	0.40	1.00	2.00
❑8, Jun 94, JKa; WW; AF, Seeds of Jupiter!; The Escape,Reprints Weird Science (EC) #8	2.00	0.40	1.00	2.00
❑9, Sep 94, The Gray Cloud of Death!; The Martian Monster,Reprints Weird Science (EC) #9	2.00	0.40	1.00	2.00
❑10, Dec 94, The Maidens Cried; Reducing Costs,Reprints Weird Science (EC) #10.	2.00	0.40	1.00	2.00
❑11, Mar 95, The Conquerors of the Moon; Only Human,Reprints Weird Science (EC) #11	2.00	0.40	1.00	2.00
❑12, Jun 95, A Goble is a Knog's Best Friend; The Last Man,Reprints Weird Science (EC) #12	2.00	0.40	1.00	2.00

	ORIG	GOOD	FINE	N-MINT
❑13, Sep 95, A Weighty Decision; Saving for the Future,Reprints Weird Science (EC) #13	2.00	0.40	1.00	2.00
❑14, There'll be Some Changes Made; Inside Story,Reprints Weird Science (EC) #14	2.00	0.40	1.00	2.00
❑15,Reprints Weird Science (EC) #15	2.50	0.50	1.25	2.50
❑16,Reprints Weird Science (EC) #16	2.50	0.50	1.25	2.50
❑17,Reprints Weird Science (EC) #17	2.50	0.50	1.25	2.50
❑18,Reprints Weird Science (EC) #18	2.50	0.50	1.25	2.50
❑19, WW; BE; JO; AW, WW (w); BE (w); JO (w); AW (w), The Precious Years; The One Who Waits,Reprints Weird Science (EC) #19	2.50	0.50	1.25	2.50
❑20, JKa; WW; JO; AW, JKa (w); WW (w); JO (w); AW (w), The Loathsome!; Surprise Package,Reprints Weird Science (EC) #20	2.50	0.50	1.25	2.50
❑21, JKa; WW; FF; JO; AW, JKa (w); WW (w); JO (w); AW (w), EC Confidential; Punishment Without Crime,Reprints Weird Science (EC) #21; EC editors put themselves in story	2.50	0.50	1.25	2.50
❑22, WW; JO; AW; GE, WW (w); JO (w); AW (w); GE (w), A New Beginning; The Headhunters,Reprints Weird Science (EC) #22; Wally Wood puts himself in story	2.50	0.50	1.25	2.50
❑Anl 1,Reprints Weird Science (EC) #1-5	8.95	1.79	4.47	8.95
❑Anl 2,Reprints Weird Science (EC) #6-10	9.95	1.99	4.97	9.95
❑Anl 3,Reprints Weird Science (EC) #11-14	10.95	2.19	5.47	10.95
❑Anl 4,Reprints Weird Science (EC) #15-18	9.95	1.99	4.97	9.95
❑Anl 5,Reprints Weird Science (EC) #19-22	10.50	2.10	5.25	10.50

WEIRD SCIENCE-FANTASY (RCP)
EC

	ORIG	GOOD	FINE	N-MINT
❑1, Nov 92, The Children; Fish Story, "The Flying Machine" Ray Bradbury adaptation; Reprints Weird Science-Fantasy #23	1.50	0.40	1.00	2.00
❑2, Feb 93, BK; WW; JO; AW, AF (c), BK (w); WW (w); JO (w); AW (w), ...For Posterity; The Teacher From Mars, "The Teacher From Mars" Eando Binder adaptation; Reprints Weird Science-Fantasy #24; "Upheaval" by Harlan Ellison (1st professional work by Harlan Ellison)	1.50	0.40	1.00	2.00
❑3, May 93, BK; WW; JO; AW, AF (c), Flying Saucer Report; A Sound of Thunder, Reprints Weird Science-Fantasy #25	1.50	0.40	1.00	2.00
❑4, Aug 93, Flying Saucer Report, UFO issue; Reprints Weird Science-Fantasy #26;	1.50	0.40	1.00	2.00
❑5, Nov 93, WW; JO, Adaptability; Close Shave, "I, Robot" story adapted from the original Adam Link tale by Eando Binder; Reprints Weird Science-Fantasy #27	2.00	0.40	1.00	2.00
❑6, Feb 94, JKa; WW; JO; AW, AF (c),Reprints Weird Science-Fantasy #28	2.00	0.40	1.00	2.00
❑7, May 94, WW; JO; AW ,Frazetta cover; Reprints Weird Science-Fantasy #29	2.00	0.40	1.00	2.00
❑8,Reprint	2.00	0.40	1.00	2.00
❑9,Reprint	2.00	0.40	1.00	2.00
❑10,Reprint	2.00	0.40	1.00	2.00
❑11,Reprint	2.00	0.40	1.00	2.00
❑Anl 1,Collects Weird Science-Fantasy (RCP) #1-5	8.95	1.79	4.47	8.95
❑Anl 2,Collects Weird Science-Fantasy (RCP) #?	12.95	2.59	6.47	12.95

WEIRD SEX
EROS

Value: Cover or less

❑1, Jan 99 .... 2.95

WEIRD SUSPENSE
ATLAS

	ORIG	GOOD	FINE	N-MINT
❑1, Feb 75, 1: The Tarantula	0.25	0.20	0.50	1.00
❑2, Apr 75	0.25	0.20	0.50	1.00
❑3, Jul 75	0.25	0.20	0.50	1.00

WEIRDSVILLE
BLINDWOLF

Value: Cover or less

- ❑1, Feb 97, Welcome to: Weirdsville 2.95
- ❑2, Apr 97 .... 2.95
- ❑3, Jun 97 .... 2.95
- ❑4, Aug 97 .... 2.95
- ❑5, Sep 97, A: Shi 2.95
- ❑6, Dec 97 .... 2.95
- ❑7 .... 2.95
- ❑8, Mar 98, An American Werewolf in Weirdsville 2.95
- ❑9, Jun 98, An American Werewolf in Weirdsville 2.95

WEIRD TALES ILLUSTRATED
MILLENNIUM

Value: Cover or less

- ❑1, Shattered Like A Glass Goblin; Party Games, full color 2.95
- ❑1/Dlx, Shattered Like A Glass Goblin; Party Games, Deluxe edition with extra stories 4.95
- ❑2 .... 2.95

WEIRD TALES OF THE MACABRE
ATLAS

	ORIG	GOOD	FINE	N-MINT
❑1, Apr 75	0.75	0.60	1.50	3.00
❑2, Apr 75	0.75	0.60	1.50	3.00

WEIRD TRIPS MAGAZINE
KITCHEN SINK

	ORIG	GOOD	FINE	N-MINT
❑1, Violence and Vegetation in	0.65	0.80	2.00	4.00

WEIRD WAR TALES
DC

	ORIG	GOOD	FINE	N-MINT
❑1, Sep 71, JKu ,52pgs.	0.25	9.00	22.50	45.00
❑2, Nov 71, MD, JKu (w), Reef of No Return; The Moon is the Murderer,52pgs.	0.25	5.60	14.00	28.00
❑3, Jan 72, Been Here Before; The Cloud That Went to War,52pgs.	0.25	4.00	10.00	20.00
❑4, Mar 72, JKu (c), Time Warp; The Unknown Sentinel,52pgs.	0.25	3.60	9.00	18.00
❑5, May 72,52pgs.	0.25	3.60	9.00	18.00
❑6, Jul 72, JKu (c)	0.20	2.40	6.00	12.00
❑7, Sep 72	0.20	2.40	6.00	12.00
❑8, Nov 72, TD, The Avenging Grave; Thou Shalt Not Kill	0.20	2.40	6.00	12.00
❑9, Dec 72, AA, The Promise; Blood Brothers	0.20	2.40	6.00	12.00
❑10, Jan 73, ATh, Who is Haunting the Haunted Chateau; The Room That Remembered	0.20	2.40	6.00	12.00
❑11, Feb 73	0.20	1.60	4.00	8.00
❑12, Mar 73, DP, God of Vengeance; Hand of Hell	0.20	1.60	4.00	8.00
❑13, Apr 73, TD; NR, The Die-Hards; Old Samurai Never Die	0.20	1.60	4.00	8.00
❑14, Jun 73, Dream of Disaster; A Phantom for a Co-Pilot	0.20	1.60	4.00	8.00
❑15, Jul 73, DP, "Ace" King Just Flew in From Hell; The Survivor	0.20	1.60	4.00	8.00
❑16, Aug 73, AA, More Dead Than Alive; The Conquerors	0.20	1.60	4.00	8.00
❑17, Sep 73, GE, Dead Man's Hands; A Gun Named Marie!	0.20	1.60	4.00	8.00
❑18, Oct 73, TD, Captain Dracula; Whim of a Phantom!	0.20	1.60	4.00	8.00
❑19, Nov 73, The Platoon That Wouldn't Die!	0.20	1.60	4.00	8.00
❑20, Dec 73	0.20	1.60	4.00	8.00
❑21, Jan 74, FR, One Hour to Kill; When Death Took a Hand	0.20	1.20	3.00	6.00
❑22, Feb 74, TD; GE, Wings of Death; Last Rites for the Living	0.20	1.20	3.00	6.00
❑23, Mar 74, AA, The Bird of Death; Day After Doomsday	0.20	1.20	3.00	6.00
❑24, Apr 74	0.20	1.20	3.00	6.00
❑25, May 74, AA, Black Magic White Death!; The Unseen Warrior	0.20	1.20	3.00	6.00
❑26, Jun 74	0.20	1.20	3.00	6.00
❑27, Jul 74	0.20	1.20	3.00	6.00
❑28, Aug 74, AA, Isle of Forgotten Warriors	0.20	1.20	3.00	6.00
❑29, Sep 74, Breaking Point; The Hunted	0.20	1.20	3.00	6.00
❑30, Oct 74	0.20	1.20	3.00	6.00
❑31, Nov 74	0.20	1.20	3.00	6.00
❑32, Dec 74	0.20	1.00	2.50	5.00
❑33, Jan 75	0.25	1.00	2.50	5.00
❑34, Feb 75, The Common Enemy; The Flying Coffins	0.25	1.00	2.50	5.00
❑35, Mar 75	0.25	1.00	2.50	5.00
❑36, Apr 75	0.50	1.00	2.50	5.00
❑37, May 75	0.25	1.00	2.50	5.00
❑38, Jun 75	0.25	1.00	2.50	5.00
❑39, Jul 75, JKu (c)	0.25	1.00	2.50	5.00
❑40, Aug 75	0.25	1.00	2.50	5.00
❑41, Sep 75	0.25	1.00	2.50	5.00
❑42, Oct 75, Old Soldiers Never Die; Twice Dead	0.25	1.00	2.50	5.00
❑43, Nov 75	0.25	1.00	2.50	5.00
❑44, Jan 76, JKu (c)	0.25	1.00	2.50	5.00
❑45, Mar 76	—	1.00	2.50	5.00
❑46, May 76	0.30	1.00	2.50	5.00
❑47, Jul 76	0.30	1.00	2.50	5.00
❑48, Sep 76	0.30	1.00	2.50	5.00
❑49, Nov 76, The Face of the Enemy; A Rite to Die	0.30	1.00	2.50	5.00
❑50, Jan 77	0.30	1.00	2.50	5.00
❑51, Mar 77, JKu (c)	0.30	0.80	2.00	4.00
❑52, Apr 77	0.30	0.80	2.00	4.00
❑53, May 77	0.30	0.80	2.00	4.00
❑54, Jul 77	0.35	0.80	2.00	4.00
❑55, Sep 77	0.35	0.80	2.00	4.00
❑56, Oct 77	0.35	0.80	2.00	4.00
❑57, Nov 77	0.35	0.80	2.00	4.00
❑58, Dec 77, JKu (c), A: Hitler	0.35	0.80	2.00	4.00
❑59, Jan 78	0.35	0.80	2.00	4.00
❑60, Feb 78	0.35	0.80	2.00	4.00
❑61, Mar 78, Mind War; The Mercenary	0.35	0.80	2.00	4.00
❑62, Apr 78	0.35	0.80	2.00	4.00
❑63, May 78	0.35	0.80	2.00	4.00
❑64, Jun 78, FM, JKu (c), Deliver Me From D-Day; Beachhead	0.35	0.80	2.00	4.00
❑65, Jul 78	0.35	0.80	2.00	4.00

	ORIG	GOOD	FINE	N-MINT
❑66, Aug 78, TS, The Iron Star	0.35	0.80	2.00	4.00
❑67, Sep 78, JKu (c)	0.50	0.80	2.00	4.00
❑68, Oct 78, FM, Rotirra-The Monster-Weapon!; Batman and the Corsair of Crime	0.50	0.80	2.00	4.00
❑69, Nov 78	0.50	0.80	2.00	4.00
❑70, Dec 78	0.40	0.80	2.00	4.00
❑71, Jan 79	0.40	0.80	2.00	4.00
❑72, Feb 79	—	0.80	2.00	4.00
❑73, Mar 79	—	0.80	2.00	4.00
❑74, Apr 79	—	0.80	2.00	4.00
❑75, May 79	—	0.80	2.00	4.00
❑76, Jun 79, JKu (c)	0.40	0.80	2.00	4.00
❑77, Jul 79	0.40	0.80	2.00	4.00
❑78, Aug 79, JKu (c)	0.40	0.80	2.00	4.00
❑79, Sep 79	0.40	0.80	2.00	4.00
❑80, Oct 79, RT; RE, An Old Man's Profession; Heads Up	0.40	0.80	2.00	4.00
❑81, Nov 79	0.40	0.80	2.00	4.00
❑82, Dec 79, HC; DN, Funeral By Fire; The Toy Battle	0.40	0.80	2.00	4.00
❑83, Jan 80	0.40	0.80	2.00	4.00
❑84, Feb 80	0.40	0.80	2.00	4.00
❑85, Mar 80	0.40	0.80	2.00	4.00
❑86, Apr 80	0.40	0.80	2.00	4.00
❑87, May 80	0.40	0.80	2.00	4.00
❑88, Jun 80	0.40	0.80	2.00	4.00
❑89, Jul 80	0.40	0.80	2.00	4.00
❑90, Aug 80	0.40	0.80	2.00	4.00
❑91, Sep 80	0.50	0.80	2.00	4.00
❑92, Oct 80, JKu (c)	0.50	0.80	2.00	4.00
❑93, Nov 80, JKu (c), 1: Creature Commandos	0.50	1.00	2.50	5.00
❑94, Dec 80	0.50	0.80	2.00	4.00
❑95, Jan 81	0.50	0.80	2.00	4.00
❑96, Feb 81, JKu (c)	0.50	0.80	2.00	4.00
❑97, Mar 81	0.50	0.80	2.00	4.00
❑98, Apr 81	0.50	0.80	2.00	4.00
❑99, May 81	0.50	0.80	2.00	4.00
❑100, Jun 81, JKu (c),Creature Commandos in War That Time Forgot	0.50	0.80	2.00	4.00
❑101, Jul 81, 1: G.I. Robot I	0.50	0.80	2.00	4.00
❑102, Aug 81,Creature Commandos captured by Hitler	0.50	0.60	1.50	3.00
❑103, Sep 81	0.50	0.60	1.50	3.00
❑104, Oct 81	0.60	0.60	1.50	3.00
❑105, Nov 81,Creature Commandos	0.60	0.60	1.50	3.00
❑106, Dec 81	0.60	0.60	1.50	3.00
❑107, Jan 82	0.60	0.60	1.50	3.00
❑108, Feb 82,Creature Commandos, G.I. Robot	0.60	0.60	1.50	3.00
❑109, Mar 82,Creature Commandos	0.60	0.60	1.50	3.00
❑110, Apr 82, 1: Dr. Medusa; 1: Doctor Medusa	0.60	0.60	1.50	3.00
❑111, May 82,G.I. Robot teams with Creature Commandos	0.60	0.60	1.50	3.00
❑112, Jun 82,Creature Commandos	0.60	0.60	1.50	3.00
❑113, Jul 82, V: Samurai Robot; 1: G.I. Robot II	0.60	0.60	1.50	3.00
❑114, Aug 82, A: Hitler,Creature Commandos	0.60	0.60	1.50	3.00
❑115, Sep 82,G.I. Robot II and Creature Commandos	0.60	0.60	1.50	3.00
❑116, Oct 82, CI, Doorway to Hell; The Lonely Robot,G.I. Robot II and Creature Commandos	0.60	0.60	1.50	3.00
❑117, Nov 82,G.I. Robot II and Creature Commandos	0.60	0.60	1.50	3.00
❑118, Dec 82	0.60	0.60	1.50	3.00
❑119, Jan 83,Creature Commandos	0.60	0.60	1.50	3.00
❑120, Feb 83,G.I. Robot	0.60	0.60	1.50	3.00
❑121, Mar 83,Creature Commandos	0.60	0.60	1.50	3.00
❑122, Apr 83,G.I. Robot vs. Sumo Robot	0.60	0.60	1.50	3.00
❑123, May 83	0.60	0.60	1.50	3.00
❑124, Jun 83,Final Issue	0.60	0.60	1.50	3.00

WEIRD WAR TALES (MINI-SERIES)
DC

Value: Cover or less

❑1, Jun 97, The Survivor; Ares	2.50
❑2, Jul 97, Looking Good, Feeling Great; Mightier	2.50
❑3, Aug 97, New Toys; Sniper's Alley	2.50
❑4, Sep 97	2.50
❑SE 1, Apr 00, Noah and Barry and Eddie and Joe; The Isihlangu	4.95

WEIRD WEST
FANTACO

Value: Cover or less

❑1	2.95
❑2	2.95
❑3	2.95

The Creature Commandos were created using horror archetypes in an attempt to scare the Axis soldiers they faced in World War II.

WEIRD WESTERN TALES
DC

	ORIG	GOOD	FINE	N-MINT
❑12, Jun 72, NA; BWr ,Series continued from All-Star Western #11	0.25	6.00	15.00	30.00
❑13, Aug 72, NA	0.20	5.00	12.50	25.00
❑14, Oct 72, ATh	0.20	4.00	10.00	20.00
❑15, Dec 72, GK; NA, Never Kill a Demon; Hang Him High	0.20	4.00	10.00	20.00
❑16, Feb 73	0.20	2.40	6.00	12.00
❑17, Apr 73	0.20	2.40	6.00	12.00
❑18, Jul 73,Jonah Hex issue	0.20	2.40	6.00	12.00
❑19, Sep 73	0.20	2.40	6.00	12.00
❑20, Nov 73	0.20	2.40	6.00	12.00
❑21, Jan 74	0.20	2.40	6.00	12.00
❑22, May 74	0.20	2.40	6.00	12.00
❑23, Jul 74	0.20	2.40	6.00	12.00
❑24, Sep 74,blind Jonah Hex	0.20	2.40	6.00	12.00
❑25, Nov 74	0.20	2.40	6.00	12.00
❑26, Jan 75	0.25	2.40	6.00	12.00
❑27, Mar 75	0.25	2.40	6.00	12.00
❑28, May 75	0.25	2.40	6.00	12.00
❑29, Jul 75, O: Jonah Hex	0.25	3.20	8.00	16.00
❑30, Sep 75	0.25	1.20	3.00	6.00
❑31, Nov 75	0.25	1.20	3.00	6.00
❑32, Jan 76	0.25	1.20	3.00	6.00
❑33, Mar 76	0.25	1.20	3.00	6.00
❑34, May 76	0.30	1.20	3.00	6.00
❑35, Jul 76	0.30	1.20	3.00	6.00
❑36, Sep 76	0.30	1.20	3.00	6.00
❑37, Nov 76	0.30	1.20	3.00	6.00
❑38, Jan 77	0.30	1.20	3.00	6.00
❑39, Mar 77, 1: Scalphunter	0.30	1.20	3.00	6.00
❑40, Jun 77	0.30	1.20	3.00	6.00
❑41, Aug 77	0.35	1.20	3.00	6.00
❑42	0.35	1.20	3.00	6.00
❑43, Dec 77	0.35	1.20	3.00	6.00
❑44	0.35	1.20	3.00	6.00
❑45	0.35	1.20	3.00	6.00
❑46, Jun 78	0.35	1.20	3.00	6.00
❑47, Aug 78	0.35	1.20	3.00	6.00
❑48, Oct 78, 1: Cinnamon	0.50	1.20	3.00	6.00
❑49	0.50	1.20	3.00	6.00
❑50	0.40	1.20	3.00	6.00
❑51	0.40	1.00	2.50	5.00
❑52, Feb 79	0.40	1.00	2.50	5.00
❑53, Mar 79	0.40	1.00	2.50	5.00
❑54, Apr 79	0.40	1.00	2.50	5.00
❑55, May 79	0.40	1.00	2.50	5.00
❑56, Jun 79	0.40	1.00	2.50	5.00
❑57, Jul 79	0.40	1.00	2.50	5.00
❑58, Aug 79	0.40	1.00	2.50	5.00
❑59, Sep 79	0.40	1.00	2.50	5.00
❑60, Oct 79	0.40	1.00	2.50	5.00
❑61, Nov 79	0.40	1.00	2.50	5.00
❑62, Dec 79	0.40	1.00	2.50	5.00
❑63, Jan 80	0.40	1.00	2.50	5.00
❑64, Feb 80	0.40	1.00	2.50	5.00
❑65, Mar 80	0.40	1.00	2.50	5.00
❑66, Apr 80	0.40	1.00	2.50	5.00
❑67, May 80	0.40	1.00	2.50	5.00
❑68, Jun 80	0.40	1.00	2.50	5.00
❑69, Jul 80	0.40	1.00	2.50	5.00
❑70, Aug 80,Final Issue	0.40	1.00	2.50	5.00

WEIRD WESTERN TALES (MINI-SERIES)
VERTIGO

Value: Cover or less

❑1, Apr 01, DaG, DaG (w), Tall Tale; Serial Hero	2.50
❑2, May 01, First Among Men; Palomino	2.50
❑3, Jun 01, Settlers; The Confession of Gabriel Winters	2.50
❑4, Jul 01	2.50

WEIRD WONDER TALES
MARVEL

	ORIG	GOOD	FINE	N-MINT
❑1, Dec 73,Reprints Mystic #6 (Eye of Doom)	0.20	0.80	2.00	4.00
❑2, Feb 74,Reprint	0.20	0.50	1.25	2.50
❑3, Apr 74,Reprint	0.20	0.50	1.25	2.50
❑4, Jun 74	0.25	0.50	1.25	2.50
❑5, Aug 74,Reprint	0.25	0.50	1.25	2.50
❑6, Oct 74	0.25	0.50	1.25	2.50
❑7, Dec 74	0.25	0.50	1.25	2.50
❑8, Feb 75	0.25	0.50	1.25	2.50
❑9, Apr 75	0.25	0.50	1.25	2.50
❑10, Jun 75	0.25	0.50	1.25	2.50
❑11, Aug 75	0.25	0.50	1.25	2.50
❑12, Oct 75	0.25	0.50	1.25	2.50
❑13, Dec 75	0.25	0.50	1.25	2.50
❑14, Feb 76	0.25	0.50	1.25	2.50
❑15, Apr 76	0.25	0.50	1.25	2.50
❑16, Jun 76	0.25	0.50	1.25	2.50
❑17, Aug 76	0.25	0.50	1.25	2.50
❑18, Oct 76	0.30	0.50	1.25	2.50
❑19, Dec 76, BK, I Am Dr. Druid!; I Challend...Groot!,Doctor Druid; Reprints from Tales to Astonish #13, Astonishing Tales #47	0.30	0.50	1.25	2.50
❑20, Jan 77,Doctor Druid	0.30	0.50	1.25	2.50
❑21, Mar 77,Doctor Druid	0.30	0.50	1.25	2.50
❑22, May 77,Doctor Druid	0.30	0.50	1.25	2.50

WEIRD WORLDS
DC

	ORIG	GOOD	FINE	N-MINT
❑1, Sep 72, The Arena of Sudden Death; Trial of Fear,continues John Carter of Mars from Tarzan #209 and Pellucidar from Korak	0.20	0.80	2.00	4.00
❑2, Nov 72,adapts Burroughs' Pellucidar and Martian novels	0.20	0.60	1.50	3.00
❑3, Jan 73,adapts Burroughs' Pellucidar and Martian novels	0.20	0.60	1.50	3.00
❑4, Mar 73,adapts Burroughs' Pellucidar and Martian novels	0.20	0.50	1.25	2.50
❑5, May 73,adapts Burroughs' Pellucidar and Martian novels	0.20	0.50	1.25	2.50
❑6, Aug 73,adapts Burroughs' Pellucidar and Martian novels	0.20	0.40	1.00	2.00
❑7, Oct 73,adapts Burroughs' Pellucidar and Martian novels; John Carter, Warlord of Mars ends	0.20	0.40	1.00	2.00
❑8, Dec 73, HC, 1: Iron Wolf	0.20	0.40	1.00	2.00
❑9, Feb 74, HC ,Iron Wolf	0.20	0.40	1.00	2.00
❑10, Nov 74, HC ,Final Issue; Iron Wolf	0.20	0.40	1.00	2.00

WELCOME BACK, KOTTER
DC

	ORIG	GOOD	FINE	N-MINT
❑1, Nov 76,based on ABC TV series	0.30	0.80	2.00	4.00
❑2, Jan 77,based on ABC TV series	0.30	0.50	1.25	2.50
❑3, Mar 77,based on ABC TV series	0.30	0.50	1.25	2.50
❑4, May 77,based on ABC TV series	0.30	0.50	1.25	2.50
❑5, Jul 77,based on ABC TV series	0.35	0.50	1.25	2.50
❑6, Sep 77,based on ABC TV series	0.35	0.50	1.25	2.50
❑7, Nov 77,based on ABC TV series	0.35	0.50	1.25	2.50
❑8, Jan 78,based on ABC TV series	0.35	0.50	1.25	2.50
❑9, Feb 78,based on ABC TV series	0.35	0.50	1.25	2.50
❑10, Mar 78,Final Issue; based on ABC TV series	0.35	0.50	1.25	2.50

WELCOME BACK TO THE HOUSE OF MYSTERY
DC

Value: Cover or less

❑1, Jul 98, JO (w), The Gourmet; Nightmare,collects stories from House of Mystery and Plop 5.95

WELCOME TO THE LITTLE SHOP OF HORRORS
ROGER CORMAN'S COSMIC COMICS

Value: Cover or less

❑1 .... 2.50

❑2 .... 2.50

❑3 .... 2.50

WENDEL
KITCHEN SINK

Value: Cover or less

❑1, b&w; adult 2.95

WENDY IN 3-D
BLACKTHORNE

Value: Cover or less

❑1 .... 2.50

WENDY THE GOOD LITTLE WITCH (VOL. 2)
HARVEY

	ORIG	GOOD	FINE	N-MINT
❑1	1.25	0.40	1.00	2.00
❑2	1.25	0.30	0.75	1.50
❑3	1.25	0.30	0.75	1.50
❑4	1.25	0.30	0.75	1.50
❑5	1.25	0.30	0.75	1.50
❑6	1.25	0.30	0.75	1.50
❑7, The Lost Monster; He's Really a Nice Monster	1.25	0.30	0.75	1.50
❑8	1.25	0.30	0.75	1.50
❑9	1.25	0.30	0.75	1.50
❑10	1.25	0.30	0.75	1.50
❑11	1.25	0.30	0.75	1.50
❑12	1.50	0.30	0.75	1.50
❑13	1.50	0.30	0.75	1.50
❑14	1.50	0.30	0.75	1.50
❑15, Aug 94	1.50	0.30	0.75	1.50

WENDY WHITEBREAD, UNDERCOVER SLUT
FANTAGRAPHICS

	ORIG	GOOD	FINE	N-MINT
❑1, b&w; adult	2.50	0.50	1.25	2.50
❑1-2, b&w; adult; 2nd Printing	—	0.59	1.48	2.95
❑, b&w; adult; 3rd Printing	—	0.59	1.48	2.95
❑1-4, b&w; adult; 4th Printing	—	0.59	1.48	2.95
❑1-5, Nov 90, b&w; adult; 5th Printing	3.95	0.79	1.98	3.95
❑2, b&w; adult	2.50	0.50	1.25	2.50

WEREWOLF
BLACKTHORNE

	ORIG	GOOD	FINE	N-MINT
❑1, b&w; TV show	2.00	1.60	4.00	8.00
❑2, Werewolf: The Call of the Sea; The Chinese Water Devils, b&w; TV show	2.00	1.00	2.50	5.00
❑3, Apr 67, Jump to Danger; The Day the World Almost Ended, O: Werewolf (Major Wiley Wolf), b&w; TV show	2.00	1.00	2.50	5.00
❑4, b&w; TV show	2.00	1.00	2.50	5.00
❑5, b&w; TV show	2.00	1.00	2.50	5.00

WEREWOLF AT LARGE
ETERNITY

Value: Cover or less

❑1, b&w 2.25

❑2, b&w 2.25

❑3, b&w 2.25

WEREWOLF BY NIGHT
MARVEL

	ORIG	GOOD	FINE	N-MINT
❑1, Sep 72	0.20	7.00	17.50	35.00
❑2, Nov 72	0.20	3.20	8.00	16.00
❑3, Jan 73	0.20	2.00	5.00	10.00
❑4, Mar 73	0.20	2.00	5.00	10.00
❑5, May 73	0.20	1.80	4.50	9.00
❑6, Jun 73	0.20	1.80	4.50	9.00
❑7, Jul 73	0.20	1.80	4.50	9.00
❑8, Aug 73	0.20	1.80	4.50	9.00
❑9, Sep 73	0.20	1.80	4.50	9.00
❑10, Oct 73	0.20	1.80	4.50	9.00
❑11, Nov 73	0.20	1.40	3.50	7.00
❑12, Dec 73	0.20	1.40	3.50	7.00
❑13, Jan 74	0.20	1.40	3.50	7.00
❑14, Feb 74	0.20	1.40	3.50	7.00
❑15, Mar 74	0.20	1.40	3.50	7.00
❑16, Apr 74	0.20	1.40	3.50	7.00
❑17, May 74	0.25	1.40	3.50	7.00
❑18, Jun 74	0.25	1.40	3.50	7.00
❑19, Jul 74	0.25	1.40	3.50	7.00
❑20, Aug 74	0.25	1.40	3.50	7.00
❑21, Sep 74	0.25	1.20	3.00	6.00
❑22, Oct 74	0.25	1.20	3.00	6.00
❑23, Nov 74	0.25	1.20	3.00	6.00
❑24, Dec 74	0.25	1.20	3.00	6.00
❑25, Jan 75	0.25	1.20	3.00	6.00
❑26, Feb 75	0.25	1.20	3.00	6.00
❑27, Mar 75	0.25	1.20	3.00	6.00
❑28, Apr 75	0.25	1.20	3.00	6.00
❑29, May 75	0.25	1.20	3.00	6.00
❑30, Jun 75	0.25	1.20	3.00	6.00
❑31, Jul 75	0.25	1.20	3.00	6.00
❑32, Aug 75, 1: Moon Knight	0.25	8.00	20.00	40.00
❑33, Sep 75, 2: Moon Knight	0.25	4.00	10.00	20.00
❑34, Oct 75, DP, Not All the Shades of Death nor Evil's Majesty	0.25	0.80	2.00	4.00
❑35, Nov 75, DP, Evil in Every Stone No Longer Hiding	0.25	0.80	2.00	4.00
❑36, Jan 76	0.25	0.80	2.00	4.00
❑37, Mar 76, DP, A: Moon Knight	0.25	1.20	3.00	6.00
❑38, May 76	0.25	0.60	1.50	3.00
❑39, Jul 76	0.25	0.60	1.50	3.00
❑40, Sep 76	0.30	0.60	1.50	3.00
❑41, Nov 76	0.30	0.60	1.50	3.00
❑42, Jan 77	0.30	0.60	1.50	3.00
❑43, Mar 77,Final Issue	0.30	0.60	1.50	3.00

WEREWOLF BY NIGHT (VOL. 2)
MARVEL

	ORIG	GOOD	FINE	N-MINT
❑1, Feb 98, Somewhere South of Heaven..	2.99	0.60	1.50	3.00
❑2, Mar 98, Life in the Fast Lane, gatefold summary	2.99	0.60	1.50	3.00
❑3, Apr 98, gatefold summary	2.99	0.60	1.50	3.00
❑4, May 98, gatefold summary	2.99	0.60	1.50	3.00
❑5, Jun 98, gatefold summary	2.99	0.60	1.50	3.00
❑6, Jul 98, A: Ghost Rider, gatefold summary	2.99	0.60	1.50	3.00

WEREWOLF IN 3-D
BLACKTHORNE

Value: Cover or less ❑1 .... 2.50

WEST COAST AVENGERS
MARVEL

	ORIG	GOOD	FINE	N-MINT
❑1, Oct 85	1.25	0.40	1.00	2.00
❑2, Nov 85	0.65	0.30	0.75	1.50
❑3, Dec 85, V: Kraven	0.65	0.30	0.75	1.50
❑4, Jan 86, 1: Master Pandemonium	0.65	0.20	0.50	1.00
❑5, Feb 86	0.75	0.20	0.50	1.00
❑6, Mar 86	0.75	0.20	0.50	1.00
❑7, Apr 86, V: Ultron	0.75	0.20	0.50	1.00
❑8, May 86, V: Rangers	0.75	0.20	0.50	1.00
❑9, Jun 86, O: Master Pandemonium	0.75	0.20	0.50	1.00
❑10, Jul 86	0.75	0.20	0.50	1.00
❑11, Aug 86	0.75	0.20	0.50	1.00
❑12, Sep 86, V: Zzzax; 1: Quantum; 1: Halflife	0.75	0.20	0.50	1.00
❑13, Oct 86, O: Hellstorm; V: Graviton	0.75	0.20	0.50	1.00
❑14, Nov 86, AM, Tigra, Tigra Burning Bright!, 1: Hellstorm	0.75	0.20	0.50	1.00
❑15, Dec 86	0.75	0.20	0.50	1.00
❑16, Jan 87	0.75	0.20	0.50	1.00
❑17, Feb 87	0.75	0.20	0.50	1.00
❑18, Mar 87	0.75	0.20	0.50	1.00
❑19, Apr 87	0.75	0.20	0.50	1.00
❑20, May 87	0.75	0.20	0.50	1.00
❑21, Jun 87, JSt; AM, Lost in Space-Time, Part 5, A: Moon Knight	0.75	0.20	0.50	1.00
❑22, Jul 87, A: Doctor Strange	0.75	0.20	0.50	1.00
❑23, Aug 87	0.75	0.20	0.50	1.00
❑24, Sep 87	0.75	0.20	0.50	1.00
❑25, Oct 87	0.75	0.20	0.50	1.00
❑26, Nov 87, V: Zodiac	0.75	0.20	0.50	1.00
❑27, Dec 87, V: Zodiac	0.75	0.20	0.50	1.00
❑28, Jan 88, AM, Double-Crossed, V: Zodiac	0.75	0.20	0.50	1.00
❑29, Feb 88	0.75	0.20	0.50	1.00
❑30, Mar 88	0.75	0.20	0.50	1.00
❑31, Apr 88, V: Arkon	0.75	0.20	0.50	1.00
❑32, May 88	0.75	0.20	0.50	1.00
❑33, Jun 88	0.75	0.20	0.50	1.00
❑34, Jul 88, V: Quicksilver	0.75	0.20	0.50	1.00
❑35, Aug 88, V: Doctor Doom	0.75	0.20	0.50	1.00
❑36, Sep 88	0.75	0.20	0.50	1.00
❑37, Oct 88	0.75	0.20	0.50	1.00
❑38, Nov 88	0.75	0.20	0.50	1.00
❑39, Dec 88, AM, Upset!	0.75	0.20	0.50	1.00
❑40, Jan 89, AM, Night Shift!	0.75	0.20	0.50	1.00
❑41, Feb 89, When Ghosts Can Die, Even Gods Must Fear!	0.75	0.20	0.50	1.00
❑42, Mar 89, JBy, JBy (w), Vision Quest	0.75	0.20	0.50	1.00
❑43, Apr 89, JBy, JBy (w), Vision Quest	0.75	0.20	0.50	1.00
❑44, May 89, JBy, JBy (w), Vision Quest, 1: U.S.Agent	0.75	0.20	0.50	1.00
❑45, Jun 89, JBy, JBy (w), Vision Quest	0.75	0.20	0.50	1.00
❑46, Jul 89, JBy, JBy (w), Franchise, 1: Big Bertha; 1: Great Lakes Avengers	0.75	0.20	0.50	1.00
❑47, Aug 89,Series continues as Avengers West Coast	0.75	0.20	0.50	1.00
❑Anl 1, ca. 86, One of Our Own!, V: Quick-silver	1.25	0.40	1.00	2.00
❑Anl 2, ca. 87	1.25	0.40	1.00	2.00
❑Anl 3, ca. 88, AM, Evolutionary War, Part 9,series continues as Avengers West Coast Annual	1.75	0.40	1.00	2.00

WEST COAST AVENGERS (LTD. SERIES)
MARVEL

	ORIG	GOOD	FINE	N-MINT
❑1, Sep 84, BH, 1: West Coast Avengers	0.75	0.50	1.25	2.50
❑2, Oct 84, BH	0.75	0.40	1.00	2.00
❑3, Nov 84, BH	0.75	0.40	1.00	2.00
❑4, Dec 84, BH	0.75	0.40	1.00	2.00

WESTERN ACTION
ATLAS

	ORIG	GOOD	FINE	N-MINT
❑1, Jun 75	0.25	0.80	2.00	4.00

WESTERN GUNFIGHTERS (2ND SERIES)
MARVEL

	ORIG	GOOD	FINE	N-MINT
❑1, Aug 70,giant	0.25	2.00	5.00	10.00
❑2, Oct 70, O: Nightwind (The Apache Kid's horse),giant	0.25	1.20	3.00	6.00
❑3, Dec 70,giant	0.25	1.20	3.00	6.00
❑4, Mar 71,giant	0.25	1.20	3.00	6.00
❑5, Jun 71,giant	0.25	1.20	3.00	6.00
❑6, Sep 71, D: Ghost Rider,giant	0.25	1.20	3.00	6.00
❑7, Jan 72, O: Night Rider ("Ghost Rider"); D: Phantom Rider I (Carter Slade); 1: Lincoln Slade as Ghost Rider,giant	0.25	1.60	4.00	8.00
❑8	0.25	1.00	2.50	5.00
❑9	0.25	1.00	2.50	5.00

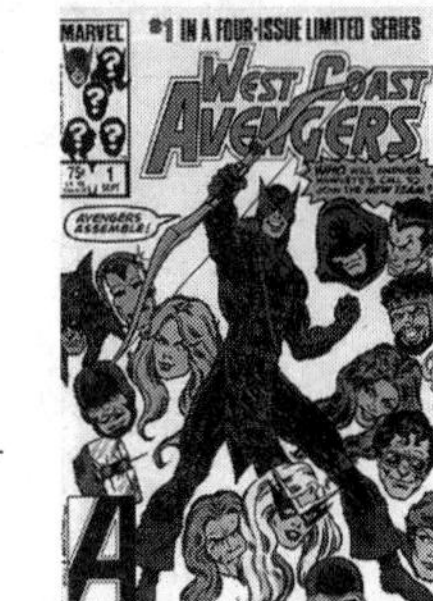

Hawkeye formed a new group of Avengers to defend the Left Coast in *West Coast Avengers.*

© 1984 Marvel Comics

	ORIG	GOOD	FINE	N-MINT
❑10, O: Black Rider	0.25	1.00	2.50	5.00
❑11	0.25	1.00	2.50	5.00
❑12, O: Matt Slade	0.25	1.00	2.50	5.00
❑13	0.25	1.00	2.50	5.00
❑14	0.25	1.00	2.50	5.00
❑15	0.25	1.00	2.50	5.00
❑16	0.25	1.00	2.50	5.00
❑17	0.25	0.80	2.00	4.00
❑18	0.25	0.80	2.00	4.00
❑19	0.25	0.80	2.00	4.00
❑20	0.25	0.80	2.00	4.00
❑21	0.25	0.80	2.00	4.00
❑22	0.25	0.80	2.00	4.00
❑23	0.25	0.80	2.00	4.00
❑24	0.25	0.80	2.00	4.00
❑25	0.25	0.80	2.00	4.00
❑26, Nov 74	0.25	0.80	2.00	4.00
❑27, Jan 75	0.25	0.80	2.00	4.00
❑28, Mar 75	0.25	0.80	2.00	4.00
❑29, May 75	0.25	0.80	2.00	4.00
❑30, Jul 75	0.25	0.80	2.00	4.00
❑31, Sep 75, A: Kid Colt; A: Apache Kid; A: Gun-Slinger	0.25	0.80	2.00	4.00
❑32, Nov 75	0.25	0.80	2.00	4.00
❑33, Jan 76,Final Issue	0.25	0.80	2.00	4.00

WESTERN KID, THE (2ND SERIES)
MARVEL

	ORIG	GOOD	FINE	N-MINT
❑1, Dec 71, Boot Hill Vengeance!	0.20	1.80	4.50	9.00
❑2, Feb 72	0.20	1.20	3.00	6.00
❑3, Apr 72	0.20	1.20	3.00	6.00
❑4, Jun 72	0.20	1.20	3.00	6.00
❑5, Aug 72	0.20	1.20	3.00	6.00

WESTERN TEAM-UP
MARVEL

	ORIG	GOOD	FINE	N-MINT
❑1, Nov 73, 1: The Dakota Kid	0.20	1.60	4.00	8.00

WESTSIDE
ANTARCTIC

Value: Cover or less ❑1, Mar 00, Blind Raise........ 2.50

WETWORKS
IMAGE

	ORIG	GOOD	FINE	N-MINT
❑1, Jun 94, 1: Wetworks; 1: Jester; 1: Dane; 1: Dozer	1.95	0.60	1.50	3.00
❑1/3D, Jun 94, 1: Wetworks; 1: Jester; 1: Dane; 1: Dozer, 3-D edition	4.95	0.99	2.47	4.95
❑1/LE, Jun 94, 1: Wetworks; 1: Jester; 1: Dozer, Special promotional edition distributed at the 1994 Chicago Comicon	1.95	0.80	2.00	4.00
❑2, Aug 94,Standard cover; Beast attacking man	1.95	0.50	1.25	2.50
❑2/A, Aug 94,alternate cover; Variant edition cover with whole team posing	1.95	0.60	1.50	3.00
❑3, Sep 94	1.95	0.50	1.25	2.50
❑4, Nov 94	2.50	0.50	1.25	2.50
❑5, Jan 95	2.50	0.50	1.25	2.50
❑6, Mar 95	2.50	0.50	1.25	2.50
❑7, Apr 95	2.50	0.50	1.25	2.50
❑8, May 95, WildStorm Rising, Part 7,bound-in trading cards	2.50	0.40	1.00	2.00
❑8/SC, trading cards	2.50	0.50	1.25	2.50
❑9, Aug 95	2.50	0.50	1.25	2.50
❑10, Aug 95	2.50	0.50	1.25	2.50
❑11, Sep 95	2.50	0.50	1.25	2.50
❑12, Nov 95, 1: Pilgrim,indicia says Nov, cover says Dec	2.50	0.50	1.25	2.50
❑13, Jan 96	2.50	0.50	1.25	2.50
❑14, Feb 96	2.50	0.50	1.25	2.50
❑15, Mar 96	2.50	0.50	1.25	2.50
❑16, Apr 96, Fire from Heaven, Part 4	2.50	0.50	1.25	2.50
❑17, May 96, Fire from Heaven, Part 11	2.50	0.50	1.25	2.50
❑18, Jul 96	2.50	0.50	1.25	2.50
❑19, Aug 96	2.50	0.50	1.25	2.50
❑20, Aug 96	2.50	0.50	1.25	2.50

	ORIG	GOOD	FINE	N-MINT
❑21, Sep 96	2.50	0.50	1.25	2.50
❑22, Oct 96	2.50	0.50	1.25	2.50
❑23, Nov 96	2.50	0.50	1.25	2.50
❑24, Dec 96	2.50	0.50	1.25	2.50
❑25, Jan 97,wraparound cover; Giant-size..	3.95	0.79	1.98	3.95
❑25/A, Jan 97,alternate wraparound cover (previous covers in background)	3.95	0.79	1.98	3.95
❑26, Feb 97	2.50	0.50	1.25	2.50
❑27, Mar 97	2.50	0.50	1.25	2.50
❑28, Apr 97	2.50	0.50	1.25	2.50
❑29, May 97	2.50	0.50	1.25	2.50
❑30, Jun 97	2.50	0.50	1.25	2.50
❑31, Jul 97	2.50	0.50	1.25	2.50
❑32, Aug 97, Sacraments of Damnation, Part 1	2.50	0.50	1.25	2.50
❑32/A, Aug 97,alternate cover (mostly b&w); Voyager pack	2.50	0.50	1.25	2.50
❑33, Sep 97, Sacraments of Damnation, Part 2	2.50	0.50	1.25	2.50
❑34, Oct 97, Sacraments of Damnation, Part 3	2.50	0.50	1.25	2.50
❑35, Nov 97, Sacraments of Damnation, Part 4	2.50	0.50	1.25	2.50
❑36, Jan 98, Maximum Security	2.50	0.50	1.25	2.50
❑37, Feb 98, Diversionary Tactics, Part 1	2.50	0.50	1.25	2.50
❑38, Mar 98, Diversionary Tactics, Part 3	2.50	0.50	1.25	2.50
❑39, Apr 98, Diversionary Tactics, Part 2	2.50	0.50	1.25	2.50
❑40, May 98, Drawn Swords, Part 1, A: StormWatch	2.50	0.50	1.25	2.50
❑41, Jun 98, Drawn Swords, Part 2	2.50	0.50	1.25	2.50
❑42, Jul 98, Flashback, Part 1	2.50	0.50	1.25	2.50
❑43, Aug 98, Flashback, Part 2	2.50	0.50	1.25	2.50
❑3D 1, Feb 98,wraparound cover; with glasses	4.95	0.99	2.47	4.95

WETWORKS SOURCEBOOK
IMAGE

Value: Cover or less

❑1, Oct 94 ... 2.50

WETWORKS/VAMPIRELLA
IMAGE

Value: Cover or less

❑1, Jul 97,crossover with Harris ... 2.95

❑1/A, Jul 97, GK (c),alternate cover; crossover with Harris ... 2.95

WHACKED!
RIVER GROUP

Value: Cover or less

❑1, Mar 94, nn; wraparound cover; Tonya Harding case parody ... 2.50

WHAT IF...? (VOL. 1)
MARVEL

	ORIG	GOOD	FINE	N-MINT
❑1, Feb 77, ...Spider-Man Joined the Fantastic Four?,Spider-Man	0.50	2.40	6.00	12.00
❑2, Apr 77, GK (c), ...The Hulk Had the Brain of Bruce Banner?,Hulk	0.50	1.20	3.00	6.00
❑3, Jun 77, KJ; GK, ...The Avengers Had Never Been?,Avengers	0.50	1.00	2.50	5.00
❑4, Aug 77, GK (c), ...The Invaders had stayed together after World War II?,Invaders	0.50	1.00	2.50	5.00
❑5, Oct 77, ...Captain America Hadn't Vanished During World War II?, 1: Captain America III (Jeffrey Mace); O: Bucky II (Fred Davis); D: Captain America II (William Nasland),Captain America	0.50	1.00	2.50	5.00
❑6, Dec 77, ...The Fantastic Four Had Different Super-Powers?,Fantastic Four	0.60	0.80	2.00	4.00
❑7, Feb 78, GK (c), ...Someone else besides Spider-Man had been bitten by the radioactive spider?,Spider-Man	0.60	0.80	2.00	4.00
❑8, Apr 78, JR (c); GK (c), ...The World Knew That Daredevil is blind?,Daredevil	0.60	0.80	2.00	4.00
❑9, Jun 78, JK (c), ...Avengers had fought evil during the 1950's?, O: Gorilla-Man; O: Venus; O: 3-D Man; O: Human Robot; O: Marvel Boy,Avengers	0.60	0.80	2.00	4.00
❑10, Aug 78, ...Jane Foster had found the hammer of Thor?,Thor	0.60	0.80	2.00	4.00
❑11, Oct 78, JK, ...The original Marvel bullpen had become the Fantastic Four?,Marvel Bullpen as Fantastic Four	0.60	0.60	1.50	3.00
❑12, Dec 78, SB, ...Rick Jones had become the Hulk?,Rick Jones as Hulk	0.60	0.60	1.50	3.00
❑13, Feb 79, JB, ...Conan the Barbarian walked the earth today?,Conan	0.60	0.80	2.00	4.00
❑14, Apr 79, ...Sgt. Fury had fought World War II in outer space?,Sgt. Fury	0.60	0.60	1.50	3.00
❑15, Jun 79, JSt; JB, ...Nova had been four other people?,Nova	0.60	0.60	1.50	3.00
❑16, Aug 79, ...Shang-Chi, Master of Kung Fu fought on the side of Fu Manchu?,Fu Manchu	0.60	0.50	1.25	2.50
❑17, Oct 79, CI, ...Ghost Rider, Spider-Woman, Captain Marvel Were Villains,Ghost Rider, Captain Marvel, Spider-Woman	0.60	0.60	1.50	3.00
❑18, Dec 79, TS, ...Dr. Strange were a disciple of Dormammu?,Doctor Strange	0.75	0.50	1.25	2.50
❑19, Feb 80, PB, ...Spider-Man had never become a crimefighter?,Spider-Man	0.75	0.50	1.25	2.50
❑20, Apr 80, ...The Avengers fought the Kree-Skrull War without Rick Jones?,Avengers	0.75	0.50	1.25	2.50
❑21, Jun 80, GC, ...The Invisible Girl of the Fantastic Four had married the Sub-Mariner?,Sub-Mariner	0.75	0.50	1.25	2.50
❑22, Aug 80, ...Doctor Doom had become a hero?,Doctor Doom	0.75	0.50	1.25	2.50
❑23, Oct 80, HT, ...The Hulk had become a barbarian?,Hulk	0.75	0.50	1.25	2.50
❑24, Dec 80, ...Spider-Man had rescued Gwen Stacy?,Spider-Man	0.75	0.50	1.25	2.50
❑25, Feb 81, ...Thor and the Avengers battled the gods?, O: Uni-Mind,Thor, Avengers	0.75	0.50	1.25	2.50
❑26, Apr 81, JBy (c), ...Captain America had been elected president?,Captain America	0.75	0.50	1.25	2.50
❑27, Jul 81, FM (c), ...Phoenix had not died?,X-Men	0.75	0.80	2.00	4.00
❑28, Aug 81, FM, FM (w), ...Daredevil became an agent of S.H.I.E.L.D.?,Daredevil	0.75	1.00	2.50	5.00
❑29, Oct 81, MG (c), ...The Avengers defeated everybody?,Avengers	0.75	0.50	1.25	2.50
❑30, Dec 81, RB, ...Spider-Man's clone lived?,Spider-Man clone, Inhumans	0.75	1.00	2.50	5.00
❑31, Feb 82, ...Wolverine had killed the Hulk?,Wolverine	1.00	1.00	2.50	5.00
❑32, Apr 82, ...The Avengers had become pawns of Korvac?,Avengers	1.00	0.50	1.25	2.50
❑33, Jun 82, DP, ...Dazzler had become the herald of Galactus?; ...Iron Man was trapped in the time of King Arthur?,Dazzler	1.00	0.50	1.25	2.50
❑34, Aug 82, FM; JBy; FH; BSz ,comedy issue	1.00	0.50	1.25	2.50
❑35, Oct 82, FM, FM (w), ...Elektra had lived?,Elektra	1.00	0.80	2.00	4.00
❑36, Dec 82, JBy, ...The Fantastic Four had not gained their super-powers?,Fantastic Four; Nova	1.00	0.50	1.25	2.50
❑37, Feb 83, ...The Beast and the King continued to mutate?,Beast; Thing; Silver Surfer	1.00	0.50	1.25	2.50
❑38, Apr 83,Daredevil, Captain America, Vision, Scarlet Witch	1.00	0.50	1.25	2.50
❑39, Jun 83, ...Thor battled Conan the Barbarian?,Thor vs. Conan	1.00	0.50	1.25	2.50
❑40, Aug 83, ...Dr. Strange had not become master of the mystic arts?,Doctor Strange	1.00	0.50	1.25	2.50
❑41, Oct 83, ...The Sub-Mariner had saved Atlantis from its destiny?,Sub-Mariner	1.00	0.50	1.25	2.50
❑42, Dec 83, ...The Invisible Girl had died?,Fantastic Four	1.00	0.50	1.25	2.50
❑43, Feb 84, ...Conan the Barbarian were stranded in the 20th century?,Conan	1.00	0.50	1.25	2.50
❑44, Apr 84, ...Captain America were revived today?,Captain America	1.00	0.50	1.25	2.50
❑45, Jun 84, ...The Hulk went berserk?,Hulk	1.00	0.50	1.25	2.50
❑46, Aug 84, ...Spider-Man's Uncle Ben had lived?,Spider-Man	1.00	0.60	1.50	3.00
❑47, Oct 84, ...Loki had found the hammer of Thor?,Final Issue; Thor, Loki	1.00	0.50	1.25	2.50
❑SE 1, Jun 88,Iron Man	1.50	0.50	1.25	2.50

WHAT IF...? (VOL. 2)
MARVEL

	ORIG	GOOD	FINE	N-MINT
❑-1, Jul 97,Flashback; Bishop	1.99	0.40	1.00	2.00
❑1, Jul 89, ...The Avengers had lost the Evolutionary War?,Avengers	1.25	0.80	2.00	4.00
❑2, Aug 89,Daredevil	1.25	0.60	1.50	3.00
❑3, Sep 89,Captain America	1.25	0.60	1.50	3.00
❑4, Oct 89,Spider-Man	1.25	0.60	1.50	3.00
❑5, Nov 89,Avengers	1.25	0.60	1.50	3.00
❑6, Nov 89,X-Men	1.25	0.60	1.50	3.00
❑7, Dec 89, RL ,Wolverine	1.25	0.60	1.50	3.00
❑8, Dec 89,Iron Man	1.25	0.50	1.25	2.50
❑9, Jan 90,X-Men	1.25	0.50	1.25	2.50
❑10, Feb 90, ...The Punisher's family hadn't been killed?,Punisher	1.25	0.50	1.25	2.50
❑11, Mar 90,Fantastic Four	1.25	0.50	1.25	2.50
❑12, Apr 90,X-Men	1.25	0.50	1.25	2.50
❑13, May 90, KB (w),X-Men	1.25	0.50	1.25	2.50
❑14, Jun 90,Captain Marvel	1.25	0.50	1.25	2.50
❑15, Jul 90,Fantastic Four, Galactus	1.25	0.50	1.25	2.50
❑16, Aug 90, ...Wolverine battled Conan?,Wolverine; Conan	1.25	0.60	1.50	3.00
❑17, Sep 90, D: Spider-Man	1.25	0.50	1.25	2.50
❑18, Oct 90,Fantastic Four, Doctor Doom ..	1.25	0.50	1.25	2.50
❑19, Nov 90,Avengers	1.25	0.50	1.25	2.50

	ORIG	GOOD	FINE	N-MINT
❑20, Dec 90,Spider-Man	1.25	0.50	1.25	2.50
❑21, Jan 91, D: Black Cat,Spider-Man	1.25	0.45	1.13	2.25
❑22, Feb 91,Silver Surfer	1.25	0.45	1.13	2.25
❑23, Mar 91, KB (w),X-Men	1.25	0.45	1.13	2.25
❑24, Apr 91,vampire Wolverine	1.25	0.70	1.75	3.50
❑25, May 91,Atlantis Attacks	1.25	0.65	1.63	3.25
❑26, Jun 91, KB (w),Punisher	1.25	0.40	1.00	2.00
❑27, Jul 91,Namor, Fantastic Four	1.25	0.40	1.00	2.00
❑28, Aug 91,Captain America	1.25	0.40	1.00	2.00
❑29, Sep 91,Captain America, Avengers	1.25	0.40	1.00	2.00
❑30, Oct 91,Fantastic Four	1.75	0.40	1.00	2.00
❑31, Nov 91,Spider-Man with cosmic powers	1.25	0.40	1.00	2.00
❑32, Dec 91,Phoenix	1.25	0.40	1.00	2.00
❑33, Jan 92,Phoenix	1.25	0.40	1.00	2.00
❑34, Feb 92, ...No One Was Watching The Watcher?,parody issue	1.25	0.40	1.00	2.00
❑35, Mar 92, Timequake, Part 1,Fantastic Four; Spider-Man; Doctor Doom	1.25	0.40	1.00	2.00
❑36, Apr 92, Timequake, Part 2,Avengers vs. Guardians of the Galaxy	1.25	0.40	1.00	2.00
❑37, May 92, Timequake, Part 3,Wolverine.	1.25	0.40	1.00	2.00
❑38, Jun 92, Timequake, Part 4,Thor	1.25	0.40	1.00	2.00
❑39, Jul 92, Timequake, Part 5,Watcher	1.25	0.40	1.00	2.00
❑40, Aug 92,X-Men	1.25	0.40	1.00	2.00
❑41, Sep 92,Avengers vs. Galactus	1.75	0.40	1.00	2.00
❑42, Oct 92,Spider-Man	1.25	0.40	1.00	2.00
❑43, Nov 92,Wolverine	1.25	0.40	1.00	2.00
❑44, Dec 92, KB (w),Venom, Punisher	1.25	0.40	1.00	2.00
❑45, Jan 93,Ghost Rider	1.25	0.40	1.00	2.00
❑46, Feb 93, KB (w), ...Cable Had Destroyed the X-Men?, Part 1,Cable	1.25	0.40	1.00	2.00
❑47, Mar 93, KB (w), ...Cable Had Destroyed the X-Men?, Part 2,Magneto	1.25	0.40	1.00	2.00
❑48, Apr 93,Daredevil	1.25	0.40	1.00	2.00
❑49, May 93,Silver Surfer	1.25	0.40	1.00	2.00
❑50, Jun 93,silver sculpted cover; Hulk, Wolverine	2.95	0.59	1.48	2.95
❑51, Jul 93,Punisher, Captain America	1.25	0.40	1.00	2.00
❑52, Aug 93,Doctor Doom	1.25	0.40	1.00	2.00
❑53, Sep 93,Spider-Man, Hulk, Iron Man 2020	1.25	0.40	1.00	2.00
❑54, Oct 93, ...Death's Head I Had Lived?, A: Charnel; A: Death's Head; A: Captain America; A: War Machine; A: Death's Head II; A: Cage; A: Fantastic Four; A: Reed Richards,Death's Head	1.25	0.40	1.00	2.00
❑55, Nov 93,Avengers	1.25	0.40	1.00	2.00
❑56, Dec 93,Avengers	1.25	0.40	1.00	2.00
❑57, Jan 94,Punisher	1.25	0.40	1.00	2.00
❑58, Feb 94, ...The Punisher had Killed Spider-Man?,Punisher, Spider-Man	1.25	0.40	1.00	2.00
❑59, Mar 94, ...Wolverine Led Alpha Flight?,Wolverine/Alpha Flight	1.25	0.40	1.00	2.00
❑60, Apr 94, KB (w),X-Men wedding	1.25	0.40	1.00	2.00
❑61, May 94, KB (w),Spider-Man	1.50	0.40	1.00	2.00
❑62, Jun 94, KB (w),Wolverine	1.50	0.40	1.00	2.00
❑63, Jul 94,War Machine	1.50	0.40	1.00	2.00
❑64, Aug 94, ...Iron Man Sold Out?,Iron Man	2.00	0.40	1.00	2.00
❑65, Sep 94	1.50	0.35	0.88	1.75
❑66, Oct 94, ...Rogue Possessed the Power of Thor?,Rogue	1.50	0.35	0.88	1.75
❑67, Nov 94,Captain America	1.50	0.35	0.88	1.75
❑68, Dec 94,Captain America	1.50	0.35	0.88	1.75
❑69, Jan 95,X-Men	1.50	0.35	0.88	1.75
❑70, Feb 95,Silver Surfer	1.50	0.35	0.88	1.75
❑71, Mar 95,Hulk	1.50	0.30	0.75	1.50
❑72, Apr 95,Spider-Man	1.50	0.30	0.75	1.50
❑73, May 95,Daredevil	1.50	0.30	0.75	1.50
❑74, Jun 95,Mr. Sinister forms The X-Men	1.50	0.30	0.75	1.50
❑75, Jul 95,Generation X	1.50	0.30	0.75	1.50
❑76, Aug 95,Flash Thompson as Spider-Man; last Watcher	1.50	0.30	0.75	1.50
❑77, Sep 95,Legion	1.50	0.30	0.75	1.50
❑78, Oct 95,New Fantastic Four remains a team	1.50	0.30	0.75	1.50
❑79, Nov 95,Storm becomes Phoenix	1.50	0.30	0.75	1.50
❑80, Dec 95, KGa, ...the Hulk Got Himself Cured?, A: Maestro,Hulk becomes The Maestro	1.50	0.30	0.75	1.50
❑81, Jan 96,Age of Apocalypse didn't end	1.50	0.30	0.75	1.50
❑82, Feb 96, ...J. Jonah Jameson Adopted Spider-Man?,J. Jonah Jameson adopts Peter Parker	1.50	0.30	0.75	1.50
❑83, Mar 96, ...Daredevil was the Disciple of Doctor Strange?,Daredevil was the disciple of Doctor Strange	1.50	0.30	0.75	1.50
❑84, Apr 96, ...Shard had Lived Instead of Bishop?,Shard lived instead of Bishop	1.50	0.30	0.75	1.50
❑85, May 96,Magneto ruled all mutants	1.50	0.30	0.75	1.50

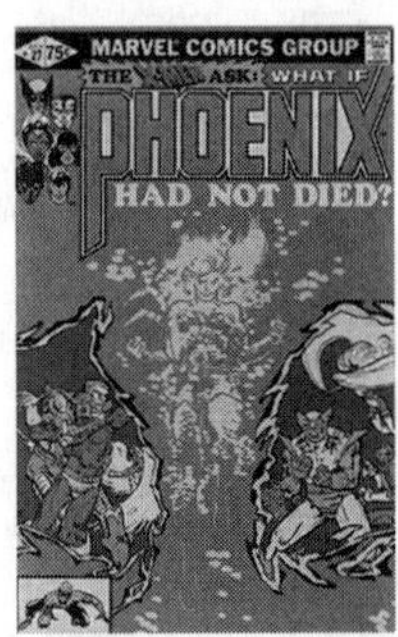

Both of Marvel's *What If?* series pondered the question of what would have happened if Phoenix had not died.

© 1981 Marvel Comics

	ORIG	GOOD	FINE	N-MINT
❑86, Jun 96,Scarlet Spider kills Spider-Man	1.50	0.30	0.75	1.50
❑87, Jul 96,Sabretooth	1.50	0.30	0.75	1.50
❑88, Aug 96,Spider-Man	1.50	0.30	0.75	1.50
❑89, Sep 96,Fantastic Four	1.50	0.30	0.75	1.50
❑90, Oct 96,Cyclops and Havok	1.50	0.30	0.75	1.50
❑91, Nov 96,Hulk	1.50	0.30	0.75	1.50
❑92, Dec 96,Joshua Guthrie and a Sentinel	1.50	0.30	0.75	1.50
❑93, Jan 97, Wolverine: A Man...No More,Wolverine	1.50	0.30	0.75	1.50
❑94, Feb 97, Juggernaut: Wanderings,Juggernaut	1.50	0.30	0.75	1.50
❑95, Mar 97, Ghost Rider: Broken Soul,Ghost Rider	1.95	0.39	0.98	1.95
❑96, Apr 97, Quicksilver: They Grow up so Quickly,Quicksilver	1.95	0.39	0.98	1.95
❑97, May 97, Black Knight: Last Light, A: Doctor Doom,Black Knight	1.95	0.39	0.98	1.95
❑98, Jun 97, Rogue: Seeds of Yesterday,Rogue, Nightcrawler	1.95	0.39	0.98	1.95
❑99, Aug 97, gatefold summary; Spider-Man	1.99	0.40	1.00	1.99
❑100, Sep 97, gatefold summary; double-sized; Gambit	2.99	0.40	1.00	1.99
❑101, Oct 97, gatefold summary; Archangel	1.99	0.40	1.00	1.99
❑102, Nov 97, gatefold summary; Daredevil	1.99	0.40	1.00	1.99
❑103, Dec 97, gatefold summary	1.99	0.40	1.00	1.99
❑104, Jan 98, gatefold summary; Impossible Man with Infinity Gauntlet	1.99	0.40	1.00	1.99
❑105, Feb 98, 1: Spider-Girl, gatefold summary; leads into Marvel 2	1.99	3.00	7.50	15.00
❑106, Mar 98, gatefold summary	1.99	0.40	1.00	1.99
❑107, Apr 98, V: Destroyer, gatefold summary; Thor as ruler of Asgard	1.99	0.40	1.00	1.99
❑108, May 98, gatefold summary; Avengers vs. Carnage	1.99	0.40	1.00	1.99
❑109, Jun 98, gatefold summary; Thing in Liddleville	1.99	0.40	1.00	1.99
❑110, Jul 98, gatefold summary; X-Men	1.99	0.40	1.00	1.99
❑111, Aug 98, gatefold summary; Wolverine as War	1.99	0.40	1.00	1.99
❑112, Sep 98, gatefold summary; Ka-Zar	1.99	0.40	1.00	1.99
❑113, Oct 98, gatefold summary; Tony Stark as Sorcerer Supreme	1.99	0.40	1.00	1.99
❑114, Nov 98, Final Issue; gatefold summary; Secret Wars 25 years later	2.50	0.50	1.25	2.50

WHAT IS...THE FACE?
ACE

Value: Cover or less

❑1, Dec 86, SD, SD (w), The Ransomed City; The Two Bottles of Relish 1.75

❑2, May 87, GT; SD, The Death Factory; The 5 Durin Brothers 1.75

❑3, Aug 87, SD 1.75

WHAT'S MICHAEL: LIVING TOGETHER
DARK HORSE

Value: Cover or less

❑1, Jul 97 .... 5.95

WHAT'S MICHAEL: MICHAEL'S ALBUM
DARK HORSE

Value: Cover or less

❑1, Apr 97 .... 5.95

WHAT'S MICHAEL: MICHAEL'S MAMBO
DARK HORSE

Value: Cover or less

❑1, Jan 98 .... 5.95

WHAT'S MICHAEL: OFF THE DEEP END
DARK HORSE

Value: Cover or less

❑1, Oct 97 .... 5.95

WHAT'S NEW?- THE COLLECTED ADVENTURES OF PHIL & DIXIE
PALLIARD

Value: Cover or less

❑1, Oct 91, PF, PF (w),color and b&w; The Collected Adventures of Phil and Dixie 7.95

❑2, full color; prestige format 7.95

WHAT'S NEW? WITH PHIL AND DIXIE
STUDIO FOGLIO

Value: Cover or less

❑3, Apr 00, PF, PF (w), The Magic Years, prestige format; collects strips from The Duelist 10.95

WHAT THE-?!
MARVEL

	ORIG	GOOD	FINE	N-MINT
❑1, Aug 88	1.25	0.80	2.00	4.00
❑2, Sep 88, JBy	1.25	0.50	1.25	2.50
❑3, Oct 88, TMc, KB (w)	1.25	0.60	1.50	3.00
❑4, Nov 88, KB (w)	1.25	0.50	1.25	2.50
❑5, Jul 89	1.50	0.50	1.25	2.50
❑6, Jan 90, JBy ,Acts of Vengeance parody	1.00	0.50	1.25	2.50
❑7, Apr 90, JBy (c)	1.25	0.50	1.25	2.50
❑8, Jul 90, JBy (c), KB (w)	1.25	0.50	1.25	2.50
❑9, Oct 90, JBy (c),wraparound cover	1.25	0.35	0.88	1.75
❑10, Jan 91, JBy (c), prestige format	1.25	0.35	0.88	1.75
❑11, Mar 91, JBy (c), O: Wolverina	1.25	0.30	0.75	1.50
❑12, May 91, JBy (c)	1.25	0.30	0.75	1.50
❑13, Jul 91, JBy (c)	1.25	0.30	0.75	1.50
❑14, Sep 91, JBy (c)	1.25	0.30	0.75	1.50
❑15, Nov 91, Strange Young fighting Frogs; Land Shark	1.25	0.30	0.75	1.50
❑16, Jan 92, Ock Around the Christmas Tree; The Grinch Who Swiped Chanuka,EC parody cover	1.25	0.30	0.75	1.50
❑17, Mar 92, KB (w)	1.25	0.30	0.75	1.50
❑18, May 92	1.25	0.30	0.75	1.50
❑19, Jul 92	1.25	0.30	0.75	1.50
❑20, Aug 92	1.25	0.30	0.75	1.50
❑21, Sep 92,Weapon X parody	1.25	0.30	0.75	1.50
❑22, Oct 92	1.25	0.30	0.75	1.50
❑23, Nov 92	1.25	0.30	0.75	1.50
❑24, Dec 92	1.25	0.30	0.75	1.50
❑25, Sum 93	2.50	0.50	1.25	2.50
❑26, Fal 93	2.50	0.50	1.25	2.50
❑27	2.50	0.50	1.25	2.50

WHEELIE AND THE CHOPPER BUNCH
CHARLTON

	ORIG	GOOD	FINE	N-MINT
❑1, JBy	5.00	1.60	4.00	8.00
❑2, JBy	3.00	1.00	2.50	5.00
❑3, JBy	3.00	0.80	2.00	4.00
❑4	2.00	0.80	2.00	4.00
❑5	2.00	0.80	2.00	4.00
❑6	2.00	0.80	2.00	4.00
❑7, Medical Mischief; The Basher Crasher,Final Issue	2.00	0.80	2.00	4.00

WHEEL OF WORLDS (NEIL GAIMAN'S...)
TEKNO

Value: Cover or less

- ❑0, Apr 95, A: Mr. Hero; A: Teknophage; A: Lady Justice; A: Adam Cain, poster; Direct Market edition; poster 2.95
- ❑0/CS, Apr 95, A: Mr. Hero; A: Teknophage; A: Lady Justice; A: Adam Cain,poster 2.95
- ❑1, May 96, RB, The Highest Bidder; the Big Bang, Chapter 1, O: Lady Justice 3.25

WHEN BEANIES ATTACK
BLATANT

Value: Cover or less

- ❑1, Mar 99 .... 2.95
- ❑1/SC,Violent cover 4.95

WHERE CREATURES ROAM
MARVEL

	ORIG	GOOD	FINE	N-MINT
❑1, Jul 70, JK	0.15	1.60	4.00	8.00
❑2, Sep 70, JK	0.15	1.00	2.50	5.00
❑3, Nov 70, JK	0.15	1.00	2.50	5.00
❑4, Jan 71, JK	0.15	1.00	2.50	5.00
❑5, Mar 71, JK	0.15	1.00	2.50	5.00
❑6, May 71, JK	0.15	1.00	2.50	5.00
❑7, Jul 71, JK	0.15	1.00	2.50	5.00
❑8, Sep 71, JK	0.15	1.00	2.50	5.00

WHERE IN THE WORLD IS CARMEN SANDIEGO?
DC

Value: Cover or less

- ❑1, Jun 96, Shop till you Drop!!!,based on computer game series 1.75
- ❑2, Sep 96 .... 1.75
- ❑3, Nov 96, Room with a Deja Vu 1.75
- ❑4, Jan 97, Stealer by Starlight,all-alien issue 1.75

WHERE MONSTERS DWELL
MARVEL

	ORIG	GOOD	FINE	N-MINT
❑1, Jan 70	0.15	2.00	5.00	10.00
❑2, Mar 70	0.15	1.20	3.00	6.00
❑3, May 70	0.15	0.80	2.00	4.00
❑4, Jul 70	0.15	0.80	2.00	4.00
❑5, Sep 70	0.15	0.80	2.00	4.00
❑6, Nov 70	0.15	0.60	1.50	3.00
❑7	0.15	0.60	1.50	3.00
❑8	0.15	0.60	1.50	3.00
❑9	0.15	0.60	1.50	3.00
❑10, SD, SD (w), Gigantuss, The Monster That Walked Like a Man!; The Frog-Man	0.15	0.60	1.50	3.00
❑11	0.15	0.60	1.50	3.00
❑12, Giant-size	0.15	0.80	2.00	4.00
❑13	0.15	0.60	1.50	3.00
❑14	0.20	0.60	1.50	3.00
❑15	0.20	0.60	1.50	3.00
❑16	0.20	0.60	1.50	3.00
❑17	0.20	0.60	1.50	3.00
❑18	0.20	0.60	1.50	3.00
❑19	0.20	0.60	1.50	3.00
❑20	0.20	0.60	1.50	3.00
❑21	0.20	0.60	1.50	3.00
❑22	0.20	0.60	1.50	3.00
❑23	0.20	0.60	1.50	3.00
❑24	0.20	0.60	1.50	3.00
❑25	0.20	0.60	1.50	3.00
❑26	0.20	0.60	1.50	3.00
❑27	0.20	0.60	1.50	3.00
❑28	0.25	0.60	1.50	3.00
❑29	0.25	0.60	1.50	3.00
❑30	0.25	0.60	1.50	3.00
❑31	0.25	0.60	1.50	3.00
❑32	0.25	0.60	1.50	3.00
❑33	0.25	0.60	1.50	3.00
❑34	0.25	0.60	1.50	3.00
❑35	0.25	0.60	1.50	3.00
❑36	0.25	0.60	1.50	3.00
❑37	0.25	0.60	1.50	3.00
❑38,Final Issue	0.25	0.60	1.50	3.00

WHILE FIFTY MILLION DIED
TOME PRESS

Value: Cover or less

- ❑1, b&w; World War II 2.95

WHISPER (VOL. 1)
CAPITAL

	ORIG	GOOD	FINE	N-MINT
❑1, Dec 83, O: Whisper	1.75	0.50	1.25	2.50
❑2, Mar 84	1.75	0.40	1.00	2.00

WHISPER (VOL. 2)
FIRST

	ORIG	GOOD	FINE	N-MINT
❑1, Jun 86, Datapanik in the Year Zero; Datapanik in the Year Zero, Part 1	1.25	0.40	1.00	2.00
❑2, Aug 86, Datapanik in the Year Zero, Part 2	1.25	0.30	0.75	1.50
❑3, Oct 86, Datapanik in the Year Zero, Part 3	1.25	0.30	0.75	1.50
❑4, Dec 86	1.25	0.30	0.75	1.50
❑5, Feb 87	1.25	0.30	0.75	1.50
❑6, Apr 87	1.25	0.30	0.75	1.50
❑7, Jun 87	1.25	0.30	0.75	1.50
❑8, Aug 87	1.75	0.35	0.88	1.75
❑9, Oct 87	1.25	0.35	0.88	1.75
❑10, Dec 87	1.75	0.35	0.88	1.75
❑11, Feb 88	1.75	0.35	0.88	1.75
❑12, Apr 88	1.75	0.35	0.88	1.75
❑13, Jun 88	1.75	0.35	0.88	1.75
❑14, Jul 88	1.75	0.35	0.88	1.75
❑15, Aug 88	1.75	0.35	0.88	1.75
❑16, Sep 88	1.75	0.35	0.88	1.75
❑17, Oct 88	1.75	0.35	0.88	1.75
❑18, Nov 88	1.95	0.39	0.98	1.95
❑19, Dec 88	1.95	0.39	0.98	1.95
❑20, Jan 89	1.95	0.39	0.98	1.95
❑21, Feb 89	1.95	0.39	0.98	1.95
❑22, Mar 89	1.95	0.39	0.98	1.95
❑23, Apr 89	1.95	0.39	0.98	1.95
❑24, May 89	1.95	0.39	0.98	1.95
❑25, Jun 89	1.95	0.39	0.98	1.95
❑26, Jul 89	1.95	0.39	0.98	1.95
❑27, Aug 89	1.95	0.39	0.98	1.95
❑28, Sep 89	1.95	0.39	0.98	1.95
❑29, Oct 89	1.95	0.39	0.98	1.95
❑30, Nov 89	1.95	0.39	0.98	1.95
❑31, Dec 89	1.95	0.39	0.98	1.95
❑32, Jan 90	1.95	0.39	0.98	1.95
❑33, Feb 90	1.95	0.39	0.98	1.95
❑34, Mar 90	1.95	0.39	0.98	1.95
❑35, Apr 90	1.95	0.39	0.98	1.95
❑36, May 90	1.95	0.39	0.98	1.95
❑37, Jun 90	1.95	0.39	0.98	1.95
❑SE 1, Nov 85, Giant-size	2.50	0.50	1.25	2.50

WHISPERS AND SHADOWS
OASIS

Value: Cover or less

- ❑1, b&w 1.50
- ❑2, b&w 1.50
- ❑3, b&w 1.50
- ❑4, b&w 1.50
- ❑5, b&w 1.50
- ❑6, b&w 1.50
- ❑7, b&w 1.50
- ❑8, b&w 1.50

WHITE DEVIL
ETERNITY

Value: Cover or less

- ❑1, b&w; adult 2.50
- ❑2, b&w; adult 2.50
- ❑3, b&w; adult 2.50
- ❑4, b&w; adult 2.50

	ORIG	GOOD	FINE	N-MINT

❑5, b&w; adult 2.50
❑6, b&w; adult 2.50
❑7, b&w; adult 2.50
❑8, b&w; adult 2.50

WHITE FANG
DISNEY

Value: Cover or less

❑1, nn; newsstand version 2.95
❑1/DM, nn; movie Adaptation 5.95

WHITE LIKE SHE
DARK HORSE

Value: Cover or less

❑1, May 94, b&w 2.95
❑2, Jun 94, b&w 2.95
❑3, Jul 94, b&w 2.95
❑4, Aug 94, b&w 2.95

WHITE ORCHID
ATLANTIS

Value: Cover or less

❑1 .... 2.95

WHITEOUT
ONI PRESS

Value: Cover or less

❑1, Jul 98 .... 2.95
❑2, Aug 98 .... 2.95
❑3, Sep 98 .... 2.95
❑4, Nov 98 .... 2.95

WHITEOUT: MELT
ONI PRESS

Value: Cover or less

❑1, Sep 99 .... 2.95
❑2, Oct 99 .... 2.95
❑3 .... 2.95
❑4 .... 2.95

WHITE RAVEN
VISIONARY

Value: Cover or less

❑1 .... 2.95

WHITE TRASH
TUNDRA

Value: Cover or less

❑1, nn 2.50
❑2 .... 3.95

WHOA, NELLIE!
FANTAGRAPHICS

Value: Cover or less

❑1, Jul 96, b&w 2.95
❑2, Aug 96, b&w 2.95
❑3, Sep 96, b&w 2.95

WHODUNNIT?
ECLIPSE

Value: Cover or less

❑1, Jun 86, DS, ME (w); DS (w), Who Shot Danny Scott? 2.00
❑2, Nov 86, DS, ME (w); DS (w), Who Slew Kangaroo? 2.00
❑3, Apr 87, DS, ME (w); DS (w), Who Offed Henry Croft? 2.00

WHO IS THE CROOKED MAN
CRUSADE

Value: Cover or less

❑1, Sep 96, The Matyr; Scarlet 7 .... 3.50

WHO REALLY KILLED JFK
REVOLUTIONARY

Value: Cover or less

❑1, Oct 93, The Kennedy Conspiracy; Who Was Lee Harvey Oswald?, b&w 2.50

WHO'S WHO IN STAR TREK
DC

Value: Cover or less

❑1, Mar 87, HC; JBy; GP 1.50
❑2, Apr 87, HC; JBy; GP ,McGivers-Vulcans 1.50

WHO'S WHO IN THE DC UNIVERSE
DC

Value: Cover or less

❑1, Aug 90 .... 4.95
❑2, Sep 90 .... 4.95
❑3, Oct 90 .... 4.95
❑4, Nov 90 .... 4.95
❑5, Dec 90 .... 4.95
❑6, Jan 91 .... 4.95
❑7, Feb 91 .... 4.95
❑8, Apr 91 .... 4.95
❑9, May 91 .... 4.95
❑10, Jun 91 .... 4.95
❑11, Jul 91 .... 4.95
❑12, Aug 91 .... 4.95
❑13, Oct 91 .... 4.95
❑14, Nov 91 .... 4.95
❑15, Jan 92 .... 4.95
❑16, Feb 92,Final Issue 4.95

WHO'S WHO IN THE DC UNIVERSE UPDATE 1993
DC

Value: Cover or less

❑1, Dec 92 .... 5.95
❑2, Jan 93 .... 5.95

WHO'S WHO IN THE IMPACT UNIVERSE
DC

Value: Cover or less

❑1, Sep 91 .... 4.95
❑2, Dec 91 .... 4.95
❑3, May 92 .... 4.95

WHO'S WHO IN THE LEGION OF SUPER-HEROES
DC

	ORIG	GOOD	FINE	N-MINT
❑1, Apr 88,Absorbancy Boy through Doctor Gym'll; Absorbancy Boy through Dr. Gym'll	1.25	0.30	0.75	1.50
❑2, Jun 88,Doctor Mayavile through High Seer; Dr. Mayavile through High Seer	1.25	0.30	0.75	1.50
❑3, Jul 88,Heroes of Lallor through Legion of Super-Rejects; plus Planets of the 30th Century	1.25	0.30	0.75	1.50
❑4, Aug 88	1.25	0.30	0.75	1.50
❑5, Sep 88,Mordru through Science Police Officer Quav; Plus Tour of Legion Headquarters	1.25	0.30	0.75	1.50
❑6, Oct 88	1.25	0.30	0.75	1.50
❑7, Nov 88	1.25	0.30	0.75	1.50

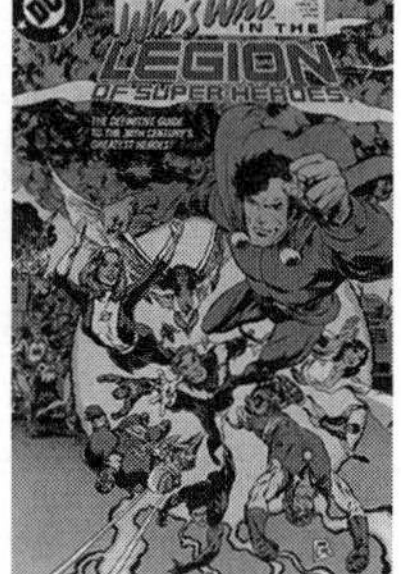

Due to the size of the group and its supporting characters, The Legion of Super-Heroes got its own seven-issue *Who's Who* series in 1988.

WHO'S WHO: THE DEFINITIVE DIRECTORY OF THE DC UNIVERSE
DC

	ORIG	GOOD	FINE	N-MINT
❑1, Mar 85, MR; GK; GP; JOy	1.00	0.30	0.75	1.50
❑2, Apr 85, GK; JK; GP; JOy	1.00	0.30	0.75	1.50
❑3, May 85, GK; JK; GP; JOy	1.00	0.30	0.75	1.50
❑4, Jun 85	1.00	0.30	0.75	1.50
❑5, Jul 85, GK; JK; GP; JOy	1.00	0.30	0.75	1.50
❑6, Aug 85, GK; JK; JOy; MW	1.00	0.30	0.75	1.50
❑7, Sep 85	1.00	0.30	0.75	1.50
❑8, Oct 85,Fatal Five-Garguax	1.00	0.30	0.75	1.50
❑9, Nov 85, GK; JK; GP; BSz	1.00	0.30	0.75	1.50
❑10, Dec 85, GK; JK; SR; GP; JOy	1.00	0.30	0.75	1.50
❑11, Jan 86	1.00	0.30	0.75	1.50
❑12, Feb 86, MR; JK; GP; JOy	1.00	0.30	0.75	1.50
❑13, Mar 86, GK; JK; GP; JSn ,Krona-Losers	1.00	0.30	0.75	1.50
❑14, Apr 86, JK; JBy; GP; BSz; JSn	1.00	0.30	0.75	1.50
❑15, May 86, JK; GP; BSz	1.00	0.30	0.75	1.50
❑16, Jun 86, GK; JK; JBy; GP	1.00	0.30	0.75	1.50
❑17, Jul 86, GK; JK; GP; JOy	1.00	0.30	0.75	1.50
❑18, Aug 86	1.00	0.30	0.75	1.50
❑19, Sep 86, GK; JK; JBy	1.00	0.30	0.75	1.50
❑20, Oct 86	1.00	0.30	0.75	1.50
❑21, Nov 86, GK; JOy; BSz; SD	1.00	0.30	0.75	1.50
❑22, Dec 86, GK; JK; JBy; JOy; SD	1.00	0.30	0.75	1.50
❑23, Jan 87	1.00	0.30	0.75	1.50
❑24, Feb 87,Tim Trench-Universo	1.00	0.30	0.75	1.50
❑25, Mar 87,Unknown Soldier-Witch Boy	1.00	0.30	0.75	1.50
❑26, Apr 87	1.00	0.30	0.75	1.50

WHO'S WHO UPDATE '87
DC

	ORIG	GOOD	FINE	N-MINT
❑1, Aug 87	1.25	0.30	0.75	1.50
❑2, Sep 87	1.25	0.30	0.75	1.50
❑3, Oct 87	1.25	0.30	0.75	1.50
❑4, Nov 87	1.25	0.30	0.75	1.50
❑5, Dec 87	1.25	0.30	0.75	1.50

WHO'S WHO UPDATE '88
DC

	ORIG	GOOD	FINE	N-MINT
❑1, Aug 88,Amazing Man to Harlequin II	1.25	0.30	0.75	1.50
❑2, Sep 88,Icemaiden to Nightwing	1.25	0.30	0.75	1.50
❑3, Oct 88,Parliament of Trees to Trident	1.25	0.30	0.75	1.50
❑4, Nov 88,Ultra-Humanite to Zuggernaut plus Supporting Characters (Abby Cable to Wade Eiling)	1.25	0.30	0.75	1.50

WHOTNOT
FANTAGRAPHICS

Value: Cover or less

❑1, b&w 2.50
❑2, b&w 2.50
❑3, b&w 2.50

WICKED
MILLENNIUM

Value: Cover or less

❑1 .... 2.50
❑2 .... 2.50
❑3, Apr 95, b&w; cover dated Mar 2.50

WICKED, THE
IMAGE

Value: Cover or less

❑1, Dec 99,Man, demoin on cover 2.95
❑1/A, Dec 99,Figure against red background on cover 2.95
❑1/B, Dec 99,Girl with glowing book on cover 2.95
❑2, Feb 00 .... 2.95
❑3 .... 2.95
❑4 .... 2.95
❑5, Jun 00 .... 2.95
❑6, Jun 00 .... 2.95
❑7, Aug 00 .... 2.95
❑Ash 1, Jul 99, Preview edition 5.00

WICKED, THE: MEDUSA'S TALE
IMAGE

Value: Cover or less

❑1, Nov 00 .... 3.95

WIDOW
AVATAR

Value: Cover or less

❑0 .... 3.95

WIDOW: FLESH AND BLOOD
GROUND ZERO

Value: Cover or less

❑1 .... 2.50
❑2 .... 2.50
❑3, Mar 93 .... 2.50

WIDOW: METAL GYPSIES
London Night

Value: Cover or less ❑1 .... 3.95

WIINDOWS
Cult

	ORIG	GOOD	FINE	N-MINT
❑1, b&w; Partial prism cover	2.50	0.70	1.75	3.50
❑2, b&w	2.50	0.60	1.50	3.00
❑3, b&w	2.50	0.60	1.50	3.00
❑4, b&w	2.50	0.50	1.25	2.50
❑5, Masterpiece in Bone, b&w	2.50	0.50	1.25	2.50
❑6, b&w	2.50	0.50	1.25	2.50
❑7, b&w	2.50	0.50	1.25	2.50
❑8, b&w	2.50	0.50	1.25	2.50
❑9, Nov 93, b&w	2.50	0.50	1.25	2.50
❑10, Dec 93, b&w	2.50	0.50	1.25	2.50
❑11, Jan 94, b&w	2.50	0.50	1.25	2.50
❑12, Feb 94, b&w	2.50	0.50	1.25	2.50
❑13, Mar 94, b&w	2.50	0.50	1.25	2.50
❑14, Apr 94, b&w	2.50	0.50	1.25	2.50
❑15, May 94, b&w	2.50	0.50	1.25	2.50
❑16, Jun 94, b&w	2.50	0.50	1.25	2.50
❑17, Jun 94, b&w	2.50	0.50	1.25	2.50

WILD ANIMALS
Pacific

Value: Cover or less ❑1 .... 1.50

WILD BILL PECOS
AC

Value: Cover or less ❑1 .... 3.50

WILDB.R.A.T.S
Fantagraphics

	ORIG	GOOD	FINE	N-MINT
❑1	2.95	0.65	1.63	3.25

WILDCARDS
Marvel

Value: Cover or less

❑1, Sep 90, prestige format; based on prose anthology series ... 4.50

❑2, Oct 90, prestige format; based on prose anthology series ... 4.50

❑3, prestige format; based on prose anthology series 4.50

❑4, prestige format; based on prose anthology series 4.50

WILDC.A.T.S
Image

	ORIG	GOOD	FINE	N-MINT
❑0, Jun 93	1.95	0.60	1.50	3.00
❑1, Aug 92, JLee, JLee(w), Resurrection Day, A: 1st; 1: Hightower; 1: WildC.A.T.s; 1: Pike; 1: Helspont; 1: Tri-Ad; 1: Gnome; 1: Spartan; 1: Grifter; 1: Maul	1.95	0.80	2.00	4.00
❑1/3D, JLee, JLee(w), Resurrection Day, 3-D edition	4.95	0.99	2.47	4.95
❑1/GO, Aug 92, JLee, JLee(w), Resurrection Day, Gold edition	—	2.00	5.00	10.00
❑1/SC, Wizard Ace edition	—	1.00	2.50	5.00
❑2, Sep 92, JLee, 1: Wetworks; 1: Black Razor,Prism cover; Coupon for Image Comics #0 enclosed	2.50	0.80	2.00	4.00
❑3, Dec 92, JLee	1.95	0.60	1.50	3.00
❑4, Mar 93, JLee, card	1.95	0.60	1.50	3.00
❑4/A, Mar 93, JLee,bagged; red trading card	2.50	0.60	1.50	3.00
❑5, Nov 93, JLee	1.95	0.50	1.25	2.50
❑6, Dec 93, JLee, Killer Instinct, Part 1	1.95	0.50	1.25	2.50
❑6/GO, Dec 93, Gold edition	1.95	0.60	1.50	3.00
❑7, Jan 94, JLee, Killer Instinct, Part 3	1.95	0.50	1.25	2.50
❑7/PL, Jan 94, Platinum edition	—	0.60	1.50	3.00
❑8, Feb 94, JLee, A: Cyclops and Jean Grey	2.50	0.50	1.25	2.50
❑9, Mar 94, JLee	2.50	0.50	1.25	2.50
❑10, Apr 94, JLee,series becomes WildC.A.T.S	2.50	0.50	1.25	2.50
❑11, Jun 94, JLee,Title changes to WildC.A.T.S	2.50	0.50	1.25	2.50
❑11/A, Jun 94,variant cover	2.50	0.50	1.25	2.50
❑12, Aug 94, 1: Savant	2.50	0.50	1.25	2.50
❑13, Sep 94	2.50	0.50	1.25	2.50
❑14, Sep 94	2.50	0.50	1.25	2.50
❑15, Nov 94	1.95	0.50	1.25	2.50
❑16, Dec 94	2.50	0.50	1.25	2.50
❑17, Jan 95, A: StormWatch	2.50	0.50	1.25	2.50
❑18, Mar 95	2.50	0.50	1.25	2.50
❑19, Apr 95	2.50	0.50	1.25	2.50
❑20, May 95, Wildstorm Rising, Part 2,with cards	2.50	0.50	1.25	2.50
❑21, Jul 95, AMo (w),1st Moore-written issue	2.50	0.50	1.25	2.50
❑22, Aug 95, AMo (w), Cat's Cradle	2.50	0.50	1.25	2.50
❑23, Sep 95, AMo (w), Cat's Eyes	2.50	0.50	1.25	2.50
❑24, Nov 95, AMo (w), Catacombs	2.50	0.50	1.25	2.50
❑25, Dec 95, AMo (w), On Earth…As It Is In Heaven,enhanced wraparound cover	4.95	0.99	2.47	4.95
❑26, Feb 96, AMo (w), Cat'spaws	2.50	0.50	1.25	2.50
❑27, Mar 96, AMo (w), Catastrophe	2.50	0.50	1.25	2.50
❑28, Apr 96, AMo (w), Cataclysm	2.50	0.50	1.25	2.50
❑29, May 96, AMo (w), Fire from Heaven, Part 7; Fire From Heaven, Chapter 7,cover says Apr, indicia says May	2.50	0.50	1.25	2.50
❑30, Jun 96, AMo (w), Fire from Heaven, Part 13; Fire From Heaven, Chapter 13	2.50	0.50	1.25	2.50
❑31, Sep 96, AMo (w), Cats & Dogs	2.50	0.50	1.25	2.50
❑32, Jan 97, AMo (w), Catharsis	2.50	0.50	1.25	2.50
❑33, Feb 97, AMo (w), Belling the Cat	2.50	0.50	1.25	2.50
❑34, Feb 97, AMo (w), Catechism	2.50	0.50	1.25	2.50
❑35, Mar 97	2.50	0.50	1.25	2.50
❑36, Mar 97	2.50	0.50	1.25	2.50
❑37, Apr 97	2.50	0.50	1.25	2.50
❑38, May 97	2.50	0.50	1.25	2.50
❑39, Jun 97	2.50	0.50	1.25	2.50
❑40, Jul 97	2.50	0.50	1.25	2.50
❑40/A, Jul 97,alternate mostly b&w cover	2.50	0.50	1.25	2.50
❑40/B, Jul 97,alternate mostly b&w cover	2.50	0.50	1.25	2.50
❑41, Aug 97	2.50	0.50	1.25	2.50
❑42, Sep 97, Brothers in Arms	2.50	0.50	1.25	2.50
❑43, Oct 97, The High Road to China	2.50	0.50	1.25	2.50
❑44, Nov 97, Paradise Lost	2.50	0.50	1.25	2.50
❑45, Jan 98, Endangered Species, Part 5	2.50	0.50	1.25	2.50
❑46, Feb 98, Endangered Species, Part 6	2.50	0.50	1.25	2.50
❑47, Mar 98	2.50	0.50	1.25	2.50
❑47/A, Mar 98, Memories of Tomorrow,alternate cover with Grifter	2.50	0.50	1.25	2.50
❑47/B, Mar 98, Memories of Tomorrow,alternate cover with Grifter	2.50	0.50	1.25	2.50
❑48, Apr 98, When Worlds Collide, Part 1	2.50	0.50	1.25	2.50
❑49, May 98, When Worlds Collide, Part 2	2.50	0.50	1.25	2.50
❑50, Jun 98, AMo (w); JRo (w), Old Feelings; The Last Goodbye, Giant-size	3.50	0.70	1.75	3.50
❑50/SC, Jun 98,chromium cover	—	0.70	1.75	3.50
❑Anl 1, Feb 98, JRo (w)	2.95	0.59	1.48	2.95
❑SE 1, Nov 93	3.50	0.70	1.75	3.50

WILDCATS (2ND SERIES)
DC

	ORIG	GOOD	FINE	N-MINT
❑1/A, Mar 99	2.50	0.50	1.25	2.50
❑1/B	2.50	0.50	1.25	2.50
❑1/C	2.50	0.50	1.25	2.50
❑1/D	2.50	0.50	1.25	2.50
❑1/E	2.50	0.50	1.25	2.50
❑1/F	2.50	0.50	1.25	2.50
❑1/G	6.95	1.39	3.47	6.95
❑1/H,DFE alternate cover	6.95	1.39	3.47	6.95
❑1/I, Euro-Edition sketch cover	—	2.00	5.00	10.00
❑1/J,Signed by Travis Charest and Richard Friend; Euro-Edition sketch cover	—	5.99	14.98	29.95
❑2, May 99	2.50	0.50	1.25	2.50
❑3, Jul 99	2.50	0.50	1.25	2.50
❑4, Sep 99, Firefight	2.50	0.50	1.25	2.50
❑5, Nov 99, Coda-Fied	2.50	0.50	1.25	2.50
❑6, Dec 99, The Chase	2.50	0.50	1.25	2.50
❑7	2.50	0.50	1.25	2.50
❑8	2.50	0.50	1.25	2.50
❑9, May 00, Set my Soul on Fire	2.50	0.50	1.25	2.50
❑10, Jun 00, Deal of the Century	2.50	0.50	1.25	2.50
❑11, Jul 00	2.50	0.50	1.25	2.50
❑12, Aug 00	2.50	0.50	1.25	2.50
❑13, Sep 00	2.50	0.50	1.25	2.50
❑14, Oct 00, Black Action Falls; Serial Boxes, Part 1	2.50	0.50	1.25	2.50
❑15, Nov 00, Serial Boxes, Part 2	2.50	0.50	1.25	2.50
❑16, Dec 00, Serial Boxes, Part 3	2.50	0.50	1.25	2.50
❑17, Jan 01, Serial Boxes, Part 4	2.50	0.50	1.25	2.50
❑18, Feb 01, Serial Boxes, Part 5	2.50	0.50	1.25	2.50
❑19, Mar 01, Serial Boxes, Part 6	2.50	0.50	1.25	2.50
❑20, Apr 01, Sodom and Modem, Part 1	2.50	0.50	1.25	2.50
❑21, May 01, Sodom and Modem, Part 2	2.50	0.50	1.25	2.50
❑22, Jun 01, Unberable Likeness	2.50	0.50	1.25	2.50
❑23	2.50	0.50	1.25	2.50
❑24	2.50	0.50	1.25	2.50
❑25	3.50	0.70	1.75	3.50
❑Anl 2000, Dec 00, Condition Dead	3.50	0.70	1.75	3.50

WILDC.A.T.S (JIM LEE'S...)
Image

	ORIG	GOOD	FINE	N-MINT
❑1, Apr 95,no cover price; informational comic for San Diego Police Dept.	—	0.40	1.00	2.00

WILDC.A.T.S ADVENTURES
Image

	ORIG	GOOD	FINE	N-MINT
❑1, Sep 94, O: WildC.A.T.s; O: Warblade	1.95	0.40	1.00	2.00
❑2, Nov 94	1.95	0.40	1.00	2.00
❑3, Nov 94	1.95	0.40	1.00	2.00
❑4, Dec 94	2.50	0.50	1.25	2.50
❑5, Jan 95	2.50	0.50	1.25	2.50
❑6, Feb 95	2.50	0.50	1.25	2.50

	ORIG	GOOD	FINE	N-MINT
❑7, Mar 95	2.50	0.50	1.25	2.50
❑8, Apr 95	2.50	0.50	1.25	2.50
❑9, May 95	2.50	0.50	1.25	2.50
❑10, Jun 95	2.50	0.50	1.25	2.50

WILDC.A.T.S ADVENTURES SOURCEBOOK
IMAGE

Value: Cover or less
❑1, Jan 95 .... 2.95

WILDC.A.T.S/ALIENS
IMAGE

Value: Cover or less
❑1, Aug 98,cardstock cover; crossover with Dark Horse 4.95
❑1/A, Aug 98,alternate cardstock cover (Zealot vs. Alien); crossover with Dark Horse 4.95

WILDCATS: LADYTRON
WILDSTORM

Value: Cover or less
❑1, Oct 00 .... 5.95

WILDCATS: MOSAIC
WILDSTORM

Value: Cover or less
❑1, Feb 00 .... 3.95

WILDC.A.T.S SOURCEBOOK
IMAGE

	ORIG	GOOD	FINE	N-MINT
❑1, Sep 93	2.50	0.50	1.25	2.50
❑1/GO, Sep 93, Gold edition	—	0.60	1.50	3.00
❑2, Nov 94	2.50	0.50	1.25	2.50

WILDC.A.T.S TRILOGY
IMAGE

Value: Cover or less
❑1, Jun 93, 1: Artemis,foil cover 2.50
❑2, Sep 93 .... 1.95
❑3, Nov 93 .... 1.95

WILDC.A.T.S/X-MEN: THE DARK AGE
IMAGE

Value: Cover or less
❑1 .... 4.95

WILDC.A.T.S/X-MEN: THE GOLDEN AGE
IMAGE

	ORIG	GOOD	FINE	N-MINT
❑1/3D-A, Sep 97, JLee(c),crossover with Marvel; with glasses	6.50	1.30	3.25	6.50
❑1/3D-B, Sep 97,scroll cover; crossover with Marvel; with glasses	6.50	1.30	3.25	6.50
❑1	4.95	0.99	2.47	4.95
❑1/A, Feb 97, JLee(c),cardstock cover; Signed by Travis Charest; crossover with Marvel	4.50	1.00	2.50	5.00
❑1/B, Feb 97,scroll cover; Signed by Jim Lee; crossover with Marvel	4.50	1.60	4.00	8.00
❑1/C, Feb 97,cardstock cover; crossover with Marvel	4.50	0.90	2.25	4.50
❑1/D, Sep 97,crossover with Marvel; with glasses	6.50	1.30	3.25	6.50
❑1/E, Sep 97,scroll cover; crossover with Marvel; with glasses	6.50	1.30	3.25	6.50

WILDC.A.T.S/X-MEN: THE MODERN AGE
IMAGE

	ORIG	GOOD	FINE	N-MINT
❑1/3D-A, Nov 97, 3-D glasses bound-in; crossover with Marvel	6.50	1.30	3.25	6.50
❑1/3D-B, Nov 97,Nightcrawler cover; 3-D glasses bound-in; crossover with Marvel.	6.50	1.30	3.25	6.50
❑1, Aug 97, JRo (w),Cardstock cover with Wolverine	4.95	0.90	2.25	4.50
❑1/A, Aug 97, JRo (w),cardstock cover; Signed by Adam Hughes; Certificate of Authenticity; crossover with Marvel	4.50	1.20	3.00	6.00
❑1/B, Aug 97, JRo (w),cardstock cover; crossover with Marvel	4.50	0.90	2.25	4.50
❑1/C, Nov 97, JRo (w), 3-D glasses bound-in; crossover with Marvel	6.50	1.30	3.25	6.50
❑1/D, Nov 97, JRo (w),Nightcrawler cover; 3-D glasses bound-in; crossover with Marvel	6.50	1.30	3.25	6.50

WILDC.A.T.S/X-MEN: THE SILVER AGE
IMAGE

	ORIG	GOOD	FINE	N-MINT
❑1/3D-B, Oct 97, 3-D glasses bound-in; crossover with Marvel; has indicia for WildC.A.T.S/X-Men: The Modern Age 3-D	6.50	1.30	3.25	6.50
❑1/3D-A, Oct 97, 3-D glasses bound-in; crossover with Marvel; has indicia for WildC.A.T.S/X-Men: The Modern Age 3-D	6.50	1.30	3.25	6.50
❑1, JLee,Jim Lee cover (Grifter standing center)	4.95	0.99	2.47	4.95
❑1/A, Jun 97, JLee; NA ,Neal Adams cover (Brood attacking); crossover with Marvel	4.50	0.99	2.47	4.95
❑1/B, Jun 97,cardstock cover; crossover with Marvel	4.50	0.90	2.25	4.50
❑1/C, JLee, 3-D edition	6.95	1.39	3.47	6.95
❑1/D, Oct 97, 3-D glasses bound-in; crossover with Marvel; has indicia for WildC.A.T.S/X-Men: The Modern Age 3-D	6.50	1.30	3.25	6.50

WILDCORE
IMAGE

	ORIG	GOOD	FINE	N-MINT
❑1, Nov 97,Three figures fighting on cover..	2.50	0.50	1.25	2.50
❑1/A, Nov 97,White background on cover; white background	2.50	0.50	1.25	2.50
❑1/B, Nov 97,alternate cover; white background	2.50	1.00	2.50	5.00

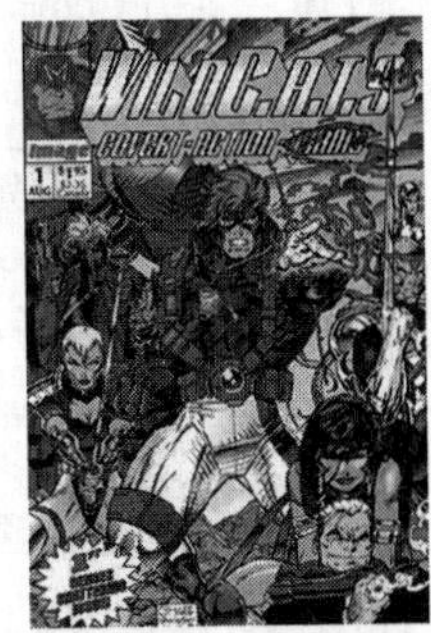

The C.A.T.S portion of the *WildC.A.T.S* title stood for Covert Action Teams.

© 1992 Jim Lee (Image)

	ORIG	GOOD	FINE	N-MINT
❑2, Dec 97,Vigor standing on cover	2.50	0.50	1.25	2.50
❑2/A, Dec 97,variant cover	2.50	0.60	1.50	3.00
❑3, Jan 98	2.50	0.50	1.25	2.50
❑4, Mar 98	2.50	0.50	1.25	2.50
❑5, Jun 98	2.50	0.50	1.25	2.50
❑6, Jul 98, Paradise Rouge	2.50	0.50	1.25	2.50
❑7, Aug 98	2.50	0.50	1.25	2.50
❑8, Oct 98	2.50	0.50	1.25	2.50
❑9, Nov 98	2.50	0.50	1.25	2.50
❑10, Dec 98	2.50	0.50	1.25	2.50
❑Ash 1, Oct 97, Preview edition	—	0.60	1.50	3.00

WILD DOG
DC

	ORIG	GOOD	FINE	N-MINT
❑1, Sep 87	0.75	0.30	0.75	1.50
❑2, Oct 87	0.75	0.30	0.75	1.50
❑3, Nov 87	0.75	0.30	0.75	1.50
❑4, Dec 87	0.75	0.30	0.75	1.50
❑SE 1, Nov 89, Dog Catcher	2.50	0.50	1.25	2.50

WILDFLOWER
SIRIUS

Value: Cover or less
❑1, Feb 98 .... 2.50
❑2, Apr 98 .... 2.50
❑3, Jun 98 .... 2.50
❑4, Aug 98 .... 2.50
❑5, Oct 98 .... 2.50

WILD FRONTIER
SHANDA

Value: Cover or less
❑1, Jan 00 .... 2.95
❑2 .... 2.95

WILD KINGDOM
MU

Value: Cover or less
❑1, Oct 91, b&w; adult 2.50
❑2, May 93, b&w; adult 2.95
❑3, Jan 95, b&w; adult 2.95
❑4, Apr 95, b&w; adult 2.95
❑5, Aug 95, b&w; adult 2.95
❑6, Dec 95, b&w; adult 2.95

WILD KNIGHTS
ETERNITY

Value: Cover or less
❑1, Mar 88 .... 1.95
❑2 .... 1.95
❑3 .... 1.95
❑4 .... 1.95
❑5 .... 1.95
❑6 .... 1.95
❑7 .... 1.95
❑8 .... 1.95
❑9 .... 1.95
❑10 .... 1.95

WILD LIFE (ANTARCTIC)
ANTARCTIC

Value: Cover or less
❑1, Feb 93, b&w 2.50
❑2, May 93, b&w 2.50
❑3, Jul 93, b&w 2.50
❑4, Nov 93, b&w 2.75
❑5, Feb 94, b&w 2.75
❑6, Apr 94, b&w 2.75
❑7, Jun 94, b&w 2.75
❑8, Aug 94, b&w 2.75
❑9, Oct 94, b&w 2.75
❑10, Dec 94, b&w 2.75
❑11, Feb 95, M.E.I.; Uni-Universe, b&w 2.75
❑12, Apr 95, Your Cake Goes Straight to My Hips; Misanthrope, b&w; Final Issue 2.75

WILD LIFE (FANTAGRAPHICS)
FANTAGRAPHICS

Value: Cover or less
❑1, Aug 94, b&w 2.75
❑2, Aug 94, b&w 2.75

WILDLIFERS
RADIO

Value: Cover or less
❑1, Sep 4.95

WILDMAN (GRASS GREEN'S...)
MEGATON

Value: Cover or less
❑1 .... 1.50
❑2 .... 1.50

WILD PERSON IN THE WOODS
G.T. LABS

Value: Cover or less
❑1 .... 2.50

WILD SIDE
UNITED PUBLICATIONS

Value: Cover or less
❑1, Jan 98, The King of Han's Bride; Zen Zebras...Stars & Stripes, b&w 3.95

ORIG GOOD FINE N-MINT

WILDSTAR
IMAGE
Value: Cover or less

❑1, Sep 95, Born to be Wild.... 2.50
❑1/A, Sep 95.......................... 2.50
❑2, Nov 95.............................. 2.50
❑3, Jan 96.............................. 2.50
❑4, Mar 96.............................. 2.50

WILD STARS
COLLECTOR'S
Value: Cover or less
❑1, b&w.................................. 1.00

WILDSTAR: SKY ZERO
IMAGE

	ORIG	GOOD	FINE	N-MINT
❑1, Mar 93, JOy ,Embossed cover; silver foil	2.50	0.60	1.50	3.00
❑1/GO, Mar 93, JOy ,Embossed cover; gold	2.50	0.80	2.00	4.00
❑2, May 93, JOy	1.95	0.40	1.00	2.00
❑3, Sep 93, JOy, A: Savage Dragon	1.95	0.50	1.25	2.50
❑4, Nov 93, JOy	1.95	0.50	1.25	2.50

WILDSTORM!
IMAGE
Value: Cover or less

❑1, Aug 95, MZ ,Anthology; color and b&w; Gen13, Grifter, Deathblow, Union, Spartan........... 2.50
❑2, Oct 95,cover says Sep, indicia says Oct; Anthology; color and b&w.................................... 2.50
❑3, Nov 95,Anthology 2.50
❑4, Dec 95, Salvage Operation; Head Problems,Anthology; StormWatch Showcase....... 2.50

WILDSTORM ANNUAL
WILDSTORM
Value: Cover or less
❑2000, Dec 00, Soul Sacrifices............................ 3.50

WILDSTORM CHAMBER OF HORRORS
IMAGE
Value: Cover or less
❑1, Oct 95, BWr, Warblade; Lord Emp,Anthology.................... 3.50

WILDSTORM FINE ARTS: THE GALLERY COLLECTION
IMAGE
Value: Cover or less
❑1, Dec 98,collects pin-up books and other art....................... 19.95

WILDSTORM HALLOWEEN '97
IMAGE
Value: Cover or less
❑1, Oct 97, Team 7, In Blood and Faith; Gen 13, ...When all the Freaks Come Out, Anthology........................... 2.50

WILDSTORM RARITIES
IMAGE
Value: Cover or less
❑1, Dec 94 .... 4.95

WILDSTORM RISING
IMAGE
Value: Cover or less
❑1, May 95, JRo (w), Wildstorm Rising, Part 1,with cards..... 2.50
❑2, Jun 95, Wildstorm Rising, Part 11,bound-in trading cards.... 2.50

WILDSTORM SAMPLER
IMAGE

	ORIG	GOOD	FINE	N-MINT
❑1, nn; no cover price; giveaway	—	0.20	0.50	1.00

WILDSTORMS PLAYER'S GUIDE
IMAGE
Value: Cover or less
❑1, Mar 96,tips on WildStorms card game........................... 1.95

WILDSTORM SPOTLIGHT
IMAGE
Value: Cover or less

❑1, Feb 97,Majestic................ 2.50
❑2, Mar 97,Loner.................... 2.50
❑3, Apr 97,Loner.................... 2.50
❑4, May 97,StormWatch; no indicia....................................... 2.50

WILDSTORM SWIMSUIT SPECIAL
IMAGE
Value: Cover or less

❑1, Dec 94............................. 2.95
❑2, Aug 95,pin-ups 2.50
❑1997, May 97,pin-ups; Wild-Storm Swimsuits '97........... 2.50

WILDSTORM THUNDERBOOK
WILDSTORM
Value: Cover or less
❑1, Oct 00, Wham!; Professionals...................... 6.95

WILDSTORM ULTIMATE SPORTS OFFICIAL PROGRAM
IMAGE
Value: Cover or less
❑1, Aug 97,pin-ups.................. 2.50

WILDSTORM UNIVERSE 97
IMAGE
Value: Cover or less

❑1, Dec 96,information on various Wildstorm characters.......... 2.50
❑2, Jan 97,information on various Wildstorm characters 2.50
❑3, Feb 97,information on various Wildstorm characters 2.50

WILDSTORM UNIVERSE SOURCEBOOK
IMAGE
Value: Cover or less

❑1, May 95............................. 2.50
❑2.. 2.50

WILD THING
MARVEL
Value: Cover or less

❑1, 1: Wild Thing,Embossed cover 2.50
❑2.. 1.75
❑3.. 1.75
❑4.. 1.75
❑5.. 1.75
❑6.. 1.75
❑7, A: Nikki Doyle; A: Liddel; A: Trout 1.75

WILD THING (2ND SERIES)
MARVEL
Value: Cover or less

❑1, Oct 99, Crash Course 1.99
❑2, Nov 99 .... 1.99
❑3, Dec 99, Awakening 1.99
❑4, Jan 99 .... 1.99

WILD THINGS
METRO
Value: Cover or less

❑1... 2.00
❑2... 2.00
❑3... 2.00

WILD THINGZ
ABC STUDIOS
Value: Cover or less

❑0/A 3.00
❑0/B,swimsuit cover............... 5.95
❑0/PL,Virgin Special Preview; limited to 300 copies 3.00

WILD THINK
WILD THINK
Value: Cover or less
❑1, Apr 87................................ 2.00

WILD TIMES: DEATHBLOW
DC
Value: Cover or less
❑1, Aug 99, Death Rides a Horse!, A: Bat Lash,set in 1899 .... 2.50

WILD TIMES: DV8
DC
Value: Cover or less
❑1, Aug 99, D-Day, A: Sgt. Rock and Easy Co.,set in 1944 .... 2.50

WILD TIMES: GEN13
DC
Value: Cover or less
❑1, Aug 99, All New All Fab, A: Teen Titans,set in 1969, 1972, and 1973 .... 2.50

WILD TIMES: GRIFTER
DC
Value: Cover or less
❑1, Aug 99, PS, just another chicago grifter,set in 1920s 2.50

WILD TIMES: WETWORKS
DC
Value: Cover or less
❑1, Aug 99, MWa (w), Still Waters Run Deep, A: Superman 2.50

WILD WEST C.O.W.-BOYS OF MOO MESA, THE
ARCHIE
Value: Cover or less

❑1... 1.25
❑2... 1.25
❑3... 1.25

WILD, WILD WEST, THE (GOLD KEY)
GOLD KEY

	ORIG	GOOD	FINE	N-MINT
❑1, Jun 66, Outlaw Empire,Photo cover; 10174-606	0.12	11.00	27.50	55.00
❑2, Aug 66,Photo cover	0.12	7.00	17.50	35.00
❑3, Jun 68,Photo cover	0.12	6.00	15.00	30.00
❑4, Dec 68,Photo cover	0.12	6.00	15.00	30.00
❑5, Apr 69,Photo cover	0.12	6.00	15.00	30.00
❑6, Jul 69,Photo cover	0.15	6.00	15.00	30.00
❑7, Oct 69,Photo cover	0.15	6.00	15.00	30.00

WILD, WILD WEST, THE (MILLENNIUM)
MILLENNIUM
Value: Cover or less

❑1, The Night of the Iron Tyrants, Part 1,TV............................ 2.95
❑2, The Night of the Iron Tyrants, Part 2,TV............................ 2.95
❑3, The Night of the Iron Tyrants, Part 3,TV 2.95
❑4, The Night of the Iron Tyrants, Part 4,TV 2.95

WILL EISNER PRESENTS
ECLIPSE
Value: Cover or less

❑1, Dec 90, 1: Mr. Mystic, b&w; Mr. Mystic................................ 2.50
❑2,Mr. Mystic.......................... 2.50
❑3,Mr. Mystic.......................... 2.50

WILL EISNER READER
DC
Value: Cover or less
❑1, Oct 00, WE, WE (w), A Sunset in Sunshine City; The Telephone........................... 9.95

WILL EISNER'S 3-D CLASSICS: SPIRIT
KITCHEN SINK
Value: Cover or less
❑1, Dec 85.............................. 2.00

WILL EISNER'S QUARTERLY
KITCHEN SINK
Value: Cover or less

❑1, Nov 83 .... 2.00
❑2, Feb 84............................... 2.00
❑3, Aug 84 .... 2.00
❑4... 2.00
❑5... 2.00
❑6... 2.00
❑7... 2.00
❑8, Mar 86............................... 2.00

WILLIAM SHATNER
CELEBRITY
Value: Cover or less
❑1... 5.95

WILLOW (ANGEL)
ANGEL
Value: Cover or less

❑0, Jun 96, b&w..................... 2.95
❑0/Nude, Jun 96,nude cardstock cover.................................. 10.00

	ORIG	GOOD	FINE	N-MINT

WILLOW (MARVEL)
MARVEL

	ORIG	GOOD	FINE	N-MINT
❏1, BH ,movie Adaptation	1.00	0.30	0.75	1.50
❏2, BH ,movie Adaptation	1.00	0.30	0.75	1.50
❏3, BH ,movie Adaptation	1.00	0.30	0.75	1.50

WILL TO POWER
DARK HORSE

	ORIG	GOOD	FINE	N-MINT
❏1, Jun 94	1.00	0.30	0.75	1.50
❏2, Jun 94	1.00	0.20	0.50	1.00
❏3, Jun 94	1.00	0.20	0.50	1.00
❏4, Jul 94, 1: Counterstrike	1.00	0.20	0.50	1.00
❏5, Jul 94	1.00	0.20	0.50	1.00
❏6, Jul 94	1.00	0.20	0.50	1.00
❏7, Jul 94	1.00	0.20	0.50	1.00
❏8, Aug 94	1.00	0.20	0.50	1.00
❏9, Aug 94	1.00	0.20	0.50	1.00
❏10, Aug 94	1.00	0.20	0.50	1.00
❏11, Aug 94	1.00	0.20	0.50	1.00
❏12, Aug 94,Final Issue	1.00	0.20	0.50	1.00

WIMMEN'S COMIX
RENEGADE

	ORIG	GOOD	FINE	N-MINT
❏1, Goldie: A Neurotic Woman; A Teenage Abortion,adult	0.50	2.00	5.00	10.00
❏2,adult	—	1.60	4.00	8.00
❏3,adult	—	1.60	4.00	8.00
❏4, Didi Glitz: She Chose Crime; Dolly Divine: Hot to Trot,adult	0.75	1.60	4.00	8.00
❏5,adult	—	1.00	2.50	5.00
❏6,adult	—	1.00	2.50	5.00
❏7,adult	—	1.00	2.50	5.00
❏8,adult	—	1.00	2.50	5.00
❏9,adult	—	0.80	2.00	4.00
❏10,adult	—	0.80	2.00	4.00
❏11, b&w; adult	2.00	0.60	1.50	3.00
❏12,adult; 3-D	2.50	0.60	1.50	3.00
❏13,adult	2.00	0.60	1.50	3.00
❏14, Feb 89, Magda Meets the Little Men in the Woods; 1st Crushed, b&w; adult; Disastrous Relationships	2.50	0.50	1.25	2.50
❏15, Aug 89, Latency Come Lately; Baby Butch Dyke, b&w; adult	2.50	0.50	1.25	2.50
❏16, Nov 90, Men; Sweet Delusions, or The Date from Hell, b&w; adult	2.50	0.50	1.25	2.50
❏17, Aug 92, b&w; adult	2.50	0.50	1.25	2.50
❏18,adult	—	0.50	1.25	2.50

WINDBURNT PLAINS OF WONDER, THE
LOHMAN HILLS

Value: Cover or less

❏1, Fal 96, nn; b&w Emma Davenport one-shot 11.95

WIND IN THE WILLOWS, THE
NBM

Value: Cover or less

❏1 .... 15.95

❏2, Feb 99 .... 15.95

WINDRAVEN
HEROIC

Value: Cover or less

❏1, b&w 2.95

WINDSOR
WIN-MIL

Value: Cover or less

❏1 .... 1.95

❏2,Flip-cover format 1.95

WINGBIRD AKUMA-SHE
VEROTIK

Value: Cover or less

❏1, Jan 98,adult; cardstock cover 3.95

WINGBIRD RETURNS
VEROTIK

Value: Cover or less

❏1, Oct 97, nn; adult; prestige format 9.95

WINGDING ORGY
EROS

Value: Cover or less

❏1 .... 3.95

❏2, Wingding Mix 3.95

WINGED TIGER, THE
CARTOONISTS ACROSS AMERICA

Value: Cover or less

❏3, Sum 99 .... 2.95

WINGING IT
SOLO

Value: Cover or less

❏1 .... 2.00

WINGS
MU

Value: Cover or less

❏1, Sep 92 .... 2.50

WINGS COMICS (A-LIST)
A-LIST

Value: Cover or less

❏1, Spr 97, Lucky Wings: The Atomic Blondshell; The Golden Ghouls, b&w; Golden Age reprint 2.95

❏2, Fal 97, b&w; Golden Age reprint 2.95

❏3, Shark Brodie; Ace of the Newsreel 2.95

❏4 .... 2.95

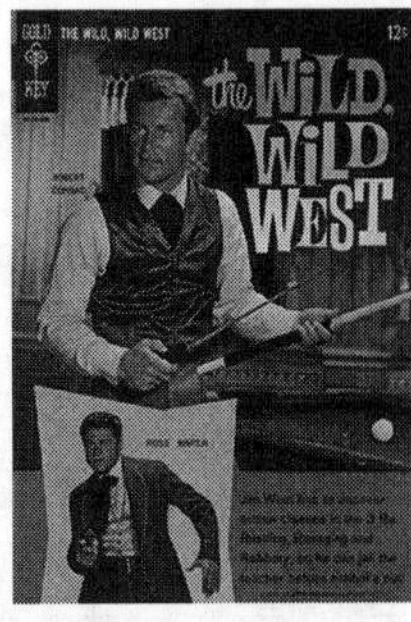

All seven issues of Gold Key's *Wild, Wild West* series featured photo covers of star Robert Conrad.

© 1966 CBS Television (Gold Key)

WINNING IN THE DESERT
APPLE

Value: Cover or less

❏1,booklet 2.95

❏2,booklet 2.95

WINTERSTAR
ECHO

Value: Cover or less

❏1, Dec 96, b&w 2.95

WINTERWORLD
ECLIPSE

	ORIG	GOOD	FINE	N-MINT
❏1	1.75	0.40	1.00	2.00
❏2	1.75	0.40	1.00	2.00
❏3	1.75	0.40	1.00	2.00

WISE SON: THE WHITE WOLF
DC

Value: Cover or less

❏1, Nov 96 .... 2.50

❏2, Dec 96, Woman in Chains 2.50

❏3, Jan 97, Once, When I Was Lost 2.50

❏4, Feb 97 .... 2.50

WISH UPON A STAR
WARP

	ORIG	GOOD	FINE	N-MINT
❏1, May 94, giveaway; no price	—	0.20	0.50	1.00

WITCH
ETERNITY

Value: Cover or less

❏1, The Love Witch, b&w; Reprint 1.95

WITCHBLADE
IMAGE

	ORIG	GOOD	FINE	N-MINT
❏0	—	1.00	2.50	5.00
❏0.5, Overstreet Fan promotional edition	—	6.00	15.00	30.00
❏1, Nov 95, 2: Witchblade	2.50	4.00	10.00	20.00
❏1/A, Nov 95,Sketch cover variant; Wizard Ace edition	2.50	1.00	2.50	5.00
❏1/B, Nov 95, Wizard Ace edition	2.50	3.00	7.50	15.00
❏2, Jan 96,Relatively scarce	2.50	3.60	9.00	18.00
❏2/A, Jan 96, Wizard Ace edition	2.50	3.00	7.50	15.00
❏2-2,2nd Printing; "Encore edition"	2.50	0.80	2.00	4.00
❏3, Mar 96	2.50	2.00	5.00	10.00
❏4, Apr 96	2.50	1.60	4.00	8.00
❏5, May 96	2.50	1.60	4.00	8.00
❏6, Jun 96, 1: Julie Pezzini	2.50	1.20	3.00	6.00
❏7, Jul 96	2.50	1.20	3.00	6.00
❏8, Aug 96	2.50	1.00	2.50	5.00
❏9, Sep 96	2.50	1.00	2.50	5.00
❏9/A, Sep 96	2.50	1.00	2.50	5.00
❏10, Nov 96, 1: The Darkness; A: Darkness	2.50	1.00	2.50	5.00
❏10/A, Nov 96, 1: The Darkness; A: Darkness,Alternate cover sold through Dynamic Forces; Signed by artists; Shows two characters back-to-back	2.50	4.00	10.00	20.00
❏10/AUT, 1: The Darkness,Signed by creators and sold through Dynamic Forces; limited to 2,500 copies	27.95	4.00	10.00	20.00
❏10/B, Nov 96, A: Darkness,alternate cover; American Entertainment alternate	2.50	1.60	4.00	8.00
❏10/C, Nov 96, A: Darkness,Dynamic Forces alternate; American Entertainment alternate	2.50	1.60	4.00	8.00
❏10/D, Nov 96, A: Darkness,Dynamic Forces alternate	2.50	1.60	4.00	8.00
❏11, Dec 96	2.50	0.80	2.00	4.00
❏12, Mar 97	2.50	0.80	2.00	4.00
❏13, Apr 97	2.50	0.70	1.75	3.50
❏14, May 97	2.50	0.70	1.75	3.50
❏14/GO, May 97, Gold logo edition	2.50	1.20	3.00	6.00
❏15, Jul 97	2.50	0.70	1.75	3.50
❏16, Aug 97	2.50	0.60	1.50	3.00
❏17, Sep 97	2.50	0.60	1.50	3.00
❏18, Nov 97, Family Ties, Part 1,continues in The Darkness #9	2.50	0.60	1.50	3.00
❏18/A, Family Ties, Part 1,variant cover	2.50	0.50	1.25	2.50
❏18/AE, Family Ties, Part 1,Green variant cover; American Entertainment Edition	—	1.00	2.50	5.00
❏19, Dec 97, Family Ties, Part 4	2.50	0.60	1.50	3.00

	ORIG	GOOD	FINE	N-MINT
❑20, Feb 98	2.50	0.60	1.50	3.00
❑21, Mar 98	2.50	0.50	1.25	2.50
❑22, May 98	2.50	0.50	1.25	2.50
❑23, Jun 98	2.50	0.50	1.25	2.50
❑24, Jul 98	2.50	0.50	1.25	2.50
❑25, Aug 98	2.95	0.50	1.25	2.50
❑26, Oct 98	2.50	0.50	1.25	2.50
❑27, Nov 98	2.50	0.50	1.25	2.50
❑28, Feb 99	2.50	0.50	1.25	2.50
❑29, Mar 99	2.50	0.50	1.25	2.50
❑30, Apr 99	2.50	0.50	1.25	2.50
❑31, May 99	2.50	0.50	1.25	2.50
❑32, Jul 99	2.50	0.50	1.25	2.50
❑33, Aug 99	2.50	0.50	1.25	2.50
❑34, Sep 99	2.50	0.50	1.25	2.50
❑35, Oct 99	2.50	0.50	1.25	2.50
❑36, Dec 99	2.50	0.50	1.25	2.50
❑37	2.50	0.50	1.25	2.50
❑38	2.50	0.50	1.25	2.50
❑39, May 00	2.50	0.50	1.25	2.50
❑40	2.50	0.50	1.25	2.50
❑41, Jul 00	2.50	0.50	1.25	2.50
❑41/A, Jul 00,e-Wanted alternate cover (Pezzini sitting)	2.50	0.60	1.50	3.00
❑42, Sep 00	2.50	0.50	1.25	2.50
❑43, Nov 00	2.50	0.50	1.25	2.50
❑44, Jan 01	2.50	0.50	1.25	2.50
❑45, Mar 01	2.50	0.50	1.25	2.50
❑46, May 01	2.50	0.50	1.25	2.50
❑47	2.50	0.50	1.25	2.50
❑48	2.50	0.50	1.25	2.50
❑49	2.50	0.50	1.25	2.50
❑50, Giant-size	4.95	0.99	2.47	4.95
❑50/A,DFE alternate cover	14.99	3.00	7.49	14.99
❑50/B	29.99	6.00	14.99	29.99
❑500, Limited edition foil cover; Given away as premium for subscription to Wizard	—	1.00	2.50	5.00
❑Dlx 1, Deluxe Collected Edition; Collects Witchblade #1-8	24.95	4.99	12.48	24.95
❑Dlx 2, Oct 00, Revelations Collected Edition; Collects Witchblade #9-17	24.95	4.99	12.48	24.95
❑Dlx 3, Oct 00,Prevailing; Collects Witchblade #20-25	14.95	2.99	7.47	14.95

WITCHBLADE/ALIENS/THE DARKNESS/PREDATOR
DARK HORSE

Value: Cover or less

❑1, Nov 00, Mindhunter 2.99

❑2, Dec 00, Mindhunter 2.99

❑3, Jan 01, Mindhunter 2.99

WITCHBLADE/DARKCHYLDE
IMAGE

Value: Cover or less

❑1, Sep 00 .... 2.50

WITCHBLADE/DARKNESS SPECIAL
IMAGE

	ORIG	GOOD	FINE	N-MINT
❑0.5/Pl, Sep 00, Platinum logo edition; Promotional giveaway when applying for Wizard credit card	—	7.00	17.50	35.00
❑1, Dec 99	3.95	0.79	1.98	3.95

WITCHBLADE: DESTINY'S CHILD
IMAGE

Value: Cover or less

❑1 .... 2.95

❑2, Jul 00 .... 2.95

❑3, Sep 00 .... 2.95

WITCHBLADE/ELEKTRA
MARVEL

	ORIG	GOOD	FINE	N-MINT
❑1, Mar 97, Devil's Reign, Part 6,crossover with Image; continues in Elektra/Cyblade #1	2.95	0.59	1.48	2.95
❑1/AE, American Entertainment Edition	—	1.00	2.50	5.00

WITCHBLADE GALLERY
IMAGE

Value: Cover or less

❑1, Nov 00 .... 2.95

WITCHBLADE INFINITY
IMAGE

Value: Cover or less

❑1, May 99 .... 3.50

WITCHBLADE ORIGIN
IMAGE

	ORIG	GOOD	FINE	N-MINT
❑1/AE, American Entertainment Edition	—	0.60	1.50	3.00

WITCHBLADE/TOMB RAIDER
IMAGE

	ORIG	GOOD	FINE	N-MINT
❑0.5, Jul 00	2.95	1.00	2.50	5.00
❑1/A, Dec 98	2.95	0.80	2.00	4.00
❑1/B, Dec 98,alternate cover (white background)	2.95	1.00	2.50	5.00
❑1/C, Dec 98,Croft standing on top of Pezzini with guns crossed on cover	2.95	1.00	2.50	5.00

WITCHCRAFT
DC

Value: Cover or less

❑1, Jun 94, JRo (w), Maiden,covers form triptych 2.95

❑2, Jul 94, JRo (w),Sex, violence-recommended for mature readers. 2.95

❑3, Aug 94, JRo (w) 2.95

WITCHCRAFT: LA TERREUR
DC

Value: Cover or less

❑1, Apr 98, JRo (w), Winter into April,covers form triptych 2.50

❑2, May 98, JRo (w),covers form triptych 2.50

❑3, Jun 98, JRo (w), Crone,covers form triptych 2.50

WITCHES' CAULDRON: THE BATTLE OF THE CHERKASSY POCKET
HERITAGE COLLECTION

Value: Cover or less

❑1, nn; b&w 3.50

WITCHFINDER, THE
IMAGE

Value: Cover or less

❑1, Sep 99,Man with torch on cover facing forward 2.95

❑1/A, Sep 99 .... 2.95

❑1/B, Sep 99,alternate cover 2.95

❑2, Nov 99 .... 2.95

WITCH HUNTER
MALIBU

Value: Cover or less

❑1, Apr 96, 1: Witch Hunter 2.50

WITCHING HOUR
DC

	ORIG	GOOD	FINE	N-MINT
❑1, Mar 69	0.12	6.00	15.00	30.00
❑2, May 69	0.12	3.00	7.50	15.00
❑3, Jul 69, BWr	0.12	2.40	6.00	12.00
❑4, Sep 69	0.12	1.60	4.00	8.00
❑5, Nov 69, BWr	0.15	2.40	6.00	12.00
❑6, Jan 70, A Face in the Crowd!; The Doll Man!	0.15	1.60	4.00	8.00
❑7, Mar 70	0.15	1.40	3.50	7.00
❑8, May 70	0.15	1.60	4.00	8.00
❑9, Jul 70	0.15	1.40	3.50	7.00
❑10, Sep 70	0.15	1.00	2.50	5.00
❑11, Nov 70	0.15	1.00	2.50	5.00
❑12, Jan 71	0.15	1.00	2.50	5.00
❑13, Mar 71, 1: Psions	0.15	1.00	2.50	5.00
❑14, May 71	0.15	1.00	2.50	5.00
❑15, Jul 71	0.15	0.80	2.00	4.00
❑16, Sep 71	0.25	0.80	2.00	4.00
❑17, Nov 71	0.25	0.80	2.00	4.00
❑18	—	0.80	2.00	4.00
❑19	—	0.80	2.00	4.00
❑20, Apr 72	—	0.80	2.00	4.00
❑21, Jun 72	—	0.60	1.50	3.00
❑22	—	0.60	1.50	3.00
❑23, Sep 72, TD; NR, Watch Over My Grave!; Death Pulls the Strings	0.20	0.60	1.50	3.00
❑24	—	0.60	1.50	3.00
❑25	—	0.60	1.50	3.00
❑26	—	0.60	1.50	3.00
❑27	—	0.60	1.50	3.00
❑28	—	0.60	1.50	3.00
❑29	—	0.60	1.50	3.00
❑30, Apr 73	0.20	0.60	1.50	3.00
❑31	0.20	0.50	1.25	2.50
❑32	0.20	0.50	1.25	2.50
❑33	0.20	0.50	1.25	2.50
❑34	0.20	0.50	1.25	2.50
❑35	0.20	0.50	1.25	2.50
❑36	0.20	0.50	1.25	2.50
❑37	0.20	0.50	1.25	2.50
❑38, Jan 74	0.50	0.50	1.25	2.50
❑39	0.20	0.50	1.25	2.50
❑40	0.20	0.50	1.25	2.50
❑41, Apr 74	0.20	0.50	1.25	2.50
❑42	—	0.50	1.25	2.50
❑43	—	0.50	1.25	2.50
❑44	—	0.50	1.25	2.50
❑45	—	0.50	1.25	2.50
❑46, The Killer Game Slithering; Burial Insurance	0.20	0.50	1.25	2.50
❑47	—	0.50	1.25	2.50
❑48	—	0.50	1.25	2.50
❑49	—	0.50	1.25	2.50
❑50	—	0.50	1.25	2.50
❑51	—	0.40	1.00	2.00
❑52	—	0.40	1.00	2.00
❑53	—	0.40	1.00	2.00
❑54	—	0.40	1.00	2.00
❑55	—	0.40	1.00	2.00
❑56	—	0.40	1.00	2.00
❑57	—	0.40	1.00	2.00
❑58	—	0.40	1.00	2.00
❑59	—	0.40	1.00	2.00
❑60	—	0.40	1.00	2.00
❑61	—	0.40	1.00	2.00
❑62	—	0.40	1.00	2.00

	ORIG	GOOD	FINE	N-MINT
❑63	—	0.40	1.00	2.00
❑64	—	0.40	1.00	2.00
❑65	—	0.40	1.00	2.00
❑66	—	0.40	1.00	2.00
❑67	—	0.40	1.00	2.00
❑68	—	0.40	1.00	2.00
❑69	—	0.40	1.00	2.00
❑70	—	0.40	1.00	2.00
❑71	—	0.40	1.00	2.00
❑72	—	0.40	1.00	2.00
❑73	—	0.40	1.00	2.00
❑74	—	0.40	1.00	2.00
❑75	—	0.40	1.00	2.00
❑76	0.35	0.40	1.00	2.00
❑77	—	0.40	1.00	2.00
❑78	—	0.40	1.00	2.00
❑79	—	0.40	1.00	2.00
❑80	—	0.40	1.00	2.00
❑81	—	0.40	1.00	2.00
❑82	—	0.40	1.00	2.00
❑83	—	0.40	1.00	2.00
❑84	—	0.40	1.00	2.00
❑85,Final Issue	—	0.40	1.00	2.00

WITCHING HOUR, THE (ANNE RICE'S...)
MILLENNIUM
Value: Cover or less

- ❑1, 92 ... 2.50
- ❑2, 93,bound-in Talamasca business card ... 2.50
- ❑3, 93 ... 2.50
- ❑4, 93 ... 2.50
- ❑5 ... 2.50
- ❑6 ... 2.50
- ❑7 ... 2.50
- ❑8 ... 2.50
- ❑9 ... 2.50
- ❑10 ... 2.50
- ❑11 ... 2.50
- ❑12 ... 2.50
- ❑13 ... 2.50

WITCHING HOUR, THE (VERTIGO)
VERTIGO

	ORIG	GOOD	FINE	N-MINT
❑1, JPH (w)	5.95	1.19	2.97	5.95
❑2, JPH (w)	5.95	1.19	2.97	5.95
❑3, JPH (w)	5.95	1.19	2.97	5.95

WITHIN OUR REACH
STAR*REACH
Value: Cover or less

- ❑1, Spider-Man: A Wolf at the Door; The Happy Prince, nn; Spider-Man, Concrete, Gift of the Magi; Christmas benefit comic ... 7.95

WIZARD OF 4TH STREET, THE (DARK HORSE)
DARK HORSE

	ORIG	GOOD	FINE	N-MINT
❑1, Caper, b&w	1.75	0.40	1.00	2.00
❑2, b&w	1.75	0.40	1.00	2.00
❑3	1.75	0.40	1.00	2.00
❑4	1.75	0.40	1.00	2.00
❑5	1.75	0.40	1.00	2.00
❑6	1.75	0.40	1.00	2.00

WIZARD OF 4TH STREET, THE (DAVID P. HOUSE)
DAVID P. HOUSE
Value: Cover or less

- ❑1 ... 1.50
- ❑2 ... 1.50
- ❑3 ... 1.50

WIZARD OF TIME, THE
DPH
Value: Cover or less

- ❑1 ... 1.50
- ❑2, Oct 86 ... 1.50

WIZARDS OF THE LAST RESORT
BLACKTHORNE
Value: Cover or less

- ❑1, Feb 87, The Odyssey of the Grey Beret ... 1.75
- ❑2 ... 1.75
- ❑3 ... 1.75
- ❑4 ... 1.75

WIZARD'S TALE, THE
IMAGE
Value: Cover or less

- ❑1 ... 19.95
- ❑1/HC,hardcover ... 29.95

WJHC
WILSON PLACE
Value: Cover or less

- ❑1, Dec 98 ... 1.95

WOGGLEBUG
ARROW
Value: Cover or less

- ❑1 ... 2.75

WOLF & RED
DARK HORSE
Value: Cover or less

- ❑1, Apr 95, Woo-ful Wolf; Lovestruck Lumberjacks,based on Tex Avery cartoons; Droopy back-up ... 2.50
- ❑2, May 95,based on Tex Avery cartoons; Screwball Squirrel back-up ... 2.50
- ❑3, Jun 95,based on Tex Avery cartoons; Droopy back-up ... 2.50

WOLFF & BYRD, COUNSELORS OF THE MACABRE
EXHIBIT A PRESS

	ORIG	GOOD	FINE	N-MINT
❑1, May 94	2.50	0.80	2.00	4.00
❑2, Jul 94	2.50	0.60	1.50	3.00

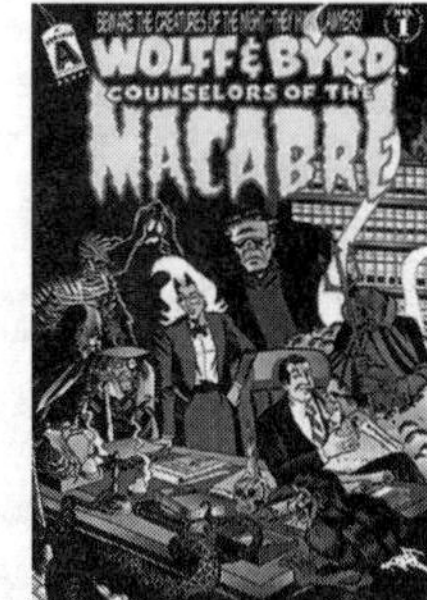

Batton Lash's *Wolff & Byrd* graduated from the newspaper page to the comics page in 1994.

	ORIG	GOOD	FINE	N-MINT
❑3, Sep 94	2.50	0.60	1.50	3.00
❑4, Nov 94	2.50	0.60	1.50	3.00
❑5, Feb 95	2.50	0.60	1.50	3.00
❑6, Apr 95	2.50	0.50	1.25	2.50
❑7, Jun 95	2.50	0.50	1.25	2.50
❑8, Sep 95	2.50	0.50	1.25	2.50
❑9, Nov 95	2.50	0.50	1.25	2.50
❑10, Feb 96	2.50	0.50	1.25	2.50
❑11, Apr 96	2.50	0.50	1.25	2.50
❑12, Aug 96	2.50	0.50	1.25	2.50
❑13, Oct 96,cover purposely upside down and backwards	2.50	0.50	1.25	2.50
❑14, Jan 97,Anne Rice parody	2.50	0.50	1.25	2.50
❑15, Mar 97	2.50	0.50	1.25	2.50
❑16, Jul 97	2.50	0.50	1.25	2.50
❑17, Oct 97,Halloween issue; reprint strips	2.50	0.50	1.25	2.50
❑18, Mar 98	2.50	0.50	1.25	2.50
❑19, Apr 98	2.50	0.50	1.25	2.50
❑20, May 98	2.50	0.50	1.25	2.50
❑21	2.50	0.50	1.25	2.50
❑22, Feb 99	2.50	0.50	1.25	2.50

WOLFF & BYRD, COUNSELORS OF THE MACABRE'S SECRETARY MAVIS
EXHIBIT A PRESS
Value: Cover or less

- ❑1, Aug 98 ... 2.95
- ❑2, Apr 99 ... 2.95

WOLFPACK
MARVEL

	ORIG	GOOD	FINE	N-MINT
❑1, Aug 88, Crusade, 1: Wolfpack	0.75	0.20	0.50	1.00
❑2, Sep 88	0.75	0.20	0.50	1.00
❑3, Oct 88	0.75	0.20	0.50	1.00
❑4, Nov 88	0.75	0.20	0.50	1.00
❑5, Dec 88	0.75	0.20	0.50	1.00
❑6, Jan 89	0.75	0.20	0.50	1.00
❑7, Feb 89	0.75	0.20	0.50	1.00
❑8, Mar 89	0.75	0.20	0.50	1.00
❑9, Apr 89	0.75	0.20	0.50	1.00
❑10, May 89	0.75	0.20	0.50	1.00
❑11, Jun 89	0.75	0.20	0.50	1.00
❑12, Jul 89	0.75	0.20	0.50	1.00

WOLF RUN-A KNOWN ASSOCIATES MYSTERY
KNOWN ASSOCIATES
Value: Cover or less

- ❑1, nn; b&w ... 2.50

WOLPH
BLACKTHORNE
Value: Cover or less

- ❑1 ... 2.00

WOLVERBROAD VS. HOBO
SPOOF
Value: Cover or less

- ❑1, b&w; parody ... 2.95

WOLVERINE
MARVEL

	ORIG	GOOD	FINE	N-MINT
❑-1, Jul 97, A Wiff of Sartre's Madeleine, A: Nick Fury; A: Carol Danvers; A: Sabretooth,Flashback; Flashback issue	1.99	0.40	1.00	2.00
❑0.5, Wizard mail-away edition	—	0.60	1.50	3.00
❑0.5/LE,Signed by Ben Raab; Blue foil	—	1.60	4.00	8.00
❑1, Nov 88	1.50	3.00	7.50	15.00
❑2, Dec 88	1.50	1.80	4.50	9.00
❑3, Jan 89	1.50	1.40	3.50	7.00
❑4, Feb 89	1.50	1.40	3.50	7.00
❑5, Mar 89, 1: Hardcase; 1: Battleaxe II; 1: Harriers; 1: Shotgun I	1.50	1.40	3.50	7.00
❑6, Apr 89	1.50	1.20	3.00	6.00
❑7, May 89, A: Hulk	1.50	1.20	3.00	6.00
❑8, Jun 89, A: Hulk	1.50	1.20	3.00	6.00
❑9, Jul 89	1.50	1.20	3.00	6.00
❑10, Aug 89, BSz, V: Sabretooth,vs. Sabretooth	1.50	2.00	5.00	10.00
❑11, Sep 89,New Costume	1.50	1.00	2.50	5.00
❑12, Sep 89	1.50	1.00	2.50	5.00
❑13, Oct 89	1.50	1.00	2.50	5.00
❑14, Oct 89	1.50	1.00	2.50	5.00

	ORIG	GOOD	FINE	N-MINT
❑15, Nov 89	1.50	1.00	2.50	5.00
❑16, Nov 89	1.50	1.00	2.50	5.00
❑17, Nov 89, JBy	1.50	1.00	2.50	5.00
❑18, Dec 89, JBy	1.50	1.00	2.50	5.00
❑19, Dec 89, JBy, Acts of Vengeance, Acts of Vengeance	1.50	1.00	2.50	5.00
❑20, Jan 90, JBy, Acts of Vengeance, Acts of Vengeance	1.50	0.80	2.00	4.00
❑21, Feb 90, KJ; JBy	1.50	0.80	2.00	4.00
❑22, Mar 90, JBy	1.50	0.80	2.00	4.00
❑23, Apr 90, JBy	1.50	0.80	2.00	4.00
❑24, May 90	1.50	0.60	1.50	3.00
❑25, Jun 90	1.50	0.60	1.50	3.00
❑26, Jul 90	1.75	0.60	1.50	3.00
❑27, Jul 90, Lazarus Project	1.75	0.60	1.50	3.00
❑28, Aug 90, Lazarus Project	1.75	0.60	1.50	3.00
❑29, Aug 90, Lazarus Project	1.75	0.60	1.50	3.00
❑30, Sep 90, Lazarus Project	1.75	0.60	1.50	3.00
❑31, Sep 90	1.75	0.50	1.25	2.50
❑32, Oct 90	1.75	0.50	1.25	2.50
❑33, Nov 90	1.75	0.50	1.25	2.50
❑34, Dec 90	1.75	0.50	1.25	2.50
❑35, Jan 91	1.75	0.50	1.25	2.50
❑36, Feb 91	1.75	0.50	1.25	2.50
❑37, Mar 91	1.75	0.50	1.25	2.50
❑38, Apr 91	1.75	0.50	1.25	2.50
❑39, May 91	1.75	0.50	1.25	2.50
❑40, Jun 91	1.75	0.50	1.25	2.50
❑41, Jul 91, A: Cable; V: Sabretooth	1.75	0.80	2.00	4.00
❑41-2, Jul 91, A: Sabretooth, 2nd Printing; Gold cover	1.75	0.35	0.88	1.75
❑42, Jul 91, A: Cable; A: Nick Fury; A: Sabretooth	1.75	0.40	1.00	2.00
❑42-2, Jul 91, A: Cable; A: Nick Fury; A: Sabretooth, 2nd Printing; Gold cover	1.75	0.35	0.88	1.75
❑43, Aug 91, A: Sabretooth	1.75	0.60	1.50	3.00
❑44, Aug 91	1.75	0.40	1.00	2.00
❑45, Sep 91, A: Sabretooth	1.75	0.50	1.25	2.50
❑46, Sep 91, A: Sabretooth	1.75	0.50	1.25	2.50
❑47, Oct 91	1.75	0.50	1.25	2.50
❑48, Nov 91, Weapon X sequel, Logan's past	1.75	0.50	1.25	2.50
❑49, Dec 91, Weapon X sequel, Logan's past	1.75	0.50	1.25	2.50
❑50, Jan 92, Weapon X sequel, 1: Shiva, diecut cover	2.50	0.80	2.00	4.00
❑51, Feb 92	1.75	0.40	1.00	2.00
❑52, Mar 92	1.75	0.40	1.00	2.00
❑53, Apr 92	1.75	0.40	1.00	2.00
❑54, May 92	1.75	0.40	1.00	2.00
❑55, Jun 92	1.75	0.40	1.00	2.00
❑56, Jul 92	1.75	0.40	1.00	2.00
❑57, Jul 92, D: Mariko Yashida	1.75	0.60	1.50	3.00
❑58, Aug 92, A: Terror	1.75	0.40	1.00	2.00
❑59, Aug 92, A: Terror	1.75	0.40	1.00	2.00
❑60, Sep 92, A: Sabretooth	1.75	0.40	1.00	2.00
❑61, Sep 92, A: Sabretooth	1.75	0.40	1.00	2.00
❑62, Oct 92, A: Sabretooth	1.75	0.40	1.00	2.00
❑63, Nov 92, A: Sabretooth	1.75	0.40	1.00	2.00
❑64, Dec 92, D: Silver Fox; A: Sabretooth	1.75	0.40	1.00	2.00
❑65, Jan 93	1.75	0.40	1.00	2.00
❑66, Feb 93	1.75	0.40	1.00	2.00
❑67, Mar 93	1.75	0.40	1.00	2.00
❑68, Apr 93	1.75	0.40	1.00	2.00
❑69, May 93	1.75	0.40	1.00	2.00
❑70, Jun 93	1.75	0.40	1.00	2.00
❑71, Jul 93	1.75	0.40	1.00	2.00
❑72, Aug 93	1.75	0.40	1.00	2.00
❑73, Sep 93	1.75	0.40	1.00	2.00
❑74, Oct 93, A: Sentinel; A: Jubilee	1.75	0.40	1.00	2.00
❑75, Nov 93, hologram; Wolverine loses adamantium skeleton	3.95	1.00	2.50	5.00
❑76, Dec 93	1.75	0.40	1.00	2.00
❑77, Jan 94, The Lady Strikes	1.75	0.40	1.00	2.00
❑78, Feb 94, D: Bloodscream; D: Cylla	1.75	0.40	1.00	2.00
❑79, Mar 94	1.75	0.40	1.00	2.00
❑80, Apr 94	1.75	0.40	1.00	2.00
❑81, May 94	1.95	0.40	1.00	2.00
❑82, Jun 94	1.95	0.40	1.00	2.00
❑83, Jul 94	1.95	0.40	1.00	2.00
❑84, Aug 94	1.95	0.40	1.00	2.00
❑85, Sep 94, Final Sanction; Final Sanction, Part 1	2.50	0.50	1.25	2.50
❑85/SC, Sep 94, Final Sanction, Part 1, enhanced cover	3.50	0.70	1.75	3.50
❑86, Oct 94	1.95	0.40	1.00	2.00
❑87, Nov 94	1.50	0.30	0.75	1.50
❑87/Dlx, Nov 94, Deluxe edition	1.95	0.40	1.00	2.00
❑88, Dec 94	1.50	0.30	0.75	1.50
❑88/Dlx, Dec 94, Deluxe edition	1.95	0.40	1.00	2.00
❑89, Jan 95	1.50	0.30	0.75	1.50
❑89/Dlx, Jan 95, Deluxe edition	1.95	0.40	1.00	2.00
❑90, Feb 95	1.50	0.30	0.75	1.50
❑90/Dlx, Feb 95, Deluxe edition	1.95	0.40	1.00	2.00
❑91, Jul 95	1.95	0.40	1.00	2.00
❑92, Aug 95	1.95	0.40	1.00	2.00
❑93, Sep 95, V: Juggernaut	1.95	0.40	1.00	2.00
❑94, Oct 95, A: Generation X	1.95	0.40	1.00	2.00
❑95, Nov 95, A: Vindicator	1.95	0.40	1.00	2.00
❑96, Dec 95, D: Cyber	1.95	0.40	1.00	2.00
❑97, Jan 96	1.95	0.40	1.00	2.00
❑98, Feb 96, Fade to Black	1.95	0.40	1.00	2.00
❑99, Mar 96	1.95	0.80	2.00	4.00
❑100, Apr 96	2.95	0.80	2.00	4.00
❑100/SC, Apr 96, enhanced cardstock cover with hologram	3.95	1.50	3.75	7.50
❑101, May 96	1.95	0.40	1.00	2.00
❑102, Jun 96	1.95	0.40	1.00	2.00
❑103, Jul 96	1.95	0.40	1.00	2.00
❑104, Aug 96	1.95	0.40	1.00	2.00
❑105, Sep 96, Onslaught: Impact 2, A: Stick	1.95	0.40	1.00	2.00
❑106, Oct 96, A: Elektra	1.95	0.40	1.00	2.00
❑107, Nov 96	1.95	0.40	1.00	2.00
❑108, Dec 96	1.95	0.40	1.00	2.00
❑109, Jan 97	1.95	0.40	1.00	2.00
❑110, Feb 97, Lesser Beasts, A: Shaman	1.95	0.40	1.00	2.00
❑111, Mar 97, Restoration	1.95	0.40	1.00	2.00
❑112, Apr 97	1.95	0.40	1.00	2.00
❑113, May 97, The Wind From The East	1.95	0.40	1.00	2.00
❑114, Jun 97, V: Deathstrike	1.95	0.40	1.00	2.00
❑115, Aug 97, Operation Zero Tolerance, gatefold summary	1.99	0.40	1.00	2.00
❑116, Sep 97, Operation Zero Tolerance, gatefold summary	1.99	0.40	1.00	2.00
❑117, Oct 97, Operation Zero Tolerance, A: Jubilee, gatefold summary	1.99	0.40	1.00	2.00
❑118, Nov 97, Operation Zero Tolerance Epilogue, A: Jubilee, gatefold summary	1.99	0.40	1.00	2.00
❑119, Dec 97, Not Dead Yet, Part 1, gatefold summary	1.99	0.40	1.00	2.00
❑120, Jan 98, Not Dead Yet, Part 2, gatefold summary	1.99	0.40	1.00	2.00
❑121, Feb 98, Not Dead Yet, Part 3	1.99	0.40	1.00	2.00
❑122, Mar 98, gatefold summary	1.99	0.40	1.00	2.00
❑123, Apr 98, gatefold summary	1.99	0.40	1.00	2.00
❑124, May 98, A: Captain America, gatefold summary	1.99	0.40	1.00	2.00
❑125, Jun 98, A: Lady Hydra, wraparound cover; gatefold summary	2.99	0.70	1.75	3.50
❑125/A, DFE alternate cover	10.00	1.20	3.00	6.00
❑125/B, DFE alternate cover; Signed by Jae Lee	19.95	2.00	5.00	10.00
❑126, Jul 98, V: Sabretooth; V: Lady Hydra, gatefold summary	1.99	0.40	1.00	1.99
❑127, Aug 98, V: Sabretooth, gatefold summary	1.99	0.40	1.00	1.99
❑128, Sep 98, A: Viper; V: Sabretooth; A: Shadow Cat, gatefold summary	1.99	0.40	1.00	1.99
❑129, Oct 98, gatefold summary	1.99	0.40	1.00	1.99
❑130, Nov 98, gatefold summary	1.99	0.40	1.00	1.99
❑131, Nov 98, gatefold summary; error on Page 6	1.99	0.40	1.00	1.99
❑131/A, Nov 98, gatefold summary; Corrected edition	1.99	0.40	1.00	1.99
❑132, Dec 98, gatefold summary	1.99	0.40	1.00	1.99
❑133, Jan 99, The Great Escape, A: Warbird, gatefold summary	1.99	0.40	1.00	1.99
❑134, Feb 99, EL (w), V: Everybody, gatefold summary	1.99	0.40	1.00	1.99
❑135, Feb 99, EL (w), A: Aria; A: Starjammers	1.99	0.40	1.00	1.99
❑136, Mar 99, EL (w), V: Collector	1.99	0.40	1.00	1.99
❑137, Apr 99, EL (w), A: Collector; A: Starjammers	1.99	0.40	1.00	1.99
❑138, May 99	1.99	0.40	1.00	1.99
❑139, Jun 99, A: Cable	1.99	0.40	1.00	1.99
❑140, Jul 99, EL (w), Vengeance, A: Nightcrawler; V: Cardiac; V: Solo	1.99	0.40	1.00	1.99
❑141, Aug 99	1.99	0.40	1.00	1.99
❑142, Sep 99	1.99	0.40	1.00	1.99
❑144, Nov 99	1.99	0.40	1.00	1.99
❑145, Dec 99	1.99	0.40	1.00	1.99
❑146, Jan 00	—	0.45	1.13	2.25
❑147, Feb 00	—	0.45	1.13	2.25
❑148, Mar 00	—	0.45	1.13	2.25
❑149, Apr 00	—	0.45	1.13	2.25
❑150, May 00, Blood Debt, Giant-size	2.99	0.60	1.50	2.99
❑151, Jun 00	—	0.45	1.13	2.25

	ORIG	GOOD	FINE	N-MINT
❑152, Jul 00	—	0.45	1.13	2.25
❑153, Aug 00	—	0.45	1.13	2.25
❑154, Sep 00	—	0.45	1.13	2.25
❑155, Oct 00, RL, RL (c), RL (w), All Along the Watchtower, Part 2, A: Deadpool	2.25	0.45	1.13	2.25
❑156, Nov 00, RL (w), Going Underground, A: Spider-Man	2.25	0.45	1.13	2.25
❑157, Dec 00, RL, RL (c), RL (w)	2.25	0.45	1.13	2.25
❑158, Jan 01, Manhunt,polybagged with Marvel Online CD-ROM	2.25	0.45	1.13	2.25
❑159, Feb 01, The Best There Is, Part 1	2.25	0.45	1.13	2.25
❑160, Mar 01, The Best There Is, Part 2	2.25	0.45	1.13	2.25
❑161, Apr 01, The Best There Is, Part 3	2.25	0.45	1.13	2.25
❑162, May 01, The Hunted	2.25	0.45	1.13	2.25
❑163, Jun 01	2.25	0.45	1.13	2.25
❑164	2.25	0.45	1.13	2.25
❑165	2.25	0.45	1.13	2.25
❑166	2.25	0.45	1.13	2.25
❑166/A	39.99	8.00	20.00	39.99
❑Anl 1995, Sep 95	3.95	0.79	1.98	3.95
❑Anl 1996, Oct 96, V: Red Ronin, nn; wraparound cover	2.95	0.59	1.48	2.95
❑Anl 1997,wraparound cover; gatefold summary	2.99	0.60	1.50	2.99
❑Anl 1999	3.50	0.70	1.75	3.50
❑SE 1, Blue Print edition	2.99	0.60	1.50	2.99

WOLVERINE (LTD. SERIES)
MARVEL

	ORIG	GOOD	FINE	N-MINT
❑1, Sep 82, FM, A: Mariko	0.60	4.00	10.00	20.00
❑2, Oct 82, FM, 1: Yukio	0.60	2.40	6.00	12.00
❑3, Nov 82, FM	0.60	2.40	6.00	12.00
❑4, Dec 82, FM	0.60	2.40	6.00	12.00

WOLVERINE AND THE PUNISHER: DAMAGING EVIDENCE
MARVEL

Value: Cover or less
- ❑1, Oct 93, A: Sniper; A: Damage ... 2.00
- ❑2, Nov 93 ... 2.00
- ❑3, Dec 93 ... 2.00

WOLVERINE BATTLES THE INCREDIBLE HULK
MARVEL

Value: Cover or less
- ❑1, nn; reprints Incredible Hulk #180 and #181 ... 4.95

WOLVERINE: BLACK RIO
MARVEL

Value: Cover or less
- ❑1 ... 5.99

WOLVERINE: BLOOD HUNGRY!
MARVEL

Value: Cover or less
- ❑1, nn; reprint stories ... 6.95

WOLVERINE: BLOODLUST
MARVEL

Value: Cover or less
- ❑1, Dec 90, nn ... 4.95

WOLVERINE: BLOODY CHOICES
MARVEL

Value: Cover or less
- ❑1 ... 7.95

WOLVERINE: DAYS OF FUTURE PAST
MARVEL

Value: Cover or less
- ❑1, Dec 97, gatefold summary; Wolverine in early 21st century ... 2.50
- ❑2, Jan 98, gatefold summary; Wolverine in early 21st century ... 2.50
- ❑3, Feb 98, gatefold summary; Wolverine in early 21st century ... 2.50

WOLVERINE: DOOMBRINGER
MARVEL

Value: Cover or less
- ❑1 ... 5.99
- ❑1/SC,foil cover ... 14.95

WOLVERINE: EVILUTION
MARVEL

Value: Cover or less
- ❑1, Direct Edition ... 5.95

WOLVERINE/GAMBIT: VICTIMS
MARVEL

Value: Cover or less
- ❑1, Sep 95, JPH (w),enhanced cardstock cover ... 2.95
- ❑2, Oct 95, JPH (w),enhanced cardstock cover ... 2.95
- ❑3, Nov 95, JPH (w),enhanced cardstock cover ... 2.95
- ❑4, Dec 95, JPH (w), A: Arcade; A: Mastermind,enhanced cardstock cover ... 2.95

WOLVERINE: GLOBAL JEOPARDY
MARVEL

Value: Cover or less
- ❑1, Dec 93, RHo, PD (w), The Heart of Animals,Embossed cover ... 2.95

WOLVERINE: INNER FURY
MARVEL

Value: Cover or less
- ❑1, Nov 92, BSz, nn ... 5.95

WOLVERINE: KILLING
MARVEL

Value: Cover or less
- ❑1, Sep 93, nn ... 5.95

Wolverine was the defender of a mutant princess, whose powers were thought to be magical, during the Middle Ages in the imaginary story *Wolverine: Rahne of Terra.*

© 1991 Marvel Comics

WOLVERINE: KNIGHT OF TERRA
MARVEL

Value: Cover or less
- ❑1, Aug 95, JDu ... 6.95

WOLVERINE POSTER MAGAZINE
MARVEL

Value: Cover or less
- ❑1,pin-ups ... 4.95

WOLVERINE/PUNISHER REVELATION
MARVEL

Value: Cover or less
- ❑1, Jun 99, Ladies in Waiting ... 2.99
- ❑2, Jul 99, Ascension ... 2.99
- ❑3, Aug 99 ... 2.99
- ❑4, Sep 99 ... 2.99
- ❑36893, Apr 01, Ladies in Waiting,2nd Printing ... 2.99
- ❑36924, May 01, Ascension,2nd Printing ... 2.99

WOLVERINE: RAHNE OF TERRA
MARVEL

Value: Cover or less
- ❑1, Aug 91, PD (w), nn; prestige format ... 5.95

WOLVERINE SAGA, THE
MARVEL

	ORIG	GOOD	FINE	N-MINT
❑1, Sep 89, O: Wolverine	3.95	0.80	2.00	4.00
❑2, Nov 89	3.95	0.80	2.00	4.00
❑3, Dec 89	3.95	0.80	2.00	4.00
❑4, Dec 89	3.95	0.80	2.00	4.00

WOLVERINE: SAVE THE TIGER!
MARVEL

Value: Cover or less
- ❑1, May 92, nn ... 2.95

WOLVERINE: THE JUNGLE ADVENTURE
MARVEL

Value: Cover or less
- ❑1, nn ... 4.50

WOLVERINE VS. NIGHT MAN
MARVEL

	ORIG	GOOD	FINE	N-MINT
❑0, limited edition	—	3.00	7.50	15.00

WOLVERINE VS. SPIDER-MAN
MARVEL

	ORIG	GOOD	FINE	N-MINT
❑1, Mar 95, Wolverine/Spider-Man: Life's End, nn; cardstock cover; One-Shot; collects story arc from Marvel Comics Presents #48-50	2.50	0.60	1.50	3.00

WOLVERINE/WITCHBLADE
IMAGE

	ORIG	GOOD	FINE	N-MINT
❑1, Mar 97, Devil's Reign, Part 5; Devil's Reign	2.95	0.90	2.25	4.50
❑1/A, Mar 97, Devil's Reign, Part 5,crossover with Marvel; continues in Witchblade/Elektra	2.95	0.59	1.48	2.95

WOMEN IN FUR
SHANDA FANTASY ARTS

Value: Cover or less
- ❑2, b&w; Anthology ... 4.50

WOMEN IN ROCK SPECIAL
REVOLUTIONARY

Value: Cover or less
- ❑1, Dec 93, b&w ... 2.50

WOMEN ON TOP
FANTAGRAPHICS

Value: Cover or less
- ❑1, b&w; adult ... 2.25

WONDERLAND
ARROW

Value: Cover or less
- ❑1 ... 2.95
- ❑2 ... 2.95
- ❑3 ... 2.95

WONDERLANDERS, THE
OKTOMICA

Value: Cover or less
- ❑1, Jan 99 ... 2.50

WONDER MAN
MARVEL

	ORIG	GOOD	FINE	N-MINT
❑1, Sep 91, poster; poster	1.00	0.30	0.75	1.50
❑2, Oct 91	1.00	0.25	0.63	1.25
❑3, Nov 91, 1: Splice	1.00	0.25	0.63	1.25
❑4, Dec 91	1.00	0.25	0.63	1.25
❑5, Jan 92, 1: Splice	1.00	0.25	0.63	1.25
❑6, Feb 92	1.25	0.25	0.63	1.25
❑7, Mar 92, Operation: Galactic Storm, Part 4,Operation Galactic Storm	1.25	0.25	0.63	1.25

	ORIG	GOOD	FINE	N-MINT
❑8, Apr 92, Operation: Galactic Storm, Part 11,Operation Galactic Storm	1.25	0.25	0.63	1.25
❑9, May 92, Operation: Galactic Storm, Part 18,Operation Galactic Storm	1.25	0.25	0.63	1.25
❑10, Jun 92	1.25	0.25	0.63	1.25
❑11, Jul 92	1.25	0.25	0.63	1.25
❑12, Aug 92	1.25	0.25	0.63	1.25
❑13, Sep 92, Infinity War	1.25	0.25	0.63	1.25
❑14, Oct 92	1.25	0.25	0.63	1.25
❑15, Nov 92	1.25	0.25	0.63	1.25
❑16, Dec 92	1.25	0.25	0.63	1.25
❑17, Jan 93	1.25	0.25	0.63	1.25
❑18, Feb 93	1.25	0.25	0.63	1.25
❑19, Mar 93	1.25	0.25	0.63	1.25
❑20, Apr 93	1.25	0.25	0.63	1.25
❑21, May 93	1.25	0.25	0.63	1.25
❑22, Jun 93	1.25	0.25	0.63	1.25
❑23, Jul 93	1.25	0.25	0.63	1.25
❑24, Aug 93	1.25	0.25	0.63	1.25
❑25, Sep 93,Embossed cover	2.95	0.59	1.48	2.95
❑26, Oct 93	1.25	0.25	0.63	1.25
❑27, Nov 93	1.25	0.25	0.63	1.25
❑28, Dec 93	1.25	0.25	0.63	1.25
❑29, Jan 94	1.25	0.25	0.63	1.25
❑Anl 1, KB (w), System Bytes	2.25	0.45	1.13	2.25
❑Anl 2,trading card	2.95	0.59	1.48	2.95

WONDER MAN (ONE-SHOT)
MARVEL

	ORIG	GOOD	FINE	N-MINT
❑1, Mar 86	1.25	0.30	0.75	1.50

WONDERS AND ODDITIES (RICK GEARY'S...)
DARK HORSE

Value: Cover or less

❑1, Dec 88, On the True Composition of Music; Suburban Romance, nn; b&w 2.00

WONDER WART-HOG, HOG OF STEEL
RIP OFF PRESS

	ORIG	GOOD	FINE	N-MINT
❑1, b&w; Reprint	2.50	0.60	1.50	3.00
❑2, Return From the Planet of the Pigs, b&w; Reprint	2.50	0.50	1.25	2.50
❑3, b&w; Reprint	2.50	0.50	1.25	2.50

WONDER WOMAN (1ST SERIES)
DC

	ORIG	GOOD	FINE	N-MINT
❑120, Feb 61	0.10	10.40	26.00	52.00
❑121	0.10	7.00	17.50	35.00
❑122, 1: Wonder Tot	0.10	7.00	17.50	35.00
❑123	0.10	7.00	17.50	35.00
❑124, 1: Wonder Family	0.10	7.00	17.50	35.00
❑125	0.10	7.00	17.50	35.00
❑126	0.10	7.00	17.50	35.00
❑127	0.12	6.00	15.00	30.00
❑128, Feb 62, O: Wonder Woman's Invisible Jet	0.12	6.00	15.00	30.00
❑129	0.12	6.00	15.00	30.00
❑130	0.12	6.00	15.00	30.00
❑131	0.12	4.00	10.00	20.00
❑132	0.12	4.00	10.00	20.00
❑133	0.12	4.00	10.00	20.00
❑134	0.12	4.00	10.00	20.00
❑135	0.12	4.00	10.00	20.00
❑136, Feb 63	0.12	4.00	10.00	20.00
❑137	0.12	4.00	10.00	20.00
❑138	0.12	4.00	10.00	20.00
❑139	0.12	4.00	10.00	20.00
❑140	0.12	4.00	10.00	20.00
❑141	0.12	4.00	10.00	20.00
❑142	0.12	4.00	10.00	20.00
❑143	0.12	4.00	10.00	20.00
❑144, Feb 64	0.12	4.00	10.00	20.00
❑145	0.12	4.00	10.00	20.00
❑146	0.12	4.00	10.00	20.00
❑147	0.12	4.00	10.00	20.00
❑148	0.12	4.00	10.00	20.00
❑149, Oct 64, The Last Day of the Amazons	0.12	4.00	10.00	20.00
❑150	0.12	4.00	10.00	20.00
❑151	0.12	3.60	9.00	18.00
❑152	0.12	3.60	9.00	18.00
❑153, Apr 65	0.12	3.60	9.00	18.00
❑154	0.12	3.60	9.00	18.00
❑155	0.12	3.60	9.00	18.00
❑156	0.12	3.60	9.00	18.00
❑157	0.12	3.60	9.00	18.00
❑158	0.12	3.60	9.00	18.00
❑159, O: Wonder Woman	0.12	3.60	9.00	18.00
❑160	0.12	3.20	8.00	16.00
❑161, Apr 66	0.12	3.20	8.00	16.00
❑162	—	3.20	8.00	16.00
❑163, Jul 66	—	3.20	8.00	16.00
❑164	—	3.20	8.00	16.00
❑165	—	3.20	8.00	16.00
❑166	—	3.20	8.00	16.00
❑167	—	3.20	8.00	16.00
❑168, Feb 67	—	3.20	8.00	16.00
❑169, Apr 67	—	3.20	8.00	16.00
❑170, Jun 67	—	3.20	8.00	16.00
❑171, Aug 67	—	2.80	7.00	14.00
❑172, Oct 67	—	2.80	7.00	14.00
❑173, Dec 67	—	2.80	7.00	14.00
❑174, Feb 68	—	2.80	7.00	14.00
❑175, Apr 68	—	2.80	7.00	14.00
❑176, Jun 68	—	2.80	7.00	14.00
❑177, Aug 68	—	2.80	7.00	14.00
❑178, Oct 68, Wonder Woman's Rival	—	2.80	7.00	14.00
❑179, Dec 68, 1: Doctor Cyber	—	2.80	7.00	14.00
❑180, Feb 69, D: Steve Trevor (Wonder Woman's boyfriend)	—	3.00	7.50	15.00
❑181, Apr 69	—	2.00	5.00	10.00
❑182, Jun 69	—	2.00	5.00	10.00
❑183, Aug 69	—	2.00	5.00	10.00
❑184, Oct 69	0.15	2.00	5.00	10.00
❑185, Dec 69	—	2.00	5.00	10.00
❑186, Feb 69	—	2.00	5.00	10.00
❑187, Apr 69	—	2.00	5.00	10.00
❑188, Jun 69	—	2.00	5.00	10.00
❑189, Aug 69	—	2.00	5.00	10.00
❑190, Oct 69	—	2.00	5.00	10.00
❑191, Dec 69	0.15	2.00	5.00	10.00
❑192, Feb 71	—	2.00	5.00	10.00
❑193, Apr 71	—	2.00	5.00	10.00
❑194, Jun 71	—	2.00	5.00	10.00
❑195, Aug 71	—	2.00	5.00	10.00
❑196, Oct 71, DG	—	2.00	5.00	10.00
❑197, Dec 71, DG	—	2.00	5.00	10.00
❑198, Feb 72, DG ,52pgs.	0.25	2.00	5.00	10.00
❑199, Apr 72, DG	0.25	2.00	5.00	10.00
❑200, Jun 72, DG	0.25	2.00	5.00	10.00
❑201, Aug 72, DG	0.20	0.80	2.00	4.00
❑202, Oct 72, DG ,Fafhrd and The Gray Mouser apperance	0.20	0.80	2.00	4.00
❑203, Dec 72, DG	0.20	0.80	2.00	4.00
❑204, Feb 73	—	0.80	2.00	4.00
❑205, Apr 73, DH; BO, Target Wonder Woman!; The Mystery of Nubia!,Suggestive cover	—	0.80	2.00	4.00
❑206, Jun 73	—	0.80	2.00	4.00
❑207, Aug 73	—	0.80	2.00	4.00
❑208, Oct 73, RE, The Titanic Trials; Chessmen of Death!	—	0.80	2.00	4.00
❑209, Dec 73	0.20	0.80	2.00	4.00
❑210, Feb 74	0.20	0.80	2.00	4.00
❑211, Apr 74	—	0.60	1.50	3.00
❑212, Jun 74	0.20	0.60	1.50	3.00
❑213, Aug 74	0.20	0.60	1.50	3.00
❑214, Oct 74	0.60	0.60	1.50	3.00
❑215, Dec 74	0.20	0.60	1.50	3.00
❑216, Feb 75	0.25	0.60	1.50	3.00
❑217, Apr 75	0.50	0.60	1.50	3.00
❑218, Jun 75	0.25	0.60	1.50	3.00
❑219, Aug 75	0.25	0.60	1.50	3.00
❑220, Oct 75	0.25	0.60	1.50	3.00
❑221, Dec 75	0.25	0.60	1.50	3.00
❑222, Feb 76	0.25	0.60	1.50	3.00
❑223, Apr 76,Return of Steve Trevor	0.30	0.60	1.50	3.00
❑224, Jun 76	0.30	0.60	1.50	3.00
❑225, Aug 76	0.30	0.60	1.50	3.00
❑226, Oct 76	0.30	0.60	1.50	3.00
❑227, Dec 76	0.30	0.60	1.50	3.00
❑228, Feb 77	0.30	0.60	1.50	3.00
❑229, Mar 77	0.30	0.60	1.50	3.00
❑230, Apr 77	0.30	0.60	1.50	3.00
❑231, May 77	0.30	0.60	1.50	3.00
❑232, Jun 77	0.35	0.60	1.50	3.00
❑233, Jul 77	0.35	0.60	1.50	3.00
❑234, Aug 77	0.35	0.60	1.50	3.00
❑235, Sep 77	0.35	0.60	1.50	3.00
❑236, Oct 77	0.35	0.60	1.50	3.00
❑237, Nov 77, 1: Kung; O: Wonder Woman	0.35	0.60	1.50	3.00
❑238, Dec 77	0.35	0.60	1.50	3.00
❑239, Jan 78	0.35	0.60	1.50	3.00
❑240, Feb 78	0.35	0.60	1.50	3.00
❑241, Mar 78	0.35	0.60	1.50	3.00
❑242, Apr 78	0.35	0.60	1.50	3.00

	ORIG	GOOD	FINE	N-MINT
❑243, May 78	0.35	0.60	1.50	3.00
❑244, Jun 78	0.35	0.60	1.50	3.00
❑245, Jul 78	0.35	0.60	1.50	3.00
❑246, Aug 78	0.35	0.60	1.50	3.00
❑247, Sep 78	0.50	0.60	1.50	3.00
❑248, Oct 78, D: Steve Trevor	0.50	0.60	1.50	3.00
❑249, Nov 78, A: Hawkgirl	0.50	0.60	1.50	3.00
❑250, Dec 78, 1: Orana (new Wonder Woman)	0.40	0.60	1.50	3.00
❑251, Jan 79	0.40	0.60	1.50	3.00
❑252, Feb 79, 1: Stacy Macklin	0.40	0.60	1.50	3.00
❑253, Mar 79	0.40	0.60	1.50	3.00
❑254, Apr 79	0.40	0.60	1.50	3.00
❑255, May 79	0.40	0.60	1.50	3.00
❑256, Jun 79	0.40	0.60	1.50	3.00
❑257, Jul 79	0.40	0.60	1.50	3.00
❑258, Aug 79	0.40	0.60	1.50	3.00
❑259, Sep 79	0.40	0.60	1.50	3.00
❑260, Oct 79	0.40	0.60	1.50	3.00
❑261, Nov 79	0.40	0.60	1.50	3.00
❑262, Dec 79	0.40	0.60	1.50	3.00
❑263, Jan 80	0.40	0.60	1.50	3.00
❑264, Feb 80	0.40	0.60	1.50	3.00
❑265, Mar 80	0.40	0.60	1.50	3.00
❑266, Apr 80	0.40	0.60	1.50	3.00
❑267, May 80, A: Animal Man	0.40	0.60	1.50	3.00
❑268, Jun 80, A: Animal Man	0.40	0.60	1.50	3.00
❑269, Jul 80	0.40	0.50	1.25	2.50
❑270, Aug 80	0.40	0.50	1.25	2.50
❑271, Sep 80, JSa, A: Huntress	0.50	0.50	1.25	2.50
❑272, Oct 80, JSa, A: Huntress	0.50	0.50	1.25	2.50
❑273, Nov 80	0.50	0.50	1.25	2.50
❑274, Dec 80, 1: Cheetah II (Deborah Domaine)	0.50	0.50	1.25	2.50
❑275, Jan 81	0.50	0.50	1.25	2.50
❑276, Feb 81	0.50	0.50	1.25	2.50
❑277, Mar 81	0.50	0.50	1.25	2.50
❑278, Apr 81	0.50	0.50	1.25	2.50
❑279, May 81	0.50	0.50	1.25	2.50
❑280, Jun 81	0.50	0.50	1.25	2.50
❑281, Jul 81, A: Joker	0.50	0.80	2.00	4.00
❑282, Aug 81, A: Joker	0.50	0.80	2.00	4.00
❑283, Sep 81, A: Joker	0.50	0.80	2.00	4.00
❑284, Oct 81	0.60	0.40	1.00	2.00
❑285, Nov 81	0.60	0.40	1.00	2.00
❑286, Dec 81	0.60	0.40	1.00	2.00
❑287, Jan 82, RT; DH, A: New Teen Titans	0.60	0.40	1.00	2.00
❑288, Feb 82, 1: The Silver Swan	0.60	0.40	1.00	2.00
❑289, Mar 82	0.60	0.40	1.00	2.00
❑290, Apr 82	0.60	0.40	1.00	2.00
❑291, May 82	0.60	0.40	1.00	2.00
❑292, Jun 82	0.60	0.40	1.00	2.00
❑293, Jul 82, GC; FMc, A: Starfire; A: Raven	0.60	0.40	1.00	2.00
❑294, Aug 82	0.60	0.40	1.00	2.00
❑295, Sep 82	0.60	0.40	1.00	2.00
❑296, Oct 82	0.60	0.40	1.00	2.00
❑297, Nov 82, 1: Aegeus	0.60	0.40	1.00	2.00
❑298, Dec 82	0.60	0.40	1.00	2.00
❑299, Jan 83	0.60	0.40	1.00	2.00
❑300, Feb 83, 1: Fury; A: New Teen Titans, 300th anniversary issue; Giant-size	1.50	0.60	1.50	3.00
❑301, Mar 83	0.60	0.40	1.00	2.00
❑302, Apr 83	0.60	0.40	1.00	2.00
❑303, May 83	0.60	0.40	1.00	2.00
❑304, Jun 83	0.60	0.40	1.00	2.00
❑305, Jul 83, 1: Circe (DC)	0.60	0.40	1.00	2.00
❑306, Aug 83	0.60	0.40	1.00	2.00
❑307, Sep 83	0.60	0.40	1.00	2.00
❑308, Oct 83	0.60	0.40	1.00	2.00
❑309, Nov 83, 1: Earthworm	0.60	0.40	1.00	2.00
❑310, Dec 83	0.75	0.40	1.00	2.00
❑311, Jan 84, DH	0.75	0.40	1.00	2.00
❑312, Feb 84, DH	0.75	0.40	1.00	2.00
❑313, Mar 84, DH	0.75	0.40	1.00	2.00
❑314, Apr 84, DH	0.75	0.40	1.00	2.00
❑315, May 84, DH	0.75	0.40	1.00	2.00
❑316, Jun 84, DH	0.75	0.40	1.00	2.00
❑317, Jul 84, DH	0.75	0.40	1.00	2.00
❑318, Aug 84, IN, KB (w)	0.75	0.40	1.00	2.00
❑319, Sep 84, DH	0.75	0.40	1.00	2.00
❑320, Oct 84, DH	0.75	0.40	1.00	2.00
❑321, Nov 84, DH	0.75	0.40	1.00	2.00
❑322, Dec 84, DH	0.75	0.40	1.00	2.00
❑323, Feb 85, DH	0.75	0.40	1.00	2.00
❑324, Apr 85, DH	0.75	0.40	1.00	2.00

George Pérez provided an updated origin for the Amazon Princess in *Wonder Woman* (2nd series) #1.

© 1987 DC Comics

	ORIG	GOOD	FINE	N-MINT
❑325, May 85, DH, A: Atomic Knight	0.75	0.40	1.00	2.00
❑326, Jul 85, DH	0.75	0.40	1.00	2.00
❑327, Sep 85, DH	0.75	0.40	1.00	2.00
❑328, Dec 85,Crisis	0.75	0.40	1.00	2.00
❑329, Feb 86,Final Issue; Giant-size; Crisis	1.25	0.40	1.00	2.00

WONDER WOMAN (2ND SERIES) DC

	ORIG	GOOD	FINE	N-MINT
❑0, Oct 94, GP, BB (c), GP (w), O: The Amazons	1.50	1.20	3.00	6.00
❑1, Feb 87, GP, GP (w), The Princess and the Power!, O: Wonder Woman (new origin); 1: Ares (DC)	0.75	0.80	2.00	4.00
❑2, Mar 87, GP, A: Steve Trevor	0.75	0.60	1.50	3.00
❑3, Apr 87, GP, 1: Decay; 1: Jack Kapatelis; 1: Vanessa Kapatelis	0.75	0.60	1.50	3.00
❑4, May 87, GP, 2: Decay	0.75	0.60	1.50	3.00
❑5, Jun 87, GP	0.75	0.60	1.50	3.00
❑6, Jul 87, GP, V: Ares	0.75	0.50	1.25	2.50
❑7, Aug 87, GP	0.75	0.50	1.25	2.50
❑8, Sep 87, GP	0.75	0.50	1.25	2.50
❑9, Oct 87, GP, 1: Cheetah	0.75	0.50	1.25	2.50
❑10, Nov 87, GP ,gatefold	0.75	0.50	1.25	2.50
❑10/A, Nov 87, GP ,no gatefold; gatefold	0.75	0.50	1.25	2.50
❑11, Dec 87, GP	0.75	0.40	1.00	2.00
❑12, Jan 88, GP ,Millennium	0.75	0.40	1.00	2.00
❑13, Feb 88, GP ,Millennium	0.75	0.40	1.00	2.00
❑14, Mar 88, GP	0.75	0.40	1.00	2.00
❑15, Apr 88, GP, 1: Ed Indelicato; 1: Silver Swan	0.75	0.40	1.00	2.00
❑16, May 88, GP	0.75	0.40	1.00	2.00
❑17, Jun 88, GP	0.75	0.40	1.00	2.00
❑18, Jul 88, GP ,Bonus Book	0.75	0.40	1.00	2.00
❑19, Aug 88, GP	0.75	0.40	1.00	2.00
❑20, Sep 88, GP	0.75	0.40	1.00	2.00
❑21, Oct 88, GP	1.00	0.40	1.00	2.00
❑22, Nov 88, GP	1.00	0.40	1.00	2.00
❑23, Dec 88, GP	1.00	0.40	1.00	2.00
❑24, Hol 88, GP	1.00	0.40	1.00	2.00
❑25, Jan 89, GP (c),Invasion!	1.00	0.40	1.00	2.00
❑26, Jan 89, GP (c),Invasion!	1.00	0.40	1.00	2.00
❑27, Feb 89, GP (c)	1.00	0.40	1.00	2.00
❑28, Mar 89, GP (c)	1.00	0.40	1.00	2.00
❑29, Apr 89, GP (c)	1.00	0.40	1.00	2.00
❑30, May 89, GP (c)	1.00	0.40	1.00	2.00
❑31, Jun 89, GP (c)	1.00	0.35	0.88	1.75
❑32, Jul 89, GP (c)	1.00	0.35	0.88	1.75
❑33, Aug 89	1.00	0.35	0.88	1.75
❑34, Sep 89	1.00	0.35	0.88	1.75
❑35, Oct 89	1.00	0.35	0.88	1.75
❑36, Nov 89	1.00	0.35	0.88	1.75
❑37, Dec 89	1.00	0.35	0.88	1.75
❑38, Jan 90	1.00	0.35	0.88	1.75
❑39, Feb 90	1.00	0.35	0.88	1.75
❑40, Mar 90	1.00	0.35	0.88	1.75
❑41, Apr 90	1.00	0.35	0.88	1.75
❑42, May 90	1.00	0.35	0.88	1.75
❑43, Jun 90	1.00	0.35	0.88	1.75
❑44, Jul 90	1.00	0.35	0.88	1.75
❑45, Aug 90	1.00	0.35	0.88	1.75
❑46, Sep 90	1.00	0.35	0.88	1.75
❑47, Oct 90, A: Troia	1.00	0.35	0.88	1.75
❑48, Nov 90	1.00	0.35	0.88	1.75
❑49, Dec 90	1.00	0.35	0.88	1.75
❑50, Jan 91, GP (c), GP (w), Embrace the Coming Dawn	1.50	0.35	0.88	1.75
❑51, Feb 91	1.00	0.30	0.75	1.50
❑52, Mar 91	1.00	0.30	0.75	1.50
❑53, Apr 91	1.00	0.30	0.75	1.50
❑54, May 91	1.00	0.30	0.75	1.50
❑55, Jun 91	1.00	0.30	0.75	1.50
❑56, Jul 91	1.00	0.30	0.75	1.50
❑57, Aug 91	1.00	0.30	0.75	1.50

	ORIG	GOOD	FINE	N-MINT
❑58, Sep 91, War of the Gods, Part 3,War of Gods	1.00	0.30	0.75	1.50
❑59, Oct 91, War of the Gods, Part 11,War of Gods	1.00	0.30	0.75	1.50
❑60, Nov 91, War of the Gods, Part 19; Lobo appearance,War of Gods	1.00	0.30	0.75	1.50
❑61, Jan 92, War of the Gods, Part 22,War of Gods	1.00	0.30	0.75	1.50
❑62, Feb 92	1.00	0.30	0.75	1.50
❑63, Jun 92, BB (c), Operation: Cheetah, Part 2	1.25	0.30	0.75	1.50
❑64, Jul 92, BB (c)	1.25	0.30	0.75	1.50
❑65, Aug 92, BB (c)	1.25	0.30	0.75	1.50
❑66, Sep 92, BB (c)	1.25	0.30	0.75	1.50
❑67, Oct 92, BB (c)	1.25	0.30	0.75	1.50
❑68, Nov 92, BB (c)	1.25	0.30	0.75	1.50
❑69, Dec 92, BB (c)	1.25	0.30	0.75	1.50
❑70, Jan 93, BB (c)	1.25	0.30	0.75	1.50
❑71, Feb 93, BB (c)	1.25	0.30	0.75	1.50
❑72, Mar 93, BB (c)	1.25	0.30	0.75	1.50
❑73, Apr 93, BB (c)	1.25	0.30	0.75	1.50
❑74, May 93, BB (c)	1.25	0.30	0.75	1.50
❑75, Jun 93, BB (c)	1.25	0.30	0.75	1.50
❑76, Jul 93, BB (c)	1.25	0.30	0.75	1.50
❑77, Aug 93, BB (c)	1.25	0.30	0.75	1.50
❑78, Sep 93, BB (c)	1.25	0.30	0.75	1.50
❑79, Oct 93, BB (c), A: Flash; V: Mayfly	1.25	0.30	0.75	1.50
❑80, Nov 93, BB (c), It's Never a Good Day to Die	1.25	0.30	0.75	1.50
❑81, Dec 93, BB (c), And then she Fell to Earth	1.25	0.30	0.75	1.50
❑82, Jan 94, BB (c), V: Ares	1.25	0.30	0.75	1.50
❑83, Feb 94, BB (c)	1.50	0.30	0.75	1.50
❑84, Mar 94, BB (c), Ares Rising: Amazon Songs	1.50	0.30	0.75	1.50
❑85, Apr 94, BB (c),Mike Deodato Jr.'s first U.S. work	1.50	2.00	5.00	10.00
❑86, May 94, BB (c)	1.50	0.80	2.00	4.00
❑87, Jun 94, BB (c)	1.50	0.60	1.50	3.00
❑88, Jul 94, BB (c), A: Superman	1.50	0.60	1.50	3.00
❑89, Aug 94, BB (c), Home	1.50	0.60	1.50	3.00
❑90, Sep 94, BB (c), The Contest	1.50	0.60	1.50	3.00
❑91, Nov 94	1.50	0.60	1.50	3.00
❑92, Dec 94	1.50	0.60	1.50	3.00
❑93, Jan 95, Violent Beginnings	1.50	0.60	1.50	3.00
❑94, Feb 95, V: Poison Ivy; V: Cheshire	1.50	0.40	1.00	2.00
❑95, Mar 95, V: Poison Ivy; V: Cheshire; V: Cheetah	1.50	0.40	1.00	2.00
❑96, Apr 95	1.50	0.40	1.00	2.00
❑97, May 95, V: Joker	1.50	0.40	1.00	2.00
❑98, Jun 95	1.75	0.40	1.00	2.00
❑99, Jul 95	1.75	0.40	1.00	2.00
❑100, Jul 95, Fall of an Amazon, D: Athena, Giant-size; Wonder Woman returns to old uniform	2.95	0.59	1.48	2.95
❑100/SC, Jul 95, D: Athena,enhanced cover; Giant-size; Wonder Woman returns to old uniform	3.95	0.80	2.00	4.00
❑101, Sep 95, JBy, JBy (w)	1.95	0.39	0.98	1.95
❑102, Oct 95, JBy, JBy (w)	1.95	0.39	0.98	1.95
❑103, Nov 95, JBy, JBy (w)	1.95	0.39	0.98	1.95
❑104, Dec 95, JBy, JBy (w)	1.95	0.39	0.98	1.95
❑105, Jan 96, JBy, JBy (w), Lifelines, Part 1	1.95	0.39	0.98	1.95
❑106, Feb 96, JBy, JBy (w), Lifelines, Part 2, A: Phantom Stranger	1.95	0.39	0.98	1.95
❑107, Mar 96, JBy, JBy (w), Lifelines, Part 3, A: Demon	1.95	0.39	0.98	1.95
❑108, Apr 96, JBy, JBy (w), Lifelines, Part 4	1.95	0.39	0.98	1.95
❑109, May 96, JBy, JBy (w), V: Flash (fake)	1.95	0.39	0.98	1.95
❑110, Jun 96, JBy, JBy (w), V: Sinestro (fake)	1.95	0.39	0.98	1.95
❑111, Jul 96, JBy, JBy (w), V: Doomsday (fake)	1.95	0.39	0.98	1.95
❑112, Aug 96, JBy, JBy (w), V: Doomsday (fake); A: Decay	1.95	0.39	0.98	1.95
❑113, Sep 96, JBy, JBy (w), A: Wonder Girl	1.95	0.39	0.98	1.95
❑114, Oct 96, JBy, JBy (w), Nightmare Alley	1.95	0.39	0.98	1.95
❑115, Nov 96, JBy, JBy (w), The Men Who Moved the World, Part 1	1.95	0.39	0.98	1.95
❑116, Dec 96, JBy, JBy (w), The Men Who Moved the World, Part 2, A: Cave Carson	1.95	0.39	0.98	1.95
❑117, Jan 97, JBy, JBy (w), The Men Who Moved the World, Part 3, 1: Invisible Plane	1.95	0.39	0.98	1.95
❑118, Feb 97, JBy, JBy (w), V: Cheetah	1.95	0.39	0.98	1.95
❑119, Mar 97, JBy, JBy (w), In the Forest of the Night, V: Cheetah	1.95	0.39	0.98	1.95
❑120, Apr 97, GP (c), Giant-size; 10th anniversary issue	2.95	0.59	1.48	2.95
❑121, May 97	1.95	0.39	0.98	1.95
❑122, Jun 97	1.95	0.39	0.98	1.95

	ORIG	GOOD	FINE	N-MINT
❑123, Jul 97, V: Artemis	1.95	0.39	0.98	1.95
❑124, Aug 97, V: Artemis	1.95	0.39	0.98	1.95
❑125, Sep 97, A: Batman; A: Green Lantern; A: Martian Manhunter; A: Flash; A: Superman; O: Demon,Diana in intensive care; Martian Manhunter; Batman; Green Lantern; Flash	1.95	0.39	0.98	1.95
❑126, Oct 97,Genesis	1.95	0.39	0.98	1.95
❑127, Nov 97, JBy, JBy (w), Transfiguration,Diana is turned into a goddess and goes to Olympus	1.95	0.39	0.98	1.95
❑128, Dec 97, JBy, JBy (w),Face cover	1.95	0.39	0.98	1.95
❑129, Jan 98	1.95	0.39	0.98	1.95
❑130, Feb 98, A: Jay Garrick; A: Justice Society of America	1.95	0.39	0.98	1.95
❑131, Mar 98, A: Jay Garrick; A: Justice Society of America	1.95	0.39	0.98	1.95
❑132, Apr 98, A: Jay Garrick; A: Justice Society of America	1.95	0.39	0.98	1.95
❑133, May 98, A: Jay Garrick; A: Justice Society of America	1.95	0.39	0.98	1.95
❑134, Jun 98, Who is Donna Troy?	1.95	0.39	0.98	1.95
❑135, Jul 98, O: Donna Troy	1.95	0.39	0.98	1.95
❑136, Aug 98,Diana returns to Earth; Return of Donna Troy	1.95	0.40	1.00	1.99
❑137, Sep 98	1.99	0.40	1.00	1.99
❑138, Oct 98	1.99	0.40	1.00	1.99
❑139, Dec 98,Diana becomes mortal again	1.99	0.40	1.00	1.99
❑139/LE	14.95	2.99	7.47	14.95
❑140, Jan 99, Trinity, Part 1, A: Batman; A: Superman	1.99	0.40	1.00	1.99
❑141, Feb 99, Trinity, Part 2, A: Oblivion; A: Batman; A: Superman	1.99	0.40	1.00	1.99
❑142, Mar 99	1.99	0.40	1.00	1.99
❑143, Apr 99, Devastation, Part 1, 1: Devastation	1.99	0.40	1.00	1.99
❑144, May 99, Devastation, Part 2, V: Devastation	1.99	0.40	1.00	1.99
❑145, Jun 99, Devastation, Part 3, V: Devastation	1.99	0.40	1.00	1.99
❑146, Jul 99, Devastation, Part 4, V: Devastation	1.99	0.40	1.00	1.99
❑147, Aug 99, Godwar, Part 1: Revolution; Godwar, Part 1	1.99	0.40	1.00	1.99
❑148, Sep 99, Godwar, Part 2	1.99	0.40	1.00	1.99
❑149, Oct 99	1.99	0.40	1.00	1.99
❑150, Nov 99, The Pandora Virus, Part 1	1.99	0.40	1.00	1.99
❑151, Dec 99, The Pandora Virus, Part 2	1.99	0.40	1.00	1.99
❑152, Jan 00	1.99	0.40	1.00	1.99
❑153, Feb 00	1.99	0.40	1.00	1.99
❑154, Mar 00	1.99	0.40	1.00	1.99
❑155, Apr 00, Three Hearts, Part 2	1.99	0.40	1.00	1.99
❑156, May 00, Devastation: The Return, Part 1	1.99	0.40	1.00	1.99
❑157, Jun 00	1.99	0.40	1.00	1.99
❑158, Jul 00	—	0.40	1.00	1.99
❑159, Aug 00	—	0.40	1.00	1.99
❑160, Sep 00, A Piece of You, Part 1	2.25	0.45	1.13	2.25
❑161, Oct 00, A Piece of You, Part 2	2.25	0.45	1.13	2.25
❑162, Nov 00, God Complex, Part 1	2.25	0.45	1.13	2.25
❑163, Dec 00, God Complex, Part 2	2.25	0.45	1.13	2.25
❑164, Jan 01, Gods of Gotham, Part 1	2.25	0.45	1.13	2.25
❑165, Feb 01, Gods of Gotham, Part 2	2.25	0.45	1.13	2.25
❑166, Mar 01, Gods of Gotham, Part 3, A: Batman	2.25	0.45	1.13	2.25
❑167, Apr 01, Gods of Gotham, Part 4	2.25	0.45	1.13	2.25
❑168, May 01, Paradise Island Lost, Part 1	2.25	0.45	1.13	2.25
❑169, Jun 01	2.25	0.45	1.13	2.25
❑170, Jul 01	2.25	0.45	1.13	2.25
❑171, Aug 01	2.25	0.45	1.13	2.25
❑172, Sep 01	2.25	0.45	1.13	2.25
❑1000000, Nov 98, Legends	1.99	0.40	1.00	1.99
❑Anl 1, ca. 88, GP (w), Amazons; The Diving Bird	1.50	0.40	1.00	2.00
❑Anl 2, ca. 89, The Game of the Name; Headline	2.00	0.40	1.00	2.00
❑Anl 3, ca. 92, Eclipso: The Darkness Within, Part 17,Eclipso	2.50	0.50	1.25	2.50
❑Anl 4, ca. 95, BA ,Year One	3.50	0.70	1.75	3.50
❑Anl 5, ca. 96, DC, JBy (w), The Unremembered,Legends of the Dead Earth; 1996 Annual	2.95	0.59	1.48	2.95
❑Anl 6, ca. 97, TP, JBy (w), City of the Dead,Pulp Heroes	3.95	0.79	1.98	3.95
❑Anl 7, ca. 98,Ghosts	2.95	0.59	1.48	2.95
❑Anl 8, Sep 99, The Thin Gold Line,JLApe	2.95	0.59	1.48	2.95
❑SE 1, Operation: Cheetah, Part 1, A: Deathstroke	1.75	0.35	0.88	1.75

ORIG GOOD FINE N-MINT

WONDER WOMAN: AMAZONIA
DC

Value: Cover or less

❑1, nn; prestige format; Oversized; Elseworlds 7.95

WONDER WOMAN: DONNA TROY
DC

Value: Cover or less

❑1, Jun 98, Why, One-Shot; Girlfrenzy 1.95

WONDER WOMAN GALLERY
DC

Value: Cover or less

❑1, nn; One-Shot; pin-ups 3.50

WONDER WOMAN PLUS
DC

Value: Cover or less

❑1, Jan 97, Heroes, A: Jesse Quick; A: Liberty Belle 2.95

WONDER WOMAN SECRET FILES
DC

Value: Cover or less

❑1, Mar 98, JBy (w), Secret Origin; Origin Epilogue, O: Wonder Woman, background on Wonder Woman and supporting cast 4.95

❑2, Jul 99, Origin of Devastation, background on Wonder Woman and supporting cast 4.95

WONDER WOMAN: THE ONCE AND FUTURE STORY
DC

Value: Cover or less

❑1, nn; prestige format one-shot; domestic violence 4.95

WONDERWORLD EXPRESS
THAT OTHER COMIX CO.

Value: Cover or less

❑1 .... 1.00

WONDERWORLDS
INNOVATION

Value: Cover or less

❑1, Reprint 3.50

WOODSTOCK: THE COMIC
MARVEL

Value: Cover or less

❑1 .... 5.95

WOODSY OWL
GOLD KEY

	ORIG	GOOD	FINE	N-MINT
❑1	0.25	1.60	4.00	8.00
❑2	0.25	1.00	2.50	5.00
❑3	0.25	0.80	2.00	4.00
❑4	0.25	0.80	2.00	4.00
❑5, Nov 74	0.25	0.80	2.00	4.00
❑6, Alias Mother Naure; Operation Hill-Kill	0.25	0.60	1.50	3.00
❑7	0.25	0.60	1.50	3.00
❑8	0.25	0.60	1.50	3.00
❑9	0.25	0.60	1.50	3.00
❑10	0.25	0.60	1.50	3.00

WOODY WOODPECKER (HARVEY)
HARVEY

	ORIG	GOOD	FINE	N-MINT
❑1	1.25	0.30	0.75	1.50
❑2	1.25	0.25	0.63	1.25
❑3, The Abominable Snowman; Big Bear & Little Bear: The Natural Expert	1.25	0.25	0.63	1.25
❑4	1.25	0.25	0.63	1.25
❑5	1.25	0.25	0.63	1.25
❑6	1.25	0.25	0.63	1.25
❑7	1.25	0.25	0.63	1.25
❑8	1.25	0.25	0.63	1.25
❑9	1.50	0.30	0.75	1.50
❑10	1.50	0.30	0.75	1.50
❑11	1.50	0.30	0.75	1.50
❑12	1.50	0.30	0.75	1.50

WOODY WOODPECKER 50TH ANNIVERSARY SPECIAL
HARVEY

Value: Cover or less

❑1, Reprint 2.50

WOODY WOODPECKER ADVENTURES
HARVEY

Value: Cover or less

❑1, The Rain Maker; Charlie Chicken: The Model Farm, Reprint 1.25

❑2 .... 1.25

❑3 .... 1.25

WOODY WOODPECKER AND FRIENDS
HARVEY

Value: Cover or less

❑1, A: Homer Pigeon; A: Conrad; A: Buzz Buzzard; A: Kathy, Reprint 1.25

❑2, Reprint 1.25

❑3, Reprint 1.25

❑4, Reprint 1.25

WOODY WOODPECKER DIGEST
HARVEY

Value: Cover or less

❑1, Reprint 1.75

WOODY WOODPECKER GIANT SIZE
HARVEY

Value: Cover or less

❑1 .... 2.25

WOODY WOODPECKER SUMMER SPECIAL
HARVEY

Value: Cover or less

❑1 .... 1.95

Wonder Woman: The Once and Future Story was a one-shot focusing on domestic abuse.

© 1996 DC Comics

ORIG GOOD FINE N-MINT

WOOFERS AND HOOTERS
FANTAGRAPHICS

Value: Cover or less

❑1, b&w; adult 2.50

WOOLWORTH'S HAPPY TIME CHRISTMAS BOOK
WHITMAN

	ORIG	GOOD	FINE	N-MINT
❑1, 1952	—	6.00	15.00	30.00

WORDS & PICTURES
MAVERICK STUDIOS

Value: Cover or less

❑1, Fal 94, b&w 3.95

❑2, Spr 95, In Vivo: The Waking Dream; Rio Grande, b&w 3.95

WORDSMITH (CALIBER)
CALIBER

Value: Cover or less

❑1 .... 2.95

❑2 .... 2.95

❑3 .... 2.95

❑4 .... 2.95

❑5 .... 2.95

❑6 .... 2.95

WORDSMITH (RENEGADE)
RENEGADE

Value: Cover or less

❑1, Aug 85, b&w 1.70

❑2, Oct 85, b&w 1.70

❑3, Dec 85, b&w 1.70

❑4, Dec 85, b&w 1.70

❑5, May 86, b&w 1.70

❑6, Aug 86 .... 1.70

❑7, Nov 86 .... 2.00

❑8, Nov 86 .... 2.00

❑9, May 87 .... 2.00

❑10, Aug 87 .... 2.00

❑11, Nov 87 .... 2.00

❑12, Jan 88 .... 2.00

WORD WARRIORS
LITERACY VOLUNTEERS

Value: Cover or less

❑1, HC (c), b&w; Ms. Tree, Jon Sable 1.50

WORGARD: VIKING BERSERKIR
STRONGHOLD STUDIOS

Value: Cover or less

❑1, Oct 97, b&w 2.95

WORKSHOP, THE
BLUE COMET

Value: Cover or less

❑1 .... 2.95

WORLD BANK, THE
PUBLIC SERVICES INTERNATIONAL

Value: Cover or less

❑1, educational comic; no indicia 2.95

WORLD BELOW, THE
DARK HORSE

Value: Cover or less

❑1, Mar 99, The Flock 2.50

❑2, Apr 99 .... 2.50

❑3, May 99 .... 2.50

❑4, Jun 99, The Stove 2.50

WORLD BELOW, THE: DEEPER AND STRANGER
DARK HORSE

Value: Cover or less

❑1, Dec 99, The Spare! 2.95

❑2, Jan 00, Zombies! 2.95

❑3, Feb 00 .... 2.95

❑4, Mar 00 .... 2.95

WORLD HARDBALL LEAGUE
TITUS

Value: Cover or less

❑1, Aug 94, Widow's Web; Legend of the Ice Bat, b&w 2.75

❑2, Jan 95, b&w 2.95

WORLD OF ARCHIE
ARCHIE

	ORIG	GOOD	FINE	N-MINT
❑1, Aug 92	1.25	0.40	1.00	2.00
❑2, Nov 92	1.25	0.30	0.75	1.50
❑3, Feb 93	1.25	0.30	0.75	1.50
❑4, May 93	1.25	0.30	0.75	1.50
❑5, Aug 93	1.25	0.30	0.75	1.50
❑6, Nov 93	1.25	0.30	0.75	1.50
❑7, Feb 94	1.25	0.30	0.75	1.50
❑8, Apr 94	1.25	0.30	0.75	1.50
❑9, Jun 94	1.25	0.30	0.75	1.50
❑10, Aug 94	1.25	0.30	0.75	1.50
❑11, Sep 94	1.50	0.30	0.75	1.50
❑12, Nov 94	1.50	0.30	0.75	1.50
❑13, Jan 95, When Rhinos Fly	1.50	0.30	0.75	1.50
❑14, Mar 95	1.50	0.30	0.75	1.50
❑15, Jun 95	1.50	0.30	0.75	1.50
❑16, Sep 95	1.50	0.30	0.75	1.50
❑17, Dec 95	1.50	0.30	0.75	1.50

	ORIG	GOOD	FINE	N-MINT
❑18, Mar 96	1.50	0.30	0.75	1.50
❑19, Jun 96	1.50	0.30	0.75	1.50
❑20, Sep 96	1.50	0.30	0.75	1.50
❑21, Dec 96, Campaign in the Neck; Not-So-Private Eye,Archie and Veronica run for class president	1.50	0.30	0.75	1.50
❑22, Mar 97	1.50	0.30	0.75	1.50

WORLD OF GINGER FOX
COMICO

Value: Cover or less

❑1 ... 6.95

❑1/HC ... 27.95

WORLD OF KRYPTON (1ST SERIES)
DC

	ORIG	GOOD	FINE	N-MINT
❑1, Jul 79, HC; MA, O: Jor-El	0.40	0.40	1.00	2.00
❑2, Aug 79, HC	0.40	0.40	1.00	2.00
❑3, Sep 79, HC	0.40	0.40	1.00	2.00

WORLD OF KRYPTON (2ND SERIES)
DC

	ORIG	GOOD	FINE	N-MINT
❑1, Dec 87, JBy (c), JBy (w), Pieces	0.75	0.40	1.00	2.00
❑2, Jan 88, JBy (w)	0.75	0.40	1.00	2.00
❑3, Feb 88, JBy (c), JBy (w)	0.75	0.40	1.00	2.00
❑4, Mar 88, JBy (c), JBy (w)	0.75	0.40	1.00	2.00

WORLD OF METROPOLIS
DC

	ORIG	GOOD	FINE	N-MINT
❑1, Aug 88	1.00	0.30	0.75	1.50
❑2, Sep 88	1.00	0.30	0.75	1.50
❑3, Oct 88	1.00	0.30	0.75	1.50
❑4, Nov 88	1.00	0.30	0.75	1.50

WORLD OF SMALLVILLE
DC

	ORIG	GOOD	FINE	N-MINT
❑1, Apr 88	0.75	0.30	0.75	1.50
❑2, May 88	0.75	0.30	0.75	1.50
❑3, Jun 88	0.75	0.30	0.75	1.50
❑4, Jul 88	0.75	0.30	0.75	1.50

WORLD OF WOOD
ECLIPSE

	ORIG	GOOD	FINE	N-MINT
❑1, WW, WW (w)	1.75	0.40	1.00	2.00
❑2, May 86, WW, WW (w), The End; The Cosmic AllWar of the Wizards	1.75	0.40	1.00	2.00
❑3, WW, WW (w), Prelude to Armageddon; The Manhunters	1.75	0.40	1.00	2.00
❑4, WW, WW (w), Kille Hawk; The Mummy	1.75	0.40	1.00	2.00
❑5, WW	1.75	0.40	1.00	2.00

WORLD OF X-RAY, THE
PYRAMID

Value: Cover or less

❑1, b&w ... 1.80

WORLD OF YOUNG MASTER
NEW COMICS

Value: Cover or less

❑1, Demonblade: Crimson Legacy,Demonblade ... 1.95

WORLDS COLLIDE
DC

	ORIG	GOOD	FINE	N-MINT
❑1, Jul 94, Worlds Collide, Part 7, 1: Rift	2.50	0.50	1.25	2.50
❑1/CS, Jul 94, Worlds Collide, Part 7, 1: Rift,enhanced cover; vinyl clings; Include press-apply stick-ons	3.95	0.80	2.00	4.00
❑1/PL, Jul 94, Platinum edition	—	0.80	2.00	4.00

WORLD'S FINEST
DC

	ORIG	GOOD	FINE	N-MINT
❑1	3.95	1.00	2.50	5.00
❑2	3.95	0.90	2.25	4.50
❑3	3.95	0.90	2.25	4.50

WORLD'S FINEST COMICS
DC

	ORIG	GOOD	FINE	N-MINT
❑115, Feb 61	0.10	16.00	40.00	80.00
❑116, Mar 61	0.10	16.00	40.00	80.00
❑117, May 61, A: Lex Luthor	0.10	16.00	40.00	80.00
❑118, Jun 61	0.10	16.00	40.00	80.00
❑119, Aug 61	0.10	16.00	40.00	80.00
❑120, Sep 61	0.10	16.00	40.00	80.00
❑121, Nov 61	0.10	16.00	40.00	80.00
❑122, Dec 61	0.12	9.00	22.50	45.00
❑123, Feb 62	0.12	9.00	22.50	45.00
❑124, Mar 62	0.12	9.00	22.50	45.00
❑125, May 62	0.12	9.00	22.50	45.00
❑126, Jun 62, A: Lex Luthor	0.12	9.00	22.50	45.00
❑127, Aug 62	0.12	9.00	22.50	45.00
❑128, Sep 62	0.12	9.00	22.50	45.00
❑129, Nov 62, A: Joker; A: Lex Luthor	0.12	9.00	22.50	45.00
❑130, Dec 62	0.12	9.00	22.50	45.00
❑131, Feb 63	0.12	9.00	22.50	45.00
❑132, Mar 63	0.12	9.00	22.50	45.00
❑133, May 63,Aqua-Girl tryout	0.12	9.00	22.50	45.00
❑134, Jun 63	0.12	9.00	22.50	45.00
❑135, Aug 63	0.12	9.00	22.50	45.00
❑136, Sep 63	0.12	9.00	22.50	45.00
❑137, Nov 63, A: Lex Luthor	0.12	9.00	22.50	45.00
❑138, Dec 63	0.12	9.00	22.50	45.00
❑139, Feb 64	0.12	9.00	22.50	45.00
❑140, Mar 64	0.12	9.00	22.50	45.00
❑141, May 64	0.12	9.00	22.50	45.00
❑142, Jun 64, CS, 1: Composite Superman; A: Legion of Super-Heroes	0.12	9.00	22.50	45.00
❑143, Aug 64, CS	0.12	6.00	15.00	30.00
❑144, Sep 64, CS	0.12	6.00	15.00	30.00
❑145, Nov 64, CS	0.12	6.00	15.00	30.00
❑146, Dec 64, CS	0.12	6.00	15.00	30.00
❑147, Feb 65, CS	0.12	6.00	15.00	30.00
❑148, Mar 65, CS, A: Lex Luthor	0.12	6.00	15.00	30.00
❑149, May 65, CS	0.12	6.00	15.00	30.00
❑150, Jun 65, CS	0.12	6.00	15.00	30.00
❑151, Aug 65,Congorilla back-up	0.12	4.80	12.00	24.00
❑152, Sep 65	0.12	4.80	12.00	24.00
❑153, Nov 65, A: Lex Luthor	0.12	4.80	12.00	24.00
❑154, Dec 65	0.12	4.80	12.00	24.00
❑155, Feb 66	0.12	4.80	12.00	24.00
❑156, Mar 66, 1: Bizarro Batman; A: Bizarro Superman; A: Joker	0.12	17.00	42.50	85.00
❑157, May 66,Imaginary story; Supersons	0.12	4.80	12.00	24.00
❑158, Jun 66, CS	0.12	4.80	12.00	24.00
❑159, Aug 66, A: Joker	0.12	4.80	12.00	24.00
❑160, Sep 66	0.12	4.80	12.00	24.00
❑161, Nov 66, Giant-size	0.25	4.80	12.00	24.00
❑162, Nov 66	0.12	3.20	8.00	16.00
❑163, Dec 66	0.12	3.20	8.00	16.00
❑164, Feb 67, CS	0.12	3.20	8.00	16.00
❑165, Mar 67	0.12	3.20	8.00	16.00
❑166, May 67, A: Joker	0.12	4.40	11.00	22.00
❑167, Jun 67,Imaginary story	0.12	3.00	7.50	15.00
❑168, Aug 67, CS	0.12	3.00	7.50	15.00
❑169, Sep 67, CS	0.12	3.00	7.50	15.00
❑170, Nov 67, Giant-size	0.25	4.40	11.00	22.00
❑171, Nov 67	0.12	3.00	7.50	15.00
❑172, Dec 67, CS, A: Lex Luthor,Imaginary story; Clark and Bruce as brothers	0.12	3.00	7.50	15.00
❑173, Feb 68, CS ,reprints from Action #241	0.12	3.00	7.50	15.00
❑174, Mar 68	0.12	3.00	7.50	15.00
❑175, May 68, NA	0.12	4.40	11.00	22.00
❑176, Jun 68, NA	0.12	4.40	11.00	22.00
❑177, Aug 68, CS, A: Joker; A: Lex Luthor	0.12	4.40	11.00	22.00
❑178, Sep 68, CS	0.12	1.80	4.50	9.00
❑179, Nov 68,80pgs.	0.25	1.80	4.50	9.00
❑180, Nov 68	0.12	1.80	4.50	9.00
❑181, Dec 68	0.12	1.80	4.50	9.00
❑182, Feb 69	0.12	1.80	4.50	9.00
❑183, Mar 69, RA, Superman's Crime of the Ages; The Ghost Planet, A: Brainiac; A: Lex Luthor,reprints story from House of Mystery #80	0.12	1.80	4.50	9.00
❑184, May 69	0.12	1.80	4.50	9.00
❑185, Jun 69	0.12	1.80	4.50	9.00
❑186, Aug 69	0.15	1.80	4.50	9.00
❑187, Sep 69, O: Green Arrow	0.15	1.80	4.50	9.00
❑188, Oct 69, Giant-size	0.25	2.00	5.00	10.00
❑189, Nov 69, A: Lex Luthor	0.15	1.80	4.50	9.00
❑190, Dec 69, A: Lex Luthor	0.15	1.80	4.50	9.00
❑191, Feb 70	0.15	1.40	3.50	7.00
❑192, Mar 70	0.15	1.40	3.50	7.00
❑193, May 70	0.15	1.40	3.50	7.00
❑194, Jun 70	0.15	1.40	3.50	7.00
❑195, Aug 70	0.15	1.40	3.50	7.00
❑196, Sep 70	0.15	1.40	3.50	7.00
❑197, Nov 70, Giant-size	0.25	1.80	4.50	9.00
❑198, Nov 70,Superman/Flash race	0.15	15.00	37.50	75.00
❑199, Dec 70,Superman/Flash race	0.15	15.00	37.50	75.00
❑200, Feb 71	0.15	1.00	2.50	5.00
❑201, Mar 71, A: Green Lantern; A: Doctor Fate	0.15	1.00	2.50	5.00
❑202, May 71	0.15	1.00	2.50	5.00
❑203, Jun 71	0.15	1.00	2.50	5.00
❑204, Aug 71, A: Wonder Woman,Green Arrow back-up; Captain Comet back-up	0.25	1.00	2.50	5.00
❑205, Sep 71, FF, A: Teen Titans,Shining Knight back-up	0.25	1.00	2.50	5.00
❑206, Nov 71, Giant-size	0.35	1.00	2.50	5.00
❑207, Nov 71	0.25	1.00	2.50	5.00
❑208, Dec 71, A: Doctor Fate	0.25	1.00	2.50	5.00
❑209, Feb 72, A: Hawkman	0.25	1.00	2.50	5.00
❑210, Mar 72	0.25	1.00	2.50	5.00
❑211, May 72	0.25	1.00	2.50	5.00
❑212, Jun 72	0.25	1.00	2.50	5.00
❑213, Sep 72	0.20	1.00	2.50	5.00
❑214, Nov 72	0.20	1.00	2.50	5.00
❑215, Jan 73	0.20	1.00	2.50	5.00
❑216, Mar 73	0.20	1.00	2.50	5.00
❑217, May 73, A: Metamorpho	0.20	1.00	2.50	5.00
❑218, Aug 73	0.20	1.00	2.50	5.00
❑219, Oct 73	0.20	1.00	2.50	5.00

	ORIG	GOOD	FINE	N-MINT
❑220, Dec 73	0.20	1.00	2.50	5.00
❑221, Feb 74, A: Super-Sons	0.20	0.80	2.00	4.00
❑222, Apr 74	0.20	0.80	2.00	4.00
❑223, Jun 74, NA, O: Deadman, Giant-size	0.60	0.80	2.00	4.00
❑224, Aug 74, Giant-size	0.60	0.80	2.00	4.00
❑225, Oct 74, Giant-size	0.60	0.80	2.00	4.00
❑226, Dec 74, NA, A: Metamorpho, Giant-size	0.60	0.80	2.00	4.00
❑227, Feb 75, A: Deadman, Giant-size	0.60	0.80	2.00	4.00
❑228, Mar 75, A: Super-Sons, Giant-size	0.60	0.80	2.00	4.00
❑229, Apr 75	0.25	0.80	2.00	4.00
❑230, May 75, Giant-size	0.50	0.80	2.00	4.00
❑231, Jul 75, A: Super-Sons	0.25	0.80	2.00	4.00
❑232, Sep 75	0.25	0.80	2.00	4.00
❑233, Oct 75	0.25	0.80	2.00	4.00
❑234, Dec 75	0.25	0.80	2.00	4.00
❑235, Jan 76	0.25	0.80	2.00	4.00
❑236, Mar 76	0.30	0.80	2.00	4.00
❑237, Apr 76	0.30	0.80	2.00	4.00
❑238, Jun 76	0.30	0.80	2.00	4.00
❑239, Jul 76	0.30	0.80	2.00	4.00
❑240, Sep 76	0.30	0.80	2.00	4.00
❑241, Oct 76	0.30	0.80	2.00	4.00
❑242, Dec 76, A: Super-Sons	0.30	0.80	2.00	4.00
❑243, Feb 77	0.30	0.80	2.00	4.00
❑244, May 77, Giant-size	1.00	0.80	2.00	4.00
❑245, Jul 77, Giant-size	1.00	0.80	2.00	4.00
❑246, Sep 77, 1: Baron Blitzkrieg; A: Justice League of America	1.00	0.80	2.00	4.00
❑247, Nov 77, KS, Giant-size	1.00	0.80	2.00	4.00
❑248, Jan 78, KS, Giant-size	1.00	0.80	2.00	4.00
❑249, Mar 78, KS, Giant-size; The Creeper begins	1.00	1.20	3.00	6.00
❑250, May 78, Giant-size	1.00	0.80	2.00	4.00
❑251, Jul 78, 1: Count Vertigo, Giant-size	1.00	0.60	1.50	3.00
❑252, Sep 78, Giant-size	1.00	0.60	1.50	3.00
❑253, Nov 78, KS, Giant-size	1.00	0.60	1.50	3.00
❑254, Jan 79, KS, Giant-size	1.00	0.60	1.50	3.00
❑255, Mar 79, SD	1.00	0.60	1.50	3.00
❑256, May 79, MA, Prey of the Harpies, Giant-size	1.00	0.60	1.50	3.00
❑257, Jul 79, RB, Attack of the In-and-Out Invaders, Giant-size	1.00	0.60	1.50	3.00
❑258, Sep 79, RB, Death Orbit, Giant-size	1.00	0.60	1.50	3.00
❑259, Nov 79, KS; MR; DG; RB; MN; DN, Stake Out Earth	1.00	0.60	1.50	3.00
❑260, Jan 80	1.00	0.60	1.50	3.00
❑261, Mar 80, JLA Databank Dossier: Hawkman	1.00	0.60	1.50	3.00
❑262, May 80, The Ghost of Adam Strange	1.00	0.60	1.50	3.00
❑263, Jul 80, A: final	1.00	0.60	1.50	3.00
❑264, Sep 80, Alone	1.00	0.60	1.50	3.00
❑265, Nov 80, This Hostage World	1.00	0.60	1.50	3.00
❑266, Jan 81, Something Sinister in Sewer Seven, 1: Lady Lunar	1.00	0.60	1.50	3.00
❑267, Mar 81, The Insect Invasion of Midway City, A: Challengers of the Unknown	1.00	0.60	1.50	3.00
❑268, May 81, Your City or Your Life	1.00	0.60	1.50	3.00
❑269, Jul 81, ... I Must Go Home Again, 1: Doctor Jymbi Humm	1.00	0.60	1.50	3.00
❑270, Aug 81, You and Me Against Our World	1.00	0.60	1.50	3.00
❑271, Sep 81, O: Superman/Batman team in World's Finest	1.00	0.60	1.50	3.00
❑272, Oct 81, Drive Me to the Moon	1.00	0.50	1.25	2.50
❑273, Nov 81, Victory?	1.00	0.50	1.25	2.50
❑274, Dec 81, Gone with the Wings	1.00	0.50	1.25	2.50
❑275, Jan 82, Matter... Matter Everywhere	1.00	0.50	1.25	2.50
❑276, Feb 82, CI, Stinging in the Rain	1.00	0.50	1.25	2.50
❑277, Mar 82, I Have My Wings and I Must Fly	1.00	0.50	1.25	2.50
❑278, Apr 82	1.00	0.50	1.25	2.50
❑279, May 82, Pirates of the Spaceways, A: Kid Eternity	1.00	0.50	1.25	2.50
❑280, Jun 82, Now You Czemm, Now You Don't, A: Kid Eternity	1.00	0.50	1.25	2.50
❑281, Jul 82, Out Into Space in Ships	1.00	0.50	1.25	2.50
❑282, Aug 82, CI, Doctor Katar and Mister Plert	1.00	0.50	1.25	2.50
❑283, Sep 82, GK; GT; FMc, V: Composite Superman	0.60	0.50	1.25	2.50
❑284, Oct 82, DS; GT, A: Legion	0.60	0.50	1.25	2.50
❑285, Nov 82	0.60	0.50	1.25	2.50
❑286, Dec 82	0.60	0.50	1.25	2.50
❑287, Jan 83	0.60	0.50	1.25	2.50
❑288, Feb 83	0.60	0.50	1.25	2.50
❑289, Mar 83	0.60	0.50	1.25	2.50
❑290, Apr 83	0.60	0.50	1.25	2.50
❑291, May 83	0.60	0.50	1.25	2.50
❑292, Jun 83	0.60	0.50	1.25	2.50
❑293, Jul 83	0.60	0.50	1.25	2.50
❑294, Aug 83	0.60	0.50	1.25	2.50
❑295, Sep 83	0.60	0.50	1.25	2.50
❑296, Oct 83	0.60	0.50	1.25	2.50
❑297, Nov 83	0.60	0.50	1.25	2.50
❑298, Dec 83	0.75	0.50	1.25	2.50

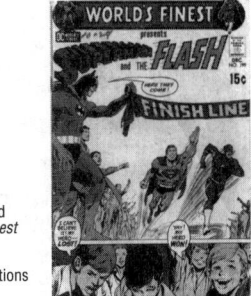

One of the Silver Age Superman and Flash races was held in *World's Finest Comics* #198 and #199.

© 1970 National Periodical Publications (DC)

	ORIG	GOOD	FINE	N-MINT
❑299, Jan 84, GC	0.75	0.50	1.25	2.50
❑300, Feb 84, RA, A: Outsiders; A: Titans; A: Justice League of America, 300th anniversary issue; Giant-size	1.25	0.60	1.50	3.00
❑301, Mar 84	0.75	0.40	1.00	2.00
❑302, Apr 84	0.75	0.40	1.00	2.00
❑303, May 84	0.75	0.40	1.00	2.00
❑304, Jun 84	0.75	0.40	1.00	2.00
❑305, Jul 84	0.75	0.40	1.00	2.00
❑306, Aug 84	0.75	0.40	1.00	2.00
❑307, Sep 84	0.75	0.40	1.00	2.00
❑308, Oct 84, KB (w)	0.75	0.40	1.00	2.00
❑309, Nov 84, KB (w), The Quantum Inheritance	0.75	0.40	1.00	2.00
❑310, Dec 84	0.75	0.40	1.00	2.00
❑311, Jan 85	0.75	0.40	1.00	2.00
❑312, Feb 85	0.75	0.40	1.00	2.00
❑313, Mar 85	0.75	0.40	1.00	2.00
❑314, Apr 85	0.75	0.40	1.00	2.00
❑315, May 85	0.75	0.40	1.00	2.00
❑316, Jun 85	0.75	0.40	1.00	2.00
❑317, Jul 85	0.75	0.40	1.00	2.00
❑318, Aug 85	0.75	0.40	1.00	2.00
❑319, Sep 85	0.75	0.40	1.00	2.00
❑320, Oct 85	0.75	0.40	1.00	2.00
❑321, Nov 85, V: Chronos	0.75	0.40	1.00	2.00
❑322, Dec 85	0.75	0.40	1.00	2.00
❑323, Jan 86,Final Issue	0.75	0.40	1.00	2.00

WORLD'S FUNNIEST COMICS
MOORDAM

Value: Cover or less

❑1, Mar 98, b&w; Cray-Baby Adventures, Mr. Beat 2.95

WORLDS OF H.P. LOVECRAFT: BEYOND THE WALL OF SLEEP
TOME

Value: Cover or less

❑1 .... 2.95

WORLDS OF H.P. LOVECRAFT, THE: DAGON
CALIBER

Value: Cover or less

❑1, b&w 2.95

WORLDS OF H.P. LOVECRAFT: THE ALCHEMIST
TOME

Value: Cover or less

❑1 .... 2.95

WORLDS OF H.P. LOVECRAFT, THE: THE MUSIC OF ERICH ZANN
CALIBER

Value: Cover or less

❑1, nn; b&w 2.95

WORLDS OF H.P. LOVECRAFT, THE: THE PICTURE IN THE HOUSE
CALIBER

Value: Cover or less

❑1, nn; b&w 2.95

WORLDS UNKNOWN
MARVEL

	ORIG	GOOD	FINE	N-MINT
❑1, May 73	0.20	1.00	2.50	5.00
❑2, Jul 73, VM, A Gun for Dinosaur!	0.20	0.80	2.00	4.00
❑3, Sep 73	0.20	0.80	2.00	4.00
❑4, Nov 73	0.20	0.60	1.50	3.00
❑5, Feb 74	0.20	0.60	1.50	3.00
❑6, Apr 74, Killdozer!	0.20	0.60	1.50	3.00
❑7, Jun 74, Golden Voyage of Sinbad; Golden Voyage of Sinbad, Part 1	0.25	0.60	1.50	3.00
❑8, Aug 74, Golden Voyage of Sinbad; Golden Voyage of Sinbad, Part 2,Final Issue	0.25	0.60	1.50	3.00

WORLD'S WORST COMICS AWARDS
KITCHEN SINK

Value: Cover or less

❑1, b&w 2.50

❑2, Jan 91, b&w 2.50

WORLD WAR II: 1946
ANTARCTIC

Value: Cover or less

❑1, Jul 99, Angels of the Luftwaffe 2.50

❑2, Born to Die 2.50

WORLD WAR II: 1946/FAMILIES OF ALTERED WARS
ANTARCTIC

Value: Cover or less

❑1, Jul 98 .... 3.95

❑1-2, Oct 98 .... 3.95

❑2, Nov 98,has indicia from #1 .... 3.95

❑2-2, Aug 98 .... 3.95

ORIG GOOD FINE N-MINT

WORLD WITHOUT END
DC
Value: Cover or less

❑1 2.50 ❑4 2.50
❑2 2.50 ❑5 2.50
❑3 2.50 ❑6 2.50

WORON'S WORLDS
ILLUSTRATION
Value: Cover or less

❑1/A, trading card 2.95
❑1/B, Adults-only cover; trading card 2.95
❑1/A-2, coupon for disk of images 3.25
❑1/B-2, coupon for disk of images 3.25
❑2/A, coupon for free print 2.95
❑2/B, Adults-only cover; coupon for free print 2.95
❑3/A, Nov 94, coupon for Woron's Female Fantasy disk 3.25
❑3/B, Nov 94, Adults-only cover; coupon for Vampires and Vixens disk 3.25

W.O.W. THE WORLD OF WARD
ALLIED AMERICAN ARTISTS
Value: Cover or less ❑1, BWa, b&w; Reprint 3.95

WRATH
MALIBU

	ORIG	GOOD	FINE	N-MINT
❑1, Jan 94, A: Mantra	1.95	0.40	1.00	2.00
❑1/LE, A: Mantra, Ultra-limited edition	—	0.60	1.50	3.00
❑2, Feb 94	1.95	0.40	1.00	2.00
❑3, Mar 94, 1: Slayer	1.95	0.40	1.00	2.00
❑4, Apr 94	1.95	0.39	0.98	1.95
❑5, May 94	1.95	0.39	0.98	1.95
❑6, Jun 94, Interludes	1.95	0.39	0.98	1.95
❑7, Jul 94, Three Strikes, 1: Doc Virtual; 1: Pierce; 1: Ogre	1.95	0.39	0.98	1.95
❑8, Oct 94, Days of Wrath, Part 2, A: Mantra; 1: Project Patriot; A: Warstrike	1.95	0.39	0.98	1.95
❑9, Dec 94, Days of Wrath, Part 3, D: Project Patriot, Final Issue	2.25	0.45	1.13	2.25
❑GS 1, Aug 94, Days of Wrath, Part 1, Giant-size Wrath #1	2.50	0.50	1.25	2.50

WRATH OF THE SPECTRE
DC
Value: Cover or less

❑1, May 88, JA, Wrath of the Spectre; Anguish of the Spectre, Reprints from Adventure Comics #431-433, 426 2.50
❑2, Jun 88, JA ,Reprint 2.50
❑3, Jul 88, JA ,Reprint 2.50
❑4, Aug 88, JA ,new stories 2.50

WRETCH, THE
CALIBER
Value: Cover or less

❑1, Jul 97, The End of the World!, b&w 2.95
❑2, Sep 97, Bad Dog, b&w 2.95
❑3, Nov 97, Snow; All the Way Down, Part 1, b&w 2.95
❑4, The Church Bus; Alarm Clock of the Beast, b&w 2.95
❑5, May 98, White Lie, Dedicated to Will Eisner 2.95
❑6, Jul 98, Doomsday 2.95

WRETCH, THE (VOL. 2)
SLAVE LABOR
Value: Cover or less

❑1, Jul 97, b&w 2.95
❑2, Sep 97, b&w 2.95
❑3, Nov 97, b&w 2.95
❑4, b&w 2.95

WRITERS' BLOC ANTHOLOGY, THE
WRITERS' BLOC

	ORIG	GOOD	FINE	N-MINT
❑1, Mis. Candice's Profession; The Gnat	—	0.60	1.50	3.00

WULF THE BARBARIAN
ATLAS

	ORIG	GOOD	FINE	N-MINT
❑1, O: Wulf	0.25	0.40	1.00	2.00
❑2	0.25	0.30	0.75	1.50
❑3	0.25	0.30	0.75	1.50
❑4	0.25	0.30	0.75	1.50

WU WEI
ANGUS
Value: Cover or less

❑1 2.50 ❑4 2.50
❑2 2.50 ❑5 2.50
❑3 2.50 ❑6 2.50

WW 2
NEC
Value: Cover or less

❑1 3.50
❑2, Nov 00, Salerno 3.50

WWF: WORLD WRESTLING FOUNDATION
VALIANT
Value: Cover or less

❑1, Ultimate Warrior's Workout, 21841 2.95
❑2, Lifestyles of the Brutal & Infamous, 21842 2.95
❑3, Out-of-the-Ring Challenges, 21843 2.95
❑4, Wait Till I Get My Hands on..., 21844 2.95

WYATT EARP
MARVEL

	ORIG	GOOD	FINE	N-MINT
❑1	0.10	22.00	55.00	110.00
❑2	0.10	13.00	32.50	65.00
❑3	0.10	9.60	24.00	48.00
❑4	0.10	9.60	24.00	48.00
❑5	0.10	9.60	24.00	48.00
❑6	0.10	9.60	24.00	48.00
❑7	0.10	9.60	24.00	48.00
❑8	0.10	9.60	24.00	48.00
❑9	0.10	9.60	24.00	48.00
❑10	0.10	9.60	24.00	48.00
❑11	0.10	8.00	20.00	40.00
❑12	0.10	8.00	20.00	40.00
❑13	0.10	8.00	20.00	40.00
❑14	0.10	8.00	20.00	40.00
❑15	0.10	8.00	20.00	40.00
❑16	0.10	8.00	20.00	40.00
❑17	0.10	8.00	20.00	40.00
❑18	0.10	8.00	20.00	40.00
❑19	0.10	8.00	20.00	40.00
❑20	0.10	8.00	20.00	40.00
❑21	0.10	5.60	14.00	28.00
❑22	0.10	5.60	14.00	28.00
❑23	0.10	5.60	14.00	28.00
❑24	0.10	5.60	14.00	28.00
❑25	0.10	5.60	14.00	28.00
❑26	0.10	5.60	14.00	28.00
❑27	0.10	5.60	14.00	28.00
❑28	0.10	5.60	14.00	28.00
❑29, Final issue of original run	0.10	5.60	14.00	28.00
❑30, Revival of old title; Series begins again	0.20	0.80	2.00	4.00
❑31, SL (w), The Man Who Out-Drew Earp; Too Many Murderers	0.20	0.80	2.00	4.00
❑32	0.20	0.80	2.00	4.00
❑33	0.20	0.80	2.00	4.00
❑34, Final Issue	0.20	0.80	2.00	4.00

WYNONNA EARP
IMAGE
Value: Cover or less

❑1, Dec 96, 1: Wynonna Earp. 2.50
❑2, Jan 97, The Bloody Badge of the Law 2.50
❑3, Feb 97, cover says Jan, indicia says Feb. 2.50
❑4, Mar 97 2.50
❑5, Apr 97, A: Beau Smith, Final Issue 2.50

WYOMING TERRITORY
ARK
Value: Cover or less ❑1, b&w 1.95

WYRD THE RELUCTANT WARRIOR
SLAVE LABOR
Value: Cover or less

❑1, Jul 99, JSn, JSn (w) 2.95
❑2, JSn, JSn (w) 2.95
❑3, JSn, JSn (w) 2.95
❑4, JSn, JSn (w) 2.95
❑5, JSn, JSn (w) 2.95
❑6, Dec 99, JSn, JSn (w), The Final Confrontation! 2.95

X

X
DARK HORSE

	ORIG	GOOD	FINE	N-MINT
❑1, Feb 94, embossed cardstock cover	2.00	0.50	1.25	2.50
❑2, Mar 94	2.00	0.50	1.25	2.50
❑3, Apr 94	2.00	0.50	1.25	2.50
❑4, May 94	2.00	0.40	1.00	2.00
❑5, Jun 94	2.00	0.40	1.00	2.00
❑6, Aug 94	2.00	0.40	1.00	2.00
❑7, Sep 94	2.00	0.40	1.00	2.00
❑8, Oct 94	2.50	0.50	1.25	2.50
❑9, Nov 94	2.50	0.50	1.25	2.50
❑10, Dec 94	2.50	0.50	1.25	2.50
❑11, Jan 95	2.50	0.50	1.25	2.50
❑12, Mar 95	2.50	0.50	1.25	2.50
❑13, Apr 95	2.50	0.50	1.25	2.50
❑14, May 95	2.50	0.50	1.25	2.50
❑15, Jun 95	2.50	0.50	1.25	2.50
❑16, Jul 95	2.50	0.50	1.25	2.50
❑17, Aug 95	2.50	0.50	1.25	2.50
❑18, Sep 95, FM (c), V: Predator	2.50	0.50	1.25	2.50
❑19, Oct 95, FM (c)	2.50	0.50	1.25	2.50
❑20, Nov 95, FM (c)	2.50	0.50	1.25	2.50
❑21, Dec 95, FM (c)	2.50	0.50	1.25	2.50
❑22, Jan 96, FM (c)	2.50	0.50	1.25	2.50
❑23, Feb 96	2.50	0.50	1.25	2.50
❑24, Mar 96	2.50	0.50	1.25	2.50
❑25, Apr 96, Final Issue	2.50	0.50	1.25	2.50
❑Hero 1, Hero Special edition #1; Included with Hero Illustrated magazine	1.00	0.20	0.50	1.00

X/1999
VIZ

	ORIG	GOOD	FINE	N-MINT
❑1, Homecoming, b&w	2.75	0.60	1.50	3.00
❑2, b&w	2.75	0.55	1.38	2.75
❑3, b&w	2.75	0.55	1.38	2.75
❑4, b&w	2.75	0.55	1.38	2.75
❑5, b&w	2.75	0.55	1.38	2.75
❑6, b&w	2.75	0.55	1.38	2.75

X-51
Marvel
Value: Cover or less

- ❑1, Sep 99, The Persistence of Memory 1.99
- ❑2, Sep 99 .... 1.99
- ❑3 .... 1.99
- ❑4, Nov 99 .... 1.99
- ❑5, Dec 99 .... 1.99

XANADU (3-D ZONE)
3-D Zone
Value: Cover or less

- ❑1, b&w 2.00
- ❑2, b&w 2.00
- ❑3, b&w 2.00
- ❑4, b&w 2.00

XANADU (THOUGHTS & IMAGES)
Thoughts & Images
Value: Cover or less

- ❑1, May 88, b&w 2.00
- ❑2, Jun 88, b&w 2.00
- ❑3, Jul 88, D: Firepetal, b&w 2.00
- ❑4, Aug 88, b&w 2.00
- ❑5, Nov 88, b&w; cover says Part Three of Five 2.00

XANADU: ACROSS DIAMOND SEAS
Mu

	ORIG	GOOD	FINE	N-MINT
❑1, b&w	2.50	0.50	1.25	2.50
❑2, Feb 94, b&w	2.50	0.50	1.25	2.50
❑3, Mar 94, b&w	2.50	0.59	1.48	2.95
❑4, Apr 94, b&w	2.50	0.59	1.48	2.95
❑5, May 94, b&w	2.95	0.59	1.48	2.95

XANADU COLOR SPECIAL
Eclipse
Value: Cover or less

- ❑1, Dec 88 .... 2.00

XANDER IN LOST UNIVERSE (GENE RODDENBERRY'S...)
Tekno
Value: Cover or less

- ❑0, Nov 95 .... 2.25
- ❑1, Dec 95 .... 2.25
- ❑2, Dec 95 .... 2.25
- ❑3, Jan 96 .... 2.25
- ❑4, Jan 96 .... 2.25
- ❑5, Feb 96 .... 2.25
- ❑6, Mar 96 .... 2.25
- ❑7, Apr 96 .... 2.25
- ❑8, May 96 .... 2.25

XANTH GRAPHIC NOVEL
Father Tree
Value: Cover or less

- ❑1, Return to Centaur 9.95

X-BABIES: MURDERAMA
Marvel
Value: Cover or less

- ❑1, Murderama 2.99

X-BABIES: REBORN
Marvel
Value: Cover or less

- ❑1, Jan 00, Beware the Babymaker 3.50

X-CALIBRE
Marvel

	ORIG	GOOD	FINE	N-MINT
❑1, Mar 95, The Infernal Gallop	1.95	0.40	1.00	2.00
❑2, Apr 95,cover says Jun	1.95	0.40	1.00	2.00
❑3, May 95	1.95	0.40	1.00	2.00
❑4, Jun 95	1.95	0.40	1.00	2.00

XENA
Brainstorm
Value: Cover or less

- ❑1 .... 2.95

XENA: WARRIOR PRINCESS (DARK HORSE)
Dark Horse

	ORIG	GOOD	FINE	N-MINT
❑1, Sep 99, The Warrior Way of Death, Part 1	2.95	0.60	1.50	3.00
❑1/SC, Sep 99, The Warrior Way of Death, Part 2,Photo cover	2.95	0.60	1.50	3.00
❑2, Oct 99, In Hell	2.95	0.60	1.50	3.00
❑2/SC, Oct 99, In Hell,Photo cover	2.95	0.60	1.50	3.00
❑3, Nov 99, Slave	2.95	0.60	1.50	3.00
❑3/SC, Nov 99, Slave,Photo cover	2.95	0.60	1.50	3.00
❑4, Dec 99	2.95	0.60	1.50	3.00
❑4/SC, Dec 99,Photo cover	2.95	0.60	1.50	3.00
❑5, Jan 00, The Slave Trail	2.95	0.60	1.50	3.00
❑5/SC, Jan 00, The Slave Trail,Photo cover	2.95	0.60	1.50	3.00
❑6, Feb 00	2.95	0.59	1.48	2.95
❑6/SC, Feb 00,Photo cover	2.95	0.59	1.48	2.95
❑7, Mar 00	2.95	0.59	1.48	2.95
❑7/SC, Mar 00,Photo cover	2.95	0.59	1.48	2.95
❑8, Apr 00	2.95	0.59	1.48	2.95
❑8/SC, Apr 00,Photo cover	2.95	0.59	1.48	2.95
❑9, May 00, If You Go Down to the Woods...	2.95	0.59	1.48	2.95
❑9/SC, May 00, If You Go Down to the Woods...,Photo cover	2.95	0.59	1.48	2.95
❑10, Jun 00, The Magnificent Seven	2.95	0.59	1.48	2.95
❑10/SC, Jun 00, The Magnificent Seven,Photo cover	2.95	0.59	1.48	2.95
❑11, Jul 00, Darkness Falls	2.95	0.59	1.48	2.95
❑11/SC, Jul 00, Darkness Falls,Photo cover	2.95	0.59	1.48	2.95
❑12, Aug 00, Darkness Falls, Part 2	2.95	0.59	1.48	2.95
❑12/SC, Aug 00, Darkness Falls, Part 2,Photo cover	2.95	0.59	1.48	2.95
❑13, Sep 00, Legion	2.95	0.59	1.48	2.95
❑13/SC, Sep 00, Legion,Photo cover	2.95	0.59	1.48	2.95

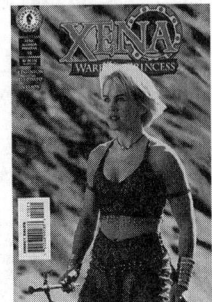

All 14 issues of Dark Horse's *Xena: Warrior Princess* featured both drawn and photo covers.

© 2000 20th Century Fox Film Corporation (Dark Horse)

	ORIG	GOOD	FINE	N-MINT
❑14, Oct 00, This Year's Model	2.99	0.60	1.50	2.99
❑14/SC, Oct 00, This Year's Model,Photo cover	2.99	0.60	1.50	2.99

XENA: WARRIOR PRINCESS (VOL. 1)
Topps

	ORIG	GOOD	FINE	N-MINT
❑0, Oct 97, The Temple of the Dragon God; Theft of the Young Lovelies, Part 3,Photo cover	2.95	0.59	1.48	2.95
❑1, Aug 97, A: Hercules,back-up Tales of Salmoneus	2.95	0.59	1.48	2.95
❑1/A, Aug 97,Photo cover of Xena poised to strike	2.95	0.59	1.48	2.95
❑1/AE, Aug 97,Photo cover; American Entertainment	—	1.40	3.50	7.00
❑1/SC, Aug 97,Photo cover of Xena walking hand in hand with Gabrielle	2.95	0.59	1.48	2.95
❑2, Sep 97	2.95	0.59	1.48	2.95
❑2/SC,Photo cover	2.95	0.59	1.48	2.95

XENA: WARRIOR PRINCESS: AND THE ORIGINAL OLYMPICS
Topps
Value: Cover or less

- ❑1, Jun 98 .... 2.95
- ❑2, Jul 98 .... 2.95
- ❑3, Aug 98 .... 2.95

XENA: WARRIOR PRINCESS: BLOODLINES
Topps
Value: Cover or less

- ❑1, May 98 .... 2.95
- ❑2, Jun 98 .... 2.95

XENA: WARRIOR PRINCESS/JOXER: WARRIOR PRINCE
Topps
Value: Cover or less

- ❑1, Nov 97 .... 2.95
- ❑1/SC, Nov 97,Photo cover 2.95
- ❑2, Dec 97 .... 2.95
- ❑2/SC, Dec 97,Photo cover 2.95
- ❑3, Jan 98 .... 2.95
- ❑3/SC, Jan 98,Photo cover 2.95

XENA: WARRIOR PRINCESS-THE DRAGON'S TEETH
Topps
Value: Cover or less

- ❑1, Dec 97 .... 2.95
- ❑1/SC, Dec 97,Photo cover 2.95
- ❑2, Jan 98 .... 2.95
- ❑2/SC, Jan 98,Photo cover 2.95
- ❑3, Feb 98 .... 2.95
- ❑3/SC, Feb 98,Photo cover 2.95

XENA: WARRIOR PRINCESS: THE ORPHEUS TRILOGY
Topps
Value: Cover or less

- ❑1, Mar 98 .... 2.95
- ❑1/SC, Mar 98,Photo cover 2.95
- ❑2, Apr 98 .... 2.95
- ❑2/SC, Apr 98,Photo cover 2.95
- ❑3, May 98 .... 2.95
- ❑3/SC, May 98,Photo cover 2.95

XENA: WARRIOR PRINCESS-THE WARRIOR WAY OF DEATH
Dark Horse
Value: Cover or less

- ❑1, Sep 99 .... 2.95
- ❑1/SC, Sep 99,Photo cover 2.95
- ❑2, Oct 99 .... 2.95
- ❑2/SC, Oct 99,Photo cover 2.95

XENA: WARRIOR PRINCESS VS. CALLISTO
Topps
Value: Cover or less

- ❑1, Feb 98 .... 2.95
- ❑1/SC, Feb 98,Photo cover 2.95
- ❑2, Mar 98 .... 2.95
- ❑2/SC, Mar 98,Photo cover 2.95
- ❑3, Mar 98 .... 2.95
- ❑3/SC, Mar 98,Photo cover 2.95

XENA, WARRIOR PRINCESS: WRATH OF HERA
Topps

	ORIG	GOOD	FINE	N-MINT
❑1	2.95	0.59	1.48	2.95
❑1/SC,Photo cover	2.95	0.60	1.50	3.00
❑2	2.95	0.59	1.48	2.95
❑2/SC,Photo cover	2.95	0.60	1.50	3.00

XENA: WARRIOR PRINCES, YEAR ONE
Topps

	ORIG	GOOD	FINE	N-MINT
❑1, O: Xena,Photo cover of Xena smiling	—	1.00	2.50	5.00
❑1/GO, O: Xena,Gold logo cover	—	2.00	5.00	10.00

XENE
Eyeball Soup Designs
Value: Cover or less

- ❑1,cardstock cover 4.95
- ❑2,cardstock cover 4.95
- ❑3, May 96, The Devil to Pay, Part 2; Hunter's Moon, Part 2,cardstock cover 4.95
- ❑4, Jul 96,cardstock cover 4.95

XENOBROOD
DC

Value: Cover or less

	ORIG
❑0, Oct 94, 1: Xenobrood	1.50
❑1, Nov 94	1.50
❑2, Dec 94	1.50
❑3, Jan 95, The Vimanian Bestiary	1.50
❑4, Feb 95	1.50
❑5, Mar 95	1.50
❑6, Apr 95,Final Issue	1.50

XENO-MEN
BLACKTHORNE

Value: Cover or less

	ORIG
❑1, 1: Xeno-Men	1.75

XENON
ECLIPSE

	ORIG	GOOD	FINE	N-MINT
❑1, Metamorphosis II	1.50	0.40	1.00	2.00
❑2, Metamorphosis II	1.50	0.40	1.00	2.00
❑3, Metamorphosis III	1.50	0.40	1.00	2.00
❑4	1.50	0.40	1.00	2.00
❑5	1.50	0.40	1.00	2.00
❑6	1.50	0.40	1.00	2.00
❑7	1.50	0.40	1.00	2.00
❑8	1.50	0.40	1.00	2.00
❑9	1.50	0.40	1.00	2.00
❑10	1.50	0.40	1.00	2.00
❑11	1.50	0.30	0.75	1.50
❑12	1.50	0.30	0.75	1.50
❑13	1.50	0.30	0.75	1.50
❑14	1.50	0.30	0.75	1.50
❑15	1.50	0.30	0.75	1.50
❑16	1.50	0.30	0.75	1.50
❑17	1.50	0.30	0.75	1.50
❑18	1.50	0.30	0.75	1.50
❑19, Sep 84	1.50	0.30	0.75	1.50
❑20	1.50	0.30	0.75	1.50
❑21	1.50	0.30	0.75	1.50
❑22, Oct 88	1.50	0.30	0.75	1.50
❑23,Final Issue	1.50	0.30	0.75	1.50

XENO'S ARROW
CUP O' TEA STUDIOS

Value: Cover or less

	ORIG
❑1, Feb 99, In My Garden, b&w	2.50

XENOTECH
MIRAGE

Value: Cover or less

	ORIG
❑1, Aug 94, Fire With Fire, 1: Chunk; 1: Pulse; 1: Starker Helm; 1: Haywire (Xenotech); 1: Xenotech; 1: Gunner, trading cards	2.75
❑1/A, Aug 94, Fire With Fire, 1: Chunk; 1: Pulse; 1: Starker Helm; 1: Haywire (Xenotech); 1: Gunner,Variant cover with monster attacking; trading cards	2.75
❑2, Oct 94, Enter Overblown!, O: Xenotech	2.75

XENOZOIC TALES
KITCHEN SINK

	ORIG	GOOD	FINE	N-MINT
❑1, Feb 87, An Archipelago of Stone	2.00	1.60	4.00	8.00
❑1-2, An Archipelago of Stone,2nd Printing	2.00	0.60	1.50	3.00
❑2, Apr 87	2.00	1.20	3.00	6.00
❑3, Jun 87	2.00	1.20	3.00	6.00
❑4, Nov 87, History Lesson; Postal Service	2.00	1.20	3.00	6.00
❑5, Feb 88, Excursion; Dog's Life	2.00	1.20	3.00	6.00
❑6, Foundling; Green Air	2.00	1.00	2.50	5.00
❑7, The Growing Pool; Crossed Currents	2.00	1.00	2.50	5.00
❑8, In the Dreamtime; Foul Weather	2.00	1.00	2.50	5.00
❑9, Last Link in the Chain; The Aqueduct	2.00	1.00	2.50	5.00
❑10, Lords of the Earth; Fields of Expertise	2.00	1.00	2.50	5.00
❑11	2.00	0.80	2.00	4.00
❑12, Two Cities; A Woman's Work	2.00	0.80	2.00	4.00
❑13	2.00	0.80	2.00	4.00
❑14, Oct 96, b&w; cardstock cover	2.95	0.80	2.00	4.00

XENYA
SANCTUARY

	ORIG	GOOD	FINE	N-MINT
❑1, Jul 94	2.95	0.59	1.48	2.95
❑2	2.95	0.59	1.48	2.95
❑3,no cover price	—	0.59	1.48	2.95

XERO
DC

	ORIG	GOOD	FINE	N-MINT
❑1, May 97, The Closer	1.75	0.40	1.00	2.00
❑2, Jun 97	1.75	0.35	0.88	1.75
❑3, Jul 97	1.75	0.35	0.88	1.75
❑4, Aug 97	1.75	0.35	0.88	1.75
❑5, Sep 97	1.75	0.35	0.88	1.75
❑6, Oct 97, The Villain; Genesis, V: Polaris,Genesis	1.75	0.35	0.88	1.75
❑7, Nov 97, The Soldier, Part 1	1.75	0.35	0.88	1.75
❑8, Dec 97, The Soldier, Part 2,Face cover.	1.95	0.39	0.98	1.95
❑9, Jan 98	1.95	0.39	0.98	1.95
❑10, Feb 98	1.95	0.39	0.98	1.95
❑11, Mar 98, The Cowboy	1.95	0.39	0.98	1.95
❑12, Apr 98,Final Issue	1.95	0.39	0.98	1.95

X-FACTOR
MARVEL

	ORIG	GOOD	FINE	N-MINT
❑-1, Jul 97, A Summer's Tale,Flashback	1.99	0.40	1.00	2.00
❑1, Feb 86, O: X-Factor; 1: Rusty Collins, Giant-size	1.25	0.80	2.00	4.00
❑2, Mar 86	0.75	0.60	1.50	3.00
❑3, Apr 86	0.75	0.60	1.50	3.00
❑4, May 86, 1: Frenzy	0.75	0.60	1.50	3.00
❑5, Jun 86, 1: Apocalypse (in shadows)	0.75	0.80	2.00	4.00
❑6, Jul 86, 1: Apocalypse (full appearance)	0.75	1.40	3.50	7.00
❑7, Aug 86, 1: Skids	0.75	0.60	1.50	3.00
❑8, Sep 86	0.75	0.60	1.50	3.00
❑9, Oct 89, Spots!,Mutant Massacre	0.75	0.60	1.50	3.00
❑10, Nov 89, Falling Angel,Mutant Massacre	0.75	0.60	1.50	3.00
❑11, Dec 89, Redemption!,Mutant Massacre	0.75	0.60	1.50	3.00
❑12, Jan 87, 1: Famine	0.75	0.50	1.25	2.50
❑13, Feb 87, A: Phoenix	0.75	0.50	1.25	2.50
❑14, Mar 87	0.75	0.50	1.25	2.50
❑15, Apr 87	0.75	0.50	1.25	2.50
❑16, May 87, O: Skids	0.75	0.50	1.25	2.50
❑17, Jun 87, 1: Rictor	0.75	0.50	1.25	2.50
❑18, Jul 87	0.75	0.50	1.25	2.50
❑19, Aug 87	0.75	0.50	1.25	2.50
❑20, Sep 87	0.75	0.50	1.25	2.50
❑21, Oct 87	0.75	0.50	1.25	2.50
❑22, Nov 87	0.75	0.50	1.25	2.50
❑23, Dec 87, 1: Archangel (cameo),registration card	0.75	1.20	3.00	6.00
❑24, Jan 88, Fall of the Mutants, Part 1, O: Apocalypse; 1: Archangel (full appearance),Fall of Mutants	0.75	2.00	5.00	10.00
❑25, Feb 88, Fall of the Mutants,Fall of Mutants	1.25	0.60	1.50	3.00
❑26, Mar 88, Fall of the Mutants,Fall of Mutants	0.75	0.60	1.50	3.00
❑27, Apr 88	0.75	0.40	1.00	2.00
❑28, May 88	1.00	0.40	1.00	2.00
❑29, Jun 88	1.00	0.40	1.00	2.00
❑30, Jul 88	1.00	0.40	1.00	2.00
❑31, Aug 88	1.00	0.40	1.00	2.00
❑32, Sep 88, A: Avengers; 1: N'astirh	1.00	0.40	1.00	2.00
❑33, Oct 88	1.00	0.40	1.00	2.00
❑34, Nov 88	1.00	0.40	1.00	2.00
❑35, Dec 88	1.00	0.40	1.00	2.00
❑36, Jan 89,Inferno	1.00	0.40	1.00	2.00
❑37, Feb 89,Inferno	1.00	0.40	1.00	2.00
❑38, Mar 89, D: Madelyn Pryor, Giant-size; Inferno	1.50	0.40	1.00	2.00
❑39, Apr 89,Inferno	1.00	0.40	1.00	2.00
❑40, May 89, RL	1.00	0.40	1.00	2.00
❑41, Jun 89	1.00	0.40	1.00	2.00
❑42, Jul 89	1.00	0.40	1.00	2.00
❑43, Aug 89, Judgment War, Part 1	1.00	0.40	1.00	2.00
❑44, Sep 89, Judgment War, Part 2	1.00	0.40	1.00	2.00
❑45, Oct 89, Judgment War, Part 3	1.00	0.40	1.00	2.00
❑46, Nov 89	1.00	0.40	1.00	2.00
❑47, Nov 89,Solo Archangel story	1.00	0.40	1.00	2.00
❑48, Dec 89, Judgment War, Part 5	1.00	0.40	1.00	2.00
❑49, Dec 89, Judgment War, Part 6	1.00	0.40	1.00	2.00
❑50, Jan 90, TMc (c), Judgment War, Part 7; Acts of Vengeance, Giant-size	1.50	0.50	1.25	2.50
❑51, Feb 90, A: Sabretooth	1.00	0.50	1.25	2.50
❑52, Mar 90, A: Sabretooth	1.00	0.50	1.25	2.50
❑53, Apr 90, A: Sabretooth	1.00	0.50	1.25	2.50
❑54, May 90, 1: Crimson	1.00	0.30	0.75	1.50
❑55, Jun 90	1.00	0.30	0.75	1.50
❑56, Jul 90	1.00	0.30	0.75	1.50
❑57, Aug 90	1.00	0.30	0.75	1.50
❑58, Sep 90	1.00	0.30	0.75	1.50
❑59, Oct 90	1.00	0.30	0.75	1.50
❑60, Nov 90, X-Tinction Agenda, Part 3	1.00	0.50	1.25	2.50
❑60-2, Nov 90, X-Tinction Agenda, Part 3,2nd Printing; Gold cover	1.00	0.30	0.75	1.50
❑61, Dec 90, X-Tinction Agenda, Part 6	1.00	0.50	1.25	2.50
❑62, Jan 91, X-Tinction Agenda, Part 9	1.00	0.50	1.25	2.50
❑63, Feb 91	1.00	0.50	1.25	2.50
❑64, Mar 91	1.00	0.50	1.25	2.50
❑65, Apr 91, Endgame, Part 1	1.00	0.50	1.25	2.50
❑66, May 91, Endgame, Part 2	1.00	0.50	1.25	2.50
❑67, Jun 91, Endgame, Part 3	1.00	0.50	1.25	2.50
❑68, Jul 91, Endgame, Part 4,Baby Nathan is sent into future	1.00	0.50	1.25	2.50
❑69, Aug 91	1.00	0.50	1.25	2.50
❑70, Sep 91,Muir Island Epilogue	1.00	0.40	1.00	2.00
❑71, Oct 91,new team; Havok, Madrox, Polaris & Wolfsbane	1.00	0.40	1.00	2.00
❑71-2,2nd Printing; Havok, Madrox, Polaris & Wolfsbane	1.00	0.30	0.75	1.50

	ORIG	GOOD	FINE	N-MINT
❑72, Nov 91	1.00	0.30	0.75	1.50
❑73, Dec 91	1.00	0.30	0.75	1.50
❑74, Jan 92	1.00	0.30	0.75	1.50
❑75, Feb 92, Giant-size	1.75	0.40	1.00	2.00
❑76, Mar 92	1.25	0.30	0.75	1.50
❑77, Apr 92	1.25	0.30	0.75	1.50
❑78, May 92	1.25	0.30	0.75	1.50
❑79, Jun 92, 1: Rhapsody	1.25	0.30	0.75	1.50
❑80, Jul 92	1.25	0.30	0.75	1.50
❑81, Aug 92	1.25	0.30	0.75	1.50
❑82, Sep 92	1.25	0.30	0.75	1.50
❑83, Oct 92	1.25	0.30	0.75	1.50
❑84/CS, Nov 92, X-Cutioner's Song; X-Cutioner's Song, Part 2, Caliban trading card	1.50	0.40	1.00	2.00
❑85/CS, Dec 92, X-Cutioner's Song, Part 6, trading card	1.50	0.40	1.00	2.00
❑86/CS, Jan 93, X-Cutioner's Song, Part 10, Dark Riders trading card	1.50	0.40	1.00	2.00
❑87, Feb 93	1.25	0.30	0.75	1.50
❑88, Mar 93	1.25	0.30	0.75	1.50
❑89, Apr 93	1.25	0.30	0.75	1.50
❑90, May 93	1.25	0.30	0.75	1.50
❑91, Jun 93	1.25	0.30	0.75	1.50
❑92, Jul 93,Hologram cover	3.50	0.80	2.00	4.00
❑93, Aug 93	1.25	0.30	0.75	1.50
❑94, Sep 93	1.25	0.30	0.75	1.50
❑95, Oct 93, A: Random; A: Polaris	1.25	0.30	0.75	1.50
❑96, Nov 93	1.25	0.30	0.75	1.50
❑97, Dec 93	1.25	0.30	0.75	1.50
❑98, Jan 94	1.25	0.30	0.75	1.50
❑99, Feb 94	1.25	0.30	0.75	1.50
❑100, Mar 94, D: Multiple Man, Giant-size	1.75	0.40	1.00	2.00
❑100/SC, Mar 94, D: Multiple Man,foil cover; Giant-size	2.95	0.60	1.50	3.00
❑101, Apr 94	1.50	0.30	0.75	1.50
❑102, May 94	1.50	0.30	0.75	1.50
❑103, Jun 94	1.50	0.30	0.75	1.50
❑104, Jul 94	1.50	0.30	0.75	1.50
❑105, Aug 94	1.50	0.30	0.75	1.50
❑106, Sep 94, Life Signs; Life Signs, Part 1	2.00	0.40	1.00	2.00
❑106/SC, Sep 94, Life Signs, Part 1,enhanced cover	2.95	0.59	1.48	2.95
❑107, Oct 94	1.50	0.30	0.75	1.50
❑108, Nov 94	1.50	0.30	0.75	1.50
❑108/Dlx, Nov 94, Deluxe edition	1.95	0.39	0.98	1.95
❑109, Dec 94, Legion Quest	1.50	0.30	0.75	1.50
❑109/Dlx, Dec 94, Deluxe edition	1.95	0.39	0.98	1.95
❑110, Jan 95, A: Lila Cheney	1.50	0.30	0.75	1.50
❑110/Dlx, Jan 95, Deluxe edition	1.95	0.39	0.98	1.95
❑111, Feb 95	1.50	0.30	0.75	1.50
❑111/Dlx, Feb 95, Deluxe edition	1.95	0.39	0.98	1.95
❑112, Jul 95	1.95	0.39	0.98	1.95
❑113, Aug 95	1.95	0.39	0.98	1.95
❑114, Sep 95	1.95	0.39	0.98	1.95
❑115, Oct 95	1.95	0.39	0.98	1.95
❑116, Nov 95	1.95	0.39	0.98	1.95
❑117, Dec 95, A: Random; A: Mystique; A: Havok; A: Wild Child; A: Cyclops	1.95	0.39	0.98	1.95
❑118, Jan 96	1.95	0.39	0.98	1.95
❑119, Feb 96, A: Shard	1.95	0.39	0.98	1.95
❑120, Mar 96, Meeting the Maker	1.95	0.39	0.98	1.95
❑121, Apr 96, The True Path	1.95	0.39	0.98	1.95
❑122, May 96	1.95	0.39	0.98	1.95
❑123, Jun 96	1.95	0.39	0.98	1.95
❑124, Jul 96	1.95	0.39	0.98	1.95
❑125, Aug 96, Onslaught: Impact 1	2.95	0.59	1.48	2.95
❑126, Sep 96, Onslaught: Impact 2,real Beast returns	1.95	0.39	0.98	1.95
❑127, Oct 96,bound-in trading cards	1.95	0.39	0.98	1.95
❑128, Nov 96	1.95	0.39	0.98	1.95
❑129, Dec 96	1.95	0.39	0.98	1.95
❑130, Jan 97, D: Graydon Creed	1.95	0.50	1.25	2.50
❑131, Feb 97, Brotherhood	1.95	0.39	0.98	1.95
❑132, Mar 97, Breakaway	1.95	0.39	0.98	1.95
❑133, Apr 97, Down Under	1.95	0.39	0.98	1.95
❑134, May 97, The Child	1.95	0.39	0.98	1.95
❑135, Jun 97, A Virtual Reality,return of Strong Guy	1.95	0.39	0.98	1.95
❑136, Aug 97, gatefold summary	1.99	0.40	1.00	1.99
❑137, Sep 97, gatefold summary	1.99	0.40	1.00	1.99
❑138, Oct 97, V: Omega Red, gatefold summary	1.99	0.40	1.00	1.99
❑139, Nov 97, gatefold summary	1.99	0.40	1.00	1.99
❑140, Dec 97, A: Xavier's Underground Enforcers, gatefold summary	1.99	0.40	1.00	1.99
❑141, Jan 98, gatefold summary	1.99	0.40	1.00	1.99

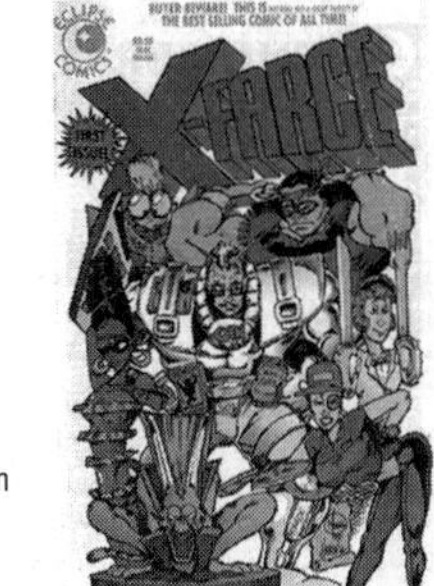

While it poked fun at Marvel's *X-Force* #1, Eclipse's *X-Farce* only had one edition as opposed to *X-Force* #1's five.

© 1991 Eclipse

	ORIG	GOOD	FINE	N-MINT
❑142, Feb 98, gatefold summary	1.99	0.40	1.00	1.99
❑143, Mar 98, gatefold summary	1.99	0.40	1.00	1.99
❑144, Apr 98, V: Random, gatefold summary	1.99	0.40	1.00	1.99
❑145, May 98, gatefold summary	1.99	0.40	1.00	1.99
❑146, Jun 98, gatefold summary; return of Multiple Man	1.99	0.40	1.00	1.99
❑147, Jul 98, gatefold summary	1.99	0.40	1.00	1.99
❑148, Aug 98, V: Mandroids, gatefold summary; return of Polaris	1.99	0.40	1.00	1.99
❑149, Sep 98,Final Issue; gatefold summary	1.99	0.40	1.00	1.99
❑Anl 1	1.25	0.60	1.50	3.00
❑Anl 2	1.25	0.60	1.50	3.00
❑Anl 3, Evolutionary War, Part 1, O: High Evolutionary	1.75	0.60	1.50	3.00
❑Anl 4, Atlantis Attacks, Part 10,Atlantis Attacks	2.00	0.50	1.25	2.50
❑Anl 5, Future Present; Days of Future Present, Part 2, A: New Mutants; A: Fantastic Four	2.00	0.50	1.25	2.50
❑Anl 6, Kings of Pain; Kings of Pain, Part 4, D: Proteus	2.00	0.50	1.25	2.50
❑Anl 7, Shattershot, Part 3,Shattershot	2.25	0.45	1.13	2.25
❑Anl 8,trading card	2.95	0.59	1.48	2.95
❑Anl 9, V: Power	2.95	0.59	1.48	2.95

X-FACTOR: PRISONER OF LOVE
MARVEL

Value: Cover or less ❑1, Aug 90, nn 4.95

X-FARCE
ECLIPSE

Value: Cover or less ❑1, Jan 92, b&w; parody 2.50

X-FARCE VS. X-CONS: X-TINCTION
PARODY PRESS

Value: Cover or less ❑1.5 .... 2.75

❑1 .... 2.75

X-FILES, THE
TOPPS

	ORIG	GOOD	FINE	N-MINT
❑-2, Sep 96, Trick of the Light; The Pit,no cover price; Reprint	10.00	1.00	2.50	5.00
❑-1, Sep 96, A Trick of the Light,no cover price; Reprint	10.00	1.00	2.50	5.00
❑0/A,forms diptych with Scully cover; adapts pilot episode	3.95	0.80	2.00	4.00
❑0/B,forms diptych with Mulder cover; adapts pilot episode	3.95	0.80	2.00	4.00
❑0/C,Scully and Mulder cover; adapts pilot episode	3.95	0.80	2.00	4.00
❑0.5, Tiptoe Through the Tulpa, Wizard promotional edition	5.00	2.00	5.00	10.00
❑1, Jan 95, Do Not Open Until X-Mas	2.95	1.60	4.00	8.00
❑1-2, Do Not Open Until X-Mas	2.50	0.50	1.25	2.50
❑2, Feb 95, Disremembrance of Things Past	2.95	1.00	2.50	5.00
❑3, Mar 95, The Return	2.95	0.80	2.00	4.00
❑3-2, The Return	2.50	0.50	1.25	2.50
❑4, Apr 95, Firebird, Part 1	2.95	0.70	1.75	3.50
❑4-2, Firebird, Part 2	2.50	0.50	1.25	2.50
❑5, May 95, Firebird, Part 2	2.95	0.60	1.50	3.00
❑6, Jun 95, Firebird, Part 3	2.95	0.60	1.50	3.00
❑7, Jul 95	2.95	0.60	1.50	3.00
❑8, Aug 95, Silent Cities of the Mind, Part 1	2.95	0.60	1.50	3.00
❑9, Sep 95, Silent Cities of the Mind, Part 2	2.95	0.60	1.50	3.00
❑10, Oct 95, Feelings of Unreality, Part 1	2.95	0.60	1.50	3.00
❑11, Nov 95, Feelings of Unreality, Part 2	2.95	0.60	1.50	3.00
❑12, Feelings of Unreality, Part 3	2.95	0.60	1.50	3.00
❑13, Feb 96	2.95	0.60	1.50	3.00
❑14, Apr 96	2.95	0.60	1.50	3.00
❑15, May 96, Home of the Brave, Part 1	2.95	0.60	1.50	3.00
❑16, May 96, Home of the Brave, Part 2	2.95	0.60	1.50	3.00
❑17, May 96, Thin Air	2.95	0.60	1.50	3.00
❑18, Jun 96, Night Lights, Part 1	2.95	0.60	1.50	3.00
❑19, Jun 96, Night Lights, Part 2	2.95	0.60	1.50	3.00
❑20, Jul 96, Family Portrait, Part 1: Gallery	2.95	0.60	1.50	3.00
❑21, Aug 96, Family Portrait, Part 2: The Camera Eye	2.95	0.60	1.50	3.00

	ORIG	GOOD	FINE	N-MINT
❑22, Sep 96, The Kanashibari	2.95	0.59	1.48	2.95
❑23, Nov 96, Donor,Donor	2.95	0.59	1.48	2.95
❑24, Dec 96, Silver Lining	2.95	0.59	1.48	2.95
❑25, Jan 97, Be Prepared, Part 1	2.95	0.59	1.48	2.95
❑26, Feb 97, Be Prepared, Part 2	2.95	0.59	1.48	2.95
❑27, Mar 97, Remote Control, Part 1	2.95	0.59	1.48	2.95
❑28, Apr 97, Remote Control, Part 2	2.95	0.59	1.48	2.95
❑29, May 97, Remote Control Conclusion	2.95	0.59	1.48	2.95
❑30, Jun 97, Surrounded, Part 1	2.95	0.59	1.48	2.95
❑31, Jul 97, Surrounded, Part 2	2.95	0.59	1.48	2.95
❑32	2.95	0.59	1.48	2.95
❑33, Soma	2.95	0.59	1.48	2.95
❑33/SC, Soma,Variant photo cover	—	1.00	2.50	5.00
❑34	2.95	0.59	1.48	2.95
❑35	2.95	0.59	1.48	2.95
❑36	2.95	0.59	1.48	2.95
❑37	2.95	0.59	1.48	2.95
❑38, Cam Ranh Bay	2.95	0.59	1.48	2.95
❑39, Scum of the Earth	2.95	0.59	1.48	2.95
❑40, Devil's Advocate	2.95	0.59	1.48	2.95
❑41	2.95	0.59	1.48	2.95
❑41/SC,Photo cover	2.95	0.59	1.48	2.95
❑Anl 1, Aug 95	3.95	0.79	1.98	3.95
❑Anl 2,E.L.F.s	3.95	0.79	1.98	3.95
❑Ash 1, Jan 95, nn; 14pgs.; no cover price; polybagged with Star Wars Galaxy #2	—	0.80	2.00	4.00
❑SE 1, Jun 95,reprints issues #1 and 2	3.95	0.99	2.47	4.95
❑SE 2, Firebird; Picasso Summer,Reprints X-Files #4-6	3.95	0.99	2.47	4.95
❑SE 3, Trepanning Opera; Silent Cities of the Mind,Reprints X-Files #7-9	3.95	0.99	2.47	4.95
❑SE 4, Nov 96, Feelings of Unreality,reprints Feelings of Unreality	4.95	0.99	2.47	4.95
❑SE 5,Reprints X-Files #13, Annual #1	—	0.99	2.47	4.95

X-FILES COMICS DIGEST, THE
TOPPS

Value: Cover or less

- ❑1, Dec 95, Big Foot, Warm Heart; The Visitor,Bradbury back-up stories 3.50
- ❑2, Apr 96, AW, The Count Saint-Germain Goes West; it Burns Me Up,Bradbury back-up stories 3.50
- ❑3, Sep 96, The Wee Folk,Bradbury back-up stories 3.95

X-FILES GROUND ZERO, THE
TOPPS

Value: Cover or less

- ❑1, Dec 97,adapts Kevin J. Anderson novel 2.95
- ❑2, Jan 98,adapts Kevin J. Anderson novel 2.95
- ❑3, Feb 98,adapts Kevin J. Anderson novel 2.95
- ❑4 ...... 2.95

X-FILES, THE: SEASON ONE
TOPPS

Value: Cover or less

- ❑1, Jul 97, Pilot Episode, prestige format; adapts pilot episode 4.95
- ❑2, Dec 97, Deep Throat, prestige format 4.95
- ❑3 ...... 4.95
- ❑4 ...... 4.95
- ❑5 ...... 4.95
- ❑6 ...... 4.95
- ❑7 ...... 4.95
- ❑8 ...... 4.95

X-FLIES BUG HUNT
TWIST AND SHOUT

Value: Cover or less

- ❑1, Dec 96, Vampires 2.95
- ❑2, Monsters 2.95
- ❑3, Aliens 2.95
- ❑4, The Truth 2.95

X-FLIES CONSPIRACY
TWIST AND SHOUT

Value: Cover or less

- ❑1, Mar 96 ...... 2.95

X-FLIES SPECIAL
TWIST AND SHOUT

Value: Cover or less

- ❑1, Sep 95, X-Flies; Bobby Ruckers 2.95

X-FORCE
MARVEL

	ORIG	GOOD	FINE	N-MINT
❑-1, Jul 97, AM, The Brothers Proudstar,Flashback; Proudstars team up	1.99	0.40	1.00	2.00
❑1/A, Aug 91, 1: G.W. Bridge,with Cable card	1.50	0.40	1.00	2.00
❑1/B, Aug 91, 1: G.W. Bridge,with Deadpool card	1.50	0.40	1.00	2.00
❑1/C, Aug 91, 1: G.W. Bridge,with Shatterstar card	1.50	0.40	1.00	2.00
❑1/D, Aug 91, 1: G.W. Bridge,with Sunspot & Gideon card	1.50	0.40	1.00	2.00
❑1/E, Aug 91, 1: G.W. Bridge,with X-Force group card	1.50	0.40	1.00	2.00
❑1-2, Aug 91,2nd Printing; Gold cover	1.50	0.30	0.75	1.50
❑2, Sep 91, RL, 1: Weapon X II (Garrison Kane)	1.00	0.50	1.25	2.50
❑3, Oct 91, RL, V: Juggernaut	1.00	0.40	1.00	2.00
❑4, Nov 91, A: Spider-Man,Sideways printing	1.00	0.40	1.00	2.00
❑5, Dec 91,Return of Brotherhood of Evil Mutants	1.00	0.40	1.00	2.00
❑6, Jan 92	1.00	0.40	1.00	2.00
❑7, Feb 92	1.25	0.40	1.00	2.00
❑8, Mar 92, 1: Grizzly II	1.25	0.40	1.00	2.00
❑9, Apr 92	1.25	0.40	1.00	2.00
❑10, May 92	1.25	0.40	1.00	2.00
❑11, Jun 92	1.25	0.40	1.00	2.00
❑12, Jul 92, RL (w), Traitors to the Cause	1.25	0.40	1.00	2.00
❑13, Aug 92	1.25	0.40	1.00	2.00
❑14, Sep 92, Payback!	1.25	0.40	1.00	2.00
❑15, Oct 92, To the Pain	1.25	0.40	1.00	2.00
❑16/CS, Nov 92, X-Cutioner's Song; X-Cutioner's Song, Part 4, Cable card	1.50	0.40	1.00	2.00
❑17/CS, Dec 92, X-Cutioner's Song, Part 8, O: Stryfe; O: Zero, trading card	1.50	0.40	1.00	2.00
❑18/CS, Jan 93, X-Cutioner's Song, Part 12, trading card	1.50	0.40	1.00	2.00
❑19, Feb 93, The Open Hand, the Closed Fist	1.25	0.30	0.75	1.50
❑20, Mar 93, Assault on Graymalkin	1.25	0.30	0.75	1.50
❑21, Apr 93	1.25	0.30	0.75	1.50
❑22, May 93, Ordinance Weighed in Blood	1.25	0.30	0.75	1.50
❑23, Jun 93, Compromising Positions	1.25	0.30	0.75	1.50
❑24, Jul 93	1.25	0.30	0.75	1.50
❑25, Aug 93,Hologram cover	3.50	0.80	2.00	4.00
❑26, Sep 93	1.25	0.30	0.75	1.50
❑27, Oct 93, A: Mutant Liberation Front	1.25	0.30	0.75	1.50
❑28, Nov 93	1.25	0.30	0.75	1.50
❑29, Dec 93, Toy Soldiers, A: Arcade	1.25	0.30	0.75	1.50
❑30, Jan 94	1.25	0.30	0.75	1.50
❑31, Feb 94	1.25	0.25	0.63	1.25
❑32, Mar 94, Child's Play	1.25	0.25	0.63	1.25
❑33, Apr 94	1.25	0.25	0.63	1.25
❑34, May 94	1.50	0.30	0.75	1.50
❑35, Jun 94, V: Nimrod	1.50	0.30	0.75	1.50
❑36, Jul 94	1.50	0.30	0.75	1.50
❑37, Aug 94	1.50	0.30	0.75	1.50
❑38, Sep 94, Life Signs, Part 2	2.00	0.40	1.00	2.00
❑38/SC, Sep 94, Life Signs, Part 2,enhanced cover	2.95	0.60	1.50	3.00
❑39, Oct 94	1.50	0.30	0.75	1.50
❑40, Nov 94	1.50	0.30	0.75	1.50
❑40/Dlx, Nov 94, Deluxe edition	1.95	0.39	0.98	1.95
❑41, Dec 94	1.50	0.30	0.75	1.50
❑41/Dlx, Dec 94, Deluxe edition	1.95	0.39	0.98	1.95
❑42, Jan 95	1.50	0.30	0.75	1.50
❑42/Dlx, Jan 95, Deluxe edition	1.95	0.39	0.98	1.95
❑43, Feb 95	1.95	0.30	0.75	1.50
❑43/Dlx, Deluxe edition	1.95	0.39	0.98	1.95
❑44, Jul 95,Cannonball to join X-Men leaves team	1.95	0.39	0.98	1.95
❑45, Aug 95	1.95	0.39	0.98	1.95
❑46, Sep 95, V: Mimic	1.95	0.39	0.98	1.95
❑47, Oct 95	1.95	0.39	0.98	1.95
❑48, Nov 95	1.95	0.39	0.98	1.95
❑49, Dec 95, JPH (w), A: Sebastian Shaw; A: Holocaust	1.50	0.30	0.75	1.50
❑49/Dlx, Dec 95, JPH (w), Direct Edition	1.95	0.39	0.98	1.95
❑50, Jan 96, JPH (w), Target: Cable,wrap-around fold-out cover; Giant-size	2.95	0.59	1.48	2.95
❑50/A, JPH (w),Variant cover by Rob Liefeld; Giant-size	2.95	0.60	1.50	3.00
❑50/SC, Jan 96, JPH (w),Special cover; Giant-size	3.95	1.00	2.50	5.00
❑51, Feb 96, JPH (w), 1: Meltdown (formerly Boomer/Boom Boom)	1.95	0.39	0.98	1.95
❑52, Mar 96, JPH (w), Bad Girls, D: Gideon; V: Blob	1.95	0.39	0.98	1.95
❑53, Apr 96	1.95	0.39	0.98	1.95
❑54, May 96	1.95	0.39	0.98	1.95
❑55, Jun 96, V: S.H.I.E.L.D.	1.95	0.39	0.98	1.95
❑56, Jul 96, JPH (w), In the Company of Strangers, Part 1	1.95	0.39	0.98	1.95
❑57, Aug 96, JPH (w), In the Company of Strangers, Part 2; Onslaught: Impact, Part 1	1.95	0.39	0.98	1.95
❑58, Sep 96, JPH (w), Onslaught: Impact 2	1.95	0.39	0.98	1.95
❑59, Oct 96, JPH (w),bound-in trading cards	1.95	0.39	0.98	1.95
❑60, Nov 96, JPH (w)	1.95	0.39	0.98	1.95
❑61, Dec 96, JPH (w), O: Shatterstar	1.95	0.39	0.98	1.95
❑62, Jan 97, Human Nature	1.95	0.39	0.98	1.95
❑63, Feb 97, Wish You Were Here,team invades Doom's castle	1.95	0.39	0.98	1.95
❑64, Mar 97, The Haunting of Castle Doom!, A: Baron Von Strucker	1.95	0.39	0.98	1.95
❑65, Apr 97, Lower East Side Story	1.95	0.39	0.98	1.95
❑66, May 97, Tragic Kingdom	1.95	0.39	0.98	1.95
❑67, Jun 97,return of Dani Moonstar	1.95	0.39	0.98	1.95

	ORIG	GOOD	FINE	N-MINT
❑68, Aug 97, Operation: Zero Tolerance, A: Vanisher, gatefold summary	1.99	0.40	1.00	1.99
❑69, Sep 97, Operation: Zero Tolerance, gatefold summary	1.99	0.40	1.00	1.99
❑70, Oct 97, gatefold summary	1.99	0.40	1.00	1.99
❑71, Nov 97, gatefold summary	1.99	0.40	1.00	1.99
❑72, Dec 97, gatefold summary	1.99	0.40	1.00	1.99
❑73, Jan 98, D: Warpath, gatefold summary	1.99	0.40	1.00	1.99
❑74, Feb 98, V: Stryfe, gatefold summary	1.99	0.40	1.00	1.99
❑75, Mar 98, A: Cannonball,wraparound cover; gatefold summary	2.99	0.40	1.00	1.99
❑76, Apr 98, gatefold summary; Domino vs. Shatterstar	1.99	0.40	1.00	1.99
❑77, May 98, gatefold summary	1.99	0.40	1.00	1.99
❑78, Jun 98, gatefold summary	1.99	0.40	1.00	1.99
❑79, Jul 98, O: Reignfire, gatefold summary	1.99	0.40	1.00	1.99
❑80, Aug 98, gatefold summary	1.99	0.40	1.00	1.99
❑81, Sep 98, gatefold summary; poster	1.99	0.40	1.00	1.99
❑82, Oct 98, gatefold summary	1.99	0.40	1.00	1.99
❑83, Nov 98, gatefold summary	1.99	0.40	1.00	1.99
❑84, Dec 98, V: New Deviants, gatefold summary	1.99	0.40	1.00	1.99
❑85, Jan 99, gatefold summary	1.99	0.40	1.00	1.99
❑86, Jan 99, gatefold summary	1.99	0.40	1.00	1.99
❑87, Feb 99, A: Hellions	1.99	0.40	1.00	1.99
❑88, Mar 99, A: Hellions; A: Christopher Bedlam; V: New Hellions	1.99	0.40	1.00	1.99
❑89, Apr 99, A: Hellions; A: Armageddon Man	1.99	0.40	1.00	1.99
❑90, May 99	1.99	0.40	1.00	1.99
❑91, Jun 99,Siryn solo tale	1.99	0.40	1.00	1.99
❑92, Jul 99,Domino vs. Halloween Jack	1.99	0.40	1.00	1.99
❑93, Aug 99	1.99	0.40	1.00	1.99
❑94, Sep 99	1.99	0.40	1.00	1.99
❑96, Nov 99	1.99	0.40	1.00	1.99
❑97, Dec 99	1.99	0.40	1.00	1.99
❑98	—	0.45	1.13	2.25
❑99	—	0.45	1.13	2.25
❑100	—	0.60	1.50	2.99
❑101	—	0.45	1.13	2.25
❑102	—	0.45	1.13	2.25
❑103	—	0.45	1.13	2.25
❑104	—	0.45	1.13	2.25
❑105	—	0.45	1.13	2.25
❑106	—	0.45	1.13	2.25
❑107	2.25	0.45	1.13	2.25
❑108, Nov 00, Shockwave, Part 3; Murder Ballads, Part 3	2.25	0.45	1.13	2.25
❑109, Nov 00, Shockwave, Part 4; Murder Ballads, Part 4	2.25	0.45	1.13	2.25
❑110, Jan 01, Rage War, Part 1	2.25	0.45	1.13	2.25
❑111, Feb 01, Rage War, Part 2	2.25	0.45	1.13	2.25
❑112, Mar 01, Rage War, Part 3	2.25	0.45	1.13	2.25
❑113, Apr 01, Rage War, Part 4	2.25	0.45	1.13	2.25
❑114	2.25	0.45	1.13	2.25
❑115	2.25	0.45	1.13	2.25
❑116	2.25	0.45	1.13	2.25
❑117	2.25	0.45	1.13	2.25
❑118	2.25	0.45	1.13	2.25
❑Anl 1, Shattershot, Part 4; The Crush,Shattershot	2.25	0.50	1.25	2.50
❑Anl 2, 1: Stronghold; 1: X-Treme; 1: Neurotap,Polybagged with trading card	2.95	0.59	1.48	2.95
❑Anl 3	2.95	0.59	1.48	2.95
❑Anl 1995, Dec 95,wraparound cover; X-Force and Cable '95	3.95	0.79	1.98	3.95
❑Anl 1996, Transmission; DTnouement,wraparound cover; X-Force and Cable '96	2.99	0.60	1.50	2.99
❑Anl 1997,wraparound cover; X-Force and Cable '97; return of Asgard	2.99	0.60	1.50	2.99
❑Anl 1998,wraparound cover; gatefold summary; X-Force/Champions '98	3.50	0.70	1.75	3.50
❑Anl 1999	3.50	0.70	1.75	3.50

X-FORCE/YOUNGBLOOD
MARVEL

Value: Cover or less

❑1, Aug 96,crossover with Image; prestige format one-shot 4.95

XIMOS: VIOLENT PAST
TRIUMPHANT

Value: Cover or less

❑1, Mar 94 ..... 2.50

❑2, Mar 94 ..... 2.50

XIOLA
XERO

	ORIG	GOOD	FINE	N-MINT
❑0	1.95	0.39	0.98	1.95
❑1, Django; Azhbane, b&w	1.95	0.39	0.98	1.95
❑2, Django; Azhbane, b&w	1.95	0.39	0.98	1.95
❑3, Django; Azhbane	1.95	0.39	0.98	1.95
❑Ash 1, b&w; no cover price	—	0.20	0.50	1.00

G.W. Bridge made his first appearance in *X-Force* #1.

XL
BLACKTHORNE

Value: Cover or less

❑1, b&w 3.50

X-LAX
THWACK! POW!

Value: Cover or less

❑1, It All Comes Out in the End!,Mini-Comic 1.25

X-MAN
MARVEL

	ORIG	GOOD	FINE	N-MINT
❑-1, Jul 97, Breeding Ground,Flashback	1.99	0.40	1.00	2.00
❑1, Mar 95	1.95	0.80	2.00	4.00
❑1-2,2nd Printing	1.95	0.45	1.13	2.25
❑2, Apr 95	1.95	0.50	1.25	2.50
❑3, May 95	1.95	0.50	1.25	2.50
❑4, Jun 95	1.95	0.50	1.25	2.50
❑5, Jul 95	1.95	0.40	1.00	2.00
❑6, Aug 95	1.95	0.40	1.00	2.00
❑7, Sep 95	1.95	0.40	1.00	2.00
❑8, Oct 95	1.95	0.40	1.00	2.00
❑9, Nov 95	1.95	0.40	1.00	2.00
❑10, Dec 95, JPH (w), V: Xavier	1.95	0.40	1.00	2.00
❑11, Jan 96, A: Rogue	1.95	0.39	0.98	1.95
❑12, Feb 96, V: Excalibur	1.95	0.39	0.98	1.95
❑13, Mar 96, The Hunted Below	1.95	0.39	0.98	1.95
❑14, Apr 96, Fallen From Grace	1.95	0.39	0.98	1.95
❑15, May 96	1.95	0.50	1.25	2.50
❑16, Jun 96, V: Holocaust	1.95	0.40	1.00	2.00
❑17, Jul 96, V: Holocaust	1.95	0.40	1.00	2.00
❑18, Aug 96	1.95	0.39	0.98	1.95
❑19, Sep 96, Onslaught: Phase 2, A: Mr. Sinister	1.95	0.39	0.98	1.95
❑20, Oct 96, V: Abomination,bound-in trading cards	1.95	0.39	0.98	1.95
❑21, Nov 96	1.95	0.39	0.98	1.95
❑22, Dec 96	1.95	0.39	0.98	1.95
❑23, Jan 97, Crash Course	1.95	0.39	0.98	1.95
❑24, Feb 97, First Noel, V: Morbius; A: Spider-Man	1.95	0.39	0.98	1.95
❑25, Mar 97, Closer to the Flame, A: Madelyne Pryor,wraparound cover; Giant-size	2.99	0.60	1.50	2.99
❑26, Apr 97, Down to Earth	1.95	0.39	0.98	1.95
❑27, May 97, Blood Brothers	1.95	0.39	0.98	1.95
❑28, Jun 97, Dance With the Devil	1.95	0.39	0.98	1.95
❑29, Aug 97, gatefold summary	1.99	0.39	0.98	1.95
❑30, Sep 97, gatefold summary	1.99	0.39	0.98	1.95
❑31, Oct 97, gatefold summary	1.99	0.40	1.00	1.99
❑32, Nov 97, gatefold summary	1.99	0.40	1.00	1.99
❑33, Dec 97, gatefold summary	1.99	0.40	1.00	1.99
❑34, Jan 98, gatefold summary	1.99	0.40	1.00	1.99
❑35, Feb 98, gatefold summary	1.99	0.40	1.00	1.99
❑36, Mar 98, gatefold summary	1.99	0.40	1.00	1.99
❑37, Apr 98, gatefold summary; Spider-Man	1.99	0.40	1.00	1.99
❑38, May 98, gatefold summary; Spider-Man	1.99	0.40	1.00	1.99
❑39, Jun 98, gatefold summary	1.99	0.40	1.00	1.99
❑40, Jul 98, gatefold summary	1.99	0.40	1.00	1.99
❑41, Aug 98, A: Madelyne Pryor, gatefold summary	1.99	0.40	1.00	1.99
❑42, Sep 98, gatefold summary	1.99	0.40	1.00	1.99
❑43, Oct 98, gatefold summary	1.99	0.40	1.00	1.99
❑44, Nov 98, V: Nemesis, gatefold summary	1.99	0.40	1.00	1.99
❑45, Dec 98, Blood Brothers, gatefold summary	1.99	0.40	1.00	1.99
❑46, Dec 98, Blood Brothers, gatefold summary	1.99	0.40	1.00	1.99
❑47, Jan 99, Blood Brothers, gatefold summary	1.99	0.40	1.00	1.99
❑48, Feb 99, The Blood of the Righteous	1.99	0.40	1.00	1.99
❑49, Mar 99	1.99	0.40	1.00	1.99
❑50, Apr 99, War of the Mutants, part 2, A: White Queen; A: Dark Beast,Story continues from Generation X #50	2.99	0.40	1.00	1.99

	ORIG	GOOD	FINE	N-MINT
❑51, May 99	1.99	0.40	1.00	1.99
❑52, Jun 99	1.99	0.40	1.00	1.99
❑53, Jul 99, A: Jean Grey; A: Cyclops	1.99	0.40	1.00	1.99
❑54, Aug 99	1.99	0.40	1.00	1.99
❑55, Sep 99	1.99	0.40	1.00	1.99
❑56, Oct 99	1.99	0.40	1.00	1.99
❑57, Nov 99	1.99	0.40	1.00	1.99
❑58, Dec 99	1.99	0.45	1.13	2.25
❑59	—	0.45	1.13	2.25
❑60	—	0.45	1.13	2.25
❑61	—	0.45	1.13	2.25
❑62	—	0.45	1.13	2.25
❑63	—	0.45	1.13	2.25
❑64	—	0.45	1.13	2.25
❑65	—	0.45	1.13	2.25
❑66	—	0.45	1.13	2.25
❑67, Sep 00, Shockwave, Part 1; The Infinities of Evil, Part 1: Further Down the Spiral	2.25	0.45	1.13	2.25
❑68, Oct 00, Shockwave, Part 2	2.25	0.45	1.13	2.25
❑69, Nov 00, Shockwave, Part 3; The Infinities of Evil, Part 3: Double Vision,polybagged with AOL CD-ROM	2.25	0.45	1.13	2.25
❑70, Dec 00, Shockwave, Part 4; The Infinities of Evil, Part 4: Worlds Without End	2.25	0.45	1.13	2.25
❑71, Jan 01, Fearful Symmetries, Part 1	2.25	0.45	1.13	2.25
❑72, Feb 01, Fearful Symmetries, Part 2	2.25	0.45	1.13	2.25
❑73, Mar 01, Fearful Symmetries, Part 3	2.25	0.45	1.13	2.25
❑74, Apr 01, Fearful Symmetries, Part 4	2.25	0.45	1.13	2.25
❑75, May 01, Till the End of the World, double-sized	2.99	0.60	1.50	2.99
❑Anl 1996, Sins of the Father; Mind Games, nn; wraparound cover	2.99	0.59	1.48	2.95
❑Anl 1997, A: Dark Beast; A: Nemesis; A: Sugar Man, nn; wraparound cover	2.99	0.60	1.50	2.99
❑Anl 1998, Call of the Wild, V: Thanos, nn; wraparound cover; X-Man/Hulk '98	2.99	0.60	1.50	2.99

X-MEN (1ST SERIES)

MARVEL

	ORIG	GOOD	FINE	N-MINT
❑1, Sep 63, JK, SL (w), X-Men, 1: Beast; 1: Magneto; 1: Iceman; 1: Marvel Girl; 1: Angel II; 1: Professor X; 1: Cyclops; 1: X-Men	0.12	1220.00	3050.00	6100.00
❑2, Nov 63, JK, SL (w), No One Can Stop the Vanisher, 1: Vanisher; 1: The Vanisher	0.12	360.00	900.00	1800.00
❑3, Jan 64, JK, SL (w), Beware of the Blob, 1: The Blob	0.12	145.00	362.50	725.00
❑4, Mar 64, JK, SL (w), 1: Brotherhood of Evil Mutants; 1: Quicksilver; 1: Scarlet Witch; 1: Mastermind; 1: Toad	0.12	130.00	325.00	650.00
❑5, May 64, JK, SL (w), A: Evil Mutants	0.12	92.00	230.00	460.00
❑6, Jul 64, JK, SL (w), A: Sub-Mariner; A: Evil Mutants	0.12	68.00	170.00	340.00
❑7, Sep 64, JK, SL (w), A: Evil Mutants; A: Blob	0.12	60.00	150.00	300.00
❑8, Nov 64, JK, SL (w), 1: Unus the Untouchable	0.12	60.00	150.00	300.00
❑9, Jan 65, JK, SL (w), 1: Lucifer	0.12	60.00	150.00	300.00
❑10, Mar 65, JK, SL (w), A: Ka-Zar	0.12	60.00	150.00	300.00
❑11, May 65, JK, SL (w), 1: Stranger; 1: The Stranger	0.12	52.00	130.00	260.00
❑12, Jul 65, JK, SL (w), 1: Juggernaut; O: Professor X	0.12	70.00	175.00	350.00
❑13, Sep 65, JK, SL (w), V: Juggernaut	0.12	48.00	120.00	240.00
❑14, Nov 65, JK, SL (w), 1: Sentinels	0.12	55.00	137.50	275.00
❑15, Dec 65, JK, SL (w), O: Beast	0.12	46.00	115.00	230.00
❑16, Jan 66, JK, SL (w), The Supreme Sacrifice!, A: Master Mold; A: Sentinels	0.12	46.00	115.00	230.00
❑17, Feb 66, JK, SL (w), ...And None Shall Survive!, V: Magneto	0.12	26.00	65.00	130.00
❑18, Mar 66, JK (c), SL (w), If Iceman Should Fail!, A: Stranger; V: Magneto	0.12	26.00	65.00	130.00
❑19, Apr 66, JK (c), 1: Mimic	0.12	26.00	65.00	130.00
❑20, May 66, JK (c), V: Lucifer; V: Unus	0.12	26.00	65.00	130.00
❑21, Jun 66, JK (c), V: Lucifer	0.12	22.00	55.00	110.00
❑22, Jul 66, JK (c), Divided - We Fall!, V: Count Nefaria	0.12	22.00	55.00	110.00
❑23, Aug 66, To Save a City, V: Count Nefaria	0.12	22.00	55.00	110.00
❑24, Sep 66, JK (c)	0.12	22.00	55.00	110.00
❑25, Oct 66, JK (c), The Power and the Pendant!, A: El Tigre	0.12	22.00	55.00	110.00
❑26, Nov 66, JK (c)	0.12	22.00	55.00	110.00
❑27, Dec 66, JK (c), Re-enter: The Mimic!, V: Puppet Master,Mimic returns	0.12	22.00	55.00	110.00
❑28, Jan 67, JK (c), 1: Banshee	0.12	30.00	75.00	150.00
❑28-2, 1: Banshee,2nd Printing	0.12	0.40	1.00	2.00
❑29, Feb 67, JK (c), V: Super-Adaptoid	0.12	22.00	55.00	110.00
❑30, Mar 67, JK (c), The Warlock Wakes!, 1: Maha Yogi	0.12	22.00	55.00	110.00
❑31, Apr 67, JK (c), 1: Cobalt Man	0.12	16.00	40.00	80.00
❑32, May 67, JK (c), V: Juggernaut	0.12	16.00	40.00	80.00
❑33, Jun 67, GK (c), V: Juggernaut	0.12	16.00	40.00	80.00
❑34, Jul 67, DA, V: Mole Man; V: Tyrannus	0.12	16.00	40.00	80.00
❑35, Aug 67, JK (c), A: Banshee; 1: Changeling; A: Spider-Man	0.12	22.00	55.00	110.00
❑36, Sep 67, RA, 1: Mekano	0.12	16.00	40.00	80.00
❑37, Oct 67, RA, JK (c); DH (c), V: Factor Three	0.12	16.00	40.00	80.00
❑38, Nov 67, DH, DA (c), V: Vanisher; V: Blob; V: Blob, Vanisher, The Origins of the X-Men back-ups begin	0.12	20.00	50.00	100.00
❑39, Dec 67, DH, GT (c), D: Mutant-Master	0.12	16.00	40.00	80.00
❑40, Jan 68, DH, GT (c), V: Frankenstein	0.12	16.00	40.00	80.00
❑41, Feb 68, DH, 1: Grotesk the Sub-Human	0.12	14.00	35.00	70.00
❑42, Mar 68, DH, JB (c), V: Grotesk; D: Changeling (disguised as Professor X)	0.12	14.00	35.00	70.00
❑43, Apr 68, GT, JB (c), The Torch is Passed ... !, V: Brotherhood of Evil Mutants	0.12	14.00	35.00	70.00
❑44, May 68, DH, Red Raven, Red Raven ...!, A: Magneto; O: Iceman; O: Red Raven; 1: Red Raven (in modern age),Return of Red Raven	0.12	14.00	35.00	70.00
❑45, Jun 68, DH, GT (c); JB (c), V: Evil Mutants; O: Iceman	0.12	14.00	35.00	70.00
❑46, Jul 68, DH, V: Juggernaut; O: Iceman	0.12	14.00	35.00	70.00
❑47, Aug 68, DH, V: Maha Yogi	0.12	14.00	35.00	70.00
❑48, Sep 68, DH, SB (c), Beware Computo Commander of the Robot Hive!, V: Quasimodo	0.12	14.00	35.00	70.00
❑49, Oct 68, JSo; DH, 1: Polaris; 1: Mesmero; 1: Mesmero, Lorna Dane	0.12	15.00	37.50	75.00
❑50, Nov 68, JSo, V: Mesmero	0.12	15.00	37.50	75.00
❑51, Dec 68, JSo, V: Mesmero	0.12	15.00	37.50	75.00
❑52, Jan 69, DH, O: Lorna Dane	0.12	10.00	25.00	50.00
❑53, Feb 69, V: Blastaar,Barry Windsor-Smith's 1st comic book art	0.12	12.00	30.00	60.00
❑54, Mar 69, DH, 1: Living Pharaoh; 1: Alex Summers (Havok); O: Havok	0.12	12.00	30.00	60.00
❑55, Apr 69, DH, O: Havok	0.12	12.00	30.00	60.00
❑56, May 69, NA, V: Living Monolith,Living Pharaoh becomes Living Monolith	0.12	12.00	30.00	60.00
❑57, Jun 69, NA, 1: Mark II Sentinels	0.12	12.00	30.00	60.00
❑58, Jul 69, NA, 1: Havok (in costume)	0.15	16.00	40.00	80.00
❑59, Aug 69, NA, 1: Dr. Karl Lykos	0.15	11.00	27.50	55.00
❑60, Sep 69, NA, 1: Sauron	0.15	12.00	30.00	60.00
❑61, Oct 69, NA, V: Sauron	0.15	12.00	30.00	60.00
❑62, Nov 69, NA, Strangers in a Savage Land!, 1: Barbarus; 1: Lupo; 1: Piper; A: Ka-Zar	0.15	12.00	30.00	60.00
❑62-2, NA, Strangers in a Savage Land!, 1: Barbarus; 1: Lupo; 1: Piper; A: Ka-Zar	0.15	0.30	0.75	1.50
❑63, Dec 69, NA, O: Lupo; V: Magneto; O: Piper; A: Ka-Zar	0.15	12.00	30.00	60.00
❑64, Jan 70, DH, SB (c), The Coming of Sun-Fire, 1: Sunfire	0.15	12.00	30.00	60.00
❑65, Feb 70, NA, A: Havok, SHIELD, Fantastic Four; D: Changeling (revealed)	0.15	12.00	30.00	60.00
❑66, Mar 70, SB, A: Hulk; A: Havok	0.15	10.00	25.00	50.00
❑67, Dec 70,reprints stories from X-Men #12 and 13	0.25	5.00	12.50	25.00
❑68, Feb 71,reprints stories from X-Men #14 and 15	0.25	5.00	12.50	25.00
❑69, Apr 71,reprints stories from X-Men #16 and 19	0.25	5.00	12.50	25.00
❑70, Jun 71,reprints stories from X-Men #17 and 18	0.25	5.00	12.50	25.00
❑71, Aug 71,reprints X-Men #20	0.15	5.00	12.50	25.00
❑72, Oct 71,reprints stories from X-Men #21 and 24	0.25	5.00	12.50	25.00
❑73, Dec 71,reprints X-Men #25	0.20	5.00	12.50	25.00
❑74, Feb 72, GK (c),reprints X-Men #26	0.20	5.00	12.50	25.00
❑75, Apr 72,reprints X-Men #27	0.20	5.00	12.50	25.00
❑76, Jun 72, GK (c),reprints X-Men #28	0.20	5.00	12.50	25.00
❑77, Aug 72,reprints X-Men #29	0.20	5.00	12.50	25.00
❑78, Oct 72, GK (c),reprints X-Men #30	0.20	5.00	12.50	25.00
❑79, Dec 72, GK (c),reprints X-Men #31	0.20	5.00	12.50	25.00
❑80, Feb 73, GK (c),reprints X-Men #32	0.20	5.00	12.50	25.00
❑81, Apr 73,reprints X-Men #33	0.20	5.00	12.50	25.00
❑82, Jun 73,reprints X-Men #34	0.20	5.00	12.50	25.00
❑83, Aug 73,reprints X-Men #35	0.20	5.00	12.50	25.00
❑84, Oct 73,reprints X-Men #36	0.20	5.00	12.50	25.00
❑85, Dec 73,reprints X-Men #37	0.20	5.00	12.50	25.00
❑86, Feb 74,reprints stories from X-Men #38 and Amazing Adult Fantasy #2	0.20	5.00	12.50	25.00
❑87, Apr 74,reprints stories from X-Men #39 and Amazing Adult Fantasy #10	0.20	5.00	12.50	25.00
❑88, Jun 74,reprints X-Men #40	0.25	5.00	12.50	25.00
❑89, Aug 74,reprints stories from X-Men #41 and Amazing Adult Fantasy #11	0.25	5.00	12.50	25.00

	ORIG	GOOD	FINE	N-MINT
❑90, Oct 74,reprints stories from X-Men #42 and Amazing Adult Fantasy #7	0.25	5.00	12.50	25.00
❑91, Dec 74,reprints stories from X-Men #43 and Amazing Adult Fantasy #7	0.25	5.00	12.50	25.00
❑92, Feb 75,reprints stories from X-Men #44 and Mystery Tales #30	0.25	5.00	12.50	25.00
❑93, Apr 75,reprints stories from X-Men #45 and Journey Into Mystery #74	0.25	5.00	12.50	25.00
❑94, Aug 75, BMc; DC, GK (c), 1: New X-Men, New X-Men begin (from Giant-Size X-Men #1); Old X-Men leave	0.25	105.00	262.50	525.00
❑95, Oct 75, DC, GK (c), D: Thunderbird	0.25	20.00	50.00	100.00
❑96, Dec 75, DC, 1: Moira MacTaggart; 1: Doctor Moira MacTaggert	0.25	16.00	40.00	80.00
❑97, Feb 76, DC, RB (c), 1: Lilandra Neramani,Cyclops vs. Havok	0.25	14.00	35.00	70.00
❑98, Apr 76, DC, A: Matt Murdock; A: Nick Fury; V: Sentinels	0.25	14.00	35.00	70.00
❑99, Jun 76, DC, 1: Black Tom Cassidy	0.25	14.00	35.00	70.00
❑100, Aug 76, DC ,Old X-Men vs. New X-Men	0.25	16.00	40.00	80.00
❑101, Oct 76, DC, A: Juggernaut; 1: Phoenix; 1: Phoenix II (Jean Grey); D: Jean Grey	0.30	12.00	30.00	60.00
❑102, Dec 76, DC, O: Storm; V: Juggernaut and Black Tom	0.30	6.00	15.00	30.00
❑103, Feb 77, DC, V: Juggernaut; V: Black Tom	0.30	6.00	15.00	30.00
❑104, Apr 77, DC, V: Magneto; 1: Muir Island; 1: Starjammers (cameo)	0.30	6.00	15.00	30.00
❑105, Jun 77, DC, A: Firelord	0.30	6.00	15.00	30.00
❑106, Aug 77, DC, A: Firelord	0.30	6.00	15.00	30.00
❑107, Oct 77, DC, 1: the Starjammers; 1: Starjammers	0.30	6.00	15.00	30.00
❑108, Dec 77, JBy, DC (c), O: Polaris; A: Fantastic Four,1st Byrne art on X-Men	0.35	11.00	27.50	55.00
❑109, Feb 78, JBy, DC (c), 1: Vindicator (Weapon Alpha); 1: Weapon Alpha	0.35	9.00	22.50	45.00
❑110, Apr 78, TD; DC, A: Warhawk	0.35	5.60	14.00	28.00
❑111, Jun 78, JBy, DC (c), A: Beast, Magneto; V: Mesmero	0.35	5.60	14.00	28.00
❑112, Aug 78, JBy, GP (c), V: Magneto	0.35	5.00	12.50	25.00
❑113, Sep 78, JBy, V: Magneto	0.35	5.00	12.50	25.00
❑114, Oct 78, JBy, V: Sauron	0.35	4.40	11.00	22.00
❑115, Nov 78, JBy, A: Ka-Zar; V: Sauron; 1: Nereel	0.35	4.40	11.00	22.00
❑116, Dec 78, JBy, A: Ka-Zar	0.35	4.40	11.00	22.00
❑117, Jan 79, JBy, DC (c), O: Professor X	0.35	4.40	11.00	22.00
❑118, Feb 79, JBy, DC (c), 1: Mariko Yashida	0.35	4.40	11.00	22.00
❑119, Mar 79, JBy, DC (c), 1: Proteus (voice only)	0.35	4.40	11.00	22.00
❑120, Apr 79, JBy, 1: Vindicator; 1: Sasquatch; 1: Northstar; 1: Snowbird; 1: Alpha Flight (cameo); 1: Aurora	0.35	8.00	20.00	40.00
❑121, May 79, JBy, DC (c), 1: Alpha Flight (full); A: Mastermind	0.40	8.00	20.00	40.00
❑122, Jun 79, JBy, DC (c), V: Arcade; 1: Hellfire Club	0.40	4.40	11.00	22.00
❑123, Jul 79, JBy, Listen-Stop Me If You've Heard It-But This One Will Kill You, V: Arcade; O: Colossus	0.40	4.40	11.00	22.00
❑124, Aug 79, JBy, JBy (w), He Only Laughs When I Hurt, A: Arcade	0.40	4.40	11.00	22.00
❑125, Sep 79, JBy, There's Something Awful on Muir Island, 1: Proteus (full appearance),Phoenix cover	0.40	4.40	11.00	22.00
❑126, Oct 79, JBy, How Sharper Than a Serpent's Tooth	0.40	4.40	11.00	22.00
❑127, Nov 79, JBy, The Quality of Hatred	0.40	4.40	11.00	22.00
❑128, Dec 79, JBy, The Action of the Tiger, D: Proteus	0.40	4.40	11.00	22.00
❑129, Jan 80, JBy, God Spare the Child, 1: Sprite II (Kitty Pryde); 1: Kitty Pryde; 1: White Queen (Emma Frost); 1: Donald Pierce (the White Bishop)	0.40	5.60	14.00	28.00
❑130, Feb 80, JBy, JR2 (c), Dazzler, 1: Dazzler	0.40	4.40	11.00	22.00
❑131, Mar 80, JBy, Run For Your Life, A: Dazzler; A: Angel, White Queen	0.40	3.60	9.00	18.00
❑132, Apr 80, JBy, And Hellfire is Their Name, A: Angel; 1: Hugh Hefner	0.40	3.60	9.00	18.00
❑133, May 80, JBy, Wolverine Alone, A: Angel; 1: Senator Edward Kelly; 1: Dark Phoenix	0.40	3.60	9.00	18.00
❑134, Jun 80, JBy, Too Late, the Heroes, A: Dark Phoenix	0.40	3.60	9.00	18.00
❑135, Jul 80, JBy, Dark Phoenix, A: Spider-Man; A: Dark Phoenix	0.40	3.60	9.00	18.00
❑136, Aug 80, JBy, Child of Light and Darkness	0.40	3.20	8.00	16.00
❑137, Sep 80, JBy, The Fate of the Phoenix, 1: Hussar; D: Phoenix II (Jean Grey); A: Angel, Giant-size	0.75	4.40	11.00	22.00
❑138, Oct 80, JBy, Elegy, A: Angel	0.50	3.00	7.50	15.00

The X-Men met The Avengers in *X-Men* (1st series) #9.

© 1965 Marvel Comics

	ORIG	GOOD	FINE	N-MINT
❑139, Nov 80, JBy, ... Something Wicked This Way Comes, 1: Stevie Hunter,Kitty Pryde joins X-Men; New costume for Wolverine	0.50	5.00	12.50	25.00
❑140, Dec 80, JBy, Rage, A: Alpha Flight	0.50	5.00	12.50	25.00
❑141, Jan 81, JBy, Days of Future Past, 1: Pyro; 1: Rachel Summers (Phoenix III); 1: Avalanche,series continues as Uncanny X-Men	0.50	5.20	13.00	26.00

X-MEN (2ND SERIES)
MARVEL

	ORIG	GOOD	FINE	N-MINT
❑-1, Jul 97, O: Magneto,Flashback	1.99	0.40	1.00	2.00
❑-1/A,Variant cover: "Magneto's Rage, Xavier's Hope...I had a Dream!"	1.95	0.50	1.25	2.50
❑1/A, Oct 91, JLee, JLee(w), Rubicon,Beast, Storm, etc. on cover	1.50	0.60	1.50	3.00
❑1/B, Oct 91, JLee, JLee(w), Rubicon,Colossus, Rogue, etc. on cover.	1.50	0.60	1.50	3.00
❑1/C, Oct 91, JLee, JLee(w), Rubicon,Cyclops, Wolverine, Iceman on cover	1.50	0.60	1.50	3.00
❑1/D, Oct 91, JLee, JLee(w), Rubicon,Magneto cover	1.50	0.60	1.50	3.00
❑1/E, Oct 91, JLee, JLee(w), Rubicon,gatefold cover	3.95	1.00	2.50	5.00
❑2, Nov 91	1.00	0.60	1.50	3.00
❑3, Dec 91	1.00	0.60	1.50	3.00
❑4, Jan 92, 1: Omega Red	1.00	0.60	1.50	3.00
❑5, Feb 92, 1: Maverick	1.25	0.60	1.50	3.00
❑6, Mar 92	1.25	0.60	1.50	3.00
❑7, Apr 92	1.25	0.60	1.50	3.00
❑8, May 92	1.25	0.60	1.50	3.00
❑9, Jun 92, A: Ghost Rider	1.25	0.60	1.50	3.00
❑10, Jul 92, A: Longshot	1.25	0.60	1.50	3.00
❑11, Aug 92	1.25	0.60	1.50	3.00
❑12, Sep 92	1.25	0.60	1.50	3.00
❑13, Oct 92	1.25	0.60	1.50	3.00
❑14/CS, Nov 92, X-Cutioner's Song; X-Cutioner's Song, Part 3, Apocalypse trading card	1.50	0.60	1.50	3.00
❑15/CS, Dec 92, X-Cutioner's Song, Part 7, trading card	1.50	0.60	1.50	3.00
❑16/CS, Jan 93, X-Cutioner's Song, Part 11, trading card	1.50	0.60	1.50	3.00
❑17, Feb 93	1.25	0.50	1.25	2.50
❑18, Mar 93	1.25	0.50	1.25	2.50
❑19, Apr 93	1.25	0.50	1.25	2.50
❑20, May 93	1.25	0.50	1.25	2.50
❑21, Jun 93, The Puzzle Box	1.25	0.40	1.00	2.00
❑22, Jul 93	1.25	0.40	1.00	2.00
❑23, Aug 93	1.25	0.40	1.00	2.00
❑24, Sep 93	1.25	0.40	1.00	2.00
❑25, Oct 93, A: Magneto,Hologram on cover; Wolverine loses adamantium skeleton	3.50	1.60	4.00	8.00
❑25/GO, A: Magneto,Hologram on cover; Gold limited edition; Wolverine loses adamantium skeleton	—	5.00	12.50	25.00
❑25/LE, A: Magneto,Black and white cover; Wolverine loses adamantium skeleton	—	5.00	12.50	25.00
❑26, Nov 93	1.25	0.40	1.00	2.00
❑27, Dec 93	1.25	0.40	1.00	2.00
❑28, Jan 94, A: Sabretooth	1.25	0.40	1.00	2.00
❑29, Feb 94	1.25	0.40	1.00	2.00
❑30, Mar 94, trading cards; Double-size; Wedding of Jean Grey and Scott Summers	1.95	0.80	2.00	4.00
❑31, Apr 94	1.25	0.35	0.88	1.75
❑32, May 94	1.50	0.35	0.88	1.75
❑33, Jun 94, A: Sabretooth	1.50	0.35	0.88	1.75
❑34, Jul 94	1.50	0.35	0.88	1.75
❑35, Aug 94, Sunset Grace	1.50	0.35	0.88	1.75
❑36, Sep 94, Generation Next, Part 2	1.50	0.35	0.88	1.75
❑36/SC, Sep 94, Generation Next, Part 2,foil cover	2.95	0.80	2.00	4.00
❑37, Oct 94, Generation Next, Part 4	1.50	0.30	0.75	1.50
❑37/SC, Oct 94, Generation Next, Part 4,enhanced cover	2.95	0.80	2.00	4.00

	ORIG	GOOD	FINE	N-MINT
❑38, Nov 94	1.50	0.30	0.75	1.50
❑38/Dlx, Nov 94, Deluxe edition	1.95	0.40	1.00	2.00
❑39, Dec 94	1.50	0.30	0.75	1.50
❑39/Dlx, Dec 94, Deluxe edition	1.95	0.40	1.00	2.00
❑40, Jan 95	1.50	0.30	0.75	1.50
❑40/Dlx, Jan 95, Deluxe edition	1.95	0.40	1.00	2.00
❑41, Feb 95	1.50	0.30	0.75	1.50
❑41/Dlx, Feb 95, Deluxe edition	1.95	0.40	1.00	2.00
❑42, Jul 95	1.95	0.40	1.00	2.00
❑43, Aug 95	1.95	0.40	1.00	2.00
❑44, Sep 95	1.95	0.40	1.00	2.00
❑45, Oct 95,enhanced wraparound gatefold cardstock cover	3.95	0.80	2.00	4.00
❑46, Nov 95,Return of X-Babies	1.95	0.40	1.00	2.00
❑47, Dec 95, A: X-babies; A: Dazzler	1.95	0.40	1.00	2.00
❑48, Jan 96, A: alternate Beast; A: Sugar Man	1.95	0.40	1.00	2.00
❑49, Feb 96	1.95	0.40	1.00	2.00
❑50, Mar 96, Full Court Press,wraparound cover; Giant-size	2.95	0.60	1.50	3.00
❑50/SC, Mar 96, Full Court Press,foil cover; Giant-size	3.95	0.80	2.00	4.00
❑51, Apr 96, MWa (w)	1.95	0.40	1.00	2.00
❑52, May 96	1.95	0.40	1.00	2.00
❑53, Jun 96,Jean Grey vs. Onslaught	1.95	0.40	1.00	2.00
❑54, Jul 96,Identity of Onslaught revealed	1.95	0.40	1.00	2.00
❑55, Aug 96	1.95	0.40	1.00	2.00
❑56, Sep 96, Onslaught: Phase 2	1.95	0.40	1.00	2.00
❑57, Oct 96	1.95	0.40	1.00	2.00
❑58, Nov 96,Gambit vs. Magneto	1.95	0.40	1.00	2.00
❑59, Dec 96, A: Hercules	1.95	0.40	1.00	2.00
❑60, Jan 97, Night	1.95	0.40	1.00	2.00
❑61, Feb 97, Bolt	1.95	0.40	1.00	2.00
❑62, Mar 97, Games of Deceit & Death, Part 1, A: Shang-Chi	1.95	0.40	1.00	2.00
❑62/A, Mar 97, A: Shang-Chi,alternate cover	1.95	0.40	1.00	2.00
❑63, Apr 97, Games of Deceit & Death, Part 2, A: Sebastian Shaw; A: Kingpin	1.95	0.40	1.00	2.00
❑64, May 97	1.95	0.40	1.00	2.00
❑65, Jun 97, Operation: Zero Tolerance	1.99	0.40	1.00	2.00
❑66, Aug 97, Operation Zero Tolerance, gatefold summary	1.99	0.40	1.00	2.00
❑67, Sep 97, Operation Zero Tolerance, gatefold summary	1.99	0.40	1.00	2.00
❑68, Oct 97, Operation Zero Tolerance, gatefold summary	1.99	0.40	1.00	2.00
❑69, Nov 97, gatefold summary	1.99	0.40	1.00	2.00
❑70, Dec 97, gatefold summary	2.99	0.60	1.50	3.00
❑71, Jan 98, gatefold summary; Cyclops and Phoenix leaves team	1.99	0.40	1.00	2.00
❑72, Feb 98, gatefold summary	1.99	0.40	1.00	2.00
❑73, Mar 98, gatefold summary	1.99	0.40	1.00	2.00
❑74, Apr 98, A: Abomination, gatefold summary	1.99	0.40	1.00	2.00
❑75, May 98,wraparound cover; gatefold summary	2.99	0.40	1.00	2.00
❑76, Jun 98, O: Maggot, gatefold summary	1.99	0.40	1.00	2.00
❑77, Jul 98, Psi-War, Part 1, gatefold summary	1.99	0.40	1.00	2.00
❑78, Aug 98, Psi-War, Part 2, gatefold summary	1.99	0.40	1.00	2.00
❑79, Sep 98, gatefold summary	1.99	0.40	1.00	2.00
❑80, Oct 98, gatefold summary; double-sized	2.99	0.60	1.50	3.00
❑81, Nov 98, gatefold summary	1.99	0.40	1.00	2.00
❑82, Dec 98, Hunt for Xavier, Part 2, gatefold summary	1.99	0.40	1.00	2.00
❑83, Jan 99, Hunt for Xavier, Part 4, gatefold summary	1.99	0.40	1.00	2.00
❑84, Feb 99, Hunt for Xavier, Part 6; The Hunt for Xavier, A: Nina, gatefold summary	1.99	0.40	1.00	2.00
❑85, Feb 99, A Tale of Two Mutants, A: Magneto	1.99	0.40	1.00	2.00
❑85/Aut, The Hunt for Xavier, A: Magneto,Signed by Alan Davis & Mark Farmer	—	5.00	12.50	25.00
❑86, Mar 99, The Magneto War, part 2, A: Magneto; A: Acolytes; A: Joseph; A: Astra	1.99	0.40	1.00	1.99
❑87, Apr 99, Magneto War; The Magneto War, part 4, A: Magneto; A: Joseph,cover says Apr; indicia says May	1.99	0.40	1.00	1.99
❑88, May 99	1.99	0.40	1.00	1.99
❑89, Jun 99	1.99	0.40	1.00	1.99
❑90, Jul 99, A: Galactus	1.99	0.40	1.00	1.99
❑91, Aug 99	1.99	0.40	1.00	1.99
❑92, Sep 99	1.99	0.40	1.00	1.99
❑93, Oct 99	1.99	0.40	1.00	1.99
❑94, Nov 99	1.99	0.40	1.00	1.99
❑95, Dec 99	1.99	0.40	1.00	1.99
❑96, Jan 00	1.99	0.40	1.00	1.99
❑97, Feb 00	—	0.45	1.13	2.25
❑98, Mar 00	—	0.45	1.13	2.25
❑99, Apr 00	—	0.45	1.13	2.25
❑100/A, May 00, End of Days,White background, team charging	2.99	0.60	1.50	2.99
❑100/B, May 00, End of Days,Nightcrawler vs. villain on cover	2.99	0.60	1.50	2.99
❑100/C, May 00, End of Days,Nightcrawler, Wolverine, Colossus, Jean Gray, Storm on cover	2.99	0.60	1.50	2.99
❑100/D, May 00, End of Days,Rogue vs. Villain on cover	2.99	0.60	1.50	2.99
❑101, Jun 00	—	0.45	1.13	2.25
❑102, Jul 00	—	0.45	1.13	2.25
❑103, Aug 00	—	0.45	1.13	2.25
❑104, Sep 00, Painted Ladies	2.25	0.45	1.13	2.25
❑105, Oct 00	2.25	0.45	1.13	2.25
❑106, Nov 00, Search and Rescue, Part 1, double-sized	2.99	0.60	1.50	2.99
❑107, Dec 00, Maximum Security; On the Yard!	2.25	0.45	1.13	2.25
❑108, Jan 01, Dream's End, Part 4: The Future is Now!	2.25	0.45	1.13	2.25
❑109, Feb 01	2.25	0.45	1.13	2.25
❑110, Mar 01	2.25	0.45	1.13	2.25
❑111, Apr 01, Prelude to Destruction, A: Magneto	2.25	0.45	1.13	2.25
❑112	2.25	0.45	1.13	2.25
❑113	2.25	0.45	1.13	2.25
❑114	2.25	0.45	1.13	2.25
❑115	2.25	0.45	1.13	2.25
❑116	2.25	0.45	1.13	2.25
❑Anl 1, Scattershot, Part 1	2.25	0.60	1.50	3.00
❑Anl 2, 1: Empyrean, trading card; trading card; Polybagged	2.95	0.60	1.50	3.00
❑Anl 3	2.95	0.59	1.48	2.95
❑Anl 1995, Oct 95	3.95	0.79	1.98	3.95
❑Anl 1996, Nov 96, nn; wraparound cover	2.99	0.60	1.50	2.99
❑Anl 1997, Not a Cloud in the Sky, nn; wraparound cover	2.99	0.60	1.50	2.99
❑Anl 1998, nn; wraparound cover; X-Men/Doctor Doom '98	2.99	0.60	1.50	2.99
❑Anl 1999, Aug 99, V: Red Skull	3.50	0.70	1.75	3.50
❑Anl 2001,2001 Annual	3.50	0.70	1.75	3.50
❑Ash 1, ashcan edition	0.75	0.15	0.38	0.75

X-MEN 2099
MARVEL

	ORIG	GOOD	FINE	N-MINT
❑1, Oct 93, 1: X-Men 2099,foil cover	1.75	0.40	1.00	2.00
❑1/GO, Oct 93, 1: X-Men 2099,foil cover; Gold edition	—	0.60	1.50	3.00
❑1-2, 1: X-Men 2099,2nd Printing; foil cover	1.75	0.35	0.88	1.75
❑2, Nov 93	1.25	0.30	0.75	1.50
❑3, Dec 93	1.25	0.30	0.75	1.50
❑4, Jan 94	1.25	0.30	0.75	1.50
❑5, Feb 94, Fall of the Hammer, Part 3	1.25	0.30	0.75	1.50
❑6, Mar 94, 1: The Freakshow	1.25	0.25	0.63	1.25
❑7, Apr 94	1.25	0.25	0.63	1.25
❑8, May 94	1.50	0.30	0.75	1.50
❑9, Jun 94	1.50	0.30	0.75	1.50
❑10, Jul 94	1.50	0.30	0.75	1.50
❑11, Aug 94	1.50	0.30	0.75	1.50
❑12, Sep 94	1.50	0.30	0.75	1.50
❑13, Oct 94	1.50	0.30	0.75	1.50
❑14, Nov 94	1.50	0.30	0.75	1.50
❑15, Dec 94	1.50	0.30	0.75	1.50
❑16, Jan 95	1.50	0.30	0.75	1.50
❑17, Feb 95	1.50	0.30	0.75	1.50
❑18, Mar 95	1.50	0.30	0.75	1.50
❑19, Apr 95	1.50	0.30	0.75	1.50
❑20, May 95	1.50	0.30	0.75	1.50
❑21, Jun 95	1.95	0.39	0.98	1.95
❑22, Jul 95	1.95	0.39	0.98	1.95
❑23, Aug 95	1.95	0.39	0.98	1.95
❑24, Sep 95	1.95	0.39	0.98	1.95
❑25, Oct 95	2.50	0.50	1.25	2.50
❑25/SC, Oct 95,enhanced wraparound cardstock cover	3.95	0.79	1.98	3.95
❑26, Nov 95	1.50	0.39	0.98	1.95
❑27, Dec 95, A: Doom; A: Herod,Story continued from 2099 Apocalypse and Doom 2099 #36	1.95	0.39	0.98	1.95
❑28, Jan 96	1.95	0.39	0.98	1.95
❑29, Feb 96, X-Nation	1.95	0.39	0.98	1.95
❑30, Mar 96, X-Nation,Story continued in X-Nation #1	1.95	0.39	0.98	1.95
❑31, Apr 96	1.95	0.39	0.98	1.95
❑32, May 96	1.95	0.39	0.98	1.95
❑33, Jun 96	1.95	0.39	0.98	1.95
❑34, Jul 96	1.95	0.39	0.98	1.95
❑35, Aug 96, A: Nostromo,Final Issue	1.95	0.39	0.98	1.95
❑SE 1, Oct 95	3.95	0.79	1.98	3.95

X-MEN 2099: OASIS
MARVEL

Value: Cover or less
❑1, Aug 96, nn 5.95

X-MEN ADVENTURES (VOL. 1)
MARVEL

	ORIG	GOOD	FINE	N-MINT
❑1, Nov 92, Night of the Sentinels	1.25	0.60	1.50	3.00
❑2, Dec 92	1.25	0.40	1.00	2.00
❑3, Jan 93	1.25	0.40	1.00	2.00
❑4, Feb 93	1.25	0.40	1.00	2.00
❑5, Mar 93	1.25	0.40	1.00	2.00
❑6, Apr 93	1.25	0.40	1.00	2.00
❑7, May 93	1.25	0.40	1.00	2.00
❑8, Jun 93	1.25	0.40	1.00	2.00
❑9, Jul 93	1.25	0.40	1.00	2.00
❑10, Aug 93	1.25	0.40	1.00	2.00
❑11, Sep 93	1.25	0.30	0.75	1.50
❑12, Oct 93, A: Apocalypse	1.25	0.30	0.75	1.50
❑13, Nov 93	1.25	0.30	0.75	1.50
❑14, Dec 93	1.25	0.30	0.75	1.50
❑15, Jan 94	1.75	0.35	0.88	1.75

X-MEN ADVENTURES (VOL. 2)
MARVEL

	ORIG	GOOD	FINE	N-MINT
❑1, Feb 94	1.25	0.40	1.00	2.00
❑2, Mar 94	1.25	0.25	0.63	1.25
❑3, Apr 94	1.25	0.25	0.63	1.25
❑4, May 94,Marvel Mart insert	1.25	0.25	0.63	1.25
❑5, Jun 94	1.25	0.25	0.63	1.25
❑6, Jul 94	1.25	0.25	0.63	1.25
❑7, Aug 94, Time Fugitives, Part 1	1.25	0.25	0.63	1.25
❑8, Sep 94, Time Fugitives, Part 2	1.25	0.25	0.63	1.25
❑9, Oct 94	1.50	0.30	0.75	1.50
❑10, Nov 94	1.50	0.30	0.75	1.50
❑11, Dec 94	1.50	0.30	0.75	1.50
❑12, Jan 95	1.50	0.30	0.75	1.50
❑13, Feb 95	1.50	0.30	0.75	1.50

X-MEN ADVENTURES (VOL. 3)
MARVEL

	ORIG	GOOD	FINE	N-MINT
❑1, Mar 95, O: Lady Deathstrike	1.50	0.40	1.00	2.00
❑2, Apr 95	1.50	0.30	0.75	1.50
❑3, May 95	1.50	0.30	0.75	1.50
❑4, Jun 95	1.50	0.30	0.75	1.50
❑5, Jul 95	1.50	0.30	0.75	1.50
❑6, Aug 95	1.50	0.30	0.75	1.50
❑7, Sep 95	1.50	0.30	0.75	1.50
❑8, Oct 95	1.50	0.30	0.75	1.50
❑9, Nov 95	1.50	0.30	0.75	1.50
❑10, Dec 95, The Dark Phoenix Saga, A: Jason Wyngarde; A: Hellfire Club; A: Dazzler	1.50	0.30	0.75	1.50
❑11, Jan 96	1.50	0.30	0.75	1.50
❑12, Feb 96	1.50	0.30	0.75	1.50
❑13, Mar 96, Crime and Punishment: The Final Fate of Phoenix	1.50	0.30	0.75	1.50

X-MEN ALPHA
MARVEL

	ORIG	GOOD	FINE	N-MINT
❑1, Feb 95, 1: X-Men (Age of Apocalypse),enhanced cover; One-Shot	3.95	1.20	3.00	6.00
❑1/GO, 1: X-Men (Age of Apocalypse), Gold edition	—	4.00	10.00	20.00

X-MEN/ALPHA FLIGHT
MARVEL

	ORIG	GOOD	FINE	N-MINT
❑1, Dec 85, 1: The Berserkers	1.50	0.80	2.00	4.00
❑2, Feb 86	1.50	0.80	2.00	4.00

X-MEN/ALPHA FLIGHT (2ND SERIES)
MARVEL

Value: Cover or less
❑1, May 98, Survivors 2.99
❑2, Jun 98 .... 2.99

X-MEN/ALPHA FLIGHT: THE GIFT
MARVEL

Value: Cover or less
❑1, May 98, nn 3.99

X-MEN & THE MICRONAUTS
MARVEL

	ORIG	GOOD	FINE	N-MINT
❑1, Jan 84,Limited Series	0.60	0.50	1.25	2.50
❑2, Feb 84	0.60	0.50	1.25	2.50
❑3, Mar 84	0.60	0.50	1.25	2.50
❑4, Apr 84	0.60	0.50	1.25	2.50

X-MEN ANNIVERSARY MAGAZINE
MARVEL

Value: Cover or less
❑1, Sep 93, Bring Me the Head of Bob Harras; Let There be X-Men, Celebrates 30th anniversary of the X-Men 3.95

X-MEN ARCHIVES
MARVEL

	ORIG	GOOD	FINE	N-MINT
❑1, Jan 95, BSz, Legion,cardstock cover; Reprints New Mutants #26	2.25	0.50	1.25	2.50
❑2, Jan 95, BSz ,cardstock cover; Reprints New Mutants #27	2.25	0.50	1.25	2.50
❑3, Jan 95, BSz, Soul War,cardstock cover; Reprints New Mutants #28	2.25	0.50	1.25	2.50
❑4, Jan 95, DC, Gold Rush,cardstock cover; Reprints Uncanny X-Men #161	2.25	0.50	1.25	2.50

Professor Xavier's efforts to form a team of mutants were told in *X-Men: Children of the Atom.*

© 1999 Marvel Characters Inc.

X-MEN ARCHIVES FEATURING CAPTAIN BRITAIN
MARVEL

Value: Cover or less
❑1, Jul 95, AMo (w),wraparound cover; reprints Captain Britain stories from British Marvel Super Heroes #377-383 .... 2.95
❑2, Aug 95, AMo (w),reprints Captain Britain stories from British Marvel Super Heroes #384-88 and The Daredevils #1 .... 2.95
❑3, Sep 95, AMo (w),reprints stories from The Daredevils #2-5 .... 2.95
❑4, Oct 95, AMo (w),reprints stories from The Daredevils #6-8 2.95
❑5, Nov 95, AMo (w),reprints stories from The Daredevils #9-11 .... 2.95
❑6, Dec 95, AMo (w),reprints stories from The Mighty World of Marvel #7-10 .... 2.95
❑7, Jan 96, AMo (w),Final Issue; reprints stories from The Mighty World of Marvel #11-13 .... 2.95

X-MEN ARCHIVES SKETCHBOOK
MARVEL

Value: Cover or less
❑1, Dec 00,character sketches 2.99

X-MEN AT THE STATE FAIR
MARVEL

	ORIG	GOOD	FINE	N-MINT
❑1,Dallas Times-Herald	—	0.40	1.00	2.00

X-MEN: BOOKS OF THE ASKANI
MARVEL

Value: Cover or less
❑1,wraparound cardstock cover; background info on Askani'son 2.95

X-MEN: CHILDREN OF THE ATOM
MARVEL

	ORIG	GOOD	FINE	N-MINT
❑1, Nov 99, SR, Childhood's End,cardstock cover	2.99	0.60	1.50	3.00
❑2, Dec 99, SR, All Children Wear the Sign,cardstock cover;	2.99	0.60	1.50	3.00
❑3,cardstock cover;	2.99	0.60	1.50	3.00
❑4, Jul 00, Child's Play,cardstock cover;	2.99	0.60	1.50	3.00
❑5, Aug 00, Where Your Children Are,cardstock cover;	2.99	0.60	1.50	2.99
❑6, Sep 00, The Great Cathedral Space,cardstock cover;	2.99	0.60	1.50	2.99

X-MEN CHRONICLES (FANTACO)
FANTACO

	ORIG	GOOD	FINE	N-MINT
❑1, Jul 81, DC (c), b&w; magazine	1.25	0.40	1.00	2.00

X-MEN CHRONICLES (MARVEL)
MARVEL

Value: Cover or less
❑1, Mar 95, Origins,Age of Apocalypse 3.95
❑2, Jun 95,Age of Apocalypse 3.95

X-MEN: CLANDESTINE
MARVEL

Value: Cover or less
❑1, Oct 96,wraparound cover . 2.95
❑2, Nov 96, The Destine's Darkest Dreams,wraparound cover .. 2.95

X-MEN CLASSIC
MARVEL

	ORIG	GOOD	FINE	N-MINT
❑46, Apr 90,Series continued from Classic X-Men #45	1.25	0.40	1.00	2.00
❑47, May 90	1.25	0.40	1.00	2.00
❑48, Jun 90	1.25	0.40	1.00	2.00
❑49, Jul 90	1.25	0.40	1.00	2.00
❑50, Aug 90	1.25	0.40	1.00	2.00
❑51, Sep 90	1.25	0.40	1.00	2.00
❑52, Oct 90	1.25	0.40	1.00	2.00
❑53, Nov 90	1.25	0.40	1.00	2.00
❑54, Dec 90	1.25	0.40	1.00	2.00
❑55, Jan 91	1.25	0.40	1.00	2.00
❑56, Feb 91	1.25	0.40	1.00	2.00
❑57, Mar 91	1.25	0.40	1.00	2.00
❑58, Apr 91	1.25	0.40	1.00	2.00
❑59, May 91	1.25	0.40	1.00	2.00
❑60, Jun 91	1.25	0.40	1.00	2.00
❑61, Jul 91	1.25	0.40	1.00	2.00
❑62, Aug 91	1.25	0.35	0.88	1.75

	ORIG	GOOD	FINE	N-MINT
❑63, Sep 91	1.25	0.35	0.88	1.75
❑64, Oct 91, BA	1.25	0.35	0.88	1.75
❑65, Nov 91	1.25	0.35	0.88	1.75
❑66, Dec 91	1.25	0.35	0.88	1.75
❑67, Jan 92	1.25	0.35	0.88	1.75
❑68, Feb 92	1.25	0.35	0.88	1.75
❑69, Mar 92	1.25	0.35	0.88	1.75
❑70, Apr 92, Giant-size	1.75	0.35	0.88	1.75
❑71, May 92	1.25	0.30	0.75	1.50
❑72, Jun 92	1.25	0.30	0.75	1.50
❑73, Jul 92	1.25	0.30	0.75	1.50
❑74, Aug 92	1.25	0.30	0.75	1.50
❑75, Sep 92	1.25	0.30	0.75	1.50
❑76, Oct 92	1.25	0.30	0.75	1.50
❑77, Nov 92	1.25	0.30	0.75	1.50
❑78, Dec 92	1.25	0.30	0.75	1.50
❑79, Jan 93	1.75	0.30	0.75	1.50
❑80, Feb 93, JR2, Decisions, 1: Valerie Cooper,Reprints Uncanny X-Men #176	1.25	0.30	0.75	1.50
❑81, Mar 93, JR2, Sanction,Reprints Uncanny X-Men #177	1.25	0.30	0.75	1.50
❑82, Apr 93, JR2, Hell Hath No Fury...,Reprints Uncanny X-Men #178	1.25	0.30	0.75	1.50
❑83, May 93, JR2, What Happened to Kitty,Reprints Uncanny X-Men #179	1.25	0.30	0.75	1.50
❑84, Jun 93, JR2, Whose Life is it, Anyway?,Reprints Uncanny X-Men #180	1.25	0.30	0.75	1.50
❑85, Jul 93, JR2, Tokyo Story,Reprints Uncanny X-Men #181	1.25	0.30	0.75	1.50
❑86, Aug 93, JR2, Madness,Reprints Uncanny X-Men #182	1.25	0.30	0.75	1.50
❑87, Sep 93, JR2, He'll Never Make Me Cry,Reprints Uncanny X-Men #183	1.25	0.30	0.75	1.50
❑88, Oct 93, JR2, The Past...of Future Days, A: Selene; A: Rachel; 1: Forge,Reprints Uncanny X-Men #184	1.25	0.30	0.75	1.50
❑89, Nov 93, JR2, Public Enemy,Reprints Uncanny X-Men #185; Storm loses powers	1.25	0.30	0.75	1.50
❑90, Dec 93, Lifedeath, double-sized; Reprints Uncanny X-Men #186	1.75	0.30	0.75	1.50
❑91, Jan 94, JR2, Wraithkill,Reprints Uncanny X-Men #187	1.25	0.30	0.75	1.50
❑92, Feb 94, JR2, Legacy of the Lost,Reprints Uncanny X-Men #188	1.25	0.30	0.75	1.50
❑93, Mar 94, JR2, Two Girls Out to Have Fun,reprints Uncanny X-Men #189	1.25	0.30	0.75	1.50
❑94, Apr 94, JR2, An Age Undreamed Of, A: Avengers; A: Spider-Man,Reprints Uncanny X-Men #190	1.25	0.30	0.75	1.50
❑95, May 94, JR2, Raiders of the Lost Temple, A: Avengers; A: Spider-Man,Reprints Uncanny X-Men #191	1.25	0.30	0.75	1.50
❑96, Jun 94, JR2, Fun'n'Games,Reprints Uncanny X-Men #192	1.25	0.30	0.75	1.50
❑97, Jul 94, JR2, Warhunt 2, double-sized; giant; Reprints Uncanny X-Men #193; 100th New X-Men	1.75	0.30	0.75	1.50
❑98, Aug 94, JR2, Juggernaut's Back in Town, A: Juggernaut,Reprints Uncanny X-Men #194	1.25	0.30	0.75	1.50
❑99, Sep 94, JR2, It Was a Dark and Stormy Night, A: Power-Pack,Reprints Uncanny X-Men #195	1.25	0.30	0.75	1.50
❑100, Oct 94, JR2, What Was That?,Reprints Uncanny X-Men #196	1.50	0.30	0.75	1.50
❑101, Nov 94, JR2, To Save Arcade?,reprints Uncanny X-Men #197	1.50	0.30	0.75	1.50
❑102, Dec 94, Lifedeath II,reprints Uncanny X-Men #198	1.50	0.30	0.75	1.50
❑103, Jan 95, JR2, The Spiral Path, 1: Phoenix III (Rachel Summers),reprints Uncanny X-Men #199	1.50	0.30	0.75	1.50
❑104, Feb 95, JR2, The Trial of Magneto, Double-size; reprints Uncanny X-Men #200	1.95	0.30	0.75	1.50
❑105, Mar 95, Duel, 1: Cable (as baby),reprints Uncanny X-Men #201; 1st Portacio art in X-Men	1.50	0.30	0.75	1.50
❑106, Apr 95,reprints Uncanny X-Men #202	1.50	0.30	0.75	1.50
❑107, May 95,reprints Uncanny X-Men #203	1.50	0.30	0.75	1.50
❑108, Jun 95,reprints Uncanny X-Men #204	1.50	0.30	0.75	1.50
❑109, Jul 95,reprints Uncanny X-Men #205	1.50	0.30	0.75	1.50
❑110, Aug 95,Final Issue; reprints Uncanny X-Men #206	1.50	0.30	0.75	1.50

X-MEN CLASSICS
MARVEL

	ORIG	GOOD	FINE	N-MINT
❑1, Dec 83,Reprint	2.00	0.70	1.75	3.50
❑2, Jan 84,Reprint	2.00	0.70	1.75	3.50
❑3, Feb 84,Reprint	2.00	0.70	1.75	3.50

X-MEN COLLECTOR'S EDITION
MARVEL

	ORIG	GOOD	FINE	N-MINT
❑2,contains fold-out poster cover; Pizza Hut giveaway in 1993	—	0.20	0.50	1.00

X-MEN: DECLASSIFIED
MARVEL

Value: Cover or less

❑1, Oct 00 ..... 3.50

X-MEN: EARTHFALL
MARVEL

Value: Cover or less

❑1, Sep 96,wraparound cover; reprints The Brood saga 2.95

X-MEN FIRSTS
MARVEL

Value: Cover or less

❑1, Feb 96,reprints Avengers Annual #10, Uncanny X-Men #221 and 266, and Incredible Hulk #181 ..... 4.95

X-MEN FOREVER
MARVEL

Value: Cover or less

❑1, Jan 01, The Destiny Pact,cardstock cover 3.50
❑2, Feb 01, Choices Once Made ...,cardstock cover 3.50
❑3, Mar 01, All of God's Creatures ...,cardstock cover 3.50
❑4, Apr 01, The Age of Innocence,cardstock cover 3.50
❑5, May 01, Iceman - Present and Accounted For,cardstock cover 3.50

X-MEN: HELLFIRE CLUB
MARVEL

Value: Cover or less

❑1, Jan 00, Witchhunt 2.50
❑2, Feb 00, Toll the Bell Liberty 2.50
❑3, Mar 00, For Want of a Soul 2.50

X-MEN: LIBERATORS
MARVEL

Value: Cover or less

❑1, Nov 98 ..... 2.99
❑1/LE 19.99
❑2, Dec 98, Home is Where the Heart Is 2.99
❑3, Jan 99 ..... 2.99
❑4, Feb 99 ..... 2.99

X-MEN: LOST TALES
MARVEL

	ORIG	GOOD	FINE	N-MINT
❑1, Apr 97, Mourning; The Big Dare,reprints back-up stories from Classic X-Men #3-5 and 12	2.99	0.60	1.50	3.00
❑2, Apr 97, Tag, Sucker; A Taste for Vengeance!,reprints back-up stories from Classic X-Men #10, 17, 21, and 23	2.99	0.60	1.50	3.00

X-MEN: MILLENNIAL VISIONS
MARVEL

Value: Cover or less

❑1, Jul 00 ..... 3.99

X-MEN MOVIE PREMIERE PREQUEL EDITION
MARVEL

	ORIG	GOOD	FINE	N-MINT
❑1, Jul 00, Toys "R" Us giveaway	—	0.40	1.00	2.00

X-MEN MOVIE PREQUEL: MAGNETO
MARVEL

Value: Cover or less

❑1, Aug 00 ..... 5.95

X-MEN MOVIE PREQUEL: ROGUE
MARVEL

Value: Cover or less

❑1, Aug 00 ..... 5.95
❑1/SC, Aug 00,Photo cover 5.95

X-MEN MOVIE PREQUEL: WOLVERINE
MARVEL

Value: Cover or less

❑1, Aug 00 ..... 5.95
❑1/SC, Aug 00,Photo cover 5.95

X-MEN MUTANT SEARCH R.U. 1?
MARVEL

	ORIG	GOOD	FINE	N-MINT
❑1, Aug 98, nn; no cover price; prototype for children's comic	—	0.40	1.00	2.00

X-MEN OMEGA
MARVEL

	ORIG	GOOD	FINE	N-MINT
❑1, Jun 95, Age of Apocalypse, nn; enhanced wraparound cover; Finale to Age of Apocalypse	3.95	1.20	3.00	6.00
❑1/GO, Age of Apocalypse,chromium cover; Gold edition; Finale to Age of Apocalypse	—	5.00	12.50	25.00

X-MEN: PHOENIX
MARVEL

Value: Cover or less

❑1, Dec 99, Askani Rising; Askani Rising, Part 1 ..... 2.50
❑2, Jan 00, Askani Rising, Part 2 ..... 2.50
❑3, Feb 00, Askani Rising, Part 3 ..... 2.50

X-MEN POSTER MAGAZINE
MARVEL

Value: Cover or less

❑1 ..... 4.95
❑2 ..... 4.95
❑3 ..... 4.95
❑4,wraparound cover 4.95

X-MEN PRIME
MARVEL

	ORIG	GOOD	FINE	N-MINT
❑1, Jul 95, nn; enhanced wraparound cover with acetate overlay	4.95	1.00	2.50	5.00

X-MEN RARITIES
MARVEL

Value: Cover or less

❑1, Jul 95, Winter Carnival; First Night, nn 5.95

X-MEN: ROAD TO ONSLAUGHT
MARVEL

Value: Cover or less

❑1, Oct 96,background on Onslaught's origins............. 2.50

X-MEN: SEARCH FOR CYCLOPS
MARVEL

Value: Cover or less

❑1, Dec 00, Lost,Single figure (red against black background) on cover.................................. 2.99
❑1/A, Oct 00, Lost,Alternate cover: Blue/white split background, man with glowing eyes kneeling at right................................ 2.99
❑2, Jan 01, Hunted 2.99
❑3, Feb 01, Am I Evil? 2.99
❑4, Mar 01, Found! 2.99

X-MEN SPECIAL EDITION
MARVEL

	ORIG	GOOD	FINE	N-MINT
❑1, Feb 83, DC, Second Genesis!, 1: Illyana Rasputin; 1: Nightcrawler; 1: Storm; 1: Colossus; 1: Thunderbird; 1: X-Men (new), reprints Giant-Size X-Men #1	2.00	0.90	2.25	4.50

X-MEN SPOTLIGHT ON...STARJAMMERS
MARVEL

Value: Cover or less

❑1, May 90, DC, Phalkon Quest, Part 1 .... 4.50
❑2, Jun 90, DC, Phalkon Quest, Part 2................................. 4.50

X-MEN: SURVIVAL GUIDE TO THE MANSION
MARVEL

Value: Cover or less

❑1, Aug 93, nn; spiralbound.... 6.95

X-MEN: THE EARLY YEARS
MARVEL

	ORIG	GOOD	FINE	N-MINT
❑1, May 94, SL (w), O: X-Men,Reprints X-Men (1st Series) #1	1.50	0.50	1.25	2.50
❑2, Jun 94, SL (w),Reprints X-Men (1st Series) #2	1.50	0.40	1.00	2.00
❑3, Jul 94, SL (w),Reprints X-Men (1st Series) #3	1.50	0.40	1.00	2.00
❑4, Aug 94, SL (w),Reprints X-Men (1st Series) #4	1.50	0.40	1.00	2.00
❑5, Sep 94, SL (w),Reprints X-Men (1st Series) #5	1.50	0.40	1.00	2.00
❑6, Oct 94, SL (w),Reprints X-Men (1st Series) #6	1.50	0.40	1.00	2.00
❑7, Nov 94, SL (w),Reprints X-Men (1st Series) #7	1.50	0.40	1.00	2.00
❑8, Dec 94, SL (w),Reprints X-Men (1st Series) #8	1.50	0.40	1.00	2.00
❑9, Jan 95, SL (w),Reprints X-Men (1st Series) #9	1.50	0.40	1.00	2.00
❑10, Feb 95, SL (w),Reprints X-Men (1st Series) #10	1.50	0.40	1.00	2.00
❑11, Mar 95, SL (w),Reprints X-Men (1st Series) #11	1.50	0.40	1.00	2.00
❑12, Apr 95, SL (w),Reprints X-Men (1st Series) #12	1.50	0.40	1.00	2.00
❑13, May 95, SL (w),Reprints X-Men (1st Series) #13	1.50	0.40	1.00	2.00
❑14, Jun 95, SL (w),Reprints X-Men (1st Series) #14	1.50	0.40	1.00	2.00
❑15, Jul 95, SL (w),Reprints X-Men (1st Series) #15	1.50	0.40	1.00	2.00
❑16, Aug 95, SL (w),Reprints X-Men (1st Series) #16	1.50	0.40	1.00	2.00
❑17, Sep 95, JK, SL (w), ...And None Shall Survive!; If Iceman Should Fail!,Final Issue; Double-size; Reprints X-Men (1st Series) #17 and #18	2.50	0.50	1.25	2.50

X-MEN: THE HIDDEN YEARS
MARVEL

Value: Cover or less

❑1, Dec 99, JBy 3.50
❑2, Jan 00, JBy 2.50
❑3, Feb 00 .... 2.50
❑4, Mar 00 .... 2.50
❑5, Apr 00 .... 2.75
❑6, May 00 .... 2.50
❑7, Jun 00 .... 2.50
❑8, Jul 00 .... 2.50
❑9, Aug 00 .... 2.50
❑10, Sep 00, TP; JBy, JBy (w), Home is Where the Hurt Is ... 2.50
❑11, Oct 00, TP; JBy, JBy (w), Destroy All Mutants!, A: Sentinels 2.50
❑12, Nov 00 .... 2.50
❑13, Dec 00, TP; JBy, JBy (w), Blood and Circuses 2.50
❑14, Jan 01, TP; JBy, JBy (w). 2.50
❑15, Feb 01, Death Be Not Proud.................................. 2.50
❑16, Mar 01, JBy, JBy (w), Echoes of a Lost Generation............ 2.50
❑17, Apr 01, TP; JBy, JBy (w), Hunter and Hunted, A: Kraven the Hunter 2.50
❑18, May 01, TP; JBy, JBy (w), Promise of a New Tomorrow 2.50
❑19.. 2.50
❑20.. 2.50
❑21 .... 2.50
❑22.. 2.50

X-MEN: THE MAGNETO WAR
MARVEL

Value: Cover or less

❑1, Mar 99, Savior Complex ... 2.99
❑2.. 2.99
❑3.. 2.99
❑4.. 2.99

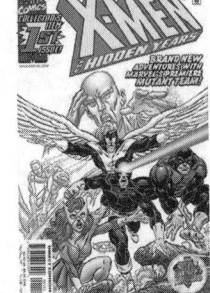

John Byrne filled in the historical gap between the events of *X-Men* (1st series) #66 and #94 in *X-Men: The Hidden Years.*

X-MEN: THE MANGA
MARVEL

Value: Cover or less

❑1, Mar 98.............................. 2.99
❑2, Apr 98 .... 2.99
❑3, Apr 98 .... 2.99
❑4, Apr 98 .... 2.99
❑5, May 98 .... 2.99
❑6, May 98 .... 2.99
❑7, Jun 98, Inside Sabretooth. 2.99
❑8, Jul 98,cover says Jun, indicia says Jul 2.99
❑9, Jul 98 .... 2.99
❑10, Aug 98 .... 2.99
❑11, Aug 98............................ 2.99
❑12, Sep 98, A: Sabretooth 2.99
❑13, Sep 98, V: Sentinels 2.99
❑14, Oct 98, A: Cable 2.99
❑15, Oct 98 .... 2.99
❑16, Nov 98,Colossus vs. Juggernaut 3.99
❑17 .... 3.99
❑18 .... 3.99
❑19 .... 3.99
❑20 .... 3.99
❑21 .... 3.99
❑22, A: Sentinels; A: Bishop.... 3.99
❑23, A: Bishop........................ 3.99
❑24, A: Nimrod; A: Gambit; A: Bishop 3.99
❑25, A: Gambit; A: Bishop....... 3.99
❑26, A: Pyro; A: Brotherhood of Evil Mutants; A: Blob; A: Avalanche,Mystique apperance 3.99

X-MEN: THE ULTRA COLLECTION
MARVEL

Value: Cover or less

❑1, Dec 94,Pin-ups 2.95
❑2, Jan 95,Pin-ups.................. 2.95
❑3, Feb 95,Pin-ups 2.95
❑4, Mar 95,Pin-ups................. 2.95
❑5, Apr 95,Pin-ups 2.95

X-MEN: THE WEDDING ALBUM
MARVEL

	ORIG	GOOD	FINE	N-MINT
❑1, nn..	2.95	0.60	1.50	3.00

X-MEN: TRUE FRIENDS
MARVEL

Value: Cover or less

❑1, Sep 99 .... 2.99
❑2, Oct 99, Royal Hunt............ 2.99
❑3, Nov 99.............................. 2.99

X-MEN ULTRA III PREVIEW
MARVEL

Value: Cover or less

❑1, Nov 95, nn; enhanced card-stock cover; previews Fleer card art 2.95

X-MEN UNIVERSE
MARVEL

Value: Cover or less

❑1, Dec 99, Beauty & The Beast; Call to Arms!,contains material originally published as Astonishing X-Men #1, Generation X #55, and Uncanny X-Men #373 .... 4.99
❑2.. 4.99
❑3.. 4.99
❑4.. 4.99
❑5.. 4.99
❑6.. 4.99
❑7 .... 4.99
❑8 .... 4.99
❑9 .... 4.99
❑10 .... 4.99
❑11 .... 4.99
❑12, Sep 00 .... 3.99
❑13, Dec 00............................ 3.99
❑14, Jan 01 .... 3.99
❑15, Feb 01 .... 3.99

X-MEN UNIVERSE: PAST, PRESENT AND FUTURE
MARVEL

Value: Cover or less

❑1, Feb 99............................. 2.99

X-MEN UNLIMITED
MARVEL

	ORIG	GOOD	FINE	N-MINT
❑1, Jun 93	3.95	1.20	3.00	6.00
❑2, Sep 93	3.95	1.00	2.50	5.00
❑3, Dec 93, A: Sabretooth	3.95	1.20	3.00	6.00
❑4, Mar 94...	3.95	1.00	2.50	5.00
❑5, Jun 94	3.95	0.90	2.25	4.50
❑6, Sep 94	3.95	0.80	2.00	4.00
❑7, Dec 94	3.95	0.80	2.00	4.00
❑8, Oct 95	3.95	0.80	2.00	4.00
❑9, Dec 95, A: Bloodscream	3.95	0.80	2.00	4.00
❑10, Mar 96, MWa (w), The Beast: Need to Know, O: Beast,Age of Apocalypse Beast imprisons and replaces real Beast..........	3.95	1.40	3.50	7.00
❑11, Jun 96,Magneto and Rogue...............	3.95	1.00	2.50	5.00
❑12, Sep 96, Onslaught: Impact, A: Doctor Strange,Juggernaut imprisoned in Cyttorak Gem	2.95	0.80	2.00	4.00
❑13, Dec 96, Fugitive From Space; Junction, A: Silver Surfer..	2.95	0.60	1.50	3.00

	ORIG	GOOD	FINE	N-MINT
❑14, Mar 97, Innocence Lost, A: Franklin Richards	2.99	0.60	1.50	3.00
❑15, Jun 97,Wolverine vs. Maverick	2.99	0.60	1.50	3.00
❑16, Sep 97	2.99	0.60	1.50	3.00
❑17, Dec 97	2.99	0.60	1.50	3.00
❑18, Apr 98	2.99	0.60	1.50	3.00
❑19, Jun 98	2.99	0.60	1.50	3.00
❑20, Sep 98	2.99	0.60	1.50	2.99
❑21, Dec 98	2.99	0.60	1.50	2.99
❑22, Jan 99	2.99	0.60	1.50	2.99
❑23, Jun 99	2.99	0.60	1.50	2.99
❑24, Sep 99	2.99	0.60	1.50	2.99
❑25, Dec 99	2.99	0.60	1.50	2.99
❑26	2.99	0.60	1.50	2.99
❑27	2.99	0.60	1.50	2.99
❑28	2.99	0.60	1.50	2.99
❑29, Dec 00, Maximum Security; Renewed Acquaintances, A: Bishop	2.99	0.60	1.50	2.99
❑30, Jan 01	2.99	0.60	1.50	2.99
❑31	—	0.60	1.50	2.99
❑32	2.50	0.50	1.25	2.50

X-MEN VS. DRACULA
MARVEL

	ORIG	GOOD	FINE	N-MINT
❑1,Reprints Uncanny X-Men Annual #6	1.75	0.40	1.00	2.00

X-MEN VS. EXILES
MALIBU

	ORIG	GOOD	FINE	N-MINT
❑0, Oct 95, limited edition	—	0.60	1.50	3.00
❑0/LE, Oct 95, limited edition; Limited edition with Certificate of Authenticity; Gold foil	—	1.00	2.50	5.00

X-MEN VS. THE AVENGERS
MARVEL

	ORIG	GOOD	FINE	N-MINT
❑1, Apr 87, A: Magneto; 1: Titanium Man II.	1.50	0.80	2.00	4.00
❑2, May 87, A: Magneto	1.50	0.60	1.50	3.00
❑3, Jun 87, A: Magneto	1.50	0.60	1.50	3.00
❑4, Jul 87, A: Magneto	1.50	0.60	1.50	3.00

X-MEN VS. THE BROOD
MARVEL

Value: Cover or less

- ❑1, Sep 96, Brood Day of Wrath part 1,wraparound cover 2.95
- ❑2, Oct 96, Brood Day of Wrath part 2,wraparound cover; Final Issue 2.95

X-MEN/WILDC.A.T.S: THE DARK AGE
MARVEL

Value: Cover or less

- ❑1/A, May 98,cardstock cover 4.50
- ❑1/B, May 98,alternate cardstock cover 4.50

X-MEN: WRATH OF APOCALYPSE
MARVEL

Value: Cover or less

- ❑1, Feb 96, Endgame, A: Cable (baby),reprints X-Factor #65-68; Nathan Summers sent into future (becomes Cable) 4.95

X-MEN: YEAR OF THE MUTANTS COLLECTOR'S PREVIEW
MARVEL

	ORIG	GOOD	FINE	N-MINT
❑1, Feb 95,One-Shot	1.95	0.40	1.00	2.00

X-NATION 2099
MARVEL

Value: Cover or less

- ❑1, Mar 96,foil cover 3.95
- ❑2, Apr 96 ..... 1.95
- ❑3, May 96 ..... 1.95
- ❑4, Jun 96 ..... 1.95
- ❑5, Jul 96 ..... 1.95
- ❑6, Aug 96,Final Issue 1.95

X-O DATABASE
VALIANT

	ORIG	GOOD	FINE	N-MINT
❑1,no cover price; polybagged with X-O TPB; armor schematics	—	0.20	0.50	1.00

X-O MANOWAR
VALIANT

	ORIG	GOOD	FINE	N-MINT
❑0, Aug 93, O: X-O Manowar,chromium cover	3.50	0.70	1.75	3.50
❑0/GO, O: X-O Manowar,chromium cover; Gold logo edition	—	1.00	2.50	5.00
❑0.5, The Wolfbridge Affair, Mini-comic from Wizard Magazine	—	0.60	1.50	3.00
❑1, Feb 92, BL, Retribution, Part 1, O: X-O Manowar; 1: Aric Dacia; 1: X-O Manowar armor	1.95	0.50	1.25	2.50
❑2, Mar 92	1.95	0.50	1.25	2.50
❑3, Apr 92, A: Solar	1.95	0.40	1.00	2.00
❑4, May 92, A: Harbinger; 1: Shadowman (cameo, out of costume)	1.95	0.40	1.00	2.00
❑5, Jun 92	1.95	0.40	1.00	2.00
❑6, Jul 92	2.25	0.45	1.13	2.25
❑7, Aug 92, FM (c), Unity, Part 5	2.25	0.45	1.13	2.25
❑8, Sep 92, Unity, Part 13	2.25	0.45	1.13	2.25
❑9, Oct 92	2.25	0.45	1.13	2.25
❑10, Nov 92	2.25	0.45	1.13	2.25
❑11, Dec 92	2.25	0.45	1.13	2.25
❑12, Jan 93, Seed of Destruction, Part 2	2.25	0.45	1.13	2.25
❑13, Feb 93, A: Solar	2.25	0.45	1.13	2.25
❑14, Mar 93, A: Turok	2.25	0.45	1.13	2.25
❑15, Apr 93, BL (w), A: Turok	2.25	0.45	1.13	2.25
❑16, May 93, Family Matters	2.25	0.45	1.13	2.25
❑17, Jun 93, Push and Shove	2.25	0.45	1.13	2.25
❑18, Jul 93, Operation: Deep Freeze, Part 1	2.25	0.45	1.13	2.25
❑19, Aug 93, Operation: Deep Freeze, Part 2, serial number coupon for contest	2.25	0.45	1.13	2.25
❑20, Sep 93, Operation: Deep Freeze, Part 3	2.25	0.45	1.13	2.25
❑21, Oct 93, Strange Bedfellows	2.25	0.45	1.13	2.25
❑22, Nov 93, White Kings and Black Knights, Part 1	2.25	0.45	1.13	2.25
❑23, Dec 93, White Kings and Black Knights, Part 2	2.25	0.45	1.13	2.25
❑24, Jan 94, Homecoming	2.25	0.45	1.13	2.25
❑25, Feb 94, Unit, Corps, God, Country, Part 1; Unit, Corps, God, Country, Part 2,with Armorines #0	3.50	0.70	1.75	3.50
❑26, Mar 94	2.25	0.45	1.13	2.25
❑27, Apr 94, The Hunt, A: Turok	2.25	0.45	1.13	2.25
❑28, May 94,trading card	2.25	0.45	1.13	2.25
❑29, Jun 94, A: Turok	2.25	0.45	1.13	2.25
❑30, Aug 94, A: Solar	2.25	0.45	1.13	2.25
❑31, Sep 94,New armor	2.25	0.45	1.13	2.25
❑32, Oct 94	2.25	0.45	1.13	2.25
❑33, Nov 94, The Chaos Effect: Delta, Part 3,Chaos Effect	2.25	0.45	1.13	2.25
❑34, Dec 94, Vengeance Trail	2.25	0.45	1.13	2.25
❑35, Jan 95, Vengeance Trail	2.25	0.45	1.13	2.25
❑36, Feb 95, Vengeance Trail	2.25	0.45	1.13	2.25
❑37, Mar 95, The Wolfbridge Affair, Part 1	2.25	0.45	1.13	2.25
❑38, Mar 95, The Wolfbridge Affair, Part 2	2.25	0.45	1.13	2.25
❑39, Mar 95, The Wolfbridge Affair, Part 3	2.25	0.45	1.13	2.25
❑40, Mar 95, The Wolfbridge Affair, Part 4	2.25	0.45	1.13	2.25
❑41, Apr 95	2.25	0.45	1.13	2.25
❑42, May 95, V: Shadowman,contains Birthquake preview	2.25	0.45	1.13	2.25
❑43, Jun 95	2.25	0.45	1.13	2.25
❑44, Jul 95,Birthquake	2.50	0.50	1.25	2.50
❑45, Jul 95,Birthquake	2.50	0.50	1.25	2.50
❑46, Aug 95	2.50	0.50	1.25	2.50
❑47, Aug 95, D: Ken Clarkson	2.50	0.50	1.25	2.50
❑48, Sep 95	2.50	0.50	1.25	2.50
❑49, Sep 95	2.50	0.50	1.25	2.50
❑50, Oct 95,cover forms diptych with X-O Manowar #50-O	2.50	0.50	1.25	2.50
❑50/A, Oct 95,cover forms diptych with X-O Manowar #50-X	2.50	0.50	1.25	2.50
❑51, Nov 95	2.50	0.50	1.25	2.50
❑52, Nov 95	2.50	0.50	1.25	2.50
❑53, Dec 95	2.50	0.50	1.25	2.50
❑54, Dec 95	2.50	0.50	1.25	2.50
❑55, Jan 96	2.50	0.50	1.25	2.50
❑56, Jan 96	2.50	0.50	1.25	2.50
❑57, Feb 96	2.50	0.50	1.25	2.50
❑58, Feb 96	2.50	0.50	1.25	2.50
❑59, Mar 96	2.50	0.50	1.25	2.50
❑60, Mar 96	2.50	0.50	1.25	2.50
❑61, Apr 96	2.50	0.50	1.25	2.50
❑62, Apr 96	2.50	0.50	1.25	2.50
❑63, May 96,Master Darque acquires X-O armor	2.50	0.50	1.25	2.50
❑64, May 96, D: Master Darque	2.50	0.50	1.25	2.50
❑65, Jun 96,X-O armor asserts control over itself	2.50	0.50	1.25	2.50
❑66, Jul 96, D: Gamin; D: Ax,Aric's armor rebels	2.50	0.50	1.25	2.50
❑67, Aug 96	2.50	0.50	1.25	2.50
❑68, Sep 96,Final Issue	2.50	0.50	1.25	2.50
❑YB 1, Apr 95, Yearbook; 1995 Yearbook	2.95	0.59	1.48	2.95

X-O MANOWAR (VOL. 2)
ACCLAIM

	ORIG	GOOD	FINE	N-MINT
❑1, Oct 96, Operation: Rebirth, Part 1; Fear Itself, D: Rand Banion,cover says Feb; indicia says Oct 96	2.50	0.50	1.25	2.50
❑1/A, Oct 96,alternate cover	2.50	0.50	1.25	2.50
❑1/SC, Fear Itself,Painted cover	2.50	0.50	1.25	2.50
❑2, Mar 97,Donovan Wylie becomes X-O	2.50	0.50	1.25	2.50
❑3, Apr 97	2.50	0.50	1.25	2.50
❑4, May 97	2.50	0.50	1.25	2.50
❑5, Jun 97	2.50	0.50	1.25	2.50
❑6, Jul 97, V: Magnus	2.50	0.50	1.25	2.50

	ORIG	GOOD	FINE	N-MINT
❑7, Aug 97, A: New Hard Corps	2.50	0.50	1.25	2.50
❑8, Sep 97	2.50	0.50	1.25	2.50
❑9, Oct 97	2.50	0.50	1.25	2.50
❑10, Nov 97, A: Bravado,Avengers #3 homage cover	2.50	0.50	1.25	2.50
❑11, Dec 97, The Past is Prologue	2.50	0.50	1.25	2.50
❑12, Jan 98	2.50	0.50	1.25	2.50
❑13, Feb 98	2.50	0.50	1.25	2.50
❑14, Mar 98	2.50	0.50	1.25	2.50
❑15, Apr 98	2.50	0.50	1.25	2.50
❑16, Jan 98, V: Quantum & Woody,no cover date, indicia says Jan	2.50	0.50	1.25	2.50
❑17, Feb 98	2.50	0.50	1.25	2.50
❑18, Mar 98,return of Rand Banion	2.50	0.50	1.25	2.50
❑19, Apr 98, 1: Master Blaster	2.50	0.50	1.25	2.50
❑20, May 98, Free Your Mind & Your Ass Will Follow	2.50	0.50	1.25	2.50
❑21, Jun 98	2.50	0.50	1.25	2.50
❑Ash 1, Oct 96, b&w; no cover price; preview of upcoming series	—	0.20	0.50	1.00

X-O MANOWAR/IRON MAN: IN HEAVY METAL
ACCLAIM

Value: Cover or less

❑1, Sep 96, The Reality Alchemists,crossover with Marvel; concludes in Iron Man/X-O Manowar: In Heavy Metal ... 2.50

XOMBI
DC

	ORIG	GOOD	FINE	N-MINT
❑0, Jan 94, Shadow War, Part 3, 1: Xombi,Shadow War	1.95	0.50	1.25	2.50
❑1, Jun 94, Silent Cathedrals, 1: Nun of the Above; 1: Catholic Girl; O: Xombi	1.75	0.40	1.00	2.00
❑1/PL, Jun 94, Silent Cathedrals,Platinum cover	—	0.60	1.50	3.00
❑2, Jul 94, Silent Cathedrals, 1: Knight of the Spoken Fire	1.75	0.35	0.88	1.75
❑3, Aug 94, Silent Cathedrals	1.75	0.35	0.88	1.75
❑4, Sep 94, Silent Cathedrals	1.75	0.35	0.88	1.75
❑5, Oct 94, Silent Cathedrals	1.75	0.35	0.88	1.75
❑6, Nov 94, Silent Cathedrals	1.75	0.35	0.88	1.75
❑7, Dec 94	1.75	0.35	0.88	1.75
❑8, Jan 95, School of Anguish, Part 2	1.75	0.35	0.88	1.75
❑9, Feb 95	1.75	0.35	0.88	1.75
❑10, Mar 95	1.75	0.35	0.88	1.75
❑11, Apr 95	1.75	0.35	0.88	1.75
❑12, May 95	1.75	0.35	0.88	1.75
❑13, Jun 95	1.75	0.35	0.88	1.75
❑14, Jul 95	2.50	0.50	1.25	2.50
❑15, Aug 95	2.50	0.50	1.25	2.50
❑16, Sep 95	2.50	0.50	1.25	2.50
❑17, Oct 95, Hidden Cities, Part 1	0.99	0.20	0.50	0.99
❑18, Nov 95, Hidden Cities, Part 2	2.50	0.50	1.25	2.50
❑19, Dec 95, Hidden Cities, Part 3	2.50	0.50	1.25	2.50
❑20, Jan 96, Hidden Cities, Part 4	2.50	0.50	1.25	2.50
❑21, Feb 96, Hidden Cities, Part 5,Final Issue; Giant-size	3.50	0.70	1.75	3.50

X: ONE SHOT TO THE HEAD
DARK HORSE

Value: Cover or less

❑1, Aug 94, nn; One-Shot ... 2.50

X-PATROL
MARVEL

Value: Cover or less

❑1, Apr 96, 1: Ferro-Man; 1: Niles Cable; 1: Beastling; 1: Elasti-Girl; 1: Shatterstarfire ... 1.95

X-RAY COMICS
SLAVE LABOR

Value: Cover or less

❑1, Feb 98, River of Sh*t!; Goth Girls ... 2.95

❑2, May 98, Redneck U.S.A.; Dead Love ... 2.95

❑3, Apr 98, Strange Air; Satan Strikes! ... 2.95

XSE
MARVEL

	ORIG	GOOD	FINE	N-MINT
❑1, Nov 96, A: Bishop and Shard	1.95	0.39	0.98	1.95
❑1/A,variant cover	—	0.50	1.25	2.50
❑2, Dec 96, Future Intense, A: Bishop and Shard	1.95	0.39	0.98	1.95
❑3, Jan 97, Future Betrayed, A: Bishop and Shard	1.95	0.39	0.98	1.95
❑4, Feb 97, A: Bishop and Shard,Final Issue	1.95	0.39	0.98	1.95

XSTACY: THE FIRST LOOK EDITION
FRESCO

Value: Cover or less

❑1, nn; b&w; promotional comic book sold at convention; also collects cartoons that ran in CBG ... 2.95

Donovan Wylie, a scientist examining the X-O technology, got first-hand experience with the alien armor when he became the new X-O Manowar.

© 1997 Acclaim

XSTACY: THE LIBRETTO
FRESCO

Value: Cover or less

❑1, nn; b&w ... 2.95

X-TERMINATORS
MARVEL

	ORIG	GOOD	FINE	N-MINT
❑1, Oct 88, 1: X-Terminators,Inferno	1.00	0.40	1.00	2.00
❑2, Nov 88,Inferno	1.00	0.40	1.00	2.00
❑3, Dec 88,Inferno	1.00	0.40	1.00	2.00
❑4, Jan 89,Inferno	1.00	0.40	1.00	2.00

X-TV
COMIC ZONE

Value: Cover or less

❑1, b&w; adult ... 2.95

❑2, b&w; adult ... 2.95

X-UNIVERSE
MARVEL

Value: Cover or less

❑1, May 95, Last Stand,foil cover ... 3.50

❑2, Jun 95,foil cover ... 3.50

XXXENOPHILE
PALLIARD

	ORIG	GOOD	FINE	N-MINT
❑1, PF, PF (w),adult	2.50	1.00	2.50	5.00
❑1-2, PF, PF (w),adult; 2nd Printing	2.50	0.59	1.48	2.95
❑2, Dec 89, PF, PF (w),adult	2.50	0.50	1.25	2.50
❑2-2, Jun 91, PF, PF (w),adult; 2nd Printing	2.50	0.59	1.48	2.95
❑3, Jul 90, PF, PF (w),adult	2.50	0.50	1.25	2.50
❑3-2, Mar 92,adult; 2nd Printing	2.50	0.60	1.50	3.00
❑4, PF, PF (w),adult	2.50	0.50	1.25	2.50
❑4-2, PF, PF (w),adult; 2nd Printing	2.95	0.59	1.48	2.95
❑5, PF (w), Hoisters,adult	2.95	0.59	1.48	2.95
❑6, PF, PF (w),adult	2.95	0.59	1.48	2.95
❑7, PF, PF (w),adult	2.95	0.59	1.48	2.95
❑8, Feb 93, PF, PF (w),adult	2.95	0.59	1.48	2.95
❑9, Jan 94, PF, PF (w),adult	2.95	0.59	1.48	2.95
❑10, Jan 95, PF, PF (w),adult; trading-card game cover; led to Xxxenophile card game	2.95	0.59	1.48	2.95
❑11, PF, PF (w),adult	2.95	0.59	1.48	2.95

XXXENOPHILE PRESENTS
PALLIARD

Value: Cover or less

❑2, Feb 93 ... 2.95

❑3, Aug 94, Utopia Unlimited, Part 1 ... 2.95

❑4, Jul 95, Incubus, Part 2 ... 2.95

XXX WOMEN
FANTAGRAPHICS

Value: Cover or less

❑1, b&w; adult ... 2.95

❑2, b&w; adult ... 2.95

❑3, b&w; adult ... 2.95

❑4, b&w; adult ... 2.95

XYZ COMICS
KITCHEN SINK

	ORIG	GOOD	FINE	N-MINT
❑1, Jun 72, Cubist be Bop; Bo Bo Bolinski in Down at the Neighborhood Bar,adult	0.50	2.00	5.00	10.00
❑1-2, Cubist be Bop; Bo Bo Bolinski in Down at the Neighborhood Bar, nn; b&w; adult; 2nd Printing	—	1.00	2.50	5.00
❑, Cubist be Bop; Bo Bo Bolinski in Down at the Neighborhood Bar, nn; b&w; adult; 3rd Printing	—	0.80	2.00	4.00
❑1-4, Cubist be Bop; Bo Bo Bolinski in Down at the Neighborhood Bar, nn; b&w; adult; 4th Printing	—	0.60	1.50	3.00
❑1-5, Cubist be Bop; Bo Bo Bolinski in Down at the Neighborhood Bar, nn; b&w; adult; 5th Printing	—	0.60	1.50	3.00
❑1-6, Cubist be Bop; Bo Bo Bolinski in Down at the Neighborhood Bar, nn; b&w; adult; 6th Printing; sixth printing	2.95	0.60	1.50	3.00
❑1-7, Jan 87, Cubist be Bop; Bo Bo Bolinski in Down at the Neighborhood Bar, nn; b&w; adult; 7th Printing; seventh printing	2.00	0.60	1.50	3.00

Y

YAHOO
FANTAGRAPHICS

	ORIG	GOOD	FINE	N-MINT
❑1, Oct 88, The Jaded Comix Bistro	2.00	0.50	1.25	2.50
❑2, Oct 89,In the Company of Longhair	2.25	0.45	1.13	2.25
❑3, Apr 90, This Perfect Day	2.00	0.40	1.00	2.00
❑4, Jan 91,Airpower Through Victory	2.50	0.50	1.25	2.50
❑5, Dec 91, How I Loved the War	2.50	0.50	1.25	2.50
❑6, Aug 92,Take It Off (Topless cover)	2.50	0.50	1.25	2.50

YAKUZA
ETERNITY
Value: Cover or less

- ❑1, Sep 87 .... 1.95
- ❑2, Nov 87 .... 1.95
- ❑3, Jan 88 .... 1.95
- ❑4, Apr 88 .... 1.95

YAK YAK
DELL

	ORIG	GOOD	FINE	N-MINT
❑1,Four-Color 1186	0.15	12.00	30.00	60.00
❑2,Four-Color 1348	0.15	12.00	30.00	60.00

YAMARA
STEVE JACKSON GAMES
Value: Cover or less

- ❑1, nn; b&w; magazine-sized; collects strips from Dragon 9.95

YARN MAN
KITCHEN SINK
Value: Cover or less

- ❑1, Oct 89, b&w 2.00

YAWN
PARODY
Value: Cover or less

- ❑1, Questionable, b&w; Spawn parody 2.50
- ❑1-2,2nd Printing 2.50

YEAH!
DC
Value: Cover or less

- ❑1, Oct 99, Everybody Say Yeah! 2.95
- ❑2, Nov 99,all copies destroyed 2.95
- ❑3, Dec 99 .... 2.95
- ❑4, Jan 00, The Origins of Yeah, Part 1 .... 2.95
- ❑5, Feb 00, The Origins of Yeah, Part 2 .... 2.95
- ❑6, Mar 00 .... 2.95
- ❑7, Apr 00, Hobo's In Love 2.95
- ❑8, May 00, Yeah! Goes to War! 2.95

YEAR IN REVIEW: SPIDER-MAN
MARVEL
Value: Cover or less

- ❑1, Feb 00 .... 2.99

YEAR OF THE MONKEY (AARON WARNER'S...)
IMAGE
Value: Cover or less

- ❑1 .... 2.95
- ❑2, Oct 97 .... 2.95

YELLOW SUBMARINE
GOLD KEY

	ORIG	GOOD	FINE	N-MINT
❑1, Feb 69, nn; adapts movie; poster	0.35	22.00	55.00	110.00

YIKES! (ALTERNATIVE)
ALTERNATIVE
Value: Cover or less

- ❑1, Nov 97,green and white 2.95
- ❑2 .... 2.95

YIKES! (WEISSMAN)
WEISSMAN
Value: Cover or less

- ❑1, b&w 2.50
- ❑2, b&w 2.50
- ❑3, b&w 2.50
- ❑4, Win 95, b&w 2.50
- ❑5,b&w with spot color 2.50

YIN FEI THE CHINESE NINJA
DR. LEUNG'S
Value: Cover or less

- ❑1 .... 1.80
- ❑2 .... 1.80
- ❑3 .... 1.80
- ❑4 .... 1.80
- ❑5 .... 1.80
- ❑6 .... 1.80

YOGI BEAR (ARCHIE)
ARCHIE
Value: Cover or less

- ❑1, May 97 .... 1.50

YOGI BEAR (CHARLTON)
CHARLTON

	ORIG	GOOD	FINE	N-MINT
❑1	—	4.40	11.00	22.00
❑2	—	3.00	7.50	15.00
❑3	—	3.00	7.50	15.00
❑4, May 71	—	2.40	6.00	12.00
❑5	—	2.40	6.00	12.00
❑6	—	2.40	6.00	12.00
❑7, Sum 71	—	3.00	7.50	15.00
❑8	—	2.40	6.00	12.00
❑9	—	2.40	6.00	12.00
❑10, Mar 72, The Sleepwalker; Christmas is Coming	0.20	2.40	6.00	12.00
❑11	—	1.60	4.00	8.00
❑12	—	1.60	4.00	8.00
❑13	0.20	1.60	4.00	8.00
❑14	—	1.60	4.00	8.00
❑15	—	1.60	4.00	8.00
❑16	—	1.60	4.00	8.00
❑17	—	1.60	4.00	8.00
❑18, Jun 73	0.20	1.60	4.00	8.00
❑19	—	1.60	4.00	8.00
❑20, Oct 73	0.20	1.60	4.00	8.00
❑21, Dec 73	0.20	1.20	3.00	6.00
❑22, Sep 74	0.25	1.20	3.00	6.00
❑23	—	1.20	3.00	6.00
❑24	—	1.20	3.00	6.00
❑25	—	1.20	3.00	6.00
❑26	—	1.20	3.00	6.00
❑27, Aug 75	0.25	1.20	3.00	6.00
❑28, Oct 75	0.25	1.20	3.00	6.00
❑29	—	1.20	3.00	6.00
❑30	—	1.20	3.00	6.00
❑31, Apr 76	0.30	1.20	3.00	6.00
❑32	—	1.20	3.00	6.00
❑33, Sep 76	0.30	1.20	3.00	6.00
❑34	—	1.20	3.00	6.00
❑35,Final Issue	—	1.20	3.00	6.00

YOGI BEAR (HARVEY)
HARVEY
Value: Cover or less

- ❑1, Sep 92 .... 1.25
- ❑2, Jan 93 .... 1.25
- ❑3, Jun 93 .... 1.25
- ❑4, Sep 93 .... 1.25
- ❑5 .... 1.50
- ❑6 .... 1.50

YOGI BEAR (MARVEL)
MARVEL

	ORIG	GOOD	FINE	N-MINT
❑1	0.35	1.20	3.00	6.00
❑2	0.35	0.80	2.00	4.00
❑3	0.35	0.80	2.00	4.00
❑4	0.35	0.80	2.00	4.00
❑5	0.35	0.80	2.00	4.00

YOGI BEAR BIG BOOK
HARVEY
Value: Cover or less

- ❑1, Nov 92 .... 1.95
- ❑2, Mar 93 .... 1.95

YOGI BEAR GIANT SIZE
HARVEY
Value: Cover or less

- ❑1, Oct 92 .... 2.25
- ❑2, Apr 93 .... 2.25

YOU AND YOUR BIG MOUTH
FANTAGRAPHICS

	ORIG	GOOD	FINE	N-MINT
❑1	—	0.50	1.25	2.50
❑2	—	0.50	1.25	2.50
❑3	—	0.50	1.25	2.50
❑4, Aug 94, b&w; Anthology	2.50	0.50	1.25	2.50

YOUNG ALL-STARS, THE
DC

	ORIG	GOOD	FINE	N-MINT
❑1, Jun 87, The Coming of the Young All-Stars, 1: Iron Munroe & Flying Fox	1.00	0.60	1.50	3.00
❑2, Jul 87	1.00	0.50	1.25	2.50
❑3, Aug 87	1.00	0.50	1.25	2.50
❑4, Sep 87	1.00	0.35	0.88	1.75
❑5, Oct 87	1.00	0.35	0.88	1.75
❑6, Nov 87	1.00	0.35	0.88	1.75
❑7, Dec 87	1.25	0.30	0.75	1.50
❑8, Jan 88, Millennium,Millennium	1.25	0.30	0.75	1.50
❑9, Feb 88, Millennium,Millennium	1.25	0.30	0.75	1.50
❑10, Mar 88, O: Iron Munro	1.25	0.30	0.75	1.50
❑11, Apr 88, O: Iron Munro	1.25	0.30	0.75	1.50
❑12, May 88	1.25	0.30	0.75	1.50
❑13, Jun 88	1.25	0.30	0.75	1.50
❑14, Jul 88	1.25	0.30	0.75	1.50
❑15, Aug 88	1.25	0.30	0.75	1.50
❑16, Sep 88, Dzyan Inheritance	1.25	0.30	0.75	1.50
❑17, Oct 88, Dzyan Inheritance	1.25	0.30	0.75	1.50
❑18, Nov 88, Dzyan Inheritance	1.25	0.30	0.75	1.50
❑19, Dec 88, Dzyan Inheritance	1.50	0.35	0.88	1.75
❑20, Dec 88, O: Flying Fox	1.50	0.35	0.88	1.75
❑21, Jan 88, Atom & Evil	1.50	0.35	0.88	1.75
❑22, Jan 89, Atom & Evil	1.50	0.35	0.88	1.75
❑23, Mar 89, Atom & Evil	1.50	0.35	0.88	1.75
❑24, Apr 89, Atom & Evil	1.50	0.35	0.88	1.75
❑25, May 89, Atom & Evil	1.50	0.35	0.88	1.75
❑26, Jun 89	1.75	0.35	0.88	1.75
❑27, Jul 89	1.75	0.35	0.88	1.75
❑28, Aug 89	1.75	0.35	0.88	1.75
❑29, Sep 89	1.75	0.35	0.88	1.75
❑30, Oct 89	1.75	0.35	0.88	1.75
❑31, Nov 89,Final Issue	1.75	0.35	0.88	1.75
❑Anl 1, A: Infinity Inc.	2.00	0.40	1.00	2.00

YOUNGBLOOD
IMAGE

	ORIG	GOOD	FINE	N-MINT
❑0, Dec 92, RL, RL (w), coupon for Image Comics #0	1.95	0.40	1.00	2.00
❑0/GO, Dec 92, RL ,gold	—	0.80	2.00	4.00
❑1, Apr 92, RL, RL (w), 1: The Four; 1: Youngblood; 1: Chapel, Flip-book; trading card; First comic by Image Comics	2.50	0.50	1.25	2.50
❑1-2, May 92, RL, RL (w), 1: The Four; 1: Youngblood; 1: Chapel,2nd Printing; gold border; First comic by Image Comics	2.50	0.40	1.00	2.00

	ORIG	GOOD	FINE	N-MINT
❑2, Jul 92, RL, 1: Berserkers; 1: Prophet; 1: Darkthorn; 1: Shadowhawk; 1: Kirby,cover says Jun, indicia says Jul; red logo	2.50	0.50	1.25	2.50
❑2/A, Jul 92, RL ,green logo	2.50	0.50	1.25	2.50
❑3, Aug 92, RL, 1: Supreme; 1: Showdown	2.50	0.50	1.25	2.50
❑4, Feb 93, RL, 1: Pitt	2.50	0.50	1.25	2.50
❑5, Jul 93,backed with Brigade #4	2.50	0.40	1.00	2.00
❑6, Jun 94, poster	1.95	0.70	1.75	3.50
❑7, Jul 94	2.50	0.50	1.25	2.50
❑8, Sep 94	2.50	0.50	1.25	2.50
❑9, Sep 94,Image X-Month	2.50	0.50	1.25	2.50
❑9/A, Sep 94,Image X-Month	2.50	0.50	1.25	2.50
❑10, Dec 94, A: Spawn; D: Chapel	2.50	0.50	1.25	2.50
❑SS 1,Super Special	2.99	0.60	1.50	2.99
❑YB 1, Jul 93, 1: Tyrax; 1: Kanan, Yearbook 1	2.50	0.50	1.25	2.50

YOUNGBLOOD (VOL. 2)
IMAGE
Value: Cover or less

- ❑1, Sep 95, Endings and Beginnings ... 2.50
- ❑2, Oct 95 ... 2.50
- ❑2/A, Oct 95,alternate cover ... 2.50
- ❑3, Nov 95,Babewatch ... 2.95
- ❑3/A, Nov 95,alternate cover; Babewatch ... 2.50
- ❑3/B, Nov 95,alternate cover; Babewatch ... 2.50
- ❑3/C, Nov 95,alternate cover; Babewatch ... 2.50
- ❑4, Jan 96, Extreme Destroyer, Part 4,polybagged with Riptide card ... 2.50
- ❑5, Feb 96, A: Jeriko ... 2.50
- ❑5/A, Feb 96, A: Jeriko,alternate cover ... 2.50
- ❑6, Mar 96, A: Angela and Glory 2.50
- ❑7, Apr 96,Shadowhunt ... 2.50
- ❑8, May 96 ... 2.50
- ❑9, Jun 96 ... 2.50
- ❑10, Jul 96,flipbook with Blindside #1 preview ... 2.50
- ❑11 ... 2.50
- ❑12 ... 2.50
- ❑13 ... 2.50
- ❑14, RL (w), Bad Intent ... 2.50
- ❑15,Final Issue ... 2.50

YOUNGBLOOD (VOL. 3)
AWESOME

	ORIG	GOOD	FINE	N-MINT
❑1/A, Feb 98, AMo (w),Blue Awesome logo, Orange Youngblood logo	2.50	0.50	1.25	2.50
❑1/B, Feb 98, AMo (w),Purple Awesome and Youngblood logos	2.50	0.50	1.25	2.50
❑1/C, Feb 98, AMo (w),Teal Awesome and Youngblood logos	2.50	0.50	1.25	2.50
❑1/D, Feb 98, AMo (w),White Awesome logo, Yellow Youngblood logo; Shaft in foreground	2.50	0.50	1.25	2.50
❑1/E, Feb 98, AMo (w),Blue Awesome logo, White Youngblood logo	2.50	0.50	1.25	2.50
❑1/F, Feb 98, AMo (w),White Awesome and Youngblood logos	2.50	0.50	1.25	2.50
❑1/G, Feb 98, AMo (w),White Awesome logo, Yellow Youngblood logo; Suprema in foreground	2.50	0.50	1.25	2.50
❑1/H, Feb 98, AMo (w),Baby Shaft on cover; Blue Awesome logo	2.50	0.50	1.25	2.50
❑1/I, Feb 98, AMo (w),Orange Awesome logo, Red Youngblood logo	2.50	0.50	1.25	2.50
❑1/J, Feb 98, AMo (w),White Awesome logo, Teal Youngblood logo; Suprema in foreground	2.50	0.50	1.25	2.50
❑1/K, Feb 98, AMo (w),3 women on cover; White Awesome logo, Teal Youngblood logo	2.50	0.50	1.25	2.50
❑1/L, Feb 98, AMo (w),Teal Awesome logo, Yellow Youngblood logo	2.50	0.50	1.25	2.50
❑1/M, Feb 98, AMo (w),Three women posing on cover, leaning against wall; A! List exclusive; Foil logo	2.50	0.70	1.75	3.50
❑1/N, AMo (w),1+ issue	2.50	0.50	1.25	2.50
❑2, Aug 98, AMo (w)	2.50	0.50	1.25	2.50

YOUNGBLOOD BATTLEZONE
IMAGE
Value: Cover or less

- ❑1, Apr 93 ... 1.95
- ❑2, Jul 94 ... 2.95

YOUNGBLOOD: STRIKEFILE
IMAGE

	ORIG	GOOD	FINE	N-MINT
❑1, Apr 93, RL, 1: Glory; 1: Giger; 1: The Allies	2.50	0.50	1.25	2.50
❑1/GO, Apr 93, Gold edition	—	0.50	1.25	2.50
❑2, Jul 93, RL	2.50	0.50	1.25	2.50
❑2/GO, Jul 93, Gold edition	—	0.50	1.25	2.50
❑3, Sep 93	2.50	0.50	1.25	2.50
❑4, Oct 93	2.50	0.50	1.25	2.50
❑5, Jul 94	2.95	0.50	1.25	2.50
❑6, Aug 94	2.95	0.50	1.25	2.50
❑7, Sep 94	2.95	0.50	1.25	2.50
❑8, Nov 94,cover says Oct	2.95	0.50	1.25	2.50
❑9, Nov 94	2.50	0.50	1.25	2.50
❑10, Dec 94	2.50	0.50	1.25	2.50
❑11, Feb 95, Extreme Sacrifice; Extreme Sacrifice, Part 0,Final Issue; polybagged with card	2.50	0.50	1.25	2.50

YOUNGBLOOD/X-FORCE
IMAGE
Value: Cover or less

- ❑1/A, Jul 96, prestige format; crossover with Marvel ... 4.95
- ❑1/B, Jul 96,alternate cover (black background) ... 4.95
- ❑1/C, Jul 96,alternate cover ... 4.95

Kurt Busiek provided historical text pieces to accompany the adventures of young Indy in *Young Indiana Jones Chronicles*.

YOUNGBROADS: STRIPFILE
PARODY PRESS
Value: Cover or less

- ❑1 ... 2.50

YOUNG BUG
ZOO ARSONIST
Value: Cover or less

- ❑1 ... 2.95
- ❑2 ... 2.95
- ❑3, Young Bug, Part 4; Good Country Insect, Part 2 ... 2.95

YOUNG CYNICS CLUB, THE
DARK HORSE
Value: Cover or less

- ❑1, Mar 93, nn; b&w ... 2.50

YOUNG DEATH
FLEETWAY
Value: Cover or less

- ❑1 ... 2.95
- ❑2 ... 2.95
- ❑3 ... 2.95

YOUNG DRACULA
CALIBER
Value: Cover or less

- ❑1, b&w ... 3.50
- ❑2, b&w ... 3.50
- ❑3, b&w; indicia says #2 ... 3.50

YOUNG DRACULA: PRAYER OF THE VAMPIRE
BONEYARD
Value: Cover or less

- ❑1 ... 2.95
- ❑2, Feb 98 ... 2.95
- ❑3 ... 2.95
- ❑4 ... 2.95

YOUNG GIRL ON GIRL: PASSION AND FASHION
ANGEL
Value: Cover or less

- ❑1 ... 3.00
- ❑1/Nude, Nude edition ... 3.95

YOUNG GUN
AC
Value: Cover or less

- ❑1, JSe, b&w; reprints Billy the Kid story ... 2.95

YOUNG HERO
AC
Value: Cover or less

- ❑1, Dec 89, b&w; reprints Daredevil #72 (1950) ... 2.50
- ❑2, Aug 90, 1: Red Devil, b&w; reprints Little Wise Guys ... 2.75

YOUNG HEROES IN LOVE
DC

	ORIG	GOOD	FINE	N-MINT
❑1, Jun 97, Your Lips! Your Eyes! Your Nuclear Breath Vision!,1st appe	1.75	0.50	1.25	2.50
❑1/LE,Signed by Dan Raspler; Wizard "Certified Authentic" edition	—	1.20	3.00	6.00
❑2, Jul 97	1.75	0.40	1.00	2.00
❑3, Aug 97, A: Superman	1.75	0.40	1.00	2.00
❑4, Sep 97	1.75	0.40	1.00	2.00
❑5, Oct 97,Genesis	1.75	0.40	1.00	2.00
❑6, Nov 97, You'll Never Walk Alone into the Furnace of Unstable Molecules!	1.75	0.40	1.00	2.00
❑7, Dec 97, Young Heroes Unplugged,Face cover	1.95	0.40	1.00	2.00
❑8, Jan 98, V: Scarecrow	1.95	0.40	1.00	2.00
❑9, Feb 98	1.95	0.40	1.00	2.00
❑10, Mar 98, Tremble in Fear-for the Beast Hunts You!	1.95	0.40	1.00	2.00
❑11, Apr 98	1.95	0.40	1.00	2.00
❑12, May 98	1.95	0.40	1.00	2.00
❑13, Jun 98	1.95	0.40	1.00	2.00
❑14, Jul 98	1.95	0.40	1.00	2.00
❑15, Aug 98	1.95	0.40	1.00	2.00
❑16, Sep 98	1.95	0.40	1.00	2.00
❑17, Oct 98	2.50	0.40	1.00	2.00
❑1000000, Nov 98, Happiness is a Warm Nanite,Final Issue	2.50	0.50	1.25	2.50

YOUNG INDIANA JONES CHRONICLES, THE
DARK HORSE

	ORIG	GOOD	FINE	N-MINT
❑1, Feb 92, Kurt Busiek (text piece), A: T.E. Lawrence	2.50	0.60	1.50	3.00
❑2, Mar 92, Kurt Busiek (text piece), A: Pancho Villa	2.50	0.50	1.25	2.50
❑3, Apr 92, Kurt Busiek (text piece), A: Teddy Roosevelt	2.50	0.50	1.25	2.50
❑4, May 92, Kurt Busiek (text piece)	2.50	0.50	1.25	2.50
❑5, Jun 92, Kurt Busiek (text piece)	2.50	0.50	1.25	2.50
❑6, Jul 92, Kurt Busiek (text piece)	2.50	0.50	1.25	2.50
❑7, Aug 92, Kurt Busiek (text piece)	2.50	0.50	1.25	2.50
❑8, Sep 92, Kurt Busiek (text piece)	2.50	0.50	1.25	2.50

	ORIG	GOOD	FINE	N-MINT
❑9, Oct 92, Kurt Busiek (text piece)	2.50	0.50	1.25	2.50
❑10, Dec 92, Kurt Busiek (text piece)	2.50	0.50	1.25	2.50
❑11, Jan 93, Kurt Busiek (text piece)	2.50	0.50	1.25	2.50
❑12, Feb 93	2.50	0.50	1.25	2.50

YOUNG INDIANA JONES CHRONICLES, THE (2ND SERIES)
HOLLYWOOD

Value: Cover or less

❑1,reprints Dark Horse issues #1 and 2 for newsstand distribution.......... 2.50
❑2,Reprint.......... 2.50
❑3,Reprint.......... 2.50

YOUNG JUSTICE
DC

	ORIG	GOOD	FINE	N-MINT
❑1, Sep 98, 1: Mighty Endowed; A: Robin; A: Impulse; 1: Supercycle; A: Martian Manhunter; A: Superboy	2.50	0.60	1.50	3.00
❑2, Oct 98, A: Ali Ben Styn; 1: Rip Roar	2.50	0.50	1.25	2.50
❑3, Dec 98, A: Mr. Mxyzptlk	2.50	0.50	1.25	2.50
❑4, Jan 99, 1: Tora; A: Arrowette; V: Harm; A: Spirit; A: Wonder Girl	2.50	0.50	1.25	2.50
❑5, Feb 99, PD (w), V: Harm	2.50	0.50	1.25	2.50
❑6, Mar 99, PD (w), A: Despero; A: Aquaman; A: Batman; A: Green Lantern; A: Martian Manhunter; A: Flash III (Wally West); A: Justice League of America; A: Superman; A: Wonder Woman	2.50	0.50	1.25	2.50
❑7, Apr 99, PD (w), A: Max Mercury; A: Nightwing,Parent/Teacher conference	2.50	0.50	1.25	2.50
❑8, May 99, A: Psyba-Rats	2.50	0.50	1.25	2.50
❑9, Jun 99, PD (w), Thug of War	2.50	0.50	1.25	2.50
❑10, Jul 99, PD (w), Kali'd Away	2.50	0.50	1.25	2.50
❑11, Aug 99, PD (w), Siege Perilous	2.50	0.50	1.25	2.50
❑12, Sep 99, PD (w), Heck's Angels, Part 1	2.50	0.50	1.25	2.50
❑13, Oct 99, PD (w), Heck's Angels, Part 3: Dis, Dat and De Other; Heck's Angels, Part 3, A: Supergirl	2.50	0.50	1.25	2.50
❑14, Nov 99, PD (w), A: Harm,Day of Judgment	2.50	0.50	1.25	2.50
❑15, Dec 99, PD (w), Unstrung	2.50	0.50	1.25	2.50
❑16, Jan 00, PD (w), Aftermath	2.50	0.50	1.25	2.50
❑17, Feb 00, PD (w), Stuff Blows Up	2.50	0.50	1.25	2.50
❑18, Mar 00, PD (w)	2.50	0.50	1.25	2.50
❑19, Apr 00, PD (w)	2.50	0.50	1.25	2.50
❑20, May 00, PD (w), Time Out	2.50	0.50	1.25	2.50
❑21, PD (w)	2.50	0.50	1.25	2.50
❑22, PD (w)	2.50	0.50	1.25	2.50
❑23, PD (w)	2.50	0.50	1.25	2.50
❑24, Oct 00, PD (w),Misprinted copies exist with duplicated ad	2.50	0.50	1.25	2.50
❑25, Nov 00, PD (w), Gold Standard	2.50	0.50	1.25	2.50
❑26, Dec 00, PD (w), From Myrg With Love	2.50	0.50	1.25	2.50
❑27, Jan 01, PD (w), Baseball Field: Myrg, or There's a Saga Born Every Minute	2.50	0.50	1.25	2.50
❑28, Feb 01, PD (w), Hitting for the Cycle	2.50	0.50	1.25	2.50
❑29, Mar 01, PD (w), Forever and a Day	2.50	0.50	1.25	2.50
❑30, Apr 01, PD (w), Round Robin	2.50	0.50	1.25	2.50
❑31, May 01, PD (w), Quiet!!!!!	2.50	0.50	1.25	2.50
❑32, Jun 01, PD (w), Anita's Date With Lobo	2.50	0.50	1.25	2.50
❑33	2.50	0.50	1.25	2.50
❑34	2.50	0.50	1.25	2.50
❑35	2.50	0.50	1.25	2.50
❑1000000, Nov 98, PD (w), Just Ice, Cubed, 1: Young Justice Legion S	2.50	0.50	1.25	2.50
❑GS 1, May 99, First Memory; The Totally O.K. Corral,80pgs.	4.95	0.99	2.47	4.95
❑SE 1, Jul 99, Road Trip,Young Justice in No Man's Land	3.95	0.79	1.98	3.95

YOUNG JUSTICE IN NO MAN'S LAND
DC

Value: Cover or less

❑1, Jul 99, A: Lagoon Boy,in Gotham City.......... 3.95

YOUNG JUSTICE SECRET FILES
DC

Value: Cover or less

❑1, Jan 99, Take Back the Night; Impulse's Trip to the Justice Cave, timeline; profiles of Young Justice members.......... 4.95

YOUNG JUSTICE: SINS OF YOUTH
DC

Value: Cover or less

❑1, May 00, PD (w), Justice for All.......... 2.50
❑2, May 00, PD (w), Sins of Youth: The Stunning Conclusion.... 2.50

YOUNG JUSTICE: THE SECRET
DC

Value: Cover or less

❑1, Jun 98,One-Shot; Girlfrenzy; leads into Young Justice: World Without Grown-Ups.......... 1.95

YOUNG LOVERS
AVALON

Value: Cover or less

❑1, Outrageous Flirt; Strength is in the Heart,Indicia reads "Rock and Roll Romance".......... 2.95

YOUNG MASTER
NEW COMICS

Value: Cover or less

❑1, Nov 87, b&w.......... 1.75
❑2, Dec 87, b&w.......... 1.75
❑3, Mar 88, b&w.......... 1.75
❑4, May 88, b&w.......... 1.75
❑5, Jul 88, b&w.......... 1.75
❑6, Oct 88, b&w.......... 1.75
❑7, Jan 89.......... 1.75
❑8, Mar 89.......... 1.95
❑9, VM.......... 1.95

YOUNGSPUD
SPOOF

Value: Cover or less

❑1.......... 2.95

YOUNG WITCHES, THE
FANTAGRAPHICS

	ORIG	GOOD	FINE	N-MINT
❑1, May 91, b&w; adult	2.25	0.50	1.25	2.50
❑2, Jun 91, b&w; adult	2.25	0.50	1.25	2.50
❑3, Jul 91, b&w; adult	2.25	0.50	1.25	2.50
❑4, Sep 91,adult	2.75	0.50	1.25	2.50

YOUNG WITCHES, THE: LONDON BABYLON
EROS

Value: Cover or less

❑1.......... 3.50
❑2.......... 3.50
❑3.......... 3.50
❑4.......... 3.50
❑5.......... 3.50
❑6.......... 3.50

YOUNG ZEN: CITY OF DEATH
EXPRESS

Value: Cover or less

❑1, b&w; cardstock cover.......... 3.25

YOUNG ZEN INTERGALACTIC NINJA
EXPRESS

Value: Cover or less

❑1, b&w; trading card.......... 3.50
❑2, b&w.......... 2.95

YOU'RE UNDER ARREST!
DARK HORSE

Value: Cover or less

❑1, Dec 95.......... 2.95
❑2, Jan 96.......... 2.95
❑3, Feb 96.......... 2.95
❑4, Mar 96.......... 2.95
❑5, Apr 96.......... 2.95
❑6, May 96.......... 2.95
❑7, Jun 96.......... 2.95
❑8, Jul 96.......... 2.95

YOUR HYTONE COMIX
APEX NOVELTIES

	ORIG	GOOD	FINE	N-MINT
❑1, Feb 71, Pete the Plumber; Mr. Natural Stops Talking, b&w; underground	0.50	1.60	4.00	8.00

Y'S GUYS
OCTOBER

Value: Cover or less

❑1, Jul 99.......... 2.95

YUMMY FUR
VORTEX

	ORIG	GOOD	FINE	N-MINT
❑1, Dec 86, b&w; adult; reprint mini-comics #1-3	1.75	1.20	3.00	6.00
❑2, b&w; adult; reprint mini-comics #4-6; no date of publication; says #4 in indicia	1.75	1.00	2.50	5.00
❑3, Feb 87, b&w; adult; reprint mini-comic #7	1.75	0.80	2.00	4.00
❑4, Apr 87, b&w; adult	1.75	0.80	2.00	4.00
❑5, Jun 87, b&w; adult	1.75	0.80	2.00	4.00
❑6, Aug 87, b&w; adult	1.75	0.60	1.50	3.00
❑7, b&w; adult	1.75	0.60	1.50	3.00
❑8, Nov 87, b&w; adult	1.75	0.60	1.50	3.00
❑9, b&w; adult	1.75	0.60	1.50	3.00
❑10, May 88, b&w; adult	1.75	0.60	1.50	3.00
❑11, Jul 88, b&w; adult	1.75	0.50	1.25	2.50
❑12, b&w; adult; no date of publication	1.75	0.50	1.25	2.50
❑13, Nov 88, b&w; adult	1.75	0.50	1.25	2.50
❑14, Jan 89, b&w; adult	1.75	0.50	1.25	2.50
❑15, Mar 89, b&w; adult	2.00	0.50	1.25	2.50
❑16, Jun 89,adult	2.00	0.50	1.25	2.50
❑17, Aug 89,adult	2.00	0.50	1.25	2.50
❑18, Oct 89,adult	2.00	0.50	1.25	2.50
❑19, Jan 90,adult	2.00	0.50	1.25	2.50
❑20, Apr 90,adult	2.00	0.50	1.25	2.50
❑21, Jun 90,adult	2.50	0.50	1.25	2.50
❑22, Sep 90,adult	2.50	0.50	1.25	2.50
❑23, Dec 90,adult	2.50	0.50	1.25	2.50
❑24,adult	2.50	0.50	1.25	2.50
❑25, Jul 91, b&w; adult	2.50	0.50	1.25	2.50
❑26, Oct 91, b&w; adult	2.50	0.50	1.25	2.50
❑27, b&w; adult	2.50	0.50	1.25	2.50
❑28, May 92, b&w; adult	2.50	0.50	1.25	2.50
❑29, Aug 92, b&w; adult	2.50	0.50	1.25	2.50
❑30, Apr 93, b&w; adult	2.50	0.50	1.25	2.50
❑31,adult	2.50	0.50	1.25	2.50
❑32, Jan 94, Matthew,adult; Final Issue; Drawn & Quarterly Publishes	2.95	0.59	1.48	2.95

YUPPIES FROM HELL
MARVEL

Value: Cover or less

❑1, b&w.......... 2.95

YUPPIES, REDNECKS AND LESBIAN BITCHES FROM MARS
EROS

Value: Cover or less

❑1.......... 2.95
❑2.......... 2.95
❑3.......... 2.95
❑4.......... 2.95
❑5.......... 2.95
❑6.......... 2.95
❑7, May 98.......... 2.95

ORIG GOOD FINE N-MINT

Z

Z
Keystone Graphics

Value: Cover or less

- ❑1, Nov 94, b&w 2.75
- ❑2, Jul 95, b&w 2.75
- ❑3, Nov 95, b&w 2.75

ZAIBATSU TEARS
Limelight

Value: Cover or less

- ❑1, b&w 2.95
- ❑2 ..... 2.95
- ❑3 ..... 2.95

ZATANNA
DC

Value: Cover or less

- ❑1, Jul 93 ..... 1.95
- ❑2, Aug 93, Zatanna gets new costume 1.95
- ❑3, Sep 93 ..... 1.95
- ❑4, Oct 93 ..... 1.95

ZATANNA SPECIAL
DC

Value: Cover or less

- ❑1, GM 2.00

ZAZA THE MYSTIC (AVALON)
Avalon

Value: Cover or less

- ❑1, Double Trouble; No Body, No Case 2.95

ZEALOT
Image

Value: Cover or less

- ❑1, Aug 95 ..... 2.50
- ❑2, Oct 95 ..... 2.50
- ❑3, Nov 95 ..... 2.50

ZELL SWORDDANCER (3-D ZONE)
3-D Zone

	ORIG	GOOD	FINE	N-MINT
❑1, b&w	—	0.40	1.00	2.00

ZELL, SWORDDANCER (THOUGHTS & IMAGES)
Thoughts & Images

Value: Cover or less

- ❑1, Jul 86, b&w 2.00

ZEN, INTERGALACTIC NINJA (1ST SERIES)
Zen

	ORIG	GOOD	FINE	N-MINT
❑1, Nov 87, b&w	1.75	0.60	1.50	3.00
❑1-2,2nd Printing	2.00	0.40	1.00	2.00
❑2, b&w	1.75	0.40	1.00	2.00
❑3, b&w	1.75	0.40	1.00	2.00
❑3-2,2nd Printing	2.00	0.40	1.00	2.00
❑4, b&w	1.75	0.40	1.00	2.00
❑5, b&w	1.75	0.40	1.00	2.00
❑6, b&w	2.00	0.40	1.00	2.00

ZEN, INTERGALACTIC NINJA (2ND SERIES)
Zen

Value: Cover or less

- ❑1, b&w 2.00
- ❑2, b&w 2.00
- ❑3, b&w 2.00
- ❑4, b&w 2.00

ZEN, INTERGALACTIC NINJA (3RD SERIES)
Zen

Value: Cover or less

- ❑1, b&w 2.25
- ❑2, b&w 2.25
- ❑3, b&w 2.25
- ❑4, b&w 2.25
- ❑5, b&w 2.25
- ❑HS 1, b&w; Flip-book 2.95

ZEN INTERGALACTIC NINJA (4TH SERIES)
Archie

Value: Cover or less

- ❑1, May 92, RA, Defend the Earth; Defend Earth, full color 1.25
- ❑2, Defend the Earth, full color 1.25
- ❑3, Defend the Earth, full color 1.25

ZEN INTERGALACTIC NINJA (5TH SERIES)
Archie

	ORIG	GOOD	FINE	N-MINT
❑1, Sep 92, RA, The Untold Origin of Zen, O: Zen Intergalactic Ninja, full color	1.25	0.25	0.63	1.25
❑2, Oct 92, Rumble in the Rainforest, Part 1, full color	1.25	0.25	0.63	1.25
❑3, Dec 92, Rumble in the Rainforest, Part 2, full color	1.25	0.25	0.63	1.25
❑4, Rumble in the Rainforest, Part 3	1.25	0.25	0.63	1.25
❑5, Defend the Earth, Part 1	1.25	0.25	0.63	1.25
❑6	—	0.25	0.63	1.25
❑7	—	0.25	0.63	1.25

ZEN INTERGALACTIC NINJA (6TH SERIES)
Express

	ORIG	GOOD	FINE	N-MINT
❑0, 1: Nira X,Gray trim around outside cover	2.50	0.60	1.50	3.00
❑0/A, Jun 93, b&w; foil cover	2.95	0.59	1.48	2.95
❑0/B, Jun 93, b&w; chromium cover	3.50	0.70	1.75	3.50
❑0/LE, 1: Nira X,Printing limited to 3,000 copies; All-gold trim	2.50	0.60	1.50	3.00
❑1, A Fire Upon the Earth, Part 1, b&w	2.95	0.60	1.50	3.00
❑1/SC, A Fire Upon the Earth, Part 1,Chromium, die-cut cover	3.95	0.79	1.98	3.95
❑2, b&w	2.95	0.60	1.50	3.00
❑3, b&w	2.95	0.60	1.50	3.00
❑4	2.50	0.60	1.50	3.00
❑Ash 1, b&w; no cover price; contains previews of Zen: Hazardous Duty and Zen: Tour of the Universe	—	0.20	0.50	1.00
❑Spr 1,Spring Spectacular	2.95	0.59	1.48	2.95

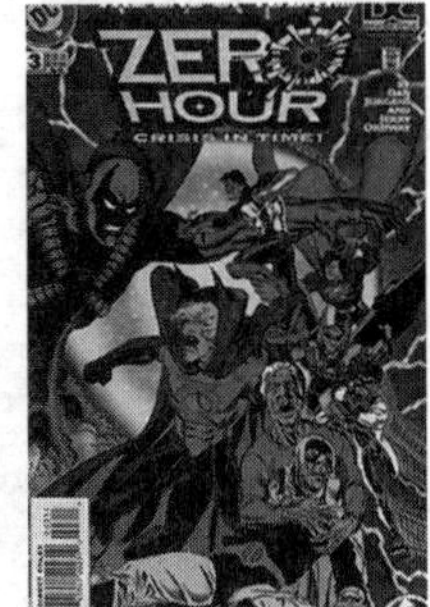

The ages of a number of DC's Golden Age characters finally caught up with them in *Zero Hour: Crisis in Time.*

ORIG GOOD FINE N-MINT

ZEN INTERGALACTIC NINJA ALL-NEW COLOR SPECIAL
Entity

Value: Cover or less

- ❑1, O: Zen Intergalactic Ninja,Chronium Cover 3.50

ZEN INTERGALACTIC NINJA COLOR
Express

Value: Cover or less

- ❑1,diecut foil cover 3.95
- ❑2 ..... 3.95
- ❑3 ..... 3.95
- ❑4 ..... 2.50
- ❑5 ..... 2.50
- ❑6 ..... 2.50
- ❑7,says #6a on cover; #7 in indicia 2.95

ZEN INTERGALACTIC NINJA COLOR (2ND SERIES)
Express

Value: Cover or less

- ❑1 ..... 2.50
- ❑2 ..... 2.50

ZEN, INTERGALACTIC NINJA EARTH DAY ANNUAL
Zen

Value: Cover or less

- ❑1, nn; b&w 2.95

ZEN INTERGALACTIC NINJA MILESTONE
Express

Value: Cover or less

- ❑1 ..... 2.95

ZEN INTERGALACTIC NINJA STARQUEST
Express

Value: Cover or less

- ❑1, b&w 2.95
- ❑2, b&w 2.95
- ❑4, b&w; cardstock cover 2.95

ZEN INTERGALACTIC NINJA SUMMER SPECIAL: VIDEO WARRIOR
Express

Value: Cover or less

- ❑1, b&w 2.95

ZEN INTERGALACTIC NINJA: TOUR OF THE UNIVERSE SPECIAL, THE AIRBRUSH ART OF DAN COTE
Express

Value: Cover or less

- ❑1,enhanced cardstock cover . 3.95

ZENITH: PHASE I
Fleetway

	ORIG	GOOD	FINE	N-MINT
❑1	1.95	0.40	1.00	2.00
❑2	1.95	0.40	1.00	2.00
❑3	1.95	0.40	1.00	2.00

ZENITH: PHASE II
Fleetway

Value: Cover or less

- ❑1 ..... 1.95
- ❑2 ..... 1.95

ZERO
Zero Comics

	ORIG	GOOD	FINE	N-MINT
❑1, Mar 75, b&w; adult	0.75	0.60	1.50	3.00
❑2, Mar 75, b&w; adult	0.75	0.60	1.50	3.00
❑3, May 76, b&w; adult	0.75	0.60	1.50	3.00

ZERO GIRL
Homage

Value: Cover or less

- ❑1, Feb 01 ..... 2.95
- ❑2, Mar 01 ..... 2.95
- ❑3, Apr 01 ..... 2.95
- ❑4, May 01 ..... 2.95
- ❑5 ..... 2.95

ZERO HOUR
Dog Soup

Value: Cover or less

- ❑1, Apr 95, nn; b&w; says Pat Leidy's Catfight on cover 2.95

ZERO HOUR: CRISIS IN TIME
DC

	ORIG	GOOD	FINE	N-MINT
❑0, Sep 94, JOy, V: Extant,contains Zero Hour checklist and new DC timeline fold-out; (#5 in sequence); (#5 in sequence)	1.50	0.40	1.00	2.00
❑1, Sep 94, JOy, 1: Jack Knight; 1: David Knight; 1: Parallax,Silver Age Atom de-aged; (#4 in sequence); (#4 in sequence)	1.50	0.60	1.50	3.00
❑2, Sep 94, JOy ,(#3 in sequence)	1.50	0.40	1.00	2.00
❑3, Sep 94, JOy, D: Hourman; D: Atom,remainder of Justice Society of America aged; (#2 in sequence); (#2 in sequence)	1.50	0.40	1.00	2.00
❑4, Sep 94, JOy ,(#1 in sequence)	1.50	0.40	1.00	2.00
❑Ash 1,Ashcan Preview	—	0.20	0.50	1.00

ZERO PATROL, THE (1ST SERIES)
Continuity

	ORIG	GOOD	FINE	N-MINT
❑1, Nov 84, NA, NA (w), 1: The Zero Patrol	1.50	0.40	1.00	2.00
❑2, NA, NA (w)	1.50	0.40	1.00	2.00

ZERO PATROL (2ND SERIES)
CONTINUITY
Value: Cover or less

❑1, NA, NA (w) 2.00
❑2, Nov 87, NA, NA (w) 2.00
❑3, Apr 88, NA, NA (w), Shaman back-up story 2.00
❑4, Mar 89, NA, NA (w) 2.00
❑5, May 89, NA, NA (w) 2.00

ZERO STREET
AMAZE INK
Value: Cover or less

❑1, 00, Erica 2.95

ZERO TOLERANCE
FIRST
Value: Cover or less

❑1, Oct 90 2.25
❑2, Nov 90 2.25
❑3, Dec 90, Vigil 2.25
❑4, Jan 91 2.25

ZERO ZERO
FANTAGRAPHICS

	ORIG	GOOD	FINE	N-MINT
❑1, Mar 95	3.95	0.80	2.00	4.00
❑2, May 95	3.95	0.80	2.00	4.00
❑3, Jul 95	3.95	0.80	2.00	4.00
❑4, Aug 95, issue number determined by back cover cartoon	3.95	0.80	2.00	4.00
❑5, Sep 95, issue number determined by back cover cartoon	3.95	0.80	2.00	4.00
❑6, Nov 95	3.95	0.80	2.00	4.00
❑7, Jan 96	3.95	0.80	2.00	4.00
❑8, Mar 96, 56pgs.; issue number determined by back cover cartoon	5.95	1.19	2.97	5.95
❑9, May 96, issue number determined by back cover cartoon	3.95	0.79	1.98	3.95
❑10, May 96, cover says Jul 96, indicia says May	3.95	0.79	1.98	3.95
❑11, Aug 96	3.95	0.79	1.98	3.95
❑12	3.95	0.79	1.98	3.95
❑13, Nov 96	3.95	0.79	1.98	3.95
❑14, Jan 97	3.95	0.79	1.98	3.95
❑15, Mar 97	3.95	0.79	1.98	3.95
❑16, Apr 97	3.95	0.79	1.98	3.95
❑17, Jun 97	3.95	0.79	1.98	3.95
❑18	3.95	0.79	1.98	3.95
❑19	3.95	0.79	1.98	3.95
❑20, Sep 97, b&w and color	3.95	0.79	1.98	3.95
❑21, Nov 97	3.95	0.79	1.98	3.95
❑22, Jan 98	3.95	0.79	1.98	3.95
❑23	3.95	0.79	1.98	3.95
❑24, Sum 98	3.95	0.79	1.98	3.95
❑25, Fal 98	3.95	0.79	1.98	3.95

ZETRAMAN
ANTARCTIC
Value: Cover or less

❑1, Sep 91, Venus Needs Men!!, b&w 1.95
❑2, Oct 91, b&w 1.95
❑3, Feb 92, b&w 1.95

ZETRAMAN: REVIVAL
ANTARCTIC
Value: Cover or less

❑1, Oct 93, Steamanetics 2.75
❑2, Dec 93 2.75
❑3, Aug 95 2.75

ZILLION
ETERNITY
Value: Cover or less

❑1, Apr 93, b&w 2.50
❑2, b&w 2.50
❑3, b&w 2.50
❑4, b&w 2.50

ZIP COMICS (COZMIC)
COZMIC

	ORIG	GOOD	FINE	N-MINT
❑1	1.00	0.80	2.00	4.00

ZIPPY QUARTERLY
FANTAGRAPHICS
Value: Cover or less

❑1, b&w 4.95
❑2, b&w 4.95
❑3, strip reprint 3.50
❑4, strip reprint 3.50
❑5, strip reprint 3.50
❑7, Aug 94, b&w; strip reprint 3.50
❑8, Nov 94, b&w; strip reprint 3.50
❑12, Dec 95, b&w; strip reprint 3.95
❑13, Aug 96, b&w; cardstock cover; strip reprint 3.95

ZÖLASTRSYA AND THE BARD
TWILIGHT TWINS
Value: Cover or less

❑1, Jan 87 1.70
❑2 1.70
❑3, wraparound photo cover 1.70
❑4, Photo cover 1.70
❑5 1.70

ZOMBIE 3-D
3-D ZONE
Value: Cover or less

❑1, nn 3.95

ZOMBIE BOY (ANTARCTIC)
ANTARCTIC
Value: Cover or less

❑1, Nov 96, b&w; wraparound cover 2.95
❑2 2.95
❑3 2.95

ZOMBIE BOY (TIMBUKTU)
TIMBUKTU
Value: Cover or less

❑1, b&w 1.50

ZOMBIE BOY RISES AGAIN
TIMBUKTU
Value: Cover or less

❑1, Jan 94, Beverly Hills Corpse; The Nosey Neighbor, b&w; Collects Zombie Boy #1 and Zombie Boy's Hoodoo Tales #1; Beverly Hillbillies cameo 2.50

ZOMBIE LOVE
ZUZUPETAL
Value: Cover or less

❑1 2.50
❑2 2.50
❑3 2.50

ZOMBIE WAR (FANTACO)
FANTACO
Value: Cover or less

❑1 3.50
❑2 3.50

ZOMBIE WAR (TUNDRA)
TUNDRA
Value: Cover or less

❑1 3.50

ZOMBIE WAR: EARTH MUST BE DESTROYED
FANTACO
Value: Cover or less

❑1, Earth Must be Destroyed!, b&w 2.95
❑1/CS, b&w; trading card 3.95
❑2, b&w 2.95
❑3, b&w 2.95
❑4, b&w 2.95

ZOMBIEWORLD: CHAMPION OF THE WORMS
DARK HORSE
Value: Cover or less

❑1, Sep 97 2.95
❑2, Oct 97 2.95
❑3, Nov 97 2.95

ZOMBIEWORLD: DEAD END
DARK HORSE
Value: Cover or less

❑1, Jan 98 2.95
❑2 2.95

ZOMBIEWORLD: EAT YOUR HEART OUT
DARK HORSE
Value: Cover or less

❑1, Apr 98, nn; One-Shot 2.95

ZOMBIEWORLD: HOME FOR THE HOLIDAYS
DARK HORSE
Value: Cover or less

❑1, Dec 97, nn; One-Shot 2.95

ZOMBIEWORLD: TREE OF DEATH
DARK HORSE
Value: Cover or less

❑1, Jun 99 2.95
❑2, Aug 99 2.95
❑3, Sep 99 2.95
❑4, Oct 99 2.95

ZOMBIEWORLD: WINTER'S DREGS
DARK HORSE
Value: Cover or less

❑1, May 98 2.95
❑2, Jun 98 2.95
❑3, Jul 98 2.95
❑4, Aug 98 2.95

ZOMBOY
INFERNO
Value: Cover or less

❑1, Aug 96, b&w 2.95

ZOMOID ILLUSTORIES
3-D ZONE
Value: Cover or less

❑1, b&w; not 3-D 2.50

ZONE
DARK HORSE

	ORIG	GOOD	FINE	N-MINT
❑1, b&w	1.95	0.40	1.00	2.00

ZONE CONTINUUM, THE
CALIBER

	ORIG	GOOD	FINE	N-MINT
❑1, b&w	2.95	0.59	1.48	2.95
❑1/A, no cover price; Orange background	—	0.40	1.00	2.00
❑1/B, no cover price; Maroon background	—	0.40	1.00	2.00
❑2, b&w	2.95	0.59	1.48	2.95

ZONE CONTINUUM (VOL. 2)
CALIBER
Value: Cover or less

❑1, b&w 2.95
❑2, b&w 2.95

ZONE ZERO
PLANET BOY
Value: Cover or less

❑1, b&w 2.95

ZOO FUNNIES (3RD SERIES)
CHARLTON

	ORIG	GOOD	FINE	N-MINT
❑1, Dec 84	0.75	0.40	1.00	2.00

ZOONIVERSE
ECLIPSE

	ORIG	GOOD	FINE	N-MINT
❑1, Aug 86	1.25	0.30	0.75	1.50
❑2, Oct 86, Yippo the Magic Zoon	1.25	0.30	0.75	1.50
❑3, Dec 86, Live at the Hall of Records	1.25	0.30	0.75	1.50
❑4, Feb 87	1.25	0.30	0.75	1.50
❑5, Apr 87	1.25	0.30	0.75	1.50
❑6, Jun 87	1.75	0.30	0.75	1.50

ZOOT!
FANTAGRAPHICS
Value: Cover or less

❑1, Nov 92, b&w 2.50
❑2, Mar 93, b&w 2.50
❑3, May 93, b&w 2.50
❑4, b&w 2.50

❑5, b&w ... 2.50
❑6, b&w ... 2.50

ZORANN: STAR-WARRIOR!
BLUE COMET

Value: Cover or less

❑0, May 94, My Enemies Blood! 2.95
❑1, b&w ... 2.00

ZORI J'S 3-D BUBBLE BATH
3-D ZONE

Value: Cover or less

❑1, nn; b&w ... 3.95

ZORI J'S SUPER-SWELL BUBBLE BATH ADVENTURE-OH BOY!
3-D ZONE

Value: Cover or less

❑1, nn; b&w ... 2.95

ZORRO (MARVEL)
MARVEL

	ORIG	GOOD	FINE	N-MINT
❑1, Dec 90, O: Zorro	1.00	0.60	1.50	3.00
❑2, Jan 91	1.00	0.40	1.00	2.00
❑3, Feb 91	1.00	0.40	1.00	2.00
❑4, Mar 91	1.00	0.40	1.00	2.00
❑5, Apr 91	1.00	0.40	1.00	2.00
❑6, May 91	1.00	0.40	1.00	2.00
❑7, Jun 91	1.00	0.40	1.00	2.00
❑8, Jul 91	1.00	0.40	1.00	2.00
❑9, Aug 91	1.00	0.40	1.00	2.00
❑10, Sep 91, ATh (c)	1.00	0.40	1.00	2.00
❑11, Oct 91, ATh (c)	1.00	0.40	1.00	2.00
❑12, Nov 91, ATh (c),Final Issue	1.00	0.40	1.00	2.00

ZORRO (TOPPS)
TOPPS

	ORIG	GOOD	FINE	N-MINT
❑0, Nov 93, 1: Buck Wylde	1.00	0.50	1.25	2.50
❑1, Jan 94, FM (c), Prequel in a Hostile Landscape, 1: Machete	2.50	0.70	1.75	3.50
❑2, Feb 94, 1: Lady Rawhide (out of costume)	2.50	1.60	4.00	8.00
❑3, Mar 94, 1: Lady Rawhide (in costume)	2.50	0.60	1.50	3.00
❑4, Apr 94, MGr (c), The Man Who Wasn't Felix Quintero, 1: Moonstalker	2.50	0.60	1.50	3.00
❑5, May 94, KG, JSt (c), The Bones Travel to the Ocean, A: Lady Rawhide	2.50	0.60	1.50	3.00
❑6, Jun 94, A Whale of a Coffin	2.50	0.60	1.50	3.00
❑7, Jul 94, PG (c), Let's Kill the Corpse, A: Lady Rawhide	2.50	0.50	1.25	2.50
❑8, Aug 94, GP, GP (c), As They Die Around You, A: Lady Rawhide	2.50	0.50	1.25	2.50
❑9, Sep 94	2.95	0.50	1.25	2.50
❑10, Oct 94, A: Lady Rawhide	2.50	0.59	1.48	2.95
❑11, Nov 94, A: Lady Rawhide,Final Issue	2.50	0.50	1.25	2.50

ZOT!
ECLIPSE

	ORIG	GOOD	FINE	N-MINT
❑1, Apr 84, 1: Zot!; 1: Jenny Weaver, full color; Color issues begin	1.50	1.00	2.50	5.00
❑2, May 84, 1: 9-Jack-9; 1: Dekko (cameo)	1.50	0.50	1.25	2.50
❑3, Jun 84, Art & Soul, Part 1, 1: Dekko (full)	1.50	0.50	1.25	2.50
❑4, Jul 84, Art & Soul, Part 2, O: Zot!	1.50	0.50	1.25	2.50
❑5, Aug 84, Sirius Business	1.50	0.50	1.25	2.50
❑6, Nov 84, It's Always Darkest…	1.50	0.50	1.25	2.50
❑7, Dec 84, DS, KB (w), Common Ground; September,The Magic Shop back-up features begin	1.50	0.50	1.25	2.50
❑8, Mar 85	1.50	0.50	1.25	2.50
❑9, May 85, Gorilla Warfare!	1.50	0.50	1.25	2.50
❑10, Jul 85, T.K.O.	1.50	0.50	1.25	2.50
❑10.5	1.50	0.50	1.25	2.50
❑11, Jan 87,Black & white issues begin	2.00	0.50	1.25	2.50
❑12, Mar 87	2.00	0.45	1.13	2.25
❑13, May 87	2.00	0.45	1.13	2.25
❑14, Jul 87	2.00	0.45	1.13	2.25
❑14.5,Adventures of Zot! in Dimension 10 1/2, The	2.00	0.45	1.13	2.25
❑15, Oct 87	2.00	0.45	1.13	2.25

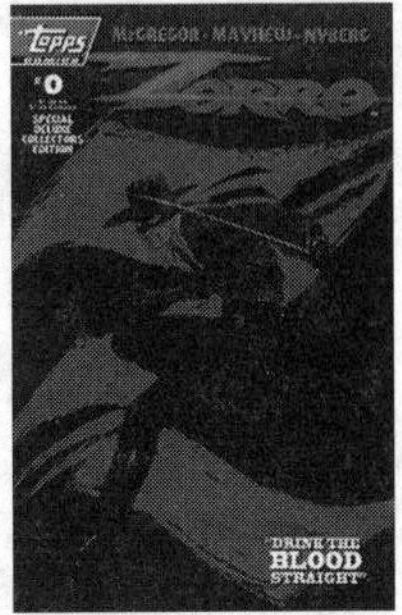

Topps' *Zorro* series introduced such characters as Buck Wylde and Lady Rawhide.

© 1993 Topps

	ORIG	GOOD	FINE	N-MINT
❑16, Dec 87	2.00	0.45	1.13	2.25
❑17, Feb 88	2.00	0.45	1.13	2.25
❑18, Apr 88	2.00	0.45	1.13	2.25
❑19, Jun 88	2.00	0.45	1.13	2.25
❑20, Jun 88	2.00	0.45	1.13	2.25
❑21, Aug 88, Can't Buy Me Love, Part 1	2.00	0.45	1.13	2.25
❑22, Oct 88, Can't Buy Me Love, Part 2; The Adventures of Zot! in Dimension 10 1/2	2.00	0.45	1.13	2.25
❑23, Nov 88	2.00	0.45	1.13	2.25
❑24, Dec 88	2.00	0.45	1.13	2.25
❑25, Feb 89	2.00	0.45	1.13	2.25
❑26, Apr 89	2.00	0.45	1.13	2.25
❑27, Jun 89	2.00	0.45	1.13	2.25
❑28, Sep 89	2.00	0.45	1.13	2.25
❑29, Dec 89, Looking for Crime; Shakedown on Astro Speedway	2.00	0.45	1.13	2.25
❑30, Mar 90	2.00	0.45	1.13	2.25
❑31, May 90	2.00	0.45	1.13	2.25
❑32, Jul 90	2.00	0.45	1.13	2.25
❑33, Oct 90	2.00	0.45	1.13	2.25
❑34, Dec 90	2.00	0.45	1.13	2.25
❑35, Mar 91	2.00	0.45	1.13	2.25
❑36, Jul 91,Final Issue	2.95	0.59	1.48	2.95
❑34973,2nd Printing	1.50	0.20	0.50	1.00

ZU
MU

Value: Cover or less

❑1, Jan 95, b&w ... 2.95
❑2, Mar 95, b&w ... 2.95
❑3, May 95, b&w ... 2.95
❑4, Jul 95, b&w ... 2.95
❑5, Sep 95, b&w ... 2.95
❑6, Nov 95, b&w ... 2.95
❑7, Jan 96, b&w ... 2.95
❑8 ... 2.95
❑9 ... 2.95
❑10 ... 2.95
❑11 ... 2.95
❑12 ... 2.95
❑13 ... 2.95
❑14 ... 2.95
❑15 ... 2.95
❑16 ... 2.95
❑17 ... 2.95
❑18 ... 2.95
❑19 ... 2.95

ZU (ONE-SHOT)
MU

Value: Cover or less

❑1, Feb 92, nn; One-Shot ... 3.95

ZUGAL
BRYAN EVANS

Value: Cover or less

❑1, The City ... 2.95

ZULUNATION
TOME PRESS

Value: Cover or less

❑1, b&w ... 2.95
❑2, b&w ... 2.95
❑3, b&w ... 2.95

ZWANNA, SON OF ZULU
DARK ZULU LIES

	ORIG	GOOD	FINE	N-MINT
❑1	1.95	0.40	1.00	2.00

ZZZ
ALAN BUNCE

Value: Cover or less

❑1, Mar 00 ... 2.35

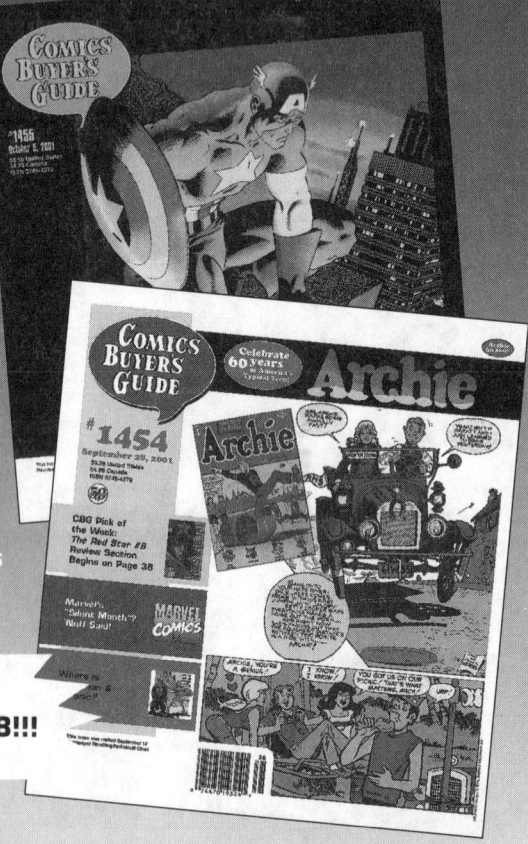